SELECTED ENVIRONMENTAL LAW STATUTES

2021–2022 Educational Edition

Updated through April 15, 2021

Compiled by Robin Kundis Craig

WEST ACADEMIC PUBLISHING

444 Cedar Street, Suite 700
St. Paul, MN 55101
1-877-888-1330

Printed in the United States of America

ISBN: 978-1-64708-863-7

TABLE OF CONTENTS

THE CODE OF THE LAWS OF THE UNITED STATES OF AMERICA

TITLE 43, PUBLIC LANDS

APPENDICES

TITLE 7

AGRICULTURE

FEDERAL INSECTICIDE, FUNGICIDE, AND RODENTICIDE ACT [FIFRA § ______]

(7 U.S.C.A. §§ 136 to 136y)

CHAPTER 6—INSECTICIDES AND ENVIRONMENTAL PESTICIDE CONTROL

SUBCHAPTER II—ENVIRONMENTAL PESTICIDE CONTROL

Sec.

SUBCHAPTER II—ENVIRONMENTAL PESTICIDE CONTROL

§ 136. Definitions

[FIFRA § 2]

For purposes of this subchapter—

(a) Active ingredient

The term "active ingredient" means—

(1) in the case of a pesticide other than a plant regulator, defoliant, desiccant, or nitrogen stabilizer, an ingredient which will prevent, destroy, repel, or mitigate any pest;

(2) in the case of a plant regulator, an ingredient which, through physiological action, will accelerate or retard the rate of growth or rate of maturation or otherwise alter the behavior of ornamental or crop plants or the product thereof;

(3) in the case of a defoliant, an ingredient which will cause the leaves or foliage to drop from a plant;

(4) in the case of a desiccant, an ingredient which will artificially accelerate the drying of plant tissue; and

(5) in the case of a nitrogen stabilizer, an ingredient which will prevent or hinder the process of nitrification, denitrification, ammonia volatilization, or urease production through action affecting soil bacteria.

(b) Administrator

The term "Administrator" means the Administrator of the Environmental Protection Agency.

(c) Adulterated

The term "adulterated" applies to any pesticide if—

(1) its strength or purity falls below the professed standard of quality as expressed on its labeling under which it is sold;

(2) any substance has been substituted wholly or in part for the pesticide; or

(3) any valuable constituent of the pesticide has been wholly or in part abstracted.

(d) Animal

The term "animal" means all vertebrate and invertebrate species, including but not limited to man and other mammals, birds, fish, and shellfish.

(e) Certified applicator, etc.

(1) Certified applicator

The term "certified applicator" means any individual who is certified under section 136i of this title as authorized to use or supervise the use of any pesticide which is classified for restricted use. Any applicator who holds or applies registered pesticides, or uses dilutions of registered pesticides consistent with subsection (ee) of this section, only to provide a service of controlling pests without delivering any unapplied pesticide to any person so served is not deemed to be a seller or distributor of pesticides under this subchapter.

(2) Private applicator

The term "private applicator" means a certified applicator who uses or supervises the use of any pesticide which is classified for restricted use for purposes of producing any agricultural commodity on property owned or rented by the applicator or the applicator's employer or (if applied without compensation other than trading of personal services between producers of agricultural commodities) on the property of another person.

(3) Commercial applicator

The term "commercial applicator" means an applicator (whether or not the applicator is a private applicator with respect to some uses) who uses or supervises the use of any pesticide which is classified for restricted use for any purpose or on any property other than as provided by paragraph (2).

(4) Under the direct supervision of a certified applicator

Unless otherwise prescribed by its labeling, a pesticide shall be considered to be applied under the direct supervision of a certified applicator if it is applied by a competent person acting under the instructions and control of a certified applicator who is available if and when needed, even though such certified applicator is not physically present at the time and place the pesticide is applied.

(f) Defoliant

The term "defoliant" means any substance or mixture of substances intended for causing the leaves or foliage to drop from a plant, with or without causing abscission.

(g) Desiccant

The term "desiccant" means any substance or mixture of substances intended for artificially accelerating the drying of plant tissue.

(h) Device

The term "device" means any instrument or contrivance (other than a firearm) which is intended for trapping, destroying, repelling, or mitigating any pest or any other form of plant or animal life (other than man and other than bacteria, virus, or other microorganism on or in living man or other living animals); but not including equipment used for the application of pesticides when sold separately therefrom.

(i) District court

The term "district court" means a United States district court, the District Court of Guam, the District Court of the Virgin Islands, and the highest court of American Samoa.

(j) Environment

The term "environment" includes water, air, land, and all plants and man and other animals living therein, and the interrelationships which exist among these.

(k) Fungus

The term "fungus" means any non-chlorophyll-bearing thallophyte (that is, any non-chlorophyll-bearing plant of a lower order than mosses and liverworts), as for example, rust, smut, mildew, mold, yeast, and bacteria, except those on or in living man or other animals and those on or in processed food, beverages, or pharmaceuticals.

(*l*) Imminent hazard

The term "imminent hazard" means a situation which exists when the continued use of a pesticide during the time required for cancellation proceeding would be likely to result in unreasonable adverse effects on the environment or will involve unreasonable hazard to the survival of a species declared endangered or threatened by the Secretary pursuant to the Endangered Species Act of 1973 [16 U.S.C.A. § 1531 et seq.].

(m) Inert ingredient

The term "inert ingredient" means an ingredient which is not active.

(n) Ingredient statement

The term "ingredient statement" means a statement which contains—

(1) the name and percentage of each active ingredient, and the total percentage of all inert ingredients, in the pesticide; and

(2) if the pesticide contains arsenic in any form, a statement of the percentages of total and water soluble arsenic, calculated as elementary arsenic.

(*o*) Insect

The term "insect" means any of the numerous small invertebrate animals generally having the body more or less obviously segmented, for the most part belonging to the class insecta, comprising six-legged, usually winged forms, as for example, beetles, bugs, bees, flies, and to other allied classes of arthropods whose members are wingless and usually have more than six legs, as for example, spiders, mites, ticks, centipedes, and wood lice.

(p) Label and labeling

(1) Label

The term "label" means the written, printed, or graphic matter on, or attached to, the pesticide or device or any of its containers or wrappers.

(2) Labeling

The term "labeling" means all labels and all other written, printed, or graphic matter—

(A) accompanying the pesticide or device at any time; or

(B) to which reference is made on the label or in literature accompanying the pesticide or device, except to current official publications of the Environmental Protection Agency, the United States Departments of Agriculture and Interior, the Department of Health and Human Services, State experiment stations, State agricultural colleges, and other similar Federal or State institutions or agencies authorized by law to conduct research in the field of pesticides.

(q) Misbranded

(1) A pesticide is misbranded if—

(A) its labeling bears any statement, design, or graphic representation relative thereto or to its ingredients which is false or misleading in any particular;

(B) it is contained in a package or other container or wrapping which does not conform to the standards established by the Administrator pursuant to section 136w(c)(3) of this title;

(C) it is an imitation of, or is offered for sale under the name of, another pesticide;

(D) its label does not bear the registration number assigned under section 136e of this title to each establishment in which it was produced;

(E) any word, statement, or other information required by or under authority of this subchapter to appear on the label or labeling is not prominently placed thereon with such conspicuousness (as compared with other words, statements, designs, or graphic matter in the labeling) and in such terms as to render it likely to be read and understood by the ordinary individual under customary conditions of purchase and use;

(F) the labeling accompanying it does not contain directions for use which are necessary for effecting the purpose for which the product is intended and if complied with, together with any requirements imposed under section 136a(d) of this title, are adequate to protect health and the environment;

(G) the label does not contain a warning or caution statement which may be necessary and if complied with, together with any requirements imposed under section 136a(d) of this title, is adequate to protect health and the environment; or

(H) in the case of a pesticide not registered in accordance with section 136a of this title and intended for export, the label does not contain, in words prominently placed thereon with such conspicuousness (as compared with other words, statements, designs, or graphic matter in the labeling) as to render it likely to be noted by the ordinary individual under customary conditions of purchase and use, the following: "Not Registered for Use in the United States of America".

(2) A pesticide is misbranded if—

(A) the label does not bear an ingredient statement on that part of the immediate container (and on the outside container or wrapper of the retail package, if there be one, through which the ingredient statement on the immediate container cannot be clearly read) which is presented or displayed under customary conditions of purchase, except that a pesticide is not misbranded under this subparagraph if—

(i) the size or form of the immediate container, or the outside container or wrapper of the retail package, makes it impracticable to place the ingredient statement on the part which is presented or displayed under customary conditions of purchase; and

(ii) the ingredient statement appears prominently on another part of the immediate container, or outside container or wrapper, permitted by the Administrator;

(B) the labeling does not contain a statement of the use classification under which the product is registered;

(C) there is not affixed to its container, and to the outside container or wrapper of the retail package, if there be one, through which the required information on the immediate container cannot be clearly read, a label bearing—

(i) the name and address of the producer, registrant, or person for whom produced;

(ii) the name, brand, or trademark under which the pesticide is sold;

(iii) the net weight or measure of the content, except that the Administrator may permit reasonable variations; and

(iv) when required by regulation of the Administrator to effectuate the purposes of this subchapter, the registration number assigned to the pesticide under this subchapter, and the use classification; and

(D) the pesticide contains any substance or substances in quantities highly toxic to man, unless the label shall bear, in addition to any other matter required by this subchapter—

(i) the skull and crossbones;

(ii) the word "poison" prominently in red on a background of distinctly contrasting color; and

(iii) a statement of a practical treatment (first aid or otherwise) in case of poisoning by the pesticide.

(r) Nematode

The term "nematode" means invertebrate animals of the phylum nemathelminthes and class nematoda, that is, unsegmented round worms with elongated, fusiform, or saclike bodies covered with cuticle, and inhabiting soil, water, plants, or plant parts; may also be called nemas or eelworms.

(s) Person

The term "person" means any individual, partnership, association, corporation, or any organized group of persons whether incorporated or not.

(t) Pest

The term "pest" means (1) any insect, rodent, nematode, fungus, weed, or (2) any other form of terrestrial or aquatic plant or animal life or virus, bacteria, or other micro-organism (except viruses, bacteria, or other micro-organisms on or in living man or other living animals) which the Administrator declares to be a pest under section 136w(c)(1) of this title.

(u) Pesticide

The term "pesticide" means (1) any substance or mixture of substances intended for preventing, destroying, repelling, or mitigating any pest, (2) any substance or mixture of substances intended for use as a plant regulator, defoliant, or desiccant, and (3) any nitrogen stabilizer, except that the term "pesticide" shall not include any article that is a "new animal drug" within the meaning of section 321(w) of Title 21, that has been determined by the Secretary of Health and Human Services not to be a new animal drug by a regulation establishing conditions of use for the article, or that is an animal feed within the meaning of section 321(x) of Title 21 bearing or containing a new animal drug. The term "pesticide" does not include liquid chemical sterilant products (including any sterilant or subordinate disinfectant claims on such products) for use on a critical or semi-critical device, as defined in section 321 of Title 21. For purposes of the preceding sentence, the term "critical device" includes any device which is introduced directly into the human body, either into or in contact with the bloodstream or normally sterile areas of the body and the term "semi-critical device" includes any device which contacts intact mucous membranes but which does not ordinarily penetrate the blood barrier or otherwise enter normally sterile areas of the body.

(v) Plant regulator

The term "plant regulator" means any substance or mixture of substances intended, through physiological action, for accelerating or retarding the rate of growth or rate of maturation, or for otherwise altering the behavior of plants or the produce thereof, but shall not include substances to the extent that they are intended as plant nutrients, trace elements, nutritional chemicals, plant inoculants, and soil amendments. Also, the term "plant regulator" shall not be required to include any of such of those nutrient mixtures or soil amendments as are commonly known as vitamin-hormone horticultural products, intended for improvement, maintenance, survival, health, and propagation of plants, and as are not for pest destruction and are nontoxic, nonpoisonous in the undiluted packaged concentration.

(w) Producer and produce

The term "producer" means the person who manufactures, prepares, compounds, propagates, or processes any pesticide or device or active ingredient used in producing a pesticide. The term "produce" means to manufacture, prepare, compound, propagate, or process any pesticide or device or active ingredient used in producing a pesticide. The dilution by individuals of formulated pesticides for their own use and according to the directions on registered labels shall not of itself result in such individuals being included in the definition of "producer" for the purposes of this subchapter.

(x) Protect health and the environment

The terms "protect health and the environment" and "protection of health and the environment" mean protection against any unreasonable adverse effects on the environment.

(y) Registrant

The term "registrant" means a person who has registered any pesticide pursuant to the provisions of this subchapter.

(z) Registration

The term "registration" includes reregistration.

(aa) State

The term "State" means a State, the District of Columbia, the Commonwealth of Puerto Rico, the Virgin Islands, Guam, the Trust Territory of the Pacific Islands, and American Samoa.

(bb) Unreasonable adverse effects on the environment

The term "unreasonable adverse effects on the environment" means (1) any unreasonable risk to man or the environment, taking into account the economic, social, and environmental costs and benefits of the use of any pesticide, or (2) a human dietary risk from residues that result from a use of a pesticide in or on any food inconsistent with the standard under section 346a of Title 21. The Administrator shall consider the risks and benefits of public health pesticides separate from the risks and benefits of other pesticides. In weighing any regulatory action concerning a public health pesticide under this subchapter, the Administrator shall weigh any risks of the pesticide against the health risks such as the diseases transmitted by the vector to be controlled by the pesticide.

(cc) Weed

The term "weed" means any plant which grows where not wanted.

(dd) Establishment

The term "establishment" means any place where a pesticide or device or active ingredient used in producing a pesticide is produced, or held, for distribution or sale.

(ee) To use any registered pesticide in a manner inconsistent with its labeling

The term "to use any registered pesticide in a manner inconsistent with its labeling" means to use any registered pesticide in a manner not permitted by the labeling, except that the term shall not include (1) applying a pesticide at any dosage, concentration, or frequency less than that specified on the labeling unless the labeling specifically prohibits deviation from the specified dosage, concentration, or frequency, (2) applying a pesticide against any target pest not specified on the labeling if the application is to the crop, animal, or site specified on the labeling, unless the Administrator has required that the labeling specifically state that the pesticide may be used only for the pests specified on the labeling after the Administrator has determined that the use of the pesticide against other pests would cause an unreasonable adverse effect on the environment, (3) employing any method of application not prohibited by the labeling unless the labeling specifically states that the product may be applied only by the methods specified on the labeling, (4) mixing a pesticide or pesticides with a fertilizer when such mixture is not prohibited by the labeling, (5) any use of a pesticide in conformance with section 136c, 136p, or 136v of this title, or (6) any use of a pesticide in a manner that the Administrator determines to be consistent with the purposes of this subchapter. After March 31, 1979, the term shall not include the use of a pesticide for agricultural or forestry purposes at a dilution less than label dosage unless before or after that date the Administrator issues a regulation or advisory opinion consistent with the study provided for in section 27(b) of the Federal Pesticide Act of 1978, which regulation or advisory opinion specifically requires the use of definite amounts of dilution.

(ff) Outstanding data requirement

(1) In general

The term "outstanding data requirement" means a requirement for any study, information, or data that is necessary to make a determination under section 136a(c)(5) of this title and which study, information, or data—

(A) has not been submitted to the Administrator; or

(B) if submitted to the Administrator, the Administrator has determined must be resubmitted because it is not valid, complete, or adequate to make a determination under section 136a(c)(5) of this title and the regulations and guidelines issued under such section.

(2) Factors

In making a determination under paragraph (1)(B) respecting a study, the Administrator shall examine, at a minimum, relevant protocols, documentation of the conduct and analysis of the study, and the results of the study to determine whether the study and the results of the study fulfill the data requirement for which the study was submitted to the Administrator.

(gg) To distribute or sell

The term "to distribute or sell" means to distribute, sell, offer for sale, hold for distribution, hold for sale, hold for shipment, ship, deliver for shipment, release for shipment, or receive and (having so received) deliver or offer to deliver. The term does not include the holding or application of registered pesticides or use dilutions thereof by any applicator who provides a service of controlling pests without delivering any unapplied pesticide to any person so served.

(hh) Nitrogen stabilizer

The term "nitrogen stabilizer" means any substance or mixture of substances intended for preventing or hindering the process of nitrification, denitrification, ammonia volatilization, or urease production through action upon soil bacteria. Such term shall not include—

(1) dicyandiamide;

(2) ammonium thiosulfate; or

(3) any substance or mixture of substances.[1]—

(A) that was not registered pursuant to section 136a of this title prior to January 1, 1992; and

(B) that was in commercial agronomic use prior to January 1, 1992, with respect to which after January 1, 1992, the distributor or seller of the substance or mixture has made no specific claim of prevention or hindering of the process of nitrification, denitrification, ammonia volatilization[2] urease production regardless of the actual use or purpose for, or future use or purpose for, the substance or mixture.

Statements made in materials required to be submitted to any State legislative or regulatory authority, or required by such authority to be included in the labeling or other literature accompanying any such substance or mixture shall not be deemed a specific claim within the meaning of this subsection.

(jj)[3] Maintenance applicator

The term "maintenance applicator" means any individual who, in the principal course of such individual's employment, uses, or supervises the use of, a pesticide not classified for restricted use (other than a ready to use consumer products pesticide); for the purpose of providing structural pest control or lawn pest control including janitors, general maintenance personnel, sanitation personnel, and grounds maintenance personnel. The term "maintenance applicator" does not include private applicators as defined in subsection (e)(2) of this section; individuals who use antimicrobial pesticides, sanitizers or disinfectants; individuals employed by Federal, State, and local governments or any political subdivisions thereof, or individuals who use pesticides not classified for restricted use in or around their homes, boats, sod farms, nurseries, greenhouses, or other noncommercial property.

(kk) Service technician

The term "service technician" means any individual who uses or supervises the use of pesticides (other than a ready to use consumer products pesticide) for the purpose of providing structural pest control or lawn pest control on the property of another for a fee. The term "service technician" does not include individuals who use antimicrobial pesticides, sanitizers or disinfectants; or who otherwise apply ready to use consumer products pesticides.

***(ll)* Minor use**

The term "minor use" means the use of a pesticide on an animal, on a commercial agricultural crop or site, or for the protection of public health where—

(1) the total United States acreage for the crop is less than 300,000 acres, as determined by the Secretary of Agriculture; or

(2) the Administrator, in consultation with the Secretary of Agriculture, determines that, based on information provided by an applicant for registration or a registrant, the use does not provide sufficient economic incentive to support the initial registration or continuing registration of a pesticide for such use and—

(A) there are insufficient efficacious alternative registered pesticides available for the use;

(B) the alternatives to the pesticide use pose greater risks to the environment or human health;

(C) the minor use pesticide plays or will play a significant part in managing pest resistance; or

(D) the minor use pesticide plays or will play a significant part in an integrated pest management program.

The status as a minor use under this subsection shall continue as long as the Administrator has not determined that, based on existing data, such use may cause an unreasonable adverse effect on the environment and the use otherwise qualifies for such status.

(mm) Antimicrobial pesticide

(1) In general

The term "antimicrobial pesticide" means a pesticide that—

(A) is intended to—

(i) disinfect, sanitize, reduce, or mitigate growth or development of microbiological organisms; or

(ii) protect inanimate objects, industrial processes or systems, surfaces, water, or other chemical substances from contamination, fouling, or deterioration caused by bacteria, viruses, fungi, protozoa, algae, or slime; and

(B) in the intended use is exempt from, or otherwise not subject to, a tolerance under section 346a of Title 21 or a food additive regulation under section 348 of Title 21.

(2) Excluded products

The term "antimicrobial pesticide" does not include—

(A) a wood preservative or antifouling paint product for which a claim of pesticidal activity other than or in addition to an activity described in paragraph (1) is made;

(B) an agricultural fungicide product; or

(C) an aquatic herbicide product.

(3) Included products

The term "antimicrobial pesticide" does include any other chemical sterilant product (other than liquid chemical sterilant products exempt under subsection (u) of this section), any other disinfectant product, any other industrial microbiocide product, and any other preservative product that is not excluded by paragraph (2).

(nn) Public health pesticide

The term "public health pesticide" means any minor use pesticide product registered for use and used predominantly in public health programs for vector control or for other recognized health protection uses, including the prevention or mitigation of viruses, bacteria, or other microorganisms (other than viruses, bacteria, or other microorganisms on or in living man or other living animal) that pose a threat to public health.

(*oo*) Vector

The term "vector" means any organism capable of transmitting the causative agent of human disease or capable of producing human discomfort or injury, including mosquitoes, flies, fleas, cockroaches, or other insects and ticks, mites, or rats.

(Act of June 25, 1947, c. 125, § 2, as added Pub. L. No. 92–516, § 2, 86 Stat. 975 (Oct. 21, 1972,); and amended by Pub. L. No. 93–205, § 13(f), 87 Stat. 903 (Dec. 28, 1973); Pub. L. No. 94–140, § 9, 89 Stat. 754 (Nov. 28, 1975); Pub. L. No. 95–396, § 1, 92 Stat. 819 (Sept. 30, 1978); Pub. L. No. 100–532, Title I, § 101, Title VI, § 601(a), Title VIII, § 801(a), 102 Stat. 2655, 2677, 2679 (Oct. 25, 1988); Pub. L. 102–237, Title X, § 1006(a)(1), (2), (b)(3)(A), (B), 105 Stat. 1894, 1895 (Dec. 13, 1991); Pub. L. No. 104–170, Title I, §§ 105(a), 120, Title II, §§ 210(a), 221, 230, Title III, § 304, 110 Stat. 1490, 1492, 1493, 1502, 1508, 1512 (Aug. 3, 1996).)

[1] So in original. Probably should not have a period.

[2] So in original. Probably should be followed by ", or."

[3] So in original. No subsec. (ii) has been enacted.

HISTORICAL AND STATUTORY NOTES

References in Text

The Endangered Species Act of 1973, referred to in subsec. (*l*), is Pub. L. No. 93–205, 87 Stat. 884 (Dec. 28, 1973), which is codified generally as chapter 35 (section 1531 et seq.) of Title 16, Conservation. For complete classification of this Act to the Code, see Short Title note set out under section 1531 of Title 16 and Tables.

Section 321 of title 21, referred to in subsec. (u), was amended and subsecs. (w) and (x) of section 321 no longer define "new animal drug" and "animal feed", but the terms are defined elsewhere in the section.

Section 27(b) of Federal Pesticide Act of 1978, referred to in subsec. (ee), is section 27(b) of Pub. L. No. 95–396, 92 Stat. 841 (Sept. 30, 1978), which is set out as a note under section 136–4 of this title.

Effective and Applicability Provisions

1991 Acts. Amendments by Pub. L. No. 102–237 effective Dec. 13, 1991, see section 1101(a) of Pub. L. No. 102–237, set out as a note under section 1421 of this title.

1988 Acts. Section 901 of Pub. L. No. 100–532 provided that: "Except as otherwise provided in this Act, the amendments made by this Act [see Short Title of 1988 Amendments note set out under this section] shall take effect on the expiration of 60 days after the date of enactment of this Act [October 25, 1988]."

1973 Acts. Amendment by Pub. L. No. 93–205 effective Dec. 28, 1973, see section 16 of Pub. L. No. 93–205, set out as a note under section 1531 of Title 16, Conservation.

1975 Acts. Section 4 of Pub. L. No. 92–516, as amended Pub. L. No. 94–140, § 4, 89 Stat. 752 (Nov. 28, 1975); Pub. L. No. 95–396, § 28, 92 Stat. 842 (Sept. 30, 1978), provided that:

"**(a)** Except as otherwise provided in the Federal Insecticide, Fungicide, and Rodenticide Act [this subchapter], as amended by this Act and as otherwise provided by this section, the amendments made by this Act [see Short Title notes set out hereunder] shall take effect at the close of the date of the enactment of this Act [Oct. 21, 1972], provided if regulations are necessary for the implementation of any provision that becomes effective on the date of enactment, such regulations shall be promulgated and shall become effective within 90 days from the date of enactment of this Act.

"**(b)** The provisions of the Federal Insecticide, Fungicide, and Rodenticide Act [this subchapter] and the regulations thereunder as such existed prior to the enactment of this Act shall remain in effect until superseded by the amendments made by this Act and regulations thereunder.

"**(c)** **(1)** Two years after the enactment of this Act the Administrator shall have promulgated regulations providing for the registration and classification of pesticides under the provisions of this Act and thereafter shall register all new applications under such provisions.

"**(2)** Any requirements that a pesticide be registered for use only by a certified applicator shall not be effective until five years from the date of enactment of this Act.

"**(3)** A period of five years from date of enactment shall be provided for certification of applicators.

"**(A)** One year after the enactment of this Act the Administrator shall have prescribed the standards for the certification of applicators.

"**(B)** Each State desiring to certify applicators shall submit a State plan to the Administrator for the purpose provided by section 4(b).

"**(C)** As promptly as possible but in no event more than one year after submission of a State plan, the Administrator shall approve the State plan or disapprove it and indicate the reasons for disapproval. Consideration of plans resubmitted by States shall be expedited.

"**(4)** One year after the enactment of this Act the Administrator shall have promulgated and shall make effective regulations relating to the registration of establishments, permits for experimental use, and the keeping of books and records under the provisions of this Act.

"**(d)** No person shall be subject to any criminal or civil penalty imposed by the Federal Insecticide, Fungicide, and Rodenticide Act, as amended by this Act, for any act (or failure to act) occurring before the expiration of 60 days after the Administrator has published effective regulations in the Federal Register and taken such other action as may be necessary to permit compliance with the provisions under which the penalty is to be imposed.

"**(e)** For purposes of determining any criminal or civil penalty or liability to any third person in respect of any act or omission occurring before the expiration of the periods referred to in this section, the Federal Insecticide, Fungicide, and Rodenticide Act shall be treated as continuing in effect as if this Act had not been enacted."

Short Title

2019 Amendments. Section 1(a) of Pub. L. No. 116–8, 133 Stat. 484 (March 8, 2019), provided that "This Act may be cited as the 'Pesticide Registration Improvement Extension Act of 2018.' "

2012 Amendments. Pub. L. No. 112–177, § 1, 126 Stat. 1327 (Sept. 28, 2012), provided that: "This Act [amending 7 U.S.C.A. §§ 136a–1, 136w–8, and 21 U.S.C.A. § 346a, and enacting provisions set out as notes under 7 U.S.C.A. § 136a–1] may be cited as the 'Pesticide Registration Improvement Extension Act of 2012'."

2007 Amendments. Pub. L. No. 110–94, § 1, 121 Stat. 1000 (Oct. 9, 2007), provided that: "This Act [amending 7 U.S.C.A. §§ 136a, 136a–1, and 136w–8 and 21 U.S.C.A. § 346a, and enacting provisions set out as a note under 7 U.S.C.A. § 136a] may be cited as the 'Pesticide Registration Improvement Renewal Act'."

2004 Amendments. Pub. L. No. 108–199, Div. G, Title V, § 501(a), 118 Stat. 419 (Jan. 23, 2004), provided that: "This section [enacting 7 U.S.C.A. § 136w–8, amending 7 U.S.C.A. §§ 136a, 136a–1, 136x, 136y, and enacting provisions set out as notes under 21 U.S.C.A. § 136a and 21 U.S.C.A. § 346a] may be cited as the 'Pesticide Registration Improvement Act of 2003'."

1996 Amendments. Pub. L. No. 104–170, § 1, 110 Stat. 1489 (Aug. 3, 1996), provided that: "This Act [enacting sections 136i–2, 136r–1, 136w–5, 136w–6, and 136w–7 of this title, amending this section and sections 136a, 136a–1, 136d, 136q, 136s, 136w, 136w–3, 136x, and 136y of this title and sections 321, 331, 333, 342, and 346a of Title 21, Food and Drugs, and enacting provisions set out as notes under section 136i–2 of this title and sections 301 and 346a of Title 21] may be cited as the 'Food Quality Protection Act of 1996'."

[Another Food Quality Protection Act of 1996 was enacted by Pub. L. No. 104–170, Title IV, 110 Stat. 1513, see section 401(a) of Pub. L. No. 104–170, set out as a note under section 301 of Title 21.]

1988 Amendments. Section 1(a) of Pub. L. No. 100–532 provided that: "This Act [enacting section 136a–1 of this title, amending sections 136, 136a, 136b, 136c, 136d, 136f, 136g, 136h, 136i, 136j, 136k, 136*l*, 136m, 136n, 136*o*, 136p, 136q, 136s, 136v, 136w, 136w–1, 136w–2, and 136y of this title, and enacting provisions set out as notes under sections 136, 136m, and 136y of this title] may be cited as the 'Federal Insecticide, Fungicide, and Rodenticide Act Amendments of 1988'."

1978 Amendments. Section 29 of Pub. L. No. 95–396 provided that: "This Act [which enacted sections 136w–1 to 136w–4 of this title, amended sections 136 to 136f, 136h, 136j, 136*l*, 136*o*, 136q, 136r, 136u to 136w, 136x, and 136y of this title, enacted provisions set out as notes under sections 136a, 136*o*, and 136w–4 of this title, and amended provisions set out as a note under this section] may be cited as the 'Federal Pesticide Act of 1978'."

1972 Acts. Section 1 of Pub. L. No. 92–516 provided: "That this Act [which amended this subchapter generally, and enacted notes set out under this section, and amended sections 1261 and 1471 of Title 15, and sections 321 and 346a of Title 21] may be cited as the 'Federal Environmental Pesticide Control Act of 1972'."

Section 1(a) of Act of June 25, 1947, c. 125, as added by Pub. L. No. 92–516, § 2, 86 Stat. 973 (Oct. 21, 1972), provided that: "This Act [which enacted this subchapter] may be cited as the 'Federal Insecticide, Fungicide, and Rodenticide Act'."

Budget Resolutions

2017 Act. Section 134(a) of Pub. L. No. 115–56, 131 Stat. 1145 (Sept. 8, 2017) provided: "The following sections of the Federal Insecticide, Fungicide, and Rodenticide Act shall continue in effect through the date specified in section 106(3) of this joint resolution [December 8, 2017]—

"(1) subparagraphs (C) through (E) of section 4(i)(1) (7 U.S.C. 136a–1(i)(1)(C)–(E));

"(2) section 4(k)(3) (7 U.S.C. 136a–1(k)(3));

"(3) section 4(k)(4) (7 U.S.C. 136a–1(k)(4)); and

"(4) section 33(c)(3)(B) (7 U.S.C. 136w–8(c)(3)(B))."

Prior Provisions

A prior section 2 of Act of June 25, 1947, was codified as section 135 of this title prior to amendment of Act of June 25, 1947 by Pub. L. No. 92–516.

Federal Compliance with Pollution Control Standards

For provisions relating to the responsibility of the head of each Executive agency for compliance with applicable pollution control standards, see Ex. Ord. No. 12088, 43 FED. REG. 47707 (Oct. 13, 1978), as amended, set out as a note under section 4321 of Title 42, The Public Health and Welfare.

Termination of Trust Territory of the Pacific Islands

For termination of Trust Territory of the Pacific Island, see note set out preceding section 1681 of Title 48.

§ 136a. Registration of pesticides

[FIFRA § 3]

(a) Requirement of registration

Except as provided by this subchapter, no person in any State may distribute or sell to any person any pesticide that is not registered under this subchapter. To the extent necessary to prevent unreasonable adverse effects on the environment, the Administrator may by regulation limit the distribution, sale, or use in any State of any pesticide that is not registered under this subchapter and that is not the subject of an experimental use permit under section 136c of this title or an emergency exemption under section 136p of this title.

(b) Exemptions

A pesticide which is not registered with the Administrator may be transferred if—

(1) the transfer is from one registered establishment to another registered establishment operated by the same producer solely for packaging at the second establishment or for use as a constituent part of another pesticide produced at the second establishment; or

(2) the transfer is pursuant to and in accordance with the requirements of an experimental use permit.

(c) Procedure for registration

(1) Statement required

Each applicant for registration of a pesticide shall file with the Administrator a statement which includes—

(A) the name and address of the applicant and of any other person whose name will appear on the labeling;

(B) the name of the pesticide;

(C) a complete copy of the labeling of the pesticide, a statement of all claims to be made for it, and any directions for its use;

(D) the complete formula of the pesticide;

(E) a request that the pesticide be classified for general use or for restricted use, or for both; and

(F) except as otherwise provided in paragraph (2)(D), if requested by the Administrator, a full description of the tests made and the results thereof upon which the claims are based, or alternatively a citation to data that appear in the public literature or that previously had been submitted to the Administrator and that the Administrator may consider in accordance with the following provisions:

(i) With respect to pesticides containing active ingredients that are initially registered under this subchapter after September 30, 1978, data submitted to support the application for the original registration of the pesticide, or an application for an amendment adding any new use to the registration and that pertains solely to such new use, shall not, without the written permission of the original data submitter, be considered by the Administrator to support an application by another person during a period of ten years following the date the Administrator first registers the pesticide, except that such permission shall not be required in the case of defensive data.

(ii) The period of exclusive data use provided under clause (i) shall be extended 1 additional year for each 3 minor uses registered after August 3, 1996, and within 7 years of the commencement of the exclusive use period, up to a total of 3 additional years for all minor uses registered by the Administrator if the Administrator, in consultation with the Secretary of Agriculture, determines that, based on information provided by an applicant for registration or a registrant, that—

(I) there are insufficient efficacious alternative registered pesticides available for the use;

(II) the alternatives to the minor use pesticide pose greater risks to the environment or human health;

(III) the minor use pesticide plays or will play a significant part in managing pest resistance; or

(IV) the minor use pesticide plays or will play a significant part in an integrated pest management program.

The registration of a pesticide for a minor use on a crop grouping established by the Administrator shall be considered for purposes of this clause 1 minor use for each representative crop for which data are provided in the crop grouping. Any additional exclusive use period under this clause shall be modified as appropriate or terminated if the registrant voluntarily cancels the product or deletes from the registration the minor uses which formed the basis for the extension of the additional exclusive use period or if the Administrator determines that the registrant is not actually marketing the product for such minor uses.

(iii) Except as otherwise provided in clause (i), with respect to data submitted after December 31, 1969, by an applicant or registrant to support an application for registration, experimental use permit, or amendment adding a new use to an existing registration, to support or maintain in effect an existing registration, or for reregistration, the Administrator may, without the permission of the original data submitter, consider any such item of data in support of an application by any other person (hereinafter in this subparagraph referred to as the "applicant") within the fifteen-year period following the date the data were originally submitted only if the applicant has made an offer to compensate the original data submitter and submitted such offer to the Administrator accompanied by evidence of delivery to the original data submitter of the offer. The terms and amount of compensation may be fixed by agreement between the original data submitter and the applicant, or, failing such agreement, binding arbitration under this subparagraph. If, at the end of ninety days after the date of delivery to the original data submitter of the offer to compensate, the original data submitter and the applicant have neither agreed on the amount and terms of compensation nor on a procedure for reaching an agreement on the amount and terms of compensation, either person may initiate binding arbitration proceedings by requesting the Federal Mediation and Conciliation Service to appoint an arbitrator from the roster of arbitrators maintained by such Service. The procedure and rules of the Service shall be applicable to the selection of such arbitrator and to such arbitration proceedings, and the findings and determination of the arbitrator shall be final and conclusive, and no official or court of the United States shall have power or jurisdiction to review any such findings and determination, except for fraud, misrepresentation, or other misconduct by one of the parties to the arbitration or the arbitrator where there is a verified complaint with supporting affidavits attesting to specific instances of such fraud, misrepresentation, or other misconduct. The parties to the arbitration shall share equally in the payment of the fee and expenses of the arbitrator. If the Administrator determines that an original data submitter has failed to participate in a procedure for reaching an agreement or in an arbitration proceeding as required by this subparagraph, or failed to comply with the terms of an agreement or arbitration decision concerning compensation under this subparagraph, the original data submitter shall forfeit the right to compensation for the use of the data in support of the application. Notwithstanding any other provision of this subchapter, if the Administrator determines that an applicant has failed to participate in a procedure for reaching an agreement or in an arbitration proceeding as required by this subparagraph, or failed to comply with the terms of an agreement or arbitration decision concerning compensation under this subparagraph, the Administrator shall deny the application or cancel the registration of the pesticide in support of which the data were used without further hearing. Before the Administrator takes action under either of the preceding two sentences, the Administrator shall furnish to the affected person, by certified mail, notice of intent to take action and allow fifteen days from the date of delivery of the notice for the affected person to respond. If a registration is denied or canceled under this subparagraph, the Administrator may make such order as the Administrator deems appropriate concerning the continued sale and use of existing stocks of such pesticide. Registration action by the Administrator shall not be delayed pending the fixing of compensation.

(iv) After expiration of any period of exclusive use and any period for which compensation is required for the use of an item of data under clauses (i), (ii), and (iii), the Administrator may consider such item of data in support of an application by any other applicant without the permission of the original data submitter and without an offer having been received to compensate the original data submitter for the use of such item of data.

(v) The period of exclusive use provided under clause (ii) shall not take effect until 1 year after August 3, 1996, except where an applicant or registrant is applying for the registration of a pesticide containing an active ingredient not previously registered.

(vi) With respect to data submitted after August 3, 1996, by an applicant or registrant to support an amendment adding a new use to an existing registration that does not retain any period of exclusive use, if such data relates solely to a minor use of a pesticide, such data shall not, without the written permission of the original data submitter, be considered by the Administrator to support an application for a minor use by another person during the period of 10 years following the date of submission of such data. The applicant or registrant at the time the new minor use is requested shall notify the Administrator that to the best of their knowledge the exclusive use period for the pesticide has expired and that the data pertaining solely to the minor use of a pesticide is eligible for the provisions of this paragraph. If the minor use registration which is supported by data submitted pursuant to this subsection is voluntarily canceled or if such data are subsequently used to support a nonminor use, the data shall no longer be subject to the exclusive use provisions of this clause but shall instead be considered by the Administrator in accordance with the provisions of clause (i), as appropriate.

(G) If the applicant is requesting that the registration or amendment to the registration of a pesticide be expedited, an explanation of the basis for the request must be submitted, in accordance with paragraph (10) of this subsection.

(2) Data in support of registration

(A) In general

The Administrator shall publish guidelines specifying the kinds of information which will be required to support the registration of a pesticide and shall revise such guidelines from time to time. If thereafter the Administrator requires any additional kind of information under subparagraph (B) of this paragraph, the Administrator shall permit sufficient time for applicants to obtain such additional information. The Administrator, in establishing standards for data requirements for the registration of pesticides with respect to minor uses, shall make such standards commensurate with the anticipated extent of use, pattern of use, the public health and agricultural need for such minor use, and the level and degree of potential beneficial or adverse effects on man and the environment. The Administrator shall not require a person to submit, in relation to a registration or reregistration of a pesticide for minor agricultural use under this subchapter, any field residue data from a geographic area where the pesticide will not be registered for such use. In the development of these standards, the Administrator shall consider the economic factors of potential national volume of use, extent of distribution, and the impact of the cost of meeting the requirements on the incentives for any potential registrant to undertake the development of the required data. Except as provided by section 136h of this title, within 30 days after the Administrator registers a pesticide under this subchapter the Administrator shall make available to the public the data called for in the registration statement together with such other scientific information as the Administrator deems relevant to the Administrator's decision.

(B) Additional data

(i) If the Administrator determines that additional data are required to maintain in effect an existing registration of a pesticide, the Administrator shall notify all existing registrants of the pesticide to which the determination relates and provide a list of such registrants to any interested person.

(ii) Each registrant of such pesticide shall provide evidence within ninety days after receipt of notification that it is taking appropriate steps to secure the additional data that are required. Two or more registrants may agree to develop jointly, or to share in the cost of developing, such data if they agree and advise the Administrator of their intent within ninety days after notification. Any registrant who agrees to share in the cost of producing the data shall be entitled to examine and rely upon such data in support of maintenance of such registration. The Administrator shall issue a notice of intent to suspend the registration of a pesticide in accordance with the procedures prescribed by clause (iv) if a registrant fails to comply with this clause.

(iii) If, at the end of sixty days after advising the Administrator of their agreement to develop jointly, or share in the cost of developing, data, the registrants have not further agreed on the terms of the data development arrangement or on a procedure for reaching such agreement, any of such registrants may initiate binding arbitration proceedings by requesting the Federal Mediation and Conciliation Service to appoint an arbitrator from the roster of arbitrators maintained by such Service. The procedure and rules of the Service shall be applicable to the selection of such arbitrator and to such arbitration proceedings, and the findings and determination of the arbitrator shall be final and conclusive, and no official or court of the United States shall have power or jurisdiction to review any such findings and determination, except for fraud, misrepresentation, or other misconduct by one of the parties to the arbitration or the arbitrator where there is a verified complaint with supporting affidavits attesting to specific instances of such fraud, misrepresentation, or other misconduct. All parties to the arbitration shall share equally in the payment of the fee and expenses of the arbitrator. The Administrator shall issue a notice of intent to suspend the registration of a pesticide in accordance with the procedures prescribed by clause (iv) if a registrant fails to comply with this clause.

(iv) Notwithstanding any other provision of this subchapter, if the Administrator determines that a registrant, within the time required by the Administrator, has failed to take appropriate steps to secure the data required under this subparagraph, to participate in a procedure for reaching agreement concerning a joint data development arrangement under this subparagraph or in an arbitration proceeding as required by this subparagraph, or to comply with the terms of an agreement or arbitration decision concerning a joint data development arrangement under this subparagraph, the Administrator may issue a notice of intent to suspend such registrant's registration of the pesticide for which additional data is required. The Administrator may include in the notice of intent to suspend such provisions as the Administrator deems appropriate concerning the continued sale and use of existing stocks of such pesticide. Any suspension proposed under this subparagraph shall become final and effective at the end of thirty days from receipt by the registrant of the notice of intent to suspend, unless during that time a request for hearing is made by a person adversely affected by the notice or the registrant has satisfied the Administrator that the registrant has complied fully with the requirements that served as a basis for the notice of intent to suspend. If a hearing is requested, a hearing shall be conducted under section 136d(d) of this title. The only matters for resolution at that hearing shall be whether the registrant has failed to take the action that served as the basis for the notice of intent to suspend the registration of the pesticide for which additional data is required, and whether the Administrator's determination with respect to the disposition of existing stocks is consistent with this subchapter. If a hearing is held, a decision after completion of such hearing shall be final. Notwithstanding any other provision of this subchapter, a hearing shall be held and a determination made within seventy-five days after receipt of a request for such hearing. Any registration suspended under this subparagraph shall be reinstated by the Administrator if the Administrator determines that the registrant has complied fully with the requirements that served as a basis for the suspension of the registration.

(v) Any data submitted under this subparagraph shall be subject to the provisions of paragraph (1)(D). Whenever such data are submitted jointly by two or more registrants, an agent shall be agreed on at the time of the joint submission to handle any subsequent data compensation matters for the joint submitters of such data.

(vi) Upon the request of a registrant the Administrator shall, in the case of a minor use, extend the deadline for the production of residue chemistry data under this subparagraph for data required solely to support that minor use until the final deadline for submission of data under section 136a–1 of this title for the other uses of the pesticide established as of August 3, 1996, if—

(I) the data to support other uses of the pesticide on a food are being provided;

(II) the registrant, in submitting a request for such an extension, provides a schedule, including interim dates to measure progress, to assure that the data production will be completed before the expiration of the extension period;

(III) the Administrator has determined that such extension will not significantly delay the Administrator's schedule for issuing a reregistration eligibility determination required under section 136a–1 of this title; and

(IV) the Administrator has determined that based on existing data, such extension would not significantly increase the risk of any unreasonable adverse effect on the environment. If the Administrator grants an extension under this clause, the Administrator shall monitor the development of the data and shall ensure that the registrant is meeting the schedule for the production of the data. If the Administrator determines that the registrant is not meeting or has not met the schedule for the production of such data, the Administrator may proceed in accordance with clause (iv) regarding the continued registration of the affected products with the minor use and shall inform the public of such action. Notwithstanding the provisions of this clause, the Administrator may take action to modify or revoke the extension under this clause if the Administrator determines that the extension for the minor use may cause an unreasonable adverse effect on the environment. In such circumstance, the Administrator shall provide, in writing to the registrant, a notice revoking the extension of time for submission of data. Such data shall instead be due in accordance with the date established by the Administrator for the submission of the data.

(vii) If the registrant does not commit to support a specific minor use of the pesticide, but is supporting and providing data in a timely and adequate fashion to support uses of the pesticide on a food, or if all uses of the pesticide are nonfood uses and the registrant does not commit to support a specific minor use of the pesticide but is supporting and providing data in a timely and adequate fashion to support other nonfood uses of the pesticide, the Administrator, at the written request of the registrant, shall not take any action pursuant to this clause in regard to such unsupported minor use until the final deadline established as of August 3, 1996, for the submission of data under section 136a–1 of this title for the supported uses identified pursuant to this clause unless the Administrator determines that the absence of the data is significant enough to cause human health or environmental concerns. On the basis of such determination, the Administrator may refuse the request for extension by the registrant. Upon receipt of the request from the registrant, the Administrator shall publish in the Federal Register a notice of the receipt of the request and the effective date upon which the uses not being supported will be voluntarily deleted from the registration pursuant to section 136d(f)(1) of this title. If the Administrator grants an extension under this clause, the Administrator shall monitor the development of the data for the uses being supported and shall ensure that the registrant is meeting the schedule for the production of such data. If the Administrator determines that the registrant is not meeting or has not met the schedule for the production of such data, the Administrator may proceed in accordance with clause (iv) of this subparagraph regarding the continued registration of the affected products with the minor and other uses and shall inform the public of such action in accordance with section 136d(f)(2) of this title. Notwithstanding the provisions of this clause, the Administrator may deny, modify, or revoke the temporary extension under this subparagraph if the Administrator determines that the continuation of the minor use may cause an unreasonable adverse effect on the environment. In the event of modification or revocation, the Administrator shall provide, in writing, to the registrant a notice revoking the temporary extension and establish a new effective date by which the minor use shall be deleted from the registration.

(viii)(I) If data required to support registration of a pesticide under subparagraph (A) is requested by a Federal or State regulatory authority, the Administrator shall, to the extent practicable, coordinate data requirements, test protocols, timetables, and standards of review and reduce burdens and redundancy caused to the registrant by multiple requirements on the registrant.

(II) The Administrator may enter into a cooperative agreement with a State to carry out subclause (I).

(III) Not later than 1 year after August 3, 1996, the Administrator shall develop a process to identify and assist in alleviating future disparities between Federal and State data requirements.

(C) Simplified procedures

Within nine months after September 30, 1978, the Administrator shall, by regulation, prescribe simplified procedures for the registration of pesticides, which shall include the provisions of subparagraph (D) of this paragraph.

(D) Exemption

No applicant for registration of a pesticide who proposes to purchase a registered pesticide from another producer in order to formulate such purchased pesticide into the pesticide that is the subject of the application shall be required to—

(i) submit or cite data pertaining to such purchased product; or

(ii) offer to pay reasonable compensation otherwise required by paragraph (1)(D) of this subsection for the use of any such data.

(E) Minor use waiver

In handling the registration of a pesticide for a minor use, the Administrator may waive otherwise applicable data requirements if the Administrator determines that the absence of such data will not prevent the Administrator from determining—

(i) the incremental risk presented by the minor use of the pesticide; and

(ii) that such risk, if any, would not be an unreasonable adverse effect on the environment.

(3) Application

(A) In general

The Administrator shall review the data after receipt of the application and shall, as expeditiously as possible, either register the pesticide in accordance with paragraph (5), or notify the applicant of the Administrator's determination that it does not comply with the provisions of the subchapter in accordance with paragraph (6).

(B) Identical or substantially similar

(i) The Administrator shall, as expeditiously as possible, review and act on any application received by the Administrator that—

(I) proposes the initial or amended registration of an end-use pesticide that, if registered as proposed, would be identical or substantially similar in composition and labeling to a currently-registered pesticide identified in the application, or that would differ in composition and labeling from such currently-registered pesticide only in ways that would not significantly increase the risk of unreasonable adverse effects on the environment; or

(II) proposes an amendment to the registration of a registered pesticide that does not require scientific review of data.

(ii) In expediting the review of an application for an action described in clause (i), the Administrator shall—

(I) review the application in accordance with section 136w–8(f)(4)(B) of this title and, if the application is found to be incomplete, reject the application;

(II) not later than the applicable decision review time established pursuant to section 136w–8(f)(4)(B) of this title, or, if no review time is established, not later than 90 days after receiving a complete application, notify the registrant if the application has been granted or denied; and

(III) if the application is denied, notify the registrant in writing of the specific reasons for the denial of the application.

(C) Minor use registration

(i) The Administrator shall, as expeditiously as possible, review and act on any complete application—

(I) that proposes the initial registration of a new pesticide active ingredient if the active ingredient is proposed to be registered solely for minor uses, or proposes a registration amendment solely for minor uses to an existing registration; or

(II) for a registration or a registration amendment that proposes significant minor uses.

(ii) For the purposes of clause (i)—

(I) the term "as expeditiously as possible" means that the Administrator shall, to the greatest extent practicable, complete a review and evaluation of all data, submitted with a complete application, within 12 months after the submission of the complete application, and the failure of the Administrator to complete such a review and evaluation under clause (i) shall not be subject to judicial review; and

(II) the term "significant minor uses" means 3 or more minor uses proposed for every nonminor use, a minor use that would, in the judgment of the Administrator, serve as a replacement for any use which has been canceled in the 5 years preceding the receipt of the application, or a minor use that in the opinion of the Administrator would avoid the reissuance of an emergency exemption under section 136p of this title for that minor use.

(D) Adequate time for submission of minor use data

If a registrant makes a request for a minor use waiver, regarding data required by the Administrator, pursuant to paragraph (2)(E), and if the Administrator denies in whole or in part such data waiver request, the registrant shall have a full-time period for providing such data. For purposes of this subparagraph, the term "full-time period" means the time period originally established by the Administrator for submission of such data, beginning with the date of receipt by the registrant of the Administrator's notice of denial.

(4) Notice of application

The Administrator shall publish in the Federal Register, promptly after receipt of the statement and other data required pursuant to paragraphs (1) and (2), a notice of each application for registration of any pesticide if it contains any new active ingredient or if it would entail a changed use pattern. The notice shall provide for a period of 30 days in which any Federal agency or any other interested person may comment.

(5) Approval of registration

The Administrator shall register a pesticide if the Administrator determines that, when considered with any restrictions imposed under subsection (d) of this section—

(A) its composition is such as to warrant the proposed claims for it;

(B) its labeling and other material required to be submitted comply with the requirements of this subchapter;

(C) it will perform its intended function without unreasonable adverse effects on the environment; and

(D) when used in accordance with widespread and commonly recognized practice it will not generally cause unreasonable adverse effects on the environment.

The Administrator shall not make any lack of essentiality a criterion for denying registration of any pesticide. Where two pesticides meet the requirements of this paragraph, one should not be registered in preference to the other. In considering an application for the registration of a pesticide, the Administrator may waive data requirements pertaining to efficacy, in which event the Administrator may register the pesticide without determining that the pesticide's composition is such as to warrant proposed claims of efficacy. If a pesticide is found to be efficacious by any State under section 136v(c) of this title, a presumption is established that the Administrator shall waive data requirements pertaining to efficacy for use of the pesticide in such State.

(6) Denial of registration

If the Administrator determines that the requirements of paragraph (5) for registration are not satisfied, the Administrator shall notify the applicant for registration of the Administrator's determination and of the Administrator's reasons (including the factual basis) therefor, and that, unless the applicant corrects the conditions and notifies the Administrator thereof during the 30-day period beginning with the day after the date on which the applicant receives the notice, the Administrator may refuse to register the pesticide. Whenever the Administrator refuses to register a pesticide, the Administrator shall notify the applicant of the Administrator's decision and of the Administrator's reasons (including the factual basis) therefor. The Administrator shall promptly publish in the Federal Register notice of such denial of registration and the reasons therefor. Upon such notification, the applicant for registration or other interested person with the concurrence of the applicant shall have the same remedies as provided for in section 136d of this title.

(7) Registration under special circumstances

Notwithstanding the provisions of paragraph (5)—

(A) The Administrator may conditionally register or amend the registration of a pesticide if the Administrator determines that (i) the pesticide and proposed use are identical or substantially similar to any currently registered pesticide and use thereof, or differ only in ways that would not significantly increase the risk of unreasonable adverse effects on the environment, and (ii) approving the registration or amendment in the manner proposed by the applicant would not significantly increase the risk of any unreasonable adverse effect on the environment. An applicant seeking conditional registration or amended registration under this subparagraph shall submit such data as would be required to obtain registration of a similar pesticide under paragraph (5). If the applicant is unable to submit an item of data because it has not yet been generated, the Administrator may register or amend the registration of the pesticide under such conditions as will require the submission of such data not later than the time such data are required to be submitted with respect to similar pesticides already registered under this subchapter.

(B) The Administrator may conditionally amend the registration of a pesticide to permit additional uses of such pesticide notwithstanding that data concerning the pesticide may be insufficient to support an unconditional amendment, if the Administrator determines that (i) the applicant has submitted satisfactory data pertaining to the proposed additional use, and (ii) amending the registration in the manner proposed by the applicant would not significantly increase the risk of any unreasonable adverse effect on the environment. Notwithstanding the foregoing provisions of this subparagraph, no registration of a pesticide may be amended to permit an additional use of such pesticide if the Administrator has issued a notice stating that such pesticide, or any ingredient thereof, meets or exceeds risk criteria associated in whole or in part with human dietary exposure enumerated in regulations issued under this subchapter, and during the pendency of any risk-benefit evaluation initiated by such notice, if (I) the additional use of such pesticide involves a major food or feed crop, or (II) the additional use of such pesticide involves a minor food or feed crop and the Administrator determines, with the concurrence of the Secretary of Agriculture, there is available an effective alternative pesticide that does not meet or exceed such risk criteria. An applicant seeking amended registration under this subparagraph shall submit such data as would be required to obtain registration of a similar pesticide under paragraph (5). If the applicant is unable to submit an item of data (other than data pertaining to the proposed additional use) because it has not yet been generated, the Administrator may amend the registration under such conditions as will require the submission of such data not later than the time such data are required to be submitted with respect to similar pesticides already registered under this subchapter.

(C) The Administrator may conditionally register a pesticide containing an active ingredient not contained in any currently registered pesticide for a period reasonably sufficient for the generation and submission of required data (which are lacking because a period reasonably sufficient for generation of the data has not elapsed since the Administrator first imposed the data requirement) on the condition that by the end of such period the Administrator receives such data and the data do not meet or exceed risk criteria enumerated in regulations issued under this subchapter, and on such other conditions as the Administrator may prescribe. A conditional registration under this subparagraph shall be granted only if the Administrator determines that use of the pesticide during such period will not cause any unreasonable adverse effect on the environment, and that use of the pesticide is in the public interest.

(8) Interim administrative review

Notwithstanding any other provision of this subchapter, the Administrator may not initiate a public interim administrative review process to develop a risk-benefit evaluation of the ingredients of a pesticide or any of its uses prior to initiating a formal action to cancel, suspend, or deny registration of such pesticide, required under this subchapter, unless such interim administrative process is based on a validated test or other significant evidence raising prudent concerns of unreasonable adverse risk to man or to the environment. Notice of the definition of the terms "validated test" and "other significant evidence" as used herein shall be published by the Administrator in the Federal Register.

(9) Labeling

(A) Additional statements

Subject to subparagraphs (B) and (C), it shall not be a violation of this subchapter for a registrant to modify the labeling of an antimicrobial pesticide product to include relevant information on product efficacy, product composition, container composition or design, or other characteristics that do not relate to any pesticidal claim or pesticidal activity.

(B) Requirements

Proposed labeling information under subparagraph (A) shall not be false or misleading, shall not conflict with or detract from any statement required by law or the Administrator as a condition of registration, and shall be substantiated on the request of the Administrator.

(C) Notification and disapproval

(i) Notification

A registration may be modified under subparagraph (A) if—

(I) the registrant notifies the Administrator in writing not later than 60 days prior to distribution or sale of a product bearing the modified labeling; and

(II) the Administrator does not disapprove of the modification under clause (ii).

(ii) Disapproval

Not later than 30 days after receipt of a notification under clause (i), the Administrator may disapprove the modification by sending the registrant notification in writing stating that the proposed language is not acceptable and stating the reasons why the Administrator finds the proposed modification unacceptable.

(iii) Restriction on sale

A registrant may not sell or distribute a product bearing a disapproved modification.

(iv) Objection

A registrant may file an objection in writing to a disapproval under clause (ii) not later than 30 days after receipt of notification of the disapproval.

(v) Final action

A decision by the Administrator following receipt and consideration of an objection filed under clause (iv) shall be considered a final agency action.

(D) Use dilution

The label or labeling required under this subchapter for an antimicrobial pesticide that is or may be diluted for use may have a different statement of caution or protective measures for use of the recommended diluted solution of the pesticide than for use of a concentrate of the pesticide if the Administrator determines that—

(i) adequate data have been submitted to support the statement proposed for the diluted solution uses; and

(ii) the label or labeling provides adequate protection for exposure to the diluted solution of the pesticide.

(10) Expedited registration of pesticides

(A) Not later than 1 year after August 3, 1996, the Administrator shall, utilizing public comment, develop procedures and guidelines, and expedite the review of an application for registration of a pesticide or an amendment to a registration that satisfies such guidelines.

(B) Any application for registration or an amendment, including biological and conventional pesticides, will be considered for expedited review under this paragraph. An application for registration or an amendment shall qualify for expedited review if use of the pesticide proposed by the application may reasonably be expected to accomplish 1 or more of the following:

(i) Reduce the risks of pesticides to human health.

(ii) Reduce the risks of pesticides to nontarget organisms.

(iii) Reduce the potential for contamination of groundwater, surface water, or other valued environmental resources.

(iv) Broaden the adoption of integrated pest management strategies, or make such strategies more available or more effective.

(C) The Administrator, not later than 30 days after receipt of an application for expedited review, shall notify the applicant whether the application is complete. If it is found to be incomplete, the Administrator may either reject the request for expedited review or ask the applicant for additional information to satisfy the guidelines developed under subparagraph (A).

(11) Interagency working group.—

(A) Definition of covered agency.—In this paragraph, the term 'covered agency' means any of the following:

(i) The Department of Agriculture.

(ii) The Department of Commerce.

(iii) The Department of the Interior.

(iv) The Council on Environmental Quality.

(v) The Environmental Protection Agency.

(B) Establishment.—The Administrator shall establish an interagency working group, to be comprised of representatives from each covered agency, to provide recommendations regarding, and to implement a strategy for improving, the consultation process required under section 7 of the Endangered Species Act of 1973 (16 U.S.C. 1536) for pesticide registration and registration review.

(C) Duties.—The interagency working group established under subparagraph (B) shall—

(i) analyze relevant Federal law (including regulations) and case law for purposes of providing an outline of the legal and regulatory framework for the consultation process referred to in that subparagraph, including—

(I) requirements under this Act and the Endangered Species Act of 1973 (16 U.S.C. 1531 et seq.);

(II) Federal case law regarding the intersection of this Act and the Endangered Species Act of 1973 (16 U.S.C. 1531 et seq.); and

(III) Federal regulations relating to the pesticide consultation process;

(ii) provide advice regarding methods of—

(I) defining the scope of actions of the covered agencies that are subject to the consultation requirement referred to in subparagraph (B); and

(II) properly identifying and classifying effects of actions of the covered agencies with respect to that consultation requirement;

(iii) identify the obligations and limitations under Federal law of each covered agency for purposes of providing a legal and regulatory framework for developing the recommendations referred to in subparagraph (B);

(iv) review practices for the consultation referred to in subparagraph (B) to identify problem areas, areas for improvement, and best practices for conducting that consultation among the covered agencies;

(v) develop scientific and policy approaches to increase the accuracy and timeliness of the process for that consultation, in accordance with requirements of this Act and the Endangered Species Act of 1973 (16 U.S.C. 1531 et seq.), including—

(I) processes to efficiently share data and coordinate analyses among the Department of Agriculture, the Department of Commerce, the Department of the Interior, and the Environmental Protection Agency;

(II) a streamlined process for identifying which actions require no consultation, informal consultation, or formal consultation;

(III) an approach that will provide clarity with respect to what constitutes the best scientific and commercial data available in the fields of pesticide use and ecological risk assessment, pursuant to section 7(a)(2) of the Endangered Species Act of 1973 (16 U.S.C. 1536(a)(2)); and

(IV) approaches that enable the Environmental Protection Agency to better assist the Department of the Interior and the Department of Commerce in carrying out obligations under that section in a timely and efficient manner; and

(vi) propose and implement a strategy to implement approaches to consultations under the Endangered Species Act of 1973 (16 U.S.C. 1531 et seq.) and document that strategy in a memorandum of understanding, revised regulations, or another appropriate format to promote durable cooperation among the covered agencies.

(D) Reports.—

(i) Progress Reports.—

(I) In general.—Not later than 18 months after the date of enactment of this paragraph, the Administrator, in coordination with the head of each other covered agency, shall submit to the Committee on Agriculture of the House of Representatives and the Committee on Agriculture, Nutrition, and Forestry of the Senate a report describing the progress of the working group in developing the recommendations under subparagraph (B).

(II) Requirements.—The report under this clause shall—

(aa) reflect the perspectives of each covered agency; and

(bb) identify areas of new consensus and continuing topics of disagreement and debate.

(ii) Results.—

(I) In general.—Not later than 1 year after the date of enactment of this paragraph, the Administrator, in coordination with the head of each other covered agency, shall submit to the Committee on Agriculture of the House of Representatives and the Committee on Agriculture, Nutrition, and Forestry of the Senate a report describing—

(aa) the recommendations developed under subparagraph (B); and

(bb) plans for implementation of those recommendations.

(II) Requirements.—The report under this clause shall—

(aa) reflect the perspectives of each covered agency; and

(bb) identify areas of consensus and continuing topics of disagreement and debate, if any.

(iii) Implementation.—Not later than 1 year after the date of submission of the report under clause (i), the Administrator, in coordination with the head of each other covered agency, shall submit to the Committee on Agriculture of the House of Representatives and the Committee on Agriculture, Nutrition, and Forestry of the Senate a report describing—

(I) the implementation of the recommendations referred to in that clause;

(II) the extent to which that implementation improved the consultation process referred to in subparagraph (B); and

(III) any additional recommendations for improvements to the process described in subparagraph (B).

(iv) Other reports.—Not later than the date that is 180 days after the date of submission of the report under clause (iii), and not less frequently than once every 180 days thereafter during the 5-year period beginning on that date, the Administrator, in coordination with the head of each other covered agency, shall submit to the Committee on Agriculture of the House of Representatives and the Committee on Agriculture, Nutrition, and Forestry of the Senate a report describing—

(I) the implementation of the recommendations referred to in that clause;

(II) the extent to which that implementation improved the consultation process referred to in subparagraph (B); and

(III) any additional recommendations for improvements to the process described in subparagraph (B).

(E) Consultation with private sector.—In carrying out the duties under this paragraph, the working group shall, as appropriate—

(i) consult with, representatives of interested industry stakeholders and nongovernmental organizations; and

(ii) take into consideration factors, such as actual and potential differences in interest between, and the views of, those stakeholders and organizations.

(F) Federal Advisory Committee Act.—The Federal Advisory Committee Act (5 U.S.C. App.) shall not apply to the working group established under this paragraph.

(G) Savings clause.—Nothing in this paragraph supersedes any provision of—

(i) this Act; or

(ii) the Endangered Species Act of 1973 (16 U.S.C. 1531 et seq.), including the requirements under section 7 of that Act (16 U.S.C. 1536).

(d) Classification of pesticides

(1) Classification for general use, restricted use, or both

(A) As a part of the registration of a pesticide the Administrator shall classify it as being for general use or for restricted use. If the Administrator determines that some of the uses for which the pesticide is registered should be for general use and that other uses for which it is registered should be for restricted use, the Administrator shall classify it for both general use and restricted use. Pesticide uses may be classified by regulation on the initial classification, and registered pesticides may be classified prior to reregistration. If some of the uses of the pesticide are classified for general use, and other uses are classified for restricted use, the directions relating to its general uses shall be clearly separated and distinguished from those directions relating to its restricted uses. The Administrator may require that its packaging and labeling for restricted uses shall be clearly distinguishable from its packaging and labeling for general uses.

(B) If the Administrator determines that the pesticide, when applied in accordance with its directions for use, warnings and cautions and for the uses for which it is registered, or for one or more of such uses, or in accordance with a widespread and commonly recognized practice, will not generally cause unreasonable adverse effects on the environment, the Administrator will classify the pesticide, or the particular use or uses of the pesticide to which the determination applies, for general use.

(C) If the Administrator determines that the pesticide, when applied in accordance with its directions for use, warnings and cautions and for the uses for which it is registered, or for one or more of such uses, or in accordance with a widespread and commonly recognized practice, may generally cause, without additional regulatory restrictions, unreasonable adverse effects on the environment, including injury to the applicator, the Administrator shall classify the pesticide, or the particular use or uses to which the determination applies, for restricted use:

(i) If the Administrator classifies a pesticide, or one or more uses of such pesticide, for restricted use because of a determination that the acute dermal or inhalation toxicity of the pesticide presents a hazard to the applicator or other persons, the pesticide shall be applied for any use to which the restricted classification applies only by or under the direct supervision of a certified applicator.

(ii) If the Administrator classifies a pesticide, or one or more uses of such pesticide, for restricted use because of a determination that its use without additional regulatory restriction may cause unreasonable adverse effects on the environment, the pesticide shall be applied for any use to which the determination applies only by or under the direct supervision of a certified applicator, or subject to such other restrictions as the Administrator may provide by regulation. Any such regulation shall be reviewable in the appropriate court of appeals upon petition of a person adversely affected filed within 60 days of the publication of the regulation in final form.

(2) Change in classification

If the Administrator determines that a change in the classification of any use of a pesticide from general use to restricted use is necessary to prevent unreasonable adverse effects on the environment, the Administrator shall notify the registrant of such pesticide of such determination at least forty-five days before making the change and shall publish the proposed change in the Federal Register. The registrant, or other interested person with the concurrence of the registrant, may seek relief from such determination under section 136d(b) of this title.

(3) Change in classification from restricted use to general use

The registrant of any pesticide with one or more uses classified for restricted use may petition the Administrator to change any such classification from restricted to general use. Such petition shall set out the basis for the registrant's position that restricted use classification is unnecessary because classification of the pesticide for general use would not cause unreasonable adverse effects on the environment. The Administrator, within sixty days after receiving such petition, shall notify the registrant whether the petition has been granted or denied. Any denial shall contain an explanation therefor and any such denial shall be subject to judicial review under section 136n of this title.

(e) Products with same formulation and claims

Products which have the same formulation, are manufactured by the same person, the labeling of which contains the same claims, and the labels of which bear a designation identifying the product as the same pesticide may be registered as a single pesticide; and additional names and labels shall be added to the registration by supplemental statements.

(f) Miscellaneous

(1) Effect of change of labeling or formulation

If the labeling or formulation for a pesticide is changed, the registration shall be amended to reflect such change if the Administrator determines that the change will not violate any provision of this subchapter.

(2) Registration not a defense

In no event shall registration of an article be construed as a defense for the commission of any offense under this subchapter. As long as no cancellation proceedings are in effect registration of a pesticide shall be prima facie evidence that the pesticide, its labeling and packaging comply with the registration provisions of the subchapter.

(3) Authority to consult other Federal agencies

In connection with consideration of any registration or application for registration under this section, the Administrator may consult with any other Federal agency.

(4) Mixtures of nitrogen stabilizers and fertilizer products

Any mixture or other combination of—

(A) 1 or more nitrogen stabilizers registered under this subchapter; and

(B) 1 or more fertilizer products,

shall not be subject to the provisions of this section or sections 136a–1, 136c, 136e, 136m, and 136*o*(a)(2) of this title if the mixture or other combination is accompanied by the labeling required under this subchapter for the nitrogen stabilizer contained in the mixture or other combination, the mixture or combination is mixed or combined in accordance with such labeling, and the mixture or combination does not contain any active ingredient other than the nitrogen stabilizer.

(g) Registration review

(1) General rule

(A) Periodic review

(i) In general

The registrations of pesticides are to be periodically reviewed.

(ii) Regulations

In accordance with this subparagraph, the Administrator shall by regulation establish a procedure for accomplishing the periodic review of registrations.

(iii) Initial registration review

The Administrator shall complete the registration review of each pesticide or pesticide case, which may be composed of 1 or more active ingredients and the products associated with the active ingredients, not later than the later of—

(I) October 1, 2022; or

(II) the date that is 15 years after the date on which the first pesticide containing a new active ingredient is registered.

(iv) Subsequent registration review

Not later than 15 years after the date on which the initial registration review is completed under clause (iii) and each 15 years thereafter, the Administrator shall complete a subsequent registration review for each pesticide or pesticide case.

(v) Cancellation

No registration shall be canceled as a result of the registration review process unless the Administrator follows the procedures and substantive requirements of section 136d of this title.

(B) Docketing

(i) In general

Subject to clause (ii), after meeting with 1 or more individuals that are not government employees to discuss matters relating to a registration review, the Administrator shall place in the docket minutes of the meeting, a list of attendees, and any documents exchanged at the meeting, not later than the earlier of—

(I) the date that is 45 days after the meeting; or

(II) the date of issuance of the registration review decision.

(ii) Protected information

The Administrator shall identify, but not include in the docket, any confidential business information the disclosure of which is prohibited by section 136h of this title.

(C) Limitation

Nothing in this subsection shall prohibit the Administrator from undertaking any other review of a pesticide pursuant to this subchapter.

(2) Data

(A) Submission required

The Administrator shall use the authority in subsection (c)(2)(B) of this section to require the submission of data when such data are necessary for a registration review.

(B) Data submission, compensation, and exemption

For purposes of this subsection, the provisions of subsections (c)(1), (c)(2)(B), and (c)(2)(D) of this section shall be utilized for and be applicable to any data required for registration review.

(h) Registration requirements for antimicrobial pesticides

(1) Evaluation of process

To the maximum extent practicable consistent with the degrees of risk presented by an antimicrobial pesticide and the type of review appropriate to evaluate the risks, the Administrator shall identify and evaluate reforms to the antimicrobial registration process that would reduce review periods existing as of August 3, 1996, for antimicrobial pesticide product registration applications and applications for amended registration of antimicrobial pesticide products, including—

(A) new antimicrobial active ingredients;

(B) new antimicrobial end-use products;

(C) substantially similar or identical antimicrobial pesticides; and

(D) amendments to antimicrobial pesticide registrations.

(2) Review time period reduction goal

Each reform identified under paragraph (1) shall be designed to achieve the goal of reducing the review period following submission of a complete application, consistent with the degree of risk, to a period of not more than—

(A) 540 days for a new antimicrobial active ingredient pesticide registration;

(B) 270 days for a new antimicrobial use of a registered active ingredient;

(C) 120 days for any other new antimicrobial product;

(D) 90 days for a substantially similar or identical antimicrobial product;

(E) 90 days for an amendment to an antimicrobial registration that does not require scientific review of data; and

(F) 120 days for an amendment to an antimicrobial registration that requires scientific review of data and that is not otherwise described in this paragraph.

(3) Implementation

(A) Proposed rulemaking

(i) Issuance

Not later than 270 days after August 3, 1996, the Administrator shall publish in the Federal Register proposed regulations to accelerate and improve the review of antimicrobial pesticide products designed to implement, to the extent practicable, the goals set forth in paragraph (2).

(ii) Requirements

Proposed regulations issued under clause (i) shall—

(I) define the various classes of antimicrobial use patterns, including household, industrial, and institutional disinfectants and sanitizing pesticides, preservatives, water treatment, and pulp and paper mill additives, and other such products intended to disinfect, sanitize, reduce, or mitigate growth or development of microbiological organisms, or protect inanimate objects, industrial processes or systems, surfaces, water, or other chemical substances from contamination, fouling, or deterioration caused by bacteria, viruses, fungi, protozoa, algae, or slime;

(II) differentiate the types of review undertaken for antimicrobial pesticides;

(III) conform the degree and type of review to the risks and benefits presented by antimicrobial pesticides and the function of review under this subchapter, considering the use patterns of the product, toxicity, expected exposure, and product type;

(IV) ensure that the registration process is sufficient to maintain antimicrobial pesticide efficacy and that antimicrobial pesticide products continue to meet product performance standards and effectiveness levels for each type of label claim made; and

(V) implement effective and reliable deadlines for process management.

(iii) Comments

In developing the proposed regulations, the Administrator shall solicit the views from registrants and other affected parties to maximize the effectiveness of the rule development process.

(B) Final regulations

(i) Issuance

The Administrator shall issue final regulations not later than 240 days after the close of the comment period for the proposed regulations.

(ii) Failure to meet goal

If a goal described in paragraph (2) is not met by the final regulations, the Administrator shall identify the goal, explain why the goal was not attained, describe the element of the regulations included instead, and identify future steps to attain the goal.

(iii) Requirements

In issuing final regulations, the Administrator shall—

(I) consider the establishment of a certification process for regulatory actions involving risks that can be responsibly managed, consistent with the degree of risk, in the most cost-efficient manner;

(II) consider the establishment of a certification process by approved laboratories as an adjunct to the review process;

(III) use all appropriate and cost-effective review mechanisms, including—

(aa) expanded use of notification and non-notification procedures;

(bb) revised procedures for application review; and

(cc) allocation of appropriate resources to ensure streamlined management of antimicrobial pesticide registrations; and

(IV) clarify criteria for determination of the completeness of an application.

(C) Expedited review

This subsection does not affect the requirements or extend the deadlines or review periods contained in subsection (c)(3) of this section.

(D) Alternative review periods

If the final regulations to carry out this paragraph are not effective 630 days after August 3, 1996, until the final regulations become effective, the review period, beginning on the date of receipt by the Agency of a complete application, shall be—

(i) 2 years for a new antimicrobial active ingredient pesticide registration;

(ii) 1 year for a new antimicrobial use of a registered active ingredient;

(iii) 180 days for any other new antimicrobial product;

(iv) 90 days for a substantially similar or identical antimicrobial product;

(v) 90 days for an amendment to an antimicrobial registration that does not require scientific review of data; and

(vi) 120 days for an amendment to an antimicrobial registration that requires scientific review of data and that is not otherwise described in this subparagraph.

(E) Wood preservatives

An application for the registration, or for an amendment to the registration, of a wood preservative product for which a claim of pesticidal activity listed in section 136(mm) of this title is made (regardless of any other pesticidal claim that is made with respect to the product) shall be reviewed by the Administrator within the same period as that established under this paragraph for an antimicrobial pesticide product application, consistent with the degree of risk posed by the use of the wood preservative product, if the application requires the applicant to satisfy the same data requirements as are required to support an application for a wood preservative product that is an antimicrobial pesticide.

(F) Notification

(i) In general

Subject to clause (iii), the Administrator shall notify an applicant whether an application has been granted or denied not later than the final day of the appropriate review period under this paragraph, unless the applicant and the Administrator agree to a later date.

(ii) Final decision

If the Administrator fails to notify an applicant within the period of time required under clause (i), the failure shall be considered an agency action unlawfully withheld or unreasonably delayed for purposes of judicial review under chapter 7 of Title 5.

(iii) Exemption

This subparagraph does not apply to an application for an antimicrobial pesticide that is filed under subsection (c)(3)(B) of this section prior to 90 days after August 3, 1996.

(iv) Limitation

Notwithstanding clause (ii), the failure of the Administrator to notify an applicant for an amendment to a registration for an antimicrobial pesticide shall not be judicially reviewable in a Federal or State court if the amendment requires scientific review of data within—

(I) the time period specified in subparagraph (D)(vi), in the absence of a final regulation under subparagraph (B); or

(II) the time period specified in paragraph (2)(F), if adopted in a final regulation under subparagraph (B).

(4) Annual report

(A) Submission

Beginning on August 3, 1996, and ending on the date that the goals under paragraph (2) are achieved, the Administrator shall, not later than March 1 of each year, prepare and submit an annual report to the Committee on Agriculture of the House of Representatives and the Committee on Agriculture, Nutrition, and Forestry of the Senate.

(B) Requirements

A report submitted under subparagraph (A) shall include a description of—

(i) measures taken to reduce the backlog of pending registration applications;

(ii) progress toward achieving reforms under this subsection; and

(iii) recommendations to improve the activities of the Agency pertaining to antimicrobial registrations.

(Act of June 25, 1947, c. 125, § 3, as added by Pub. L. No. 92–516, § 2, 86 Stat. 979 (Oct. 21, 1972); and amended by Pub. L. No. 94–140, § 12, 89 Stat. 755 (Nov. 28, 1975); Pub. L. No. 95–396, §§ 2(a), 3–8, 92 Stat. 820, 824–827 (Sept. 30, 1978,); Pub. L. No. 100–532, Title I, §§ 102(b), 103, Title VI, § 601(b)(1), Title VIII, § 801(b), 102 Stat. 2667, 2677, 2680 (Oct. 25, 1988); Pub. L. No. 101–624, Title XIV, § 1492, 104 Stat. 3628 (Nov. 28, 1990); Pub. L. No. 102–237, Title X, § 1006(a)(3), (b)(1), (2), (c), 105 Stat. 1894 to 1896 (Dec. 13, 1991); Pub. L. No. 104–170, Title I, §§ 105(b), 106(b), Title II, §§ 210(b), (c)(1), (d), (e), (f)(2), 222 to 224, 231, 250, 110 Stat. 1491, 1494 to 1497, 1499, 1503, 1504, 1508, 1510 (Aug. 3, 1996); Pub. L. No. 108–199, Div. G, Title V, § 501(b), 118 Stat. 419 (Jan. 23, 2004);

Pub. L. No. 110–94, §§ 2, 3, 121 Stat. 1000 (Oct. 9, 2007); Pub. L. No. 115–334, § 10115, 132 Stat. 4490, 4914–4917 (Dec. 20, 2018).)

HISTORICAL AND STATUTORY NOTES

Codifications

Section 1006(c) of Pub. L. No. 102–237 provided that the phrase sought to be struck out of subsec. (c)(2)(D) of this section by section 102(b)(2)(A) of Pub. L. No. 100–532 is to be deemed to be "an end-use product", rather than "an end use product", as such phrase appeared in section 102(b)(2)(A) of Pub. L. No. 100–532.

Effective and Applicability Provisions

2007 Acts. Pub. L. No. 110–94, § 6, 121 Stat. 1007 (Oct. 9, 2007), provided that: "This Act and the amendments made by this Act [amending 7 U.S.C.A. §§ 136a, 136a–1, and 136w–8 and 21 U.S.C.A. § 346a, and enacting provisions set out as a note under 7 U.S.C.A. § 136a] take effect on October 1, 2007."

2004 Acts. Pub. L. No. 108–199, Div. G, Title V, § 501(h), 118 Stat. 434 (Jan. 23, 2004), provided that: "Except as otherwise provided in this section and the amendments made by this section, this section and the amendments made by this section [enacting 7 U.S.C.A. § 136w–8, amending this section and 7 U.S.C.A. §§ 136a–1, 136x, and 136y, and enacting provisions set out as a note under 7 U.S.C.A. § 136] take effect on the date that is 60 days after the date of enactment of this Act [Jan. 23, 2004]."

1991 Acts. Amendments by Pub. L. No. 102–237 effective Dec. 13, 1991, see section 1101(a) of Pub. L. No. 102–237, set out as a note under section 1421 of this title.

1988 Acts. Amendment by Pub. L. No. 100–532 effective on expiration of 60 days after October 25, 1988, see section 901 of Pub. L. No. 100–532, set out as a note under section 136 of this title.

1978 Acts. Section 2(b) of Pub. L. No. 95–396 provided that: "The amendment to section 3(c)(1)(D) of the Federal Insecticide, Fungicide, and Rodenticide Act [subsec. (c)(1)(D) of this section] made by this section shall apply with respect to all applications for registration approved after the date of enactment of this Act [Sept. 30, 1978]."

1972 Acts. Section effective at the close of Oct. 21, 1972, except if regulations are necessary for the implementation of any provision that becomes effective on Oct. 21, 1972, and continuation in effect of the provisions of subchapter I of this chapter and regulations thereunder as in effect prior to Oct. 21, 1972, until superseded by provisions of Pub. L. No. 92–516 and regulations thereunder, see section 4 of Pub. L. No. 92–516, set out as a note under section 136 of this title.

Severability of Provisions

If any provision of Pub. L. No. 101–624 or the application thereof to any person or circumstance is held invalid, such invalidity not to affect other provisions or applications of Pub. L. No. 101–624 which can be given effect without regard to the invalid provision or application, see section 2519 of Pub. L. No. 101–624, set out as a note under section 1421 of this title.

Prior Provisions

A prior section 3 of Act of June 25, 1947, was codified as section 135a of this title prior to amendment of Act of June 25, 1947, by Pub. L. 92–516.

Reports to Congress

Pub. L. No. 113–79, § 10013, 128 Stat. 951–52 (Feb. 7, 2014), provided that:

"(a) In general.—Not later than 180 days and 1 year after the date of enactment of this Act, the Administrator of the Environmental Protection Agency and Secretaries of Commerce, Agriculture and the Interior shall submit to the Committees on Agriculture and Natural Resources of the House of Representatives and the Committees on Agriculture, Nutrition, and Forestry and Environment and Public Works of the Senate, 2 reports that describe approaches and actions taken by the Environmental Protection Agency, the United States Fish and Wildlife Service, and the National Marine Fisheries Service—

"(1) to implement recommendations, including an analysis of how any identified delays to implementation will be overcome, of the 2013 Expert Report authored by the National Research Council of the National Academies entitled "Assessing Risks to Endangered and Threatened Species from Pesticides";

"(2) to otherwise minimize delays in integrating—

"(A) the pesticide registration and registration review requirements of sections 3 and 33 of the Federal Insecticide, Fungicide, and Rodenticide Act (**7 U.S.C. 136a**, 136w–8); and

"(B) the species and habitat protection processes described in sections 7 and 10 of the Endangered Species Act of 1973 (16 U.S.C. 1536, 1539); and

"(3) to ensure public participation and transparency during the development, implementation, and evaluation of the approaches to implement the recommendations contained in the report described in paragraph (1).

"(b) **Requirement for final report.**—In addition to the requirements of subsection (a), the final report submitted to Congress under that subsection shall—

"(1) inform Congress of specific actions that have been and will be taken to address the recommendations identified in subsection (a)(1), including an evaluation to establish that—

"(A) the approaches utilize the best available science;

"(B) reasonable and prudent alternatives within biological opinions are technologically and economically feasible;

"(C) reasonable and prudent measures are necessary and appropriate; and

"(D) the agencies ensure public participation and transparency in the development of reasonable and prudent alternatives and reasonable and prudent measures; and

"(2) update the study and report required by subsections (b) and (c) of section 1010 of Public Law 100–478 (**7 U.S.C. 136a** note)."

Pesticides Labeling Program; Education, Study and Report to Congress

Pub. L. No. 100–478, Title I, § 1010, 102 Stat. 2313 (Oct. 7, 1988), provided that:

"(a) **Education.** The Administrator of the Environmental Protection Agency in cooperation with the Secretary of Agriculture and the Secretary of the Interior, promptly upon enactment of this Act [which was approved Oct. 7, 1988], shall conduct a program to inform and educate fully persons engaged in agricultural food and fiber commodity production of any proposed pesticide labeling program or requirements that may be imposed by the Administrator in compliance with the Endangered Species Act (16 U.S.C. 1531 et seq.) [section 1531 et seq. of Title 16, Conservation]. The Administrator also shall provide the public with notice of, and opportunity for comment on, the elements of any such program and requirements based on compliance with the Endangered Species Act, including (but not limited to) an identification of any pesticides affected by the program; an explanation of the restriction or prohibition on the user or applicator of any such pesticide; an identification of those geographic areas affected by any pesticide restriction or prohibition; an identification of the effects of any restricted or prohibited pesticide on endangered or threatened species; and an identification of the endangered or threatened species along with a general description of the geographic areas in which such species are located wherein the application of a pesticide will be restricted, prohibited, or its use otherwise limited, unless the Secretary of the Interior determines that the disclosure of such information may create a substantial risk of harm to such species or its habitat.

"(b) **Study.** The Administrator of the Environmental Protection Agency, jointly with the Secretary of Agriculture and the Secretary of the Interior, shall conduct a study to identify reasonable and prudent means available to the Administrator to implement the endangered species pesticides labeling program which would comply with the Endangered Species Act of 1973, as amended, and which would allow persons to continue production of agricultural food and fiber commodities. Such study shall include investigation by the Administrator of the best available methods to develop maps and the best available alternatives to mapping as means of identifying those circumstances in which use of pesticides may be restricted; identification of alternatives to prohibitions on pesticide use, including, but not limited to, alternative pesticides and application methods and other agricultural practices which can be used in lieu of any pesticides whose use may be restricted by the labeling program; examination of methods to improve coordination among the Environmental Protection Agency, Department of Agriculture, and Department of the Interior in administration of the labeling program; and analysis of the means of implementing the endangered species pesticides labeling program or alternatives to such a program, if any, to promote the conservation of endangered or threatened species and to minimize the impacts to persons engaged in agricultural food and fiber commodity production and other affected pesticide users and applicators.

"(c) Report. The Administrator of the Environmental Protection Agency in cooperation with the Secretary of Agriculture and the Secretary of the Interior shall submit a report within one year of the date of enactment of this Act [Oct. 7, 1988], presenting the results of the study conducted pursuant to subsection (b) of this section to the Committee on Merchant Marine and Fisheries and the Committee on Agriculture of the United States House of Representatives, and the Committee on Environment and Public Works and the Committee on Agriculture, Nutrition, and Forestry of the United States Senate."

Biological Pesticide Handling Study

Section 1498 of Pub. L. No. 101–624 provided that:

"(a) Study.—Not later than September 30, 1992, the National Academy of Sciences shall conduct a study of the biological control programs and registration procedures utilized by the Food and Drug Administration, the Animal and Plant Health Inspection Service, and the Environmental Protection Agency.

"(b) Development of procedures.—Not later than 1 year after the completion of the study under subsection (a), the agencies and offices described in such subsection shall develop and implement a common process for reviewing and approving biological control applications that are submitted to such agencies and offices that shall be based on the study conducted under such subsection and the recommendation of the National Academy of Sciences, and other public comment."

§ 136a–1. Reregistration of registered pesticides

[FIFRA § 4]

(a) General rule

The Administrator shall reregister, in accordance with this section, each registered pesticide containing any active ingredient contained in any pesticide first registered before November 1, 1984, except for any pesticide as to which the Administrator has determined, after November 1, 1984, and before the effective date of this section, that—

(1) there are no outstanding data requirements; and

(2) the requirements of section 136a(c)(5) of this title have been satisfied.

(b) Reregistration phases

Reregistrations of pesticides under this section shall be carried out in the following phases:

(1) The first phase shall include the listing under subsection (c) of this section of the active ingredients of the pesticides that will be reregistered.

(2) The second phase shall include the submission to the Administrator under subsection (d) of this section of notices by registrants respecting their intention to seek reregistration, identification by registrants of missing and inadequate data for such pesticides, and commitments by registrants to replace such missing or inadequate data within the applicable time period.

(3) The third phase shall include submission to the Administrator by registrants of the information required under subsection (e) of this section.

(4) The fourth phase shall include an independent, initial review by the Administrator under subsection (f) of this section of submissions under phases two and three, identification of outstanding data requirements, and the issuance, as necessary, of requests for additional data.

(5) The fifth phase shall include the review by the Administrator under subsection (g) of this section of data submitted for reregistration and appropriate regulatory action by the Administrator.

(c) Phase one

(1) Priority for reregistration

For purposes of the reregistration of the pesticides described in subsection (a) of this section, the Administrator shall list the active ingredients of pesticides and shall give priority to, among others, active ingredients (other than active ingredients for which registration standards have been issued before the effective date of this section) that—

(A) are in use on or in food or feed and may result in postharvest residues;

(B) may result in residues of potential toxicological concern in potable ground water, edible fish, or shellfish;

(C) have been determined by the Administrator before the effective date of this section to have significant outstanding data requirements; or

(D) are used on crops, including in greenhouses and nurseries, where worker exposure is most likely to occur.

(2) Reregistration lists

For purposes of reregistration under this section, the Administrator shall by order—

(A) not later than 70 days after the effective date of this section, list pesticide active ingredients for which registration standards have been issued before such effective date;

(B) not later than 4 months after such effective date, list the first 150 pesticide active ingredients, as determined under paragraph (1);

(C) not later than 7 months after such effective date, list the second 150 pesticide active ingredients, as determined under paragraph (1); and

(D) not later than 10 months after such effective date, list the remainder of the pesticide active ingredients, as determined under paragraph (1).

Each list shall be published in the Federal Register.

(3) Judicial review

The content of a list issued by the Administrator under paragraph (2) shall not be subject to judicial review.

(4) Notice to registrants

On the publication of a list of pesticide active ingredients under paragraph (2), the Administrator shall send by certified mail to the registrants of the pesticides containing such active ingredients a notice of the time by which the registrants are to notify the Administrator under subsection (d) of this section whether the registrants intend to seek or not to seek reregistration of such pesticides.

(d) Phase two

(1) In general

The registrant of a pesticide that contains an active ingredient listed under subparagraph (B), (C), or (D) of subsection (c)(2) of this section shall submit to the Administrator, within the time period prescribed by paragraph (4), the notice described in paragraph (2) and any information, commitment, or offer described in paragraph (3).

(2) Notice of intent to seek or not to seek reregistration

(A) The registrant of a pesticide containing an active ingredient listed under subparagraph (B), (C), or (D) of subsection (c)(2) of this section shall notify the Administrator by certified mail whether the registrant intends to seek or does not intend to seek reregistration of the pesticide.

(B) If a registrant submits a notice under subparagraph (A) of an intention not to seek reregistration of a pesticide, the Administrator shall publish a notice in the Federal Register stating that such a notice has been submitted.

(3) Missing or inadequate data

Each registrant of a pesticide that contains an active ingredient listed under subparagraph (B), (C), or (D) of subsection (c)(2) of this section and for which the registrant submitted a notice under paragraph (2) of an intention to seek reregistration of such pesticide shall submit to the Administrator—

(A) in accordance with regulations issued by the Administrator under section 136a of this title, an identification of—

(i) all data that are required by regulation to support the registration of the pesticide with respect to such active ingredient;

(ii) data that were submitted by the registrant previously in support of the registration of the pesticide that are inadequate to meet such regulations; and

(iii) data identified under clause (i) that have not been submitted to the Administrator; and

(B) either—

(i) a commitment to replace the data identified under subparagraph (A)(ii) and submit the data identified under subparagraph (A)(iii) within the applicable time period prescribed by paragraph (4)(B); or

(ii) an offer to share in the cost to be incurred by a person who has made a commitment under clause (i) to replace or submit the data and an offer to submit to arbitration as described by section 136a(c)(2)(B) of this title with regard to such cost sharing.

For purposes of a submission by a registrant under subparagraph (A)(ii), data are inadequate if the data are derived from a study with respect to which the registrant is unable to make the certification prescribed by subsection (e)(1)(G) of this section that the registrant possesses or has access to the raw data used in or generated by such study. For purposes of a submission by a registrant under such subparagraph, data shall be considered to be inadequate if the data are derived from a study submitted before January 1, 1970, unless it is demonstrated to the satisfaction of the Administrator that such data should be considered to support the registration of the pesticide that is to be reregistered.

(4) Time periods

(A) A submission under paragraph (2) or (3) shall be made—

(i) in the case of a pesticide containing an active ingredient listed under subsection (c)(2)(B) of this section, not later than 3 months after the date of publication of the listing of such active ingredient;

(ii) in the case of a pesticide containing an active ingredient listed under subsection (c)(2)(C) of this section, not later than 3 months after the date of publication of the listing of such active ingredient; and

(iii) in the case of a pesticide containing an active ingredient listed under subsection (c)(2)(D) of this section, not later than 3 months after the date of publication of the listing of such active ingredient.

On application, the Administrator may extend a time period prescribed by this subparagraph if the Administrator determines that factors beyond the control of the registrant prevent the registrant from complying with such period.

(B) A registrant shall submit data in accordance with a commitment entered into under paragraph (3)(B) within a reasonable period of time, as determined by the Administrator, but not more than 48 months after the date the registrant submitted the commitment. The Administrator, on application of a registrant, may extend the period prescribed by the preceding sentence by no more than 2 years if extraordinary circumstances beyond the control of the registrant prevent the registrant from submitting data within such prescribed period. Upon application of a registrant, the Administrator shall, in the case of a minor use, extend the deadline for the production of residue chemistry data under this subparagraph for data required solely to support that minor use until the final deadline for submission of data under this section for the other uses of the pesticide established as of August 3, 1996, if—

(i) the data to support other uses of the pesticide on a food are being provided;

(ii) the registrant, in submitting a request for such an extension provides a schedule, including interim dates to measure progress, to assure that the data production will be completed before the expiration of the extension period;

(iii) the Administrator has determined that such extension will not significantly delay the Administrator's schedule for issuing a reregistration eligibility determination required under this section; and

(iv) the Administrator has determined that based on existing data, such extension would not significantly increase the risk of any unreasonable adverse effect on the environment. If the Administrator grants an extension under this subparagraph, the Administrator shall monitor the development of the data and shall ensure that the registrant is meeting the schedule for the production of the data. If the Administrator determines that the registrant is not meeting or has not met the schedule for the production of such data, the Administrator may proceed in accordance with clause (iv) of section 136a(c)(2)(B) of this title or other provisions of this section, as appropriate, regarding the continued registration of the affected products with the minor use and shall inform the public of such action. Notwithstanding the provisions of this subparagraph, the Administrator may take action to modify or revoke the extension under this subparagraph if the Administrator determines that the extension for the minor use may cause an unreasonable adverse effect on the environment. In such circumstance, the Administrator shall provide written notice to the registrant revoking the extension of time for submission of data. Such data shall instead be due in accordance with the date then established by the Administrator for submission of the data.

(5) Cancellation and removal

(A) If the registrant of a pesticide does not submit a notice under paragraph (2) or (3) within the time prescribed by paragraph (4)(A), the Administrator shall issue a notice of intent to cancel the registration of such registrant for such pesticide and shall publish the notice in the Federal Register and allow 60 days for the submission of comments on the notice. On expiration of such 60 days, the Administrator, by order and without a hearing, may cancel the registration or take such other action, including extension of applicable time periods, as may be necessary to enable reregistration of such pesticide by another person.

(B) (i) If—

(I) no registrant of a pesticide containing an active ingredient listed under subsection (c)(2) of this section notifies the Administrator under paragraph (2) that the registrant intends to seek reregistration of any pesticide containing that active ingredient;

(II) no such registrant complies with paragraph (3)(A); or

(III) no such registrant makes a commitment under paragraph (3)(B) to replace or submit all data described in clauses (ii) and (iii) of paragraph (3)(A);

the Administrator shall publish in the Federal Register a notice of intent to remove the active ingredient from the list established under subsection (c)(2) of this section and a notice of intent to cancel the registrations of all pesticides containing such active ingredient and shall provide 60 days for comment on such notice.

(ii) After the 60-day period has expired, the Administrator, by order, may cancel any such registration without hearing, except that the Administrator shall not cancel a registration under this subparagraph if—

(I) during the comment period a person acquires the rights of the registrant in that registration;

(II) during the comment period that person furnishes a notice of intent to reregister the pesticide in accordance with paragraph (2); and

(III) not later than 120 days after the publication of the notice under this subparagraph, that person has complied with paragraph (3) and the fee prescribed by this section of this section has been paid.

(6) Suspensions and penalties

The Administrator shall issue a notice of intent to suspend the registration of a pesticide in accordance with the procedures prescribed by section 136a(c)(2)(B)(iv) of this title if the Administrator determines that (A) progress is insufficient to ensure the submission of the data required for such pesticide under a commitment made under paragraph (3)(B) within the time period prescribed by paragraph (4)(B) or (B) the registrant has not submitted such data to the Administrator within such time period. If the registrant does not commit to support a specific minor use of the pesticide, but is supporting and providing data in a timely and adequate fashion to support uses of the pesticide on a food, or if all uses of the pesticide are nonfood uses and the registrant does not commit to support a specific minor use of the pesticide but is supporting and providing data in a timely and adequate fashion to support other nonfood uses of the pesticide, the Administrator, at the written request of the registrant, shall not take any action pursuant to this paragraph in regard to such unsupported minor use until the final deadline established as of August 3, 1996, for the submission of data under this section for the supported uses identified pursuant to this paragraph unless the Administrator determines that the absence of the data is significant enough to cause human health or environmental concerns. On such a determination the Administrator may refuse the request for extension by the registrant. Upon receipt of the request from the registrant, the Administrator shall publish in the Federal Register a notice of the receipt of the request and the effective date upon which the uses not being supported will be voluntarily deleted from the registration pursuant to section 136d(f)(1) of this title. If the Administrator grants an extension under this paragraph, the Administrator shall monitor the development of the data for the uses being supported and shall ensure that the registrant is meeting the schedule for the production of such data. If the Administrator determines that the registrant is not meeting or has not met the schedule for the production of such data, the Administrator may proceed in accordance with section 136a(c)(2)(B)(iv) of this title regarding the continued registration of the affected products with the minor and other uses and shall inform the public of such action in accordance with section 136d(f)(2) of this title. Notwithstanding this subparagraph, the Administrator may deny, modify, or revoke the temporary extension under this paragraph if the Administrator determines that the continuation of the minor use may cause an unreasonable adverse effect on the environment. In the event of modification or revocation, the Administrator shall provide, in writing, to the registrant a notice revoking the temporary extension and establish a new effective date by which the minor use shall be deleted from the registration.

(e) Phase three

(1) Information about studies

Each registrant of a pesticide that contains an active ingredient listed under subparagraph (B), (C), or (D) of subsection (c)(2) of this section who has submitted a notice under subsection (d)(2) of this section of an intent to seek the reregistration of such pesticide shall submit, in accordance with the guidelines issued under paragraph (4), to the Administrator—

(A) a summary of each study concerning the active ingredient previously submitted by the registrant in support of the registration of a pesticide containing such active ingredient and considered by the registrant to be adequate to meet the requirements of section 136a of this title and the regulations issued under such section;

(B) a summary of each study concerning the active ingredient previously submitted by the registrant in support of the registration of a pesticide containing such active ingredient that may not comply with the requirements of section 136a of this title and the regulations issued under such section but which the registrant asserts should be deemed to comply with such requirements and regulations;

(C) a reformat of the data from each study summarized under subparagraph (A) or (B) by the registrant concerning chronic dosing, oncogenicity, reproductive effects, mutagenicity, neurotoxicity, teratogenicity, or residue chemistry of the active ingredient that were submitted to the Administrator before January 1, 1982;

(D) where data described in subparagraph (C) are not required for the active ingredient by regulations issued under section 136a of this title, a reformat of acute and subchronic dosing data submitted by the registrant to the Administrator before January 1, 1982, that the registrant considers to be adequate to meet the requirements of section 136a of this title and the regulations issued under such section;

(E) an identification of data that are required to be submitted to the Administrator under section 136d(a)(2) of this title, indicating an adverse effect of the pesticide;

(F) an identification of any other information available that in the view of the registrant supports the registration;

(G) a certification that the registrant or the Administrator possesses or has access to the raw data used in or generated by the studies that the registrant summarized under subparagraph (A) or (B);

(H) either—

(i) a commitment to submit data to fill each outstanding data requirement identified by the registrant; or

(ii) an offer to share in the cost of developing such data to be incurred by a person who has made a commitment under clause (i) to submit such data, and an offer to submit to arbitration as described by section 136a(c)(2)(B) of this title with regard to such cost sharing; and

(I) evidence of compliance with section 136a(c)(1)(D)(ii) of this title and regulations issued thereunder with regard to previously submitted data as if the registrant were now seeking the original registration of the pesticide.

A registrant who submits a certification under subparagraph (G) that is false shall be considered to have violated this subchapter and shall be subject to the penalties prescribed by section 136*l* of this title.

(2) Time periods

(A) The information required by paragraph (1) shall be submitted to the Administrator—

(i) in the case of a pesticide containing an active ingredient listed under subsection (c)(2)(B) of this section, not later than 12 months after the date of publication of the listing of such active ingredient;

(ii) in the case of a pesticide containing an active ingredient listed under subsection (c)(2)(C) of this section, not later than 12 months after the date of publication of the listing of such active ingredient; and

(iii) in the case of a pesticide containing an active ingredient listed under subsection (c)(2)(D) of this section, not later than 12 months after the date of publication of the listing of such active ingredient.

(B) A registrant shall submit data in accordance with a commitment entered into under paragraph (1)(H) within a reasonable period of time, as determined by the Administrator, but not more than 48 months after the date the registrant submitted the commitment under such paragraph. The Administrator, on application of a registrant, may extend the period prescribed by the preceding sentence by no more than 2 years if extraordinary circumstances beyond the control of the registrant prevent the registrant from submitting data within such prescribed period. Upon application of a registrant, the Administrator shall, in the case of a minor use, extend the deadline for the production of residue chemistry data under this subparagraph for data required solely to support that minor use until the final deadline for submission of data under this section for the other uses of the pesticide established as of August 3, 1996, if—

(i) the data to support other uses of the pesticide on a food are being provided;

(ii) the registrant, in submitting a request for such an extension provides a schedule, including interim dates to measure progress, to assure that the data production will be completed before the expiration of the extension period;

(iii) the Administrator has determined that such extension will not significantly delay the Administrator's schedule for issuing a reregistration eligibility determination required under this section; and

(iv) the Administrator has determined that based on existing data, such extension would not significantly increase the risk of any unreasonable adverse effect on the environment. If the Administrator grants an extension under this subparagraph, the Administrator shall monitor the development of the data and shall ensure that the registrant is meeting the schedule for the production of the data. If the Administrator determines that the registrant is not meeting or has not met the schedule for the production of such data, the Administrator may proceed in accordance with clause (iv) of section 136a(c)(2)(B) of this title or other provisions of this section, as appropriate, regarding the continued registration of the affected products with the minor use and shall inform the public of such action. Notwithstanding the provisions of this subparagraph, the Administrator may take action to modify or revoke the extension under this subparagraph if the Administrator determines that the extension for the minor use may cause an unreasonable adverse effect on the environment. In such circumstance, the Administrator shall provide written notice to the registrant revoking the extension of time for submission of data. Such data shall instead be due in accordance with the date then established by the Administrator for submission of the data.

(3) Cancellation

(A) If the registrant of a pesticide fails to submit the information required by paragraph (1) within the time prescribed by paragraph (2), the Administrator, by order and without hearing, shall cancel the registration of such pesticide. If the registrant does not commit to support a specific minor use of the pesticide, but is supporting and providing data in a timely and adequate fashion to support uses of the pesticide on a food, or if all uses of the pesticide are nonfood uses and the registrant does not commit to support a specific minor use of the pesticide but is supporting and providing data in a timely and adequate fashion to support other nonfood uses of the pesticide, the Administrator, at the written request of the registrant, shall not take any action pursuant to this subparagraph in regard to such unsupported minor use until the final deadline established as of August 3, 1996, for the submission of data under this section for the supported uses identified pursuant to this subparagraph unless the Administrator determines that the absence of the data is significant enough to cause human health or environmental concerns. On the basis of such determination, the Administrator may refuse the request for extension by the registrant. Upon receipt of the request from the registrant, the Administrator shall publish in the Federal Register a notice of the receipt of the request and the effective date upon which the uses not being supported will be voluntarily deleted from the registration pursuant to section 136d(f)(1) of this title. If the Administrator grants an extension under this subparagraph, the Administrator shall monitor the development of the data for the uses being supported and shall ensure that the registrant is meeting the schedule for the production of such data. If the Administrator determines that the registrant is not meeting or has not met the schedule for the production of such data, the Administrator may proceed in accordance with section 136a(c)(2)(B)(iv) of this title regarding the continued registration of the affected products with the minor and other uses and shall inform the public of such action in accordance with section 136d(f)(2) of this title. Notwithstanding this subparagraph, the Administrator may deny, modify, or revoke the temporary extension under this subparagraph if the Administrator determines that the continuation of the minor use may cause an unreasonable adverse effect on the environment. In the event of modification or revocation, the Administrator shall provide, in writing, to the registrant a notice revoking the temporary extension and establish a new effective date by which the minor use shall be deleted from the registration.

(B) **(i)** If the registrant of a pesticide submits the information required by paragraph (1) within the time prescribed by paragraph (2) and such information does not conform to the guidelines for submissions established by the Administrator, the Administrator shall determine whether the registrant made a good faith attempt to conform its submission to such guidelines.

(ii) If the Administrator determines that the registrant made a good faith attempt to conform its submission to such guidelines, the Administrator shall provide the registrant a reasonable period of time to make any necessary changes or corrections.

(iii) (I) If the Administrator determines that the registrant did not make a good faith attempt to conform its submission to such guidelines, the Administrator may issue a notice of intent to cancel the registration. Such a notice shall be sent to the registrant by certified mail.

(II) The registration shall be canceled without a hearing or further notice at the end of 30 days after receipt by the registrant of the notice unless during that time a request for a hearing is made by the registrant.

(III) If a hearing is requested, a hearing shall be conducted under section 136d(d) of this title, except that the only matter for resolution at the hearing shall be whether the registrant made a good faith attempt to conform its submission to such guidelines. The hearing shall be held and a determination made within 75 days after receipt of a request for hearing.

(4) Guidelines

(A) Not later than 1 year after the effective date of this section, the Administrator, by order, shall issue guidelines to be followed by registrants in—

(i) summarizing studies;

(ii) reformatting studies;

(iii) identifying adverse information; and

(iv) identifying studies that have been submitted previously that may not meet the requirements of section 136a of this title or regulations issued under such section, under paragraph (1).

(B) Guidelines issued under subparagraph (A) shall not be subject to judicial review.

(5) Monitoring

The Administrator shall monitor the progress of registrants in acquiring and submitting the data required under paragraph (1).

(f) Phase four

(1) Independent review and identification of outstanding data requirements

(A) The Administrator shall review the submissions of all registrants of pesticides containing a particular active ingredient under subsections (d)(3) and (e)(1) of this section to determine if such submissions identified all the data that are missing or inadequate for such active ingredient. To assist the review of the Administrator under this subparagraph, the Administrator may require a registrant seeking reregistration to submit complete copies of studies summarized under subsection (e)(1) of this section.

(B) The Administrator shall independently identify and publish in the Federal Register the outstanding data requirements for each active ingredient that is listed under subparagraph (B), (C), or (D) of subsection (c)(2) of this section and that is contained in a pesticide to be reregistered under this section. The Administrator, at the same time, shall issue a notice under section 136a(c)(2)(B) of this title for the submission of the additional data that are required to meet such requirements.

(2) Time periods

(A) The Administrator shall take the action required by paragraph (1)—

(i) in the case of a pesticide containing an active ingredient listed under subsection (c)(2)(B) of this section, not later than 18 months after the date of the listing of such active ingredient;

(ii) in the case of a pesticide containing an active ingredient listed under subsection (c)(2)(C) of this section, not later than 24 months after the date of the listing of such active ingredient; and

(iii) in the case of a pesticide containing an active ingredient listed under subsection (c)(2)(D) of this section, not later than 33 months after the date of the listing of such active ingredient.

(B) If the Administrator issues a notice to a registrant under paragraph (1)(B) for the submission of additional data, the registrant shall submit such data within a reasonable period of time, as determined by the Administrator, but not to exceed 48 months after the issuance of such notice. The Administrator, on application of a registrant, may extend the period prescribed by the preceding sentence by no more than 2 years if extraordinary circumstances beyond the control of the registrant prevent the registrant from submitting data within such prescribed period. Upon application of a registrant, the Administrator shall, in the case of a minor use, extend the deadline for the production of residue chemistry data under this subparagraph for data required solely to support that minor use until the final deadline for submission of data under this section for the other uses of the pesticide established as of August 3, 1996, if—

(i) the data to support other uses of the pesticide on a food are being provided;

(ii) the registrant, in submitting a request for such an extension provides a schedule, including interim dates to measure progress, to assure that the data production will be completed before the expiration of the extension period;

(iii) the Administrator has determined that such extension will not significantly delay the Administrator's schedule for issuing a reregistration eligibility determination required under this section; and

(iv) the Administrator has determined that based on existing data, such extension would not significantly increase the risk of any unreasonable adverse effect on the environment. If the Administrator grants an extension under this subparagraph, the Administrator shall monitor the development of the data and shall ensure that the registrant is meeting the schedule for the production of the data. If the Administrator determines that the registrant is not meeting or has not met the schedule for the production of such data, the Administrator may proceed in accordance with clause (iv) of section 136a(c)(2)(B) of this title or other provisions of this section, as appropriate, regarding the continued registration of the affected products with the minor use and shall inform the public of such action. Notwithstanding the provisions of this subparagraph, the Administrator may take action to modify or revoke the extension under this subparagraph if the Administrator determines that the extension for the minor use may cause an unreasonable adverse effect on the environment. In such circumstance, the Administrator shall provide written notice to the registrant revoking the extension of time for submission of data. Such data shall instead be due in accordance with the date then established by the Administrator for submission of the data.

(3) Suspensions and penalties

The Administrator shall issue a notice of intent to suspend the registration of a pesticide in accordance with the procedures prescribed by section 136a(c)(2)(B)(iv) of this title if the Administrator determines that (A) tests necessary to fill an outstanding data requirement for such pesticide have not been initiated within 1 year after the issuance of a notice under paragraph (1)(B), or (B) progress is insufficient to ensure submission of the data referred to in clause (A) within the time period prescribed by paragraph (2)(B) or the required data have not been submitted to the Administrator within such time period. If the registrant does not commit to support a specific minor use of the pesticide, but is supporting and providing data in a timely and adequate fashion to support uses of the pesticide on a food, or if all uses of the pesticide are nonfood uses and the registrant does not commit to support a specific minor use of the pesticide but is supporting and providing data in a timely and adequate fashion to support other nonfood uses of the pesticide, the Administrator, at the written request of the registrant, shall not take any action pursuant to this paragraph in regard to such unsupported minor use until the final deadline established as of August 3, 1996, for the submission of data under this section for the supported uses identified pursuant to this paragraph unless the Administrator determines that the absence of the data is significant enough to cause human health or environmental concerns. On such a determination the Administrator may refuse the request for extension by the registrant. Upon receipt of the request from the registrant, the Administrator shall publish in the Federal Register a notice of the receipt of the request and the effective date upon which the uses not being supported will be voluntarily deleted from the registration pursuant to section 136d(f)(1) of this title. If the Administrator grants an extension under this paragraph, the Administrator shall monitor the development of the data for the uses being supported and shall ensure that the registrant is meeting the schedule for the production of such data. If the Administrator determines that the registrant is not meeting or has not met the schedule for the production of such data, the Administrator may proceed in accordance with section 136a(c)(2)(B)(iv) of this title regarding the continued registration of the affected products with the minor and other uses and shall inform the public of such action in accordance with section 136d(f)(2) of this title. Notwithstanding this subparagraph, the Administrator may deny, modify, or revoke the temporary extension under this paragraph if the Administrator determines that the continuation of the minor use may cause an unreasonable adverse effect on the environment. In the event of modification or revocation, the Administrator shall provide, in writing, to the registrant a notice revoking the temporary extension and establish a new effective date by which the minor use shall be deleted from the registration.

(g) Phase five

(1) Data review

The Administrator shall conduct a thorough examination of all data submitted under this section concerning an active ingredient listed under subsection (c)(2) of this section and of all other available data found by the Administrator to be relevant.

(2) Reregistration and other actions

(A) In general

The Administrator shall make a determination as to eligibility for reregistration—

(i) for all active ingredients subject to reregistration under this section for which tolerances or exemptions from tolerances are required under the Federal Food, Drug, and Cosmetic Act (21 U.S.C. 301 et seq.), not later than the last date for tolerance reassessment established under section 408(q)(1)(C) of that Act (21 U.S.C. 346a(q)(1)(C)); and

(ii) for all other active ingredients subject to reregistration under this section, not later than October 3, 2008.

(B) Product-specific data

(i) In general

Before reregistering a pesticide, the Administrator shall obtain any needed product-specific data regarding the pesticide by use of section 136a(c)(2)(B) of this title and shall review such data within 90 days after its submission.

(ii) Timing

(I) In general

Subject to subclause (II), the Administrator shall require that data under this subparagraph be submitted to the Administrator not later than 8 months after a determination of eligibility under subparagraph (A) has been made for each active ingredient of the pesticide, unless the Administrator determines that a longer period is required for the generation of the data.

(II) Extraordinary circumstances

In the case of extraordinary circumstances, the Administrator may provide such a longer period, of not more than 2 additional years, for submission of data to the Administrator under this subparagraph.

(C) After conducting the review required by paragraph (1) for each active ingredient of a pesticide and the review required by subparagraph (B) of this paragraph, the Administrator shall determine whether to reregister a pesticide by determining whether such pesticide meets the requirements of section 136a(c)(5) of this title. If the Administrator determines that a pesticide is eligible to be reregistered, the Administrator shall reregister such pesticide within 6 months after the submission of the data concerning such pesticide under subparagraph (B).

(D) Determination to not reregister

(i) In general

If after conducting a review under paragraph (1) or subparagraph (B) of this paragraph the Administrator determines that a pesticide should not be reregistered, the Administrator shall take appropriate regulatory action.

(ii) Timing for regulatory action

Regulatory action under clause (i) shall be completed as expeditiously as possible.

(E) As soon as the Administrator has sufficient information with respect to the dietary risk of a particular active ingredient, but in any event no later than the time the Administrator makes a determination under subparagraph (C) or (D) with respect to pesticides containing a particular active ingredient, the Administrator shall—

(i) reassess each associated tolerance and exemption from the requirement for a tolerance issued under section 408 of the Federal Food, Drug, and Cosmetic Act (21 U.S.C. 346a);

(ii) determine whether such tolerance or exemption meets the requirements of that Act [21 U.S.C.A. § 301 et seq.];

(iii) determine whether additional tolerances or exemptions should be issued;

(iv) publish in the Federal Register a notice setting forth the determinations made under this subparagraph; and

(v) commence promptly such proceedings under this subchapter and section 408 of the Federal Food, Drug, and Cosmetic Act [21 U.S.C.A. § 346a] as are warranted by such determinations.

(h) Compensation of data submitter

If data that are submitted by a registrant under subsection (d), (e), (f), or (g) of this section are used to support the application of another person under section 136a of this title, the registrant who submitted such data shall be entitled to compensation for the use of such data as prescribed by section 136a(c)(1)(D) of this title. In determining the amount of such compensation, the fees paid by the registrant under this section shall be taken into account.

(i) Fees

(1) Maintenance fee

(A) In general

Subject to other provisions of this paragraph, each registrant of a pesticide shall pay an annual fee by January 15 of each year for each registration, except that no fee shall be charged for more than 200 registrations held by any registrant.

(B) In the case of a pesticide that is registered for a minor agricultural use, the Administrator may reduce or waive the payment of the fee imposed under this paragraph if the Administrator determines that the fee would significantly reduce the availability of the pesticide for the use.

(C) Total amount of fees

The amount of each fee prescribed under subparagraph (A) shall be adjusted by the Administrator to a level that will result in the collection under this paragraph of, to the extent practicable, an average amount of $31,000,000 for each of fiscal years 2019 through 2023.

(D) Maximum amount of fees for registrants

The maximum annual fee payable under this paragraph by—

(i) a registrant holding not more than 50 pesticide registrations shall be $129,400 for each of fiscal years 2019 through 2023; and

(ii) a registrant holding over 50 registrations shall be $207,000 for each of fiscal years 2019 through 2023.

(E) Maximum amount of fees for small businesses

(i) In general

For a small business, the maximum annual fee payable under this paragraph by—

(I) a registrant holding not more than 50 pesticide registrations shall be $79,100 for each of fiscal years 2019 through 2023; and

(II) a registrant holding over 50 pesticide registrations shall be $136,800 for each of fiscal years 2019 through 2023.

(ii) Definition of small business

(I) In general—

In clause (i), the term "small business" means a corporation, partnership, or unincorporated business that—

(aa) has 500 or fewer employees; and

(bb) during the 3-year period prior to the most recent maintenance fee billing cycle, had an average annual global gross revenue from pesticides that did not exceed $60,000,000.

(II) Affiliates

(aa) In general

In the case of a business entity with 1 or more affiliates, the gross revenue limit under subclause (I)(bb) shall apply to the gross revenue for the entity and all of the affiliates of the entity, including parents and subsidiaries, if applicable.

(bb) Affiliated persons

For the purpose of item (aa), persons are affiliates of each other if, directly or indirectly, either person controls or has the power to control the other person, or a third person controls or has the power to control both persons.

(cc) Indicia of control

For the purpose of item (aa), indicia of control include interlocking management or ownership, identity of interests among family members, shared facilities and equipment, and common use of employees.

(F) Fee reduction for certain small businesses

(i) Definition

In this subparagraph, the term "qualified small business entity" means a corporation, partnership, or unincorporated business that—

(I) has 500 or fewer employees;

(II) during the 3-year period prior to the most recent maintenance fee billing cycle, had an average annual global gross revenue from all sources that did not exceed $10,000,000; and

(III) holds not more than 5 pesticide registrations under this paragraph.

(ii) Waiver

Except as provided in clause (iii), the Administrator shall waive 25 percent of the fee under this paragraph applicable to the first registration of any qualified small business entity under this paragraph.

(iii) Limitation

The Administrator shall not grant a waiver under clause (ii) to a qualified small business entity if the Administrator determines that the entity has been formed or manipulated primarily for the purpose of qualifying for the waiver.

(G) The Administrator shall exempt any public health pesticide from the payment of the fee prescribed under this paragraph if, in consultation with the Secretary of Health and Human Services, the Administrator determines, based on information supplied by the registrant, that the economic return to the registrant from sales of the pesticide does not support the registration or reregistration of the pesticide.

(H) If any fee prescribed by this paragraph with respect to the registration of a pesticide is not paid by a registrant by the time prescribed, the Administrator, by order and without hearing, may cancel the registration.

(I) The authority provided under this paragraph shall terminate on September 30, 2023.

(2) Other fees

Except as provided in section 136w–8 of this title, during the period beginning on the effective date of the Pesticide Registration Improvement Extension Act of 2018 and ending on September 30, 2025, the Administrator may not levy any other fees for the registration of a pesticide under this Act or any other action covered under a table specified in section 33(b)(3), except as provided in paragraph (1).

(j) Exemption of certain registrants

The requirements of subsections (d), (e), (f), and (i) of this section (other than subsection (i)(1) of this section) regarding data concerning an active ingredient and fees for review of such data shall not apply to any person who is the registrant of a pesticide to the extent that, under section 136a(c)(2)(D) of this title, the person would not be required to submit or cite such data to obtain an initial registration of such pesticide.

(k) Reregistration and expedited processing fund

(1) Establishment

There shall be established in the Treasury of the United States a reregistration and expedited processing fund which shall be known as the Reregistration and Expedited Processing Fund.

(2) Source and use

(A) All moneys derived from fees collected by the Administrator under subsection (i) of this section shall be deposited in the Reregistration and Expedited Processing Fund and shall be available to the Administrator, without fiscal year limitation, specifically to offset the costs of reregistration and expedited processing of the applications specified in paragraph (3), to offset the costs of registration review under section 3(g), including the costs associated with any review under the Endangered Species Act of 1973 (16 U.S.C. 1531 et seq.) required as part of the registration review, to offset the costs associated with tracking and implementing registration review decisions, including registration review decisions designed to reduce risk, for the purposes specified in paragraphs (4) and (5), and to enhance the information systems capabilities to improve the tracking of pesticide registration decisions. The Administrator shall, prior to expending any such moneys derived from fees—

(i) effective October 1, 1997, adopt specific and cost accounting rules and procedures as approved by the Government Accountability Office and the Inspector General of the Environmental Protection Agency to ensure that moneys derived from fees are allocated solely for the purposes specified in the first sentence of this subparagraph;

(ii) prohibit the use of such moneys derived from fees to pay for any costs other than those necessary to achieve the purposes specified in the first sentence of this subparagraph; and

(iii) ensure that personnel and facility costs associated with the functions to be carried out under this paragraph do not exceed agency averages for comparable personnel and facility costs.

(B) The Administrator shall also—

(i) complete the review of unreviewed reregistration studies required to support the reregistration eligibility decisions scheduled for completion in accordance with subsection (*l*)(2) of this section; and

(ii) contract for such outside assistance as may be necessary for review of required studies, using a generally accepted competitive process for the selection of vendors of such assistance.

(3) Review of inert ingredients; expedited processing of similar applications

(A) For each of fiscal years 2018 through 2023, the Administrator shall use between 1/9 and 1/8 of the maintenance fees collected in such fiscal year to obtain sufficient personnel and resources—

(i) to review and evaluate inert ingredients; and

(ii) to ensure the expedited processing and review of any application that—

(I) proposes the initial or amended registration of an end-use pesticide that, if registered as proposed, would be identical or substantially similar in composition and labeling to a currently-registered pesticide identified in the application, or that would differ in composition and labeling from any such currently-registered pesticide only in ways that would not significantly increase the risk of unreasonable adverse effects on the environment;

(II) proposes an amendment to the registration of a registered pesticide that does not require scientific review of data; or

(III) proposes the initial or amended registration of an end use pesticide that, if registered as proposed, would be used for a public health pesticide.

(B) Any amounts made available under subparagraph (A) shall be used to obtain sufficient personnel and resources to carry out the activities described in such subparagraph that are in addition to the personnel and resources available to carry out such activities on October 25, 1988.

(C) So long as the Administrator has not met the time frames specified in clause (ii) of section 136a(c)(3)(B) of this title with respect to any application subject to section 136a(c)(3)(B) of this title that was received prior to August 3, 1996, the Administrator shall use the full amount of the fees specified in subparagraph (A) for the purposes specified therein. Once all applications subject to section 136a(c)(3)(B) of this title that were received prior to August 3, 1996, have been acted upon, no limitation shall be imposed by the preceding sentence of this subparagraph so long as the Administrator meets the time frames specified in the clause (ii) of section 136a(c)(3)(B) of this title on 90 percent of affected applications in a fiscal year. Should the Administrator not meet such time frames in a fiscal year, the limitations imposed by the first sentence of this subparagraph shall apply until all overdue applications subject to section 136a(c)(3)(B) of this title have been acted upon.

(4) Expedited rulemaking and guidance development for certain product performance data requirements.—

(A) Set-aside.—For each of fiscal years 2018 through 2023, the Administrator shall use not more than $500,000 of the amounts made available to the Administrator in the Reregistration and Expedited Processing Fund for the activities described in subparagraph (B).

(B) Products claiming efficacy against invertebrate pests of significant public health or economic importance.—The Administrator shall use amounts made available under subparagraph (A) to develop, receive comments with respect to, finalize, and implement the necessary rulemaking and guidance for product performance data requirements to evaluate products claiming efficacy against the following invertebrate pests of significant public health or economic importance (in order of importance):

(i) Bed bugs.

(ii) Premise (including crawling insects, flying insects, and baits).

(iii) Pests of pets (including pet pests controlled by spot-ons, collars, shampoos, powders, or dips).

(iv) Fire ants.

(C) Deadlines for guidance.—The Administrator shall develop, and publish guidance required by subparagraph (B), with respect to claims of efficacy against pests described in such subparagraph as follows:

(i) With respect to bed bugs, issue final guidance not later than 30 days after the effective date of the Pesticide Registration Improvement Extension Act of 2018.

(ii) With respect to pests specified in clause (ii) of such subparagraph—

(I) submit draft guidance to the Scientific Advisory Panel and for public comment not later than June 30, 2018; and

(II) complete any response to comments received with respect to such draft guidance and finalize the guidance not later than September 30, 2019.

(iii) With respect to pests specified in clauses (iii) and (iv) of such subparagraph—

(I) submit draft guidance to the Scientific Advisory Panel and for public comment not later than June 30, 2019; and

(II) complete any response to comments received with respect to such draft guidance and finalize the guidance not later than March 31, 2021.

(D) Revision.—The Administrator shall revise the guidance required by subparagraph (B) from time to time, but shall permit applicants and registrants sufficient time to obtain data that meet the requirements specified in such revised guidance.

(E) Deadline for product performance data requirements.—The Administrator shall, not later than September 30, 2021, issue regulations prescribing product performance data requirements for any pesticide intended for preventing, destroying, repelling, or mitigating any invertebrate pest of significant public health or economic importance specified in clauses (i) through (iv) of subparagraph (B).

(5) Good laboratory practices inspections.—

(A) Set-aside.—For each of fiscal years 2018 through 2023, the Administrator shall use not more than $500,000 of the amounts made available to the Administrator in the Reregistration and Expedited Processing Fund for the activities described in subparagraph (B).

(B) Activities.—The Administrator shall use amounts made available under subparagraph (A) for enhancements to the good laboratory practices standards compliance monitoring program established under part 160 of title 40 of the Code of Federal Regulations (or successor regulations), with respect to laboratory inspections and data audits conducted in support of pesticide product registrations under this Act. As part of such monitoring program, the Administrator shall make available to each laboratory inspected under such program in support of such registrations a preliminary summary of inspection observations not later than 60 days after the date on which such an inspection is completed.

(6) Unused funds

Money in the fund not currently needed to carry out this section shall be—

(A) maintained on hand or on deposit;

(B) invested in obligations of the United States or guaranteed thereby; or

(C) invested in obligations, participations, or other instruments that are lawful investments for fiduciary, trust, or public funds.

(7) Accounting and performance

The Administrator shall take all steps necessary to ensure that expenditures from fees authorized by subsection (i)(1)(C)(ii) of this section are used only for the purposes described in paragraphs (2), (3), (4), and (5) and to carry out the goals established under subsection (*l*) of this section. The Reregistration and Expedited Processing Fund shall be designated as an Environmental Protection Agency component for purposes of section 3515(c) of Title 31. The annual audit required under section 3521 of such title of the financial statements of activities under this subchapter under section 3515(b) of such title shall include an audit of the fees collected under subsection (i)(1)(C) of this section and disbursed, of the amount appropriated to match such fees, and of the Administrator's attainment of performance measures and goals established under subsection (*l*) of this section. Such an audit shall also include a review of the reasonableness of the overhead allocation and adequacy of disclosures of direct and indirect costs associated with carrying out the reregistration and expedited processing of the applications specified in paragraph (3), and the basis for and accuracy of all costs paid with moneys derived from such fees. The Inspector General shall conduct the annual audit and report the findings and recommendations of such audit to the Administrator and to the Committees on Agriculture of the House of Representatives and the Senate. The cost of such audit shall be paid for out of the fees collected under subsection (i)(1)(C) of this section.

(*l*) Performance measures and goals

The Administrator shall establish and publish annually in the Federal Register performance measures and goals. Such measures and goals shall include—

(1) the number of products reregistered, canceled, or amended, the status of reregistration, the number and type of data requests under section 136a(c)(2)(B) of this title issued to support product reregistration by active ingredient, the progress in reducing the number of unreviewed, required reregistration studies, the aggregate status of tolerances reassessed, and the number of applications for registration submitted under subsection (k)(3) of this section that were approved or disapproved;

(2) the future schedule for reregistrations, including the projection for such schedules that will be issued under subsection (g)(2)(A) and (B) of this section in the current fiscal year and the succeeding fiscal year; and

(3) the projected year of completion of the reregistrations under this section.

(m) Judicial review

Any failure of the Administrator to take any action required by this section shall be subject to judicial review under the procedures prescribed by section 136n(b) of this title.

(n) Authorization of funds to develop public health data

(1) "Secretary" defined

For the purposes of this section, "Secretary" means the Secretary of Health and Human Services, acting through the Public Health Service.

(2) Consultation

In the case of a pesticide registered for use in public health programs for vector control or for other uses the Administrator determines to be human health protection uses, the Administrator shall, upon timely request by the registrant or any other interested person, or on the Administrator's own initiative may, consult with the Secretary prior to taking final action to suspend registration under section 136a(c)(2)(B)(iv) of this title, or cancel a registration under section 136a–1, 136d(e), or 136d(f) of this title. In consultation with the Secretary, the Administrator shall prescribe the form and content of requests under this section.

(3) Benefits to support family

The Administrator, after consulting with the Secretary, shall make a determination whether the potential benefits of continued use of the pesticide for public health or health protection purposes are of such significance as to warrant a commitment by the Secretary to conduct or to arrange for the conduct of the studies required by the Administrator to support continued registration under section 136a of this title or reregistration under this section.

(4) Additional time

If the Administrator determines that such a commitment is warranted and in the public interest, the Administrator shall notify the Secretary and shall, to the extent necessary, amend a notice issued under section 136a(c)(2)(B) of this title to specify additional reasonable time periods for submission of the data.

(5) Arrangements

The Secretary shall make such arrangements for the conduct of required studies as the Secretary finds necessary and appropriate to permit submission of data in accordance with the time periods prescribed by the Administrator. Such arrangements may include Public Health Service intramural research activities, grants, contracts, or cooperative agreements with academic, public health, or other organizations qualified by experience and training to conduct such studies.

(6) Support

The Secretary may provide for support of the required studies using funds authorized to be appropriated under this section, the Public Health Service Act [42 U.S.C.A. § 201 et seq.], or other appropriate authorities. After a determination is made under subsection (d) of this section, the Secretary shall notify the Committees on Appropriations of the House of Representatives and the Senate of the sums required to conduct the necessary studies.

(7) Authorization of appropriations

There is authorized to be appropriated to carry out the purposes of this section $12,000,000 for fiscal year 1997, and such sums as may be necessary for succeeding fiscal years.

(Act of June 25, 1947, c. 125, § 4, formerly § 3A, as added and renumbered § 4, Pub. L. No. 100–532, Title I, § 102(a), Title VIII, § 801(q)(2)(A), 102 Stat. 2655, 2683 (Oct. 25, 1988); and amended by Pub. L. No. 101–624, Title XIV, § 1493, 104 Stat. 3628 (Nov. 28, 1990); Pub. L. No. 102–237, Title X, § 1006(a)(4), (e), (f), 105 Stat. 1895 to 1897 (Dec. 13, 1991); Pub. L. No. 104–170, Title I, § 103, Title II, §§ 210(c)(2), (f)(1), 232, 237, Title V, § 501, 110 Stat. 1490, 1496, 1498, 1508, 1509, 1536 (Aug. 3, 1996); Pub. L. No. 107–73, Title III, 115 Stat. 686 (Nov. 26, 2001); Pub. L. No. 108–7, Div. K, Title III, 117 Stat. 513 (Feb. 20, 2003); Pub. L. No. 108–199, Div. G, Title V, § 501(c), (d)(1), (e), 118 Stat. 419, 422 (Jan. 23, 2004); Pub. L. No. 108–271, § 8(b), 118 Stat. 814 (July 7, 2004); Pub. L. No. 110–94, § 4(a) to (c), (d)(1), (e), 121 Stat. 1001, 1002 (Oct. 9, 2007); Pub. L. No. 112–177, § 2(a)(1), (2)(A), (4), 126 Stat. 1327, 1329 (Sept. 28, 2012); Pub. L. No. 116–8, §§ 2, 3 133 Stat. 484, 484–487 (Mar. 8, 2019).)

HISTORICAL AND STATUTORY NOTES

References in Text

The effective date of this section, referred to in subsec. (c), is 60 days after Oct. 25, 1988, see section 901 of Pub. L. No. 100–532, set out as a note under section 136 of this title.

Section 136a(c)(1)(D), referred to in subsecs. (e)(1)(I) and (h), was redesignated section 136a(c)(1)(F) of this title by Pub. L. No. 102–237, Title X, § 1006(a)(3)(b), Dec. 13, 1991, 105 Stat. 1894.

The Federal Food, Drug, and Cosmetic Act, referred to in subsec. (g)(2)(A) and (E), is Act of June 25, 1938, c. 675, 52 Stat. 1040, as amended, which is codified generally as chapter 9 of Title 21, 21 U.S.C.A. § 301 et seq. For complete classification, see 21 U.S.C.A. § 301 and Tables.

Subsection (i)(5)(C)(ii) of this section, referred to in subsec. (k)(5), was repealed and a new subsec. (i)(5)(C)(ii) was added by Pub. L. No. 108–199, Div. G, Title V, § 501(c)(2), Jan. 23, 2004, 118 Stat. 420.

The Public Health Service Act, referred to in subsec. (n)(6), is Act of July 1, 1944, c. 373, 58 Stat. 682, as amended, which is codified generally as chapter 6A (section 201 et seq.) of Title 42, The Public Health and Welfare.

For complete classification of this Act to the Code, see Short Title note set out under section 201 of Title 42 and Tables.

Codifications

Amendment to subsec. (i)(5)(C) by Pub. L. No. 110–94, § 4(a), directed striking out "amount of" and all that follows through the end of clause (v) and inserting "amount of $22,000,000 for each of fiscal years 2008 through 2012". The language "amount of" appeared once in the subparagraph heading and twice in the subparagraph text, and the directive was executed to the third location as the probable intent of Congress.

Pub. L. No. 108–199, Div. G, Title V, § 501(c)(2), which directed that "Section 4(i)(5)(C) of the Federal Insecticide, fungicide, and Rodenticide Act (7 U.S.C. § 136(a)–1(i)(5)(C)" be amended by "striking (C)(i) The" and inserting text, was executed to subsec. (i)(5)(C) of this section, despite the parenthetical reference to "(7 U.S.C. 136(a)–1(i)(5)(C)", as the probable intent of Congress.

Effective and Applicability Provisions

2012 Acts. Pub. L. No. 112–177, § 2(c), Sept. 28, 2012, 126 Stat. 1407, provided that: "This section and the amendments made by this section [amending this section, 7 U.S.C.A. § 136w–8, and 21 U.S.C.A. § 346a, and enacting provisions set out as notes under this section] take effect on October 1, 2012."

2007 Acts. Amendments by Pub. L. No. 110–94 effective Oct. 1, 2007, see Pub. L. No. 110–94, § 6, set out as a note under 7 U.S.C.A. § 136a.

2004 Acts. Amendments made by section 501 of Pub. L. No. 108–199 effective 60 days after Jan. 23, 2004, except as otherwise provided, see Pub. L. No. 108–199, § 501(h), set out as a note under 7 U.S.C.A. § 136a.

1991 Acts. Amendments by Pub. L. No. 102–237 effective Dec. 13, 1991, see section 1101(a) of Pub. L. No. 102–237, set out as a note under section 1421 of this title.

1988 Acts. Section effective on expiration of 60 days after October 25, 1988, see section 901 of Pub. L. No. 100–532, set out as a note under section 136 of this title.

Severability of Provisions

If any provision of Pub. L. No. 101–624 or the application thereof to any person or circumstance is held invalid, such invalidity not to affect other provisions or applications of Pub. L. No. 101–624 which can be given effect without regard to the invalid provision or application, see section 2519 of Pub. L. No. 101–624, set out as a note under section 1421 of this title.

Prior Provisions

A prior section 4 of Act of June 25, 1947, which was codified as 7 U.S.C.A. § 136b was transferred to section 11(a)–(c) of Act of June 25, 1947, which is codified as 7 U.S.C.A. § 136*i*(a)–(c).

Another prior section 4 of Act of June 25, 1947, was codified as section 135b of this title prior to amendment of Act of June 25, 1947, by Pub. L. No. 92–516.

Budget Resolutions

2017. Section 134(b)(1) of Pub. L. No. 115–56, 131 Stat. 1145 (Sept. 8, 2017), provided: "Section 4(i)(1)(I) of the Federal Insecticide, Fungicide, and Rodenticide Act (7 U.S.C. 136a–1(i)(1)(I)) shall be applied by substituting the date specified in section 106(3) of this joint resolution [December 8, 2017] for 'September 30, 2017.' "

Relationship of Pub. L. No. 112–177 to Other Laws

Pub. L. No. 112–177, § 2(d), Sept. 28, 2012, 126 Stat. 1407, provided that: "In the case of any conflict between this section (including the amendments made by this section) [amending this section, 7 U.S.C.A. § 136w–8, and 21 U.S.C.A. § 346a, and enacting provisions set out as notes under this section] and a joint resolution making continuing appropriations for fiscal year 2013 (including any amendments made by such a joint resolution), this section and the amendments made by this section [amending this section, 7 U.S.C.A. § 136w–8, and 21 U.S.C.A. § 346a, and enacting provisions set out as notes under this section] shall control."

Adjustment of Maximum Annual Fee Payable by Pesticide Registrants

Pub. L. No. 108–11, Title II, Apr. 16, 2003, 117 Stat. 603, provided that: "Within 30 days of enactment of this Act [within 30 days of Apr. 16, 2003], the Administrator of the Environmental Protection Agency shall adjust each 'maximum annual fee payable' pursuant to 7 U.S.C. 136a–1(i)(5)(D) and (E) [subsec. (i)(5)(D) and (E) of this section] in a manner such that maintenance fee collections made to reach the level authorized in division K of Public Law

108–7 [Pub. L. No. 108–7, Div. K, Feb. 20, 2003, 117 Stat. 474; see Tables for complete classification] shall be established in the same proportion as those maintenance fee collections authorized in Public Law 107–73 [Pub. L. No. 107–73, Nov. 26, 2001, 115 Stat. 651; see Tables for complete classification]."

§ 136b. Transferred

[FIFRA Former § 4]

HISTORICAL AND STATUTORY NOTES

Codifications

Act of June 25, 1947, c. 125, § 4, as added by Pub. L. No. 92–516, § 2, 86 Stat. 983 (Oct. 21, 1972); and amended by Pub. L. No. 94–140, §§ 5, 11, 89 Stat. 753, 754 (Nov. 28, 1975); Pub. L. No. 95–396, § 9, 92 Stat. 827 (Sept. 30, 1978); Pub. L. No. 100–532, Title VIII, § 801(c), (q)(1)(A), (B), 102 Stat. 2681, 2683 (Oct. 25, 1988). This section, which related to use of restricted use pesticides and certification of applicators, was transferred to subsecs. (a) to (c) of section 11 of Act of June 25, 1947, by section 801(q)(1)(A) of Pub. L. No. 100–532 and is now codified as 7 U.S.C.A. § 136*i*(a) to (c).

§ 136c. Experimental use permits

[FIFRA § 5]

(a) Issuance

Any person may apply to the Administrator for an experimental use permit for a pesticide. An application for an experimental use permit for a covered application under section 33(b) shall conform with the requirements of that section. The Administrator shall review the application. After completion of the review, but not later than one hundred and twenty days after receipt of the application and all required supporting data (or in the case of an application for an experimental use permit for a covered application under section 33(b), not later than the last day of the applicable timeframe for such application specified in such section), the Administrator shall either issue the permit or notify the applicant of the Administrator's determination not to issue the permit and the reasons therefor. The applicant may correct the application or request a waiver of the conditions for such permit within thirty days of receipt by the applicant of such notification. The Administrator may issue an experimental use permit only if the Administrator determines that the applicant needs such permit in order to accumulate information necessary to register a pesticide under section 136a of this title. An application for an experimental use permit may be filed at any time.

(b) Temporary tolerance level

If the Administrator determines that the use of a pesticide may reasonably be expected to result in any residue on or in food or feed, the Administrator may establish a temporary tolerance level for the residue of the pesticide before issuing the experimental use permit.

(c) Use under permit

Use of a pesticide under an experimental use permit shall be under the supervision of the Administrator, and shall be subject to such terms and conditions and be for such period of time as the Administrator may prescribe in the permit.

(d) Studies

When any experimental use permit is issued for a pesticide containing any chemical or combination of chemicals which has not been included in any previously registered pesticide, the Administrator may specify that studies be conducted to detect whether the use of the pesticide under the permit may cause unreasonable adverse effects on the environment. All results of such studies shall be reported to the Administrator before such pesticide may be registered under section 136a of this title.

(e) Revocation

The Administrator may revoke any experimental use permit, at any time, if the Administrator finds that its terms or conditions are being violated, or that its terms and conditions are inadequate to avoid unreasonable adverse effects on the environment.

(f) State issuance of permits

Notwithstanding the foregoing provisions of this section, the Administrator shall, under such terms and conditions as the Administrator may by regulations prescribe, authorize any State to issue an experimental use permit for a pesticide. All provisions of section 136i of this title relating to State plans shall apply with equal force to a State plan for the issuance of experimental use permits under this section.

(g) Exemption for agricultural research agencies

Notwithstanding the foregoing provisions of this section, the Administrator may issue an experimental use permit for a pesticide to any public or private agricultural research agency or educational institution which applies for such permit. Each permit shall not exceed more than a one-year period or such other specific time as the Administrator may prescribe. Such permit shall be issued under such terms and conditions restricting the use of the pesticide as the Administrator may require. Such pesticide may be used only by such research agency or educational institution for purposes of experimentation.

(Act of June 25, 1947, c. 125, § 5, as added by Pub. L. No. 92–516, § 2, 86 Stat. 983 (Oct. 21, 1972); and amended by Pub. L. No. 94–140, § 10, 89 Stat. 754 (Nov. 28, 1975); Pub. L. No. 95–396, § 10, 92 Stat. 828 (Sept. 30, 1978); Pub. L. No. 100–532, Title VIII, § 801(d), (q)(1)(D), 102 Stat. 2681, 2683 (Oct. 25, 1988); Pub. L. No. 102–237, Title X, § 1006(b)(1), 105 Stat. 1895 (Dec. 13, 1991); Pub. L. No. 116–8, § 4 133 Stat. 484, 487 (Mar. 8, 2019).)

HISTORICAL AND STATUTORY NOTES

Effective and Applicability Provisions

1991 Acts. Amendment by section 1006(b)(1) of Pub. L. No. 102–237 effective Dec. 13, 1991, see section 1101(a) of Pub. L. No. 102–237, set out as a note under section 1421 of this title.

1988 Acts. Amendment by Pub. L. No. 100–532 effective on expiration of 60 days after October 25, 1988, see section 901 of Pub. L. No. 100–532, set out as a note under section 136 of this title.

1972 Acts. Section effective at the close of Oct. 21, 1972, except if regulations are necessary for the implementation of any provision that becomes effective on Oct. 21, 1972, and continuation in effect of the provisions of subchapter I of this chapter and regulations thereunder as in effect prior to Oct. 21, 1972, until superseded by provisions of Pub. L. No. 92–516 and regulations thereunder, see section 4 of Pub. L. No. 92–516, set out as a note under section 136 of this title.

Prior Provisions

A prior section 5 of Act of June 25, 1947, was codified as section 135c of this title prior to amendment of Act of June 25, 1947, by Pub. L. No.92–516.

§ 136d. Administrative review; suspension

[FIFRA § 6]

(a) Existing stocks and information

(1) Existing stocks

The Administrator may permit the continued sale and use of existing stocks of a pesticide whose registration is suspended or canceled under this section, or section 136a or 136a–1 of this title, to such extent, under such conditions, and for such uses as the Administrator determines that such sale or use is not inconsistent with the purposes of this subchapter.

(2) Information

If at any time after the registration of a pesticide the registrant has additional factual information regarding unreasonable adverse effects on the environment of the pesticide, the registrant shall submit such information to the Administrator.

(b) Cancellation and change in classification

If it appears to the Administrator that a pesticide or its labeling or other material required to be submitted does not comply with the provisions of this subchapter or, when used in accordance with widespread and commonly recognized practice, generally causes unreasonable adverse effects on the environment, the Administrator may issue a notice of the Administrator's intent either—

(1) to cancel its registration or to change its classification together with the reasons (including the factual basis) for the Administrator's action, or

(2) to hold a hearing to determine whether or not its registration should be canceled or its classification changed.

Such notice shall be sent to the registrant and made public. In determining whether to issue any such notice, the Administrator shall include among those factors to be taken into account the impact of the action proposed in such notice on production and prices of agricultural commodities, retail food prices, and otherwise on the agricultural economy. At least 60 days prior to sending such notice to the registrant or making public such notice, whichever occurs first, the Administrator shall provide the Secretary of Agriculture with a copy of such notice and an analysis of such impact on the agricultural economy. If the Secretary comments in writing to the Administrator regarding the notice and analysis within 30 days after receiving them, the Administrator shall publish in the Federal Register (with the notice) the comments of the Secretary and the response of the Administrator with regard to the Secretary's comments. If the Secretary does not comment in writing to the Administrator regarding the notice and analysis within 30 days after receiving them, the Administrator may notify the registrant and make public the notice at any time after such 30-day period notwithstanding the foregoing 60-day time requirement. The time requirements imposed by the preceding 3 sentences may be waived or modified to the extent agreed upon by the Administrator and the Secretary. Notwithstanding any other provision of this subsection and section 136w(d) of this title, in the event that the Administrator determines that suspension of a pesticide registration is necessary to prevent an imminent hazard to human health, then upon such a finding the Administrator may waive the requirement of notice to and consultation with the Secretary of Agriculture pursuant to this subsection and of submission to the Scientific Advisory Panel pursuant to section 136w(d) of this title and proceed in accordance with subsection (c) of this section. When a public health use is affected, the Secretary of Health and Human Services should provide available benefits and use information, or an analysis thereof, in accordance with the procedures followed and subject to the same conditions as the Secretary of Agriculture in the case of agricultural pesticides. The proposed action shall become final and effective at the end of 30 days from receipt by the registrant, or publication, of a notice issued under paragraph (1), whichever occurs later, unless within that time either (i) the registrant makes the necessary corrections, if possible, or (ii) a request for a hearing is made by a person adversely affected by the notice. In the event a hearing is held pursuant to such a request or to the Administrator's determination under paragraph (2), a decision pertaining to registration or classification issued after completion of such hearing shall be final. In taking any final action under this subsection, the Administrator shall consider restricting a pesticide's use or uses as an alternative to cancellation and shall fully explain the reasons for these restrictions, and shall include among those factors to be taken into account the impact of such final action on production and prices of agricultural commodities, retail food prices, and otherwise on the agricultural economy, and the Administrator shall publish in the Federal Register an analysis of such impact.

(c) Suspension

(1) Order

If the Administrator determines that action is necessary to prevent an imminent hazard during the time required for cancellation or change in classification proceedings, the Administrator may, by order, suspend the registration of the pesticide immediately. Except as provided in paragraph (3), no order of suspension may be issued under this subsection unless the Administrator has issued, or at the same time issues, a notice of intention to cancel the registration or change the classification of the pesticide under subsection (b) of this section. Except as provided in paragraph (3), the Administrator shall notify the registrant prior to issuing any suspension order. Such notice shall include findings pertaining to the question of "imminent hazard". The registrant shall then have an opportunity, in accordance with the provisions of paragraph (2), for an expedited hearing before the Administrator on the question of whether an imminent hazard exists.

(2) Expedite hearing

If no request for a hearing is submitted to the Administrator within five days of the registrant's receipt of the notification provided for by paragraph (1), the suspension order may be issued and shall take effect and shall not be reviewable by a court. If a hearing is requested, it shall commence within five days of the receipt of the request for such hearing unless the registrant and the Administrator agree that it shall commence at a later time. The hearing shall be held in accordance with the provisions of subchapter II of chapter 5 of Title 5, except that the presiding officer need not be a certified administrative law judge. The presiding officer shall have ten days from the conclusion of the presentation of evidence to submit recommended findings and conclusions to the Administrator, who shall then have seven days to render a final order on the issue of suspension.

(3) Emergency order

Whenever the Administrator determines that an emergency exists that does not permit the Administrator to hold a hearing before suspending, the Administrator may issue a suspension order in advance of notification to the registrant. The Administrator may issue an emergency order under this paragraph before issuing a notice of intention to cancel the registration or change the classification of the pesticide under subsection (b) of this section and the Administrator shall proceed to issue the notice under subsection (b) of this section within 90 days of issuing an emergency order. If the Administrator does not issue a notice under subsection (b) of this section within 90 days of issuing an emergency order, the emergency order shall expire. In the case of an emergency order, paragraph (2) shall apply except that (A) the order of suspension shall be in effect pending the expeditious completion of the remedies provided by that paragraph and the issuance of a final order on suspension, and (B) no party other than the registrant and the Administrator shall participate except that any person adversely affected may file briefs within the time allotted by the Agency's rules. Any person so filing briefs shall be considered a party to such proceeding for the purposes of section 136n(b) of this title.

(4) Judicial review

A final order on the question of suspension following a hearing shall be reviewable in accordance with section 136n of this title, notwithstanding the fact that any related cancellation proceedings have not been completed. Any order of suspension entered prior to a hearing before the Administrator shall be subject to immediate review in an action by the registrant or other interested person with the concurrence of the registrant in an appropriate district court, solely to determine whether the order of suspension was arbitrary, capricious or an abuse of discretion, or whether the order was issued in accordance with the procedures established by law. The effect of any order of the court will be only to stay the effectiveness of the suspension order, pending the Administrator's final decision with respect to cancellation or change in classification. This action may be maintained simultaneously with any administrative review proceedings under this section. The commencement of proceedings under this paragraph shall not operate as a stay of order, unless ordered by the court.

(d) Public hearings and scientific review

In the event a hearing is requested pursuant to subsection (b) of this section or determined upon by the Administrator pursuant to subsection (b) of this section, such hearing shall be held after due notice for the purpose of receiving evidence relevant and material to the issues raised by the objections filed by the applicant or other interested parties, or to the issues stated by the Administrator, if the hearing is called by the Administrator rather than by the filing of objections. Upon a showing of relevance and reasonable scope of evidence sought by any party to a public hearing, the Hearing Examiner shall issue a subpena to compel testimony or production of documents from any person. The Hearing Examiner shall be guided by the principles of the Federal Rules of Civil Procedure in making any order for the protection of the witness or the content of documents produced and shall order the payment of reasonable fees and expenses as a condition to requiring testimony of the witness. On contest, the subpena may be enforced by an appropriate United States district court in accordance with the principles stated herein. Upon the request of any party to a public hearing and when in the Hearing Examiner's judgment it is necessary or desirable, the Hearing Examiner shall at any time before the hearing record is closed refer to a Committee of the National Academy of Sciences the relevant questions of scientific fact involved in the public hearing. No member of any committee of the National Academy of Sciences established to carry out the functions of this section shall have a financial or other conflict of interest with respect to any matter considered by such committee. The

Committee of the National Academy of Sciences shall report in writing to the Hearing Examiner within 60 days after such referral on these questions of scientific fact. The report shall be made public and shall be considered as part of the hearing record. The Administrator shall enter into appropriate arrangements with the National Academy of Sciences to assure an objective and competent scientific review of the questions presented to Committees of the Academy and to provide such other scientific advisory services as may be required by the Administrator for carrying out the purposes of this subchapter. As soon as practicable after completion of the hearing (including the report of the Academy) but not later than 90 days thereafter, the Administrator shall evaluate the data and reports before the Administrator and issue an order either revoking the Administrator's notice of intention issued pursuant to this section, or shall issue an order either canceling the registration, changing the classification, denying the registration, or requiring modification of the labeling or packaging of the article. Such order shall be based only on substantial evidence of record of such hearing and shall set forth detailed findings of fact upon which the order is based.

(e) Conditional registration

(1) The Administrator shall issue a notice of intent to cancel a registration issued under section 136a(c)(7) of this title if (A) the Administrator, at any time during the period provided for satisfaction of any condition imposed, determines that the registrant has failed to initiate and pursue appropriate action toward fulfilling any condition imposed, or (B) at the end of the period provided for satisfaction of any condition imposed, that condition has not been met. The Administrator may permit the continued sale and use of existing stocks of a pesticide whose conditional registration has been canceled under this subsection to such extent, under such conditions, and for such uses as the Administrator may specify if the Administrator determines that such sale or use is not inconsistent with the purposes of this subchapter and will not have unreasonable adverse effects on the environment.

(2) A cancellation proposed under this subsection shall become final and effective at the end of thirty days from receipt by the registrant of the notice of intent to cancel unless during that time a request for hearing is made by a person adversely affected by the notice. If a hearing is requested, a hearing shall be conducted under subsection (d) of this section. The only matters for resolution at that hearing shall be whether the registrant has initiated and pursued appropriate action to comply with the condition or conditions within the time provided or whether the condition or conditions have been satisfied within the time provided, and whether the Administrator's determination with respect to the disposition of existing stocks is consistent with this subchapter. A decision after completion of such hearing shall be final. Notwithstanding any other provision of this section, a hearing shall be held and a determination made within seventy-five days after receipt of a request for such hearing.

(f) General provisions

(1) Voluntary cancellation

(A) A registrant may, at any time, request that a pesticide registration of the registrant be canceled or amended to terminate one or more pesticide uses.

(B) Before acting on a request under subparagraph (A), the Administrator shall publish in the Federal Register a notice of the receipt of the request and provide for a 30-day period in which the public may comment.

(C) In the case of a pesticide that is registered for a minor agricultural use, if the Administrator determines that the cancellation or termination of uses would adversely affect the availability of the pesticide for use, the Administrator—

(i) shall publish in the Federal Register a notice of the receipt of the request and make reasonable efforts to inform persons who so use the pesticide of the request; and

(ii) may not approve or reject the request until the termination of the 180-day period beginning on the date of publication of the notice in the Federal Register, except that the Administrator may waive the 180-day period upon the request of the registrant or if the Administrator determines that the continued use of the pesticide would pose an unreasonable adverse effect on the environment.

(D) Subject to paragraph (3)(B), after complying with this paragraph, the Administrator may approve or deny the request.

(2) Publication of notice

A notice of denial of registration, intent to cancel, suspension, or intent to suspend issued under this subchapter or a notice issued under subsection (c)(4) or (d)(5)(A) of section 136a–1 of this title shall be published in the Federal Register and shall be sent by certified mail, return receipt requested, to the registrant's or applicant's address of record on file with the Administrator. If the mailed notice is returned to the Administrator as undeliverable at that address, if delivery is refused, or if the Administrator otherwise is unable to accomplish delivery of the notice to the registrant or applicant after making reasonable efforts to do so, the notice shall be deemed to have been received by the registrant or applicant on the date the notice was published in the Federal Register.

(3) Transfer of registration of pesticides registered for minor agricultural uses

In the case of a pesticide that is registered for a minor agricultural use:

(A) During the 180-day period referred to in paragraph (1)(C)(ii), the registrant of the pesticide may notify the Administrator of an agreement between the registrant and a person or persons (including persons who so use the pesticide) to transfer the registration of the pesticide, in lieu of canceling or amending the registration to terminate the use.

(B) An application for transfer of registration, in conformance with any regulations the Administrator may adopt with respect to the transfer of the pesticide registrations, must be submitted to the Administrator within 30 days of the date of notification provided pursuant to subparagraph (A). If such an application is submitted, the Administrator shall approve the transfer and shall not approve the request for voluntary cancellation or amendment to terminate use unless the Administrator determines that the continued use of the pesticide would cause an unreasonable adverse effect on the environment.

(C) If the Administrator approves the transfer and the registrant transfers the registration of the pesticide, the Administrator shall not cancel or amend the registration to delete the use or rescind the transfer of the registration, during the 180-day period beginning on the date of the approval of the transfer unless the Administrator determines that the continued use of the pesticide would cause an unreasonable adverse effect on the environment.

(D) The new registrant of the pesticide shall assume the outstanding data and other requirements for the pesticide that are pending at the time of the transfer.

(4) Utilization of data for voluntarily canceled pesticide

When an application is filed with the Administrator for the registration of a pesticide for a minor use and another registrant subsequently voluntarily cancels its registration for an identical or substantially similar pesticide for an identical or substantially similar use, the Administrator shall process, review, and evaluate the pending application as if the voluntary cancellation had not yet taken place except that the Administrator shall not take such action if the Administrator determines that such minor use may cause an unreasonable adverse effect on the environment. In order to rely on this subsection, the applicant must certify that it agrees to satisfy any outstanding data requirements necessary to support the reregistration of the pesticide in accordance with the data submission schedule established by the Administrator.

(g) Notice for stored pesticides with canceled or suspended registrations

(1) In general

Any producer or exporter of pesticides, registrant of a pesticide, applicant for registration of a pesticide, applicant for or holder of an experimental use permit, commercial applicator, or any person who distributes or sells any pesticide, who possesses any pesticide which has had its registration canceled or suspended under this section shall notify the Administrator and appropriate State and local officials of—

(A) such possession,

(B) the quantity of such pesticide such person possesses, and

(C) the place at which such pesticide is stored.

(2) **Copies**

The Administrator shall transmit a copy of each notice submitted under this subsection to the regional office of the Environmental Protection Agency which has jurisdiction over the place of pesticide storage identified in the notice.

(h) Judicial review

Final orders of the Administrator under this section shall be subject to judicial review pursuant to section 136n of this title.

(Act of June 25, 1947, c. 125, § 6, as added by Pub. L. No. 92–516, § 2, 86 Stat. 984 (Oct. 21, 1972); and amended by Pub. L. No 94–140, § 1, 89 Stat. 751 (Nov. 28, 1975); Pub. L. No. 95–251, § 2(a)(2), 92 Stat. 183, 184 (Mar. 27, 1978); Pub. L. No. 95–396, §§ 11, 12, 92 Stat. 828 (Sept. 30, 1978); Pub. L. No. 98–620, Title IV, § 402(4)(A), 98 Stat. 3357 (Nov. 8, 1984); Pub. L. No. 100–532, Title II, § 201, Title IV, § 404, Title VIII, § 801(e), (q)(2)(B), 102 Stat. 2668, 2673, 2681, 2683 (Oct. 25, 1988); Pub. L. No. 101–624, Title XIV, § 1494, 104 Stat. 3628 (Nov. 28, 1990); Pub. L. No. 102–237, Title X, § 1006(a)(5), (b)(1), (2), (3)(C) to (E), 105 Stat. 1895, 1896 (Dec. 13, 1991); Pub. L. No. 104–170, Title I, §§ 102, 106(a), Title II, §§ 210(g), (h), 233, 110 Stat. 1489, 1491, 1500, 1509 (Aug. 3, 1996).)

HISTORICAL AND STATUTORY NOTES

Codifications

"Subchapter II of chapter 5 of Title 5", referred to in subsec. (c)(2), was in the original "subchapter II of Title 5", and has been editorially changed as the probable intent of Congress.

Effective and Applicability Provisions

1988 Acts. Amendment by Pub. L. No. 100–532 effective on expiration of 60 days after October 25, 1988, see section 901 of Pub. L. No. 100–532, set out as a note under section 136 of this title.

1984 Acts. Amendment by Pub. L. No. 98–620 not to apply to cases pending on Nov. 8, 1984, see section 403 of Pub. L. No. 98–620, set out as a note under section 1657 of Title 28, Judiciary and Judicial Procedure.

1972 Acts. Section effective at the close of Oct. 21, 1972, except if regulations are necessary for the implementation of any provision that becomes effective on Oct. 21, 1972, and continuation in effect of the provisions of subchapter I of this chapter and regulations thereunder as in effect prior to Oct. 21, 1972, until superseded by provisions of Pub. L. No. 92–516 and regulations thereunder, see section 4 of Pub. L. No. 92–516, set out as a note under section 136 of this title.

Change of Name

In subsec. (d), "Administrative Law Judge" and "Administrative Law Judge's" were substituted for "Hearing Examiner" and "Hearing Examiner's", respectively, on authority of section 3 of Pub. L. No. 95–251, which provided that any reference in any law, regulation, or order to a hearing examiner appointed under section 3105 of Title 5, Government Organization and Employees, be deemed a reference to an administrative law judge.

Severability of Provisions

If any provision of Pub. L. No. 101–624 or the application thereof to any person or circumstance is held invalid, such invalidity not to affect other provisions or applications of Pub. L. No. 101–624 which can be given effect without regard to the invalid provision or application, see section 2519 of Pub. L. No. 101–624, set out as a note under section 1421 of this title.

Prior Provisions

A prior section 6 of Act of June 25, 1947, was codified as section 135d of this title prior to amendment of Act of June 25, 1947, by Pub. L. No. 92–516.

§ 136e. Registration of establishments

[FIFRA § 7]

(a) Requirement

No person shall produce any pesticide subject to this subchapter or active ingredient used in producing a pesticide subject to this subchapter in any State unless the establishment in which it is produced is registered with the Administrator. The application for registration of any establishment shall include the name and address of the establishment and of the producer who operates such establishment.

(b) Registration

Whenever the Administrator receives an application under subsection (a) of this section, the Administrator shall register the establishment and assign it an establishment number.

(c) Information required

(1) Any producer operating an establishment registered under this section shall inform the Administrator within 30 days after it is registered of the types and amounts of pesticides and, if applicable, active ingredients used in producing pesticides—

(A) which the producer is currently producing;

(B) which the producer has produced during the past year; and

(C) which the producer has sold or distributed during the past year.

The information required by this paragraph shall be kept current and submitted to the Administrator annually as required under such regulations as the Administrator may prescribe.

(2) Any such producer shall, upon the request of the Administrator for the purpose of issuing a stop sale order pursuant to section 136k of this title, inform the Administrator of the name and address of any recipient of any pesticide produced in any registered establishment which the producer operates.

(d) Confidential records and information

Any information submitted to the Administrator pursuant to subsection (c) of this section other than the names of the pesticides or active ingredients used in producing pesticides produced, sold, or distributed at an establishment shall be considered confidential and shall be subject to the provisions of section 136h of this title.

(Act of June 25, 1947, c. 125, § 7, as added by Pub. L. No. 92–516, § 2, 86 Stat. 987 (Oct. 21, 1972); and amended by Pub. L. No. 95–396, § 13, 92 Stat. 829 (Sept. 30, 1978); Pub. L. No. 102–237, Title X, § 1006(b)(1), (3)(F), (G), 105 Stat. 1895, 1896 (Dec. 13, 1991).)

HISTORICAL AND STATUTORY NOTES

Effective and Applicability Provisions

1991 Acts. Amendments by Pub. L. No. 102–237 effective Dec. 13, 1991, see section 1101(a) of Pub. L. No. 102–237, set out as a note under section 1421 of this title.

1972 Acts. Section effective at the close of Oct. 21, 1972, except if regulations are necessary for the implementation of any provision that becomes effective on Oct. 21, 1972, and continuation in effect of the provisions of subchapter I of this chapter and regulations thereunder as in effect prior to Oct. 21, 1972, until superseded by provisions of Pub. L. No. 92–516 and regulations thereunder, see section 4 of Pub. L. No. 92–516, set out as a note under section 136 of this title.

Prior Provisions

A prior section 7 of Act of June 25, 1947, was codified as section 135e of this title prior to amendment of Act of June 25, 1947, by Pub. L. No. 92–516.

§ 136f. Books and records

[FIFRA § 8]

(a) Requirements

The Administrator may prescribe regulations requiring producers, registrants, and applicants for registration to maintain such records with respect to their operations and the pesticides and devices produced as the Administrator determines are necessary for the effective enforcement of this subchapter and to make the records available for inspection and copying in the same manner as provided in subsection (b) of this section. No records required under this subsection shall extend to financial data, sales data other than shipment data, pricing data, personnel data, and research data (other than data relating to registered pesticides or to a pesticide for which an application for registration has been filed).

(b) Inspection

For the purposes of enforcing the provisions of this subchapter, any producer, distributor, carrier, dealer, or any other person who sells or offers for sale, delivers or offers for delivery any pesticide or device subject to this subchapter, shall, upon request of any officer or employee of the Environmental Protection Agency or of any State or political subdivision, duly designated by the Administrator, furnish or permit such person at all reasonable times to have access to, and to copy: (1) all records showing the delivery, movement, or holding of such pesticide or device, including the quantity, the date of shipment and receipt, and the name of the consignor and consignee; or (2) in the event of the inability of any person to produce records containing such information, all other records and information relating to such delivery, movement, or holding of the pesticide or device. Any inspection with respect to any records and information referred to in this subsection shall not extend to financial data, sales data other than shipment data, pricing data, personnel data; and research data (other than data relating to registered pesticides or to a pesticide for which an application for registration has been filed). Before undertaking an inspection under this subsection, the officer or employee must present to the owner, operator, or agent in charge of the establishment or other place where pesticides or devices are held for distribution or sale, appropriate credentials and a written statement as to the reason for the inspection, including a statement as to whether a violation of the law is suspected. If no violation is suspected, an alternate and sufficient reason shall be given in writing. Each such inspection shall be commenced and completed with reasonable promptness.

(Act of June 25, 1947, c. 125, § 8, as added by Pub. L. No. 92–516, § 2, 86 Stat. 987 (Oct. 21, 1972); and amended by Pub. L. No. 95–396, § 14, 92 Stat. 829 (Sept. 30, 1978); Pub. L. No. 100–532, Title III, § 301, 102 Stat. 2668 (Oct. 25, 1988); Pub. L. No. 102–237, Title X, § 1006(b)(1), 105 Stat. 1895 (Dec. 13, 1991).)

HISTORICAL AND STATUTORY NOTES

Effective and Applicability Provisions

1991 Acts. Amendment by section 1006(b)(1) of Pub. L. No. 102–237 effective Dec. 13, 1991, see section 1101(a) of Pub. L. No. 102–237, set out as a note under section 1421 of this title.

1988 Acts. Amendment by Pub. L. No. 100–532 effective on expiration of 60 days after October 25, 1988, see section 901 of Pub. L. No. 100–532, set out as a note under section 136 of this title.

1972 Acts. Section effective at the close of Oct. 21, 1972, except if regulations are necessary for the implementation of any provision that becomes effective on Oct. 21, 1972, and continuation in effect of the provisions of subchapter I of this chapter and regulations thereunder as in effect prior to Oct. 21, 1972, until superseded by provisions of Pub. L. No. 92–516 and regulations thereunder, see section 4 of Pub. L. No. 92–516, set out as a note under section 136 of this title.

Prior Provisions

A prior section 8 of Act of June 25, 1947, was codified as section 135f of this title prior to amendment of Act of June 25, 1947, by Pub. L. No. 92–516.

§ 136g. Inspection of establishments, etc.

[FIFRA § 9]

(a) In general

(1) For purposes of enforcing the provisions of this subchapter, officers or employees of the Environmental Protection Agency or of any State duly designated by the Administrator are authorized to enter at reasonable times (A) any establishment or other place where pesticides or devices are held for distribution or sale for the purpose of inspecting and obtaining samples of any pesticides or devices, packaged, labeled, and released for shipment, and samples of any containers or labeling for such pesticides or devices, or (B) any place where there is being held any pesticide the registration of which has been suspended or canceled for the purpose of determining compliance with section 136q of this title.

(2) Before undertaking such inspection, the officers or employees must present to the owner, operator, or agent in charge of the establishment or other place where pesticides or devices are held for distribution or sale, appropriate credentials and a written statement as to the reason for the inspection, including a statement as to whether a violation of the law is suspected. If no violation is suspected, an alternate and sufficient reason shall be given in writing. Each such inspection shall be commenced and completed with reasonable promptness. If the officer or employee obtains any samples, prior to leaving the premises, the officer or employee shall give to the owner, operator, or agent in charge a receipt describing the samples obtained and, if requested, a portion of each such sample equal in volume or weight to the portion retained. If an analysis is made of such samples, a copy of the results of such analysis shall be furnished promptly to the owner, operator, or agent in charge.

(b) Warrants

For purposes of enforcing the provisions of this subchapter and upon a showing to an officer or court of competent jurisdiction that there is reason to believe that the provisions of this subchapter have been violated, officers or employees duly designated by the Administrator are empowered to obtain and to execute warrants authorizing—

(1) entry, inspection, and copying of records for purposes of this section or section 136f of this title;

(2) inspection and reproduction of all records showing the quantity, date of shipment, and the name of consignor and consignee of any pesticide or device found in the establishment which is adulterated, misbranded, not registered (in the case of a pesticide) or otherwise in violation of this subchapter and in the event of the inability of any person to produce records containing such information, all other records and information relating to such delivery, movement, or holding of the pesticide or device; and

(3) the seizure of any pesticide or device which is in violation of this subchapter.

(c) Enforcement

(1) Certification of facts to Attorney General

The examination of pesticides or devices shall be made in the Environmental Protection Agency or elsewhere as the Administrator may designate for the purpose of determining from such examinations whether they comply with the requirements of this subchapter. If it shall appear from any such examination that they fail to comply with the requirements of this subchapter, the Administrator shall cause notice to be given to the person against whom criminal or civil proceedings are contemplated. Any person so notified shall be given an opportunity to present the person's views, either orally or in writing, with regard to such contemplated proceedings, and if in the opinion of the Administrator it appears that the provisions of this subchapter have been violated by such person, then the Administrator shall certify the facts to the Attorney General, with a copy of the results of the analysis or the examination of such pesticide for the institution of a criminal proceeding pursuant to section 136*l*(b) of this title or a civil proceeding under section 136*l*(a) of this title, when the Administrator determines that such action will be sufficient to effectuate the purposes of this subchapter.

(2) Notice not required

The notice of contemplated proceedings and opportunity to present views set forth in this subsection are not prerequisites to the institution of any proceeding by the Attorney General.

(3) Warning notices

Nothing in this subchapter shall be construed as requiring the Administrator to institute proceedings for prosecution of minor violations of this subchapter whenever the Administrator believes that the public interest will be adequately served by a suitable written notice of warning.

(Act of June 25, 1947, c. 125, § 9, as added by Pub. L. No. 92–516, § 2, 86 Stat. 1988 (Oct. 21, 1972); and amended by Pub. L. No. 100–532, Title III, § 302, 102 Stat. 2669 (Oct. 25, 1988); Pub. L. No. 102–237, Title X, § 1006(b)(1), (3)(H), (I), 105 Stat. 1895, 1896 (Dec. 13, 1991).)

HISTORICAL AND STATUTORY NOTES

Effective and Applicability Provisions

1991 Acts. Amendments by Pub. L. No. 102–237 effective Dec. 13, 1991, see section 1101(a) of Pub. L. No. 102–237, set out as a note under section 1421 of this title.

1988 Acts. Amendment by Pub. L. No. 100–532 effective on expiration of 60 days after October 25, 1988, see section 901 of Pub. L. No. 100–532, set out as a note under section 136 of this title.

1972 Acts. Section effective at the close of Oct. 21, 1972, except if regulations are necessary for the implementation of any provision that becomes effective on Oct. 21, 1972, and continuation in effect of the provisions of subchapter I of this chapter and regulations thereunder as in effect prior to Oct. 21, 1972, until superseded by provisions of Pub. L. No. 92–516 and regulations thereunder, see section 4 of Pub. L. No. 92–516, set out as a note under section 136 of this title.

Prior Provisions

A prior section 9 of Act of June 25, 1947, was codified as section 135g of this title prior to amendment of Act of June 25, 1947, by Pub. L. No. 92–516.

§ 136h. Protection of trade secrets and other information

[FIFRA § 10]

(a) In general

In submitting data required by this subchapter, the applicant may (1) clearly mark any portions thereof which in the applicant's opinion are trade secrets or commercial or financial information and (2) submit such market material separately from other material required to be submitted under this subchapter.

(b) Disclosure

Notwithstanding any other provision of this subchapter and subject to the limitations in subsections (d) and (e) of this section, the Administrator shall not make public information which in the Administrator's judgment contains or relates to trade secrets or commercial or financial information obtained from a person and privileged or confidential, except that, when necessary to carry out the provisions of this subchapter, information relating to formulas of products acquired by authorization of this subchapter may be revealed to any Federal agency consulted and may be revealed at a public hearing or in findings of fact issued by the Administrator.

(c) Disputes

If the Administrator proposes to release for inspection information which the applicant or registrant believes to be protected from disclosure under subsection (b) of this section, the Administrator shall notify the applicant or registrant, in writing, by certified mail. The Administrator shall not thereafter make available for inspection such data until thirty days after receipt of the notice by the applicant or registrant. During this period, the applicant or registrant may institute an action in an appropriate district court for a declaratory judgment as to whether such information is subject to protection under subsection (b) of this section.

(d) Limitations

(1) All information concerning the objectives, methodology, results, or significance of any test or experiment performed on or with a registered or previously registered pesticide or its separate ingredients, impurities, or degradation products, and any information concerning the effects of such pesticide on any organism or the behavior of such pesticide in the environment, including, but not limited to, data on safety to fish and wildlife, humans and other mammals, plants, animals, and soil, and studies on persistence, translocation and fate in the environment, and metabolism, shall be available for disclosure to the public. The use of such data for any registration purpose shall be governed by section 136a of this title. This paragraph does not authorize the disclosure of any information that—

(A) discloses manufacturing or quality control processes,

(B) discloses the details of any methods for testing, detecting, or measuring the quantity of any deliberately added inert ingredient of a pesticide, or

(C) discloses the identity or percentage quantity of any deliberately added inert ingredient of a pesticide,

unless the Administrator has first determined that disclosure is necessary to protect against an unreasonable risk of injury to health or the environment.

(2) Information concerning production, distribution, sale, or inventories of a pesticide that is otherwise entitled to confidential treatment under subsection (b) of this section may be publicly disclosed in connection with a public proceeding to determine whether a pesticide, or any ingredient of a pesticide, causes unreasonable adverse effects on health or the environment, if the Administrator determines that such disclosure is necessary in the public interest.

(3) If the Administrator proposes to disclose information described in clause (A), (B), or (C) of paragraph (1) or in paragraph (2) of this subsection, the Administrator shall notify by certified mail the submitter of such information of the intent to release such information. The Administrator may not release such information, without the submitter's consent, until thirty days after the submitter has been furnished such notice. Where the Administrator finds that disclosure of information described in clause (A), (B), or (C) of paragraph (1) of this subsection is necessary to avoid or lessen an imminent and substantial risk of injury to the public health, the Administrator may set such shorter period of notice (but not less than ten days) and such method of notice as the Administrator finds appropriate. During such period the data submitter may institute an action in an appropriate district court to enjoin or limit the proposed disclosure. The court may enjoin disclosure, or limit the disclosure or the parties to whom disclosure shall be made, to the extent that—

(A) in the case of information described in clause (A), (B), or (C)of paragraph (1) of this subsection, the proposed disclosure is not required to protect against an unreasonable risk of injury to health or the environment; or

(B) in the case of information described in paragraph (2) of this subsection, the public interest in availability of the information in the public proceeding does not outweigh the interests in preserving the confidentiality of the information.

(e) Disclosure to contractors

Information otherwise protected from disclosure to the public under subsection (b) of this section may be disclosed to contractors with the United States and employees of such contractors if, in the opinion of the Administrator, such disclosure is necessary for the satisfactory performance by the contractor of a contract with the United States for the performance of work in connection with this subchapter and under such conditions as the Administrator may specify. The Administrator shall require as a condition to the disclosure of information under this subsection that the person receiving it take such security precautions respecting the information as the Administrator shall by regulation prescribe.

(f) Penalty for disclosure by Federal employees

(1) Any officer or employee of the United States or former officer or employee of the United States who, by virtue of such employment or official position, has obtained possession of, or has access to, material the disclosure of which is prohibited by subsection (b) of this section, and who, knowing that disclosure of such material is prohibited by such subsection, willfully discloses the material in any manner to any person not entitled to receive it, shall be fined not more than $10,000 or imprisoned for not more than one year, or both. Section 1905 of Title 18 shall not apply with respect to the publishing, divulging, disclosure, or making known of, or making available, information reported or otherwise obtained under this subchapter. Nothing in this subchapter shall preempt any civil remedy under State or Federal law for wrongful disclosure of trade secrets.

(2) For the purposes of this section, any contractor with the United States who is furnished information as authorized by subsection (e) of this section, or any employee of any such contractor, shall be considered to be an employee of the United States.

(g) Disclosure to foreign and multinational pesticide producers

(1) The Administrator shall not knowingly disclose information submitted by an applicant or registrant under this subchapter to any employee or agent of any business or other entity engaged in the production, sale, or distribution of pesticides in countries other than the United States or in addition to the United States or to any other person who intends to deliver such data to such foreign or multinational business or entity unless the applicant or registrant has consented to such disclosure. The Administrator shall require an affirmation from any person who intends to inspect data that such person does not seek access to the data for purposes of delivering it or offering it for sale to any such business or entity or its agents or employees and will not purposefully deliver or negligently cause the data to be delivered to such business or entity or its agents or employees. Notwithstanding any other provision of this subsection, the Administrator may disclose information to any person in connection with a public proceeding under law or regulation, subject to restrictions on the availability of information contained elsewhere in this subchapter, which information is relevant to a determination by the Administrator with respect to whether a pesticide, or any ingredient of a pesticide, causes unreasonable adverse effects on health or the environment.

(2) The Administrator shall maintain records of the names of persons to whom data are disclosed under this subsection and the persons or organizations they represent and shall inform the applicant or registrant of the names and affiliations of such persons.

(3) Section 1001 of Title 18 shall apply to any affirmation made under paragraph (1) of this subsection.

(Act of June 25, 1947, c. 125, § 10, as added by Pub. L. No. 92–516, § 2, 86 Stat. 989 (Oct. 21, 1972); and amended by Pub. L. No. 95–396, § 15, 92 Stat. 829 (Sept. 30, 1978); Pub. L. No. 98–620, Title IV, § 402(4)(B), 98 Stat. 3357 (Nov. 8, 1984); Pub. L. No. 100–532, Title VIII, § 801(f), 102 Stat. 2682 (Oct. 25, 1988); Pub. L. No. 102–237, Title X, § 1006(b)(1), (2), (3)(J), 105 Stat. 1895, 1896 (Dec. 13, 1991).)

HISTORICAL AND STATUTORY NOTES

Effective and Applicability Provisions

1991 Acts. Amendments by Pub. L. No. 102–237 effective Dec. 13, 1991, see section 1101(a) of Pub. L. No. 102–237, set out as a note under section 1421 of this title.

1988 Acts. Amendment by Pub. L. No. 100–532 effective 60 days after October 25, 1988, see section 901 of Pub. L. No. 100–532, set out as a note under section 136 of this title.

1984 Acts. Amendment by Pub. L. No. 98–620 not to apply to cases pending on Nov. 8, 1984, see section 403 of Pub. L. No. 98–620, set out as a note under section 1657 of Title 28, Judiciary and Judicial Procedure.

1972 Acts. Section effective at the close of Oct. 21, 1972, except if regulations are necessary for the implementation of any provision that becomes effective on Oct. 21, 1972, and continuation in effect of the provisions of subchapter I of this chapter and regulations thereunder as in effect prior to Oct. 21, 1972, until superseded by provisions of Pub. L. No. 92–516 and regulations thereunder, see section 4 of Pub. L. No. 92–516, set out as a note under section 136 of this title.

Prior Provision

A prior section 10 of Act of June 25, 1947, was codified as section 135h of this title prior to amendment of Act of June 25, 1947, by Pub. L. No. 92–516.

§ 136i. Use of restricted use pesticides; applicators

[FIFRA § 11]

(a) Certification procedure

(1) Federal certification

In any State for which a State plan for applicator certification has not been approved by the Administrator, the Administrator, in consultation with the Governor of such State, shall conduct a program for the certification of applicators of pesticides. Such program shall conform to the requirements imposed upon the States under the provisions of subsection (a)(2) of this section and shall not require private applicators to take any examination to establish competency in the use of pesticides. Prior to the implementation of the program, the Administrator shall publish in the Federal Register for review and comment a summary of the Federal plan for applicator certification and shall make generally available within the State copies of the plan. The Administrator shall hold public hearings at one or more locations within the State if so requested by the Governor of such State during the thirty days following publication of the Federal Register notice inviting comment on the Federal plan. The hearings shall be held within thirty days following receipt of the request from the Governor. In any State in which the Administrator conducts a certification program, the Administrator may require any person engaging in the commercial application, sale, offering for sale, holding for sale, or distribution of any pesticide one or more uses of which have been classified for restricted use to maintain such records and submit such reports concerning the commercial application, sale, or distribution of such pesticide as the Administrator may by regulation prescribe. Subject to paragraph (2), the Administrator shall prescribe standards for the certification of applicators of pesticides. Such standards shall provide that to be certified, an individual must be determined to be competent with respect to the use and handling of the pesticides, or to the use and handling of the pesticide or class of pesticides covered by such individual's certification. The certification standard for a private applicator shall, under a State plan submitted for approval, be deemed fulfilled by the applicator completing a certification form. The Administrator shall further assure that such form contains adequate information and affirmations to carry out the intent of this subchapter, and may include in the form an affirmation that the private applicator has completed a training program approved by the Administrator so long as the program does not require the private applicator to take, pursuant to a requirement prescribed by the Administrator, any examination to establish competency in the use of the pesticide. The Administrator may require any pesticide dealer participating in a certification program to be licensed under a State licensing program approved by the Administrator.

(2) State certification

If any State, at any time, desires to certify applicators of pesticides, the Governor of such State shall submit a State plan for such purpose. The Administrator shall approve the plan submitted by any State, or any modification thereof, if such plan in the Administrator's judgment—

(A) designates a State agency as the agency responsible for administering the plan throughout the State;

(B) contains satisfactory assurances that such agency has or will have the legal authority and qualified personnel necessary to carry out the plan;

(C) gives satisfactory assurances that the State will devote adequate funds to the administration of the plan;

(D) provides that the State agency will make such reports to the Administrator in such form and containing such information as the Administrator may from time to time require; and

(E) contains satisfactory assurances that State standards for the certification of applicators of pesticides conform with those standards prescribed by the Administrator under paragraph (1).

Any State certification program under this section shall be maintained in accordance with the State plan approved under this section.

(b) State plans

If the Administrator rejects a plan submitted under subsection (a)(2) of this section, the Administrator shall afford the State submitting the plan due notice and opportunity for hearing before so doing. If the Administrator approves a plan submitted under subsection (a)(2) of this section, then such State shall certify applicators of pesticides with respect to such State. Whenever the Administrator determines that a State is not administering the certification program in accordance with the plan approved under this section, the Administrator shall so notify the State and provide for a hearing at the request of the State, and, if appropriate corrective action is not taken within a reasonable time, not to exceed ninety days, the Administrator shall withdraw approval of such plan.

(c) Instruction in integrated pest management techniques

Standards prescribed by the Administrator for the certification of applicators of pesticides under subsection (a) of this section, and State plans submitted to the Administrator under subsection (a) of this section, shall include provisions for making instructional materials concerning integrated pest management techniques available to individuals at their request in accordance with the provisions of section 136u(c) of this title, but such plans may not require that any individual receive instruction concerning such techniques or to be shown to be competent with respect to the use of such techniques. The Administrator and States implementing such plans shall provide that all interested individuals are notified on the availability of such instructional materials.

(d) In general

No regulations prescribed by the Administrator for carrying out the provisions of this subchapter shall require any private applicator to maintain any records or file any reports or other documents.

(e) Separate standards

When establishing or approving standards for licensing or certification, the Administrator shall establish separate standards for commercial and private applicators.

(Act of June 25, 1947, c. 125, § 11, formerly §§ 4 and 11, as added by Pub. L. No. 92–516, § 2, 86 Stat. 983, 989 (Oct. 21, 1972); and amended by Pub. L. No. 94–140, §§ 5, 11, 89 Stat. 753, 754 (Nov. 28, 1975); Pub. L. No. 95–396, § 9, 92 Stat. 827 (Sept. 30, 1978); renumbered § 11 and amended by Pub. L. No. 100–532, Title VIII, § 801(c), (q)(1)(A) to (C), 102 Stat. 2681, 2683 (Oct. 25, 1988); Pub. L. No. 102–237, Title X, § 1006(a)(6), (b)(1), (2), (3)(K), 105 Stat. 1895, 1896 (Dec. 13, 1991).)

HISTORICAL AND STATUTORY NOTES

Codifications

Pub. L. No. 100–332, § 801(q)(1)(A), transferred subsecs. (a) to (c) of section 4 of Act of June 25, 1947, which was codified as section 136b of this title, to subsecs. (a) to (c) of this section.

Effective and Applicability Provisions

1991 Acts. Amendments by Pub. L. No. 102–237 effective Dec. 13, 1991, see section 1101(a) of Pub. L. No. 102–237, set out as a note under section 1421 of this title.

1988 Acts. Amendment by Pub. L. No. 100–532 effective on expiration of 60 days after October 25, 1988, see section 901 of Pub. L. No. 100–532, set out as a note under section 136 of this title.

1972 Acts. Section effective at the close of Oct. 21, 1972, except if regulations are necessary for the implementation of any provision that becomes effective on Oct. 21, 1972, and continuation in effect of the provisions of subchapter I of this chapter and regulations thereunder as in effect prior to Oct. 21, 1972, until superseded by provisions of Pub. L. No. 92–516 and regulations thereunder, see section 4 of Pub. L. No. 92–516, set out as a note under section 136 of this title.

Prior Provisions

A prior section 11 of Act of June 25, 1947, was codified as section 135i of this title prior to amendment of Act of June 25, 1947, by Pub. L. No. 92–516.

§ 136i–1. Pesticide recordkeeping

(a) Requirements

(1) The Secretary of Agriculture, in consultation with the Administrator of the Environmental Protection Agency, shall require certified applicators of restricted use pesticides (of the type described under section 136a(d)(1)(C) of this title) to maintain records comparable to records maintained by commercial applicators of pesticides in each State. If there is no State requirement for the maintenance of records, such applicator shall maintain records that contain the product name, amount, approximate date of application, and location of application of each such pesticide used for a 2-year period after such use.

(2) Within 30 days of a pesticide application, a commercial certified applicator shall provide a copy of records maintained under paragraph (1) to the person for whom such application was provided.

(b) Access

Records maintained under subsection (a) of this section shall be made available to any Federal or State agency that deals with pesticide use or any health or environmental issue related to the use of pesticides, on the request of such agency. Each such Federal agency shall conduct surveys and record the data from individual applicators to facilitate statistical analysis for environmental and agronomic purposes, but in no case may a government agency release data, including the location from which the data was derived, that would directly or indirectly reveal the identity of individual producers. In the case of Federal agencies, such access to records maintained under subsection (a) of this section shall be through the Secretary of Agriculture, or the Secretary's designee. State agency requests for access to records maintained under subsection (a) of this section shall be through the lead State agency so designated by the State.

(c) Health care personnel

When a health professional determines that pesticide information maintained under this section is necessary to provide medical treatment or first aid to an individual who may have been exposed to pesticides for which the information is maintained, upon request persons required to maintain records under subsection (a) of this section shall promptly provide record and available label information to that health professional. In the case of an emergency, such record information shall be provided immediately.

(d) Penalty

The Secretary of Agriculture shall be responsible for the enforcement of subsections (a), (b), and (c) of this section. A violation of such subsection shall—

(1) in the case of the first offense, be subject to a fine of not more than $500; and

(2) in the case of subsequent offenses, be subject to a fine of not less than $1,000 for each violation, except that the penalty shall be less than $1,000 if the Secretary determines that the person made a good faith effort to comply with such subsection.

(e) Federal or State provisions

The requirements of this section shall not affect provisions of other Federal or State laws.

(f) Surveys and reports

The Secretary of Agriculture and the Administrator of the Environmental Protection Agency, shall survey the records maintained under subsection (a) of this section to develop and maintain a data base that is sufficient to enable the Secretary and the Administrator to publish annual comprehensive reports concerning agricultural and nonagricultural pesticide use. The Secretary and Administrator shall enter into a memorandum of understanding to define their respective responsibilities under this subsection in order to avoid duplication of effort. Such reports shall be transmitted to Congress not later than April 1 of each year.

(g) Regulations

The Secretary of Agriculture and the Administrator of the Environmental Protection Agency shall promulgate regulations on their respective areas of responsibility implementing this section within 180 days after November 28, 1990.

(As added by Pub. L. No. 101–624, Title XIV, § 1491, 104 Stat. 3627 (Nov. 28, 1990); and amended by Pub. L. No. 102–237, Title X, § 1006(d), 105 Stat. 1896 (Dec. 13, 1991).)

HISTORICAL AND STATUTORY NOTES

Codifications

This section was enacted as part of the Food, Agriculture, Conservation and Trade Act of 1990, and not as part of the Federal Insecticide, Fungicide, and Rodenticide Act, which comprises this subchapter.

Effective and Applicability Provisions

1991 Acts. Amendment by Pub. L. No. 102–237 effective Dec. 13, 1991, see section 1101(a) of Pub. L. No. 102–237, set out as a note under section 1421 of this title.

Severability of Provisions

If any provision of Pub. L. No. 101–624 or the application thereof to any person or circumstance is held invalid, such invalidity not to affect other provisions or applications of Pub. L. No. 101–624 which can be given effect without regard to the invalid provision or application, see section 2519 of Pub. L. No. 101–624, set out as a note under section 1421 of this title.

§ 136i–2. Collection of pesticide use information

(a) In general

The Secretary of Agriculture shall collect data of statewide or regional significance on the use of pesticides to control pests and diseases of major crops and crops of dietary significance, including fruits and vegetables.

(b) Collection

The data shall be collected by surveys of farmers or from other sources offering statistically reliable data.

(c) Coordination

The Secretary of Agriculture shall, as appropriate, coordinate with the Administrator of the Environmental Protection Agency in the design of the surveys and make available to the Administrator the aggregate results of the surveys to assist the Administrator.

(As added by Pub. L. No. 104–170, Title III, § 302, 110 Stat. 1512 (Aug. 3, 1996).)

HISTORICAL AND STATUTORY NOTES

Codifications

This section was enacted as part of the Food Quality Protection Act of 1996 and not as part of the Federal Insecticide, Fungicide, and Rodenticide Act of 1996, which comprises this subchapter.

Pesticide Use Information Study

Section 305 of Pub. L. No. 104–170 provided that:

"(a) The Secretary of Agriculture shall, in consultation with the Administrator of the Environmental Protection Agency, prepare a report to Congress evaluating the current status and potential improvements in Federal pesticide use information gathering activities. This report shall at least include—

"(1) an analysis of the quality and reliability of the information collected by the Department of Agriculture, the Environmental Protection Agency, and other Federal agencies regarding the agricultural use of pesticides; and

"(2) an analysis of options to increase the effectiveness of national pesticide use information collection, including an analysis of costs, burdens placed on agricultural producers and other pesticide users, and effectiveness in tracking risk reduction by those options.

"(b) The Secretary shall submit this report to Congress not later than 1 year following the date of enactment of this section [August 3, 1996]."

§ 136j. Unlawful acts

[FIFRA § 12]

(a) In general

(1) Except as provided by subsection (b) of this section, it shall be unlawful for any person in any State to distribute or sell to any person—

(A) any pesticide that is not registered under section 136a of this title or whose registration has been canceled or suspended, except to the extent that distribution or sale otherwise has been authorized by the Administrator under this subchapter;

(B) any registered pesticide if any claims made for it as a part of its distribution or sale substantially differ from any claims made for it as a part of the statement required in connection with its registration under section 136a of this title;

(C) any registered pesticide the composition of which differs at the time of its distribution or sale from its composition as described in the statement required in connection with its registration under section 136a of this title;

(D) any pesticide which has not been colored or discolored pursuant to the provisions of section 136w(c)(5) of this title;

(E) any pesticide which is adulterated or misbranded; or

(F) any device which is misbranded.

(2) It shall be unlawful for any person—

(A) to detach, alter, deface, or destroy, in whole or in part, any labeling required under this subchapter;

(B) to refuse to—

(i) prepare, maintain, or submit any records required by or under section 136c, 136e, 136f, 136i, or 136q of this title;

(ii) submit any reports required by or under section 136c, 136d, 136e, 136f, 136i, or 136q of this title; or

(iii) allow any entry, inspection, copying of records, or sampling authorized by this subchapter;

(C) to give a guaranty or undertaking provided for in subsection (b) of this section which is false in any particular, except that a person who receives and relies upon a guaranty authorized under subsection (b) of this section may give a guaranty to the same effect, which guaranty shall contain, in addition to the person's own name and address, the name and address of the person residing in the United States from whom the person received the guaranty or undertaking;

(D) to use for the person's own advantage or to reveal, other than to the Administrator, or officials or employees of the Environmental Protection Agency or other Federal executive agencies, or to the courts, or to physicians, pharmacists, and other qualified persons, needing such information for the performance of their duties, in accordance with such directions as the Administrator may prescribe, any information acquired by authority of this subchapter which is confidential under this subchapter;

(E) who is a registrant, wholesaler, dealer, retailer, or other distributor to advertise a product registered under this subchapter for restricted use without giving the classification of the product assigned to it under section 136a of this title;

(F) to distribute or sell, or to make available for use, or to use, any registered pesticide classified for restricted use for some or all purposes other than in accordance with section 136a(d) of this title and any regulations thereunder, except that it shall not be unlawful to sell, under regulations issued by the Administrator, a restricted use pesticide to a person who is not a certified applicator for application by a certified applicator;

(G) to use any registered pesticide in a manner inconsistent with its labeling;

(H) to use any pesticide which is under an experimental use permit contrary to the provisions of such permit;

(I) to violate any order issued under section 136k of this title;

(J) to violate any suspension order issued under section 136a(c)(2)(B), 136a–1, or 136d of this title;

(K) to violate any cancellation order issued under this subchapter or to fail to submit a notice in accordance with section 136d(g) of this title;

(L) who is a producer to violate any of the provisions of section 136e of this title;

(M) to knowingly falsify all or part of any application for registration, application for experimental use permit, any information submitted to the Administrator pursuant to section 136e of this title, any records required to be maintained pursuant to this subchapter, any report filed under this subchapter, or any information marked as confidential and submitted to the Administrator under any provision of this subchapter;

(N) who is a registrant, wholesaler, dealer, retailer, or other distributor to fail to file reports required by this subchapter;

(O) to add any substance to, or take any substance from, any pesticide in a manner that may defeat the purpose of this subchapter;

(P) to use any pesticide in tests on human beings unless such human beings (i) are fully informed of the nature and purposes of the test and of any physical and mental health consequences which are reasonably foreseeable therefrom, and (ii) freely volunteer to participate in the test;

(Q) to falsify all or part of any information relating to the testing of any pesticide (or any ingredient, metabolite, or degradation product thereof), including the nature of any protocol, procedure, substance, organism, or equipment used, observation made, or conclusion or opinion formed, submitted to the Administrator, or that the person knows will be furnished to the Administrator or will become a part of any records required to be maintained by this subchapter;

(R) to submit to the Administrator data known to be false in support of a registration; or

(S) to violate any regulation issued under section 136a(a) or 136q of this title.

(b) Exemptions

The penalties provided for a violation of paragraph (1) of subsection (a) of this section shall not apply to—

(1) any person who establishes a guaranty signed by, and containing the name and address of, the registrant or person residing in the United States from whom the person purchased or received in good faith the pesticide in the same unbroken package, to the effect that the pesticide was lawfully registered at the time of sale and delivery to the person, and that it complies with the other requirements of this subchapter, and in such case the guarantor shall be subject to the penalties which would otherwise attach to the person holding the guaranty under the provisions of this subchapter;

(2) any carrier while lawfully shipping, transporting, or delivering for shipment any pesticide or device, if such carrier upon request of any officer or employee duly designated by the Administrator shall permit such officer or employee to copy all of its records concerning such pesticide or device;

(3) any public official while engaged in the performance of the official duties of the public official;

(4) any person using or possessing any pesticide as provided by an experimental use permit in effect with respect to such pesticide and such use or possession; or

(5) any person who ships a substance or mixture of substances being put through tests in which the purpose is only to determine its value for pesticide purposes or to determine its toxicity or other properties and from which the user does not expect to receive any benefit in pest control from its use.

(Act of June 25, 1947, c. 125, § 12, as added by Pub. L. No. 92–516, § 2, 86 Stat. 989 (Oct. 21, 1972); and amended by Pub. L. No. 95–396, § 16, 92 Stat. 832 (Sept. 30, 1978); Pub. L. No. 100–532, Title VI, §§ 601(b)(2), 603, Title VIII, § 801(g), (q)(2)(B), 102 Stat. 2677, 2678, 2682, 2683 (Oct. 25, 1988); Pub. L. No. 102–237, Title X, § 1006(a)(7), (b)(3)(L) to (O), 105 Stat. 1895, 1896 (Dec. 13, 1991).)

HISTORICAL AND STATUTORY NOTES

Effective and Applicability Provisions

1991 Acts. Amendments by Pub. L. No. 102–237 effective Dec. 13, 1991, see section 1101(a) of Pub. L. No. 102–237, set out as a note under section 1421 of this title.

1988 Acts. Amendment by Pub. L. No. 100–532 effective on expiration of 60 days after October 25, 1988, see section 901 of Pub. L. No. 100–532, set out as a note under section 136 of this title.

1972 Acts. Section effective at the close of Oct. 21, 1972, except if regulations are necessary for the implementation of any provision that becomes effective on Oct. 21, 1972, and continuation in effect of the provisions of subchapter I of this chapter and regulations thereunder as in effect prior to Oct. 21, 1972, until superseded by provisions of Pub. L. No. 92–516 and regulations thereunder, see section 4 of Pub. L. No. 92–516, set out as a note under section 136 of this title.

Prior Provisions

A prior section 12 of Act of June 25, 1947, was codified as section 135j of this title prior to amendment by Pub. L. No. 92–516.

§ 136k. Stop sale, use, removal, and seizure

[FIFRA § 13]

(a) Stop sale, etc., orders

Whenever any pesticide or device is found by the Administrator in any State and there is reason to believe on the basis of inspection or tests that such pesticide or device is in violation of any of the provisions of this subchapter, or that such pesticide or device has been or is intended to be distributed or sold in violation of any such provisions, or when the registration of the pesticide has been canceled by a final order or has been suspended, the Administrator may issue a written or printed "stop sale, use, or removal" order to any person who owns, controls, or has custody of such pesticide or device, and after receipt of such order no person shall sell, use, or remove the pesticide or device described in the order except in accordance with the provisions of the order.

(b) Seizure

Any pesticide or device that is being transported or, having been transported, remains unsold or in original unbroken packages, or that is sold or offered for sale in any State, or that is imported from a foreign country, shall be liable to be proceeded against in any district court in the district where it is found and seized for confiscation by a process in rem for condemnation if—

(1) in the case of a pesticide—

(A) it is adulterated or misbranded;

(B) it is not registered pursuant to the provisions of section 136a of this title;

(C) its labeling fails to bear the information required by this subchapter;

(D) it is not colored or discolored and such coloring or discoloring is required under this subchapter; or

(E) any of the claims made for it or any of the directions for its use differ in substance from the representations made in connection with its registration;

(2) in the case of a device, it is misbranded; or

(3) in the case of a pesticide or device, when used in accordance with the requirements imposed under this subchapter and as directed by the labeling, it nevertheless causes unreasonable adverse effects on the environment.

In the case of a plant regulator, defoliant, or desiccant, used in accordance with the label claims and recommendations, physical or physiological effects on plants or parts thereof shall not be deemed to be injury, when such effects are the purpose for which the plant regulator, defoliant, or desiccant was applied.

(c) Disposition after condemnation

If the pesticide or device is condemned it shall, after entry of the decree, be disposed of by destruction or sale as the court may direct and the proceeds, if sold, less the court costs, shall be paid into the Treasury of the United States, but the pesticide or device shall not be sold contrary to the provisions of this subchapter or the laws of the jurisdiction in which it is sold. On payment of the costs of the condemnation proceedings and the execution and delivery of a good and sufficient bond conditioned that the pesticide or device shall not be sold or otherwise disposed of contrary to the provisions of the subchapter or the laws of any jurisdiction in which sold, the court may direct that such pesticide or device be delivered to the owner thereof. The proceedings of such condemnation cases shall conform, as near as may be to the proceedings in admiralty, except that either party may demand trial by jury of any issue of fact joined in any case, and all such proceedings shall be at the suit of and in the name of the United States.

(d) Court costs, etc.—When a decree of condemnation is entered against the pesticide or device, court costs and fees, storage, and other proper expenses shall be awarded against the person, if any, intervening as claimant of the pesticide or device.

(Act of June 25, 1947, c. 125, § 13, as added by Pub. L. No. 92–516, § 2, 86 Stat. 991 (Oct. 21, 1972); and amended by Pub. L. No. 100–532, Title VIII, § 801(h), 102 Stat. 2682 (Oct. 25, 1988).)

HISTORICAL AND STATUTORY NOTES

Effective and Applicability Provisions

1988 Acts. Amendment by Pub. L. No. 100–532 effective on expiration of 60 days after October 25, 1988, see section 901 of Pub. L. No. 100–532, set out as a note under section 136 of this title.

1972 Acts. Section effective at the close of Oct. 21, 1972, except if regulations are necessary for the implementation of any provision that becomes effective on Oct. 21, 1972, and continuation in effect of the provisions of subchapter I of this chapter and regulations thereunder as in effect prior to Oct. 21, 1972, until superseded by provisions of Pub. L. No. 92–516 and regulations thereunder, see section 4 of Pub. L. No. 92–516, set out as a note under section 136 of this title.

Prior Provision

A prior section 13 of Act of June 25, 1947, was codified as section 135k of this title prior to amendment of Act of June 25, 1947, by Pub. L. No. 92–516.

§ 136*l*. Penalties

[FIFRA § 14]

(a) Civil penalties

(1) In general

Any registrant, commercial applicator, wholesaler, dealer, retailer, or other distributor who violates any provision of this subchapter may be assessed a civil penalty by the Administrator of not more than $5,000 for each offense.

(2) Private applicator

Any private applicator or other person not included in paragraph (1) who violates any provision of this subchapter subsequent to receiving a written warning from the Administrator or following a citation for a prior violation, may be assessed a civil penalty by the Administrator of not more than $1,000 for each offense, except that any applicator not included under paragraph (1) of this subsection who holds or applies registered pesticides, or uses dilutions of registered pesticides, only to provide a service of controlling pests without delivering any unapplied pesticide to any person so served, and who violates any provision of this subchapter may be assessed a civil penalty by the Administrator of not more than $500 for the first offense nor more than $1,000 for each subsequent offense.

(3) Hearing

No civil penalty shall be assessed unless the person charged shall have been given notice and opportunity for a hearing on such charge in the county, parish, or incorporated city of the residence of the person charged.

(4) Determination of penalty

In determining the amount of the penalty, the Administrator shall consider the appropriateness of such penalty to the size of the business of the person charged, the effect on the person's ability to continue in business, and the gravity of the violation. Whenever the Administrator finds that the violation occurred despite the exercise of due care or did not cause significant harm to health or the environment, the Administrator may issue a warning in lieu of assessing a penalty.

(5) References to Attorney General

In case of inability to collect such civil penalty or failure of any person to pay all, or such portion of such civil penalty as the Administrator may determine, the Administrator shall refer the matter to the Attorney General, who shall recover such amount by action in the appropriate United States district court.

(b) Criminal penalties

(1) In general

(A) Any registrant, applicant for a registration, or producer who knowingly violates any provision of this subchapter shall be fined not more than $50,000 or imprisoned for not more than 1 year, or both.

(B) Any commercial applicator of a restricted use pesticide, or any other person not described in subparagraph (A) who distributes or sells pesticides or devices, who knowingly violates any provision of this subchapter shall be fined not more than $25,000 or imprisoned for not more than 1 year, or both.

(2) Private applicator

Any private applicator or other person not included in paragraph (1) who knowingly violates any provision of this subchapter shall be guilty of a misdemeanor and shall on conviction be fined not more than $1,000, or imprisoned for not more than 30 days, or both.

(3) Disclosure of information

Any person, who, with intent to defraud, uses or reveals information relative to formulas of products acquired under the authority of section 136a of this title, shall be fined not more than $10,000, or imprisoned for not more than three years, or both.

(4) Acts of officers, agents, etc.

When construing and enforcing the provisions of this subchapter, the act, omission, or failure of any officer, agent, or other person acting for or employed by any person shall in every case be also deemed to be the act, omission, or failure of such person as well as that of the person employed.

(Act of June 25, 1947, c. 125, § 14, as added by Pub. L. No. 92–516, § 2, 86 Stat. 992 (Oct. 21, 1972); and amended by Pub. L. No. 95–396, § 17, 92 Stat. 832 (Sept. 30, 1978); Pub. L. No. 100–532, Title VI, § 604, 102 Stat. 2678 (Oct. 25, 1988); Pub. L. No. 102–237, Title X, § 1006(a)(8), 105 Stat. 1895 (Dec. 13, 1991).)

HISTORICAL AND STATUTORY NOTES

Effective and Applicability Provisions

1991 Acts. Amendments by section 1006(a)(8) of Pub. L. No. 102–237 effective Dec. 13, 1991, see section 1101(a) of Pub. L. No. 102–237, set out as a note under section 1421 of this title.

1988 Acts. Amendment by Pub. L. No. 100–532 effective on expiration of 60 days after October 25, 1988, see section 901 of Pub. L. No. 100–532, set out as a note under section 136 of this title.

1972 Acts. Section effective at the close of Oct. 21, 1972, except if regulations are necessary for the implementation of any provision that becomes effective on Oct. 21, 1972, and continuation in effect of the provisions of subchapter I of this chapter and regulations thereunder as in effect prior to Oct. 21, 1972, until superseded by provisions of Pub. L. No. 92–516 and regulations thereunder, see section 4 of Pub. L. No. 92–516, set out as a note under section 136 of this title.

§ 136m. Indemnities

[FIFRA § 15]

(a) General indemnification

(1) In general

Except as otherwise provided in this section, if—

(A) the Administrator notifies a registrant under section 136d(c)(1) of this title that the Administrator intends to suspend a registration or that an emergency order of suspension of a registration under section 136d(c)(3) of this title has been issued;

(B) the registration in question is suspended under section 136d(c) of this title, and thereafter is canceled under section 136d(b), 136d(d), or 136d(f) of this title; and

(C) any person who owned any quantity of the pesticide immediately before the notice to the registrant under subparagraph (A) suffered losses by reason of suspension or cancellation of the registration;

the Administrator shall make an indemnity payment to the person.

(2) Exception

Paragraph (1) shall not apply if the Administrator finds that the person—

(A) had knowledge of facts that, in themselves, would have shown that the pesticide did not meet the requirements of section 136a(c)(5) of this title for registration; and

(B) continued thereafter to produce the pesticide without giving timely notice of such facts to the Administrator.

(3) Report

If the Administrator takes an action under paragraph (1) that requires the payment of indemnification, the Administrator shall report to the Committee on Agriculture of the House of Representatives, the Committee on Agriculture, Nutrition, and Forestry of the Senate, and the Committees on Appropriations of the House of Representatives and the Senate on—

(A) the action taken that requires the payment of indemnification;

(B) the reasons for taking the action;

(C) the estimated cost of the payment; and

(D) a request for the appropriation of funds for the payment.

(4) Appropriation

The Administrator may not make a payment of indemnification under paragraph (1) unless a specific line item appropriation of funds has been made in advance for the payment.

(b) Indemnification of end users, dealers, and distributors

(1) End users

If—

(A) the Administrator notifies a registrant under section 136d(c)(1) of this title that the Administrator intends to suspend a registration or that an emergency order of suspension of a registration under section 136d(c)(3) of this title has been issued;

(B) the registration in question is suspended under section 136d(c) of this title, and thereafter is canceled under section 136d(b), 136d(d), or 136d(f) of this title; and

(C) any person who, immediately before the notice to the registrant under subparagraph (A), owned any quantity of the pesticide for purposes of applying or using the pesticide as an end user, rather than for purposes of distributing or selling it or further processing it for distribution or sale, suffered a loss by reason of the suspension or cancellation of the pesticide;

the person shall be entitled to an indemnity payment under this subsection for such quantity of the pesticide.

(2) Dealers and distributors

(A) Any registrant, wholesaler, dealer, or other distributor (hereinafter in this paragraph referred to as a "seller") of a registered pesticide who distributes or sells the pesticide directly to any person not described as an end user in paragraph (1)(C) shall, with respect to any quantity of the pesticide that such person cannot use or resell as a result of the suspension or cancellation of the pesticide, reimburse such person for the cost of first acquiring the pesticide from the seller (other than the cost of transportation, if any), unless the seller provided to the person at the time of distribution or sale a notice, in writing, that the pesticide is not subject to reimbursement by the seller.

(B) If—

(i) the Administrator notifies a registrant under section 136d(c)(1) of this title that the Administrator intends to suspend a registration or that an emergency order of suspension of a registration under section 136d(c)(3) of this title has been issued;

(ii) the registration in question is suspended under section 136d(c) of this title, and thereafter is canceled under section 136d(b), 136d(d), or 136d(f) of this title;

(iii) any person who, immediately before the notice to the registrant under clause (i)—

(I) had not been notified in writing by the seller, as provided under subparagraph (A), that any quantity of the pesticide owned by such person is not subject to reimbursement by the seller in the event of suspension or cancellation of the pesticide; and

(II) owned any quantity of the pesticide for purposes of—

(aa) distributing or selling it; or

(bb) further processing it for distribution or sale directly to an end user;

suffered a loss by reason of the suspension or cancellation of the pesticide; and

(iv) the Administrator determines on the basis of a claim of loss submitted to the Administrator by the person, that the seller—

(I) did not provide the notice specified in subparagraph (A) to such person; and

(II) is and will continue to be unable to provide reimbursement to such person, as provided under subparagraph (A), for the loss referred to in clause (iii), as a result of the insolvency or bankruptcy of the seller and the seller's resulting inability to provide such reimbursement;

the person shall be entitled to an indemnity payment under this subsection for such quantity of the pesticide.

(C) If an indemnity payment is made by the United States under this paragraph, the United States shall be subrogated to any right that would otherwise be held under this paragraph by a seller who is unable to make a reimbursement in accordance with this paragraph with regard to reimbursements that otherwise would have been made by the seller.

(3) Source

Any payment required to be made under paragraph (1) or (2) shall be made from the appropriation provided under section 1304 of Title 31.

(4) Administrative settlement

An administrative settlement of a claim for such indemnity may be made in accordance with the third paragraph of section 2414 of Title 28 and shall be regarded as if it were made under that section for purposes of section 1304 of Title 31.

(c) Amount of payment

(1) In general

The amount of an indemnity payment under subsection (a) or (b) of this section to any person shall be determined on the basis of the cost of the pesticide owned by the person (other than the cost of transportation, if any) immediately before the issuance of the notice to the registrant referred to in subsection (a)(1)(A), (b)(1)(A), or (b)(2)(B)(i) of this section, except that in no event shall an indemnity payment to any person exceed the fair market value of the pesticide owned by the person immediately before the issuance of the notice.

(2) Special rule

Notwithstanding any other provision of this subchapter, the Administrator may provide a reasonable time for use or other disposal of the pesticide. In determining the quantity of any pesticide for which indemnity shall be paid under this section, proper adjustment shall be made for any pesticide used or otherwise disposed of by the owner.

(Act of June 25, 1947, c. 125, § 15, as added by Pub. L. No. 92–516, § 2, 86 Stat. 993 (Oct. 21, 1972); and amended by Pub. L. No. 100–532, Title V, § 501(a), 102 Stat. 2674 (Oct. 25, 1988).)

HISTORICAL AND STATUTORY NOTES

Effective and Applicability Provisions

1988 Acts. Section 501(a) of Pub. L. No. 100–532 provided in part that amendment by Pub. L. No. 100–532 is effective 180 days after October 25, 1988.

1971 Acts. Section effective at the close of Oct. 21, 1972, except if regulations are necessary for the implementation of any provision that becomes effective on Oct. 21, 1972, and continuation in effect of the provisions of subchapter I of this chapter and regulations thereunder as in effect prior to Oct. 21, 1972, until superseded by provisions of Pub. L. No. 92–516 and regulations thereunder, see section 4 of Pub. L. No. 92–516, set out as a note under section 136 of this title.

Interim Payments

Section 501(b) of Pub. L. No. 100–532 provided that:

"(1) Source.—Any obligation of the Administrator to pay an indemnity arising under section 15 [this section], as it existed prior to the effective date of the amendment made by this section [see Effective Date note under section], shall be made from the appropriation provided under section 1304 of title 31, United States Code [section 1304 of Title 31, Money and Finance].

"(2) Administrative settlement.—An administrative settlement of a claim for such indemnity may be made in accordance with the third paragraph of section 2414 of title 28, United States Code [section 2414 of Title 28, Judiciary and Judicial Procedure], and shall be regarded as if it were made under that section for purposes of section 1304 of title 31, United States Code [section 1304 of Title 31]."

[Section 901 of Pub. L. No. 100–532 provided that this provision be effective 60 days after October 25, 1988].

§ 136n. Administrative procedure; judicial review

[FIFRA § 16]

(a) District court review

Except as otherwise provided in this subchapter, the refusal of the Administrator to cancel or suspend a registration or to change a classification not following a hearing and other final actions of the Administrator not committed to the discretion of the Administrator by law are judicially reviewable by the district courts of the United States.

(b) Review by court of appeals

In the case of actual controversy as to the validity of any order issued by the Administrator following a public hearing, any person who will be adversely affected by such order and who had been a party to the proceedings may obtain judicial review by filing in the United States court of appeals for the circuit wherein such person resides or has a place of business, within 60 days after the entry of such order, a petition praying that the order be set aside in whole or in part. A copy of the petition shall be forthwith transmitted by the clerk of the court to the Administrator or any officer designated by the Administrator for that purpose, and thereupon the Administrator shall file in the court the record of the proceedings on which the Administrator based the Administrator's order, as provided in section 2112 of Title 28. Upon the filing of such petition the court shall have exclusive jurisdiction to affirm or set aside the order complained of in whole or in part. The court shall consider all evidence of record. The order of the Administrator shall be sustained if it is supported by substantial evidence when considered on the record as a whole. The judgment of the court affirming or setting aside, in whole or in part, any order under this section shall be final, subject to review by the Supreme Court of the United States upon certiorari or certification as provided in section 1254 of Title 28. The commencement of proceedings under this section shall not, unless specifically ordered by the court to the contrary, operate as a stay of an order.

(c) Jurisdiction of district courts

The district courts of the United States are vested with jurisdiction specifically to enforce, and to prevent and restrain violations of, this subchapter.

(d) Notice of judgments

The Administrator shall, by publication in such manner as the Administrator may prescribe, give notice of all judgments entered in actions instituted under the authority of this subchapter.

(Act of June 25, 1947, c. 125, § 16, as added by Pub. L. No. 92–516, § 2, 86 Stat. 994 (Oct. 21, 1972); and amended by Pub. L. No. 98–620, Title IV, § 402(4)(C), 98 Stat. 3357 (Nov. 8, 1984); Pub. L. No. 100–532, Title VIII, § 801(i), 102 Stat. 2682 (Oct. 25, 1988); Pub. L. No. 102–237, Title X, § 1006(b)(1), (2), (3)(P), 105 Stat. 1895, 1896 (Dec. 13, 1991).)

HISTORICAL AND STATUTORY NOTES

Effective and Applicability Provisions

1991 Acts. Amendments by Pub. L. No. 102–237 effective Dec. 13, 1991, see section 1101(a) of Pub. L. No. 102–237, set out as a note under section 1421 of this title.

1988 Acts. Amendment by Pub. L. No. 100–532 effective on expiration of 60 days after October 25, 1988, see section 901 of Pub. L. No. 100–532, set out as a note under section 136 of this title.

1984 Acts. Amendment by Pub. L. No. 98–620 not to apply to cases pending on Nov. 8, 1984, see section 403 of Pub. L. No. 98–620, set out as a note under section 1657 of Title 28, Judiciary and Judicial Procedure.

1972 Acts. Section effective at the close of Oct. 21, 1972, except if regulations are necessary for the implementation of any provision that becomes effective on Oct. 21, 1972, and continuation in effect of the provisions of subchapter I of this chapter and regulations thereunder as in effect prior to Oct. 21, 1972, until superseded by provisions of Pub. L. No. 92–516 and regulations thereunder, see section 4 of Pub. L. No. 92–516, set out as a note under section 136 of this title.

§ 136*o*. Imports and exports

[FIFRA § 17]

(a) Pesticides and devices intended for export

Notwithstanding any other provision of this subchapter, no pesticide or device or active ingredient used in producing a pesticide intended solely for export to any foreign country shall be deemed in violation of this subchapter—

(1) when prepared or packed according to the specifications or directions of the foreign purchaser, except that producers of such pesticides and devices and active ingredients used in producing pesticides shall be subject to sections 136(p), 136(q)(1)(A), (C), (D), (E), (G), and (H), 136(q)(2)(A), (B), (C)(i) and (iii), and (D), 136e, and 136f of this title; and

(2) in the case of any pesticide other than a pesticide registered under section 136a or sold under section 136d(a)(1) of this title, if, prior to export, the foreign purchaser has signed a statement acknowledging that the purchaser understands that such pesticide is not registered for use in the United States and cannot be sold in the United States under this subchapter.

A copy of that statement shall be transmitted to an appropriate official of the government of the importing country.

(b) Cancellation notices furnished to foreign governments

Whenever a registration, or a cancellation or suspension of the registration of a pesticide becomes effective, or ceases to be effective, the Administrator shall transmit through the State Department notification thereof to the governments of other countries and to appropriate international agencies. Such notification shall, upon request, include all information related to the cancellation or suspension of the registration of the pesticide and information concerning other pesticides that are registered under section 136a of this title and that could be used in lieu of such pesticide.

(c) Importation of pesticides and devices

(1) In general.—The Secretary of the Treasury shall notify the Administrator of the arrival of pesticides and devices and shall deliver to the Administrator, upon the Administrator's request, samples of pesticides or devices which are being imported into the United States, giving notice to the owner or consignee, who may appear before the Administrator and have the right to introduce testimony. If it appears from the examination of a sample that it is adulterated, or misbranded or otherwise violates the provisions set forth in this subchapter, or is otherwise injurious to health or the environment, the pesticide or device may be refused admission, and the Secretary of the Treasury shall refuse delivery to the consignee and shall cause the destruction of any pesticide or device refused delivery which shall not be exported by the consignee within 90 days from the date of notice of such refusal under such regulations as the Secretary of the Treasury may prescribe. The Secretary of the Treasury may deliver to the consignee such pesticide or device pending examination and decision in the matter on execution of bond for the amount of the full invoice value of such pesticide or device, together with the duty thereon, and on refusal to return such pesticide or device for any cause to the custody of the Secretary of the Treasury, when demanded, for the purpose of excluding them from the country, or for any other purpose, said consignee shall forfeit the full amount of said bond. All charges for storage, cartage, and labor on pesticides or devices which are refused admission or delivery shall be paid by the owner or consignee, and in default of such payment shall constitute a lien against any future importation made by such owner or consignee.

(2) Importation of seed.—Notwithstanding any other provision of law, no person is required to notify the Administrator of the arrival of a plant-incorporated protectant (as defined in section 174.3 of title 40, Code of Federal Regulations (or any successor regulation)) that is contained in a seed, if—

(A) that plant-incorporated protectant is registered under section 136a of this title;

(B) the Administrator has issued an experimental use permit for that plant-incorporated protectant under section 136c of this title; or

(C) the seed is covered by a permit (as defined in part 340 of title 7, Code of Federal Regulations (or any successor regulation)) or a notification.

(3) Cooperation.—

(A) In general.—In response to a request from the Administrator, the Secretary of Agriculture shall provide to the Administrator a list of seed containing plant-incorporated protectants (as defined in section 174.3 of title 40, Code of Federal Regulations (or any successor regulation)) if the importation of that seed into the United States has been approved under a permit or notification referred to in paragraph (2).

(B) Contents.—The list under subparagraph (A) shall be provided in a form and at such intervals as may be agreed to by the Secretary and the Administrator.

(4) Applicability.—Nothing in this subsection precludes or limits the authority of the Secretary of Agriculture with respect to the importation or movement of plants, plant products, or seeds under—

(A) the Plant Protection Act (7 U.S.C. 7701 et seq.); and

(B) the Federal Seed Act (7 U.S.C. 1551 et seq.).

(d) Cooperation in international efforts

(1) In general

The Administrator shall, in cooperation with the Department of State and any other appropriate Federal agency, participate and cooperate in any international efforts to develop improved pesticide research and regulations.

(2) Department of State expenses

Any expenses incurred by an employee of the Environmental Protection Agency who participates in any international technical, economic, or policy review board, committee, or other official body that is meeting in relation to an international treaty shall be paid by the Department of State.

(e) Regulations

The Secretary of the Treasury, in consultation with the Administrator, shall prescribe regulations for the enforcement of subsection (c) of this section.

(Act of June 25, 1947, c. 125, § 17, as added by Pub. L. No. 92–516, § 2, 86 Stat. 995 (Oct. 21, 1972); and amended by Pub. L. No. 95–396, § 18(a), 92 Stat. 833 (Sept. 30, 1978); Pub. L. No. 100–532, Title VIII, § 801(j), 102 Stat. 2682 (Oct. 25, 1988); Pub. L. No. 102–237, Title X, § 1006(a)(9), (b)(2), 105 Stat. 1895 (Dec. 13, 1991); Pub. L. No. 110–234, Title XIV, § 14209(a), 122 Stat. 1463 (May 22, 2008); Pub. L. No. 110–246, § 4(a), Title XIV, § 14209(a), 122 Stat. 1664, 2225 (June 18, 2008); Pub. L. No. 113–79, Title X, § 10008, 128 Stat. 948 (Feb. 7, 2014).)

HISTORICAL AND STATUTORY NOTES

References in Text

The Plant Protection Act, referred to in subsec. (c)(4)(A), is Pub. L. No. 106–224, Title IV, June 20, 2000, 114 Stat. 438, which is codified principally to chapter 104 of this title, 7 U.S.C.A. § 7701 et seq. For complete classification, see Short Title note set out under 7 U.S.C.A. § 7701 and Tables.

The Federal Seed Act, referred to in subsec. (c)(4)(B), is Act of Aug. 9, 1939, c. 615, 53 Stat. 1275, which is codified generally to chapter 37 of this title, 7 U.S.C.A. § 1551 et seq. For complete classification, see 7 U.S.C.A. § 1551 and Tables.

Codifications

The authorities provided by each provision of, and each amendment made by, Pub. L. No. 110–246, as in effect on Sept. 30, 2012, to continue, and the Secretary of Agriculture to carry out the authorities, until the later of Sept. 30, 2013, or the date specified in the provision of, or amendment made by, Pub. L. No. 110–246, see section 701(a) of Pub. L. No. 112–240, set out in a note under 7 U.S.C.A. § 8701.

Pub. L. No. 113–79, Title X, § 10008(1), which directed the amendment of subsec. (c) by striking "The Secretary" and inserting paragraph heading (1) reading "In General" and the words "The Secretary" to follow, was executed by striking "The Secretary" the first place it appeared in subsec. (c) and inserting the specified paragraph heading (1) and the words "The Secretary" as the probably intent of Congress. The phrase "The Secretary" appeared a second time in former subsec. (c) at the beginning of the third sentence.

Pub. L. No. 110–234 and Pub. L. No. 110–246 made identical amendments to this section. The amendments made by Pub. L. No. 110–234 were repealed by section 4(a) of Pub. L. No. 110–246.

Effective and Applicability Provisions

2008 Acts. Amendments by Pub. L. No. 110–246, except as otherwise provided, shall take effect on the earlier of June 18, 2008, or May 22, 2008, see Pub. L. No. 110–246, § 4(b), set out in a Repeal of Duplicative Enactment note under 7 U.S.C.A. § 8701.

1991 Acts. Amendments by Pub. L. No. 102–237 effective Dec. 13, 1991, see section 1101(a) of Pub. L. No. 102–237, set out as a note under section 1421 of this title.

1988 Acts. Amendment by Pub. L. No. 100–532 effective on expiration of 60 days after October 25, 1988, see section 901 of Pub. L. No. 100–532, set out as a note under section 136 of this title.

1978 Acts. Pub. L. No. 95–396, § 18(b), Sept. 30, 1978, 92 Stat. 833, provided that: "The amendment made by subsection (a)(1) of this section [amending subsec. (a) of this section] shall become effective one hundred and eighty days after the date of enactment of this Act [Sept. 30, 1978]."

1972 Acts. Section effective at the close of Oct. 21, 1972, except if regulations are necessary for the implementation of any provision that becomes effective on Oct. 21, 1972, and continuation in effect of the provisions of subchapter I of this chapter and regulations thereunder as in effect prior to Oct. 21, 1972, until superseded by provisions of Pub. L. No. 92–516 and regulations thereunder, see section 4 of Pub. L. No. 92–516, set out as a note under section 136 of this title.

Repeals

Pub. L. No. 110–234 was repealed effective May 22, 2008, see Repeal of Duplicative Enactment by Pub. L. No. 110–246, § 4(a), set out in a note under 7 U.S.C.A. § 8701.

§ 136p. Exemption of Federal and State agencies

[FIFRA § 18]

The Administrator may, at the Administrator's discretion, exempt any Federal or State agency from any provision of this subchapter if the Administrator determines that emergency conditions exist which require such exemption. The Administrator, in determining whether or not such emergency conditions exist, shall consult with the Secretary of Agriculture and the Governor of any State concerned if they request such determination.

(Act of June 25, 1947, c. 125, § 18, as added by Pub. L. No. 92–516, § 2, 86 Stat. 995 (Oct. 21, 1972); and amended by Pub. L. No. 94–140, § 8, 89 Stat. 754 (Nov. 28, 1975); Pub. L. No. 100–532, Title VIII, § 801(k), 102 Stat. 2682 (Oct. 25, 1988); Pub. L. No. 102–237, Title X, § 1006(b)(1), (2), 105 Stat. 1895 (Dec. 13, 1991).)

HISTORICAL AND STATUTORY NOTES

Effective and Applicability Provisions

1991 Acts. Amendments by Pub. L. No. 102–237 effective Dec. 13, 1991, see section 1101(a) of Pub. L. No. 102–237, set out as a note under section 1421 of this title.

1988 Acts. Amendment by Pub. L. No. 100–532 effective on expiration of 60 days after October 25, 1988, see section 901 of Pub. L. No. 100–532, set out as a note under section 136 of this title.

1972 Acts. Section effective at the close of Oct. 21, 1972, except if regulations are necessary for the implementation of any provision that becomes effective on Oct. 21, 1972, and continuation in effect of the provisions of subchapter I of this chapter and regulations thereunder as in effect prior to Oct. 21, 1972, until superseded by provisions of Pub. L. No. 92–516 and regulations thereunder, see section 4 of Pub. L. No. 92–516, set out as a note under section 136 of this title.

§ 136q. Storage, disposal, transportation, and recall

[FIFRA § 19]

(a) Storage, disposal, and transportation

(1) Data requirements and registration of pesticides

The Administrator may require under section 136a or 136d of this title that—

(A) the registrant or applicant for registration of a pesticide submit or cite data or information regarding methods for the safe storage and disposal of excess quantities of the pesticide to support the registration or continued registration of a pesticide;

(B) the labeling of a pesticide contain requirements and procedures for the transportation, storage, and disposal of the pesticide, any container of the pesticide, any rinsate containing the pesticide, or any other material used to contain or collect excess or spilled quantities of the pesticide; and

(C) the registrant of a pesticide provide evidence of sufficient financial and other resources to carry out a recall plan under subsection (b) of this section, and provide for the disposition of the pesticide, in the event of suspension and cancellation of the pesticide.

(2) Pesticides

The Administrator may by regulation, or as part of an order issued under section 136d of this title or an amendment to such an order—

(A) issue requirements and procedures to be followed by any person who stores or transports a pesticide the registration of which has been suspended or canceled;

(B) issue requirements and procedures to be followed by any person who disposes of stocks of a pesticide the registration of which has been suspended; and

(C) issue requirements and procedures for the disposal of any pesticide the registration of which has been canceled.

(3) Containers, rinsates, and other materials

The Administrator may by regulation, or as part of an order issued under section 136d of this title or an amendment to such an order—

(A) issue requirements and procedures to be followed by any person who stores or transports any container of a pesticide the registration of which has been suspended or canceled, any rinsate containing the pesticide, or any other material used to contain or collect excess or spilled quantities of the pesticide;

(B) issue requirements and procedures to be followed by any person who disposes of stocks of any container of a pesticide the registration of which has been suspended, any rinsate containing the pesticide, or any other material used to contain or collect excess or spilled quantities of the pesticide; and

(C) issue requirements and procedures for the disposal of any container of a pesticide the registration of which has been canceled, any rinsate containing the pesticide, or any other material used to contain or collect excess or spilled quantities of the pesticide.

(4) Container recycling

The Secretary may promulgate a regulation for the return and recycling of disposable pesticide containers used for the distribution or sale of registered pesticide products in interstate commerce. Any such regulation requiring recycling of disposable pesticide containers shall not apply to antimicrobial pesticides (as defined in section 136 of this title) or other pesticide products intended for non-agricultural uses.

(b) Recalls

(1) In general

If the registration of a pesticide has been suspended and canceled under section 136d of this title, and if the Administrator finds that recall of the pesticide is necessary to protect health or the environment, the Administrator shall order a recall of the pesticide in accordance with this subsection.

(2) Voluntary recall

If, after determining under paragraph (1) that a recall is necessary, the Administrator finds that voluntary recall by the registrant and others in the chain of distribution may be as safe and effective as a mandatory recall, the Administrator shall request the registrant of the pesticide to submit, within 60 days of the request, a plan for the voluntary recall of the pesticide. If such a plan is requested and submitted, the Administrator shall approve the plan and order the registrant to conduct the recall in accordance with the plan unless the Administrator determines, after an informal hearing, that the plan is inadequate to protect health or the environment.

(3) Mandatory recall

If, after determining under paragraph (1) that a recall is necessary, the Administrator does not request the submission of a plan under paragraph (2) or finds such a plan to be inadequate, the Administrator shall issue a regulation that prescribes a plan for the recall of the pesticide. A regulation issued under this paragraph may apply to any person who is or was a registrant, distributor, or seller of the pesticide, or any successor in interest to such a person.

(4) Recall procedure

A regulation issued under this subsection may require any person that is subject to the regulation to—

(A) arrange to make available one or more storage facilities to receive and store the pesticide to which the recall program applies, and inform the Administrator of the location of each such facility;

(B) accept and store at such a facility those existing stocks of such pesticide that are tendered by any other person who obtained the pesticide directly or indirectly from the person that is subject to such regulation;

(C) on the request of a person making such a tender, provide for proper transportation of the pesticide to a storage facility; and

(D) take such reasonable steps as the regulation may prescribe to inform persons who may be holders of the pesticide of the terms of the recall regulation and how those persons may tender the pesticide and arrange for transportation of the pesticide to a storage facility.

(5) Contents of recall plan

A recall plan established under this subsection shall include—

(A) the level in the distribution chain to which the recall is to extend, and a schedule for recall; and

(B) the means to be used to verify the effectiveness of the recall.

(6) Requirements or procedures

No requirement or procedure imposed in accordance with paragraph (2) of subsection (a) of this section may require the recall of existing stocks of the pesticide except as provided by this subsection.

(c) Storage costs

(1) Submission of plan

A registrant who wishes to become eligible for reimbursement of storage costs incurred as a result of a recall prescribed under subsection (b) of this section for a pesticide whose registration has been suspended and canceled shall, as soon as practicable after the suspension of the registration of the pesticide, submit to the Administrator a plan for the storage and disposal of the pesticide that meets criteria established by the Administrator by regulation.

(2) Reimbursement

Within a reasonable period of time after such storage costs are incurred and paid by the registrant, the Administrator shall reimburse the registrant, on request, for—

(A) none of the costs incurred by the registrant before the date of submission of the plan referred to in paragraph (1) to the Administrator;

(B) 100 percent of the costs incurred by the registrant after the date of submission of the plan to the Administrator or the date of cancellation of the registration of the pesticide, whichever is later, but before the approval of the plan by the Administrator;

(C) 50 percent of the costs incurred by the registrant during the 1-year period beginning on the date of the approval of the plan by the Administrator or the date of cancellation of the registration of the pesticide, whichever is later;

(D) none of the costs incurred by the registrant during the 3-year period beginning on the 366th day following approval of the plan by the Administrator or the date of cancellation of the registration of the pesticide, whichever is later; and

(E) 25 percent of the costs incurred by the registrant during the period beginning on the first day of the 5th year following the date of the approval of the plan by the Administrator or the date of cancellation of the registration of the pesticide, whichever is later, and ending on the date that a disposal permit for the pesticide is issued by a State or an alternative plan for disposal of the pesticide in accordance with applicable law has been developed.

(d) Administration of storage, disposal, transportation, and recall programs

(1) Voluntary agreements

Nothing in this section shall be construed as preventing or making unlawful any agreement between a seller and a buyer of any pesticide or other substance regarding the ultimate allocation of the costs of storage, transportation, or disposal of a pesticide.

(2) Rule and regulation review

Section 136w(a)(4) of this title shall not apply to any regulation issued under subsection (a)(2) or (b) of this section.

(3) Limitations

No registrant shall be responsible under this section for a pesticide the registration of which is held by another person. No distributor or seller shall be responsible under this section for a pesticide that the distributor or seller did not hold or sell.

(4) Seizure and penalties

If the Administrator finds that a person who is subject to a regulation or order under subsection (a)(2) or (b) of this section has failed substantially to comply with that regulation or order, the Administrator may take action under section 136k or 136*l* of this title or obtain injunctive relief under section 136n(c) of this title against such person or any successor in interest of any such person.

(e) Container design

(1) Procedures

(A) Not later than 3 years after the effective date of this subsection, the Administrator shall, in consultation with the heads of other interested Federal agencies, promulgate regulations for the design of pesticide containers that will promote the safe storage and disposal of pesticides.

(B) The regulations shall ensure, to the fullest extent practicable, that the containers—

(i) accommodate procedures used for the removal of pesticides from the containers and the rinsing of the containers;

(ii) facilitate the safe use of the containers, including elimination of splash and leakage of pesticides from the containers;

(iii) facilitate the safe disposal of the containers; and

(iv) facilitate the safe refill and reuse of the containers.

(2) Compliance

The Administrator shall require compliance with the regulations referred to in paragraph (1) not later than 5 years after the effective date of this subsection.

(f) Pesticide residue removal

(1) Procedures

(A) Not later than 3 years after the effective date of this subsection, the Administrator shall, in consultation with the heads of other interested Federal agencies, promulgate regulations prescribing procedures and standards for the removal of pesticides from containers prior to disposal.

(B) The regulations may—

(i) specify, for each major type of pesticide container, procedures and standards providing for, at a minimum, triple rinsing or the equivalent degree of pesticide removal;

(ii) specify procedures that can be implemented promptly and easily in various circumstances and conditions;

(iii) provide for reuse, whenever practicable, or disposal of rinse water and residue; and

(iv) be coordinated with requirements for the rinsing of containers imposed under the Solid Waste Disposal Act (42 U.S.C. 6901 et seq.).

(C) The Administrator may, at the discretion of the Administrator, exempt products intended solely for household use from the requirements of this subsection.

(2) Compliance

Effective beginning 5 years after the effective date of this subsection, a State may not exercise primary enforcement responsibility under section 136w–1 of this title, or certify an applicator under section 136i of this title, unless the Administrator determines that the State is carrying out an adequate program to ensure compliance with this subsection.

(3) Solid Waste Disposal Act

Nothing in this subsection shall affect the authorities or requirements concerning pesticide containers under the Solid Waste Disposal Act (42 U.S.C. 6901).

(g) Pesticide container study

(1) Study

(A) The Administrator shall conduct a study of options to encourage or require—

(i) the return, refill, and reuse of pesticide containers;

(ii) the development and use of pesticide formulations that facilitate the removal of pesticide residues from containers; and

(iii) the use of bulk storage facilities to reduce the number of pesticide containers requiring disposal.

(B) In conducting the study, the Administrator shall—

(i) consult with the heads of other interested Federal agencies, State agencies, industry groups, and environmental organizations; and

(ii) assess the feasibility, costs, and environmental benefits of encouraging or requiring various measures or actions.

(2) Report

Not later than 2 years after the effective date of this subsection, the Administrator shall submit to Congress a report describing the results of the study required under paragraph (1).

(h) Relationship to Solid Waste Disposal Act

(1) In general

Nothing in this section shall diminish the authorities or requirements of the Solid Waste Disposal Act (42 U.S.C. 6901 et seq.).

(2) Antimicrobial products

A household, industrial, or institutional antimicrobial product that is not subject to regulation under the Solid Waste Disposal Act (42 U.S.C. 6901 et seq.) shall not be subject to the provisions of subsections (a), (e), and (f) of this section, unless the Administrator determines that such product must be subject to such provisions to prevent an unreasonable adverse effect on the environment.

(Act of June 25, 1947, c. 125, § 19, as added by Pub. L. No. 92–516, § 2, 86 Stat. 995 (Oct. 21, 1972); and amended by Pub. L. No. 95–396, § 19, 92 Stat. 833 (Sept. 30, 1978); Pub. L. No. 100–532, Title IV, §§ 401–403, Title VIII, § 801(q)(1)(D), 102 Stat. 2669 to 2672, 2683 (Oct. 25, 1988); Pub. L. No. 104–170, Title II, § 225, 110 Stat. 1507 (Aug. 3, 1996); Pub. L. No. 110–234, Title XIV, § 14209(b), 122 Stat. 1463 (May 22, 2008); Pub. L. No. 110–246, § 4(a), Title XIV, § 14209(b), 122 Stat. 1664, 2225 (June 18, 2008).)

HISTORICAL AND STATUTORY NOTES

References in Text

The effective date of this subsection, referred to in text, is 60 days after Oct. 25, 1988, the effective date of Pub. L. No. 100–532. See section 901 of Pub. L. No. 100–532, set out as a note under 7 U.S.C.A. § 136.

The Solid Waste Disposal Act, referred to in text, is Title II of Pub. L. No. 89–272, Oct. 20, 1965, 79 Stat. 997, as amended generally by Pub. L. No. 94–580, § 2, Oct. 21, 1976, 90 Stat. 2795, which is codified generally to chapter 82 (section 6901 et seq.) of Title 42. For complete classification of this Act to the Code, see Short Title of 1965 Acts note set out under section 6901 of Title 42, The Public Health and Welfare, and Tables.

Codifications

The authorities provided by each provision of, and each amendment made by, Pub. L. No. 110–246, as in effect on Sept. 30, 2012, to continue, and the Secretary of Agriculture to carry out the authorities, until the later of Sept. 30, 2013, or the date specified in the provision of, or amendment made by, Pub. L. No. 110–246, see section 701(a) of Pub. L. No. 112–240, set out in a note under 7 U.S.C.A. § 8701.

Effective and Applicability Provisions

2008 Acts. Amendments by Pub. L. No. 110–246, except as otherwise provided, shall take effect on the earlier of June 18, 2008, or May 22, 2008, see Pub. L. No. 110–246, § 4(b), set out in a Repeal of Duplicative Enactment note under 7 U.S.C.A. § 8701.

1988 Acts. Amendment by Pub. L. No. 100–532 effective on expiration of 60 days after October 25, 1988, see section 901 of Pub. L. No. 100–532, set out as a note under section 136 of this title.

1972 Acts. Section effective at the close of Oct. 21, 1972, except if regulations are necessary for the implementation of any provision that becomes effective on Oct. 21, 1972, and continuation in effect of the provisions of subchapter I of this chapter and regulations thereunder as in effect prior to Oct. 21, 1972, until superseded by provisions of Pub. L. No. 92–516 and regulations thereunder, see section 4 of Pub. L. No. 92–516, set out as a note under section 136 of this title.

Repeals

Pub. L. No. 110–234 was repealed effective May 22, 2008, see Repeal of Duplicative Enactment by Pub. L. No. 110–246, § 4(a), set out in a note under 7 U.S.C.A. § 8701.

§ 136r. Research and monitoring

[FIFRA § 20]

(a) Research

The Administrator shall undertake research including research by grant or contract with other Federal agencies, universities, or others as may be necessary to carry out the purposes of this subchapter, and the Administrator shall conduct research into integrated pest management in coordination with the Secretary of Agriculture. The Administrator shall also take care to ensure that such research does not duplicate research being undertaken by any other Federal agency.

(b) National monitoring plan

The Administrator shall formulate and periodically revise, in cooperation with other Federal, State, or local agencies, a national plan for monitoring pesticides.

(c) Monitoring

The Administrator shall undertake such monitoring activities, including, but not limited to monitoring in air, soil, water, man, plants, and animals, as may be necessary for the implementation of this subchapter and of the national pesticide monitoring plan. The Administrator shall establish procedures for the monitoring of man and animals and their environment for incidential[1] pesticide exposure, including, but not limited to, the quantification of incidental human and environmental pesticide pollution and the secular trends thereof, and identification of the sources of contamination and their relationship to human and environmental effects. Such activities shall be carried out in cooperation with other Federal, State, and local agencies.

(Act of June 25, 1947, c. 125, § 20, as added by Pub. L. No. 92–516, § 2, 86 Stat. 996 (Oct. 21, 1972); and amended by Pub. L. No. 95–396, § 20, 92 Stat. 834 (Sept. 30, 1978); Pub. L. No. 102–237, Title X, § 1006(a)(10), (b)(1), 105 Stat. 1895 (Dec. 13, 1991).)

[1] So in original. Probably should read "incidental".

HISTORICAL AND STATUTORY NOTES

Effective and Applicability Provisions

1991 Acts. Amendments by section 1006(a)(10), (b)(1) of Pub. L. No. 102–237 effective Dec. 13, 1991, see section 1101(a) of Pub. L. No. 102–237, set out as a note under section 1421 of this title.

1972 Acts. Section effective at the close of Oct. 21, 1972, except if regulations are necessary for the implementation of any provision that becomes effective on Oct. 21, 1972, and continuation in effect of the provisions of subchapter I of this chapter and regulations thereunder as in effect prior to Oct. 21, 1972, until superseded by provisions of Pub. L. No. 92–516 and regulations thereunder, see section 4 of Pub. L. No. 92–516, set out as a note under section 136 of this title.

Award of Grants

Pub. L. No. 106–74, Title III, 113 Stat. 1081 (Oct. 20, 1999), provided in part "[t]hat notwithstanding 7 U.S.C. 136r [this section] and 15 U.S.C. 2609, beginning in fiscal year 2000 and thereafter, grants awarded under section 20 of the Federal Insecticide, Fungicide, and Rodenticide Act, as amended, [this section] and section 10 of the Toxic Substances Control Act, as amended, [15 U.S.C.A. § 2609] shall be available for research, development, monitoring, public education, training, demonstrations, and studies."

§ 136r–1. Integrated Pest Management

The Secretary of Agriculture, in cooperation with the Administrator, shall implement research, demonstration, and education programs to support adoption of Integrated Pest Management. Integrated Pest Management is a sustainable approach to managing pests by combining biological, cultural, physical, and chemical tools in a way that minimizes economic, health, and environmental risks. The Secretary of Agriculture and the Administrator shall make information on Integrated Pest Management widely available to pesticide users, including Federal agencies. Federal agencies shall use Integrated Pest Management techniques in carrying out pest management activities and shall promote Integrated Pest Management through procurement and regulatory policies, and other activities.

(Added by Pub. L. No. 104–170, Title III, § 303, 110 Stat. 1512 (Aug. 3, 1996).)

HISTORICAL AND STATUTORY NOTES

Codifications

This section was enacted as part of the Food Quality Protection Act of 1996 and not as part of the Federal Insecticide, Fungicide, and Rodenticide Act of 1996, which comprises this subchapter.

§ 136s. Solicitation of comments; notice of public hearings

[FIFRA § 21]

(a) Secretary of Agriculture

The Administrator, before publishing regulations under this subchapter, shall solicit the views of the Secretary of Agriculture in accordance with the procedure described in section 136w(a) of this title.

(b) Secretary of Health and Human Services

The Administrator, before publishing regulations under this subchapter for any public health pesticide, shall solicit the views of the Secretary of Health and Human Services in the same manner as the views of the Secretary of Agriculture are solicited under section 136w(a)(2) of this title.

(c) Views

In addition to any other authority relating to public hearings and solicitation of views, in connection with the suspension or cancellation of a pesticide registration or any other actions authorized under this subchapter, the Administrator may, at the Administrator's discretion, solicit the views of all interested persons, either orally or in writing, and seek such advice from scientists, farmers, farm organizations, and other qualified persons as the Administrator deems proper.

(d) Notice

In connection with all public hearings under this subchapter the Administrator shall publish timely notice of such hearings in the Federal Register.

(Act of June 25, 1947, c. 125, § 21, as added by Pub. L. No. 92–516, § 2, 86 Stat. 996 (Oct. 21, 1972); and amended by Pub. L. No. 94–140, § 2(b), 89 Stat. 752 (Nov. 28, 1975); Pub. L. No. 100–532, Title VIII, § 801(*l*), 102 Stat. 2682 (Oct. 25, 1988); Pub. L. No. 102–237, Title X, § 1006(b)(1), (2), 105 Stat. 1895 (Dec. 13, 1991); Pub. L. No. 104–170, Title II, § 234, 110 Stat. 1509 (Aug. 3, 1996).)

HISTORICAL AND STATUTORY NOTES

Effective and Applicability Provisions

1991 Acts. Amendments by Pub. L. No. 102–237 effective Dec. 13, 1991, see section 1101(a) of Pub. L. No. 102–237, set out as a note under section 1421 of this title.

1988 Acts. Amendment by Pub. L. No. 100–532 effective on expiration of 60 days after October 25, 1988, see section 901 of Pub. L. No. 100–532, set out as a note under section 136 of this title.

1972 Acts. Section effective at the close of Oct. 21, 1972, except if regulations are necessary for the implementation of any provision that becomes effective on Oct. 21, 1972, and continuation in effect of the provisions of subchapter I of this chapter and regulations thereunder as in effect prior to Oct. 21, 1972, until superseded by provisions of Pub. L. No. 92–516 and regulations thereunder, see section 4 of Pub. L. No. 92–516, set out as a note under section 136 of this title.

§ 136t. Delegation and cooperation

[FIFRA § 22]

(a) Delegation.

All authority vested in the Administrator by virtue of the provisions of this subchapter may with like force and effect be executed by such employees of the Environmental Protection Agency as

(b) Cooperation.

The Administrator shall cooperate with Department of Agriculture, any other Federal agency, and any appropriate agency of any State or any political subdivision thereof, in carrying out the provisions of this subchapter, and in securing uniformity of regulations.

(Act of June 25, 1947, c. 125, § 22, as added by Pub. L. No. 92–516, § 2, 86 Stat. 996 (Oct. 21, 1972).)

HISTORICAL AND STATUTORY NOTES

Effective and Applicability Provisions

1972 Acts. Section effective at the close of Oct. 21, 1972, except if regulations are necessary for the implementation of any provision that becomes effective on Oct. 21, 1972, and continuation in effect of the provisions of subchapter I of this chapter and regulations thereunder as in effect prior to Oct. 21, 1972, until superseded by provisions of Pub. L. No. 92–516, and regulations thereunder, see section 4 of Pub. L. No. 92–516, set out as a note under section 136 of this title.

§ 136u. State cooperation, aid, and training

[FIFRA § 23]

(a) Cooperative agreements

The Administrator may enter into cooperative agreements with States and Indian tribes—

(1) to delegate to any State or Indian tribe the authority to cooperate in the enforcement of this subchapter through the use of its personnel or facilities, to train personnel of the State or Indian tribe to cooperate in the enforcement of this subchapter, and to assist States and Indian tribes in implementing cooperative enforcement programs through grants-in-aid; and

(2) to assist States in developing and administering State programs, and Indian tribes that enter into cooperative agreements, to train and certify applicators consistent with the standards the Administrator prescribes.

Effective with the fiscal year beginning October 1, 1978, there are authorized to be appropriated annually such funds as may be necessary for the Administrator to provide through cooperative agreements an amount equal to 50 percent of the anticipated cost to each State or Indian tribe, as agreed to under such cooperative agreements, of conducting training and certification programs during such fiscal year. If funds sufficient to pay 50 percent of the costs for any year are not appropriated, the share of each State and Indian tribe shall be reduced in a like proportion in allocating available funds.

(b) Contracts for training

In addition, the Administrator may enter into contracts with Federal, State, or Indian tribal agencies for the purpose of encouraging the training of certified applicators.

(c) Information and education

The Administrator shall, in cooperation with the Secretary of Agriculture, use the services of the cooperative State extension services to inform and educate pesticide users about accepted uses and other regulations made under this subchapter.

(Act of June 25, 1947, c. 125, § 23, as added by Pub. L. No. 92–516, § 2, 86 Stat. 996 (Oct. 21, 1972); and amended by Pub. L. No. 95–396, § 21, 92 Stat. 834 (Sept. 30, 1978).)

HISTORICAL AND STATUTORY NOTES

State and Tribal Assistance Grants

Pub. L. No. 105–276, Title III, 112 Stat. 2499 (Oct. 21, 1998), provided in part: "That beginning in fiscal year 1999 and thereafter, pesticide program implementation grants under section 23(a)(1) of the Federal Insecticide, Fungicide and Rodenticide Act, as amended [subsec. (a)(1) of this section], shall be available for pesticide program development and implementation, including enforcement and compliance activities."

§ 136v. Authority of States

[FIFRA § 24]

(a) In general

A State may regulate the sale or use of any federally registered pesticide or device in the State, but only if and to the extent the regulation does not permit any sale or use prohibited by this subchapter.

(b) Uniformity

Such State shall not impose or continue in effect any requirements for labeling or packaging in addition to or different from those required under this subchapter.

(c) Additional uses

(1) A State may provide registration for additional uses of federally registered pesticides formulated for distribution and use within that State to meet special local needs in accord with the purposes of this subchapter and if registration for such use has not previously been denied, disapproved, or canceled by the Administrator. Such registration shall be deemed registration under section 136a of this title for all purposes of this subchapter, but shall authorize distribution and use only within such State.

(2) A registration issued by a State under this subsection shall not be effective for more than ninety days if disapproved by the Administrator within that period. Prior to disapproval, the Administrator shall, except as provided in paragraph (3) of this subsection, advise the State of the Administrator's intention to disapprove and the reasons therefor, and provide the State time to respond. The Administrator shall not prohibit or disapprove a registration issued by a State under this subsection (A) on the basis of lack of essentiality of a pesticide or (B) except as provided in paragraph (3) of this subsection, if its composition and use patterns are similar to those of a federally registered pesticide.

(3) In no instance may a State issue a registration for a food or feed use unless there exists a tolerance or exemption under the Federal Food, Drug, and Cosmetic Act [21 U.S.C.A. § 301 et seq.] that permits the residues of the pesticides on the food or feed. If the Administrator determines that a registration issued by a State is inconsistent with the Federal Food, Drug, and Cosmetic Act, or the use of, a pesticide under a registration issued by a State constitutes an imminent hazard, the Administrator may immediately disapprove the registration.

(4) If the Administrator finds, in accordance with standards set forth in regulations issued under section 136w of this title, that a State is not capable of exercising adequate controls to assure that State registration under this section will be in accord with the purposes of this subchapter or has failed to exercise adequate controls, the Administrator may suspend the authority of the State to register pesticides until such time as the Administrator is satisfied that the State can and will exercise adequate controls. Prior to any such suspension, the Administrator shall advise the State of the Administrator's intention to suspend and the reasons therefor and provide the State time to respond.

(Act of June 25, 1947, c. 125, § 24, as added by Pub. L. No. 92–516, § 2, 86 Stat. 997 (Oct. 21, 1972); and amended by Pub. L. No. 95–396, § 22, 92 Stat. 835 (Sept. 30, 1978); Pub. L. No. 100–532, Title VIII, § 801(m), 102 Stat. 2682 (Oct. 25, 1988).)

HISTORICAL AND STATUTORY NOTES

References in Text

The Federal Food, Drug, and Cosmetic Act, referred to in subsec. (c)(3), is Act of June 25, 1938, c. 675, 52 Stat. 1040, as amended, which is codified generally to chapter 9 (section 301 et seq.) of Title 21, Food and Drugs. For complete classification of this Act to the Code, see section 301 of Title 21 and Tables.

Effective and Applicability Provisions

1988 Acts. Amendment by Pub. L. No. 100–532 effective on expiration of 60 days after October 25, 1988, see section 901 of Pub. L. No. 100–532, set out as a note under section 136 of this title.

1972 Acts. Section effective at the close of Oct. 21, 1972, except if regulations are necessary for the implementation of any provision that becomes effective on Oct. 21, 1972, and continuation in effect of the provisions of subchapter I of this chapter and regulations thereunder as in effect prior to Oct. 21, 1972, until superseded by provisions of Pub. L. No. 92–516 and regulations thereunder, see section 4 of Pub. L. No. 92–516, set out as a note under section 136 of this title.

§ 136w. Authority of Administrator

[FIFRA § 25]

(a) In general

(1) Regulations

The Administrator is authorized, in accordance with the procedure described in paragraph (2), to prescribe regulations to carry out the provisions of this subchapter. Such regulations shall take into account the difference in concept and usage between various classes of pesticides, including public health pesticides, and differences in environmental risk and the appropriate data for evaluating such risk between agricultural, nonagricultural, and public health pesticides.

(2) Procedure

(A) Proposed regulations

At least 60 days prior to signing any proposed regulation for publication in the Federal Register, the Administrator shall provide the Secretary of Agriculture with a copy of such regulation. If the Secretary comments in writing to the Administrator regarding any such regulation within 30 days after receiving it, the Administrator shall publish in the Federal Register (with the proposed regulation) the comments of the Secretary and the response of the Administrator with regard to the Secretary's comments. If the Secretary does not comment in writing to the Administrator regarding the regulation within 30 days after receiving it, the Administrator may sign such regulation for publication in the Federal Register any time after such 30-day period notwithstanding the foregoing 60-day time requirement.

(B) Final regulations

At least 30 days prior to signing any regulation in final form for publication in the Federal Register, the Administrator shall provide the Secretary of Agriculture with a copy of such regulation. If the Secretary comments in writing to the Administrator regarding any such final regulation within 15 days after receiving it, the Administrator shall publish in the Federal Register (with the final regulation) the comments of the Secretary, if requested by the Secretary, and the response of the Administrator concerning the Secretary's comments. If the Secretary does not comment in writing to the Administrator regarding the regulation within 15 days after receiving it, the Administrator may sign such regulation for publication in the Federal Register at any time after such 15-day period notwithstanding the foregoing 30-day time requirement. In taking any final action under this subsection, the Administrator shall include among those factors to be taken into account the effect of the regulation on production and prices of agricultural commodities, retail food prices, and otherwise on the agricultural economy, and the Administrator shall publish in the Federal Register an analysis of such effect.

(C) Time requirements

The time requirements imposed by subparagraphs (A) and (B) may be waived or modified to the extent agreed upon by the Administrator and the Secretary.

(D) Publication in the Federal Register

The Administrator shall, simultaneously with any notification to the Secretary of Agriculture under this paragraph prior to the issuance of any proposed or final regulation, publish such notification in the Federal Register.

(3) Congressional committees

At such time as the Administrator is required under paragraph (2) of this subsection to provide the Secretary of Agriculture with a copy of proposed regulations and a copy of the final form of regulations, the Administrator shall also furnish a copy of such regulations to the Committee on Agriculture of the House of Representatives and the Committee on Agriculture, Nutrition, and Forestry of the Senate.

(4) Congressional review of regulations

Simultaneously with the promulgation of any rule or regulation under this subchapter, the Administrator shall transmit a copy thereof to the Secretary of the Senate and the Clerk of the House of Representatives. The rule or regulation shall not become effective until the passage of 60 calendar days after the rule or regulation is so transmitted.

(b) Exemption of pesticides

The Administrator may exempt from the requirements of this subchapter by regulation any pesticide which the Administrator determines either (1) to be adequately regulated by another Federal agency, or (2) to be of a character which is unnecessary to be subject to this subchapter in order to carry out the purposes of this subchapter.

(c) Other authority

The Administrator, after notice and opportunity for hearing, is authorized—

(1) to declare a pest any form of plant or animal life (other than man and other than bacteria, virus, and other micro-organisms on or in living man or other living animals) which is injurious to health or the environment;

(2) to determine any pesticide which contains any substance or substances in quantities highly toxic to man;

(3) to establish standards (which shall be consistent with those established under the authority of the Poison Prevention Packaging Act (Public Law 91–601) [15 U.S.C.A. § 1471 et seq.]) with respect to the package, container, or wrapping in which a pesticide or device is enclosed for use or consumption, in order to protect children and adults from serious injury or illness resulting from accidental ingestion or contact with pesticides or devices regulated by this subchapter as well as to accomplish the other purposes of this subchapter;

(4) to specify those classes of devices which shall be subject to any provision of section 136(q)(1) or section 136e of this title upon the Administrator's determination that application of such provision is necessary to effectuate the purposes of this subchapter;

(5) to prescribe regulations requiring any pesticide to be colored or discolored if the Administrator determines that such requirement is feasible and is necessary for the protection of health and the environment; and

(6) to determine and establish suitable names to be used in the ingredient statement.

(d) Scientific advisory panel

(1) In general

The Administrator shall submit to an advisory panel for comment as to the impact on health and the environment of the action proposed in notices of intent issued under section 136d(b) of this title and of the proposed and final form of regulations issued under subsection (a) of this section within the same time periods as provided for the comments of the Secretary of Agriculture under such section 136d(b) and subsection (a) of this section. The time requirements for notices of intent and proposed and final forms of regulation may not be modified or waived unless in addition to meeting the requirements of section 136d(b) of this title or subsection (a) of this section, as applicable, the advisory panel has failed to comment on the proposed action within the prescribed time period or has agreed to the modification or waiver. The Administrator shall also solicit from the advisory panel comments, evaluations, and recommendations for operating guidelines to improve the effectiveness and quality of scientific analyses made by personnel of the Environmental Protection Agency that lead to decisions by the Administrator in carrying out the provisions of this subchapter. The comments, evaluations, and recommendations of the advisory panel submitted under this subsection and the response of the Administrator shall be published in the Federal Register in the same manner as provided for publication of the comments of the Secretary of Agriculture under such sections. The chairman of the advisory panel, after consultation with the Administrator, may create temporary subpanels on specific projects to assist the full advisory panel in expediting and preparing its evaluations, comments, and recommendations. The subpanels may be composed of scientists other than members of the advisory panel, as deemed necessary for the purpose of evaluating scientific studies relied upon by the Administrator with respect to proposed action. Such additional scientists shall be selected by the advisory panel. The panel referred to in this subsection shall consist of 7 members appointed by the Administrator from a list of 12 nominees, 6 nominated by the National Institutes of Health and 6 by the National Science Foundation, utilizing a system of staggered terms of appointment. Members of the panel shall be selected on the basis of their professional qualifications to assess the effects of the impact of pesticides on health and the environment. To the extent feasible to insure multidisciplinary representation, the panel membership shall include representation from the disciplines of toxicology, pathology, environmental biology, and related sciences. If a vacancy occurs on the panel due to expiration of a term, resignation, or any other reason, each replacement shall be selected by the Administrator from a group of 4 nominees, 2 submitted by each of the nominating entities named in this subsection. The Administrator may extend the term of a panel member until the new member is appointed to fill the vacancy. If a vacancy occurs due to resignation, or reason other than expiration of a term, the Administrator shall appoint a member to serve during the unexpired term utilizing the nomination process set forth in this subsection. Should the list of nominees provided under this subsection be unsatisfactory, the Administrator may request an additional set of nominees from the nominating entities. The Administrator may require such information from the nominees to the advisory panel as the Administrator deems necessary, and the Administrator shall publish in the Federal Register the name, address, and professional affiliations of each nominee. Each member of the panel shall receive per diem compensation at a rate not in excess of that fixed for GS–18 of the General Schedule as may be determined by the Administrator, except that any such member who holds another office or position under the Federal Government the compensation for which exceeds such rate may elect to receive compensation at the rate provided for such other office or position in lieu of the compensation provided by this subsection. In order to assure the objectivity of the advisory panel, the Administrator shall promulgate regulations regarding conflicts of interest with respect to the members of the panel. The advisory panel established under this section shall be permanent. In performing the functions assigned by this subchapter, the panel shall consult and coordinate its activities with the Science Advisory Board established under the Environmental Research, Development, and Demonstration Authorization Act of 1978 [42 U.S.C.A. § 4365]. Whenever the Administrator exercises authority under section 136d(c) of this title to immediately suspend the registration of any pesticide to prevent an imminent hazard, the Administrator shall promptly submit to the advisory panel for comment, as to the impact on health and the environment, the action taken to suspend the registration of such pesticide.

(2) Science Review Board

There is established a Science Review Board to consist of 60 scientists who shall be available to the Scientific Advisory Panel to assist in reviews conducted by the Panel. Members of the Board shall be selected in the same manner as members of temporary subpanels created under paragraph (1). Members of the Board shall be compensated in the same manner as members of the Panel.

(e) Peer review

The Administrator shall, by written procedures, provide for peer review with respect to the design, protocols, and conduct of major scientific studies conducted under this subchapter by the Environmental Protection Agency or by any other Federal agency, any State or political subdivision thereof, or any institution or individual under grant, contract, or cooperative agreement from or with the Environmental Protection Agency. In such procedures, the Administrator shall also provide for peer review, using the advisory panel established under subsection (d) of this section or appropriate experts appointed by the Administrator from a current list of nominees maintained by such panel, with respect to the results of any such scientific studies relied upon by the Administrator with respect to actions the Administrator may take relating to the change in classification, suspension, or cancellation of a pesticide. Whenever the Administrator determines that circumstances do not permit the peer review of the results of any such scientific study prior to the Administrator's exercising authority under section 136d(c) of this title to immediately suspend the registration of any pesticide to prevent an imminent hazard, the Administrator shall promptly thereafter provide for the conduct of peer review as provided in this sentence. The evaluations and relevant documentation constituting the peer review that relate to the proposed scientific studies and the results of the completed scientific studies shall be included in the submission for comment forwarded by the Administrator to the advisory panel as provided in subsection (d) of this section. As used in this subsection, the term "peer review" shall mean an independent evaluation by scientific experts, either within or outside the Environmental Protection Agency, in the appropriate disciplines.

(Act of June 25, 1947, c. 125, § 25, as added by Pub. L. No. 92–516, § 2, 86 Stat. 997 (Oct. 21, 1972); and amended by Pub. L. No. 94–140, §§ 2(a), 6, 7, 89 Stat. 751, 753 (Nov. 28, 1975); Pub. L. No. 95–396, § 23, 92 Stat. 836 (Sept.

30, 1978); Pub. L. No. 96–539, §§ 1, 2(a), 4, 94 Stat. 3194, 3195 (Dec. 17, 1980); Pub. L. No. 98–201, § 1, 97 Stat. 1379 (Dec. 2, 1983); Pub. L. No. 98–620, Title IV, § 402(4)(D), 98 Stat. 3357 (Nov. 8, 1984); Pub. L. No. 100–352, § 6(i), 102 Stat. 664 (June 27, 1988); Pub. L. No. 100–532, Title VI, §§ 602, 605, Title VIII, § 801(n), 102 Stat. 2678, 2679, 2683 (Oct. 25, 1988); Pub. L. No. 102–237, Title X, § 1006(b)(1), (2), 105 Stat. 1895 (Dec. 13, 1991); Pub. L. No. 104–170, Title I, § 104, Title II, § 235, 110 Stat. 1490, 1509 (Aug. 3, 1996).)

HISTORICAL AND STATUTORY NOTES

References in Text

The Poison Prevention Packaging Act, referred to in subsec. (c)(3), is Pub. L. No. 91–601, 84 Stat. 1670 (Dec. 30, 1970), which is codified generally to chapter 39A (section 1471 et seq.) of Title 15, Commerce and Trade. For complete classification of this Act to the Code, see Short Title note set out under section 1471 of Title 15 and Tables.

Reference in subsec. (c)(4) to "section 136(q)(1)" was, in the original, a reference to "paragraph 2(q)(1)" and has been editorially translated as "section 136(q)(1)" as the probable intent of Congress.

GS-18 of the General Schedule, referred to in subsec. (d)(1), is codified as section 5332 of Title 5, Government Organization and Employees.

The Environmental Research, Development, and Demonstration Authorization Act of 1978, referred to in subsec. (d)(1), is Pub. L. No. 95–155, Nov. 8, 1977, 91 Stat. 1257, as amended. Provisions of the Act establishing the Science Advisory Board are codified as section 4365 of Title 42, The Public Health and Welfare. For complete classification of this Act to the Code, see Tables.

Effective and Applicability Provisions

1991 Acts. Amendments by Pub. L. No. 102–237 effective Dec. 13, 1991, see section 1101(a) of Pub. L. No. 102–237, set out as a note under section 1421 of this title.

1988 Acts. Amendment by Pub. L. No. 100–532 effective on expiration of 60 days after October 25, 1988, see section 901 of Pub. L. No. 100–532, set out as a note under section 136 of this title.

Amendment by Pub. L. No. 100–352 effective ninety days after June 27, 1988, except that such amendment not apply to cases pending in the Supreme Court on such effective date or affect the right to review or the manner of reviewing the judgment or decree of a court which was entered before such effective date, see section 7 of Pub. L. No. 100–352, set out as a note under section 1254 of Title 28, Judiciary and Judicial Procedure.

1984 Acts. Amendment by Pub. L. No. 98–620 not to apply to cases pending on Nov. 8, 1984, see section 403 of Pub. L. No. 98–620, set out as a note under section 1657 of Title 28, Judiciary and Judicial Procedure.

1980 Acts. Section 2(b) of Pub. L. No. 96–539 provided that: "The provisions of this section [amending subsec. (e) of this section] shall become effective upon publication in the Federal Register of final procedures for peer review as provided in this section, but in no event shall such provisions become effective later than one year after the date of enactment of this Act [Dec. 17, 1980]."

1972 Acts. Section effective at the close of Oct. 21, 1972, except if regulations are necessary for the implementation of any provision that becomes effective on Oct. 21, 1972, and continuation in effect of the provisions of subchapter I of this chapter and regulations thereunder as in effect prior to Oct. 1, 1972, until superseded by provisions of Pub. L. No. 92–516 and regulations thereunder, see section 4 of Pub. L. No. 92–516, set out as a note under section 136 of this title.

Transfer of Functions

Any reference in any provision of law enacted before Jan. 4, 1995, to a function, duty, or authority of the Clerk of the House of Representatives treated as referring, with respect to that function, duty, or authority, to the officer of the House of Representatives exercising that function, duty, or authority, as determined by the Committee on House Oversight of the House of Representatives, see section 2(1) of Pub. L. No. 104–14, set out as a note preceding section 21 of Title 2, The Congress.

FIFRA User Fees

Pub. L. No. 101–508, Title I, § 1204(e), 104 Stat. 1388 (Nov. 5, 1990), provided that: "Notwithstanding any provision of the Omnibus Budget Reconciliation Act of 1990, [for classification of Pub. L. No. 101–508, see Tables], nothing in this title [for classifications of Pub. L. No. 101–508, Title I, see Agricultural Reconciliation Act of 1990, set out as a Short Title note under section 1421 of this title and Tables], or the other provisions of this Act shall be construed to require or authorize the Administrator of the Environmental Protection Agency to assess or collect any fees of charges for services and activities authorized under the Federal Insecticide, Fungicide and Rodenticide Act (7 U.S.C. 136 et seq.) [this subchapter]."

Agricultural Worker Protection Standard and Certification of Pesticide Applicators

Pub. L. No. 116–8, § 7, 133 Stat. 578–579 (Mar. 8, 2019), provided that:

"**(a) In General.**—Except as provided in subsection (b), during the period beginning on the date of enactment of this Act and ending not earlier than October 1, 2021, the Administrator of the Environmental Protection Agency (referred to in this section as the "Administrator")—

"**(1)** shall carry out—

"**(A)** the final rule of the Administrator entitled "Pesticides; Agricultural Worker Protection Standard Revisions" (80 Fed. Reg. 67496 (November 2, 2015)); and

"**(B)** the final rule of the Administrator entitled "Pesticides; Certification of Pesticide Applicators" (82 Fed. Reg. 952 (January 4, 2017)); and

"**(2)** shall not revise or develop revisions to the rules described in subparagraphs (A) and (B) of paragraph (1).

"**(b) Exceptions.**—Prior to October 1, 2021, the Administrator may propose, and after a notice and public comment period of not less than 90 days, promulgate revisions to the final rule described in subsection (a)(1)(A) addressing application exclusion zones under part 170 of title 40, Code of Federal Regulations, consistent with the Federal Insecticide, Fungicide, and Rodenticide Act (7 U.S.C. 136 et seq.)

"**(c) GAO Report.**—The Comptroller General of the United States shall—

"**(1)** conduct a study on the use of the designated representative, including the effect of that use on the availability of pesticide application and hazard information and worker health and safety; and

"**(2)** not later than October 1, 2021, make publically available a report describing the study under paragraph (1), including any recommendations to prevent the misuse of pesticide application and hazard information, if that misuse is identified."

References to other Laws to GS–16, 17, or 18 Pay Rates

References in laws to the rates of pay for GS–16, 17, or 18, or to maximum rates of pay under the General Schedule, to be considered references to rates payable under specified sections of Title 5, Government Organization and Employees, see section 529 [title I, § 101(c)(1)] of Pub. L. No. 101–509, set out in a note under section 5376 of Title 5.

§ 136w–1. State primary enforcement responsibility

[FIFRA § 26]

(a) In general

For the purposes of this subchapter, a State shall have primary enforcement responsibility for pesticide use violations during any period for which the Administrator determines that such State—

(1) has adopted adequate pesticide use laws and regulations, except that the Administrator may not require a State to have pesticide use laws that are more stringent than this subchapter;

(2) has adopted and is implementing adequate procedures for the enforcement of such State laws and regulations; and

(3) will keep such records and make such reports showing compliance with paragraphs (1) and (2) of this subsection as the Administrator may require by regulation.

(b) Special rules

Notwithstanding the provisions of subsection (a) of this section, any State that enters into a cooperative agreement with the Administrator under section 136u of this title for the enforcement of pesticide use restrictions shall have the primary enforcement responsibility for pesticide use violations. Any State that has a plan approved by the Administrator in accordance with the requirements of section 136i of this title that the Administrator determines meets the criteria set out in subsection (a) of this section shall have the primary enforcement responsibility for pesticide use violations. The Administrator shall make such determinations with respect to State plans under section 136i of this title in effect on September 30, 1978, not later than six months after that date.

(c) Administrator

The Administrator shall have primary enforcement responsibility for those States that do not have primary enforcement responsibility under this subchapter. Notwithstanding the provisions of section 136(e)(1) of this title, during any period when the Administrator has such enforcement responsibility, section 136f(b) of this title shall apply to the books and records of commercial applicators and to any applicator who holds or applies pesticides, or uses dilutions of pesticides, only to provide a service of controlling pests without delivering any unapplied pesticide to any person so served, and section 136g(a) of this title shall apply to the establishment or other place where pesticides or devices are held for application by such persons with respect to pesticides or devices held for such application.

(Act of June 25, 1947, c. 125, § 26, as added Pub. L. No. 95–396, § 24(2), 92 Stat. 836 (Sept. 30, 1978); and amended by Pub. L. No. 100–532, Title VIII, § 801(*o*), (q)(1)(D), 102 Stat. 2683 (Oct. 25, 1988); Pub. L. No. 102–237, Title X, § 1006(a)(11), 105 Stat. 1895 (Dec. 13, 1991).)

HISTORICAL AND STATUTORY NOTES

Effective and Applicability Provisions

1991 Acts. Amendment by section 1006(a)(11) of Pub. L. No. 102–237 effective Dec. 13, 1991, see section 1101(a) of Pub. L. No. 102–237, set out as a note under section 1421 of this title.

1988 Acts. Amendment by Pub. L. No. 100–532 effective on expiration of 60 days after October 25, 1988, see section 901 of Pub. L. No. 100–532, set out as a note under section 136 of this title.

Prior Provisions

A prior section 26 of the Federal Insecticide, Fungicide, and Rodenticide Act, Act of June 25, 1947, c. 125, as added Oct. 21, 1972, Pub. L. No. 92–516, § 2, 86 Stat. 998, as amended, relating to severability of environmental pesticide control provisions, was redesignated as section 34 of that Act by Pub. L. No. 108–199, Div. G, Title V, § 501(f)(1), Jan. 23, 2004, 118 Stat. 422, and is codified as 7 U.S.C.A. § 136x.

§ 136w–2. Failure by the State to assure enforcement of State pesticide use regulations

[FIFRA § 27]

(a) Referral

Upon receipt of any complaint or other information alleging or indicating a significant violation of the pesticide use provisions of this subchapter, the Administrator shall refer the matter to the appropriate State officials for their investigation of the matter consistent with the requirements of this subchapter. If, within thirty days, the State has not commenced appropriate enforcement action, the Administrator may act upon the complaint or information to the extent authorized under this subchapter.

(b) Notice

Whenever the Administrator determines that a State having primary enforcement responsibility for pesticide use violations is not carrying out (or cannot carry out due to the lack of adequate legal authority) such responsibility, the Administrator shall notify the State. Such notice shall specify those aspects of the administration of the State program that are determined to be inadequate. The State shall have ninety days after receipt of the notice to correct any deficiencies. If after that time the Administrator determines that the State program remains inadequate, the Administrator may rescind, in whole or in part, the State's primary enforcement responsibility for pesticide use violations.

(c) Construction

Neither section 136w–1 of this title nor this section shall limit the authority of the Administrator to enforce this subchapter, where the Administrator determines that emergency conditions exist that require immediate action on the part of the Administrator and the State authority is unwilling or unable adequately to respond to the emergency.

(Act of June 25, 1947, c. 125, § 27, as added by Pub. L. No. 95–396, § 24(2), 92 Stat. 837 (Sept. 30, 1978); and amended by Pub. L. No. 100–532, Title VIII, § 801(p), 102 Stat. 2683 (Oct. 25, 1988).)

HISTORICAL AND STATUTORY NOTES

Effective and Applicability Provisions

1988 Acts. Amendment by Pub. L. No. 100–532 effective on expiration of 60 days after October 25, 1988, see section 901 of Pub. L. No. 100–532, set out as a note under section 136 of this title.

Prior Provisions

A prior section 27 of the Federal Insecticide, Fungicide, and Rodenticide Act, Act of June 25, 1947, c. 125, as added Oct. 21, 1972, Pub. L. No. 92–516, § 2, 86 Stat. 998, and amended, relating to authorization of appropriations for environmental pesticide control, was redesignated as section 35 of that Act by Pub. L. No. 108–199, Title V, § 501(f)(1), 118 Stat. 422 (Jan. 23, 2004), and is codified as 7 U.S.C.A. § 136y.

§ 136w–3. Identification of pests; cooperation with Department of Agriculture's program

[FIFRA § 28]

(a) In general

The Administrator, in coordination with the Secretary of Agriculture, shall identify those pests that must be brought under control. The Administrator shall also coordinate and cooperate with the Secretary of Agriculture's research and implementation programs to develop and improve the safe use and effectiveness of chemical, biological, and alternative methods to combat and control pests that reduce the quality and economical production and distribution of agricultural products to domestic and foreign consumers.

(b) Pest control availability

(1) In general

The Administrator, in cooperation with the Secretary of Agriculture, shall identify—

(A) available methods of pest control by crop or animal;

(B) minor pest control problems, both in minor crops and minor or localized problems in major crops; and

(C) factors limiting the availability of specific pest control methods, such as resistance to control methods and regulatory actions limiting the availability of control methods.

(2) Report

The Secretary of Agriculture shall, not later than 180 days after November 28, 1990, and annually thereafter, prepare a report and send the report to the Administrator. The report shall—

(A) contain the information described in paragraph (1);

(B) identify the crucial pest control needs where a shortage of control methods is indicated by the information described in paragraph (1); and

(C) describe in detail research and extension efforts designed to address the needs identified in subparagraph (B).

(c) Integrated pest management

The Administrator, in cooperation with the Secretary of Agriculture, shall develop approaches to the control of pests based on integrated pest management that respond to the needs of producers, with a special emphasis on minor pests.

(d) Public health pests

The Administrator, in coordination with the Secretary of Agriculture and the Secretary of Health and Human Services, shall identify pests of significant public health importance and, in coordination with the Public Health Service, develop and implement programs to improve and facilitate the safe and necessary use of chemical, biological, and other methods to combat and control such pests of public health importance.

(Act of June 25, 1947, c. 125, § 28, as added by Pub. L. No. 95–396, § 24(2), 92 Stat. 838 (Sept. 30, 1978); and amended by Pub. L. No. 101–624, Title XIV, § 1495, 104 Stat. 3629 (Nov. 28, 1990); Pub. L. No. 104–127, Title VIII, § 862(b)(1), 110 Stat. 1174 (Apr. 4, 1996); Pub. L. No. 104–170, Title II, § 236, 110 Stat. 1509 (Aug. 3, 1996).)

HISTORICAL AND STATUTORY NOTES

Severability of Provisions

If any provision of Pub. L. No. 101–624 or the application thereof to any person or circumstance is held invalid, such invalidity not to affect other provisions or applications of Pub. L. No. 101–624 which can be given effect without regard to the invalid provision or application, see section 2519 of Pub. L. No. 101–624, set out as a note under section 1421 of this title.

§ 136w–4. Omitted

HISTORICAL AND STATUTORY NOTES

This section, Act of June 25, 1947, c. 125, § 29, as added by Pub. L. No. 95–396, § 24(2), 92 Stat. 838 (Sept. 30, 1978), required the Administrator of the Environmental Protection Agency to submit an annual report to Congress relating to filing of applications for conditional registration under 7 U.S.C.A. § 136a(c)(7)(B), (C). It terminated, effective May 15, 2000, pursuant to Pub. L. No. 104–66, § 3003, as amended, set out as a note under 31 U.S.C.A. § 1113. See also page 164 of House Document No. 103–7.

§ 136w–5. Minimum requirements for training of maintenance applicators and service technicians

[FIFRA § 30]

Each State may establish minimum requirements for training of maintenance applicators and service technicians. Such training may include instruction in the safe and effective handling and use of pesticides in accordance with the Environmental Protection Agency approved labeling, and instruction in integrated pest management techniques. The authority of the Administrator with respect to minimum requirements for training of maintenance applicators and service technicians shall be limited to ensuring that each State understands the provisions of this section.

(Act of June 25, 1947, c. 125, § 30, as added by Pub. L. No. 104–170, Title I, § 121(2), 110 Stat. 1492 (Aug. 3, 1996).)

HISTORICAL AND STATUTORY NOTES

Prior Provisions

A prior section 30 of the Federal Insecticide, Fungicide, and Rodenticide Act, Act of June 25, 1947, c. 125, § 34, formerly § 26, as added by Pub. L. No. 92–516, § 2, 86 Stat. 998 (Oct. 21, 1972), renumbered § 30 by Pub. L. No. 95–396, § 24(1), 92 Stat. 836 (, Sept. 30, 1978), as amended, relating to severability of environmental pesticide control provisions, was redesignated as section 34 of that Act by Pub. L. No. 108–199, Div. G, Title V, § 501(f)(1), 118 Stat. 422 (Jan. 23, 2004), and is codified as 7 U.S.C.A. § 136x.

§ 136w–6. Environmental Protection Agency minor use program

[FIFRA § 31]

(a) The Administrator shall assure coordination of minor use issues through the establishment of a minor use program within the Office of Pesticide Programs. Such office shall be responsible for coordinating the development of minor use programs and policies and consulting with growers regarding minor use issues and registrations and amendments which are submitted to the Environmental Protection Agency.

(b) The Office of Pesticide Programs shall prepare a public report concerning the progress made on the registration of minor uses, including implementation of the exclusive use as an incentive for registering new minor uses, within 3 years of the passage of the Food Quality Protection Act of 1996.

(Act of June 25, 1947, c. 125, § 31, as added by Pub. L. No. 104–170, Title II, § 210(i), 110 Stat. 1500 (Aug. 3, 1996).)

HISTORICAL AND STATUTORY NOTES

References in Text

The passage of the Food Quality Protection Act of 1996, referred to in subsec. (b), probably means the date of enactment of Pub. L. No. 104–170, which was approved Aug. 3, 1996.

Prior Provisions

A prior section 31 of the Federal Insecticide, Fungicide, and Rodenticide Act, Act of June 25, 1947, c. 125, formerly § 27, as added by Pub. L. No. 92–516, § 2, 86 Stat. 998 (Oct. 21, 1972), as amended; renumbered § 31 and amended by Pub. L. No. 95–396, §§ 24(1), (25), 92 Stat. 836 (Sept. 30, 1978), as amended, relating to authorization of appropriations for environmental pesticide control, was redesignated as section 35 of that Act by Pub. L. No. 108–199, Div. G, Title V, § 501(f)(1), 118 Stat. 422 (Jan. 23, 2004), and is codified as 7 U.S.C.A. § 136y.

§ 136w–7. Department of Agriculture minor use program

[FIFRA § 32]

(a) In general

The Secretary of Agriculture (hereinafter in this section referred to as the "Secretary") shall assure the coordination of the responsibilities of the Department of Agriculture related to minor uses of pesticides, including—

(1) carrying out the Inter-Regional Project Number 4 (IR-4) as described in section 2 of Public Law 89–106 (7 U.S.C. 450i(e)) and the national pesticide resistance monitoring program established under section 1651 of the Food, Agriculture, Conservation, and Trade Act of 1990 (7 U.S.C. 5882);

(2) supporting integrated pest management research;

(3) consulting with growers to develop data for minor uses; and

(4) providing assistance for minor use registrations, tolerances, and reregistrations with the Environmental Protection Agency.

(b) Minor use pesticide data and revolving fund

(1) Minor use pesticide data

(A) Grant authority

The Secretary, in consultation with the Administrator, shall establish a program to make grants for the development of data to support minor use pesticide registrations and reregistrations. The amount of any such grant shall not exceed 1/2 of the cost of the project for which the grant is made.

(B) Applicants

Any person who wants to develop data to support minor use pesticide registrations and reregistrations may apply for a grant under subparagraph (A). Priority shall be given to an applicant for such a grant who does not directly receive funds from the sale of pesticides registered for minor uses.

(C) Data ownership

Any data that is developed under a grant under subparagraph (A) shall be jointly owned by the Department of Agriculture and the person who received the grant. Such a person shall enter into an agreement with the Secretary under which such person shall share any fee paid to such person under section 136a(c)(1)(F) of this title.

(2) Minor Use Pesticide Data Revolving Fund

(A) Establishment

There is established in the Treasury of the United States a revolving fund to be known as the Minor Use Pesticide Data Revolving Fund. The Fund shall be available without fiscal year limitation to carry out the authorized purposes of this subsection.

(B) Contents of the Fund

There shall be deposited in the Fund—

(i) such amounts as may be appropriated to support the purposes of this subsection; and

(ii) fees collected by the Secretary for any data developed under a grant under paragraph (1)(A).

(C) Authorizations of appropriations

There are authorized to be appropriated for each fiscal year to carry out the purposes of this subsection $10,000,000 to remain available until expended.

(Act of June 25, 1947, c. 125, § 32, as added by Pub. L. No. 104–170, Title II, § 210(j), 110 Stat. 1501 (Aug. 3, 1996).)

HISTORICAL AND STATUTORY NOTES

References in Text

Section 2 of Pub. L. No. 89–106, referred to in subsec. (a)(1), is Pub. L. No. 89–106, § 2, 79 Stat. 431 (Aug. 4, 1965,), which is codified as 7 U.S.C.A. § 450i.

Section 1651 of the Food, Agriculture, Conservation, and Trade Act of 1990, referred to in subsec. (a)(1), was codified as section 5882 of this title prior to repeal by Pub. L. No. 104–127, Title VIII, § 862(a), 110 Stat. 1174 (Apr. 4, 1996).

§ 136w–8. Pesticide registration service fees

[FIFRA § 33]

(a) Definition of costs

In this section, the term "costs", when used with respect to review and decisionmaking pertaining to an application for which registration service fees are paid under this section, means—

(1) costs to the extent that—

(A) officers and employees provide direct support for the review and decisionmaking for covered pesticide applications, associated tolerances, and corresponding risk and benefits information and analyses;

(B) persons and organizations under contract with the Administrator engage in the review of the applications, and corresponding risk and benefits information and assessments; and

(C) advisory committees and other accredited persons or organizations, on the request of the Administrator, engage in the peer review of risk or benefits information associated with covered pesticide applications;

(2) costs of management of information, and the acquisition, maintenance, and repair of computer and telecommunication resources (including software), used to support review of pesticide applications, associated tolerances, and corresponding risk and benefits information and analyses; and

(3) costs of collecting registration service fees under subsections (b) and (c) of this section and reporting, auditing, and accounting under this section.

(b) Fees

(1) In general

Effective beginning on the effective date of the Pesticide Registration Improvement Act of 2003, the Administrator shall assess and collect covered pesticide registration service fees in accordance with this section.

(2) Covered applications

(A) In general

An application for the registration of a pesticide covered by this subchapter that is received by the Administrator on or after the effective date of the Pesticide Registration Improvement Act of 2003 or for any other action covered by a table specified in paragraph (3) shall be subject to a registration service fee under this section.

(B) Existing applications

(i) In general

Subject to clause (ii), an application for the registration of a pesticide that was submitted to the Administrator before the effective date of the Pesticide Registration Improvement Act of 2003 and is pending on that effective date shall be subject to a service fee under this section if the application is for the registration of a new active ingredient that is not listed in the Registration Division 2003 Work Plan of the Office of Pesticide Programs of the Environmental Protection Agency.

(ii) Tolerance or exemption fees

The amount of any fee otherwise payable for an application described in clause (i) under this section shall be reduced by the amount of any fees paid to support the related petition for a pesticide tolerance or exemption under the Federal Food, Drug, and Cosmetic Act (21 U.S.C. 301 et seq.).

(C) Documentation

An application subject to a registration service fee under this section shall be submitted with documentation certifying—

(i) payment of the registration service fee; or

(ii) payment of at least 25 percent of the registration service fee and a request for a waiver from or reduction of the remaining amount of the registration service fee.

(D) Payment

The registration service fee required under this subsection shall be due upon submission of the application.

(E) Applications subject to additional fees

An application may be subject to additional fees if—

(i) the applicant identified the incorrect registration service fee and decision review period;

(ii) after review of a waiver request, the Administrator denies the waiver request; or

(iii) after review of the application, the Administrator determines that a different registration service fee and decision review period apply to the application.

(F) Effect of failure to pay fees

The Administrator shall reject any application submitted without the required registration service fee.

(G) Non-refundable portion of fees

(i) In general

The Administrator shall retain 25 percent of the applicable registration service fee.

(ii) Limitation

Any waiver, refund, credit or other reduction in the registration service fee shall not exceed 75 percent of the registration service fee.

(H) Collection of unpaid fees

In any case in which the Administrator does not receive payment of a registration service fee (or applicable portion of the registration service fee) by the date that is 30 days after the fee is due, the fee shall be treated as a claim of the United States Government subject to subchapter II of chapter 37 of Title 31.

(3) Schedule of covered applications and other actions and their registration service fees.—Subject to paragraph (6), the schedule of registration applications and other covered actions and their corresponding registration service fees shall be as follows:

TABLE 1.—REGISTRATION DIVISION—NEW ACTIVE INGREDIENTS

EPA No.	New CR No.	Action	Decision Review Time (Months)(1)	Registration Service Fee ($)
R010	1	New Active Ingredient, Food use. (2)(3)	24	753,082
R020	2	New Active Ingredient, Food use; reduced risk. (2)(3)	18	627,568
R040	3	New Active Ingredient, Food use; Experimental Use Permit application; establish temporary tolerance; submitted before application for registration; credit 45% of fee toward new active ingredient application that follows. (3)	18	462,502
R060	4	New Active Ingredient, Non-food use; outdoor. (2)(3)	21	523,205
R070	5	New Active Ingredient, Non-food use; outdoor; reduced risk. (2)(3)	16	436,004
R090	6	New Active Ingredient, Non-food use; outdoor; Experimental Use Permit application; submitted before application for registration; credit 45% of fee toward new active ingredient application that follows. (3)	16	323,690
R110	7	New Active Ingredient, Non-food use; indoor. (2)(3)	20	290,994
R120	8	New Active Ingredient, Non-food use; indoor; reduced risk. (2)(3)	14	242,495
R121	9	New Active Ingredient, Non-food use; indoor; Experimental Use Permit application; submitted before application for registration; credit 45% of fee toward new active ingredient application that follows. (3)	18	182,327
R122	10	Enriched isomer(s) of registered mixed-isomer active ingredient. (2)(3)	18	317,128
R123	11	New Active Ingredient, Seed treatment only; includes agricultural and non-agricultural seeds; residues not expected in raw agricultural commodities. (2)(3)	18	471,861
R125	12	New Active Ingredient, Seed treatment; Experimental Use Permit application; submitted before application for registration; credit 45% of fee toward new active ingredient application that follows. (3)	16	323,690

(1) A decision review time that would otherwise end on a Saturday, Sunday, or federal holiday, will be extended to end on the next business day.

(2) All requests for new uses (food and/or nonfood) contained in any application for a new active ingredient or a first food use are covered by the base fee for that new active ingredient or first food use application and retain the same

decision time review period as the new active ingredient or first food use application. The application must be received by the agency in one package. The base fee for the category covers a maximum of five new products. Each application for an additional new product registration and new inert approval that is submitted in the new active ingredient application package or first food use application package is subject to the registration service fee for a new product or a new inert approval. All such associated applications that are submitted together will be subject to the new active ingredient or first food use decision review time. In the case of a new active ingredient application, until that new active ingredient is approved, any subsequent application for another new product containing the same active ingredient or an amendment to the proposed labeling will be deemed a new active ingredient application, subject to the registration service fee and decision review time for a new active ingredient. In the case of a first food use application, until that first food use is approved, any subsequent application for an additional new food use or uses will be subject to the registration service fee and decision review time for a first food use. Any information that (a) was neither requested nor required by the Agency, and (b) is submitted by the applicant at the applicant's initiative to support the application after completion of the technical deficiency screening, and (c) is not itself a covered registration application, must be assessed 25% of the full registration service fee for the new active ingredient or first food use application.

(3) Where the action involves approval of a new or amended label, on or before the end date of the decision review time, the Agency shall provide to the applicant a draft accepted label, including any changes made by the Agency that differ from the applicant-submitted label and relevant supporting data reviewed by the Agency. The applicant will notify the Agency that the applicant either (a) agrees to all of the terms associated with the draft accepted label as amended by the Agency and requests that it be issued as the accepted final Agency-stamped label; or (b) does not agree to one or more of the terms of the draft accepted label as amended by the Agency and requests additional time to resolve the difference(s); or (c) withdraws the application without prejudice for subsequent resubmission, but forfeits the associated registration service fee. For cases described in (b), the applicant shall have up to 30 calendar days to reach agreement with the Agency on the final terms of the Agency-accepted label. If the applicant agrees to all of the terms of the accepted label as in (a), including upon resolution of differences in (b), the Agency shall provide an accepted final Agency-stamped label to the registrant within 2 business days following the registrant's written or electronic confirmation of agreement to the Agency.

TABLE 2.—REGISTRATION DIVISION—NEW USES

EPA No.	New CR No.	Action	Decision Review Time (Months)(1)	Registration Service Fee ($)
R130	13	First food use; indoor; food/food handling. (2) (3)	21	191,444
R140	14	Additional food use; Indoor; food/food handling. (3) (4)	15	44,672
R150	15	First food use. (2)(3)	21	317,104
R155	16 (new)	First food use, Experimental Use Permit application; a.i. registered for non-food outdoor use. (3)(4)	21	264,253
R160	17	First food use; reduced risk. (2)(3)	16	264,253
R170	18	Additional food use. (3) (4)	15	79,349
R175	19	Additional food uses covered within a crop group resulting from the conversion of existing approved crop group(s) to one or more revised crop groups. (3)(4)	10	66,124
R180	20	Additional food use; reduced risk. (3)(4)	10	66,124
R190	21	Additional food uses; 6 or more submitted in one application. (3)(4)	15	476,090
R200	22	Additional Food Use; 6 or more submitted in one application; Reduced Risk. (3)(4)	10	396,742
R210	23	Additional food use; Experimental Use Permit application; establish temporary tolerance; no credit toward new use registration. (3)(4)	12	48,986
R220	24	Additional food use; Experimental Use Permit application; crop destruct basis; no credit toward new use registration. (3)(4)	6	19,838
R230	25	Additional use; non-food; outdoor. (3) (4)	15	31,713

EPA No.	New CR No.	Action	Decision Review Time (Months)(1)	Registration Service Fee ($)
R240	26	Additional use; non-food; outdoor; reduced risk. (3)(4)	10	26,427
R250	27	Additional use; non-food; outdoor; Experimental Use Permit application; no credit toward new use registration. (3)(4)	6	19,838
R251	28	Experimental Use Permit application which requires no changes to the tolerance(s); non-crop destruct basis. (3)	8	19,838
R260	29	New use; non-food; indoor. (3) (4)	12	15,317
R270	30	New use; non-food; indoor; reduced risk. (3)(4)	9	12,764
R271	31	New use; non-food; indoor; Experimental Use Permit application; no credit toward new use registration. (3)(4)	6	9,725
R273	32	Additional use; seed treatment; limited uptake into Raw Agricultural Commodities; includes crops with established tolerances (e.g., for soil or foliar application); includes food and/or non-food uses. (3)(4)	12	50,445
R274	33	Additional uses; seed treatment only; 6 or more submitted in one application; limited uptake into raw agricultural commodities; includes crops with established tolerances (e.g., for soil or foliar application); includes food and/or non-food uses. (3)(4)	12	302,663

(1) A decision review time that would otherwise end on a Saturday, Sunday, or federal holiday, will be extended to end on the next business day.

(2) All requests for new uses (food and/or nonfood) contained in any application for a new active ingredient or a first food use are covered by the base fee for that new active ingredient or first food use application and retain the same decision time review period as the new active ingredient or first food use application. The application must be received by the agency in one package. The base fee for the category covers a maximum of five new products. Each application for an additional new product registration and new inert approval that is submitted in the new active ingredient application package or first food use application package is subject to the registration service fee for a new product or a new inert approval. All such associated applications that are submitted together will be subject to the new active ingredient or first food use decision review time. In the case of a new active ingredient application, until that new active ingredient is approved, any subsequent application for another new product containing the same active ingredient or an amendment to the proposed labeling will be deemed a new active ingredient application, subject to the registration service fee and decision review time for a new active ingredient. In the case of a first food use application, until that first food use is approved, any subsequent application for an additional new food use or uses will be subject to the registration service fee and decision review time for a first food use. Any information that (a) was neither requested nor required by the Agency, and (b) is submitted by the applicant at the applicant's initiative to support the application after completion of the technical deficiency screening, and (c) is not itself a covered registration application, must be assessed 25% of the full registration service fee for the new active ingredient or first food use application.

(3) Where the action involves approval of a new or amended label, on or before the end date of the decision review time, the Agency shall provide to the applicant a draft accepted label, including any changes made by the Agency that differ from the applicant-submitted label and relevant supporting data reviewed by the Agency. The applicant will notify the Agency that the applicant either (a) agrees to all of the terms associated with the draft accepted label as amended by the Agency and requests that it be issued as the accepted final Agency-stamped label; or (b) does not agree to one or more of the terms of the draft accepted label as amended by the Agency and requests additional time to resolve the difference(s); or (c) withdraws the application without prejudice for subsequent resubmission, but forfeits the associated registration service fee. For cases described in (b), the applicant shall have up to 30 calendar days to reach agreement with the Agency on the final terms of the Agency-accepted label. If the applicant agrees to all of the terms of the accepted label as in (a), including upon resolution of differences in (b), the Agency shall provide an accepted final Agency-stamped label to the registrant within 2 business days following the registrant's written or electronic confirmation of agreement to the Agency.

(4) Amendment applications to add the new use(s) to registered product labels are covered by the base fee for the new use(s). All items in the covered application must be submitted together in one package. Each application for an additional new product registration and new inert approval(s) that is submitted in the new use application package is subject to the

registration service fee for a new product or a new inert approval. However, if a new use application only proposes to register the new use for a new product and there are no amendments in the application, then review of one new product application is covered by the new use fee. All such associated applications that are submitted together will be subject to the new use decision review time. Any application for a new product or an amendment to the proposed labeling (a) submitted subsequent to submission of the new use application and (b) prior to conclusion of its decision review time and (c) containing the same new uses, will be deemed a separate new-use application, subject to a separate registration service fee and new decision review time for a new use. If the new-use application includes non-food (indoor and/or outdoor), and food (outdoor and/or indoor) uses, the appropriate fee is due for each type of new use and the longest decision review time applies to all of the new uses requested in the application. Any information that (a) was neither requested nor required by the Agency, and (b) is submitted by the applicant at the applicant's initiative to support the application after completion of the technical deficiency screen, and (c) is not itself a covered registration application, must be assessed 25% of the full registration service fee for the new use application.

TABLE 3.—REGISTRATION DIVISION—IMPORT AND OTHER TOLERANCES

EPA No.	New CR No.	Action	Decision Review Time (Months)(1)	Registration Service Fee ($)
R280	34	Establish import tolerance; new active ingredient or first food use. (2)	21	319,072
R290	35	Establish Import tolerance; Additional new food use.	15	63,816
R291	36	Establish import tolerances; additional food uses; 6 or more crops submitted in one petition.	15	382,886
R292	37	Amend an established tolerance (e.g., decrease or increase) and/or harmonize established tolerances with Codex MRLs; domestic or import; applicant-initiated.	11	45,341
R293	38	Establish tolerance(s) for inadvertent residues in one crop; applicant-initiated.	12	53,483
R294	39	Establish tolerances for inadvertent residues; 6 or more crops submitted in one application; applicant-initiated.	12	320,894
R295	40	Establish tolerance(s) for residues in one rotational crop in response to a specific rotational crop application; submission of corresponding label amendments which specify the necessary plant-back restrictions; applicant-initiated. (3) (4)	15	66,124
R296	41	Establish tolerances for residues in rotational crops in response to a specific rotational crop petition; 6 or more crops submitted in one application; submission of corresponding label amendments which specify the necessary plant-back restrictions; applicant-initiated. (3) (4)	15	396,742
R297	42	Amend 6 or more established tolerances (e.g., decrease or increase) in one petition; domestic or import; applicant-initiated.	11	272,037
R298	43	Amend an established tolerance (e.g., decrease or increase); domestic or import; submission of corresponding amended labels (requiring science review). (3) (4)	13	58,565
R299	44	Amend 6 or more established tolerances (e.g., decrease or increase); domestic or import; submission of corresponding amended labels (requiring science review). (3) (4)	13	285,261

(1) A decision review time that would otherwise end on a Saturday, Sunday, or federal holiday, will be extended to end on the next business day.

(2) All requests for new uses (food and/or nonfood) contained in any application for a new active ingredient or a first food use are covered by the base fee for that new active ingredient or first food use application and retain the same

decision time review period as the new active ingredient or first food use application. The application must be received by the agency in one package. The base fee for the category covers a maximum of five new products. Each application for an additional new product registration and new inert approval that is submitted in the new active ingredient application package or first food use application package is subject to the registration service fee for a new product or a new inert approval. All such associated applications that are submitted together will be subject to the new active ingredient or first food use decision review time. In the case of a new active ingredient application, until that new active ingredient is approved, any subsequent application for another new product containing the same active ingredient or an amendment to the proposed labeling will be deemed a new active ingredient application, subject to the registration service fee and decision review time for a new active ingredient. In the case of a first food use application, until that first food use is approved, any subsequent application for an additional new food use or uses will be subject to the registration service fee and decision review time for a first food use. Any information that (a) was neither requested nor required by the Agency, and (b) is submitted by the applicant at the applicant's initiative to support the application after completion of the technical deficiency screening, and (c) is not itself a covered registration application, must be assessed 25% of the full registration service fee for the new active ingredient or first food use application.

(3) Where the action involves approval of a new or amended label, on or before the end date of the decision review time, the Agency shall provide to the applicant a draft accepted label, including any changes made by the Agency that differ from the applicant-submitted label and relevant supporting data reviewed by the Agency. The applicant will notify the Agency that the applicant either (a) agrees to all of the terms associated with the draft accepted label as amended by the Agency and requests that it be issued as the accepted final Agency-stamped label; or (b) does not agree to one or more of the terms of the draft accepted label as amended by the Agency and requests additional time to resolve the difference(s); or (c) withdraws the application without prejudice for subsequent resubmission, but forfeits the associated registration service fee. For cases described in (b), the applicant shall have up to 30 calendar days to reach agreement with the Agency on the final terms of the Agency-accepted label. If the applicant agrees to all of the terms of the accepted label as in (a), including upon resolution of differences in (b), the Agency shall provide an accepted final Agency-stamped label to the registrant within 2 business days following the registrant's written or electronic confirmation of agreement to the Agency.

(4) Amendment applications to add the revised use pattern(s) to registered product labels are covered by the base fee for the category. All items in the covered application must be submitted together in one package. Each application for an additional new product registration and new inert approval(s) that is submitted in the amendment application package is subject to the registration service fee for a new product or a new inert approval. However, if an amendment application only proposes to register the amendment for a new product and there are no amendments in the application, then review of one new product application is covered by the base fee. All such associated applications that are submitted together will be subject to the category decision review time.

TABLE 4.—REGISTRATION DIVISION—NEW PRODUCTS

EPA No.	New CR No.	Action	Decision Review Time (Months)(1)	Registration Service Fee ($)
R300	45	New product; or similar combination product (already registered) to an identical or substantially similar in composition and use to a registered product; registered source of active ingredient; no data review on acute toxicity, efficacy or CRP-only product chemistry data; cite-all data citation, or selective data citation where applicant owns all required data, or applicant submits specific authorization letter from data owner. Category also includes 100% re-package of registered end-use or manufacturing-use product that requires no data submission nor data matrix. (2)(3)	4	1,582
R301	46	New product; or similar combination product (already registered) to an identical or substantially similar in composition and use to a registered product; registered source of active ingredient; selective data citation only for data on product chemistry and/or acute toxicity and/or public health pest efficacy (identical data citation and claims to cited product(s)), where applicant does not own all required data and does not have a specific authorization letter from data owner. (2)(3)	4	1,897

EPA No.	New CR No.	Action	Decision Review Time (Months)(1)	Registration Service Fee ($)
R310	47	New end-use or manufacturing-use product with registered source(s) of active ingredient(s); includes products containing two or more registered active ingredients previously combined in other registered products; excludes products requiring or citing an animal safety study; requires review of data package within RD only; includes data and/or waivers of data for only: • product chemistry and/or • acute toxicity and/or • child resistant packaging and/or • pest(s) requiring efficacy (4)—for up to 3 target pests. (2)(3)	7	7,301
R314	48	New end use product containing up to three registered active ingredients never before registered as this combination in a formulated product; new product label is identical or substantially similar to the labels of currently registered products which separately contain the respective component active ingredients; excludes products requiring or citing an animal safety study; requires review of data package within RD only; includes data and/or waivers of data for only: • product chemistry and/or • acute toxicity and/or • child resistant packaging and/or • pest(s) requiring efficacy (4)—for up to 3 target pests. (2)(3)	8	8,626
R319	49	New end use product containing up to three registered active ingredients never before registered as this combination in a formulated product; new product label is identical or substantially similar to the labels of currently registered products which separately contain the respective component active ingredients; excludes products requiring or citing an animal safety study; requires review of data package within RD only; includes data and/or waivers of data for only: • product chemistry and/or • acute toxicity and/or • child resistant packaging and/or • pest(s) requiring efficacy (4)—for 4 to 7 target pests. (2)(3)	10	12,626
R318	50 (new)	New end use product containing four or more registered active ingredients never before registered as this combination in a formulated product; new product label is identical or substantially similar to the labels of currently registered products which separately contain the respective component active ingredients; excludes products requiring or citing an animal safety study; requires review of data package within RD only; includes data and/or waivers of data for only: • product chemistry and/or • acute toxicity and/or • child resistant packaging and/or • pest(s) requiring efficacy (4)—for up to 3 target pests. (2)(3)	9	13,252

EPA No.	New CR No.	Action	Decision Review Time (Months)(1)	Registration Service Fee ($)
R321	51 (new)	New end use product containing four or more registered active ingredients never before registered as this combination in a formulated product; new product label is identical or substantially similar to the labels of currently registered products which separately contain the respective component active ingredients; excludes products requiring or citing an animal safety study; requires review of data package within RD only; includes data and/or waivers of data for only: • product chemistry and/or • acute toxicity and/or • child resistant packaging and/or • pest(s) requiring efficacy (4)—for 4 to 7 target pests. (2)(3)	11	17,252
R315	52	New end-use, on-animal product, registered source of active ingredient(s), with the submission of data and/or waivers for only: • animal safety and • pest(s) requiring efficacy (4) and/or • product chemistry and/or • acute toxicity and/or • child resistant packaging. (2) (3)	9	9,820
R316	53 (new)	New end-use or manufacturing product with registered source(s) of active ingredient(s) including products containing two or more registered active ingredients previously combined in other registered products; excludes products requiring or citing an animal safety study; and requires review of data and/or waivers for only: • product chemistry and/or • acute toxicity and/or • child resistant packaging and/or • pest(s) requiring efficacy (4)—for greater than 3 and up to 7 target pests. (2)(3)	9	11,301
R317	54 (new)	New end-use or manufacturing product with registered source(s) of active ingredient(s) including products containing 2 or more registered active ingredients previously combined in other registered products; excludes products requiring or citing an animal safety study; and requires review of data and/or waivers for only: • product chemistry and/or • acute toxicity and/or • child resistant packaging and/or • pest(s) requiring efficacy (4)—for greater than 7 target pests. (2)(3)	10	15,301
R320	55	New product; new physical form; requires data review in science divisions. (2)(3)	12	13,226
R331	56	New product; repack of identical registered end-use product as a manufacturing-use product, or identical registered	3	2,530

EPA No.	New CR No.	Action	Decision Review Time (Months)(1)	Registration Service Fee ($)
		manufacturing-use product as an end use product; same registered uses only. (2)(3)		
R332	57	New manufacturing-use product; registered active ingredient; unregistered source of active ingredient; submission of completely new generic data package; registered uses only; requires review in RD and science divisions. (2)(3)	24	283,215
R333	58	New product; MUP or End use product with unregistered source of active ingredient; requires science data review; new physical form; etc. Cite-all or selective data citation where applicant owns all required data. (2)(3)	10	19,838
R334	59	New product; MUP or End use product with unregistered source of the active ingredient; requires science data review; new physical form; etc. Selective data citation. (2)(3)	11	23,100

(1) A decision review time that would otherwise end on a Saturday, Sunday, or federal holiday, will be extended to end on the next business day.

(2) An application for a new end-use product using a source of active ingredient that (a) is not yet registered but (b) has an application pending with the Agency for review, will be considered an application for a new product with an unregistered source of active ingredient.

(3) Where the action involves approval of a new or amended label, on or before the end date of the decision review time, the Agency shall provide to the applicant a draft accepted label, including any changes made by the Agency that differ from the applicant-submitted label and relevant supporting data reviewed by the Agency. The applicant will notify the Agency that the applicant either (a) agrees to all of the terms associated with the draft accepted label as amended by the Agency and requests that it be issued as the accepted final Agency-stamped label; or (b) does not agree to one or more of the terms of the draft accepted label as amended by the Agency and requests additional time to resolve the difference(s); or (c) withdraws the application without prejudice for subsequent resubmission, but forfeits the associated registration service fee. For cases described in (b), the applicant shall have up to 30 calendar days to reach agreement with the Agency on the final terms of the Agency-accepted label. If the applicant agrees to all of the terms of the accepted label as in (a), including upon resolution of differences in (b), the Agency shall provide an accepted final Agency-stamped label to the registrant within 2 business days following the registrant's written or electronic confirmation of agreement to the Agency.

(4) For the purposes of classifying proposed registration actions into PRIA categories, "pest(s) requiring efficacy are: public health pests listed in PR Notice 2002–1, livestock pests (e.g. Horn flies, Stable flies), wood-destroying pests (e.g. termites, carpenter ants, wood-boring beetles) and certain invasive species (e.g. Asian Longhorned beetle, Emerald Ashborer). This list may be updated/refined as invasive pest needs arise. To determine the number of pests for the PRIA categories, pests have been placed into groups (general; e.g., cockroaches) and pest specific (specifically a test species). If seeking a label claim against a pest group (general), use the group listing below and each group will count as 1. The general pests groups are: mites, dust mites, chiggers, ticks, hard ticks, soft ticks, cattle ticks, scorpions, spiders, centipedes, lice, fleas, cockroaches, keds, bot flies, screwworms, filth flies, blow flies, house flies, flesh flies, mosquitoes, biting flies, horse flies, stable flies, deer flies, sand flies, biting midges, black flies, true bugs, bed bugs, stinging bees, wasps, yellow jackets, hornets, ants (excluding carpenter ants), fire and harvester ants, wood destroying beetles, carpenter ants, termites, subterranean termites, dry wood termites, arboreal termites, damp wood termites and invasive species. If seeking a claim against a specific pest without a general claim then each specific pest will count as 1.

TABLE 5.—REGISTRATION DIVISION—AMENDMENTS

EPA No.	New CR No.	Action	Decision Review Time (Months)(1)	Registration Service Fee ($)
R340	60	Amendment requiring data review within RD (e.g., changes to precautionary label statements); includes adding/modifying pest(s)	4	4,988

EPA No.	New CR No.	Action	Decision Review Time (Months)(1)	Registration Service Fee ($)
		claims for up to 2 target pests, excludes products requiring or citing an animal safety study. (2)(3)(4)		
R341	61 (new)	Amendment requiring data review within RD (e.g., changes to precautionary label statements), includes adding/modifying pest(s) claims for greater than 2 target pests, excludes products requiring or citing an animal safety study. (2)(3)(4)	6	5,988
R345	62	Amending on-animal products previously registered, with the submission of data and/or waivers for only: • animal safety and • pest(s) requiring efficacy (4) and/or • product chemistry and/or • acute toxicity and/or • child resistant packaging. (2)(3)	7	8,820
R350	63	Amendment requiring data review in science divisions (e.g., changes to REI, or PPE, or PHI, or use rate, or number of applications; or add aerial application; or modify GW/SW advisory statement). (2)(3)	9	13,226
R351	64	Amendment adding a new unregistered source of active ingredient. (2)(3)	8	13,226
R352	65	Amendment adding already approved uses; selective method of support; does not apply if the applicant owns all cited data. (2) (3)	8	13,226
R371	66	Amendment to Experimental Use Permit; (does not include extending a permit's time period). (3)	6	10,090

(1) A decision review time that would otherwise end on a Saturday, Sunday, or federal holiday, will be extended to end on the next business day.

(2) (a) EPA-initiated amendments shall not be charged registration service fees.

(b) Registrant-initiated fast-track amendments are to be completed within the timelines specified in FIFRA Section 3(c)(3)(B) and are not subject to registration service fees.

(c) Registrant-initiated fast-track amendments handled by the Antimicrobials Division are to be completed within the timelines specified in FIFRA Section 3(h) and are not subject to registration service fees.

(d) Registrant initiated amendments submitted by notification under PR Notices, such as PR Notice 98–10, continue under PR Notice timelines and are not subject to registration service fees.

(e) Submissions with data and requiring data review are subject to registration service fees.

(3) Where the action involves approval of a new or amended label, on or before the end date of the decision review time, the Agency shall provide to the applicant a draft accepted label, including any changes made by the Agency that differ from the applicant-submitted label and relevant supporting data reviewed by the Agency. The applicant will notify the Agency that the applicant either (a) agrees to all of the terms associated with the draft accepted label as amended by the Agency and requests that it be issued as the accepted final Agency-stamped label; or (b) does not agree to one or more of the terms of the draft accepted label as amended by the Agency and requests additional time to resolve the difference(s); or (c) withdraws the application without prejudice for subsequent resubmission, but forfeits the associated registration service fee. For cases described in (b), the applicant shall have up to 30 calendar days to reach agreement with the Agency on the final terms of the Agency-accepted label. If the applicant agrees to all of the terms of the accepted label as in (a), including upon resolution of differences in (b), the Agency shall provide an accepted final Agency-stamped label to the registrant within 2 business days following the registrant's written or electronic confirmation of agreement to the Agency.

(4) For the purposes of classifying proposed registration actions into PRIA categories, "pest(s) requiring efficacy" are: public health pests listed in PR Notice 2002–1, livestock pests (e.g. Horn flies, Stable flies), wood-destroying pests (e.g.

termites, carpenter ants, wood-boring beetles) and certain invasive species (e.g. Asian Longhorned beetle, Emerald Ashborer). This list may be updated/refined as invasive pest needs arise. To determine the number of pests for the PRIA categories, pests have been placed into groups (general; e.g., cockroaches) and pest specific (specifically a test species). If seeking a label claim against a pest group (general), use the group listing below and each group will count as 1. The general pests groups are: mites, dust mites, chiggers, ticks, hard ticks, soft ticks, cattle ticks, scorpions, spiders, centipedes, lice, fleas, cockroaches, keds, bot flies, screwworms, filth flies, blow flies, house flies, flesh flies, mosquitoes, biting flies, horse flies, stable flies, deer flies, sand flies, biting midges, black flies, true bugs, bed bugs, stinging bees, wasps, yellow jackets, hornets, ants (excluding carpenter ants), fire and harvester ants, wood destroying beetles, carpenter ants, termites, subterranean termites, dry wood termites, arboreal termites, damp wood termites and invasive species. If seeking a claim against a specific pest without a general claim then each specific pest will count as 1.

TABLE 6.—REGISTRATION DIVISION—OTHER ACTIONS

EPA No.	New CR No.	Action	Decision Review Time (Months)(1)	Registration Service Fee ($)
R124	67	Conditional Ruling on Pre-application Study Waivers; applicant-initiated.	6	2,530
R272	68	Review of Study Protocol applicant-initiated; excludes DART, pre-registration conference, Rapid Response review, DNT protocol review, protocol needing HSRB review.	3	2,530
R275	69	Rebuttal of agency reviewed protocol, applicant initiated.	3	2,530
R370	70	Cancer reassessment; applicant-initiated.	18	198,250

(1) A decision review time that would otherwise end on a Saturday, Sunday, or federal holiday, will be extended to end on the next business day.

TABLE 7.—ANTIMICROBIALS DIVISION—NEW ACTIVE INGREDIENTS

EPA No.	New CR No.	Action	Decision Review Time (Months)(1)	Registration Service Fee ($)
A380	71	New Active Ingredient; Indirect Food use; establish tolerance or tolerance exemption if required. (2)(3)	24	137,841
A390	72	New Active Ingredient; Direct Food use; establish tolerance or tolerance exemption if required. (2)(3)	24	229,733
A410	73	New Active Ingredient Non-food use.(2)(3)	21	229,733
A431	74	New Active Ingredient, Non-food use; low-risk. (2)(3)	12	80,225

(1) A decision review time that would otherwise end on a Saturday, Sunday, or federal holiday, will be extended to end on the next business day.

(2) All requests for new uses (food and/or nonfood) contained in any application for a new active ingredient or a first food use are covered by the base fee for that new active ingredient or first food use application and retain the same decision time review period as the new active ingredient or first food use application. The application must be received by the agency in one package. The base fee for the category covers a maximum of five new products. Each application for an additional new product registration and new inert approval that is submitted in the new active ingredient application package or first food use application package is subject to the registration service fee for a new product or a new inert approval. All such associated applications that are submitted together will be subject to the new active ingredient or first food use decision review time. In the case of a new active ingredient application, until that new active ingredient is approved, any subsequent application for another new product containing the same active ingredient or an amendment to the proposed labeling will be deemed a new active ingredient application, subject to the registration service fee and decision review time for a new active ingredient. In the case of a first food use application, until that first food use is approved, any subsequent application for an additional new food use or uses will be subject to the registration service fee

and decision review time for a first food use. Any information that (a) was neither requested nor required by the Agency, and (b) is submitted by the applicant at the applicant's initiative to support the application after completion of the technical deficiency screening, and (c) is not itself a covered registration application, must be assessed 25% of the full registration service fee for the new active ingredient or first food use application.

(3) Where the action involves approval of a new or amended label, on or before the end date of the decision review time, the Agency shall provide to the applicant a draft accepted label, including any changes made by the Agency that differ from the applicant-submitted label and relevant supporting data reviewed by the Agency. The applicant will notify the Agency that the applicant either (a) agrees to all of the terms associated with the draft accepted label as amended by the Agency and requests that it be issued as the accepted final Agency-stamped label; or (b) does not agree to one or more of the terms of the draft accepted label as amended by the Agency and requests additional time to resolve the difference(s); or (c) withdraws the application without prejudice for subsequent resubmission, but forfeits the associated registration service fee. For cases described in (b), the applicant shall have up to 30 calendar days to reach agreement with the Agency on the final terms of the Agency-accepted label. If the applicant agrees to all of the terms of the accepted label as in (a), including upon resolution of differences in (b), the Agency shall provide an accepted final Agency-stamped label to the registrant within 2 business days following the registrant's written or electronic confirmation of agreement to the Agency.

TABLE 8.—ANTIMICROBIALS DIVISION—NEW USES

EPA No.	New CR No.	Action	Decision Review Time (Months)(1)	Registration Service Fee ($)
A440	75	New Use, Indirect Food Use, establish tolerance or tolerance exemption. (2)(3)(4)	21	31,910
A441	76	Additional Indirect food uses; establish tolerances or tolerance exemptions if required; 6 or more submitted in one application. (3)(4)(5)	21	114,870
A450	77	New use, Direct food use, establish tolerance or tolerance exemption. (2)(3)(4)	21	95,724
A451	78	Additional Direct food uses; establish tolerances or tolerance exemptions if required; 6 or more submitted in one application. (3)(4)(5)	21	182,335
A500	79	New use, non-food. (4)(5)	12	31,910
A501	80	New use, non-food; 6 or more submitted in one application. (4)(5)	15	76,583

(1) A decision review time that would otherwise end on a Saturday, Sunday, or federal holiday, will be extended to end on the next business day.

(2) All requests for new uses (food and/or nonfood) contained in any application for a new active ingredient or a first food use are covered by the base fee for that new active ingredient or first food use application and retain the same decision time review period as the new active ingredient or first food use application. The application must be received by the agency in one package. The base fee for the category covers a maximum of five new products. Each application for an additional new product registration and new inert approval that is submitted in the new active ingredient application package or first food use application package is subject to the registration service fee for a new product or a new inert approval. All such associated applications that are submitted together will be subject to the new active ingredient or first food use decision review time. In the case of a new active ingredient application, until that new active ingredient is approved, any subsequent application for another new product containing the same active ingredient or an amendment to the proposed labeling will be deemed a new active ingredient application, subject to the registration service fee and decision review time for a new active ingredient. In the case of a first food use application, until that first food use is approved, any subsequent application for an additional new food use or uses will be subject to the registration service fee and decision review time for a first food use. Any information that (a) was neither requested nor required by the Agency, and (b) is submitted by the applicant at the applicant's initiative to support the application after completion of the technical deficiency screening, and (c) is not itself a covered registration application, must be assessed 25% of the full registration service fee for the new active ingredient or first food use application.

(3) If EPA data rules are amended to newly require clearance under section 408 of the FFDCA for an ingredient of an antimicrobial product where such ingredient was not previously subject to such a clearance, then review of the data for

such clearance of such product is not subject to a registration service fee for the tolerance action for two years from the effective date of the rule.

(4) Where the action involves approval of a new or amended label, on or before the end date of the decision review time, the Agency shall provide to the applicant a draft accepted label, including any changes made by the Agency that differ from the applicant-submitted label and relevant supporting data reviewed by the Agency. The applicant will notify the Agency that the applicant either (a) agrees to all of the terms associated with the draft accepted label as amended by the Agency and requests that it be issued as the accepted final Agency-stamped label; or (b) does not agree to one or more of the terms of the draft accepted label as amended by the Agency and requests additional time to resolve the difference(s); or (c) withdraws the application without prejudice for subsequent resubmission, but forfeits the associated registration service fee. For cases described in (b), the applicant shall have up to 30 calendar days to reach agreement with the Agency on the final terms of the Agency-accepted label. If the applicant agrees to all of the terms of the accepted label as in (a), including upon resolution of differences in (b), the Agency shall provide an accepted final Agency-stamped label to the registrant within 2 business days following the registrant's written or electronic confirmation of agreement to the Agency.

(5) Amendment applications to add the new use(s) to registered product labels are covered by the base fee for the new use(s). All items in the covered application must be submitted together in one package. Each application for an additional new product registration and new inert approval(s) that is submitted in the new use application package is subject to the registration service fee for a new product or a new inert approval. However, if a new use application only proposes to register the new use for a new product and there are no amendments in the application, then review of one new product application is covered by the new use fee. All such associated applications that are submitted together will be subject to the new use decision review time. Any application for a new product or an amendment to the proposed labeling (a) submitted subsequent to submission of the new use application and (b) prior to conclusion of its decision review time and (c) containing the same new uses, will be deemed a separate new-use application, subject to a separate registration service fee and new decision review time for a new use. If the new-use application includes non-food (indoor and/or outdoor), and food (outdoor and/or indoor) uses, the appropriate fee is due for each type of new use and the longest decision review time applies to all of the new uses requested in the application. Any information that (a) was neither requested nor required by the Agency, and (b) is submitted by the applicant at the applicant's initiative to support the application after completion of the technical deficiency screen, and (c) is not itself a covered registration application, must be assessed 25% of the full registration service fee for the new use application.

TABLE 9.—ANTIMICROBIALS DIVISION—NEW PRODUCTS AND AMENDMENTS

EPA No.	New CR No.	Action	Decision Review Time (Months)(1)	Registration Service Fee ($)
A530	81	New product, identical or substantially similar in composition and use to a registered product; no data review or only product chemistry data; cite all data citation or selective data citation where applicant owns all required data; or applicant submits specific authorization letter from data owner. Category also includes 100% re-package of registered end-use or manufacturing use product that requires no data submission nor data matrix. (2)(3)	4	1,278
A531	82	New product; identical or substantially similar in composition and use to a registered product; registered source of active ingredient: selective data citation only for data on product chemistry and/or acute toxicity and/or public health pest efficacy, where applicant does not own all required data and does not have a specific authorization letter from data owner. (2)(3)	4	1,824
A532	83	New product; identical or substantially similar in composition and use to a registered product; registered active ingredient; unregistered source of active ingredient; cite-all data citation except for product chemistry; product chemistry data submitted. (2)(3)	5	5,107
A540	84	New end use product; FIFRA § 2(mm) uses only; up to 25 public health organisms. (2)(3)(5)(6)	5	5,107

EPA No.	New CR No.	Action	Decision Review Time (Months)(1)	Registration Service Fee ($)
A541	85 (new)	New end use product; FIFRA § 2(mm) uses only; 26–50 public health organisms. (2)(3)(5)(6)	7	8,500
A542	86 (new)	New end use product; FIFRA § 2(mm) uses only; ≥ 51 public health organisms. (2)(3)(5)	10	15,000
A550	87	New end-use product; uses other than FIFRA § 2(mm); non-FQPA product. (2)(3)(5)	9	13,226
A560	88	New manufacturing use product; registered active ingredient; selective data citation. (2)(3)	6	12,596
A565	89 (new)	New manufacturing-use product; registered active ingredient; unregistered source of active ingredient; submission of new generic data package; registered uses only; requires science review. (2)(3)	12	18,234
A570	90	Label amendment requiring data review; up to 25 public health organisms. (3)(4)(5)(6)	4	3,831
A573	91 (new)	Label amendment requiring data review; 26–50 public health organisms. (2)(3)(5)(7)	6	6,350
A574	92 (new)	Label amendment requiring data review; ≥ 51 public health organisms. (2)(3)(5)(7)	9	11,000
A572	93	New Product or amendment requiring data review for risk assessment by Science Branch (e.g., changes to REI, or PPE, or use rate). (2)(3)(4)	9	13,226

(1) A decision review time that would otherwise end on a Saturday, Sunday, or federal holiday, will be extended to end on the next business day.

(2) An application for a new end-use product using a source of active ingredient that (a) is not yet registered but (b) has an application pending with the Agency for review, will be considered an application for a new product with an unregistered source of active ingredient.

(3) Where the action involves approval of a new or amended label, on or before the end date of the decision review time, the Agency shall provide to the applicant a draft accepted label, including any changes made by the Agency that differ from the applicant-submitted label and relevant supporting data reviewed by the Agency. The applicant will notify the Agency that the applicant either (a) agrees to all of the terms associated with the draft accepted label as amended by the Agency and requests that it be issued as the accepted final Agency-stamped label; or (b) does not agree to one or more of the terms of the draft accepted label as amended by the Agency and requests additional time to resolve the difference(s); or (c) withdraws the application without prejudice for subsequent resubmission, but forfeits the associated registration service fee. For cases described in (b), the applicant shall have up to 30 calendar days to reach agreement with the Agency on the final terms of the Agency-accepted label. If the applicant agrees to all of the terms of the accepted label as in (a), including upon resolution of differences in (b), the Agency shall provide an accepted final Agency-stamped label to the registrant within 2 business days following the registrant's written or electronic confirmation of agreement to the Agency.

(4) (a) EPA-initiated amendments shall not be charged registration service fees.

(b) Registrant-initiated fast-track amendments are to be completed within the timelines specified in FIFRA Section 3(c)(3)(B) and are not subject to registration service fees.

(c) Registrant-initiated fast-track amendments handled by the Antimicrobials Division are to be completed within the timelines specified in FIFRA Section 3(h) and are not subject to registration service fees.

(d) Registrant initiated amendments submitted by notification under PR Notices, such as PR Notice 98–10, continue under PR Notice timelines and are not subject to registration service fees.

(e) Submissions with data and requiring data review are subject to registration service fees.

(5) The applicant must identify the substantially similar product if opting to use cite-all or the selective method to support acute toxicity data requirements.

(6) Once a submission for a new product with public health organisms has been submitted and classified in either A540 or A541, additional organisms submitted for the same product before expiration of the first submission's original decision review time period will result in reclassification of both the original and subsequent submission into the appropriate new category based on the sum of the number of organisms in both submissions. A reclassification would result in a new PRIA start date and require additional fees to meet the fee of the new category.

(7) Once a submission for a label amendment with public health organisms has been submitted and classified in either A570 or A573, additional organisms submitted for the same product before expiration of the first submission's original decision review time period will result in reclassification of both the original and subsequent submission into the appropriate new category based on the sum of the number of organisms in both submissions. A reclassification would result in a new PRIA start date and require additional fees to meet the fee of the new category.

TABLE 10.—ANTIMICROBIALS DIVISION—EXPERIMENTAL USE PERMITS AND OTHER ACTIONS

EPA No.	New CR No.	Action	Decision Review Time (Months)(1)	Registration Service Fee ($)
A520	94	Experimental Use Permit application, non-food use. (2)	9	6,383
A521	95	Review of public health efficacy study protocol within AD, per AD Internal Guidance for the Efficacy Protocol Review Process; Code will also include review of public health efficacy study protocol and data review for devices making pesticidal claims; applicant-initiated; Tier 1.	4	4,726
A522	96	Review of public health efficacy study protocol outside AD by members of AD Efficacy Protocol Review Expert Panel; Code will also include review of public health efficacy study protocol and data review for devices making pesticidal claims; applicant-initiated; Tier 2.	12	12,156
A537	97 (new)	New Active Ingredient/New Use, Experimental Use Permit application; Direct food use; Establish tolerance or tolerance exemption if required. Credit 45% of fee toward new active ingredient/new use application that follows.	18	153,156
A538	98 (new)	New Active Ingredient/New Use, Experimental Use Permit application; Indirect food use; Establish tolerance or tolerance exemption if required Credit 45% of fee toward new active ingredient/new use application that follows.	18	95,724
A539	99 (new)	New Active Ingredient/New Use, Experimental Use Permit application; Nonfood use. Credit 45% of fee toward new active ingredient/new use application that follows.	15	92,163
A529	100	Amendment to Experimental Use Permit; requires data review or risk assessment. (2)	9	11,429
A523	101	Review of protocol other than a public health efficacy study (i.e., Toxicology or Exposure Protocols).	9	12,156
A571	102	Science reassessment: Cancer risk, refined ecological risk, and/or endangered species; applicant-initiated.	18	95,724
A533	103 (new)	Exemption from the requirement of an Experimental Use Permit. (2)	4	2,482
A534	104 (new)	Rebuttal of agency reviewed protocol, applicant initiated.	4	4,726

EPA No.	New CR No.	Action	Decision Review Time (Months)(1)	Registration Service Fee ($)
A535	105 (new)	Conditional Ruling on Pre-application Study Waiver or Data Bridging Argument; applicant-initiated.	6	2,409
A536	106 (new)	Conditional Ruling on Pre-application Direct Food, Indirect Food, Nonfood use determination; applicant-initiated.	4	2,482

(1) A decision review time that would otherwise end on a Saturday, Sunday, or federal holiday, will be extended to end on the next business day.

(2) Where the action involves approval of a new or amended label, on or before the end date of the decision review time, the Agency shall provide to the applicant a draft accepted label, including any changes made by the Agency that differ from the applicant-submitted label and relevant supporting data reviewed by the Agency. The applicant will notify the Agency that the applicant either (a) agrees to all of the terms associated with the draft accepted label as amended by the Agency and requests that it be issued as the accepted final Agency-stamped label; or (b) does not agree to one or more of the terms of the draft accepted label as amended by the Agency and requests additional time to resolve the difference(s); or (c) withdraws the application without prejudice for subsequent resubmission, but forfeits the associated registration service fee. For cases described in (b), the applicant shall have up to 30 calendar days to reach agreement with the Agency on the final terms of the Agency-accepted label. If the applicant agrees to all of the terms of the accepted label as in (a), including upon resolution of differences in (b), the Agency shall provide an accepted final Agency-stamped label to the registrant within 2 business days following the registrant's written or electronic confirmation of agreement to the Agency.

TABLE 11.—BIOPESTICIDES DIVISION—NEW ACTIVE INGREDIENTS

EPA No.	New CR No.	Action	Decision Review Time (Months)(1)	Registration Service Fee ($)
B580	107	New active ingredient; food use; petition to establish a tolerance. (2)(3)	20	51,053
B590	108	New active ingredient; food use; petition to establish a tolerance exemption. (2)(3)	18	31,910
B600	109	New active ingredient; non-food use. (2)(3)	13	19,146
B610	110	New active ingredient; Experimental Use Permit application; petition to establish a temporary tolerance or temporary tolerance exemption. (3)	10	12,764
B611	111	New active ingredient; Experimental Use Permit application; petition to establish permanent tolerance exemption. (3)	12	12,764
B612	112	New active ingredient; no change to a permanent tolerance exemption. (2)(3)	10	17,550
B613	113	New active ingredient; petition to convert a temporary tolerance or a temporary tolerance exemption to a permanent tolerance or tolerance exemption. (2)(3)	11	17,550
B620	114	New active ingredient; Experimental Use Permit application; non-food use including crop destruct. (3)	7	6,383

(1) A decision review time that would otherwise end on a Saturday, Sunday, or federal holiday, will be extended to end on the next business day.

(2) All requests for new uses (food and/or nonfood) contained in any application for a new active ingredient or a first food use are covered by the base fee for that new active ingredient or first food use application and retain the same decision time review period as the new active ingredient or first food use application. The application must be received by the agency in one package. The base fee for the category covers a maximum of five new products. Each application for an additional new product registration and new inert approval that is submitted in the new active ingredient application

package or first food use application package is subject to the registration service fee for a new product or a new inert approval. All such associated applications that are submitted together will be subject to the new active ingredient or first food use decision review time. In the case of a new active ingredient application, until that new active ingredient is approved, any subsequent application for another new product containing the same active ingredient or an amendment to the proposed labeling will be deemed a new active ingredient application, subject to the registration service fee and decision review time for a new active ingredient. In the case of a first food use application, until that first food use is approved, any subsequent application for an additional new food use or uses will be subject to the registration service fee and decision review time for a first food use. Any information that (a) was neither requested nor required by the Agency, and (b) is submitted by the applicant at the applicant's initiative to support the application after completion of the technical deficiency screening, and (c) is not itself a covered registration application, must be assessed 25% of the full registration service fee for the new active ingredient or first food use application.

(3) Where the action involves approval of a new or amended label, on or before the end date of the decision review time, the Agency shall provide to the applicant a draft accepted label, including any changes made by the Agency that differ from the applicant-submitted label and relevant supporting data reviewed by the Agency. The applicant will notify the Agency that the applicant either (a) agrees to all of the terms associated with the draft accepted label as amended by the Agency and requests that it be issued as the accepted final Agency-stamped label; or (b) does not agree to one or more of the terms of the draft accepted label as amended by the Agency and requests additional time to resolve the difference(s); or (c) withdraws the application without prejudice for subsequent resubmission, but forfeits the associated registration service fee. For cases described in (b), the applicant shall have up to 30 calendar days to reach agreement with the Agency on the final terms of the Agency-accepted label. If the applicant agrees to all of the terms of the accepted label as in (a), including upon resolution of differences in (b), the Agency shall provide an accepted final Agency-stamped label to the registrant within 2 business days following the registrant's written or electronic confirmation of agreement to the Agency.

TABLE 12.—BIOPESTICIDES DIVISION—NEW USES

EPA No.	New CR No.	Action	Decision Review Time (Months)(1)	Registration Service Fee ($)
B630	115	First food use; petition to establish a tolerance exemption. (2)(4)	13	12,764
B631	116	New food use; petition to amend an established tolerance. (3)(4)	12	12,764
B640	117	First food use; petition to establish a tolerance. (2)(4)	19	19,146
B643	118	New Food use; petition to amend an established tolerance exemption. (3)(4)	10	12,764
B642	119	First food use; indoor; food/food handling. (2)(4)	12	31,910
B644	120	New use, no change to an established tolerance or tolerance exemption. (3)(4)	8	12,764
B650	121	New use; non-food. (3)(4)	7	6,383
B645	122 (new)	New food use; Experimental Use Permit application; petition to amend or add a tolerance exemption. (4)	12	12,764
B646	123 (new)	New use; non-food use including crop destruct; Experimental Use Permit application. (4)	7	6,383

(1) A decision review time that would otherwise end on a Saturday, Sunday, or federal holiday, will be extended to end on the next business day.

(2) All requests for new uses (food and/or nonfood) contained in any application for a new active ingredient or a first food use are covered by the base fee for that new active ingredient or first food use application and retain the same decision time review period as the new active ingredient or first food use application. The application must be received by the agency in one package. The base fee for the category covers a maximum of five new products. Each application for an additional new product registration and new inert approval that is submitted in the new active ingredient application package or first food use application package is subject to the registration service fee for a new product or a new inert approval. All such associated applications that are submitted together will be subject to the new active ingredient or first food use decision review time. In the case of a new active ingredient application, until that new active ingredient is approved, any subsequent application for another new product containing the same active ingredient or an amendment

to the proposed labeling will be deemed a new active ingredient application, subject to the registration service fee and decision review time for a new active ingredient. In the case of a first food use application, until that first food use is approved, any subsequent application for an additional new food use or uses will be subject to the registration service fee and decision review time for a first food use. Any information that (a) was neither requested nor required by the Agency, and (b) is submitted by the applicant at the applicant's initiative to support the application after completion of the technical deficiency screening, and (c) is not itself a covered registration application, must be assessed 25% of the full registration service fee for the new active ingredient or first food use application.

(3) Amendment applications to add the new use(s) to registered product labels are covered by the base fee for the new use(s). All items in the covered application must be submitted together in one package. Each application for an additional new product registration and new inert approval(s) that is submitted in the new use application package is subject to the registration service fee for a new product or a new inert approval. However, if a new use application only proposes to register the new use for a new product and there are no amendments in the application, then review of one new product application is covered by the new use fee. All such associated applications that are submitted together will be subject to the new use decision review time. Any application for a new product or an amendment to the proposed labeling (a) submitted subsequent to submission of the new use application and (b) prior to conclusion of its decision review time and (c) containing the same new uses, will be deemed a separate new-use application, subject to a separate registration service fee and new decision review time for a new use. If the new-use application includes non-food (indoor and/or outdoor), and food (outdoor and/or indoor) uses, the appropriate fee is due for each type of new use and the longest decision review time applies to all of the new uses requested in the application. Any information that (a) was neither requested nor required by the Agency, and (b) is submitted by the applicant at the applicant's initiative to support the application after completion of the technical deficiency screen, and (c) is not itself a covered registration application, must be assessed 25% of the full registration service fee for the new use application.

(4) Where the action involves approval of a new or amended label, on or before the end date of the decision review time, the Agency shall provide to the applicant a draft accepted label, including any changes made by the Agency that differ from the applicant-submitted label and relevant supporting data reviewed by the Agency. The applicant will notify the Agency that the applicant either (a) agrees to all of the terms associated with the draft accepted label as amended by the Agency and requests that it be issued as the accepted final Agency-stamped label; or (b) does not agree to one or more of the terms of the draft accepted label as amended by the Agency and requests additional time to resolve the difference(s); or (c) withdraws the application without prejudice for subsequent resubmission, but forfeits the associated registration service fee. For cases described in (b), the applicant shall have up to 30 calendar days to reach agreement with the Agency on the final terms of the Agency-accepted label. If the applicant agrees to all of the terms of the accepted label as in (a), including upon resolution of differences in (b), the Agency shall provide an accepted final Agency-stamped label to the registrant within 2 business days following the registrant's written or electronic confirmation of agreement to the Agency.

TABLE 13.—BIOPESTICIDES DIVISION—NEW PRODUCTS

EPA No.	New CR No.	Action	Decision Review Time (Months)(1)	Registration Service Fee ($)
B652	124	New product; registered source of active ingredient; requires petition to amend established tolerance or tolerance exemption; requires 1) submission of product specific data; or 2) citation of previously reviewed and accepted data; or 3) submission or citation of data generated at government expense; or 4) submission or citation of scientifically-sound rationale based on publicly available literature or other relevant information that addresses the data requirement; or 5) submission of a request for a data requirement to be waived supported by a scientifically-sound rationale explaining why the data requirement does not apply. (2)(3)	13	12,764
B660	125	New product; registered source of active ingredient(s); identical or substantially similar in composition and use to a registered product. No data review, or only product chemistry data; cite-all data citation, or selective data citation where applicant owns all required data or authorization from data owner is demonstrated. Category includes 100% re-package of registered end-use or manufacturing-use product that requires no data submission or	4	1,278

EPA No.	New CR No.	Action	Decision Review Time (Months)(1)	Registration Service Fee ($)
		data matrix. For microbial pesticides, the active ingredient(s) must not be re-isolated. (2)(3)		
B670	126	New product; registered source of active ingredient(s); requires: 1) submission of product specific data; or 2) citation of previously reviewed and accepted data; or 3) submission or citation of data generated at government expense; or 4) submission or citation of a scientifically-sound rationale based on publicly available literature or other relevant information that addresses the data requirement; or 5) submission of a request for a data requirement to be waived supported by a scientifically-sound rationale explaining why the data requirement does not apply. (2)(3)	7	5,107
B671	127	New product; unregistered source of active ingredient(s); requires a petition to amend an established tolerance or tolerance exemption; requires: 1) submission of product specific data; or 2) citation of previously reviewed and accepted data; or 3) submission or citation of data generated at government expense; or 4) submission or citation of a scientifically-sound rationale based on publicly available literature or other relevant information that addresses the data requirement; or 5) submission of a request for a data requirement to be waived supported by a scientifically-sound rationale explaining why the data requirement does not apply. (2)(3)	17	12,764
B672	128	New product; unregistered source of active ingredient(s); non-food use or food use requires: 1) submission of product specific data; or 2) citation of previously reviewed and accepted data; or 3) submission or citation of data generated at government expense; or 4) submission or citation of a scientifically-sound rationale based on publicly available literature or other relevant information that addresses the data requirement; or 5) submission of a request for a data requirement to be waived supported by a scientifically-sound rationale explaining why the data requirement does not apply. (2)(3)	13	9,118
B673	129	New product MUP/EP; unregistered source of active ingredient(s); citation of Technical Grade Active Ingredient (TGAI) data previously reviewed and accepted by the Agency. Requires an Agency determination that the cited data supports the new product. (2)(3)	10	5,107
B674	130	New product MUP; Repack of identical registered end-use product as a manufacturing-use product; same registered uses only. (2)(3)	4	1,278
B675	131	New Product MUP; registered source of active ingredient; submission of completely new generic data package; registered uses only. (2)(3)	10	9,118
B676	132	New product; more than one active ingredient where one active ingredient is an unregistered source; product chemistry data must be submitted; requires: 1) submission of product specific data, and 2) citation of previously reviewed and accepted data; or 3) submission or citation of data generated at government expense; or 4) submission or citation of a scientifically-sound rationale based on publicly available literature or other relevant information that addresses the data requirement; or 5) submission of a request for a data requirement to be waived supported by a scientifically-	13	9,118

EPA No.	New CR No.	Action	Decision Review Time (Months)(1)	Registration Service Fee ($)
		sound rationale explaining why the data requirement does not apply. (2)(3)		
B677	133	New end-use non-food animal product with submission of two or more target animal safety studies; includes data and/or waivers of data for only: • product chemistry and/or • acute toxicity and/or • public health pest efficacy and/or • animal safety studies and/or • child resistant packaging. (2)(3)	10	8,820

(1) A decision review time that would otherwise end on a Saturday, Sunday, or federal holiday, will be extended to end on the next business day.

(2) An application for a new end-use product using a source of active ingredient that (a) is not yet registered but (b) has an application pending with the Agency for review, will be considered an application for a new product with an unregistered source of active ingredient.

(3) Where the action involves approval of a new or amended label, on or before the end date of the decision review time, the Agency shall provide to the applicant a draft accepted label, including any changes made by the Agency that differ from the applicant-submitted label and relevant supporting data reviewed by the Agency. The applicant will notify the Agency that the applicant either (a) agrees to all of the terms associated with the draft accepted label as amended by the Agency and requests that it be issued as the accepted final Agency-stamped label; or (b) does not agree to one or more of the terms of the draft accepted label as amended by the Agency and requests additional time to resolve the difference(s); or (c) withdraws the application without prejudice for subsequent resubmission, but forfeits the associated registration service fee. For cases described in (b), the applicant shall have up to 30 calendar days to reach agreement with the Agency on the final terms of the Agency-accepted label. If the applicant agrees to all of the terms of the accepted label as in (a), including upon resolution of differences in (b), the Agency shall provide an accepted final Agency-stamped label to the registrant within 2 business days following the registrant's written or electronic confirmation of agreement to the Agency.

TABLE 14.—BIOPESTICIDES DIVISION—AMENDMENTS

EPA No.	New CR No.	Action	Decision Review Time (Months)(1)	Registration Service Fee ($)
B621	134	Amendment; Experimental Use Permit; no change to an established temporary tolerance or tolerance exemption. (3)	7	5,107
B622	135	Amendment; Experimental Use Permit; petition to amend an established or temporary tolerance or tolerance exemption. (3)	11	12,764
B641	136	Amendment of an established tolerance or tolerance exemption.	13	12,764
B680	137	Amendment; registered sources of active ingredient(s); no new use(s); no changes to an established tolerance or tolerance exemption. Requires data submission. (2)(3)	5	5,107
B681	138	Amendment; unregistered source of active ingredient(s). Requires data submission. (2)(3)	7	6,079
B683	139	Label amendment; requires review/update of previous risk assessment(s) without data submission (e.g., labeling changes to REI, PPE, PHI). (2)(3)	6	5,107
B684	140	Amending non-food animal product that includes submission of target animal safety data; previously registered. (2)(3)	8	8,820

EPA No.	New CR No.	Action	Decision Review Time (Months)(1)	Registration Service Fee ($)
B685	141 (new)	Amendment; add a new biochemical unregistered source of active ingredient or a new microbial production site. Requires submission of analysis of samples data and source/production site-specific manufacturing process description. (3)	5	5,107

(1) A decision review time that would otherwise end on a Saturday, Sunday, or federal holiday, will be extended to end on the next business day.

(2) (a) EPA-initiated amendments shall not be charged registration service fees.

(b) Registrant-initiated fast-track amendments are to be completed within the timelines specified in FIFRA Section 3(c)(3)(B) and are not subject to registration service fees.

(c) Registrant-initiated fast-track amendments handled by the Antimicrobials Division are to be completed within the timelines specified in FIFRA Section 3(h) and are not subject to registration service fees.

(d) Registrant initiated amendments submitted by notification under PR Notices, such as PR Notice 98–10, continue under PR Notice timelines and are not subject to registration service fees.

(e) Submissions with data and requiring data review are subject to registration service fees.

(3) Where the action involves approval of a new or amended label, on or before the end date of the decision review time, the Agency shall provide to the applicant a draft accepted label, including any changes made by the Agency that differ from the applicant-submitted label and relevant supporting data reviewed by the Agency. The applicant will notify the Agency that the applicant either (a) agrees to all of the terms associated with the draft accepted label as amended by the Agency and requests that it be issued as the accepted final Agency-stamped label; or (b) does not agree to one or more of the terms of the draft accepted label as amended by the Agency and requests additional time to resolve the difference(s); or (c) withdraws the application without prejudice for subsequent resubmission, but forfeits the associated registration service fee. For cases described in (b), the applicant shall have up to 30 calendar days to reach agreement with the Agency on the final terms of the Agency-accepted label. If the applicant agrees to all of the terms of the accepted label as in (a), including upon resolution of differences in (b), the Agency shall provide an accepted final Agency-stamped label to the registrant within 2 business days following the registrant's written or electronic confirmation of agreement to the Agency.

TABLE 15.—BIOPESTICIDES DIVISION—SCLP

EPA No.	New CR No.	Action	Decision Review Time (Months)(1)	Registration Service Fee ($)
B690	142	New active ingredient; food or non-food use. (2)(6)	7	2,554
B700	143	Experimental Use Permit application; new active ingredient or new use. (6)	7	1,278
B701	144	Extend or amend Experimental Use Permit. (6)	4	1,278
B710	145	New product; registered source of active ingredient(s); identical or substantially similar in composition and use to a registered product; no change in an established tolerance or tolerance exemption. No data review, or only product chemistry data; cite-all data citation, or selective data citation where applicant owns all required data or authorization from data owner is demonstrated. Category includes 100% re-package of registered end-use or manufacturing-use product that requires no data submission or data matrix. (3)(6)	4	1,278
B720	146	New product; registered source of active ingredient(s); requires: 1) submission of product specific data; or 2) citation of previously reviewed and accepted data; or 3) submission or citation of data generated at government expense; or 4) submission or citation of	5	1,278

EPA No.	New CR No.	Action	Decision Review Time (Months)(1)	Registration Service Fee ($)
		a scientifically-sound rationale based on publicly available literature or other relevant information that addresses the data requirement; or 5) submission of a request for a data requirement to be waived supported by a scientifically-sound rationale explaining why the data requirement does not apply. (3)(6)		
B721	147	New product; unregistered source of active ingredient. (3)(6)	7	2,676
B722	148	New use and/or amendment; petition to establish a tolerance or tolerance exemption. (4)(5)(6)	7	2,477
B730	149	Label amendment requiring data submission. (4)(6)	5	1,278

(1) A decision review time that would otherwise end on a Saturday, Sunday, or federal holiday, will be extended to end on the next business day.

(2) All requests for new uses (food and/or nonfood) contained in any application for a new active ingredient or a first food use are covered by the base fee for that new active ingredient or first food use application and retain the same decision time review period as the new active ingredient or first food use application. The application must be received by the agency in one package. The base fee for the category covers a maximum of five new products. Each application for an additional new product registration and new inert approval that is submitted in the new active ingredient application package or first food use application package is subject to the registration service fee for a new product or a new inert approval. All such associated applications that are submitted together will be subject to the new active ingredient or first food use decision review time. In the case of a new active ingredient application, until that new active ingredient is approved, any subsequent application for another new product containing the same active ingredient or an amendment to the proposed labeling will be deemed a new active ingredient application, subject to the registration service fee and decision review time for a new active ingredient. In the case of a first food use application, until that first food use is approved, any subsequent application for an additional new food use or uses will be subject to the registration service fee and decision review time for a first food use. Any information that (a) was neither requested nor required by the Agency, and (b) is submitted by the applicant at the applicant's initiative to support the application after completion of the technical deficiency screening, and (c) is not itself a covered registration application, must be assessed 25% of the full registration service fee for the new active ingredient or first food use application.

(3) An application for a new end-use product using a source of active ingredient that (a) is not yet registered but (b) has an application pending with the Agency for review, will be considered an application for a new product with an unregistered source of active ingredient.

(4) (a) EPA-initiated amendments shall not be charged registration service fees. (b) Registrant-initiated fast-track amendments are to be completed within the timelines specified in FIFRA Section 3(c)(3)(B) and are not subject to registration service fees. (c) Registrant-initiated fast-track amendments handled by the Antimicrobials Division are to be completed within the timelines specified in FIFRA Section 3(h) and are not subject to registration service fees. (d) Registrant initiated amendments submitted by notification under PR Notices, such as PR Notice 98–10, continue under PR Notice timelines and are not subject to registration service fees. (e) Submissions with data and requiring data review are subject to registration service fees.

(5) Amendment applications to add the new use(s) to registered product labels are covered by the base fee for the new use(s). All items in the covered application must be submitted together in one package. Each application for an additional new product registration and new inert approval(s) that is submitted in the new use application package is subject to the registration service fee for a new product or a new inert approval. However, if a new use application only proposes to register the new use for a new product and there are no amendments in the application, then review of one new product application is covered by the new use fee. All such associated applications that are submitted together will be subject to the new use decision review time. Any application for a new product or an amendment to the proposed labeling (a) submitted subsequent to submission of the new use application and (b) prior to conclusion of its decision review time and (c) containing the same new uses, will be deemed a separate new-use application, subject to a separate registration service fee and new decision review time for a new use. If the new-use application includes non-food (indoor and/or outdoor), and food (outdoor and/or indoor) uses, the appropriate fee is due for each type of new use and the longest decision review time applies to all of the new uses requested in the application. Any information that (a) was neither requested nor required by the Agency, and (b) is submitted by the applicant at the applicant's initiative to support the application after

completion of the technical deficiency screen, and (c) is not itself a covered registration application, must be assessed 25% of the full registration service fee for the new use application.

(6) Where the action involves approval of a new or amended label, on or before the end date of the decision review time, the Agency shall provide to the applicant a draft accepted label, including any changes made by the Agency that differ from the applicant-submitted label and relevant supporting data reviewed by the Agency. The applicant will notify the Agency that the applicant either (a) agrees to all of the terms associated with the draft accepted label as amended by the Agency and requests that it be issued as the accepted final Agency-stamped label; or (b) does not agree to one or more of the terms of the draft accepted label as amended by the Agency and requests additional time to resolve the difference(s); or (c) withdraws the application without prejudice for subsequent resubmission, but forfeits the associated registration service fee. For cases described in (b), the applicant shall have up to 30 calendar days to reach agreement with the Agency on the final terms of the Agency-accepted label. If the applicant agrees to all of the terms of the accepted label as in (a), including upon resolution of differences in (b), the Agency shall provide an accepted final Agency-stamped label to the registrant within 2 business days following the registrant's written or electronic confirmation of agreement to the Agency.

TABLE 16.—BIOPESTICIDES DIVISION—OTHER ACTIONS

EPA No.	New CR No.	Action	Decision Review Time (Months)(1)	Registration Service Fee ($)
B614	150	Pre-application; Conditional Ruling on rationales for addressing a data requirement in lieu of data; applicant-initiated; applies to one rationale at a time.	3	2,530
B615	151	Rebuttal of agency reviewed protocol, applicant initiated.	3	2,530
B682	152	Protocol review; applicant initiated; excludes time for HSRB review.	3	2,432

(1) A decision review time that would otherwise end on a Saturday, Sunday, or federal holiday, will be extended to end on the next business day.

TABLE 17.—BIOPESTICIDES DIVISION—PIP

EPA No.	New CR No.	Action	Decision Review Time (Months)(1)	Registration Service Fee ($)
B740	153	Experimental Use Permit application; no petition for tolerance/tolerance exemption. Includes: 1. non-food/feed use(s) for a new (2) or registered (3) PIP (12); 2. food/feed use(s) for a new or registered PIP with crop destruct (12); 3. food/feed use(s) for a new or registered PIP in which an established tolerance/tolerance exemption exists for the intended use(s). (4)(12)	6	95,724
B741	154 (new)	Experimental Use Permit application; no petition for tolerance/tolerance exemption. Includes: 1. non-food/feed use(s) for a new (2) or registered (3) PIP; 2. food/feed use(s) for a new or registered PIP with crop destruct; 3. food/feed use(s) for a new or registered PIP in which an established tolerance/tolerance exemption exists for the intended use(s); SAP Review. (12)	12	159,538
B750	155	Experimental Use Permit application; with a petition to establish a temporary or permanent tolerance/tolerance exemption for the	9	127,630

EPA No.	New CR No.	Action	Decision Review Time (Months)(1)	Registration Service Fee ($)
		active ingredient. Includes new food/feed use for a registered (3) PIP. (4)(12)		
B770	156	Experimental Use Permit application; new (2) PIP; with petition to establish a temporary tolerance/tolerance exemption for the active ingredient; credit 75% of B771 fee toward registration application for a new active ingredient that follows; SAP review. (5)(12)	15	191,444
B771	157	Experimental Use Permit application; new (2) PIP; with petition to establish a temporary tolerance/tolerance exemption for the active ingredient; credit 75% of B771 fee toward registration application for a new active ingredient that follows. (12)	10	127,630
B772	158	Application to amend or extend an Experimental Use Permit; no petition since the established tolerance/tolerance exemption for the active ingredient is unaffected. (12)	3	12,764
B773	159	Application to amend or extend an Experimental Use Permit; with petition to extend a temporary tolerance/tolerance exemption for the active ingredient. (12)	5	31,910
B780	160	Registration application; new (2) PIP; non-food/feed. (12)	12	159,537
B790	161	Registration application; new (2) PIP; non-food/feed; SAP review. (5)(12)	18	223,351
B800	162	Registration application; new (2) PIP; with petition to establish permanent tolerance/tolerance exemption for the active ingredient based on an existing temporary tolerance/tolerance exemption. (12)	13	172,300
B810	163	Registration application; new (2) PIP; with petition to establish permanent tolerance/tolerance exemption for the active ingredient based on an existing temporary tolerance/tolerance exemption. SAP review. (5)(12)	19	236,114
B820	164	Registration application; new (2) PIP; with petition to establish or amend a permanent tolerance/tolerance exemption of an active ingredient. (12)	15	204,208
B840	165	Registration application; new (2) PIP; with petition to establish or amend a permanent tolerance/tolerance exemption of an active ingredient. SAP review. (5)(12)	21	268,022
B851	166	Registration application; new event of a previously registered PIP active ingredient(s); no petition since permanent tolerance/tolerance exemption is already established for the active ingredient(s). (12)	9	127,630
B870	167	Registration application; registered (3) PIP; new product; new use; no petition since a permanent tolerance/tolerance exemption is already established for the active ingredient(s). (4) (12)	9	38,290
B880	168	Registration application; registered (3) PIP; new product or new terms of registration; additional data submitted; no petition since a permanent tolerance/tolerance exemption is already established for the active ingredient(s). (6) (7) (12)	9	31,910
B881	169	Registration application; registered (3) PIP; new product or new terms of registration; additional data submitted; no petition since a permanent tolerance/tolerance exemption is already established for the active ingredient(s). SAP review. (5)(6)(7)(12)	15	95,724

EPA No.	New CR No.	Action	Decision Review Time (Months)(1)	Registration Service Fee ($)
B882	170 (new)	Registration application; new (2) PIP, seed increase with negotiated acreage cap and time-limited registration; with petition to establish a permanent tolerance/tolerance exemption for the active ingredient based on an existing temporary tolerance/tolerance exemption; SAP Review. (8)(12)	15	191,444
B883	171	Registration application; new (2) PIP, seed increase with negotiated acreage cap and time-limited registration; with petition to establish a permanent tolerance/tolerance exemption for the active ingredient based on an existing temporary tolerance/tolerance exemption. (8) (12)	9	127,630
B884	172	Registration application; new (2) PIP, seed increase with negotiated acreage cap and time-limited registration; with petition to establish a permanent tolerance/tolerance exemption for the active ingredient. (8)(12)	12	159,537
B885	173	Registration application; registered (3) PIP, seed increase; breeding stack of previously approved PIPs, same crop; no petition since a permanent tolerance/tolerance exemption is already established for the active ingredient(s). (9)(12)	6	31,910
B886	174 (new)	Registration application; new (2) PIP, seed increase with negotiated acreage cap and time-limited registration; with petition to establish a permanent tolerance/tolerance exemption for the active ingredient. SAP Review. (8) (12)	18	223,351
B890	175	Application to amend a seed increase registration; converts registration to commercial registration; no petition since permanent tolerance/tolerance exemption is already established for the active ingredient(s). (12)	9	63,816
B891	176	Application to amend a seed increase registration; converts registration to a commercial registration; no petition since a permanent tolerance/tolerance exemption already established for the active ingredient(s); SAP review. (5)(12)	15	127,630
B900	177	Application to amend a registration, including actions such as extending an expiration date, modifying an IRM plan, or adding an insect to be controlled. (10)(11)(12)	6	12,764
B901	178	Application to amend a registration, including actions such as extending an expiration date, modifying an IRM plan, or adding an insect to be controlled. SAP review. (10) (11) (12)	12	76,578
B902	179	PIP Protocol review.	3	6,383
B903	180	Inert ingredient tolerance exemption; e.g., a marker such as NPT II; reviewed in BPPD.	6	63,816
B904	181	Import tolerance or tolerance exemption; processed commodities/food only (inert or active ingredient).	9	127,630
B905	182 (new)	SAP Review.	6	63,816
B906	183 (new)	Petition to establish a temporary tolerance/tolerance exemption for one or more active ingredients.	3	31,907
B907	184 (new)	Petition to establish a temporary tolerance/tolerance exemption for one or more active ingredients based on an existing temporary tolerance/tolerance exemption.	3	12,764

EPA No.	New CR No.	Action	Decision Review Time (Months)(1)	Registration Service Fee ($)
B908	185 (new)	Petition to establish a temporary tolerance/tolerance exemption for one or more active ingredients or inert ingredients.	3	44,671

(1) A decision review time that would otherwise end on a Saturday, Sunday, or federal holiday, will be extended to end on the next business day.

(2) New PIP = a PIP with an active ingredient that has not been registered.

(3) Registered PIP = a PIP with an active ingredient that is currently registered.

(4) Transfer registered PIP through conventional breeding for new food/feed use, such as from field corn to sweet corn.

(5) The scientific data involved in this category are complex. EPA often seeks technical advice from the Scientific Advisory Panel on risks that pesticides pose to wildlife, farm workers, pesticide applicators, non-target species, as well as insect resistance, and novel scientific issues surrounding new technologies. The scientists of the SAP neither make nor recommend policy decisions. They provide advice on the science used to make these decisions. Their advice is invaluable to the EPA as it strives to protect humans and the environment from risks posed by pesticides. Due to the time it takes to schedule and prepare for meetings with the SAP, additional time and costs are needed.

(6) Registered PIPs stacked through conventional breeding.

(7) Deployment of a registered PIP with a different IRM plan (e.g., seed blend).

(8) The negotiated acreage cap will depend upon EPA's determination of the potential environmental exposure, risk(s) to non-target organisms, and the risk of targeted pest developing resistance to the pesticidal substance. The uncertainty of these risks may reduce the allowable acreage, based upon the quantity and type of non-target organism data submitted and the lack of insect resistance management data, which is usually not required for seed-increase registrations. Registrants are encouraged to consult with EPA prior to submission of a registration application in this category.

(9) Application can be submitted prior to or concurrently with an application for commercial registration.

(10) For example, IRM plan modifications that are applicant-initiated.

(11) EPA-initiated amendments shall not be charged fees.

(12) Where the action involves approval of a new or amended label, on or before the end date of the decision review time, the Agency shall provide to the applicant a draft accepted label, including any changes made by the Agency that differ from the applicant-submitted label and relevant supporting data reviewed by the Agency. The applicant will notify the Agency that the applicant either (a) agrees to all of the terms associated with the draft accepted label as amended by the Agency and requests that it be issued as the accepted final Agency-stamped label; or (b) does not agree to one or more of the terms of the draft accepted label as amended by the Agency and requests additional time to resolve the difference(s); or (c) withdraws the application without prejudice for subsequent resubmission, but forfeits the associated registration service fee. For cases described in (b), the applicant shall have up to 30 calendar days to reach agreement with the Agency on the final terms of the Agency-accepted label. If the applicant agrees to all of the terms of the accepted label as in (a), including upon resolution of differences in (b), the Agency shall provide an accepted final Agency-stamped label to the registrant within 2 business days following the registrant's written or electronic confirmation of agreement to the Agency.

TABLE 18.—INERT INGREDIENTS

EPA No.	New CR No.	Action	Decision Review Time (Months)(1)	Registration Service Fee ($)
I001	186	Approval of new food use inert ingredient. (2)(3)	13	27,000
I002	187	Amend currently approved inert ingredient tolerance or exemption from tolerance; new data. (2)	11	7,500
I003	188	Amend currently approved inert ingredient tolerance or exemption from tolerance; no new data. (2)	9	3,308
I004	189	Approval of new non-food use inert ingredient. (2)	6	11,025

EPA No.	New CR No.	Action	Decision Review Time (Months)(1)	Registration Service Fee ($)
I005	190	Amend currently approved non-food use inert ingredient with new use pattern; new data. (2)	6	5,513
I006	191	Amend currently approved non-food use inert ingredient with new use pattern; no new data. (2)	3	3,308
I007	192	Approval of substantially similar non-food use inert ingredients when original inert is compositionally similar with similar use pattern. (2)	4	1,654
I008	193	Approval of new or amended polymer inert ingredient, food use. (2)	5	3,749
I009	194	Approval of new or amended polymer inert ingredient, non-food use. (2)	4	3,087
I010	195	Petition to amend a single tolerance exemption descriptor, or single non-food use descriptor, to add ≤ 10 CASRNs; no new data. (2)	6	1,654
I011	196 (new)	Approval of new food use safener with tolerance or exemption from tolerance. (2)(8)	24	597,683
I012	197 (new)	Approval of new non-food use safener. (2)(8)	21	415,241
I013	198 (new)	Approval of additional food use for previously approved safener with tolerance or exemption from tolerance. (2)	15	62,975
I014	199 (new)	Approval of additional non-food use for previously approved safener. (2)	15	25,168
I015	200 (new)	Approval of new generic data for previously approved food use safener. (2)	24	269,728
I016	201 (new)	Approval of amendment(s) to tolerance and label for previously approved safener. (2)	13	55,776

(1) A decision review time that would otherwise end on a Saturday, Sunday, or federal holiday, will be extended to end on the next business day.

(2) If another covered application is submitted that depends upon an application to approve an inert ingredient, each application will be subject to its respective registration service fee. The decision review time line for both submissions will be the longest of the associated applications. If the application covers multiple ingredients grouped by EPA into one chemical class, a single registration service fee will be assessed for approval of those ingredients.

(3) If EPA data rules are amended to newly require clearance under section 408 of the FFDCA for an ingredient of an antimicrobial product where such ingredient was not previously subject to such a clearance, then review of the data for such clearance of such product is not subject to a registration service fee for the tolerance action for two years from the effective date of the rule.

(4) Any other covered application that is associated with and dependent on the HSRB review will be subject to its separate registration service fee. The decision review times for the associated actions run concurrently, but will end at the date of the latest review time.

(5) Any other covered application that is associated with and dependent on the SAP review will be subject to its separate registration service fee. The decision review time for the associated action will be extended by the decision review time for the SAP review.

(6) An application for a new end-use product using a source of active ingredient that (a) is not yet registered but (b) has an application pending with the Agency for review, will be considered an application for a new product with an unregistered source of active ingredient.

(7) Where the action involves approval of a new or amended label, on or before the end date of the decision review time, the Agency shall provide to the applicant a draft accepted label, including any changes made by the Agency that differ from the applicant-submitted label and relevant supporting data reviewed by the Agency. The applicant will notify the Agency that the applicant either (a) agrees to all of the terms associated with the draft accepted label as amended by the Agency and requests that it be issued as the accepted final Agency-stamped label; or (b) does not agree to one or more of the terms of the draft accepted label as amended by the Agency and requests additional time to resolve the difference(s); or (c) withdraws the application without prejudice for subsequent resubmission, but forfeits the associated registration service fee. For cases described in (b), the applicant shall have up to 30 calendar days to reach agreement with the Agency on the final terms of the Agency-accepted label. If the applicant agrees to all of the terms of the accepted label as in (a), including upon resolution of differences in (b), the Agency shall provide an accepted final Agency-stamped label to the registrant within 2 business days following the registrant's written or electronic confirmation of agreement to the Agency.

(8) If a new safener is submitted in the same package as a new active ingredient, and that new active ingredient is determined to be reduced risk, then the safener would get the same reduced timeframe as the new active ingredient.

TABLE 19.—EXTERNAL REVIEW AND MISCELLANEOUS ACTIONS

EPA No.	New CR No.	Action	Decision Review Time (Months)(1)	Registration Service Fee ($)
M001	202	Study protocol requiring Human Studies Review Board review as defined in 40 CFR Part 26 in support of an active ingredient. (4)	9	7,938
M002	203	Completed study requiring Human Studies Review Board review as defined in 40 CFR Part 26 in support of an active ingredient. (4)	9	7,938
M003	204	External technical peer review of new active ingredient, product, or amendment (e.g., consultation with FIFRA Scientific Advisory Panel) for an action with a decision timeframe of less than 12 months. Applicant initiated request based on a requirement of the Administrator, as defined by FIFRA § 25(d), in support of a novel active ingredient, or unique use pattern or application technology. Excludes PIP active ingredients. (5)	12	63,945
M004	205	External technical peer review of new active ingredient, product, or amendment (e.g., consultation with FIFRA Scientific Advisory Panel) for an action with a decision timeframe of greater than 12 months. Applicant initiated request based on a requirement of the Administrator, as defined by FIFRA § 25(d), in support of a novel active ingredient, or unique use pattern or application technology. Excludes PIP active ingredients. (5)	18	63,945
M005	206	New Product: Combination, Contains a combination of active ingredients from a registered and/or unregistered source; conventional, antimicrobial and/or biopesticide. Requires coordination with other regulatory divisions to conduct review of data, label and/or verify the validity of existing data as cited. Only existing uses for each active ingredient in the combination product. (6)(7)	9	22,050
M006	207	Request for up to 5 letters of certification (Gold Seal) for one actively registered product (excludes distributor products). (8)	1	277
M007	208	Request to extend Exclusive Use of data as provided by FIFRA Section 3(c)(1)(F)(ii).	12	5,513
M008	209	Request to grant Exclusive Use of data as provided by FIFRA Section 3(c)(1)(F)(vi) for a minor use, when a FIFRA Section 2(ll)(2) determination is required.	15	1,654
M009	210 (new)	Non-FIFRA Regulated Determination: Applicant initiated, per product.	4	2,363

EPA No.	New CR No.	Action	Decision Review Time (Months)(1)	Registration Service Fee ($)
M010	211 (new)	Conditional ruling on pre-application, product substantial similarity.	4	2,363
M011	212 (new)	Label amendment to add the DfE logo; requires data review; no other label changes. (9)	4	3,648

(1) A decision review time that would otherwise end on a Saturday, Sunday, or federal holiday, will be extended to end on the next business day.

(2) If another covered application is submitted that depends upon an application to approve an inert ingredient, each application will be subject to its respective registration service fee. The decision review time line for both submissions will be the longest of the associated applications. If the application covers multiple ingredients grouped by EPA into one chemical class, a single registration service fee will be assessed for approval of those ingredients.

(3) If EPA data rules are amended to newly require clearance under section 408 of the FFDCA for an ingredient of an antimicrobial product where such ingredient was not previously subject to such a clearance, then review of the data for such clearance of such product is not subject to a registration service fee for the tolerance action for two years from the effective date of the rule.

(4) Any other covered application that is associated with and dependent on the HSRB review will be subject to its separate registration service fee. The decision review times for the associated actions run concurrently, but will end at the date of the latest review time.

(5) Any other covered application that is associated with and dependent on the SAP review will be subject to its separate registration service fee. The decision review time for the associated action will be extended by the decision review time for the SAP review.

(6) An application for a new end-use product using a source of active ingredient that (a) is not yet registered but (b) has an application pending with the Agency for review, will be considered an application for a new product with an unregistered source of active ingredient.

(7) Where the action involves approval of a new or amended label, on or before the end date of the decision review time, the Agency shall provide to the applicant a draft accepted label, including any changes made by the Agency that differ from the applicant-submitted label and relevant supporting data reviewed by the Agency. The applicant will notify the Agency that the applicant either (a) agrees to all of the terms associated with the draft accepted label as amended by the Agency and requests that it be issued as the accepted final Agency-stamped label; or (b) does not agree to one or more of the terms of the draft accepted label as amended by the Agency and requests additional time to resolve the difference(s); or (c) withdraws the application without prejudice for subsequent resubmission, but forfeits the associated registration service fee. For cases described in (b), the applicant shall have up to 30 calendar days to reach agreement with the Agency on the final terms of the Agency-accepted label. If the applicant agrees to all of the terms of the accepted label as in (a), including upon resolution of differences in (b), the Agency shall provide an accepted final Agency-stamped label to the registrant within 2 business days following the registrant's written or electronic confirmation of agreement to the Agency.

(8) Due to low fee and short time frame this category is not eligible for small business waivers. Gold seal applies to one registered product.

(9) This category includes amendments the sole purpose of which is to add DfE (or equivalent terms that do not use "safe" or derivatives of "safe") logos to a label. DfE is a voluntary program. A label bearing a DfE logo is not considered an Agency endorsement because the ingredients in the qualifying product must meet objective, scientific criteria established and widely publicized by EPA.

---

(4) Pending pesticide registration applications

(A) In general

An applicant that submitted a registration application to the Administrator before the effective date of the Pesticide Registration Improvement Act of 2003, but that is not required to pay a registration service fee under paragraph (2)(B), may, on a voluntary basis, pay a registration service fee in accordance with paragraph (2)(B).

(B) Voluntary fee

The Administrator may not compel payment of a registration service fee for an application described in subparagraph (A).

(C) Documentation

An application for which a voluntary registration service fee is paid under this paragraph shall be submitted with documentation certifying—

(i) payment of the registration service fee; or

(ii) a request for a waiver from or reduction of the registration service fee.

(5) Resubmission of covered applications

If a covered application is submitted by a person that paid the fee for the application under paragraph (2), is determined by the Administrator to be complete, and is not approved or is withdrawn (without a waiver or refund), the submission of the same covered application by the same person (or a licensee, assignee, or successor of the person) shall not be subject to a fee under paragraph (2).

(6) Fee adjustment

(A) In general

Effective for a covered application received during the period beginning on October 1, 2019, and ending on September 30, 2021, the Administrator shall increase by 5 percent the registration service fee payable for the application under paragraph (3).

(B) Additional adjustment

Effective for a covered application received on or after October 1, 2021, the Administrator shall increase by an additional 5 percent the registration service fee in effect as of September 30, 2021.

(C) Publication

The Administrator shall publish in the Federal Register the service fee schedules revised pursuant to this paragraph.

(7) Waivers and reductions

(A) In general

An applicant for a covered application may request the Administrator to waive or reduce the amount of a registration service fee payable under this section under the circumstances described in subparagraphs (D) through (G), except that no waiver or fee reduction shall be provided in connection with a request for a letter of certification (commonly referred to as a Gold Seal letter).

(B) Documentation

(i) In general

A request for a waiver from or reduction of the registration service fee shall be accompanied by appropriate documentation demonstrating the basis for the waiver or reduction.

(ii) Certification

The applicant shall provide to the Administrator a written certification, signed by a responsible officer, that the documentation submitted to support the waiver or reduction request is accurate.

(iii) Inaccurate documentation

An application shall be subject to the applicable registration service fee payable under paragraph (3) if, at any time, the Administrator determines that—

(I) the documentation supporting the waiver or reduction request is not accurate; or

(II) based on the documentation or any other information, the waiver or reduction should not have been granted or should not be granted.

(C) Determination to grant or deny request

As soon as practicable, but not later than 60 days, after the date on which the Administrator receives a request for a waiver or reduction of a registration service fee under this paragraph, the Administrator shall—

(i) determine whether to grant or deny the request; and

(ii) notify the applicant of the determination.

(D) Minor uses

(i) In general

The Administrator may exempt from, or waive a portion of, the registration service fee for an application for minor uses for a pesticide.

(ii) Supporting documentation

An applicant requesting a waiver or exemption under this subparagraph shall provide supporting documentation that demonstrates, to the satisfaction of the Administrator, that anticipated revenues from the uses that are the subject of the application would be insufficient to justify imposition of the full application fee.

(E) IR-4 exemption

The Administrator shall exempt an application from the registration service fee if the Administrator determines that—

(i) the application is solely associated with a tolerance petition submitted in connection with the Inter-Regional Project Number 4 (IR-4) as described in section 2 of Public Law 89–106 (7 U.S.C. 450i(e)); and

(ii) the exemption is in the public interest.

(F) Small businesses

(i) In general

The Administrator shall waive 50 percent of the registration service fees payable by an entity for a covered application under this section if the entity is a small business (as defined in section 136a–1(i)(1)(E)(ii) of this title) at the time of application.

(ii) Waiver of fees

The Administrator shall waive 75 percent of the registration service fees payable by an entity under this section if the entity—

(I) is a small business (as defined in section 136a–1(i)(1)(E)(ii) of this title) at the time of application; and

(II) has average annual global gross revenues described in section 136a–1(i)(1)(E)(ii)(I)(bb) of this title that does not exceed $10,000,000, at the time of application.

(iii) Formation for waiver

The Administrator shall not grant a waiver under this subparagraph if the Administrator determines that the entity submitting the application has been formed or manipulated primarily for the purpose of qualifying for the waiver.

(iv) Documentation

An entity requesting a waiver under this subparagraph shall provide to the Administrator—

(I) documentation demonstrating that the entity is a small business (as defined in section 136a–1(i)(1)(E)(ii) of this title) at the time of application; and

(II) if the entity is requesting a waiver of 75 percent of the applicable registration service fees payable under this section, documentation demonstrating that the entity has an average annual global gross revenue described in section 136a–1(i)(1)(E)(ii)(I)(bb) of this title that does not exceed $10,000,000, at the time of application.

(G) Federal and State agency exemptions

An agency of the Federal Government or a State government shall be exempt from covered registration service fees under this section.

(8) Refunds

(A) Early withdrawals

If, during the first 60 days after the beginning of the applicable decision time review period under subsection (f)(3) of this section, a covered application is withdrawn by the applicant, the Administrator shall refund all but 25 percent.[1] of the total registration service fee payable under paragraph (3) for the application.

(B) Withdrawals after the first 60 days of decision review time period

(i) In general

If a covered application is withdrawn after the first 60 days of the applicable decision time review period, the Administrator shall determine what portion, if any, of the total registration service fee payable under paragraph (3) for the application may be refunded based on the proportion of the work completed at the time of withdrawal.

(ii) Timing

The Administrator shall—

(I) make the determination described in clause (i) not later than 90 days after the date the application is withdrawn; and

(II) provide any refund as soon as practicable after the determination.

(C) Discretionary refunds

(i) In general

In the case of a covered application that has been filed with the Administrator and has not been withdrawn by the applicant, but for which the Administrator has not yet made a final determination, the Administrator may refund a portion of a covered registration service fee if the Administrator determines that the refund is justified.

(ii) Basis

The Administrator may provide a refund for an application under this subparagraph—

(I) on the basis that, in reviewing the application, the Administrator has considered data submitted in support of another covered application;

(II) on the basis that the Administrator completed portions of the review of the application before the effective date of this section; or

(III) on the basis that the Administrator rejected the application under subsection (f)(4)(B).

(D) Credited fees

In determining whether to grant a refund under this paragraph, the Administrator shall take into account any portion of the registration service fees credited under paragraph (2) or (4).

(c) Pesticide Registration Fund

(1) Establishment

There is established in the Treasury of the United States a Pesticide Registration Fund to be used in carrying out this section (referred to in this section as the "Fund"), consisting of—

(A) such amounts as are deposited in the Fund under paragraph (2);

(B) any interest earned on investment of amounts in the Fund under paragraph (5); and

(C) any proceeds from the sale or redemption of investments held in the Fund.

(2) Deposits in Fund

Subject to paragraph (4), the Administrator shall deposit fees collected under this section in the Fund.

(3) Expenditures from Fund

(A) In general

Subject to subparagraphs (B) and (C) and paragraph (4), the Administrator may make expenditures from the Fund—

(i) to cover the costs associated with the review and decisionmaking pertaining to all applications for which registration service fees have been paid under this section; and

(ii) to otherwise carry out this section.

(B) Worker protection, pesticide grants, and pesticide safety education

(i) In general

For each of fiscal years 2013 through 2023, the Administrator shall use approximately $^1/_{17}$ of the amount in the Fund (but not less than $1,000,000) to enhance scientific and regulatory activities relating to worker protection, with an emphasis on field-worker populations in the United States.

(ii) Partnership grants

Of the amounts in the Fund, the Administrator shall use for partnership grants, for each of fiscal years 2013 through 2023, $500,000.

(iii) Pesticide safety education program

Of the amounts in the Fund, the Administrator shall use $500,000 for each of fiscal years 2013 through 2023 to carry out the pesticide safety education program.

(4) Collections and appropriations Acts

The fees authorized by this section and amounts deposited in the Fund—

(A) shall be collected and made available for obligation only to the extent provided in advance in appropriations Acts; and

(B) shall be available without fiscal year limitation.

(5) Unused funds

(A) In general

Amounts in the Fund not currently needed to carry out this section shall be—

(i) maintained readily available or on deposit;

(ii) invested in obligations of the United States or guaranteed by the United States; or

(iii) invested in obligations, participations, or other instruments that are lawful investments for fiduciary, trust, or public funds.

(B) Use of investment income

After consultation with the Secretary of the Treasury, the Administrator may use income from investments described in clauses (ii) and (iii) of subparagraph (A) to carry out this section.

(d) Assessment of fees

(1) Definition of covered functions

In this subsection, the term "covered functions" means functions of the Office of Pesticide Programs of the Environmental Protection Agency, as identified in key programs and projects of the final operating plan for the Environmental Protection Agency submitted as part of the budget process for fiscal year 2002, regardless of any subsequent transfer of 1 or more of the functions to another office or agency or the subsequent transfer of a new function to the Office of Pesticide Programs.

(2) Minimum amount of appropriations

Registration service fees may not be assessed for a fiscal year under this section unless the amount of appropriations for salaries, contracts, and expenses for the functions (as in existence in fiscal year 2012) of the Office of Pesticide Programs of the Environmental Protection Agency for the fiscal year (excluding the amount of any fees appropriated for the fiscal year) are equal to or greater than the amount of appropriations for covered functions for fiscal year 2012 (excluding the amount of any fees appropriated for the fiscal year).

(3) Use of fees

Registration service fees authorized by this section shall be available, in the aggregate, only to defray increases in the costs associated with the review and decisionmaking for the review of pesticide registration applications and associated tolerances (including increases in the number of full-time equivalent positions in the Environmental Protection Agency engaged in those activities) over the costs for fiscal year 2002, excluding costs paid from fees appropriated for the fiscal year.

(4) Subsequent authority

If the Administrator does not assess registration service fees under subsection (b) of this section during any portion of a fiscal year as the result of paragraph (2) and is subsequently permitted to assess the fees under subsection (b) of this section during the fiscal year, the Administrator shall assess and collect the fees, without any modification in rate, at any time during the fiscal year, notwithstanding any provisions of subsection (b) of this section relating to the date fees are to be paid.

(e) Reforms to reduce decision time review periods

To the maximum extent practicable consistent with the degrees of risk presented by pesticides and the type of review appropriate to evaluate risks, the Administrator shall identify and evaluate reforms to the pesticide registration process under this subchapter with the goal of reducing decision review periods in effect on the effective date of the Pesticide Registration Improvement Extension Act of 2018 for pesticide registration actions for covered pesticide registration applications (including reduced risk applications). Such reforms shall include identifying opportunities for streamlining review processes for applications for a new active ingredient or a new use and providing prompt feedback to applicants during such review process.

(f) Decision time review periods

(1) In general

Not later than 30 days after the effective date of the Pesticide Registration Improvement Extension Act of 2018, the Administrator shall make publicly available a schedule of decision review periods for covered pesticide registration actions or for any other action covered by a table specified in subsection (b)(3) and corresponding registration service fees under this subchapter.

(2) Report

The schedule shall be the same as the applicable schedule provided under subsection (b)(3).

(3) Applications subject to decision time review periods

The decision time review periods specified in paragraph (1) shall apply to—

(A) covered pesticide registration applications subject to registration service fees under subsection (b)(2) of this section;

(B) covered pesticide registration applications for which an applicant has voluntarily paid registration service fees under subsection (b)(4) of this section; and

(C) applications for any other action covered by a table specified in subsection (b)(3).

(4) Start of decision time review period

(A) In general

Except as provided in subparagraphs (C), (D), and (E), in the case of a covered application accompanied by the registration service fee required under this section, the decision time review period begins 21 days after the date on which the Administrator receives the covered application and fee.

(B) Initial content and preliminary technical screenings

(i) Screenings

(I) Initial content

Not later than 21 days after receiving an application and the required registration service fee, the Administrator shall conduct an initial screening of the contents of the application in accordance with clause (iii).

(II) Preliminary technical screening

After conducting the initial content screening described in subclause (I) and in accordance with clause (iv), the Administrator shall conduct a preliminary technical screening—

(aa) not later than 45 days after the date on which the decision time review period begins (for applications with decision time review periods of not more than 180 days); and

(bb) not later than 90 days after the date on which the decision time review period begins (for applications with decision time review periods greater than 180 days).

(ii) Rejection

(I) In general

If the Administrator determines at any time before the Administrator completes the preliminary technical screening under clause (i)(II) that the application failed the initial content or preliminary technical screening and the applicant does not correct the failure before the date that is 10 business days after the applicant receives a notification of the failure, the Administrator shall reject the application.

(II) Written notification

The Administrator shall make every effort to provide a written notification of a rejection under subclause (I) during the 10-day period that begins on the date the Administrator completes the preliminary technical screening.

(iii) Requirements of initial content screening

In conducting an initial content screening of an application, the Administrator shall determine whether—

(I) **(aa)** the applicable registration service fee has been paid; or

(bb) at least 25 percent of the applicable registration service fee has been paid and the application contains a waiver or refund request for the outstanding amount and documentation establishing the basis for the waiver request; and

(II) the application appears to contain all the necessary forms, data, and draft labeling, formatted in accordance with guidance published by the Administrator.

(iv) Requirements of preliminary technical screening

In conducting a preliminary technical screening of an application, the Administrator shall determine if—

(I) the application and the data and information submitted with the application are accurate and complete; and

(II) the application, data, and information are consistent with the proposed labeling and any proposal for a tolerance or exemption from the requirement for a tolerance under section 408 of the Federal Food, Drug, and Cosmetic Act (21 U.S.C. 346a), and are such that, subject to full review under the standards of this Act, could result in the granting of the application.

(C) Applications with waiver or reduction requests

(i) In general

In the case of an application submitted with a request for a waiver or reduction of registration service fees under subsection (b)(7) of this section, the decision time review period shall be determined in accordance with this subparagraph.

(ii) Request granted with no additional fees required

If the Administrator grants the waiver or reduction request and no additional fee is required, the decision time review period begins on the earlier of—

(I) the date on which the Administrator grants the request; or

(II) the date that is 60 days after the date of receipt of the application.

(iii) Request granted with additional fees required

If the Administrator grants the waiver or reduction request, in whole or in part, but an additional registration service fee is required, the decision time review period begins on the date on which the Administrator receives certification of payment of the applicable registration service fee.

(iv) Request denied

If the Administrator denies the waiver or reduction request, the decision time review period begins on the date on which the Administrator receives certification of payment of the applicable registration service fee.

(D) Pending applications

(i) In general

The start of the decision time review period for applications described in clause (ii) shall be the date on which the Administrator receives certification of payment of the applicable registration service fee.

(ii) Applications

Clause (i) applies to—

(I) covered pesticide registration applications for which voluntary fees have been paid under subsection (b)(4) of this section; and

(II) covered pesticide registration applications received on or after the effective date of the Pesticide Registration Improvement Act of 2003 but submitted without the applicable registration service fee required under this section due to the inability of the Administrator to assess fees under subsection (d)(1) of this section.

(E) 2003 work plan

In the case of a covered pesticide registration application listed in the Registration Division 2003 Work Plan of the Office of Pesticide Programs of the Environmental Protection Agency, the decision time review period begins on the date that is 30 days after the effective date of the Pesticide Registration Improvement Act of 2003.

(5) Extension of decision time review period

The Administrator and the applicant may mutually agree in writing to extend a decision time review period under this subsection.

(g) Judicial review

(1) In general

Any applicant adversely affected by the failure of the Administrator to make a determination on the application of the applicant for registration of a new active ingredient or new use for which a registration service fee is paid under this section may obtain judicial review of the failure solely under this section.

(2) Scope

(A) In general

In an action brought under this subsection, the only issue on review is whether the Administrator failed to make a determination on the application specified in paragraph (1) by the end of the applicable decision time review period required under subsection (f) of this section for the application.

(B) Other actions

No other action authorized or required under this section shall be judicially reviewable by a Federal or State court.

(3) Timing

(A) In general

A person may not obtain judicial review of the failure of the Administrator to make a determination on the application specified in paragraph (1) before the expiration of the 2-year period that begins on the date on which the decision time review period for the application ends.

(B) Meeting with Administrator

To be eligible to seek judicial review under this subsection, a person seeking the review shall first request in writing, at least 120 days before filing the complaint for judicial review, a decision review meeting with the Administrator.

(4) Remedies

The Administrator may not be required or permitted to refund any portion of a registration service fee paid in response to a complaint that the Administrator has failed to make a determination on the covered pesticide registration application specified in paragraph (1) by the end of the applicable decision review period.

(h) Accounting

The Administrator shall—

(1) provide an annual accounting of the registration service fees paid to the Administrator and disbursed from the Fund, by providing financial statements in accordance with—

(A) the Chief Financial Officers Act of 1990 (Public Law 101–576; 104 Stat. 2838) and amendments made by that Act; and

(B) the Government Management Reform Act of 1994 (Public Law 103–356; 108 Stat. 3410) and amendments made by that Act;

(2) provide an accounting describing expenditures from the Fund authorized under subsection (c) of this section; and

(3) provide an annual accounting describing collections and expenditures authorized under subsection (d) of this section.

(i) Auditing

(1) Financial statements of agencies

For the purpose of section 3515(c) of Title 31, the Fund shall be considered a component of an executive agency.

(2) Components

The annual audit required under sections 3515(b) and 3521 of that title of the financial statements of activities under this section shall include an analysis of—

(A) the fees collected under subsection (b) of this section and disbursed;

(B) compliance with subsection (f) of this section;

(C) the amount appropriated to meet the requirements of subsection (d)(1) of this section; and

(D) the reasonableness of the allocation of the overhead allocation of costs associated with the review and decisionmaking pertaining to applications under this section.

(3) Inspector General

The Inspector General of the Environmental Protection Agency shall—

(A) conduct the annual audit required under this subsection; and

(B) report the findings and recommendations of the audit to the Administrator and to the appropriate committees of Congress.

(j) Personnel levels

All full-time equivalent positions supported by fees authorized and collected under this section shall not be counted against the agency-wide personnel level goals of the Environmental Protection Agency.

(k) Reports

(1) In general

Not later than March 1, 2005, and each March 1 thereafter through March 1, 2023, the Administrator shall publish an annual report describing actions taken under this section.

(2) Contents

The report shall include—

(A) a review of the progress made in carrying out each requirement of subsections (e) and (f) of this section, including—

(i) the number of applications reviewed, including the decision times for each application specified in subsection (f) of this section;

(ii) the number of label amendments that have been reviewed using electronic means;

(iii) the amount of money from the Reregistration and Expedited Processing Fund used to carry out inert ingredient review and review of similar applications under section 136a–1(k)(3) of this title;

(iv) the number of applications completed for identical or substantially similar applications under section 136a(c)(3)(B) of this title, including the number of such applications completed within 90 days pursuant to that section;

(v) the number of actions pending in each category of actions described in subsection (f)(3) of this section, as well as the number of inert ingredients;

(vi) to the extent determined appropriate by the Administrator and consistent with the authorities of the Administrator and limitations on delegation of functions by the Administrator, recommendations for—

(I) expanding the use of self-certification in all appropriate areas of the registration process;

(II) providing for accreditation of outside reviewers and the use of outside reviewers to conduct the review of major portions of applications;

(III) reviewing the scope of use of the notification process to cover broader categories of registration actions;

(IV) providing for electronic submission and review of labels, including process improvements to further enhance the procedures used in electronic label review; and

(V) the allowance and use of summaries of acute toxicity studies;

(vii) the use of performance-based contracts, other contracts, and procurement to ensure that—

(I) the goals of this subchapter for the timely review of applications for registration are met; and

(II) the registration program is administered in the most productive and cost effective manner practicable; and

(viii) the number of extensions of decision time review periods agreed to under subsection (f)(5) along with a description of the reason that the Administrator was unable to make a decision within the initial decision time review period;

(B) a description of the staffing and resources relating to the costs associated with the review and decisionmaking pertaining to applications;

(C) a review of the progress in meeting the timeline requirements of section 136a–1(g) of this title;

(D) a review of the progress in carrying out section 136a(g) of this title, including—

(i) the number of pesticides or pesticide cases reviewed and the number of registration review decisions completed, including—

(I) the number of cases cancelled;

(II) the number of cases requiring risk mitigation measures;

(III) the number of cases removing risk mitigation measures;

(IV) the number of cases with no risk mitigation needed; and

(V) the number of cases in which risk mitigation has been fully implemented;

(ii) a description of the staffing and resources relating to the costs associated with the review and decision making relating to reregistration and registration review for compliance with the deadlines specified in this subchapter;

(iii) to the extent determined appropriate by the Administrator and consistent with the authorities of the Administrator and limitations on delegation of functions by the Administrator, recommendations for—

(I) process improvements in the handling of registration review under section 136a(g) of this title;

(II) providing for accreditation of outside reviewers and the use of outside reviewers in the registration review process; and

(III) streamlining the registration review process, consistent with section 136a(g) of this title;

(E) a review of the progress in meeting the timeline requirements for the review of antimicrobial pesticide products under section 136a(h) of this title;

(F) a review of the progress in carrying out the review of inert ingredients, including the number of applications pending, the number of new applications, the number of applications reviewed, staffing, and resources devoted to the review of inert ingredients and recommendations to improve the timeliness of review of inert ingredients;

(G) a review of the progress made toward—

(i) carrying out paragraphs (4) and (5) of section 4(k) of this title and the amounts from the Reregistration and Expedited Processing Fund used for the purposes described in those paragraphs;

(ii) implementing enhancements to—

(I) the electronic tracking of covered applications;

(II) the electronic tracking of conditional registrations;

(III) the endangered species database;

(IV) the electronic review of labels submitted with covered applications; and

(V) the electronic review and assessment of confidential statements of formula submitted with covered applications; and

(iii) facilitating public participation in certain registration actions and the registration review process by providing electronic notification to interested parties of additions to the public docket;

(H) the number of applications rejected by the Administrator under the initial content and preliminary technical screening conducted under subsection (f)(4);

(I) a review of the progress made in updating the Pesticide Incident Data System, including progress toward making the information contained in the System available to the public (as the Administrator determines is appropriate);

(J) an assessment of the public availability of summary pesticide usage data;

(K) a review of the progress made in developing, updating, and implementing product performance test guidelines for pesticide products that are intended to control invertebrate pests of significant public health importance and, by regulation, prescribing product performance data requirements for such pesticide products registered under section 3;

(L) a review of the progress made in the priority review and approval of new pesticides to control invertebrate public health pests that may transmit vector-borne disease for use in the United States, including each territory or possession of the United States, and United States military installations globally;

(M) a review of the progress made in implementing enhancements to the good laboratory practices standards compliance monitoring program established under part 160 of title 40 of the Code of Federal Regulations (or successor regulations);

(N) the number of approvals for active ingredients, new uses, and pesticide end use products granted in connection with the Design for the Environment program (or any successor program) of the Environmental Protection Agency; and

(O) with respect to funds in the Pesticide Registration Fund reserved under subsection (c)(3), a review that includes—

(i) a description of the amount and use of such funds—

(I) to carry out activities relating to worker protection under clause (i) of subsection (c)(3)(B);

(II) to award partnership grants under clause (ii) of such subsection; and

(III) to carry out the pesticide safety education program under clause (iii) of such subsection;

(ii) an evaluation of the appropriateness and effectiveness of the activities, grants, and program described in clause (i);

(iii) a description of how stakeholders are engaged in the decision to fund such activities, grants, and program; and

(iv) with respect to activities relating to worker protection carried out under subparagraph (B)(i) of such subsection, a summary of the analyses from stakeholders, including from worker community-based organizations, on the appropriateness and effectiveness of such activities.

(3) Method

The Administrator shall publish a report required by this subsection by such method as the Administrator determines to be the most effective for efficiently disseminating the report, including publication of the report on the Internet site of the Environmental Protection Agency.

(4) Other report

(A) Scope

In addition to the annual report described in paragraph (1), not later than October 1, 2016, the Administrator shall submit to the Committee on Agriculture of the House of Representatives and the Committee on Agriculture, Nutrition, and Forestry of the Senate a report that includes an analysis of the impact of maintenance fees on small businesses that have—

(i) 10 or fewer employees; and

(ii) annual global gross revenue that does not exceed $2,000,000.

(B) Information required

In conducting the analysis described in subparagraph (A), the Administrator shall collect, and include in the report under that subparagraph, information on—

(i) the number of small businesses described in subparagraph (A) that are paying maintenance fees; and

(ii) the number of registrations each company holds.

(*l*) Savings clause

Nothing in this section affects any other duties, obligations, or authorities established by any other section of this subchapter, including the right to judicial review of duties, obligations, or authorities established by any other section of this subchapter.

(m) Termination of effectiveness

(1) In general

Except as provided in paragraph (2), the authority provided by this section terminates on September 30, 2023.

(2) Phase out

(A) Fiscal year 2024

During fiscal year 2024, the requirement to pay and collect registration service fees applies, except that the level of registration service fees payable under this section shall be reduced 40 percent below the level in effect on September 30, 2023.

(B) Fiscal year 2025

During fiscal year 2025, the requirement to pay and collect registration service fees applies, except that the level of registration service fees payable under this section shall be reduced 70 percent below the level in effect on September 30, 2023.

(C) September 30, 2025

Effective September 30, 2025, the requirement to pay and collect registration service fees terminates.

(D) Decision review periods

(i) Pending applications

In the case of an application received under this section before September 30, 2023, the application shall be reviewed in accordance with subsection (f) of this section.

(ii) New applications

In the case of an application received under this section on or after September 30, 2023, subsection (f) of this section shall not apply to the application.

(Act of June 25, 1947, c. 125, § 33, as added by Pub. L. No. 108–199, Div. G, Title V, § 501(f)(2), 118 Stat. 422 (Jan. 23, 2004); and amended by Pub. L. No. 110–94, § 5, 121 Stat. 1002 (Oct. 9, 2007); Pub. L. No. 110–193, § 1(a), 122 Stat. 649 (Mar. 6, 2008); Pub. L. No. 112–177, § 2(a)(2)(B), (b), 126 Stat. 1328, 1330 (Sept. 28, 2012); Pub. L. No. 116–8, §§ 5, 6, 133 Stat. 484. 487–578 (Mar. 8, 2019).)

[1] So in original. Period probably should not appear.

HISTORICAL AND STATUTORY NOTES

References in Text

The effective date of the Pesticide Registration Improvement Act of 2003, referred to in text, is the effective date of Pub. L. No. 108–199, Div. G, Title V, § 501, 118 Stat. 419 (Jan. 23, 2004), which is 60 days after Jan. 23, 2004, unless otherwise provided, see Pub. L. No. 108–199, Div. G, Title V, § 501(h), set out as a note under 7 U.S.C.A. § 136a.

This subchapter, referred to in text, originally read "this Act", meaning the Federal Insecticide, Fungicide and Rodenticide Act (FIFRA), Act of June 25, 1947, c. 125, as amended generally by Pub. L. No. 92–516, 86 Stat. 973 (Oct. 21, 1972), which is codified principally to this subchapter. Section 3 of FIFRA, referred to in subsec. (b)(3), is codified as 7 U.S.C.A. § 136a. For complete classification, see Short Title note set out under 7 U.S.C.A. § 136 and Tables.

The Federal Food, Drug, and Cosmetic Act (FDCA, FFDCA), referred to in subsec. (b)(2)(B)(ii), is Act of June 25, 1938, c. 675, 52 Stat. 1040, as amended, which is principally codified as chapter 9 of Title 21, 21 U.S.C.A. § 301 et seq. Section 408 of FFDCA, referred to in subsec. (b)(3), is codified as 21 U.S.C.A. § 346a. For complete classification, see Short Title set out at 21 U.S.C.A. § 301 and Tables.

Subchapter II of chapter 37 of Title 31, referred to in subsec. (b)(2)(H), is 31 U.S.C.A. § 711 et seq.

Section 2 of Pub. L. No. 89–106, referred to in subsec. (b)(7)(E)(i), is Pub. L. No. 89–106, § 2, 79 Stat. 431 (Aug. 4, 1965), which is codified as 7 U.S.C.A. § 450i.

The effective date of this section, referred to in subsec. (b)(8)(C)((ii)(II), is the effective date of Pub. L. No. 108–199, Div. G, Title V, § 501, 118 Stat. 419 (Jan. 23, 2004), which is 60 days after Jan. 23, 2004, unless otherwise provided, see Pub. L. No. 108–199, Div. G, Title V, § 501(h), set out as a note under 7 U.S.C.A. § 136a.

The effective date of the Pesticide Registration Improvement Extension Act of 2012, referred to in subsecs. (e), (f)(1), is the effective date of Pub. L. No. 112–177, 126 Stat. 1327 (Sept. 28, 2012), which is Oct. 1, 2012, see Pub. L. No. 112–177, § 2(c), set out as a note under 7 U.S.C.A. § 136a–1.

The Chief Financial Officers Act of 1990, referred to in subsec. (h)(1)(A), is Pub. L. No. 101–576, Nov. 15, 1990, 104 Stat. 2838. For complete classification, see Short Title note set out under 31 U.S.C.A. § 501 and Tables.

The Government Management Reform Act of 1994, referred to in subsec. (h)(1)(B), is Pub. L. No. 103–356, Oct. 13, 1994, 108 Stat. 3410. For complete classification, see Short Title note set out under 31 U.S.C.A. § 3301 and Tables.

Effective and Applicability Provisions

2012 Acts. Amendments by Pub. L. No. 112–177, § 2, take effect on Oct. 1, 2012, see Pub. L. No. 112–177, § 2(c), set out as a note under 7 U.S.C.A. § 136a–1.

2008 Acts. Pub. L. No. 110–193, § 1(b), 122 Stat. 650 (Mar. 6, 2008), provided that: "The amendments made by subsection (a) [amending this section] take effect on October 1, 2007."

2007 Acts. Amendments by Pub. L. No. 110–94 were effective Oct. 1, 2007, see Pub. L. No. 110–94, § 6, set out as a note under 7 U.S.C.A. § 136a.

2004 Acts. Section became effective 60 days after Jan. 23, 2004, except as otherwise provided, see Pub. L. No. 108–199, Div. G, Title V, § 501(h), set out as a note under 7 U.S.C.A. § 136a.

Prior Provisions

A prior section 33 of the Federal Insecticide, Fungicide, and Rodenticide Act, Act of June 25, 1947, c. 125, § 34, formerly § 26, as added by Pub. L. No. 92–516, § 2, 86 Stat. 998 (Oct. 21, 1972), renumbered § 30 by Pub. L. No. 95–396, § 24(1) (Sept. 30, 1978), renumbered § 33 by Pub. L. No. 104–170, Title I, § 121(1), 110 Stat. 1492 (Aug. 3, 1996), as amended, relating to severability of environmental pesticide control provisions, was redesignated as section 34 of that Act by Pub. L. No. 108–199, Div. G, Title V, § 501(f)(1), 118 Stat. 422 (Jan. 23, 2004), and is codified to 7 U.S.C.A. § 136x.

Budget Resolutions

2020. Pub. L. No. 116–260, 135 Stat 1182, 1515 (Dec. 27, 2020) provided that: "The Administrator of the Environmental Protection Agency is authorized to collect and obligate pesticide registration service fees in accordance with section 33 of the Federal Insecticide, Fungicide, and Rodenticide Act (7 U.S.C. 136w–8). Notwithstanding section 33(d)(2) of the Federal Insecticide, Fungicide, and Rodenticide Act (FIFRA) (7 U.S.C. 136w–8(d)(2)), the Administrator of the Environmental Protection Agency may assess fees under section 33 of FIFRA (7 U.S.C. 136w–8) for fiscal year 2021."

2019. Pub. L. No. 116–94, 133 Stat. 2534, 2723 (Dec. 20, 2019), provided that: "The Administrator of the Environmental Protection Agency is authorized to collect and obligate pesticide registration service fees in accordance with section 33 of the Federal Insecticide, Fungicide, and Rodenticide Act, as amended by Public Law 116–8, the Pesticide Registration Improvement Extension Act of 2018. Notwithstanding section 33(d)(2) of the Federal Insecticide, Fungicide, and Rodenticide Act (FIFRA) (7 U.S.C. 136w–8(d)(2)), the Administrator of the Environmental Protection Agency may assess fees under section 33 of FIFRA (7 U.S.C. 136w–8) for fiscal year 2020."

Pub. L. No. 116–6, 133 Stat. 13, 240 (Feb. 15, 2019), provided that: "The Administrator of the Environmental Protection Agency is authorized to collect and obligate pesticide registration service fees in accordance with section 33 of the Federal Insecticide, Fungicide, and Rodenticide Act, as amended by Public Law 112–177, the Pesticide Registration Improvement Extension Act of 2012. Notwithstanding section 33(d)(2) of the Federal Insecticide, Fungicide, and Rodenticide Act (FIFRA) (7 U.S.C. 136w–8(d)(2)), the Administrator of the Environmental Protection Agency may assess fees under section 33 of FIFRA (7 U.S.C. 136w–8) for fiscal year 2019."

2017. Section 134(b)(2) of Pub. L. No. 115–56, 131 Stat. 1145 (Sept. 8, 2017), provided: "Notwithstanding section 33(m)(2) of the Federal Insecticide, Fungicide, and Rodenticide Act (7 U.S.C. 136w–8(m)(2)), section 33(m)(1) of such Act (7 U.S.C. 136w–8(m)(1)) shall be applied by substituting the date specified in section 106(3) of this joint resolution [December 8, 2017] for 'September 30, 2017.' "

Pub. L. No. 115–31, 131 Stat. 475 (May 5, 2017), provided: "Notwithstanding section 33(d)(2) of the Federal Insecticide, Fungicide, and Rodenticide Act (FIFRA) (7 U.S.C. 136w–8(d)(2)), the Administrator of the

Environmental Protection Agency may assess fees under section 33 of FIFRA (7 U.S.C. 136w–8) for fiscal year 2017."

Relationship of Pub. L. No. 112–177 to Other Laws

In case of any conflict between the amendments made by Pub. L. No. 112–177, § 2, and a joint resolution making continuing appropriations for fiscal year 2013, the amendments made by § 2 of Pub. L. No. 112–177 shall control, see Pub. L. No. 112–177, § 2(d), set out as a note under 7 U.S.C.A. § 136a–1.

Administrative Provisions—Environmental Protection Agency

Pub. L. No. 113–235, Title II, 128 Stat. 2426 (Dec. 16, 2014), provided in part that "[t]he Administrator of the Environmental Protection Agency is authorized to collect and obligate pesticide registration service fees in accordance with section 33 of the Federal Insecticide, Fungicide, and Rodenticide Act, as amended by Public Law 112–177, the Pesticide Registration Improvement Extension Act of 2012" and that "[n]otwithstanding section 33(d)(2) of the Federal Insecticide, Fungicide, and Rodenticide Act (FIFRA) (7 U.S.C. 136w–8(d)(2)), the Administrator of the Environmental Protection Agency may assess fees under section 33 of FIFRA (7 U.S.C. 136w–8) for fiscal year 2015."

Administrative Provisions—Environmental Protection Agency

Pub. L. No. 113–76, Title II, 128 Stat. 320 (Jan. 17, 2014), provided in part that "[t]he Administrator of the Environmental Protection Agency is authorized to collect and obligate pesticide registration service fees in accordance with section 33 of the Federal Insecticide, Fungicide, and Rodenticide Act, as amended by Public Law 112–177, the Pesticide Registration Improvement Extension Act of 2012" and that "[n]otwithstanding section 33(d)(2) of the Federal Insecticide, Fungicide, and Rodenticide Act (FIFRA) (7 U.S.C. 136w–8(d)(2)), the Administrator of the Environmental Protection Agency may assess fees under section 33 of FIFRA (7 U.S.C. 136w–8) for fiscal year 2014."

Fee Assessment in 2013

Pub. L. No. 113–6, § 1407, 127 Stat. 420 (Mar. 26, 2013), provided that: "Notwithstanding subsection (d)(2) of section 33 of the Federal Insecticide, Fungicide, and Rodenticide Act (7 U.S.C. 136w–8), the Administrator of the Environmental Protection Agency may assess pesticide registration service fees under such section for fiscal year 2013."

§ 136x. Severability

[FIFRA § 34]

If any provision of this subchapter or the application thereof to any person or circumstance is held invalid, the invalidity shall not affect other provisions or applications of this subchapter which can be given effect without regard to the invalid provision or application, and to this end the provisions of this subchapter are severable.

(Act of June 25, 1947, c. 125, § 34, formerly § 26, as added by Pub. L. No. 92–516, § 2, 86 Stat. 998 (Oct. 21, 1972); and renumbered § 30 by Pub. L. No. 95–396, § 24(1), 92 Stat. 836 (Sept. 30, 1978); and renumbered § 33 by Pub. L. No. 104–170, Title I, § 121(1), 110 Stat. 1492 (Aug. 3, 1996); and renumbered § 34 by Pub. L. No. 108–199, Div. G, Title V, § 501(f)(1), 118 Stat. 422 (Jan. 23, 2004).)

HISTORICAL AND STATUTORY NOTES

Effective and Applicability Provisions

2004 Acts. Amendments made by Pub. L. No. 108–199, § 501, redesignating section 33 of the Federal Insecticide, Fungicide, and Rodenticide Act [this section] as section 34 of that Act, to take effect 60 days after Jan. 23, 2004, except as otherwise provided, see Pub. L. No. 108–199, § 501(h), set out as a note under 7 U.S.C.A. § 136a.

1972 Acts. Section effective at the close of Oct. 21, 1972, except if regulations are necessary for the implementation of any provision that becomes effective on Oct. 21, 1972, and continuation in effect of the provisions of subchapter I of this chapter and regulations thereunder as in effect prior to Oct. 21, 1972, until superseded by provisions of Pub. L. No. 92–516 and regulations thereunder, see section 4 of Pub. L. No. 92–516, set out as a note under section 136 of this title.

Prior Provisions

A prior section 34 of the Federal Insecticide, Fungicide, and Rodenticide Act, Act of June 25, 1947, c. 125, formerly § 27, as added by Pub. L. No. 92–516, § 2, 86 Stat. 998 (Oct. 21, 1972), as amended; renumbered § 31 and amended by Pub. L. No. 95–396, §§ 24(1), (25), 92 Stat. 836 (Sept. 30, 1978), as amended; and renumbered § 34 by Pub. L. No. 104–170, Title I, § 121(1), 110 Stat. 1492 (Aug. 3, 1996), relating to authorization of appropriations for environmental pesticide control, was redesignated as section 35 of that Act by Pub. L. No. 108–199, Div. G, Title V, § 501(f)(1), 118 Stat. 422 (Jan. 23, 2004), and is codified to 7 U.S.C.A. § 136y.

§ 136y. Authorization of appropriations

[FIFRA § 35]

There is authorized to be appropriated to carry out this subchapter (other than section 136u(a) of this title)—

(1) $83,000,000 for fiscal year 1989, of which not more than $13,735,500 shall be available for research under this subchapter;

(2) $95,000,000 for fiscal year 1990, of which not more than $14,343,600 shall be available for research under this subchapter; and

(3) $95,000,000 for fiscal year 1991, of which not more than $14,978,200 shall be available for research under this subchapter.

(Act of June 25, 1947, c. 125, § 35, formerly § 27, as added by Pub. L. No. 92–516, § 2, 86 Stat. 998 (Oct. 21, 1972); and amended by Pub. L. No. 94–51, 89 Stat. 257 (July 2, 1975); Pub. L. No. 94–109, 89 Stat. 571 (Oct. 10, 1975); Pub. L. No. 94–140, § 3, 89 Stat. 752 (Nov. 28, 1975); renumbered § 31 and amended by Pub. L. No. 95–396, §§ 24(1), 25, 92 Stat. 836, 838 (Sept. 30, 1978); Pub. L. No. 96–539, § 3, 94 Stat. 3195 (Dec. 17, 1980); Pub. L. No. 98–201, § 2, 97 Stat. 1380 (Dec. 2, 1983); Pub. L. No. 99–198, Title XVII, § 1768, 99 Stat. 1656 (Dec. 23, 1985); Pub. L. No. 100–532, Title VII, § 701, 102 Stat. 2679 (Oct. 25, 1988); renumbered § 34 by Pub. L. No. 104–170, Title I, § 121(1), 110 Stat. 1492 (Aug. 3, 1996); renumbered § 35 by Pub. L. No. 108–199, Div. G, Title V, § 501(f)(1), 118 Stat. 422 (Jan. 23, 2004).)

HISTORICAL AND STATUTORY NOTES

Codifications

Another section 1768(a) to (f) of Pub. L. No. 99–198 enacted sections 154a and 159 and amended sections 151, 154, and 157 of Title 21, Food and Drugs.

Effective and Applicability Provisions

2004 Acts. Amendments made by Pub. L. No. 108–199, § 501(f)(1), redesignating section 34 of the Federal Insecticide, Fungicide, and Rodenticide Act [this section] as section 35 of that Act, to take effect 60 days after Jan. 23, 2004, except as otherwise provided, see Pub. L. No. 108–199, § 501(h), set out as a note under 7 U.S.C.A. § 136a.

1988 Acts. Section 701 of Pub. L. No. 100–532 provided in part that amendment by Pub. L. No. 100–532 be effective Oct. 1, 1988.

1972 Acts. Section effective at the close of Oct. 21, 1972, except if regulations are necessary for the implementation of any provision that becomes effective on Oct. 21, 1972, and continuation in effect of the provisions of subchapter I of this chapter and regulations thereunder as in effect prior to Oct. 21, 1972, until superseded by provisions of Pub. L. No. 92–516 and regulations thereunder, see section 4 of Pub. L. No. 92–516, set out as a note under section 136 of this title.

TITLE 15

COMMERCE AND TRADE

TOXIC SUBSTANCES CONTROL ACT
[TSCA § ______]

(15 U.S.C.A. §§ 2601 to 2697)

CHAPTER 53—TOXIC SUBSTANCES CONTROL

SUBCHAPTER I—CONTROL OF TOXIC SUBSTANCES

Sec.
2601. Findings, policy, and intent.
2602. Definitions.
2603. Testing of chemical substances and mixtures.
2604. Manufacturing and processing notices.
2605. Prioritization, Risk Evaluation, and Regulation of Chemical Substances and Mixtures.
2606. Imminent hazards.
2607. Reporting and retention of information.
2608. Relationship to other Federal laws.
2609. Research, development, collection, dissemination, and utilization of information.
2610. Inspections and subpoenas.
2611. Exports.
2612. Entry into customs territory of the United States.
2613. Confidential information.
2614. Prohibited acts.
2615. Penalties.
2616. Specific enforcement and seizure.
2617. Preemption.
2618. Judicial review.
2619. Citizens' civil actions.
2620. Citizens' petitions.
2621. National defense waiver.
2622. Employee protection.
2623. Employment effects.
2624. Repealed.
2625. Administration.
2626. Development and evaluation of test methods.
2627. State programs.
2628. Authorization of appropriations.
2629. Annual report.

SUBCHAPTER II—ASBESTOS HAZARD EMERGENCY RESPONSE

2641. Congressional findings and purpose.
2642. Definitions.
2643. EPA regulations.
2644. Requirements if EPA fails to promulgate regulations.
2645. Submission to State Governor.
2646. Contractor and laboratory accreditation.
2647. Enforcement.

SUBCHAPTER III—INDOOR RADON ABATEMENT

SUBCHAPTER IV—LEAD EXPOSURE REDUCTION

SUBCHAPTER V—HEALTHY HIGH-PERFORMANCE SCHOOLS

SUBCHAPTER VI—FORMALDEHYDE STANDARDS FOR COMPOSITE WOOD PRODUCTS

SUBCHAPTER I—CONTROL OF TOXIC SUBSTANCES

§ 2601. Findings, policy, and intent

[TSCA § 2]

(a) Findings

The Congress finds that—

(1) human beings and the environment are being exposed each year to a large number of chemical substances and mixtures;

(2) among the many chemical substances and mixtures which are constantly being developed and produced, there are some whose manufacture, processing, distribution in commerce, use, or disposal may present an unreasonable risk of injury to health or the environment; and

(3) the effective regulation of interstate commerce in such chemical substances and mixtures also necessitates the regulation of intrastate commerce in such chemical substances and mixtures.

(b) Policy

It is the policy of the United States that—

(1) adequate information should be developed with respect to the effect of chemical substances and mixtures on health and the environment and that the development of such information should be the responsibility of those who manufacture and those who process such chemical substances and mixtures;

(2) adequate authority should exist to regulate chemical substances and mixtures which present an unreasonable risk of injury to health or the environment, and to take action with respect to chemical substances and mixtures which are imminent hazards; and

(3) authority over chemical substances and mixtures should be exercised in such a manner as not to impede unduly or create unnecessary economic barriers to technological innovation while fulfilling the primary purpose of this chapter to assure that such innovation and commerce in such chemical substances and mixtures do not present an unreasonable risk of injury to health or the environment.

(c) Intent of Congress

It is the intent of Congress that the Administrator shall carry out this chapter in a reasonable and prudent manner, and that the Administrator shall consider the environmental, economic, and social impact of any action the Administrator takes or proposes as provided under this chapter.

(Pub. L. No. 94–469, Title I, § 2, 90 Stat. 2003 (Oct. 11, 1976); renumbered Title I, Pub. L. No. 99–519, § 3(c)(1), 100 Stat. 2989 (Oct. 22, 1986); as amended by Pub. L. No. 114–182, §§ 2, 19(b), 130 Stat. 448, 505 (June 22, 2016).)

HISTORICAL AND STATUTORY NOTES

Effective and Applicability Provisions

1976 Acts. Section 31 of Title I of Pub. L. No. 94–469; remanded Title I, Pub. L. No. 99–519, § 3(c), 100 Stat. 2989 (Oct. 22, 1986), provided that: "Except as provided in section 4(f) [section 2603(f) of this title], this Act [enacting this chapter] shall take effect on January 1, 1977."

Short Title

2016 Amendments. Pub. L. No. 114–182, § 1, 130 Stat. 448 (June 22, 2016), provided that: "This Act may be cited as the 'Frank R. Lautenberg Chemical Safety for the 21st Century Act'."

2010 Amendments. Pub. L. No. 111–199, § 1, 124 Stat. 1359 (July 7, 2010), provided that: "This Act [enacting subchapter VI of this chapter, 15 U.S.C.A. § 2697, and enacting provisions set out as a note under 15 U.S.C.A. § 2697] may be cited as the 'Formaldehyde Standards for Composite Wood Products Act'."

2008 Amendments. Pub. L. No. 110–414, § 1, 122 Stat. 4341 (Oct. 14, 2008), provided that: "This Act [enacting 42 U.S.C.A. § 6939f, amending 15 U.S.C.A. §§ 2605 and 2611, and enacting provisions set out as a note under 15 U.S.C.A. § 2611] may be cited as the 'Mercury Export Ban Act of 2008'."

1992 Amendments. Pub. L. No. 102–550, Title X, § 1021(c), 106 Stat. 3924 (Oct. 28, 1992), provided that: "This subtitle [subtitle B (§ 1021) of Title X of Pub. L. No. 102–550, enacting sections 2681 to 2692 of this title and amending sections 2606, 2610, 2612, 2615, 2616, 2618, and 2619 of this title] may be cited as the 'Lead-Based Paint Exposure Reduction Act'."

1986 Amendments. Section 1 of Pub. L. No. 99–519 provided that: "This Act [enacting sections 2641 to 2654 of this title, and section 4022 of Title 20, Education, amending sections 2614, 2618, and 2619 of this title and sections 4014 and 4021 of Title 20, and enacting provisions set out as a note under section 4014 of Title 20] may be cited as the 'Asbestos Hazard Emergency Response Act of 1986'."

1976 Acts. Section 1 of Pub. L. No. 94–469 provided that: "This Act [enacting this chapter and provisions set out as notes under this section] may be cited as the 'Toxic Substances Control Act'."

Federal Compliance with Pollution Control Standards

For provisions relating to the responsibility of the head of each Executive agency for compliance with applicable pollution control standards, see Ex. Ord. No. 12088, Oct. 13, 1978, 43 FED. REG. 47707, set out as a note under section 4321 of Title 42, The Public Health and Welfare.

Modification of Definition of Sport Fishing Equipment under Toxic Substances Control Act

Section 108 of the America's Conservation Enhancement Act, Pub. L. No. 116–188, 134 Stat. 905, 920 (Oct. 30, 2020), provided that:

"(a) Prohibition.—During the 5-year period beginning on the date of enactment of this Act, the Administrator of the Environmental Protection Agency shall not take any action to regulate the lead content of sport fishing equipment or sport fishing equipment components under the Toxic Substances Control Act (15 U.S.C. 2601 et seq.).

"(b) Definition of Sport Fishing Equipment.—In this section, the term "sport fishing equipment" means any sport fishing equipment (as such term is defined in section 4162(a) of the Internal Revenue Code of 1986) the sale of which is subject to the tax imposed by section 4161(a) of such Code (determined without regard to any exemptions from such tax provided by section 4162 or 4221 or any other provision of such Code)."

Funding Prohibitions on Regulation of Lead Content

Section 438 of Pub. L. No. 116–260, 134 Stat. 1182, 1547 (Dec. 27, 2020), provided that: "None of the funds made available by this or any other Act may be used to regulate the lead content of ammunition, ammunition components, or fishing tackle under the Toxic Substances Control Act (15 U.S.C. 2601 et seq.) or any other law."

Section 439 of Pub. L. No. 116–94, 133 Stat. 2751 (Dec. 20, 2019), provided: "None of the funds made available by this or any other Act may be used to regulate the lead content of ammunition, ammunition components, or fishing tackle under **the Toxic Substances Control Act** (15 U.S.C. 2601 et seq.) or any other law."

Section 418 of Pub. L. No. 116–6, 133 Stat. 13, 262 (Feb. 15, 2019), provided that: "None of the funds made available by this or any other Act may be used to regulate the lead content of ammunition, ammunition components, or fishing tackle under the Toxic Sub stances Control Act (**15 U.S.C. 2601** et seq.) or any other law."

Section 420 of Pub. L. No. 115–31, 131 Stat. 499–500 (May 5, 2017), provided: "None of the funds made available by this or any other Act may be used to regulate the lead content of ammunition, ammunition components, or fishing tackle under the Toxic Substances Control Act (15 U.S.C. 2601 et seq.) or any other law."

Section 420 of Pub. L. No. 114–113, 129 Stat. 2579 (Dec. 15, 2015), provided that "[n]one of the funds made available by this or any other Act may be used to regulate the lead content of ammunition, ammunition components, or fishing tackle under the Toxic Substances Control Act (15 U.S.C. 2601 et seq.) or any other law."

Retroactivity

Section 20 of Pub. L. No. 114–182, 130 Stat. 510 (June 22, 2016), provided that "[n]othing in sections 1 through 19, or the amendments made by sections 1 through 19, shall be interpreted to apply retroactively to any State, Federal, or maritime legal action filed before the date of enactment of this Act."

§ 2602. Definitions

[TSCA § 3]

As used in this chapter:

(1) the[1] term "Administrator" means the Administrator of the Environmental Protection Agency.

(2) **(A)** Except as provided in subparagraph (B), the term "chemical substance" means any organic or inorganic substance of a particular molecular identity, including—

(i) any combination of such substances occurring in whole or in part as a result of a chemical reaction or occurring in nature and

(ii) any element or uncombined radical.

(B) Such term does not include—

(i) any mixture,

(ii) any pesticide (as defined in the Federal Insecticide, Fungicide, and Rodenticide Act) [7 U.S.C.A. § 136 et seq.] when manufactured, processed, or distributed in commerce for use as a pesticide,

(iii) tobacco or any tobacco product,

(iv) any source material, special nuclear material, or byproduct material (as such terms are defined in the Atomic Energy Act of 1954 [42 U.S.C.A. § 2011 et seq.] and regulations issued under such Act),

(v) any article the sale of which is subject to the tax imposed by section 4181 of the Internal Revenue Code of 1986 [26 U.S.C.A. 4181] (determined without regard to any exemptions from such tax provided by section 4182 or 4221 or any other provision of such code), and

(vi) any food, food additive, drug, cosmetic, or device (as such terms are defined in section 201 of the Federal Food, Drug, and Cosmetic Act (21 U.S.C.A. 321]) when manufactured, processed, or distributed in commerce for use as a food, food additive, drug, cosmetic, or device.

The term "food" as used in clause (vi) of this subparagraph includes poultry and poultry products (as defined in sections 4(e) and 4(f) of the Poultry Products Inspection Act [21 U.S.C. 453(e) and (f)]), meat and meat food products (as defined in section 1(j) of the Federal Meat Inspection Act [21 U.S.C. 601(j)]), and eggs and egg products (as defined in section 4 of the Egg Products Inspection Act [21 U.S.C. 1033]).

(3) The term "commerce" means trade, traffic, transportation, or other commerce (A) between a place in a State and any place outside of such State, or (B) which affects trade, traffic, transportation, or commerce described in clause (A).

(4) The term "conditions of use" means the circumstances, as determined by the Administrator, under which a chemical substance is intended, known, or reasonably foreseen to be manufactured, processed, distributed in commerce, used, or disposed of.

(5) The terms "distribute in commerce" and "distribution in commerce" when used to describe an action taken with respect to a chemical substance or mixture or article containing a substance or mixture mean to sell, or the sale of, the substance, mixture, or article in commerce; to introduce or deliver for introduction into commerce, or the introduction or delivery for introduction into commerce of, the substance, mixture, or article; or to hold, or the holding of, the substance, mixture, or article after its introduction into commerce.

(6) The term "environment" includes water, air, and land and the interrelationship which exists among and between water, air, and land and all living things.

(7) The term "guidance" means any significant written guidance of general applicability prepared by the Administrator.

(8) The term "health and safety study" means any study of any effect of a chemical substance or mixture on health or the environment or on both, including underlying information and epidemiological studies, studies of occupational exposure to a chemical substance or mixture, toxicological, clinical, and ecological studies of a chemical substance or mixture, and any test performed pursuant to this chapter.

(9) The term "manufacture" means to import into the customs territory of the United States (as defined in general note 2 of the Harmonized Tariff Schedule of the United States), produce, or manufacture.

(10) The term "mixture" means any combination of two or more chemical substances if the combination does not occur in nature and is not, in whole or in part, the result of a chemical reaction; except that such term does include any combination which occurs, in whole or in part, as a result of a chemical reaction if none of the chemical substances comprising the combination is a new chemical substance and if the combination could have been manufactured for commercial purposes without a chemical reaction at the time the chemical substances comprising the combination were combined.

(11) The term "new chemical substance" means any chemical substance which is not included in the chemical substance list compiled and published under section 2607(b) of this title.

(12) The term "potentially exposed or susceptible subpopulation" means a group of individuals within the general population identified by the Administrator who, due to either greater susceptibility or greater exposure, may be at greater risk than the general population of adverse health effects from exposure to a chemical substance or mixture, such as infants, children, pregnant women, workers, or the elderly.

(13) The term "process" means the preparation of a chemical substance or mixture, after its manufacture, for distribution in commerce—

(A) in the same form or physical state as, or in a different form or physical state from, that in which it was received by the person so preparing such substance or mixture, or

(B) as part of an article containing the chemical substance or mixture.

(14) The term "processor" means any person who processes a chemical substance or mixture.

(15) The term "protocols and methodologies for the development of test data" means a prescription of—

(A) the—

(i) health and environmental effects, and

(ii) information relating to toxicity, persistence, and other characteristics which affect health and the environment,

for which information for a chemical substance or mixture are to be developed and any analysis that is to be performed on such information, and

(B) to the extent necessary to assure that information respecting such effects and characteristics are reliable and adequate—

(i) the manner in which such information is to be developed,

(ii) the specification of any test protocol or methodology to be employed in the development of such information, and

(iii) such other requirements as are necessary to provide such assurance.

(16) The term "State" means any State of the United States, the District of Columbia, the Commonwealth of Puerto Rico, the Virgin Islands, Guam, the Canal Zone, American Samoa, the Northern Mariana Islands, or any other territory or possession of the United States.

(17) The term "United States", when used in the geographic sense, means all of the States.

(Pub. L. No. 94–469, Title I, § 3, 90 Stat. 2004 (Oct. 11, 1976); as amended by Pub. L. No. 99–514, § 2, 100 Stat. 2095 (Oct. 22, 1986); renumbered Title I by Pub. L. No. 99–519, § 3(c)(1), 100 Stat. 2989 (Oct. 22, 1986); amended by Pub. L. No. 100–418, Title I, § 1214(e)(1), 102 Stat. 1156 (Aug. 23, 1988); Pub. L. No. 114–182, §§ 3, 19(c) 130 Stat. 449, 505 (June 22, 2016).)

[1] So in original. Probably should be capitalized.

HISTORICAL AND STATUTORY NOTES

References in Text

The Federal Insecticide, Fungicide, and Rodenticide Act, referred to in par. (2)(B)(ii), is Act of June 25, 1947, c. 125, as amended generally by Pub. L. No. 92–516, 86 Stat. 973 (Oct. 21, 1972), which is codified generally to subchapter II (§ 136 et seq.) of chapter 6 of Title 7, Agriculture. For complete classification of this Act to the Code, see Short Title note set out under section 136 of Title 7 and Tables.

The Atomic Energy Act of 1954, referred to in par. (2)(B)(iv), is Act of Aug. 30, 1954, c. 1073, 68 Stat. 919, as amended, which is codified generally to chapter 23 (§ 2011 et seq.) of Title 42, The Public Health and Welfare. For complete classification of this Act to the Code, see Short Title note set out under section 2011 of Title 42 and Tables.

The Harmonized Tariff Schedule of the United States, referred to in par. (7), is not set out in the Code. See Publication of Harmonized Tariff Schedule note set out under section 1202 of Title 19, Customs Duties.

For definition of Canal Zone, Governor of the Canal Zone, and Panama Canal Company, referred to in par. (13), see section 3602(b) of Title 22, Foreign Relations and Intercourse.

Effective and Applicability Provisions

1988 Acts. Amendment by Pub. L. No. 100–418 effective Jan. 1, 1989, and applicable with respect to articles entered on or after such date, see section 1217(b)(1) of Pub. L. No. 100–418, set out as an Effective Date note under section 3001 of Title 19, Customs Duties.

Retroactivity

Section 20 of Pub. L. No. 114–182, 130 Stat. 510 (June 22, 2016), provided that "[n]othing in sections 1 through 19, or the amendments made by sections 1 through 19, shall be interpreted to apply retroactively to any State, Federal, or maritime legal action filed before the date of enactment of this Act."

§ 2603. Testing of chemical substances and mixtures

[TSCA § 4]

(a) Testing requirements

(1) If the Administrator finds

(A) (i) (I) the manufacture, distribution in commerce, processing, use, or disposal of a chemical substance or mixture, or that any combination of such activities, may present an unreasonable risk of injury to health or the environment,

(II) there is insufficient information and experience upon which the effects of such manufacture, distribution in commerce, processing, use, or disposal of such substance or mixture or of any combination of such activities on health or the environment can reasonably be determined or predicted, and

(III) testing of such substance or mixture with respect to such effects is necessary to develop such information; or

(ii) (I) a chemical substance or mixture is or will be produced in substantial quantities, and (aa) it enters or may reasonably be anticipated to enter the environment in substantial quantities or (bb) there is or may be significant or substantial human exposure to such substance or mixture,

(II) there is insufficient information and experience upon which the effects of the manufacture, distribution in commerce, processing, use, or disposal of such substance or mixture or of any combination of such activities on health or the environment can reasonably be determined or predicted, and

(III) testing of such substance or mixture with respect to such effects is necessary to develop such information; and

(B) in the case of a mixture, the effects which the mixture's manufacture, distribution in commerce, processing, use, or disposal or any combination of such activities may have on health or the environment may not be reasonably and more efficiently determined or predicted by testing the chemical substances which comprise the mixture;

the Administrator shall by rule, or, in the case of a chemical substance or mixture described in subparagraph (A)(i), by rule, order, or consent agreement, require that testing be conducted on such substance or mixture to develop information with respect to the health and environmental effects for which there is an insufficiency of information and experience and which is relevant to a determination that the manufacture, distribution in commerce, processing, use, or disposal of such substance or mixture, or that any combination of such activities, does or does not present an unreasonable risk of injury to health or the environment.

(2) Additional testing authority.—In addition to the authority provided under paragraph (1), the Administrator may, by rule, order, or consent agreement—

(A) require the development of new information relating to a chemical substance or mixture if the Administrator determines that the information is necessary—

(i) to review a notice under section 5 or to perform a risk evaluation under section 6(b);

(ii) to implement a requirement imposed in a rule, order, or consent agreement under subsection (e) or (f) of section 5 or in a rule promulgated under section 6(a);

(iii) at the request of a Federal implementing authority under another Federal law, to meet the regulatory testing needs of that authority with regard to toxicity and exposure; or

(iv) pursuant to section 12(a)(2); and

(B) require the development of new information for the purposes of prioritizing a chemical substance under section 6(b) only if the Administrator determines that such information is necessary to establish the priority of the substance, subject to the limitations that—

(i) not later than 90 days after the date of receipt of information regarding a chemical substance complying with a rule, order, or consent agreement under this subparagraph, the Administrator shall designate the chemical substance as a high-priority substance or a low-priority substance; and

(ii) information required by the Administrator under this subparagraph shall not be required for the purposes of establishing or implementing a minimum information requirement of broader applicability.

(3) Statement of need.—When requiring the development of new information relating to a chemical substance or mixture under paragraph (2), the Administrator shall identify the need for the new information, describe how information reasonably available to the Administrator was used to inform the decision to require new information, explain the basis for any decision that requires the use of vertebrate animals, and, as applicable, explain why issuance of an order is warranted instead of promulgating a rule or entering into a consent agreement.

(4) Tiered testing.—When requiring the development of new information under this subsection, the Administrator shall employ a tiered screening and testing process, under which the results of screening-level tests or assessments of available information inform the decision as to whether 1 or more additional tests are necessary, unless information available to the Administrator justifies more advanced testing of potential health or environmental effects or potential exposure without first conducting screening-level testing.

(b) Testing requirement rule

(1) Testing rule, order, or consent agreement.—A rule, order, or consent agreement under subsection (a) of this section shall include—

(A) identification of the chemical substance or mixture for which testing is required under the rule, order, or consent agreement,

(B) protocols and methodologies for the development of information for such substance or mixture, and

(C) with respect to chemical substances which are not new chemical substances and to mixtures, a specification of the period (which period may not be of unreasonable duration) within which the persons required to conduct the testing shall submit to the Administrator information developed in accordance with the standards referred to in subparagraph (B).

In determining the protocols and methodologies and period to be included, pursuant to subparagraphs (B) and (C), in a rule, order, or consent agreement under subsection (a) of this section, the Administrator's considerations shall include the relative costs of the various test protocols and methodologies which may be required under the rule, order, or consent agreement and the reasonably foreseeable availability of the facilities and personnel needed to perform the testing required under the rule, order, or consent agreement. Any such rule, order, or consent agreement may require the submission to the Administrator of preliminary information during the period prescribed under subparagraph (C).

(2) **(A)** The health and environmental effects for which protocols and methodologies for the development of information may be prescribed include carcinogenesis, mutagenesis, teratogenesis, behavioral disorders, cumulative or synergistic effects, and any other effect which may present an unreasonable risk of injury to health or the environment. Protocols and methodologies for the development of information may also be prescribed for the assessment of exposure or exposure potential to humans or the environment. The characteristics of chemical substances and mixtures for which such protocols and methodologies may be prescribed include persistence, acute toxicity, subacute toxicity, chronic toxicity, and any other characteristic which may present such a risk. The methodologies that may be prescribed in such protocols and methodologies include epidemiologic studies, serial or tiered testing, in vitro tests, and whole animal tests, except that before prescribing epidemiologic studies of employees, the Administrator shall consult with the Director of the National Institute for Occupational Safety and Health.

(B) from time to time, but not less than once each 12 months, the Administrator shall review the adequacy of the protocols and methodologies for development of information prescribed in rules, orders, and consent agreements under subsection (a) of this section and shall, if necessary, institute proceedings to make appropriate revisions of such standards.

(3) **(A)** A rule or order under subsection (a) of this section respecting a chemical substance or mixture shall require the persons described in subparagraph (B) or (C), as applicable to conduct tests and submit information to the Administrator on such substance or mixture, except that the Administrator may permit two or more of such persons to designate one such person or a qualified third party to conduct such tests and submit such information on behalf of the persons making the designation.

(B) The following persons shall be required to conduct tests and submit data on a chemical substance or mixture subject to a rule under subsection (a)(1) of this section:

(i) Each person who manufactures or intends to manufacture such substance or mixture if the Administrator makes a finding described in subsection (a)(1)(A)(i)(II) or (a)(1)(A)(ii)(II) of this section with respect to the manufacture of such substance or mixture.

(ii) Each person who processes or intends to process such substance or mixture if the Administrator makes a finding described in subsection (a)(1)(A)(i)(II) or (a)(1)(A)(ii)(II) of this section with respect to the processing of such substance or mixture.

(iii) Each person who manufactures or processes or intends to manufacture or process such substance or mixture if the Administrator makes a finding described in subsection (a)(1)(A)(i)(II) or (a)(1)(A)(ii)(II) of this section with respect to the distribution in commerce, use, or disposal of such substance or mixture.

(C) A rule or order under paragraph (1) or (2) of subsection (a) may require the development of information by any person who manufactures or processes, or intends to manufacture or process, a chemical substance or mixture subject to the rule or order.

(4) Any rule, order, or consent agreement under subsection (a) of this section requiring the testing of and submission of information for a particular chemical substance or mixture shall expire at the end of the reimbursement period (as defined in subsection (c)(3)(B) of this section) which is applicable to information for such substance or mixture unless the Administrator repeals the rule or order or modifies the consent agreement to terminate the requirement before such date; and a rule, order, or consent agreement under subsection (a) of this section requiring the testing of and submission of information for a category of chemical substances or mixtures shall expire with respect to a chemical substance or mixture included in the category at the end of the reimbursement period (as so defined) which is applicable to information for such substance or mixture unless the Administrator before such date repeals or modifies the application of the rule, order, or consent agreement to such substance or mixture or repeals the rule or order or modifies the consent agreement to terminate the requirement.

(c) Exemption

(1) Any person required by a rule or order under subsection (a) of this section to conduct tests and submit information on a chemical substance or mixture may apply to the Administrator (in such form and manner as the Administrator shall prescribe) for an exemption from such requirement.

(2) If, upon receipt of an application under paragraph (1), the Administrator determines that—

(A) the chemical substance or mixture with respect to which such application was submitted is equivalent to a chemical substance or mixture for which information has been submitted to the Administrator in accordance with a rule, order, or consent agreement under subsection (a) or for which information is being developed pursuant to such a rule, order, or consent agreement, and

(B) submission of information by the applicant on such substance or mixture would be duplicative of data which has been submitted to the Administrator in accordance with such rule, order, or consent agreement or which is being developed pursuant to such rule, order, or consent agreement,

the Administrator shall exempt, in accordance with paragraph (3) or (4), the applicant from conducting tests and submitting information on such substance or mixture under the rule or order with respect to which such application was submitted.

(3) **(A)** If the exemption under paragraph (2) of any person from the requirement to conduct tests and submit information on a chemical substance or mixture is granted on the basis of the existence of previously submitted information and if such exemption is granted during the reimbursement period for such information (as prescribed by subparagraph (B)), then (unless such person and the persons referred to in clauses (i) and (ii) agree on the amount and method of reimbursement) the Administrator shall order the person granted the exemption to provide fair and equitable reimbursement (in an amount determined under rules of the Administrator)—

(i) to the person who previously submitted such information, for a portion of the costs incurred by such person in complying with the requirement to submit such data, and

(ii) to any other person who has been required under this subparagraph to contribute with respect to such costs, for a portion of the amount such person was required to contribute.

In promulgating rules for the determination of fair and equitable reimbursement to the persons described in clauses (i) and (ii) for costs incurred with respect to a chemical substance or mixture, the Administrator shall, after consultation with the Attorney General and the Federal Trade Commission, consider all relevant factors, including the effect on the competitive position of the person required to provide reimbursement in relation to the person to be reimbursed and the share of the market for such substance or mixture of the person required to provide reimbursement in relation to the share of such market of the persons to be reimbursed. An order under this subparagraph shall, for purposes of judicial review, be considered final agency action.

(B) For purposes of subparagraph (A), the reimbursement period for any information for a chemical substance or mixture is a period—

(i) beginning on the date such information is submitted in accordance with a rule, order, or consent agreement under subsection (a) of this section, and

(ii) ending—

(I) five years after the date referred to in clause (i), or

(II) at the expiration of a period which begins on the date referred to in clause (i) and which is equal to the period which the Administrator determines was necessary to develop such information,

whichever is later.

(4) **(A)** If the exemption under paragraph (2) of any person from the requirement to conduct tests and submit information on a chemical substance or mixture is granted on the basis of the fact that information is being developed by one or more persons pursuant to a rule, order, or consent agreement promulgated under subsection (a) of this section, then (unless such person and the persons referred to in clauses (i) and (ii) agree on the amount and method of reimbursement) the Administrator shall order the person granted the exemption to provide fair and equitable reimbursement (in an amount determined under rules of the Administrator)—

(i) to each such person who is developing such information, for a portion of the costs incurred by each such person in complying with such rule, order, or consent agreement, and

(ii) to any other person who has been required under this subparagraph to contribute with respect to the costs of complying with such rule, order, or consent agreement, for a portion of the amount such person was required to contribute.

In promulgating rules for the determination of fair and equitable reimbursement to the persons described in clauses (i) and (ii) for costs incurred with respect to a chemical substance or mixture, the Administrator shall, after consultation with the Attorney General and the Federal Trade Commission, consider the factors described in the second sentence of paragraph (3)(A). An order under this subparagraph shall, for purposes of judicial review, be considered final agency action.

(B) If any exemption is granted under paragraph (2) on the basis of the fact that one or more persons are developing information pursuant to a rule, order, or consent agreement promulgated under subsection (a) of this section and if after such exemption is granted the Administrator determines that no such person has complied with such rule, order, or consent agreement the Administrator shall (i) after providing written notice to the person who holds such exemption and an opportunity for a hearing, by order terminate such exemption, and (ii) notify in writing such person of the requirements of the rule, order, or consent agreement with respect to which such exemption was granted.

(d) Notice

Upon the receipt of any information pursuant to a rule, order, or consent agreement under subsection (a) of this section, the Administrator shall publish a notice of the receipt of such information in the Federal Register within 15 days of its receipt. Subject to section 2613 of this title, each such notice shall (1) identify the chemical substance or mixture for which information has been received; (2) list the uses or intended uses of such substance or mixture and the information required by the applicable standards for the development of information; and (3) describe the nature of the information developed. Except as otherwise provided in section 2613 of this title, such information shall be made available by the Administrator for examination by any person.

(e) Priority list

(1) **(A)** There is established a committee to make recommendations to the Administrator respecting the chemical substances and mixtures to which the Administrator should give priority consideration for the development of information under subsection (a) of this section. In making such a recommendation with respect to any chemical substance or mixture, the committee shall consider all relevant factors, including—

(i) the quantities in which the substance or mixture is or will be manufactured,

(ii) the quantities in which the substance or mixture enters or will enter the environment,

(iii) the number of individuals who are or will be exposed to the substance or mixture in their places of employment and the duration of such exposure,

(iv) the extent to which human beings are or will be exposed to the substance or mixture,

(v) the extent to which the substance or mixture is closely related to a chemical substance or mixture which is known to present an unreasonable risk of injury to health or the environment,

(vi) the existence of information concerning the effects of the substance or mixture on health or the environment,

(vii) the extent to which testing of the substance or mixture may result in the development of information upon which the effects of the substance or mixture on health or the environment can reasonably be determined or predicted, and

(viii) the reasonably foreseeable availability of facilities and personnel for performing testing on the substance or mixture.

The recommendations of the committee shall be in the form of a list of chemical substances and mixtures which shall be set forth, either by individual substance or mixture or by groups of substances or mixtures, in the order in which the committee determines the Administrator should take action under subsection (a) of this section with respect to the substances and mixtures. In establishing such list, the committee shall give priority attention to those chemical substances and mixtures which are known to cause or contribute to or which are suspected of causing or contributing to cancer, gene mutations, or birth defects. The committee shall designate chemical substances and mixtures on the list with respect to which the committee determines the Administrator should, within 12 months of the date on which such substances and mixtures are first designated, initiate a proceeding under subsection (a) of this section. The total number of chemical substances and mixtures on the list which are designated under the preceding sentence may not, at any time, exceed 50.

(B) As soon as practicable but not later than nine months after January 1, 1977, the committee shall publish in the Federal Register and transmit to the Administrator the list and designations required by subparagraph (A) together with the reasons for the committee's inclusion of each chemical substance or mixture on the list. At least every six months after the date of the transmission to the Administrator of the list pursuant to the preceding[1] sentence, the committee shall make such revisions in the list as it determines to be necessary and shall transmit them to the Administrator together with the committee's reasons for the revisions. Upon receipt of any such revision, the Administrator shall publish in the Federal Register the list with such revision, the reasons for such revision, and the designations made under subparagraph (A). The Administrator shall provide reasonable opportunity to any interested person to file with the Administrator written comments on the committee's list, any revision of such list by the committee, and designations made by the committee, and shall make such comments available to the public. Within the 12-month period beginning on the date of the first inclusion on the list of a chemical substance or mixture designated by the committee under subparagraph (A) issue an order, enter into a consent agreement, or initiate a rulemaking proceeding under subsection (a), or, if such an order or consent agreement is not issued or such a proceeding is not initiated within such period, publish in the Federal Register the Administrator's reason for not issuing such an order, entering into such a consent agreement, or initiating such a proceeding.

(2) **(A)** The committee established by paragraph (1)(A) shall consist of ten members as follows:

(i) One member appointed by the Administrator from the Environmental Protection Agency.

(ii) One member appointed by the Secretary of Labor from officers or employees of the Department of Labor engaged in the Secretary's activities under the Occupational Safety and Health Act of 1970 [29 U.S.C.A. § 651 et seq.].

(iii) One member appointed by the Chairman of the Council on Environmental Quality from the Council or its officers or employees.

(iv) One member appointed by the Director of the National Institute for Occupational Safety and Health from officers or employees of the Institute.

(v) One member appointed by the Director of the National Institute of Environmental Health Sciences from officers or employees of the Institute.

(vi) One member appointed by the Director of the National Cancer Institute from officers or employees of the Institute.

(vii) One member appointed by the Director of the National Science Foundation from officers or employees of the Foundation.

(viii) One member appointed by the Secretary of Commerce from officers or employees of the Department of Commerce.

(ix) One member appointed by the Chairman of the Consumer Product Safety Commission from Commissioners or employees of the Commission.

(x) One member appointed by the Commissioner of Food and Drugs from employees of the Food and Drug Administration.

(B) (i) An appointed member may designate an individual to serve on the committee on the member's behalf. Such a designation may be made only with the approval of the applicable appointing authority and only if the individual is from the entity from which the member was appointed.

(ii) No individual may serve as a member of the committee for more than four years in the aggregate. If any member of the committee leaves the entity from which the member was appointed, such member may not continue as a member of the committee, and the member's position shall be considered to be vacant. A vacancy in the committee shall be filled in the same manner in which the original appointment was made.

(iii) Initial appointments to the committee shall be made not later than the 60th day after January 1, 1977. Not later than the 90th day after such date the members of the committee shall hold a meeting for the selection of a chairperson from among their number.

(C) (i) No member of the committee, or designee of such member, shall accept employment or compensation from any person subject to any requirement of this chapter or of any rule promulgated or order issued thereunder, for a period of at least 12 months after termination of service on the committee.

(ii) No person, while serving as a member of the committee, or designee of such member, may own any stocks or bonds, or have any pecuniary interest, of substantial value in any person engaged in the manufacture, processing, or distribution in commerce of any chemical substance or mixture subject to any requirement of this chapter or of any rule promulgated or order issued thereunder.

(iii) The Administrator, acting through attorneys of the Environmental Protection Agency, or the Attorney General may bring an action in the appropriate district court of the United States to restrain any violation of this subparagraph.

(D) The Administrator shall provide the committee such administrative support services as may be necessary to enable the committee to carry out its function under this subsection.

(f) Required actions

Upon the receipt of—

(1) any information required to be submitted under this chapter, or

(2) any other information available to the Administrator,

which indicates to the Administrator that there may be a reasonable basis to conclude that a chemical substance or mixture presents a significant risk of serious or widespread harm to human beings, the Administrator shall, within the 180-day period beginning on the date of the receipt of such information, initiate applicable action under section 2604, 2605, or 2606 of this title to prevent or reduce to a sufficient extent such risk or publish in the Federal Register a finding that such risk is not unreasonable, made without consideration of costs or other nonrisk factors. For good cause shown the Administrator may extend such period for an additional period of not more than 90 days. The Administrator shall publish in the Federal Register notice of any such extension and the reasons therefor. A finding by the Administrator that a risk is not unreasonable shall be considered agency action for purposes of judicial review under chapter 7 of Title 5. This subsection shall not take effect until two years after January 1, 1977.

(g) Petition for Protocols and Methodologies for the Development of Information

A person intending to manufacture or process a chemical substance for which notice is required under section 2604(a) of this title and who is not required under a rule, order, or consent agreement under subsection (a) of this section to conduct tests and submit information on such substance may petition the Administrator to prescribe protocols and methodologies for the development of information for such substance. The Administrator shall by order either grant or deny any such petition within 60 days of its receipt. If the petition is granted, the Administrator shall prescribe such protocols and methodologies for such substance within 75 days of the date the petition is granted. If the petition is denied, the Administrator shall publish, subject to section 2613 of this title, in the Federal Register the reasons for such denial.

(h) Reduction of Testing on Vertebrates.—

(1) In general.—The Administrator shall reduce and replace, to the extent practicable, scientifically justified, and consistent with the policies of this title, the use of vertebrate animals in the testing of chemical substances or mixtures under this title by—

(A) prior to making a request or adopting a requirement for testing using vertebrate animals, and in accordance with subsection (a)(3), taking into consideration, as appropriate and to the extent practicable and scientifically justified, reasonably available existing information, including—

(i) toxicity information;

(ii) computational toxicology and bioinformatics; and

(iii) high-throughput screening methods and the prediction models of those methods; and

(B) encouraging and facilitating—

(i) the use of scientifically valid test methods and strategies that reduce or replace the use of vertebrate animals while providing information of equivalent or better scientific quality and relevance that will support regulatory decisions under this title;

(ii) the grouping of 2 or more chemical substances into scientifically appropriate categories in cases in which testing of a chemical substance would provide scientifically valid and useful information on other chemical substances in the category; and

(iii) the formation of industry consortia to jointly conduct testing to avoid unnecessary duplication of tests, provided that such consortia make all information from such testing available to the Administrator.

(2) Implementation of alternative testing methods.—To promote the development and timely incorporation of new scientifically valid test methods and strategies that are not based on vertebrate animals, the Administrator shall—

(A) not later than 2 years after the date of enactment of the Frank R. Lautenberg Chemical Safety for the 21st Century Act, develop a strategic plan to promote the development and implementation of alternative test methods and strategies to reduce, refine, or replace vertebrate animal testing and provide information of equivalent or better scientific quality and relevance for assessing risks of injury to health or the environment of chemical substances or mixtures through, for example—

(i) computational toxicology and bioinformatics;

(ii) high-throughput screening methods;

(iii) testing of categories of chemical substances;

(iv) tiered testing methods;

(v) in vitro studies;

(vi) systems biology;

(vii) new or revised methods identified by validation bodies such as the Interagency Coordinating Committee on the Validation of Alternative Methods or the Organization for Economic Co-operation and Development; or

(viii) industry consortia that develop information submitted under this title;

(B) as practicable, ensure that the strategic plan developed under subparagraph (A) is reflected in the development of requirements for testing under this section;

(C) include in the strategic plan developed under subparagraph (A) a list, which the Administrator shall update on a regular basis, of particular alternative test methods or strategies the Administrator has identified that do not require new vertebrate animal testing and are scientifically reliable, relevant, and capable of providing information of equivalent or better scientific reliability and quality to that which would be obtained from vertebrate animal testing;

(D) provide an opportunity for public notice and comment on the contents of the plan developed under subparagraph (A), including the criteria for considering scientific reliability and relevance of the test methods and strategies that may be identified pursuant to subparagraph (C);

(E) beginning on the date that is 5 years after the date of enactment of the Frank R. Lautenberg Chemical Safety for the 21st Century Act, and every 5 years thereafter, submit to Congress a report that describes the progress made in implementing the plan developed under subparagraph (A) and goals for future alternative test methods and strategies implementation; and

(F) prioritize and, to the extent consistent with available resources and the Administrator's other responsibilities under this title, carry out performance assessment, validation, and translational studies to accelerate the development of scientifically valid test methods and strategies that reduce, refine, or replace the use of vertebrate animals, including minimizing duplication, in any testing under this title.

(3) Voluntary testing.—

(A) In general.—Any person developing information for submission under this title on a voluntary basis and not pursuant to any request or requirement by the Administrator shall first attempt to develop the information by means of an alternative test method or strategy identified by the Administrator pursuant to paragraph (2)(C), if the Administrator has identified such a test method or strategy for the development of such information, before conducting new vertebrate animal testing.

(B) Effect of paragraph.—Nothing in this paragraph shall, under any circumstance, limit or restrict the submission of any existing information to the Administrator.

(C) Relationship to other law.—A violation of this paragraph shall not be a prohibited act under section 15.

(D) Review of means.—This paragraph authorizes, but does not require, the Administrator to review the means by which a person conducted testing described in subparagraph (A).

(Pub. L. No. 94–469, Title I, § 4, 90 Stat. 2006 (Oct. 11, 1976); renumbered Title I by Pub. L. No. 99–519, § 3(c)(1), 100 Stat. 2989 (Oct. 22, 1986); and amended by Pub. L. No. 114–182, §§ 4, 19(d) 130 Stat. 449–454, 505–506 (June 22, 2016).)

1 So in original. Probably should be "preceding".

HISTORICAL AND STATUTORY NOTES

References in Text

The Occupational Safety and Health Act of 1970, referred to in text, is Pub. L. No. 91–596, 84 Stat. 1590 (Dec. 29, 1970), as amended, which is codified principally to chapter 15 (§ 651 et seq.) of Title 29, Labor. For complete classification of this Act to the Code, see Short Title note set out under section 651 of Title 29 and Tables.

Effective and Applicability Provisions

1976 Acts. Section effective Jan. 1, 1977, except as provided in subsec. (f) of this section, see section 31 of Pub. L. No. 94–469, set out as a note under section 2601 of this title.

Retroactivity

Section 20 of Pub. L. No. 114–182, 130 Stat. 510 (June 22, 2016), provided that "[n]othing in sections 1 through 19, or the amendments made by sections 1 through 19, shall be interpreted to apply retroactively to any State, Federal, or maritime legal action filed before the date of enactment of this Act."

§ 2604. Manufacturing and processing notices

[TSCA § 5]

(a) In general

(1) (A) Except as provided in subparagraph (B) of this paragraph and subsection (h) of this section, no person may—

(i) manufacture a new chemical substance on or after the 30th day after the date on which the Administrator first publishes the list required by section 2607(b) of this title, or

(ii) manufacture or process any chemical substance for a use which the Administrator has determined, in accordance with paragraph (2), is a significant new use.

(B) A person may take the actions described in subparagraph (A) if—

(i) such person submits to the Administrator, at least 90 days before such manufacture or processing, a notice, in accordance with subsection (d), of such person's intention to manufacture or process such substance and such person complies with any applicable requirement of, or imposed pursuant to, subsection (b), (e), or (f); and

(ii) the Administrator—

(I) conducts a review of the notice; and

(II) makes a determination under subparagraph (A), (B), or (C) of paragraph (3) and takes the actions required in association with that determination under such subparagraph within the applicable review period."; and

(2) A determination by the Administrator that a use of a chemical substance is a significant new use with respect to which notification is required under paragraph (1) shall be made by a rule promulgated after a consideration of all relevant factors, including—

(A) the projected volume of manufacturing and processing of a chemical substance,

(B) the extent to which a use changes the type or form of exposure of human beings or the environment to a chemical substance,

(C) the extent to which a use increases the magnitude and duration of exposure of human beings or the environment to a chemical substance, and

(D) the reasonably anticipated manner and methods of manufacturing, processing, distribution in commerce, and disposal of a chemical substance.

(3) Review and determination.—Within the applicable review period, subject to section 18, the Administrator shall review such notice and determine—

(A) that the relevant chemical substance or significant new use presents an unreasonable risk of injury to health or the environment, without consideration of costs or other nonrisk factors, including an unreasonable risk to a potentially exposed or susceptible subpopulation identified as relevant by the Administrator under the conditions of use, in which case the Administrator shall take the actions required under subsection (f);

(B) that—

(i) the information available to the Administrator is insufficient to permit a reasoned evaluation of the health and environmental effects of the relevant chemical substance or significant new use; or

(ii) **(I)** in the absence of sufficient information to permit the Administrator to make such an evaluation, the manufacture, processing, distribution in commerce, use, or disposal of such substance, or any combination of such activities, may present an unreasonable risk of injury to health or the environment, without consideration of costs or other nonrisk factors, including an unreasonable risk to a potentially exposed or susceptible subpopulation identified as relevant by the Administrator; or

(II) such substance is or will be produced in substantial quantities, and such substance either enters or may reasonably be anticipated to enter the environment in substantial quantities or there is or may be significant or substantial human exposure to the substance,

in which case the Administrator shall take the actions required under subsection (e); or

(C) that the relevant chemical substance or significant new use is not likely to present an unreasonable risk of injury to health or the environment, without consideration of costs or other nonrisk factors, including an unreasonable risk to a potentially exposed or susceptible subpopulation identified as relevant by the Administrator under the conditions of use, in which case the submitter of the notice may commence manufacture of the chemical substance or manufacture or processing for a significant new use.

(4) Failure to render determination.—

(A) Failure to render determination.—If the Administrator fails to make a determination on a notice under paragraph (3) by the end of the applicable review period and the notice has not been withdrawn by the submitter, the Administrator shall refund to the submitter all applicable fees charged to the submitter for review of the notice pursuant to section 26(b), and the Administrator shall not be relieved of any requirement to make such determination.

(B) Limitations.—**(i)** A refund of applicable fees under subparagraph (A) shall not be made if the Administrator certifies that the submitter has not provided information required under subsection (b) or has otherwise unduly delayed the process such that the Administrator is unable to render a determination within the applicable review period.

(ii) A failure of the Administrator to render a decision shall not be deemed to constitute a withdrawal of the notice.

(iii) Nothing in this paragraph shall be construed as relieving the Administrator or the submitter of the notice from any requirement of this section.

(5) Article consideration.—The Administrator may require notification under this section for the import or processing of a chemical substance as part of an article or category of articles under paragraph (1)(A)(ii) if the Administrator makes an affirmative finding in a rule under paragraph (2) that the reasonable potential for exposure to the chemical substance through the article or category of articles subject to the rule justifies notification.

(b) Submission of Information

(1) (A) If (i) a person is required by subsection (a)(1) of this section to submit a notice to the Administrator before beginning the manufacture or processing of a chemical substance, and (ii) such person is required to submit information for such substance pursuant to a rule, order, or consent agreement under section 2603 of this title before the submission of such notice, such person shall submit to the Administrator such information in accordance with such rule, order, or consent agreement at the time notice is submitted in accordance with subsection (a)(1) of this section.

(B) If—

(i) a person is required by subsection (a)(1) of this section to submit a notice to the Administrator, and

(ii) such person has been granted an exemption under section 2603(c) of this title from the requirements of a rule or order under section 2603 of this title before the submission of such notice,

such person may not, before the expiration of the 90 day period which begins on the date of the submission in accordance with such rule, order, or consent agreement of the information the submission or development of which was the basis for the exemption, manufacture such substance if such person is subject to subsection (a)(1)(A)(i) of this section or manufacture or process such substance for a significant new use if the person is subject to subsection (a)(1)(A)(ii) of this section.

(2) (A) If a person—

(i) is required by subsection (a)(1) of this section to submit a notice to the Administrator before beginning the manufacture or processing of a chemical substance listed under paragraph (4), and

(ii) is not required by a rule, order, or consent agreement under section 2603 of this title before the submission of such notice to submit information for such substance,

such person may submit to the Administrator information prescribed by subparagraph (B) at the time notice is submitted in accordance with subsection (a)(1) of this section.

(B) Information submitted pursuant to subparagraph (A) shall be information which the person submitting the information believes shows that—

(i) in the case of a substance with respect to which notice is required under subsection (a)(1)(A)(i) of this section, the manufacture, processing, distribution in commerce, use, and disposal of the chemical substance or any combination of such activities will not present an unreasonable risk of injury to health or the environment, or

(ii) in the case of a chemical substance with respect to which notice is required under subsection (a)(1)(A)(ii) of this section, the intended significant new use of the chemical substance will not present an unreasonable risk of injury to health or the environment.

(3) Information submitted paragraph (1) or (2) of this subsection or under subsection (e) shall be made available, subject to section 2613 of this title, for examination by interested persons.

(4) (A) (i) The Administrator may, by rule, compile and keep current a list of chemical substances with respect to which the Administrator finds that the manufacture, processing, distribution in commerce, use, or disposal, or any combination of such activities, presents or may present an unreasonable risk of injury to health or the environment, without consideration of costs or other nonrisk factors.

(ii) In making a finding under clause (i) that the manufacture, processing, distribution in commerce, use, or disposal of a chemical substance or any combination of such activities presents or may present an unreasonable risk of injury to health or the environment, the Administrator shall consider all relevant factors, including—

(I) the effects of the chemical substance on health and the magnitude of human exposure to such substance; and

(II) the effects of the chemical substance on the environment and the magnitude of environmental exposure to such substance.

(B) The Administrator shall, in prescribing a rule under subparagraph (A) which lists any chemical substance, identify those uses, if any, which the Administrator determines, by rule under subsection (a)(2) of this section, would constitute a significant new use of such substance.

(C) Any rule under subparagraph (A), and any substantive amendment or repeal of such a rule, shall be promulgated pursuant to the procedures specified in section 553 of Title 5.

(c) Extension of review period

The Administrator may for good cause extend for additional periods (not to exceed in the aggregate 90 days) the period, prescribed by subsection (a) or (b) of this section. Subject to section 2613 of this title, such an extension and the reasons therefor shall be published in the Federal Register and shall constitute a final agency action subject to judicial review.

(d) Content of notice; publications in the Federal Register

(1) The notice required by subsection (a) of this section shall include—

(A) insofar as known to the person submitting the notice or insofar as reasonably ascertainable, the information described in subparagraphs (A), (B), (C), (D), (F), and (G) of section 2607(a)(2) of this title, and

(B) in such form and manner as the Administrator may prescribe, any information in the possession or control of the person giving such notice which are related to the effect of any manufacture, processing, distribution in commerce, use, or disposal of such substance or any article containing such substance, or of any combination of such activities, on health or the environment, and

(C) a description of any other information concerning the environmental and health effects of such substance, insofar as known to the person making the notice or insofar as reasonably ascertainable.

Such a notice shall be made available, subject to section 2613 of this title, for examination by interested persons.

(2) Subject to section 2613 of this title, not later than five days (excluding Saturdays, Sundays and legal holidays) after the date of the receipt of a notice under subsection (a) of this section or of information under subsection (b) of this section, the Administrator shall publish in the Federal Register a notice which—

(A) identifies the chemical substance for which notice or information has been received;

(B) lists the uses of such substance identified in the notice; and

(C) in the case of the receipt of information under subsection (b) of this section, describes the nature of the tests performed on such substance and any information which was developed pursuant to subsection (b) of this section or a rule, order, or consent agreement under section 2603 of this title.

A notice under this paragraph respecting a chemical substance shall identify the chemical substance by generic class unless the Administrator determines that more specific identification is required in the public interest.

(3) At the beginning of each month the Administrator shall publish a list in the Federal Register of (A) each chemical substance for which notice has been received under subsection (a) of this section and for which the applicable review period has not expired, and (B) each chemical substance for which such period has expired since the last publication in the Federal Register of such list.

(e) Regulation pending development of information

(1) **(A)** If the Administrator determines that—

(i) the information available to the Administrator is insufficient to permit a reasoned evaluation of the health and environmental effects of a chemical substance with respect to which notice is required by subsection (a) of this section; or

(ii) **(I)** in the absence of sufficient information to permit the Administrator to make such an evaluation, the manufacture, processing, distribution in commerce, use, or disposal of such substance, or any combination of such activities, may present an unreasonable risk of injury to health or the environment, without consideration of costs or other nonrisk factors, including an unreasonable risk to a potentially exposed subpopulation identified as relevant by the Administrator under the conditions of use; or

(II) such substance is or will be produced in substantial quantities, and such substance either enters or may reasonably be anticipated to enter the environment in substantial quantities or there is or may be significant or substantial human exposure to the substance,

the Administrator shall issue an order, to take effect on the expiration of the applicable review period, to prohibit or limit the manufacture, processing, distribution in commerce, use, or disposal of such substance or to prohibit or limit any combination of such activities to the extent necessary to protect against an unreasonable risk of injury to health or the environment, without consideration of costs or other nonrisk factors, including an unreasonable risk to a potentially exposed or susceptible subpopulation identified as relevant by the Administrator under the conditions of use, and the submitter of the notice may commence manufacture of the chemical substance, or manufacture or processing of the chemical substance for a significant new use, including while any required information is being developed, only in compliance with the order.

(B) An order may not be issued under subparagraph (A) respecting a chemical substance (i) later than 45 days before the expiration of the applicable review period of this section, and (ii) unless the Administrator has, on or before the issuance of the order, notified, in writing, each manufacturer or processor, as the case may be, of such substance of the determination which underlies such order.

(f) Protection against unreasonable risks

(1) If the Administrator determines that a chemical substance or significant new use with respect to which notice is required by subsection (a) of this section presents an unreasonable risk of injury to health or environment, without consideration of costs or other nonrisk factors, including an unreasonable risk to a potentially exposed subpopulation identified as relevant by the Administrator under the conditions of use, the Administrator shall, before the expiration of the applicable review period, take the action authorized by paragraph (2) or (3) to the extent necessary to protect against such risk.

(2) The Administrator may issue a proposed rule under section 2605(a) of this title to apply to a chemical substance with respect to which a finding was made under paragraph (1)—

(A) a requirement limiting the amount of such substance which may be manufactured, processed, or distributed in commerce,

(B) a requirement described in paragraph (2), (3), (4), (5), (6), or (7) of section 2605(a) of this title, or

(C) any combination of the requirements referred to in subparagraph (B).

Such a proposed rule shall be effective upon its publication in the Federal Register. Section 6(d)(3)(B) of this title shall apply with respect to such rule.

(3) **(A)** Administrator may issue an order to prohibit or limit the manufacture, processing, or distribution in commerce of a substance with respect to which a finding was made under paragraph (1). Such order shall take effect on the expiration of the applicable review period.

(B) The provisions of subparagraph (B) of subsection (e)(1) of this section shall apply with respect to an order issued under subparagraph (A).

(4) Treatment of nonconforming uses.—Not later than 90 days after taking an action under paragraph (2) or (3) or issuing an order under subsection (e) relating to a chemical substance with respect to which the Administrator has made a determination under subsection (a)(3)(A) or (B), the Administrator shall consider whether to promulgate a rule pursuant to subsection (a)(2) that identifies as a significant new use any manufacturing, processing, use, distribution in commerce, or disposal of the chemical substance that does not conform to the restrictions imposed by the action or order, and, as applicable, initiate such a rulemaking or publish a statement describing the reasons of the Administrator for not initiating such a rulemaking.

(5) Workplace exposures.—To the extent practicable, the Administrator shall consult with the Assistant Secretary of Labor for Occupational Safety and Health prior to adopting any prohibition or other restriction relating to a chemical substance with respect to which the Administrator has made a determination under subsection (a)(3)(A) or (B) to address workplace exposures.

(g) Statement of Administrator finding.—If the Administrator finds in accordance with subsection (a)(3)(C) that a chemical substance or significant new use is not likely to present an unreasonable risk of injury to health or the environment, then notwithstanding any remaining portion of the applicable review period, the submitter of the notice may commence manufacture of the chemical substance or manufacture or processing for the significant new use, and the Administrator shall make public a statement of the Administrator's finding. Such a statement shall be submitted for publication in the Federal Register as soon as is practicable before the expiration of such period. Publication of such statement in accordance with the preceding sentence is not a prerequisite to the manufacturing or processing of the substance with respect to which the statement is to be published.

(h) Exemptions

(1) The Administrator may, upon application, exempt any person from any requirement of subsection (a) or (b) of this section to permit such person to manufacture or process a chemical substance for test marketing purposes—

(A) upon a showing by such person satisfactory to the Administrator that the manufacture, processing, distribution in commerce, use, and disposal of such substance, and that any combination of such activities, for such purposes will not present any unreasonable risk of injury to health or the environment, including an unreasonable risk to a potentially exposed or susceptible subpopulation identified by the Administrator for the specific conditions of use identified in the application, and

(B) under such restrictions as the Administrator considers appropriate.

(2) (A) The Administrator may, upon application, exempt any person from the requirement of subsection (b)(2) of this section to submit information for a chemical substance. If, upon receipt of an application under the preceding sentence, the Administrator determines that—

(i) the chemical substance with respect to which such application was submitted is equivalent to a chemical substance for which information has been submitted to the Administrator as required by subsection (b)(2) of this section, and

(ii) submission of information by the applicant on such substance would be duplicative of information which has been submitted to the Administrator in accordance with such subsection,

the Administrator shall exempt the applicant from the requirement to submit such information on such substance. No exemption which is granted under this subparagraph with respect to the submission of information for a chemical substance may take effect before the beginning of the reimbursement period applicable to such information.

(B) If the Administrator exempts any person, under subparagraph (A), from submitting information required under subsection (b)(2) of this section for a chemical substance because of the existence of previously submitted information and if such exemption is granted during the reimbursement period for such information, then (unless such person and the persons referred to in clauses (i) and (ii) agree on the amount and method of reimbursement) the Administrator shall order the person granted the exemption to provide fair and equitable reimbursement (in an amount determined under rules of the Administrator)—

(i) to the person who previously submitted the information on which the exemption was based, for a portion of the costs incurred by such person in complying with the requirement under subsection (b)(2) of this section to submit such information, and

(ii) to any other person who has been required under this subparagraph to contribute with respect to such costs, for a portion of the amount such person was required to contribute.

In promulgating rules for the determination of fair and equitable reimbursement to the persons described in clauses (i) and (ii) for costs incurred with respect to a chemical substance, the Administrator shall, after consultation with the Attorney General and the Federal Trade Commission, consider all relevant factors, including the effect on the competitive position of the person required to provide reimbursement in relation to the persons to be reimbursed and the share of the market for such substance of the person required to provide reimbursement in relation to the share of such market of the persons to be reimbursed. For purposes of judicial review, an order under this subparagraph shall be considered final agency action.

(C) For purposes of this paragraph, the reimbursement period for any previously submitted information for a chemical substance is a period—

(i) beginning on the date of the termination of the prohibition, imposed under this section, on the manufacture or processing of such substance by the person who submitted such information to the Administrator, and

(ii) ending—

(I) five years after the date referred to in clause (i), or

(II) at the expiration of a period which begins on the date referred to in clause (i) and is equal to the period which the Administrator determines was necessary to develop such information,

whichever is later.

(3) The requirements of subsections (a) and (b) of this section do not apply with respect to the manufacturing or processing of any chemical substance which is manufactured or processed, or proposed to be manufactured or processed, only in small quantities (as defined by the Administrator by rule) solely for purposes of—

(A) scientific experimentation or analysis, or

(B) chemical research on, or analysis of such substance or another substance, including such research or analysis for the development of a product,

if all persons engaged in such experimentation, research, or analysis for a manufacturer or processor are notified (in such form and manner as the Administrator may prescribe) of any risk to health which the manufacturer, processor, or the Administrator has reason to believe may be associated with such chemical substance.

(4) The Administrator may, upon application and by rule, exempt the manufacturer of any new chemical substance from all or part of the requirements of this section if the Administrator determines that the manufacture, processing, distribution in commerce, use, or disposal of such chemical substance, or that any combination of such activities, will not present an unreasonable risk of injury to health or the environment, including an unreasonable risk to a potentially exposed or susceptible subpopulation identified by the Administrator under the conditions of use.

(5) The Administrator may, upon application, make the requirements of subsections (a) and (b) of this section inapplicable with respect to the manufacturing or processing of any chemical substance (A) which exists temporarily as a result of a chemical reaction in the manufacturing or processing of a mixture or another chemical substance, and (B) to which there is no, and will not be, human or environmental exposure.

(6) Immediately upon receipt of an application under paragraph (1) or (5) the Administrator shall publish in the Federal Register notice of the receipt of such application. The Administrator shall give interested persons an opportunity to comment upon any such application and shall, within 45 days of its receipt, either approve or deny the application. The Administrator shall publish in the Federal Register notice of the approval or denial of such an application.

(i) Definitions.—

(1) For purposes of this section, the terms "manufacture" and "process" mean manufacturing or processing for commercial purposes.

(2) For purposes of this Act, the term "requirement" as used in this section shall not displace any statutory or common law.

(3) For purposes of this section, the term "applicable review period" means the period starting on the date the Administrator receives a notice under subsection (a)(1) and ending 90 days after that date, or on such date as is provided for in subsection (b)(1) or (c).

(Pub. L. No. 94–469, Title I, § 5, 90 Stat. 2012 (Oct. 11, 1976); renumbered Title I by Pub. L. No. 99–519, § 3(c)(1), 100 Stat. 2989 (Oct. 22, 1986); and amended by Pub. L. No. 114–182, §§ 5, 19(d) 130 Stat. 454–460, 506–507 (June 22, 2016).)

Retroactivity

Section 20 of Pub. L. No. 114–182, 130 Stat. 510 (June 22, 2016), provided that "[n]othing in sections 1 through 19, or the amendments made by sections 1 through 19, shall be interpreted to apply retroactively to any State, Federal, or maritime legal action filed before the date of enactment of this Act."

§ 2605. Prioritization, Risk Evaluation, and Regulation of Chemical Substances and Mixtures

[TSCA § 6]

(a) Scope of regulation

If the Administrator determines in accordance with subsection (b)(4)(A) that the manufacture, processing, distribution in commerce, use, or disposal of a chemical substance or mixture, or that any combination of such activities, presents an unreasonable risk of injury to health or the environment, the Administrator shall by rule and subject to section 18, and in accordance with subsection (c)(2) apply one or more of the following requirements to such substance or mixture to the extent necessary so that the chemical substance or mixture no longer presents such risk:

(1) A requirement (A) prohibiting or otherwise restricting the manufacturing, processing, or distribution in commerce of such substance or mixture, or (B) limiting the amount of such substance or mixture which may be manufactured, processed, or distributed in commerce.

(2) A requirement—

(A) prohibiting or otherwise restricting the manufacture, processing, or distribution in commerce of such substance or mixture for (i) a particular use or (ii) a particular use in a concentration in excess of a level specified by the Administrator in the rule imposing the requirement, or

(B) limiting the amount of such substance or mixture which may be manufactured, processed, or distributed in commerce for (i) a particular use or (ii) a particular use in a concentration in excess of a level specified by the Administrator in the rule imposing the requirement.

(3) A requirement that such substance or mixture or any article containing such substance or mixture be marked with or accompanied by clear and adequate minimum warnings and instructions with respect to its use, distribution in commerce, or disposal or with respect to any combination of such activities. The form and content of such minimum warnings and instructions shall be prescribed by the Administrator.

(4) A requirement that manufacturers and processors of such substance or mixture make and retain records of the processes used to manufacture or process such substance or mixture or monitor or conduct tests which are reasonable and necessary to assure compliance with the requirements of any rule applicable under this subsection.

(5) A requirement prohibiting or otherwise regulating any manner or method of commercial use of such substance or mixture.

(6) (A) A requirement prohibiting or otherwise regulating any manner or method of disposal of such substance or mixture, or of any article containing such substance or mixture, by its manufacturer or processor or by any other person who uses, or disposes of, it for commercial purposes.

(B) A requirement under subparagraph (A) may not require any person to take any action which would be in violation of any law or requirement of, or in effect for, a State or political subdivision, and shall require each person subject to it to notify each State and political subdivision in which a required disposal may occur of such disposal.

(7) A requirement directing manufacturers or processors of such substance or mixture (A) to give notice of such determination to distributors in commerce of such substance or mixture and, to the extent reasonably ascertainable, to other persons in possession of such substance or mixture or exposed to such substance or mixture, (B) to give public notice of such determination, and (C) to replace or repurchase such substance or mixture as elected by the person to which the requirement is directed.

Any requirement (or combination of requirements) imposed under this subsection may be limited in application to specified geographic areas.

(b) Risk evaluations.—

(1) Prioritizination for risk evaluations.—

(A) Establishment of process.—Not later than 1 year after the date of enactment of the Frank R. Lautenberg Chemical Safety for the 21st Century Act, the Administrator shall establish, by rule, a risk-based screening process, including criteria for designating chemical substances as high-priority substances for risk evaluations or low-priority substances for which risk evaluations are not warranted at the time. The process to designate the priority of chemical substances shall include a consideration of the hazard and exposure potential of a chemical substance or a category of chemical substances (including consideration of persistence and bioaccumulation, potentially exposed or susceptible subpopulations and storage near significant sources of drinking water), the conditions of use or significant changes in the conditions of use of the chemical substance, and the volume or significant changes in the volume of the chemical substance manufactured or processed.

(B) Identification of priorities for risk evaluation.—

(i) High-priority substances.—The Administrator shall designate as a high-priority substance a chemical substance that the Administrator concludes, without consideration of costs or other nonrisk factors, may present an unreasonable risk of injury to health or the environment because of a potential hazard and a potential route of exposure under the conditions of use, including an unreasonable risk to a potentially exposed or susceptible subpopulation identified as relevant by the Administrator.

(ii) Low-priority substances.—The Administrator shall designate a chemical substance as a low-priority substance if the Administrator concludes, based on information sufficient to establish, without consideration of costs or other nonrisk factors, that such substance does not meet the standard identified in clause (i) for designating a chemical substance a high-priority substance.

(C) Information request and review and proposed and final prioritization designation.—The rulemaking required in subparagraph (A) shall ensure that the time required to make a priority designation of a chemical substance be no shorter than nine months and no longer than 1 year, and that the process for such designations includes—

(i) a requirement that the Administrator request interested persons to submit relevant information on a chemical substance that the Administrator has initiated the prioritization process on, before proposing a priority designation for the chemical substance, and provide 90 days for such information to be provided;

(ii) a requirement that the Administrator publish each proposed designation of a chemical substance as a high- or low-priority substance, along with an identification of the information, analysis, and basis used to make the proposed designations, and provide 90 days for public comment on each such proposed designation; and

(iii) a process by which the Administrator may extend the deadline in clause (i) for up to three months in order to receive or evaluate information required to be submitted in accordance with section 4(a)(2)(B), subject to the limitation that if the information available to the Administrator at the end of such an extension remains insufficient to enable the designation of the chemical substance as a low-priority substance, the Administrator shall designate the chemical substance as a high-priority substance.

(2) Initial risk evaluations and subsequent designations of high- and low-priority substances.—

(A) Initial risk evaluations.—Not later than 180 days after the date of enactment of the Frank R. Lautenberg Chemical Safety for the 21st Century Act, the Administrator shall ensure that risk evaluations are being conducted on 10 chemical substances drawn from the 2014 update of the TSCA Work Plan for Chemical Assessments and shall publish the list of such chemical substances during the 180 day period.

(B) Additional risk evaluations.—Not later than three and one half years after the date of enactment of the Frank R. Lautenberg Chemical Safety for the 21st Century Act, the Administrator shall ensure that risk evaluations are being conducted on at least 20 high-priority substances and that at least 20 chemical substances have been designated as low-priority substances, subject to the limitation that at least 50 percent of all chemical substances on which risk evaluations are being conducted by the Administrator are drawn from the 2014 update of the TSCA Work Plan for Chemical Assessments.

(C) Continuing designations and risk evaluations.—The Administrator shall continue to designate priority substances and conduct risk evaluations in accordance with this subsection at a pace consistent with the ability of the Administrator to complete risk evaluations in accordance with the deadlines under paragraph (4)(G).

(D) Preference.—In designating high-priority substances, the Administrator shall give preference to—

(i) chemical substances that are listed in the 2014 update of the TSCA Work Plan for Chemical Assessments as having a Persistence and Bioaccumulation Score of 3; and

(ii) chemical substances that are listed in the 2014 update of the TSCA Work Plan for Chemical Assessments that are known human carcinogens and have high acute and chronic toxicity.

(E) Metals and metal compounds.—In identifying priorities for risk evaluation and conducting risk evaluations of metals and metal compounds, the Administrator shall use the Framework for Metals Risk Assessment of the Office of the Science Advisor, Risk Assessment Forum, and dated March 2007, or a successor document that addresses metals risk assessment and is peer reviewed by the Science Advisory Board.

(3) Initiation of risk evaluations; designations.—

(A) Risk evaluation initiation.—Upon designating a chemical substance as a high-priority substance, the Administrator shall initiate a risk evaluation on the substance.

(B) Revision.—The Administrator may revise the designation of a low-priority substance based on information made available to the Administrator.

(C) Ongoing designations.—The Administrator shall designate at least one high-priority substance upon the completion of each risk evaluation (other than risk evaluations for chemical substances designated under paragraph (4)(C)(ii)).

(4) Risk evaluation process and deadlines.—

(A) In general.—The Administrator shall conduct risk evaluations pursuant to this paragraph to determine whether a chemical substance presents an unreasonable risk of injury to health or the environment, without consideration of costs or other nonrisk factors, including an unreasonable risk to a potentially exposed or susceptible subpopulation identified as relevant to the risk evaluation by the Administrator, under the conditions of use.

(B) Establishment of process.—Not later than 1 year after the date of enactment of the Frank R. Lautenberg Chemical Safety for the 21st Century Act, the Administrator shall establish, by rule, a process to conduct risk evaluations in accordance with subparagraph (A).

(C) Requirement.—The Administrator shall conduct and publish risk evaluations, in accordance with the rule promulgated under subparagraph (B), for a chemical substance—

(i) that has been identified under paragraph (2)(A) or designated under paragraph (1)(B)(i); and

(ii) subject to subparagraph (E), that a manufacturer of the chemical substance has requested, in a form and manner and using the criteria prescribed by the Administrator in the rule promulgated under subparagraph (B), be subjected to a risk evaluation.

(D) Scope.—The Administrator shall, not later than 6 months after the initiation of a risk evaluation, publish the scope of the risk evaluation to be conducted, including the hazards, exposures, conditions of use, and the potentially exposed or susceptible subpopulations the Administrator expects to consider, and, for each designation of a high-priority substance, ensure not less than 12 months between the initiation of the prioritization process for the chemical substance and the publication of the scope of the risk evaluation for the chemical substance, and for risk evaluations conducted on chemical substances that have been identified under paragraph (2)(A) or selected under subparagraph (E)(iv)(II) of this paragraph, ensure not less than 3 months before the Administrator publishes the scope of the risk evaluation.

(E) Limitation and criteria.—

(i) Percentage requirements.—The Administrator shall ensure that, of the number of chemical substances that undergo a risk evaluation under clause (i) of subparagraph (C), the number of chemical substances undergoing a risk evaluation under clause (ii) of subparagraph (C) is—

(I) not less than 25 percent, if sufficient requests are made under clause (ii) of subparagraph (C); and

(II) not more than 50 percent.

(ii) Requested risk evaluations.—Requests for risk evaluations under subparagraph (C)(ii) shall be subject to the payment of fees pursuant to section 26(b), and the Administrator shall not expedite or otherwise provide special treatment to such risk evaluations.

(iii) Preference.—In deciding whether to grant requests under subparagraph (C)(ii), the Administrator shall give preference to requests for risk evaluations on chemical substances for which the Administrator determines that restrictions imposed by 1 or more States have the potential to have a significant impact on interstate commerce or health or the environment.

(iv) Exceptions.—

(I) Chemical substances for which requests have been granted under subparagraph (C)(ii) shall not be subject to section 18(b).

(II) Requests for risk evaluations on chemical substances which are made under subparagraph (C)(ii) and that are drawn from the 2014 update of the TSCA Work Plan for Chemical Assessments shall be granted at the discretion of the Administrator and not be subject to clause (i)(II).

(F) Requirements.—In conducting a risk evaluation under this subsection, the Administrator shall—

(i) integrate and assess available information on hazards and exposures for the conditions of use of the chemical substance, including information that is relevant to specific risks of injury to health or the environment and information on potentially exposed or susceptible subpopulations identified as relevant by the Administrator;

(ii) describe whether aggregate or sentinel exposures to a chemical substance under the conditions of use were considered, and the basis for that consideration;

(iii) not consider costs or other nonrisk factors;

(iv) take into account, where relevant, the likely duration, intensity, frequency, and number of exposures under the conditions of use of the chemical substance; and

(v) describe the weight of the scientific evidence for the identified hazard and exposure.

(G) Deadlines.—The Administrator—

(i) shall complete a risk evaluation for a chemical substance as soon as practicable, but not later than 3 years after the date on which the Administrator initiates the risk evaluation under subparagraph (C); and

(ii) may extend the deadline for a risk evaluation for not more than 6 months.

(H) Notice and comment.—The Administrator shall provide no less than 30 days public notice and an opportunity for comment on a draft risk evaluation prior to publishing a final risk evaluation.";

(c) Promulgation of subsection (a) rules.—

(1) Deadlines.—If the Administrator determines that a chemical substance presents an unreasonable risk of injury to health or the environment in accordance with subsection (b)(4)(A), the Administrator—

(A) shall propose in the Federal Register a rule under subsection (a) for the chemical substance not later than 1 year after the date on which the final risk evaluation regarding the chemical substance is published;

(B) shall publish in the Federal Register a final rule not later than 2 years after the date on which the final risk evaluation regarding the chemical substance is published; and

(C) may extend the deadlines under this paragraph for not more than 2 years, subject to the condition that the aggregate length of extensions under this subparagraph and subsection (b)(4)(G)(ii) does not exceed 2 years, and subject to the limitation that the Administrator may not extend a deadline for the publication of a proposed or final rule regarding a chemical substance drawn from the 2014 update of the TSCA Work Plan for Chemical Assessments or a chemical substance that, with respect to persistence and bioaccumulation, scores high for 1 and either high or moderate for the other, pursuant to the TSCA Work Plan Chemicals Methods Document published by the Administrator in February 2012 (or a successor scoring system), without adequate public justification that demonstrates, following a review of the information reasonably available to the Administrator, that the Administrator cannot complete the proposed or final rule without additional information regarding the chemical substance.

(2) Requirements for rule.—

(A) Statement of effects.—In proposing and promulgating a rule under subsection (a) with respect to a chemical substance or mixture, the Administrator shall consider and publish a statement based on reasonably available information with respect to—

(i) the effects of the chemical substance or mixture on health and the magnitude of the exposure of human beings to the chemical substance or mixture;

(ii) the effects of the chemical substance or mixture on the environment and the magnitude of the exposure of the environment to such substance or mixture;

(iii) the benefits of the chemical substance or mixture for various uses; and

(iv) the reasonably ascertainable economic consequences of the rule, including consideration of—

(I) the likely effect of the rule on the national economy, small business, technological innovation, the environment, and public health;

(II) the costs and benefits of the proposed and final regulatory action and of the 1 or more primary alternative regulatory actions considered by the Administrator; and

(III) the cost effectiveness of the proposed regulatory action and of the 1 or more primary alternative regulatory actions considered by the Administrator.

(B) Selecting requirements.—In selecting among prohibitions and other restrictions, the Administrator shall factor in, to the extent practicable, the considerations under subparagraph (A) in accordance with subsection (a).

(C) Consideration of alternatives.—Based on the information published under subparagraph (A), in deciding whether to prohibit or restrict in a manner that substantially prevents a specific condition of use of a chemical substance or mixture, and in setting an appropriate transition period for such action, the Administrator shall consider, to the extent practicable, whether technically and economically feasible alternatives that benefit health or the environment, compared to the use so proposed to be prohibited or restricted, will be reasonably available as a substitute when the proposed prohibition or other restriction takes effect.

(D) Replacement parts.—

(i) In general.—The Administrator shall exempt replacement parts for complex durable goods and complex consumer goods that are designed prior to the date of publication in the Federal Register of the rule under subsection (a), unless the Administrator finds that such replacement parts contribute significantly to the risk, identified in a risk evaluation conducted under subsection (b)(4)(A), to the general population or to an identified potentially exposed or susceptible subpopulation.

(ii) Definitions.—In this subparagraph—

(I) the term "complex consumer goods" means electronic or mechanical devices composed of multiple manufactured components, with an intended useful life of 3 or more years, where the product is typically not consumed, destroyed, or discarded after a single use, and the components of which would be impracticable to redesign or replace; and

(II) the term "complex durable goods" means manufactured goods composed of 100 or more manufactured components, with an intended useful life of 5 or more years, where the product is typically not consumed, destroyed, or discarded after a single use.

(E) Articles.—In selecting among prohibitions and other restrictions, the Administrator shall apply such prohibitions or other restrictions to an article or category of articles containing the chemical substance or mixture only to the extent necessary to address the identified risks from exposure to the chemical substance or mixture from the article or category of articles so that the substance or mixture does not present an unreasonable risk of injury to health or the environment identified in the risk evaluation conducted in accordance with subsection (b)(4)(A).

(3) Procedures.—When prescribing a rule under subsection (a) the Administrator shall proceed in accordance with section 553 of title 5, United States Code (without regard to any reference in such section to sections 556 and 557 of such title), and shall also—

(A) publish a notice of proposed rulemaking stating with particularity the reason for the proposed rule;

(B) allow interested persons to submit written data, views, and arguments, and make all such submissions publicly available;

(C) promulgate a final rule based on the matter in the rulemaking record; and

(D) make and publish with the rule the determination described in subsection (a)

(d) Effective date

(1) In general.—In any rule under subsection (a), the Administrator shall—

(A) specify the date on which it shall take effect, which date shall be as soon as practicable;

(B) except as provided in subparagraphs (C) and (D), specify mandatory compliance dates for all of the requirements under a rule under subsection (a), which shall be as soon as practicable, but not later than 5 years after the date of promulgation of the rule, except in a case of a use exempted under subsection (g);

(C) specify mandatory compliance dates for the start of ban or phase-out requirements under a rule under subsection (a), which shall be as soon as practicable, but not later than 5 years after the date of promulgation of the rule, except in the case of a use exempted under subsection (g);

(D) specify mandatory compliance dates for full implementation of ban or phase-out requirements under a rule under subsection (a), which shall be as soon as practicable; and

(E) provide for a reasonable transition period.

(2) Variability.—As determined by the Administrator, the compliance dates established under paragraph (1) may vary for different affected persons.

(3) (A) The Administrator may declare a proposed rule under subsection (a) of this section to be effective, and compliance with the proposed requirements to be mandatory, upon publication in the Federal Register of the proposed rule and until the compliance dates applicable to such requirements in a final rule promulgated under section 6(a) or until the Administrator revokes such proposed rule, in accordance with subparagraph (B), if—

(i) the Administrator determines that—

(I) the manufacture, processing, distribution in commerce, use, or disposal of the chemical substance or mixture subject to such proposed rule or any combination of such activities is likely to result in an unreasonable risk of serious or widespread injury to health or the environment before such effective date without consideration of costs or other non-risk factors; and

(II) making such proposed rule so effective is necessary to protect the public interest; and

(ii) in the case of a proposed rule to prohibit the manufacture, processing, or distribution of a chemical substance or mixture because of the risk determined under clause (i)(I), a court has in an action under section 2606 of this title granted relief with respect to such risk associated with such substance or mixture.

Such a proposed rule which is made so effective shall not, for purposes of judicial review, be considered final agency action.

(B) If the Administrator makes a proposed rule effective upon its publication in the Federal Register, the Administrator shall, as expeditiously as possible, give interested persons prompt notice of such action in accordance with subsection (c), and either promulgate such rule (as proposed or with modifications) or revoke it.

(e) Polychlorinated biphenyls

(1) Within six months after January 1, 1977, the Administrator shall promulgate rules to—

(A) prescribe methods for the disposal of polychlorinated biphenyls, and

(B) require polychlorinated biphenyls to be marked with clear and adequate warnings, and instructions with respect to their processing, distribution in commerce, use, or disposal or with respect to any combination of such activities.

Requirements prescribed by rules under this paragraph shall be consistent with the requirements of paragraphs (2) and (3).

(2) **(A)** Except as provided under subparagraph (B), effective one year after January 1, 1977, no person may manufacture, process, or distribute in commerce or use any polychlorinated biphenyl in any manner other than in a totally enclosed manner.

(B) The Administrator may by rule authorize the manufacture, processing, distribution in commerce or use (or any combination of such activities) of any polychlorinated biphenyl in a manner other than in a totally enclosed manner if the Administrator finds that such manufacture, processing, distribution in commerce, or use (or combination of such activities) will not present an unreasonable risk of injury to health or the environment.

(C) For the purposes of this paragraph, the term "totally enclosed manner" means any manner which will ensure that any exposure of human beings or the environment to a polychlorinated biphenyl will be insignificant as determined by the Administrator by rule.

(3) **(A)** Except as provided in subparagraphs (B) and (C)—

(i) no person may manufacture any polychlorinated biphenyl after two years after January 1, 1977, and

(ii) no person may process or distribute in commerce any polychlorinated biphenyl after two and one-half years after such date.

(B) Any person may petition the Administrator for an exemption from the requirements of subparagraph (A), and the Administrator may grant by rule such an exemption if the Administrator finds that—

(i) an unreasonable risk of injury to health or environment would not result, and

(ii) good faith efforts have been made to develop a chemical substance which does not present an unreasonable risk of injury to health or the environment and which may be substituted for such polychlorinated biphenyl.

An exemption granted under this subparagraph shall be subject to such terms and conditions as the Administrator may prescribe and shall be in effect for such period (but not more than one year from the date it is granted) as the Administrator may prescribe.

(C) Subparagraph (A) shall not apply to the distribution in commerce of any polychlorinated biphenyl if such polychlorinated biphenyl was sold for purposes other than resale before two and one half years after October 11, 1976.

(D) Omitted

(4) Any rule under paragraph (1), (2)(B), or (3)(B) shall be promulgated in accordance with paragraph (3) of subsection (c) of this section.

(5) This subsection does not limit the authority of the Administrator, under any other provision of this chapter or any other Federal law, to take action respecting any polychlorinated biphenyl.

(f) **Mercury**

(1) **Prohibition on sale, distribution, or transfer of elemental mercury by Federal agencies**

Except as provided in paragraph (2), effective beginning on October 14, 2008, no Federal agency shall convey, sell, or distribute to any other Federal agency, any State or local government agency, or any private individual or entity any elemental mercury under the control or jurisdiction of the Federal agency.

(2) Exceptions

Paragraph (1) shall not apply to—

(A) a transfer between Federal agencies of elemental mercury for the sole purpose of facilitating storage of mercury to carry out this chapter; or

(B) a conveyance, sale, distribution, or transfer of coal.

(3) Leases of Federal coal

Nothing in this subsection prohibits the leasing of coal.

(g) Exemptions.—

(1) Criteria for exemption.—The Administrator may, as part of a rule promulgated under subsection (a), or in a separate rule, grant an exemption from a requirement of a subsection (a) rule for a specific condition of use of a chemical substance or mixture, if the Administrator finds that—

(A) the specific condition of use is a critical or essential use for which no technically and economically feasible safer alternative is available, taking into consideration hazard and exposure;

(B) compliance with the requirement, as applied with respect to the specific condition of use, would significantly disrupt the national economy, national security, or critical infrastructure; or

(C) the specific condition of use of the chemical substance or mixture, as compared to reasonably available alternatives, provides a substantial benefit to health, the environment, or public safety.

(2) Exemption analysis and statement.—In proposing an exemption under this subsection, the Administrator shall analyze the need for the exemption, and shall make public the analysis and a statement describing how the analysis was taken into account.

(3) Period of exemption.—The Administrator shall establish, as part of a rule under this subsection, a time limit on any exemption for a time to be determined by the Administrator as reasonable on a case-by-case basis, and, by rule, may extend, modify, or eliminate an exemption if the Administrator determines, on the basis of reasonably available information and after adequate public justification, the exemption warrants extension or modification or is no longer necessary.

(4) Conditions.—As part of a rule promulgated under this subsection, the Administrator shall include conditions, including reasonable recordkeeping, monitoring, and reporting requirements, to the extent that the Administrator determines the conditions are necessary to protect health and the environment while achieving the purposes of the exemption.

(h) Chemicals that are persistent, bioaccumulative, and toxic.—

(1) Expedited action.—Not later than 3 years after the date of enactment of the Frank R. Lautenberg Chemical Safety for the 21st Century Act, the Administrator shall propose rules under subsection (a) with respect to chemical substances identified in the 2014 update of the TSCA Work Plan for Chemical Assessments—

(A) that the Administrator has a reasonable basis to conclude are toxic and that with respect to persistence and bioaccumulation score high for one and either high or moderate for the other, pursuant to the TSCA Work Plan Chemicals Methods Document published by the Administrator in February 2012 (or a successor scoring system), and are not a metal or a metal compound, and for which the Administrator has not completed a Work Plan Problem Formulation, initiated a review under section 5, or entered into a consent agreement under section 4, prior to the date of enactment of the Frank R. Lautenberg Chemical Safety for the 21st Century Act; and

(B) exposure to which under the conditions of use is likely to the general population or to a potentially exposed or susceptible subpopulation identified by the Administrator, or the environment, on the basis of an exposure and use assessment conducted by the Administrator.

(2) No risk evaluation required.—The Administrator shall not be required to conduct risk evaluations on chemical substances that are subject to paragraph (1).

(3) Final rule.—Not later than 18 months after proposing a rule pursuant to paragraph (1), the Administrator shall promulgate a final rule under subsection (a).

(4) Selecting restrictions.—In selecting among prohibitions and other restrictions promulgated in a rule under subsection (a) pursuant to paragraph (1), the Administrator shall address the risks of injury to health or the environment that the Administrator determines are presented by the chemical substance and shall reduce exposure to the substance to the extent practicable.

(5) Relationship to subsection (b).—If, at any time prior to the date that is 90 days after the date of enactment of the Frank R. Lautenberg Chemical Safety for the 21st Century Act, the Administrator makes a designation under subsection (b)(1)(B)(i), or receives a request under subsection (b)(4)(C)(ii), such chemical substance shall not be subject to this subsection, except that in selecting among prohibitions and other restrictions promulgated in a rule pursuant to subsection (a), the Administrator shall both ensure that the chemical substance meets the rulemaking standard under subsection (a) and reduce exposure to the substance to the extent practicable.

(i) Final agency action.—Under this section and subject to section 18—

(1) a determination by the Administrator under subsection (b)(4)(A) that a chemical substance does not present an unreasonable risk of injury to health or the environment shall be issued by order and considered to be a final agency action, effective beginning on the date of issuance of the order; and

(2) a final rule promulgated under subsection (a), including the associated determination by the Administrator under subsection (b)(4)(A) that a chemical substance presents an unreasonable risk of injury to health or the environment, shall be considered to be a final agency action, effective beginning on the date of promulgation of the final rule.

(j) Definition.—For the purposes of this Act, the term "requirement" as used in this section shall not displace statutory or common law.

(Pub. L. No. 94–469, Title I, § 6, 90 Stat. 2020 (Oct. 11, 1976); renumbered Title I by Pub. L. No. 99–519, § 3(c)(1), 100 Stat. 2989 (Oct. 22, 1986); and amended by Pub. L. No. 109–364, Div. A, Title III, § 317(a), 120 Stat. 2142 (Oct. 17, 2006); Pub. L. No. 110–414, § 3, 122 Stat. 4342 (Oct. 14, 2008); Pub. L. No. 114–182, § 6, 130 Stat. 460–470 (June 22, 2016).)

HISTORICAL AND STATUTORY NOTES

References in Text

This chapter, referred to in text, originally read "this Act", meaning the Toxic Substances Control Act, Pub. L. No. 94–469, 90 Stat. 2003 (Oct. 11, 1976), which principally enacted this chapter. See Short Title note set out under 15 U.S.C.A. § 2601 and Tables.

Sunset Provisions

Pub. L. No. 109–364, Div. A, Title III, § 317(b), 120 Stat. 2142 (Oct. 17, 2006), provided that: "The amendments made by subsection (a) [amending subsec. (e)(3)(A), (B), and (D) of this section] shall cease to have effect on September 30, 2012. The termination of the authority to grant exemptions pursuant to such amendments shall not effect the validity of any exemption granted prior to such date."

Retroactivity

Section 20 of Pub. L. No. 114–182, 130 Stat. 510 (June 22, 2016), provided that "[n]othing in sections 1 through 19, or the amendments made by sections 1 through 19, shall be interpreted to apply retroactively to any State, Federal, or maritime legal action filed before the date of enactment of this Act."

§ 2606. Imminent hazards

[TSCA § 7]

(a) Actions authorized and required

(1) The Administrator may commence a civil action in an appropriate district court of the United States—

(A) for seizure of an imminently hazardous chemical substance or mixture or any article containing such a substance or mixture,

(B) for relief (as authorized by subsection (b) of this section) against any person who manufactures, processes, distributes in commerce, or uses, or disposes of, an imminently hazardous chemical substance or mixture or any article containing such a substance or mixture, or

(C) for both such seizure and relief.

A civil action may be commenced under this paragraph notwithstanding the existence of a determination under section 5 or 6, a rule under section 4, 5, or 6 or title IV, an order under section 4, 5, or 6 or title IV, or a consent agreement under section 4, and notwithstanding the pendency of any administrative or judicial proceeding under any provision of this chapter.

(2) If the Administrator has not made a rule under section 6(a) of this title immediately effective (as authorized by section 6(d)(3)(A)(i) of this title) with respect to an imminently hazardous chemical substance or mixture, the Administrator shall commence in a district court of the United States with respect to such substance or mixture or article containing such substance or mixture a civil action described in subparagraph (A), (B), or (C) of paragraph (1).

(b) Relief authorized

(1) The district court of the United States in which an action under subsection (a) of this section is brought shall have jurisdiction to grant such temporary or permanent relief as may be necessary to protect health or the environment from the unreasonable risk (as identified by the Administrator without consideration of costs or other nonrisk factors) associated with the chemical substance, mixture, or article involved in such action.

(2) In the case of an action under subsection (a) of this section brought against a person who manufactures, processes, or distributes in commerce a chemical substance or mixture or an article containing a chemical substance or mixture, the relief authorized by paragraph (1) may include the issuance of a mandatory order requiring (A) in the case of purchasers of such substance, mixture, or article known to the defendant, notification to such purchasers of the risk associated with it; (B) public notice of such risk; (C) recall; (D) the replacement or repurchase of such substance, mixture, or article; or (E) any combination of the actions described in the preceding clauses.

(3) In the case of an action under subsection (a) of this section against a chemical substance, mixture, or article, such substance, mixture, or article may be proceeded against by process of libel for its seizure and condemnation. Proceedings in such an action shall conform as nearly as possible to proceedings in rem in admiralty.

(c) Venue and consolidation

(1) (A) An action under subsection (a) of this section against a person who manufactures, processes, or distributes a chemical substance or mixture or an article containing a chemical substance or mixture may be brought in the United States District Court for the District of Columbia, or for any judicial district in which any of the defendants is found, resides, or transacts business; and process in such an action may be served on a defendant in any other district in which such defendant resides or may be found. An action under subsection (a) of this section against a chemical substance, mixture, or article may be brought in any United States district court within the jurisdiction of which the substance, mixture, or article is found.

(B) In determining the judicial district in which an action may be brought under subsection (a) of this section in instances in which such action may be brought in more than one judicial district, the Administrator shall take into account the convenience of the parties.

(C) Subpeonas[1] requiring attendance of witnesses in an action brought under subsection (a) of this section may be served in any judicial district.

(2) Whenever proceedings under subsection (a) of this section involving identical chemical substances, mixtures, or articles are pending in courts in two or more judicial districts, they shall be consolidated for trial by order of any such court upon application reasonably made by any party in interest, upon notice to all parties in interest.

(d) Action under section 2605

Where appropriate, concurrently with the filing of an action under subsection (a) of this section or as soon thereafter as may be practicable, the Administrator shall initiate a proceeding for the promulgation of a rule under section 2605(a) of this title.

(e) Representation

Notwithstanding any other provision of law, in any action under subsection (a) of this section, the Administrator may direct attorneys of the Environmental Protection Agency to appear and represent the Administrator in such an action.

(f) "Imminently hazardous chemical substance or mixture" defined

For the purposes of subsection (a) of this section, the term "imminently hazardous chemical substance or mixture" means a chemical substance or mixture which presents an imminent and unreasonable risk of serious or widespread injury to health or the environment, without consideration of costs or other nonrisk factors. Such a risk to health or the environment shall be considered imminent if it is shown that the manufacture, processing, distribution in commerce, use, or disposal of the chemical substance or mixture, or that any combination of such activities, is likely to result in such injury to health or the environment before a final rule under section 2605 of this title can protect against such risk.

(Pub. L. No. 94–469, Title I, § 7, 90 Stat. 2026 (Oct. 11, 1976); renumbered Title I by Pub. L. No. 99–519, § 3(c)(1), 100 Stat. 2989 (Oct. 22, 1986); and amended by Pub. L. No. 102–550, Title X, § 1021(b)(1), 106 Stat. 3923 (Oct. 28, 1992); Pub. L. No. 114–182, §§ 7, 19(f) 130 Stat. 470, 507 (June 22, 2016).)

[1] So in original. Probably should be "subpoenas".

Retroactivity

Section 20 of Pub. L. No. 114–182, 130 Stat. 510 (June 22, 2016), provided that "[n]othing in sections 1 through 19, or the amendments made by sections 1 through 19, shall be interpreted to apply retroactively to any State, Federal, or maritime legal action filed before the date of enactment of this Act."

§ 2607. Reporting and retention of information

[TSCA § 8]

(a) Reports

(1) The Administrator shall promulgate rules under which—

(A) each person (other than a small manufacturer or processor) who manufactures or processes or proposes to manufacture or process a chemical substance (other than a chemical substance described in subparagraph (B)(ii)) shall maintain such records, and shall submit to the Administrator such reports, as the Administrator may reasonably require, and

(B) each person (other than a small manufacturer or processor) who manufactures or processes or proposes to manufacture or process—

(i) a mixture, or

(ii) a chemical substance in small quantities (as defined by the Administrator by rule) solely for purposes of scientific experimentation or analysis or chemical research on, or analysis of, such substance or another substance, including any such research or analysis for the development of a product,

shall maintain records and submit to the Administrator reports but only to the extent the Administrator determines the maintenance of records or submission of reports, or both, is necessary for the effective enforcement of this chapter.

The Administrator may not require in a rule promulgated under this paragraph the maintenance of records or the submission of reports with respect to changes in the proportions of the components of a mixture unless the Administrator finds that the maintenance of such records or the submission of such reports, or both, is necessary for the effective enforcement of this chapter. For purposes of the compilation of the list of chemical substances required under subsection (b) of this section, the Administrator shall promulgate rules pursuant to this subsection not later than 180 days after January 1, 1977.

(2) The Administrator may require under paragraph (1) maintenance of records and reporting with respect to the following insofar as known to the person making the report or insofar as reasonably ascertainable:

(A) The common or trade name, the chemical identity, and the molecular structure of each chemical substance or mixture for which such a report is required.

(B) The categories or proposed categories of use of each such substance or mixture.

(C) The total amount of each such substance and mixture manufactured or processed, reasonable estimates of the total amount to be manufactured or processed, the amount manufactured or processed for each of its categories of use, and reasonable estimates of the amount to be manufactured or processed for each of its categories of use or proposed categories of use.

(D) A description of the byproducts resulting from the manufacture, processing, use, or disposal of each such substance or mixture.

(E) All existing information concerning the environmental and health effects of such substance or mixture.

(F) The number of individuals exposed, and reasonable estimates of the number who will be exposed, to such substance or mixture in their places of employment and the duration of such exposure.

(G) In the initial report under paragraph (1) on such substance or mixture, the manner or method of its disposal, and in any subsequent report on such substance or mixture, any change in such manner or method.

(3) **(A)** **(i)** The Administrator may by rule require a small manufacturer or processor of a chemical substance to submit to the Administrator such information respecting the chemical substance as the Administrator may require for publication of the first list of chemical substances required by subsection (b) of this section.

(ii) The Administrator may by rule require a small manufacturer or processor of a chemical substance or mixture—

(I) subject to a rule proposed or promulgated under section 2603, 2604(b)(4), or 2605 of this title, an order in effect under section 4 or 5(e), or a consent agreement under section 4, or

(II) with respect to which relief has been granted pursuant to a civil action brought under section 2604 or 2606 of this title,

to maintain such records on such substance or mixture, and to submit to the Administrator such reports on such substance or mixture, as the Administrator may reasonably require. A rule under this clause requiring reporting may require reporting with respect to the matters referred to in paragraph (2).

(B) The Administrator, after consultation with the Administrator of the Small Business Administration, shall by rule prescribe standards for determining the manufacturers and processors which qualify as small manufacturers and processors for purposes of this paragraph and paragraph (1).

(C) Not later than 180 days after the date of enactment of the Frank R. Lautenberg Chemical Safety for the 21st Century Act, and not less frequently than once every 10 years thereafter, the Administrator, after consultation with the Administrator of the Small Business Administration, shall—

(i) review the adequacy of the standards prescribed under subparagraph (B); and

(ii) after providing public notice and an opportunity for comment, make a determination as to whether revision of the standards is warranted.

(4) Contents.—The rules promulgated pursuant to paragraph (1)—

(A) may impose differing reporting and recordkeeping requirements on manufacturers and processors; and

(B) shall include the level of detail necessary to be reported, including the manner by which use and exposure information may be reported.

(5) Administration.—In carrying out this section, the Administrator shall, to the extent feasible—

(A) not require reporting which is unnecessary or duplicative;

(B) minimize the cost of compliance with this section and the rules issued thereunder on small manufacturers and processors; and

(C) apply any reporting obligations to those persons likely to have information relevant to the effective implementation of this title.

(6) Negotiated rulemaking.—(A) The Administrator shall enter into a negotiated rulemaking pursuant to subchapter III of chapter 5 of title 5, United States Code, to develop and publish, not later than 3 years after the date of enactment of the Frank R. Lautenberg Chemical Safety for the 21st Century Act, a proposed rule providing for limiting the reporting requirements, under this subsection, for manufacturers of any inorganic byproducts, when such byproducts, whether by the byproduct manufacturer or by any other person, are subsequently recycled, reused, or reprocessed.

(B) Not later than 3 and one-half years after such date of enactment, the Administrator shall publish a final rule resulting from such negotiated rulemaking.

(7) PFAS Data.—Not later than January 1, 2023, the Administrator shall promulgate a rule in accordance with this subsection requiring each person who has manufactured a chemical substance that is a perfluoroalkyl or polyfluoroalkyl substance in any year since January 1, 2011, to submit to the Administrator a report that includes, for each year since January 1, 2011, the information described in subparagraphs (A) through (G) of paragraph (2).

(b) Inventory

(1) The Administrator shall compile, keep current, and publish a list of each chemical substance which is manufactured or processed in the United States. Such list shall at least include each chemical substance which any person reports, under section 2604 of this title or subsection (a) of this section, is manufactured or processed in the United States. Such list may not include any chemical substance which was not manufactured or processed in the United States within three years before the effective date of the rules promulgated pursuant to the last sentence of subsection (a)(1) of this section. In the case of a chemical substance for which a notice is submitted in accordance with section 2604 of this title, such chemical substance shall be included in such list as of the earliest date (as determined by the Administrator) on which such substance was manufactured or processed in the United States. The Administrator shall first publish such a list not later than 315 days after January 1, 1977. The Administrator shall not include in such list any chemical substance which is manufactured or processed only in small quantities (as defined by the Administrator by rule) solely for purposes of scientific experimentation or analysis or chemical research on, or analysis of, such substance or another substance, including such research or analysis for the development of a product.

(2) To the extent consistent with the purposes of this chapter, the Administrator may, in lieu of listing, pursuant to paragraph (1), a chemical substance individually, list a category of chemical substances in which such substance is included.

(3) Nomenclature.—

(A) In general.—In carrying out paragraph (1), the Administrator shall—

(i) maintain the use of Class 2 nomenclature in use on the date of enactment of the Frank R. Lautenberg Chemical Safety for the 21st Century Act;

(ii) maintain the use of the Soap and Detergent Association Nomenclature System, published in March 1978 by the Administrator in section 1 of addendum III of the document entitled 'Candidate List of Chemical Substances', and further described in the appendix A of volume I of the 1985 edition of the **Toxic Substances Control Act** Substances Inventory (EPA Document No. EPA–560/7–85–002a); and

(iii) treat the individual members of the categories of chemical substances identified by the Administrator as statutory mixtures, as defined in Inventory descriptions established by the Administrator, as being included on the list established under paragraph (1).

(B) Multiple nomenclature listings.—If a manufacturer or processor demonstrates to the Administrator that a chemical substance appears multiple times on the list published under paragraph (1) under different CAS numbers, the Administrator may recognize the multiple listings as a single chemical substance.

(4) Chemical substances in commerce.—

(A) Rules.—

(i) In general.—Not later than 1 year after the date of enactment of the Frank R. Lautenberg Chemical Safety for the 21st Century Act, the Administrator, by rule, shall require manufacturers, and may require processors, subject to the limitations under subsection (a)(5)(A), to notify the Administrator, by not later than 180 days after the date on which the final rule is published in the Federal Register, of each chemical substance on the list published under paragraph (1) that the manufacturer or processor, as applicable, has manufactured or processed for a nonexempt commercial purpose during the 10-year period ending on the day before the date of enactment of the Frank R. Lautenberg Chemical Safety for the 21st Century Act.

(ii) Active substances.—The Administrator shall designate chemical substances for which notices are received under clause (i) to be active substances on the list published under paragraph (1).

(iii) Inactive substances.—The Administrator shall designate chemical substances for which no notices are received under clause (i) to be inactive substances on the list published under paragraph (1).

(iv) Limitation.—No chemical substance on the list published under paragraph (1) shall be removed from such list by reason of the implementation of this subparagraph, or be subject to section 5(a)(1)(A)(i) by reason of a change to active status under paragraph (5)(B).

(B) Confidential chemical substances.—In promulgating a rule under subparagraph (A), the Administrator shall—

(i) maintain the list under paragraph (1), which shall include a confidential portion and a nonconfidential portion consistent with this section and section 14;

(ii) require any manufacturer or processor of a chemical substance on the confidential portion of the list published under paragraph (1) that seeks to maintain an existing claim for protection against disclosure of the specific chemical identity of the chemical substance as confidential pursuant to section 14 to submit a notice under subparagraph (A) that includes such request;

(iii) require the substantiation of those claims pursuant to section 14 and in accordance with the review plan described in subparagraph (C); and

(iv) move any active chemical substance for which no request was received to maintain an existing claim for protection against disclosure of the specific chemical identity of the chemical substance as confidential from the confidential portion of the list published under paragraph (1) to the nonconfidential portion of that list.

(C) Review plan.—Not later than 1 year after the date on which the Administrator compiles the initial list of active substances pursuant to subparagraph (A), the Administrator shall promulgate a rule that establishes a plan to review all claims to protect the specific chemical identities of chemical substances on the confidential portion of the list published under paragraph (1) that are asserted pursuant to subparagraph (B).

(D) Requirements of a review plan.—In establishing the review plan under subparagraph (C), the Administrator shall—

(i) require, at a time specified by the Administrator, all manufacturers or processors asserting claims under subparagraph (B) to substantiate the claim, in accordance with section 14, unless the manufacturer or processor has substantiated the claim in a submission made to the Administrator during the 5-year period ending on the last day of the of the time period specified by the Administrator; and

(ii) in accordance with section 14—

(I) review each substantiation—

(aa) submitted pursuant to clause (i) to determine if the claim qualifies for protection from disclosure; and

(bb) submitted previously by a manufacturer or processor and relied on in lieu of the substantiation required pursuant to clause (i), if the substantiation has not been previously reviewed by the Administrator, to determine if the claim warrants protection from disclosure;

(II) approve, approve in part and deny in part, or deny each claim; and

(III) except as provided in this section and section 14, protect from disclosure information for which the Administrator approves such a claim for a period of 10 years, unless, prior to the expiration of the period—

(aa) the person notifies the Administrator that the person is withdrawing the claim, in which case the Administrator shall not protect the information from disclosure; or

(bb) the Administrator otherwise becomes aware that the information does not qualify for protection from disclosure, in which case the Administrator shall take the actions described in section 14(g)(2).

(E) Timeline for completion of reviews.—

(i) In general.—The Administrator shall implement the review plan so as to complete reviews of all claims specified in subparagraph (C) not later than 5 years after the date on which the Administrator compiles the initial list of active substances pursuant to subparagraph (A).

(ii) Considerations.—

(I) In general.—The Administrator may extend the deadline for completion of the reviews for not more than 2 additional years, after an adequate public justification, if the Administrator determines that the extension is necessary based on the number of claims needing review and the available resources.

(II) Annual review goal and results.—At the beginning of each year, the Administrator shall publish an annual goal for reviews and the number of reviews completed in the prior year.

(5) Active and inactive substances.—

(A) In general.—The Administrator shall keep designations of active substances and inactive substances on the list published under paragraph (1) current.

(B) Change to active status.—

(i) **In general.**—Any person that intends to manufacture or process for a nonexempt commercial purpose a chemical substance that is designated as an inactive substance shall notify the Administrator before the date on which the inactive substance is manufactured or processed.

(ii) **Confidential chemical identity.**—If a person submitting a notice under clause (i) for an inactive substance on the confidential portion of the list published under paragraph (1) seeks to maintain an existing claim for protection against disclosure of the specific chemical identity of the inactive substance as confidential, the person shall, consistent with the requirements of section 14—

(I) in the notice submitted under clause (i), assert the claim; and

(II) by not later than 30 days after providing the notice under clause (i), substantiate the claim.

(iii) **Active status.**—On receiving a notification under clause (i), the Administrator shall—

(I) designate the applicable chemical substance as an active substance;

(II) pursuant to section 14, promptly review any claim and associated substantiation submitted pursuant to clause (ii) for protection against disclosure of the specific chemical identity of the chemical substance and approve, approve in part and deny in part, or deny the claim;

(III) except as provided in this section and section 14, protect from disclosure the specific chemical identity of the chemical substance for which the Administrator approves a claim under subclause (II) for a period of 10 years, unless, prior to the expiration of the period—

(aa) the person notifies the Administrator that the person is withdrawing the claim, in which case the Administrator shall not protect the information from disclosure; or

(bb) the Administrator otherwise becomes aware that the information does not qualify for protection from disclosure, in which case the Administrator shall take the actions described in section 14(g)(2); and

(IV) pursuant to section 6(b), review the priority of the chemical substance as the Administrator determines to be necessary.

(C) **Category status.**—The list of inactive substances shall not be considered to be a category for purposes of section 26(c).

(6) **Interim list of active substances.**—Prior to the promulgation of the rule required under paragraph (4)(A), the Administrator shall designate the chemical substances reported under part 711 of title 40, Code of Federal Regulations (as in effect on the date of enactment of the Frank R. Lautenberg Chemical Safety for the 21st Century Act), during the reporting period that most closely preceded the date of enactment of the Frank R. Lautenberg Chemical Safety for the 21st Century Act, as the interim list of active substances for the purposes of section 6(b).

(7) **Public information.**—Subject to this subsection and section 14, the Administrator shall make available to the public—

(A) each specific chemical identity on the nonconfidential portion of the list published under paragraph (1) along with the Administrator's designation of the chemical substance as an active or inactive substance;

(B) the unique identifier assigned under section 14, accession number, generic name, and, if applicable, premanufacture notice case number for each chemical substance on the confidential portion of the list published under paragraph (1) for which a claim of confidentiality was received; and

(C) the specific chemical identity of any active substance for which—

(i) a claim for protection against disclosure of the specific chemical identity of the active substance was not asserted, as required under this subsection or section 14;

(ii) all claims for protection against disclosure of the specific chemical identity of the active substance have been denied by the Administrator; or

(iii) the time period for protection against disclosure of the specific chemical identity of the active substance has expired.

(8) Limitation.—No person may assert a new claim under this subsection or section 14 for protection from disclosure of a specific chemical identity of any active or inactive substance for which a notice is received under paragraph (4)(A)(i) or (5)(B)(i) that is not on the confidential portion of the list published under paragraph (1).

(9) Certification.—Under the rules promulgated under this subsection, manufacturers and processors, as applicable, shall be required—

(A) to certify that each notice or substantiation the manufacturer or processor submits complies with the requirements of the rule, and that any confidentiality claims are true and correct; and

(B) to retain a record documenting compliance with the rule and supporting confidentiality claims for a period of 5 years beginning on the last day of the submission period.

(10) Mercury.—

(A) Definition of mercury.—In this paragraph, notwithstanding section 3(2)(B), the term 'mercury' means—

(i) elemental mercury; and

(ii) a mercury compound.

(B) Publication.—Not later than April 1, 2017, and every 3 years thereafter, the Administrator shall carry out and publish in the Federal Register an inventory of mercury supply, use, and trade in the United States.

(C) Process.—In carrying out the inventory under subparagraph (B), the Administrator shall—

(i) identify any manufacturing processes or products that intentionally add mercury; and

(ii) recommend actions, including proposed revisions of Federal law or regulations, to achieve further reductions in mercury use.

(D) Reporting.—

(i) In general.—To assist in the preparation of the inventory under subparagraph (B), any person who manufactures mercury or mercury-added products or otherwise intentionally uses mercury in a manufacturing process shall make periodic reports to the Administrator, at such time and including such information as the Administrator shall determine by rule promulgated not later than 2 years after the date of enactment of this paragraph.

(ii) Coordination.—To avoid duplication, the Administrator shall coordinate the reporting under this subparagraph with the Interstate Mercury Education and Reduction Clearinghouse.

(iii) Exemption.—Clause (i) shall not apply to a person engaged in the generation, handling, or management of mercury-containing waste, unless that person manufactures or recovers mercury in the management of that waste.

(c) Records

Any person who manufactures, processes, or distributes in commerce any chemical substance or mixture shall maintain records of significant adverse reactions to health or the environment, as determined by the Administrator by rule, alleged to have been caused by the substance or mixture. Records of such adverse reactions to the health of employees shall be retained for a period of 30 years from the date such reactions were first reported to or known by the person maintaining such records. Any other record of such adverse reactions shall be retained for a period of five years from the date the information contained in the record was first reported to or known by the person maintaining the record. Records required to be maintained under this subsection shall include records of consumer allegations of personal injury or harm to health, reports of occupational disease or injury, and reports or complaints of injury to the environment submitted to the manufacturer, processor, or distributor in commerce from any source. Upon request of any duly designated representative of the Administrator, each person who is required to maintain records under this subsection shall permit the inspection of such records and shall submit copies of such records.

(d) Health and safety studies

The Administrator shall promulgate rules under which the Administrator shall require any person who manufactures, processes, or distributes in commerce or who proposes to manufacture, process, or distribute in commerce any chemical substance or mixture (or with respect to paragraph (2), any person who has possession of a study) to submit to the Administrator—

(1) lists of health and safety studies (A) conducted or initiated by or for such person with respect to such substance or mixture at any time, (B) known to such person, or (C) reasonably ascertainable by such person, except that the Administrator may exclude certain types or categories of studies from the requirements of this subsection if the Administrator finds that submission of lists of such studies are unnecessary to carry out the purposes of this chapter; and

(2) copies of any study contained on a list submitted pursuant to paragraph (1) or otherwise known by such person.

(e) Notice to Administrator of substantial risks

Any person who manufactures, processes, or distributes in commerce a chemical substance or mixture and who obtains information which reasonably supports the conclusion that such substance or mixture presents a substantial risk of injury to health or the environment shall immediately inform the Administrator of such information unless such person has actual knowledge that the Administrator has been adequately informed of such information.

(f) "Manufacture" and "process" defined

For purposes of this section, the terms "manufacture" and "process" mean manufacture or process for commercial purposes.

(Pub. L. No. 94–469, Title I, § 8, 90 Stat. 2027 (Oct. 11, 1976); renumbered Title I by Pub. L. No. 99–519, § 3(c)(1), 100 Stat. 2989 (Oct. 22, 1986); and amended by Pub. L. No. 114–182, §§ 8, 19(g) 130 Stat. 470–476, 507 (June 22, 2016); Pub. L. No. 116–92, § 7351, 133 Stat. 2289 (Dec. 20, 2019).)

HISTORICAL AND STATUTORY NOTES

Asbestos Information

Pub. L. No. 100–577, 102 Stat. 2901 (Oct. 31, 1988), provided that:

"Section 1. Short title.

"This Act may be cited as the 'Asbestos Information Act of 1988'.

"Sec. 2. Submission of information by manufacturers.

"Within 90 days after the date of the enactment of this Act [Oct. 31, 1988], any person who manufactured or processed, before the date of the enactment of this Act, asbestos or asbestos-containing material that was prepared for sale for use as surfacing material, thermal system insulation, or miscellaneous material in buildings (or whose corporate predecessor manufactured or processed such asbestos or material) shall submit to the Administrator of the Environmental Protection Agency the years of manufacture, the types or classes of product, and, to the extent available, other identifying characteristics reasonably necessary to identify or distinguish the asbestos or asbestos-containing material. Such person also may submit to the Administrator protocols for samples of asbestos and asbestos-containing material.

"Sec. 3. Publication of information.

"Within 30 days after the date of the enactment of this Act [Oct. 31, 1988], the Administrator shall publish a notice in the Federal Register that explains how, when, and where the information specified in section 2 is to be submitted. The Administrator shall receive and organize the information submitted under section 2 and, within 180 days after the date of the enactment of this Act, shall publish the information. In carrying out this section, the Administrator may not—

"(1) review the information submitted under section 2 for accuracy, or

"(2) analyze such information to determine whether it is reasonably necessary to identify or distinguish the particular asbestos or asbestos-containing material.

"Sec. 4. Definitions.

"In this Act:

"(1) The term 'asbestos' means—

"(A) chrysotile, amosite, or crocidolite, or

"(B) in fibrous form, tremolite, anthophyllite, or actinolite.

"(2) The term 'asbestos-containing material' means any material containing more than one percent asbestos by weight.

"(3) The term 'identifying characteristics' means a description of asbestos or asbestos-containing material, including—

"(A) the mineral or chemical constituents (or both) of the asbestos or material by weight or volume (or both),

"(B) the types or classes of the product in which the asbestos or material is contained,

"(C) the designs, patterns, or textures of the product in which the asbestos or material is contained, and

"(D) the means by which the product in which the asbestos or material is contained may be distinguishable from other products containing asbestos or asbestos-containing material.

"(4) The term 'miscellaneous material' means building material on structural components, structural members, or fixtures, such as floor and ceiling tiles. The term does not include surfacing material or thermal system insulation.

"(5) The term 'protocol' means any procedure for taking, handling, and preserving samples of asbestos and asbestos-containing material and for testing and analyzing such samples for the purpose of determining the person who manufactured or processed for sale such samples and the identifying characteristics of such samples.

"(6) The term 'surfacing material' means material in a building that is sprayed on surfaces, troweled on surfaces, or otherwise applied to surfaces for acoustical, fireproofing, or other purposes, such as acoustical plaster on ceilings and fireproofing material on structural members.

"(7) The term 'thermal system insulation' means material in a building applied to pipes, fittings, boilers, breeching, tanks, ducts, or other structural components to prevent heat loss or gain or water condensation, or for other purposes."

Retroactivity

Section 20 of Pub. L. No. 114–182, 130 Stat. 510 (June 22, 2016), provided that "[n]othing in sections 1 through 19, or the amendments made by sections 1 through 19, shall be interpreted to apply retroactively to any State, Federal, or maritime legal action filed before the date of enactment of this Act."

PFAS Regulation

Section 7352 of Pub. L. No. 116–92, 133 Stat 2289 (Dec. 20, 2019) provided that "[n]ot later than June 22, 2020, the Administrator shall take final action on the proposed rule entitled 'Long-Chain Perfluoroalkyl Carboxylate and Perfluoroalkyl Sulfonate Chemical Substances; Significant New Use Rule' (80 Fed. Reg. 2885 (January 21, 2015))."

§ 2608. Relationship to other Federal laws

[TSCA § 9]

(a) Laws not administered by the Administrator

(1) If the Administrator determines that the manufacture, processing, distribution in commerce, use, or disposal of a chemical substance or mixture, or that any combination of such activities, presents an unreasonable risk of injury to health or the environment, without consideration of costs or other nonrisk factors, including an unreasonable risk to a potentially exposed or susceptible subpopulation identified as relevant by the Administrator, under the conditions of use, and determines, in the Administrator's discretion, that such risk may be prevented or reduced to a sufficient extent by action taken under a Federal law not administered by the Administrator, the Administrator shall submit to the agency which administers such law a report which describes such risk and includes in such description a specification of the activity or combination of activities which the Administrator has reason to believe so presents such risk. Such report shall also request such agency—

(A) **(i)** to determine if the risk described in such report may be prevented or reduced to a sufficient extent by action taken under such law, and

(ii) if the agency determines that such risk may be so prevented or reduced, to issue an order declaring whether or not the activity or combination of activities specified in the description of such risk presents such risk; and

(B) to respond to the Administrator with respect to the matters described in subparagraph (A).

Any report of the Administrator shall include a detailed statement of the information on which it is based and shall be published in the Federal Register. The agency receiving a request under such a report shall make the requested determination, issue the requested order, and make the requested response within such time as the Administrator specifies in the request, but such time specified may not be less than 90 days from the date the request was made. The response of an agency shall be accompanied by a detailed statement of the findings and conclusions of the agency and shall be published in the Federal Register.

(2) If the Administrator makes a report under paragraph (1) with respect to a chemical substance or mixture and the agency to which such report was made either—

(A) issues an order, within the time period specified by the Administrator in the report, declaring that the activity or combination of activities specified in the description of the risk described in the report does not present the risk described in the report, or

(B) responds within the time period specified by the Administrator in the report and initiates, within 90 days of the publication in the Federal Register of the response of the agency under paragraph (1), action under the law (or laws) administered by such agency to protect against such risk associated with such activity or combination of activities,

the Administrator may not take any action under section 6(a) or 7 of this title with respect to such risk.

(3) The Administrator shall take the actions described in paragraph (4) if the Administrator makes a report under paragraph (1) with respect to a chemical substance or mixture and the agency to which the report was made does not—

(A) issue the order described in paragraph (2)(A) within the time period specified by the Administrator in the report; or

(B) **(i)** respond under paragraph (1) within the timeframe specified by the Administrator in the report; and

(ii) initiate action within 90 days of publication in the Federal Register of the response described in clause (i).

(4) If an agency to which a report is submitted under paragraph (1) does not take the actions described in subparagraph (A) or (B) of paragraph (3), the Administrator shall—

(A) initiate or complete appropriate action under section 6(a); or

(B) take any action authorized or required under section 7, as applicable.

(5) This subsection shall not relieve the Administrator of any obligation to take any appropriate action under section 6(a) or 7 to address risks from the manufacture, processing, distribution in commerce, use, or disposal of a chemical substance or mixture, or any combination of those activities, that are not identified in a report issued by the Administrator under paragraph (1).";

(6) If the Administrator has initiated action under section 6(a) or 7 of this title with respect to a risk associated with a chemical substance or mixture which was the subject of a report made to an agency under paragraph (1), such agency shall before taking action under the law (or laws) administered by it to protect against such risk consult with the Administrator for the purpose of avoiding duplication of Federal action against such risk.

(b) Laws administered by the Administrator

(1) The Administrator shall coordinate actions taken under this chapter with actions taken under other Federal laws administered in whole or in part by the Administrator. If the Administrator determines that a risk to health or the environment associated with a chemical substance or mixture could be eliminated or reduced to a sufficient extent by actions taken under the authorities contained in such other Federal laws, the Administrator shall use such authorities to protect against such risk unless the Administrator determines, in the Administrator's discretion, that it is in the public interest to protect against such risk by actions taken under this chapter. This subsection shall not be construed to relieve the Administrator of any requirement imposed on the Administrator by such other Federal laws.

(2) In making a determination under paragraph (1) that it is in the public interest for the Administrator to take an action under this title with respect to a chemical substance or mixture rather than under another law administered in whole or in part by the Administrator, the Administrator shall consider, based on information reasonably available to the Administrator, all relevant aspects of the risk described in paragraph (1) and a comparison of the estimated costs and efficiencies of the action to be taken under this title and an action to be taken under such other law to protect against such risk.

(c) Occupational safety and health

In exercising any authority under this chapter, the Administrator shall not, for purposes of section 653(b)(1) of Title 29, be deemed to be exercising statutory authority to prescribe or enforce standards or regulations affecting occupational safety and health.

(d) Coordination

In administering this chapter, the Administrator shall consult and coordinate with the Secretary of Health and Human Services and the heads of any other appropriate Federal executive department or agency, any relevant independent regulatory agency, and any other appropriate instrumentality of the Federal Government for the purpose of achieving the maximum enforcement of this chapter while imposing the least burdens of duplicative requirements on those subject to the chapter and for other purposes. The Administrator shall, in the report required by section 2629 of this title, report annually to the Congress on actions taken to coordinate with such other Federal departments, agencies, or instrumentalities, and on actions taken to coordinate the authority under this chapter with the authority granted under other Acts referred to in subsection (b) of this section.

(e) Exposure information.—In addition to the requirements of subsection (a), if the Administrator obtains information related to exposures or releases of a chemical substance or mixture that may be prevented or reduced under another Federal law, including a law not administered by the Administrator, the Administrator shall make such information available to the relevant Federal agency or office of the Environmental Protection Agency.

(Pub. L. No. 94–469, Title I, § 9, 90 Stat. 2030 (Oct. 11, 1976); as amended by Pub. L. No. 96–88, Title V, § 509(b), 93 Stat. 695 (Oct. 17, 1979); and renumbered Title I by Pub. L. No. 99–519, § 3(c)(1), 100 Stat. 2989 (Oct. 22, 1986); and amended by Pub. L. No. 114–182, §§ 9, 19(h), 130 Stat. 476–477, 507 (June 22, 2016).)

HISTORICAL AND STATUTORY NOTES

Change of Name

"Secretary of Health and Human Services" was substituted for "Secretary of Health, Education, and Welfare" in subsec. (d), pursuant to section 509(b) of Pub. L. No. 96–88 which is codified as section 3508 of Title 20, Education.

Termination of Reporting Requirements

For termination, effective May 15, 2000, of provisions in subsec. (d) of this section relating to reporting certain coordinating actions annually to Congress in the report required by 15 U.S.C.A. § 2629, see Pub. L. No. 104–66, § 3003, as amended, set out as a note under 31 U.S.C.A. § 1113, and page 90 of House Document No. 103–7.

Retroactivity

Section 20 of Pub. L. No. 114–182, 130 Stat. 510 (June 22, 2016), provided that "[n]othing in sections 1 through 19, or the amendments made by sections 1 through 19, shall be interpreted to apply retroactively to any State, Federal, or maritime legal action filed before the date of enactment of this Act."

§ 2609. Research, development, collection, dissemination, and utilization of information

[TSCA § 10]

(a) Authority

The Administrator shall, in consultation and cooperation with the Secretary of Health and Human Services and with other heads of appropriate departments and agencies, conduct such research, development, and monitoring as is necessary to carry out the purposes of this chapter. The Administrator may enter into contracts and may make grants for research, development, and monitoring under this subsection. Contracts may be entered into under this subsection without regard to section 3324(a) and (b) of Title 31 and section 6101 of Title 41.

(b) Information systems

(1) The Administrator shall establish, administer, and be responsible for the continuing activities of an interagency committee which shall design, establish, and coordinate an efficient and effective system, within the Environmental Protection Agency, for the collection, dissemination to other Federal departments and agencies, and use of information submitted to the Administrator under this chapter.

(2) (A) The Administrator shall, in consultation and cooperation with the Secretary of Health and Human Services and other heads of appropriate departments and agencies design, establish, and coordinate an efficient and effective system for the retrieval of toxicological and other scientific information which could be useful to the Administrator in carrying out the purposes of this chapter. Systematized retrieval shall be developed for use by all Federal and other departments and agencies with responsibilities in the area of regulation or study of chemical substances and mixtures and their effect on health or the environment.

(B) The Administrator, in consultation and cooperation with the Secretary of Health and Human Services, may make grants and enter into contracts for the development of an information retrieval system described in subparagraph (A). Contracts may be entered into under this subparagraph without regard to section 3324(a) and (b) of Title 31 and section 6101 of Title 41.

(c) Screening techniques

The Administrator shall coordinate, with the Assistant Secretary for Health of the Department of Health and Human Services, research undertaken by the Administrator and directed toward the development of rapid, reliable, and economical screening techniques for carcinogenic, mutagenic, teratogenic, and ecological effects of chemical substances and mixtures.

(d) Monitoring

The Administrator shall, in consultation and cooperation with the Secretary of Health and Human Services, establish and be responsible for research aimed at the development, in cooperation with local, State, and Federal agencies, of monitoring techniques and instruments which may be used in the detection of toxic chemical substances and mixtures and which are reliable, economical, and capable of being implemented under a wide variety of conditions.

(e) Basic research

The Administrator shall, in consultation and cooperation with the Secretary of Health and Human Services, establish research programs to develop the fundamental scientific basis of the screening and monitoring techniques described in subsections (c) and (d) of this section, the bounds of the reliability of such techniques, and the opportunities for their improvement.

(f) Training

The Administrator shall establish and promote programs and workshops to train or facilitate the training of Federal laboratory and technical personnel in existing or newly developed screening and monitoring techniques.

(g) Exchange of research and development results

The Administrator shall, in consultation with the Secretary of Health and Human Services and other heads of appropriate departments and agencies, establish and coordinate a system for exchange among Federal, State, and local authorities of research and development results respecting toxic chemical substances and mixtures, including a system to facilitate and promote the development of standard information format and analysis and consistent testing procedures.

(Pub. L. No. 94–469, Title I, § 10, 90 Stat. 2031 (Oct. 11, 1976); as amended by Pub. L. No. 96–88, Title V, § 509(b), 93 Stat. 695 (Oct. 17, 1979); and renumbered Title I by Pub. L. No. 99–519, § 3(c)(1), 100 Stat. 2989 (Oct. 22, 1986); and amended by Pub. L. No. 114–182, § 19(i), 130 Stat. 507 (June 22, 2016).)

HISTORICAL AND STATUTORY NOTES

Codifications

In subsecs. (a) and (b)(2)(B), "section 6101 of Title 41" substituted for "section 5 of Title 41" on authority of Pub. L. No. 111–350, § 6(c), 124 Stat. 3854 (Jan. 4, 2011), which Act enacted Title 41, Public Contracts.

In subsecs. (a) and (b)(2)(B), "section 3324(a) and (b) of Title 31" was substituted for references to section 3648 of the Revised Statutes (31 U.S.C. 529) on authority of Pub. L. No. 97–258, § 4(b), 96 Stat. 1067 (Sept. 13, 1982), the first section of which enacted Title 31, Money and Finance.

Change of Name

"Secretary of Health and Human Services" was substituted for "Secretary of Health, Education, and Welfare" in subsecs. (a), (b), (d), (e), and (g), and "Department of Health and Human Services" was substituted for "Department of Health, Education, and Welfare" in subsec. (c), pursuant to section 509(b) of Pub. L. No. 96–88, which is codified as section 3508(b) of Title 20, Education.

Availability of Grants

Grants awarded under this section are available for research, development, monitoring, public education, training, demonstrations, and studies, beginning in fiscal year 2000 and thereafter, see provisions of Pub. L. No. 106–74, Title III, set out as a note under 7 U.S.C.A. § 136r.

Retroactivity

Section 20 of Pub. L. No. 114–182, 130 Stat. 510 (June 22, 2016), provided that "[n]othing in sections 1 through 19, or the amendments made by sections 1 through 19, shall be interpreted to apply retroactively to any State, Federal, or maritime legal action filed before the date of enactment of this Act."

§ 2610. Inspections and subpoenas

[TSCA § 11]

(a) In general

For purposes of administering this chapter, the Administrator, and any duly designated representative of the Administrator, may inspect any establishment, facility, or other premises in which chemical substances, mixtures, or products subject to subchapter IV of this chapter are manufactured, processed, stored, or held before or after their distribution in commerce and any conveyance being used to transport chemical substances, mixtures, such products, or such articles in connection with distribution in commerce. Such an inspection may only be made upon the presentation of appropriate credentials and of a written notice to the owner, operator, or agent in charge of the premises or conveyance to be inspected. A separate notice shall be given for each such inspection, but a notice shall not be required for each entry made during the period covered by the inspection. Each such inspection shall be commenced and completed with reasonable promptness and shall be conducted at reasonable times, within reasonable limits, and in a reasonable manner.

(b) Scope

(1) Except as provided in paragraph (2), an inspection conducted under subsection (a) of this section shall extend to all things within the premises or conveyance inspected (including records, files, papers, processes, controls, and facilities) bearing on whether the requirements of this chapter applicable to the chemical substances, mixtures, or products subject to subchapter IV of this chapter within such premises or conveyance have been complied with.

(2) No inspection under subsection (a) of this section shall extend to—

(A) financial information,

(B) sales information (other than shipment data),

(C) pricing information,

(D) personnel information, or

(E) research information (other than data required by this chapter or under a rule promulgated, order issued, or consent agreement entered into thereunder),

unless the nature and extent of such information are described with reasonable specificity in the written notice required by subsection (a) of this section for such inspection.

(c) Subpoenas

In carrying out this chapter, the Administrator may by subpoena require the attendance and testimony of witnesses and the production of reports, papers, documents, answers to questions, and other information that the Administrator deems necessary. Witnesses shall be paid the same fees and mileage that are paid witnesses in the courts of the United States. In the event of contumacy, failure, or refusal of any person to obey any such subpoena, any district court of the United States in which venue is proper shall have jurisdiction to order any such person to comply with such subpoena. Any failure to obey such an order of the court is punishable by the court as a contempt thereof.

(Pub. L. No. 94–469, Title I, § 11, 90 Stat. 2032 (Oct. 11, 1976); renumbered Title I by Pub. L. No. 99–519, § 3(c)(1), 100 Stat. 2989 (Oct. 22, 1986); and amended by Pub. L. No. 102–550, Title X, § 1021(b)(2), (3), 106 Stat. 3923 (Oct. 28, 1992); Pub. L. No. 114–182, § 19(j), 130 Stat. 507–508 (June 22, 2016).)

Retroactivity

Section 20 of Pub. L. No. 114–182, 130 Stat. 510 (June 22, 2016), provided that "[n]othing in sections 1 through 19, or the amendments made by sections 1 through 19, shall be interpreted to apply retroactively to any State, Federal, or maritime legal action filed before the date of enactment of this Act."

§ 2611. Exports

[TSCA § 12]

(a) In general

(1) Except as provided in paragraph (2) and subsections (b) and (c) of this section, this chapter (other than section 2607 of this title) shall not apply to any chemical substance, mixture, or to an article containing a chemical substance or mixture, if—

(A) it can be shown that such substance, mixture, or article is being manufactured, processed, or distributed in commerce for export from the United States, unless such substance, mixture, or article was, in fact, manufactured, processed, or distributed in commerce, for use in the United States, and

(B) such substance, mixture, or article (when distributed in commerce), or any container in which it is enclosed (when so distributed), bears a stamp or label stating that such substance, mixture, or article is intended for export.

(2) Paragraph (1) shall not apply to any chemical substance, mixture, or article if the Administrator finds that the substance, mixture, or article presents an unreasonable risk of injury to health within the United States or to the environment of the United States. The Administrator may require, under section 2603 of this title, testing of any chemical substance or mixture exempted from this chapter by paragraph (1) for the purpose of determining whether or not such substance or mixture presents an unreasonable risk of injury to health within the United States or to the environment of the United States.

(b) Notice

(1) If any person exports or intends to export to a foreign country a chemical substance or mixture for which the submission of information is required under section 2603 or 2604(b) of this title, such person shall notify the Administrator of such exportation or intent to export and the Administrator shall furnish to the government of such country notice of the availability of the information submitted to the Administrator under such section for such substance or mixture.

(2) If any person exports or intends to export to a foreign country a chemical substance or mixture for which an order has been issued under section 2604 of this title or a rule has been proposed or promulgated under section 2604 or 2605 of this title, or with respect to which an action is pending, or relief has been granted under section 2604 or 2606 of this title, such person shall notify the Administrator of such exportation or intent to export and the Administrator shall furnish to the government of such country notice of such rule, order, action, or relief.

(c) Prohibition on export of elemental mercury and mercury compounds

(1) Prohibition

Effective January 1, 2013, the export of elemental mercury from the United States is prohibited.

(2) Inapplicability of subsection (a)

Subsection (a) shall not apply to this subsection.

(3) Report to Congress on mercury compounds

(A) Report

Not later than one year after October 14, 2008, the Administrator shall publish and submit to Congress a report on mercuric chloride, mercurous chloride or calomel, mercuric oxide, and other mercury compounds, if any, that may currently be used in significant quantities in products or processes. Such report shall include an analysis of—

(i) the sources and amounts of each of the mercury compounds imported into the United States or manufactured in the United States annually;

(ii) the purposes for which each of these compounds are used domestically, the amount of these compounds currently consumed annually for each purpose, and the estimated amounts to be consumed for each purpose in 2010 and beyond;

(iii) the sources and amounts of each mercury compound exported from the United States annually in each of the last three years;

(iv) the potential for these compounds to be processed into elemental mercury after export from the United States; and

(v) other relevant information that Congress should consider in determining whether to extend the export prohibition to include one or more of these mercury compounds.

(B) Procedure

For the purpose of preparing the report under this paragraph, the Administrator may utilize the information gathering authorities of this subchapter, including sections 2609 and 2610 of this title.

(4) Essential use exemption

(A) Any person residing in the United States may petition the Administrator for an exemption from the prohibition in paragraph (1), and the Administrator may grant by rule, after notice and opportunity for comment, an exemption for a specified use at an identified foreign facility if the Administrator finds that—

(i) nonmercury alternatives for the specified use are not available in the country where the facility is located;

(ii) there is no other source of elemental mercury available from domestic supplies (not including new mercury mines) in the country where the elemental mercury will be used;

(iii) the country where the elemental mercury will be used certifies its support for the exemption;

(iv) the export will be conducted in such a manner as to ensure the elemental mercury will be used at the identified facility as described in the petition, and not otherwise diverted for other uses for any reason;

(v) the elemental mercury will be used in a manner that will protect human health and the environment, taking into account local, regional, and global human health and environmental impacts;

(vi) the elemental mercury will be handled and managed in a manner that will protect human health and the environment, taking into account local, regional, and global human health and environmental impacts; and

(vii) the export of elemental mercury for the specified use is consistent with international obligations of the United States intended to reduce global mercury supply, use, and pollution.

(B) Each exemption issued by the Administrator pursuant to this paragraph shall contain such terms and conditions as are necessary to minimize the export of elemental mercury and ensure that the conditions for granting the exemption will be fully met, and shall contain such other terms and conditions as the Administrator may prescribe. No exemption granted pursuant to this paragraph shall exceed three years in duration and no such exemption shall exceed 10 metric tons of elemental mercury.

(C) The Administrator may by order suspend or cancel an exemption under this paragraph in the case of a violation described in subparagraph (D).

(D) A violation of this subsection or the terms and conditions of an exemption, or the submission of false information in connection therewith, shall be considered a prohibited act under section 2614 of this title, and shall be subject to penalties under section 2615 of this title, injunctive relief under section 2616 of this title, and citizen suits under section 2619 of this title.

(5) Consistency with trade obligations

Nothing in this subsection affects, replaces, or amends prior law relating to the need for consistency with international trade obligations.

(6) Export of coal

Nothing in this subsection shall be construed to prohibit the export of coal.

(7) Prohibition on export of certain mercury compounds.—

(A) In general.—Effective January 1, 2020, the export of the following mercury compounds is prohibited:

(i) Mercury (I) chloride or calomel.

(ii) Mercury (II) oxide.

(iii) Mercury (II) sulfate.

(iv) Mercury (II) nitrate.

(v) Cinnabar or mercury sulphide.

(vi) Any mercury compound that the Administrator adds to the list published under subparagraph (B) by rule, on determining that exporting that mercury compound for the purpose of regenerating elemental mercury is technically feasible.

(B) Publication.—Not later than 90 days after the date of enactment of the Frank R. Lautenberg Chemical Safety for the 21st Century Act, and as appropriate thereafter, the Administrator shall publish in the Federal Register a list of the mercury compounds that are prohibited from export under this paragraph.

(C) Petition.—Any person may petition the Administrator to add a mercury compound to the list published under subparagraph (B).

(D) Environmentally sound disposal.—This paragraph does not prohibit the export of mercury compounds on the list published under subparagraph (B) to member countries of the Organization for Economic Co-operation and Development for environmentally sound disposal, on the condition that no mercury or mercury compounds so exported are to be recovered, recycled, or reclaimed for use, or directly reused, after such export.

(E) Report.—Not later than 5 years after the date of enactment of the Frank R. Lautenberg Chemical Safety for the 21st Century Act, the Administrator shall evaluate any exports of mercury compounds on the list published under subparagraph (B) for disposal that occurred after such date of enactment and shall submit to Congress a report that—

(i) describes volumes and sources of mercury compounds on the list published under subparagraph (B) exported for disposal;

(ii) identifies receiving countries of such exports;

(iii) describes methods of disposal used after such export;

(iv) identifies issues, if any, presented by the export of mercury compounds on the list published under subparagraph (B);

(v) includes an evaluation of management options in the United States for mercury compounds on the list published under subparagraph (B), if any, that are commercially available and comparable in cost and efficacy to methods being utilized in such receiving countries; and

(vi) makes a recommendation regarding whether Congress should further limit or prohibit the export of mercury compounds on the list published under subparagraph (B) for disposal.

(F) Effect on other law.—Nothing in this paragraph shall be construed to affect the authority of the Administrator under the Solid Waste Disposal Act (42 U.S.C. 6901 et seq.).

(Pub. L. No. 94–469, Title I, § 12, 90 Stat. 2033 (Oct. 11, 1976); renumbered Title I by Pub. L. No. 99–519, § 3(c)(1), 100 Stat. 2989 (Oct. 22, 1986); and amended by Pub. L. No. 110–414, § 4, 122 Stat. 4342 (Oct. 14, 2008); Pub. L. No. 114–182, §§ 10(a), (b), 19(k), 130 Stat. 477–478, 508 (June 22, 2016).)

HISTORICAL AND STATUTORY NOTES

References in Text

This subchapter, referred to in subsec. (c)(3)(B), originally read "this title", meaning Title I of the Toxic Substances Control Act, Pub. L. No. 94–469, Title I, §§ 1 to 30, 90 Stat. 2003 (Oct. 11, 1976), which is codified to this subchapter.

Findings

Pub. L. No. 110–414, § 2, 122 Stat. 4341 (Oct. 14, 2008), provided that: "Congress finds that—

"(1) mercury is highly toxic to humans, ecosystems, and wildlife;

"(2) as many as 10 percent of women in the United States of childbearing age have mercury in the blood at a level that could put a baby at risk;

"(3) as many as 630,000 children born annually in the United States are at risk of neurological problems related to mercury;

"(4) the most significant source of mercury exposure to people in the United States is ingestion of mercury-contaminated fish;

"(5) The Environmental Protection Agency reports that, as of 2004—

"(A) 44 States have fish advisories covering over 13,000,000 lake acres and over 750,000 river miles;

"(B) in 21 States the freshwater advisories are statewide; and

"(C) in 12 States the coastal advisories are statewide;

"(6) the long-term solution to mercury pollution is to minimize global mercury use and releases to eventually achieve reduced contamination levels in the environment, rather than reducing fish consumption since uncontaminated fish represents a critical and healthy source of nutrition worldwide;

"(7) mercury pollution is a transboundary pollutant, depositing locally, regionally, and globally, and affecting water bodies near industrial sources (including the Great Lakes) and remote areas (including the Arctic Circle);

"(8) the free trade of elemental mercury on the world market, at relatively low prices and in ready supply, encourages the continued use of elemental mercury outside of the United States, often involving highly dispersive activities such as artisinal gold mining;

"(9) the intentional use of mercury is declining in the United States as a consequence of process changes to manufactured products (including batteries, paints, switches, and measuring devices), but those uses remain substantial in the developing world where releases from the products are extremely likely due to the limited pollution control and waste management infrastructures in those countries;

"(10) the member countries of the European Union collectively are the largest source of elemental mercury exports globally;

"(11) the European Commission has proposed to the European Parliament and to the Council of the European Union a regulation to ban exports of elemental mercury from the European Union by 2011;

"(12) the United States is a net exporter of elemental mercury and, according to the United States Geological Survey, exported 506 metric tons of elemental mercury more than the United States imported during the period of 2000 through 2004; and

"(13) banning exports of elemental mercury from the United States will have a notable effect on the market availability of elemental mercury and switching to affordable mercury alternatives in the developing world."

Retroactivity

Section 20 of Pub. L. No. 114–182, 130 Stat. 510 (June 22, 2016), provided that "[n]othing in sections 1 through 19, or the amendments made by sections 1 through 19, shall be interpreted to apply retroactively to any State, Federal, or maritime legal action filed before the date of enactment of this Act."

§ 2612. Entry into customs territory of the United States

[TSCA § 13]

(a) In general

(1) The Secretary of the Treasury shall refuse entry into the customs territory of the United States (as defined in general note 2 of the Harmonized Tariff Schedule of the United States) of any chemical substance, mixture, or article containing a chemical substance or mixture offered for such entry if—

(A) it fails to comply with any rule in effect under this chapter, or

(B) it is offered for entry in violation of section 2604 of this title, 2605 of this title, or subchapter IV of this chapter, a rule or order under section 2604 of this title, 2605 of this title, or subchapter IV of this chapter, or an order issued in a civil action brought under section 2604 of this title, 2606 of this title or subchapter IV of this chapter.

(2) If a chemical substance, mixture, or article is refused entry under paragraph (1), the Secretary of the Treasury shall notify the consignee of such entry refusal, shall not release it to the consignee, and shall cause its disposal or storage (under such rules as the Secretary of the Treasury may prescribe) if it has not been exported by the consignee within 90 days from the date of receipt of notice of such refusal, except that the Secretary of the Treasury may, pending a review by the Administrator of the entry refusal, release to the consignee such substance, mixture, or article on execution of bond for the amount of the full invoice of such substance, mixture, or article (as such value is set forth in the customs entry), together with the duty thereon. On failure to return such substance, mixture, or article for any cause to the custody of the Secretary of the Treasury when demanded, such consignee shall be liable to the United States for liquidated damages equal to the full amount of such bond. All charges for storage, cartage, and labor on and for disposal of substances, mixtures, or articles which are refused entry or release under this section shall be paid by the owner or consignee, and in default of such payment shall constitute a lien against any future entry made by such owner or consignee.

(b) Rules

The Secretary of the Treasury, after consultation with the Administrator, shall issue rules for the administration of subsection (a) of this section.

(Pub. L. No. 94–469, Title I, § 13, 90 Stat. 2034 (Oct. 11, 1976); renumbered Title I by Pub. L. No. 99–519, § 3(c)(1), 100 Stat. 2989 (Oct. 22, 1986); and amended by Pub. L. No. 100–418, Title I, § 1214(e)(2), 102 Stat. 1156 (Aug. 23, 1988); Pub. L. No. 102–550, Title X, § 1021(b)(4), 106 Stat. 3923 (Oct. 28, 1992).)

HISTORICAL AND STATUTORY NOTES

References in Text

The Harmonized Tariff Schedule of the United States, referred to in subsec. (a), is not set out in the Code. See Publication of Harmonized Tariff Schedules note set out under section 1202 of Title 19, Customs Duties.

Effective and Applicability Provisions

1988 Acts. Amendment by Pub. L. No. 100–418 effective Jan. 1, 1989, and applicable with respect to articles entered on or after such date, see section 1217(b)(1) of Pub. L. No. 100–418, set out as an Effective Date note under section 3001 of Title 19, Customs Duties.

Retroactivity

Section 20 of Pub. L. No. 114–182, 130 Stat. 510 (June 22, 2016), provided that "[n]othing in sections 1 through 19, or the amendments made by sections 1 through 19, shall be interpreted to apply retroactively to any State, Federal, or maritime legal action filed before the date of enactment of this Act."

§ 2613. Confidential information

[TSCA § 14]

(a) In general.—Except as provided in this section, the Administrator shall not disclose information that is exempt from disclosure pursuant to subsection (a) of section 552 of title 5, United States Code, by reason of subsection (b)(4) of that section—

(1) that is reported to, or otherwise obtained by, the Administrator under this Act; and

(2) for which the requirements of subsection (c) are met. In any proceeding under section 552(a) of title 5, United States Code, to obtain information the disclosure of which has been denied because of the provisions of this subsection, the Administrator may not rely on section 552(b)(3) of such title to sustain the Administrator's action.

(b) Information not protected from disclosure.—

(1) Mixed confidential and nonconfidential information.—Information that is protected from disclosure under this section, and which is mixed with information that is not protected from disclosure under this section, does not lose its protection from disclosure notwithstanding that it is mixed with information that is not protected from disclosure.

(2) Information from health and safety studies.—Subsection (a) does not prohibit the disclosure of—

(A) any health and safety study which is submitted under this Act with respect to—

(i) any chemical substance or mixture which, on the date on which such study is to be disclosed has been offered for commercial distribution; or

(ii) any chemical substance or mixture for which testing is required under section 4 or for which notification is required under section 5; and

(B) any information reported to, or otherwise obtained by, the Administrator from a health and safety study which relates to a chemical substance or mixture described in clause (i) or (ii) of subparagraph (A).

This paragraph does not authorize the disclosure of any information, including formulas (including molecular structures) of a chemical substance or mixture, that discloses processes used in the manufacturing or processing of a chemical substance or mixture or, in the case of a mixture, the portion of the mixture comprised by any of the chemical substances in the mixture.

(3) Other information not protected from disclosure.—Subsection (a) does not prohibit the disclosure of—

(A) any general information describing the manufacturing volumes, expressed as specific aggregated volumes or, if the Administrator determines that disclosure of specific aggregated volumes would reveal confidential information, expressed in ranges; or

(B) a general description of a process used in the manufacture or processing and industrial, commercial, or consumer functions and uses of a chemical substance, mixture, or article containing a chemical substance or mixture, including information specific to an industry or industry sector that customarily would be shared with the general public or within an industry or industry sector.

(4) Bans and phase-outs.—

(A) In general.—If the Administrator promulgates a rule pursuant to section 6(a) that establishes a ban or phase-out of a chemical substance or mixture, the protection from disclosure of any information under this section with respect to the chemical substance or mixture shall be presumed to no longer apply, subject to subsection (g)(1)(E) and subparagraphs (B) and (C) of this paragraph.

(B) Limitations.—

(i) Critical use.—In the case of a chemical substance or mixture for which a specific condition of use is subject to an exemption pursuant to section 6(g), if the Administrator establishes a ban or phase-out described in subparagraph (A) with respect to the chemical substance or mixture, the presumption against protection under such subparagraph shall only apply to information that relates solely to any conditions of use of the chemical substance or mixture to which the exemption does not apply.

(ii) Export.—In the case of a chemical substance or mixture for which there is manufacture, processing, or distribution in commerce that meets the conditions of section 12(a)(1), if the Administrator establishes a ban or phase-out described in subparagraph (A) with respect to the chemical substance or mixture, the presumption against protection under such subparagraph shall only apply to information that relates solely to any other manufacture, processing, or distribution in commerce of the chemical substance or mixture for the conditions of use subject to the ban or phase-out, unless the Administrator makes the determination in section 12(a)(2).

(iii) Specific conditions of use.—In the case of a chemical substance or mixture for which the Administrator establishes a ban or phase-out described in subparagraph (A) with respect to a specific condition of use of the chemical substance or mixture, the presumption against protection under such subparagraph shall only apply to information that relates solely to the condition of use of the chemical substance or mixture for which the ban or phase-out is established.

(C) Request for nondisclosure.—

(i) In general.—A manufacturer or processor of a chemical substance or mixture subject to a ban or phase-out described in this paragraph may submit to the Administrator, within 30 days of receiving a notification under subsection (g)(2)(A), a request, including documentation supporting such request, that some or all of the information to which the notice applies should not be disclosed or that its disclosure should be delayed, and the Administrator shall review the request under subsection (g)(1)(E).

(ii) Effect of no request or denial.—If no request for nondisclosure or delay is submitted to the Administrator under this subparagraph, or the Administrator denies such a request under subsection (g)(1)(A), the information shall not be protected from disclosure under this section.

(5) Certain requests.—If a request is made to the Administrator under section 552(a) of title 5, United States Code, for information reported to or otherwise obtained by the Administrator under this Act that is not protected from disclosure under this subsection, the Administrator may not deny the request on the basis of section 552(b)(4) of title 5, United States Code.

(c) Requirements for confidentiality claims.—

(1) Assertion of claims.—

(A) In general.—A person seeking to protect from disclosure any information that person submits under this Act (including information described in paragraph (2)) shall assert to the Administrator a claim for protection from disclosure concurrent with submission of the information, in accordance with such rules regarding a claim for protection from disclosure as the Administrator has promulgated or may promulgate pursuant to this title.

(B) Inclusion.—An assertion of a claim under subparagraph (A) shall include a statement that the person has—

(i) taken reasonable measures to protect the confidentiality of the information;

(ii) determined that the information is not required to be disclosed or otherwise made available to the public under any other Federal law;

(iii) a reasonable basis to conclude that disclosure of the information is likely to cause substantial harm to the competitive position of the person; and

(iv) a reasonable basis to believe that the information is not readily discoverable through reverse engineering.

(C) Additional requirements for claims regarding chemical identity information.—In the case of a claim under subparagraph (A) for protection from disclosure of a specific chemical identity, the claim shall include a structurally descriptive generic name for the chemical substance that the Administrator may disclose to the public, subject to the condition that such generic name shall—

(i) be consistent with guidance developed by the Administrator under paragraph (4)(A); and

(ii) describe the chemical structure of the chemical substance as specifically as practicable while protecting those features of the chemical structure—

(I) that are claimed as confidential; and

(II) the disclosure of which would be likely to cause substantial harm to the competitive position of the person.

(2) Information generally not subject to substantiation requirements.—Subject to subsection (f), the following information shall not be subject to substantiation requirements under paragraph (3):

(A) Specific information describing the processes used in manufacture or processing of a chemical substance, mixture, or article.

(B) Marketing and sales information.

(C) Information identifying a supplier or customer.

(D) In the case of a mixture, details of the full composition of the mixture and the respective percentages of constituents.

(E) Specific information regarding the use, function, or application of a chemical substance or mixture in a process, mixture, or article.

(F) Specific production or import volumes of the manufacturer or processor.

(G) Prior to the date on which a chemical substance is first offered for commercial distribution, the specific chemical identity of the chemical substance, including the chemical name, molecular formula, Chemical Abstracts Service number, and other information that would identify the specific chemical substance, if the specific chemical identity was claimed as confidential at the time it was submitted in a notice under section 5.

(3) Substantiation requirements.—Except as provided in paragraph (2), a person asserting a claim to protect information from disclosure under this section shall substantiate the claim, in accordance with such rules as the Administrator has promulgated or may promulgate pursuant to this section.

(4) Guidance.—The Administrator shall develop guidance regarding—

(A) the determination of structurally descriptive generic names, in the case of claims for the protection from disclosure of specific chemical identity; and

(B) the content and form of the statements of need and agreements required under paragraphs (4), (5), and (6) of subsection (d).

(5) Certification.—An authorized official of a person described in paragraph (1)(A) shall certify that the statement required to assert a claim submitted pursuant to paragraph (1)(B), and any information required to substantiate a claim submitted pursuant to paragraph (3), are true and correct.

(d) Exceptions to protections from disclosure.—Information described in subsection (a)—

(1) shall be disclosed to an officer or employee of the United States—

(A) in connection with the official duties of that person under any Federal law for the protection of health or the environment; or

(B) for a specific Federal law enforcement purpose;

(2) shall be disclosed to a contractor of the United States and employees of that contractor—

(A) if, in the opinion of the Administrator, the disclosure is necessary for the satisfactory performance by the contractor of a contract with the United States for the performance of work in connection with this Act; and

(B) subject to such conditions as the Administrator may specify;

(3) shall be disclosed if the Administrator determines that disclosure is necessary to protect health or the environment against an unreasonable risk of injury to health or the environment, without consideration of costs or other nonrisk factors, including an unreasonable risk to a potentially exposed or susceptible subpopulation identified as relevant by the Administrator under the conditions of use;

(4) shall be disclosed to a State, political subdivision of a State, or tribal government, on written request, for the purpose of administration or enforcement of a law, if such entity has 1 or more applicable agreements with the Administrator that are consistent with the guidance developed under subsection (c)(4)(B) and ensure that the entity will take appropriate measures, and has adequate authority, to maintain the confidentiality of the information in accordance with procedures comparable to the procedures used by the Administrator to safeguard the information;

(5) shall be disclosed to a health or environmental professional employed by a Federal or State agency or tribal government or a treating physician or nurse in a nonemergency situation if such person provides a written statement of need and agrees to sign a written confidentiality agreement with the Administrator, subject to the conditions that—

(A) the statement of need and confidentiality agreement are consistent with the guidance developed under subsection (c)(4)(B);

(B) the statement of need shall be a statement that the person has a reasonable basis to suspect that—

(i) the information is necessary for, or will assist in—

(I) the diagnosis or treatment of 1 or more individuals; or

(II) responding to an environmental release or exposure; and

(ii) 1 or more individuals being diagnosed or treated have been exposed to the chemical substance or mixture concerned, or an environmental release of or exposure to the chemical substance or mixture concerned has occurred; and

(C) the person will not use the information for any purpose other than the health or environmental needs asserted in the statement of need, except as otherwise may be authorized by the terms of the agreement or by the person who has a claim under this section with respect to the information;

(6) shall be disclosed in the event of an emergency to a treating or responding physician, nurse, agent of a poison control center, public health or environmental official of a State, political subdivision of a State, or tribal government, or first responder (including any individual duly authorized by a Federal agency, State, political subdivision of a State, or tribal government who is trained in urgent medical care or other emergency procedures, including a police officer, firefighter, or emergency medical technician) if such person requests the information, subject to the conditions that such person shall—

(A) have a reasonable basis to suspect that—

(i) a medical, public health, or environmental emergency exists;

(ii) the information is necessary for, or will assist in, emergency or first-aid diagnosis or treatment; or

(iii) 1 or more individuals being diagnosed or treated have likely been exposed to the chemical substance or mixture concerned, or a serious environmental release of or exposure to the chemical substance or mixture concerned has occurred; and

(B) if requested by a person who has a claim with respect to the information under this section—

(i) provide a written statement of need and agree to sign a confidentiality agreement, as described in paragraph (5); and

(ii) submit to the Administrator such statement of need and confidentiality agreement as soon as practicable, but not necessarily before the information is disclosed;

(7) may be disclosed if the Administrator determines that disclosure is relevant in a proceeding under this Act, subject to the condition that the disclosure is made in such a manner as to preserve confidentiality to the extent practicable without impairing the proceeding;

(8) shall be disclosed if the information is required to be made public under any other provision of Federal law; and

(9) shall be disclosed as required pursuant to discovery, subpoena, other court order, or any other judicial process otherwise allowed under applicable Federal or State law.

(e) Duration of protection from disclosure.—

(1) In general.—Subject to paragraph (2), subsection (f)(3), and section 8(b), the Administrator shall protect from disclosure information described in subsection (a)—

(A) in the case of information described in subsection (c)(2), until such time as—

(i) the person that asserted the claim notifies the Administrator that the person is withdrawing the claim, in which case the information shall not be protected from disclosure under this section; or

(ii) the Administrator becomes aware that the information does not qualify for protection from disclosure under this section, in which case the Administrator shall take any actions required under subsections (f) and (g); and

(B) in the case of information other than information described in subsection (c)(2)—

(i) for a period of 10 years from the date on which the person asserts the claim with respect to the information submitted to the Administrator; or

(ii) if applicable before the expiration of such 10-year period, until such time as—

(I) the person that asserted the claim notifies the Administrator that the person is withdrawing the claim, in which case the information shall not be protected from disclosure under this section; or

(II) the Administrator becomes aware that the information does not qualify for protection from disclosure under this section, in which case the Administrator shall take any actions required under subsections (f) and (g).

(2) Extensions.—

(A) In general.—In the case of information other than information described in subsection (c)(2), not later than the date that is 60 days before the expiration of the period described in paragraph (1)(B)(i), the Administrator shall provide to the person that asserted the claim a notice of the impending expiration of the period.

(B) Request.—

(i) In general.—Not later than the date that is 30 days before the expiration of the period described in paragraph (1)(B)(i), a person reasserting the relevant claim shall submit to the Administrator a request for extension substantiating, in accordance with subsection (c)(3), the need to extend the period.

(ii) Action by Administrator.—Not later than the date of expiration of the period described in paragraph (1)(B)(i), the Administrator shall, in accordance with subsection (g)(1)—

(I) review the request submitted under clause (i);

(II) make a determination regarding whether the claim for which the request was submitted continues to meet the relevant requirements of this section; and

(III) (aa) grant an extension of 10 years; or

(bb) deny the request.

(C) No limit on number of extensions.—There shall be no limit on the number of extensions granted under this paragraph, if the Administrator determines that the relevant request under subparagraph (B)(i)—

(i) establishes the need to extend the period; and

(ii) meets the requirements established by the Administrator.

(f) Review and resubstantiation.—

(1) Discretion of Administrator.—The Administrator may require any person that has claimed protection for information from disclosure under this section, whether before, on, or after the date of enactment of the Frank R. Lautenberg Chemical Safety for the 21st Century Act, to reassert and substantiate or resubstantiate the claim in accordance with this section—

(A) after the chemical substance is designated as a high-priority substance under section 6(b);

(B) for any chemical substance designated as an active substance under section 8(b)(5)(B)(iii); or

(C) if the Administrator determines that disclosure of certain information currently protected from disclosure would be important to assist the Administrator in conducting risk evaluations or promulgating rules under section 6.

(2) Review required.—The Administrator shall review a claim for protection of information from disclosure under this section and require any person that has claimed protection for that information, whether before, on, or after the date of enactment of the Frank R. Lautenberg Chemical Safety for the 21st Century Act, to reassert and substantiate or resubstantiate the claim in accordance with this section—

(A) as necessary to determine whether the information qualifies for an exemption from disclosure in connection with a request for information received by the Administrator under section 552 of title 5, United States Code;

(B) if the Administrator has a reasonable basis to believe that the information does not qualify for protection from disclosure under this section; or

(C) for any chemical substance the Administrator determines under section 6(b)(4)(A) presents an unreasonable risk of injury to health or the environment.

(3) Period of protection.—If the Administrator requires a person to reassert and substantiate or resubstantiate a claim under this subsection, and determines that the claim continues to meet the relevant requirements of this section, the Administrator shall protect the information subject to the claim from disclosure for a period of 10 years from the date of such determination, subject to any subsequent requirement by the Administrator under this subsection.

(g) Duties of Administrator.—

(1) Determination.—

(A) In general.—Except for claims regarding information described in subsection (c)(2), the Administrator shall, subject to subparagraph (C), not later than 90 days after the receipt of a claim under subsection (c), and not later than 30 days after the receipt of a request for extension of a claim under subsection (e) or a request under subsection (b)(4)(C), review and approve, approve in part and deny in part, or deny the claim or request.

(B) Reasons for denial.—If the Administrator denies or denies in part a claim or request under subparagraph (A) the Administrator shall provide to the person that asserted the claim or submitted the request a written statement of the reasons for the denial or denial in part of the claim or request.

(C) Subsets.—The Administrator shall—

(i) except with respect to information described in subsection (c)(2)(G), review all claims or requests under this section for the protection from disclosure of the specific chemical identity of a chemical substance; and

(ii) review a representative subset, comprising at least 25 percent, of all other claims or requests for protection from disclosure under this section.

(D) Effect of failure to act.—The failure of the Administrator to make a decision regarding a claim or request for protection from disclosure or extension under this section shall not have the effect of denying or eliminating a claim or request for protection from disclosure.

(E) Determination of requests under subsection (b)(4)(C).—With respect to a request submitted under subsection (b)(4)(C), the Administrator shall, with the objective of ensuring that information relevant to the protection of health and the environment is disclosed to the extent practicable, determine whether the documentation provided by the person rebuts what shall be the presumption of the Administrator that the public interest in the disclosure of the information outweighs the public or proprietary interest in maintaining the protection for all or a portion of the information that the person has requested not be disclosed or for which disclosure be delayed.

(2) Notification.—

(A) In general.—Except as provided in subparagraph (B) and subsections (b), (d), and (e), if the Administrator denies or denies in part a claim or request under paragraph (1), concludes, in accordance with this section, that the information does not qualify for protection from disclosure, intends to disclose information pursuant to subsection (d), or promulgates a rule under section 6(a) establishing a ban or phase-out with respect to a chemical substance or mixture, the Administrator shall notify, in writing, the person that asserted the claim or submitted the request of the intent of the Administrator to disclose the information or not protect the information from disclosure under this section. The notice shall be furnished by certified mail (return receipt requested), by personal delivery, or by other means that allows verification of the fact and date of receipt.

(B) Disclosure of information.—Except as provided in subparagraph (C), the Administrator shall not disclose information under this subsection until the date that is 30 days after the date on which the person that asserted the claim or submitted the request receives notification under subparagraph (A).

(C) Exceptions.—

(i) Fifteen day notification.—For information the Administrator intends to disclose under subsections (d)(3), (d)(4), (d)(5), and (j), the Administrator shall not disclose the information until the date that is 15 days after the date on which the person that asserted the claim or submitted the request receives notification under subparagraph (A), except that, with respect to information to be disclosed under subsection (d)(3), if the Administrator determines that disclosure of the information is necessary to protect against an imminent and substantial harm to health or the environment, no prior notification shall be necessary.

(ii) Notification as soon as practicable.—For information the Administrator intends to disclose under paragraph (6) of subsection (d), the Administrator shall notify the person that submitted the information that the information has been disclosed as soon as practicable after disclosure of the information.

(iii) No notification required.—Notification shall not be required—

(I) for the disclosure of information under paragraphs (1), (2), (7), or (8) of subsection (d); or

(II) for the disclosure of information for which—

(aa) the Administrator has provided to the person that asserted the claim a notice under subsection (e)(2)(A); and

(bb) such person does not submit to the Administrator a request under subsection (e)(2)(B) on or before the deadline established in subsection (e)(2)(B)(i).

(D) Appeals.—

(i) Action to restrain disclosure.—If a person receives a notification under this paragraph and believes the information is protected from disclosure under this section, before the date on which the information is to be disclosed pursuant to subparagraph (B) or (C) the person may bring an action to restrain disclosure of the information in—

(I) the United States district court of the district in which the complainant resides or has the principal place of business; or

(II) the United States District Court for the District of Columbia.

(ii) No disclosure.—

(I) In general.—Subject to subsection (d), the Administrator shall not disclose information that is the subject of an appeal under this paragraph before the date on which the applicable court rules on an action under clause (i).

(II) Exception.—Subclause (I) shall not apply to disclosure of information described under subsections (d)(4) and (j).

(3) Request and notification systems.—The Administrator, in consultation with the Director of the Centers for Disease Control and Prevention, shall develop a request and notification system that, in a format and language that is readily accessible and understandable, allows for expedient and swift access to information disclosed pursuant to paragraphs (5) and (6) of subsection (d).

(4) Unique identifier.—The Administrator shall—

(A) (i) develop a system to assign a unique identifier to each specific chemical identity for which the Administrator approves a request for protection from disclosure, which shall not be either the specific chemical identity or a structurally descriptive generic term; and

(ii) apply that identifier consistently to all information relevant to the applicable chemical substance;

(B) annually publish and update a list of chemical substances, referred to by their unique identifiers, for which claims to protect the specific chemical identity from disclosure have been approved, including the expiration date for each such claim;

(C) ensure that any nonconfidential information received by the Administrator with respect to a chemical substance included on the list published under subparagraph (B) while the specific chemical identity of the chemical substance is protected from disclosure under this section identifies the chemical substance using the unique identifier; and

(D) for each claim for protection of a specific chemical identity that has been denied by the Administrator or expired, or that has been withdrawn by the person who asserted the claim, and for which the Administrator has used a unique identifier assigned under this paragraph to protect the specific chemical identity in information that the Administrator has made public, clearly link the specific chemical identity to the unique identifier in such information to the extent practicable.

(h) Criminal penalty for wrongful disclosure.—

(1) Individuals subject to penalty.—

(A) In general.—Subject to subparagraph (C) and paragraph (2), an individual described in subparagraph (B) shall be fined under title 18, United States Code, or imprisoned for not more than 1 year, or both.

(B) Description.—An individual referred to in subparagraph (A) is an individual who—

(i) pursuant to this section, obtained possession of, or has access to, information protected from disclosure under this section; and

(ii) knowing that the information is protected from disclosure under this section, willfully discloses the information in any manner to any person not entitled to receive that information.

(C) Exception.—This paragraph shall not apply to any medical professional (including an emergency medical technician or other first responder) who discloses any information obtained under paragraph (5) or (6) of subsection (d) to a patient treated by the medical professional, or to a person authorized to make medical or health care decisions on behalf of such a patient, as needed for the diagnosis or treatment of the patient.

(2) Other laws.—Section 1905 of title 18, United States Code, shall not apply with respect to the publishing, divulging, disclosure, or making known of, or making available, information reported to or otherwise obtained by the Administrator under this Act.

(i) Applicability.—

(1) In general.—Except as otherwise provided in this section, section 8, or any other applicable Federal law, the Administrator shall have no authority—

(A) to require the substantiation or resubstantiation of a claim for the protection from disclosure of information reported to or otherwise obtained by the Administrator under this Act prior to the date of enactment of the Frank R. Lautenberg Chemical Safety for the 21st Century Act; or

(B) to impose substantiation or resubstantiation requirements, with respect to the protection of information described in subsection (a), under this Act that are more extensive than those required under this section.

(2) Actions prior to promulgation of rules.—Nothing in this Act prevents the Administrator from reviewing, requiring substantiation or resubstantiation of, or approving, approving in part, or denying any claim for the protection from disclosure of information before the effective date of such rules applicable to those claims as the Administrator may promulgate after the date of enactment of the Frank R. Lautenberg Chemical Safety for the 21st Century Act.

(j) Access by Congress.—Notwithstanding any limitation contained in this section or any other provision of law, all information reported to or otherwise obtained by the Administrator (or any representative of the Administrator) under this Act shall be made available, upon written request of any duly authorized committee of the Congress, to such committee.

(Pub. L. No. 94–469, Title I, § 14, 90 Stat. 2034 (Oct. 11, 1976); renumbered Title I by Pub. L. No. 99–519, § 3(c)(1), 100 Stat. 2989 (Oct. 22, 1986); and amended by Pub. L. No. 114–182, § 11, 130 Stat. 481–492 (June 22, 2016).)

Retroactivity

Section 20 of Pub. L. No. 114–182, 130 Stat. 510 (June 22, 2016), provided that "[n]othing in sections 1 through 19, or the amendments made by sections 1 through 19, shall be interpreted to apply retroactively to any State, Federal, or maritime legal action filed before the date of enactment of this Act."

§ 2614. Prohibited acts

[TSCA § 15]

It shall be unlawful for any person to—

(1) fail or refuse to comply with any requirement of this title or any rule promulgated, order issued, or consent agreement entered into under this title, or any requirement of subchapter II of this chapter or any rule promulgated or order issued under subchapter II of this chapter;

(2) use for commercial purposes a chemical substance or mixture which such person knew or had reason to know was manufactured, processed, or distributed in commerce in violation of section 2604 or 2605 of this title, a rule or order under section 2604 or 2605 of this title, or an order issued in action brought under section 2604 or 2606 of this title;

(3) fail or refuse to (A) establish or maintain records, (B) submit reports, notices, or other information, or (C) permit access to or copying of records, as required by this chapter or a rule thereunder; or

(4) fail or refuse to permit entry or inspection as required by section 2610 of this title.

(Pub. L. No. 94–469, Title I, § 15, 90 Stat. 2036 (Oct. 11, 1976); renumbered Title I and amended by Pub. L. No. 99–519, § 3(b)(1), (c)(1), 100 Stat. 2988, 2989 (Oct. 22, 1986), and amended by Pub. L. No. 114–182, § 19(*l*), 130 Stat. 508 (June 22, 2016).)

Retroactivity

Section 20 of Pub. L. No. 114–182, 130 Stat. 510 (June 22, 2016), provided that "[n]othing in sections 1 through 19, or the amendments made by sections 1 through 19, shall be interpreted to apply retroactively to any State, Federal, or maritime legal action filed before the date of enactment of this Act."

§ 2615. Penalties

[TSCA § 16]

(a) Civil

(1) Any person who violates a provision of section 2614 or 2689 of this title shall be liable to the United States for a civil penalty in an amount not to exceed $37,500 for each such violation. Each day such a violation continues shall, for purposes of this subsection, constitute a separate violation of section 2614 or 2689 of this title.

(2) **(A)** A civil penalty for a violation of section 2614 or 2689 of this title shall be assessed by the Administrator by an order made on the record after opportunity (provided in accordance with this subparagraph) for a hearing in accordance with section 554 of Title 5. Before issuing such an order, the Administrator shall give written notice to the person to be assessed a civil penalty under such order of the Administrator's proposal to issue such order and provide such person an opportunity to request, within 15 days of the date the notice is received by such person, such a hearing on the order.

(B) In determining the amount of a civil penalty, the Administrator shall take into account the nature, circumstances, extent, and gravity of the violation or violations and, with respect to the violator, ability to pay, effect on ability to continue to do business, any history of prior such violations, the degree of culpability, and such other matters as justice may require.

(C) The Administrator may compromise, modify, or remit, with or without conditions, any civil penalty which may be imposed under this subsection. The amount of such penalty, when finally determined, or the amount agreed upon in compromise, may be deducted from any sums owing by the United States to the person charged.

(3) Any person who requested in accordance with paragraph (2)(A) a hearing respecting the assessment of a civil penalty and who is aggrieved by an order assessing a civil penalty may file a petition for judicial review of such order with the United States Court of Appeals for the District of Columbia Circuit or for any other circuit in which such person resides or transacts business. Such a petition may only be filed within the 30-day period beginning on the date the order making such assessment was issued.

(4) If any person fails to pay an assessment of a civil penalty—

(A) after the order making the assessment has become a final order and if such person does not file a petition for judicial review of the order in accordance with paragraph (3), or

(B) after a court in an action brought under paragraph (3) has entered a final judgment in favor of the Administrator, the Attorney General shall recover the amount assessed (plus interest at currently prevailing rates from the date of the expiration of the 30-day period referred to in paragraph (3) or the date of such final judgment, as the case may be) in an action brought in any appropriate district court of the United States. In such an action, the validity, amount, and appropriateness of such penalty shall not be subject to review.

(b) Criminal

(1) In general.—Any person who knowingly or willfully violates any provision of section 2614 or 2689 of this title, shall, in addition to or in lieu of any civil penalty which may be imposed under subsection (a) of this section for such violation, be subject, upon conviction, to a fine of not more than $50,000 for each day of violation, or to imprisonment for not more than one year, or both.

(2) Imminent danger of death or serious bodily injury.—

(A) In general.—Any person who knowingly and willfully violates any provision of section 15 or 409, and who knows at the time of the violation that the violation places an individual in imminent danger of death or serious bodily injury, shall be subject on conviction to a fine of not more than $250,000, or imprisonment for not more than 15 years, or both.

(B) Organizations.—Notwithstanding the penalties described in subparagraph (A), an organization that commits a knowing violation described in subparagraph (A) shall be subject on conviction to a fine of not more than $1,000,000 for each violation.

(C) Incorporation of corresponding provisions.—Subparagraphs (B) through (F) of section 113(c)(5) of the Clean Air Act (42 U.S.C. 7413(c)(5)(B)–(F)) shall apply to the prosecution of a violation under this paragraph.

(Pub. L. No. 94–469, Title I, § 16, 90 Stat. 2037 (Oct. 11, 1976); renumbered Title I by Pub. L. No. 99–519, § 3(c)(1), 100 Stat. 2989 (Oct. 22, 1986); and amended by Pub. L. No. 102–550, Title X, § 1021(b)(5), 106 Stat. 3923 (Oct. 28, 1992); Pub. L. No. 114–182, § 12, 130 Stat. 492 (June 22, 2016).)

Retroactivity

Section 20 of Pub. L. No. 114–182, 130 Stat. 510 (June 22, 2016), provided that "[n]othing in sections 1 through 19, or the amendments made by sections 1 through 19, shall be interpreted to apply retroactively to any State, Federal, or maritime legal action filed before the date of enactment of this Act."

§ 2616. Specific enforcement and seizure

[TSCA § 17]

(a) Specific enforcement

(1) The district courts of the United States shall have jurisdiction over civil actions to—

(A) restrain any violation of section 2614 or 2689 of this title,

(B) restrain any person from taking any action prohibited by section 2604 of this title, 2605 of this title, or subchapter IV of this subchapter, or by a rule or order under section 2604 of this title, 2605 of this title, or subchapter IV of this chapter,

(C) compel the taking of any action required by or under this chapter, or

(D) direct any manufacturer or processor of a chemical substance, mixture, or product subject to subchapter IV of this subchapter manufactured or processed in violation of section 2604 of this title, 2605 of this title, or subchapter IV of this chapter, or a rule or order under section 2604 of this title, 2605 of this title, or subchapter IV of this chapter, and distributed in commerce, (i) to give notice of such fact to distributors in commerce of such substance, mixture, or product and, to the extent reasonably ascertainable, to other persons in possession of such substance, mixture, or product or exposed to such substance, mixture, or product, (ii) to give public notice of such risk of injury, and (iii) to either replace or repurchase such substance, mixture, or product, whichever the person to which the requirement is directed elects.

(2) A civil action described in paragraph (1) may be brought—

(A) in the case of a civil action described in subparagraph (A) of such paragraph, in the United States district court for the judicial district wherein any act, omission, or transaction constituting a violation of section 2614 of this title occurred or wherein the defendant is found or transacts business, or

(B) in the case of any other civil action described in such paragraph, in the United States district court for the judicial district wherein the defendant is found or transacts business.

In any such civil action process may be served on a defendant in any judicial district in which a defendant resides or may be found. Subpoenas requiring attendance of witnesses in any such action may be served in any judicial district.

(b) Seizure

Any chemical substance, mixture, or product subject to subchapter IV of this chapter which was manufactured, processed, or distributed in commerce in violation of this chapter or any rule promulgated or order issued under this chapter or any article containing such a substance or mixture shall be liable to be proceeded against, by process of libel, for the seizure and condemnation of such substance, mixture, product, or article, in any district court of the United States within the jurisdiction of which such substance, mixture, product, or article is found. Such proceedings shall conform as nearly as possible to proceedings in rem in admiralty.

(Pub. L. No. 94–469, Title I, § 17, 90 Stat. 2037 (Oct. 11, 1976); renumbered Title I by Pub. L. No. 99–519, § 3(c)(1), 100 Stat. 2989 (Oct. 22, 1986); and amended by Pub. L. No. 102–550, Title X, § 1021(b)(6), (7), 106 Stat. 3923 (Oct. 28, 1992).)

HISTORICAL AND STATUTORY NOTES

Federal Rules of Civil Procedure

Admiralty and maritime rules of practice (which included libel procedures) were superseded, and civil and admiralty procedures in United States district courts were unified, effective July 1, 1966, see rule 1 and Supplemental Rules for Certain Admiralty and Maritime Claims, Title 28, Appendix, Judiciary and Judicial Procedure.

Retroactivity

Section 20 of Pub. L. No. 114–182, 130 Stat. 510 (June 22, 2016), provided that "[n]othing in sections 1 through 19, or the amendments made by sections 1 through 19, shall be interpreted to apply retroactively to any State, Federal, or maritime legal action filed before the date of enactment of this Act."

§ 2617. Preemption

[TSCA § 18]

(a) In general.—

(1) Establishment or enforcement.—Except as otherwise provided in subsections (c), (d), (e), (f), and (g), and subject to paragraph (2), no State or political subdivision of a State may establish or continue to enforce any of the following:

(A) Development of information.—A statute or administrative action to require the development of information about a chemical substance or category of chemical substances that is reasonably likely to produce the same information required under section 4, 5, or 6 in—

(i) a rule promulgated by the Administrator;

(ii) a consent agreement entered into by the Administrator; or

(iii) an order issued by the Administrator.

(B) Chemical substances found not to present an unreasonable risk or restricted.—A statute, criminal penalty, or administrative action to prohibit or otherwise restrict the manufacture, processing, or distribution in commerce or use of a chemical substance—

(i) for which the determination described in section 6(i)(1) is made, consistent with the scope of the risk evaluation under section (6)(b)(4)(D); or

(ii) for which a final rule is promulgated under section 6(a), after the effective date of the rule issued under section 6(a) for the chemical substance, consistent with the scope of the risk evaluation under section (6)(b)(4)(D).

(C) Significant new use.—A statute or administrative action requiring the notification of a use of a chemical substance that the Administrator has specified as a significant new use and for which the Administrator has required notification pursuant to a rule promulgated under section 5.

(2) Effective date of preemption.—Under this subsection, Federal preemption of statutes and administrative actions applicable to specific chemical substances shall not occur until the effective date of the applicable action described in paragraph (1) taken by the Administrator.

(b) New statutes, criminal penalties, or administrative actions creating prohibitions or other restrictions.—

(1) In general.—Except as provided in subsections (c), (d), (e), (f), and (g), beginning on the date on which the Administrator defines the scope of a risk evaluation for a chemical substance under section 6(b)(4)(D) and ending on the date on which the deadline established pursuant to section 6(b)(4)(G) for completion of the risk evaluation expires, or on the date on which the Administrator publishes the risk evaluation under section 6(b)(4)(C), whichever is earlier, no State or political subdivision of a State may establish a statute, criminal penalty, or administrative action prohibiting or otherwise restricting the manufacture, processing, distribution in commerce, or use of such chemical substance that is a high-priority substance designated under section 6(b)(1)(B)(i).

(2) Effect of subsection.—This subsection does not restrict the authority of a State or political subdivision of a State to continue to enforce any statute enacted, criminal penalty assessed, or administrative action taken, prior to the date on which the Administrator defines and publishes the scope of a risk evaluation under section 6(b)(4)(D).

(c) Scope of preemption.—Federal preemption under subsections (a) and (b) of statutes, criminal penalties, and administrative actions applicable to specific chemical substances shall apply only to—

(1) with respect to subsection (a)(1)(A), the chemical substances or category of chemical substances subject to a rule, order, or consent agreement under section 4, 5, or 6;

(2) with respect to subsection (b), the hazards, exposures, risks, and uses or conditions of use of such chemical substances included in the scope of the risk evaluation pursuant to section 6(b)(4)(D);

(3) with respect to subsection (a)(1)(B), the hazards, exposures, risks, and uses or conditions of use of such chemical substances included in any final action the Administrator takes pursuant to section 6(a) or 6(i)(1); or

(4) with respect to subsection (a)(1)(C), the uses of such chemical substances that the Administrator has specified as significant new uses and for which the Administrator has required notification pursuant to a rule promulgated under section 5.

(d) Exceptions.—

(1) No preemption of statutes and administrative actions.—

(A) In general.—Nothing in this Act, nor any amendment made by the Frank R. Lautenberg Chemical Safety for the 21st Century Act, nor any rule, standard of performance, risk evaluation, or scientific assessment implemented pursuant to this Act, shall affect the right of a State or a political subdivision of a State to adopt or enforce any rule, standard of performance, risk evaluation, scientific assessment, or any other protection for public health or the environment that—

(i) is adopted or authorized under the authority of any other Federal law or adopted to satisfy or obtain authorization or approval under any other Federal law;

(ii) implements a reporting, monitoring, or other information obligation for the chemical substance not otherwise required by the Administrator under this Act or required under any other Federal law;

(iii) is adopted pursuant to authority under a law of the State or political subdivision of the State related to water quality, air quality, or waste treatment or disposal, except to the extent that the action—

(I) imposes a restriction on the manufacture, processing, distribution in commerce, or use of a chemical substance; and

(II) (aa) addresses the same hazards and exposures, with respect to the same conditions of use as are included in the scope of the risk evaluation published pursuant to section 6(b)(4)(D), but is inconsistent with the action of the Administrator; or

(bb) would cause a violation of the applicable action by the Administrator under section 5 or 6; or

(iv) subject to subparagraph (B), is identical to a requirement prescribed by the Administrator.

(B) Identical requirements.—

(i) In general.—The penalties and other sanctions applicable under a law of a State or political subdivision of a State in the event of noncompliance with the identical requirement shall be no more stringent than the penalties and other sanctions available to the Administrator under section 16 of this Act.

(ii) Penalties.—In the case of an identical requirement—

(I) a State or political subdivision of a State may not assess a penalty for a specific violation for which the Administrator has assessed an adequate penalty under section 16; and

(II) if a State or political subdivision of a State has assessed a penalty for a specific violation, the Administrator may not assess a penalty for that violation in an amount that would cause the total of the penalties assessed for the violation by the State or political subdivision of a State and the Administrator combined to exceed the maximum amount that may be assessed for that violation by the Administrator under section 16.

(2) Applicability to certain rules or orders.—

(A) Prior rules and orders.—Nothing in this section shall be construed as modifying the preemptive effect under this section, as in effect on the day before the effective date of the Frank R. Lautenberg Chemical Safety for the 21st Century Act, of any rule or order promulgated or issued under this Act prior to that effective date.

(B) Certain chemical substances and mixtures.—With respect to a chemical substance or mixture for which any rule or order was promulgated or issued under section 6 prior to the effective date of the Frank R. Lautenberg Chemical Safety for the 21st Century Act with respect to manufacturing, processing, distribution in commerce, use, or disposal of the chemical substance or mixture, nothing in this section shall be construed as modifying the preemptive effect of this section as in effect prior to the enactment of the Frank R. Lautenberg Chemical Safety for the 21st Century Act of any rule or order that is promulgated or issued with respect to such chemical substance or mixture under section 6 after that effective date, unless the latter rule or order is with respect to a chemical substance or mixture containing a chemical substance and follows a designation of that chemical substance as a high-priority substance under section 6(b)(1)(B)(i), the identification of that chemical substance under section 6(b)(2)(A), or the selection of that chemical substance for risk evaluation under section 6(b)(4)(E)(iv)(II).

(e) Preservation of certain laws.—

(1) In general.—Nothing in this Act, subject to subsection (g) of this section, shall—

(A) be construed to preempt or otherwise affect the authority of a State or political subdivision of a State to continue to enforce any action taken or requirement imposed or requirement enacted relating to a specific chemical substance before April 22, 2016, under the authority of a law of the State or political subdivision of the State that prohibits or otherwise restricts manufacturing, processing, distribution in commerce, use, or disposal of a chemical substance; or

(B) be construed to preempt or otherwise affect any action taken pursuant to a State law that was in effect on August 31, 2003.

(2) Effect of subsection.—This subsection does not affect, modify, or alter the relationship between Federal law and laws of a State or political subdivision of a State pursuant to any other Federal law.

(f) Waivers.—

(1) Discretionary exemptions.—Upon application of a State or political subdivision of a State, the Administrator may, by rule, exempt from subsection (a), under such conditions as may be prescribed in the rule, a statute, criminal penalty, or administrative action of that State or political subdivision of the State that relates to the effects of exposure to a chemical substance under the conditions of use if the Administrator determines that—

(A) compelling conditions warrant granting the waiver to protect health or the environment;

(B) compliance with the proposed requirement of the State or political subdivision of the State would not unduly burden interstate commerce in the manufacture, processing, distribution in commerce, or use of a chemical substance;

(C) compliance with the proposed requirement of the State or political subdivision of the State would not cause a violation of any applicable Federal law, rule, or order; and

(D) in the judgment of the Administrator, the proposed requirement of the State or political subdivision of the State is designed to address a risk of a chemical substance, under the conditions of use, that was identified—

(i) consistent with the best available science;

(ii) using supporting studies conducted in accordance with sound and objective scientific practices; and

(iii) based on the weight of the scientific evidence.

(2) Required exemptions.—Upon application of a State or political subdivision of a State, the Administrator shall exempt from subsection (b) a statute or administrative action of a State or political subdivision of a State that relates to the effects of exposure to a chemical substance under the conditions of use if the Administrator determines that—

(A) (i) compliance with the proposed requirement of the State or political subdivision of the State would not unduly burden interstate commerce in the manufacture, processing, distribution in commerce, or use of a chemical substance;

(ii) compliance with the proposed requirement of the State or political subdivision of the State would not cause a violation of any applicable Federal law, rule, or order; and

(iii) the State or political subdivision of the State has a concern about the chemical substance or use of the chemical substance based in peer-reviewed science; or

(B) no later than the date that is 18 months after the date on which the Administrator has initiated the prioritization process for a chemical substance under the rule promulgated pursuant to section 6(b)(1)(A), or the date on which the Administrator publishes the scope of the risk evaluation for a chemical substance under section 6(b)(4)(D), whichever is sooner, the State or political subdivision of the State has enacted a statute or proposed or finalized an administrative action intended to prohibit or otherwise restrict the manufacture, processing, distribution in commerce, or use of the chemical substance.

(3) Determination of a waiver request.—The duty of the Administrator to grant or deny a waiver application shall be nondelegable and shall be exercised—

(A) not later than 180 days after the date on which an application under paragraph (1) is submitted; and

(B) not later than 110 days after the date on which an application under paragraph (2) is submitted.

(4) Failure to make a determination.—If the Administrator fails to make a determination under paragraph (3)(B) during the 110-day period beginning on the date on which an application under paragraph (2) is submitted, the statute or administrative action of the State or political subdivision of the State that was the subject of the application shall not be considered to be an existing statute or administrative action for purposes of subsection (b) by reason of the failure of the Administrator to make a determination.

(5) Notice and comment.—Except in the case of an application approved under paragraph (9), the application of a State or political subdivision of a State under this subsection shall be subject to public notice and comment.

(6) Final agency actions.—The decision of the Administrator on the application of a State or political subdivision of a State shall be—

(A) considered to be a final agency action; and

(B) subject to judicial review.

(7) Duration of waivers.—A waiver granted under paragraph (2) or approved under paragraph (9) shall remain in effect until such time as the Administrator publishes the risk evaluation under section 6(b).

(8) Judicial review of waivers.—Not later than 60 days after the date on which the Administrator makes a determination on an application of a State or political subdivision of a State under paragraph (1) or (2), any person may file a petition for judicial review in the United States Court of Appeals for the District of Columbia Circuit, which shall have exclusive jurisdiction over the determination.

(9) Approval.—

(A) Automatic approval.—If the Administrator fails to meet the deadline established under paragraph (3)(B), the application of a State or political subdivision of a State under paragraph (2) shall be automatically approved, effective on the date that is 10 days after the deadline.

(B) Requirements.—Notwithstanding paragraph (6), approval of a waiver application under subparagraph (A) for failure to meet the deadline under paragraph (3)(B) shall not be considered final agency action or be subject to judicial review or public notice and comment.

(g) Savings.—

(1) No preemption of common law or statutory causes of action for civil relief or criminal conduct.—

(A) In general.—Nothing in this Act, nor any amendment made by the Frank R. Lautenberg Chemical Safety for the 21st Century Act, nor any standard, rule, requirement, standard of performance, risk evaluation, or scientific assessment implemented pursuant to this Act, shall be construed to preempt, displace, or supplant any State or Federal common law rights or any State or Federal statute creating a remedy for civil relief, including those for civil damage, or a penalty for a criminal conduct.

(B) Clarification of no preemption.—Notwithstanding any other provision of this Act, nothing in this Act, nor any amendments made by the Frank R. Lautenberg Chemical Safety for the 21st Century Act, shall preempt or preclude any cause of action for personal injury, wrongful death, property damage, or other injury based on negligence, strict liability, products liability, failure to warn, or any other legal theory of liability under any State law, maritime law, or Federal common law or statutory theory.

(2) No effect on private remedies.—

(A) In general.—Nothing in this Act, nor any amendments made by the Frank R. Lautenberg Chemical Safety for the 21st Century Act, nor any rules, regulations, requirements, risk evaluations, scientific assessments, or orders issued pursuant to this Act shall be interpreted as, in either the plaintiff's or defendant's favor, dispositive in any civil action.

(B) Authority of courts.—This Act does not affect the authority of any court to make a determination in an adjudicatory proceeding under applicable State or Federal law with respect to the admission into evidence or any other use of this Act or rules, regulations, requirements, standards of performance, risk evaluations, scientific assessments, or orders issued pursuant to this Act.

(Pub. L. No. 94–469, Title I, § 18, 90 Stat. 2038 (Oct. 11, 1976); renumbered Title I by Pub. L. No. 99–519, § 3(c)(1), 100 Stat. 2989 (Oct. 22, 1986); and amended by Pub. L. No. 114–182, § 13, 130 Stat. 492–498 (June 22, 2016).)

HISTORICAL AND STATUTORY NOTES

References in Text

The Clean Air Act, referred to in subsec. (a)(2)(B), is Act of July 14, 1955, c. 360, 69 Stat. 322, as amended, codified generally to chapter 85 (§ 7401 et seq.) of Title 42, the Public Health and Welfare. For complete classification of this Act to the Code, see Short Title note set out under section 7401 of Title 42 and Tables.

Retroactivity

Section 20 of Pub. L. No. 114–182, 130 Stat. 510 (June 22, 2016), provided that "[n]othing in sections 1 through 19, or the amendments made by sections 1 through 19, shall be interpreted to apply retroactively to any State, Federal, or maritime legal action filed before the date of enactment of this Act."

§ 2618. Judicial review

[TSCA § 19]

(a) In general

(1) (A) Except as otherwise provided in this title, not later than 60 days after the date on which a rule is promulgated under this title, title II, or title IV, or the date on which an order is issued under section 4, 5(e), 5(f), or 6(i)(1), of this chapter, any person may file a petition for judicial review of such rule or order with the United States Court of Appeals for the District of Columbia Circuit or for the circuit in which such person resides or in which such person's principal place of business is located. Courts of appeals of the United States shall have exclusive jurisdiction of any action to obtain judicial review (other than in an enforcement proceeding) of such a rule or order if any district court of the United States would have had jurisdiction of such action but for this subparagraph.

(B) Except as otherwise provided in this title, courts of appeals of the United States shall have exclusive jurisdiction of any action to obtain judicial review (other than in an enforcement proceeding) of an order issued under this title, other than an order under section 4, 5(e), 5(f), or 6(i)(1) of this title if any district court of the United States would have had jurisdiction of such action but for this subparagraph.

(C) (i) Not later than 60 days after the publication of a designation under section 6(b)(1)(B)(ii), any person may commence a civil action to challenge the designation.

(ii) The United States Court of Appeals for the District of Columbia Circuit shall have exclusive jurisdiction over a civil action filed under this subparagraph.

(2) Copies of any petition filed under paragraph (1)(A) shall be transmitted forthwith to the Administrator and to the Attorney General by the clerk of the court with which such petition was filed. The provisions of section 2112 of Title 28 shall apply to the filing of the record of proceedings on which the Administrator based the rule or order being reviewed under this section and to the transfer of proceedings between United States courts of appeals.

(b) Additional submissions and presentations; modifications

If in an action under this section to review a rule, or an order under section 4, 5(e), 5(f), or 6(i)(1), the petitioner or the Administrator applies to the court for leave to make additional oral submissions or written presentations respecting such rule or order and shows to the satisfaction of the court that such submissions and presentations would be material and that there were reasonable grounds for the submissions and failure to make such submissions and presentations in the proceeding before the Administrator, the court may order the Administrator to provide additional opportunity to make such submissions and presentations. The Administrator may modify or set aside the rule or order being reviewed or make a new rule or order by reason of the additional submissions and presentations and shall file such modified or new rule or order with the return of such submissions and presentations. The court shall thereafter review such new or modified rule or order.

(c) Standard of review

(1) (A) Upon the filing of a petition under subsection (a)(1) of this section for judicial review of a rule or order, the court shall have jurisdiction (i) to grant appropriate relief, including interim relief, as provided in chapter 7 of Title 5 and (ii) except as otherwise provided in subparagraph (B), to review such rule or order in accordance with chapter 7 of Title 5.

(B) Section 706 of Title 5 shall apply to review of a rule or order under this section, except that—

(i) in the case of review of—

(I) a rule under section 4(a), 5(b)(4), 6(a) (including review of the associated determination under section 6(b)(4)(A)), or 6(e), the standard for review prescribed by paragraph (2)(E) of such section 706 shall not apply and the court shall hold unlawful and set aside such rule if the court finds that the rule is not supported by substantial evidence in the rulemaking record taken as a whole; and

(II) an order under section 4, 5(e), 5(f), or 6(i)(1), the standard for review prescribed by paragraph (2)(E) of such section 706 shall not apply and the court shall hold unlawful and set aside such order if the court finds that the order is not supported by substantial evidence in the record taken as a whole; and

(ii) the court may not review the contents and adequacy of any statement of basis and purpose required by section 553(c) of title 5, United States Code, to be incorporated in the rule or order, except as part of the record, taken as a whole.

(2) The judgment of the court affirming or setting aside, in whole or in part, any rule or order reviewed in accordance with this section shall be final, subject to review by the Supreme Court of the United States upon certiorari or certification, as provided in section 1254 of Title 28.

(d) Fees and costs

The decision of the court in an action commenced under subsection (a) of this section, or of the Supreme Court of the United States on review of such a decision, may include an award of costs of suit and reasonable fees for attorneys and expert witnesses if the court determines that such an award is appropriate.

(e) Other remedies

The remedies as provided in this section shall be in addition to and not in lieu of any other remedies provided by law.

(Pub. L. No. 94–469, Title I, § 19, 90 Stat. 2039 (Oct. 11, 1976); renumbered Title I and amended by Pub. L. No. 99–519, § 3(b)(2), (c)(1), 100 Stat. 2989 (Oct. 22, 1986); and amended by Pub. L. No. 102–550, Title X, § 1021(b)(8), 106 Stat. 3923 (Oct. 28, 1992); Pub. L. No. 114–182, §§ 14, 19(m) 130 Stat. 498, 508–509 (June 22, 2016).)

Retroactivity

Section 20 of Pub. L. No. 114–182, 130 Stat. 510 (June 22, 2016), provided that "[n]othing in sections 1 through 19, or the amendments made by sections 1 through 19, shall be interpreted to apply retroactively to any State, Federal, or maritime legal action filed before the date of enactment of this Act."

§ 2619. Citizens' civil actions

[TSCA § 20]

(a) In general

Except as provided in subsection (b)of this section, any person may commence a civil action—

(1) against any person (including (A) the United States, and (B) any other governmental instrumentality or agency to the extent permitted by the eleventh amendment to the Constitution) who is alleged to be in violation of this chapter or any rule promulgated under section 2603, 2604, or 2605 of this title, or subchapter II or IV of this chapter, or order issued under section 4 or 5 of this title or subchapter II or IV of this chapter to restrain such violation, or

(2) against the Administrator to compel the Administrator to perform any act or duty under this chapter which is not discretionary.

Any civil action under paragraph (1) shall be brought in the United States district court for the district in which the alleged violation occurred or in which the defendant resides or in which the defendant's principal place of business is located. Any action brought under paragraph (2) shall be brought in the United States District Court for the District of Columbia, or the United States district court for the judicial district in which the plaintiff is domiciled. The district courts of the United States shall have jurisdiction over suits brought under this section, without regard to the amount in controversy or the citizenship of the parties. In any civil action under this subsection process may be served on a defendant in any judicial district in which the defendant resides or may be found and subpoenas for witnesses may be served in any judicial district.

(b) Limitation

No civil action may be commenced—

(1) under subsection (a)(1) of this section to restrain a violation of this chapter or rule or order under this chapter—

(A) before the expiration of 60 days after the plaintiff has given notice of such violation (i) to the Administrator, and (ii) to the person who is alleged to have committed such violation, or

(B) if the Administrator has commenced and is diligently prosecuting a proceeding for the issuance of an order under section 2615(a)(2) of this title to require compliance with this chapter or with such rule or order or if the Attorney General has commenced and is diligently prosecuting a civil action in a court of the United States to require compliance with this chapter or with such rule or order, but if such proceeding or civil action is commenced after the giving of notice, any person giving such notice may intervene as a matter of right in such proceeding or action;

(2) under subsection (a)(2) of this section before the expiration of 60 days after the plaintiff has given notice to the Administrator of the alleged failure of the Administrator to perform an act or duty which is the basis for such action or, in the case of an action under such subsection for the failure of the Administrator to file an action under section 2606 of this title, before the expiration of ten days after such notification, except that no prior notification shall be required in the case of a civil action brought to compel a decision by the Administrator pursuant to section 18(f)(3)(B); or

(3) in the case of a civil action brought to compel a decision by the Administrator pursuant to section 18(f)(3)(B), after the date that is 60 days after the deadline specified in section 18(f)(3)(B).".

Notice under this subsection shall be given in such manner as the Administrator shall prescribe by rule.

(c) General

(1) In any action under this section, the Administrator, if not a party, may intervene as a matter of right.

(2) The court, in issuing any final order in any action brought pursuant to subsection (a) of this section, may award costs of suit and reasonable fees for attorneys and expert witnesses if the court determines that such an award is appropriate. Any court, in issuing its decision in an action brought to review such an order, may award costs of suit and reasonable fees for attorneys if the court determines that such an award is appropriate.

(3) Nothing in this section shall restrict any right which any person (or class of persons) may have under any statute or common law to seek enforcement of this chapter or any rule or order under this chapter or to seek any other relief.

(d) Consolidation

When two or more civil actions brought under subsection (a) of this section involving the same defendant and the same issues or violations are pending in two or more judicial districts, such pending actions, upon application of such defendants to such actions which is made to a court in which any such action is brought, may, if such court in its discretion so decides, be consolidated for trial by order (issued after giving all parties reasonable notice and opportunity to be heard) of such court and tried in—

(1) any district which is selected by such defendant and in which one of such actions is pending,

(2) a district which is agreed upon by stipulation between all the parties to such actions and in which one of such actions is pending, or

(3) a district which is selected by the court and in which one of such actions is pending.

The court issuing such an order shall give prompt notification of the order to the other courts in which the civil actions consolidated under the order are pending.

(Pub. L. No. 94–469, Title I, § 20, 90 Stat. 2041 (Oct. 11, 1976); renumbered Title I and amended by Pub. L. No. 99–519, § 3(b)(3), (c)(1), 100 Stat. 2989 (Oct. 22, 1986); and amended by Pub. L. No. 102–550, Title X, § 1021(b)(9), 106 Stat. 3923 (Oct. 28, 1992); Pub. L. No. 114–182, §§ 15, 19(n) 130 Stat. 498, 509 (June 22. 2016).)

§ 2620. Citizens' petitions

[TSCA § 21]

(a) In general

Any person may petition the Administrator to initiate a proceeding for the issuance, amendment, or repeal of a rule under section 2603, 2605, or 2607 of this title or an order under section 4 or 5(e) or (f)of this title.

(b) Procedures

(1) Such petition shall be filed in the principal office of the Administrator and shall set forth the facts which it is claimed establish that it is necessary to issue, amend, or repeal a rule under section 2603, 2605, or 2607 of this title or an order under section 4 or 5(e) or (f) of this title.

(2) The Administrator may hold a public hearing or may conduct such investigation or proceeding as the Administrator deems appropriate in order to determine whether or not such petition should be granted.

(3) Within 90 days after filing of a petition described in paragraph (1), the Administrator shall either grant or deny the petition. If the Administrator grants such petition, the Administrator shall promptly commence an appropriate proceeding in accordance with section 2603, 2604, 2605, or 2607 of this title. If the Administrator denies such petition, the Administrator shall publish in the Federal Register the Administrator's reasons for such denial.

(4) (A) If the Administrator denies a petition filed under this section (or if the Administrator fails to grant or deny such petition within the 90-day period) the petitioner may commence a civil action in a district court of the United States to compel the Administrator to initiate a rulemaking proceeding as requested in the petition. Any such action shall be filed within 60 days after the Administrator's denial of the petition or, if the Administrator fails to grant or deny the petition within 90 days after filing the petition, within 60 days after the expiration of the 90-day period.

(B) In an action under subparagraph (A) respecting a petition to initiate a proceeding to issue a rule under section 2603, 2605, or 2607 of this title or an order under section 4 or 5(e) or (f) of this title, the petitioner shall be provided an opportunity to have such petition considered by the court in a de novo proceeding. If the petitioner demonstrates to the satisfaction of the court by a preponderance of the evidence that—

(i) in the case of a petition to initiate a proceeding for the issuance of a rule under section 2603 of this title or an order under section 4 or 5(e) of this title—

(I) information available to the Administrator is insufficient to permit a reasoned evaluation of the health and environmental effects of the chemical substance to be subject to such rule or order; and

(II) in the absence of such information, the substance may present an unreasonable risk to health or the environment, or the substance is or will be produced in substantial quantities and it enters or may reasonably be anticipated to enter the environment in substantial quantities or there is or may be significant or substantial human exposure to it; or

(ii) in the case of a petition to initiate a proceeding for the issuance of a rule section 6(a) or 8 or an order under section 5(f), the chemical substance or mixture to be subject to such rule or order presents an unreasonable risk of injury to health or the environment, without consideration of costs or other nonrisk factors, including an unreasonable risk to a potentially exposed or susceptible subpopulation, under the conditions of use.

the court shall order the Administrator to initiate the action requested by the petitioner. If the court finds that the extent of the risk to health or the environment alleged by the petitioner is less than the extent of risks to health or the environment with respect to which the Administrator is taking action under this chapter and there are insufficient resources available to the Administrator to take the action requested by the petitioner, the court may permit the Administrator to defer initiating the action requested by the petitioner until such time as the court prescribes.

(C) The court in issuing any final order in any action brought pursuant to subparagraph (A) may award costs of suit and reasonable fees for attorneys and expert witnesses if the court determines that such an award is appropriate. Any court, in issuing its decision in an action brought to review such an order, may award costs of suit and reasonable fees for attorneys if the court determines that such an award is appropriate.

(5) The remedies under this section shall be in addition to, and not in lieu of, other remedies provided by law.

(Pub. L. No. 94–469, Title I, § 21, 90 Stat. 2042 (Oct. 11, 1976); renumbered Title I by Pub. L. No. 99–519, § 3(c)(1), 100 Stat. 2989 (Oct. 22, 1986); and amended by Pub. L. No. 114–182, § 19(*o*), 130 Stat. 509–510 (June 22, 2016).)

§ 2621. National defense waiver

[TSCA § 22]

The Administrator shall waive compliance with any provision of this chapter upon a request and determination by the President that the requested waiver is necessary in the interest of national defense. The Administrator shall maintain a written record of the basis upon which such waiver was granted and make such record available for in camera examination when relevant in a judicial proceeding under this chapter. Upon the issuance of such a waiver, the Administrator shall publish in the Federal Register a notice that the waiver was granted for national defense purposes, unless, upon the request of the President, the Administrator determines to omit such publication because the publication itself would be contrary to the interests of national defense, in which event the Administrator shall submit notice thereof to the Armed Services Committees of the Senate and the House of Representatives.

(Pub. L. No. 94–469, Title I, § 22, 90 Stat. 2044 (Oct. 11, 1976); renumbered Title I by Pub. L. No. 99–519, § 3(c)(1), 100 Stat. 2989 (Oct. 22, 1986).)

HISTORICAL AND STATUTORY NOTES

Change of Name

Committee on Armed Services of the House of Representatives changed to the Committee on National Security of the House of Representatives, see section 1(a)(1) of Pub. L. No. 104–14, set out as a note preceding section 21 of Title 2, The Congress.

§ 2622. Employee protection

[TSCA § 23]

(a) In general

No employer may discharge any employee or otherwise discriminate against any employee with respect to the employee's compensation, terms, conditions, or privileges of employment because the employee (or any person acting pursuant to a request of the employee) has—

(1) commenced, caused to be commenced, or is about to commence or cause to be commenced a proceeding under this chapter;

(2) testified or is about to testify in any such proceeding; or

(3) assisted or participated or is about to assist or participate in any manner in such a proceeding or in any other action to carry out the purposes of this chapter.

(b) Remedy

(1) Any employee who believes that the employee has been discharged or otherwise discriminated against by any person in violation of subsection (a) of this section may, within 30 days after such alleged violation occurs, file (or have any person file on the employee's behalf) a complaint with the Secretary of Labor (hereinafter in this section referred to as the "Secretary") alleging such discharge or discrimination. Upon receipt of such a complaint, the Secretary shall notify the person named in the complaint of the filing of the complaint.

(2) (A) Upon receipt of a complaint filed under paragraph (1), the Secretary shall conduct an investigation of the violation alleged in the complaint. Within 30 days of the receipt of such complaint, the Secretary shall complete such investigation and shall notify in writing the complainant (and any person acting on behalf of the complainant) and the person alleged to have committed such violation of the results of the investigation conducted pursuant to this paragraph. Within ninety days of the receipt of such complaint the Secretary shall, unless the proceeding on the complaint is terminated by the Secretary on the basis of a settlement entered into by the Secretary and the person alleged to have committed such violation, issue an order either providing the relief prescribed by subparagraph (B) or denying the complaint. An order of the Secretary shall be made on the record after notice and opportunity for agency hearing. The Secretary may not enter into a settlement terminating a proceeding on a complaint without the participation and consent of the complainant.

(B) If in response to a complaint filed under paragraph (1) the Secretary determines that a violation of subsection (a) of this section has occurred, the Secretary shall order (i) the person who committed such violation to take affirmative action to abate the violation, (ii) such person to reinstate the complainant to the complainant's former position together with the compensation (including back pay), terms, conditions, and privileges of the complainant's employment, (iii) compensatory damages, and (iv) where appropriate, exemplary damages. If such an order issued, the Secretary, at the request of the complainant, shall assess against the person against whom the order is issued a sum equal to the aggregate amount of all costs and expenses (including attorney's fees) reasonably incurred, as determined by the Secretary, by the complainant for, or in connection with, the bringing of the complaint upon which the order was issued.

(c) Review

(1) Any employee or employer adversely affected or aggrieved by an order issued under subsection (b) of this section may obtain review of the order in the United States Court of Appeals for the circuit in which the violation, with respect to which the order was issued, allegedly occurred. The petition for review must be filed within sixty days from the issuance of the Secretary's order. Review shall conform to chapter 7 of Title 5.

(2) An order of the Secretary, with respect to which review could have been obtained under paragraph (1), shall not be subject to judicial review in any criminal or other civil proceeding.

(d) Enforcement

Whenever a person has failed to comply with an order issued under subsection (b)(2) of this section, the Secretary shall file a civil action in the United States district court for the district in which the violation was found to occur to enforce such order. In actions brought under this subsection, the district courts shall have jurisdiction to grant all appropriate relief, including injunctive relief and compensatory and exemplary damages.

(e) Exclusion

Subsection (a) of this section shall not apply with respect to any employee who, acting without direction from the employee's employer (or any agent of the employer), deliberately causes a violation of any requirement of this chapter.

(Pub. L. No. 94–469, Title I, § 23, 90 Stat. 2044 (Oct. 11, 1976); and amended by Pub. L. No. 98–620, Title IV, § 402(19), 98 Stat. 3358 (Nov. 8, 1984); renumbered Title I by Pub. L. No. 99–519, § 3(c)(1), 100 Stat. 2989 (Oct. 22, 1986).)

HISTORICAL AND STATUTORY NOTES

Effective and Applicability Provisions

1984 Acts. Amendment by Pub. L. No. 98–620 not applicable to cases pending on Nov. 8, 1984, see section 403 of Pub. L. No. 98–620, set out as an Effective Date note under section 1657 of Title 28, Judiciary and Judicial Procedure.

§ 2623. Employment effects

[TSCA § 24]

(a) In general

The Administrator shall evaluate on a continuing basis the potential effects on employment (including reductions in employment or loss of employment from threatened plant closures)of—

(1) the issuance of a rule or order under section 2603, 2604, or 2605 of this title, or

(2) a requirement of section 2604 or 2605 of this title.

(b) Investigations

(1) Any employee (or any representative of an employee) may request the Administrator to make an investigation of—

(A) a discharge or layoff or threatened discharge or layoff of the employee, or

(B) adverse or threatened adverse effects on the employee's employment,

allegedly resulting from a rule or order under section 2603, 2604, or 2605 of this title or a requirement of section 2604 or 2605 of this title. Any such request shall be made in writing, shall set forth with reasonable particularity the grounds for the request, and shall be signed by the employee, or representative of such employee, making the request.

(2) **(A)** Upon receipt of a request made in accordance with paragraph (1) the Administrator shall (i) conduct the investigation requested, and (ii) if requested by any interested person, hold public hearings on any matter involved in the investigation unless the Administrator, by order issued within 45 days of the date such hearings are requested, denies the request for the hearings because the Administrator determines there are no reasonable grounds for holding such hearings. If the Administrator makes such a determination, the Administrator shall notify in writing the person requesting the hearing of the determination and the reasons therefor and shall publish the determination and the reasons therefor in the Federal Register.

(B) If public hearings are to be held on any matter involved in an investigation conducted under this subsection—

(i) at least five days' notice shall be provided the person making the request for the investigation and any person identified in such request, and

(ii) each employee who made or for whom was made a request for such hearings and the employer of such employee shall be required to present information respecting the applicable matter referred to in paragraph (1)(A) or (1)(B) together with the basis for such information.

(3) Upon completion of an investigation under paragraph (2), the Administrator shall make findings of fact, shall make such recommendations as the Administrator deems appropriate, and shall make available to the public such findings and recommendations.

(4) This section shall not be construed to require the Administrator to amend or repeal any rule or order in effect under this chapter.

(Pub. L. No. 94–469, Title I, § 24, 90 Stat. 2045 (Oct. 11, 1976); renumbered Title I by Pub. L. No. 99–519, § 3(c)(1), 100 Stat. 2989 (Oct. 22, 1986); and amended by Pub. L. No. 114–182, § 19(p), 130 Stat. 510 (June 22, 2016).)

§ 2624. Repealed. Pub. L. No. 114–182, § 16, 130 Stat. 499 (June 22, 2016).

[TSCA § 25]

(Pub. L. No. 94–469, Title I, § 25, 90 Stat. 2046 (Oct. 11, 1976); as amended by Pub. L. No. 96–88, Title V, § 509(b), 93 Stat. 695 (Oct. 17, 1979); renumbered Title I by Pub. L. No. 99–519, § 3(c)(1), 100 Stat. 2989 (Oct. 22, 1986); repealed by Pub. L. No. 114–182, § 16, 130 Stat. 499 (June 22, 2016).)

§ 2625. Administration

[TSCA § 26]

(a) Cooperation of Federal agencies

Upon request by the Administrator, each Federal department and agency is authorized—

(1) to make its services, personnel, and facilities available (with or without reimbursement) to the Administrator to assist the Administrator in the administration of this chapter; and

(2) to furnish to the Administrator such information, data, estimates, and statistics, and to allow the Administrator access to all information in its possession as the Administrator may reasonably determine to be necessary for the administration of this chapter.

(b) Fees

(1) The Administrator may, by rule, require the payment from any person required to submit information under section 4 or a notice or other information to be reviewed by the Administrator under section 5, or who manufactures or processes a chemical substance that is the subject of a risk evaluation under section 6(b), of a fee that is sufficient and not more than reasonably necessary to defray the cost related to such chemical substance of administering sections 4, 5, and 6, and collecting, processing, reviewing, and providing access to and protecting from disclosure as appropriate under section 14 information on chemical substances under this title, including contractor costs incurred by the Administrator. In setting a fee under this paragraph, the Administrator shall take into account the ability to pay of the person required to pay such fee and the cost to the Administrator of carrying out the activities described in this paragraph. Such rules may provide for sharing such a fee in any case in which the expenses of testing are shared under section 2603 or 2604 of this title

(2) The Administrator, after consultation with the Administrator of the Small Business Administration, shall by rule prescribe standards for determining the persons which qualify as small business concerns for purposes of paragraph (4).

(c) Action with respect to categories

(1) Any action authorized or required to be taken by the Administrator under any provision of this chapter with respect to a chemical substance or mixture may be taken by the Administrator in accordance with that provision with respect to a category of chemical substances or mixtures. Whenever the Administrator takes action under a provision of this chapter with respect to a category of chemical substances or mixtures, any reference in this chapter to a chemical substance or mixture (insofar as it relates to such action) shall be deemed to be a reference to each chemical substance or mixture in such category.

(2) For purposes of paragraph (1):

(A) The term "category of chemical substances" means a group of chemical substances the members of which are similar in molecular structure, in physical, chemical, or biological properties, in use, or in mode of entrance into the human body or into the environment, or the members of which are in some other way suitable for classification as such for purposes of this chapter, except that such term does not mean a group of chemical substances which are grouped together solely on the basis of their being new chemical substances.

(B) The term "category of mixtures" means a group of mixtures the members of which are similar in molecular structure, in physical, chemical, or biological properties, in use, or in the mode of entrance into the human body or into the environment, or the members of which are in some other way suitable for classification as such for purposes of this chapter.

(3) Fund.—

(A) Establishment.—There is established in the Treasury of the United States a fund, to be known as the TSCA Service Fee Fund (in this paragraph referred to as the 'Fund'), consisting of such amounts as are deposited in the Fund under this paragraph.

(B) Collection and deposit of fees.—Subject to the conditions of subparagraph (C), the Administrator shall collect the fees described in this subsection and deposit those fees in the Fund.

(C) Use of funds by Administrator.—Fees authorized under this section shall be collected and available for obligation only to the extent and in the amount provided in advance in appropriations Acts, and shall be available without fiscal year limitation for use in defraying the costs of the activities described in paragraph (1).

(D) Accounting and auditing.—

(i) Accounting.—The Administrator shall biennially prepare and submit to the Committee on Environment and Public Works of the Senate and the Committee on Energy and Commerce of the House of Representatives a report that includes an accounting of the fees paid to the Administrator under this paragraph and amounts disbursed from the Fund for the period covered by the report, as reflected by financial statements provided in accordance with sections 3515 and 3521 of title 31, United States Code.

(ii) Auditing.—

(I) In general.—For the purpose of section 3515(c) of title 31, United States Code, the Fund shall be considered a component of a covered executive agency.

(II) Components of audit.—The annual audit required in accordance with sections 3515 and 3521 of title 31, United States Code, of the financial statements of activities carried out using amounts from the Fund shall include an analysis of—

(aa) the fees collected and amounts disbursed under this subsection;

(bb) the reasonableness of the fees in place as of the date of the audit to meet current and projected costs of administering the provisions of this title for which the fees may be used; and

(cc) the number of requests for a risk evaluation made by manufacturers under section 6(b)(4)(C)(ii).

(III) Federal responsibility.—The Inspector General of the Environmental Protection Agency shall conduct the annual audit described in subclause (II) and submit to the Administrator a report that describes the findings and any recommendations of the Inspector General resulting from the audit.

(4) Amount and adjustment of fees; refunds.—In setting fees under this section, the Administrator shall—

(A) prescribe lower fees for small business concerns, after consultation with the Administrator of the Small Business Administration;

(B) set the fees established under paragraph (1) at levels such that the fees will, in aggregate, provide a sustainable source of funds to annually defray—

(i) the lower of—

(I) 25 percent of the costs to the Administrator of carrying out sections 4, 5, and 6, and of collecting, processing, reviewing, and providing access to and protecting from disclosure as appropriate under section 14 information on chemical substances under this title, other than the costs to conduct and complete risk evaluations under section 6(b); or

(II) $25,000,000 (subject to adjustment pursuant to subparagraph (F)); and

(ii) the costs of risk evaluations specified in subparagraph (D);

(C) reflect an appropriate balance in the assessment of fees between manufacturers and processors, and allow the payment of fees by consortia of manufacturers or processors;

(D) notwithstanding subparagraph (B)—

(i) except as provided in clause (ii), for chemical substances for which the Administrator has granted a request from a manufacturer pursuant to section 6(b)(4)(C)(ii), establish the fee at a level sufficient to defray the full costs to the Administrator of conducting the risk evaluation under section 6(b);

(ii) for chemical substances for which the Administrator has granted a request from a manufacturer pursuant to section 6(b)(4)(C)(ii), and which are included in the 2014 update of the TSCA Work Plan for Chemical Assessments, establish the fee at a level sufficient to defray 50 percent of the costs to the Administrator of conducting the risk evaluation under section 6(b); and

(iii) apply fees collected pursuant to clauses (i) and (ii) only to defray the costs described in those clauses;

(E) prior to the establishment or amendment of any fees under paragraph (1), consult and meet with parties potentially subject to the fees or their representatives, subject to the condition that no obligation under the Federal Advisory Committee Act (5 U.S.C. App.) or subchapter II of chapter 5 of title 5, United States Code, is applicable with respect to such meetings;

(F) beginning with the fiscal year that is 3 years after the date of enactment of the Frank R. Lautenberg Chemical Safety for the 21st Century Act, and every 3 years thereafter, after consultation with parties potentially subject to the fees and their representatives pursuant to subparagraph (E), increase or decrease the fees established under paragraph (1) as necessary to adjust for inflation and to ensure that funds deposited in the Fund are sufficient to defray—

(i) approximately but not more than 25 percent of the costs to the Administrator of carrying out sections 4, 5, and 6, and of collecting, processing, reviewing, and providing access to and protecting from disclosure as appropriate under section 14 information on chemical substances under this title, other than the costs to conduct and complete risk evaluations requested under section 6(b)(4)(C)(ii); and

(ii) the costs of risk evaluations specified in subparagraph (D); and

(G) if a notice submitted under section 5 is not reviewed or such a notice is withdrawn, refund the fee or a portion of the fee if no substantial work was performed on the notice.

(5) **Minimum amount of appropriations.**—Fees may not be assessed for a fiscal year under this section unless the amount of appropriations for the Chemical Risk Review and Reduction program project of the Environmental Protection Agency for the fiscal year (excluding the amount of any fees appropriated for the fiscal year) are equal to or greater than the amount of appropriations for that program project for fiscal year 2014.

(6) **Termination.**—The authority provided by this subsection shall terminate at the conclusion of the fiscal year that is 10 years after the date of enactment of the Frank R. Lautenberg Chemical Safety for the 21st Century Act unless otherwise reauthorized or modified by Congress.

(d) Assistance office

The Administrator shall establish in the Environmental Protection Agency an identifiable office to provide technical and other nonfinancial assistance to manufacturers and processors of chemical substances and mixtures respecting the requirements of this chapter applicable to such manufacturers and processors, the policy of the Agency respecting the application of such requirements to such manufacturers and processors, and the means and methods by which such manufacturers and processors may comply with such requirements.

(e) Financial disclosures

(1) Except as provided under paragraph (3), each officer or employee of the Environmental Protection Agency and the Department of Health and Human Services who—

(A) performs any function or duty under this chapter, and

(B) has any known financial interest (i) in any person subject to this chapter or any rule or order in effect under this chapter, or (ii) in any person who applies for or receives any grant or contract under this chapter,

shall, on February 1, 1978, and on February 1 of each year thereafter, file with the Administrator or the Secretary of Health and Human Services (hereinafter in this subsection referred to as the "Secretary"), as appropriate, a written statement concerning all such interests held by such officer or employee during the preceding calendar year. Such statement shall be made available to the public.

(2) The Administrator and the Secretary shall—

(A) act within 90 days of January 1, 1977—

(i) to define the term "known financial interests" for purposes of paragraph (1), and

(ii) to establish the methods by which the requirement to file written statements specified in paragraph (1) will be monitored and enforced, including appropriate provisions for review by the Administrator and the Secretary of such statements; and

(B) report to the Congress on June 1, 1978, and on June 1 of each year thereafter with respect to such statements and the actions taken in regard thereto during the preceding calendar year.

(3) The Administrator may by rule identify specific positions with the Environmental Protection Agency, and the Secretary may by rule identify specific positions with the Department of Health and Human Services, which are of a nonregulatory or nonpolicymaking nature, and the Administrator and the Secretary may by rule provide that officers or employees occupying such positions shall be exempt from the requirements of paragraph (1).

(4) This subsection does not supersede any requirement of chapter 11 of Title 18.

(5) Any officer or employee who is subject to, and knowingly violates, this subsection or any rule issued thereunder, shall be fined not more than $2,500 or imprisoned not more than one year, or both.

(f) Statement of basis and purpose

Any final order issued under this chapter shall be accompanied by a statement of its basis and purpose. The contents and adequacy of any such statement shall not be subject to judicial review in any respect.

(g) Assistant Administrator

(1) The President, by and with the advice and consent of the Senate, shall appoint an Assistant Administrator for Toxic Substances of the Environmental Protection Agency. Such Assistant Administrator shall be a qualified individual who is, by reason of background and experience, especially qualified to direct a program concerning the effects of chemicals on human health and the environment. Such Assistant Administrator shall be responsible for (A) the collection of information, (B) the preparation of studies, (C) the making of recommendations to the Administrator for regulatory and other actions to carry out the purposes and to facilitate the administration of this chapter, and (D) such other functions as the Administrator may assign or delegate.

(2) The Assistant Administrator to be appointed under paragraph (1) shall be in addition to the Assistant Administrators of the Environmental Protection Agency authorized by section 1(d) of Reorganization Plan No. 3 of 1970.

(h) Scientific standards.—In carrying out sections 4, 5, and 6, to the extent that the Administrator makes a decision based on science, the Administrator shall use scientific information, technical procedures, measures, methods, protocols, methodologies, or models, employed in a manner consistent with the best available science, and shall consider as applicable—

(1) the extent to which the scientific information, technical procedures, measures, methods, protocols, methodologies, or models employed to generate the information are reasonable for and consistent with the intended use of the information;

(2) the extent to which the information is relevant for the Administrator's use in making a decision about a chemical substance or mixture;

(3) the degree of clarity and completeness with which the data, assumptions, methods, quality assurance, and analyses employed to generate the information are documented;

(4) the extent to which the variability and uncertainty in the information, or in the procedures, measures, methods, protocols, methodologies, or models, are evaluated and characterized; and

(5) the extent of independent verification or peer review of the information or of the procedures, measures, methods, protocols, methodologies, or models.

(i) Weight of scientific evidence.—The Administrator shall make decisions under sections 4, 5, and 6 based on the weight of the scientific evidence.

(j) Availability of information.—Subject to section 14, the Administrator shall make available to the public—

(1) all notices, determinations, findings, rules, consent agreements, and orders of the Administrator under this title;

(2) any information required to be provided to the Administrator under section 4;

(3) a nontechnical summary of each risk evaluation conducted under section 6(b);

(4) a list of the studies considered by the Administrator in carrying out each such risk evaluation, along with the results of those studies; and

(5) each designation of a chemical substance under section 6(b), along with an identification of the information, analysis, and basis used to make the designations.

(k) Reasonably available information.—In carrying out sections 4, 5, and 6, the Administrator shall take into consideration information relating to a chemical substance or mixture, including hazard and exposure information, under the conditions of use, that is reasonably available to the Administrator.

(*l*) Policies, procedures, and guidance.—

(1) Development.—Not later than 2 years after the date of enactment of the Frank R. Lautenberg Chemical Safety for the 21st Century Act, the Administrator shall develop any policies, procedures, and guidance the Administrator determines are necessary to carry out the amendments to this Act made by the Frank R. Lautenberg Chemical Safety for the 21st Century Act.

(2) Review.—Not later than 5 years after the date of enactment of the Frank R. Lautenberg Chemical Safety for the 21st Century Act, and not less frequently than once every 5 years thereafter, the Administrator shall—

(A) review the adequacy of the policies, procedures, and guidance developed under paragraph (1), including with respect to animal, nonanimal, and epidemiological test methods and procedures for assessing and determining risk under this title; and

(B) revise such policies, procedures, and guidance as the Administrator determines necessary to reflect new scientific developments or understandings.

(3) Testing of chemical substances and mixtures.—The policies, procedures, and guidance developed under paragraph (1) applicable to testing chemical substances and mixtures shall—

(A) address how and when the exposure level or exposure potential of a chemical substance or mixture would factor into decisions to require new testing, subject to the condition that the Administrator shall not interpret the lack of exposure information as a lack of exposure or exposure potential; and

(B) describe the manner in which the Administrator will determine that additional information is necessary to carry out this title, including information relating to potentially exposed or susceptible populations.

(4) Chemical substances with completed risk assessments.—With respect to a chemical substance listed in the 2014 update to the TSCA Work Plan for Chemical Assessments for which the Administrator has published a completed risk assessment prior to the date of enactment of the Frank R. Lautenberg Chemical Safety for the 21st Century Act, the Administrator may publish proposed and final rules under section 6(a) that are consistent with the scope of the completed risk assessment for the chemical substance and consistent with other applicable requirements of section 6.

(5) Guidance.—Not later than 1 year after the date of enactment of the Frank R. Lautenberg Chemical Safety for the 21st Century Act, the Administrator shall develop guidance to assist interested persons in developing and submitting draft risk evaluations which shall be considered by the Administrator. The guidance shall, at a minimum, address the quality of the information submitted and the process to be followed in developing draft risk evaluations for consideration by the Administrator.

(m) Report to Congress.—

(1) Initial report.—Not later than 6 months after the date of enactment of the Frank R. Lautenberg Chemical Safety for the 21st Century Act, the Administrator shall submit to the Committees on Energy and Commerce and Appropriations of the House of Representatives and the Committees on Environment and Public Works and Appropriations of the Senate a report containing an estimation of—

(A) the capacity of the Environmental Protection Agency to conduct and publish risk evaluations under section 6(b)(4)(C)(i), and the resources necessary to conduct the minimum number of risk evaluations required under section 6(b)(2);

(B) the capacity of the Environmental Protection Agency to conduct and publish risk evaluations under section 6(b)(4)(C)(ii), the likely demand for such risk evaluations, and the anticipated schedule for accommodating that demand;

(C) the capacity of the Environmental Protection Agency to promulgate rules under section 6(a) as required based on risk evaluations conducted and published under section 6(b); and

(D) the actual and anticipated efforts of the Environmental Protection Agency to increase the Agency's capacity to conduct and publish risk evaluations under section 6(b).

(2) Subsequent reports.—The Administrator shall update and resubmit the report described in paragraph (1) not less frequently than once every 5 years.

(n) Annual plan.—

(1) In general.—The Administrator shall inform the public regarding the schedule and the resources necessary for the completion of each risk evaluation as soon as practicable after initiating the risk evaluation.

(2) Publication of plan.—At the beginning of each calendar year, the Administrator shall publish an annual plan that—

(A) identifies the chemical substances for which risk evaluations are expected to be initiated or completed that year and the resources necessary for their completion;

(B) describes the status of each risk evaluation that has been initiated but not yet completed; and

(C) if the schedule for completion of a risk evaluation has changed, includes an updated schedule for that risk evaluation.

(*o*) Consultation with Science Advisory Committee on chemicals.—

(1) Establishment.—Not later than 1 year after the date of enactment of the Frank R. Lautenberg Chemical Safety for the 21st Century Act, the Administrator shall establish an advisory committee, to be known as the Science Advisory Committee on Chemicals (referred to in this subsection as the 'Committee').

(2) Purpose.—The purpose of the Committee shall be to provide independent advice and expert consultation, at the request of the Administrator, with respect to the scientific and technical aspects of issues relating to the implementation of this title.

(3) Composition.—The Committee shall be composed of representatives of such science, government, labor, public health, public interest, animal protection, industry, and other groups as the Administrator determines to be advisable, including representatives that have specific scientific expertise in the relationship of chemical exposures to women, children, and other potentially exposed or susceptible subpopulations.

(4) Schedule.—The Administrator shall convene the Committee in accordance with such schedule as the Administrator determines to be appropriate, but not less frequently than once every 2 years.

(p) Prior actions.—

(1) Rules, orders, and exemptions.—Nothing in the Frank R. Lautenberg Chemical Safety for the 21st Century Act eliminates, modifies, or withdraws any rule promulgated, order issued, or exemption established pursuant to this Act before the date of enactment of the Frank R. Lautenberg Chemical Safety for the 21st Century Act.

(2) Prior-initiated evaluations.—Nothing in this Act prevents the Administrator from initiating a risk evaluation regarding a chemical substance, or from continuing or completing such risk evaluation, prior to the effective date of the policies, procedures, and guidance required to be developed by the Administrator pursuant to the amendments made by the Frank R. Lautenberg Chemical Safety for the 21st Century Act.

(3) Actions completed prior to completion of policies, procedures, and guidance.—Nothing in this Act requires the Administrator to revise or withdraw a completed risk evaluation, determination, or rule under this Act solely because the action was completed prior to the development of a policy, procedure, or guidance pursuant to the amendments made by the Frank R. Lautenberg Chemical Safety for the 21st Century Act.

(Pub. L. No. 94–469, Title I, § 26, 90 Stat. 2046 (Oct. 11, 1976); as amended by Pub. L. No. 96–88, Title V, § 509(b), 93 Stat. 695 (Oct. 17, 1979); Pub. L. No. 98–80, § 2(c)(2)(A), 97 Stat. 485 (Aug. 23, 1983); renumbered Title I, Pub.

L. No. 99–519, § 3(c)(1), 100 Stat. 2989 (Oct. 22, 1986); and as amended by Pub. L. No. 114–182, §§ 17, 19(q), 130 Stat. 499–505, 510 (June 22, 2016).)

HISTORICAL AND STATUTORY NOTES

References in Text

Reorganization Plan No. 3 of 1970, referred to in text, is set out in the Appendix to Title 5, Government Organization and Employees.

Change of Name

"Department of Health and Human Services" was substituted for "Department of Health, Education, and Welfare" in subsec. (e)(1) and (3), and "Secretary of Health and Human Services" was substituted for "Secretary of Health, Education, and Welfare" in subsec. (e)(1), pursuant to § 509(b) of Pub. L. No. 96–88 which is codified as § 3508(b) of Title 20, Education.

Termination of Reporting Requirements

For termination, effective May 15, 2000, of provisions in subsec. (e)(2)(B) of this section relating to annual report to Congress, see Pub. L. No. 104–66, § 3003, as amended, set out as a note under 31 U.S.C.A. § 1113, and pages 93 and 164 of House Document No. 103–7.

§ 2626. Development and evaluation of test methods

[TSCA § 27]

(a) In general

The Secretary of Health and Human Services, in consultation with the Administrator and acting through the Assistant Secretary for Health, may conduct, and make grants to public and nonprofit private entities and enter into contracts with public and private entities for, projects for the development and evaluation of inexpensive and efficient methods (1) for determining and evaluating the health and environmental effects of chemical substances and mixtures, and their toxicity, persistence, and other characteristics which affect health and the environment, and (2) which may be used for the development of information to meet the requirements of rules, orders, or consent agreements under section 2603 of this title. The Administrator shall consider such methods in prescribing under section 2603 of this title protocols and methodologies for the development of information.

(b) Approval by Secretary

No grant may be made or contract entered into under subsection (a) of this section unless an application therefor has been submitted to and approved by the Secretary. Such an application shall be submitted in such form and manner and contain such information as the Secretary may require. The Secretary may apply such conditions to grants and contracts under subsection (a) of this section as the Secretary determines are necessary to carry out the purposes of such subsection. Contracts may be entered into under such subsection without regard to section 3324(a) and (b) of Title 31 and section 6101 of Title 41.

(Pub. L. No. 94–469, Title I, § 27, 90 Stat. 2049 (Oct. 11, 1976); as amended by Pub. L. No. 96–88, Title V, § 509(b), 93 Stat. 695 (Oct. 17, 1979); renumbered Title I by Pub. L. No. 99–519, § 3(c)(1), 100 Stat. 2989 (Oct. 22, 1986); and amended by Pub. L. No. 104–66, Title I, § 1061(a), 109 Stat. 719 (Dec. 21, 1995); Pub. L. No. 114–182, § 19(r), 130 Stat. 510 (June 22, 2016).)

HISTORICAL AND STATUTORY NOTES

Codifications

In subsec. (b), "section 6101 of Title 41" substituted for "section 5 of Title 41" on authority of Pub. L. No. 111–350, § 6(c), 124 Stat. 3854 (Jan. 4, 2011), which Act enacted Title 41, Public Contracts.

In subsec. (b), "section 3324(a) and (b) of Title 31" was substituted for reference to section 3648 of the Revised Statutes (31 U.S.C. 529) on authority of Pub. L. No. 97–258, § 4(b), 96 Stat. 1067 (Sept. 13, 1982), the first section of which enacted Title 31, Money and Finance.

Change of Name

"Secretary of Health and Human Services" was substituted for "Secretary of Health, Education, and Welfare" in subsec. (a), pursuant to § 509(b) of Pub. L. No. 96–88 which is codified as § 3508(b) of Title 20, Education.

§ 2627. State programs

[TSCA § 28]

(a) In general

For the purpose of complementing (but not reducing) the authority of, or actions taken by, the Administrator under this chapter, the Administrator may make grants to States for the establishment and operation of programs to prevent or eliminate unreasonable risks within the States to health or the environment which are associated with a chemical substance or mixture and with respect to which the Administrator is unable or is not likely to take action under this chapter for their prevention or elimination. The amount of a grant under this subsection shall be determined by the Administrator, except that no grant for any State program may exceed 75 per centum of the establishment and operation costs (as determined by the Administrator) of such program during the period for which the grant is made.

(b) Approval by Administrator

(1) No grant may be made under subsection (a) of this section unless an application therefor is submitted to and approved by the Administrator. Such an application shall be submitted in such form and manner as the Administrator may require and shall—

(A) set forth the need of the applicant for a grant under subsection (a) of this section,

(B) identify the agency or agencies of the State which shall establish or operate, or both, the program for which the application is submitted,

(C) describe the actions proposed to be taken under such program,

(D) contain or be supported by assurances satisfactory to the Administrator that such program shall, to the extent feasible, be integrated with other programs of the applicant for environmental and public health protection,

(E) provide for the making of such reports and evaluations as the Administrator may require, and

(F) contain such other information as the Administrator may prescribe.

(2) The Administrator may approve an application submitted in accordance with paragraph (1) only if the applicant has established to the satisfaction of the Administrator a priority need, as determined under rules of the Administrator, for the grant for which the application has been submitted. Such rules shall take into consideration the seriousness of the health effects in a State which are associated with chemical substances or mixtures, including cancer, birth defects, and gene mutations, the extent of the exposure in a State of human beings and the environment to chemical substances and mixtures, and the extent to which chemical substances and mixtures are manufactured, processed, used, and disposed of in a State.

(Pub. L. No. 94–469, Title I, § 28, 90 Stat. 2049 (Oct. 11, 1976); as amended by Pub. L. No. 97–129, § 1(a), 95 Stat. 1686 (Dec. 29, 1981); renumbered Title I, Pub. L. No. 99–519, § 3(c)(1), 100 Stat. 2989 (Oct. 22, 1986); and amended by Pub. L. No. 114–182, § 18, 130 Stat. 505 (June 22, 2016).)

§ 2628. Authorization of appropriations

[TSCA § 29]

There are authorized to be appropriated to the Administrator for purposes of carrying out this chapter (other than sections 2626 and 2627 of this title and subsections (a) and (c) through (g) of section 2609 of this title) $58,646,000 for the fiscal year 1982 and $62,000,000 for the fiscal year 1983. No part of the funds appropriated under this section may be used to construct any research laboratories.

(Pub. L. No. 94–469, Title I, § 29, 90 Stat. 2050 (Oct. 11, 1976); as amended by Pub. L. No. 97–129, § 1(b), 95 Stat. 1686 (Dec. 29, 1981); renumbered Title I by Pub. L. No. 99–519, § 3(c)(1), 100 Stat. 2989 (Oct. 22, 1986).)

§ 2629. Annual report

[TSCA § 30]

The Administrator shall prepare and submit to the President and the Congress on or before January 1, 1978, and on or before January 1 of each succeeding year a comprehensive report on the administration of this chapter during the preceding fiscal year. Such reports shall include—

(1) a list of the testing required under section 2603 of this title during the year for which the report is made and an estimate of the costs incurred during such year by the persons required to perform such tests;

(2) the number of notices received during such year under section 2604 of this title, the number of such notices received during such year under such section for chemical substances subject to a rule, order or consent agreement, and a summary of any action taken during such year under section 2604(g) of this title;

(3) a list of rules issued during such year under section 2605 of this title;

(4) a list, with a brief statement of the issues, of completed or pending judicial actions under this chapter and administrative actions under section 2615 of this title during such year;

(5) a summary of major problems encountered in the administration of this chapter; and

(6) such recommendations for additional legislation as the Administrator deems necessary to carry out the purposes of this chapter.

(Pub. L. No. 94–469, Title I, § 30, 90 Stat. 2050 (Oct. 11, 1976); renumbered Title I by Pub. L. No. 99–519, § 3(c)(1), 100 Stat. 2989 (Oct. 22, 1986); and amended by Pub. L. No. 114–182, § 19(s), 130 Stat. 510 (June 22, 2016).)

HISTORICAL AND STATUTORY NOTES

Termination of Reporting Requirements

For termination, effective May 15, 2000, of provisions in this section relating to submitting annual report to Congress, see Pub. L. No. 104–66, § 3003, as amended, set out as a note under 31 U.S.C.A. § 1113, and page 163 of House Document No. 103–7.

SUBCHAPTER II—ASBESTOS HAZARD EMERGENCY RESPONSE

§ 2641. Congressional findings and purpose

[TSCA § 201]

(a) Findings

The Congress finds the following:

(1) The Environmental Protection Agency's rule on local educational agency inspection for, and notification of, the presence of friable asbestos-containing material in school buildings includes neither standards for the proper identification of asbestos-containing material and appropriate response actions with respect to friable asbestos-containing material, nor a requirement that response actions with respect to friable asbestos-containing material be carried out in a safe and complete manner once actions are found to be necessary. As a result of the lack of regulatory guidance from the Environmental Protection Agency, some schools have not undertaken response action while many others have undertaken expensive projects without knowing if their action is necessary, adequate, or safe. Thus, the danger of exposure to asbestos continues to exist in schools, and some exposure actually may have increased due to the lack of Federal standards and improper response action.

(2) There is no uniform program for accrediting persons involved in asbestos identification and abatement, nor are local educational agencies required to use accredited contractors for asbestos work.

(3) The guidance provided by the Environmental Protection Agency in its "Guidance for Controlling Asbestos-Containing Material in Buildings" is insufficient in detail to ensure adequate responses. Such guidance is intended to be used only until the regulations required by this subchapter become effective.

(4) Because there are no Federal standards whatsoever regulating daily exposure to asbestos in other public and commercial buildings, persons in addition to those comprising the Nation's school population may be exposed daily to asbestos.

(b) Purpose

The purpose of this subchapter is—

(1) to provide for the establishment of Federal regulations which require inspection for asbestos-containing material and implementation of appropriate response actions with respect to asbestos-containing material in the Nation's schools in a safe and complete manner;

(2) to mandate safe and complete periodic reinspection of school buildings following response actions, where appropriate; and

(3) to require the Administrator to conduct a study to find out the extent of the danger to human health posed by asbestos in public and commercial buildings and the means to respond to any such danger.

(Pub. L. No. 94–469, Title II, § 201, as added by Pub. L. No. 99–519, § 2, 100 Stat. 2970 (Oct. 22, 1986).)

§ 2642. Definitions

[TSCA § 202]

For purposes of this subchapter—

(1) Accredited asbestos contractor

The term "accredited asbestos contractor" means a person accredited pursuant to the provisions of section 2646 of this title.

(2) Administrator

The term "Administrator" means the Administrator of the Environmental Protection Agency.

(3) Asbestos

The term "asbestos" means asbestiform varieties of—

(A) chrysotile (serpentine),

(B) crocidolite (riebeckite),

(C) amosite (cummingtonite-grunerite),

(D) anthophyllite,

(E) tremolite, or

(F) actinolite.

(4) Asbestos-containing material

The term "asbestos-containing material" means any material which contains more than 1 percent asbestos by weight.

(5) EPA guidance document

The term "Guidance for Controlling Asbestos-Containing Material in Buildings", means the Environmental Protection Agency document with such title as in effect on March 31, 1986.

(6) Friable asbestos-containing material

The term "friable asbestos-containing material" means any asbestos-containing material applied on ceilings, walls, structural members, piping, duct work, or any other part of a building which when dry may be crumbled, pulverized, or reduced to powder by hand pressure. The term includes non-friable asbestos-containing material after such previously non-friable material becomes damaged to the extent that when dry it may be crumbled, pulverized, or reduced to powder by hand pressure.

(7) Local educational agency

The term "local educational agency" means—

(A) any local educational agency as defined in section 7801 of Title 20,

(B) the owner of any private, nonprofit elementary or secondary school building, and

(C) the governing authority of any school operated under the defense dependents' education system provided for under the Defense Dependents' Education Act of 1978 (20 U.S.C. 921 et seq.).

(8) Most current guidance document

The term "most current guidance document" means the Environmental Protection Agency's "Guidance for Controlling Asbestos-Containing Material in Buildings" as modified by the Environmental Protection Agency after March 31, 1986.

(9) Non-profit elementary or secondary school

The term "non-profit elementary or secondary school" means any elementary or secondary school (as defined in section 7801 of Title 20) owned and operated by one or more nonprofit corporations or associations no part of the net earnings of which inures, or may lawfully inure, to the benefit of any private shareholder or individual.

(10) Public and commercial building

The term "public and commercial building" means any building which is not a school building, except that the term does not include any residential apartment building of fewer than 10 units.

(11) Response action

The term "response action" means methods that protect human health and the environment from asbestos-containing material. Such methods include methods described in chapters 3 and 5 of the Environmental Protection Agency's "Guidance for Controlling Asbestos-Containing Materials in Buildings".

(12) School

The term "school" means any elementary or secondary school as defined in section 7801 of Title 20.

(13) School building

The term "school building" means—

(A) any structure suitable for use as a classroom, including a school facility such as a laboratory, library, school eating facility, or facility used for the preparation of food,

(B) any gymnasium or other facility which is specially designed for athletic or recreational activities for an academic course in physical education,

(C) any other facility used for the instruction of students or for the administration of educational or research programs, and

(D) any maintenance, storage, or utility facility, including any hallway, essential to the operation of any facility described in subparagraphs (A), (B), or (C).

(14) State

The term "State" means a State, the District of Columbia, the Commonwealth of Puerto Rico, Guam, American Samoa, the Northern Marianas, the Trust Territory of the Pacific Islands, and the Virgin Islands.

(Pub. L. No. 94–469, Title II, § 202, as added by Pub. L. No. 99–519, § 2, 100 Stat. 2971 (Oct. 22, 1986); and amended by Pub. L. No. 103–382, Title III, § 391(c)(1) to (3), 108 Stat. 4022 (Oct. 20, 1994); Pub. L. No. 107–110, Title X, § 1076(f)(1), 105 Stat. 2091 (Jan. 8, 2002).)

HISTORICAL AND STATUTORY NOTES

References in Text

The Defense Dependent's Education Act of 1978, referred to in par. (7)(C), is Title XIV of Pub. L. No. 95–561, 92 Stat. 2365 (Nov. 1, 1978), as amended, which is codified principally to chapter 25A (§ 921 et seq.) of Title 20, Education. For complete classification of this Act to the Code, see Short Title note set out under section 921 of Title 20 and Tables.

Effective and Applicability Provisions

2002 Acts. Except as otherwise provided, amendments by Pub. L. No. 107–110 effective Jan. 8, 2002, see Pub. L. No. 107–110, § 5, set out as a note under 20 U.S.C.A. § 6301.

Termination of Trust Territory of the Pacific Islands

For termination of Trust Territory of the Pacific Islands, see note set out preceding section 1681 of Title 48, Territories and Insular Possessions.

§ 2643. EPA regulations

[TSCA § 203]

(a) In general

Within 360 days after October 22, 1986, the Administrator shall promulgate regulations as described in subsections (b) through (i) of this section. With respect to regulations described in subsections (b), (c), (d), (e), (f), (g), and (i) of this section, the Administrator shall issue an advanced notice of proposed rulemaking within 60 days after October 22, 1986, and shall propose regulations within 180 days after October 22, 1986. Any regulation promulgated under this section must protect human health and the environment.

(b) Inspection

The Administrator shall promulgate regulations which prescribe procedures, including the use of personnel accredited under section 2646(b) or (c) of this title and laboratories accredited under section 2646(d) of this title, for determining whether asbestos-containing material is present in a school building under the authority of a local educational agency. The regulations shall provide for the exclusion of any school building, or portion of a school building, if (1) an inspection of such school building (or portion) was completed before the effective date of the regulations, and (2) the inspection meets the procedures and other requirements of the regulations under this subchapter or of the "Guidance for Controlling Asbestos-Containing Materials in Buildings" (unless the Administrator determines that an inspection in accordance with the guidance document is inadequate). The regulations shall require inspection of any school building (or portion of a school building) that is not excluded by the preceding sentence.

(c) Circumstances requiring response actions

(1) The Administrator shall promulgate regulations which define the appropriate response action in a school building under the authority of a local educational agency in at least the following circumstances:

(A) Damage

Circumstances in which friable asbestos-containing material or its covering is damaged, deteriorated, or delaminated.

(B) Significant damage

Circumstances in which friable asbestos-containing material or its covering is significantly damaged, deteriorated, or delaminated.

(C) Potential damage

Circumstances in which—

(i) friable asbestos-containing material is in an area regularly used by building occupants, including maintenance personnel, in the course of their normal activities, and

(ii) there is a reasonable likelihood that the material or its covering will become damaged, deteriorated, or delaminated.

(D) Potential significant damage

Circumstances in which—

(i) friable asbestos-containing material is in an area regularly used by building occupants, including maintenance personnel, in the course of their normal activities, and

(ii) there is a reasonable likelihood that the material or its covering will become significantly damaged, deteriorated, or delaminated.

(2) In promulgating such regulations, the Administrator shall consider and assess the value of various technologies intended to improve the decisionmaking process regarding response actions and the quality of any work that is deemed necessary, including air monitoring and chemical encapsulants.

(d) Response actions

(1) In general

The Administrator shall promulgate regulations describing a response action in a school building under the authority of a local educational agency, using the least burdensome methods which protect human health and the environment. In determining the least burdensome methods, the Administrator shall take into account local circumstances, including occupancy and use patterns within the school building and short- and long-term costs.

(2) Response action for damaged asbestos

In the case of a response action for the circumstances described in subsection (c)(1)(A) of this section, methods for responding shall include methods identified in chapters 3 and 5 of the "Guidance for Controlling Asbestos-Containing Material in Buildings".

(3) Response action for significantly damaged asbestos

In the case of a response action for the circumstances described in subsection (c)(1)(B) of this section, methods for responding shall include methods identified in chapter 5 of the "Guidance for Controlling Asbestos-Containing Material in Buildings".

(4) Response action for potentially damaged asbestos

In the case of a response action for the circumstances described in subsection (c)(1)(C) of this section, methods for responding shall include methods identified in chapters 3 and 5 of the "Guidance for Controlling Asbestos-Containing Material in Buildings", unless preventive measures will eliminate the reasonable likelihood that the asbestos-containing material will become damaged, deteriorated, or delaminated.

(5) Response action for potentially significantly damaged asbestos

In the case of a response action for the circumstances described in subsection (c)(1)(D) of this section, methods for responding shall include methods identified in chapter 5 of the "Guidance for Controlling Asbestos-Containing Material in Buildings", unless preventive measures will eliminate the reasonable likelihood that the asbestos-containing material will become significantly damaged, deteriorated, or delaminated.

(6) "Preventive measures" defined

For purposes of this section, the term "preventive measures" means actions which eliminate the reasonable likelihood of asbestos-containing material becoming damaged, deteriorated, or delaminated, or significantly damaged[1] deteriorated, or delaminated (as the case may be) or which protect human health and the environment.

(7) EPA information or advisory

The Administrator shall, not later than 30 days after November 28, 1990, publish and distribute to all local education agencies and State Governors information or an advisory to—

(A) facilitate public understanding of the comparative risks associated with in-place management of asbestos-containing building materials and removals;

(B) promote the least burdensome response actions necessary to protect human health, safety, and the environment; and

(C) describe the circumstances in which asbestos removal is necessary to protect human health.

Such information or advisory shall be based on the best available scientific evidence and shall be revised, republished, and redistributed as appropriate, to reflect new scientific findings.

(e) Implementation

The Administrator shall promulgate regulations requiring the implementation of response actions in school buildings under the authority of a local educational agency and, where appropriate, for the determination of when a response action is completed. Such regulations shall include standards for the education and protection of both workers and building occupants for the following phases of activity:

(1) Inspection.

(2) Response Action.[2]

(3) Post-response action, including any periodic reinspection of asbestos-containing material and long-term surveillance activity.

(f) Operations and maintenance

The Administrator shall promulgate regulations to require implementation of an operations and maintenance and repair program as described in chapter 3 of the "Guidance for Controlling Asbestos-Containing Materials in Buildings" for all friable asbestos-containing material in a school building under the authority of a local educational agency.

(g) Periodic surveillance

The Administrator shall promulgate regulations to require the following:

(1) An identification of the location of friable and non-friable asbestos in a school building under the authority of a local educational agency.

(2) Provisions for surveillance and periodic reinspection of such friable and non-friable asbestos.

(3) Provisions for education of school employees, including school service and maintenance personnel, about the location of and safety procedures with respect to such friable and non-friable asbestos.

(h) Transportation and disposal

The Administrator shall promulgate regulations which prescribe standards for transportation and disposal of asbestos-containing waste material to protect human health and the environment. Such regulations shall include such provisions related to the manner in which transportation vehicles are loaded and unloaded as will assure the physical integrity of containers of asbestos-containing waste material.

(i) Management plans

(1) In general

The Administrator shall promulgate regulations which require each local educational agency to develop an asbestos management plan for school buildings under its authority, to begin implementation of such plan within 990 days after October 22, 1986, and to complete implementation of such plan in a timely fashion. The regulations shall require that each plan include the following elements, wherever relevant to the school building:

(A) An inspection statement describing inspection and response action activities carried out before October 22, 1986.

(B) A description of the results of the inspection conducted pursuant to regulations under subsection (b) of this section, including a description of the specific areas inspected.

(C) A detailed description of measures to be taken to respond to any friable asbestos-containing material pursuant to the regulations promulgated under subsections (c), (d), and (e) of this section, including the location or locations at which a response action will be taken, the method or methods of response action to be used, and a schedule for beginning and completing response actions.

(D) A detailed description of any asbestos-containing material which remains in the school building once response actions are undertaken pursuant to the regulations promulgated under subsections (c), (d), and (e) of this section.

(E) A plan for periodic reinspection and long-term surveillance activities developed pursuant to regulations promulgated under subsection (g) of this section, and a plan for operations and maintenance activities developed pursuant to regulations promulgated under subsection (f) of this section.

(F) With respect to the person or persons who inspected for asbestos-containing material and who will design or carry out response actions with respect to the friable asbestos-containing material, one of the following statements:

(i) If the State has adopted a contractor accreditation plan under section 2646(b) of this title, a statement that the person (or persons) is accredited under such plan.

(ii) A statement that the local educational agency used (or will use) persons who have been accredited by another State which has adopted a contractor accreditation plan under section 2646(b) of this title or is accredited pursuant to an Administrator-approved course under section 2646(c) of this title.

(G) A list of the laboratories that analyzed any bulk samples of asbestos-containing material found in the school building or air samples taken to detect asbestos in the school building and a statement that each laboratory has been accredited pursuant to the accreditation program under section 2646(d) of this title.

(H) With respect to each consultant who contributed to the management plan, the name of the consultant and one of the following statements:

(i) If the State has adopted a contractor accreditation plan under section 2646(b) of this title, a statement that the consultant is accredited under such plan.

(ii) A statement that the contractor is accredited by another State which has adopted a contractor accreditation plan under section 2646(b) of this title or is accredited pursuant to an Administrator-approved course under section 2646(c) of this title.

(I) An evaluation of resources needed to successfully complete response actions and carry out reinspection, surveillance, and operation and maintenance activities.

(2) Statement by contractor

A local educational agency may require each management plan to contain a statement signed by an accredited asbestos contractor that such contractor has prepared or assisted in the preparation of such plan, or has reviewed such plan, and that such plan is in compliance with the applicable regulations and standards promulgated or adopted pursuant to this section and other applicable provisions of law. Such a statement may not be signed by a contractor who, in addition to preparing or assisting in preparing the management plan, also implements (or will implement) the management plan.

(3) Warning labels

(A) The regulations shall require that each local educational agency which has inspected for and discovered any asbestos-containing material with respect to a school building shall attach a warning label to any asbestos-containing material still in routine maintenance areas (such as boiler rooms) of the school building, including—

(i) friable asbestos-containing material which was responded to by a means other than removal, and

(ii) asbestos-containing material for which no response action was carried out.

(B) The warning label shall read, in print which is readily visible because of large size or bright color, as follows: **"CAUTION: ASBESTOS. HAZARDOUS. DO NOT DISTURB WITHOUT PROPER TRAINING AND EQUIPMENT."**

(4) Plan may be submitted in stages

A local educational agency may submit a management plan in stages, with each submission of the agency covering only a portion of the school buildings under the agency's authority, if the agency determines that such action would expedite the identification and abatement of hazardous asbestos-containing material in the school buildings under the authority of the agency.

(5) Public availability

A copy of the management plan developed under the regulations shall be available in the administrative offices of the local educational agency for inspection by the public, including teachers, other school personnel, and parents. The local educational agency shall notify parent, teacher, and employee organizations of the availability of such plan.

(6) Submission to State Governor

Each plan developed under this subsection shall be submitted to the State Governor under section 2645 of this title.

(j) Changes in regulations

Changes may be made in the regulations promulgated under this section only by rule in accordance with section 553 of Title 5. Any such change must protect human health and the environment.

(k) Changes in guidance document

Any change made in the "Guidance for Controlling Asbestos-Containing Material in Buildings" shall be made only by rule in accordance with section 553 of Title 5, unless a regulation described in this section dealing with the same subject matter is in effect. Any such change must protect human health and the environment.

(*l*) Treatment of Department of Defense schools

(1) Secretary to act in lieu of Governor

In the administration of this subchapter, any function, duty, or other responsibility imposed on a Governor of a State shall be carried out by the Secretary of Defense with respect to any school operated under the defense dependents' education system provided for under the Defense Dependents' Education Act of 1978 (20 U.S.C. 921 et seq.).

(2) Regulations

The Secretary of Defense, in cooperation with the Administrator, shall, to the extent feasible and consistent with the national security, take such action as may be necessary to provide for the identification, inspection, and management (including abatement) of asbestos in any building used by the Department of Defense as an overseas school for dependents of members of the Armed Forces. Such identification, inspection, and management (including abatement) shall, subject to the preceding sentence, be carried out in a manner comparable to the manner in which a local educational agency is required to carry out such activities with respect to a school building under this subchapter.

(m) Waiver

The Administrator, upon request by a Governor and after notice and comment and opportunity for a public hearing in the affected State, may waive some or all of the requirements of this section and section 2644 of this title with respect to such State if it has established and is implementing a program of asbestos inspection and management that contains requirements that are at least as stringent as the requirements of this section and section 2644 of this title.

(Pub. L. No. 94–469, Title II, § 203, as added by Pub. L. No. 99–519, § 2, 100 Stat. 2972 (Oct. 22, 1986); and amended by Pub. L. No. 101–637, § 13, 104 Stat. 4593 (Nov. 28, 1990).)

[1] So in original. Probably should be followed by a comma.

[2] So in original. Probably should not be capitalized.

HISTORICAL AND STATUTORY NOTES

References in Text

The Defense Dependents' Education Act of 1978, referred to in subsec. (*l*)(1), is Title XIV of Pub. L. No. 95–561, 92 Stat. 2365 (Nov. 1, 1978), as amended, which is codified principally to chapter 25A (§ 921 et seq.) of Title 20, Education. For complete classification of this Act to the Code, see Short Title note set out under section 921 of Title 20 and Tables.

§ 2644. Requirements if EPA fails to promulgate regulations

[TSCA § 204]

(a) In general

(1) Failure to promulgate

If the Administrator fails to promulgate within the prescribed period—

(A) regulations described in section 2643(b) of this title (relating to inspection);

(B) regulations described in section 2643(c), (d), (e), (f), (g), and (i) of this title (relating to responding to asbestos); or

(C) regulations described in section 2643(h) of this title (relating to transportation and disposal);

each local educational agency shall carry out the requirements described in this section in subsection (b); subsections (c), (d), and (e); or subsection (f); respectively, in accordance with the Environmental Protection Agency's most current guidance document.

(2) Stay by court

If the Administrator has promulgated regulations described in paragraph (1)(A), (B), or (C) within the prescribed period, but the effective date of such regulations has been stayed by a court for a period of more than 30 days, a local educational agency shall carry out the pertinent requirements described in this subsection in accordance with the Environmental Protection Agency's most current guidance document.

(3) Effective period

The requirements of this section shall be in effect until such time as the Administrator promulgates the pertinent regulations or until the stay is lifted (as the case may be).

(b) Inspection

(1) Except as provided in paragraph (2), the local educational agency, within 540 days after October 22, 1986, shall conduct an inspection for asbestos-containing material, using personnel accredited under section 2646(b) or (c) of this title and laboratories accredited under section 2646(d) of this title, in each school building under its authority.

(2) The local educational agency may exclude from the inspection requirement in paragraph (1) any school building, or portion of a school building, if (A) an inspection of such school building (or portion) was completed before the date on which this section goes into effect, and (B) the inspection meets the inspection requirements of this section.

(c) Operation and maintenance

The local educational agency shall, within 720 days after October 22, 1986, develop and begin implementation of an operation and maintenance plan with respect to friable asbestos-containing material in a school building under its authority. Such plan shall provide for the education of school service and maintenance personnel about safety procedures with respect to asbestos-containing material, including friable asbestos-containing material.

(d) Management plan

(1) In general

The local educational agency shall—

(A) develop a management plan for responding to asbestos-containing material in each school building under its authority and submit such plan to the Governor under section 2645 of this title within 810 days after October 22, 1986,

(B) begin implementation of such plan within 990 days after October 22, 1986, and

(C) complete implementation of such plan in a timely fashion.

(2) Plan requirements

The management plan shall—

(A) include the elements listed in section 2643(i)(1) of this title, including an inspection statement as described in paragraph (3) of this section,[1]

(B) provide for the attachment of warning labels as described in section 2643(i)(3) of this title,

(C) be prepared in accordance with the most current guidance document,

(D) meet the standard described in paragraph (4) for actions described in that paragraph, and

(E) be submitted to the State Governor under section 2645 of this title.

(3) Inspection statement

The local educational agency shall complete an inspection statement, covering activities carried out before October 22, 1986, which meets the following requirements:

(A) The statement shall include the following information:

(i) The dates of inspection.

(ii) The name, address, and qualifications of each inspector.

(iii) A description of the specific areas inspected.

(iv) A list of the laboratories that analyzed any bulk samples of asbestos-containing material or air samples of asbestos found in any school building and a statement describing the qualifications of each laboratory.

(v) The results of the inspection.

(B) The statement shall state whether any actions were taken with respect to any asbestos-containing material found to be present, including a specific reference to whether any actions were taken in the boiler room of the building. If any such action was taken, the following items of information shall be included in the statement:

(i) The location or locations at which the action was taken.

(ii) A description of the method of action.

(iii) The qualifications of the persons who conducted the action.

(4) Standard

The ambient interior concentration of asbestos after the completion of actions described in the most current guidance document, other than the type of action described in sections 2643(f) of this title and subsection (c) of this section, shall not exceed the ambient exterior concentration, discounting any contribution from any local stationary source. Either a scanning electron microscope or a transmission electron microscope shall be used to determine the ambient interior concentration. In the absence of reliable measurements, the ambient exterior concentration shall be deemed to be—

(A) less than 0.003 fibers per cubic centimeter if a scanning electron microscope is used, and

(B) less than 0.005 fibers per cubic centimeter if a transmission electron microscope is used.

(5) Public availability

A copy of the management plan shall be available in the administrative offices of the local educational agency for inspection by the public, including teachers, other school personnel, and parents. The local educational agency shall notify parent, teacher, and employee organizations of the availability of such plan.

(e) Building occupant protection

The local educational agency shall provide for the protection of building occupants during each phase of activity described in this section.

(f) Transportation and disposal

The local educational agency shall provide for the transportation and disposal of asbestos in accordance with the most recent version of the Environmental Protection Agency's "Asbestos Waste Management Guidance" (or any successor to such document).

(Pub. L. No. 94–469, Title II, § 204, as added by Pub. L. No. 99–519, § 2, 100 Stat. 2977 (Oct. 22, 1986).)

[1] So in original. Probably should be "subsection,".

§ 2645. Submission to State Governor

[TSCA § 205]

(a) Submission

Within 720 days after October 22, 1986 (or within 810 days if there are no regulations under section 2643(i) of this title), a local educational agency shall submit a management plan developed pursuant to regulations promulgated under section 2643(i) of this title (or under section 2644(d) of this title if there are no regulations) to the Governor of the State in which the local educational agency is located.

(b) Governor requirements

Within 360 days after October 22, 1986, the Governor of each State—

(1) shall notify local educational agencies in the State of where to submit their management plans under this section, and

(2) may establish administrative procedures for reviewing management plans submitted under this section.

If the Governor establishes procedures under paragraph (2), the Governor shall designate to carry out the reviews those State officials who are responsible for implementing environmental protection or other public health programs, or with authority over asbestos programs, in the State.

(c) Management plan review

(1) Review of plan

The Governor may disapprove a management plan within 90 days after the date of receipt of the plan if the plan—

(A) does not conform with the regulations under section 2643(i) of this title (or with section 2644(d) of this title if there are no regulations),

(B) does not assure that contractors who are accredited pursuant to this subchapter will be used to carry out the plan, or

(C) does not contain a response action schedule which is reasonable and timely, taking into account circumstances relevant to the speed at which the friable asbestos-containing material in the school buildings under the local educational agency's authority should be responded to, including human exposure to the asbestos while the friable asbestos-containing material remains in the school building, and the ability of the local educational agency to continue to provide educational services to the community.

(2) Revision of plan

If the State Governor disapproves a plan, the State Governor shall explain in writing to the local educational agency the reasons why the plan was disapproved and the changes that need to be made in the plan. Within 30 days after the date on which notice is received of disapproval of its plan, the local educational agency shall revise the plan to conform with the State Governor's suggested changes. The Governor may extend the 30-day period for not more than 90 days.

(d) Deferral of submission

(1) Request for deferral

A local educational agency may request a deferral, to May 9, 1989, of the deadline under subsection (a) of this section. Upon approval of such a request, the deadline under subsection (a) of this section is deferred until May 9, 1989, for the local educational agency which submitted the request. Such a request may cover one or more schools under the authority of the agency and shall include a list of all the schools covered by the request. A local educational agency shall file any such request with the State Governor by October 12, 1988, and shall include with the request either of the following statements:

(A) A statement—

(i) that the State in which the agency is located has requested from the Administrator, before June 1, 1988, a waiver under section 2643(m) of this title; and

(ii) that gives assurance that the local educational agency has carried out the notification and, in the case of a public school, public meeting required by paragraph (2).

(B) A statement, the accuracy of which is sworn to by a responsible official of the agency (by notarization or other means of certification), that includes the following with respect to each school for which a deferral is sought in the request:

(i) A statement that, in spite of the fact that the local educational agency has made a good faith effort to meet the deadline for submission of a management plan under subsection (a) of this section, the agency will not be able to meet the deadline. The statement shall include a brief explanation of the reasons why the deadline cannot be met.

(ii) A statement giving assurance that the local educational agency has made available for inspection by the public, at each school for which a deferral is sought in the request, at least one of the following documents:

(I) A solicitation by the local educational agency to contract with an accredited asbestos contractor for inspection or management plan development.

(II) A letter attesting to the enrollment of school district personnel in an Environmental Protection Agency-accredited training course for inspection and management plan development.

(III) Documentation showing that an analysis of suspected asbestos-containing material from the school is pending at an accredited laboratory.

(IV) Documentation showing that an inspection or management plan has been completed in at least one other school under the local educational agency's authority.

(iii) A statement giving assurance that the local educational agency has carried out the notification and, in the case of a public school, public meeting required by paragraph (2).

(iv) A proposed schedule outlining all significant activities leading up to submission of a management plan by May 9, 1989, including inspection of the school (if not completed at the time of the request) with a deadline of no later than December 22, 1988, for entering into a signed contract with an accredited asbestos contractor for inspection (unless such inspections are to be performed by school personnel), laboratory analysis of material from the school suspected of containing asbestos, and development of the management plan.

(2) Notification and public meeting

Before filing a deferral request under paragraph (1), a local educational agency shall notify affected parent, teacher, and employee organizations of its intent to file such a request. In the case of a deferral request for a public school, the local educational agency shall discuss the request at a public meeting of the school board with jurisdiction over the school, and affected parent, teacher, and employee organizations shall be notified in advance of the time and place of such meeting.

(3) Response by Governor

(A) Not later than 30 days after the date on which a Governor receives a deferral request under paragraph (1) from a local educational agency, the Governor shall respond to the local educational agency in writing by acknowledging whether the request is complete or incomplete. If the request is incomplete, the Governor shall identify in the response the items that are missing from the request.

(B) A local educational agency may correct any deficiencies in an incomplete deferral request and refile the request with the Governor. In any case in which the local educational agency decides to refile the request, the agency shall refile the request, and the Governor shall respond to such refiled request in the manner described in subparagraph (A), no later than 15 days after the local educational agency has received a response from the Governor under subparagraph (A).

(C) Approval of a deferral request under this subsection occurs only upon the receipt by a local educational agency of a written acknowledgment from the Governor that the agency's deferral request is complete.

(4) Submission and review of plan

A local educational agency whose deferral request is approved shall submit a management plan to the Governor not later than May 9, 1989. Such management plan shall include a copy of the deferral request and the statement accompanying such request. Such management plan shall be reviewed in accordance with subsection (c) of this section, except that the Governor may extend the 30-day period for revision of the plan under subsection (c)(2) of this section for only an additional 30 days (for a total of 60 days).

(5) Implementation of plan

The approval of a deferral request from a local educational agency shall not be considered to be a waiver or exemption from the requirement under section 2643(i) of this title for the local educational agency to begin implementation of its management plan by July 9, 1989.

(6) EPA notice

(A) Not later than 15 days after July 18, 1988, the Administrator shall publish in the Federal Register the following:

(i) A notice describing the opportunity to file a request for deferral under this subsection.

(ii) A list of the State offices (including officials (if available) in each State as designated under subsection (b) of this section) with which deferral requests should be filed.

(B) As soon as practicable, but in no event later than 30 days, after July 18, 1988, the Administrator shall mail a notice describing the opportunity to file a request for deferral under this subsection to each local educational agency and to each State office in the list published under subparagraph (A).

(e) Status reports

(1) Not later than December 31, 1988, the Governor of each State shall submit to the Administrator a written statement on the status of management plan submissions and deferral requests by local educational agencies in the State. The statement shall be made available to local educational agencies in the State and shall contain the following:

(A) A list containing each local educational agency that submitted a management plan by October 12, 1988.

(B) A list containing each local educational agency whose deferral request was approved.

(C) A list containing each local educational agency that failed to submit a management plan by October 12, 1988, and whose deferral request was disapproved.

(D) A list containing each local educational agency that failed to submit a management plan by October 12, 1988, and did not submit a deferral request.

(2) Not later than December 31, 1989, the Governor of each State shall submit to the Administrator an updated version of the written statement submitted under paragraph (1). The statement shall be made available to local educational agencies in the State and shall contain the following:

(A) A list containing each local educational agency whose management plan was submitted and not disapproved as of October 9, 1989.

(B) A list containing each local educational agency whose management plan was submitted and disapproved, and which remains disapproved, as of October 9, 1989.

(C) A list containing each local educational agency that submitted a management plan after May 9, 1989, and before October 10, 1989.

(D) A list containing each local educational agency that failed to submit a management plan as of October 9, 1989.

(Pub. L. No. 94–469, Title II, § 205, as added by Pub. L. No. 99–519, § 2, 100 Stat. 2979 (Oct. 22, 1986); and amended by Pub. L. No. 100–368, §§ 1(a), 2, 102 Stat. 829, 831 (July 18, 1988).)

§ 2646. Contractor and laboratory accreditation [TSCA § 206]

(a) Contractor accreditation

A person may not—

(1) inspect for asbestos-containing material in a school building under the authority of a local educational agency or in a public or commercial building,

(2) prepare a management plan for such a school, or

(3) design or conduct response actions, other than the type of action described in sections 2643(f) and 2644(c) of this title, with respect to friable asbestos-containing material in such a school or in a public or commercial building,

unless such person is accredited by a State under subsection (b) of this section or is accredited pursuant to an Administrator-approved course under subsection (c) of this section.

(b) Accreditation by State

(1) Model plan

(A) Persons to be accredited

Within 180 days after October 22, 1986, the Administrator, in consultation with affected organizations, shall develop a model contractor accreditation plan for States to give accreditation to persons in the following categories:

(i) Persons who inspect for asbestos-containing material in school buildings under the authority of a local educational agency or in public or commercial buildings.

(ii) Persons who prepare management plans for such schools.

(iii) Persons who design or carry out response actions, other than the type of action described in sections 2643(f) and 2644(c) of this title, with respect to friable asbestos-containing material in such schools or in public or commercial buildings.

(B) Plan requirements

The plan shall include a requirement that any person in a category listed in paragraph (1) achieve a passing grade on an examination and participate in continuing education to stay informed about current asbestos inspection and response action technology. The examination shall demonstrate the knowledge of the person in areas that the Administrator prescribes as necessary and appropriate in each of the categories. Such examinations may include requirements for knowledge in the following areas:

(i) Recognition of asbestos-containing material and its physical characteristics.

(ii) Health hazards of asbestos and the relationship between asbestos exposure and disease.

(iii) Assessing the risk of asbestos exposure through a knowledge of percentage weight of asbestos-containing material, friability, age, deterioration, location and accessibility of materials, and advantages and disadvantages of dry and wet response action methods.

(iv) Respirators and their use, care, selection, degree of protection afforded, fitting, testing, and maintenance and cleaning procedures.

(v) Appropriate work practices and control methods, including the use of high efficiency particle absolute vacuums, the use of amended water, and principles of negative air pressure equipment use and procedures.

(vi) Preparing a work area for response action work, including isolating work areas to prevent bystander or public exposure to asbestos, decontamination procedures, and procedures for dismantling work areas after completion of work.

(vii) Establishing emergency procedures to respond to sudden releases.

(viii) Air monitoring requirements and procedures.

(ix) Medical surveillance program requirements.

(x) Proper asbestos waste transportation and disposal procedures.

(xi) Housekeeping and personal hygiene practices, including the necessity of showers, and procedures to prevent asbestos exposure to an employee's family.

(2) State adoption of plan

Each State shall adopt a contractor accreditation plan at least as stringent as the model plan developed by the Administrator under paragraph (1), within 180 days after the commencement of the first regular session of the legislature of such State which is convened following the date on which the Administrator completes development of the model plan. In the case of a school operated under the defense dependents' education system provided for under the Defense Dependents' Education Act of

1978 (20 U.S.C. 921 et seq.), the Secretary of Defense shall adopt a contractor accreditation plan at least as stringent as that model.

(c) Accreditation by Administrator-approved course

(1) Course approval

Within 180 days after October 22, 1986, the Administrator shall ensure that any Environmental Protection Agency-approved asbestos training course is consistent with the model plan (including testing requirements) developed under subsection (b) of this section. A contractor may be accredited by taking and passing such a course.

(2) Treatment of persons with previous EPA asbestos training

A person who—

(A) completed an Environmental Protection Agency-approved asbestos training course before October 22, 1986, and

(B) passed (or passes) an asbestos test either before or after October 22, 1986,

may be accredited under paragraph (1) if the Administrator determines that the course and test are equivalent to the requirements of the model plan developed under subsection (b) of this section. If the Administrator so determines, the person shall be considered accredited for the purposes of this subchapter until a date that is one year after the date on which the State in which such person is employed establishes an accreditation program pursuant to subsection (b) of this section.

(3) Lists of courses

The Administrator, in consultation with affected organizations, shall publish (and revise as necessary)—

(A) a list of asbestos courses and tests in effect before October 22, 1986, which qualify for equivalency treatment under paragraph (2), and

(B) a list of asbestos courses and tests which the Administrator determines under paragraph (1) are consistent with the model plan and which will qualify a contractor for accreditation under such paragraph.

(d) Laboratory accreditation

(1) The Administrator shall provide for the development of an accreditation program for laboratories by the National Institute of Standards and Technology in accordance with paragraph (2). The Administrator shall transfer such funds as are necessary to the National Institute of Standards and Technology to carry out such program.

(2) The National Institute of Standards and Technology, upon request by the Administrator, shall, in consultation with affected organizations—

(A) within 360 days after October 22, 1986, develop an accreditation program for laboratories which conduct qualitative and semi-quantitative analyses of bulk samples of asbestos-containing material, and

(B) within 720 days after October 22, 1986, develop an accreditation program for laboratories which conduct analyses of air samples of asbestos from school buildings under the authority of a local educational agency.

(3) A laboratory which plans to carry out any such analysis shall comply with the requirements of the accreditation program.

(e) Financial assistance contingent on use of accredited persons

(1) A school which is an applicant for financial assistance under section 505 of the Asbestos School Hazard Abatement Act of 1984 [20 U.S.C.A. § 4014] is not eligible for such assistance unless the school, in carrying out the requirements of this subchapter—

(A) uses a person (or persons)—

(i) who is accredited by a State which has adopted an accreditation plan based on the model plan developed under subsection (b) of this section, or

(ii) who is accredited pursuant to an Administrator-approved course under subsection (c) of this section, and

(B) uses a laboratory (or laboratories) which is accredited under the program developed under subsection (d) of this section.

(2) This subsection shall apply to any financial assistance provided under the Asbestos School Hazard Abatement Act of 1984 [20 U.S.C.A. § 4011 et seq.] for activities performed after the following dates:

(A) In the case of activities performed by persons, after the date which is one year after October 22, 1986.

(B) In the case of activities performed by laboratories, after the date which is 180 days after the date on which a laboratory accreditation program is completed under subsection (d) of this section.

(f) List of EPA-approved courses

Not later than August 31, 1988, and every three months thereafter until August 31, 1991, the Administrator shall publish in the Federal Register a list of all Environmental Protection Agency-approved asbestos training courses for persons to achieve accreditation in each category described in subsection (b)(1)(A) of this section and for laboratories to achieve accreditation. The Administrator may continue publishing such a list after August 31, 1991, at such times as the Administrator considers it useful. The list shall include the name and address of each approved trainer and, to the extent available, a list of all the geographic sites where training courses will take place. The Administrator shall provide a copy of the list to each State official on the list published by the Administrator under section 2645(d)(6) of this title and to each regional office of the Environmental Protection Agency.

(Pub. L. No. 94–469, Title II, § 206, as added by Pub. L. No. 99–519, § 2, 100 Stat. 2980 (Oct. 22, 1986); and amended by Pub. L. No. 100–368, § 3, 102 Stat. 832 (July 18, 1988); Pub. L. No. 100–418, Title V, § 5115(c), 102 Stat. 1433 (Aug. 23, 1988); Pub. L. No. 101–637, § 15(a)(1), (2), 104 Stat. 4596 (Nov. 28, 1990).)

HISTORICAL AND STATUTORY NOTES

References in Text

The Defense Dependents' Education Act of 1978, referred to in subsec. (b)(2), is Title XIV of Pub. L. No. 95–561, 92 Stat. 2365 (Nov. 1, 1978), as amended, which is codified principally to chapter 25A (§ 921 et seq.) of Title 20, Education. For complete classification of this Act to the Code, see Short Title note set out under section 921 of Title 20 and Tables.

The Asbestos School Hazard Abatement Act of 1984, referred to in subsec. (e)(2), is Title V of Pub. L. No. 98–377, 98 Stat. 1287 (Aug. 11, 1984), as amended, which is codified generally to subchapter V (§ 4011 et seq.) of chapter 52 of Title 20. For complete classification of this Act to the Code, see Short Title note set out under section 4011 of Title 20 and Tables.

Effective and Applicability Provisions

1990 Acts. Section 15(c) of Pub. L. No. 101–637 provided that: "This section [amending this section and section 2647 of this title and enacting provisions set out as notes under this section] shall take effect upon the expiration of the 12-month period following the date of the enactment of this Act [Nov. 28, 1990]. The Administrator may extend the effective date for a period not to exceed one year if the Administrator determines that accredited asbestos contractors are needed to perform school-site abatement required under the Asbestos Hazard Emergency Response Act [of 1986] (15 U.S.C. 2641) and such an extension is necessary to ensure effective implementation of section 203 of the Toxic Substances Control Act [15 U.S.C.A. § 2643]."

Revision of Model Contractor Accreditation Program

Section 15(a)(3) of Pub. L. No. 101–637 provided that: "Not later than one year after the date of the enactment of this Act [Nov. 28, 1990], the Administrator of the Environmental Protection Agency shall revise the model contractor accreditation plan promulgated under section 206(b)(1) of the Toxic Substances Control Act (15 U.S.C.

2646(b)(1)) to increase the minimum number of hours of training, including additional hours of hands-on health and safety training, required for asbestos abatement workers and to make such other changes as may be necessary to implement the amendments made by paragraphs (1) and (2) [amending this section]."

EPA Administrator Not Exercising "Statutory Authority" Under OSHA Law in Exercising Authority Under this Chapter

Section 15(b) of Pub. L. No. 101–637 provided that: "In exercising any authority under the Toxic Substances Control Act [15 U.S.C.A. § 2601 et seq.] in connection with the amendment made by subsection (a) of this section [amending this section and section 2647 of this title], the Administrator of the Environmental Protection Agency shall not, for purposes of section 4(b)(1) of the Occupational Safety and Health Act of 1970 (29 U.S.C. 653(b)(1)), be considered to be exercising statutory authority to prescribe or enforce standards or regulations affecting occupational safety and health."

§ 2647. Enforcement

[TSCA § 207]

(a) Penalties

Any local educational agency—

(1) which fails to conduct an inspection pursuant to regulations under section 2643(b) of this title or under section 2644(b) of this title,

(2) which knowingly submits false information to the Governor regarding any inspection pursuant to regulations under section 2643(i) of this title or knowingly includes false information in any inspection statement under section 2644(d)(3) of this title,

(3) which fails to develop a management plan pursuant to regulations under section 2643(i) of this title or under section 2644(d) of this title,

(4) which carries out any activity prohibited by section 2655 of this title, or

(5) which knowingly submits false information to the Governor regarding a deferral request under section 2645(d) of this title.[1]

is liable for a civil penalty of not more than $5,000 for each day during which the violation continues. Any civil penalty under this subsection shall be assessed and collected in the same manner, and subject to the same provisions, as in the case of civil penalties assessed and collected under section 2615 of this title. For purposes of this subsection, a "violation" means a failure to comply with respect to a single school building. The court shall order that any civil penalty collected under this subsection be used by the local educational agency for purposes of complying with this subchapter. Any portion of a civil penalty remaining unspent after compliance by a local educational agency is completed shall be deposited into the Asbestos Trust Fund established by section 4022 of Title 20.

(b) Relationship to subchapter I of this chapter

A local educational agency is not liable for any civil penalty under subchapter I of this chapter for failing or refusing to comply with any rule promulgated or order issued under this subchapter.

(c) Enforcement considerations

(1) In determining the amount of a civil penalty to be assessed under subsection (a) of this section against a local educational agency, the Administrator shall consider—

(A) the significance of the violation;

(B) the culpability of the violator, including any history of previous violations under this chapter;

(C) the ability of the violator to pay the penalty; and

(D) the ability of the violator to continue to provide educational services to the community.

(2) Any action ordered by a court in fashioning relief under section 2619 of this title shall be consistent with regulations promulgated under section 2643 of this title (or with the requirements of section 2644 of this title if there are no regulations).

(d) Citizen complaints

Any person may file a complaint with the Administrator or with the Governor of the State in which the school building is located with respect to asbestos-containing material in a school building. If the Administrator or Governor receives a complaint under this subsection containing allegations which provide a reasonable basis to believe that a violation of this chapter has occurred, the Administrator or Governor shall investigate and respond (including taking enforcement action where appropriate) to the complaint within a reasonable period of time.

(e) Citizen petitions

(1) Any person may petition the Administrator to initiate a proceeding for the issuance, amendment, or repeal of a regulation or order under this subchapter.

(2) Such petition shall be filed in the principal office of the Administrator and shall set forth the facts which it is claimed establish that it is necessary to issue, amend, or repeal a regulation or order under this subchapter.

(3) The Administrator may hold a public hearing or may conduct such investigation or proceeding as the Administrator deems appropriate in order to determine whether or not such petition should be granted.

(4) Within 90 days after filing of a petition described in paragraph (1), the Administrator shall either grant or deny the petition. If the Administrator grants such petition, the Administrator shall promptly commence an appropriate proceeding in accordance with this subchapter. If the Administrator denies such petition, the Administrator shall publish in the Federal Register the Administrator's reasons for such denial. The granting or denial of a petition under this subsection shall not affect any deadline or other requirement of this subchapter.

(f) Citizen civil actions with respect to EPA regulations

(1) Any person may commence a civil action without prior notice against the Administrator to compel the Administrator to meet the deadlines in section 2643 of this title for issuing advanced notices of proposed rulemaking, proposing regulations, and promulgating regulations. Any such action shall be brought in the district court of the United States for the District of Columbia.

(2) In any action brought under paragraph (1) in which the court finds the Administrator to be in violation of any deadline in section 2643 of this title, the court shall set forth a schedule for promulgating the regulations required by section 2643 of this title and shall order the Administrator to comply with such schedule. The court may extend any deadline (which has not already occurred) in section 2644(b), (c), or (d) of this title for a period of not more than 6 months, if the court-ordered schedule will result in final promulgation of the pertinent regulations within the extended period. Such deadline extensions may not be granted by the court beginning 720 days after October 22, 1986.

(3) Section 2619 of this title shall apply to civil actions described in this subsection, except to the extent inconsistent with this subsection.

(g) Failure to attain accreditation; penalty

Any contractor who—

(1) inspects for asbestos-containing material in a school, public or commercial building;

(2) designs or conducts response actions with respect to friable asbestos-containing material in a school, public or commercial building; or

(3) employs individuals to conduct response actions with respect to friable asbestos-containing material in a school, public or commercial building;

and who fails to obtain the accreditation under section 2646 of this title, or in the case of employees to require or provide for the accreditation required, is liable for a civil penalty of not more than $5,000 for each day during which the violation continues, unless such contractor is a direct employee of the Federal Government.

(Pub. L. No. 94–469, Title II, § 207, as added by Pub. L. No. 99–519, § 2, 100 Stat. 2983 (Oct. 22, 1986); and amended by Pub. L. No. 100–368, § 5, 102 Stat. 833 (July 18, 1988); Pub. L. No. 101–637, § 15(a)(4), 104 Stat. 4596 (Nov. 28, 1990).)

[1] So in original. The period probably should be a comma.

HISTORICAL AND STATUTORY NOTES

Effective and Applicability Provisions

1990 Acts. Amendment by Pub. L. No. 101–637 effective upon expiration of 12-month period following Nov. 28, 1990, with provisions for extension, see section 15(c) of Pub. L. No. 101–637, set out as a note under section 2646 of this title.

EPA Administrator Not Exercising "Statutory Authority" Under OSHA Law in Exercising Authority Under this Chapter

In exercising any authority under this chapter in connection with amendment made by Pub. L. No. 101–637, Administrator of Environmental Protection Agency not, for purposes of section 653(b)(1) of Title 29, Labor, to be considered to be exercising statutory authority to prescribe or enforce standards or regulations affecting occupational safety and health, see section 15(b) of Pub. L. No. 101–637, set out as a note under section 2646 of this title.

§ 2648. Emergency authority

[TSCA § 208]

(a) Emergency action

(1) Authority

Whenever—

(A) the presence of airborne asbestos or the condition of friable asbestos-containing material in a school building governed by a local educational agency poses an imminent and substantial endangerment to human health or the environment, and

(B) the local educational agency is not taking sufficient action (as determined by the Administrator or the Governor) to respond to the airborne asbestos or friable asbestos-containing material,

the Administrator or the Governor of a State is authorized to act to protect human health or the environment.

(2) Limitations on Governor's action

The Governor of a State shall notify the Administrator within a reasonable period of time before the Governor plans to take an emergency action under this subsection. After such notification, if the Administrator takes an emergency action with respect to the same hazard, the Governor may not carry out (or continue to carry out, if the action has been started) the emergency action.

(3) Notification

The following notification shall be provided before an emergency action is taken under this subsection:

(A) In the case of a Governor taking the action, the Governor shall notify the local educational agency concerned.

(B) In the case of the Administrator taking the action, the Administrator shall notify both the local educational agency concerned and the Governor of the State in which such agency is located.

(4) Cost recovery

The Administrator or the Governor of a State may seek reimbursement for all costs of an emergency action taken under this subsection in the United States District Court for the District of Columbia or for the district in which the emergency action occurred. In any action seeking reimbursement from a local educational agency, the action shall be brought in the United States District Court for the district in which the local educational agency is located.

(b) Injunctive relief

Upon receipt of evidence that the presence of airborne asbestos or the condition of friable asbestos-containing material in a school building governed by a local educational agency poses an imminent and substantial endangerment to human health or the environment—

(1) the Administrator may request the Attorney General to bring suit, or

(2) the Governor of a State may bring suit,

to secure such relief as may be necessary to respond to the hazard. The district court of the United States in the district in which the response will be carried out shall have jurisdiction to grant such relief, including injunctive relief.

(Pub. L. No. 94–469, Title II, § 208, as added by Pub. L. No. 99–519, § 2, 100 Stat. 2985 (Oct. 22, 1986).)

§ 2649. State and Federal law

[TSCA § 209]

(a) No preemption

Nothing in this subchapter shall be construed, interpreted, or applied to preempt, displace, or supplant any other State or Federal law, whether statutory or common.

(b) Cost and damage awards

Nothing in this subchapter or any standard, regulation, or requirement promulgated pursuant to this subchapter shall be construed or interpreted to preclude any court from awarding costs and damages associated with the abatement, including the removal, of asbestos-containing material, or a portion of such costs, at any time prior to the actual date on which such material is removed.

(c) State may establish more requirements

Nothing in this subchapter shall be construed or interpreted as preempting a State from establishing any additional liability or more stringent requirements with respect to asbestos in school buildings within such State.

(d) No Federal cause of action

Nothing in this subchapter creates a cause of action or in any other way increases or diminishes the liability of any person under any other law.

(e) Intent of Congress

It is not the intent of Congress that this subchapter or rules, regulations, or orders issued pursuant to this subchapter be interpreted as influencing, in either the plaintiff's or defendant's favor, the disposition of any civil action for damages relating to asbestos. This subsection does not affect the authority of any court to make a determination in an adjudicatory proceeding under applicable State law with respect to the admission into evidence or any other use of this subchapter or rules, regulations, or orders issued pursuant to this subchapter.

(Pub. L. No. 94–469, Title II, § 209, as added by Pub. L. No. 99–519, § 2, 100 Stat. 2986 (Oct. 22, 1986).)

§ 2650. Asbestos contractors and local educational agencies

[TSCA § 210]

(a) Study

(1) General requirement

The Administrator shall conduct a study on the availability of liability insurance and other forms of assurance against financial loss which are available to local educational agencies and asbestos contractors with respect to actions required under this subchapter. Such study shall examine the following:

(A) The extent to which liability insurance and other forms of assurance against financial loss are available to local educational agencies and asbestos contractors.

(B) The extent to which the cost of insurance or other forms of assurance against financial loss has increased and the extent to which coverage has become less complete.

(C) The extent to which any limitation in the availability of insurance or other forms of assurance against financial loss is the result of factors other than standards of liability in applicable law.

(D) The extent to which the existence of the regulations required by subsections (c) and (d) of section 2643 of this title and the accreditation of contractors under section 2646 of this title has affected the availability or cost of insurance or other forms of assurance against financial loss.

(E) The extent to which any limitation on the availability of insurance or other forms of assurance against financial loss is inhibiting inspections for asbestos-containing material or the development or implementation of management plans under this subchapter.

(F) Identification of any other impediments to the timely completion of inspections or the development and implementation of management plans under this subchapter.

(2) Interim report

Not later than April 1, 1988, the Administrator shall submit to the Congress an interim report on the progress of the study required by this subsection, along with preliminary findings based on information collected to that date.

(3) Final report

Not later than October 1, 1990, the Administrator shall submit to the Congress a final report on the study required by this subsection, including final findings based on the information collected.

(b) State action

On the basis of the interim report or the final report of the study required by subsection (a) of this section, a State may enact or amend State law to establish or modify a standard of liability for local educational agencies or asbestos contractors with respect to actions required under this subchapter.

(Pub. L. No. 94–469, Title II, § 210, as added by Pub. L. No. 99–519, § 2, 100 Stat. 2986 (Oct. 22, 1986).)

§ 2651. Public protection

[TSCA § 211]

(a) Public protection

No State or local educational agency may discriminate against a person in any way, including firing a person who is an employee, because the person provided information relating to a potential violation of this subchapter to any other person, including a State or the Federal Government.

(b) Labor Department review

Any public or private employee or representative of employees who believes he or she has been fired or otherwise discriminated against in violation of subsection (a) of this section may within 90 days after the alleged violation occurs apply to the Secretary of Labor for a review of the firing or alleged discrimination. The review shall be conducted in accordance with section 660(c) of Title 29.

(Pub. L. No. 94–469, Title II, § 211, as added by Pub. L. No. 99–519, § 2, 100 Stat. 2987 (Oct. 22, 1986).)

§ 2652. Asbestos Ombudsman

[TSCA § 212]

(a) Appointment

The Administrator shall appoint an Asbestos Ombudsman, who shall carry out the duties described in subsection (b) of this section.

(b) Duties

The duties of the Asbestos Ombudsman are—

(1) to receive complaints, grievances, and requests for information submitted by any person with respect to any aspect of this subchapter,

(2) to render assistance with respect to the complaints, grievances, and requests received, and

(3) to make such recommendations to the Administrator as the Ombudsman considers appropriate.

(Pub. L. No. 94–469, Title II, § 212, as added by Pub. L. No. 99–519, § 2, 100 Stat. 2987 (Oct. 22, 1986).)

§ 2653. EPA study of asbestos-containing material in public buildings

[TSCA § 213]

Within 360 days after October 22, 1986, the Administrator shall conduct and submit to the Congress the results of a study which shall—

(1) assess the extent to which asbestos-containing materials are present in public and commercial buildings;

(2) assess the condition of asbestos-containing material in commercial buildings and the likelihood that persons occupying such buildings, including service and maintenance personnel, are, or may be, exposed to asbestos fibers;

(3) consider and report on whether public and commercial buildings should be subject to the same inspection and response action requirements that apply to school buildings;

(4) assess whether existing Federal regulations adequately protect the general public, particularly abatement personnel, from exposure to asbestos during renovation and demolition of such buildings; and

(5) include recommendations that explicitly address whether there is a need to establish standards for, and regulate asbestos exposure in, public and commercial buildings.

(Pub. L. No. 94–469, Title II, § 213, as added by Pub. L. No. 99–519, § 2, 100 Stat. 2987 (Oct. 22, 1986).)

§ 2654. Transitional rules

[TSCA § 214]

Any regulation of the Environmental Protection Agency under subchapter I of this chapter which is inconsistent with this subchapter shall not be in effect after October 22, 1986. Any advanced notice of proposed rulemaking, any proposed rule, and any regulation of the Environmental Protection Agency in effect before October 22, 1986, which is consistent with the regulations required under section 2643 of this title shall remain in effect and may be used to meet the requirements of section 2643 of this title, except that any such regulation shall be enforced under this chapter.

(Pub. L. No. 94–469, Title II, § 214, as added by Pub. L. No. 99–519, § 2, 100 Stat. 2988 (Oct. 22, 1986).)

§ 2655. Worker protection

[TSCA § 215]

(a) Prohibition on certain activities

Until the local educational agency with authority over a school has submitted a management plan (for the school) which the State Governor has not disapproved as of the end of the period for review and revision of the plan under section 2645 of this title, the local educational agency may not do either of the following in the school:

(1) Perform, or direct an employee to perform, renovations or removal of building materials, except emergency repairs, in the school, unless—

(A) the school is carrying out work under a grant awarded under section 4014 of Title 20; or

(B) an inspection that complies with the requirements of regulations promulgated under section 2643 of this title has been carried out in the school and the agency complies with the following sections of title 40 of the Code of Federal Regulations:

(i) Paragraphs (g), (h), and (i) of section 763.90 (response actions).

(ii) Appendix D to subpart E of part 763 (transport and disposal of asbestos waste).

(2) Perform, or direct an employee to perform, operations and maintenance activities in the school, unless the agency complies with the following sections of title 40 of the Code of Federal Regulations:

(A) Section 763.91 (operations and maintenance), including appendix B to subpart E of part 763.

(B) Paragraph (a)(2) of section 763.92 (training and periodic surveillance).

(b) Employee training and equipment

Any school employee who is directed to conduct emergency repairs involving any building material containing asbestos or suspected of containing asbestos, or to conduct operations and maintenance activities, in a school—

(1) shall be provided the proper training to safely conduct such work in order to prevent potential exposure to asbestos; and

(2) shall be provided the proper equipment and allowed to follow work practices that are necessary to safely conduct such work in order to prevent potential exposure to asbestos.

(c) "Emergency repair" defined

For purposes of this section, the term "emergency repair" means a repair in a school building that was not planned and was in response to a sudden, unexpected event that threatens either—

(1) the health or safety of building occupants; or

(2) the structural integrity of the building.

(Pub. L. No. 94–469, Title II, § 215, as added by Pub. L. No. 100–368, § 4(a), 102 Stat. 832 (July 18, 1988).)

HISTORICAL AND STATUTORY NOTES

Effective and Applicability Provisions

1988 Acts. Section 4(c) of Pub. L. No. 100–368 provided that: "Section 215 of the Toxic Substances Control Act [this section], as added by subsection (a), shall take effect on October 12, 1988."

§ 2656. Training grants

[TSCA § 216]

(a) Grants

The Administrator is authorized to award grants under this section to nonprofit organizations that demonstrate experience in implementing and operating health and safety asbestos training and education programs for workers who are or will be engaged in asbestos-related activities (including State and local governments, colleges and universities, joint labor-management trust funds, and nonprofit government employee organizations) to establish and, or, operate asbestos training programs on a not-for-profit basis. Applications for grants under this subsection shall be submitted in such form and manner, and contain such information, as the Administrator prescribes.

(b) Authorization

Of such sums as are authorized to be appropriated pursuant to section 4021(a) of Title 20 for the fiscal years 1991, 1992, 1993, 1994, and 1995, not more than $5,000,000 are authorized to be appropriated to carry out this section in each such fiscal year.

(Pub. L. No. 94–469, Title II, § 216, as added by Pub. L. No. 101–637, § 16(a)(1), 104 Stat. 4597 (Nov. 28, 1990).)

HISTORICAL AND STATUTORY NOTES

Effective and Applicability Provisions

1990 Acts. Section 16(b) of Pub. L. No. 101–637 provided that: "Section 216 of the Toxic Substances Control Act [this section], as added by subsection (a), shall take effect on the date of the enactment of this Act [Nov. 28, 1990]."

SUBCHAPTER III—INDOOR RADON ABATEMENT

§ 2661. National goal

[TSCA § 301]

The national long-term goal of the United States with respect to radon levels in buildings is that the air within buildings in the United States should be as free of radon as the ambient air outside of buildings.

(Pub. L. No. 94–469, Title III, § 301, as added by Pub. L. No. 100–551, § 1(a), 102 Stat. 2755 (Oct. 28, 1988).)

HISTORICAL AND STATUTORY NOTES

Report on Recommended Policy for Dealing with Radon in Assisted Housing

Pub. L. No. 100–628, Title X, § 1091, 102 Stat. 3283 (Nov. 7, 1988), provided that:

"**(a) Purposes.**—The purposes of this section are—

"**(1)** to require the Department of Housing and Urban Development to develop an effective departmental policy for dealing with radon contamination that utilizes any Environmental Protection Agency guidelines and standards to ensure that occupants of housing covered by this section are not exposed to hazardous levels of radon; and

"**(2)** to require the Department of Housing and Urban Development to assist the Environmental Protection Agency in reducing radon contamination.

"**(b) Program.**—

"**(1) Applicability.**—The housing covered by this section is—

"**(A)** multifamily housing owned by the Department of Housing and Urban Development;

"**(B)** public housing and Indian housing assisted under the United States Housing Act of 1937 [42 U.S.C.A. § 1437 et seq.];

"**(C)** housing receiving project-based assistance under section 8 of the United States Housing Act of 1937 [42 U.S.C.A. § 1437f];

"**(D)** housing assisted under section 236 of the National Housing Act [12 U.S.C.A. § 1715z–1]; and

"**(E)** housing assisted under section 221(d)(3) of the National Housing Act [12 U.S.C.A. § 1715*l*(d)(3)].

"**(2) In general.**—The Secretary of Housing and Urban Development shall develop and recommend to the Congress a policy for dealing with radon contamination that specifies programs for education, research, testing, and mitigation of radon hazards in housing covered by this section.

"**(3) Standards.**—In developing the policy, the Secretary shall utilize any guidelines, information, or standards established by the Environmental Protection Agency for—

"**(A)** testing residential and nonresidential structures for radon;

"**(B)** identifying elevated radon levels;

"**(C)** identifying when remedial actions should be taken; and

"**(D)** identifying geographical areas that are likely to have elevated levels of radon.

"**(4) Coordination.**—In developing the policy, the Secretary shall coordinate the efforts of the Department of Housing and Urban Development with the Environmental Protection Agency, and other appropriate Federal agencies, and shall consult with State and local governments, the housing industry, consumer groups, health organizations, appropriate professional organizations, and other appropriate experts.

"**(5) Report.**—The Secretary shall submit a report to the Congress within 1 year after the date of the enactment of this Act [Nov. 7, 1988] that describes the Secretary's recommended policy for dealing with radon contamination and the Secretary's reasons for recommending such policy. The report shall include an estimate of the housing covered by this section that is likely to have hazardous levels of radon.

"**(c) Cooperation with Environmental Protection Agency.**—Within 6 months after the date of the enactment of this Act [Nov. 7, 1988], the Secretary and the Administrator of the Environmental Protection Agency shall enter into a memorandum of understanding describing the Secretary's plan to assist the Administrator in carrying out the Environmental Protection Agency's authority to assess the extent of radon contamination in the United States and assist in the development of measures to avoid and reduce radon contamination.

"**(d) Definitions.**—For purposes of this section:

"**(1) Administrator.**—The term 'Administrator' means the Administrator of the Environmental Protection Agency.

"**(2) Secretary.**—The term 'Secretary' means the Secretary of Housing and Urban Development.

"**(e) Authorization.**—Funds available for housing covered by this section shall be available to carry out this section with respect to such housing."

§ 2662. Definitions

[TSCA § 302]

For purposes of this subchapter:

(1) The term "local educational agency" means—

(A) any local educational agency as defined in section 7801 of Title 20;

(B) the owner of any nonprofit elementary or secondary school building; and

(C) the governing authority of any school operated pursuant to section 241 of Title 20, as in effect before enactment of the Improving America's Schools Act of 1994, or successor authority, relating to impact aid for children who reside on Federal property.

(2) The term "nonprofit elementary or secondary school" has the meaning given such term by section 2642(8)[1] of this title,

(3) The term "radon" means the radioactive gaseous element and its short-lived decay products produced by the disintegration of the element radium occurring in air, water, soil, or other media.

(4) The term "school building" has the meaning given such term by section 2642(13) of this title.

(Pub. L. No. 94–469, Title III, § 302, as added by Pub. L. No. 100–551, § 1(a), 102 Stat. 2755 (Oct. 28, 1988); and amended by Pub. L. No. 103–382, Title III, §§ 391(c)(4), 392(b)(2), 108 Stat. 4022, 4026 (Oct. 20, 1994); Pub. L. No. 107–110, Title X, § 1076(f)(2), 115 Stat. 2091 (Jan. 8, 2002).)

[1] So in original. Probably should be "2642(9)".

HISTORICAL AND STATUTORY NOTES

References in Text

Section 241 of Title 20, as in effect before enactment of the Improving America's Schools Act of 1994, referred to in par. (1)(C), means section 241 of Title 20, Education, prior to its repeal by Pub. L. No. 103–382 Title III, § 331(b), 108 Stat. 3965 (Oct. 20, 1994).

Effective and Applicability Provisions

2002 Acts. Except as otherwise provided, amendments by Pub. L. No. 107–110 effective Jan. 8, 2002, see Pub. L. No. 107–110, § 5, set out as a note under 20 U.S.C.A. § 6301.

§ 2663. EPA citizen's guide

[TSCA § 303]

(a) Publication

In order to make continuous progress toward the long-term goal established in section 2661 of this title, the Administrator of the Environmental Protection Agency shall, not later than June 1, 1989, publish and make available to the public an updated version of its document titled "A Citizen's Guide to Radon". The Administrator shall revise and republish the guide as necessary thereafter.

(b) Information included

(1) Action levels

The updated citizen's guide published as provided in subsection (a) of this section shall include a description of a series of action levels indicating the health risk associated with different levels of radon exposure.

(2) Other information

The updated citizen's guide shall also include information with respect to each of the following:

(A) The increased health risk associated with the exposure of potentially sensitive populations to different levels of radon.

(B) The increased health risk associated with the exposure to radon of persons engaged in potentially risk-increasing behavior.

(C) The cost and technological feasibility of reducing radon concentrations within existing and new buildings.

(D) The relationship between short-term and long-term testing techniques and the relationship between (i) measurements based on both such techniques, and (ii) the actions[1] levels set forth as provided in paragraph (1).

(E) Outdoor radon levels around the country.

(Pub. L. No. 94–469, Title III, § 303, as added by Pub. L. No. 100–551, § 1(a), 102 Stat. 2755 (Oct. 28, 1988).)

[1] So in original. Probably should be "action".

§ 2664. Model construction standards and techniques

[TSCA § 304]

The Administrator of the Environmental Protection Agency shall develop model construction standards and techniques for controlling radon levels within new buildings. To the maximum extent possible, these standards and techniques should be developed with the assistance of organizations involved in establishing national building construction standards and techniques. The Administrator shall make a draft of the document containing the model standards and techniques available for public review and comment. The model standards and techniques shall provide for geographic differences in construction types and materials, geology, weather, and other variables that may affect radon levels in new buildings. The Administrator shall make final model standards and techniques available to the public by June 1, 1990. The Administrator shall work to ensure that organizations responsible for developing national model building codes, and authorities which regulate building construction within States or political subdivisions within States, adopt the Agency's model standards and techniques.

(Pub. L. No. 94–469, Title III, § 304, as added by Pub. L. No. 100–551, § 1(a), 102 Stat. 2756 (Oct. 28, 1988).)

§ 2665. Technical assistance to States for radon programs

[TSCA § 305]

(a) Required activities

The Administrator (or another Federal department or agency designated by the Administrator) shall develop and implement activities designed to assist State radon programs. These activities may include, but are not limited to, the following:

(1) Establishment of a clearinghouse of radon related information, including mitigation studies, public information materials, surveys of radon levels, and other relevant information.

(2) Operation of a voluntary proficiency program for rating the effectiveness of radon measurement devices and methods, the effectiveness of radon mitigation devices and methods, and the effectiveness of private firms and individuals offering radon-related architecture, design, engineering, measurement, and mitigation services. The proficiency program under this subparagraph shall be in operation within one year after October 28, 1988.

(3) Design and implementation of training seminars for State and local officials and private and professional firms dealing with radon and addressing topics such as monitoring, analysis, mitigation, health effects, public information, and program design.

(4) Publication of public information materials concerning radon health risks and methods of radon mitigation.

(5) Operation of cooperative projects between the Environmental Protection Agency's Radon Action Program and the State's radon program. Such projects shall include the Home Evaluation Program, in which the Environmental Protection Agency evaluates homes and States demonstrate mitigation methods in these homes. To the maximum extent practicable, consistent with the objectives of the evaluation and demonstration, homes of low-income persons should be selected for evaluation and demonstration.

(6) Demonstration of radon mitigation methods in various types of structures and in various geographic settings and publication of findings. In the case of demonstration of such methods in homes, the Administrator should select homes of low-income persons, to the maximum extent practicable and consistent with the objectives of the demonstration.

(7) Establishment of a national data base with data organized by State concerning the location and amounts of radon.

(8) Development and demonstration of methods of radon measurement and mitigation that take into account unique characteristics, if any, of nonresidential buildings housing child care facilities.

(b) Discretionary assistance

Upon request of a State, the Administrator (or another Federal department or agency designated by the Administrator) may provide technical assistance to such State in development or implementation of programs addressing radon. Such assistance may include, but is not limited to, the following:

(1) Design and implementation of surveys of the location and occurrence of radon within a State.

(2) Design and implementation of public information and education programs.

(3) Design and implementation of State programs to control radon in existing or new structures.

(4) Assessment of mitigation alternatives in unusual or unconventional structures.

(5) Design and implementation of methods for radon measurement and mitigation for nonresidential buildings housing child care facilities.

(c) Information provided to professional organizations

The Administrator, or another Federal department or agency designated by the Administrator, shall provide appropriate information concerning technology and methods of radon assessment and mitigation to professional organizations representing private firms involved in building design, engineering, and construction.

(d) Proficiency rating program and training seminar

(1) Authorization

There is authorized to be appropriated not more than $1,500,000 for the purposes of initially establishing the proficiency rating program under subsection (a)(2) of this section and the training seminars under subsection (a)(3) of this section.

(2) Charge imposed

To cover the operating costs of such proficiency rating program and training seminars, the Administrator shall impose on persons applying for a proficiency rating and on private and professional firms participating in training seminars such charges as may be necessary to defray the costs of the program or seminars. No such charge may be imposed on any State or local government.

(3) Special account

Funds derived from the charges imposed under paragraph (2) of this subsection shall be deposited in a special account in the Treasury. Amounts in the special account are authorized to be appropriated only for purposes of administering such proficiency rating program or training seminars or for reimbursement of funds appropriated to the Administrator to initially establish such program or seminars.

(4) Reimbursement of general fund

During the first three years of the program and seminars, the Administrator shall make every effort, consistent with the goals and successful operation of the program and seminars, to set charges imposed under paragraph (2) of this subsection so that an amount in excess of operation costs is collected. Such excess amount shall be used to reimburse the General Fund of the Treasury for the full amount appropriated to initially establish the program and seminars.

(5) Research

The Administrator shall, in conjunction with other Federal agencies, conduct research to develop, test, and evaluate radon and radon progeny measurement methods and protocols. The purpose of such research shall be to assess the ability of those methods and protocols to accurately assess exposure to radon progeny. Such research shall include—

(A) conducting comparisons among radon and radon progeny measurement techniques;

(B) developing measurement protocols for different building types under varying operating conditions; and

(C) comparing the exposures estimated by stationary monitors and protocols to those measured by personal monitors, and issue guidance documents that—

(i) provide information on the results of research conducted under this paragraph; and

(ii) describe model State radon measurement and mitigation programs.

(6) Mandatory proficiency testing program study

(A) The Administrator shall conduct a study to determine the feasibility of establishing a mandatory proficiency testing program that would require that—

(i) any product offered for sale, or device used in connection with a service offered to the public, for the measurement of radon meets minimum performance criteria; and

(ii) any operator of a device, or person employing a technique, used in connection with a service offered to the public for the measurement of radon meets a minimum level of proficiency.

(B) The study shall also address procedures for—

(i) ordering the recall of any product sold for the measurement of radon which does not meet minimum performance criteria;

(ii) ordering the discontinuance of any service offered to the public for the measurement of radon which does not meet minimum performance criteria; and

(iii) establishing adequate quality assurance requirements for each company offering radon measurement services to the public to follow.

The study shall identify enforcement mechanisms necessary to the success of the program. The Administrator shall report the findings of the study with recommendations to Congress by March 1, 1991.

(7) User fee

In addition to any charge imposed pursuant to paragraph (2) of this subsection, the Administrator shall collect user fees from persons seeking certification under the radon proficiency program in an amount equal to $1,500,000 to cover the Environmental Protection Agency's cost of conducting research pursuant to paragraph (5) for each of the fiscal years 1991, 1992, 1993, 1994, and 1995. Such funds shall be deposited in the account established pursuant to paragraph (3).

(e) Authorization

(1) There is authorized to be appropriated for the purposes of carrying out sections 2663, 2664, and 2665 of this title an amount not to exceed $3,000,000 for each of fiscal years 1989, 1990, and 1991.

(2) No amount appropriated under this subsection may be used by the Environmental Protection Agency to administer the grant program under section 2666 of this title.

(3) No amount appropriated under this subsection may be used to cover the costs of the proficiency rating program under subsection (a)(2) of this section.

(Pub. L. No. 94–469, Title III, § 305, as added by Pub. L. No. 100–551, § 1(a), 102 Stat. 2756 (Oct. 28, 1988); and amended by Pub. L. No. 101–508, Title X, § 10202, 104 Stat. 1388–393 (Nov. 5, 1990); Pub. L. No. 104–66, Title II, § 2021(*l*), 109 Stat. 728 (Dec. 21, 1995).)

§ 2666. Grant assistance to States for radon programs

[TSCA § 306]

(a) In general

For each fiscal year, upon application of the Governor of a State, the Administrator may make a grant, subject to such terms and conditions as the Administrator considers appropriate, under this section to the State for the purpose of assisting the State in the development and implementation of programs for the assessment and mitigation of radon.

(b) Application

An application for a grant under this section in any fiscal year shall contain such information as the Administrator shall require, including each of the following:

(1) A description of the seriousness and extent of radon exposure in the State.

(2) An identification of the State agency which has the primary responsibility for radon programs and which will receive the grant, a description of the roles and responsibilities of the lead State agency and any other State agencies involved in radon programs, and description of the roles and responsibilities of any municipal, district, or areawide organization involved in radon programs.

(3) A description of the activities and programs related to radon which the State proposes in such year.

(4) A budget specifying Federal and State funding of each element of activity of the grant application.

(5) A 3-year plan which outlines long range program goals and objectives, tasks necessary to achieve them, and resource requirements for the entire 3-year period, including anticipated State funding levels and desired Federal funding levels. This clause shall apply only for the initial year in which a grant application is made.

(c) Eligible activities

Activities eligible for grant assistance under this section are the following:

(1) Survey of radon levels, including special surveys of geographic areas or classes of buildings (such as, among others, public buildings, school buildings, high-risk residential construction types).

(2) Development of public information and educational materials concerning radon assessment, mitigation, and control programs.

(3) Implementation of programs to control radon in existing and new structures.

(4) Purchase by the State of radon measurement equipment or devices.

(5) Purchase and maintenance of analytical equipment connected to radon measurement and analysis, including costs of calibration of such equipment.

(6) Payment of costs of Environmental Protection Agency-approved training programs related to radon for permanent State or local employees.

(7) Payment of general overhead and program administration costs.

(8) Development of a data storage and management system for information concerning radon occurrence, levels, and programs.

(9) Payment of costs of demonstration of radon mitigation methods and technologies as approved by the Administrator, including State participation in the Environmental Protection Agency Home Evaluation Program.

(10) A toll-free radon hotline to provide information and technical assistance.

(d) Preference to certain States

Beginning in fiscal year 1991, the Administrator shall give a preference for grant assistance under this section to States that have made reasonable efforts to ensure the adoption, by the authorities which regulate building construction within that State or political subdivisions within States, of the model construction standards and techniques for new buildings developed under section 2664 of this title.

(e) Priority activities and projects

The Administrator shall support eligible activities contained in State applications with the full amount of available funds. In the event that State applications for funds exceed the total funds available in a fiscal year, the Administrator shall give priority to activities or projects proposed by States based on each of the following criteria:

(1) The seriousness and extent of the radon contamination problem to be addressed.

(2) The potential for the activity or project to bring about reduction in radon levels.

(3) The potential for development of innovative radon assessment techniques, mitigation measures as approved by the Administrator, or program management approaches which may be of use to other States.

(4) Any other uniform criteria that the Administrator deems necessary to promote the goals of the grant program and that the Administrator provides to States before the application process.

(f) Federal share

The Federal share of the cost of radon program activities implemented with Federal assistance under this section in any fiscal year shall not exceed 75 percent of the costs incurred by the State in implementing such program in the first year of a grant to such State, 60 percent in the second year, and 50 percent in the third year. Federal assistance shall be made on the condition that the non-Federal share is provided from non-Federal funds.

(g) Assistance to local governments

States may, at the Governor's discretion, use funds from grants under this section to assist local governments in implementation of activities eligible for assistance under paragraphs (2), (3), and (6) of subsection (c) of this section.

(h) Information

(1) The Administrator may request such information, data, and reports developed by the State as he considers necessary to make the determination of continuing eligibility under this section.

(2) Any State receiving funds under this section shall provide to the Administrator all radon-related information generated in its activities, including the results of radon surveys, mitigation demonstration projects, and risk communication studies.

(3) Any State receiving funds under this section shall maintain, and make available to the public, a list of firms and individuals within the State that have received a passing rating under the Environmental Protection Agency proficiency rating program referred to in section 2665(a)(2) of this title. The list shall also include the address and phone number of such firms and individuals, together with the proficiency rating received by each. The Administrator shall make such list available to the public at appropriate locations in each State which does not receive funds under this section unless the State assumes such responsibility.

(i) Limitations

(1) No grant may be made under this section in any fiscal year to a State which in the preceding fiscal year received a grant under this section unless the Administrator determines that such State satisfactorily implemented the activities funded by the grant in such preceding fiscal year.

(2) The costs of implementing paragraphs (4) and (9) of subsection (c) of this section shall not in the aggregate exceed 50 percent of the amount of any grant awarded under this section to a State in a fiscal year. In implementing such paragraphs, a State should make every effort, consistent with the goals and successful operation of the State radon program, to give a preference to low-income persons.

(3) The costs of general overhead and program administration under subsection (c)(7) of this section shall not exceed 25 percent of the amount of any grant awarded under this section to a State in a fiscal year.

(4) A State may use funds received under this section for financial assistance to persons only to the extent such assistance is related to demonstration projects or the purchase and analysis of radon measurement devices.

(j) Authorization

(1) There is authorized to be appropriated for grant assistance under this section an amount not to exceed $10,000,000 for each of fiscal years 1989, 1990, and 1991.

(2) There is authorized to be appropriated for the purpose of administering the grant program under this section such sums as may be necessary for each of such fiscal years.

(3) Notwithstanding any other provision of this section, not more than 10 percent of the amount appropriated to carry out this section may be used to make grants to any one State.

(4) Funds not obligated to States in the fiscal year for which funds are appropriated under this section shall remain available for obligation during the next fiscal year.

(5) No amount appropriated under this subsection may be used to cover the costs of the proficiency rating program under section 2665(a)(2) of this title.

(Pub. L. No. 94–469, Title III, § 306, as added Pub. L. No. 100–551, § 1(a), 102 Stat. 2758 (Oct. 28, 1988).)

HISTORICAL AND STATUTORY NOTES

Federal Share of Cost

Pub. L. No. 109–54, Title II, 119 Stat. 531 (Aug. 2, 2005), provided in part that: "Beginning in fiscal year 2006 and thereafter, and notwithstanding section 306 of the Toxic Substances Control Act [this section], the Federal share of the cost of radon program activities implemented with Federal assistance under section 306 [this section] shall not exceed 60 percent in the third and subsequent grant years."

§ 2667. Radon in schools

[TSCA § 307]

(a) Study of radon in schools

(1) Authority

The Administrator shall conduct a study for the purpose of determining the extent of radon contamination in the Nation's school buildings.

(2) List of high probability areas

In carrying out such study, the Administrator shall identify and compile a list of areas within the United States which the Administrator determines have a high probability of including schools which have elevated levels of radon.

(3) Basis of list

In compiling such list, the Administrator shall make such determinations on the basis of, among other things, each of the following:

(A) Geological data.

(B) Data on high radon levels in homes and other structures nearby any such school.

(C) Physical characteristics of the school buildings.

(4) Survey

In conducting such study the Administrator shall design a survey which when completed allows Congress to characterize the extent of radon contamination in schools in each State. The survey shall include testing from a representative sample of schools in each high-risk area identified in paragraph (1) and shall include additional testing, to the extent resources are available for such testing. The survey also shall include any reliable testing data supplied by States, schools, or other parties.

(5) Assistance

(A) The Administrator shall make available to the appropriate agency of each State, as designated by the Governor of such State, a list of high risk areas within each State, including a delineation of such areas and any other data available to the Administrator for schools in that State. To assist such agencies, the Administrator also shall provide guidance and data detailing the risks associated with high radon levels, technical guidance and related information concerning testing for radon within schools, and methods of reducing radon levels.

(B) In addition to the assistance authorized by subparagraph (A), the Administrator is authorized to make available to the appropriate agency of each State, as designated by the Governor of such State, devices suitable for use by such agencies in conducting tests for radon within the schools under the jurisdiction of any such State agency. The Administrator is authorized to make available to such agencies the use of laboratories of the Environmental Protection Agency, or to recommend laboratories, to evaluate any such devices for the presence of radon levels.

(6) Diagnostic and remedial efforts

The Administrator is authorized to select, from high-risk areas identified in paragraph (2), school buildings for purposes of enabling the Administrator to undertake diagnostic and remedial efforts to reduce the levels of radon in such school buildings. Such diagnostic and remedial efforts shall be carried out with a view to developing technology and expertise for the purpose of making such technology and expertise available to any local educational agency and the several States.

(7) Status report

On or before October 1, 1989, the Administrator shall submit to the Congress a status report with respect to action taken by the Administrator in conducting the study required by this section, including the results of the Administrator's diagnostic and remedial work. On or before October 1, 1989, the Administrator shall submit a final report setting forth the results of the study conducted pursuant to this section, including the results of the Administrator's diagnostic and remedial work, and the recommendations of the Administrator.

(b) Authorization

For the purpose of carrying out the provisions of paragraph (6) of subsection (a) of this section, there are authorized to be appropriated such sums, not to exceed $500,000, as may be necessary. For the purpose of carrying out the provisions of this section other than such paragraph (6), there are authorized to be appropriated such sums, not to exceed $1,000,000, as may be necessary.

(Pub. L. No. 94–469, Title III, § 307, as added by Pub. L. No. 100–551, § 1(a), 102 Stat. 2761 (Oct. 28, 1988).)

§ 2668. Regional radon training centers

[TSCA § 308]

(a) Funding program

Upon application of colleges, universities, institutions of higher learning, or consortia of such institutions, the Administrator may make a grant or cooperative agreement, subject to such terms and conditions as the Administrator considers appropriate, under this section to the applicant for the purpose of establishing and operating a regional radon training center.

(b) Purpose of centers

The purpose of a regional radon training center is to develop information and provide training to Federal and State officials, professional and private firms, and the public regarding the health risks posed by radon and demonstrated methods of radon measurement and mitigation.

(c) Applications

Any colleges, universities, institutions of higher learning or consortia of such institutions may submit an application for funding under this section. Such applications shall be submitted to the Administrator in such form and containing such information as the Administrator may require.

(d) Selection criteria

The Administrator shall support at least 3 eligible applications with the full amount of available funds. The Administrator shall select recipients of funding under this section to ensure that funds are equitably allocated among regions of the United States, and on the basis of each of the following criteria:

(1) The extent to which the applicant's program will promote the purpose described in subsection (b) of this section.

(2) The demonstrated expertise of the applicant regarding radon measurement and mitigation methods and other radon-related issues.

(3) The demonstrated expertise of the applicant in radon training and in activities relating to information development and dissemination.

(4) The seriousness of the radon problem in the region.

(5) The geographical coverage of the proposed center.

(6) Any other uniform criteria that the Administrator deems necessary to promote the purpose described in subsection (b) of this section and that the Administrator provides to potential applicants prior to the application process.

(e) Termination of funding

No funding may be given under this section in any fiscal year to an applicant which in the preceding fiscal year received funding under this section unless the Administrator determines that the recipient satisfactorily implemented the activities that were funded in the preceding year.

(f) Authorization

There is authorized to be appropriated to carry out the program under this section not to exceed $1,000,000 for each of fiscal years 1989, 1990, and 1991.

(Pub. L. No. 94–469, Title III, § 308, as added by Pub. L. No. 100–551, § 1(a), 102 Stat. 2762 (Oct. 28, 1988).)

§ 2669. Study of radon in Federal buildings

[TSCA § 309]

(a) Study requirement

The head of each Federal department or agency that owns a Federal building shall conduct a study for the purpose of determining the extent of radon contamination in such buildings. Such study shall include, in the case of a Federal building using a nonpublic water source (such as a well or other groundwater), radon contamination of the water.

(b) High-risk Federal buildings

(1) The Administrator shall identify and compile a list of areas within the United States which the Administrator, in consultation with Federal departments and agencies, determines have a high probability of including Federal buildings which have elevated levels of radon.

(2) In compiling such list, the Administrator shall make such determinations on the basis of, among other things, the following:

(A) Geological data.

(B) Data on high radon levels in homes and other structures near any such Federal building.

(C) Physical characteristics of the Federal buildings.

(c) Study designs

Studies required under subsection (a) of this section shall be based on design criteria specified by the Administrator. The head of each Federal department or agency conducting such a study shall submit, not later than July 1, 1989, a study design to the Administrator for approval. The study design shall follow the most recent Environmental Protection Agency guidance documents, including "A Citizen's Guide to Radon"; the "Interim Protocol for Screening and Follow Up: Radon and Radon Decay Products Measurements"; the "Interim Indoor Radon & Radon Decay Product Measurement Protocol"; and any other recent guidance documents. The study design shall include testing data from a representative sample of Federal buildings in each high-risk area identified in subsection (b) of this section. The study design also shall include additional testing data to the extent resources are available, including any reliable data supplied by Federal agencies, States, or other parties.

(d) Information on risks and testing

(1) The Administrator shall provide to the departments or agencies conducting studies under subsection (a) of this section the following:

(A) Guidance and data detailing the risks associated with high radon levels.

(B) Technical guidance and related information concerning testing for radon within Federal buildings and water supplies.

(C) Technical guidance and related information concerning methods for reducing radon levels.

(2) In addition to the assistance required by paragraph (1), the Administrator is authorized to make available, on a cost reimbursable basis, to the departments or agencies conducting studies under subsection (a) of this section devices suitable for use by such departments or agencies in conducting tests for radon within Federal buildings. For the purpose of assisting such departments or agencies in evaluating any such devices for the presence of radon levels, the Administrator is authorized to recommend laboratories or to make available to such departments or agencies, on a cost reimbursable basis, the use of laboratories of the Environmental Protection Agency.

(e) Study deadline

Not later than June 1, 1990, the head of each Federal department or agency conducting a study under subsection (a) of this section shall complete the study and provide the study to the Administrator.

(f) Report to Congress

Not later than October 1, 1990, the Administrator shall submit a report to the Congress describing the results of the studies conducted pursuant to subsection (a) of this section.

(Pub. L. No. 94–469, Title III, § 309, as added by Pub. L. No. 100–551, § 1(a), 102 Stat. 2763 (Oct. 28, 1988).)

§ 2670. Regulations

[TSCA § 310]

The Administrator is authorized to issue such regulations as may be necessary to carry out the provisions of this subchapter.

(Pub. L. No. 94–469, Title III, § 310, as added by Pub. L. No. 100–551, § 1(a), 102 Stat. 2764 (Oct. 28, 1988).)

§ 2671. Additional authorizations

[TSCA § 311]

Amounts authorized to be appropriated in this subchapter for purposes of carrying out the provisions of this subchapter are in addition to amounts authorized to be appropriated under other provisions of law for radon-related activities.

(Pub. L. No. 94–469, Title III, § 311, as added by Pub. L. No. 100–551, § 1(a), 102 Stat. 2764 (Oct. 28, 1988).)

SUBCHAPTER IV—LEAD EXPOSURE REDUCTION

§ 2681. Definitions

[TSCA § 401]

For the purposes of this subchapter:

(1) Abatement

The term "abatement" means any set of measures designed to permanently eliminate lead-based paint hazards in accordance with standards established by the Administrator under this subchapter. Such term includes—

(A) the removal of lead-based paint and lead-contaminated dust, the permanent containment or encapsulation of lead-based paint, the replacement of lead-painted surfaces or fixtures, and the removal or covering of lead-contaminated soil; and

(B) all preparation, cleanup, disposal, and postabatement clearance testing activities associated with such measures.

(2) Accessible surface

The term "accessible surface" means an interior or exterior surface painted with lead-based paint that is accessible for a young child to mouth or chew.

(3) Deteriorated paint

The term "deteriorated paint" means any interior or exterior paint that is peeling, chipping, chalking or cracking or any paint located on an interior or exterior surface or fixture that is damaged or deteriorated.

(4) Evaluation

The term "evaluation" means risk assessment, inspection, or risk assessment and inspection.

(5) Friction surface

The term "friction surface" means an interior or exterior surface that is subject to abrasion or friction, including certain window, floor, and stair surfaces.

(6) Impact surface

The term "impact surface" means an interior or exterior surface that is subject to damage by repeated impacts, for example, certain parts of door frames.

(7) Inspection

The term "inspection" means (A) a surface-by-surface investigation to determine the presence of lead-based paint, as provided in section 4822(c) of Title 42, and (B) the provision of a report explaining the results of the investigation.

(8) Interim controls

The term "interim controls" means a set of measures designed to reduce temporarily human exposure or likely exposure to lead-based paint hazards, including specialized cleaning, repairs, maintenance, painting, temporary containment, ongoing monitoring of lead-based paint hazards or potential hazards, and the establishment and operation of management and resident education programs.

(9) Lead-based paint

The term "lead-based paint" means paint or other surface coatings that contain lead in excess of 1.0 milligrams per centimeter squared or 0.5 percent by weight or (A) in the case of paint or other surface coatings on target housing, such lower level as may be established by the Secretary of Housing and Urban Development, as defined in section 4822(c) of Title 42, or (B) in the case of any other paint or surface coatings, such other level as may be established by the Administrator.

(10) Lead-based paint hazard

The term "lead-based paint hazard" means any condition that causes exposure to lead from lead-contaminated dust, lead-contaminated soil, lead-contaminated paint that is deteriorated or present in accessible surfaces, friction surfaces, or impact surfaces that would result in adverse human health effects as established by the Administrator under this subchapter.

(11) Lead-contaminated dust

The term "lead-contaminated dust" means surface dust in residential dwellings that contains an area or mass concentration of lead in excess of levels determined by the Administrator under this subchapter to pose a threat of adverse health effects in pregnant women or young children.

(12) Lead-contaminated soil

The term "lead-contaminated soil" means bare soil on residential real property that contains lead at or in excess of the levels determined to be hazardous to human health by the Administrator under this subchapter.

(13) Reduction

The term "reduction" means measures designed to reduce or eliminate human exposure to lead-based paint hazards through methods including interim controls and abatement.

(14) Residential dwelling

The term "residential dwelling" means—

(A) a single-family dwelling, including attached structures such as porches and stoops; or

(B) a single-family dwelling unit in a structure that contains more than 1 separate residential dwelling unit, and in which each such unit is used or occupied, or intended to be used or occupied, in whole or in part, as the home or residence of 1 or more persons.

(15) Residential real property

The term "residential real property" means real property on which there is situated 1 or more residential dwellings used or occupied, or intended to be used or occupied, in whole or in part, as the home or residence of 1 or more persons.

(16) Risk assessment

The term "risk assessment" means an on-site investigation to determine and report the existence, nature, severity and location of lead-based paint hazards in residential dwellings, including—

(A) information gathering regarding the age and history of the housing and occupancy by children under age 6;

(B) visual inspection;

(C) limited wipe sampling or other environmental sampling techniques;

(D) other activity as may be appropriate; and

(E) provision of a report explaining the results of the investigation.

(17) Target housing

The term "target housing" means any housing constructed prior to 1978, except housing for the elderly or persons with disabilities or any 0-bedroom dwelling (unless any child who is less than 6 years of age resides or is expected to reside in such housing). In the case of jurisdictions which banned the sale or use of lead-based paint prior to 1978, the Secretary of Housing and Urban Development, at the Secretary's discretion, may designate an earlier date.

(Pub. L. No. 94–469, Title IV, § 401, as added by Pub. L. No. 102–550, Title X, § 1021(a), 106 Stat. 3912 (Oct. 28, 1992), and amended by Pub. L. No. 115–31, § 237(c) 131 Stat. 789 (May 5, 2017).)

§ 2682. Lead-based paint activities training and certification [TSCA § 402]

(a) Regulations

(1) In general

Not later than 18 months after October 28, 1992, the Administrator shall, in consultation with the Secretary of Labor, the Secretary of Housing and Urban Development, and the Secretary of Health and Human Services (acting through the Director of the National Institute for Occupational Safety and Health), promulgate final regulations governing lead-based paint activities to ensure that individuals engaged in such activities are properly trained; that training programs are accredited; and that contractors engaged in such activities are certified. Such regulations shall contain standards for performing lead-based paint activities, taking into account reliability, effectiveness, and safety. Such regulations shall require that all risk assessment, inspection, and abatement activities performed in target housing shall be performed by certified contractors, as such term is defined in section 4851b of Title 42. The provisions of this section shall supersede the provisions set forth under the heading "Lead Abatement Training and Certification" and under the heading "Training Grants" in title III of the Act entitled "An Act making appropriations for the Departments of Veterans Affairs and Housing and Urban Development, and for sundry independent agencies, commissions, corporations, and offices for the fiscal year ending September 30, 1992, and for other purposes", Public Law 102–139 [105 Stat. 765, 42 U.S.C.A. 4822 note], and upon October 28, 1992, the provisions set forth in such public law under such headings shall cease to have any force and effect.

(2) Accreditation of training programs

Final regulations promulgated under paragraph (1) shall contain specific requirements for the accreditation of lead-based paint activities training programs for workers, supervisors, inspectors and planners, and other individuals involved in lead-based paint activities, including, but not limited to, each of the following:

(A) Minimum requirements for the accreditation of training providers.

(B) Minimum training curriculum requirements.

(C) Minimum training hour requirements.

(D) Minimum hands-on training requirements.

(E) Minimum trainee competency and proficiency requirements.

(F) Minimum requirements for training program quality control.

(3) Accreditation and certification fees

The Administrator (or the State in the case of an authorized State program) shall impose a fee on—

(A) persons operating training programs accredited under this subchapter; and

(B) lead-based paint activities contractors certified in accordance with paragraph (1).

The fees shall be established at such level as is necessary to cover the costs of administering and enforcing the standards and regulations under this section which are applicable to such programs and contractors. The fee shall not be imposed on any State, local government, or nonprofit training program. The Administrator (or the State in the case of an authorized State program) may waive the fee for lead-based paint activities contractors under subparagraph (A) for the purpose of training their own employees.

(b) Lead-based paint activities

For purposes of this subchapter, the term "lead-based paint activities" means—

(1) in the case of target housing, risk assessment, inspection, and abatement; and

(2) in the case of any public building constructed before 1978, commercial building, bridge, or other structure or superstructure, identification of lead-based paint and materials containing lead-based paint, deleading, removal of lead from bridges, and demolition.

For purposes of paragraph (2), the term "deleading" means activities conducted by a person who offers to eliminate lead-based paint or lead-based paint hazards or to plan such activities.

(c) Renovation and remodeling

(1) Guidelines

In order to reduce the risk of exposure to lead in connection with renovation and remodeling of target housing, public buildings constructed before 1978, and commercial buildings, the Administrator shall, within 18 months after October 28, 1992, promulgate guidelines for the conduct of such renovation and remodeling activities which may create a risk of exposure to dangerous levels of lead. The Administrator shall disseminate such guidelines to persons engaged in such renovation and remodeling through hardware and paint stores, employee organizations, trade groups, State and local agencies, and through other appropriate means.

(2) Study of certification

The Administrator shall conduct a study of the extent to which persons engaged in various types of renovation and remodeling activities in target housing, public buildings constructed before 1978, and commercial buildings are exposed to lead in the conduct of such activities or disturb lead and create a lead-based paint hazard on a regular or occasional basis. The Administrator shall complete such study and publish the results thereof within 30 months after October 28, 1992.

(3) Certification determination

Within 4 years after October 28, 1992, the Administrator shall revise the regulations under subsection (a) of this section to apply the regulations to renovation or remodeling activities in target housing, public buildings constructed before 1978, and commercial buildings that create lead-based paint hazards. In determining which contractors are engaged in such activities, the Administrator shall utilize the results of the study under paragraph (2) and consult with the representatives of labor organizations, lead-based paint activities contractors, persons engaged in remodeling and renovation, experts in lead health effects, and others. If the Administrator determines that any category of contractors engaged in renovation or remodeling does not require certification, the Administrator shall publish an explanation of the basis for that determination.

(Pub. L. No. 94–469, Title IV, § 402, as added by Pub. L. No. 102–550, Title X, § 1021(a), 106 Stat. 3914 (Oct. 28, 1992).)

§ 2683. Identification of dangerous levels of lead

[TSCA § 403]

Within 18 months after October 28, 1992, the Administrator shall promulgate regulations which shall identify, for purposes of this subchapter and the Residential Lead-Based Paint Hazard Reduction Act of 1992 [42 U.S.C.A. § 4851 et seq.], lead-based paint hazards, lead-contaminated dust, and lead-contaminated soil.

(Pub. L. No. 94–469, Title IV, § 403, as added by Pub. L. No. 102–550, Title X, § 1021(a), 106 Stat. 3916 (Oct. 28, 1992).)

HISTORICAL STATUTORY NOTES

References in Text

The Residential Lead-Based Paint Hazard Reduction Act of 1992, referred to in text, is Title X of Pub. L. No. 102–550, 106 Stat. 3897 (Oct. 28, 1992), which is codified principally to chapter 63A (§ 4851 et seq.) of Title 42, The Public Health and Welfare. For complete classification of this Act to the Code, see Short Title note set out under section 4851 of Title 42 and Tables.

§ 2684. Authorized State programs

[TSCA § 404]

(a) Approval

Any State which seeks to administer and enforce the standards, regulations, or other requirements established under section 2682 or 2686 of this title, or both, may, after notice and opportunity for public hearing, develop and submit to the Administrator an application, in such form as the Administrator shall require, for authorization of such a State program. Any such State may also certify to the Administrator at the time of submitting such program that the State program meets the requirements of paragraphs (1) and (2) of subsection (b) of this section. Upon submission of such certification, the State program shall be deemed to be authorized under this section, and shall apply in such State in lieu of the corresponding Federal program under section 2682 or 2686 of this title, or both, as the case may be, until such time as the Administrator disapproves the program or withdraws the authorization.

(b) Approval or disapproval

Within 180 days following submission of an application under subsection (a) of this section, the Administrator shall approve or disapprove the application. The Administrator may approve the application only if, after notice and after opportunity for public hearing, the Administrator finds that—

(1) the State program is at least as protective of human health and the environment as the Federal program under section 2682 or 2686 of this title, or both, as the case may be, and

(2) such State program provides adequate enforcement.

Upon authorization of a State program under this section, it shall be unlawful for any person to violate or fail or refuse to comply with any requirement of such program.

(c) Withdrawal of authorization

If a State is not administering and enforcing a program authorized under this section in compliance with standards, regulations, and other requirements of this subchapter, the Administrator shall so notify the State and, if corrective action is not completed within a reasonable time, not to exceed 180 days, the Administrator shall withdraw authorization of such program and establish a Federal program pursuant to this subchapter.

(d) Model State program

Within 18 months after October 28, 1992, the Administrator shall promulgate a model State program which may be adopted by any State which seeks to administer and enforce a State program under this subchapter. Such model program shall, to the extent practicable, encourage States to utilize existing State and local certification and accreditation programs and procedures. Such program shall encourage reciprocity among the States with respect to the certification under section 2682 of this title.

(e) Other State requirements

Nothing in this subchapter shall be construed to prohibit any State or political subdivision thereof from imposing any requirements which are more stringent than those imposed by this subchapter.

(f) State and local certification

The regulations under this subchapter shall, to the extent appropriate, encourage States to seek program authorization and to use existing State and local certification and accreditation procedures, except that a State or local government shall not require more than 1 certification under this section for any lead-based paint activities contractor to carry out lead-based paint activities in the State or political subdivision thereof.

(g) Grants to States

The Administrator is authorized to make grants to States to develop and carry out authorized State programs under this section. The grants shall be subject to such terms and conditions as the Administrator may establish to further the purposes of this subchapter.

(h) Enforcement by Administrator

If a State does not have a State program authorized under this section and in effect by the date which is 2 years after promulgation of the regulations under section 2682 or 2686 of this title, the Administrator shall, by such date, establish a Federal program for section 2682 or 2686 of this title (as the case may be) for such State and administer and enforce such program in such State.

(Pub. L. No. 94–469, Title IV, § 404, as added by Pub. L. No. 102–550, Title X, § 1021(a), 106 Stat. 3916 (Oct. 28, 1992).)

§ 2685. Lead abatement and measurement

[TSCA § 405]

(a) Program to promote lead exposure abatement

The Administrator, in cooperation with other appropriate Federal departments and agencies, shall conduct a comprehensive program to promote safe, effective, and affordable monitoring, detection, and abatement of lead-based paint and other lead exposure hazards.

(b) Standards for environmental sampling laboratories

(1) The Administrator shall establish protocols, criteria, and minimum performance standards for laboratory analysis of lead in paint films, soil, and dust. Within 2 years after October 28, 1992, the Administrator, in consultation with the Secretary of Health and Human Services, shall establish a program to certify laboratories as qualified to test substances for lead content unless the Administrator determines, by the date specified in this paragraph, that effective voluntary accreditation programs are in place and operating on a nationwide basis at the time of such determination. To be certified under such program, a laboratory shall, at a minimum, demonstrate an ability to test substances accurately for lead content.

(2) Not later than 24 months after October 28, 1992, and annually thereafter, the Administrator shall publish and make available to the public a list of certified or accredited environmental sampling laboratories.

(3) If the Administrator determines under paragraph (1) that effective voluntary accreditation programs are in place for environmental sampling laboratories, the Administrator shall review the performance and effectiveness of such programs within 3 years after such determination. If, upon such review, the Administrator determines that the voluntary accreditation programs are not effective in assuring the quality and consistency of laboratory analyses, the Administrator shall, not more than 12 months thereafter, establish a certification program that meets the requirements of paragraph (1).

(c) Exposure studies

(1) The Secretary of Health and Human Services (hereafter in this subsection referred to as the "Secretary"), acting through the Director of the Centers for Disease Control,[1] (CDC), and the Director of the National Institute of Environmental Health Sciences, shall jointly conduct a study of the sources of lead exposure in children who have elevated blood lead levels (or other indicators of elevated lead body burden), as defined by the Director of the Centers for Disease Control.

(2) The Secretary, in consultation with the Director of the National Institute for Occupational Safety and Health, shall conduct a comprehensive study of means to reduce hazardous occupational lead abatement exposures. This study shall include, at a minimum, each of the following—

(A) Surveillance and intervention capability in the States to identify and prevent hazardous exposures to lead abatement workers.

(B) Demonstration of lead abatement control methods and devices and work practices to identify and prevent hazardous lead exposures in the workplace.

(C) Evaluation, in consultation with the National Institute of Environmental Health Sciences, of health effects of low and high levels of occupational lead exposures on reproductive, neurological, renal, and cardiovascular health.

(D) Identification of high risk occupational settings to which prevention activities and resources should be targeted.

(E) A study assessing the potential exposures and risks from lead to janitorial and custodial workers.

(3) The studies described in paragraphs (1) and (2) shall, as appropriate, examine the relative contributions to elevated lead body burden from each of the following:

(A) Drinking water.

(B) Food.

(C) Lead-based paint and dust from lead-based paint.

(D) Exterior sources such as ambient air and lead in soil.

(E) Occupational exposures, and other exposures that the Secretary determines to be appropriate.

(4) Not later than 30 months after October 28, 1992, the Secretary shall submit a report to the Congress concerning the studies described in paragraphs (1) and (2).

(d) Public education

(1) The Administrator, in conjunction with the Secretary of Health and Human Services, acting through the Director of the Agency for Toxic Substances and Disease Registry, and in conjunction with the Secretary of Housing and Urban Development, shall sponsor public education and outreach activities to increase public awareness of—

(A) the scope and severity of lead poisoning from household sources;

(B) potential exposure to sources of lead in schools and childhood day care centers;

(C) the implications of exposures for men and women, particularly those of childbearing age;

(D) the need for careful, quality, abatement and management actions;

(E) the need for universal screening of children;

(F) other components of a lead poisoning prevention program;

(G) the health consequences of lead exposure resulting from lead-based paint hazards;

(H) risk assessment and inspection methods for lead-based paint hazards; and

(I) measures to reduce the risk of lead exposure from lead-based paint.

(2) The activities described in paragraph (1) shall be designed to provide educational services and information to—

(A) health professionals;

(B) the general public, with emphasis on parents of young children;

(C) homeowners, landlords, and tenants;

(D) consumers of home improvement products;

(E) the residential real estate industry; and

(F) the home renovation industry.

(3) In implementing the activities described in paragraph (1), the Administrator shall assure coordination with the President's Commission on Environmental Quality's education and awareness campaign on lead poisoning.

(4) The Administrator, in consultation with the Chairman of the Consumer Product Safety Commission, shall develop information to be distributed by retailers of home improvement products to provide consumers with practical information related to the hazards of renovation and remodeling where lead-based paint may be present.

(e) Technical assistance

(1) Clearinghouse

Not later than 6 months after October 28, 1992, the Administrator shall establish, in consultation with the Secretary of Housing and Urban Development and the Director of the Centers for Disease Control, a National Clearinghouse on Childhood Lead Poisoning (hereinafter in this section referred to as "Clearinghouse"). The Clearinghouse shall—

(A) collect, evaluate, and disseminate current information on the assessment and reduction of lead-based paint hazards, adverse health effects, sources of exposure, detection and risk assessment methods, environmental hazards abatement, and clean-up standards;

(B) maintain a rapid-alert system to inform certified lead-based paint activities contractors of significant developments in research related to lead-based paint hazards; and

(C) perform any other duty that the Administrator determines necessary to achieve the purposes of this chapter.

(2) Hotline

Not later than 6 months after October 28, 1992, the Administrator, in cooperation with other Federal agencies and with State and local governments, shall establish a single lead-based paint hazard hotline to provide the public with answers to questions about lead poisoning prevention and referrals to the Clearinghouse for technical information.

(f) Products for lead-based paint activities

Not later than 30 months after October 28, 1992, the President shall, after notice and opportunity for comment, establish by rule appropriate criteria, testing protocols, and performance characteristics as are necessary to ensure, to the greatest extent possible and consistent with the purposes and policy of this subchapter, that lead-based paint hazard evaluation and reduction products introduced into commerce after a period specified in the rule are effective for the intended use described by the manufacturer. The rule shall identify the types or classes of products that are subject to such rule. The President, in implementation of the rule, shall, to the maximum extent possible, utilize independent testing laboratories, as appropriate, and consult with such entities and others in developing the rules. The President may delegate the authorities under this subsection to the Environmental Protection Agency or the Secretary of Commerce or such other appropriate agency.

(Pub. L. No. 94–469, Title IV, § 405, as added by Pub. L. No. 102–550, Title X, § 1021(a), 106 Stat. 3917 (Oct. 28, 1992).)

[1] So in original. The comma probably should not appear.

HISTORICAL AND STATUTORY NOTES

Termination of Reporting Requirements

For termination of reporting provisions of this section pertaining to lead abatement and measurement, effective May 15, 2000, see Pub. L. No. 104–66, § 3003, as amended, set out as a note under 31 U.S.C.A. § 1113, and the 7th item on page 104 of House Document No. 103–7.

§ 2686. Lead hazard information pamphlet

[TSCA § 406]

(a) Lead hazard information pamphlet

Not later than 2 years after October 28, 1992, after notice and opportunity for comment, the Administrator of the Environmental Protection Agency, in consultation with the Secretary of Housing and Urban Development and with the Secretary of Health and Human Services, shall publish, and from time to time revise, a lead hazard information pamphlet to be used in connection with this subchapter and section 4852d of Title 42. The pamphlet shall—

(1) contain information regarding the health risks associated with exposure to lead;

(2) provide information on the presence of lead-based paint hazards in federally assisted, federally owned, and target housing;

(3) describe the risks of lead exposure for children under 6 years of age, pregnant women, women of childbearing age, persons involved in home renovation, and others residing in a dwelling with lead-based paint hazards;

(4) describe the risks of renovation in a dwelling with lead-based paint hazards;

(5) provide information on approved methods for evaluating and reducing lead-based paint hazards and their effectiveness in identifying, reducing, eliminating, or preventing exposure to lead-based paint hazards;

(6) advise persons how to obtain a list of contractors certified pursuant to this subchapter in lead-based paint hazard evaluation and reduction in the area in which the pamphlet is to be used;

(7) state that a risk assessment or inspection for lead-based paint is recommended prior to the purchase, lease, or renovation of target housing;

(8) state that certain State and local laws impose additional requirements related to lead-based paint in housing and provide a listing of Federal, State, and local agencies in each State, including address and telephone number, that can provide information about applicable laws and available governmental and private assistance and financing; and

(9) provide such other information about environmental hazards associated with residential real property as the Administrator deems appropriate.

(b) Renovation of target housing

Within 2 years after October 28, 1992, the Administrator shall promulgate regulations under this subsection to require each person who performs for compensation a renovation of target housing to provide a lead hazard information pamphlet to the owner and occupant of such housing prior to commencing the renovation.

(Pub. L. No. 94–469, Title IV, § 406, as added by Pub. L. No. 102–550, Title X, § 1021(a), 106 Stat. 3920 (Oct. 28, 1992).)

§ 2687. Regulations

[TSCA § 407]

The regulations of the Administrator under this subchapter shall include such recordkeeping and reporting requirements as may be necessary to insure the effective implementation of this subchapter. The regulations may be amended from time to time as necessary.

(Pub. L. No. 94–469, Title IV, § 407, as added by Pub. L. No. 102–550, Title X, § 1021(a), 106 Stat. 3921 (Oct. 28, 1992).)

§ 2688. Control of lead-based paint hazards at Federal facilities

[TSCA § 408]

Each department, agency, and instrumentality of executive, legislative, and judicial branches of the Federal Government (1) having jurisdiction over any property or facility, or (2) engaged in any activity resulting, or which may result, in a lead-based paint hazard, and each officer, agent, or employee thereof, shall be subject to, and comply with, all Federal, State, interstate, and local requirements, both substantive and procedural (including any requirement for certification, licensing, recordkeeping, or reporting or any provisions for injunctive relief and such sanctions as may be imposed by a court to enforce such relief) respecting lead-based paint, lead-based paint activities, and lead-based paint hazards in the same manner, and to the same extent as any nongovernmental entity is subject to such requirements, including the payment of reasonable service charges. The Federal, State, interstate, and local substantive and procedural requirements referred to in this subsection include, but are not limited to, all administrative orders and all civil and administrative penalties and fines regardless of whether such penalties or fines are punitive or coercive in nature, or whether imposed for isolated, intermittent or continuing violations. The United States hereby expressly waives any immunity otherwise applicable to the United States with respect to any such substantive or procedural requirement (including, but not limited to, any injunctive relief, administrative order, or civil or administrative penalty or fine referred to in the preceding sentence, or reasonable service charge). The reasonable service charges referred to in this section include, but are not limited to, fees or charges assessed for certification and licensing, as well as any other nondiscriminatory charges that are assessed in connection with a Federal, State, interstate, or local lead-based paint, lead-based paint activities, or lead-based paint hazard activities program. No agent, employee, or officer of the United States shall be personally liable for any civil penalty under any Federal, State, interstate, or local law relating to lead-based paint, lead-based paint activities, or lead-based paint hazards with respect to any act or omission within the scope of his official duties.

(Pub. L. No. 94–469, Title IV, § 408, as added by Pub. L. No. 102–550, Title X, § 1021(a), 106 Stat. 3921 (Oct. 28, 1992).)

§ 2689. Prohibited acts

[TSCA § 409]

It shall be unlawful for any person to fail or refuse to comply with a provision of this subchapter or with any rule or order issued under this subchapter.

(Pub. L. No. 94–469, Title IV, § 409, as added by Pub. L. No. 102–550, Title X, § 1021(a), 106 Stat. 3921 (Oct. 28, 1992).)

§ 2690. Relationship to other Federal law

[TSCA § 410]

Nothing in this subchapter shall affect the authority of other appropriate Federal agencies to establish or enforce any requirements which are at least as stringent as those established pursuant to this subchapter.

(Pub. L. No. 94–469, Title IV, § 410, as added by Pub. L. No. 102–550, Title X, § 1021(a), 106 Stat. 3921 (Oct. 28, 1992).)

§ 2691. General provisions relating to administrative proceedings

[TSCA § 411]

(a) Applicability

This section applies to the promulgation or revision of any regulation issued under this subchapter.

(b) Rulemaking docket

Not later than the date of proposal of any action to which this section applies, the Administrator shall establish a rulemaking docket for such action (hereinafter in this subsection referred to as a "rule"). Whenever a rule applies only within a particular State, a second (identical) docket shall be established in the appropriate regional office of the Environmental Protection Agency.

(c) Inspection and copying

(1) The rulemaking docket required under subsection (b) of this section shall be open for inspection by the public at reasonable times specified in the notice of proposed rulemaking. Any person may copy documents contained in the docket. The Administrator shall provide copying facilities which may be used at the expense of the person seeking copies, but the Administrator may waive or reduce such expenses in such instances as the public interest requires. Any person may request copies by mail if the person pays the expenses, including personnel costs to do the copying.

(2) **(A)** Promptly upon receipt by the agency, all written comments and documentary information on the proposed rule received from any person for inclusion in the docket during the comment period shall be placed in the docket. The transcript of public hearings, if any, on the proposed rule shall also be included in the docket promptly upon receipt from the person who transcribed such hearings. All documents which become available after the proposed rule has been published and which the Administrator determines are of central relevance to the rulemaking shall be placed in the docket as soon as possible after their availability.

(B) The drafts of proposed rules submitted by the Administrator to the Office of Management and Budget for any interagency review process prior to proposal of any such rule, all documents accompanying such drafts, and all written comments thereon by other agencies and all written responses to such written comments by the Administrator shall be placed in the docket no later than the date of proposal of the rule. The drafts of the final rule submitted for such review process prior to promulgation and all such written comments thereon, all documents accompanying such drafts, and written responses thereto shall be placed in the docket no later than the date of promulgation.

(d) Explanation

(1) The promulgated rule shall be accompanied by an explanation of the reasons for any major changes in the promulgated rule from the proposed rule.

(2) The promulgated rule shall also be accompanied by a response to each of the significant comments, criticisms, and new data submitted in written or oral presentations during the comment period.

(3) The promulgated rule may not be based (in part or whole) on any information or data which has not been placed in the docket as of the date of such promulgation.

(e) Judicial review

The material referred to in subsection (c)(2)(B) of this section shall not be included in the record for judicial review.

(f) Effective date

The requirements of this section shall take effect with respect to any rule the proposal of which occurs after 90 days after October 28, 1992.

(Pub. L. No. 94–469, Title IV, § 411, as added by Pub. L. No. 102–550, Title X, § 1021(a), 106 Stat. 3922 (Oct. 28, 1992).)

§ 2692. Authorization of appropriations

[TSCA § 412]

There are authorized to be appropriated to carry out the purposes of this subchapter such sums as may be necessary.

(Pub. L. No. 94–469, Title IV, § 412, as added by Pub. L. No. 102–550, Title X, § 1021(a), 106 Stat. 3923 (Oct. 28, 1992).)

SUBCHAPTER V—HEALTHY HIGH-PERFORMANCE SCHOOLS

§ 2695. Grants for healthy school environments

[TSCA § 501]

(a) In general

The Administrator, in consultation with the Secretary of Education, may provide grants to States for use in—

(1) providing technical assistance for programs of the Environmental Protection Agency (including the Tools for Schools Program and the Healthy School Environmental Assessment Tool) to schools for use in addressing environmental issues; and

(2) development and implementation of State school environmental health programs that include—

(A) standards for school building design, construction, and renovation; and

(B) identification of ongoing school building environmental problems, including contaminants, hazardous substances, and pollutant emissions, in the State and recommended solutions to address those problems, including assessment of information on the exposure of children to environmental hazards in school facilities.

(b) Sunset

The authority of the Administrator to carry out this section shall expire 5 years after December 19, 2007.

(Pub. L. No. 94–469, Title V, § 501, as added by Pub. L. No. 110–140, Title IV, § 461(a), 121 Stat. 1640 (Dec. 19, 2007).)

HISTORICAL AND STATUTORY NOTES

Effective and Applicability Provisions

Enactment by Pub. L. 110–140 effective on the date that is 1 day after December 19, 2007, see Pub. L. No. 110–140, § 1601, set out as a note under 2 U.S.C.A. § 1824.

§ 2695a. Model guidelines for siting of school facilities

[TSCA § 502]

Not later than 18 months after December 19, 2007, the Administrator, in consultation with the Secretary of Education and the Secretary of Health and Human Services, shall issue voluntary school site selection guidelines that account for—

(1) the special vulnerability of children to hazardous substances or pollution exposures in any case in which the potential for contamination at a potential school site exists;

(2) modes of transportation available to students and staff;

(3) the efficient use of energy; and

(4) the potential use of a school at the site as an emergency shelter.

(Pub. L. No. 94–469, Title V, § 502, as added by Pub. L. No. 110–140, Title IV, § 461(a), 121 Stat. 1640 (Dec. 19, 2007).)

HISTORICAL AND STATUTORY NOTES

Effective and Applicability Provisions

Enactment by Pub. L. 110–140 effective on the date that is 1 day after December 19, 2007, see Pub. L. No. 110–140, § 1601, set out as a note under 2 U.S.C.A. § 1824.

§ 2695b. Public outreach

[TSCA § 503]

(a) Reports

The Administrator shall publish and submit to Congress an annual report on all activities carried out under this subchapter, until the expiration of authority described in section 2695(b) of this title.

(b) Public outreach

The Federal Director appointed under section 17092(a) of Title 42 (in this subchapter referred to as the "Federal Director") shall ensure, to the maximum extent practicable, that the public clearinghouse established under section 17083(1) of Title 42 receives and makes available information on the exposure of children to environmental hazards in school facilities, as provided by the Administrator.

(Pub. L. No. 94–469, Title V, § 503, as added by Pub. L. No. 110–140, Title IV, § 461(a), 121 Stat. 1640 (Dec. 19, 2007).)

HISTORICAL AND STATUTORY NOTES

References in Text

This subchapter, referred to in subsecs. (a), (b), originally read "this title," meaning Title V of the Toxic Substances Control Act, Pub. L. No. 94–469, Title V, §§ 501 to 505, as added by Pub. L. No. 110–140, Title IV, § 461(a), 121 Stat. 1640 (Dec. 19, 2007), which is codified as this subchapter.

Effective and Applicability Provisions

Enactment by Pub. L. 110–140 effective on the date that is 1 day after December 19, 2007, see Pub. L. No. 110–140, § 1601, set out as a note under 2 U.S.C.A. § 1824.

§ 2695c. Environmental health program

[TSCA § 504]

(a) In general

Not later than 2 years after December 19, 2007, the Administrator, in consultation with the Secretary of Education, the Secretary of Health and Human Services, and other relevant agencies, shall issue voluntary guidelines for use by the State in developing and implementing an environmental health program for schools that—

(1) takes into account the status and findings of Federal initiatives established under this subchapter or subtitle C of title IV of the Energy Independence and Security Act of 2007 and other relevant Federal law with respect to school facilities, including relevant updates on trends in the field, such as the impact of school facility environments on student and staff—

(A) health, safety, and productivity; and

(B) disabilities or special needs;

(2) takes into account studies using relevant tools identified or developed in accordance with section 492 of the Energy Independence and Security Act of 2007;

(3) takes into account, with respect to school facilities, each of—

(A) environmental problems, contaminants, hazardous substances, and pollutant emissions, including—

(i) lead from drinking water;

(ii) lead from materials and products;

(iii) asbestos;

(iv) radon;

(v) the presence of elemental mercury releases from products and containers;

(vi) pollutant emissions from materials and products; and

(vii) any other environmental problem, contaminant, hazardous substance, or pollutant emission that present or may present a risk to the health of occupants of the school facilities or environment;

(B) natural day lighting;

(C) ventilation choices and technologies;

(D) heating and cooling choices and technologies;

(E) moisture control and mold;

(F) maintenance, cleaning, and pest control activities;

(G) acoustics; and

(H) other issues relating to the health, comfort, productivity, and performance of occupants of the school facilities;

(4) provides technical assistance on siting, design, management, and operation of school facilities, including facilities used by students with disabilities or special needs;

(5) collaborates with federally funded pediatric environmental health centers to assist in on-site school environmental investigations;

(6) assists States and the public in better understanding and improving the environmental health of children; and

(7) takes into account the special vulnerability of children in low-income and minority communities to exposures from contaminants, hazardous substances, and pollutant emissions.

(b) Public outreach

The Federal Director and Commercial Director shall ensure, to the maximum extent practicable, that the public clearinghouse established under section 17083 of Title 42 receives and makes available—

(1) information from the Administrator that is contained in the report described in section 2695b(a) of this title; and

(2) information on the exposure of children to environmental hazards in school facilities, as provided by the Administrator.

(Pub. L. No. 94–469, Title V, § 504, as added by Pub. L. No. 110–140, Title IV, § 461(a), 121 Stat. 1641 (Dec. 19, 2007).)

HISTORICAL AND STATUTORY NOTES

References in Text

This subchapter, referred to in subsec. (a)(1), originally read "this title", meaning Title V of the Toxic Substances Control Act, Pub. L. No. 94–469, Title V, §§ 501 to 505, as added by Pub. L. No. 110–140, Title IV, 461, 121 Stat. 1640 (Dec. 19, 2007), which is codified as this subchapter.

Subtitle C of title IV of the Energy Independence and Security Act of 2007, referred to in subsec. (a)(1), is Pub. L. No. 110–140, Title IV, §§ 431 to 441, 121 Stat. 1607 (Dec. 19, 2007), which enacted Part C of Subchapter III of Chapter 152 of Title 42, 42 U.S.C.A. §§ 17091 to 17096, and amended 42 U.S.C.A. §§ 6832, 6834, 8253, and 8254, and enacted provisions set out as notes under 42 U.S.C.A. § 6834.

Section 492 of the Energy Independence and Security Act of 2007, referred to in subsec. (a)(2), is Pub. L. No. 110–140, Title IV, 492, 121 Stat. 1651 (Dec. 19, 2007), which enacted 42 U.S.C.A. § 17122.

Effective and Applicability Provisions

Enactment by Pub. L. 110–140 effective on the date that is 1 day after December 19, 2007, see Pub. L. No. 110–140, § 1601, set out as a note under 2 U.S.C.A. § 1824.

§ 2695d. Authorization of appropriations

[TSCA § 505]

There are authorized to be appropriated to carry out this subchapter $1,000,000 for fiscal year 2009, and $1,500,000 for each of fiscal years 2010 through 2013, to remain available until expended.

(Pub. L. No. 94–469, Title V, § 505, as added by Pub. L. No. 110–140, Title V, § 461(a), 121 Stat. 1642 (Dec. 19, 2007).)

HISTORICAL AND STATUTORY NOTES

References in Text

This subchapter, referred to in text, originally read "this title", meaning Title V of the Toxic Substances Control Act, Pub. L. No. 94–469, Title V, §§ 501 to 505, as added by Pub. L. No. 110–140, Title IV, § 461(a), Dec. 19, 2007, 121 Stat. 1640, which is codified as this subchapter.

Effective and Applicability Provisions

Enactment by Pub. L. 110–140 effective on the date that is 1 day after December 19, 2007, see Pub. L. No. 110–140, § 1601, set out as a note under 2 U.S.C.A. § 1824.

SUBCHAPTER VI—FORMALDEHYDE STANDARDS FOR COMPOSITE WOOD PRODUCTS

§ 2697. Formaldehyde standards

[TSCA § 601]

(a) Definitions

In this section:

(1) Finished good

(A) In general

The term "finished good" means any good or product (other than a panel) containing—

(i) hardwood plywood;

(ii) particleboard; or

(iii) medium-density fiberboard.

(B) Exclusions

The term "finished good" does not include—

(i) any component part or other part used in the assembly of a finished good; or

(ii) any finished good that has previously been sold or supplied to an individual or entity that purchased or acquired the finished good in good faith for purposes other than resale, such as—

(I) an antique; or

(II) secondhand furniture.

(2) Hardboard

The term "hardboard" has such meaning as the Administrator shall establish, by regulation, pursuant to subsection (d).

(3) Hardwood plywood

(A) In general

The term "hardwood plywood" means a hardwood or decorative panel that is—

(i) intended for interior use; and

(ii) composed of (as determined under the standard numbered ANSI/HPVA HP–1–2009) an assembly of layers or plies of veneer, joined by an adhesive with—

(I) lumber core;

(II) particleboard core;

(III) medium-density fiberboard core;

(IV) hardboard core; or

(V) any other special core or special back material.

(B) Exclusions

The term "hardwood plywood" does not include—

(i) military-specified plywood;

(ii) curved plywood; or

(iii) any other product specified in—

(I) The standard entitled "Voluntary Product Standard—Structural Plywood" and numbered PS 1–07; or

(II) The standard entitled "Voluntary Product Standard—Performance Standard for Wood-Based Structural-Use Panels" and numbered PS 2–04.

(C) Laminated products

(i) Rulemaking

(I) In general

The Administrator shall conduct a rulemaking process pursuant to subsection (d) that uses all available and relevant information from State authorities, industry, and other available sources of such information, and analyzes that information to determine, at the discretion of the Administrator, whether the definition of the term "hardwood plywood" should exempt engineered veneer or any laminated product.

(II) Modification

The Administrator may modify any aspect of the definition contained in clause (ii) before including that definition in the regulations promulgated pursuant to subclause (I).

(ii) Laminated product

The term "laminated product" means a product—

(I) in which a wood veneer is affixed to—

(aa) a particleboard platform;

(bb) a medium-density fiberboard platform; or

(cc) a veneer-core platform; and

(II) that is—

(aa) a component part;

(bb) used in the construction or assembly of a finished good; and

(cc) produced by the manufacturer or fabricator of the finished good in which the product is incorporated.

(4) Manufactured home

The term "manufactured home" has the meaning given the term in section 3280.2 of title 24, Code of Federal Regulations (as in effect on the date of promulgation of regulations pursuant to subsection (d)).

(5) Medium-density fiberboard

The term "medium-density fiberboard" means a panel composed of cellulosic fibers made by dry forming and pressing a resinated fiber mat (as determined under the standard numbered ANSI A208.2–2009).

(6) Modular home

The term "modular home" means a home that is constructed in a factory in 1 or more modules—

(A) each of which meet applicable State and local building codes of the area in which the home will be located; and

(B) that are transported to the home building site, installed on foundations, and completed.

(7) No-added formaldehyde-based resin

(A) In general

(i) The term "no-added formaldehyde-based resin" means a resin formulated with no added formaldehyde as part of the resin cross-linking structure in a composite wood product that meets the emission standards in subparagraph (C) as measured by—

(I) one test conducted pursuant to test method ASTM E–1333–96 (2002) or, subject to clause (ii), ASTM D–6007–02; and

(II) 3 months of routine quality control tests pursuant to ASTM D–6007–02 or ASTM D–5582 or such other routine quality control test methods as may be established by the Administrator through rulemaking.

(ii) Test results obtained under clause (i)(I) or (II) by any test method other than ASTM E–1333–96 (2002) must include a showing of equivalence by means established by the Administrator through rulemaking.

(B) Inclusions

The term "no-added formaldehyde-based resin" may include any resin made from—

(i) soy;

(ii) polyvinyl acetate; or

(iii) methylene diisocyanate.

(C) Emission standards

The following are the emission standards for composite wood products made with no-added formaldehyde-based resins under this paragraph:

(i) No higher than 0.04 parts per million of formaldehyde for 90 percent of the 3 months of routine quality control testing data required under subparagraph (A)(ii).

(ii) No test result higher than 0.05 parts per million of formaldehyde for hardwood plywood and 0.06 parts per million for particleboard, medium-density fiberboard, and thin medium-density fiberboard.

(8) Particleboard

(A) In general

The term "particleboard" means a panel composed of cellulosic material in the form of discrete particles (as distinguished from fibers, flakes, or strands) that are pressed together with resin (as determined under the standard numbered ANSI A208.1–2009).

(B) Exclusions

The term "particleboard" does not include any product specified in the standard entitled "Voluntary Product Standard—Performance Standard for Wood-Based Structural-Use Panels" and numbered PS 2–04.

(9) Recreational vehicle

The term "recreational vehicle" has the meaning given the term in section 3282.8 of title 24, Code of Federal Regulations (as in effect on the date of promulgation of regulations pursuant to subsection (d)).

(10) Ultra low-emitting formaldehyde resin

(A) In general

(i) The term "ultra low-emitting formaldehyde resin" means a resin in a composite wood product that meets the emission standards in subparagraph (C) as measured by—

(I) 2 quarterly tests conducted pursuant to test method ASTM E–1333–96 (2002) or, subject to clause (ii), ASTM D–6007–02; and

(II) 6 months of routine quality control tests pursuant to ASTM D–6007–02 or ASTM D–5582 or such other routine quality control test methods as may be established by the Administrator through rulemaking.

(ii) Test results obtained under clause (i)(I) or (II) by any test method other than ASTM E–1333–96 (2002) must include a showing of equivalence by means established by the Administrator through rulemaking.

(B) Inclusions

The term "ultra low-emitting formaldehyde resin" may include—

(i) melamine-urea-formaldehyde resin;

(ii) phenol formaldehyde resin; and

(iii) resorcinol formaldehyde resin.

(C) Emission standards

(i) The Administrator may, pursuant to regulations issued under subsection (d), reduce the testing requirements for a manufacturer only if its product made with ultra low-emitting formaldehyde resin meets the following emission standards:

(I) For hardwood plywood, no higher than 0.05 parts per million of formaldehyde.

(II) For medium-density fiberboard—

(aa) no higher than 0.06 parts per million of formaldehyde for 90 percent of 6 months of routine quality control testing data required under subparagraph (A)(ii); and

(bb) no test result higher than 0.09 parts per million of formaldehyde.

(III) For particleboard—

(aa) no higher than 0.05 parts per million of formaldehyde for 90 percent of 6 months of routine quality control testing data required under subparagraph (A)(ii); and

(bb) no test result higher than 0.08 parts per million of formaldehyde.

(IV) For thin medium-density fiberboard—

(aa) no higher than 0.08 parts per million of formaldehyde for 90 percent of 6 months of routine quality control testing data required under subparagraph (A)(ii); and

(bb) no test result higher than 0.11 parts per million of formaldehyde.

(ii) The Administrator may not, pursuant to regulations issued under subsection (d), exempt a manufacturer from third party certification requirements unless its product made with ultra low-emitting formaldehyde resin meets the following emission standards:

(I) No higher than 0.04 parts per million of formaldehyde for 90 percent of 6 months of routine quality control testing data required under subparagraph (A)(ii).

(II) No test result higher than 0.05 parts per million of formaldehyde for hardwood plywood and 0.06 parts per million for particleboard, medium-density fiberboard, and thin medium-density fiberboard.

(b) Requirement

(1) In general

Except as provided in an applicable sell-through regulation promulgated pursuant to subsection (d), effective beginning on the date that is 180 days after the date of promulgation of those regulations, the emission standards described in paragraph (2), shall apply to hardwood plywood, medium-density fiberboard, and particleboard sold, supplied, offered for sale, or manufactured in the United States.

(2) Emission standards

The emission standards referred to in paragraph (1), based on test method ASTM E–1333–96 (2002), are as follows:

(A) For hardwood plywood with a veneer core, 0.05 parts per million of formaldehyde.

(B) For hardwood plywood with a composite core—

(i) 0.08 parts per million of formaldehyde for any period after the effective date described in paragraph (1) and before July 1, 2012; and

(ii) 0.05 parts per million of formaldehyde, effective on the later of the effective date described in paragraph (1) or July 1, 2012.

(C) For medium-density fiberboard—

(i) 0.21 parts per million of formaldehyde for any period after the effective date described in paragraph (1) and before July 1, 2011; and

(ii) 0.11 parts per million of formaldehyde, effective on the later of the effective date described in paragraph (1) or July 1, 2011.

(D) For thin medium-density fiberboard—

(i) 0.21 parts per million of formaldehyde for any period after the effective date described in paragraph (1) and before July 1, 2012; and

(ii) 0.13 parts per million of formaldehyde, effective on the later of the effective date described in paragraph (1) or July 1, 2012.

(E) For particleboard—

(i) 0.18 parts per million of formaldehyde for any period after the effective date described in paragraph (1) and before July 1, 2011; and

(ii) 0.09 parts per million of formaldehyde, effective on the later of the effective date described in paragraph (1) or July 1, 2011.

(3) Compliance with emission standards

(A) Compliance with the emission standards described in paragraph (2) shall be measured by—

(i) quarterly tests shall be conducted pursuant to test method ASTM E–1333–96 (2002) or, subject to subparagraph (B), ASTM D–6007–02; and

(ii) quality control tests shall be conducted pursuant to ASTM D–6007–02, ASTM D–5582, or such other test methods as may be established by the Administrator through rulemaking.

(B) Test results obtained under subparagraph (A)(i) or (ii) by any test method other than ASTM E–1333–96 (2002) must include a showing of equivalence by means established by the Administrator through rulemaking.

(C) Except where otherwise specified, the Administrator shall establish through rulemaking the number and frequency of tests required to demonstrate compliance with the emission standards.

(4) Applicability

The formaldehyde emission standard referred to in paragraph (1) shall apply regardless of whether an applicable hardwood plywood, medium-density fiberboard, or particleboard is—

(A) in the form of an unfinished panel; or

(B) incorporated into a finished good.

(c) Exemptions

The formaldehyde emission standard referred to in subsection (b)(1) shall not apply to—

(1) hardboard;

(2) structural plywood, as specified in the standard entitled "Voluntary Product Standard—Structural Plywood" and numbered PS 1–07;

(3) structural panels, as specified in the standard entitled "Voluntary Product Standard—Performance Standard for Wood-Based Structural-Use Panels" and numbered PS 2–04;

(4) structural composite lumber, as specified in the standard entitled "Standard Specification for Evaluation of Structural Composite Lumber Products" and numbered ASTM D 5456–06;

(5) oriented strand board;

(6) glued laminated lumber, as specified in the standard entitled "Structural Glued Laminated Timber" and numbered ANSI A190.1–2002;

(7) prefabricated wood I-joists, as specified in the standard entitled "Standard Specification for Establishing and Monitoring Structural Capacities of Prefabricated Wood I-Joists" and numbered ASTM D 5055–05;

(8) finger-jointed lumber;

(9) wood packaging (including pallets, crates, spools, and dunnage);

(10) composite wood products used inside a new—

(A) vehicle (other than a recreational vehicle) constructed entirely from new parts that has never been—

(i) the subject of a retail sale; or

(ii) registered with the appropriate State agency or authority responsible for motor vehicles or with any foreign state, province, or country;

(B) rail car;

(C) boat;

(D) aerospace craft; or

(E) aircraft;

(11) windows that contain composite wood products, if the window product contains less than 5 percent by volume of hardwood plywood, particleboard, or medium-density fiberboard, combined, in relation to the total volume of the finished window product; or

(12) exterior doors and garage doors that contain composite wood products, if—

(A) the doors are made from composite wood products manufactured with no-added formaldehyde-based resins or ultra low-emitting formaldehyde resins; or

(B) the doors contain less than 3 percent by volume of hardwood plywood, particleboard, or medium-density fiberboard, combined, in relation to the total volume of the finished exterior door or garage door.

(d) Regulations

(1) In general

Not later than January 1, 2013, the Administrator shall promulgate regulations to implement the standards required under subsection (b) in a manner that ensures compliance with the emission standards described in subsection (b)(2).

(2) Inclusions

The regulations promulgated pursuant to paragraph (1) shall include provisions relating to—

(A) labeling;

(B) chain of custody requirements;

(C) sell-through provisions;

(D) ultra low-emitting formaldehyde resins;

(E) no-added formaldehyde-based resins;

(F) finished goods;

(G) third-party testing and certification;

(H) auditing and reporting of third-party certifiers;

(I) recordkeeping;

(J) enforcement;

(K) laminated products; and

(L) exceptions from the requirements of regulations promulgated pursuant to this subsection for products and components containing de minimis amounts of composite wood products.

The Administrator shall not provide under subparagraph (L) exceptions to the formaldehyde emission standard requirements in subsection (b).

(3) Sell-through provisions

(A) In general

Sell-through provisions established by the Administrator under this subsection, with respect to composite wood products and finished goods containing regulated composite wood products (including recreational vehicles, manufactured homes, and modular homes), shall—

(i) be based on a designated date of manufacture (which shall be no earlier than the date 180 days following the promulgation of the regulations pursuant to this subsection) of the composite wood product or finished good, rather than date of sale of the composite wood product or finished good; and

(ii) provide that any inventory of composite wood products or finished goods containing regulated composite wood products, manufactured before the designated date of manufacture of the composite wood products or finished goods, shall not be subject to the formaldehyde emission standard requirements under subsection (b)(1).

(B) Implementing regulations

The regulations promulgated under this subsection shall—

(i) prohibit the stockpiling of inventory to be sold after the designated date of manufacture; and

(ii) not require any labeling or testing of composite wood products or finished goods containing regulated composite wood products manufactured before the designated date of manufacture.

(C) Definition

For purposes of this paragraph, the term "stockpiling" means manufacturing or purchasing a composite wood product or finished good containing a regulated composite wood product between July 7, 2010, and the date 180 days following the promulgation of the regulations pursuant to this subsection at a rate which is significantly greater (as determined by the Administrator) than the rate at which such product or good was manufactured or purchased during a base period (as determined by the Administrator) ending before July 7, 2010.

(4) Import regulations

Not later than July 1, 2013, the Administrator, in coordination with the Commissioner of Customs and Border Protection and other appropriate Federal departments and agencies, shall revise regulations promulgated pursuant to section 2612 of this title as the Administrator determines to be necessary to ensure compliance with this section.

(5) Successor standards and test methods

The Administrator may, after public notice and opportunity for comment, substitute an industry standard or test method referenced in this section with its successor version.

(e) Prohibited acts

An individual or entity that violates any requirement under this section (including any regulation promulgated pursuant to subsection (d)) shall be considered to have committed a prohibited act under section 2614 of this title.

(Pub. L. No. 94–469, Title VI, § 601, as added by Pub. L. No. 111–199, § 2(a), 124 Stat. 1359 (July 7, 2010).)

HISTORICAL AND STATUTORY NOTES

Modification of Regulation

Pub. L. No. 111–199, § 4, 124 Stat. 1367 (July 7, 2010), provided that: "Not later than 180 days after the date of promulgation of regulations pursuant to section 601(d) of the Toxic Substances Control Act (as amended by section 2) [subsection (d) of this section], the Secretary of Housing and Urban Development shall update the regulation contained in section 3280.308 of title 24, Code of Federal Regulations (as in effect on the date of enactment of this Act [July 7, 2010]), to ensure that the regulation reflects the standards established by section 601 of the Toxic Substances Control Act [this section]."

Change of Customs Reference

Pub. L. No. 114–125, § 801(d)(2), 130 Stat. 206 (Feb. 24, 2016), provided that: "On and after the date of the enactment of this Act, any reference in law or regulations to the 'Commissioner of Customs' or the 'Commissioner of the Customs Service' shall be deemed to be a reference to the Commissioner of U.S. Customs and Border Protection."

TITLE 16

CONSERVATION

MULTIPLE-USE SUSTAINED-YIELD ACT OF 1960 [MUSYA § ____]

(16 U.S.C.A. §§ 528 to 531)

CHAPTER 2—NATIONAL FORESTS

§ 528. Development and administration of renewable surface resources for multiple use and sustained yield of products and services; Congressional declaration of policy and purpose

[MUSYA § 1]

It is the policy of the Congress that the national forests are established and shall be administered for outdoor recreation, range, timber, watershed, and wildlife and fish purposes. The purposes of sections 528 to 531 of this title are declared to be supplemental to, but not in derogation of, the purposes for which the national forests were established as set forth in section 475 of this title. Nothing herein shall be construed as affecting the jurisdiction or responsibilities of the several States with respect to wildlife and fish on the national forests. Nothing herein shall be construed so as to affect the use or administration of the mineral resources of national forest lands or to affect the use or administration of Federal lands not within national forests.

(Pub. L. No. 86–517, § 1, 74 Stat. 215 (June 12, 1960).)

HISTORICAL AND STATUTORY NOTES

Short Title

1960 Acts. Pub. L. No. 86–517, § 5, as added by Pub. L. No. 94–588, § 19, 90 Stat. 2962 (Oct. 22, 1976), provided that: "This Act [enacting sections 528 to 531 of this title] may be cited as the 'Multiple-Use Sustained-Yield Act of 1960'."

Pilot Program of Charges and Fees for Harvest of Forest Botanical Products

Section 339 of Pub. L. No. 106–113, Div. B, § 1000(a)(3), 113 Stat. 1535, 1501A–199 (Nov. 29, 1999), as amended by Pub. L. No. 108–108, Title III, § 335, 117 Stat. 1312 (Nov. 10, 2003); Pub. L. No. 111–88, Div. A, Title IV, § 420, 123 Stat. 2960 (Oct. 30, 2009); Pub. L. No. 113–76, Div. G, Title IV, § 432, 128 Stat. 345 (Jan. 17, 2014); Pub. L. No. 116–94, § 431, 133 Stat. 2534, 2749 (Dec. 20, 2019); Pub. L. No. 116–260, § 429, 134 Stat. 1182, 1542 (Dec. 27, 2020), provides that:

"(a) Definition of forest botanical product.—For purposes of this section, the term 'forest botanical product' means any naturally occurring mushrooms, fungi, flowers, seeds, roots, bark, leaves, and other vegetation (or portion thereof) that grow on National Forest System lands. The term does not include trees, except as provided in regulations issued under this section by the Secretary of Agriculture.

"(b) Recovery of fair market value for products.—The Secretary of Agriculture shall develop and implement a pilot program to charge and collect fees under subsection (c) [of this note] for forest botanical products harvested on National Forest System lands. The Secretary shall establish appraisal methods and bidding procedures to determine the fair market value of forest botanical products harvested under the pilot program.

"(c) Fees.—

"(1) Imposition and collection.—Under the pilot program, the Secretary of Agriculture shall charge and collect from a person who harvests forest botanical products on National Forest System lands a fee in an amount established by the Secretary to recover at least a portion of the fair market value of the harvested forest botanical products and a portion of the costs incurred by the Department of Agriculture associated with granting, modifying, or monitoring the authorization for harvest of the forest botanical products, including the costs of any environmental or other analysis.

"(2) Security.—The Secretary may require a person assessed a fee under this subsection to provide security to ensure that the Secretary receives the fees imposed under this subsection from the person.

"(d) Sustainable harvest levels for forest botanical products.—The Secretary of Agriculture shall conduct appropriate analyses to determine whether and how the harvest of forest botanical products on National Forest System lands can be conducted on a sustainable basis. The Secretary may not permit under the pilot program the harvest of forest botanical products at levels in excess of sustainable harvest levels, as defined pursuant to the Multiple-Use Sustained-Yield Act of 1960 (16 U.S.C. 528 et seq.). The Secretary shall establish procedures and timeframes to monitor and revise the harvest levels established for forest botanical products.

"(e) Waiver authority.—

"(1) Personal use.—The Secretary of Agriculture shall establish a personal use harvest level for each forest botanical product, and the harvest of a forest botanical product below that level by a person for personal use shall not be subject to a fee under subsection (c) [of this note].

"(2) Other exceptions.—The Secretary may also waive the application of subsection (b) or (c) [of this note] pursuant to such regulations as the Secretary may prescribe.

"(f) Deposit and use of funds.—

"(1) Deposit.—Funds collected under the pilot program in accordance with subsection (c) [of this note] shall be deposited into a special account in the Treasury of the United States.

"(2) Funds available.—Funds deposited into the special account in accordance with paragraph (1) shall be available for expenditure by the Secretary of Agriculture under paragraph (3) without further appropriation, and shall remain available for expenditure until the date specified in subsection (h)(2) [of this note].

"(3) Authorized uses.—The funds made available under paragraph (2) shall be expended at units of the National Forest System in proportion to the fees collected at that unit under subsection (c) [of this note] to pay for the costs of conducting inventories of forest botanical products, determining sustainable levels of harvest, monitoring and assessing the impacts of harvest levels and methods, conducting restoration activities, including any necessary vegetation, and covering costs of the Department of Agriculture described in subsection (c)(1) [of this note].

"(4) Treatment of fees.—Funds collected under subsection (c) [of this note] shall not be taken into account for the purposes of the following laws:

"(A) The sixth paragraph under the heading 'Forest Service in the Act of May 23, 1908 (16 U.S.C. 500) and section 13 of the Act of March 1, 1911 (commonly known as the Weeks Act; 16 U.S.C. 500).

"(B) The fourteenth paragraph under the heading 'Forest Service in the Act of March 4, 1913 (16 U.S.C. 501).

"(C) Section 33 of the Bankhead-Jones Farm Tenant Act (7 U.S.C. 1012).

"(D) The Act of August 8, 1937, and the Act of May 24, 1939 (43 U.S.C. 1181a et seq.) [43 U.S.C.A. §§ 1181a et seq., 1181f–1 et seq.].

"(E) Section 6 of the Act of June 14, 1926 (commonly known as the Recreation and Public Purposes Act; 43 U.S.C. 869–4).

"(F) Chapter 69 of title 31, United States Code [31 U.S.C.A. § 6901 et seq.].

"(G) Section 401 of the Act of June 15, 1935 (16 U.S.C. 715s).

"(H) Section 4 of the Land and Water Conservation Fund Act of 1965 (16 U.S.C. 460*l*–6a).

"(I) Any other provision of law relating to revenue allocation.

"(g) Reporting requirements.—As soon as practicable after the end of each fiscal year in which the Secretary of Agriculture collects fees under subsection (c) [of this note] or expends funds from the special account under subsection (f) [of this note], the Secretary shall submit to the Congress a report summarizing the activities of the Secretary under the pilot program, including the funds generated under subsection (c) [of this note], the expenses incurred to carry out the pilot program, and the expenditures made from the special account during that fiscal year.

"(h) Duration of pilot program.—

"(1) Collection of fees.—The Secretary of Agriculture may collect fees under the authority of subsection (c) [of this note] through fiscal year 2021.

"(2) Use of special account.—The Secretary may make expenditures from the special account under subsection (f) [of this note] until September 30 of the fiscal year following the last fiscal year specified in paragraph (1). After that date, amounts remaining in the special account shall be transferred to the general fund of the Treasury."

[Pub. L. No. 108–108, § 335(3), purporting to amend subsec. (d)(1) of this note, was executed to subsec. (e)(1) of this note as the probable intent of Congress.]

§ 529. Authorization of development and administration; consideration to relative values of resources; areas of wilderness

[MUSYA § 2]

The Secretary of Agriculture is authorized and directed to develop and administer the renewable surface resources of the national forests for multiple use and sustained yield of the several products and services obtained therefrom. In the administration of the national forests due consideration shall be given to the relative values of the various resources in particular areas. The establishment and maintenance of areas of wilderness are consistent with the purposes and provisions of sections 528 to 531 of this title.

(Pub. L. No. 86–517, § 2, 74 Stat. 215 (June 12, 1960).)

HISTORICAL AND STATUTORY NOTES

Transfer of Functions

Enforcement functions of Secretary or other official in Department of Agriculture, insofar as they involve lands and programs under jurisdiction of that Department, related to compliance with the provisions of sections 528 to 531 of this title with respect to pre-construction, construction, and initial operation of transportation system for Canadian and Alaskan natural gas were transferred to the Federal Inspector, Office of Federal Inspector for the Alaska Natural Gas Transportation System, until the first anniversary of date of initial operation of the Alaska Natural Gas Transportation System, see Reorg. Plan No. 1 of 1979, §§ 102(f), 203(a), 44 Fed. Reg. 33663, 33666, 93 Stat. 1373, 1376, eff. July 1, 1979, set out in Appendix 1 to Title 5, Government Organization and Employees.

§ 530. Cooperation for purposes of development and administration with State and local governmental agencies and others

[MUSYA § 3]

In the effectuation of sections 528 to 531 of this title the Secretary of Agriculture is authorized to cooperate with interested State and local governmental agencies and others in the development and management of the national forests.

(Pub. L. No. 86–517, § 3, 74 Stat. 215 (June 12, 1960).)

HISTORICAL AND STATUTORY NOTES

Transfer of Functions

Enforcement functions of Secretary or other official in Department of Agriculture, insofar as they involve lands and programs under jurisdiction of that Department, related to compliance with the provisions of sections

528 to 531 of this title with respect to pre-construction, construction, and initial operation of transportation system for Canadian and Alaskan natural gas were transferred to the Federal Inspector, Office of Federal Inspector for the Alaska Natural Gas Transportation System, until the first anniversary of date of initial operation of the Alaska Natural Gas Transportation System, see Reorg. Plan No. 1 of 1979, §§ 102(f), 203(a), 44 Fed. Reg. 33663, 33666, 93 Stat. 1373, 1376, eff. July 1, 1979, set out in Appendix 1 to Title 5, Government Organization and Employees.

§ 531. Definitions

[MUSYA § 4]

As used in sections 528 to 531 of this title the following terms shall have the following meanings:

(a) "Multiple use" means: The management of all the various renewable surface resources of the national forests so that they are utilized in the combination that will best meet the needs of the American people; making the most judicious use of the land for some or all of these resources or related services over areas large enough to provide sufficient latitude for periodic adjustments in use to conform to changing needs and conditions; that some land will be used for less than all of the resources; and harmonious and coordinated management of the various resources, each with the other, without impairment of the productivity of the land, with consideration being given to the relative values of the various resources, and not necessarily the combination of uses that will give the greatest dollar return or the greatest unit output.

(b) "Sustained yield of the several products and services" means the achievement and maintenance in perpetuity of a high-level annual or regular periodic output of the various renewable resources of the national forests without impairment of the productivity of the land.

(Pub. L. No. 86–517, § 4, 74 Stat. 215 (June 12, 1960).)

COASTAL ZONE MANAGEMENT ACT OF 1972
[CZMA § ______]

(16 U.S.C.A. §§ 1451 to 1466)

CHAPTER 33—COASTAL ZONE MANAGEMENT

Sec.

§ 1451. Congressional findings

[CZMA § 302]

The Congress finds that—

(a) There is a national interest in the effective management, beneficial use, protection, and development of the coastal zone.

(b) The coastal zone is rich in a variety of natural, commercial, recreational, ecological, industrial, and esthetic resources of immediate and potential value to the present and future well-being of the Nation.

(c) The increasing and competing demands upon the lands and waters of our coastal zone occasioned by population growth and economic development, including requirements for industry, commerce, residential development, recreation, extraction of mineral resources and fossil fuels, transportation and navigation, waste disposal, and harvesting of fish, shellfish, and other living marine resources, have resulted in the loss of living marine resources, wildlife, nutrient-rich areas, permanent and adverse changes to ecological systems, decreasing open space for public use, and shoreline erosion.

(d) The habitat areas of the coastal zone, and the fish, shellfish, other living marine resources, and wildlife therein, are ecologically fragile and consequently extremely vulnerable to destruction by man's alterations.

(e) Important ecological, cultural, historic, and esthetic values in the coastal zone which are essential to the well-being of all citizens are being irretrievably damaged or lost.

(f) New and expanding demands for food, energy, minerals, defense needs, recreation, waste disposal, transportation, and industrial activities in the Great Lakes, territorial sea, exclusive economic zone, and Outer Continental Shelf are placing stress on these areas and are creating the need for resolution of serious conflicts among important and competing uses and values in coastal and ocean waters;[1]

(g) Special natural and scenic characteristics are being damaged by ill-planned development that threatens these values.

(h) In light of competing demands and the urgent need to protect and to give high priority to natural systems in the coastal zone, present state and local institutional arrangements for planning and regulating land and water uses in such areas are inadequate.

(i) The key to more effective protection and use of the land and water resources of the coastal zone is to encourage the states to exercise their full authority over the lands and waters in the coastal zone by assisting the states, in cooperation with Federal and local governments and other vitally affected interests, in developing land and water use programs for the coastal zone, including unified policies, criteria, standards, methods, and processes for dealing with land and water use decisions of more than local significance.

(j) The national objective of attaining a greater degree of energy self-sufficiency would be advanced by providing Federal financial assistance to meet state and local needs resulting from new or expanded energy activity in or affecting the coastal zone.

(k) Land uses in the coastal zone, and the uses of adjacent lands which drain into the coastal zone, may significantly affect the quality of coastal waters and habitats, and efforts to control coastal water pollution from land use activities must be improved.

(*l*) Because global warming may result in a substantial sea level rise with serious adverse effects in the coastal zone, coastal states must anticipate and plan for such an occurrence.

(m) Because of their proximity to and reliance upon the ocean and its resources, the coastal states have substantial and significant interests in the protection, management, and development of the resources of the exclusive economic zone that can only be served by the active participation of coastal states in all Federal programs affecting such resources and, wherever appropriate, by the development of state ocean resource plans as part of their federally approved coastal zone management programs.

(Pub. L. No. 89–454, Title III, § 302, as added by Pub. L. No. 92–583, 86 Stat. 1280 (Oct. 27, 1972); and amended by Pub. L. No. 94–370, § 2, 90 Stat. 1013 (July 26, 1976); Pub. L. No. 96–464, § 2, 94 Stat. 2060 (Oct. 17, 1980); Pub. L. No. 101–508, Title VI, § 6203(a), 104 Stat. 1388–300 (Nov. 5, 1990).)

[1] So in original. Probably should be a period.

HISTORICAL AND STATUTORY NOTES

Short Title

2009 Amendments. Pub. L. No. 111–11, Title XII, § 12501, 123 Stat. 1442 (Mar. 30, 2009), provided that: "This Act [Subtitle E of Title XII of Pub. L. No. 111–11 (§§ 12501, 12502) 123 Stat. 1422 (Mar. 30, 2009), enacting 16 U.S.C.A. § 1456–1] may be cited as the 'Coastal and Estuarine Land Conservation Program Act'."

2004 Amendments. Pub. L. No. 108–456, Title I, § 101, 118 Stat. 3630 (Dec. 10, 2004), provided that: "This title [enacting provisions set out as a note under this section and amending provisions set out as notes under this section] may be cited as the 'Harmful Algal Bloom and Hypoxia Amendments Act of 2004'."

1996 Amendments. Pub. L. No. 104–150, § 1, 110 Stat. 1380 (June 3, 1996), provided that: "This Act [enacting section 1465 of this title, amending sections 1454, 1455a, 1456a, 1456b, 1461, and 1464 of this title, and enacting provisions set out as a note under section 1454 of this title] may be cited as the 'Coastal Zone Protection Act of 1996'."

1990 Amendments. Section 6201 of Pub. L. No. 101–508 provided that: "This subtitle [enacting sections 1455b, 1456c and 1460 of this title, amending this section and sections 1452, 1453, 1454, 1455, 1455a, 1456, 1456a, 1456b, 1458, 1461 and 1464 of this title, and enacting provisions set out as notes under this section and section 1455 of this title] may be cited as the 'Coastal Zone Act Reauthorization Amendments of 1990'."

1986 Amendments. Pub. L. No. 99–272, Title VI, § 6041, 100 Stat. 124 (Apr. 7, 1986), provided that: "This subtitle [amending sections 1455, 1455a, 1456a, 1458, 1461, and 1464 of this title, repealing sections 1456c and

1460 of this title and repealing provisions set out as a note under this section] may be cited as the 'Coastal Zone Management Reauthorization Act of 1985'."

1980 Amendments. Section 1 of Pub. L. No. 96–464 provided: "That this Act [enacting sections 1455a and 1463a of this title, amending sections 1451, 1452, 1453, 1455, 1456a, 1456b, 1458, 1461, 1462, and 1464 of this title, and enacting provisions set out as notes under sections 1455, 1458, and 1463a of this title] may be cited as the 'Coastal Zone Management Improvement Act of 1980'."

1976 Amendments. Section 1 of Pub. L. No. 94–370 provided: "That this Act [which enacted section 1511a of Title 15, Commerce and Trade, and sections 1456a to 1456c of this title, amended section 5316 of Title 5, Government Organization and Employees, and sections 1451, 1453 to 1456, and 1457 to 1464 of this title, and enacted provisions set out as notes under section 1511a of Title 15 and section 1462 of this title] may be cited as the 'Coastal Zone Management Act Amendments of 1976'."

1972 Amendments. Section 301 of Pub. L. No. 89–454, as added by Pub. L. No. 92–583, provided that: "This title [enacting this chapter] may be cited as the 'Coastal Zone Management Act of 1972'."

Harmful Algal Bloom and Hypoxia Research and Control Amendments Act of 2014

Pub. L. 113–124, 128 Stat. 1379 (June 30, 2014), enacted the Harmful Algal Bloom and Hypoxia Research and Control Amendments Act of 2014, which provided as follows:

"SECTION 1. Short title.

"This Act may be cited as the 'Harmful Algal Bloom and Hypoxia Research and Control Amendments Act of 2014'."

"SEC. 2 References to the Harmful Algal Bloom and Hypoxia Research and Control Act of 1998.

"Except as otherwise expressly provided, whenever in this Act an amendment or repeal is expressed in terms of an amendment to, or repeal of, a section or other provision, the reference shall be considered to be made to a section or other provision of the Harmful Algal Bloom and Hypoxia Research and Control Act of 1998 (16 U.S.C. 1451 note)."

* * *

"SEC. 4 National harmful algal bloom and hyposix program.

"The Act is amended by inserting after section 603 the following:

" 'SEC. 603A National harmful algal bloom and hypoxia program.

" '(a) Establishment.—Not later than 1 year after the date of enactment of the Harmful Algal Bloom and Hypoxia Research and Control Amendments Act of 2014, the Under Secretary, acting through the Task Force, shall maintain and enhance a national harmful algal bloom and hypoxia program, including—

" '(1) a statement of objectives, including understanding, detecting, predicting, controlling, mitigating, and responding to marine and freshwater harmful algal bloom and hypoxia events; and

" '(2) the comprehensive research plan and action strategy under section 603B.

" '(b) Periodic revision.—The Task Force shall periodically review and revise the Program, as necessary.

" '(c) Task Force functions.—The Task Force shall—

" '(1) coordinate interagency review of the objectives and activities of the Program;

" '(2) expedite the interagency review process by ensuring timely review and dispersal of required reports and assessments under this title;

" '(3) support the implementation of the Action Strategy, including the coordination and integration of the research of all Federal programs, including ocean and Great Lakes science and management programs and centers, that address the chemical, biological, and physical components of marine and freshwater harmful algal blooms and hypoxia;

" '(4) support the development of institutional mechanisms and financial instruments to further the objectives and activities of the Program;

" '(5) review the Program's distribution of Federal funding to address the objectives and activities of the Program;

" '(6) promote the development of new technologies for predicting, monitoring, and mitigating harmful algal bloom and hypoxia conditions; and

" '(7) establish such interagency working groups as it considers necessary.

" '(d) **Lead Federal agency.**—Except as provided in subsection (h), the National Oceanic and Atmospheric Administration shall have primary responsibility for administering the Program.

" '(e) **Program duties.**—In administering the Program, the Under Secretary shall—

" '(1) promote the Program;

" '(2) prepare work and spending plans for implementing the research and activities identified under the Action Strategy;

" '(3) administer peer-reviewed, merit-based, competitive grant funding—

" '(A) to maintain and enhance baseline monitoring programs established by the Program;

" '(B) to support the projects maintained and established by the Program; and

" '(C) to address the research and management needs and priorities identified in the Action Strategy;

" '(4) coordinate with and work cooperatively with regional, State, tribal, and local government agencies and programs that address marine and freshwater harmful algal blooms and hypoxia;

" '(5) coordinate with the Secretary of State to support international efforts on marine and freshwater harmful algal bloom and hypoxia information sharing, research, prediction, mitigation, control, and response activities;

" '(6) identify additional research, development, and demonstration needs and priorities relating to monitoring, prevention, control, mitigation, and response to marine and freshwater harmful algal blooms and hypoxia, including methods and technologies to protect the ecosystems affected by marine and freshwater harmful algal blooms and hypoxia;

" '(7) integrate, coordinate, and augment existing education programs to improve public understanding and awareness of the causes, impacts, and mitigation efforts for marine and freshwater harmful algal blooms and hypoxia;

" '(8) facilitate and provide resources to train State and local coastal and water resource managers in the methods and technologies for monitoring, preventing, controlling, and mitigating marine and freshwater harmful algal blooms and hypoxia;

" '(9) support regional efforts to control and mitigate outbreaks through—

" '(A) communication of the contents of the Action Strategy and maintenance of online data portals for other information about harmful algal blooms and hypoxia to State, tribal, and local stakeholders; and

" '(B) overseeing the development, review, and periodic updating of the Action Strategy;

" '(10) convene at least 1 meeting of the Task Force each year; and

" '(11) perform such other tasks as may be delegated by the Task Force.

" '(f) **National Oceanic and Atmospheric Administration activities.**—The Under Secretary shall—

" '(1) maintain and enhance the existing competitive programs at the National Oceanic and Atmospheric Administration relating to harmful algal blooms and hypoxia;

" '(2) carry out marine and Great Lakes harmful algal bloom and hypoxia events response activities;

" '(3) develop and enhance, including with respect to infrastructure as necessary, critical observations, monitoring, modeling, data management, information dissemination, and operational forecasts relevant to harmful algal blooms and hypoxia events;

" '(4) enhance communication and coordination among Federal agencies carrying out marine and freshwater harmful algal bloom and hypoxia activities and research;

" '(5) to the greatest extent practicable, leverage existing resources and expertise available from local research universities and institutions; and

" '(6) increase the availability to appropriate public and private entities of—

"(A) analytical facilities and technologies;

"(B) operational forecasts; and

"(C) reference and research materials.

" '(g) Cooperative efforts.—The Under Secretary shall work cooperatively and avoid duplication of effort with other offices, centers, and programs within the National Oceanic and Atmospheric Administration, other agencies on the Task Force, and States, tribes, and nongovernmental organizations concerned with marine and freshwater issues to coordinate harmful algal bloom and hypoxia (and related) activities and research.

" '(h) Freshwater.—With respect to the freshwater aspects of the Program, the Administrator, through the Task Force, shall carry out the duties otherwise assigned to the Under Secretary under this section, except the activities described in subsection (f).

" '(1) Participation.—The Administrator's participation under this section shall include—

" '(A) research on the ecology and impacts of freshwater harmful algal blooms; and

" '(B) forecasting and monitoring of and event response to freshwater harmful algal blooms in lakes, rivers, estuaries (including their tributaries), and reservoirs.

" '(2) Nonduplication.—The Administrator shall ensure that activities carried out under this title focus on new approaches to addressing freshwater harmful algal blooms and are not duplicative of existing research and development programs authorized by this title or any other law.

" '(i) Integrated coastal and ocean observation systems.—The collection of monitoring and observation data under this title shall comply with all data standards and protocols developed pursuant to the Integrated Coastal and Ocean Observation System Act of 2009 (33 U.S.C. 3601 et seq.). Such data shall be made available through the system established under that Act.". ' "

"SEC. 5 Comprehensive research plan and action strategy.

"The Act, as amended by section 4 of this Act, is further amended by inserting after section 603A the following:

" 'SEC. 603B Comprehensive research plan and action strategy.

" '(a) In general.—Not later than 1 year after the date of enactment of the Harmful Algal Bloom and Hypoxia Research and Control Amendments Act of 2014, the Under Secretary, through the Task Force, shall develop and submit to Congress a comprehensive research plan and action strategy to address marine and freshwater harmful algal blooms and hypoxia. The Action Strategy shall identify—

" '(1) the specific activities to be carried out by the Program and the timeline for carrying out those activities;

" '(2) the roles and responsibilities of each Federal agency in the Task Force in carrying out the activities under paragraph (1); and

" '(3) the appropriate regions and subregions requiring specific research and activities to address harmful algal blooms and hypoxia.

" '(b) Regional focus.—The regional and subregional parts of the Action Strategy shall identify—

" '(1) regional priorities for ecological, economic, and social research on issues related to the impacts of harmful algal blooms and hypoxia;

" '(2) research, development, and demonstration activities needed to develop and advance technologies and techniques for minimizing the occurrence of harmful algal blooms and hypoxia and improving capabilities to detect, predict, monitor, control, mitigate, respond to, and remediate harmful algal blooms and hypoxia;

" '(3) ways to reduce the duration and intensity of harmful algal blooms and hypoxia, including deployment of response technologies in a timely manner;

" '(4) research and methods to address human health dimensions of harmful algal blooms and hypoxia;

" '(5) mechanisms, including the potential costs and benefits of those mechanisms, to protect ecosystems that may be or have been affected by harmful algal bloom and hypoxia events;

" '(6) mechanisms by which data, information, and products may be transferred between the Program and the State, tribal, and local governments and research entities;

" '(7) communication and information dissemination methods that State, tribal, and local governments may undertake to educate and inform the public concerning harmful algal blooms and hypoxia; and

" '(8) roles that Federal agencies may have to assist in the implementation of the Action Strategy, including efforts to support local and regional scientific assessments under section 603(e).

" '(c) Utilizing available studies and information.—In developing the Action Strategy, the Under Secretary shall utilize existing research, assessments, reports, and program activities, including—

" '(1) those carried out under existing law; and

" '(2) other relevant peer-reviewed and published sources.

" '(d) Development of the action strategy.—In developing the Action Strategy, the Under Secretary shall, as appropriate—

" '(1) coordinate with—

" '(A) State coastal management and planning officials;

" '(B) tribal resource management officials; and

" '(C) water management and watershed officials from both coastal States and noncoastal States with water sources that drain into water bodies affected by harmful algal blooms and hypoxia; and

" '(2) consult with—

" '(A) public health officials;

" '(B) emergency management officials;

" '(C) science and technology development institutions;

" '(D) economists;

" '(E) industries and businesses affected by marine and freshwater harmful algal blooms and hypoxia;

" '(F) scientists with expertise concerning harmful algal blooms or hypoxia from academic or research institutions; and

" '(G) other stakeholders.

" '(e) Federal Register.—The Under Secretary shall publish the Action Strategy in the Federal Register.

" '(f) **Periodic revision.**—The Under Secretary, in coordination and consultation with the individuals and entities under subsection (d), shall periodically review and revise the Action Strategy prepared under this section, as necessary.". ' "

"SEC. 6 Reporting.

"Section 603 is amended by adding at the end the following:

" '(j) **Report.**—Not later than 2 years after the date the Action Strategy is submitted under section 603B, the Under Secretary shall submit a report to Congress that describes—

" '(1) the proceedings of the annual Task Force meetings;

" '(2) the activities carried out under the Program, including the regional and subregional parts of the Action Strategy;

" '(3) the budget related to the activities under paragraph (2);

" '(4) the progress made on implementing the Action Strategy; and

" '(5) any need to revise or terminate research and activities under the Program.". ' "

"SEC. 7 Northern Gulf of Mexico hypoxia.

"Section 604 is amended to read as follows:

" 'SEC. 604 Northern Gulf of Mexico hypoxia.

" '(a) **Initial progress reports.**—Beginning not later than 12 months after the date of enactment of the Harmful Algal Bloom and Hypoxia Research and Control Amendments Act of 2014, and biennially thereafter, the Administrator, through the Mississippi River/Gulf of Mexico Watershed Nutrient Task Force, shall submit a progress report to the appropriate congressional committees and the President that describes the progress made by activities directed by the Mississippi River/Gulf of Mexico Watershed Nutrient Task Force and carried out or funded by the Environmental Protection Agency and other State and Federal partners toward attainment of the goals of the Gulf Hypoxia Action Plan 2008.

" '(b) **Contents.**—Each report required under this section shall—

" '(1) assess the progress made toward nutrient load reductions, the response of the hypoxic zone and water quality throughout the Mississippi/Atchafalaya River Basin, and the economic and social effects;

" '(2) evaluate lessons learned; and

" '(3) recommend appropriate actions to continue to implement or, if necessary, revise the strategy set forth in the Gulf Hypoxia Action Plan 2008.". ' "

"SEC. 8 Great Lakes hypoxia and harmful algal blooms.

"Section 605 is amended to read as follows:

" 'SEC. 605 Great Lakes hypoxia and harmful algal blooms.

" '(a) **Integrated assessments.**—Not later than 18 months after the date of enactment of the Harmful Algal Bloom and Hypoxia Research and Control Amendments Act of 2014, the Task Force, in accordance with the authority under section 603, shall complete and submit to the Congress and the President an integrated assessment that examines the causes, consequences, and approaches to reduce hypoxia and harmful algal blooms in the Great Lakes, including the status of and gaps within current research, monitoring, management, prevention, response, and control activities by—

" '(1) Federal agencies;

" '(2) State agencies;

" '(3) regional research consortia;

" '(4) academia;

" '(5) private industry; and

" '(6) nongovernmental organizations.

" '**(b) Plan.**—

" '**(1) In general.**—Not later than 2 years after the date of enactment of the Harmful Algal Bloom and Hypoxia Research and Control Amendments Act of 2014, the Task Force shall develop and submit to the Congress a plan, based on the integrated assessment under subsection (a), for reducing, mitigating, and controlling hypoxia and harmful algal blooms in the Great Lakes.

" '**(2) Contents.**—The plan shall—

" '(A) address the monitoring needs identified in the integrated assessment under subsection (a);

" '(B) develop a timeline and budgetary requirements for deployment of future assets;

" '(C) identify requirements for the development and verification of Great Lakes hypoxia and harmful algal bloom models, including—

" '(i) all assumptions built into the models; and

" '(ii) data quality methods used to ensure the best available data are utilized; and

" '(D) describe efforts to improve the assessment of the impacts of hypoxia and harmful algal blooms by—

" '(i) characterizing current and past biological conditions in ecosystems affected by hypoxia and harmful algal blooms; and

" '(ii) quantifying effects, including economic effects, at the population and community levels.

" '**(3) Requirements.**—In developing the plan, the Task Force shall—

" '(A) coordinate with State and local governments;

" '(B) consult with representatives from academic, agricultural, industry, and other stakeholder groups, including relevant Canadian agencies;

" '(C) ensure that the plan complements and does not duplicate activities conducted by other Federal or State agencies;

" '(D) identify critical research for reducing, mitigating, and controlling hypoxia events and their effects;

" '(E) evaluate cost-effective, incentive-based partnership approaches;

" '(F) ensure that the plan is technically sound and cost effective;

" '(G) utilize existing research, assessments, reports, and program activities;

" '(H) publish a summary of the proposed plan in the Federal Register at least 180 days prior to submitting the completed plan to Congress; and

" '(I) after submitting the completed plan to Congress, provide biennial progress reports on the activities toward achieving the objectives of the plan.". ' "

"**SEC. 9 Application with other laws.**

"The Act is amended by adding after section 606 the following:

" '**SEC. 607 Effect on other Federal authority.**

" '**(a) Authority preserved.**—Nothing in this title supersedes or limits the authority of any agency to carry out its responsibilities and missions under other laws.

" '**(b) Regulatory authority.**—Nothing in this title may be construed as establishing new regulatory authority for any agency.". ' "

"SEC. 10 Definitions; conforming amendment.

"(a) In general.—The Act, as amended by section 9 of this Act, is further amended by adding after section 607 the following:

" 'SEC. 608 Definitions.

" 'In this title:

" '(1) Action strategy.—The term 'Action Strategy' means the comprehensive research plan and action strategy established under section 603B.

" '(2) Administrator.—The term 'Administrator' means the Administrator of the Environmental Protection Agency.

" '(3) Harmful algal bloom.—The term 'harmful algal bloom' means marine and freshwater phytoplankton that proliferate to high concentrations, resulting in nuisance conditions or harmful impacts on marine and aquatic ecosystems, coastal communities, and human health through the production of toxic compounds or other biological, chemical, and physical impacts of the algae outbreak.

" '(4) Hypoxia.—The term 'hypoxia' means a condition where low dissolved oxygen in aquatic systems causes stress or death to resident organisms.

" '(5) Program.—The term 'Program' means the national harmful algal bloom and hypoxia program established under section 603A.

" '(6) State.—The term 'State' means each of the several States of the United States, the District of Columbia, the Commonwealth of Puerto Rico, the Virgin Islands, Guam, American Samoa, the Commonwealth of the Northern Mariana Islands, any other territory or possession of the United States, and any Indian tribe.

" '(7) Task Force.—The term 'Task Force' means the Inter-Agency Task Force on Harmful Algal Blooms and Hypoxia under section 603(a).

" '(8) Under Secretary.—The term 'Under Secretary' means the Under Secretary of Commerce for Oceans and Atmosphere.

" '(9) United States coastal waters.—The term 'United States coastal waters' includes the Great Lakes.".'

"(b) Conforming amendment.—Section 603(a) is amended by striking '(hereinafter referred to as the 'Task Force')'."

"SEC. 11 Authorization of appropriations.

"The Act is further amended by adding after section 608 the following:

" 'SEC. 609 Authorization of appropriations.

" '(a) In general.—There is authorized to be appropriated to the Under Secretary to carry out sections 603A and 603B $20,500,000 for each of fiscal years 2014 through 2018.

" '(b) Extramural research activities.—The Under Secretary shall ensure that a substantial portion of funds appropriated pursuant to subsection (a) that are used for research purposes are allocated to extramural research activities. For each fiscal year, the Under Secretary shall publish a list of all grant recipients and the amounts for all of the funds allocated for research purposes, specifying those allocated for extramural research activities.' "

Hypoxia Assessment

Pub. L. No. 110–114, Title V, § 5022, 121 Stat. 1203 (Nov. 8, 2007), provided that: "The Secretary [of the Army] may participate with Federal, State, and local agencies, non-Federal and nonprofit entities, regional researchers, and other interested parties to assess hypoxia in the Gulf of Mexico."

Task Force; Consultation

Pub. L. No. 108–456, Title I, § 102, 118 Stat. 3630 (Dec. 10, 2004), provided that: "In developing the assessments, reports, and plans under the amendments made by this title [Pub. L. No. 108–456, Title I, 118 Stat. 3630 (Dec. 10, 2004), enacting this note and provisions set out as a note under this section and amending provisions set out as a note under this section], the Task Force shall consult with the coastal States, Indian tribes, local governments, appropriate industries (including fisheries, agriculture, and fertilizer), academic institutions, and nongovernmental organizations with expertise in coastal zone science and management."

Harmful Algal Blooms and Hypoxia Research and Control

Pub. L. No. 105–383, Title VI, 112 Stat. 3447 (Nov. 13, 1998), as amended by Pub. L. No. 108–456, Title I, §§ 102 to 105, 118 Stat. 3630 (Dec. 10, 2004); Pub. L. No. 110–161, Div. B, Title V, § 528, 121 Stat. 1930 (Dec. 26, 2007), provided that:

"Sec. 601. Short Title.

"This title [Title VI of Pub. L. No. 105–383, 112 Stat. 3447 (Nov. 13, 1998), enacting provisions set out as notes under this section] may be cited as the 'Harmful Algal Bloom and Hypoxia Research and Control Act of 1998'.

"Sec. 602. Findings.

"The Congress finds that—

"(1) the recent outbreak of the harmful microbe *Pfiesteria piscicida* in the coastal waters of the United States is one example of potentially harmful algal blooms composed of naturally occurring species that reproduce explosively and that are increasing in frequency and intensity in the Nation's coastal waters;

"(2) other recent occurrences of harmful algal blooms include red tides in the Gulf of Mexico and the Southeast; brown tides in New York and Texas; ciguatera fish poisoning in Hawaii, Florida, Puerto Rico, and the United States Virgin Islands; and shellfish poisonings in the Gulf of Maine, the Pacific Northwest, and the Gulf of Alaska;

"(3) in certain cases, harmful algal blooms have resulted in fish kills, the deaths of numerous endangered West Indian manatees, beach and shellfish bed closures, threats to public health and safety, and concern among the public about the safety of seafood;

"(4) according to some scientists, the factors causing or contributing to harmful algal blooms may include excessive nutrients in coastal waters, other forms of pollution, the transfer of harmful species through ship ballast water, and ocean currents;

"(5) harmful algal blooms may have been responsible for an estimated $1,000,000,000 in economic losses during the past decade;

"(6) harmful algal blooms and blooms of non-toxic algal species may lead to other damaging marine conditions such as hypoxia (reduced oxygen concentrations), which are harmful or fatal to fish, shellfish, and benthic organisms;

"(7) according to the National Oceanic and Atmospheric Administration in the Department of Commerce, 53 percent of United States estuaries experience hypoxia for at least part of the year and a 7,000 square mile area in the Gulf of Mexico off Louisiana and Texas suffers from hypoxia;

"(8) according to some scientists, a factor believed to cause hypoxia is excessive nutrient loading into coastal waters;

"(9) there is a need to identify more workable and effective actions to reduce nutrient loadings to coastal waters;

"(10) the National Oceanic and Atmospheric Administration, through its ongoing research, education, grant, and coastal resource management programs, possesses a full range of capabilities necessary to support a near and long-term comprehensive effort to prevent, reduce, and control harmful algal blooms and hypoxia;

"(11) funding for the research and related programs of the National Oceanic and Atmospheric Administration will aid in improving the Nation's understanding and capabilities for addressing the human and environmental costs associated with harmful algal blooms and hypoxia; and

"(12) other Federal agencies such as the Environmental Protection Agency, the Department of Agriculture, and the National Science Foundation, along with the States, Indian tribes, and local governments, conduct important work related to the prevention, reduction, and control of harmful algal blooms and hypoxia.

"Sec. 603. Assessments.

"(a) **Establishment of Inter-Agency Task Force.**—The President, through the Committee on Environment and Natural Resources of the National Science and Technology Council, shall establish an Inter-Agency Task Force on Harmful Algal Blooms and Hypoxia (hereinafter referred to as the 'Task Force"). The Task Force shall consist of the following representatives from—

"(1) the Department of Commerce (who shall serve as Chairman of the Task Force);

"(2) the Environmental Protection Agency;

"(3) the Department of Agriculture;

"(4) the Department of the Interior;

"(5) the Department of the Navy;

"(6) the Department of Health and Human Services;

"(7) the National Science Foundation;

"(8) the National Aeronautics and Space Administration;

"(9) the Food and Drug Administration;

"(10) the Office of Science and Technology Policy;

"(11) the Council on Environmental Quality; and

"(12) such other Federal agencies as the President considers appropriate.

"(b) **Assessment of harmful algal blooms**—

"(1) Not later than 12 months after the date of enactment of this title [Nov. 13, 1998], the Task Force, in cooperation with the coastal States, Indian tribes, and local governments, industry (including agricultural organizations), academic institutions, and non-governmental organizations with expertise in coastal zone management, shall complete and submit to the Congress an assessment which examines the ecological and economic consequences of harmful algal blooms, alternatives for reducing, mitigating, and controlling harmful algal blooms, and the social and economic costs and benefits of such alternatives.

"(2) The assessment shall—

"(A) identify alternatives for preventing unnecessary duplication of effort among Federal agencies and departments with respect to harmful algal blooms; and

"(B) provide for Federal cooperation and coordination with and assistance to the coastal States, Indian tribes, and local governments in the prevention, reduction, management, mitigation, and control of harmful algal blooms and their environmental and public health impacts.

"(c) **Assessment of hypoxia.**—

"(1) Not later than 12 months after the date of enactment of this title [Nov. 13, 1998], the Task Force, in cooperation with the States, Indian tribes, local governments, industry, agricultural, academic institutions, and non-governmental organizations with expertise in watershed and coastal zone management, shall complete and submit to the Congress an assessment which examines the ecological and economic consequences of hypoxia in United States coastal waters, alternatives for reducing, mitigating, and controlling hypoxia, and the social and economic costs and benefits of such alternatives.

"(2) The assessment shall—

"(A) establish needs, priorities, and guidelines for a peer-reviewed, inter-agency research program on the causes, characteristics, and impacts of hypoxia;

"(B) identify alternatives for preventing unnecessary duplication of effort among Federal agencies and departments with respect to hypoxia; and

"(C) provide for Federal cooperation and coordination with and assistance to the States, Indian tribes, and local governments in the prevention, reduction, management, mitigation, and control of hypoxia and its environmental impacts.

"(d) Report to Congress on harmful algal bloom impacts—

"(1) Development.—Not later than 12 months after the date of enactment of the Harmful Algal Bloom and Hypoxia Amendments Act of 2004 [Dec. 10, 2004], the President, in consultation with the chief executive officers of the States, shall develop and submit to the Congress a report that describes and evaluates the effectiveness of measures described in paragraph (2) that may be utilized to protect environmental and public health from impacts of harmful algal blooms. In developing the report, the President shall consult with the Task Force, the coastal States, Indian tribes, local governments, appropriate industries (including fisheries, agriculture, and fertilizer), academic institutions, and nongovernmental organizations with expertise in coastal zone science and management, and also consider the scientific assessments developed under this Act [this note].

"(2) Requirements.—The report shall—

"(A) review techniques for prediction of the onset, course, and impacts of harmful algal blooms including evaluation of their accuracy and utility in protecting environmental and public health and provisions for their development;

"(B) identify innovative research and development methods for the prevention, control, and mitigation of harmful algal blooms and provisions for their development; and

"(C) include incentive-based partnership approaches regarding subparagraphs (A) and (B) where practicable.

"(3) Publication and opportunity for comment.—At least 90 days before submitting the report to the Congress, the President shall cause a summary of the proposed plan to be published in the Federal Register for a public comment period of not less than 60 days.

"(4) Federal assistance.—The Secretary of Commerce, in coordination with the Task Force and to the extent of funds available, shall provide for Federal cooperation with and assistance to the coastal States, Indian tribes, and local governments regarding the measures described in paragraph (2), as requested.

"(e) Local and regional scientific assessments.—

"(1) In general.—The Secretary of Commerce, in coordination with the Task Force and appropriate State, Indian tribe, and local governments, to the extent of funds available, shall provide for local and regional scientific assessments of hypoxia and harmful algal blooms, as requested by States, Indian tribes, and local governments, or for affected areas as identified by the Secretary. If the Secretary receives multiple requests, the Secretary shall ensure, to the extent practicable, that assessments under this subsection cover geographically and ecologically diverse locations with significant ecological and economic impacts from hypoxia or harmful algal blooms. The Secretary shall establish a procedure for reviewing requests for local and regional assessments. The Secretary shall ensure, through consultation with Sea Grant Programs, that the findings of the assessments are communicated to the appropriate State, Indian tribe, and local governments, and to the general public.

"(2) Purpose.—Local and regional assessments shall examine—

"(A) the causes and ecological consequences, and the economic cost, of hypoxia or harmful algal blooms in that area;

"(B) potential methods to prevent, control, and mitigate hypoxia or harmful algal blooms in that area and the potential ecological and economic costs and benefits of such methods; and

"(C) other topics the Task Force considers appropriate.

"(f) Scientific assessment of freshwater harmful algal blooms—(1) Not later than 24 months after the date of enactment of the Harmful Algal Bloom and Hypoxia Amendments Act of 2004 [Dec. 10, 2004] the Task Force shall complete and submit to Congress a scientific assessment of current knowledge about harmful algal blooms in freshwater, such as the Great Lakes and upper reaches of estuaries, including a research plan for coordinating Federal efforts to better understand freshwater harmful algal blooms.

"(2) The freshwater harmful algal bloom scientific assessment shall—

"(A) examine the causes and ecological consequences, and the economic costs, of harmful algal blooms with significant effects on freshwater, including estimations of the frequency and occurrence of significant events;

"(B) establish priorities and guidelines for a competitive, peer-reviewed, merit-based interagency research program, as part of the Ecology and Oceanography of Harmful Algal Blooms (ECOHAB) project, to better understand the causes, characteristics, and impacts of harmful algal blooms in freshwater locations; and

"(C) identify ways to improve coordination and to prevent unnecessary duplication of effort among Federal agencies and departments with respect to research on harmful algal blooms in freshwater locations.

"(g) Scientific assessments of hypoxia—(1) Not less than once every 5 years the Task Force shall complete and submit to the Congress a scientific assessment of hypoxia in United States coastal waters including the Great Lakes. The first such assessment shall be completed not less than 24 months after the date of enactment of the Harmful Algal Bloom and Hypoxia Amendments Act of 2004 [Dec. 10, 2004].

"(2) The assessments under this subsection shall—

"(A) examine the causes and ecological consequences, and the economic costs, of hypoxia;

"(B) describe the potential ecological and economic costs and benefits of possible policy and management actions for preventing, controlling, and mitigating hypoxia;

"(C) evaluate progress made by, and the needs of, Federal research programs on the causes, characteristics, and impacts of hypoxia, including recommendations of how to eliminate significant gaps in hypoxia modeling and monitoring data; and

"(D) identify ways to improve coordination and to prevent unnecessary duplication of effort among Federal agencies and departments with respect to research on hypoxia.

"(h) Scientific assessments of harmful algal blooms—(1) Not less than once every 5 years the Task Force shall complete and submit to Congress a scientific assessment of harmful algal blooms in United States coastal waters. The first such assessment shall be completed not later than 24 months after the date of enactment of the Harmful Algal Bloom and Hypoxia Amendments Act of 2004 [Dec. 10, 2004] and shall consider only marine harmful algal blooms. All subsequent assessments shall examine both marine and freshwater harmful algal blooms, including those in the Great Lakes and upper reaches of estuaries.

"(2) The assessments under this subsection shall—

"(A) examine the causes and ecological consequences, and economic costs, of harmful algal blooms;

"(B) describe the potential ecological and economic costs and benefits of possible actions for preventing, controlling, and mitigating harmful algal blooms;

"(C) evaluate progress made by, and the needs of, Federal research programs on the causes, characteristics, and impacts of harmful algal blooms; and

"(D) identify ways to improve coordination and to prevent unnecessary duplication of effort among Federal agencies and departments with respect to research on harmful algal blooms.

"(i) National scientific research, development, demonstration, and technology transfer plan on reducing impacts from harmful algal blooms—(1) Not later than 12 months after the date of enactment of the Harmful Algal Bloom and Hypoxia Amendments Act of 2004 [Dec. 10, 2004], the Task Force shall develop and submit to Congress a plan providing for a comprehensive and coordinated national research program to develop and demonstrate prevention, control, and mitigation methods to reduce the impacts of harmful algal blooms on coastal ecosystems (including the Great Lakes), public health, and the economy.

"(2) The plan shall—

"(A) establish priorities and guidelines for a competitive, peer reviewed, merit based interagency research, development, demonstration, and technology transfer program on methods for the prevention, control, and mitigation of harmful algal blooms;

"(B) identify ways to improve coordination and to prevent unnecessary duplication of effort among Federal agencies and departments with respect to the actions described in paragraph (1); and

"(C) include to the maximum extent practicable diverse institutions, including Historically Black Colleges and Universities and those serving large proportions of Hispanics, Native Americans, Asian Pacific Americans, and other underrepresented populations.

"(3) The Secretary of Commerce, in conjunction with other appropriate Federal agencies, shall establish a research, development, demonstration, and technology transfer program that meets the priorities and guidelines established under paragraph (2)(A). The Secretary shall ensure, through consultation with Sea Grant Programs, that the results and findings of the program are communicated to State, Indian tribe, and local governments, and to the general public.

"Sec. 604. Northern Gulf of Mexico Hypoxia.

"(a) Assessment report.—Not later than May 30, 1999, the Task Force shall complete and submit to Congress and the President an integrated assessment of hypoxia in the northern Gulf of Mexico that examines: the distribution, dynamics, and causes; ecological and economic consequences; sources and loads of nutrients transported by the Mississippi River to the Gulf of Mexico; effects of reducing nutrient loads; methods for reducing nutrient loads; and the social and economic costs and benefits of such methods.

"(b) Submission of a plan.—No later than March 30, 2000, the President, in conjunction with the chief executive officers of the States, shall develop and submit to Congress a plan, based on the integrated assessment submitted under subsection (a), for reducing, mitigating, and controlling hypoxia in the northern Gulf of Mexico. In developing such plan, the President shall consult with State, Indian tribe, and local governments, academic, agricultural, industry, and environmental groups and representatives. Such plan shall include incentive-based partnership approaches. The plan shall also include the social and economic costs and benefits of the measures for reducing, mitigating, and controlling hypoxia. At least 90 days before the President submits such plan to the Congress, a summary of the proposed plan shall be published in the Federal Register for a public comment period of not less than 60 days.

"Sec. 605. Authorization of Appropriations.

"There are authorized to be appropriated to the Secretary of Commerce for research, education, and monitoring activities related to the prevention, reduction, and control of harmful algal blooms and hypoxia, $15,000,000 for fiscal year 1999, $18,250,000 for fiscal year 2000, $19,000,000 for fiscal year 2001, $23,500,000 for fiscal year 2005, $24,500,000 for fiscal year 2006, $25,000,000 for fiscal year 2007, and $30,000,000 for each of fiscal years 2008 through 2010, to remain available until expended. The Secretary shall consult with the States on a regular basis regarding the development and implementation of the activities authorized under this section. Of such amounts for each fiscal year—

"(1) $1,500,000 for fiscal year 1999, $1,500,000 for fiscal year 2000, $2,000,000 for fiscal year 2001, and $2,500,000 for each of fiscal years 2005 through 2010 may be used to enable the National Oceanic and Atmospheric Administration to carry out research and assessment activities, including procurement of necessary research equipment, at research laboratories of the National Ocean Service and the National Marine Fisheries Service;

"(2) $4,000,000 for fiscal year 1999, $5,500,000 for fiscal year 2000, $5,500,000 for fiscal year 2001, and $6,500,000, of which $1,000,000 shall be used for the research program described in section 603(f)(2)(B) [section 603(f)(2)(B) of this note], for each of fiscal years 2005 through 2010 may be used to carry out the Ecology and Oceanography of Harmful Algal Blooms (ECOHAB) project under the Coastal Ocean Program established under section 201(c) of Public Law 102–567 [Pub. L. No. 102–567, 106 Stat. 4280 (Oct. 29, 1992), which was not codified as the Code];

"(3) $1,000,000 for fiscal year 1999, $2,000,000 for fiscal year 2000, $2,000,000 for fiscal year 2001, and $3,000,000 for each of fiscal years 2005 through 2010 may be used by the National Ocean Service of the National Oceanic and Atmospheric Administration to carry out a peer-reviewed research project on management measures that can be taken to prevent, reduce, control, and mitigate harmful algal blooms and to carry out section 603(d) [section 603(d) of this note];

"(4) $5,500,000 for each of the fiscal years 1999, 2000, 2001, and $6,000,000 for each of fiscal years 2005 through 2010 may be used to carry out Federal and State annual monitoring and analysis activities for harmful algal blooms administered by the National Ocean Service of the National Oceanic and Atmospheric Administration;

"(5) $3,000,000 for fiscal year 1999, $3,750,000 for fiscal year 2000, $4,000,000 for fiscal year 2001, $4,000,000 for fiscal year 2005, $5,000,000 for fiscal year 2006, $5,500,000 for fiscal year 2007, and $6,000,000 for each of fiscal years 2008 through 2010 may be used for activities related to research and monitoring on hypoxia by the National Ocean Service and the Office of Oceanic and Atmospheric Research of the National Oceanic and Atmospheric Administration; and

"(6) $1,500,000 for each of fiscal years 2005 through 2010 to carry out section 603(e) [section 603(e) of this note].

"Sec. 606. Protection of States' Rights.

"(a) Nothing in this title shall be interpreted to adversely affect existing State regulatory or enforcement power which has been granted to any State through the Clean Water Act [Act of June 30, 1948, c. 758, 62 Stat. 1155; which is codified generally to 33 U.S.C.A. § 1251 et seq.] or Coastal Zone Management Act of 1972 [Pub. L. No. 92–583, 86 Stat. 1280 (Oct. 27, 1972), which is codified generally as 16 U.S.C.A. § 1451 et seq.].

"(b) Nothing in this title shall be interpreted to expand the regulatory or enforcement power of the Federal Government which has been delegated to any State through the Clean Water Act or Coastal Zone Management Act of 1972."

Findings and Purposes of the Coastal Zone Act Reauthorization Amendments of 1990

Section 6202 of Pub. L. No. 101–508 provided that:

"(a) Findings.—Congress finds and declares the following:

"(1) Our oceans, coastal waters, and estuaries constitute a unique resource. The condition of the water quality in and around the coastal areas is significantly declining. Growing human pressures on the coastal ecosystem will continue to degrade this resource until adequate actions and policies are implemented.

"(2) Almost one-half of our total population now lives in coastal areas. By 2010, the coastal population will have grown from 80,000,000 in 1960 to 127,000,000 people, an increase of approximately 60 percent, and population density in coastal counties will be among the highest in the Nation.

"(3) Marine resources contribute to the Nation's economic stability. Commercial and recreational fishery activities support an industry with an estimated value of $12,000,000,000 a year.

"(4) Wetlands play a vital role in sustaining the coastal economy and environment. Wetlands support and nourish fishery and marine resources. They also protect the Nation's shores from storm and wave damage. Coastal wetlands contribute an estimated $5,000,000,000 to the production of fish and shellfish in the United States coastal waters. Yet, 50 percent of the Nation's coastal wetlands have been destroyed, and more are likely to decline in the near future.

"(5) Nonpoint source pollution is increasingly recognized as a significant factor in coastal water degradation. In urban areas, storm water and combined sewer overflow are linked to major coastal problems, and in rural areas, run-off from Agricultural activities may add to coastal pollution.

"(6) Coastal planning and development control measures are essential to protect coastal water quality, which is subject to continued ongoing stresses. Currently, not enough is being done to manage and protect our coastal resources.

"(7) Global warming results from the accumulation of man-made gases, released into the atmosphere from such activities as the burning of fossil fuels, deforestation, and the production of chlorofluorocarbons, which trap solar heat in the atmosphere and raise temperatures worldwide. Global warming could result in significant global sea level rise by 2050 resulting from ocean expansion, the melting of snow and ice, and the gradual melting of the polar ice cap. Sea level rise will result in the loss of natural resources such as beaches, dunes, estuaries, and wetlands, and will contribute to the salinization of drinking water supplies. Sea level rise will also result in damage to properties, infrastructures, and public works. There is a growing need to plan for sea level rise.

"(8) There is a clear link between coastal water quality and land use activities along the shore. State management programs under the Coastal Zone Management Act of 1972 (16 U.S.C. 1451 et seq.) [this chapter] are among the best tools for protecting coastal resources and must play a larger role, particularly in improving coastal zone water quality.

"(9) All coastal States should have coastal zone management programs in place that conform to the Coastal Zone Management Act of 1972, as amended by this Act [this chapter].

"(b) Purpose.—It is the purpose of Congress in this subtitle [subtitle C (sections 6201–6217) of title VI of P.L. 101–508, see Short Title of 1990 amendment note under this section] to enhance the effectiveness of the Coastal Zone Management Act of 1972 [this chapter] by increasing our understanding of the coastal environment and expanding the ability of State coastal zone management programs to address coastal environmental problems."

Establishment of Positions and Fixing of Compensation by Secretary of Commerce; Appointments

Section 15(c) of Pub. L. No. 94–370, 90 Stat. 1013 (July 26, 1976), which related to establishment and compensation of four new positions without regard to the provisions of chapter 51 of Title 5, was repealed by Pub. L. No. 99–272, Title VI, § 6045(3), 100 Stat. 127 (Apr. 7, 1986).

§ 1452. Congressional declaration of policy

[CZMA § 303]

The Congress finds and declares that it is the national policy—

(1) to preserve, protect, develop, and where possible, to restore or enhance, the resources of the Nation's coastal zone for this and succeeding generations;

(2) to encourage and assist the states to exercise effectively their responsibilities in the coastal zone through the development and implementation of management programs to achieve wise use of the land and water resources of the coastal zone, giving full consideration to ecological, cultural, historic, and esthetic values as well as the needs for compatible economic development, which programs should at least provide for—

(A) the protection of natural resources, including wetlands, floodplains, estuaries, beaches, dunes, barrier islands, coral reefs, and fish and wildlife and their habitat, within the coastal zone,

(B) the management of coastal development to minimize the loss of life and property caused by improper development in flood-prone, storm surge, geological hazard, and erosion-prone areas and in areas likely to be affected by or vulnerable to sea level rise, land subsidence, and saltwater intrusion, and by the destruction of natural protective features such as beaches, dunes, wetlands, and barrier islands,

(C) the management of coastal development to improve, safeguard, and restore the quality of coastal waters, and to protect natural resources and existing uses of those waters,

(D) priority consideration being given to coastal-dependent uses and orderly processes for siting major facilities related to national defense, energy, fisheries development, recreation, ports and transportation, and the location, to the maximum extent practicable, of new commercial and industrial developments in or adjacent to areas where such development already exists,

(E) public access to the coasts for recreation purposes,

(F) assistance in the redevelopment of deteriorating urban waterfronts and ports, and sensitive preservation and restoration of historic, cultural, and esthetic coastal features,

(G) the coordination and simplification of procedures in order to ensure expedited governmental decisionmaking for the management of coastal resources,

(H) continued consultation and coordination with, and the giving of adequate consideration to the views of, affected Federal agencies,

(I) the giving of timely and effective notification of, and opportunities for public and local government participation in, coastal management decisionmaking,

(J) assistance to support comprehensive planning, conservation, and management for living marine resources, including planning for the siting of pollution control and aquaculture facilities within the coastal zone, and improved coordination between State and Federal coastal zone management agencies and State and wildlife agencies, and

(K) the study and development, in any case in which the Secretary considers it to be appropriate, of plans for addressing the adverse effects upon the coastal zone of land subsidence and of sea level rise; and

(3) to encourage the preparation of special area management plans which provide for increased specificity in protecting significant natural resources, reasonable coastal-dependent economic growth, improved protection of life and property in hazardous areas, including those areas likely to be affected by land subsidence, sea level rise, or fluctuating water levels of the Great Lakes, and improved predictability in governmental decisionmaking;

(4) to encourage the participation and cooperation of the public, state and local governments, and interstate and other regional agencies, as well as of the Federal agencies having programs affecting the coastal zone, in carrying out the purposes of this chapter;

(5) to encourage coordination and cooperation with and among the appropriate Federal, State, and local agencies, and international organizations where appropriate, in collection, analysis, synthesis, and dissemination of coastal management information, research results, and technical assistance, to support State and Federal regulation of land use practices affecting the coastal and ocean resources of the United States; and

(6) to respond to changing circumstances affecting the coastal environment and coastal resource management by encouraging States to consider such issues as ocean uses potentially affecting the coastal zone.

(Pub. L. No. 89–454, Title III, § 303, as added by Pub. L. No. 92–583, 86 Stat. 1281 (Oct. 27, 1972); and amended by Pub. L. No. 96–464, § 3, 94 Stat. 2060 (Oct. 17, 1980); Pub. L. No. 101–508, Title VI, § 6203(b), 104 Stat. 1388–301 (Nov. 5, 1990); Pub. L. No. 102–587, Title II, § 2205(b)(2), 106 Stat. 5050 (Nov. 4, 1992).)

§ 1453. Definitions

[CZMA § 304]

For purposes of this chapter—

(1) The term "coastal zone" means the coastal waters (including the lands therein and thereunder) and the adjacent shorelands (including the waters therein and thereunder), strongly influenced by each other and in proximity to the shorelines of the several coastal states, and includes islands, transitional and intertidal areas, salt marshes, wetlands, and beaches. The zone extends, in Great Lakes waters, to the international boundary between the United States and Canada and, in other areas, seaward to the outer limit of State title and ownership under the Submerged Lands Act (43 U.S.C. 1301 et seq.), the Act of March 2, 1917, (48 U.S.C. 749) [48 U.S.C.A. § 731 et seq.], the Covenant to Establish a Commonwealth of the Northern Mariana Islands in Political Union with the United States of America, as approved by the Act of March 24, 1976 (48 U.S.C. 1801 et seq.), or section 1 of the Act of November 20, 1963 (48 U.S.C. 1705), as applicable. The zone extends inland from the shorelines only to the extent necessary to control shorelands, the uses of which have a direct and significant impact on the coastal waters, and to control those geographical areas which are likely to be affected by or vulnerable to sea level rise. Excluded from the coastal zone are lands the use of which is by law subject solely to the discretion of or which is held in trust by the Federal Government, its officers or agents.

(2) The term "coastal resource of national significance" means any coastal wetland, beach, dune, barrier island, reef, estuary, or fish and wildlife habitat, if any such area is determined by a coastal state to be of substantial biological or natural storm protective value.

(3) The term "coastal waters" means (A) in the Great Lakes area, the waters within the territorial jurisdiction of the United States consisting of the Great Lakes, their connecting waters, harbors, roadsteads, and estuary-type areas such as bays, shallows, and marshes and (B) in other areas, those waters, adjacent to the shorelines, which contain a measurable quantity or percentage of sea water, including, but not limited to, sounds, bays, lagoons, bayous, ponds, and estuaries.

(4) The term "coastal state" means a state of the United States in, or bordering on, the Atlantic, Pacific, or Arctic Ocean, the Gulf of Mexico, Long Island Sound, or one or more of the Great Lakes. For the purposes of this chapter, the term also includes Puerto Rico, the Virgin Islands, Guam, the Commonwealth of the Northern Mariana Islands, and the Trust Territories of the Pacific Islands, and American Samoa.

(5) The term "coastal energy activity" means any of the following activities if, and to the extent that (A) the conduct, support, or facilitation of such activity requires and involves the siting, construction, expansion, or operation of any equipment or facility; and (B) any technical requirement exists which, in the determination of the Secretary, necessitates that the siting, construction, expansion, or operation of such equipment or facility be carried out in, or in close proximity to, the coastal zone of any coastal state;

(i) Any outer Continental Shelf energy activity.

(ii) Any transportation, conversion, treatment, transfer, or storage of liquefied natural gas.

(iii) Any transportation, transfer, or storage of oil, natural gas, or coal (including, but not limited to, by means of any deepwater port, as defined in section 1502(10) of Title 33).

For purposes of this paragraph, the siting, construction, expansion, or operation of any equipment or facility shall be "in close proximity to" the coastal zone of any coastal state if such siting, construction, expansion, or operation has, or is likely to have, a significant effect on such coastal zone.

(6) The term "energy facilities" means any equipment or facility which is or will be used primarily—

(A) in the exploration for, or the development, production, conversion, storage, transfer, processing, or transportation of, any energy resource; or

(B) for the manufacture, production, or assembly of equipment, machinery, products, or devices which are involved in any activity described in subparagraph (A).

The term includes, but is not limited to (i) electric generating plants; (ii) petroleum refineries and associated facilities; (iii) gasification plants; (iv) facilities used for the transportation, conversion, treatment, transfer, or storage of liquefied natural gas; (v) uranium enrichment or nuclear fuel processing facilities; (vi) oil and gas facilities, including platforms, assembly plants, storage depots, tank farms, crew and supply bases, and refining complexes; (vii) facilities including deepwater ports, for the transfer of petroleum; (viii) pipelines and transmission facilities; and (ix) terminals which are associated with any of the foregoing.

(6a) The term "enforceable policy" means State policies which are legally binding through constitutional provisions, laws, regulations, land use plans, ordinances, or judicial or administrative decisions, by which a State exerts control over private and public land and water uses and natural resources in the coastal zone.

(7) The term "estuary" means that part of a river or stream or other body of water having unimpaired connection with the open sea, where the sea water is measurably diluted with fresh water derived from land drainage. The term includes estuary-type areas of the Great Lakes.

(8) The term "estuarine sanctuary" means a research area which may include any part or all of an estuary and any island, transitional area, and upland in, adjoining, or adjacent to such estuary, and which constitutes to the extent feasible a natural unit, set aside to provide scientists and students the opportunity to examine over a period of time the ecological relationships within the area.

(9) The term "Fund" means the Coastal Zone Management Fund established under section 1456a(b) of this title.

(10) The term "land use" means activities which are conducted in, or on the shorelands within, the coastal zone, subject to the requirements outlined in section 1456(g) of this title.

(11) The term "local government" means any political subdivision of, or any special entity created by, any coastal state which (in whole or part) is located in, or has authority over, such state's coastal zone and which (A) has authority to levy taxes, or to establish and collect user fees, or (B) provides any public facility or public service which is financed in whole or part by taxes or user fees. The term includes, but is not limited to, any school district, fire district, transportation authority, and any other special purpose district or authority.

(12) The term "management program" includes, but is not limited to, a comprehensive statement in words, maps, illustrations, or other media of communication, prepared and adopted by the state in accordance with the provisions of this chapter, setting forth objectives, policies, and standards to guide public and private uses of lands and waters in the coastal zone.

(13) The term "outer Continental Shelf energy activity" means any exploration for, or any development or production of, oil or natural gas from the outer Continental Shelf (as defined in section 1331(a) of Title 43) or the siting, construction, expansion, or operation of any new or expanded energy facilities directly required by such exploration, development, or production.

(14) The term "person" means any individual; any corporation, partnership, association, or other entity organized or existing under the laws of any state; the Federal Government; any state, regional, or local government; or any entity of any such Federal, state, regional, or local government.

(15) The term "public facilities and public services" means facilities or services which are financed, in whole or in part, by any state or political subdivision thereof, including, but not limited to, highways and secondary roads, parking, mass transit, docks, navigation aids, fire and police protection, water supply, waste collection and treatment (including drainage), schools and education, and hospitals and health care. Such term may also include any other facility or service so financed which the Secretary finds will support increased population.

(16) The term "Secretary" means the Secretary of Commerce.

(17) The term "special area management plan" means a comprehensive plan providing for natural resource protection and reasonable coastal-dependent economic growth containing a detailed and comprehensive statement of policies; standards and criteria to guide public and private uses of lands and waters; and mechanisms for timely implementation in specific geographic areas within the coastal zone.

(18) The term "water use" means a use, activity, or project conducted in or on waters within the coastal zone.

(Pub. L. No. 89–454, Title III, § 304, as added by Pub. L. No. 92–583, 86 Stat. 1281 (Oct. 27, 1972); and amended by Pub. L. No. 94–370, § 3, 90 Stat. 1013 (July 26, 1976); Pub. L. No. 96–464, § 4, 94 Stat. 2061 (Oct. 17, 1980); Pub. L. No. 101–508, Title VI, § 6204, 104 Stat. 1388–302 (Nov. 5, 1990); Pub. L. No. 102–587, Title II, § 2205(b)(3)–(7), 106 Stat. 5050, 5051 (Nov. 4, 1992).)

HISTORICAL AND STATUTORY NOTES

References in Text

The Submerged Lands Act, referred to in par. (1), is Act May 22, 1953, c. 65, 67 Stat. 29, as amended, which is codified generally to subchapters I and II (sections 1301 et seq., 1311 et seq.) of chapter 29 of Title 43, Public Lands. For complete classification of this Act to the Code, see Short Title note set out under section 1301 of Title 43 and Tables.

The Act of March 2, 1917, referred to in par. (1) is Act Mar. 2, 1917, c. 145, 39 Stat. 961, as amended, known as the Puerto Rican Federal Relations Act and also popularly known as the Jones Act, which is codified principally to chapter 4 (section 731 et seq.) of Title 48, Territories and Insular Possessions. Section 8 of this Act is codified as section 749 of Title 48. For complete classification of this Act to the Code, see Short Title note set out under section 731 of Title 48 and Tables.

The Act of March 24, 1976, referred to in par. (1), is Pub. L. No. 94–241, 90 Stat. 263 (Mar. 24, 1976), as amended, which is codified as a note entitled "Covenant to Establish Commonwealth of Northern Mariana Islands in Political Union with the United States of America" under section 1681 of Title 48, Territories and Insular Possessions.

Section 1 of the Act of November 20, 1963, referred to in par. (1), is section 1 of Pub. L. No. 88–183, 77 Stat. 338 (Nov. 20, 1963), which was formerly codified as section 1701 of Title 48, Possessions and Insular Territories. Such section, which related to the authority of the Secretary of the Interior to transfer tidelands, submerged lands, and filled lands to the governments of Guam, Virgin Islands and American Samoa, was repealed by Pub. L. No. 93–435, § 5, 88 Stat. 1212 (Oct. 5, 1974). Similar provisions were enacted by section 1 of Pub. L. No. 93–435, 88 Stat. 1210 (Oct. 5, 1974), as amended, and are codified as section 1705 of Title 48.

Section 1502 of Title 33, referred to in par. (5)(iii), was subsequently amended, and the definition of "deepwater port" was transferred to 33 U.S.C.A. § 1502(9).

Codifications

Amendment of par. (1) by section 6204(a) of Pub. L. No. 101–508 was executed to the second sentence of par. (1), notwithstanding directory language reciting that it be executed to the third sentence, as the probable intent of Congress.

Termination of Trust Territory of the Pacific Islands

For termination of Trust Territory of the Pacific Islands, see note set out preceding section 1681 of Title 48.

§ 1454. Submittal of state program for approval

[CZMA § 305]

Any coastal state which has completed the development of its management program shall submit such program to the Secretary for review and approval pursuant to section 1455 of this title.

(Pub. L. No. 89–454, Title III, § 305, as added by Pub. L. No. 92–583, 86 Stat. 1282 (Oct. 27, 1972); and amended by Pub. L. No. 93–612, § 1(1), 88 Stat. 1974 (Jan. 2, 1975); Pub. L. No. 94–370, § 4, 90 Stat. 1015 (July 26, 1976); Pub. L. No. 101–508, Title VI, § 6205, 104 Stat. 1388–302 (Nov. 5, 1990); Pub. L. No. 102–587, Title II, § 2205(b)(1)(A), 106 Stat. 5050 (Nov. 4, 1992); Pub. L. No. 104–150, § 2(a), (b)(1), 110 Stat. 1380 (June 3, 1996).)

HISTORICAL AND STATUTORY NOTES

Effective and Applicability Provisions

1996 Acts. Section 2(b)(3) of Pub. L. No. 104–150 provided that: "This subsection [amending this section and section 1456a of this title] shall take effect on October 1, 1999."

§ 1455. Administrative grants

[CZMA § 306]

(a) Authorization; matching funds

The Secretary may make grants to any coastal state for the purpose of administering that state's management program, if the state matches any such grant according to the following ratios of Federal-to-State contributions for the applicable fiscal year:

(1) For those States for which programs were approved prior to November 5, 1990, 1 to 1 for any fiscal year.

(2) For programs approved after November 5, 1990, 4 to 1 for the first fiscal year, 2.3 to 1 for the second fiscal year, 1.5 to 1 for the third fiscal year, and 1 to 1 for each fiscal year thereafter.

(b) Grants to coastal states; requirements

The Secretary may make a grant to a coastal state under subsection (a) of this section only if the Secretary finds that the management program of the coastal state meets all applicable requirements of this chapter and has been approved in accordance with subsection (d) of this section.

(c) Allocation of grants to coastal states

Grants under this section shall be allocated to coastal states with approved programs based on rules and regulations promulgated by the Secretary which shall take into account the extent and nature of the shoreline and area covered by the program, population of the area, and other relevant factors. The Secretary shall establish, after consulting with the coastal states, maximum and minimum grants for any fiscal year to promote equity between coastal states and effective coastal management.

(d) Mandatory adoption of State management program for coastal zone

Before approving a management program submitted by a coastal state, the Secretary shall find the following:

(1) The State has developed and adopted a management program for its coastal zone in accordance with rules and regulations promulgated by the Secretary, after notice, and with the opportunity of full participation by relevant Federal agencies, State agencies, local governments, regional organizations, port authorities, and other interested parties and individuals, public and private, which is adequate to carry out the purposes of this chapter and is consistent with the policy declared in section 1452 of this title.

(2) The management program includes each of the following required program elements:

(A) An identification of the boundaries of the coastal zone subject to the management program.

(B) A definition of what shall constitute permissible land uses and water uses within the coastal zone which have a direct and significant impact on the coastal waters.

(C) An inventory and designation of areas of particular concern within the coastal zone.

(D) An identification of the means by which the State proposes to exert control over the land uses and water uses referred to in subparagraph (B), including a list of relevant State constitutional provisions, laws, regulations, and judicial decisions.

(E) Broad guidelines on priorities of uses in particular areas, including specifically those uses of lowest priority.

(F) A description of the organizational structure proposed to implement such management program, including the responsibilities and interrelationships of local, areawide, State, regional, and interstate agencies in the management process.

(G) A definition of the term "beach" and a planning process for the protection of, and access to, public beaches and other public coastal areas of environmental, recreational, historical, esthetic, ecological, or cultural value.

(H) A planning process for energy facilities likely to be located in, or which may significantly affect, the coastal zone, including a process for anticipating the management of the impacts resulting from such facilities.

(I) A planning process for assessing the effects of, and studying and evaluating ways to control, or lessen the impact of, shoreline erosion, and to restore areas adversely affected by such erosion.

(3) The State has—

(A) coordinated its program with local, areawide, and interstate plans applicable to areas within the coastal zone—

(i) existing on January 1 of the year in which the State's management program is submitted to the Secretary; and

(ii) which have been developed by a local government, an areawide agency, a regional agency, or an interstate agency; and

(B) established an effective mechanism for continuing consultation and coordination between the management agency designated pursuant to paragraph (6) and with local governments, interstate agencies, regional agencies, and areawide agencies within the coastal zone to assure the full participation of those local governments and agencies in carrying out the purposes of this chapter; except that the Secretary shall not find any mechanism to be effective for purposes of this subparagraph unless it requires that—

(i) the management agency, before implementing any management program decision which would conflict with any local zoning ordinance, decision, or other action, shall send a notice of the management program decision to any local government whose zoning authority is affected;

(ii) within the 30-day period commencing on the date of receipt of that notice, the local government may submit to the management agency written comments on the management program decision, and any recommendation for alternatives; and

(iii) the management agency, if any comments are submitted to it within the 30-day period by any local government—

(I) shall consider the comments;

(II) may, in its discretion, hold a public hearing on the comments; and

(III) may not take any action within the 30-day period to implement the management program decision.

(4) The State has held public hearings in the development of the management program.

(5) The management program and any changes thereto have been reviewed and approved by the Governor of the State.

(6) The Governor of the State has designated a single State agency to receive and administer grants for implementing the management program.

(7) The State is organized to implement the management program.

(8) The management program provides for adequate consideration of the national interest involved in planning for, and managing the coastal zone, including the siting of facilities such as energy facilities which are of greater than local significance. In the case of energy facilities, the Secretary shall find that the State has given consideration to any applicable national or interstate energy plan or program.

(9) The management program includes procedures whereby specific areas may be designated for the purpose of preserving or restoring them for their conservation, recreational, ecological, historical, or esthetic values.

(10) The State, acting through its chosen agency or agencies (including local governments, areawide agencies, regional agencies, or interstate agencies) has authority for the management of the coastal zone in accordance with the management program. Such authority shall include power—

(A) to administer land use and water use regulations to control development[1] to ensure compliance with the management program, and to resolve conflicts among competing uses; and

(B) to acquire fee simple and less than fee simple interests in land, waters, and other property through condemnation or other means when necessary to achieve conformance with the management program.

(11) The management program provides for any one or a combination of the following general techniques for control of land uses and water uses within the coastal zone:

(A) State establishment of criteria and standards for local implementation, subject to administrative review and enforcement.

(B) Direct State land and water use planning and regulation.

(C) State administrative review for consistency with the management program of all development plans, projects, or land and water use regulations, including exceptions and variances thereto, proposed by any State or local authority or private developer, with power to approve or disapprove after public notice and an opportunity for hearings.

(12) The management program contains a method of assuring that local land use and water use regulations within the coastal zone do not unreasonably restrict or exclude land uses and water uses of regional benefit.

(13) The management program provides for—

(A) the inventory and designation of areas that contain one or more coastal resources of national significance; and

(B) specific and enforceable standards to protect such resources.

(14) The management program provides for public participation in permitting processes, consistency determinations, and other similar decisions.

(15) The management program provides a mechanism to ensure that all State agencies will adhere to the program.[1]

(16) The management program contains enforceable policies and mechanisms to implement the applicable requirements of the Coastal Nonpoint Pollution Control Program of the State required by section 1455b of this title.

(e) Amendment or modification of State management program for coastal zone

A coastal state may amend or modify a management program which it has submitted and which has been approved by the Secretary under this section, subject to the following conditions:

(1) The State shall promptly notify the Secretary of any proposed amendment, modification, or other program change and submit it for the Secretary's approval. The Secretary may suspend all or part of any grant made under this section pending State submission of the proposed amendments, modification, or other program change.

(2) Within 30 days after the date the Secretary receives any proposed amendment, the Secretary shall notify the State whether the Secretary approves or disapproves the amendment, or whether the Secretary finds it is necessary to extend the review of the proposed amendment for a period not to exceed 120 days after the date the Secretary received the proposed amendment. The Secretary may extend this period only as necessary to meet the requirements of the National Environmental Policy Act of 1969 (42 U.S.C. 4321 et seq.). If the Secretary does not notify the coastal state that the Secretary approves or disapproves the amendment within that period, then the amendment shall be conclusively presumed as approved.

(3)(A) Except as provided in subparagraph (B), a coastal state may not implement any amendment, modification, or other change as part of its approved management program unless the amendment, modification, or other change is approved by the Secretary under this subsection.

(B) The Secretary, after determining on a preliminary basis, that an amendment, modification, or other change which has been submitted for approval under this subsection is likely to meet the program approval standards in this section, may permit the State to expend funds awarded under this section to begin implementing the proposed amendment, modification, or change. This preliminary approval shall not extend for more than 6 months and may not be renewed. A proposed amendment, modification, or change which has been given preliminary approval and is not finally approved under this paragraph shall not be considered an enforceable policy for purposes of section 1456 of this title.

(Pub. L. No. 89–454, Title III, § 306, as added by Pub. L. No. 92–583, 86 Stat. 1283 (Oct. 27, 1972); and amended by Pub. L. No. 93–612, § 1(2), 88 Stat. 1974 (Jan. 2, 1975); Pub. L. No. 94–370, § 5, 90 Stat. 1017 (July 26, 1976); Pub. L. No. 96–464, § 5(a), 94 Stat. 2062 (Oct. 17, 1980); Pub. L. No. 99–272, Title VI, § 6043(b)(1), (c), 100 Stat. 124, 125 (Apr. 7, 1986); Pub. L. No. 101–508, Title VI, § 6206(a), 104 Stat. 1388–303 (Nov. 5, 1990); Pub. L. No. 102–587, Title II, § 2205(b)(1)(A), (B), (8), 106 Stat. 5050, 5051 (Nov. 4, 1992).)

[1] So in original. Probably should be followed by a comma.

HISTORICAL AND STATUTORY NOTES

References in Text

The National Environmental Policy Act of 1969, referred to in subsec. (e)(2), is Pub. L. No. 91–190, 83 Stat. 852 (Jan. 1, 1970), as amended, which is codified generally to chapter 55 (section 4321 et seq.) of Title 42, The Public Health and Welfare. For complete classification of this Act to the Code, see Short Title note set out under section 4321 of Title 42 and Tables.

Effective and Applicability Provisions

1980 Acts. Section 5(b) of Pub. L. No. 96–464 provided that: "The amendments made by subsection (a) (1) and (2) of this section [amending subsecs. (a) and (b) of this section] apply with respect to grants made after September 30, 1980, under section 306 of the Coastal Zone Management Act of 1972 [this section] and, within two hundred and seventy days after such date, the Secretary of Commerce shall issue regulations relating to the administration of subsection (a) of such section 306 (as so amended by such subsection (a(1)) [subsec. (a) of this section]."

Additional Program Requirements

Section 6206(b) of Pub. L. No. 101–508 provided that:

"Each State which submits a management program for approval under section 306 of the Coastal Zone Management Act of 1972 [this section], as amended by this subtitle (including a State which submitted a program before the date of enactment of this Act [Nov. 5, 1990]), shall demonstrate to the Secretary—

"(1) that the program complies with section 306(d)(14) and (15) of that Act [subsec. (d)(14) and (15) of this section] by not later than 3 years after the date of the enactment of this Act [Nov. 5, 1990]; and

"(2) that the program complies with section 306(d)(16) of that Act [subsec. (d)(16) of this section], by not later than 30 months after the date of publication of final guidance under section 6217(g) of this Act [section 1455b(g) of this title]."

Limitations on Federal Financial Increases

Pub. L. No. 113–6, 127 Stat. 239 (Mar. 26, 2013), provided in part that "in allocating grants under sections 306 and 306A of the Coastal Zone Management Act of 1972, as amended, no coastal State shall receive more than 5 percent or less than 1 percent of increased funds appropriated over the previous fiscal year. . . ."

§ 1455a. Coastal resource improvement program

[CZMA § 306A]

(a) Definitions

For purposes of this section—

(1) The term "eligible coastal state" means a coastal state that for any fiscal year for which a grant is applied for under this section—

(A) has a management program approved under section 1455 of this title; and

(B) in the judgment of the Secretary, is making satisfactory progress in activities designed to result in significant improvement in achieving the coastal management objectives specified in section 1452(2)(A) through (K) of this title.

(2) The term "urban waterfront and port" means any developed area that is densely populated and is being used for, or has been used for, urban residential recreational, commercial, shipping or industrial purposes.

(b) Resource management improvement grants

The Secretary may make grants to any eligible coastal state to assist that state in meeting one or more of the following objectives:

(1) The preservation or restoration of specific areas of the state that (A) are designated under the management program procedures required by section 1455(d)(9) of this title because of their conservation recreational, ecological, or esthetic values, or (B) contain one or more coastal resources of national significance, or for the purpose of restoring and enhancing shellfish production by the purchase and distribution of clutch material on publicly owned reef tracts.

(2) The redevelopment of deteriorating and underutilized urban waterfronts and ports that are designated in the state's management program pursuant to section 1455(d)(2)(C) of this title as areas of particular concern.

(3) The provision of access to public beaches and other public coastal areas and to coastal waters in accordance with the planning process required under section 1455(d)(2)(G) of this title.

(4) The development of a coordinated process among State agencies to regulate and issue permits for aquaculture facilities in the coastal zone.

(c) Uses, terms and conditions of grants

(1) Each grant made by the Secretary under this section shall be subject to such terms and conditions as may be appropriate to ensure that the grant is used for purposes consistent with this section.

(2) Grants made under this section may be used for—

(A) the acquisition of fee simple and other interests in land;

(B) low-cost construction projects determined by the Secretary to be consistent with the purposes of this section, including but not limited to, paths, walkways, fences, parks, and the rehabilitation of historic buildings and structures; except that not more than 50 per centum of any grant made under this section may be used for such construction projects;

(C) in the case of grants made for objectives described in subsection (b) (2) of this section—

(i) the rehabilitation or acquisition of piers to provide increased public use, including compatible commercial activity,

(ii) the establishment of shoreline stabilization measures including the installation or rehabilitation of bulkheads for the purpose of public safety or increasing public access and use, and

(iii) the removal or replacement of pilings where such action will provide increased recreational use of urban waterfront areas,

but activities provided for under this paragraph shall not be treated as construction projects subject to the limitations in paragraph (B);

(D) engineering designs, specifications, and other appropriate reports; and

(E) educational, interpretive, and management costs and such other related costs as the Secretary determines to be consistent with the purposes of this section.

(d) State matching contributions; ratio; maximum amount of grants

(1) The Secretary may make grants to any coastal state for the purpose of carrying out the project or purpose for which such grants are awarded, if the state matches any such grant according to the following ratios of Federal to state contributions for the applicable fiscal year: 4 to 1 for fiscal year 1986; 2.3 to 1 for fiscal year 1987; 1.5 to 1 for fiscal year 1988; and 1 to 1 for each fiscal year after fiscal year 1988.

(2) Grants provided under this section may be used to pay a coastal state's share of costs required under any other Federal program that is consistent with the purposes of this section.

(3) The total amount of grants made under this section to any eligible coastal state for any fiscal year may not exceed an amount equal to 10 per centum of the total amount appropriated to carry out this section for such fiscal year.

(e) Allocation of grants to local governments and other agencies

With the approval of the Secretary, an eligible coastal state may allocate to a local government, an areawide agency designated under section 3334 of Title 42, a regional agency, or an interstate agency, a portion of any grant made under this section for the purpose of carrying out this section; except that such an allocation shall not relieve that state of the responsibility for ensuring that any funds so allocated are applied in furtherance of the state's approved management program.

(f) Other technical and financial assistance

In addition to providing grants under this section, the Secretary shall assist eligible coastal states and their local governments in identifying and obtaining other sources of available Federal technical and financial assistance regarding the objectives of this section.

(Pub. L. No. 89–454, Title III, § 306A, as added by Pub. L. No. 96–464, § 6, 94 Stat. 2062 (Oct. 17, 1980); and amended by Pub. L. No. 99–272, Title VI, § 6043(b)(2), 100 Stat. 124 (Apr. 7, 1986); Pub. L. No. 101–508, Title VI, §§ 6207, 6216(a), 104 Stat. 1388–307, 1388–314 (Nov. 5, 1990); Pub. L. No. 102–587, Title II, § 2205(b)(9) to (12), 106 Stat. 5051 (Nov. 4, 1992); Pub. L. No. 104–150, § 7(1), 110 Stat. 1381 (June 3, 1996).)

HISTORICAL AND STATUTORY NOTES

Codifications

Section 6216a of Pub. L. No. 101–508 directed the amendment of section 306a(b)(1) of the Coastal Zone Management Act of 1972. There is no such section of such Act. Section 306A(b)(1) of such Act is codified as subsec. (b)(1) of this section, and such amendment was executed to such subsec. as the probable intent of Congress.

§ 1455b. Protecting coastal waters

(a) In general

(1) Program development

Not later than 30 months after the date of the publication of final guidance under subsection (g) of this section, each State for which a management program has been approved pursuant to section 306 of the Coastal Zone Management Act of 1972 [16 U.S.C.A. § 1455] shall prepare and submit to the Secretary and the Administrator a Coastal Nonpoint Pollution Control Program for approval pursuant to this section. The purpose of the program shall be to develop and implement management measures for nonpoint source pollution to restore and protect coastal waters, working in close conjunction with other State and local authorities.

(2) Program coordination

A State program under this section shall be coordinated closely with State and local water quality plans and programs developed pursuant to sections 1288, 1313, 1329, and 1330 of Title 33 and with State plans developed pursuant to the Coastal Zone Management Act of 1972, as amended by this Act [16 U.S.C.A. § 1451 et seq.]. The program shall serve as an update and expansion of the State nonpoint source management program developed under section 1329 of Title 33, as the program under that section relates to land and water uses affecting coastal waters.

(b) Program contents

Each State program under this section shall provide for the implementation, at a minimum, of management measures in conformity with the guidance published under subsection (g) of this section, to protect coastal waters generally, and shall also contain the following:

(1) Identifying land uses

The identification of, and a continuing process for identifying, land uses which, individually or cumulatively, may cause or contribute significantly to a degradation of—

(A) those coastal waters where there is a failure to attain or maintain applicable water quality standards or protect designated uses, as determined by the State pursuant to its water quality planning processes; or

(B) those coastal waters that are threatened by reasonably foreseeable increases in pollution loadings from new or expanding sources.

(2) Identifying critical coastal areas

The identification of, and a continuing process for identifying, critical coastal areas adjacent to coastal waters referred to in paragraph (1)(A) and (B), within which any new land uses or substantial expansion of existing land uses shall be subject to management measures in addition to those provided for in subsection (g) of this section.

(3) Management measures

The implementation and continuing revision from time to time of additional management measures applicable to the land uses and areas identified pursuant to paragraphs (1) and (2) that are necessary to achieve and maintain applicable water quality standards under section 1313 of Title 33 and protect designated uses.

(4) Technical assistance

The provision of technical and other assistance to local governments and the public for implementing the measures referred to in paragraph (3), which may include assistance in developing ordinances and regulations, technical guidance, and modeling to predict and assess the effectiveness of such measures, training, financial incentives, demonstration projects, and other innovations to protect coastal water quality and designated uses.

(5) Public participation

Opportunities for public participation in all aspects of the program, including the use of public notices and opportunities for comment, nomination procedures, public hearings, technical and financial assistance, public education, and other means.

(6) Administrative coordination

The establishment of mechanisms to improve coordination among State agencies and between State and local officials responsible for land use programs and permitting, water quality permitting and enforcement, habitat protection, and public health and safety, through the use of joint project review, memoranda of agreement, or other mechanisms.

(7) State coastal zone boundary modification

A proposal to modify the boundaries of the State coastal zone as the coastal management agency of the State determines is necessary to implement the recommendations made pursuant to subsection (e) of this section. If the coastal management agency does not have the authority to modify such boundaries, the program shall include recommendations for such modifications to the appropriate State authority.

(c) Program submission, approval, and implementation

(1) Review and approval

Within 6 months after the date of submission by a State of a program pursuant to this section, the Secretary and the Administrator shall jointly review the program. The program shall be approved if—

(A) the Secretary determines that the portions of the program under the authority of the Secretary meet the requirements of this section and the Administrator concurs with that determination; and

(B) the Administrator determines that the portions of the program under the authority of the Administrator meet the requirements of this section and the Secretary concurs with that determination.

(2) Implementation of approved program

If the program of a State is approved in accordance with paragraph (1), the State shall implement the program, including the management measures included in the program pursuant to subsection (b) of this section, through—

(A) changes to the State plan for control of nonpoint source pollution approved under section 1329 of Title 33; and

(B) changes to the State coastal zone management program developed under section 306 of the Coastal Zone Management Act of 1972, as amended by this Act [16 U.S.C.A. § 1455].

(3) Withholding coastal management assistance

If the Secretary finds that a coastal State has failed to submit an approvable program as required by this section, the Secretary shall withhold for each fiscal year until such a program is submitted a portion of grants otherwise available to the State for the fiscal year under section 306 of the Coastal Zone Management Act of 1972 [16 U.S.C.A. § 1455], as follows:

(A) 10 percent for fiscal year 1996.

(B) 15 percent for fiscal year 1997.

(C) 20 percent for fiscal year 1998.

(D) 30 percent for fiscal year 1999 and each fiscal year thereafter.

The Secretary shall make amounts withheld under this paragraph available to coastal States having programs approved under this section.

(4) Withholding water pollution control assistance

If the Administrator finds that a coastal State has failed to submit an approvable program as required by this section, the Administrator shall withhold from grants available to the State under section 1329 of Title 33, for each fiscal year until such a program is submitted, an amount equal to a percentage of the grants awarded to the State for the preceding fiscal year under that section, as follows:

(A) For fiscal year 1996, 10 percent of the amount awarded for fiscal year 1995.

(B) For fiscal year 1997, 15 percent of the amount awarded for fiscal year 1996.

(C) For fiscal year 1998, 20 percent of the amount awarded for fiscal year 1997.

(D) For fiscal year 1999 and each fiscal year thereafter, 30 percent of the amount awarded for fiscal year 1998 or other preceding fiscal year.

The Administrator shall make amounts withheld under this paragraph available to States having programs approved pursuant to this subsection.

(d) Technical assistance

The Secretary and the Administrator shall provide technical assistance to coastal States and local governments in developing and implementing programs under this section. Such assistance shall include—

(1) methods for assessing water quality impacts associated with coastal land uses;

(2) methods for assessing the cumulative water quality effects of coastal development;

(3) maintaining and from time to time revising an inventory of model ordinances, and providing other assistance to coastal States and local governments in identifying, developing, and implementing pollution control measures; and

(4) methods to predict and assess the effects of coastal land use management measures on coastal water quality and designated uses.

(e) Inland coastal zone boundaries

(1) Review

The Secretary, in consultation with the Administrator of the Environmental Protection Agency, shall, within 18 months after November 5, 1990, review the inland coastal zone boundary of each coastal State program which has been approved or is proposed for approval under section 306 of the Coastal Zone Management Act of 1972 [16 U.S.C.A. § 1455], and evaluate whether the State's coastal zone boundary extends inland to the extent necessary to control the land and water uses that have a significant impact on coastal waters of the State.

(2) Recommendation

If the Secretary, in consultation with the Administrator, finds that modifications to the inland boundaries of a State's coastal zone are necessary for that State to more effectively manage land and water uses to protect coastal waters, the Secretary, in consultation with the Administrator, shall recommend appropriate modifications in writing to the affected State.

(f) Financial assistance

(1) In general

Upon request of a State having a program approved under section 306 of the Coastal Zone Management Act of 1972 [16 U.S.C.A. § 1455], the Secretary, in consultation with the Administrator, may provide grants to the State for use for developing a State program under this section.

(2) Amount

The total amount of grants to a State under this subsection shall not exceed 50 percent of the total cost to the State of developing a program under this section.

(3) State share

The State share of the cost of an activity carried out with a grant under this subsection shall be paid from amounts from non-Federal sources.

(4) Allocation

Amounts available for grants under this subsection shall be allocated among States in accordance with regulations issued pursuant to section 306(c) of the Coastal Zone Management Act of 1972 [16 U.S.C.A. § 1455(c)], except that the Secretary may use not more than 25 percent of amounts available for such grants to assist States which the Secretary, in consultation with the Administrator, determines are making exemplary progress in preparing a State program under this section or have extreme needs with respect to coastal water quality.

(g) Guidance for coastal nonpoint source pollution control

(1) In general

The Administrator, in consultation with the Secretary and the Director of the United States Fish and Wildlife Service and other Federal agencies, shall publish (and periodically revise thereafter) guidance for specifying management measures for sources of nonpoint pollution in coastal waters.

(2) Content

Guidance under this subsection shall include, at a minimum—

(A) a description of a range of methods, measures, or practices, including structural and nonstructural controls and operation and maintenance procedures, that constitute each measure;

(B) a description of the categories and subcategories of activities and locations for which each measure may be suitable;

(C) an identification of the individual pollutants or categories or classes of pollutants that may be controlled by the measures and the water quality effects of the measures;

(D) quantitative estimates of the pollution reduction effects and costs of the measures;

(E) a description of the factors which should be taken into account in adapting the measures to specific sites or locations; and

(F) any necessary monitoring techniques to accompany the measures to assess over time the success of the measures in reducing pollution loads and improving water quality.

(3) Publication

The Administrator, in consultation with the Secretary, shall publish—

(A) proposed guidance pursuant to this subsection not later than 6 months after November 5, 1990; and

(B) final guidance pursuant to this subsection not later than 18 months after November 5, 1990.

(4) Notice and comment

The Administrator shall provide to coastal States and other interested persons an opportunity to provide written comments on proposed guidance under this subsection.

(5) Management measures

For purposes of this subsection, the term "management measures" means economically achievable measures for the control of the addition of pollutants from existing and new categories and classes of nonpoint sources of pollution, which reflect the greatest degree of pollutant reduction achievable through the application of the best available nonpoint pollution control practices, technologies, processes, siting criteria, operating methods, or other alternatives.

(h) Authorization of appropriations

(1) Administrator

There is authorized to be appropriated to the Administrator for use for carrying out this section not more than $1,000,000 for each of fiscal years 1992, 1993, and 1994.

(2) Secretary

(A) Of amounts appropriated to the Secretary for a fiscal year under section 318(a)(4) of the Coastal Zone Management Act of 1972, as amended by this Act, not more than $1,000,000 shall be available for use by the Secretary for carrying out this section for that fiscal year, other than for providing in the form of grants under subsection (f) of this section.

(B) There is authorized to be appropriated to the Secretary for use for providing in the form of grants under subsection (f) of this section not more than—

(i) $6,000,000 for fiscal year 1992;

(ii) $12,000,000 for fiscal year 1993;

(iii) $12,000,000 for fiscal year 1994; and

(iv) $12,000,000 for fiscal year 1995.

(i) Definitions

In this section—

(1) the term "Administrator" means the Administrator of the Environmental Protection Agency;

(2) the term "coastal state" has the meaning given the term "coastal State" under section 304 of the Coastal Zone Management Act of 1972 (16 U.S.C. 1453) [16 U.S.C.A. § 1453];

(3) each of the terms "coastal waters" and "coastal zone" has the meaning that term has in the Coastal Zone Management Act of 1972 [16 U.S.C.A. § 1451 et seq.];

(4) the term "coastal management agency" means a State agency designated pursuant to section 306(d)(6) of the Coastal Zone Management Act of 1972 [16 U.S.C.A. § 1455(d)(6)];

(5) the term "land use" includes a use of waters adjacent to coastal waters; and

(6) the term "Secretary" means the Secretary of Commerce.

(Pub. L. No. 101–508, Title VI, § 6217, 104 Stat. 1388–314 (Nov. 5, 1990); Pub. L. No. 102–587, Title II, § 2205(b)(24), 106 Stat. 5052 (Nov. 4, 1992).)

HISTORICAL AND STATUTORY NOTES

References in Text

The Coastal Zone Management Act of 1972, referred to in subsecs. (a)(2) and (i)(3), is Pub. L. No. 89–454, Title III (section 301 et seq.), as added Pub. L. No. 92–583, 86 Stat. 1280 (Oct. 27, 1972), as amended, which is codified generally to this chapter.

Section 306 of the Coastal Zone Management Act of 1972, referred to in subsecs. (a)(1), (c)(2)(B), (3), (e)(1) and (f)(1), is section 306 of this same Act, which is codified as section 1455 of this title.

Section 306(c) of the Coastal Zone Management Act of 1972, referred to in subsec. (f)(4), is section 1455(c) of this same Act, which is codified as section 1455(c) of this title.

Section 304 of the Coastal Management Act of 1972, referred to in subsec. (i)(2), is section 304 of this same Act, which is codified as section 1453 of this title.

Section 306(d)(6) of the Coastal Zone Management Act of 1972, referred to in subsec. (i)(4), is section 306(d)(6) of this same Act, which is codified as section 1455(d)(6) of this title.

Section 318(a)(4) of the Coastal Zone Management Act of 1972, referred to in subsec. (h)(2)(A), which is section 318(a)(4) of this same Act and which was codified as section 1464(a)(4) of this title, was amended generally by Pub. L. No. 104–150, § 4(1), 110 Stat. 1381 (June 3, 1996), and, as so amended, does not contain a par. (4).

As amended by this Act, referred to in subsecs. (a)(2), (c)(2)(B) and (h)(2), is a reference to the amendment of the Coastal Zone Management Act of 1972 by Pub. L. No. 101–508, Title VI, Subtitle C (section 6201 et seq.), 104 Stat. 1388–299 (Nov. 5, 1990), known as the Coastal Zone Act Reauthorization Amendments of 1990, which is codified generally to this chapter.

For complete classification of these Acts to the Code, see Short Title notes set out under section 1451 of this title and Tables.

Codifications

Section was enacted as part of the Coastal Zone Act Reauthorization Amendments of 1990, and not as part of the Coastal Zone Management Act of 1972, which comprises this chapter.

§ 1456. Coordination and cooperation

[CZMA § 307]

(a) Federal agencies

In carrying out his functions and responsibilities under this chapter, the Secretary shall consult with, cooperate with, and, to the maximum extent practicable, coordinate his activities with other interested Federal agencies.

(b) Adequate consideration of views of Federal agencies

The Secretary shall not approve the management program submitted by a state pursuant to section 1455 of this title unless the views of Federal agencies principally affected by such program have been adequately considered.

(c) Consistency of Federal activities with State management programs; Presidential exemption; certification

(1)(A) Each Federal agency activity within or outside the coastal zone that affects any land or water use or natural resource of the coastal zone shall be carried out in a manner which is consistent to the maximum extent practicable with the enforceable policies of approved State management programs. A Federal agency activity shall be subject to this paragraph unless it is subject to paragraph (2) or (3).

(B) After any final judgment, decree, or order of any Federal court that is appealable under section 1291 or 1292 of Title 28, or under any other applicable provision of Federal law, that a specific Federal agency activity is not in compliance with subparagraph (A), and certification by the Secretary that mediation under subsection (h) of this section is not likely to result in such compliance, the President may, upon written request from the Secretary, exempt from compliance those elements of the Federal agency activity that are found by the Federal court to be inconsistent with an approved State program, if the President determines that the activity is in the paramount interest of the United States. No such exemption shall be granted on the basis of a lack of appropriations unless the President has specifically requested such appropriations as part of the budgetary process, and the Congress has failed to make available the requested appropriations.

(C) Each Federal agency carrying out an activity subject to paragraph (1) shall provide a consistency determination to the relevant State agency designated under section 1455(d)(6) of this title at the earliest practicable time, but in no case later than 90 days before final approval of the Federal activity unless both the Federal agency and the State agency agree to a different schedule.

(2) Any Federal agency which shall undertake any development project in the coastal zone of a state shall insure that the project is, to the maximum extent practicable, consistent with the enforceable policies of approved state management programs.

(3)(A) After final approval by the Secretary of a state's management program, any applicant for a required Federal license or permit to conduct an activity, in or outside of the coastal zone, affecting any land or water use or natural resource of the coastal zone of that state shall provide in the application to the licensing or permitting agency a certification that the proposed activity complies with the enforceable policies of the state's approved program and that such activity will be conducted in a manner consistent with the program. At the same time, the applicant shall furnish to the state or its designated agency a copy of the certification, with all necessary information and data. Each coastal state shall establish procedures for public notice in the case of all such certifications and, to the extent it deems appropriate, procedures for public hearings in connection therewith. At the earliest practicable time, the state or its designated agency shall notify the Federal agency concerned that the state concurs with or objects to the applicant's certification. If the state or its designated agency fails to furnish the required notification within six months after receipt of its copy of the applicant's certification, the state's concurrence with the certification shall be conclusively presumed. No license or permit shall be granted by the Federal agency until the state or its designated agency has concurred with the applicant's certification or until, by the state's failure to act, the concurrence is conclusively presumed, unless the Secretary, on his own initiative or upon appeal by the applicant, finds, after providing a reasonable opportunity for detailed comments from the Federal agency involved and from the state, that the activity is consistent with the objectives of this chapter or is otherwise necessary in the interest of national security.

(B) After the management program of any coastal state has been approved by the Secretary under section 1455 of this title, any person who submits to the Secretary of the Interior any plan for the exploration or development of, or production from, any area which has been leased under the Outer Continental Shelf Lands Act (43 U.S.C. 1331 et seq.) and regulations under such Act shall, with respect to any exploration, development, or production described in such plan and affecting any land or water use or natural resource of the coastal zone of such state, attach to such plan a certification that each activity which is described in detail in such plan complies with the enforceable policies of such state's approved management program and will be carried out in a manner consistent with such program. No Federal official or agency shall grant such person any license or permit for any activity described in detail in such plan until such state or its designated agency receives a copy of such certification and plan, together with any other necessary data and information, and until—

(i) such state or its designated agency, in accordance with the procedures required to be established by such state pursuant to subparagraph (A), concurs with such person's certification and notifies the Secretary and the Secretary of the Interior of such concurrence;

(ii) concurrence by such state with such certification is conclusively presumed as provided for in subparagraph (A), except if such state fails to concur with or object to such certification within three months after receipt of its copy of such certification and supporting information, such state shall provide the Secretary, the appropriate federal agency, and such person with a written statement describing the status of review and the basis for further delay in issuing a final decision, and if such statement is not so provided, concurrence by such state with such certification shall be conclusively presumed; or

(iii) the Secretary finds, pursuant to subparagraph (A), that each activity which is described in detail in such plan is consistent with the objectives of this chapter or is otherwise necessary in the interest of national security.

If a state concurs or is conclusively presumed to concur, or if the Secretary makes such a finding, the provisions of subparagraph (A) are not applicable with respect to such person, such state, and any Federal license or permit which is required to conduct any activity affecting land uses or water uses in the coastal zone of such state which is described in detail in the plan to which such concurrence or finding applies. If such state objects to such certification and if the Secretary fails to make a finding under clause (iii) with respect to such certification, or if such person fails substantially to comply with such plan as submitted, such person shall submit an amendment to such plan, or a new plan, to the Secretary of the Interior. With respect to any amendment or new plan submitted to the Secretary of the Interior pursuant to the preceding sentence, the applicable time period for purposes of concurrence by conclusive presumption under subparagraph (A) is 3 months.

(d) Application of local governments for Federal assistance; relationship of activities with approved management programs

State and local governments submitting applications for Federal assistance under other Federal programs, in or outside of the coastal zone, affecting any land or water use of natural resource of the coastal zone shall indicate the views of the appropriate state or local agency as to the relationship of such activities to the approved management program for the coastal zone. Such applications shall be submitted and coordinated in accordance with the provisions of section 6506 of Title 31. Federal agencies shall not approve proposed projects that are inconsistent with the enforceable policies of a coastal state's management program, except upon a finding by the Secretary that such project is consistent with the purposes of this chapter or necessary in the interest of national security.

(e) Construction with other laws

Nothing in this chapter shall be construed—

(1) to diminish either Federal or state jurisdiction, responsibility, or rights in the field of planning, development, or control of water resources, submerged lands, or navigable waters; nor to displace, supersede, limit, or modify any interstate compact or the jurisdiction or responsibility of any legally established joint or common agency of two or more states or of two or more states and the Federal Government; nor to limit the authority of Congress to authorize and fund projects;

(2) as superseding, modifying, or repealing existing laws applicable to the various Federal agencies; nor to affect the jurisdiction, powers, or prerogatives of the International Joint Commission, United States and Canada, the Permanent Engineering Board, and the United States operating entity or entities established pursuant to the Columbia River Basin Treaty, signed at Washington, January 17, 1961, or the International Boundary and Water Commission, United States and Mexico.

(f) Construction with existing requirements of water and air pollution programs

Notwithstanding any other provision of this chapter, nothing in this chapter shall in any way affect any requirement (1) established by the Federal Water Pollution Control Act, as amended [33 U.S.C.A. § 1251 et seq.], or the Clean Air Act, as amended [42 U.S.C.A. § 7401 et seq.], or (2) established by the Federal Government or by any state or local government pursuant to such Acts. Such requirements shall be incorporated in any program developed pursuant to this chapter and shall be the water pollution control and air pollution control requirements applicable to such program.

(g) Concurrence with programs which affect inland areas

When any state's coastal zone management program, submitted for approval or proposed for modification pursuant to section 1455 of this title, includes requirements as to shorelands which also would be subject to any Federally supported national land use program which may be hereafter enacted, the Secretary, prior to approving such program, shall obtain the concurrence of the Secretary of the Interior, or such other Federal official as may be designated to administer the national land use program, with respect to that portion of the coastal zone management program affecting such inland areas.

(h) Mediation of disagreements

In case of serious disagreement between any Federal agency and a coastal state—

(1) in the development or the initial implementation of a management program under section 1454 of this title; or

(2) in the administration of a management program approved under section 1455 of this title;

the Secretary, with the cooperation of the Executive Office of the President, shall seek to mediate the differences involved in such disagreement. The process of such mediation shall, with respect to any disagreement described in paragraph (2), include public hearings which shall be conducted in the local area concerned.

(i) Application fee for appeals

(1) With respect to appeals under subsections (c)(3) and (d) of this section which are submitted after November 5, 1990, the Secretary shall collect an application fee of not less than $200 for minor appeals and not less than $500 for major appeals, unless the Secretary, upon consideration of an applicant's request for a fee waiver, determines that the applicant is unable to pay the fee.

(2)(A) The Secretary shall collect such other fees as are necessary to recover the full costs of administering and processing such appeals under subsection (c) of this section.

(B) If the Secretary waives the application fee under paragraph (1) for an applicant, the Secretary shall waive all other fees under this subsection for the applicant.

(3) Fees collected under this subsection shall be deposited into the Coastal Zone Management Fund established under section 1456a of this title.

(Pub. L. No. 89–454, Title III, § 307, as added by Pub. L. No. 92–583, 86 Stat. 1285 (Oct. 27, 1972); and amended by Pub. L. No. 94–370, § 6, 90 Stat. 1018 (July 26, 1976); Pub. L. No. 95–372, Title V, § 504, 92 Stat. 693 (Sept. 18, 1978); Pub. L. No. 101–508, Title VI, § 6208, 104 Stat. 1388–307 (Nov. 5, 1990); Pub. L. No. 102–587, Title II, § 2205(b)(13), (14), 106 Stat. 5051 (Nov. 4, 1992).)

HISTORICAL AND STATUTORY NOTES

References in Text

The Outer Continental Shelf Lands Act, referred to in subsec. (c)(3)(B), is Act Aug. 7, 1953, c. 345, 67 Stat. 462, as amended, which is codified generally to subchapter III (section 1331 et seq.) of chapter 29 of Title 43, Public Lands. For complete classification of this Act to the Code, see Short Title note set out under section 1331 of Title 43 and Tables.

The Federal Water Pollution Control Act, referred to in subsec. (f), is Act of June 30, 1948, c. 758, as amended generally by Pub. L. No. 92–500, § 2, 86 Stat. 816 (Oct. 18, 1972), which is codified generally to chapter 26 (section 1251 et seq.) of Title 33, Navigation and Navigable Waters. For complete classification of this Act to the Code, see Short Title note set out under section 1251 of Title 33 and Tables.

The Clean Air Act, referred to in subsec. (f), is Act of July 14, 1955, c. 360, as amended generally by Pub. L. No. 88–206, 77 Stat. 392 (Dec. 17, 1963), and later by Pub. L. No. 95–95, 91 Stat. 685 (Aug. 7, 1977). The Clean Air Act was originally codified as chapter 15B (section 1857 et seq.) of Title 42, The Public Health and Welfare. On enactment of Pub. L. No. 95–95, the Act was recodified as chapter 85 (section 7401 et seq.) of Title 42. For complete classification of this Act to the Code, see Short Title note set out under section 7401 of Title 42 and Tables.

Codifications

Amendment of subsec. (c)(3)(B) by Pub. L. No. 101–508, Title VI, § 6208(b)(3), was executed following "with," notwithstanding directory language which recited that it be executed following "complies," as the probable intent of Congress.

In subsec. (d), "section 6506 of Title 31" was substituted for "Title IV of the Intergovernmental Coordination [Cooperation] Act of 1968 [42 U.S.C.A. § 4231 et seq.]" on authority of Pub. L. No. 97–258, § 4(b), 96 Stat. 1067 (Sept. 13, 1982), the first section of which enacted Title 31, Money and Finance.

§ 1456a. Coastal Zone Management Fund

[CZMA § 308]

(a)(1) The obligations of any coastal state or unit of general purpose local government to repay loans made pursuant to this section as in effect before November 5, 1990, and any repayment schedule established pursuant to this chapter as in effect before November 5, 1990, are not altered by any provision of this chapter. Such loans shall be repaid under authority of this subsection and the Secretary may issue regulations governing such repayment. If the Secretary finds that any coastal state or unit of local government is unable to meet its obligations pursuant to this subsection because the actual increases in employment and related population resulting from coastal energy activity and the facilities associated with such activity do not provide adequate revenues to enable such State or unit to meet such obligations in accordance with the appropriate repayment schedule, the Secretary shall, after review of the information submitted by such State or unit, take any of the following actions:

(A) Modify the terms and conditions of such loan.

(B) Refinance the loan.

(C) Recommend to the Congress that legislation be enacted to forgive the loan.

(2) Loan repayments made pursuant to this subsection shall be retained by the Secretary as offsetting collections, and shall be deposited into the Coastal Zone Management Fund established under subsection (b) of this section.

(b)(1) The Secretary shall establish and maintain a fund, to be known as the "Coastal Zone Management Fund", which shall consist of amounts retained and deposited into the Fund under subsection (a) of this section and fees deposited into the Fund under section 1456(i)(3) of this title.

(2) Subject to amounts provided in appropriation Acts, amounts in the Fund shall be available to the Secretary for use for the following:

(A) Expenses incident to the administration of this chapter, in an amount not to exceed for each of fiscal years 1997, 1998, and 1999 the higher of—

(i) $4,000,000; or

(ii) 8 percent of the total amount appropriated under this chapter for the fiscal year.

(B) After use under subparagraph (A)—

(i) projects to address management issues which are regional in scope, including interstate projects;

(ii) demonstration projects which have high potential for improving coastal zone management, especially at the local level;

(iii) emergency grants to State coastal zone management agencies to address unforeseen or disaster-related circumstances;

(iv) appropriate awards recognizing excellence in coastal zone management as provided in section 1460 of this title; and

(v) to provide financial support to coastal states for use for investigating and applying the public trust doctrine to implement State management programs approved under section 1455 of this title.

(Pub. L. No. 89–454, Title III, § 308, as added by Pub. L. No. 94–370, § 7, 90 Stat. 1019 (July 26, 1976); and amended by Pub. L. No. 95–372, Title V, §§ 501, 503(a) to (d), 92 Stat. 690, 692, 693 (Sept. 18, 1978); Pub. L. No. 96–464, § 7, 94 Stat. 2064 (Oct. 17, 1980); Pub. L. No. 99–272, Title VI, § 6047, 100 Stat. 128 (Apr. 7, 1986); Pub. L. No. 101–508, Title VI, § 6209, 104 Stat. 1388–308 (Nov. 5, 1990); Pub. L. No. 102–587, Title II, § 2205(b)(1)(A),

(B), (15) to (18), 106 Stat. 5050, 5052 (Nov. 4, 1992); Pub. L. No. 104–150, §§ 2(b)(2), 5, 110 Stat. 1380, 1381 (June 3, 1996).)

HISTORICAL AND STATUTORY NOTES

Codifications

Section 2(b)(2) of Pub. L. No. 104–150 directed the amendment of section 308(b)(2)(B) of the Coastal Zone Management Act of 1972 (16 U.S.C. 1457(b)(2)(B)). Section 308 of such Act is section 308 of Pub. L. No. 89–454, Title III, as added Pub. L. No. 94–370, § 7, 90 Stat. 1019 (July 26, 1976), as amended, which is codified as section 1456a of this title [this section]. Such amendment was executed to this section as the probable intent of Congress.

Section 1460 of this title, referred to in subsec. (b)(2)(B)(iv), was in the original section 314. Translation was made to section 1460 of this title as the probable intent of Congress.

Effective and Applicability Provisions

1996 Acts. Amendments by section 2(b)(2) of Pub. L. No. 104–150 effective Oct. 1, 1999, see section 2(b)(3) of Pub. L. No. 104–150, set out as a note under section 1454 of this title.

Rescission of Balances

Pub. L. No. 112–55, Div. B, Title I, § 109, 125 Stat. 602 (Nov. 18, 2011), provided that: "All balances in the Coastal Zone Management Fund, whether unobligated or unavailable, are hereby permanently rescinded, and notwithstanding section 308(b) of the Coastal Zone Management Act of 1972, as amended (16 U.S.C. 1456a), any future payments to the Fund made pursuant to sections 307 (16 U.S.C. 1456) and 308 (16 U.S.C. 1456a) of the Coastal Zone Management Act of 1972, as amended, shall, in this fiscal year and any future fiscal years, be treated in accordance with the Federal Credit Reform Act of 1990, as amended [Pub. L. No. 93–344, Title V, as added by Pub. L. No. 101–508, Title XIII, § 13201(a), 104 Stat. 1388–609 (Nov. 5, 1990), enacting subchapter III of chapter 17A of Title 2, 2 U.S.C.A. § 661 et seq.]."

Extension of Loan Making Authority Under Subsection (d)(1); Amount of Loan

Pub. L. No. 99–626, § 6, 100 Stat. 3506 (Nov. 7, 1986), provided that: "The authority of the Secretary of Commerce to make loans under paragraph (1) of subsection (d) of section 308 of the Coastal Zone Management Act of 1972 (Public Law 92–583, 16 U.S.C. 1451, et seq.) as amended [subsec. (d)(1) of this section], shall extend to September 30, 1987, for loans made to eligible States or units pursuant to and in accord with agreements entered into between the Secretary and any State prior to September 30, 1986, that provided for a total sum of loans to be made to that State or its units, but such loan authority shall be limited to $7,000,000."

§ 1456b. Coastal zone enhancement grants

[CZMA § 309]

(a) "Coastal zone enhancement objective" defined

For purposes of this section, the term "coastal zone enhancement objective" means any of the following objectives:

(1) Protection, restoration, or enhancement of the existing coastal wetlands base, or creation of new coastal wetlands.

(2) Preventing or significantly reducing threats to life and destruction of property by eliminating development and redevelopment in high-hazard areas, managing development in other hazard areas, and anticipating and managing the effects of potential sea level rise and Great Lakes level rise.

(3) Attaining increased opportunities for public access, taking into account current and future public access needs, to coastal areas of recreational, historical, aesthetic, ecological, or cultural value.

(4) Reducing marine debris entering the Nation's coastal and ocean environment by managing uses and activities that contribute to the entry of such debris.

(5) Development and adoption of procedures to assess, consider, and control cumulative and secondary impacts of coastal growth and development, including the collective effect on various individual uses or activities on coastal resources, such as coastal wetlands and fishery resources.

(6) Preparing and implementing special area management plans for important coastal areas.

(7) Planning for the use of ocean resources.

(8) Adoption of procedures and enforceable policies to help facilitate the siting of energy facilities and Government facilities and energy-related activities and Government activities which may be of greater than local significance.

(9) Adoption of procedures and policies to evaluate and facilitate the siting of public and private aquaculture facilities in the coastal zone, which will enable States to formulate, administer, and implement strategic plans for marine aquaculture.

(b) Limits on grants

(1) Subject to the limitations and goals established in this section, the Secretary may make grants to coastal states to provide funding for development and submission for Federal approval of program changes that support attainment of one or more coastal zone enhancement objectives.

(2)(A) In addition to any amounts provided under section 1455 of this title, and subject to the availability of appropriations, the Secretary may make grants under this subsection to States for implementing program changes approved by the Secretary in accordance with section 1455(e) of this title.

(B) Grants under this paragraph to implement a program change may not be made in any fiscal year after the second fiscal year that begins after the approval of that change by the Secretary.

(c) Evaluation of State proposals by Secretary

The Secretary shall evaluate and rank State proposals for funding under this section, and make funding awards based on those proposals, taking into account the criteria established by the Secretary under subsection (d) of this section. The Secretary shall ensure that funding decisions under this section take into consideration the fiscal and technical needs of proposing States and the overall merit of each proposal in terms of benefits to the public.

(d) Promulgation of regulations by Secretary

Within 12 months following November 5, 1990, and consistent with the notice and participation requirements established in section 1463 of this title, the Secretary shall promulgate regulations concerning coastal zone enhancement grants that establish—

(1) specific and detailed criteria that must be addressed by a coastal state (including the State's priority needs for improvement as identified by the Secretary after careful consultation with the State) as part of the State's development and implementation of coastal zone enhancement objectives;

(2) administrative or procedural rules or requirements as necessary to facilitate the development and implementation of such objectives by coastal states; and

(3) other funding award criteria as are necessary or appropriate to ensure that evaluations of proposals, and decisions to award funding, under this section are based on objective standards applied fairly and equitably to those proposals.

(e) No State contribution required

A State shall not be required to contribute any portion of the cost of any proposal for which funding is awarded under this section.

(f) Funding

Beginning in fiscal year 1991, not less than 10 percent and not more than 20 percent of the amounts appropriated to implement sections 1455 and 1455a of this title shall be retained by the Secretary for use in implementing this section, up to a maximum of $10,000,000 annually.

(g) Eligibility; suspension of State for noncompliance

If the Secretary finds that the State is not undertaking the actions committed to under the terms of the grant, the Secretary shall suspend the State's eligibility for further funding under this section for at least one year.

(Pub. L. No. 89–454, Title III, § 309, as added by Pub. L. No. 94–370, § 8, 90 Stat. 1028 (July 26, 1976); and amended by Pub. L. No. 96–464, § 8, 94 Stat. 2064 (Oct. 17, 1980); Pub. L. No. 101–508, Title VI, § 6210, 104 Stat. 1388–309 (Nov. 5, 1990); Pub. L. No. 102–587, Title II, § 2205(b)(1)(B), 106 Stat. 5050 (Nov. 4, 1992); Pub. L. No. 104–150, §§ 3, 7(2), 110 Stat. 1380, 1382 (June 3, 1996).)

HISTORICAL AND STATUTORY NOTES

Codifications

Section 6210 of Pub. L. No. 101–508 directed the amendment of section 309 of the Coastal Zone Management Act of 1972 (16 U.S.C. 1452b). Section 309 of such Act is this section, and such amendment was executed to this section as the probable intent of Congress.

§ 1456c. Technical assistance

[CZMA § 310]

(a) The Secretary shall conduct a program of technical assistance and management-oriented research necessary to support the development and implementation of State coastal management program amendments under section 1456b of this title, and appropriate to the furtherance of international cooperative efforts and technical assistance in coastal zone management. Each department, agency, and instrumentality of the executive branch of the Federal Government may assist the Secretary, on a reimbursable basis or otherwise, in carrying out the purposes of this section, including the furnishing of information to the extent permitted by law, the transfer of personnel with their consent and without prejudice to their position and rating, and the performance of any research, study, and technical assistance which does not interfere with the performance of the primary duties of such department, agency, or instrumentality. The Secretary may enter into contracts or other arrangements with any qualified person for the purposes of carrying out this subsection.

(b)(1) The Secretary shall provide for the coordination of technical assistance, studies, and research activities under this section with any other such activities that are conducted by or subject to the authority of the Secretary.

(2) The Secretary shall make the results of research and studies conducted pursuant to this section available to coastal states in the form of technical assistance publications, workshops, or other means appropriate.

(3) The Secretary shall consult with coastal states on a regular basis regarding the development and implementation of the program established by this section.

(Pub. L. No. 89–454, Title III, § 310, as added by Pub. L. No. 101–508, Title VI, § 6211, 104 Stat. 1388–311 (Nov. 5, 1990).)

HISTORICAL AND STATUTORY NOTES

Prior Provisions

A prior section 1456c, Pub. L. No. 89–454, Title III, § 310, as added by Pub. L. No. 94–370, § 9, 90 Stat. 1029 (July 26, 1976), which related to research and technical assistance for coastal zone management, was repealed by Pub. L. No. 99–272, Title VI, § 6045(1), 100 Stat. 127 (Apr. 7, 1986).

§ 1456d. Coastal and Estuarine Land Conservation Program

The Secretary shall establish a Coastal and Estuarine Land Conservation Program, for the purpose of protecting important coastal and estuarine areas that have significant conservation, recreation, ecological, historical, or aesthetic values, or that are threatened by conversion from their natural or recreational state to other uses: *Provided further,* That by September 30, 2002, the Secretary shall issue guidelines for this program delineating the criteria for grant awards: *Provided further,* That the Secretary shall distribute these funds in consultation with the States' Coastal Zone Managers' or Governors' designated representatives based on demonstrated need and ability to successfully leverage funds, and shall give priority to lands which can be effectively managed and protected and which have significant ecological value: *Provided further,* That grants funded under this program shall require a 100 percent match from other sources.

(Pub. L. No. 107–77, Title II, 115 Stat. 776 (Nov. 28, 2001).)

HISTORICAL AND STATUTORY NOTES

Codifications

This section was enacted as part of the Department of Commerce and Related Agencies Appropriations Act, 2002, and also as part of the Departments of Commerce, Justice and State, the Judiciary, and Related Agencies Appropriations Act, 2002, and not as part of the Coastal Zone Management Act of 1972 which comprises this chapter.

National Oceanic and Atmospheric Administration, Procurement, Acquisition and Construction

Pub. L. No. 108–7, Div. B, Title II, 117 Stat. 75 (Feb. 20, 2003), provided in part: "That the Secretary shall establish a Coastal and Estuarine Land Conservation Program, for the purpose of protecting important coastal and estuarine areas that have significant conservation, recreation, ecological, historical, or aesthetic values, or that are threatened by conversion from their natural or recreational state to other uses."

Similar provisions were contained in the following Appropriations Acts: Pub. L. No. 107–77, Title II, 115 Stat. 776 (Nov. 28, 2001).

§ 1456–1. Authorization of the Coastal and Estuarine Land Conservation Program

[CZMA § 307A]

(a) In general

The Secretary may conduct a Coastal and Estuarine Land Conservation Program, in cooperation with appropriate State, regional, and other units of government, for the purposes of protecting important coastal and estuarine areas that have significant conservation, recreation, ecological, historical, or aesthetic values, or that are threatened by conversion from their natural, undeveloped, or recreational state to other uses or could be managed or restored to effectively conserve, enhance, or restore ecological function. The program shall be administered by the National Ocean Service of the National Oceanic and Atmospheric Administration through the Office of Ocean and Coastal Resource Management.

(b) Property acquisition grants

The Secretary shall make grants under the program to coastal states with approved coastal zone management plans or National Estuarine Research Reserve units for the purpose of acquiring property or interests in property described in subsection (a) that will further the goals of—

(1) a Coastal Zone Management Plan or Program approved under this chapter;

(2) a National Estuarine Research Reserve management plan;

(3) a regional or State watershed protection or management plan involving coastal states with approved coastal zone management programs; or

(4) a State coastal land acquisition plan that is consistent with an approved coastal zone management program.

(c) Grant process

The Secretary shall allocate funds to coastal states or National Estuarine Research Reserves under this section through a competitive grant process in accordance with guidelines that meet the following requirements:

(1) The Secretary shall consult with the coastal state's coastal zone management program, any National Estuarine Research Reserve in that State, and the lead agency designated by the Governor for coordinating the implementation of this section (if different from the coastal zone management program).

(2) Each participating coastal state, after consultation with local governmental entities and other interested stakeholders, shall identify priority conservation needs within the State, the values to be protected by inclusion of lands in the program, and the threats to those values that should be avoided.

(3) Each participating coastal state shall to the extent practicable ensure that the acquisition of property or easements shall complement working waterfront needs.

(4) The applicant shall identify the values to be protected by inclusion of the lands in the program, management activities that are planned and the manner in which they may affect the values identified, and any other information from the landowner relevant to administration and management of the land.

(5) Awards shall be based on demonstrated need for protection and ability to successfully leverage funds among participating entities, including Federal programs, regional organizations, State and other governmental units, landowners, corporations, or private organizations.

(6) The governor, or the lead agency designated by the governor for coordinating the implementation of this section, where appropriate in consultation with the appropriate local government, shall determine that the application is consistent with the State's or territory's approved coastal zone plan, program, and policies prior to submittal to the Secretary.

(7)(A) Priority shall be given to lands described in subsection (a) that can be effectively managed and protected and that have significant ecological value.

(B) Of the projects that meet the standard in subparagraph (A), priority shall be given to lands that—

(i) are under an imminent threat of conversion to a use that will degrade or otherwise diminish their natural, undeveloped, or recreational state; and

(ii) serve to mitigate the adverse impacts caused by coastal population growth in the coastal environment.

(8) In developing guidelines under this section, the Secretary shall consult with coastal states, other Federal agencies, and other interested stakeholders with expertise in land acquisition and conservation procedures.

(9) Eligible coastal states or National Estuarine Research Reserves may allocate grants to local governments or agencies eligible for assistance under section 1455a(e) of this title.

(10) The Secretary shall develop performance measures that the Secretary shall use to evaluate and report on the program's effectiveness in accomplishing its purposes, and shall submit such evaluations to Congress triennially.

(d) Limitations and private property protections

(1) A grant awarded under this section may be used to purchase land or an interest in land, including an easement, only from a willing seller. Any such purchase shall not be the result of a forced taking under this section. Nothing in this section requires a private property owner to participate in the program under this section.

(2) Any interest in land, including any easement, acquired with a grant under this section shall not be considered to create any new liability, or have any effect on liability under any other law, of any private property owner with respect to any person injured on the private property.

(3) Nothing in this section requires a private property owner to provide access (including Federal, State, or local government access) to or use of private property unless such property or an interest in such property (including a conservation easement) has been purchased with funds made available under this section.

(e) Recognition of authority to control land use

Nothing in this chapter modifies the authority of Federal, State, or local governments to regulate land use.

(f) Matching requirements

(1) In general

The Secretary may not make a grant under the program unless the Federal funds are matched by non-Federal funds in accordance with this subsection.

(2) Cost share requirement

(A) In general

Grant funds under the program shall require a 100 percent match from other non-Federal sources.

(B) Waiver of requirement

The Secretary may grant a waiver of subparagraph (A) for underserved communities, communities that have an inability to draw on other sources of funding because of the small population or low income of the community, or for other reasons the Secretary deems appropriate and consistent with the purposes of the program.

(3) Other Federal funds

Where financial assistance awarded under this section represents only a portion of the total cost of a project, funding from other Federal sources may be applied to the cost of the project. Each portion shall be subject to match requirements under the applicable provision of law.

(4) Source of matching cost share

For purposes of paragraph (2)(A), the non-Federal cost share for a project may be determined by taking into account the following:

(A) The value of land or a conservation easement may be used by a project applicant as non-Federal match, if the Secretary determines that—

(i) the land meets the criteria set forth in section 2(b)[1] and is acquired in the period beginning 3 years before the date of the submission of the grant application and ending 3 years after the date of the award of the grant;

(ii) the value of the land or easement is held by a non-governmental organization included in the grant application in perpetuity for conservation purposes of the program; and

(iii) the land or easement is connected either physically or through a conservation planning process to the land or easement that would be acquired.

(B) The appraised value of the land or conservation easement at the time of the grant closing will be considered and applied as the non-Federal cost share.

(C) costs associated with land acquisition, land management planning, remediation, restoration, and enhancement may be used as non-Federal match if the activities are identified in the plan and expenses are incurred within the period of the grant award, or, for lands described in (A)[1], within the same time limits described therein. These costs may include either cash or in-kind contributions.

(g) Reservation of funds for National Estuarine Research Reserve sites

No less than 15 percent of funds made available under this section shall be available for acquisitions benefitting National Estuarine Research Reserves.

(h) Limit on administrative costs

No more than 5 percent of the funds made available to the Secretary under this section shall be used by the Secretary for planning or administration of the program. The Secretary shall provide a report to Congress with an account of all expenditures under this section for fiscal year 2009 and triennially thereafter.

(i) Title and management of acquired property

If any property is acquired in whole or in part with funds made available through a grant under this section, the grant recipient shall provide—

(1) such assurances as the Secretary may require that—[1]

(A) the title to the property will be held by the grant recipient or another appropriate public agency designated by the recipient in perpetuity;

(B) the property will be managed in a manner that is consistent with the purposes for which the land entered into the program and shall not convert such property to other uses; and

(C) if the property or interest in land is sold, exchanged, or divested, funds equal to the current value will be returned to the Secretary in accordance with applicable Federal law for redistribution in the grant process; and

(2) certification that the property (including any interest in land) will be acquired from a willing seller.

(j) Requirement for property used for non-Federal match

If the grant recipient elects to use any land or interest in land held by a non-governmental organization as a non-Federal match under subsection (g), the grant recipient must to the Secretary's satisfaction demonstrate in the grant application that such land or interest will satisfy the same requirements as the lands or interests in lands acquired under the program.

(k) Definitions

In this section:

(1) Conservation easement

The term "conservation easement" includes an easement or restriction, recorded deed, or a reserve interest deed where the grantee acquires all rights, title, and interest in a property, that do not conflict with the goals of this section except those rights, title, and interests that may run with the land that are expressly reserved by a grantor and are agreed to at the time of purchase.

(2) Interest in property

The term "interest in property" includes a conservation easement.

(*l*) Authorization of appropriations

There are authorized to be appropriated to the Secretary to carry out this section $60,000,000 for each of fiscal years 2009 through 2013.

(Pub. L. No. 89–454, Title III, § 307A, as added by Pub. L. No. 111–11, Title XII, § 12502, 123 Stat. 1442 (Mar. 30, 2009).)

[1] So in original.

HISTORICAL AND STATUTORY NOTES

References in Text

This chapter, referred to in text, originally read "this title", meaning Title III of Pub. L. No. 89–454, known as the Coastal Zone Management Act of 1972, as amended, which is principally codified as this chapter. For complete classification, see Short Title note set out under 42 U.S.C.A. § 1451 and Tables.

§ 1457. Public hearings

[CZMA § 311]

All public hearings required under this chapter must be announced at least thirty days prior to the hearing date. At the time of the announcement, all agency materials pertinent to the hearings, including documents, studies, and other data, must be made available to the public for review and study. As similar materials are subsequently developed, they shall be made available to the public as they become available to the agency.

(Pub. L. No. 89–454, Title III, § 311, formerly, § 308, as added by Pub. L. No. 92–583, 86 Stat. 1287 (Oct. 27, 1972), and renumbered by Pub. L. No. 94–370, § 7, 90 Stat. 1019 (July 26, 1976).)

§ 1458. Review of performance

[CZMA § 312]

(a) Evaluation of adherence with terms of grants

The Secretary shall conduct a continuing review of the performance of coastal states with respect to coastal management. Each review shall include a written evaluation with an assessment and detailed findings concerning the extent to which the state has implemented and enforced the program approved by the Secretary, addressed the coastal management needs identified in section 1452(2)(A) through (K) of this title, and adhered to the terms of any grant, loan, or cooperative agreement funded under this chapter.

(b) Public participation; notice of meetings; reports

In evaluating a coastal state's performance, the Secretary shall conduct the evaluation in an open and public manner, and provide full opportunity for public participation, including holding public meetings in the State being evaluated and providing opportunities for the submission of written and oral comments by the public. The Secretary shall provide the public with at least 45 days' notice of such public meetings by placing a notice in the Federal Register, by publication of timely notices in newspapers of general circulation within the State being evaluated, and by communications with persons and organizations known to be interested in the evaluation. Each evaluation shall be prepared in report form and shall include written responses to the written comments received during the evaluation process. The final report of the evaluation shall be completed within 120 days after the last public meeting held in the State being evaluated. Copies of the evaluation shall be immediately provided to all persons and organizations participating in the evaluation process.

(c) Suspension of financial assistance for noncompliance; notification of Governor; length of suspension

(1) The Secretary may suspend payment of any portion of financial assistance extended to any coastal state under this chapter, and may withdraw any unexpended portion of such assistance, if the Secretary determines that the coastal state is failing to adhere to (A) the management program or a State plan developed to manage a national estuarine reserve established under section 1461 of this title, or a portion of the program or plan approved by the Secretary, or (B) the terms of any grant or cooperative agreement funded under this chapter.

(2) Financial assistance may not be suspended under paragraph (1) unless the Secretary provides the Governor of the coastal state with—

(A) written specifications and a schedule for the actions that should be taken by the State in order that such suspension of financial assistance may be withdrawn; and

(B) written specifications stating how those funds from the suspended financial assistance shall be expended by the coastal state to take the actions referred to in subparagraph (A).

(3) The suspension of financial assistance may not last for less than 6 months or more than 36 months after the date of suspension.

(d) Withdrawal of approval of program

The Secretary shall withdraw approval of the management program of any coastal state and shall withdraw financial assistance available to that State under this chapter as well as any unexpended portion of such assistance, if the Secretary determines that the coastal state has failed to take the actions referred to in subsection (c)(2)(A) of this section.

(e) Notice and hearing

Management program approval and financial assistance may not be withdrawn under subsection (d) of this section, unless the Secretary gives the coastal state notice of the proposed withdrawal and an opportunity for a public hearing on the proposed action. Upon the withdrawal of management program approval under this subsection (d) of this section, the Secretary shall provide the coastal state with written specifications of the actions that should be taken, or not engaged in, by the state in order that such withdrawal may be canceled by the Secretary.

(Pub. L. No. 89–454, Title III, § 312, formerly § 309, as added by Pub. L. No. 92–583, 86 Stat. 1287 (Oct. 27, 1972), and renumbered and amended by Pub. L. No. 94–370, §§ 7, 10, 90 Stat. 1019, 1029 (July 26, 1976); Pub. L. No. 96–464, § 9(a), 94 Stat. 2065 (Oct. 17, 1980); Pub. L. No. 99–272, Title VI, § 6043(a), 100 Stat. 124 (Apr. 7, 1986); Pub. L. No. 101–508, Title VI, §§ 6212, 6216(b), 104 Stat. 1388–311, 1388–314 (Nov. 5, 1990); Pub. L. No. 102–587, Title II, § 2205(b)(1)(A), (C), 106 Stat. 5050 (Nov. 4, 1992).)

HISTORICAL AND STATUTORY NOTES

Issuance of Regulations

Section 9(b) of Pub. L. No. 96–464 provided that: "Within two hundred and seventy days after the date of the enactment of this Act [Oct. 17, 1980], the Secretary of Commerce shall issue such regulations as may be necessary or appropriate to administer section 312 of the Coastal Zone Management Act of 1972 (as amended by subsection (a) of this section) [this section]."

§ 1459. Records and audit

[CZMA § 313]

(a) Maintenance of records by recipients of grants or financial assistance

Each recipient of a grant under this chapter or of financial assistance under section 1456a of this title, as in effect before November 5, 1990, shall keep such records as the Secretary shall prescribe, including records which fully disclose the amount and disposition of the funds received under the grant and of the proceeds of such assistance, the total cost of the project or undertaking supplied by other sources, and such other records as will facilitate an effective audit.

(b) Access by Secretary and Comptroller General to records, books, etc., of recipients of grants or financial assistance for audit and examination

The Secretary and the Comptroller General of the United States, or any of their duly authorized representatives, shall—

(1) after any grant is made under this chapter or any financial assistance is provided under section 1456a of this title, as in effect before November 5, 1990; and

(2) until the expiration of 3 years after—

(A) completion of the project, program, or other undertaking for which such grant was made or used, or

(B) repayment of the loan or guaranteed indebtedness for which such financial assistance was provided,

have access for purposes of audit and examination to any record, book, document, and paper which belongs to or is used or controlled by, any recipient of the grant funds or any person who entered into any transaction relating to such financial assistance and which is pertinent for purposes of determining if the grant funds or the proceeds of such financial assistance are being, or were, used in accordance with the provisions of this chapter.

(Pub. L. No. 89–454, Title III, § 313, formerly § 310, as added by Pub. L. No. 92–583, 86 Stat. 1287 (Oct. 27, 1972); and renumbered and amended by Pub. L. No. 94–370, §§ 7, 11, 90 Stat. 1019, 1030 (July 26, 1976); Pub. L. No. 102–587, Title II, § 2205(b)(19), 106 Stat. 5052 (Nov. 4, 1992).)

HISTORICAL AND STATUTORY NOTES

Codifications

Another section 313 of Pub. L. No. 89–454, Title III, as added by Pub. L. No. 101–508, Title VI, § 6213, 104 Stat. 1388–312 (Nov. 5, 1990), is codified as section 1460 of this title.

§ 1460. Walter B. Jones excellence in coastal zone management awards

[CZMA § 314]

(a) Establishment

The Secretary shall, using sums in the Coastal Zone Management Fund established under section 1456a of this title and other amounts available to carry out this chapter (other than amounts appropriated to carry out sections 1454, 1455, 1455a, 1456b, 1456c, and 1461 of this title), implement a program to promote excellence in coastal zone management by identifying and acknowledging outstanding accomplishments in the field.

(b) Annual selection of recipients

The Secretary shall select annually—

(1) one individual, other than an employee or officer of the Federal Government, whose contribution to the field of coastal zone management has been the most significant;

(2) 5 local governments which have made the most progress in developing and implementing the coastal zone management principles embodied in this chapter; and

(3) up to 10 graduate students whose academic study promises to contribute materially to development of new or improved approaches to coastal zone management.

(c) Solicitation of nominations for local government recipients

In making selections under subsection (b)(2) of this section the Secretary shall solicit nominations from the coastal states, and shall consult with experts in local government planning and land use.

(d) Solicitation of nominations for graduate student recipients

In making selections under subsection (b)(3) of this section the Secretary shall solicit nominations from coastal states and the National Sea Grant College Program.

(e) Funding; types of awards

Using sums in the Coastal Zone Management Fund established under section 1456a of this title and other amounts available to carry out this chapter (other than amounts appropriated to carry out sections 1454, 1455, 1455a, 1456b, 1456c, and 1461 of this title), the Secretary shall establish and execute appropriate awards, to be known as the "Walter B. Jones Awards," including—

(1) cash awards in an amount not to exceed $5,000 each;

(2) research grants; and

(3) public ceremonies to acknowledge such awards.

(Pub. L. No. 89–454, Title III, § 314, formerly § 313, as added by Pub. L. No. 101–508, Title VI, § 6213, 104 Stat. 1388–312 (Nov. 5, 1990); and renumbered § 314 and amended by Pub. L. No. 102–587, Title II, § 2205(b)(20), 106 Stat. 5052 (Nov. 4, 1992).)

HISTORICAL AND STATUTORY NOTES

Prior Provisions

A prior section 1460, Pub. L. No. 89–454, Title III, § 314, formerly § 311, as added by Pub. L. No. 92–583, 86 Stat. 1287 (Oct. 27, 1972), and renumbered by Pub. L. No. 94–370, § 7, 90 Stat. 1019 (July 26, 1976), which related to the establishment of the Coastal Zone Management Advisory Committee, was repealed by Pub. L. No. 99–272, Title VI, § 6045(2), 100 Stat. 127 (Apr. 7, 1986).

§ 1461. National Estuarine Research Reserve System

[CZMA § 315]

(a) Establishment of System

There is established the National Estuarine Research Reserve System (hereinafter referred to in this section as the "System") that consists of—

(1) each estuarine sanctuary designated under this section as in effect before April 7, 1986; and

(2) each estuarine area designated as a national estuarine reserve under subsection (b) of this section.

Each estuarine sanctuary referred to in paragraph (1) is hereby designated as a national estuarine reserve.

(b) Designation of national estuarine reserves

After April 7, 1986, the Secretary may designate an estuarine area as a national estuarine reserve if—

(1) the Governor of the coastal state in which the area is located nominates the area for that designation; and

(2) the Secretary finds that—

(A) the area is a representative estuarine ecosystem that is suitable for long-term research and contributes to the biogeographical and typological balance of the System;

(B) the law of the coastal state provides long-term protection for reserve resources to ensure a stable environment for research;

(C) designation of the area as a reserve will serve to enhance public awareness and understanding of estuarine areas, and provide suitable opportunities for public education and interpretation; and

(D) the coastal state in which the area is located has complied with the requirements of any regulations issued by the Secretary to implement this section.

(c) Estuarine research guidelines

The Secretary shall develop guidelines for the conduct of research within the System that shall include—

(1) a mechanism for identifying, and establishing priorities among, the coastal management issues that should be addressed through coordinated research within the System;

(2) the establishment of common research principles and objectives to guide the development of research programs within the System;

(3) the identification of uniform research methodologies which will ensure comparability of data, the broadest application of research results, and the maximum use of the System for research purposes;

(4) the establishment of performance standards upon which the effectiveness of the research efforts and the value of reserves within the System in addressing the coastal management issues identified in paragraph (1) may be measured; and

(5) the consideration of additional sources of funds for estuarine research than the funds authorized under this chapter, and strategies for encouraging the use of such funds within the System, with particular emphasis on mechanisms established under subsection (d) of this section.

In developing the guidelines under this section, the Secretary shall consult with prominent members of the estuarine research community.

(d) Promotion and coordination of estuarine research

The Secretary shall take such action as is necessary to promote and coordinate the use of the System for research purposes including—

(1) requiring that the National Oceanic and Atmospheric Administration, in conducting or supporting estuarine research, give priority consideration to research that uses the System; and

(2) consulting with other Federal and State agencies to promote use of one or more reserves within the System by such agencies when conducting estuarine research.

(e) Financial assistance

(1) The Secretary may, in accordance with such rules and regulations as the Secretary shall promulgate, make grants—

(A) to a coastal state—

(i) for purposes of acquiring such lands and waters, and any property interests therein, as are necessary to ensure the appropriate long-term management of an area as a national estuarine reserve,

(ii) for purposes of operating or managing a national estuarine reserve and constructing appropriate reserve facilities, or

(iii) for purposes of conducting educational or interpretive activities; and

(B) to any coastal state or public or private person for purposes of supporting research and monitoring within a national estuarine reserve that are consistent with the research guidelines developed under subsection (c) of this section.

(2) Financial assistance provided under paragraph (1) shall be subject to such terms and conditions as the Secretary considers necessary or appropriate to protect the interests of the United States, including requiring coastal states to execute suitable title documents setting forth the property interest or interests of the United States in any lands and waters acquired in whole or part with such financial assistance.

(3)(A) The amount of the financial assistance provided under paragraph (1)(A)(i) with respect to the acquisition of lands and waters, or interests therein, for any one national estuarine reserve may not exceed an amount equal to 50 percent of the costs of the lands, waters, and interests therein or $5,000,000, whichever amount is less.

(B) The amount of the financial assistance provided under paragraph (1)(A)(ii) and (iii) and paragraph (1)(B) may not exceed 70 percent of the costs incurred to achieve the purposes described in those paragraphs with respect to a reserve; except that the amount of the financial assistance provided under paragraph (1)(A)(iii) may be up to 100 percent of any costs for activities that benefit the entire System.

(C) Notwithstanding subparagraphs (A) and (B), financial assistance under this subsection provided from amounts recovered as a result of damage to natural resources located in the coastal zone may be used to pay 100 percent of the costs of activities carried out with the assistance.

(f) Evaluation of System performance

(1) The Secretary shall periodically evaluate the operation and management of each national estuarine reserve, including education and interpretive activities, and the research being conducted within the reserve.

(2) If evaluation under paragraph (1) reveals that the operation and management of the reserve is deficient, or that the research being conducted within the reserve is not consistent with the research guidelines developed under subsection (c) of this section, the Secretary may suspend the eligibility of that reserve for financial assistance under subsection (e) of this section until the deficiency or inconsistency is remedied.

(3) The Secretary may withdraw the designation of an estuarine area as a national estuarine reserve if evaluation under paragraph (1) reveals that—

(A) the basis for any one or more of the findings made under subsection (b)(2) of this section regarding that area no longer exists; or

(B) a substantial portion of the research conducted within the area, over a period of years, has not been consistent with the research guidelines developed under subsection (c) of this section.

(g) Report

The Secretary shall include in the report required under section 1462 of this title information regarding—

(1) new designations of national estuarine reserves;

(2) any expansion of existing national estuarine reserves;

(3) the status of the research program being conducted within the System; and

(4) a summary of the evaluations made under subsection (f) of this section.

(Pub. L. No. 89–454, Title III, § 315, formerly § 312, as added by Pub. L. No. 92–583, 86 Stat. 1288 (Oct. 27, 1972); and renumbered and amended by Pub. L. No. 94–370, §§ 7, 12, 90 Stat. 1019, 1030 (July 26, 1976); Pub. L. No. 96–464, § 11, 94 Stat. 2067 (Oct. 17, 1980); Pub. L. No. 99–272, Title VI, § 6044, 100 Stat. 125 (Apr. 7, 1986); Pub. L. No. 101–508, Title VI, § 6214, 104 Stat. 1388–313 (Nov. 5, 1990); Pub. L. No. 102–587, Title II, § 2205(b)(1)(A), (B), (21), (22), 106 Stat. 5050, 5052 (Nov. 4, 1992); Pub. L. No. 104–150, § 6, 110 Stat. 1381 (June 3, 1996).)

§ 1462. Coastal zone management reports [CZMA § 316]

(a) Biennial reports

The Secretary shall consult with the Congress on a regular basis concerning the administration of this chapter and shall prepare and submit to the President for transmittal to the Congress a report summarizing the administration of this chapter during each period of two consecutive fiscal years. Each report, which shall be transmitted to the Congress not later than April 1 of the year following the close of the biennial period to which it pertains, shall include, but not be restricted to (1) an identification of the state programs approved pursuant to this chapter during the preceding Federal fiscal year and a description of those programs; (2) a listing of the states participating in the provisions of this chapter and a description of the status of each state's programs and its accomplishments during the preceding Federal fiscal year; (3) an itemization of the allocation of funds to the various coastal states and a breakdown of the major projects and areas on which these funds were expended; (4) an identification of any state programs which have been reviewed and disapproved, and a statement of the reasons for such action; (5) a summary of evaluation findings prepared in accordance with subsection (a) of section 1458 of this title, and a description of any sanctions imposed under subsections (c) and (d) of section 1458 of this title; (6) a listing of all activities and projects which, pursuant to the provisions of subsection (c) or subsection (d) of section 1456 of this title, are not consistent with an applicable approved state management program; (7) a summary of the regulations issued by the Secretary or in effect during the preceding Federal fiscal year; (8) a summary of a coordinated national strategy and program for the Nation's coastal zone including identification and discussion of Federal, regional, state, and local responsibilities and functions therein; (9) a summary of outstanding problems arising in the administration of this chapter in order of priority; (10) a description of the economic, environmental, and social consequences of energy activity affecting the coastal zone and an evaluation of the effectiveness of financial assistance under section 1456a of this title in dealing with such consequences; (11) a description and evaluation of applicable interstate and regional planning and coordination mechanisms developed by the coastal states; (12) a summary and evaluation of the research, studies, and training conducted in support of coastal zone management; and (13) such other information as may be appropriate.

(b) Recommendations for legislation

The report required by subsection (a) of this section shall contain such recommendations for additional legislation as the Secretary deems necessary to achieve the objectives of this chapter and enhance its effective operation.

(c) Review of other Federal programs; report to Congress

(1) The Secretary shall conduct a systematic review of Federal programs, other than this chapter, that affect coastal resources for purposes of identifying conflicts between the objectives and administration of such programs and the purposes and policies of this chapter. Not later than 1 year after October 17, 1980, the Secretary shall notify each Federal agency having appropriate jurisdiction of any conflict between its program and the purposes and policies of this chapter identified as a result of such review.

(2) The Secretary shall promptly submit a report to the Congress consisting of the information required under paragraph (1) of this subsection. Such report shall include recommendations for changes necessary to resolve existing conflicts among Federal laws and programs that affect the uses of coastal resources.

(Pub. L. No. 89–454, Title III, § 316, formerly § 313, as added by Pub. L. No. 92–583, 86 Stat. 1288 (Oct. 27, 1972); and renumbered and amended by Pub. L. No. 94–370, §§ 7, 13, 90 Stat. 1019, 1030 (July 26, 1976); Pub. L. No. 96–464, § 10, 94 Stat. 2066 (Oct. 17, 1980); Pub. L. No. 102–587, Title II, § 2205(b)(23), 106 Stat. 5052 (Nov. 4, 1992).)

HISTORICAL AND STATUTORY NOTES

Termination of Reporting Requirements

For termination, effective May 15, 2000, of provisions of law requiring submittal to Congress of any annual, semiannual, or other regular periodic report listed in House Document No. 103–7 (in which the report required by subsec. (a) of this section is listed on page 53), see Pub. L. No. 104–66, § 3003, as amended, set out as a note under 31 U.S.C.A. § 1113.

Shellfish Sanitation

Section 16 of Pub. L. No. 94–370 provided that:

"(a) The Secretary of Commerce shall—

"(1) undertake a comprehensive review of all aspects of the molluscan shellfish industry, including, but not limited to, the harvesting, processing, and transportation of such shellfish; and

"(2) evaluate the impact of Federal law concerning water quality on the molluscan shellfish industry.

The Secretary of Commerce shall, not later than April 30, 1977, submit a report to the Congress of the findings, comments, and recommendations (if any) which result from such review and evaluation.

"(b) The Secretary of Health, Education, and Welfare [now Health and Human Services] shall not promulgate final regulations concerning the national shellfish safety program before June 30, 1977. At least 60 days prior to the promulgation of any such regulations, the Secretary of Health, Education, and Welfare, in consultation with the Secretary of Commerce, shall publish an analysis (1) of the economic impact of such regulations on the domestic shellfish industry, and (2) the cost of such national shellfish safety program relative to the benefits that it is expected to achieve."

§ 1463. Rules and regulations

[CZMA § 317]

The Secretary shall develop and promulgate, pursuant to section 553 of Title 5, after notice and opportunity for full participation by relevant Federal agencies, state agencies, local governments, regional organizations, port authorities, and other interested parties, both public and private, such rules and regulations as may be necessary to carry out the provisions of this chapter.

(Pub. L. No. 89–454, Title III, § 317, formerly § 314, as added by Pub. L. No. 92–583, 86 Stat. 1288 (Oct. 27, 1972); and renumbered by Pub. L. No. 94–370, § 7, 90 Stat. 1019 (July 26, 1976).)

§ 1463a. Omitted

HISTORICAL AND STATUTORY NOTES

Codifications

This section was created by Pub. L. No. 96–464, § 12(a) to (g), 94 Stat. 2067 (Oct. 17, 1980); and Pub. L. No. 98–620, Title IV, § 402(20), 98 Stat. 3358 (Nov. 8, 1984), and set forth procedures and definitions applicable to Congressional disapproval for final rules. It was omitted pursuant to section 12(h) of Pub. L. No. 96–464 providing that this section shall cease to have any force or effect after Sept. 30, 1985.

§ 1463b. National Coastal Resources Research and Development Institute

(a) Establishment by Secretary; administration

The Secretary of Commerce shall provide for the establishment of a National Coastal Resources Research and Development Institute (hereinafter in this section referred to as the "Institute") to be administered by the Oregon State Marine Science Center.

(b) Purposes of Institute

The Institute shall conduct research and carry out educational and demonstration projects designed to promote the efficient and responsible development of ocean and coastal resources, including arctic resources. Such projects shall be based on biological, geological, genetic, economic and other scientific research applicable to the purposes of this section and shall include studies on the economic diversification and environmental protection of the Nation's coastal areas.

(c) Determination of Institute policies

(1) The policies of the Institute shall be determined by a Board of Governors composed of—

(A) two representatives appointed by the Governor of Oregon;

(B) one representative appointed by the Governor of Alaska;

(C) one representative appointed by the Governor of Washington;

(D) one representative appointed by the Governor of California; and

(E) one representative appointed by the Governor of Hawaii.

(2) Such policies shall include the selection, on a nationally competitive basis, of the research, projects, and studies to be supported by the Institute in accordance with the purposes of this section.

(d) Establishment of Advisory Council; functions and composition

(1) The Board of Governors shall establish an Advisory Council composed of specialists in ocean and coastal resources from the academic community.

(2) To the maximum extent practicable, the Advisory Council shall be composed of such specialists from every coastal region of the Nation.

(3) The Advisory Council shall provide such advice to the Board of Governors as such Board shall request, including recommendations regarding the support of research, projects, and studies in accordance with the purposes of this section.

(e) Administration of Institute

The Institute shall be administered by a Director who shall be appointed by the Chancellor of the Oregon Board of Higher Education in consultation with the Board of Governors.

(f) Evaluation of Institute by Secretary

The Secretary of Commerce shall conduct an ongoing evaluation of the activities of the Institute to ensure that funds received by the Institute under this section are used in a manner consistent with the provisions of this section.

(g) Report to Secretary

The Institute shall report to the Secretary of Commerce on its activities within 2 years after July 17, 1984.

(h) Access to Institute books, records, and documents

The Comptroller General of the United States, and any of his duly authorized representatives, shall have access, for the purpose of audit and examination, to any books, documents, papers and records of the Institute that are pertinent to the funds received under this section.

(i) Status of Institute employees

Employees of the Institute shall not, by reason of such employment, be considered to be employees of the Federal Government for any purpose.

(j) Authorization of appropriations

For the purposes of this section, there are authorized to be appropriated in each fiscal year $5,000,000, commencing with fiscal year 1985.

(Pub. L. No. 98–364, Title II, § 201, 98 Stat. 443 (July 17, 1984).)

HISTORICAL AND STATUTORY NOTES

Codifications

This section was not enacted as part of the Coastal Zone Management Act of 1972, which comprises this chapter.

§ 1464. Authorization of appropriations

[CZMA § 318]

(a) Sums appropriated to Secretary

There are authorized to be appropriated to the Secretary, to remain available until expended—

(1) for grants under sections 1455, 1455a, and 1456b of this title—

(A) $47,600,000 for fiscal year 1997;

(B) $49,000,000 for fiscal year 1998; and

(C) $50,500,000 for fiscal year 1999; and

(2) for grants under section 1461 of this title—

(A) $4,400,000 for fiscal year 1997;

(B) $4,500,000 for fiscal year 1998; and

(C) $4,600,000 for fiscal year 1999.

(b) Limitations

Federal funds received from other sources shall not be used to pay a coastal state's share of costs under section 1455 or 1456b of this title.

(c) Reversion to Secretary of unobligated State funds; availability of funds

The amount of any grant, or portion of a grant, made to a State under any section of this chapter which is not obligated by such State during the fiscal year, or during the second fiscal year after the fiscal year, for which it was first authorized to be obligated by such State shall revert to the Secretary. The Secretary shall add such reverted amount to those funds available for grants under the section for such reverted amount was originally made available.

(Pub. L. No. 89–454, Title III, § 318, formerly § 315, as added by Pub. L. No. 92–583, 86 Stat. 1289 (Oct. 27, 1972); and amended by Pub. L. No. 93–612, § 1(3), 88 Stat. 1974 (Jan. 2, 1975); renumbered and amended by Pub. L. No. 94–370, §§ 7, 14, 90 Stat. 1019, 1031 (July 26, 1976); amended by Pub. L. No. 95–372, Title V, §§ 502, 503(e), (f),

92 Stat. 692, 693 (Sept. 18, 1978); Pub. L. No. 96–464, § 13, 94 Stat. 2070 (Oct. 17, 1980); Pub. L. No. 99–272, Title VI, § 6046, 100 Stat. 127 (Apr. 7, 1986); Pub. L. No. 99–626, § 7, 100 Stat. 3506 (Nov. 7, 1986); Pub. L. No. 101–508, Title VI, § 6215, 104 Stat. 1388–313 (Nov. 5, 1990); Pub. L. No. 104–150, § 4, 110 Stat. 1381 (June 3, 1996).)

HISTORICAL AND STATUTORY NOTES

Codifications

Amendment to this section by section 6046 of Pub. L. No. 99–272, which directed that this section be amended by revising par. (1), striking former par. (2), renumbering former pars. (3) to (6) as (2) to (5), respectively, and revising pars. (3) to (5), as so renumbered, has been executed to pars. (1) to (6) of subsec. (a) of this section as the probable intent of Congress.

§ 1465. Appeals to the Secretary

[CZMA § 319]

(a) Notice

Not later than 30 days after the date of the filing of an appeal to the Secretary of a consistency determination under section 1456 of this title, the Secretary shall publish an initial notice in the Federal Register.

(b) Closure of record

(1) In general

Not later than the end of the 160-day period beginning on the date of publication of an initial notice under subsection (a) of this section, except as provided in paragraph (3), the Secretary shall immediately close the decision record and receive no more filings on the appeal.

(2) Notice

After closing the administrative record, the Secretary shall immediately publish a notice in the Federal Register that the administrative record has been closed.

(3) Exception

(A) In general

Subject to subparagraph (B), during the 160-day period described in paragraph (1), the Secretary may stay the closing of the decision record—

(i) for a specific period mutually agreed to in writing by the appellant and the State agency; or

(ii) as the Secretary determines necessary to receive, on an expedited basis—

(I) any supplemental information specifically requested by the Secretary to complete a consistency review under this chapter; or

(II) any clarifying information submitted by a party to the proceeding related to information in the consolidated record compiled by the lead Federal permitting agency.

(B) Applicability

The Secretary may only stay the 160-day period described in paragraph (1) for a period not to exceed 60 days.

(c) Deadline for decision

(1) In general

Not later than 60 days after the date of publication of a Federal Register notice stating when the decision record for an appeal has been closed, the Secretary shall issue a decision or publish a notice in the Federal Register explaining why a decision cannot be issued at that time.

(2) Subsequent decision

Not later than 15 days after the date of publication of a Federal Register notice explaining why a decision cannot be issued within the 60-day period, the Secretary shall issue a decision.

(Pub. L. No. 89–454, Title III, § 319, as added by Pub. L. No. 104–150, § 8, 110 Stat. 1382 (June 3, 1996); Pub. L. No. 109–58, Title III, § 381, 119 Stat. 737 (Aug. 8, 2005).)

HISTORICAL AND STATUTORY NOTES

References in Text

This chapter, referred to in subsec. (b), originally read "this Act", and was translated as reading "this title", meaning Title III of Pub. L. No. 89–454, known as the Coastal Zone Management Act of 1972, as amended, which is principally codified as this chapter. For complete classification, see Short Title note set out under 42 U.S.C.A. § 1451 and Tables.

§ 1466. Appeals relating to offshore mineral development

For any Federal administrative agency proceeding that is an appeal or review under section 319 of the Coastal Zone Management Act of 1972 (16 U.S.C. 1465) related to any Federal authorization for the permitting, approval, or other authorization of an energy project, the lead Federal permitting agency for the project shall, with the cooperation of Federal and State administrative agencies, maintain a consolidated record of all decisions made or actions taken by the lead agency or by another Federal or State administrative agency or officer. Such record shall be the initial record for appeals or reviews under that Act, provided that the record may be supplemented as expressly provided pursuant to section 319 of that Act.

(Pub. L. No. 109–58, Title III, § 382, 119 Stat. 738 (Aug. 8, 2005).)

HISTORICAL AND STATUTORY NOTES

References in Text

That Act, referred to in text, probably means the Coastal Zone Management Act of 1972, also known as the CZMA, Pub. L. No. 89–454, Title III, as added by Pub. L. No. 92–483, 86 Stat. 1280 (Oct. 27, 1972), as amended, which is principally codified as this chapter. Section 319 of the Coastal Zone Management Act of 1972 is codified as 16 U.S.C.A. § 1465. For complete classification, see Short Title note set out under 42 U.S.C.A. § 1451 and Tables.

Codifications

Section was enacted as part of the Energy Policy Act of 2005, and not as part of the Coastal Zone Management Act of 1972, which otherwise comprises this chapter.

ENDANGERED SPECIES ACT OF 1973
[ESA § _____]

(16 U.S.C.A. §§ 1531 to 1544)

CHAPTER 35—ENDANGERED SPECIES

§ 1531. Congressional findings and declaration of purposes and policy

[ESA § 2]

(a) Findings

The Congress finds and declares that—

(1) various species of fish, wildlife, and plants in the United States have been rendered extinct as a consequence of economic growth and development untempered by adequate concern and conservation;

(2) other species of fish, wildlife, and plants have been so depleted in numbers that they are in danger of or threatened with extinction;

(3) these species of fish, wildlife, and plants are of esthetic, ecological, educational, historical, recreational, and scientific value to the Nation and its people;

(4) the United States has pledged itself as a sovereign state in the international community to conserve to the extent practicable the various species of fish or wildlife and plants facing extinction, pursuant to—

(A) migratory bird treaties with Canada and Mexico;

(B) the Migratory and Endangered Bird Treaty with Japan;

(C) the Convention on Nature Protection and Wildlife Preservation in the Western Hemisphere;

(D) the International Convention for the Northwest Atlantic Fisheries;

(E) the International Convention for the High Seas Fisheries of the North Pacific Ocean;

(F) the Convention on International Trade in Endangered Species of Wild Fauna and Flora; and

(G) other international agreements; and

(5) encouraging the States and other interested parties, through Federal financial assistance and a system of incentives, to develop and maintain conservation programs which meet national and international standards is a key to meeting the Nation's international commitments and to better safeguarding, for the benefit of all citizens, the Nation's heritage in fish, wildlife, and plants.

(b) Purposes

The purposes of this chapter are to provide a means whereby the ecosystems upon which endangered species and threatened species depend may be conserved, to provide a program for the conservation of such endangered species and threatened species, and to take such steps as may be appropriate to achieve the purposes of the treaties and conventions set forth in subsection (a) of this section.

(c) Policy

(1) It is further declared to be the policy of Congress that all Federal departments and agencies shall seek to conserve endangered species and threatened species and shall utilize their authorities in furtherance of the purposes of this chapter.

(2) It is further declared to be the policy of Congress that Federal agencies shall cooperate with State and local agencies to resolve water resource issues in concert with conservation of endangered species.

(Pub. L. No. 93–205, § 2, 87 Stat. 884(Dec. 28, 1973); as amended by Pub. L. No. 96–159, § 1, 93 Stat. 1225 (Dec. 28, 1979); Pub. L. No. 97–304, § 9(a), 96 Stat. 1426 (Oct. 13, 1982); Pub. L. No. 100–478, Title I, § 1013(a), 102 Stat. 2315 (Oct. 7, 1988).)

HISTORICAL AND STATUTORY NOTES

References in Text

This chapter, referred to in subsecs. (b) and (c)(1), in the original read "this Act", meaning the Endangered Species Act of 1973, Pub. L. No. 93–205, 81 Stat. 884 (Dec. 28, 1973), as amended, which is codified principally to this chapter. For complete classification, see Short Title note set out below and Tables.

Effective and Applicability Provisions

1973 Acts. Section 16 of Pub. L. No. 93–205 provided that: "This Act [enacting this chapter, amending sections 460k–1, 460*l*–9, 668dd, 715i, 715s, 1362, 1371, 1372, and 1402 of this title and section 136 of Title 7, Agriculture, repealing sections 668aa to 668cc–6 of this title, and enacting provisions set out as notes under this section] shall take effect on the date of its enactment [Dec. 28, 1973]."

Short Title

1982 Amendments. Section 1 of Pub. L. No. 97–304 provided: "That this Act [amending sections 1531, 1532, 1533, 1535, 1536, 1537a, 1538, 1539, 1540, and 1542 of this title and enacting provisions set out as notes under sections 1533, 1537a, and 1539 of this title] may be cited as the 'Endangered Species Act Amendments of 1982'."

1978 Amendments. Pub. L. No. 95–632, § 1, 92 Stat. 3751 (Nov. 10, 1978), provided: "That this Act [amending sections 1532 to 1536, 1538 to 1540, and 1542 of this title] may be cited as the 'Endangered Species Act Amendments of 1978'."

1973 Acts. Section 1 of Pub. L. No. 93–205 provided: "That this Act [enacting this chapter, amending sections 460k–1, 460*l*–9, 668dd, 715i, 715s, 1362, 1371, 1372 and 1402 of this title and section 136 of Title 7, Agriculture, repealing sections 668aa to 668cc–6 of this title, and enacting provisions set out as notes under this section] may be cited as the 'Endangered Species Act of 1973'."

Relationship to Endangered Species Act of 1973

Pub. L. No. 102–251, Title III, § 305, 106 Stat. 66 (Mar. 9, 1992), as amended by Pub. L. No. 104–208, Div. A, Title I, § 101(a) [Title II, § 211(b)], 110 Stat. 3009–41 (Sept. 30, 1996), provided that: "The special areas defined in section 3(24) of the Magnuson-Stevens Fishery Conservation and Management Act (16 U.S.C. 1802(24)) [section 1802(24) of this title] shall be considered places that are subject to the jurisdiction of the United States for the purposes of the Endangered Species Act of 1973 (16 U.S.C. 1531 et seq.) [this chapter]."

[Amendment by Pub. L. No. 104–208, Div. A, Title I, § 101(a) [Title II, § 211(b)], 110 Stat. 3009–41 (Sept. 30, 1996), effective 15 days after Oct. 11, 1996, see Pub. L. No. 104–208, Div. A, Title I, § 101(a) [Title II, § 211(b)], 110 Stat. 3009–41 (Sept. 30, 1996), set out as a note under section 1801 of this title.]

[Section 305 of Pub. L. No. 102–251 effective on the date on which the Agreement between the United States and the Union of Soviet Socialist Republics on the Maritime Boundary, signed June 1, 1990, enters into force for the United States, with authority to prescribe implementing regulations effective Mar. 9, 1992, but with no such regulation to be effective until the date on which the Agreement enters into force for the United States, see section 308 of Pub. L. No. 102–251, set out as a note under section 773 of this title.]

Endangered Salmon Predation Prevention Act

Pub. L. No. 115–329, 132 Stat. 4475 (Dec. 18, 2018), amends the Marine Mammal Protection Act to allow sea lions to be killed to prevent their predation on ESA-listed species of salmon, steelhead, and eulachon in the Columbia River.

Recovering Species Report and Listing Requirements

Section 8102 of Pub. L. No. 116–9, 133 Stat. 809 (Mar. 12, 2019), requires the Secretary of the Interior to submit a report to Congress by September 30, 2021, that identifies "the listing status under the Endangered Species Act of 1973 . . . of the Colorado pikeminnow, humpback chub, razorback sucker, and bonytail" and the projected listing status of each of these species as of September 30, 2023.

Endangered Species Act Reports

Section 301 of the America's Conservation Enhancement Act, Pub. L. No. 116–188, 134 Stat. 905. 938–39 (Oct. 30, 2020), provided that:

(a) Definition of Secretaries.—In this section, the term "Secretaries" means—

(1) the Secretary of Agriculture;

(2) the Secretary of Commerce, acting through the Assistant Administrator of the National Marine Fisheries Service; and

(3) the Secretary of the Interior, acting through the Director of the United States Fish and Wildlife Service.

(b) Study.—To assess factors affecting successful conservation activities under the Endangered Species Act of 1973 (16 U.S.C. 1531 et seq.), the Secretaries shall carry out a study—

(1) **(A)** to review any factors that threaten or endanger a species, such as wildlife disease, for which a listing under *939 the Endangered Species Act of 1973 (16 U.S.C. 1531 et seq.) would not **contribute to the conservation of the species; and**

(B) to identify additional conservation measures that can be taken to protect and conserve a species described in subparagraph (A);

(2) to review any barriers to—

(A) the delivery of Federal, State, local, or private funds for such conservation activities, including statutory or regulatory impediments, staffing needs, and other relevant considerations; or

(B) the implementation of conservation agreements, plans, or other cooperative agreements, including agreements focused on voluntary activities, multispecies efforts, and other relevant considerations;

(3) to review factors that impact the ability of the Federal Government to successfully implement the Endangered Species Act of 1973 (16 U.S.C. 1531 et seq.);

(4) to develop recommendations regarding methods to address barriers identified under paragraph (2), if any;

(5) to review determinations under the Endangered Species Act of 1973 (16 U.S.C. 1531 et seq.) in which a species is determined to be recovered by the Secretary of the Interior, acting through the Director of the United States Fish and Wildlife Service, or the Secretary of Commerce, acting through the Assistant Administrator of the National Marine Fisheries Service, but remains listed under that Act, including—

(A) an explanation of the factors preventing a delisting or downlisting of the species; and

(B) recommendations regarding methods to address the factors described in subparagraph (A); and

(6) to review any determinations under the Endangered Species Act of 1973 (16 U.S.C. 1531 et seq.) in which a species has been identified as needing listing or uplisting under that Act but remains unlisted or listed as a threatened species, respectively, including—

(A) an explanation of the factors preventing a listing or uplisting of the species; and

(B) recommendations regarding methods to address the factors described in subparagraph (A).

(c) Report.—Not later than 1 year after the date of enactment of this Act, the Secretaries shall submit to the Committees on Appropriations and Environment and Public Works of the Senate and the Committees on Appropriations and Natural Resources of the House of Representatives and make publicly available a report describing the results of the study under subsection (b).

Section 302 of the same Act, 134 Stat. at 939–41, provides that:

(a) Reports on Expenditures.—

(1) Federal Departments and Agencies.—

(A) In General.—At the determination of the Comptroller General of the United States (referred to in this section as the "Comptroller General"), to facilitate the preparation of the reports from the Comptroller General under paragraph (2), the head of each Federal department and agency shall submit to the Comptroller General data and other relevant information that describes the amounts expended or disbursed (including through loans, loan guarantees, grants, or any other financing mechanism) by the department or agency as a direct result of any provision of the Endangered Species Act of 1973 (16 U.S.C. 1531 et seq.) (including any regulation promulgated pursuant to that Act) during—

(i) with respect to the first report under paragraph (2), the 3 fiscal years preceding the date of submission of the report; and

(ii) with respect to the second report under paragraph (2), the 2 fiscal years preceding the date of submission of the report.

(B) Requirements.—Data and other relevant information submitted under subparagraph (A) shall describe, with respect to the applicable amounts—

(i) the programmatic office of the department or agency on behalf of which each amount was expended or disbursed;

(ii) the provision of the Endangered Species Act of 1973 (16 U.S.C. 1531 et seq.) (or regulation promulgated pursuant to that Act) pursuant to which each amount was expended or disbursed; and

(iii) the project or activity carried out using each amount, in detail sufficient to reflect the breadth, scope, and purpose of the project or activity.

(2) Comptroller General.—Not later than 2 years and 4 years after the date of enactment of this Act, the Comptroller General shall submit to the Committees on Appropriations, Commerce, Science, and Transportation, and Environment and Public Works of the Senate and the Committee on Appropriations and Natural Resources of the House of Representatives a report that describes—

(A) the aggregate amount expended or disbursed by all Federal departments and agencies as a direct result of any provision of the Endangered Species Act of 1973 (16 U.S.C. 1531 et seq.) (including any regulation promulgated pursuant to that Act) during—

(i) with respect to the first report, the 3 fiscal years preceding the date of submission of the report; and

(ii) with respect to the second report, the 2 fiscal years preceding the date of submission of the report;

(B) the provision of the Endangered Species Act of 1973 (16 U.S.C. 1531 et seq.) (or regulation promulgated pursuant to that Act) pursuant to which each such amount was expended or disbursed; and

(C) with respect to each relevant department or agency—

(i) the total amount expended or disbursed by the department or agency as described in subparagraph (A); and

(ii) the information described in clauses (i) through (iii) of paragraph (1)(B).

(b) Report on Conservation Activities.—

(1) Federal Departments and Agencies.—At the determination of the Comptroller General, to facilitate the preparation of the report under paragraph (2), the head of each Federal department and agency shall submit to the Comptroller General data and other relevant information that describes the conservation activities by the Federal department or agency as a direct result of any provision of the Endangered Species Act of 1973 (16 U.S.C. 1531 et seq.) (including any regulation promulgated pursuant to that Act) during—

(A) with respect to the first report under paragraph (2), the 3 fiscal years preceding the date of submission of the report; and

(B) with respect to the second report under paragraph (2), the 2 fiscal years preceding the date of submission of the report.

(2) Comptroller General.—Not later than 2 years and 4 years after the date of enactment of this Act, the Comptroller General shall submit to the Committees on Commerce, Science, and Transportation and Environment and Public Works of the Senate and the Committee on Natural Resources of the House of Representatives a report that—

(A) describes the conservation activities by all Federal departments and agencies for species listed as a threatened species or endangered species under the Endangered Species Act of 1973 (16 U.S.C. 1531 et seq.), as reported under paragraph (1), during—

(i) with respect to the first report, the 3 fiscal years preceding the date of submission of the report; and

(ii) with respect to the second report, the 2 fiscal years preceding the date of submission of the report;

(B) is organized into categories with respect to whether a recovery plan for a species has been established;

(C) includes conservation outcomes associated with the conservation activities; and

(D) as applicable, describes the conservation activities that required interaction between Federal agencies and between Federal agencies and State and Tribal agencies and units of local government pursuant to the Endangered Species Act of 1973 (16 U.S.C. 1531 et seq.).

§ 1532. Definitions

[ESA § 3]

For the purposes of this chapter—

(1) The term "alternative courses of action" means all alternatives and thus is not limited to original project objectives and agency jurisdiction.

(2) The term "commercial activity" means all activities of industry and trade, including, but not limited to, the buying or selling of commodities and activities conducted for the purpose of facilitating such buying and selling: *Provided, however*, That it does not include exhibition of commodities by museums or similar cultural or historical organizations.

(3) The terms "conserve", "conserving", and "conservation" mean to use and the use of all methods and procedures which are necessary to bring any endangered species or threatened species to the point at which the measures provided pursuant to this chapter are no longer necessary. Such methods and procedures include, but are not limited to, all activities associated with scientific resources management such as research, census, law enforcement, habitat acquisition and maintenance, propagation, live trapping, and transplantation, and, in the extraordinary case where population pressures within a given ecosystem cannot be otherwise relieved, may include regulated taking.

(4) The term "Convention" means the Convention on International Trade in Endangered Species of Wild Fauna and Flora, signed on March 3, 1973, and the appendices thereto.

(5) **(A)** The term "critical habitat" for a threatened or endangered species means—

(i) the specific areas within the geographical area occupied by the species, at the time it is listed in accordance with the provisions of section 1533 of this title, on which are found those physical or biological features (I) essential to the conservation of the species and (II) which may require special management considerations or protection; and

(ii) specific areas outside the geographical area occupied by the species at the time it is listed in accordance with the provisions of section 1533 of this title, upon a determination by the Secretary that such areas are essential for the conservation of the species.

(B) Critical habitat may be established for those species now listed as threatened or endangered species for which no critical habitat has heretofore been established as set forth in subparagraph (A) of this paragraph.

(C) Except in those circumstances determined by the Secretary, critical habitat shall not include the entire geographical area which can be occupied by the threatened or endangered species.

(6) The term "endangered species" means any species which is in danger of extinction throughout all or a significant portion of its range other than a species of the Class Insecta determined by the Secretary to constitute a pest whose protection under the provisions of this chapter would present an overwhelming and overriding risk to man.

(7) The term "Federal agency" means any department, agency, or instrumentality of the United States.

(8) The term "fish or wildlife" means any member of the animal kingdom, including without limitation any mammal, fish, bird (including any migratory, nonmigratory, or endangered bird for which protection is also afforded by treaty or other international agreement), amphibian, reptile, mollusk, crustacean, arthropod or other invertebrate, and includes any part, product, egg, or offspring thereof, or the dead body or parts thereof.

(9) The term "foreign commerce" includes, among other things, any transaction—

(A) between persons within one foreign country;

(B) between persons in two or more foreign countries;

(C) between a person within the United States and a person in a foreign country; or

(D) between persons within the United States, where the fish and wildlife in question are moving in any country or countries outside the United States.

(10) The term "import" means to land on, bring into, or introduce into, or attempt to land on, bring into, or introduce into, any place subject to the jurisdiction of the United States, whether or not such landing, bringing, or introduction constitutes an importation within the meaning of the customs laws of the United States.

(11) Repealed. [Pub. L. No. 97–304, § 4(b), 96 Stat. 1420 (Oct. 13, 1982).]

(12) The term "permit or license applicant" means, when used with respect to an action of a Federal agency for which exemption is sought under section 1536 of this title, any person whose application to such agency for a permit or license has been denied primarily because of the application of section 1536(a) of this title to such agency action.

(13) The term "person" means an individual, corporation, partnership, trust, association, or any other private entity; or any officer, employee, agent, department, or instrumentality of the Federal Government, of any State, municipality, or political subdivision of a State, or of any foreign government; any State, municipality, or political subdivision of a State; or any other entity subject to the jurisdiction of the United States.

(14) The term "plant" means any member of the plant kingdom, including seeds, roots and other parts thereof.

(15) The term "Secretary" means, except as otherwise herein provided, the Secretary of the Interior or the Secretary of Commerce as program responsibilities are vested pursuant to the provisions of Reorganization Plan Numbered 4 of 1970; except that with respect to the enforcement of the provisions of this chapter and the Convention which pertain to the importation or exportation of terrestrial plants, the term also means the Secretary of Agriculture.

(16) The term "species" includes any subspecies of fish or wildlife or plants, and any distinct population segment of any species of vertebrate fish or wildlife which interbreeds when mature.

(17) The term "State" means any of the several States, the District of Columbia, the Commonwealth of Puerto Rico, American Samoa, the Virgin Islands, Guam, and the Trust Territory of the Pacific Islands.

(18) The term "State agency" means any State agency, department, board, commission, or other governmental entity which is responsible for the management and conservation of fish, plant, or wildlife resources within a State.

(19) The term "take" means to harass, harm, pursue, hunt, shoot, wound, kill, trap, capture, or collect, or to attempt to engage in any such conduct.

(20) The term "threatened species" means any species which is likely to become an endangered species within the foreseeable future throughout all or a significant portion of its range.

(21) The term "United States", when used in a geographical context, includes all States.

(Pub. L. No. 93–205, § 3, 87 Stat. 885 (Dec. 28, 1973); as amended by Pub. L. No. 94–359, § 5, 90 Stat. 913 (July 12, 1976); Pub. L. No. 95–632, § 2, 92 Stat. 3751 (Nov. 10, 1978); Pub. L. No. 96–159, § 2, 93 Stat. 1225 (Dec. 28, 1979); Pub. L. No. 97–304, § 4(b), 96 Stat. 1420 (Oct. 13, 1982); Pub. L. No. 100–478, Title I, § 1001, 102 Stat. 2306 (Oct. 7, 1988).)

HISTORICAL AND STATUTORY NOTES

References in Text

This chapter, referred to in text, in the original read "this Act", meaning the Endangered Species Act of 1973, which is codified principally to this chapter. For complete classification, see Short Title note set out under section 1531 of this title and Tables.

The customs laws of the United States, referred to in par. (10), are codified generally to Title 19.

Reorganization Plan No. 4 of 1970, referred to in par. (15), is Reorg. Plan No. 4 of 1970, eff. Oct. 3, 1970, 35 Fed. Reg. 15627, 84 Stat. 2090, which is set out in the Appendix to Title 5, Government Organization and Employees.

Effective and Applicability Provisions

1973 Acts. Section effective Dec. 28, 1973, see section 16 of Pub. L. No. 93–205, set out as an Effective Date note under section 1531 of this title.

Termination of Trust Territory of the Pacific Islands

For termination of Trust Territory of the Pacific Islands, see note set out preceding 48 U.S.C.A. § 1681.

§ 1533. Determination of endangered species and threatened species

[ESA § 4]

(a) Generally

(1) The Secretary shall by regulation promulgated in accordance with subsection (b) of this section determine whether any species is an endangered species or a threatened species because of any of the following factors:

(A) the present or threatened destruction, modification, or curtailment of its habitat or range;

(B) overutilization for commercial, recreational, scientific, or educational purposes;

(C) disease or predation;

(D) the inadequacy of existing regulatory mechanisms; or

(E) other natural or manmade factors affecting its continued existence.

(2) With respect to any species over which program responsibilities have been vested in the Secretary of Commerce pursuant to Reorganization Plan Numbered 4 of 1970—

(A) in any case in which the Secretary of Commerce determines that such species should—

(i) be listed as an endangered species or a threatened species, or

(ii) be changed in status from a threatened species to an endangered species,

he shall so inform the Secretary of the Interior, who shall list such species in accordance with this section;

(B) in any case in which the Secretary of Commerce determines that such species should—

(i) be removed from any list published pursuant to subsection (c) of this section, or

(ii) be changed in status from an endangered species to a threatened species,

he shall recommend such action to the Secretary of the Interior, and the Secretary of the Interior, if he concurs in the recommendation, shall implement such action; and

(C) the Secretary of the Interior may not list or remove from any list any such species, and may not change the status of any such species which are listed, without a prior favorable determination made pursuant to this section by the Secretary of Commerce.

(3) **(A)** The Secretary, by regulation promulgated in accordance with subsection (b) of this section and to the maximum extent prudent and determinable—

(i) shall, concurrently with making a determination under paragraph (1) that a species is an endangered species or a threatened species, designate any habitat of such species which is then considered to be critical habitat; and

(ii) may, from time-to-time thereafter as appropriate, revise such designation.

(B) **(i)** The Secretary shall not designate as critical habitat any lands or other geographical areas owned or controlled by the Department of Defense, or designated for its use, that are subject to an integrated natural resources management plan prepared under section 670a of this title, if the Secretary determines in writing that such plan provides a benefit to the species for which critical habitat is proposed for designation.

(ii) Nothing in this paragraph affects the requirement to consult under section 1536(a)(2) of this title with respect to an agency action (as that term is defined in that section).

(iii) Nothing in this paragraph affects the obligation of the Department of Defense to comply with section 1538 of this title, including the prohibition preventing extinction and taking of endangered species and threatened species.

(b) Basis for determinations

(1) **(A)** The Secretary shall make determinations required by subsection (a) (1) of this section solely on the basis of the best scientific and commercial data available to him after conducting a review of the status of the species and after taking into account those efforts, if any, being made by any State or foreign nation, or any political subdivision of a State or foreign nation, to protect such species, whether by predator control, protection of habitat and food supply, or other conservation practices, within any area under its jurisdiction, or on the high seas.

(B) In carrying out this section, the Secretary shall give consideration to species which have been—

(i) designated as requiring protection from unrestricted commerce by any foreign nation, or pursuant to any international agreement; or

(ii) identified as in danger of extinction, or likely to become so within the foreseeable future, by any State agency or by any agency of a foreign nation that is responsible for the conservation of fish or wildlife or plants.

(2) The Secretary shall designate critical habitat, and make revisions thereto, under subsection (a)(3) of this section on the basis of the best scientific data available and after taking into consideration the economic impact, the impact on national security, and any other relevant impact, of specifying any particular area as critical habitat. The Secretary may exclude any area from critical habitat if he determines that the benefits of such exclusion outweigh the benefits of specifying such area as part of the critical habitat, unless he determines, based on the best scientific and commercial data available, that the failure to designate such area as critical habitat will result in the extinction of the species concerned.

(3) **(A)** To the maximum extent practicable, within 90 days after receiving the petition of an interested person under section 553(e) of Title 5, to add a species to, or to remove a species from, either of the lists published under subsection (c) of this section, the Secretary shall make a finding as to whether the petition presents substantial scientific or commercial information indicating that the petitioned action may be warranted. If such a petition is found to present such information, the Secretary shall promptly commence a review of the status of the species concerned. The Secretary shall promptly publish each finding made under this subparagraph in the Federal Register.

(B) Within 12 months after receiving a petition that is found under subparagraph (A) to present substantial information indicating that the petitioned action may be warranted, the Secretary shall make one of the following findings:

(i) The petitioned action is not warranted, in which case the Secretary shall promptly publish such finding in the Federal Register.

(ii) The petitioned action is warranted, in which case the Secretary shall promptly publish in the Federal Register a general notice and the complete text of a proposed regulation to implement such action in accordance with paragraph (5).

(iii) The petitioned action is warranted, but that—

(I) the immediate proposal and timely promulgation of a final regulation implementing the petitioned action in accordance with paragraphs (5) and (6) is precluded by pending proposals to determine whether any species is an endangered species or a threatened species, and

(II) expeditious progress is being made to add qualified species to either of the lists published under subsection (c) of this section and to remove from such lists species for which the protections of this chapter are no longer necessary,

in which case the Secretary shall promptly publish such finding in the Federal Register, together with a description and evaluation of the reasons and data on which the finding is based.

(C) **(i)** A petition with respect to which a finding is made under subparagraph (B)(iii) shall be treated as a petition that is resubmitted to the Secretary under subparagraph (A) on the date of such finding and that presents substantial scientific or commercial information that the petitioned action may be warranted.

(ii) Any negative finding described in subparagraph (A) and any finding described in subparagraph (B)(i) or (iii) shall be subject to judicial review.

(iii) The Secretary shall implement a system to monitor effectively the status of all species with respect to which a finding is made under subparagraph (B)(iii) and shall make prompt use of the authority under paragraph 7[1] to prevent a significant risk to the well being of any such species.

(D) **(i)** To the maximum extent practicable, within 90 days after receiving the petition of an interested person under section 553(e) of Title 5, to revise a critical habitat designation, the Secretary shall make a finding as to whether the petition presents substantial scientific information indicating that the revision may be warranted. The Secretary shall promptly publish such finding in the Federal Register.

(ii) Within 12 months after receiving a petition that is found under clause (i) to present substantial information indicating that the requested revision may be warranted, the Secretary shall determine how he intends to proceed with the requested revision, and shall promptly publish notice of such intention in the Federal Register.

(4) Except as provided in paragraphs (5) and (6) of this subsection, the provisions of section 553 of Title 5 (relating to rulemaking procedures), shall apply to any regulation promulgated to carry out the purposes of this chapter.

(5) With respect to any regulation proposed by the Secretary to implement a determination, designation, or revision referred to in subsection (a)(1) or (3) of this section, the Secretary shall—

(A) not less than 90 days before the effective date of the regulation—

(i) publish a general notice and the complete text of the proposed regulation in the Federal Register, and

(ii) give actual notice of the proposed regulation (including the complete text of the regulation) to the State agency in each State in which the species is believed to occur, and to each county or equivalent jurisdiction in which the species is believed to occur, and invite the comment of such agency, and each such jurisdiction, thereon;

(B) insofar as practical, and in cooperation with the Secretary of State, give notice of the proposed regulation to each foreign nation in which the species is believed to occur or whose citizens harvest the species on the high seas, and invite the comment of such nation thereon;

(C) give notice of the proposed regulation to such professional scientific organizations as he deems appropriate;

(D) publish a summary of the proposed regulation in a newspaper of general circulation in each area of the United States in which the species is believed to occur; and

(E) promptly hold one public hearing on the proposed regulation if any person files a request for such a hearing within 45 days after the date of publication of general notice.

(6) **(A)** Within the one-year period beginning on the date on which general notice is published in accordance with paragraph (5)(A)(i) regarding a proposed regulation, the Secretary shall publish in the Federal Register—

(i) if a determination as to whether a species is an endangered species or a threatened species, or a revision of critical habitat, is involved, either—

(I) a final regulation to implement such determination,

(II) a final regulation to implement such revision or a finding that such revision should not be made,

(III) notice that such one-year period is being extended under subparagraph (B)(i), or

(IV) notice that the proposed regulation is being withdrawn under subparagraph (B)(ii), together with the finding on which such withdrawal is based; or

(ii) subject to subparagraph (C), if a designation of critical habitat is involved, either—

(I) a final regulation to implement such designation, or

(II) notice that such one-year period is being extended under such subparagraph.

(B) **(i)** If the Secretary finds with respect to a proposed regulation referred to in subparagraph (A)(i) that there is substantial disagreement regarding the sufficiency or accuracy of the available data relevant to the determination or revision concerned, the Secretary may extend the one-year period specified in subparagraph (A) for not more than six months for purposes of soliciting additional data.

(ii) If a proposed regulation referred to in subparagraph (A)(i) is not promulgated as a final regulation within such one-year period (or longer period if extension under clause (i) applies) because the Secretary finds that there is not sufficient evidence to justify the action proposed by the regulation, the Secretary shall immediately withdraw the regulation. The finding on which a withdrawal is based shall be subject to judicial review. The Secretary may not propose a regulation that has previously been withdrawn under this clause unless he determines that sufficient new information is available to warrant such proposal.

(iii) If the one-year period specified in subparagraph (A) is extended under clause (i) with respect to a proposed regulation, then before the close of such extended period the Secretary shall publish in the Federal Register either a final regulation to implement the determination or revision concerned, a finding that the revision should not be made, or a notice of withdrawal of the regulation under clause (ii), together with the finding on which the withdrawal is based.

(C) A final regulation designating critical habitat of an endangered species or a threatened species shall be published concurrently with the final regulation implementing the determination that such species is endangered or threatened, unless the Secretary deems that—

(i) it is essential to the conservation of such species that the regulation implementing such determination be promptly published; or

(ii) critical habitat of such species is not then determinable, in which case the Secretary, with respect to the proposed regulation to designate such habitat, may extend the one-year period specified in subparagraph (A) by not more than one additional year, but not later than the close of such additional year the Secretary must publish a final regulation, based on such data as may be available at that time, designating, to the maximum extent prudent, such habitat.

(7) Neither paragraph (4), (5), or (6) of this subsection nor section 553 of Title 5 shall apply to any regulation issued by the Secretary in regard to any emergency posing a significant risk to the well-being of any species of fish or wildlife or plants, but only if—

(A) at the time of publication of the regulation in the Federal Register the Secretary publishes therein detailed reasons why such regulation is necessary; and

(B) in the case such regulation applies to resident species of fish or wildlife, or plants, the Secretary gives actual notice of such regulation to the State agency in each State in which such species is believed to occur.

Such regulation shall, at the discretion of the Secretary, take effect immediately upon the publication of the regulation in the Federal Register. Any regulation promulgated under the authority of this paragraph shall cease to have force and effect at the close of the 240-day period following the date of publication unless, during such 240-day period, the rulemaking procedures which would apply to such regulation without regard to this paragraph are complied with. If at any time after issuing an emergency regulation the Secretary determines, on the basis of the best appropriate data available to him, that substantial evidence does not exist to warrant such regulation, he shall withdraw it.

(8) The publication in the Federal Register of any proposed or final regulation which is necessary or appropriate to carry out the purposes of this chapter shall include a summary by the Secretary of the data on which such regulation is based and shall show the relationship of such data to such regulation; and if such regulation designates or revises critical habitat, such summary shall, to the maximum extent practicable, also include a brief description and evaluation of those activities (whether public or private) which, in the opinion of the Secretary, if undertaken may adversely modify such habitat, or may be affected by such designation.

(c) Lists

(1) The Secretary of the Interior shall publish in the Federal Register a list of all species determined by him or the Secretary of Commerce to be endangered species and a list of all species determined by him or the Secretary of Commerce to be threatened species. Each list shall refer to the species contained therein by scientific and common name or names, if any, specify with respect to each such species over what portion of its range it is endangered or threatened, and specify any critical habitat within such range. The Secretary shall from time to time revise each list published under the authority of this subsection to reflect recent determinations, designations, and revisions made in accordance with subsections (a) and (b) of this section.

(2) The Secretary shall—

(A) conduct, at least once every five years, a review of all species included in a list which is published pursuant to paragraph (1) and which is in effect at the time of such review; and

(B) determine on the basis of such review whether any such species should—

(i) be removed from such list;

(ii) be changed in status from an endangered species to a threatened species; or

(iii) be changed in status from a threatened species to an endangered species.

Each determination under subparagraph (B) shall be made in accordance with the provisions of subsections (a) and (b) of this section.

(d) Protective regulations

Whenever any species is listed as a threatened species pursuant to subsection (c) of this section, the Secretary shall issue such regulations as he deems necessary and advisable to provide for the conservation of such species. The Secretary may by regulation prohibit with respect to any threatened species any act prohibited under section 1538(a)(1) of this title, in the case of fish or wildlife, or section 1538(a)(2) of this title, in the case of plants, with respect to endangered species; except that with respect to the taking of resident species of fish or wildlife, such regulations shall apply in any State which has entered into a cooperative agreement pursuant to section 1535(c) of this title only to the extent that such regulations have also been adopted by such State.

(e) Similarity of appearance cases

The Secretary may, by regulation of commerce or taking, and to the extent he deems advisable, treat any species as an endangered species or threatened species even though it is not listed pursuant to this section if he finds that—

(A) such species so closely resembles in appearance, at the point in question, a species which has been listed pursuant to such section that enforcement personnel would have substantial difficulty in attempting to differentiate between the listed and unlisted species;

(B) the effect of this substantial difficulty is an additional threat to an endangered or threatened species; and

(C) such treatment of an unlisted species will substantially facilitate the enforcement and further the policy of this chapter.

(f) Recovery plans

(1) The Secretary shall develop and implement plans (hereinafter in this subsection referred to as "recovery plans") for the conservation and survival of endangered species and threatened species listed pursuant to this section, unless he finds that such a plan will not promote the conservation of the species. The Secretary, in developing and implementing recovery plans, shall, to the maximum extent practicable—

(A) give priority to those endangered species or threatened species, without regard to taxonomic classification, that are most likely to benefit from such plans, particularly those species that are, or may be, in conflict with construction or other development projects or other forms of economic activity;

(B) incorporate in each plan—

(i) a description of such site-specific management actions as may be necessary to achieve the plan's goal for the conservation and survival of the species;

(ii) objective, measurable criteria which, when met, would result in a determination, in accordance with the provisions of this section, that the species be removed from the list; and

(iii) estimates of the time required and the cost to carry out those measures needed to achieve the plan's goal and to achieve intermediate steps toward that goal.

(2) The Secretary, in developing and implementing recovery plans, may procure the services of appropriate public and private agencies and institutions, and other qualified persons. Recovery teams appointed pursuant to this subsection shall not be subject to the Federal Advisory Committee Act.

(3) The Secretary shall report every two years to the Committee on Environment and Public Works of the Senate and the Committee on Merchant Marine and Fisheries of the House of Representatives on the status of efforts to develop and implement recovery plans for all species listed pursuant to this section and on the status of all species for which such plans have been developed.

(4) The Secretary shall, prior to final approval of a new or revised recovery plan, provide public notice and an opportunity for public review and comment on such plan. The Secretary shall consider all information presented during the public comment period prior to approval of the plan.

(5) Each Federal agency shall, prior to implementation of a new or revised recovery plan, consider all information presented during the public comment period under paragraph (4).

(g) Monitoring

(1) The Secretary shall implement a system in cooperation with the States to monitor effectively for not less than five years the status of all species which have recovered to the point at which the measures provided pursuant to this chapter are no longer necessary and which, in accordance with the provisions of this section, have been removed from either of the lists published under subsection (c) of this section.

(2) The Secretary shall make prompt use of the authority under paragraph 7[1] of subsection (b) of this section to prevent a significant risk to the well being of any such recovered species.

(h) Agency guidelines; publication in Federal Register; scope; proposals and amendments: notice and opportunity for comments

The Secretary shall establish, and publish in the Federal Register, agency guidelines to insure that the purposes of this section are achieved efficiently and effectively. Such guidelines shall include, but are not limited to—

(1) procedures for recording the receipt and the disposition of petitions submitted under subsection (b)(3) of this section;

(2) criteria for making the findings required under such subsection with respect to petitions;

(3) a ranking system to assist in the identification of species that should receive priority review under subsection (a)(1) of this section; and

(4) a system for developing and implementing, on a priority basis, recovery plans under subsection (f) of this section.

The Secretary shall provide to the public notice of, and opportunity to submit written comments on, any guideline (including any amendment thereto) proposed to be established under this subsection.

(i) Submission to State agency of justification for regulations inconsistent with State agency's comments or petition

If, in the case of any regulation proposed by the Secretary under the authority of this section, a State agency to which notice thereof was given in accordance with subsection (b)(5)(A)(ii) of this section files comments disagreeing with all or part of the proposed regulation, and the Secretary issues a final regulation which is in conflict with such comments, or if the Secretary fails to adopt a regulation pursuant to an action petitioned by a State agency under subsection (b)(3) of this section, the Secretary shall submit to the State agency a written justification for his failure to adopt regulations consistent with the agency's comments or petition.

(Pub. L. No. 93–205, § 4, 87 Stat. 886 (Dec. 28, 1973); as amended by Pub. L. No. 94–359, § 1, 90 Stat. 911 (July 12, 1976); Pub. L. No. 95–632, §§ 11, 13, 92 Stat. 3764, 3766 (Nov. 10, 1978); Pub. L. No. 96–159, § 3, 93 Stat. 1225 (Dec. 28, 1979); Pub. L. No. 97–304, § 2(a), 96 Stat. 1411 (Oct. 13, 1982); Pub. L. No. 100–478, Title I, §§ 1002 to 1004, 102 Stat. 2306 (Oct. 7, 1988); Pub. L. No. 108–136, Div. A, Title III, § 318, 117 Stat. 1433 (Nov. 24, 2003).)

[1] So in original. Probably should be "paragraph (7)".

HISTORICAL AND STATUTORY NOTES

References in Text

Reorganization Plan No. 4 of 1970, referred to in subsec. (a)(2), is Reorg. Plan No. 4 of 1970, eff. Oct. 3, 1970, 35 Fed. Reg. 15627, 84 Stat. 2090, which is set out in the Appendix to Title 5, Government Organization and Employees.

This chapter, referred to in subsecs. (b)(3)(B)(iii)(II), (4), (8), (e)(C) and (g)(1), in the original read "this Act", meaning the Endangered Species Act of 1973, which is codified principally to this chapter. For complete classification, see Short Title note set out under section 1531 of this title and Tables.

The Federal Advisory Committee Act, referred to in subsec. (f)(2), is set out in Appendix 2 to Title 5, Government Organization and Employees.

Effective and Applicability Provisions

1982 Acts. Section 2(b) of Pub. L. No. 97–304 provided that:

"(1) Any petition filed under section 4(c)(2) of the Endangered Species Act of 1973 [subsec. (c)(2) of this section] (as in effect on the day before the date of the enactment of this Act) [Oct. 13, 1982] and any regulation proposed under section 4(f) of such Act of 1973 [subsec. (f) of this section] (as in effect on such day) that is pending on such date of enactment [Oct. 13, 1982] shall be treated as having been filed or proposed on such date of enactment [Oct. 13, 1982] under section 4(b) of such Act of 1973 [subsec. (b) of this section] (as amended by subsection (a)); and the procedural requirements specified in such section 4(b) [subsec. (b) of this section] (as so amended) regarding such petition or proposed regulation shall be deemed to be complied with to the extent that like requirements under such section 4 [this section] (as in effect before the date of the enactment of this Act) [Oct. 13, 1982] were complied with before such date of enactment [Oct. 13, 1982].

"(2) Any regulation proposed after, or pending on, the date of the enactment of this Act [Oct. 13, 1982] to designate critical habitat for a species that was determined before such date of enactment [Oct. 13, 1982] to be endangered or threatened shall be subject to the procedures set forth in section 4 of such Act of 1973 [this section] (as amended by subsection (a)) for regulations proposing revisions to critical habitat instead of those for regulations proposing the designation of critical habitat.

"(3) Any list of endangered species or threatened species (as in effect under section 4(c) of such Act of 1973 [subsec. (c) of this section] on the day before the date of the enactment of this Act) [Oct. 13, 1982] shall remain in effect unless and until determinations regarding species and designations and revisions of critical habitats that require changes to such list are made in accordance with subsection (b)(5) of such Act of 1973 [subsec. (b)(5) of this section] (as added by subsection (a)).

"(4) Section 4(a)(3)(A) of such Act of 1973 [subsec. (a)(3)(A) of this section] (as added by subsection (a)) shall not apply with respect to any species which was listed as an endangered species or a threatened species before November 10, 1978."

1973 Acts. Section effective Dec. 28, 1973, see section 16 of Pub. L. No. 93–205, set out as an Effective Date note under section 1531 of this title.

Abolition of House Committee on Merchant Marine and Fisheries

Committee on Merchant Marine and Fisheries of House of Representatives abolished and its jurisdiction transferred by House Resolution No. 6, One Hundred Fourth Congress, Jan. 4, 1995. Committee on Merchant Marine and Fisheries of the House of Representatives treated as referring to the Committee on Resources of the House of Representatives, in the case of a provision of law relating to fisheries, wildlife, international fishing agreements, marine affairs (including coastal zone management) except for measures relating to oil and other pollution of navigable waters, or oceanography by section 1(b)(3) of Pub. L. No. 104–14, set out as a note preceding 2 U.S.C.A. § 21. Committee on Resources of the House of Representatives, changed to Committee on Natural Resources of the House of Representatives by House Resolution No. 6, One Hundred Tenth Congress, Jan. 5, 2007.

Fiscal Limitations on Listing Species

Section 116 of Pub. L. No. 116–260, 134 Stat. 1182, 1506 (Dec. 27, 2020), provided that:

"None of the funds made available by this or any other Act may be used by the Secretary of the Interior to write or issue pursuant to section 4 of the Endangered Species Act of 1973 (16 U.S.C. 1533)—

"**(1)** a proposed rule for greater sage-grouse (*Centrocercus urophasianus*);

"**(2)** a proposed rule for the Columbia basin distinct population segment of greater sage-grouse."

Section 116 of Pub. L. No. 116–94, 133 Stat. 2715 (Dec. 20, 2019), provided that:

"None of the funds made available by this or any other Act may be used by the Secretary of the Interior to write or issue pursuant to section 4 of the Endangered Species Act of 1973 (16 U.S.C. 1533)—

"**(1)** a proposed rule for greater sage-grouse (Centrocercus urophasianus);

"**(2)** a proposed rule for the Columbia basin distinct population segment of greater sage-grouse."

Section 120 of Pub. L. No. 11–6, 133 Stat. 13, 233 (Feb. 15, 2019), provided that:

"None of the funds made available by this or any other Act may be used by the Secretary of the Interior to write or issue pursuant to section 4 of the Endangered Species Act of 1973 (16 U.S.C. 1533)—

"**(1)** a proposed rule for greater sage-grouse (*Centrocercus urophasianus*);

"**(2)** a proposed rule for the Columbia basin distinct population segment of greater sage-grouse."

Pub. L. No. 113–76, 128 Stat. 292 (Jan. 17, 2014), provided as follows:

"For necessary expenses of the United States Fish and Wildlife Service, as authorized by law, and for scientific and economic studies, general administration, and for the performance of other authorized functions related to such resources, $1,188,339,000, to remain available until September 30, 2015 except as otherwise provided herein: *Provided,* That not to exceed $20,515,000 shall be used for implementing subsections (a), (b), (c), and (e) of section 4 of the Endangered Species Act of 1973 (16 U.S.C. 1533) (except for processing petitions, developing and issuing proposed and final regulations, and taking any other steps to implement actions described in subsection (c)(2)(A), (c)(2)(B)(i), or (c)(2)(B)(ii)), of which not to exceed $4,605,000 shall be used for any activity regarding the designation of critical habitat, pursuant to subsection (a)(3), excluding litigation support, for species listed pursuant to subsection (a)(1) prior to October 1, 2012; of which not to exceed $1,501,000 shall be used for any activity regarding petitions to list species that are indigenous to the United States pursuant to subsections (b)(3)(A) and (b)(3)(B); and, of which not to exceed $1,504,000 shall be used for implementing subsections (a), (b), (c), and (e) of section 4 of the Endangered Species Act of 1973 (16 U.S.C. 1533) for species that are not indigenous to the United States."

Pub. L. No. 113–235, 128 Stat. 2399 (Dec. 16, 2014), provided as follows:

"For necessary expenses of the United States Fish and Wildlife Service, as authorized by law, and for scientific and economic studies, general administration, and for the performance of other authorized functions related to such resources, $1,207,658,000, to remain available until September 30, 2016 except as otherwise provided herein: *Provided,* That not to exceed $20,515,000 shall be used for implementing subsections (a), (b), (c), and (e) of section 4 of the Endangered Species Act of 1973 (16 U.S.C. 1533) (except for processing petitions, developing and issuing proposed and final regulations, and taking any other steps to implement actions described in subsection (c)(2)(A), (c)(2)(B)(i), or (c)(2)(B)(ii)), of which not to exceed $4,605,000 shall be used for any activity regarding the designation of critical habitat, pursuant to subsection (a)(3), excluding litigation support, for species listed pursuant to subsection (a)(1) prior to October 1, 2012; of which not to exceed $1,501,000 shall be used for any activity regarding petitions to list species that are indigenous to the United States pursuant to subsections (b)(3)(A) and (b)(3)(B); and, of which not to exceed $1,504,000 shall be used for implementing subsections (a), (b), (c), and (e) of section 4 of the Endangered Species Act of 1973 (16 U.S.C. 1533) for species that are not indigenous to the United States."

In addition, Section 122 of Pub. L. No. 113–235, 128 Stat. 2421–22, provided that:

"None of the funds made available by this or any other Act may be used by the Secretary of the Interior to write or issue pursuant to section 4 of the Endangered Species Act of 1973 (16 U.S.C. 1533)—

"(1) a proposed rule for greater sage-grouse (*Centrocercus urophasianus*);

"(2) a proposed rule for the Columbia basin distinct population segment of greater sage-grouse;

"(3) a final rule for the bi-state distinct population segment of greater sage-grouse; or

"(4) a final rule for Gunnison sage-grouse (*Centrocercus minimus*)."

§ 1534. Land acquisition

[ESA § 5]

(a) Implementation of conservation program; authorization of Secretary and Secretary of Agriculture

The Secretary, and the Secretary of Agriculture with respect to the National Forest System, shall establish and implement a program to conserve fish, wildlife, and plants, including those which are listed as endangered species or threatened species pursuant to section 1533 of this title. To carry out such a program, the appropriate Secretary—

(1) shall utilize the land acquisition and other authority under the Fish and Wildlife Act of 1956, as amended [16 U.S.C.A. § 742a et seq.], the Fish and Wildlife Coordination Act, as amended [16 U.S.C.A. § 661 et seq.], and the Migratory Bird Conservation Act [16 U.S.C.A. § 715 et seq.], as appropriate; and

(2) is authorized to acquire by purchase, donation, or otherwise, lands, waters, or interest therein, and such

authority shall be in addition to any other land acquisition authority vested in him.

(b) Availability of funds for acquisition of lands, waters, etc.

Funds made available pursuant to the Land and Water Conservation Fund Act of 1965, as amended [16 U.S.C.A. § 460*l*–4 et seq.], may be used for the purpose of acquiring lands, waters, or interests therein under subsection (a) of this section.

(Pub. L. No. 93–205, § 5, 87 Stat. 889 (Dec. 28, 1973); as amended by Pub. L. No. 95–632, § 12, 92 Stat. 3766 (Nov. 10, 1978).)

HISTORICAL AND STATUTORY NOTES

References in Text

The Fish and Wildlife Act of 1956, as amended, referred to in subsec. (a)(1), is codified generally as sections 742a to 742d and 742e to 742j–2 of this title. For complete classification, see Short Title note set out under section 742a of this title and Tables.

The Fish and Wildlife Coordination Act, as amended, referred to in subsec. (a)(1), is codified generally as sections 661 to 666c of this title. For complete classification, see Short Title note set out under section 661 of this title and Tables volume.

The Migratory Bird Conservation Act, referred to in subsec. (a)(1), is codified generally as subchapter III of chapter 7 of this title (16 U.S.C.A. § 715 et seq.). For complete classification, see section 715 of this title and Tables volume.

The Land and Water Conservation Fund Act of 1965, as amended, referred to in subsec. (b), is codified as section 460*l*–4 et seq. of this title. For complete classification, see Short Title note set out under section 460*l*–4 of this title and Tables volume.

Effective and Applicability Provisions

1973 Acts. Section effective Dec. 28, 1973, see section 16 of Pub. L. No. 93–205, set out as an Effective Date note under section 1531 of this title.

§ 1535. Cooperation with States

[ESA § 6]

(a) Generally

In carrying out the program authorized by this chapter, the Secretary shall cooperate to the maximum extent practicable with the States. Such cooperation shall include consultation with the States concerned before acquiring any land or water, or interest therein, for the purpose of conserving any endangered species or threatened species.

(b) Management agreements

The Secretary may enter into agreements with any State for the administration and management of any area established for the conservation of endangered species or threatened species. Any revenues derived from the administration of such areas under these agreements shall be subject to the provisions of section 715s of this title.

(c) Cooperative agreements

(1) In furtherance of the purposes of this chapter, the Secretary is authorized to enter into a cooperative agreement in accordance with this section with any State which establishes and maintains an adequate and active program for the conservation of endangered species and threatened species. Within one hundred and twenty days after the Secretary receives a certified copy of such a proposed State program, he shall make a determination whether such program is in accordance with this chapter. Unless he determines, pursuant to this paragraph, that the State program is not in accordance with this chapter, he shall enter into a cooperative agreement with the State for the purpose of assisting in implementation of the State program. In order for a State program to be deemed an adequate and active program for the conservation of endangered species and threatened species, the Secretary must find, and annually thereafter reconfirm such finding, that under the State program—

(A) authority resides in the State agency to conserve resident species of fish or wildlife determined by the State agency or the Secretary to be endangered or threatened;

(B) the State agency has established acceptable conservation programs, consistent with the purposes and policies of this chapter, for all resident species of fish or wildlife in the State which are deemed by the Secretary to be endangered or threatened, and has furnished a copy of such plan and program together with all pertinent details, information, and data requested to the Secretary;

(C) the State agency is authorized to conduct investigations to determine the status and requirements for survival of resident species of fish and wildlife;

(D) the State agency is authorized to establish programs, including the acquisition of land or aquatic habitat or interests therein, for the conservation of resident endangered or threatened species of fish or wildlife; and

(E) provision is made for public participation in designating resident species of fish or wildlife as endangered or threatened; or that under the State program—

(i) the requirements set forth in subparagraphs (C), (D), and (E) of this paragraph are complied with, and

(ii) plans are included under which immediate attention will be given to those resident species of fish and wildlife which are determined by the Secretary or the State agency to be endangered or threatened and which the Secretary and the State agency agree are most urgently in need of conservation programs; except that a cooperative agreement entered into with a State whose program is deemed adequate and active pursuant to clause (i) and this clause shall not affect the applicability of prohibitions set forth in or authorized pursuant to section 1533(d) of this title or section 1538(a) (1) of this title with respect to the taking of any resident endangered or threatened species.

(2) In furtherance of the purposes of this chapter, the Secretary is authorized to enter into a cooperative agreement in accordance with this section with any State which establishes and maintains an adequate and active program for the conservation of endangered species and threatened species of plants. Within one hundred and twenty days after the Secretary receives a certified copy of such a proposed State program, he shall make a determination whether such program is in accordance with this chapter. Unless he determines, pursuant to this paragraph, that the State program is not in accordance with this chapter, he shall enter into a cooperative agreement with the State for the purpose of assisting in implementation of the State program. In order for a State program to be deemed an adequate and active program for the conservation of endangered species of plants and threatened species of plants, the Secretary must find, and annually thereafter reconfirm such finding, that under the State program—

(A) authority resides in the State agency to conserve resident species of plants determined by the State agency or the Secretary to be endangered or threatened;

(B) the State agency has established acceptable conservation programs, consistent with the purposes and policies of this chapter, for all resident species of plants in the State which are deemed by the Secretary to be endangered or threatened, and has furnished a copy of such plan and program together with all pertinent details, information, and data requested to the Secretary;

(C) the State agency is authorized to conduct investigations to determine the status and requirements for survival of resident species of plants; and

(D) provision is made for public participation in designating resident species of plants as endangered or threatened; or

that under the State program—

(i) the requirements set forth in subparagraphs (C) and (D) of this paragraph are complied with, and

(ii) plans are included under which immediate attention will be given to those resident species of plants which are determined by the Secretary or the State agency to be endangered or threatened and which the Secretary and the State agency agree are most urgently in need of conservation programs; except that a cooperative agreement entered into with a State whose program is deemed adequate and active pursuant to clause (i) and this clause shall not affect the applicability of prohibitions set forth in or authorized pursuant to section 1533(d) or section 1538(a)(1) of this title with respect to the taking of any resident endangered or threatened species.

(d) Allocation of funds

(1) The Secretary is authorized to provide financial assistance to any State, through its respective State agency, which has entered into a cooperative agreement pursuant to subsection (c) of this section to assist in development of programs for the conservation of endangered and threatened species or to assist in monitoring the status of candidate species pursuant to subparagraph (C) of section 1533(b)(3) of this title and recovered species pursuant to section 1533(g) of this title. The Secretary shall allocate each annual appropriation made in accordance with the provisions of subsection (i) of this section to such States based on consideration of—

(A) the international commitments of the United States to protect endangered species or threatened species;

(B) the readiness of a State to proceed with a conservation program consistent with the objectives and purposes of this chapter;

(C) the number of endangered species and threatened species within a State;

(D) the potential for restoring endangered species and threatened species within a State;

(E) the relative urgency to initiate a program to restore and protect an endangered species or threatened species in terms of survival of the species;

(F) the importance of monitoring the status of candidate species within a State to prevent a significant risk to the well being of any such species; and

(G) the importance of monitoring the status of recovered species within a State to assure that such species do not return to the point at which the measures provided pursuant to this chapter are again necessary.

So much of the annual appropriation made in accordance with provisions of subsection (i) of this section allocated for obligation to any State for any fiscal year as remains unobligated at the close thereof is authorized to be made available to that State until the close of the succeeding fiscal year. Any amount allocated to any State which is unobligated at the end of the period during which it is available for expenditure is authorized to be made available for expenditure by the Secretary in conducting programs under this section.

(2) Such cooperative agreements shall provide for (A) the actions to be taken by the Secretary and the States; (B) the benefits that are expected to be derived in connection with the conservation of endangered or threatened species; (C) the estimated cost of these actions; and (D) the share of such costs to be borne by the Federal Government and by the States; except that—

(i) the Federal share of such program costs shall not exceed 75 percent of the estimated program cost stated in the agreement; and

(ii) the Federal share may be increased to 90 percent whenever two or more States having a common interest in one or more endangered or threatened species, the conservation of which may be enhanced by cooperation of such States, enter jointly into an agreement with the Secretary.

The Secretary may, in his discretion, and under such rules and regulations as he may prescribe, advance funds to the State for financing the United States pro rata share agreed upon in the cooperative agreement. For the purposes of this section, the non-Federal share may, in the discretion of the Secretary, be in the form of money or real property, the value of which will be determined by the Secretary, whose decision shall be final.

(e) Review of State programs

Any action taken by the Secretary under this section shall be subject to his periodic review at no greater than annual intervals.

(f) Conflicts between Federal and State laws

Any State law or regulation which applies with respect to the importation or exportation of, or interstate or foreign commerce in, endangered species or threatened species is void to the extent that it may effectively (1) permit what is prohibited by this chapter or by any regulation which implements this chapter, or (2) prohibit what is authorized pursuant to an exemption or permit provided for in this chapter or in any regulation which implements this chapter. This chapter shall not otherwise be construed to void any State law or regulation which is intended to conserve migratory, resident, or introduced fish or wildlife, or to permit or prohibit sale of such fish or wildlife. Any State law or regulation respecting the taking of an endangered species or threatened species may be more restrictive than the exemptions or permits provided for in this chapter or in any regulation which implements this chapter but not less restrictive than the prohibitions so defined.

(g) Transition

(1) For purposes of this subsection, the term "establishment period" means, with respect to any State, the period beginning on December 28, 1973, and ending on whichever of the following dates first occurs: (A) the date of the close of the 120-day period following the adjournment of the first regular session of the legislature of such State which commences after December 28, 1973, or (B) the date of the close of the 15-month period following December 28, 1973.

(2) The prohibitions set forth in or authorized pursuant to sections 1533(d) and 1538(a)(1)(B) of this title shall not apply with respect to the taking of any resident endangered species or threatened species (other than species listed in Appendix I to the Convention or otherwise specifically covered by any other treaty or Federal law) within any State—

(A) which is then a party to a cooperative agreement with the Secretary pursuant to subsection (c) of this section (except to the extent that the taking of any such species is contrary to the law of such State); or

(B) except for any time within the establishment period when—

(i) the Secretary applies such prohibition to such species at the request of the State, or

(ii) the Secretary applies such prohibition after he finds, and publishes his finding, that an emergency exists posing a significant risk to the well-being of such species and that the prohibition must be applied to protect such species. The Secretary's finding and publication may be made without regard to the public hearing or comment provisions of section 553 of Title 5 or any other provision of this chapter; but such prohibition shall expire 90 days after the date of its imposition unless the Secretary further extends such prohibition by publishing notice and a statement of justification of such extension.

(h) Regulations

The Secretary is authorized to promulgate such regulations as may be appropriate to carry out the provisions of this section relating to financial assistance to States.

(i) Appropriations

(1) To carry out the provisions of this section for fiscal years after September 30, 1988, there shall be deposited into a special fund known as the cooperative endangered species conservation fund, to be administered by the Secretary, an amount equal to 5 percent of the combined amounts covered each fiscal year into the Federal aid to wildlife restoration fund under section 669b of this title, and paid, transferred, or otherwise credited each fiscal year to the Sport Fishing Restoration Account established under 1016 of the Act of July 18, 1984.

(2) Amounts deposited into the special fund are authorized to be appropriated annually and allocated in accordance with subsection (d) of this section.

(Pub. L. No. 93–205, § 6, 87 Stat. 889 (Dec. 28, 1973); as amended by Pub. L. No. 95–212, 91 Stat. 1493 (Dec. 19, 1977); Pub. L. No. 95–632, § 10, 92 Stat. 3762 (Nov. 10, 1978); Pub. L. No. 96–246, 94 Stat. 348 (May 23, 1980); Pub. L. No. 97–304, §§ 3, 8(b), 96 Stat. 1416, 1426 (Oct. 13, 1982); Pub. L. No. 100–478, Title I, § 1005, 102 Stat. 2307 (Oct. 7, 1988).)

HISTORICAL AND STATUTORY NOTES

References in Text

This chapter, referred to in subsecs. (a), (c), (d)(1)(B), (G), (f), and (g)(2)(B)(ii), in the original read "this Act", meaning the Endangered Species Act of 1973, which is codified principally in this chapter. For complete classification, see Short Title note set out under section 1531 of this title and Tables.

Section 1016 of the Act of July 18, 1984, referred to in subsec. (i), probably means Pub. L. No. 98–369, Div. A, Title X, § 1016, 98 Stat. 1019, (July 18, 1984), which enacted section 9504 of Title 26, Internal Revenue Code, amended section 9503 of Title 26, repealed section 13107 of Title 46, Shipping, and enacted provisions set out as a note under section 9504 of Title 26.

Effective and Applicability Provisions

1973 Acts. Section effective Dec. 28, 1973, see section 16 of Pub. L. No. 93–205, set out as an Effective Date note under section 1531 of this title.

Cooperative Agreements With States Unaffected by 1981 Amendment of Marine Mammal Protection Act

Nothing in the amendment of section 109 of the Marine Mammal Protection Act of 1972 [section 1379 of this title] by section 4(a) of Pub. L. No. 97–58 to be construed as affecting in any manner, or to any extent, any cooperative agreement entered into by a State under subsec. (c) of this section before, on, or after Oct. 9, 1981, see section 4(b) of Pub. L. No. 97–58, set out as a note under section 1379 of this title.

§ 1536. Interagency cooperation

[ESA § 7]

(a) Federal agency actions and consultations

(1) The Secretary shall review other programs administered by him and utilize such programs in furtherance of the purposes of this chapter. All other Federal agencies shall, in consultation with and with the assistance of the Secretary, utilize their authorities in furtherance of the purposes of this chapter by carrying out programs for the conservation of endangered species and threatened species listed pursuant to section 1533 of this title.

(2) Each Federal agency shall, in consultation with and with the assistance of the Secretary, insure that any action authorized, funded, or carried out by such agency (hereinafter in this section referred to as an "agency action") is not likely to jeopardize the continued existence of any endangered species or threatened species or result in the destruction or adverse modification of habitat of such species which is determined by the Secretary, after consultation as appropriate with affected States, to be critical, unless such agency has been granted an exemption for such action by the Committee pursuant to subsection (h) of this section. In fulfilling the requirements of this paragraph each agency shall use the best scientific and commercial data available.

(3) Subject to such guidelines as the Secretary may establish, a Federal agency shall consult with the Secretary on any prospective agency action at the request of, and in cooperation with, the prospective permit or license applicant if the applicant has reason to believe that an endangered species or a threatened species may be present in the area affected by his project and that implementation of such action will likely affect such species.

(4) Each Federal agency shall confer with the Secretary on any agency action which is likely to jeopardize the continued existence of any species proposed to be listed under section 1533 of this title or result in the destruction or adverse modification of critical habitat proposed to be designated for such species. This paragraph does not require a limitation on the commitment of resources as described in subsection (d) of this section.

(b) Opinion of Secretary

(1) (A) Consultation under subsection (a) (2) f this section with respect to any agency action shall be concluded within the 90-day period beginning on the date on which initiated or, subject to subparagraph (B), within such other period of time as is mutually agreeable to the Secretary and the Federal agency.

(B) In the case of an agency action involving a permit or license applicant, the Secretary and the Federal agency may not mutually agree to conclude consultation within a period exceeding 90 days unless the Secretary, before the close of the 90th day referred to in subparagraph (A)—

(i) if the consultation period proposed to be agreed to will end before the 150th day after the date on which consultation was initiated, submits to the applicant a written statement setting forth—

(I) the reasons why a longer period is required,

(II) the information that is required to complete the consultation, and

(III) the estimated date on which consultation will be completed; or

(ii) if the consultation period proposed to be agreed to will end 150 or more days after the date on which consultation was initiated, obtains the consent of the applicant to such period.

The Secretary and the Federal agency may mutually agree to extend a consultation period established under the preceding sentence if the Secretary, before the close of such period, obtains the consent of the applicant to the extension.

(2) Consultation under subsection (a) (3) of this section shall be concluded within such period as is agreeable to the Secretary, the Federal agency, and the applicant concerned.

(3) **(A)** Promptly after conclusion of consultation under paragraph (2) or (3) of subsection (a) of this section, the Secretary shall provide to the Federal agency and the applicant, if any, a written statement setting forth the Secretary's opinion, and a summary of the information on which the opinion is based, detailing how the agency action affects the species or its critical habitat. If jeopardy or adverse modification is found, the Secretary shall suggest those reasonable and prudent alternatives which he believes would not violate subsection (a) (2) of this section and can be taken by the Federal agency or applicant in implementing the agency action.

(B) Consultation under subsection (a) (3) of this section, and an opinion issued by the Secretary incident to such consultation, regarding an agency action shall be treated respectively as a consultation under subsection (a) (2) of this section, and as an opinion issued after consultation under such subsection, regarding that action if the Secretary reviews the action before it is commenced by the Federal agency and finds, and notifies such agency, that no significant changes have been made with respect to the action and that no significant change has occurred regarding the information used during the initial consultation.

(4) If after consultation under subsection (a)(2) of this section, the Secretary concludes that—

(A) the agency action will not violate such subsection, or offers reasonable and prudent alternatives which the Secretary believes would not violate such subsection;

(B) the taking of an endangered species or a threatened species incidental to the agency action will not violate such subsection; and

(C) if an endangered species or threatened species of a marine mammal is involved, the taking is authorized pursuant to section 1371(a)(5) of this title;

the Secretary shall provide the Federal agency and the applicant concerned, if any, with a written statement that—

(i) specifies the impact of such incidental taking on the species,

(ii) specifies those reasonable and prudent measures that the Secretary considers necessary or appropriate to minimize such impact,

(iii) in the case of marine mammals, specifies those measures that are necessary to comply with section 1371(a)(5) of this title with regard to such taking, and

(iv) sets forth the terms and conditions (including, but not limited to, reporting requirements) that must be complied with by the Federal agency or applicant (if any), or both, to implement the measures specified under clauses (ii) and (iii).

(c) Biological assessment

(1) To facilitate compliance with the requirements of subsection (a) (2) of this section, each Federal agency shall, with respect to any agency action of such agency for which no contract for construction has been entered into and for which no construction has begun on November 10, 1978, request of the Secretary information whether any species which is listed or proposed to be listed may be present in the area of such proposed action. If the Secretary advises, based on the best scientific and commercial data available, that such species may be present, such agency shall conduct a biological assessment for the purpose of identifying any endangered species or threatened species which is likely to be affected by such action. Such assessment shall be completed within 180 days after the date on which initiated (or within such other period as is mutually agreed to by the Secretary and such agency, except that if a permit or license applicant is involved, the 180-day period may not be extended unless such agency provides the applicant, before the close of such period, with a written statement setting forth the estimated length of the proposed extension and the reasons therefor) and, before any contract for construction is entered into and before construction is begun with respect to such action. Such assessment may be undertaken as part of a Federal agency's compliance with the requirements of section 102 of the National Environmental Policy Act of 1969 (42 U.S.C. 4332).

(2) Any person who may wish to apply for an exemption under subsection (g) of this section for that action may conduct a biological assessment to identify any endangered species or threatened species which is likely to be affected by such action. Any such biological assessment must, however, be conducted in cooperation with the Secretary and under the supervision of the appropriate Federal agency.

(d) Limitation on commitment of resources

After initiation of consultation required under subsection (a) (2) of this section, the Federal agency and the permit or license applicant shall not make any irreversible or irretrievable commitment of resources with respect to the agency action which has the effect of foreclosing the formulation or implementation of any reasonable and prudent alternative measures which would not violate subsection (a) (2) of this section.

(e) Endangered Species Committee

(1) There is established a committee to be known as the Endangered Species Committee (hereinafter in this section referred to as the "Committee").

(2) The Committee shall review any application submitted to it pursuant to this section and determine in accordance with subsection (h) of this section whether or not to grant an exemption from the requirements of subsection (a) (2) of this section for the action set forth in such application.

(3) The Committee shall be composed of seven members as follows:

(A) The Secretary of Agriculture.

(B) The Secretary of the Army.

(C) The Chairman of the Council of Economic Advisors.

(D) The Administrator of the Environmental Protection Agency.

(E) The Secretary of the Interior.

(F) The Administrator of the National Oceanic and Atmospheric Administration.

(G) The President, after consideration of any recommendations received pursuant to subsection (g) (2) (B) of this section shall appoint one individual from each affected State, as determined by the Secretary, to be a member of the Committee for the consideration of the application for exemption for an agency action with respect to which such recommendations are made, not later than 30 days after an application is submitted pursuant to this section.

(4) **(A)** Members of the Committee shall receive no additional pay on account of their service on the Committee.

(B) While away from their homes or regular places of business in the performance of services for the Committee, members of the Committee shall be allowed travel expenses, including per diem in lieu of subsistence, in the same manner as persons employed intermittently in the Government service are allowed expenses under section 5703 of Title 5.

(5) **(A)** Five members of the Committee or their representatives shall constitute a quorum for the transaction of any function of the Committee, except that, in no case shall any representative be considered in determining the existence of a quorum for the transaction of any function of the Committee if that function involves a vote by the Committee on any matter before the Committee.

(B) The Secretary of the Interior shall be the Chairman of the Committee.

(C) The Committee shall meet at the call of the Chairman or five of its members.

(D) All meetings and records of the Committee shall be open to the public.

(6) Upon request of the Committee, the head of any Federal agency is authorized to detail, on a nonreimbursable basis, any of the personnel of such agency to the Committee to assist it in carrying out its duties under this section.

(7) **(A)** The Committee may for the purpose of carrying out its duties under this section hold such hearings, sit and act at such times and places, take such testimony, and receive such evidence, as the Committee deems advisable.

(B) When so authorized by the Committee, any member or agent of the Committee may take any action which the Committee is authorized to take by this paragraph.

(C) Subject to the Privacy Act [5 U.S.C.A. § 552a], the Committee may secure directly from any Federal agency information necessary to enable it to carry out its duties under this section. Upon request of the Chairman of the Committee, the head of such Federal agency shall furnish such information to the Committee.

(D) The Committee may use the United States mails in the same manner and upon the same conditions as a Federal agency.

(E) The Administrator of General Services shall provide to the Committee on a reimbursable basis such administrative support services as the Committee may request.

(8) In carrying out its duties under this section, the Committee may promulgate and amend such rules, regulations, and procedures, and issue and amend such orders as it deems necessary.

(9) For the purpose of obtaining information necessary for the consideration of an application for an exemption under this section the Committee may issue subpenas for the attendance and testimony of witnesses and the production of relevant papers, books, and documents.

(10) In no case shall any representative, including a representative of a member designated pursuant to paragraph (3) (G) of this subsection, be eligible to cast a vote on behalf of any member.

(f) Promulgation of regulations; form and contents of exemption application

Not later than 90 days after November 10, 1978, the Secretary shall promulgate regulations which set forth the form and manner in which applications for exemption shall be submitted to the Secretary and the information to be contained in such applications. Such regulations shall require that information submitted in an application by the head of any Federal agency with respect to any agency action include, but not be limited to—

(1) a description of the consultation process carried out pursuant to subsection (a) (2) of this section between the head of the Federal agency and the Secretary; and

(2) a statement describing why such action cannot be altered or modified to conform with the requirements of subsection (a) (2) of this section.

(g) Application for exemption; report to Committee

(1) A Federal agency, the Governor of the State in which an agency action will occur, if any, or a permit or license applicant may apply to the Secretary for an exemption for an agency action of such agency if, after consultation under subsection (a) (2) of this section, the Secretary's opinion under subsection (b) of this section indicates that the agency action would violate subsection (a) (2) of this section. An application for an exemption shall be considered initially by the Secretary in the manner provided for in this subsection, and shall be considered by the Committee for a final determination under subsection (h) of this section after a report is made pursuant to paragraph (5). The applicant for an exemption shall be referred to as the "exemption applicant" in this section.

(2) (A) An exemption applicant shall submit a written application to the Secretary, in a form prescribed under subsection (f) of this section, not later than 90 days after the completion of the consultation process; except that, in the case of any agency action involving a permit or license applicant, such application shall be submitted not later than 90 days after the date on which the Federal agency concerned takes final agency action with respect to the issuance of the permit or license. For purposes of the preceding sentence, the term "final agency action" means (i) a disposition by an agency with respect to the issuance of a permit or license that is subject to administrative review, whether or not such disposition is subject to judicial review; or (ii) if administrative review is sought with respect to such disposition, the decision resulting after such review. Such application shall set forth the reasons why the exemption applicant considers that the agency action meets the requirements for an exemption under this subsection.

(B) Upon receipt of an application for exemption for an agency action under paragraph (1), the Secretary shall promptly (i) notify the Governor of each affected State, if any, as determined by the Secretary, and request the Governors so notified to recommend individuals to be appointed to the Endangered Species Committee for consideration of such application; and (ii) publish notice of receipt of the application in the Federal Register, including a summary of the information contained in the application and a description of the agency action with respect to which the application for exemption has been filed.

(3) The Secretary shall within 20 days after the receipt of an application for exemption, or within such other period of time as is mutually agreeable to the exemption applicant and the Secretary—

(A) determine that the Federal agency concerned and the exemption applicant have—

(i) carried out the consultation responsibilities described in subsection (a) of this section in good faith and made a reasonable and responsible effort to develop and fairly consider modifications or reasonable and prudent alternatives to the proposed agency action which would not violate subsection (a) (2) of this section;

(ii) conducted any biological assessment required by subsection (c) of this section; and

(iii) to the extent determinable within the time provided herein, refrained from making any irreversible or irretrievable commitment of resources prohibited by subsection (d) of this section; or

(B) deny the application for exemption because the Federal agency concerned or the exemption applicant have not met the requirements set forth in subparagraph (A) (i), (ii), and (iii).

The denial of an application under subparagraph (B) shall be considered final agency action for purposes of chapter 7 of Title 5.

(4) If the Secretary determines that the Federal agency concerned and the exemption applicant have met the requirements set forth in paragraph (3) (A) (i), (ii), and (iii) he shall, in consultation with the Members of the Committee, hold a hearing on the application for exemption in accordance with sections 554, 555, and 556 (other than subsection (b) (1) and (2) thereof) of Title 5 and prepare the report to be submitted pursuant to paragraph (5).

(5) Within 140 days after making the determinations under paragraph (3) or within such other period of time as is mutually agreeable to the exemption applicant and the Secretary, the Secretary shall submit to the Committee a report discussing—

(A) the availability of reasonable and prudent alternatives to the agency action, and the nature and extent of the benefits of the agency action and of alternative courses of action consistent with conserving the species or the critical habitat;

(B) a summary of the evidence concerning whether or not the agency action is in the public interest and is of national or regional significance;

(C) appropriate reasonable mitigation and enhancement measures which should be considered by the Committee; and

(D) whether the Federal agency concerned and the exemption applicant refrained from making any irreversible or irretrievable commitment of resources prohibited by subsection (d) of this section.

(6) To the extent practicable within the time required for action under subsection (g) of this section, and except to the extent inconsistent with the requirements of this section, the consideration of any application for an exemption under this section and the conduct of any hearing under this subsection shall be in accordance with sections 554, 555, and 556 (other than subsection (b) (3) of section 556) of Title 5.

(7) Upon request of the Secretary, the head of any Federal agency is authorized to detail, on a nonreimbursable basis, any of the personnel of such agency to the Secretary to assist him in carrying out his duties under this section.

(8) All meetings and records resulting from activities pursuant to this subsection shall be open to the public.

(h) Grant of exemption

(1) The Committee shall make a final determination whether or not to grant an exemption within 30 days after receiving the report of the Secretary pursuant to subsection (g) (5) of this section. The Committee shall grant an exemption from the requirements of subsection (a) (2) of this section for an agency action if, by a vote of not less than five of its members voting in person—

(A) it determines on the record, based on the report of the Secretary, the record of the hearing held under subsection (g) (4) of this section and on such other testimony or evidence as it may receive, that—

(i) there are no reasonable and prudent alternatives to the agency action;

(ii) the benefits of such action clearly outweigh the benefits of alternative courses of action consistent with conserving the species or its critical habitat, and such action is in the public interest;

(iii) the action is of regional or national significance; and

(iv) neither the Federal agency concerned nor the exemption applicant made any irreversible or irretrievable commitment of resources prohibited by subsection (d) of this section; and

(B) it establishes such reasonable mitigation and enhancement measures, including, but not limited to, live propagation, transplantation, and habitat acquisition and improvement, as are necessary and appropriate to minimize the adverse effects of the agency action upon the endangered species, threatened species, or critical habitat concerned.

Any final determination by the Committee under this subsection shall be considered final agency action for purposes of chapter 7 of Title 5.

(2) **(A)** Except as provided in subparagraph (B), an exemption for an agency action granted under paragraph (1) shall constitute a permanent exemption with respect to all endangered or threatened species for the purposes of completing such agency action—

(i) regardless whether the species was identified in the biological assessment; and

(ii) only if a biological assessment has been conducted under subsection (c) of this section with respect to such agency action.

(B) An exemption shall be permanent under subparagraph (A) unless—

(i) the Secretary finds, based on the best scientific and commercial data available, that such exemption would result in the extinction of a species that was not the subject of consultation under subsection (a) (2) of this section or was not identified in any biological assessment conducted under subsection (c) of this section, and

(ii) the Committee determines within 60 days after the date of the Secretary's finding that the exemption should not be permanent.

If the Secretary makes a finding described in clause (i), the Committee shall meet with respect to the matter within 30 days after the date of the finding.

(i) Review by Secretary of State; violation of international treaty or other international obligation of United States

Notwithstanding any other provision of this chapter, the Committee shall be prohibited from considering for exemption any application made to it, if the Secretary of State, after a review of the proposed agency action and its potential implications, and after hearing, certifies, in writing, to the Committee within 60 days of any application made under this section that the granting of any such exemption and the carrying out of such action would be in violation of an international treaty obligation or other international obligation of the United States. The Secretary of State shall, at the time of such certification, publish a copy thereof in the Federal Register.

(j) Exemption for national security reasons

Notwithstanding any other provision of this chapter, the Committee shall grant an exemption for any agency action if the Secretary of Defense finds that such exemption is necessary for reasons of national security.

(k) Exemption decision not considered major Federal action; environmental impact statement

An exemption decision by the Committee under this section shall not be a major Federal action for purposes of the National Environmental Policy Act of 1969 [42 U.S.C.A. § 4321 et seq.]: *Provided*, That an environmental impact statement which discusses the impacts upon endangered species or threatened species or their critical habitats shall have been previously prepared with respect to any agency action exempted by such order.

(*l*) Committee order granting exemption; cost of mitigation and enhancement measures; report by applicant to Council on Environmental Quality

(1) If the Committee determines under subsection (h) of this section that an exemption should be granted with respect to any agency action, the Committee shall issue an order granting the exemption and specifying the mitigation and enhancement measures established pursuant to subsection (h) of this section which shall be carried out and paid for by the exemption applicant in implementing the agency action. All necessary mitigation and enhancement measures shall be authorized prior to the implementing of the agency action and funded concurrently with all other project features.

(2) The applicant receiving such exemption shall include the costs of such mitigation and enhancement measures within the overall costs of continuing the proposed action. Notwithstanding the preceding sentence the costs of such measures shall not be treated as project costs for the purpose of computing benefit-cost or other ratios for the proposed action. Any applicant may request the Secretary to carry out such mitigation and enhancement measures. The costs incurred by the Secretary in carrying out any such measures shall be paid by the applicant receiving the exemption. No later than one year after the granting of an exemption, the exemption applicant shall submit to the Council on Environmental Quality a report describing its compliance with the mitigation and enhancement measures prescribed by this section. Such a report shall be submitted annually until all such mitigation and enhancement measures have been completed. Notice of the public availability of such reports shall be published in the Federal Register by the Council on Environmental Quality.

(m) Notice requirement for citizen suits not applicable

The 60-day notice requirement of section 1540(g) of this title shall not apply with respect to review of any final determination of the Committee under subsection (h) of this section granting an exemption from the requirements of subsection (a) (2) of this section.

(n) Judicial review

Any person, as defined by section 1532(13) of this title, may obtain judicial review, under chapter 7 of Title 5, of any decision of the Endangered Species Committee under subsection (h) of this section in the United States Court of Appeals for (1) any circuit wherein the agency action concerned will be, or is being, carried out, or (2) in any case in which the agency action will be, or is being, carried out outside of any circuit, the District of Columbia, by filing in such court within 90 days after the date of issuance of the decision, a written petition for review. A copy of such petition shall be transmitted by the clerk of the court to the Committee and the Committee shall file in the court the record in the proceeding, as provided in section 2112 of Title 28. Attorneys designated by the Endangered Species Committee may appear for, and represent the Committee in any action for review under this subsection.

(*o*) Exemption as providing exception on taking of endangered species

Notwithstanding sections 1533(d) and 1538(a)(1)(B) and (C) of this title, sections 1371 and 1372 of this title, or any regulation promulgated to implement any such section—

(1) any action for which an exemption is granted under subsection (h) of this section shall not be considered to be a taking of any endangered species or threatened species with respect to any activity which is necessary to carry out such action; and

(2) any taking that is in compliance with the terms and conditions specified in a written statement provided under subsection (b)(4)(iv) of this section shall not be considered to be a prohibited taking of the species concerned.

(p) Exemptions in Presidentially declared disaster areas

In any area which has been declared by the President to be a major disaster area under the Disaster Relief and Emergency Assistance Act [42 U.S.C.A. § 5121 et seq.], the President is authorized to make the determinations required by subsections (g) and (h) of this section for any project for the repair or replacement of a public facility substantially as it existed prior to the disaster under section 405 or 406 of the Disaster Relief and Emergency Assistance Act [42 U.S.C.A. §§ 5171 or 5172], and which the President determines (1) is necessary to prevent the recurrence of such a natural disaster and to reduce the potential loss of human life, and (2) to involve an emergency situation which does not allow the ordinary procedures of this section to be followed. Notwithstanding any other provision of this section, the Committee shall accept the determinations of the President under this subsection.

(Pub. L. No. 93–205, § 7, 87 Stat. 892 (Dec. 28, 1973); as amended by Pub. L. No. 95–632, § 3, 92 Stat. 3752 (Nov. 10, 1978); Pub. L. No. 96–159, § 4, 93 Stat. 1226 (Dec. 28, 1979); Pub. L. No. 97–304, §§ 4(a), 8(b), 96 Stat. 1417, 1426 (Oct. 13, 1982); Pub. L. No. 99–659, Title IV, § 411(b), (c), 100 Stat. 3742 (Nov. 14, 1986); Pub. L. No. 100–707, Title I, § 109(g), 102 Stat. 4709 (Nov. 23, 1988).)

HISTORICAL AND STATUTORY NOTES

References in Text

This chapter, referred to in subsecs. (a)(1) and (j), in the original read "this Act", meaning the Endangered Species Act of 1973, which is codified principally to this chapter. For complete classification, see Short Title note set out under section 1531 of this title and Tables.

The Privacy Act, referred to in subsec. (e)(7)(C), is enacted section 552a of Title 5, Government Organization and Employees, and provisions set out as notes under section 552a of Title 5. For complete classification, see Short Title note set out under section 552a of Title 5 and Tables volume.

The National Environmental Policy Act of 1969, referred to in subsec. (k), is codified generally to chapter 55 of Title 42 (42 U.S.C.A. § 4321 et seq.). Section 102 of the National Environmental Policy Act of 1969, referred to in subsec. (c)(1), is codified as section 4332 of Title 42. For complete classification, see Short Title note set out under section 4321 of Title 42 and Tables.

The Disaster Relief and Emergency Assistance Act, redesignated "The Robert T. Stafford Disaster Relief and Emergency Assistance Act" by Pub. L. No. 93–288, § 1, as amended by 100–707, § 102(a), referred to in subsec. (p), is codified principally to chapter 68 of Title 42, (42 U.S.C.A. § 5121 et seq.). Sections 405 and 406 of the Disaster and Emergency Assistance Act are codified as sections 5171 and 5172 of Title 42. For complete classification, see Short Title note set out under section 5121 of Title 42 and Tables.

Effective and Applicability Provisions

1973 Acts. Section effective Dec. 28, 1973, see section 16 of Pub. L. No. 93–205, set out as an Effective Date note under section 1531 of this title.

Deferral of Agency Action

Pub. L. No. 105–18, Title II, § 3003, 111 Stat. 176 (June 12, 1997), provided that:

"(a) Consultation and conferencing.—As provided by regulations issued under the Endangered Species Act (16 U.S.C. 1531 et seq.) [this chapter] for emergency situations, formal consultation or conferencing under section 7(a)(2) or section 7(a)(4) of the Act [subsec. (a)(2) or (a)(4) of this section] for any action authorized, funded or carried out by any Federal agency to repair a Federal or non-Federal flood control project, facility or structure may be deferred by the Federal agency authorizing, funding or carrying out the action, if the agency determines that the repair is needed to respond to an emergency causing an imminent threat to human lives and property in 1996 or 1997. Formal consultation or conferencing shall be deferred until the imminent threat to human lives and property has been abated. For purposes of this section, the term repair shall include preventive and remedial measures to restore the project, facility or structure to remove an imminent threat to human lives and property.

"(b) Reasonable and prudent measures.—Any reasonable and prudent measures specified under section 7 of the Endangered Species Act (16 U.S.C. 1536)[this section] to minimize the impact of an action taken under this section shall be related both in nature and extent to the effect of the action taken to repair the flood control project, facility or structure."

Translocation of California Sea Otters

Pub. L. No. 99–625, § 1, 100 Stat. 3500 (Nov. 7, 1986), provided that:

"(a) Definitions.—For purposes of this section—

"(1) The term 'Act' means the Endangered Species Act of 1973 (16 U.S.C. 1531 et seq.) [this chapter].

"(2) The term 'agency action' has the meaning given that term in section 7(a)(2) of the Act [subsec. (a)(2) of this section].

"(3) The term 'experimental population' means the population of sea otters provided for under a plan developed under subsection (b).

"(4) The phrase 'parent population' means the population of sea otters existing in California on the date on which proposed regulations setting forth a proposed plan under subsection (b) are issued.

"(5) The phrase 'prospective action' refers to any prospective agency action that—

"(A) may affect either the experimental population or the parent population; and

"(B) has evolved to the point where meaningful consultation under section 7(a)(2) or (3) of the Act [subsec. (a)(2) or (3) of this section] can take place.

"(6) The term 'Secretary' means the Secretary of the Interior.

"(7) The term 'Service' means the United States Fish and Wildlife Service.

"(b) Plan specifications.—The Secretary may develop and implement, in accordance with this section, a plan for the relocation and management of a population of California sea otters from the existing range of the parent population to another location. The plan, which must be developed by regulation and administered by the Service in cooperation with the appropriate State agency, shall include the following:

"(1) The number, age, and sex of sea otters proposed to be relocated.

"(2) The manner in which the sea otters will be captured, translocated, released, monitored, and protected.

"(3) The specification of a zone (hereinafter referred to as the 'translocation zone') to which the experimental population will be relocated. The zone must have appropriate characteristics for furthering the conservation of the species.

"(4) The specification of a zone (hereinafter referred to as the 'management zone') that—

"(A) surrounds the translocation zone; and

"(B) does not include the existing range of the parent population or adjacent range where expansion is necessary for the recovery of the species.

The purpose of the management zone is to (i) facilitate the management of sea otters and the containment of the experimental population within the translocation zone, and (ii) to prevent, to the maximum extent feasible, conflict with other fishery resources within the management zone by the experimental population. Any sea otter found within the management zone shall be treated as a member of the experimental population. The Service shall use all feasible non-lethal means and measures to capture any sea otter found within the management zone and return it to either the translocation zone or to the range of the parent population.

"(5) Measures, including an adequate funding mechanism, to isolate and contain the experimental population.

"(6) A description of the relationship of the implementation of the plan to the status of the species under the Act [this chapter] and to determinations of the Secretary under section 7 of the Act [this section].

"(c) Status of members of the experimental population.—(1) Any member of the experimental population shall be treated while within the translocation zone as a threatened species for purposes of the Act [this chapter], except that—

"(A) section 7 of the Act [this section] shall only apply to agency actions that—

"(i) are undertaken within the translocation zone,

"(ii) are not defense-related agency actions, and

"(iii) are initiated after the date of the enactment of this section; and

"(B) with respect to defense-related actions within the translocation zone, members of the experimental population shall be treated as members of a species that is proposed to be listed under section 4 of the Act [16 U.S.C.A. § 1533].

For purposes of this paragraph, the term 'defense-related agency action' means an agency action proposed to be carried out directly by a military department.

"(2) For purposes of section 7 of the Act [this section], any member of the experimental population shall be treated while within the management zone as a member of a species that is proposed to be listed under section 4 of the Act [16 U.S.C.A. § 1533]. Section 9 of the Act [16 U.S.C.A. § 1538] applies to members of the experimental population; except that any incidental taking of such a member during the course of an otherwise lawful activity within the management zone, may not be treated as a violation of the Act [this chapter] or the Marine Mammal Protection Act of 1972 [16 U.S.C.A. § 1361 et seq.].

"(d) **Implementation of plan.**—The Secretary shall implement the plan developed under subsection (b)—

"(1) after the Secretary provides an opinion under section 7(b) of the Act [subsec. (b) of this section] regarding each prospective action for which consultation was initiated by a Federal agency or requested by a prospective permit or license applicant before April 1, 1986; or

"(2) if no consultation under section 7(a)(2) or (3) [subsec. (a)(2) or (3) of this section] regarding any prospective action is initiated or requested by April 1, 1986, at any time after that date.

"(e) **Consultation and effect of opinion.**—A Federal agency shall promptly consult with the Secretary, under section 7(a)(3) of the Act [subsec. (a)(3) of this section], at the request of, and in cooperation with, any permit or license applicant regarding any prospective action. The time limitations applicable to consultations under section 7(a)(2) of the Act [subsec. (a)(2) of this section] apply to consultations under the preceding sentence. In applying section 7(b)(3)(B) [subsec. (b)(3)(B) of this section] with respect to an opinion on a prospective action that is provided after consultation under section 7(a)(3), that opinion shall be treated as the opinion issued after consultation under section 7(a)(2) unless the Secretary finds, after notice and opportunity for comment in accordance with section 553 of title 5, United States Code [5 U.S.C.A. § 553], that a significant change has been made with respect to the action or that a significant change has occurred regarding the information used during the initial consultation. The interested party may petition the Secretary to make a finding under the preceding sentence. The Secretary may implement any reasonable and prudent alternatives specified in any opinion referred to in this subsection through appropriate agreements with any such Federal agency, prospective permit or license applicant, or other interested party.

"(f) **Construction.**—For purposes of implementing the plan, no act by the Service, an authorized State agency, or an authorized agent of the Service or such an agency with respect to a sea otter that is necessary to effect the relocation or management of any sea otter under the plan may be treated as a violation of any provision of the Act [this chapter] or the Marine Mammal Protection Act of 1972 (16 U.S.C. 1361 et seq.) [16 U.S.C.A. § 1361 et seq.]."

§ 1537. International cooperation

[ESA § 8]

(a) Financial assistance

As a demonstration of the commitment of the United States to the worldwide protection of endangered species and threatened species, the President may, subject to the provisions of section 1306 of Title 31, use foreign currencies accruing to the United States Government under the Food for Peace Act [7 U.S.C.A. § 1691 et seq.] or any other law to provide to any foreign country (with its consent) assistance in the development and management of programs in that country which the Secretary determines to be necessary or useful for the conservation of any endangered species or threatened species listed by the Secretary pursuant to section 1533 of this title. The President shall provide assistance (which includes, but is not limited to, the acquisition, by lease or otherwise, of lands, waters, or interests therein) to foreign countries under this section under such terms and conditions as he deems appropriate. Whenever foreign currencies are available for the provision of assistance under this section, such currencies shall be used in preference to funds appropriated under the authority of section 1542 of this title.

(b) Encouragement of foreign programs

In order to carry out further the provisions of this chapter, the Secretary, through the Secretary of State, shall encourage—

(1) foreign countries to provide for the conservation of fish or wildlife and plants including endangered species and threatened species listed pursuant to section 1533 of this title;

(2) the entering into of bilateral or multilateral agreements with foreign countries to provide for such conservation; and

(3) foreign persons who directly or indirectly take fish or wildlife or plants in foreign countries or on the high seas for importation into the United States for commercial or other purposes to develop and carry out with such assistance as he may provide, conservation practices designed to enhance such fish or wildlife or plants and their habitat.

(c) Personnel

After consultation with the Secretary of State, the Secretary may—

(1) assign or otherwise make available any officer or employee of his department for the purpose of cooperating with foreign countries and international organizations in developing personnel resources and programs which promote the conservation of fish or wildlife or plants; and

(2) conduct or provide financial assistance for the educational training of foreign personnel, in this country or abroad, in fish, wildlife, or plant management, research and law enforcement and to render professional assistance abroad in such matters.

(d) Investigations

After consultation with the Secretary of State and the Secretary of the Treasury, as appropriate, the Secretary may conduct or cause to be conducted such law enforcement investigations and research abroad as he deems necessary to carry out the purposes of this chapter.

(Pub. L. No. 93–205, § 8, 87 Stat. 892 (Dec. 28, 1973); as amended by Pub. L. No. 96–159, § 5, 93 Stat. 1228 (Dec. 28, 1979); Pub. L. No. 110–246, Title III, § 3001(b)(1)(A), (b)(2)(N), 122 Stat. 1820 (June 18, 2008).)

HISTORICAL AND STATUTORY NOTES

References in Text

The Food for Peace Act, referred to in subsec. (a), is Act of July 10, 1954, c. 469, 68 Stat. 454, as amended, formerly known as the Agricultural Trade Development and Assistance Act of 1954, which is principally codified as chapter 41 of this title, 7 U.S.C.A. § 1691 et seq. For complete classification, see Short Title note set out under 7 U.S.C.A. § 1691 and Tables.

This chapter, referred to in subsecs. (b) and (d), in the original read "this Act", meaning the Endangered Species Act of 1973, which is codified principally to this chapter. For complete classification, see Short Title note set out under section 1531 of this title and Tables.

Codifications

The authorities provided by each provision of, and each amendment made by, Pub. L. No. 110–246, as in effect on Sept. 30, 2012, to continue, and the Secretary of Agriculture to carry out the authorities, until the later of Sept. 30, 2013, or the date specified in the provision of, or amendment made by, Pub. L. No. 110–246, see section 701(a) of Pub. L. No. 112–240, set out in a note under 7 U.S.C.A. § 8701.

In subsec. (a), "section 1306 of Title 31" was substituted for "section 1415 of the Supplemental Appropriation Act, 1953 (31 U.S.C. 724)" on authority of Pub. L. No. 97–258, § 4(b), 96 Stat. 1067 (Sept. 13, 1982), the first section of which enacted Title 31.

Effective and Applicability Provisions

2008 Acts. Amendments by Pub. L. No. 110–246, except as otherwise provided, shall take effect on the earlier of June 18, 2008, or May 22, 2008, see Pub. L. No. 110–246, § 4(b), set out in a Repeal of Duplicative Enactment note under 7 U.S.C.A. § 8701.

1973 Acts. Section effective Dec. 28, 1973, see section 16 of Pub. L. No. 93–205, set out as an Effective Date note under section 1531 of this title.

Conservation of Sea Turtles; Importation of Shrimp

Pub. L. No. 101–162, Title VI, § 609, 103 Stat. 1037 (Nov. 21, 1989), provided that:

"(a) The Secretary of State, in consultation with the Secretary of Commerce, shall, with respect to those species of sea turtles the conservation of which is the subject of regulations promulgated by the Secretary of Commerce on June 29, 1987—

"(1) initiate negotiations as soon as possible for the development of bilateral or multilateral agreements with other nations for the protection and conservation of such species of sea turtles;

"(2) initiate negotiations as soon as possible with all foreign governments which are engaged in, or which have persons or companies engaged in, commercial fishing operations which, as determined by the Secretary of Commerce, may affect adversely such species of sea turtles, for the purpose of entering into bilateral and multilateral treaties with such countries to protect such species of sea turtles;

"(3) encourage such other agreements to promote the purposes of this section with other nations for the protection of specific ocean and land regions which are of special significance to the health and stability of such species of sea turtles;

"(4) initiate the amendment of any existing international treaty for the protection and conservation of such species of sea turtles to which the United States is a party in order to make such treaty consistent with the purposes and policies of this section; and

"(5) provide to the Congress by not later than one year after the date of enactment of this section [Nov. 21, 1989]

"(A) a list of each nation which conducts commercial shrimp fishing operations within the geographic range of distribution of such sea turtles;

"(B) a list of each nation which conducts commercial shrimp fishing operations which may affect adversely such species of sea turtles; and

"(C) a full report on—

"(i) the results of his efforts under this section; and

"(ii) the status of measures taken by each nation listed pursuant to paragraph (A) or (B) to protect and conserve such sea turtles.

"(b) (1) In general.—The importation of shrimp or products from shrimp which have been harvested with commercial fishing technology which may affect adversely such species of sea turtles shall be prohibited not later than May 1, 1991, except as provided in paragraph (2).

"(2) Certification procedure.—The ban on importation of shrimp or products from shrimp pursuant to paragraph (1) shall not apply if the President shall determine and certify to the Congress not later than May 1, 1991, and annually thereafter that—

"(A) the government of the harvesting nation has provided documentary evidence of the adoption of a regulatory program governing the incidental taking of such sea turtles in the course of such harvesting that is comparable to that of the United States; and

"(B) the average rate of that incidental taking by the vessels of the harvesting nation is comparable to the average rate of incidental taking of sea turtles by United States vessels in the course of such harvesting; or

"(C) the particular fishing environment of the harvesting nation does not pose a threat of the incidental taking of such sea turtles in the course of such harvesting."

[For termination, effective May 15, 2000, of reporting provisions of Pub. L. No. 101–162, § 609(b)(2), set out above, see Pub. L. No. 104–66, § 3003, as amended, set out as a note under 31 U.S.C.A. § 1113, and the 8th item on page 21 of House Document No. 103–7.]

§ 1537a. Convention implementation

[ESA § 8A]

(a) Management Authority and Scientific Authority

The Secretary of the Interior (hereinafter in this section referred to as the "Secretary") is designated as the Management Authority and the Scientific Authority for purposes of the Convention and the respective functions of each such Authority shall be carried out through the United States Fish and Wildlife Service.

(b) Management Authority functions

The Secretary shall do all things necessary and appropriate to carry out the functions of the Management Authority under the Convention.

(c) Scientific Authority functions; determinations

(1) The Secretary shall do all things necessary and appropriate to carry out the functions of the Scientific Authority under the Convention.

(2) The Secretary shall base the determinations and advice given by him under Article IV of the Convention with respect to wildlife upon the best available biological information derived from professionally accepted wildlife management practices; but is not required to make, or require any State to make, estimates of population size in making such determinations or giving such advice.

(d) Reservations by the United States under Convention

If the United States votes against including any species in Appendix I or II of the Convention and does not enter a reservation pursuant to paragraph (3) of Article XV of the Convention with respect to that species, the Secretary of State, before the 90th day after the last day on which such a reservation could be entered, shall submit to the Committee on Merchant Marine and Fisheries of the House of Representatives, and to the Committee on the Environment and Public Works of the Senate, a written report setting forth the reasons why such a reservation was not entered.

(e) Wildlife Preservation in Western Hemisphere

(1) The Secretary of the Interior (hereinafter in this subsection referred to as the "Secretary"), in cooperation with the Secretary of State, shall act on behalf of, and represent, the United States in all regards as required by the Convention on Nature Protection and Wildlife Preservation in the Western Hemisphere (56 Stat. 1354, T.S. 982, hereinafter in this subsection referred to as the "Western Convention"). In the discharge of these responsibilities, the Secretary and the Secretary of State shall consult with the Secretary of Agriculture, the Secretary of Commerce, and the heads of other agencies with respect to matters relating to or affecting their areas of responsibility.

(2) The Secretary and the Secretary of State shall, in cooperation with the contracting parties to the Western Convention and, to the extent feasible and appropriate, with the participation of State agencies, take such steps as are necessary to implement the Western Convention. Such steps shall include, but not be limited to—

(A) cooperation with contracting parties and international organizations for the purpose of developing personnel resources and programs that will facilitate implementation of the Western Convention;

(B) identification of those species of birds that migrate between the United States and other contracting parties, and the habitats upon which those species depend, and the implementation of cooperative measures to ensure that such species will not become endangered or threatened; and

(C) identification of measures that are necessary and appropriate to implement those provisions of the Western Convention which address the protection of wild plants.

(3) No later than September 30, 1985, the Secretary and the Secretary of State shall submit a report to Congress describing those steps taken in accordance with the requirements of this subsection and identifying the principal remaining actions yet necessary for comprehensive and effective implementation of the Western Convention.

(4) The provisions of this subsection shall not be construed as affecting the authority, jurisdiction, or responsibility of the several States to manage, control, or regulate resident fish or wildlife under State law or regulations.

(Pub. L. No. 93–205, § 8A, as added by Pub. L. No. 96–159, § 6(a) (1), 93 Stat. 1228 (Dec. 28, 1979); and amended by Pub. L. No. 97–304, § 5, 96 Stat. 1421 (Oct. 13, 1982).)

HISTORICAL AND STATUTORY NOTES

Effective and Applicability Provisions

1982 Acts. Section 5(b) of Pub. L. No. 97–304 provided that: "The amendment made by paragraph (1) of subsection (a) [enacting subsec. (c) (2) of this section] shall take effect January 1, 1981."

Abolition of House Committee on Merchant Marine and Fisheries

Committee on Merchant Marine and Fisheries of House of Representatives abolished and its jurisdiction transferred by House Resolution No. 6, 104th Congress, Jan. 4, 1995. Committee on Merchant Marine and Fisheries of the House of Representatives treated as referring to the Committee on Resources of the House of Representatives, in the case of a provision of law relating to fisheries, wildlife, international fishing agreements, marine affairs (including coastal zone management) except for measures relating to oil and other pollution of navigable waters, or oceanography by section 1(b)(3) of Pub. L. No. 104–14, set out as a note preceding 2 U.S.C.A. § 21. Committee on Resources of the House of Representatives, changed to Committee on Natural Resources of the House of Representatives by House Resolution No. 6, 110th Congress, Jan. 5, 2007.

Endangered Species Scientific Authority; Interim Performance of Functions of Commission

Section 6(b) of Pub. L. No. 96–159, provided that until such time as the Chairman, Members, and Executive Secretary of the International Convention Advisory Commission are appointed, but not later than 90 days after Dec. 28, 1979, the functions of the Commission be carried out by the Endangered Species Scientific Authority as established by Exec. Order No. 11911, formerly set out as a note under section 1537 of this title, with staff and administrative support being provided by the Secretary of the Interior as set forth in that Executive order.

§ 1538. Prohibited acts

[ESA § 9]

(a) Generally

(1) Except as provided in sections 1535(g)(2) and 1539 of this title, with respect to any endangered species of fish or wildlife listed pursuant to section 1533 of this title it is unlawful for any person subject to the jurisdiction of the United States to—

(A) import any such species into, or export any such species from the United States;

(B) take any such species within the United States or the territorial sea of the United States;

(C) take any such species upon the high seas;

(D) possess, sell, deliver, carry, transport, or ship, by any means whatsoever, any such species taken in violation of subparagraphs (B) and (C);

(E) deliver, receive, carry, transport, or ship in interstate or foreign commerce, by any means whatsoever and in the course of a commercial activity, any such species;

(F) sell or offer for sale in interstate or foreign commerce any such species; or

(G) violate any regulation pertaining to such species or to any threatened species of fish or wildlife listed pursuant to section 1533 of this title and promulgated by the Secretary pursuant to authority provided by this chapter.

(2) Except as provided in sections 1535(g)(2) and 1539 of this title, with respect to any endangered species of plants listed pursuant to section 1533 of this title, it is unlawful for any person subject to the jurisdiction of the United States to—

(A) import any such species into, or export any such species from, the United States;

(B) remove and reduce to possession any such species from areas under Federal jurisdiction; maliciously damage or destroy any such species on any such area; or remove, cut, dig up, or damage or destroy any such species on any other area in knowing violation of any law or regulation of any State or in the course of any violation of a State criminal trespass law;

(C) deliver, receive, carry, transport, or ship in interstate or foreign commerce, by any means whatsoever and in the course of a commercial activity, any such species;

(D) sell or offer for sale in interstate or foreign commerce any such species; or

(E) violate any regulation pertaining to such species or to any threatened species of plants listed pursuant to section 1533 of this title and promulgated by the Secretary pursuant to authority provided by this chapter.

(b) Species held in captivity or controlled environment

(1) The provisions of subsections (a)(1)(A) and (a)(1)(G) of this section shall not apply to any fish or wildlife which was held in captivity or in a controlled environment on (A) December 28, 1973, or (B) the date of the publication in the Federal Register of a final regulation adding such fish or wildlife species to any list published pursuant to subsection (c) of section 1533 of this title: *Provided,* That such holding and any subsequent holding or use of the fish or wildlife was not in the course of a commercial activity. With respect to any act prohibited by subsections (a)(1)(A and (a)(1)(G) of this section which occurs after a period of 180 days from (i) December 28, 1973, or (ii) the date of publication in the Federal Register of a final regulation adding such fish or wildlife species to any list published pursuant to subsection (c) of section 1533 of this title, there shall be a rebuttable presumption that the fish or wildlife involved in such act is not entitled to the exemption contained in this subsection.

(2) **(A)** The provisions of subsection (a) (1) of this section shall not apply to—

(i) any raptor legally held in captivity or in a controlled environment on November 10, 1978; or

(ii) any progeny of any raptor described in clause (i);

until such time as any such raptor or progeny is intentionally returned to a wild state.

(B) Any person holding any raptor or progeny described in subparagraph (A) must be able to demonstrate that the raptor or progeny does, in fact, qualify under the provisions of this paragraph, and shall maintain and submit to the Secretary, on request, such inventories, documentation, and records as the Secretary may by regulation require as being reasonably appropriate to carry out the purposes of this paragraph. Such requirements shall not unnecessarily duplicate the requirements of other rules and regulations promulgated by the Secretary.

(c) Violation of Convention

(1) It is unlawful for any person subject to the jurisdiction of the United States to engage in any trade in any specimens contrary to the provisions of the Convention, or to possess any specimens traded contrary to the provisions of the Convention, including the definitions of terms in article I thereof.

(2) Any importation into the United States of fish or wildlife shall, if—

(A) such fish or wildlife is not an endangered species listed pursuant to section 1533 of this title but is listed in Appendix II to the Convention,

(B) the taking and exportation of such fish or wildlife is not contrary to the provisions of the Convention and all other applicable requirements of the Convention have been satisfied,

(C) the applicable requirements of subsections (d), (e), and (f) of this section have been satisfied, and

(D) such importation is not made in the course of a commercial activity,

be presumed to be an importation not in violation of any provision of this chapter or any regulation issued pursuant to this chapter.

(d) Imports and exports

(1) In general

It is unlawful for any person, without first having obtained permission from the Secretary, to engage in business—

(A) as an importer or exporter of fish or wildlife (other than shellfish and fishery products which (i) are not listed pursuant to section 1533 of this title as endangered species or threatened species, and (ii) are imported for purposes of human or animal consumption or taken in waters under the jurisdiction of the United States or on the high seas for recreational purposes) or plants; or

(B) as an importer or exporter of any amount of raw or worked African elephant ivory.

(2) Requirements

Any person required to obtain permission under paragraph (1) of this subsection shall—

(A) keep such records as will fully and correctly disclose each importation or exportation of fish, wildlife, plants, or African elephant ivory made by him and the subsequent disposition made by him with respect to such fish, wildlife, plants, or ivory;

(B) at all reasonable times upon notice by a duly authorized representative of the Secretary, afford such representative access to his place of business, an opportunity to examine his inventory of imported fish, wildlife, plants, or African elephant ivory and the records required to be kept under subparagraph (A) of this paragraph, and to copy such records; and

(C) file such reports as the Secretary may require.

(3) Regulations

The Secretary shall prescribe such regulations as are necessary and appropriate to carry out the purposes of this subsection.

(4) Restriction on consideration of value or amount of African elephant ivory imported or exported

In granting permission under this subsection for importation or exportation of African elephant ivory, the Secretary shall not vary the requirements for obtaining such permission on the basis of the value or amount of ivory imported or exported under such permission.

(e) Reports

It is unlawful for any person importing or exporting fish or wildlife (other than shellfish and fishery products which (1) are not listed pursuant to section 1533 of this title as endangered or threatened species, and (2) are imported for purposes of human or animal consumption or taken in waters under the jurisdiction of the United States or on the high seas for recreational purposes) or plants to fail to file any declaration or report as the Secretary deems necessary to facilitate enforcement of this chapter or to meet the obligations of the Convention.

(f) Designation of ports

(1) It is unlawful for any person subject to the jurisdiction of the United States to import into or export from the United States any fish or wildlife (other than shellfish and fishery products which (A) are not listed pursuant to section 1533 of this title as endangered species or threatened species, and (B) are imported for purposes of human or animal consumption or taken in waters under the jurisdiction of the United States or on the high seas for recreational purposes) or plants, except at a port or ports designated by the Secretary of the Interior. For the purpose of facilitating enforcement of this chapter and reducing the costs thereof, the Secretary of the Interior, with approval of the Secretary of the Treasury and after notice and opportunity for public hearing, may, by regulation, designate ports and change such designations. The Secretary of the Interior, under such terms and conditions as he may prescribe, may permit the importation or exportation at nondesignated ports in the interest of the health or safety of the fish or wildlife or plants, or for other reasons if, in his discretion, he deems it appropriate and consistent with the purpose of this subsection.

(2) Any port designated by the Secretary of the Interior under the authority of section 668cc–4(d) of this title, shall, if such designation is in effect on December 27, 1973, be deemed to be a port designated by the Secretary under paragraph (1) of this subsection until such time as the Secretary otherwise provides.

(g) Violations

It is unlawful for any person subject to the jurisdiction of the United States to attempt to commit, solicit another to commit, or cause to be committed, any offense defined in this section.

(Pub. L. No. 93–205, § 9, 87 Stat. 893 (Dec. 28, 1973); as amended by Pub. L. No. 95–632, § 4, 92 Stat. 3760 (Nov. 10, 1978); Pub. L. No. 97–304, § 9(b), 96 Stat. 1426 (Oct. 13, 1982); Pub. L. No. 100–478, Title I, § 1006, Title II, § 2301, 102 Stat. 2308, 2321 (Oct. 7, 1988); Pub. L. No. 100–653, Title IX, § 905, 102 Stat. 3835 (Nov. 14, 1988).)

HISTORICAL AND STATUTORY NOTES

References in Text

This chapter, referred to in subsec. (a)(1)(G), (2)(E), (c)(2), (e), and (f)(1), in the original read "this Act", meaning the Endangered Species Act of 1973, which is codified principally to this chapter. For complete classification, see Short Title note set out under section 1531 of this title and Tables.

Section 668cc–4(d) of this title, referred to in subsec. (f)(2), was repealed by Pub. L. No. 93–205, § 14, 87 Stat. 903 (Dec. 28, 1973).

Effective and Applicability Provisions

1973 Acts. Section effective Dec. 28, 1973, see section 16 of Pub. L. No. 93–205, set out as an Effective Date note under section 1531 of this title.

Human Activities Within Proximity of Whales

Pub. L. No. 103–238, § 17, 108 Stat. 559 (Apr. 30, 1994), provided that:

"(a) Lawful approaches.—In waters of the United States surrounding the State of Hawaii, it is lawful for a person subject to the jurisdiction of the United States to approach, by any means other than an aircraft, no closer than 100 yards to a humpback whale, regardless of whether the approach is made in waters designated under section 222.31 of title 50, Code of Federal Regulations, as cow/calf waters.

"(b) Termination of legal effect of certain regulations.—Subsection (b) of section 222.31 of title 50, Code of Federal Regulations, shall cease to be in force and effect."

§ 1539. Exceptions

[ESA § 10]

(a) Permits

(1) The Secretary may permit, under such terms and conditions as he shall prescribe—

(A) any act otherwise prohibited by section 1538 of this title for scientific purposes or to enhance the propagation or survival of the affected species, including, but not limited to, acts necessary for the establishment and maintenance of experimental populations pursuant to subsection (j) of this section; or

(B) any taking otherwise prohibited by section 1538(a)(1)(B) of this title if such taking is incidental to, and not the purpose of, the carrying out of an otherwise lawful activity.

(2) **(A)** No permit may be issued by the Secretary authorizing any taking referred to in paragraph (1)(B) unless the applicant therefor submits to the Secretary a conservation plan that specifies—

(i) the impact which will likely result from such taking;

(ii) what steps the applicant will take to minimize and mitigate such impacts, and the funding that will be available to implement such steps;

(iii) what alternative actions to such taking the applicant considered and the reasons why such alternatives are not being utilized; and

(iv) such other measures that the Secretary may require as being necessary or appropriate for purposes of the plan.

(B) If the Secretary finds, after opportunity for public comment, with respect to a permit application and the related conservation plan that—

(i) the taking will be incidental;

(ii) the applicant will, to the maximum extent practicable, minimize and mitigate the impacts of such taking;

(iii) the applicant will ensure that adequate funding for the plan will be provided;

(iv) the taking will not appreciably reduce the likelihood of the survival and recovery of the species in the wild; and

(v) the measures, if any, required under subparagraph (A)(iv) will be met;

and he has received such other assurances as he may require that the plan will be implemented, the Secretary shall issue the permit. The permit shall contain such terms and conditions as the Secretary deems necessary or appropriate to carry out the purposes of this paragraph, including, but not limited to, such reporting requirements as the Secretary deems necessary for determining whether such terms and conditions are being complied with.

(C) The Secretary shall revoke a permit issued under this paragraph if he finds that the permittee is not complying with the terms and conditions of the permit.

(b) Hardship exemptions

(1) If any person enters into a contract with respect to a species of fish or wildlife or plant before the date of the publication in the Federal Register of notice of consideration of that species as an endangered species and the subsequent listing of that species as an endangered species pursuant to section 1533 of this title will cause undue economic hardship to such person under the contract, the Secretary, in order to minimize such hardship, may exempt such person from the application of section 1538(a) of this title to the extent the Secretary deems appropriate if such person applies to him for such exemption and includes with such application such information as the Secretary may require to prove such hardship; except that (A) no such exemption shall be for a duration of more than one year from the date of publication in the Federal Register of notice of consideration of the species concerned, or shall apply to a quantity of fish or wildlife or plants in excess of that specified by the Secretary; (B) the one-year period for those species of fish or wildlife listed by the Secretary as endangered prior to December 28, 1973, shall expire in accordance with the terms of section 668cc–3 of this title; and (C) no such exemption may be granted for the importation or exportation of a specimen listed in Appendix I of the Convention which is to be used in a commercial activity.

(2) As used in this subsection, the term "undue economic hardship" shall include, but not be limited to:

(A) substantial economic loss resulting from inability caused by this chapter to perform contracts with respect to species of fish and wildlife entered into prior to the date of publication in the Federal Register of a notice of consideration of such species as an endangered species;

(B) substantial economic loss to persons who, for the year prior to the notice of consideration of such species as an endangered species, derived a substantial portion of their income from the lawful taking of any listed species, which taking would be made unlawful under this chapter; or

(C) curtailment of subsistence taking made unlawful under this chapter by persons (i) not reasonably able to secure other sources of subsistence; and (ii) dependent to a substantial extent upon hunting and fishing for subsistence; and (iii) who must engage in such curtailed taking for subsistence purposes.

(3) The Secretary may make further requirements for a showing of undue economic hardship as he deems fit. Exceptions granted under this section may be limited by the Secretary in his discretion as to time, area, or other factor of applicability.

(c) Notice and review

The Secretary shall publish notice in the Federal Register of each application for an exemption or permit which is made under this section. Each notice shall invite the submission from interested parties, within thirty days after the date of the notice, of written data, views, or arguments with respect to the application; except that such thirty-day period may be waived by the Secretary in an emergency situation where the health or life of an endangered animal is threatened and no reasonable alternative is available to the applicant, but notice of any such waiver shall be published by the Secretary in the Federal Register within ten days following the issuance of the exemption or permit. Information received by the Secretary as a part of any application shall be available to the public as a matter of public record at every stage of the proceeding.

(d) Permit and exemption policy

The Secretary may grant exceptions under subsections (a)(1)(A) and (b) of this section only if he finds and publishes his finding in the Federal Register that (1) such exceptions were applied for in good faith, (2) if granted and exercised will not operate to the disadvantage of such endangered species, and (3) will be consistent with the purposes and policy set forth in section 1531 of this title.

(e) Alaska natives

(1) Except as provided in paragraph (4) of this subsection the provisions of this chapter shall not apply with respect to the taking of any endangered species or threatened species, or the importation of any such species taken pursuant to this section, by—

(A) any Indian, Aleut, or Eskimo who is an Alaskan Native who resides in Alaska; or

(B) any non-native permanent resident of an Alaskan native village;

if such taking is primarily for subsistence purposes. Non-edible byproducts of species taken pursuant to this section may be sold in interstate commerce when made into authentic native articles of handicrafts and clothing; except that the provisions of this subsection shall not apply to any non-native resident of an Alaskan native village found by the Secretary to be not primarily dependent upon the taking of fish and wildlife for consumption or for the creation and sale of authentic native articles of handicrafts and clothing.

(2) Any taking under this subsection may not be accomplished in a wasteful manner.

(3) As used in this subsection—

(i) The term "subsistence" includes selling any edible portion of fish or wildlife in native villages and towns in Alaska for native consumption within native villages or towns; and

(ii) The term "authentic native articles of handicrafts and clothing" means items composed wholly or in some significant respect of natural materials, and which are produced, decorated, or fashioned in the exercise of traditional native handicrafts without the use of pantographs, multiple carvers, or other mass copying devices. Traditional native handicrafts include, but are not limited to, weaving, carving, stitching, sewing, lacing, beading, drawing, and painting.

(4) Notwithstanding the provisions of paragraph (1) of this subsection, whenever the Secretary determines that any species of fish or wildlife which is subject to taking under the provisions of this subsection is an endangered species or threatened species, and that such taking materially and negatively affects the threatened or endangered species, he may prescribe regulations upon the taking of such species by any such Indian, Aleut, Eskimo, or non-Native Alaskan resident of an Alaskan native village. Such regulations may be established with reference to species, geographical description of the area included, the season for taking, or any other factors related to the reason for establishing such regulations and consistent with the policy of this chapter. Such regulations shall be prescribed after a notice and hearings in the affected judicial districts of Alaska and as otherwise required by section 1373 of this title, and shall be removed as soon as the Secretary determines that the need for their impositions has disappeared.

(f) Pre-Act endangered species parts exemption; application and certification; regulation; validity of sales contract; separability; renewal of exemption; expiration of renewal certification

(1) As used in this subsection—

(A) The term "pre-Act endangered species part" means—

(i) any sperm whale oil, including derivatives thereof, which was lawfully held within the United States on December 28, 1973, in the course of a commercial activity; or

(ii) any finished scrimshaw product, if such product or the raw material for such product was lawfully held within the United States on December 28, 1973, in the course of a commercial activity.

(B) The term "scrimshaw product" means any art form which involves the substantial etching or engraving of designs upon, or the substantial carving of figures, patterns, or designs from, any bone or tooth of any marine mammal of the order Cetacea. For purposes of this subsection, polishing or the adding of minor superficial markings does not constitute substantial etching, engraving, or carving.

(2) The Secretary, pursuant to the provisions of this subsection, may exempt, if such exemption is not in violation of the Convention, any pre-Act endangered species part from one or more of the following prohibitions:

(A) The prohibition on exportation from the United States set forth in section 1538(a)(1)(A) of this title.

(B) Any prohibition set forth in section 1538(a)(1)(E) or (F) of this title.

(3) Any person seeking an exemption described in paragraph (2) of this subsection shall make application therefor to the Secretary in such form and manner as he shall prescribe, but no such application may be considered by the Secretary unless the application—

(A) is received by the Secretary before the close of the one-year period beginning on the date on which regulations promulgated by the Secretary to carry out this subsection first take effect;

(B) contains a complete and detailed inventory of all pre-Act endangered species parts for which the applicant seeks exemption;

(C) is accompanied by such documentation as the Secretary may require to prove that any endangered species part or product claimed by the applicant to be a pre-Act endangered species part is in fact such a part; and

(D) contains such other information as the Secretary deems necessary and appropriate to carry out the purposes of this subsection.

(4) If the Secretary approves any application for exemption made under this subsection, he shall issue to the applicant a certificate of exemption which shall specify—

(A) any prohibition in section 1538(a) of this title which is exempted;

(B) the pre-Act endangered species parts to which the exemption applies;

(C) the period of time during which the exemption is in effect, but no exemption made under this subsection shall have force and effect after the close of the three-year period beginning on the date of issuance of the certificate unless such exemption is renewed under paragraph (8); and

(D) any term or condition prescribed pursuant to paragraph (5)(A) or (B), or both, which the Secretary deems necessary or appropriate.

(5) The Secretary shall prescribe such regulations as he deems necessary and appropriate to carry out the purposes of this subsection. Such regulations may set forth—

(A) terms and conditions which may be imposed on applicants for exemptions under this subsection (including, but not limited to, requirements that applicants register inventories, keep complete sales records, permit duly authorized agents of the Secretary to inspect such inventories and records, and periodically file appropriate reports with the Secretary); and

(B) terms and conditions which may be imposed on any subsequent purchaser of any pre-Act endangered species part covered by an exemption granted under this subsection;

to insure that any such part so exempted is adequately accounted for and not disposed of contrary to the provisions of this chapter. No regulation prescribed by the Secretary to carry out the purposes of this subsection shall be subject to section 1533(f)(2)(A)(i) of this title.

(6) **(A)** Any contract for the sale of pre-Act endangered species parts which is entered into by the Administrator of General Services prior to the effective date of this subsection and pursuant to the notice published in the Federal Register on January 9, 1973, shall not be rendered invalid by virtue of the fact that fulfillment of such contract may be prohibited under section 1538(a)(1)(F) of this title.

(B) In the event that this paragraph is held invalid, the validity of the remainder of this chapter, including the remainder of this subsection, shall not be affected.

(7) Nothing in this subsection shall be construed to—

(A) exonerate any person from any act committed in violation of paragraphs (1)(A), (1)(E), or (1)(F) of section 1538(a) of this title prior to July 12, 1976; or

(B) immunize any person from prosecution for any such act.

(8) **(A)** **(i)**[1] Any valid certificate of exemption which was renewed after October 13, 1982, and was in effect on March 31, 1988, shall be deemed to be renewed for a six-month period beginning on October 7, 1988. Any person holding such a certificate may apply to the Secretary for one additional renewal of such certificate for a period not to exceed 5 years beginning on October 7, 1988.

(B) If the Secretary approves any application for renewal of an exemption under this paragraph, he shall issue to the applicant a certificate of renewal of such exemption which shall provide that all terms, conditions, prohibitions, and other regulations made applicable by the previous certificate shall remain in effect during the period of the renewal.

(C) No exemption or renewal of such exemption made under this subsection shall have force and effect after the expiration date of the certificate of renewal of such exemption issued under this paragraph.

(D) No person may, after January 31, 1984, sell or offer for sale in interstate or foreign commerce, any pre-Act finished scrimshaw product unless such person holds a valid certificate of exemption issued by the Secretary under this subsection, and unless such product or the raw material for such product was held by such person on October 13, 1982.

(g) Burden of proof

In connection with any action alleging a violation of section 1538 of this title, any person claiming the benefit of any exemption or permit under this chapter shall have the burden of proving that the exemption or permit is applicable, has been granted, and was valid and in force at the time of the alleged violation.

(h) Certain antique articles; importation; port designation; application for return of articles

(1) Sections 1533(d) and 1538(a) and (c) of this title do not apply to any article which—

(A) is not less than 100 years of age;

(B) is composed in whole or in part of any endangered species or threatened species listed under section 1533 of this title;

(C) has not been repaired or modified with any part of any such species on or after December 28, 1973; and

(D) is entered at a port designated under paragraph (3).

(2) Any person who wishes to import an article under the exception provided by this subsection shall submit to the customs officer concerned at the time of entry of the article such documentation as the Secretary of the Treasury, after consultation with the Secretary of the Interior, shall by regulation require as being necessary to establish that the article meets the requirements set forth in paragraph (1)(A), (B), and (C).

(3) The Secretary of the Treasury, after consultation with the Secretary of the Interior, shall designate one port within each customs region at which articles described in paragraph (1)(A), (B), and (C) must be entered into the customs territory of the United States.

(4) Any person who imported, after December 27, 1973, and on or before November 10, 1978, any article described in paragraph (1) which—

(A) was not repaired or modified after the date of importation with any part of any endangered species or threatened species listed under section 1533 of this title;

(B) was forfeited to the United States before November 10, 1978, or is subject to forfeiture to the United States on such date of enactment, pursuant to the assessment of a civil penalty under section 1540 of this title; and

(C) is in the custody of the United States on November 10, 1978;

may, before the close of the one-year period beginning on November 10, 1978, make application to the Secretary for return of the article. Application shall be made in such form and manner, and contain such documentation, as the Secretary prescribes. If on the basis of any such application which is timely filed, the Secretary is satisfied that the requirements of this paragraph are met with respect to the article concerned, the Secretary shall return the article to the applicant and the importation of such article shall, on and after the date of return, be deemed to be a lawful importation under this chapter.

(i) Noncommercial transshipments

Any importation into the United States of fish or wildlife shall, if—

(1) such fish or wildlife was lawfully taken and exported from the country of origin and country of reexport, if any;

(2) such fish or wildlife is in transit or transshipment through any place subject to the jurisdiction of the United States en route to a country where such fish or wildlife may be lawfully imported and received;

(3) the exporter or owner of such fish or wildlife gave explicit instructions not to ship such fish or wildlife through any place subject to the jurisdiction of the United States, or did all that could have reasonably been done to prevent transshipment, and the circumstances leading to the transshipment were beyond the exporter's or owner's control;

(4) the applicable requirements of the Convention have been satisfied; and

(5) such importation is not made in the course of a commercial activity,

be an importation not in violation of any provision of this chapter or any regulation issued pursuant to this chapter while such fish or wildlife remains in the control of the United States Customs Service.

(j) Experimental populations

(1) For purposes of this subsection, the term "experimental population" means any population (including any offspring arising solely therefrom) authorized by the Secretary for release under paragraph (2), but only when, and at such times as, the population is wholly separate geographically from nonexperimental populations of the same species.

(2) **(A)** The Secretary may authorize the release (and the related transportation) of any population (including eggs, propagules, or individuals) of an endangered species or a threatened species outside the current range of such species if the Secretary determines that such release will further the conservation of such species.

(B) Before authorizing the release of any population under subparagraph (A), the Secretary shall by regulation identify the population and determine, on the basis of the best available information, whether or not such population is essential to the continued existence of an endangered species or a threatened species.

(C) For the purposes of this chapter, each member of an experimental population shall be treated as a threatened species; except that—

(i) solely for purposes of section 1536 of this title (other than subsection (a)(1) thereof), an experimental population determined under subparagraph (B) to be not essential to the continued existence of a species shall be treated, except when it occurs in an area within the National Wildlife Refuge System or the National Park System, as a species proposed to be listed under section 1533 of this title; and

(ii) critical habitat shall not be designated under this chapter for any experimental population determined under subparagraph (B) to be not essential to the continued existence of a species.

(3) The Secretary, with respect to populations of endangered species or threatened species that the Secretary authorized, before October 13, 1982, for release in geographical areas separate from the other populations of such species, shall determine by regulation which of such populations are an experimental population for the purposes of this subsection and whether or not each is essential to the continued existence of an endangered species or a threatened species.

(Pub. L. No. 93–205, § 10, 87 Stat. 896 (Dec. 28, 1973); as amended by Pub. L. No. 94–359, §§ 2, 3, 90 Stat. 911, 912 (July 12, 1976); Pub. L. No. 95–632, § 5, 92 Stat. 3760 (Nov. 10, 1978); Pub. L. No. 96–159, § 7, 93 Stat. 1230 (Dec. 28, 1979); Pub. L. No. 97–304, § 6(1) to (3), (4)(A), (5), (6), 96 Stat. 1422 to 1424 (Oct. 13, 1982); Pub. L. No. 100–478, Title I, §§ 1011, 1013(b), (c), 102 Stat. 2314, 2315 (Oct. 7, 1988).)

[1] So in original. No cl. (ii) has been enacted.

HISTORICAL AND STATUTORY NOTES

References in Text

Section 668cc–3 of this title, referred to in subsec. (b), was repealed by Pub. L. No. 93–205, § 14, 87 Stat. 903 (Dec. 28, 1973).

This chapter, referred to in subsecs. (b)(2), (e)(1), (4), (f)(5), (6)(B), (g), (h)(4), (i), (j)(2)(C)(ii), in the original read "this Act", meaning the Endangered Species Act of 1973, which is codified principally to this chapter. For complete classification, see Short Title note set out under section 1531 of this title and Tables.

Pre-Act, referred to in subsec. (f), means the period prior to the effective date of the Endangered Species Act of 1973, Dec. 28, 1973. See section 16 of Pub. L. No. 93–205, set out as an Effective Date note under section 1531 of this title.

Subsec. (f) of section 1533 of this title, referred to in subsec. (f)(5), which related to promulgation of regulations by the Secretary was struck out, and subsec. (g) of section 1533 of this title was redesignated as subsec. (f), by Pub. L. No. 97–304, § 2(a)(4)(B), (C), 96 Stat. 1415 (Oct. 13, 1982). For provisions related to promulgation of regulations, see subsecs. (b) and (h) of section 1533 of this title.

Effective date of this subsection, referred to in subsec. (f)(6)(A), probably means the date of enactment of subsec. (f) by section 2 of Pub. L. No. 94–359, July 12, 1976.

Effective and Applicability Provisions

1982 Acts. Section 6(4)(B) of Pub. L. No. 97–304 provided that: "The amendment made by subparagraph (A) [amending subsec. (h)(1) of this section] shall take effect of January 1, 1981."

1973 Acts. Section effective Dec. 28, 1973, see section 16 of Pub. L. No. 93–205, set out as an Effective Date note under section 1531 of this title.

Transfer of Functions

For transfer of functions, personnel, assets, and liabilities of the United States Customs Service of the Department of the Treasury, including functions of the Secretary of the Treasury relating thereto, to the Secretary of Homeland Security, and for treatment of related references, see 6 U.S.C.A. §§ 203(1), 551(d), 552(d) and 557, and the Department of Homeland Security Reorganization Plan of November 25, 2002, as modified, set out as a note under 6 U.S.C.A. § 542.

Scrimshaw Exemptions

Pub. L. No. 103–238, § 18, 108 Stat. 559 (Apr. 30, 1994), provided that: "Notwithstanding any other provision of law, any valid certificate of exemption renewed by the Secretary (or deemed to be renewed) under section 10(f)(8) of the Endangered Species Act of 1973 (16 U.S.C. 1539(f)(8) [subsec. (f)(8) of this section]) for any person holding such a certificate with respect to the possession of pre-Act finished scrimshaw products or raw material for such products shall remain valid for a period not to exceed 5 years beginning on the date of enactment of this Act [Apr. 30, 1994]."

§ 1540. Penalties and enforcement

[ESA § 11]

(a) Civil penalties

(1) Any person who knowingly violates, and any person engaged in business as an importer or exporter of fish, wildlife, or plants who violates, any provision of this chapter, or any provision of any permit or certificate issued hereunder, or of any regulation issued in order to implement subsection (a)(1)(A), (B), (C), (D), (E), or (F), (a)(2)(A), (B), (C), or (D), (c), (d) (other than regulation relating to recordkeeping or filing of reports), (f) or (g) of section 1538 of this title, may be assessed a civil penalty by the Secretary of not more than $25,000 for each violation. Any person who knowingly violates, and any person engaged in business as an importer or exporter of fish, wildlife, or plants who violates, any provision of any other regulation issued under this chapter may be assessed a civil penalty by the Secretary of not more than $12,000 for each such violation. Any person who otherwise violates any provision of this chapter, or any regulation, permit, or certificate issued hereunder, may be assessed a civil penalty by the Secretary of not more than $500 for each such violation. No penalty may be assessed under this subsection unless such person is given notice and opportunity for a hearing with respect to such violation. Each violation shall be a separate offense. Any such civil penalty may be remitted or mitigated by the Secretary. Upon any failure to pay a penalty assessed under this subsection, the Secretary may request the Attorney General to institute a civil action in a district court of the United States for any district in which such person is found, resides, or transacts business to collect the penalty and such court shall have jurisdiction to hear and decide any such action. The court shall hear such action on the record made before the Secretary and shall sustain his action if it is supported by substantial evidence on the record considered as a whole.

(2) Hearings held during proceedings for the assessment of civil penalties authorized by paragraph (1) of this subsection shall be conducted in accordance with section 554 of Title 5. The Secretary may issue subpenas for the attendance and testimony of witnesses and the production of relevant papers, books, and documents, and administer oaths. Witnesses summoned shall be paid the same fees and mileage that are paid to witnesses in the courts of the United States. In case of contumacy or refusal to obey a subpena served upon any person pursuant to this paragraph, the district court of the United States for any district in which such person is found or resides or transacts business, upon application by the United States and after notice to such person, shall have jurisdiction to issue an order requiring such person to appear and give testimony before the Secretary or to appear and produce documents before the Secretary, or both, and any failure to obey such order of the court may be punished by such court as a contempt thereof.

(3) Notwithstanding any other provision of this chapter, no civil penalty shall be imposed if it can be shown by a preponderance of the evidence that the defendant committed an act based on a good faith belief that he was acting to protect himself or herself, a member of his or her family, or any other individual from bodily harm, from any endangered or threatened species.

(b) Criminal violations

(1) Any person who knowingly violates any provision of this chapter, of any permit or certificate issued hereunder, or of any regulation issued in order to implement subsection (a)(1)(A), (B), (C), (D), (E), or (F); (a)(2)(A), (B), (C), or (D), (c), (d) (other than a regulation relating to recordkeeping, or filing of reports), (f), or (g) of section 1538 of this title shall, upon conviction, be fined not more than $50,000 or imprisoned for not more than one year, or both. Any person who knowingly violates any provision of any other regulation issued under this chapter shall, upon conviction, be fined not more than $25,000 or imprisoned for not more than six months, or both.

(2) The head of any Federal agency which has issued a lease, license, permit, or other agreement authorizing a person to import or export fish, wildlife, or plants, or to operate a quarantine station for imported wildlife, or authorizing the use of Federal lands, including grazing of domestic livestock, to any person who is convicted of a criminal violation of this chapter or any regulation, permit, or certificate issued hereunder may immediately modify, suspend, or revoke each lease, license, permit or other agreement. The Secretary shall also suspend for a period of up to one year, or cancel, any Federal hunting or fishing permits or stamps issued to any person who is convicted of a criminal violation of any provision of this chapter or any regulation, permit, or certificate issued hereunder. The United States shall not be liable for the payments of any compensation, reimbursement, or damages in connection with the modification, suspension, or revocation of any leases, licenses, permits, stamps, or other agreements pursuant to this section.

(3) Notwithstanding any other provision of this chapter, it shall be a defense to prosecution under this subsection if the defendant committed the offense based on a good faith belief that he was acting to protect himself or herself, a member of his or her family, or any other individual, from bodily harm from any endangered or threatened species.

(c) District court jurisdiction

The several district courts of the United States, including the courts enumerated in section 460 of Title 28, shall have jurisdiction over any actions arising under this chapter. For the purpose of this chapter, American Samoa shall be included within the judicial district of the District Court of the United States for the District of Hawaii.

(d) Rewards and incidental expenses

The Secretary or the Secretary of the Treasury shall pay, from sums received as penalties, fines, or forfeitures of property for any violation of this chapter or any regulation issued hereunder (1) a reward to any person who furnishes information which leads to an arrest, a criminal conviction, civil penalty assessment, or forfeiture of property for any violation of this chapter or any regulation issued hereunder, and (2) the reasonable and necessary costs incurred by any person in providing temporary care for any fish, wildlife, or plant pending the disposition of any civil or criminal proceeding alleging a violation of this chapter with respect to that fish, wildlife, or plant. The amount of the reward, if any, is to be designated by the Secretary or the Secretary of the Treasury, as appropriate. Any officer or employee of the United States or any State or local government who furnishes information or renders service in the performance of his official duties is ineligible for payment under this subsection. Whenever the balance of sums received under this section and section 3375(d) of this title, as penalties or fines, or from forfeitures of property, exceed $500,000, the Secretary of the Treasury shall deposit an amount equal to such excess balance in the cooperative endangered species conservation fund established under section 1535(i) of this title.

(e) Enforcement

(1) The provisions of this chapter and any regulations or permits issued pursuant thereto shall be enforced by the Secretary, the Secretary of the Treasury, or the Secretary of the Department in which the Coast Guard is operating, or all such Secretaries. Each such Secretary may utilize by agreement, with or without reimbursement, the personnel, services, and facilities of any other Federal agency or any State agency for purposes of enforcing this chapter.

(2) The judges of the district courts of the United States and the United States magistrate judges may, within their respective jurisdictions, upon proper oath or affirmation showing probable cause, issue such warrants or other process as may be required for enforcement of this chapter and any regulation issued thereunder.

(3) Any person authorized by the Secretary, the Secretary of the Treasury, or the Secretary of the Department in which the Coast Guard is operating, to enforce this chapter may detain for inspection and inspect any package, crate, or other container, including its contents, and all accompanying documents, upon importation or exportation. Such person may make arrests without a warrant for any violation of this chapter if he has reasonable grounds to believe that the person to be arrested is committing the violation in his presence or view, and may execute and serve any arrest warrant, search warrant, or other warrant or civil or criminal process issued by any officer or court of competent jurisdiction for enforcement of this chapter. Such person so authorized may search and seize, with or without a warrant, as authorized by law. Any fish, wildlife, property, or item so seized shall be held by any person authorized by the Secretary, the Secretary of the Treasury, or the Secretary of the Department in which the Coast Guard is operating pending disposition of civil or criminal proceedings, or the institution of an action in rem for forfeiture of such fish, wildlife, property, or item pursuant to paragraph (4) of this subsection; except that the Secretary may, in lieu of holding such fish, wildlife, property, or item, permit the owner or consignee to post a bond or other surety satisfactory to the Secretary, but upon forfeiture of any such property to the United States, or the abandonment or waiver of any claim to any such property, it shall be disposed of (other than by sale to the general public) by the Secretary in such a manner, consistent with the purposes of this chapter, as the Secretary shall by regulation prescribe.

(4) **(A)** All fish or wildlife or plants taken, possessed, sold, purchased, offered for sale or purchase, transported, delivered, received, carried, shipped, exported, or imported contrary to the provisions of this chapter, any regulation made pursuant thereto, or any permit or certificate issued hereunder shall be subject to forfeiture to the United States.

(B) All guns, traps, nets, and other equipment, vessels, vehicles, aircraft, and other means of transportation used to aid the taking, possessing, selling, purchasing, offering for sale or purchase, transporting, delivering, receiving, carrying, shipping, exporting, or importing of any fish or wildlife or plants in violation of this chapter, any regulation made pursuant thereto, or any permit or certificate issued thereunder shall be subject to forfeiture to the United States upon conviction of a criminal violation pursuant to subsection (b)(1) of this section.

(5) All provisions of law relating to the seizure, forfeiture, and condemnation of a vessel for violation of the customs laws, the disposition of such vessel or the proceeds from the sale thereof, and the remission or mitigation of such forfeiture, shall apply to the seizures and forfeitures incurred, or alleged to have been incurred, under the provisions of this chapter, insofar as such provisions of law are applicable and not inconsistent with the provisions of this chapter; except that all powers, rights, and duties conferred or imposed by the customs laws upon any officer or employee of the Treasury Department shall, for the purposes of this chapter, be exercised or performed by the Secretary or by such persons as he may designate.

(6) The Attorney General of the United States may seek to enjoin any person who is alleged to be in violation of any provision of this chapter or regulation issued under authority thereof.

(f) Regulations

The Secretary, the Secretary of the Treasury, and the Secretary of the Department in which the Coast Guard is operating, are authorized to promulgate such regulations as may be appropriate to enforce this chapter, and charge reasonable fees for expenses to the Government connected with permits or certificates authorized by this chapter including processing applications and reasonable inspections, and with the transfer, board, handling, or storage of fish or wildlife or plants and evidentiary items seized and forfeited under this chapter. All such fees collected pursuant to this subsection shall be deposited in the Treasury to the credit of the appropriation which is current and chargeable for the cost of furnishing the services. Appropriated funds may be expended pending reimbursement from parties in interest.

(g) Citizen suits

(1) Except as provided in paragraph (2) of this subsection any person may commence a civil suit on his own behalf—

(A) to enjoin any person, including the United States and any other governmental instrumentality or agency (to the extent permitted by the eleventh amendment to the Constitution), who is alleged to be in violation of any provision of this chapter or regulation issued under the authority thereof; or

(B) to compel the Secretary to apply, pursuant to section 1535(g)(2)(B)(ii) of this title, the prohibitions set forth in or authorized pursuant to section 1533(d) or 1538(a)(1)(B) of this title with respect to the taking of any resident endangered species or threatened species within any State; or

(C) against the Secretary where there is alleged a failure of the Secretary to perform any act or duty under section 1533 of this title which is not discretionary with the Secretary.

The district courts shall have jurisdiction, without regard to the amount in controversy or the citizenship of the parties, to enforce any such provision or regulation, or to order the Secretary to perform such act or duty, as the case may be. In any civil suit commenced under subparagraph (B) the district court shall compel the Secretary to apply the prohibition sought if the court finds that the allegation that an emergency exists is supported by substantial evidence.

(2) (A) No action may be commenced under subparagraph (1)(A) of this section—

(i) prior to sixty days after written notice of the violation has been given to the Secretary, and to any alleged violator of any such provision or regulation;

(ii) if the Secretary has commenced action to impose a penalty pursuant to subsection (a) of this section; or

(iii) if the United States has commenced and is diligently prosecuting a criminal action in a court of the United States or a State to redress a violation of any such provision or regulation.

(B) No action may be commenced under subparagraph (1)(B) of this section—

(i) prior to sixty days after written notice has been given to the Secretary setting forth the reasons why an emergency is thought to exist with respect to an endangered species or a threatened species in the State concerned; or

(ii) if the Secretary has commenced and is diligently prosecuting action under section 1535(g)(2)(B)(ii) of this title to determine whether any such emergency exists.

(C) No action may be commenced under subparagraph (1) (C) of this section prior to sixty days after written notice has been given to the Secretary; except that such action may be brought immediately after such notification in the case of an action under this section respecting an emergency posing a significant risk to the well-being of any species of fish or wildlife or plants.

(3) (A) Any suit under this subsection may be brought in the judicial district in which the violation occurs.

(B) In any such suit under this subsection in which the United States is not a party, the Attorney General, at the request of the Secretary, may intervene on behalf of the United States as a matter of right.

(4) The court, in issuing any final order in any suit brought pursuant to paragraph (1) of this subsection, may award costs of litigation (including reasonable attorney and expert witness fees) to any party, whenever the court determines such award is appropriate.

(5) The injunctive relief provided by this subsection shall not restrict any right which any person (or class of persons) may have under any statute or common law to seek enforcement of any standard or limitation or to seek any other relief (including relief against the Secretary or a State agency).

(h) Coordination with other laws

The Secretary of Agriculture and the Secretary shall provide for appropriate coordination of the administration of this chapter with the administration of the animal quarantine laws (as defined in section 136a(f) of Title 21) and section 306 of the Tariff Act of 1930 (19 U.S.C. 1306). Nothing in this chapter or any amendment made by this chapter shall be construed as superseding or limiting in any manner the functions of the Secretary of Agriculture under any other law relating to prohibited or restricted importations or possession of animals and other articles and no proceeding or determination under this chapter shall preclude any proceeding or be considered determinative of any issue of fact or law in any proceeding under any Act administered by the Secretary of Agriculture. Nothing in this chapter shall be construed as superseding or limiting in any manner the functions and responsibilities of the Secretary of the Treasury under the Tariff Act of 1930 [19 U.S.C.A. § 1202 et seq.], including, without limitation, section 527 of that Act (19 U.S.C. 1527), relating to the importation of wildlife taken, killed, possessed, or exported to the United States in violation of the laws or regulations of a foreign country.

(Pub. L. No. 93–205, § 11, 87 Stat. 897 (Dec. 28, 1973); as mended by Pub. L. No. 94–359, § 4, 90 Stat. 913 (July 12, 1976); Pub. L. No. 95–632, §§ 6 to 8, 92 Stat. 3761, 3762 (Nov. 10, 1978); Pub. L. No. 97–79, § 9(e), 95 Stat. 1079 (Nov. 16, 1981); Pub. L. No. 97–304, §§ 7, 9(c), 96 Stat. 1425, 1427 (Oct. 13, 1982); Pub. L. No. 98–327, § 4, 98 Stat. 271 (June 25, 1984); Pub. L. No. 100–478, Title I, § 1007, 102 Stat. 2309 (Oct. 7, 1988); Pub. L. No. 101–650, Title III, § 321, 104 Stat. 5117 (Dec. 1, 1990); Pub. L. No. 107–171, Title X, § 10418(b)(3), 116 Stat. 508 (May 13, 2002).)

HISTORICAL AND STATUTORY NOTES

References in Text

This chapter, referred to in text, in the original read "this Act", meaning the Endangered Species Act of 1973, which is codified principally to this chapter. For complete classification, see Short Title note set out under section 1531 of this title and Tables.

The customs laws, referred to in subsec. (e)(5), are codified generally to Title 19.

The amendments made by this chapter, referred to in subsec. (h), refer to the amendments made by Pub. L. No. 93–205, which amended 16 U.S.C.A. §§ 460k–1, 460*l*–9, 668dd, 715i, 715s, 1362, 1371, 1372, and 1402 and 7 U.S.C.A. § 136, and repealed 16 U.S.C.A. §§ 668aa to 668cc–6.

The Tariff Act of 1930, referred to in subsec. (h), also known as the Smoot-Hawley Act, is Act of June 17, 1930, ch. 497, 46 Stat. 590, which is codified generally to chapter 4 of Title 19 (19 U.S.C.A. § 1202 et seq.). For complete classification, see section 1654 of Title 19 and Tables. Section 306 of the Tariff Act, Act of June 17, 1930, c. 497, Title III, § 306, 46 Stat. 689; Sept. 2, 1958, as amended, was repealed by Pub. L. No. 107–171, Title X, § 10418(a)(5), 116 Stat. 507 (May 13, 2002).

Effective and Applicability Provisions

1981 Acts. Section 9(f) of Pub. L. No. 97–79 provided that: "The amendment specified in subsection 9(e) of this Act [amending subsec. (d) of this section] shall take effect beginning in fiscal year 1983."

1973 Acts. Section effective Dec. 28, 1973, see section 16 of Pub. L. No. 93–205, set out as an Effective Date note under section 1531 of this title.

Change of Name

"United States magistrate judges" substituted for "United States magistrates" in subsec. (e)(2) pursuant to section 321 of Pub. L. No. 101–650, set out as a note under 28 U.S.C.A. § 631.

Transfer of Functions

For transfer of authorities, functions, personnel, and assets of the Coast Guard, including the authorities and functions of the Secretary of Transportation relating thereto, to the Department of Homeland Security, and for treatment of related references, see 6 U.S.C.A. §§ 468(b), 551(d), 552(d) and 557, and the Department of Homeland Security Reorganization Plan of November 25, 2002, as modified, set out as a note under 6 U.S.C.A. § 542.

For transfer of functions of the Secretary of Agriculture relating to agricultural import and entry inspection activities under this section to the Secretary of Homeland Security, and for treatment of related references, see 6 U.S.C.A. §§ 231, 551(d), 552(d) and 557, and the Department of Homeland Security Reorganization Plan of November 25, 2002, as modified, set out as a note under 6 U.S.C.A. § 542.

§ 1541. Endangered plants

[ESA § 12]

The Secretary of the Smithsonian Institution, in conjunction with other affected agencies, is authorized and directed to review (1) species of plants which are now or may become endangered or threatened and (2) methods of adequately conserving such species, and to report to Congress, within one year after December

28, 1973, the results of such review including recommendations for new legislation or the amendment of existing legislation.

(Pub. L. No. 93–205, § 12, 87 Stat. 901 (Dec. 28, 1973).)

HISTORICAL AND STATUTORY NOTES

Effective and Applicability Provisions

1973 Acts. Section effective Dec. 28, 1973, see section 16 of Pub. L. No. 93–205, set out as an Effective Date note under section 1531 of this title.

§ 1542. Authorization of appropriations

[ESA § 15]

(a) In general

Except as provided in subsections (b), (c), and (d) of this section, there are authorized to be appropriated—

(1) not to exceed $35,000,000 for fiscal year 1988, $36,500,000 for fiscal year 1989, $38,000,000 for fiscal year 1990, $39,500,000 for fiscal year 1991, and $41,500,000 for fiscal year 1992 to enable the Department of the Interior to carry out such functions and responsibilities as it may have been given under this chapter;

(2) not to exceed $5,750,000 for fiscal year 1988, $6,250,000 for each of fiscal years 1989 and 1990, and $6,750,000 for each of fiscal years 1991 and 1992 to enable the Department of Commerce to carry out such functions and responsibilities as it may have been given under this chapter; and

(3) not to exceed $2,200,000 for fiscal year 1988, $2,400,000 for each of fiscal years 1989 and 1990, and $2,600,000 for each of fiscal years 1991 and 1992, to enable the Department of Agriculture to carry out its functions and responsibilities with respect to the enforcement of this chapter and the Convention which pertain to the importation or exportation of plants.

(b) Exemptions

There are authorized to be appropriated to the Secretary to assist him and the Endangered Species Committee in carrying out their functions under sections[1] 1536(e), (g), and (h) of this title not to exceed $600,000 for each of fiscal years 1988, 1989, 1990, 1991, and 1992.

(c) Convention implementation

There are authorized to be appropriated to the Department of the Interior for purposes of carrying out section 1537a(e) of this title not to exceed $400,000 for each of fiscal years 1988, 1989, and 1990, and $500,000 for each of fiscal years 1991 and 1992, and such sums shall remain available until expended.

(Pub. L. No. 93–205, § 15, 87 Stat. 903 (Dec. 28, 1973); Pub. L. No. 94–325, 90 Stat. 724 (June 30, 1976); Pub. L. No. 95–632, § 9, 92 Stat. 3762 (Nov. 10, 1978); Pub. L. No. 96–159, § 8, 93 Stat. 1230 (Dec. 28, 1979); Pub. L. No. 97–304, § 8(a), 96 Stat. 1425 (Oct. 13, 1982); Pub. L. No. 100–478, Title I, § 1009, 102 Stat. 2312 (Oct. 7, 1988).)

[1] So in original. Probably should be "section".

HISTORICAL AND STATUTORY NOTES

References in Text

This chapter, referred to in subsec. (a) in the original read "this Act", meaning the Endangered Species Act of 1973, which is codified principally to this chapter. For complete classification, see Short Title note set out under section 1531 of this title and Tables.

Effective and Applicability Provisions

1973 Acts. Section effective Dec. 28, 1973, see section 16 of Pub. L. No. 93–205, set out as an Effective Date note under section 1531 of this title.

§ 1543. Construction with Marine Mammal Protection Act of 1972

[ESA § 17]

Except as otherwise provided in this chapter, no provision of this chapter shall take precedence over any more restrictive conflicting provision of the Marine Mammal Protection Act of 1972 [16 U.S.C.A. § 1361 et seq.].

(Pub. L. No. 93–205, § 17, 87 Stat. 903 (Dec. 28, 1973).)

HISTORICAL AND STATUTORY NOTES

References in Text

This chapter, referred to in text, in the original read "this Act", meaning the Endangered Species Act of 1973, which is codified principally to this chapter. For complete classification, see Short Title note set out under section 1531 of this title and Tables.

The Marine Mammal Protection Act of 1972, referred to in text, is codified generally as chapter 31 of this title (16 U.S.C.A. § 1361 et seq.). For complete classification, see Short Title note set out under section 1361 of this title and Tables.

Effective and Applicability Provisions

1973 Acts. Section effective Dec. 28, 1973, see section 16 of Pub. L. No. 93–205, set out as an Effective Date note under section 1531 of this title.

§ 1544. Annual cost analysis by Fish and Wildlife Service

[ESA § 18]

Notwithstanding section 3003 of Public Law 104–66 (31 U.S.C. 1113 note; 109 Stat. 734), on or before January 15, 1990, and each January 15 thereafter, the Secretary of the Interior, acting through the Fish and Wildlife Service, shall submit to the Congress an annual report covering the preceding fiscal year which shall contain—

(1) an accounting on a species by species basis of all reasonably identifiable Federal expenditures made primarily for the conservation of endangered or threatened species pursuant to this chapter; and

(2) an accounting on a species by species basis of all reasonably identifiable expenditures made primarily for the conservation of endangered or threatened species pursuant to this chapter by States receiving grants under section 1535 of this title.

(Pub. L. No. 93–205, § 18, as added by Pub. L. No. 100–478, Title I, § 1012, 102 Stat. 2314 (Oct. 7, 1988); and amended by Pub. L. No. 106–201, § 1(a), 114 Stat. 307 (May 18, 2000).)

HISTORICAL AND STATUTORY NOTES

References in Text

Section 3003 of Public Law 104–66, referred to in text, is the Federal Reports Elimination and Sunset Act of 1995, Pub. L. No. 104–66, Title III, § 3003, 109 Stat. 734 (Dec. 21, 1995), as amended, set out as a note under 31 U.S.C.A. § 1113, which, with reference to the 6th item on page 107 of House Document No. 103–7, had eliminated reporting requirements of this section.

This chapter, referred to in pars. (1), (2), in the original read "this Act", meaning the Endangered Species Act of 1973, which is codified principally to this chapter. For complete classification, see Short Title note set out under section 1531 of this title and Tables.

Effective and Applicability Provisions

2000 Acts. Pub. L. No. 106–201, § 1(b), 114 Stat. 307 (May 18, 2000), provided that:

"The amendment made by this section [amending this section] takes effect on the earlier of—

"(1) the date of enactment of this Act [May 18, 2000]; or

"(2) December 19, 1999."

FOREST AND RANGELAND RESOURCES

CHAPTER 36—FOREST AND RANGELAND RENEWABLE RESOURCES PLANNING

SUBCHAPTER I—PLANNING

SUBCHAPTER II—RESEARCH

SUBCHAPTER III—EXTENSION PROGRAMS

FOREST AND RANGELAND RENEWABLE RESOURCES PLANNING ACT OF 1974 [FRRRPA § ____]

(16 U.S.C.A. §§ 1600 to 1614)

SUBCHAPTER I—PLANNING

§ 1600. Congressional findings

[FRRRPA § 2]

The Congress finds that—

(1) the management of the Nation's renewable resources is highly complex and the uses, demand for, and supply of the various resources are subject to change over time;

(2) the public interest is served by the Forest Service, Department of Agriculture, in cooperation with other agencies, assessing the Nation's renewable resources, and developing and preparing a national renewable resource program, which is periodically reviewed and updated;

(3) to serve the national interest, the renewable resource program must be based on a comprehensive assessment of present and anticipated uses, demand for, and supply of renewable resources from the Nation's public and private forests and rangelands, through analysis of environmental and economic impacts, coordination of multiple use and sustained yield opportunities as provided in the Multiple-Use Sustained-Yield Act of 1960 (74 Stat. 215; 16 U.S.C. 528–531), and public participation in the development of the program;

(4) the new knowledge derived from coordinated public and private research programs will promote a sound technical and ecological base for effective management, use, and protection of the Nation's renewable resources;

(5) inasmuch as the majority of the Nation's forests and rangeland is under private, State, and local governmental management and the Nation's major capacity to produce goods and services is based on these nonfederally managed renewable resources, the Federal Government should be a catalyst to encourage and assist these owners in the efficient long-term use and improvement of these lands and their renewable resources consistent with the principles of sustained yield and multiple use;

(6) the Forest Service, by virtue of its statutory authority for management of the National Forest System, research and cooperative programs, and its role as an agency in the Department of Agriculture, has both a responsibility and an opportunity to be a leader in assuring that the Nation maintains a natural resource conservation posture that will meet the requirements of our people in perpetuity; and

(7) recycled timber product materials are as much a part of our renewable forest resources as are the trees from which they originally came, and in order to extend our timber and timber fiber resources and reduce pressures for timber production from Federal lands, the Forest Service should expand its research in the use of recycled and waste timber product materials, develop techniques for the substitution of these secondary materials for primary materials, and promote and encourage the use of recycled timber product materials.

(Pub. L. No. 93–378, § 2, as added by Pub. L. No. 94–588, § 2, 90 Stat. 2949 (Oct. 22, 1976).)

HISTORICAL AND STATUTORY NOTES

References in Text

The Multiple-Use Sustained-Yield Act of 1960, referred to in par. (3), is Pub. L. No. 86–517, 74 Stat. 215 (June 12, 1960), which is codified as section 528 to 531 of this title. For complete classification of this Act to the Code, see Short Title note set out under section 528 of this title and Tables.

Short Title

1988 Amendments. Pub. L. No. 100–521, § 1, 102 Stat. 2601 (Oct. 24, 1988), provided that: "This Act [amending section 1642 of this title and enacting provisions set out as a note under section 1642 of this title] may be cited as the 'Forest Ecosystems and Atmospheric Pollution Research Act of 1988'."

1987 Amendments. Pub. L. No. 100–231, § 1, 101 Stat. 1565 (Jan. 5, 1988), provided that: "This Act [amending sections 1674 and 1675 of this title and provisions set out as a note under section 1671 of this title] may be cited as the 'Renewable Resources Extension Act Amendments of 1987'."

1980 Amendments. Pub. L. No. 96–554, § 1, 94 Stat. 3257 (Dec. 19, 1980), provided: "That this Act [enacting subchapter IV of this chapter and provision set out as a note under section 1681 of this title] may be cited as the 'Wood Residue Utilization Act of 1980'."

1978 Amendments. Pub. L. No. 95–307, § 1, 92 Stat. 353 (June 30, 1978), provided: "That this Act [enacting subchapter II of this chapter, repealing sections 581 to 581i of this title, and enacting provisions set out as a note under sections 1641 of this title] may be cited as the 'Forest and Rangeland Renewable Resources Research Act of 1978'."

Pub. L. No. 95–306, § 1, 92 Stat. 349 (June 30, 1978), provided: "That this Act [enacting subchapter III of this chapter and provisions set out as a note under section 1671 of this title] may be cited as the 'Renewable Resources Extension Act of 1978'."

1976 Amendments. Section 1 of Pub. L. No. 94–588 provided: "That this Act [enacting this section and sections 472a, 576b, 1611, 1612, 1613, and 1614 of this title, amending sections 500, 515, 516, 518, 1602, 1604, 1606, 1608, 1609, and 1610 of this title, repealing sections 476, 513, 513 note, and 514 of this title, and enacting provisions set out as notes under this section and sections 476, 528, and 594–2 of this title] may be cited as the 'National Forest Management Act of 1976'."

1974 Acts. Section 1 of Pub. L. No. 93–378 provided: "That this Act [which enacted this subchapter and amended section 581h of this title] may be cited as the 'Forest and Rangeland Renewable Resources Planning Act of 1974'."

Separability of Provisions

Section 21 of Pub. L. No. 94–588 provided that: "If any provision of this Act [see Short Title of 1976 Amendment note set out above] or the application thereof to any person or circumstances is held invalid, the validity of the remainder of the Act and of the application of such provision to other persons and circumstances shall not be affected thereby."

§ 1601. Renewable Resource Assessment

[FRRRPA § 3]

(a) Preparation by Secretary of Agriculture; time of preparation, updating and contents

In recognition of the vital importance of America's renewable resources of the forest, range, and other associated lands to the Nation's social and economic well-being, and of the necessity for a long term perspective in planning and undertaking related national renewable resource programs administered by the Forest Service, the Secretary of Agriculture (referred to in this Act as the 'Secretary') shall prepare a Renewable Resource Assessment (hereinafter called the "Assessment"). The Assessment shall be prepared not later than December 31, 1975, and shall be updated during 1979 and each tenth year thereafter, and shall include but not be limited to—

(1) an analysis of present and anticipated uses, demand for, and supply of the renewable resources, with consideration of the international resource situation, and an emphasis of pertinent supply and demand and price relationship trends;

(2) an inventory, based on information developed by the Forest Service and other Federal agencies, of present and potential renewable resources, and an evaluation of opportunities for improving their yield of tangible and intangible goods and services, together with estimates of investment costs and direct and indirect returns to the Federal Government;

(3) a description of Forest Service programs and responsibilities in research, cooperative programs and management of the National Forest System, their interrelationships, and the relationship of these programs and responsibilities to public and private activities;

(4) a discussion of important policy considerations, laws, regulations, and other factors expected to influence and affect significantly the use, ownership, and management of forest, range, and other associated lands; and[1]

(5) an analysis of the potential effects of global climate change on the condition of renewable resources on the forests and rangelands of the United States; and

(6) an analysis of the rural and urban forestry opportunities to mitigate the buildup of atmospheric carbon dioxide and reduce the risk of global climate change,[2]

(b) Omitted

(c) Contents of Assessments

The Secretary shall report in the 1979 and subsequent Assessments on:

(1) the additional fiber potential in the National Forest System including, but not restricted to, forest mortality, growth, salvage potential, potential increased forest products sales, economic constraints, alternate markets, contract considerations, and other multiple use considerations;

(2) the potential for increased utilization of forest and wood product wastes in the National Forest System and on other lands, and of urban wood wastes and wood product recycling, including recommendations to the Congress for actions which would lead to increased utilization of material now being wasted both in the forests and in manufactured products; and

(3) the milling and other wood fiber product fabrication facilities and their location in the United States, noting the public and private forested areas that supply such facilities, assessing the degree of utilization into product form of harvested trees by such facilities, and setting forth the technology appropriate to the facilities to improve utilization either individually or in aggregate units of harvested trees and to reduce wasted wood fibers. The Secretary shall set forth a program to encourage the adoption by these facilities of these technologies for improving wood fiber utilization.

(d)[3] Public involvement; consultation with governmental departments and agencies

In developing the reports required under subsection (c) of this section, the Secretary shall provide opportunity for public involvement and shall consult with other interested governmental departments and agencies.

(d)[3] Congressional policy of multiple use sustained yield management; examination and certification of lands; estimate of appropriations necessary for reforestation and other treatment; budget requirements; authorization of appropriations

(1) It is the policy of the Congress that all forested lands in the National Forest System shall be maintained in appropriate forest cover with species of trees, degree of stocking, rate of growth, and conditions of stand designed to secure the maximum benefits of multiple use sustained yield management in accordance with land management plans. Accordingly, the Secretary is directed to identify and report to the Congress annually at the time of submission of the President's budget together with the annual report provided for under section 1606(c) of this title, beginning with submission of the President's budget for fiscal year 1978, the amount and location by forests and States and by productivity class, where practicable, of all lands in the National Forest System where objectives of land management plans indicate the need to reforest areas that have been cut-over or

otherwise denuded or deforested, and all lands with stands of trees that are not growing at their best potential rate of growth. All national forest lands treated from year to year shall be examined after the first and third growing seasons and certified by the Secretary in the report provided for under this subsection as to stocking rate, growth rate in relation to potential and other pertinent measures. Any lands not certified as satisfactory shall be returned to the backlog and scheduled for prompt treatment. The level and types of treatment shall be those which secure the most effective mix of multiple use benefits.

(2) Notwithstanding the provisions of section 1607 of this title, the Secretary shall annually for eight years following October 22, 1976, transmit to the Congress in the manner provided in this subsection an estimate of the sums necessary to be appropriated, in addition to the funds available from other sources, to replant and otherwise treat an acreage equal to the acreage to be cut over that year, plus a sufficient portion of the backlog of lands found to be in need of treatment to eliminate the backlog within the eight-year period. After such eight-year period, the Secretary shall transmit annually to the Congress an estimate of the sums necessary to replant and otherwise treat all lands being cut over and maintain planned timber production on all other forested lands in the National Forest System so as to prevent the development of a backlog of needed work larger than the needed work at the beginning of the fiscal year. The Secretary's estimate of sums necessary, in addition to the sums available under other authorities, for accomplishment of the reforestation and other treatment of National Forest System lands under this section shall be provided annually for inclusion in the President's budget and shall also be transmitted to the Speaker of the House and the President of the Senate together with the annual report provided for under section 1606(c) of this title at the time of submission of the President's budget to the Congress beginning with the budget for fiscal year 1978. The sums estimated as necessary for reforestation and other treatment shall include moneys needed to secure seed, grow seedlings, prepare sites, plant trees, thin, remove deleterious growth and underbrush, build fence to exclude livestock and adverse wildlife from regeneration areas and otherwise establish and improve growing forests to secure planned production of trees and other multiple use values.

(3) Effective for the fiscal year beginning October 1, 1977, and each fiscal year thereafter, there is hereby authorized to be appropriated for the purpose of reforesting and treating lands in the National Forest System $200,000,000 annually to meet requirements of this subsection (d). All sums appropriated for the purposes of this subsection shall be available until expended.

(e) Report on herbicides and pesticides

The Secretary shall submit an annual report to the Congress on the amounts, types, and uses of herbicides and pesticides used in the National Forest System, including the beneficial or adverse effects of such uses.

(Pub. L. No. 93–378, § 3, formerly § 2, 88 Stat. 476 (Aug. 17, 1974); renumbered § 3 and amended by Pub. L. No. 94–588, §§ 2 to 4, 90 Stat. 2949, 2950 (Oct. 22, 1976); and amended by Pub. L. No. 101–624, Title XXIV, § 2408(a), 104 Stat. 4061 (Nov. 28, 1990); Pub. L. No. 115–141, § 208(1), 132 Stat. 348, 1066 (Mar. 23, 2018).)

[1] So in original. The word "and" probably should not appear.

[2] So in original. The comma should probably be a period.

[3] So in original. Two subsecs. (d) have been enacted.

HISTORICAL AND STATUTORY NOTES

Codifications

Subsec. (b) of this section, omitted from this codification, amended section 581h of this title.

Termination of Reporting Requirements

For termination, effective May 15, 2000, of provisions in subsecs. (d)(1) and (e) of this section relating to submitting annual reports to Congress, see Pub. L. No. 104–66, § 3003, as amended, set out as a note under 31 U.S.C.A. § 1113 and pages 45 and 47 of House Document No. 103–7.

Transfer of Functions

The enforcement functions of the Secretary of Agriculture or other appropriate officer or entity in the Department of Agriculture, insofar as they involve lands and programs under the jurisdiction of that Department, related to compliance with system activities requiring coordination and approval under general authorities of this chapter as they relate to pre-construction, construction, and initial operation of an approved transportation system for the transport of Canadian natural gas and Alaskan natural gas as such terms are defined in the Alaskan Natural Gas Transportation Act of 1976, section 719 et seq. of Title 15, Commerce and Trade, were transferred to the Federal Inspector for the Alaska Natural Gas Transportation System, effective July 1, 1979, until the first anniversary of the date of initial operation of the Alaska Natural Gas Transportation System, pursuant to sections 102(f) and 203(a) of 1979 Reorg. Plan No. 1, June 12, 1979, 44 Fed. Reg. 33665, 33666, 93 Stat. 1373, set out in Appendix 1 to Title 5.

Severability of Provisions

If any provision of Pub. L. No. 101–624 or the application thereof to any person or circumstance is held invalid, such invalidity not to affect other provisions or applications of Pub. L. No. 101–624 which can be given effect without regard to the invalid provision or application, see section 2519 of Pub. L. No. 101–624, set out as a note under section 1421 of Title 7, Agriculture.

Presidential Commission on State and Private Forests

Pub. L. No. 101–624, Title XII, § 1245, 104 Stat. 3548 (Nov. 28, 1990), as amended by Pub. L. No. 102–237, Title X, § 1018(b), 105 Stat. 1905 (Dec. 13, 1991), provided that:

"(a) Establishment.—The President shall establish a Commission on State and Private Forests (hereafter in this section referred to as the 'Commission') which shall assess the status of the State and private forest lands of the United States, the problems affecting these lands, and the potential contribution of these lands to the renewable natural resource needs of the United States associated with their improved management and protection.

"(b) Composition.—The Commission shall be composed of 25 members to be appointed by the President, including Federal, State, and local officials, timber industry representatives, nonindustrial private forest landowners, conservationists, and community leaders. No more than five members shall be appointed from any one State. Not fewer than 20 members shall be appointed by the President from nominations submitted by the following Members of Congress:

"(1) The chairman of the Committee on Agriculture of the House of Representatives.

"(2) The ranking minority member of the Committee on Agriculture of the House of Representatives.

"(3) The chairman of the Committee on Agriculture, Nutrition, and Forestry of the Senate.

"(4) The ranking minority member of the Committee on Agriculture, Nutrition, and Forestry of the Senate.

"(c) Vacancy.—A vacancy on the Commission shall be filled by appointment by the President in the manner provided in subsection (b).

"(d) Chairperson.—The Commission shall elect a chairperson from among the members of the Commission by a majority vote.

"(e) Meetings.—The Commission shall meet at the call of the chairperson or a majority of the members of the Commission.

"(f) Duties.—

"(1) Study.—The Commission shall conduct a study that shall include—

"(A) an assessment using existing inventories of the current status of the State and private forest lands of the United States, including—

"(i) ownership status and past and future trends;

"(ii) the production of timber and nontimber resources from such lands; and

"(iii) landowner attitudes toward the protection and management of these lands;

"(B) a review of the problems affecting the State and private forest lands of the United States, including—

"(i) resource losses to insects, disease, fire, and damaging weather;

"(ii) inadequate reforestation;

"(iii) fragmentation and conversion of the forest land base; and

"(iv) management options;

"(C) constraints on, and opportunities for, providing multiresource outputs from forest lands;

"(D) administrative and legislative recommendations for addressing the problems and capitalizing on the potential of these lands for contributing to the renewable natural resource needs of the United States.

"(2) Findings and recommendations.—On the basis of its study, the Commission shall make findings and develop recommendations for consideration by the President with respect to the future demands placed on State and private forests in meeting both commodity and noncommodity needs of the United States in anticipation of impending changes in the management of the national forests, especially with regard to timber harvest. This assessment should focus on the role of State and private forest lands and help to identify means of improving their contribution to meeting the timber and nontimber needs of the United States.

"(3) Report.—The Commission shall submit to the President, not later than December 1, 1992, a report containing its findings and recommendations. The President shall submit the report to the Committee on Agriculture of the House of Representatives and the Committee on Agriculture, Nutrition, and Forestry of the Senate, and the report is authorized to be printed as a House Document.

"(g) Operations in general—

"(1) Agency cooperation.—The heads of executive agencies, the General Accounting Office [now Government Accountability Office], the Office of Technology Assessment, and the Congressional Budget Office shall cooperate with the Commission.

"(2) Compensation.—Members of the Commission shall serve without compensation for work on the Commission. While away from their homes or regular places of business in the performance of duties of the Commission, members of the Commission shall be allowed travel expenses, including per diem in lieu of subsistence, as authorized by law for persons serving intermittently in the Government service under section 5703 of title 5 of the United States Code. [Section 5703 of Title 5, Government Organization and Employees].

"(3) Director.—To the extent there are sufficient funds available to the Commission and subject to such rules as may be adopted by the Commission, the Commission, without regard to the provisions of title 5 of the United States Code [Title 5] governing appointments in the competitive service and without regard to the provisions of chapter 51 and subchapter III of chapter 53 of such title [chapter 51 and subchapter III of chapter 53 of Title V] relating to the classification and General Schedule pay rates, may—

"(A) appoint and fix the compensation of a director; and

"(B) appoint and fix the compensation of such additional personnel as the Commission determines necessary to assist it to carry out its duties and functions.

"(4) Staff and services.—On the request of the Commission, the heads of executive agencies, the Comptroller General, and the Director of the Office of Technology Assessment may furnish the Commission with such office, personnel or support services as the head of the agency, or office, and the chairperson of the Commission agree are necessary to assist the Commission to carry out its duties and functions. The Commission shall not be required to pay, or reimburse, any agency for office, personnel or support services provided by this subsection.

"(5) Exemptions.—

"(A) FACA.—The Commission shall be exempt from sections 7(d), 10(e), 10(f), and 14 of the Federal Advisory Committee Act (5 U.S.C. App. 2, 1 et seq. [sections 7(d), 10(e), 10(f), and 14 of Appendix 2 of Title 5].

"(B) Title 5.—The Commission shall be exempt from the requirements of sections 4301 through 4305 of title 5 of the United States Code [sections 4301 through 4305 of Title 5].

"(h) Authorization of appropriations and spending authority.—

"(1) Authorization of appropriations.—There is authorized to be appropriated such sums as are necessary to implement this section.

"(2) Spending authority.—Any spending authority (as defined in section 401 of the Congressional Budget Act of 1974 [section 651 of Title 2, The Congress]) provided in this title [Title XII of Pub. L. No. 101–624, Nov. 28, 1990, 104 Stat. 3521, for distribution of which see Short Title note set out under section 2101 of this title and Tables] shall be effective for any fiscal year only to such extent or in such amounts as are provided in appropriation Acts.

"(i) Termination.—The Presidential Commission on State and Private Forests shall cease to exist 90 days following the submission of its report to the President."

[Amendment by Pub. L. No. 102–237 effective Dec. 13, 1991, see section 1101(a) of Pub. L. No. 102–237, set out as a note under section 1421 of Title 7, Agriculture.]

[For termination, effective May 15, 2000, of reporting provisions of Pub. L. No. 101–624, § 1245(f)(3), set out above, see Pub. L. No. 104–66, § 3003, as amended, set out as a note under 31 U.S.C.A. § 1113, and the 5th item on page 31 of House Document No. 103–7.]

Non-Violation for Planning Delays

Section 407 of Pub. L. No. 116–94. 133 Stat. 2743 (Dec. 20, 2019), provided that:

"The Secretary of Agriculture shall not be considered to be in violation of subparagraph 6(f)(5)(A) of the Forest and Rangeland Renewable Resources Planning Act of 1974 (16 U.S.C. 1604(f)(5)(A)) solely because more than 15 years have passed without revision of the plan for a unit of the National Forest System. Nothing in this section exempts the Secretary from any other requirement of the Forest and Rangeland Renewable Resources Planning Act (16 U.S.C. 1600 et seq.) or any other law: Provided, That if the Secretary is not acting expeditiously and in good faith, within the funding available, to revise a plan for a unit of the National Forest System, this section shall be void with respect to such plan and a court of proper jurisdiction may order completion of the plan on an accelerated basis."

§ 1602. Renewable Resource Program; preparation by Secretary of Agriculture and transmittal to President; purpose and development of program; time of preparation, updating and contents

[FRRRPA § 4]

In order to provide for periodic review of programs for management and administration of the National Forest System, for research, for cooperative State and private Forest Service programs, and for conduct of other Forest Service activities in relation to the findings of the Assessment, the Secretary, utilizing information available to the Forest Service and other agencies within the Department of Agriculture, including data prepared pursuant to section 1010a of Title 7, shall prepare and transmit to the President a recommended Renewable Resource Program (hereinafter called the "Program"). The Program transmitted to the President may include alternatives, and shall provide in appropriate detail for protection, management, and development of the National Forest System, including forest development roads and trails; for cooperative Forest Service programs; and for research. The Program shall be developed in accordance with principles set forth in the Multiple-Use Sustained-Yield Act of June 12, 1960 (74 Stat. 215; 16 U.S.C. 528–531), and the National Environmental Policy Act of 1969 (83 Stat. 852) [42 U.S.C.A. § 4321 et seq.]. The Program shall be prepared not later than December 31, 1975, to cover the four-year period beginning October 1, 1976, and at least each of the four fiscal decades next following such period, and shall be updated no later than during the first half of the fiscal year ending September 30, 1980, and the first half of each fifth fiscal year thereafter to cover at least each of the four fiscal decades beginning next after such updating. The Program shall include, but not be limited to—

(1) an inventory of specific needs and opportunities for both public and private program investments. The inventory shall differentiate between activities which are of a capital nature and those which are of an operational nature;

(2) specific identification of Program outputs, results anticipated, and benefits associated with investments in such a manner that the anticipated costs can be directly compared with the total related benefits and direct and indirect returns to the Federal Government;

(3) a discussion of priorities for accomplishment of inventoried Program opportunities, with specified costs, outputs, results, and benefits;

(4) a detailed study of personnel requirements as needed to implement and monitor existing and ongoing programs; and

(5) Program recommendations which—

(A) evaluate objectives for the major Forest Service programs in order that multiple-use and sustained-yield relationships among and within the renewable resources can be determined;

(B) explain the opportunities for owners of forests and rangeland to participate in programs to improve and enhance the condition of the land and the renewable resource products therefrom;

(C) recognize the fundamental need to protect and, where appropriate, improve the quality of soil, water, and air resources;

(D) state national goals that recognize the interrelationships between and interdependence within the renewable resources;

(E) evaluate the impact of the export and import of raw logs upon domestic timber supplies and prices; and

(F) account for the effects of global climate change on forest and rangeland conditions, including potential effects on the geographic ranges of species, and on forest and rangeland products.

(Pub. L. No. 93–378, § 4, formerly § 3, 88 Stat. 477 (Aug. 17, 1974), renumbered and amended by Pub. L. No. 94–588, §§ 2, 5, 90 Stat. 2949, 2951 (Oct. 22, 1976); and amended by Pub. L. No. 101–624, Title XXIV, § 2408(b), 104 Stat. 4061 (Nov. 28, 1990); Pub. L. No. 115–141, § 208(2), 132 Stat. 348, 1066–1067 (Mar. 23, 2018).)

HISTORICAL AND STATUTORY NOTES

References in Text

The Multiple-Use Sustained-Yield Act of 1960, referred to in text, is codified as sections 528 to 531 of this title. For complete classification, see Short Title note set out under section 528 of this title and Tables.

The National Environmental Policy Act of 1969, referred to in text, is codified generally as chapter 55 of Title 42 (42 U.S.C.A. § 4321 et seq.). For complete classification, see Short Title note set out under section 4321 of Title 42 and Tables.

Transfer of Functions

For transfer of certain enforcement functions of Secretary or other official in Department of Agriculture under this subchapter to Federal Inspector, Office of Federal Inspector for the Alaska Natural Gas Transportation System, see Transfer of Functions note set out under section 1601 of this title.

Severability of Provisions

If any provision of Pub. L. No. 101–624 or the application thereof to any person or circumstance is held invalid, such invalidity not to affect other provisions or applications of Pub. L. No. 101–624 which can be given effect without regard to the invalid provision or application, see section 2519 of Pub. L. No. 101–624, set out as a note under section 1421 of Title 7, Agriculture.

§ 1603. National Forest System resource inventories; development, maintenance, and updating by Secretary of Agriculture as part of Assessment

[FRRRPA § 5]

As a part of the Assessment, the Secretary shall develop and maintain on a continuing basis a comprehensive and appropriately detailed inventory of all National Forest System lands and renewable resources. This inventory shall be kept current so as to reflect changes in conditions and identify new and emerging resources and values.

(Pub. L. No. 93–378, § 5, formerly § 4, 88 Stat. 477 (Aug. 17, 1974), renumbered by Pub. L. No. 94–588, § 2, 90 Stat. 2949 (Oct. 22, 1976); Pub. L. No. 115–141, § 208(2), 132 Stat. 348, 1066–1067 (Mar. 23, 2018).)

§ 1604. National Forest System land and resource management plans

[FRRRPA § 6]

(a) Development, maintenance, and revision by Secretary of Agriculture as part of program; coordination

As a part of the Program provided for by section 1602 of this title, the Secretary shall develop, maintain, and, as appropriate, revise land and resource management plans for units of the National Forest System, coordinated with the land and resource management planning processes of State and local governments and other Federal agencies.

(b) Criteria

In the development and maintenance of land management plans for use on units of the National Forest System, the Secretary shall use a systematic interdisciplinary approach to achieve integrated consideration of physical, biological, economic, and other sciences.

(c) Incorporation of standards and guidelines by Secretary; time of completion; progress reports; existing management plans

The Secretary shall begin to incorporate the standards and guidelines required by this section in plans for units of the National Forest System as soon as practicable after October 22, 1976, and shall attempt to complete such incorporation for all such units by no later than September 30, 1985. The Secretary shall report to the Congress on the progress of such incorporation in the annual report required by section 1606(c) of this title. Until such time as a unit of the National Forest System is managed under plans developed in accordance with this subchapter, the management of such unit may continue under existing land and resource management plans.

(d) Public participation in management plans; availability of plans; public meetings

The Secretary shall provide for public participation in the development, review, and revision of land management plans including, but not limited to, making the plans or revisions available to the public at convenient locations in the vicinity of the affected unit for a period of at least three months before final adoption, during which period the Secretary shall publicize and hold public meetings or comparable processes at locations that foster public participation in the review of such plans or revisions.

(e) Required assurances

In developing, maintaining, and revising plans for units of the National Forest System pursuant to this section, the Secretary shall assure that such plans—

(1) provide for multiple use and sustained yield of the products and services obtained therefrom in accordance with the Multiple-Use Sustained-Yield Act of 1960 [16 U.S.C.A. §§ 528–531], and, in particular, include coordination of outdoor recreation, range, timber, watershed, wildlife and fish, and wilderness; and

(2) determine forest management systems, harvesting levels, and procedures in the light of all of the uses set forth in subsection (c)(1) of this section, the definition of the terms "multiple use" and "sustained yield" as provided in the Multiple-Use Sustained-Yield Act of 1960, and the availability of lands and their suitability for resource management.

(f) Required provisions

Plans developed in accordance with this section shall—

(1) form one integrated plan for each unit of the National Forest System, incorporating in one document or one set of documents, available to the public at convenient locations, all of the features required by this section;

(2) be embodied in appropriate written material, including maps and other descriptive documents, reflecting proposed and possible actions, including the planned timber sale program and the proportion of probable methods of timber harvest within the unit necessary to fulfill the plan;

(3) be prepared by an interdisciplinary team. Each team shall prepare its plan based on inventories of the applicable resources of the forest;

(4) be amended in any manner whatsoever after final adoption after public notice, and, if such amendment would result in a significant change in such plan, in accordance with the provisions of subsections (e) and (f) of this section and public involvement comparable to that required by subsection (d) of this section; and

(5) be revised (A) from time to time when the Secretary finds conditions in a unit have significantly changed, but at least every fifteen years, and (B) in accordance with the provisions of subsections (e) and (f) of this section and public involvement comparable to that required by subsection (d) of this section.

(g) Promulgation of regulations for development and revision of plans; environmental considerations; resource management guidelines; guidelines for land management plans

As soon as practicable, but not later than two years after October 22, 1976, the Secretary shall in accordance with the procedures set forth in section 553 of Title 5, promulgate regulations, under the principles of the Multiple-Use Sustained-Yield Act of 1960 [16 U.S.C.A. §§ 528 to 531], that set out the process for the development and revision of the land management plans, and the guidelines and standards prescribed by this subsection. The regulations shall include, but not be limited to—

(1) specifying procedures to insure that land management plans are prepared in accordance with the National Environmental Policy Act of 1969 [42 U.S.C.A. § 4321 et seq.], including, but not limited to, direction on when and for what plans an environmental impact statement required under section 102(2)(C) of that Act [42 U.S.C.A. § 4332(2)(C)] shall be prepared;

(2) specifying guidelines which—

(A) require the identification of the suitability of lands for resource management;

(B) provide for obtaining inventory data on the various renewable resources, and soil and water, including pertinent maps, graphic material, and explanatory aids; and

(C) provide for methods to identify special conditions or situations involving hazards to the various resources and their relationship to alternative activities;

(3) specifying guidelines for land management plans developed to achieve the goals of the Program which—

(A) insure consideration of the economic and environmental aspects of various systems of renewable resource management, including the related systems of silviculture and protection of forest resources, to provide for outdoor recreation (including wilderness), range, timber, watershed, wildlife, and fish;

(B) provide for diversity of plant and animal communities based on the suitability and capability of the specific land area in order to meet overall multiple-use objectives, and within the multiple-use objectives of a land management plan adopted pursuant to this section, provide, where appropriate, to the degree practicable, for steps to be taken to preserve the diversity of tree species similar to that existing in the region controlled by the plan;

(C) insure research on and (based on continuous monitoring and assessment in the field) evaluation of the effects of each management system to the end that it will not produce substantial and permanent impairment of the productivity of the land;

(D) permit increases in harvest levels based on intensified management practices, such as reforestation, thinning, and tree improvement if (i) such practices justify increasing the harvests in accordance with the Multiple-Use Sustained-Yield Act of 1960, and (ii) such harvest levels are decreased at the end of each planning period if such practices cannot be successfully implemented or funds are not received to permit such practices to continue substantially as planned;

(E) insure that timber will be harvested from National Forest System lands only where—

(i) soil, slope, or other watershed conditions will not be irreversibly damaged;

(ii) there is assurance that such lands can be adequately restocked within five years after harvest;

(iii) protection is provided for streams, streambanks, shorelines, lakes, wetlands, and other bodies of water from detrimental changes in water temperatures, blockages of water courses, and deposits of sediment, where harvests are likely to seriously and adversely affect water conditions or fish habitat; and

(iv) the harvesting system to be used is not selected primarily because it will give the greatest dollar return or the greatest unit output of timber; and

(F) insure that clearcutting, seed tree cutting, shelterwood cutting, and other cuts designed to regenerate an evenaged stand of timber will be used as a cutting method on National Forest System lands only where—

(i) for clearcutting, it is determined to be the optimum method, and for other such cuts it is determined to be appropriate, to meet the objectives and requirements of the relevant land management plan;

(ii) the interdisciplinary review as determined by the Secretary has been completed and the potential environmental, biological, esthetic, engineering, and economic impacts on each advertised sale area have been assessed, as well as the consistency of the sale with the multiple use of the general area;

(iii) cut blocks, patches, or strips are shaped and blended to the extent practicable with the natural terrain;

(iv) there are established according to geographic areas, forest types, or other suitable classifications the maximum size limits for areas to be cut in one harvest operation, including provision to exceed the established limits after appropriate public notice and review by the responsible Forest Service officer one level above the Forest Service officer who normally would approve the harvest proposal: *Provided*, That such limits shall not apply to the size of areas harvested as a result of natural catastrophic conditions such as fire, insect and disease attack, or windstorm; and

(v) such cuts are carried out in a manner consistent with the protection of soil, watershed, fish, wildlife, recreation, and esthetic resources, and the regeneration of the timber resource.

(h) Scientific committee to aid in promulgation of regulations; termination; revision committees; clerical and technical assistance; compensation of committee members

(1) In carrying out the purposes of subsection (g) of this section, the Secretary shall appoint a committee of scientists who are not officers or employees of the Forest Service. The committee shall provide scientific and technical advice and counsel on proposed guidelines and procedures to assure that an effective interdisciplinary approach is proposed and adopted. The committee shall terminate upon promulgation of the regulations, but the Secretary may, from time to time, appoint similar committees when considering revisions of the regulations. The views of the committees shall be included in the public information supplied when the regulations are proposed for adoption.

(2) Clerical and technical assistance, as may be necessary to discharge the duties of the committee, shall be provided from the personnel of the Department of Agriculture.

(3) While attending meetings of the committee, the members shall be entitled to receive compensation at a rate of $100 per diem, including traveltime, and while away from their homes or regular places of business they may be allowed travel expenses, including per diem in lieu of subsistence, as authorized by section 5703 of Title 5, for persons in the Government service employed intermittently.

(i) Consistency of resource plans, permits, contracts, and other instruments with land management plans; revision

Resource plans and permits, contracts, and other instruments for the use and occupancy of National Forest System lands shall be consistent with the land management plans. Those resource plans and permits, contracts, and other such instruments currently in existence shall be revised as soon as practicable to be made consistent with such plans. When land management plans are revised, resource plans and permits, contracts, and other instruments, when necessary, shall be revised as soon as practicable. Any revision in present or future permits, contracts, and other instruments made pursuant to this section shall be subject to valid existing rights.

(j) Effective date of land management plans and revisions

Land management plans and revisions shall become effective thirty days after completion of public participation and publication of notification by the Secretary as required under subsection (d) of this section.

(k) Development of land management plans

In developing land management plans pursuant to this subchapter, the Secretary shall identify lands within the management area which are not suited for timber production, considering physical, economic, and other pertinent factors to the extent feasible, as determined by the Secretary, and shall assure that, except for salvage sales or sales necessitated to protect other multiple-use values, no timber harvesting shall occur on such lands for a period of 10 years. Lands once identified as unsuitable for timber production shall continue to be treated for reforestation purposes, particularly with regard to the protection of other multiple-use values. The Secretary shall review his decision to classify these lands as not suited for timber production at least every 10 years and shall return these lands to timber production whenever he determines that conditions have changed so that they have become suitable for timber production.

(*l*) Program evaluation; process for estimating long-term costs and benefits; summary of data included in annual report

The Secretary shall—

(1) formulate and implement, as soon as practicable, a process for estimating long-terms[1] costs and benefits to support the program evaluation requirements of this subchapter. This process shall include requirements to provide information on a representative sample basis of estimated expenditures associated with the reforestation, timber stand improvement, and sale of timber from the National Forest System, and shall provide a comparison of these expenditures to the return to the Government resulting from the sale of timber; and

(2) include a summary of data and findings resulting from these estimates as a part of the annual report required pursuant to section 1606(c) of this title, including an identification on a representative sample basis of those advertised timber sales made below the estimated expenditures for such timber as determined by the above cost process; and[2]

(m) Establishment of standards to ensure culmination of mean annual increment of growth; silvicultural practices; salvage harvesting; exceptions

The Secretary shall establish—

(1) standards to insure that, prior to harvest, stands of trees throughout the National Forest System shall generally have reached the culmination of mean annual increment of growth (calculated on the basis of cubic measurement or other methods of calculation at the discretion of the Secretary): *Provided*, That these standards shall not preclude the use of sound silvicultural practices, such as thinning or other stand improvement measures: *Provided further*, That these standards shall not preclude the Secretary from salvage or sanitation harvesting of timber stands which are substantially damaged by fire, windthrow or other catastrophe, or which are in imminent danger from insect or disease attack; and

(2) exceptions to these standards for the harvest of particular species of trees in management units after consideration has been given to the multiple uses of the forest including, but not limited to, recreation, wildlife habitat, and range and after completion of public participation processes utilizing the procedures of subsection (d) of this section.

(Pub. L. No. 93–378, § 6, formerly § 5, 88 Stat. 477 (Aug. 17, 1974); renumbered § 6 and amended by Pub. L. No. 94–588, §§ 2, 6, 12(a), 90 Stat. 2949, 2952, 2958 (Oct. 22, 1976); Pub. L. No. 115–141, § 208(2), 132 Stat. 348, 1066–1067 (Mar. 23, 2018).)

[1] So in original. Probably should be "long-term".

[2] So in original. The "; and" probably should be a period.

HISTORICAL AND STATUTORY NOTES

References in Text

The Multiple-Use Sustained-Yield Act of 1960, referred to in subsecs. (e) and (g), is codified as sections 528 to 531 of this title. For complete classification, see Short Title note set out under section 528 of this title and Tables.

The National Environmental Policy Act of 1969, referred to in subsec. (g)(1), is codified generally as chapter 55 of Title 42 (42 U.S.C.A. § 4321 et seq.). For complete classification, see Short Title note set out under section 4321 of Title 42 and Tables.

Transfer of Functions

For transfer of certain enforcement functions of Secretary or other official in Department of Agriculture under this subchapter to Federal Inspector, Office of Federal Inspector for the Alaska Natural Gas Transportation System, see Transfer of Functions note set out under section 1601 of this title.

Non-Violation for Time Lag in Revision of Forest Plans

Section 407 of Pub. L. No. 116–260, 134 Stat. 1182, 1536 (Dec. 27, 2020, provided that: "The Secretary of Agriculture shall not be considered to be in violation of subparagraph 6(f)(5)(A) of the Forest and Rangeland Renewable Resources Planning Act of 1974 (16 U.S.C. 1604(f)(5)(A)) solely because more than 15 years have passed without revision of the plan for a unit of the National Forest System. Nothing in this section exempts the Secretary from any other requirement of the Forest and Rangeland Renewable Resources Planning Act (16 U.S.C. 1600 et seq.) or any other law: Provided, That if the Secretary is not acting expeditiously and in good faith, within the funding available, to revise a plan for a unit of the National Forest System, this section shall be void with respect to such plan and a court of proper jurisdiction may order completion of the plan on an accelerated basis."

Section 407 of Pub. L. No. 116–94, 133 Stat. 2534, 2743 (Dec. 20, 2019), provided that: "The Secretary of Agriculture shall not be considered to be in violation of subparagraph 6(f)(5)(A) of the Forest and Rangeland Renewable Resources Planning Act of 1974 (16 U.S.C. 1604(f)(5)(A)) solely because more than 15 years have passed without revision of the plan for a unit of the National Forest System. Nothing in this section exempts the Secretary from any other requirement of the Forest and Rangeland Renewable Resources Planning Act (16 U.S.C. 1600 et seq.) or any other law: Provided, That if the Secretary is not acting expeditiously and in good faith, within the funding available, to revise a plan for a unit of the National Forest System, this section shall be void with respect to such plan and a court of proper jurisdiction may order completion of the plan on an accelerated basis."

Section 407 of Pub. L. No. 116–6, 133 Stat. 13, 259 (Feb. 1. 2019), provided that: "The Secretary of Agriculture shall not be considered to be in violation of subparagraph 6(f)(5)(A) of the Forest and Rangeland Renewable Resources Planning Act of 1974 (16 U.S.C. 1604(f)(5)(A)) solely because more than 15 years have passed with out revision of the plan for a unit of the National Forest System. Nothing in this section exempts the Secretary from any other requirement of the Forest and Rangeland Renewable Resources Planning Act (16 U.S.C. 1600 et seq.) or any other law: Provided, That if the Secretary is not acting expeditiously and in good faith, within the funding available, to revise a plan for a unit of the National Forest System, this section shall be void with respect to such plan and a court of proper jurisdiction may order completion of the plan on an accelerated basis."

Section 407 of Pub. L. No. 113–76, 128 Stat. 338 (Jan. 17, 2014), provided that: "The Secretary of Agriculture shall not be considered to be in violation of subparagraph 6(f)(5)(A) of the Forest and Rangeland Renewable Resources Planning Act of 1974 (16 U.S.C. 1604(f)(5)(A)) [subsec. (f)(5)(A) of this section] solely because more than 15 years have passed without revision of the plan for a unit of the National Forest System. Nothing in this section exempts the Secretary from any other requirement of the Forest and Rangeland Renewable Resources Planning Act (16 U.S.C. 1600 et seq.) [Pub. L. No. 93–378, 88 Stat. 476 (Aug. 17, 1974), as amended, which is codified generally to subchapter I (§ 1600 et seq.) of this chapter, 16 U.S.C.A. § 1600 et seq.; for complete classification, see Short Title note set out under section 1600 of this title and Tables] or any other law: *Provided,* That if the Secretary is not acting expeditiously and in good faith, within the funding available, to revise a plan for a unit of the National

Forest System, this section shall be void with respect to such plan and a court of proper jurisdiction may order completion of the plan on an accelerated basis."

Similar provisions were contained in the following prior Appropriations Acts:

Pub. L. No. 112–74, Div. E, Title IV, § 409, 125 Stat. 1039 (Dec. 23, 2011).

Pub. L. No. 111–88, Div. A, Title IV, § 410, 123 Stat. 2957 (Oct. 30, 2009).

Pub. L. No. 111–8, Div. E, Title IV, § 410, 123 Stat. 746 (Mar. 11, 2009).

Pub. L. No. 110–161, Div. F, Title IV, § 410, 121 Stat. 2146 (Dec. 26, 2007).

Pub. L. No. 109–54, Title IV, § 415, 119 Stat. 551 (Aug. 2, 2005).

Pub. L. No. 108–447, Div. E, Title III, § 320, 118 Stat. 3097 (Dec. 8, 2004).

Pub. L. No. 108–108, Title III, § 320, 117 Stat. 1306 (Nov. 10, 2003).

Pub. L. No. 108–7, Div. F, Title III, § 320, 117 Stat. 274 (Feb. 20, 2003).

Pub. L. No. 107–63, Title III, § 327, 115 Stat. 470 (Nov. 5, 2001).

Forest Land and Resource Management Plans of Forest Service and Bureau of Land Management

Pub. L. No. 101–121, Title III, § 312, 103 Stat. 743 (Oct. 23, 1989), provided that: "The Forest Service and Bureau of Land Management are to continue to complete as expeditiously as possible development of their respective Forest Land and Resource Management Plans to meet all applicable statutory requirements. Notwithstanding the date in section 6(c) of the NFMA (16 U.S.C. 1600) [subsec. (c) of this section], the Forest Service, and the Bureau of Land Management under separate authority, may continue the management of lands within their jurisdiction under existing land and resource management plans pending the completion of new plans. Nothing shall limit judicial review of particular activities on these lands: *Provided, however,* That there shall be no challenges to any existing plan on the sole basis that the plan in its entirety is outdated, or in the case of the Bureau of Land Management, solely on the basis that the plan does not incorporate information available subsequent to the completion of the existing plan: *Provided further,* That any and all particular activities to be carried out under existing plans may nevertheless be challenged."

Similar provisions were contained in the following prior Appropriations Acts:

Pub. L. No. 100–446, Title III, § 314, 102 Stat. 1825 (Sept. 27, 1988).

Pub. L. No. 100–202, § 101(g)[Title III, § 314], 101 Stat. 1329–254 (Dec. 22, 1987).

Pub. L. No. 99–591, Title I, § 101(h)[Title II, § 201], 100 Stat. 3341–268 (Oct. 30, 1986).

Pub. L. No. 99–500, Title I, § 101(h)[Title II, § 201], 100 Stat. 1783–268 (Oct. 18, 1986).

Expeditious Completion of Management Plans; Continuation of Present Plans Pending Development of New Plans; Judicial Review

Pub. L. No. 99–500, Title I, § 101(h) [Title II, § 201], 100 Stat. 1783–268 (Oct. 18, 1986), provided in part that: "The Forest Service is to continue to complete as expeditiously as possible development of land and resource management plans to meet the requirements of the National Forest Management Act of 1976 (NFMA) [Pub. L. No. 94–588, 90 Stat. 2949 (Oct. 22, 1976)]. Notwithstanding the date in section 6(c) of the NFMA (16 U.S.C. 1600) [probably means section 6(c) of Pub. L. No. 93–378 which is codified as subsec. (c) of this section], the Forest Service may continue the management of units of the National Forest System under existing land and resource management plans pending the completion of plans developed in accordance with the Act [this chapter]. Nothing shall limit judicial review of particular activities on management units of the National Forest System: *Provided, however,* That there shall be no challenges to any existing plan on the sole basis that the plan in its entirety is outdated: *Provided further,* That any and all particular activities to be carried out under existing plans may nevertheless be challenged."

[An identical provision is contained in Pub. L. No. 99–591, Title I, § 101(h) [Title II, § 201], 100 Stat. 3341–268 (Oct. 30, 1986).]

Forest Management Plans

Section 407 of Pub. L. 115–31, 131 Stat. 495 (May 5, 2017), provided: "The Secretary of Agriculture shall not be considered to be in violation of subparagraph 6(f)(5)(A) of the Forest and Rangeland Renewable Resources Planning Act of 1974 (16 U.S.C. 1604(f)(5)(A)) solely because more than 15 years have passed without revision of the plan for a unit of the National Forest System. Nothing in this section exempts the Secretary from any other requirement of the Forest and Rangeland Renewable Resources Planning Act (16 U.S.C. 1600 et seq.) or any other law: *Provided*, That if the Secretary is not acting expeditiously and in good faith, within the funding available, to revise a plan for a unit of the National Forest System, this section shall be void with respect to such plan and a court of proper jurisdiction may order completion of the plan on an accelerated basis."

Section 407 of Pub. L. No. 113–76, Title IV, 128 Stat. 338–39 (Jan. 17, 2014), provided: "The Secretary of Agriculture shall not be considered to be in violation of subparagraph 6(f)(5)(A) of the Forest and Rangeland Renewable Resources Planning Act of 1974 (16 U.S.C. 1604(f)(5)(A)) solely because more than 15 years have passed without revision of the plan for a unit of the National Forest System. Nothing in this section exempts the Secretary from any other requirement of the Forest and Rangeland Renewable Resources Planning Act (16 U.S.C. 1600 et seq.) or any other law: *Provided,* That if the Secretary is not acting expeditiously and in good faith, within the funding available, to revise a plan for a unit of the National Forest System, this section shall be void with respect to such plan and a court of proper jurisdiction may order completion of the plan on an accelerated basis."

[A nearly identical provision is contained in Pub. L. No. 113–235, Title IV, § 408, 128 Stat. 2445 (Dec. 16, 2014).]

Forest Service Pre-Decisional Objection Process

Pub. L. No. 113–79, Title VIII, § 8006(b), 128 Stat. 912 (Feb. 7, 2014), provided that: "Section 428 of division E of the Consolidated Appropriations Act, 2012 (16 U.S.C. 6515 note; Public Law 112–74) shall not apply to any project or activity implementing a land and resource management plan developed under section 6 of the Forest and Rangeland Renewable Resources Planning Act of 1974 (16 U.S.C. 1604) that is categorically excluded from documentation in an environmental assessment or an environmental impact statement under the National Environmental Policy Act of 1969 (42 U.S.C. 4321 et seq.)."

§ 1605. Protection, use and management of renewable resources on non-Federal lands; utilization of Assessment, surveys and Program by Secretary of Agriculture to assist States, etc.

[FRRRPA § 7]

The Secretary may utilize the Assessment, resource surveys, and Program prepared pursuant to this subchapter to assist States and other organizations in proposing the planning for the protection, use, and management of renewable resources on non-Federal land.

(Pub. L. No. 93–378, § 7, formerly § 6, 88 Stat. 478 (Aug. 17, 1974), renumbered by Pub. L. No. 94–588, § 2, 90 Stat. 2949 (Oct. 22, 1976); Pub. L. No. 115–141, § 208(2), 132 Stat. 348, 1066–1067 (Mar. 23, 2018).)

§ 1606. Budget requests by President for Forest Service activities

[FRRRPA § 8]

(a) Transmittal to Speaker of House and President of Senate of Assessment, Program and Statement of Policy used in framing requests; time for transmittal; implementation by President of programs established under Statement of Policy unless Statement subsequently disapproved by Congress; time for disapproval

On the date Congress first convenes in 1976 and thereafter following each updating of the Assessment and the Program, the President shall transmit to the Speaker of the House of Representatives and the President of the Senate, when Congress convenes, the Assessment as set forth in section 1601 of this title and the Program as set forth in section 1602 of this title, together with a detailed Statement of Policy intended to be used in framing budget requests by that Administration for Forest Service activities for the five- or ten-year program period beginning during the term of such Congress for such further action deemed appropriate by the Congress. Following the transmission of such Assessment, Program, and Statement of Policy, the President shall, subject to other actions of the Congress, carry out programs already established by law in accordance with such Statement of Policy or any subsequent amendment or modification thereof approved by the Congress, unless, before the end of the first period of ninety calendar days of continuous session of Congress after the date on which the President of the Senate and the Speaker of the House are recipients of the transmission of such Assessment, Program, and Statement of Policy, either House adopts a resolution reported by the appropriate committee of jurisdiction disapproving the Statement of Policy. For the purpose of this subsection, the continuity of a session shall be deemed to be broken only by an adjournment sine die, and the days on which either House is not in session because of an adjournment of more than three days to a day certain shall be excluded in the computation of the ninety-day period. Notwithstanding any other provision of this subchapter, Congress may revise or modify the Statement of Policy transmitted by the President, and the revised or modified Statement of Policy shall be used in framing budget requests.

(b) Contents of requests to show extent of compliance of projected programs and policies with policies approved by Congress; requests not conforming to approved policies; expenditure of appropriations

Commencing with the fiscal budget for the year ending September 30, 1977, requests presented by the President to the Congress governing Forest Service activities shall express in qualitative and quantitative terms the extent to which the programs and policies projected under the budget meet the policies approved by the Congress in accordance with subsection (a) of this section. In any case in which such budget so presented recommends a course which fails to meet the policies so established, the President shall specifically set forth the reason or reasons for requesting the Congress to approve the lesser programs or policies presented. Amounts appropriated to carry out the policies approved in accordance with subsection (a) of this section shall be expended in accordance with the Congressional Budget and Impoundment Control Act of 1974.

(c) Annual evaluation report to Congress of Program components; time of submission; status of major research programs; application of findings; status, etc., of cooperative forestry assistance programs and activities

For the purpose of providing information that will aid Congress in its oversight responsibilities and improve the accountability of agency expenditures and activities, the Secretary shall prepare an annual report which evaluates the component elements of the Program required to be prepared by section 1602 of this title which shall be furnished to the Congress at the time of submission of the annual fiscal budget commencing with the third fiscal year after August 17, 1974. With regard to the research component of the program, the report shall include, but not be limited to, a description of the status of major research programs, significant findings, and how these findings will be applied in National Forest System management and in cooperative State and private Forest Service programs. With regard to the cooperative forestry assistance part of the Program, the report shall include, but not be limited to, a description of the status, accomplishments, needs, and work backlogs for the programs and activities conducted under the Cooperative Forestry Assistance Act of 1978 [16 U.S.C.A. § 2101 et seq.].

(d) Required contents of annual evaluation report

These annual evaluation reports shall set forth progress in implementing the Program required to be prepared by section 1602 of this title, together with accomplishments of the Program as they relate to the objectives of the Assessment. Objectives should be set forth in qualitative and quantitative terms and accomplishments should be reported accordingly. The report shall contain appropriate measurements of pertinent costs and benefits. The evaluation shall assess the balance between economic factors and environmental quality factors. Program benefits shall include, but not be limited to, environmental quality factors such as esthetics, public access, wildlife habitat, recreational and wilderness use, and economic factors such as the excess of cost savings over the value of foregone benefits and the rate of return on renewable resources.

(e) Additional required contents of annual evaluation report

The reports shall indicate plans for implementing corrective action and recommendations for new legislation where warranted.

(f) Form of annual evaluation report

The reports shall be structured for Congress in concise summary form with necessary detailed data in appendices.

(Pub. L. No. 93–378, § 8, formerly § 7, 88 Stat. 478 (Aug. 17, 1974); renumbered § 8 and amended by Pub. L. No. 94–588, §§ 2, 7, 12(b), 90 Stat. 2949, 2956, 2958 (Oct. 22, 1976); and amended by Pub. L. No. 95–313, § 15, formerly

§ 12, 92 Stat. 374 (July 1, 1978); renumbered § 15 by Pub. L. No. 101–624, Title XII, § 1215(1), 104 Stat. 3525 (Nov. 28, 1990); Pub. L. No. 115–141, § 208(2), 132 Stat. 348, 1066–1067 (Mar. 23, 2018).)

HISTORICAL AND STATUTORY NOTES

References in Text

Congressional Budget and Impoundment Control Act of 1974, referred to in subsec. (b), is Pub. L. No. 93–344, 88 Stat. 297 (July 12, 1974), as amended. For complete classification, see Short Title note set out under section 621 of Title 2 and Tables.

The Cooperative Forestry Assistance Act of 1978, referred to in subsec. (c), is codified principally to chapter 41 of this title (16 U.S.C.A. § 2101 et seq.). For complete classification, see Short Title note set out under section 2101 of this title and Tables.

Effective and Applicability Provisions

1978 Acts. Amendment by Pub. L. No. 95–313 effective Oct. 1, 1978, see section 17 of Pub. L. No. 95–313, set out as a note under section 2101 of this title.

Termination of Reporting Requirements

For termination, effective May 15, 2000, of provisions in subsecs. (a) and (c) of this section relating to transmitting an updated Assessment, Program, and Statement of Policy to the Speaker of the House of Representatives and the President of the Senate and furnishing an annual report to Congress, see Pub. L. No. 104–66, § 3003, as amended, set out as a note under 31 U.S.C.A. § 1113, and pages 45 and 48 of House Document No. 103–7.

Statement of Policy

Pub. L. No. 96–514, Title III, § 310, 94 Stat. 2984 (Dec. 12, 1980), provided that:

"The Statement of Policy transmitted by the President to the Speaker of the House of Representatives and the President of the Senate on June 19, 1980, as required under section 8 of the Forest and Rangeland Renewable Resources Planning Act of 1974 [this section], is revised and modified to read as follows:

"STATEMENT OF POLICY

"BASIC PRINCIPLES

"It is the policy of the United States—

"(1) forests and rangeland, in all ownerships, should be managed to maximize their net social and economic contributions to the Nation's well being, in an environmentally sound manner.

"(2) the Nation's forested land, except such public land that is determined by law or policy to be maintained in its existing or natural state, should be managed at levels that realize its capabilities to satisfy the Nation's need for food, fiber, energy, water, soil stability, wildlife and fish, recreation, and esthetic values.

"(3) the productivity of suitable forested land, in all ownerships, should be maintained and enhanced to minimize the inflationary impacts of wood product prices on the domestic economy and permit a net export of forest products by the year 2030.

"(4) in order to achieve this goal, it is recognized that in the major timber growing regions most of the commercial timber lands will have to be brought to and maintained, where possible, at 90 percent of their potential level of growth, consistent with the provisions of the National Forest Management Act of 1976 on Federal lands, so that all resources are utilized in the combination that will best meet the needs of the American people.

"(5) forest and rangeland protection programs should be improved to more adequately protect forest and rangeland resources from fire, erosion, insects, disease, and the introduction or spread of noxious weeds, insects, and animals.

"(6) the Federal agencies carrying out the policies contained in this Statement will cooperate and coordinate their efforts to accomplish the goals contained in this Statement and will consult, coordinate, and cooperate with the planning efforts of the States.

"(7) in carrying out the Assessment and the Program under the Forest and Rangeland Renewable Resources Planning Act of 1974 [this subchapter] and the Appraisal and the Program under the Soil and Water

Resources Conservation Act of 1977 [section 2001 et seq. of this title], the Secretary of Agriculture shall assure that resource and economic information and evaluation data will be continually improved so that the best possible information is always available for use by Federal agencies and the public.

"Range Land Data Base and Its Improvement

"The data on and understanding of the cover and condition of range lands is less refined than the data on and understanding of commercial forest land. Range lands have significant value in the production of water and protection of watersheds; the production of fish and wildlife food and habitat; recreation; and the production of livestock forage. An adequate data base on the cover and condition of range lands should be developed by the year 1990. Currently, cattle production from these lands is annually estimated at 213 million animal unit months of livestock forage. These lands should be maintained and enhanced, including their water and other resource values, so that they can annually provide 310 million animal units months of forage by the year 2030, along with other benefits.

"General Acceptance of High Bound Program

"Congress generally accepts the 'high-bound' program described on pages 7 through 18 of the 1980 Report to Congress on the Nation's Renewable Resources prepared by the Secretary of Agriculture. However, Congress finds that the 'high-bound' program may not be sufficient to accomplish the goals contained in this statement, particularly in the areas of range and watershed resources, State and private forest cooperation and timber management.

"State and Private Lands

"States and owners of private forest and rangelands will be encouraged, consistent with their individual objectives, to manage their land in support of this Statement of Policy. The State and private forestry and range programs of the Forest Service will be essential to the furtherance of this Statement of Policy.

"Funding the Goals

"In order to accomplish the policy goals contained in this statement by the year 2030, the Federal Government should adequately fund programs of research (including cooperative research), extension, cooperative forestry assistance and protection, and improved management of the forest and rangelands. The Secretary of Agriculture shall continue his efforts to evaluate the cost-effectiveness of the renewable resource programs."

Statement of Purposes of Amendment by Cooperative Forestry Assistance Act of 1978

Section 12 of Pub. L. No. 95–313 provided in part that the amendment of subsec. (c) of this section by Pub. L. No. 95–313 is to insure that Congress has adequate information to implement its oversight responsibilities and to provide accountability for expenditures and activities under the Cooperative Forestry Assistance Act of 1978. See Short Title note set out under section 2101 of this title for distribution of the Cooperative Forestry Assistance Act of 1978 in the Code.

§ 1606a. Reforestation Trust Fund

(a) Establishment; source of funds

There is established in the Treasury of the United States a trust fund, to be known as the Reforestation Trust Fund (hereinafter in this section referred to as the "Trust Fund"), consisting of such amounts as are transferred to the Trust Fund under subsection (b) (1) of this section and any interest earned on investment of amounts in the Trust Fund under subsection (c) (2) of this section.

(b) Transfer of certain tariff receipts to Trust Fund; fiscal year limitation; quarterly transfers; adjustment of estimates

(1) Subject to the limitation in paragraph (2), the Secretary of the Treasury shall transfer to the Trust Fund an amount equal to the sum of the tariffs received in the Treasury after January 1, 1989, under headings 4401 through 4412 and subheadings 4418.50.00, 4418.90.20, 4420.10.00, 4420.90.80, 4421.90.10 through 4421.90.20, and 4421.90.70 of chapter 44, subheadings 6808.00.00 and 6809.11.00 of chapter 68 and subheading 9614.10.00 of chapter 96 of the Harmonized Tariff Schedule of the United States.

(2) The Secretary shall not transfer more than $30,000,000 to the Trust Fund for any fiscal year.

(3) The amounts required to be transferred to the Trust Fund under paragraph (1) shall be transferred at least quarterly from the general fund of the Treasury to the Trust Fund on the basis of estimates made by the Secretary of the Treasury. Proper adjustment shall be made in the amounts subsequently transferred to the extent prior estimates were in excess of or less than the amounts required to be transferred.

(c) Report to Congress; printing as House and Senate document; investments; sale and redemption of obligations; credits for Trust Fund

(1) It shall be the duty of the Secretary of the Treasury to hold the Trust Fund, and (after consultation with the Secretary of Agriculture) to report to the Congress each year on the financial condition and the results of the operations of the Trust Fund during the preceding fiscal year and on its expected condition and operations during the next fiscal year. Such report shall be printed as both a House and Senate document of the session of the Congress to which the report is made.

(2) (A) It shall be the duty of the Secretary of the Treasury to invest such portion of the Trust Fund as is not, in his judgment, required to meet current withdrawals. Such investments may be made only in interest-bearing obligations of the United States or in obligations guaranteed as to both principal and interest by the United States. For such purpose, such obligations may be acquired (i) on original issue at the issue price, or (ii) by purchase of outstanding obligations at the market price. The purposes for which obligations of the United States may be issued under chapter 31 of Title 31 are hereby extended to authorize the issuance at par of special obligations exclusively to the Trust Fund. Such special obligations shall bear interest at a rate equal to the average rate of interest, computed as to the end of the calendar month next preceding the date of such issue, borne by all marketable interest-bearing obligations of the United States then forming a part of the Public Debt; except that where such average rate is not a multiple of one-eighth of 1 percent, the rate of interest of such special obligations shall be the multiple of one-eighth of 1 percent next lower than such average rate. Such special obligations shall be issued only if the Secretary of the Treasury determines that the purchase of other interest-bearing obligations of the United States, or of obligations guaranteed as to both principal and interest by the United States on original issue or at the market price, is not in the public interest.

(B) Any obligation acquired by the Trust Fund (except special obligations issued exclusively to the Trust Fund) may be sold by the Secretary of the Treasury at the market price, and such special obligations may be redeemed at par plus accrued interest.

(C) The interest on, and the proceeds from the sale or redemption of, any obligations held in the Trust Fund shall be credited to and form a part of the Trust Fund.

(d) Obligations from Trust Fund

The Secretary of Agriculture is on and after December 19, 1985, authorized to obligate such sums as are available in the Trust Fund (including any amounts not obligated in previous fiscal years) for—

(1) reforestation and timber stand improvement as specified in section 1601(d) of this title and other forest stand improvement activities to enhance forest health and reduce hazardous fuel loads of forest stands in the National Forest System; and

(2) properly allocable administrative costs of the Federal Government for the activities specified above.

(Pub. L. No. 96–451, Title III, § 303, 94 Stat. 1991 (Oct. 14, 1980); Pub. L. No. 97–424, Title IV, § 422, 96 Stat. 2164 (Jan. 6, 1983); Pub. L. No. 99–190, § 101(d) [Title II, § 201], 99 Stat. 1245 (Dec. 19, 1985); Pub. L. No. 100–418, Title I, § 1214(r), 102 Stat. 1160 (Aug. 23, 1988); Pub. L. No. 105–83, Title III, § 322, 111 Stat. 1596 (Nov. 14, 1997).)

HISTORICAL AND STATUTORY NOTES

Codifications

Section was not enacted as part of the Forest and Rangeland Renewable Resources Planning Act of 1974, which comprises this subchapter.

In subsec. (c)(2)(A), "chapter 31 of Title 31" was substituted for "the Second Liberty Bond Act, as amended" on authority of Pub. L. No. 97–258, § 4(b), 96 Stat. 1067 (Sept. 13, 1982), the first section of which enacted Title 31, Money and Finance.

Effective and Applicability Provisions

1988 Acts. Amendment by Pub. L. No. 100–418, effective Jan. 1, 1989, and applicable with respect to articles entered on or after such date, see section 1217(b)(1) of Pub. L. No. 100–418, set out as a note under section 3001 of Title 19, Customs Duties.

Termination of Reporting Requirements

For termination, effective May 15, 2000, of provisions in subsec. (c)(1) of this section relating to reporting to Congress each year, see Pub. L. No. 104–66, § 3003, as amended, set out as a note under 31 U.S.C.A. § 1113, and page 143 of House Document No. 103–7.

§ 1607. National Forest System renewable resources; development and administration by Secretary of Agriculture in accordance with multiple use and sustained yield concepts for products and services; target year for operational posture of resources; budget requests

[FRRRPA § 9]

The Secretary shall take such action as will assure that the development and administration of the renewable resources of the National Forest System are in full accord with the concepts for multiple use and sustained yield of products and services as set forth in the Multiple-Use Sustained-Yield Act of 1960 [16 U.S.C.A. §§ 528–531]. To further these concepts, the Congress hereby sets the year 2000 as the target year when the renewable resources of the National Forest System shall be in an operating posture whereby all backlogs of needed treatment for their restoration shall be reduced to a current basis and the major portion of planned intensive multiple-use sustained-yield management procedures shall be installed and operating on an environmentally-sound basis. The annual budget shall contain requests for funds for an orderly program to eliminate such backlogs: *Provided,* That when the Secretary finds that (1) the backlog of areas that will benefit by such treatment has been eliminated, (2)the cost of treating the remainder of such area exceeds the economic and environmental benefits to be secured from their treatment, or (3) the total supplies of the renewable resources of the United States are adequate to meet the future needs of the American people, the budget request for these elements of restoration may be adjusted accordingly.

(Pub. L. No. 93–378, § 9, formerly § 8, 88 Stat. 479 (Aug. 17, 1974); renumbered by Pub. L. No. 94–588, § 2, 90 Stat. 2949 (Oct. 22, 1976); Pub. L. No. 115–141, § 208(2), 132 Stat. 348, 1066–1067 (Mar. 23, 2018).)

HISTORICAL AND STATUTORY NOTES

References in Text

The Multiple-Use Sustained-Yield Act of 1960, referred to in text, is codified as sections 528 to 531 of this title. For complete classification, see Short Title note set out under section 528 of this title and Tables.

Transfer of Functions

For transfer of certain enforcement functions of Secretary or other official in Department of Agriculture under this subchapter to Federal Inspector, Office of Federal Inspector for the Alaska Natural Gas Transportation System, see Transfer of Functions note set out under section 1601 of this title.

§ 1608. National Forest Transportation System

[FRRRPA § 10]

(a) Congressional declaration of policy; time for development; method of financing; financing of forest development roads

The Congress declares that the installation of a proper system of transportation to service the National Forest System, as is provided for in sections 532 to 538 of this title, shall be carried forward in time to meet anticipated needs on an economical and environmentally sound basis, and the method chosen for financing the construction and maintenance of the transportation system should be such as to enhance local, regional, and national benefits: *Provided*, That limitations on the level of obligations for construction of forest roads by timber purchasers shall be established in annual appropriation Acts.

(b) Construction of temporary roadways in connection with timber contracts, and other permits or leases

Unless the necessity for a permanent road is set forth in the forest development road system plan, any road constructed on land of the National Forest System in connection with a timber contract or other permit or lease shall be designed with the goal of reestablishing vegetative cover on the roadway and areas where the vegetative cover has been disturbed by the construction of the road, within ten years after the termination of the contract, permit, or lease either through artificial or natural means. Such action shall be taken unless it is later determined that the road is needed for use as a part of the National Forest Transportation System.

(c) Standards of roadway construction

Roads constructed on National Forest System lands shall be designed to standards appropriate for the intended uses, considering safety, cost of transportation, and impacts on land and resources.

(Pub. L. No. 93–378, § 10, formerly § 9, 88 Stat. 479 (Aug. 17, 1974); renumbered and amended by Pub. L. No. 94–588, §§ 2, 8, 90 Stat. 2949, 2956 (Oct. 22, 1976); and amended by Pub. L. No. 97–100, Title II, § 201, 95 Stat. 1405 (Dec. 23, 1981).)

HISTORICAL AND STATUTORY NOTES

Transfer of Functions

For transfer of certain enforcement functions of Secretary or other official in Department of Agriculture under this subchapter to Federal Inspector, Office of Federal Inspector for the Alaska Natural Gas Transportation System, see Transfer of Functions note set out under section 1601 of this title.

County Payment Mitigation.—Transportation System Moratorium.

Pub. L. No. 105–174, § 3006, 112 Stat. 85 (May 1, 1998), provided that:

"(a) (1) This section provides compensation for loss of revenues that would have been provided to counties if no road moratorium, as described in subsection (a)(2) [of this note], were implemented or no substitute sales offered as described in subsection (b)(1) [of this note]. This section does not endorse or prohibit the road building moratorium nor does it affect the applicability of existing law to any moratorium.

"(2) The Chief of the Forest Service, Department of Agriculture, in his sole discretion, may offer any timber sales that were scheduled October 1, 1997, or thereafter, to be offered in fiscal year 1998 or fiscal year 1999 even if such sales would have been delayed or halted as a result of any moratorium (resulting from the Federal Register proposal of January 28, 1998, pages 4351–4354) [63 Fed. Reg. 4351] on construction of roads in roadless areas within the National Forest System adopted as policy or by regulation that would otherwise be applicable to such sales.

"(3) Any sales offered pursuant to subsection (a)(2) shall.—

"(A) comply with all applicable laws and regulations and be consistent with applicable land and resource management plans, except any regulations or plan amendments which establish or implement the moratorium referred to in subsection (a)(2); and

"(B) be subject to administrative appeals pursuant to part 215 of title 36 of the Code of Federal Regulations [36 C.F.R. 215] and to judicial review.

"(b) (1) For any previously scheduled sales that are not offered pursuant to subsection (a)(2) [of this note], the Chief may, to the extent practicable, offer substitute sales within the same State in fiscal year 1998 or fiscal year 1999. Such substitute sales shall be subject to the requirements of subsection (a)(3) [of this note].

"(2) (A) The Chief shall pay as soon as practicable after fiscal year 1998 and fiscal year 1999 to any State in which sales previously scheduled to be offered that are referred to in, but not offered pursuant to, subsection (a)(2) [of this note] would have occurred, 25 percent of any anticipated receipts from such sales that—

"(i) were scheduled from fiscal year 1998 or fiscal year 1999 sales in the absence of any moratorium referred to in subsection (a)(2) [of this note]; and

"(ii) are not offset by revenues received in such fiscal years from substitute projects authorized pursuant to subsection (b)(1) [of this note].

"(B) After reporting the amount of funds required to make any payments required by subsection (b)(2)(A) [of this note], and the source from which such funds are to be derived, to the Committees on Appropriations of the House of Representatives and the Senate, the Chief shall make any payments required by subsection (b)(2)(A) [of this note] from any funds available to the Forest Service in fiscal year 1998 or fiscal year 1999, subject to approval of the Committees on Appropriations of the House of Representatives and the Senate, that are not specifically earmarked for another purpose by the applicable appropriation Act or a committee or conference report thereon.

"(C) Any State which receives payments required by subsection (b)(2)(A) [of this note] shall expend such funds only in the manner, and for the purposes, prescribed in section 500 of title 16, United States Code.

"(c) (1) During the term of the moratorium referred to in subsection (a)(2) [of this note], the Chief shall prepare and submit to the Committees on Appropriations of the House of Representatives and the Senate a report on each of the following—

"(A) a study of whether standards and guidelines in existing land and resource management plans compel or encourage entry into roadless areas within the National Forest System for the purpose of constructing roads or undertaking any other ground-disturbing activities;

"(B) an inventory of all roads within the National Forest System and the uses which they serve, in a format that will inform and facilitate the development of a long-term Forest Service transportation policy; and

"(C) a comprehensive and detailed analysis of the economic and social effects of the moratorium referred to in subsection (a)(2) [of this note] on county, State, and regional levels."

§ 1609. National Forest System

[FRRRPA § 11]

(a) Congressional declaration of constituent elements and purposes; lands etc., included within; return of lands to public domain

Congress declares that the National Forest System consists of units of federally owned forest, range, and related lands throughout the United States and its territories, united into a nationally significant system dedicated to the long-term benefit for present and future generations, and that it is the purpose of this section to include all such areas into one integral system. The "National Forest System" shall include all national forest lands reserved or withdrawn from the public domain of the United States, all national forest lands acquired through purchase, exchange, donation, or other means, the national grasslands and land utilization projects administered under title III of the Bankhead-Jones Farm Tenant Act [7 U.S.C.A. § 1010 et seq.], and other lands, waters, or interests therein which are administered by the Forest Service or are designated for administration through the Forest Service as a part of the system. Notwithstanding the provisions of section 473 of this title, no land now or hereafter reserved or withdrawn from the public domain as national forests pursuant to section 471 of this title, or any act supplementary to and amendatory thereof, shall be returned to the public domain except by an act of Congress.

(b) Location of Forest Service offices

The on-the-ground field offices, field supervisory offices, and regional offices of the Forest Service shall be so situated as to provide the optimum level of convenient, useful services to the public, giving priority to the maintenance and location of facilities in rural areas and towns near the national forest and Forest Service program locations in accordance with the standards in section 2204b–1(b) of Title 7.

(Pub. L. No. 93–378, § 11, formerly § 10, 88 Stat. 480 (Aug. 17, 1974); renumbered and amended by Pub. L. No. 94–588, §§ 2, 9, 90 Stat. 2949, 2957 (Oct. 22, 1976).)

HISTORICAL AND STATUTORY NOTES

References in Text

The Bankhead-Jones Farm Tenant Act, referred to in subsec. (a), is Act of July 22, 1937, c. 517, 50 Stat. 522, as amended. Title III of the Bankhead-Jones Farm Tenant Act is codified generally as subchapter III of chapter 33 of Title 7 (7 U.S.C.A. § 1010 et seq.). For complete classification, see Short Title note set out under section 1000 of Title 7 and Tables.

Section 471 of this title, referred to in subsec. (a), was repealed by Pub. L. No. 94–579, Title VII, § 704(a), 90 Stat. 2792 (Oct. 21, 1976).

Transfer of Functions

For transfer of certain enforcement functions of Secretary or other official in Department of Agriculture under this subchapter to Federal Inspector, Office of Federal Inspector for the Alaska Natural Gas Transportation System, see Transfer of Functions note set out under section 1601 of this title.

Land Conveyances Involving Joliet Army Ammunition Plant, Illinois

Pub. L. No. 104–106, Div. B, Title XXIX, 110 Stat. 594 (Feb. 10, 1996), as amended by Pub. L. No. 106–65, Div. B, Title XXVIII, § 2842, 113 Stat. 863 (Oct. 5, 1999), provided for the conversion of the Joliet Army Ammunition Plant to the Midewin National Tallgrass Prairie, Illinois, and the conveyance of certain real property at the Arsenal for a national cemetery, a Will County, Illinois, landfill for waste generated in the county to be closed and capped after 23 years of operation, and industrial parks to replace all or a part of lost economic activity, with provisions prohibiting construction of title to restrict or lessen the degree of cleanup required to be carried out under environmental laws, and provisions authorizing retention of real property used for environmental cleanup by the Secretary of the Army until the transfer occurs.

§ 1610. Implementation of provisions by Secretary of Agriculture; utilization of information and data of other organizations; avoidance of duplication of planning, etc.; "renewable resources" defined

[FRRRPA § 12]

In carrying out this subchapter, the Secretary shall utilize information and data available from other Federal, State, and private organizations and shall avoid duplication and overlap of resource assessment and program planning efforts of other Federal agencies. The term "renewable resources" shall be construed to involve those matters within the scope of responsibilities and authorities of the Forest Service on August 17, 1974 and on the date of enactment of any legislation amendatory or supplementary thereto.

(Pub. L. No. 93–378, § 12, formerly § 11, 88 Stat. 480 (Aug. 17, 1974); renumbered and amended by Pub. L. No. 94–588, §§ 2, 10, 90 Stat. 2949, 2957 (Oct. 22, 1976); Pub. L. No. 115–141, § 208(2), 132 Stat. 348, 1066–1067 (Mar. 23, 2018).)

HISTORICAL AND STATUTORY NOTES

Transfer of Functions

For transfer of certain enforcement functions of Secretary or other official in Department of Agriculture under this subchapter to Federal Inspector, Office of Federal Inspector for the Alaska Natural Gas Transportation System, see Transfer of Functions note set out under section 1601 of this title.

§ 1611. Timber

[FRRRPA § 13]

(a) Limitations on removal; variations in allowable sale quantity; public participation

The Secretary shall limit the sale of timber from each national forest to a quantity equal to or less than a quantity which can be removed from such forest annually in perpetuity on a sustained-yield basis: *Provided*, That, in order to meet overall multiple-use objectives, the Secretary may establish an allowable sale quantity for any decade which departs from the projected long-term average sale quantity that would otherwise be established: *Provided further*, That any such planned departure must be consistent with the multiple-use management objectives of the land management plan. Plans for variations in the allowable sale quantity must be made with public participation as required by section 1604(d) of this title. In addition, within any decade, the Secretary may sell a quantity in excess of the annual allowable sale quantity established pursuant to this section in the case of any national forest so long as the average sale quantities of timber from such national forest over the decade covered by the plan do not exceed such quantity limitation. In those cases where a forest has less than two hundred thousand acres of commercial forest land, the Secretary may use two or more forests for purposes of determining the sustained yield.

(b) Salvage harvesting

Nothing in subsection (a) of this section shall prohibit the Secretary from salvage or sanitation harvesting of timber stands which are substantially damaged by fire, windthrow, or other catastrophe, or which are in imminent danger from insect or disease attack. The Secretary may either substitute such timber for timber that would otherwise be sold under the plan or, if not feasible, sell such timber over and above the plan volume.

(Pub. L. No. 93–378, § 13, as added by Pub. L. No. 94–588, § 11, 90 Stat. 2957 (Oct. 22, 1976); Pub. L. No. 115–141, § 208(2), 132 Stat. 348, 1066–1067 (Mar. 23, 2018).)

HISTORICAL AND STATUTORY NOTES

Transfer of Functions

For transfer of certain enforcement functions of Secretary or other official in Department of Agriculture under this subchapter to Federal Inspector, Office of Federal Inspector for the Alaska Natural Gas Transportation System, see Transfer of Functions note set out under section 1601 of this title.

Emergency Salvage Timber Sale Program

Pub. L. No. 104–19, Title II, § 2001, 109 Stat. 240 (July 27, 1995), as amended by Pub. L. No. 104–134, Title I, § 101(c)[Title III, § 316], 110 Stat. 1321–202 (Apr. 26, 1996); and renumbered Title I by Pub. L. No. 104–140, § 1(a), 110 Stat. 1327 (May 2, 1996), provided that:

"(a) Definitions.—For purposes of this section:

"(1) The term 'appropriate committees of Congress' means the Committee on Resources, the Committee on Agriculture, and the Committee on Appropriations of the House of Representatives and the Committee on Energy and Natural Resources, the Committee on Agriculture, Nutrition, and Forestry, and the Committee on Appropriations of the Senate.

"(2) The term 'emergency period' means the period beginning on the date of the enactment of this section [July 27, 1995] and ending on December 31, 1996.

"(3) The term 'salvage timber sale' means a timber sale for which an important reason for entry includes the removal of disease- or insect-infested trees, dead, damaged, or down trees, or trees affected by fire or imminently susceptible to fire or insect attack. Such term also includes the removal of associated trees or trees lacking the characteristics of a healthy and viable ecosystem for the purpose of ecosystem improvement or rehabilitation, except that any such sale must include an identifiable salvage component of trees described in the first sentence.

"(4) The term 'Secretary concerned' means—

"(A) the Secretary of Agriculture, with respect to lands within the National Forest System; and

"(B) the Secretary of the Interior, with respect to Federal lands under the jurisdiction of the Bureau of Land Management.

"(b) Completion of salvage timber sales.—

"(1) Salvage timber sales.—Using the expedited procedures provided in subsection (c), the Secretary concerned shall prepare, advertise, offer, and award contracts during the emergency period for salvage timber sales from Federal lands described in subsection (a)(4). During the emergency period, the Secretary concerned is to achieve, to the maximum extent feasible, a salvage timber sale volume level above the programmed level to reduce the backlogged volume of salvage timber. The preparation, advertisement, offering, and awarding of such contracts shall be performed utilizing subsection (c) and notwithstanding any other provision of law, including a law under the authority of which any judicial order may be outstanding on or after the date of the enactment of this Act [July 27, 1995].

"(2) Use of salvage sale funds.—To conduct salvage timber sales under this subsection, the Secretary concerned may use salvage sale funds otherwise available to the Secretary concerned.

"(3) Sales in preparation.—Any salvage timber sale in preparation on the date of the enactment of this Act [July 27, 1995] shall be subject to the provisions of this section.

"(c) Expedited procedures for emergency salvage timber sales.—

"(1) Sale documentation.—

"(A) Preparation.—For each salvage timber sale conducted under subsection (b), the Secretary concerned shall prepare a document that combines an environmental assessment under section 102(2) of the National Environmental Policy Act of 1969 (42 U.S.C. 4332(2)) [section 4332(2) of Title 42, The Public Health and Welfare] (including regulations implementing such section) and a biological evaluation under section 7(a)(2) of the Endangered Species Act of 1973 (16 U.S.C. 1536(a)(2)) [section 1536(a)(2) of this title] and other applicable Federal law and implementing regulations. A document embodying decisions relating to salvage timber sales proposed under authority of this section shall, at the sole discretion of the Secretary concerned and to the extent the Secretary concerned considers appropriate and feasible, consider the environmental effects of the salvage timber sale and the effect, if any, on threatened or endangered species, and to the extent the Secretary concerned, at his sole discretion, considers appropriate and feasible, be consistent with any standards and guidelines from the management plans applicable to the National Forest or Bureau of Land Management District on which the salvage timber sale occurs.

"(B) Use of existing materials.—In lieu of preparing a new document under this paragraph, the Secretary concerned may use a document prepared pursuant to the National Environmental Policy Act of 1969 (42 U.S.C. 4321 et seq.) [section 4321 et seq. of Title 42] before the date of the enactment of this Act [July 27, 1995], a biological evaluation written before such date, or information collected for such a document or evaluation if the document, evaluation, or information applies to the Federal lands covered by the proposed sale.

"(C) Scope and content.—The scope and content of the documentation and information prepared, considered, and relied on under this paragraph is at the sole discretion of the Secretary concerned.

"(2) Reporting requirements.—Not later than August 30, 1995, the Secretary concerned shall submit a report to the appropriate committees of Congress on the implementation of this section. The report shall be updated and resubmitted to the appropriate committees of Congress every six months thereafter until the completion of all salvage timber sales conducted under subsection (b). Each report shall contain the following:

"(A) The volume of salvage timber sales sold and harvested, as of the date of the report, for each National Forest and each district of the Bureau of Land Management.

"(B) The available salvage volume contained in each National Forest and each district of the Bureau of Land Management.

"(C) A plan and schedule for an enhanced salvage timber sale program for fiscal years 1995, 1996, and 1997 using the authority provided by this section for salvage timber sales.

"(D) A description of any needed resources and personnel, including personnel reassignments, required to conduct an enhanced salvage timber sale program through fiscal year 1997.

"(E) A statement of the intentions of the Secretary concerned with respect to the salvage timber sale volume levels specified in the joint explanatory statement of managers accompanying the conference report on H.R. 1158, House Report 104–124.

"(3) Advancement of sales authorized.—The Secretary concerned may begin salvage timber sales under subsection (b) intended for a subsequent fiscal year before the start of such fiscal year if the Secretary concerned determines that performance of such salvage timber sales will not interfere with salvage timber sales intended for a preceding fiscal year.

"(4) Decisions.—The Secretary concerned shall design and select the specific salvage timber sales to be offered under subsection (b) on the basis of the analysis contained in the document or documents prepared pursuant to paragraph (1) to achieve, to the maxi um extent feasible, a salvage timber sale volume level above the program level.

"(5) Sale preparation.—

"(A) Use of available authorities.—The Secretary concerned shall make use of all available authority, including the employment of private contractors and the use of expedited fire contracting procedures, to prepare and advertise salvage timber sales under subsection (b).

"(B) Exemptions.—The preparation, solicitation, and award of salvage timber sales under subsection (b) shall be exempt from—

"(i) the requirements of the Competition in Contracting Act (41 U.S.C. 253 et seq.) [probably means the Competition in Contracting Act of 1984, Pub. L. No. 98–369, Div. B, Title VIII, July 18, 1984, 98 Stat. 1175; see Tables for complete classification] and the implementing regulations in the Federal Acquisition Regulation issued pursuant to section 25(c) of the Office of Federal Procurement Policy Act (41 U.S.C. 421(c)) [see, now, section 1303 of Title 41] and any departmental acquisition regulations; and

"(ii) the notice and publication requirements in section 18 of such Act (41 U.S.C. 416) [see, now, section 1708 of Title 41] and 8(e) of the Small Business Act (15 U.S.C. 637(e)) [section 637(e) of Title 15, Commerce and Trade] and the implementing regulations in the Federal Acquisition Regulations and any departmental acquisition regulations.

"(C) Incentive payment recipients; report.—The provisions of section 3(d)(1) of the Federal Workforce Restructuring Act of 1994 (Public Law 103–226; 5 U.S.C. 5597 note) [set out as a note under section 5597 of Title 5, Government Organization and Employees] shall not apply to any former employee of the Secretary concerned who received a voluntary separation incentive payment authorized by such Act [Pub. L. No. 103–226, 108 Stat. 111 (Mar. 30, 1994), for classifications to which see Short Title note under section 2101 of Title 5 and Tables] and accepts employment pursuant to this paragraph. The Director of the Office of Personnel Management and the Secretary concerned shall provide a summary report to the appropriate committees of Congress, the Committee on Government Reform and Oversight of the House of Representatives [now Committee on Homeland Security and Governmental Affairs of Senate], and the Committee on Governmental Affairs of the Senate [now Committee on Homeland Security and Governmental Affairs of Senate] regarding the number of incentive payment recipients who were rehired, their terms of reemployment, their job classifications, and an explanation, in the judgment of the agencies involved of how such reemployment without repayment of the incentive payments received is consistent with the original waiver provisions of such Act. This report shall not be conducted in a manner that would delay the rehiring of any former employees under this paragraph, or affect the normal confidentiality of Federal employees.

"(6) Cost considerations.—Salvage timber sales undertaken pursuant to this section shall not be precluded because the costs of such activities are likely to exceed the revenues derived from such activities.

"(7) Effect of salvage sales.—The Secretary concerned shall not substitute salvage timber sales conducted under subsection (b) for planned non-salvage timber sales.

"(8) Reforestation of salvage timber sale parcels.—The Secretary concerned shall plan and implement reforestation of each parcel of land harvested under a salvage timber sale conducted under subsection (b) as expeditiously as possible after completion of the harvest on the parcel, but in no case later than any applicable restocking period required by law or regulation.

"(9) Effect on judicial decisions.—The Secretary concerned may conduct salvage timber sales under subsection (b) notwithstanding any decision, restraining order, or injunction issued by a United States court before the date of the enactment of this section [July 27, 1995].

"(d) Direction to complete timber sales on lands covered by option 9.—Notwithstanding any other law (including a law under the authority of which any judicial order may be outstanding on or after the date of enactment of this Act [July 27, 1995]), the Secretary concerned shall expeditiously prepare, offer, and award timber sale contracts on Federal lands described in the 'Record of Decision for Amendments to Forest Service and Bureau of Land Management Planning Documents Within the Range of the Northern Spotted Owl', signed by the Secretary of the Interior and the Secretary of Agriculture on April 13, 1994. The Secretary concerned may conduct timber sales under this subsection notwithstanding any decision, restraining order, or injunction issued by a United States court before the date of the enactment of this section. The issuance of any regulation pursuant to section 4(d) of the Endangered Species Act of 1973 (16 U.S.C. 1533(d)) [section

1533(d) of this title] to ease or reduce restrictions on non-Federal lands within the range of the northern spotted owl shall be deemed to satisfy the requirements of section 102(2)(C) of the National Environmental Policy Act of 1969 (42 U.S.C. 4332(2)(C)) [section 4332(2)(C) of Title 42], given the analysis included in the Final Supplemental Impact Statement on the Management of the Habitat for Late Successional and Old Growth Forest Related Species Within the Range of the Northern Spotted Owl, prepared by the Secretary of Agriculture and the Secretary of the Interior in 1994, which is, or may be, incorporated by reference in the administrative record of any such regulation. The issuance of any such regulation pursuant to section 4(d) of the Endangered Species Act of 1973 (16 U.S.C. 1533(d)) shall not require the preparation of an environmental impact statement under section 102(2)(C) of the National Environmental Policy Act of 1969 (42 U.S.C. 4332(2)(C)).

"(e) Administrative review.—Salvage timber sales conducted under subsection (b), timber sales conducted under subsection (d), and any decision of the Secretary concerned in connection with such sales, shall not be subject to administrative review.

"(f) Judicial review.—

"(1) Place and time of filing.—A salvage timber sale to be conducted under subsection (b), and a timber sale to be conducted under subsection (d), shall be subject to judicial review only in the United States district court for the district in which the affected Federal lands are located. Any challenge to such sale must be filed in such district court within 15 days after the date of initial advertisement of the challenged sale. The Secretary concerned may not agree to, and a court may not grant, a waiver of the requirements of this paragraph.

"(2) Effect of filing on agency action.—For 45 days after the date of the filing of a challenge to a salvage timber sale to be conducted under subsection (b) or a timber sale to be conducted under subsection (d), the Secretary concerned shall take no action to award the challenged sale.

"(3) Prohibition on restraining orders, preliminary injunctions, and relief pending review.—No restraining order, preliminary injunction, or injunction pending appeal shall be issued by any court of the United States with respect to any decision to prepare, advertise, offer, award, or operate a salvage timber sale pursuant to subsection (b) or any decision to prepare, advertise, offer, award, or operate a timber sale pursuant to subsection (d). Section 705 of title 5, United States Code, shall not apply to any challenge to such a sale.

"(4) Standard of review.—The courts shall have authority to enjoin permanently, order modification of, or void an individual salvage timber sale if it is determined by a review of the record that the decision to prepare, advertise, offer, award, or operate such sale was arbitrary and capricious or otherwise not in accordance with applicable law (other than those laws specified in subsection (i)).

"(5) Time for decision.—Civil actions filed under this subsection shall be assigned for hearing at the earliest possible date. The court shall render its final decision relative to any challenge within 45 days from the date such challenge is brought, unless the court determines that a longer period of time is required to satisfy the requirement of the United States Constitution. In order to reach a decision within 45 days, the district court may assign all or part of any such case or cases to one or more Special Masters, for prompt review and recommendations to the court.

"(6) Procedures.—Notwithstanding any other provision of law, the court may set rules governing the procedures of any proceeding brought under this subsection which set page limits on briefs and time limits on filing briefs and motions and other actions which are shorter than the limits specified in the Federal rules of civil or appellate procedure.

"(7) Appeal.—Any appeal from the final decision of a district court in an action brought pursuant to this subsection shall be filed not later than 30 days after the date of decision.

"(g) Exclusion of certain Federal lands.—

"(1) Exclusion.—The Secretary concerned may not select, authorize, or undertake any salvage timber sale under subsection (b) with respect to lands described in paragraph (2).

"(2) Description of excluded lands.—The lands referred to in paragraph (1) are as follows:

"(A) Any area on Federal lands included in the National Wilderness Preservation System.

"(B) Any roadless area on Federal lands designated by Congress for wilderness study in Colorado or Montana.

"(C) Any roadless area on Federal lands recommended by the Forest Service or Bureau of Land Management for wilderness designation in its most recent land management plan in effect as of the date of the enactment of this Act [July 27, 1995].

"(D) Any area on Federal lands on which timber harvesting for any purpose is prohibited by statute.

"(h) Rulemaking.—The Secretary concerned is not required to issue formal rules under section 553 of title 5, United States Code, to implement this section or carry out the authorities provided by this section.

"(i) Effect on other laws.—The documents and procedures required by this section for the preparation, advertisement, offering, awarding, and operation of any salvage timber sale subject to subsection (b) and any timber sale under subsection (d) shall be deemed to satisfy the requirements of the following applicable Federal laws (and regulations implementing such laws):

"(1) The Forest and Rangeland Renewable Resources Planning Act of 1974 (16 U.S.C. 1600 et seq.) [section 1600 et seq. of this title].

"(2) The Federal Land Policy and Management Act of 1976 (43 U.S.C. 1701 et seq.) [section 1701 et seq. of Title 43, Public Lands].

"(3) The National Environmental Policy Act of 1969 (42 U.S.C. 4321 et seq.) [section 4321 et seq. of Title 42].

"(4) The Endangered Species Act of 1973 (16 U.S.C. 1531 et seq.) [section 1531 et seq. of this title].

"(5) The National Forest Management Act of 1976 (16 U.S.C. 472a et seq.) [Pub. L. No. 94–588, Oct. 22, 1976, 90 Stat. 2949, for classifications to which see Short Title note under section 1600 of this Title and Tables].

"(6) The Multiple-Use Sustained-Yield Act of 1960 (16 U.S.C. 528 et seq.) [section 528 et seq. of this title].

"(7) Any compact, executive agreement, convention, treaty, and international agreement, and implementing legislation related thereto.

"(8) All other applicable Federal environmental and natural resource laws.

"(j) Expiration date.—The authority provided by subsections (b) and (d) shall expire on December 31, 1996. The terms and conditions of this section shall continue in effect with respect to salvage timber sale contracts offered under subsection (b) and timber sale contracts offered under subsection (d) until the completion of performance of the contracts.

"(k) Award and release of previously offered and unawarded timber sale contracts.—

"(1) Award and release required.—Notwithstanding any other provision of law, within 45 days after the date of the enactment of this Act [July 27, 1995], the Secretary concerned shall act to award, release, and permit to be completed in fiscal years 1995 and 1996, with no change in originally advertised terms, volumes, and bid prices, all timber sale contracts offered or awarded before that date in any unit of the National Forest System or district of the Bureau of Land Management subject to section 318 of Public Law 101–121 (103 Stat. 745) [not codified as the Code]. The return of the bid bond of the high bidder shall not alter the responsibility of the Secretary concerned to comply with this paragraph.

"(2) Threatened or endangered bird species.—No sale unit shall be released or completed under this subsection if any threatened or endangered bird species is known to be nesting within the acreage that is the subject of the sale unit.

"(3) Alternative offer in case of delay.—If for any reason a sale cannot be released and completed under the terms of this subsection within 45 days after the date of the enactment of this Act [July 27, 1995], the Secretary concerned shall provide the purchaser an equal volume of timber, of like kind and value, which shall be subject to the terms of the original contract and shall not count against current allowable sale quantities.

"(*l*) Effect on plans, policies, and activities.—Compliance with this section shall not require or permit any administrative action, including revisions, amendment, consultation, supplementation, or other action, in or for any land management plan, standard, guideline, policy, regional guide, or multiforest plan because of implementation or impacts, site-specific or cumulative, of activities authorized or required by this section, except that any such administrative action with respect to salvage timber sales is permitted to the extent necessary, at the sole discretion of the Secretary concerned, to meet the salvage timber sale goal specified in subsection (b)(1) of this section or to reflect the effects of the salvage program. The Secretary concerned shall not rely on salvage timber sales as the basis for administrative action limiting other multiple use activities nor be required to offer a particular salvage timber sale. No project decision shall be required to be halted or delayed by such documents or guidance, implementation, or impacts."

Timber Sales Pipeline Restoration Funds

Pub. L. No. 104–134, Title I, § 101(c)[Title III, § 327], 110 Stat. 1321–206 (Apr. 26, 1996); renumbered Title I by Pub. L. No. 104–140, § 1(a), 110 Stat. 1327 (May 2, 1996), provided that:

"(a) The Secretary of Agriculture and the Secretary of the Interior shall each establish a Timber Sales Pipeline Restoration Fund (hereinafter 'Agriculture Fund' and 'Interior Fund' or 'Funds'). Any revenues received from sales released under section 2001(k) of the fiscal year 1995 Supplemental Appropriations for Disaster Assistance and Rescissions Act [probably means section 2001(k) of Pub. L. No. 104–19, set out as a note under this section], minus the funds necessary to make payments to States or local governments under other law concerning the distribution of revenues derived from the affected lands, which are in excess of $37,500,000 (hereinafter 'excess revenues') shall be deposited into the Funds. The distribution of excess revenues between the Agriculture Fund and Interior Fund shall be calculated by multiplying the total of excess revenues times a fraction with a denominator of the total revenues received from all sales released under such section 2001(k) and numerators of the total revenues received from such sales on lands within the National Forest System and the total revenues received from such sales on lands administered by the Bureau of Land Management, respectively: *Provided,* That revenues or portions thereof from sales released under such section 2001(k), minus the amounts necessary for State and local government payments and other necessary deposits, may be deposited into the Funds immediately upon receipt thereof and subsequently redistributed between the Funds or paid into the United States Treasury as miscellaneous receipts as may be required when the calculation of excess revenues is made.

"(b) (1) from the funds deposited into the Agriculture Fund and into the Interior Fund pursuant to subsection (a)—

"(A) seventy-five percent shall be available, without fiscal year limitation or further appropriation, for preparation of timber sales, other than salvage sales as defined in section 2001(a)(3) of the fiscal year 1995 Supplemental Appropriations for Disaster Assistance and Rescissions Act [probably means section 2001(a)(3) of Pub. L. No. 104–19, set out as a note under this section], which—

"(i) are situated on lands within the National Forest System and lands administered by the Bureau of Land Management, respectively; and

"(ii) are in addition to timber sales for which funds are otherwise available in this Act [probably means Pub. L. No. 104–134, Title I, § 101(c), Apr. 26, 1996, 104 Stat. 1321–156; renumbered Title I Pub. L. No. 104–140, § 1(a), May 2, 1996, 104 Stat. 1327, known as the Department of the Interior and Related Agencies Appropriations Act, 1996, see Tables for classification] or other appropriations Acts; and

"(B) twenty-five percent shall be available, without fiscal year limitation or further appropriation, to expend on the backlog of recreation projects on lands within the National Forest System and lands administered by the Bureau of Land Management, respectively.

"(2) Expenditures under this subsection for preparation of timber sales may include expenditures for Forest Service activities within the forest land management budget line item and associated timber roads, and Bureau of Land Management activities within the Oregon and California grant lands account and the forestry management area account, as determined by the Secretary concerned.

"(c) Revenues received from any timber sale prepared under subsection (b) or under this subsection, minus the amounts necessary for State and local government payments and other necessary deposits, shall be deposited into the Fund from which funds were expended on such sale. Such deposited revenues shall be available for preparation of additional timber sales and completion of additional recreation projects in accordance with the requirements set forth in subsection (b).

"(d) The Secretary concerned shall terminate all payments into the Agriculture Fund or the Interior Fund, and pay any unobligated funds in the affected Fund into the United States Treasury as miscellaneous receipts, whenever the Secretary concerned makes a finding, published in the Federal Register, that sales sufficient to achieve the total allowable sales quantity of the National Forest System for the Forest Service or the allowable sales level for the Oregon and California grant lands for the Bureau of Land Management, respectively, have been prepared.

"(e) Any timber sales prepared and recreation projects completed under this section shall comply with all applicable environmental and natural resource laws and regulations.

"(f) The Secretary concerned shall report annually to the Committees on Appropriations of the United States Senate and the House of Representatives on expenditures made from the Fund for timber sales and recreation projects, revenues received into the Fund from timber sales, and timber sale preparation and recreation project work undertaken during the previous year and projected for the next year under the Fund. Such information shall be provided for each Forest Service region and Bureau of Land Management State office.

"(g) The authority of this section shall terminate upon the termination of both Funds in accordance with the provisions of subsection (d)."

§ 1612. Public participation

[FRRRPA § 14]

(a) Adequate notice and opportunity to comment

In exercising his authorities under this subchapter and other laws applicable to the Forest Service, the Secretary, by regulation, shall establish procedures, including public hearings where appropriate, to give the Federal, State, and local governments and the public adequate notice and an opportunity to comment upon the formulation of standards, criteria, and guidelines applicable to Forest Service programs.

(b) Advisory boards

In providing for public participation in the planning for and management of the National Forest System, the Secretary, pursuant to the Federal Advisory Committee Act (86 Stat. 770) and other applicable law, shall establish and consult such advisory boards as he deems necessary to secure full information and advice on the execution of his responsibilities. The membership of such boards shall be representative of a cross section of groups interested in the planning for and management of the National Forest System and the various types of use and enjoyment of the lands thereof.

(Pub. L. No. 93–378, § 14, as added by Pub. L. No. 94–588, § 11, 90 Stat. 2958 (Oct. 22, 1976).)

HISTORICAL AND STATUTORY NOTES

References in Text

The Federal Advisory Committee Act, referred to in text, is set out in Appendix 2 to Title 5.

Transfer of Functions

For transfer of certain enforcement functions of Secretary or other official in Department of Agriculture under this subchapter to Federal Inspector, Office of Federal Inspector for the Alaska Natural Gas Transportation System, see Transfer of Functions note set out under section 1601 of this title.

Forest Service Decision Making and Appeals Reform

Pub. L. No. 102–381, Title III, § 322, 106 Stat. 1419 (Oct. 5, 1992), which provided for the Secretary of Agriculture to establish a notice and comment process for proposed actions of the Forest Service concerning certain land and resource management projects and required modification of the procedure for appeals of decisions concerning such projects, was repealed by Pub. L. No. 113–79, Title VIII, § 8006(a), 128 Stat. 913 (Feb. 7, 2014).

§ 1613. Promulgation of regulations

[FRRRPA § 15]

The Secretary shall prescribe such regulations as he determines necessary and desirable to carry out the provisions of this subchapter.

(Pub. L. No. 93–378, § 15, as added by Pub. L. No. 94–588, § 11, 90 Stat. 2958 (Oct. 22, 1976); Pub. L. No. 115–141, § 208(2), 132 Stat. 348, 1066–1067 (Mar. 23, 2018).)

HISTORICAL AND STATUTORY NOTES

Transfer of Functions

For transfer of certain enforcement functions of Secretary or other official in Department of Agriculture under this subchapter to Federal Inspector, Office of Federal Inspector for the Alaska Natural Gas Transportation System, see Transfer of Functions note set out under section 1601 of this title.

§ 1614. Severability

[FRRRPA § 16]

If any provision of this subchapter or the application thereof to any person or circumstances is held invalid, the validity of the remainder of this subchapter and of the application of such provision to other persons and circumstances shall not be affected thereby.

(Pub. L. No. 93–378, § 16, as added by Pub. L. No. 94–588, § 11, 90 Stat. 2958 (Oct. 22, 1976).)

FOREST AND RANGELAND RENEWABLE RESOURCES RESEARCH ACT OF 1978 [FRRRRA § ______]

(16 U.S.C.A. §§ 1641 to 1650)

SUBCHAPTER II—RESEARCH

§ 1641. Findings and purpose

[FRRRRA § 2]

(a) Findings

Congress finds the following:

(1) Forests and rangeland, and the resources of forests and rangeland, are of strategic economic and ecological importance to the United States, and the Federal Government has an important and substantial role in ensuring the continued health, productivity, and sustainability of the forests and rangeland of the United States.

(2) Over 75 percent of the productive commercial forest land in the United States is privately owned, with some 60 percent owned by small nonindustrial private owners. These 10,000,000 nonindustrial private owners are critical to providing both commodity and noncommodity values to the citizens of the United States.

(3) The National Forest System manages only 17 percent of the commercial timberland of the United States, with over half of the standing softwoods inventory located on that land. Dramatic changes in Federal agency policy during the early 1990's have significantly curtailed the management of this vast timber resource, causing abrupt shifts in the supply of timber from public to private ownership. As a result of these shifts in supply, some 60 percent of total wood production in the United States is now coming from private forest land in the southern United States.

(4) At the same time that pressures are building for the removal of even more land from commercial production, the Federal Government is significantly reducing its commitment to productivity-related research regarding forests and rangeland, which is critically needed by the private sector for the sustained management of remaining available timber and forage resources for the benefit of all species.

(5) Uncertainty over the availability of the United States timber supply, increasing regulatory burdens, and the lack of Federal Government support for research is causing domestic wood and paper producers to move outside the United States to find reliable sources of wood supplies, which in turn results in a worsening of the United States trade balance, the loss of employment and infrastructure investments, and an increased risk of infestations of exotic pests and diseases from imported wood products.

(6) Wood and paper producers in the United States are being challenged not only by shifts in Federal Government policy, but also by international competition from tropical countries where growth rates of trees far exceed those in the United States. Wood production per acre will need to quadruple from 1996 levels for the United States forestry sector to remain internationally competitive on an ever decreasing forest land base.

(7) Better and more frequent forest inventorying and analysis is necessary to identify productivity-related forestry research needs and to provide forest managers with the current data necessary to make timely and effective management decisions.

(b) Relationship to other law

This subchapter shall be deemed to complement the policies and direction set forth in the Forest and Rangeland Renewable Resources Planning Act of 1974 [16 U.S.C.A. § 1600 et seq.].

(c) Purpose

It is the purpose of this subchapter to authorize the Secretary to expand research activities to encompass international forestry and natural resource issues on a global scale.

(Pub. L. No. 95–307, § 2, 92 Stat. 353 (June 30, 1978); as amended by Pub. L. No. 101–513, Title VI, § 611(a)(1), formerly § 607(a)(1), 104 Stat. 2072 (Nov. 5, 1990); renumbered § 611(a)(1) by Pub. L. No. 102–574, § 2(a)(1), 106 Stat. 4593 (Oct. 29, 1992); and amended by Pub. L. No. 105–185, Title II, § 253(a), 112 Stat. 558 (June 23, 1998).)

HISTORICAL AND STATUTORY NOTES

References in Text

The Forest and Rangeland Renewable Resources Planning Act of 1974, referred to in subsec. (b), is codified principally as subchapter I of this chapter (16 U.S.C.A. § 1600 et seq.). For complete classification, see Short Title note set out under section 1600 of this title and Tables.

This subchapter, referred to in subsec. (c), in the original read "this Act", meaning the Forest and Rangeland Renewable Resources Research Act of 1978, which enacted this subchapter, repealed sections 581 to 581i of this title, and enacted provisions set out as a note under section 1641 of this title. For complete classification, see Short Title note set out under section 1600 of this title and Tables.

Effective and Applicability Provisions

1990 Acts. Section 9 of Pub. L. No. 95–307 which provided that Pub. L. No. 95–307 (enacting this subchapter, repealing sections 581 to 581i of this title, and enacting provisions set out as a note under section 1600 of this title) is effective Oct. 1, 1978, was amended generally by Pub. L. No. 101–624 and codified as section 1648 of this title.

Short Title

1978 Acts. For Short Title of Pub. L. No. 95–307, 92 Stat. 353 (June 30, 1978), as the Forest and Rangeland Renewable Resources Research Act of 1978, see short title note set out under section 1600 of this title.

§ 1642. Investigations, experiments, tests, and other activities [FRRRRA § 3]

(a) Authorization; scope and purposes of activities

The Secretary is authorized to conduct, support, and cooperate in investigations, experiments, tests, and other activities the Secretary deems necessary to obtain, analyze, develop, demonstrate, and disseminate scientific information about protecting, managing, and utilizing forest and rangeland renewable resources in rural, suburban, and urban areas. The activities conducted, supported, or cooperated in by the Secretary under this subchapter shall include, but not be limited to, the five major areas of renewable resource research identified in paragraphs (1) through (5) of this subsection.

(1) Renewable resource management research shall include, as appropriate, research activities related to managing, reproducing, planting, and growing vegetation on forests and rangelands for timber, forage, water, fish and wildlife, aesthetics, recreation, wilderness, energy production, activities related to energy conservation, and other purposes, including activities for encouraging improved reforestation of forest lands from which timber has been harvested; determining the role of forest and rangeland management in the productive use of forests and rangelands, in diversified agriculture, and in mining, transportation, and other industries; and developing alternatives for the management of forests and rangelands that will make possible the most effective use of their multiple products and services.

(2) Renewable resource environmental research shall include, as appropriate, research activities related to understanding and managing surface and subsurface water flow, preventing and controlling erosion, and restoring damaged or disturbed soils on forest and rangeland watersheds; maintaining and improving wildlife and fish habitats; managing vegetation to reduce air and water pollution, provide amenities, and for other purposes; and understanding, predicting, and modifying weather, climatic, and other environmental conditions that affect the protection and management of forests and rangelands.

(3) Renewable resource protection research shall include, as appropriate, research activities related to protecting vegetation and other forest and rangeland resources, including threatened and endangered flora and fauna, as well as wood and wood products in storage or use, from fires, insects, diseases, noxious plants, animals, air pollutants, and other agents through biological, chemical, and mechanical control methods and systems; and protecting people, natural resources, and property from fires in rural areas.

(4) Renewable resource utilization research shall include, as appropriate, research activities related to harvesting, transporting, processing, marketing, distributing, and utilizing wood and other materials derived from forest and rangeland renewable resources; recycling and fully utilizing wood fiber; producing and conserving energy; and testing forest products, including necessary fieldwork associated therewith.

(5) Renewable resource assessment research shall include, as appropriate, research activities related to developing and applying scientific knowledge and technology in support of the survey and analysis of forest and rangeland renewable resources described in subsection (b) of this section.

(b) Development of periodic Renewable Resource Assessment through survey and analysis of conditions; implementation; authorization of appropriations

(1) To ensure the availability of adequate data and scientific information for development of the periodic Renewable Resource Assessment provided for in section 1601 of this title, the Secretary of Agriculture shall make and keep current a comprehensive survey and analysis of the present and prospective conditions of and requirements for renewable resources of the forests and rangelands of the United States and of the supplies of such renewable resources, including a determination of the present and potential productivity of the land, and of such other facts as may be necessary and useful in the determination of ways and means needed to balance the demand for and supply of these renewable resources, benefits, and uses in meeting the needs of the people of the United States. The Secretary shall conduct the survey and analysis under such plans as the Secretary may determine to be fair and equitable, and cooperate with appropriate officials of each State and, either through them or directly, with private or other entities.

(2) In implementing this subsection, the Secretary is authorized to develop and implement improved methods of survey and analysis of forest inventory information, for which purposes there are hereby authorized to be appropriated annually $10,000,000.

(c) Program of research and study relative to health and productivity of domestic forest ecosystems; advisory committee; reports

(1) The Secretary, acting through the United States Forest Service, shall establish not later than 180 days after October 24, 1988, a 10-year program (hereinafter in this subsection referred to as the "Program") to—

(A) increase the frequency of forest inventories in matters that relate to atmospheric pollution and conduct such surveys as are necessary to monitor long-term trends in the health and productivity of domestic forest ecosystems;

(B) determine the scope of the decline in the health and productivity of domestic forest ecosystems;

(C) accelerate and expand existing research efforts (including basic forest ecosystem research) to evaluate the effects of atmospheric pollutants on forest ecosystems and their role in the decline in domestic forest health and productivity;

(D) study the relationship between atmospheric pollution and other climatological, chemical, physical, and biological factors that may affect the health and productivity of domestic forest ecosystems;

(E) develop recommendations for solving or mitigating problems related to the effects of atmospheric pollution on the health and productivity of domestic forest ecosystems;

(F) foster cooperation among Federal, State, and private researchers and encourage the exchange of scientific information on the effects of atmospheric pollutants on forest ecosystems among the United States, Canada, European nations, and other nations;

(G) support the long-term funding of research programs and related efforts to determine the causes of declines in the health and productivity of domestic forest ecosystems and the effects of atmospheric pollutants on the health and productivity of domestic forest ecosystems; and

(H) enlarge the Eastern Hardwood Cooperative by devoting additional resources to field analysis of the response of hardwood species to atmospheric pollution, and other factors that may affect the health and productivity of these ecosystems.

(2) The Secretary shall establish a committee to advise the Secretary in developing and carrying out the Program, which shall be composed of scientists with training and experience in various disciplines, including atmospheric, ecological, and biological sciences. Such scientists shall be selected from among individuals who are actively performing research for Federal or State agencies or for private industries, institutions, or organizations.

(3) The Secretary shall coordinate the Program with existing research efforts of Federal and State agencies and private industries, institutions, or organizations.

(4) The Secretary shall submit to the President and to Congress the following reports:

(A) Not less than 30 days before establishing the Program, the Secretary shall submit an initial program report—

(i) discussing existing information about declining health and productivity of forest ecosystems on public and private lands in North America and Europe;

(ii) outlining the findings and status of all current research and monitoring efforts in North America and Europe on the causes and effects of atmospheric pollution on the health and productivity of forest ecosystems;

(iii) describing the Program; and

(iv) estimating the cost of implementing the Program for each fiscal year of its duration.

(B) Not later than January 15, 1990, and January 15 of each year thereafter, during which the Program is in operation following the year in which the initial program report is submitted, the Secretary shall submit an annual report—

(i) updating information about declining health and productivity of forest ecosystems on public and private lands in North America and Europe;

(ii) updating the findings and status of all current research and monitoring efforts in North America and Europe on the causes and effects of atmospheric pollution on the health and productivity of forest ecosystems, including efforts conducted under the Program;

(iii) recommending additional research and monitoring efforts to be undertaken under the Program to determine the effects of atmospheric pollution on the health and productivity of domestic forest ecosystems; and

(iv) recommending methods for solving or mitigating problems stemming from the effects of atmospheric pollution on the health and productivity of domestic forest ecosystems.

(C) Not later than 10 years after the date on which the initial program report is submitted, the Secretary shall submit a final report—

(i) reviewing existing information about declining health and productivity of forest ecosystems on public and private lands in North America and Europe;

(ii) reviewing the nature and findings of all research and monitoring efforts conducted under the Program and any other relevant research and monitoring efforts related to the effects of atmospheric pollution on forest ecosystem; and

(iii) making final recommendations for solving or mitigating problems stemming from the effects of atmospheric pollution on the health and productivity of domestic forest ecosystems.

(d) High priority forestry and rangeland research and education

(1) In general

The Secretary may conduct, support, and cooperate in forestry and rangeland research and education that is of the highest priority to the United States and to users of public and private forest land and rangeland in the United States.

(2) Priorities

The research and education priorities include the following:

(A) The biology of forest organisms and rangeland organisms.

(B) Functional characteristics and cost-effective management of forest and rangeland ecosystems.

(C) Interactions between humans and forests and rangeland.

(D) Wood and forage as a raw material.

(E) International trade, competition, and cooperation.

(3) Northeastern States research cooperative

At the request of the Governor of the State of Maine, New Hampshire, New York, or Vermont, the Secretary may cooperate with the northeastern States of New Hampshire, New York, Maine, and Vermont, land-grant colleges and universities of those States, natural resources and forestry schools of those States, other Federal agencies, and other interested persons in those States to coordinate and improve ecological and economic research relating to agricultural research, extension, and education, including—

(A) research on ecosystem health, forest management, product development, economics, and related fields;

(B) research to assist those States and landowners in those States to achieve sustainable forest management;

(C) technology transfer to the wood products industry of technologies that promote efficient processing, pollution prevention, and energy conservation;

(D) dissemination of existing and new information to landowners, public and private resource managers, State forest citizen advisory committees, and the general public through professional associations, publications, and other information clearinghouse activities; and

(E) analysis of strategies for the protection of areas of outstanding ecological significance or high biological diversity, and strategies for the provision of important recreational opportunities and traditional uses, including strategies for areas identified through State land conservation planning processes.

(e) Forest inventory and analysis

(1) Program required

In compliance with other applicable provisions of law, the Secretary shall establish a program to inventory and analyze, in a timely manner, public and private forests and their resources in the United States.

(2) Annual state inventory

(A) In general

Not later than the end of each full fiscal year beginning after June 23, 1998, the Secretary shall prepare for each State, in cooperation with the State forester for the State, an inventory of forests and their resources in the State.

(B) Sample plots

For purposes of preparing the inventory for a State, the Secretary shall measure annually 20 percent of all sample plots that are included in the inventory program for that State.

(C) Compilation of inventory

On completion of the inventory for a year, the Secretary shall make available to the public a compilation of all data collected for that year from measurements of sample plots as well as any analysis made of the samples.

(3) 5-year reports

Not more often than every 5 full fiscal years after June 23, 1998, the Secretary shall prepare, publish, and make available to the public a report, prepared in cooperation with State foresters, that—

(A) contains a description of each State inventory of forests and their resources, incorporating all sample plot measurements conducted during the 5 years covered by the report;

(B) displays and analyzes on a nationwide basis the results of the annual reports required by paragraph (2); and

(C) contains an analysis of forest health conditions and trends over the previous 2 decades, with an emphasis on such conditions and trends during the period subsequent to the immediately preceding report under this paragraph.

(4) National standards and definitions

To ensure uniform and consistent data collection for all forest land that is publicly or privately owned and for each State, the Secretary shall develop, in consultation with State foresters and Federal land management agencies not under the jurisdiction of the Secretary, and publish national standards and definitions to be applied in inventorying and analyzing forests and their resources under this subsection. The standards shall include a core set of variables to be measured on all sample plots under paragraph (2) and a standard set of tables to be included in the reports under paragraph (3).

(5) Protection for private property rights

The Secretary shall obtain authorization from property owners prior to collecting data from sample plots located on private property pursuant to paragraphs (2) and (3).

(6) Strategic plan

Not later than 180 days after June 23, 1998, the Secretary shall prepare and submit to Congress a strategic plan to implement and carry out this subsection, including the annual updates required by paragraph (2) and the reports required by paragraph (3), that shall describe in detail—

(A) the financial resources required to implement and carry out this subsection, including the identification of any resources required in excess of the amounts provided for forest inventorying and analysis in recent appropriations Acts;

(B) the personnel necessary to implement and carry out this subsection, including any personnel in addition to personnel currently performing inventorying and analysis functions;

(C) the organization and procedures necessary to implement and carry out this subsection, including proposed coordination with Federal land management agencies and State foresters;

(D) the schedules for annual sample plot measurements in each State inventory required by paragraph (2) within the first 5-year interval after June 23, 1998;

(E) the core set of variables to be measured in each sample plot under paragraph (2) and the standard set of tables to be used in each State and national report under paragraph (3); and

(F) the process for employing, in coordination with the Secretary of Energy and the Administrator of the National Aeronautics and Space Administration, remote sensing, global positioning systems, and other advanced technologies to carry out this subsection, and the subsequent use of the technologies.

(Pub. L. No. 95–307, § 3, 92 Stat. 353 (June 30, 1978); as amended by Pub. L. No. 96–294, Title II, § 254, 94 Stat. 707 (June 30, 1980); Pub. L. No. 100–521, § 3, 102 Stat. 2601 (Oct. 24, 1988); Pub. L. No. 101–624, Title XII, § 1241(a), 104 Stat. 3544 (Nov. 28, 1990); Pub. L. No. 105–185, Title II, § 253(b), (c), 112 Stat. 559 (June 23, 1998); Pub. L. No. 105–277, Div. A, § 101(a) [Title VII, § 753(a)], 112 Stat. 2681–32 (Oct. 21, 1998).)

HISTORICAL AND STATUTORY NOTES

References in Text

This subchapter, referred to in subsec. (a), in the original read "this Act", meaning the Forest and Rangeland Renewable Resources Research Act of 1978, which enacted this subchapter, repealed sections 581 to 581i of this title, and enacted provisions set out as a note under section 1641 of this title. For complete classification, see Short Title note set out under section 1600 of this title and Tables.

Effective and Applicability Provisions

1998 Acts. Amendment of this section by Pub. L. No. 105–277, § 101(a) [Title VII, § 753] effective on the date of enactment of the Agricultural Research, Extension, and Education Reform Act of 1998 [June 23, 1998], see Pub. L. No. 105–277, § 101(a) [Title VII, § 753(f)] set out as a note under section 343 of Title 7.

Termination of Reporting Requirements

For termination of reporting provisions of this section, effective May 15, 2000, see Pub. L. No. 104–66, § 3003, as amended, set out as a note under 31 U.S.C.A. § 1113, and the 7th item on page 47 of House Document No. 103–7.

Severability of Provisions

If any provision of Pub. L. No. 101–624 or the application thereof to any person or circumstance is held invalid, such invalidity not to affect other provisions or applications of Pub. L. No. 101–624 which can be given effect without regard to the invalid provision or application, see section 2519 of Pub. L. No. 101–624, set out as a note under section 1421 of Title 7, Agriculture.

Semiarid Agroforestry Research Center

Section 1243 of Pub. L. No. 101–624 provided that:

"(a) Semiarid Agroforestry Research, Development, and Demonstration Center.—The Secretary of Agriculture shall establish at the Forestry Sciences Laboratory of the United States Forest Service, in Lincoln, Nebraska, a Semiarid Agroforestry Research, Development, and Demonstration Center (hereafter referred to in this section as the 'Center') and appoint a Director to manage and coordinate the program established at the Center under subsection (b).

"(b) Program.—The Secretary shall establish a program at the Center and seek the participation of Federal or State governmental entities, land-grant colleges or universities, State agricultural experiment stations, State and private foresters, the National Arbor Day Foundation, and other nonprofit foundations in such program to conduct or assist research, investigations, studies, and surveys to—

"(1) develop sustainable agroforestry systems on semiarid lands that minimize topsoil loss and water contamination and stabilize or enhance crop productivity;

"(2) adapt, demonstrate, document, and model the effectiveness of agroforestry systems under different farming systems and soil or climate conditions;

"(3) develop dual use agroforestry systems compatible with paragraphs (1) and (2) which would provide high-value forestry products for commercial sale from semiarid land;

"(4) develop and improve the drought and pest resistance characteristics of trees for conservation forestry and agroforestry applications in semiarid regions, including the introduction and breeding of trees suited for the Great Plains region of the United States;

"(5) develop technology transfer programs that increase farmer and public acceptance of sustainable agroforestry systems;

"(6) develop improved windbreak and shelterbelt technologies for drought preparedness, soil and water conservation, environmental quality, and biological diversity on semiarid lands;

"(7) develop technical and economic concepts for sustainable agroforestry on semiarid lands, including the conduct of economic analyses of the costs and benefits of agroforestry systems and the development of models to predict the economic benefits under soil or climate conditions;

"(8) provide international leadership in the development and exchange of agroforestry practices on semiarid lands worldwide;

"(9) support research on the effects of agroforestry systems on semiarid lands in mitigating nonpoint source water pollution;

"(10) support research on the design, establishment, and maintenance of tree and shrub plantings to regulate the deposition of snow along roadways; and

"(11) conduct sociological, demographic, and economic studies as needed to develop strategies for increasing the use of forestry conservation and agroforestry practices.

"(c) Information collection and dissemination.—The Secretary shall establish at the Center a program, to be known as the National Clearinghouse on Agroforestry Conservation and Promotion to—

"(1) collect, analyze, and disseminate information on agroforestry conservation technologies and practices; and

"(2) promote the use of such information by landowners and those organizations associated with forestry and tree promotion.

"(d) Authorization of Appropriations.—There are authorized to be appropriated $5,000,000 for each of fiscal years 2019 through 2023 to carry out this section."

(as amended by Pub. L. No. 115–334, § 8502, 132 Stat. 4490, 4847 (Dec. 20, 2018)).

Southern Forest Regeneration Program

Section 1242 of Pub. L. No. 101–624 provided that:

"(a) Establishment.—The Secretary of Agriculture shall make a grant to a State for the establishment, within such State, of a center, to be known as the "Southern Forest Regeneration Center" (hereafter referred to in this section as the "Center"), to study forest regeneration problems and forest productivity in the southern region of the United States.

"(b) **Duties of Center.**—The Center shall study forest regeneration problems and forest productivity in the southern region of the United States, including—

"(1) nursery management concerns that will lead to improved seedling quality;

"(2) forest management practices that account for environmental stresses; and

"(3) the development of low-cost forest regeneration methods that provide options for wood products, species diversity, wildlife habitat, and production of clean air and water.

"(c) **Establishment of other Programs.**—The Secretary of Agriculture may establish other programs in other regions of the United States, or a comprehensive National program, to carry out the purposes of this section as the Secretary determines appropriate.

"(d) **Authorization of Appropriations.**—There are authorized to be appropriated such sums as may be necessary to carry out this section."

Forest Ecosystems and Atmospheric Pollution Research; Congressional Statement of Findings

Section 2 of Pub. L. No. 100–521 provided that: "Congress finds that—

"(1) the health and productivity of forests in certain regions of the United States are declining;

"(2) there is a special concern about the decline of certain hardwood species, particularly sugar maples and oaks, in the eastern United States and the effects of atmospheric pollutants on the health and productivity of these forests;

"(3) declines in the productivity of certain commercially important Southern pine species have been measured;

"(4) existing research indicates that atmospheric pollution, including ozone, acidic deposition, and heavy metals, may contribute to this decline;

"(5) there is an urgent need to expand and better coordinate existing Federal, State, and private research, including research by private industry, to determine the cause of changes in the health and productivity of domestic forest ecosystems and to monitor and evaluate the effects of atmospheric pollutants on such ecosystems; and

"(6) such research and monitoring should not impede efforts to control atmospheric pollutants."

Revision of Strategic Plan for Forest Inventory and Analysis: REPEALED

Pub. L. No. 113–79, § 8301, 128 Stat. 922–23 (Feb. 7, 2014) provided that:

"(a) **Revision Required.**—Not later than 180 days after the date of enactment of this Act, the Secretary shall revise the strategic plan for forest inventory and analysis initially prepared pursuant to section 3(e) of the Forest and Rangeland Renewable Resources Research Act of 1978 (16 U.S.C. 1642(e)) to address the requirements imposed by subsection (b).

"(b) **Elements of Revised Strategic Plan.**—In revising the strategic plan, the Secretary shall describe in detail the organization, procedures, and funding needed to achieve each of the following:

"(1) Complete the transition to a fully annualized forest inventory program and include inventory and analysis of interior Alaska.

"(2) Implement an annualized inventory of trees in urban settings, including the status and trends of trees and forests, and assessments of their ecosystem services, values, health, and risk to pests and diseases.

"(3) Report information on renewable biomass supplies and carbon stocks at the local, State, regional, and national level, including by ownership type.

"(4) Engage State foresters and other users of information from the forest inventory and analysis in reevaluating the list of core data variables collected on forest inventory and analysis plots with an emphasis on demonstrated need.

"(5) Improve the timeliness of the timber product output program and accessibility of the annualized information on that database.

"(6) Foster greater cooperation among the forest inventory and analysis program, research station leaders, and State foresters and other users of information from the forest inventory and analysis.

"(7) Promote availability of and access to non-Federal resources to improve information analysis and information management.

"(8) Collaborate with the Natural Resources Conservation Service, National Aeronautics and Space Administration, National Oceanic and Atmospheric Administration, and United States Geological Survey to integrate remote sensing, spatial analysis techniques, and other new technologies in the forest inventory and analysis program.

"(9) Understand and report on changes in land cover and use.

"(10) Expand existing programs to promote sustainable forest stewardship through increased understanding, in partnership with other Federal agencies, of the over 10,000,000 family forest owners, their demographics, and the barriers to forest stewardship.

"(11) Implement procedures to improve the statistical precision of estimates at the sub-State level.

"(c) **Submission of Revised Strategic Plan.**—The Secretary shall submit the revised strategic plan to the Committee on Agriculture of the House of Representatives and the Committee on Agriculture, Nutrition, and Forestry of the Senate."

This section was repealed by Pub. L. No. 115–334, § 8501, 132 Stat. 4490, 4847 (Dec. 20, 2018).

§ 1643. Implementation of provisions

[FRRRRA § 4(A)–(C)]

(a) Establishment and maintenance of research facilities; acquisition, expenditures, etc., for property

In implementing this subchapter, the Secretary is authorized to establish and maintain a system of experiment stations, research laboratories, experimental areas, and other forest and rangeland research facilities. The Secretary is authorized, with donated or appropriated funds, to acquire by lease, donation, purchase, exchange, or otherwise, land or interests in land within the United States needed to implement this subchapter, to make necessary expenditures to examine, appraise, and survey such property, and to do all things incident to perfecting title thereto in the United States.

(b) Acceptance, holding, and administration of gifts, donations, and bequests; use and investment of gifts, proceeds, etc.; funding requirements

In implementing this subchapter, the Secretary is authorized to accept, hold, and administer gifts, donations, and bequests of money, real property, or personal property from any source not otherwise prohibited by law and to use such gifts, donations, and bequests to (1) establish or operate any forest and rangeland research facility within the United States, or (2) perform any forest and rangeland renewable resource research activity authorized by this subchapter. Such gifts, donations, and bequests, or the proceeds thereof, and money appropriated for these purposes shall be deposited in the Treasury in a special fund. At the request of the Secretary, the Secretary of the Treasury may invest or reinvest any money in the fund that in the opinion of the Secretary is not needed for current operations. Such investments shall be in public debt securities with maturities suitable for the needs of the fund and bearing interest at prevailing market rates. There are hereby authorized to be expended from such fund such amounts as may be specified in annual appropriation Acts, which shall remain available until expended.

(c) Cooperation with international, Federal, State, and other governmental agencies, public and private agencies, etc.; funding requirements for contributions from cooperators

In implementing this subchapter, the Secretary may cooperate with international, Federal, State, and other governmental agencies, with public or private agencies, institutions, universities, and organizations, and with businesses and individuals in the United States and in other countries. The Secretary may receive money and other contributions from cooperators under such conditions as the Secretary may prescribe. Any money contributions received under this subsection shall be credited to the applicable appropriation or fund to be used for the same purposes and shall remain available until expended as the Secretary may direct for use in conducting research activities authorized by this subchapter and in making refunds to contributors.

(Pub. L. No. 95–307, § 4(a)–(c), 92 Stat. 354 (June 30, 1978); as amended by Pub. L. No. 101–513, Title VI, § 611(a)(2), formerly § 607(a)(2), 104 Stat. 2072 (Nov. 5, 1990); and renumbered § 611(a)(2) by Pub. L. No. 102–574, § 2(a)(1), 106 Stat. 4593 (Oct. 29, 1992).)

HISTORICAL AND STATUTORY NOTES

References in Text

This subchapter, referred to in text, in the original read "this Act", meaning the Forest and Rangeland Renewable Resources Research Act of 1978, which enacted this subchapter, repealed sections 581 to 581i of this title, and enacted provisions set out as a note under section 1641 of this title. For complete classification, see Short Title note set out under section 1600 of this title and Tables.

§ 1644. Forestry and rangeland competitive research grants

[FRRRRA § 5]

(a) Competitive grant authority

In addition to any grants made under other laws, the Secretary is authorized to make competitive grants that will further research activities authorized by this subchapter to Federal, State, and other governmental agencies, public or private agencies, institutions, universities, and organizations, and businesses and individuals in the United States. In making these grants, the Secretary shall emphasize basic and applied research activities that are important to achieving the purposes of this subchapter, and shall obtain, through review by qualified scientists and other methods, participation in research activities by scientists throughout the United States who have expertise in matters related to forest and rangeland renewable resources. Grants under this section shall be made at the discretion of the Secretary under whatever conditions the Secretary may prescribe, after publicly soliciting research proposals, allowing sufficient time for submission of the proposals, and considering qualitative, quantitative, financial, administrative, and other factors that the Secretary deems important in judging, comparing, and accepting the proposals. The Secretary may reject any or all proposals received under this section if the Secretary determines that it is in the public interest to do so.

(b) Emphasis on certain high priority forestry research

The Secretary may use up to 5 percent of the amounts made available for research under section 1642 of this title to make competitive grants regarding forestry research in the high priority research areas identified under section 1642(d) of this title.

(c) Emphasis on certain high priority rangeland research

The Secretary may use up to 5 percent of the amounts made available for research under section 1642 of this title to make competitive grants regarding rangeland research in the high priority research areas identified under section 1642(d) of this title.

(d) Priorities

In making grants under subsections (b) and (c) of this section, the Secretary shall give priority to research proposals under which—

(1) the proposed research will be collaborative research organized through a center of scientific excellence;

(2) the applicant agrees to provide matching funds (in the form of direct funding or in-kind support) in an amount equal to not less than 50 percent of the grant amount; and

(3) the proposed research will be conducted as part of an existing private and public partnership or cooperative research effort and involves several interested research partners.

(Pub. L. No. 95–307, § 5, 92 Stat. 355 (June 30, 1978); Pub. L. No. 105–185, Title II, § 253(d), 112 Stat. 561 (June 23, 1998).)

HISTORICAL AND STATUTORY NOTES

References in Text

This subchapter, referred to in text, in the original read "this Act", meaning the Forest and Rangeland Renewable Resources Research Act of 1978, which enacted this subchapter, repealed sections 581 to 581i of this title, and enacted provisions set out as a note under section 1641 of this title. For complete classification, see Short Title note set out under section 1600 of this title and Tables.

§ 1645. General provisions

[FRRRRA § 6]

(a) Availability of funds to cooperators and grantees

The Secretary may make funds available to cooperators and grantees under this subchapter without regard to the provisions of section 3324(a) and (b) of Title 31, which prohibits advances of public money.

(b) Coordination of cooperative aid and grants with other aid and grant authorities

To avoid duplication, the Secretary shall coordinate cooperative aid and grants under this subchapter with cooperative aid and grants the Secretary makes under any other authority.

(c) Dissemination of knowledge and technology developed from research activities; cooperation with specified entities

The Secretary shall use the authorities and means available to the Secretary to disseminate the knowledge and technology developed from research activities conducted under or supported by this subchapter. In meeting this responsibility, the Secretary shall cooperate, as the Secretary deems appropriate, with the entities identified in subsection (d) (3) of this section and with others.

(d) Additional implementative authorities

In implementing this subchapter, the Secretary, as the Secretary deems appropriate and practical, shall—

(1) use, and encourage cooperators and grantees to use, the best available scientific skills from a variety of disciplines within and outside the fields of agriculture and forestry;

(2) seek, and encourage cooperators and grantees to seek, a proper mixture of short-term and long-term research and a proper mixture of basic and applied research;

(3) avoid unnecessary duplication and coordinate activities under this section among agencies of the Department of Agriculture and with other affected Federal departments and agencies, State agricultural experiment stations, State extension services, State foresters or equivalent State officials, forestry schools, and private research organizations; and

(4) encourage the development, employment, retention, and exchange of qualified scientists and other specialists through postgraduate, postdoctoral, and other training, national and international exchange of scientists, and other incentives and programs to improve the quality of forest and rangeland renewable resources research.

(e) Construction of statutory provisions

This subchapter shall be construed as supplementing all other laws relating to the Department of Agriculture and shall not be construed as limiting or repealing any existing law or authority of the Secretary except as specifically cited in this subchapter.

(f) Definitions

For the purposes of this subchapter, the terms "United States" and "State" shall include each of the several States, the District of Columbia, the Commonwealth of Puerto Rico, the Virgin Islands of the United States, the Commonwealth of the Northern Mariana Islands, the Trust Territory of the Pacific Islands, and the territories and possessions of the United States.

(Pub. L. No. 95–307, § 6, 92 Stat. 355 (June 30, 1978).)

HISTORICAL AND STATUTORY NOTES

References in Text

This subchapter, referred to in text, in the original read "this Act", meaning the Forest and Rangeland Renewable Resources Research Act of 1978, which enacted this subchapter, repealed sections 581 to 581i of this title, and enacted provisions set out as a note under section 1641 of this title. For complete classification, see Short Title note set out under section 1600 of this title and Tables.

Codifications

In subsec. (a), "section 3324(a) and (b) of Title 31" was substituted for "section 3648 of the Revised Statutes (31 U.S.C. 529)" on authority of Pub. L. No. 97–258, § 4(b), 96 Stat. 1067 (Sept. 13, 1982), the first section of which enacted Title 31, Money and Finance.

Termination of Trust Territory of the Pacific Islands

For termination of Trust Territory of the Pacific Islands, see note set out preceding 48 U.S.C.A. § 1681.

§ 1646. Authorization of appropriations

[FRRRRA § 7]

There are authorized to be appropriated annually such sums as may be needed to implement this subchapter. Funds appropriated under this subchapter shall remain available until expended.

(Pub. L. No. 95–307, § 7, 92 Stat. 356 (June 30, 1978).)

HISTORICAL AND STATUTORY NOTES

References in Text

This subchapter, referred to in text, in the original read "this Act", meaning the Forest and Rangeland Renewable Resources Research Act of 1978, which enacted this subchapter, repealed sections 581 to 581i of this title, and enacted provisions set out as a note under section 1641 of this title. For complete classification, see Short Title note set out under section 1600 of this title and Tables.

§ 1647. Other Federal programs

[FRRRRA § 8]

(a) Repeal of statutory authorities relating to investigation, experiments, and tests in reforestation and forest products

The Act of May 22, 1928, known as the McSweeney-McNary Act (45 Stat. 699–702, as amended; 16 U.S.C. 581, 581a, 581b–581i), is hereby repealed.

(b) Force and effect of cooperative and other agreements under repealed statutory authorities relating to investigation, etc., in reforestation and forest products

Contracts and cooperative and other agreements under the McSweeney-McNary Act shall remain in effect until revoked or amended by their own terms or under other provisions of law.

(c) Issuance of rules and regulations for implementation of provisions and coordination with agricultural research, extension, and teaching provisions

The Secretary is authorized to issue such rules and regulations as the Secretary deems necessary to implement the provisions of this subchapter and to coordinate this subchapter with title XIV of the Food and Agriculture Act of 1977 [7 U.S.C.A. § 3101 et seq.].

(d) Availability of funds appropriated under repealed statutory authorities relating to investigation, etc., in reforestation and forest products

Funds appropriated under the authority of the McSweeney-McNary Act shall be available for expenditure for the programs authorized under this subchapter.

(Pub. L. No. 95–307, § 8, 92 Stat. 356 (June 30, 1978).)

HISTORICAL AND STATUTORY NOTES

References in Text

This subchapter, referred to in text, in the original read "this Act", meaning the Forest and Rangeland Renewable Resources Research Act of 1978, which enacted this subchapter, repealed sections 581 to 581i of this title, and enacted provisions set out as a note under section 1641 of this title. For complete classification, see Short Title note set out under section 1600 of this title and Tables.

The Food and Agriculture Act of 1977, referred to in subsec. (c), is Pub. L. No. 95–113, 91 Stat. 913 (Sept. 29, 1977), as amended. Title XIV of the Food and Agriculture Act of 1977, known as the "National Agricultural Research, Extension, and Teaching Policy Act of 1977", is codified principally as chapter 64 of Title 7 (7 U.S.C.A. § 3101 et seq.). For complete classification of this title to the Code, see Short Title note set out under section 3101 of Title 7 and Tables.

§ 1648. Repealed. Pub. L. No. 115–334, § 8201, 132 Stat. 4490, 4839 (Dec. 20, 2018).

§ 1649. Repealed. Pub. L. No. 115–334, § 8202, 132 Stat. 4490, 4839 (Dec. 20, 2018).

§ 1649a. Repealed. Pub. L. No. 113–79, Title VIII, § 8004, 128 Stat. 913 (Feb. 7, 2014).

§ 1650. Hardwood technology transfer and applied research

(a) Authority of Secretary

The Secretary of Agriculture (hereinafter the "Secretary") is hereby and hereafter authorized to conduct technology transfer and development, training, dissemination of information and applied research in the management, processing and utilization of the hardwood forest resource. This authority is in addition to any other authorities which may be available to the Secretary including, but not limited to, the Cooperative Forestry Assistance Act of 1978, as amended (16 U.S.C. 2101 et seq.), and the Forest and Rangeland Renewable Resources Act of 1978, as amended (16 U.S.C. 1600–1614).[1]

(b) Grants, contracts, and cooperative agreements; gifts and donations

In carrying out this authority, the Secretary may enter into grants, contracts, and cooperative agreements with public and private agencies, organizations, corporations, institutions and individuals. The Secretary may accept gifts and donations pursuant to section 2269 of Title 7 including gifts and donations from a donor that conducts business with any agency of the Department of Agriculture or is regulated by the Secretary of Agriculture.

(c) Use of assets of Wood Education and Resource Center; establishment of Institute of Hardwood Technology Transfer and Applied Research

The Secretary is hereby and hereafter authorized to operate and utilize the assets of the Wood Education and Resource Center (previously named the Robert C. Byrd Hardwood Technology Center in West Virginia) as part of a newly formed "Institute of Hardwood Technology Transfer and Applied Research" (hereinafter the "Institute"). The Institute, in addition to the Wood Education and Resource Center, will consist of a Director, technology transfer specialists from State and Private Forestry, the Forestry Sciences Laboratory in Princeton, West Virginia, and any other organizational unit of the Department of Agriculture as the Secretary deems appropriate. The overall management of the Institute will be the responsibility of the Forest Service, State and Private Forestry.

(d) Generation of revenue; deposit into Hardwood Technology Transfer and Applied Research Fund

The Secretary is hereby and hereafter authorized to generate revenue using the authorities provided herein. Any revenue received as part of the operation of the Institute shall be deposited into a special fund in the Treasury of the United States, known as the "Hardwood Technology Transfer and Applied Research Fund", which shall be available to the Secretary until expended, without further appropriation, in furtherance of the purposes of this section, including upkeep, management, and operation of the Institute and the payment of salaries and expenses.

(e) Authorization of appropriations

There are hereby and hereafter authorized to be appropriated such sums as necessary to carry out the provisions of this section.

(Pub. L. No. 106–113, Div. B, § 1000(a)(3) [Title III, § 332], 113 Stat. 1535, 1501A–197 (Nov. 29, 1999).)

[1] So in original.

HISTORICAL AND STATUTORY NOTES

Codifications

Section was enacted as part of the Department of the Interior and Related Agencies Appropriations Act, 2000, and not as part of the Forest and Rangeland Renewable Resources Research Act of 1978 which comprises this subchapter.

Temporary Authority to Conduct Hardwood Technology Transfer and Applied Research

Pub. L. No. 105–277, Div. A, § 101(e) [Title III, § 343], 112 Stat. 2681–297 (Oct. 21, 1998), provided that:

"(a) The Secretary of Agriculture (hereinafter the 'Secretary') is hereby authorized to conduct technology transfer and development, training, dissemination of information and applied research in the management, processing and utilization of the hardwood forest resource. This authority is in addition to any other authorities which may be available to the Secretary including, but not limited to, the Cooperative Forestry Assistance Act of 1978, as amended (16 U.S.C. 2101 et. seq.), and the Forest and Rangeland Renewable Resources Act of 1978, as amended (16 U.S.C. 1600–1614).

"(b) In carrying out this authority, the Secretary may enter into grants, contracts, and cooperative agreements with public and private agencies, organizations, corporations, institutions and individuals. The Secretary may accept gifts and donations pursuant to the Act of October 10, 1978 (7 U.S.C. 2269) including gifts and donations from a donor that conducts business with any agency of the Department of Agriculture or is regulated by the Secretary of Agriculture.

"(c) The Secretary is authorized, on such terms and conditions as the Secretary may prescribe, to assume all rights, title, and interest, including all outstanding assets, of the Robert C. Byrd Hardwood Technology Center, Inc. (hereinafter the 'Center'), a nonprofit corporation existing under the laws of the State of West Virginia: *Provided,* That the Board of Directors of the Center requests such an action and dissolves the corporation consistent with the Articles of Incorporation and the laws of the State of West Virginia.

"(d) The Secretary is authorized to operate and utilize the assets of the Center as part of a newly formed 'Institute of Hardwood Technology Transfer and Applied Research' (hereinafter the 'Institute'). The Institute, in addition to the Center, will consist of a Director, technology transfer specialists from State and Private Forestry, the Forestry Sciences Laboratory in Princeton, West Virginia, and any other organizational unit of the Department of Agriculture as the Secretary deems appropriate. The overall management of the Institute will be the responsibility of the USDA Forest Service, State and Private Forestry.

"(e) The Secretary is authorized to generate revenue using the authorities provided herein. Any revenue received as part of the operation of the Institute shall be deposited into a special fund in the Treasury of the United States, known as the 'Hardwood Technology Transfer and Applied Research Fund', which shall be available to the Secretary until expended, without further appropriation, in furtherance of the purposes of this section, including upkeep, management, and operation of the Institute and the payment of salaries and expenses.

"(f) There are hereby authorized to be appropriated such sums as necessary to carry out the provisions of this section [this note]."

RENEWABLE RESOURCES EXTENSION ACT OF 1978 [RREA § _____]

(16 U.S.C.A. §§ 1671 to 1676)

SUBCHAPTER III—EXTENSION PROGRAMS

Effective Date

For the period during which this subchapter is effective, see Section 8 of Pub. L. No. 95–306, as amended, set out as an Effective and Applicability Provisions note under 16 U.S.C.A. § 1671.

§ 1671. Congressional statement of findings

[RREA § 2]

Congress finds that—

(1) the extension program of the Department of Agriculture and the extension activities of each State provide useful and productive educational programs for private forest and range landowners and processors and consumptive and nonconsumptive users of forest and rangeland renewable resources, and these educational programs complement research and assistance programs conducted by the Department of Agriculture;

(2) to meet national goals, it is essential that all forest and rangeland renewable resources (hereinafter in this subchapter referred to as "renewable resources"), including fish and wildlife, forage, outdoor recreation opportunities, timber, and water, be fully considered in designing educational programs for landowners, processors, and users;

(3) more efficient utilization and marketing of renewable resources extend available supplies of such resources, provide products to consumers at prices less than they would otherwise be, and promote reasonable returns on the investments of landowners, processors, and users;

(4) trees and forests in urban areas improve the esthetic quality, reduce noise, filter impurities from the air and add oxygen to it, save energy by moderating temperature extremes, control wind and water erosion, and provide habitat for wildlife; and

(5) trees and shrubs used as shelterbelts protect farm lands from wind and water erosion, promote moisture accumulation in the soil, and provide habitat for wildlife.

(Pub. L. No. 95–306, § 2, 92 Stat. 349 (June 30, 1978).)

Effective Date

For the period during which this subchapter is effective, see Section 8 of Pub. L. No. 95–306, as amended, set out as an Effective and Applicability Provisions note under this section.

HISTORICAL AND STATUTORY NOTES

Codifications

The authorities provided by each provision of, and each amendment made by, Pub. L. No. 110–246, as in effect on Sept. 30, 2012, to continue, and the Secretary of Agriculture to carry out the authorities, until the later of Sept. 30, 2013, or the date specified in the provision of, or amendment made by, Pub. L. No. 110–246, see section 701(a) of Pub. L. No. 112–240, set out in a note under 7 U.S.C.A. § 8701.

Effective and Applicability Provisions

1978 Acts. Pub. L. No. 95–306, § 8, 92 Stat. 352 (June 30, 1978), as amended by Pub. L. No. 100–231, § 2(2), 101 Stat. 1565 (Jan. 5, 1988); Pub. L. No. 107–171, Title VIII, § 8101(b)(2), 116 Stat. 475 (May 13, 2002); Pub. L. No. 110–234, Title VII, § 7413(b), 122 Stat. 1256 (May 22, 2008); Pub. L. No. 110–246, Title VII, § 7413(b), 122 Stat. 2017 (June 18, 2008); Pub. L. No. 113–79, § 7405(b), 128 Stat. 898 (Feb. 7. 2014), amended § 8 of the Renewable Resources Extension Act of 1978 so that the act's provisions "shall be effective for the period beginning October 1, 1978, and ending September 30, 2018." [For provisions extending the authorities provided by and amendments made by the Food, Conservation, and Energy Act of 2008, Pub. L. No. 110–246, 122 Stat. 1651 (June

18, 2008), see Pub. L. No. 112–240, Title VII, § 701, 126 Stat. 2362 (Jan. 2, 2013), set out as a note under 7 U.S.C.A. § 8701.]

[Amendments by Pub. L. No. 110–246, except as otherwise provided, shall take effect on the earlier of June 18, 2008, or May 22, 2008, see Pub. L. No. 110–246, § 4(b), set out in a Repeal of Duplicative Enactment note under 7 U.S.C.A. § 8701; Pub. L. No. 110–234 repealed effective May 22, 2008, see Repeal of Duplicative Enactment by Pub. L. No. 110–246, § 4(a), set out in a note under 7 U.S.C.A. § 8701.]

2018 Extension. Pub. L. No. 115–334, § 7509, 132 Stat. 4409, 4824 (Dec. 20, 2018), extended the effective date of and appropriations for this subchapter to September 30, 2023.

Short Title

1978 Acts. For Short Title of Renewable Resources Extension Act of 1978, see short title note set out under section 1600 of this title.

§ 1672. General program authorization

[RREA § 3]

(a) Types of programs; preconditions and cooperation with State program directors, etc.

The Secretary of Agriculture (hereinafter in this subchapter referred to as the "Secretary"), under conditions the Secretary may prescribe and in cooperation with the State directors of cooperative extension service programs and eligible colleges and universities, shall—

(1) provide educational programs that enable individuals to recognize, analyze, and resolve problems dealing with renewable resources, including forest- and range-based outdoor recreation opportunities, trees and forests in urban areas, and trees and shrubs in shelterbelts;

(2) use educational programs to disseminate the results of research on renewable resources;

(3) conduct educational programs that transfer the best available technology to those involved in the management and protection of forests and rangelands and the processing and use of their associated renewable resources;

(4) develop and implement educational programs that give special attention to the educational needs of small, private nonindustrial forest landowners;

(5) develop and implement educational programs in range and fish and wildlife management;

(6) assist in providing continuing education programs for professionally trained individuals in fish and wildlife, forest, range, and watershed management and related fields;

(7) help forest and range landowners in securing technical and financial assistance to bring appropriate expertise to bear on their problems;

(8) help identify areas of needed research regarding renewable resources;

(9) in cooperation with State foresters or equivalent State officials, promote public understanding of the energy conservation, economic, social, environmental, and psychological values of trees and open space in urban and community area environments and expand knowledge of the ecological relationships and benefits of trees and related resources in urban and community environments; and

(10) conduct a comprehensive natural resource and environmental education program for landowners and managers, public officials, and the public, with particular emphasis on youth.

(b) "Eligible colleges and universities" defined

As used in this subchapter, the term "eligible colleges and universities" means colleges and universities eligible to be supported and maintained, in whole or in part, with funds made available under the provisions of the Act of July 2, 1862 (12 Stat. 503–505, as amended; 7 U.S.C. 301–305, 307, 308), and the Act of August 30, 1890 (26 Stat. 417–419, as amended; 7 U.S.C. 321–326, 328), including Tuskegee Institute, and colleges and universities eligible for assistance under the Act of October 10, 1962 (76 Stat. 806–807, as amended; 16 U.S.C. 582a, 582a–1–582a–7).

(c) Use of appropriate educational methods required; scope of methods

In implementing this section, all appropriate educational methods may be used, including, but not limited to, meetings, short courses, workshops, tours, demonstrations, publications, news releases, and radio and television programs.

(Pub. L. No. 95–306, § 3, 92 Stat. 349 (June 30, 1978); Pub. L. No. 101–624, Title XII, §§ 1219(b)(1), 1251(b), 104 Stat. 3538, 3552 (Nov. 28, 1990); Pub. L. No. 102–237, Title X, § 1018(d), 105 Stat. 1905 (Dec. 13, 1991).)

Effective Date

For the period during which this subchapter is effective, see Section 8 of Pub. L. No. 95–306, as amended, set out as an Effective and Applicability Provisions note under 16 U.S.C.A. § 1671.

HISTORICAL AND STATUTORY NOTES

References in Text

The Act of July 2, 1862 (12 Stat. 503–505, as amended; 7 U.S.C. 301–305, 307, 308), referred to in subsec. (b), is popularly known as the Morrill Act and also as the First Morrill Act, which is codified generally as subchapter I of chapter 13 of Title 7 (7 U.S.C.A. § 301 et seq.). For complete classification, see Short Title note set out under section 301 of Title 7 and Tables.

The Act of August 30, 1890 (26 Stat. 417–419, as amended; 7 U.S.C. 321–326, 328), referred to in subsec. (b), is popularly known as the Agricultural College Act of 1890 and also as the Second Morrill Act, which is codified generally as subchapter II of chapter 13 of Title 7 (7 U.S.C.A. § 321 et seq.). For complete classification, see Short Title note set out under section 321 of Title 7 and Tables.

The Act of October 10, 1962 (76 Stat. 806–807, as amended), referred to in subsec. (b), is the McIntire-Stennis Act of 1962, which is codified principally as subchapter III of chapter 3 of this title (16 U.S.C.A. § 582a et seq.). For complete classification, see Short Title note set out under section 582a of this title and Tables.

Effective and Applicability Provisions

1991 Acts. Amendments by Pub. L. No. 102–237 effective Dec. 13, 1991, see section 1101(a) of Pub. L. No. 102–237, set out as a note under section 1421 of Title 7, Agriculture.

1978 Acts. Amendments by Pub. L. No. 95–306 effective for the period beginning October 1, 1978, and ending September 30, 2018, see Pub. L. No. 95–306, § 8, as amended, set out as a note under 16 U.S.C.A. § 1671.

Severability of Provisions

If any provision of Pub. L. No. 101–624 or the application thereof to any person or circumstance is held invalid, such invalidity not to affect other provisions or applications of Pub. L. No. 101–624 which can be given effect without regard to the invalid provision or application, see section 2519 of Pub. L. No. 101–624, set out as a note under section 1421 of Title 7, Agriculture.

§ 1673. State programs

[RREA § 4]

(a) Development by State program director, etc., of comprehensive and coordinated program by mutual agreement; consultations; review procedure

The State director of cooperative extension programs (hereinafter in this subchapter referred to as the "State director") and the administrative heads of extension for eligible colleges and universities in each State shall jointly develop, by mutual agreement, a single comprehensive and coordinated renewable resources extension program in which the role of each eligible college and university is well-defined. In meeting this responsibility, the State director and the administrative heads of extension for eligible colleges and universities shall consult and seek agreement with the administrative technical representatives and the forestry representatives provided for by the Secretary in implementation of the Act of October 10, 1962 (76 Stat. 806–807, as amended; 16 U.S.C. 582a, 582a–1–582a–7), in the State. Each State's renewable resources extension program shall be submitted to the Secretary annually. The National Agricultural Research, Extension, Education, and Economics Advisory Board established under section 3123 of Title 7 shall review and make recommendations to the Secretary pertaining to programs conducted under this subchapter.

(b) Encouragement by State director, etc., of cooperation between county and State extension staffs and appropriate Federal and State agencies and organizations

The State director and the administrative heads of extension for eligible colleges and universities in each State shall encourage close cooperation between extension staffs at the county and State levels, and State and Federal research organizations dealing with renewable resources, State and Federal agencies that manage forests and rangelands and their associated renewable resources, State and Federal agencies that have responsibilities associated with the processing or use of renewable resources, and other agencies or organizations the State director and administrative heads of extension deem appropriate.

(c) Administration and coordination of program by State director; exception

Each State renewable resources extension program shall be administered and coordinated by the State director, except that, in States having colleges eligible to receive funds under the Act of August 30, 1890 (26 Stat. 417–419, as amended; 7 U.S.C. 321–326, 328), including Tuskegee Institute, the State renewable resources extension program shall be administered by the State director and the administrative head or heads of extension for the college or colleges eligible to receive such funds.

(d) Appointment and use of advisory committees by State director, etc.; composition of advisory committees

In meeting the provisions of this section, each State director and administrative heads of extension for eligible colleges and universities shall appoint and use one or more advisory committees comprised of forest and range landowners, professionally trained individuals in fish and wildlife, forest, range, and watershed management, and related fields, as appropriate, and other suitable persons.

(e) "State" defined

For the purposes of this subchapter, the term "State" means any one of the fifty States, the Commonwealth of Puerto Rico, Guam, the District of Columbia, and the Virgin Islands of the United States.

(Pub. L. No. 95–306, § 4, 92 Stat. 350 (June 30, 1978); Pub. L. No. 104–127, Title VIII, § 802(b)(3), 110 Stat. 1159 (Apr. 4, 1996).)

Effective Date

For the period during which this subchapter is effective, see Section 8 of Pub. L. No. 95–306, as amended, set out as an Effective and Applicability Provisions note under 16 U.S.C.A. § 1671.

HISTORICAL AND STATUTORY NOTES

References in Text

The Act of October 10, 1962 (76 Stat. 806–807, as amended), referred to in subsec. (a), is the McIntire-Stennis Act of 1962, which is codified generally as subchapter III of chapter 3 of this title (16 U.S.C.A. § 582a et seq.). For complete classification, see Short Title note set out under section 582a of this title and Tables.

The Act of August 30, 1890 (26 Stat. 417–419, as amended; 7 U.S.C. 321–326, 328), referred to in subsec. (c), is popularly known as the Agricultural College Act of 1890 and also as the Second Morrill Act, which is codified principally as subchapter II of chapter 13 of Title 7 (7 U.S.C.A. § 321 et seq.). For complete classification, see Short Title note set out under section 321 of Title 7 and Tables.

Effective and Applicability Provisions

1978 Acts. Amendments by Pub. L. No. 95–306 effective for the period beginning October 1, 1978, and ending September 30, 2018, see Pub. L. No. 95–306, § 8, as amended, set out as a note under 16 U.S.C.A. § 1671.

§ 1674. Renewable Resources Extension Program plan

[RREA § 5]

(a) Preparation and submission to Congress; purposes; contents

The Secretary shall prepare a five-year plan for implementing this subchapter, which is to be called the "Renewable Resources Extension Program" and shall submit such plan to the Committee on Agriculture of the House of Representatives and the Committee on Agriculture, Nutrition, and Forestry of the Senate no later than the last day of the first half of the fiscal year ending September 30, 1980, and the last day of the first half of each fifth fiscal year thereafter. The Renewable Resources Extension Program shall provide national emphasis and direction as well as guidance to State directors and administrative heads of extension for eligible colleges and universities in the development of their respective State renewable resources extension programs, which are to be appropriate in terms of the conditions, needs, and opportunities in each State. The Renewable Resources Extension Program shall contain, but not be limited to, brief outlines of general extension programs for fish and wildlife management (for both game and nongame species), range management, timber management (including brief outlines of general extension programs for timber utilization, timber harvesting, timber marketing, wood utilization, and wood products marketing), and watershed management (giving special attention to water quality protection), as well as brief outlines of general extension programs for recognition and enhancement of forest- and range-based outdoor recreation opportunities, for urban and community forestry activities, and for planting and management of trees and shrubs in shelterbelts, and give special attention to water quality protection and natural resource and environmental education for landowners and managers, public officials, and the public.

(b) Considerations governing preparation

In preparing the Renewable Resources Extension Program, the Secretary shall take into account the respective capabilities of private forests and rangelands for yielding renewable resources and the relative needs for such resources identified in the periodic Renewable Resource Assessment provided for in section 1601 of this title and the periodic appraisal of land and water resources provided for in section 2004 of this title.

(c) Omitted

(d) Review of activities and evaluation of progress

To assist Congress and the public in evaluating the Renewable Resources Extension Program, the program shall include a review of activities undertaken in response to the preceding five-year plan and an evaluation of the progress made toward accomplishing the goals and objectives set forth in such preceding plan. Such review and evaluation shall be displayed in the program, for the Nation as a whole, and for each State.

(Pub. L. No. 95–306, § 5, 92 Stat. 351 (June 30, 1978); as amended by Pub. L. No. 100–231, § 3, 101 Stat. 1565 (Jan. 5, 1988); Pub. L. No. 101–624, Title XII, §§ 1219(b)(2), 1251(c), 104 Stat. 3539, 3553 (Nov. 28, 1990).)

Effective Date

For the period during which this subchapter is effective, see Section 8 of Pub. L. No. 95–306, as amended, set out as an Effective and Applicability Provisions note under 16 U.S.C.A. § 1671.

HISTORICAL AND STATUTORY NOTES

Codifications

Subsec. (c) of this section, which required the Secretary to furnish Congress with an annual report on the Renewable Resources Extension Program at the time of submission of each annual fiscal budget, terminated, effective May 15, 2000, pursuant to Pub. L. No. 104–66, Title III, § 3003, 109 Stat. 734 (Dec. 21, 1995), as amended, set out as a note under 31 U.S.C.A. § 1113. See, also, House Document No. 103–7, page 45.

Effective and Applicability Provisions

1978 Acts. Amendments by Pub. L. No. 95–306 effective for the period beginning October 1, 1978, and ending September 30, 2018, see Pub. L. No. 95–306, § 8, as amended, set out as a note under 16 U.S.C.A. § 1671.

Severability of Provisions

If any provision of Pub. L. No. 101–624 or the application thereof to any person or circumstance is held invalid, such invalidity not to affect other provisions or applications of Pub. L. No. 101–624 which can be given effect without regard to the invalid provision or application, see section 2519 of Pub. L. No. 101–624, set out as a note under section 1421 of Title 7, Agriculture.

§ 1674a. Expanded programs

[RREA § 5A]

(a) In general

The Secretary, acting through the National Institute of Food and Agriculture and the State cooperative extension services, and in consultation with State foresters or equivalent State officials, school boards, and universities, shall expand forestry and natural resources education programs conducted under this subchapter for private forest owners and managers, public officials, youth, and the general public, and shall include guidelines for the transfer of technology.

(b) Activities

(1) In general

In expanding the programs conducted under this subchapter, the Secretary shall ensure that activities are undertaken to promote policies and practices that enhance the health, vitality, productivity, economic value, and environmental attributes of the forest lands of the United States.

(2) Types

The activities referred to in paragraph (1) shall include—

(A) demonstrating and teaching landowners and forest managers the concepts of multiple-use and sustainable natural resource management;

(B) conducting comprehensive environmental education programs that assist citizens to participate in environmentally positive activities such as tree planting, recycling, erosion prevention, and waste management; and

(C) educational programs and materials that will improve the capacity of schools, local governments and resource agencies to deliver forestry and natural resources information to young people, environmentally concerned citizens, and action groups.

(Pub. L. No. 95–306, § 5A, as added by Pub. L. No. 101–624, Title XII, § 1251(a), 104 Stat. 3552 (Nov. 28, 1990); and amended by Pub. L. No. 110–234, Title VII, § 7511(c)(34), 122 Stat. 1270 (May 22, 2008); Pub. L. No. 110–246, § 4(a), Title VII, § 7511(c)(34), 122 Stat. 1664, 2032 (June 18, 2008).)

Effective Date

For the period during which this subchapter is effective, see Section 8 of Pub. L. No. 95–306, as amended, set out as an Effective and Applicability Provisions note under 16 U.S.C.A. § 1671.

HISTORICAL AND STATUTORY NOTES

Codifications

The authorities provided by each provision of, and each amendment made by, Pub. L. No. 110–246, as in effect on Sept. 30, 2012, to continue, and the Secretary of Agriculture to carry out the authorities, until the later of Sept. 30, 2013, or the date specified in the provision of, or amendment made by, Pub. L. No. 110–246, see section 701(a) of Pub. L. No. 112–240, set out in a note under 7 U.S.C.A. § 8701.

Pub. L. No. 110–234, Title VII, § 7511(c)(34), 122 Stat. 1270 (May 22, 2008), and Pub. L. No. 110–246, Title VII, § 7511(c)(34), 122 Stat. 2032 (June 18, 2008), made identical amendments, which directed that section 5(a) of the Renewable Resources Extension Act of 1978, Pub. L. No. 95–306, 92 Stat. 349 (June 30, 1978), is amended by striking "Extension Service" and inserting "National Institute of Food and Agriculture" was executed to section 5A of Pub. L. No. 95–306 (codified as this section) as the probable intent of Congress.

Effective and Applicability Provisions

2008 Acts. Amendments by Pub. L. No. 110–246, except as otherwise provided, shall take effect on the earlier of June 18, 2008, or May 22, 2008, see Pub. L. No. 110–246, § 4(b), set out in a Repeal of Duplicative Enactment note under 7 U.S.C.A. § 8701.

Amendments by Pub. L. No. 110–234, Title VII, § 7511(c)(34), and Pub. L. No. 110–246, Title VII, § 7511(c)(34), effective on October 1, 2009, see Pub. L. No. 110–234, Title VII, § 7511(c), and Pub. L. No. 110–246, Title VII, § 7511(c), set out as a note under 7 U.S.C.A. § 1522.

1978 Acts. Amendments by Pub. L. No. 95–306 effective for the period beginning October 1, 1978, and ending September 30, 2018, see Pub. L. No. 95–306, § 8, as amended, set out as a note under 16 U.S.C.A. § 1671.

Repeals

Pub. L. No. 110–234 repealed effective May 22, 2008, see Repeal of Duplicative Enactment by Pub. L. No. 110–246, § 4(a), set out in a note under 7 U.S.C.A. § 8701.

Severability of Provisions

If any provision of Pub. L. No. 101–624 or the application thereof to any person or circumstance is held invalid, such invalidity not to affect other provisions or applications of Pub. L. No. 101–624 which can be given effect without regard to the invalid provision or application, see section 2519 of Pub. L. No. 101–624, set out as a note under section 1421 of Title 7, Agriculture.

§ 1674b. Sustainable Forestry Outreach Initiative

[RREA § 5B]

The Secretary shall establish a program, to be known as the "Sustainable Forestry Outreach Initiative", to educate landowners concerning the following:

(1) The value and benefits of practicing sustainable forestry.

(2) The importance of professional forestry advice in achieving sustainable forestry objectives.

(3) The variety of public and private sector resources available to assist the landowners in planning for and practicing sustainable forestry.

(Pub. L. No. 95–306, § 5B, as added by Pub. L. No. 107–171, Title VIII, § 8101(a), 116 Stat. 474 (May 13, 2002).)

Effective Date

For the period during which this subchapter is effective, see Section 8 of Pub. L. No. 95–306, as amended, set out as an Effective and Applicability Provisions note under 16 U.S.C.A. § 1671.

HISTORICAL AND STATUTORY NOTES

Effective and Applicability Provisions

1978 Acts. Amendments by Pub. L. No. 95–306 effective for the period beginning October 1, 1978, and ending September 30, 2018, see Pub. L. No. 95–306, § 8, as amended, set out as a note under 16 U.S.C.A. § 1671.

§ 1675. Authorization of appropriations; criteria for eligibility of States for funds

[RREA § 6]

There is authorized to be appropriated to carry out this subchapter $30,000,000 for each of fiscal years 2002 through 2023. Generally, States shall be eligible for funds appropriated under this subchapter according to the respective capabilities of their private forests and rangelands for yielding renewable resources and relative needs for such resources identified in the periodic Renewable Resource Assessment provided for in section 1601 of this title and the periodic appraisal of land and water resources provided for in section 2004 of this title.

(Pub. L. No. 95–306, § 6, 92 Stat. 352 (June 30, 1978); as amended by Pub. L. No. 100–231, § 2(1), 101 Stat. 1565 (Jan. 5, 1988); Pub. L. No. 105–185, Title III, § 301(h), 112 Stat. 563 (June 23, 1998); Pub. L. No. 107–171, Title VIII, § 8101(b)(1), 116 Stat. 474 (May 13, 2002); Pub. L. No. 110–234, Title VII, § 7413(a), 122 Stat. 1256 (May 22, 2008); Pub. L. No. 110–246, § 4(a), Title VII, § 7413(a), 122 Stat. 1664, 2017 (June 18, 2008); Pub. L. No. 113–79, Title VII, § 7405(a), 128 Stat. 898 (Feb. 7, 2014); Pub. L. No. 115–334, § 7509(a), 132 Stat. 4490, 4824 (Dec. 20, 2018).)

Effective Date

For the period during which this subchapter is effective, see Section 8 of Pub. L. No. 95–306, as amended, set out as an Effective and Applicability Provisions note under 16 U.S.C.A. § 1671.

HISTORICAL AND STATUTORY NOTES

References in Text

This subchapter, referred to in text, originally read "this Act", meaning the Renewable Resources Extension Act of 1978, or RREA, Pub. L. No. 95–306, 92 Stat. 349 (June 30, 1978), which is principally codified as this subchapter. For complete classification, see short title note set out under 16 U.S.C.A. § 1600 and Tables.

Codifications

The authorities provided by each provision of, and each amendment made by, Pub. L. No. 110–246, as in effect on Sept. 30, 2012, to continue, and the Secretary of Agriculture to carry out the authorities, until the later of Sept. 30, 2013, or the date specified in the provision of, or amendment made by, Pub. L. No. 110–246, see section 701(a) of Pub. L. No. 112–240, set out in a note under 7 U.S.C.A. § 8701.

Effective and Applicability Provisions

2008 Acts. Amendments by Pub. L. No. 110–246, except as otherwise provided, shall take effect on the earlier of June 18, 2008, or May 22, 2008, see Pub. L. No. 110–246, § 4(b), set out in a Repeal of Duplicative Enactment note under 7 U.S.C.A. § 8701.

1978 Acts. Amendments by Pub. L. No. 95–306 effective for the period beginning October 1, 1978, and ending September 30, 2018, see Pub. L. No. 95–306, § 8, as amended, set out as a note under 16 U.S.C.A. § 1671.

Repeals

Pub. L. No. 110–234 repealed effective May 22, 2008, see Repeal of Duplicative Enactment by Pub. L. No. 110–246, § 4(a), set out in a note under 7 U.S.C.A. § 8701.

§ 1676. Issuance of rules and regulations for implementation of provisions and coordination with agricultural, research, extension, and teaching provisions

[RREA § 7]

The Secretary is authorized to issue such rules and regulations as the Secretary deems necessary to implement the provisions of this subchapter and to coordinate this subchapter with title XIV of the Food and Agriculture Act of 1977 [7 U.S.C.A. § 3101 et seq.].

(Pub. L. No. 95–306, § 7, 92 Stat. 352 (June 30, 1978).)

Effective Date

For the period during which this subchapter is effective, see Section 8 of Pub. L. No. 95–306, as amended, set out as an Effective and Applicability Provisions note under 16 U.S.C.A. § 1671.

HISTORICAL AND STATUTORY NOTES

References in Text

The Food and Agriculture Act of 1977, referred to in text, is Pub. L. No. 95–113, 91 Stat. 913 (Sept. 29, 1977), as amended. Title XIV of the Food and Agriculture Act of 1977, known as the "National Agricultural Research, Extension, and Teaching Policy Act of 1977", is codified principally as chapter 64 of Title 7 (7 U.S.C.A. § 3101 et seq.). For complete classification, see Short Title note set out under section 3101 of Title 7 and Tables.

Effective and Applicability Provisions

1978 Acts. Amendments by Pub. L. No. 95–306 effective for the period beginning October 1, 1978, and ending September 30, 2018, see Pub. L. No. 95–306, § 8, as amended, set out as a note under 16 U.S.C.A. § 1671.

WOOD RESIDUE UTILIZATION ACT OF 1980
[WRUA § ______]

(16 U.S.C.A. §§ 1681 to 1687)

SUBCHAPTER IV—WOOD RESIDUE UTILIZATION

§ 1681. Congressional statement of purpose

[WRUA § 2]

The purpose of this subchapter is to develop, demonstrate, and make available information on feasible methods that have potential for commercial application to increase and improve utilization, in residential, commercial, and industrial or powerplant applications, of wood residues resulting from timber harvesting and forest protection and management activities occurring on public and private forest lands, and from the manufacture of forest products, including woodpulp.

(Pub. L. No. 96–554, § 2, 94 Stat. 3257 (Dec. 19, 1980).)

HISTORICAL AND STATUTORY NOTES

Effective and Applicability Provisions

1980 Acts. Section 9 of Pub. L. No. 96–554 provided that: "This Act [enacting this subchapter and provision set out as a note under section 1600 of this title] shall become effective October 1, 1981."

Short Title

1980 Acts. For Short Title of Pub. L. No. 96–554, Dec. 19, 1980, 94 Stat. 3257, as the Wood Residue Utilization Act of 1980, see short title note set out under section 1600 of this title.

§ 1682. Pilot projects and demonstrations

[WRUA § 3]

(a) Establishment, implementation

The Secretary may establish pilot projects and demonstrations to carry out the purposes of this subchapter. The pilot projects and demonstrations established under this section (1) may be operated by the Secretary; or (2) may be carried out through contracts or agreements with owners of private forest lands or other persons, or in conjunction with projects, contracts, or agreements entered into under any other authority which the Secretary may possess: *Provided,* That nothing contained in this subchapter shall abrogate or modify provisions of existing contracts or agreements, including contracts or agreements for the sale of national forest timber, except to the extent such changes are mutually agreed to by the parties to such contracts or agreements.

(b) Scope; residue removal credits

Pilot projects and demonstrations carried out under this section may include, but are not limited to (1) establishment and operation of utilization demonstration areas; (2) establishment and operation of fuel wood concentration and distribution centers; and (3) construction of access roads needed to facilitate wood residue utilization: *Provided,* That residue removal credits may be utilized by the Secretary only as provided in section 1683 of this title.

(Pub. L. No. 96–554, § 3, 94 Stat. 3257 (Dec. 19, 1980).)

§ 1683. Pilot projects; requirements; residue removal credits as compensation; implementation guidelines

[WRUA § 4]

The Secretary may carry out pilot wood residue utilization projects under which purchasers of National Forest System timber under contracts awarded prior to October 1, 1986, may, except as otherwise provided in this section, be required to remove wood residues not purchased by them to points of prospective use in return for compensation in the form of "residue removal credits." Such projects may be carried out where the Secretary identifies situations in which pilot wood residue utilization projects on the National Forest System can provide important information on various methods and approaches to increasing the utilization, in residential, commercial, and industrial or powerplant applications, of wood residues and where such information cannot reasonably be obtained unless the pilot projects are done in conjunction with normal National Forest timber sale activities. The residue removal credits shall be applied against the amount payable for the timber purchased and shall represent the anticipated cost of removal of wood residues. The following guidelines shall apply to projects carried out under this section:

(1) Except in cases where wood residue removal is determined to be necessary for fire prevention, site preparation for regeneration, wildlife habitat improvement, or other land management purposes, the Secretary may not provide for removal of wood residues in instances where the anticipated cost of removal would exceed the anticipated value.

(2) The residue removal credits authorized by this section shall not exceed the amount payable by the purchaser for timber after the application of all other designated charges and credits.

(3) The Secretary may sell the wood residues removed to points of prospective use for not less than their appraised value.

(4) Pilot projects, demonstrations, and other programs established pursuant to this subchapter shall be carried out in a manner which does not result in an adverse effect on the furnishing of timber, free of charge, under any other provision of law.

(5) Wood residues shall be collected grom a site so as to avoid soil depletion or erosion giving full consideration to the protection of wildlife habitat.

(6) For the purposes of section 500 of this title, (A)any residue removal credit applied under this section shall be considered as "money received" or "moneys received", respectively, and (B) the "money received" or "moneys received", respectively, from the sales of wood residues removed to points of prospective use shall be the proceeds of the sales less the sum of any residue removal credit applied with respect to such residues plus any costs incurred by the Forest Service in processing and storing such residues.

(Pub. L. No. 96–554, § 4, 94 Stat. 3257 (Dec. 19, 1980).)

§ 1684. Annual reports

[WRUA § 5]

The Secretary shall make annual reports to the Congress on the programs authorized by this subchapter. These reports shall be submitted with the reports required under section 1606(c) of this title.

(Pub. L. No. 96–554, § 5, 94 Stat. 3258 (Dec. 19, 1980).)

§ 1685. Regulations

[WRUA § 6]

The Secretary shall issue such regulations as the Secretary deems necessary to implement the provisions of this subchapter.

(Pub. L. No. 96–554, § 6, 94 Stat. 3258 (Dec. 19, 1980).)

§ 1686. Definitions

[WRUA § 7]

For purposes of this subchapter, the term:

(1) "Anticipated cost of removal" means the projected cost of removal of wood residues from timber sales areas to points of prospective use, as determined by the Secretary at the time of advertisement of the timber sales contract in accordance with appropriate appraisal and sale procedures.

(2) "Anticipated value" means the projected value of wood residues as fuel or other merchantable wood products, as determined by the Secretary at the time of advertisement of the timber sales contract in accordance with appropriate appraisal and sale procedures.

(3) "Points of prospective use" means the locations where the wood residues are sold or otherwise put to use, as determined by the Secretary in accordance with appropriate appraisal and sale procedures.

(4) "Person" means an individual, partnership, joint-stock company, corporation, association, trust, estate, or any other legal entity, or any agency of Federal or State government or of a political subdivision of a State.

(5) "Secretary" means the Secretary of Agriculture.

(6) "Wood residues" includes, but is not limited to, logging slash, down timber material, woody plants, and standing live or dead trees which do not meet utilization standards because of size, species, merchantable volume, or economic selection criteria and which, in the case of live trees, are surplus to growing stock needs.

(Pub. L. No. 96–554, § 7, 94 Stat. 3258 (Dec. 19, 1980).)

§ 1687. Authorization of appropriations

[WRUA § 8]

There is hereby authorized to be appropriated not to exceed $25,000,000 for each of the fiscal years 1982, 1983, 1984, 1985, and 1986 to carry out the pilot projects and demonstrations authorized by section 1682 of this title, the residue removal credits authorized by section 1683 of this title, and the other provisions of this subchapter: *Provided,* That not to exceed $2,500,000 of such amount may be appropriated for administrative expenses to carry out this subchapter for the period beginning October 1, 1981, and ending September 30, 1986. Such sums shall be in addition to those provided under other provisions of law and shall remain available until expended.

(Pub. L. No. 96–554, § 8, 94 Stat. 3259 (Dec. 19, 1980).)

TITLE 30

MINERAL LANDS AND MINING

CHAPTER 25—SURFACE MINING CONTROL AND RECLAMATION

SUBCHAPTER I—STATEMENT OF FINDINGS AND POLICY

SUBCHAPTER II—OFFICE OF SURFACE MINING RECLAMATION AND ENFORCEMENT

SUBCHAPTER III—STATE MINING AND MINERAL RESOURCES RESEARCH INSTITUTES

SUBCHAPTER IV—ABANDONED MINE RECLAMATIONS

SUBCHAPTER V—CONTROL OF THE ENVIRONMENTAL IMPACTS OF SURFACE COAL MINING

SUBCHAPTER VI—DESIGNATION OF LANDS UNSUITABLE FOR NONCOAL MINING

SUBCHAPTER VII—ADMINISTRATIVE AND MISCELLANEOUS PROVISIONS

SURFACE MINING CONTROL AND RECLAMATION ACT OF 1977 [SMCRA § ____]

(30 U.S.C.A. §§ 1201, 1202, 1211)

SUBCHAPTER I—STATEMENT OF FINDINGS AND POLICY

§ 1201. Congressional findings

[SMCRA § 101]

The Congress finds and declares that—

(a) extraction of coal and other minerals from the earth can be accomplished by various methods of mining, including surface mining;

(b) coal mining operations presently contribute significantly to the Nation's energy requirements; surface coal mining constitutes one method of extraction of the resource; the overwhelming percentage of the Nation's coal reserves can only be extracted by underground mining methods, and it is, therefore, essential to the national interest to insure the existence of an expanding and economically healthy underground coal mining industry;

(c) many surface mining operations result in disturbances of surface areas that burden and adversely affect commerce and the public welfare by destroying or diminishing the utility of land for commercial, industrial, residential, recreational, agricultural, and forestry purposes, by causing erosion and landslides, by contributing to floods, by polluting the water, by destroying fish and wildlife habitats, by impairing natural beauty, by damaging the property of citizens, by creating hazards dangerous to life and property by degrading the quality of life in local communities, and by counteracting governmental programs and efforts to conserve soil, water, and other natural resources;

(d) the expansion of coal mining to meet the Nation's energy needs makes even more urgent the establishment of appropriate standards to minimize damage to the environment and to productivity of the soil and to protect the health and safety of the public.[1]

(e) surface mining and reclamation technology are now developed so that effective and reasonable regulation of surface coal mining operations by the States and by the Federal Government in accordance with the requirements of this chapter is an appropriate and necessary means to minimize so far as practicable the adverse social, economic, and environmental effects of such mining operations;

(f) because of the diversity in terrain, climate, biologic, chemical, and other physical conditions in areas subject to mining operations, the primary governmental responsibility for developing, authorizing, issuing, and enforcing regulations for surface mining and reclamation operations subject to this chapter should rest with the States;

(g) surface mining and reclamation standards are essential in order to insure that competition in interstate commerce among sellers of coal produced in different States will not be used to undermine the ability of the several States to improve and maintain adequate standards on coal mining operations within their borders;

(h) there are a substantial number of acres of land throughout major regions of the United States disturbed by surface and underground coal on which little or no reclamation was conducted, and the impacts from these unreclaimed lands impose social and economic costs on residents in nearby and adjoining areas as well as continuing to impair environmental quality;

(i) while there is a need to regulate surface mining operations for minerals other than coal, more data and analyses are needed to serve as a basis for effective and reasonable regulation of such operations;

(j) surface and underground coal mining operations affect interstate commerce, contribute to the economic well-being, security, and general welfare of the Nation and should be conducted in an environmentally sound manner; and

(k) the cooperative effort established by this chapter is necessary to prevent or mitigate adverse environmental effects of present and future surface coal mining operations.[1]

(Pub. L. No. 95–87, Title I, § 101, 91 Stat. 447 (Aug. 3, 1977).)

[1] So in original. The period probably should be a semicolon.

HISTORICAL AND STATUTORY NOTES

References in Text

This chapter, referred to in subsecs. (e), (f), and (k), was in the original "this Act", meaning Pub. L. No. 95–87, 91 Stat. 445 (Aug. 3, 1977), as amended, which enacted this chapter and amended section 1114 of Title 18, Crimes and Criminal Procedure. For complete classification of this Act to the Code, see Short Title note set out below and Tables.

Short Title

2020 Amendments. Pub. L. No. 116–260, Div. Y, § 1, 134 Stat. 2417 (Dec. 27, 2020), provided that: "This division may be cited as the 'American Miner Benefits Improvement Act of 2020.' "

2019 Amendments. Section 101 of pub. L. No. 116–94, 133 Stat. 3091 (Dec. 20, 2019), provided that: "This division may be cited as the 'Bipartisan American Miners Act of 2019.' "

2006 Amendments. Pub. L. No. 109–432, Div. C, Title II, § 200, 120 Stat. 3006 (Dec. 20, 2006), provided that: "This title [enacting 30 U.S.C.A. § 1244, amending 26 U.S.C.A. §§ 9701, 9702, 9704 to 9707, 9711, 9712, and 9721, and 30 U.S.C.A. §§ 1231, 1232, 1233, 1236, 1238, 1240a, 1260, 1300, and 1302, and enacting provisions set out as notes under 26 U.S.C.A. §§ 9701, 9704, and 9712, and 30 U.S.C.A. § 1232] may be cited as the 'Surface Mining Control and Reclamation Act Amendments of 2006'."

1990 Amendments. Pub. L. No. 101–508, Title VI, Subtitle A, § 6001, 104 Stat. 1388–289 (Nov. 5, 1990), provided that: "This subtitle [enacting section 1240a of this title, amending sections 1231, 1232, 1233, 1234, 1235, 1236, 1237, 1239, 1257 and 1302 of this title, and enacting provisions set out as a note under section 1231 of this title] may be cited as the 'Abandoned Mine Reclamation Act of 1990'."

Pub. L. No. 101–498, § 1, 104 Stat. 1207 (Nov. 2, 1990), provided that: "This Act [enacting section 1230a of this title] may be cited as the 'Strategic and Critical Minerals Act of 1990'."

1988 Amendments. Pub. L. No. 100–483, § 13, 102 Stat. 2341 (Oct. 12, 1988), provided that: "This Act [amending sections 1221(a)(1), (a)(2)(A), (b), 1222(a), 1224(a), 1226(d), 1229(a)(7), (e), and 1230(b) of this title; and enacting note provisions set out under this section and section 1229 of this title] may be cited as the 'Mining and Mineral Resources Research Institute Amendments of 1988'."

1977 Amendments. Section 1 of Pub. L. No. 95–87 provided: "That this Act [which enacted this chapter and amended section 1114 of Title 18] may be cited as the 'Surface Mining Control and Reclamation Act of 1977'."

Pub. L. No. 98–409, § 11, as added by Pub. L. No. 100–483, § 12, 102 Stat. 2341 (Oct. 12, 1988), and amended by Pub. L. No. 104–312, § 1(b), 110 Stat. 3819 (Oct. 19, 1996), provided that: "This Act [enacting subchapter III of this chapter] may be cited as the 'Mining and Mineral Resources Institutes Act'."

§ 1202. Statement of purpose

[SMCRA § 102]

It is the purpose of this chapter to—

(a) establish a nationwide program to protect society and the environment from the adverse effects of surface coal mining operations;

(b) assure that the rights of surface landowners and other persons with a legal interest in the land or appurtenances thereto are fully protected from such operations;

(c) assure that surface mining operations are not conducted where reclamation as required by this chapter is not feasible;

(d) assure that surface coal mining operations are so conducted as to protect the environment;

(e) assure that adequate procedures are undertaken to reclaim surface areas as contemporaneously as possible with the surface coal mining operations;

(f) assure that the coal supply essential to the Nation's energy requirements, and to its economic and social well-being is provided and strike a balance between protection of the environment and agricultural productivity and the Nation's need for coal as an essential source of energy;

(g) assist the States in developing and implementing a program to achieve the purposes of this chapter;

(h) promote the reclamation of mined areas left without adequate reclamation prior to August 3, 1977, and which continue, in their unreclaimed condition, to substantially degrade the quality of the environment, prevent or damage the beneficial use of land or water resources, or endanger the health or safety of the public;

(i) assure that appropriate procedures are provided for the public participation in the development, revision, and enforcement of regulations, standards, reclamation plans, or programs established by the Secretary or any State under this chapter;

(j) provide a means for development of the data and analyses necessary to establish effective and reasonable regulation of surface mining operations for other minerals;

(k) encourage the full utilization of coal resources through the development and application of underground extraction technologies;

(*l*) stimulate, sponsor, provide for and/or supplement present programs for the conduct of research investigations, experiments, and demonstrations, in the exploration, extraction, processing, development, and production of minerals and the training of mineral engineers and scientists in the field of mining, minerals resources, and technology, and the establishment of an appropriate research and training center in various States; and

(m) wherever necessary, exercise the full reach of Federal constitutional powers to insure the protection of the public interest through effective control of surface coal mining operations.

(Pub. L. No. 95–87, Title I, § 102, 91 Stat. 448 (Aug. 3, 1977).)

HISTORICAL AND STATUTORY NOTES

References in Text

This chapter, referred to in the introductory text and pars. (c), (g), and (i), was in the original "this Act", meaning Pub. L. No. 95–87, 91 Stat. 445 (Aug. 3, 1977), as amended, which enacted this chapter and amended section 1114 of Title 18, Crimes and Criminal Procedure. For complete classification of this Act to the Code, see Short Title note set out under section 1201 of this title and Tables.

SUBCHAPTER II—OFFICE OF SURFACE MINING RECLAMATION AND ENFORCEMENT

§ 1211. Office of Surface Mining Reclamation and Enforcement

[SMCRA § 201]

(a) Establishment

There is established in the Department of the Interior, the Office of Surface Mining Reclamation and Enforcement (hereinafter referred to as the "Office").

(b) Appointment, compensation, duties, etc., of Director; employees

The Office shall have a Director who shall be appointed by the President, by and with the advice and consent of the Senate, and shall be compensated at the rate provided for level V of the Executive Schedule under section 5315[1] of Title 5, and such other employees as may be required. Pursuant to section 5108 of Title 5, and after consultation with the Secretary, the Director of the Office of Personnel Management shall determine the necessary number of positions in general schedule employees in grade 16, 17, and 18 to perform functions of this subchapter and shall allocate such positions to the Secretary. The Director shall have the responsibilities provided under subsection (c) of this section and those duties and responsibilities relating to the functions of the Office which the Secretary may assign, consistent with this chapter. Employees of the Office shall be recruited on the basis of their professional competence and capacity to administer the provisions of this chapter. The Office may use, on a reimbursable basis when appropriate, employees of the Department and other Federal agencies to administer the provisions of this chapter, providing that no legal authority, program, or function in any Federal agency which has as its purpose promoting the development or use of coal or other mineral resources or regulating the health and safety of miners under provisions of the Federal Coal Mine Health and Safety Act of 1969 (83 Stat. 742) [30 U.S.C.A. § 801 et seq.], shall be transferred to the Office.

(c) Duties of Secretary

The Secretary, acting through the Office, shall—

(1) administer the programs for controlling surface coal mining operations which are required by this chapter; review and approve or disapprove State programs for controlling surface coal mining operations and reclaiming abandoned mined lands; make those investigations and inspections necessary to insure compliance with this chapter; conduct hearings, administer oaths, issue subpenas, and compel the attendance of witnesses and production of written or printed material as provided for in this chapter; issue cease-and-desist orders; review and vacate or modify or approve orders and decisions; and order the suspension, revocation, or withholding of any permit for failure to comply with any of the provisions of this chapter or any rules and regulations adopted pursuant thereto;

(2) publish and promulgate such rules and regulations as may be necessary to carry out the purposes and provisions of this chapter;

(3) administer the State grant-in-aid program for the development of State programs for surface and mining and reclamation operations provided for in subchapter V of this chapter;

(4) administer the program for the purchase and reclamation of abandoned and unreclaimed mined areas pursuant to subchapter IV of this chapter;

(5) administer the surface mining and reclamation research and demonstration project authority provided for in this chapter;

(6) consult with other agencies of the Federal Government having expertise in the control and reclamation of surface mining operations and assist States, local governments, and other eligible agencies in the coordination of such programs;

(7) maintain a continuing study of surface mining and reclamation operations in the United States;

(8) develop and maintain an Information and Data Center on Surface Coal Mining, Reclamation, and Surface Impacts of Underground Mining, which will make such data available to the public and the Federal, regional, State, and local agencies conducting or concerned with land use planning and agencies concerned with surface and underground mining and reclamation operations;

(9) assist the States in the development of State programs for surface coal mining and reclamation operations which meet the requirements of this chapter, and at the same time, reflect local requirements and local environmental and agricultural conditions;

(10) assist the States in developing objective scientific criteria and appropriate procedures and institutions for determining those areas of a State to be designated unsuitable for all or certain types of surface coal mining pursuant to section 1272 of this title;

(11) monitor all Federal and State research programs dealing with coal extraction and use and recommend to Congress the research and demonstration projects and necessary changes in public policy which are designated to (A) improve feasibility of underground coal mining, and (B) improve surface mining and reclamation techniques directed at eliminating adverse environmental and social impacts;

(12) cooperate with other Federal agencies and State regulatory authorities to minimize duplication of inspections, enforcement, and administration of this chapter; and

(13) perform such other duties as may be provided by law and relate to the purposes of this chapter.

(d) Restriction on use of Federal coal mine health and safety inspectors

The Director shall not use either permanently or temporarily any person charged with responsibility of inspecting coal mines under the Federal Coal Mine Health and Safety Act of 1969 [30 U.S.C.A. § 801 et seq.], unless he finds and publishes such finding in the Federal Register, that such activities would not interfere with such inspections under the 1969 Act.

(e) Repealed. Pub. L. No. 96–511, § 4(b), 94 Stat. 2826 (Dec. 11, 1980).

(f) Conflict of interest; penalties; rules and regulations; report to Congress

No employee of the Office or any other Federal employee performing any function or duty under this chapter shall have a direct or indirect financial interest in underground or surface coal mining operations. Whoever knowingly violates the provisions of the above sentence shall, upon conviction, be punished by a fine of not more than $2,500, or by imprisonment for not more than one year, or both. The Director shall (1) within sixty days after August 3, 1977, publish regulations, in accordance with section 553 of Title 5, to establish the methods by which the provisions of this subsection will be monitored and enforced, including appropriate provisions for the filing by such employees and the review of statements and supplements thereto concerning their financial interests which may be affected by this subsection, and (2) report to the Congress as part of the annual report (section 1296 of this title) on the actions taken and not taken during the preceding calendar year under this subsection.

(g) Petition for issuance, amendment, or repeal of rule; filing; hearing or investigation; notice of denial

(1) After the Secretary has adopted the regulations required by section 1251 of this title, any person may petition the Director to initiate a proceeding for the issuance, amendment, or repeal of a rule under this chapter.

(2) Such petitions shall be filed in the principal office of the Director and shall set forth the facts which it is claimed established that it is necessary to issue, amend, or repeal a rule under this chapter.

(3) The Director may hold a public hearing or may conduct such investigation or proceeding as the Director deems appropriate in order to determine whether or not such petition should be granted.

(4) Within ninety days after filing of a petition described in paragraph (1), the Director shall either grant or deny the petition. If the Director grants such petition, the Director shall promptly commence an appropriate proceeding in accordance with the provisions of this chapter. If the Director denies such petition, the Director shall so notify the petitioner in writing setting forth the reasons for such denial.

(Pub. L. No. 95–87, Title II, § 201, 91 Stat. 449 (Aug. 3, 1977); as amended by Pub. L. No. 95–240, Title I, § 100, 92 Stat. 109 (Mar. 7, 1978); 1978 Reorg. Plan No. 2, § 102, eff. Jan. 1, 1979, 43 Fed. Reg. 36037, 92 Stat. 3783; Pub. L. No. 96–511, § 4(b), 94 Stat. 2826 (Dec. 11, 1980).)

[1] So in original. Probably should be "section 5316".

HISTORICAL AND STATUTORY NOTES

References in Text

This chapter, referred to in text, was in the original "this Act", meaning Pub. L. No. 95–87, 91 Stat. 445 (Aug. 3, 1977), as amended, which enacted this chapter and amended section 1114 of Title 18, Crimes and Criminal Procedure. For complete classification of this Act to the Code, see Short Title note set out under section 1201 of this title and Tables.

The general schedule, referred to in subsec. (b), is set out under section 5332 of Title 5, Government Organization and Employees.

The Federal Coal Mine Health and Safety Act of 1969, referred to in subsecs. (b) and (d), is Pub. L. No. 91–173, 83 Stat. 742 (Dec. 30, 1969), as amended, which was redesignated the Federal Mine Safety and Health Act of 1977 by Pub. L. No. 95–164, Title I, § 101, 91 Stat. 1290 (Nov. 9, 1977), and is codified principally as chapter 22 (section 801 et seq.) of this title. For complete classification of this Act to the Code, see Short Title note set out under section 801 of this title and Tables.

Effective and Applicability Provisions

1980 Acts. Amendment by Pub. L. No. 96–511 effective on Apr. 1, 1981, see section 5 of Pub. L. No. 96–511, set out as a note under section 3501 of Title 44, Public Printing and Documents.

Termination of Reporting Requirements

For termination of reporting provisions of subsec. (f) of this section, effective May 15, 2000, see Pub. L. No. 104–66, § 3003, as amended, set out as a note under 31 U.S.C.A. § 1113, and page 109 of House Document No. 103–7.

Transfer of Functions

"The Director of the Office of Personnel Management" was substituted for "a majority of members of the Civil Service Commission" in subsec. (b) pursuant to Reorg. Plan No. 2 of 1978, § 102, 43 Fed. Reg. 36037, 92 Stat. 3783, set out under section 1101 of Title 5, Government Organization and Employees, which transferred all functions vested by statute in the United States Civil Service Commission to the Director of the Office of Personnel Management (except as otherwise specified), effective Jan. 1, 1979, as provided by section 1–102 of Ex. Ord. No. 12107, Dec. 28, 1978, 44 FED. REG. 1055, set out under section 1101 of Title 5.

Travel and Per Diem Expenses of State and Tribal Personnel Attending Sponsored Training

Pub. L. No. 100–446, Title I, 102 Stat. 1793 (Sept. 27, 1988), provided in part: "That notwithstanding any other provisions of law, appropriations for the Office of Surface Mining Reclamation and Enforcement may, hereafter, provide for the travel and per diem expenses of State and tribal personnel attending OSMRE sponsored training.".

Similar provisions were contained in the following subsequent Appropriations Acts:

Pub. L. No. 113–76, Div. G, Title I, 128 Stat. 298 (Jan. 17, 2014).

Pub. L. No. 112–74, Div. E, Title I, 125 Stat. 995 (Dec. 23, 2011).

Pub. L. No. 111–88, Div. A, Title I, 123 Stat. 2915 (Oct. 30, 2009).

Pub. L. No. 111–8, Div. E, Title I, 123 Stat. 712 (Mar. 11, 2009).

Pub. L. No. 110–161, Div. F, Title I, 121 Stat. 2109 (Dec. 26, 2007).

Pub. L. No. 109–54, Title I, 119 Stat. 512 (Aug. 2, 2005).

Pub. L. No. 108–447, Div. E, Title I, 118 Stat. 3054 (Dec. 8, 2004).

Pub. L. No. 108–108, Title I, 117 Stat. 1256 (Nov. 10, 2003).

Pub. L. No. 108–7, Div. F, Title I, 117 Stat. 230 (Feb. 20, 2003).

Pub. L. No. 107–63, Title I, 115 Stat. 429 (Nov. 5, 2001).

Pub. L. No. 106–291, Title I, 114 Stat. 933 (Oct. 11, 2000).

Pub. L. No. 106–113, Div. B, § 1000(a)(3) [Title I], 113 Stat. 1535, 1501A–147 (Nov. 29, 1999).

Pub. L. No. 105–277, Div. A, § 101(e) [Title I], 112 Stat. 2681–244 (Oct. 21, 1998).

Pub. L. No. 105–83, Title I, 111 Stat. 1553 (Nov. 14, 1997).

Pub. L. No. 104–208, Div. A, Title I, § 101(d) [Title I], 110 Stat. 3009–191 (Sept. 30, 1996).

Pub. L. No. 104–134, Title I, § 101(c) [Title I], 110 Stat. 1321–168 (Apr. 26, 1996); renumbered Title I by Pub. L. No. 104–140, § 1(a), 110 Stat. 1327 (May 26, 1996).

Pub. L. No. 103–332, Title I, 108 Stat. 2510 (Sept. 30, 1994).

Pub. L. No. 103–138, Title I, 107 Stat. 1389 (Nov. 11, 1993).

Pub. L. No. 102–381, Title I, 106 Stat. 1387 (Oct. 5, 1992).

Pub. L. No. 102–154, Title I, 105 Stat. 1002 (Nov. 13, 1991).

Pub. L. No. 101–512, Title I, 104 Stat. 1927 (Nov. 5, 1990).

Pub. L. No. 101–121, Title I, 103 Stat. 712 (Oct. 23, 1989).

Pub. L. No. 100–446, Title I, 102 Stat. 1793 (Sept. 27, 1988).

Fiscal Limitations

Pub. L. No. 113–76, 128 Stat. 298–99 (Jan. 17, 2014), provided that:

"For necessary expenses to carry out the provisions of the Surface Mining Control and Reclamation Act of 1977, Public Law 95–87, $122,713,000, to remain available until September 30, 2015: *Provided,* That appropriations for the Office of Surface Mining Reclamation and Enforcement may provide for the travel and per diem expenses of State and tribal personnel attending Office of Surface Mining Reclamation and Enforcement sponsored training: *Provided further,* That, in fiscal year 2014, up to $40,000 collected by the Office of Surface Mining from permit fees pursuant to section 507 of Public Law 95–87 (30 U.S.C. 1257) shall be credited to this account as discretionary offsetting collections, to remain available until expended: *Provided further,* That the sum herein appropriated shall be reduced as collections are received during the fiscal year so as to result in a final fiscal year 2014 appropriation estimated at not more than $122,713,000: *Provided further,* That, in subsequent fiscal years, all amounts collected by the Office of Surface Mining from permit fees pursuant to section 507 of Public Law 95–87 (30 U.S.C. 1257) shall be credited to this account as discretionary offsetting collections, to remain available until expended."

MINING AND MINERAL RESOURCES RESEARCH INSTITUTE ACT OF 1984 [MMRRIA § ______]

(30 U.S.C.A. §§ 1221 to 1230a)

SUBCHAPTER III—STATE MINING AND MINERAL RESOURCES RESEARCH INSTITUTES

HISTORICAL AND STATUTORY NOTES

Codifications

Subchapter was not enacted as part of the Surface Mining Control and Reclamation Act of 1977 which comprises this chapter.

§ 1221. Authorization of State allotments to institutes

[MMRRIA § 1]

(a) **(1)** There are authorized to be appropriated to the Secretary of the Interior (hereafter in this subchapter referred to as the "Secretary") funds adequate to provide for each participating State $400,000 for each of the fiscal years ending September 30, 1990, through September 30, 1994, to assist the States in carrying on the work of a competent and qualified mining and mineral resources research institute or center (hereafter in this subchapter referred to as the "institute") at one public college or university in the State which meets the eligibility criteria established in section 1230 of this title.

(2) **(A)** Funds appropriated under this section shall be made available for grants to be matched on a basis of no less than 2 non-Federal dollars for each Federal dollar.

(B) If there is more than one such eligible college or university in a State, funds appropriated under this subchapter shall, in the absence of a designation to the contrary by act of the legislature of the State, be granted to one such college or university designated by the Governor of the State.

(C) Where a State does not have a public college or university eligible under section 1230 of this title, the Committee on Mining and Mineral Resources Research established in section 1229 of this title (hereafter in this subchapter referred to as the "Committee") may allocate the State's allotment to one private college or university which it determines to be eligible under such section.

(b) It shall be the duty of each institute to plan and conduct, or arrange for a component or components of the college or university with which it is affiliated to conduct research, investigations, demonstrations, and experiments of either, or both, a basic or practical nature in relation to mining and mineral resources, and to provide for the training of mineral engineers and scientists through such research, investigations, demonstrations, and experiments. The subject of such research, investigation, demonstration, experiment, and training may include exploration; extraction; processing; development; production of fuel and nonfuel mineral resources; mining and mineral technology; supply and demand for minerals; conservation and best use of available supplies of minerals; the economic, legal, social, engineering, recreational, biological, geographic, ecological, and other aspects of mining, mineral resources, and mineral reclamation. Such research, investigation, demonstration, experiment and training shall consider the interrelationship with the natural environment, the varying conditions and needs of the respective States, and mining and mineral resources research projects being conducted by agencies of the Federal and State Governments and other institutes.

(Pub. L. 98–409, § 1, 98 Stat. 1536 (Aug. 29, 1984); as amended by Pub. L. No. 100–483, §§ 2–4, 102 Stat. 2339 (Oct. 12, 1988).)

HISTORICAL AND STATUTORY NOTES

Codifications

Section was not enacted as part of the Surface Mining Control and Reclamation Act of 1977 which comprises this chapter.

Prior Provisions

A prior section 1221, Pub. L. No. 95–87, Title III, § 301, 91 Stat. 451 (Aug. 3, 1977), contained provisions similar to this section covering fiscal years 1978 through 1984.

Short Title

For popular name of Pub. L. No. 98–409, which is codified as this subchapter, as the "Mining and Mineral Resources Research Institute Act of 1984", see section 11 of Pub. L. No. 98–409, set out as a note under section 1201 of this title.

§ 1222. Research funds to institutes

[MMRRIA § 2]

(a) Authorization of appropriations

There is authorized to be appropriated to the Secretary not more than $15,000,000 for each of the fiscal years ending September 30, 1990, through September 30, 1994, which shall remain available until expended. Such funds when appropriated shall be made available to an institute or to institutes participating in a generic mineral technology center to meet the necessary expenses for purposes of—

(1) specific mineral research and demonstration projects of broad application, which could not otherwise be undertaken, including the expenses of planning and coordinating regional mining and mineral resources research projects by two or more institutes; and

(2) research into any aspects of mining and mineral resources problems related to the mission of the Department of the Interior, which are deemed by the Committee to be desirable and are not otherwise being studied.

There is authorized to be appropriated to the Secretary not more than $1,800,000 for each of the fiscal years after fiscal year 1996 to be made available by the Secretary to an institute or institutes experienced in investigating the continental shelf regions of the United States, the deep seabed and near shore environments of islands, and the Arctic and cold water regions as a source for nonfuel minerals. Such funds are to be used by the institute or institutes to assist in developing domestic technological capabilities required for the location of, and the efficient and environmentally sound recovery of, minerals (other than oil and gas) from the Nation's shallow and deep seabed.

(b) Application for funds; contents

Each application for funds under subsection (a) of this section shall state, among other things, the nature of the project to be undertaken; the period during which it will be pursued; the qualifications of the personnel who will direct and conduct it; the estimated costs; the importance of the project to the Nation, region, or State concerned; its relation to other known research projects theretofore pursued or being pursued; the extent to which the proposed project will provide opportunity for the training of mining and mineral engineers and scientists; and the extent of participation by nongovernmental sources in the project.

(c) Research facilities; selection of institutes; designation of funds for scholarships and fellowships

The Committee shall review all such funding applications and recommend to the Secretary the use of the institutes, insofar as practicable, to perform special research. Recommendations shall be made without regard to the race, religion, or sex of the personnel who will conduct and direct the research, and on the basis of the facilities available in relation to the particular needs of the research project; special geographic, geologic, or climatic conditions within the immediate vicinity of the institute; any other special requirements of the research project; and the extent to which such project will provide an opportunity for training individuals as mineral engineers and scientists. The Committee shall recommend to the Secretary the designation and utilization of such portions of the funds authorized to be appropriated by this section as it deems appropriate for the purpose of providing scholarships, graduate fellowships, and postdoctoral fellowships.

(d) Requirements for receipt of funds

No funds shall be made available under subsection (a) of this section except for a project approved by the Secretary and all funds shall be made available upon the basis of merit of the project, the need for the knowledge which it is expected to produce when completed, and the opportunity it provides for the training of individuals as mineral engineers and scientists.

(e) Restriction on application of funds

No funds made available under this section shall be applied to the acquisition by purchase or lease of any land or interests therein, or the rental, purchase, construction, preservation, or repair of any building.

(Pub. L. No. 98–409, § 2, 98 Stat. 1537 (Aug. 29, 1984); Pub. L. No. 100–483, § 5, 102 Stat. 2339 (Oct. 12, 1988); Pub. L. No. 104–312, § 1(a), 110 Stat. 3819 (Oct. 19, 1996).)

HISTORICAL AND STATUTORY NOTES

Codifications

Section was not enacted as part of the Surface Mining Control and Reclamation Act of 1977 which comprises this chapter.

Prior Provisions

A prior section 1222, Pub. L. No. 95–87, Title III, § 302, 91 Stat. 452 (Aug. 3, 1977), contained provisions similar to this section covering fiscal years 1978 through 1984.

§ 1223. Funding criteria

[MMRRIA § 3]

(a) Funds available to institutes under sections 1221 and 1222 of this title shall be paid at such times and in such amounts during each fiscal year as determined by the Secretary, and upon vouchers approved by him. Each institute shall—

(1) set forth its plan to provide for the training of individuals as mineral engineers and scientists under a curriculum appropriate to the field of mineral resources and mineral engineering and related fields;

(2) set forth policies and procedures which assure that Federal funds made available under this subchapter for any fiscal year will supplement and, to the extent practicable, increase the level of funds that would, in the absence of such Federal funds, be made available for purposes of this subchapter, and in no case supplant such funds; and

(3) have an officer appointed by its governing authority who shall receive and account for all funds paid under the provisions of this subchapter and shall make an annual report to the Secretary on or before the first day of September of each year, on work accomplished and the status of projects underway, together with a detailed statement of the amounts received under any provisions of this subchapter during the preceding fiscal year, and of its disbursements on schedules prescribed by the Secretary.

If any of the funds received by the authorized receiving officer of any institute under the provisions of this subchapter shall by any action or contingency be found by the Secretary to have been improperly diminished, lost, or misapplied, such funds shall be replaced by the State concerned and until so replaced no subsequent appropriation shall be allotted or paid to any institute of such State.

(b) The institutes are authorized and encouraged to plan and conduct programs under this subchapter in cooperation with each other and with such other agencies and individuals as may contribute to the solution of the mining and mineral resources problems involved. Moneys appropriated pursuant to this subchapter shall be available for paying the necessary expenses of planning, coordinating, and conducting such cooperative research.

(Pub. L. No. 98–409, § 3, 98 Stat. 1538 (Aug. 29, 1984).)

HISTORICAL AND STATUTORY NOTES

Codifications

Section was not enacted as part of the Surface Mining Control and Reclamation Act of 1977 which comprises this chapter.

Prior Provisions

A prior section 1223, Pub. L. No. 95–87, Title III, § 303, 91 Stat. 453 (Aug. 3, 1977), contained provisions similar to this section covering fiscal years 1978 through 1984.

§ 1224. Duties of Secretary

[MMRRIA § 4]

(a) Consulting with other agencies; prescribing rules and regulations; furnishing advice and assistance; coordinating research

The Secretary, acting through the Director of the United States Bureau of Mines, shall administer this subchapter and, after full consultation with other interested Federal agencies, shall prescribe such rules and regulations as may be necessary to carry out its provisions. The Secretary shall furnish such advice and assistance as will best promote the purposes of this subchapter, shall participate in coordinating research initiated under this subchapter by the institutes, shall indicate to them such lines of inquiry that seem most important, and shall encourage and assist in the establishment and maintenance of cooperation by and between the institutes and between them and other research organizations, the United States Department of the Interior, and other Federal establishments.

(b) Annual ascertainment of compliance

On or before the first day of July in each year beginning after August 29, 1984, the Secretary shall ascertain whether the requirements of section 1223(a) of this title have been met as to each institute and State.

(Pub. L. No. 98–409, § 4, 98 Stat. 1538 (Aug. 29, 1984); as amended by Pub. L. No. 100–483, § 6, 102 Stat. 2340 (Oct. 12, 1988); Pub. L. No. 102–285, § 10(b), 106 Stat. 172 (May 18, 1992).)

HISTORICAL AND STATUTORY NOTES

Codifications

Section was not enacted as part of the Surface Mining Control and Reclamation Act of 1977 which comprises this chapter.

Subsec. (c) of this section, which required the Secretary to submit annual reports to Congress on the receipts, expenditures, and work of the institutes in all States under the provisions of this subchapter, terminated, effective May 15, 2000, pursuant to Pub. L. No. 104–66, § 3003, as amended, which is set out as a note under 31 U.S.C.A. § 1113. See, also, House Document No. 103–7, page 109.

Change of Name

"United States Bureau of Mines" substituted for "Bureau of Mines" in subsec. (a) pursuant to section 10(b) of Pub. L. No. 102–285, set out as a note under 30 U.S.C.A. § 1. For provisions relating to closure and transfer of functions of the United States Bureau of Mines, see Transfer of Functions note set out under 30 U.S.C.A. § 1.

Prior Provisions

A prior section 1224, Pub. L. No. 95–87, Title III, § 304, 91 Stat. 454 (Aug. 3, 1977), contained provisions similar to this section covering fiscal years 1978 through 1984.

§ 1225. Effect on colleges and universities

[MMRRIA § 5]

Nothing in this subchapter shall be construed to impair or modify the legal relationship existing between any of the colleges or universities under whose direction an institute is established and the government of the State in which it is located, and nothing in this subchapter shall in any way be construed to authorize Federal control or direction of education at any college or university.

(Pub. L. No. 98–409, § 5, 98 Stat. 1539 (Aug. 29, 1984).)

HISTORICAL AND STATUTORY NOTES

Codifications

Section was not enacted as part of the Surface Mining Control and Reclamation Act of 1977 which comprises this chapter.

Prior Provisions

A prior section 1225, Pub. L. No. 95–87, Title III, § 305, 91 Stat. 454 (Aug. 3, 1977), contained provisions similar to this section covering fiscal years 1978 through 1984.

§ 1226. Research

[MMRRIA § 6]

(a) Coordination with existing programs; availability of information to public

The Secretary shall obtain the continuing advice and cooperation of all agencies of the Federal Government concerned with mining and mineral resources, of State and local governments, and of private institutions and individuals to assure that the programs authorized by this subchapter will supplement and not be redundant with respect to established mining and minerals research programs, and to stimulate research in otherwise neglected areas, and to contribute to a comprehensive nationwide program of mining and minerals research, with due regard for the protection and conservation of the environment. The Secretary shall make generally available information and reports on projects completed, in progress, or planned under the provisions of this subchapter, in addition to any direct publication of information by the institutes themselves.

(b) Effect on Federal agencies

Nothing in this subchapter is intended to give or shall be construed as giving the Secretary any authority over mining and mineral resources research conducted by any agency of the Federal Government, or as repealing or diminishing existing authorities or responsibilities of any agency of the Federal Government to plan and conduct, contract for, or assist in research in its area of responsibility and concern with regard to mining and mineral resources.

(c) Availability of results to public

No research, demonstration, or experiment shall be carried out under this subchapter by an institute financed by grants under this subchapter, unless all uses, products, processes, patents, and other developments resulting therefrom, with such exception or limitation, if any, as the Secretary may find necessary in the public interest, are made available promptly to the general public. Patentable inventions shall be governed by the provisions of Public Law 96–517. Nothing contained in this section shall deprive the owner of any background patent relating to any such activities of any rights which that owner may have under that patent.

(d) Authorization of appropriations

(1) There is authorized to be appropriated to the Secretary $450,000 for each of the fiscal years ending September 30, 1990, through September 30, 1994, to administer this subchapter. No funds may be withheld by the Secretary for administrative expenses from those authorized to be appropriated by sections 1221 and 1222 of this title.

(2) There are authorized to be appropriated to the Secretary such sums as are necessary for the printing and publishing of the results of activities carried out by institutes and generic mineral technology centers under this subchapter, but such appropriations shall not exceed $550,000 in any single fiscal year.

(Pub. L. No. 98–409, § 6, 98 Stat. 1539 (Aug. 29, 1984); as amended by Pub. L. No. 100–483, § 7, 102 Stat. 2340 (Oct. 12, 1988).)

HISTORICAL AND STATUTORY NOTES

References in Text

Public Law 96–517, referred to in subsec. (c), is Pub. L. No. 96–517, 94 Stat. 3015 (Dec. 12, 1980). Section 6(a) of Pub. L. No. 96–517, relating to patent rights in inventions made with Federal assistance, is codified as chapter 18 (section 200 et seq.) of Title 35, Patents. For complete classification of this Act to the Code, see Tables.

Codifications

Section was not enacted as part of the Surface Mining Control and Reclamation Act of 1977 which comprises this chapter.

Prior Provisions

A prior section 1226, Pub. L. No. 95–87, Title III, § 306, 91 Stat. 454 (Aug. 3, 1977), contained provisions similar to this section covering fiscal years 1978 through 1984.

§ 1227. Center for cataloging

[MMRRIA § 7]

The Secretary shall establish a center for cataloging current and projected scientific research in all fields of mining and mineral resources. Each Federal agency doing mining and mineral resources research shall cooperate by providing the cataloging center with information on work underway or scheduled by it. The cataloging center shall classify and maintain for public use a catalog of mining and mineral resources research and investigation projects in progress or scheduled by all Federal agencies and by such non-Federal agencies of government, colleges, universities, private institutions, firms, and individuals as may make such information available.

(Pub. L. No. 98–409, § 7, 98 Stat. 1540 (Aug. 29, 1984).)

HISTORICAL AND STATUTORY NOTES

Codifications

Section was not enacted as part of the Surface Mining Control and Reclamation Act of 1977 which comprises this chapter.

Prior Provisions

A prior section 1227, Pub. L. No. 95–87, Title III, § 307, 91 Stat. 455 (Aug. 3, 1977), contained provisions similar to this section covering fiscal years 1978 through 1984.

§ 1228. Interagency cooperation

[MMRRIA § 8]

The President shall, by such means as he deems appropriate, clarify agency responsibility for Federal mining and mineral resources research and provide for interagency coordination of such research, including the research authorized by this subchapter. Such coordination shall include—

(1) continuing review of the adequacy of the Government-wide program in mining and mineral resources research;

(2) identification and elimination of duplication and overlap between agency programs;

(3) identification of technical needs in various mining and mineral resources research categories;

(4) recommendations with respect to allocation of technical effort among Federal agencies;

(5) review of technical manpower needs, and findings concerning management policies to improve the quality of the Government-wide research effort; and

(6) actions to facilitate interagency communication at management levels.

(Pub. L. No. 98–409, § 8, 98 Stat. 1540 (Aug. 29, 1984).)

HISTORICAL AND STATUTORY NOTES

Codifications

Section was not enacted as part of the Surface Mining Control and Reclamation Act of 1977 which comprises this chapter.

Prior Provisions

A prior section 1228, Pub. L. No. 95–87, Title III, § 308, 91 Stat. 455 (Aug. 3, 1977), contained provisions similar to this section covering fiscal years 1978 through 1984.

§ 1229. Committee on Mining and Mineral Resources Research [MMRRIA § 9]

(a) Appointment; composition

The Secretary shall appoint a Committee on Mining and Mineral Resources Research composed of—

(1) the Assistant Secretary of the Interior responsible for minerals and mining research, or his delegate;

(2) the Director, United States Bureau of Mines, or his delegate;

(3) the Director, United States Geological Survey, or his delegate;

(4) the Director of the National Science Foundation, or his delegate;

(5) the President, National Academy of Sciences, or his delegate;

(6) the President, National Academy of Engineering, or his delegate; and

(7) not more than 7 other persons who are knowledgeable in the fields of mining and mineral resources research, including two university administrators involved in the conduct of programs authorized by this subchapter, 3 representatives from the mining industry, a working miner, and a representative from the conservation community. In making these 7 appointments, the Secretary shall consult with interested groups.

(b) Consultation and recommendations

The Committee shall consult with, and make recommendations to, the Secretary on all matters relating to mining and mineral resources research and the determinations that are required to be made under this subchapter. The Secretary shall consult with, and consider recommendations of, such Committee in such matters.

(c) Compensation, travel, subsistence and related expenses

Committee members, other than officers or employees of Federal, State, or local governments, shall be, for each day (including traveltime) during which they are performing Committee business, paid at a rate fixed by the Secretary but not[1] excess of the daily equivalent of the maximum rate of pay for grade GS–18 of the General Schedule under section 5332 of Title 5, and shall be fully reimbursed for travel, subsistence, and related expenses.

(d) Chairmanship of Committee

The Committee shall be jointly chaired by the Assistant Secretary of the Interior responsible for minerals and mining and a person to be elected by the Committee from among the members referred to in paragraphs (5), (6), and (7) of subsection (a) of this section.

(e) National plan for research

The Committee shall develop a national plan for research in mining and mineral resources, considering ongoing efforts in the universities, the Federal Government, and the private sector, and shall formulate and recommend a program to implement the plan utilizing resources provided for under this subchapter. The Committee shall submit such plan to the Secretary, the President, and the Congress on or before March 1, 1986, and shall submit an annual update of such plan by January 15 of each calendar year.

(f) Application of Federal Advisory Committee Act

Section 10 of the Federal Advisory Committee Act (5 U.S.C. App.) shall not apply to the Committee.

(Pub. L. No. 98–409, § 9, 98 Stat. 1540 (Aug. 29, 1984); Pub. L. No. 100–483, §§ 8, 9, 102 Stat. 2340 (Oct. 12, 1988); Pub. L. No. 102–285, § 10(b), 106 Stat. 172 (May 18, 1992).)

[1] So in original. Probably should be followed by "in".

HISTORICAL AND STATUTORY NOTES

References in Text

The Federal Advisory Committee Act, referred to in subsec. (f), is Pub. L. No. 92–463, 86 Stat. 770 (Oct. 6, 1972), as amended, which is set out in the Appendix to Title 5, Government Organization and Employees.

Codifications

Section was not enacted as part of the Surface Mining Control and Reclamation Act of 1977 which comprises this chapter.

Termination of Reporting Requirements

For termination, effective May 15, 2000, of provisions in subsec. (e) of this section relating to the requirement to submit annual updates of the national plan to Congress, see Pub. L. No. 104–66, § 3003, as amended, set out as a note under 31 U.S.C.A. § 1113, and page 157 of House Document No. 103–7.

Change of Name

"United States Bureau of Mines" substituted for "Bureau of Mines" in subsec. (a)(2) pursuant to section 10(b) of Pub. L. No. 102–285, set out as a note under 30 U.S.C.A. § 1. For provisions relating to closure and transfer of functions of the United States Bureau of Mines, see Transfer of Functions note set out under 30 U.S.C.A. § 1.

Prior Provisions

A prior section 1229, Pub. L. No. 95–87, Title III, § 309, 91 Stat. 455 (Aug. 3, 1977), contained provisions similar to this section covering fiscal years 1978 through 1984.

Reports to Congressional Committees

Section 11 of Pub. L. No. 100–483 provided that:

"(a) Report on Programs.—The Committee on Mining and Mineral Resources Research established under section 9 of the Mining and Mineral Resources Research Institute Act of 1984 (30 U.S.C. 1229) [this section] shall submit a report by January 15, 1992, to the Committee on Interior and Insular Affairs [now Committee on Natural Resources] of the United States House of Representatives and the Committee on Energy and Natural Resources of the United States Senate on the programs established under that Act [this subchapter]. Such report may be submitted in conjunction with the annual plan update required by section 9(e) of such Act (30 U.S.C. 1229(e)) [subsec. (e) of this section] and shall include, but not necessarily be limited to, each of the following:

"(1) A review of the activities of the institutes and generic mineral technology centers established under the Mining and Mineral Resources Research Institute Act of 1984 [this subchapter].

"(2) A review of each institute's eligibility pursuant to section 10 of the Mining and Mineral Resources Research Institute Act of 1984 (30 U.S.C. 1230) [section 1230 of this title].

"(3) A review of each generic mineral technology center's eligibility. In conducting such review the committee shall consider the following criteria:

"(A) Relevance and effectiveness of the research conducted.

"(B) Need for further research in the generic area.

"(4) Recommendations on establishing a mechanism by which new generic mineral technology centers can be established and existing centers can be phased-out or consolidated upon the completion of their mission.

"(b) Report on Proposal for Center.—The committee shall submit a proposal to establish a Generic Mineral Technology Center on Strategic and Critical Minerals to the Committee on Interior and Insular Affairs [now Committee on Natural Resources] of the United States House of Representatives and the Committee on Energy and Natural Resources of the United States Senate by January 15, 1990."

§ 1230. Eligibility criteria

[MMRRIA § 10]

(a) The Committee shall determine the eligibility of a college or university to participate as a mining and mineral resources research institute under this subchapter using criteria which include—

(1) the presence of a substantial program of graduate instruction and research in mining or mineral extraction or closely related fields which has a demonstrated history of achievement;

(2) evidence of institutional commitment for the purposes of this subchapter;

(3) evidence that such institution has or can obtain significant industrial cooperation in activities within the scope of this subchapter; and

(4) the presence of an engineering program in mining or minerals extraction that is accredited by the Accreditation Board for Engineering and Technology, or evidence of equivalent institutional capability as determined by the Committee.

(b) **(1)** Notwithstanding the provisions of subsection (a) of this section, those colleges or universities which, on October 12, 1988, have a mining or mineral resources research institute program which has been found to be eligible pursuant to this subchapter shall continue to be eligible subject to review at least once during the period authorized by the Mining and Mineral Resources Research Institute Amendments of 1988, under the provisions of subsection (a) of this section. The results of such review shall be submitted by January 15, 1992, pursuant to section 11(a)(2) of the Mining and Mineral Resources Research Institute Amendments of 1988.

(2) Generic mineral technology centers established by the Secretary under this subchapter are to be composed of institutes eligible pursuant to subsection (a) of this section. Existing generic mineral technology centers shall continue to be eligible under this subchapter subject to at least one review prior to January 15, 1992, pursuant to section 11(a)(3) of the Mining and Mineral Resources Research Institute Amendments of 1988.

(Pub. L. No. 98–409, § 10, 98 Stat. 1541 (Aug. 29, 1984); as amended by Pub. L. No. 100–483, § 10, 102 Stat. 2340 (Oct. 12, 1988).)

HISTORICAL AND STATUTORY NOTES

References in Text

The Mining and Mineral Resources Research Institute Amendments of 1988, referred to in subsec. (b)(1), is Pub. L. No. 100–483, 102 Stat. 2341 (Oct. 12, 1988), which amended this subchapter. Section 11(a)(2), (3) of such Amendments of 1988, referred to in subsec. (b)(1), (2), is set out as a note under section 1229 of this title. For complete classification of this Act to the Code, see Short Title of 1988 Amendment note under section 1201 of this title and Tables.

Codifications

Section was not enacted as part of the Surface Mining Control and Reclamation Act of 1977 which comprises this chapter.

§ 1230a. Strategic Resources Generic Mineral Technology Center

[MMRRIA § 12]

(a) Establishment

The Secretary of[1] Interior is authorized and directed to establish a Strategic Resources Mineral Technology Center (hereinafter referred to as the "center") for the purpose of improving existing, and developing new, technologies that will decrease the dependence of the United States on supplies of strategic and critical minerals.

(b) Functions

The center shall—

(1) provide for studies and technology development in the areas of mineral extraction and refining processes, product substitution and conservation of mineral resources through recycling and advanced processing and fabrication methods;

(2) identify new deposits of strategic and critical mineral resources; and

(3) facilitate the transfer of information, studies, and technologies developed by the center to the private sector.

(c) Criteria

The Secretary shall establish the center referred to in subsection (a) of this section at a university that—

(1) does not currently host a generic mineral technology center;

(2) has established advanced degree programs in geology and geological engineering, and metallurgical and mining engineering;

(3) has expertise in materials and advanced processing research; and

(4) is located west of the 100th meridian.

(d) Authorization of appropriations

There is authorized to be appropriated such sums as may be necessary to carry out this section.

(Pub. L. No. 98–409, § 12, as added by Pub. L. No. 101–498, § 2, 104 Stat. 1207 (Nov. 2, 1990).)

[1] So in original. Probably should be "of the".

SURFACE MINING CONTROL AND RECLAMATION ACT OF 1977 [SMCRA § ______]

(30 U.S.C.A. §§ 1231 to 1244, 1251 to 1279, 1281, 1291 to 1309b, 1311 to 1316, 1321 to 1328)

SUBCHAPTER IV—ABANDONED MINE RECLAMATIONS

§ 1231. Abandoned Mine Reclamation Fund

[SMCRA § 401]

(a) Establishment; administration; State funds

There is created on the books of the Treasury of the United States a trust fund to be known as the Abandoned Mine Reclamation Fund (hereinafter referred to as the "fund") which shall be administered by the Secretary of the Interior. State abandoned mine reclamation funds (State funds) generated by grants from this subchapter shall be established by each State pursuant to an approved State program.

(b) Sources of deposits to fund

The fund shall consist of amounts deposited in the fund, from time to time derived from—

(1) the reclamation fees levied under section 1232 of this title;

(2) any user charge imposed on or for land reclaimed pursuant to this subchapter, after expenditures for maintenance have been deducted;

(3) donations by persons, corporations, associations, and foundations for the purposes of this subchapter;

(4) recovered moneys as provided for in this subchapter; and

(5) interest credited to the fund under subsection (e) of this section.

(c) Use of moneys

Moneys in the fund may be used for the following purposes:

(1) reclamation and restoration of land and water resources adversely affected by past coal mining, including but not limited to reclamation and restoration of abandoned surface mine areas, abandoned coal processing areas, and abandoned coal refuse disposal areas; sealing and filling abandoned deep mine entries and voids; planting of land adversely affected by past coal mining to prevent erosion and sedimentation; prevention, abatement, treatment, and control of water pollution created by coal mine drainage including restoration of stream beds, and construction and operation of water treatment plants; prevention, abatement, and control of burning coal refuse disposal areas and burning coal in situ; prevention, abatement, and control of coal mine subsidence; and establishment of self-sustaining, individual State administered programs to insure private property against damages caused by land subsidence resulting from underground coal mining in those States which have reclamation plans approved in accordance with section 1253 of this title: *Provided*, That funds used for this purpose shall not exceed $3,000,000 of the funds made available to any State under section 1232(g)(1) of this title;

(2) acquisition and filling of voids and sealing of tunnels, shafts, and entryways under section 1239 of this title;

(3) acquisition of land as provided for in this subchapter;

(4) enforcement and collection of the reclamation fee provided for in section 1232 of this title;

(5) restoration, reclamation, abatement, control, or prevention of adverse effects of coal mining which constitutes an emergency as provided for in this subchapter;

(6) grants to the States to accomplish the purposes of this subchapter;

(7) administrative expenses of the United States and each State to accomplish the purposes of this subchapter;

(8) for use under section 1240a of this title;

(9) for the purpose of section 1257(c) of this title, except that not more than $10,000,000 shall annually be available for such purpose;

(10) for the purpose described in section 1232(h) of this title; and

(11) all other necessary expenses to accomplish the purposes of this subchapter.

(12) Redesignated (10)

(13) Redesignated (11)

(d) Availability of moneys; no fiscal year limitation

(1) In general

Moneys from the fund for expenditures under subparagraphs (A) through (D) of section 1232(g)(3) of this title shall be available only when appropriated for those subparagraphs.

(2) No fiscal year limitation

Appropriations described in paragraph (1) shall be made without fiscal year limitation.

(3) Other purposes

Moneys from the fund shall be available for all other purposes of this subchapter without prior appropriation as provided in subsection (f) of this section.

(e) Interest

The Secretary of the Interior shall notify the Secretary of the Treasury as to what portion of the fund is not, in his judgment, required to meet current withdrawals. The Secretary of the Treasury shall invest such portion of the fund in public debt securities with maturities suitable for achieving the purposes of the transfers under section 1232(h) of this title and bearing interest at rates determined by the Secretary of the Treasury, taking into consideration current market yields on outstanding marketable obligations of the

United States of comparable maturities. The income on such investments shall be credited to, and form a part of, the fund for the purpose of the transfers under section 1232(h) of this title.

(f) General limitation on obligation authority

(1) In general

from amounts deposited into the fund under subsection (b) of this section, the Secretary shall distribute during each fiscal year beginning after September 30, 2007, an amount determined under paragraph (2).

(2) Amounts

(A) For fiscal years 2008 through 2022

For each of fiscal years 2008 through 2022, the amount distributed by the Secretary under this subsection shall be equal to—

(i) the amounts deposited into the fund under paragraphs (1), (2), and (4) of subsection (b) of this section for the preceding fiscal year that were allocated under paragraphs (1) and (5) of section 1232(g) of this title; plus

(ii) the amount needed for the adjustment under section 1232(g)(8) of this title for the current fiscal year.

(B) Fiscal years 2023 and thereafter

For fiscal year 2023 and each fiscal year thereafter, to the extent that funds are available, the Secretary shall distribute an amount equal to the amount distributed under subparagraph (A) during fiscal year 2022.

(3) Distribution

(A) In general

Except as provided in subparagraph (B), for each fiscal year, of the amount to be distributed to States and Indian tribes pursuant to paragraph (2), the Secretary shall distribute—

(i) the amounts allocated under paragraph (1) of section 1232(g) of this title, the amounts allocated under paragraph (5) of section 1232(g) of this title, and any amount reallocated under section 1240a(h)(3) of this title in accordance with section 1240a(h)(2) of this title, for grants to States and Indian tribes under section 1232(g)(5) of this title; and

(ii) the amounts allocated under section 1232(g)(8) of this title.

(B) Exclusion

Beginning on October 1, 2007, certified States shall be ineligible to receive amounts under section 1232(g)(1) of this title.

(4) Availability

Amounts in the fund available to the Secretary for obligation under this subsection shall be available until expended.

(5) Addition

(A) In general

Subject to subparagraph (B), the amount distributed under this subsection for each fiscal year shall be in addition to the amount appropriated from the fund during the fiscal year.

(B) Exceptions

Notwithstanding paragraph (3), the amount distributed under this subsection for the first 4 fiscal years beginning on and after October 1, 2007, shall be equal to the following percentage of the amount otherwise required to be distributed:

(i) 50 percent in fiscal year 2008.

(ii) 50 percent in fiscal year 2009.

(iii) 75 percent in fiscal year 2010.

(iv) 75 percent in fiscal year 2011.

(Pub. L. No. 95–87, Title IV, § 401, 91 Stat. 456 (Aug. 3, 1977); as amended by Pub. L. No. 98–473, Title I, § 101(c), 98 Stat. 1875 (Oct. 12, 1984); Pub. L. No. 101–508, Title VI, § 6002, 104 Stat. 1388–289 (Nov. 5, 1990); Pub. L. No. 102–486, Title XIX, § 19143(b)(3)(A), Title XXV, § 2504(c)(1), 106 Stat. 3056, 3105 (Oct. 24, 1992); Pub. L. No. 109–432, Div. C, Title II, § 201(a), 120 Stat. 3006 (Dec. 20, 2006).)

HISTORICAL AND STATUTORY NOTES

References in Text

This subchapter, referred to in text, originally read "this title", meaning Pub. L. No. 95–87, Title IV, 91 Stat. 456 (Aug. 3, 1977), as amended, which enacted this subchapter.

Effective and Applicability Provisions

1990 Acts. Section 6014 of Pub. L. No. 101–508 provided that: "The amendments made by this subtitle [enacting section 1240a of this title, amending this section and sections 1232 to 1237, 1239, 1257 and 1302 of this title, and enacting provisions set out as notes under this section] shall take effect at the beginning of the first fiscal year immediately following the fiscal year in which this subtitle is enacted [Pub. L. No. 101–508 was approved on Nov. 5, 1990; the next fiscal year began on Oct. 1, 1991]."

Savings Provisions

Section 6013 of Pub. L. No. 101–508 provided that: "Nothing in this subtitle [Subtitle A (section 6001 et seq.) of Pub. L. No. 101–508, Title VI, 104 Stat. 1388–289 (Nov. 5, 1990), for distribution of which, see Short Title of 1990 Amendment note set out under section 1201 of title and Tables] shall be construed to affect the certifications made by the State of Wyoming, the State of Montana, and the State of Louisiana to the Secretary of the Interior prior to the date of enactment of this subtitle [Nov. 5, 1990] that such State has completed the reclamation of eligible abandoned coal mine lands."

Abandoned Mine Reclamation Fund; Donations for Projects Under the Appalachian Clean Streams Initiative and Under the Western Mine Lands Restoration Partnership Initiative

Pub. L. No. 105–277, § 101(e) [Title I], 112 Stat. 2681–245 (Oct. 21, 1998), provided in part that: "[H]ereafter, donations received to support projects under the Appalachian Clean Streams Initiative and under the Western Mine Lands Restoration Partnerships Initiative, pursuant to 30 U.S.C. 1231 [this section], shall be credited to this account and remain available until expended without further appropriation for projects sponsored under these initiatives, directly through agreements with other Federal agencies, or through grants to States, and funding to local governments, or tax exempt private entities."

Abandoned Mine Reclamation Research and Development

Pub. L. No. 99–509, Title III, § 3501, 100 Stat. 1891 (Oct. 21, 1986), provided that: "After the enactment of this Act [Oct. 21, 1986], the research and demonstration authorities of the Department of the Interior under the provisions of section 401(c)(6) of the Surface Mining Control and Reclamation Act of 1977 (Public Law 95–87) [subsec. (c)(6) of this section] shall be transferred to, and carried out by, the Director of the Bureau of Mines. Research and demonstration projects under such provision shall be selected by a panel appointed by the Director of the Bureau of Mines to be comprised of 9 persons, including 4 representatives of State abandoned mine reclamation programs, 4 representatives of the Bureau of Mines, and one representative of the Office of Surface Mining Reclamation and Enforcement."

[Pub. L. No. 102–285, § 10(b), 106 Stat. 172 (May 18, 1992), provided that, on and after May 18, 1992, the Bureau of Mines is redesignated and shall thereafter be known as the United States Bureau of Mines. See note under section 1 of Title 30, Mineral Lands and Mining.]

§ 1232. Reclamation fee

[SMCRA § 402]

(a) Payment; rate

All operators of coal mining operations subject to the provisions of this chapter shall pay to the Secretary of the Interior, for deposit in the fund, a reclamation fee of 28 cents per ton of coal produced by surface coal mining and 12 cents per ton of coal produced by underground mining or 10 per centum of the value of the coal at the mine, as determined by the Secretary, whichever is less, except that the reclamation fee for lignite coal shall be at a rate of 2 per centum of the value of the coal at the mine, or 8 cents per ton, whichever is less.

(b) Due date

Such fee shall be paid no later than thirty days after the end of each calendar quarter beginning with the first calendar quarter occurring after August 3, 1977, and ending September 30, 2021.

(c) Submission of statement

Together with such reclamation fee, all operators of coal mine operations shall submit a statement of the amount of coal produced during the calendar quarter, the method of coal removal and the type of coal, the accuracy of which shall be sworn to by the operator and notarized. Such statement shall include an identification of the permittee of the surface coal mining operation, any operator in addition to the permittee, the owner of the coal, the preparation plant, tripple,[1] or loading point for the coal, and the person purchasing the coal from the operator. The report shall also specify the number of the permit required under section 1256 of this title and the mine safety and health identification number. Each quarterly report shall contain a notification of any changes in the information required by this subsection since the date of the preceding quarterly report. The information contained in the quarterly reports under this subsection shall be maintained by the Secretary in a computerized database.

(d) Penalty

(1) Any person, corporate officer, agent or director, on behalf of a coal mine operator, who knowingly makes any false statement, representation or certification, or knowingly fails to make any statement, representation or certification required in this section shall, upon conviction, be punished by a fine of not more than $10,000, or by imprisonment for not more than one year, or both.

(2) The Secretary shall conduct such audits of coal production and the payment of fees under this subchapter as may be necessary to ensure full compliance with the provisions of this subchapter. For purposes of performing such audits the Secretary (or any duly designated officer, employee, or representative of the Secretary) shall, at all reasonable times, upon request, have access to, and may copy, all books, papers, and other documents of any person subject to the provisions of this subchapter. The Secretary may at any time conduct audits of any surface coal mining and reclamation operation, including without limitation, tipples and preparation plants, as may be necessary in the judgment of the Secretary to ensure full and complete payment of the fees under this subchapter.

(e) Civil action to recover fee

Any portion of the reclamation fee not properly or promptly paid pursuant to this section shall be recoverable, with statutory interest, from coal mine operators, in any court of competent jurisdiction in any action at law to compel payment of debts.

(f) Cooperation from other agencies

All Federal and State agencies shall fully cooperate with the Secretary of the Interior in the enforcement of this section. Whenever the Secretary believes that any person has not paid the full amount of the fee payable under subsection (a) of this section the Secretary shall notify the Federal agency responsible for ensuring compliance with the provisions of section 4121 of Title 26.

(g) Allocation of funds

(1) Except as provided in subsection (h) of this section, moneys deposited into the fund shall be allocated by the Secretary to accomplish the purposes of this subchapter as follows:

(A) 50 percent of the reclamation fees collected annually in any State (other than fees collected with respect to Indian lands) shall be allocated annually by the Secretary to the State, subject to such State having each of the following:

(i) An approved abandoned mine reclamation program pursuant to section 1235 of this title.

(ii) Lands and waters which are eligible pursuant to section 1234 of this title (in the case of a State not certified under section 1240a(a) of this title) or pursuant to section 1240a(b) of this title (in the case of a State certified under section 1240a(a) of this title).

(B) 50 percent of the reclamation fees collected annually with respect to Indian lands shall be allocated annually by the Secretary to the Indian tribe having jurisdiction over such lands, subject to such tribe having each of the following:

(i) an[2] approved abandoned mine reclamation program pursuant to section 1235 of this title.

(ii) Lands and waters which are eligible pursuant to section 1234 of this title (in the case of an Indian tribe not certified under section 1240a(a) of this title) or pursuant to section 1240a(b) of this title (in the case of a tribe certified under section 1240a(a) of this title).

(C) The funds allocated by the Secretary under this paragraph to States and Indian tribes shall only be used for annual reclamation project construction and program administration grants.

(D) To the extent not expended within 3 years after the date of any grant award under this paragraph (except for grants awarded during fiscal years 2008, 2009, and 2010 to the extent not expended within 5 years), such grant shall be available for expenditure by the Secretary under paragraph (5).

(2) In making the grants referred to in paragraph (1)(C) and the grants referred to in paragraph (5), the Secretary shall ensure strict compliance by the States and Indian tribes with the priorities described in section 1233(a) of this title until a certification is made under section 1240a(a) of this title.

(3) Amounts available in the fund which are not allocated to States and Indian tribes under paragraph (1) or allocated under paragraph (5) are authorized to be expended by the Secretary for any of the following:

(A) For the purpose of section 1257(c) of this title, either directly or through grants to the States, subject to the limitation contained in section 1231(c)(9) of this title.

(B) For the purpose of section 1240 of this title (relating to emergencies).

(C) For the purpose of meeting the objectives of the fund set forth in section 1233(a) of this title for eligible lands and waters pursuant to section 1234 of this title in States and on Indian lands where the State or Indian tribe does not have an approved abandoned mine reclamation program pursuant to section 1235 of this title.

(D) For the administration of this subchapter by the Secretary.

(E) For the purpose of paragraph (8).

(4) **(A)** Amounts available in the fund which are not allocated under paragraphs (1), (2), and (5) or expended under paragraph (3) in any fiscal year are authorized to be expended by the Secretary under this paragraph for the reclamation or drainage abatement of lands and waters within unreclaimed sites which are mined for coal or which were affected by such mining, wastebanks, coal processing or other coal mining processes and left in an inadequate reclamation status.

(B) Funds made available under this paragraph may be used for reclamation or drainage abatement at a site referred to in subparagraph (A) if the Secretary makes either of the following findings:

(i) A finding that the surface coal mining operation occurred during the period beginning on August 4, 1977, and ending on or before the date on which the Secretary approved a State program pursuant to section 1253 of this title for a State in which the site is located, and that any funds for reclamation or abatement which are available pursuant to a bond or other form of financial guarantee or from any other source are not sufficient to provide for adequate reclamation or abatement at the site.

(ii) A finding that the surface coal mining operation occurred during the period beginning on August 4, 1977, and ending on or before November 5, 1990, and that the surety of such mining operator became insolvent during such period, and as of November 5, 1990, funds immediately available from proceedings relating to such insolvency, or from any financial guarantee or other source are not sufficient to provide for adequate reclamation or abatement at the site.

(C) In determining which sites to reclaim pursuant to this paragraph, the Secretary shall follow the priorities stated in paragraphs (1) and (2) of section 1233(a) of this title. The Secretary shall ensure that priority is given to those sites which are in the immediate vicinity of a residential area or which have an adverse economic impact upon a local community.

(D) Amounts collected from the assessment of civil penalties under section 1268 of this title are authorized to be appropriated to carry out this paragraph.

(E) Any State may expend grants made available under paragraphs (1) and (5) for reclamation and abatement of any site referred to in subparagraph (A) if the State, with the concurrence of the Secretary, makes either of the findings referred to in clause (i) or (ii) of subparagraph (B) and if the State determines that the reclamation priority of the site is the same or more urgent than the reclamation priority for eligible lands and waters pursuant to section 1234 of this title under the priorities stated in paragraphs (1) and (2) of section 1233(a) of this title.

(F) For the purposes of the certification referred to in section 1240a(a) of this title, sites referred to in subparagraph (A) of this paragraph shall be considered as having the same priorities as those stated in section 1233(a) of this title for eligible lands and waters pursuant to section 1234 of this title. All sites referred to in subparagraph (A) of this paragraph within any State shall be reclaimed prior to such State making the certification referred to in section 1240a(a) of this title.

(5) **(A)** The Secretary shall allocate 60 percent of the amount in the fund after making the allocation referred to in paragraph (1) for making additional annual grants to States and Indian tribes which are not certified under section 1240a(a) of this title to supplement grants received by such States and Indian tribes pursuant to paragraph (1)(C) until the priorities stated in paragraphs (1) and (2) of section 1233(a) of this title have been achieved by such State or Indian tribe. The allocation of such funds for the purpose of making such expenditures shall be through a formula based on the amount of coal historically produced in the State or from the Indian lands concerned prior to August 3, 1977. Funds made available under paragraph (3) or (4) of this subsection for any State or Indian tribe shall not be deducted against any allocation of funds to the State or Indian tribe under paragraph (1) or under this paragraph.

(B) Any amount that is reallocated and available under section 1240a(h)(3) of this title shall be in addition to amounts that are allocated under subparagraph (A).

(6) **(A)** Any State with an approved abandoned mine reclamation program pursuant to section 1235 of this title may receive and retain, without regard to the 3-year limitation referred to in paragraph (1)(D), up to 30 percent of the total of the grants made annually to the State under paragraphs (1) and (5) if those amounts are deposited into an acid mine drainage abatement and treatment fund established under State law, from which amounts (together with all interest earned on the amounts) are expended by the State for the abatement of the causes and the treatment of the effects of acid mine drainage in a comprehensive manner within qualified hydrologic units affected by coal mining practices.

(B) In this paragraph, the term "qualified hydrologic unit" means a hydrologic unit—

(i) in which the water quality has been significantly affected by acid mine drainage from coal mining practices in a manner that adversely impacts biological resources; and

(ii) that contains land and water that are—

(I) eligible pursuant to section 1234 of this title and include any of the priorities described in section 1233(a) of this title; and

(II) the subject of expenditures by the State from the forfeiture of bonds required under section 1259 of this title or from other States sources to abate and treat acid mine drainage.

(7) In complying with the priorities described in section 1233(a) of this title, any State or Indian tribe may use amounts available in grants made annually to the State or tribe under paragraphs (1) and (5) for the reclamation of eligible land and water described in section 1233(a)(3) of this title before the completion of reclamation projects under paragraphs (1) and (2) of section 1233(a) of this title only if the expenditure of funds for the reclamation is done in conjunction with the expenditure before, on, or after December 20, 2006 of funds for reclamation projects under paragraphs (1) and (2) of section 1233(a) of this title.

(8) (A) In making funds available under this subchapter, the Secretary shall ensure that the grant awards total not less than $3,000,000 annually to each State and each Indian tribe having an approved abandoned mine reclamation program pursuant to section 1235 of this title and eligible land and water pursuant to section 1234 of this title, so long as an allocation of funds to the State or tribe is necessary to achieve the priorities stated in paragraphs (1) and (2) of section 1233(a) of this title.

(B) Notwithstanding any other provision of law, this paragraph applies to the States of Tennessee and Missouri.

(h) Transfers of interest earned by fund

(1) In general

(A) Transfers to Combined Benefit Fund

As soon as practicable after the beginning of fiscal year 2007 and each fiscal year thereafter, and before making any allocation with respect to the fiscal year under subsection (g) of this section, the Secretary shall use an amount not to exceed the amount of interest that the Secretary estimates will be earned and paid to the fund during the fiscal year to transfer to the Combined Benefit Fund such amounts as are estimated by the trustees of such fund to offset the amount of any deficit in net assets in the Combined Benefit Fund as of October 1, 2006, and to make the transfer described in paragraph (2)(A).

(B) Transfers to 1992 and 1993 plans

As soon as practicable after the beginning of fiscal year 2008 and each fiscal year thereafter, and before making any allocation with respect to the fiscal year under subsection (g) of this section, the Secretary shall use an amount not to exceed the amount of interest that the Secretary estimates will be earned and paid to the fund during the fiscal year (reduced by the amount used under subparagraph (A)) to make the transfers described in paragraphs (2)(B) and (2)(C).

(2) Transfers described

The transfers referred to in paragraph (1) are the following:

(A) United Mine Workers of America Combined Benefit Fund

A transfer to the United Mine Workers of America Combined Benefit Fund equal to the amount that the trustees of the Combined Benefit Fund estimate will be expended from the fund for the fiscal year in which the transfer is made, reduced by—

(i) the amount the trustees of the Combined Benefit Fund estimate the Combined Benefit Fund will receive during the fiscal year in—

(I) required premiums; and

(II) payments paid by Federal agencies in connection with benefits provided by the Combined Benefit Fund; and

(ii) the amount the trustees of the Combined Benefit Fund estimate will be expended during the fiscal year to provide health benefits to beneficiaries who are unassigned beneficiaries solely as a result of the application of section 9706(h)(1) of Title 26, but only to the extent that such amount does not exceed the amounts described in subsection (i)(1)(A) that the Secretary estimates will be available to pay such estimated expenditures.

(B) United Mine Workers of America 1992 Benefit Plan

A transfer to the United Mine Workers of America 1992 Benefit Plan, in an amount equal to the difference between—

(i) the amount that the trustees of the 1992 UMWA Benefit Plan estimate will be expended from the 1992 UMWA Benefit Plan during the next calendar year to provide the benefits required by the 1992 UMWA Benefit Plan on December 20, 2006; minus

(ii) the amount that the trustees of the 1992 UMWA Benefit Plan estimate the 1992 UMWA Benefit Plan will receive during the next calendar year in—

(I) required monthly per beneficiary premiums, including the amount of any security provided to the 1992 UMWA Benefit Plan that is available for use in the provision of benefits; and

(II) payments paid by Federal agencies in connection with benefits provided by the 1992 UMWA Benefit Plan.

(C) Multiemployer Health Benefit Plan

(i) Transfer to the plan.—A transfer to the Multiemployer Health Benefit Plan established after July 20, 1992, by the parties that are the settlors of the 1992 UMWA Benefit Plan referred to in subparagraph (B) (referred to in this subparagraph and subparagraph (D) as "the Plan"), in an amount equal to the excess (if any) of—

(I) the amount that the trustees of the Plan estimate will be expended from the Plan during the next calendar year, to provide benefits no greater than those provided by the Plan as of December 31, 2006; over

(II) the amount that the trustees estimated the Plan will receive during the next calendar year in payments paid by Federal agencies in connection with benefits provided by the Plan.

(ii) Calculation of excess.—The excess determined under clause (i) shall be calculated by taking into account only—

(I) those beneficiaries actually enrolled in the Plan as of May 5, 2017, who are eligible to receive health benefits under the Plan on the first day of the calendar year for which the transfer is made, other than those beneficiaries enrolled in the Plan under the terms of a participation agreement with the current or former employer of such beneficiaries;

(II) those beneficiaries whose health benefits, defined as those benefits payable, following death or retirement or upon a finding of disability, directly by an employer in the bituminous coal industry under a coal wage agreement (as defined in section 9701(b)(1) of Title 26), or a related coal wage agreement, would be denied or reduced as a result of a bankruptcy proceeding commenced in 2012, 2015, 2018, or 2019, orany year thereafter.

For purposes of subclause (I), a beneficiary enrolled in the Plan as of May 5, 2017, shall be deemed to have been eligible to receive health benefits under the Plan on January 1, 2020 (or, in the case of any such health benefits confirmed in any bankruptcy proceeding, would be subsequently denied or reduced); and

(III) the cost of administering the resolution of disputes process administered (as of the date of the enactment of the American Miners Benefits Improvement Act of 2020) by the Trustees of the Plan.

(iii) Eligibility of certain retirees.—Individuals referred to in clause (ii)(II) shall be treated as eligible to receive health benefits under the Plan.

(iv) Requirements for transfer.—The amount of the transfer otherwise determined under this subparagraph for a fiscal year shall be reduced by any amount transferred for the fiscal year to the Plan, to pay benefits required under the Plan, from a voluntary employees' beneficiary association established as a result of a bankruptcy proceeding described in clause (ii).

(v) Veba transfer.—The administrator of such voluntary employees' beneficiary association shall transfer to the Plan any amounts received as a result of such bankruptcy proceeding, reduced by an amount for administrative costs of such association.

(vi) Related Coal Wage Agreement.—For purposes of clause (ii), the term 'related coal wage agreement' means an agreement between the United Mine Workers of America and an employer in the bituminous coal industry that—

(I) is a signatory operator; or

(II) is or was a debtor in a bankruptcy proceeding that was consolidated, administratively or otherwise, with the bankruptcy proceeding of a signatory operator or a related person to a signatory operator (as those terms are defined in section 9701(c) of the Internal Revenue Code of 1986).

(D) Individuals considered enrolled

For purposes of subparagraph (C), any individual who was eligible to receive benefits from the Plan as of the date of enactment of this subsection, even though benefits were being provided to the individual pursuant to a settlement agreement approved by order of a bankruptcy court entered on or before September 30, 2004, will be considered to be actually enrolled in the Plan and shall receive benefits from the Plan beginning on December 31, 2006.

(3) Adjustment

If, for any fiscal year, the amount of a transfer under subparagraph (A), (B), or (C) of paragraph (2) is more or less than the amount required to be transferred under that subparagraph, the Secretary shall appropriately adjust the amount transferred under that subparagraph for the next fiscal year.

(4) Additional amounts

(A) Previously credited interest

Notwithstanding any other provision of law, any interest credited to the fund that has not previously been transferred to the Combined Benefit Fund referred to in paragraph (2)(A) under this section—

(i) shall be held in reserve by the Secretary until such time as necessary to make the payments under subparagraphs (A) and (B) of subsection (i)(1) of this section, as described in clause (ii); and

(ii) in the event that the amounts described in subsection (i)(1) are insufficient to make the maximum payments described in subparagraphs (A) and (B) of subsection (i)(1) of this section, shall be used by the Secretary to supplement the payments so that the maximum amount permitted under those paragraphs is paid.

(B) Previously allocated amounts

All amounts allocated under subsection (g)(2) of this section before December 20, 2006, for the program described in section 1236 of this title but not appropriated before that date, shall be available to the Secretary to make the transfers described in paragraph (2).

(C) Adequacy of previously credited interest

The Secretary shall—

(i) consult with the trustees of the plans described in paragraph (2) at reasonable intervals; and

(ii) notify Congress if a determination is made that the amounts held in reserve under subparagraph (A) are insufficient to meet future requirements under subparagraph (A)(ii).

(D) Additional reserve amounts

In addition to amounts held in reserve under subparagraph (A), there is authorized to be appropriated such sums as may be necessary for transfer to the fund to carry out the purposes of subparagraph (A)(ii).

(E) Inapplicability of cap

The limitation described in subsection (i)(3)(A) of this section shall not apply to payments made from the reserve fund under this paragraph.

(5) Limitations

(A) Availability of funds for next fiscal year

The Secretary may make transfers under subparagraphs (B) and (C) of paragraph (2) for a calendar year only if the Secretary determines, using actuarial projections provided by the trustees of the Combined Benefit Fund referred to in paragraph (2)(A), that amounts will be available under paragraph (1), after the transfer, for the next fiscal year for making the transfer under paragraph (2)(A).

(B) Rate of contributions of obligors

(i) In general

(I) Rate

A transfer under paragraph (2)(C) shall not be made for a calendar year unless the persons that are obligated to contribute to the plan referred to in paragraph (2)(C) on the date of the transfer are obligated to make the contributions at rates that are no less than those in effect on the date which is 30 days before December 20, 2006.

(II) Application

The contributions described in subclause (I) shall be applied first to the provision of benefits to those plan beneficiaries who are not described in paragraph (2)(C)(ii).

(ii) Initial contributions

(I) In general

From December 20, 2006, through December 31, 2010, the persons that, on December 20, 2006, are obligated to contribute to the plan referred to in paragraph (2)(C) shall be obligated, collectively, to make contributions equal to the amount described in paragraph (2)(C), less the amount actually transferred due to the operation of subparagraph (C).

(II) First calendar year

Calendar year 2006 is the first calendar year for which contributions are required under this clause.

(III) Amount of contribution for 2006

Except as provided in subclause (IV), the amount described in paragraph (2)(C) for calendar year 2006 shall be calculated as if paragraph (2)(C) had been in effect during 2005.

(IV) Limitation

The contributions required under this clause for calendar year 2006 shall not exceed the amount necessary for solvency of the plan described in paragraph (2)(C), measured as of December 31, 2006, and taking into account all assets held by the plan as of that date.

(iii) Division

The collective annual contribution obligation required under clause (ii) shall be divided among the persons subject to the obligation, and applied uniformly, based on the hours worked for which contributions referred to in clause (i) would be owed.

(C) Phase-in of transfers

For each of calendar years 2008 through 2010, the transfers required under subparagraphs (B) and (C) of paragraph (2) shall equal the following amounts:

(i) For calendar year 2008, the Secretary shall make transfers equal to 25 percent of the amounts that would otherwise be required under subparagraphs (B) and (C) of paragraph (2).

(ii) For calendar year 2009, the Secretary shall make transfers equal to 50 percent of the amounts that would otherwise be required under subparagraphs (B) and (C) of paragraph (2).

(iii) For calendar year 2010, the Secretary shall make transfers equal to 75 percent of the amounts that would otherwise be required under subparagraphs (B) and (C) of paragraph (2).

(i) Funding

(1) In general

Subject to paragraph (3), out of any funds in the Treasury not otherwise appropriated, the Secretary of the Treasury shall transfer to the plans described in subsection (h)(2) of this section such sums as are necessary to pay the following amounts:

(A) To the Combined Fund (as defined in section 9701(a)(5) of Title 26 and referred to in this paragraph as the "Combined Fund"), the amount that the trustees of the Combined Fund estimate will be expended from premium accounts maintained by the Combined Fund for the fiscal year to provide benefits for beneficiaries who are unassigned beneficiaries solely as a result of the application of section 9706(h)(1) of Title 26, subject to the following limitations:

(i) For fiscal year 2008, the amount paid under this subparagraph shall equal—

(I) the amount described in subparagraph (A); minus

(II) the amounts required under section 9706(h)(3)(A) of Title 26.

(ii) For fiscal year 2009, the amount paid under this subparagraph shall equal—

(I) the amount described in subparagraph (A); minus

(II) the amounts required under section 9706(h)(3)(B) of Title 26.

(iii) For fiscal year 2010, the amount paid under this subparagraph shall equal—

(I) the amount described in subparagraph (A); minus

(II) the amounts required under section 9706(h)(3)(C) of Title 26.

(B) On certification by the trustees of any plan described in subsection (h)(2) of this section that the amount available for transfer by the Secretary pursuant to this section (determined after application of any limitation under subsection (h)(5) of this section) is less than the amount required to be transferred, to the plan the amount necessary to meet the requirement of subsection (h)(2) of this section.

(C) To the Combined Fund, $9,000,000 on October 1, 2007, $9,000,000 on October 1, 2008, $9,000,000 on October 1, 2009, and $9,000,000 on October 1, 2010 (which amounts shall not be exceeded) to provide a refund of any premium (as described in section 9704(a) of Title 26) paid on or before September 7, 2000, to the Combined Fund, plus interest on the premium calculated at the rate of 7.5 percent per year, on a proportional basis and to be paid not later than 60 days after the date on which each payment is received by the Combined Fund, to those signatory operators (to the extent that the Combined Fund has not previously returned the premium amounts to the operators), or any related persons to the operators (as defined in section 9701(c) of Title 26), or their heirs, successors, or assigns who have been denied the refunds as the result of final judgments or settlements if—

(i) prior to December 20, 2006, the signatory operator (or any related person to the operator)—

(I) had all of its beneficiary assignments made under section 9706 of Title 26 voided by the Commissioner of the Social Security Administration; and

(II) was subject to a final judgment or final settlement of litigation adverse to a claim by the operator that the assignment of beneficiaries under section 9706 of Title 26 was unconstitutional as applied to the operator; and

(ii) on or before September 7, 2000, the signatory operator (or any related person to the operator) had paid to the Combined Fund any premium amount that had not been refunded.

(2) Payments to States and Indian tribes

Subject to paragraph (3), out of any funds in the Treasury not otherwise appropriated, the Secretary of the Treasury shall transfer to the Secretary of the Interior for distribution to States and Indian tribes such sums as are necessary to pay amounts described in paragraphs (1)(A) and (2)(A) of section 1240a(h) of this title.

(3) Limitations

(A) Cap

The total amount transferred under this subsection for any fiscal year shall not exceed $750,000,000.

(B) Insufficient amounts

In a case in which the amount required to be transferred without regard to this paragraph exceeds the maximum annual limitation in subparagraph (A), the Secretary shall adjust the transfers of funds under paragraph (1) so that—

(i) each such transfer for the fiscal year is a percentage of the amount described;

(ii) the amount is determined without regard to subsection (h)(5)(A) of this section; and

(iii) the percentage transferred is the same for all transfers made under paragraph (1) for the fiscal year.

(C) Increase in Limitation to Account for Calculation of Health Benefit Plan Excess.—The dollar limitation under subparagraph (A) shall be increased by the amount of the cost to provide benefits which are taken into account under subsection (h)(2)(C)(ii) solely by reason of the amendments made by section 2(a) of the American Miner Benefits Improvement Act of 2020.

(4) Additional Amounts.—

(A) Calculation.—If the dollar limitation specified in paragraph (3)(A) exceeds the aggregate amount required to be transferred under paragraphs (1) and (2) for a fiscal year, the Secretary of the Treasury shall transfer an additional amount equal to the difference between such dollar limitation and such aggregate amount to the trustees of the 1974 UMWA Pension Plan to pay benefits required under that plan.

(B) Cessation of Transfers.—The transfers described in subparagraph (A) shall cease as of the first fiscal year beginning after the first plan year for which the funded percentage (as defined in section 432(j)(2) of the Internal Revenue Code of 1986) of the 1974 UMWA Pension Plan is at least 100 percent.

(C) Prohibition on Benefit Increases, Etc.—During a fiscal year in which the 1974 UMWA Pension Plan is receiving transfers under subparagraph (A), no amendment of such plan which increases the liabilities of the plan by reason of any increase in benefits, any change in the accrual of benefits, or any change in the rate at which benefits become nonforfeitable under the plan may be adopted unless the amendment is required as a condition of qualification under part I of subchapter D of chapter 1 of the Internal Revenue Code of 1986.

(D) Critical Status to Be Maintained.—Until such time as the 1974 UMWA Pension Plan ceases to be eligible for the transfers described in subparagraph (A)—

(i) the Plan shall be treated as if it were in critical status for purposes of sections 412(b)(3), 432(e)(3), and 4971(g)(1)(A) of the Internal Revenue Code of 1986 and sections 302(b)(3) and 305(e)(3) of the Employee Retirement Income Security Act;

(ii) the Plan shall maintain and comply with its rehabilitation plan under section 432(e) of such Code and section 305(e) of such Act, including any updates thereto; and

(iii) the provisions of subsections (c) and (d) of section 432 of such Code and subsections (c) and (d) of section 305 of such Act shall not apply.

(E) Treatment of Transfers for Purposes of Withdrawal Liability under ERISA.—The amount of any transfer made under subparagraph (A) (and any earnings attributable thereto) shall be disregarded in determining the unfunded vested benefits of the 1974 UMWA Pension Plan and the allocation of such unfunded vested benefits to an employer for purposes of determining the employer's withdrawal liability under section 4201 of the Employee Retirement Income Security Act of 1974.

(F) Requirement to Maintain Contribution Rate.—A transfer under subparagraph (A) shall not be made for a fiscal year unless the persons that are obligated to contribute to the 1974 UMWA Pension Plan on the date of the transfer are obligated to make the contributions at rates that are no less than those in effect on the date which is 30 days before the date of enactment of the Bipartisan American Miners Act of 2019.

(G) Enhanced Annual Reporting.—

(i) In General.—Not later than the 90th day of each plan year beginning after the date of enactment of the Bipartisan American Miners Act of 2019, the trustees of the 1974 UMWA Pension Plan shall file with the Secretary of the Treasury or the Secretary's delegate and the Pension Benefit Guaranty Corporation a report (including appropriate documentation and actuarial certifications from the plan actuary, as required by the Secretary of the Treasury or the Secretary's delegate) that contains—

(I) whether the plan is in endangered or critical status under section 305 of the Employee Retirement Income Security Act of 1974 and section 432 of the Internal Revenue Code of 1986 as of the first day of such plan year;

(II) the funded percentage (as defined in section 432(j)(2) of such Code) as of the first day of such plan year, and the underlying actuarial value of assets and liabilities taken into account in determining such percentage;

(III) the market value of the assets of the plan as of the last day of the plan year preceding such plan year;

(IV) the total value of all contributions made during the plan year preceding such plan year;

(V) the total value of all benefits paid during the plan year preceding such plan year;

(VI) cash flow projections for such plan year and either the 6 or 10 succeeding plan years, at the election of the trustees, and the assumptions relied upon in making such projections;

(VII) funding standard account projections for such plan year and the 9 succeeding plan years, and the assumptions relied upon in making such projections;

(VIII) the total value of all investment gains or losses during the plan year preceding such plan year;

(IX) any significant reduction in the number of active participants during the plan year preceding such plan year, and the reason for such reduction;

(X) a list of employers that withdrew from the plan in the plan year preceding such plan year, and the resulting reduction in contributions;

(XI) a list of employers that paid withdrawal liability to the plan during the plan year preceding such plan year and, for each employer, a total assessment of the withdrawal liability paid, the annual payment amount, and the number of years remaining in the payment schedule with respect to such withdrawal liability;

(XII) any material changes to benefits, accrual rates, or contribution rates during the plan yea preceding such plan year;

(XIII) any scheduled benefit increase or decrease in the plan year preceding such plan year having a material effect on liabilities of the plan;

(XIV) details regarding any funding improvement plan or rehabilitation plan and updates to such plan;

(XV) the number of participants and beneficiaries during the plan year preceding such plan year who are active participants, the number of participants and beneficiaries in pay status, and the number of terminated vested participants and beneficiaries;

(XVI) the information contained on the most recent annual funding notice submitted by the plan under section 101(f) of the Employee Retirement Income Security Act of 1974;

(XVII) the information contained on the most recent Department of Labor Form 5500 of the plan; and

(XVIII) copies of the plan document and amendments, other retirement benefit or ancillary benefit plans relating to the plan and contribution obligations under such plans, a breakdown of administrative expenses of the plan, participant census data and distribution of benefits, the most recent actuarial valuation report as of the plan year, copies of collective bargaining agreements, and financial reports, and such other information as the Secretary of the Treasury or the Secretary's delegate, in consultation with the Secretary of Labor and the Director of the Pension Benefit Guaranty Corporation, may require.

(ii) Electronic Submission.—The report required under clause (i) shall be submitted electronically.

(iii) Information Sharing.—The Secretary of the Treasury or the Secretary's delegate shall share the information in the report under clause (i) with the Secretary of Labor.

(iv) Penalty.—Any failure to file the report required under clause (i) on or before the date described in such clause shall be treated as a failure to file a report required to be filed under section 6058(a) of the Internal Revenue Code of 1986, except that section 6652(e) of such Code shall be applied with respect to any such failure by substituting '$100' for '$25'. The preceding sentence shall not apply if the Secretary of the Treasury or the Secretary's delegate determines that reasonable diligence has been exercised by the trustees of such plan in attempting to timely file such report.

(H) 1974 UMWA Pension Plan Defined.—For purposes of this paragraph, the term '1974 UMWA Pension Plan' has the meaning given the term in section 9701(a)(3) of the Internal Revenue Code of 1986, but without regard to the limitation on participation to individuals who retired in 1976 and thereafter.

(5) Availability of funds

Funds shall be transferred under paragraphs (1) and (2) beginning in fiscal year 2008 and each fiscal year thereafter, and shall remain available until expended.

(Pub. L. No. 95–87, Title IV, § 402, 91 Stat. 457 (Aug. 3, 1977); as amended by Pub. L. No. 100–34, Title I, § 101, 101 Stat. 300 (May 7, 1987); Pub. L. No. 101–508, Title VI, §§ 6003, 6004, 104 Stat. 1388–290, 1388–291 (Nov. 5, 1990); Pub. L. No. 102–285, § 10(b), 106 Stat. 172 (May 18, 1992); Pub. L. No. 102–486, Title XIX, § 19143(b)(1), (2), (3)(B), Title XXV, § 2515, 106 Stat. 3056, 3113 (Oct. 24, 1992); Pub. L. No. 108–447, Div. E, Title I, § 135(a), 118 Stat. 3068 (Dec. 8, 2004); Pub. L. No. 109–13, Div. A, Title VI, § 6035, 119 Stat. 289 (May 11, 2005); Pub. L. No. 109–54, Title I, § 129, 119 Stat. 525 (Aug. 2, 2005); Pub. L. No. 109–234, Title VII, § 7007, 120 Stat. 483 (June 15, 2006); Pub. L. No. 109–432, Div. C, Title II, § 202(a)(1), (2), (b) to (d), 120 Stat. 3008 (Dec. 20, 2006); Pub. L. No. 110–343, Div. C, Title VI, § 602, 122 Stat. 3911 (Oct. 3, 2008); Pub. L. No. 114–254, § 167, 130 Stat. 1009 (Dec. 10, 2016); Pub. L. No. 115–30, § 202(a), (b), 131 Stat. 134 (April 28, 2017); Pub. L. No. 115–31, § 104, 131 Stat. 803–804 (May 5, 2017); Pub. L. No. 116–94, §§ 103(a), 104, 133 Stat. 3091–95 (Dec. 20, 2019); Publ. L. No. 116–260, Div. Y, §§ 1,2, 134 Stat. 1182, 2417–18 (Dec. 27, 2020).)

[1] So in original. Probably should be "tipple,".

[2] So in original. Probably should be capitalized.

HISTORICAL AND STATUTORY NOTES

References in Text

This chapter, referred to in subsec. (a), was in the original "this Act", meaning Pub. L. No. 95–87, 91 Stat. 445 (Aug. 3, 1977), as amended, which enacted this chapter and amended 18 U.S.C.A. § 1114. For complete classification of this Act to the Code, see Short Title note set out under 30 U.S.C.A. § 1201 and Tables.

This subchapter, referred to in text, originally read "this title", meaning Pub. L. No. 95–87, Title IV, 91 Stat. 456 (Aug. 3, 1977), as amended, which enacted this subchapter.

Codifications

November 5, 1990, referred to in subsec. (g)(4)(B)(ii), was in the original "the date of enactment of this paragraph", which was translated as meaning the date of enactment of Pub. L. No. 101–508, which amended this section generally, to reflect the probable intent of Congress.

In subsec. (g)(2), "chapter 69 of Title 31" was substituted for "the Act of October 20, 1976, Public Law 94–565 (90 Stat. 2662) [31 U.S.C.A. § 1601 et seq.]" on authority of Pub. L. No. 97–258, § 4(b), 96 Stat. 1067 (Sept. 13, 1982), the first section of which enacted Title 31, Money and Finance.

Effective and Applicability Provisions

2020 Amendments. Pub. L. No. 116–260, Div. Y, § 2(c), 134 Stat. 2418 (Dec. 27, 2020), provided for the amendments to 30 U.S.C. § 1232(h), (i) that

2019 Amendments. Pub. L. No. 116–94, § 103(b), 133 Stat. 3093 (Dec. 20, 2019), provided for the amendments to 30 U.S.C. § 1232(i) that:

"**Application.—**

"**(1) In General.**—Except as provided in paragraph (2), the amendments made by this section shall take effect on the date of the enactment of this Act.

(2) Subsection (a)(3).—The amendment made by subsection (a)(3) shall apply to denials and reductions after December 31, 2019.

"**Effective Dates.—**

"**(1) In General.**—The amendments made by this section shall apply to fiscal years beginning after September 30, 2016.

"**(2) Reporting Requirements.**—Section 402(i)(4)(G) of the Surface Mining Control and Reclamation Act of 1977 (30 U.S.C. 1232(i)(4)(G)), as added by this section, shall apply to plan years beginning after the date of the enactment of this Act."

2017 Act. Pub. L. No. 115–31, § 104(b), 131 Stat. 804 (May 5, 2017), provided: "The amendments made by this section shall apply to fiscal years beginning after September 30, 2016."

2006 Acts. Pub. L. No. 109–432, Div. C, Title II, § 202(a)(1), 120 Stat. 3008 (Dec. 20, 2006), provided in part that amendments to subsec. (a) by section 202(a)(1) are "[e]ffective October 1, 2007".

Pub. L. No. 109–432, Div. C, Title II, § 202(a)(2), 120 Stat. 3008 (Dec. 20, 2006), provided in part that amendments to subsec. (a) by section 202(a)(2) are "[e]ffective October 1, 2012".

Pub. L. No. 109–432, Div. C, Title II, § 202(b), 120 Stat. 3008 (Dec. 20, 2006), provided in part that amendments to subsec. (b) by section 202(b) are "[e]ffective September 30, 2007".

1990 Acts. Amendment by Pub. L. No. 101–508 effective Oct. 1, 1991, see section 6014 of Pub. L. No. 101–508, set out as a note under section 1231 of this title.

Change of Name

"United States Bureau of Mines" substituted for "Bureau of Mines" in subsec. (g)(7)(C) pursuant to section 10(b) of Pub. L. No. 102–285, set out as a note under 30 U.S.C.A. § 1. For provisions relating to closure and transfer of functions of the United States Bureau of Mines, see Transfer of Functions note set out under 30 U.S.C.A. § 1.

Savings Provisions

Nothing in Subtitle A (section 6001 et seq.) of Title VI of Pub. L. No. 101–508, shall be construed to affect the certifications made by the States of Wyoming, Montana, and Louisiana to the Secretary of the Interior prior to Nov. 5, 1990, that each such State has completed the reclamation of eligible abandoned coal mine lands, see section 6013 of Pub. L. No. 101–508, set out as a note under section 1231 of this title.

Name of Provision

Pub. L. No. 115–30, § 202(a), 131 Stat. 134 (April 28, 2017), provided: "This section may be cited as the 'Further Continued Health Benefits for Miners Act'."

Pub. L. No. 114–254, § 167(a), 130 Stat. 1009, provided: "This section may be cited as the 'Continued Health Benefits for Miners Act'."

§ 1233. Objectives of fund

[SMCRA § 403]

(a) Priorities

Expenditure of moneys from the fund on lands and water eligible pursuant to section 1234 of this title for the purposes of this subchapter, except as provided for under section 1240a of this title, shall reflect the following priorities in the order stated:

(1) (A) the protection;[1] of public health, safety, and property from extreme danger of adverse effects of coal mining practices;

(B) the restoration of land and water resources and the environment that—

(i) have been degraded by the adverse effects of coal mining practices; and

(ii) are adjacent to a site that has been or will be remediated under subparagraph (A);

(2) (A) the protection of public health and safety from adverse effects of coal mining practices;

(B) the restoration of land and water resources and the environment that—

(i) have been degraded by the adverse effects of coal mining practices; and

(ii) are adjacent to a site that has been or will be remediated under subparagraph (A); and

(3) the restoration of land and water resources and the environment previously degraded by adverse effects of coal mining practices including measures for the conservation and development of soil, water (excluding channelization), woodland, fish and wildlife, recreation resources, and agricultural productivity.

(4), (5) Repealed. Pub. L. No. 109–432, Div. C, Title II, § 203(1)(D), 120 Stat. 3016 (Dec. 20, 2006).

(b) Water supply restoration

(1) Any State or Indian tribe not certified under section 1240a(a) of this title may expend funds allocated to such State or Indian tribe in any year through the grants made available under paragraphs (1) and (5) of section 1232(g) of this title for the purpose of protecting, repairing, replacing, constructing, or enhancing facilities relating to water supply, including water distribution facilities and treatment plants, to replace water supplies adversely affected by coal mining practices.

(2) If the adverse effect on water supplies referred to in this subsection occurred both prior to and after August 3, 1977, or as the case may be, the dates (and under the criteria) set forth under section 1232(g)(4)(B) of this title, section 1234 of this title shall not be construed to prohibit a State or Indian tribe referred to in paragraph (1) from using funds referred to in such paragraph for the purposes of this subsection if the State or Indian tribe determines that such adverse effects occurred predominantly prior to August 3, 1977, or as the case may be, the dates (and under the criteria) set forth under section 1232(g)(4)(B) of this title.

(c) Inventory

For the purposes of assisting in the planning and evaluation of reclamation projects pursuant to section 1235 of this title, and assisting in making the certification referred to in section 1240a(a) of this title, the Secretary shall maintain an inventory of eligible lands and waters pursuant to section 1234 of this title which meet the priorities stated in paragraphs (1) and (2) of subsection (a) of this section. Under standardized procedures established by the Secretary, States and Indian tribes with approved abandoned mine reclamation programs pursuant to section 1235 of this title may offer amendments, subject to the approval of the Secretary, to update the inventory as it applies to eligible lands and waters under the jurisdiction of such States or tribes. The Secretary shall provide such States and tribes with the financial and technical assistance necessary for the purpose of making inventory amendments. The Secretary shall compile and maintain an inventory for States and Indian lands in the case when a State or Indian tribe does not have an approved abandoned mine reclamation program pursuant to section 1235 of this title. On a regular basis, but not less than annually, the projects completed under this subchapter shall be so noted on the inventory under standardized procedures established by the Secretary.

(Pub. L. No. 95–87, Title IV, § 403, 91 Stat. 458 (Aug. 3, 1977); as amended by Pub. L. No. 101–508, Title VI, § 6005, 104 Stat. 1388–294 (Nov. 5, 1990); Pub. L. No. 102–486, Title XXV, § 2504(c)(2), (e), 106 Stat. 3105, 3106 (Oct. 24, 1999); Pub. L. No. 109–432, Div. C, Title II, § 203, 120 Stat. 3015 (Dec. 20, 2006).)

[1] So in original. The semicolon probably should not appear.

HISTORICAL AND STATUTORY NOTES

Effective and Applicability Provisions

1990 Acts. Amendment by Pub. L. No. 101–508 effective Oct. 1, 1991, see section 6014 of Pub. L. No. 101–508, set out as a note under section 1231 of this title.

Savings Provisions

Nothing in Subtitle A (section 6001 et seq.) of Title VI of Pub. L. No. 101–508, shall be construed to affect the certifications made by the States of Wyoming, Montana, and Louisiana to the Secretary of the Interior prior to Nov. 5, 1990, that each such State has completed the reclamation of eligible abandoned coal mine lands, see section 6013 of Pub. L. No. 101–508, set out as a note under section 1231 of this title.

§ 1234. Eligible lands and water

[SMCRA § 404]

Lands and water eligible for reclamation or drainage abatement expenditures under this subchapter are those which were mined for coal or which were affected by such mining, wastebanks, coal processing, or other coal mining processes, except as provided for under section 1240a of this title, and abandoned or left in an inadequate reclamation status prior to August 3, 1977, and for which there is no continuing reclamation responsibility under State or other Federal laws. For other provisions relating to lands and waters eligible for such expenditures, see section 1232(g)(4) of this title, section 1233(b)(1) of this title, and section 1239 of this title. Surface coal mining operations on lands eligible for remining shall not affect the eligibility of such lands for reclamation and restoration under this subchapter after the release of the bond or deposit for any such operation as provided under section 1269 of this title. In the event the bond or deposit for a surface coal mining operation on lands eligible for remining is forfeited, funds available under this subchapter may be used if the amount of such bond or deposit is not sufficient to provide for adequate reclamation or abatement, except that if conditions warrant the Secretary shall immediately exercise his authority under section 1240 of this title.

(Pub. L. No. 95–87, Title IV, § 404, 91 Stat. 459 (Aug. 3, 1977); as amended by Pub. L. No. 101–508, Title VI, § 6006, 104 Stat. 1388–295 (Nov. 5, 1990); Pub. L. No. 102–486, Title XXV, § 2503(d), 106 Stat. 3103 (Oct. 24, 1992).)

HISTORICAL AND STATUTORY NOTES

Effective and Applicability Provisions

1990 Acts. Amendment by Pub. L. No. 101–508 effective Oct. 1, 1991, see section 6014 of Pub. L. No. 101–508, set out as a note under section 1231 of this title.

Savings Provisions

Nothing in Subtitle A (section 6001 et seq.) of Title VI of Pub. L. No. 101–508, shall be construed to affect the certifications made by the States of Wyoming, Montana, and Louisiana to the Secretary of the Interior prior to Nov. 5, 1990, that each such State has completed the reclamation of eligible abandoned coal mine lands, see section 6013 of Pub. L. No. 101–508, set out as a note under section 1231 of this title.

§ 1235. State reclamation program

[SMCRA § 405]

(a) Promulgation of regulations

Not later than the end of the one hundred and eighty-day period immediately following August 3, 1977, the Secretary shall promulgate and publish in the Federal Register regulations covering implementation of an abandoned mine reclamation program incorporating the provisions of this subchapter and establishing procedures and requirements for preparation, submission, and approval of State programs consisting of the plan and annual submissions of projects.

(b) Submission of State Reclamation Plan and annual projects

Each State having within its borders coal mined lands eligible for reclamation under this subchapter, may submit to the Secretary a State Reclamation Plan and annual projects to carry out the purposes of this subchapter.

(c) Restriction

The Secretary shall not approve, fund, or continue to fund a State abandoned mine reclamation program unless that State has an approved State regulatory program pursuant to section 1253 of this title.

(d) Approval of State program; withdrawal

If the Secretary determines that a State has developed and submitted a program for reclamation of abandoned mines and has the ability and necessary State legislation to implement the provisions of this subchapter, sections 1232 and 1240 of this title excepted, the Secretary shall approve such State program and shall grant to the State exclusive responsibility and authority to implement the provisions of the approved program: *Provided,* That the Secretary shall withdraw such approval and authorization if he determines upon the basis of information provided under this section that the State program is not in compliance with the procedures, guidelines, and requirements established under subsection (a) of this section.

(e) Contents of State Reclamation Plan

Each State Reclamation Plan shall generally identify the areas to be reclaimed, the purposes for which the reclamation is proposed, the relationship of the lands to be reclaimed and the proposed reclamation to surrounding areas, the specific criteria for ranking and identifying projects to be funded, and the legal authority and programmatic capability to perform such work in conformance with the provisions of this subchapter.

(f) Annual application for support; contents

On an annual basis, each State having an approved State Reclamation Plan may submit to the Secretary an application for the support of the State program and implementation of specific reclamation projects. Such annual requests shall include such information as may be requested by the Secretary including:

(1) a general description of each proposed project;

(2) a priority evaluation of each proposed project;

(3) a statement of the estimated benefits in such terms as: number of acres restored, miles of stream improved, acres of surface lands protected from subsidence, population protected from subsidence, air pollution, hazards of mine and coal refuse disposal area fires;

(4) an estimate of the cost for each proposed project;

(5) in the case of proposed research and demonstration projects, a description of the specific techniques to be evaluated or objective to be attained;

(6) an identification of lands or interest therein to be acquired and the estimated cost; and

(7) in each year after the first in which a plan is filed under this subchapter, an inventory of each project funded under the previous year's grant: which inventory shall include details of financial expenditures on such project together with a brief description of each such project, including project locations, landowner's name, acreage, type of reclamation performed.

(g) Costs

The costs for each proposed project under this section shall include: actual construction costs, actual operation and maintenance costs of permanent facilities, planning and engineering costs, construction inspection costs, and other necessary administrative expenses.

(h) Grant of funds

Upon approval of State Reclamation Plan by the Secretary and of the surface mine regulatory program pursuant to section 1253 of this title, the Secretary shall grant, on an annual basis, funds to be expended in such State pursuant to section 1232(g) of this title and which are necessary to implement the State reclamation program as approved by the Secretary.

(i) Program monitorship

The Secretary, through his designated agents, will monitor the progress and quality of the program. The States shall not be required at the start of any project to submit complete copies of plans and specifications.

(j) Annual report to Secretary

The Secretary shall require annual and other reports as may be necessary to be submitted by each State administering the approved State reclamation program with funds provided under this subchapter. Such reports shall include that information which the Secretary deems necessary to fulfill his responsibilities under this subchapter.

(k) Eligible lands of Indian tribes

Indian tribes having within their jurisdiction eligible lands pursuant to section 1234 of this title or from which coal is produced, shall be considered as a "State" for the purposes of this subchapter except for purposes of subsection (c) of this section with respect to the Navajo, Hopi and Crow Indian Tribes.

(*l*) State liability

No State shall be liable under any provision of Federal law for any costs or damages as a result of action taken or omitted in the course of carrying out a State abandoned mine reclamation plan approved under this section. This subsection shall not preclude liability for cost or damages as a result of gross negligence or intentional misconduct by the State. For purposes of the preceding sentence, reckless, willful, or wanton misconduct shall constitute gross negligence.

(Pub. L. No. 95–87, Title IV, § 405, 91 Stat. 459 (Aug. 3, 1977); Pub. L. No. 100–71, Title I, 101 Stat. 416 (July 11, 1987); Pub. L. No. 101–508, Title VI, §§ 6007, 6012(d)(1), (2), 104 Stat. 1388–295, 1388–298 (Nov. 5, 1990).)

HISTORICAL AND STATUTORY NOTES

Effective and Applicability Provisions

1990 Acts. Amendment by Pub. L. No. 101–508 effective Oct. 1, 1991, see section 6014 of Pub. L. No. 101–508, set out as a note under section 1231 of this title.

Savings Provisions

Nothing in Subtitle A (section 6001 et seq.) of Title VI of Pub. L. No. 101–508, shall be construed to affect the certifications made by the States of Wyoming, Montana, and Louisiana to the Secretary of the Interior prior to Nov. 5, 1990, that each such State has completed the reclamation of eligible abandoned coal mine lands, see section 6013 of Pub. L. No. 101–508, set out as a note under section 1231 of this title.

Grant of Funds to States Under Surface Mining Control and Reclamation Act

Pub. L. No. 97–377, Title I, § 150, 96 Stat. 1918 (Dec. 21, 1982), provided that: "Within 60 days of receipt of a complete abandoned mine reclamation fund grant application from any eligible State under the provisions of the Surface Mining Control and Reclamation Act (91 Stat. 460) the Secretary of Interior shall grant to such State any and all funds available for such purposes in the applicable appropriations Act."

§ 1236. Reclamation of rural lands

[SMCRA § 406]

(a) Agreements with landowners for conservation treatment

In order to provide for the control and prevention of erosion and sediment damages from unreclaimed mined lands, and to promote the conservation and development of soil and water resources of unreclaimed mined lands and lands affected by mining, the Secretary of Agriculture is authorized to enter into agreements of not more than ten years with landowners (including owners of water rights), residents, and tenants, and individually or collectively, determined by him to have control for the period of the agreement of lands in question therein, providing for land stabilization, erosion, and sediment control, and reclamation through conservation treatment, including measures for the conservation and development of soil, water (excluding stream channelization), woodland, wildlife, and recreation resources, and agricultural productivity of such lands. Such agreements shall be made by the Secretary with the owners, including owners of water rights, residents, or tenants (collectively or individually) of the lands in question.

(b) Conservation and development plans

The landowner, including the owner of water rights, resident, or tenant shall furnish to the Secretary of Agriculture a conservation and development plan setting forth the proposed land uses and conservation treatment which shall be mutually agreed by the Secretary of Agriculture and the landowner, including owner of water rights, resident, or tenant to be needed on the lands for which the plan was prepared. In those instances where it is determined that the water rights or water supply of a tenant, landowner, including owner of water rights, resident, or tenant have been adversely affected by a surface or underground coal mine operation which has removed or disturbed a stratum so as to significantly affect the hydrologic balance, such plan may include proposed measures to enhance water quality or quantity by means of joint action with other affected landowners, including owner of water rights, residents, or tenants in consultation with appropriate State and Federal agencies.

(c) Agreement to effect plan

Such plan shall be incorporated in an agreement under which the landowner, including owner of water rights, resident, or tenant shall agree with the Secretary of Agriculture to effect the land uses and conservation treatment provided for in such plan on the lands described in the agreement in accordance with the terms and conditions thereof.

(d) Financial and other assistance; determination by Secretary

In return for such agreement by the landowner, including owner of water rights, resident, or tenant, the Secretary of Agriculture is authorized to furnish financial and other assistance to such landowner, including owner of water rights, resident, or tenant, in such amounts and subject to such conditions as the Secretary of Agriculture determines are appropriate in the public interest for carrying out the land use and conservation treatment set forth in the agreement. Grants made under this section, depending on the income-producing potential of the land after reclaiming, shall provide up to 80 per centum of the cost of carrying out such land uses and conservation treatment on not more than one hundred and twenty acres of land occupied by such owner, including water rights owners, resident, or tenant, or on not more than one hundred and twenty acres of land which has been purchased jointly by such landowners, including water rights owners, residents, or tenants, under an agreement for the enhancement of water quality or quantity or on land which has been acquired by an appropriate State or local agency for the purpose of implementing such agreement; except the Secretary may reduce the matching cost share where he determines that (1) the main benefits to be derived from the project are related to improving offsite water quality, offsite esthetic values, or other offsite benefits, and (2) the matching share requirement would place a burden on the landowner which would probably prevent him from participating in the program: *Provided, however*, That the Secretary of Agriculture may allow for land use and conservation treatment on such lands occupied by any such owner in excess of such one hundred and twenty acre limitation up to three hundred and twenty acres, but in such event the amount of the grant to such landowner to carry out such reclamation on such lands shall be reduced proportionately. Notwithstanding any other provision of this section with regard to acreage limitations, the Secretary of Agriculture may carry out reclamation treatment projects to control erosion and improve water quality on all lands within a hydrologic unit, consisting of not more than 25,000 acres, if the Secretary determines that treatment of such lands as a hydrologic unit will achieve greater reduction in the adverse effects of past surface mining practices than would be achieved if reclamation was done on individual parcels of land.

(e) Termination of agreements

The Secretary of Agriculture may terminate any agreement with a landowner including water rights owners, operator, or occupier by mutual agreement if the Secretary of Agriculture determines that such termination would be in the public interest, and may agree to such modification of agreements previously entered into hereunder as he deems desirable to carry out the purposes of this section or to facilitate the practical administration of the program authorized herein.

(f) Preservation and surrender of history and allotments

Notwithstanding any other provision of law, the Secretary of Agriculture, to the extent he deems it desirable to carry out the purposes of this section, may provide in any agreement hereinunder for (1) preservation for a period not to exceed the period covered by the agreement and an equal period thereafter of the cropland, crop acreage, and allotment history applicable to land covered by the agreement for the purpose of any Federal program under which such history is used as a basis for an allotment or other limitation on the production of such crop; or (2) surrender of any such history and allotments.

(g) Rules and regulations

The Secretary of Agriculture shall be authorized to issue such rules and regulations as he determines are necessary to carry out the provisions of this section.

(h) Utilization of Natural Resources Conservation Service

In carrying out the provisions of this section, the Secretary of Agriculture shall utilize the services of the Natural Resources Conservation Service.

(i) There are authorized to be appropriated to the Secretary of Agriculture, from amounts in the Treasury other than amounts in the fund, such sums as may be necessary to carry out this section.

(Pub. L. No. 95–87, Title IV, § 406, 91 Stat. 460 (Aug. 3, 1977); as amended by Pub. L. No. 97–98, Title XV, § 1551, 95 Stat. 1344 (Dec. 22, 1981); Pub. L. No. 101–508, Title VI, §§ 6008, 6012(c), (d)(3), 104 Stat. 1388–295, 1388–298 (Nov. 5, 1990); Pub. L. No. 109–432, Div. C, Title II, § 204, 120 Stat. 3016 (Dec. 20, 2006).)

HISTORICAL AND STATUTORY NOTES

Effective and Applicability Provisions

1990 Acts. Amendment by Pub. L. No. 101–508 effective Oct. 1, 1991, see section 6014 of Pub. L. No. 101–508, set out as a note under section 1231 of this title.

Savings Provisions

Nothing in Subtitle A (section 6001 et seq.) of Title VI of Pub. L. No. 101–508, shall be construed to affect the certifications made by the States of Wyoming, Montana, and Louisiana to the Secretary of the Interior prior to Nov. 5, 1990, that each such State has completed the reclamation of eligible abandoned coal mine lands, see section 6013 of Pub. L. No. 101–508, set out as a note under section 1231 of this title.

§ 1237. Acquisition and reclamation of land adversely affected by past coal mining practices

[SMCRA § 407]

(a) Findings of fact; notice; right of entry

If the Secretary or the State pursuant to an approved State program, makes a finding of fact that—

(1) land or water resources have been adversely affected by past coal mining practices; and

(2) the adverse effects are at a stage where, in the public interest, action to restore, reclaim, abate, control, or prevent should be taken; and

(3) the owners of the land or water resources where entry must be made to restore, reclaim, abate, control, or prevent the adverse effects of past coal mining practices are not known, or readily available; or

(4) the owners will not give permission for the United States, the States, political subdivisions, their agents, employees, or contractors to enter upon such property to restore, reclaim, abate, control, or prevent the adverse effects of past coal mining practices;

then, upon giving notice by mail to the owners if known or if not known by posting notice upon the premises and advertising once in a newspaper of general circulation in the municipality in which the land lies, the Secretary, his agents, employees, or contractors, or the State pursuant to an approved State program, shall have the right to enter upon the property adversely affected by past coal mining practices and any other property to have access to such property to do all things necessary or expedient to restore, reclaim, abate, control, or prevent the adverse effects. Such entry shall be construed as an exercise of the police power for the protection of public health, safety, and general welfare and shall not be construed as an act of condemnation of property nor of trespass thereon. The moneys expended for such work and the benefits accruing to any such premises so entered upon shall be chargeable against such land and shall mitigate or offset any claim in or any action brought by any owner of any interest in such premises for any alleged damages by virtue of such entry: *Provided, however*, That this provision is not intended to create new rights of action or eliminate existing immunities.

(b) Studies or exploratory work

The Secretary, his agents, employees, or contractors or the State pursuant to an approved State program, shall have the right to enter upon any property for the purpose of conducting studies or exploratory work to determine the existence of adverse effects of past coal mining practices and to determine the feasibility of restoration, reclamation, abatement, control, or prevention of such adverse effects. Such entry shall be construed as an exercise of the police power for the protection of public health, safety, and general welfare and shall not be construed as an act of condemnation of property nor trespass thereon.

(c) Requirements for acquisition of affected land

The Secretary or the State pursuant to an approved State program, may acquire any land, by purchase, donation, or condemnation, which is adversely affected by past coal mining practices if the Secretary determines that acquisition of such land is necessary to successful reclamation and that—

(1) the acquired land, after restoration, reclamation, abatement, control, or prevention of the adverse effects of past coal mining practices, will serve recreation and historic purposes, conservation and reclamation purposes or provide open space benefits; and

(2) permanent facilities such as a treatment plant or a relocated stream channel will be constructed on the land for the restoration, reclamation, abatement, control, or prevention of the adverse effects of past coal mining practices; or

(3) acquisition of coal refuse disposal sites and all coal refuse thereon will serve the purposes of this subchapter or that public ownership is desirable to meet emergency situations and prevent recurrences of the adverse effects of past coal mining practices.

(d) Title to affected land; value

Title to all lands acquired pursuant to this section shall be in the name of the United States or, if acquired by a State pursuant to an approved program, title shall be in the name of the State. The price paid for land acquired under this section shall reflect the market value of the land as adversely affected by past coal mining practices.

(e) State participation; grants

States are encouraged as part of their approved State programs, to reclaim abandoned and unreclaimed mined lands within their boundaries and, if necessary, to acquire or to transfer such lands to the Secretary or the appropriate State regulatory authority under appropriate Federal regulations. The Secretary is authorized to make grants on a matching basis to States in such amounts as he deems appropriate for the purpose of carrying out the provisions of this subchapter but in no event shall any grant exceed 90 per centum of the cost of acquisition of the lands for which the grant is made. When a State has made any such land available to the Federal Government under this subchapter, such State shall have a preference right to purchase such lands after reclamation at fair market value less the State portion of the original acquisition price. Notwithstanding the provisions of paragraph (1) of subsection (c) of this section, reclaimed land may be sold to the State or local government in which it is located at a price less than fair market value, which in no case shall be less than the cost to the United States of the purchase and reclamation of the land, as negotiated by the Secretary, to be used for a valid public purpose. If any land sold to a State or local government under this paragraph is not used for a valid public purpose as specified by the Secretary in the terms of the sales agreement then all right, title, and interest in such land shall revert to the United States. Money received from such sale shall be deposited in the fund.

(f) Rules and regulations

The Secretary, in formulating regulations for making grants to the States to acquire land pursuant to this section, shall specify that acquired land meet the criteria provided for in subsections (c) and (d) of this section. The Secretary may provide by regulation that money derived from the lease, rental, or user charges of such acquired land and facilities thereon will be deposited in the fund.

(g) Public sale; notice and hearing

(1) Where land acquired pursuant to this section is deemed to be suitable for industrial, commercial, residential, or recreational development, the Secretary may sell or authorize the States to sell such land by public sale under a system of competitive bidding, at not less than fair market value and under such other regulations promulgated to insure that such lands are put to proper use consistent with local and State land use plans, if any, as determined by the Secretary.

(2) The Secretary or the State pursuant to an approved State program, when requested after appropriate public notice shall hold a public hearing, with the appropriate notice, in the county or counties or the appropriate subdivisions of the State in which lands acquired pursuant to this section are located. The hearings shall be held at a time which shall afford local citizens and governments the maximum opportunity to participate in the decision concerning the use or disposition of the lands after restoration, reclamation, abatement, control, or prevention of the adverse effects of past coal mining practices.

(h) Construction or rehabilitation of housing for disabled, displaced, or dislocated persons; grants

In addition to the authority to acquire land under subsection (d) of this section the Secretary is authorized to use money in the fund to acquire land by purchase, donation, or condemnation, and to reclaim and transfer acquired land to any State or to a political subdivision thereof, or to any person, firm, association, or corporation, if he determines that such is an integral and necessary element of an economically feasible plan for the project to construct or rehabilitate housing for persons disabled as the result of employment in the mines or work incidental thereto, persons displaced by acquisition of land pursuant to this section, or persons dislocated as the result of adverse effects of coal mining practices which constitute an emergency as provided in section 1240 of this title or persons dislocated as the result of natural disasters or catastrophic failures from any cause. Such activities shall be accomplished under such terms and conditions as the Secretary shall require, which may include transfers of land with or without monetary consideration: *Provided*, That, to the extent that the consideration is below the fair market value of the land transferred, no portion of the difference between the fair market value and the consideration shall accrue as a profit to such persons, firm, association, or corporation. No part of the funds provided under this subchapter may be used to pay the actual construction costs of housing. The Secretary may carry out the purposes of this subsection directly or he may make grants and commitments for grants, and may advance money under such terms and conditions as he may require to any State, or any department, agency, or instrumentality of a State, or any public body or nonprofit organization designated by a State.

(Pub. L. No. 95–87, Title IV, § 407, 91 Stat. 462 (Aug. 3, 1977); as amended by Pub. L. No. 101–508, Title VI, § 6012(d)(4)–(7), 104 Stat. 1388–298 (Nov. 5, 1990).)

HISTORICAL AND STATUTORY NOTES

Effective and Applicability Provisions

1990 Acts. Amendment by Pub. L. No. 101–508 effective Oct. 1, 1991, see section 6014 of Pub. L. No. 101–508, set out as a note under section 1231 of this title.

Savings Provisions

Nothing in Subtitle A (section 6001 et seq.) of Title VI of Pub. L. No. 101–508, shall be construed to affect the certifications made by the States of Wyoming, Montana, and Louisiana to the Secretary of the Interior prior to Nov. 5, 1990, that each such State has completed the reclamation of eligible abandoned coal mine lands, see section 6013 of Pub. L. No. 101–508, set out as a note under section 1231 of this title.

§ 1238. Liens

[SMCRA § 408]

(a) Filing of statement and appraisal

Within six months after the completion of projects to restore, reclaim, abate, control, or prevent adverse effects of past coal mining practices on privately owned land, the Secretary or the State, pursuant to an approved State program, shall itemize the moneys so expended and may file a statement thereof in the office of the county in which the land lies which has the responsibility under local law for the recording of judgments against land, together with a notarized appraisal by an independent appraiser of the value of the land before the restoration, reclamation, abatement, control, or prevention of adverse effects of past coal mining practices if the moneys so expended shall result in a significant increase in property value. Such statement shall constitute a lien upon the said land. The lien shall not exceed the amount determined by the appraisal to be the increase in the market value of the land as a result of the restoration, reclamation, abatement, control, or prevention of the adverse effects of past coal mining practices. No lien shall be filed against the property of any person, in accordance with this subsection, who neither consented to nor participated in nor exercised control over the mining operation which necessitated the reclamation performed hereunder.

(b) Petition

The landowner may proceed as provided by local law to petition within sixty days of the filing of the lien, to determine the increase in the market value of the land as a result of the restoration, reclamation, abatement, control, or prevention of the adverse effects of past coal mining practices. The amount reported to be the increase in value of the premises shall constitute the amount of the lien and shall be recorded with the statement herein provided. Any party aggrieved by the decision may appeal as provided by local law.

(c) Recordation

The lien provided in this section shall be entered in the county office in which the land lies and which has responsibility under local law for the recording of judgments against land. Such statement shall constitute a lien upon the said land as of the date of the expenditure of the moneys and shall have priority as a lien second only to the lien of real estate taxes imposed upon said land.

(Pub. L. No. 95–87, Title IV, § 408, 91 Stat. 465 (Aug. 3, 1977); as amended by Pub. L. No. 109–432, Div. C, Title II, § 205, 120 Stat. 3016 (Dec. 20, 2006).)

§ 1239. Filling voids and sealing tunnels [SMCRA § 409]

(a) Congressional declaration of hazardous conditions

The Congress declares that voids, and open and abandoned tunnels, shafts, and entryways resulting from any previous mining operation, constitute a hazard to the public health or safety and that surface impacts of any underground or surface mining operation may degrade the environment. The Secretary, at the request of the Governor of any State, or the the[1] governing body of an Indian tribe, is authorized to fill such voids, seal such abandoned tunnels, shafts, and entryways, and reclaim surface impacts of underground or surface mines which the Secretary determines could endanger life and property, constitute a hazard to the public health and safety, or degrade the environment. State regulatory authorities are authorized to carry out such work pursuant to an approved abandoned mine reclamation program.

(b) Limitation on funds

Funds available for use in carrying out the purpose of this section shall be limited to those funds which must be allocated to the respective States or Indian tribes under the provisions of paragraphs (1) and (5) of section 1232(g) of this title.

(c) Limitation on expenditures

(1) The Secretary may make expenditures and carry out the purposes of this section in such States where requests are made by the Governor or governing body of an Indian tribe for those reclamation projects which meet the priorities stated in section 1233(a)(1) of this title, except that for the purposes of this section the reference to coal in section 1233(a)(1) of this title shall not apply.

(2) The provisions of section 1234 of this title shall apply to this section, with the exception that such mined lands need not have been mined for coal.

(3) The Secretary shall not make any expenditures for the purposes of this section in those States which have made the certification referred to in section 1240a(a) of this title.

(d) Disposal of mine wastes

In those instances where mine waste piles are being reworked for conservation purposes, the incremental costs of disposing of the wastes from such operations by filling voids and sealing tunnels may be eligible for funding providing that the disposal of these wastes meets the purposes of this section.

(e) Land acquisition

The Secretary may acquire by purchase, donation, easement, or otherwise such interest in land as he determines necessary to carry out the provisions of this section.

(Pub. L. No. 95–87, Title IV, § 409, 91 Stat. 465 (Aug. 3, 1977); Pub. L. No. 101–508, Title VI, § 6009, 104 Stat. 1388–296 (Nov. 5, 1990).)

[1] So in original.

HISTORICAL AND STATUTORY NOTES

Effective and Applicability Provisions

1990 Amendments. Amendment by Pub. L. No. 101–508 effective Oct. 1, 1991, see section 6014 of Pub. L. No. 101–508, set out as note under section 1231 of this title.

Savings Provisions

Nothing in Subtitle A (section 6001 et seq.) of Title VI of Pub. L. No. 101–508, shall be construed to affect the certifications made by the States of Wyoming, Montana, and Louisiana to the Secretary of the Interior prior to Nov. 5, 1990, that each such State has completed the reclamation of eligible abandoned coal mine lands, see section 6013 of Pub. L. No. 101–508, set out as a note under section 1231 of this title.

§ 1240. Emergency powers

[SMCRA § 410]

(a) The Secretary is authorized to expend moneys from the fund for the emergency restoration, reclamation, abatement, control, or prevention of adverse effects of coal mining practices, on eligible lands, if the Secretary makes a finding of fact that—

(1) an emergency exists constituting a danger to the public health, safety, or general welfare; and

(2) no other person or agency will act expeditiously to restore, reclaim, abate, control, or prevent the adverse effects of coal mining practices.

(b) The Secretary, his agents, employees, and contractors shall have the right to enter upon any land where the emergency exists and any other land to have access to the land where the emergency exists to restore, reclaim, abate, control, or prevent the adverse effects of coal mining practices and to do all things necessary or expedient to protect the public health, safety, or general welfare. Such entry shall be construed as an exercise of the police power and shall not be construed as an act of condemnation of property nor of trespass thereof. The moneys expended for such work and the benefits accruing to any such premises so entered upon shall be chargeable against such land and shall mitigate or offset any claim in or any action brought by any owner of any interest in such premises for any alleged damages by virtue of such entry: *Provided, however,* That this provision is not intended to create new rights of action or eliminate existing immunities.

(Pub. L. No. 95–87, Title IV, § 410, 91 Stat. 466 (Aug. 3, 1977).)

§ 1240a. Certification

[SMCRA § 411]

(a) Certification of completion of coal reclamation

(1) The Governor of a State, or the head of a governing body of an Indian tribe, with an approved abandoned mine reclamation program under section 1235 of this title may certify to the Secretary that all of the priorities stated in section 1233(a) of this title for eligible lands and waters pursuant to section 1234 of this title have been achieved. The Secretary, after notice in the Federal Register and opportunity for public comment, shall concur with such certification if the Secretary determines that such certification is correct.

(2) **(A)** The Secretary may, on the initiative of the Secretary, make the certification referred to in paragraph (1) on behalf of any State or Indian tribe referred to in paragraph (1) if on the basis of the inventory referred to in section 1233(c) of this title all reclamation projects relating to the priorities described in section 1233(a of this title for eligible land and water pursuant to section 1234 of this title in the State or tribe have been completed.

(B) The Secretary shall only make the certification after notice in the Federal Register and opportunity for public comment.

(b) Eligible lands, waters, and facilities

If the Secretary has concurred in a State or tribal certification under subsection (a) of this section, for purposes of determining the eligibility of lands and waters for annual grants under section 1232(g)(1) of this title, section 1234 of this title shall not apply, and eligible lands, waters, and facilities shall be those—

(1) which were mined or processed for minerals or which were affected by such mining or processing, and abandoned or left in an inadequate reclamation status prior to August 3, 1977; and

(2) for which there is no continuing reclamation responsibility under State or other Federal laws. In determining the eligibility under this subsection of Federal lands, waters, and facilities under the jurisdiction of the Forest Service or Bureau of Land Management, in lieu of the August 3, 1977, date referred to in paragraph (1) the applicable date shall be August 28, 1974, and November 26, 1980, respectively.

(c) Priorities

Expenditures of moneys for lands, waters, and facilities referred to in subsection (b) of this section shall reflect the following objectives and priorities in the order stated (in lieu of the priorities set forth in section 1233 of this title):

(1) The protection of public health, safety, general welfare, and property from extreme danger of adverse effects of mineral mining and processing practices.

(2) The protection of public health, safety, and general welfare from adverse effects of mineral mining and processing practices.

(3) The restoration of land and water resources and the environment previously degraded by the adverse effects of mineral mining and processing practices.

(d) Specific sites and areas not eligible

Sites and areas designated for remedial action pursuant to the Uranium Mill Tailings Radiation Control Act of 1978 (42 U.S.C. 7901 and following) or which have been listed for remedial action pursuant to the Comprehensive Environmental Response Compensation and Liability Act of 1980 (42 U.S.C. 9601 and following) shall not be eligible for expenditures from the Fund under this section.

(e) Utilities and other facilities

Reclamation projects involving the protection, repair, replacement, construction, or enhancement of utilities, such as those relating to water supply, roads, and such other facilities serving the public adversely affected by mineral mining and processing practices, and the construction of public facilities in communities impacted by coal or other mineral mining and processing practices, shall be deemed part of the objectives set forth, and undertaken as they relate to, the priorities stated in subsection (c) of this section.

(f) Public facilities related to coal or minerals industry

Notwithstanding subsection (e) of this section, where the Secretary has concurred in the certification referenced in subsection (a) of this section and where the Governor of a State or the head of a governing body of an Indian tribe determines there is a need for activities or construction of specific public facilities related to the coal or minerals industry in States impacted by coal or minerals development and the Secretary concurs in such need, then the State or Indian tribe, as the case may be, may use annual grants made available under section 1232(g)(1) of this title to carry out such activities or construction.

(g) Application of other provisions

The provisions of sections 1237 and 1238 of this title shall apply to subsections (a) through (e) of this section, except that for purposes of this section the references to coal in sections 1237 and 1238 of this title shall not apply.

(h) Payments to States and Indian tribes

(1) In general

(A) Payments

(i) In general

Notwithstanding section 1231(f)(3)(B) of this title, from funds referred to in section 1232(i)(2) of this title, the Secretary shall make payments to States or Indian tribes for the amount due for the aggregate unappropriated amount allocated to the State or Indian tribe under subparagraph (A) or (B) of section 1232(g)(1) of this title.

(ii) Conversion as equivalent payments

Amounts allocated under subparagraph (A) or (B) of section 1232(g)(1) of this title shall be reallocated to the allocation established in section 1232(g)(5) of this title in amounts equivalent to payments made to States or Indian tribes under this paragraph.

(B) Amount due

In this paragraph, the term "amount due" means the unappropriated amount allocated to a State or Indian tribe before October 1, 2007, under subparagraph (A) or (B) of section 1232(g)(1) of this title.

(C) Schedule

Payments under subparagraph (A) shall be made in 7 equal annual installments, beginning with fiscal year 2008.

(D) Use of funds

(i) Certified States and Indian tribes

A State or Indian tribe that makes a certification under subsection (a) of this section in which the Secretary concurs shall use any amounts provided under this paragraph for the purposes established by the State legislature or tribal council of the Indian tribe, with priority given for addressing the impacts of mineral development.

(ii) Uncertified States and Indian tribes

A State or Indian tribe that has not made a certification under subsection (a) of this section in which the Secretary has concurred shall use any amounts provided under this paragraph for the purposes described in section 1233 of this title.

(2) Subsequent State and Indian tribe share for certified States and Indian tribes

(A) In general

Notwithstanding section 1231(f)(3)(B) of this title, from funds referred to in section 1232(i)(2) of this title, the Secretary shall pay to each certified State or Indian tribe an amount equal to the sum of the aggregate unappropriated amount allocated on or after October 1, 2007, to the certified State or Indian tribe under subparagraph (A) or (B) of section 1232(g)(1) of this title.

(B) Certified State or Indian tribe defined

In this paragraph the term "certified State or Indian tribe" means a State or Indian tribe for which a certification is made under subsection (a) of this section in which the Secretary concurs.

(3) Manner of payment

(A) In general

Subject to subparagraph (B), payments to States or Indian tribes under this subsection shall be made without regard to any limitation in section 1231(d) of this title and concurrently with payments to States under that section.

(B) Initial payments

The first 3 payments made to any State or Indian tribe shall be reduced to 25 percent, 50 percent, and 75 percent, respectively, of the amounts otherwise required under paragraph (2)(A).

(C) Installments

Amounts withheld from the first 3 annual installments as provided under subparagraph (B) shall be paid in 2 equal annual installments beginning with fiscal year 2018.

(4) Reallocation

(A) In general

The annual amount allocated under subparagraph (A) or (B) of section 1232(g)(1) of this title to any State or Indian tribe that makes a certification under subsection (a) of this section in which the Secretary concurs shall be reallocated and available for grants under section 1232(g)(5) of this title.

(B) Allocation

The grants shall be allocated based on the amount of coal historically produced before August 3, 1977, in the same manner as under section 1232(g)(5) of this title.

(5) Limitation on annual payments

Notwithstanding any other provision of this subsection, the total annual payment to a certified State or Indian tribe under this subsection shall be not more than $15,000,000.

(6) Supplemental funding

(A) Waiver of limitation

Notwithstanding paragraph (5), the limitation on the total annual payments to a certified State or Indian tribe under this subsection shall not apply for fiscal years 2014 and 2015.

(B) Limitation on waiver

Notwithstanding subparagraph (A), the total annual payment to a certified State or Indian tribe under this subsection for fiscal year 2014 shall not be more than $28,000,000 and for fiscal year 2015 shall not be more than $75,000,000.

(C) Insufficient amounts

If the total annual payment to a certified State or Indian tribe under paragraphs (1) and (2) is limited by subparagraph (B), the Secretary shall—

(i) give priority to making payments under paragraph (2); and

(ii) use any remaining funds to make payments under paragraph (1).

(Pub. L. No. 95–87, Title IV, § 411, as added by Pub. L. No. 101–508, Title VI, § 6010(2), 104 Stat. 1388–296 (Nov. 5, 1990); and amended by Pub. L. No. 109–432, Div. C, Title II, § 206, 120 Stat. 3016 (Dec. 20, 2006); Pub. L. No. 112–141, Div. F, Title I, § 100125, 126 Stat. 915 (July 6, 2012); Pub. L. No. 112–175, § 142, 126 Stat. 1321 (Sept. 28, 2012); Pub. L. No. 113–40, § 10(d), 127 Stat. 546 (Oct. 2, 2013).)

HISTORICAL AND STATUTORY NOTES

References in Text

The Uranium Mill Tailings Radiation Control Act of 1978, referred to in subsec. (d), is Pub. L. No. 95–604, 92 Stat. 3021 (Nov. 8, 1978), as amended, which is codified principally as chapter 88 (section 7901 et seq.) of Title 42, The Public Health and Welfare. For complete classification of this Act to the Code, see Short Title note set out under section 7901 of Title 42 and Tables.

The Comprehensive Environmental Response Compensation and Liability Act of 1980, referred to in subsec. (d), is Pub. L. No. 96–510, 94 Stat. 2767 (Dec. 11, 1980), as amended, which is codified principally as chapter 103 (sections 9601 et seq.) of Title 42, The Public Health and Welfare. For complete classification of this Act to the Code, see Short Title note set out under section 9601 of Title 42 and Tables.

Codifications

Another section 411 of Pub. L. No. 95–87 is codified as section 1241 of this title. Such section is redesignated section 412 of Pub. L. No. 95–87, eff. Oct. 1, 1991, pursuant to sections 6010(1) and 6014 of Pub. L. No. 101–508. Such section remains codified as section 1241 of this title after such redesignation on Oct. 1, 1991.

Effective and Applicability Provisions

1990 Acts. Section effective Oct. 1, 1991, see section 6014 of Pub. L. No. 101–508, set out as a note under section 1231 of this title.

Savings Provisions

Nothing in Subtitle A (section 6001 et seq.) of Title VI of Pub. L. No. 101–508, shall be construed to affect the certifications made by the States of Wyoming, Montana, and Louisiana to the Secretary of the Interior prior to Nov. 5, 1990, that each such State has completed the reclamation of eligible abandoned coal mine lands, see section 6013 of Pub. L. No. 101–508, set out as note under section 1231 of this title.

Prior Provisions

A prior section 411 of Pub. L. No. 95–87 was renumbered section 412 and was codified as section 1241 of this title, prior to being omitted from the Code.

§ 1241. Omitted

HISTORICAL AND STATUTORY NOTES

This section was created by Pub. L. No. 95–87, Title IV, § 412, formerly § 411, 91 Stat. 466 (Aug. 3, 1977), renumbered § 412 by Pub. L. No.101–508, Title VI, § 6010(1), 104 Stat. 1388–296 (Nov. 5, 1990), and required the Secretary of the Interior or the State pursuant to an approved State program to annually submit to Congress reports on operations under the fund together with recommendations for future use of the fund. It was terminated, effective May 15, 2000, pursuant to Pub. L. No. 104–66, § 3003, as amended, which is set out as a note under 31 U.S.C.A. § 1113. See, also, page 109 of House Document No. 103–7.

§ 1242. Powers of Secretary or State

[SMCRA § 413]

(a) Engage in work, promulgate rules and regulations, etc., to implement and administer this subchapter

The Secretary or the State pursuant to an approved State program, shall have the power and authority, if not granted it otherwise, to engage in any work and to do all things necessary or expedient, including promulgation of rules and regulations, to implement and administer the provisions of this subchapter.

(b) Engage in cooperative projects

The Secretary or the State pursuant to an approved State program, shall have the power and authority to engage in cooperative projects under this subchapter with any other agency of the United States of America, any State and their governmental agencies.

(c) Request for action to restrain interference with regard to this subchapter

The Secretary or the State pursuant to an approved State program, may request the Attorney General, who is hereby authorized to initiate, in addition to any other remedies provided for in this subchapter, in any court of competent jurisdiction, an action in equity for an injunction to restrain any interference with the exercise of the right to enter or to conduct any work provided in this subchapter.

(d) Construct and operate plants for control and treatment of water pollution resulting from mine drainage

The Secretary or the State pursuant to an approved State program, shall have the power and authority to construct and operate a plant or plants for the control and treatment of water pollution resulting from mine drainage. The extent of this control and treatment may be dependent upon the ultimate use of the water: *Provided*, That the above provisions of this paragraph shall not be deemed in any way to repeal or supersede any portion of the Federal Water Pollution Control Act (33 U.S.C.A. 1151, et seq. as amended) [33 U.S.C.A. § 1251 et seq.] and no control or treatment under this subsection shall in any way be less than that required under the Federal Water Pollution Control Act. The construction of a plant or plants may include major interceptors and other facilities appurtenant to the plant.

(e) Transfer funds

The Secretary may transfer funds to other appropriate Federal agencies, in order to carry out the reclamation activities authorized by this subchapter.

(Pub. L. No. 95–87, Title IV, § 413, formerly § 412, 91 Stat. 466 (Aug. 3, 1977); as renumbered by Pub. L. No. 101–508, Title VI, § 6010(1), 104 Stat. 1388–296 (Nov. 5, 1990).)

HISTORICAL AND STATUTORY NOTES

References in Text

The Federal Water Pollution Control Act (33 U.S.C.A. 1151, et seq. as amended), referred to in subsec. (d), is Act of June 30, 1948, c. 758, 62 Stat. 1155, formerly codified as chapter 23 (section 1151 et seq.) of Title 33, Navigation and Navigable Waters, which was completely revised by Pub. L. No. 92–500, § 2, 86 Stat. 816 (Oct. 18, 1972), and is now codified generally as chapter 26 (section 1251 et seq.) of Title 33. For complete classification of this Act to the Code, see Short Title note set out under section 1251 of Title 33 and Tables.

§ 1243. Interagency cooperation

[SMCRA § 414]

All departments, boards, commissioners, and agencies of the United States of America shall cooperate with the Secretary by providing technical expertise, personnel, equipment, materials, and supplies to implement and administer the provisions of this subchapter.

(Pub. L. No. 95–87, Title IV, § 414, formerly § 413, 91 Stat. 467 (Aug. 3, 1977); as renumbered by Pub. L. No. 101–508, Title VI, § 6010(1), 104 Stat. 1388–296 (Nov. 5, 1990).)

§ 1244. Remining incentives

[SMCRA § 415]

(a) In general

Notwithstanding any other provision of this chapter, the Secretary may, after opportunity for public comment, promulgate regulations that describe conditions under which amounts in the fund may be used to provide incentives to promote remining of eligible land under section 1234 of this title in a manner that leverages the use of amounts from the fund to achieve more reclamation with respect to the eligible land than would be achieved without the incentives.

(b) Requirements

Any regulations promulgated under subsection (a) of this section shall specify that the incentives shall apply only if the Secretary determines, with the concurrence of the State regulatory authority referred to in subchapter V of this chapter, that, without the incentives, the eligible land would not be likely to be remined and reclaimed.

(c) Incentives

(1) In general

Incentives that may be considered for inclusion in the regulations promulgated under subsection (a) of this section include, but are not limited to—

(A) a rebate or waiver of the reclamation fees required under section 1232(a) of this title; and

(B) the use of amounts in the fund to provide financial assurance for remining operations in lieu of all or a portion of the performance bonds required under section 1259 of this title.

(2) Limitations

(A) Use

A rebate or waiver under paragraph (1)(A) shall be used only for operations that—

(i) remove or reprocess abandoned coal mine waste; or

(ii) conduct remining activities that meet the priorities specified in paragraph (1) or (2) of section 1233(a) of this title.

(B) Amount

The amount of a rebate or waiver provided as an incentive under paragraph (1)(A) to remine or reclaim eligible land shall not exceed the estimated cost of reclaiming the eligible land under this section.

(Pub. L. No. 95–87, Title IV, § 415, as added by Pub. L. No. 109–432, Div. C, Title II, § 207, 120 Stat. 3018 (Dec. 20, 2006).)

HISTORICAL AND STATUTORY NOTES

References in Text

This chapter, referred to in subsec. (a), originally read "this Act", meaning the Surface Mining Control and Reclamation Act of 1977, or the SMCRA, Pub. L. No. 95–87, 91 Stat. 445 (Aug. 3, 1977), as amended, which is principally codified as this chapter. For complete classification, see Tables.

Subchapter V of this chapter, referee to in subsec. (b), originally read "title V", meaning the Surface Mining Control and Reclamation Act of 1977, Pub. L. No. 95–87, Title V, § 501, 91 Stat. 467 (Aug. 3, 1977), which is codified as subchapter V of this chapter, 30 U.S.C.A. § 1251 et seq.

SUBCHAPTER V—CONTROL OF THE ENVIRONMENTAL IMPACTS OF SURFACE COAL MINING

§ 1251. Environmental protection standards

[SMCRA § 501]

(a) Not later than the end of the ninety-day period immediately following August 3, 1977, the Secretary shall promulgate and publish in the Federal Register regulations covering an interim regulatory procedure for surface coal mining and reclamation operations setting mining and reclamation performance standards based on and incorporating the provisions set out in section 1252(c) of this title. The issuance of the interim regulations shall be deemed not to be a major Federal action within the meaning of section 4332(2)(c) of Title 42. Such regulations, which shall be concise and written in plain, understandable language shall not be promulgated and published by the Secretary until he has—

(A) published proposed regulations in the Federal Register and afforded interested persons and State and local governments a period of not less than thirty days after such publication to submit written comments thereon;

(B) obtained the written concurrence of the Administrator of the Environmental Protection Agency with respect to those regulations promulgated under this section which relate to air or water quality standards promulgated under the authority of the Federal Water Pollution Control Act, as amended [33 U.S.C.A. § 1251 et seq.]; and the Clean Air Act, as amended [42 U.S.C.A. § 7401 et seq.]; and

(C) held at least one public hearing on the proposed regulations.

The date, time, and place of any hearing held on the proposed regulations shall be set out in the publication of the proposed regulations. The Secretary shall consider all comments and relevant data presented at such hearing before final promulgation and publication of the regulations.

(b) Not later than one year after August 3, 1977, the Secretary shall promulgate and publish in the Federal Register regulations covering a permanent regulatory procedure for surface coal mining and reclamation operations performance standards based on and conforming to the provisions of this subchapter and establishing procedures and requirements for preparation, submission, and approval of State programs; and development and implementation of Federal programs under the subchapter. The Secretary shall promulgate these regulations, which shall be concise and written in plain, understandable language in accordance with the procedures in subsection (a) of this section.

(Pub. L. No. 95–87, Title V, § 501, 91 Stat. 467 (Aug. 3, 1977).)

HISTORICAL AND STATUTORY NOTES

References in Text

The Federal Water Pollution Control Act, as amended, referred to in subsec. (a)(B), is Act of June 30, 1948, c. 758, 62 Stat. 1155, formerly codified as chapter 23 (section 1151 et seq.) of Title 33, Navigation and Navigable Waters, which was completely revised by Pub. L. No. 92–500, § 2, 86 Stat. 816 (Oct. 18, 1972), and is codified generally as chapter 26 (section 1251 et seq.) of Title 33. For complete classification of this Act to the Code, see Short Title note set out under section 1251 of Title 33 and Tables.

The Clean Air Act, as amended, referred to in subsec. (a)(B), is Act of July 14, 1955, c. 360, as amended generally by Pub. L. No. 88–206, 77 Stat. 392 (Dec. 17, 1963), and later by Pub. L. No. 95–95, 91 Stat. 685 (Aug. 7, 1977). The Clean Air Act was originally codified as chapter 15B (section 1857 et seq.) of Title 42, The Public Health and Welfare. On enactment of Pub. L. No. 95–95, the Act was recodified as chapter 85 (section 7401 et seq.) of Title 42. For complete classification of this Act to the Code, see Short Title note set out under section 7401 of Title 42 and Tables volume.

§ 1251a. Abandoned coal refuse sites

(1) Notwithstanding any other provision of the Surface Mining Control and Reclamation Act of 1977 [30 U.S.C.A. § 1201 et seq.] to the contrary, the Secretary of the Interior shall, within one year after October 24, 1992, publish proposed regulations in the Federal Register, and after opportunity for public comment publish final regulations, establishing environmental protection performance and reclamation standards, and separate permit systems applicable to operations for the on-site reprocessing of abandoned coal refuse and operations for the removal of abandoned coal refuse on lands that would otherwise be eligible for expenditure under section 404 and section 402(g)(4) of the Surface Mining Control and Reclamation Act of 1977 [30 U.S.C.A. §§ 1234 and 1232(g)(4)].

(2) The standards and permit systems referred to in paragraph (1) shall distinguish between those operations which reprocess abandoned coal refuse on-site, and those operations which completely remove abandoned coal refuse from a site for the direct use of such coal refuse, or for the reprocessing of such coal refuse, at another location. Such standards and permit systems shall be premised on the distinct differences between operations for the on-site reprocessing, and operations for the removal, of abandoned coal refuse and other types of surface coal mining operations.

(3) The Secretary of the Interior may devise a different standard than any of those set forth in section 515 and section 516 of the Surface Mining Control and Reclamation Act of 1977 [30 U.S.C.A. §§ 1265 and 1266], and devise a separate permit system, if he determines, on a standard-by-standard basis, that a different standard may facilitate the on-site reprocessing, or the removal, of abandoned coal refuse in a manner that would provide the same level of environmental protection as under section 515 and section 516.

(4) Not later than 30 days prior to the publication of the proposed regulations referred to in this section, the Secretary shall submit a report to the Committee on Interior and Insular Affairs of the United States House of Representatives, and the Committee on Energy and Natural Resources of the United States Senate containing a detailed description of any environmental protection performance and reclamation standards, and separate permit systems, devised pursuant to this section.

(Pub. L. No. 102–486, Title XXV, § 2503(e), 106 Stat. 3103 (Oct. 24, 1992).)

HISTORICAL AND STATUTORY NOTES

References in Text

The Surface Mining Control and Reclamation Act of 1977, referred to in paragraphs (1) and (3), is Pub. L. No. 95–87, 91 Stat. 445 (Aug. 3, 1977), as amended, which is codified generally to this chapter. For complete classification of this Act to the Code, see Short Title note set out under section 1201 of this title and Tables.

Codifications

Section was not enacted as part of the Surface Mining Control and Reclamation Act of 1977 which comprises this chapter.

Change of Name

Committee on Interior and Insular Affairs of the House of Representatives changed to Committee on Natural Resources of the House of Representatives on Jan. 5, 1993, by House Resolution No. 5, One Hundred Third Congress.

§ 1252. Initial regulatory procedures

[SMCRA § 502]

(a) State regulation

No person shall open or develop any new or previously mined or abandoned site for surface coal mining operations on lands on which such operations are regulated by a State unless such person has obtained a permit from the State's regulatory authority.

(b) Interim standards

All surface coal mining operations on lands on which such operations are regulated by a State which commence operations pursuant to a permit issued on or after six months from August 3, 1977, shall comply, and such permits shall contain terms requiring compliance with, the provisions set out in subsection (c) of this section. Prior to final disapproval of a State program or prior to promulgation of a Federal program or a Federal lands program pursuant to this chapter, a State may issue such permits.

(c) Full compliance with environmental protection performance standards

On and after nine months from August 3, 1977, all surface coal mining operations on lands on which such operations are regulated by a State shall comply with the provisions of subsections (b)(2), (b)(3), (b)(5), (b)(10), (b)(13), (b)(15), (b)(19), and (d) of section 1265 of this title or, where a surface coal mining operation will remove an entire coal seam or seams running through the upper fraction of a mountain, ridge, or hill by removing all of the overburden and creating a level plateau or a gently rolling contour with no highwalls remaining, such operation shall comply with the requirements of section 1265(c)(4) and (5) of this title without regard to the requirements of section 1265(b)(3) or (d)(2) and (3) of this title, with respect to lands from which overburden and the coal seam being mined have not been removed: *Provided, however,* That surface coal mining operations in operation pursuant to a permit issued by a State before August 3, 1977, issued to a person as defined in section 1291(19) of this title in existence prior to May 2, 1977 and operated by a person whose total annual production of coal from surface and underground coal mining operations does not exceed one hundred thousand tons shall not be subject to the provisions of this subsection except with reference to the provision of section 1265(d)(1) of this title until January 1, 1979.

(d) Permit application

Not later than two months following the approval of a State program pursuant to section 1253 of this title or the implementation of a Federal program pursuant to section 1254 of this title, regardless of litigation contesting that approval or implementation, all operators of surface coal mines in expectation of operating such mines after the expiration of eight months from the approval of a State program or the implementation of a Federal program, shall file an application for a permit with the regulatory authority. Such application shall cover those lands to be mined after the expiration of eight months from the approval of a State program or the implementation of a Federal program. The regulatory authority shall process such applications and grant or deny a permit within eight months after the date of approval of the State program or the implementation of the Federal program, unless specially enjoined by a court of competent jurisdiction, but in no case later than forty-two months from August 3, 1977.

(e) Federal enforcement program

Within six months after August 3, 1977, the Secretary shall implement a Federal enforcement program which shall remain in effect in each State as surface coal mining operations are required to comply with the provisions of this chapter, until the State program has been approved pursuant to this chapter or until a Federal program has been implemented pursuant to this chapter. The enforcement program shall—

(1) include inspections of surface coal mine sites which may be made (but at least one inspection for every site every six months), without advance notice to the mine operator and for the purpose of ascertaining compliance with the standards of subsections (b) and (c) above. The Secretary shall order any necessary enforcement action to be implemented pursuant to the Federal enforcement provision of this subchapter to correct violations identified at the inspections;

(2) provide that upon receipt of inspection reports indicating that any surface coal mining operation has been found in violation of subsections (b) and (c) above, during not less than two consecutive State inspections or upon receipt by the Secretary of information which would give rise to reasonable belief that such standards are being violated by any surface coal mining operation, the Secretary shall order the immediate inspection of such operation by Federal inspectors and the necessary enforcement actions, if any, to be implemented pursuant to the Federal enforcement provisions of this subchapter. When the Federal inspection results from information provided to the Secretary by any person, the Secretary shall notify such person when the Federal inspection is proposed to be carried out and such person shall be allowed to accompany the inspector during the inspection;

(3) provide that the State regulatory agency file with the Secretary and with a designated Federal office centrally located in the county or area in which the inspected surface coal mine is located copies of inspection reports made;

(4) provide that moneys authorized by section 1302 of this title shall be available to the Secretary prior to the approval of a State program pursuant to this chapter to reimburse the State for conducting those inspections in which the standards of this chapter are enforced and for the administration of this section.[1]

(5) for purposes of this section, the term "Federal inspector" means personnel of the Office of Surface Mining Reclamation and Enforcement and such additional personnel of the United States Geological Survey, Bureau of Land Management, or of the Mining Enforcement and Safety Administration so designated by the Secretary, or such other personnel of the Forest Service, Soil Conservation Service, or the Agricultural Stabilization and Conservation Service as arranged by appropriate agreement with the Secretary on a reimbursable or other basis;[2]

(f) Interim period

Following the final disapproval of a State program, and prior to promulgation of a Federal program or a Federal lands program pursuant to this chapter, including judicial review of such a program, existing surface coal mining operations may continue surface mining operations pursuant to the provisions of this section. During such period no new permits shall be issued by the State whose program has been disapproved. Permits which lapse during such period may continue in full force and effect until promulgation of a Federal program or a Federal lands program.

(Pub. L. No. 95–87, Title V, § 502, 91 Stat. 468 (Aug. 3, 1977).)

[1] So in original. The period probably should be a semicolon.

[2] So in original. The semicolon probably should be a period.

HISTORICAL AND STATUTORY NOTES

References in Text

This chapter, referred to in the introductory text of subsec. (e) and in subsecs. (e)(4) and (f), was in the original "this Act", meaning Pub. L. No. 95–87, 91 Stat. 445 (Aug. 3, 1977), as amended, which enacted this chapter and amended section 1114 of Title 18, Crimes and Criminal Procedure. For complete classification of this Act to the Code, see Short Title note set out under section 1201 of this title and Tables.

§ 1253. State programs

[SMCRA § 503]

(a) Regulation of surface coal mining and reclamation operations; submittal to Secretary; time limit; demonstration of effectiveness

Each State in which there are or may be conducted surface coal mining operations on non-Federal lands, and which wishes to assume exclusive jurisdiction over the regulation of surface coal mining and reclamation operations, except as provided in sections 1271 and 1273 of this title and subchapter IV of this chapter, shall submit to the Secretary, by the end of the eighteenth-month period beginning on August 3, 1977, a State program which demonstrates that such State has the capability of carrying out the provisions of this chapter and meeting its purposes through—

(1) a State law which provides for the regulation of surface coal mining and reclamation operations in accordance with the requirements of this chapter;

(2) a State law which provides sanctions for violations of State laws, regulations, or conditions of permits concerning surface coal mining and reclamation operations, which sanctions shall meet the minimum requirements of this chapter, including civil and criminal actions, forfeiture of bonds, suspensions, revocations, and withholding of permits, and the issuance of cease-and-desist orders by the State regulatory authority or its inspectors;

(3) a State regulatory authority with sufficient administrative and technical personnel, and sufficient funding to enable the State to regulate surface coal mining and reclamation operations in accordance with the requirements of this chapter;

(4) a State law which provides for the effective implementations, maintenance, and enforcement of a permit system, meeting the requirements of this subchapter for the regulations of surface coal mining and reclamation operations for coal on lands within the State;

(5) establishment of a process for the designation of areas as unsuitable for surface coal mining in accordance with section 1272 of this title provided that the designation of Federal lands unsuitable for mining shall be performed exclusively by the Secretary after consultation with the State; and[1]

(6) establishment for the purposes of avoiding duplication, of a process for coordinating the review and issuance of permits for surface coal mining and reclamation operations with any other Federal or State permit process applicable to the proposed operations; and

(7) rules and regulations consistent with regulations issued by the Secretary pursuant to this chapter.

(b) Approval of program

The Secretary shall not approve any State program submitted under this section until he has—

(1) solicited and publicly disclosed the views of the Administrator of the Environmental Protection Agency, the Secretary of Agriculture, and the heads of other Federal agencies concerned with or having special expertise pertinent to the proposed State program;

(2) obtained the written concurrence of the Administrator of the Environmental Protection Agency with respect to those aspects of a State program which relate to air or water quality standards promulgated under the authority of the Federal Water Pollution Control Act, as amended [33 U.S.C.A. § 1251 et seq.], and the Clean Air Act, as amended [42 U.S.C.A. § 7401 et seq.];

(3) held at least one public hearing on the State program within the State; and

(4) found that the State has the legal authority and qualified personnel necessary for the enforcement of the environmental protection standards.

The Secretary shall approve or disapprove a State program, in whole or in part, within six full calendar months after the date such State program was submitted to him.

(c) Notice of disapproval

If the Secretary disapproves any proposed State program in whole or in part, he shall notify the State in writing of his decision and set forth in detail the reasons therefor. The State shall have sixty days in which to resubmit a revised State program or portion thereof. The Secretary shall approve or disapprove the resubmitted State program or portion thereof within sixty days from the date of resubmission.

(d) Inability of State to take action

For the purposes of this section and section 1254 of this title, the inability of a State to take any action the purpose of which is to prepare, submit or enforce a State program, or any portion thereof, because the action is enjoined by the issuance of an injunction by any court of competent jurisdiction shall not result in a loss of eligibility for financial assistance under subchapters IV and VII of this chapter or in the imposition of a Federal program. Regulation of the surface coal mining and reclamation operations covered or to be covered by the State program subject to the injunction shall be conducted by the State pursuant to section 1252 of this title, until such time as the injunction terminates or for one year, whichever is shorter, at which time the requirements of this section and section 1254 of this title shall again be fully applicable.

(Pub. L. No. 95–87, Title V, § 503, 91 Stat. 470 (Aug. 3, 1977).)

[1] So in original.

HISTORICAL AND STATUTORY NOTES

References in Text

This chapter, referred to in subsec. (a), was in the original "this Act", meaning Pub. L. No. 95–87, 91 Stat. 445 (Aug. 3, 1977), as amended, which enacted this chapter and amended section 1114 of Title 18, Crimes and Criminal Procedure. For complete classification of this Act to the Code, see Short Title note set out under section 1201 of this title and Tables volume.

The Federal Water Pollution Control Act, as amended, referred to in subsec. (b)(2), is Act of June 30, 1948, c. 758, 62 Stat. 1155, formerly codified as chapter 23 (section 1151 et seq.) of Title 33, Navigation and Navigable Waters, which was completely revised by Pub. L. No. 92–500, § 2, 86 Stat. 816 (Oct. 18, 1972), and is codified generally to chapter 26 (section 1251 et seq.) of Title 33. For complete classification of this Act to the Code, see Short Title note set out under section 1251 of Title 33 and Tables volume.

The Clean Air Act, as amended, referred to in subsec. (b)(2), is Act of July 14, 1955, c. 360, as amended generally by Pub. L. No. 88–206, 77 Stat. 392 (Dec. 17, 1963), and later by Pub. L. No. 95–95, 91 Stat. 685 (Aug. 7, 1977). The Clean Air Act was originally codified as chapter 15B (section 1857 et seq.) of Title 42, The Public Health and Welfare. On enactment of Pub. L. No. 95–95, the Act was recodified as chapter 85 (section 7401 et seq.) of Title 42. For complete classification of this Act to the Code, see Short Title note set out under section 7401 of Title 42 and Tables volume.

§ 1254. Federal programs

[SMCRA § 504]

(a) Promulgation and implementation by Secretary for State

The Secretary shall prepare and, subject to the provisions of this section, promulgate and implement a Federal program for a State no later than thirty-four months after August 3, 1977, if such State—

(1) fails to submit a State program covering surface coal mining and reclamation operations by the end of the eighteen-month period beginning on August 3, 1977;

(2) fails to resubmit an acceptable State program within sixty days of disapproval of a proposed State program: *Provided*, That the Secretary shall not implement a Federal program prior to the expiration of the initial period allowed for submission of a State program as provided for in clause (1) of this subsection; or

(3) fails to implement, enforce, or maintain its approved State program as provided for in this chapter.

If State compliance with clause (1) of this subsection requires an act of the State legislature, the Secretary may extend the period of submission of a State program up to an additional six months. Promulgation and implementation of a Federal program vests the Secretary with exclusive jurisdiction for the regulation and control of surface coal mining and reclamation operations taking place on lands within any State not in compliance with this chapter. After promulgation and implementation of a Federal program the Secretary shall be the regulatory authority. If a Federal program is implemented for a State, section 1272(a), (c), and (d) of this title shall not apply for a period of one year following the date of such implementation. In promulgating and implementing a Federal program for a particular State the Secretary shall take into consideration the nature of that State's terrain, climate, biological, chemical, and other relevant physical conditions.

(b) Federal enforcement of State program

In the event that a State has a State program for surface coal mining, and is not enforcing any part of such program, the Secretary may provide for the Federal enforcement, under the provisions of section 1271 of this title, of that part of the State program not being enforced by such State.

(c) Notice and hearing

Prior to promulgation and implementation of any proposed Federal program, the Secretary shall give adequate public notice and hold a public hearing in the affected State.

(d) Review of permits

Permits issued pursuant to a previously approved State program shall be valid but reviewable under a Federal program. Immediately following promulgation of a Federal program, the Secretary shall undertake to review such permits to determine that the requirements of this chapter are not violated. If the Secretary determines any permit to have been granted contrary to the requirements of this chapter, he shall so advise the permittee and provide him an opportunity for hearing and a reasonable opportunity for submission of a new application and reasonable time, within a time limit prescribed in regulations promulgated pursuant to section 1251(b) of this title, to conform ongoing surface mining and reclamation operations to the requirements of the Federal program.

(e) Submission of State program after implementation of Federal program

A State which has failed to obtain the approval of a State program prior to implementation of a Federal program may submit a State program at any time after such implementation. Upon the submission of such a program, the Secretary shall follow the procedures set forth in section 1253(b) of this title and shall approve or disapprove the State program within six months after its submittal. Approval of a State program shall be based on the determination that the State has the capability of carrying out the provisions of this chapter and meeting its purposes through the criteria set forth in section 1253(a)(1) through (6) of this title. Until a State program is approved as provided under this section, the Federal program shall remain in effect and all actions taken by the Secretary pursuant to such Federal program, including the terms and conditions of any permit issued thereunder shall remain in effect.

(f) Validity of Federal program permits under superseding State program

Permits issued pursuant to the Federal program shall be valid under any superseding State program: *Provided,* That the Federal permittee shall have the right to apply for a State permit to supersede his Federal permit. The State regulatory authority may review such permits to determine that the requirements of this chapter and the approved State program are not violated. Should the State program contain additional requirements not contained in the Federal program, the permittee will be provided opportunity for hearing and a reasonable time, within a time limit prescribed in regulations promulgated pursuant to section 1251 of this title, to conform ongoing surface mining and reclamation operations to the additional State requirements.

(g) Preemption of State statutes or regulations

Whenever a Federal program is promulgated for a State pursuant to this chapter, any statutes or regulations of such State which are in effect to regulate surface mining and reclamation operations subject to this chapter shall, insofar as they interfere with the achievement of the purposes and the requirements of this chapter and the Federal program, be preempted and superseded by the Federal program. The Secretary shall set forth any State law or regulation which is preempted and superseded by the Federal program.

(h) Coordination of issuance and review of Federal program permits with any other Federal or State permit process

Any Federal program shall include a process for coordinating the review and issuance of permits for surface mining and reclamation operations with any other Federal or State permit process applicable to the proposed operation.

(Pub. L. No. 95–87, Title V, § 504, 91 Stat. 471 (Aug. 3, 1977).)

HISTORICAL AND STATUTORY NOTES

References in Text

This chapter, referred to in subsecs. (a), (d), (e), (f), and (g), was in the original "this Act", meaning Pub. L. No. 95–87, 91 Stat. 445 (Aug. 3, 1977), as amended, which enacted this chapter and amended section 1114 of Title 18, Crimes and Criminal Procedure. For complete classification of this Act to the Code, see Short Title note set out under section 1201 of this title and Tables.

§ 1255. State laws

[SMCRA § 505]

(a) No State law or regulation in effect on August 3, 1977, or which may become effective thereafter, shall be superseded by any provision of this chapter or any regulation issued pursuant thereto, except insofar as such State law or regulation is inconsistent with the provisions of this chapter.

(b) Any provision of any State law or regulation in effect upon August 3, 1977, or which may become effective thereafter, which provides for more stringent land use and environmental controls and regulations of surface coal mining and reclamation operation than do the provisions of this chapter or any regulation issued pursuant thereto shall not be construed to be inconsistent with this chapter. The Secretary shall set forth any State law or regulation which is construed to be inconsistent with this chapter. Any provision of any State law or regulation in effect on August 3, 1977, or which may become effective thereafter, which provides for the control and regulation of surface mining and reclamation operations for which no provision is contained in this chapter shall not be construed to be inconsistent with this chapter.

(Pub. L. No. 95–87, Title V, § 505, 91 Stat. 473 (Aug. 3, 1977).)

HISTORICAL AND STATUTORY NOTES

References in Text

This chapter, referred to in text, was in the original "this Act", meaning Pub. L. No. 95–87, 91 Stat. 455 (Aug. 3, 1977), as amended, which enacted this chapter and amended section 1114 of Title 18, Crimes and Criminal Procedure. For complete classification of this Act to the Code, see Short Title note set out under section 1201 of this title and Tables.

§ 1256. Permits

[SMCRA § 506]

(a) Persons engaged in surface coal mining within State; time limit; exception

No later than eight months from the date on which a State program is approved by the Secretary, pursuant to section 1253 of this title, or no later than eight months from the date on which the Secretary has promulgated a Federal program for a State not having a State program pursuant to section 1254 of this title, no person shall engage in or carry out on lands within a State any surface coal mining operations unless such person has first obtained a permit issued by such State pursuant to an approved State program or by the Secretary pursuant to a Federal program; except a person conducting surface coal mining operations under a permit from the State regulatory authority, issued in accordance with the provisions of section 1252 of this title, may conduct such operations beyond such period if an application for a permit has been filed in accordance with the provisions of this chapter, but the initial administrative decision has not been rendered.

(b) Term

All permits issued pursuant to the requirements of this chapter shall be issued for a term not to exceed five years: *Provided,* That if the applicant demonstrates that a specified longer term is reasonably needed to allow the applicant to obtain necessary financing for equipment and the opening of the operation and if the application is full and complete for such specified longer term, the regulatory authority may grant a permit for such longer term. A successor in interest to a permittee who applies for a new permit within thirty days of succeeding to such interest and who is able to obtain the bond coverage of the original permittee may continue surface coal mining and reclamation operations according to the approved mining and reclamation plan of the original permittee until such successor's application is granted or denied.

(c) Termination

A permit shall terminate if the permittee has not commenced the surface coal mining operations covered by such permit within three years of the issuance of the permit: *Provided,* That the regulatory authority may grant reasonable extensions of time upon a showing that such extensions are necessary by reason of litigation precluding such commencement or threatening substantial economic loss to the permittee, or by reason of conditions beyond the control and without the fault or negligence of the permittee: *Provided further,* That in the case of a coal lease issued under the Federal Mineral Leasing Act, as amended [30 U.S.C.A. § 181 et seq.], extensions of time may not extend beyond the period allowed for diligent development in accordance with section 7 of that Act [30 U.S.C.A. § 207]: *Provided further,* That with respect to coal to be mined for use in a synthetic fuel facility or specific major electric generating facility, the permittee shall be deemed to have commenced surface mining operations at such time as the construction of the synthetic fuel or generating facility is initiated.

(d) Renewal

(1) Any valid permit issued pursuant to this chapter shall carry with it the right of successive renewal upon expiration with respect to areas within the boundaries of the existing permit. The holders of the permit may apply for renewal and such renewal shall be issued (provided that on application for renewal the burden shall be on the opponents of renewal), subsequent to fulfillment of the public notice requirements of sections 1263 and 1264 of this title unless it is established that and written findings by the regulatory authority are made that—

(A) the terms and conditions of the existing permit are not being satisfactorily met;

(B) the present surface coal mining and reclamation operation is not in compliance with the environmental protection standards of this chapter and the approved State plan or Federal program pursuant to this chapter; or

(C) the renewal requested substantially jeopardizes the operator's continuing responsibility on existing permit areas;

(D) the operator has not provided evidence that the performance bond in effect for said operation will continue in full force and effect for any renewal requested in such application as well as any additional bond the regulatory authority might require pursuant to section 1259 of this title; or

(E) any additional revised or updated information required by the regulatory authority has not been provided. Prior to the approval of any renewal of permit the regulatory authority shall provide notice to the appropriate public authorities.

(2) If an application for renewal of a valid permit includes a proposal to extend the mining operation beyond the boundaries authorized in the existing permit, the portion of the application for renewal of a valid permit which addresses any new land areas shall be subject to the full standards applicable to new applications under this chapter: *Provided, however,* That if the surface coal mining operations authorized by a permit issued pursuant to this chapter were not subject to the standards contained in section 1260(b)(5)(A) and (B) of this title by reason of complying with the proviso of section 1260(b)(5) of this title, then the portion of the application for renewal of the permit which addresses any new land areas previously identified in the reclamation plan submitted pursuant to section 1258 of this title shall not be subject to the standards contained in section 1260(b)(5)(A) and (B) of this title.

(3) Any permit renewal shall be for a term not to exceed the period of the original permit established by this chapter. Application for permit renewal shall be made at least one hundred and twenty days prior to the expiration of the valid permit.

(Pub. L. No. 95–87, Title V, § 506, 91 Stat. 473 (Aug. 3, 1977).)

HISTORICAL AND STATUTORY NOTES

References in Text

This chapter, referred to in subsecs. (a), (b), and (d), was in the original "this Act", meaning Pub. L. No. 95–87, 91 Stat. 445 (Aug. 3, 1977), as amended, which enacted this chapter and amended section 1114 of Title 18, Crimes and Criminal Procedure. For complete classification of this Act to the Code, see Short Title note set out under section 1201 of this title and Tables.

§ 1257. Application requirements

[SMCRA § 507]

(a) Fee

Each application for a surface coal mining and reclamation permit pursuant to an approved State program or a Federal program under the provisions of this chapter shall be accompanied by a fee as determined by the regulatory authority. Such fee may be less than but shall not exceed the actual or anticipated cost of reviewing, administering, and enforcing such permit issued pursuant to a State or Federal program. The regulatory authority may develop procedures so as to enable the cost of the fee to be paid over the term of the permit.

(b) Submittal; contents

The permit application shall be submitted in a manner satisfactory to the regulatory authority and shall contain, among other things—

(1) the names and addresses of (A) the permit applicant; (B) every legal owner of record of the property (surface and mineral), to be mined; (C) the holders of record of any leasehold interest in the property; (D) any purchaser of record of the property under a real estate contract; and (E) the operator if he is a person different from the applicant; and (F) if any of these are business entities other than a single proprietor, the names and addresses of the principals, officers, and resident agent;

(2) the names and addresses of the owners of record of all surface and subsurface areas adjacent to any part of the permit area;

(3) a statement of any current or previous surface coal mining permits in the United States held by the applicant and the permit identification and each pending application;

(4) if the applicant is a partnership, corporation, association, or other business entity, the following where applicable: the names and addresses of every officer, partner, director, or person performing a function similar to a director, of the applicant, together with the name and address of any person owning, of record 10 per centum or more of any class of voting stock of the applicant and a list of all names under which the applicant, partner, or principal shareholder previously operated a surface mining operation within the United States within the five-year period preceding the date of submission of the application;

(5) a statement of whether the applicant, any subsidiary, affiliate, or persons controlled by or under common control with the applicant, has ever held a Federal or State mining permit which in the five-year period prior to the date of submission of the application has been suspended or revoked or has had a mining bond or similar security deposited in lieu of bond forefeited[1] and, if so, a brief explanation of the facts involved;

(6) a copy of the applicant's advertisement to be published in a newspaper of general circulation in the locality of the proposed site at least once a week for four successive weeks, and which includes the ownership, a description of the exact location and boundaries of the proposed site sufficient so that the proposed operation is readily locatable by local residents, and the location of where the application is available for public inspection;

(7) a description of the type and method of coal mining operation that exists or is proposed, the engineering techniques proposed or used, and the equipment used or proposed to be used;

(8) the anticipated or actual starting and termination dates of each phase of the mining operation and number of acres of land to be affected;

(9) the applicant shall file with the regulatory authority on an accurate map or plan, to an appropriate scale, clearly showing the land to be affected as of the date of the application, the area of land within the permit area upon which the applicant has the legal right to enter and commence surface mining operations and shall provide to the regulatory authority a statement of those documents upon which the applicant bases his legal right to enter and commence surface mining operations on the area affected, and whether that right is the subject of pending court litigation: *Provided*, That nothing in this chapter shall be construed as vesting in the regulatory authority the jurisdiction to adjudicate property title disputes.[2]

(10) the name of the watershed and location of the surface stream or tributary into which surface and pit drainage will be discharged;

(11) a determination of the probable hydrologic consequences of the mining and reclamation operations, both on and off the mine site, with respect to the hydrologic regime, quantity and quality of water in surface and ground water systems including the dissolved and suspended solids under seasonal flow conditions and the collection of sufficient data for the mine site and surrounding areas so that an assessment can be made by the regulatory authority of the probable cumulative impacts of all anticipated mining in the area upon the hydrology of the area and particularly upon water availability: *Provided, however*, That this determination shall not be required until such time as hydrologic information on the general area prior to mining is made available from an appropriate Federal or State agency: *Provided further*, That the permit shall not be approved until such information is available and is incorporated into the application;

(12) when requested by the regulatory authority, the climatological factors that are peculiar to the locality of the land to be affected, including the average seasonal precipitation, the average direction and velocity of prevailing winds, and the seasonal temperature ranges;

(13) accurate maps to an appropriate scale clearly showing (A) the land to be affected as of the date of application and (B) all types of information set forth on topographical maps of the United States Geological Survey of a scale of 1:24,000 or 1:25,000 or larger, including all manmade features and significant known archeological sites existing on the date of application. Such a map or plan shall among other things specified by the regulatory authority show all boundaries of the land to be affected, the boundary lines and names of present owners of record of all surface areas abutting the permit area, and the location of all buildings within one thousand feet of the permit area;

(14) cross-section maps or plans of the land to be affected including the actual area to be mined, prepared by or under the direction of and certified by a qualified registered professional engineer, or professional geologist with assistance from experts in related fields such as land surveying and landscape architecture, showing pertinent elevation and location of test borings or core samplings and depicting the following information: the nature and depth of the various strata of overburden; the location of subsurface water, if encountered, and its quality; the nature and thickness of any coal or rider seam above the coal seam to be mined; the nature of the stratum immediately beneath the coal seam to be mined; all mineral crop lines and the strike and dip of the coal to be mined, within the area of land to be affected; existing or previous surface mining limits; the location and extent of known workings of any underground mines, including mine openings to the surface; the location of aquifers; the estimated elevation of the water table; the location of spoil, waste, or refuse areas and top-soil preservation areas; the location of all impoundments for waste or erosion control; any settling or water treatment facility; constructed or natural drainways and the location of any discharges to any surface body of water on the area of land to be affected or adjacent thereto; and profiles at appropriate cross sections of the anticipated final surface configuration that will be achieved pursuant to the operator's proposed reclamation plan;

(15) a statement of the result of test borings or core samplings from the permit area, including logs of the drill holes; the thickness of the coal seam found, an analysis of the chemical properties of such coal; the sulfur content of any coal seam; chemical analysis of potentially acid or toxic forming sections of the overburden; and chemical analysis of the stratum lying immediately underneath the coal to be mined except that the provisions of this paragraph (15) may be waived by the regulatory authority with respect to the specific application by a written determination that such requirements are unnecessary;

(16) for those lands in the permit application which a reconnaissance inspection suggests may be prime farm lands, a soil survey shall be made or obtained according to standards established by the Secretary of Agriculture in order to confirm the exact location of such prime farm lands, if any; and

(17) information pertaining to coal seams, test borings, core samplings, or soil samples as required by this section shall be made available to any person with an interest which is or may be adversely affected: *Provided,* That information which pertains only to the analysis of the chemical and physical properties of the coal (excepting information regarding such mineral or elemental content which is potentially toxic in the environment) shall be kept confidential and not made a matter of public record.

(c) Assistance to small coal operators

(1) If the regulatory authority finds that the probable total annual production at all locations of a coal surface mining operator will not exceed 300,000 tons, the cost of the following activities, which shall be performed by a qualified public or private laboratory or such other public or private qualified entity designated by the regulatory authority, shall be assumed by the regulatory authority upon the written request of the operator in connection with a permit application:

(A) The determination of probable hydrologic consequences required by subsection (b)(11) of this section, including the engineering analyses and designs necessary for the determination.

(B) The development of cross-section maps and plans required by subsection (b)(14) of this section.

(C) The geologic drilling and statement of results of test borings and core samplings required by subsection (b)(15) of this section.

(D) The collection of archaeological information required by subsection (b)(13) of this section and any other archaeological and historical information required by the regulatory authority, and the preparation of plans necessitated thereby.

(E) Pre-blast surveys required by section 1265(b)(15)(E) of this title.

(F) The collection of site-specific resource information and production of protection and enhancement plans for fish and wildlife habitats and other environmental values required by the regulatory authority under this chapter.

(2) The Secretary shall provide or assume the cost of training coal operators that meet the qualifications stated in paragraph (1) concerning the preparation of permit applications and compliance with the regulatory program, and shall ensure that qualified coal operators are aware of the assistance available under this subsection.

(d) Reclamation plan

Each applicant for a permit shall be required to submit to the regulatory authority as part of the permit application a reclamation plan which shall meet the requirements of this chapter.

(e) Public inspection

Each applicant for a surface coal mining and reclamation permit shall file a copy of his application for public inspection with the recorder at the courthouse of the county or an appropriate public office approved by the regulatory authority where the mining is proposed to occur, except for that information pertaining to the coal seam itself.

(f) Insurance certificate

Each applicant for a permit shall be required to submit to the regulatory authority as part of the permit application a certificate issued by an insurance company authorized to do business in the United States certifying that the applicant has a public liability insurance policy in force for the surface mining and reclamation operations for which such permit is sought, or evidence that the applicant has satisfied other State or Federal self-insurance requirements. Such policy shall provide for personal injury and property damage protection in an amount adequate to compensate any persons damaged as a result of surface coal mining and reclamation operations including use of explosives and entitled to compensation under the applicable provisions of State law. Such policy shall be maintained in full force and effect during the terms of the permit or any renewal, including the length of all reclamation operations.

(g) Blasting plan

Each applicant for a surface coal mining and reclamation permit shall submit to the regulatory authority as part of the permit application a blasting plan which shall outline the procedures and standards by which the operator will meet the provisions of section 1265(b)(15) of this title.

(h) Reimbursement of costs

A coal operator that has received assistance pursuant to subsection (c)(1) or (2) of this section shall reimburse the regulatory authority for the cost of the services rendered if the program administrator finds that the operator's actual and attributed annual production of coal for all locations exceeds 300,000 tons during the 12 months immediately following the date on which the operator is issued the surface coal mining and reclamation permit.

(Pub. L. No. 95–87, Title V, § 507, 91 Stat. 474 (Aug. 3, 1977); as amended by Pub. L. No. 101–508, Title VI, § 6011, 104 Stat. 1388–297 (Nov. 5, 1990); Pub. L. No. 102–486, Title XXV, § 2513, 106 Stat. 3112 (Oct. 24, 1992).)

[1] So in original. Probably should be "forfeited".

[2] So in original. The period probably should be a semicolon.

HISTORICAL AND STATUTORY NOTES

References in Text

This chapter, referred to in subsecs. (a), (b)(9), and (d), was in the original "this Act", meaning Pub. L. No. 95–87, 91 Stat. 445 (Aug. 3, 1977), as amended, which enacted this chapter and amended section 1114 of Title 18, Crimes and Criminal Procedure. For complete classification of this Act to the Code, see Short Title note set out under section 1201 of this title and Tables.

This chapter, referred to in subsec. (c)(1)(F), was in the original "this Act", meaning Pub. L. No. 95–87, 91 Stat. 445 (Aug. 3, 1977), as amended, which enacted this chapter and amended section 1114 of Title 18, Crimes and Criminal Procedure. For complete classification of this Act to the Code, see Short Title note set out under section 1201 of this title and Tables.

Effective and Applicability Provisions

1990 Acts. Amendment by Pub. L. No. 101–508 effective Oct. 1, 1991, see section 6014 of Pub. L. No. 101–508, set out as a note under section 1231 of this title.

Savings Provisions

Nothing in Subtitle A (section 6001 et seq.) of Title VI of Pub. L. No. 101–508, shall be construed to affect the certifications made by the States of Wyoming, Montana, and Louisiana to the Secretary of the Interior prior to Nov. 5, 1990, that each such State has completed the reclamation of eligible abandoned coal mine lands, see section 6013 of Pub. L. No. 101–508, set out as a note under section 1231 of this title.

Preparation of Cross-Sections, Maps, and Plans by or Under Direction of Qualified Registered Professional Engineers, Geologists, or Land Surveyors

Pub. L. No. 98–146, Title I, § 115, 97 Stat. 938 (Nov. 4, 1983), provided that: "Notwithstanding section 507(b)(14) of the Surface Mining Control and Reclamation Act of 1977 (Public Law 95–87) [subsec. (b)(14) of this section], cross-sections, maps or plans of land to be affected by an application for a surface mining and reclamation permit shall be prepared by or under the direction of a qualified registered professional engineer or geologist, or qualified registered professional land surveyor in any State which authorizes land surveyors to prepare and certify such maps or plans."

Office of Surface Mining Reclamation and Enforcement

Pub. L. No. 113–76, Div. G, Title I, 128 Stat. 299 (Jan. 17, 2014), provided in part: "That, in subsequent fiscal years, all amounts collected by the Office of Surface Mining from permit fees pursuant to section 507 of Public Law 95–87 (30 U.S.C. 1257) shall be credited to this account [Office of Surface Mining Reclamation and Enforcement and Regulation and Technology] as discretionary offsetting collections, to remain available until expended."

Similar provisions were contained in the following prior appropriations Act:

Pub. L. No. 112–74, Div. E, Title I, 125 Stat. 996 (Dec. 23, 2011).

Fiscal Limitations

Pub. L. No. 113–76, 128 Stat. 298–99 (Jan. 17, 2014), provided that:

"For necessary expenses to carry out the provisions of the Surface Mining Control and Reclamation Act of 1977, Public Law 95–87, $122,713,000, to remain available until September 30, 2015: *Provided,* That appropriations for the Office of Surface Mining Reclamation and Enforcement may provide for the travel and per diem expenses of State and tribal personnel attending Office of Surface Mining Reclamation and Enforcement sponsored training: *Provided further,* That, in fiscal year 2014, up to $40,000 collected by the Office of Surface Mining from permit fees pursuant to section 507 of Public Law 95–87 (30 U.S.C. 1257) shall be credited to this account as discretionary offsetting collections, to remain available until expended: *Provided further,* That the sum herein appropriated shall be reduced as collections are received during the fiscal year so as to result in a final fiscal year 2014 appropriation estimated at not more than $122,713,000: *Provided further,* That, in subsequent fiscal years, all amounts collected by the Office of Surface Mining from permit fees pursuant to section 507 of Public Law 95–87 (30 U.S.C. 1257) shall be credited to this account as discretionary offsetting collections, to remain available until expended."

§ 1258. Reclamation plan requirements

[SMCRA § 508]

(a) Each reclamation plan submitted as part of a permit application pursuant to any approved State program or a Federal program under the provisions of this chapter shall include, in the degree of detail necessary to demonstrate that reclamation required by the State or Federal program can be accomplished, a statement of:

(1) the identification of the lands subject to surface coal mining operations over the estimated life of those operations and the size, sequence, and timing of the subareas for which it is anticipated that individual permits for mining will be sought;

(2) the condition of the land to be covered by the permit prior to any mining including:

(A) the uses existing at the time of the application, and if the land has a history of previous mining, the uses which preceded any mining; and

(B) the capability of the land prior to any mining to support a variety of uses giving consideration to soil and foundation characteristics, topography, and vegetative cover, and, if applicable, a soil survey prepared pursuant to section 1257(b)(16) of this title; and

(C) the productivity of the land prior to mining, including appropriate classification as prime farm lands, as well as the average yield of food, fiber, forage, or wood products from such lands obtained under high levels of management;

(3) the use which is proposed to be made of the land following reclamation, including a discussion of the utility and capacity of the reclaimed land to support a variety of alternative uses and the relationship of such use to existing land use policies and plans, and the comments of any owner of the surface, State and local governments or agencies thereof which would have to initiate, implement, approve or authorize the proposed use of the land following reclamation;

(4) a detailed description of how the proposed postmining land use is to be achieved and the necessary support activities which may be needed to achieve the proposed land use;

(5) the engineering techniques proposed to be used in mining and reclamation and a description of the major equipment; a plan for the control of surface water drainage and of water accumulation; a plan, where appropriate, for backfilling, soil stabilization, and compacting, grading, and appropriate revegetation; a plan for soil reconstruction, replacement, and stabilization, pursuant to the performance standards in section 1265(b)(7)(A), (B), (C), and (D) of this title, for those food, forage, and forest lands identified in section 1265(b)(7) of this title; an estimate of the cost per acre of the reclamation, including a statement as to how the permittee plans to comply with each of the requirements set out in section 1265 of this title;

(6) the consideration which has been given to maximize the utilization and conservation of the solid fuel resource being recovered so that reaffecting the land in the future can be minimized;

(7) a detailed estimated timetable for the accomplishment of each major step in the reclamation plan;

(8) the consideration which has been given to making the surface mining and reclamation operations consistent with surface owner plans, and applicable State and local land use plans and programs;

(9) the steps to be taken to comply with applicable air and water quality laws and regulations and any applicable health and safety standards;

(10) the consideration which has been given to developing the reclamation plan in a manner consistent with local physical environmental, and climatological conditions;

(11) all lands, interests in lands, or options on such interests held by the applicant or pending bids on interests in lands by the applicant, which lands are contiguous to the area to be covered by the permit;

(12) the results of test boring which the applicant has made at the area to be covered by the permit, or other equivalent information and data in a form satisfactory to the regulatory authority, including the location of subsurface water, and an analysis of the chemical properties including acid forming properties of the mineral and overburden: *Provided,* That information which pertains only to the analysis of the chemical and physical properties of the coal (excepting information regarding such mineral or elemental contents which is potentially toxic in the environment) shall be kept confidential and not made a matter of public record;

(13) a detailed description of the measures to be taken during the mining and reclamation process to assure the protection of:

(A) the quality of surface and ground water systems, both on- and off-site, from adverse effects of the mining and reclamation process;

(B) the rights of present users to such water; and

(C) the quantity of surface and ground water systems, both on- and off-site, from adverse effects of the mining and reclamation process or to provide alternative sources of water where such protection of quantity cannot be assured;

(14) such other requirements as the regulatory authority shall prescribe by regulations.

(b) Any information required by this section which is not on public file pursuant to State law shall be held in confidence by the regulatory authority.

(Pub. L. No. 95–87, Title V, § 508, 91 Stat. 478 (Aug. 3, 1977).)

HISTORICAL AND STATUTORY NOTES

References in Text

This chapter, referred to in subsec. (a), was in the original "this Act", meaning Pub. L. No. 95–87, 91 Stat. 445 (Aug. 3, 1977), as amended, which enacted this chapter and amended section 1114 of Title 18, Crimes and Criminal Procedure. For complete classification of this Act to the Code, see Short Title note set out under section 1201 of this title and Tables.

§ 1259. Performance bonds

[SMCRA § 509]

(a) Filing with regulatory authority; scope; number and amount

After a surface coal mining and reclamation permit application has been approved but before such a permit is issued, the applicant shall file with the regulatory authority, on a form prescribed and furnished by the regulatory authority, a bond for performance payable, as appropriate, to the United States or to the State, and conditional upon faithful performance of all the requirements of this chapter and the permit. The bond shall cover that area of land within the permit area upon which the operator will initiate and conduct surface coal mining and reclamation operations within the initial term of the permit. As succeeding increments of surface coal mining and reclamation operations are to be initiated and conducted within the permit area, the permittee shall file with the regulatory authority an additional bond or bonds to cover such increments in accordance with this section. The amount of the bond required for each bonded area shall depend upon the reclamation requirements of the approved permit; shall reflect the probable difficulty of reclamation giving consideration to such factors as topography, geology of the site, hydrology, and revegetation potential, and shall be determined by the regulatory authority. The amount of the bond shall be sufficient to assure the completion of the reclamation plan if the work had to be performed by the regulatory authority in the event of forfeiture and in no case shall the bond for the entire area under one permit be less than $10,000.

(b) Liability period; execution

Liability under the bond shall be for the duration of the surface coal mining and reclamation operation and for a period coincident with operator's responsibility for revegetation requirements in section 1265 of this title. The bond shall be executed by the operator and a corporate surety licensed to do business in the State where such operation is located, except that the operator may elect to deposit cash, negotiable bonds of the United States Government or such State, or negotiable certificates of deposit of any bank organized or transacting business in the United States. The cash deposit or market value of such securities shall be equal to or greater than the amount of the bond required for the bonded area.

(c) Bond of applicant without separate surety; alternate system

The regulatory authority may accept the bond of the applicant itself without separate surety when the applicant demonstrates to the satisfaction of the regulatory authority the existence of a suitable agent to receive service of process and a history of financial solvency and continuous operation sufficient for authorization to self-insure or bond such amount or in lieu of the establishment of a bonding program, as set forth in this section, the Secretary may approve as part of a State or Federal program an alternative system that will achieve the objectives and purposes of the bonding program pursuant to this section.

(d) Deposit of cash or securities

Cash or securities so deposited shall be deposited upon the same terms as the terms upon which surety bonds may be deposited. Such securities shall be security for the repayment of such negotiable certificate of deposit.

(e) Adjustments

The amount of the bond or deposit required and the terms of each acceptance of the applicant's bond shall be adjusted by the regulatory authority from time to time as affected land acreages are increased or decreased or where the cost of future reclamation changes.

(Pub. L. No. 95–87, Title V, § 509, 91 Stat. 479 (Aug. 3, 1977).)

HISTORICAL AND STATUTORY NOTES

References in Text

This chapter, referred to in subsec. (a), was in the original "this Act", meaning Pub. L. No. 95–87, 91 Stat. 445 (Aug. 3, 1977), as amended, which enacted this chapter and amended section 1114 of Title 18, Crimes and Criminal Procedure. For complete classification of this Act to the Code, see Short Title note set out under section 1201 of this title and Tables.

§ 1260. Permit approval or denial

[SMCRA § 510]

(a) Basis for decision; notification of applicant and local government officials; burden of proof

Upon the basis of a complete mining application and reclamation plan or a revision or renewal thereof, as required by this chapter and pursuant to an approved State program or Federal program under the provisions of this chapter, including public notification and an opportunity for a public hearing as required by section 1263 of this title, the regulatory authority shall grant, require modification of, or deny the application for a permit in a reasonable time set by the regulatory authority and notify the applicant in writing. The applicant for a permit, or revision of a permit, shall have the burden of establishing that his application is in compliance with all the requirements of the applicable State or Federal program. Within ten days after the granting of a permit, the regulatory authority shall notify the local governmental officials in the local political subdivision in which the area of land to be affected is located that a permit has been issued and shall describe the location of the land.

(b) Requirements for approval

No permit or revision application shall be approved unless the application affirmatively demonstrates and the regulatory authority finds in writing on the basis of the information set forth in the application or from information otherwise available which will be documented in the approval, and made available to the applicant, that—

(1) the permit application is accurate and complete and that all the requirements of this chapter and the State or Federal program have been complied with;

(2) the applicant has demonstrated that reclamation as required by this chapter and the State or Federal program can be accomplished under the reclamation plan contained in the permit application;

(3) the assessment of the probable cumulative impact of all anticipated mining in the area on the hydrologic balance specified in section 1257(b) of this title has been made by the regulatory authority and the proposed operation thereof has been designed to prevent material damage to hydrologic balance outside permit area;

(4) the area proposed to be mined is not included within an area designated unsuitable for surface coal mining pursuant to section 1272 of this title or is not within an area under study for such designation in an administrative proceeding commenced pursuant to section 1272(a)(4)(D) or section 1272(c) of this title (unless in such an area as to which an administrative proceeding has commenced pursuant to section 1272(a)(4)(D) of this title, the operator making the permit application demonstrates that, prior to January 1, 1977, he has made substantial legal and financial commitments in relation to the operation for which he is applying for a permit);

(5) the proposed surface coal mining operation, if located west of the one hundredth meridian west longitude, would—

(A) not interrupt, discontinue, or preclude farming on alluvial valley floors that are irrigated or naturally subirrigated, but, excluding undeveloped range lands which are not significant to farming on said alluvial valley floors and those lands as to which the regulatory authority finds that if the farming that will be interrupted, discontinued, or precluded is of such small acreage as to be of negligible impact on the farm's agricultural production, or

(B) not materially damage the quantity or quality of water in surface or underground water systems that supply these valley floors in (A) of subsection (b)(5) of this section:

Provided, That this paragraph (5) shall not affect those surface coal mining operations which in the year preceding August 3, 1977, (I) produced coal in commercial quantities, and were located within or adjacent to alluvial valley floors or (II) had obtained specific permit approval by the State regulatory authority to conduct surface coal mining operations within said alluvial valley floors.

With respect to such surface mining operations which would have been within the purview of the foregoing proviso but for the fact that no coal was so produced in commercial quantities and no such specific permit approval was so received, the Secretary, if he determines that substantial financial and legal commitments were made by an operator prior to January 1, 1977, in connection with any such operation, is authorized, in accordance with such regulations as the Secretary may prescribe, to enter into an agreement with that operator pursuant to which the Secretary may, notwithstanding any other provision of law, lease other Federal coal deposits to such operator in exchange for the relinquishment by such operator of his Federal lease covering coal deposits involving such mining operations, or pursuant to section 1716 of Title 43, convey to the fee holder of any such coal deposits involving such mining operations the fee title to other available Federal coal deposits in exchange for the fee title to such deposits so involving such mining operations. It is the policy of the Congress that the Secretary shall develop and carry out a coal exchange program to acquire private fee coal precluded from being mined by the restrictions of this paragraph (5) in exchange for Federal coal which is not so precluded. Such exchanges shall be made under section 1716 of Title 43;

(6) in cases where the private mineral estate has been severed from the private surface estate, the applicant has submitted to the regulatory authority—

(A) the written consent of the surface owner to the extraction of coal by surface mining methods; or

(B) a conveyance that expressly grants or reserves the right to extract the coal by surface mining methods; or

(C) if the conveyance does not expressly grant the right to extract coal by surface mining methods, the surface-subsurface legal relationship shall be determined in accordance with State law: *Provided,* That nothing in this chapter shall be construed to authorize the regulatory authority to adjudicate property rights disputes.

(c) Schedule of violations

The applicant shall file with his permit application a schedule listing any and all notices of violations of this chapter and any law, rule, or regulation of the United States, or of any department or agency in the United States pertaining to air or water environmental protection incurred by the applicant in connection with any surface coal mining operation during the three-year period prior to the date of application. The schedule shall also indicate the final resolution of any such notice of violation. Where the schedule or other information available to the regulatory authority indicates that any surface coal mining operation owned or controlled by the applicant is currently in violation of this chapter or such other laws referred to[1] this subsection, the permit shall not be issued until the applicant submits proof that such violation has been corrected or is in the process of being corrected to the satisfaction of the regulatory authority, department, or agency which has jurisdiction over such violation and no permit shall be issued to an applicant after a finding by the regulatory authority, after opportunity for hearing, that the applicant, or the operator specified in the application, controls or has controlled mining operations with a demonstrated pattern of willful violations of this chapter of such nature and duration with such resulting irreparable damage to the environment as to indicate an intent not to comply with the provisions of this chapter.

(d) Prime farmland mining permit

(1) In addition to finding the application in compliance with subsection (b) of this section, if the area proposed to be mined contains prime farmland pursuant to section 1257(b)(16) of this title, the regulatory authority shall, after consultation with the Secretary of Agriculture, and pursuant to regulations issued hereunder by the Secretary of[2] Interior with the concurrence of the Secretary of Agriculture, grant a permit to mine on prime farmland if the regulatory authority finds in writing that the operator has the technological capability to restore such mined area, within a reasonable time, to equivalent or higher levels of yield as non-mined prime farmland in the surrounding area under equivalent levels of management and can meet the soil reconstruction standards in section 1265(b)(7) of this title. Except for compliance with subsection (b) of this section, the requirements of this paragraph (1) shall apply to all permits issued after August 3, 1977.

(2) Nothing in this subsection shall apply to any permit issued prior to August 3, 1977, or to any revisions or renewals thereof, or to any existing surface mining operations for which a permit was issued prior to August 3, 1977.

(e) Modification of prohibition

After October 24, 1992, the prohibition of subsection (c) of this section shall not apply to a permit application due to any violation resulting from an unanticipated event or condition at a surface coal mining operation on lands eligible for remining under a permit held by the person making such application. As used in this subsection, the term "violation" has the same meaning as such term has under subsection (c) of this section.

(Pub. L. No. 95–87, Title V, § 510, 91 Stat. 480 (Aug. 3, 1977); as amended by Pub. L. No. 102–486, Title XXV, § 2503(a), 106 Stat. 3102 (Oct. 24, 1992); Pub. L. No. 109–432, Div. C, Title II, § 208, 120 Stat. 3019 (Dec. 20, 2006).)

[1] So in original. Probably should be followed by "in".

[2] So in original. Probably should be "of the".

HISTORICAL AND STATUTORY NOTES

References in Text

This chapter, referred to in subsecs. (a), (b), and (c), was in the original "this Act", meaning Pub. L. No. 95–87, 91 Stat. 445 (Aug. 3, 1977), as amended, which enacted this chapter and amended section 1114 of Title 18, Crimes and Criminal Procedure. For complete classification of this Act to the Code, see Short Title note set out under section 1201 of this title and Tables.

§ 1261. Revision of permits

[SMCRA § 511]

(a) Application and revised reclamation plan; requirements; extensions to area covered

(1) During the term of the permit the permittee may submit an application for a revision of the permit, together with a revised reclamation plan, to the regulatory authority.

(2) An application for a revision of a permit shall not be approved unless the regulatory authority finds that reclamation as required by this chapter and the State or Federal program can be accomplished under the revised reclamation plan. The revision shall be approved or disapproved within a period of time established by the State or Federal program. The regulatory authority shall establish guidelines for a determination of the scale or extent of a revision request for which all permit application information requirements and procedures, including notice and hearings, shall apply: *Provided,* That any revisions which propose significant alterations in the reclamation plan shall, at a minimum, be subject to notice and hearing requirements.

(3) Any extensions to the area covered by the permit except incidental boundary revisions must be made by application for another permit.

(b) Transfer, assignment, or sale of rights under permit

No transfer, assignment, or sale of the rights granted under any permit issued pursuant to this chapter shall be made without the written approval of the regulatory authority.

(c) Review of outstanding permits

The regulatory authority shall within a time limit prescribed in regulations promulgated by the regulatory authority, review outstanding permits and may require reasonable revision or modification of the permit provisions during the term of such permit: *Provided,* That such revision or modification shall be based upon a written finding and subject to notice and hearing requirements established by the State or Federal program.

(Pub. L. No. 95–87, Title V, § 511, 91 Stat. 483 (Aug. 3, 1977).)

HISTORICAL AND STATUTORY NOTES

References in Text

This chapter, referred to in subsecs. (a)(2), and (b), was in the original "this Act", meaning Pub. L. No. 95–87, 91 Stat. 445 (Aug. 3, 1977), as amended, which enacted this chapter and amended section 1114 of Title 18, Crimes and Criminal Procedure. For complete classification of this Act to the Code, see Short Title note set out under section 1201 of this title and Tables.

§ 1262. Coal exploration permits

[SMCRA § 512]

(a) Regulations; contents

Each State or Federal program shall include a requirement that coal exploration operations which substantially disturb the natural land surface be conducted in accordance with exploration regulations issued by the regulatory authority. Such regulations shall include, at a minimum (1) the requirement that prior to conducting any exploration under this section, any person must file with the regulatory authority notice of intention to explore and such notice shall include a description of the exploration area and the period of supposed exploration and (2) provisions for reclamation in accordance with the performance standards in section 1265 of this title of all lands disturbed in exploration, including excavations, roads, drill holes, and the removal of necessary facilities and equipment.

(b) Confidential information

Information submitted to the regulatory authority pursuant to this subsection as confidential concerning trade secrets or privileged commercial or financial information which relates to the competitive rights of the person or entity intended to explore the described area shall not be available for public examination.

(c) Penalties

Any person who conducts any coal exploration activities which substantially disturb the natural land surface in violation of this section or regulations issued pursuant thereto shall be subject to the provisions of section 1268 of this title.

(d) Limitation on removal of coal

No operator shall remove more than two hundred and fifty tons of coal pursuant to an exploration permit without the specific written approval of the regulatory authority.

(e) Law governing exploration of Federal lands

Coal exploration on Federal lands shall be governed by section 4 of the Federal Coal Leasing Amendments Act of 1975 (90 Stat. 1085).

(Pub. L. No. 95–87, Title V, § 512, 91 Stat. 483 (Aug. 3, 1977).)

HISTORICAL AND STATUTORY NOTES

References in Text

Section 4 of the Federal Coal Leasing Amendments Act of 1975 (90 Stat. 1085), referred to in subsec. (e), is section 4 of Pub. L. No. 94–377, 90 Stat. 1085 (Aug. 4, 1976), redesignated the Federal Coal Leasing Amendments Act of 1976, which amended section 201(b) of this title.

§ 1263. Public notice and public hearings

[SMCRA § 513]

(a) Submittal of advertisement to regulatory authority; notification of local governmental bodies

At the time of submission of an application for a surface coal mining and reclamation permit, or revision of an existing permit, pursuant to the provisions of this chapter or an approved State program, the applicant shall submit to the regulatory authority a copy of his advertisement of the ownership, precise location, and boundaries of the land to be affected. At the time of submission such advertisement shall be placed by the applicant in a local newspaper of general circulation in the locality of the proposed surface mine at least once a week for four consecutive weeks. The regulatory authority shall notify various local governmental bodies, planning agencies, and sewage and water treatment authorities, of[1] water companies in the locality in which the proposed surface mining will take place, notifying them of the operator's intention to surface mine a particularly described tract of land and indicating the application's permit number and where a copy of the proposed mining and reclamation plan may be inspected. These local bodies, agencies, authorities, or companies may submit written comments within a reasonable period established by the regulatory authority on the mining applications with respect to the effect of the proposed operation on the environment which are within their area of responsibility. Such comments shall immediately be transmitted to the applicant by the regulatory authority and shall be made available to the public at the same locations as are the mining applications.

(b) Objections to permit applications; informal conference; record

Any person having an interest which is or may be adversely affected or the officer or head of any Federal, State, or local governmental agency or authority shall have the right to file written objections to the proposed initial or revised application for a permit for surface coal mining and reclamation operation with the regulatory authority within thirty days after the last publication of the above notice. Such objections shall immediately be transmitted to the applicant by the regulatory authority and shall be made available to the public. If written objections are filed and an informal conference requested, the regulatory authority shall then hold an informal conference in the locality of the proposed mining, if requested within a reasonable time of the receipt of such objections or request. The date, time and location of such informal conference shall be advertised by the regulatory authority in a newspaper of general circulation in the locality at least two weeks prior to the scheduled conference date. The regulatory authority may arrange with the applicant upon request by any party to the administrative proceeding access to the proposed mining area for the purpose of gathering information relevant to the proceeding. An electronic or stenographic record shall be made of the conference proceeding, unless waived by all parties. Such record shall be maintained and shall be accessible to the parties until final release of the applicant's performance bond. In the event all parties requesting the informal conference stipulate agreement prior to the requested informal conference and withdraw their request, such informal conference need not be held.

(c) Prior Federal coal lease hearing as evidence

Where the lands included in an application for a permit are the subject of a Federal coal lease in connection with which hearings were held and determinations were made under section 201(a)(3)(A), (B) and (C) of this title, such hearings shall be deemed as to the matters covered to satisfy the requirements of this section and section 1264 of this title and such determinations shall be deemed to be a part of the record and conclusive for purposes of sections 1260, 1264 of this title and this section.

(Pub. L. No. 95–87, Title V, § 513, 91 Stat. 484 (Aug. 3, 1977).)

[1] So in original. Probably should be "or".

HISTORICAL AND STATUTORY NOTES

References in Text

This chapter, referred to in subsec. (a), was in the original "this Act", meaning Pub. L. No. 95–87, 91 Stat. 445 (Aug. 3, 1977), as amended, which enacted this chapter and amended section 1114 of Title 18, Crimes and Criminal Procedure. For complete classification of this Act to the Code, see Short Title note set out under section 1201 of this title and Tables.

§ 1264. Decisions of regulatory authority and appeals

[SMCRA § 514]

(a) Issuance of findings within 60 days after informal conference

If an informal conference has been held pursuant to section 1263(b) of this title, the regulatory authority shall issue and furnish the applicant for a permit and persons who are parties to the administrative proceedings with the written finding of the regulatory authority, granting or denying the permit in whole or in part and stating the reasons therefor, within the sixty days of said hearings.

(b) Decision without informal conference; notification within a reasonable time

If there has been no informal conference held pursuant to section 1263(b) of this title, the regulatory authority shall notify the applicant for a permit within a reasonable time as determined by the regulatory authority and set forth in regulations, taking into account the time needed for proper investigation of the site, the complexity of the permit application, and whether or not written objection to the application has been filed, whether the application has been approved or disapproved in whole or part.

(c) Request for rehearing on reasons for final determination; time; issuance of decision

If the application is approved, the permit shall be issued. If the application is disapproved, specific reasons therefor must be set forth in the notification. Within thirty days after the applicant is notified of the final decision of the regulatory authority on the permit application, the applicant or any person with an interest which is or may be adversely affected may request a hearing on the reasons for the final determination. The regulatory authority shall hold a hearing within thirty days of such request and provide notification to all interested parties at the time that the applicant is so notified. If the Secretary is the regulatory authority the hearing shall be of record and governed by section 554 of Title 5. Where the regulatory authority is the State, such hearing shall be of record, adjudicatory in nature and no person who presided at a conference under section 1263(b) of this title shall either preside at the hearing or participate in this decision thereon or in any administrative appeal therefrom. Within thirty days after the hearing the regulatory authority shall issue and furnish the applicant, and all persons who participated in the hearing, with the written decision of the regulatory authority granting or denying the permit in whole or in part and stating the reasons therefor.

(d) Temporary relief

Where a hearing is requested pursuant to subsection (c) of this section, the Secretary, where the Secretary is the regulatory authority, or the State hearing authority may, under such conditions as it may prescribe, grant such temporary relief as it deems appropriate pending final determination of the proceedings if—

(1) all parties to the proceedings have been notified and given an opportunity to be heard on a request for temporary relief;

(2) the person requesting such relief shows that there is a substantial likelihood that he will prevail on the merits of the final determination of the proceeding; and

(3) such relief will not adversely affect the public health or safety or cause significant imminent environmental harm to land, air, or water resources.

(e) Power of regulatory authority with respect to rehearing

For the purpose of such hearing, the regulatory authority may administer oaths, subpoena witnesses, or written or printed materials, compel attendance of the witness, or production of the materials, and take evidence including but not limited to site inspections of the land to be affected and other surface coal mining operations carried on by the applicant in the general vicinity of the proposed operation. A verbatim record of each public hearing required by this chapter shall be made, and a transcript made available on the motion of any party or by order of the regulatory authority.

(f) Right to appeal in accordance with section 1276 of this title

Any applicant or any person with an interest which is or may be adversely affected who has participated in the administrative proceedings as an objector, and who is aggrieved by the decision of the regulatory authority, or if the regulatory authority fails to act within the time limits specified in this chapter shall have the right to appeal in accordance with section 1276 of this title.

(Pub. L. No. 95–87, Title V, § 514, 91 Stat. 485 (Aug. 3, 1977).)

HISTORICAL AND STATUTORY NOTES

References in Text

This chapter, referred to in subsecs. (e), and (f), was in the original "this Act", meaning Pub. L. No. 95–87, 91 Stat. 445 (Aug. 3, 1977), as amended, which enacted this chapter and amended section 1114 of Title 18, Crimes and Criminal Procedure. For complete classification of this Act to the Code, see Short Title note set out under section 1201 of this title and Tables.

§ 1265. Environmental protection performance standards

[SMCRA § 515]

(a) Permit requirement

Any permit issued under any approved State or Federal program pursuant to this chapter to conduct surface coal mining operations shall require that such surface coal mining operations will meet all applicable performance standards of this chapter, and such other requirements as the regulatory authority shall promulgate.

(b) General standards

General performance standards shall be applicable to all surface coal mining and reclamation operations and shall require the operation as a minimum to—

(1) conduct surface coal mining operations so as to maximize the utilization and conservation of the solid fuel resource being recovered so that reaffecting the land in the future through surface coal mining can be minimized;

(2) restore the land affected to a condition capable of supporting the uses which it was capable of supporting prior to any mining, or higher or better uses of which there is reasonable likelihood, so long as such use or uses do not present any actual or probable hazard to public health or safety or pose any actual or probable threat of water diminution or pollution, and the permit applicants' declared proposed land use following reclamation is not deemed to be impractical or unreasonable, inconsistent with applicable land use policies and plans, involves unreasonable delay in implementation, or is violative of Federal, State, or local law;

(3) except as provided in subsection (c) of this section with respect to all surface coal mining operations backfill, compact (where advisable to insure stability or to prevent leaching of toxic materials), and grade in order to restore the approximate original contour of the land with all highwalls, spoil piles, and depressions eliminated (unless small depressions are needed in order to retain moisture to assist revegetation or as otherwise authorized pursuant to this chapter): *Provided, however*, That in surface coal mining which is carried out at the same location over a substantial period of time where the operation transects the coal deposit, and the thickness of the coal deposits relative to the volume of the overburden is large and where the operator demonstrates that the overburden and other spoil and waste materials at a particular point in the permit area or otherwise available from the entire permit area is insufficient, giving due consideration to volumetric expansion, to restore the approximate original contour, the operator, at a minimum, shall backfill, grade, and compact (where advisable) using all available overburden and other spoil and waste materials to attain the lowest practicable grade but not more than the angle of repose, to provide adequate drainage and to cover all acid-forming and other toxic materials, in order to achieve an ecologically sound land use compatible with the surrounding region: *And provided further*, That in surface coal mining where the volume of overburden is large relative to the thickness of the coal deposit and where the operator demonstrates that due to volumetric expansion the amount of overburden and other spoil and waste materials removed in the course of the mining operation is more than sufficient to restore the approximate original contour, the operator shall after restoring the approximate contour, backfill, grade, and compact (where advisable) the excess overburden and other spoil and waste materials to attain the lowest grade but not more than the angle of repose, and to cover all acid-forming and other toxic materials, in order to achieve an ecologically sound land use compatible with the surrounding region and that such overburden or spoil shall be shaped and graded in such a way as to prevent slides, erosion, and water pollution and is revegetated in accordance with the requirements of this chapter;

(4) stabilize and protect all surface areas including spoil piles affected by the surface coal mining and reclamation operation to effectively control erosion and attendant air and water pollution;

(5) remove the topsoil from the land in a separate layer, replace it on the backfill area, or if not utilized immediately, segregate it in a separate pile from other spoil and when the topsoil is not replaced on a backfill area within a time short enough to avoid deterioration of the topsoil, maintain a successful cover by quick growing plant or other means thereafter so that the topsoil is preserved from wind and water erosion, remains free of any contamination by other acid or toxic material, and is in a usable condition for sustaining vegetation when restored during reclamation, except if topsoil is of insufficient quantity or of poor quality for sustaining vegetation, or if other strata can be shown to be more suitable for vegetation requirements, then the operator shall remove, segregate, and preserve in a like manner such other strata which is best able to support vegetation;

(6) restore the topsoil or the best available subsoil which is best able to support vegetation;

(7) for all prime farm lands as identified in section 1257(b)(16) of this title to be mined and reclaimed, specifications for soil removal, storage, replacement, and reconstruction shall be established by the Secretary of Agriculture, and the operator shall, as a minimum, be required to—

(A) segregate the A horizon of the natural soil, except where it can be shown that other available soil materials will create a final soil having a greater productive capacity; and if not utilized immediately, stockpile this material separately from other spoil, and provide needed protection from wind and water erosion or contamination by other acid or toxic material;

(B) segregate the B horizon of the natural soil, or underlying C horizons or other strata, or a combination of such horizons or other strata that are shown to be both texturally and chemically suitable for plant growth and that can be shown to be equally or more favorable for plant growth than the B horizon, in sufficient quantities to create in the regraded final soil a root zone of comparable depth and quality to that which existed in the natural soil; and if not utilized immediately, stockpile this material separately from other spoil, and provide needed protection from wind and water erosion or contamination by other acid or toxic material;

(C) replace and regrade the root zone material described in (B) above with proper compaction and uniform depth over the regraded spoil material; and

(D) redistribute and grade in a uniform manner the surface soil horizon described in subparagraph (A);

(8) create, if authorized in the approved mining and reclamation plan and permit, permanent impoundments of water on mining sites as part of reclamation activities only when it is adequately demonstrated that—

(A) the size of the impoundment is adequate for its intended purposes;

(B) the impoundment dam construction will be so designed as to achieve necessary stability with an adequate margin of safety compatible with that of structures constructed under Public Law 83–566 (16 U.S.C. 1006);

(C) the quality of impounded water will be suitable on a permanent basis for its intended use and that discharges from the impoundment will not degrade the water quality below water quality standards established pursuant to applicable Federal and State law in the receiving stream;

(D) the level of water will be reasonably stable;

(E) final grading will provide adequate safety and access for proposed water users; and

(F) such water impoundments will not result in the diminution of the quality or quantity of water utilized by adjacent or surrounding landowners for agricultural, industrial[1] recreational, or domestic uses;

(9) conducting[2] any augering operation associated with surface mining in a manner to maximize recoverability of mineral reserves remaining after the operation and reclamation are complete; and seal all auger holes with an impervious and noncombustible material in order to prevent drainage except where the regulatory authority determines that the resulting impoundment of water in such auger holes may create a hazard to the environment or the public health or safety: *Provided*, That the permitting authority may prohibit augering if necessary to maximize the utilization, recoverability or conservation of the solid fuel resources or to protect against adverse water quality impacts;

(10) minimize the disturbances to the prevailing hydrologic balance at the mine-site and in associated offsite areas and to the quality and quantity of water in surface and ground water systems both during and after surface coal mining operations and during reclamation by—

(A) avoiding acid or other toxic mine drainage by such measures as, but not limited to—

(i) preventing or removing water from contact with toxic producing deposits;

(ii) treating drainage to reduce toxic content which adversely affects downstream water upon being released to water courses;

(iii) casing, sealing, or otherwise managing boreholes, shafts, and wells and keep[3] acid or other toxic drainage from entering ground and surface waters;

(B) **(i)** conducting surface coal mining operations so as to prevent, to the extent possible using the best technology currently available, additional contributions of suspended solids to streamflow, or runoff outside the permit area, but in no event shall contributions be in excess of requirements set by applicable State or Federal law;

(ii) constructing any siltation structures pursuant to subparagraph (B)(i) of this subsection prior to commencement of surface coal mining operations, such structures to be certified by a qualified registered engineer or a qualified registered professional land surveyor in any State which authorizes land surveyors to prepare and certify such maps or plans to be constructed as designed and as approved in the reclamation plan;

(C) cleaning out and removing temporary or large settling ponds or other siltation structures from drainways after disturbed areas are revegetated and stabilized; and depositing the silt and debris at a site and in a manner approved by the regulatory authority;

(D) restoring recharge capacity of the mined area to approximate premining conditions;

(E) avoiding channel deepening or enlargement in operations requiring the discharge of water from mines;

(F) preserving throughout the mining and reclamation process the essential hydrologic functions of alluvial valley floors in the arid and semiarid areas of the country; and

(G) such other actions as the regulatory authority may prescribe;

(11) with respect to surface disposal of mine wastes, tailings, coal processing wastes, and other wastes in areas other than the mine working or excavations, stabilize all waste piles in designated areas through construction in compacted layers including the use of incombustible and impervious materials if necessary and assure the final contour of the waste pile will be compatible with natural surroundings and that the site can and will be stabilized and revegetated according to the provisions of this chapter;

(12) refrain from surface coal mining within five hundred feet from active and abandoned underground mines in order to prevent breakthroughs and to protect health or safety of miners: *Provided*, That the regulatory authority shall permit an operator to mine near, through or partially through an abandoned underground mine or closer to an active underground mine if (A) the nature, timing, and sequencing of the approximate coincidence of specific surface mine activities with specific underground mine activities are jointly approved by the regulatory authorities concerned with surface mine regulation and the health and safety of underground miners, and (B) such operations will result in improved resource recovery, abatement of water pollution, or elimination of hazards to the health and safety of the public;

(13) design, locate, construct, operate, maintain, enlarge, modify, and remove or abandon, in accordance with the standards and criteria developed pursuant to subsection (f) of this section, all existing and new coal mine waste piles consisting of mine wastes, tailings, coal processing wastes, or other liquid and solid wastes, and used either temporarily or permanently as dams or embankments;

(14) insure that all debris, acid-forming materials, toxic materials, or materials constituting a fire hazard are treated or buried and compacted or otherwise disposed of in a manner designed to prevent contamination of ground or surface waters and that contingency plans are developed to prevent sustained combustion;

(15) insure that explosives are used only in accordance with existing State and Federal law and the regulations promulgated by the regulatory authority, which shall include provisions to—

(A) provide adequate advance written notice to local governments and residents who might be affected by the use of such explosives by publication of the planned blasting schedule in a newspaper of general circulation in the locality and by mailing a copy of the proposed blasting schedule to every resident living within one-half mile of the proposed blasting site and by providing daily notice to resident/occupiers in such areas prior to any blasting;

(B) maintain for a period of at least three years and make available for public inspection upon request a log detailing the location of the blasts, the pattern and depth of the drill holes, the amount of explosives used per hole, and the order and length of delay in the blasts;

(C) limit the type of explosives and detonating equipment, the size, the timing and frequency of blasts based upon the physical conditions of the site so as to prevent (i) injury to persons, (ii) damage to public and private property outside the permit area, (iii) adverse impacts on any underground mine, and (iv) change in the course, channel, or availability of ground or surface water outside the permit area;

(D) require that all blasting operations be conducted by trained and competent persons as certified by the regulatory authority;

(E) provide that upon the request of a resident or owner of a man-made dwelling or structure within one-half mile of any portion of the permitted area the applicant or permittee shall conduct a pre-blasting survey of such structures and submit the survey to the regulatory authority and a copy to the resident or owner making the request. The area of the survey shall be decided by the regulatory authority and shall include such provisions as the Secretary shall promulgate.

(16) insure that all reclamation efforts proceed in an environmentally sound manner and as contemporaneously as practicable with the surface coal mining operations: *Provided, however*, That where the applicant proposes to combine surface mining operations with underground mining operations to assure maximum practical recovery of the mineral resources, the regulatory authority may grant a variance for specific areas within the reclamation plan from the requirement that reclamation efforts proceed as contemporaneously as practicable to permit underground mining operations prior to reclamation:

(A) if the regulatory authority finds in writing that:

(i) the applicant has presented, as part of the permit application, specific, feasible plans for the proposed underground mining operations;

(ii) the proposed underground mining operations are necessary or desirable to assure maximum practical recovery of the mineral resource and will avoid multiple disturbance of the surface;

(iii) the applicant has satisfactorily demonstrated that the plan for the underground mining operations conforms to requirements for underground mining in the jurisdiction and that permits necessary for the underground mining operations have been issued by the appropriate authority;

(iv) the areas proposed for the variance have been shown by the applicant to be necessary for the implementing of the proposed underground mining operations;

(v) no substantial adverse environmental damage, either on-site or off-site, will result from the delay in completion of reclamation as required by this chapter;

(vi) provisions for the off-site storage of spoil will comply with paragraph (22);

(B) if the Secretary has promulgated specific regulations to govern the granting of such variances in accordance with the provisions of this subsection and section 1251 of this title, and has imposed such additional requirements as he deems necessary;

(C) if variances granted under the provisions of this subsection are to be reviewed by the regulatory authority not more than three years from the date of issuance of the permit; and

(D) if liability under the bond filed by the applicant with the regulatory authority pursuant to section 1259(b) of this title shall be for the duration of the underground mining operations and until the requirements of this subsection and section 1269 of this title have been fully complied with.[4]

(17) insure that the construction, maintenance, and postmining conditions of access roads into and across the site of operations will control or prevent erosion and siltation, pollution of water, damage to fish or wildlife or their habitat, or public or private property;

(18) refrain from the construction of roads or other access ways up a stream bed or drainage channel or in such proximity to such channel so as to seriously alter the normal flow of water;

(19) establish on the regraded areas, and all other lands affected, a diverse, effective, and permanent vegetative cover of the same seasonal variety native to the area of land to be affected and capable of self-regeneration and plant succession at least equal in extent of cover to the natural vegetation of the area; except, that introduced species may be used in the revegetation process where desirable and necessary to achieve the approved postmining land use plan;

(20) (A) assume the responsibility for successful revegetation, as required by paragraph (19) above, for a period of five full years after the last year of augmented seeding, fertilizing, irrigation, or other work in order to assure compliance with paragraph (19) above, except in those areas or regions of the country where the annual average precipitation is twenty-six inches or less, then the operator's assumption of responsibility and liability will extend for a period of ten full years after the last year of augmented seeding, fertilizing, irrigation, or other work: *Provided*, That when the regulatory authority approves a long-term intensive agricultural postmining land use, the applicable five- or ten-year period of responsibility for revegetation shall commence at the date of initial planting for such long-term intensive agricultural postmining land use: *Provided further*, That when the regulatory authority issues a written finding approving a long-term, intensive, agricultural postmining land use as part of the mining and reclamation plan, the authority may grant exception to the provisions of paragraph (19) above;

(B) on lands eligible for remining assume the responsibility for successful revegetation for a period of two full years after the last year of augmented seeding, fertilizing, irrigation, or other work in order to assure compliance with the applicable standards, except in those areas or regions of the country where the annual average precipitation is twenty-six inches or less, then the operator's assumption of responsibility and liability will be extended for a period of five full years after the last year of augmented seeding, fertilizing, irrigation, or other work in order to assure compliance with the applicable standards.

(21) protect offsite areas from slides or damage occurring during the surface coal mining and reclamation operations, and not deposit spoil material or locate any part of the operations or waste accumulations outside the permit area;

(22) place all excess spoil material resulting from coal surface mining and reclamation activities in such a manner that—

(A) spoil is transported and placed in a controlled manner in position for concurrent compaction and in such a way to assure mass stability and to prevent mass movement;

(B) the areas of disposal are within the bonded permit areas and all organic matter shall be removed immediately prior to spoil placement;

(C) appropriate surface and internal drainage systems and diversion ditches are used so as to prevent spoil erosion and movement;

(D) the disposal area does not contain springs, natural water courses or wet weather seeps unless lateral drains are constructed from the wet areas to the main underdrains in such a manner that filtration of the water into the spoil pile will be prevented;

(E) if placed on a slope, the spoil is placed upon the most moderate slope among those upon which, in the judgment of the regulatory authority, the spoil could be placed in compliance with all the requirements of this chapter, and shall be placed, where possible, upon, or above, a natural terrace, bench, or berm, if such placement provides additional stability and prevents mass movement;

(F) where the toe of the spoil rests on a downslope, a rock toe buttress, of sufficient size to prevent mass movement, is constructed;

(G) the final configuration is compatible with the natural drainage pattern and surroundings and suitable for intended uses;

(H) design of the spoil disposal area is certified by a qualified registered professional engineer in conformance with professional standards; and

(I) all other provisions of this chapter are met.[4]

(23) meet such other criteria as are necessary to achieve reclamation in accordance with the purposes of this chapter, taking into consideration the physical, climatological, and other characteristics of the site; and[5]

(24) to the extent possible using the best technology currently available, minimize disturbances and adverse impacts of the operation on fish, wildlife, and related environmental values, and achieve enhancement of such resources where practicable;

(25) provide for an undisturbed natural barrier beginning at the elevation of the lowest coal seam to be mined and extending from the outslope for such distance as the regulatory authority shall determine shall be retained in place as a barrier to slides and erosion.

(c) Procedures; exception to original contour restoration requirements

(1) Each State program may and each Federal program shall include procedures pursuant to which the regulatory authority may permit surface mining operations for the purposes set forth in paragraph (3) of this subsection.

(2) Where an applicant meets the requirements of paragraphs (3) and (4) of this subsection a permit without regard to the requirement to restore to approximate original contour set forth in subsection (b)(3 or (d)(2) and (3) of this section may be granted for the surface mining of coal where the mining operation will remove an entire coal seam or seams running through the upper fraction of a mountain, ridge, or hill (except as provided in subsection (c)(4)(A) hereof) by removing all of the overburden and creating a level plateau or a gently rolling contour with no highwalls remaining, and capable of supporting postmining uses in accord with the requirements of this subsection.

(3) In cases where an industrial, commercial, agricultural, residential or public facility (including recreational facilities) use is proposed or[6] the postmining use of the affected land, the regulatory authority may grant a permit for a surface mining operation of the nature described in subsection (c)(2) of this section where—

(A) after consultation with the appropriate land use planning agencies, if any, the proposed postmining land use is deemed to constitute an equal or better economic or public use of the affected land, as compared with premining use;

(B) the applicant presents specific plans for the proposed postmining land use and appropriate assurances that such use will be—

(i) compatible with adjacent land uses;

(ii) obtainable according to data regarding expected need and market;

(iii) assured of investment in necessary public facilities;

(iv) supported by commitments from public agencies where appropriate;

(v) practicable with respect to private financial capability for completion of the proposed use;

(vi) planned pursuant to a schedule attached to the reclamation plan so as to integrate the mining operation and reclamation with the postmining land use; and

(vii) designed by a registered engineer in conformance with professional standards established to assure the stability, drainage, and configuration necessary for the intended use of the site;

(C) the proposed use would be consistent with adjacent land uses, and existing State and local land use plans and programs;

(D) the regulatory authority provides the governing body of the unit of general-purpose government in which the land is located and any State or Federal agency which the regulatory agency, in its discretion, determines to have an interest in the proposed use, an opportunity of not more than sixty days to review and comment on the proposed use;

(E) all other requirements of this chapter will be met.

(4) In granting any permit pursuant to this subsection the regulatory authority shall require that—

(A) the toe of the lowest coal seam and the overburden associated with it are retained in place as a barrier to slides and erosion;

(B) the reclaimed area is stable;

(C) the resulting plateau or rolling contour drains inward from the outslopes except at specified points;

(D) no damage will be done to natural watercourses;

(E) spoil will be placed on the mountaintop bench as is necessary to achieve the planned postmining land use: *Provided*, That all excess spoil material not retained on the mountaintop shall be placed in accordance with the provisions of subsection (b)(22) of this section;

(F) insure stability of the spoil retained on the mountaintop and meet the other requirements of this chapter;[7]

(5) The regulatory authority shall promulgate specific regulations to govern the granting of permits in accord with the provisions of this subsection, and may impose such additional requirements as he deems to be necessary.

(6) All permits granted under the provisions of this subsection shall be reviewed not more than three years from the date of issuance of the permit, unless the applicant affirmatively demonstrates that the proposed development is proceeding in accordance with the terms of the approved schedule and reclamation plan.

(d) Steep-slope surface coal mining standards

The following performance standards shall be applicable to steep-slope surface coal mining and shall be in addition to those general performance standards required by this section: *Provided, however*, That the provisions of this subsection (d) shall not apply to those situations in which an operator is mining on flat or gently rolling terrain, on which an occasional steep slope is encountered through which the mining operation is to proceed, leaving a plain or predominantly flat area or where an operator is in compliance with provisions of subsection (c) hereof:

(1) Insure that when performing surface coal mining on steep slopes, no debris, abandoned or disabled equipment, spoil material, or waste mineral matter be placed on the downslope below the bench or mining cut: *Provided*, That spoil material in excess of that required for the reconstruction of the approximate original contour under the provisions of subsection (b)(3) or (d)(2) of this section shall be permanently stored pursuant to subsection (b)(22) of this section.

(2) Complete backfilling with spoil material shall be required to cover completely the highwall and return the site to the appropriate original contour, which material will maintain stability following mining and reclamation.

(3) The operator may not disturb land above the top of the highwall unless the regulatory authority finds that such disturbance will facilitate compliance with the environmental protection standards of this section: *Provided, however*, That the land disturbed above the highwall shall be limited to that amount necessary to facilitate said compliance.

(4) For the purposes of this subsection (d), the term "steep slope" is any slope above twenty degrees or such lesser slope as may be defined by the regulatory authority after consideration of soil, climate, and other characteristics of a region or State.

(e) Variances to original contour restoration requirements

(1) Each State program may and each Federal program shall include procedures pursuant to which the regulatory authority may permit variances for the purposes set forth in paragraph (3) of this subsection, provided that the watershed control of the area is improved; and further provided complete backfilling with spoil material shall be required to cover completely the highwall which material will maintain stability following mining and reclamation.

(2) Where an applicant meets the requirements of paragraphs (3) and (4) of this subsection a variance from the requirement to restore to approximate original contour set forth in subsection (d)(2) of this section may be granted for the surface mining of coal where the owner of the surface knowingly requests in writing, as a part of the permit application that such a variance be granted so as to render the land, after reclamation, suitable for an industrial, commercial, residential, or public use (including recreational facilities) in accord with the further provisions of (3) and (4) of this subsection.

(3) **(A)** After consultation with the appropriate land use planning agencies, if any, the potential use of the affected land is deemed to constitute an equal or better economic or public use;

(B) is designed and certified by a qualified registered professional engineer in conformance with professional standards established to assure the stability, drainage, and configuration necessary for the intended use of the site; and

(C) after approval of the appropriate state environmental agencies, the watershed of the affected land is deemed to be improved.

(4) In granting a variance pursuant to this subsection the regulatory authority shall require that only such amount of spoil will be placed off the mine bench as is necessary to achieve the planned postmining land use, insure stability of the spoil retained on the bench, meet all other requirements of this chapter, and all spoil placement off the mine bench must comply with subsection (b)(22) of this section.

(5) The regulatory authority shall promulgate specific regulations to govern the granting of variances in accord with the provisions of this subsection, and may impose such additional requirements as he deems to be necessary.

(6) All exceptions granted under the provisions of this subsection shall be reviewed not more than three years from the date of issuance of the permit, unless the permittee affirmatively demonstrates that the proposed development is proceeding in accordance with the terms of the reclamation plan.

(f) Standards and criteria for coal mine waste piles

The Secretary, with the written concurrence of the Chief of Engineers, shall establish within one hundred and thirty-five days from August 3, 1977, standards and criteria regulating the design, location, construction, operation, maintenance, enlargement, modification, removal, and abandonment of new and existing coal mine waste piles referred to in subsection (b)(13) of this section and section 1266(b)(5) of this title. Such standards and criteria shall conform to the standards and criteria used by the Chief of Engineers to insure that flood control structures are safe and effectively perform their intended function. In addition to engineering and other technical specifications the standards and criteria developed pursuant to this subsection must include provisions for: review and approval of plans and specifications prior to construction, enlargement, modification, removal, or abandonment; performance of periodic inspections during construction; issuance of certificates of approval upon completion of construction; performance of periodic safety inspections; and issuance of notices for required remedial or maintenance work.

(Pub. L. No. 95–87, Title V, § 515, 91 Stat. 486 (Aug. 3, 1977); as amended by Pub. L. No. 99–500, Title I, § 101(h) [Title I, § 123], 100 Stat. 3341–267 (Oct. 18, 1986); Pub. L. No. 99–591, Title I, § 101(h) [Title I, § 123], 100 Stat. 3341–267 (Oct. 30, 1986); Pub. L. No. 102–486, Title XXV, § 2503(b), 106 Stat. 3102 (Oct. 24, 1992).)

[1] So in original. Probably should be followed by a comma.

[2] So in original. Probably should be "conduct."

[3] So in original. Probably should be "keeping."

[4] So in original. The period probably should be a semicolon.

[5] So in original. The word "and" probably should appear at end of par. (24).

[6] So in original. Probably should be "for."

[7] So in original. The semicolon probably should be a period.

HISTORICAL AND STATUTORY NOTES

References in Text

This chapter, referred to in subsecs. (a), (b), and (c), was in the original "this Act", meaning Pub. 95–87, 91 Stat. 445 (Aug. 3, 1977), as amended, which enacted this chapter and amended section 1114 of Title 18, Crimes and Criminal Procedure. For complete classification of this Act to the Code, see Short Title note set out under section 1201 of this title and Tables.

Public Law 83–566, referred to in subsec. (b)(8)(B), is Act Aug. 4, 1954, c. 656, 68 Stat. 666, as amended, known as the Watershed Protection and Flood Prevention Act, which is codified generally to chapter 18 (section 1001 et seq.) of Title 16, Conservation. For complete classification of this Act to the Code, see Short Title note set out under section 1001 of Title 16 and Tables volume.

§ 1266. Surface effects of underground coal mining operations

[SMCRA § 516]

(a) Rules and regulations

The Secretary shall promulgate rules and regulations directed toward the surface effects of underground coal mining operations, embodying the following requirements and in accordance with the procedures established under section 1251 of this title: *Provided, however,* That in adopting any rules and regulations the Secretary shall consider the distinct difference between surface coal mining and underground coal mining. Such rules and regulations shall not conflict with nor supersede any provision of the Federal Coal Mine Health and Safety Act of 1969 [30 U.S.C.A. § 801 et seq.] nor any regulation issued pursuant thereto, and shall not be promulgated until the Secretary has obtained the written concurrence of the head of the department which administers such Act.

(b) Permit requirements

Each permit issued under any approved State or Federal program pursuant to this chapter and relating to underground coal mining shall require the operator to—

(1) adopt measures consistent with known technology in order to prevent subsidence causing material damage to the extent technologically and economically feasible, maximize mine stability, and maintain the value and reasonably foreseeable use of such surface lands, except in those instances where the mining technology used requires planned subsidence in a predictable and controlled manner: *Provided,* That nothing in this subsection shall be construed to prohibit the standard method of room and pillar mining;

(2) seal all portals, entryways, drifts, shafts, or other openings between the surface and underground mine working when no longer needed for the conduct of the mining operations;

(3) fill or seal exploratory holes no longer necessary for mining, maximizing to the extent technologically and economically feasible return of mine and processing waste, tailings, and any other waste incident to the mining operation, to the mine workings or excavations;

(4) with respect to surface disposal of mine wastes, tailings, coal processing wastes, and other wastes in areas other than the mine workings or excavations, stabilize all waste piles created by the permittee from current operations through construction in compacted layers including the use of incombustible and impervious materials if necessary and assure that the leachate will not degrade below water quality standards established pursuant to applicable Federal and State law surface or ground waters and that the final contour of the waste accumulation will be compatible with natural surroundings and that the site is stabilized and revegetated according to the provisions of this section;

(5) design, locate, construct, operate, maintain, enlarge, modify, and remove, or abandon, in accordance with the standards and criteria developed pursuant to section 1265(f) of this title, all existing and new coal mine waste piles consisting of mine wastes, tailings, coal processing wastes, or other liquid and solid wastes and used either temporarily or permanently as dams or embankments;

(6) establish on regraded areas and all other lands affected, a diverse and permanent vegetative cover capable of self-regeneration and plant succession and at least equal in extent of cover to the natural vegetation of the area;

(7) protect offsite areas from damages which may result from such mining operations;

(8) eliminate fire hazards and otherwise eliminate conditions which constitute a hazard to health and safety of the public;

(9) minimize the disturbances of the prevailing hydrologic balance at the minesite and in associated offsite areas and to the quantity of water in surface ground water systems both during and after coal mining operations and during reclamation by—

(A) avoiding acid or other toxic mine drainage by such measures as, but not limited to—

(i) preventing or removing water from contact with toxic producing deposits;

(ii) treating drainage to reduce toxic content which adversely affects downstream water upon being released to water courses;

(iii) casing, sealing, or otherwise managing boreholes, shafts, and wells to keep acid or other toxic drainage from entering ground and surface waters; and

(B) conducting surface coal mining operations so as to prevent, to the extent possible using the best technology currently available, additional contributions of suspended solids to streamflow or runoff outside the permit area (but in no event shall such contributions be in excess of requirements set by applicable State or Federal law), and avoiding channel deepening or enlargement in operations requiring the discharge of water from mines;

(10) with respect to other surface impacts not specified in this subsection including the construction of new roads or the improvement or use of existing roads to gain access to the site of such activities and for haulage, repair areas, storage areas, processing areas, shipping areas, and other areas upon which are sited structures, facilities, or other property or materials on the surface, resulting from or incident to such activities, operate in accordance with the standards established under section 1265 of this title for such effects which result from surface coal mining operations: *Provided*, That the Secretary shall make such modifications in the requirements imposed by this paragraph as are necessary to accommodate the distinct difference between surface and underground coal mining;

(11) to the extent possible using the best technology currently available, minimize disturbances and adverse impacts of the operation on fish, wildlife, and related environmental values, and achieve enhancement of such resources where practicable;

(12) locate openings for all new drift mines working acid-producing or iron-producing coal seams in such a manner as to prevent a gravity discharge of water from the mine.

(c) Suspension of underground coal mining operations in urbanized areas

In order to protect the stability of the land, the regulatory authority shall suspend underground coal mining under urbanized areas, cities, towns, and communities and adjacent to industrial or commercial buildings, major impoundments, or permanent streams if he finds imminent danger to inhabitants of the urbanized areas, cities, towns, and communities.

(d) Applicability of this subchapter to surface operations and surface impacts incident to underground coal mining operations

The provisions of this subchapter relating to State and Federal programs, permits, bonds, inspections and enforcement, public review, and administrative and judicial review shall be applicable to surface operations and surface impacts incident to an underground coal mine with such modifications to the permit application requirements, permit approval or denial procedures, and bond requirements as are necessary to accommodate the distinct difference between surface and underground coal mining. The Secretary shall promulgate such modifications in accordance with the rulemaking procedure established in section 1251 of this title.

(Pub. L. No. 95–87, Title V, § 516, 91 Stat. 495 (Aug. 3, 1977).)

HISTORICAL AND STATUTORY NOTES

References in Text

The Federal Coal Mine Health and Safety Act of 1969, referred to in subsec. (a), is Pub. L. No. 91–173, 83 Stat. 742 (Dec. 30, 1969), as amended, which was redesignated the Federal Mine Safety and Health Act of 1977 by Pub. L. No. 95–164, Title I, § 101, 91 Stat. 1290 (Nov. 9, 1977), and is codified principally as chapter 22 (section 801 et seq.) of this title. For complete classification of this Act to the Code, see Short Title note set out under section 801 of this title and Tables.

This chapter, referred to in subsec. (b), was in the original, "this Act", meaning Pub. L. No. 95–87, 91 Stat. 445 (Aug. 3, 1977), as amended, which enacted this chapter and amended section 1114 of Title 18, Crimes and Criminal Procedure. For complete classification of this Act to the Code, see Short Title note set out under section 1201 of this title and Tables volume.

§ 1267. Inspections and monitoring

[SMCRA § 517]

(a) Inspections of surface coal mining and reclamation operations

The Secretary shall cause to be made such inspections of any surface coal mining and reclamation operations as are necessary to evaluate the administration of approved State programs, or to develop or enforce any Federal program, and for such purposes authorized representatives of the Secretary shall have a right of entry to, upon, or through any surface coal mining and reclamation operations.

(b) Records and reports; monitoring systems; evaluation of results

For the purpose of developing or assisting in the development, administration, and enforcement of any approved State or Federal program under this chapter or in the administration and enforcement of any permit under this chapter, or of determining whether any person is in violation of any requirement of any such State or Federal program or any other requirement of this chapter—

(1) the regulatory authority shall require any permittee to (A) establish and maintain appropriate records, (B) make monthly reports to the regulatory authority, (C) install, use, and maintain any necessary monitoring equipment or methods, (D) evaluate results in accordance with such methods, at such locations, intervals, and in such manner as a regulatory authority shall prescribe, and (E) provide such other information relative to surface coal mining and reclamation operations as the regulatory authority deems reasonable and necessary;

(2) for those surface coal mining and reclamation operations which remove or disturb strata that serve as aquifers which significantly insure the hydrologic balance of water use either on or off the mining site, the regulatory authority shall specify those—

(A) monitoring sites to record the quantity and quality of surface drainage above and below the minesite as well as in the potential zone of influence;

(B) monitoring sites to record level, amount, and samples of ground water and aquifers potentially affected by the mining and also directly below the lowermost (deepest) coal seam to be mined;

(C) records of well logs and borehole data to be maintained; and

(D) monitoring sites to record precipitation.

The monitoring data collection and analysis required by this section shall be conducted according to standards and procedures set forth by the regulatory authority in order to assure their reliability and validity; and

(3) the authorized representatives of the regulatory authority, without advance notice and upon presentation of appropriate credentials (A) shall have the right of entry to, upon, or through any surface coal mining and reclamation operations or any premises in which any records required to be maintained under paragraph (1) of this subsection are located; and (B) may at reasonable times, and without delay, have access to and copy any records, inspect any monitoring equipment or method of operation required under this chapter.

(c) Inspection intervals

The inspections by the regulatory authority shall (1) occur on an irregular basis averaging not less than one partial inspection per month and one complete inspection per calendar quarter for the surface coal mining and reclamation operation covered by each permit; (2) occur without prior notice to the permittee or his agents or employees except for necessary onsite meetings with the permittee; and (3) include the filing of inspection reports adequate to enforce the requirements of and to carry out the terms and purposes of this chapter.

(d) Maintenance of sign

Each permittee shall conspicuously maintain at the entrances to the surface coal mining and reclamation operations a clearly visible sign which sets forth the name, business address, and phone number of the permittee and the permit number of the surface coal mining and reclamation operations.

(e) Violations

Each inspector, upon detection of each violation of any requirement of any State or Federal program or of this chapter, shall forthwith inform the operator in writing, and shall report in writing any such violation to the regulatory authority.

(f) Availability of information to public

Copies of any records, reports, inspection materials, or information obtained under this subchapter by the regulatory authority shall be made immediately available to the public at central and sufficient locations in the county, multicounty, and State area of mining so that they are conveniently available to residents in the areas of mining.

(g) Conflict of interest; penalty; publication of regulations; report to Congress

No employee of the State regulatory authority performing any function or duty under this chapter shall have a direct or indirect financial interest in any underground or surface coal mining operation. Whoever knowingly violates the provisions of this subsection shall, upon conviction, be punished by a fine of not more than $2,500, or by imprisonment of not more than one year, or by both. The Secretary shall (1) within sixty days after August 3, 1977, publish in the Federal Register, in accordance with section 553 of Title 5, regulations to establish methods by which the provisions of this subsection will be monitored and enforced by the Secretary and such State regulatory authority, including appropriate provisions for the filing by such employees and the review of statements and supplements thereto concerning any financial interest which may be affected by this subsection, and (2) report to the Congress as part of the Annual Report (section 1296 of this title) on actions taken and not taken during the preceding year under this subsection.

(h) Review; procedures for inspections

(1) Any person who is or may be adversely affected by a surface mining operation may notify the Secretary or any representative of the Secretary responsible for conducting the inspection, in writing, of any violation of this chapter which he has reason to believe exists at the surface mining site. The Secretary shall, by regulation, establish procedures for informal review of any refusal by a representative of the Secretary to issue a citation with respect to any such alleged violation. The Secretary shall furnish such persons requesting the review a written statement of the reasons for the Secretary's final disposition of the case.

(2) The Secretary shall also, by regulation, establish procedures to insure that adequate and complete inspections are made. Any such person may notify the Secretary of any failure to make such inspections, after which the Secretary shall determine whether adequate and complete inspections have been made. The Secretary shall furnish such persons a written statement of the reasons for the Secretary's determination that adequate and complete inspections have or have not been conducted.

(Pub. L. No. 95–87, Title V, § 517, 91 Stat. 498 (Aug. 3, 1977).)

HISTORICAL AND STATUTORY NOTES

References in Text

This chapter, referred to in subsecs. (b), (c), (e), (g), and (h)(1), was in the original "this Act", meaning Pub. L. No. 95–87, 91 Stat. 445 (Aug. 3, 1977), as amended, which enacted this chapter and amended section 1114 of Title 18, Crimes and Criminal Procedure. For complete classification of this Act to the Code, see Short Title note set out under section 1201 of this title and Tables.

Termination of Reporting Requirements

For termination of reporting provisions of subsec. (g) of this section, effective May 15, 2000, see Pub. L. No. 104–66, § 3003, as amended, set out as a note under 31 U.S.C.A. § 1113, and page 109 of House Document No. 103–7.

For termination, effective May 15, 2000, of provisions in subsec. (g) of this section relating to requirement to report to Congress on actions taken and not taken under subsec. (g), see Pub. L. No. 104–66, § 3003, as amended, set out as a note under 31 U.S.C.A. § 1113, and House Document No. 103–7, page 109.

§ 1268. Penalties

[SMCRA § 518]

(a) Civil penalties for violations of permit conditions and provisions of this subchapter

In the enforcement of a Federal program or Federal lands program, or during Federal enforcement pursuant to section 1252 of this title or during Federal enforcement of a State program pursuant to section 1271 of this title, any permittee who violates any permit condition or who violates any other provision of this subchapter, may be assessed a civil penalty by the Secretary, except that if such violation leads to the issuance of a cessation order under section 1271 of this title, the civil penalty shall be assessed. Such penalty shall not exceed $5,000 for each violation. Each day of continuing violation may be deemed a separate violation for purposes of penalty assessments. In determining the amount of the penalty, consideration shall be given to the permittee's history of previous violations at the particular surface coal mining operation; the seriousness of the violation, including any irreparable harm to the environment and any hazard to the health or safety of the public; whether the permittee was negligent; and the demonstrated good faith of the permittee charged in attempting to achieve rapid compliance after notification of the violation.

(b) Hearing

A civil penalty shall be assessed by the Secretary only after the person charged with a violation described under subsection (a) of this section has been given an opportunity for a public hearing. Where such a public hearing has been held, the Secretary shall make findings of fact, and he shall issue a written decision as to the occurrence of the violation and the amount of the penalty which is warranted, incorporating, when appropriate, an order therein requiring that the penalty be paid. When appropriate, the Secretary shall consolidate such hearings with other proceedings under section 1271 of this title. Any hearing under this section shall be of record and shall be subject to section 554 of Title 5. Where the person charged with such a violation fails to avail himself of the opportunity for a public hearing, a civil penalty shall be assessed by the Secretary after the Secretary has determined that a violation did occur, and the amount of the penalty which is warranted, and has issued an order requiring that the penalty be paid.

(c) Notice of violation; action required of violator; waiver of legal rights

Upon the issuance of a notice or order charging that a violation of this chapter has occurred, the Secretary shall inform the operator within thirty days of the proposed amount of said penalty. The person charged with the penalty shall then have thirty days to pay the proposed penalty in full or, if the person wishes to contest either the amount of the penalty or the fact of the violation, forward the proposed amount to the Secretary for placement in an escrow account. If through administrative or judicial review of the proposed penalty, it is determined that no violation occurred, or that the amount of the penalty should be reduced, the Secretary shall within thirty days remit the appropriate amount to the person, with interest at the rate of 6 percent, or at the prevailing Department of the Treasury rate, whichever is greater. Failure to forward the money to the Secretary within thirty days shall result in a waiver of all legal rights to contest the violation or the amount of the penalty.

(d) Civil action to recover civil penalties

Civil penalties owed under this chapter, may be recovered in a civil action brought by the Attorney General at the request of the Secretary in any appropriate district court of the United States.

(e) Willful violations

Any person who willfully and knowingly violates a condition of a permit issued pursuant to a Federal program, a Federal lands program or Federal enforcement pursuant to section 1252 of this title or during Federal enforcement of a State program pursuant to section 1271 of this title or fails or refuses to comply with any order issued under section 1271 or section 1276 of this title, or any order incorporated in a final decision issued by the Secretary under this chapter, except an order incorporated in a decision issued under subsection (b) of this section or section 1294 of this title, shall, upon conviction, be punished by a fine of not more than $10,000, or by imprisonment for not more than one year or both.

(f) Corporate violations

Whenever a corporate permittee violates a condition of a permit issued pursuant to a Federal program, a Federal lands program or Federal enforcement pursuant to section 1252 of this title or Federal enforcement of a State program pursuant to section 1271 of this title or fails or refuses to comply with any order issued under section 1271 of this title, or any order incorporated in a final decision issued by the Secretary under this chapter except an order incorporated in a decision issued under subsection (b) of this section or section 1293 of this title, any director, officer, or agent of such corporation who willfully and knowingly authorized, ordered, or carried out such violation, failure, or refusal shall be subject to the same civil penalties, fines, and imprisonment that may be imposed upon a person under subsections (a) and (e) of this section.

(g) False statements, representations, or certifications

Whoever knowingly makes any false statement, representation, or certification, or knowingly fails to make any statement, representation, or certification in any application, record, report, plant, or other document filed or required to be maintained pursuant to a Federal program or a Federal lands program or any order of decision issued by the Secretary under this chapter, shall, upon conviction, be punished by a fine of not more than $10,000, or by imprisonment for not more than one year or both.

(h) Failure to correct violation

Any operator who fails to correct a violation for which a citation has been issued under section 1271(a) of this title within the period permitted for its correction (which period shall not end until the entry of a final order by the Secretary, in the case of any review proceedings under section 1275 of this title initiated by the operator wherein the Secretary orders, after an expedited hearing, the suspension of the abatement requirements of the citation after determining that the operator will suffer irreparable loss or damage from the application of those requirements, or until the entry of an order of the court, in the case of any review proceedings under section 1276 of this title initiated by the operator wherein the court orders the suspension of the abatement requirements of the citation), shall be assessed a civil penalty of not less than $750 for each day during which such failure or violation continues.

(i) Effect on additional enforcement right or procedure available under State law

As a condition of approval of any State program submitted pursuant to section 1253 of this title, the civil and criminal penalty provisions thereof shall, at a minimum, incorporate penalties no less stringent than those set forth in this section, and shall contain the same or similar procedural requirements relating thereto. Nothing herein shall be construed so as to eliminate any additional enforcement right or procedures which are available under State law to a State regulatory authority but which are not specifically enumerated herein.

(Pub. L. No. 95–87, Title V, § 518, 91 Stat. 499 (Aug. 3, 1977).)

HISTORICAL AND STATUTORY NOTES

References in Text

This chapter, referred to in subsecs. (c) to (g), was in the original "this Act", meaning Pub. L. No. 95–87, 91 Stat. 445 (Aug. 3, 1977), as amended, which enacted this chapter and amended section 1114 of Title 18, Crimes and Criminal Procedure. For complete classification of this Act to the Code, see Short Title note set out under section 1201 of this title and Tables.

§ 1269. Release of performance bonds or deposits

[SMCRA § 519]

(a) Filing of request; submittal of copy of advertisement; notification by letter of intent to seek release

The permittee may file a request with the regulatory authority for the release of all or part of a performance bond or deposit. Within thirty days after any application for bond or deposit release has been filed with the regulatory authority, the operator shall submit a copy of an advertisement placed at least once a week for four successive weeks in a newspaper of general circulation in the locality of the surface coal mining operation. Such advertisement shall be considered part of any bond release application and shall contain a notification of the precise location of the land affected, the number of acres, the permit and the date approved, the amount of the bond filed and the portion sought to be released, and the type and appropriate dates of reclamation work performed, and a description of the results achieved as they relate to the operator's approved reclamation plan. In addition, as part of any bond release application, the applicant shall submit copies of letters which he has sent to adjoining property owners, local governmental bodies, planning agencies, and sewage and water treatment authorities, or water companies in the locality in which the surface coal mining and reclamation activities took place, notifying them of his intention to seek release from the bond.

(b) Inspection and evaluation; notification of decision

Upon receipt of the notification and request, the regulatory authority shall within thirty days conduct an inspection and evaluation of the reclamation work involved. Such evaluation shall consider, among other things, the degree of difficulty to complete any remaining reclamation, whether pollution of surface and subsurface water is occurring, the probability of continuance of future occurrence of such pollution, and the estimated cost of abating such pollution. The regulatory authority shall notify the permittee in writing of its decision to release or not to release all or part of the performance bond or deposit within sixty days from the filing of the request, if no public hearing is held pursuant to subsection (f) of this section, and if there has been a public hearing held pursuant to subsection (f) of this section, within thirty days thereafter.

(c) Requirements for release

The regulatory authority may release in whole or in part said bond or deposit if the authority is satisfied the reclamation covered by the bond or deposit or portion thereof has been accomplished as required by this chapter according to the following schedule:

(1) When the operator completes the backfilling, regrading, and drainage control of a bonded area in accordance with his approved reclamation plan, the release of 60 per centum of the bond or collateral for the applicable permit area.

(2) After revegetation has been established on the regraded mined lands in accordance with the approved reclamation plan. When determining the amount of bond to be released after successful revegetation has been established, the regulatory authority shall retain that amount of bond for the revegetated area which would be sufficient for a third party to cover the cost of reestablishing revegetation and for the period specified for operator responsibility in section 1265 of this title of reestablishing revegetation. No part of the bond or deposit shall be released under this paragraph so long as the lands to which the release would be applicable are contributing suspended solids to streamflow or runoff outside the permit area in excess of the requirements set by section 1265(b)(10) of this title or until soil productivity for prime farm lands has returned to equivalent levels of yield as nonmined land of the same soil type in the surrounding area under equivalent management practices as determined from the soil survey performed pursuant to section 1257(b)(16) of this title. Where a silt dam is to be retained as a permanent impoundment pursuant to section 1265(b)(8) of this title, the portion of bond may be released under this paragraph so long as provisions for sound future maintenance by the operator or the landowner have been made with the regulatory authority.

(3) When the operator has completed successfully all surface coal mining and reclamation activities, the release of the remaining portion of the bond, but not before the expiration of the period specified for operator responsibility in section 1265 of this title: *Provided, however,* That no bond shall be fully released until all reclamation requirements of this chapter are fully met.

(d) Notice of disapproval

If the regulatory authority disapproves the application for release of the bond or portion thereof, the authority shall notify the permittee, in writing, stating the reasons for disapproval and recommending corrective actions necessary to secure said release and allowing opportunity for a public hearing.

(e) Notice to municipality

When any application for total or partial bond release is filed with the regulatory authority, the regulatory authority shall notify the municipality in which a surface coal mining operation is located by certified mail at least thirty days prior to the release of all or a portion of the bond.

(f) Objections to release; hearing

Any person with a valid legal interest which might be adversely affected by release of the bond or the responsible officer or head of any Federal, State, or local governmental agency which has jurisdiction by law or special expertise with respect to any environmental, social, or economic impact involved in the operation, or is authorized to develop and enforce environmental standards with respect to such operations shall have the right to file written objections to the proposed release from bond to the regulatory authority within thirty days after the last publication of the above notice. If written objections are filed, and a hearing requested, the regulatory authority shall inform all the interested parties, of the time and place of the hearing, and hold a public hearing in the locality of the surface coal mining operation proposed for bond release within thirty days of the request for such hearing. The date, time, and location of such public hearings shall be advertised by the regulatory authority in a newspaper of general circulation in the locality for two consecutive weeks, and shall hold a public hearing in the locality of the surface coal mining operation proposed for bond release or at the State capital at the option of the objector, within thirty days of the request for such hearing.

(g) Informal conference

Without prejudice to the rights of the objectors, the applicant, or the responsibilities of the regulatory authority pursuant to this section, the regulatory authority may establish an informal conference as provided in section 1263 of this title to resolve such written objections.

(h) Power of regulatory authority with respect to informal conference

For the purpose of such hearing the regulatory authority shall have the authority and is hereby empowered to administer oaths, subpena witnesses, or written or printed materials, compel the attendance of witnesses, or production of the materials, and take evidence including but not limited to inspections of the land affected and other surface coal mining operations carried on by the applicant in the general vicinity. A verbatim record of each public hearing required by this chapter shall be made, and a transcript made available on the motion of any party or by order of the regulatory authority.

(Pub. L. No. 95–87, Title V, § 519, 91 Stat. 501 (Aug. 3, 1977).)

HISTORICAL AND STATUTORY NOTES

References in Text

This chapter, referred to in subsecs. (c) and (h), was in the original "this Act", meaning Pub. L. No. 95–87, 91 Stat. 445 (Aug. 3, 1977), as amended, which enacted this chapter and amended section 1114 of Title 18, Crimes and Criminal Procedure. For complete classification of this Act to the Code, see Short Title note set out under section 1201 of this title and Tables.

§ 1270. Citizens suits

[SMCRA § 520]

(a) Civil action to compel compliance with this chapter

Except as provided in subsection (b) of this section, any person having an interest which is or may be adversely affected may commence a civil action on his own behalf to compel compliance with this chapter—

(1) against the United States or any other governmental instrumentality or agency to the extent permitted by the eleventh amendment to the Constitution which is alleged to be in violation of the provisions of this chapter or of any rule, regulation, order or permit issued pursuant thereto, or against any other person who is alleged to be in violation of any rule, regulation, order or permit issued pursuant to this subchapter; or

(2) against the Secretary or the appropriate State regulatory authority to the extent permitted by the eleventh amendment to the Constitution where there is alleged a failure of the Secretary or the appropriate State regulatory authority to perform any act or duty under this chapter which is not discretionary with the Secretary or with the appropriate State regulatory authority.

The district courts shall have jurisdiction, without regard to the amount in controversy or the citizenship of the parties.

(b) Limitation on bringing of action

No action may be commenced—

(1) under subsection (a)(1) of this section—

(A) prior to sixty days after the plaintiff has given notice in writing of the violation (i) to the Secretary, (ii) to the State in which the violation occurs, and (iii) to any alleged violator; or

(B) if the Secretary or the State has commenced and is diligently prosecuting a civil action in a court of the United States or a State to require compliance with the provisions of this chapter, or any rule, regulation, order, or permit issued pursuant to this chapter, but in any such action in a court of the United States any person may intervene as a matter of right; or

(2) under subsection (a)(2) of this section prior to sixty days after the plaintiff has given notice in writing of such action to the Secretary, in such manner as the Secretary shall by regulation prescribe, or to the appropriate State regulatory authority, except that such action may be brought immediately after such notification in the case where the violation or order complained of constitutes an imminent threat to the health or safety of the plaintiff or would immediately affect a legal interest of the plaintiff.

(c) Venue; intervention

(1) Any action respecting a violation of this chapter or the regulations thereunder may be brought only in the judicial district in which the surface coal mining operation complained of is located.

(2) In such action under this section, the Secretary, or the State regulatory authority, if not a party, may intervene as a matter of right.

(d) Costs; filing of bonds

The court, in issuing any final order in any action brought pursuant to subsection (a) of this section, may award costs of litigation (including attorney and expert witness fees) to any party, whenever the court determines such award is appropriate. The court may, if a temporary restraining order or preliminary injunction is sought require the filing of a bond or equivalent security in accordance with the Federal Rules of Civil Procedure.

(e) Effect on other enforcement methods

Nothing in this section shall restrict any right which any person (or class of persons) may have under any statute or common law to seek enforcement of any of the provisions of this chapter and the regulations thereunder, or to seek any other relief (including relief against the Secretary or the appropriate State regulatory authority).

(f) Action for damages

Any person who is injured in his person or property through the violation by any operator of any rule, regulation, order, or permit issued pursuant to this chapter may bring an action for damages (including reasonable attorney and expert witness fees) only in the judicial district in which the surface coal mining operation complained of is located. Nothing in this subsection shall affect the rights established by or limits imposed under State Workmen's Compensation laws.

(Pub. L. No. 95–87, Title V, § 520, 91 Stat. 503 (Aug. 3, 1977).)

HISTORICAL AND STATUTORY NOTES

References in Text

This chapter, referred to in subsecs. (a) to (c), (e), and (f), was in the original "this Act", meaning Pub. L. No. 95–87, 91 Stat. 445 (Aug. 3, 1977), as amended, which enacted this chapter and amended section 1114 of Title 18, Crimes and Criminal Procedure. For complete classification of this Act to the Code, see Short Title note set out under section 1201 of this title and Tables.

The Federal Rules of Civil Procedure, referred to in subsec. (d), are set out in the Appendix to Title 28, Judiciary and Judicial Procedure.

§ 1271. Enforcement

[SMCRA § 521]

(a) Notice of violation; Federal inspection; waiver of notification period; cessation order; affirmative obligation on operator; suspension or revocation of permits; contents of notices and orders

(1) Whenever, on the basis of any information available to him, including receipt of information from any person, the Secretary has reason to believe that any person is in violation of any requirement of this chapter or any permit condition required by this chapter, the Secretary shall notify the State regulatory authority, if one exists, in the State in which such violation exists. If no such State authority exists or the State regulatory authority fails within ten days after notification to take appropriate action to cause said violation to be corrected or to show good cause for such failure and transmit notification of its action to the Secretary, the Secretary shall immediately order Federal inspection of the surface coal mining operation at which the alleged violation is occurring unless the information available to the Secretary is a result of a previous Federal inspection of such surface coal mining operation. The ten-day notification period shall be waived when the person informing the Secretary provides adequate proof that an imminent danger of significant environmental harm exists and that the State has failed to take appropriate action. When the Federal inspection results from information provided to the Secretary by any person, the Secretary shall notify such person when the Federal inspection is proposed to be carried out and such person shall be allowed to accompany the inspector during the inspection.

(2) When, on the basis of any Federal inspection, the Secretary or his authorized representative determines that any condition or practices exist, or that any permittee is in violation of any requirement of this chapter or any permit condition required by this chapter, which condition, practice, or violation also creates an imminent danger to the health or safety of the public, or is causing, or can reasonably be expected to cause significant, imminent environmental harm to land, air, or water resources, the Secretary or his authorized representative shall immediately order a cessation of surface coal mining and reclamation operations or the portion thereof relevant to the condition, practice, or violation. Such cessation order shall remain in effect until the Secretary or his authorized representative determines that the condition, practice, or violation has been abated, or until modified, vacated, or terminated by the Secretary or his authorized representative pursuant to paragraph (5) f this subsection. Where the Secretary finds that the ordered cessation of surface coal mining and reclamation operations, or any portion thereof, will not completely abate the imminent danger to health or safety of the public or the significant imminent environmental harm to land, air, or water resources, the Secretary shall, in addition to the cessation order, impose affirmative obligations on the operator requiring him to take whatever steps the Secretary deems necessary to abate the imminent danger or the significant environmental harm.

(3) When, on the basis of a Federal inspection which is carried out during the enforcement of a Federal program or a Federal lands program, Federal inspection pursuant to section 1252, or section 1254(b) of this title, or during Federal enforcement of a State program in accordance with subsection (b) of this section, the Secretary or his authorized representative determines that any permittee is in violation of any requirement of this chapter or any permit condition required by this chapter; but such violation does not create an imminent danger to the health or safety of the public, or cannot be reasonably expected to cause significant, imminent environmental harm to land, air, or water resources, the Secretary or authorized representative shall issue a notice to the permittee or his agent fixing a reasonable time but not more than ninety days for the abatement of the violation and providing opportunity for public hearing.

If, upon expiration of the period of time as originally fixed or subsequently extended, for good cause shown and upon the written finding of the Secretary or his authorized representative, the Secretary or his authorized representative finds that the violation has not been abated, he shall immediately order a cessation of surface coal mining and reclamation operations or the portion thereof relevant to the violation. Such cessation order shall remain in effect until the Secretary or his authorized representative determines that the violation has been abated, or until modified, vacated, or terminated by the Secretary or his authorized representative pursuant to paragraph (5) of this subsection. In the order of cessation issued by the Secretary under this subsection, the Secretary shall determine the steps necessary to abate the violation in the most expeditious manner possible, and shall include the necessary measures in the order.

(4) When, on the basis of a Federal inspection which is carried out during the enforcement of a Federal program or a Federal lands program, Federal inspection pursuant to section 1252 or section 1254 of this title or during Federal enforcement of a State program in accordance with subsection (b) of this section, the Secretary or his authorized representative determines that a pattern of violations of any requirements of this chapter or any permit conditions required by this chapter exists or has existed, and if the Secretary or his authorized representative also find that such violations are caused by the unwarranted failure of the permittee to comply with any requirements of this chapter or any permit conditions, or that such violations are willfully caused by the permittee, the Secretary or his authorized representative shall forthwith issue an order to the permittee to show cause as to why the permit should not be suspended or revoked and shall provide opportunity for a public hearing. If a hearing is requested the Secretary shall inform all interested parties of the time and place of the hearing. Upon the permittee's failure to show cause as to why the permit should not be suspended or revoked, the Secretary or his authorized representative shall forthwith suspend or revoke the permit.

(5) Notices and orders issued pursuant to this section shall set forth with reasonable specificity the nature of the violation and the remedial action required, the period of time established for abatement, and a reasonable description of the portion of the surface coal mining and reclamation operation to which the notice or order applies. Each notice or order issued under this section shall be given promptly to the permittee or his agent by the Secretary or his authorized representative who issues such notice or order, and all such notices and orders shall be in writing and shall be signed by such authorized representatives. Any notice or order issued pursuant to this section may be modified, vacated, or terminated by the Secretary or his authorized representative. A copy of any such order or notice shall be sent to the State regulatory authority in the State in which the violation occurs: *Provided,* That any notice or order issued pursuant to this section which requires cessation of mining by the operator shall expire within thirty days of actual notice to the operator unless a public hearing is held at the site or within such reasonable proximity to the site that any viewings of the site can be conducted during the course of public hearing.

(b) Inadequate State enforcement; notice and hearing

Whenever on the basis of information available to him, the Secretary has reason to believe that violations of all or any part of an approved State program result from a failure of the State to enforce such State program or any part thereof effectively, he shall after public notice and notice to the State, hold a hearing thereon in the State within thirty days of such notice. If as a result of said hearing the Secretary finds that there are violations and such violations result from a failure of the State to enforce all or any part of the State program effectively, and if he further finds that the State has not adequately demonstrated its capability and intent to enforce such State program, he shall give public notice of such finding. During the period beginning with such public notice and ending when such State satisfies the Secretary that it will enforce this chapter, the Secretary shall enforce, in the manner provided by this chapter, any permit condition required under this chapter, shall issue new or revised permits in accordance with requirements of this chapter, and may issue such notices and orders as are necessary for compliance therewith: *Provided*, That in the case of a State permittee who has met his obligations under such permit and who did not willfully secure the issuance of such permit through fraud or collusion, the Secretary shall give the permittee a reasonable time to conform ongoing surface mining and reclamation to the requirements of this chapter before suspending or revoking the State permit.

(c) Civil action for relief

The Secretary may request the Attorney General to institute a civil action for relief, including a permanent or temporary injunction, restraining order, or any other appropriate order in the district court of the United States for the district in which the surface coal mining and reclamation operation is located or in which the permittee thereof has his principal office, whenever such permittee or his agent (A) violates or fails or refuses to comply with any order or decision issued by the Secretary under this chapter, or (B) interferes with, hinders, or delays the Secretary or his authorized representatives in carrying out the provisions of this chapter, or (C) refuses to admit such authorized representative to the mine, or (D) refuses to permit inspection of the mine by such authorized representative, or (E) refuses to furnish any information or report requested by the Secretary in furtherance of the provisions of this chapter, or (F) refuses to permit access to, and copying of, such records as the Secretary determines necessary in carrying out the provisions of this chapter. Such court shall have jurisdiction to provide such relief as may be appropriate. Temporary restraining orders shall be issued in accordance with rule 65 of the Federal Rules of Civil Procedure, as amended. Any relief granted by the court to enforce an order under clause (A) of this section shall continue in effect until the completion or final termination of all proceedings for review of such order under this subchapter, unless, prior thereto, the district court granting such relief sets it aside or modifies it.

(d) Sanctions; effect on additional enforcement rights under State law

As a condition of approval of any State program submitted pursuant to section 1253 of this title, the enforcement provisions thereof shall, at a minimum, incorporate sanctions no less stringent than those set forth in this section, and shall contain the same or similar procedural requirements relating thereto. Nothing herein shall be construed so as to eliminate any additional enforcement rights or procedures which are available under State law to a State regulatory authority but which are not specifically enumerated herein.

(Pub. L. No. 95–87, Title V, § 521, 91 Stat. 504 (Aug. 3, 1977).)

HISTORICAL AND STATUTORY NOTES

References in Text

This chapter, referred to in subsecs. (a) to (c), was in the original "this Act", Meaning Pub. L. No. 95–87, 91 Stat. 445 (Aug. 3, 1977), as amended, which enacted this chapter and amended section 1114 of Title 18, Crimes and Criminal Procedure. For complete classification of this Act to the Code, see Short title note set out under section 1201 of this title and Tables.

Rule 65 of the Federal Rules of Civil Procedure, referred to in subsec. (c), is set out in the Appendix to Title 28, Judiciary and Judicial Procedure.

§ 1272. Designating areas unsuitable for surface coal mining [SMCRA § 522]

(a) Establishment of State planning process; standards; State process requirements; integration with present and future land use planning and regulation processes; savings provisions

(1) To be eligible to assume primary regulatory authority pursuant to section 1253 of this title, each State shall establish a planning process enabling objective decisions based upon competent and scientifically sound data and information as to which, if any, land areas of a State are unsuitable for all or certain types of surface coal mining operations pursuant to the standards set forth in paragraphs (2) and (3) of this subsection but such designation shall not prevent the mineral exploration pursuant to the chapter of any area so designated.

(2) Upon petition pursuant to subsection (c) of this section, the State regulatory authority shall designate an area as unsuitable for all or certain types of surface coal mining operations if the State regulatory authority determines that reclamation pursuant to the requirements of this chapter is not technologically and economically feasible.

(3) Upon petition pursuant to subsection (c) of this section, a surface area may be designated unsuitable for certain types of surface coal mining operations if such operations will—

(A) be incompatible with existing State or local land use plans or programs; or

(B) affect fragile or historic lands in which such operations could result in significant damage to important historic, cultural, scientific, and esthetic values and natural systems; or

(C) affect renewable resource lands in which such operations could result in a substantial loss or reduction of long-range productivity of water supply or of food or fiber products, and such lands to include aquifers and aquifer recharge areas; or

(D) affect natural hazard lands in which such operations could substantially endanger life and property, such lands to include areas subject to frequent flooding and areas of unstable geology.

(4) To comply with this section, a State must demonstrate it has developed or is developing a process which includes—

(A) a State agency responsible for surface coal mining lands review;

(B) a data base and an inventory system which will permit proper evaluation of the capacity of different land areas of the State to support and permit reclamation of surface coal mining operations;

(C) a method or methods for implementing land use planning decisions concerning surface coal mining operations; and

(D) proper notice, opportunities for public participation, including a public hearing prior to making any designation or redesignation, pursuant to this section.

(5) Determinations of the unsuitability of land for surface coal mining, as provided for in this section, shall be integrated as closely as possible with present and future land use planning and regulation processes at the Federal, State, and local levels.

(6) The requirements of this section shall not apply to lands on which surface coal mining operations are being conducted on August 3, 1977, or under a permit issued pursuant to this chapter, or where substantial legal and financial commitments in such operation were in existence prior to January 4, 1977.

(b) Review of Federal lands

The Secretary shall conduct a review of the Federal lands to determine, pursuant to the standards set forth in paragraphs (2) and (3) of subsection (a) of this section, whether there are areas on Federal lands which are unsuitable for all or certain types of surface coal mining operations: *Provided, however*, That the Secretary may permit surface coal mining on Federal lands prior to the completion of this review. When the

Secretary determines an area on Federal lands to be unsuitable for all or certain types of surface coal mining operations, he shall withdraw such area or condition any mineral leasing or mineral entries in a manner so as to limit surface coal mining operations on such area. Where a Federal program has been implemented in a State pursuant to section 1254 of this title, the Secretary shall implement a process for designation of areas unsuitable for surface coal mining for non-Federal lands within such State and such process shall incorporate the standards and procedures of this section. Prior to designating Federal lands unsuitable for such mining, the Secretary shall consult with the appropriate State and local agencies.

(c) Petition; intervention; decision

Any person having an interest which is or may be adversely affected shall have the right to petition the regulatory authority to have an area designated as unsuitable for surface coal mining operations, or to have such a designation terminated. Such a petition shall contain allegations of facts with supporting evidence which would tend to establish the allegations. Within ten months after receipt of the petition the regulatory authority shall hold a public hearing in the locality of the affected area, after appropriate notice and publication of the date, time, and location of such hearing. After a person having an interest which is or may be adversely affected has filed a petition and before the hearing, as required by this subsection, any person may intervene by filing allegations of facts with supporting evidence which would tend to establish the allegations. Within sixty days after such hearing, the regulatory authority shall issue and furnish to the petitioner and any other party to the hearing, a written decision regarding the petition, and the reasons therefore.[1] In the event that all the petitioners stipulate agreement prior to the requested hearing, and withdraw their request, such hearing need not be held.

(d) Statement

Prior to designating any land areas as unsuitable for surface coal mining operations, the regulatory authority shall prepare a detailed statement on (i) the potential coal resources of the area, (ii) the demand for coal resources, and (iii) the impact of such designation on the environment, the economy, and the supply of coal.

(e) Prohibition on certain Federal public and private surface coal mining operations

After August 3, 1977, and subject to valid existing rights no surface coal mining operations except those which exist on August 3, 1977, shall be permitted—

(1) on any lands within the boundaries of units of the National Park System, the National Wildlife Refuge Systems, the National System of Trails, the National Wilderness Preservation System, the Wild and Scenic Rivers System, including study rivers designated under section 1276(a) of Title 16 and National Recreation Areas designated by Act of Congress;

(2) on any Federal lands within the boundaries of any national forest: *Provided, however*, That surface coal mining operations may be permitted on such lands if the Secretary finds that there are no significant recreational, timber, economic, or other values which may be incompatible with such surface mining operations and—

(A) surface operations and impacts are incident to an underground coal mine; or

(B) where the Secretary of Agriculture determines, with respect to lands which do not have significant forest cover within those national forests west of the 100th meridian, that surface mining is in compliance with the Multiple-Use Sustained-Yield Act of 1960 [16 U.S.C.A. §§ 528–531], the Federal Coal Leasing Amendments Act of 1975, the National Forest Management Act of 1976, and the provisions of this chapter: *And provided further*, That no surface coal mining operations may be permitted within the boundaries of the Custer National Forest;

(3) which will adversely affect any publicly owned park or places included in the National Register of Historic Sites unless approved jointly by the regulatory authority and the Federal, State, or local agency with jurisdiction over the park or the historic site;

(4) within one hundred feet of the outside right-of-way line of any public road, except where mine access roads or haulage roads join such right-of-way line and except that the regulatory authority may permit such roads to be relocated or the area affected to lie within one hundred feet of such road, if after public notice and opportunity for public hearing in the locality a written finding is made that the interests of the public and the landowners affected thereby will be protected; or

(5) within three hundred feet from any occupied dwelling, unless waived by the owner thereof, nor within three hundred feet of any public building, school, church, community, or institutional building, public park, or within one hundred feet of a cemetery.

(Pub. L. No. 95–87, Title V, § 522, 91 Stat. 507 (Aug. 3, 1977).)

[1] So in original. Probably should be "therefor.

HISTORICAL AND STATUTORY NOTES

References in Text

The chapter and this chapter, referred to in subsecs. (a)(1), (a)(2), (a)(6), and (e)(2)(B), were in the original "the Act" and "this Act", respectively, meaning Pub. L. No. 95–87, 91 Stat. 445 (Aug. 3, 1977), as amended, which enacted this chapter and amended section 1114 of Title 18, Crimes and Criminal Procedure. For complete classification of this Act to the Code, see Short Title note set out under section 1201 of this title and Tables.

The Multiple-Use Sustained-Yield Act of 1960, referred to in subsec. (e)(2)(B), is Pub. L. No. 86–517, 74 Stat. 215 (June 12, 1960), as amended, which is codified as sections 528 to 531 of Title 16, Conservation. For complete classification of this Act to the Code, see Short Title note set out under section 528 of Title 16 and Tables volume.

The Federal Coal Leasing Amendments Act of 1975, referred to in subsec. (e)(2)(B), is Pub. L. No. 94–377, 90 Stat. 1083 (Aug. 4, 1976), which was redesignated the Federal Coal Leasing Amendments Act of 1976 by Pub. L. No. 95–554, § 8, 92 Stat. 2075 (Oct. 30, 1978), and which enacted sections 202a, 208–1, and 208–2 of this title, amended sections 184, 191, 201, 203, 207, 209, and 352 of this title, repealed sections 201–1 and 204 of this title, and enacted provisions set out as notes under sections 181, 184, 201, 201–1, 203, and 204 of this title. For complete classification of this Act to the Code, see Short Title of 1976 Amendment note set out under section 181 of this title and Tables volume.

The National Forest Management Act of 1976, referred to in subsec. (e)(2)(B), is Pub. L. No. 94–588, 90 Stat. 2949 (Oct. 22, 1976), as amended, which enacted sections 472a, 521b, 1600, and 1611 to 1614 of Title 16, Conservation, amended sections 500, 515, 516, 518, 576b, 581h, and 1601 to 1610 of Title 16, repealed sections 476, 513, and 514 of Title 16, enacted provisions set out as notes under sections 476, 513, 528, 594–2, and 1600 of Title 16. For complete classification of this Act to the Code, see Short Title of 1976 Amendment note set out under section 1600 of Title 16 and Tables volume.

§ 1273. Federal lands

[SMCRA § 523]

(a) Promulgation and implementation of Federal lands program

No later than one year after August 3, 1977, the Secretary shall promulgate and implement a Federal lands program which shall be applicable to all surface coal mining and reclamation operations taking place pursuant to any Federal law on any Federal lands: *Provided*, That except as provided in section 1300 of this title the provisions of this chapter shall not be applicable to Indian lands. The Federal lands program shall, at a minimum, incorporate all of the requirements of this chapter and shall take into consideration the diverse physical, climatological, and other unique characteristics of the Federal lands in question. Where Federal lands in a State with an approved State program are involved, the Federal lands program shall, at a minimum, include the requirements of the approved State program: *Provided*, That the Secretary shall retain his duties under sections 201(a), (2)(B)[1] and 201(a)(3) of this title, and shall continue to be responsible for designation of Federal lands as unsuitable for mining in accordance with section 1272(b) of this title.

(b) Incorporation of requirements into any lease, permit, or contract issued by Secretary which may involve surface coal mining and reclamation operations

The requirements of this chapter and the Federal lands program or an approved State program for State regulation of surface coal mining on Federal lands under subsection (c) of this section, whichever is applicable, shall be incorporated by reference or otherwise in any Federal mineral lease, permit, or contract issued by the Secretary which may involve surface coal mining and reclamation operations. Incorporation of such requirements shall not, however, limit in any way the authority of the Secretary to subsequently issue new regulations, revise the Federal lands program to deal with changing conditions or changed technology, and to require any surface mining and reclamation operations to conform with the requirements of this chapter and the regulations issued pursuant to this chapter.

(c) State cooperative agreements

Any State with an approved State program may elect to enter into a cooperative agreement with the Secretary to provide for State regulation of surface coal mining and reclamation operations on Federal lands within the State, provided the Secretary determines in writing that such State has the necessary personnel and funding to fully implement such a cooperative agreement in accordance with the provision of this chapter. States with cooperative agreements existing on August 3, 1977, may elect to continue regulation on Federal lands within the State, prior to approval by the Secretary of their State program, or imposition of a Federal program, provided that such existing cooperative agreement is modified to fully comply with the initial regulatory procedures set forth in section 1252 of this title. Nothing in this subsection shall be construed as authorizing the Secretary to delegate to the States his duty to approve mining plans on Federal lands, to designate certain Federal lands as unsuitable for surface coal mining pursuant to section 1272 of this title, or to regulate other activities taking place on Federal lands.

(d) Development of program to assure no unreasonable denial to any class of coal purchasers

The Secretary shall develop a program to assure that with respect to the granting of permits, leases, or contracts for coal owned by the United States, that no class of purchasers of the mined coal shall be unreasonably denied purchase thereof.

(Pub. L. No. 95–87, Title V, § 523, 91 Stat. 510 (Aug. 3, 1977).)

[1] So in original. Probably should be "201(a)(2)(B)."

HISTORICAL AND STATUTORY NOTES

References in Text

This chapter, referred to in subsecs. (a) to (c), was in the original "this Act", meaning Pub. L. No. 95–87, 91 Stat. 445 (Aug. 3, 1977), as amended, which enacted this chapter and amended section 1114 of Title 18, Crimes and Criminal Procedure. For complete classification of this Act to the Code, see Short Title note set out under section 1201 of this title and Tables.

§ 1274. Public agencies, public utilities, and public corporations

[SMCRA § 524]

Any agency, unit, or instrumentality of Federal, State, or local government, including any publicly owned utility or publicly owned corporation of Federal, State, or local government, which proposes to engage in surface coal mining operations which are subject to the requirements of this chapter shall comply with the provisions of this subchapter.

(Pub. L. No. 95–87, Title V, § 524, 91 Stat. 511 (Aug. 3, 1977).)

HISTORICAL AND STATUTORY NOTES

References in Text

This chapter, referred to in text, was in the original "this Act", meaning Pub. L. No. 95–87, 91 Stat. 445 (Aug. 3, 1977), as amended, which enacted this chapter and amended section 1114 of Title 18, Crimes and Criminal Procedure. For complete classification of this Act to the Code, see Short Title note set out under section 1201 of this title and Tables.

§ 1275. Review by Secretary

[SMCRA § 525]

(a) Application for review of order or notice; investigation; hearing; notice

(1) A permittee issued a notice or order by the Secretary pursuant to the provisions of paragraphs (2) and (3) of subsection (a) of section 1271 of this title, or pursuant to a Federal program or the Federal lands program or any person having an interest which is or may be adversely affected by such notice or order or by any modification, vacation, or termination of such notice or order, may apply to the Secretary for review of the notice or order within thirty days of receipt thereof or within thirty days of its modification, vacation, or termination. Upon receipt of such application, the Secretary shall cause such investigation to be made as he deems appropriate. Such investigation shall provide an opportunity for a public hearing, at the request of the applicant or the person having an interest which is or may be adversely affected, to enable the applicant or such person to present information relating to the issuance and continuance of such notice or order or the modification, vacation, or termination thereof. The filing of an application for review under this subsection shall not operate as a stay of any order or notice.

(2) The permittee and other interested persons shall be given written notice of the time and place of the hearing at least five days prior thereto. Any such hearing shall be of record and shall be subject to section 554 of Title 5.

(b) Findings of fact; issuance of decision

Upon receiving the report of such investigation, the Secretary shall make findings of fact, and shall issue a written decision, incorporating therein an order vacating, affirming, modifying, or terminating the notice or order, or the modification, vacation, or termination of such notice or order complained of and incorporate his findings therein. Where the application for review concerns an order for cessation of surface coal mining and reclamation operations issued pursuant to the provisions of paragraph (2) or (3) of subsection (a) of section 1271 of this title, the Secretary shall issue the written decision within thirty days of the receipt of the application for review, unless temporary relief has been granted by the Secretary pursuant to subsection (c) of this section or by the court pursuant to subsection (c) of section 1276 of this title.

(c) Temporary relief; issuance of order or decision granting or denying relief

Pending completion of the investigation and hearing required by this section, the applicant may file with the Secretary a written request that the Secretary grant temporary relief from any notice or order issued under section 1271 of this title, a Federal program or the Federal lands program together with a detailed statement giving reasons for granting such relief. The Secretary shall issue an order or decision granting or denying such relief expeditiously: *Provided,* That where the applicant requests relief from an order for cessation of coal mining and reclamation operations issued pursuant to paragraph (2) or (3) of subsection (a) of section 1271 of this title, the order or decision on such a request shall be issued within five days of its receipt. The Secretary may grant such relief, under such conditions as he may prescribe, if—

(1) a hearing has been held in the locality of the permit area on the request for temporary relief in which all parties were given an opportunity to be heard;

(2) the applicant shows that there is substantial likelihood that the findings of the Secretary will be favorable to him; and

(3) such relief will not adversely affect the health or safety of the public or cause significant, imminent environmental harm to land, air, or water resources.

(d) Notice and hearing with respect to section 1271 order to show cause

Following the issuance of an order to show cause as to why a permit should not be suspended or revoked pursuant to section 1271 of this title, the Secretary shall hold a public hearing after giving written notice of the time, place, and date thereof. Any such hearing shall be of record and shall be subject to section 554 of Title 5. Within sixty days following the public hearing, the Secretary shall issue and furnish to the permittee and all other parties to the hearing a written decision, and the reasons therefor, concerning suspension or revocation of the permit. If the Secretary revokes the permit, the permittee shall immediately cease surface coal mining operations on the permit area and shall complete reclamation within a period specified by the Secretary, or the Secretary shall declare as forfeited the performance bonds for the operation.

(e) Costs

Whenever an order is issued under this section, or as a result of any administrative proceeding under this chapter, at the request of any person, a sum equal to the aggregate amount of all costs and expenses (including attorney fees) as determined by the Secretary to have been reasonably incurred by such person for or in connection with his participation in such proceedings, including any judicial review of agency actions, may be assessed against either party as the court, resulting from judicial review or the Secretary, resulting from administrative proceedings, deems proper.

(Pub. L. No. 95–87, Title V, § 525, 91 Stat. 511 (Aug. 3, 1977).)

HISTORICAL AND STATUTORY NOTES

References in Text

This chapter, referred to in subsec. (e), was in the original "this Act", meaning Pub. L. No. 95–87, 91 Stat. 445 (Aug. 3, 1977), as amended, which enacted this chapter and amended section 1114 of Title 18, Crimes and Criminal Procedure. For complete classification of this Act to the Code, see Short Title note set out under section 1201 of this title and Tables.

§ 1276. Judicial review

[SMCRA § 526]

(a) Review by United States District Court; venue; filing of petition; time

(1) Any action of the Secretary to approve or disapprove a State program or to prepare or promulgate a Federal program pursuant to this chapter shall be subject to judicial review by the United States District Court for the District which includes the capital of the State whose program is at issue. Any action by the Secretary promulgating national rules or regulations including standards pursuant to sections 1251, 1265, 1266, and 1273 of this title shall be subject to judicial review in the United States District Court for the District of Columbia Circuit. Any other action constituting rulemaking by the Secretary shall be subject to judicial review only by the United States District Court for the District in which the surface coal mining operation is located. Any action subject to judicial review under this subsection shall be affirmed unless the court concludes that such action is arbitrary, capricious, or otherwise inconsistent with law. A petition for review of any action subject to judicial review under this subsection shall be filed in the appropriate Court within sixty days from the date of such action, or after such date if the petition is based solely on grounds arising after the sixtieth day. Any such petition may be made by any person who participated in the administrative proceedings and who is aggrieved by the action of the Secretary.

(2) Any order or decision issued by the Secretary in a civil penalty proceeding or any other proceeding required to be conducted pursuant to section 554 of Title 5 shall be subject to judicial review on or before 30 days from the date of such order or decision in accordance with subsection (b) of this section in the United States District Court for the district in which the surface coal mining operation is located. In the case of a proceeding to review an order or decision issued by the Secretary under the penalty section of this chapter, the court shall have jurisdiction to enter an order requiring payment of any civil penalty assessment enforced by its judgment. This availability of review established in this subsection shall not be construed to limit the operations of rights established in section 1270 of this title.

(b) Evidence; conclusiveness of findings; orders

The court shall hear such petition or complaint solely on the record made before the Secretary. Except as provided in subsection (a) of this section, the findings of the Secretary if supported by substantial evidence on the record considered as a whole, shall be conclusive. The court may affirm, vacate, or modify any order or decision or may remand the proceedings to the Secretary for such further action as it may direct.

(c) Temporary relief; prerequisites

In the case of a proceeding to review any order or decision issued by the Secretary under this chapter, including an order or decision issued pursuant to subsection (c) or (d) of section 1275 of this title pertaining to any order issued under paragraph (2), (3), or (4) of subsection (a) of section 1271 of this title for cessation of coal mining and reclamation operations, the court may, under such conditions as it may prescribe, grant such temporary relief as it deems appropriate pending final determination of the proceedings if—

(1) all parties to the proceedings have been notified and given an opportunity to be heard on a request for temporary relief;

(2) the person requesting such relief shows that there is a substantial likelihood that he will prevail on the merits of the final determination of the proceeding; and

(3) such relief will not adversely affect the public health or safety or cause significant imminent environmental harm to land, air, or water resources.

(d) Stay of action, order, or decision of Secretary

The commencement of a proceeding under this section shall not, unless specifically ordered by the court, operate as a stay of the action, order, or decision of the Secretary.

(e) Action of State regulatory authority

Action of the State regulatory authority pursuant to an approved State program shall be subject to judicial review by a court of competent jurisdiction in accordance with State law, but the availability of such review shall not be construed to limit the operation of the rights established in section 1270 of this title except as provided therein.

(Pub. L. No. 95–87, Title V, § 526, 91 Stat. 512 (Aug. 3, 1977).)

HISTORICAL AND STATUTORY NOTES

References in Text

This chapter, referred to in subsecs. (a) and (c), was in the original "this Act", meaning Pub. L. No. 95–87, 91 Stat. 445 (Aug. 3, 1977), as amended, which enacted this chapter and amended section 1114 of Title 18, Crimes and Criminal Procedure. For complete classification of this Act to the Code, see Short Title note set out under section 1201 of this title and Tables.

§ 1277. Special bituminous coal mines

[SMCRA § 527]

(a) Issuance of separate regulations; criteria

The regulatory authority is authorized to issue separate regulations for those special bituminous coal surface mines located west of the 100th meridian west longitude which meet the following criteria:

(1) the excavation of the specific mine pit takes place on the same relatively limited site for an extended period of time;

(2) the excavation of the specific mine pit follows a coal seam having an inclination of fifteen degrees or more from the horizontal, and continues in the same area proceeding downward with lateral expansion of the pit necessary to maintain stability or as necessary to accommodate the orderly expansion of the total mining operation;

(3) the excavation of the specific mine pit involves the mining of more than one coal seam and mining has been initiated on the deepest coal seam contemplated to be mined in the current operation;

(4) the amount of material removed is large in proportion to the surface area disturbed;

(5) there is no practicable alternative method of mining the coal involved;

(6) there is no practicable method to reclaim the land in the manner required by this chapter; and

(7) the specific mine pit has been actually producing coal since January 1, 1972, in such manner as to meet the criteria set forth in this section, and, because of past duration of mining, is substantially committed to a mode of operation which warrants exceptions to some provisions of this subchapter.

(b) New bituminous coal surface mines

Such separate regulations shall also contain a distinct part to cover and pertain to new bituminous coal surface mines which may be developed after August 3, 1977, on lands immediately adjacent to lands upon which are located special bituminous mines existing on January 1, 1972. Such new mines shall meet the criteria of subsection (a) of this section except for paragraphs (3) and (7), and all requirements of State law, notwithstanding in whole or part the regulations issued pursuant to subsection (c) of this section. In the event of an amendment or revision to the State's regulatory program, regulations, or decisions made thereunder governing such mines, the Secretary shall issue such additional regulations as necessary to meet the purposes of this chapter.

(c) Scope of alternative regulations

Such alternative regulations may pertain only to the standards governing onsite handling of spoils, elimination of depressions capable of collecting water, creation of impoundments, and regrading to the approximate original contour and shall specify that remaining highwalls are stable. All other performance standards in this subchapter shall apply to such mines.

(Pub. L. No. 95–87, Title V, § 527, 91 Stat. 513 (Aug. 3, 1977).)

HISTORICAL AND STATUTORY NOTES

References in Text

This chapter, referred to in subsecs. (a)(6) and (b), was in the original "this Act", meaning Pub. L. No. 95–87, 91 Stat. 445 (Aug. 3, 1977), as amended, which enacted this chapter and amended section 1114 of Title 18, Crimes and Criminal Procedure. For complete classification of this Act to the Code, see Short Title note set out under section 1201 of this title and Tables.

§ 1278. Surface mining operations not subject to this chapter

[SMCRA § 528]

The provisions of this chapter shall not apply to any of the following activities:

(1) the extraction of coal by a landowner for his own noncommercial use from land owned or leased by him; and

(2) the extraction of coal as an incidental part of Federal, State or local government-financed highway or other construction under regulations established by the regulatory authority.

(Pub. L. No. 95–87, Title V, § 528, 91 Stat. 514 (Aug. 3, 1977); as amended by Pub. L. No. 100–34, Title II, § 201(a), 101 Stat. 300 (May 7, 1987).)

HISTORICAL AND STATUTORY NOTES

References in Text

This chapter, referred to in text, was in the original "this Act", meaning Pub. L. No. 95–87, 91 Stat. 445 (Aug. 3, 1977), as amended, which enacted this chapter and amended section 1114 of Title 18, Crimes and Criminal Procedure. For complete classification of this Act to the Code, see Short Title note set out under section 1201 of this title and Tables.

Effective and Applicability Provisions

1987 Acts. Section 201(b) to (e) of Pub. L. No. 100–34 provided that:

"(b) Effective date for new operations.—The amendments made by this section [amending pars. (1) to (3) of this section] shall take effect on the date 30 days after the enactment of this Act [May 7, 1987] with respect to each operator commencing surface coal mining operations on or after such date.

"(c) Effective date for existing operations.—The amendments made by this section [amending pars. (1) to (3) of this section] shall take effect on the date 6 months after the enactment of this Act [May 7, 1987] with respect to each operator commencing surface coal mining operations pursuant to an authorization under State law before the date 30 days after the enactment of this Act [May 7, 1987]. Nothing in this Act [probably means section, which amended pars. (1) to (3) of this section and enacted this note] shall preclude reclamation activities pursuant to State law or regulations at the site of any surface coal mine which was exempt from the Surface Mining Control and Reclamation Act of 1977 [this chapter] under section 528(2) of that Act [par. (2) of this section], as in effect before the enactment of this Act [May 7, 1987].

"(d) Effect on State law.—To the extent that any provision of a State law, or of a State regulation, adopted pursuant to the exception under section 528(2) of the Surface Mining Control and Reclamation Act of 1977 [par. (2) of this section] as in effect before the enactment of this Act [May 7, 1987], is inconsistent with the amendments made by this section [amending pars. (1) to (3) of this section], such provision shall be of no further force and effect after the effective date of such amendments.

"(e) Definition.—For purposes of this section, the term 'surface coal mining operations' has the meaning provided by section 701(28) of the Surface Mining Control and Reclamation Act of 1977 [section 1291(28) of this title]."

§ 1279. Anthracite coal mines

[SMCRA § 529]

(a) The Secretary is authorized to and shall issue separate regulations according to time schedules established in this chapter for anthracite coal surface mines, if such mines are regulated by environmental protection standards of the State in which they are located. Such alternative regulations shall adopt, in each instance, the environmental protection provisions of the State regulatory program in existence on August 3, 1977, in lieu of sections 1265 and 1266 of this title. Provisions of sections 1259 and 1269 of this title are applicable except for specified bond limits and period of revegetation responsibility. All other provisions of this chapter apply and the regulation issued by the Secretary of Interior for each State anthracite regulatory program shall so reflect: *Provided, however,* That upon amendment of a State's regulatory program for anthracite mining or regulations thereunder in force in lieu of the above-cited sections of this chapter, the Secretary shall issue such additional regulations as necessary to meet the purposes of this chapter.

(b) Omitted.

(Pub. L. No. 95–87, Title V, § 529, 91 Stat. 514 (Aug. 3, 1977).)

HISTORICAL AND STATUTORY NOTES

References in Text

This chapter, referred to in text, was in the original "this Act", meaning Pub. L. No. 95–87, 91 Stat. 445 (Aug. 3, 1977), as amended, which enacted this chapter and amended section 1114 of Title 18, Crimes and Criminal Procedure. For complete classification of this Act to the Code, see Short Title note set out under section 1201 of this title and Tables.

Codifications

Subsec. (b) of this section, shown as omitted, which required the Secretary of the Interior to submit biennial reports to Congress on the effectiveness of State anthracite regulatory programs operating in conjunction with this chapter with respect to protecting the environment, terminated, effective May 15, 2000, pursuant to Pub. L. No. 104–66, § 3003, as amended, which is set out as a note under 31 U.S.C.A. § 1113. See, also, House Document No. 103–7, page 109.

SUBCHAPTER VI—DESIGNATION OF LANDS UNSUITABLE FOR NONCOAL MINING

§ 1281. Designation procedures

[SMCRA § 601]

(a) Review of Federal land areas for unsuitability for noncoal mining

With respect to Federal lands within any State, the Secretary of Interior may, and if so requested by the Governor of such State shall, review any area within such lands to assess whether it may be unsuitable for mining operations for minerals or materials other than coal, pursuant to the criteria and procedures of this section.

(b) Criteria considered in determining designations

An area of Federal land may be designated under this section as unsuitable for mining operations if (1) such area consists of Federal land of a predominantly urban or suburban character, used primarily for residential or related purposes, the mineral estate of which remains in the public domain, or (2) such area consists of Federal land where mining operations would have an adverse impact on lands used primarily for residential or related purposes.

(c) Petition for exclusion; contents; hearing; temporary land withdrawal

Any person having an interest which is or may be adversely affected shall have the right to petition the Secretary to seek exclusion of an area from mining operations pursuant to this section or the redesignation of an area or part thereof as suitable for such operations. Such petition shall contain allegations of fact with supporting evidence which would tend to substantiate the allegations. The petitioner shall be granted a hearing within a reasonable time and finding with reasons therefor upon the matter of their petition. In any instance where a Governor requests the Secretary to review an area, or where the Secretary finds the national interest so requires, the Secretary may temporarily withdraw the area to be reviewed from mineral entry or leasing pending such review: *Provided, however*, That such temporary withdrawal be ended as promptly as practicable and in no event shall exceed two years.

(d) Limitation on designations; rights preservation; regulations

In no event is a land area to be designated unsuitable for mining operations under this section on which mining operations are being conducted prior to the holding of a hearing on such petition in accordance with subsection (c) of this section. Valid existing rights shall be preserved and not affected by such designation. Designation of an area as unsuitable for mining operations under this section shall not prevent subsequent mineral exploration of such area, except that such exploration shall require the prior written consent of the holder of the surface estate, which consent shall be filed with the Secretary. The Secretary may promulgate, with respect to any designated area, regulations to minimize any adverse effects of such exploration.

(e) Statement

Prior to any designation pursuant to this section, the Secretary shall prepare a detailed statement on (i) the potential mineral resources of the area, (ii) the demand for such mineral resources, and (iii) the impact of such designation or the absence of such designation on the environment, economy, and the supply of such mineral resources.

(f) Area withdrawal

When the Secretary designates an area of Federal lands as unsuitable for all or certain types of mining operations for minerals and materials other than coal pursuant to this section he may withdraw such area from mineral entry or leasing, or condition such entry or leasing so as to limit such mining operations in accordance with his determination, if the Secretary also determines, based on his analysis pursuant to subsection (e) of this section, that the benefits resulting from such designation would be greater than the benefits to the regional or national economy which could result from mineral development of such area.

(g) Right to appeal

Any party with a valid legal interest who has appeared in the proceedings in connection with the Secretary's determination pursuant to this section and who is aggrieved by the Secretary's decision (or by his failure to act within a reasonable time) shall have the right of appeal for review by the United States district court for the district in which the pertinent area is located.

(Pub. L. No. 95–87, Title VI, § 601, 91 Stat. 515 (Aug. 3, 1977).)

SUBCHAPTER VII—ADMINISTRATIVE AND MISCELLANEOUS PROVISIONS

§ 1291. Definitions

[SMCRA § 701]

For the purposes of this chapter—

(1) "alluvial valley floors" means the unconsolidated stream laid deposits holding streams where water availability is sufficient for subirrigation or flood irrigation agricultural activities but does not include upland areas which are generally overlain by a thin veneer of colluvial deposits composed chiefly of debris from sheet erosion, deposits by unconcentrated runoff or slope wash, together with talus, other mass movement accumulation and windblown deposits;

(2) "approximate original contour" means that surface configuration achieved by backfilling and grading of the mined area so that the reclaimed area, including any terracing or access roads, closely resembles the general surface configuration of the land prior to mining and blends into and complements the drainage pattern of the surrounding terrain, with all highwalls and spoil piles eliminated; water impoundments may be permitted where the regulatory authority determines that they are in compliance with section 1265(b)(8) of this title;

(3) "commerce" means trade, traffic, commerce, transportation, transmission, or communication among the several States, or between a State and any other place outside thereof, or between points in the same State which directly or indirectly affect interstate commerce;

(4) "Federal lands" means any land, including mineral interests, owned by the United States without regard to how the United States acquired ownership of the land and without regard to the agency having responsibility for management thereof, except Indian lands: *Provided,* That for the purposes of this chapter lands or mineral interests east of the one hundredth meridian west longitude owned by the United States and entrusted to or managed by the Tennessee Valley Authority shall not be subject to sections 1304 (Surface Owner Protection) and 1305 (Federal Lessee Protection) of this title.[1]

(5) "Federal lands program" means a program established by the Secretary pursuant to section 1273 of this title to regulate surface coal mining and reclamation operations on Federal lands;

(6) "Federal program" means a program established by the Secretary pursuant to section 1254 of this title to regulate surface coal mining and reclamation operations on lands within a State in accordance with the requirements of this chapter;

(7) "fund" means the Abandoned Mine Reclamation Fund established pursuant to section 1231 of this title;

(8) "imminent danger to the health and safety of the public" means the existence of any condition or practice, or any violation of a permit or other requirement of this chapter in a surface coal mining and reclamation operation, which condition, practice, or violation could reasonably be expected to cause substantial physical harm to persons outside the permit area before such condition, practice, or violation can be abated. A reasonable expectation of death or serious injury before abatement exists if a rational person, subjected to the same conditions or practices giving rise to the peril, would not expose himself or herself to the danger during the time necessary for abatement;

(9) "Indian lands" means all lands, including mineral interests, within the exterior boundaries of any Federal Indian reservation, notwithstanding the issuance of any patent, and including rights-of-way, and all lands including mineral interests held in trust for or supervised by an Indian tribe;

(10) "Indian tribe" means any Indian tribe, band, group, or community having a governing body recognized by the Secretary;

(11) "lands within any State" or "lands within such State" means all lands within a State other than Federal lands and Indian lands;

(12) "Office" means the Office of Surface Mining Reclamation and Enforcement established pursuant to subchapter II of this chapter;

(13) "operator" means any person, partnership, or corporation engaged in coal mining who removes or intends to remove more than two hundred and fifty tons of coal from the earth by coal mining within twelve consecutive calendar months in any one location;

(14) "other minerals" means clay, stone, sand, gravel, metalliferous and nonmetalliferous ores, and any other solid material or substances of commercial value excavated in solid form from natural deposits on or in the earth, exclusive of coal and those minerals which occur naturally in liquid or gaseous form;

(15) "permit" means a permit to conduct surface coal mining and reclamation operations issued by the State regulatory authority pursuant to a State program or by the Secretary pursuant to a Federal program;

(16) "permit applicant" or "applicant" means a person applying for a permit;

(17) "permit area" means the area of land indicated on the approved map submitted by the operator with his application, which area of land shall be covered by the operator's bond as required by section 1259 of this title and shall be readily identifiable by appropriate markers on the site;

(18) "permittee" means a person holding a permit;

(19) "person" means an individual, partnership, association, society, joint stock company, firm, company, corporation, or other business organization;

(20) the term "prime farmland" shall have the same meaning as that previously prescribed by the Secretary of Agriculture on the basis of such factors as moisture availability, temperature regime, chemical balance, permeability, surface layer composition, susceptibility to flooding, and erosion characteristics, and which historically have been used for intensive agricultural purposes, and as published in the Federal Register.[1]

(21) "reclamation plan" means a plan submitted by an applicant for a permit under a State program or Federal program which sets forth a plan for reclamation of the proposed surface coal mining operations pursuant to section 1258 of this title;

(22) "regulatory authority" means the State regulatory authority where the State is administering this chapter under an approved State program or the Secretary where the Secretary is administering this chapter under a Federal program;

(23) "Secretary" means the Secretary of the Interior, except where otherwise described;

(24) "State" means a State of the United States, the District of Columbia, the Commonwealth of Puerto Rico, the Virgin Islands, American Samoa, and Guam;

(25) "State program" means a program established by a State pursuant to section 1253 of this title to regulate surface coal mining and reclamation operations, on lands within such State in accord with the requirements of this chapter and regulations issued by the Secretary pursuant to this chapter;

(26) "State regulatory authority" means the department or agency in each State which has primary responsibility at the State level for administering this chapter;

(27) "surface coal mining and reclamation operations" means surface mining operations and all activities necessary and incident to the reclamation of such operations after August 3, 1977;

(28) "surface coal mining operations" means—

(A) activities conducted on the surface of lands in connection with a surface coal mine or subject to the requirements of section 1266 of this title surface operations and surface impacts incident to an underground coal mine, the products of which enter commerce or the operations of which directly or indirectly affect interstate commerce. Such activities include excavation for the purpose of obtaining coal including such common methods as contour, strip, auger, mountaintop removal, box cut, open pit, and area mining, the uses of explosives and blasting, and in situ distillation or retorting, leaching or other chemical or physical processing, and the cleaning, concentrating, or other processing or preparation, loading of coal for interstate commerce at or near the mine site: *Provided, however*, That such activities do not include the extraction of coal incidental to the extraction of other minerals where coal does not exceed $16^2/_3$ per centum of the tonnage of minerals removed for purposes of commercial use or sale or coal explorations subject to section 1262 of this title; and

(B) the areas upon which such activities occur or where such activities disturb the natural land surface. Such areas shall also include any adjacent land the use of which is incidental to any such activities, all lands affected by the construction of new roads or the improvement or use of existing roads to gain access to the site of such activities and for haulage, and excavations, workings, impoundments, dams, ventilation shafts, entryways, refuse banks, dumps, stockpiles, overburden piles, spoil banks, culm banks, tailings, holes or depressions, repair areas, storage areas, processing areas, shipping areas and other areas upon which are sited structures, facilities, or other property or materials on the surface, resulting from or incident to such activities; and[2]

(29) "unwarranted failure to comply" means the failure of a permittee to prevent the occurrence of any violation of his permit or any requirement of this chapter due to indifference, lack of diligence, or lack of reasonable care, or the failure to abate any violation of such permit or the chapter due to indifference, lack of diligence, or lack of reasonable care;

(30) "lignite coal" means consolidated lignitic coal having less than 8,300 British thermal units per pound, moist and mineral matter free;

(31) the term "coal laboratory", as used in subchapter VIII of this chapter, means a university coal research laboratory established and operated pursuant to a designation made under section 1311 of this title;

(32) the term "institution of higher education" as used in subchapters VIII and IX of this chapter, means any such institution as defined by section 1001 of Title 20;

(33) the term "unanticipated event or condition" as used in section 1260(e) of this title means an event or condition encountered in a remining operation that was not contemplated by the applicable surface coal mining and reclamation permit; and

(34) the term "lands eligible for remining" means those lands that would otherwise be eligible for expenditures under section 1234 of this title or under section 1232(g)(4) of this title.

(Pub. L. No. 95–87, Title VII, § 701, 91 Stat. 516 (Aug. 3, 1977); as amended by Pub. L. No. 102–486, Title XXV, § 2503(c), 106 Stat. 3103 (Oct. 24, 1992); Pub. L. No. 105–244, Title I, § 102(a)(10), 112 Stat. 1620 (Oct. 7, 1998).)

[1] So in original. The period probably should be a semicolon.

[2] So in original. The word "and" probably should not appear.

HISTORICAL AND STATUTORY NOTES

References in Text

This chapter, referred to in text, was in the original "this Act", meaning Pub. L. No. 95–87, 91 Stat. 445 (Aug. 3, 1977), as amended, which enacted this chapter and amended section 1114 of Title 18, Crimes and Criminal Procedure. For complete classification of this Act to the Code, see Short Title note set out under section 1201 of this title and Tables.

Section 1001 of Title 20, referred to in par. (32), was in the original "section 101 of the Higher Education Act of 1968" and was translated as reading "section 101 of the Higher Education Act of 1965", meaning section 101 of Pub. L. No. 89–329, to reflect the probable intent of Congress because section 101 was added to the Higher Education Act of 1965 by Pub. L. No. 105–244.

Effective and Applicability Provisions

1998 Acts. Amendment by Pub. L. No. 105–244 effective Oct. 1, 1998, except as otherwise provided, see section 3 of Pub. L. No. 105–244, set out as a note under section 1001 of Title 20.

§ 1292. Other Federal laws

[SMCRA § 702]

(a) Construction of chapter as superseding, amending, modifying, or repealing certain laws

Nothing in this chapter shall be construed as superseding, amending, modifying, or repealing the Mining and Minerals Policy Act of 1970 (30 U.S.C. 21a), the National Environmental Policy Act of 1969 (42 U.S.C. 4321–47), or any of the following Acts or with any rule or regulation promulgated thereunder, including, but not limited to—

(1) The Federal Metal and Nonmetallic Mine Safety Act (30 U.S.C. 721–740).

(2) The Federal Coal Mine Health and Safety Act of 1969 (83 Stat. 742) [30 U.S.C.A. § 801 et seq.].

(3) The Federal Water Pollution Control Act (79 Stat. 903), as amended [33 U.S.C.A. § 1251 et seq.], the State laws enacted pursuant thereto, or other Federal laws relating to preservation of water quality.

(4) The Clean Air Act, as amended [42 U.S.C.A. § 7401 et seq.].

(5) The Solid Waste Disposal Act [42 U.S.C.A. § 6901 et seq.].

(6) The Refuse Act of 1899 (33 U.S.C. 407).

(7) The Fish and Wildlife Coordination Act of 1934 (16 U.S.C. 661–666c).

(8) The Mineral Leasing Act of 1920, as amended (30 U.S.C. 181 et seq.).

(b) Effect on authority of Secretary or heads of other Federal agencies

Nothing in this chapter shall affect in any way the authority of the Secretary or the heads of other Federal agencies under other provisions of law to include in any lease, license, permit, contract, or other instrument such conditions as may be appropriate to regulate surface coal mining and reclamation operations on land under their jurisdiction.

(c) Cooperation

To the greatest extent practicable each Federal agency shall cooperate with the Secretary and the States in carrying out the provisions of this chapter.

(d) Major Federal action

Approval of the State programs, pursuant to section 1253(b) of this title, promulgation of Federal programs, pursuant to section 1254 of this title, and implementation of the Federal lands programs, pursuant to section 1273 of this title, shall not constitute a major action within the meaning of section 102(2)(C) of the National Environmental Policy Act of 1969 (42 U.S.C. 4332). Adoption of regulations under section 1251(b) of this title shall constitute a major action within the meaning of section 102(2)(C) of the National Environmental Policy Act of 1969 (42 U.S.C. 4332).

(Pub. L. No. 95–87, Title VII, § 702, 91 Stat. 519 (Aug. 3, 1977).)

HISTORICAL AND STATUTORY NOTES

References in Text

This chapter, referred to in subsecs. (a) to (c), was in the original "this Act", meaning Pub. L. No. 95–87, 91 Stat. 445 (Aug. 3, 1977), as amended, which enacted this chapter and amended section 1114 of Title 18, Crimes and Criminal Procedure. For complete classification of this Act to the Code, see Short Title note set out under section 1201 of this title and Tables.

The Mining and Minerals Policy Act of 1970 (30 U.S.C. 21a), referred to in subsec. (a), is Pub. L. No. 91–631, 84 Stat. 1876 (Dec. 31, 1970), which enacted section 21a of this title and provisions set out as a note under section 21a of this title. For complete classification of this Act to the Code, see Short Title note set out under section 21a of this title and Tables volume.

The National Environmental Policy Act of 1969 (42 U.S.C. 4321–47), referred to in subsec. (a), is Pub. L. No. 91–190, 83 Stat. 852 (Jan. 1, 1970), as amended, which is codified generally as chapter 55 (section 4321 et seq.) of Title 42, The Public Health and Welfare. For complete classification of this Act to the Code, see Short Title note set out under section 4321 of Title 42 and Tables volume.

The Federal Metal and Nonmetallic Mine Safety Act (30 U.S.C. 721–740), referred to in subsec. (a)(1), is Pub. L. No. 89–577, 80 Stat. 772 (Sept. 16, 1966), which was codified generally as chapter 21 (section 721 et seq.) of this title and was repealed by Pub. L. No. 95–164, Title III, § 306(a), 91 Stat. 1322 (Nov. 9, 1977).

The Federal Coal Mine Health and Safety Act of 1969 (83 Stat. 742), referred to in subsec. (a)(2), is Pub. L. No. 91–173, 83 Stat. 742 (Dec. 30, 1969), as amended, which was redesignated the Federal Mine Safety and Health Act of 1977 by Pub. L. No. 95–164, Title I, § 101, 91 Stat. 1290 (Nov. 9, 1977), and is codified principally as chapter 22 (section 801 et seq.) of this title. For complete classification of this Act to the Code, see Short Title note set out under section 801 of this title and Tables volume.

The Federal Water Pollution Control Act (79 Stat. 903), as amended, referred to in subsec. (a)(3), is Act of June 30, 1948, c. 758, 62 Stat. 1155, as amended, formerly codified as chapter 23 (section 1151 et seq.) of Title 33,

Navigation and Navigable Waters, which was completely revised by Pub. L. No. 92–500, § 2, 86 Stat. 816 (Oct. 18, 1972), and is now codified generally as chapter 26 (section 1251 et seq.) of Title 33. For complete classification of this Act to the Code, see Short Title note set out under section 1251 of Title 33 and Tables volume.

The Clean Air Act, as amended, referred to in subsec. (a)(4), is Act of July 14, 1955, c. 360, as amended generally by Pub. L. No. 88–206, 77 Stat. 392 (Dec. 17, 1963), and later by Pub. L. No. 95–95, 91 Stat. 685 (Aug. 7, 1977). The Clean Air Act was originally codified as chapter 15B (section 1857 et seq.) of Title 42, The Public Health and Welfare. On enactment of Pub. L. No. 95–95, the Act was recodified as chapter 85 (section 7401 et seq.) of Title 42. For complete classification of this Act to the Code, see Short Title note set out under section 7401 of Title 42 and Tables volume.

The Solid Waste Disposal Act, referred to in subsec. (a)(5), is Title II of Pub. L. No. 89–272, 79 Stat. 997 (Oct. 20, 1965), as amended generally by Pub. L. No. 94–580, § 2, 90 Stat. 2795 (Oct. 21, 1976), which is codified generally as chapter 82 (section 6901 et seq.) of Title 42. For complete classification of this Act to the Code, see Short Title note set out under section 6901 of Title 42 and Tables volume.

The Refuse Act of 1899 (33 U.S.C. 407), referred to in subsec. (a)(6), probably means Act Mar. 3, 1899, c. 425, § 13, 30 Stat. 1152, which enacted section 407 of Title 33, Navigation and Navigable Waters.

The Fish and Wildlife Coordination Act of 1934 (16 U.S.C. 661–666c), referred to in subsec. (a)(7), is Act Of Mar. 10, 1934, c. 55, 48 Stat. 401, as amended, which is codified generally as sections 661 to 666c of Title 16, Conservation. For complete classification of this Act to the Code, see Short Title note set out under section 661 of Title 16 and Tables volume.

The Mineral Leasing Act of 1920, as amended (30 U.S.C. 181 et seq.), referred to in subsec. (a)(8), is Act of Feb. 25, 1920, c. 85, 41 Stat. 437, as amended, which is codified principally as chapter 3A (section 181 et seq.) of this title. For complete classification of this Act to the Code, see Short Title note set out under section 181 of this title and Tables volume.

§ 1293. Employee protection

[SMCRA § 703]

(a) Retaliatory practices prohibited

No person shall discharge, or in any other way discriminate against, or cause to be fired or discriminated against, any employee or any authorized representative of employees by reason of the fact that such employee or representative has filed, instituted, or caused to be filed or instituted any proceeding under this chapter, or has testified or is about to testify in any proceeding resulting from the administration or enforcement of the provisions of this chapter.

(b) Review by Secretary; investigation; notice; hearing; findings of fact; judicial review

Any employee or a representative of employees who believes that he has been fired or otherwise discriminated against by any person in violation of subsection (a) of this section may, within thirty days after such alleged violation occurs, apply to the Secretary for a review of such firing or alleged discrimination. A copy of the application shall be sent to the person or operator who will be the respondent. Upon receipt of such application, the Secretary shall cause such investigation to be made as he deems appropriate. Such investigation shall provide an opportunity for a public hearing at the request of any party to such review to enable the parties to present information relating to the alleged violation. The parties shall be given written notice of the time and place of the hearing at least five days prior to the hearing. Any such hearing shall be of record and shall be subject to section 554 of Title 5. Upon receiving the report of such investigation the Secretary shall make findings of fact. If he finds that a violation did occur, he shall issue a decision incorporating therein his findings and an order requiring the party committing the violation to take such affirmative action to abate the violation as the Secretary deems appropriate, including, but not limited to, the rehiring or reinstatement of the employee or representative of employees to his former position with compensation. If he finds that there was no violation, he will issue a finding. Orders issued by the Secretary under this subsection shall be subject to judicial review in the same manner as orders and decisions of the Secretary are subject to judicial review under this chapter.

(c) Costs

Whenever an order is issued under this section to abate any violation, at the request of the applicant a sum equal to the aggregate amount of all costs and expenses (including attorneys' fees) to have been reasonably incurred by the applicant for, or in connection with, the institution and prosecution of such proceedings, shall be assessed against the persons committing the violation.

(Pub. L. No. 95–87, Title VII, § 703, 91 Stat. 520 (Aug. 3, 1977).)

HISTORICAL AND STATUTORY NOTES

References in Text

This chapter, referred to in subsecs. (a) and (b), was in the original "this Act", meaning Pub. L. No. 95–87, 91 Stat. 445 (Aug. 3, 1977), as amended, which enacted this chapter and amended section 1114 of Title 18, Crimes and Criminal Procedure. For complete classification of this Act to the Code, see Short Title note set out under section 1201 of this title and Tables.

§ 1294. Penalty

[SMCRA § 704]

Any person who shall, except as permitted by law, willfully resist, prevent, impede, or interfere with the Secretary or any of his agents in the performance of duties pursuant to this chapter shall be punished by a fine of not more than $5,000 or by imprisonment for not more than one year, or both.

(Pub. L. No. 95–87, Title VII, § 704, 91 Stat. 520 (Aug. 3, 1977).)

HISTORICAL AND STATUTORY NOTES

References in Text

This chapter, referred to in text, was in the original "this Act", meaning Pub. L. No. 95–87, 91 Stat. 445 (Aug. 3, 1977), as amended, which enacted this chapter and amended section 1114 of Title 18, Crimes and Criminal Procedure. For complete classification of this Act to the Code, see Short Title note set out under section 1201 of this title and Tables.

Codifications

Section 704 of Pub. L. No. 95–87 also amended section 1114 of Title 18, Crimes and Criminal Procedure.

§ 1295. Grants to States

[SMCRA § 705]

(a) Assisting any State in development, administration, and enforcement of State programs under this chapter

The Secretary is authorized to make annual grants to any State for the purpose of assisting such State in developing, administering, and enforcing State programs under this chapter. Except as provided in subsection (c) of this section, such grants shall not exceed 80 per centum of the total costs incurred during the first year, 60 per centum of total costs incurred during the second year, and 50 per centum of the total costs incurred during each year thereafter.

(b) Assisting any State in development, administration, and enforcement of its State programs

The Secretary is authorized to cooperate with and provide assistance to any State for the purpose of assisting it in the development, administration, and enforcement of its State programs. Such cooperation and assistance shall include—

(1) technical assistance and training including provision of necessary curricular and instruction materials, in the development, administration, and enforcement of the State programs; and

(2) assistance in preparing and maintaining a continuing inventory of information on surface coal mining and reclamation operations for each State for the purposes of evaluating the effectiveness of the State programs. Such assistance shall include all Federal departments and agencies making available data relevant to surface coal mining and reclamation operations and to the development, administration, and enforcement of State programs concerning such operations.

(c) Increases in annual grants

If, in accordance with section 1273(d) of this title, a State elects to regulate surface coal mining and reclamation operations on Federal lands, the Secretary may increase the amount of the annual grants under subsection (a) of this section by an amount which he determines is approximately equal to the amount the Federal Government would have expended for such regulation if the State had not made such election.

(Pub. L. No. 95–87, Title VII, § 705, 91 Stat. 520 (Aug. 3, 1977).)

HISTORICAL AND STATUTORY NOTES

References in Text

This chapter, referred to in subsec. (a), was in the original "this Act", meaning Pub. L. No. 95–87, 91 Stat. 445 (Aug. 3, 1977), as amended, which enacted this chapter and amended section 1114 of Title 18, Crimes and Criminal Procedure. For complete classification of this Act to the Code, see Short Title note set out under section 1201 of this title and Tables.

Termination of Reporting Requirements

For termination of reporting provisions authorized by this section, effective May 15, 2000, see Pub. L. No. 104–66, § 3003, as amended, set out as a note under 31 U.S.C.A. § 1113, and page 109 of House Document No. 103–7.

§ 1296. Annual report to President and Congress

[SMCRA § 706]

The Secretary shall submit annually to the President and the Congress a report concerning activities conducted by him, the Federal Government, and the States pursuant to this chapter. Among other matters, the Secretary shall include in such report recommendations for additional administrative or legislative action as he deems necessary and desirable to accomplish the purposes of this chapter.

(Pub. L. No. 95–87, Title VII, § 706, 91 Stat. 521 (Aug. 3, 1977).)

HISTORICAL AND STATUTORY NOTES

References in Text

This chapter, referred to in text, was in the original "this Act", meaning Pub. L. No. 95–87, 91 Stat. 445 (Aug. 3, 1977), as amended, which enacted this chapter and amended section 1114 of Title 18, Crimes and Criminal Procedure. For complete classification of this Act to the Code, see Short Title note set out under section 1201 of this title and Tables.

Termination of Reporting Requirements

For termination, effective May 15, 2000, of provisions in this section relating to requirement to submit a report annually to Congress, see Pub. L. No. 104–66, § 3003, as amended, set out as a note under 31 U.S.C.A. § 1113, and House Document No. 103–7, page 109.

§ 1297. Separability

[SMCRA § 707]

If any provision of this chapter or the applicability thereof to any person or circumstances is held invalid, the remainder of this chapter and the application of such provision to other persons or circumstances shall not be affected thereby.

(Pub. L. No. 95–87, Title VII, § 707, 91 Stat. 521 (Aug. 3, 1977).)

HISTORICAL AND STATUTORY NOTES

References in Text

This chapter, referred to in text, was in the original "this Act", meaning Pub. L. No. 95–87, 91 Stat. 445 (Aug. 3, 1977), as amended, which enacted this chapter and amended section 1114 of Title 18, Crimes and Criminal Procedure. For complete classification of this Act to the Code, see Short Title note set out under section 1201 of this title and Tables.

§ 1298. Alaskan surface coal mine study

[SMCRA § 708]

(a) Contract with National Academy of Sciences—National Academy of Engineering

The Secretary is directed to contract to such extent or in such amounts as are provided in advance in appropriation Acts with the National Academy of Sciences—National Academy of Engineering for an in-depth study of surface coal mining conditions in the State of Alaska in order to determine which, if any, of the provisions of this chapter should be modified with respect to surface coal mining operations in Alaska.

(b) Report to President and Congress

The Secretary shall report on the findings of the study to the President and Congress no later than two years after August 3, 1977.

(c) Draft of legislation

The Secretary shall include in his report a draft of legislation to implement any changes recommended to this chapter.

(d) Modification of applicability of environmental protection provisions of this chapter to surface coal mining operations in Alaska; publication in Federal Register; hearing

Until one year after the Secretary has made this report to the President and Congress, or three years after August 3, 1977, whichever comes first, the Secretary is authorized to modify the applicability of any environmental protection provision of this chapter, or any regulation issued pursuant thereto, to any surface coal mining operation in Alaska from which coal has been mined during the year preceding August 3, 1977, if he determines that it is necessary to insure the continued operation of such surface coal mining operation. The Secretary may exercise this authority only after he has (1) published notice of proposed modification in the Federal Register and in a newspaper of general circulation in the area of Alaska in which the affected surface coal mining operation is located, and (2) held a public hearing on the proposed modification in Alaska.

(e) Interim regulations

In order to allow new mines in Alaska to continue orderly development, the Secretary is authorized to issue interim regulations pursuant to section 1251(b) of this title including those modifications to the environmental standards as required based on the special physical, hydrological and climatic conditions in Alaska but with the purpose of protecting the environment to an extent equivalent to those standards for the other coal regions.

(f) Authorization of appropriations

There is authorized to be appropriated for the purpose of this section $250,000: *Provided*, That no new budget authority is authorized to be appropriated for fiscal year 1977.

(Pub. L. No. 95–87, Title VII, § 708, 91 Stat. 521 (Aug. 3, 1977).)

HISTORICAL AND STATUTORY NOTES

References in Text

This chapter, referred to in subsecs. (a), (c), and (d), was in the original "this Act", meaning Pub. L. No. 95–87, 91 Stat. 445 (Aug. 3, 1977), as amended, which enacted this chapter and amended section 1114 of Title 18, Crimes and Criminal Procedure. For complete classification of this Act to the Code, see Short Title note set out under section 1201 of this title and Tables.

§ 1299. Study of reclamation standards for surface mining of other minerals

[SMCRA § 709]

(a) Contract with National Academy of Sciences-National Academy of Engineering; requirements

The Chairman of the Council on Environmental Quality is directed to contract to such extent or in such amounts as are provided in appropriation Acts with the National Academy of Sciences—National Academy of Engineering, other Government agencies or private groups as appropriate, for an in-depth study of current and developing technology for surface and open pit mining and reclamation for minerals other than coal designed to assist in the establishment of effective and reasonable regulation of surface and open pit mining and reclamation for minerals other than coal. The study shall—

(1) assess the degree to which the requirements of this chapter can be met by such technology and the costs involved;

(2) identify areas where the requirements of this chapter cannot be met by current and developing technology;

(3) in those instances describe requirements most comparable to those of this chapter which could be met, the costs involved, and the differences in reclamation results between these requirements and those of this chapter; and

(4) discuss alternative regulatory mechanisms designed to insure the achievement of the most beneficial postmining land use for areas affected by surface and open pit mining.

(b) Submittal of study with legislative recommendation to President and Congress

The study together with specific legislative recommendations shall be submitted to the President and the Congress no later than eighteen months after August 3, 1977: *Provided*, That, with respect to surface or open pit mining for sand and gravel the study shall be submitted no later than twelve months after August 3, 1977: *Provided further*, That with respect to mining for oil shale and tar sands that a preliminary report shall be submitted no later than twelve months after August 3, 1977.

(c) Authorization of appropriations

There are authorized to be appropriated for the purpose of this section $500,000: *Provided*, That no new budget authority is authorized to be appropriated for fiscal year 1977.

(Pub. L. No. 95–87, Title VII, § 709, 91 Stat. 522 (Aug. 3, 1977).)

HISTORICAL AND STATUTORY NOTES

References in Text

This chapter, referred to in subsec. (a), was in the original "this Act", meaning Pub. L. No. 95–87, 91 Stat. 445 (Aug. 3, 1977), as amended, which enacted this chapter and amended section 1114 of Title 18, Crimes and Criminal Procedure. For complete classification of this Act to the Code, see Short title note set out under section 1201 of this title and Tables.

§ 1300. Indian lands

[SMCRA § 710]

(a) Study of regulation of surface mining; consultation with tribe; proposed legislation

The Secretary is directed to study the question of the regulation of surface mining on Indian lands which will achieve the purpose of this chapter and recognize the special jurisdictional status of these lands. In carrying out this study the Secretary shall consult with Indian tribes. The study report shall include proposed legislation designed to allow Indian tribes to elect to assume full regulatory authority over the administration and enforcement of regulation of surface mining of coal on Indian lands.

(b) Submittal of study to Congress

The study report required by subsection (a) of this section together with drafts of proposed legislation and the view of each Indian tribe which would be affected shall be submitted to the Congress as soon as possible but not later than January 1, 1978.

(c) Compliance with interim environmental protection standards of this chapter

On and after one hundred and thirty-five days from August 3, 1977, all surface coal mining operations on Indian lands shall comply with requirements at least as stringent as those imposed by subsections (b)(2), (b)(3), (b)(5), (b)(10), (b)(13), (b)(19), and (d) of section 1265 of this title and the Secretary shall incorporate the requirements of such provisions in all existing and new leases issued for coal on Indian lands.

(d) Compliance with permanent environmental protection standards of this chapter

On and after thirty months from August 3, 1977, all surface coal mining operations on Indian lands shall comply with requirements at least as stringent as those imposed by sections 1257, 1258, 1259, 1260, 1265, 1266, 1267, and 1269 of this title and the Secretary shall incorporate the requirements of such provisions in all existing and new leases issued for coal on Indian lands.

(e) Inclusion and enforcement of terms and conditions of leases

With respect to leases issued after August 3, 1977, the Secretary shall include and enforce terms and conditions in addition to those required by subsections (c) and (d) of this section as may be requested by the Indian tribe in such leases.

(f) Approval of changes in terms and conditions of leases

Any change required by subsection (c) or (d) of this section in the terms and conditions of any coal lease on Indian lands existing on August 3, 1977, shall require the approval of the Secretary.

(g) Participation of tribes

The Secretary shall provide for adequate participation by the various Indian tribes affected in the study authorized in this section and not more than $700,000 of the funds authorized in section 1302(a) of this title shall be reserved for this purpose.

(h) Jurisdictional status

The Secretary shall analyze and make recommendations regarding the jurisdictional status of Indian Lands[1] outside the exterior boundaries of Indian reservations: *Provided*, That nothing in this chapter shall change the existing jurisdictional status of Indian Lands[1].

(i) Grants

The Secretary shall make grants to the Navajo, Hopi, Northern Cheyenne, and Crow tribes to assist such tribes in developing regulations and programs for regulating surface coal mining and reclamation operations on Indian lands. Grants made under this subsection shall be used to establish an office of surface mining regulation for each such tribe. Each such office shall—

(1) develop tribal regulations and program policies with respect to surface mining;

(2) assist the Office of Surface Mining Reclamation and Enforcement established by section 1211 of this title in the inspection and enforcement of surface mining activities on Indian lands, including, but not limited to, permitting, mine plan review, and bond release; and

(3) sponsor employment training and education in the area of mining and mineral resources.

(j) Tribal regulatory authority

(1) Tribal regulatory programs

(A) In general

Notwithstanding any other provision of law, an Indian tribe may apply for, and obtain the approval of, a tribal program under section 1233 of this title regulating in whole or in part surface coal mining and reclamation operations on reservation land under the jurisdiction of the Indian tribe using the procedures of section 1234(e) of this title.

(B) **References to State**

For purposes of this subsection and the implementation and administration of a tribal program under subchapter V of this chapter, any reference to a 'State' in this chapter shall be considered to be a reference to a 'tribe".

(2) **Conflicts of interest**

(A) **In general**

The fact that an individual is a member of an Indian tribe does not in itself constitute a violation of section 1211(f) of this title.

(B) **Employees of tribal regulatory authority**

Any employee of a tribal regulatory authority shall not be eligible for a per capita distribution of any proceeds from coal mining operations conducted on Indian reservation lands under this chapter.

(3) **Sovereign immunity**

To receive primary regulatory authority under section 1234(e) of this title, an Indian tribe shall waive sovereign immunity for purposes of section 1270 of this title and paragraph (4).

(4) **Judicial review**

(A) **Civil actions**

(i) **In general**

After exhausting all tribal remedies with respect to a civil action arising under a tribal program approved under section 1254(e) of this title, an interested party may file a petition for judicial review of the civil action in the United States circuit court for the circuit in which the surface coal mining operation named in the petition is located.

(ii) **Scope of review**

(I) **Questions of law**

The United States circuit court shall review de novo any questions of law under clause (i).

(II) **Findings of fact**

The United States circuit court shall review findings of fact under clause (i) using a clearly erroneous standard.

(B) **Criminal actions**

Any criminal action brought under section 1268 of this title with respect to surface coal mining or reclamation operations on Indian reservation lands shall be brought in—

(i) the United States District Court for the District of Columbia; or

(ii) the United States district court in which the criminal activity is alleged to have occurred.

(5) **Grants**

(A) **In general**

Except as provided in subparagraph (B), grants for developing, administering, and enforcing tribal programs approved in accordance with section 1254(e) of this title shall be provided to an Indian tribe in accordance with section 1295 of this title.

(B) **Exception**

Notwithstanding subparagraph (A), the Federal share of the costs of developing, administering, and enforcing an approved tribal program shall be 100 percent.

(6) Report

Not later than 18 months after the date on which a tribal program is approved under subsection (e) of section 1254 of this title, the Secretary shall submit to the appropriate committees of Congress a report, developed in cooperation with the applicable Indian tribe, on the tribal program that includes a recommendation of the Secretary on whether primary regulatory authority under that subsection should be expanded to include additional Indian lands.

(Pub. L. No. 95–87, Title VII, § 710, 91 Stat. 523 (Aug. 3, 1977); as amended by Pub. L. No. 102–486, Title XXV, § 2514, 106 Stat. 3112 (Oct. 24, 1992); Pub. L. No. 109–432, Div. C, Title II, § 209, 120 Stat. 3019 (Dec. 20, 2006).)

[1] So in original. Probably should be "lands".

HISTORICAL AND STATUTORY NOTES

References in Text

This chapter, referred to in text, originally read "this Act", meaning the Surface Mining Control and Reclamation Act of 1977, or the SMCRA, Pub. L. No. 95–87, 91 Stat. 445 (Aug. 3, 1977), as amended, which is principally codified as this chapter. For complete classification, see Tables.

Subchapter V of this chapter, referee to in subsec. (j)(1)(B), (2)(B), originally read "title V", meaning the Surface Mining Control and Reclamation Act of 1977, Pub. L. No. 95–87, Title V, § 501, 91 Stat. 467 (Aug. 3, 1977), which is codified as subchapter V of this chapter, 30 U.S.C.A. § 1251 et seq.

§ 1301. Environmental practices

[SMCRA § 711]

In order to encourage advances in mining and reclamation practices or to allow post-mining land use for industrial, commercial, residential, or public use (including recreational facilities), the regulatory authority with approval by the Secretary may authorize departures in individual cases on an experimental basis from the environmental protection performance standards promulgated under sections 1265 and 1266 of this title. Such departures may be authorized if (i) the experimental practices are potentially more or at least as environmentally protective, during and after mining operations, as those required by promulgated standards; (ii) the mining operations approved for particular land-use or other purposes are not larger or more numerous than necessary to determine the effectiveness and economic feasibility of the experimental practices; and (iii) the experimental practices do not reduce the protection afforded public health and safety below that provided by promulgated standards.

(Pub. L. No. 95–87, Title VII, § 711, 91 Stat. 523 (Aug. 3, 1977).)

§ 1302. Authorization of appropriations

[SMCRA § 712]

There is authorized to be appropriated to the Secretary for the purposes of this chapter the following sums; and all such funds appropriated shall remain available until expended:

(a) For the implementation and funding of sections 1252, 1273, and 1300 of this title, there are authorized to be appropriated to the Secretary of the Interior the sum of $10,000,000 for the fiscal year ending September 30, 1978, $25,000,000 for each of the two succeeding fiscal years, and in such fiscal years such additional amounts as may be necessary for increases in salary, pay, retirement, other employee benefits authorized by law, and other nondiscretionary costs.

(b) For the implementation and funding of section 1257(c) of this title, see the provisions of section 1231(c)(9) of this title.

(c) For the implementation and funding of section 1295 of this title and for the administrative and other purposes of this chapter, except as otherwise provided for in this chapter, authorization is provided for the sum of $20,000,000 for the fiscal year ending September 30, 1978, and $30,000,000 for each of the two succeeding fiscal years and such funds that are required thereafter.

(d) In order that the implementation of the requirements of this chapter may be initiated in a timely and orderly manner, the Secretary is authorized, subject to the approval of the appropriation Committees of the House and of the Senate, to utilize not to exceed $2,000,000 of the appropriations otherwise available to him for the fiscal year ending September 30, 1977, for the administration and other purposes of the chapter.

(Pub. L. No. 95–87, Title VII, § 712, 91 Stat. 524 (Aug. 3, 1977); as amended by Pub. L. No. 95–343, § 1, 92 Stat. 473 (Aug. 11, 1978); Pub. L. No. 101–508, Title VI, § 6012(b), 104 Stat. 1388–298 (Nov. 5, 1990); Pub. L. No. 109–432, Div. C, Title II, § 201(b), 120 Stat. 3008 (Dec. 20, 2006).)

HISTORICAL AND STATUTORY NOTES

References in Text

This chapter, referred to in text, was in the original "this Act", meaning Pub. L. No. 95–87, 91 Stat. 445 (Aug. 3, 1977), as amended, which enacted this chapter and amended section 1114 of Title 18, Crimes and Criminal Procedure. For complete classification of this Act to the Code, see Short Title note set out under section 1201 of this title and Tables.

Effective and Applicability Provisions

1990 Acts. Amendment by Pub. L. No. 101–508 effective Oct. 1, 1991, see section 6014 of Pub. L. No. 101–508, set out as a note under section 1231 of this title.

Savings Provisions

Nothing in Subtitle A (section 6001 et seq.) of Title VI of Pub. L. No. 101–508, shall be construed to affect the certifications made by the States of Wyoming, Montana, and Louisiana to the Secretary of the Interior prior to Nov. 5, 1990, that each such State has completed the reclamation of eligible abandoned coal mine lands, see section 6013 of Pub. L. No. 101–508, set out as a note under section 1231 of this title.

Crediting Additional Amount from Performance Bond Forfeitures

Pub. L. No. 105–277, Div. A, § 101(e) [Title I], 112 Stat. 2681–244 (Oct. 21, 1998), provided in part that: "Notwithstanding 31 U.S.C. 3302, an additional amount shall be credited to this account, to remain available until expended, from performance bond forfeitures in fiscal year 1999 and thereafter."

Cost-based Fees for Products of the Mine Map Repository; Collection and Credit to Program Account

Pub. L. No. 105–277, Div. A, § 101(e) [Title I], 112 Stat. 2681–244 (Oct. 21, 1998), provided in part that: "Beginning in fiscal year 1999 and thereafter, cost-based fees for the products of the Mine Map Repository shall be established (and revised as needed) in Federal Register Notices, and shall be collected and credited to this account, to be available until expended for the costs of administering this program."

§ 1303. Coordination of regulatory and inspection activities

[SMCRA § 713]

(a) The President shall, to the extent appropriate, and in keeping with the particular enforcement requirements of each Act referred to herein, insure the coordination of regulatory and inspection activities among the departments, agencies, and instrumentalities to which such activities are assigned by this chapter, by the Clean Air Act [42 U.S.C.A. § 7401 et seq.], by the Water Pollution Control Act [33 U.S.C.A. § 1251 et seq.], by the Department of Energy Organization Act [42 U.S.C.A. § 7101 et seq.], and by existing or subsequently enacted Federal mine safety and health laws, except that no such coordination shall be required with respect to mine safety and health inspections, advance notice of which is or may be prohibited by existing or subsequently enacted Federal mine safety and health laws.

(b) The President may execute the coordination required by this section by means of an Executive order, or by any other mechanism he determines to be appropriate.

(Pub. L. No. 95–87, Title VII, § 713, 91 Stat. 524 (Aug. 3, 1977).)

HISTORICAL AND STATUTORY NOTES

References in Text

This chapter, referred to in subsec. (a), was in the original "this Act", meaning Pub. L. No. 95–87, 91 Stat. 445 (Aug. 3, 1977), as amended, which enacted this chapter and amended section 1114 of Title 18, Crimes and

Criminal Procedure. For complete classification of this Act to the Code, see Short Title note set out under section 1201 of this title and Tables.

The Clean Air Act, referred to in subsec. (a), is Act of July 14, 1955, c. 360, as amended generally by Pub. L. No. 88–206, 77 Stat. 392 (Dec. 17, 1963), and later by Pub. L. No. 95–95, 91 Stat. 685 (Aug. 7, 1977). The Clean Air Act was originally codified as chapter 15B (section 1857 et seq.) of Title 42, The Public Health and Welfare. On enactment of Pub. L. No. 95–95, the Act was recodified as chapter 85 (section 7401 et seq.) of Title 42. For complete classification of this Act to the Code, see Short Title note set out under section 7401 of Title 42 and Tables volume.

The Water Pollution Control Act, referred to in subsec. (a), probably means Act of June 30, 1948, c. 758, 62 Stat. 1155, known as the Federal Water Pollution Control Act, formerly codified as chapter 23 (section 1151 et seq.) of Title 33, Navigation and Navigable Waters, which was completely revised by Pub. L. No. 92–500, § 2, 86 Stat. 816 (Oct. 18, 1972), and is codified generally as chapter 26 (section 1251 et seq.) of Title 33. For complete classification of this Act to the Code, see Short Title note set out under section 1251 of Title 33 and Tables volume.

The Department of Energy Organization Act, referred to in subsec. (a), is Pub. L. No. 95–91, 91 Stat. 565 (Aug. 4, 1977), as amended, which is codified principally as chapter 84 (section 7101 et seq.) of Title 42, The Public Health and Welfare. For complete classification of this Act to the Code, see Short Title note set out under section 7101 of Title 42 and Tables volume.

§ 1304. Surface owner protection

[SMCRA § 714]

(a) Applicability

The provisions of this section shall apply where coal owned by the United States under land the surface rights to which are owned by a surface owner as defined in this section is to be mined by methods other than underground mining techniques.

(b) Lease of coal deposits governed by section 201 of this title

Any coal deposits subject to this section shall be offered for lease pursuant to section 201(a) of this title.

(c) Consent to lease by surface owner

The Secretary shall not enter into any lease of Federal coal deposits until the surface owner has given written consent to enter and commence surface mining operations and the Secretary has obtained evidence of such consent. Valid written consent given by any surface owner prior to August 3, 1977, shall be deemed sufficient for the purposes of complying with this section.

(d) Preferences

In order to minimize disturbance to surface owners from surface coal mining of Federal coal deposits and to assist in the preparation of comprehensive land-use plans required by section 201(a) of this title, the Secretary shall consult with any surface owner whose land is proposed to be included in a leasing tract and shall ask the surface owner to state his preference for or against the offering of the deposit under his land for lease. The Secretary shall, in his discretion but to the maximum extent practicable, refrain from leasing coal deposits for development by methods other than underground mining techniques in those areas where a significant number of surface owners have stated a preference against the offering of the deposits for lease.

(e) "Surface owner" defined

For the purpose of this section the term "surface owner" means the natural person or persons (or corporation, the majority stock of which is held by a person or persons who meet the other requirements of this section) who—

(1) hold legal or equitable title to the land surface;

(2) have their principal place of residence on the land; or personally conduct farming or ranching operations upon a farm or ranch unit to be affected by surface coal mining operations; or receive directly a significant portion of their income, if any, from such farming or ranching operations; and

(3) have met the conditions of paragraphs (1) and (2) for a period of at least three years prior to the granting of the consent.

In computing the three-year period the Secretary may include periods during which title was owned by a relative of such person by blood or marriage during which period such relative would have met the requirements of this subsection.

(f) Exception

This section shall not apply to Indian lands.

(g) Effect on property rights of United States or any other landowner

Nothing in this section shall be construed as increasing or diminishing any property rights by the United States or by any other landowner.

(Pub. L. No. 95–87, Title VII, § 714, 91 Stat. 524 (Aug. 3, 1977).)

§ 1305. Federal lessee protection

[SMCRA § 715]

In those instances where the coal proposed to be mined by surface coal mining operations is owned by the Federal Government and the surface is subject to a lease or a permit issued by the Federal Government, the application for a permit shall include either:

(1) the written consent of the permittee or lessee of the surface lands involved to enter and commence surface coal mining operations on such land, or in lieu thereof;

(2) evidence of the execution of a bond or undertaking to the United States or the State, whichever is applicable, for the use and benefit of the permittee or lessee of the surface lands involved to secure payment of any damages to the surface estate which the operations will cause to the crops, or to the tangible improvements of the permittee or lessee of the surface lands as may be determined by the parties involved, or as determined and fixed in an action brought against the operator or upon the bond in a court of competent jurisdiction. This bond is in addition to the performance bond required for reclamation under this chapter.

(Pub. L. No. 95–87, Title VII, § 715, 91 Stat. 525 (Aug. 3, 1977).)

HISTORICAL AND STATUTORY NOTES

References in Text

This chapter, referred to in text, was in the original "this Act", meaning Pub. L. No. 95–87, 91 Stat. 445 (Aug. 3, 1977), as amended, which enacted this chapter and amended section 1114 of Title 18, Crimes and Criminal Procedure. For complete classification of this Act to the Code, see Short Title note set out under section 1201 of this title and Tables.

§ 1306. Effect on rights of owner of coal in Alaska to conduct surface mining operations

[SMCRA § 716]

Nothing in this chapter shall be construed as increasing or diminishing the rights of any owner of coal in Alaska to conduct or authorize surface coal mining operations for coal which has been or is hereafter conveyed out of Federal ownership to the State of Alaska or pursuant to the Alaska Native Claims Settlement Act [43 U.S.C.A. § 1601 et seq.]: *Provided,* That such surface coal mining operations meet the requirements of this chapter.

(Pub. L. No. 95–87, Title VII, § 716, 91 Stat. 526 (Aug. 3, 1977).)

HISTORICAL AND STATUTORY NOTES

References in Text

This chapter, referred to in text, was in the original "this Act", meaning Pub. L. No. 95–87, 91 Stat. 445 (Aug. 3, 1977), as amended, which enacted this chapter and amended section 1114 of Title 18, Crimes and Criminal Procedure. For complete classification of this Act to the Code, see Short Title note set out under section 1201 of this title and Tables.

The Alaska Native Claims Settlement Act, referred to in text, is Pub. L. No. 92–203, 85 Stat. 688 (Dec. 18, 1971), as amended, which is codified generally as chapter 33 (section 1601 et seq.) of Title 43, Public Lands. For complete classification of this Act to the Code, see Short Title note set out under section 1601 of Title 43 and Tables volume.

§ 1307. Water rights and replacement

[SMCRA § 717]

(a) Nothing in this chapter shall be construed as affecting in any way the right of any person to enforce or protect, under applicable law, his interest in water resources affected by a surface coal mining operation.

(b) The operator of a surface coal mine shall replace the water supply of an owner of interest in real property who obtains all or part of his supply of water for domestic, agricultural, industrial, or other legitimate use from an underground or surface source where such supply has been affected by contamination, diminution, or interruption proximately resulting from such surface coal mine operation.

(Pub. L. No. 95–87, Title VII, § 717, 91 Stat. 526 (Aug. 3, 1977).)

HISTORICAL AND STATUTORY NOTES

References in Text

This chapter, referred to in subsec. (a), was in the original "this Act", meaning Pub. L. No. 95–87, 91 Stat. 445 (Aug. 3, 1977), as amended, which enacted this chapter and amended section 1114 of Title 18, Crimes and Criminal Procedure. For complete classification of this Act to the Code, see Short Title note set out under section 1201 of this title and Tables.

§ 1308. Advance appropriations

[SMCRA § 718]

Notwithstanding any other provision of this chapter, no authority to make payments under this chapter shall be effective except to such extent or in such amounts as are provided in advance in appropriation Acts.

(Pub. L. No. 95–87, Title VII, § 718, 91 Stat. 526 (Aug. 3, 1977).)

HISTORICAL AND STATUTORY NOTES

References in Text

This chapter, referred to in text, was in the original "this Act", meaning Pub. L. No. 95–87, 91 Stat. 445 (Aug. 3, 1977), as amended, which enacted this chapter and amended section 1114 of Title 18, Crimes and Criminal Procedure. For complete classification of this Act to the Code, see Short Title note set out under section 1201 of this title and Tables.

§ 1308a. Use of Civil Penalty Funds[1]

That, in fiscal year 2009 and thereafter, the Secretary of the Interior, pursuant to regulations, may use directly or through grants to States, moneys collected for civil penalties assessed under section 1268 of this title, to reclaim lands adversely affected by coal mining practices after August 3, 1977, to remain available until expended.

(Pub. L. No. 111–8, Div. E, Title I, 123 Stat. 712 (Mar. 11, 2009).)

[1] Editorially supplied.

HISTORICAL AND STATUTORY NOTES

Codifications

Section is based on a proviso in the paragraph under the subheading "Regulation and Technology" under the heading "Office of Surface Mining Reclamation and Enforcement" in the Department of the Interior, Environment, and Related Agencies Appropriations Act, 2009, Pub. L. No. 111–8, Div. E, 123 Stat. 701 (Mar. 11, 2009).

§ 1308b. Computer hardware, software and other technical equipment; transfer of title

With funds available for the Technical Innovation and Professional Services program in this or any other Act with respect to any fiscal year, the Secretary may transfer title for computer hardware, software and other technical equipment to State and tribal regulatory and reclamation programs.

(Pub. L. No. 113–76, Div. G, Title I, 128 Stat. 299 (Jan. 17, 2014).)

HISTORICAL AND STATUTORY NOTES

References in Text

This Act, referred to in text, is Pub. L. No. 113–76, Div. G, 128 Stat. 289 (Jan. 17, 2014), known as the Department of the Interior, Environment, and Related Agencies Appropriations Act, 2014. For complete classification of this Act to the Code, see Tables.

Codifications

Section was enacted as part of the Department of the Interior, Environment, and Related Agencies Appropriations Act, 2014, and also as part of the Consolidated Appropriations Act, 2014, and not as part of the Surface Mining Control and Reclamation Act of 1977 which comprises this chapter.

§ 1309. Certification and training of blasters

[SMCRA § 719]

In accordance with this chapter, the Secretary of the Interior (or the approved State regulatory authority as provided for in section 1253 of this title) shall promulgate regulations requiring the training, examination, and certification of persons engaging in or directly responsible for blasting or use of explosives in surface coal mining operations.

(Pub. L. No. 95–87, Title VII, § 719, 91 Stat. 526 (Aug. 3, 1977).)

HISTORICAL AND STATUTORY NOTES

References in Text

This chapter, referred to in text, was in the original "this Act", meaning Pub. L. No. 95–87, 91 Stat. 445 (Aug. 3, 1977), as amended, which enacted this chapter and amended section 1114 of Title 18, Crimes and Criminal Procedure. For complete classification of this Act to the Code, see Short Title note set out under section 1201 of this title and Tables.

§ 1309a. Subsidence

[SMCRA § 720]

(a) Requirements

Underground coal mining operations conducted after October 24, 1992, shall comply with each of the following requirements:

(1) Promptly repair, or compensate for, material damage resulting from subsidence caused to any occupied residential dwelling and structures related thereto, or non-commercial building due to underground coal mining operations. Repair of damage shall include rehabilitation, restoration, or replacement of the damaged occupied residential dwelling and structures related thereto, or non-commercial building. Compensation shall be provided to the owner of the damaged occupied residential dwelling and structures related thereto or non-commercial building and shall be in the full amount of the diminution in value resulting from the subsidence. Compensation may be accomplished by the purchase, prior to mining, of a noncancellable premium-prepaid insurance policy.

(2) Promptly replace any drinking, domestic, or residential water supply from a well or spring in existence prior to the application for a surface coal mining and reclamation permit, which has been affected by contamination, diminution, or interruption resulting from underground coal mining operations.

Nothing in this section shall be construed to prohibit or interrupt underground coal mining operations.

(b) Regulations

Within one year after October 24, 1992, the Secretary shall, after providing notice and opportunity for public comment, promulgate final regulations to implement subsection (a) of this section.

(Pub. L. No. 95–87, Title VII, § 720, as added by Pub. L. No. 102–486, Title XXV, § 2504(a)(1), 106 Stat. 3104 (Oct. 24, 1992).)

HISTORICAL AND STATUTORY NOTES

Review of Existing Requirements and Report to Congress

Section 2504(a)(2) of Pub. L. No. 102–486 provided that:

"(A) The Secretary of the Interior shall review existing requirements related to underground coal mine subsidence and natural gas and petroleum pipeline safety. Such review shall consider the following with respect to subsidence: notification; mitigation; coordination; requirements of the Natural Gas Pipeline Safety Act and the Hazardous Liquid Pipeline Safety Act [section 1671 et seq. and section 2001 et seq. of Appendix to Title 49, Transportation]; and the status of Federal, State and local laws, as well as common law, with respect to prevention or mitigation of damage from subsidence.

"(B) The review shall also include a survey of the status of Federal, State, and local laws, as well as common law, with respect to the responsibilities of the relevant parties for costs resulting from damage due to subsidence or from mitigation efforts undertaken to prevent damage from subsidence.

"(C) In conducting the review, the Secretary of the Interior shall consult with the Secretary of Transportation, the Attorney General of the United States, appropriate officials of relevant States, and owners and representatives of natural gas and petroleum pipeline companies and coal companies.

"(D) The Secretary of the Interior shall submit a report detailing the results of the review to the Committee on Energy and Natural Resources of the United States Senate and the Committee on Interior and Insular Affairs [now Committee on Natural Resources] of the United States House of Representatives within 18 months of enactment of this Act [Oct. 24, 1992]. Where appropriate, the Secretary of the Interior shall commence a rulemaking to address any deficiencies in existing law determined in the review under subparagraph (A) regarding notification, coordination and mitigation."

§ 1309b. Research

[SMCRA § 721]

The Office of Surface Mining Reclamation and Enforcement is authorized to conduct studies, research and demonstration projects relating to the implementation of, and compliance with, subchapter V of this chapter, and provide technical assistance to states[1] for that purpose. Prior to approving any such studies, research or demonstration projects the Director, Office of Surface Mining Reclamation and Enforcement, shall first consult with the Director, Bureau of Mines, and obtain a determination from such Director that the Bureau of Mines is not already conducting like or similar studies, research or demonstration projects. Studies, research and demonstration projects for the purposes of subchapter IV of this chapter shall only be conducted in accordance with section 1231(c)(6) of this title.

(Pub. L. No. 95–87, Title VII, § 721, as added by Pub. L. No. 102–486, Title XXV, § 2504(c)(3), 106 Stat. 3105 (Oct. 24, 1992).)

[1] So in original. Probably should be capitalized.

SUBCHAPTER VIII—UNIVERSITY COAL RESEARCH LABORATORIES

§ 1311. Establishment of university coal research laboratories

[SMCRA § 801]

(a) Designation by Secretary of Energy

The Secretary of Energy, after consultation with the National Academy of Engineering, shall designate thirteen institutions of higher education at which university coal research laboratories will be established and operated. Ten such designations shall be made as provided in subsection (e) of this section and the remaining three shall be made in fiscal year 1980.

(b) Criteria

In making designations under this section, the Secretary of Energy shall consider the following criteria:

(1) Those ten institutions of higher education designated as provided in subsection (e) of this section shall be located in a State with abundant coal reserves.

(2) The institution of higher education shall have experience in coal research, expertise in several areas of coal research, and potential or currently active, outstanding programs in coal research.

(3) The institution of higher education has the capacity to establish and operate the coal laboratories to be assisted under this subchapter.

(c) Location of coal laboratories

Not more than one coal laboratory established pursuant to this subchapter shall be located in a single State and at least one coal laboratory shall be established within each of the major coal provinces recognized by the United States Bureau of Mines, including Alaska.

(d) Period for submission of applications for designation; contents

The Secretary of Energy shall establish a period, not in excess of ninety days after August 3, 1977, for the submission of applications for designation under this section. Any institution of higher education desiring to be designated under this subchapter shall submit an application to the Secretary of Energy in such form, at such time, and containing or accompanied by such information as the Secretary of Energy may reasonably require. Each application shall—

(1) describe the facilities to be established for coal energy resources and conversion research and research on related environmental problems including facilities for interdisciplinary academic research projects by the combined efforts of specialists such as mining engineers, mineral engineers, geochemists, mineralogists, mineral economists, fuel scientists, combustion engineers, mineral preparation engineers, coal petrographers, geologists, chemical engineers, civil engineers, mechanical engineers, and ecologists;

(2) set forth a program for the establishment of a test laboratory for coal characterization which, in addition, may be used as a site for the exchange of coal research activities by representatives of private industry engaged in coal research and characterization;

(3) set forth a program for providing research and development activities for students engaged in advanced study in any discipline which is related to the development of adequate energy supplies in the United States. The research laboratory shall be associated with an ongoing educational and research program on extraction and utilization of coal.

(e) Time limit

The Secretary of Energy shall designate the ten institutions of higher education under this section not later than ninety days after the date on which such applications are to be submitted.

(Pub. L. No. 95–87, Title VIII, § 801, 91 Stat. 526 (Aug. 3, 1977); as amended by Pub. L. No. 95–617, Title VI, § 604(a), (c), 92 Stat. 3166, 3167 (Nov. 9, 1978); Pub. L. No. 102–285, § 10(b), 106 Stat. 172 (May 18, 1992).)

HISTORICAL AND STATUTORY NOTES

Change of Name

"United States Bureau of Mines" substituted for "Bureau of Mines" in subsec. (c) pursuant to section 10(b) of Pub. L. No. 102–285, set out as a note under 30 U.S.C.A. § 1. For provisions relating to closure and transfer of functions of the United States Bureau of Mines, see Transfer of Functions note set out under 30 U.S.C.A. § 1.

§ 1312. Financial assistance

[SMCRA § 802]

(a) The Secretary of Energy is authorized to make grants to any institution of higher education designated under section 1311 of this title to pay the Federal share of the cost of establishing (including the construction of such facilities as may be necessary) and maintaining a coal laboratory.

(b) Each institution of higher education designated pursuant to section 1311 of this title shall submit an application to the Secretary of Energy. Each such application shall—

(1) set forth the program to be conducted at the coal laboratory which includes the purposes set forth in section 1311(d) of this title;

(2) provide assurances that the university will pay from non-Federal sources the remaining costs of carrying out the program set forth;

(3) provide such fiscal control and fund accounting procedures as may be necessary to assure the proper disbursement of and accounting for Federal funds received under this subchapter;

(4) provide for making an annual report which shall include a description of the activities conducted at the coal laboratory and an evaluation of the success of such activities, and such other necessary reports in such form and containing such information as the Secretary of Energy may require, and for keeping such records and affording such access thereto as may be necessary to assure the correctness and verification of such reports; and

(5) set forth such policies and procedures as will insure that Federal funds made available under this section for any fiscal year will be so used as to supplement and, to the extent practical, increase the level of funds that would, in the absence of such Federal funds, be made available for the purposes of the activities described in subsections (d)(1), (2), and (3) of section 1311 of this title, and in no case supplant such funds.

(Pub. L. No. 95–87, Title VIII, § 802, 91 Stat. 527 (Aug. 3, 1977); as amended by Pub. L. No. 95–617, Title VI, § 604(c), 92 Stat. 3167 (Nov. 9, 1978).)

§ 1313. Limitation on payments

[SMCRA § 803]

(a) No institutions of higher education may receive more than $4,000,000 for the construction of its coal research laboratory, including initially installed fixed equipment, nor may it receive more than $1,500,000 for initially installed movable equipment, nor may it receive more than $500,000 for new program startup expenses.

(b) No institution of higher education may receive more than $1,500,000 per year from the Federal Government for operating expenses.

(Pub. L. No. 95–87, Title VIII, § 803, 91 Stat. 528 (Aug. 3, 1977).)

§ 1314. Payments; Federal share of operating expenses

[SMCRA § 804]

(a) From the amounts appropriated pursuant to section 1316 of this title, the Secretary of Energy shall pay to each institution of higher education having an application approved under this subchapter an amount equal to the Federal share of the cost of carrying out that application. Such payments may be in installments, by way of reimbursement, or by way of advance with necessary adjustments on account of underpayments or overpayments.

(b) The Federal share of operating expenses for any fiscal year shall not exceed 50 per centum of the cost of the operation of a coal research laboratory.

(Pub. L. No. 95–87, Title VIII, § 804, 91 Stat. 528 (Aug. 3, 1977); as amended by Pub. L. No. 95–617, Title VI, § 604(c), 92 Stat. 3167 (Nov. 9, 1978).)

§ 1315. Advisory Council on Coal Research

[SMCRA § 805]

(a) Establishment; members

There is established an Advisory Council on Coal Research which shall be composed of—

(1) the Secretary of Energy, who shall be Chairman;

(2) the Director of the United States Bureau of Mines of the Department of the Interior;

(3) the President of the National Academy of Sciences;

(4) the President of the National Academy of Engineering;

(5) the Director of the United States Geological Survey; and

(6) six members appointed by the Secretary of Energy from among individuals who, by virtue of experience or training, are knowledgeable in the field of coal research and mining, and who are representatives of institutions of higher education, industrial users of coal and coal-derived fuels, the coal industry, mine workers, nonindustrial consumer groups, and institutions concerned with the preservation of the environment.

(b) Furnishing advice to Secretary of Energy

The Advisory Council shall advise the Secretary of Energy with respect to the general administration of this subchapter, and furnish such additional advice as he may request.

(c) Annual report to President; transmittal to Congress

The Advisory Council shall make an annual report of its findings and recommendations (including recommendations for changes in the provisions of this subchapter) to the President not later than December 31 of each calendar year. The President shall transmit each such report to the Congress.

(d) Compensation and travel expenses

(1) Members of the Council who are not regular officers or employees of the United States Government shall, while serving on business of the Council, be entitled to receive compensation at rates fixed by the Secretary of Energy but not exceeding the daily rate prescribed for GS–18 of the General Schedule under section 5332 of Title 5 and while so serving away from their homes or regular places of business, they may be allowed travel expenses, including per diem in lieu of subsistence, as authorized by section 5703 of Title 5 for persons in the Government service employed intermittently.

(2) Members of the Council who are officers or employees of the Government shall be reimbursed for travel, subsistence, and other necessary expenses incurred by them in carrying out their duties on the Council.

(e) Alternate members

Whenever a member of the Council appointed under clauses (1) through (5) is unable to attend a meeting, that member shall appoint an appropriate alternate to represent him for that meeting.

(Pub. L. No. 95–87, Title VIII, § 805, 91 Stat. 528 (Aug. 3, 1977); as amended by Pub. L. No. 95–617, Title VI, § 604(c), 92 Stat. 3167 (Nov. 9, 1978); Pub. L. No. 102–285, § 10(b), 106 Stat. 172 (May 18, 1992).)

HISTORICAL AND STATUTORY NOTES

Change of Name

"United States Bureau of Mines" substituted for "Bureau of Mines" in subsec. (a)(2) pursuant to section 10(b) of Pub. L. No. 102–285, set out as a note under 30 U.S.C.A. § 1. For provisions relating to closure and transfer of functions of the United States Bureau of Mines, see Transfer of Functions note set out under 30 U.S.C.A. § 1.

Termination of Reporting Requirements

For termination, effective May 15, 2000, of provisions in subsec. (c) of this section relating to requirement that the President transmit each annual report to Congress, see Pub. L. No. 104–66, § 3003, as amended, set out as a note under 31 U.S.C.A. § 1113, and House Document No. 103–7, page 153.

Termination of Advisory Committees

Advisory committees established after Jan. 5, 1973, to terminate not later than the expiration of the two-year period beginning on the date of their establishment, unless, in the case of a committee established by the President or an officer of the Federal Government, such committee is renewed by appropriate action prior to the expiration of such two-year period, or in the case of a committee established by the Congress, its duration is otherwise provided for by law. See section 14 of Pub. L. No. 92–463, 86 Stat. 776 (Oct. 6, 1972), set out in Appendix 2 to Title 5, Government Organization and Employees.

§ 1316. Authorization of appropriations

[SMCRA § 806]

(a) For the ten institutions referred to in the last sentence of section 1311(a) of this title, there are authorized to be appropriated not to exceed $30,000,000 for the fiscal year ending September 30, 1979 (including the cost of construction, equipment, and startup expenses), and not to exceed $7,500,000 for the fiscal year 1980 and for each fiscal year thereafter through the fiscal year ending before October 1, 1984, to carry out the provisions of this subchapter.

(b) For the three remaining institutions referred to in the last sentence of section 1311(a) of this title, there are authorized to be appropriated not to exceed $6,500,000 for the fiscal year 1980 (including the cost of construction, equipment, and startup expenses), and not to exceed $2,000,000 for each fiscal year after fiscal year 1980 ending before October 1, 1984, to carry out the provisions of this subchapter.

(Pub. L. No. 95–87, Title VIII, § 806, 91 Stat. 529 (Aug. 3, 1977); as amended by Pub. L. No. 95–617, Title VI, § 604(b), 92 Stat. 3166 (Nov. 9, 1978).)

SUBCHAPTER IX—ENERGY RESOURCE GRADUATE FELLOWSHIPS

§ 1321. Fellowship awards

[SMCRA § 901]

(a) Graduate study and research in areas of applied science and engineering relating to production, conservation, and utilization of fuels and energy

The Secretary of Energy is authorized to award under the provisions of this subchapter not to exceed one thousand fellowships for the fiscal year ending September 30, 1979, and each of the five succeeding fiscal years. Fellowships shall be awarded under the provisions of this subchapter for graduate study and research in those areas of applied science and engineering that are related to the production, conservation, and utilization of fuels and energy. Fellowships shall be awarded to students in programs leading to master's degrees. Such fellowships may be awarded for graduate study and research at any institution of higher education, library, archive, or any other research center approved by the Secretary of Energy after consultation with the Secretary of Education.

(b) Term

Such fellowships shall be awarded for such periods as the Secretary of Energy may determine, but not to exceed two years.

(c) Replacement awards

In addition to the number of fellowships authorized to be awarded by subsection (a) of this section, the Secretary of Energy is authorized to award fellowships equal to the number previously awarded during any fiscal year under this subchapter but vacated prior to the end of the period for which they were awarded; except that each fellowship awarded under this subsection shall be for such period of graduate work or research, not in excess of the remainder of the period for which the fellowship which it replaces was awarded as the Secretary of Energy may determine.

(Pub. L. No. 95–87, Title IX, § 901, 91 Stat. 529 (Aug. 3, 1977); as amended by Pub. L. No. 95–91, Title III, § 301(a), Title VII, §§ 703, 707, 91 Stat. 577, 606, 607 (Aug. 4, 1977); Pub. L. No. 96–88, Title III, § 301(a)(1), Title V, § 507, 93 Stat. 677, 692 (Oct. 17, 1979).)

HISTORICAL AND STATUTORY NOTES

Transfer of Functions

"Secretary of Energy" was substituted for "Administrator ERDA" and "Administrator", meaning the Administrator of the Energy Research and Development Administration, in text pursuant to sections 301(a), 703, and 707 of Pub. L. No. 95–91, which are codified as sections 7151(a), 7293, 7297 of Title 42, The Public Health and Welfare, and which terminated the Energy Research and Development Administration and transferred its functions and the functions of the Administrator thereof (with certain exceptions) to the Secretary of Energy.

"Secretary of Education" was substituted for "Commissioner of Education" in subsec. (a), pursuant to sections 301(a)(1) and 507 of Pub. L. No. 96–88, which are codified as sections 3441(a)(1) and 3507 of Title 20, Education, and which transferred all functions of the Commissioner of Education to the Secretary of Education.

§ 1322. Fellowship recipients

[SMCRA § 902]

Recipients of fellowships under this subchapter shall be—

(a) persons who have been accepted by an institution of higher education for graduate study leading to an advanced degree or for a professional degree, and

(b) persons who plan a career in the field of energy resources, production, or utilization.

(Pub. L. No. 95–87, Title IX, § 902, 91 Stat. 530 (Aug. 3, 1977).)

§ 1323. Distribution of fellowships

[SMCRA § 903]

In awarding fellowships under the provisions of this subchapter, the Secretary of Energy shall endeavor to provide equitable distribution of such fellowships throughout the Nation, except that the Secretary of Energy shall give special attention to institutions of higher education, libraries, archives, or other research centers which have a demonstrated capacity to offer courses of study or research in the field of energy resources and conservation and conversion and related disciplines. In carrying out his responsibilities under this section, the Secretary of Energy shall take into consideration the projected need for highly trained engineers and scientists in the field of energy sources.

(Pub. L. No. 95–87, Title IX, § 903, 91 Stat. 530 (Aug. 3, 1977); as amended by Pub. L. No. 95–91, Title III, § 301(a), Title VII, §§ 703, 707, 91 Stat. 577, 606, 607 (Aug. 4, 1977).)

HISTORICAL AND STATUTORY NOTES

Transfer of Functions

"Secretary of Energy" was substituted for "Administrator", meaning the Administrator of the Energy Research and Development Administration, in text pursuant to sections 301(a), 703, and 707 of Pub. L. No. 95–91, which are codified as sections 7151(a), 7293, 7297 of Title 42, The Public Health and Welfare, and which terminated the Energy Research and Development Administration and transferred its functions and the functions of the Administrator thereof (with certain exceptions) to the Secretary of Energy.

§ 1324. Stipends and allowances

[SMCRA § 904]

(a) Each person awarded a fellowship under this subchapter shall receive a stipend of not more than $10,000 for each academic year of study. An additional amount of $500 for each such calendar year of study shall be paid to such person on account of each of his dependents.

(b) In addition to the amount paid to such person pursuant to subsection (a) of this section there shall be paid to the institution of higher education at which each such person is pursuing his course of study, 100 per centum of the amount paid to such person less the amount paid on account of such person's dependents, to such person less any amount charged such person for tuition.

(Pub. L. No. 95–87, Title IX, § 904, 91 Stat. 530 (Aug. 3, 1977).)

§ 1325. Limitation on fellowships

[SMCRA § 905]

No fellowship shall be awarded under this subchapter for study at a school or department of divinity. For the purpose of this section, the term "school or department of divinity" means an institution or department or branch of an institution, whose program is specifically for the education of students to prepare them to become ministers of religion or to enter upon some other religious vocation or to prepare them to teach theological subjects.

(Pub. L. No. 95–87, Title IX, § 905, 91 Stat. 530 (Aug. 3, 1977).)

§ 1326. Fellowship conditions

[SMCRA § 906]

(a) A person awarded a fellowship under the provisions of this subchapter shall continue to receive the payments provided in section 1324(a) of this title only during such periods as the Secretary of Energy finds that he is maintaining satisfactory proficiency in, and devoting essentially full time to, study or research in the field in which such fellowship was awarded, in an institution of higher education, and is not engaging in gainful employment other than part-time employment in teaching, research, or similar activities, approved by the Secretary of Energy.

(b) The Secretary of Energy shall require reports containing such information in such forms and to be filed at such times as he determines necessary from each person awarded a fellowship under the provisions of this subchapter. Such reports shall be accompanied by a certificate from an appropriate official at the institution of higher education, library, archive, or other research center approved by the Secretary of Energy, stating that such person is making satisfactory progress in, and is devoting essentially full time to the research for which the fellowship was awarded.

(Pub. L. No. 95–87, Title IX, § 906, 91 Stat. 530 (Aug. 3, 1977); as amended by Pub. L. No. 95–91, Title III, § 301(a), Title VII, §§ 703, 707, 91 Stat. 577, 606, 607 (Aug. 4, 1977).)

HISTORICAL AND STATUTORY NOTES

Transfer of Functions

"Secretary of Energy" was substituted for "Administrator", meaning the Administrator of the Energy Research and Development Administration, in text pursuant to sections 301(a), 703, and 707 of Pub. L. No. 95–91, which are codified as sections 7151(a), 7293, 7297 of Title 42, The Public Health and Welfare, and which terminated the Energy Research and Development Administration and transferred its functions and the functions of the Administrator thereof (with certain exceptions) to the Secretary of Energy.

§ 1327. Authorization of appropriations

[SMCRA § 907]

There are authorized to be appropriated $11,000,000 for the fiscal year ending September 30, 1979, and for each of the five succeeding fiscal years. For payments for the initial awarding of fellowships awarded under this subchapter, there are authorized to be appropriated for the fiscal year ending September 30, 1979, and for each of the five succeeding fiscal years, such sums as may be necessary in order that fellowships already awarded might be completed.

(Pub. L. No. 95–87, Title IX, § 907, 91 Stat. 531 (Aug. 3, 1977).)

§ 1328. Research, development projects, etc., relating to alternative coal mining technologies

[SMCRA § 908]

(a) Authority of Secretary of the Interior to conduct, promote, etc.

The Secretary of the Interior is authorized to conduct and promote the coordination and acceleration of, research, studies, surveys, experiments, demonstration projects, and training relating to—

(1) the development and application of coal mining technologies which provide alternatives to surface disturbance and which maximize the recovery of available coal resources, including the improvement of present underground mining methods, methods for the return of underground mining wastes to the mine void, methods for the underground mining of thick coal seams and very deep seams; and

(2) safety and health in the application of such technologies, methods, and means.

(b) Contracts and grants

In conducting the activities authorized by this section, the Secretary of the Interior may enter into contracts with and make grants to qualified institutions, agencies, organizations, and persons.

(c) Authorization of appropriations

There are authorized to be appropriated to the Secretary of the Interior, to carry out the purposes of this section, $35,000,000 for each fiscal year beginning with the fiscal year 1979, and for each year thereafter for the next four years.

(d) Publication in Federal Register; report to Congress

At least sixty days before any funds are obligated for any research studies, surveys, experiments or demonstration projects to be conducted or financed under this chapter in any fiscal year, the Secretary of the Interior in consultation with the heads of other Federal agencies having the authority to conduct or finance such projects, shall determine and publish such determinations in the Federal Register that such projects are not being conducted or financed by any other Federal agency. On December 31 of each calendar year, the Secretary shall report to the Congress on the research studies, surveys, experiments or demonstration projects, conducted or financed under this chapter, including, but not limited to, a statement of the nature and purpose of each project, the Federal cost thereof, the identity and affiliation of the persons engaged in such projects, the expected completion date of the projects and the relationship of the projects to other such projects of a similar nature.

(e) Availability of information to public

Subject to the patent provisions of section 306(d) of this Act, all information and data resulting from any research studies, surveys, experiments, or demonstration projects conducted or financed under this chapter shall be promptly made available to the public.

(Pub. L. No. 95–87, Title IX, § 908, 91 Stat. 531 (Aug. 3, 1977); as amended by Pub. L. No. 95–91, Title III, § 301(a), Title VII, §§ 703, 707, 91 Stat. 577, 606, 607 (Aug. 4, 1977); Pub. L. No. 97–257, Title I, § 100, 96 Stat. 841 (Sept. 10, 1982).)

HISTORICAL AND STATUTORY NOTES

References in Text

This chapter, referred to in subsecs. (d) and (e), was in the original "this Act", meaning Pub. L. No. 95–87, 91 Stat. 445 (Aug. 3, 1977), as amended, which enacted this chapter and amended section 1114 of Title 18, Crimes and Criminal Procedure. For complete classification of this Act to the Code, see Short Title note set out under section 1201 of this title and Tables.

Section 306(d) of this Act, referred to in subsec. (e), was codified as section 1226(d) of this title and was omitted from the Code pursuant to the replacement of subchapter III (section 1221 et seq.) of this chapter by Pub. L. No. 98–409. See section 1226(c) of this title.

Termination of Reporting Requirements

For termination, effective May 15, 2000, of provisions in subsec. (d) of this section relating to requirement that on Dec. 31 of each calendar year, the Secretary report to Congress on research studies, surveys, experiments or demonstration projects, conducted or financed under this chapter, see Pub. L. No. 104–66, § 3003, as amended, set out as a note under 31 U.S.C.A. § 1113, and House Document No. 103–7, page 109.

Transfer of Functions

"Secretary of the Interior" was substituted for "Secretary of Energy" in subsecs. (a) to (d) pursuant to section 100 of Pub. L. No. 97–257, which is set out as a note under section 7152 of Title 42, The Public Health and Welfare, and which transferred to, and vested in, the Secretary of the Interior all functions vested in, or delegated to, the Secretary of Energy and the Department of Energy under this section.

Previously, "Secretary of Energy" was substituted for "Administrator", meaning the Administrator of the Energy Research and Development Administration, in subsecs. (a) to (d) pursuant to sections 301(a), 703, and 707 of Pub. L. No. 95–91, which are codified as sections 7151(a), 7293, 7297 of Title 42, and which terminated the Energy Research and Development Administration and transferred its functions and the functions of the Administrator thereof (with certain exceptions) to the Secretary of Energy.

TITLE 33

NAVIGATION AND NAVIGABLE WATERS

WATER POLLUTION PREVENTION AND CONTROL

FEDERAL WATER POLLUTION CONTROL ACT [FWPCA § ____]

(33 U.S.C.A. §§ 1251 to 1388)

CHAPTER 26—WATER POLLUTION PREVENTION AND CONTROL

SUBCHAPTER I—RESEARCH AND RELATED PROGRAMS

SUBCHAPTER II—GRANTS FOR CONSTRUCTION OF TREATMENT WORKS

SUBCHAPTER III—STANDARDS AND ENFORCEMENT

SUBCHAPTER I—RESEARCH AND RELATED PROGRAMS

§ 1251. Congressional declaration of goals and policy

[FWPCA § 101]

(a) Restoration and maintenance of chemical, physical and biological integrity of Nation's waters; national goals for achievement of objective

The objective of this chapter is to restore and maintain the chemical, physical, and biological integrity of the Nation's waters. In order to achieve this objective it is hereby declared that, consistent with the provisions of this chapter—

(1) it is the national goal that the discharge of pollutants into the navigable waters be eliminated by 1985;

(2) it is the national goal that wherever attainable, an interim goal of water quality which provides for the protection and propagation of fish, shellfish, and wildlife and provides for recreation in and on the water be achieved by July 1, 1983;

(3) it is the national policy that the discharge of toxic pollutants in toxic amounts be prohibited;

(4) it is the national policy that Federal financial assistance be provided to construct publicly owned waste treatment works;

(5) it is the national policy that areawide waste treatment management planning processes be developed and implemented to assure adequate control of sources of pollutants in each State;

(6) it is the national policy that a major research and demonstration effort be made to develop technology necessary to eliminate the discharge of pollutants into the navigable waters, waters of the contiguous zone, and the oceans; and

(7) it is the national policy that programs for the control of nonpoint sources of pollution be developed and implemented in an expeditious manner so as to enable the goals of this chapter to be met through the control of both point and nonpoint sources of pollution.

(b) Congressional recognition, preservation, and protection of primary responsibilities and rights of States

It is the policy of the Congress to recognize, preserve, and protect the primary responsibilities and rights of States to prevent, reduce, and eliminate pollution, to plan the development and use (including restoration, preservation, and enhancement) of land and water resources, and to consult with the Administrator in the exercise of his authority under this chapter. It is the policy of Congress that the States manage the construction grant program under this chapter and implement the permit programs under sections 1342 and 1344 of this title. It is further the policy of the Congress to support and aid research relating to the prevention, reduction, and elimination of pollution, and to provide Federal technical services and financial aid to State and interstate agencies and municipalities in connection with the prevention, reduction, and elimination of pollution.

(c) Congressional policy toward Presidential activities with foreign countries

It is further the policy of Congress that the President, acting through the Secretary of State and such national and international organizations as he determines appropriate, shall take such action as may be necessary to insure that to the fullest extent possible all foreign countries shall take meaningful action for the prevention, reduction, and elimination of pollution in their waters and in international waters and for the achievement of goals regarding the elimination of discharge of pollutants and the improvement of water quality to at least the same extent as the United States does under its laws.

(d) Administrator of Environmental Protection Agency to administer chapter

Except as otherwise expressly provided in this chapter, the Administrator of the Environmental Protection Agency (hereinafter in this chapter called "Administrator") shall administer this chapter.

(e) Public participation in development, revision, and enforcement of any regulation, etc.

Public participation in the development, revision, and enforcement of any regulation, standard, effluent limitation, plan, or program established by the Administrator or any State under this chapter shall be provided for, encouraged, and assisted by the Administrator and the States. The Administrator, in cooperation with the States, shall develop and publish regulations specifying minimum guidelines for public participation in such processes.

(f) Procedures utilized for implementing chapter

It is the national policy that to the maximum extent possible the procedures utilized for implementing this chapter shall encourage the drastic minimization of paperwork and interagency decision procedures, and the best use of available manpower and funds, so as to prevent needless duplication and unnecessary delays at all levels of government.

(g) Authority of States over water

It is the policy of Congress that the authority of each State to allocate quantities of water within its jurisdiction shall not be superseded, abrogated or otherwise impaired by this chapter. It is the further policy of Congress that nothing in this chapter shall be construed to supersede or abrogate rights to quantities of water which have been established by any State. Federal agencies shall co-operate with State and local agencies to develop comprehensive solutions to prevent, reduce and eliminate pollution in concert with programs for managing water resources.

(June 30, 1948, c. 758, Title I, § 101, as added by Pub. L. No. 92–500, § 2, 86 Stat. 816 (Oct. 18, 1972); and amended by Pub. L. No. 95–217, §§ 5(a), 26(b), 91 Stat. 1567, 1575 (Dec. 27, 1977); Pub. L. No. 100–4, Title III, § 316(b), 101 Stat. 60 (Feb. 4, 1987).)

HISTORICAL AND STATUTORY NOTES

Codifications

The Federal Water Pollution Control Act, comprising this chapter, was originally enacted by Act of June 30, 1948, c. 758, 62 Stat. 1155, and amended by Act of July 17, 1952, c. 927, 66 Stat. 755; Act of July 9, 1956, c. 518, 70 Stat. 498; Pub. L. No. 86–70, 73 Stat. 141 (June 25, 1959); Pub. L. No. 86–624, 74 Stat. 411 (July 12, 1960); Pub. L. No. 87–88, 75 Stat. 204 (July 20, 1961); Pub. L. No. 89–234, 79 Stat. 903 (Oct. 2, 1965); Pub. L. No. 89–753, 80 Stat. 1246 (Nov. 3, 1966); Pub. L. No. 91–224, 84 Stat. 91 (Apr. 3, 1970); Pub. L. No. 91–611, 84 Stat. 1818 (Dec. 31, 1970); Pub. L. No. 92–50, 85 Stat. 124 (July 9, 1971); Pub. L. No. 92–137, 85 Stat. 379 (Oct. 13, 1971); Pub. L. No. 92–240, 86 Stat. 47 (Mar. 1, 1972), and was formerly codified first as section 466 et seq. of this title and later to section 1151 et seq. of this title. The Act is shown herein, however, as having been added by Pub. L. No. 92–500 without reference to such intervening amendments because of the extensive amendment, reorganization, and expansion of the Act's provisions by Pub. L. No. 92–500.

Savings Provisions

Section 4 of Pub. L. No. 92–500 provided that:

"(a) No suit, action, or other proceeding lawfully commenced by or against the Administrator or any other officer or employee of the United States in his official capacity or in relation to the discharge of his official duties under the Federal Water Pollution Control Act as in effect immediately prior to the date of enactment of this Act [Oct. 18, 1972] shall abate by reason of the taking effect of the amendment made by section 2 of this Act [which enacted this chapter]. The court may, on its own motion or that of any party made at any time within twelve months after such taking effect, allow the same to be maintained by or against the Administrator or such officer or employee.

"(b) All rules, regulations, orders, determinations, contracts, certifications, authorizations, delegations or other actions duly issued, made, or taken by or pursuant to the Federal Water Pollution Control Act as in effect immediately prior to the date of enactment of this Act [Oct. 18, 1972], and pertaining to any functions, powers, requirements, and duties under the Federal Water Pollution Control Act as in effect immediately prior to the date of enactment of this Act [Oct. 18, 1972], shall continue in full force and effect after the date of enactment of this Act [Oct. 18, 1972] until modified or rescinded in accordance with the Federal Water Pollution Control Act as amended by this Act [this chapter].

"(c) The Federal Water Pollution Control Act as in effect immediately prior to the date of enactment of this Act [Oct. 18, 1972] shall remain applicable to all grants made from funds authorized for the fiscal year ending June 30, 1972, and prior fiscal years, including any increases in the monetary amount of any such grant which may be paid from authorizations for fiscal years beginning after June 30, 1972, except as specifically otherwise provided in section 202 of the Federal Water Pollution Control Act as amended by this Act [section 1282 of this title] and in subsection (c) of section 3 of this Act."

Severability of Provisions

Section 512 of Act of June 30, 1948, c. 758, Title V, as added by Pub. L. No. 92–500, § 2, 86 Stat. 894 (Oct. 18, 1972), provided that: "If any provision of this Act [this chapter], or the application of any provision of this Act [this chapter] to any person or circumstance, is held invalid, the application of such provision to other persons or circumstances, and the remainder of this Act [this chapter], shall not be affected thereby."

Short Title

2021 Amendments. Section 1 of Pub. L. No. 116–294, 134 Stat. 4899 (Jan. 5, 2021), provided that "This Act may be cited as the 'Great Lakes Restoration Initiative Act of 2019' or the 'GLRI Act of 2019.' " Section 1 of Pub.

L. No. 116–337, 134 Stat. 5120 (Jan. 13, 2021), provided that: "This Act may be cited as the 'Protect and Restore America's Estuaries Act.' "

2008 Amendments. Pub. L. No. 110–365, § 1, 122 Stat. 4021 (Oct. 8, 2008), provided that: "This Act [amending 33 U.S.C.A. §§ 1268 and 1271a, and enacting provisions set out as a note under this section] may be cited as the 'Great Lakes Legacy Reauthorization Act of 2008'."

Pub. L. No. 110–288, § 1, 122 Stat. 2650 (July 29, 2008), provided that: "This Act [amending 33 U.S.C.A. §§ 1322, 1342, and 1362] may be cited as the 'Clean Boating Act of 2008'."

2002 Amendments. Pub. L. No. 107–303, § 1(a), 116 Stat. 2355 (Nov. 27, 2002), provided that: "This Act [enacting 33 U.S.C.A. § 1271a, amending 33 U.S.C.A. §§ 1254, 1266, 1268, 1270, 1285, 1290, 1324, 1329, 1330 and 1375, enacting provisions set out as notes under this section, 31 U.S.C.A. § 1113 and 33 U.S.C.A. § 1254, and repealing provisions set out as a note under 20 U.S.C.A. § 50] may be cited as the 'Great Lakes and Lake Champlain Act of 2002'."

Pub. L. No. 107–303, Title I, § 101, 116 Stat. 2355 (Nov. 27, 2002), provided that: "This Title [enacting 33 U.S.C.A. § 1271a, and amending 33 U.S.C.A. § 1268] may be cited as the 'Great Lakes Legacy Act of 2002'."

Pub. L. No. 107–303, Title II, § 201, 116 Stat. 2358 (Nov. 27, 2002), provided that: "This Title [amending 33 U.S.C.A. § 1270] may be cited as the 'Daniel Patrick Moynihan Lake Champlain Basin Program Act of 2002'."

2000 Amendments. Pub. L. No. 106–457, Title VI, § 601, 114 Stat. 1975 (Nov. 7, 2000), provided that: "This title [enacting section 1300 of this title] may be cited as the 'Alternative Water Sources Act of 2000'."

Pub. L. No. 106–457, Title V, § 501, 114 Stat. 1973 (Nov. 7, 2000), provided that: "This title [enacting section 1273 of this title] may be cited as the 'Lake Pontchartrain Basin Restoration Act of 2000'."

Pub. L. No. 106–457, Title IV, § 401, 114 Stat. 1973 (Nov. 7, 2000), provided that: "This title [amending section 1269 of this title] may be cited as the 'Long Island Sound Restoration Act'."

Pub. L. No. 106–457, Title II, § 201, 114 Stat. 1967 (Nov. 7, 2000), provided that: "This title [amending section 1267 of this title and enacting provisions set out as a note under section 1267 of this title] may be cited as the 'Chesapeake Bay Restoration Act of 2000'."

Pub. L. No. 106–284, § 1, 114 Stat. 870 (Oct. 10, 2000), provided that: "This Act [enacting sections 1346 and 1375a of this title and amending sections 1254, 1313, 1314, 1362, and 1377 of this title] may be cited as the 'Beaches Environmental Assessment and Coastal Health Act of 2000'."

1994 Amendments. Pub. L. No. 103–431, § 1, 108 Stat. 4396 (Oct. 31, 1994), provided that: "This Act [amending section 1311 of this title] may be cited as the 'Ocean Pollution Reduction Act'."

1990 Amendments. Pub. L. No. 101–596, § 1, 104 Stat. 3000 (Nov. 16, 1990), provided that: "This Act [enacting sections 1269 and 1270 and amending sections 1268 and 1324 of this title, and enacting note provisions under this section and section 1270 of this title] may be cited as the 'Great Lakes Critical Programs Act of 1990'."

Pub. L. No. 101–596, Title II, § 201, 104 Stat. 3004 (Nov. 16, 1990), provided that: "This part [enacting section 1269 and amending section 1416 of this title] may be cited as the 'Long Island Sound Improvement Act of 1990'."

Pub. L. No. 101–596, Title III, § 301, 104 Stat. 3006 (Nov. 16, 1990), provided that: "This title [enacting section 1270 and amending section 1324(d)(2) of this title and enacting note provision under section 1270 of this title] may be cited as the 'Lake Champlain Special Designation Act of 1990'."

1988 Amendments. Pub. L. No. 100–653, Title X, § 1001, 102 Stat. 3835 (Nov. 14, 1988), provided that: "This title [amending section 1330(a)(2)(B) of this title and enacting provisions set out as notes under section 1330 of this title] may be cited as the 'Massachusetts Bay Protection Act of 1988'."

1987 Amendments. Section 1(a) of Pub. L. No. 100–4 provided that: "This Act [enacting sections 1254a, 1267, 1268, 1281b, 1329, 1330, 1377, 1381, 1382, 1383, 1384, 1385, 1386, 1387, and 1414a of this title, amending sections 1251, 1254, 1256, 1262, 1281, 1282, 1283, 1284, 1285, 1287, 1288, 1291, 1311, 1312, 1313, 1314, 1317, 1318, 1319, 1321, 1322, 1324, 1342, 1344, 1345, 1361, 1362, 1365, 1369, 1375, and 1376 of this title, and enacting provisions set out as notes under sections 1251, 1284, 1311, 1317, 1319, 1330, 1342, 1345, 1362, 1375, and 1414a of this title and section 1962d–20 of Title 42, The Public Health and Welfare] may be cited as the 'Water Quality Act of 1987'."

1981 Amendments. Pub. L. No. 97–117, § 1, 95 Stat. 1623 (Dec. 29, 1981), provided that: "This Act [enacting sections 1298, 1299, and 1313a of this title, amending sections 1281 to 1285, 1287, 1291, 1292, 1296, 1311, and

1314 of this title, and enacting provisions set out as notes under sections 1311 and 1375 of this title] may be cited as the 'Municipal Wastewater Treatment Construction Grant Amendments of 1981'."

1977 Amendments. Section 1 of Pub. L. No. 95–217 provided: "That this Act [enacting sections 1281a, 1294 to 1296, and 1297 of this title, amending sections 1251, 1252, 1254 to 1256, 1259, 1262, 1263, 1281, 1282 to 1288, 1291, 1292, 1311, 1314, 1315, 1317 to 1319, 1321 to 1324, 1328, 1341, 1342, 1344, 1345, 1362, 1364, 1375, and 1376 of this title, enacting provisions set out as notes under sections 1251, 1284, 1286, 1314, 1321, 1342, 1344, and 1376 of this title, and amending a provision set out as a note under this section] may be cited as the 'Clean Water Act of 1977'."

1972 Amendments. Section 1 of Pub. L. No. 92–500 provided: "That this Act [enacting this chapter, amending section 24 of Title 12, Banks and Banking, sections 633 and 636 of Title 15, Commerce and Trade, and section 711 of former Title 31, Money and Finance, and enacting provisions set out as notes under this section and sections 1281 and 1361 of this title] may be cited as the 'Federal Water Pollution Control Act Amendments of 1972'."

1948 Acts. Section 519, formerly section 518, of Act of June 30, 1948, c. 758, Title V, as added by Pub. L. No. 92–500, § 2, 86 Stat. 896 (Oct. 18, 1972), and amended by Pub. L. No. 95–217, § 2, 91 Stat. 1566 (Dec. 27, 1977), and renumbered by Pub. L. No. 100–4, Title V, § 506, 101 Stat. 76 (Feb. 4, 1987), provided that: "This Act [enacting this chapter] may be cited as the 'Federal Water Pollution Control Act' (commonly referred to as the Clean Water Act)."

Standards

For provisions relating to the responsibility of the head of each Executive agency for compliance with applicable pollution control standards, see Ex. Ord. No. 12088, Oct. 13, 1978, 43 Fed. Reg. 47707, set out as a note under section 4321 of Title 42, The Public Health and Welfare.

Seafood Processing Study; Submittal of Results to Congress Not Later Than January 1, 1979

Pub. L. No. 95–217, § 74, 91 Stat. 1609 (Dec. 27, 1977), provided that the Administrator of the Environmental Protection Agency conduct a study to examine the geographical, hydrological, and biological characteristics of marine waters to determine the effects of seafood processes which dispose of untreated natural wastes into such waters and to include in this study an examination of technologies which may be used in such processes to facilitate the use of the nutrients in these wastes or to reduce the discharge of such wastes into the marine environment and to submit the result of this study to Congress not later than Jan. 1, 1979.

Oversight Study

Section 5 of Pub. L. No. 92–500 authorized the Comptroller General of the United States to conduct a study and review of the research, pilot, and demonstration programs related to prevention and control of water pollution conducted, supported, or assisted by any Federal agency pursuant to any federal law or regulation and assess conflicts between these programs and their coordination and efficacy, and to report to Congress thereon by Oct. 1, 1973.

International Trade Study

Section 6 of Pub. L. No. 92–500 provided that:

"(a) The Secretary of Commerce, in cooperation with other interested Federal agencies and with representatives of industry and the public, shall undertake immediately an investigation and study to determine—

"(1) the extent to which pollution abatement and control programs will be imposed on, or voluntarily undertaken by, United States manufacturers in the near future and the probable short- and long-range effects of the costs of such programs (computed to the greatest extent practicable on an industry-by-industry basis) on (A) the production costs of such domestic manufacturers, and (B) the market prices of the goods produced by them;

"(2) the probable extent to which pollution abatement and control programs will be implemented in foreign industrial nations in the near future and the extent to which the production costs (computed to the greatest extent practicable on an industry-by-industry basis) of foreign manufacturers will be affected by the costs of such programs;

"(3) the probable competitive advantage which any article manufactured in a foreign nation will likely have in relation to a comparable article made in the United States if that foreign nation—

"(A) does not require its manufacturers to implement pollution abatement and control programs,

"(B) requires a lesser degree of pollution abatement and control in its programs, or

"(C) in any way reimburses or otherwise subsidizes its manufacturers for the costs of such program;

"(4) alternative means by which any competitive advantage accruing to the products of any foreign nation as a result of any factor described in paragraph (3) may be (A) accurately and quickly determined, and (B) equalized, for example, by the imposition of a surcharge or duty, on a foreign product in an amount necessary to compensate for such advantage; and

"(5) the impact, if any, which the imposition of a compensating tariff of other equalizing measure may have in encouraging foreign nations to implement pollution and abatement control programs.

"(b) The Secretary shall make an initial report to the President and Congress within six months after the date of enactment of this section [Oct. 18, 1972] of the results of the study and investigation carried out pursuant to this section and shall make additional reports thereafter at such times as he deems appropriate taking into account the development of relevant data, but not less than once every twelve months."

International Agreements

Section 7 of Pub. L. No. 92–500 provided that: "The President shall undertake to enter into international agreement to apply uniform standards of performance for the control of the discharge and emission of pollutants from new sources, uniform controls over the discharge and emission of toxic pollutants, and uniform controls over the discharge of pollutants into the ocean. For this purpose the President shall negotiate multilateral treaties, conventions, resolutions, or other agreements, and formulate, present, or support proposals at the United Nations and other appropriate international forums."

National Policies and Goal Study

Section 10 of Pub. L. No. 92–500 authorized the President to make a full and complete investigation and study of all national policies and goals established by law to determine what the relationship should be between these policies and goals, taking into account the resources of the Nation, and to report the results of his investigation and study together with his recommendations to Congress not later than two years after Oct. 18, 1972.

Efficiency Study

Section 11 of Pub. L. No. 92–500 authorized the President, by utilization of the General Accounting Office, to conduct a full and complete investigation and study of ways and means of most effectively using all of the various resources, facilities, and personnel of the Federal Government in order to most efficiently carry out the provisions of this chapter and to report the results of his investigation and study together with his recommendations to Congress not later than two hundred and seventy days after Oct. 18, 1972.

Sex Discrimination

Section 13 of Pub. L. No. 92–500 provided that: "No person in the United States shall on the ground of sex be excluded from participation in, be denied the benefits of, or be subjected to discrimination under any program or activity receiving Federal Assistance under this Act [see Short Title note above], the Federal Water Pollution Control Act [this chapter], or the Environmental Financing Act [set out as a note under section 1281 of this title]. This section shall be enforced through agency provisions and rules similar to those already established, with respect to racial and other discrimination, under title VI of the Civil Rights Act of 1964 [section 2000d et seq. of Title 42, The Public Health and Welfare]. However, this remedy is not exclusive and will not prejudice or cut off any other legal remedies available to a discriminatee."

Prevention, Control, and Abatement of Environmental Pollution at Federal Facilities

Ex. Ord. No. 12088, Oct. 13, 1978, 43 Fed. Reg. 47707, set out as a note under section 4321 of Title 42, The Public Health and Welfare, provides for the prevention, control, and abatement of environmental pollution at federal facilities.

National Shellfish Indicator Program

Pub. L. No. 102–567, Title III, § 308, 106 Stat. 4286 (Oct. 29, 1992), as amended by Pub. L. No. 105–362, Title II, § 201(b), 112 Stat. 3282 (Nov. 10, 1998), provided that:

"(a) Establishment of a research program.—The Secretary of Commerce, in cooperation with the Secretary of Health and Human Services and the Administrator of the Environmental Protection Agency, shall establish and administer a 5-year national shellfish research program (hereafter in this section referred to as the 'Program') for the purpose of improving existing classification systems for shellfish growing waters using the latest technological advancements in microbiology and epidemiological methods. Within 12 months after the date of enactment of this Act [Oct. 29, 1992], the Secretary of Commerce, in cooperation with the advisory committee established under subsection (b) and the Consortium, shall develop a comprehensive 5-year plan for the Program which shall at a minimum provide for—

"(1) an environmental assessment of commercial shellfish growing areas in the United States, including an evaluation of the relationships between indicators of fecal contamination and human enteric pathogens;

"(2) the evaluation of such relationships with respect to potential health hazards associated with human consumption of shellfish;

"(3) a comparison of the current microbiological methods used for evaluating indicator bacteria and human enteric pathogens in shellfish and shellfish growing waters with new technological methods designed for this purpose;

"(4) the evaluation of current and projected systems for human sewage treatment in eliminating viruses and other human enteric pathogens which accumulate in shellfish;

"(5) the design of epidemiological studies to relate microbiological data, sanitary survey data, and human shellfish consumption data to actual hazards to health associated with such consumption; and

"(6) recommendations for revising Federal shellfish standards and improving the capabilities of Federal and State agencies to effectively manage shellfish and ensure the safety of shellfish intended for human consumption.

"(b) Advisory committee.—(1) For the purpose of providing oversight of the Program on a continuing basis, an advisory committee (hereafter in this section referred to as the 'Committee') shall be established under a memorandum of understanding between the Interstate Shellfish Sanitation Conference and the National Marine Fisheries Service.

"(2) The Committee shall—

"(A) identify priorities for achieving the purpose of the Program;

"(B) review and recommend approval or disapproval of Program work plans and plans of operation;

"(C) review and comment on all subcontracts and grants to be awarded under the Program;

"(D) receive and review progress reports from the Consortium and program subcontractors and grantees; and

"(E) provide such other advice on the Program as is appropriate.

"(3) The Committee shall consist of at least ten members and shall include—

"(A) three members representing agencies having authority under State law to regulate the shellfish industry, of whom one shall represent each of the Atlantic, Pacific, and Gulf of Mexico shellfish growing regions;

"(B) three members representing persons engaged in the shellfish industry in the Atlantic, Pacific, and Gulf of Mexico shellfish growing regions (who shall be appointed from among at least six recommendations by the industry members of the Interstate Shellfish Sanitation Conference Executive Board), of whom one shall represent the shellfish industry in each region;

"(C) three members, of whom one shall represent each of the following Federal agencies: the National Oceanic and Atmospheric Administration, the Environmental Protection Agency, and the Food and Drug Administration; and

"(D) one member representing the Shellfish Institute of North America.

"(4) The Chairman of the Committee shall be selected from among the Committee members described in paragraph (3)(A).

"(5) The Committee shall establish and maintain a subcommittee of scientific experts to provide advice, assistance, and information relevant to research funded under the Program, except that no individual who is awarded, or whose application is being considered for, a grant or subcontract under the Program may serve on such subcommittee. The membership of the subcommittee shall, to the extent practicable, be regionally balanced with experts who have scientific knowledge concerning each of the Atlantic, Pacific, and Gulf of Mexico shellfish growing regions. Scientists from the National Academy of Sciences and appropriate Federal agencies (including the National Oceanic and Atmospheric Administration, Food and Drug Administration, Centers for Disease Control, National Institutes of Health, Environmental Protection Agency, and National Science Foundation) shall be considered for membership on the subcommittee.

"(6) Members of the Committee and its scientific subcommittee established under this subsection shall not be paid for serving on the Committee or subcommittee, but shall receive travel expenses as authorized by section 5703 of title 5, United States Code [section 5703 of Title 5, Government Organization and Employees].

"(c) **Contract with consortium.**—Within 30 days after the date of enactment of this Act [Oct. 29, 1992], the Secretary of Commerce shall seek to enter into a cooperative agreement or contract with the Consortium under which the Consortium will—

"(1) be the academic administrative organization and fiscal agent for the Program;

"(2) award and administer such grants and subcontracts as are approved by the Committee under subsection (b);

"(3) develop and implement a scientific peer review process for evaluating grant and subcontractor applications prior to review by the Committee;

"(4) in cooperation with the Secretary of Commerce and the Committee, procure the services of a scientific project director;

"(5) develop and submit budgets, progress reports, work plans, and plans of operation for the Program to the Secretary of Commerce and the Committee; and

"(6) make available to the Committee such staff, information, and assistance as the Committee may reasonably require to carry out its activities.

"(d) **Authorization of appropriations.—(1)** Of the sums authorized under section 4(a) of the National Oceanic and Atmospheric Administration Marine Fisheries Program Authorization Act (Public Law 98–210; 97 Stat. 1409) [section 4(a) of Pub. L. No. 98–210, 97 Stat. 1409 (Dec. 6, 1983), which is not codified in the Code], there are authorized to be appropriated to the Secretary of Commerce $5,200,000 for each of the fiscal years 1993 through 1997 for carrying out the Program. Of the amounts appropriated pursuant to this authorization, not more than 5 percent of such appropriation may be used for administrative purposes by the National Oceanic and Atmospheric Administration. The remaining 95 percent of such appropriation shall be used to meet the administrative and scientific objectives of the Program.

"(2) The Interstate Shellfish Sanitation Conference shall not administer appropriations authorized under this section, but may be reimbursed from such appropriations for its expenses in arranging for travel, meetings, workshops, or conferences necessary to carry out the Program.

"(e) **Definitions.**—As used in this section, the term—

"(1) 'Consortium' means the Louisiana Universities Marine Consortium; and

"(2) 'shellfish' means any species of oyster, clam, or mussel that is harvested for human consumption."

Definition of "Administrator"

Section 1(d) of Pub. L. No. 100–4 provided that: "For purposes of this Act [see Short Title of 1987 Amendment note set out above], the term 'Administrator' means the Administrator of the Environmental Protection Agency."

Limitation on Payments

Section 2 of Pub. L. No. 100–4 provided that: "No payments may be made under this Act [see Short Title of 1987 Amendment note set out above] except to the extent provided in advance in appropriation Acts."

Contiguous Zone of United States

For extension of contiguous zone of United States, see Proc. No. 7219, set out as a note under 43 U.S.C.A. § 1331.

§ 1252. Comprehensive programs for water pollution control

[FWPCA § 102]

(a) Preparation and development

The Administrator shall, after careful investigation, and in cooperation with other Federal agencies, State water pollution control agencies, interstate agencies, and the municipalities and industries involved, prepare or develop comprehensive programs for preventing, reducing, or eliminating the pollution of the navigable waters and ground waters and improving the sanitary condition of surface and underground waters. In the development of such comprehensive programs due regard shall be given to the improvements which are necessary to conserve such waters for the protection and propagation of fish and aquatic life and wildlife, recreational purposes, and the withdrawal of such waters for public water supply, agricultural, industrial, and other purposes. For the purpose of this section, the Administrator is authorized to make joint investigations with any such agencies of the condition of any waters in any State or States, and of the discharges of any sewage, industrial wastes, or substance which may adversely affect such waters.

(b) Planning for reservoirs; storage for regulation of streamflow

(1) In the survey or planning of any reservoir by the Corps of Engineers, Bureau of Reclamation, or other Federal agency, consideration shall be given to inclusion of storage for regulation of streamflow, except that any such storage and water releases shall not be provided as a substitute for adequate treatment or other methods of controlling waste at the source.

(2) The need for and the value of storage for regulation of streamflow (other than for water quality) including but not limited to navigation, salt water intrusion, recreation, esthetics, and fish and wildlife, shall be determined by the Corps of Engineers, Bureau of Reclamation, or other Federal agencies.

(3) The need for, the value of, and the impact of, storage for water quality control shall be determined by the Administrator, and his views on these matters shall be set forth in any report or presentation to Congress proposing authorization or construction of any reservoir including such storage.

(4) The value of such storage shall be taken into account in determining the economic value of the entire project of which it is a part, and costs shall be allocated to the purpose of regulation of streamflow in a manner which will insure that all project purposes, share equitably in the benefit of multiple-purpose construction.

(5) Costs of regulation of streamflow features incorporated in any Federal reservoir or other impoundment under the provisions of this chapter shall be determined and the beneficiaries identified and if the benefits are widespread or national in scope, the costs of such features shall be nonreimbursable.

(6) No license granted by the Federal Energy Regulatory Commission for a hydroelectric power project shall include storage for regulation of streamflow for the purpose of water quality control unless the Administrator shall recommend its inclusion and such reservoir storage capacity shall not exceed such proportion of the total storage required for the water quality control plan as the drainage area of such reservoir bears to the drainage area of the river basin or basins involved in such water quality control plan.

(c) Basins; grants to State agencies

(1) The Administrator shall, at the request of the Governor of a State, or a majority of the Governors when more than one State is involved, make a grant to pay not to exceed 50 per centum of the administrative expenses of a planning agency for a period not to exceed three years, which period shall begin after October 18, 1972, if such agency provides for adequate representation of appropriate State, interstate, local, or (when appropriate) international interests in the basin or portion thereof involved and is capable of developing an effective, comprehensive water quality control plan for a basin or portion thereof.

(2) Each planning agency receiving a grant under this subsection shall develop a comprehensive pollution control plan for the basin or portion thereof which—

(A) is consistent with any applicable water quality standards, effluent and other limitations, and thermal discharge regulations established pursuant to current law within the basin;

(B) recommends such treatment works as will provide the most effective and economical means of collection, storage, treatment, and elimination of pollutants and recommends means to encourage both municipal and industrial use of such works;

(C) recommends maintenance and improvement of water quality within the basin or portion thereof and recommends methods of adequately financing those facilities as may be necessary to implement the plan; and

(D) as appropriate, is developed in cooperation with, and is consistent with any comprehensive plan prepared by the Water Resources Council, any areawide waste management plans developed pursuant to section 1288 of this title, and any State plan developed pursuant to section 1313(e) of this title.

(3) For the purposes of this subsection the term "basin" includes, but is not limited to, rivers and their tributaries, streams, coastal waters, sounds, estuaries, bays, lakes, and portions thereof as well as the lands drained thereby.

(June 30, 1948, c. 758, Title I, § 102, as added by Pub. L. No. 92–500, § 2, 86 Stat. 817 (Oct. 18, 1972); and amended by Pub. L. No. 95–91, Title IV, § 402(a)(1)(A), 91 Stat. 583 (Aug. 4, 1977); Pub. L. No. 95–217, § 5(b), 91 Stat. 1567 (Dec. 27, 1977); Pub. L. No. 104–66, Title II, § 2021(a), 109 Stat. 726 (Dec. 21, 1995).)

HISTORICAL AND STATUTORY NOTES

Transfer of Functions

"Federal Energy Regulatory Commission" was substituted for "Federal Power Commission" in subsec. (b)(6) on authority of Pub. L. No. 95–91, Title IV, § 402(a)(1)(A), 91 Stat. 583 (Aug. 4, 1977), which is codified as section 7172(a)(1)(A) of Title 42, The Public Health and Welfare.

Environmental Dredging

Pub. L. No. 101–640, Title III, § 312, 104 Stat. 4639 (Nov. 28, 1990), which was formerly set out as a note under this section, is now set out as section 1272 of this title.

§ 1252a. Reservoir projects, water storage; modification; storage for other than for water quality, opinion of Federal agency, committee resolutions of approval; provisions inapplicable to projects with certain prescribed water quality benefits in relation to total project benefits

In the case of any reservoir project authorized for construction by the Corps of Engineers, Bureau of Reclamation, or other Federal agency when the Administrator of the Environmental Protection Agency determines pursuant to section 1252(b) of this title that any storage in such project for regulation of streamflow for water quality is not needed, or is needed in a different amount, such project may be modified accordingly by the head of the appropriate agency, and any storage no longer required for water quality may be utilized for other authorized purposes of the project when, in the opinion of the head of such agency, such use is justified. Any such modification of a project where the benefits attributable to water quality are 15 per centum or more but not greater than 25 per centum of the total project benefits shall take effect only upon the adoption of resolutions approving such modification by the appropriate committees of the Senate and House of Representatives. The provisions of the section shall not apply to any project where the benefits attributable to water quality exceed 25 per centum of the total project benefits.

(Pub. L. No. 93–251, Title I, § 65, 88 Stat. 30 (Mar. 7, 1974).)

HISTORICAL AND STATUTORY NOTES

Codifications

This section was not enacted as part of the Federal Water Pollution Control Act which comprises this chapter.

§ 1253. Interstate cooperation and uniform laws

[FWPCA § 103]

(a) The Administrator shall encourage cooperative activities by the States for the prevention, reduction, and elimination of pollution, encourage the enactment of improved and, so far as practicable, uniform State laws relating to the prevention, reduction, and elimination of pollution; and encourage compacts between States for the prevention and control of pollution.

(b) The consent of the Congress is hereby given to two or more States to negotiate and enter into agreements or compacts, not in conflict with any law or treaty of the United States, for (1) cooperative effort and mutual assistance for the prevention and control of pollution and the enforcement of their respective laws relating thereto, and (2) the establishment of such agencies, joint or otherwise, as they may deem desirable for making effective such agreements and compacts. No such agreement or compact shall be binding or obligatory upon any State a party thereto unless and until it has been approved by the Congress.

(June 30, 1948, c. 758, Title I, § 103, as added by Pub. L. No. 92–500, § 2, 86 Stat. 818 (Oct. 18, 1972).)

§ 1254. Research, investigations, training, and information

[FWPCA § 104]

(a) Establishment of national programs; cooperation; investigations; water quality surveillance system; reports

The Administrator shall establish national programs for the prevention, reduction, and elimination of pollution and as part of such programs shall—

(1) in cooperation with other Federal, State, and local agencies, conduct and promote the coordination and acceleration of, research, investigations, experiments, training, demonstrations, surveys, and studies relating to the causes, effects, extent, prevention, reduction, and elimination of pollution;

(2) encourage, cooperate with, and render technical services to pollution control agencies and other appropriate public or private agencies, institutions, and organizations, and individuals, including the general public, in the conduct of activities referred to in paragraph (1) of this subsection;

(3) conduct, in cooperation with State water pollution control agencies and other interested agencies, organizations and persons, public investigations concerning the pollution of any navigable waters, and report on the results of such investigations;

(4) establish advisory committees composed of recognized experts in various aspects of pollution and representatives of the public to assist in the examination and evaluation of research progress and proposals and to avoid duplication of research;

(5) in cooperation with the States, and their political subdivisions, and other Federal agencies establish, equip, and maintain a water quality surveillance system for the purpose of monitoring the quality of the navigable waters and ground waters and the contiguous zone and the oceans and the Administrator shall, to the extent practicable, conduct such surveillance by utilizing the resources of the National Aeronautics and Space Administration, the National Oceanic and Atmospheric Administration, the United States Geological Survey, and the Coast Guard, and shall report on such quality in the report required under subsection (a) of section 1375 of this title; and

(6) initiate and promote the coordination and acceleration of research designed to develop the most effective practicable tools and techniques for measuring the social and economic costs and benefits of activities which are subject to regulation under this chapter; and shall transmit a report on the results of such research to the Congress not later than January 1, 1974.

(b) Authorized activities of Administrator

In carrying out the provisions of subsection (a) of this section the Administrator is authorized to—

(1) collect and make available, through publications and other appropriate means, the results of and other information, including appropriate recommendations by him in connection therewith, pertaining to such research and other activities referred to in paragraph (1) of subsection (a) of this section;

(2) cooperate with other Federal departments and agencies, State water pollution control agencies, interstate agencies, other public and private agencies, institutions, organizations, industries involved, and individuals, in the preparation and conduct of such research and other activities referred to in paragraph (1) of subsection (a) of this section;

(3) make grants to State water pollution control agencies, interstate agencies, other public or nonprofit private agencies, institutions, organizations, and individuals, for purposes stated in paragraph (1) of subsection (a) of this section;

(4) contract with public or private agencies, institutions, organizations, and individuals, without regard to section 3324(a) and (b) of Title 31 and section 6101 of Title 41, referred to in paragraph (1) of subsection (a) of this section;

(5) establish and maintain research fellowships at public or nonprofit private educational institutions or research organizations;

(6) collect and disseminate, in cooperation with other Federal departments and agencies, and with other public or private agencies, institutions, and organizations having related responsibilities, basic data on chemical, physical, and biological effects of varying water quality and other information pertaining to pollution and the prevention, reduction, and elimination thereof;

(7) develop effective and practical processes, methods, and prototype devices for the prevention, reduction, and elimination of pollution; and

(8) make grants to nonprofit organizations—

(A) to provide technical assistance to rural, small, and tribal municipalities for the purpose of assisting, in consultation with the State in which the assistance is provided, such municipalities and tribal governments in the planning, developing, and acquisition of financing for eligible projects and activities described in section 603(c);

(B) to provide technical assistance and training for rural, small, and tribal publicly owned treatment works and decentralized wastewater treatment systems to enable such treatment works and systems to protect water quality and achieve and maintain compliance with the requirements of this Act; and

(C) to disseminate information to rural, small, and tribal municipalities and municipalities that meet the affordability criteria established under section 603(i)(2) by the State in which the municipality is located with respect to planning, design, construction, and operation of publicly owned treatment works and decentralized wastewater treatment systems.

(c) Research and studies on harmful effects of pollutants; cooperation with Secretary of Health and Human Services

In carrying out the provisions of subsection (a) of this section the Administrator shall conduct research on, and survey the results of other scientific studies on, the harmful effects on the health or welfare of persons caused by pollutants. In order to avoid duplication of effort, the Administrator shall, to the extent practicable, conduct such research in cooperation with and through the facilities of the Secretary of Health and Human Services.

(d) Sewage treatment; identification and measurement of effects of pollutants; augmented streamflow

In carrying out the provisions of this section the Administrator shall develop and demonstrate under varied conditions (including conducting such basic and applied research, studies, and experiments as may be necessary):

(1) Practicable means of treating municipal sewage, and other waterborne wastes to implement the requirements of section 1281 of this title;

(2) Improved methods and procedures to identify and measure the effects of pollutants, including those pollutants created by new technological developments; and

(3) Methods and procedures for evaluating the effects on water quality of augmented streamflows to control pollution not susceptible to other means of prevention, reduction, or elimination.

(e) Field laboratory and research facilities

The Administrator shall establish, equip, and maintain field laboratory and research facilities, including, but not limited to, one to be located in the northeastern area of the United States, one in the Middle Atlantic area, one in the southeastern area, one in the midwestern area, one in the southwestern area, one in the Pacific Northwest, and one in the State of Alaska, for the conduct of research, investigations, experiments, field demonstrations and studies, and training relating to the prevention, reduction and elimination of pollution. Insofar as practicable, each such facility shall be located near institutions of higher learning in which graduate training in such research might be carried out. In conjunction with the development of criteria under section 1343 of this title, the Administrator shall construct the facilities authorized for the National Marine Water Quality Laboratory established under this subsection.

(f) Great Lakes water quality research

The Administrator shall conduct research and technical development work, and make studies, with respect to the quality of the waters of the Great Lakes, including an analysis of the present and projected future water quality of the Great Lakes under varying conditions of waste treatment and disposal, an evaluation of the water quality needs of those to be served by such waters, an evaluation of municipal, industrial, and vessel waste treatment and disposal practices with respect to such waters, and a study of alternate means of solving pollution problems (including additional waste treatment measures) with respect to such waters.

(g) Treatment works pilot training programs; employment needs forecasting; training projects and grants; research fellowships; technical training; report to the President and transmittal to Congress

(1) For the purpose of providing an adequate supply of trained personnel to operate and maintain existing and future treatment works and related activities, and for the purpose of enhancing substantially the proficiency of those engaged in such activities, the Administrator shall finance pilot programs, in cooperation with State and interstate agencies, municipalities, educational institutions, and other organizations and individuals, of manpower development and training and retraining of persons in, on entering into, the field of operation and maintenance of treatment works and related activities. Such program and any funds expended for such a program shall supplement, not supplant, other manpower and training programs and funds available for the purposes of this paragraph. The Administrator is authorized, under such terms and conditions as he deems appropriate, to enter into agreements with one or more States, acting jointly or severally, or with other public or private agencies or institutions for the development and implementation of such a program.

(2) The Administrator is authorized to enter into agreements with public and private agencies and institutions, and individuals to develop and maintain an effective system for forecasting the supply of, and demand for, various professional and other occupational categories needed for the prevention, reduction, and elimination of pollution in each region, State, or area of the United States and, from time to time, to publish the results of such forecasts.

(3) In furtherance of the purposes of this chapter, the Administrator is authorized to—

(A) make grants to public or private agencies and institutions and to individuals for training projects, and provide for the conduct of training by contract with public or private agencies and institutions and with individuals without regard to section 3324(a) and (b) of Title 31 and section 6101 of Title 41;

(B) establish and maintain research fellowships in the Environmental Protection Agency with such stipends and allowances, including traveling and subsistence expenses, as he may deem necessary to procure the assistance of the most promising research fellows; and

(C) provide, in addition to the program established under paragraph (1) of this subsection, training in technical matters relating to the causes, prevention, reduction, and elimination of pollution for personnel of public agencies and other persons with suitable qualifications.

(4) The Administrator shall submit, through the President, a report to the Congress not later than December 31, 1973, summarizing the actions taken under this subsection and the effectiveness of such actions, and setting forth the number of persons trained, the occupational categories for which training was provided, the effectiveness of other Federal, State, and local training programs in this field, together with estimates of future needs, recommendations on improving training programs, and such other information and recommendations, including legislative recommendations, as he deems appropriate.

(h) Lake pollution

The Administrator is authorized to enter into contracts with, or make grants to, public or private agencies and organizations and individuals for (A) the purpose of developing and demonstrating new or improved methods for the prevention, removal, reduction, and elimination of pollution in lakes, including the undesirable effects of nutrients and vegetation, and (B) the construction of publicly owned research facilities for such purpose.

(i) Oil pollution control studies

The Administrator, in cooperation with the Secretary of the Department in which the Coast Guard is operating, shall—

(1) engage in such research, studies, experiments, and demonstrations as he deems appropriate, relative to the removal of oil from any waters and to the prevention, control, and elimination of oil and hazardous substances pollution;

(2) publish from time to time the results of such activities; and

(3) from time to time, develop and publish in the Federal Register specifications and other technical information on the various chemical compounds used in the control of oil and hazardous substances spills.

In carrying out this subsection, the Administrator may enter into contracts with, or make grants to, public or private agencies and organizations and individuals.

(j) Solid waste disposal equipment for vessels

The Secretary of the department in which the Coast Guard is operating shall engage in such research, studies, experiments, and demonstrations as he deems appropriate relative to equipment which is to be installed on board a vessel and is designed to receive, retain, treat, or discharge human body wastes and the wastes from toilets and other receptacles intended to receive or retain body wastes with particular emphasis on equipment to be installed on small recreational vessels. The Secretary of the department in which the Coast Guard is operating shall report to Congress the results of such research, studies, experiments, and demonstrations prior to the effective date of any regulations established under section 1322 of this title. In carrying out this subsection the Secretary of the department in which the Coast Guard is operating may enter into contracts with, or make grants to, public or private organizations and individuals.

(k) Land acquisition

In carrying out the provisions of this section relating to the conduct by the Administrator of demonstration projects and the development of field laboratories and research facilities, the Administrator may acquire land and interests therein by purchase, with appropriated or donated funds, by donation, or by exchange for acquired or public lands under his jurisdiction which he classifies as suitable for disposition. The values of the properties so exchanged either shall be approximately equal, or if they are not approximately equal, the values shall be equalized by the payment of cash to the grantor or to the Administrator as the circumstances require.

(*l*) Collection and dissemination of scientific knowledge on effects and control of pesticides in water

(1) The Administrator shall, after consultation with appropriate local, State, and Federal agencies, public and private organizations, and interested individuals, as soon as practicable but not later than January 1, 1973, develop and issue to the States for the purpose of carrying out this chapter the latest scientific knowledge available in indicating the kind and extent of effects on health and welfare which may be expected from the presence of pesticides in the water in varying quantities. He shall revise and add to such information whenever necessary to reflect developing scientific knowledge.

(2) The President shall, in consultation with appropriate local, State, and Federal agencies, public and private organizations, and interested individuals, conduct studies and investigations of methods to control the release of pesticides into the environment which study shall include examination of the persistency of pesticides in the water environment and alternatives thereto. The President shall submit reports, from time to time, on such investigations to Congress together with his recommendations for any necessary legislation.

(m) Waste oil disposal study

(1) The Administrator shall, in an effort to prevent degradation of the environment from the disposal of waste oil, conduct a study of (A) the generation of used engine, machine, cooling, and similar waste oil, including quantities generated, the nature and quality of such oil, present collecting methods and disposal practices, and alternate uses of such oil; (B) the long-term, chronic biological effects of the disposal of such waste oil; and (C) the potential market for such oils, including the economic and legal factors relating to the sale of products made from such oils, the level of subsidy, if any, needed to encourage the purchase by public and private nonprofit agencies of products from such oil, and the practicability of Federal procurement, on a priority basis, of products made from such oil. In conducting such study, the Administrator shall consult with affected industries and other persons.

(2) The Administrator shall report the preliminary results of such study to Congress within six months after October 18, 1972, and shall submit a final report to Congress within 18 months after such date.

(n) Comprehensive studies of effects of pollution on estuaries and estuarine zones

(1) The Administrator shall, in cooperation with the Secretary of the Army, the Secretary of Agriculture, the Water Resources Council, and with other appropriate Federal, State, interstate, or local public bodies and private organizations, institutions, and individuals, conduct and promote, and encourage contributions to, continuing comprehensive studies of the effects of pollution, including sedimentation, in the estuaries and estuarine zones of the United States on fish and wildlife, on sport and commercial fishing, on recreation, on water supply and water power, and on other beneficial purposes. Such studies shall also consider the effect of demographic trends, the exploitation of mineral resources and fossil fuels, land and industrial development, navigation, flood and erosion control, and other uses of estuaries and estuarine zones upon the pollution of the waters therein.

(2) In conducting such studies, the Administrator shall assemble, coordinate, and organize all existing pertinent information on the Nation's estuaries and estuarine zones; carry out a program of investigations and surveys to supplement existing information in representative estuaries and estuarine zones; and identify the problems and areas where further research and study are required.

(3) The Administrator shall submit to Congress, from time to time, reports of the studies authorized by this subsection but at least one such report during any six-year period. Copies of each such report shall be made available to all interested parties, public and private.

(4) For the purpose of this subsection, the term "estuarine zones" means an environmental system consisting of an estuary and those transitional areas which are consistently influenced or affected by water from an estuary such as, but not limited to, salt marshes, coastal and intertidal areas, bays, harbors, lagoons, inshore waters, and channels, and the term "estuary" means all or part of the mouth of a river or stream or other body of water having unimpaired natural connection with open sea and within which the sea water is measurably diluted with fresh water derived from land drainage.

(*o*) Methods of reducing total flow of sewage and unnecessary water consumption; reports

(1) The Administrator shall conduct research and investigations on devices, systems, incentives, pricing policy, and other methods of reducing the total flow of sewage, including, but not limited to, unnecessary water consumption in order to reduce the requirements for, and the costs of, sewage and waste treatment services. Such research and investigations shall be directed to develop devices, systems, policies, and methods capable of achieving the maximum reduction of unnecessary water consumption.

(2) The Administrator shall report the preliminary results of such studies and investigations to the Congress within one year after October 18, 1972, and annually thereafter in the report required under subsection (a) of section 1375 of this title. Such report shall include recommendations for any legislation that may be required to provide for the adoption and use of devices, systems, policies, or other methods of reducing water consumption and reducing the total flow of sewage. Such report shall include an estimate of the benefits to be derived from adoption and use of such devices, systems, policies, or other methods and also shall reflect estimates of any increase in private, public, or other cost that would be occasioned thereby.

(p) Agricultural pollution

In carrying out the provisions of subsection (a) of this section the Administrator shall, in cooperation with the Secretary of Agriculture, other Federal agencies, and the States, carry out a comprehensive study and research program to determine new and improved methods and the better application of existing methods of preventing, reducing, and eliminating pollution from agriculture, including the legal, economic, and other implications of the use of such methods.

(q) Sewage in rural areas; national clearinghouse for alternative treatment information; clearinghouse on small flows

(1) The Administrator shall conduct a comprehensive program of research and investigation and pilot project implementation into new and improved methods of preventing, reducing, storing, collecting, treating, or otherwise eliminating pollution from sewage in rural and other areas where collection of sewage in conventional, communitywide sewage collection systems is impractical, uneconomical, or otherwise infeasible, or where soil conditions or other factors preclude the use of septic tank and drainage field systems.

(2) The Administrator shall conduct a comprehensive program of research and investigation and pilot project implementation into new and improved methods for the collection and treatment of sewage and other liquid wastes combined with the treatment and disposal of solid wastes.

(3) The Administrator shall establish, either within the Environmental Protection Agency, or through contract with an appropriate public or private non-profit organization, a national clearinghouse which shall (A) receive reports and information resulting from research, demonstrations, and other projects funded under this chapter related to paragraph (1) of this subsection and to subsection (e)(2) of section 1255 of this title; (B) coordinate and disseminate such reports and information for use by Federal and State agencies, municipalities, institutions, and persons in developing new and improved methods pursuant to this subsection; and (C) provide for the collection and dissemination of reports and information relevant to this subsection from other Federal and State agencies, institutions, universities, and persons.

(4) Small flows clearinghouse

Notwithstanding section 1285(d) of this title, from amounts that are set aside for a fiscal year under section 1285(i) of this title and are not obligated by the end of the 24-month period of availability for such amounts under section 1285(d) of this title, the Administrator shall make available $1,000,000 or such unobligated amount, whichever is less, to support a national clearinghouse within the Environmental Protection Agency to collect and disseminate information on small flows of sewage and innovative or alternative wastewater treatment processes and techniques, consistent with paragraph (3). This paragraph shall apply with respect to amounts set aside under section 1285(i) of this title for which the 24-month period of availability referred to in the preceding sentence ends on or after September 30, 1986.

(r) Research grants to colleges and universities

The Administrator is authorized to make grants to colleges and universities to conduct basic research into the structure and function of freshwater aquatic ecosystems, and to improve understanding of the ecological characteristics necessary to the maintenance of the chemical, physical, and biological integrity of freshwater aquatic ecosystems.

(s) River Study Centers

The Administrator is authorized to make grants to one or more institutions of higher education (regionally located and to be designated as "River Study Centers") for the purpose of conducting and reporting on interdisciplinary studies on the nature of river systems, including hydrology, biology, ecology, economics, the relationship between river uses and land uses, and the effects of development within river basins on river systems and on the value of water resources and water related activities. No such grant in any fiscal year shall exceed $1,000,000.

(t) Thermal discharges

The Administrator shall, in cooperation with State and Federal agencies and public and private organizations, conduct continuing comprehensive studies of the effects and methods of control of thermal discharges. In evaluating alternative methods of control the studies shall consider (1) such data as are available on the latest available technology, economic feasibility including cost-effectiveness analysis, and (2) the total impact on the environment, considering not only water quality but also air quality, land use, and effective utilization and conservation of freshwater and other natural resources. Such studies shall consider methods of minimizing adverse effects and maximizing beneficial effects of thermal discharges. The results of these studies shall be reported by the Administrator as soon as practicable, but not later than 270 days after October 18, 1972, and shall be made available to the public and the States, and considered as they become available by the Administrator in carrying out section 1326 of this title and by the States in proposing thermal water quality standards.

(u) Authorization of appropriations

There is authorized to be appropriated (1) not to exceed $100,000,000 per fiscal year for the fiscal year ending June 30, 1973, the fiscal year ending June 30, 1974, and the fiscal year ending June 30, 1975, not to exceed $14,039,000 for the fiscal year ending September 30, 1980, not to exceed $20,697,000 for the fiscal year ending September 30, 1981, not to exceed $22,770,000 for the fiscal year ending September 30, 1982, such sums as may be necessary for fiscal years 1983 through 1985, and not to exceed $22,770,000 per fiscal year for each of the fiscal years 1986 through 1990, for carrying out the provisions of this section, other than subsections (g)(1) and (2), (p), (r), and (t) of this section, except that such authorizations are not for any research, development, or demonstration activity pursuant to such provisions; (2) not to exceed $7,500,000 for fiscal years 1973, 1974, and 1975, $2,000,000 for fiscal year 1977, $3,000,000 for fiscal year 1978, $3,000,000 for fiscal year 1979, $3,000,000 for fiscal year 1980, $3,000,000 for fiscal year 1981, $3,000,000 for fiscal year 1982, such sums as may be necessary for fiscal years 1983 through 1985, and $3,000,000 per fiscal year for each of the fiscal years 1986 through 1990, for carrying out the provisions of subsection (g)(1) of this section; (3) not to exceed $2,500,000 for fiscal years 1973, 1974, and 1975, $1,000,000 for fiscal year 1977, $1,500,000 for fiscal year 1978, $1,500,000 for fiscal year 1979, $1,500,000 for fiscal year 1980, $1,500,000 for fiscal year 1981, $1,500,000 for fiscal year 1982, such sums as may be necessary for fiscal years 1983 through 1985, and $1,500,000 per fiscal year for each of the fiscal years 1986 through 1990, for carrying out the provisions of subsection (g)(2) of this section; (4) not to exceed $10,000,000 for each of the fiscal years ending June 30, 1973, June 30, 1974, and June 30, 1975, for carrying out the provisions of subsection (p) of this section; (5) not to exceed $15,000,000 per fiscal year for the fiscal years ending June 30, 1973, June 30, 1974, and June 30, 1975, for carrying out the provisions of subsection (r) of this section; (6) not to exceed $10,000,000 per fiscal year for the fiscal years ending June 30, 1973, June 30, 1974, and June 30, 1975, for carrying out the provisions of subsection (t) of this section; and (7) not to exceed $25,000,000 for each of fiscal years 2019 through 2023 for carrying out subsections (b)(3), (b)(8), and (g).

(v) Studies concerning pathogen indicators in coastal recreation waters

Not later than 18 months after October 10, 2000, after consultation and in cooperation with appropriate Federal, State, tribal, and local officials (including local health officials), the Administrator shall initiate, and, not later than 3 years after October 10, 2000, shall complete, in cooperation with the heads of other Federal agencies, studies to provide additional information for use in developing—

(1) an assessment of potential human health risks resulting from exposure to pathogens in coastal recreation waters, including nongastrointestinal effects;

(2) appropriate and effective indicators for improving detection in a timely manner in coastal recreation waters of the presence of pathogens that are harmful to human health;

(3) appropriate, accurate, expeditious, and cost-effective methods (including predictive models) for detecting in a timely manner in coastal recreation waters the presence of pathogens that are harmful to human health; and

(4) guidance for State application of the criteria for pathogens and pathogen indicators to be published under section 1314(a)(9) of this title to account for the diversity of geographic and aquatic conditions.

(w) Nonprofit organization.—For purposes of subsection (b)(8), the term "nonprofit organization" means a nonprofit organization that the Administrator determines, after consultation with the States regarding what small publicly owned treatments works in the State find to be most beneficial and effective, is qualified and experienced in providing on-site training and technical assistance to small publicly owned treatment works.

(June 30, 1948, c. 758, Title I, § 104, as added by Pub. L. No. 92–500, § 2, 86 Stat. 819 (Oct. 18, 1972); and amended by Pub. L. No. 93–207, § 1(1), 87 Stat. 906 (Dec. 28, 1973); Pub. L. No. 93–592, § 1, 88 Stat. 1924 (Jan. 2, 1975); Pub. L. No. 95–217, §§ 4(a), (b), 6, 7, 91 Stat. 1566, 1567 (Dec. 27, 1977); Pub. L. No. 95–576, § 1(a), 92 Stat. 2467 (Nov. 2, 1978); Pub. L. No. 96–88, Title V, § 509(b), 93 Stat. 695 (Oct. 17, 1979); Pub. L. No. 96–483, § 1(a), 94 Stat. 2360 (Oct. 21, 1980); Pub. L. No. 100–4, Title I, §§ 101(a), 102, 101 Stat. 8, 9 (Feb. 4, 1987); Pub. L. No. 102–154, Title I, 105 Stat. 1000 (Nov. 13, 1991); Pub. L. No. 102–285, § 10(a), 106 Stat. 171 (May 18, 1992); Pub. L. No. 105–362, Title V, § 501(a)(1), (d)(2)(A), 112 Stat. 3283, 3284 (Nov. 10, 1998); Pub. L. No. 106–284, § 3(a), 114 Stat. 871 (Oct. 10, 2000); Pub. L. No. 107–303, Title III, § 302(b)(1), 116 Stat. 2361 (Nov. 27, 2002); Pub. L. No. 115–270, § 4103, 132 Stat. 3765, 3872–3873 (Oct. 23, 2018).)

HISTORICAL AND STATUTORY NOTES

Codifications

In subsecs. (b)(4) and (g)(3)(A), "section 3324(a) and (b) of Title 31 and section 6101 of Title 41" substituted for references to sections 3648 and 3709 of the Revised Statutes on authority of Pub. L. No. 97–258, § 4(b), 96 Stat. 1067 (Sept. 13, 1982), which Act enacted Title 31, Money and Finance, and Pub. L. No. 111–350, § 6(c), 124 Stat. 3854 (Jan. 4, 2011), which Act enacted Title 41, Public Contracts.

Effective and Applicability Provisions

2002 Acts. Pub. L. No. 107–303, Title III, § 302(b), 116 Stat. 2361 (Nov. 27, 2002), provided that:

"(1) In general.—Effective November 10, 1998, section 501 of the Federal Reports Elimination Act of 1998 (Public Law 105–362; 112 Stat. 3283) [Pub. L. No. 105–362, Title V, § 501, 112 Stat. 3283 (Nov. 10, 1998), see Tables for complete classification] is amended by striking subsections (a), (b), (c), and (d) [amending this section and 33 U.S.C.A. §§ 1266, 1285, 1290, 1324, 1329, 1330, and 1375].

"(2) Applicability.—The Federal Water Pollution Control Act (33 U.S.C. 1254(n)(3)) shall be applied and administered on and after the date of enactment of this Act [Nov. 27, 2002] as if the amendments made by subsections (a), (b), (c), and (d) of section 501 of the Federal Reports Elimination Act of 1998 (Public Law 105–362; 112 Stat. 3283) [Pub. L. No. 105–362, Title V, § 501(a) to (d), 112 Stat. 3283 (Nov. 10, 1998), amending this section and 33 U.S.C.A. §§ 1266, 1285, 1290, 1324, 1329, 1330, and 1375] had not been enacted."

Change of Name

Pub. L. No. 102–285, § 10(a), 106 Stat. 171 (May 18, 1992), redesignated the Geological Survey and provided that on and after May 18, 1992, it shall be known as the United States Geological Survey. An earlier statute [Pub.

L. No. 102–154, Title I, 105 Stat. 1000 (Nov. 13, 1991)] had provided for the identical change of name effective on and after Nov. 13, 1991. See note under section 31 of Title 43, Public Lands.

"Secretary of Health and Human Services" was substituted for "Secretary of Health, Education, and Welfare" in subsec. (c) pursuant to section 509(b) of Pub. L. No. 96–88 which is codified as section 3508(b) of Title 20, Education.

Transfer of Functions

Enforcement functions of Secretary or other official in Department of Agriculture, insofar as they involve lands and programs under jurisdiction of that Department, related to compliance with this chapter with respect to pre-construction, construction, and initial operation of transportation system for Canadian and Alaskan natural gas were transferred to the Federal Inspector, Office of Federal Inspector for the Alaska Natural Gas Transportation System, until the first anniversary of date of initial operation of the Alaska Natural Gas Transportation System, see Reorg. Plan No. 1 of 1979, §§ 102(f), 203(a), 44 Fed. Reg. 33663, 33666, 93 Stat. 1373, 1376, effective July 1, 1979, set out in Appendix 1 to Title 5, Government Organization and Employees.

Termination of Reporting Requirements

Reporting requirement of subsec. (n)(3) of this section excepted from termination under Pub. L. No. 104–66, § 3003(a)(1), as amended, set out as a note under 31 U.S.C.A. § 1113, see Pub. L. No. 107–303, § 302(a), set out as a note under 31 U.S.C.A. § 1113.

Columbia River Basin System; Protection from Oil Spills and Discharges; Criteria for Evaluation and Report to Congress by Commandant of Coast Guard in Consultation With Federal, Etc., Agencies

Pub. L. 95–308, § 8, 92 Stat. 359 (June 30, 1978), set forth Congressional findings and declarations and evaluation criteria with respect to protection from oil spills and discharges and betterment of the Columbia River Basin system, with such evaluation by the Commandant of the Coast Guard to begin within 180 days after June 30, 1978, and immediate submission of the evaluation to appropriate Congressional committees.

Contiguous Zone of United States

For extension of contiguous zone of United States, see Proc. No. 7219, set out as a note under 43 U.S.C.A. § 1331.

§ 1254a. Research on effects of pollutants

In carrying out the provisions of section 1254(a) of this title, the Administrator shall conduct research on the harmful effects on the health and welfare of persons caused by pollutants in water, in conjunction with the United States Fish and Wildlife Service, the National Oceanic and Atmospheric Administration, and other Federal, State, and interstate agencies carrying on such research. Such research shall include, and shall place special emphasis on, the effect that bioaccumulation of these pollutants in aquatic species has upon reducing the value of aquatic commercial and sport industries. Such research shall further study methods to reduce and remove these pollutants from the relevant affected aquatic species so as to restore and enhance these valuable resources.

(Pub. L. No. 100–4, Title I, § 105, 101 Stat. 15 (Feb. 4, 1987).)

HISTORICAL AND STATUTORY NOTES

Codifications

Section was enacted as part of the Water Quality Act of 1987, and not as part of the Federal Water Pollution Control Act, which comprises this chapter.

Definition

Administrator means the Administrator of the Environmental Protection Agency, see section 1(d) of Pub. L. No. 100–4, set out as a note under 33 U.S.C.A. § 1251.

§ 1255. Grants for research and development

[FWPCA § 105]

(a) Demonstration projects covering storm waters, advanced waste treatment and water purification methods, and joint treatment systems for municipal and industrial wastes

The Administrator is authorized to conduct in the Environmental Protection Agency, and to make grants to any State, municipality, or intermunicipal or interstate agency for the purpose of assisting in the development of—

(1) any project which will demonstrate a new or improved method of preventing, reducing, and eliminating the discharge into any waters of pollutants from sewers which carry storm water or both storm water and pollutants; or

(2) any project which will demonstrate advanced waste treatment and water purification methods (including the temporary use of new or improved chemical additives which provide substantial immediate improvements to existing treatment processes), or new or improved methods of joint treatment systems for municipal and industrial wastes;

and to include in such grants such amounts as are necessary for the purpose of reports, plans, and specifications in connection therewith.

(b) Demonstration projects for advanced treatment and environmental enhancement techniques to control pollution in river basins

The Administrator is authorized to make grants to any State or States or interstate agency to demonstrate, in river basins or portions thereof, advanced treatment and environmental enhancement techniques to control pollution from all sources, within such basins or portions thereof, including nonpoint sources, together with in stream[1] water quality improvement techniques.

(c) Research and demonstration projects for prevention of water pollution by industry

In order to carry out the purposes of section 1311 of this title, the Administrator is authorized to (1) conduct in the Environmental Protection Agency, (2) make grants to persons, and (3) enter into contracts with persons, for research and demonstration projects for prevention of pollution of any waters by industry including, but not limited to, the prevention, reduction, and elimination of the discharge of pollutants. No grant shall be made for any project under this subsection unless the Administrator determines that such project will develop or demonstrate a new or improved method of treating industrial wastes or otherwise prevent pollution by industry, which method shall have industrywide application.

(d) Accelerated and priority development of waste management and waste treatment methods and identification and measurement methods

In carrying out the provisions of this section, the Administrator shall conduct, on a priority basis, an accelerated effort to develop, refine, and achieve practical application of:

(1) waste management methods applicable to point and nonpoint sources of pollutants to eliminate the discharge of pollutants, including, but not limited to, elimination of runoff of pollutants and the effects of pollutants from inplace or accumulated sources;

(2) advanced waste treatment methods applicable to point and nonpoint sources, including inplace or accumulated sources of pollutants, and methods for reclaiming and recycling water and confining pollutants so they will not migrate to cause water or other environmental pollution; and

(3) improved methods and procedures to identify and measure the effects of pollutants on the chemical, physical, and biological integrity of water, including those pollutants created by new technological developments.

(e) Research and demonstration projects covering agricultural pollution and pollution from sewage in rural areas; dissemination of information

(1) The Administrator is authorized to (A) make, in consultation with the Secretary of Agriculture, grants to persons for research and demonstration projects with respect to new and improved methods of preventing, reducing, and eliminating pollution from agriculture, and (B) disseminate, in cooperation with the Secretary of Agriculture, such information obtained under this subsection, section 1254(p) of this title, and section 1314 of this title as will encourage and enable the adoption of such methods in the agricultural industry.

(2) The Administrator is authorized, (A) in consultation with other interested Federal agencies, to make grants for demonstration projects with respect to new and improved methods of preventing, reducing, storing, collecting, treating, or otherwise eliminating pollution from sewage in rural and other areas where collection of sewage in conventional, community-wide sewage collection systems is impractical, uneconomical, or otherwise infeasible, or where soil conditions or other factors preclude the use of septic tank and drainage field systems, and (B) in cooperation with other interested Federal and State agencies, to disseminate such information obtained under this subsection as will encourage and enable the adoption of new and improved methods developed pursuant to this subsection.

(f) Limitations

Federal grants under subsection (a) of this section shall be subject to the following limitations:

(1) No grant shall be made for any project unless such project shall have been approved by the appropriate State water pollution control agency or agencies and by the Administrator;

(2) No grant shall be made for any project in an amount exceeding 75 per centum of cost thereof as determined by the Administrator; and

(3) No grant shall be made for any project unless the Administrator determines that such project will serve as a useful demonstration for the purpose set forth in clause (1) or (2) of subsection (a) of this section.

(g) Maximum grants

Federal grants under subsections (c) and (d) of this section shall not exceed 75 per centum of the cost of the project.

(h) Authorization of appropriations

For the purpose of this section there is authorized to be appropriated $75,000,000 per fiscal year for the fiscal year ending June 30, 1973, the fiscal year ending June 30, 1974, and the fiscal year ending June 30, 1975, and from such appropriations at least 10 per centum of the funds actually appropriated in each fiscal year shall be available only for the purposes of subsection (e) of this section.

(i) Assistance for research and demonstration projects

The Administrator is authorized to make grants to a municipality to assist in the costs of operating and maintaining a project which received a grant under this section, section 1254 of this title, or section 1263 of this title prior to December 27, 1977, so as to reduce the operation and maintenance costs borne by the recipients of services from such project to costs comparable to those for projects assisted under subchapter II of this chapter.[1]

(j) Assistance for recycle, reuse, and land treatment projects

The Administrator is authorized to make a grant to any grantee who received an increased grant pursuant to section 1282(a)(2) of this title. Such grant may pay up to 100 per centum of the costs of technical evaluation of the operation of the treatment works, costs of training of persons (other than employees of the grantee), and costs of disseminating technical information on the operation of the treatment works.

(June 30, 1948, c. 758, Title I, § 105, as added by Pub. L. No. 92–500, § 2, 86 Stat. 825 (Oct. 18, 1972); and amended by Pub. L. No. 93–592, § 2, 88 Stat. 1925 (Jan. 2, 1975); Pub. L. No. 95–217, §§ 8, 9, 91 Stat. 1568 (Dec. 27, 1977).)

[1] So in original.

HISTORICAL AND STATUTORY NOTES

Transfer of Functions

Enforcement functions of Secretary or other official in Department of Agriculture, insofar as they involve lands and programs under jurisdiction of that Department, related to compliance with this chapter with respect to pre-construction, construction, and initial operation of transportation system for Canadian and Alaskan natural gas were transferred to the Federal Inspector, Office of Federal Inspector for the Alaska Natural Gas Transportation System, until the first anniversary of date of initial operation of the Alaska Natural Gas Transportation System, see Reorg. Plan No. 1 of 1979, §§ 102(f), 203(a), 44 Fed. Reg. 33663, 33666, 93 Stat. 1373, 1376, effective July 1, 1979, set out in Appendix 1 to Title 5, Government Organization and Employees.

§ 1256. Grants for pollution control programs

[FWPCA § 106]

(a) Authorization of appropriations for State and interstate programs

There are hereby authorized to be appropriated the following sums, to remain available until expended, to carry out the purposes of this section—

(1) $60,000,000 for the fiscal year ending June 30, 1973; and

(2) $75,000,000 for the fiscal year ending June 30, 1974, and the fiscal year ending June 30, 1975, $100,000,000 per fiscal year for the fiscal years 1977, 1978, 1979, and 1980, $75,000,000 per fiscal year for the fiscal years 1981 and 1982, such sums as may be necessary for fiscal years 1983 through 1985, and $75,000,000 per fiscal year for each of the fiscal years 1986 through 1990;

for grants to States and to interstate agencies to assist them in administering programs for the prevention, reduction, and elimination of pollution, including enforcement directly or through appropriate State law enforcement officers or agencies.

(b) Allotments

From the sums appropriated in any fiscal year, the Administrator shall make allotments to the several States and interstate agencies in accordance with regulations promulgated by him on the basis of the extent of the pollution problem in the respective States.

(c) Maximum annual payments

The Administrator is authorized to pay to each State and interstate agency each fiscal year either—

(1) the allotment of such State or agency for such fiscal year under subsection (b) of this section, or

(2) the reasonable costs as determined by the Administrator of developing and carrying out a pollution program by such State or agency during such fiscal year,

which ever amount is the lesser.

(d) Limitations

No grant shall be made under this section to any State or interstate agency for any fiscal year when the expenditure of non-Federal funds by such State or interstate agency during such fiscal year for the recurrent expenses of carrying out its pollution control program are less than the expenditure by such State or interstate agency of non-Federal funds for such recurrent program expenses during the fiscal year ending June 30, 1971.

(e) Grants prohibited to States not establishing water quality monitoring procedures or adequate emergency and contingency plans

Beginning in fiscal year 1974 the Administrator shall not make any grant under this section to any State which has not provided or is not carrying out as a part of its program—

(1) the establishment and operation of appropriate devices, methods, systems, and procedures necessary to monitor, and to compile and analyze data on (including classification according to eutrophic condition), the quality of navigable waters and to the extent practicable, ground waters including biological monitoring; and provision for annually updating such data and including it in the report required under section 1315 of this title;

(2) authority comparable to that in section 1364 of this title and adequate contingency plans to implement such authority.

(f) Conditions

Grants shall be made under this section on condition that—

(1) Such State (or interstate agency) files with the Administrator within one hundred and twenty days after October 18, 1972:

(A) a summary report of the current status of the State pollution control program, including the criteria used by the State in determining priority of treatment works; and

(B) such additional information, data, and reports as the Administrator may require.

(2) No federally assumed enforcement as defined in section 1319(a)(2) of this title is in effect with respect to such State or interstate agency.

(3) Such State (or interstate agency) submits within one hundred and twenty days after October 18, 1972, and before October 1 of each year thereafter for the Administrator's approval of its program for the prevention, reduction, and elimination of pollution in accordance with purposes and provisions of this chapter in such form and content as the Administrator may prescribe.

(g) Reallotment of unpaid allotments

Any sums allotted under subsection (b) of this section in any fiscal year which are not paid shall be reallotted by the Administrator in accordance with regulations promulgated by him.

(June 30, 1948, c. 758, Title I, § 106, as added by Pub. L. No. 92–500, § 2, 86 Stat. 827 (Oct. 18, 1972); and amended by Pub. L. No. 93–592, § 3, 88 Stat. 1925 (Jan. 2, 1975); Pub. L. No. 94–273, § 3(20), 90 Stat. 377 (Apr. 21, 1976); Pub. L. No. 95–217, § 4(c), 91 Stat. 1566 (Dec. 27, 1977); Pub. L. No. 96–483, § 1(b), 94 Stat. 2360 (Oct. 21, 1980); Pub. L. No. 100–4, Title I, § 101(b), 101 Stat. 9 (Feb. 4, 1987).)

§ 1257. Mine water pollution control demonstrations

[FWPCA § 107]

(a) Comprehensive approaches to elimination or control of mine water pollution

The Administrator in cooperation with the Appalachian Regional Commission and other Federal agencies is authorized to conduct, to make grants for, or to contract for, projects to demonstrate comprehensive approaches to the elimination or control of acid or other mine water pollution resulting from active or abandoned mining operations and other environmental pollution affecting water quality within all or part of a watershed or river basin, including siltation from surface mining. Such projects shall demonstrate the engineering and economic feasibility and practicality of various abatement techniques which will contribute substantially to effective and practical methods of acid or other mine water pollution elimination or control, and other pollution affecting water quality, including techniques that demonstrate the engineering and economic feasibility and practicality of using sewage sludge materials and other municipal wastes to diminish or prevent pollution affecting water quality from acid, sedimentation, or other pollutants and in such projects to restore affected lands to usefulness for forestry, agriculture, recreation, or other beneficial purposes.

(b) Consistency of projects with objectives of Appalachian Regional Development Act of 1965

Prior to undertaking any demonstration project under this section in the Appalachian region (as defined in section 14102 of Title 40), the Appalachian Regional Commission shall determine that such demonstration project is consistent with the objectives of subtitle IV of Title 40.

(c) Watershed selection

The Administrator, in selecting watersheds for the purposes of this section, shall be satisfied that the project area will not be affected adversely by the influx of acid or other mine water pollution from nearby sources.

(d) Conditions upon Federal participation

Federal participation in such projects shall be subject to the conditions—

(1) that the State shall acquire any land or interests therein necessary for such project; and

(2) that the State shall provide legal and practical protection to the project area to insure against any activities which will cause future acid or other mine water pollution.

(e) Authorization of appropriations

There is authorized to be appropriated $30,000,000 to carry out the provisions of this section, which sum shall be available until expended.

(June 30, 1948, c. 758, Title I, § 107, as added by Pub. L. No. 92–500, § 2, 86 Stat. 828 (Oct. 18, 1972).)

HISTORICAL AND STATUTORY NOTES

References in Text

Subtitle IV of Title 40, referred to in subsec. (b), is chapters 141, 143, 145, and 147 of Title 40, 40 U.S.C.A. §§ 14101 et seq., 14301 et seq., 14501 et seq., and 14701 et seq., respectively.

Codifications

In subsec. (b), "section 14102 of Title 40" substituted for "section 403 of the Appalachian Regional Development Act of 1965, as amended [40 App.U.S.C.A. § 403]" and "subtitle IV of Title 40" substituted for "the Appalachian Regional Development Act of 1965, as amended [40 App.U.S.C.A. § 1 et seq.]" on authority of Pub. L. No. 107–217, § 5(c), 116 Stat. 1301 (Aug. 21, 2002), which is set out as a note preceding 40 U.S.C.A. § 101. Pub. L. No. 107–217, § 1, enacted Title 40 into positive law. The Appalachian Regional Development Act of 1965, is Pub. L. No. 89–4, 79 Stat. 5 (Mar. 9, 1965), as amended, which was repealed by Pub. L. No. 107–217, § 6(b), 116 Stat. 1317 (Aug. 21, 2002), and its substance reenacted as subtitle IV of Title 40, consisting of chapters 141, 143, 145, and 147 of Title 40, 40 U.S.C.A. §§ 14101 et seq., 14301 et seq., 14501 et seq., and 14701 et seq., respectively. Former 40 U.S.C.A. § 403 was reenacted as 40 U.S.C.A. § 14102.

§ 1257a. State demonstration programs for cleanup of abandoned mines for use as waste disposal sites; authorization of appropriations

The Administrator of the Environmental Protection Agency is authorized to make grants to States to undertake a demonstration program for the cleanup of State-owned abandoned mines which can be used as hazardous waste disposal sites. The State shall pay 10 per centum of project costs. At a minimum, the Administrator shall undertake projects under such program in the States of Ohio, Illinois, and West Virginia. There are authorized to be appropriated $10,000,000 per fiscal year for each of the fiscal years ending September 30, 1982, September 30, 1983, and September 30, 1984, to carry out this section. Such projects shall be undertaken in accordance with all applicable laws and regulations.

(Pub. L. No. 96–483, § 12, 94 Stat. 2363 (Oct. 21, 1980).)

HISTORICAL AND STATUTORY NOTES

Codifications

This section was not enacted as part of the Federal Water Pollution Control Act, which comprises this chapter.

§ 1258. Pollution control in the Great Lakes

[FWPCA § 108]

(a) Demonstration projects

The Administrator, in cooperation with other Federal departments, agencies, and instrumentalities is authorized to enter into agreements with any State, political subdivision, interstate agency, or other public agency, or combination thereof, to carry out one or more projects to demonstrate new methods and techniques and to develop preliminary plans for the elimination or control of pollution, within all or any part of the watersheds of the Great Lakes. Such projects shall demonstrate the engineering and economic feasibility and practicality of removal of pollutants and prevention of any polluting matter from entering into the Great Lakes in the future and other reduction and remedial techniques which will contribute substantially to effective and practical methods of pollution prevention, reduction, or elimination.

(b) Conditions of Federal participation

Federal participation in such projects shall be subject to the condition that the State, political subdivision, interstate agency, or other public agency, or combination thereof, shall pay not less than 25 per centum of the actual project costs, which payment may be in any form, including, but not limited to, land or interests therein that is needed for the project, and personal property or services the value of which shall be determined by the Administrator.

(c) Authorization of appropriations

There is authorized to be appropriated $20,000,000 to carry out the provisions of subsections (a) and (b) of this section, which sum shall be available until expended.

(d) Lake Erie demonstration program

(1) In recognition of the serious conditions which exist in Lake Erie, the Secretary of the Army, acting through the Chief of Engineers, is directed to design and develop a demonstration waste water management program for the rehabilitation and environmental repair of Lake Erie. Prior to the initiation of detailed engineering and design, the program, along with the specific recommendations of the Chief of Engineers, and recommendations for its financing, shall be submitted to the Congress for statutory approval. This authority is in addition to, and not in lieu of, other waste water studies aimed at eliminating pollution emanating from select sources around Lake Erie.

(2) This program is to be developed in cooperation with the Environmental Protection Agency, other interested departments, agencies, and instrumentalities of the Federal Government, and the States and their political subdivisions. This program shall set forth alternative systems for managing waste water on a regional basis and shall provide local and State governments with a range of choice as to the type of system to be used for the treatment of waste water. These alternative systems shall include both advanced waste treatment technology and land disposal systems including aerated treatment-spray irrigation technology and will also include provisions for the disposal of solid wastes, including sludge. Such program should include measures to control point sources of pollution, area sources of pollution, including acid-mine drainage, urban runoff and rural runoff, and in place sources of pollution, including bottom loads, sludge banks, and polluted harbor dredgings.

(e) Authorization of appropriations for Lake Erie demonstration program

There is authorized to be appropriated $5,000,000 to carry out the provisions of subsection (d) of this section, which sum shall be available until expended.

(June 30, 1948, c. 758, Title I, § 108, as added by Pub. L. No. 92–500, § 2, 86 Stat. 828 (Oct. 18, 1972).)

§ 1259. Training grants and contracts

[FWPCA § 109]

(a) The Administrator is authorized to make grants to or contracts with institutions of higher education, or combinations of such institutions, to assist them in planning, developing, strengthening, improving, or carrying out programs or projects for the preparation of undergraduate students to enter an occupation which involves the design, operation, and maintenance of treatment works, and other facilities whose purpose is water quality control. Such grants or contracts may include payment of all or part of the cost of programs or projects such as—

(A) planning for the development or expansion of programs or projects for training persons in the operation and maintenance of treatment works;

(B) training and retraining of faculty members;

(C) conduct of short-term or regular session institutes for study by persons engaged in, or preparing to engage in, the preparation of students preparing to enter an occupation involving the operation and maintenance of treatment works;

(D) carrying out innovative and experimental programs of cooperative education involving alternate periods of full-time or part-time academic study at the institution and periods of full-time or part-time employment involving the operation and maintenance of treatment works; and

(E) research into, and development of, methods of training students or faculty, including the preparation of teaching materials and the planning of curriculum.

(b) **(1)** The Administrator may pay 100 per centum of any additional cost of construction of treatment works required for a facility to train and upgrade waste treatment works operation and maintenance personnel and for the costs of other State treatment works operator training programs, including mobile training units, classroom rental, specialized instructors, and instructional material.

(2) The Administrator shall make no more than one grant for such additional construction in any State (to serve a group of States, where, in his judgment, efficient training programs require multi-State programs), and shall make such grant after consultation with and approval by the State or States on the basis of (A) the suitability of such facility for training operation and maintenance personnel for treatment works throughout such State or States; and (B) a commitment by the State agency or agencies to carry out at such facility a program of training approved by the Administrator. In any case where a grant is made to serve two or more States, the Administrator is authorized to make an additional grant for a supplemental facility in each such State.

(3) The Administrator may make such grant out of the sums allocated to a State under section 1285 of this title, except that in no event shall the Federal cost of any such training facilities exceed $500,000.

(4) The Administrator may exempt a grant under this section from any requirement under section 1284(a)(3) of this title. Any grantee who received a grant under this section prior to enactment of the Clean Water Act of 1977 shall be eligible to have its grant increased by funds made available under such Act.

(June 30, 1948, c. 758, Title I, § 109, as added by Pub. L. No. 92–500, § 2, 86 Stat. 829 (Oct. 18, 1972); and amended by Pub. L. No. 95–217, § 10, 91 Stat. 1568 (Dec. 27, 1977).)

HISTORICAL AND STATUTORY NOTES

References in Text

Prior to the date of enactment of the Clean Water Act of 1977, referred to in subsec. (b)(4), means prior to the enactment of Pub. L. No. 95–217, 91 Stat. 1566 (Dec. 27, 1977), which was approved Dec. 27, 1977.

Such Act, referred to in subsec. (b)(4), means Pub. L. No. 95–217, 91 Stat. 1566 (Dec. 27, 1977), as amended, known as the Clean Water Act of 1977. For complete classification of this Act to the Code, see Short Title of 1977 Amendment note set out under section 1251 of this title and Tables volume.

§ 1260. Applications; allocation

[FWPCA § 110]

(1) A grant or contract authorized by section 1259 of this title may be made only upon application to the Administrator at such time or times and containing such information as he may prescribe, except that no such application shall be approved unless it—

(A) sets forth programs, activities, research, or development for which a grant is authorized under section 1259 of this title and describes the relation to any program set forth by the applicant in an application, if any, submitted pursuant to section 1261 of this title;

(B) provides such fiscal control and fund accounting procedures as may be necessary to assure proper disbursement of and accounting for Federal funds paid to the applicant under this section; and

(C) provides for making such reports, in such form and containing such information, as the Administrator may require to carry out his functions under this section, and for keeping such records and for affording such access thereto as the Administrator may find necessary to assure the correctness and verification of such reports.

(2) The Administrator shall allocate grants or contracts under section 1259 of this title in such manner as will most nearly provide an equitable distribution of the grants or contracts throughout the United States among institutions of higher education which show promise of being able to use funds effectively for the purpose of this section.

(3) (A) Payments under this section may be used in accordance with regulations of the Administrator, and subject to the terms and conditions set forth in an application approved under paragraph (1), to pay part of the compensation of students employed in connection with the operation and maintenance of treatment works, other than as an employee in connection with the operation and maintenance of treatment works or as an employee in any branch of the Government of the United States, as part of a program for which a grant has been approved pursuant to this section.

(B) Departments and agencies of the United States are encouraged, to the extent consistent with efficient administration, to enter into arrangements with institutions of higher education for the full-time, part-time, or temporary employment, whether in the competitive or excepted service, of students enrolled in programs set forth in applications approved under paragraph (1).

(June 30, 1948, c. 758, Title I, § 110, as added by Pub. L. No. 92–500, § 2, 86 Stat. 830 (Oct. 18, 1972).)

§ 1261. Scholarships

[FWPCA § 111]

(1) The Administrator is authorized to award scholarships in accordance with the provisions of this section for undergraduate study by persons who plan to enter an occupation involving the operation and maintenance of treatment works. Such scholarships shall be awarded for such periods as the Administrator may determine but not to exceed four academic years.

(2) The Administrator shall allocate scholarships under this section among institutions of higher education with programs approved under the provisions of this section for the use of individuals accepted into such programs in such manner and according to such plan as will insofar as practicable—

(A) provide an equitable distribution of such scholarships throughout the United States; and

(B) attract recent graduates of secondary schools to enter an occupation involving the operation and maintenance of treatment works.

(3) The Administrator shall approve a program of any institution of higher education for the purposes of this section only upon application by the institution and only upon his finding—

(A) that such program has a principal objective the education and training of persons in the operation and maintenance of treatment works;

(B) that such program is in effect and of high quality, or can be readily put into effect and may reasonably be expected to be of high quality;

(C) that the application describes the relation of such program to any program, activity, research, or development set forth by the applicant in an application, if any, submitted pursuant to section 1260 of this title; and

(D) that the application contains satisfactory assurances that (i) the institution will recommend to the Administrator for the award of scholarships under this section, for study in such program, only persons who have demonstrated to the satisfaction of the institution a serious intent, upon completing the program, to enter an occupation involving the operation and maintenance of treatment works, and (ii) the institution will make reasonable continuing efforts to encourage recipients of scholarships under this section, enrolled in such program, to enter occupations involving the operation and maintenance of treatment works upon completing the program.

(4) (A) The Administrator shall pay to persons awarded scholarships under this section such stipends (including such allowances for subsistence and other expenses for such persons and their dependents) as he may determine to be consistent with prevailing practices under comparable federally supported programs.

(B) The Administrator shall (in addition to the stipends paid to persons under paragraph (1)) pay to the institution of higher education at which such person is pursuing his course of study such amount as he may determine to be consistent with prevailing practices under comparable federally supported programs.

(5) A person awarded a scholarship under the provisions of this section shall continue to receive the payments provided in this section only during such periods as the Administrator finds that he is maintaining satisfactory proficiency and devoting full time to study or research in the field in which such scholarship was awarded in an institution of higher education, and is not engaging in gainful employment other than employment approved by the Administrator by or pursuant to regulation.

(6) The Administrator shall by regulation provide that any person awarded a scholarship under this section shall agree in writing to enter and remain in an occupation involving the design, operation, or maintenance of treatment works for such period after completion of his course of studies as the Administrator determines appropriate.

(June 30, 1948, c. 758, Title I, § 111, as added by Pub. L. No. 92–500, § 2, 86 Stat. 831 (Oct. 18, 1972).)

§ 1262. Definitions and authorizations

[FWPCA § 112]

(a) As used in sections 1259 through 1262 of this title—

(1) The term "institution of higher education" means an educational institution described in the first sentence of section 1001 of Title 20 (other than an institution of any agency of the United States) which is accredited by a nationally recognized accrediting agency or association approved by the Administrator for this purpose. For purposes of this subsection, the Administrator shall publish a list of nationally recognized accrediting agencies or associations which he determines to be reliable authority as to the quality of training offered.

(2) The term "academic year" means an academic year or its equivalent, as determined by the Administrator.

(b) The Administrator shall annually report his activities under sections 1259 through 1262 of this title, including recommendations for needed revisions in the provisions thereof.

(c) There are authorized to be appropriated $25,000,000 per fiscal year for the fiscal years ending June 30, 1973, June 30, 1974, and June 30, 1975, $6,000,000 for the fiscal year ending September 30, 1977, $7,000,000 for the fiscal year ending September 30, 1978, $7,000,000 for the fiscal year ending September 30, 1979, $7,000,000 for the fiscal year ending September 30, 1980, $7,000,000 for the fiscal year ending September 30, 1981, $7,000,000 for the fiscal year ending September 30, 1982, such sums as may be necessary for fiscal years 1983 through 1985, and $7,000,000 per fiscal year for each of the fiscal years 1986 through 1990, to carry out sections 1259 through 1262 of this title.

(June 30, 1948, c. 758, Title I, § 112, as added by Pub. L. No. 92–500, § 2, 86 Stat. 832 (Oct. 18, 1972); and amended by Pub. L. No. 93–592, § 4, 88 Stat. 1925 (Jan. 2, 1975); Pub. L. No. 95–217, § 4(d), 91 Stat. 1566 (Dec. 27, 1977); Pub. L. No. 96–483, § 1(c), 94 Stat. 2360 (Oct. 21, 1980); Pub. L. No. 100–4, Title I, § 101(c), 101 Stat. 9 (Feb. 4, 1987); Pub. L. No. 105–244, Title I, § 102(a)(11) (Oct. 7, 1998).)

HISTORICAL AND STATUTORY NOTES

Effective and Applicability Provisions

1998 Acts. Amendment by Pub. L. No. 105–244 effective Oct. 1, 1998, except as otherwise provided, see section 3 of Pub. L. No. 105–244, set out as a note under section 1001 of Title 20.

§ 1263. Alaska village demonstration projects

[FWPCA § 113]

(a) Central community facilities for safe water; elimination or control of pollution

The Administrator is authorized to enter into agreements with the State of Alaska to carry out one or more projects to demonstrate methods to provide for central community facilities for safe water and elimination or control of pollution in those native villages of Alaska without such facilities. Such project shall include provisions for community safe water supply systems, toilets, bathing and laundry facilities, sewage disposal facilities, and other similar facilities, and educational and informational facilities and programs relating to health and hygiene. Such demonstration projects shall be for the further purpose of developing preliminary plans for providing such safe water and such elimination or control of pollution for all native villages in such State.

(b) Utilization of personnel and facilities of Department of Health and Human Services

In carrying out this section the Administrator shall cooperate with the Secretary of Health and Human Services for the purpose of utilizing such of the personnel and facilities of that Department as may be appropriate.

(c) Omitted

(d) Authorization of appropriations

There is authorized to be appropriated not to exceed $2,000,000 to carry out this section. In addition, there is authorized to be appropriated to carry out this section not to exceed $200,000 for the fiscal year ending September 30, 1978, and $220,000 for the fiscal year ending September 30, 1979.

(e) Study to develop comprehensive program for achieving sanitation services; report to Congress

The Administrator is authorized to coordinate with the Secretary of the Department of Health and Human Services, the Secretary of the Department of Housing and Urban Development, the Secretary of the Department of the Interior, the Secretary of the Department of Agriculture, and the heads of any other departments or agencies he may deem appropriate to conduct a joint study with representatives of the State of Alaska and the appropriate Native organizations (as defined in Public Law 92–203) to develop a comprehensive program for achieving adequate sanitation services in Alaska villages. This study shall be coordinated with the programs and projects authorized by sections 1254(q) and 1255(e)(2) of this title. The Administrator shall submit a report of the results of the study, together with appropriate supporting data and such recommendations as he deems desirable, to the Committee on Environment and Public Works of the Senate and to the Committee on Public Works and Transportation of the House of Representatives not later than December 31, 1979. The Administrator shall also submit recommended administrative actions, procedures, and any proposed legislation necessary to implement the recommendations of the study no later than June 30, 1980.

(f) Technical, financial, and management assistance

The Administrator is authorized to provide technical, financial and management assistance for operation and maintenance of the demonstration projects constructed under this section, until such time as the recommendations of subsection (e) of this section are implemented.

(g) "Village" and "sanitation services" defined

For the purpose of this section, the term "village" shall mean an incorporated or unincorporated community with a population of ten to six hundred people living within a two-mile radius. The term "sanitation services" shall mean water supply, sewage disposal, solid waste disposal and other services necessary to maintain generally accepted standards of personal hygiene and public health.

(June 30, 1948, c. 758, Title I, § 113, as added by Pub. L. No. 92–500, § 2, 86 Stat. 832 (Oct. 18, 1972); and amended by Pub. L. No. 95–217, § 11, 91 Stat. 1568 (Dec. 27, 1977); Pub. L. No. 96–88, Title V, § 509(b), 93 Stat. 695 (Oct. 17, 1979).)

HISTORICAL AND STATUTORY NOTES

References in Text

Public Law 92–203, referred to in subsec. (e), is Pub. L. No. 92–203, 85 Stat. 688 (Dec. 18, 1971), as amended, known as the Alaska Native Claims Settlement Act, which is codified generally to chapter 33 (section 1601 et seq.)

of Title 43, Public Lands. For complete classification of this Act to the Code, see Short Title note set out under section 1601 of Title 43 and Tables.

Codifications

Subsec. (c), authorized the Administrator to report to Congress the results of the demonstration project accompanied by his recommendations for the establishment of a statewide project not later than July 1, 1973.

Change of Name

"Secretary of Health and Human Services" was substituted for "Secretary of Health, Education, and Welfare" in subsec. (b), and "Secretary of the Department of Health and Human Services" was substituted for "Secretary of the Department of Health, Education, and Welfare" in subsec. (e), pursuant to section 509(b) of Pub. L. 96–88 which is codified as section 3508(b) of Title 20, Education.

Any reference in any provision of law enacted before Jan. 4, 1995, to the Committee on Public Works and Transportation of the House of Representatives treated as referring to the Committee on Transportation and Infrastructure of the House of Representatives, see section 1(a)(9) of Pub. L. No. 104–14, set out as a note preceding section 21 of Title 2, The Congress.

Corps Capability Study, Alaska

Pub. L. No. 104–303, Title IV, § 401, 110 Stat. 3740 (Oct. 12, 1996), provided that: "Not later than 18 months after the date of the enactment of this Act [Oct. 12, 1996], the Secretary shall report to Congress on the advisability and capability of the Corps of Engineers to implement rural sanitation projects for rural and Native villages in Alaska."

§ 1263a. Grants to Alaska to improve sanitation in rural and Native villages

(a) In general

The Administrator of the Environmental Protection Agency may make grants to the State of Alaska for the benefit of rural and Native villages in Alaska to pay the Federal share of the cost of—

(1) the development and construction of public water systems and wastewater systems to improve the health and sanitation conditions in the villages; and

(2) training, technical assistance, and educational programs relating to the operation and management of sanitation services in rural and Native villages.

(b) Federal share

The Federal share of the cost of the activities described in subsection (a) of this section shall be 50 percent.

(c) Administrative expenses

The State of Alaska may use an amount not to exceed 4 percent of any grant made available under this subsection[1] for administrative expenses necessary to carry out the activities described in subsection (a) of this section.

(d) Consultation with the State of Alaska

The Administrator shall consult with the State of Alaska on a method of prioritizing the allocation of grants under subsection (a) of this section according to the needs of, and relative health and sanitation conditions in, each eligible village.

(e) Authorization of appropriations

There are authorized to be appropriated to carry out this section $40,000,000 for each of fiscal years 2001 through 2005.

(Pub. L. No. 104–182, Title III, § 303, 110 Stat. 1683 (Aug. 6, 1996); as amended by Pub. L. No. 106–457, Title IX, § 903, 114 Stat. 1982 (Nov. 7, 2000).)

[1] So in original. Probably should be "section".

HISTORICAL AND STATUTORY NOTES

Codifications

This section was enacted as part of the Safe Drinking Water Act Amendments of 1996, and not as part of The Federal Water Pollution Control Act, which comprises this chapter.

Effective and Applicability Provisions

1996 Acts. Section effective Aug. 6, 1996, except as otherwise specifically provided, see section 2(b) of Pub. L. No. 104–182, set out as a note under section 300f of Title 42, The Public Health and Welfare.

§ 1264. Omitted

HISTORICAL AND STATUTORY NOTES

Codifications

Section, Act of June 30, 1948, c. 758, Title I, § 114, as added by Pub. L. No. 92–500, § 2, 86 Stat. 833 (Oct. 18, 1972), authorized the Administrator, in consultation with the Tahoe Regional Planning Agency, the Secretary of Agriculture, other Federal agencies, representatives of State and local governments, and members of the public, to conduct a thorough and complete study on the need of extending Federal oversight and control in order to preserve the fragile ecology of Lake Tahoe and to report the results of this study to Congress not later than one year after Oct. 18, 1972.

§ 1265. In-place toxic pollutants

[FWPCA § 115]

The Administrator is directed to identify the location of in-place pollutants with emphasis on toxic pollutants in harbors and navigable waterways and is authorized, acting through the Secretary of the Army, to make contracts for the removal and appropriate disposal of such materials from critical port and harbor areas. There is authorized to be appropriated $15,000,000 to carry out the provisions of this section, which sum shall be available until expended.

(June 30, 1948, c. 758, Title I, § 115, as added by Pub. L. No. 92–500, § 2, 86 Stat. 833 (Oct. 18, 1972).)

§ 1266. Hudson River reclamation demonstration project

[FWPCA § 116]

(a) The Administrator is authorized to enter into contracts and other agreements with the State of New York to carry out a project to demonstrate methods for the selective removal of polychlorinated biphenyls contaminating bottom sediments of the Hudson River, treating such sediments as required, burying such sediments in secure landfills, and installing monitoring systems for such landfills. Such demonstration project shall be for the purpose of determining the feasibility of indefinite storage in secure landfills of toxic substances and of ascertaining the improvement of the rate of recovery of a toxic contaminated national waterway. No pollutants removed pursuant to this paragraph shall be placed in any landfill unless the Administrator first determines that disposal of the pollutants in such landfill would provide a higher standard of protection of the public health, safety, and welfare than disposal of such pollutants by any other method including, but not limited to, incineration or a chemical destruction process.

(b) The Administrator is authorized to make grants to the State of New York to carry out this section from funds allotted to such State under section 1285(a) of this title, except that the amount of any such grant shall be equal to 75 per centum of the cost of the project and such grant shall be made on condition that non-Federal sources provide the remainder of the cost of such project. The authority of this section shall be available until September 30, 1983. Funds allotted to the State of New York under section 1285(a) of this title shall be available under this subsection only to the extent that funds are not available, as determined by the Administrator, to the State of New York for the work authorized by this section under section 1265 or 1321 of this title or a comprehensive hazardous substance response and clean up fund. Any funds used under the authority of this subsection shall be deducted from any estimate of the needs of the State of New

York prepared under section 1375(b) of this title. The Administrator may not obligate or expend more than $20,000,000 to carry out this section.

(June 30, 1948, c. 758, Title I, § 116, as added by Pub. L. No. 96–483, § 10, 94 Stat. 2363 (Oct. 21, 1980); and amended by Pub. L. No. 105–362, Title V, § 501(d)(2)(B), 112 Stat. 3284 (Nov. 10, 1998); Pub. L. No. 107–303, Title III, § 302(b)(1), 116 Stat. 2361 (Nov. 27, 2002).)

HISTORICAL AND STATUTORY NOTES

Effective and Applicability Provisions

2002 Acts. Effective November 10, 1998, section 501 of the Federal Reports Elimination Act of 1998 [Pub. L. No. 105–362, Title V, § 501, 112 Stat. 3283 (Nov. 10, 1998)] is amended by striking subsections (a), (b), (c), and (d) [amending this section and others, see Tables for complete classification]. The Federal Water Pollution Control Act (33 U.S.C.A. § 1254(n)(3)) shall be applied and administered on and after Nov. 27, 2002 as if the amendments made by subsections (a), (b), (c), and (d) of Pub. L. No. 105–362, § 501, had not been enacted, see Pub. L. No. 107–303, § 302(b)(2), set out as a note under 33 U.S.C.A. § 1254.

§ 1267. Chesapeake Bay

[FWPCA § 117]

(a) Definitions

In this section, the following definitions apply:

(1) Administrative cost

The term “administrative cost” means the cost of salaries and fringe benefits incurred in administering a grant under this section.

(2) Chesapeake Bay Agreement

The term “Chesapeake Bay Agreement” means the formal, voluntary agreements executed to achieve the goal of restoring and protecting the Chesapeake Bay ecosystem and the living resources of the Chesapeake Bay ecosystem and signed by the Chesapeake Executive Council.

(3) Chesapeake Bay ecosystem

The term “Chesapeake Bay ecosystem” means the ecosystem of the Chesapeake Bay and its watershed.

(4) Chesapeake Bay Program

The term “Chesapeake Bay Program” means the program directed by the Chesapeake Executive Council in accordance with the Chesapeake Bay Agreement.

(5) Chesapeake Executive Council

The term “Chesapeake Executive Council” means the signatories to the Chesapeake Bay Agreement.

(6) Signatory jurisdiction

The term “signatory jurisdiction” means a jurisdiction of a signatory to the Chesapeake Bay Agreement.

(b) Continuation of Chesapeake Bay Program

(1) In general

In cooperation with the Chesapeake Executive Council (and as a member of the Council), the Administrator shall continue the Chesapeake Bay Program.

(2) **Program Office**

(A) **In general**

The Administrator shall maintain in the Environmental Protection Agency a Chesapeake Bay Program Office.

(B) **Function**

The Chesapeake Bay Program Office shall provide support to the Chesapeake Executive Council by—

(i) implementing and coordinating science, research, modeling, support services, monitoring, data collection, and other activities that support the Chesapeake Bay Program;

(ii) developing and making available, through publications, technical assistance, and other appropriate means, information pertaining to the environmental quality and living resources of the Chesapeake Bay ecosystem;

(iii) in cooperation with appropriate Federal, State, and local authorities, assisting the signatories to the Chesapeake Bay Agreement in developing and implementing specific action plans to carry out the responsibilities of the signatories to the Chesapeake Bay Agreement;

(iv) coordinating the actions of the Environmental Protection Agency with the actions of the appropriate officials of other Federal agencies and State and local authorities in developing strategies to—

(I) improve the water quality and living resources in the Chesapeake Bay ecosystem; and

(II) obtain the support of the appropriate officials of the agencies and authorities in achieving the objectives of the Chesapeake Bay Agreement; and

(v) implementing outreach programs for public information, education, and participation to foster stewardship of the resources of the Chesapeake Bay.

(c) **Interagency agreements**

The Administrator may enter into an interagency agreement with a Federal agency to carry out this section.

(d) **Technical assistance and assistance grants**

(1) **In general**

In cooperation with the Chesapeake Executive Council, the Administrator may provide technical assistance, and assistance grants, to nonprofit organizations, State and local governments, colleges, universities, and interstate agencies to carry out this section, subject to such terms and conditions as the Administrator considers appropriate.

(2) **Federal share**

(A) **In general**

Except as provided in subparagraph (B), the Federal share of an assistance grant provided under paragraph (1) shall be determined by the Administrator in accordance with guidance issued by the Administrator.

(B) **Small watershed grants program**

The Federal share of an assistance grant provided under paragraph (1) to carry out an implementing activity under subsection (g)(2) of this section shall not exceed 75 percent of eligible project costs, as determined by the Administrator.

(3) Non-Federal share

An assistance grant under paragraph (1) shall be provided on the condition that non-Federal sources provide the remainder of eligible project costs, as determined by the Administrator.

(4) Administrative costs

Administrative costs shall not exceed 10 percent of the annual grant award.

(e) Implementation and monitoring grants

(1) In general

If a signatory jurisdiction has approved and committed to implement all or substantially all aspects of the Chesapeake Bay Agreement, on the request of the chief executive of the jurisdiction, the Administrator—

(A) shall make a grant to the jurisdiction for the purpose of implementing the management mechanisms established under the Chesapeake Bay Agreement, subject to such terms and conditions as the Administrator considers appropriate; and

(B) may make a grant to a signatory jurisdiction for the purpose of monitoring the Chesapeake Bay ecosystem.

(2) Proposals

(A) In general

A signatory jurisdiction described in paragraph (1) may apply for a grant under this subsection for a fiscal year by submitting to the Administrator a comprehensive proposal to implement management mechanisms established under the Chesapeake Bay Agreement.

(B) Contents

A proposal under subparagraph (A) shall include—

(i) a description of proposed management mechanisms that the jurisdiction commits to take within a specified time period, such as reducing or preventing pollution in the Chesapeake Bay and its watershed or meeting applicable water quality standards or established goals and objectives under the Chesapeake Bay Agreement; and

(ii) the estimated cost of the actions proposed to be taken during the fiscal year.

(3) Approval

If the Administrator finds that the proposal is consistent with the Chesapeake Bay Agreement and the national goals established under section 1251(a) of this title, the Administrator may approve the proposal for an award.

(4) Federal share

The Federal share of a grant under this subsection shall not exceed 50 percent of the cost of implementing the management mechanisms during the fiscal year.

(5) Non-Federal share

A grant under this subsection shall be made on the condition that non-Federal sources provide the remainder of the costs of implementing the management mechanisms during the fiscal year.

(6) Administrative costs

Administrative costs shall not exceed 10 percent of the annual grant award.

(7) Reporting

On or before October 1 of each fiscal year, the Administrator shall make available to the public a document that lists and describes, in the greatest practicable degree of detail—

(A) all projects and activities funded for the fiscal year;

(B) the goals and objectives of projects funded for the previous fiscal year; and

(C) the net benefits of projects funded for previous fiscal years.

(f) Federal facilities and budget coordination

(1) Subwatershed planning and restoration

A Federal agency that owns or operates a facility (as defined by the Administrator) within the Chesapeake Bay watershed shall participate in regional and subwatershed planning and restoration programs.

(2) Compliance with Agreement

The head of each Federal agency that owns or occupies real property in the Chesapeake Bay watershed shall ensure that the property, and actions taken by the agency with respect to the property, comply with the Chesapeake Bay Agreement, the Federal Agencies Chesapeake Ecosystem Unified Plan, and any subsequent agreements and plans.

(3) Budget coordination

(A) In general

As part of the annual budget submission of each Federal agency with projects or grants related to restoration, planning, monitoring, or scientific investigation of the Chesapeake Bay ecosystem, the head of the agency shall submit to the President a report that describes plans for the expenditure of the funds under this section.

(B) Disclosure to the Council

The head of each agency referred to in subparagraph (A) shall disclose the report under that subparagraph with the Chesapeake Executive Council as appropriate.

(g) Chesapeake Bay Program

(1) Management strategies

The Administrator, in coordination with other members of the Chesapeake Executive Council, shall ensure that management plans are developed and implementation is begun by signatories to the Chesapeake Bay Agreement to achieve and maintain—

(A) the nutrient goals of the Chesapeake Bay Agreement for the quantity of nitrogen and phosphorus entering the Chesapeake Bay and its watershed;

(B) the water quality requirements necessary to restore living resources in the Chesapeake Bay ecosystem;

(C) the Chesapeake Bay Basinwide Toxins Reduction and Prevention Strategy goal of reducing or eliminating the input of chemical contaminants from all controllable sources to levels that result in no toxic or bioaccumulative impact on the living resources of the Chesapeake Bay ecosystem or on human health;

(D) habitat restoration, protection, creation, and enhancement goals established by Chesapeake Bay Agreement signatories for wetlands, riparian forests, and other types of habitat associated with the Chesapeake Bay ecosystem; and

(E) the restoration, protection, creation, and enhancement goals established by the Chesapeake Bay Agreement signatories for living resources associated with the Chesapeake Bay ecosystem.

(2) Small watershed grants program

The Administrator, in cooperation with the Chesapeake Executive Council, shall—

(A) establish a small watershed grants program as part of the Chesapeake Bay Program; and

(B) offer technical assistance and assistance grants under subsection (d) of this section to local governments and nonprofit organizations and individuals in the Chesapeake Bay region to implement—

(i) cooperative tributary basin strategies that address the water quality and living resource needs in the Chesapeake Bay ecosystem; and

(ii) locally based protection and restoration programs or projects within a watershed that complement the tributary basin strategies, including the creation, restoration, protection, or enhancement of habitat associated with the Chesapeake Bay ecosystem.

(h) Study of Chesapeake Bay Program

(1) In general

Not later than April 22, 2003, and every 5 years thereafter, the Administrator, in coordination with the Chesapeake Executive Council, shall complete a study and submit to Congress a comprehensive report on the results of the study.

(2) Requirements

The study and report shall—

(A) assess the state of the Chesapeake Bay ecosystem;

(B) compare the current state of the Chesapeake Bay ecosystem with its state in 1975, 1985, and 1995;

(C) assess the effectiveness of management strategies being implemented on November 7, 2000, and the extent to which the priority needs are being met;

(D) make recommendations for the improved management of the Chesapeake Bay Program either by strengthening strategies being implemented on November 7, 2000, or by adopting new strategies; and

(E) be presented in such a format as to be readily transferable to and usable by other watershed restoration programs.

(i) Special study of living resource response

(1) In general

Not later than 180 days after November 7, 2000, the Administrator shall commence a 5-year special study with full participation of the scientific community of the Chesapeake Bay to establish and expand understanding of the response of the living resources of the Chesapeake Bay ecosystem to improvements in water quality that have resulted from investments made through the Chesapeake Bay Program.

(2) Requirements

The study shall—

(A) determine the current status and trends of living resources, including grasses, benthos, phytoplankton, zooplankton, fish, and shellfish;

(B) establish to the extent practicable the rates of recovery of the living resources in response to improved water quality condition;

(C) evaluate and assess interactions of species, with particular attention to the impact of changes within and among trophic levels; and

(D) recommend management actions to optimize the return of a healthy and balanced ecosystem in response to improvements in the quality and character of the waters of the Chesapeake Bay.

(3) Annual Survey.—The Administrator shall carry out an annual survey of sea grasses in the Chesapeake Bay.

(j) Authorization of Appropriations.—There are authorized to be appropriated to carry out this section—

(1) for fiscal year 2021, $90,000,000;

(2) for fiscal year 2022, $90,500,000;

(3) for fiscal year 2023, $91,000,000;

(4) for fiscal year 2024, $91,500,000; and

(5) for fiscal year 2025, $92,000,000.

(June 30, 1948, c. 758, Title I, § 117, as added by Pub. L. No. 100–4, Title I, § 103, 101 Stat. 10 (Feb. 4, 1987); and amended by Pub. L. No. 106–457, Title II, § 203, 114 Stat. 1967 (Nov. 7, 2000); Pub. L. No. 114–322, § 5007, 130 Stat 1896 (Dec. 16, 2016); Pub. L. No. 116–188, § 109, 134 Stat. 905, 920 (Oct. 30, 2020).)

HISTORICAL AND STATUTORY NOTES

Codifications

November 7, 2000, referred to in subsecs. (h)(2)(C), (D), and (i)(1), originally read "the date of enactment of this section", which was translated as meaning the date of enactment of Pub. L. No. 106–457, which amended this section generally, to reflect the probable intent of Congress.

Findings and Purposes

Pub. L. No. 106–457, Title II, § 202, 114 Stat. 1967 (Nov. 7, 2000), provided that:

"(a) Findings.—Congress finds that—

"(1) the Chesapeake Bay is a national treasure and a resource of worldwide significance;

"(2) over many years, the productivity and water quality of the Chesapeake Bay and its watershed were diminished by pollution, excessive sedimentation, shoreline erosion, the impacts of population growth and development in the Chesapeake Bay watershed, and other factors;

"(3) the Federal Government (acting through the Administrator of the Environmental Protection Agency), the Governor of the State of Maryland, the Governor of the Commonwealth of Virginia, the Governor of the Commonwealth of Pennsylvania, the Chairperson of the Chesapeake Bay Commission, and the mayor of the District of Columbia, as Chesapeake Bay Agreement signatories, have committed to a comprehensive cooperative program to achieve improved water quality and improvements in the productivity of living resources of the Bay;

"(4) the cooperative program described in paragraph (3) serves as a national and international model for the management of estuaries; and

"(5) there is a need to expand Federal support for monitoring, management, and restoration activities in the Chesapeake Bay and the tributaries of the Bay in order to meet and further the original and subsequent goals and commitments of the Chesapeake Bay Program.

"(b) Purposes.—The purposes of this title [Pub. L. No. 106–457, Title II, Nov. 7, 2000, 114 Stat. 1957, amending this section and enacting this note] are—

"(1) to expand and strengthen cooperative efforts to restore and protect the Chesapeake Bay; and

"(2) to achieve the goals established in the Chesapeake Bay Agreement."

Nutrient Loading Resulting from Dredged Material Disposal.

Pub. L. No. 106–53, Title IV, § 457, 113 Stat. 332 (Aug. 17, 1999), provided that:

"(a) Study.—The Secretary shall conduct a study of nutrient loading that occurs as a result of discharges of dredged material into open-water sites in the Chesapeake Bay.

"(b) Report.—Not later than 18 months after the date of enactment of this Act [Aug. 17, 1999], the Secretary shall submit to Congress a report on the results of the study."

Chesapeake Watershed Investments for Landscape Defense.

Section 111 of Pub. L. No. 116–188, 134 Stat. 921–24 (Oct. 30, 2020), provided that:

"(a) Definitions.—In this section:

"(1) Chesaapeake Bay Agreements.—The term "Chesapeake Bay agreements" means the formal, voluntary agreements

"(A) executed to achieve the goal of restoring and protecting the Chesapeake Bay watershed ecosystem and the living resources of the Chesapeake Bay watershed ecosystem; and

"(B) signed by the Chesapeake Executive Council.

"(2) **Chesapeake Bay Program.**—The term "Chesapeake Bay program" means the program directed by the Chesapeake Executive Council in accordance with the Chesapeake Bay agreements.

"(3) **Chesapeake Bay Watershed.**—The term "Chesapeake Bay watershed" means the region that covers—

"(A) the Chesapeake Bay;

"(B) the portions of the States of Delaware, Maryland, New York, Pennsylvania, Virginia, and West Virginia that drain into the Chesapeake Bay; and

"(C) the District of Columbia.

"(4) **Chesapeake Executive Council.**—The term "Chesapeake Executive Council" means the council comprised of—

"(A) the Governors of each of the States of Delaware, Maryland, New York, Pennsylvania, Virginia, and West Virginia;

"(B) the Mayor of the District of Columbia;

"(C) the Chair of the Chesapeake Bay Commission; and

"(D) the Administrator of the Environmental Protection Agency.

"(5) **Chesapeake Wild Program.**—The term "Chesapeake WILD program" means the nonregulatory program established by the Secretary under subsection (b)(1).

"(6) **Grant Program.**—The term "grant program" means the Chesapeake Watershed Investments for Landscape Defense grant program established by the Secretary under subsection (c)(1).

"(7) **Restoration and Protection Activity.**—The term "restoration and protection activity" means an activity carried out for the conservation, stewardship, and enhancement of habitat for fish and wildlife—

"(A) to preserve and improve ecosystems and ecological processes on which the fish and wildlife depend; and

"(B) for use and enjoyment by the public.

"(8) **Secretary.**—The term "Secretary" means the Secretary of the Interior, acting through the Director of the United States Fish and Wildlife Service.

"(b) **Program Establishment.**—

"(1) **Establishment.**—Not later than 180 days after the date of enactment of this Act, the Secretary shall establish a nonregulatory program, to be known as the "Chesapeake Watershed Investments for Landscape Defense program".

"(2) **Purposes.**—The purposes of the Chesapeake WILD program are—

"(A) coordinating restoration and protection activities among Federal, State, local, and regional entities and conservation partners throughout the Chesapeake Bay watershed;

"(B) engaging other agencies and organizations to build a broader range of partner support, capacity, and potential funding for projects in the Chesapeake Bay watershed;

"(C) carrying out coordinated restoration and protection activities, and providing for technical assistance, throughout the Chesapeake Bay watershed—

"(i) to sustain and enhance restoration and protection activities;

"(ii) to improve and maintain water quality to support fish and wildlife, habitats of fish and wildlife, and drinking water for people;

"(iii) to sustain and enhance water management for volume and flood damage mitigation improvements to benefit fish and wildlife habitat;

"(iv) to improve opportunities for public access and recreation in the Chesapeake Bay watershed consistent with the ecological needs of fish and wildlife habitat;

"(v) to facilitate strategic planning to maximize the resilience of natural ecosystems and habitats under changing watershed conditions;

"(vi) to engage the public through outreach, education, and citizen involvement to increase capacity and support for coordinated restoration and protection activities in the Chesapeake Bay watershed;

"(vii) to sustain and enhance vulnerable communities and fish and wildlife habitat;

"(viii) to conserve and restore fish, wildlife, and plant corridors; and

"(ix) to increase scientific capacity to support the planning, monitoring, and research activities necessary to carry out coordinated restoration and protection activities.

"(3) **Duties.**—In carrying out the Chesapeake WILD program, the Secretary shall—

"(A) draw on existing plans for the Chesapeake Bay watershed, or portions of the Chesapeake Bay watershed, including the Chesapeake Bay agreements, and work in consultation with applicable management entities, including Chesapeake Bay program partners, such as the Federal Government, State and local governments, the Chesapeake Bay Commission, and other regional organizations, as appropriate, to identify, prioritize, and implement restoration and protection activities within the Chesapeake Bay watershed;

"(B) adopt a Chesapeake Bay watershed-wide strategy that—

"(i) supports the implementation of a shared set of science-based restoration and protection activities developed in accordance with subparagraph (A); and

"(ii) targets cost-effective projects with measurable results; and

"(C) establish the grant program in accordance with subsection (c).

"(4) **Coordination.**—In establishing the Chesapeake WILD program, the Secretary shall consult, as appropriate, with—

"(A) the heads of Federal agencies, including—

"(i) the Administrator of the Environmental Protection Agency;

"(ii) the Administrator of the National Oceanic and Atmospheric Administration;

"(iii) the Chief of the Natural Resources Conservation Service;

"(iv) the Chief of Engineers;

"(v) the Director of the United States Geological Survey;

"(vi) the Secretary of Transportation;

"(vii) the Chief of the Forest Service; and

"(viii) the head of any other applicable agency;

"(B) the Governors of each of the States of Delaware, Maryland, New York, Pennsylvania, Virginia, and West Virginia and the Mayor of the District of Columbia;

"(C) fish and wildlife joint venture partnerships; and

"(D) other public agencies and organizations with authority for the planning and implementation of conservation strategies in the Chesapeake Bay watershed.

"(c) **Grants and Technical Assistance.**—

"(1) **Chesapeake Wild Grant Program.**—To the extent that funds are made available to carry out this subsection, the Secretary shall establish and carry out, as part of the Chesapeake WILD program, a voluntary grant and technical assistance program, to be known as the "Chesapeake Watershed Investments for Landscape Defense grant program", to provide competitive matching grants of varying amounts and technical assistance to eligible entities described in paragraph (2) to carry out activities described in subsection (b)(2).

"(2) **Eligible Entities.**—The following entities are eligible to receive a grant and technical assistance under the grant program:

"(A) A State.

"(B) The District of Columbia.

"(C) A unit of local government.

"(D) A nonprofit organization.

"(E) An institution of higher education as such term is defined in section 101(a) of the Higher Education Act of 1965 (20 U.S.C. 1001(a)).

"(F) Any other entity that the Secretary determines to be appropriate in accordance with the criteria established under paragraph (3).

"(3) **Criteria.**—The Secretary, in consultation with officials and entities described in subsection (b)(4), shall establish criteria for the grant program to help ensure that activities funded under this subsection—

"(A) accomplish 1 or more of the purposes described in subsection (b)(2); and

"(B) advance the implementation of priority actions or needs identified in the Chesapeake Bay watershed-wide strategy adopted under subsection (b)(3)(B).

"(4) **Cost Sharing.**—

"(A) **Department of the Interiors Share.**—The Department of the Interior share of the cost of a project funded under the grant program shall not exceed 50 percent of the total cost of the project, as determined by the Secretary.

"(B) **Non-Department of the Interior Share.**—

"(i) **In General.**—The non-Department of the Interior share of the cost of a project funded under the grant program may be provided in cash or in the form of an in-kind contribution of services or materials.

"(ii) **Other Federal Funding.**—Non-Department of the Interior Federal funds may be used for not more than 25 percent of the total cost of a project funded under the grant program.

"(5) **Administration.**—The Secretary may enter into an agreement to manage the grant program with an organization that offers grant management services.

"(d) **Reporting.**—Not later than 180 days after the date of enactment of this Act, and annually thereafter, the Secretary shall submit to Congress a report describing the implementation of this section, including a description of each project that has received funding under this section.

"(e) **Authorization of Appropriations.**—

"(1) **In General.**—There is authorized to be appropriated to carry out this section $15,000,000 for each of fiscal years 2021 through 2025.

"(2) **Supplement, Not Supplant.**—Funds made available under paragraph (1) shall supplement, and not supplant, funding for other activities conducted by the Secretary in the Chesapeake Bay watershed.

§ 1268. Great Lakes

[FWPCA § 118]

(a) Findings, purpose, and definitions

(1) Findings

The Congress finds that—

(A) the Great Lakes are a valuable national resource, continuously serving the people of the United States and other nations as an important source of food, fresh water, recreation, beauty, and enjoyment;

(B) the United States should seek to attain the goals embodied in the Great Lakes Water Quality Agreement of 1978, as amended by the Water Quality Agreement of 1987 and any other agreements and amendments, with particular emphasis on goals related to toxic pollutants; and

(C) the Environmental Protection Agency should take the lead in the effort to meet those goals, working with other Federal agencies and State and local authorities.

(2) Purpose

It is the purpose of this section to achieve the goals embodied in the Great Lakes Water Quality Agreement of 1978, as amended by the Water Quality Agreement of 1987 and any other agreements and amendments, through improved organization and definition of mission on the part of the Agency, funding of State grants for pollution control in the Great Lakes area, and improved accountability for implementation of such agreement.

(3) Definitions

For purposes of this section, the term—

(A) "Agency" means the Environmental Protection Agency;

(B) "Great Lakes" means Lake Ontario, Lake Erie, Lake Huron (including Lake St. Clair), Lake Michigan, and Lake Superior, and the connecting channels (Saint Mary's River, Saint Clair River, Detroit River, Niagara River, and Saint Lawrence River to the Canadian Border);

(C) "Great Lakes System" means all the streams, rivers, lakes, and other bodies of water within the drainage basin of the Great Lakes;

(D) "Program Office" means the Great Lakes National Program Office established by this section;

(E) "Research Office" means the Great Lakes Research Office established by subsection (d) of this section;

(F) "area of concern" means a geographic area located within the Great Lakes, in which beneficial uses are impaired and which has been officially designated as such under Annex 2 of the Great Lakes Water Quality Agreement;

(G) "Great Lakes States" means the States of Illinois, Indiana, Michigan, Minnesota, New York, Ohio, Pennsylvania, and Wisconsin;

(H) "Great Lakes Water Quality Agreement" means the bilateral agreement, between the United States and Canada which was signed in 1978 and amended by the Protocol of 1987;

(I) "Lakewide Management Plan" means a written document which embodies a systematic and comprehensive ecosystem approach to restoring and protecting the beneficial uses of the open waters of each of the Great Lakes, in accordance with article VI and Annex 2 of the Great Lakes Water Quality Agreement;

(J) "Remedial Action Plan" means a written document which embodies a systematic and comprehensive ecosystem approach to restoring and protecting the beneficial uses of areas of concern, in accordance with article VI and Annex 2 of the Great Lakes Water Quality Agreement;

(K) "site characterization" means a process for monitoring and evaluating the nature and extent of sediment contamination in accordance with the Environmental Protection Agency's guidance for the assessment of contaminated sediment in an area of concern located wholly or partially within the United States; and

(L) "potentially responsible party" means an individual or entity that may be liable under any Federal or State authority that is being used or may be used to facilitate the cleanup and protection of the Great Lakes.

(b) Great Lakes National Program Office

The Great Lakes National Program Office (previously established by the Administrator) is hereby established within the Agency. The Program Office shall be headed by a Director who, by reason of management experience and technical expertise relating to the Great Lakes, is highly qualified to direct the development of programs and plans on a variety of Great Lakes issues. The Great Lakes National Program Office shall be located in a Great Lakes State.

(c) Great Lakes management

(1) Functions

The Program Office shall—

(A) in cooperation with appropriate Federal, State, tribal, and international agencies, and in accordance with section 1251(e) of this title, develop and implement specific action plans to carry out the responsibilities of the United States under the Great Lakes Water Quality Agreement of 1978, as amended by the Water Quality Agreement of 1987 and any other agreements and amendments;[1]

(B) establish a Great Lakes system-wide surveillance network to monitor the water quality of the Great Lakes, with specific emphasis on the monitoring of toxic pollutants;

(C) serve as the liaison with, and provide information to, the Canadian members of the International Joint Commission and the Canadian counterpart to the Agency;

(D) coordinate actions of the Agency (including actions by headquarters and regional offices thereof) aimed at improving Great Lakes water quality; and

(E) coordinate actions of the Agency with the actions of other Federal agencies and State and local authorities, so as to ensure the input of those agencies and authorities in developing water quality strategies and obtain the support of those agencies and authorities in achieving the objectives of such agreement.

(2) Great Lakes water quality guidance

(A) By June 30, 1991, the Administrator, after consultation with the Program Office, shall publish in the Federal Register for public notice and comment proposed water quality guidance for the Great Lakes System. Such guidance shall conform with the objectives and provisions of the Great Lakes Water Quality Agreement, shall be no less restrictive than the provisions of this chapter and national water quality criteria and guidance, shall specify numerical limits on pollutants in ambient Great Lakes waters to protect human health, aquatic life, and wildlife, and shall provide guidance to the Great Lakes States on minimum water quality standards, antidegradation policies, and implementation procedures for the Great Lakes System.

(B) By June 30, 1992, the Administrator, in consultation with the Program Office, shall publish in the Federal Register, pursuant to this section and the Administrator's authority under this chapter, final water quality guidance for the Great Lakes System.

(C) Within two years after such Great Lakes guidance is published, the Great Lakes States shall adopt water quality standards, antidegradation policies, and implementation procedures for waters within the Great Lakes System which are consistent with such guidance. If a Great Lakes State fails to adopt such standards, policies, and procedures, the Administrator shall promulgate them not later than the end of such two-year period. When reviewing any Great Lakes State's water quality plan, the agency shall consider the extent to which the State has complied with the Great Lakes guidance issued pursuant to this section.

(3) Remedial action plans

(A) For each area of concern for which the United States has agreed to draft a Remedial Action Plan, the Program Office shall ensure that the Great Lakes State in which such area of concern is located—

(i) submits a Remedial Action Plan to the Program Office by June 30, 1991;

(ii) submits such Remedial Action Plan to the International Joint Commission by January 1, 1992; and

(iii) includes such Remedial Action Plans within the State's water quality plan by January 1, 1993.

(B) For each area of concern for which Canada has agreed to draft a Remedial Action Plan, the Program Office shall, pursuant to subparagraph (c)(1)(C) of this section, work with Canada to assure the submission of such Remedial Action Plans to the International Joint Commission by June 30, 1991, and to finalize such Remedial Action Plans by January 1, 1993.

(C) For any area of concern designated as such subsequent to November 16, 1990, the Program Office shall (i) if the United States has agreed to draft the Remedial Action Plan, ensure that the Great Lakes State in which such area of concern is located submits such Plan to the Program Office within two years of the area's designation, submits it to the International Joint Commission no later than six months after submitting it to the Program Office, and includes such Plan in the State's water quality plan no later than one year after submitting it to the Commission; and (ii) if Canada has agreed to draft the Remedial Action Plan, work with Canada, pursuant to subparagraph (c)(1)(C) of this section, to ensure the submission of such Plan to the International Joint Commission within two years of the area's designation and the finalization of such Plan no later than eighteen months after submitting it to such Commission.

(D) The Program Office shall compile formal comments on individual Remedial Action Plans made by the International Joint Commission pursuant to section 4(d) of Annex 2 of the Great Lakes Water Quality Agreement and, upon request by a member of the public, shall make such comments available for inspection and copying. The Program Office shall also make available, upon request, formal comments made by the Environmental Protection Agency on individual Remedial Action Plans.

(E) Report

Not later than 1 year after the date of enactment of this subparagraph, the Administrator shall submit to Congress a report on such actions, time periods, and resources as are necessary to fulfill the duties of the Agency relating to oversight of Remedial Action Plans under—

(i) this paragraph; and

(ii) the Great Lakes Water Quality Agreement.

(4) Lakewide Management Plans

The Administrator, in consultation with the Program Office shall—

(A) by January 1, 1992, publish in the Federal Register a proposed Lakewide Management Plan for Lake Michigan and solicit public comments;

(B) by January 1, 1993, submit a proposed Lakewide Management Plan for Lake Michigan to the International Joint Commission for review; and

(C) by January 1, 1994, publish in the Federal Register a final Lakewide Management Plan for Lake Michigan and begin implementation.

Nothing in this subparagraph shall preclude the simultaneous development of Lakewide Management Plans for the other Great Lakes.

(5) Spills of oil and hazardous materials

The Program Office, in consultation with the Coast Guard, shall identify areas within the Great Lakes which are likely to experience numerous or voluminous spills of oil or other hazardous materials from land based facilities, vessels, or other sources and, in consultation with the Great Lakes States, shall identify weaknesses in Federal and State programs and systems to prevent and respond to such spills. This information shall be included on at least a biennial basis in the report required by this section.

(6) 5-year plan and program

The Program Office shall develop, in consultation with the States, a five-year plan and program for reducing the amount of nutrients introduced into the Great Lakes. Such program shall incorporate any management program for reducing nutrient runoff from nonpoint sources established under section 1329 of this title and shall include a program for monitoring nutrient runoff into, and ambient levels in, the Great Lakes.

(7) 5-year study and demonstration projects

(A) The Program Office shall carry out a five-year study and demonstration projects relating to the control and removal of toxic pollutants in the Great Lakes, with emphasis on the removal of toxic pollutants from bottom sediments. In selecting locations for conducting demonstration projects under this paragraph, priority consideration shall be given to projects at the following locations: Saginaw Bay, Michigan; Sheboygan Harbor, Wisconsin; Grand Calumet River, Indiana; Ashtabula River, Ohio; and Buffalo River, New York.

(B) Focus areas.—In carrying out the Initiative, the Administrator shall prioritize programs and projects, to be carried out in coordination with non-Federal partners, that address the priority areas described in the Initiative Action Plan, including—

(i) the remediation of toxic substances and areas of concern;

(ii) the prevention and control of invasive species and the impacts of invasive species;

(iii) the protection and restoration of nearshore health and the prevention and mitigation of nonpoint source pollution;

(iv) habitat and wildlife protection and restoration, including wetlands restoration and preservation; and

(v) accountability, monitoring, evaluation, communication, and partnership activities.

(C) Projects.—

(i) In general.—In carrying out the Initiative, the Administrator shall collaborate with other Federal partners, including the Great Lakes Interagency Task Force established by Executive Order No. 13340 (69 Fed. Reg. 29043), to select the best combination of programs and projects for Great Lakes protection and restoration using appropriate principles and criteria, including whether a program or project provides—

(I) the ability to achieve strategic and measurable environmental outcomes that implement the Initiative Action Plan and the Great Lakes Water Quality Agreement;

(II) the feasibility of—

(aa) prompt implementation;

(bb) timely achievement of results; and

(cc) resource leveraging; and

(III) the opportunity to improve interagency, intergovernmental, and interorganizational coordination and collaboration to reduce duplication and streamline efforts.

(ii) Outreach.—In selecting the best combination of programs and projects for Great Lakes protection and restoration under clause (i), the Administrator shall consult with the Great Lakes States and Indian tribes and solicit input from other non-Federal stakeholders.

(iii) Harmful algal bloom coordinator.—The Administrator shall designate a point person from an appropriate Federal partner to coordinate, with Federal partners and Great Lakes States, Indian tribes, and other non-Federal stakeholders, projects and activities under the Initiative involving harmful algal blooms in the Great Lakes.

(D) Implementation of projects

(i) In general.—Subject to subparagraph (J)(ii), funds made available to carry out the Initiative shall be used to strategically implement—

(I) Federal projects;

(II) projects carried out in coordination with States, Indian tribes, municipalities, institutions of higher education, and other organizations; and

(III) operations and activities of the Program Office, including remediation of sediment contamination in areas of concern.";

(ii) Transfer of funds

With amounts made available for the Initiative each fiscal year, the Administrator may—

(I) transfer not more than the total amount appropriated under subparagraph (J)(i) for the fiscal year to the head of any Federal department or agency, with the concurrence of the department or agency head, to carry out activities to support the Initiative and the Great Lakes Water Quality Agreement; and

(II) enter into an interagency agreement with the head of any Federal department or agency to carry out activities described in subclause (I).

(iii) Agreements with non-Federal entities.—

(I) In general.—The Administrator, or the head of any other Federal department or agency receiving funds under clause (ii)(I), may make a grant to, or otherwise enter into an agreement with, a qualified non-Federal entity, as determined by the Administrator or the applicable head of the other Federal department or agency receiving funds, for planning, research, monitoring, outreach, or implementation of a project selected under subparagraph (C), to support the Initiative Action Plan or the Great Lakes Water Quality Agreement.

(II) Qualified non-Federal entity.—For purposes of this clause, a qualified non-Federal entity may include a governmental entity, nonprofit organization, institution, or individual."; and

(E) Scope.—

(i) In general.—Projects may be carried out under the Initiative on multiple levels, including—

(I) locally;

(II) Great Lakes-wide; or

(III) Great Lakes basin-wide.

(ii) Limitation.—No funds made available to carry out the Initiative may be used for any water infrastructure activity (other than a green infrastructure project that improves habitat and other ecosystem functions in the Great Lakes) for which financial assistance is received—

(I) from a State water pollution control revolving fund established under title VI;

(II) from a State drinking water revolving loan fund established under section 1452 of the Safe Drinking Water Act (42 U.S.C. 300j–12); or

(III) pursuant to the Water Infrastructure Finance and Innovation Act of 2014 (33 U.S.C. 3901 et seq.).

(F) Activities by other Federal agencies.—Each relevant Federal department or agency shall, to the maximum extent practicable—

(i) maintain the base level of funding for the Great Lakes activities of that department or agency without regard to funding under the Initiative; and

(ii) identify new activities and projects to support the environmental goals of the Initiative.

(G) Revision of initiative action plan.—

(i) In general.—Not less often than once every 5 years, the Administrator, in conjunction with the Great Lakes Interagency Task Force, shall review, and revise as appropriate, the Initiative Action Plan to guide the activities of the Initiative in addressing the restoration and protection of the Great Lakes system.

(ii) Outreach.—In reviewing and revising the Initiative Action Plan under clause (i), the Administrator shall consult with the Great Lakes States and Indian tribes and solicit input from other non-Federal stakeholders.

(H) Monitoring and reporting.—The Administrator shall—

(i) establish and maintain a process for monitoring and periodically reporting to the public on the progress made in implementing the Initiative Action Plan;

(ii) make information about each project carried out under the Initiative Action Plan available on a public website; and

(iii) provide to the Committee on Transportation and Infrastructure of the House of Representatives and the Committee on Environment and Public Works of the Senate a yearly detailed description of the progress of the Initiative and amounts transferred to participating Federal departments and agencies under subparagraph (D)(ii).

(I) Initiative action plan defined.—In this paragraph, the term 'Initiative Action Plan' means the comprehensive, multiyear action plan for the restoration of the Great Lakes, first developed pursuant to the Joint Explanatory Statement of the Conference Report accompanying the Department of the Interior, Environment, and Related Agencies Appropriations Act, 2010 (Public Law 111–88).

(J) Funding.—

(i) In general.—There are authorized to be appropriated to carry out this paragraph—

(I) $300,000,000 for each of fiscal years 2017 through 2021;

(II) $375,000,000 for fiscal year 2022;

(III) $400,000,000 for fiscal year 2023;

(IV) $425,000,000 for fiscal year 2024;

(V) $450,000,000 for fiscal year 2025; and

(VI) $475,000,000 for fiscal year 2026.

(ii) Limitation.—Nothing in this paragraph creates, expands, or amends the authority of the Administrator to implement programs or projects under—

(I) this section;

(II) the Initiative Action Plan; or

(III) the Great Lakes Water Quality Agreement.

(8) Administrator's responsibility

The Administrator shall ensure that the Program Office enters into agreements with the various organizational elements of the Agency involved in Great Lakes activities and the appropriate State agencies specifically delineating—

(A) the duties and responsibilities of each such element in the Agency with respect to the Great Lakes;

(B) the time periods for carrying out such duties and responsibilities; and

(C) the resources to be committed to such duties and responsibilities.

(9) Budget item

The Administrator shall, in the Agency's annual budget submission to Congress, include a funding request for the Program Office as a separate budget line item.

(10) Confined disposal facilities

(A) The Administrator, in consultation with the Assistant Secretary of the Army for Civil Works, shall develop and implement, within one year of November 16, 1990, management plans for every Great Lakes confined disposal facility.

(B) The plan shall provide for monitoring of such facilities, including

(i) water quality at the site and in the area of the site;

(ii) sediment quality at the site and in the area of the site;

(iii) the diversity, productivity, and stability of aquatic organisms at the site and in the area of the site; and

(iv) such other conditions as the Administrator deems appropriate.

(C) The plan shall identify the anticipated use and management of the site over the following twenty-year period including the expected termination of dumping at the site, the anticipated need for site management, including pollution control, following the termination of the use of the site.

(D) The plan shall identify a schedule for review and revision of the plan which shall not be less frequent than five years after adoption of the plan and every five years thereafter.

(11) Remediation of sediment contamination in areas of concern

(A) In general

In accordance with this paragraph, the Administrator, acting through the Program Office, may carry out projects that meet the requirements of subparagraph (B).

(B) Eligible projects

A project meets the requirements of this subparagraph if the project is to be carried out in an area of concern located wholly or partially in the United States and the project—

(i) monitors or evaluates contaminated sediment;

(ii) subject to subparagraph (D), implements a plan to remediate contaminated sediment, including activities to restore aquatic habitat that are carried out in conjunction with a project for the remediation of contaminated sediment; or

(iii) prevents further or renewed contamination of sediment.

(C) Priority

In selecting projects to carry out under this paragraph, the Administrator shall give priority to a project that—

(i) constitutes remedial action for contaminated sediment;

(ii) (I) has been identified in a Remedial Action Plan submitted under paragraph (3); and

(II) is ready to be implemented;

(iii) will use an innovative approach, technology, or technique that may provide greater environmental benefits, or equivalent environmental benefits at a reduced cost; or

(iv) includes remediation to be commenced not later than 1 year after the date of receipt of funds for the project.

(D) Limitations

The Administrator may not carry out a project under this paragraph for remediation of contaminated sediments located in an area of concern—

(i) if an evaluation of remedial alternatives for the area of concern has not been conducted, including a review of the short-term and long-term effects of the alternatives on human health and the environment;

(ii) if the Administrator determines that the area of concern is likely to suffer significant further or renewed contamination from existing sources of pollutants causing sediment contamination following completion of the project;

(iii) unless each non-Federal sponsor for the project has entered into a written project agreement with the Administrator under which the party agrees to carry out its responsibilities and requirements for the project; or

(iv) unless the Administrator provides assurance that the Agency has conducted a reasonable inquiry to identify potentially responsible parties connected with the site.

(E) Non-Federal share

(i) In general

The non-Federal share of the cost of a project carried out under this paragraph shall be at least 35 percent.

(ii) In-kind contributions

(I) In general

The non-Federal share of the cost of a project carried out under this paragraph may include the value of an in-kind contribution provided by a non-Federal sponsor.

(II) Credit

A project agreement described in subparagraph (D)(iii) may provide, with respect to a project, that the Administrator shall credit toward the non-Federal share of the cost of the project the value of an in-kind contribution made by the non-Federal sponsor, if the Administrator determines that the material or service provided as the in-kind contribution is integral to the project.

(III) Work performed before project agreement

In any case in which a non-Federal sponsor is to receive credit under subclause (II) for the cost of work carried out by the non-Federal sponsor and such work has not been carried out by the non-Federal sponsor as of Oct. 8, 2008, the Administrator and the non-Federal sponsor shall enter into an agreement under which the non-Federal sponsor shall carry out such work, and only work carried out following the execution of the agreement shall be eligible for credit.

(IV) Limitation

Credit authorized under this clause for a project carried out under this paragraph—

(aa) shall not exceed the non-Federal share of the cost of the project; and

(bb) shall not exceed the actual and reasonable costs of the materials and services provided by the non-Federal sponsor, as determined by the Administrator.

(V) Inclusion of certain contributions

In this subparagraph, the term "in-kind contribution" may include the costs of planning (including data collection), design, construction, and materials that are provided by the non-Federal sponsor for implementation of a project under this paragraph.

(iii) **Treatment of credit between projects**

Any credit provided under this subparagraph towards the non-Federal share of the cost of a project carried out under this paragraph may be applied towards the non-Federal share of the cost of any other project carried out under this paragraph by the same non-Federal sponsor for a site within the same area of concern.

(iv) **Non-Federal share**

The non-Federal share of the cost of a project carried out under this paragraph—

(I) may include monies paid pursuant to, or the value of any in-kind contribution performed under, an administrative order on consent or judicial consent decree; but

(II) may not include any funds paid pursuant to, or the value of any in-kind contribution performed under, a unilateral administrative order or court order.

(v) **Operation and maintenance**

The non-Federal share of the cost of the operation and maintenance of a project carried out under this paragraph shall be 100 percent.

(F) **Site characterization**

(i) **In general**

The Administrator, in consultation with any affected State or unit of local government, shall carry out at Federal expense the site characterization of a project under this paragraph for the remediation of contaminated sediment.

(ii) **Limitation**

For purposes of clause (i), the Administrator may carry out one site assessment per discrete site within a project at Federal expense.

(G) **Coordination**

In carrying out projects under this paragraph, the Administrator shall coordinate with the Secretary of the Army, and with the Governors of States in which the projects are located, to ensure that Federal and State assistance for remediation in areas of concern is used as efficiently as practicable.

(H) **Authorization of appropriations**

(i) **In general**

In addition to other amounts authorized under this section, there is authorized to be appropriated to carry out this paragraph $50,000,000 for each of fiscal years 2004 through 2010.

(ii) **Availability**

Funds made available under clause (i) shall remain available until expended.

(iii) **Allocation of funds**

Not more than 20 percent of the funds appropriated pursuant to clause (i) for a fiscal year may be used to carry out subparagraph (F).

(12) **Public information program**

(A) **In general**

The Administrator, acting through the Program Office and in coordination with States, Indian tribes, local governments, and other entities, may carry out a public information program to provide information relating to the remediation of contaminated sediment to the public in areas of concern that are located wholly or partially in the United States.

(B) Authorization of appropriations

There is authorized to be appropriated to carry out this paragraph $1,000,000 for each of fiscal years 2004 through 2010.

(d) Great Lakes research

(1) Establishment of Research Office

There is established within the National Oceanic and Atmospheric Administration the Great Lakes Research Office.

(2) Identification of issues

The Research Office shall identify issues relating to the Great Lakes resources on which research is needed. The Research Office shall submit a report to Congress on such issues before the end of each fiscal year which shall identify any changes in the Great Lakes system with respect to such issues.

(3) Inventory

The Research Office shall identify and inventory Federal, State, university, and tribal environmental research programs (and, to the extent feasible, those of private organizations and other nations) relating to the Great Lakes system, and shall update that inventory every four years.

(4) Research exchange

The Research Office shall establish a Great Lakes research exchange for the purpose of facilitating the rapid identification, acquisition, retrieval, dissemination, and use of information concerning research projects which are ongoing or completed and which affect the Great Lakes System.

(5) Research program

The Research Office shall develop, in cooperation with the Coordination Office, a comprehensive environmental research program and data base for the Great Lakes system. The data base shall include, but not be limited to, data relating to water quality, fisheries, and biota.

(6) Monitoring

The Research Office shall conduct, through the Great Lakes Environmental Research Laboratory, the National Sea Grant College program, other Federal laboratories, and the private sector, appropriate research and monitoring activities which address priority issues and current needs relating to the Great Lakes.

(7) Location

The Research Office shall be located in a Great Lakes State.

(e) Research and management coordination

(1) Joint plan

Before October 1 of each year, the Program Office and the Research Office shall prepare a joint research plan for the fiscal year which begins in the following calendar year.

(2) Contents of plan

Each plan prepared under paragraph (1) shall—

(A) identify all proposed research dedicated to activities conducted under the Great Lakes Water Quality Agreement of 1978, as amended by the Water Quality Agreement of 1987 and any other agreements and amendments;[1]

(B) include the Agency's assessment of priorities for research needed to fulfill the terms of such Agreement; and

(C) identify all proposed research that may be used to develop a comprehensive environmental data base for the Great Lakes System and establish priorities for development of such data base.

(3) Health research report

(A) Not later than September 30, 1994, the Program Office, in consultation with the Research Office, the Agency for Toxic Substances and Disease Registry, and Great Lakes States shall submit to the Congress a report assessing the adverse effects of water pollutants in the Great Lakes System on the health of persons in Great Lakes States and the health of fish, shellfish, and wildlife in the Great Lakes System. In conducting research in support of this report, the Administrator may, where appropriate, provide for research to be conducted under cooperative agreements with Great Lakes States.

(B) There is authorized to be appropriated to the Administrator to carry out this section not to exceed $3,000,000 for each of fiscal years 1992, 1993, and 1994.

(f) Interagency cooperation

The head of each department, agency, or other instrumentality of the Federal Government which is engaged in, is concerned with, or has authority over programs relating to research, monitoring, and planning to maintain, enhance, preserve, or rehabilitate the environmental quality and natural resources of the Great Lakes, including the Chief of Engineers of the Army, the Chief of the Soil Conservation Service, the Commandant of the Coast Guard, the Director of the Fish and Wildlife Service, and the Administrator of the National Oceanic and Atmospheric Administration, shall submit an annual report to the Administrator with respect to the activities of that agency or office affecting compliance with the Great Lakes Water Quality Agreement of 1978, as amended by the Water Quality Agreement of 1987 and any other agreements and amendments.[1]

(g) Relationship to existing Federal and State laws and international treaties

Nothing in this section shall be construed—

(1) to affect the jurisdiction, powers, or prerogatives of any department, agency, or officer of the Federal Government or of any State government, or of any tribe, nor any powers, jurisdiction, or prerogatives of any international body created by treaty with authority relating to the Great Lakes; or

(2) to affect any other Federal or State authority that is being used or may be used to facilitate the cleanup and protection of the Great Lakes.

(h) Authorizations of Great Lakes appropriations

There are authorized to be appropriated to the Administrator to carry out this section not to exceed—

(1) $11,000,000 per fiscal year for the fiscal years 1987, 1988, 1989, and 1990, and $25,000,000 for fiscal year 1991;

(2) such sums as are necessary for each of fiscal years 1992 through 2003; and

(3) $25,000,000 for each of fiscal years 2004 through 2008.

(June 30, 1948, c. 758, Title I, § 118, as added by Pub. L. No. 100–4, Title I, § 104, 101 Stat. 11 (Feb. 4, 1987); and amended by Pub. L. No. 100–688, Title I, § 1008, 102 Stat. 4151 (Nov. 18, 1988); Pub. L. No. 101–596, Title I, §§ 101–106, 104 Stat. 3000–3004 (Nov. 16, 1990); Pub. L. No. 107–303, Title I, §§ 102, 103, 104, 105, 116 Stat. 2355, 2356, 2357, 2358 (Nov. 27, 2002); Pub. L. No. 110–365, §§ 2, 3, 122 Stat. 4021 (Oct. 8, 2008); Pub. L. No. 113–188, § 701, 128 Stat. 2019 (Nov. 26, 2014); Pub. L. No. 114–113, § 426, 129 Stat. 2581 (Dec. 18, 2015); Pub. L. No. 114–332, § 5005, 130 Stat. 1889–92 (Dec. 16, 2016); Pub. L. No. 116–294, § 2, 134 Stat. 4899 (Jan. 5, 2021).)

[1] So in original.

HISTORICAL AND STATUTORY NOTES

References in Text

The date of enactment of this subparagraph, referred to in subsec. (c)(3)(E), is Nov. 27, 2002, the date of enactment of Pub. L. No. 107–303, 116 Stat. 2355, which enacted such subparagraph (E).

Codifications

November 16, 1990, referred to in subsec. (c)(3)(C), (7)(C), was in the original "the enactment of this Act", and "the date of the enactment of this title" which were translated as meaning the date of enactment of Pub. L. No. 101–596, Title I of which enacted subsec. (c)(3), (7)(C), to reflect the probable intent of Congress.

Termination of Reporting Requirements

Reporting requirement of subsec. (c)(10) of this section excepted from termination under Pub. L. No. 104–66, § 3003(a)(1), as amended, set out as a note under 31 U.S.C.A. § 1113, and page 163 of House Document No. 103–7, see Pub. L. No. 107–303, § 302(a), set out as a note under 31 U.S.C.A. § 1113.

Reporting requirement of subsec. (d)(2) of this section excepted from termination under Pub. L. No. 104–66, § 3003(a)(1), as amended, set out as a note under 31 U.S.C.A. § 1113, see Pub. L. No. 107–74, set out as a note under 31 U.S.C.A. § 1113.

For termination, effective May 15, 2000, of reporting provisions of subsec. (e) of this section relating to adverse effects of water pollutants in the Great Lakes System on the health of persons in the Great Lakes States, see Pub. L. No. 104–66, § 3003, as amended, set out as a note under 31 U.S.C.A. § 1113, and the 17th item on page 164 of House Document No. 103–7.

Administrative Provisions

Pub. L. No. 108–447, Div. I, Title III, 118 Stat. 3332 (Dec. 8, 2004), provided that: "The Administrator may hereafter receive and use funds contributed by a non-Federal sponsor as its share of the cost of a project to carry out a project under paragraph (c)(12) of section 118 of the Federal Water Pollution Control Act [subsec. (c)(12) of this section, Act of June 30, 1948, c.758, Title I, § 118, as added by Pub. L. No. 100–4, Title I, § 104, 101 Stat. 11 (Feb. 4, 1987), and amended], as amended."

Great Lakes Remedial Action Plans and Sediment Remediation

Pub. L. No. 101–640, Title IV, § 401, 104 Stat. 4644 (Nov. 28, 1990), as amended by Pub. L. No. 104–303, Title V, § 515, 110 Stat. 3763 (Oct. 12, 1996); Pub. L. No. 106–53, Title V, § 505, 113 Stat. 338 (Aug. 17, 1999); Pub. L. No. 106–541, Title III, § 344, 114 Stat. 2613 (Dec. 11, 2000); Pub. L. No. 110–114, § 5012, 121 Stat. 1195 (Nov. 8, 2007), provided that:

"(a) Great Lakes remedial action plans.—

"(1) In general.—The Secretary may provide technical, planning, and engineering assistance to State and local governments and nongovernmental entities designated by a State or local government in the development and implementation of remedial action plans for Areas of Concern in the Great Lakes identified under the Great Lakes Water Quality Agreement of 1978.

"(2) Non-Federal share.—

"(A) In general.—Non-Federal interests shall contribute, in cash or by providing in-kind contributions, 35 percent of costs of activities for which assistance is provided under paragraph (1).

"(B) Contributions by entities.—Nonprofit public or private entities may contribute all or a portion of the non-Federal share.

"(b) Sediment remediation projects.—

"(1) In general.—The Secretary, in consultation with the Administrator of the Environmental Protection Agency (acting through the Great Lakes National Program Office), may conduct pilot- and full-scale projects of promising technologies to remediate contaminated sediments in freshwater coastal regions in the Great Lakes basin. The Secretary shall conduct not fewer than 3 full-scale projects under this subsection.

"(2) Site selection for projects.—In selecting the sites for the technology projects, the Secretary shall give priority consideration to Saginaw Bay, Michigan, Sheboygan Harbor, Wisconsin, Grand Calumet River, Indiana, Ashtabula River, Ohio, Buffalo River, New York, and Duluth-Superior Harbor, Minnesota and Wisconsin.

"(3) Non-Federal share.—Non-Federal interests shall contribute 35 percent of costs of projects under this subsection. Such costs may be paid in cash or by providing in-kind contributions.

"(c) **Authorization of appropriations.**—There is authorized to be appropriated to the Secretary to carry out this section $10,000,000 for each of fiscal years 2001 through 2012."

§ 1268a. Great Lakes restoration activities; submission of report

(a) For purposes of this section the following definitions apply:

(1) The terms "Great Lakes" and "Great Lakes State" have the same meanings as such terms have in section 1962d–22 of Title 42.

(2) The term "Great Lakes restoration activities" means any Federal or State activity primarily or entirely within the Great Lakes watershed that seeks to improve the overall health of the Great Lakes ecosystem.

(b) Hereafter, not later than 45 days after submission of the budget of the President to Congress, the Director of the Office of Management and Budget, in coordination with the Governor of each Great Lakes State and the Great Lakes Interagency Task Force, shall submit to the appropriate authorizing and appropriating committees of the Senate and the House of Representatives a financial report, certified by the Secretary of each agency that has budget authority for Great Lakes restoration activities, containing—

(1) an interagency budget crosscut report that—

(A) displays the budget proposed, including any planned interagency or intra-agency transfer, for each of the Federal agencies that carries out Great Lakes restoration activities in the upcoming fiscal year, separately reporting the amount of funding to be provided under existing laws pertaining to the Great Lakes ecosystem; and

(B) identifies all expenditures in each of the 5 prior fiscal years by the Federal Government and State governments for Great Lakes restoration activities;

(2) a detailed accounting of all funds received and obligated by all Federal agencies and, to the extent available, State agencies using Federal funds, for Great Lakes restoration activities during the current and previous fiscal years;

(3) a budget for the proposed projects (including a description of the project, authorization level, and project status) to be carried out in the upcoming fiscal year with the Federal portion of funds for activities; and

(4) a listing of all projects to be undertaken in the upcoming fiscal year with the Federal portion of funds for activities.

(Pub. L. No. 113–76, Div. E, Title VII, § 738, 128 Stat. 238 (Jan. 17, 2014).)

HISTORICAL AND STATUTORY NOTES

Codifications

Section was enacted as part of the Financial Services and General Government Appropriations Act, 2014, and also as part of the Consolidated Appropriations Act, 2014, and not as part of the Federal Water Pollution Control Act which comprises this chapter.

§ 1269. Long Island Sound

[FWPCA § 119]

(a) Office of Management Conference of the Long Island Sound Study

The Administrator shall continue the Management Conference of the Long Island Sound Study (hereinafter referred to as the "Conference") as established pursuant to section 1330 of this title, and shall establish an office (hereinafter referred to as the "Office") to be located on or near Long Island Sound.

(b) Administration and staffing of Office

The Office shall be headed by a Director, who shall be detailed by the Administrator, following consultation with the Administrators of EPA regions I and II, from among the employees of the Agency who are in civil service. The Administrator shall delegate to the Director such authority and detail such additional staff as may be necessary to carry out the duties of the Director under this section.

(c) Duties of Office

The Office shall assist the conference study in carrying out its goals. Specifically, the Office shall—

(1) assist and support the implementation of the Comprehensive Conservation and Management Plan for Long Island Sound developed pursuant to section 1330 of this title, including efforts to establish, within the process for granting watershed general permits, a system for promoting innovative methodologies and technologies that are cost-effective and consistent with the goals of the Plan;

(2) conduct or commission studies deemed necessary for strengthened implementation of the Comprehensive Conservation and Management Plan including, but not limited to—

(A) population growth and the adequacy of wastewater treatment facilities;

(B) the use of biological methods for nutrient removal in sewage treatment plants;

(C) contaminated sediments, and dredging activities;

(D) nonpoint source pollution abatement and land use activities in the Long Island Sound watershed;

(E) wetland protection and restoration;

(F) atmospheric deposition of acidic and other pollutants into Long Island Sound;

(G) water quality requirements to sustain fish, shellfish, and wildlife populations, and the use of indicator species to assess environmental quality;

(H) State water quality programs, for their adequacy pursuant to implementation of the Comprehensive Conservation and Management Plan;

(I) options for long-term financing of wastewater treatment projects and water pollution control programs;

(J) environmental vulnerabilities of the Long Island Sound watershed, including—

(i) the identification and assessment of such vulnerabilities in the watershed;

(ii) the development and implementation of adaptation strategies to reduce such vulnerabilities; and

(iii) the identification and assessment of the effects of sea level rise on water quality, habitat, and infrastructure; and

(3) coordinate the grant, research and planning programs authorized under this section;

(4) develop and implement strategies to increase public education and awareness with respect to the ecological health and water quality conditions of Long Island Sound;

(5) provide administrative and technical support to the conference study;

(6) collect and make available to the public (including on a publicly accessible website) publications, and other forms of information the conference study determines to be appropriate, relating to the environmental quality of Long Island Sound;

(7) monitor the progress made toward meeting the identified goals, actions, and schedules of the Comprehensive Conservation and Management Plan, including through the implementation and support of a monitoring system for the ecological health and water quality conditions of Long Island Sound; and

(8) convene conferences and meetings for legislators from State governments and political subdivisions thereof for the purpose of making recommendations for coordinating legislative efforts to facilitate the environmental restoration of Long Island Sound and the implementation of the Comprehensive Conservation and Management Plan.

(d) Grants

(1) The Administrator is authorized to make grants for projects and studies which will help implement the Long Island Sound Comprehensive Conservation and Management Plan. Special emphasis shall be given to implementation, research and planning, enforcement, and citizen involvement and education.

(2) State, interstate, and regional water pollution control agencies, and other public or nonprofit private agencies, institutions, and organizations held to be eligible for grants pursuant to this subsection.

(3) Citizen involvement and citizen education grants under this subsection shall not exceed 95 per centum of the costs of such work. All other grants under this subsection shall not exceed 60 percent of the research, studies, or work. All grants shall be made on the condition that the non-Federal share of such costs are provided from non-Federal sources.

(e) Assistance to distressed communities

(1) Eligible communities

For the purposes of this subsection, a distressed community is any community that meets affordability criteria established by the State in which the community is located, if such criteria are developed after public review and comment.

(2) Priority

In making assistance available under this section for the upgrading of wastewater treatment facilities, the Administrator may give priority to a distressed community.

(f) Report.—

(1) In general.—Not later than 2 years after the date of enactment of this Act, and biennially thereafter, the Director of the Office, in consultation with the Governor of each Long Island Sound State, shall submit to Congress a report that—

(A) summarizes and assesses the progress made by the Office and the Long Island Sound States in implementing the Long Island Sound Comprehensive Conservation and Management Plan, including an assessment of the progress made toward meeting the performance goals and milestones contained in the Plan;

(B) assesses the key ecological attributes that reflect the health of the ecosystem of the Long Island Sound watershed;

(C) describes any substantive modifications to the Long Island Sound Comprehensive Conservation and Management Plan made during the 2-year period preceding the date of submission of the report;

(D) provides specific recommendations to improve progress in restoring and protecting the Long Island Sound watershed, including, as appropriate, proposed modifications to the Long Island Sound Comprehensive Conservation and Management Plan;

(E) identifies priority actions for implementation of the Long Island Sound Comprehensive Conservation and Management Plan for the 2-year period following the date of submission of the report; and

(F) describes the means by which Federal funding and actions will be coordinated with the actions of the Long Island Sound States and other entities.

(2) Public availability.—The Administrator shall make the report described in paragraph (1) available to the public, including on a publicly accessible website.

(g) Federal entities.—

(1) Coordination.—The Administrator shall coordinate the actions of all Federal departments and agencies that affect water quality in the Long Island Sound watershed in order to improve the water quality and living resources of the watershed.

(2) Methods.—In carrying out this section, the Administrator, acting through the Director of the Office, may—

(A) enter into interagency agreements; and

(B) make intergovernmental personnel appointments.

(4)[1] **Consistency with comprehensive conservation and management plan.**—To the maximum extent practicable, the head of each Federal department or agency that owns or occupies real property, or carries out activities, within the Long Island Sound watershed shall ensure that the property and all activities carried out by the department or agency are consistent with the Long Island Sound Comprehensive Conservation and Management Plan (including any related subsequent agreements and plans).

(h) Authorizations

(1) There is authorized to be appropriated to the Administrator to carry out this section $40,000,000 for each of fiscal years 2019 through 2023.

(2) There is authorized to be appropriated to the Administrator for the implementation of subsection (d) of this section not to exceed $40,000,000 for each of fiscal years 2001 through 2010.

(June 30, 1948, c. 758, Title I, § 119, as added by Pub. L. No. 101–596, Title II, § 202, 104 Stat. 3004 (Nov. 16, 1990); and amended by Pub. L. No. 104–303, Title IV, § 583, 110 Stat. 3791 (Oct. 12, 1996); Pub. L. No. 106–457, Title IV, §§ 402 to 404, 114 Stat. 1973 (Nov. 7, 2000); Pub. L. No. 109–137, § 1, 119 Stat. 2646 (Dec. 22, 2005); Pub. L. No. 115–270, § 4104(a), (c)(1), 132 Stat. 3765, 3873–3875 (Oct. 23, 2018).)

[1] So numbered in Pub. L. No. 115–270, § 4104.

HISTORICAL AND STATUTORY NOTES

References in Text

The Marine Protection, Research, and Sanctuaries Act, referred to in subsec. (c)(4), probably means the Marine Protection, Research and Sanctuaries Act of 1972, Pub. L. No. 92–532, 86 Stat. 1052 (Oct. 23, 1972), as amended, which is codified principally as chapters 32 and 32A of Title 16 [16 U.S.C.A. §§ 1431 et seq., 1447 et seq.] and chapters 27 and 41 of this title [33 U.S.C.A. §§ 1401 et seq. 2801 et seq.] See Short Title note set out under 33 U.S.C.A § 1401 and Tables for complete classification.

Termination of Reporting Requirements

Reporting requirement of subsec. (c)(7) of this section excepted from termination under Pub. L. No. 104–66, § 3003(a)(1), as amended, set out as a note under 31 U.S.C.A. § 1113, and page 163 of House Document No. 103–7, see Pub. L. No. 107–303, § 302(a).

Long Island Sound Stewardship Initiative

Pub. L. No. 109–359, 120 Stat. 2049 (Oct. 16, 2006), provided that:

"Sec. 1. Short title.

"This Act [enacting this note] may be cited as the 'Long Island Sound Stewardship Act of 2006'.

"Sec. 2. Findings and purpose.

"(a) Findings.—Congress finds that—

"(1) Long Island Sound is a national treasure of great cultural, environmental, and ecological importance;

"(2) 8,000,000 people live within the Long Island Sound watershed and 28,000,000 people (approximately 10 percent of the population of the United States) live within 50 miles of Long Island Sound;

"(3) activities that depend on the environmental health of Long Island Sound contribute more than $5,000,000,000 each year to the regional economy;

"(4) the portion of the shoreline of Long Island Sound that is accessible to the general public (estimated at less than 20 percent of the total shoreline) is not adequate to serve the needs of the people living in the area;

"**(5)** existing shoreline facilities are in many cases overburdened and underfunded;

"**(6)** large parcels of open space already in public ownership are strained by the effort to balance the demand for recreation with the needs of sensitive natural resources;

"**(7)** approximately 1/3 of the tidal marshes of Long Island Sound have been filled, and much of the remaining marshes have been ditched, diked, or impounded, reducing the ecological value of the marshes; and

"**(8)** much of the remaining exemplary natural landscape is vulnerable to further development.

"**(b) Purpose.**—The purpose of this Act [this note] is to establish the Long Island Sound Stewardship Initiative to identify, protect, and enhance upland sites within the Long Island Sound ecosystem with significant ecological, educational, open space, public access, or recreational value through a bi-State network of sites best exemplifying these values.

"**Sec. 3. Definitions.**

"In this Act [this note], the following definitions apply:

"**(1) Administrator.**—The term 'Administrator' means the Administrator of the Environmental Protection Agency.

"**(2) Advisory committee.**—The term 'Advisory Committee' means the Long Island Sound Stewardship Advisory Committee established by section 8 [of this note].

"**(3) Region.**—The term 'Region' means the Long Island Sound Stewardship Initiative Region established by section 4(a) [of this note].

"**(4) State.**—The term 'State' means each of the States of Connecticut and New York.

"**(5) Stewardship.**—The term 'stewardship' means land acquisition, land conservation agreements, site planning, plan implementation, land and habitat management, public access improvements, site monitoring, and other activities designed to enhance and preserve natural resource-based recreation and ecological function of upland areas.

"**(6) Stewardship site.**—The term 'stewardship site' means any area of State, local, or tribal government, or privately owned land within the Region that is designated by the Administrator under section 5(a) [of this note].

"**(7) Systematic site selection.**—The term 'systematic site selection' means a process of selecting stewardship sites that—

"**(A)** has explicit goals, methods, and criteria;

"**(B)** produces feasible, repeatable, and defensible results;

"**(C)** provides for consideration of natural, physical, and biological patterns;

"**(D)** addresses replication, connectivity, species viability, location, and public recreation values;

"**(E)** uses geographic information systems technology and algorithms to integrate selection criteria; and

"**(F)** will result in achieving the goals of stewardship site selection at the lowest cost.

"**(8) Qualified applicants.**—The term 'qualified applicant' means a non-Federal person that owns title to property located within the borders of the Region.

"**(9) Threat.**—The term 'threat' means a threat that is likely to destroy or seriously degrade a conservation target or a recreation area.

"**Sec. 4. Long Island Sound Stewardship Initiative Region.**

"**(a) Establishment.**—There is established in the States of Connecticut and New York the Long Island Sound Stewardship Initiative Region.

"**(b) Boundaries.**—The Region consists of the immediate coastal upland areas along—

"**(1)** Long Island Sound between mean high water and the inland boundary, as described on the map entitled 'Long Island Sound Stewardship Region' and dated April 21, 2004; and

"(2) the Peconic Estuary as described on the map entitled 'Peconic Estuary Program Study Area Boundaries' and included in the Comprehensive Conservation and Management Plan for the Peconic Estuary Program and dated November 15, 2001.

"Sec. 5. Designation of stewardship sites.

"(a) In general.—The Administrator may designate a stewardship site in accordance with this Act [this note] any area that contributes to accomplishing the purpose of this Act.

"(b) Publication of list of recommended sites.—The Administrator shall—

"(1) publish in the Federal Register and make available in general circulation in the States of Connecticut and New York the list of sites recommended by the Advisory Committee; and

"(2) Provide a 90-day period for—

"(A) the submission of public comment on the list; and

"(B) an opportunity for owners of such sites to decline designation of such sites as stewardship sites.

"(c) Opinion regarding owner's responsibilities.—The Administrator may not designate an area as a stewardship site under this Act unless the Administrator provides to the owner of the area, and the owner acknowledges to the Administrator receipt of, a comprehensive opinion in plain English setting forth expressly the responsibility of the owner that arises from such designation.

"(d) Designation of stewardship sites.—Not later than 150 days after receiving from the Advisory Committee its list of recommended sites, the Administrator—

"(1) shall review the recommendations of the Advisory Committee; and

"(2) may designate as a stewardship site any site included in the list.

"Sec. 6. Recommendations by advisory committee.

"(a) In general.—The Advisory Committee shall—

"(1) In accordance with this section [of this note], evaluate applications—

"(A) for designation of areas as stewardship sites;

"(B) to develop management plans to address threats to stewardship sites; and

"(C) to act on opportunities to protect and enhance stewardship sites;

"(2) develop recommended guidelines, criteria, schedules, and due dates for the submission of applications and the evaluation by the Advisory Committee of information to recommend areas for designation as stewardship sites that fulfill terms of a multi-year management plan;

"(3) recommend to the Administrator a list of sites for designation as stewardship sites that further the purpose of this Act [this note];

"(4) develop management plans to address threats to stewardship sites;

"(5) raise awareness of the values of and threats to stewardship sites;

"(6) recommend that the Administrator award grants to qualified applicants; and

"(7) recommend to the Administrator ways to leverage additional resources for improved stewardship of the Region.

"(b) Identification of sites.—

"(1) In general.—Any qualified applicant may submit an application to the Advisory Committee to have a site recommended to the Administrator for designation as a stewardship site.

"(2) Identification.—The Advisory Committee shall review each application submitted under this subsection to determine whether the site exhibits values that promote the purpose of this Act.

"(3) Natural resource-based recreation areas.—In reviewing an application for recommendation of a recreation area for designation as a stewardship site, the Advisory Committee may use a selection technique that includes consideration of—

"(A) public access;

"(B) community support;

"(C) high population density;

"(D) environmental justice (as defined in section 385.3 of title 33, Code of Federal Regulations (or successor regulations));

"(E) open spaces; and

"(F) cultural, historic, and scenic characteristics.

"(4) Natural areas with ecological value.—In reviewing an application for recommendation of a natural area with ecological value for designation as a stewardship site, the Advisory Committee may use a selection technique that includes consideration of—

"(A) measurable conservation targets for the Region; and

"(B) Prioritizing new sites using systematic site selection, which shall include consideration of—

"(i) ecological uniqueness;

"(ii) species viability;

"(iii) habitat heterogeneity;

"(iv) size;

"(v) quality;

"(vi) open spaces;

"(vii) land cover;

"(viii) scientific, research, or educational value; and

"(ix) threats.

"(5) Deviation from process.—The Advisory Committee may accept an application to recommend a site other than as provided in this subsection, if the Advisory Committee—

"(A) determines that the site makes significant ecological or recreational contributions to the Region; and

"(B) provides to the Administrator the reasons for deviating from the process otherwise described in this subsection.

"(c) Submission of list of recommended sites.—

"(1) In general.—After completion of the site identification process set forth in subsection (b), the Advisory Committee shall submit to the Administrator its list of sites recommended for designation as stewardship sites.

"(2) Limitation.—The Advisory Committee shall not include a site in the list submitted under this subsection unless, prior to submission of the list, the owner of the site is—

"(A) notified of the inclusion of the site in the list; and

"(B) allowed to decline inclusion of the site in the list.

"(3) Public comment.—In identifying sites for inclusion in the list, the Advisory Committee shall provide an opportunity for submission of, and consider, public comments.

"Sec. 7. Grants and assistance.

"(a) In general.—The Administrator may provide grants, subject to the availability of appropriations, and other assistance for projects to fulfill the purpose of this Act [this note].

"(b) Federal share.—The Federal share of the cost of an activity carried out using any assistance or grant under this Act shall not exceed 60 percent of the total cost of the activity.

"Sec. 8. Long Island Sound Stewardship Advisory Committee.

"(a) Establishment.—There is established a committee to be known as the 'Long Island Sound Stewardship Advisory Committee'.

"(b) Membership.—

"(1) In general.—The Administrator may appoint the members of the Advisory Committee in accordance with this subsection and the guidance in section 320(c) of the Federal Water Pollution Control Act (33 U.S.C. 1330(c)), except that the Governor of each State may appoint 2 members of the Advisory Committee.

"(2) Additional members.—In addition to the other members appointed under this subsection, the Advisory Committee may include—

"(A) a representative of the Regional Plan Association;

"(B) a representative of marine trade organizations; and

"(C) a representative of private landowner interests.

"(3) Consideration of interests.—In appointing members of the Advisory Committee, the Administrator shall consider—

"(A) Federal, State, and local government interests and tribal interests;

"(B) the interests of nongovernmental organizations;

"(C) academic interests;

"(D) private interests including land, agriculture, and business interests; and

"(E) recreational and commercial fishing interests.

"(4) Chairperson.—In addition to the other members appointed under this subsection, the Administrator may appoint as a member of the Advisory Committee an individual to serve as the Chairperson, who may be the Director of the Long Island Sound Office of the Environmental Protection Agency.

"(5) Completion of appointments.—The Administrator shall complete the appointment of all members of the Advisory Committee by not later than 180 days after the date of enactment of this Act [Oct. 16, 2006].

"(A) Vacancies.—A vacancy on the Advisory Committee—

"(i) shall be filled not later than 90 days after the vacancy occurs;

"(ii) shall not affect the powers of the Advisory Committee; and

"(iii) shall be filled in the same manner as the original appointment was made.

"(c) Term.—

"(1) In general.—A member of the Advisory Committee shall be appointed for a term of 4 years.

"(2) Multiple terms.—An individual may be appointed as a member of the Advisory Committee for more than 1 term.

"(d) Powers.—The Advisory Committee may hold such hearings, meet and act at such times and places, take such testimony, and receive such evidence as the Advisory Committee considers advisable to carry out this Act [this note].

"(e) Meetings.—

"(1) In general.—The Advisory Committee shall meet at the call of the Chairperson, but no fewer than 4 times each year.

"(2) Initial meeting.—Not later than 30 days after the date on which all members of the Advisory Committee have been appointed, the Chairperson shall call the initial meeting of the Advisory Committee.

"(3) **Quorum.**—A majority of the members of the Advisory Committee shall constitute a quorum, but a lesser number of members may hold hearings.

"(f) **Adaptive management.**—

"(1) **In general.**—The Advisory Committee shall use an adaptive management framework to identify the best policy initiatives and actions through—

"(A) definition of strategic goals;

"(B) definition of policy options for methods to achieve strategic goals;

"(C) establishment of measures of success;

"(D) identification of uncertainties;

"(E) development of informative models of policy implementation;

"(F) separation of the landscape into geographic units;

"(G) monitoring key responses at different spatial and temporal scales; and

"(H) evaluation of outcomes and incorporation into management strategies.

"(2) **Application of adaptive management framework.**—The Advisory Committee shall apply the adaptive management framework to the process for making recommendations under subsections (b) through (f) of section 6 [sic] to the Administrator regarding sites that should be designated as stewardship sites.

"(3) **Adaptive management.**—The adaptive management framework required by this subsection shall consist of a scientific process—

"(A) For—

"(i) developing predictive models;

"(ii) making management policy decisions based upon the model outputs;

"(iii) revising the management policies as data become available with which to evaluate the policies; and

"(iv) acknowledging uncertainty, complexity, and variance in the spatial and temporal aspects of natural systems; and

"(B) that requires that management be viewed as experimental.

"(g) **Termination of advisory committee.**—The Advisory Committee shall terminate on December 31, 2021.

"Sec. 9. Reports.

"(a) **Administrator.**—The Administrator shall publish and make available to the public on the Internet and in paper form—

"(1) Not later than 1 year after the date of enactment of this Act [Oct 16, 2006], a report that—

"(A) assesses the role of this Act [this note] in protecting the Long Island Sound;

"(B) establishes in coordination with the Advisory Committee guidelines, criteria, schedules, and due dates for evaluating information to designate stewardship sites;

"(C) includes information about any grants that are available for the purchase of land or property rights to protect stewardship sites; and

"(D) accounts for funds received and expended during the previous fiscal year;

"(2) an update of such report, at least every other year; and

"(3) information on funding and any new stewardship sites more frequently than every other year.

"(b) **Advisory committee.**—

"(1) **Report.**—For each of fiscal years 2007 through 2011, the Advisory Committee shall submit to the Administrator and the decisionmaking body of the Long Island Sound Study Management Conference established under section 320 of the Federal Water Pollution Control Act (33 U.S.C. 1330), an annual report that contains—

"**(A)** a detailed statement of the findings and conclusions of the Advisory Committee since the last report under this subsection;

"**(B)** a description of all sites recommended by the Advisory Committee to the Administrator for designation as stewardship sites;

"**(C)** the recommendations of the Advisory Committee for such legislation and administrative actions as the Advisory Committee considers appropriate; and

"**(D)** in accordance with paragraph (2), the recommendations of the Advisory Committee for the awarding of grants.

"**(2) Recommendation for grants.**—

"**(A) In general.**—The Advisory Committee shall recommend that the Administrator award grants to qualified applicants to help to secure and improve the open space, public access, or ecological values of stewardship sites, through—

"**(i)** purchase of the property of a stewardship site;

"**(ii)** purchase of relevant property rights to a stewardship site; or

"**(iii)** entering into any other binding legal arrangement that ensures that the values of a stewardship site are sustained, including entering into an arrangement with a land manager or property owner to develop or implement a management plan that is necessary for the conservation of natural resources.

"**(B) Equitable distribution of funds.**—The Advisory Committee shall exert due diligence to ensure that its recommendations result in an equitable distribution of funds between the States.

"**Sec. 10. Private property protection; no regulatory authority.**

"**(a) Access to private property.**—Nothing in this Act [this note]—

"**(1)** requires any private property owner to allow public access (including Federal, State, or local government access) to the private property; or

"**(2)** modifies the application of any provision of Federal, State, or local law with regard to public access to or use of private property, except as entered into by voluntary agreement of the owner or custodian of the property.

"**(b) Liability.**—Establishment of the Region does not create any liability, or have any effect on any liability under any other law, of any private property owner with respect to any person injured on the private property.

"**(c) Recognition of authority to control land use.**—Nothing in this Act modifies the authority of Federal, State, or local governments to regulate land use.

"**(d) Participation of private property owners not required.**—Nothing in this Act requires the owner of any private property located within the boundaries of the Region to participate in any land conservation, financial or technical assistance, or other programs established under this Act.

"**(e) Purchase of land or interest in land from willing sellers only.**—Funds appropriated to carry out this Act may be used to purchase land or interests in land only from willing sellers.

"**(f) Manner of acquisition.**—All acquisitions of land under this Act shall be made in a voluntary manner and shall not be the result of forced takings.

"**(g) Effect of establishment.**—

"**(1) In general.**—The boundaries of the Region represent the area within which Federal funds appropriated for the purpose of this Act may be expended.

"**(2) Regulatory authority.**—The establishment of the Region and the boundaries of the Region do not provide any regulatory authority not in existence immediately before the enactment of this Act [Oct. 16, 2006] on land use in the Region by any management entity, except for such property rights as may be purchased from or donated by the owner of the property (including public lands donated by a State or local government).

"Sec. 11. Authorization of appropriations.

"(a) In general.—There is authorized to be appropriated to the Administrator $25,000,000 for each of fiscal years 2019 through 2023 to carry out this Act [this note], including for—

"(1) acquisition of land and interests in land;

"(2) development and implementation of site management plans;

"(3) site enhancements to reduce threats or promote stewardship; and

"(4) administrative expenses of the Advisory Committee and the Administrator.

"(b) Use of funds.—Amounts made available to the Administrator under this section [of this note] each fiscal year shall be used by the Administrator after reviewing the recommendations included in the annual reports of the Advisory Committee under section 9 [of this note].

"(c) Authorization of gifts, devises, and bequests for system.—In furtherance of the purpose of this Act, the Administrator may accept and use any gift, devise, or bequest of real or personal property, proceeds therefrom, or interests therein, to carry out this Act. Such acceptance may be subject to the terms of any restrictive or affirmative covenant, or condition of servitude, if such terms are considered by the Administrator to be in accordance with law and compatible with the purpose for which acceptance is sought.

"(d) Limitation on administrative costs.—Of the amount available each fiscal year to carry out this Act, not more than 8 percent may be used for administrative costs."

(as amended by Pub. L. No. 115–270, § 4104(b), (c)(2) 132 Stat. 3875 (Oct. 23, 2018).)

§ 1270. Lake Champlain Basin Program

[WPCA § 120]

(a) Establishment

(1) In general

There is established a Lake Champlain Management Conference to develop a comprehensive pollution prevention, control, and restoration plan for Lake Champlain. The Administrator shall convene the management conference within ninety days of November 16, 1990.

(2) Implementation

The Administrator—

(A) may provide support to the State of Vermont, the State of New York, and the New England Interstate Water Pollution Control Commission for the implementation of the Lake Champlain Basin Program; and

(B) shall coordinate actions of the Environmental Protection Agency under subparagraph (A) with the actions of other appropriate Federal agencies.";

(b) Membership

The Members of the Management Conference shall be comprised of—

(1) the Governors of the States of Vermont and New York;

(2) each interested Federal agency, not to exceed a total of five members;

(3) the Vermont and New York Chairpersons of the Vermont, New York, Quebec Citizens Advisory Committee for the Environmental Management of Lake Champlain;

(4) four representatives of the State legislature of Vermont;

(5) four representatives of the State legislature of New York;

(6) six persons representing local governments having jurisdiction over any land or water within the Lake Champlain basin, as determined appropriate by the Governors; and

(7) eight persons representing affected industries, nongovernmental organizations, public and private educational institutions, and the general public, as determined appropriate by the trigovernmental Citizens Advisory Committee for the Environmental Management of Lake Champlain, but not to be current members of the Citizens Advisory Committee.

(c) Technical Advisory Committee

(1) The Management Conference shall, not later than one hundred and twenty days after November 16, 1990, appoint a Technical Advisory Committee.

(2) Such Technical Advisory Committee shall consist of officials of: appropriate departments and agencies of the Federal Government; the State governments of New York and Vermont; and governments of political subdivisions of such States; and public and private research institutions.

(d) Research program

The Management Conference shall establish a multi-disciplinary environmental research program for Lake Champlain. Such research program shall be planned and conducted jointly with the Lake Champlain Research Consortium.

(e) Pollution prevention, control, and restoration plan

(1) Not later than three years after November 16, 1990, the Management Conference shall publish a pollution prevention, control, and restoration plan for Lake Champlain.

(2) The Plan developed pursuant to this section shall—

(A) identify corrective actions and compliance schedules addressing point and nonpoint sources of pollution necessary to restore and maintain the chemical, physical, and biological integrity of water quality, a balanced, indigenous population of shellfish, fish and wildlife, recreational, and economic activities in and on the lake;

(B) incorporate environmental management concepts and programs established in State and Federal plans and programs in effect at the time of the development of such plan;

(C) clarify the duties of Federal and State agencies in pollution prevention and control activities, and to the extent allowable by law, suggest a timetable for adoption by the appropriate Federal and State agencies to accomplish such duties within a reasonable period of time;

(D) describe the methods and schedules for funding of programs, activities, and projects identified in the Plan, including the use of Federal funds and other sources of funds;

(E) include a strategy for pollution prevention and control that includes the promotion of pollution prevention and management practices to reduce the amount of pollution generated in the Lake Champlain basin; and

(F) be reviewed and revised, as necessary, at least once every 5 years, in consultation with the Administrator and other appropriate Federal agencies.

(3) The Administrator, in cooperation with the Management Conference, shall provide for public review and comment on the draft Plan. At a minimum, the Management Conference shall conduct one public meeting to hear comments on the draft plan in the State of New York and one such meeting in the State of Vermont.

(4) Not less than one hundred and twenty days after the publication of the Plan required pursuant to this section, the Administrator shall approve such plan if the plan meets the requirements of this section and the Governors of the States of New York and Vermont concur.

(5) Upon approval of the plan, such plan shall be deemed to be an approved management program for the purposes of section 1329(h) of this title and such plan shall be deemed to be an approved comprehensive conservation and management plan pursuant to section 1330 of this title.

(f) Grant assistance

(1) The Administrator may, in consultation with participants in the Lake Champlain Basin Program, make grants to State, interstate, and regional water pollution control agencies, and public or nonprofit agencies, institutions, and organizations.

(2) Grants under this subsection shall be made for assisting research, surveys, studies, and modeling and technical and supporting work necessary for the development and implementation of the Plan.

(3) The amount of grants to any person under this subsection for a fiscal year shall not exceed 75 per centum of the costs of such research, survey, study and work and shall be made available on the condition that non-Federal share of such costs are provided from non-Federal sources.

(4) The Administrator may establish such requirements for the administration of grants as he determines to be appropriate.

(g) Definitions

In this section:

(1) Lake Champlain Basin Program

The term "Lake Champlain Basin Program" means the coordinated efforts among the Federal Government, State governments, and local governments to implement the Plan.

(2) Lake Champlain drainage basin

The term "Lake Champlain drainage basin" means all or part of Clinton, Franklin, Hamilton, Warren, Essex, and Washington counties in the State of New York and all or part of Franklin, Grand Isle, Chittenden, Addison, Rutland, Bennington, Lamoille, Orange, Washington, Orleans, and Caledonia counties in Vermont, that contain all of the streams, rivers, lakes, and other bodies of water, including wetlands, that drain into Lake Champlain.

(3) Plan

The term "Plan" means the plan developed under subsection (e) of this section.

(h) No effect on certain authority

Nothing in this section—

(1) affects the jurisdiction or powers of—

(A) any department or agency of the Federal Government or any State government; or

(B) any international organization or entity related to Lake Champlain created by treaty or memorandum to which the United States is a signatory;

(2) provides new regulatory authority for the Environmental Protection Agency; or

(3) affects section 304 of the Great Lakes Critical Programs Act of 1990 (Public Law 101–596; 33 U.S.C. 1270 note).

(i) Authorization

There are authorized to be appropriated to the Environmental Protection Agency to carry out this section—

(1) $2,000,000 for each of fiscal years 1991, 1992, 1993, 1994, and 1995;

(2) such sums as are necessary for each of fiscal years 1996 through 2003; and

(3) $11,000,000 for each of fiscal years 2004 through 2008.

(June 30, 1948, c. 758, Title I, § 120, as added by Pub. L. No. 101–596, Title III, § 303, 104 Stat. 3006 (Nov. 16, 1990); and amended by Pub. L. No. 107–303, Title II, § 202, 116 Stat. 2358 (Nov. 27, 2002).)

HISTORICAL AND STATUTORY NOTES

References in Text

Section 304 of the Great Lakes Critical Programs Act of 1990, referred to in subsec. (h)(3), is section 304 of Pub. L. No. 101–596, 104 Stat. 3008 (Nov. 16, 1990), which is set out as a note under this section.

Federal Program Coordination

Section 304 of Pub. L. No. 101–596, as amended Pub. L. No. 104–127, Title III, § 336(a)(2)(F), 110 Stat. 1005 (Apr. 4, 1996), provided that:

"(a) Designation of Lake Champlain as a priority area under the Environmental Quality Incentives Program.—

"(1) In general.—Notwithstanding any other provision of law, the Lake Champlain basin, as defined under section 120(h) of the Federal Water Pollution Control Act [section 1270(h) of this title], shall be designated by the Secretary of Agriculture as a priority area under the environmental quality incentives program established under subchapter A of chapter 4 of Title 16.

"(2) Technical assistance reimbursement.—To carry out the purposes of this subsection, the technical assistance reimbursement from the Agricultural Stabilization and Conservation Service authorized under the Soil Conservation and Domestic Allotment Act [section 590a of Title 16], shall be increased from 5 per centum to 10 per centum.

"(3) Comprehensive agricultural monitoring.—The Secretary, in consultation with the Management Conference and appropriate State and Federal agencies, shall develop a comprehensive agricultural monitoring and evaluation network for all major drainages within the Lake Champlain basin.

"(4) Allocation of funds.—In allocating funds under this subsection, the Secretary of Agriculture shall consult with the Management Conference established under section 120 of the Federal Water Pollution Control Act [section 1270 of this title] and to the extent allowable by law, allocate funds to those agricultural enterprises located at sites that the Management Conference determines to be priority sites, on the basis of a concern for ensuring implementation of nonpoint source pollution controls throughout the Lake Champlain basin.

"(b) Cooperation of the United States Geological Survey of the Department of the Interior.—For the purpose of enhancing and expanding basic data collection and monitoring in operation in the Lake Champlain basin, as defined under section 120 of the Federal Water Pollution Control Act [section 1270 of this title], the Secretary of the Interior, acting through the heads of water resources divisions of the New York and New England districts of the United States Geological Survey, shall—

"(1) in cooperation with appropriate universities and private research institutions, and the appropriate officials of the appropriate departments and agencies of the States of New York and Vermont, develop an integrated geographic information system of the Lake Champlain basin;

"(2) convert all partial recording sites in the Lake Champlain basin to continuous monitoring stations with full gauging capabilities and status; and

"(3) establish such additional continuous monitoring station sites in the Lake Champlain basin as are necessary to carry out basic data collection and monitoring, as defined by the Secretary of the Interior, including groundwater mapping, and water quality and sediment data collection.

"(c) Cooperation of the United States Fish and Wildlife Service of the Department of the Interior.—

"(1) Resource conservation program.—The Secretary of the Interior, acting through the United States Fish and Wildlife Service, in cooperation with the Lake Champlain Fish and Wildlife Management Cooperative and the Management Conference established pursuant to this subsection shall—

"(A) establish and implement a fisheries resources restoration, development and conservation program, including dedicating a level of hatchery production within the Lake Champlain basin at or above the level that existed immediately preceding the date of enactment of this Act [Nov. 16, 1990]; and

"(B) conduct a wildlife species and habitat assessment survey in the Lake Champlain basin, including—

"(i) a survey of Federal threatened and endangered species, listed or proposed for listing under the Endangered Species Act of 1973 (16 U.S.C. 1531 et seq.), New York State and State of Vermont threatened and endangered species and other species of special concern, migratory nongame species of management concern, and national resources plan species;

"(ii) a survey of wildlife habitats such as islands, wetlands, and riparian areas; and

"(iii) a survey of migratory bird populations breeding, migrating and wintering within the Lake Champlain basin.

"(2) To accomplish the purposes of paragraph (1), the Director of the United States Fish and Wildlife Service is authorized to carry out activities related to—

"(A) controlling sea lampreys and other nonindigenous aquatic animal nuisances;

"(B) improving the health of fishery resources;

"(C) conducting investigations about and assessing the status of fishery resources, and disseminating that information to all interested parties; and

"(D) conducting and periodically updating a survey of the fishery resources and their habitats and food chains in the Lake Champlain basin.

"(d) Authorizations.—(1) There is authorized to be appropriated to the Department of Agriculture $2,000,000 for each of fiscal years 1991, 1992, 1993, 1994, and 1995 to carry out subsection (a) of this section.

"(2) There is authorized to be appropriated to the Department of Interior $1,000,000 for each of fiscal years 1991, 1992, 1993, 1994, and 1995 to carry out subsections (b) and (c) of this section."

(as amended by Pub. L. No. 115–334, § 2301(d)(2)(F), 132 Stat. 4490, 4554 (Dec. 20, 2018).)

§ 1271. Sediment survey and monitoring

[NCSAMA § 503]

(a) Survey

(1) In general

The Administrator, in consultation with the Administrator of the National Oceanic and Atmospheric Administration and the Secretary, shall conduct a comprehensive national survey of data regarding aquatic sediment quality in the United States. The Administrator shall compile all existing information on the quantity, chemical and physical composition, and geographic location of pollutants in aquatic sediment, including the probable source of such pollutants and identification of those sediments which are contaminated pursuant to section 501(b)(4).

(2) Report

Not later than 24 months after October 31, 1992, the Administrator shall report to the Congress the findings, conclusions, and recommendations of such survey, including recommendations for actions necessary to prevent contamination of aquatic sediments and to control sources of contamination.

(b) Monitoring

(1) In general

The Administrator, in consultation with the Administrator of the National Oceanic and Atmospheric Administration and the Secretary, shall conduct a comprehensive and continuing program to assess aquatic sediment quality. The program conducted pursuant to this subsection shall, at a minimum—

(A) identify the location of pollutants in aquatic sediment;

(B) identify the extent of pollutants in sediment and those sediments which are contaminated pursuant to section 501(b)(4);

(C) establish methods and protocols for monitoring the physical, chemical, and biological effects of pollutants in aquatic sediment and of contaminated sediment;

(D) develop a system for the management, storage, and dissemination of data concerning aquatic sediment quality;

(E) provide an assessment of aquatic sediment quality trends over time;

(F) identify locations where pollutants in sediment may pose a threat to the quality of drinking water supplies, fisheries resources, and marine habitats; and

(G) establish a clearing house for information on technology, methods, and practices available for the remediation, decontamination, and control of sediment contamination.

(2) Report

The Administrator shall submit to Congress a report on the findings of the monitoring under paragraph (1) on the date that is 2 years after the date specified in subsection (a)(2) of this section and biennially thereafter.

(Pub. L. No. 102–580, Title V, § 503, Oct. 31, 1992, 106 Stat. 4865.)

HISTORICAL AND STATUTORY NOTES

References in Text

Section 501(b)(4), referred to in subsecs. (a)(1) and (b)(1)(B), is section 501(b)(4) of Pub. L. No. 102–580, Title V, Oct. 31, 1992, 106 Stat. 4864, which is codified in a note entitled "Definitions" and set out under this section.

Codifications

Section was enacted as part of the Water Resources Development Act of 1992 and the National Contaminated Sediment Assessment and Management Act, and not as part of the Federal Water Pollution Control Act, which comprises this chapter.

Short Title

1992 Acts. Section 501(a) of Pub. L. No. 102–580 provided that: "This title [Pub. L. No. 102–580, Title V, Oct. 31, 1992, 106 Stat. 4864, which enacted this section, amended sections 1412, 1413, 1414, 1415, 1416, 1420 and 1421 of this title, and enacted provisions set out as notes under section 1271 of this title; for distribution of Pub. L. No. 102–580 to the Code, see Short Title note set out under section 2201 of this title and Tables] may be cited as the 'National Contaminated Sediment Assessment and Management Act'."

"Secretary" Defined

Secretary means the Secretary of the Army, see section 2 of Pub. L. No. 100–676, set out as a note under 33 U.S.C.A. § 2201.

Authorization of Appropriations

Section 509(b) of Pub. L. No. 102–580 provided that: "There is authorized to be appropriated to the Administrator to carry out sections 502 [set out as a note under this section] and 503 [this section] such sums as may be necessary."

Availability of Contaminated Sediments Information

Section 327 of Pub. L. No. 102–580 directed the Secretary to conduct a national study on information currently available on contaminated sediments of surface waters of United States, compile information obtained in such study for the purpose of identifying the location and nature of contaminated sediments in the Nation, and, not later than 1 year after Oct. 31, 1992, to transmit to the Committee on Public Works and Transportation of the House of Representatives and the Committee on Environment and Public Works of the Senate a report on the results of the study.

Definitions

Section 501(b) of Pub. L. No. 102–580 provided that: "For the purposes of sections 502 [set out as a note under this section] and 503 of this title [this section]—

"(1) the term 'aquatic sediment' means sediment underlying the navigable waters of the United States;

"(2) the term 'navigable waters' has the same meaning as in section 502(7) of the Federal Water Pollution Control Act (33 U.S.C. 1362(7) [section 1362(7) of this title]);

"(3) the term 'pollutant' has the same meaning as in section 502(6) of the Federal Water Pollution Control Act (33 U.S.C. 1362(6) [section 1362(6) of this title]); except that such term does not include dredge spoil, rock, sand, or cellar dirt;

"(4) the term 'contaminated sediment' means aquatic sediment which—

"(A) contains chemical substances in excess of appropriate geochemical, toxicological or sediment quality criteria or measures; or

"(B) is otherwise considered by the Administrator to pose a threat to human health or the environment; and

"(5) the term 'Administrator' means the Administrator of the Environmental Protection Agency."

National Contaminated Sediment Task Force

Section 502 of Pub. L. No. 102–580 provided that:

"Sec. 502. National contaminated sediment task force.

"(a) Establishment.—There is established a National Contaminated Sediment Task Force (hereinafter referred to in this section as the 'Task Force'). The Task Force shall—

"(1) advise the Administrator and the Secretary in the implementation of this title [Pub. L. No. 102–580, Title V, Oct. 31, 1992, 106 Stat. 4864, which enacted this section, amended sections 1412, 1413, 1414, 1415, 1416, 1420 and 1421 of this title, and enacted provisions set out as notes under section 1271 of this title; for distribution of Pub. L. No. 102–580 to the Code, see Short Title note set out under section 2201 of this title and Tables];

"(2) review and comment on reports concerning aquatic sediment quality and the extent and seriousness of aquatic sediment contamination throughout the Nation;

"(3) review and comment on programs for the research and development of aquatic sediment restoration methods, practices, and technologies;

"(4) review and comment on the selection of pollutants for development of aquatic sediment criteria and the schedule for the development of such criteria;

"(5) advise appropriate officials in the development of guidelines for restoration of contaminated sediment;

"(6) make recommendations to appropriate officials concerning practices and measures—

"(A) to prevent the contamination of aquatic sediments; and

"(B) to control sources of sediment contamination; and

"(7) review and assess the means and methods for locating and constructing permanent, cost-effective long-term disposal sites for the disposal of dredged material that is not suitable for ocean dumping (as determined under the Marine Protection, Research, and Sanctuaries Act of 1972 (33 U.S.C. 1401 et seq.) [section 1401 et seq. of this title]).

"(b) Membership.—

"(1) In general.—The membership of the Task Force shall include 1 representative of each of the following:

"(A) The Administrator.

"(B) The Secretary.

"(C) The National Oceanic and Atmospheric Administration.

"(D) The United States Fish and Wildlife Service.

"(E) The Geological Survey.

"(F) The Department of Agriculture.

"(2) Additional members.—Additional members of the Task Force shall be jointly selected by the Administrator and the Secretary, and shall include—

"(A) not more than 3 representatives of States;

"(B) not more than 3 representatives of ports, agriculture, and manufacturing; and

"(C) not more than 3 representatives of public interest organizations with a demonstrated interest in aquatic sediment contamination.

"(3) Cochairmen.—The Administrator and the Secretary shall serve as cochairmen of the Task Force.

"(4) Clerical and technical assistance.—Such clerical and technical assistance as may be necessary to discharge the duties of the Task Force shall be provided by the personnel of the Environmental Protection Agency and the Army Corps of Engineers.

"(5) Compensation for additional members.—The additional members of the Task Force selected under paragraph (2) shall, while attending meetings or conferences of the Task Force, be compensated at a rate to be fixed by the cochairmen, but not to exceed the daily equivalent of the base rate of pay in effect for grade GS–15 of the General Schedule under section 5332 of title 5, United States Code [section 5332 of Title 5, Government Organization and Employees], for each day (including travel time) during which they are engaged in the actual performance of duties vested in the Task Force. While away from their homes or regular places of business in the performance of services for the Task Force, such members shall be allowed travel expenses, including per diem in lieu of subsistence, in the same manner as persons employed intermittently in the Government service are allowed expenses under section 5703(b) of title 5, United States Code [section 5703(b) of Title 5].

"(c) Report.—Within 2 years after the date of the enactment of this Act [Oct. 31, 1992], the Task Force shall submit to Congress a report stating the findings and recommendations of the Task Force."

§ 1271a. Research and development program

(a) In general

In coordination with other Federal, State, and local officials, the Administrator of the Environmental Protection Agency may conduct research on the development and use of innovative approaches, technologies, and techniques for the remediation of sediment contamination in areas of concern that are located wholly or partially in the United States.

(b) Authorization of appropriations

(1) In general

In addition to any amounts authorized under other provisions of law, there is authorized to be appropriated to carry out this section $3,000,000 for each of fiscal years 2004 through 2010.

(2) Availability

Funds appropriated under paragraph (1) shall remain available until expended.

(Pub. L. No. 107–303, Title I, § 106, Nov. 27, 2002, 116 Stat. 2358; Pub. L. No. 110–365, § 4, Oct. 8, 2008, 122 Stat. 4023.)

HISTORICAL AND STATUTORY NOTES

Codifications

Section was enacted as part of the Great Lakes and Lake Champlain Act of 2002 and as part of the Great Lakes Legacy Act of 2002 and not as part of the Federal Water Pollution Control Act which otherwise comprises this chapter.

§ 1272. Environmental dredging

(a) Operation and maintenance of navigation projects

Whenever necessary to meet the requirements of the Federal Water Pollution Control Act [33 U.S.C.A. § 1251 et seq.], the Secretary, in consultation with the Administrator of the Environmental Protection Agency, may remove and remediate, as part of operation and maintenance of a navigation project, contaminated sediments outside the boundaries of and adjacent to the navigation channel.

(b) Nonproject specific

(1) In general

The Secretary may remove and remediate contaminated sediments from the navigable waters of the United States for the purpose of environmental enhancement and water quality improvement if such removal and remediation is requested by a non-Federal sponsor and the sponsor agrees to pay 35 percent of the cost of such removal and remediation.

(2) Maximum amount

The Secretary may not expend more than $50,000,000 in a fiscal year to carry out this subsection.

(c) Joint plan requirement

The Secretary may only remove and remediate contaminated sediments under subsection (b) of this section in accordance with a joint plan developed by the Secretary and interested Federal, State, and local government officials. Such plan must include an opportunity for public comment, a description of the work to be undertaken, the method to be used for dredged material disposal, the roles and responsibilities of the Secretary and non-Federal sponsors, and identification of sources of funding.

(d) Disposal costs

Costs of disposal of contaminated sediments removed under this section shall be a[1] shared as a cost of construction.

(e) Limitation on statutory construction

Nothing in this section shall be construed to affect the rights and responsibilities of any person under the Comprehensive Environmental Response, Compensation, and Liability Act of 1980 [42 U.S.C.A. § 9601 et seq.].

(f) Priority work

In carrying out this section, the Secretary shall give priority to work in the following areas:

(1) Brooklyn Waterfront, New York.

(2) Buffalo Harbor and River, New York.

(3) Ashtabula River, Ohio.

(4) Mahoning River, Ohio.

(5) Lower Fox River, Wisconsin.

(6) Passaic River and Newark Bay, New Jersey.

(7) Snake Creek, Bixby, Oklahoma.

(8) Willamette River, Oregon.

(g) Nonprofit entities

Notwithstanding section 1962d–5b of Title 42, for any project carried out under this section, a non-Federal sponsor may include a nonprofit entity, with the consent of the affected local government.

(Pub. L. No. 101–640, Title III, § 312, 104 Stat. 4639 (Nov. 28, 1990); Pub. L. No. 104–303, Title II, § 205, 110 Stat. 3679 (Oct. 12, 1996); Pub. L. No. 106–53, Title II, § 224, 113 Stat. 297 (Aug. 17, 1999); Pub. L. No. 106–541, Title II, § 210(a), 114 Stat. 2592 (Dec. 11, 2000).)

[1] So in original.

HISTORICAL AND STATUTORY NOTES

References in Text

The Federal Water Pollution Control Act, as amended, referred to in text, probably means Act of June 30, 1948, c. 758, as amended generally by Pub. L. No. 92–500, § 2, Oct. 18, 1972, 86 Stat. 816, which is codified generally to this chapter 26 (section 1251 et seq.). For complete classification of this Act to the Code, see Short Title note set out under section 1251 of this title and Tables.

The Comprehensive Environmental Response, Compensation, and Liability Act, as amended, referred to in subsec. (e), is Pub. L. No. 96–510, Dec. 11, 1980, 94 Stat. 2767, as amended, which is codified principally to chapter 103 (section 9601 et seq.) of Title 42, The Public Health and Welfare. For complete classification of this Act to the Code, see Short Title note set out under section 9601 of Title 42 and Tables.

Codifications

Section was formerly set out as a note under section 1252 of this title.

Section was enacted as part of the Water Resources Development Act of 1990 and not as part of the Federal Water Pollution Control Act, which comprises this chapter.

§ 1273. Lake Pontchartrain Basin

[FWPCA § 121]

(a) Establishment of Restoration Program

The Administrator shall establish within the Environmental Protection Agency the Lake Pontchartrain Basin Restoration Program.

(b) Purpose

The purpose of the program shall be to restore the ecological health of the Basin by developing and funding restoration projects and related scientific and public education projects.

(c) Duties

In carrying out the program, the Administrator shall—

(1) provide administrative and technical assistance to a management conference convened for the Basin under section 1330 of this title;

(2) assist and support the activities of the management conference, including the implementation of recommendations of the management conference;

(3) support environmental monitoring of the Basin and research to provide necessary technical and scientific information;

(4) develop a comprehensive research plan to address the technical needs of the program;

(5) coordinate the grant, research, and planning programs authorized under this section; and

(6) collect and make available to the public publications, and other forms of information the management conference determines to be appropriate, relating to the environmental quality of the Basin.

(d) Grants

The Administrator may make grants to pay not more than 75 percent of the costs—

(1) for restoration projects and studies recommended by a management conference convened for the Basin under section 1330 of this title; and

(2) for public education projects recommended by the management conference.

(e) Definitions

In this section, the following definitions apply:

(1) Basin

The term "Basin" means the Lake Pontchartrain Basin, a 5,000 square mile watershed encompassing 16 parishes in the State of Louisiana and 4 counties in the State of Mississippi.

(2) Program

The term "program" means the Lake Pontchartrain Basin Restoration Program established under subsection (a) of this section.

(f) Authorization of appropriations

(1) In general

There is authorized to be appropriated to carry out this section $20,000,000 for each of fiscal years 2001 through 2012 and the amount appropriated for fiscal year 2009 for each of fiscal years 2013 through 2017. Such sums shall remain available until expended.

(2) Public education projects

Not more than 15 percent of the amount appropriated pursuant to paragraph (1) in a fiscal year may be expended on grants for public education projects under subsection (d)(2) of this section.

(June 30, 1948, c. 758, Title I, § 121, as added by Pub. L. No. 106–457, Title V, § 502, 114 Stat. 1973 (Nov. 7, 2000); Pub. L. No. 109–392, § 1, 120 Stat. 2703 (Dec. 12, 2006,); and amended by Pub. L. No. 112–237, § 1, 126 Stat. 1628 (Dec. 28, 2012).)

HISTORICAL AND STATUTORY NOTES

Codifications

Another section 121 of the Federal Water Pollution Control Act, which was added by of Pub. L. No. 106–554, § 1(a)(4) [Div. B, Title I, § 112(b)], and was codified as 33 U.S.C.A. § 1274, was redesignated as section 122 of the Federal Water Pollution Control Act by Pub. L. No. 109–392, § 2, 120 Stat. 2703.

Lake Pontchartrain, Louisiana

Pub. L. No. 110–114, Title V, § 5084, Nov. 8, 2007, 121 Stat. 1228, provided that: "For purposes of carrying out section 121 of the Federal Water Pollution Control Act (33 U.S.C. 1273), the Lake Pontchartrain, Louisiana, basin stakeholders conference convened by the Environmental Protection Agency, National Oceanic and Atmospheric Administration, and United States Geological Survey on February 25, 2002, shall be treated as being a management conference convened under section 320 of such Act (33 U.S.C. 1330)."

§ 1274. Watershed pilot projects

[FWPCA § 122]

(a) In general

The Administrator, in coordination with the States, may provide technical assistance and grants to a municipality or municipal entity to carry out pilot projects relating to the following areas:

(1) Watershed management of wet weather discharges

The management of municipal combined sewer overflows, sanitary sewer overflows, and stormwater discharges, on an integrated watershed or subwatershed basis for the purpose of demonstrating the effectiveness of a unified wet weather approach.

(2) Stormwater best management practices

The control of pollutants from municipal separate storm sewer systems for the purpose of demonstrating and determining controls that are cost-effective and that use innovative technologies to manage, reduce, treat, recapture, or reuse municipal stormwater, including techniques that utilize infiltration, evapotranspiration, and reuse of stormwater onsite.

(3) **Watershed partnerships.**—Efforts of municipalities and property owners to demonstrate cooperative ways to address nonpoint sources of pollution to reduce adverse impacts on water quality.

(4) **Integrated water resource plan.**—The development of an integrated water resource plan for the coordinated management and protection of surface water, ground water, and stormwater resources on a watershed or subwatershed basis to meet the objectives, goals, and policies of this Act.

(5) **Municipality-Wide stormwater management planning.**—The development of a municipality-wide plan that identifies the most effective placement of stormwater technologies and management approaches, to reduce water quality impairments from stormwater on a municipality-wide basis.

(6) **Increased resilience of treatment works.**—Efforts to assess future risks and vulnerabilities of publicly owned treatment works to manmade or natural disasters, including extreme weather events and sea-level rise, and to carry out measures, on a systemwide or area-wide basis, to increase the resiliency of publicly owned treatment works.

(b) Administration

The Administrator, in coordination with the States, shall provide municipalities participating in a pilot project under this section the ability to engage in innovative practices, including the ability to unify separate wet weather control efforts under a single permit.

(c) Report to Congress

Not later than October 1, 2015, the Administrator shall transmit to Congress a report on the results of the pilot projects conducted under this section and their possible application nationwide.

(June 30, 1948, c. 758, Title I, § 122, formerly § 121, as added by Pub. L. No. 106–554, § 1(a)(4) [Div. B, Title I, § 112(b)], 114 Stat. 2763, 2763A–225 (Dec. 21, 2000); and renumbered § 122 by Pub. L. No. 109–392, § 2, 120 Stat. 2703 (Dec. 12, 2006); and amended by Pub. L. No. 113–121, § 5011, 128 Stat. 1327–28 (June 10, 2014).)

HISTORICAL AND STATUTORY NOTES

Codifications

Prior to redesignation as section 122 of the Federal Water Pollution Control Act by Pub. L. No. 109–392, § 2, 120 Stat. 2703, this section was designated as section 121 of the Federal Water Pollution Control Act. Another section 121 of the Federal Water Pollution Control Act, added by Pub. L. No. 106–457, § 502, is codified as 33 U.S.C.A. § 1274.

§ 1275. Columbia River Basin Restoration [FWPCA § 123]

(a) Definitions.—In this section, the following definitions apply:

(1) **Columbia River Basin.**—The term 'Columbia River Basin' means the entire United States portion of the Columbia River watershed.

(2) **Estuary partnership.**—The term 'Estuary Partnership' means the Lower Columbia Estuary Partnership, an entity created by the States of Oregon and Washington and the Environmental Protection Agency under section 320.

(3) **Estuary plan.**—

(A) **In general.**—The term 'Estuary Plan' means the Estuary Partnership Comprehensive Conservation and Management Plan adopted by the Environmental Protection Agency and the Governors of Oregon and Washington on October 20, 1999, under section 320.

(B) **Inclusion.**—The term 'Estuary Plan' includes any amendments to the plan.

(4) **Lower Columbia River estuary.**—The term 'Lower Columbia River Estuary' means the mainstem Columbia River from the Bonneville Dam to the Pacific Ocean and tidally influenced portions of tributaries to the Columbia River in that region.

(5) Middle and Upper Columbia River Basin.—The term 'Middle and Upper Columbia River Basin' means the region consisting of the United States portion of the Columbia River Basin above Bonneville Dam.

(6) Program.—The term 'Program' means the Columbia River Basin Restoration Program established under subsection (b)(1)(A).

(b) Columbia River Basin restoration program.—

(1) Establishment.—

(A) In general.—The Administrator shall establish within the Environmental Protection Agency a Columbia River Basin Restoration Program.

(B) Effect.—

(i) The establishment of the Program does not modify any legal or regulatory authority or program in effect as of the date of enactment of this section, including the roles of Federal agencies in the Columbia River Basin.

(ii) This section does not create any new regulatory authority.

(2) Scope of program.—The Program shall consist of a collaborative stakeholder-based program for environmental protection and restoration activities throughout the Columbia River Basin.

(3) Duties.—The Administrator shall—

(A) assess trends in water quality, including trends that affect uses of the water of the Columbia River Basin;

(B) collect, characterize, and assess data on water quality to identify possible causes of environmental problems; and

(C) provide grants in accordance with subsection (d) for projects that assist in—

(i) eliminating or reducing pollution;

(ii) cleaning up contaminated sites;

(iii) improving water quality;

(iv) monitoring to evaluate trends;

(v) reducing runoff;

(vi) protecting habitat; or

(vii) promoting citizen engagement or knowledge.

(c) Stakeholder working group.—

(1) Establishment.—The Administrator shall establish a Columbia River Basin Restoration Working Group (referred to in this subsection as the 'Working Group').

(2) Membership.—

(A) In general.—Membership in the Working Group shall be on a voluntary basis and any person invited by the Administrator under this subsection may decline membership.

(B) Invited representatives.—The Administrator shall invite, at a minimum, representatives of—

(i) each State located in whole or in part in the Columbia River Basin;

(ii) the Governors of each State located in whole or in part in the Columbia River Basin;

(iii) each federally recognized Indian tribe in the Columbia River Basin;

(iv) local governments in the Columbia River Basin;

(v) industries operating in the Columbia River Basin that affect or could affect water quality;

(vi) electric, water, and wastewater utilities operating in the Columba River Basin;

(vii) private landowners in the Columbia River Basin;

(viii) soil and water conservation districts in the Columbia River Basin;

(ix) nongovernmental organizations that have a presence in the Columbia River Basin;

(x) the general public in the Columbia River Basin; and

(xi) the Estuary Partnership.

(3) **Geographic representation.**—The Working Group shall include representatives from—

(A) each State located in whole or in part in the Columbia River Basin; and

(B) each of the lower, middle, and upper basins of the Columbia River.

(4) **Duties and responsibilities.**—The Working Group shall—

(A) recommend and prioritize projects and actions; and

(B) review the progress and effectiveness of projects and actions implemented.

(5) **Lower Columbia River estuary.**—

(A) **Estuary partnership.**—The Estuary Partnership shall perform the duties and fulfill the responsibilities of the Working Group described in paragraph (4) as those duties and responsibilities relate to the Lower Columbia River Estuary for such time as the Estuary Partnership is the management conference for the Lower Columbia River National Estuary Program under section 320.

(B) **Designation.**—If the Estuary Partnership ceases to be the management conference for the Lower Columbia River National Estuary Program under section 320, the Administrator may designate the new management conference to assume the duties and responsibilities of the Working Group described in paragraph (4) as those duties and responsibilities relate to the Lower Columbia River Estuary.

(C) **Incorporation.**—If the Estuary Partnership is removed from the National Estuary Program, the duties and responsibilities for the lower 146 miles of the Columbia River pursuant to this section shall be incorporated into the duties of the Working Group.

(d) **Grants.**—

(1) **In general.**—The Administrator shall establish a voluntary, competitive Columbia River Basin program to provide grants to State governments, tribal governments, regional water pollution control agencies and entities, local government entities, nongovernmental entities, or soil and water conservation districts to develop or implement projects authorized under this section for the purpose of environmental protection and restoration activities throughout the Columbia River Basin.

(2) **Federal share.**—

(A) **In general.**—Except as provided in subparagraph (B), the Federal share of the cost of any project or activity carried out using funds from a grant provided to any person (including a State, tribal, or local government or interstate or regional agency) under this subsection for a fiscal year—

(i) shall not exceed 75 percent of the total cost of the project or activity; and

(ii) shall be made on condition that the non-Federal share of such total cost shall be provided from non-Federal sources.

(B) **Exceptions.**—With respect to cost-sharing for a grant provided under this subsection—

(i) a tribal government may use Federal funds for the non-Federal share; and

(ii) the Administrator may increase the Federal share under such circumstances as the Administrator determines to be appropriate.

(3) Allocation.—In making grants using funds appropriated to carry out this section, the Administrator shall—

(A) provide not less than 25 percent of the funds to make grants for projects, programs, and studies in the Lower Columbia River Estuary;

(B) provide not less than 25 percent of the funds to make grants for projects, programs, and studies in the Middle and Upper Columbia River Basin, including the Snake River Basin; and

(C) retain not more than 5 percent of the funds for the Environmental Protection Agency for purposes of implementing this section.

(4) Reporting.—

(A) In general.—Each grant recipient under this subsection shall submit to the Administrator reports on progress being made in achieving the purposes of this section.

(B) Requirements.—The Administrator shall establish requirements and timelines for recipients of grants under this subsection to report on progress made in achieving the purposes of this section.

(5) Relationship to other funding.—

(A) In general.—Nothing in this subsection limits the eligibility of the Estuary Partnership to receive funding under section 320(g).

(B) Limitation.—None of the funds made available under this subsection may be used for the administration of a management conference under section 320.

(6) Authorization of appropriations.—There is authorized to be appropriated to carry out this subsection $30,000,000 for each of fiscal years 2020 and 2021.

(e) Annual budget plan.—The President, as part of the annual budget submission of the President to Congress under section 1105(a) of title 31, United States Code, shall submit information regarding each Federal agency involved in protection and restoration of the Columbia River Basin, including an interagency crosscut budget that displays for each Federal agency—

(1) the amounts obligated for the preceding fiscal year for protection and restoration projects, programs, and studies relating to the Columbia River Basin;

(2) the estimated budget for the current fiscal year for protection and restoration projects, programs, and studies relating to the Columbia River Basin; and

(3) the proposed budget for protection and restoration projects, programs, and studies relating to the Columbia River Basin.

(June 30, 1948, c. 758, Title I, § 123, as added by Pub. L. No. 114–322, § 5010, 130 Stat. 1898–1902 (Dec. 16, 2016); and amended by Pub. L. No. 115–270, § 4105, 132 Stat. 3765, 3875 (Oct. 23, 2018).)

SUBCHAPTER II—GRANTS FOR CONSTRUCTION OF TREATMENT WORKS

§ 1281. Congressional declaration of purpose

[FWPCA § 201]

(a) Development and implementation of waste treatment management plans and practices

It is the purpose of this subchapter to require and to assist the development and implementation of waste treatment management plans and practices which will achieve the goals of this chapter.

(b) Application of technology: confined disposal of pollutants; consideration of advanced techniques

Waste treatment management plans and practices shall provide for the application of the best practicable waste treatment technology before any discharge into receiving waters, including reclaiming and recycling of water, and confined disposal of pollutants so they will not migrate to cause water or other environmental pollution and shall provide for consideration of advanced waste treatment techniques.

(c) Waste treatment management area and scope

To the extent practicable, waste treatment management shall be on an areawide basis and provide control or treatment of all point and nonpoint sources of pollution, including in place or accumulated pollution sources.

(d) Waste treatment management construction of revenue producing facilities

The Administrator shall encourage waste treatment management which results in the construction of revenue producing facilities providing for—

(1) the recycling of potential sewage pollutants through the production of agriculture, silviculture, or aquaculture products, or any combination thereof;

(2) the confined and contained disposal of pollutants not recycled;

(3) the reclamation of wastewater; and

(4) the ultimate disposal of sludge in a manner that will not result in environmental hazards.

(e) Waste treatment management integration of facilities

The Administrator shall encourage waste treatment management which results in integrating facilities for sewage treatment and recycling with facilities to treat, dispose of, or utilize other industrial and municipal wastes, including but not limited to solid waste and waste heat and thermal discharges. Such integrated facilities shall be designed and operated to produce revenues in excess of capital and operation and maintenance costs and such revenues shall be used by the designated regional management agency to aid in financing other environmental improvement programs.

(f) Waste treatment management "open space" and recreational considerations

The Administrator shall encourage waste treatment management which combines "open space" and recreational considerations with such management.

(g) Grants to construct publicly owned treatment works

(1) The Administrator is authorized to make grants to any State, municipality, or intermunicipal or interstate agency for the construction of publicly owned treatment works. On and after October 1, 1984, grants under this subchapter shall be made only for projects for secondary treatment or more stringent treatment, or any cost effective alternative thereto, new interceptors and appurtenances, and infiltration-in-flow correction. Notwithstanding the preceding sentences, the Administrator may make grants on and after October 1, 1984, for (A) any project within the definition set forth in section 1292(2) of this title, other than for a project referred to in the preceding sentence, and (B) any purpose for which a grant may be made under sections[1] 1329(h) and (i) of this title (including any innovative and alternative approaches for the control of nonpoint sources of pollution), except that not more than 20 per centum (as determined by the Governor of the State) of the amount allotted to a State under section 1285 of this title for any fiscal year shall be obligated in such State under authority of this sentence.

(2) The Administrator shall not make grants from funds authorized for any fiscal year beginning after June 30, 1974, to any State, municipality, or intermunicipal or interstate agency for the erection, building, acquisition, alteration, remodeling, improvement, or extension of treatment works unless the grant applicant has satisfactorily demonstrated to the Administrator that—

(A) alternative waste management techniques have been studied and evaluated and the works proposed for grant assistance will provide for the application of the best practicable waste treatment technology over the life of the works consistent with the purposes of this subchapter; and

(B) as appropriate, the works proposed for grant assistance will take into account and allow to the extent practicable the application of technology at a later date which will provide for the reclaiming or recycling of water or otherwise eliminate the discharge of pollutants.

(3) The Administrator shall not approve any grant after July 1, 1973, for treatment works under this section unless the applicant shows to the satisfaction of the Administrator that each sewer collection system discharging into such treatment works is not subject to excessive infiltration.

(4) The Administrator is authorized to make grants to applicants for treatment works grants under this section for such sewer system evaluation studies as may be necessary to carry out the requirements of paragraph (3) of this subsection. Such grants shall be made in accordance with rules and regulations promulgated by the Administrator. Initial rules and regulations shall be promulgated under this paragraph not later than 120 days after October 18, 1972.

(5) The Administrator shall not make grants from funds authorized for any fiscal year beginning after September 30, 1978, to any State, municipality, or intermunicipal or interstate agency for the erection, building, acquisition, alteration, remodeling, improvement, or extension of treatment works unless the grant applicant has satisfactorily demonstrated to the Administrator that innovative and alternative wastewater treatment processes and techniques which provide for the reclaiming and reuse of water, otherwise eliminate the discharge of pollutants, and utilize recycling techniques, land treatment, new or improved methods of waste treatment management for municipal and industrial waste (discharged into municipal systems) and the confined disposal of pollutants, so that pollutants will not migrate to cause water or other environmental pollution, have been fully studied and evaluated by the applicant taking into account subsection (d) of this section and taking into account and allowing to the extent practicable the more efficient use of energy and resources.

(6) The Administrator shall not make grants from funds authorized for any fiscal year beginning after September 30, 1978, to any State, municipality, or intermunicipal or interstate agency for the erection, building, acquisition, alteration, remodeling, improvement, or extension of treatment works unless the grant applicant has satisfactorily demonstrated to the Administrator that the applicant has analyzed the potential recreation and open space opportunities in the planning of the proposed treatment works.

(h) Grants to construct privately owned treatment works

A grant may be made under this section to construct a privately owned treatment works serving one or more principal residences or small commercial establishments constructed prior to, and inhabited on, December 27, 1977, where the Administrator finds that—

(1) a public body otherwise eligible for a grant under subsection (g) of this section has applied on behalf of a number of such units and certified that public ownership of such works is not feasible;

(2) such public body has entered into an agreement with the Administrator which guarantees that such treatment works will be properly operated and maintained and will comply with all other requirements of section 1284 of this title and includes a system of charges to assure that each recipient of waste treatment services under such a grant will pay its proportionate share of the cost of operation and maintenance (including replacement); and

(3) the total cost and environmental impact of providing waste treatment services to such residences or commercial establishments will be less than the cost of providing a system of collection and central treatment of such wastes.

(i) Waste treatment management methods, processes, and techniques to reduce energy requirements

The Administrator shall encourage waste treatment management methods, processes, and techniques which will reduce total energy requirements.

(j) Grants for treatment works utilizing processes and techniques of guidelines under section 1314(d)(3) of this title

The Administrator is authorized to make a grant for any treatment works utilizing processes and techniques meeting the guidelines promulgated under section 1314(d)(3) of this title, if the Administrator determines it is in the public interest and if in the cost effectiveness study made of the construction grant application for the purpose of evaluating alternative treatment works, the life cycle cost of the treatment works for which the grant is to be made does not exceed the life cycle cost of the most cost effective alternative by more than 15 per centum.

(k) Limitation on use of grants for publicly owned treatment works

No grant made after November 15, 1981, for a publicly owned treatment works, other than for facility planning and the preparation of construction plans and specifications, shall be used to treat, store, or convey the flow of any industrial user into such treatment works in excess of a flow per day equivalent to fifty thousand gallons per day of sanitary waste. This subsection shall not apply to any project proposed by a grantee which is carrying out an approved project to prepare construction plans and specifications for a facility to treat wastewater, which received its grant approval before May 15, 1980. This subsection shall not be in effect after November 15, 1981.

(*l*) Grants for facility plans, or plans, specifications, and estimates for proposed project for construction of treatment works; limitations, allotments, advances, etc.

(1) After December 29, 1981, Federal grants shall not be made for the purpose of providing assistance solely for facility plans, or plans, specifications, and estimates for any proposed project for the construction of treatment works. In the event that the proposed project receives a grant under this section for construction, the Administrator shall make an allowance in such grant for non-Federal funds expended during the facility planning and advanced engineering and design phase at the prevailing Federal share under section 1282(a) of this title, based on the percentage of total project costs which the Administrator determines is the general experience for such projects.

(2) (A) Each State shall use a portion of the funds allotted to such State each fiscal year, but not to exceed 10 per centum of such funds, to advance to potential grant applicants under this subchapter the costs of facility planning or the preparation of plans, specifications, and estimates.

(B) Such an advance shall be limited to the allowance for such costs which the Administrator establishes under paragraph (1) of this subsection, and shall be provided only to a potential grant applicant which is a small community and which in the judgment of the State would otherwise be unable to prepare a request for a grant for construction costs under this section.

(C) In the event a grant for construction costs is made under this section for a project for which an advance has been made under this paragraph, the Administrator shall reduce the amount of such grant by the allowance established under paragraph (1) of this subsection. In the event no such grant is made, the State is authorized to seek repayment of such advance on such terms and conditions as it may determine.

(m) Grants for State of California projects

(1) Notwithstanding any other provisions of this subchapter, the Administrator is authorized to make a grant from any funds otherwise allotted to the State of California under section 1285 of this title to the project (and in the amount) specified in Order WQG 81–1 of the California State Water Resources Control Board.

(2) Notwithstanding any other provision of this chapter, the Administrator shall make a grant from any funds otherwise allotted to the State of California to the city of Eureka, California, in connection with project numbered C–06–2772, for the purchase of one hundred and thirty-nine acres of property as environmental mitigation for siting of the proposed treatment plant.

(3) Notwithstanding any other provision of this chapter, the Administrator shall make a grant from any funds otherwise allotted to the State of California to the city of San Diego, California, in connection with that city's aquaculture sewage process (total resources recovery system) as an innovative and alternative waste treatment process.

(n) Water quality problems; funds, scope, etc.

(1) On and after October 1, 1984, upon the request of the Governor of an affected State, the Administrator is authorized to use funds available to such State under section 1285 of this title to address water quality problems due to the impacts of discharges from combined storm water and sanitary sewer overflows, which are not otherwise eligible under this subsection, where correction of such discharges is a major priority for such State.

(2) Beginning fiscal year 1983, the Administrator shall have available $200,000,000 per fiscal year in addition to those funds authorized in section 1287 of this title to be utilized to address water quality problems of marine bays and estuaries subject to lower levels of water quality due to the impacts of discharges from combined storm water and sanitary sewer overflows from adjacent urban complexes, not otherwise eligible under this subsection. Such sums may be used as deemed appropriate by the Administrator as provided in paragraphs (1) and (2) of this subsection, upon the request of and demonstration of water quality benefits by the Governor of an affected State.

(*o*) Capital financing plan

The Administrator shall encourage and assist applicants for grant assistance under this subchapter to develop and file with the Administrator a capital financing plan which, at a minimum—

(1) projects the future requirements for waste treatment services within the applicant's jurisdiction for a period of no less than ten years;

(2) projects the nature, extent, timing, and costs of future expansion and reconstruction of treatment works which will be necessary to satisfy the applicant's projected future requirements for waste treatment services; and

(3) sets forth with specificity the manner in which the applicant intends to finance such future expansion and reconstruction.

(p) Time limit on resolving certain disputes

In any case in which a dispute arises with respect to the awarding of a contract for construction of treatment works by a grantee of funds under this subchapter and a party to such dispute files an appeal with the Administrator under this subchapter for resolution of such dispute, the Administrator shall make a final decision on such appeal within 90 days of the filing of such appeal.

(June 30, 1948, c. 758, Title II, § 201, as added by Pub. L. No. 92–500, § 2, 86 Stat. 833 (Oct. 18, 1972); and amended by Pub. L. No. 95–217, §§ 12–16, 91 Stat. 1569, 1570 (Dec. 27, 1977); Pub. L. No. 96–483, §§ 2(d), 3, 94 Stat. 2361 (Oct. 21, 1980); Pub. L. No. 97–117, §§ 2(a), 3(a), 4–6, 10(c), 95 Stat. 1623–1626 (Dec. 29, 1981); Pub. L. No. 100–4, Title II, § 201, Title III, § 316(c), 101 Stat. 15, 60 (Feb. 4, 1987).)

[1] So in original. Probably should be "section".

HISTORICAL AND STATUTORY NOTES

Effective and Applicability Provisions

1980 Acts. Section 2(g) of Pub. L. No. 96–483, provided that: "The amendments made by this section [amending sections 1281, 1284, and 1293 of this title enacting provisions set out as notes under section 1284 of this title, and amending provisions set out as a note under section 1284 of this title] shall take effect on December 27, 1977."

Environmental Protection Agency State and Tribal Assistance Grants

Pub. L. No. 105–174, Title III, 112 Stat. 92 (May 1, 1998), provided, in part, that: "Notwithstanding any other provision of law, eligible recipients of the funds appropriated to the Environmental Protection Agency in the State and Tribal Assistance Grants account since fiscal year 1997 and hereafter for multi-media or single media grants, other than Performance Partnership Grants authorized pursuant to Public Law 104–134 and Public Law 105–65, for pollution prevention, control, and abatement and related activities have been and shall be those entities eligible for grants under the Agency's organic statutes."

Grants to Indian Tribes for Pollution Prevention, Control and Abatement

Pub. L. No. 105–65, Title III, 111 Stat. 1373 (Oct. 27, 1997), provided in part that: "$745,000,000 for grants to States, federally recognized tribes, and air pollution control agencies for multi-media or single media pollution prevention, control and abatement and related activities pursuant to the provisions set forth under this heading in Public Law 104–134 [Omnibus Consolidated Recissions and Appropriations Act of 1996, Pub. L. No. 104–134, 111 Stat. 1321 (April 26, 1996), for classification of which see Tables], provided that eligible recipients of these funds and the funds made available for this purpose since fiscal year 1996 and hereafter include States, federally recognized tribes, interstate agencies, tribal consortia, and air pollution control agencies, as provided in authorizing statutes, subject to such terms and conditions as the Administrator shall establish, and for making grants under section 103 of the Clean Air Act [section 7403 of Title 42] for particulate matter monitoring and data collection activities:"

Multi-media or Single Media Pollution Control Prevention

Pub. L. No. 105–65, Title III, 111 Stat. 1374 (Oct. 27, 1997), provided in part that: "hereafter from funds appropriated under this heading, the Administrator is authorized to make grants to federally recognized Indian governments for the development of multi-media environmental programs: That, hereafter, the funds available under this heading for grants to States, federally recognized tribes, and air pollution control agencies for multi-media or single media pollution prevention, control and abatement and related activities may also be used for the direct implementation by the Federal Government of a program required by law in the absence of an acceptable State or tribal program:"

Similar provisions were contained in the following prior Acts:

Pub. L. No. 104–204, Title III, 110 Stat. 2912 (Sept. 26, 1996).

Pub. L. No. 104–134, Title I, § 101(e), [Title III] 110 Stat. 1321–299 (April 26, 1996), renumbered Title I by Pub. L. No. 104–140, § 1(a), 110 Stat. 1327 (May 2, 1996).

Pub. L. No. 103–327, Title III, 108 Stat. 2320 (Sept. 28, 1994).

Pub. L. No. 103–124, Title III, 107 Stat. 1293 (Oct. 28, 1993).

Pub. L. No. 102–389, Title III, 106 Stat. 1597 (Oct. 6, 1992).

Pub. L. No. 102–139, Title III, 105 Stat. 762 (Oct. 28, 1991).

Pub. L. No. 101–507, Title III, 104 Stat. 1372 (Nov. 5, 1990).

Privatization of Infrastructure Assets

Pub. L. No. 104–303, Title V, § 586, 110 Stat. 3791 (Oct. 12, 1996), provided that:

"(a) In general.—Notwithstanding the provisions of title II of the Federal Water Pollution Control Act (33 U.S.C. 1281 et seq.) [Act of June 30, 1948, c. 758, for complete classification to the Code, see Short Title note under section 1251 of this title], Executive Order 12803 [set out as a note under section 601 of Title 5, Government Organization and Employees], or any other law or authority, an entity that received Federal grant assistance for an infrastructure asset under the Federal Water Pollution Control Act shall not be required to repay any portion of the grant upon the lease or concession of the asset only if—

"(1) ownership of the asset remains with the entity that received the grant; and

"(2) the Administrator of the Environmental Protection Agency determines that the lease or concession furthers the purposes of such Act and approves the lease or concession.

"(b) Limitation.—The Administrator shall not approve a total of more than 5 leases and concessions under this section [this note]."

Grants to States to Administer Completion and Closeout of Construction Grants Program

Pub. L. No. 104–204, Title III, 110 Stat. 2912 (Sept. 26, 1996), provided: "That notwithstanding any other provision of law, beginning in fiscal year 1997 the Administrator may make grants to States, from funds available for obligation in the State under title II of the Federal Water Pollution Control Act [this subchapter], as amended, for administering the completion and closeout of the State's construction grants program, based on a budget annually negotiated with the State."

Wastewater Assistance to Colonias

Pub. L. No. 104–182, Title III, § 307, 110 Stat. 1688 (Aug. 6, 1996), provided that:

"(a) Definitions.—As used in this section:

"(1) Border State.—The term 'border State' means Arizona, California, New Mexico, and Texas.

"(2) Eligible community.—The term 'eligible community' means a low-income community with economic hardship that—

"**(A)** is commonly referred to as a colonia;

"**(B)** is located along the United States-Mexico border (generally in an unincorporated area); and

"**(C)** lacks basic sanitation facilities such as household plumbing or a proper sewage disposal system.

"**(3) Treatment works.**—The term 'treatment works' has the meaning provided in section 212(2) of the Federal Water Pollution Control Act (33 U.S.C. 1292(2)) [section 1292(2) of this title].

"**(b) Grants for wastewater assistance.**—The Administrator of the Environmental Protection Agency and the heads of other appropriate Federal agencies are authorized to award grants to a border State to provide assistance to eligible communities for the planning, design, and construction or improvement of sewers, treatment works, and appropriate connections for wastewater treatment.

"**(c) Use of funds.**—Each grant awarded pursuant to subsection (b) shall be used to provide assistance to one or more eligible communities with respect to which the residents are subject to a significant health risk (as determined by the Administrator or the head of the Federal agency making the grant) attributable to the lack of access to an adequate and affordable treatment works for wastewater.

"**(d) Cost sharing.**—The amount of a grant awarded pursuant to this section shall not exceed 50 percent of the costs of carrying out the project that is the subject of the grant.

"**(e) Authorization of appropriations.**—There are authorized to be appropriated to carry out this section $25,000,000 for each of the fiscal years 1997 through 1999."

[Provisions effective Aug. 6, 1996, see section 2(b) of Pub. L. No. 104–182, set out as a note under section 300f of Title 42, The Public Health and Welfare.]

Authorization to Make Grants to Indian Tribes for Pollution Prevention, Control and Abatement

Pub. L. No. 104–134, Title I, § 101(e)[Title III], 110 Stat. 1321–299 (Apr. 26, 1996); renumbered Title I by Pub. L. No. 104–140, § 1(a), 110 Stat. 1327 (May 2, 1996), provided in part: "That beginning in fiscal year 1996 and each fiscal year thereafter, and notwithstanding any other provision of law, the Administrator is authorized to make grants annually from funds appropriated under this heading, subject to such terms and conditions as the Administrator shall establish, to any State or federally recognized Indian tribe for multimedia or single media pollution prevention, control and abatement and related environmental activities at the request of the Governor or other appropriate State official or the tribe[.]"

State Management of Construction Grant Activities

Pub. L. No. 104–134, Title I, § 101(e)[Title III], 110 Stat. 1321–299 (Apr. 26, 1996); renumbered Title I by Pub. L. No. 104–140, § 1(a), 110 Stat. 1327 (May 2, 1996), provided in part: "That of the funds appropriated in the Construction Grants and Water Infrastructure/State Revolving Funds accounts since the appropriation for the fiscal year ending September 30, 1992, and hereafter, for making grants for wastewater treatment works construction projects, portions may be provided by the recipients to States for managing construction grant activities, on condition that the States agree to reimburse the recipients from State funding sources[.]"

Grants to Trust Territory of the Pacific Islands, American Samoa, Guam, the Northern Mariana Islands, and the Virgin Islands; Waiver by Administrator of Limitations Relating to Collector Sewers

Pub. L. No. 99–396, § 12(b), 100 Stat. 841 (Aug. 27, 1986), provided that: "In awarding grants to the Trust Territory of the Pacific Islands, American Samoa, Guam, the Northern Mariana Islands and the Virgin Islands under section 201(g)(1) of the Clean Water Act (33 U.S.C. 1251 et seq.) [subsec. (g)(1) of this section], the Administrator of the Environmental Protection Agency may waive limitations regarding grant eligibility for sewerage facilities and related appurtenances, insofar as such limitations relate to collector sewers, based upon a determination that applying such limitations could hinder the alleviation of threats to public health and water quality. In making such a determination, the Administrator shall take into consideration the public health and water quality benefits to be derived and the availability of alternate funding sources. The Administrator shall not award grants under this section for the operation and maintenance of sewerage facilities, for construction of facilities which are not an essential component of the sewerage facilities, or any other activities or facilities which are not concerned with the management of wastewater to alleviate threats to public health and water quality."

Environmental Financing Authority

Section 12 of Pub. L. No. 92–500, as amended by Pub. L. No. 97–258, § 4(b), 96 Stat. 1067 (Sept. 13, 1982), provided that:

"(a) [Short Title] This section may be cited as the 'Environmental Financing Act of 1972.'

"(b) [Establishment] There is hereby created a body corporate to be known as the Environmental Financing Authority, which shall have succession until dissolved by Act of Congress. The Authority shall be subject to the general supervision and direction of the Secretary of the Treasury. The Authority shall be an instrumentality of the United States Government and shall maintain such offices as may be necessary or appropriate in the conduct of its business.

"(c) [Congressional Declaration of Purpose] The purpose of this section is to assure that inability to borrow necessary funds on reasonable terms does not prevent any State or local public body from carrying out any project for construction of waste treatment works determined eligible for assistance pursuant to subsection (e) of this section.

"(d) [Board of Directors] (1) The Authority shall have a Board of Directors consisting of five persons, one of whom shall be the Secretary of the Treasury or his designee as Chairman of the Board, and four of whom shall be appointed by the President from among the officers or employees of the Authority or of any department or agency of the United States Government.

"(2) The Board of Directors shall meet at the call of its Chairman. The Board shall determine the general policies which shall govern the operations of the Authority. The Chairman of the Board shall select and effect the appointment of qualified persons to fill the offices as may be provided for in the bylaws, with such executive functions, powers, and duties as may be prescribed by the bylaws or by the Board of Directors, and such persons shall be the executive officers of the Authority and shall discharge all such executive functions, powers, and duties. The members of the Board, as such, shall not receive compensation for their services.

"(e) [Purchase of State and Local Obligations] (1) Until July 1, 1975, the Authority is authorized to make commitments to purchase, and to purchase on terms and conditions determined by the Authority, any obligation or participation therein which is issued by a State or local public body to finance the non-Federal share of the cost of any project for the construction of waste treatment works which the Administrator of the Environmental Protection Agency has determined to be eligible for Federal financial assistance under the Federal Water Pollution Control Act [this chapter].

"(2) No commitment shall be entered into, and no purchase shall be made, unless the Administrator of the Environmental Protection Agency (A) has certified that the public body is unable to obtain on reasonable terms sufficient credit to finance its actual needs; (B) has approved the project as eligible under the Federal Water Pollution Control Act [this chapter]; and (C) has agreed to guarantee timely payment of principal and interest on the obligation. The Administrator is authorized to guarantee such timely payments and to issue regulations as he deems necessary and proper to protect such guarantees. Appropriations are hereby authorized to be made to the Administrator in such sums as are necessary to make payments under such guarantees, and such payments are authorized to be made from such appropriations.

"(3) No purchase shall be made of obligations issued to finance projects, the permanent financing of which occurred prior to the enactment of this section [Oct. 18, 1972].

"(4) Any purchase by the Authority shall be upon such terms and conditions as to yield a return at a rate determined by the Secretary of the Treasury taking into consideration (A) the current average yield on outstanding marketable obligations of the United States of comparable maturity or in its stead whenever the Authority has sufficient of its own long-term obligations outstanding, the current average yield on outstanding obligations of the Authority of comparable maturity; and (B) the market yields on municipal bonds.

"(5) The Authority is authorized to charge fees for its commitments and other services adequate to cover all expenses and to provide for the accumulation of reasonable contingency reserves and such fees shall be included in the aggregate project costs.

"(f) [Initial Capital] To provide initial capital to the Authority the Secretary of the Treasury is authorized to advance the funds necessary for this purpose. Each such advance shall be upon such terms and conditions as to yield a return at a rate not less than a rate determined by the Secretary of the Treasury taking into consideration the current average yield on outstanding marketable obligations of the United States of comparable maturities. Interest payments on such advances may be deferred, at the discretion of the Secretary, but any such deferred payments shall themselves bear interest at the rate specified in this section. There is authorized to be appropriated not to exceed $100,000,000, which shall be available for the purposes of this subsection.

"(g) [Issuance of Obligations] (1) The Authority is authorized, with the approval of the Secretary of the Treasury, to issue and have outstanding obligations having such maturities and bearing such rate or rates of interest as may be determined by the Authority. Such obligations may be redeemable at the option of the Authority before maturity in such manner as may be stipulated therein.

"(h) [Interest Differential] The Secretary of the Treasury is authorized and directed to make annual payments to the Authority in such amounts as are necessary to equal the amount by which the dollar amount of interest expense accrued by the Authority on account of its obligations exceeds the dollar amount of interest income accrued by the Authority on account of obligations purchased by it pursuant to subsection (e) of this section.

"(i) [Powers] The Authority shall have power—

"(1) to sue and be sued, complain and defend, in its corporate name;

"(2) to adopt, alter, and use a corporate seal, which shall be judicially noticed;

"(3) to adopt, amend, and repeal by-laws, rules, and regulations as may be necessary for the conduct of its business;

"(4) to conduct its business, carry on its operations, and have offices and exercise the powers granted by this section in any State without regard to any qualification or similar statute in any State;

"(5) to lease, purchase, or otherwise acquire, own, hold, improve, use, or otherwise deal in and with any property, real, personal, or mixed, or any interest therein, wherever situated;

"(6) to accept gifts or donations of services, or of property, real, personal, or mixed, tangible or intangible, in aid of any of the purposes of the Authority;

"(7) to sell, convey, mortgage, pledge, lease, exchange, and otherwise dispose of its property and assets;

"(8) to appoint such officers, attorneys, employees, and agents as may be required, to define their duties, to fix and to pay such compensation for their services as may be determined, subject to the civil service and classification laws, to require bonds for them and pay the premium thereof; and

"(9) to enter into contracts, to execute instruments, to incur liabilities, and to do all things as are necessary or incidental to the proper management of its affairs and the proper conduct of its business.

"(j) [Tax Exemptions; Exceptions] The Authority, its property, its franchise, capital, reserves, surplus, security holdings, and other funds, and its income shall be exempt from all taxation now or hereafter imposed by the United States or by any State or local taxing authority; except that (A) any real property and any tangible personal property of the Authority shall be subject to Federal, State, and local taxation to the same extent according to its value as other such property is taxed, and (B) any and all obligations issued by the Authority shall be subject both as to principal and interest to Federal, State, and local taxation to the same extent as the obligations of private corporations are taxed.

"(k) [Nature of Obligations] All obligations issued by the Authority shall be lawful investments, and may be accepted as security for all fiduciary, trust, and public funds, the investment or deposit of which shall be under authority or control of the United States or of any officer or officers thereof. All obligations issued by the Authority pursuant to this section shall be deemed to be exempt securities within the meaning of laws administered by the Securities and Exchange Commission, to the same extent as securities which are issued by the United States.

"(*l*) [Preparation of Obligations by Secretary of Treasury] In order to furnish obligations for delivery by the Authority, the Secretary of the Treasury is authorized to prepare such obligations in such form as the Authority may approve, such obligations when prepared to be held in the Treasury subject to delivery upon order by the Authority. The engraved plates, dies, bed pieces, and so forth, executed in connection therewith, shall remain in the custody of the Secretary of the Treasury. The Authority shall reimburse the Secretary of the Treasury for any expenditures made in the preparation, custody, and delivery of such obligations.

"(m) [Annual Report to Congress] The Authority shall, as soon as practicable after the end of each fiscal year, transmit to the President and the Congress an annual report of its operations and activities.

"(n) [Subsec. (n) amended section 24 of Title 12, Banks and Banking, and is not set out herein.]

"(*o*) [Financial Controls] The budget and audit provisions of chapter 91 of title 31 shall be applicable to the Environmental Financing Authority in the same manner as they are applied to the wholly owned Government corporations. (As amended Pub. L. No. 97–258, § 4(b), Sept. 13, 1982, 96 Stat. 1067.)

"(p) [Subsec. (p) amended section 711 of Title 31, Money and Finance, and is not set out herein.]"

§ 1281a. Total treatment system funding

Notwithstanding any other provision of law, in any case where the Administrator of the Environmental Protection Agency finds that the total of all grants made under section 1281 of this title for the same treatment works exceeds the actual construction costs for such treatment works (as defined in this chapter) such excess amount shall be a grant of the Federal share (as defined in this chapter) of the cost of construction of a sewage collection system if—

(1) such sewage collection system was constructed as part of the same total treatment system as the treatment works for which such grants under section 1281 of this title were approved, and

(2) an application for assistance for the construction of such sewage collection system was filed in accordance with section 3102 of Title 42 before all such grants under section 1281 of this title were made and such grant under section 3102 of Title 42 could not be approved due to lack of funding under such section 3102 of Title 42.

The total of all grants for sewage collection systems made under this section shall not exceed $2,800,000.

(Pub. L. No. 95–217, § 78, 91 Stat. 1611 (Dec. 27, 1977).)

HISTORICAL AND STATUTORY NOTES

References in Text

Section 3102 of title 42, referred to in par. (2), was omitted from the Code pursuant to 42 U.S.C.A. § 5316, which terminated the authority to make grants or loans under that section after Jan. 1, 1975.

Codifications

This section was enacted as part of the Clean Water Act of 1977, Pub. L. No. 95–217, and not as part of the Federal Water Pollution Control Act, June 30, 1948, c. 758, as added by Pub. L. No. 92–500, 86 Stat. 816 (Oct. 18, 1972), which comprises this chapter.

§ 1281b. Availability of Farmers Home Administration funds for non-Federal share

Notwithstanding any other provision of law, Federal assistance made available by the Farmers Home Administration to any political subdivision of a State may be used to provide the non-Federal share of the cost of any construction project carried out under section 1281 of this title.

(Pub. L. No. 100–4, Title II, § 202(f), 101 Stat. 16 (Feb. 4, 1987).)

HISTORICAL AND STATUTORY NOTES

Codifications

This section was enacted as part of the Water Quality Act of 1987, and not as part of the Federal Water Pollution Control Act, which comprises this chapter.

§ 1282. Federal share

[FWPCA § 202]

(a) Amount of grants for treatment works

(1) The amount of any grant for treatment works made under this chapter from funds authorized for any fiscal year beginning after June 30, 1971, and ending before October 1, 1984, shall be 75 per centum of the cost of construction thereof (as approved by the Administrator), and for any fiscal year beginning on or after October 1, 1984, shall be 55 per centum of the cost of construction thereof (as approved by the Administrator), unless modified to a lower percentage rate uniform throughout a State by the Governor of that State with the concurrence of the Administrator. Within ninety days after October 21, 1980, the Administrator shall issue guidelines for concurrence in any such modification, which shall provide for the consideration of the unobligated balance of sums allocated to the State under section 1285 of this title, the need for assistance under this subchapter in such State, and the availability of State grant assistance to replace the Federal share reduced by such modification. The payment of any such reduced Federal share shall not constitute an obligation on the part of the United States or a claim on the part of any State or grantee to reimbursement for the portion of the Federal share reduced in any such State. Any grant (other than for reimbursement) made prior to October 18, 1972, from any funds authorized for any fiscal year beginning after June 30, 1971, shall, upon the request of the applicant, be increased to the applicable percentage under this section. Notwithstanding the first sentence of this paragraph, in any case where a primary, secondary, or advanced waste treatment facility or its related interceptors or a project for infiltration-in-flow correction has received a grant for erection, building, acquisition, alteration, remodeling, improvement, extension, or correction before October 1, 1984, all segments and phases of such facility, interceptors, and project for infiltration-in-flow correction shall be eligible for grants at 75 per centum of the cost of construction thereof for any grant made pursuant to a State obligation which obligation occurred before October 1, 1990. Notwithstanding the first sentence of this paragraph, in the case of a project for which an application for a grant under this subchapter has been made to the Administrator before October 1, 1984, and which project is under judicial injunction on such date prohibiting its construction, such project shall be eligible for grants at 75 percent of the cost of construction thereof. Notwithstanding the first sentence of this paragraph, in the case of the Wyoming Valley Sanitary Authority project mandated by judicial order under a proceeding begun prior to October 1, 1984, and a project for wastewater treatment for Altoona, Pennsylvania, such projects shall be eligible for grants at 75 percent of the cost of construction thereof.

(2) The amount of any grant made after September 30, 1978, and before October 1, 1981, for any eligible treatment works or significant portion thereof utilizing innovative or alternative wastewater treatment processes and techniques referred to in section 1281(g)(5) of this title shall be 85 per centum of the cost of construction thereof, unless modified by the Governor of the State with the concurrence of the Administrator to a percentage rate no less than 15 per centum greater than the modified uniform percentage rate in which the Administrator has concurred pursuant to paragraph (1) of this subsection. The amount of any grant made after September 30, 1981, for any eligible treatment works or unit processes and techniques thereof utilizing innovative or alternative wastewater treatment processes and techniques referred to in section 1281(g)(5) of this title shall be a percentage of the cost of construction thereof equal to 20 per centum greater than the percentage in effect under paragraph (1) of this subsection for such works or unit processes and techniques, but in no event greater than 85 per centum of the cost of construction thereof. No grant shall be made under this paragraph for construction of a treatment works in any State unless the proportion of the State contribution to the non-Federal share of construction costs for all treatment works in such State receiving a grant under this paragraph is the same as or greater than the proportion of the State contribution (if any) to the non-Federal share of construction costs for all treatment works receiving grants in such State under paragraph (1) of this subsection.

(3) In addition to any grant made pursuant to paragraph (2) of this subsection, the Administrator is authorized to make a grant to fund all of the costs of the modification or replacement of any facilities constructed with a grant made pursuant to paragraph (2) if the Administrator finds that such facilities have not met design performance specifications unless such failure is attributable to negligence on the part of any person and if such failure has significantly increased capital or operating and maintenance expenditures. In addition, the Administrator is authorized to make a grant to fund all of the costs of the modification or replacement of biodisc equipment (rotating biological contactors) in any publicly owned treatment works if the Administrator finds that such equipment has failed to meet design performance specifications, unless such failure is attributable to negligence on the part of any person, and if such failure has significantly increased capital or operating and maintenance expenditures.

(4) For the purposes of this section, the term "eligible treatment works" means those treatment works in each State which meet the requirements of section 1281(g)(5) of this title and which can be fully funded from funds available for such purpose in such State.

(b) Amount of grants for construction of treatment works not commenced prior to July 1, 1971

The amount of the grant for any project approved by the Administrator after January 1, 1971, and before July 1, 1971, for the construction of treatment works, the actual erection, building or acquisition of which was not commenced prior to July 1, 1971, shall, upon the request of the applicant, be increased to the applicable percentage under subsection (a) of this section for grants for treatment works from funds for fiscal years beginning after June 30, 1971, with respect to the cost of such actual erection, building, or acquisition. Such increased amount shall be paid from any funds allocated to the State in which the treatment works is located without regard to the fiscal year for which such funds were authorized. Such increased amount shall be paid for such project only if—

(1) a sewage collection system that is a part of the same total waste treatment system as the treatment works for which such grant was approved is under construction or is to be constructed for use in conjunction with such treatment works, and if the cost of such sewage collection system exceeds the cost of such treatment works, and

(2) the State water pollution control agency or other appropriate State authority certifies that the quantity of available ground water will be insufficient, inadequate, or unsuitable for public use, including the ecological preservation and recreational use of surface water bodies, unless effluents from publicly-owned treatment works after adequate treatment are returned to the ground water consistent with acceptable technological standards.

(c) Availability of sums allotted to Puerto Rico

Notwithstanding any other provision of law, sums allotted to the Commonwealth of Puerto Rico under section 1285 of this title for fiscal year 1981 shall remain available for obligation for the fiscal year for which authorized and for the period of the next succeeding twenty-four months. Such sums and any unobligated funds available to Puerto Rico from allotments for fiscal years ending prior to October 1, 1981, shall be available for obligation by the Administrator of the Environmental Protection Agency only to fund the following systems: Aguadilla, Arecibo, Mayaguez, Carolina, and Camuy Hatillo. These funds may be used by the Commonwealth of Puerto Rico to fund the non-Federal share of the costs of such projects. To the extent that these funds are used to pay the non-Federal share, the Commonwealth of Puerto Rico shall repay to the Environmental Protection Agency such amounts on terms and conditions developed and approved by the Administrator in consultation with the Governor of the Commonwealth of Puerto Rico. Agreement on such terms and conditions, including the payment of interest to be determined by the Secretary of the Treasury, shall be reached prior to the use of these funds for the Commonwealth's non-Federal share. No Federal funds awarded under this provision shall be used to replace local governments funds previously expended on these projects.

(June 30, 1948, c. 758, Title II, § 202, as added by Pub. L. No. 92–500, § 2, 86 Stat. 834 (Oct. 18, 1972); and amended by Pub. L. No. 95–217, § 17, 91 Stat. 1571 (Dec. 27, 1977); Pub. L. No. 96–483, § 9, 94 Stat. 2362 (Oct. 21, 1980); Pub. L. No. 97–117, §§ 7, 8(a), (b), 95 Stat. 1625 (Dec. 29, 1981); Pub. L. No. 97–357, Title V, § 501, 96 Stat. 1712 (Oct. 19, 1982); Pub. L. No. 100–4, Title II, § 202(a)–(d), 101 Stat. 15, 16 (Feb. 4, 1987).)

HISTORICAL AND STATUTORY NOTES

Promulgation of Federal Shares

Act of July 9, 1956, c. 518, § 4, 70 Stat. 507, authorized the Surgeon General to promulgate Federal shares under the Federal Water Pollution Control Grant Program as soon as possible after July 9, 1956, in the manner specified in the Water Pollution Control Act, Act of June 30, 1948, c. 758, 62 Stat. 1155, and provided that such shares were to be conclusive for the purposes of section 5 of Act of June 30, 1948.

§ 1283. Plans, specifications, estimates, and payments

[FWPCA § 203]

(a) Submission; contractual nature of approval by Administrator; agreement on eligible costs; single grant

(1) Each applicant for a grant shall submit to the Administrator for his approval, plans, specifications, and estimates for each proposed project for the construction of treatment works for which a grant is applied for under section 1281(g)(1) of this title from funds allotted to the State under section 1285 of this title and which otherwise meets the requirements of this chapter. The Administrator shall act upon such plans, specifications, and estimates as soon as practicable after the same have been submitted, and his approval of any such plans, specifications, and estimates shall be deemed a contractual obligation of the United States for the payment of its proportional contribution to such project.

(2) Agreement on eligible costs

(A) Limitation on modifications

Before taking final action on any plans, specifications, and estimates submitted under this subsection after the 60th day following February 4, 1987, the Administrator shall enter into a written agreement with the applicant which establishes and specifies which items of the proposed project are eligible for Federal payments under this section. The Administrator may not later modify such eligibility determinations unless they are found to have been made in violation of applicable Federal statutes and regulations.

(B) Limitation on effect

Eligibility determinations under this paragraph shall not preclude the Administrator from auditing a project pursuant to section 1361 of this title, or other authority, or from withholding or recovering Federal funds for costs which are found to be unreasonable, unsupported by adequate documentation, or otherwise unallowable under applicable Federal cost principles, or which are incurred on a project which fails to meet the design specifications or effluent limitations contained in the grant agreement and permit pursuant to section 1342 of this title for such project.

(3) In the case of a treatment works that has an estimated total cost of $8,000,000 or less (as determined by the Administrator), and the population of the applicant municipality is twenty-five thousand or less (according to the most recent United States census), upon completion of an approved facility plan, a single grant may be awarded for the combined Federal share of the cost of preparing construction plans and specifications, and the building and erection of the treatment works.

(b) Periodic payments

The Administrator shall, from time to time as the work progresses, make payments to the recipient of a grant for costs of construction incurred on a project. These payments shall at no time exceed the Federal share of the cost of construction incurred to the date of the voucher covering such payment plus the Federal share of the value of the materials which have been stockpiled in the vicinity of such construction in conformity to plans and specifications for the project.

(c) Final payments

After completion of a project and approval of the final voucher by the Administrator, he shall pay out of the appropriate sums the unpaid balance of the Federal share payable on account of such project.

(d) Projects eligible

Nothing in this chapter shall be construed to require, or to authorize the Administrator to require, that grants under this chapter for construction of treatment works be made only for projects which are operable units usable for sewage collection, transportation, storage, waste treatment, or for similar purposes without additional construction.

(e) Technical and legal assistance in administration and enforcement of contracts; intervention in civil actions

At the request of a grantee under this subchapter, the Administrator is authorized to provide technical and legal assistance in the administration and enforcement of any contract in connection with treatment works assisted under this subchapter, and to intervene in any civil action involving the enforcement of such a contract.

(f) Design/build projects

(1) Agreement

Consistent with State law, an applicant who proposes to construct waste water treatment works may enter into an agreement with the Administrator under this subsection providing for the preparation of construction plans and specifications and the erection of such treatment works, in lieu of proceeding under the other provisions of this section.

(2) Limitation on projects

Agreements under this subsection shall be limited to projects under an approved facility plan which projects are—

(A) treatment works that have an estimated total cost of $8,000,000 or less; and

(B) any of the following types of waste water treatment systems: aerated lagoons, trickling filters, stabilization ponds, land application systems, sand filters, and subsurface disposal systems.

(3) Required terms

An agreement entered into under this subsection shall—

(A) set forth an amount agreed to as the maximum Federal contribution to the project, based upon a competitively bid document of basic design data and applicable standard construction specifications and a determination of the federally eligible costs of the project at the applicable Federal share under section 1282 of this title;

(B) set forth dates for the start and completion of construction of the treatment works by the applicant and a schedule of payments of the Federal contribution to the project;

(C) contain assurances by the applicant that (i) engineering and management assistance will be provided to manage the project; (ii) the proposed treatment works will be an operable unit and will meet all the requirements of this subchapter; and (iii) not later than 1 year after the date specified as the date of completion of construction of the treatment works, the treatment works will be operating so as to meet the requirements of any applicable permit for such treatment works under section 1342 of this title;

(D) require the applicant to obtain a bond from the contractor in an amount determined necessary by the Administrator to protect the Federal interest in the project; and

(E) contain such other terms and conditions as are necessary to assure compliance with this subchapter (except as provided in paragraph (4) of this subsection).

(4) Limitation on application

Subsections (a), (b), and (c) of this section shall not apply to grants made pursuant to this subsection.

(5) Reservation to assure compliance

The Administrator shall reserve a portion of the grant to assure contract compliance until final project approval as defined by the Administrator. If the amount agreed to under paragraph (3)(A) exceeds the cost of designing and constructing the treatment works, the Administrator shall reallot the amount of the excess to the State in which such treatment works are located for the fiscal year in which such audit is completed.

(6) Limitation on obligations

The Administrator shall not obligate more than 20 percent of the amount allotted to a State for a fiscal year under section 1285 of this title for grants pursuant to this subsection.

(7) Allowance

The Administrator shall determine an allowance for facilities planning for projects constructed under this subsection in accordance with section 1281(*l*) of this title.

(8) Limitation on Federal contributions

In no event shall the Federal contribution for the cost of preparing construction plans and specifications and the building and erection of treatment works pursuant to this subsection exceed the amount agreed upon under paragraph (3).

(9) Recovery action

In any case in which the recipient of a grant made pursuant to this subsection does not comply with the terms of the agreement entered into under paragraph (3), the Administrator is authorized to take such action as may be necessary to recover the amount of the Federal contribution to the project.

(10) Prevention of double benefits

A recipient of a grant made pursuant to this subsection shall not be eligible for any other grants under this subchapter for the same project.

(June 30, 1948, c. 758, Title II, § 203, as added by Pub. L. No. 92–500, § 2, 86 Stat. 835 (Oct. 18, 1972); and amended by Pub. L. No. 93–243, § 2, 87 Stat. 1069 (Jan. 2, 1974); Pub. L. No. 95–217, §§ 18, 19, 91 Stat. 1571, 1572 (Dec. 27, 1977); Pub. L. No. 96–483, § 6, 94 Stat. 2362 (Oct. 21, 1980); Pub. L. No. 97–117, § 9, 95 Stat. 1626 (Dec. 29, 1981); Pub. L. No. 100–4, Title II, §§ 203, 204, 101 Stat. 16, 17 (Feb. 4, 1987).)

§ 1284. Limitations and conditions

[FWPCA § 204]

(a) Determinations by Administrator

Before approving grants for any project for any treatment works under section 1281(g)(1) of this title the Administrator shall determine—

(1) that any required areawide waste treatment management plan under section 1288 of this title (A) is being implemented for such area and the proposed treatment works are included in such plan, or (B) is being developed for such area and reasonable progress is being made toward its implementation and the proposed treatment works will be included in such plan;

(2) that (A) the State in which the project is to be located (i) is implementing any required plan under section 1313(e) of this title and the proposed treatment works are in conformity with such plan, or (ii) is developing such a plan and the proposed treatment works will be in conformity with such plan, and (B) such State is in compliance with section 1315(b) of this title;

(3) that such works have been certified by the appropriate State water pollution control agency as entitled to priority over such other works in the State in accordance with any applicable State plan under section 1313(e) of this title, except that any priority list developed pursuant to section 1313(e)(3)(H) of this title may be modified by such State in accordance with regulations promulgated by the Administrator to give higher priority for grants for the Federal share of the cost of preparing construction drawings and specifications for any treatment works utilizing processes and techniques meeting the guidelines promulgated under section 1314(d)(3) of this title and for grants for the combined Federal share of the cost of preparing construction drawings and specifications and the building and erection of any treatment works meeting the requirements of the next to last sentence of section 1283(a) of this title which utilizes processes and techniques meeting the guidelines promulgated under section 1314(d)(3) of this title.[1]

(4) that the applicant proposing to construct such works agrees to pay the non-Federal costs of such works and has made adequate provisions satisfactory to the Administrator for assuring proper and efficient operation, including the employment of trained management and operations personnel, and the maintenance of such works in accordance with a plan of operation approved by the State water pollution control agency or, as appropriate, the interstate agency, after construction thereof;

(5) that the size and capacity of such works relate directly to the needs to be served by such works, including sufficient reserve capacity. The amount of reserve capacity provided shall be approved by the Administrator on the basis of a comparison of the cost of constructing such reserves as a part of the works to be funded and the anticipated cost of providing expanded capacity at a date when such capacity will be required, after taking into account, in accordance with regulations promulgated by the Administrator, efforts to reduce total flow of sewage and unnecessary water consumption. The amount of reserve capacity eligible for a grant under this subchapter shall be determined by the Administrator taking into account the projected population and associated commercial and industrial establishments within the jurisdiction of the applicant to be served by such treatment works as identified in an approved facilities plan, an areawide plan under section 1288 of this title, or an applicable municipal master plan of development. For the purpose of this paragraph, section 1288 of this title, and any such plan, projected population shall be determined on the basis of the latest information available from the United States Department of Commerce or from the States as the Administrator, by regulation, determines appropriate. Beginning October 1, 1984, no grant shall be made under this subchapter to construct that portion of any treatment works providing reserve capacity in excess of existing needs (including existing needs of residential, commercial, industrial, and other users) on the date of approval of a grant for the erection, building, acquisition, alteration, remodeling, improvement, or extension of a project for secondary treatment or more stringent treatment or new interceptors and appurtenances, except that in no event shall reserve capacity of a facility and its related interceptors to which this subsection applies be in excess of existing needs on October 1, 1990. In any case in which an applicant proposes to provide reserve capacity greater than that eligible for Federal financial assistance under this subchapter, the incremental costs of the additional reserve capacity shall be paid by the applicant;

(6) that no specification for bids in connection with such works shall be written in such a manner as to contain proprietary, exclusionary, or discriminatory requirements other than those based upon performance, unless such requirements are necessary to test or demonstrate a specific thing or to provide for necessary interchangeability of parts and equipment. When in the judgment of the grantee, it is impractical or uneconomical to make a clear and accurate description of the technical requirements, a "brand name or equal" description may be used as a means to define the performance or other salient requirements of a procurement, and in doing so the grantee need not establish the existence of any source other than the brand or source so named.

(b) Additional determinations; issuance of guidelines; approval by Administrator; system of charges

(1) Notwithstanding any other provision of this subchapter, the Administrator shall not approve any grant for any treatment works under section 1281(g)(1) of this title after March 1, 1973, unless he shall first have determined that the applicant (A) has adopted or will adopt a system of charges to assure that each recipient of waste treatment services within the applicant's jurisdiction, as determined by the Administrator, will pay its proportionate share (except as otherwise provided in this paragraph) of the costs of operation and maintenance (including replacement) of any waste treatment services provided by the applicant; and (B) has legal, institutional, managerial, and financial capability to insure adequate construction, operation, and maintenance of treatment works throughout the applicant's jurisdiction, as determined by the Administrator. In any case where an applicant which, as of December 27, 1977, uses a system of dedicated ad valorem taxes and the Administrator determines that the applicant has a system of charges which results in the distribution of operation and maintenance costs for treatment works within the applicant's jurisdiction, to each user class, in proportion to the contribution to the total cost of operation and maintenance of such works by each user class (taking into account total waste water loading of such works, the constituent elements of the wastes, and other appropriate factors), and such applicant is otherwise in compliance with clause (A) of this paragraph with respect to each industrial user, then such dedicated ad valorem tax system shall be deemed to be the user charge system meeting the requirements of clause (A) of this paragraph for the residential user class and such small non-residential user classes as defined by the Administrator. In defining small non-residential users, the Administrator shall consider the volume of wastes discharged into the treatment works by such users and the constituent elements of such wastes as well as such other factors as he deems appropriate. A system of user charges which imposes a lower charge for low-income residential users (as defined by the Administrator) shall be deemed to be a user charge system meeting the requirements of clause (A) of this paragraph if the Administrator determines that such system was adopted after public notice and hearing.

(2) The Administrator shall, within one hundred and eighty days after October 18, 1972, and after consultation with appropriate State, interstate, municipal, and intermunicipal agencies, issue guidelines applicable to payment of waste treatment costs by industrial and nonindustrial recipients of waste treatment services which shall establish (A) classes of users of such services, including categories of industrial users; (B) criteria against which to determine the adequacy of charges imposed on classes and categories of users reflecting all factors that influence the cost of waste treatment, including strength, volume, and delivery flow rate characteristics of waste; and (C) model systems and rates of user charges typical of various treatment works serving municipal-industrial communities.

(3) Approval by the Administrator of a grant to an interstate agency established by interstate compact for any treatment works shall satisfy any other requirement that such works be authorized by Act of Congress.

(4) A system of charges which meets the requirement of clause (A) of paragraph (1) of this subsection may be based on something other than metering the sewage or water supply flow of residential recipients of waste treatment services, including ad valorem taxes. If the system of charges is based on something other than metering the Administrator shall require (A) the applicant to establish a system by which the necessary funds will be available for the proper operation and maintenance of the treatment works; and (B) the applicant to establish a procedure under which the residential user will be notified as to that portion of his total payment which will be allocated to the cost of the waste treatment services.

(c) Applicability of reserve capacity restrictions to primary, secondary, or advanced waste treatment facilities or related interceptors

The next to the last sentence of paragraph (5) of subsection (a) of this section shall not apply in any case where a primary, secondary, or advanced waste treatment facility or its related interceptors has received a grant for erection, building, acquisition, alteration, remodeling, improvement, or extension before October 1, 1984, and all segments and phases of such facility and interceptors shall be funded based on a 20-year reserve capacity in the case of such facility and a 20-year reserve capacity in the case of such interceptors, except that, if a grant for such interceptors has been approved prior to December 29, 1981, such interceptors shall be funded based on the approved reserve capacity not to exceed 40 years.

(d) Engineering requirements; certification by owner and operator; contractual assurances, etc.

(1) A grant for the construction of treatment works under this subchapter shall provide that the engineer or engineering firm supervising construction or providing architect engineering services during construction shall continue its relationship to the grant applicant for a period of one year after the completion of construction and initial operation of such treatment works. During such period such engineer or engineering firm shall supervise operation of the treatment works, train operating personnel, and prepare curricula and training material for operating personnel. Costs associated with the implementation of this paragraph shall be eligible for Federal assistance in accordance with this subchapter.

(2) On the date one year after the completion of construction and initial operation of such treatment works, the owner and operator of such treatment works shall certify to the Administrator whether or not such treatment works meet the design specifications and effluent limitations contained in the grant agreement and permit pursuant to section 1342 of this title for such works. If the owner and operator of such treatment works cannot certify that such treatment works meet such design specifications and effluent limitations, any failure to meet such design specifications and effluent limitations shall be corrected in a timely manner, to allow such affirmative certification, at other than Federal expense.

(3) Nothing in this section shall be construed to prohibit a grantee under this subchapter from requiring more assurances, guarantees, or indemnity or other contractual requirements from any party to a contract pertaining to a project assisted under this subchapter, than those provided under this subsection.

(June 30, 1948, c. 758, Title II, § 204, as added by Pub. L. No. 92–500, § 2, 86 Stat. 835 (Oct. 18, 1972); and amended by Pub. L. No. 95–217, §§ 20–24, 91 Stat. 1572, 1573 (Dec. 27, 1977); Pub. L. No. 96–483, § 2(a), (b), 94 Stat. 2360, 2361 (Oct. 21, 1980); Pub. L. No. 97–117, §§ 10(a), (b), 11, 12, 95 Stat. 1626, 1627 (Dec. 29, 1981); Pub. L. No. 100–4, Title II, § 205(a)–(c), 101 Stat. 18 (Feb. 4, 1987).)

[1] So in original. The period probably should be a semicolon.

HISTORICAL AND STATUTORY NOTES

Effective and Applicability Provisions

1987 Acts. Section 205(d) of Pub. L. No. 100–4 provided that: "This section [amending subsecs. (a)(1), (2), and (b)(1) of this section shall take effect on the date of the enactment of this Act [Feb. 4, 1987], except that the amendments made by subsections (a) [amending subsec. (a)(1) of this section] and (b) [amending subsec. (a)(2) of this section] shall take effect on the last day of the two-year period beginning on such date of enactment [Feb. 4, 1987]."

1980 Acts. Amendment by Pub. L. No. 96–483 effective Dec. 27, 1977, see section 2(g) of Pub. L. No. 96–483, set out as a note under section 1281 of this title.

Elimination of Inapplicable Conditions or Requirements from Certain Grants

Section 2(c) of Pub. L. No. 96–483 provided that: "The Administrator of the Environmental Protection Agency shall take such action as may be necessary to remove from any grant made under section 201(g)(1) of the Federal Water Pollution Control Act [section 1281(g)(1) of this title] after March 1, 1973, and prior to the date of enactment of this Act [Oct. 21, 1980], any condition or requirement no longer applicable as a result of the repeals made by subsections (a) and (b) of this section [amending subsec. (b) of this section] or release any grant recipient of the obligations established by such conditions of other requirement."

Section 2(c) of Pub. L. No. 96–483, set out above, effective Dec. 27, 1977, see section 2(g) of Pub. L. No. 96–483, set out as a note under section 1281 of this title.

Cost Recovery; Suspension of Grant Requirements That Industrial Users Make Payments

Section 75 of Pub. L. No. 95–217, as amended by Pub. L. No. 96–148, § 1(a), (b), 93 Stat. 1088 (Dec. 16, 1979); and amended by Pub. L. No. 96–483, § 2(f), 94 Stat. 2361 (Oct. 21, 1980), authorized the Administrator of the Environmental Protection Agency to study and report to Congress not later than the last day of the twelfth month which begins after Dec. 27, 1977, cost recovery procedures from industrial users of treatment works to the extent construction costs are attributable to the Federal share of the cost of construction.

§ 1285. Allotment of grant funds

[FWPCA § 205]

(a) Funds for fiscal years during period June 30, 1972, and September 30, 1977; determination of amount

Sums authorized to be appropriated pursuant to section 1287 of this title for each fiscal year beginning after June 30, 1972, and before September 30, 1977, shall be allotted by the Administrator not later than the January 1st immediately preceding the beginning of the fiscal year for which authorized, except that the allotment for fiscal year 1973 shall be made not later than 30 days after October 18, 1972. Such sums shall be allotted among the States by the Administrator in accordance with regulations promulgated by him, in the ratio that the estimated cost of constructing all needed publicly owned treatment works in each State bears to the estimated cost of construction of all needed publicly owned treatment works in all of the States. For the fiscal years ending June 30, 1973, and June 30, 1974, such ratio shall be determined on the basis of table III of House Public Works Committee Print No. 92–50. For the fiscal year ending June 30, 1975, such ratio shall be determined one-half on the basis of table I of House Public Works Committee Print Numbered

93–28 and one-half on the basis of table II of such print, except that no State shall receive an allotment less than that which it received for the fiscal year ending June 30, 1972, as set forth in table III of such print. Allotments for fiscal years which begin after the fiscal year ending June 30, 1975, shall be made only in accordance with a revised cost estimate made and submitted to Congress in accordance with section 1375(b) of this title and only after such revised cost estimate shall have been approved by law specifically enacted after October 18, 1972.

(b) Availability and use of funds allotted for fiscal years during period June 30, 1972, and September 30, 1977; reallotment

(1) Any sums allotted to a State under subsection (a) of this section shall be available for obligation under section 1283 of this title on and after the date of such allotment. Such sums shall continue available for obligation in such State for a period of one year after the close of the fiscal year for which such sums are authorized. Any amounts so allotted which are not obligated by the end of such one-year period shall be immediately reallotted by the Administrator, in accordance with regulations promulgated by him, generally on the basis of the ratio used in making the last allotment of sums under this section. Such reallotted sums shall be added to the last allotments made to the States. Any sum made available to a State by reallotment under this subsection shall be in addition to any funds otherwise allotted to such State for grants under this subchapter during any fiscal year.

(2) Any sums which have been obligated under section 1283 of this title and which are released by the payment of the final voucher for the project shall be immediately credited to the State to which such sums were last allotted. Such released sums shall be added to the amounts last allotted to such State and shall be immediately available for obligation in the same manner and to the same extent as such last allotment.

(c) Funds for fiscal years during period October 1, 1977, and September 30, 1981; funds for fiscal years 1982 to 1990; determination of amount

(1) Sums authorized to be appropriated pursuant to section 1287 of this title for the fiscal years during the period beginning October 1, 1977, and ending September 30, 1981, shall be allotted for each such year by the Administrator not later than the tenth day which begins after December 27, 1977. Notwithstanding any other provision of law, sums authorized for the fiscal years ending September 30, 1978, September 30, 1979, September 30, 1980, and September 30, 1981, shall be allotted in accordance with table 3 of Committee Print Numbered 95–30 of the Committee on Public Works and Transportation of the House of Representatives.

(2) Sums authorized to be appropriated pursuant to section 1287 of this title for the fiscal years 1982, 1983, 1984, and 1985 shall be allotted for each such year by the Administrator not later than the tenth day which begins after December 29, 1981. Notwithstanding any other provision of law, sums authorized for the fiscal year ending September 30, 1982, shall be allotted in accordance with table 3 of Committee Print Numbered 95–30 of the Committee on Public Works and Transportation of the House of Representatives. Sums authorized for the fiscal years ending September 30, 1983, September 30, 1984, September 30, 1985, and September 30, 1986, shall be allotted in accordance with the following table:

States	Fiscal years 1983 through 1985[1]
Alabama	.011398
Alaska	.006101
Arizona	.006885
Arkansas	.006668
California	.072901
Colorado	.008154
Connecticut	.012487
Delaware	.004965

States	Fiscal years 1983 through 1985[1]
District of Columbia	.004965
Florida	.034407
Georgia	.017234
Hawaii	.007895
Idaho	.004965
Illinois	.046101
Indiana	.024566
Iowa	.013796
Kansas	.009201
Kentucky	.012973
Louisiana	.011205
Maine	.007788
Maryland	.024653
Massachusetts	.034608
Michigan	.043829
Minnesota	.018735
Mississippi	.009184
Missouri	.028257
Montana	.004965
Nebraska	.005214
Nevada	.004965
New Hampshire	.010186
New Jersey	.041654
New Mexico	.004965
New York	.113097
North Carolina	.018396
North Dakota	.004965
Ohio	.057383
Oklahoma	.008235
Oregon	.011515
Pennsylvania	.040377
Rhode Island	.006750
South Carolina	.010442
South Dakota	.004965
Tennessee	.014807
Texas	.038726
Utah	.005371
Vermont	.004965
Virginia	.020861
Washington	.017726
West Virginia	.015890
Wisconsin	.027557
Wyoming	.004965
Samoa	.000915
Guam	.000662

States	Fiscal years 1983 through 1985[1]
Northern Marianas	.000425
Puerto Rico	.013295
Pacific Trust Territories	.001305
Virgin Islands	.000531
United States totals	.999996

(3) Fiscal years 1987–1990

Sums authorized to be appropriated pursuant to section 1287 of this title for the fiscal years 1987, 1988, 1989, and 1990 shall be allotted for each such year by the Administrator not later than the 10th day which begins after February 4, 1987. Sums authorized for such fiscal years shall be allotted in accordance with the following table:

States:	
Alabama	.011309
Alaska	.006053
Arizona	.006831
Arkansas	.006616
California	.072333
Colorado	.008090
Connecticut	.012390
Delaware	.004965
District of Columbia	.004965
Florida	.034139
Georgia	.017100
Hawaii	.007833
Idaho	.004965
Illinois	.045741
Indiana	.024374
Iowa	.013688
Kansas	.009129
Kentucky	.012872
Louisiana	.011118
Maine	.007829
Maryland	.024461
Massachusetts	.034338
Michigan	.043487
Minnesota	.018589
Mississippi	.009112
Missouri	.028037
Montana	.004965
Nebraska	.005173
Nevada	.004965
New Hampshire	.010107
New Jersey	.041329
New Mexico	.004965

States:	
New York	.111632
North Carolina	.018253
North Dakota	.004965
Ohio	.056936
Oklahoma	.008171
Oregon	.011425
Pennsylvania	.040062
Rhode Island	.006791
South Carolina	.010361
South Dakota	.004965
Tennessee	.014692
Texas	.046226
Utah	.005329
Vermont	.004965
Virginia	.020698
Washington	.017588
West Virginia	.015766
Wisconsin	.027342
Wyoming	.004965
American Samoa	.000908
Guam	.000657
Northern Marianas	.000422
Puerto Rico	.013191
Pacific Trust Territories	.001295
Virgin Islands	.000527

(d) Availability and use of funds; reallotment

Sums allotted to the States for a fiscal year shall remain available for obligation for the fiscal year for which authorized and for the period of the next succeeding twelve months. The amount of any allotment not obligated by the end of such twenty-four-month period shall be immediately reallotted by the Administrator on the basis of the same ratio as applicable to sums allotted for the then current fiscal year, except that none of the funds reallotted by the Administrator for fiscal year 1978 and for fiscal years thereafter shall be allotted to any State which failed to obligate any of the funds being reallotted. Any sum made available to a State by reallotment under this subsection shall be in addition to any funds otherwise allotted to such State for grants under this subchapter during any fiscal year.

(e) Minimum allotment; additional appropriations; ratio of amount available

For the fiscal years 1978, 1979, 1980, 1981, 1982, 1983, 1984, 1985, 1986, 1987, 1988, 1989, and 1990, no State shall receive less than one-half of 1 per centum of the total allotment under subsection (c) of this section, except that in the case of Guam, Virgin Islands, American Samoa, and the Trust Territories not more than thirty-three one-hundredths of 1 per centum in the aggregate shall be allotted to all four of these jurisdictions. For the purpose of carrying out this subsection there are authorized to be appropriated, subject to such amounts as are provided in appropriation Acts, not to exceed $75,000,000 for each of fiscal years 1978, 1979, 1980, 1981, 1982, 1983, 1984, 1985, 1986, 1987, 1988, 1989, and 1990. If for any fiscal year the amount appropriated under authority of this subsection is less than the amount necessary to carry out this subsection, the amount each State receives under this subsection for such year shall bear the same ratio to the amount such State would have received under this subsection in such year if the amount necessary to carry it out had been appropriated as the amount appropriated for such year bears to the amount necessary to carry out this subsection for such year.

(f) Omitted

(g) Reservation of funds; State management assistance

(1) The Administrator is authorized to reserve each fiscal year not to exceed 2 per centum of the amount authorized under section 1287 of this title for purposes of the allotment made to each State under this section on or after October 1, 1977, except in the case of any fiscal year beginning on or after October 1, 1981, and ending before October 1, 1994, in which case the percentage authorized to be reserved shall not exceed 4 per centum.[2] or $400,000 whichever amount is the greater. Sums so reserved shall be available for making grants to such State under paragraph (2) of this subsection for the same period as sums are available from such allotment under subsection (d) of this section, and any such grant shall be available for obligation only during such period. Any grant made from sums reserved under this subsection which has not been obligated by the end of the period for which available shall be added to the amount last allotted to such State under this section and shall be immediately available for obligation in the same manner and to the same extent as such last allotment. Sums authorized to be reserved by this paragraph shall be in addition to and not in lieu of any other funds which may be authorized to carry out this subsection.

(2) The Administrator is authorized to grant to any State from amounts reserved to such State under this subsection, the reasonable costs of administering any aspects of sections 1281, 1283, 1284, and 1292 of this title the responsibility for administration of which the Administrator has delegated to such State. The Administrator may increase such grant to take into account the reasonable costs of administering an approved program under section 1342 or 1344 of this title, administering a state wide waste treatment management planning program under section 1288(b)(4) of this title, and managing waste treatment construction grants for small communities.

(h) Alternate systems for small communities

The Administrator shall set aside from funds authorized for each fiscal year beginning on or after October 1, 1978, a total (as determined by the Governor of the State) of not less than 4 percent nor more than 7½ percent of the sums allotted to any State with a rural population of 25 per centum or more of the total population of such State, as determined by the Bureau of the Census. The Administrator may set aside no more than 7½ percent of the sums allotted to any other State for which the Governor requests such action. Such sums shall be available only for alternatives to conventional sewage treatment works for municipalities having a population of three thousand five hundred or less, or for the highly dispersed sections of larger municipalities, as defined by the Administrator.

(i) Set-aside for innovative and alternative projects

Not less than ½ of 1 percent of funds allotted to a State for each of the fiscal years ending September 30, 1979, through September 30, 1990, under subsection (c) of this section shall be expended only for increasing the Federal share of grants for construction of treatment works utilizing innovative processes and techniques pursuant to section 1282(a)(2) of this title. Including the expenditures authorized by the preceding sentence, a total of 2 percent of the funds allotted to a State for each of the fiscal years ending September 30, 1979, and September 30, 1980, and 3 percent of the funds allotted to a State for the fiscal year ending September 30, 1981, under subsection (c) of this section shall be expended only for increasing grants for construction of treatment works pursuant to section 1282(a)(2) of this title. Including the expenditures authorized by the first sentence of this subsection, a total (as determined by the Governor of the State) of not less than 4 percent nor more than 7½ percent of the funds allotted to such State under subsection (c) of this section for each of the fiscal years ending September 30, 1982, through September 30, 1990, shall be expended only for increasing the Federal share of grants for construction of treatment works pursuant to section 1282(a)(2) of this title.

(j) Water quality management plan; reservation of funds for nonpoint source management

(1) The Administrator shall reserve each fiscal year not to exceed 1 per centum of the sums allotted and available for obligation to each State under this section for each fiscal year beginning on or after October 1, 1981, or $100,000, whichever amount is the greater.

(2) Such sums shall be used by the Administrator to make grants to the States to carry out water quality management planning, including, but not limited to—

(A) identifying most cost effective and locally acceptable facility and non-point measures to meet and maintain water quality standards;

(B) developing an implementation plan to obtain State and local financial and regulatory commitments to implement measures developed under subparagraph (A);

(C) determining the nature, extent, and causes of water quality problems in various areas of the State and interstate region, and reporting on these annually; and

(D) determining those publicly owned treatment works which should be constructed with assistance under this subchapter, in which areas and in what sequence, taking into account the relative degree of effluent reduction attained, the relative contributions to water quality of other point or nonpoint sources, and the consideration of alternatives to such construction, and implementing section 1313(e) of this title.

(3) In carrying out planning with grants made under paragraph (2) of this subsection, a State shall develop jointly with local, regional, and interstate entities, a plan for carrying out the program and give funding priority to such entities and designated or undesignated public comprehensive planning organizations to carry out the purposes of this subsection. In giving such priority, the State shall allocate at least 40 percent of the amount granted to such State for a fiscal year under paragraph (2) of this subsection to regional public comprehensive planning organizations in such State and appropriate interstate organizations for the development and implementation of the plan described in this paragraph. In any fiscal year for which the Governor, in consultation with such organizations and with the approval of the Administrator, determines that allocation of at least 40 percent of such amount to such organizations will not result in significant participation by such organizations in water quality management planning and not significantly assist in development and implementation of the plan described in this paragraph and achieving the goals of this chapter, the allocation to such organization may be less than 40 percent of such amount.

(4) All activities undertaken under this subsection shall be in coordination with other related provisions of this chapter.

(5) Nonpoint source reservation

In addition to the sums reserved under paragraph (1), the Administrator shall reserve each fiscal year for each State 1 percent of the sums allotted and available for obligation to such State under this section for each fiscal year beginning on or after October 1, 1986, or $100,000, whichever is greater, for the purpose of carrying out section 1329 of this title. Sums so reserved in a State in any fiscal year for which such State does not request the use of such sums, to the extent such sums exceed $100,000, may be used by such State for other purposes under this subchapter.

(k) New York City Convention Center

The Administrator shall allot to the State of New York from sums authorized to be appropriated for the fiscal year ending September 30, 1982, an amount necessary to pay the entire cost of conveying sewage from the Convention Center of the city of New York to the Newtown sewage treatment plant, Brooklyn-Queens area, New York. The amount allotted under this subsection shall be in addition to and not in lieu of any other amounts authorized to be allotted to such State under this chapter.

(*l*) Marine estuary reservation

(1) Reservation of funds

(A) General rule

Prior to making allotments among the States under subsection (c) of this section, the Administrator shall reserve funds from sums appropriated pursuant to section 1287 of this title for each fiscal year beginning after September 30, 1986.

(B) Fiscal years 1987 and 1988

For each of fiscal years 1987 and 1988 the reservation shall be 1 percent of the sums appropriated pursuant to section 1287 of this title for such fiscal year.

(C) Fiscal years 1989 and 1990

For each of fiscal years 1989 and 1990 the reservation shall be 1½ percent of the funds appropriated pursuant to section 1287 of this title for such fiscal year.

(2) Use of funds

Of the sums reserved under this subsection, two-thirds shall be available to address water quality problems of marine bays and estuaries subject to lower levels of water quality due to the impacts of discharges from combined storm water and sanitary sewer overflows from adjacent urban complexes, and one-third shall be available for the implementation of section 1330 of this title, relating to the national estuary program.

(3) Period of availability

Sums reserved under this subsection shall be subject to the period of availability for obligation established by subsection (d) of this section.

(4) Treatment of certain body of water

For purposes of this section and section 1281(n) of this title, Newark Bay, New Jersey, and the portion of the Passaic River up to Little Falls, in the vicinity of Beatties Dam, shall be treated as a marine bay and estuary.

(m) Discretionary deposits into State water pollution control revolving funds

(1) From construction grant allotments

In addition to any amounts deposited in a water pollution control revolving fund established by a State under subchapter VI of this chapter, upon request of the Governor of such State, the Administrator shall make available to the State for deposit, as capitalization grants, in such fund in any fiscal year beginning after September 30, 1986, such portion of the amounts allotted to such State under this section for such fiscal year as the Governor considers appropriate; except that (A) in fiscal year 1987, such deposit may not exceed 50 percent of the amounts allotted to such State under this section for such fiscal year, and (B) in fiscal year 1988, such deposit may not exceed 75 percent of the amounts allotted to such State under this section for this fiscal year.

(2) Notice requirement

The Governor of a State may make a request under paragraph (1) for a deposit into the water pollution control revolving fund of such State—

(A) in fiscal year 1987 only if no later than 90 days after February 4, 1987, and

(B) in each fiscal year thereafter only if 90 days before the first day of such fiscal year,

the State provides notice of its intent to make such deposit.

(3) Exception

Sums reserved under section 1285(j) of this title shall not be available for obligation under this subsection.

(June 30, 1948, c. 758, Title II, § 205, as added by Pub. L. No. 92–500, § 2, 86 Stat. 837 (Oct. 18, 1972); and amended by Pub. L. No. 93–243, § 1, 87 Stat. 1069 (Jan. 2, 1974); Pub. L. No. 95–217, §§ 25, 26(a), 27, 28, 91 Stat. 1574, 1575 (Dec. 27, 1977); Pub. L. No. 96–483, § 11, 94 Stat. 2363 (Oct. 21, 1980); Pub. L. No. 97–117, §§ 8(c), 13 to 16, 95 Stat. 1625, 1627 to 1629 (Dec. 29, 1981); Pub. L. No. 100–4, Title II, §§ 206(a) to (c), 207 to 210, 212(b), Title III, § 316(d), 101 Stat. 19 to 21, 27, 60 (Feb. 4, 1987); Pub. L. No. 105–362, Title V, § 501(d)(2)(C), 112 Stat. 3284 (Nov. 10, 1998); Pub. L. No. 107–303, Title III, § 302(b)(1), 116 Stat. 2361 (Nov. 27, 2002).)

[1] So in original. Probably should be "1986".

[2] So in original. The period probably should be a comma.

HISTORICAL AND STATUTORY NOTES

Codifications

Subsec. (f) provided that sums made available for obligation between Jan. 1, 1975, and Mar. 1, 1975, be available for obligation until Sept. 30, 1978.

Effective and Applicability Provisions

2002 Acts. Effective November 10, 1998, section 501 of the Federal Reports Elimination Act of 1998 [Pub. L. No. 105–362, Title V, § 501, 112 Stat. 3283 (Nov. 10, 1998)] is amended by striking subsections (a), (b), (c), and (d) [amending this section and others, see Tables for complete classification]. The Federal Water Pollution Control Act (33 U.S.C.A. § 1254(n)(3)) shall be applied and administered on and after Nov. 27, 2002 as if the amendments made by subsections (a), (b), (c), and (d) of Pub. L. No. 105–362, § 501, had not been enacted, see Pub. L. No. 107–303, § 302(b)(2), set out as a note under 33 U.S.C.A. § 1254.

Change of Name

Any reference in any provision of law enacted before Jan. 4, 1995, to the Committee on Public Works and Transportation of the House of Representatives treated as referring to the Committee on Transportation and Infrastructure of the House of Representatives, see section 1(a)(9) of Pub. L. No. 104–14, set out as a note preceding section 21 of Title 2, The Congress.

Termination of Trust Territory of the Pacific Islands

For termination of Trust Territory of the Pacific Islands, see note set out preceding 48 U.S.C.A. § 1681.

Period of July 1, 1975, through September, 30, 1976, Considered as One Year

Period of July 1, 1975, through Sept. 30, 1976, considered as one year for purposes of subsec. (b)(1) of this section, see section 206(5) of Pub. L. No. 94–274, Title II, 90 Stat. 394 (Apr. 21, 1976), set out as an note under section 246 of Title 42, The Public Health and Welfare.

Limitation on Authorization of Appropriations and Allotment to States for Fiscal Year 1982

Pub. L. No. 97–35, Title XVIII, § 1801(b), 95 Stat. 764 (Aug. 13, 1981), authorized an appropriation to the Administrator of the Environmental Protection Agency for the fiscal year ending Sept. 30, 1982, not to exceed $40,000,000 to carry out section 1285(g) of this title. The Administrator was to make such authorization available to the States in accordance with such section 1285(g) in the same manner and to the same extent as would be the case if $2,000,000,000 had been authorized under section 1287 of this title, using the same allotment table as was applicable to the fiscal year ending Sept. 30, 1981.

Availability of Allotted Sums in Subsequent Years; Reallotment of Unobligated Sums

Section 7 of Pub. L. No. 96–483 provided that: "Notwithstanding section 205(d) of the Federal Water Pollution Control Act (33 U.S.C. 1285) [subsec. (d) of this section], sums allotted to the States for the fiscal year 1979 shall remain available for obligation for the fiscal year for which authorized and for the period of the next succeeding twenty-four months. The amount of any allotment not obligated by the end of such thirty-six month period shall be immediately reallotted by the Administrator on the basis of the same ratio as applicable to sums allotted for the then current fiscal year, except that none of the funds reallotted by the Administrator for fiscal year 1979 shall be allotted to any State which failed to obligate any of the funds being reallotted. Any sum made available to a State by reallotment under this section shall be in addition to any funds otherwise allotted to such State for grants under title II of the Federal Water Pollution Control Act [this subchapter] during any fiscal year. This section shall take effect on September 30, 1980."

Period of July 1, 1975, through September 30, 1976, Considered as One Year

Period of July 1, 1975, through Sept. 30, 1976, considered as one year for purposes of subsec. (b)(1) of this section, see section 206(5) of Pub. L. No. 94–274, Title II, Apr. 21, 1976, 90 Stat. 394, set out as a note under section 289c–2 of Title 42, The Public Health and Welfare.

§ 1286. Reimbursement and advanced construction

[FWPCA § 206]

(a) Publicly owned treatment works construction initiated after June 30, 1966, but before July 1, 1973; reimbursement formula

Any publicly owned treatment works in a State on which construction was initiated after June 30, 1966, but before July 1, 1973, which was approved by the appropriate State water pollution control agency and which the Administrator finds meets the requirements of section 1158 of this title in effect at the time of the initiation of construction shall be reimbursed a total amount equal to the difference between the amount of Federal financial assistance, if any, received under such section 1158 of this title for such project and 50 per centum of the cost of such project, or 55 per centum of the project cost where the Administrator also determines that such treatment works was constructed in conformity with a comprehensive metropolitan treatment plan as described in section 1158(f) of this title as in effect immediately prior to October 18, 1972. Nothing in this subsection shall result in any such works receiving Federal grants from all sources in excess of 80 per centum of the cost of such project.

(b) Publicly owned treatment works construction initiated between June 30, 1956, and June 30, 1966; reimbursement formula

Any publicly owned treatment works constructed with or eligible for Federal financial assistance under this Act in a State between June 30, 1956, and June 30, 1966, which was approved by the State water pollution control agency and which the Administrator finds meets the requirements of section 1158 of this title prior to October 18, 1972 but which was constructed without assistance under such section 1158 of this title or which received such assistance in an amount less than 30 per centum of the cost of such project shall qualify for payments and reimbursement of State or local funds used for such project from sums allocated to such State under this section in an amount which shall not exceed the difference between the amount of such assistance, if any, received for such project and 30 per centum of the cost of such project.

(c) Application for reimbursement

No publicly owned treatment works shall receive any payment or reimbursement under subsection (a) or (b) of this section unless an application for such assistance is filed with the Administrator within the one year period which begins on October 18, 1972. Any application filed within such one year period may be revised from time to time, as may be necessary.

(d) Allocation of funds

The Administrator shall allocate to each qualified project under subsection (a) of this section each fiscal year for which funds are appropriated under subsection (e) of this section an amount which bears the same ratio to the unpaid balance of the reimbursement due such project as the total of such funds for such year bears to the total unpaid balance of reimbursement due all such approved projects on the date of enactment of such appropriation. The Administrator shall allocate to each qualified project under subsection (b) of this section each fiscal year for which funds are appropriated under subsection (e) of this section an amount which bears the same ratio to the unpaid balance of the reimbursement due such project as the total of such funds for such year bears to the total unpaid balance of reimbursement due all such approved projects on the date of enactment of such appropriation.

(e) Authorization of appropriations

There is authorized to be appropriated to carry out subsection (a) of this section not to exceed $2,600,000,000 and, to carry out subsection (b) of this section, not to exceed $750,000,000. The authorizations contained in this subsection shall be the sole source of funds for reimbursements authorized by this section.

(f) Additional funds

(1) In any case where a substantial portion of the funds allotted to a State for the current fiscal year under this subchapter have been obligated under section 1281(g) of this title, or will be so obligated in a timely manner (as determined by the Administrator), and there is construction of any treatment works project without the aid of Federal funds and in accordance with all procedures and all requirements applicable to treatment works projects, except those procedures and requirements which limit construction of projects to those constructed with the aid of previously allotted Federal funds, the Administrator, upon his approval of an application made under this subsection therefor, is authorized to pay the Federal share of the cost of construction of such project when additional funds are allotted to the State under this subchapter if prior to the construction of the project the Administrator approves plans, specifications, and estimates therefor in the same manner as other treatment works projects. The Administrator may not approve an application under this subsection unless an authorization is in effect for the first fiscal year in the period for which the application requests payment and such requested payment for that fiscal year does not exceed the State's expected allotment from such authorization. The Administrator shall not be required to make such requested payment for any fiscal year—

(A) to the extent that such payment would exceed such State's allotment of the amount appropriated for such fiscal year; and

(B) unless such payment is for a project which, on the basis of an approved funding priority list of such State, is eligible to receive such payment based on the allotment and appropriation for such fiscal year.

To the extent that sufficient funds are not appropriated to pay the full Federal share with respect to a project for which obligations under the provisions of this subsection have been made, the Administrator shall reduce the Federal share to such amount less than 75 per centum as such appropriations do provide.

(2) In determining the allotment for any fiscal year under this subchapter, any treatment works project constructed in accordance with this section and without the aid of Federal funds shall not be considered completed until an application under the provisions of this subsection with respect to such project has been approved by the Administrator, or the availability of funds from which this project is eligible for reimbursement has expired, whichever first occurs.

(June 30, 1948, c. 758, Title II, § 206, as added by Pub. L. No. 92–500, § 2, 86 Stat. 838 (Oct. 18, 1972); and amended by Pub. L. No. 93–207, § 1(2), 87 Stat. 906 (Dec. 28, 1973); Pub. L. No. 95–217, § 29(a), 91 Stat. 1576 (Dec. 27, 1977); Pub. L. No. 96–483, § 5, 94 Stat. 2361 (Oct. 21, 1980).)

HISTORICAL AND STATUTORY NOTES

References in Text

Section 1158 of this title, referred to in subsecs. (a) and (b), refers to section 8 of Act of June 30, 1948, c. 758, 62 Stat. 1158, prior to the supersedure and reenactment of Act of June 30, 1948, by Pub. L. No. 92–500, 86 Stat. 816 (Oct. 18, 1972). Provisions of section 1158 of this title are now covered by this subchapter.

This Act, referred to in subsec. (b), means Act of June 30, 1948, c. 758, 62 Stat. 1155, prior to the supersedure and reenactment of Act of June 30, 1948 by Pub. L. No. 92–500, 86 Stat. 816 (Oct. 18, 1972). Act of June 30, 1948, c. 758, as added by Act Oct. 18, 1972, Pub. L. No. 92–500, 86 Stat. 816, enacted this chapter.

Applications for Assistance for Publicly Owned Treatment Works Where Grants Were Made Before July 2, 1972, and on Which Construction Was Initiated Before July 1, 1973

Section 29(b) of Pub. L. 95–217 provided that applications for assistance for publicly owned treatment works for which a grant was made under this chapter before July 1, 1972, and on which construction was initiated before July 1, 1973, be filed not later than the ninetieth day after Dec. 27, 1977.

Application for Assistance

Section 2 of Pub. L. No. 93–207 provided that notwithstanding the requirements of subsec. (c) of this section, applications for assistance under this section could have been filed with the Administrator until Jan. 31, 1974.

Allocation of Construction Grants Appropriated for the Year Ending June 30, 1973; Interim Payments; Limitations

Section 3 of Pub. L. No. 93–207 provided that: "Funds available for reimbursement under Public Law 92–399 [making appropriations for Agriculture-Environmental and Consumer protection programs for the fiscal year ending June 30, 1973] shall be allocated in accordance with subsection (d) of section 206 of the Federal Water Pollution Control Act (86 Stat. 838) [subsec. (d) of this section], pro rata among all projects eligible under subsection (a) of such section 206 [subsec. (a) of this section] for which applications have been submitted and approved by the Administrator pursuant to such Act [this chapter]. Notwithstanding the provisions of subsection (d) of such section 206, (1) the Administrator is authorized to make interim payments to each such project for which an application has been approved on the basis of estimates of maximum pro rata entitlement of all applicants under section 206(a) and (2) for the purpose of determining allocation of sums available under Public Law 92–399, the unpaid balance of reimbursement due such projects shall be computed as of January 31, 1974. Upon completion by the Administrator of his audit and approval of all projects for which an application has been filed under subsection (a) of such section 206, the Administrator shall, within the limits of appropriated funds, allocate to each such qualified project the amount remaining, if any, of its total entitlement. Amounts allocated to projects which are later determined to be in excess of entitlement shall be available for reallocation, until expended, to other qualified projects under subsection (a) of such section 206. In no event, however, shall any payments exceed the Federal share of the cost of construction incurred to the date of the voucher covering such payment plus the Federal share of the value of the materials which have been stockpiled in the vicinity of such construction in conformity to plans and specifications for the project."

§ 1287. Authorization of appropriations

[FWPCA § 207]

There is authorized to be appropriated to carry out this subchapter, other than sections 1286(e), 1288 and 1289 of this title, for the fiscal year ending June 30, 1973, not to exceed $5,000,000,000, for the fiscal year ending June 30, 1974, not to exceed $6,000,000,000, and for the fiscal year ending June 30, 1975, not to exceed $7,000,000,000, and subject to such amounts as are provided in appropriation Acts, for the fiscal year ending September 30, 1977, $1,000,000,000 for the fiscal year ending September 30, 1978, $4,500,000,000 and for the fiscal years ending September 30, 1979, September 30, 1980, not to exceed $5,000,000,000; for the fiscal year ending September 30, 1981, not to exceed $2,548,837,000; and for the fiscal years ending September 30, 1982, September 30, 1983, September 30, 1984, and September 30, 1985, not to exceed $2,400,000,000 per fiscal year; and for each of the fiscal years ending September 30, 1986, September 30, 1987, and September 30, 1988, not to exceed $2,400,000,000; and for each of the fiscal years ending September 30, 1989, and September 30, 1990, not to exceed $1,200,000,000.

(June 30, 1948, c. 758, Title II, § 207, as added by Pub. L. No. 92–500, § 2, 86 Stat. 839 (Oct. 18, 1972); and amended by Pub. L. No. 93–207, § 1(3), 87 Stat. 906 (Dec. 28, 1973); Pub. L. No. 95–217, § 30, 91 Stat. 1576 (Dec. 27, 1977); Pub. L. No. 97–35, Title XVIII, § 1801(a), 95 Stat. 764 (Aug. 13, 1981); Pub. L. No. 97–117, § 17, 95 Stat. 1630 (Dec. 29, 1981); Pub. L. No. 100–4, Title II, § 211, 101 Stat. 21 (Feb. 4, 1987).)

HISTORICAL AND STATUTORY NOTES

Additional Authorization of Appropriations

Pub. L. No. 94–369, Title III, § 301, 90 Stat. 1011 (July 22, 1976), provided for authorization to carry out this subchapter, other than sections 1286, 1288, and 1289, for the fiscal year ending Sept. 30, 1977, not to exceed $700,000,000, which sum (subject to amounts provided in appropriation Acts) was to be allotted to each State listed in column 1 of table IV contained in House Public Works and Transportation Committee Print numbered 94–25 in accordance with the percentages provided for such State (if any) in column 5 of such table, and such sum to be in addition to, and not in lieu of, any funds otherwise authorized and to be available until expended.

§ 1288. Areawide waste treatment management

[FWPCA § 208]

(a) Identification and designation of areas having substantial water quality control problems

For the purpose of encouraging and facilitating the development and implementation of areawide waste treatment management plans—

(1) The Administrator, within ninety days after October 18, 1972, and after consultation with appropriate Federal, State, and local authorities, shall by regulation publish guidelines for the identification of those areas which, as a result of urban-industrial concentrations or other factors, have substantial water quality control problems.

(2) The Governor of each State, within sixty days after publication of the guidelines issued pursuant to paragraph (1) of this subsection, shall identify each area within the State which, as a result of urban-industrial concentrations or other factors, has substantial water quality control problems. Not later than one hundred and twenty days following such identification and after consultation with appropriate elected and other officials of local governments having jurisdiction in such areas, the Governor shall designate (A) the boundaries of each such area, and (B) a single representative organization, including elected officials from local governments or their designees, capable of developing effective areawide waste treatment management plans for such area. The Governor may in the same manner at any later time identify any additional area (or modify an existing area) for which he determines areawide waste treatment management to be appropriate, designate the boundaries of such area, and designate an organization capable of developing effective areawide waste treatment management plans for such area.

(3) With respect to any area which, pursuant to the guidelines published under paragraph (1) of this subsection, is located in two or more States, the Governors of the respective States shall consult and cooperate in carrying out the provisions of paragraph (2), with a view toward designating the boundaries of the interstate area having common water quality control problems and for which areawide waste treatment management plans would be most effective, and toward designating, within one hundred and eighty days after publication of guidelines issued pursuant to paragraph (1) of this subsection, of a single representative organization capable of developing effective areawide waste treatment management plans for such area.

(4) If a Governor does not act, either by designating or determining not to make a designation under paragraph (2) of this subsection, within the time required by such paragraph, or if, in the case of an interstate area, the Governors of the States involved do not designate a planning organization within the time required by paragraph (3) of this subsection, the chief elected officials of local governments within an area may by agreement designate (A) the boundaries for such an area, and (B) a single representative organization including elected officials from such local governments, or their designees, capable of developing an areawide waste treatment management plan for such area.

(5) Existing regional agencies may be designated under paragraphs (2), (3), and (4) of this subsection.

(6) The State shall act as a planning agency for all portions of such State which are not designated under paragraphs (2), (3), or (4) of this subsection.

(7) Designations under this subsection shall be subject to the approval of the Administrator.

(b) Planning process

(1) (A) Not later than one year after the date of designation of any organization under subsection (a) of this section such organization shall have in operation a continuing areawide waste treatment management planning process consistent with section 1281 of this title. Plans prepared in accordance with this process shall contain alternatives for waste treatment management, and be applicable to all wastes generated within the area involved. The initial plan prepared in accordance with such process shall be certified by the Governor and submitted to the Administrator not later than two years after the planning process is in operation.

(B) For any agency designated after 1975 under subsection (a) of this section and for all portions of a State for which the State is required to act as the planning agency in accordance with subsection (a)(6) of this section, the initial plan prepared in accordance with such process shall be certified by the Governor and submitted to the Administrator not later than three years after the receipt of the initial grant award authorized under subsection (f) of this section.

(2) Any plan prepared under such process shall include, but not be limited to—

(A) the identification of treatment works necessary to meet the anticipated municipal and industrial waste treatment needs of the area over a twenty-year period, annually updated (including an analysis of alternative waste treatment systems), including any requirements for the acquisition of land for treatment purposes; the necessary waste water collection and urban storm water runoff systems; and a program to provide the necessary financial arrangements for the development of such treatment works, and an identification of open space and recreation opportunities that can be expected to result from improved water quality, including consideration of potential use of lands associated with treatment works and increased access to water-based recreation;

(B) the establishment of construction priorities for such treatment works and time schedules for the initiation and completion of all treatment works;

(C) the establishment of a regulatory program to—

(i) implement the waste treatment management requirements of section 1281(c) of this title,

(ii) regulate the location, modification, and construction of any facilities within such area which may result in any discharge in such area, and

(iii) assure that any industrial or commercial wastes discharged into any treatment works in such area meet applicable pretreatment requirements;

(D) the identification of those agencies necessary to construct, operate, and maintain all facilities required by the plan and otherwise to carry out the plan;

(E) the identification of the measures necessary to carry out the plan (including financing), the period of time necessary to carry out the plan, the costs of carrying out the plan within such time, and the economic, social, and environmental impact of carrying out the plan within such time;

(F) a process to (i) identify, if appropriate, agriculturally and silviculturally related nonpoint sources of pollution, including return flows from irrigated agriculture, and their cumulative effects, runoff from manure disposal areas, and from land used for livestock and crop production, and (ii) set forth procedures and methods (including land use requirements) to control to the extent feasible such sources;

(G) a process to (i) identify, if appropriate, mine-related sources of pollution including new, current, and abandoned surface and underground mine runoff, and (ii) set forth procedures and methods (including land use requirements) to control to the extent feasible such sources;

(H) a process to (i) identify construction activity related sources of pollution, and (ii) set forth procedures and methods (including land use requirements) to control to the extent feasible such sources;

(I) a process to (i) identify, if appropriate, salt water intrusion into rivers, lakes, and estuaries resulting from reduction of fresh water flow from any cause, including irrigation, obstruction, ground water extraction, and diversion, and (ii) set forth procedures and methods to control such intrusion to the extent feasible where such procedures and methods are otherwise a part of the waste treatment management plan;

(J) a process to control the disposition of all residual waste generated in such area which could affect water quality; and

(K) a process to control the disposal of pollutants on land or in subsurface excavations within such area to protect ground and surface water quality.

(3) Areawide waste treatment management plans shall be certified annually by the Governor or his designee (or Governors or their designees, where more than one State is involved) as being consistent with applicable basin plans and such areawide waste treatment management plans shall be submitted to the Administrator for his approval.

(4) **(A)** Whenever the Governor of any State determines (and notifies the Administrator) that consistency with a statewide regulatory program under section 1313 of this title so requires, the requirements of clauses (F) through (K) of paragraph (2) of this subsection shall be developed and submitted by the Governor to the Administrator for approval for application to a class or category of activity throughout such State.

(B) Any program submitted under subparagraph (A) of this paragraph which, in whole or in part, is to control the discharge or other placement of dredged or fill material into the navigable waters shall include the following:

(i) A consultation process which includes the State agency with primary jurisdiction over fish and wildlife resources.

(ii) A process to identify and manage the discharge or other placement of dredged or fill material which adversely affects navigable waters, which shall complement and be coordinated with a State program under section 1344 of this title conducted pursuant to this chapter.

(iii) A process to assure that any activity conducted pursuant to a best management practice will comply with the guidelines established under section 1344(b)(1) of this title, and sections 1317 and 1343 of this title.

(iv) A process to assure that any activity conducted pursuant to a best management practice can be terminated or modified for cause including, but not limited to, the following:

(I) violation of any condition of the best management practice;

(II) change in any activity that requires either a temporary or permanent reduction or elimination of the discharge pursuant to the best management practice.

(v) A process to assure continued coordination with Federal and Federal-State water-related planning and reviewing processes, including the National Wetlands Inventory.

(C) If the Governor of a State obtains approval from the Administrator of a statewide regulatory program which meets the requirements of subparagraph (B) of this paragraph and if such State is administering a permit program under section 1344 of this title, no person shall be required to obtain an individual permit pursuant to such section, or to comply with a general permit issued pursuant to such section, with respect to any appropriate activity within such State for which a best management practice has been approved by the Administrator under the program approved by the Administrator pursuant to this paragraph.

(D) (i) Whenever the Administrator determines after public hearing that a State is not administering a program approved under this section in accordance with the requirements of this section, the Administrator shall so notify the State, and if appropriate corrective action is not taken within a reasonable time, not to exceed ninety days, the Administrator shall withdraw approval of such program. The Administrator shall not withdraw approval of any such program unless he shall first have notified the State, and made public, in writing, the reasons for such withdrawal.

(ii) In the case of a State with a program submitted and approved under this paragraph, the Administrator shall withdraw approval of such program under this subparagraph only for a substantial failure of the State to administer its program in accordance with the requirements of this paragraph.

(c) Regional operating agencies

(1) The Governor of each State, in consultation with the planning agency designated under subsection (a) of this section, at the time a plan is submitted to the Administrator, shall designate one or more waste treatment management agencies (which may be an existing or newly created local, regional, or State agency or political subdivision) for each area designated under subsection (a) of this section and submit such designations to the Administrator.

(2) The Administrator shall accept any such designation, unless, within 120 days of such designation, he finds that the designated management agency (or agencies) does not have adequate authority—

(A) to carry out appropriate portions of an areawide waste treatment management plan developed under subsection (b) of this section;

(B) to manage effectively waste treatment works and related facilities serving such area in conformance with any plan required by subsection (b) of this section;

(C) directly or by contract, to design and construct new works, and to operate and maintain new and existing works as required by any plan developed pursuant to subsection (b) of this section;

(D) to accept and utilize grants, or other funds from any source, for waste treatment management purposes;

(E) to raise revenues, including the assessment of waste treatment charges;

(F) to incur short- and long-term indebtedness;

(G) to assure in implementation of an areawide waste treatment management plan that each participating community pays its proportionate share of treatment costs;

(H) to refuse to receive any wastes from any municipality or subdivision thereof, which does not comply with any provisions of an approved plan under this section applicable to such area; and

(I) to accept for treatment industrial wastes.

(d) Conformity of works with area plan

After a waste treatment management agency having the authority required by subsection (c) of this section has been designated under such subsection for an area and a plan for such area has been approved under subsection (b) of this section, the Administrator shall not make any grant for construction of a publicly owned treatment works under section 1281(g)(1) of this title within such area except to such designated agency and for works in conformity with such plan.

(e) Permits not to conflict with approved plans

No permit under section 1342 of this title shall be issued for any point source which is in conflict with a plan approved pursuant to subsection (b) of this section.

(f) Grants

(1) The Administrator shall make grants to any agency designated under subsection (a) of this section for payment of the reasonable costs of developing and operating a continuing areawide waste treatment management planning process under subsection (b) of this section.

(2) For the two-year period beginning on the date the first grant is made under paragraph (1) of this subsection to an agency, if such first grant is made before October 1, 1977, the amount of each such grant to such agency shall be 100 per centum of the costs of developing and operating a continuing areawide waste treatment management planning process under subsection (b) of this section, and thereafter the amount granted to such agency shall not exceed 75 per centum of such costs in each succeeding one-year period. In the case of any other grant made to an agency under such paragraph (1) of this subsection, the amount of such grant shall not exceed 75 per centum of the costs of developing and operating a continuing areawide waste treatment management planning process in any year.

(3) Each applicant for a grant under this subsection shall submit to the Administrator for his approval each proposal for which a grant is applied for under this subsection. The Administrator shall act upon such proposal as soon as practicable after it has been submitted, and his approval of that proposal shall be deemed a contractual obligation of the United States for the payment of its contribution to such proposal, subject to such amounts as are provided in appropriation Acts. There is authorized to be appropriated to carry out this subsection not to exceed $50,000,000 for the fiscal year ending June 30, 1973, not to exceed $100,000,000 for the fiscal year ending June 30, 1974, not to exceed $150,000,000 per fiscal year for the fiscal years ending June 30, 1975, September 30, 1977, September 30, 1978, September 30, 1979, and September 30, 1980, not to exceed $100,000,000 per fiscal year for the fiscal years ending September 30, 1981, and September 30, 1982, and such sums as may be necessary for fiscal years 1983 through 1990.

(g) Technical assistance by Administrator

The Administrator is authorized, upon request of the Governor or the designated planning agency, and without reimbursement, to consult with, and provide technical assistance to, any agency designated under subsection (a) of this section in the development of areawide waste treatment management plans under subsection (b) of this section.

(h) Technical assistance by Secretary of the Army

(1) The Secretary of the Army, acting through the Chief of Engineers, in cooperation with the Administrator is authorized and directed, upon request of the Governor or the designated planning organization, to consult with, and provide technical assistance to, any agency designed[1] under subsection (a) of this section in developing and operating a continuing areawide waste treatment management planning process under subsection (b) of this section.

(2) There is authorized to be appropriated to the Secretary of the Army, to carry out this subsection, not to exceed $50,000,000 per fiscal year for the fiscal years ending June 30, 1973, and June 30, 1974.

(i) State best management practices program

(1) The Secretary of the Interior, acting through the Director of the United States Fish and Wildlife Service, shall, upon request of the Governor of a State, and without reimbursement, provide technical assistance to such State in developing a statewide program for submission to the Administrator under subsection (b)(4)(B) of this section and in implementing such program after its approval.

(2) There is authorized to be appropriated to the Secretary of the Interior $6,000,000 to complete the National Wetlands Inventory of the United States, by December 31, 1981, and to provide information from such Inventory to States as it becomes available to assist such States in the development and operation of programs under this chapter.

(j) Agricultural cost sharing

(1) The Secretary of Agriculture, with the concurrence of the Administrator, and acting through the Soil Conservation Service and such other agencies of the Department of Agriculture as the Secretary may designate, is authorized and directed to establish and administer a program to enter into contracts, subject to such amounts as are provided in advance by appropriation acts, of not less than five years nor more than ten years with owners and operators having control of rural land for the purpose of installing and maintaining measures incorporating best management practices to control nonpoint source pollution for improved water quality in those States or areas for which the Administrator has approved a plan under subsection (b) of this section where the practices to which the contracts apply are certified by the management agency designated under subsection (c)(1) of this section to be consistent with such plans and will result in improved water quality. Such contracts may be entered into during the period ending not later than September 31, 1988. Under such contracts the land owner or operator shall agree—

(i) to effectuate a plan approved by a soil conservation district, where one exists, under this section for his farm, ranch, or other land substantially in accordance with the schedule outlined therein unless any requirement thereof is waived or modified by the Secretary;

(ii) to forfeit all rights to further payments or grants under the contract and refund to the United States all payments and grants received thereunder, with interest, upon his violation of the contract at any stage during the time he has control of the land if the Secretary, after considering the recommendations of the soil conservation district, where one exists, and the Administrator, determines that such violation is of such a nature as to warrant termination of the contract, or to make refunds or accept such payment adjustments as the Secretary may deem appropriate if he determines that the violation by the owner or operator does not warrant termination of the contract;

(iii) upon transfer of his right and interest in the farm, ranch, or other land during the contract period to forfeit all rights to further payments or grants under the contract and refund to the United States all payments or grants received thereunder, with interest, unless the transferee of any such land agrees with the Secretary to assume all obligations of the contract;

(iv) not to adopt any practice specified by the Secretary on the advice of the Administrator in the contract as a practice which would tend to defeat the purposes of the contract;

(v) to such additional provisions as the Secretary determines are desirable and includes in the contract to effectuate the purposes of the program or to facilitate the practical administration of the program.

(2) In return for such agreement by the landowner or operator the Secretary shall agree to provide technical assistance and share the cost of carrying out those conservation practices and measures set forth in the contract for which he determines that cost sharing is appropriate and in the public interest and which are approved for cost sharing by the agency designated to implement the plan developed under subsection (b) of this section. The portion of such cost (including labor) to be shared shall be that part which the Secretary determines is necessary and appropriate to effectuate the installation of the water quality management practices and measures under the contract, but not to exceed 50 per centum of the total cost of the measures set forth in the contract; except the Secretary may increase the matching cost share where he determines that (1) the main benefits to be derived from the measures are related to improving offsite water quality, and (2) the matching share requirement would place a burden on the landowner which would probably prevent him from participating in the program.

(3) The Secretary may terminate any contract with a landowner or operator by mutual agreement with the owner or operator if the Secretary determines that such termination would be in the public interest, and may agree to such modification of contracts previously entered into as he may determine to be desirable to carry out the purposes of the program or facilitate the practical administration thereof or to accomplish equitable treatment with respect to other conservation, land use, or water quality programs.

(4) In providing assistance under this subsection the Secretary will give priority to those areas and sources that have the most significant effect upon water quality. Additional investigations or plans may be made, where necessary, to supplement approved water quality management plans, in order to determine priorities.

(5) The Secretary shall, where practicable, enter into agreements with soil conservation districts, State soil and water conservation agencies, or State water quality agencies to administer all or part of the program established in this subsection under regulations developed by the Secretary. Such agreements shall provide for the submission of such reports as the Secretary deems necessary, and for payment by the United States of such portion of the costs incurred in the administration of the program as the Secretary may deem appropriate.

(6) The contracts under this subsection shall be entered into only in areas where the management agency designated under subsection (c)(1) of this section assures an adequate level of participation by owners and operators having control of rural land in such areas. Within such areas the local soil conservation district, where one exists, together with the Secretary of Agriculture, will determine the priority of assistance among individual land owners and operators to assure that the most critical water quality problems are addressed.

(7) The Secretary, in consultation with the Administrator and subject to section 1314(k) of this title, shall, not later than September 30, 1978, promulgate regulations for carrying out this subsection and for support and cooperation with other Federal and non-Federal agencies for implementation of this subsection.

(8) This program shall not be used to authorize or finance projects that would otherwise be eligible for assistance under the terms of Public Law 83–566 [16 U.S.C.A. § 1001 et seq.].

(9) There are hereby authorized to be appropriated to the Secretary of Agriculture $200,000,000 for fiscal year 1979, $400,000,000 for fiscal year 1980, $100,000,000 for fiscal year 1981, $100,000,000 for fiscal year 1982, and such sums as may be necessary for fiscal years 1983 through 1990, to carry out this subsection. The program authorized under this subsection shall be in addition to, and not in substitution of, other programs in such area authorized by this or any other public law.

(June 30, 1948, c. 758, Title II, § 208, as added by Pub. L. No. 92–500, § 2, 86 Stat. 839 (Oct. 18, 1972); and amended by Pub. L. No. 95–217, §§ 4(e), 31, 32, 33(a), 34, 35, 91 Stat. 1566, 1576–1579 (Dec. 27, 1977); Pub. L. No. 96–483, § 1(d), (e), 94 Stat. 2360 (Oct. 21, 1980); Pub. L. No. 100–4, Title I, § 101(d), (e), 101 Stat. 9 (Feb. 4, 1987).)

[1] So in original. Probably should be "designated".

HISTORICAL AND STATUTORY NOTES

References in Text

Public Law 83–566, referred to in subsec. (j)(8), is Act Aug. 4, 1954, c. 656, 68 Stat. 666, as amended, known as the Watershed Protection and Flood Prevention Act, which is codified generally as chapter 18 (section 1001 et seq.) of Title 16, Conservation. For complete classification of this Act to the Code, see Short Title note set out under section 1001 of Title 16 and Tables.

Transfer of Functions

Enforcement functions of Secretary or other official in Department of Agriculture, insofar as they involve lands and programs under jurisdiction of that Department, related to compliance with this chapter with respect to pre-construction, construction, and initial operation of transportation system for Canadian and Alaskan natural gas were transferred to the Federal Inspector, Office of Federal Inspector for the Alaska Natural Gas Transportation System, until the first anniversary of date of initial operation of the Alaska Natural Gas Transportation System, see Reorg. Plan No. 1 of 1979, §§ 102(f), 203(a), 44 Fed. Reg. 33663, 33666, 93 Stat. 1373, 1376, effective July 1, 1979, set out in Appendix 1 to Title 5, Government Organization and Employees.

§ 1289. Basin planning

[FWPCA § 209]

(a) Preparation of Level B plan

The President, acting through the Water Resources Council, shall, as soon as practicable, prepare a Level B plan under the Water Resources Planning Act [42 U.S.C.A. § 1962 et seq.] for all basins in the United States. All such plans shall be completed not later than January 1, 1980, except that priority in the preparation of such plans shall be given to those basins and portions thereof which are within those areas designated under paragraphs (2), (3), and (4) of subsection (a) of section 1288 of this title.

(b) Reporting requirements

The President, acting through the Water Resources Council, shall report annually to Congress on progress being made in carrying out this section. The first such report shall be submitted not later than January 31, 1973.

(c) Authorization of appropriations

There is authorized to be appropriated to carry out this section not to exceed $200,000,000.

(June 30, 1948, c. 758, Title II, § 209, as added by Pub. L. No. 92–500, § 2, 86 Stat. 843 (Oct. 18, 1972).)

HISTORICAL AND STATUTORY NOTES

References in Text

The Water Resources Planning Act, referred to in subsec. (a), is Pub. L. No. 89–80, 79 Stat. 244 (July 22, 1965), as amended, which is codified generally to chapter 19B (section 1962 et seq.) of Title 42, The Public Health and Welfare. For complete classification of this Act to the Code, see Short Title note set out under section 1962 of Title 42 and Tables.

Termination of Reporting Requirements

Reporting requirement of subsec. (b) of this section excepted from termination under Pub. L. No. 104–66, § 3003(a)(1), as amended, set out as a note under 31 U.S.C.A. § 1113, and page 195 of House Document No. 103–7, see Pub. L. No. 107–303, § 302(a).

§ 1290. Annual survey

[FWPCA § 210]

The Administrator shall annually make a survey to determine the efficiency of the operation and maintenance of treatment works constructed with grants made under this chapter, as compared to the efficiency planned at the time the grant was made. The results of such annual survey shall be included in the report required under section 1375(a) of this title.

(June 30, 1948, c. 758, Title II, § 210, as added by Pub. L. No. 92–500, § 2, 86 Stat. 843 (Oct. 18, 1972); and amended by Pub. L. No. 105–362, Title V, § 501(d)(2)(D), 112 Stat. 3284 (Nov. 10, 1998); Pub. L. No. 107–303, Title III, § 302(b)(1), 116 Stat. 2361 (Nov. 27, 2002).)

HISTORICAL AND STATUTORY NOTES

Effective and Applicability Provisions

2002 Acts. Effective November 10, 1998, section 501 of the Federal Reports Elimination Act of 1998 [Pub. L. No. 105–362, Title V, § 501, 112 Stat. 3283 (Nov. 10, 1998)] is amended by striking subsections (a), (b), (c), and (d) [amending this section and others, see Tables for complete classification]. The Federal Water Pollution Control Act (33 U.S.C.A. § 1254(n)(3)) shall be applied and administered on and after Nov. 27, 2002 as if the amendments made by subsections (a), (b), (c), and (d) of Pub. L. No. 105–362, § 501, had not been enacted, see Pub. L. No. 107–303, § 302(b)(2), set out as a note under 33 U.S.C.A. § 1254.

§ 1291. Sewage collection systems

[FWPCA § 211]

(a) Existing and new systems

No grant shall be made for a sewage collection system under this subchapter unless such grant (1) is for replacement or major rehabilitation of an existing collection system and is necessary to the total integrity and performance of the waste treatment works servicing such community, or (2) is for a new collection system in an existing community with sufficient existing or planned capacity adequately to treat such collected sewage and is consistent with section 1281 of this title.

(b) Use of population density as test

If the Administrator uses population density as a test for determining the eligibility of a collector sewer for assistance it shall be only for the purpose of evaluating alternatives and determining the needs for such system in relation to ground or surface water quality impact.

(c) Pollutant discharges from separate storm sewer systems

No grant shall be made under this subchapter from funds authorized for any fiscal year during the period beginning October 1, 1977, and ending September 30, 1990, for treatment works for control of pollutant discharges from separate storm sewer systems.

(June 30, 1948, c. 758, Title II, § 211, as added by Pub. L. No. 92–500, § 2, 86 Stat. 843 (Oct. 18, 1972); and amended by Pub. L. No. 95–217, § 36, 91 Stat. 1581 (Dec. 27, 1977); Pub. L. No. 97–117, § 2(b), 95 Stat. 1623 (Dec. 29, 1981); Pub. L. No. 100–4, Title II, § 206(d), 101 Stat. 20 (Feb. 4, 1987).)

§ 1292. Definitions

[FWPCA § 212]

As used in this subchapter—

(1) The term "construction" means any one or more of the following: preliminary planning to determine the feasibility of treatment works, engineering, architectural, legal, fiscal, or economic investigations or studies, surveys, designs, plans, working drawings, specifications, procedures, field testing of innovative or alternative waste water treatment processes and techniques meeting guidelines promulgated under section 1314(d)(3) of this title, or other necessary actions, erection, building, acquisition, alteration, remodeling, improvement, or extension of treatment works, or the inspection or supervision of any of the foregoing items.

(2) (A) The term "treatment works" means any devices and systems used in the storage, treatment, recycling, and reclamation of municipal sewage or industrial wastes of a liquid nature to implement section 1281 of this title, or necessary to recycle or reuse water at the most economical cost over the estimated life of the works, including intercepting sewers, outfall sewers, sewage collection systems, pumping, power, and other equipment, and their appurtenances; extensions, improvements, remodeling, additions, and alterations thereof; elements essential to provide a reliable recycled supply such as standby treatment units and clear well facilities; and acquisition of the land that will be an integral part of the treatment process (including land used for the storage of treated wastewater in land treatment systems prior to land application) or will be used for ultimate disposal of residues resulting from such treatment and acquisition of land, and interests in land, that are necessary for construction.

(B) In addition to the definition contained in subparagraph (A) of this paragraph, "treatment works" means any other method or system for preventing, abating, reducing, storing, treating, separating, or disposing of municipal waste, including storm water runoff, or industrial waste, including waste in combined storm water and sanitary sewer systems. Any application for construction grants which includes wholly or in part such methods or systems shall, in accordance with guidelines published by the Administrator pursuant to subparagraph (C) of this paragraph, contain adequate data and analysis demonstrating such proposal to be, over the life of such works, the most cost efficient alternative to comply with sections 1311 or 1312 of this title, or the requirements of section 1281 of this title.

(C) For the purposes of subparagraph (B) of this paragraph, the Administrator shall, within one hundred and eighty days after October 18, 1972, publish and thereafter revise no less often than annually, guidelines for the evaluation of methods, including cost-effective analysis, described in subparagraph (B) of this paragraph.

(3) The term "replacement" as used in this subchapter means those expenditures for obtaining and installing equipment, accessories, or appurtenances during the useful life of the treatment works necessary to maintain the capacity and performance for which such works are designed and constructed.

[June 30, 1948, c. 758, Title II, § 212, as added by Pub. L. No. 92–500, § 2, 86 Stat. 844 (Oct. 18, 1972); and amended by Pub. L. No. 95–217, § 37, 91 Stat. 1581 (Dec. 27, 1977); Pub. L. No. 97–117, § 8(d), 95 Stat. 1626 (Dec. 29, 1981); Pub. L. No. 113–121, § 5012(a), 128 Stat. 1328 (June 10, 2014).]

Effective and Applicability Provisions

2014 Amendments. Pub. L. No. 113–121, § 5012(c), 128 Stat. 1328 (June 10, 2014), provided that the amendments made in § 5012 "shall take effect on October 1, 2014."

§ 1293. Loan guarantees

[FWPCA § 213]

(a) State or local obligations issued exclusively to Federal Financing Bank for publicly owned treatment works; determination of eligibility of project by Administrator

Subject to the conditions of this section and to such terms and conditions as the Administrator determines to be necessary to carry out the purposes of this subchapter, the Administrator is authorized to guarantee, and to make commitments to guarantee, the principal and interest (including interest accruing between the date of default and the date of the payment in full of the guarantee) of any loan, obligation, or participation therein of any State, municipality, or intermunicipal or interstate agency issued directly and exclusively to the Federal Financing Bank to finance that part of the cost of any grant-eligible project for the construction of publicly owned treatment works not paid for with Federal financial assistance under this subchapter (other than this section), which project the Administrator has determined to be eligible for such financial assistance under this subchapter, including, but not limited to, projects eligible for reimbursement under section 1286 of this title.

(b) Conditions for issuance

No guarantee, or commitment to make a guarantee, may be made pursuant to this section—

(1) unless the Administrator certifies that the issuing body is unable to obtain on reasonable terms sufficient credit to finance its actual needs without such guarantee; and

(2) unless the Administrator determines that there is a reasonable assurance of repayment of the loan, obligation, or participation therein.

A determination of whether financing is available at reasonable rates shall be made by the Secretary of the Treasury with relationship to the current average yield on outstanding marketable obligations of municipalities of comparable maturity.

(c) Fees for application investigation and issuance of commitment guarantee

The Administrator is authorized to charge reasonable fees for the investigation of an application for a guarantee and for the issuance of a commitment to make a guarantee.

(d) Commitment for repayment

The Administrator, in determining whether there is a reasonable assurance of repayment, may require a commitment which would apply to such repayment. Such commitment may include, but not be limited to, any funds received by such grantee from the amounts appropriated under section 1286 of this title.

(June 30, 1948, c. 758, Title II, § 213, as added by Pub. L. No. 94–558, 90 Stat. 2639 (Oct. 19, 1976); and amended by Pub. L. No. 96–483, § 2(e), 94 Stat. 2361 (Oct. 21, 1980).)

HISTORICAL AND STATUTORY NOTES

Effective and Applicability Provisions

1980 Acts. Amendment by Pub. L. No. 96–483 effective Dec. 27, 1977, see section 2(g) of Pub. L. No. 96–483, set out as a note under section 1281 of this title.

§ 1293a. Contained spoil disposal facilities

(a) Construction, operation, and maintenance; period; conditions; requirements

The Secretary of the Army, acting through the Chief of Engineers, is authorized to construct, operate, and maintain, subject to the provisions of subsection (c) of this section, contained spoil disposal facilities of sufficient capacity for a period not to exceed ten years, to meet the requirements of this section. Before establishing each such facility, the Secretary of the Army shall obtain the concurrence of appropriate local governments and shall consider the views and recommendations of the Administrator of the Environmental Protection Agency and shall comply with requirements of section 1171 of this title, and of the National Environmental Policy Act of 1969 [42 U.S.C.A. § 4321 et seq.]. Section 401 of this title shall not apply to any facility authorized by this section.

(b) Time for establishment; consideration of area needs; requirements

The Secretary of the Army, acting through the Chief of Engineers, shall establish the contained spoil disposal facilities authorized in subsection (a) of this section at the earliest practicable date, taking into consideration the views and recommendations of the Administrator of the Environmental Protection Agency as to those areas which, in the Administrator's judgment, are most urgently in need of such facilities and pursuant to the requirements of the National Environmental Policy Act of 1969 [42 U.S.C.A. § 4321 et seq.] and the Federal Water Pollution Control Act [33 U.S.C.A. § 1251 et seq.].

(c) Written agreement requirement; terms of agreement

Prior to construction of any such facility, the appropriate State or States, interstate agency, municipality, or other appropriate political subdivision of the State shall agree in writing to (1) furnish all lands, easements, and rights-of-way necessary for the construction, operation, and maintenance of the facility; (2) contribute to the United States 25 per centum of the construction costs, such amount to be payable either in cash prior to construction, in installments during construction, or in installments, with interest at a rate to be determined by the Secretary of the Treasury, as of the beginning of the fiscal year in which construction is initiated, on the basis of the computed average interest rate payable by the Treasury upon its outstanding marketable public obligations, which are neither due or callable for redemption for fifteen years from date of issue; (3) hold and save the United States free from damages due to construction, operation, and maintenance of the facility; and (4) except as provided in subsection (f) of this section, maintain the facility after completion of its use for disposal purposes in a manner satisfactory to the Secretary of the Army.

(d) Waiver of construction costs contribution from non-Federal interests; findings of participation in waste treatment facilities for general geographical area and compliance

with water quality standards; waiver of payments in event of written agreement before occurrence of findings

The requirement for appropriate non-Federal interest or interests to furnish an agreement to contribute 25 per centum of the construction costs as set forth in subsection (c) of this section shall be waived by the Secretary of the Army upon a finding by the Administrator of the Environmental Protection Agency that for the area to which such construction applies, the State or States involved, interstate agency, municipality, and other appropriate political subdivision of the State and industrial concerns are participating in and in compliance with an approved plan for the general geographical area of the dredging activity for construction, modification, expansion, or rehabilitation of waste treatment facilities and the Administrator has found that applicable water quality standards are not being violated. In the event such findings occur after the appropriate non-Federal interest or interests have entered into the agreement required by subsection (c) of this section, any payments due after the date of such findings as part of the required local contribution of 25 per centum of the construction costs shall be waived by the Secretary of the Army.

(e) Federal payment of costs for disposal of dredged spoil from project

Notwithstanding any other provision of law, all costs of disposal of dredged spoil from the project for the Great Lakes connecting channels, Michigan, shall be borne by the United States.

(f) Title to lands, easements, and rights-of-way; retention by non-Federal interests; conveyance of facilities; agreement of transferee

The participating non-Federal interest or interests shall retain title to all lands, easements, and rights-of-way furnished by it pursuant to subsection (c) of this section. A spoil disposal facility owned by a non-Federal interest or interests may be conveyed to another party only after completion of the facility's use for disposal purposes and after the transferee agrees in writing to use or maintain the facility in a manner which the Secretary of the Army determines to be satisfactory.

(g) Federal licenses or permits; charges; remission of charge

Any spoil disposal facilities constructed under the provisions of this section shall be made available to Federal licensees or permittees upon payment of an appropriate charge for such use. Twenty-five per centum of such charge shall be remitted to the participating non-Federal interest or interests except for those excused from contributing to the construction costs under subsections (d) and (e) of this section.

(h) Provisions applicable to Great Lakes and their connecting channels

This section, other than subsection (i), shall be applicable only to the Great Lakes and their connecting channels.

(i) Research, study, and experimentation program relating to dredged spoil extended to navigable waters, etc.; cooperative program; scope of program; utilization of facilities and personnel of Federal agency

The Chief of Engineers, under the direction of the Secretary of the Army, is hereby authorized to extend to all navigable waters, connecting channels, tributary streams, other waters of the United States and waters contiguous to the United States, a comprehensive program of research, study, and experimentation relating to dredged spoil. This program shall be carried out in cooperation with other Federal and State agencies, and shall include, but not be limited to, investigations on the characteristics of dredged spoil, and alternative methods of its disposal. To the extent that such study shall include the effects of such dredge spoil on water quality, the facilities and personnel of the Environmental Protection Agency shall be utilized.

(j) Period for depositing dredged materials

The Secretary of the Army, acting through the Chief of Engineers, is authorized to continue to deposit dredged materials into a contained spoil disposal facility constructed under this section until the Secretary determines that such facility is no longer needed for such purpose or that such facility is completely full.

(k) Study and monitoring program

(1) Study

The Secretary of the Army, acting through the Chief of Engineers, shall conduct a study of the materials disposed of in contained spoil disposal facilities constructed under this section for the purpose of determining whether or not toxic pollutants are present in such facilities and for the purpose of determining the concentration levels of each of such pollutants in such facilities.

(2) Report

Not later than 1 year after November 17, 1988, the Secretary shall transmit to Congress a report on the results of the study conducted under paragraph (1).

(3) Inspection and monitoring program

The Secretary shall conduct a program to inspect and monitor contained spoil disposal facilities constructed under this section for the purpose of determining whether or not toxic pollutants are leaking from such facilities.

(4) Toxic pollutant defined

For purposes of this subsection, the term "toxic pollutant" means those toxic pollutants referred to in section 1311(b)(2)(C) and 1311(b)(2)(D) of this title and such other pollutants as the Secretary, in consultation with the Administrator of the Environmental Protection Agency, determines are appropriate based on their effects on human health and the environment.

(Pub. L. No. 91–611, Title I, § 123, 84 Stat. 1823 (Dec. 31, 1970); as amended by Pub. L. No. 93–251, Title I, § 23, 88 Stat. 20 (Mar. 7, 1974); Pub. L. No. 100–676, § 24, 102 Stat. 4027 (Nov. 17, 1988).)

HISTORICAL AND STATUTORY NOTES

References in Text

Section 1171 of this title, referred to in subsec. (a), was omitted as superseded.

The National Environmental Policy Act of 1969, referred to in subsecs. (a) and (b), is Pub. L. No. 91–190, 83 Stat. 852 (Jan. 1, 1970), as amended, which is codified generally as chapter 55 (section 4321 et seq.) of Title 42, The Public Health and Welfare. For complete classification of this Act to the Code, see Short Title note set out under section 4321 of Title 42 and Tables volume.

The Federal Water Pollution Control Act, referred to in subsec. (b), is Act of June 30, 1948, c. 758, as amended generally by Pub. L. No. 92–500, § 2, 86 Stat. 816 (Oct. 18, 1972), which is codified generally as chapter 26 (section 1251 et seq.) of this title. For complete classification of this Act to the Code, see Short Title note set out under section 1251 of this title and Tables volume.

Codifications

This section was formerly codified as section 1165a of this title.

This section was not enacted as part of the Federal Water Pollution Control Act, which comprises this chapter.

Great Lakes Confined Disposal Facilities

Pub. L. No. 104–303, Title V, § 513, 110 Stat. 3762 (Oct. 12, 1996), provided that:

"**(a) Assessment.**—Pursuant to the responsibilities of the Secretary under section 123 of the River and Harbor Act of 1970 (33 U.S.C. 1293a) [this section], the Secretary shall conduct an assessment of the general conditions of confined disposal facilities in the Great Lakes.

"**(b) Report.**—Not later than 3 years after the date of the enactment of this Act [Oct. 12, 1996], the Secretary shall transmit to Congress a report on the results of the assessment conducted under subsection (a), including the following:

"**(1)** A description of the cumulative effects of confined disposal facilities in the Great Lakes.

"**(2)** Recommendations for specific remediation actions for each confined disposal facility in the Great Lakes.

"**(3)** An evaluation of, and recommendations for, confined disposal facility management practices and technologies to conserve capacity at such facilities and to minimize adverse environmental effects at such facilities throughout the Great Lakes system."

§ 1294. Public information and education on recycling and reuse of wastewater, use of land treatment, and reduction of wastewater volume

[FWPCA § 214]

The Administrator shall develop and operate within one year of December 27, 1977, a continuing program of public information and education on recycling and reuse of wastewater (including sludge), the use of land treatment, and methods for the reduction of wastewater volume.

(June 30, 1948, c. 758, Title II, § 214, as added by Pub. L. No. 95–217, § 38, 91 Stat. 1581 (Dec. 27, 1977).)

§ 1295. Requirements for American materials

[FWPCA § 215]

Notwithstanding any other provision of law, no grant for which application is made after February 1, 1978, shall be made under this subchapter for any treatment works unless only such unmanufactured articles, materials, and supplies as have been mined or produced in the United States, and only such manufactured articles, materials, and supplies as have been manufactured in the United States, substantially all from articles, materials, or supplies mined, produced, or manufactured, as the case may be, in the United States will be used in such treatment works. This section shall not apply in any case where the Administrator determines, based upon those factors the Administrator deems relevant, including the available resources of the agency, it to be inconsistent with the public interest (including multilateral government procurement agreements) or the cost to be unreasonable, or if articles, materials, or supplies of the class or kind to be used or the articles, materials, or supplies from which they are manufactured are not mined, produced, or manufactured, as the case may be, in the United States in sufficient and reasonably available commercial quantities and of a satisfactory quality.

(June 30, 1948, c. 758, Title II, § 215, as added by Pub. L. No. 95–217, § 39, 91 Stat. 1581 (Dec. 27, 1977).)

§ 1296. Determination of priority of projects

[FWPCA § 216]

Notwithstanding any other provision of this chapter, the determination of the priority to be given each category of projects for construction of publicly owned treatment works within each State shall be made solely by that State, except that if the Administrator, after a public hearing, determines that a specific project will not result in compliance with the enforceable requirements of this chapter, such project shall be removed from the State's priority list and such State shall submit a revised priority list. These categories shall include, but not be limited to (A) secondary treatment, (B) more stringent treatment, (C) infiltration-in-flow correction, (D) major sewer system rehabilitation, (E) new collector sewers and appurtenances, (F) new interceptors and appurtenances, and (G) correction of combined sewer overflows. Not less than 25 per centum of funds allocated to a State in any fiscal year under this subchapter for construction of publicly owned treatment works in such State shall be obligated for those types of projects referred to in clauses (D), (E), (F), and (G) of this section, if such projects are on such State's priority list for that year and are otherwise eligible for funding in that fiscal year. It is the policy of Congress that projects for wastewater treatment and management undertaken with Federal financial assistance under this chapter by any State, municipality, or intermunicipal or interstate agency shall be projects which, in the estimation of the State, are designed to achieve optimum water quality management, consistent with the public health and water quality goals and requirements of this chapter.

(June 30, 1948, c. 758, Title II, § 216, as added by Pub. L. No. 95–217, § 40, 91 Stat. 1582 (Dec. 27, 1977); and amended by Pub. L. No. 97–117, § 18, 95 Stat. 1630 (Dec. 29, 1981).)

§ 1297. Guidelines for cost-effectiveness analysis

[FWPCA § 217]

Any guidelines for cost-effectiveness analysis published by the Administrator under this subchapter shall provide for the identification and selection of cost effective alternatives to comply with the objective and goals of this chapter and sections 1281(b), 1281(d), 1281(g)(2)(A), and 1311(b)(2)(B) of this title.

(June 30, 1948, c. 758, Title II, § 217, as added by Pub. L. No. 95–217, § 41, 91 Stat. 1582 (Dec. 27, 1977).)

§ 1298. Cost effectiveness

[FWPCA § 218]

(a) Congressional statement of policy

It is the policy of Congress that a project for waste treatment and management undertaken with Federal financial assistance under this chapter by any State, municipality, or intermunicipal or interstate agency shall be considered as an overall waste treatment system for waste treatment and management, and shall be that system which constitutes the most economical and cost-effective combination of devices and systems used in the storage, treatment, recycling, and reclamation of municipal sewage or industrial wastes of a liquid nature to implement section 1281 of this title, or necessary to recycle or reuse water at the most economical cost over the estimated life of the works, including intercepting sewers, outfall sewers, sewage collection systems, pumping power, and other equipment, and their appurtenances; extension, improvements, remodeling, additions, and alterations thereof; elements essential to provide a reliable recycled supply such as standby treatment units and clear well facilities; and any works, including site acquisition of the land that will be an integral part of the treatment process (including land use for the storage of treated wastewater in land treatment systems prior to land application) or which is used for ultimate disposal of residues resulting from such treatment; water efficiency measures and devices; and any other method or system for preventing, abating, reducing, storing, treating, separating, or disposing of municipal waste, including storm water runoff, or industrial waste, including waste in combined storm water and sanitary sewer systems; to meet the requirements of this chapter.

(b) Determination by Administrator as prerequisite to approval of grant

In accordance with the policy set forth in subsection (a) of this section, before the Administrator approves any grant to any State, municipality, or intermunicipal or interstate agency for the erection, building, acquisition, alteration, remodeling, improvement, or extension of any treatment works the Administrator shall determine that the facilities plan of which such treatment works are a part constitutes the most economical and cost-effective combination of treatment works over the life of the project to meet the requirements of this chapter, including, but not limited to, consideration of construction costs, operation, maintenance, and replacement costs.

(c) Value engineering review

In furtherance of the policy set forth in subsection (a) of this section, the Administrator shall require value engineering review in connection with any treatment works, prior to approval of any grant for the erection, building, acquisition, alteration, remodeling, improvement, or extension of such treatment works, in any case in which the cost of such erection, building, acquisition, alteration, remodeling, improvement, or extension is projected to be in excess of $10,000,000. For purposes of this subsection, the term "value engineering review" means a specialized cost control technique which uses a systematic and creative approach to identify and to focus on unnecessarily high cost in a project in order to arrive at a cost saving without sacrificing the reliability or efficiency of the project.

(d) Projects affected

This section applies to projects for waste treatment and management for which no treatment works including a facilities plan for such project have received Federal financial assistance for the preparation of construction plans and specifications under this chapter before December 29, 1981.

(June 30, 1948, c. 758, Title II, § 218, as added by Pub. L. No. 97–117, § 19, 95 Stat. 1630 (Dec. 29, 1981).)

§ 1299. State certification of projects

[FWPCA § 219]

Whenever the Governor of a State which has been delegated sufficient authority to administer the construction grant program under this subchapter in that State certifies to the Administrator that a grant application meets applicable requirements of Federal and State law for assistance under this subchapter, the Administrator shall approve or disapprove such application within 45 days of the date of receipt of such application. If the Administrator does not approve or disapprove such application within 45 days of receipt, the application shall be deemed approved. If the Administrator disapproves such application the Administrator shall state in writing the reasons for such disapproval. Any grant approved or deemed approved under this section shall be subject to amounts provided in appropriation Acts.

(June 30, 1948, c. 758, Title II, § 219, as added by Pub. L. No. 97–117, § 20, 95 Stat. 1631 (Dec. 29, 1981).)

§ 1300. Pilot program for alternative water source projects

[FWPCA § 220]

(a) Policy

Nothing in this section shall be construed to affect the application of section 1251(g) of this title and all of the provisions of this section shall be carried out in accordance with the provisions of section 1251(g) of this title.

(b) In general

The Administrator may establish a pilot program to make grants to State, interstate, and intrastate water resource development agencies (including water management districts and water supply authorities), local government agencies, private utilities, and nonprofit entities for alternative water source projects to meet critical water supply needs.

(c) Eligible entity

The Administrator may make grants under this section to an entity only if the entity has authority under State law to develop or provide water for municipal, industrial, and agricultural uses in an area of the State that is experiencing critical water supply needs.

(d) Selection of projects

(1) Limitation

A project that has received funds under the reclamation and reuse program conducted under the Reclamation Projects Authorization and Adjustment Act of 1992 (43 U.S.C. 390h et seq.) shall not be eligible for grant assistance under this section.

(2) Additional consideration

In making grants under this section, the Administrator shall consider whether the project is located within the boundaries of a State or area referred to in section 391 of Title 43, and within the geographic scope of the reclamation and reuse program conducted under the Reclamation Projects Authorization and Adjustment Act of 1992 (43 U.S.C. 390h et seq.).

(3) Geographical distribution

Alternative water source projects selected by the Administrator under this section shall reflect a variety of geographical and environmental conditions.

(e) Committee resolution procedure

(1) In general

No appropriation shall be made for any alternative water source project under this section, the total Federal cost of which exceeds $3,000,000, if such project has not been approved by a resolution adopted by the Committee on Transportation and Infrastructure of the House of Representatives or the Committee on Environment and Public Works of the Senate.

(2) Requirements for securing consideration

For purposes of securing consideration of approval under paragraph (1), the Administrator shall provide to a committee referred to in paragraph (1) such information as the committee requests and the non-Federal sponsor shall provide to the committee information on the costs and relative needs for the alternative water source project.

(f) Uses of grants

Amounts from grants received under this section may be used for engineering, design, construction, and final testing of alternative water source projects designed to meet critical water supply needs. Such amounts may not be used for planning, feasibility studies or for operation, maintenance, replacement, repair, or rehabilitation.

(g) Cost sharing

The Federal share of the eligible costs of an alternative water source project carried out using assistance made available under this section shall not exceed 50 percent.

(h) Reports

On or before September 30, 2004, the Administrator shall transmit to Congress a report on the results of the pilot program established under this section, including progress made toward meeting the critical water supply needs of the participants in the pilot program.

(i) Definitions

In this section, the following definitions apply:

(1) Alternative water source project

The term "alternative water source project" means a project designed to provide municipal, industrial, and agricultural water supplies in an environmentally sustainable manner by conserving, managing, reclaiming, or reusing water or wastewater or by treating wastewater. Such term does not include water treatment or distribution facilities.

(2) Critical water supply needs

The term "critical water supply needs" means existing or reasonably anticipated future water supply needs that cannot be met by existing water supplies, as identified in a comprehensive statewide or regional water supply plan or assessment projected over a planning period of at least 20 years.

(j) Authorization of appropriations

There is authorized to be appropriated to carry out this section a total of $75,000,000 for fiscal years 2002 through 2004. Such sums shall remain available until expended.

(June 30, 1948, c. 758, Title II, § 220, as added by Pub. L. No. 106–457, Title VI, § 602, 114 Stat. 1975 (Nov. 7, 2000).)

HISTORICAL AND STATUTORY NOTES

References in Text

The Reclamation Projects Authorization and Adjustment Act of 1992, referred to in subsec. (d)(1), (2), is Pub. L. No. 102–575, 106 Stat. 4600 (Oct. 30, 1992), as amended. Provisions relating to the reclamation and reuse program are codified principally as 43 U.S.C.A. § 390h et seq. See Short Title of 1992 Amendment note set out under 43 U.S.C.A. § 371 and Tables for complete classification.

Section 1 of the Reclamation Act of June 17, 1902, referred to in subsec. (d)(2), probably means Act of June 17, 1902, c. 1093, § 1, 32 Stat. 388, which is codified as section 391 of Title 43.

§ 1301. Sewer overflow and stormwater reuse municipal grants [FWPCA § 221]

(a) In general

(1) Grants to States.—The Administrator may make grants to States for the purpose of providing grants to a municipality or municipal entity for planning, design, and construction of—

(A) treatment works to intercept, transport, control, treat, or reuse municipal combined sewer overflows, sanitary sewer overflows, or stormwater; and

(B) any other measures to manage, reduce, treat, or recapture stormwater or subsurface drainage water eligible for assistance under section 603(c).

(2) Direct municipal grants.—Subject to subsection (g), the Administrator may make a direct grant to a municipality or municipal entity for the purposes described in paragraph (1).

(b) Prioritization

In selecting from among municipalities applying for grants under subsection (a) of this section, a State or the Administrator shall give priority to an applicant that—

(1) is a municipality that is a financially distressed community under subsection (c) of this section;

(2) has implemented or is complying with an implementation schedule for the nine minimum controls specified in the CSO control policy referred to in section 1342(q)(1) of this title and has begun implementing a long-term municipal combined sewer overflow control plan or a separate sanitary sewer overflow control plan;

(3) is requesting a grant for a project that is on a State's intended use plan pursuant to section 1386(c) of this title; or

(4) is an Alaska Native Village.

(c) Financially distressed community

(1) Definition

In subsection (b) of this section, the term "financially distressed community" means a community that meets affordability criteria established by the State in which the community is located, if such criteria are developed after public review and comment.

(2) Consideration of impact on water and sewer rates

In determining if a community is a distressed community for the purposes of subsection (b) of this section, the State shall consider, among other factors, the extent to which the rate of growth of a community's tax base has been historically slow such that implementing a plan described in subsection (b)(2) of this section would result in a significant increase in any water or sewer rate charged by the community's publicly owned wastewater treatment facility.

(3) Information to assist States

The Administrator may publish information to assist States in establishing affordability criteria under paragraph (1).

(d) Cost-sharing

The Federal share of the cost of activities carried out using amounts from a grant made under subsection (a) of this section shall be not less than 55 percent of the cost. The non-Federal share of the cost may include, in any amount, public and private funds and in-kind services, and may include, notwithstanding section 1383(h) of this title, financial assistance, including loans, from a State water pollution control revolving fund.

(e) Administrative requirements

A project that receives assistance under this section shall be carried out subject to the same requirements as a project that receives assistance from a State water pollution control revolving fund under title VI, except to the extent that the Governor of the State in which the project is located determines that a requirement of title VI is inconsistent with the purposes of this section. For the purposes of this subsection, a Governor may not determine that the requirements of title VI relating to the application of section 513 are inconsistent with the purposes of this section.

(f) Authorization of appropriations

(1) In general.—There is authorized to be appropriated to carry out this section $225,000,000 for each of fiscal years 2019 through 2020.

(2) Minimum allocations.—To the extent there are sufficient eligible project applications, the Administrator shall ensure that a State uses not less than 20 percent of the amount of the grants made to the State under subsection (a) in a fiscal year to carry out projects to intercept, transport, control, treat, or reuse municipal combined sewer overflows, sanitary sewer overflows, or stormwater through the use of green infrastructure, water and energy efficiency improvements, and other environmentally innovative activities.

(g) Allocation of funds

(1) Fiscal Year 2019.—Subject to subsection (h), the Administrator shall use the amounts appropriated to carry out this section for fiscal year 2019 for making grants to municipalities and municipal entities under subsection (a)(2) in accordance with the criteria set forth in subsection (b).

(2) Fiscal Year 2020 and thereafter.—Subject to subsection (h), the Administrator shall use the amounts appropriated to carry out this section for fiscal year 2020 and each fiscal year thereafter for making grants to States under subsection (a)(1) in accordance with a formula to be established by the Administrator, after providing notice and an opportunity for public comment, that allocates to each State a proportional share of such amounts based on the total needs of the State for municipal combined sewer overflow controls, sanitary sewer overflow controls, and stormwater identified in the most recent detailed estimate and comprehensive study submitted pursuant to section 516 and any other information the Administrator considers appropriate.

(h) Administrative expenses

Of the amounts appropriated to carry out this section for each fiscal year—

(1) the Administrator may retain an amount not to exceed 1 percent for the reasonable and necessary costs of administering this section; and

(2) the Administrator, or a State, may retain an amount not to exceed 4 percent of any grant made to a municipality or municipal entity under subsection (a) of this section, for the reasonable and necessary costs of administering the grant.

(i) Reports

Not later than December 31, 2003, and periodically thereafter, the Administrator shall transmit to Congress a report containing recommended funding levels for grants under this section. The recommended funding levels shall be sufficient to ensure the continued expeditious implementation of municipal combined sewer overflow and sanitary sewer overflow controls nationwide.

(June 30, 1948, c. 758, Title II, § 221, as added by Pub. L. No. 106–554, § 1(a)(4) [Div. B, Title I, § 112(c)], 114 Stat. 2763, 2763A–225 (Dec. 21, 2000); and amended by Pub. L. No. 115–270, § 4106, 132 Stat. 3765, 3875–3876 (Oct. 23, 2018).)

HISTORICAL AND STATUTORY NOTES

References in Text

Section 1375 of this title, referred to in subsec. (g)(2)(B), was amended by Pub. L. No. 105–362, Title V, § 501(d)(1), 112 Stat. 3283 (Nov. 10, 1998), and, as so amended, no longer contains subsections.

Information on CSOS and SSOS.—

Pub. L. No. 106–554, § 1(a)(4) [Div. B, Title I, § 112(d)], 114 Stat. 2763, 2763a–227 (Dec. 21, 2000), provided that:

"(1) Report to Congress.—Not later than 3 years after December 21, 2000, the Administrator of the Environmental Protection Agency shall transmit to Congress a report summarizing—

"(A) the extent of the human health and environmental impacts caused by municipal combined sewer overflows and sanitary sewer overflows, including the location of discharges causing such impacts, the volume of pollutants discharged, and the constituents discharged;

"(B) the resources spent by municipalities to address these impacts; and

"(C) an evaluation of the technologies used by municipalities to address these impacts.

"(2) Technology clearinghouse.—After transmitting a report under paragraph (1), the Administrator shall maintain a clearinghouse of cost-effective and efficient technologies for addressing human health and environmental impacts due to municipal combined sewer overflows and sanitary sewer overflows."

SUBCHAPTER III—STANDARDS AND ENFORCEMENT

§ 1311. Effluent limitations

[FWPCA § 301]

(a) Illegality of pollutant discharges except in compliance with law

Except as in compliance with this section and sections 1312, 1316, 1317, 1328, 1342, and 1344 of this title, the discharge of any pollutant by any person shall be unlawful.

(b) Timetable for achievement of objectives

In order to carry out the objective of this chapter there shall be achieved—

(1) (A) not later than July 1, 1977, effluent limitations for point sources, other than publicly owned treatment works, (i) which shall require the application of the best practicable control technology currently available as defined by the Administrator pursuant to section 1314(b) of this title, or (ii) in the case of a discharge into a publicly owned treatment works which meets the requirements of subparagraph (B) of this paragraph, which shall require compliance with any applicable pretreatment requirements and any requirements under section 1317 of this title; and

(B) for publicly owned treatment works in existence on July 1, 1977, or approved pursuant to section 1283 of this title prior to June 30, 1974 (for which construction must be completed within four years of approval), effluent limitations based upon secondary treatment as defined by the Administrator pursuant to section 1314(d)(1) of this title; or,

(C) not later than July 1, 1977, any more stringent limitation, including those necessary to meet water quality standards, treatment standards, or schedules of compliance, established pursuant to any State law or regulations (under authority preserved by section 1370 of this title) or any other Federal law or regulation, or required to implement any applicable water quality standard established pursuant to this chapter.

(2) (A) for pollutants identified in subparagraphs (C), (D), and (F) of this paragraph, effluent limitations for categories and classes of point sources, other than publicly owned treatment works, which (i) shall require application of the best available technology economically achievable for such category or class, which will result in reasonable further progress toward the national goal of eliminating the discharge of all pollutants, as determined in accordance with regulations issued by the Administrator pursuant to section 1314(b)(2) of this title, which such effluent limitations shall require the elimination of discharges of all pollutants if the Administrator finds, on the basis of information available to him (including information developed pursuant to section 1325 of this title), that such elimination is technologically and economically achievable for a category or class of point sources as determined in accordance with regulations issued by the Administrator pursuant to section 1314(b)(2) of this title, or (ii) in the case of the introduction of a pollutant into a publicly owned treatment works which meets the requirements of subparagraph (B) of this paragraph, shall require compliance with any applicable pretreatment requirements and any other requirement under section 1317 of this title;

(B) Repealed. Pub. L. No. 97–117, § 21(b), Dec. 29, 1981, 95 Stat. 1632.

(C) with respect to all toxic pollutants referred to in table 1 of Committee Print Numbered 95–30 of the Committee on Public Works and Transportation of the House of Representatives compliance with effluent limitations in accordance with subparagraph (A) of this paragraph as expeditiously as practicable but in no case later than three years after the date such limitations are promulgated under section 1314(b) of this title, and in no case later than March 31, 1989;

(D) for all toxic pollutants listed under paragraph (1) of subsection (a) of section 1317 of this title which are not referred to in subparagraph (C) of this paragraph compliance with effluent limitations in accordance with subparagraph (A) of this paragraph as expeditiously as practicable, but in no case later than three years after the date such limitations are promulgated under section 1314(b) of this title, and in no case later than March 31, 1989;

(E) as expeditiously as practicable but in no case later than three years after the date such limitations are promulgated under section 1314(b) of this title, and in no case later than March 31, 1989, compliance with effluent limitations for categories and classes of point sources, other than publicly owned treatment works, which in the case of pollutants identified pursuant to section 1314(a)(4) of this title shall require application of the best conventional pollutant control technology as determined in accordance with regulations issued by the Administrator pursuant to section 1314(b)(4) of this title; and

(F) for all pollutants (other than those subject to subparagraphs (C), (D), or (E) of this paragraph) compliance with effluent limitations in accordance with subparagraph (A) of this paragraph as expeditiously as practicable but in no case later than 3 years after the date such limitations are established, and in no case later than March 31, 1989.

(3) (A) for effluent limitations under paragraph (1)(A)(i) of this subsection promulgated after January 1, 1982, and requiring a level of control substantially greater or based on fundamentally different control technology than under permits for an industrial category issued before such date, compliance as expeditiously as practicable but in no case later than three years after the date such limitations are promulgated under section 1314(b) of this title, and in no case later than March 31, 1989; and

(B) for any effluent limitation in accordance with paragraph (1)(A)(i), (2)(A)(i), or (2)(E) of this subsection established only on the basis of section 1342(a)(1) of this title in a permit issued after February 4, 1987, compliance as expeditiously as practicable but in no case later than three years after the date such limitations are established, and in no case later than March 31, 1989.

(c) Modification of timetable

The Administrator may modify the requirements of subsection (b)(2)(A) of this section with respect to any point source for which a permit application is filed after July 1, 1977, upon a showing by the owner or operator of such point source satisfactory to the Administrator that such modified requirements (1) will represent the maximum use of technology within the economic capability of the owner or operator; and (2) will result in reasonable further progress toward the elimination of the discharge of pollutants.

(d) Review and revision of effluent limitations

Any effluent limitation required by paragraph (2) of subsection (b) of this section shall be reviewed at least every five years and, if appropriate, revised pursuant to the procedure established under such paragraph.

(e) All point discharge source application of effluent limitations

Effluent limitations established pursuant to this section or section 1312 of this title shall be applied to all point sources of discharge of pollutants in accordance with the provisions of this chapter.

(f) Illegality of discharge of radiological, chemical, or biological warfare agents, high-level radioactive waste, or medical waste

Notwithstanding any other provisions of this chapter it shall be unlawful to discharge any radiological, chemical, or biological warfare agent, any high-level radioactive waste, or any medical waste, into the navigable waters.

(g) Modifications for certain nonconventional pollutants

(1) General authority

The Administrator, with the concurrence of the State, may modify the requirements of subsection (b)(2)(A) of this section with respect to the discharge from any point source of ammonia, chlorine, color, iron, and total phenols (4AAP) (when determined by the Administrator to be a pollutant covered by subsection (b)(2)(F) of this section) and any other pollutant which the Administrator lists under paragraph (4) of this subsection.

(2) Requirements for granting modifications

A modification under this subsection shall be granted only upon a showing by the owner or operator of a point source satisfactory to the Administrator that—

(A) such modified requirements will result at a minimum in compliance with the requirements of subsection (b)(1)(A) or (C) of this section, whichever is applicable;

(B) such modified requirements will not result in any additional requirements on any other point or nonpoint source; and

(C) such modification will not interfere with the attainment or maintenance of that water quality which shall assure protection of public water supplies, and the protection and propagation of a balanced population of shellfish, fish, and wildlife, and allow recreational activities, in and on the water and such modification will not result in the discharge of pollutants in quantities which may reasonably be anticipated to pose an unacceptable risk to human health or the environment because of bioaccumulation, persistency in the environment, acute toxicity, chronic toxicity (including carcinogenicity, mutagenicity or teratogenicity), or synergistic propensities.

(3) Limitation on authority to apply for subsection (c) modification

If an owner or operator of a point source applies for a modification under this subsection with respect to the discharge of any pollutant, such owner or operator shall be eligible to apply for modification under subsection (c) of this section with respect to such pollutant only during the same time period as he is eligible to apply for a modification under this subsection.

(4) Procedures for listing additional pollutants

(A) General authority

Upon petition of any person, the Administrator may add any pollutant to the list of pollutants for which modification under this section is authorized (except for pollutants identified pursuant to section 1314(a)(4) of this title, toxic pollutants subject to section 1317(a) of this title, and the thermal component of discharges) in accordance with the provisions of this paragraph.

(B) Requirements for listing

(i) Sufficient information

The person petitioning for listing of an additional pollutant under this subsection shall submit to the Administrator sufficient information to make the determinations required by this subparagraph.

(ii) Toxic criteria determination

The Administrator shall determine whether or not the pollutant meets the criteria for listing as a toxic pollutant under section 1317(a) of this title.

(iii) Listing as toxic pollutant

If the Administrator determines that the pollutant meets the criteria for listing as a toxic pollutant under section 1317(a) of this title, the Administrator shall list the pollutant as a toxic pollutant under section 1317(a) of this title.

(iv) Nonconventional criteria determination

If the Administrator determines that the pollutant does not meet the criteria for listing as a toxic pollutant under such section and determines that adequate test methods and sufficient data are available to make the determinations required by paragraph (2) of this subsection with respect to the pollutant, the Administrator shall add the pollutant to the list of pollutants specified in paragraph (1) of this subsection for which modifications are authorized under this subsection.

(C) Requirements for filing of petitions

A petition for listing of a pollutant under this paragraph—

(i) must be filed not later than 270 days after the date of promulgation of an applicable effluent guideline under section 1314 of this title;

(ii) may be filed before promulgation of such guideline; and

(iii) may be filed with an application for a modification under paragraph (1) with respect to the discharge of such pollutant.

(D) Deadline for approval of petition

A decision to add a pollutant to the list of pollutants for which modifications under this subsection are authorized must be made within 270 days after the date of promulgation of an applicable effluent guideline under section 1314 of this title.

(E) Burden of proof

The burden of proof for making the determinations under subparagraph (B) shall be on the petitioner.

(5) Removal of pollutants

The Administrator may remove any pollutant from the list of pollutants for which modifications are authorized under this subsection if the Administrator determines that adequate test methods and sufficient data are no longer available for determining whether or not modifications may be granted with respect to such pollutant under paragraph (2) of this subsection.

(h) Modification of secondary treatment requirements

The Administrator, with the concurrence of the State, may issue a permit under section 1342 of this title which modifies the requirements of subsection (b)(1)(B) of this section with respect to the discharge of any pollutant from a publicly owned treatment works into marine waters, if the applicant demonstrates to the satisfaction of the Administrator that—

(1) there is an applicable water quality standard specific to the pollutant for which the modification is requested, which has been identified under section 1314(a)(6) of this title;

(2) the discharge of pollutants in accordance with such modified requirements will not interfere, alone or in combination with pollutants from other sources, with the attainment or maintenance of that water quality which assures protection of public water supplies and the protection and propagation of a balanced, indigenous population of shellfish, fish, and wildlife, and allows recreational activities, in and on the water;

(3) the applicant has established a system for monitoring the impact of such discharge on a representative sample of aquatic biota, to the extent practicable, and the scope of such monitoring is limited to include only those scientific investigations which are necessary to study the effects of the proposed discharge;

(4) such modified requirements will not result in any additional requirements on any other point or nonpoint source;

(5) all applicable pretreatment requirements for sources introducing waste into such treatment works will be enforced;

(6) in the case of any treatment works serving a population of 50,000 or more, with respect to any toxic pollutant introduced into such works by an industrial discharger for which pollutant there is no applicable pretreatment requirement in effect, sources introducing waste into such works are in compliance with all applicable pretreatment requirements, the applicant will enforce such requirements, and the applicant has in effect a pretreatment program which, in combination with the treatment of discharges from such works, removes the same amount of such pollutant as would be removed if such works were to apply secondary treatment to discharges and if such works had no pretreatment program with respect to such pollutant;

(7) to the extent practicable, the applicant has established a schedule of activities designed to eliminate the entrance of toxic pollutants from nonindustrial sources into such treatment works;

(8) there will be no new or substantially increased discharges from the point source of the pollutant to which the modification applies above that volume of discharge specified in the permit;

(9) the applicant at the time such modification becomes effective will be discharging effluent which has received at least primary or equivalent treatment and which meets the criteria established under section 1314(a)(1) of this title after initial mixing in the waters surrounding or adjacent to the point at which such effluent is discharged.

For the purposes of this subsection the phrase "the discharge of any pollutant into marine waters" refers to a discharge into deep waters of the territorial sea or the waters of the contiguous zone, or into saline estuarine waters where there is strong tidal movement and other hydrological and geological characteristics which the Administrator determines necessary to allow compliance with paragraph (2) of this subsection, and section 1251(a)(2) of this title. For the purposes of paragraph (9), "primary or equivalent treatment" means treatment by screening, sedimentation, and skimming adequate to remove at least 30 percent of the biological oxygen demanding material and of the suspended solids in the treatment works influent, and disinfection, where appropriate. A municipality which applies secondary treatment shall be eligible to receive a permit pursuant to this subsection which modifies the requirements of subsection (b)(1)(B) of this section with respect to the discharge of any pollutant from any treatment works owned by such municipality into marine waters. No permit issued under this subsection shall authorize the discharge of sewage sludge into marine waters. In order for a permit to be issued under this subsection for the discharge of a pollutant into marine waters, such marine waters must exhibit characteristics assuring that water providing dilution does not contain significant amounts of previously discharged effluent from such treatment works. No permit issued under this subsection shall authorize the discharge of any pollutant into saline estuarine waters which at the time of application do not support a balanced indigenous population of shellfish, fish and wildlife, or allow recreation in and on the waters or which exhibit ambient water quality below applicable water quality standards adopted for the protection of public water supplies, shellfish, fish and wildlife or recreational activities or such other standards necessary to assure support and protection of such uses. The prohibition contained in the preceding sentence shall apply without regard to the presence or absence of a causal relationship between such characteristics and the applicant's current or proposed discharge. Notwithstanding any other provisions of this subsection, no permit may be issued under this subsection for discharge of a pollutant into the New York Bight Apex consisting of the ocean waters of the Atlantic Ocean westward of 73 degrees 30 minutes west longitude and northward of 40 degrees 10 minutes north latitude.

(i) Municipal time extensions

(1) Where construction is required in order for a planned or existing publicly owned treatment works to achieve limitations under subsection (b)(1)(B) or (b)(1)(C) of this section, but (A) construction cannot be completed within the time required in such subsection, or (B) the United States has failed to make financial assistance under this chapter available in time to achieve such limitations by the time specified in such subsection, the owner or operator of such treatment works may request the

Administrator (or if appropriate the State) to issue a permit pursuant to section 1342 of this title or to modify a permit issued pursuant to that section to extend such time for compliance. Any such request shall be filed with the Administrator (or if appropriate the State) within 180 days after February 4, 1987. The Administrator (or if appropriate the State) may grant such request and issue or modify such a permit, which shall contain a schedule of compliance for the publicly owned treatment works based on the earliest date by which such financial assistance will be available from the United States and construction can be completed, but in no event later than July 1, 1988, and shall contain such other terms and conditions, including those necessary to carry out subsections (b) through (g) of section 1281 of this title, section 1317 of this title, and such interim effluent limitations applicable to that treatment works as the Administrator determines are necessary to carry out the provisions of this chapter.

(2) **(A)** Where a point source (other than a publicly owned treatment works) will not achieve the requirements of subsections (b)(1)(A) and (b)(1)(C) of this section and—

(i) if a permit issued prior to July 1, 1977, to such point source is based upon a discharge into a publicly owned treatment works; or

(ii) if such point source (other than a publicly owned treatment works) had before July 1, 1977, a contract (enforceable against such point source) to discharge into a publicly owned treatment works; or

(iii) if either an application made before July 1, 1977, for a construction grant under this chapter for a publicly owned treatment works, or engineering or architectural plans or working drawings made before July 1, 1977, for a publicly owned treatment works, show that such point source was to discharge into such publicly owned treatment works,

and such publicly owned treatment works is presently unable to accept such discharge without construction, and in the case of a discharge to an existing publicly owned treatment works, such treatment works has an extension pursuant to paragraph (1) of this subsection, the owner or operator of such point source may request the Administrator (or if appropriate the State) to issue or modify such a permit pursuant to such section 1342 of this title to extend such time for compliance. Any such request shall be filed with the Administrator (or if appropriate the State) within 180 days after December 27, 1977, or the filing of a request by the appropriate publicly owned treatment works under paragraph (1) of this subsection, whichever is later. If the Administrator (or if appropriate the State) finds that the owner or operator of such point source has acted in good faith, he may grant such request and issue or modify such a permit, which shall contain a schedule of compliance for the point source to achieve the requirements of subsections (b)(1)(A) and (C) of this section and shall contain such other terms and conditions, including pretreatment and interim effluent limitations and water conservation requirements applicable to that point source, as the Administrator determines are necessary to carry out the provisions of this chapter.

(B) No time modification granted by the Administrator (or if appropriate the State) pursuant to paragraph (2)(A) of this subsection shall extend beyond the earliest date practicable for compliance or beyond the date of any extension granted to the appropriate publicly owned treatment works pursuant to paragraph (1) of this subsection, but in no event shall it extend beyond July 1, 1988; and no such time modification shall be granted unless (i) the publicly owned treatment works will be in operation and available to the point source before July 1, 1988, and will meet the requirements of subsections (b)(1)(B) and (C) of this section after receiving the discharge from that point source; and (ii) the point source and the publicly owned treatment works have entered into an enforceable contract requiring the point source to discharge into the publicly owned treatment works, the owner or operator of such point source to pay the costs required under section 1284 of this title, and the publicly owned treatment works to accept the discharge from the point source; and (iii) the permit for such point source requires that point source to meet all requirements under section 1317(a) and (b) of this title during the period of such time modification.

(j) Modification procedures

(1) Any application filed under this section for a modification of the provisions of—

(A) subsection (b)(1)(B) of this section under subsection (h) of this section shall be filed not later that[1] the 365th day which begins after December 29, 1981, except that a publicly owned treatment works which prior to December 31, 1982, had a contractual arrangement to use a portion of the capacity of an ocean outfall operated by another publicly owned treatment works which has applied for or received modification under subsection (h) of this section, may apply for a modification of subsection (h) of this section in its own right not later than 30 days after February 4, 1987, and except as provided in paragraph (5);

(B) subsection (b)(2)(A) of this section as it applies to pollutants identified in subsection (b)(2)(F) of this section shall be filed not later than 270 days after the date of promulgation of an applicable effluent guideline under section 1314 of this title or not later than 270 days after December 27, 1977, whichever is later.

(2) Subject to paragraph (3) of this section, any application for a modification filed under subsection (g) of this section shall not operate to stay any requirement under this chapter, unless in the judgment of the Administrator such a stay or the modification sought will not result in the discharge of pollutants in quantities which may reasonably be anticipated to pose an unacceptable risk to human health or the environment because of bioaccumulation, persistency in the environment, acute toxicity, chronic toxicity (including carcinogenicity, mutagenicity, or teratogenicity), or synergistic propensities, and that there is a substantial likelihood that the applicant will succeed on the merits of such application. In the case of an application filed under subsection (g) of this section, the Administrator may condition any stay granted under this paragraph on requiring the filing of a bond or other appropriate security to assure timely compliance with the requirements from which a modification is sought.

(3) Compliance requirements under subsection (g)

(A) Effect of filing

An application for a modification under subsection (g) of this section and a petition for listing of a pollutant as a pollutant for which modifications are authorized under such subsection shall not stay the requirement that the person seeking such modification or listing comply with effluent limitations under this chapter for all pollutants not the subject of such application or petition.

(B) Effect of disapproval

Disapproval of an application for a modification under subsection (g) of this section shall not stay the requirement that the person seeking such modification comply with all applicable effluent limitations under this chapter.

(4) Deadline for subsection (g) decision

An application for a modification with respect to a pollutant filed under subsection (g) of this section must be approved or disapproved not later than 365 days after the date of such filing; except that in any case in which a petition for listing such pollutant as a pollutant for which modifications are authorized under such subsection is approved, such application must be approved or disapproved not later than 365 days after the date of approval of such petition.

(5) Extension of application deadline

(A) In general

In the 180-day period beginning on October 31, 1994, the city of San Diego, California, may apply for a modification pursuant to subsection (h) of this section of the requirements of subsection (b)(1)(B) of this section with respect to biological oxygen demand and total suspended solids in the effluent discharged into marine waters.

(B) Application

An application under this paragraph shall include a commitment by the applicant to implement a waste water reclamation program that, at a minimum, will—

(i) achieve a system capacity of 45,000,000 gallons of reclaimed waste water per day by January 1, 2010; and

(ii) result in a reduction in the quantity of suspended solids discharged by the applicant into the marine environment during the period of the modification.

(C) Additional conditions

The Administrator may not grant a modification pursuant to an application submitted under this paragraph unless the Administrator determines that such modification will result in removal of not less than 58 percent of the biological oxygen demand (on an annual average) and not less than 80 percent of total suspended solids (on a monthly average) in the discharge to which the application applies.

(D) Preliminary decision deadline

The Administrator shall announce a preliminary decision on an application submitted under this paragraph not later than 1 year after the date the application is submitted.

(k) Innovative technology

In the case of any facility subject to a permit under section 1342 of this title which proposes to comply with the requirements of subsection (b)(2)(A) or (b)(2)(E) of this section by replacing existing production capacity with an innovative production process which will result in an effluent reduction significantly greater than that required by the limitation otherwise applicable to such facility and moves toward the national goal of eliminating the discharge of all pollutants, or with the installation of an innovative control technique that has a substantial likelihood for enabling the facility to comply with the applicable effluent limitation by achieving a significantly greater effluent reduction than that required by the applicable effluent limitation and moves toward the national goal of eliminating the discharge of all pollutants, or by achieving the required reduction with an innovative system that has the potential for significantly lower costs than the systems which have been determined by the Administrator to be economically achievable, the Administrator (or the State with an approved program under section 1342 of this title, in consultation with the Administrator) may establish a date for compliance under subsection (b)(2)(A) or (b)(2)(E) of this section no later than two years after the date for compliance with such effluent limitation which would otherwise be applicable under such subsection, if it is also determined that such innovative system has the potential for industrywide application.

(*l*) Toxic pollutants

Other than as provided in subsection (n) of this section, the Administrator may not modify any requirement of this section as it applies to any specific pollutant which is on the toxic pollutant list under section 1317(a)(1) of this title.

(m) Modification of effluent limitation requirements for point sources

(1) The Administrator, with the concurrence of the State, may issue a permit under section 1342 of this title which modifies the requirements of subsections (b)(1)(A) and (b)(2)(E) of this section, and of section 1343 of this title, with respect to effluent limitations to the extent such limitations relate to biochemical oxygen demand and pH from discharges by an industrial discharger in such State into deep waters of the territorial seas, if the applicant demonstrates and the Administrator finds that—

(A) the facility for which modification is sought is covered at the time of the enactment of this subsection by National Pollutant Discharge Elimination System permit number CA0005894 or CA0005282;

(B) the energy and environmental costs of meeting such requirements of subsections (b)(1)(A) and (b)(2)(E) of this section and section 1343 of this title exceed by an unreasonable amount the benefits to be obtained, including the objectives of this chapter;

(C) the applicant has established a system for monitoring the impact of such discharges on a representative sample of aquatic biota;

(D) such modified requirements will not result in any additional requirements on any other point or nonpoint source;

(E) there will be no new or substantially increased discharges from the point source of the pollutant to which the modification applies above that volume of discharge specified in the permit;

(F) the discharge is into waters where there is strong tidal movement and other hydrological and geological characteristics which are necessary to allow compliance with this subsection and section 1251(a)(2) of this title;

(G) the applicant accepts as a condition to the permit a contractual[2] obligation to use funds in the amount required (but not less than $250,000 per year for ten years) for research and development of water pollution control technology, including but not limited to closed cycle technology;

(H) the facts and circumstances present a unique situation which, if relief is granted, will not establish a precedent or the relaxation of the requirements of this chapter applicable to similarly situated discharges; and

(I) no owner or operator of a facility comparable to that of the applicant situated in the United States has demonstrated that it would be put at a competitive disadvantage to the applicant (or the parent company or any subsidiary thereof) as a result of the issuance of a permit under this subsection.

(2) The effluent limitations established under a permit issued under paragraph (1) shall be sufficient to implement the applicable State water quality standards, to assure the protection of public water supplies and protection and propagation of a balanced, indigenous population of shellfish, fish, fauna, wildlife, and other aquatic organisms, and to allow recreational activities in and on the water. In setting such limitations, the Administrator shall take into account any seasonal variations and the need for an adequate margin of safety, considering the lack of essential knowledge concerning the relationship between effluent limitations and water quality and the lack of essential knowledge of the effects of discharges on beneficial uses of the receiving waters.

(3) A permit under this subsection may be issued for a period not to exceed five years, and such a permit may be renewed for one additional period not to exceed five years upon a demonstration by the applicant and a finding by the Administrator at the time of application for any such renewal that the provisions of this subsection are met.

(4) The Administrator may terminate a permit issued under this subsection if the Administrator determines that there has been a decline in ambient water quality of the receiving waters during the period of the permit even if a direct cause and effect relationship cannot be shown: *Provided,* That if the effluent from a source with a permit issued under this subsection is contributing to a decline in ambient water quality of the receiving waters, the Administrator shall terminate such permit.

(n) Fundamentally different factors

(1) General rule

The Administrator, with the concurrence of the State, may establish an alternative requirement under subsection (b)(2) of this section or section 1317(b) of this title for a facility that modifies the requirements of national effluent limitation guidelines or categorical pretreatment standards that would otherwise be applicable to such facility, if the owner or operator of such facility demonstrates to the satisfaction of the Administrator that—

(A) the facility is fundamentally different with respect to the factors (other than cost) specified in section 1314(b) or 1314(g) of this title and considered by the Administrator in establishing such national effluent limitation guidelines or categorical pretreatment standards;

(B) the application—

(i) is based solely on information and supporting data submitted to the Administrator during the rulemaking for establishment of the applicable national effluent limitation guidelines or categorical pretreatment standard specifically raising the factors that are fundamentally different for such facility; or

(ii) is based on information and supporting data referred to in clause (i) and information and supporting data the applicant did not have a reasonable opportunity to submit during such rulemaking;

(C) the alternative requirement is no less stringent than justified by the fundamental difference; and

(D) the alternative requirement will not result in a non-water quality environmental impact which is markedly more adverse than the impact considered by the Administrator in establishing such national effluent limitation guideline or categorical pretreatment standard.

(2) Time limit for applications

An application for an alternative requirement which modifies the requirements of an effluent limitation or pretreatment standard under this subsection must be submitted to the Administrator within 180 days after the date on which such limitation or standard is established or revised, as the case may be.

(3) Time limit for decision

The Administrator shall approve or deny by final agency action an application submitted under this subsection within 180 days after the date such application is filed with the Administrator.

(4) Submission of information

The Administrator may allow an applicant under this subsection to submit information and supporting data until the earlier of the date the application is approved or denied or the last day that the Administrator has to approve or deny such application.

(5) Treatment of pending applications

For the purposes of this subsection, an application for an alternative requirement based on fundamentally different factors which is pending on February 4, 1987, shall be treated as having been submitted to the Administrator on the 180th day following February 4, 1987. The applicant may amend the application to take into account the provisions of this subsection.

(6) Effect of submission of application

An application for an alternative requirement under this subsection shall not stay the applicant's obligation to comply with the effluent limitation guideline or categorical pretreatment standard which is the subject of the application.

(7) Effect of denial

If an application for an alternative requirement which modifies the requirements of an effluent limitation or pretreatment standard under this subsection is denied by the Administrator, the applicant must comply with such limitation or standard as established or revised, as the case may be.

(8) Reports

By January 1, 1997, and January 1 of every odd-numbered year thereafter, the Administrator shall submit to the Committee on Environment and Public Works of the Senate and the Committee on Transportation and Infrastructure of the House of Representatives a report on the status of applications for alternative requirements which modify the requirements of effluent limitations under section 1311 or 1314 of this title or any national categorical pretreatment standard under section 1317(b) of this title filed before, on, or after February 4, 1987.

(*o*) Application fees

The Administrator shall prescribe and collect from each applicant fees reflecting the reasonable administrative costs incurred in reviewing and processing applications for modifications submitted to the Administrator pursuant to subsections (c), (g), (i), (k), (m), and (n) of this section, section 1314(d)(4) of this title, and section 1326(a) of this title. All amounts collected by the Administrator under this subsection shall be deposited into a special fund of the Treasury entitled "Water Permits and Related Services" which shall thereafter be available for appropriation to carry out activities of the Environmental Protection Agency for which such fees were collected.

(p) Modified permit for coal remining operations

(1) In general

Subject to paragraphs (2) through (4) of this subsection, the Administrator, or the State in any case which the State has an approved permit program under section 1342(b) of this title, may issue a permit under section 1342 of this title which modifies the requirements of subsection (b)(2)(A) of this section with respect to the pH level of any pre-existing discharge, and with respect to pre-existing discharges of iron and manganese from the remined area of any coal remining operation or with respect to the pH level or level of iron or manganese in any pre-existing discharge affected by the remining operation. Such modified requirements shall apply the best available technology economically achievable on a case-by-case basis, using best professional judgment, to set specific numerical effluent limitations in each permit.

(2) Limitations

The Administrator or the State may only issue a permit pursuant to paragraph (1) if the applicant demonstrates to the satisfaction of the Administrator or the State, as the case may be, that the coal remining operation will result in the potential for improved water quality from the remining operation but in no event shall such a permit allow the pH level of any discharge, and in no event shall such a permit allow the discharges of iron and manganese, to exceed the levels being discharged from the remined area before the coal remining operation begins. No discharge from, or affected by, the remining operation shall exceed State water quality standards established under section 1313 of this title.

(3) Definitions

For purposes of this subsection—

(A) Coal remining operation

The term "coal remining operation" means a coal mining operation which begins after February 4, 1987 at a site on which coal mining was conducted before August 3, 1977.

(B) Remined area

The term "remined area" means only that area of any coal remining operation on which coal mining was conducted before August 3, 1977.

(C) Pre-existing discharge

The term "pre-existing discharge" means any discharge at the time of permit application under this subsection.

(4) Applicability of strip mining laws

Nothing in this subsection shall affect the application of the Surface Mining Control and Reclamation Act of 1977 [30 U.S.C.A. § 1201 et seq.] to any coal remining operation, including the application of such Act to suspended solids.

(June 30, 1948, c. 758, Title III, § 301, as added by Pub. L. No. 92–500, § 2, 86 Stat. 844 (Oct. 18, 1972); and amended by Pub. L. No. 95–217, §§ 42–47, 53(c), 91 Stat. 1582–1586, 1590 (Dec. 27, 1977); Pub. L. No. 97–117, §§ 21, 22(a)–(d), 95 Stat. 1631, 1632 (Dec. 29, 1981); Pub. L. No. 97–440, 96 Stat. 2289 (Jan. 8, 1983); Pub. L. No. 100–4, Title III, §§ 301(a) to (e), 302(a) to (d), 303(a), (b)(1), (c) to (f), 304(a), 305, 306(a), (b), 307, 101 Stat. 29–37 (Feb. 4, 1987); Pub. L. No. 100–688, Title III, § 3202(b), 102 Stat. 4154 (Nov. 18, 1988); Pub. L. No. 103–431, § 2, 108 Stat. 4396 (Oct. 31, 1994); Pub. L. No. 104–66, Title II, § 2021(b), 109 Stat. 727 (Dec. 21, 1995).)

[1] So in original. Probably should be "than."

[2] So in original. Probably should be "contractual."

HISTORICAL AND STATUTORY NOTES

References in Text

The Surface Mining Control and Reclamation Act of 1977, referred to in subsec. (p)(4), is Pub. L. No. 95–87, 91 Stat. 445 (Aug. 3, 1977), as amended, which is codified generally as chapter 25 (section 1201 et seq.) of Title 30, Mineral Lands and Mining. For complete classification of this Act to the Code, see Short Title note set out under section 1201 of Title 30 and Tables.

Change of Name

Any reference in any provision of law enacted before Jan. 4, 1995, to the Committee on Public Works and Transportation of the House of Representatives treated as referring to the Committee on Transportation and Infrastructure of the House of Representatives, see section 1(a)(9) of Pub. L. No. 104–14, set out as a note preceding section 21 of Title 2, The Congress.

Effective and Applicability Provisions

1987 Acts. Section 302(e) of Pub. L. No. 100–4 provided that:

"(1) General Rule.—Except as provided in paragraph (2), the amendments made by this section [amending subsecs. (g) and (j) of this section] shall apply to all requests for modifications under section 301(g) of the Federal Water Pollution Control Act [subsec. (g) of this section] pending on the date of the enactment of this Act [Feb. 4, 1987] and shall not have the effect of extending the deadline established in section 301(j)(1)(B) of such Act [subsec. (j)(1)(B) of this section].

"(2) Exception.—The amendments made by this section [amending subsecs. (g) and (j) of this section] shall not affect any application for a modification with respect to the discharge of ammonia, chlorine, color, iron, or total phenols (4AAP) under section 301(g) of the Federal Water Pollution Control Act [subsec. (g) of this section] pending on the date of the enactment of this Act [Feb. 4, 1987]; except that the Administrator must approve or disapprove such application not later than 365 days after the date of such enactment [Feb. 4, 1987]."

Section 303(b)(2) of Pub. L. No. 100–4 provided that: "The amendment made by subsection (b) [amending subsec. (h)(3) of this section] shall only apply to modifications and renewals of modifications which are tentatively or finally approved after the date of the enactment of this Act [Feb. 4, 1987]."

Section 303(g) of Pub. L. No. 100–4 provided that: "The amendments made by subsections (a) [amending subsec. (h)(2) of this section], (c) [enacting subsec. (h)(6) of this section and redesignating former subsec. (h)(6) and (7) as (h)(7) and (8)], (d) [enacting subsec. (h)(9) of this section and inserting provision defining primary and equivalent treatment in provision following subsec. (h)(9)], and (e) [inserting provision relating to issuance of permit to discharge pollutants into marine waters in provision following subsec. (h)(9)] of this section shall not apply to an application for a permit under section 301(h) of the Federal Water Pollution Control Act [subsec. (h) of this title] which has been tentatively or finally approved by the Administrator before the date of the enactment of this Act [Feb. 4, 1987]; except that such amendments shall apply to all renewals of such permits after such date of enactment."

Section 304(b) of Pub. L. No. 100–4 provided that: "The amendment made by subsection (a) [amending subsec. (i)(1) of this section] shall not apply to those treatment works which are subject to a compliance schedule established before the date of the enactment of this Act [Feb. 4, 1987] by a court order or a final administrative order."

1981 Acts. Section 22(e) of Pub. L. No. 97–117 provided that: "The amendments made by this section [amending subsecs. (h) and (j)(1)(A) of this section] shall take effect on the date of enactment of this Act [Dec. 29, 1981], except that no applicant, other than the city of Avalon, California, who applies after the date of enactment of this Act for a permit pursuant to subsection (h) of section 301 of the Federal Water Pollution Control Act [subsec. (h) of this section] which modifies the requirements of subsection (b)(1)(B) of section 301 of such Act [subsec. (b)(1)(B) of this section] shall receive such permit during the one-year period which begins on the date of enactment of this Act."

Phosphate Fertilizer Effluent Limitation

Amendment by section 306(a), (b) of Pub. L. No. 100–4 not to be construed (A) to require the Administrator to permit the discharge of gypsum or gypsum waste into the navigable waters, (B) to affect the procedures and standards applicable to the Administrator in issuing permits under section 1342(a)(1)(B) of this title, and (C) to affect the authority of any State to deny or condition certification under section 1314 of this title with respect to the issuance of permits under section 1342(a)(1)(B) of this title, see section 306(c) of Pub. L. No. 100–4, set out as a note under 33 U.S.C.A. § 1342.

Territorial Sea and Contiguous Zone of United States

For extension of territorial sea and contiguous zone of United States, see Proc. No. 5928 and Proc. No. 7219, respectively, set out as notes under 43 U.S.C.A. § 1331.

Deadlines for Regulations for Certain Toxic Pollutants

Section 301(f) of Pub. L. No. 100–4 provided that: "The Administrator shall promulgate final regulations establishing effluent limitations in accordance with sections 301(b)(2)(A) and 307(b)(1) of the Federal Water Pollution Control Act [subsec. (b)(2)(A) of this section and section 1317(b)(1) of this title] for all toxic pollutants referred to in table 1 of Committee Print Numbered 95–30 of the Committee on Public Works and Transportation of the House of Representatives which are discharged from the categories of point sources in accordance with the following table:

"Category	Date by which the final regulation shall be promulgated
"Organic chemicals and plastics and synthetic fibers	December 31, 1986.
"Pesticides	December 31, 1986."

[Any reference in any provision of law enacted before Jan. 4, 1995, to the Committee on Public Works and Transportation of the House of Representatives treated as referring to the Committee on Transportation and Infrastructure of the House of Representatives, see section 1(a)(9) of Pub. L. No. 104–14, set out as a note preceding section 21 of Title 2, The Congress.]

Discharges from Point Sources in United States Virgin Islands Attributable to Manufacture of Rum; Exemption from Federal Water Pollution Control Requirements; Conditions

Pub. L. 98–67, Title II, § 214(g), 97 Stat. 393 (Aug. 5, 1983), provided that:

"Any discharge from a point source in the United States Virgin Islands in existence on the date of the enactment of this subsection [Aug. 5, 1983] which discharge is attributable to the manufacture of rum (as defined in paragraphs (3) of section 7652(c) of the Internal Revenue Code of 1954 [section 7652(c)(3) of Title 26, Internal Revenue Code]) shall not be subject to the requirements of section 301 [this section] (other than toxic pollutant discharges), section 306 [section 1316 of this title] or section 403 [section 1343 of this title] of the Federal Water Pollution Control Act if—

"(1) such discharge occurs at least one thousand five hundred feet into the territorial sea from the line of ordinary low water from that portion of the coast which is in direct contact with the sea, and

"(2) the Governor of the United States Virgin Islands determines that such discharge will not interfere with the attainment or maintenance of that water quality which shall assure protection of public water supplies, and the protection and propagation of a balanced population of shellfish, fish, and wildlife, and allow recreational activities, in and on the water and will not result in the discharge of pollutants in quantities which may reasonably be anticipated to pose an unacceptable risk to human health or the environment because of bioaccumulation, persistency in the environment, acute toxicity, chronic toxicity (including carcinogenicity, mutagenicity, or teratogenicity), or synergistic propensities."

Certain Municipal Compliance Deadlines Unaffected; Exception

Section 21(a) of Pub. L. No. 97–117 provided in part that: "The amendment made by this subsection [amending subsec. (i)(1) and (2)(B) of this section] shall not be interpreted or applied to extend the date for compliance with section 301(b)(1)(B) or (C) of the Federal Water Pollution Control Act [subsec. (b)(1)(B) or (C) of this section] beyond schedules for compliance in effect as of the date of enactment of this Act [Dec. 29, 1981], except in cases where reductions in the amount of financial assistance under this Act [Pub. L. No. 97–117, see Short Title of 1981 Amendment set out under section 1251 of this title] or changed conditions affecting the rate of construction beyond the control of the owner or operator will make it impossible to complete construction by July 1, 1983."

§ 1312. Water quality related effluent limitations

[FWPCA § 302]

(a) Establishment

Whenever, in the judgment of the Administrator or as identified under section 1314(*l*) of this title, discharges of pollutants from a point source or group of point sources, with the application of effluent limitations required under section 1311(b)(2) of this title, would interfere with the attainment or maintenance of that water quality in a specific portion of the navigable waters which shall assure protection of public health, public water supplies, agricultural and industrial uses, and the protection and propagation of a balanced population of shellfish, fish and wildlife, and allow recreational activities in and on the water, effluent limitations (including alternative effluent control strategies) for such point source or sources shall be established which can reasonably be expected to contribute to the attainment or maintenance of such water quality.

(b) Modifications of effluent limitations

(1) Notice and hearing

Prior to establishment of any effluent limitation pursuant to subsection (a) of this section, the Administrator shall publish such proposed limitation and within 90 days of such publication hold a public hearing.

(2) Permits

(A) No reasonable relationship

The Administrator, with the concurrence of the State, may issue a permit which modifies the effluent limitations required by subsection (a) of this section for pollutants other than toxic pollutants if the applicant demonstrates at such hearing that (whether or not technology or other alternative control strategies are available) there is no reasonable relationship between the economic and social costs and the benefits to be obtained (including attainment of the objective of this chapter) from achieving such limitation.

(B) Reasonable progress

The Administrator, with the concurrence of the State, may issue a permit which modifies the effluent limitations required by subsection (a) of this section for toxic pollutants for a single period not to exceed 5 years if the applicant demonstrates to the satisfaction of the Administrator that such modified requirements (i) will represent the maximum degree of control within the economic capability of the owner and operator of the source, and (ii) will result in reasonable further progress beyond the requirements of section 1311(b)(2) of this title toward the requirements of subsection (a) of this section.

(c) Delay in application of other limitations

The establishment of effluent limitations under this section shall not operate to delay the application of any effluent limitation established under section 1311 of this title.

(June 30, 1948, c. 758, Title III, § 302, as added by Pub. L. No. 92–500, § 2, 86 Stat. 846 (Oct. 18, 1972); and amended by Pub. L. No. 100–4, Title III, § 308(e), 101 Stat. 39 (Feb. 4, 1987).)

§ 1313. Water quality standards and implementation plans

[FWPCA § 303]

(a) Existing water quality standards

(1) In order to carry out the purpose of this chapter, any water quality standard applicable to interstate waters which was adopted by any State and submitted to, and approved by, or is a waiting approval by, the Administrator pursuant to this Act as in effect immediately prior to October 18, 1972, shall remain in effect unless the Administrator determined that such standard is not consistent with the applicable requirements of this Act as in effect immediately prior to October 18, 1972. If the

Administrator makes such a determination he shall, within three months after October 18, 1972, notify the State and specify the changes needed to meet such requirements. If such changes are not adopted by the State within ninety days after the date of such notification, the Administrator shall promulgate such changes in accordance with subsection (b) of this section.

(2) Any State which, before October 18, 1972, has adopted, pursuant to its own law, water quality standards applicable to intrastate waters shall submit such standards to the Administrator within thirty days after October 18, 1972. Each such standard shall remain in effect, in the same manner and to the same extent as any other water quality standard established under this chapter unless the Administrator determines that such standard is inconsistent with the applicable requirements of this Act as in effect immediately prior to October 18, 1972. If the Administrator makes such a determination he shall not later than the one hundred and twentieth day after the date of submission of such standards, notify the State and specify the changes needed to meet such requirements. If such changes are not adopted by the State within ninety days after such notification, the Administrator shall promulgate such changes in accordance with subsection (b) of this section.

(3) **(A)** Any State which prior to October 18, 1972, has not adopted pursuant to its own laws water quality standards applicable to intrastate waters shall, not later than one hundred and eighty days after October 18, 1972, adopt and submit such standards to the Administrator.

(B) If the Administrator determines that any such standards are consistent with the applicable requirements of this Act as in effect immediately prior to October 18, 1972, he shall approve such standards.

(C) If the Administrator determines that any such standards are not consistent with the applicable requirements of this Act as in effect immediately prior to October 18, 1972, he shall, not later than the ninetieth day after the date of submission of such standards, notify the State and specify the changes to meet such requirements. If such changes are not adopted by the State within ninety days after the date of notification, the Administrator shall promulgate such standards pursuant to subsection (b) of this section.

(b) Proposed regulations

(1) The Administrator shall promptly prepare and publish proposed regulations setting forth water quality standards for a State in accordance with the applicable requirements of this Act as in effect immediately prior to October 18, 1972, if—

(A) the State fails to submit water quality standards within the times prescribed in subsection (a) of this section.

(B) a water quality standard submitted by such State under subsection (a) of this section is determined by the Administrator not to be consistent with the applicable requirements of subsection (a) of this section.

(2) The Administrator shall promulgate any water quality standard published in a proposed regulation not later than one hundred and ninety days after the date he publishes any such proposed standard, unless prior to such promulgation, such State has adopted a water quality standard which the Administrator determines to be in accordance with subsection (a) of this section.

(c) Review; revised standards; publication

(1) The Governor of a State or the State water pollution control agency of such State shall from time to time (but at least once each three year period beginning with October 18, 1972) hold public hearings for the purpose of reviewing applicable water quality standards and, as appropriate, modifying and adopting standards. Results of such review shall be made available to the Administrator.

(2) **(A)** Whenever the State revises or adopts a new standard, such revised or new standard shall be submitted to the Administrator. Such revised or new water quality standard shall consist of the designated uses of the navigable waters involved and the water quality criteria for such waters based upon such uses. Such standards shall be such as to protect the public health or welfare, enhance the quality of water and serve the purposes of this chapter. Such standards shall be established taking into consideration their use and value for public water supplies, propagation of fish and wildlife, recreational purposes, and agricultural, industrial, and other purposes, and also taking into consideration their use and value for navigation.

(B) Whenever a State reviews water quality standards pursuant to paragraph (1) of this subsection, or revises or adopts new standards pursuant to this paragraph, such State shall adopt criteria for all toxic pollutants listed pursuant to section 1317(a)(1) of this title for which criteria have been published under section 1314(a) of this title, the discharge or presence of which in the affected waters could reasonably be expected to interfere with those designated uses adopted by the State, as necessary to support such designated uses. Such criteria shall be specific numerical criteria for such toxic pollutants. Where such numerical criteria are not available, whenever a State reviews water quality standards pursuant to paragraph (1), or revises or adopts new standards pursuant to this paragraph, such State shall adopt criteria based on biological monitoring or assessment methods consistent with information published pursuant to section 1314(a)(8) of this title. Nothing in this section shall be construed to limit or delay the use of effluent limitations or other permit conditions based on or involving biological monitoring or assessment methods or previously adopted numerical criteria.

(3) If the Administrator, within sixty days after the date of submission of the revised or new standard, determines that such standard meets the requirements of this chapter, such standard shall thereafter be the water quality standard for the applicable waters of that State. If the Administrator determines that any such revised or new standard is not consistent with the applicable requirements of this chapter, he shall not later than the ninetieth day after the date of submission of such standard notify the State and specify the changes to meet such requirements. If such changes are not adopted by the State within ninety days after the date of notification, the Administrator shall promulgate such standard pursuant to paragraph (4) of this subsection.

(4) The Administrator shall promptly prepare and publish proposed regulations setting forth a revised or new water quality standard for the navigable waters involved—

(A) if a revised or new water quality standard submitted by such State under paragraph (3) of this subsection for such waters is determined by the Administrator not to be consistent with the applicable requirements of this chapter, or

(B) in any case where the Administrator determines that a revised or new standard is necessary to meet the requirements of this chapter.

The Administrator shall promulgate any revised or new standard under this paragraph not later than ninety days after he publishes such proposed standards, unless prior to such promulgation, such State has adopted a revised or new water quality standard which the Administrator determines to be in accordance with this chapter.

(d) Identification of areas with insufficient controls; maximum daily load; certain effluent limitations revision

(1) **(A)** Each State shall identify those waters within its boundaries for which the effluent limitations required by section 1311(b)(1)(A) and section 1311(b)(1)(B) of this title are not stringent enough to implement any water quality standard applicable to such waters. The State shall establish a priority ranking for such waters, taking into account the severity of the pollution and the uses to be made of such waters.

(B) Each State shall identify those waters or parts thereof within its boundaries for which controls on thermal discharges under section 1311 of this title are not stringent enough to assure protection and propagation of a balanced indigenous population of shellfish, fish, and wildlife.

(C) Each State shall establish for the waters identified in paragraph (1)(A) of this subsection, and in accordance with the priority ranking, the total maximum daily load, for those pollutants which the Administrator identifies under section 1314(a)(2) of this title as suitable for such calculation. Such load shall be established at a level necessary to implement the applicable water quality standards with seasonal variations and a margin of safety which takes into account any lack of knowledge concerning the relationship between effluent limitations and water quality.

(D) Each State shall estimate for the waters identified in paragraph (1)(B) of this subsection the total maximum daily thermal load required to assure protection and propagation of a balanced, indigenous population of shellfish, fish, and wildlife. Such estimates shall take into account the normal water temperatures, flow rates, seasonal variations, existing sources of heat input, and the dissipative capacity of the identified waters or parts thereof. Such estimates shall include a calculation of the maximum heat input that can be made into each such part and shall include a margin of safety which takes into account any lack of knowledge concerning the development of thermal water quality criteria for such protection and propagation in the identified waters or parts thereof.

(2) Each State shall submit to the Administrator from time to time, with the first such submission not later than one hundred and eighty days after the date of publication of the first identification of pollutants under section 1314(a)(2)(D) of this title, for his approval the waters identified and the loads established under paragraphs (1)(A), (1)(B), (1)(C), and (1)(D) of this subsection. The Administrator shall either approve or disapprove such identification and load not later than thirty days after the date of submission. If the Administrator approves such identification and load, such State shall incorporate them into its current plan under subsection (e) of this section. If the Administrator disapproves such identification and load, he shall not later than thirty days after the date of such disapproval identify such waters in such State and establish such loads for such waters as he determines necessary to implement the water quality standards applicable to such waters and upon such identification and establishment the State shall incorporate them into its current plan under subsection (e) of this section.

(3) For the specific purpose of developing information, each State shall identify all waters within its boundaries which it has not identified under paragraph (1)(A) and (1)(B) of this subsection and estimate for such waters the total maximum daily load with seasonal variations and margins of safety, for those pollutants which the Administrator identifies under section 1314(a)(2) of this title as suitable for such calculation and for thermal discharges, at a level that would assure protection and propagation of a balanced indigenous population of fish, shellfish, and wildlife.

(4) Limitations on revision of certain effluent limitations

(A) Standard not attained

For waters identified under paragraph (1)(A) where the applicable water quality standard has not yet been attained, any effluent limitation based on a total maximum daily load or other waste load allocation established under this section may be revised only if (i) the cumulative effect of all such revised effluent limitations based on such total maximum daily load or waste load allocation will assure the attainment of such water quality standard, or (ii) the designated use which is not being attained is removed in accordance with regulations established under this section.

(B) Standard attained

For waters identified under paragraph (1)(A) where the quality of such waters equals or exceeds levels necessary to protect the designated use for such waters or otherwise required by applicable water quality standards, any effluent limitation based on a total maximum daily load or other waste load allocation established under this section, or any water quality standard established under this section, or any other permitting standard may be revised only if such revision is subject to and consistent with the antidegradation policy established under this section.

(e) Continuing planning process

(1) Each State shall have a continuing planning process approved under paragraph (2) of this subsection which is consistent with this chapter.

(2) Each State shall submit not later than 120 days after October 18, 1972, to the Administrator for his approval a proposed continuing planning process which is consistent with this chapter. Not later than thirty days after the date of submission of such a process the Administrator shall either approve or disapprove such process. The Administrator shall from time to time review each State's approved planning process for the purpose of insuring that such planning process is at all times consistent with this chapter. The Administrator shall not approve any State permit program under subchapter IV of this chapter for any State which does not have an approved continuing planning process under this section.

(3) The Administrator shall approve any continuing planning process submitted to him under this section which will result in plans for all navigable waters within such State, which include, but are not limited to, the following:

(A) effluent limitations and schedules of compliance at least as stringent as those required by section 1311(b)(1), section 1311(b)(2), section 1316, and section 1317 of this title, and at least as stringent as any requirements contained in any applicable water quality standard in effect under authority of this section;

(B) the incorporation of all elements of any applicable area-wide waste management plans under section 1288 of this title, and applicable basin plans under section 1289 of this title;

(C) total maximum daily load for pollutants in accordance with subsection (d) of this section;

(D) procedures for revision;

(E) adequate authority for intergovernmental cooperation;

(F) adequate implementation, including schedules of compliance, for revised or new water quality standards, under subsection (c) of this section;

(G) controls over the disposition of all residual waste from any water treatment processing;

(H) an inventory and ranking, in order of priority, of needs for construction of waste treatment works required to meet the applicable requirements of sections 1311 and 1312 of this title.

(f) Earlier compliance

Nothing in this section shall be construed to affect any effluent limitation, or schedule of compliance required by any State to be implemented prior to the dates set forth in sections 1311(b)(1) and 1311(b)(2) of this title nor to preclude any State from requiring compliance with any effluent limitation or schedule of compliance at dates earlier than such dates.

(g) Heat standards

Water quality standards relating to heat shall be consistent with the requirements of section 1326 of this title.

(h) Thermal water quality standards

For the purposes of this chapter the term "water quality standards" includes thermal water quality standards.

(i) Coastal recreation water quality criteria

(1) Adoption by States

(A) Initial criteria and standards

Not later than 42 months after October 10, 2000, each State having coastal recreation waters shall adopt and submit to the Administrator water quality criteria and standards for the coastal recreation waters of the State for those pathogens and pathogen indicators for which the Administrator has published criteria under section 1314(a) of this title.

(B) New or revised criteria and standards

Not later than 36 months after the date of publication by the Administrator of new or revised water quality criteria under section 1314(a)(9) of this title, each State having coastal recreation waters shall adopt and submit to the Administrator new or revised water quality standards for the coastal recreation waters of the State for all pathogens and pathogen indicators to which the new or revised water quality criteria are applicable.

(2) Failure of States to adopt

(A) In general

If a State fails to adopt water quality criteria and standards in accordance with paragraph (1)(A) that are as protective of human health as the criteria for pathogens and pathogen indicators for coastal recreation waters published by the Administrator, the Administrator shall promptly propose regulations for the State setting forth revised or new water quality standards for pathogens and pathogen indicators described in paragraph (1)(A) for coastal recreation waters of the State.

(B) Exception

If the Administrator proposes regulations for a State described in subparagraph (A) under subsection (c)(4)(B) of this section, the Administrator shall publish any revised or new standard under this subsection not later than 42 months after October 10, 2000.

(3) Applicability

Except as expressly provided by this subsection, the requirements and procedures of subsection (c) of this section apply to this subsection, including the requirement in subsection (c)(2)(A) of this section that the criteria protect public health and welfare.

(June 30, 1948, c. 758, Title III, § 303, as added by Pub. L. No. 92–500, § 2, 86 Stat. 846 (Oct. 18, 19720; and amended by Pub. L. No. 100–4, Title III, § 308(d), Title IV, § 404(b), 101 Stat. 39, 68 (Feb. 4, 1987); Pub. L. No. 106–284, § 2, 114 Stat. 870 (Oct. 10, 2000).)

HISTORICAL AND STATUTORY NOTES

References in Text

This Act, referred to in subsecs. (a)(1), (2), (3)(B), (C), (b)(1), means Act of June 30, 1948, c. 758, 62 Stat. 1155, prior to the supersedure and reenactment of Act of June 30, 1948 by Pub. L. No. 92–500, 86 Stat. 816 (Oct. 18, 1972). Act of June 30, 1948, c. 758, as added by Pub. L. No. 92–500, 86 Stat. 816 (Oct. 18, 1972), enacted this chapter.

§ 1313a. Revised water quality standards

The review, revision, and adoption or promulgation of revised or new water quality standards pursuant to section 303(c) of the Federal Water Pollution Control Act [33 U.S.C.A. § 1313(c)] shall be completed by the date three years after December 29, 1981. No grant shall be made under title II of the Federal Water Pollution Control Act [33 U.S.C.A. § 1281 et seq.] after such date until water quality standards are reviewed and revised pursuant to section 303(c), except where the State has in good faith submitted such revised water quality standards and the Administrator has not acted to approve or disapprove such submission within one hundred and twenty days of receipt.

(Pub. L. No. 97–117, § 24, 95 Stat. 1632 (Dec. 29, 1981).)

HISTORICAL AND STATUTORY NOTES

References in Text

The Federal Water Pollution Control Act, referred to in text, is Act of June 30, 1948, c. 758, as amended generally by Pub. L. No. 92–500, § 2, 86 Stat. 816 (Oct. 18, 1972). Title II of the Federal Water Pollution Control Act is codified generally as subchapter II (section 1281 et seq.) of this chapter. For complete classification of this Act to the Code, see Short Title note set out under section 1251 of this title and Tables.

Codifications

This section was enacted as part of the Municipal Wastewater Treatment Construction Grant Amendments of 1981, and not as part of the Federal Water Pollution Control Act, which comprises this chapter.

§ 1314. Information and guidelines

[FWPCA § 304]

(a) Criteria development and publication

(1) The Administrator, after consultation with appropriate Federal and State agencies and other interested persons, shall develop and publish, within one year after October 18, 1972 (and from time to time thereafter revise) criteria for water quality accurately reflecting the latest scientific knowledge (A) on the kind and extent of all identifiable effects on health and welfare including, but not limited to, plankton, fish, shellfish, wildlife, plant life, shorelines, beaches, esthetics, and recreation which may be expected from the presence of pollutants in any body of water, including ground water; (B) on the concentration and dispersal of pollutants, or their byproducts, through biological, physical, and chemical processes; and (C) on the effects of pollutants on biological community diversity, productivity, and stability, including information on the factors affecting rates of eutrophication and rates of organic and inorganic sedimentation for varying types of receiving waters.

(2) The Administrator, after consultation with appropriate Federal and State agencies and other interested persons, shall develop and publish, within one year after October 18, 1972 (and from time to time thereafter revise) information (A) on the factors necessary to restore and maintain the chemical, physical, and biological integrity of all navigable waters, ground waters, waters of the contiguous zone, and the oceans; (B) on the factors necessary for the protection and propagation of shellfish, fish, and wildlife for classes and categories of receiving waters and to allow recreational activities in and on the water; and (C) on the measurement and classification of water quality; and (D) for the purpose of section 1313 of this title, on and the identification of pollutants suitable for maximum daily load measurement correlated with the achievement of water quality objectives.

(3) Such criteria and information and revisions thereof shall be issued to the States and shall be published in the Federal Register and otherwise made available to the public.

(4) The Administrator shall, within 90 days after December 27, 1977, and from time to time thereafter, publish and revise as appropriate information identifying conventional pollutants, including but not limited to, pollutants codified as biological oxygen demanding, suspended solids, fecal coliform, and pH. The thermal component of any discharge shall not be identified as a conventional pollutant under this paragraph.

(5) **(A)** The Administrator, to the extent practicable before consideration of any request under section 1311(g) of this title and within six months after December 27, 1977, shall develop and publish information on the factors necessary for the protection of public water supplies, and the protection and propagation of a balanced population of shellfish, fish and wildlife, and to allow recreational activities, in and on the water.

(B) The Administrator, to the extent practicable before consideration of any application under section 1311(h) of this title and within six months after December 27, 1977, shall develop and publish information on the factors necessary for the protection of public water supplies, and the protection and propagation of a balanced indigenous population of shellfish, fish and wildlife, and to allow recreational activities, in and on the water.

(6) The Administrator shall, within three months after December 27, 1977, and annually thereafter, for purposes of section 1311(h) of this title publish and revise as appropriate information identifying each water quality standard in effect under this chapter or State law, the specific pollutants associated with such water quality standard, and the particular waters to which such water quality standard applies.

(7) **Guidance to states**

The Administrator, after consultation with appropriate State agencies and on the basis of criteria and information published under paragraphs (1) and (2) of this subsection, shall develop and publish, within 9 months after February 4, 1987, guidance to the States on performing the identification required by subsection (*l*)(1) of this section.

(8) Information on water quality criteria

The Administrator, after consultation with appropriate State agencies and within 2 years after February 4, 1987, shall develop and publish information on methods for establishing and measuring water quality criteria for toxic pollutants on other bases than pollutant-by-pollutant criteria, including biological monitoring and assessment methods.

(9) Revised criteria for coastal recreation waters

(A) In general

Not later than 5 years after October 10, 2000, after consultation and in cooperation with appropriate Federal, State, tribal, and local officials (including local health officials), the Administrator shall publish new or revised water quality criteria for pathogens and pathogen indicators (including a revised list of testing methods, as appropriate), based on the results of the studies conducted under section 1254(v) of this title, for the purpose of protecting human health in coastal recreation waters.

(B) Reviews

Not later than the date that is 5 years after the date of publication of water quality criteria under this paragraph, and at least once every 5 years thereafter, the Administrator shall review and, as necessary, revise the water quality criteria.

(b) Effluent limitation guidelines

For the purpose of adopting or revising effluent limitations under this chapter the Administrator shall, after consultation with appropriate Federal and State agencies and other interested persons, publish within one year of October 18, 1972, regulations, providing guidelines for effluent limitations, and, at least annually thereafter, revise, if appropriate, such regulations. Such regulations shall—

(1) (A) identify, in terms of amounts of constituents and chemical, physical, and biological characteristics of pollutants, the degree of effluent reduction attainable through the application of the best practicable control technology currently available for classes and categories of point sources (other than publicly owned treatment works); and

(B) specify factors to be taken into account in determining the control measures and practices to be applicable to point sources (other than publicly owned treatment works) within such categories or classes. Factors relating to the assessment of best practicable control technology currently available to comply with subsection (b)(1) of section 1311 of this title shall include consideration of the total cost of application of technology in relation to the effluent reduction benefits to be achieved from such application, and shall also take into account the age of equipment and facilities involved, the process employed, the engineering aspects of the application of various types of control techniques, process changes, non-water quality environmental impact (including energy requirements), and such other factors as the Administrator deems appropriate;

(2) (A) identify, in terms of amounts of constituents and chemical, physical, and biological characteristics of pollutants, the degree of effluent reduction attainable through the application of the best control measures and practices achievable including treatment techniques, process and procedure innovations, operating methods, and other alternatives for classes and categories of point sources (other than publicly owned treatment works); and

(B) specify factors to be taken into account in determining the best measures and practices available to comply with subsection (b)(2) of section 1311 of this title to be applicable to any point source (other than publicly owned treatment works) within such categories or classes. Factors relating to the assessment of best available technology shall take into account the age of equipment and facilities involved, the process employed, the engineering aspects of the application of various types of control techniques, process changes, the cost of achieving such effluent reduction, non-water quality environmental impact (including energy requirements), and such other factors as the Administrator deems appropriate;

(3) identify control measures and practices available to eliminate the discharge of pollutants from categories and classes of point sources, taking into account the cost of achieving such elimination of the discharge of pollutants; and

(4) **(A)** identify, in terms of amounts of constituents and chemical, physical, and biological characteristics of pollutants, the degree of effluent reduction attainable through the application of the best conventional pollutant control technology (including measures and practices) for classes and categories of point sources (other than publicly owned treatment works); and

(B) specify factors to be taken into account in determining the best conventional pollutant control technology measures and practices to comply with section 1311(b)(2)(E) of this title to be applicable to any point source (other than publicly owned treatment works) within such categories or classes. Factors relating to the assessment of best conventional pollutant control technology (including measures and practices) shall include consideration of the reasonableness of the relationship between the costs of attaining a reduction in effluents and the effluent reduction benefits derived, and the comparison of the cost and level of reduction of such pollutants from the discharge from publicly owned treatment works to the cost and level of reduction of such pollutants from a class or category of industrial sources, and shall take into account the age of equipment and facilities involved, the process employed, the engineering aspects of the application of various types of control techniques, process changes, non-water quality environmental impact (including energy requirements), and such other factors as the Administrator deems appropriate.

(c) Pollution discharge elimination procedures

The Administrator, after consultation, with appropriate Federal and State agencies and other interested persons, shall issue to the States and appropriate water pollution control agencies within 270 days after October 18, 1972 (and from time to time thereafter) information on the processes, procedures, or operating methods which result in the elimination or reduction of the discharge of pollutants to implement standards of performance under section 1316 of this title. Such information shall include technical and other data, including costs, as are available on alternative methods of elimination or reduction of the discharge of pollutants. Such information, and revisions thereof, shall be published in the Federal Register and otherwise shall be made available to the public.

(d) Secondary treatment information; alternative waste treatment management techniques; innovative and alternative wastewater treatment processes; facilities deemed equivalent of secondary treatment

(1) The Administrator, after consultation with appropriate Federal and State agencies and other interested persons, shall publish within sixty days after October 18, 1972 (and from time to time thereafter) information, in terms of amounts of constituents and chemical, physical, and biological characteristics of pollutants, on the degree of effluent reduction attainable through the application of secondary treatment.

(2) The Administrator, after consultation with appropriate Federal and State agencies and other interested persons, shall publish within nine months after October 18, 1972 (and from time to time thereafter) information on alternative waste treatment management techniques and systems available to implement section 1281 of this title.

(3) The Administrator, after consultation with appropriate Federal and State agencies and other interested persons, shall promulgate within one hundred and eighty days after December 27, 1977, guidelines for identifying and evaluating innovative and alternative wastewater treatment processes and techniques referred to in section 1281(g)(5) of this title.

(4) For the purposes of this subsection, such biological treatment facilities as oxidation ponds, lagoons, and ditches and trickling filters shall be deemed the equivalent of secondary treatment. The Administrator shall provide guidance under paragraph (1) of this subsection on design criteria for such facilities, taking into account pollutant removal efficiencies and, consistent with the objectives of this chapter, assuring that water quality will not be adversely affected by deeming such facilities as the equivalent of secondary treatment.

(e) Best management practices for industry

The Administrator, after consultation with appropriate Federal and State agencies and other interested persons, may publish regulations, supplemental to any effluent limitations specified under subsections (b) and (c) of this section for a class or category of point sources, for any specific pollutant which the Administrator is charged with a duty to regulate as a toxic or hazardous pollutant under section 1317(a)(1) or 1321 of this title, to control plant site runoff, spillage or leaks, sludge or waste disposal, and drainage from raw material storage which the Administrator determines are associated with or ancillary to the industrial manufacturing or treatment process within such class or category of point sources and may contribute significant amounts of such pollutants to navigable waters. Any applicable controls established under this subsection shall be included as a requirement for the purposes of section 1311, 1312, 1316, 1317, or 1343 of this title, as the case may be, in any permit issued to a point source pursuant to section 1342 of this title.

(f) Identification and evaluation of nonpoint sources of pollution; processes, procedures, and methods to control pollution

The Administrator, after consultation with appropriate Federal and State agencies and other interested persons, shall issue to appropriate Federal agencies, the States, water pollution control agencies, and agencies designated under section 1288 of this title, within one year after October 18, 1972 (and from time to time thereafter) information including (1) guidelines for identifying and evaluating the nature and extent of nonpoint sources of pollutants, and (2) processes, procedures, and methods to control pollution resulting from—

(A) agricultural and silvicultural activities, including runoff from fields and crop and forest lands;

(B) mining activities, including runoff and siltation from new, currently operating, and abandoned surface and underground mines;

(C) all construction activity, including runoff from the facilities resulting from such construction;

(D) the disposal of pollutants in wells or in subsurface excavations;

(E) salt water intrusion resulting from reductions of fresh water flow from any cause, including extraction of ground water, irrigation, obstruction, and diversion; and

(F) changes in the movement, flow, or circulation of any navigable waters or ground waters, including changes caused by the construction of dams, levees, channels, causeways, or flow diversion facilities.

Such information and revisions thereof shall be published in the Federal Register and otherwise made available to the public.

(g) Guidelines for pretreatment of pollutants

(1) For the purpose of assisting States in carrying out programs under section 1342 of this title, the Administrator shall publish, within one hundred and twenty days after October 18, 1972, and review at least annually thereafter and, if appropriate, revise guidelines for pretreatment of pollutants which he determines are not susceptible to treatment by publicly owned treatment works. Guidelines under this subsection shall be established to control and prevent the discharge into the navigable waters, the contiguous zone, or the ocean (either directly or through publicly owned treatment works) of any pollutant which interferes with, passes through, or otherwise is incompatible with such works.

(2) When publishing guidelines under this subsection, the Administrator shall designate the category or categories of treatment works to which the guidelines shall apply.

(h) Test procedures guidelines

The Administrator shall, within one hundred and eighty days from October 18, 1972, promulgate guidelines establishing test procedures for the analysis of pollutants that shall include the factors which must be provided in any certification pursuant to section 1341 of this title or permit application pursuant to section 1342 of this title.

(i) Guidelines for monitoring, reporting, enforcement, funding, personnel, and manpower

The Administrator shall (1) within sixty days after October 18, 1972, promulgate guidelines for the purpose of establishing uniform application forms and other minimum requirements for the acquisition of information from owners and operators of point-sources of discharge subject to any State program under section 1342 of this title, and (2) within sixty days from October 18, 1972, promulgate guidelines establishing the minimum procedural and other elements of any State program under section 1342 of this title, which shall include:

(A) monitoring requirements;

(B) reporting requirements (including procedures to make information available to the public);

(C) enforcement provisions; and

(D) funding, personnel qualifications, and manpower requirements (including a requirement that no board or body which approves permit applications or portions thereof shall include, as a member, any person who receives, or has during the previous two years received, a significant portion of his income directly or indirectly from permit holders or applicants for a permit).

(j) Lake restoration guidance manual

The Administrator shall, within 1 year after February 4, 1987, and biennially thereafter, publish and disseminate a lake restoration guidance manual describing methods, procedures, and processes to guide State and local efforts to improve, restore, and enhance water quality in the Nation's publicly owned lakes.

(k) Agreements with Secretaries of Agriculture, Army, and the Interior to provide maximum utilization of programs to achieve and maintain water quality; transfer of funds; authorization of appropriations

(1) The Administrator shall enter into agreements with the Secretary of Agriculture, the Secretary of the Army, and the Secretary of the Interior, and the heads of such other departments, agencies, and instrumentalities of the United States as the Administrator determines, to provide for the maximum utilization of other Federal laws and programs for the purpose of achieving and maintaining water quality through appropriate implementation of plans approved under section 1288 of this title and nonpoint source pollution management programs approved under section 1329 of this title.

(2) The Administrator is authorized to transfer to the Secretary of Agriculture, the Secretary of the Army, and the Secretary of the Interior and the heads of such other departments, agencies, and instrumentalities of the United States as the Administrator determines, any funds appropriated under paragraph (3) of this subsection to supplement funds otherwise appropriated to programs authorized pursuant to any agreement under paragraph (1).

(3) There is authorized to be appropriated to carry out the provisions of this subsection, $100,000,000 per fiscal year for the fiscal years 1979 through 1983 and such sums as may be necessary for fiscal years 1984 through 1990.

(*l*) Individual control strategies for toxic pollutants

(1) State list of navigable waters and development of strategies

Not later than 2 years after February 4, 1987, each State shall submit to the Administrator for review, approval, and implementation under this subsection—

(A) a list of those waters within the State which after the application of effluent limitations required under section 1311(b)(2) of this title cannot reasonably be anticipated to attain or maintain (i) water quality standards for such waters reviewed, revised, or adopted in accordance with section 1313(c)(2)(B) of this title, due to toxic pollutants, or (ii) that water quality which shall assure protection of public health, public water supplies, agricultural and industrial uses, and the protection and propagation of a balanced population of shellfish, fish and wildlife, and allow recreational activities in and on the water;

(B) a list of all navigable waters in such State for which the State does not expect the applicable standard under section 1313 of this title will be achieved after the requirements of sections

1311(b), 1316, and 1317(b) of this title are met, due entirely or substantially to discharges from point sources of any toxic pollutants listed pursuant to section 1317(a) of this title;

(C) for each segment of the navigable waters included on such lists, a determination of the specific point sources discharging any such toxic pollutant which is believed to be preventing or impairing such water quality and the amount of each such toxic pollutant discharged by each such source; and

(D) for each such segment, an individual control strategy which the State determines will produce a reduction in the discharge of toxic pollutants from point sources identified by the State under this paragraph through the establishment of effluent limitations under section 1342 of this title and water quality standards under section 1313(c)(2)(B) of this title, which reduction is sufficient, in combination with existing controls on point and nonpoint sources of pollution, to achieve the applicable water quality standard as soon as possible, but not later than 3 years after the date of the establishment of such strategy.

(2) Approval or disapproval

Not later than 120 days after the last day of the 2-year period referred to in paragraph (1), the Administrator shall approve or disapprove the control strategies submitted under paragraph (1) by any State.

(3) Administrator's action

If a State fails to submit control strategies in accordance with paragraph (1) or the Administrator does not approve the control strategies submitted by such State in accordance with paragraph (1), then, not later than 1 year after the last day of the period referred to in paragraph (2), the Administrator, in cooperation with such State and after notice and opportunity for public comment, shall implement the requirements of paragraph (1) in such State. In the implementation of such requirements, the Administrator shall, at a minimum, consider for listing under this subsection any navigable waters for which any person submits a petition to the Administrator for listing not later than 120 days after such last day.

(m) Schedule for review of Guidelines

(1) Publication

Within 12 months after February 4, 1987, and biennially thereafter, the Administrator shall publish in the Federal Register a plan which shall—

(A) establish a schedule for the annual review and revision of promulgated effluent guidelines, in accordance with subsection (b) of this section;

(B) identify categories of sources discharging toxic or nonconventional pollutants for which guidelines under subsection (b)(2) of this section and section 1316 of this title have not previously been published; and

(C) establish a schedule for promulgation of effluent guidelines for categories identified in subparagraph (B), under which promulgation of such guidelines shall be no later than 4 years after February 4, 1987, for categories identified in the first published plan or 3 years after the publication of the plan for categories identified in later published plans.

(2) Public review

The Administrator shall provide for public review and comment on the plan prior to final publication.

(June 30, 1948, c. 758, Title III, § 304, as added by Pub. L. No. 92–500, § 2, 86 Stat. 850 (Oct. 18, 1972); and amended by Pub. L. No. 95–217, §§ 48–51, 62(b), 91 Stat. 1587, 1588, 1598 (Dec. 27, 1977); Pub. L. No. 97–117, § 23, 95 Stat. 1632 (Dec. 29, 1981); Pub. L. No. 100–4, Title I, § 101(f), Title III, §§ 308(a), (c), (f), 315(c), 316(e), 101 Stat. 9, 38–40, 52, 61 (Feb. 4, 1987); Pub. L. No. 106–284, § 3(b), 114 Stat. 871 (Oct. 10, 2000).)

HISTORICAL AND STATUTORY NOTES

References in Text

December 27, 1977, referred to in subsec. (d)(3), was in the original "the date of enactment of this subsection", and has been editorially translated as December 27, 1977, the date of enactment of Pub. L. No. 95–217, which added par. (3) to subsec. (d), as the probable intent of Congress.

Codifications

Section 50 of Pub. L. No. 95–217 provided in part that, upon the enactment of subsec. (e) of this section by Pub. L. No. 95–217 and the concurrent redesignation of former subsecs. (e) to (j) of this section as (f) to (k), respectively, all references to former subsecs. (e) to (j) be changed to (f) to (k), respectively.

Transfer of Functions

Enforcement functions of Secretary or other official in Department of Agriculture, insofar as they involve lands and programs under jurisdiction of that Department, relating to compliance with this chapter with respect to pre-construction, construction, and initial operation of transportation system for Canadian and Alaskan natural gas were transferred to the Federal Inspector, Office of Federal Inspector for the Alaska Natural Gas Transportation System, until the first anniversary of the date of initial operation of the Alaska Natural Gas Transportation System, see Reorg. Plan No. 1 of 1979, §§ 102(f), 203(a), 44 Fed. Reg. 33663, 33666, 93 Stat. 1373, 1376, effective July 1, 1979, set out in Appendix 1 to Title 5, Government Organization and Employees.

Stormwater Infrastructure Funding

Pub. L. No. 115–270, §§ 4101, 4102 132 Stat. 3765, 3870–3872 (Oct. 23, 2018), provided that:

"Sec. 4101. Stormwater Infrastructure Funding Task Force.

"(a) In general.—Not later than 180 days after the date of enactment of this Act, the Administrator of the Environmental Protection Agency shall establish a stormwater infrastructure ***3871** funding task force composed of representatives of Federal, State, and local governments and private (including nonprofit) entities to conduct a study on, and develop recommendations to improve, the availability of public and private sources of funding for the construction, rehabilitation, and operation and maintenance of stormwater infrastructure to meet the requirements of the Federal Water Pollution Control Act (33 U.S.C. 1251 et seq.).

"(b) Considerations.—In carrying out subsection (a), the task force shall—

"(1) identify existing Federal, State, and local public sources and private sources of funding for stormwater infrastructure; and

"(2) consider—

"(A) how funding for stormwater infrastructure from such sources has been made available, and utilized, in each State to address stormwater infrastructure needs identified pursuant to section 516(b)(1) of the Federal Water Pollution Control Act (33 U.S.C. 1375(b)(1));

"(B) how the source of funding affects the affordability of the infrastructure (as determined based on the considerations used to assess the financial capability of municipalities under the integrated planning guidelines described in the Integrated Municipal Stormwater and Wastewater Planning Approach Framework, issued by the Environmental Protection Agency on June 5, 2012, and dated May, 2012), including consideration of the costs associated with financing the infrastructure; and

"(C) whether such sources of funding are sufficient to support capital expenditures and long-term operation and maintenance costs necessary to meet the stormwater infrastructure needs of municipalities.

"(c) Report.—Not later than 18 months after the date of enactment of this Act, the Administrator shall submit to Congress a report that describes the results of the study conducted, and the recommendations developed, under subsection (a).

"(d) State defined.—In this section, the term "State" has the meaning given that term in section 502 of the Federal Water Pollution Control Act (33 U.S.C. 1362).

"Sec. 4102. Wastewater Technology Clearinghouse.

"(a) In general.—

"(1) In general.—The Administrator of the Environmental Protection Agency shall—

"(A) for each of the programs described in paragraph (2), update the information for those programs to include information on cost-effective and alternative wastewater recycling and treatment technologies, including onsite and decentralized systems; and

"(B) disseminate to units of local government and nonprofit organizations seeking Federal funds for wastewater technology information on the cost effectiveness of alternative wastewater treatment and recycling technologies, including onsite and decentralized systems.

"(2) Programs described.—The programs referred to in paragraph (1)(A) are programs that provide technical assistance for wastewater management, including—

"(A) programs for nonpoint source management under section 319 of the Federal Water Pollution Control Act (33 U.S.C. 1329); and

"(B) the permit program for the disposal of sewer sludge under section 405 of the Federal Water Pollution Control Act (33 U.S.C. 1345).

"(b) Report to Congress.—Not later than 1 year after the date of enactment of this Act, and not less frequently than every 3 years thereafter, the Administrator of the Environmental Protection Agency shall submit to Congress a report that describes—

"(1) the type and amount of information provided under subsection (a) to units of local government and nonprofit organizations regarding alternative wastewater treatment and recycling technologies;

"(2) the States and regions that have made greatest use of alternative wastewater treatment and recycling technologies; and

"(3) the actions taken by the Administrator to assist States in the deployment of alternative wastewater treatment and recycling technologies, including onsite and decentralized systems."

Contiguous Zone of United States

For extension of contiguous zone of United States, see Proc. No. 7219, set out as a note under 43 U.S.C.A. § 1331.

Review of Effluent Guidelines Promulgated Prior to December 27, 1977

Section 73 of Pub. L. No. 95–217 provided that: "Within 90 days after the date of enactment of this Act [Dec. 27, 1977], the Administrator shall review every effluent guideline promulgated prior to the date of enactment of this Act which is final or interim final (other than those applicable to industrial categories listed in table 2 of Committee Print Numbered 95–30 of the Committee on Public Works and Transportation of the House of Representatives) and which applies to those pollutants identified pursuant to section 304(a)(4) of the Federal Water Pollution Control Act [subsec. (a)(4) of this section]. The Administrator shall review every guideline applicable to industrial categories listed in such table 2 on or before July 1, 1980. Upon completion of each such review the Administrator is authorized to make such adjustments in any such guidelines as may be necessary to carry out section 304(b)(4) of such Act [subsec. (b)(4 of this section]. The Administrator shall publish the results of each such review, including, with respect to each such guideline, the determination to adjust or not to adjust such guideline. Any such determination by the Administrator shall be final except that if, on judicial review in accordance with section 509 of such Act [section 1369 of this title], it is determined that the Administrator either did not comply with the requirements of this section or the determination of the Administrator was based on arbitrary and capricious action in applying section 304(b)(4) of such Act [subsec. (b)(4) of this section] to such guideline, the Administrator shall make a further review and redetermination of any such guideline."

[Any reference in any provision of law enacted before Jan. 4, 1995, to the Committee on Public Works and Transportation of the House of Representatives treated as referring to the Committee on Transportation and Infrastructure of the House of Representatives, see section 1(a)(9) of Pub. L. No. 104–14, set out as a note preceding section 21 of Title 2, The Congress].

§ 1315. State reports on water quality

[FWPCA § 305]

(a) Omitted

(b) **(1)** Each State shall prepare and submit to the Administrator by April 1, 1975, and shall bring up to date by April 1, 1976, and biennially thereafter, a report which shall include—

(A) a description of the water quality of all navigable waters in such State during the preceding year, with appropriate supplemental descriptions as shall be required to take into account seasonal, tidal, and other variations, correlated with the quality of water required by the objective of this chapter (as identified by the Administrator pursuant to criteria published under section 1314(a) of this title) and the water quality described in subparagraph (B) of this paragraph;

(B) an analysis of the extent to which all navigable waters of such State provide for the protection and propagation of a balanced population of shellfish, fish, and wildlife, and allow recreational activities in and on the water;

(C) an analysis of the extent to which the elimination of the discharge of pollutants and a level of water quality which provides for the protection and propagation of a balanced population of shellfish, fish, and wildlife and allows recreational activities in and on the water, have been or will be achieved by the requirements of this chapter, together with recommendations as to additional action necessary to achieve such objectives and for what waters such additional action is necessary;

(D) an estimate of (i) the environmental impact, (ii) the economic and social costs necessary to achieve the objective of this chapter in such State, (iii) the economic and social benefits of such achievement, and (iv) an estimate of the date of such achievement; and

(E) a description of the nature and extent of nonpoint sources of pollutants, and recommendations as to the programs which must be undertaken to control each category of such sources, including an estimate of the costs of implementing such programs.

(2) The Administrator shall transmit such State reports, together with an analysis thereof, to Congress on or before October 1, 1975, and October 1, 1976, and biennially thereafter.

(June 30, 1948, c. 758, Title III, § 305, as added by Pub. L. No. 92–500, § 2, 86 Stat. 853 (Oct. 18, 1972); and amended by Pub. L. No. 95–217, § 52, 91 Stat. 1589 (Dec. 27, 1977).)

HISTORICAL AND STATUTORY NOTES

Codifications

Subsec. (a), shown as omitted, authorized the Administrator, in cooperation with the States and Federal agencies, to prepare a report describing the specific quality, during 1973, of all navigable waters and waters of the contiguous zone, including an inventory of all point sources of discharge of pollutants into these waters, and identifying those navigable waters capable of supporting fish and wildlife populations and allowing recreational activities, those which could reasonably be expected to attain this level by 1977 or 1983, and those which could attain this level sooner, and submit this report to Congress on or before Jan. 1, 1974.

Termination of Reporting Requirements

Reporting requirement of subsec. (b) of this section excepted from termination under Pub. L. No. 104–66, § 3003(a)(1), as amended, set out as a note under 31 U.S.C.A. § 1113, and page 165 of House Document No. 103–7, see Pub. L. No. 107–303, § 302(a).

§ 1316. National standards of performance

[FWPCA § 306]

(a) Definitions

For purposes of this section:

(1) The term "standard of performance" means a standard for the control of the discharge of pollutants which reflects the greatest degree of effluent reduction which the Administrator determines to be achievable through application of the best available demonstrated control technology, processes, operating methods, or other alternatives, including, where practicable, a standard permitting no discharge of pollutants.

(2) The term "new source" means any source, the construction of which is commenced after the publication of proposed regulations prescribing a standard of performance under this section which will be applicable to such source, if such standard is thereafter promulgated in accordance with this section.

(3) The term "source" means any building, structure, facility, or installation from which there is or may be the discharge of pollutants.

(4) The term "owner or operator" means any person who owns, leases, operates, controls, or supervises a source.

(5) The term "construction" means any placement, assembly, or installation of facilities or equipment (including contractual obligations to purchase such facilities or equipment) at the premises where such equipment will be used, including preparation work at such premises.

(b) Categories of sources; Federal standards of performance for new sources

(1) (A) The Administrator shall, within ninety days after October 18, 1972, publish (and from time to time thereafter shall revise) a list of categories of sources, which shall, at the minimum, include:

pulp and paper mills;

paperboard, builders paper and board mills;

meat product and rendering processing;

dairy product processing;

grain mills;

canned and preserved fruits and vegetables processing;

canned and preserved seafood processing;

sugar processing;

textile mills;

cement manufacturing;

feedlots;

electroplating;

organic chemicals manufacturing;

inorganic chemicals manufacturing;

plastic and synthetic materials manufacturing;

soap and detergent manufacturing;

fertilizer manufacturing;

petroleum refining;

iron and steel manufacturing;

nonferrous metals manufacturing;

phosphate manufacturing;

steam electric powerplants;

ferroalloy manufacturing;

leather tanning and finishing;

glass and asbestos manufacturing;

rubber processing; and

timber products processing.

(B) As soon as practicable, but in no case more than one year, after a category of sources is included in a list under subparagraph (A) of this paragraph, the Administrator shall propose and publish regulations establishing Federal standards of performance for new sources within such category. The Administrator shall afford interested persons an opportunity for written comment on such proposed regulations. After considering such comments, he shall promulgate, within one hundred and twenty days after publication of such proposed regulations, such standards with such adjustments as he deems appropriate. The Administrator shall, from time to time, as technology and alternatives change, revise such standards following the procedure required by this subsection for promulgation of such standards. Standards of performance, or revisions thereof, shall become effective upon promulgation. In establishing or revising Federal standards of performance for new sources under this section, the Administrator shall take into consideration the cost of achieving such effluent reduction, and any non-water quality, environmental impact and energy requirements.

(2) The Administrator may distinguish among classes, types, and sizes within categories of new sources for the purpose of establishing such standards and shall consider the type of process employed (including whether batch or continuous).

(3) The provisions of this section shall apply to any new source owned or operated by the United States.

(c) State enforcement of standards of performance

Each State may develop and submit to the Administrator a procedure under State law for applying and enforcing standards of performance for new sources located in such State. If the Administrator finds that the procedure and the law of any State require the application and enforcement of standards of performance to at least the same extent as required by this section, such State is authorized to apply and enforce such standards of performance (except with respect to new sources owned or operated by the United States).

(d) Protection from more stringent standards

Notwithstanding any other provision of this chapter, any point source the construction of which is commenced after October 18, 1972, and which is so constructed as to meet all applicable standards of performance shall not be subject to any more stringent standard of performance during a ten-year period beginning on the date of completion of such construction or during the period of depreciation or amortization of such facility for the purposes of section 167 or 169 (or both) of Title 26, whichever period ends first.

(e) Illegality of operation of new sources in violation of applicable standards of performance

After the effective date of standards of performance promulgated under this section, it shall be unlawful for any owner or operator of any new source to operate such source in violation of any standard of performance applicable to such source.

(June 30, 1948, c. 758, Title III, § 306, as added by Pub. L. No. 92–500, § 2, 86 Stat. 854 (Oct. 18, 1972).)

HISTORICAL AND STATUTORY NOTES

Exemption For Discharges from Point Sources in United States Virgin Islands Attributable to Manufacture of Rum; Conditions

Discharges from point sources in the United States Virgin Islands in existence on Aug. 5, 1983, attributable to the manufacture of rum not to be subject to the requirements of this section under certain conditions, see section 214(g) of Pub. L. No. 98–67, set out as a note under section 1311 of this title.

Exemption for Fort Allen in Puerto Rico

For provisions relating to the prohibition of an exemption from this section for Fort Allen in Puerto Rico, in its use as temporary housing for Haitian refugees, see section 1–101 of Ex. Ord. No. 12327, Oct. 1, 1981, 46 Fed. Reg. 48893, set out as a note under section 2601 of Title 22, Foreign Relations and Intercourse.

§ 1317. Toxic and pretreatment effluent standards

[FWPCA § 307]

(a) Toxic pollutant list; revision; hearing; promulgation of standards; effective date; consultation

(1) On and after December 27, 1977, the list of toxic pollutants or combination of pollutants subject to this chapter shall consist of those toxic pollutants listed in table 1 of Committee Print Numbered 95–30 of the Committee on Public Works and Transportation of the House of Representatives, and the Administrator shall publish, not later than the thirtieth day after December 27, 1977, that list. from time to time thereafter, the Administrator may revise such list and the Administrator is authorized to add to or remove from such list any pollutant. The Administrator in publishing any revised list, including the addition or removal of any pollutant from such list, shall take into account toxicity of the pollutant, its persistence, degradability, the usual or potential presence of the affected organisms in any waters, the importance of the affected organisms, and the nature and extent of the effect of the toxic pollutant on such organisms. A determination of the Administrator under this paragraph shall be final except that if, on judicial review, such determination was based on arbitrary and capricious action of the Administrator, the Administrator shall make a redetermination.

(2) Each toxic pollutant listed in accordance with paragraph (1) of this subsection shall be subject to effluent limitations resulting from the application of the best available technology economically achievable for the applicable category or class of point sources established in accordance with sections 1311(b)(2)(A) and 1314(b)(2) of this title. The Administrator, in his discretion, may publish in the Federal Register a proposed effluent standard (which may include a prohibition) establishing requirements for a toxic pollutant which, if an effluent limitation is applicable to a class or category of point sources, shall be applicable to such category or class only if such standard imposes more stringent requirements. Such published effluent standard (or prohibition) shall take into account the toxicity of the pollutant, its persistence, degradability, the usual or potential presence of the affected organisms in any waters, the importance of the affected organisms and the nature and extent of the effect of the toxic pollutant on such organisms, and the extent to which effective control is being or may be achieved under other regulatory authority. The Administrator shall allow a period of not less than sixty days following publication of any such proposed effluent standard (or prohibition) for written comment by interested persons on such proposed standard. In addition, if within thirty days of publication of any such proposed effluent standard (or prohibition) any interested person so requests, the Administrator shall hold a public hearing in connection therewith. Such a public hearing shall provide an opportunity for oral and written presentations, such cross-examination as the Administrator determines is appropriate on disputed issues of material fact, and the transcription of a verbatim record which shall be available to the public. After consideration of such comments and any information and material presented at any public hearing held on such proposed standard or prohibition, the Administrator shall promulgate such standard (or prohibition) with such modification as the Administrator finds are justified. Such promulgation by the Administrator shall be made within two hundred and seventy days after publication of proposed standard (or prohibition). Such standard (or prohibition) shall be final except that if, on judicial review, such standard was not based on substantial evidence, the Administrator shall promulgate a revised standard. Effluent limitations shall be established in accordance with sections 1311(b)(2)(A) and 1314(b)(2) of this title for every toxic pollutant referred to in table 1 of Committee Print Numbered 95–30 of the Committee on Public Works and Transportation of the House of Representatives as soon as practicable after December 27, 1977, but no later than July 1, 1980. Such effluent limitations or effluent standards (or prohibitions) shall be established for every other toxic pollutant listed under paragraph (1) of this subsection as soon as practicable after it is so listed.

(3) Each such effluent standard (or prohibition) shall be reviewed and, if appropriate, revised at least every three years.

(4) Any effluent standard promulgated under this section shall be at that level which the Administrator determines provides an ample margin of safety.

(5) When proposing or promulgating any effluent standard (or prohibition) under this section, the Administrator shall designate the category or categories of sources to which the effluent standard (or prohibition) shall apply. Any disposal of dredged material may be included in such a category of sources after consultation with the Secretary of the Army.

(6) Any effluent standard (or prohibition) established pursuant to this section shall take effect on such date or dates as specified in the order promulgating such standard, but in no case, more than one year from the date of such promulgation. If the Administrator determines that compliance within one year from the date of promulgation is technologically infeasible for a category of sources, the Administrator may establish the effective date of the effluent standard (or prohibition) for such category at the earliest date upon which compliance can be feasibly attained by sources within such category, but in no event more than three years after the date of such promulgation.

(7) Prior to publishing any regulations pursuant to this section the Administrator shall, to the maximum extent practicable within the time provided, consult with appropriate advisory committees, States, independent experts, and Federal departments and agencies.

(b) Pretreatment standards; hearing; promulgation; compliance period; revision; application to State and local laws

(1) The Administrator shall, within one hundred and eighty days after October 18, 1972, and from time to time thereafter, publish proposed regulations establishing pretreatment standards for introduction of pollutants into treatment works (as defined in section 1292 of this title) which are publicly owned for those pollutants which are determined not to be susceptible to treatment by such treatment works or which would interfere with the operation of such treatment works. Not later than ninety days after such publication, and after opportunity for public hearing, the Administrator shall promulgate such pretreatment standards. Pretreatment standards under this subsection shall specify a time for compliance not to exceed three years from the date of promulgation and shall be established to prevent the discharge of any pollutant through treatment works (as defined in section 1292 of this title) which are publicly owned, which pollutant interferes with, passes through, or otherwise is incompatible with such works. If, in the case of any toxic pollutant under subsection (a) of this section introduced by a source into a publicly owned treatment works, the treatment by such works removes all or any part of such toxic pollutant and the discharge from such works does not violate that effluent limitation or standard which would be applicable to such toxic pollutant if it were discharged by such source other than through a publicly owned treatment works, and does not prevent sludge use or disposal by such works in accordance with section 1345 of this title, then the pretreatment requirements for the sources actually discharging such toxic pollutant into such publicly owned treatment works may be revised by the owner or operator of such works to reflect the removal of such toxic pollutant by such works.

(2) The Administrator shall, from time to time, as control technology, processes, operating methods, or other alternatives change, revise such standards following the procedure established by this subsection for promulgation of such standards.

(3) When proposing or promulgating any pretreatment standard under this section, the Administrator shall designate the category or categories of sources to which such standard shall apply.

(4) Nothing in this subsection shall affect any pretreatment requirement established by any State or local law not in conflict with any pretreatment standard established under this subsection.

(c) New sources of pollutants into publicly owned treatment works

In order to insure that any source introducing pollutants into a publicly owned treatment works, which source would be a new source subject to section 1316 of this title if it were to discharge pollutants, will not cause a violation of the effluent limitations established for any such treatment works, the Administrator shall promulgate pretreatment standards for the category of such sources simultaneously with the promulgation of standards of performance under section 1316 of this title for the equivalent category of new sources. Such pretreatment standards shall prevent the discharge of any pollutant into such treatment works, which pollutant may interfere with, pass through, or otherwise be incompatible with such works.

(d) Operation in violation of standards unlawful

After the effective date of any effluent standard or prohibition or pretreatment standard promulgated under this section, it shall be unlawful for any owner or operator of any source to operate any source in violation of any such effluent standard or prohibition or pretreatment standard.

(e) Compliance date extension for innovative pretreatment systems

In the case of any existing facility that proposes to comply with the pretreatment standards of subsection (b) of this section by applying an innovative system that meets the requirements of section 1311(k) of this title, the owner or operator of the publicly owned treatment works receiving the treated effluent from such facility may extend the date for compliance with the applicable pretreatment standard established under this section for a period not to exceed 2 years—

(1) if the Administrator determines that the innovative system has the potential for industrywide application, and

(2) if the Administrator (or the State in consultation with the Administrator, in any case in which the State has a pretreatment program approved by the Administrator)—

(A) determines that the proposed extension will not cause the publicly owned treatment works to be in violation of its permit under section 1342 of this title or of section 1345 of this title or to contribute to such a violation, and

(B) concurs with the proposed extension.

(June 30, 1948, c. 758, Title III, § 307, as added by Pub. L. No. 92–500, § 2, 86 Stat. 856 (Oct. 18, 1972); and amended by Pub. L. No. 95–217, §§ 53(a), (b), 54(a), 91 Stat. 1589–1591 (Dec. 27, 1977); Pub. L. No. 100–4, Title III, § 309(a), 101 Stat. 41 (Feb. 4, 1987).)

HISTORICAL AND STATUTORY NOTES

Change of Name

Any reference in any provision of law enacted before Jan. 4, 1995, to the Committee on Public Works and Transportation of the House of Representatives treated as referring to the Committee on Transportation and Infrastructure of the House of Representatives, see section 1(a)(9) of Pub. L. No. 104–14, set out as a note preceding section 21 of Title 2, The Congress.

Increase in EPA Employees

Section 309(b) of Pub. L. No. 100–4 provided that: "The Administrator shall take such actions as may be necessary to increase the number of employees of the Environmental Protection Agency in order to effectively implement pretreatment requirements under section 307 of the Federal Water Pollution Control Act [this section]."

Exemption for Fort Allen in Puerto Rico

For provisions relating to the prohibition of an exemption from this section for Fort Allen in Puerto Rico, in its use as temporary housing for Haitian refugees, see section 1–101 of Ex. Ord. No. 12327, Oct. 1, 1981, 46 Fed. Reg. 48893, set out as a note under section 2601 of Title 22, Foreign Relations and Intercourse.

§ 1318. Records and reports; inspections

[FWPCA § 308]

(a) Maintenance; monitoring equipment; entry; access to information

Whenever required to carry out the objective of this chapter, including but not limited to (1) developing or assisting in the development of any effluent limitation, or other limitation, prohibition, or effluent standard, pretreatment standard, or standard of performance under this chapter; (2) determining whether any person is in violation of any such effluent limitation, or other limitation, prohibition or effluent standard, pretreatment standard, or standard of performance; (3) any requirement established under this section; or (4) carrying out sections 1315, 1321, 1342, 1344 (relating to State permit programs), 1345, and 1364 of this title—

(A) the Administrator shall require the owner or operator of any point source to (i) establish and maintain such records, (ii) make such reports, (iii) install, use, and maintain such monitoring equipment or methods (including where appropriate, biological monitoring methods), (iv) sample such effluents (in accordance with such methods, at such locations, at such intervals, and in such manner as the Administrator shall prescribe), and (v) provide such other information as he may reasonably require; and

(B) the Administrator or his authorized representative (including an authorized contractor acting as a representative of the Administrator), upon presentation of his credentials—

(i) shall have a right of entry to, upon, or through any premises in which an effluent source is located or in which any records required to be maintained under clause (A) of this subsection are located, and

(ii) may at reasonable times have access to and copy any records, inspect any monitoring equipment or method required under clause (A), and sample any effluents which the owner or operator of such source is required to sample under such clause.

(b) Availability to public; trade secrets exception; penalty for disclosure of confidential information

Any records, reports, or information obtained under this section (1) shall, in the case of effluent data, be related to any applicable effluent limitations, toxic, pretreatment, or new source performance standards, and (2) shall be available to the public, except that upon a showing satisfactory to the Administrator by any person that records, reports, or information, or particular part thereof (other than effluent data), to which the Administrator has access under this section, if made public would divulge methods or processes entitled to protection as trade secrets of such person, the Administrator shall consider such record, report, or information, or particular portion thereof confidential in accordance with the purposes of section 1905 of Title 18. Any authorized representative of the Administrator (including an authorized contractor acting as a representative of the Administrator) who knowingly or willfully publishes, divulges, discloses, or makes known in any manner or to any extent not authorized by law any information which is required to be considered confidential under this subsection shall be fined not more than $1,000 or imprisoned not more than 1 year, or both. Nothing in this subsection shall prohibit the Administrator or an authorized representative of the Administrator (including any authorized contractor acting as a representative of the Administrator) from disclosing records, reports, or information to other officers, employees, or authorized representatives of the United States concerned with carrying out this chapter or when relevant in any proceeding under this chapter.

(c) Application of State law

Each State may develop and submit to the Administrator procedures under State law for inspection, monitoring, and entry with respect to point sources located in such State. If the Administrator finds that the procedures and the law of any State relating to inspection, monitoring, and entry are applicable to at least the same extent as those required by this section, such State is authorized to apply and enforce its procedures for inspection, monitoring, and entry with respect to point sources located in such State (except with respect to point sources owned or operated by the United States).

(d) Access by Congress

Notwithstanding any limitation contained in this section or any other provision of law, all information reported to or otherwise obtained by the Administrator (or any representative of the Administrator) under this chapter shall be made available, upon written request of any duly authorized committee of Congress, to such committee.

(June 30, 1948, c. 758, Title III, § 308, as added by Pub. L. No. 92–500, § 2, 86 Stat. 858 (Oct. 18, 1972); and amended by Pub. L. No. 95–217, § 67(c)(1), 91 Stat. 1606 (Dec. 27, 1977); Pub. L. No. 100–4, Title III, § 310, Title IV, § 406(d)(1), 101 Stat. 41, 73 (Feb. 4, 1987).)

§ 1319. Enforcement

[FWPCA § 309]

(a) State enforcement; compliance orders

(1) Whenever, on the basis of any information available to him, the Administrator finds that any person is in violation of any condition or limitation which implements section 1311, 1312, 1316, 1317, 1318, 1322(p), 1328, or 1345 of this title in a permit issued by a State under an approved permit program under section 1342 or 1344 of this title, he shall proceed under his authority in paragraph (3) of this subsection or he shall notify the person in alleged violation and such State of such finding. If beyond the thirtieth day after the Administrator's notification the State has not commenced appropriate enforcement action, the Administrator shall issue an order requiring such person to comply with such condition or limitation or shall bring a civil action in accordance with subsection (b) of this section.

(2) Whenever, on the basis of information available to him, the Administrator finds that violations of permit conditions or limitations as set forth in paragraph (1) of this subsection are so widespread that such violations appear to result from a failure of the State to enforce such permit conditions or limitations effectively, he shall so notify the State. If the Administrator finds such failure extends beyond the thirtieth day after such notice, he shall give public notice of such finding. During the period beginning with such public notice and ending when such State satisfies the Administrator that it will enforce such conditions and limitations (hereafter referred to in this section as the period of "federally assumed enforcement"), except where an extension has been granted under paragraph (5)(B) of this subsection, the Administrator shall enforce any permit condition or limitation with respect to any person—

(A) by issuing an order to comply with such condition or limitation, or

(B) by bringing a civil action under subsection (b) of this section.

(3) Whenever on the basis of any information available to him the Administrator finds that any person is in violation of section 1311, 1312, 1316, 1317, 1318, 1322(p), 1328, or 1345 of this title, or is in violation of any permit condition or limitation implementing any of such sections in a permit issued under section 1342 of this title by him or by a State or in a permit issued under section 1344 of this title by a State, he shall issue an order requiring such person to comply with such section or requirement, or he shall bring a civil action in accordance with subsection (b) of this section.

(4) A copy of any order issued under this subsection shall be sent immediately by the Administrator to the State in which the violation occurs and other affected States. In any case in which an order under this subsection (or notice to a violator under paragraph (1) of this subsection) is issued to a corporation, a copy of such order (or notice) shall be served on any appropriate corporate officers. An order issued under this subsection relating to a violation of section 1318 of this title shall not take effect until the person to whom it is issued has had an opportunity to confer with the Administrator concerning the alleged violation.

(5) **(A)** Any order issued under this subsection shall be by personal service, shall state with reasonable specificity the nature of the violation, and shall specify a time for compliance not to exceed thirty days in the case of a violation of an interim compliance schedule or operation and maintenance requirement and not to exceed a time the Administrator determines to be reasonable in the case of a violation of a final deadline, taking into account the seriousness of the violation and any good faith efforts to comply with applicable requirements.

(B) The Administrator may, if he determines (i) that any person who is a violator of, or any person who is otherwise not in compliance with, the time requirements under this chapter or in any permit issued under this chapter, has acted in good faith, and has made a commitment (in the form of contracts or other securities) of necessary resources to achieve compliance by the earliest possible date after July 1, 1977, but not later than April 1, 1979; (ii) that any extension under this provision will not result in the imposition of any additional controls on any other point or nonpoint source; (iii) that an application for a permit under section 1342 of this title was filed for such person prior to December 31, 1974; and (iv) that the facilities necessary for compliance with such requirements are under construction, grant an extension of the date referred to in section 1311(b)(1)(A) of this title to a date which will achieve compliance at the earliest time possible but not later than April 1, 1979.

(6) Whenever, on the basis of information available to him, the Administrator finds (A) that any person is in violation of section 1311(b)(1)(A) or (C) of this title, (B) that such person cannot meet the requirements for a time extension under section 1311(i)(2) of this title, and (C) that the most expeditious and appropriate means of compliance with this chapter by such person is to discharge into a publicly owned treatment works, then, upon request of such person, the Administrator may issue an order requiring such person to comply with this chapter at the earliest date practicable, but not later than July 1, 1983, by discharging into a publicly owned treatment works if such works concur with such order. Such order shall include a schedule of compliance.

(b) Civil actions

The Administrator is authorized to commence a civil action for appropriate relief, including a permanent or temporary injunction, for any violation for which he is authorized to issue a compliance order under subsection (a) of this section. Any action under this subsection may be brought in the district court of the United States for the district in which the defendant is located or resides or is doing business, and such court shall have jurisdiction to restrain such violation and to require compliance. Notice of the commencement of such action shall be given immediately to the appropriate State.

(c) Criminal penalties

(1) Negligent violations

Any person who—

(A) negligently violates section 1311, 1312, 1316, 1317, 1318, 1321(b)(3), 1322(p), 1328, or 1345 of this title, or any permit condition or limitation implementing any of such sections in a permit issued under section 1342 of this title by the Administrator or by a State, or any requirement imposed in a pretreatment program approved under section 1342(a)(3) or 1342(b)(8) of this title or in a permit issued under section 1344 of this title by the Secretary of the Army or by a State; or

(B) negligently introduces into a sewer system or into a publicly owned treatment works any pollutant or hazardous substance which such person knew or reasonably should have known could cause personal injury or property damage or, other than in compliance with all applicable Federal, State, or local requirements or permits, which causes such treatment works to violate any effluent limitation or condition in any permit issued to the treatment works under section 1342 of this title by the Administrator or a State;

shall be punished by a fine of not less than $2,500 nor more than $25,000 per day of violation, or by imprisonment for not more than 1 year, or by both. If a conviction of a person is for a violation committed after a first conviction of such person under this paragraph, punishment shall be by a fine of not more than $50,000 per day of violation, or by imprisonment of not more than 2 years, or by both.

(2) Knowing violations

Any person who—

(A) knowingly violates section 1311, 1312, 1316, 1317, 1318, 1321(b)(3), 1322(p), 1328, or 1345 of this title, or any permit condition or limitation implementing any of such sections in a permit issued under section 1342 of this title by the Administrator or by a State, or any requirement imposed in a pretreatment program approved under section 1342(a)(3) or 1342(b)(8) of this title or in a permit issued under section 1344 of this title by the Secretary of the Army or by a State; or

(B) knowingly introduces into a sewer system or into a publicly owned treatment works any pollutant or hazardous substance which such person knew or reasonably should have known could cause personal injury or property damage or, other than in compliance with all applicable Federal, State, or local requirements or permits, which causes such treatment works to violate any effluent limitation or condition in a permit issued to the treatment works under section 1342 of this title by the Administrator or a State;

shall be punished by a fine of not less than $5,000 nor more than $50,000 per day of violation, or by imprisonment for not more than 3 years, or by both. If a conviction of a person is for a violation committed after a first conviction of such person under this paragraph, punishment shall be by a fine of not more than $100,000 per day of violation, or by imprisonment of not more than 6 years, or by both.

(3) Knowing endangerment

(A) General rule

Any person who knowingly violates section 1311, 1312, 1313, 1316, 1317, 1318, 1321(b)(3), 1322(p), 1328, or 1345 of this title, or any permit condition or limitation implementing any of such sections in a permit issued under section 1342 of this title by the Administrator or by a State, or in a permit issued under section 1344 of this title by the Secretary of the Army or by a State, and who knows at that time that he thereby places another person in imminent danger of death or serious bodily injury, shall, upon conviction, be subject to a fine of not more than $250,000 or imprisonment of not more than 15 years, or both. A person which is an organization shall, upon conviction of violating this subparagraph, be subject to a fine of not more than $1,000,000. If a conviction of a person is for a violation committed after a first conviction of such person under this paragraph, the maximum punishment shall be doubled with respect to both fine and imprisonment.

(B) Additional provisions

For the purpose of subparagraph (A) of this paragraph—

(i) in determining whether a defendant who is an individual knew that his conduct placed another person in imminent danger of death or serious bodily injury—

(I) the person is responsible only for actual awareness or actual belief that he possessed; and

(II) knowledge possessed by a person other than the defendant but not by the defendant himself may not be attributed to the defendant;

except that in proving the defendant's possession of actual knowledge, circumstantial evidence may be used, including evidence that the defendant took affirmative steps to shield himself from relevant information;

(ii) it is an affirmative defense to prosecution that the conduct charged was consented to by the person endangered and that the danger and conduct charged were reasonably foreseeable hazards of—

(I) an occupation, a business, or a profession; or

(II) medical treatment or medical or scientific experimentation conducted by professionally approved methods and such other person had been made aware of the risks involved prior to giving consent;

and such defense may be established under this subparagraph by a preponderance of the evidence;

(iii) the term "organization" means a legal entity, other than a government, established or organized for any purpose, and such term includes a corporation, company, association, firm, partnership, joint stock company, foundation, institution, trust, society, union, or any other association of persons; and

(iv) the term "serious bodily injury" means bodily injury which involves a substantial risk of death, unconsciousness, extreme physical pain, protracted and obvious disfigurement, or protracted loss or impairment of the function of a bodily member, organ, or mental faculty.

(4) False statements

Any person who knowingly makes any false material statement, representation, or certification in any application, record, report, plan, or other document filed or required to be maintained under this chapter or who knowingly falsifies, tampers with, or renders inaccurate any monitoring device or method required to be maintained under this chapter, shall upon conviction, be punished by a fine of not more than $10,000, or by imprisonment for not more than 2 years, or by both. If a conviction of a person is for a violation committed after a first conviction of such person under this paragraph, punishment shall be by a fine of not more than $20,000 per day of violation, or by imprisonment of not more than 4 years, or by both.

(5) Treatment of single operational upset

For purposes of this subsection, a single operational upset which leads to simultaneous violations of more than one pollutant parameter shall be treated as a single violation.

(6) Responsible corporate officer as "person"

For the purpose of this subsection, the term "person" means, in addition to the definition contained in section 1362(5) of this title, any responsible corporate officer.

(7) Hazardous substance defined

For the purpose of this subsection, the term "hazardous substance" means (A) any substance designated pursuant to section 1321(b)(2)(A) of this title, (B) any element, compound, mixture, solution, or substance designated pursuant to section 9602 of Title 42, (C) any hazardous waste having the characteristics identified under or listed pursuant to section 3001 of the Solid Waste Disposal Act [42 U.S.C.A. § 6921] (but not including any waste the regulation of which under the Solid Waste Disposal Act [42 U.S.C.A. § 6901 et seq.] has been suspended by Act of Congress), (D) any toxic pollutant listed under section 1317(a) of this title, and (E) any imminently hazardous chemical substance or mixture with respect to which the Administrator has taken action pursuant to section 2606 of Title 15.

(d) Civil penalties; factors considered in determining amount

Any person who violates section 1311, 1312, 1316, 1317, 1318, 1322(p), 1328, or 1345 of this title, or any permit condition or limitation implementing any of such sections in a permit issued under section 1342 of this title by the Administrator, or by a State,[1] or in a permit issued under section 1344 of this title by a State, or any requirement imposed in a pretreatment program approved under section 1342(a)(3) or 1342(b)(8) of this title, and any person who violates any order issued by the Administrator under subsection (a) of this section, shall be subject to a civil penalty not to exceed $25,000 per day for each violation. In determining the amount of a civil penalty the court shall consider the seriousness of the violation or violations, the economic benefit (if any) resulting from the violation, any history of such violations, any good-faith efforts to comply with the applicable requirements, the economic impact of the penalty on the violator, and such other matters as justice may require. For purposes of this subsection, a single operational upset which leads to simultaneous violations of more than one pollutant parameter shall be treated as a single violation.

(e) State liability for judgments and expenses

Whenever a municipality is a party to a civil action brought by the United States under this section, the State in which such municipality is located shall be joined as a party. Such State shall be liable for payment of any judgment, or any expenses incurred as a result of complying with any judgment, entered against the municipality in such action to the extent that the laws of that State prevent the municipality from raising revenues needed to comply with such judgment.

(f) Wrongful introduction of pollutant into treatment works

Whenever, on the basis of any information available to him, the Administrator finds that an owner or operator of any source is introducing a pollutant into a treatment works in violation of subsection (d) of section 1317 of this title, the Administrator may notify the owner or operator of such treatment works and the State of such violation. If the owner or operator of the treatment works does not commence appropriate enforcement action within 30 days of the date of such notification, the Administrator may commence a civil action for appropriate relief, including but not limited to, a permanent or temporary injunction, against the owner or operator of such treatment works. In any such civil action the Administrator shall join the owner or operator of such source as a party to the action. Such action shall be brought in the district court of the United States in the district in which the treatment works is located. Such court shall have jurisdiction to restrain such violation and to require the owner or operator of the treatment works and the owner or operator of the source to take such action as may be necessary to come into compliance with this chapter. Notice of commencement of any such action shall be given to the State. Nothing in this subsection shall be construed to limit or prohibit any other authority the Administrator may have under this chapter.

(g) Administrative penalties

(1) Violations

Whenever on the basis of any information available—

(A) the Administrator finds that any person has violated section 1311, 1312, 1316, 1317, 1318, 1322(p), 1328, or 1345 of this title, or has violated any permit condition or limitation implementing any of such sections in a permit issued under section 1342 of this title by the Administrator or by a State, or in a permit issued under section 1344 of this title by a State, or

(B) the Secretary of the Army (hereinafter in this subsection referred to as the "Secretary") finds that any person has violated any permit condition or limitation in a permit issued under section 1344 of this title by the Secretary,

the Administrator or Secretary, as the case may be, may, after consultation with the State in which the violation occurs, assess a class I civil penalty or a class II civil penalty under this subsection.

(2) Classes of penalties

(A) Class I

The amount of a class I civil penalty under paragraph (1) may not exceed $10,000 per violation, except that the maximum amount of any class I civil penalty under this subparagraph shall not exceed $25,000. Before issuing an order assessing a civil penalty under this subparagraph, the Administrator or the Secretary, as the case may be, shall give to the person to be assessed such penalty written notice of the Administrator's or Secretary's proposal to issue such order and the opportunity to request, within 30 days of the date the notice is received by such person, a hearing on the proposed order. Such hearing shall not be subject to section 554 or 556 of Title 5, but shall provide a reasonable opportunity to be heard and to present evidence.

(B) Class II

The amount of a class II civil penalty under paragraph (1) may not exceed $10,000 per day for each day during which the violation continues; except that the maximum amount of any class II civil penalty under this subparagraph shall not exceed $125,000. Except as otherwise provided in this subsection, a class II civil penalty shall be assessed and collected in the same manner, and subject to the same provisions, as in the case of civil penalties assessed and collected after notice and opportunity for a hearing on the record in accordance with section 554 of Title 5. The Administrator and the Secretary may issue rules for discovery procedures for hearings under this subparagraph.

(3) Determining amount

In determining the amount of any penalty assessed under this subsection, the Administrator or the Secretary, as the case may be, shall take into account the nature, circumstances, extent and gravity of the violation, or violations, and, with respect to the violator, ability to pay, any prior history of such violations, the degree of culpability, economic benefit or savings (if any) resulting from the violation, and such other matters as justice may require. For purposes of this subsection, a single operational upset which leads to simultaneous violations of more than one pollutant parameter shall be treated as a single violation.

(4) Rights of interested persons

(A) Public notice

Before issuing an order assessing a civil penalty under this subsection the Administrator or Secretary, as the case may be, shall provide public notice of and reasonable opportunity to comment on the proposed issuance of such order.

(B) Presentation of evidence

Any person who comments on a proposed assessment of a penalty under this subsection shall be given notice of any hearing held under this subsection and of the order assessing such penalty. In any hearing held under this subsection, such person shall have a reasonable opportunity to be heard and to present evidence.

(C) Rights of interested persons to a hearing

If no hearing is held under paragraph (2) before issuance of an order assessing a penalty under this subsection, any person who commented on the proposed assessment may petition, within 30 days after the issuance of such order, the Administrator or Secretary, as the case may be, to set aside such order and to provide a hearing on the penalty. If the evidence presented by the petitioner in support of the petition is material and was not considered in the issuance of the order, the Administrator or Secretary shall immediately set aside such order and provide a hearing in accordance with paragraph (2)(A) in the case of a class I civil penalty and paragraph (2)(B) in the case of a class II civil penalty. If the Administrator or Secretary denies a hearing under this subparagraph, the Administrator or Secretary shall provide to the petitioner, and publish in the Federal Register, notice of and the reasons for such denial.

(5) Finality of order

An order issued under this subsection shall become final 30 days after its issuance unless a petition for judicial review is filed under paragraph (8) or a hearing is requested under paragraph (4)(C). If such a hearing is denied, such order shall become final 30 days after such denial.

(6) Effect of order

(A) Limitation on actions under other sections

Action taken by the Administrator or the Secretary, as the case may be, under this subsection shall not affect or limit the Administrator's or Secretary's authority to enforce any provision of this chapter; except that any violation—

(i) with respect to which the Administrator or the Secretary has commenced and is diligently prosecuting an action under this subsection,

(ii) with respect to which a State has commenced and is diligently prosecuting an action under a State law comparable to this subsection, or

(iii) for which the Administrator, the Secretary, or the State has issued a final order not subject to further judicial review and the violator has paid a penalty assessed under this subsection, or such comparable State law, as the case may be,

shall not be the subject of a civil penalty action under subsection (d) of this section or section 1321(b) of this title or section 1365 of this title.

(B) Applicability of limitation with respect to citizen suits

The limitations contained in subparagraph (A) on civil penalty actions under section 1365 of this title shall not apply with respect to any violation for which—

(i) a civil action under section 1365(a)(1) of this title has been filed prior to commencement of an action under this subsection, or

(ii) notice of an alleged violation of section 1365(a)(1) of this title has been given in accordance with section 1365(b)(1)(A) of this title prior to commencement of an action under this subsection and an action under section 1365(a)(1) of this title with respect to such alleged violation is filed before the 120th day after the date on which such notice is given.

(7) Effect of action on compliance

No action by the Administrator or the Secretary under this subsection shall affect any person's obligation to comply with any section of this chapter or with the terms and conditions of any permit issued pursuant to section 1342 or 1344 of this title.

(8) Judicial review

Any person against whom a civil penalty is assessed under this subsection or who commented on the proposed assessment of such penalty in accordance with paragraph (4) may obtain review of such assessment—

(A) in the case of assessment of a class I civil penalty, in the United States District Court for the District of Columbia or in the district in which the violation is alleged to have occurred, or

(B) in the case of assessment of a class II civil penalty, in United States Court of Appeals for the District of Columbia Circuit or for any other circuit in which such person resides or transacts business,

by filing a notice of appeal in such court within the 30-day period beginning on the date the civil penalty order is issued and by simultaneously sending a copy of such notice by certified mail to the Administrator or the Secretary, as the case may be, and the Attorney General. The Administrator or the Secretary shall promptly file in such court a certified copy of the record on which the order was issued. Such court shall not set aside or remand such order unless there is not substantial evidence in the record, taken as a whole, to support the finding of a violation or unless the Administrator's or Secretary's assessment of the penalty constitutes an abuse of discretion and shall not impose additional civil penalties for the same violation unless the Administrator's or Secretary's assessment of the penalty constitutes an abuse of discretion.

(9) Collection

If any person fails to pay an assessment of a civil penalty—

(A) after the order making the assessment has become final, or

(B) after a court in an action brought under paragraph (8) has entered a final judgment in favor of the Administrator or the Secretary, as the case may be,

the Administrator or the Secretary shall request the Attorney General to bring a civil action in an appropriate district court to recover the amount assessed (plus interest at currently prevailing rates from the date of the final order or the date of the final judgment, as the case may be). In such an action, the validity, amount, and appropriateness of such penalty shall not be subject to review. Any person who fails to pay on a timely basis the amount of an assessment of a civil penalty as described in the first sentence of this paragraph shall be required to pay, in addition to such amount and interest, attorneys fees and costs for collection proceedings and a quarterly nonpayment penalty for each quarter during which such failure to pay persists. Such nonpayment penalty shall be in an amount equal to 20 percent of the aggregate amount of such person's penalties and nonpayment penalties which are unpaid as of the beginning of such quarter.

(10) Subpoenas

The Administrator or Secretary, as the case may be, may issue subpoenas for the attendance and testimony of witnesses and the production of relevant papers, books, or documents in connection with hearings under this subsection. In case of contumacy or refusal to obey a subpoena issued pursuant to this paragraph and served upon any person, the district court of the United States for any district in which such person is found, resides, or transacts business, upon application by the United States and after notice to such person, shall have jurisdiction to issue an order requiring such person to appear and give testimony before the administrative law judge or to appear and produce documents before the administrative law judge, or both, and any failure to obey such order of the court may be punished by such court as a contempt thereof.

(11) Protection of existing procedures

Nothing in this subsection shall change the procedures existing on the day before February 4, 1987, under other subsections of this section for issuance and enforcement of orders by the Administrator.

(h) Implementation of integrated plans.—

(1) In general.—In conjunction with an enforcement action under subsection (a) or (b) relating to municipal discharges, the Administrator shall inform a municipality of the opportunity to develop an integrated plan, as defined in section 1342(s).

(2) Modification.—Any municipality under an administrative order under subsection (a) or settlement agreement (including a judicial consent decree) under subsection (b) that has developed an integrated plan consistent with section 1342(s) may request a modification of the administrative order or settlement agreement based on that integrated plan.

(June 30, 1948, c. 758, Title III, § 309, as added by Pub. L. No. 92–500, § 2, 86 Stat. 859 (Oct. 18, 1972); and amended by Pub. L. No. 95–217, §§ 54(b), 55, 56, 67(c)(2), 91 Stat. 1591, 1592, 1606 (Dec. 27, 1977); Pub. L. No. 100–4, Title III, §§ 312, 313(a)(1), (b)(1), (c), 314(a), 101 Stat. 42, 45, 46 (Feb. 4, 1987); Pub. L. No. 101–380, Title IV, § 4301(c), 104 Stat. 537 (Aug. 18, 1990); Pub. L. No. 115–282, § 312(k)(2), 132 Stat. 4192, 4356 (Dec. 4, 2018); Pub. L. No. 115–436, § 3(b), 132 Stat. 5558, 5560 (Jan. 14, 2019).)

[1] So in original.

HISTORICAL AND STATUTORY NOTES

References in Text

The Solid Waste Disposal Act, referred to in subsec. (c)(7) is Title II of Pub. L. No. 89–272, as amended generally by Pub. L. No. 94–580, § 2, 90 Stat. 2795 (Oct. 21, 1976), which is codified generally as chapter 82 (section 6901 et seq.) of Title 42, The Public Health and Welfare. Section 3001 of the Solid Waste Disposal Act is codified as section 6921 of Title 42. For complete classification of this Act to the Code, see Short Title note set out under section 6901 of Title 42 and Tables.

Savings Provisions

Section 313(a)(2) of Pub. L. No. 100–4 provided that: "No State shall be required before July 1, 1988, to modify a permit program approved or submitted under section 402 of the Federal Water Pollution Control Act [section 1342 of this title] as a result of the amendment made by paragraph (1) [amending subsec. (d) of this section by inserting reference to requirements imposed in a pretreatment program approved under section 1342(a)(3) or (b)(8) of this title]."

Report on Integrated Plans

Pub. L. No. 115–436, § 3(c), 132 Stat. 5558, 5560 (Jan. 14, 2019), provided that: "Not later than 2 years after the date of enactment of this Act, the Administrator shall submit to the Committee on Environment and Public Works of the Senate and the Committee on Transportation and Infrastructure of the House of Representatives, and make publicly available, a report on each integrated plan developed and implemented through a permit, order, or judicial consent decree pursuant to the Federal Water Pollution Control Act since the date of publication of the "Integrated Municipal Stormwater and Wastewater Planning Approach Framework" issued by the Environmental Protection Agency and dated June 5, 2012, including a description of the control measures, levels of control, estimated costs, and compliance schedules for the requirements implemented through such an integrated plan."

Deposit of Certain Penalties Into Oil Spill Liability Trust Fund

Penalties paid pursuant to this section and sections 1321 and 1501 et seq., respectively, of this title, deposited in the Oil Spill Liability Trust Fund created under section 9509 of Title 26, Internal Revenue Code, see section 4304 of Pub. L. No. 101–380, set out as a note under section 9509 of Title 26.

Increased Penalties Not Required Under State Programs

Section 313(b)(2) of Pub. L. No. 100–4 provided that: "The Federal Water Pollution Control Act [this chapter] shall not be construed as requiring a State to have a civil penalty for violations described in section 309(d) of such Act [subsec. (d) of this section] which has the same monetary amount as the civil penalty established by such section, as amended by paragraph (1) [amending subsec. (d) of this section by increasing the penalty to $25,000]. Nothing in this paragraph shall affect the Administrator's authority to establish or adjust by regulation a minimum acceptable State civil penalty."

Actions by Surgeon General Relating to Interstate Pollution

Act of July 9, 1956, c. 518, § 5, 70 Stat. 507, provided that actions by the Surgeon General with respect to water pollutants under section 2(d) of Act of June 30, 1948, c. 758, 62 Stat. 1155, as in effect prior to July 9, 1956, which had been completed prior to such date, would still be subject to the terms of section 2(d) of Act of June 30, 1948, in effect prior to the July 9, 1956 amendment, but that actions with respect to such pollutants would nevertheless subsequently be possible in accordance with the terms of Act of June 30, 1948, as amended by Act of July 9, 1956.

§ 1320. International pollution abatement

[FWPCA § 310]

(a) Hearing; participation by foreign nations

Whenever the Administrator, upon receipts of reports, surveys, or studies from any duly constituted international agency, has reason to believe that pollution is occurring which endangers the health or welfare of persons in a foreign country, and the Secretary of State requests him to abate such pollution, he shall give formal notification thereof to the State water pollution control agency of the State or States in which such discharge or discharges originate and to the appropriate interstate agency, if any. He shall also promptly call such a hearing, if he believes that such pollution is occurring in sufficient quantity to warrant such action, and if such foreign country has given the United States essentially the same rights with respect to the prevention and control of pollution occurring in that country as is given that country by this subsection. The Administrator, through the Secretary of State, shall invite the foreign country which may be adversely affected by the pollution to attend and participate in the hearing, and the representative of such country shall, for the purpose of the hearing and any further proceeding resulting from such hearing, have all the rights of a State water pollution control agency. Nothing in this subsection shall be construed to modify, amend, repeal, or otherwise affect the provisions of the 1909 Boundary Waters Treaty between Canada and the United States or the Water Utilization Treaty of 1944 between Mexico and the United States (59 Stat. 1219), relative to the control and abatement of pollution in waters covered by those treaties.

(b) Functions and responsibilities of Administrator not affected

The calling of a hearing under this section shall not be construed by the courts, the Administrator, or any person as limiting, modifying, or otherwise affecting the functions and responsibilities of the Administrator under this section to establish and enforce water quality requirements under this chapter.

(c) Hearing board; composition; findings of fact; recommendations; implementation of board's decision

The Administrator shall publish in the Federal Register a notice of a public hearing before a hearing board of five or more persons appointed by the Administrator. A majority of the members of the board and the chairman who shall be designated by the Administrator shall not be officers or employees of Federal, State, or local governments. On the basis of the evidence presented at such hearing, the board shall within sixty days after completion of the hearing make findings of fact as to whether or not such pollution is occurring and shall thereupon by decision, incorporating its findings therein, make such recommendations to abate the pollution as may be appropriate and shall transmit such decision and the record of the hearings to the Administrator. All such decisions shall be public. Upon receipt of such decision, the Administrator shall promptly implement the board's decision in accordance with the provisions of this chapter.

(d) Report by alleged polluter

In connection with any hearing called under this subsection, the board is authorized to require any person whose alleged activities result in discharges causing or contributing to pollution to file with it in such forms as it may prescribe, a report based on existing data, furnishing such information as may reasonably be required as to the character, kind, and quantity of such discharges and the use of facilities or other means to prevent or reduce such discharges by the person filing such a report. Such report shall be made under oath or otherwise, as the board may prescribe, and shall be filed with the board within such reasonable period as it may prescribe, unless additional time is granted by it. Upon a showing satisfactory to the board by the person filing such report that such report or portion thereof (other than effluent data), to which the Administrator has access under this section, if made public would divulge trade secrets or secret processes of such person, the board shall consider such report or portion thereof confidential for the purposes of section 1905 of Title 18. If any person required to file any report under this paragraph shall fail to do so within the time fixed by the board for filing the same, and such failure shall continue for thirty days after notice of such default, such person shall forfeit to the United States the sum of $1,000 for each and every day of the continuance of such failure, which forfeiture shall be payable into the Treasury of the United States, and shall be recoverable in a civil suit in the name of the United States in the district court of the United States where such person has his principal office or in any district in which he does business. The Administrator may upon application therefor remit or mitigate any forfeiture provided for under this subsection.

(e) Compensation of board members

Board members, other than officers or employees of Federal, State, or local governments, shall be for each day (including travel-time) during which they are performing board business, entitled to receive compensation at a rate fixed by the Administrator but not in excess of the maximum rate of pay for grade GS–18, as provided in the General Schedule under section 5332 of Title 5, and shall, notwithstanding the limitations of sections 5703 and 5704 of Title 5, be fully reimbursed for travel, subsistence and related expenses.

(f) Enforcement proceedings

When any such recommendation adopted by the Administrator involves the institution of enforcement proceedings against any person to obtain the abatement of pollution subject to such recommendation, the Administrator shall institute such proceedings if he believes that the evidence warrants such proceedings. The district court of the United States shall consider and determine de novo all relevant issues, but shall receive in evidence the record of the proceedings before the conference or hearing board. The court shall have jurisdiction to enter such judgment and orders enforcing such judgment as it deems appropriate or to remand such proceedings to the Administrator for such further action as it may direct.

(June 30, 1948, c. 758, Title III, § 310, as added by Pub. L. No. 92–500, § 2, 86 Stat. 860 (Oct. 18, 1972).)

HISTORICAL AND STATUTORY NOTES

References in Other Laws to GS–16, 17, or 18 Pay Rates

References in laws to the rates of pay for GS–16, 17, or 18, or to maximum rates of pay under the General Schedule, to be considered references to rates payable under specified sections of Title 5, see section 529 [Title I, § 101(c)(1)] of Pub. L. No. 101–509, set out in a note under 5 U.S.C.A. § 5376.

§ 1321. Oil and hazardous substance liability

[FWPCA § 311]

(a) Definitions

For the purpose of this section, the term—

(1) "oil" means oil of any kind or in any form, including, but not limited to, petroleum, fuel oil, sludge, oil refuse, and oil mixed with wastes other than dredged spoil;

(2) "discharge" includes, but is not limited to, any spilling, leaking, pumping, pouring, emitting, emptying or dumping, but excludes (A) discharges in compliance with a permit under section 1342 of this title, (B) discharges resulting from circumstances identified and reviewed and made a part of the public record with respect to a permit issued or modified under section 1342 of this title, and subject to a condition in such permit,[1] (C) continuous or anticipated intermittent discharges from a point source, identified in a permit or permit application under section 1342 of this title, which are caused by events occurring within the scope of relevant operating or treatment systems, and (D) discharges incidental to mechanical removal authorized by the President under subsection (c) of this section;

(3) "vessel" means every description of watercraft or other artificial contrivance used, or capable of being used, as a means of transportation on water other than a public vessel;

(4) "public vessel" means a vessel owned or bareboat-chartered and operated by the United States, or by a State or political subdivision thereof, or by a foreign nation, except when such vessel is engaged in commerce;

(5) "United States" means the States, the District of Columbia, the Commonwealth of Puerto Rico, the Commonwealth of the Northern Mariana Islands, Guam, American Samoa, the Virgin Islands, and the Trust Territory of the Pacific Islands;

(6) "owner or operator" means (A) in the case of a vessel, any person owning, operating, or chartering by demise, such vessel, and (B) in the case of an onshore facility, and an offshore facility, any person owning or operating such onshore facility or offshore facility, and (C) in the case of any abandoned offshore facility, the person who owned or operated such facility immediately prior to such abandonment;

(7) "person" includes an individual, firm, corporation, association, and a partnership;

(8) "remove" or "removal" refers to containment and removal of the oil or hazardous substances from the water and shorelines or the taking of such other actions as may be necessary to prevent, minimize, or mitigate damage to the public health or welfare, including, but not limited to, fish, shellfish, wildlife, and public and private property, shorelines, and beaches;

(9) "contiguous zone" means the entire zone established or to be established by the United States under article 24 of the Convention on the Territorial Sea and the Contiguous Zone;

(10) "onshore facility" means any facility (including, but not limited to, motor vehicles and rolling stock) of any kind located in, on, or under, any land within the United States other than submerged land;

(11) "offshore facility" means any facility of any kind located in, on, or under, any of the navigable waters of the United States, any facility of any kind which is subject to the jurisdiction of the United States and is located in, on, or under any other waters, other than a vessel or a public vessel, and, for the purposes of applying subsections (b), (c), (e), and (*o*), any foreign offshore unit (as defined in section 1001 of the Oil Pollution Act) or any other facility located seaward of the exclusive economic zone;

(12) "act of God" means an act occasioned by an unanticipated grave natural disaster;

(13) "barrel" means 42 United States gallons at 60 degrees Fahrenheit;

(14) "hazardous substance" means any substance designated pursuant to subsection (b)(2) of this section;

(15) "inland oil barge" means a non-self-propelled vessel carrying oil in bulk as cargo and certificated to operate only in the inland waters of the United States, while operating in such waters;

(16) "inland waters of the United States" means those waters of the United States lying inside the baseline from which the territorial sea is measured and those waters outside such baseline which are a part of the Gulf Intracoastal Waterway;

(17) "otherwise subject to the jurisdiction of the United States" means subject to the jurisdiction of the United States by virtue of United States citizenship, United States vessel documentation or numbering, or as provided for by international agreement to which the United States is a party;

(18) "Area Committee" means an Area Committee established under subsection (j) of this section;

(19) "Area Contingency Plan" means an Area Contingency Plan prepared under subsection (j) of this section;

(20) "Coast Guard District Response Group" means a Coast Guard District Response Group established under subsection (j) of this section;

(21) "Federal On-Scene Coordinator" means a Federal On-Scene Coordinator designated in the National Contingency Plan;

(22) "National Contingency Plan" means the National Contingency Plan prepared and published under subsection (d) of this section;

(23) "National Response Unit" means the National Response Unit established under subsection (j) of this section;

(24) "worst case discharge" means—

(A) in the case of a vessel, a discharge in adverse weather conditions of its entire cargo; and

(B) in the case of an offshore facility or onshore facility, the largest foreseeable discharge in adverse weather conditions;

(25) "removal costs" means—

(A) the costs of removal of oil or a hazardous substance that are incurred after it is discharged; and

(B) in any case in which there is a substantial threat of a discharge of oil or a hazardous substance, the costs to prevent, minimize, or mitigate that threat;

(26) "nontank vessel" means a self-propelled vessel that—

(A) is at least 400 gross tons as measured under section 14302 of Title 46, or, for vessels not measured under that section, as measured under section 14502 of that title;

(B) is not a tank vessel;

(C) carries oil of any kind as fuel for main propulsion; and

(D) operates on the navigable waters of the United States, as defined in section 2101(23) of that title;

(27) the term "best available science" means science that—

(A) maximizes the quality, objectivity, and integrity of information, including statistical information;

(B) uses peer-reviewed and publicly available data; and

(C) clearly documents and communicates risks and uncertainties in the scientific basis for such projects;

(28) the term "Chairperson" means the Chairperson of the Council;

(29) the term "coastal political subdivision" means any local political jurisdiction that is immediately below the State level of government, including a county, parish, or borough, with a coastline that is contiguous with any portion of the United States Gulf of Mexico;

(30) the term "Comprehensive Plan" means the comprehensive plan developed by the Council pursuant to subsection (t);

(31) the term "Council" means the Gulf Coast Ecosystem Restoration Council established pursuant to subsection (t);

(32) the term "Deepwater Horizon oil spill" means the blowout and explosion of the mobile offshore drilling unit *Deepwater Horizon* that occurred on April 20, 2010, and resulting hydrocarbon releases into the environment;

(33) the term "Gulf Coast region" means—

(A) in the Gulf Coast States, the coastal zones (as that term is defined in section 304 of the Coastal Zone Management Act of 1972 (16 U.S.C. 1453)), except that, in this section, the term "coastal zones" includes land within the coastal zones that is held in trust by, or the use of which is by law subject solely to the discretion of, the Federal Government or officers or agents of the Federal Government) that border the Gulf of Mexico;

(B) any adjacent land, water, and watersheds, that are within 25 miles of the coastal zones described in subparagraph (A) of the Gulf Coast States; and

(C) all Federal waters in the Gulf of Mexico;

(34) the term "Gulf Coast State" means any of the States of Alabama, Florida, Louisiana, Mississippi, and Texas; and

(35) the term "Trust Fund" means the Gulf Coast Restoration Trust Fund established pursuant to section 1602 of the Resources and Ecosystems Sustainability, Tourist Opportunities, and Revived Economies of the Gulf Coast States Act of 2012.

(b) Congressional declaration of policy against discharges of oil or hazardous substances; designation of hazardous substances; study of higher standard of care incentives and report to Congress; liability; penalties; civil actions: penalty limitations, separate offenses, jurisdiction, mitigation of damages and costs, recovery of removal costs, alternative remedies, and withholding clearance of vessels

(1) The Congress hereby declares that it is the policy of the United States that there should be no discharges of oil or hazardous substances into or upon the navigable waters of the United States, adjoining shorelines, or into or upon the waters of the contiguous zone, or in connection with activities under the Outer Continental Shelf Lands Act [43 U.S.C.A. § 1331 et seq.] or the Deepwater Port Act of 1974 [33 U.S.C.A. § 1501 et seq.], or which may affect natural resources belonging to, appertaining to, or under the exclusive management authority of the United States (including resources under the Magnuson-Stevens Fishery Conservation and Management Act [16 U.S.C.A. § 1801 et seq.]).

(2) (A) The Administrator shall develop, promulgate, and revise as may be appropriate, regulations designating as hazardous substances, other than oil as defined in this section, such elements and compounds which, when discharged in any quantity into or upon the navigable waters of the United States or adjoining shorelines or the waters of the contiguous zone or in connection with activities under the Outer Continental Shelf Lands Act [43 U.S.C.A. § 1331 et seq.] or the Deepwater Port Act of 1974 [33 U.S.C.A. § 1501 et seq.], or which may affect natural resources belonging to, appertaining to, or under the exclusive management authority of the United States (including resources under the Magnuson-Stevens Fishery Conservation and Management Act [16 U.S.C.A. § 1801 et seq.]), present an imminent and substantial danger to the public health or welfare, including, but not limited to, fish, shellfish, wildlife, shorelines, and beaches.

(B) The Administrator shall within 18 months after the date of enactment of this paragraph, conduct a study and report to the Congress on methods, mechanisms, and procedures to create incentives to achieve a higher standard of care in all aspects of the management and movement of hazardous substances on the part of owners, operators, or persons in charge of onshore facilities, offshore facilities, or vessels. The Administrator shall include in such study (1) limits of liability, (2) liability for third party damages, (3) penalties and fees, (4) spill prevention plans, (5) current practices in the insurance and banking industries, and (6) whether the penalty enacted in subclause (bb) of clause (iii) of subparagraph (B) of subsection (b)(2) of section 311 of Public Law 92–500 should be enacted.

(3) The discharge of oil or hazardous substances (i) into or upon the navigable waters of the United States, adjoining shorelines, or into or upon the waters of the contiguous zone, or (ii) in connection with activities under the Outer Continental Shelf Lands Act [43 U.S.C.A. § 1331 et seq.] or the Deepwater Port Act of 1974 [33 U.S.C.A. § 1501 et seq.], or which may affect natural resources belonging to, appertaining to, or under the exclusive management authority of the United States (including resources under the Magnuson-Stevens Fishery Conservation and Management Act [16 U.S.C.A. § 1801 et seq.]), in such quantities as may be harmful as determined by the President under paragraph (4) of this subsection, is prohibited, except (A) in the case of such discharges into the waters of the contiguous zone or which may affect natural resources belonging to, appertaining to, or under the exclusive management authority of the United States (including resources under the Magnuson-Stevens Fishery Conservation and Management Act), where permitted under the Protocol of 1978 Relating to the International Convention for the Prevention of Pollution from Ships, 1973, and (B) where permitted in quantities and at times and locations or under such circumstances or conditions as the President may, by regulation, determine not to be harmful. Any regulations issued under this subsection shall be consistent with maritime safety and with marine and navigation laws and regulations and applicable water quality standards.

(4) The President shall by regulation determine for the purposes of this section those quantities of oil and any hazardous substances the discharge of which may be harmful to the public health or welfare or the environment of the United States, including but not limited to fish, shellfish, wildlife, and public and private property, shorelines, and beaches.

(5) Any person in charge of a vessel or of an onshore facility or an offshore facility shall, as soon as he has knowledge of any discharge of oil or a hazardous substance from such vessel or facility in violation of paragraph (3) of this subsection, immediately notify the appropriate agency of the United States Government of such discharge. The Federal agency shall immediately notify the appropriate State agency of any State which is, or may reasonably be expected to be, affected by the discharge of oil or a hazardous substance. Any such person (A) in charge of a vessel from which oil or a hazardous substance is discharged in violation of paragraph (3)(i) of this subsection, or (B) in charge of a vessel from which oil or a hazardous substance is discharged in violation of paragraph (3)(ii) of this subsection and who is otherwise subject to the jurisdiction of the United States at the time of the discharge, or (C) in charge of an onshore facility or an offshore facility, who fails to notify immediately such agency of such discharge shall, upon conviction, be fined in accordance with Title 18, or imprisoned for not more than 5 years, or both. Notification received pursuant to this paragraph shall not be used against any such natural person in any criminal case, except a prosecution for perjury or for giving a false statement.

(6) Administrative penalties

(A) Violations

Any owner, operator, or person in charge of any vessel, onshore facility, or offshore facility—

(i) from which oil or a hazardous substance is discharged in violation of paragraph (3), or

(ii) who fails or refuses to comply with any regulation issued under subsection (j) of this section to which that owner, operator, or person in charge is subject,

may be assessed a class I or class II civil penalty by the Secretary of the department in which the Coast Guard is operating, the Secretary of Transportation, or the Administrator.

(B) Classes of penalties

(i) Class I

The amount of a class I civil penalty under subparagraph (A) may not exceed $10,000 per violation, except that the maximum amount of any class I civil penalty under this subparagraph shall not exceed $25,000. Before assessing a civil penalty under this clause, the Administrator or Secretary, as the case may be, shall give to the person to be assessed such penalty written notice of the Administrator's or Secretary's proposal to assess the penalty and the opportunity to request, within 30 days of the date the notice is received by such person, a hearing on the proposed penalty. Such hearing shall not be subject to section 554 or 556 of Title 5, but shall provide a reasonable opportunity to be heard and to present evidence.

(ii) Class II

The amount of a class II civil penalty under subparagraph (A) may not exceed $10,000 per day for each day during which the violation continues; except that the maximum amount of any class II civil penalty under this subparagraph shall not exceed $125,000. Except as otherwise provided in this subsection, a class II civil penalty shall be assessed and collected in the same manner, and subject to the same provisions, as in the case of civil penalties assessed and collected after notice and opportunity for a hearing on the record in accordance with section 554 of Title 5. The Administrator and Secretary may issue rules for discovery procedures for hearings under this paragraph.

(C) Rights of interested persons

(i) Public notice

Before issuing an order assessing a class II civil penalty under this paragraph the Administrator or Secretary, as the case may be, shall provide public notice of and reasonable opportunity to comment on the proposed issuance of such order.

(ii) Presentation of evidence

Any person who comments on a proposed assessment of a class II civil penalty under this paragraph shall be given notice of any hearing held under this paragraph and of the order assessing such penalty. In any hearing held under this paragraph, such person shall have a reasonable opportunity to be heard and to present evidence.

(iii) Rights of interested persons to a hearing

If no hearing is held under subparagraph (B) before issuance of an order assessing a class II civil penalty under this paragraph, any person who commented on the proposed assessment may petition, within 30 days after the issuance of such order, the Administrator or Secretary, as the case may be, to set aside such order and to provide a hearing on the penalty. If the evidence presented by the petitioner in support of the petition is material and was not considered in the issuance of the order, the Administrator or Secretary shall immediately set aside such order and provide a hearing in accordance with subparagraph (B)(ii). If the Administrator or Secretary denies a hearing under this clause, the Administrator or Secretary shall provide to the petitioner, and publish in the Federal Register, notice of and the reasons for such denial.

(D) Finality of order

An order assessing a class II civil penalty under this paragraph shall become final 30 days after its issuance unless a petition for judicial review is filed under subparagraph (G) or a hearing is requested under subparagraph (C)(iii). If such a hearing is denied, such order shall become final 30 days after such denial.

(E) Effect of order

Action taken by the Administrator or Secretary, as the case may be, under this paragraph shall not affect or limit the Administrator's or Secretary's authority to enforce any provision of this chapter; except that any violation—

(i) with respect to which the Administrator or Secretary has commenced and is diligently prosecuting an action to assess a class II civil penalty under this paragraph, or

(ii) for which the Administrator or Secretary has issued a final order assessing a class II civil penalty not subject to further judicial review and the violator has paid a penalty assessed under this paragraph,

shall not be the subject of a civil penalty action under section 1319(d), 1319(g), or 1365 of this Title or under paragraph (7).

(F) Effect of action on compliance

No action by the Administrator or Secretary under this paragraph shall affect any person's obligation to comply with any section of this chapter.

(G) Judicial review

Any person against whom a civil penalty is assessed under this paragraph or who commented on the proposed assessment of such penalty in accordance with subparagraph (C) may obtain review of such assessment—

(i) in the case of assessment of a class I civil penalty, in the United States District Court for the District of Columbia or in the district in which the violation is alleged to have occurred, or

(ii) in the case of assessment of a class II civil penalty, in United States Court of Appeals for the District of Columbia Circuit or for any other circuit in which such person resides or transacts business,

by filing a notice of appeal in such court within the 30-day period beginning on the date the civil penalty order is issued and by simultaneously sending a copy of such notice by certified mail to the Administrator or Secretary, as the case may be, and the Attorney General. The Administrator or Secretary shall promptly file in such court a certified copy of the record on which the order was issued. Such court shall not set aside or remand such order unless there is not substantial evidence in the record, taken as a whole, to support the finding of a violation or unless the Administrator's or Secretary's assessment of the penalty constitutes an abuse of discretion and shall not impose additional civil penalties for the same violation unless the Administrator's or Secretary's assessment of the penalty constitutes an abuse of discretion.

(H) Collection

If any person fails to pay an assessment of a civil penalty—

(i) after the assessment has become final, or

(ii) after a court in an action brought under subparagraph (G) has entered a final judgment in favor of the Administrator or Secretary, as the case may be,

the Administrator or Secretary shall request the Attorney General to bring a civil action in an appropriate district court to recover the amount assessed (plus interest at currently prevailing rates from the date of the final order or the date of the final judgment, as the case may be). In such an action, the validity, amount, and appropriateness of such penalty shall not be subject to review. Any person who fails to pay on a timely basis the amount of an assessment of a civil penalty as described in the first sentence of this subparagraph shall be required to pay, in addition to such amount and interest, attorneys fees and costs for collection proceedings and a quarterly nonpayment penalty for each quarter during which such failure to pay persists. Such nonpayment penalty shall be in an amount equal to 20 percent of the aggregate amount of such person's penalties and nonpayment penalties which are unpaid as of the beginning of such quarter.

(I) Subpoenas

The Administrator or Secretary, as the case may be, may issue subpoenas for the attendance and testimony of witnesses and the production of relevant papers, books, or documents in connection with hearings under this paragraph. In case of contumacy or refusal to obey a subpoena issued pursuant to this subparagraph and served upon any person, the district court of the United States for any district in which such person is found, resides, or transacts business, upon application by the United States and after notice to such person, shall have jurisdiction to issue an order requiring such person to appear and give testimony before the administrative law judge or to appear and produce documents before the administrative law judge, or both, and any failure to obey such order of the court may be punished by such court as a contempt thereof.

(7) Civil penalty action

(A) Discharge, generally

Any person who is the owner, operator, or person in charge of any vessel, onshore facility, or offshore facility from which oil or a hazardous substance is discharged in violation of paragraph (3), shall be subject to a civil penalty in an amount up to $25,000 per day of violation or an amount up to $1,000 per barrel of oil or unit of reportable quantity of hazardous substances discharged.

(B) Failure to remove or comply

Any person described in subparagraph (A) who, without sufficient cause—

(i) fails to properly carry out removal of the discharge under an order of the President pursuant to subsection (c) of this section; or

(ii) fails to comply with an order pursuant to subsection (e)(1)(B) of this section;

shall be subject to a civil penalty in an amount up to $25,000 per day of violation or an amount up to 3 times the costs incurred by the Oil Spill Liability Trust Fund as a result of such failure.

(C) Failure to comply with regulation

Any person who fails or refuses to comply with any regulation issued under subsection (j) of this section shall be subject to a civil penalty in an amount up to $25,000 per day of violation.

(D) Gross negligence

In any case in which a violation of paragraph (3) was the result of gross negligence or willful misconduct of a person described in subparagraph (A), the person shall be subject to a civil penalty of not less than $100,000, and not more than $3,000 per barrel of oil or unit of reportable quantity of hazardous substance discharged.

(E) Jurisdiction

An action to impose a civil penalty under this paragraph may be brought in the district court of the United States for the district in which the defendant is located, resides, or is doing business, and such court shall have jurisdiction to assess such penalty.

(F) Limitation

A person is not liable for a civil penalty under this paragraph for a discharge if the person has been assessed a civil penalty under paragraph (6) for the discharge.

(8) Determination of amount

In determining the amount of a civil penalty under paragraphs (6) and (7), the Administrator, Secretary, or the court, as the case may be, shall consider the seriousness of the violation or violations, the economic benefit to the violator, if any, resulting from the violation, the degree of culpability involved, any other penalty for the same incident, any history of prior violations, the nature, extent, and degree of success of any efforts of the violator to minimize or mitigate the effects of the discharge, the economic impact of the penalty on the violator, and any other matters as justice may require.

(9) Mitigation of damage

In addition to establishing a penalty for the discharge of oil or a hazardous substance, the Administrator or the Secretary of the department in which the Coast Guard is operating may act to mitigate the damage to the public health or welfare caused by such discharge. The cost of such mitigation shall be deemed a cost incurred under subsection (c) of this section for the removal of such substance by the United States Government.

(10) Recovery of removal costs

Any costs of removal incurred in connection with a discharge excluded by subsection (a)(2)(C) of this section shall be recoverable from the owner or operator of the source of the discharge in an action brought under section 1319(b) of this Title.

(11) Limitation

Civil penalties shall not be assessed under both this section and section 1319 of this Title for the same discharge.

(12) Withholding clearance

If any owner, operator, or person in charge of a vessel is liable for a civil penalty under this subsection, or if reasonable cause exists to believe that the owner, operator, or person in charge may be subject to a civil penalty under this subsection, the Secretary of the Treasury, upon the request of the Secretary of the department in which the Coast Guard is operating or the Administrator, shall with respect to such vessel refuse or revoke—

(A) the clearance required by section 60105 of Title 46;

(B) a permit to proceed under section 313 of the Appendix to Title 46; and

(C) a permit to depart required under section 1443 of Title 19;

as applicable. Clearance or a permit refused or revoked under this paragraph may be granted upon the filing of a bond or other surety satisfactory to the Secretary of the department in which the Coast Guard is operating or the Administrator.

(c) Federal removal authority

(1) General removal requirement

(A) The President shall, in accordance with the National Contingency Plan and any appropriate Area Contingency Plan, ensure effective and immediate removal of a discharge, and mitigation or prevention of a substantial threat of a discharge, of oil or a hazardous substance—

(i) into or on the navigable waters;

(ii) on the adjoining shorelines to the navigable waters;

(iii) into or on the waters of the exclusive economic zone; or

(iv) that may affect natural resources belonging to, appertaining to, or under the exclusive management authority of the United States.

(B) In carrying out this paragraph, the President may—

(i) remove or arrange for the removal of a discharge, and mitigate or prevent a substantial threat of a discharge, at any time;

(ii) direct or monitor all Federal, State, and private actions to remove a discharge; and

(iii) remove and, if necessary, destroy a vessel discharging, or threatening to discharge, by whatever means are available.

(2) Discharge posing substantial threat to public health or welfare

(A) If a discharge, or a substantial threat of a discharge, of oil or a hazardous substance from a vessel, offshore facility, or onshore facility is of such a size or character as to be a substantial threat to the public health or welfare of the United States (including but not limited to fish, shellfish, wildlife, other natural resources, and the public and private beaches and shorelines of the United States), the President shall direct all Federal, State, and private actions to remove the discharge or to mitigate or prevent the threat of the discharge.

(B) In carrying out this paragraph, the President may, without regard to any other provision of law governing contracting procedures or employment of personnel by the Federal Government—

(i) remove or arrange for the removal of the discharge, or mitigate or prevent the substantial threat of the discharge; and

(ii) remove and, if necessary, destroy a vessel discharging, or threatening to discharge, by whatever means are available.

(3) Actions in accordance with National Contingency Plan

(A) Each Federal agency, State, owner or operator, or other person participating in efforts under this subsection shall act in accordance with the National Contingency Plan or as directed by the President.

(B) An owner or operator participating in efforts under this subsection shall act in accordance with the National Contingency Plan and the applicable response plan required under subsection (j) of this section, or as directed by the President, except that the owner or operator may deviate from the applicable response plan if the President or the Federal On-Scene Coordinator determines that deviation from the response plan would provide for a more expeditious or effective response to the spill or mitigation of its environmental effects.

(4) Exemption from liability

(A) A person is not liable for removal costs or damages which result from actions taken or omitted to be taken in the course of rendering care, assistance, or advice consistent with the National Contingency Plan or as otherwise directed by the President relating to a discharge or a substantial threat of a discharge of oil or a hazardous substance.

(B) Subparagraph (A) does not apply—

(i) to a responsible party;

(ii) to a response under the Comprehensive Environmental Response, Compensation, and Liability Act of 1980 (42 U.S.C. 9601 et seq.);

(iii) with respect to personal injury or wrongful death; or

(iv) if the person is grossly negligent or engages in willful misconduct.

(C) A responsible party is liable for any removal costs and damages that another person is relieved of under subparagraph (A).

(5) Obligation and liability of owner or operator not affected

Nothing in this subsection affects—

(A) the obligation of an owner or operator to respond immediately to a discharge, or the threat of a discharge, of oil; or

(B) the liability of a responsible party under the Oil Pollution Act of 1990 [33 U.S.C.A. § 2701 et seq.].

(6) "Responsible party" defined

For purposes of this subsection, the term "responsible party" has the meaning given that term under section 1001 of the Oil Pollution Act of 1990 [33 U.S.C.A. § 2701].

(d) National Contingency Plan

(1) Preparation by President

The President shall prepare and publish a National Contingency Plan for removal of oil and hazardous substances pursuant to this section.

(2) Contents

The National Contingency Plan shall provide for efficient, coordinated, and effective action to minimize damage from oil and hazardous substance discharges, including containment, dispersal, and removal of oil and hazardous substances, and shall include, but not be limited to, the following:

(A) Assignment of duties and responsibilities among Federal departments and agencies in coordination with State and local agencies and port authorities including, but not limited to, water pollution control and conservation and trusteeship of natural resources (including conservation of fish and wildlife).

(B) Identification, procurement, maintenance, and storage of equipment and supplies.

(C) Establishment or designation of Coast Guard strike teams, consisting of—

(i) personnel who shall be trained, prepared, and available to provide necessary services to carry out the National Contingency Plan;

(ii) adequate oil and hazardous substance pollution control equipment and material; and

(iii) a detailed oil and hazardous substance pollution and prevention plan, including measures to protect fisheries and wildlife.

(D) A system of surveillance and notice designed to safeguard against as well as ensure earliest possible notice of discharges of oil and hazardous substances and imminent threats of such discharges to the appropriate State and Federal agencies.

(E) Establishment of a national center to provide coordination and direction for operations in carrying out the Plan.

(F) Procedures and techniques to be employed in identifying, containing, dispersing, and removing oil and hazardous substances.

(G) A schedule, prepared in cooperation with the States, identifying—

(i) dispersants, other chemicals, and other spill mitigating devices and substances, if any, that may be used in carrying out the Plan,

(ii) the waters in which such dispersants, other chemicals, and other spill mitigating devices and substances may be used, and

(iii) the quantities of such dispersant, other chemicals, or other spill mitigating device or substance which can be used safely in such waters,

which schedule shall provide in the case of any dispersant, chemical, spill mitigating device or substance, or waters not specifically identified in such schedule that the President, or his delegate, may, on a case-by-case basis, identify the dispersants, other chemicals, and other spill mitigating devices and substances which may be used, the waters in which they may be used, and the quantities which can be used safely in such waters.

(H) A system whereby the State or States affected by a discharge of oil or hazardous substance may act where necessary to remove such discharge and such State or States may be reimbursed in accordance with the Oil Pollution Act of 1990 [33 U.S.C.A. § 2701 et seq.], in the case of any discharge of oil from a vessel or facility, for the reasonable costs incurred for that removal, from the Oil Spill Liability Trust Fund.

(I) Establishment of criteria and procedures to ensure immediate and effective Federal identification of, and response to, a discharge, or the threat of a discharge, that results in a substantial threat to the public health or welfare of the United States, as required under subsection (c)(2) of this section.

(J) Establishment of procedures and standards for removing a worst case discharge of oil, and for mitigating or preventing a substantial threat of such a discharge.

(K) Designation of the Federal official who shall be the Federal On-Scene Coordinator for each area for which an Area Contingency Plan is required to be prepared under subsection (j) of this section.

(L) Establishment of procedures for the coordination of activities of—

(i) Coast Guard strike teams established under subparagraph (C);

(ii) Federal On-Scene Coordinators designated under subparagraph (K);

(iii) District Response Groups established under subsection (j) of this section; and

(iv) Area Committees established under subsection (j) of this section.

(M) A fish and wildlife response plan, developed in consultation with the United States Fish and Wildlife Service, the National Oceanic and Atmospheric Administration, and other interested parties (including State fish and wildlife conservation officials), for the immediate and effective protection, rescue, and rehabilitation of, and the minimization of risk of damage to, fish and wildlife resources and their habitat that are harmed or that may be jeopardized by a discharge.

(3) Revisions and amendments

The President may, from time to time, as the President deems advisable, revise or otherwise amend the National Contingency Plan.

(4) Actions in accordance with National Contingency Plan

After publication of the National Contingency Plan, the removal of oil and hazardous substances and actions to minimize damage from oil and hazardous substance discharges shall, to the greatest extent possible, be in accordance with the National Contingency Plan.

(e) Civil enforcement

(1) Orders protecting public health

In addition to any action taken by a State or local government, when the President determines that there may be an imminent and substantial threat to the public health or welfare of the United States, including fish, shellfish, and wildlife, public and private property, shorelines, beaches, habitat, and other living and nonliving natural resources under the jurisdiction or control of the United States, because of an actual or threatened discharge of oil or a hazardous substance from a vessel or facility in violation of subsection (b) of this section, the President may—

(A) require the Attorney General to secure any relief from any person, including the owner or operator of the vessel or facility, as may be necessary to abate such endangerment; or

(B) after notice to the affected State, take any other action under this section, including issuing administrative orders, that may be necessary to protect the public health and welfare.

(2) Jurisdiction of district courts

The district courts of the United States shall have jurisdiction to grant any relief under this subsection that the public interest and the equities of the case may require.

(f) Liability for actual costs of removal

(1) Except where an owner or operator can prove that a discharge was caused solely by (A) an act of God, (B) an act of war, (C) negligence on the part of the United States Government, or (D) an act or omission of a third party without regard to whether any such act or omission was or was not negligent, or any combination of the foregoing clauses, such owner or operator of any vessel from which oil or a hazardous substance is discharged in violation of subsection (b)(3) of this section shall, notwithstanding any other provision of law, be liable to the United States Government for the actual costs incurred under subsection (c) of this section for the removal of such oil or substance by the United States Government in an amount not to exceed, in the case of an inland oil barge $125 per gross ton of such barge, or $125,000, whichever is greater, and in the case of any other vessel, $150 per gross ton of such vessel (or, for a vessel carrying oil or hazardous substances as cargo, $250,000), whichever is greater, except that where the United States can show that such discharge was the result of willful negligence or willful misconduct within the privity and knowledge of the owner, such owner or operator shall be liable to the United States Government for the full amount of such costs. Such costs shall constitute a maritime lien on such vessel which may be recovered in an action in rem in the district court of the United States for any district within which any vessel may be found. The United States may also bring an action against the owner or operator of such vessel in any court of competent jurisdiction to recover such costs.

(2) Except where an owner or operator of an onshore facility can prove that a discharge was caused solely by (A) an act of God, (B) an act of war, (C) negligence on the part of the United States Government, or (D) an act or omission of a third party without regard to whether any such act or omission was or was not negligent, or any combination of the foregoing clauses, such owner or operator of any such facility from which oil or a hazardous substance is discharged in violation of subsection (b)(3) of this section shall be liable to the United States Government for the actual costs incurred under subsection (c) of this section for the removal of such oil or substance by the United States Government in an amount not to exceed $50,000,000, except that where the United States can show that such discharge was the result of willful negligence or willful misconduct within the privity and knowledge of the owner, such owner or operator shall be liable to the United States Government for the full amount of such costs. The United States may bring an action against the owner or operator of such facility in any court of competent jurisdiction to recover such costs. The Administrator is authorized, by regulation, after consultation with the Secretary of Commerce and the Small Business Administration, to establish reasonable and equitable classifications of those onshore facilities having a total fixed storage capacity of 1,000 barrels or less which he determines because of size, type, and location do not present a substantial risk of the discharge of oil or a hazardous substance in violation of subsection (b)(3) of this section, and apply with respect to such classifications differing limits of liability which may be less than the amount contained in this paragraph.

(3) Except where an owner or operator of an offshore facility can prove that a discharge was caused solely by (A) an act of God, (B) an act of war, (C) negligence on the part of the United States Government, or (D) an act or omission of a third party without regard to whether any such act or omission was or was not negligent, or any combination of the foregoing clauses, such owner or operator of any such facility from which oil or a hazardous substance is discharged in violation of subsection (b)(3) of this section shall, notwithstanding any other provision of law, be liable to the United States Government for the actual costs incurred under subsection (c) of this section for the removal of such oil or substance by the United States Government in an amount not to exceed $50,000,000, except that where the United States can show that such discharge was the result of willful negligence or willful misconduct within the privity and knowledge of the owner, such owner or operator shall be liable to the United States Government for the full amount of such costs. The United States may bring an action against the owner or operator of such a facility in any court of competent jurisdiction to recover such costs.

(4) The costs of removal of oil or a hazardous substance for which the owner or operator of a vessel or onshore or offshore facility is liable under subsection (f) of this section shall include any costs or expenses incurred by the Federal Government or any State government in the restoration or replacement of natural resources damaged or destroyed as a result of a discharge of oil or a hazardous substance in violation of subsection (b) of this section.

(5) The President, or the authorized representative of any State, shall act on behalf of the public as trustee of the natural resources to recover for the costs of replacing or restoring such resources. Sums recovered shall be used to restore, rehabilitate, or acquire the equivalent of such natural resources by the appropriate agencies of the Federal Government, or the State government.

(g) Third party liability

Where the owner or operator of a vessel (other than an inland oil barge) carrying oil or hazardous substances as cargo or an onshore or offshore facility which handles or stores oil or hazardous substances in bulk, from which oil or a hazardous substance is discharged in violation of subsection (b) of this section, alleges that such discharge was caused solely by an act or omission of a third party, such owner or operator shall pay to the United States Government the actual costs incurred under subsection (c) of this section for removal of such oil or substance and shall be entitled by subrogation to all rights of the United States Government to recover such costs from such third party under this subsection. In any case where an owner or operator of a vessel, of an onshore facility, or of an offshore facility, from which oil or a hazardous substance is discharged in violation of subsection (b)(3) of this section, proves that such discharge of oil or hazardous substance was caused solely by an act or omission of a third party, or was caused solely by such an act or omission in combination with an act of God, an act of war, or negligence on the part of the United States Government, such third party shall, notwithstanding any other provision of law, be liable to the United States Government for the actual costs incurred under subsection (c) of this section for removal of such oil or substance by the United States Government, except where such third party can prove that such discharge was caused solely by (A) an act of God, (B) an act of war, (C) negligence on the part of the United States Government, or (D) an act or omission of another party without regard to whether such act or omission was or was not negligent, or any combination of the foregoing clauses. If such third party was the owner or operator of a vessel which caused the discharge of oil or a hazardous substance in violation of subsection (b)(3) of this section, the liability of such third party under this subsection shall not exceed, in the case of an inland oil barge $125 per gross ton of such barge, or $125,000, whichever is greater, and in the case of any other vessel, $150 per gross ton of such vessel (or, for a vessel carrying oil or hazardous substances as cargo, $250,000), whichever is greater. In any other case the liability of such third party shall not exceed the limitation which would have been applicable to the owner or operator of the vessel or the onshore or offshore facility from which the discharge actually occurred if such owner or operator were liable. If the United States can show that the discharge of oil or a hazardous substance in violation of subsection (b)(3) of this section was the result of willful negligence or willful misconduct within the privity and knowledge of such third party, such third party shall be liable to the United States Government for the full amount of such removal costs. The United States may bring an action against the third party in any court of competent jurisdiction to recover such removal costs.

(h) Rights against third parties who caused or contributed to discharge

The liabilities established by this section shall in no way affect any rights which (1) the owner or operator of a vessel or of an onshore facility or an offshore facility may have against any third party whose acts may in any way have caused or contributed to such discharge, or (2) The United States Government may have against any third party whose actions may in any way have caused or contributed to the discharge of oil or hazardous substance.

(i) Recovery of removal costs

In any case where an owner or operator of a vessel or an onshore facility or an offshore facility from which oil or a hazardous substance is discharged in violation of subsection (b)(3) of this section acts to remove such oil or substance in accordance with regulations promulgated pursuant to this section, such owner or operator shall be entitled to recover the reasonable costs incurred in such removal upon establishing, in a suit which may be brought against the United States Government in the United States Court of Federal Claims, that such discharge was caused solely by (A) an act of God, (B) an act of war, (C) negligence on the part of the United States Government, or (D) an act or omission of a third party without regard to whether such act or omission was or was not negligent, or of any combination of the foregoing causes.

(j) National Response System

(1) In general

Consistent with the National Contingency Plan required by subsection (c)(2) of this section, as soon as practicable after October 18, 1972, and from time to time thereafter, the President shall issue regulations consistent with maritime safety and with marine and navigation laws (A) establishing methods and procedures for removal of discharged oil and hazardous substances, (B) establishing criteria for the development and implementation of local and regional oil and hazardous substance removal contingency plans, (C) establishing procedures, methods, and equipment and other requirements for equipment to prevent discharges of oil and hazardous substances from vessels and from onshore facilities and offshore facilities, and to contain such discharges, and (D) governing the inspection of vessels carrying cargoes of oil and hazardous substances and the inspection of such cargoes in order to reduce the likelihood of discharges of oil from vessels in violation of this section.

(2) National Response Unit

The Secretary of the department in which the Coast Guard is operating shall establish a National Response Unit at Elizabeth City, North Carolina. The Secretary, acting through the National Response Unit—

(A) shall compile and maintain a comprehensive computer list of spill removal resources, personnel, and equipment that is available worldwide and within the areas designated by the President pursuant to paragraph (4), and of information regarding previous spills, including data from universities, research institutions, State governments, and other nations, as appropriate, which shall be disseminated as appropriate to response groups and area committees, and which shall be available to Federal and State agencies and the public;

(B) shall provide technical assistance, equipment, and other resources requested by a Federal On-Scene Coordinator;

(C) shall coordinate use of private and public personnel and equipment to remove a worst case discharge, and to mitigate or prevent a substantial threat of such a discharge, from a vessel, offshore facility, or onshore facility operating in or near an area designated by the President pursuant to paragraph (4);

(D) may provide technical assistance in the preparation of Area Contingency Plans required under paragraph (4);

(E) shall administer Coast Guard strike teams established under the National Contingency Plan;

(F) shall maintain on file all Area Contingency Plans approved by the President under this subsection; and

(G) shall review each of those plans that affects its responsibilities under this subsection.

(3) Coast Guard District Response Groups

(A) The Secretary of the department in which the Coast Guard is operating shall establish in each Coast Guard district a Coast Guard District Response Group.

(B) Each Coast Guard District Response Group shall consist of—

(i) the Coast Guard personnel and equipment, including firefighting equipment, of each port within the district;

(ii) additional prepositioned equipment; and

(iii) a district response advisory staff.

(C) Coast Guard district response groups—

(i) shall provide technical assistance, equipment, and other resources when required by a Federal On-Scene Coordinator;

(ii) shall maintain all Coast Guard response equipment within its district;

(iii) may provide technical assistance in the preparation of Area Contingency Plans required under paragraph (4); and

(iv) shall review each of those plans that affect its area of geographic responsibility.

(4) Area Committees and Area Contingency Plans

(A) There is established for each area designated by the President an Area Committee comprised of members appointed by the President from qualified—

(i) personnel of Federal, State, and local agencies; and

(ii) members of federally recognized Indian tribes, where applicable.

(B) Each Area Committee, under the direction of the Federal On-Scene Coordinator for its area, shall—

(i) prepare for its area the Area Contingency Plan required under subparagraph (C);

(ii) work with State, local, and tribal officials to enhance the contingency planning of those officials and to assure preplanning of joint response efforts, including appropriate procedures for mechanical recovery, dispersal, shoreline cleanup, protection of sensitive environmental areas, and protection, rescue, and rehabilitation of fisheries and wildlife, including advance planning with respect to the closing and reopening of fishing areas following a discharge; and

(iii) work with State, local, and tribal officials to expedite decisions for the use of dispersants and other mitigating substances and devices.

(C) Each Area Committee shall prepare and submit to the President for approval an Area Contingency Plan for its area. The Area Contingency Plan shall—

(i) when implemented in conjunction with the National Contingency Plan, be adequate to remove a worst case discharge, and to mitigate or prevent a substantial threat of such a discharge, from a vessel, offshore facility, or onshore facility operating in or near the area;

(ii) describe the area covered by the plan, including the areas of special economic or environmental importance that might be damaged by a discharge;

(iii) describe in detail the responsibilities of an owner or operator and of Federal, State, and local agencies in removing a discharge, and in mitigating or preventing a substantial threat of a discharge;

(iv) list the equipment (including firefighting equipment), dispersants or other mitigating substances and devices, and personnel available to an owner or operator and Federal, State, and local agencies, and tribal governments to ensure an effective and immediate removal of a discharge, and to ensure mitigation or prevention of a substantial threat of a discharge;

(v) compile a list of local scientists, both inside and outside Federal Government service, with expertise in the environmental effects of spills of the types of oil typically transported in the area, who may be contacted to provide information or, where appropriate, participate in meetings of the scientific support team convened in response to a spill, and describe the procedures to be followed for obtaining an expedited decision regarding the use of dispersants;

(vi) describe in detail how the plan is integrated into other Area Contingency Plans and vessel, offshore facility, and onshore facility response plans approved under this subsection, and into operating procedures of the National Response Unit;

(vii) include a framework for advance planning and decisionmaking with respect to the closing and reopening of fishing areas following a discharge, including protocols and standards for closing and reopening of fishing areas;

(viii) include any other information the President requires; and

(ix) be updated periodically by the Area Committee.

(D) The President shall—

(i) review and approve Area Contingency Plans under this paragraph; and

(ii) periodically review Area Contingency Plans so approved.

(5) Tank vessel, nontank vessel, and facility response plans

(A) (i) The President shall issue regulations which require an owner or operator of a tank vessel or facility described in subparagraph (C) to prepare and submit to the President a plan for responding, to the maximum extent practicable, to a worst case discharge, and to a substantial threat of such a discharge, of oil or a hazardous substance.

(ii) The President shall also issue regulations which require an owner or operator of a nontank vessel to prepare and submit to the President a plan for responding, to the maximum extent practicable, to a worst case discharge, and to a substantial threat of such a discharge, of oil.

(B) The Secretary of the Department in which the Coast Guard is operating may issue regulations which require an owner or operator of a tank vessel, a nontank vessel, or a facility described in subparagraph (C) that transfers noxious liquid substances in bulk to or from a vessel to prepare and submit to the Secretary a plan for responding, to the maximum extent practicable, to a worst case discharge, and to a substantial threat of such a discharge, of a noxious liquid substance that is not designated as a hazardous substance or regulated as oil in any other law or regulation. For purposes of this paragraph, the term "noxious liquid substance" has the same meaning when that term is used in the MARPOL Protocol described in section 1901(a)(3) of this title.

(C) The tank vessels, nontank vessels, and facilities referred to in subparagraphs (A) and (B) are the following:

(i) A tank vessel, as defined under section 2101 of Title 46.

(ii) A nontank vessel.

(iii) An offshore facility.

(iv) An onshore facility that, because of its location, could reasonably be expected to cause substantial harm to the environment by discharging into or on the navigable waters, adjoining shorelines, or the exclusive economic zone.

(D) A response plan required under this paragraph shall—

(i) be consistent with the requirements of the National Contingency Plan and Area Contingency Plans;

(ii) identify the qualified individual having full authority to implement removal actions, and require immediate communications between that individual and the appropriate Federal official and the persons providing personnel and equipment pursuant to clause (iii);

(iii) identify, and ensure by contract or other means approved by the President the availability of, private personnel and equipment necessary to remove to the maximum extent practicable a worst case discharge (including a discharge resulting from fire or explosion), and to mitigate or prevent a substantial threat of such a discharge;

(iv) describe the training, equipment testing, periodic unannounced drills, and response actions of persons on the vessel or at the facility, to be carried out under the plan to ensure the safety of the vessel or facility and to mitigate or prevent the discharge, or the substantial threat of a discharge;

(v) be updated periodically; and

(vi) be resubmitted for approval of each significant change.

(E) With respect to any response plan submitted under this paragraph for an onshore facility that, because of its location, could reasonably be expected to cause significant and substantial harm to the environment by discharging into or on the navigable waters or adjoining shorelines or the exclusive economic zone, and with respect to each response plan submitted under this paragraph for a tank vessel, nontank vessel, or offshore facility, the President shall—

(i) promptly review such response plan;

(ii) require amendments to any plan that does not meet the requirements of this paragraph;

(iii) approve any plan that meets the requirements of this paragraph;

(iv) review each plan periodically thereafter; and

(v) in the case of a plan for a nontank vessel, consider any applicable State-mandated response plan in effect on August 9, 2004 and ensure consistency to the extent practicable.

(F) A tank vessel, nontank vessel, offshore facility, or onshore facility required to prepare a response plan under this subsection may not handle, store, or transport oil unless—

(i) in the case of a tank vessel, nontank vessel, offshore facility, or onshore facility for which a response plan is reviewed by the President under subparagraph (E), the plan has been approved by the President; and

(ii) the vessel or facility is operating in compliance with the plan.

(G) Notwithstanding subparagraph (E), the President may authorize a tank vessel, nontank vessel, offshore facility, or onshore facility to operate without a response plan approved under this paragraph, until not later than 2 years after the date of the submission to the President of a plan for the tank vessel, nontank vessel, or facility, if the owner or operator certifies that the owner or operator has ensured by contract or other means approved by the President the availability of private personnel and equipment necessary to respond, to the maximum extent practicable, to a worst case discharge or a substantial threat of such a discharge.

(H) The owner or operator of a tank vessel, nontank vessel, offshore facility, or onshore facility may not claim as a defense to liability under title I of the Oil Pollution Act of 1990 [33 U.S.C.A. § 2701 et seq.] that the owner or operator was acting in accordance with an approved response plan.

(I) The Secretary shall maintain, in the Vessel Identification System established under chapter 125 of Title 46, the dates of approval and review of a response plan under this paragraph for each tank vessel and nontank vessel that is a vessel of the United States.

(6) Equipment requirements and inspection

The President may require—

(A) periodic inspection of containment booms, skimmers, vessels, and other major equipment used to remove discharges; and

(B) vessels operating on navigable waters and carrying oil or a hazardous substance in bulk as cargo, and nontank vessels carrying oil of any kind as fuel for main propulsion, to carry appropriate removal equipment that employs the best technology economically feasible and that is compatible with the safe operation of the vessel.

(7) Area drills

The President shall periodically conduct drills of removal capability, without prior notice, in areas for which Area Contingency Plans are required under this subsection and under relevant tank vessel, nontank vessel, and facility response plans. The drills may include participation by Federal, State, and local agencies, the owners and operators of vessels and facilities in the area, and private industry. The President may publish annual reports on these drills, including assessments of the effectiveness of the plans and a list of amendments made to improve plans.

(8) United States Government not liable

The United States Government is not liable for any damages arising from its actions or omissions relating to any response plan required by this section.

(k) Repealed. Pub. L. No. 101–380, Title I, § 2002(b)(2), 104 Stat. 507 (Aug. 18, 1990).

(*l*) Administration

The President is authorized to delegate the administration of this section to the heads of those Federal departments, agencies, and instrumentalities which he determines to be appropriate. Each such department, agency, and instrumentality, in order to avoid duplication of effort, shall, whenever appropriate, utilize the personnel, services, and facilities of other Federal departments, agencies, and instrumentalities.

(m) Administrative provisions

(1) For vessels

Anyone authorized by the President to enforce the provisions of this section with respect to any vessel may, except as to public vessels—

(A) board and inspect any vessel upon the navigable waters of the United States or the waters of the contiguous zone,

(B) with or without a warrant, arrest any person who in the presence or view of the authorized person violates the provisions of this section or any regulation issued thereunder, and

(C) execute any warrant or other process issued by an officer or court of competent jurisdiction.

(2) For facilities

(A) Recordkeeping

Whenever required to carry out the purposes of this section, the Administrator, the Secretary of Transportation, or the Secretary of the Department in which the Coast Guard is operating shall require the owner or operator of a facility to which this section applies to establish and maintain such records, make such reports, install, use, and maintain such monitoring equipment and methods, and provide such other information as the Administrator or Secretary, as the case may be, may require to carry out the objectives of this section.

(B) Entry and inspection

Whenever required to carry out the purposes of this section, the Administrator, the Secretary of Transportation, or the Secretary of the Department in which the Coast Guard is operating or an authorized representative of the Administrator or Secretary, upon presentation of appropriate credentials, may—

(i) enter and inspect any facility to which this section applies, including any facility at which any records are required to be maintained under subparagraph (A); and

(ii) at reasonable times, have access to and copy any records, take samples, and inspect any monitoring equipment or methods required under subparagraph (A).

(C) Arrests and execution of warrants

Anyone authorized by the Administrator or the Secretary of the department in which the Coast Guard is operating to enforce the provisions of this section with respect to any facility may—

(i) with or without a warrant, arrest any person who violates the provisions of this section or any regulation issued thereunder in the presence or view of the person so authorized; and

(ii) execute any warrant or process issued by an officer or court of competent jurisdiction.

(D) Public access

Any records, reports, or information obtained under this paragraph shall be subject to the same public access and disclosure requirements which are applicable to records, reports, and information obtained pursuant to section 1318 of this title.

(n) Jurisdiction

The several district courts of the United States are invested with jurisdiction for any actions, other than actions pursuant to subsection (i)(1) of this section, arising under this section. In the case of Guam and the Trust Territory of the Pacific Islands, such actions may be brought in the district court of Guam, and in the case of the Virgin Islands such actions may be brought in the district court of the Virgin Islands. In the case of American Samoa and the Trust Territory of the Pacific Islands, such actions may be brought in the District Court of the United States for the District of Hawaii and such court shall have jurisdiction of such actions. In the case of the Canal Zone, such actions may be brought in the United States District Court for the District of the Canal Zone.

(*o*) Obligation for damages unaffected; local authority not preempted; existing Federal authority not modified or affected

(1) Nothing in this section shall affect or modify in any way the obligations of any owner or operator of any vessel, or of any owner or operator of any onshore facility or offshore facility to any person or agency under any provision of law for damages to any publicly owned or privately owned property resulting from a discharge of any oil or hazardous substance or from the removal of any such oil or hazardous substance.

(2) Nothing in this section shall be construed as preempting any State or political subdivision thereof from imposing any requirement or liability with respect to the discharge of oil or hazardous substance into any waters within such State, or with respect to any removal activities related to such discharge.

(3) Nothing in this section shall be construed as affecting or modifying any other existing authority of any Federal department, agency, or instrumentality, relative to onshore or offshore facilities under this chapter or any other provision of law, or to affect any State or local law not in conflict with this section.

(p) Repealed. Pub. L. No. 101–380, Title II, § 2002(b)(4), 104 Stat. 507 (Aug. 18, 1990).

(q) Establishment of maximum limit of liability with respect to onshore or offshore facilities

The President is authorized to establish, with respect to any class or category of onshore or offshore facilities, a maximum limit of liability under subsections (f)(2) and (3) of this section of less than $50,000,000, but not less than $8,000,000.

(r) Liability limitations not to limit liability under other legislation

Nothing in this section shall be construed to impose, or authorize the imposition of, any limitation on liability under the Outer Continental Shelf Lands Act [43 U.S.C.A. § 1331 et seq.] or the Deepwater Port Act of 1974 [33 U.S.C.A. § 1501 et seq.].

(s) Oil Spill Liability Trust Fund

The Oil Spill Liability Trust Fund established under section 9509 of Title 26 shall be available to carry out subsections (b), (c), (d), (j), and (*l*) of this section as those subsections apply to discharges, and substantial threats of discharges, of oil. Any amounts received by the United States under this section shall be deposited in the Oil Spill Liability Trust Fund except as provided in subsection (t).

(t) Gulf Coast restoration and recovery

(1) State allocation and expenditures

(A) In general

Of the total amounts made available in any fiscal year from the Trust Fund, 35 percent shall be available, in accordance with the requirements of this section, to the Gulf Coast States in equal shares for expenditure for ecological and economic restoration of the Gulf Coast region in accordance with this subsection.

(B) Use of funds

(i) Eligible activities in the Gulf Coast region

Subject to clause (iii), amounts provided to the Gulf Coast States under this subsection may only be used to carry out 1 or more of the following activities in the Gulf Coast region:

(I) Restoration and protection of the natural resources, ecosystems, fisheries, marine and wildlife habitats, beaches, and coastal wetlands of the Gulf Coast region.

(II) Mitigation of damage to fish, wildlife, and natural resources.

(III) Implementation of a federally approved marine, coastal, or comprehensive conservation management plan, including fisheries monitoring.

(IV) Workforce development and job creation.

(V) Improvements to or on State parks located in coastal areas affected by the Deepwater Horizon oil spill.

(VI) Infrastructure projects benefitting the economy or ecological resources, including port infrastructure.

(VII) Coastal flood protection and related infrastructure.

(VIII) Planning assistance.

(IX) Administrative costs of complying with this subsection.

(ii) Activities to promote tourism and seafood in the Gulf Coast region

Amounts provided to the Gulf Coast States under this subsection may be used to carry out 1 or more of the following activities:

(I) Promotion of tourism in the Gulf Coast Region, including recreational fishing.

(II) Promotion of the consumption of seafood harvested from the Gulf Coast Region.

(iii) Limitation

(I) In general

Of the amounts received by a Gulf Coast State under this subsection, not more than 3 percent may be used for administrative costs eligible under clause (i)(IX).

(II) Claims for compensation

Activities funded under this subsection may not be included in any claim for compensation paid out by the Oil Spill Liability Trust Fund after July 6, 2012.

(C) Coastal political subdivisions

(i) Distribution

In the case of a State where the coastal zone includes the entire State—

(I) 75 percent of funding shall be provided directly to the 8 disproportionately affected counties impacted by the Deepwater Horizon oil spill; and

(II) 25 percent shall be provided directly to nondisproportionately impacted counties within the State.

(ii) Nondisproportionately impacted counties

The total amounts made available to coastal political subdivisions in the State of Florida under clause (i)(II) shall be distributed according to the following weighted formula:

(I) 34 percent based on the weighted average of the population of the county.

(II) 33 percent based on the weighted average of the county per capita sales tax collections estimated for fiscal year 2012.

(III) 33 percent based on the inverse proportion of the weighted average distance from the Deepwater Horizon oil rig to each of the nearest and farthest points of the shoreline.

(D) Louisiana

(i) In general

Of the total amounts made available to the State of Louisiana under this paragraph:

(I) 70 percent shall be provided directly to the State in accordance with this subsection.

(II) 30 percent shall be provided directly to parishes in the coastal zone (as defined in section 304 of the Coastal Zone Management Act of 1972 (16 U.S.C. 1453)) of the State of Louisiana according to the following weighted formula:

(aa) 40 percent based on the weighted average of miles of the parish shoreline oiled.

(bb) 40 percent based on the weighted average of the population of the parish.

(cc) 20 percent based on the weighted average of the land mass of the parish.

(ii) Conditions

(I) Land use plan

As a condition of receiving amounts allocated under this paragraph, the chief executive of the eligible parish shall certify to the Governor of the State that the parish has completed a comprehensive land use plan.

(II) Other conditions

A coastal political subdivision receiving funding under this paragraph shall meet all of the conditions in subparagraph (E).

(E) Conditions

As a condition of receiving amounts from the Trust Fund, a Gulf Coast State, including the entities described in subparagraph (F), or a coastal political subdivision shall—

(i) agree to meet such conditions, including audit requirements, as the Secretary of the Treasury determines necessary to ensure that amounts disbursed from the Trust Fund will be used in accordance with this subsection;

(ii) certify in such form and in such manner as the Secretary of the Treasury determines necessary that the project or program for which the Gulf Coast State or coastal political subdivision is requesting amounts—

(I) is designed to restore and protect the natural resources, ecosystems, fisheries, marine and wildlife habitats, beaches, coastal wetlands, or economy of the Gulf Coast;

(II) carries out 1 or more of the activities described in clauses (i) and (ii) of subparagraph (B);

(III) was selected based on meaningful input from the public, including broad-based participation from individuals, businesses, and nonprofit organizations; and

(IV) in the case of a natural resource protection or restoration project, is based on the best available science;

(iii) certify that the project or program and the awarding of a contract for the expenditure of amounts received under this paragraph are consistent with the standard procurement rules and regulations governing a comparable project or program in that State, including all applicable competitive bidding and audit requirements; and

(iv) develop and submit a multiyear implementation plan for the use of such amounts, which may include milestones, projected completion of each activity, and a mechanism to evaluate the success of each activity in helping to restore and protect the Gulf Coast region impacted by the Deepwater Horizon oil spill.

(F) Approval by State entity, task force, or agency

The following Gulf Coast State entities, task forces, or agencies shall carry out the duties of a Gulf Coast State pursuant to this paragraph:

(i) Alabama

(I) In general

In the State of Alabama, the Alabama Gulf Coast Recovery Council, which shall be comprised of only the following:

(aa) The Governor of Alabama, who shall also serve as Chairperson and preside over the meetings of the Alabama Gulf Coast Recovery Council.

(bb) The Director of the Alabama State Port Authority, who shall also serve as Vice Chairperson and preside over the meetings of the Alabama Gulf Coast Recovery Council in the absence of the Chairperson.

(cc) The Chairman of the Baldwin County Commission.

(dd) The President of the Mobile County Commission.

(ee) The Mayor of the city of Bayou La Batre.

(ff) The Mayor of the town of Dauphin Island.

(gg) The Mayor of the city of Fairhope.

(hh) The Mayor of the city of Gulf Shores.

(ii) The Mayor of the city of Mobile.

(jj) The Mayor of the city of Orange Beach.

(II) Vote

Each member of the Alabama Gulf Coast Recovery Council shall be entitled to 1 vote.

(III) Majority vote

All decisions of the Alabama Gulf Coast Recovery Council shall be made by majority vote.

(IV) Limitation on administrative expenses

Administrative duties for the Alabama Gulf Coast Recovery Council may only be performed by public officials and employees that are subject to the ethics laws of the State of Alabama.

(ii) Louisiana

In the State of Louisiana, the Coastal Protection and Restoration Authority of Louisiana.

(iii) Mississippi

In the State of Mississippi, the Mississippi Department of Environmental Quality.

(iv) Texas

In the State of Texas, the Office of the Governor or an appointee of the Office of the Governor.

(G) Compliance with eligible activities

If the Secretary of the Treasury determines that an expenditure by a Gulf Coast State or coastal political subdivision of amounts made available under this subsection does not meet one of the activities described in clauses (i) and (ii) of subparagraph (B), the Secretary shall make no additional amounts from the Trust Fund available to that Gulf Coast State or coastal political subdivision until such time as an amount equal to the amount expended for the unauthorized use—

(i) has been deposited by the Gulf Coast State or coastal political subdivision in the Trust Fund; or

(ii) has been authorized by the Secretary of the Treasury for expenditure by the Gulf Coast State or coastal political subdivision for a project or program that meets the requirements of this subsection.

(H) Compliance with conditions

If the Secretary of the Treasury determines that a Gulf Coast State or coastal political subdivision does not meet the requirements of this paragraph, including the conditions of subparagraph (E), where applicable, the Secretary of the Treasury shall make no amounts from the Trust Fund available to that Gulf Coast State or coastal political subdivision until all conditions of this paragraph are met.

(I) Public input

In meeting any condition of this paragraph, a Gulf Coast State may use an appropriate procedure for public consultation in that Gulf Coast State, including consulting with one or more established task forces or other entities, to develop recommendations for proposed projects and programs that would restore and protect the natural resources, ecosystems, fisheries, marine and wildlife habitats, beaches, coastal wetlands, and economy of the Gulf Coast.

(J) Previously approved projects and programs

A Gulf Coast State or coastal political subdivision shall be considered to have met the conditions of subparagraph (E) for a specific project or program if, before July 6, 2012—

(i) the Gulf Coast State or coastal political subdivision has established conditions for carrying out projects and programs that are substantively the same as the conditions described in subparagraph (E); and

(ii) the applicable project or program carries out 1 or more of the activities described in clauses (i) and (ii) of subparagraph (B).

(K) Local preference

In awarding contracts to carry out a project or program under this paragraph, a Gulf Coast State or coastal political subdivision may give a preference to individuals and companies that reside in, are headquartered in, or are principally engaged in business in the State of project execution.

(L) Unused funds

Funds allocated to a State or coastal political subdivision under this paragraph shall remain in the Trust Fund until such time as the State or coastal political subdivision develops and submits a plan identifying uses for those funds in accordance with subparagraph (E)(iv).

(M) Judicial review

If the Secretary of the Treasury determines that a Gulf Coast State or coastal political subdivision does not meet the requirements of this paragraph, including the conditions of subparagraph (E), the Gulf Coast State or coastal political subdivision may obtain expedited judicial review within 90 days after that decision in a district court of the United States, of appropriate jurisdiction and venue, that is located within the State seeking the review.

(N) Cost-sharing

(i) In general

A Gulf Coast State or coastal political subdivision may use, in whole or in part, amounts made available under this paragraph to that Gulf Coast State or coastal political subdivision to satisfy the non-Federal share of the cost of any project or program authorized by Federal law that is an eligible activity described in clauses (i) and (ii) of subparagraph (B).

(ii) Effect on other funds

The use of funds made available from the Trust Fund to satisfy the non-Federal share of the cost of a project or program that meets the requirements of clause (i) shall not affect the priority in which other Federal funds are allocated or awarded.

(2) Council establishment and allocation

(A) In general

Of the total amount made available in any fiscal year from the Trust Fund, 30 percent shall be disbursed to the Council to carry out the Comprehensive Plan.

(B) Council expenditures

(i) In general

In accordance with this paragraph, the Council shall expend funds made available from the Trust Fund to undertake projects and programs, using the best available science, that would restore and protect the natural resources, ecosystems, fisheries, marine and wildlife habitats, beaches, coastal wetlands, and economy of the Gulf Coast.

(ii) Allocation and expenditure procedures

The Secretary of the Treasury shall develop such conditions, including audit requirements, as the Secretary of the Treasury determines necessary to ensure that amounts disbursed from the Trust Fund to the Council to implement the Comprehensive Plan will be used in accordance with this paragraph.

(iii) Administrative expenses

Of the amounts received by the Council under this paragraph, not more than 3 percent may be used for administrative expenses, including staff.

(C) Gulf Coast Ecosystem Restoration Council

(i) Establishment

There is established as an independent entity in the Federal Government a council to be known as the "Gulf Coast Ecosystem Restoration Council".

(ii) Membership

The Council shall consist of the following members, or in the case of a Federal agency, a designee at the level of the Assistant Secretary or the equivalent:

(I) The Secretary of the Interior.

(II) The Secretary of the Army.

(III) The Secretary of Commerce.

(IV) The Administrator of the Environmental Protection Agency.

(V) The Secretary of Agriculture.

(VI) The head of the department in which the Coast Guard is operating.

(VII) The Governor of the State of Alabama.

(VIII) The Governor of the State of Florida.

(IX) The Governor of the State of Louisiana.

(X) The Governor of the State of Mississippi.

(XI) The Governor of the State of Texas.

(iii) Alternate

A Governor appointed to the Council by the President may designate an alternate to represent the Governor on the Council and vote on behalf of the Governor.

(iv) Chairperson

From among the Federal agency members of the Council, the representatives of States on the Council shall select, and the President shall appoint, 1 Federal member to serve as Chairperson of the Council.

(v) Presidential appointment

All Council members shall be appointed by the President.

(vi) Council actions

(I) In general

The following actions by the Council shall require the affirmative vote of the Chairperson and a majority of the State members to be effective:

(aa) Approval of a Comprehensive Plan and future revisions to a Comprehensive Plan.

(bb) Approval of State plans pursuant to paragraph (3)(B)(iv).

(cc) Approval of reports to Congress pursuant to clause (vii)(VII).

(dd) Approval of transfers pursuant to subparagraph (E)(ii)(I).

(ee) Other significant actions determined by the Council.

(II) Quorum

A majority of State members shall be required to be present for the Council to take any significant action.

(III) Affirmative vote requirement considered met

For approval of State plans pursuant to paragraph (3)(B)(iv), the certification by a State member of the Council that the plan satisfies all requirements of clauses (i) and (ii) of paragraph (3)(B), when joined by an affirmative vote of the Federal Chairperson of the Council, shall be considered to satisfy the requirements for affirmative votes under subclause (I).

(IV) Public transparency

Appropriate actions of the Council, including significant actions and associated deliberations, shall be made available to the public via electronic means prior to any vote.

(vii) Duties of Council

The Council shall—

(I) develop the Comprehensive Plan and future revisions to the Comprehensive Plan;

(II) identify as soon as practicable the projects that—

(aa) have been authorized prior to July 6, 2012 but not yet commenced; and

(bb) if implemented quickly, would restore and protect the natural resources, ecosystems, fisheries, marine and wildlife habitats, beaches, barrier islands, dunes, and coastal wetlands of the Gulf Coast region;

(III) establish such other 1 or more advisory committees as may be necessary to assist the Council, including a scientific advisory committee and a committee to advise the Council on public policy issues;

(IV) collect and consider scientific and other research associated with restoration of the Gulf Coast ecosystem, including research, observation, and monitoring carried out pursuant to sections 1604 and 1605 of the Resources and Ecosystems Sustainability, Tourist Opportunities, and Revived Economies of the Gulf Coast States Act of 2012;

(V) develop standard terms to include in contracts for projects and programs awarded pursuant to the Comprehensive Plan that provide a preference to individuals and companies that reside in, are headquartered in, or are principally engaged in business in a Gulf Coast State;

(VI) prepare an integrated financial plan and recommendations for coordinated budget requests for the amounts proposed to be expended by the Federal agencies represented on the Council for projects and programs in the Gulf Coast States; and

(VII) submit to Congress an annual report that—

(aa) summarizes the policies, strategies, plans, and activities for addressing the restoration and protection of the Gulf Coast region;

(bb) describes the projects and programs being implemented to restore and protect the Gulf Coast region, including—

(AA) a list of each project and program;

(BB) an identification of the funding provided to projects and programs identified in subitem (AA);

(CC) an identification of each recipient for funding identified in subitem (BB); and

(DD) a description of the length of time and funding needed to complete the objectives of each project and program identified in subitem (AA);

(cc) makes such recommendations to Congress for modifications of existing laws as the Council determines necessary to implement the Comprehensive Plan;

(dd) reports on the progress on implementation of each project or program—

(AA) after 3 years of ongoing activity of the project or program, if applicable; and

(BB) on completion of the project or program;

(ee) includes the information required to be submitted under section 1605(c)(4) of the Resources and Ecosystems Sustainability, Tourist Opportunities, and Revived Economies of the Gulf Coast States Act of 2012; and

(ff) submits the reports required under item (dd) to—

(AA) the Committee on Science, Space, and Technology, the Committee on Natural Resources, the Committee on Transportation and Infrastructure, and the Committee on Appropriations of the House of Representatives; and

(BB) the Committee on Environment and Public Works, the Committee on Commerce, Science, and Transportation, the Committee on Energy and Natural Resources, and the Committee on Appropriations of the Senate.

(viii) Application of Federal Advisory Committee Act

The Council, or any other advisory committee established under this subparagraph, shall not be considered an advisory committee under the Federal Advisory Committee Act (5 U.S.C. App.).

(ix) Sunset

The authority for the Council, and any other advisory committee established under this subparagraph, shall terminate on the date all funds in the Trust Fund have been expended.

(D) Comprehensive plan

(i) Proposed plan

(I) In general

Not later than 180 days after July 6, 2012, the Chairperson, on behalf of the Council and after appropriate public input, review, and comment, shall publish a proposed plan to restore and protect the natural resources, ecosystems, fisheries, marine and wildlife habitats, beaches, and coastal wetlands of the Gulf Coast region.

(II) Inclusions

The proposed plan described in subclause (I) shall include and incorporate the findings and information prepared by the President's Gulf Coast Restoration Task Force.

(ii) Publication

(I) Initial plan

Not later than 1 year after July 6, 2012 and after notice and opportunity for public comment, the Chairperson, on behalf of the Council and after approval by the Council, shall publish in the Federal Register the initial Comprehensive Plan to restore and protect the natural resources, ecosystems, fisheries, marine and wildlife habitats, beaches, and coastal wetlands of the Gulf Coast region.

(II) Cooperation with Gulf Coast Restoration Task Force

The Council shall develop the initial Comprehensive Plan in close coordination with the President's Gulf Coast Restoration Task Force.

(III) Considerations

In developing the initial Comprehensive Plan and subsequent updates, the Council shall consider all relevant findings, reports, or research prepared or funded under section 1604 or 1605 of the Resources and Ecosystems Sustainability, Tourist Opportunities, and Revived Economies of the Gulf Coast States Act of 2012.

(IV) Contents

The initial Comprehensive Plan shall include—

(aa) such provisions as are necessary to fully incorporate in the Comprehensive Plan the strategy, projects, and programs recommended by the President's Gulf Coast Restoration Task Force;

(bb) a list of any project or program authorized prior to July 6, 2012 but not yet commenced, the completion of which would further the purposes and goals of this subsection and of the Resources and Ecosystems Sustainability, Tourist Opportunities, and Revived Economies of the Gulf Coast States Act of 2012;

(cc) a description of the manner in which amounts from the Trust Fund projected to be made available to the Council for the succeeding 10 years will be allocated; and

(dd) subject to available funding in accordance with clause (iii), a prioritized list of specific projects and programs to be funded and carried out during the 3-year period immediately following the date of publication of the initial Comprehensive Plan, including a table that illustrates the distribution of projects and programs by the Gulf Coast State.

(V) Plan updates

The Council shall update—

(aa) the Comprehensive Plan every 5 years in a manner comparable to the manner established in this subparagraph for each 5-year period for which amounts are expected to be made available to the Gulf Coast States from the Trust Fund; and

(bb) the 3-year list of projects and programs described in subclause (IV)(dd) annually.

(iii) Restoration priorities

Except for projects and programs described in clause (ii)(IV)(bb), in selecting projects and programs to include on the 3-year list described in clause (ii)(IV)(dd), based on the best available science, the Council shall give highest priority to projects that address 1 or more of the following criteria:

(I) Projects that are projected to make the greatest contribution to restoring and protecting the natural resources, ecosystems, fisheries, marine and wildlife habitats, beaches, and coastal wetlands of the Gulf Coast region, without regard to geographic location within the Gulf Coast region.

(II) Large-scale projects and programs that are projected to substantially contribute to restoring and protecting the natural resources, ecosystems, fisheries, marine and wildlife habitats, beaches, and coastal wetlands of the Gulf Coast ecosystem.

(III) Projects contained in existing Gulf Coast State comprehensive plans for the restoration and protection of natural resources, ecosystems, fisheries, marine and wildlife habitats, beaches, and coastal wetlands of the Gulf Coast region.

(IV) Projects that restore long-term resiliency of the natural resources, ecosystems, fisheries, marine and wildlife habitats, beaches, and coastal wetlands most impacted by the Deepwater Horizon oil spill.

(E) Implementation

(i) In general

The Council, acting through the Federal agencies represented on the Council and Gulf Coast States, shall expend funds made available from the Trust Fund to carry out projects and programs adopted in the Comprehensive Plan.

(ii) Administrative responsibility

(I) In general

Primary authority and responsibility for each project and program included in the Comprehensive Plan shall be assigned by the Council to a Gulf Coast State represented on the Council or a Federal agency.

(II) Transfer of amounts

Amounts necessary to carry out each project or program included in the Comprehensive Plan shall be transferred by the Secretary of the Treasury from the Trust Fund to that Federal agency or Gulf Coast State as the project or program is implemented, subject to such conditions as the Secretary of the Treasury, in consultation with the Secretary of the Interior and the Secretary of Commerce, established pursuant to section 1602 of the Resources and Ecosystems Sustainability, Tourist Opportunities, and Revived Economies of the Gulf Coast States Act of 2012.

(III) Limitation on transfers

(aa) Grants to nongovernmental entities

In the case of funds transferred to a Federal or State agency under subclause (II), the agency shall not make 1 or more grants or cooperative agreements to a nongovernmental entity if the total amount provided to the entity would equal or exceed 10 percent of the total amount provided to the agency for that particular project or program, unless the 1 or more grants have been reported in accordance with item (bb).

(bb) Reporting of grantees

At least 30 days prior to making a grant or entering into a cooperative agreement described in item (aa), the name of each grantee, including the amount and purpose of each grant or cooperative agreement, shall be published in the Federal Register and delivered to the congressional committees listed in subparagraph (C)(vii)(VII)(ff).

(cc) Annual reporting of grantees

Annually, the name of each grantee, including the amount and purposes of each grant or cooperative agreement, shall be published in the Federal Register and delivered to Congress as part of the report submitted pursuant to subparagraph (C)(vii)(VII).

(IV) Project and program limitation

The Council, a Federal agency, or a State may not carry out a project or program funded under this paragraph outside of the Gulf Coast region.

(F) Coordination

The Council and the Federal members of the Council may develop memoranda of understanding establishing integrated funding and implementation plans among the member agencies and authorities.

(3) Oil spill restoration impact allocation

(A) In general

(i) Disbursement

Of the total amount made available from the Trust Fund, 30 percent shall be disbursed pursuant to the formula in clause (ii) to the Gulf Coast States on the approval of the plan described in subparagraph (B)(i).

(ii) Formula

Subject to subparagraph (B), for each Gulf Coast State, the amount disbursed under this paragraph shall be based on a formula established by the Council by regulation that is based on a weighted average of the following criteria:

(I) 40 percent based on the proportionate number of miles of shoreline in each Gulf Coast State that experienced oiling on or before April 10, 2011, compared to the total number of miles of shoreline that experienced oiling as a result of the Deepwater Horizon oil spill.

(II) 40 percent based on the inverse proportion of the average distance from the mobile offshore drilling unit *Deepwater Horizon* at the time of the explosion to the nearest and farthest point of the shoreline that experienced oiling of each Gulf Coast State.

(III) 20 percent based on the average population in the 2010 decennial census of coastal counties bordering the Gulf of Mexico within each Gulf Coast State.

(iii) Minimum allocation

The amount disbursed to a Gulf Coast State for each fiscal year under clause (ii) shall be at least 5 percent of the total amounts made available under this paragraph.

(B) Disbursement of funds

(i) In general

The Council shall disburse amounts to the respective Gulf Coast States in accordance with the formula developed under subparagraph (A) for projects, programs, and activities that will improve the ecosystems or economy of the Gulf Coast region, subject to the condition that each Gulf Coast State submits a plan for the expenditure of amounts disbursed under this paragraph that meets the following criteria:

(I) All projects, programs, and activities included in the plan are eligible activities pursuant to clauses (i) and (ii) of paragraph (1)(B).

(II) The projects, programs, and activities included in the plan contribute to the overall economic and ecological recovery of the Gulf Coast.

(III) The plan takes into consideration the Comprehensive Plan and is consistent with the goals and objectives of the Plan, as described in paragraph (2)(B)(i).

(ii) Funding

(I) In general

Except as provided in subclause (II), the plan described in clause (i) may use not more than 25 percent of the funding made available for infrastructure projects eligible under subclauses (VI) and (VII) of paragraph (1)(B)(i).

(II) Exception

The plan described in clause (i) may propose to use more than 25 percent of the funding made available for infrastructure projects eligible under subclauses (VI) and (VII) of paragraph (1)(B)(i) if the plan certifies that—

(aa) ecosystem restoration needs in the State will be addressed by the projects in the proposed plan; and

(bb) additional investment in infrastructure is required to mitigate the impacts of the Deepwater Horizon Oil Spill to the ecosystem or economy.

(iii) Development

The plan described in clause (i) shall be developed by—

(I) in the State of Alabama, the Alabama Gulf Coast Recovery Council established under paragraph (1)(F)(i);

(II) in the State of Florida, a consortia[2] of local political subdivisions that includes at a minimum 1 representative of each affected county;

(III) in the State of Louisiana, the Coastal Protection and Restoration Authority of Louisiana;

(IV) in the State of Mississippi, the Office of the Governor or an appointee of the Office of the Governor; and

(V) in the State of Texas, the Office of the Governor or an appointee of the Office of the Governor.

(iv) Approval

Not later than 60 days after the date on which a plan is submitted under clause (i), the Council shall approve or disapprove the plan based on the conditions of clause (i).

(C) Disapproval

If the Council disapproves a plan pursuant to subparagraph (B)(iv), the Council shall—

(i) provide the reasons for disapproval in writing; and

(ii) consult with the State to address any identified deficiencies with the State plan.

(D) Failure to submit adequate plan

If a State fails to submit an adequate plan under this paragraph, any funds made available under this paragraph shall remain in the Trust Fund until such date as a plan is submitted and approved pursuant to this paragraph.

(E) Judicial review

If the Council fails to approve or take action within 60 days on a plan, as described in subparagraph (B)(iv), the State may obtain expedited judicial review within 90 days of that decision in a district court of the United States, of appropriate jurisdiction and venue, that is located within the State seeking the review.

(F) Cost-sharing

(i) In general

A Gulf Coast State or coastal political subdivision may use, in whole or in part, amounts made available to that Gulf Coast State or coastal political subdivision under this paragraph to satisfy the non-Federal share of any project or program that—

(I) is authorized by other Federal law; and

(II) is an eligible activity described in clause (i) or (ii) of paragraph (1)(B).

(ii) Effect on other funds

The use of funds made available from the Trust Fund under this paragraph to satisfy the non-Federal share of the cost of a project or program described in clause (i) shall not affect the priority in which other Federal funds are allocated or awarded.

(4) Authorization of interest transfers

Of the total amount made available for any fiscal year from the Trust Fund that is equal to the interest earned by the Trust Fund and proceeds from investments made by the Trust Fund in the preceding fiscal year—

(A) 50 percent shall be divided equally between—

(i) the Gulf Coast Ecosystem Restoration Science, Observation, Monitoring, and Technology program authorized in section 1604 of the Resources and Ecosystems Sustainability, Tourist Opportunities, and Revived Economies of the Gulf Coast States Act of 2012; and

(ii) the centers of excellence research grants authorized in section 1605 of that Act; and

(B) 50 percent shall be made available to the Gulf Coast Ecosystem Restoration Council to carry out the Comprehensive Plan pursuant to paragraph (2).

(June 30, 1948, c. 758, Title III, § 311, as added by Pub. L. No. 92–500, § 2, 86 Stat. 862 (Oct. 18, 1972); and amended by Pub. L. No. 93–207, § 1(4), 87 Stat. 906 (Dec. 28, 1973); Pub. L. No. 95–217, §§ 57, 58(a) to (g), (i), (k) to (m), 91 Stat. 1593–1596 (Dec. 27, 1977); Pub. L. No. 95–576, § 1(b), 92 Stat. 2467 (Nov. 2, 1978); Pub. L. No. 96–478, § 13(b), 94 Stat. 2303 (Oct. 21, 1980); Pub. L. No. 96–483, § 8, 94 Stat. 2362 (Oct. 21, 1980); Pub. L. No. 96–561, Title II, § 238(b), 94 Stat. 3300 (Dec. 22, 1980); Pub. L. No. 97–164, Title I, § 161(5), 96 Stat. 49 (Apr. 2, 1982); Pub. L. No. 100–4, Title V, § 502(b), 101 Stat. 75 (Feb. 4, 1987); Pub. L. No. 101–380, Title II, § 2002(b), Title IV, §§ 4201(a), (b), (b)[(c)], 4202(a), (c), 4204, 4301(a), (b), 4305, 4306, 104 Stat. 507, 523 to 527, 532, 533, 540, 541 (Aug. 18, 1990); Pub. L. No. 102–388, Title III, § 349, 106 Stat. 1554 (Oct. 6, 1992); Pub. L. No. 102–572, Title IX, § 902(b)(1), 106 Stat. 4516 (Oct. 29, 1992); Pub. L. No. 104–208, Div. A, Title I, § 101(a) [Title II, § 211(b)], 110 Stat. 3009–41 (Sept. 30, 1996); Pub. L. No. 104–324, Title XI, §§ 1143, 1144, 110 Stat. 3992 (Oct. 19, 1996); Pub. L. No. 105–383, Title IV, § 411, 112 Stat. 3432 (Nov. 13, 1998); Pub. L. No. 108–293, Title VII, § 701(a), (b), (d),

118 Stat. 1067, 1068 (Aug. 9, 2004); Pub. L. No. 109–241, Title VI, § 608, Title IX, § 901(i), 120 Stat. 558, 564 (July 11, 2006); Pub. L. No. 112–90, § 10, 125 Stat. 1912 (Jan. 3, 2012); Pub. L. No. 112–141, Div. A, Title I, § 1603, 126 Stat. 589 (July 6, 2012); Pub. L. No. 113–281, § 313, 128 Stat. 3048–49 (Dec. 18, 2014); Pub. L. No. 115–91, § 3508(2), 131 Stat. 1916 (Dec. 12, 2017); Pub. L. No.115–232, § 3541(b)(5), 132 Stat. 1636, 2323 (Aug. 13, 2018).)

[1] So in original. The second comma probably should not appear.

[2] So in original. Probably be "consortium."

HISTORICAL AND STATUTORY NOTES

References in Text

The Resources and Ecosystems Sustainability, Tourist Opportunities, and Revived Economies of the Gulf Coast States Act of 2012, referred to in subsecs. (a)(35) and (t)(2)(C)(vii)(IV), (VII)(ee), (D)(ii)(III), (IV)(bb), (E)(ii)(II), and (4)(A), is Pub. L. No. 112–141, Div. A, Title I, Subtitle F, § 1601 et seq., 126 Stat. 588 (July 6, 2012), which enacted this subsection, amended subsec. (a)(25)(B), (26)(D), (a)(27) to (35), and (s) of this section, and enacted provisions set out as a note under this section. Section 1602 is set out in a note under this section. Sections 1604 and 1605 are set out in a note under this section. For complete classification, see Tables.

The Outer Continental Shelf Lands Act, referred to in subsecs. (b)(1), (2)(A), (3), and (r), is Act of Aug. 7, 1953, c. 345, 67 Stat. 462, as amended, which is codified generally as subchapter III (section 1331 et seq.) of chapter 29 of Title 43, Public Lands. For complete classification of this Act to the Code, see Short Title note set out under section 1331 of Title 43 and Tables.

The Deepwater Port Act of 1974, referred to in subsecs. (b)(1), (2)(A), (3), and (r), is Pub. L. No. 93–627, 88 Stat. 2126 (Jan. 3, 1975), as amended, which is codified generally as chapter 29 (section 1501 et seq.) of this title. For complete classification of this Act to the Code, see Short Title note set out under section 1501 of this title and Tables volume.

The Magnuson-Stevens Fishery Conservation and Management Act, referred to in subsec. (b)(1), (2)(A), and (3), is Pub. L. 94–265, 90 Stat. 331 (Apr. 13, 1976), as amended, which is codified principally as chapter 38 (section 1801 et seq.) of Title 16, Conservation. For complete classification of this Act to the Code, see Short Title note set out under section 1801 of Title 16 and Tables.

The date of enactment of this paragraph, referred to in subsec. (b)(2)(B), probably means the date of enactment of Pub. L. 95–576, which amended subsec. (b)(2)(B) and which was approved Nov. 2, 1978.

Section 313 of the Appendix to Title 46, referred to in subsec. (b)(12)(B), was repealed by Pub. L. No. 103–182, Title VI, § 690(a)(21), 107 Stat. 2223 (Dec. 8, 1993).

The penalty enacted in subclause (bb) of clause (iii) of subparagraph (B) of subsection (b)(2) of section 311 of Public Law 92–500, referred to in subsec. (b)(2)(B), probably means the penalty provision of subsec. (b)(2)(B)(iii)(bb) of this section as added by Pub. L. No. 92–500, § 2, 86 Stat. 864 (Oct. 18, 1972), prior to the amendment to subsec. (b)(2)(B) by section 1(b)(3) of Pub. L. No. 95–576. Prior to amendment, subsec. (b)(2)(B)(iii)(bb) read as follows: "a penalty determined by the number of units discharged multiplied by the amount established for such unit under clause (iv) of this subparagraph, but such penalty shall not be more than $5,000,000 in the case of a discharge from a vessel and $500,000 in the case of a discharge from an onshore or offshore facility."

Section 1443 of Title 19, referred to in subsec. (b)(12)(C), was repealed by Pub. L. No. 103–182, Title VI, § 690(b)(6), 107 Stat. 2223 (Dec. 8, 1993).

The Comprehensive Environmental Response, Compensation, and Liability Act of 1980, referred to in subsec. (c)(4)(B)(ii), is Pub. L. No. 96–510, 94 Stat. 2767 (Dec. 11, 1980), as amended, which is principally codified as chapter 103 (section 9601 et seq.) of Title 42, Public Health and Welfare. For complete classification of this Act to the Code, see Short Title note set out under section 9601 of Title 42 and Tables.

The Oil Pollution Act of 1990, referred to in subsecs. (c)(5)(B), (c)(6), (d)(2)(H) and (j)(5)(G), is Pub. L. No. 101–380, 104 Stat. 484 (Aug. 18, 1990), which is principally codified as chapter 40 (section 2701 et seq.) of this title. Section 1001 of the Act is codified as section 2701 of this title. For complete classification of this Act to the Code, see Short Title note set out under section 2701 of this title and Tables.

Par. (3) of section 1901(a) of this title, referred to in subsec. (j)(5)(B), was redesignated par. (4) by Pub. L. No. 110–280, § 3(1), 122 Stat. 2611 (July 21, 2008).

The Federal Advisory Committee Act, referred to in subsec. (t)(2)(C)(viii), is Pub. L. No. 92–463, 86 Stat. 770 (Oct. 6, 1972), as amended, which is set out in Appendix 2 to Title 5, 5 App. 2 U.S.C.A. § 1 et seq.

Codifications

"Section 60105 of Title 46" substituted in subsec. (b)(12)(A) for "section 91 of the Appendix to Title 46" on authority of Pub. L. No. 109–304, § 18(c), 120 Stat. 1709 (Oct. 6, 2006), which completed the codification of T. 46, Shipping, as positive law.

"Not later than 2 years after August 18, 1990", appearing in subsec. (j)(6), was, in the original, "not later than 2 years after the date of enactment of this section", and was editorially translated according to the probable intent of Congress in enacting subsec. (j)(6) by Pub. L. No. 101–380, 104 Stat. 484, which was approved Aug. 18, 1990.

Effective and Applicability Provisions

2012 Acts. Except as otherwise provided, Divisions A, B, C (other than amendments to 16 U.S.C.A. § 777c and 49 U.S.C.A. § 31104, and provisions set out as notes under 49 U.S.C.A. §§ 31100 and 31301), and E of Pub. L. No. 112–141, take effect on Oct. 1, 2012, see Pub. L. No. 112–141, § 3(a), set out as a note under 23 U.S.C.A. § 101.

2006 Acts. Pub. L. No. 109–241, Title IX, § 901(i)(2), 120 Stat. 564 (July 11, 2006), in part provided that the amendment by Pub. L. No. 109–241, § 901(i)(2), is '[e]ffective August 9, 2004'."

1996 Acts. Amendment by Pub. L. No. 104–208, Div. A, Title I, § 101(a) [Title II, § 211(b)], 110 Stat. 3009–41 (Sept. 30, 1996), effective 15 days after Oct. 11, 1996, see Pub. L. No. 104–208, Div. A, Title I, § 101(a) [Title II, § 211(b)], 110 Stat. 3009–41 (Sept. 30, 1996), set out as a note under section 1801 of Title 16, Conservation.

1992 Acts. Amendment by Title IX of Pub. L. No. 102–572 were effective Oct. 29, 1992, see section 911 of Pub. L. No. 102–572, set out as a note under section 171 of Title 28, Judiciary and Judicial Procedure.

1982 Acts. Amendment by Pub. L. No. 97–164 were effective Oct. 1, 1982, see section 402 of Pub. L. No. 97–164, set out as a note under section 171 of Title 28, Judiciary and Judicial Procedure.

1980 Acts. Amendment by Pub. L. No. 96–561 were effective 15 days after Dec. 22, 1980, see section 238 of Pub. L. No. 96–561, set out as a Short Title note under section 1801 of Title 16, Conservation.

Amendment by Pub. L. No. 96–478 were effective Oct. 2, 1983, see section 14(a) of Pub. L. No. 96–478, set out as a note under section 1901 of this title.

1977 Acts. Section 58(h) of Pub. L. No. 95–217 provided that: "The amendments made by paragraphs (5) and (6) of subsection (d) of this section [substituting "$50,000,000' for "$8,000,000' in subsec. (f)(2) and substituting "$50,000,000' for "$8,000,000' in subsec. (f)(3) of this section] shall take effect 180 days after the date of enactment of the Clean Water Act of 1977 [Dec. 27, 1977]."

Transfer of Functions

For transfer of authorities, functions, personnel, and assets of the Coast Guard, including the authorities and functions of the Secretary of Transportation relating thereto, to the Department of Homeland Security, and for treatment of related references, see 6 U.S.C.A. §§ 468(b), 551(d), 552(d), and 557 and the Department of Homeland Security Reorganization Plan of November 25, 2002, as modified, set out as a note under 6 U.S.C.A. § 542.

Enforcement functions of Administrator or other official of the Environmental Protection Agency under this section relating to spill prevention, containment and countermeasure plans with respect to pre-construction, construction, and initial operation of transportation system for Canadian and Alaskan natural gas were transferred to the Federal Inspector, Office of Federal Inspector for the Alaska Natural Gas Transportation System, until the first anniversary of the date of initial operation of the Alaska Natural Gas Transportation System, see Reorganization Plan No. 1 of 1979, §§ 102(a), 203(a), 44 Fed. Reg. 33663, 33666, 93 Stat. 1373, 1376, effective July 1, 1979, set out in the Appendix to Title 5, 5 USCA App. 1 Reorg. Plan 1 1979. Office of Federal Inspector for the Alaska Natural Gas Transportation System abolished and functions and authority vested in Inspector transferred to Secretary of Energy by section 3012(b) of Pub. L. No. 102–486, set out as an Abolition of Office of Federal Inspector note under 15 U.S.C.A. § 719e. Functions and authority vested in Secretary of Energy subsequently transferred to Federal Coordinator for Alaska Natural Gas Transportation Projects by 15 U.S.C.A. § 720d(f).

Delegation of Functions

For delegation of certain functions of President under this section, see Ex. Ord. No. 12580, Jan. 23, 1987, 52 Fed. Reg. 2923, as amended, set out as a note under 42 U.S.C.A. § 9615.

Arctic Planning Requirements

Pub. L. No. 115–282, § 823, 132 Stat. 4192, 4311–4312 (Dec. 4, 2018), provided:

"(a) Alternative planning criteria.—

"(1) In general.—For purposes of the Oil Pollution Act of 1990 (33 U.S.C. 2701 et seq.), the Commandant of the Coast Guard may approve a vessel response plan under section 311 of the Federal Water Pollution Control Act (33 U.S.C. 1321) for a vessel operating in any area covered by the Captain of the Port Zone (as established by the Commandant) that includes the Arctic, if the Commandant verifies that—

"(A) equipment required to be available for response under the plan has been tested and proven capable of operating in the environmental conditions expected in the area in which it is intended to be operated; and

"(B) the operators of such equipment have conducted training on the equipment within the area covered by such Captain of the Port Zone.

"(2) Post-approval requirements.—In approving a vessel response plan under paragraph (1), the Commandant shall—

"(A) require that the oil spill removal organization identified in the vessel response plan conduct regular exercises and drills using the response resources identified in the plan in the area covered by the Captain of the Port Zone that includes the Arctic; and

"(B) allow such oil spill removal organization to take credit for a response to an actual spill or release in the area covered by such Captain of the Port Zone, instead of conducting an exercise or drill required under subparagraph (A), if the oil spill removal organization—

"(i) documents which exercise or drill requirements were met during the response; and

"(ii) submits a request for credit to, and receives approval from, the Commandant.

"(b) Report.—

"(1) In general.—Not later than 120 days after the date of enactment of this Act, the Commandant of the Coast Guard shall submit to the Committee on Commerce, Science, and Transportation of the Senate and the Committee on Transportation and Infrastructure of the House of Representatives a report on the oil spill prevention and response capabilities for the area covered by the Captain of the Port Zone (as established by the Commandant) that includes the Arctic.

"(2) Contents.—The report submitted under paragraph (1) shall include the following:

"(A) A description of equipment and assets available for response under the vessel response plans approved for vessels operating in the area covered by the Captain of the Port Zone, including details on any providers of such equipment and assets.

"(B) A description of the location of such equipment and assets, including an estimate of the time to deploy the equipment and assets.

"(C) A determination of how effectively such equipment and assets are distributed throughout the area covered by the Captain of the Port Zone.

"(D) A statement regarding whether the ability to maintain and deploy such equipment and assets is taken into account when measuring the equipment and assets available throughout the area covered by the Captain of the Port Zone.

"(E) A validation of the port assessment visit process and response resource inventory for response under the vessel response plans approved for vessels operating in the area covered by the Captain of the Port Zone.

"(F) A determination of the compliance rate with Federal vessel response plan regulations in the area covered by the Captain of the Port Zone during the previous 3 years.

"(G) A description of the resources needed throughout the area covered by the Captain of the Port Zone to conduct port assessments, exercises, response plan reviews, and spill responses.

"(c) Definition of Arctic.—In this section, the term 'Arctic' has the meaning given the term under section 112 of the Arctic Research and Policy Act of 1984 (15 U.S.C. 4111)."

Vessel Response Plan Audit

Pub. L. No. 115–282, § 824, 132 Stat. 4192, 4312–4313 (Dec. 4, 2018), provided:

"(a) In general.—Not later than 1 year after the date of enactment of this Act, the Comptroller General of the United States shall complete and submit to the Committee on Commerce, Science, and Transportation of the Senate and the Committee on Transportation and Infrastructure of the House of Representatives a comprehensive review of the processes and resources used by the Coast Guard to implement vessel response plan requirements under section 311 of the Federal Water Pollution Control Act (33 U.S.C. 1321).

"(b) Required elements of review.—The review required under subsection (a) shall, at a minimum, include—

"(1) a study, or an audit if appropriate, of the processes the Coast Guard uses—

"(A) to approve the vessel response plans referred to in subsection (a);

"(B) to approve alternate planning criteria used in lieu of National Planning Criteria in approving such plans;

"(C) to verify compliance with such plans; and

"(D) to act in the event of a failure to comply with the requirements of such plans;

"(2) an examination of all Federal and State agency resources used by the Coast Guard in carrying out the processes identified under paragraph (1), including—

"(A) the current staffing model and organization;

"(B) data, software, simulators, systems, or other technology, including those pertaining to weather, oil spill trajectory modeling, and risk management;

"(C) the total amount of time per fiscal year expended by Coast Guard personnel to approve and verify compliance with vessel response plans; and

"(D) the average amount of time expended by the Coast Guard for approval of, and verification of compliance with, a single vessel response plan;

"(3) an analysis of how, including by what means or methods, the processes identified under paragraph (1)—

"(A) ensure compliance with applicable law;

"(B) are implemented by the Coast Guard, including at the district and sector levels;

"(C) are informed by public comment and engagement with States, Indian Tribes, and other regional stakeholders;

"(D) ensure availability and adequate operational capability and capacity of required assets and equipment, including in cases in which contractual obligations may limit the availability of such assets and equipment for response;

"(E) provide for adequate asset and equipment mobilization time requirements, particularly with respect to—

"(i) calculation and establishment of such requirements;

"(ii) verifying compliance with such requirements; and

"(iii) factoring in weather, including specific regional adverse weather as defined in section 155.1020 of title 33, Code of Federal Regulations, in calculating, establishing, and verifying compliance with such requirements;

"(F) ensure response plan updates and vessel compliance when changes occur in response planning criteria, asset and equipment mobilization times, or regional response needs, such as trends in transportation of high gravity oils or changes in vessel traffic volume; and

"(G) enable effective action by the Coast Guard in the event of a failure to comply with response plan requirements;

"(4) a determination regarding whether asset and equipment mobilization time requirements under approved vessel response plans can be met by the vessels to which they apply; and

"(5) recommendations for improving the processes identified under paragraph (1), including recommendations regarding the sufficiency of Coast Guard resources dedicated to those processes."

Coast Guard Response Plan Requirements

Pub. L. No. 113–281, § 317, 128 Stat. 3050–51 (Dec. 18, 2014), provided that:

"(a) **Vessel Response Plan Contents.**—The Secretary of the department in which the Coast Guard is operating shall require that each vessel response plan prepared for a mobile offshore drilling unit includes information from the facility response plan prepared for the mobile offshore drilling unit regarding the planned response to a worst case discharge, and to a threat of such a discharge."

"(b) **Definitions.**—In this section:

"(1) **Mobile Offshore Drilling Unit.**—The term "mobile offshore drilling unit" has the meaning given that term in section 1001 of the Oil Pollution Act of 1990 (33 U.S.C. 2701).

"(2) **Response Plan.**—The term "response plan" means a response plan prepared under section 311(j) of the Federal Water Pollution Control Act (33 U.S.C. 1321(j)).

"(3) **Worst Case Discharge.**—The term "worst case discharge" has the meaning given that term under section 311(a) of the Federal Water Pollution Control Act (33 U.S.C. 1321(a))."

"(c) **Rule of Construction.**—Nothing in this section shall be construed to require the Coast Guard to review or approve a facility response plan for a mobile offshore drilling unit."

Gulf Coast Restoration

Pub. L. No. 112–141, Div. A, Title I, §§ 1601 to 1608, 126 Stat. 588 (July 6, 2012), provided that:

"Sec. 1601. Short title.

"This subtitle [Subtitle F of Title I of Div. A of Pub. L. No. 112–141 (§ 1601 et seq.), 126 Stat. 588 (July 6, 2012), which enacted this note and enacted subsec. (t) of this section, and amended subsec. (a)(25)(B), (26)(D), (a)(27) to (35), and subsec. (s) of this section] may be cited as the 'Resources and Ecosystems Sustainability, Tourist Opportunities, and Revived Economies of the Gulf Coast States Act of 2012'.

"Sec. 1602. Gulf Coast Restoration Trust Fund.

"(a) **Establishment.**—There is established in the Treasury of the United States a trust fund to be known as the 'Gulf Coast Restoration Trust Fund' (referred to in this section as the 'Trust Fund'), consisting of such amounts as are deposited in the Trust Fund under this Act [Moving Ahead for Progress in the 21st Century Act of the MAP–21, Pub. L. No. 112–141, 126 Stat. 405 (July 6, 2012)] or any other provision of law.

"(b) **Transfers.**—The Secretary of the Treasury shall deposit in the Trust Fund an amount equal to 80 percent of all administrative and civil penalties paid by responsible parties after the date of enactment of this Act [Pursuant to § 3(b) of Pub. L. No. 112–141, July 6, 2012, 126 Stat. 413, except as otherwise provided, any reference to 'the date of enactment of the MAP–21' (Pub. L. No. 112–141) in divisions A, B, C, and E of Pub. L. No. 112–141, (other than amendments to 16 U.S.C.A. § 777c and 49 U.S.C.A. § 31104, and provisions set out as notes under 49 U.S.C.A. §§ 31100 and 31301) shall be deemed to be a reference to the effective date of such divisions, see provisions set out as a bracketed note under this note and § 3(a) and (b) of Pub. L. No. 112–141, set out as notes under 23 U.S.C.A. § 101] in connection with the explosion on, and sinking of, the mobile offshore drilling unit *Deepwater Horizon* pursuant to a court order, negotiated settlement, or other instrument in accordance with section 311 of the Federal Water Pollution Control Act (33 U.S.C. 1321).

"(c) **Expenditures.**—Amounts in the Trust Fund, including interest earned on advances to the Trust Fund and proceeds from investment under subsection (d), shall—

"(1) be available for expenditure, without further appropriation, solely for the purpose and eligible activities of this subtitle and the amendments made by this subtitle [Subtitle F of Title I of Div. A of Pub. L. No. 112–141 (§ 1601 et seq.), July 6, 2012, 126 Stat. 588, which enacted this note and enacted subsec. (t) of this section, and amended subsec. (a)(25)(B), (26)(D), (a)(27) to (35), and subsec. (s) of this section]; and

"(2) remain available until expended, without fiscal year limitation.

"(d) Investment.—Amounts in the Trust Fund shall be invested in accordance with section 9702 of title 31, United States Code, and any interest on, and proceeds from, any such investment shall be available for expenditure in accordance with this subtitle and the amendments made by this subtitle [Subtitle F of Title I of Div. A of Pub. L. No. 112–141 (§ 1601 et seq.), 126 Stat. 588 (July 6, 2012), which enacted this note and enacted subsec. (t) of this section, and amended subsec. (a)(25)(B), (26)(D), (a)(27) to (35), and subsec. (s) of this section].

"(e) Administration.—Not later than 180 days after the date of enactment of this Act [Pursuant to § 3(b) of Pub. L. No. 112–141, 126 Stat. 413 (July 6, 2012), except as otherwise provided, any reference to 'the date of enactment of the MAP–21' (Pub. L. No. 112–141) in divisions A, B, C, and E of Pub. L. No. 112–141, (other than amendments to 16 U.S.C.A. § 777c and 49 U.S.C.A. § 31104, and provisions set out as notes under 49 U.S.C.A. §§ 31100 and 31301) shall be deemed to be a reference to the effective date of such divisions, see provisions set out as a bracketed note under this note and § 3(a) and (b) of Pub. L. No. 112–141, set out as notes under 23 U.S.C.A. § 101], after providing notice and an opportunity for public comment, the Secretary of the Treasury, in consultation with the Secretary of the Interior and the Secretary of Commerce, shall establish such procedures as the Secretary determines to be necessary to deposit amounts in, and expend amounts from, the Trust Fund pursuant to this subtitle [Subtitle F of Title I of Div. A of Pub. L. No. 112–141 (§ 1601 et seq.), 126 Stat. 588 (July 6, 2012), which enacted this note and enacted subsec. (t) of this section, and amended subsec. (a)(25)(B), (26)(D), (a)(27) to (35), and subsec. (s) of this section], including—

"(1) procedures to assess whether the programs and activities carried out under this subtitle and the amendments made by this subtitle [Subtitle F of Title I of Div. A of Pub. L. No. 112–141 (§ 1601 et seq.), 126 Stat. 588 (July 6, 2012), which enacted this note and enacted subsec. (t) of this section, and amended subsec. (a)(25)(B), (26)(D), (a)(27) to (35), and subsec. (s) of this section] achieve compliance with applicable requirements, including procedures by which the Secretary of the Treasury may determine whether an expenditure by a Gulf Coast State or coastal political subdivision (as those terms are defined in section 311 of the Federal Water Pollution Control Act (33 U.S.C. 1321)) pursuant to such a program or activity achieves compliance;

"(2) auditing requirements to ensure that amounts in the Trust Fund are expended as intended; and

"(3) procedures for identification and allocation of funds available to the Secretary under other provisions of law that may be necessary to pay the administrative expenses directly attributable to the management of the Trust Fund.

"(f) Sunset.—The authority for the Trust Fund shall terminate on the date all funds in the Trust Fund have been expended.

[Sec. 1603. Omitted. Enacts subsec. (t) of this section and amends subsec. (a)(25)(B), (26)(D), (a)(27) to (35), and subsec. (s) of this section.]

"Sec. 1604. Gulf Coast Ecosystem Restoration Science, Observation, Monitoring, and Technology program.

"(a) Definitions.—In this section:

"(1) Administrator.—The term 'Administrator' means the Administrator of the National Oceanic and Atmospheric Administration.

"(2) Commission.—The term 'Commission' means the Gulf States Marine Fisheries Commission.

"(3) Director.—The term 'Director' means the Director of the United States Fish and Wildlife Service.

"(4) Program.—The term 'program' means the Gulf Coast Ecosystem Restoration Science, Observation, Monitoring, and Technology program established under this section.

"(b) Establishment of program.—

"(1) In general.—Not later than 180 days after the date of enactment of this Act [Pursuant to § 3(b) of Pub. L. No. 112–141, 126 Stat. 413 (July 6, 2012), except as otherwise provided, any reference to 'the date of enactment of the MAP–21' (Pub. L. No. 112–141) in divisions A, B, C, and E of Pub. L. No. 112–141, (other than amendments to 16 U.S.C.A. § 777c and 49 U.S.C.A. § 31104, and provisions set out as notes under 49 U.S.C.A. §§ 31100 and 31301) shall be deemed to be a reference to the effective date of such divisions, see provisions set out as a bracketed note under this note and § 3(a) and (b) of Pub. L. No. 112–141, set out as notes under 23 U.S.C.A. § 101], the Administrator, in consultation with the Director, shall establish the Gulf Coast Ecosystem Restoration Science, Observation, Monitoring, and Technology program to carry out research, observation, and monitoring to support, to the maximum extent practicable, the long-term sustainability of the ecosystem, fish stocks, fish habitat, and the recreational, commercial, and charter fishing industry in the Gulf of Mexico.

"(2) Expenditure of funds.—For each fiscal year, amounts made available to carry out this subsection may be expended for, with respect to the Gulf of Mexico—

"(A) marine and estuarine research;

"(B) marine and estuarine ecosystem monitoring and ocean observation;

"(C) data collection and stock assessments;

"(D) Pilot programs for—

"(i) fishery independent data; and

"(ii) reduction of exploitation of spawning aggregations; and

"(E) cooperative research.

"(3) Cooperation with the Commission.—For each fiscal year, amounts made available to carry out this subsection may be transferred to the Commission to establish a fisheries monitoring and research program, with respect to the Gulf of Mexico.

"(4) Consultation.—The Administrator and the Director shall consult with the Regional Gulf of Mexico Fishery Management Council and the Commission in carrying out the program.

"(c) Species included.—The research, monitoring, assessment, and programs eligible for amounts made available under the program shall include all marine, estuarine, aquaculture, and fish species in State and Federal waters of the Gulf of Mexico.

"(d) Research priorities.—In distributing funding under this subsection, priority shall be given to integrated, long-term projects that—

"(1) build on, or are coordinated with, related research activities; and

"(2) address current or anticipated marine ecosystem, fishery, or wildlife management information needs.

"(e) Duplication.—In carrying out this section, the Administrator, in consultation with the Director, shall seek to avoid duplication of other research and monitoring activities.

"(f) Coordination with other programs.—The Administrator, in consultation with the Director, shall develop a plan for the coordination of projects and activities between the program and other existing Federal and State science and technology programs in the States of Alabama, Florida, Louisiana, Mississippi, and Texas, as well as between the centers of excellence.

"(g) Limitation on expenditures.—

"(1) In general.—Not more than 3 percent of funds provided in subsection (h) shall be used for administrative expenses.

"(2) NOAA.—The funds provided in subsection (h) may not be used—

"(A) for any existing or planned research led by the National Oceanic and Atmospheric Administration, unless agreed to in writing by the grant recipient;

"(B) to implement existing regulations or initiate new regulations promulgated or proposed by the National Oceanic and Atmospheric Administration; or

"(C) to develop or approve a new limited access privilege program (as that term is used in section 303A of the Magnuson-Stevens Fishery Conservation and Management Act (16 U.S.C. 1853a)) for any fishery under the jurisdiction of the South Atlantic, Mid-Atlantic, New England, or Gulf of Mexico Fishery Management Councils.

"(h) **Funding.**—Of the total amount made available for each fiscal year for the Gulf Coast Restoration Trust Fund established under section 1602, 2.5 percent shall be available to carry out the program.

"(i) **Sunset.**—The program shall cease operations when all funds in the Gulf Coast Restoration Trust Fund established under section 1602 have been expended.

"Sec. 1605. Centers of excellence research grants.

"(a) In general.—Of the total amount made available for each fiscal year from the Gulf Coast Restoration Trust Fund established under section 1602 [of this note], 2. 5 percent shall be made available to the Gulf Coast States (as defined in section 311(a) of the Federal Water Pollution Control Act (as added by section 1603 of the Resources and Ecosystems Sustainability, Tourist Opportunities, and Revived Economies of the Gulf Coast States Act of 2012) [subsec. (a) of this section]), in equal shares, exclusively for grants in accordance with subsection (c) to establish centers of excellence to conduct research only on the Gulf Coast Region (as defined in section 311 of the Federal Water Pollution Control Act (33. U.S.C. 1321) [this section]).

"(b) Approval by State entity, task force, or agency.—The duties of a Gulf Coast State under this section shall be carried out by the applicable Gulf Coast State entities, task forces, or agencies listed in section 311(t)(1)(F) of the Federal Water Pollution Control Act (as added by section 1603 of the Resources and Ecosystems Sustainability, Tourist Opportunities, and Revived Economies of the Gulf Coast States Act of 2012 [subsec. (t)(1)(F) of this section]), and for the State of Florida, a consortium of public and private research institutions within the State, which shall include the Florida Department of Environmental Protection and the Florida Fish and Wildlife Conservation Commission, for that Gulf Coast State.

"(c) Grants.—

"(1) In general.—A Gulf Coast State shall use the amounts made available to carry out this section to award competitive grants to nongovernmental entities and consortia in the Gulf Coast region (including public and private institutions of higher education) for the establishment of centers of excellence as described in subsection (d).

"(2) Application.—To be eligible to receive a grant under this subsection, an entity or consortium described in paragraph (1) shall submit to a Gulf Coast State an application at such time, in such manner, and containing such information as the Gulf Coast State determines to be appropriate.

"(3) Priority.—In awarding grants under this subsection, a Gulf Coast State shall give priority to entities and consortia that demonstrate the ability to establish the broadest cross-section of participants with interest and expertise in any discipline described in subsection (d) on which the proposal of the center of excellence will be focused.

"(4) Reporting.—

"(A) In general.—Each Gulf Coast State shall provide annually to the Gulf Coast Ecosystem Restoration Council established under section 311(t)(2)(C) of the Federal Water Pollution Control Act (as added by section 1603 of the Resources and Ecosystems Sustainability, Tourist Opportunities, and Revived Economies of the Gulf Coast States Act of 2012) [subsec. (t)(2)(C) of this section]) information regarding all grants, including the amount, discipline or disciplines, and recipients of the grants, and in the case of any grant awarded to a consortium, the membership of the consortium.

"(B) Inclusion.—The Gulf Coast Ecosystem Restoration Council shall include the information received under subparagraph (A) in the annual report to Congress of the Council required under section 311(t)(2)(C)(vii)(VII) of the Federal Water Pollution Control Act (as added by section 1603 of the Resources and Ecosystems Sustainability, Tourist Opportunities, and Revived Economies of the Gulf Coast States Act of 2012) [subsec. (t)(2)(C)(vii)(VII) of this section].

"(d) Disciplines.—Each center of excellence shall focus on science, technology, and monitoring in at least 1 of the following disciplines:

"(1) Coastal and deltaic sustainability, restoration and protection, including solutions and technology that allow citizens to live in a safe and sustainable manner in a coastal delta in the Gulf Coast Region.

"(2) Coastal fisheries and wildlife ecosystem research and monitoring in the Gulf Coast Region.

"(3) Offshore energy development, including research and technology to improve the sustainable and safe development of energy resources in the Gulf of Mexico.

"(4) Sustainable and resilient growth, economic and commercial development in the Gulf Coast Region.

"(5) Comprehensive observation, monitoring, and mapping of the Gulf of Mexico.

"Sec. 1606. Effect.

"(a) Definition of Deepwater Horizon oil spill.—In this section, the term 'Deepwater Horizon oil spill' has the meaning given the term in section 311(a) of the Federal Water Pollution Control Act (33 U.S.C. 1321(a)).

"(b) Effect and application.—Nothing in this subtitle or any amendment made by this subtitle [Subtitle F of Title I of Div. A of Pub. L. No. 112–141 (§ 1601 et seq.), 126 Stat. 588 (July 6, 2012), which enacted this note and enacted subsec. (t) of this section, and amended subsec. (a)(25)(B), (26)(D), (a)(27) to (35), and subsec. (s) of this section]—

"(1) supersedes or otherwise affects any other provision of Federal law, including, in particular, laws providing recovery for injury to natural resources under the Oil Pollution Act of 1990 (33 U.S.C. 2701 et seq.) [Pub. L. No. 101–380, Aug. 18, 1990, 104 Stat. 484, which is codified principally to chapter 40 of Title 33, 33 U.S.C.A. § 2701 et seq.; for complete classification, see Short Title note set out under 33 U.S.C.A. § 2701 and Tables] and laws for the protection of public health and the environment; or

"(2) applies to any fine collected under section 311 of the Federal Water Pollution Control Act (33 U.S.C. 1321) for any incident other than the Deepwater Horizon oil spill.

"(c) Use of funds.—Funds made available under this subtitle may be used only for eligible activities specifically authorized by this subtitle and the amendments made by this subtitle [Subtitle F of Title I of Div. A of Pub. L. No. 112–141 (§ 1601 et seq.), July 6, 2012, 126 Stat. 588, which enacted this note and enacted subsec. (t) of this section, and amended subsec. (a)(25)(B), (26)(D), (a)(27) to (35), and subsec. (s) of this section].

"Sec. 1607. Restoration and protection activity limitations.

"(a) Willing seller.—Funds made available under this subtitle [Subtitle F of Title I of Div. A of Pub. L. No. 112–141 (§ 1601 et seq.), July 6, 2012, 126 Stat. 588, which enacted this note and enacted subsec. (t) of this section, and amended subsec. (a)(25)(B), (26)(D), (a)(27) to (35), and subsec. (s) of this section] may only be used to acquire land or interests in land by purchase, exchange, or donation from a willing seller.

"(b) Acquisition of Federal land.—None of the funds made available under this subtitle [Subtitle F of Title I of Div. A of Pub. L. No. 112–141 (§ 1601 et seq.), July 6, 2012, 126 Stat. 588, which enacted this note and enacted subsec. (t) of this section, and amended subsec. (a)(25)(B), (26)(D), (a)(27) to (35), and subsec. (s) of this section] may be used to acquire land in fee title by the Federal Government unless—

"(1) the land is acquired by exchange or donation; or

"(2) the acquisition is necessary for the restoration and protection of the natural resources, ecosystems, fisheries, marine and wildlife habitats, beaches, and coastal wetlands of the Gulf Coast region and has the concurrence of the Governor of the State in which the acquisition will take place.

"Sec. 1608. Inspector General.

"The Office of the Inspector General of the Department of the Treasury shall have authority to conduct, supervise, and coordinate audits and investigations of projects, programs, and activities funded under this subtitle and the amendments made by this subtitle [Subtitle F of Title I of Div. A of Pub. L. No. 112–141 (§ 1601 et seq.), July 6, 2012, 126 Stat. 588, which enacted this note and enacted subsec. (t) of this section, and amended subsec. (a)(25)(B), (26)(D), (a)(27) to (35), and subsec. (s) of this section]."

[Except as otherwise provided, Divisions A, B, C (other than amendments to 16 U.S.C.A. § 777c and 49 U.S.C.A. § 31104, and provisions set out as notes under 49 U.S.C.A. §§ 31100 and 31301), and E of Pub. L. No. 112–141, take effect on Oct. 1, 2012, see Pub. L. No. 112–141, § 3(a), set out as a note under 23 U.S.C.A. § 101.]

Rulemakings

Pub. L. No. 111–281, Title VII, § 701(a), (b), 124 Stat. 2980 (Oct. 15, 2010), provided that:

"(a) Status report.—

"(1) In general.—Not later than 90 days after the date of enactment of this Act [Oct. 15, 2010], the Secretary of the department in which the Coast Guard is operating shall provide a report to the Senate Committee on Commerce, Science, and Transportation and the House of Representatives Committee on Transportation and Infrastructure on the status of all Coast Guard rulemakings required or otherwise being developed (but for which no final rule has been issued as of the date of enactment of this Act [Oct. 15, 2010]) under section 311 of the Federal Water Pollution Control Act (33 U.S.C. 1321).

"(2) Information required.—The Secretary shall include in the report required in paragraph (1)—

"(A) A detailed explanation with respect to each such rulemaking as to—

"(i) what steps have been completed;

"(ii) what areas remain to be addressed; and

"(iii) the cause of any delays; and

"(B) the date by which a final rule may reasonably be expected to be issued.

"(b) Final rules.—The Secretary shall issue a final rule in each pending rulemaking described in subsection (a) as soon as practicable, but in no event later than 18 months after the date of enactment of this Act [Oct. 15, 2010]."

Implementation Date

Pub. L. No. 108–293, Title VII, § 701(c), 118 Stat. 1068 (Aug. 9, 2004), provided that: "No later than one year after the date of enactment of this Act [Aug. 9, 2004], the owner or operator of a nontank vessel (as defined section 311(j)(9) of the Federal Water Pollution Control Act (33 U.S.C. 1321(j)(9) [sic; see section 311(a)(26) of that Act, which is codified as subsec. (a)(26) of this section], as amended by this section [Pub. L. No. 108–293, § 701(a)(3), which added par. (26) of subsec. (a) of this section]) shall prepare and submit a vessel response plan for such vessel."

Termination of Trust Territory of the Pacific Islands

For termination of Trust Territory of the Pacific Islands, see note set out preceding 48 U.S.C.A. § 1681.

Termination of United States District Court for the District of the Canal Zone

For termination of the United States District Court for the District of the Canal Zone at end of the "transition period", being the 30-month period beginning Oct. 1, 1979, and ending midnight Mar. 31, 1982, see Paragraph 5 of Article XI of the Panama Canal Treaty of 1977 and sections 2101 and 2201 to 2203 of Pub. L. No. 96–70, Title II, 93 Stat. 493 (Sept. 27, 1979), formerly codified as 22 U.S.C.A. §§ 3831 and 3841 to 3843, respectively.

Territorial Sea and Contiguous Zone of United States

For extension of territorial sea and contiguous zone of United States, see Proc. No. 5928 and Proc. No. 7219, respectively, set out as notes under 43 U.S.C.A. § 1331.

Deposit of Certain Penalties Into Oil Spill Liability Trust Fund

Penalties paid pursuant to this section and sections 1319(c) and 1501 et seq., respectively, of this title, deposited in the Oil Spill Liability Trust Fund created under section 9509 of Title 26, Internal Revenue Code, see section 4304 of Pub. L. No. 101–380, set out as a note under section 9509 of Title 26.

Report on Oil Spill Responder Immunity

Pub. L. No. 107–295, Title IV, § 440, 116 Stat. 2130 (Nov. 25, 2002), provided that:

"(a) Report to Congress.—Not later than January 1, 2004, the Secretary of the department in which the Coast Guard is operating, jointly with the Secretary of Commerce and the Secretary of the Interior, and after consultation with the Administrator of the Environmental Protection Agency and the Attorney General, shall submit a report to the Committee on Commerce, Science, and Transportation of the Senate and the Committee on Transportation and Infrastructure of the House of Representatives on the immunity from criminal and civil penalties provided under existing law of a private responder (other than a responsible party) in the case of the incidental take of federally listed fish or wildlife that results from, but is not the purpose of, carrying out an otherwise lawful activity conducted by that responder during an oil spill removal activity where the responder was acting in a manner consistent with the National Contingency Plan or as otherwise directed by the Federal On-Scene Coordinator for the spill, and on the circumstances under which such penalties have been or could be imposed on a private responder. The report shall take into consideration the procedures under the Inter-Agency Memorandum for addressing incidental takes.

"(b) Definitions.—In this section—

"(1) the term 'Federal On-Scene Coordinator' has the meaning given that term in section 311 of the Federal Water Pollution Control Act (33 U.S.C. 1321);

"(2) the term 'incidental take' has the meaning given that term in the Inter-Agency Memorandum;

"(3) the term 'Inter-Agency Memorandum' means the Inter-Agency Memorandum of Agreement Regarding Oil Spill Planning and Response Activities under the Federal Water Pollution Control Act's National Oil and Hazardous Substances Pollution Contingency Plan [40 C.F.R. § 300.1 et seq.] and the Endangered Species Act [Pub. L. No. 93–205, Dec. 28, 1973, 87 Stat. 884, as amended, which is codified principally to 16 U.S.C.A. § 1531 et seq.; see Tables for complete classification], effective on July 22, 2001;

"(4) the terms 'National Contingency Plan', 'removal', and 'responsible party' have the meanings given those terms under section 1001 of the Oil Pollution Act of 1990 (33 U.S.C. 2701); and

"(5) the term 'private responder' means a nongovernmental entity or individual that is carrying out an oil spill removal activity at the direction of a Federal agency or a responsible party."

Implementation of National Planning and Response System

Section 4202(b) of Pub. L. No. 101–380 provided that:

"(1) Area Committees and Contingency Plans.—(A) Not later than 6 months after the date of the enactment of this Act [Aug. 18, 1990], the President shall designate the areas for which Area Committees are established under section 311(j)(4) of the Federal Water Pollution Control Act [subsec. (j)(4) of this section], as amended by this Act. In designating such areas, the President shall ensure that all navigable waters, adjoining shorelines, and waters of the exclusive economic zone are subject to an Area Contingency Plan under that section.

"(B) Not later than 18 months after the date of the enactment of this Act [Aug. 18, 1990], each Area Committee established under that section [subsec. (j)(4) of this section] shall submit to the President the Area Contingency Plan required under that section.

"(C) Not later than 24 months after the date of the enactment of this Act [Aug. 18, 1990], the President shall—

"(i) promptly review each plan;

"(ii) require amendments to any plan that does not meet the requirements of section 311(j)(4) of the Federal Water Pollution Control Act [subsec. (j)(4) of this section]; and

"(iii) approve each plan that meets the requirements of that section.

"(2) National Response Unit.—Not later than one year after the date of the enactment of this Act [Aug. 18, 1990], the Secretary of the department in which the Coast Guard is operating shall establish a National Response Unit in accordance with section 311(j)(2) of the Federal Water Pollution Control Act, as amended by this Act [subsec. (j)(2) of this section].

"(3) Coast Guard District Response Groups.—Not later than 1 year after the date of the enactment of this Act [Aug. 18, 1990], the Secretary of the department in which the Coast Guard is operating shall establish Coast Guard District Response Groups in accordance with section 311(j)(3) of the Federal Water Pollution Control Act, as amended by this Act [subsec. (j)(3) of this section].

"(4) Tank vessel and facility response plans; transition provision; effective date of prohibition.—

"(A) Not later than 24 months after the date of the enactment of this Act [Aug. 18, 1990], the President shall issue regulations for tank vessel and facility response plans under section 311(j)(5) of the Federal Water Pollution Control Act, as amended by this Act [subsec. (j)(5) of this section].

"(B) During the period beginning 30 months after the date of the enactment of this paragraph [Aug. 18, 1990], and ending 36 months after that date of enactment, a tank vessel or facility for which a response plan is required to be prepared under section 311(j)(5) of the Federal Water Pollution Control Act, [subsec. (j)(5) of this section], as amended by this Act, may not handle, store, or transport oil unless the owner or operator thereof has submitted such a plan to the President.

"(C) Subparagraph (E) of section 311(j)(5) of the Federal Water Pollution Control Act [subsec. (j)(5) of this section], as amended by this Act, shall take effect 36 months after the date of the enactment of this Act [Aug. 18, 1990]."

Oil Spill Liability Under Oil Pollution Act of 1990

Section 2002(a) of Pub. L. No. 101–380 provided that: "Subsections (f), (g), (h), and (i) of section 311 of the Federal Water Pollution Control Act (33 U.S.C. 1321) [subsecs. (f), (g), (h), and (i) of this section] shall not apply with respect to any incident for which liability is established under section 1002 of this Act [section 2702 of this title]."

Transfer to Oil Spill Liability Trust Fund of Moneys Remaining in Revolving Fund Upon Its Repeal

Section 2002(b)(2) of Pub. L. No. 101–380 provided that: "Subsection (k) [of this section] is repealed. Any amounts remaining in the revolving fund established under that subsection shall be deposited in the [Oil Spill Liability Trust] Fund. The [Oil Spill Liability Trust] Fund shall assume all liability incurred by the revolving fund established under that subsection."

Revision of National Contingency Plan

Section 4201(c) of Pub. L. No. 101–380 provided that: "Not later than one year after the date of the enactment of this Act [Aug. 18, 1990], the President shall revise and republish the National Contingency Plan prepared under section 311(c)(2) of the Federal Water Pollution Control Act [subsec. (c)(2) of this section] (as in effect immediately before the date of the enactment of this Act [Aug. 18, 1990]) to implement the amendments made by this section [amending subsecs. (a), (c), and (d) of this section] and section 4202 [amending subsecs. (j) and (*o*) of this section]."

Designation of Federal Trustees for Natural Resources

For designation by the President, in accordance with subsec. (f)(5) of this section, of the Secretaries of Defense, Interior, Agriculture, Commerce and Energy as among those to be designated in the National Contingency Plan as Federal Trustees for natural resources, see section 1(c) of Ex. Ord. No. 12580, Jan. 23, 1987, 52 Fed. Reg. 2923, set out as a note under section 9615 of Title 42, The Public Health and Welfare.

Allowable Delay in Establishing Financial Responsibility for Increases in Amounts Under 1977 Amendment

Section 58(j) of Pub. L. No. 95–217 provided that: "No vessel subject to the increased amounts which result from the amendments made by subsections (d)(2), (d)(3), and (d)(4) of this section [amending subsecs. (f)(1), (g), and (p)(1) of this section] shall be required to establish any evidence of financial responsibility under section 311(p) of the Federal Water Pollution Control Act [subsec. (p) of this section] for such increased amounts before October 1, 1978."

§ 1321a. Prevention of small oil spills

(a) Prevention and education program

The Under Secretary of Commerce for Oceans and Atmosphere, in consultation with the Secretary of the Department in which the Coast Guard is operating and other appropriate agencies, shall establish an oil spill prevention and education program for small vessels. The program shall provide for assessment, outreach, and training and voluntary compliance activities to prevent and improve the effective response to oil spills from vessels and facilities not required to prepare a vessel response plan under the Federal Water Pollution Control Act (33 U.S.C. 1251 et seq.), including recreational vessels, commercial fishing vessels, marinas, and aquaculture facilities. The Under Secretary may provide grants to sea grant colleges and institutes designated under section 1126 of this title and to State agencies, tribal governments, and other appropriate entities to carry out—

(1) regional assessments to quantify the source, incidence and volume of small oil spills, focusing initially on regions in the country where, in the past 10 years, the incidence of such spills is estimated to be the highest;

(2) voluntary, incentive-based clean marina programs that encourage marina operators, recreational boaters, and small commercial vessel operators to engage in environmentally sound operating and maintenance procedures and best management practices to prevent or reduce pollution from oil spills and other sources;

(3) cooperative oil spill prevention education programs that promote public understanding of the impacts of spilled oil and provide useful information and techniques to minimize pollution, including methods to remove oil and reduce oil contamination of bilge water, prevent accidental spills during maintenance and refueling and properly cleanup and dispose of oil and hazardous substances; and

(4) support for programs, including outreach and education to address derelict vessels and the threat of such vessels sinking and discharging oil and other hazardous substances, including outreach and education to involve efforts to the owners of such vessels.

(b) Authorization of appropriations

There are authorized to be appropriated to the Under Secretary of Commerce for Oceans and Atmosphere to carry out this section, $10,000,000 for each of fiscal years 2010 through 2014.

(Pub. L. No. 111–281, Title VII, § 705, 124 Stat. 2983 (Oct. 15, 2010).)

HISTORICAL AND STATUTORY NOTES

References in Text

The Federal Water Pollution Control Act, referred to in subsec. (a), commonly referred to as the Clean Water Act, is Act of June 30, 1948, c. 758, 62 Stat. 1155, as amended, which is principally codified as chapter 26 of Title 33, 33 U.S.C.A. § 1251 et seq. For complete classification, see Short Title note set out under 33 U.S.C.A. § 1251 and Tables.

Codifications

Section was enacted as part of the Coast Guard Authorization Act of 2010 and not as part of the Federal Water Pollution Control Act, which otherwise comprises this chapter.

§ 1321b. Improved coordination with tribal governments

(a) In general

Within 6 months after October 15, 2010, the Secretary of the Department in which the Coast Guard is operating shall complete the development of a tribal consultation policy, which recognizes and protects to the maximum extent practicable tribal treaty rights and trust assets in order to improve the Coast Guard's consultation and coordination with the tribal governments of federally recognized Indian tribes with respect to oil spill prevention, preparedness, response and natural resource damage assessment.

(b) Inclusion of tribal government

The Secretary of the Department in which the Coast Guard is operating shall ensure that, as soon as practicable after identifying an oil spill that is likely to have a significant impact on natural or cultural resources owned or directly utilized by a federally recognized Indian tribe, the Coast Guard will—

(1) ensure that representatives of the tribal government of the affected tribes are included as part of the incident command system established by the Coast Guard to respond to the spill;

(2) share information about the oil spill with the tribal government of the affected tribe; and

(3) to the extent practicable, involve tribal governments in deciding how to respond to the spill.

(c) Cooperative arrangements

The Coast Guard may enter into memoranda of agreement and associated protocols with Indian tribal governments in order to establish cooperative arrangements for oil pollution prevention, preparedness, and response. Such memoranda may be entered into prior to the development of the tribal consultation and coordination policy to provide Indian tribes grant and contract assistance. Such memoranda of agreement and associated protocols with Indian tribal governments may include—

(1) arrangements for the assistance of the tribal government to participate in the development of the National Contingency Plan and local Area Contingency Plans to the extent they affect tribal lands, cultural and natural resources;

(2) arrangements for the assistance of the tribal government to develop the capacity to implement the National Contingency Plan and local Area Contingency Plans to the extent they affect tribal lands, cultural and natural resources;

(3) provisions on coordination in the event of a spill, including agreements that representatives of the tribal government will be included as part of the regional response team co-chaired by the Coast Guard and the Environmental Protection Agency to establish policies for responding to oil spills;

(4) arrangements for the Coast Guard to provide training of tribal incident commanders and spill responders for oil spill preparedness and response;

(5) demonstration projects to assist tribal governments in building the capacity to protect tribal treaty rights and trust assets from oil spills; and

(6) such additional measures the Coast Guard determines to be necessary for oil pollution prevention, preparedness, and response.

(d) Funding for tribal participation

Subject to the availability of appropriations, the Commandant of the Coast Guard shall provide assistance to participating tribal governments in order to facilitate the implementation of cooperative arrangements under subsection (c) and ensure the participation of tribal governments in such arrangements. There are authorized to be appropriated to the Commandant $500,000 for each of fiscal years 2010 through 2014 to be used to carry out this section.

(Pub. L. No. 111–281, Title VII, § 706, 124 Stat. 2983 (Oct. 15, 2010).)

HISTORICAL AND STATUTORY NOTES

Codifications

This section was enacted as part of the Coast Guard Authorization Act of 2010 and not as part of the Federal Water Pollution Control Act, which otherwise comprises this chapter.

§ 1321c. International efforts on enforcement

The Secretary of the department in which the Coast Guard is operating, in consultation with the heads of other appropriate Federal agencies, shall ensure that the Coast Guard pursues stronger enforcement in the International Maritime Organization of agreements related to oil discharges, including joint enforcement operations, training, and stronger compliance mechanisms.

(Pub. L. No. 111–281, Title VII, § 709, 124 Stat. 2986 (Oct. 15, 2010).)

HISTORICAL NOTES AND STATUTORY NOTES

Codifications

This section was enacted as part of the Coast Guard Authorization Act of 2010 and not as part of the Federal Water Pollution Control Act, which otherwise comprises this chapter.

§ 1322. Marine sanitation devices; discharges incidental to the normal operation of vessels

[FWPCA § 312]

(a) Definitions

In this section, the term—

(1) "new vessel" includes every description of watercraft or other artificial contrivance used, or capable of being used, as a means of transportation on the navigable waters, the construction of which is initiated after promulgation of standards and regulations under this section;

(2) "existing vessel" includes every description of watercraft or other artificial contrivance used, or capable of being used, as a means of transportation on the navigable waters, the construction of which is initiated before promulgation of standards and regulations under this section;

(3) "public vessel" means a vessel owned or bareboat chartered and operated by the United States, by a State or political subdivision thereof, or by a foreign nation, except when such vessel is engaged in commerce;

(4) "United States" includes the States, the District of Columbia, the Commonwealth of Puerto Rico, the Virgin Islands, Guam, American Samoa, the Canal Zone, and the Trust Territory of the Pacific Islands;

(5) "marine sanitation device" includes any equipment for installation on board a vessel which is designed to receive, retain, treat, or discharge sewage, and any process to treat such sewage;

(6) "sewage" means human body wastes and the wastes from toilets and other receptacles intended to receive or retain body wastes except that, with respect to commercial vessels on the Great Lakes, such term shall include graywater;

(7) "manufacturer" means any person engaged in the manufacturing, assembling, or importation of marine sanitation devices, marine pollution control device equipment, or of vessels subject to standards and regulations promulgated under this section;

(8) "person" means an individual, partnership, firm, corporation, association, or agency of the United States, but does not include an individual on board a public vessel;

(9) "discharge" includes, but is not limited to, any spilling, leaking, pumping, pouring, emitting, emptying or dumping;

(10) "commercial vessels" means those vessels used in the business of transporting property for compensation or hire, or in transporting property in the business of the owner, lessee, or operator of the vessel;

(11) "graywater" means galley, bath, and shower water;

(12) "discharge incidental to the normal operation of a vessel"—

(A) means a discharge, including—

(i) graywater, bilge water, cooling water, weather deck runoff, ballast water, oil water separator effluent, and any other pollutant discharge from the operation of a marine propulsion system, shipboard maneuvering system, crew habitability system, or installed major equipment, such as an aircraft carrier elevator or a catapult, or from a protective, preservative, or absorptive application to the hull of the vessel; and

(ii) a discharge in connection with the testing, maintenance, and repair of a system described in clause (i) whenever the vessel is waterborne; and

(B) does not include—

(i) a discharge of rubbish, trash, garbage, or other such material discharged overboard;

(ii) an air emission resulting from the operation of a vessel propulsion system, motor driven equipment, or incinerator; or

(iii) a discharge that is not covered by part 122.3 of title 40, Code of Federal Regulations (as in effect on February 10, 1996);

(13) "marine pollution control device" means, except as provided in subsection (p), any equipment or management practice, for installation or use on board a vessel of the Armed Forces, that is—

(A) designed to receive, retain, treat, control, or discharge a discharge incidental to the normal operation of a vessel; and

(B) determined by the Administrator and the Secretary of Defense to be the most effective equipment or management practice to reduce the environmental impacts of the discharge consistent with the considerations set forth in subsection (n)(2)(B) of this section; and

(14) "vessel of the Armed Forces" means—

(A) any vessel owned or operated by the Department of Defense, other than a time or voyage chartered vessel; and

(B) any vessel owned or operated by the Department of Transportation that is designated by the Secretary of the department in which the Coast Guard is operating as a vessel equivalent to a vessel described in subparagraph (A).

(b) Federal standards of performance

(1) As soon as possible, after October 18, 1972, and subject to the provisions of section 1254(j) of this title, the Administrator, after consultation with the Secretary of the department in which the Coast Guard is operating, after giving appropriate consideration to the economic costs involved, and within the limits of available technology, shall promulgate Federal standards of performance for marine sanitation devices (hereafter in this section referred to as "standards") which shall be designed to prevent the discharge of untreated or inadequately treated sewage into or upon the navigable waters from new vessels and existing vessels, except vessels not equipped with installed toilet facilities. Such standards and standards established under subsection (c)(1)(B) of this section shall be consistent with maritime safety and the marine and navigation laws and regulations and shall be coordinated with the regulations issued under this subsection by the Secretary of the department in which the Coast Guard is operating. The Secretary of the department in which the Coast Guard is operating shall promulgate regulations, which are consistent with standards promulgated under this subsection and subsection (c) of this section and with maritime safety and the marine and navigation laws and regulations governing the design, construction, installation, and operation of any marine sanitation device on board such vessels.

(2) Any existing vessel equipped with a marine sanitation device on the date of promulgation of initial standards and regulations under this section, which device is in compliance with such initial standards and regulations, shall be deemed in compliance with this section until such time as the device is replaced or is found not to be in compliance with such initial standards and regulations.

(c) Initial standards; effective dates; revision; waiver

(1) **(A)** Initial standards and regulations under this section shall become effective for new vessels two years after promulgation; and for existing vessels five years after promulgation. Revisions of standards and regulations shall be effective upon promulgation, unless another effective date is specified, except that no revision shall take effect before the effective date of the standard or regulation being revised.

(B) The Administrator shall, with respect to commercial vessels on the Great Lakes, establish standards which require at a minimum the equivalent of secondary treatment as defined under section 1314(d) of this title. Such standards and regulations shall take effect for existing vessels after such time as the Administrator determines to be reasonable for the upgrading of marine sanitation devices to attain such standard.

(2) The Secretary of the department in which the Coast Guard is operating with regard to his regulatory authority established by this section, after consultation with the Administrator, may distinguish among classes, type, and sizes of vessels as well as between new and existing vessels, and may waive applicability of standards and regulations as necessary or appropriate for such classes, types, and sizes of vessels (including existing vessels equipped with marine sanitation devices on the date of promulgation of the initial standards required by this section), and, upon application, for individual vessels.

(d) Vessels owned and operated by the United States

The provisions of this section and the standards and regulations promulgated hereunder apply to vessels owned and operated by the United States unless the Secretary of Defense finds that compliance would not be in the interest of national security. With respect to vessels owned and operated by the Department of Defense, regulations under the last sentence of subsection (b)(1) of this section and certifications under subsection (g)(2) of this section shall be promulgated and issued by the Secretary of Defense.

(e) Pre-promulgation consultation

Before the standards and regulations under this section are promulgated, the Administrator and the Secretary of the department in which the Coast Guard is operating shall consult with the Secretary of State; the Secretary of Health and Human Services; the Secretary of Defense; the Secretary of the Treasury; the Secretary of Commerce; other interested Federal agencies; and the States and industries interested; and otherwise comply with the requirements of section 553 of Title 5.

(f) Regulation by States or political subdivisions thereof; complete prohibition upon discharge of sewage

(1) (A) Except as provided in subparagraph (B), after the effective date of the initial standards and regulations promulgated under this section, no State or political subdivision thereof shall adopt or enforce any statute or regulation of such State or political subdivision with respect to the design, manufacture, or installation or use of any marine sanitation device on any vessel subject to the provisions of this section.

(B) A State may adopt and enforce a statute or regulation with respect to the design, manufacture, or installation or use of any marine sanitation device on a houseboat, if such statute or regulation is more stringent than the standards and regulations promulgated under this section. For purposes of this paragraph, the term "houseboat" means a vessel which, for a period of time determined by the State in which the vessel is located, is used primarily as a residence and is not used primarily as a means of transportation.

(2) If, after promulgation of the initial standards and regulations and prior to their effective date, a vessel is equipped with a marine sanitation device in compliance with such standards and regulations and the installation and operation of such device is in accordance with such standards and regulations, such standards and regulations shall, for the purposes of paragraph (1) of this subsection, become effective with respect to such vessel on the date of such compliance.

(3) After the effective date of the initial standards and regulations promulgated under this section, if any State determines that the protection and enhancement of the quality of some or all of the waters within such State require greater environmental protection, such State may completely prohibit the discharge from all vessels of any sewage, whether treated or not, into such waters, except that no such prohibition shall apply until the Administrator determines that adequate facilities for the safe and sanitary removal and treatment of sewage from all vessels are reasonably available for such water to which such prohibition would apply. Upon application of the State, the Administrator shall make such determination within 90 days of the date of such application.

(4) (A) If the Administrator determines upon application by a State that the protection and enhancement of the quality of specified waters within such State requires such a prohibition, he shall by regulation completely prohibit the discharge from a vessel of any sewage (whether treated or not) into such waters.

(B) Upon application by a State, the Administrator shall, by regulation, establish a drinking water intake zone in any waters within such State and prohibit the discharge of sewage from vessels within that zone.

(g) Sales limited to certified devices; certification of test device; recordkeeping; reports

(1) No manufacturer of a marine sanitation device or marine pollution control device equipment shall sell, offer for sale, or introduce or deliver for introduction in interstate commerce, or import into the United States for sale or resale any marine sanitation device or marine pollution control device equipment manufactured after the effective date of the standards and regulations promulgated under this section unless such device or equipment is in all material respects substantially the same as a test device or equipment certified under this subsection.

(2) Upon application of the manufacturer, the Secretary of the department in which the Coast Guard is operating shall so certify a marine sanitation device or marine pollution control device equipment if he determines, in accordance with the provisions of this paragraph, that it meets the appropriate standards and regulations promulgated under this section. The Secretary of the department in which the Coast Guard is operating shall test or require such testing of the device or equipment in accordance with procedures set forth by the Administrator as to standards of performance and for such other purposes as may be appropriate. If the Secretary of the department in which the Coast Guard is operating determines that the device or equipment is satisfactory from the standpoint of safety and any other requirements of maritime law or regulation, and after consideration of the design, installation, operation, material, or other appropriate factors, he shall certify the device or equipment. Any device or equipment manufactured by such manufacturer which is in all material respects substantially the same as the certified test device or equipment shall be deemed to be in conformity with the appropriate standards and regulations established under this section.

(3) Every manufacturer shall establish and maintain such records, make such reports, and provide such information as the Administrator or the Secretary of the department in which the Coast Guard is operating may reasonably require to enable him to determine whether such manufacturer has acted or is acting in compliance with this section and regulations issued thereunder and shall, upon request of an officer or employee duly designated by the Administrator or the Secretary of the department in which the Coast Guard is operating, permit such officer or employee at reasonable times to have access to and copy such records. All information reported to or otherwise obtained by the Administrator or the Secretary of the department in which the Coast Guard is operating or their representatives pursuant to this subsection which contains or relates to a trade secret or other matter referred to in section 1905 of Title 18 shall be considered confidential for the purpose of that section, except that such information may be disclosed to other officers or employees concerned with carrying out this section. This paragraph shall not apply in the case of the construction of a vessel by an individual for his own use.

(h) Sale and resale of properly equipped vessels; operability of certified marine sanitation devices.—

(1) In general.—Subject to paragraph (2), after the effective date of standards and regulations promulgated under this section, it shall be unlawful—

(A) for the manufacturer of any vessel subject to such standards and regulations to manufacture for sale, to sell or offer for sale, or to distribute for sale or resale any such vessel unless it is equipped with a marine sanitation device or marine pollution control device equipment which is in all material respects substantially the same as the appropriate test device or equipment certified pursuant to this section;

(B) for any person, prior to the sale or delivery of a vessel subject to such standards and regulations to the ultimate purchaser, wrongfully to remove or render inoperative any certified marine sanitation device or element of design of such device or certified marine pollution control device equipment or element of design of such equipment installed in such vessel;

(C) for any person to fail or refuse to permit access to or copying of records or to fail to make reports or provide information required under this section; and

(D) for a vessel subject to such standards and regulations to operate on the navigable waters of the United States, if such vessel is not equipped with an operable marine sanitation device certified pursuant to this section.

(2) Effect of subsection.—Nothing in this subsection requires certification of a marine pollution control device for use on any vessel of the Armed Forces.".

(i) Jurisdiction to restrain violations; contempts

The district courts of the United States shall have jurisdictions to restrain violations of subsection (g)(1) of this section and subsections (h)(1) through (3) of this section. Actions to restrain such violations shall be brought by, and in, the name of the United States. In case of contumacy or refusal to obey a subpena served upon any person under this subsection, the district court of the United States for any district in which such person is found or resides or transacts business, upon application by the United States and after notice to such person, shall have jurisdiction to issue an order requiring such person to appear and give testimony or to appear and produce documents, and any failure to obey such order of the court may be punished by such court as a contempt thereof.

(j) Penalties

Any person who violates subsection (g)(1) of this section, clause (1) or (2) of subsection (h) of this section, or subsection (n)(8) of this section shall be liable to a civil penalty of not more than $5,000 for each violation. Any person who violates clause (4) of subsection (h) of this section or any regulation issued pursuant to this section shall be liable to a civil penalty of not more than $2,000 for each violation. Each violation shall be a separate offense. The Secretary of the department in which the Coast Guard is operating may assess and compromise any such penalty. No penalty shall be assessed until the person charged shall have been given notice and an opportunity for a hearing on such charge. In determining the amount of the penalty, or the amount agreed upon in compromise, the gravity of the violation, and the demonstrated good faith of the person charged in attempting to achieve rapid compliance, after notification of a violation, shall be considered by said Secretary.

(k) Enforcement authority

(1) Administrator.—This section shall be enforced by the Administrator, to the extent provided in section 1319.

(2) Secretary.—

(A) In general.—This section shall be enforced by the Secretary of the department in which the Coast Guard is operating, who may use, by agreement, with or without reimbursement, law enforcement officers or other personnel and facilities of the Administrator, other Federal agencies, or the States to carry out the provisions of this section.

(B) Inspections.—For purposes of ensuring compliance with this section, the Secretary—

(i) may carry out an inspection (including the taking of ballast water samples) of any vessel at any time; and

(ii) shall—

(I) establish procedures for—

(aa) reporting violations of this section; and

(bb) accumulating evidence regarding those violations; and

(II) use appropriate and practicable measures of detection and environmental monitoring of vessels.

(C) Detention.—The Secretary may detain a vessel if the Secretary—

(i) has reasonable cause to believe that the vessel—

(I) has failed to comply with an applicable requirement of this section; or

(II) is being operated in violation of such a requirement; and

(ii) the Secretary provides to the owner or operator of the vessel a notice of the intent to detain.

(3) States.—

(A) In general.—This section may be enforced by a State or political subdivision of a State (including the attorney general of a State), including by filing a civil action in an appropriate Federal district court to enforce any violation of subsection (p).

(B) Jurisdiction.—The appropriate Federal district court shall have jurisdiction with respect to a civil action filed pursuant to subparagraph (A), without regard to the amount in controversy or the citizenship of the parties—

(i) to enforce the requirements of this section; and

(ii) to apply appropriate civil penalties under this section or section 309(d), as appropriate.

(*l*) Boarding and inspection of vessels; execution of warrants and other process

Anyone authorized by the Secretary of the department in which the Coast Guard is operating to enforce the provisions of this section may, except as to public vessels, (1) board and inspect any vessel upon the navigable waters of the United States and (2) execute any warrant or other process issued by an officer or court of competent jurisdiction.

(m) Enforcement in United States possessions

In the case of Guam and the Trust Territory of the Pacific Islands, actions arising under this section may be brought in the district court of Guam, and in the case of the Virgin Islands such actions may be brought in the district court of the Virgin Islands. In the case of American Samoa and the Trust Territory of the Pacific Islands, such actions may be brought in the District Court of the United States for the District of Hawaii and such court shall have jurisdiction of such actions. In the case of the Canal Zone, such actions may be brought in the District Court for the District of the Canal Zone.

(n) Uniform National Discharge Standards for Vessels of Armed Forces

(1) Applicability

This subsection shall apply to vessels of the Armed Forces and discharges, other than sewage, incidental to the normal operation of a vessel of the Armed Forces, unless the Secretary of Defense finds that compliance with this subsection would not be in the national security interests of the United States.

(2) Determination of discharges required to be controlled by marine pollution control devices

(A) In general

The Administrator and the Secretary of Defense, after consultation with the Secretary of the department in which the Coast Guard is operating, the Secretary of Commerce, and interested States, shall jointly determine the discharges incidental to the normal operation of a vessel of the Armed Forces for which it is reasonable and practicable to require use of a marine pollution control device to mitigate adverse impacts on the marine environment. Notwithstanding subsection (a)(1) of section 553 of Title 5, the Administrator and the Secretary of Defense shall promulgate the determinations in accordance with such section. The Secretary of Defense shall require the use of a marine pollution control device on board a vessel of the Armed Forces in any case in which it is determined that the use of such a device is reasonable and practicable.

(B) Considerations

In making a determination under subparagraph (A), the Administrator and the Secretary of Defense shall take into consideration—

(i) the nature of the discharge;

(ii) the environmental effects of the discharge;

(iii) the practicability of using the marine pollution control device;

(iv) the effect that installation or use of the marine pollution control device would have on the operation or operational capability of the vessel;

(v) applicable United States law;

(vi) applicable international standards; and

(vii) the economic costs of the installation and use of the marine pollution control device.

(3) Performance standards for marine pollution control devices

(A) In general

For each discharge for which a marine pollution control device is determined to be required under paragraph (2), the Administrator and the Secretary of Defense, in consultation with the Secretary of the department in which the Coast Guard is operating, the Secretary of State, the Secretary of Commerce, other interested Federal agencies, and interested States, shall jointly promulgate Federal standards of performance for each marine pollution control device required with respect to the discharge. Notwithstanding subsection (a)(1) of section 553 of Title 5, the

Administrator and the Secretary of Defense shall promulgate the standards in accordance with such section.

(B) Considerations

In promulgating standards under this paragraph, the Administrator and the Secretary of Defense shall take into consideration the matters set forth in paragraph (2)(B).

(C) Classes, types, and sizes of vessels

The standards promulgated under this paragraph may—

(i) distinguish among classes, types, and sizes of vessels;

(ii) distinguish between new and existing vessels; and

(iii) provide for a waiver of the applicability of the standards as necessary or appropriate to a particular class, type, age, or size of vessel.

(4) Regulations for use of marine pollution control devices

The Secretary of Defense, after consultation with the Administrator and the Secretary of the department in which the Coast Guard is operating, shall promulgate such regulations governing the design, construction, installation, and use of marine pollution control devices on board vessels of the Armed Forces as are necessary to achieve the standards promulgated under paragraph (3).

(5) Deadlines; effective date

(A) Determinations

The Administrator and the Secretary of Defense shall—

(i) make the initial determinations under paragraph (2) not later than 2 years after February 10, 1996; and

(ii) every 5 years—

(I) review the determinations; and

(II) if necessary, revise the determinations based on significant new information.

(B) Standards

The Administrator and the Secretary of Defense shall—

(i) promulgate standards of performance for a marine pollution control device under paragraph (3) not later than 2 years after the date of a determination under paragraph (2) that the marine pollution control device is required; and

(ii) every 5 years—

(I) review the standards; and

(II) if necessary, revise the standards, consistent with paragraph (3)(B) and based on significant new information.

(C) Regulations

The Secretary of Defense shall promulgate regulations with respect to a marine pollution control device under paragraph (4) as soon as practicable after the Administrator and the Secretary of Defense promulgate standards with respect to the device under paragraph (3), but not later than 1 year after the Administrator and the Secretary of Defense promulgate the standards. The regulations promulgated by the Secretary of Defense under paragraph (4) shall become effective upon promulgation unless another effective date is specified in the regulations.

(D) Petition for review

The Governor of any State may submit a petition requesting that the Secretary of Defense and the Administrator review a determination under paragraph (2) or a standard under paragraph (3), if there is significant new information, not considered previously, that could reasonably result in a change to the particular determination or standard after consideration of the matters set forth in paragraph (2)(B). The petition shall be accompanied by the scientific and technical information on which the petition is based. The Administrator and the Secretary of Defense shall grant or deny the petition not later than 2 years after the date of receipt of the petition.

(6) Effect on other laws

(A) Prohibition on regulation by States or political subdivisions of States

Beginning on the effective date of—

(i) a determination under paragraph (2) that it is not reasonable and practicable to require use of a marine pollution control device regarding a particular discharge incidental to the normal operation of a vessel of the Armed Forces; or

(ii) regulations promulgated by the Secretary of Defense under paragraph (4);

except as provided in paragraph (7), neither a State nor a political subdivision of a State may adopt or enforce any statute or regulation of the State or political subdivision with respect to the discharge or the design, construction, installation, or use of any marine pollution control device required to control discharges from a vessel of the Armed Forces.

(B) Federal laws

This subsection shall not affect the application of section 1321 of this title to discharges incidental to the normal operation of a vessel.

(7) Establishment of State no-discharge zones

(A) State prohibition

(i) In general

After the effective date of—

(I) a determination under paragraph (2) that it is not reasonable and practicable to require use of a marine pollution control device regarding a particular discharge incidental to the normal operation of a vessel of the Armed Forces; or

(II) regulations promulgated by the Secretary of Defense under paragraph (4);

if a State determines that the protection and enhancement of the quality of some or all of the waters within the State require greater environmental protection, the State may prohibit 1 or more discharges incidental to the normal operation of a vessel, whether treated or not treated, into the waters. No prohibition shall apply until the Administrator makes the determinations described in subclauses (II) and (III) of subparagraph (B)(i).

(ii) Documentation

To the extent that a prohibition under this paragraph would apply to vessels of the Armed Forces and not to other types of vessels, the State shall document the technical or environmental basis for the distinction.

(B) Prohibition by the Administrator

(i) In general

Upon application of a State, the Administrator shall by regulation prohibit the discharge from a vessel of 1 or more discharges incidental to the normal operation of a vessel, whether treated or not treated, into the waters covered by the application if the Administrator determines that—

(I) the protection and enhancement of the quality of the specified waters within the State require a prohibition of the discharge into the waters;

(II) adequate facilities for the safe and sanitary removal of the discharge incidental to the normal operation of a vessel are reasonably available for the waters to which the prohibition would apply; and

(III) the prohibition will not have the effect of discriminating against a vessel of the Armed Forces by reason of the ownership or operation by the Federal Government, or the military function, of the vessel.

(ii) Approval or disapproval

The Administrator shall approve or disapprove an application submitted under clause (i) not later than 90 days after the date on which the application is submitted to the Administrator. Notwithstanding clause (i)(II), the Administrator shall not disapprove an application for the sole reason that there are not adequate facilities to remove any discharge incidental to the normal operation of a vessel from vessels of the Armed Forces.

(C) Applicability to foreign flagged vessels

A prohibition under this paragraph—

(i) shall not impose any design, construction, manning, or equipment standard on a foreign flagged vessel engaged in innocent passage unless the prohibition implements a generally accepted international rule or standard; and

(ii) that relates to the prevention, reduction, and control of pollution shall not apply to a foreign flagged vessel engaged in transit passage unless the prohibition implements an applicable international regulation regarding the discharge of oil, oily waste, or any other noxious substance into the waters.

(8) Prohibition relating to vessels of the Armed Forces

After the effective date of the regulations promulgated by the Secretary of Defense under paragraph (4), it shall be unlawful for any vessel of the Armed Forces subject to the regulations to—

(A) operate in the navigable waters of the United States or the waters of the contiguous zone, if the vessel is not equipped with any required marine pollution control device meeting standards established under this subsection; or

(B) discharge overboard any discharge incidental to the normal operation of a vessel in waters with respect to which a prohibition on the discharge has been established under paragraph (7).

(9) Enforcement

This subsection shall be enforceable, as provided in subsections (j) and (k) of this section, against any agency of the United States responsible for vessels of the Armed Forces notwithstanding any immunity asserted by the agency.

(*o*) Management practices for recreational vessels

(1) Applicability

This subsection applies to any discharge, other than a discharge of sewage, from a recreational vessel that is—

(A) incidental to the normal operation of the vessel; and

(B) exempt from permitting requirements under section 1342(r) of this title.

(2) Determination of discharges subject to management practices

(A) Determination

(i) In general

The Administrator, in consultation with the Secretary of the department in which the Coast Guard is operating, the Secretary of Commerce, and interested States, shall determine the discharges incidental to the normal operation of a recreational vessel for which it is reasonable and practicable to develop management practices to mitigate adverse impacts on the waters of the United States.

(ii) Promulgation

The Administrator shall promulgate the determinations under clause (i) in accordance with section 553 of Title 5.

(iii) Management practices

The Administrator shall develop management practices for recreational vessels in any case in which the Administrator determines that the use of those practices is reasonable and practicable.

(B) Considerations

In making a determination under subparagraph (A), the Administrator shall consider—

(i) the nature of the discharge;

(ii) the environmental effects of the discharge;

(iii) the practicability of using a management practice;

(iv) the effect that the use of a management practice would have on the operation, operational capability, or safety of the vessel;

(v) applicable Federal and State law;

(vi) applicable international standards; and

(vii) the economic costs of the use of the management practice.

(C) Timing

The Administrator shall—

(i) make the initial determinations under subparagraph (A) not later than 1 year after July 29, 2008; and

(ii) every 5 years thereafter—

(I) review the determinations; and

(II) if necessary, revise the determinations based on any new information available to the Administrator.

(3) Performance standards for management practices

(A) In general

For each discharge for which a management practice is developed under paragraph (2), the Administrator, in consultation with the Secretary of the department in which the Coast Guard is operating, the Secretary of Commerce, other interested Federal agencies, and interested States, shall promulgate, in accordance with section 553 of Title 5, Federal standards of performance for each management practice required with respect to the discharge.

(B) Considerations

In promulgating standards under this paragraph, the Administrator shall take into account the considerations described in paragraph (2)(B).

(C) Classes, types, and sizes of vessels

The standards promulgated under this paragraph may—

(i) distinguish among classes, types, and sizes of vessels;

(ii) distinguish between new and existing vessels; and

(iii) provide for a waiver of the applicability of the standards as necessary or appropriate to a particular class, type, age, or size of vessel.

(D) Timing

The Administrator shall—

(i) promulgate standards of performance for a management practice under subparagraph (A) not later than 1 year after the date of a determination under paragraph (2) that the management practice is reasonable and practicable; and

(ii) every 5 years thereafter—

(I) review the standards; and

(II) if necessary, revise the standards, in accordance with subparagraph (B) and based on any new information available to the Administrator.

(4) Regulations for the use of management practices

(A) In general

The Secretary of the department in which the Coast Guard is operating shall promulgate such regulations governing the design, construction, installation, and use of management practices for recreational vessels as are necessary to meet the standards of performance promulgated under paragraph (3).

(B) Regulations

(i) In general

The Secretary shall promulgate the regulations under this paragraph as soon as practicable after the Administrator promulgates standards with respect to the practice under paragraph (3), but not later than 1 year after the date on which the Administrator promulgates the standards.

(ii) Effective date

The regulations promulgated by the Secretary under this paragraph shall be effective upon promulgation unless another effective date is specified in the regulations.

(iii) Consideration of time

In determining the effective date of a regulation promulgated under this paragraph, the Secretary shall consider the period of time necessary to communicate the existence of the regulation to persons affected by the regulation.

(5) Effect of other laws

This subsection shall not affect the application of section 1321 of this title to discharges incidental to the normal operation of a recreational vessel.

(6) Prohibition relating to recreational vessels

After the effective date of the regulations promulgated by the Secretary of the department in which the Coast Guard is operating under paragraph (4), the owner or operator of a recreational vessel shall neither operate in nor discharge any discharge incidental to the normal operation of the vessel into, the waters of the United States or the waters of the contiguous zone, if the owner or operator of the vessel is not using any applicable management practice meeting standards established under this subsection.

(p) Uniform national standard for discharges incidental to normal operations of vessels.—

(1) Definitions.—In this subsection:

(A) Aquatic nuisance species.—The term "aquatic nuisance species" means a nonindigenous species that threatens—

(i) the diversity or abundance of a native species;

(ii) the ecological stability of—

(I) waters of the United States; or

(II) waters of the contiguous zone; or

(iii) a commercial, agricultural, aquacultural, or recreational activity that is dependent on—

(I) waters of the United States; or

(II) waters of the contiguous zone.

(B) Ballast water.—

(i) In general.—The term "ballast water" means any water, suspended matter, and other materials taken onboard a vessel—

(I) to control or maintain trim, draught, stability, or stresses of the vessel, regardless of the means by which any such water or suspended matter is carried; or

(II) during the cleaning, maintenance, or other operation of a ballast tank or ballast water management system of the vessel.

(ii) Exclusion.—The term "ballast water" does not include any substance that is added to the water described in clause (i) that is directly related to the operation of a properly functioning ballast water management system.

(C) Ballast water discharge standard.—The term "ballast water discharge standard" means—

(i) the numerical ballast water discharge standard established by section 151.1511 or 151.2030 of title 33, Code of Federal Regulations (or successor regulations); or

(ii) if a standard referred to in clause (i) is superseded by a numerical standard of performance under this subsection, that superseding standard.

(D) Ballast water exchange.—The term "ballast water exchange" means the replacement of water in a ballast water tank using 1 of the following methods:

(i) Flow-through exchange, in which ballast water is flushed out by pumping in midocean water at the bottom of the tank if practicable, and continuously overflowing the tank from the top, until 3 full volumes of water have been changed to minimize the number of original organisms remaining in the tank.

(ii) Empty and refill exchange, in which ballast water taken on in ports, estuarine waters, or territorial waters is pumped out until the pump loses suction, after which the ballast tank is refilled with midocean water.

(E) Ballast water management system.—The term "ballast water management system" means any marine pollution control device (including all ballast water treatment equipment, ballast tanks, pipes, pumps, and all associated control and monitoring equipment) that processes ballast water—

(i) to kill, render nonviable, or remove organisms; or

(ii) to avoid the uptake or discharge of organisms.

(F) Best available technology economically achievable.—The term "best available technology economically achievable" means—

(i) best available technology economically achievable (within the meaning of section 1311(b)(2)(A));

(ii) best available technology (within the meaning of section 13144(b)(2)(B)); and

(iii) best available technology, as determined in accordance with section 125.3(d)(3) of title 40, Code of Federal Regulations (or successor regulations).

(G) Best conventional pollutant control technology.—The term "best conventional pollutant control technology" means—

(i) best conventional pollutant control technology (within the meaning of section 1311(b)(2)(E));

(ii) best conventional pollutant control technology (within the meaning of section 1314(b)(4)); and

(iii) best conventional pollutant control technology, as determined in accordance with section 125.3(d)(2) of title 40, Code of Federal Regulations (or successor regulations).

(H) Best management practice.—

(i) In general.—The term "best management practice" means a schedule of activities, prohibitions of practices, maintenance procedures, and other management practices to prevent or reduce the pollution of—

(I) the waters of the United States; or

(II) the waters of the contiguous zone.

(ii) Inclusions.—The term "best management practice" includes any treatment requirement, operating procedure, or practice to control—

(I) vessel runoff;

(II) spillage or leaks;

(III) sludge or waste disposal; or

(IV) drainage from raw material storage.

(I) Best practicable control technology currently available.—The term "best practicable control technology currently available" means—

(i) best practicable control technology currently available (within the meaning of section 1311(b)(1)(A));

(ii) best practicable control technology currently available (within the meaning of section 1314(b)(1)); and

(iii) best practicable control technology currently available, as determined in accordance with section 125.3(d)(1) of title 40, Code of Federal Regulations (or successor regulations).

(J) Captain of the Port Zone.—The term "Captain of the Port Zone" means a Captain of the Port Zone established by the Secretary pursuant to sections 92, 93, and 633 of title 14, United States Code.

(K) Empty ballast tank.—The term "empty ballast tank" means a tank that—

(i) has previously held ballast water that has been drained to the limit of the functional or operational capabilities of the tank (such as loss of suction);

(ii) is recorded as empty on a vessel log; and

(iii) contains unpumpable residual ballast water and sediment.

(L) Great Lakes Commission.—The term "Great Lakes Commission" means the Great Lakes Commission established by article IV A of the Great Lakes Compact to which Congress granted consent in the Act of July 24, 1968 (Public Law 90–419; 82 Stat. 414).

(M) Great Lakes State.—The term "Great Lakes State" means any of the States of—

(i) Illinois;

(ii) Indiana;

(iii) Michigan;

(iv) Minnesota;

(v) New York;

(vi) Ohio;

(vii) Pennsylvania; and

(viii) Wisconsin.

(N) Great Lakes System.—The term "Great Lakes System" has the meaning given the term in section 1268(a)(3).

(O) Internal waters.—The term "internal waters" has the meaning given the term in section 2.24 of title 33, Code of Federal Regulations (or a successor regulation).

(P) Marine pollution control device.—The term "marine pollution control device" means any equipment or management practice (or combination of equipment and a management practice), for installation or use onboard a vessel, that is—

(i) designed to receive, retain, treat, control, or discharge a discharge incidental to the normal operation of a vessel; and

(ii) determined by the Administrator and the Secretary to be the most effective equipment or management practice (or combination of equipment and a management practice) to reduce the environmental impacts of the discharge, consistent with the factors for consideration described in paragraphs (4) and (5).

(Q) Nonindigenous species.—The term "nonindigenous species" means an organism of a species that enters an ecosystem beyond the historic range of the species.

(R) Organism.—The term "organism" includes—

(i) an animal, including fish and fish eggs and larvae;

(ii) a plant;

(iii) a pathogen;

(iv) a microbe;

(v) a virus;

(vi) a prokaryote (including any archean or bacterium);

(vii) a fungus; and

(viii) a protist.

(S) Pacific Region.—

(i) In general.—The term "Pacific Region" means any Federal or State water—

(I) adjacent to the State of Alaska, California, Hawaii, Oregon, or Washington; and

(II) extending from shore.

(ii) Inclusion.—The term "Pacific Region" includes the entire exclusive economic zone (as defined in section 1001 of the Oil Pollution Act of 1990 (33 U.S.C. 2701)) adjacent to each State described in clause (i)(I).

(T) Port or place of destination.—The term "port or place of destination" means a port or place to which a vessel is bound to anchor or moor.

(U) Render nonviable.—The term "render nonviable", with respect to an organism in ballast water, means the action of a ballast water management system that renders the organism permanently incapable of reproduction following treatment.

(V) Saltwater flush.—

(i) In general.—The term "saltwater flush" means—

(I) **(aa)** the addition of as much midocean water into each empty ballast tank of a vessel as is safe for the vessel and crew; and

(bb) the mixing of the flushwater with residual ballast water and sediment through the motion of the vessel; and

(II) the discharge of that mixed water, such that the resultant residual water remaining in the tank—

(aa) has the highest salinity possible; and

(bb) is at least 30 parts per thousand.

(ii) Multiple sequences.—For purposes of clause (i), a saltwater flush may require more than 1 fill-mix-empty sequence, particularly if only small quantities of water can be safely taken onboard a vessel at 1 time.

(W) Secretary.—The term "Secretary" means the Secretary of the department in which the Coast Guard is operating.

(X) Small Vessel General Permit.—The term "Small Vessel General Permit" means the permit that is the subject of the notice of final permit issuance entitled "Final National Pollutant Discharge Elimination System (NPDES) Small Vessel General Permit for Discharges Incidental to the Normal Operation of Vessels Less Than 79 Feet" (79 Fed. Reg. 53702 (September 10, 2014)).

(Y) Small vessel or fishing vessel.—The term "small vessel or fishing vessel" means a vessel that is—

(i) less than 79 feet in length; or

(ii) a fishing vessel, fish processing vessel, or fish tender vessel (as those terms are defined in section 2101 of title 46, United States Code), regardless of the length of the vessel.

(Z) Vessel General Permit.—The term "Vessel General Permit" means the permit that is the subject of the notice of final permit issuance entitled "Final National Pollutant Discharge Elimination System (NPDES) General Permit for Discharges Incidental to the Normal Operation of a Vessel" (78 Fed. Reg. 21938 (April 12, 2013)).

(2) Applicability.—

(A) In general.—Except as provided in subparagraph (B), this subsection applies to—

(i) any discharge incidental to the normal operation of a vessel; and

(ii) any discharge incidental to the normal operation of a vessel (such as most graywater) that is commingled with sewage, subject to the conditions that—

(I) nothing in this subsection prevents a State from regulating sewage discharges; and

(II) any such commingled discharge shall comply with all applicable requirements of—

(aa) this subsection; and

(bb) any law applicable to discharges of sewage.

(B) Exclusion.—This subsection does not apply to any discharge incidental to the normal operation of a vessel—

(i) from—

(I) a vessel of the Armed Forces subject to subsection (n);

(II) a recreational vessel subject to subsection (*o*);

(III) a small vessel or fishing vessel, except that this subsection shall apply to any discharge of ballast water from a small vessel or fishing vessel; or

(IV) a floating craft that is permanently moored to a pier, including a 'floating' casino, hotel, restaurant, or bar;

(ii) of ballast water from a vessel—

(I) that continuously takes on and discharges ballast water in a flow-through system, if the Administrator determines that system cannot materially contribute to the spread or introduction of an aquatic nuisance species into waters of the United States;

(II) in the National Defense Reserve Fleet that is scheduled for disposal, if the vessel does not have an operable ballast water management system;

(III) that discharges ballast water consisting solely of water taken onboard from a public or commercial source that, at the time the water is taken onboard, meets the applicable requirements or permit requirements of the Safe Drinking Water Act (42 U.S.C. 300f et seq.);

(IV) that carries all permanent ballast water in sealed tanks that are not subject to discharge; or

(V) that only discharges ballast water into a reception facility; or

(iii) that results from, or contains material derived from, an activity other than the normal operation of the vessel, such as material resulting from an industrial or manufacturing process onboard the vessel.

(3) Continuation in effect of existing requirements.—

(A) Vessel General Permit.—Notwithstanding the expiration date of the Vessel General Permit or any other provision of law, all provisions of the Vessel General Permit shall remain in force and effect, and shall not be modified, until the applicable date described in subparagraph (C).

(B) Nonindigenous Aquatic Nuisance Prevention and Control Act regulations.— Notwithstanding section 903(a)(2)(A) of the Vessel Incidental Discharge Act of 2018, all regulations promulgated by the Secretary pursuant to section 1101 of the Nonindigenous Aquatic Nuisance Prevention and Control Act of 1990 (16 U.S.C. 4711) (as in effect on the day before the date of enactment of this subsection), including the regulations contained in subparts C and D of part 151 of title 33, Code of Federal Regulations, and subpart 162.060 of part 162 of title 46, Code of Federal Regulations (as in effect on the day before that date of enactment), shall remain in force and effect until the applicable date described in subparagraph (C).

(C) Repeal on existence of final, effective, and enforceable requirements.—Effective beginning on the date on which the requirements promulgated by the Secretary under subparagraphs (A), (B), and (C) of paragraph (5) with respect to every discharge incidental to the normal operation of a vessel that is subject to regulation under this subsection are final, effective, and enforceable, the requirements of the Vessel General Permit and the regulations described in subparagraph (B) shall have no force or effect.

(4) National standards of performance for marine pollution control devices and water quality orders.—

(A) Establishment.—

(i) In general.—Not later than 2 years after the date of enactment of this subsection, the Administrator, in concurrence with the Secretary (subject to clause (ii)), and in consultation with interested Governors (subject to clause (iii)), shall promulgate Federal standards of performance for marine pollution control devices for each type of discharge incidental to the normal operation of a vessel that is subject to regulation under this subsection.

(ii) Concurrence with Secretary.—

(I) Request.—The Administrator shall submit to the Secretary a request for written concurrence with respect to a proposed standard of performance under clause (i).

(II) Effect of failure to concur.—A failure by the Secretary to concur with the Administrator under clause (i) by the date that is 60 days after the date on which the Administrator submits a request for concurrence under subclause (I) shall not prevent the Administrator from promulgating the relevant standard of performance in accordance with the deadline under clause (i), subject to the condition that the Administrator shall include in the administrative record of the promulgation—

(aa) documentation of the request submitted under subclause (I); and

(bb) the response of the Administrator to any written objections received from the Secretary relating to the proposed standard of performance during the 60-day period beginning on the date of submission of the request.

(iii) Consultation with Governors.—

(I) In general.—The Administrator, in promulgating a standard of performance under clause (i), shall develop the standard of performance—

(aa) in consultation with interested Governors; and

(bb) in accordance with the deadlines under that clause.

(II) Process.—The Administrator shall develop a process for soliciting input from interested Governors, including information sharing relevant to such process, to allow interested Governors to inform the development of standards of performance under clause (i).

(III) Objection by Governors.—

(aa) Submission.—An interested Governor that objects to a proposed standard of performance under clause (i) may submit to the Administrator in writing a detailed objection to the proposed standard of performance, describing the scientific, technical, or operational factors that form the basis of the objection.

(bb) Response.—Before finalizing a standard of performance under clause (i) that is subject to an objection under item (aa) from 1 or more interested Governors, the Administrator shall provide a written response to each interested Governor that submitted an objection under that item that details the scientific, technical, or operational factors that form the basis for that standard of performance.

(cc) Judicial review.—A response of the Administrator under item (bb) shall not be subject to judicial review.

(iv) Procedure.—The Administrator shall promulgate the standards of performance under this subparagraph in accordance with—

(I) this paragraph; and

(II) section 553 of title 5, United States Code.

(B) Stringency.—

(i) In general.—Subject to clause (iii), the standards of performance promulgated under this paragraph shall require—

(I) with respect to conventional pollutants, toxic pollutants, and nonconventional pollutants (including aquatic nuisance species), the application of the best practicable control technology currently available;

(II) with respect to conventional pollutants, the application of the best conventional pollutant control technology; and

(III) with respect to toxic pollutants and nonconventional pollutants (including aquatic nuisance species), the application of the best available technology economically achievable for categories and classes of vessels, which shall result in reasonable **progress toward the national goal of eliminating discharges of all pollutants.**

(ii) Best management practices.—The Administrator shall require the use of best management practices to control or abate any discharge incidental to the normal operation of a vessel if—

(I) numeric standards of performance are infeasible under clause (i); or

(II) the best management practices are reasonably necessary—

(aa) to achieve the standards of performance; or

(bb) to carry out the purpose and intent of this subsection.

(iii) Minimum requirements.—Subject to subparagraph (D)(ii)(II), the combination of any equipment or best management practice comprising a marine pollution control device shall not be less stringent than the following provisions of the Vessel General Permit:

(I) All requirements contained in parts 2.1 and 2.2 (relating to effluent limits and related requirements), including with respect to waters subject to Federal protection, in whole or in part, for conservation purposes.

(II) All requirements contained in part 5 (relating to vessel class-specific requirements) that concern effluent limits and authorized discharges (within the meaning of that part), including with respect to waters subject to Federal protection, in whole or in part, for conservation purposes.

(C) Classes, types, and sizes of vessels.—The standards promulgated under this paragraph may distinguish—

(i) among classes, types, and sizes of vessels; and

(ii) between new vessels and existing vessels.

(D) Review and revision.—

(i) In general.—Not less frequently than once every 5 years, the Administrator, in consultation with the Secretary, shall—

(I) review the standards of performance in effect under this paragraph; and

(II) if appropriate, revise those standards of performance—

(aa) in accordance with subparagraphs (A) through (C); and

(bb) as necessary to establish requirements for any discharge that is subject to regulation under this subsection.

(ii) Maintaining protectiveness.—

(I) In general.—Except as provided in subclause (II), the Administrator shall not revise a standard of performance under this subsection to be less stringent than an applicable existing requirement.

(II) Exceptions.—The Administrator may revise a standard of performance to be less stringent than an applicable existing requirement—

(aa) if information becomes available that—

(AA) was not reasonably available when the Administrator promulgated the initial standard of performance or comparable requirement of the Vessel General Permit, as applicable (including the subsequent scarcity or unavailability of materials used to control the relevant discharge); and

(BB) would have justified the application of a less-stringent standard of performance at the time of promulgation; or

(bb) if the Administrator determines that a material technical mistake or misinterpretation of law occurred when promulgating the existing standard of performance or comparable requirement of the Vessel General Permit, as applicable.

(E) Best management practices for aquatic nuisance species emergencies and further protection of water quality.—

(i) In general.—Notwithstanding any other provision of this subsection, the Administrator, in concurrence with the Secretary (subject to clause (ii)), and in consultation with States, may require, by order, the use of an emergency best management practice for any region or category of vessels in any case in which the Administrator determines that such a best management practice—

(I) is necessary to reduce the reasonably foreseeable risk of introduction or establishment of an aquatic nuisance species; or

(II) will mitigate the adverse effects of a discharge that contributes to a violation of a water quality requirement under section 303, other than a requirement based on the presence of an aquatic nuisance species.

(ii) Concurrence with Secretary.—

(I) Request.—The Administrator shall submit to the Secretary a request for written concurrence with respect to an order under clause (i).

(II) Effect of failure to concur.—A failure by the Secretary to concur with the Administrator under clause (i) by the date that is 60 days after the date on which the Administrator submits a request for concurrence under subclause (I) shall not prevent the Administrator from issuing the relevant order, subject to the condition that the Administrator shall include in the administrative record of the issuance—

(aa) documentation of the request submitted under subclause (I); and

(bb) the response of the Administrator to any written objections received from the Secretary relating to the proposed order during the 60-day period beginning on the date of submission of the request.

(iii) Duration.—An order issued by the Administrator under clause (i) shall expire not later than the date that is 4 years after the date of issuance.

(iv) Extensions.—The Administrator may reissue an order under clause (i) for such subsequent periods of not longer than 4 years as the Administrator determines to be appropriate.

(5) Implementation, compliance, and enforcement requirements.—

(A) Establishment.—

(i) In general.—As soon as practicable, but not later than 2 years, after the date on which the Administrator promulgates any new or revised standard of performance under paragraph (4) with respect to a discharge, the Secretary, in consultation with States, shall promulgate the regulations required under this paragraph with respect to that discharge.

(ii) Minimum requirements.—Subject to subparagraph (C)(ii)(II), the regulations promulgated under this paragraph shall not be less stringent with respect to ensuring, monitoring, and enforcing compliance than—

(I) the requirements contained in part 3 of the Vessel General Permit (relating to corrective actions);

(II) the requirements contained in part 4 of the Vessel General Permit (relating to inspections, monitoring, reporting, and recordkeeping), including with respect to waters subject to Federal protection, in whole or in part, for conservation purposes;

(III) the requirements contained in part 5 of the Vessel General Permit (relating to vessel class-specific requirements) regarding monitoring, inspection, and educational and training requirements (within the meaning of that part), including with respect to waters subject to Federal protection, in whole or in part, for conservation purposes; and

(IV) any comparable, existing requirements promulgated under the Nonindigenous Aquatic Nuisance Prevention and Control Act of 1990 (16 U.S.C. 4701 et seq.) (including section 1101 of that Act (16 U.S.C. 4711) (as in effect on the day before the date of enactment of this subsection)) applicable to that discharge.

(iii) Coordination with States.—The Secretary, in coordination with the Governors of the States, shall develop, publish, and periodically update inspection, monitoring, data management, and enforcement procedures for the enforcement by States of Federal standards and requirements under this subsection.

(iv) Effective date.—In determining the effective date of a regulation promulgated under this paragraph, the Secretary shall take into consideration the period of time necessary—

(I) to communicate to affected persons the applicability of the regulation; and

(II) for affected persons reasonably to comply with the regulation.

(v) Procedure.—The Secretary shall promulgate the regulations under this subparagraph in accordance with—

(I) this paragraph; and

(II) section 553 of title 5, United States Code.

(B) Implementation regulations for marine pollution control devices.—The Secretary shall promulgate such regulations governing the design, construction, testing, approval, installation, and use of marine pollution control devices as are necessary to ensure compliance with the standards of performance promulgated under paragraph (4).

(C) Compliance assurance.—

(i) In general.—The Secretary shall promulgate requirements (including requirements for vessel owners and operators with respect to inspections, monitoring, reporting, sampling, and recordkeeping) to ensure, monitor, and enforce compliance with—

(I) the standards of performance promulgated by the Administrator under paragraph (4); and

(II) the implementation regulations promulgated by the Secretary under subparagraph (B).

(ii) Maintaining protectiveness.—

(I) In general.—Except as provided in subclause (II), the Secretary shall not revise a requirement under this subparagraph or subparagraph (B) to be less stringent with respect to ensuring, monitoring, or enforcing compliance than an applicable existing requirement.

(II) Exceptions.—The Secretary may revise a requirement under this subparagraph or subparagraph (B) to be less stringent than an applicable existing requirement—

(aa) in accordance with this subparagraph or subparagraph (B), as applicable;

(bb) if information becomes available that—

(AA) the Administrator determines was not reasonably available when the Administrator promulgated the existing requirement of the Vessel General Permit, or that the Secretary determines was not reasonably available when the Secretary promulgated the existing requirement under the Nonindigenous Aquatic Nuisance Prevention and Control Act of 1990 (16 U.S.C. 4701 et seq.) or the applicable existing requirement under this subparagraph, as applicable (including subsequent scarcity or unavailability of materials used to control the relevant discharge); and

(BB) would have justified the application of a less-stringent requirement at the time of promulgation; or

(cc) if the Administrator determines that a material technical mistake or misinterpretation of law occurred when promulgating an existing requirement of the Vessel General Permit, or if the Secretary determines that a material mistake or misinterpretation of law occurred when promulgating an existing requirement under the Nonindigenous Aquatic Nuisance Prevention and Control Act of 1990 (16 U.S.C. 4701 et seq.) or this subsection.

(D) Data availability.—Beginning not later than 1 year after the date of enactment of this subsection, the Secretary shall provide to the Governor of a State, on request by the Governor, access to Automated Identification System arrival data for inbound vessels to specific ports or places of destination in the State.

(6) Additional provisions regarding ballast water.—

(A) In general.—In addition to the other applicable requirements of this subsection, the requirements of this paragraph shall apply with respect to any discharge incidental to the normal operation of a vessel that is a discharge of ballast water.

(B) Empty ballast tanks.—

(i) Requirements.—Except as provided in clause (ii), the owner or operator of a vessel with empty ballast tanks bound for a port or place of destination subject to the jurisdiction of the United States shall, prior to arriving at that port or place of destination, conduct a ballast water exchange or saltwater flush—

(I) not less than 200 nautical miles from any shore for a voyage originating outside the United States or Canadian exclusive economic zone; or

(II) not less than 50 nautical miles from any shore for a voyage originating within the United States or Canadian exclusive economic zone.

(ii) Exceptions.—Clause (i) shall not apply—

(I) if the unpumpable residual waters and sediments of an empty ballast tank were subject to treatment, in compliance with applicable requirements, through a type-approved ballast water management system approved by the Secretary;

(II) except as otherwise required under this subsection, if the unpumpable residual waters and sediments of an empty ballast tank were sourced within—

(aa) the same port or place of destination; or

(bb) contiguous portions of a single Captain of the Port Zone;

(III) if complying with an applicable requirement of clause (i)—

(aa) would compromise the safety of the vessel; or

(bb) is otherwise prohibited by any Federal, Canadian, or international law (including regulations) pertaining to vessel safety;

(IV) if design limitations of the vessel prevent a ballast water exchange or saltwater flush from being conducted in accordance with clause (i); or

(V) if the vessel is operating exclusively within the internal waters of the United States or Canada.

(C) Period of use of installed ballast water management systems.—

(i) In general.—Except as provided in clause (ii), a vessel shall be deemed to be in compliance with a standard of performance for a marine pollution control device that is a ballast water management system if the ballast water management system—

(I) is maintained in proper working condition, as determined by the Secretary;

(II) is maintained and used in accordance with manufacturer specifications;

(III) continues to meet the ballast water discharge standard applicable to the vessel at the time of installation, as determined by the Secretary; and

(IV) has in effect a valid type-approval certificate issued by the Secretary.

(ii) Limitation.—Clause (i) shall cease to apply with respect to any vessel on, as applicable—

(I) the expiration of the service life, as determined by the Secretary, of—

(aa) the ballast water management system; or

(bb) the vessel;

(II) the completion of a major conversion (as defined in section 2101 of title 46, United States Code) of the vessel; or

(III) a determination by the Secretary that there are other type-approved systems for the vessel or category of vessels, with respect to the use of which the environmental, health, and economic benefits would exceed the costs.

(D) Review of ballast water management system type-approval testing methods.—

(i) Definition of live; living.—Notwithstanding any other provision of law (including regulations), for purposes of section 151.1511 of title 33, and part 162 of title 46, Code of Federal Regulations (or successor regulations), the terms 'live' and 'living' shall not—

(I) include an organism that has been rendered nonviable; or

(II) preclude the consideration of any method of measuring the concentration of organisms in ballast water that are capable of reproduction.

(ii) Draft policy.—Not later than 180 days after the date of enactment of this subsection, the Secretary, in coordination with the Administrator, shall publish a draft policy letter, based on the best available science, describing type-approval testing methods and protocols for ballast water management systems, if any, that—

(I) render nonviable organisms in ballast water; and

(II) may be used in addition to the methods established under subpart 162.060 of title 46, Code of Federal Regulations (or successor regulations)—

(aa) to measure the concentration of organisms in ballast water that are capable of reproduction;

(bb) to certify the performance of each ballast water management system under this subsection; and

(cc) to certify laboratories to evaluate applicable treatment technologies.

(iii) Public comment.—The Secretary shall provide a period of not more than 60 days for public comment regarding the draft policy letter published under clause (ii).

(iv) Final policy.—

(I) In general.—Not later than 1 year after the date of enactment of this subsection, the Secretary, in coordination with the Administrator, shall publish a final policy letter describing type-approval testing methods, if any, for ballast water management systems that render nonviable organisms in ballast water.

(II) Method of evaluation.—The ballast water management systems under subclause (I) shall be evaluated by measuring the concentration of organisms in ballast water that are capable of reproduction based on the best available science that may be used in addition to the methods established under subpart 162.060 of title 46, Code of Federal Regulations (or successor regulations).

(III) Revisions.—The Secretary shall revise the final policy letter under subclause (I) in any case in which the Secretary, in coordination with the Administrator, determines that additional testing methods are capable of measuring the concentration of organisms in ballast water that have not been rendered nonviable.

(v) Factors for consideration.—In developing a policy letter under this subparagraph, the Secretary, in coordination with the Administrator—

(I) shall take into consideration a testing method that uses organism grow-out and most probable number statistical analysis to determine the concentration of organisms in ballast water that are capable of reproduction; and

(II) shall not take into consideration a testing method that relies on a staining method that measures the concentration of—

(aa) organisms greater than or equal to 10 micrometers; and

(bb) organisms less than or equal to 50 micrometers.

(E) Intergovernmental response framework.—

(i) In general.—The Secretary, in consultation with the Administrator and acting in coordination with, or through, the Aquatic Nuisance Species Task Force established by section 1201(a) of the Nonindigenous Aquatic Nuisance Prevention and Control Act of 1990 (16 U.S.C. 4721(a)), shall establish a framework for Federal and intergovernmental response to aquatic nuisance species risks from discharges from vessels subject to ballast water and incidental discharge compliance requirements under this subsection, including the introduction, spread, and establishment of aquatic nuisance species populations.

(ii) Ballast discharge risk response.—The Administrator, in coordination with the Secretary and taking into consideration information from the National Ballast Information Clearinghouse developed under section 1102(f) of the Nonindigenous Aquatic Nuisance Prevention and Control Act of 1990 (16 U.S.C. 4712(f)), shall establish a risk assessment and response framework using ballast water discharge data and aquatic nuisance species monitoring data for the purposes of—

(I) identifying and tracking populations of aquatic invasive species;

(II) evaluating the risk of any aquatic nuisance species population tracked under subclause (I) establishing and spreading in waters of the United States or waters of the contiguous zone; and

(III) establishing emergency best management practices that may be deployed rapidly, in a local or regional manner, to respond to emerging aquatic nuisance species threats.

(7) Petitions by Governors for review.—

(A) In general.—The Governor of a State (or a designee) may submit to the Administrator or the Secretary a petition—

(i) to issue an order under paragraph (4)(E); or

(ii) to review any standard of performance, regulation, or policy promulgated under paragraph (4), (5), or (6), respectively, if there exists new information that could reasonably result in a change to—

(I) the standard of performance, regulation, or policy; or

(II) a determination on which the standard of performance, regulation, or policy was based.

(B) Inclusions.—A petition under subparagraph (A) shall include a description of any applicable scientific or technical information that forms the basis of the petition.

(C) Determination.—

(i) Timing.—The Administrator or the Secretary, as applicable, shall grant or deny—

(I) a petition under subparagraph (A)(i) by not later than the date that is 180 days after the date on which the petition is submitted; and

(II) a petition under subparagraph (A)(ii) by not later than the date that is 1 year after the date on which the petition is submitted.

(ii) Effect of grant.—If the Administrator or the Secretary determines under clause (i) to grant a petition—

(I) in the case of a petition under subparagraph (A)(i), the Administrator shall immediately issue the relevant order under paragraph (4)(E); or

(II) in the case of a petition under subparagraph (A)(ii), the Administrator or Secretary shall publish in the Federal Register, by not later than 30 days after the date of that determination, a notice of proposed rulemaking to revise the relevant standard, requirement, regulation, or policy under paragraph (4), (5), or (6), as applicable.

(iii) Notice of denial.—If the Administrator or the Secretary determines under clause (i) to deny a petition, the Administrator or Secretary shall publish in the Federal Register, by not later than 30 days after the date of that determination, a detailed explanation of the scientific, technical, or operational factors that form the basis of the determination.

(iv) Review.—A determination by the Administrator or the Secretary under clause (i) to deny a petition shall be—

(I) considered to be a final agency action; and

(II) subject to judicial review in accordance with section 509, subject to clause (v).

(v) Exceptions.—

(I) Venue.—Notwithstanding section 509(b), a petition for review of a determination by the Administrator or the Secretary under clause (i) to deny a petition submitted by the Governor of a State under subparagraph (A) may be filed in any United States district court of competent jurisdiction.

(II) Deadline for filing.—Notwithstanding section 509(b), a petition for review of a determination by the Administrator or the Secretary under clause (i) shall be filed by not later than 180 days after the date on which the justification for the determination is published in the Federal Register under clause (iii).

(8) Prohibition.—

(A) In general.—It shall be unlawful for any person to violate—

(i) a provision of the Vessel General Permit in force and effect under paragraph (3)(A);

(ii) a regulation promulgated pursuant to section 1101 of the Nonindigenous Aquatic Nuisance Prevention and Control Act of 1990 (16 U.S.C. 4711) (as in effect on the day before the date of enactment of this subsection) in force and effect under paragraph (3)(B); or

(iii) an applicable requirement or regulation under this subsection.

(B) Compliance with regulations.—Effective beginning on the effective date of a regulation promulgated under paragraph (4), (5), (6), or (10), as applicable, it shall be unlawful for the owner or operator of a vessel subject to the regulation—

(i) to discharge any discharge incidental to the normal operation of the vessel into waters of the United States or waters of the contiguous zone, except in compliance with the regulation; or

(ii) to operate in waters of the United States or waters of the contiguous zone, if the vessel is not equipped with a required marine pollution control device that complies with the requirements established under this subsection, unless—

(I) the owner or operator of the vessel denotes in an entry in the official logbook of the vessel that the equipment was not operational; and

(II) either—

(aa) the applicable discharge was avoided; or

(bb) an alternate compliance option approved by the Secretary as meeting the applicable standard was employed.

(C) Affirmative defense.—No person shall be found to be in violation of this paragraph if—

(i) the violation was in the interest of ensuring the safety of life at sea, as determined by the Secretary; and

(ii) the applicable emergency circumstance was not the result of negligence or malfeasance on the part of—

(I) the owner or operator of the vessel;

(II) the master of the vessel; or

(III) the person in charge of the vessel.

(D) Treatment.—Each day of continuing violation of an applicable requirement of this subsection shall constitute a separate offense.

(E) In rem liability.—A vessel operated in violation of this subsection is liable in rem for any civil penalty assessed for the violation.

(F) Revocation of clearance.—The Secretary shall withhold or revoke the clearance of a vessel required under section 60105 of title 46, United States Code, if the owner or operator of the vessel is in violation of this subsection.

(9) Effect on other laws.—

(A) State authority.—

(i) In general.—Except as provided in clauses (ii) through (v) and paragraph (10), effective beginning on the date on which the requirements promulgated by the Secretary under subparagraphs (A), (B), and (C) of paragraph (5) with respect to every discharge incidental to the normal operation of a vessel that is subject to regulation under this subsection are final, effective, and enforceable, no State, political subdivision of a State, or interstate agency may adopt or enforce any law, regulation, or other requirement of the State, political subdivision, or interstate agency with respect to any such discharge.

(ii) Identical or lesser State laws.—Clause (i) shall not apply to any law, regulation, or other requirement of a State, political subdivision of a State, or interstate agency in effect on or after the date of enactment of this subsection—

(I) that is identical to a Federal requirement under this subsection applicable to the relevant discharge; or

(II) compliance with which would be achieved concurrently in achieving compliance with a Federal requirement under this subsection applicable to the relevant discharge.

(iii) State enforcement of Federal requirements.—A State may enforce any standard of performance or other Federal requirement of this subsection in accordance with subsection (k) or other applicable Federal authority.

(iv) Exception for certain fees.—

(I) In general.—Subject to subclauses (II) and (III), a State that assesses any fee pursuant to any State or Federal law relating to the regulation of a discharge incidental to the normal operation of a vessel before the date of enactment of this subsection may assess or retain a fee to cover the costs of administration, inspection, monitoring, and enforcement activities by the State to achieve compliance with the applicable requirements of this subsection.

(II) Maximum amount.—

(aa) In general.—Except as provided in item (bb), a State may assess a fee for activities under this clause equal to not more than $1,000 against the owner or operator of a vessel that—

(AA) has operated outside of that State; and

(BB) arrives at a port or place of destination in the State (excluding movement entirely within a single port or place of destination).

(bb) Vessels engaged in coastwise trade.—A State may assess against the owner or operator of a vessel registered in accordance with applicable Federal law and lawfully engaged in the coastwise trade not more than $5,000 in fees under this clause per vessel during a calendar year.

(III) Adjustment for inflation.—

(aa) In general.—A State may adjust the amount of a fee authorized under this clause not more frequently than once every 5 years to reflect the percentage by which the Consumer Price Index for All Urban Consumers published by the Department of Labor for the month of October immediately preceding the date of adjustment exceeds the Consumer Price Index for All Urban Consumers published by the Department of Labor for the month of October that immediately precedes the date that is 5 years before the date of adjustment.

(bb) Effect of subclause.—Nothing in this subclause prevents a State from adjusting a fee in effect before the date of enactment of this subsection to the applicable maximum amount under subclause (II).

(cc) Applicability.—This subclause applies only to increases in fees to amounts greater than the applicable maximum amount under subclause (II).

(v) Alaska graywater.—Clause (i) shall not apply with respect to any discharge of graywater (as defined in section 1414 of the Consolidated Appropriations Act, 2001 (Public Law 106–554; 114 Stat. 2763A–323)) from a passenger vessel (as defined in section 2101 of title 46, United States Code) in the State of Alaska (including all waters in the Alexander Archipelago) carrying 50 or more passengers.

(vi) Preservation of authority.—Nothing in this subsection preempts any State law, public initiative, referendum, regulation, requirement, or other State action, except as expressly provided in this subsection.

(B) Established regimes.—Except as expressly provided in this subsection, nothing in this subsection affects the applicability to a vessel of any other provision of Federal law, including—

(i) this section;

(ii) section 311;

(iii) the Act to Prevent Pollution from Ships (33 U.S.C. 1901 et seq.); and

(iv) title X of the Coast Guard Authorization Act of 2010 (33 U.S.C. 3801 et seq.).

(C) Permitting.—Effective beginning on the date of enactment of this subsection—

(i) the Small Vessel General Permit is repealed; and

(ii) the Administrator, or a State in the case of a permit program approved under section 402, shall not require, or in any way modify, a permit under that section for—

(I) any discharge that is subject to regulation under this subsection;

(II) any discharge incidental to the normal operation of a vessel from a small vessel or fishing vessel, regardless of whether that discharge is subject to regulation under this subsection; or

(III) any discharge described in paragraph (2)(B)(ii).

(D) No effect on civil or criminal actions.—Nothing in this subsection, or any standard, regulation, or requirement established under this subsection, modifies or otherwise affects, preempts, or displaces—

(i) any cause of action; or

(ii) any provision of Federal or State law establishing a remedy for civil relief or criminal penalty.

(E) No effect on certain Secretarial authority.—Nothing in this subsection affects the authority of the Secretary of Commerce or the Secretary of the Interior to administer any land or waters under the administrative control of the Secretary of Commerce or the Secretary of the Interior, respectively.

(F) No limitation on State inspection authority.—Nothing in this subsection limits the authority of a State to inspect a vessel pursuant to paragraph (5)(A)(iii) in order to monitor compliance with an applicable requirement of this section.

(10) Additional regional requirements.—

(A) Minimum Great Lakes system requirements.—

(i) In general.—Except as provided in clause (ii), the owner or operator of a vessel entering the St. Lawrence Seaway through the mouth of the St. Lawrence River shall conduct a complete ballast water exchange or saltwater flush—

(I) not less than 200 nautical miles from any shore for a voyage originating outside the United States or Canadian exclusive economic zone; or

(II) not less than 50 nautical miles from any shore for a voyage originating within the United States or Canadian exclusive economic zone.

(ii) Exceptions.—Clause (i) shall not apply to a vessel if—

(I) complying with an applicable requirement of clause (i)—

(aa) would compromise the safety of the vessel; or

(bb) is otherwise prohibited by any Federal, Canadian, or international law (including regulations) pertaining to vessel safety;

(II) design limitations of the vessel prevent a ballast water exchange from being conducted in accordance with an applicable requirement of clause (i);

(III) the vessel—

(aa) is certified by the Secretary as having no residual ballast water or sediments onboard; or

(bb) retains all ballast water while in waters subject to the requirement; or

(IV) empty ballast tanks on the vessel are sealed and certified by the Secretary in a manner that ensures that—

(aa) no discharge or uptake occurs; and

(bb) any subsequent discharge of ballast water is subject to the requirement.

(B) Enhanced Great Lakes System requirements.—

(i) Petitions by Governors for proposed enhanced standards and requirements.—

(I) In general.—The Governor of a Great Lakes State (or a State employee designee) may submit a petition in accordance with subclause (II) to propose that other Governors of Great Lakes States endorse an enhanced standard of performance or other requirement with respect to any discharge that—

(aa) is subject to regulation under this subsection; and

(bb) occurs within the Great Lakes System.

(II) Submission.—A Governor shall submit a petition under subclause (I), in writing, to—

(aa) the Executive Director of the Great Lakes Commission, in such manner as may be prescribed by the Great Lakes Commission;

(bb)the Governor of each other Great Lakes State; and

(cc) the Director of the Great Lakes National Program Office established by section 118(b).

(III) Preliminary assessment by Great Lakes Commission.—

(aa) In general.—After the date of receipt of a petition under subclause (II)(aa), the Great Lakes Commission (acting through the Great Lakes Panel on Aquatic Nuisance Species, to the maximum extent practicable) may develop a preliminary assessment regarding each enhanced standard of performance or other requirement described in the petition.

(bb) Provisions.—The preliminary assessment developed by the Great Lakes Commission under item (aa)—

(AA) may be developed in consultation with relevant experts and stakeholders;

(BB) may be narrative in nature;

(CC) may include the preliminary views, if any, of the Great Lakes Commission on the propriety of the proposed enhanced standard of performance or other requirement;

(DD) shall be submitted, in writing, to the Governor of each Great Lakes State and the Director of the Great Lakes National Program Office and published on the internet website of the Great Lakes National Program Office; and

(EE) except as provided in clause (iii), shall not be taken into consideration, or provide a basis for review, by the Administrator or the Secretary for purposes of that clause.

(ii) Proposed enhanced standards and requirements.—

(I) Publication in Federal Register.—

(aa) Request by Governor.—Not earlier than the date that is 90 days after the date on which the Executive Director of the Great Lakes Commission receives from a Governor of a Great Lakes State a petition under clause (i)(II)(aa), the Governor may request the Director of the Great Lakes National Program Office to publish, for a period requested by the Governor of not less than 30 days, and the Director shall so publish, in the Federal Register for public comment—

(AA) a copy of the petition; and

(BB) if applicable as of the date of publication, any preliminary assessment of the Great Lakes Commission developed under clause (i)(III) relating to the petition.

(bb) Review of public comments.—On receipt of a written request of a Governor of a Great Lakes State, the Director of the Great Lakes National Program Office shall make available all public comments received in response to the notice under item (aa).

(cc) No response required.—Notwithstanding any other provision of law, a Governor of a Great Lakes State or the Director of the Great Lakes National Program Office shall not be required to provide a response to any comment received in response to the publication of a petition or preliminary assessment under item (aa).

(dd) Purpose.—Any public comments received in response to the publication of a petition or preliminary assessment under item (aa) shall be used solely for the purpose of providing information and feedback to the Governor of each Great Lakes State regarding the decision to endorse the proposed standard or requirement.

(ee) Effect of petition.—A proposed standard or requirement developed under subclause (II) may differ from the proposed standard or requirement described in a petition published under item (aa).

(II) Coordination to develop proposed standard or requirement.—After the expiration of the public comment period for the petition under subclause (I), any interested Governor of a Great Lakes State may work in coordination with the Great Lakes Commission to develop a proposed standard of performance or other requirement applicable to a discharge referred to in the petition.

(III) Requirements.—A proposed standard of performance or other requirement under subclause (II)—

(aa) shall be developed—

(AA) in consultation with representatives from the Federal and provincial governments of Canada;

(BB) after notice and opportunity for public comment on the petition published under subclause (I); and

(CC) taking into consideration the preliminary assessment, if any, of the Great Lakes Commission under clause (i)(III);

(bb) shall be specifically endorsed in writing by—

(AA) the Governor of each Great Lakes State, if the proposed standard or requirement would impose any additional equipment requirement on a vessel; or

(BB) not fewer than 5 Governors of Great Lakes States, if the proposed standard or requirement would not impose any additional equipment requirement on a vessel; and

(cc) in the case of a proposed requirement to prohibit 1 or more types of discharge regulated under this subsection, whether treated or not treated, into waters within the Great Lakes System, shall not apply outside the waters of the Great Lakes States of the Governors endorsing the proposed requirement under item (bb).

(iii) Promulgation by Administrator and Secretary.—

(I) Submission.—

(aa) In general.—The Governors endorsing a proposed standard or requirement under clause (ii)(III)(bb) may jointly submit to the Administrator and the Secretary for approval each proposed standard of performance or other requirement developed and endorsed pursuant to clause (ii).

(bb) Inclusion.—Each submission under item (aa) shall include an explanation regarding why the applicable standard of performance or other requirement is—

(AA) at least as stringent as a comparable standard of performance or other requirement under this subsection;

(BB) in accordance with maritime safety; and

(CC) in accordance with applicable maritime and navigation laws and regulations.

(cc) Withdrawal.—

(AA) In general.—The Governor of any Great Lakes State that endorses a proposed standard or requirement under clause (ii)(III)(bb) may withdraw the endorsement by not later than the date that is 90 days after the date on which the Administrator and the Secretary receive the proposed standard or requirement.

(BB) Effect on Federal review.—If, after the withdrawal of an endorsement under subitem (AA), the proposed standard or requirement does not have the applicable number of endorsements under clause (ii)(III)(bb), the Administrator and the Secretary shall terminate the review under this clause.

(dd) Dissenting opinions.—The Governor of a Great Lakes State that does not endorse a proposed standard or requirement under clause (ii)(III)(bb) may submit to the Administrator and the Secretary any dissenting opinions of the Governor.

(II) Joint notice.—On receipt of a proposed standard of performance or other requirement under subclause (I), the Administrator and the Secretary shall publish in the Federal Register a joint notice that, at minimum—

(aa) states that the proposed standard or requirement is publicly available; and

(bb) provides an opportunity for public comment regarding the proposed standard or requirement during the 90-day period beginning on the date of receipt by the Administrator and the Secretary of the proposed standard or requirement.

(III) Review.—

(aa) In general.—As soon as practicable after the date of publication of a joint notice under subclause (II)—

(AA) the Administrator shall commence a review of each proposed standard of performance or other requirement covered by the notice to determine whether that standard or requirement is at least as stringent as comparable standards and requirements under this subsection; and

(BB) the Secretary shall commence a review of each proposed standard of performance or other requirement covered by the notice to determine whether that standard or requirement is in accordance with maritime safety and applicable maritime and navigation laws and regulations.

(bb) Consultation.—In carrying out item (aa), the Administrator and the Secretary—

(AA) shall consult with the Governor of each Great Lakes State and representatives from the Federal and provincial governments of Canada;

(BB) shall take into consideration any relevant data or public comments received under subclause (II)(bb); and

(CC) shall not take into consideration any preliminary assessment by the Great Lakes Commission under clause (i)(III), or any dissenting opinion under subclause (I)(dd), except to the extent that such an assessment or opinion is relevant to the criteria for the applicable determination under item (aa).

(IV) Approval or disapproval.—Not later than 180 days after the date of receipt of each proposed standard of performance or other requirement under subclause (I), the Administrator and the Secretary shall—

(aa) determine, as applicable, whether each proposed standard or other requirement satisfies the criteria under subclause (III)(aa);

(bb) approve each proposed standard or other requirement, unless the Administrator or the Secretary, as applicable, determines under item (aa) that the proposed standard or other requirement does not satisfy the criteria under subclause (III)(aa); and

(cc) submit to the Governor of each Great Lakes State, and publish in the Federal Register, a notice of the determination under item (aa).

(V) Action on disapproval.—

(aa) Rationale and recommendations.—If the Administrator and the Secretary disapprove a proposed standard of performance or other requirement under subclause (IV)(bb), the notices under subclause (IV)(cc) shall include—

(AA) a description of the reasons why the standard or requirement is, as applicable, less stringent than a comparable standard or requirement under this subsection, inconsistent with maritime safety, or inconsistent with applicable maritime and navigation laws and regulations; and

(BB) any recommendations regarding changes the Governors of the Great Lakes States could make to conform the disapproved portion of the standard or requirement to the requirements of this subparagraph.

(bb) Review.—Disapproval of a proposed standard or requirement by the Administrator and the Secretary under this subparagraph shall be considered to be a final agency action subject to judicial review under section 509.

(VI) Action on approval.—On approval by the Administrator and the Secretary of a proposed standard of performance or other requirement under subclause (IV)(bb)—

(aa) the Administrator shall establish, by regulation, the proposed standard or requirement within the Great Lakes System in lieu of any comparable standard or other requirement promulgated under paragraph (4); and

(bb) the Secretary shall establish, by regulation, any requirements necessary to implement, ensure compliance with, and enforce the standard or requirement under item (aa), or to apply the proposed requirement, within the Great Lakes System in lieu of any comparable requirement promulgated under paragraph (5).

(VII) No judicial review for certain actions.—An action or inaction of a Governor of a Great Lakes State or the Great Lakes Commission under this subparagraph shall not be subject to judicial review.

(VIII) Great Lakes Compact.—Nothing in this subsection limits, alters, or amends the Great Lakes Compact to which Congress granted consent in the Act of July 24, 1968 (Public Law 90–419; 82 Stat. 414).

(IX) Authorization of appropriations.—There is authorized to be appropriated to the Great Lakes Commission $5,000,000, to be available until expended.

(C) Minimum Pacific Region requirements.—

(i) Definition of commercial vessel.—In this subparagraph, the term 'commercial vessel' means a vessel operating between—

(I) 2 ports or places of destination within the Pacific Region; or

(II) a port or place of destination within the Pacific Region and a port or place of destination on the Pacific Coast of Canada or Mexico north of parallel 20 degrees north latitude, inclusive of the Gulf of California.

(ii) Ballast water exchange.—

(I) In general.—Except as provided in subclause (II) and clause (iv), the owner or operator of a commercial vessel shall conduct a complete ballast water exchange in waters more than 50 nautical miles from shore.

(II) Exemptions.—Subclause (I) shall not apply to a commercial vessel—

(aa) using, in compliance with applicable requirements, a type-approved ballast water management system approved by the Secretary; or

(bb) voyaging—

(AA) between or to a port or place of destination in the State of Washington, if the ballast water to be discharged from the commercial vessel originated solely from waters located between the parallel 46 degrees north latitude, including the internal waters of the Columbia River, and the internal waters of Canada south of parallel 50 degrees north latitude, including the waters of the Strait of Georgia and the Strait of Juan de Fuca;

(BB) between ports or places of destination in the State of Oregon, if the ballast water to be discharged from the commercial vessel originated solely from waters located between the parallel 40 degrees north latitude and the parallel 50 degrees north latitude;

(CC) between ports or places of destination in the State of California within the San Francisco Bay area east of the Golden Gate Bridge, including the Port of Stockton and the Port of Sacramento, if the ballast water to be discharged from the commercial vessel originated solely from ports or places within that area;

(DD) between the Port of Los Angeles, the Port of Long Beach, and the El Segundo offshore marine oil terminal, if the ballast water to be discharged from the commercial vessel originated solely from the Port of Los Angeles, the Port of Long Beach, or the El Segundo offshore marine oil terminal;

(EE) between a port or place of destination in the State of Alaska within a single Captain of the Port Zone;

(FF) between ports or places of destination in different counties of the State of Hawaii, if the vessel may conduct a complete ballast water exchange in waters that are more than 10 nautical miles from shore and at least 200 meters deep; or

(GG) between ports or places of destination within the same county of the State of Hawaii, if the vessel does not transit outside State marine waters during the voyage.

(iii) Low-salinity ballast water.—

(I) In general.—Except as provided in subclause (II) and clause (iv), the owner or operator of a commercial vessel that transports ballast water sourced from waters with a measured salinity of less than 18 parts per thousand and voyages to a Pacific Region port or place of destination with a measured salinity of less than 18 parts per thousand shall conduct a complete ballast water exchange—

(aa) not less than 50 nautical miles from shore, if the ballast water was sourced from a Pacific Region port or place of destination; or

(bb) more than 200 nautical miles from shore, if the ballast water was not sourced from a Pacific Region port or place of destination.

(II) Exception.—Subclause (I) shall not apply to a commercial vessel voyaging to a port or place of destination in the Pacific Region that is using, in compliance with applicable requirements, a type-approved ballast water management system approved by the Secretary to achieve standards of performance of—

(aa) less than 1 organism per 10 cubic meters, if that organism—

(AA) is living, or has not been rendered nonviable; and

(BB) is 50 or more micrometers in minimum dimension;

(bb)less than 1 organism per 10 milliliters, if that organism—

(AA) is living, or has not been rendered nonviable; and

(BB) is more than 10, but less than 50, micrometers in minimum dimension;

(cc) concentrations of indicator microbes that are less than—

(AA) 1 colony-forming unit of toxicogenic Vibrio cholera (serotypes O1 and O139) per 100 milliliters or less than 1 colony-forming unit of that microbe per gram of wet weight of zoological samples;

(BB) 126 colony-forming units of escherichia coli per 100 milliliters; and

(CC) 33 colony-forming units of intestinal enterococci per 100 milliliters; and

(dd) concentrations of such additional indicator microbes and viruses as may be specified in the standards of performance established by the Administrator under paragraph (4).

(iv) General exceptions.—The requirements of clauses (ii) and (iii) shall not apply to a commercial vessel if—

(I) complying with the requirement would compromise the safety of the commercial vessel;

(II) design limitations of the commercial vessel prevent a ballast water exchange from being conducted in accordance with clause (ii) or (iii), as applicable;

(III) the commercial vessel—

(aa) is certified by the Secretary as having no residual ballast water or sediments onboard; or

(bb) retains all ballast water while in waters subject to those requirements; or

(IV) empty ballast tanks on the commercial vessel are sealed and certified by the Secretary in a manner that ensures that—

(aa) no discharge or uptake occurs; and

(bb) any subsequent discharge of ballast water is subject to those requirements.

(D) Establishment of State No-Discharge Zones.—

(i) State prohibition.—Subject to clause (ii), after the effective date of regulations promulgated by the Secretary under paragraph (5), if any State determines that the protection and enhancement of the quality of some or all of the waters within the State require greater environmental protection, the State may prohibit 1 or more types of discharge regulated under this subsection, whether treated or not treated, into such waters.

(ii) Applicability.—A prohibition by a State under clause (i) shall not apply until the date on which the Administrator makes the applicable determinations described in clause (iii).

(iii) Prohibition by Administrator.—

(I) Determination.—On application of a State, the Administrator, in concurrence with the Secretary (subject to subclause (II)), shall, by regulation, prohibit the discharge from a vessel of 1 or more discharges subject to regulation under this subsection, whether treated or not treated, into the waters covered by the application if the Administrator determines that—

(aa) prohibition of the discharge would protect and enhance the quality of the specified waters within the State;

(bb) adequate facilities for the safe and sanitary removal and treatment of the discharge are reasonably available for the water and all vessels to which the prohibition would apply;

(cc) the discharge can be safely collected and stored until a vessel reaches a discharge facility or other location; and

(dd) in the case of an application for the prohibition of discharges of ballast water in a port (or in any other location where cargo, passengers, or fuel are loaded and unloaded)—

(AA) the adequate facilities described in item (bb) are reasonably available for commercial vessels, after considering, at a minimum, water depth, dock size, pumpout facility capacity and flow rate, availability of year-round operations, proximity to navigation routes, and the ratio of pumpout facilities to the population and discharge capacity of commercial vessels operating in those waters; and

(BB) the prohibition will not unreasonably interfere with the safe loading and unloading of cargo, passengers, or fuel.

(II) Concurrence with the Secretary.—

(aa) Request.—The Administrator shall submit to the Secretary a request for written concurrence with respect to a prohibition under subclause (I).

(bb) Effect of failure to concur.—A failure by the Secretary to concur with the Administrator under subclause (I) by the date that is 60 days after the date on which the Administrator submits a request for concurrence under item (aa) shall not prevent the Administrator from prohibiting the relevant discharge in accordance with subclause (III), subject to the condition that the Administrator shall include in the administrative record of the promulgation—

(AA) documentation of the request submitted under item (aa); and

(BB) the response of the Administrator to any written objections received from the Secretary relating to the proposed standard of performance during the 60-day period beginning on the date of submission of the request.

(III) Timing.—The Administrator shall approve or disapprove an application submitted under subclause (I) by not later than 90 days after the date on which the application is submitted to the Administrator.

(E) Maintenance in effect of more stringent standards.—In any case in which a requirement established under this paragraph is more stringent or environmentally protective than a comparable requirement established under paragraph (4), (5), or (6), the more-stringent or more-protective requirement shall control.

(June 30, 1948, c. 758, Title III, § 312, as added by Pub. L. No. 92–500, § 2, 86 Stat. 871 (Oct. 18, 1972); and amended by Pub. L. No. 95–217, § 59, 91 Stat. 1596 (Dec. 27, 1977); Pub. L. No. 96–88, Title V, § 509(b), 93 Stat. 695 (Oct. 17, 1979); Pub. L. No. 100–4, Title III, § 311, 101 Stat. 42 (Feb. 4, 1987); Pub. L. No. 104–106, Div. A, Title III, § 325(b) to (c)(2), 110 Stat. 254 (Feb. 10, 1996); Pub. L. No. 110–288, § 4, 122 Stat. 2650 (July 29, 2008); Pub. L. No. 115–282, § 903(a)(1), (c)(1), 132 Stat. 4192, 4324–4354, 4355–4356 (Dec. 4, 2018).)

HISTORICAL AND STATUTORY NOTES

References in Text

For definition of Canal Zone, referred to in subsecs. (a)(4) and (m), see section 3602(b) of Title 22, Foreign Relations and Intercourse.

Change of Name

"Secretary of Health and Human Services" was substituted for "Secretary of Health, Education, and Welfare" in subsec. (e) pursuant to section 509(b) of Pub. L. No. 96–88 which is codified as section 3508(b) of Title 20, Education.

Termination of Trust Territory of the Pacific Islands

For termination of Trust Territory of the Pacific Islands, see note set out preceding 48 U.S.C.A. § 1681.

Termination of United States District Court for the District of the Canal Zone

For termination of the United States District Court for the District of the Canal Zone at end of the "transition period", being the 30-month period beginning Oct. 1, 1979, and ending midnight Mar. 31, 1982, see Paragraph 5 of Article XI of the Panama Canal Treaty of 1977 and sections 2101 and 2201 to 2203 of Pub. L. No. 96–70, Title II, 93 Stat. 493 (Sept. 27, 1979), formerly codified as 22 U.S.C.A. §§ 3831 and 3841 to 3843, respectively.

Contiguous Zone of United States

For extension of contiguous zone of United States, see Proc. No. 7219, set out as a note under 43 U.S.C.A. § 1331.

Purposes of National Discharge Standards

Section 325(a) of Pub. L. No. 104–106 provided that: "The purposes of this section [section 325 of Pub. L. No. 104–106, which enacted subsec. (n) of this section, amended subsecs. (a) and (j) of this section and section 1362(6)(A) of this title, and enacted provisions set out as a note under this section] are to—

"(1) enhance the operational flexibility of vessels of the Armed Forces domestically and internationally;

"(2) stimulate the development of innovative vessel pollution control technology; and

"(3) advance the development by the United States Navy of environmentally sound ships."

Cooperation in National Discharge Standards Development

Section 325(d) of Pub. L. No. 104–106 provided that: "The Administrator of the Environmental Protection Agency and the Secretary of Defense may, by mutual agreement, with or without reimbursement, provide for the use of information, reports, personnel, or other resources of the Environmental Protection Agency or the Department of Defense to carry out section 312(n) of the Federal Water Pollution Control Act (as added by subsection (b) [subsec. (n) of this section]), including the use of the resources—

"(1) to determine—

"(A) the nature and environmental effect of discharges incidental to the normal operation of a vessel of the Armed Forces;

"(B) the practicability of using marine pollution control devices on vessels of the Armed Forces; and

"(C) the effect that installation or use of marine pollution control devices on vessels of the Armed Forces would have on the operation or operational capability of the vessels; and

"(2) to establish performance standards for marine pollution control devices on vessels of the Armed Forces."

Construction, Renovation, Operation, and Maintenance of Pumpout Stations and Waste Reception Facilities

Pub. L. No. 102–587, Title V, Subtitle F, § 5601 et seq., 106 Stat. 5086 (Nov. 4, 1992), as amended Pub. L. No. 109–59, Title X, § 10131, 119 Stat. 1931 (Aug. 10, 2005), provided that:

"Sec. 5601. Short title.

"This subtitle [subtitle F, §§ 5601 to 5608, of Title V of Pub. L. No. 102–587, amending sections 777c and 777g of Title 16, Conservation and enacting this note] may be cited as the 'Clean Vessel Act of 1992'.

"Sec. 5602. Findings; purpose.

"(a) Findings.—The Congress finds the following:

"(1) The discharge of untreated sewage by vessels is prohibited under Federal law in all areas within the navigable waters of the United States.

"(2) The discharge of treated sewage by vessels is prohibited under either Federal or State law in many of the United States bodies of water where recreational boaters operate.

"(3) There is currently an inadequate number of pumpout stations for type III marine sanitation devices where recreational vessels normally operate.

"(4) Sewage discharged by recreational vessels because of an inadequate number of pumpout stations is a substantial contributor to localized degradation of water quality in the United States.

"(b) Purpose.—The purpose of this subtitle is to provide funds to States for the construction, renovation, operation, and maintenance of pumpout stations and waste reception facilities.

"Sec. 5603. Determination and plan regarding State marine sanitation device pumpout station needs.

"(a) Survey.—Within 3 months after the notification under section 5605(b), each coastal State shall conduct a survey to determine—

"(1) the number and location of all operational pumpout stations and waste reception facilities at public and private marinas, mooring areas, docks, and other boating access facilities within the coastal zone of the State; and

"(2) the number of recreational vessels in the coastal waters of the State with type III marine sanitation devices or portable toilets, and the areas of those coastal waters where those vessels congregate.

"(b) Plan.—Within 6 months after the notification under section 5605(b), and based on the survey conducted under subsection (a), each coastal State shall—

"(1) develop and submit to the Secretary of the Interior a plan for any construction or renovation of pumpout stations and waste reception facilities that are necessary to ensure that, based on the guidance issued under section 5605(a), there are pumpout stations and waste reception facilities in the State that are adequate and reasonably available to meet the needs of recreational vessels using the coastal waters of the State; and

"(2) submit to the Secretary of the Interior with that plan a list of all stations and facilities in the coastal zone of the State which are operational on the date of submittal.

"(c) Plan approval.—

"(1) In general.—Not later than 60 days after a plan is submitted by a State under subsection (b), the Secretary of the Interior shall approve or disapprove the plan, based on—

"(A) the adequacy of the survey conducted by the State under subsection (a); and

"(B) the ability of the plan, based on the guidance issued under section 5605(a), to meet the construction and renovation needs of the recreational vessels identified in the survey.

"(2) Notification of State; modification.—The Secretary of the Interior shall promptly notify the affected Governor of the approval or disapproval of a plan. If a plan is disapproved, the Secretary of the Interior shall recommend necessary modifications and return the plan to the affected Governor.

"(3) **Resubmittal.**—Not later than 60 days after receiving a plan returned by the Secretary of the Interior, the Governor shall make the appropriate changes and resubmit the plan.

"(d) **Indication of stations and facilities on NOAA charts.**—

"(1) **In general.**—The Under Secretary of Commerce for Oceans and Atmosphere shall indicate, on charts published by the National Oceanic and Atmospheric Administration for the use of operators of recreational vessels, the locations of pumpout stations and waste reception facilities.

"(2) **Notification of NOAA.**—

"(A) **Lists of stations and facilities.**—The Secretary of the Interior shall transmit to the Under Secretary of Commerce for Oceans and Atmosphere each list of operational stations and facilities submitted by a State under subsection (b)(2), by not later than 30 days after the date of receipt of that list.

"(B) **Completion of project.**—The Director of the United States Fish and Wildlife Service shall notify the Under Secretary of the location of each station or facility at which a construction or renovation project is completed by a State with amounts made available under the Act of August 9, 1950 (16 U.S.C. 777a et seq.), as amended by this subtitle [section 777 et seq. of Title 16, Conservation], by not later than 30 days after the date of notification by a State of the completion of the project.

"Sec. 5604. Funding.

"(a) **[Omitted.** Subsec. (a) amended section 777c of Title 16, Conservation]

"(b) **[Omitted.** Subsec. (b) amended section 777g of Title 16, Conservation]

"(c) **Grant program.**—

"(1) **Matching grants.**—The Secretary of the Interior may obligate an amount not to exceed the amount made available under section 4(b)(2) of the Act of August 9, 1950 (16 U.S.C. 777c(b)(2), as amended by this Act) [section 777c(b)(2) of Title 16], to make grants to—

"(A) coastal States to pay not more than 75 percent of the cost to a coastal State of—

"(i) conducting a survey under section 5603(a);

"(ii) developing and submitting a plan and accompanying list under section 5603(b);

"(iii) constructing and renovating pumpout stations and waste reception facilities; and

"(iv) conducting a program to educate recreational boaters about the problem of human body waste discharges from vessels and inform them of the location of pumpout stations and waste reception facilities.

"(B) inland States, which can demonstrate to the Secretary of the Interior that there are an inadequate number of pumpout stations and waste reception facilities to meet the needs of recreational vessels in the waters of that State, to pay 75 percent of the cost to that State of—

"(i) constructing and renovating pumpout stations and waste reception facilities in the inland State; and

"(ii) conducting a program to educate recreational boaters about the problem of human body waste discharges from vessels and inform them of the location of pumpout stations and waste reception facilities.

"(2) **Priority.**—In awarding grants under this subsection, the Secretary of the Interior shall give priority consideration to grant applications that—

"(A) provide for public/private partnership efforts to develop and operate pumpout stations and waste reception facilities; and

"(B) propose innovative ways to increase the availability and use of pumpout stations and waste reception facilities.

"(d) **Disclaimer.**—Nothing in this subtitle shall be interpreted to preclude a State from carrying out the provisions of this subtitle with funds other than those described in this section.

"Sec. 5605. Guidance and notification.

"(a) Issuance of guidance.—Not later than 3 months after the date of the enactment of this subtitle [Nov. 4, 1992], the Secretary of the Interior shall, after consulting with the Administrator of the Environmental Protection Agency, the Under Secretary of Commerce for Oceans and Atmosphere, and the Commandant of the Coast Guard, issue for public comment pumpout station and waste reception facility guidance. The Secretary of the Interior shall finalize the guidance not later than 6 months after the date of enactment of this subtitle [Nov. 4, 1992]. The guidance shall include—

"(1) guidance regarding the types of pumpout stations and waste reception facilities that may be appropriate for construction, renovation, operation, or maintenance with amounts available under the Act of August 9, 1950 (16 U.S.C. 777a et seq.) [section 777 et seq. of Title 16], as amended by this subtitle, and appropriate location of the stations and facilities within a marina or boatyard;

"(2) guidance defining what constitutes adequate and reasonably available pumpout stations and waste reception facilities in boating areas;

"(3) guidance on appropriate methods for disposal of vessel sewage from pumpout stations and waste reception facilities;

"(4) guidance on appropriate connector fittings to facilitate the sanitary and expeditious discharge of sewage from vessels;

"(5) guidance on the waters most likely to be affected by the discharge of sewage from vessels; and

"(6) other information that is considered necessary to promote the establishment of pumpout facilities to reduce sewage discharges from vessels and to protect United States waters.

"(b) Notification.—Not later than one month after the guidance issued under subsection (a) is finalized, the Secretary of the Interior shall provide notification in writing to the fish and wildlife, water pollution control, and coastal zone management authorities of each State, of—

"(1) the availability of amounts under the Act of August 9, 1950 (16 U.S.C. 777a et seq.) [section 777 et seq. of Title 16] to implement the Clean Vessel Act of 1992 [subtitle F of Title V of Pub. L. No. 102–587 amending sections 777c and 777g of Title 16 and enacting this note]; and

"(2) the guidance developed under subsection (a).

"Sec. 5606. Effect on State funding eligibility.

"This subtitle shall not be construed or applied to jeopardize any funds available to a coastal State under the Act of August 9, 1950 (16 U.S.C. 777a et seq.) [section 777 et seq. of Title 16], if the coastal State is, in good faith, pursuing a survey and plan designed to meet the purposes of this subtitle.

"Sec. 5607. Applicability.

"The requirements of section 5603 shall not apply to a coastal State if within six months after the date of enactment of this subtitle [Nov. 4, 1992] the Secretary of the Interior certifies that—

"(1) the State has developed and is implementing a plan that will ensure that there will be pumpout stations and waste reception facilities adequate to meet the needs of recreational vessels in the coastal waters of the State; or

"(2) existing pumpout stations and waste reception facilities in the coastal waters of the State are adequate to meet those needs.

"Sec. 5608. Definitions.

"For the purposes of this subtitle the term:

"(1) 'coastal State'—

"(A) means a State of the United States in, or bordering on the Atlantic, Pacific, or Arctic Ocean; the Gulf of Mexico; Long Island Sound; or one or more of the Great Lakes;

"(B) includes Puerto Rico, the Virgin Islands, Guam, the Commonwealth of the Northern Mariana Islands, and American Samoa; and

"(C) does not include a State for which the ratio of the number of recreational vessels in the State numbered under chapter 123 of title 46, United States Code [section 12301 et seq. of Title 46,

Shipping], to number of miles of shoreline (as that term is defined in section 926.2(d) of title 15, Code of Federal Regulations, as in effect on January 1, 1991), is less than one.

"(2) 'coastal waters' means—

"(A) in the Great Lakes area, the waters within the territorial jurisdiction of the United States consisting of the Great Lakes, their connecting waters, harbors, roadsteads, and estuary-type areas such as bays, shallows, and marshes; and

"(B) in other areas, those waters, adjacent to the shorelines, which contain a measurable percentage of sea water, including sounds, bay, lagoons, bayous, ponds, and estuaries.

"(3) 'coastal zone' has the same meaning that term has in section 304(1) of the Coastal Zone Management Act of 1972 (16 U.S.C. 1453(1)) [section 1453(1) of Title 16];

"(4) 'inland State' means a State which is not a coastal state;

"(5) 'type III marine sanitation device' means any equipment for installation on board a vessel which is specifically designed to receive, retain, and discharge human body wastes;

"(6) 'pumpout station' means a facility that pumps or receives human body wastes out of type III marine sanitation devices installed on board vessels;

"(7) 'recreational vessel' means a vessel—

"(A) manufactured for operation, or operated, primarily for pleasure; or

"(B) leased, rented, or chartered to another for the latter's pleasure; and

"(8) 'waste reception facility' means a facility specifically designed to receive wastes from portable toilets carried on vessels, and does not include lavatories."

[Amendments by Pub. L. No. 109–59, §§ 10101 to 10143, effective Oct. 1, 2005, see 2005 Effective and Applicability Provisions note regarding Pub. L. No. 109–59, § 10102, set out under 16 U.S.C.A. § 777b.]

[Except as otherwise provided, during the period beginning on Aug. 10, 2005, and ending upon the expiration of fiscal year 2005, provisions of law amended by the Sportfishing and Recreational Boating Safety Act of 2005, Pub. L. No. 109–59, §§ 10101 to 10143, as amended by Pub. L. No. 109–74, to be considered to read as such laws read immediately before the enactment of that Act, see Pub. L. No. 109–74, § 101(b), set out as a note under 16 U.S.C.A. § 777b.]

§ 1323. Federal facilities pollution control

[FWPCA § 313]

(a) Each department, agency, or instrumentality of the executive, legislative, and judicial branches of the Federal Government (1) having jurisdiction over any property or facility, or (2) engaged in any activity resulting, or which may result, in the discharge or runoff of pollutants, and each officer, agent, or employee thereof in the performance of his official duties, shall be subject to, and comply with, all Federal, State, interstate, and local requirements, administrative authority, and process and sanctions respecting the control and abatement of water pollution in the same manner, and to the same extent as any nongovernmental entity including the payment of reasonable service charges. The preceding sentence shall apply (A) to any requirement whether substantive or procedural (including any recordkeeping or reporting requirement, any requirement respecting permits and any other requirement, whatsoever), (B) to the exercise of any Federal, State, or local administrative authority, and (C) to any process and sanction, whether enforced in Federal, State, or local courts or in any other manner. This subsection shall apply notwithstanding any immunity of such agencies, officers, agents, or employees under any law or rule of law. Nothing in this section shall be construed to prevent any department, agency, or instrumentality of the Federal Government, or any officer, agent, or employee thereof in the performance of his official duties, from removing to the appropriate Federal district court any proceeding to which the department, agency, or instrumentality or officer, agent, or employee thereof is subject pursuant to this section, and any such proceeding may be removed in accordance with section 1441 et seq. of Title 28. No officer, agent, or employee of the United States shall be personally liable for any civil penalty arising from the performance of his official duties, for which he is not otherwise liable, and the United States shall be liable only for those civil penalties arising under Federal law or imposed by a State or local court to enforce an order or the process of such court. The President may exempt any effluent source of any department, agency, or instrumentality in the executive branch from compliance with any such a requirement if he determines it to be in the paramount interest of the United States to do so; except that no exemption may be granted from the requirements of section 1316 or 1317 of this title. No such exemptions shall be granted due to lack of appropriation unless the President shall have specifically requested such appropriation as a part of the budgetary process and the Congress shall have failed to make available such requested appropriation. Any exemption shall be for a period not in excess of one year, but additional exemptions may be granted for periods of not to exceed one year upon the President's making a new determination. The President shall report each January to the Congress all exemptions from the requirements of this section granted during the preceding calendar year, together with his reason for granting such exemption. In addition to any such exemption of a particular effluent source, the President may, if he determines it to be in the paramount interest of the United States to do so, issue regulations exempting from compliance with the requirements of this section any weaponry, equipment, aircraft, vessels, vehicles, or other classes or categories of property, and access to such property, which are owned or operated by the Armed Forces of the United States (including the Coast Guard) or by the National Guard of any State and which are uniquely military in nature. The President shall reconsider the need for such regulations at three-year intervals.

(b) **(1)** The Administrator shall coordinate with the head of each department, agency, or instrumentality of the Federal Government having jurisdiction over any property or facility utilizing federally owned wastewater facilities to develop a program of cooperation for utilizing wastewater control systems utilizing those innovative treatment processes and techniques for which guidelines have been promulgated under section 1314(d)(3) of this title. Such program shall include an inventory of property and facilities which could utilize such processes and techniques.

(2) Construction shall not be initiated for facilities for treatment of wastewater at any Federal property or facility after September 30, 1979, if alternative methods for wastewater treatment at such property or facility utilizing innovative treatment processes and techniques, including but not limited to methods utilizing recycle and reuse techniques and land treatment are not utilized, unless the life cycle cost of the alternative treatment works exceeds the life cycle cost of the most cost effective alternative by more than 15 per centum. The Administrator may waive the application of this paragraph in any case where the Administrator determines it to be in the public interest, or that compliance with this paragraph would interfere with the orderly compliance with conditions of a permit issued pursuant to section 1342 of this title.

(c) **Reasonable service charges**

(1) **In general**

For the purposes of this chapter, reasonable service charges described in subsection (a) include any reasonable nondiscriminatory fee, charge, or assessment that is—

(A) based on some fair approximation of the proportionate contribution of the property or facility to stormwater pollution (in terms of quantities of pollutants, or volume or rate of stormwater discharge or runoff from the property or facility); and

(B) used to pay or reimburse the costs associated with any stormwater management program (whether associated with a separate storm sewer system or a sewer system that manages a combination of stormwater and sanitary waste), including the full range of programmatic and structural costs attributable to collecting stormwater, reducing pollutants in stormwater, and reducing the volume and rate of stormwater discharge, regardless of whether that reasonable fee, charge, or assessment is denominated a tax.

(2) **Limitation on accounts**

(A) **Limitation**

The payment or reimbursement of any fee, charge, or assessment described in paragraph (1) shall not be made using funds from any permanent authorization account in the Treasury.

(B) Reimbursement or payment obligation of Federal Government

Each department, agency, or instrumentality of the executive, legislative, and judicial branches of the Federal Government, as described in subsection (a), shall not be obligated to pay or reimburse any fee, charge, or assessment described in paragraph (1), except to the extent and in an amount provided in advance by any appropriations Act to pay or reimburse the fee, charge, or assessment.

(June 30, 1948, c. 758, Title III, § 313, as added by Pub. L. No. 92–500, § 2, 86 Stat. 875 (Oct. 18, 1972); and amended by Pub. L. No. 95–217, §§ 60, 61(a), 91 Stat. 1597, 1598 (Dec. 27, 1977); Pub. L. No. 111–378, § 1, 124 Stat. 4128 (Jan. 4, 2011).)

HISTORICAL AND STATUTORY NOTES

References in Text

This chapter, referred to in subsec. (c)(1), originally read "this Act", meaning the Federal Water Pollution Control Act, commonly referred to as the Clean Water Act, Act of June 30, 30 1948, c. 758, 62 Stat. 1155, as amended, which is principally codified as chapter 26 of Title 33, 33 U.S.C.A. § 1251 et seq. For completion classification, see Short Title note set out under 33 U.S.C.A. § 1251 and Tables.

Termination of Reporting Requirements

Reporting requirement of subsec. (a) of this section excepted from termination under Pub. L. No. 104–66, § 3003(a)(1), as amended, set out as a note under 31 U.S.C.A. § 1113, see Pub. L. No. 107–303, § 302(a), set out as a note under 31 U.S.C.A. § 1113.

Marine Guidance Systems

Pub. L. No. 105–383, Title IV, § 425(b), 112 Stat. 3441 (Nov. 13, 1998), provided that: "The Secretary of Transportation shall, within 12 months after the date of the enactment of this Act [Nov. 13, 1998], evaluate and report to the Congress on the suitability of marine sector laser lighting, cold cathode lighting, and ultraviolet enhanced vision technologies for use in guiding marine vessels and traffic."

Exemption for Fort Allen in Puerto Rico

For provisions relating to the exemption for Fort Allen in Puerto Rico, in its use as temporary housing for Haitian refugees, from compliance with provisions of this chapter relating to effluent sources located at Fort Allen, with exceptions, see sections 1–101 and 1–105 of Ex. Ord. No. 12327, Oct. 1, 1981, 46 Fed. Reg. 48893, set out as a note under section 2601 of Title 22, Foreign Relations and Intercourse.

Federal Compliance with Pollution Control Standards

For provisions relating to the responsibility of the head of each Executive agency for compliance with applicable pollution control standards, see Ex. Ord. No. 12088, Oct. 13, 1978, 43 Fed. Reg. 47707, set out as a note under section 4321 of Title 42, Public Health and Welfare.

§ 1324. Clean lakes

[FWPCA § 314]

(a) Establishment and scope of program

(1) State program requirements

Each State on a biennial basis shall prepare and submit to the Administrator for his approval—

(A) an identification and classification according to eutrophic condition of all publicly owned lakes in such State;

(B) a description of procedures, processes, and methods (including land use requirements), to control sources of pollution of such lakes;

(C) a description of methods and procedures, in conjunction with appropriate Federal agencies, to restore the quality of such lakes;

(D) methods and procedures to mitigate the harmful effects of high acidity, including innovative methods of neutralizing and restoring buffering capacity of lakes and methods of removing from lakes toxic metals and other toxic substances mobilized by high acidity;

(E) a list and description of those publicly owned lakes in such State for which uses are known to be impaired, including those lakes which are known not to meet applicable water quality standards or which require implementation of control programs to maintain compliance with applicable standards and those lakes in which water quality has deteriorated as a result of high acidity that may reasonably be due to acid deposition; and

(F) an assessment of the status and trends of water quality in lakes in such State, including but not limited to, the nature and extent of pollution loading from point and nonpoint sources and the extent to which the use of lakes is impaired as a result of such pollution, particularly with respect to toxic pollution.

(2) Submission as part of 1315(b)(1) report

The information required under paragraph (1) shall be included in the report required under section 1315(b)(1) of this title, beginning with the report required under such section by April 1, 1988.

(3) Report of Administrator

Not later than 180 days after receipt from the States of the biennial information required under paragraph (1), the Administrator shall submit to the Committee on Public Works and Transportation of the House of Representatives and the Committee on Environment and Public Works of the Senate a report on the status of water quality in lakes in the United States, including the effectiveness of the methods and procedures described in paragraph (1)(D).

(4) Eligibility requirement

Beginning after April 1, 1988, a State must have submitted the information required under paragraph (1) in order to receive grant assistance under this section.

(b) Financial assistance to States

The Administrator shall provide financial assistance to States in order to carry out methods and procedures approved by him under subsection (a) of this section. The Administrator shall provide financial assistance to States to prepare the identification and classification surveys required in subsection (a)(1) of this section.

(c) Maximum amount of grant; authorization of appropriations

(1) The amount granted to any State for any fiscal year under subsection (b) of this section shall not exceed 70 per centum of the funds expended by such State in such year for carrying out approved methods and procedures under subsection (a) of this section.

(2) There is authorized to be appropriated $50,000,000 for each of fiscal years 2001 through 2005 for grants to States under subsection (b) of this section which such sums shall remain available until expended. The Administrator shall provide for an equitable distribution of such sums to the States with approved methods and procedures under subsection (a) of this section.

(d) Demonstration program

(1) General requirements

The Administrator is authorized and directed to establish and conduct at locations throughout the Nation a lake water quality demonstration program. The program shall, at a minimum—

(A) develop cost effective technologies for the control of pollutants to preserve or enhance lake water quality while optimizing multiple lakes uses;

(B) control nonpoint sources of pollution which are contributing to the degradation of water quality in lakes;

(C) evaluate the feasibility of implementing regional consolidated pollution control strategies;

(D) demonstrate environmentally preferred techniques for the removal and disposal of contaminated lake sediments;

(E) develop improved methods for the removal of silt, stumps, aquatic growth, and other obstructions which impair the quality of lakes;

(F) construct and evaluate silt traps and other devices or equipment to prevent or abate the deposit of sediment in lakes; and

(G) demonstrate the costs and benefits of utilizing dredged material from lakes in the reclamation of despoiled land.

(2) Geographical requirements

Demonstration projects authorized by this subsection shall be undertaken to reflect a variety of geographical and environmental conditions. As a priority, the Administrator shall undertake demonstration projects at Lake Champlain, New York and Vermont; Lake Houston, Texas; Beaver Lake, Arkansas; Greenwood Lake and Belcher Creek, New Jersey; Deal Lake, New Jersey; Alcyon Lake, New Jersey; Gorton's Pond, Rhode Island; Lake Washington, Rhode Island; Lake Bomoseen, Vermont; Sauk Lake, Minnesota; Otsego Lake, New York; Oneida Lake, New York; Raystown Lake, Pennsylvania; Swan Lake, Itasca County, Minnesota; Walker Lake, Nevada; Lake Tahoe, California and Nevada; Ten Mile Lakes, Oregon; Woahink Lake, Oregon; Highland Lake, Connecticut; Lily Lake, New Jersey; Strawbridge Lake, New Jersey; Baboosic Lake, New Hampshire; French Pond, New Hampshire; Dillon Reservoir, Ohio; Tohopekaliga Lake, Florida; Lake Apopka, Florida; Lake George, New York; Lake Wallenpaupack, Pennsylvania; Lake Allatoona, Georgia; and Lake Worth, Texas.

(3) Reports

Notwithstanding section 3003 of the Federal Reports Elimination and Sunset Act of 1995 (31 U.S.C. 1113 note; 109 Stat. 734–736), by January 1, 1997, and January 1 of every odd-numbered year thereafter, the Administrator shall report to the Committee on Transportation and Infrastructure of the House of Representatives and the Committee on Environment and Public Works of the Senate on work undertaken pursuant to this subsection. Upon completion of the program authorized by this subsection, the Administrator shall submit to such committees a final report on the results of such program, along with recommendations for further measures to improve the water quality of the Nation's lakes.

(4) Authorization of appropriations

(A) In general

There is authorized to be appropriated to carry out this subsection not to exceed $40,000,000 for fiscal years beginning after September 30, 1986, to remain available until expended.

(B) Special authorizations

(i) Amount

There is authorized to be appropriated to carry out subsection (b) of this section with respect to subsection (a)(1)(D) of this section not to exceed $25,000,000 for fiscal years beginning after September 30, 1986, to remain available until expended.

(ii) Distribution of funds

The Administrator shall provide for an equitable distribution of sums appropriated pursuant to this subparagraph among States carrying out approved methods and procedures. Such distribution shall be based on the relative needs of each such State for the mitigation of the harmful effects on lakes and other surface waters of high acidity that may reasonably be due to acid deposition or acid mine drainage.

(iii) Grants as additional assistance

The amount of any grant to a State under this subparagraph shall be in addition to, and not in lieu of, any other Federal financial assistance.

(June 30, 1948, c. 758, Title III, § 314, as added by Pub. L. No. 92–500, § 2, 86 Stat. 875 (Oct. 18, 1972); and amended by Pub. L. No. 95–217, §§ 4(f), 62(a), 91 Stat. 1567, 1598 (Dec. 27, 1977); Pub. L. No. 96–483, § 1(f), 94 Stat. 2360 (Oct. 21, 1980); Pub. L. No. 100–4, Title I, § 101(g), Title III, § 315(a), (b), (d), 101 Stat. 9, 49, 50, 52 (Feb. 4, 1987); Pub. L. No. 101–596, Title III, § 302, 104 Stat. 3006 (Nov. 16, 1990); Pub. L. No. 104–66, Title II, § 2021(c), 109 Stat. 727 (Dec. 21, 1995); Pub. L. No. 105–362, Title V, § 501(b), 112 Stat. 3283 (Nov. 10, 1998); Pub. L. No. 106–457, Title VII, §§ 701, 702, 114 Stat. 1976 (Nov. 7, 2000); Pub. L. No. 107–303, Title III, § 302(b)(1), 116 Stat. 2361 (Nov. 27, 2002).)

HISTORICAL AND STATUTORY NOTES

References in Text

Section 3003 of the Federal Reports Elimination and Sunset Act of 1995, referred to in subsec. (d)(3), is Pub. L. No. 104–66, Title III, § 3003, 109 Stat. 734 (Dec. 21, 1995), which is set out as a note under section 1113 of Title 31.

Effective and Applicability Provisions

2002 Acts. Effective November 10, 1998, section 501 of the Federal Reports Elimination Act of 1998 [Pub. L. No. 105–362, Title V, § 501, 112 Stat. 3283 (Nov. 10, 1998)] is amended by striking subsections (a), (b), (c), and (d) [amending this section and others, see Tables for complete classification]. The Federal Water Pollution Control Act (33 U.S.C.A. § 1254(n)(3)) shall be applied and administered on and after Nov. 27, 2002 as if the amendments made by subsections (a), (b), (c), and (d) of Pub. L. No. 105–362, § 501, had not been enacted, see Pub. L. No. 107–303, § 302(b)(2), set out as a note under 33 U.S.C.A. § 1254.

Change of Name

Any reference in any provision of law enacted before Jan. 4, 1995, to the Committee on Public Works and Transportation of the House of Representatives treated as referring to the Committee on Transportation and Infrastructure of the House of Representatives, see section 1(a)(9) of Pub. L. No. 104–14, set out as a note preceding section 21 of Title 2, The Congress.

Termination of Reporting Requirements

Reporting requirement of subsec. (a) of this section excepted from termination under Pub. L. No. 104–66, § 3003(a)(1), as amended, set out as a note under 31 U.S.C.A. § 1113, see Pub. L. No. 107–303, § 302(a).

§ 1325. National Study Commission

[FWPCA § 315]

(a) Establishment

There is established a National Study Commission, which shall make a full and complete investigation and study of all of the technological aspects of achieving, and all aspects of the total economic, social, and environmental effects of achieving or not achieving, the effluent limitations and goals set forth for 1983 in section 1311(b)(2) of this title.

(b) Membership; chairman

Such Commission shall be composed of fifteen members, including five members of the Senate, who are members of the Environment and Public Works committee, appointed by the President of the Senate, five members of the House, who are members of the Public Works and Transportation committee, appointed by the Speaker of the House, and five members of the public appointed by the President. The Chairman of such Commission shall be elected from among its members.

(c) Contract authority

In the conduct of such study, the Commission is authorized to contract with the National Academy of Sciences and the National Academy of Engineering (acting through the National Research Council), the National Institute of Ecology, Brookings Institution, and other nongovernmental entities, for the investigation of matters within their competence.

(d) Cooperation of departments, agencies, and instrumentalities of executive branch

The heads of the departments, agencies and instrumentalities of the executive branch of the Federal Government shall cooperate with the Commission in carrying out the requirements of this section, and shall furnish to the Commission such information as the Commission deems necessary to carry out this section.

(e) Report to Congress

A report shall be submitted to the Congress of the results of such investigation and study, together with recommendations, not later than three years after October 18, 1972.

(f) Compensation and allowances

The members of the Commission who are not officers or employees of the United States, while attending conferences or meetings of the Commission or while otherwise serving at the request of the Chairman shall be entitled to receive compensation at a rate not in excess of the maximum rate of pay for Grade GS–18, as provided in the General Schedule under section 5332 of Title 5, including traveltime and while away from their homes or regular places of business they may be allowed travel expenses, including per diem in lieu of subsistence as authorized by law for persons in the Government service employed intermittently.

(g) Appointment of personnel

In addition to authority to appoint personnel subject to the provisions of Title 5 governing appointments in the competitive service, and to pay such personnel in accordance with the provisions of chapter 51 and subchapter III of chapter 53 of such title relating to classification and General Schedule pay rates, the Commission shall have authority to enter into contracts with private or public organizations who shall furnish the Commission with such administrative and technical personnel as may be necessary to carry out the purpose of this section. Personnel furnished by such organizations under this subsection are not, and shall not be considered to be, Federal employees for any purposes, but in the performance of their duties shall be guided by the standards which apply to employees of the legislative branches under rules 41 and 43 of the Senate and House of Representatives, respectively.

(h) Authorization of appropriation

There is authorized to be appropriated, for use in carrying out this section, not to exceed $17,250,000.

(June 30, 1948, c. 758, Title III, § 315, as added by Pub. L. No. 92–500, § 2, 86 Stat. 875 (Oct. 18, 1972); and amended by Pub. L. No. 93–207, § 1(5), 87 Stat. 906 (Dec. 28, 1973); Pub. L. No. 93–592, § 5, 88 Stat. 1925 (Jan. 2, 1975); Pub. L. No. 94–238, 90 Stat. 250 (Mar. 23, 1976); H.Res. 988 (Oct. 8, 1974); S.Res. 4 (Feb. 4, 1977).)

HISTORICAL AND STATUTORY NOTES

References in Text

Travel expenses, including per diem in lieu of subsistence as authorized by law, referred to in subsec. (f), probably refers to the allowances authorized by section 5703 of Title 5, Government Organization and Employees.

The General Schedule, referred to in subsec. (g), is set out under section 5332 of Title 5.

The Rules of the House of Representatives for the One Hundred Sixth Congress were adopted and amended generally by House Resolution No. 5, One Hundred Sixth Congress, Jan. 6, 1999. Provisions formerly appearing in rule 43, referred to in subsec. (g), were contained in rule XXIV, which was subsequently renumbered Rule XXIII by House Resolution No. 5, One Hundred Seventh Congress, Jan. 3, 2001.

Change of Name

The Committee on Public Works of the Senate was abolished and replaced by the Committee on Environment and Public Works of the Senate, effective Feb. 11, 1977. See Rule XXV of the Standing Rules of the Senate, as amended by Senate Resolution 4 (popularly cited as the "Committee System Reorganization Amendments of 1977"), approved Feb. 4, 1977.

Any reference in any provision of law enacted before Jan. 4, 1995, to the Committee on Public Works and Transportation of the House of Representatives treated as referring to the Committee on Transportation and Infrastructure of the House of Representatives, see section 1(a)(9) of Pub. L. No. 104–14, set out as a note preceding section 21 of Title 2, The Congress.

The Committee on Public Works of the House of Representatives was changed to the Committee on Public Works and Transportation of the House of Representatives, effective Jan. 3, 1975, by House Resolution 988, 93d Congress.

References in Other Laws to GS–16, 17, or 18 Pay Rates

References in laws to the rates of pay for GS–16, 17, or 18, or to maximum rates of pay under the General Schedule, to be considered references to rates payable under specified sections of Title 5, see section 529 [Title I, § 101(c)(1)] of Pub. L. No. 101–509, set out in a note under 5 U.S.C.A. § 5376.

§ 1326. Thermal discharges

[FWPCA § 316]

(a) Effluent limitations that will assure protection and propagation of balanced, indigenous population of shellfish, fish, and wildlife

With respect to any point source otherwise subject to the provisions of section 1311 of this title or section 1316 of this title, whenever the owner or operator of any such source, after opportunity for public hearing, can demonstrate to the satisfaction of the Administrator (or, if appropriate, the State) that any effluent limitation proposed for the control of the thermal component of any discharge from such source will require effluent limitations more stringent than necessary to assure the projection and propagation of a balanced, indigenous population of shellfish, fish, and wildlife in and on the body of water into which the discharge is to be made, the Administrator (or, if appropriate, the State) may impose an effluent limitation under such sections for such plant, with respect to the thermal component of such discharge (taking into account the interaction of such thermal component with other pollutants), that will assure the protection and propagation of a balanced, indigenous population of shellfish, fish, and wildlife in and on that body of water.

(b) Cooling water intake structures

Any standard established pursuant to section 1311 of this title or section 1316 of this title and applicable to a point source shall require that the location, design, construction, and capacity of cooling water intake structures reflect the best technology available for minimizing adverse environmental impact.

(c) Period of protection from more stringent effluent limitations following discharge point source modification commenced after October 18, 1972

Notwithstanding any other provision of this chapter, any point source of a discharge having a thermal component, the modification of which point source is commenced after October 18, 1972, and which, as modified, meets effluent limitations established under section 1311 of this title or, if more stringent, effluent limitations established under section 1313 of this title and which effluent limitations will assure protection and propagation of a balanced, indigenous population of shellfish, fish, and wildlife in or on the water into which the discharge is made, shall not be subject to any more stringent effluent limitation with respect to the thermal component of its discharge during a ten year period beginning on the date of completion of such modification or during the period of depreciation or amortization of such facility for the purpose of section 167 or 169 (or both) of Title 26, whichever period ends first.

(June 30, 1948, c. 758, Title III, § 316, as added by Pub. L. No. 92–500, § 2, 86 Stat. 876 (Oct. 18, 1972); and amended by Pub. L. No. 99–514, § 2, 100 Stat. 2095 (Oct. 22, 1986).)

§ 1327. Omitted

HISTORICAL AND STATUTORY NOTES

Codifications

Section, Act of June 30, 1948, c. 758, Title III, § 317, as added by Pub. L. No. 92–500, § 2, 86 Stat. 877 (Oct. 18, 1972), authorized the Administrator to investigate and study the feasibility of alternate methods of financing the cost of preventing, controlling, and abating pollution as directed by the Water Quality Improvement Act of 1970 and to report to Congress, not later than two years after Oct. 18, 1972, the results of his investigation and study accompanied by his recommendations for financing these programs for the fiscal years beginning after 1976.

§ 1328. Aquaculture

[FWPCA § 318]

(a) Authority to permit discharge of specific pollutants

The Administrator is authorized, after public hearings, to permit the discharge of a specific pollutant or pollutants under controlled conditions associated with an approved aquaculture project under Federal or State supervision pursuant to section 1342 of this title.

(b) Procedures and guidelines

The Administrator shall by regulation establish any procedures and guidelines which the Administrator deems necessary to carry out this section. Such regulations shall require the application to such discharge of each criterion, factor, procedure, and requirement applicable to a permit issued under section 1342 of this title, as the Administrator determines necessary to carry out the objective of this chapter.

(c) State administration

Each State desiring to administer its own permit program within its jurisdiction for discharge of a specific pollutant or pollutants under controlled conditions associated with an approved aquaculture project may do so if upon submission of such program the Administrator determines such program is adequate to carry out the objective of this chapter.

(June 30, 1948, c. 758, Title III, § 318, as added by Pub. L. No. 92–500, § 2, 86 Stat. 877 (Oct. 18, 1972); and amended by Pub. L. No. 95–217, § 63, 91 Stat. 1599 (Dec. 27, 1977).)

§ 1329. Nonpoint source management programs

[FWPCA § 319]

(a) State assessment reports

(1) Contents

The Governor of each State shall, after notice and opportunity for public comment, prepare and submit to the Administrator for approval, a report which—

(A) identifies those navigable waters within the State which, without additional action to control nonpoint sources of pollution, cannot reasonably be expected to attain or maintain applicable water quality standards or the goals and requirements of this chapter;

(B) identifies those categories and subcategories of nonpoint sources or, where appropriate, particular nonpoint sources which add significant pollution to each portion of the navigable waters identified under subparagraph (A) in amounts which contribute to such portion not meeting such water quality standards or such goals and requirements;

(C) describes the process, including intergovernmental coordination and public participation, for identifying best management practices and measures to control each category and subcategory of nonpoint sources and, where appropriate, particular nonpoint sources identified under subparagraph (B) and to reduce, to the maximum extent practicable, the level of pollution resulting from such category, subcategory, or source; and

(D) identifies and describes State and local programs for controlling pollution added from nonpoint sources to, and improving the quality of, each such portion of the navigable waters, including but not limited to those programs which are receiving Federal assistance under subsections (h) and (i) of this section.

(2) Information used in preparation

In developing the report required by this section, the State (A) may rely upon information developed pursuant to sections 1288, 1313(e), 1314(f), 1315(b), and 1324 of this title, and other information as appropriate, and (B) may utilize appropriate elements of the waste treatment management plans developed pursuant to sections 1288(b) and 1313 of this title, to the extent such elements are consistent with and fulfill the requirements of this section.

(b) State management programs

(1) In general

The Governor of each State, for that State or in combination with adjacent States, shall, after notice and opportunity for public comment, prepare and submit to the Administrator for approval a management program which such State proposes to implement in the first four fiscal years beginning after the date of submission of such management program for controlling pollution added from nonpoint sources to the navigable waters within the State and improving the quality of such waters.

(2) Specific contents

Each management program proposed for implementation under this subsection shall include each of the following:

(A) An identification of the best management practices and measures which will be undertaken to reduce pollutant loadings resulting from each category, subcategory, or particular nonpoint source designated under paragraph (1)(B), taking into account the impact of the practice on ground water quality.

(B) An identification of programs (including, as appropriate, nonregulatory or regulatory programs for enforcement, technical assistance, financial assistance, education, training, technology transfer, and demonstration projects) to achieve implementation of the best management practices by the categories, subcategories, and particular nonpoint sources designated under subparagraph (A).

(C) A schedule containing annual milestones for (i) utilization of the program implementation methods identified in subparagraph (B), and (ii) implementation of the best management practices identified in subparagraph (A) by the categories, subcategories, or particular nonpoint sources designated under paragraph (1)(B). Such schedule shall provide for utilization of the best management practices at the earliest practicable date.

(D) A certification of the attorney general of the State or States (or the chief attorney of any State water pollution control agency which has independent legal counsel) that the laws of the State or States, as the case may be, provide adequate authority to implement such management program or, if there is not such adequate authority, a list of such additional authorities as will be necessary to implement such management program. A schedule and commitment by the State or States to seek such additional authorities as expeditiously as practicable.

(E) Sources of Federal and other assistance and funding (other than assistance provided under subsections (h) and (i) of this section) which will be available in each of such fiscal years for supporting implementation of such practices and measures and the purposes for which such assistance will be used in each of such fiscal years.

(F) An identification of Federal financial assistance programs and Federal development projects for which the State will review individual assistance applications or development projects for their effect on water quality pursuant to the procedures set forth in Executive Order 12372 as in effect on September 17, 1983, to determine whether such assistance applications or development projects would be consistent with the program prepared under this subsection; for the purposes of this subparagraph, identification shall not be limited to the assistance programs or development projects subject to Executive Order 12372 but may include any programs listed in the most recent Catalog of Federal Domestic Assistance which may have an effect on the purposes and objectives of the State's nonpoint source pollution management program.

(3) Utilization of local and private experts

In developing and implementing a management program under this subsection, a State shall, to the maximum extent practicable, involve local public and private agencies and organizations which have expertise in control of nonpoint sources of pollution.

(4) Development on watershed basis

A State shall, to the maximum extent practicable, develop and implement a management program under this subsection on a watershed-by-watershed basis within such State.

(c) Administrative provisions

(1) Cooperation requirement

Any report required by subsection (a) of this section and any management program and report required by subsection (b) of this section shall be developed in cooperation with local, substate regional, and interstate entities which are actively planning for the implementation of nonpoint source pollution controls and have either been certified by the Administrator in accordance with section 1288 of this title, have worked jointly with the State on water quality management planning under section 1285(j) of this title, or have been designated by the State legislative body or Governor as water quality management planning agencies for their geographic areas.

(2) Time period for submission of reports and management programs

Each report and management program shall be submitted to the Administrator during the 18-month period beginning on February 4, 1987.

(d) Approval or disapproval of reports and management programs

(1) Deadline

Subject to paragraph (2), not later than 180 days after the date of submission to the Administrator of any report or management program under this section (other than subsections (h), (i), and (k) of this section), the Administrator shall either approve or disapprove such report or management program, as the case may be. The Administrator may approve a portion of a management program under this subsection. If the Administrator does not disapprove a report, management program, or portion of a management program in such 180-day period, such report, management program, or portion shall be deemed approved for purposes of this section.

(2) Procedure for disapproval

If, after notice and opportunity for public comment and consultation with appropriate Federal and State agencies and other interested persons, the Administrator determines that—

(A) the proposed management program or any portion thereof does not meet the requirements of subsection (b)(2) of this section or is not likely to satisfy, in whole or in part, the goals and requirements of this chapter;

(B) adequate authority does not exist, or adequate resources are not available, to implement such program or portion;

(C) the schedule for implementing such program or portion is not sufficiently expeditious; or

(D) the practices and measures proposed in such program or portion are not adequate to reduce the level of pollution in navigable waters in the State resulting from nonpoint sources and to improve the quality of navigable waters in the State;

the Administrator shall within 6 months of the receipt of the proposed program notify the State of any revisions or modifications necessary to obtain approval. The State shall thereupon have an additional 3 months to submit its revised management program and the Administrator shall approve or disapprove such revised program within three months of receipt.

(3) Failure of State to submit report

If a Governor of a State does not submit the report required by subsection (a) of this section within the period specified by subsection (c)(2) of this section, the Administrator shall, within 30 months after February 4, 1987, prepare a report for such State which makes the identifications required by paragraphs (1)(A) and (1)(B) of subsection (a) of this section. Upon completion of the requirement of the preceding sentence and after notice and opportunity for comment, the Administrator shall report to Congress on his actions pursuant to this section.

(e) Local management programs; technical assistance

If a State fails to submit a management program under subsection (b) of this section or the Administrator does not approve such a management program, a local public agency or organization which has expertise in, and authority to, control water pollution resulting from nonpoint sources in any area of such State which the Administrator determines is of sufficient geographic size may, with approval of such State, request the Administrator to provide, and the Administrator shall provide, technical assistance to such agency or organization in developing for such area a management program which is described in subsection (b) of this section and can be approved pursuant to subsection (d) of this section. After development of such management program, such agency or organization shall submit such management program to the Administrator for approval. If the Administrator approves such management program, such agency or organization shall be eligible to receive financial assistance under subsection (h) of this section for implementation of such management program as if such agency or organization were a State for which a report submitted under subsection (a) of this section and a management program submitted under subsection (b) of this section were approved under this section. Such financial assistance shall be subject to the same terms and conditions as assistance provided to a State under subsection (h) of this section.

(f) Technical assistance for States

Upon request of a State, the Administrator may provide technical assistance to such State in developing a management program approved under subsection (b) of this section for those portions of the navigable waters requested by such State.

(g) Interstate management conference

(1) Convening of conference; notification; purpose

If any portion of the navigable waters in any State which is implementing a management program approved under this section is not meeting applicable water quality standards or the goals and requirements of this chapter as a result, in whole or in part, of pollution from nonpoint sources in another State, such State may petition the Administrator to convene, and the Administrator shall convene, a management conference of all States which contribute significant pollution resulting from nonpoint sources to such portion. If, on the basis of information available, the Administrator determines that a State is not meeting applicable water quality standards or the goals and requirements of this chapter as a result, in whole or in part, of significant pollution from nonpoint sources in another State, the Administrator shall notify such States. The Administrator may convene a management conference under this paragraph not later than 180 days after giving such notification, whether or not the State which is not meeting such standards requests such conference. The purpose of such conference shall be to develop an agreement among such States to reduce the level of pollution in such portion resulting from nonpoint sources and to improve the water quality of such portion. Nothing in such agreement shall supersede or abrogate rights to quantities of water which have been established by interstate water compacts, Supreme Court decrees, or State water laws. This subsection shall not apply to any pollution which is subject to the Colorado River Basin Salinity Control Act [43 U.S.C.A. § 1571 et seq.]. The requirement that the Administrator convene a management conference shall not be subject to the provisions of section 1365 of this title.

(2) State management program requirement

To the extent that the States reach agreement through such conference, the management programs of the States which are parties to such agreements and which contribute significant pollution to the navigable waters or portions thereof not meeting applicable water quality standards or goals and requirements of this chapter will be revised to reflect such agreement. Such management programs shall be consistent with Federal and State law.

(h) Grant program

(1) Grants for implementation of management programs

Upon application of a State for which a report submitted under subsection (a) of this section and a management program submitted under subsection (b) of this section is approved under this section, the Administrator shall make grants, subject to such terms and conditions as the Administrator considers appropriate, under this subsection to such State for the purpose of assisting the State in implementing such management program. Funds reserved pursuant to section 1285(j)(5) of this title may be used to develop and implement such management program.

(2) Applications

An application for a grant under this subsection in any fiscal year shall be in such form and shall contain such other information as the Administrator may require, including an identification and description of the best management practices and measures which the State proposes to assist, encourage, or require in such year with the Federal assistance to be provided under the grant.

(3) Federal share

The Federal share of the cost of each management program implemented with Federal assistance under this subsection in any fiscal year shall not exceed 60 percent of the cost incurred by the State in implementing such management program and shall be made on condition that the non-Federal share is provided from non-Federal sources.

(4) Limitation on grant amounts

Notwithstanding any other provision of this subsection, not more than 15 percent of the amount appropriated to carry out this subsection may be used to make grants to any one State, including any grants to any local public agency or organization with authority to control pollution from nonpoint sources in any area of such State.

(5) Priority for effective mechanisms

For each fiscal year beginning after September 30, 1987, the Administrator may give priority in making grants under this subsection, and shall give consideration in determining the Federal share of any such grant, to States which have implemented or are proposing to implement management programs which will—

(A) control particularly difficult or serious nonpoint source pollution problems, including, but not limited to, problems resulting from mining activities;

(B) implement innovative methods or practices for controlling nonpoint sources of pollution, including regulatory programs where the Administrator deems appropriate;

(C) control interstate nonpoint source pollution problems; or

(D) carry out ground water quality protection activities which the Administrator determines are part of a comprehensive nonpoint source pollution control program, including research, planning, ground water assessments, demonstration programs, enforcement, technical assistance, education, and training to protect ground water quality from nonpoint sources of pollution.

(6) Availability for obligation

The funds granted to each State pursuant to this subsection in a fiscal year shall remain available for obligation by such State for the fiscal year for which appropriated. The amount of any such funds not obligated by the end of such fiscal year shall be available to the Administrator for granting to other States under this subsection in the next fiscal year.

(7) Limitation on use of funds

States may use funds from grants made pursuant to this section for financial assistance to persons only to the extent that such assistance is related to the costs of demonstration projects.

(8) Satisfactory progress

No grant may be made under this subsection in any fiscal year to a State which in the preceding fiscal year received a grant under this subsection unless the Administrator determines that such State made satisfactory progress in such preceding fiscal year in meeting the schedule specified by such State under subsection (b)(2) of this section.

(9) Maintenance of effort

No grant may be made to a State under this subsection in any fiscal year unless such State enters into such agreements with the Administrator as the Administrator may require to ensure that such

State will maintain its aggregate expenditures from all other sources for programs for controlling pollution added to the navigable waters in such State from nonpoint sources and improving the quality of such waters at or above the average level of such expenditures in its two fiscal years preceding February 4, 1987.

(10) Request for information

The Administrator may request such information, data, and reports as he considers necessary to make the determination of continuing eligibility for grants under this section.

(11) Reporting and other requirements

Each State shall report to the Administrator on an annual basis concerning (A) its progress in meeting the schedule of milestones submitted pursuant to subsection (b)(2)(C) of this section, and (B) to the extent that appropriate information is available, reductions in nonpoint source pollutant loading and improvements in water quality for those navigable waters or watersheds within the State which were identified pursuant to subsection (a)(1)(A) of this section resulting from implementation of the management program.

(12) Limitation on administrative costs

For purposes of this subsection, administrative costs in the form of salaries, overhead, or indirect costs for services provided and charged against activities and programs carried out with a grant under this subsection shall not exceed in any fiscal year 10 percent of the amount of the grant in such year, except that costs of implementing enforcement and regulatory activities, education, training, technical assistance, demonstration projects, and technology transfer programs shall not be subject to this limitation.

(i) Grants for protecting groundwater quality

(1) Eligible applicants and activities

Upon application of a State for which a report submitted under subsection (a) of this section and a plan submitted under subsection (b) of this section is approved under this section, the Administrator shall make grants under this subsection to such State for the purpose of assisting such State in carrying out groundwater quality protection activities which the Administrator determines will advance the State toward implementation of a comprehensive nonpoint source pollution control program. Such activities shall include, but not be limited to, research, planning, groundwater assessments, demonstration programs, enforcement, technical assistance, education and training to protect the quality of groundwater and to prevent contamination of groundwater from nonpoint sources of pollution.

(2) Applications

An application for a grant under this subsection shall be in such form and shall contain such information as the Administrator may require.

(3) Federal share; maximum amount

The Federal share of the cost of assisting a State in carrying out groundwater protection activities in any fiscal year under this subsection shall be 50 percent of the costs incurred by the State in carrying out such activities, except that the maximum amount of Federal assistance which any State may receive under this subsection in any fiscal year shall not exceed $150,000.

(4) Report

The Administrator shall include in each report transmitted under subsection (m) of this section a report on the activities and programs implemented under this subsection during the preceding fiscal year.

(j) Authorization of appropriations

There is authorized to be appropriated to carry out subsections (h) and (i) of this section not to exceed $70,000,000 for fiscal year 1988, $100,000,000 per fiscal year for each of fiscal years 1989 and 1990, and $130,000,000 for fiscal year 1991; except that for each of such fiscal years not to exceed $7,500,000 may be made available to carry out subsection (i) of this section. Sums appropriated pursuant to this subsection shall remain available until expended.

(k) Consistency of other programs and projects with management programs

The Administrator shall transmit to the Office of Management and Budget and the appropriate Federal departments and agencies a list of those assistance programs and development projects identified by each State under subsection (b)(2)(F) of this section for which individual assistance applications and projects will be reviewed pursuant to the procedures set forth in Executive Order 12372 as in effect on September 17, 1983. Beginning not later than sixty days after receiving notification by the Administrator, each Federal department and agency shall modify existing regulations to allow States to review individual development projects and assistance applications under the identified Federal assistance programs and shall accommodate, according to the requirements and definitions of Executive Order 12372, as in effect on September 17, 1983, the concerns of the State regarding the consistency of such applications or projects with the State nonpoint source pollution management program.

(*l*) Collection of information

The Administrator shall collect and make available, through publications and other appropriate means, information pertaining to management practices and implementation methods, including, but not limited to, (1) information concerning the costs and relative efficiencies of best management practices for reducing nonpoint source pollution; and (2) available data concerning the relationship between water quality and implementation of various management practices to control nonpoint sources of pollution.

(m) Reports of Administrator

(1) Annual reports

Not later than January 1, 1988, and each January 1 thereafter, the Administrator shall transmit to the Committee on Public Works and Transportation of the House of Representatives and the Committee on Environment and Public Works of the Senate, a report for the preceding fiscal year on the activities and programs implemented under this section and the progress made in reducing pollution in the navigable waters resulting from nonpoint sources and improving the quality of such waters.

(2) Final report

Not later than January 1, 1990, the Administrator shall transmit to Congress a final report on the activities carried out under this section. Such report, at a minimum, shall—

(A) describe the management programs being implemented by the States by types and amount of affected navigable waters, categories and subcategories of nonpoint sources, and types of best management practices being implemented;

(B) describe the experiences of the States in adhering to schedules and implementing best management practices;

(C) describe the amount and purpose of grants awarded pursuant to subsections (h) and (i) of this section;

(D) identify, to the extent that information is available, the progress made in reducing pollutant loads and improving water quality in the navigable waters;

(E) indicate what further actions need to be taken to attain and maintain in those navigable waters (i) applicable water quality standards, and (ii) the goals and requirements of this chapter;

(F) include recommendations of the Administrator concerning future programs (including enforcement programs) for controlling pollution from nonpoint sources; and

(G) identify the activities and programs of departments, agencies, and instrumentalities of the United States which are inconsistent with the management programs submitted by the States and recommend modifications so that such activities and programs are consistent with and assist the States in implementation of such management programs.

(n) Set aside for administrative personnel

Not less than 5 percent of the funds appropriated pursuant to subsection (j) of this section for any fiscal year shall be available to the Administrator to maintain personnel levels at the Environmental Protection Agency at levels which are adequate to carry out this section in such year.

(June 30, 1948, c. 758, Title III, § 319, as added by Pub. L. No. 100–4, Title III, § 316(a), 101 Stat. 52 (Feb. 4, 1987); and amended by Pub. L. No. 105–362, Title V, § 501(c), 112 Stat. 3283 (Nov. 10, 1998); Pub. L. No. 107–303, Title III, § 302(b)(1), 116 Stat. 2361 (Nov. 27, 2002).)

HISTORICAL AND STATUTORY NOTES

References in Text

Executive Order 12372, referred to in subsecs. (b)(2)(F) and (k), is Ex. Ord. No. 12372, July 14, 1982, 47 Fed. Reg. 30959, as amended, which is set out as a note under section 6506 of Title 31, Money and Finance.

The Colorado River Basin Salinity Control Act, referred to in subsec. (g)(1), is Pub. L. No. 93–320, 88 Stat. 266 (June 24, 1974), as amended, which is codified principally to chapter 32A (section 1571 et seq.) of Title 43, Public Lands. For complete classification of this Act to the Code, see Short Title note set out under section 1571 of Title 43 and Tables.

Effective and Applicability Provisions

2002 Acts. Effective November 10, 1998, section 501 of the Federal Reports Elimination Act of 1998 [Pub. L. No. 105–362, Title V, § 501, 112 Stat. 3283 (Nov. 10, 1998)] is amended by striking subsections (a), (b), (c), and (d) [amending this section and others, see Tables for complete classification]. The Federal Water Pollution Control Act (33 U.S.C.A. § 1254(n)(3)) shall be applied and administered on and after Nov. 27, 2002 as if the amendments made by subsections (a), (b), (c), and (d) of Pub. L. No. 105–362, § 501, had not been enacted, see Pub. L. No. 107–303, § 302(b)(2), set out as a note under 33 U.S.C.A. § 1254.

Change of Name

Any reference in any provision of law enacted before Jan. 4, 1995, to the Committee on Public Works and Transportation of the House of Representatives treated as referring to the Committee on Transportation and Infrastructure of the House of Representatives, see section 1(a)(9) of Pub. L. No. 104–14, set out as a note preceding section 21 of Title 2, The Congress.

§ 1330. National estuary program

[FWPCA § 320]

(a) Management conference

(1) Nomination of estuaries

The Governor of any State may nominate to the Administrator an estuary lying in whole or in part within the State as an estuary of national significance and request a management conference to develop a comprehensive management plan for the estuary. The nomination shall document the need for the conference, the likelihood of success, and information relating to the factors in paragraph (2).

(2) Convening of conference

(A) In general

In any case where the Administrator determines, on his own initiative or upon nomination of a State under paragraph (1), that the attainment or maintenance of that water quality in an estuary which assures protection of public water supplies and the protection and propagation of a balanced, indigenous population of shellfish, fish, and wildlife, and allows recreational activities, in and on the water, requires the control of point and nonpoint sources of pollution to supplement existing controls of pollution in more than one State, the Administrator shall select such estuary and convene a management conference.

(B) Priority consideration

The Administrator shall give priority consideration under this section to Long Island Sound, New York and Connecticut; Narragansett Bay, Rhode Island; Buzzards Bay, Massachusetts; Massachusetts Bay, Massachusetts (including Cape Cod Bay and Boston Harbor); Puget Sound,

Washington; New York-New Jersey Harbor, New York and New Jersey; Delaware Bay, Delaware and New Jersey; Delaware Inland Bays, Delaware; Albemarle Sound, North Carolina; Sarasota Bay, Florida; San Francisco Bay, California; Santa Monica Bay, California; Galveston Bay, Texas; Barataria-Terrebonne Bay estuary complex, Louisiana; Indian River Lagoon, Florida; Lake Pontchartrain Basin, Louisiana and Mississippi; Peconic Bay, New York; Casco Bay, Maine; Tampa Bay, Florida; Coastal Bend, Texas; San Juan Bay, Puerto Rico; Tillamook Bay, Oregon; Piscataqua Region, New Hampshire; Barnegat Bay, New Jersey; Maryland Coastal Bays, Maryland; Charlotte Harbor, Florida; Mobile Bay, Alabama; Morro Bay, California; and Lower Columbia River, Oregon and Washington.

(3) Boundary dispute exception

In any case in which a boundary between two States passes through an estuary and such boundary is disputed and is the subject of an action in any court, the Administrator shall not convene a management conference with respect to such estuary before a final adjudication has been made of such dispute.

(b) Purposes of conference

The purposes of any management conference convened with respect to an estuary under this subsection shall be to—

(1) assess trends in water quality, natural resources, and uses of the estuary;

(2) collect, characterize, and assess data on toxics, nutrients, and natural resources within the estuarine zone to identify the causes of environmental problems;

(3) develop the relationship between the in place loads and point and nonpoint loadings of pollutants to the estuarine zone and the potential uses of the zone, water quality, and natural resources;

(4) develop a comprehensive conservation and management plan that—

(A) recommends priority corrective actions and compliance schedules addressing point and nonpoint sources of pollution to restore and maintain the chemical, physical, and biological integrity of the estuary, including restoration and maintenance of water quality, a balanced indigenous population of shellfish, fish and wildlife, and recreational activities in the estuary, and assure that the designated uses of the estuary are protected;

(B) addresses the effects of recurring extreme weather events on the estuary, including the identification and assessment of vulnerabilities in the estuary and the development and implementation of adaptation strategies; and

(C) increases public education and awareness of the ecological health and water quality conditions of the estuary;

(5) develop plans for the coordinated implementation of the plan by the States as well as Federal and local agencies participating in the conference;

(6) monitor the effectiveness of actions taken pursuant to the plan; and

(7) review all Federal financial assistance programs and Federal development projects in accordance with the requirements of Executive Order 12372, as in effect on September 17, 1983, to determine whether such assistance program or project would be consistent with and further the purposes and objectives of the plan prepared under this section.

For purposes of paragraph (7), such programs and projects shall not be limited to the assistance programs and development projects subject to Executive Order 12372, but may include any programs listed in the most recent Catalog of Federal Domestic Assistance which may have an effect on the purposes and objectives of the plan developed under this section.

(c) Members of conference

The members of a management conference convened under this section shall include, at a minimum, the Administrator and representatives of—

(1) each State and foreign nation located in whole or in part in the estuarine zone of the estuary for which the conference is convened;

(2) international, interstate, or regional agencies or entities having jurisdiction over all or a significant part of the estuary;

(3) each interested Federal agency, as determined appropriate by the Administrator;

(4) local governments having jurisdiction over any land or water within the estuarine zone, as determined appropriate by the Administrator; and

(5) affected industries, public and private educational institutions, nonprofit organizations, and the general public, as determined appropriate by the Administrator.

(d) Utilization of existing data

In developing a conservation and management plan under this section, the management conference shall survey and utilize existing reports, data, and studies relating to the estuary that have been developed by or made available to Federal, interstate, State, and local agencies.

(e) Period of conference

A management conference convened under this section shall be convened for a period not to exceed 5 years. Such conference may be extended by the Administrator, and if terminated after the initial period, may be reconvened by the Administrator at any time thereafter, as may be necessary to meet the requirements of this section.

(f) Approval and implementation of plans

(1) Approval

Not later than 120 days after the completion of a conservation and management plan and after providing for public review and comment, the Administrator shall approve such plan if the plan meets the requirements of this section and the affected Governor or Governors concur.

(2) Implementation

Upon approval of a conservation and management plan under this section, such plan shall be implemented. Funds authorized to be appropriated under subchapters II and VI of this chapter and section 1329 of this title may be used in accordance with the applicable requirements of this chapter to assist States with the implementation of such plan.

(g) Grants

(1) Recipients

The Administrator is authorized to make grants to State, interstate, and regional water pollution control agencies and entities, State coastal zone management agencies, interstate agencies, other public or nonprofit private agencies, institutions, organizations, and individuals.

(2) Purposes

Grants under this subsection shall be made to pay for activities necessary for the development and implementation of a comprehensive conservation and management plan under this section.

(3) Federal share

The Federal share of a grant to any person (including a State, interstate, or regional agency or entity) under this subsection for a fiscal year—

(A) shall not exceed—

(i) 75 percent of the annual aggregate costs of the development of a comprehensive conservation and management plan; and

(ii) 50 percent of the annual aggregate costs of the implementation of the plan; and

(B) shall be made on condition that the non-Federal share of the costs are provided from non-Federal sources.

(4) Competitive awards.—

(A) In general.—Using the amounts made available under subsection (i)(2)(B), the Administrator shall make competitive awards under this paragraph.

(B) Application for awards.—The Administrator shall solicit applications for awards under this paragraph from State, interstate, and regional water pollution control agencies and entities, State coastal zone management agencies, interstate agencies, other public or nonprofit private agencies, institutions, organizations, and individuals.

(C) Selection of recipients.—In selecting award recipients under this paragraph, the Administrator shall select recipients that are best able to address urgent, emerging, and challenging issues that threaten the ecological and economic well-being of the estuaries selected by the Administrator under subsection(a)(2), or that relate to the coastal resiliency of such estuaries. Such issues shall include—

(i) extensive seagrass habitat losses resulting in significant impacts on fisheries and water quality;

(ii) recurring harmful algae blooms;

(iii) unusual marine mammal mortalities;

(iv) invasive exotic species that may threaten wastewater systems and cause other damage;

(v) jellyfish proliferation limiting community access to water during peak tourism seasons;

(vi) stormwater runoff;

(vii) accelerated land loss; and

(viii) flooding that may be related to sea level rise, extreme weather, or wetland degradation or loss; and

(ix) low dissolved oxygen conditions in estuarine waters and related nutrient management.

(h) Grant reporting

Any person (including a State, interstate, or regional agency or entity) that receives a grant under subsection (g) of this section shall report to the Administrator not later than 18 months after receipt of such grant and biennially thereafter on the progress being made under this section.

(i) Authorization of appropriations.—

(1) In general.—There is authorized to be appropriated to the Administrator $26,500,000 for each of fiscal years 2017 through 2021, and $50,000,000 for each of fiscal years 2022 through 2026, for—

(A) expenses relating to the administration of grants or awards by the Administrator under this section, including the award and oversight of grants and awards, except that such expenses may not exceed 5 percent of the amount appropriated under this subsection for a fiscal year; and

(B) making grants and awards under subsection (g).

(2) Allocations.—

(A) Conservation and management plans.—Not less than 80 percent of the amount made available under this subsection for a fiscal year shall be used by the Administrator to provide grant assistance for the development, implementation, and monitoring of each of the conservation and management plans eligible for grant assistance under subsection (g)(2).

(B) Competitive awards.—Not less than 15 percent of the amount made available under this subsection for a fiscal year shall be used by the Administrator for making competitive awards described in subsection (g)(4).

(j) Research

(1) Programs

In order to determine the need to convene a management conference under this section or at the request of such a management conference, the Administrator shall coordinate and implement, through the National Marine Pollution Program Office and the National Marine Fisheries Service of the National Oceanic and Atmospheric Administration, as appropriate, for one or more estuarine zones—

(A) a long-term program of trend assessment monitoring measuring variations in pollutant concentrations, marine ecology, and other physical or biological environmental parameters which may affect estuarine zones, to provide the Administrator the capacity to determine the potential and actual effects of alternative management strategies and measures;

(B) a program of ecosystem assessment assisting in the development of (i) baseline studies which determine the state of estuarine zones and the effects of natural and anthropogenic changes, and (ii) predictive models capable of translating information on specific discharges or general pollutant loadings within estuarine zones into a set of probable effects on such zones;

(C) a comprehensive water quality sampling program for the continuous monitoring of nutrients, chlorine, acid precipitation dissolved oxygen, and potentially toxic pollutants (including organic chemicals and metals) in estuarine zones, after consultation with interested State, local, interstate, or international agencies and review and analysis of all environmental sampling data presently collected from estuarine zones; and

(D) a program of research to identify the movements of nutrients, sediments and pollutants through estuarine zones and the impact of nutrients, sediments, and pollutants on water quality, the ecosystem, and designated or potential uses of the estuarine zones.

(2) Reports

The Administrator, in cooperation with the Administrator of the National Oceanic and Atmospheric Administration, shall submit to the Congress no less often than biennially a comprehensive report on the activities authorized under this subsection including—

(A) a listing of priority monitoring and research needs;

(B) an assessment of the state and health of the Nation's estuarine zones, to the extent evaluated under this subsection;

(C) a discussion of pollution problems and trends in pollutant concentrations with a direct or indirect effect on water quality, the ecosystem, and designated or potential uses of each estuarine zone, to the extent evaluated under this subsection; and

(D) an evaluation of pollution abatement activities and management measures so far implemented to determine the degree of improvement toward the objectives expressed in subsection (b)(4) of this section.

(k) Definitions

For purposes of this section, the terms "estuary" and "estuarine zone" have the meanings such terms have in section 1254(n)(4) of this title, except that the term "estuarine zone" shall also include associated aquatic ecosystems and those portions of tributaries draining into the estuary up to the historic height of migration of anadromous fish or the historic head of tidal influence, whichever is higher.

(June 30, 1948, c. 758, Title III, § 320, as added by Pub. L. No. 100–4, Title III, § 317(b), 101 Stat. 61 (Feb. 4, 1987); and amended by Pub. L. No. 100–202, Title II, § 101(f), 101 Stat. 1329–197 (Dec. 22, 1987); Pub. L. No. 100–653, Title X, § 1004, 102 Stat. 3836 (Nov. 14, 1988); Pub. L. No. 100–688, Title II, § 2001, 102 Stat. 4152 (Nov. 18, 1988); Pub. L. No. 105–362, Title V, § 501(a)(2), 112 Stat. 3283 (Nov. 10, 1998); Pub. L. No. 106–457, Title III, §§ 301 to 303, 114 Stat. 1972 (Nov. 7, 2000); Pub. L. No. 107–303, Title III, § 302(b)(1), 116 Stat. 2361 (Nov. 27, 2002); Pub. L. No. 108–399, § 1, 118 Stat. 2253 (Oct. 30, 2004); Pub. L. No. 114–162, §§ 1, 2, 130 Stat 409–10 (May 20, 2016); Pub. L. No. 116–337, §§ 2–6, 134 Stat. 5120–21 (Jan. 13, 2021).)

HISTORICAL AND STATUTORY NOTES

References in Text

Executive Order 12372, referred to in subsec. (b). is Ex. Ord. No. 12372, July 14, 1982, 47 Fed. Reg. 30959, as amended, which is set out as a note under section 6506 of Title 31, Money and Finance.

Codifications

Pub. L. No. 100–653 and section 2001(1) of Pub. L. No. 100–688 made an identical amendment to subsection (a)(2)(B).

Effective and Applicability Provisions

2002 Acts. Effective November 10, 1998, section 501 of the Federal Reports Elimination Act of 1998 [Pub. L. No. 105–362, Title V, § 501, 112 Stat. 3283 (Nov. 10, 1998)] is amended by striking subsections (a), (b), (c), and (d) [amending this section and others, see Tables for complete classification]. The Federal Water Pollution Control Act (33 U.S.C.A. § 1254(n)(3)) shall be applied and administered on and after Nov. 27, 2002 as if the amendments made by subsections (a), (b), (c), and (d) of Pub. L. No. 105–362, § 501, had not been enacted, see Pub. L. No. 107–303, § 302(b)(2), set out as a note under 33 U.S.C.A. § 1254.

Termination of Reporting Requirements

Reporting requirement of subsec. (j)(2) of this section excepted from termination under Pub. L. No. 104–66, § 3003(a)(1), as amended, set out as a note under 31 U.S.C.A. § 1113, and page 162 of House Document No. 103–7, see Pub. L. No. 107–303, § 302(a).

Massachusetts Bay Protection; Massachusetts Bay Defined

Pub. L. No. 100–653, § 1002, 102 Stat. 3831 (Nov. 14, 1988), provided that: "For purposes of this title [amending subsec. (a)(2)(B) of this section and enacting note provisions under sections 1251 and 1330 of this title], the term 'Massachusetts Bay' includes Massachusetts Bay, Cape Cod Bay, and Boston Harbor, consisting of an area extending from Cape Ann, Massachusetts south to the northern reach of Cape Cod, Massachusetts."

Massachusetts Bay Protection; Congressional Findings and Purpose

Pub. L. No. 100–653, § 1003, 102 Stat. 3831 (Nov. 14, 1988), provided that:

"(a) Findings.—The Congress finds and declares that—

"(1) Massachusetts Bay comprises a single major estuarine and oceanographic system extending from Cape Ann, Massachusetts south to the northern reaches of Cape Cod, encompassing Boston Harbor, Massachusetts Bay, and Cape Cod Bay;

"(2) several major riverine systems, including the Charles, Neoponset, and Mystic Rivers, drain the watersheds of eastern Massachusetts into the Bay;

"(3) the shorelines of Massachusetts Bay, first occupied in the middle 1600's, are home to over 4 million people and support a thriving industrial and recreational economy;

"(4) Massachusetts Bay supports important commercial fisheries, including lobsters, finfish, and shellfisheries, and is home to or frequented by several endangered species and marine mammals;

"(5) Massachusetts Bay also constitutes an important recreational resource, providing fishing, swimming, and boating opportunities to the region;

"(6) rapidly expanding coastal populations and pollution pose increasing threats to the long-term health and integrity of Massachusetts Bay;

"(7) while the cleanup of Boston Harbor will contribute significantly to improving the overall environmental quality of Massachusetts Bay, expanded efforts encompassing the entire ecosystem will be necessary to ensure its long-term health;

"(8) the concerted efforts of all levels of Government, the private sector, and the public at large will be necessary to protect and enhance the environmental integrity of Massachusetts Bay; and

"(9) the designation of Massachusetts Bay as an Estuary of National Significance and the development of a comprehensive plan for protecting and restoring the Bay may contribute significantly to its long-term health and environmental integrity.

"(b) Purpose.—The purpose of this title [amending subsec. (a)(2)(B) of this section and enacting note provisions under sections 1251 and 1330 of this title] is to protect and enhance the environmental quality of Massachusetts Bay by providing for its designation as an Estuary of National Significance and by providing for the preparation of a comprehensive restoration plan for the Bay."

Massachusetts Bay Protection; Funding Sources

Pub. L. No. 100–653, § 1005, 102 Stat. 3832 (Nov. 14, 1988), provided that: "Within one year of enactment [Nov. 14, 1988], the Administrator of the United States Environmental Protection Agency, and the Governor of Massachusetts shall undertake to identify and make available sources of funding to support activities pertaining to Massachusetts Bay undertaken pursuant to or authorized by section 320 of the Clean Water Act [this section], and shall make every effort to coordinate existing research, monitoring or control efforts with such activities."

Purposes and Policies of National Estuary Program

Pub. L. No. 100–4, § 317(a), 101 Stat. 7 (Feb. 4, 1987), provided that:

"(1) Findings.—Congress finds and declares that—

"(A) the Nation's estuaries are of great importance for fish and wildlife resources and recreation and economic opportunity;

"(B) maintaining the health and ecological integrity of these estuaries is in the national interest;

"(C) increasing coastal population, development, and other direct and indirect uses of these estuaries threaten their health and ecological integrity;

"(D) long-term planning and management will contribute to the continued productivity of these areas, and will maximize their utility to the Nation; and

"(E) better coordination among Federal and State programs affecting estuaries will increase the effectiveness and efficiency of the national effort to protect, preserve, and restore these areas.

"(2) Purposes.—The purposes of this section [enacting this section and enacting this provision] are to—

"(A) identify nationally significant estuaries that are threatened by pollution, development, or overuse;

"(B) promote comprehensive planning for, and conservation and management of, nationally significant estuaries;

"(C) encourage the preparation of management plans for estuaries of national significance; and

"(D) enhance the coordination of estuarine research."

SUBCHAPTER IV—PERMITS AND LICENSES

§ 1341. Certification

[FWPCA § 401]

(a) Compliance with applicable requirements; application; procedures; license suspension

(1) Any applicant for a Federal license or permit to conduct any activity including, but not limited to, the construction or operation of facilities, which may result in any discharge into the navigable waters, shall provide the licensing or permitting agency a certification from the State in which the discharge originates or will originate, or, if appropriate, from the interstate water pollution control agency having jurisdiction over the navigable waters at the point where the discharge originates or will originate, that any such discharge will comply with the applicable provisions of sections 1311, 1312, 1313, 1316, and 1317 of this title. In the case of any such activity for which there is not an applicable effluent limitation or other limitation under sections 1311(b) and 1312 of this title, and there is not an applicable standard under sections 1316 and 1317 of this title, the State shall so certify, except that any such certification shall not be deemed to satisfy section 1371(c) of this title. Such State or interstate agency shall establish procedures for public notice in the case of all applications for certification by it and, to the extent it deems appropriate, procedures for public hearings in connection with specific applications. In any case where a State or interstate agency has no authority to give such a certification, such certification shall be from the Administrator. If the State, interstate agency, or Administrator, as the case may be, fails or refuses to act on a request for certification, within a reasonable period of time (which shall not exceed one year) after receipt of such request, the certification requirements of this subsection shall be waived with respect to such Federal application. No license or permit shall be granted until the certification required by this section has been obtained or has been waived as provided in the preceding sentence. No license or permit shall be granted if certification has been denied by the State, interstate agency, or the Administrator, as the case may be.

(2) Upon receipt of such application and certification the licensing or permitting agency shall immediately notify the Administrator of such application and certification. Whenever such a discharge may affect, as determined by the Administrator, the quality of the waters of any other State, the Administrator within thirty days of the date of notice of application for such Federal license or permit shall so notify such other State, the licensing or permitting agency, and the applicant. If, within sixty days after receipt of such notification, such other State determines that such discharge will affect the quality of its waters so as to violate any water quality requirements in such State, and within such sixty-day period notifies the Administrator and the licensing or permitting agency in writing of its objection to the issuance of such license or permit and requests a public hearing on such objection, the licensing or permitting agency shall hold such a hearing. The Administrator shall at such hearing submit his evaluation and recommendations with respect to any such objection to the licensing or permitting agency. Such agency, based upon the recommendations of such State, the Administrator, and upon any additional evidence, if any, presented to the agency at the hearing, shall condition such license or permit in such manner as may be necessary to insure compliance with applicable water quality requirements. If the imposition of conditions cannot insure such compliance such agency shall not issue such license or permit.

(3) The certification obtained pursuant to paragraph (1) of this subsection with respect to the construction of any facility shall fulfill the requirements of this subsection with respect to certification in connection with any other Federal license or permit required for the operation of such facility unless, after notice to the certifying State, agency, or Administrator, as the case may be, which shall be given by the Federal agency to whom application is made for such operating license or permit, the State, or if appropriate, the interstate agency or the Administrator, notifies such agency within sixty days after receipt of such notice that there is no longer reasonable assurance that there will be compliance with the applicable provisions of sections 1311, 1312, 1313, 1316, and 1317 of this title because of changes since the construction license or permit certification was issued in (A) the construction or operation of the facility, (B) the characteristics of the waters into which such discharge is made, (C) the water quality criteria applicable to such waters or (D) applicable effluent limitations or other requirements. This paragraph shall be inapplicable in any case where the applicant for such operating license or permit has failed to provide the certifying State, or, if appropriate, the interstate agency or the Administrator, with notice of any proposed changes in the construction or operation of the facility with respect to which a construction license or permit has been granted, which changes may result in violation of section 1311, 1312, 1313, 1316, or 1317 of this title.

(4) Prior to the initial operation of any federally licensed or permitted facility or activity which may result in any discharge into the navigable waters and with respect to which a certification has been obtained pursuant to paragraph (1) of this subsection, which facility or activity is not subject to a Federal operating license or permit, the licensee or permittee shall provide an opportunity for such certifying State, or, if appropriate, the interstate agency or the Administrator to review the manner in which the facility or activity shall be operated or conducted for the purposes of assuring that applicable effluent limitations or other limitations or other applicable water quality requirements will not be violated. Upon notification by the certifying State, or if appropriate, the interstate agency or the Administrator that the operation of any such federally licensed or permitted facility or activity will violate applicable effluent limitations or other limitations or other water quality requirements such Federal agency may, after public hearing, suspend such license or permit. If such license or permit is suspended, it shall remain suspended until notification is received from the certifying State, agency, or Administrator, as the case may be, that there is reasonable assurance that such facility or activity will not violate the applicable provisions of section 1311, 1312, 1313, 1316, or 1317 of this title.

(5) Any Federal license or permit with respect to which a certification has been obtained under paragraph (1) of this subsection may be suspended or revoked by the Federal agency issuing such license or permit upon the entering of a judgment under this chapter that such facility or activity has been operated in violation of the applicable provisions of section 1311, 1312, 1313, 1316, or 1317 of this title.

(6) Except with respect to a permit issued under section 1342 of this title, in any case where actual construction of a facility has been lawfully commenced prior to April 3, 1970, no certification shall be required under this subsection for a license or permit issued after April 3, 1970, to operate such facility, except that any such license or permit issued without certification shall terminate April 3, 1973, unless prior to such termination date the person having such license or permit submits to the Federal agency which issued such license or permit a certification and otherwise meets the requirements of this section.

(b) Compliance with other provisions of law setting applicable water quality requirements

Nothing in this section shall be construed to limit the authority of any department or agency pursuant to any other provision of law to require compliance with any applicable water quality requirements. The Administrator shall, upon the request of any Federal department or agency, or State or interstate agency, or applicant, provide, for the purpose of this section, any relevant information on applicable effluent limitations, or other limitations, standards, regulations, or requirements, or water quality criteria, and shall, when requested by any such department or agency or State or interstate agency, or applicant, comment on any methods to comply with such limitations, standards, regulations, requirements, or criteria.

(c) Authority of Secretary of the Army to permit use of spoil disposal areas by Federal licensees or permittees

In order to implement the provisions of this section, the Secretary of the Army, acting through the Chief of Engineers, is authorized, if he deems it to be in the public interest, to permit the use of spoil disposal areas under his jurisdiction by Federal licensees or permittees, and to make an appropriate charge for such use. Moneys received from such licensees or permittees shall be deposited in the Treasury as miscellaneous receipts.

(d) Limitations and monitoring requirements of certification

Any certification provided under this section shall set forth any effluent limitations and other limitations, and monitoring requirements necessary to assure that any applicant for a Federal license or permit will comply with any applicable effluent limitations and other limitations, under section 1311 or 1312 of this title, standard of performance under section 1316 of this title, or prohibition, effluent standard, or pretreatment standard under section 1317 of this title, and with any other appropriate requirement of State law set forth in such certification, and shall become a condition on any Federal license or permit subject to the provisions of this section.

(June 30, 1948, c. 758, Title IV, § 401, as added by Pub. L. No. 92–500, § 2, 86 Stat. 877 (Oct. 18, 1972); and amended by Pub. L. No. 95–217, §§ 61(b), 64, 91 Stat. 1598, 1599 (Dec. 27, 1977).)

HISTORICAL AND STATUTORY NOTES

Restrictions on Uses of Funding

Pub. L. No. 115–31, § 105, 131 Stat. 306 (May 5, 2017), provided: "None of the funds in this Act shall be used for an open lake placement alternative for dredged material, after evaluating the least costly, environmentally acceptable manner for the disposal or management of dredged material originating from Lake Erie or tributaries thereto, unless it is approved under a State water quality certification pursuant to section 401 of the Federal Water Pollution Control Act (33 U.S.C. 1341); Provided further, That until an open lake placement alternative for dredged material is approved under a State water quality certification, the Corps of Engineers shall continue upland placement of such dredged material consistent with the requirements of section 101 of the Water Resources Development Act of 1986 (33 U.S.C. 2211)."

Administration of Refuse Act Permit Program

Administration of Refuse Act Permit Program to regulate discharge of pollutants and other refuse matter into navigable waters of the United States or their tributaries, see Ex. Ord. No. 11574, Dec. 23, 1970, 35 Fed. Reg. 19627, set out as a note under section 407 of this title.

§ 1342. National pollutant discharge elimination system

[FWPCA § 402]

(a) Permits for discharge of pollutants

(1) Except as provided in sections 1328 and 1344 of this title, the Administrator may, after opportunity for public hearing, issue a permit for the discharge of any pollutant, or combination of pollutants, notwithstanding section 1311(a) of this title, upon condition that such discharge will meet either (A) all applicable requirements under sections 1311, 1312, 1316, 1317, 1318, and 1343 of this title, or (B) prior to the taking of necessary implementing actions relating to all such requirements, such conditions as the Administrator determines are necessary to carry out the provisions of this chapter.

(2) The Administrator shall prescribe conditions for such permits to assure compliance with the requirements of paragraph (1) of this subsection, including conditions on data and information collection, reporting, and such other requirements as he deems appropriate.

(3) The permit program of the Administrator under paragraph (1) of this subsection, and permits issued thereunder, shall be subject to the same terms, conditions, and requirements as apply to a State permit program and permits issued thereunder under subsection (b) of this section.

(4) All permits for discharges into the navigable waters issued pursuant to section 407 of this title shall be deemed to be permits issued under this subchapter, and permits issued under this subchapter shall be deemed to be permits issued under section 407 of this title, and shall continue in force and effect for their term unless revoked, modified, or suspended in accordance with the provisions of this chapter.

(5) No permit for a discharge into the navigable waters shall be issued under section 407 of this title after October 18, 1972. Each application for a permit under section 407 of this title, pending on October 18, 1972, shall be deemed to be an application for a permit under this section. The Administrator shall authorize a State, which he determines has the capability of administering a permit program which will carry out the objective of this chapter to issue permits for discharges into the navigable waters within the jurisdiction of such State. The Administrator may exercise the authority granted him by the preceding sentence only during the period which begins on October 18, 1972, and ends either on the ninetieth day after the date of the first promulgation of guidelines required by section 1314(i)(2) of this title, or the date of approval by the Administrator of a permit program for such State under subsection (b) of this section, whichever date first occurs, and no such authorization to a State shall extend beyond the last day of such period. Each such permit shall be subject to such conditions as the Administrator determines are necessary to carry out the provisions of this chapter. No such permit shall issue if the Administrator objects to such issuance.

(b) State permit programs

At any time after the promulgation of the guidelines required by subsection (i)(2) of section 1314 of this title, the Governor of each State desiring to administer its own permit program for discharges into navigable waters within its jurisdiction may submit to the Administrator a full and complete description of the program it proposes to establish and administer under State law or under an interstate compact. In addition, such State shall submit a statement from the attorney general (or the attorney for those State water pollution control agencies which have independent legal counsel), or from the chief legal officer in the case of an interstate agency, that the laws of such State, or the interstate compact, as the case may be, provide adequate authority to carry out the described program. The Administrator shall approve each such submitted program unless he determines that adequate authority does not exist:

(1) To issue permits which—

(A) apply, and insure compliance with, any applicable requirements of sections 1311, 1312, 1316, 1317, and 1343 of this title;

(B) are for fixed terms not exceeding five years; and

(C) can be terminated or modified for cause including, but not limited to, the following:

(i) violation of any condition of the permit;

(ii) obtaining a permit by misrepresentation, or failure to disclose fully all relevant facts;

(iii) change in any condition that requires either a temporary or permanent reduction or elimination of the permitted discharge;

(D) control the disposal of pollutants into wells;

(2) **(A)** To issue permits which apply, and insure compliance with, all applicable requirements of section 1318 of this title; or

(B) To inspect, monitor, enter, and require reports to at least the same extent as required in section 1318 of this title;

(3) To insure that the public, and any other State the waters of which may be affected, receive notice of each application for a permit and to provide an opportunity for public hearing before a ruling on each such application;

(4) To insure that the Administrator receives notice of each application (including a copy thereof) for a permit;

(5) To insure that any State (other than the permitting State), whose waters may be affected by the issuance of a permit may submit written recommendations to the permitting State (and the Administrator) with respect to any permit application and, if any part of such written recommendations are not accepted by the permitting State, that the permitting State will notify such affected State (and the Administrator) in writing of its failure to so accept such recommendations together with its reasons for so doing;

(6) To insure that no permit will be issued if, in the judgment of the Secretary of the Army acting through the Chief of Engineers, after consultation with the Secretary of the department in which the Coast Guard is operating, anchorage and navigation of any of the navigable waters would be substantially impaired thereby;

(7) To abate violations of the permit or the permit program, including civil and criminal penalties and other ways and means of enforcement;

(8) To insure that any permit for a discharge from a publicly owned treatment works includes conditions to require the identification in terms of character and volume of pollutants of any significant source introducing pollutants subject to pretreatment standards under section 1317(b) of this title into such works and a program to assure compliance with such pretreatment standards by each such source, in addition to adequate notice to the permitting agency of (A) new introductions into such works of pollutants from any source which would be a new source as defined in section 1316 of this title if such source were discharging pollutants, (B) new introductions of pollutants into such works from a source which would be subject to section 1311 of this title if it were discharging such pollutants, or (C) a substantial change in volume or character of pollutants being introduced into such works by a source introducing pollutants into such works at the time of issuance of the permit. Such notice shall include information on the quality and quantity of effluent to be introduced into such treatment works and any anticipated impact of such change in the quantity or quality of effluent to be discharged from such publicly owned treatment works; and

(9) To insure that any industrial user of any publicly owned treatment works will comply with sections 1284(b), 1317, and 1318 of this title.

(c) Suspension of Federal program upon submission of State program; withdrawal of approval of State program; return of State program to Administrator

(1) Not later than ninety days after the date on which a State has submitted a program (or revision thereof) pursuant to subsection (b) of this section, the Administrator shall suspend the issuance of permits under subsection (a) of this section as to those discharges subject to such program unless he determines that the State permit program does not meet the requirements of subsection (b) of this section or does not conform to the guidelines issued under section 1314(i)(2) of this title. If the

Administrator so determines, he shall notify the State of any revisions or modifications necessary to conform to such requirements or guidelines.

(2) Any State permit program under this section shall at all times be in accordance with this section and guidelines promulgated pursuant to section 1314(i)(2) of this title.

(3) Whenever the Administrator determines after public hearing that a State is not administering a program approved under this section in accordance with requirements of this section, he shall so notify the State and, if appropriate corrective action is not taken within a reasonable time, not to exceed ninety days, the Administrator shall withdraw approval of such program. The Administrator shall not withdraw approval of any such program unless he shall first have notified the State, and made public, in writing, the reasons for such withdrawal.

(4) Limitations on partial permit program returns and withdrawals

A State may return to the Administrator administration,[1] and the Administrator may withdraw under paragraph (3) of this subsection approval, of—

(A) a State partial permit program approved under subsection (n)(3) of this section only if the entire permit program being administered by the State department or agency at the time is returned or withdrawn; and

(B) a State partial permit program approved under subsection (n)(4) of this section only if an entire phased component of the permit program being administered by the State at the time is returned or withdrawn.

(d) Notification of Administrator

(1) Each State shall transmit to the Administrator a copy of each permit application received by such State and provide notice to the Administrator of every action related to the consideration of such permit application, including each permit proposed to be issued by such State.

(2) No permit shall issue (A) if the Administrator within ninety days of the date of his notification under subsection (b)(5) of this section objects in writing to the issuance of such permit, or (B) if the Administrator within ninety days of the date of transmittal of the proposed permit by the State objects in writing to the issuance of such permit as being outside the guidelines and requirements of this chapter. Whenever the Administrator objects to the issuance of a permit under this paragraph such written objection shall contain a statement of the reasons for such objection and the effluent limitations and conditions which such permit would include if it were issued by the Administrator.

(3) The Administrator may, as to any permit application, waive paragraph (2) of this subsection.

(4) In any case where, after December 27, 1977, the Administrator, pursuant to paragraph (2) of this subsection, objects to the issuance of a permit, on request of the State, a public hearing shall be held by the Administrator on such objection. If the State does not resubmit such permit revised to meet such objection within 30 days after completion of the hearing, or, if no hearing is requested within 90 days after the date of such objection, the Administrator may issue the permit pursuant to subsection (a) of this section for such source in accordance with the guidelines and requirements of this chapter.

(e) Waiver of notification requirement

In accordance with guidelines promulgated pursuant to subsection (i)(2) of section 1314 of this title, the Administrator is authorized to waive the requirements of subsection (d) of this section at the time he approves a program pursuant to subsection (b) of this section for any category (including any class, type, or size within such category) of point sources within the State submitting such program.

(f) Point source categories

The Administrator shall promulgate regulations establishing categories of point sources which he determines shall not be subject to the requirements of subsection (d) of this section in any State with a program approved pursuant to subsection (b) of this section. The Administrator may distinguish among classes, types, and sizes within any category of point sources.

(g) Other regulations for safe transportation, handling, carriage, storage, and stowage of pollutants

Any permit issued under this section for the discharge of pollutants into the navigable waters from a vessel or other floating craft shall be subject to any applicable regulations promulgated by the Secretary of the department in which the Coast Guard is operating, establishing specifications for safe transportation, handling, carriage, storage, and stowage of pollutants.

(h) Violation of permit conditions; restriction or prohibition upon introduction of pollutant by source not previously utilizing treatment works

In the event any condition of a permit for discharges from a treatment works (as defined in section 1292 of this title) which is publicly owned is violated, a State with a program approved under subsection (b) of this section or the Administrator, where no State program is approved or where the Administrator determines pursuant to section 1319(a) of this title that a State with an approved program has not commenced appropriate enforcement action with respect to such permit, may proceed in a court of competent jurisdiction to restrict or prohibit the introduction of any pollutant into such treatment works by a source not utilizing such treatment works prior to the finding that such condition was violated.

(i) Federal enforcement not limited

Nothing in this section shall be construed to limit the authority of the Administrator to take action pursuant to section 1319 of this title.

(j) Public information

A copy of each permit application and each permit issued under this section shall be available to the public. Such permit application or permit, or portion thereof, shall further be available on request for the purpose of reproduction.

(k) Compliance with permits

Compliance with a permit issued pursuant to this section shall be deemed compliance, for purposes of sections 1319 and 1365 of this title, with sections 1311, 1312, 1316, 1317, and 1343 of this title, except any standard imposed under section 1317 of this title for a toxic pollutant injurious to human health. Until December 31, 1974, in any case where a permit for discharge has been applied for pursuant to this section, but final administrative disposition of such application has not been made, such discharge shall not be a violation of (1) section 1311, 1316, or 1342 of this title, or (2) section 407 of this title, unless the Administrator or other plaintiff proves that final administrative disposition of such application has not been made because of the failure of the applicant to furnish information reasonably required or requested in order to process the application. For the 180-day period beginning on October 18, 1972, in the case of any point source discharging any pollutant or combination of pollutants immediately prior to such date which source is not subject to section 407 of this title, the discharge by such source shall not be a violation of this chapter if such a source applies for a permit for discharge pursuant to this section within such 180-day period.

(*l*) Limitation on permit requirement

(1) Agricultural return flows

The Administrator shall not require a permit under this section for discharges composed entirely of return flows from irrigated agriculture, nor shall the Administrator directly or indirectly, require any State to require such a permit.

(2) Stormwater runoff from oil, gas, and mining operations

The Administrator shall not require a permit under this section, nor shall the Administrator directly or indirectly require any State to require a permit, for discharges of stormwater runoff from mining operations or oil and gas exploration, production, processing, or treatment operations or transmission facilities, composed entirely of flows which are from conveyances or systems of conveyances (including but not limited to pipes, conduits, ditches, and channels) used for collecting and conveying precipitation runoff and which are not contaminated by contact with, or do not come into contact with, any overburden, raw material, intermediate products, finished product, byproduct, or waste products located on the site of such operations.

(3) Silvicultural activities

(A) NPDES permit requirements for silvicultural activities

The Administrator shall not require a permit under this section nor directly or indirectly require any State to require a permit under this section for a discharge from runoff resulting from the conduct of the following silviculture activities conducted in accordance with standard industry practice: nursery operations, site preparation, reforestation and subsequent cultural treatment, thinning, prescribed burning, pest and fire control, harvesting operations, surface drainage, or road construction and maintenance.

(B) Other requirements

Nothing in this paragraph exempts a discharge from silvicultural activity from any permitting requirement under section 1344 of this title, existing permitting requirements under section 1342 of this title, or from any other federal law.

(C) The authorization provided in Section 505(a) does not apply to any non-permitting program established under 402(p)(6) for the silviculture activities listed in 402(*l*)(3)(A), or to any other limitations that might be deemed to apply to the silviculture activities listed in 402(*l*)(3)(A).

(m) Additional pretreatment of conventional pollutants not required

To the extent a treatment works (as defined in section 1292 of this title) which is publicly owned is not meeting the requirements of a permit issued under this section for such treatment works as a result of inadequate design or operation of such treatment works, the Administrator, in issuing a permit under this section, shall not require pretreatment by a person introducing conventional pollutants identified pursuant to section 1314(a)(4) of this title into such treatment works other than pretreatment required to assure compliance with pretreatment standards under subsection (b)(8) of this section and section 1317(b)(1) of this title. Nothing in this subsection shall affect the Administrator's authority under sections 1317 and 1319 of this title, affect State and local authority under sections 1317(b)(4) and 1370 of this title, relieve such treatment works of its obligations to meet requirements established under this chapter, or otherwise preclude such works from pursuing whatever feasible options are available to meet its responsibility to comply with its permit under this section.

(n) Partial permit program

(1) State submission

The Governor of a State may submit under subsection (b) of this section a permit program for a portion of the discharges into the navigable waters in such State.

(2) Minimum coverage

A partial permit program under this subsection shall cover, at a minimum, administration of a major category of the discharges into the navigable waters of the State or a major component of the permit program required by subsection (b) of this section.

(3) Approval of major category partial permit programs

The Administrator may approve a partial permit program covering administration of a major category of discharges under this subsection if—

(A) such program represents a complete permit program and covers all of the discharges under the jurisdiction of a department or agency of the State; and

(B) the Administrator determines that the partial program represents a significant and identifiable part of the State program required by subsection (b) of this section.

(4) Approval of major component partial permit programs

The Administrator may approve under this subsection a partial and phased permit program covering administration of a major component (including discharge categories) of a State permit program required by subsection (b) of this section if—

(A) the Administrator determines that the partial program represents a significant and identifiable part of the State program required by subsection (b) of this section; and

(B) the State submits, and the Administrator approves, a plan for the State to assume administration by phases of the remainder of the State program required by subsection (b) of this section by a specified date not more than 5 years after submission of the partial program under this subsection and agrees to make all reasonable efforts to assume such administration by such date.

(*o*) Anti-backsliding

(1) General prohibition

In the case of effluent limitations established on the basis of subsection (a)(1)(B) of this section, a permit may not be renewed, reissued, or modified on the basis of effluent guidelines promulgated under section 1314(b) of this title subsequent to the original issuance of such permit, to contain effluent limitations which are less stringent than the comparable effluent limitations in the previous permit. In the case of effluent limitations established on the basis of section 1311(b)(1)(C) or section 1313(d) or (e) of this title, a permit may not be renewed, reissued, or modified to contain effluent limitations which are less stringent than the comparable effluent limitations in the previous permit except in compliance with section 1313(d)(4) of this title.

(2) Exceptions

A permit with respect to which paragraph (1) applies may be renewed, reissued, or modified to contain a less stringent effluent limitation applicable to a pollutant if—

(A) material and substantial alterations or additions to the permitted facility occurred after permit issuance which justify the application of a less stringent effluent limitation;

(B) **(i)** information is available which was not available at the time of permit issuance (other than revised regulations, guidance, or test methods) and which would have justified the application of a less stringent effluent limitation at the time of permit issuance; or

(ii) the Administrator determines that technical mistakes or mistaken interpretations of law were made in issuing the permit under subsection (a)(1)(B) of this section;

(C) a less stringent effluent limitation is necessary because of events over which the permittee has no control and for which there is no reasonably available remedy;

(D) the permittee has received a permit modification under section 1311(c), 1311(g), 1311(h), 1311(i), 1311(k), 1311(n), or 1326(a) of this title; or

(E) the permittee has installed the treatment facilities required to meet the effluent limitations in the previous permit and has properly operated and maintained the facilities but has nevertheless been unable to achieve the previous effluent limitations, in which case the limitations in the reviewed, reissued, or modified permit may reflect the level of pollutant control actually achieved (but shall not be less stringent than required by effluent guidelines in effect at the time of permit renewal, reissuance, or modification).

Subparagraph (B) shall not apply to any revised waste load allocations or any alternative grounds for translating water quality standards into effluent limitations, except where the cumulative effect of such revised allocations results in a decrease in the amount of pollutants discharged into the concerned waters, and such revised allocations are not the result of a discharger eliminating or substantially reducing its discharge of pollutants due to complying with the requirements of this chapter or for reasons otherwise unrelated to water quality.

(3) Limitations

In no event may a permit with respect to which paragraph (1) applies be renewed, reissued, or modified to contain an effluent limitation which is less stringent than required by effluent guidelines in effect at the time the permit is renewed, reissued, or modified. In no event may such a permit to discharge into waters be renewed, reissued, or modified to contain a less stringent effluent limitation if the implementation of such limitation would result in a violation of a water quality standard under section 1313 of this title applicable to such waters.

(p) Municipal and industrial stormwater discharges

(1) General rule

Prior to October 1, 1994, the Administrator or the State (in the case of a permit program approved under this section) shall not require a permit under this section for discharges composed entirely of stormwater.

(2) Exceptions

Paragraph (1) shall not apply with respect to the following stormwater discharges:

(A) A discharge with respect to which a permit has been issued under this section before February 4, 1987.

(B) A discharge associated with industrial activity.

(C) A discharge from a municipal separate storm sewer system serving a population of 250,000 or more.

(D) A discharge from a municipal separate storm sewer system serving a population of 100,000 or more but less than 250,000.

(E) A discharge for which the Administrator or the State, as the case may be, determines that the stormwater discharge contributes to a violation of a water quality standard or is a significant contributor of pollutants to waters of the United States.

(3) Permit requirements

(A) Industrial discharges

Permits for discharges associated with industrial activity shall meet all applicable provisions of this section and section 1311 of this title.

(B) Municipal discharge

Permits for discharges from municipal storm sewers—

(i) may be issued on a system- or jurisdiction-wide basis;

(ii) shall include a requirement to effectively prohibit non-stormwater discharges into the storm sewers; and

(iii) shall require controls to reduce the discharge of pollutants to the maximum extent practicable, including management practices, control techniques and system, design and engineering methods, and such other provisions as the Administrator or the State determines appropriate for the control of such pollutants.

(4) Permit application requirements

(A) Industrial and large municipal discharges

Not later than 2 years after February 4, 1987, the Administrator shall establish regulations setting forth the permit application requirements for stormwater discharges described in paragraphs (2)(B) and (2)(C). Applications for permits for such discharges shall be filed no later than 3 years after February 4, 1987. Not later than 4 years after February 4, 1987, the Administrator or the State, as the case may be, shall issue or deny each such permit. Any such permit shall provide for compliance as expeditiously as practicable, but in no event later than 3 years after the date of issuance of such permit.

(B) Other municipal discharges

Not later than 4 years after February 4, 1987, the Administrator shall establish regulations setting forth the permit application requirements for stormwater discharges described in paragraph (2)(D). Applications for permits for such discharges shall be filed no later than 5 years after February 4, 1987. Not later than 6 years after February 4, 1987, the Administrator or the State, as the case may be, shall issue or deny each such permit. Any such permit shall provide for compliance as expeditiously as practicable, but in no event later than 3 years after the date of issuance of such permit.

(5) Studies

The Administrator, in consultation with the States, shall conduct a study for the purposes of—

(A) identifying those stormwater discharges or classes of stormwater discharges for which permits are not required pursuant to paragraphs (1) and (2) of this subsection;

(B) determining, to the maximum extent practicable, the nature and extent of pollutants in such discharges; and

(C) establishing procedures and methods to control stormwater discharges to the extent necessary to mitigate impacts on water quality.

Not later than October 1, 1988, the Administrator shall submit to Congress a report on the results of the study described in subparagraphs (A) and (B). Not later than October 1, 1989, the Administrator shall submit to Congress a report on the results of the study described in subparagraph (C).

(6) Regulations

Not later than October 1, 1993, the Administrator, in consultation with State and local officials, shall issue regulations (based on the results of the studies conducted under paragraph (5)) which designate stormwater discharges, other than those discharges described in paragraph (2), to be regulated to protect water quality and shall establish a comprehensive program to regulate such designated sources. The program shall, at a minimum, (A) establish priorities, (B) establish requirements for State stormwater management programs, and (C) establish expeditious deadlines. The program may include performance standards, guidelines, guidance, and management practices and treatment requirements, as appropriate.

(q) Combined sewer overflows

(1) Requirement for permits, orders, and decrees

Each permit, order, or decree issued pursuant to this chapter after December 21, 2000 for a discharge from a municipal combined storm and sanitary sewer shall conform to the Combined Sewer Overflow Control Policy signed by the Administrator on April 11, 1994 (in this subsection referred to as the "CSO control policy").

(2) Water quality and designated use review guidance

Not later than July 31, 2001, and after providing notice and opportunity for public comment, the Administrator shall issue guidance to facilitate the conduct of water quality and designated use reviews for municipal combined sewer overflow receiving waters.

(3) Report

Not later than September 1, 2001, the Administrator shall transmit to Congress a report on the progress made by the Environmental Protection Agency, States, and municipalities in implementing and enforcing the CSO control policy.

(r) Discharges incidental to the normal operation of recreational vessels

No permit shall be required under this chapter by the Administrator (or a State, in the case of a permit program approved under subsection (b)) for the discharge of any graywater, bilge water, cooling water, weather deck runoff, oil water separator effluent, or effluent from properly functioning marine engines, or any other discharge that is incidental to the normal operation of a vessel, if the discharge is from a recreational vessel.

(s) Integrated plans.—

(1) Definition of integrated plan.—In this subsection, the term 'integrated plan' means a plan developed in accordance with the Integrated Municipal Stormwater and Wastewater Planning Approach Framework, issued by the Environmental Protection Agency and dated June 5, 2012.

(2) In general.—The Administrator (or a State, in the case of a permit program approved by the Administrator) shall inform municipalities of the opportunity to develop an integrated plan that may be incorporated into a permit under this section.

(3) Scope.—

(A) Scope of permit incorporating integrated plan.—A permit issued under this section that incorporates an integrated plan may integrate all requirements under this Act addressed in the integrated plan, including requirements relating to—

(i) a combined sewer overflow;

(ii) a capacity, management, operation, and maintenance program for sanitary sewer collection systems;

(iii) a municipal stormwater discharge;

(iv) a municipal wastewater discharge; and

(v) a water quality-based effluent limitation to implement an applicable wasteload allocation in a total maximum daily load.

(B) Inclusions in integrated plan.—An integrated plan incorporated into a permit issued under this section may include the implementation of—

(i) projects, including innovative projects, to reclaim, recycle, or reuse water; and

(ii) green infrastructure.

(4) Compliances schedules.—

(A) In general.—A permit issued under this section that incorporates an integrated plan may include a schedule of compliance, under which actions taken to meet any applicable water quality-based effluent limitation may be implemented over more than 1 permit term if the schedule of compliance—

(i) is authorized by State water quality standards; and

(ii) meets the requirements of section 122.47 of title 40, Code of Federal Regulations (as in effect on the date of enactment of this subsection).

(B) Time for compliance.—For purposes of subparagraph (A)(ii), the requirement of section 122.47 of title 40, Code of Federal Regulations, for compliance by an applicable statutory deadline under this Act does not prohibit implementation of an applicable water quality-based effluent limitation over more than 1 permit term.

(C) Review.—A schedule of compliance incorporated into a permit issued under this section may be reviewed at the time the permit is renewed to determine whether the schedule should be modified.

(5) Existing authorities retained.—

(A) Applicable standards.—Nothing in this subsection modifies any obligation to comply with applicable technology and water quality-based effluent limitations under this Act.

(B) Flexibility.—Nothing in this subsection reduces or eliminates any flexibility available under this Act, including the authority of a State to revise a water quality standard after a use attainability analysis under section 131.10(g) of title 40, Code of Federal Regulations (or a successor regulation), subject to the approval of the Administrator under section 303(c).

(6) Clarification of State authority.—

(A) In general.—Nothing in section 301(b)(1)(C) precludes a State from authorizing in the water quality standards of the State the issuance of a schedule of compliance to meet water quality-based effluent limitations in permits that incorporate provisions of an integrated plan.

(B) Transition rule.—In any case in which a discharge is subject to a judicial order or consent decree, as of the date of enactment of this subsection, resolving an enforcement action under this Act, any schedule of compliance issued pursuant to an authorization in a State water quality standard may not revise a schedule of compliance in that order or decree to be less stringent, unless the order or decree is modified by agreement of the parties and the court.

(June 30, 1948, c. 758, Title IV, § 402, as added by Pub. L. No. 92–500, § 2, 86 Stat. 880 (Oct. 18, 1972); and amended by Pub. L. No. 95–217, §§ 33(c), 50, 54(c)(1), 65, 66, 91 Stat. 1577, 1588, 1591, 1599, 1600 (Dec. 27, 1977); Pub. L. No. 100–4, Title IV, §§ 401 to 404(a), (c), formerly (d), 405, 101 Stat. 65 to 67, 69 (Feb. 4, 1987); Pub. L. No. 102–580, Title III, § 364, 106 Stat. 4862 (Oct. 31, 1992); Pub. L. No. 104–66, Title II, § 2021(e)(2), 109 Stat. 727 (Dec. 21, 1995); Pub. L. No. 106–554, § 1(a)(4) [Div. B, Title I, § 112(a)], 114 Stat. 2763, 2763A–224 (Dec. 21, 2000); Pub. L. No. 110–288, § 2, 122 Stat. 2650 (July 29, 2008); Pub. L. No. 113–79, Title XII, § 12313, 128 Stat. 992 (Feb. 7, 2014); Pub. L. No. 115–436, § 3(a), 132 Stat. 5558, 5558–5560 (Jan. 14, 2019).)

[1] So in original.

HISTORICAL AND STATUTORY NOTES

References in Text

This chapter, referred to in subsecs. (q) and (r), originally read "this Act", meaning the Federal Water Pollution Control Act, June 30, 1948, c. 758, 62 Stat. 1155, which is codified principally as this chapter. See Tables for complete classification.

Transfer of Functions

Enforcement functions of Administrator or other official of the Environmental Protection Agency under this section relating to compliance with national pollutant discharge elimination system permits with respect to pre-construction, construction, and initial operation of transportation system for Canadian and Alaskan natural gas were transferred to the Federal Inspector, Office of Federal Inspector for the Alaska Natural Gas Transportation System, until the first anniversary of the date of initial operation of the Alaska Natural Gas Transportation System, see Reorg. Plan No. 1 of 1979, §§ 102(a), 203(a), 44 Fed. Reg. 33663, 33666, 93 Stat. 1373, 1376, effective July 1, 1979, set out in Appendix 1 to Title 5, Government Organization and Employees.

Permits for Discharges from Certain Vessels

Pub. L. No. 110–299, §§ 1, 2, 122 Stat. 2995 (July 31, 2008), as amended by Pub. L. No. 111–215, § 1, 124 Stat. 2347 (July 30, 2010); Pub. L. No. 112–213, Title VII, § 703, 126 Stat. 1580 (Dec. 20, 2012); Pub. L. No. 113–281, § 602, 128 Stat. 3061 (Dec. 18, 2014); Pub. L. No. 115–100, § 1, 131 Stat. 2245 (Jan. 3, 2018), created permit requirements for certain vessels. Congress repealed this law in Pub. L. No. 115–282, § 903(a)(2)(A), 132 Stat. 4354 (Dec. 4, 2018).

Stormwater Infrastructure Funding Task Force

Pub. L. No. 115–270, § 4101, 132 Stat. 3765, 3870–3871 (Oct. 23, 2018), provided that:

"(a) In general.—Not later than 180 days after the date of enactment of this Act, the Administrator of the Environmental Protection Agency shall establish a stormwater infrastructure ***3871** funding task force composed of representatives of Federal, State, and local governments and private (including nonprofit) entities to conduct a study on, and develop recommendations to improve, the availability of public and private sources of funding for the construction, rehabilitation, and operation and maintenance of stormwater infrastructure to meet the requirements of the Federal Water Pollution Control Act (**33 U.S.C. 1251** et seq.).

"(b) Considerations.—In carrying out subsection (a), the task force shall—

"(1) identify existing Federal, State, and local public sources and private sources of funding for stormwater infrastructure; and

"(2) consider—

"(A) how funding for stormwater infrastructure from such sources has been made available, and utilized, in each State to address stormwater infrastructure needs identified pursuant to section 516(b)(1) of the Federal Water Pollution Control Act (33 U.S.C. 1375(b)(1));

"(B) how the source of funding affects the affordability of the infrastructure (as determined based on the considerations used to assess the financial capability of municipalities under the integrated planning guidelines described in the Integrated Municipal Stormwater and Wastewater Planning Approach Framework, issued by the Environmental Protection Agency on June 5, 2012, and dated May, 2012), including consideration of the costs associated with financing the infrastructure; and

"(C) whether such sources of funding are sufficient to support capital expenditures and long-term operation and maintenance costs necessary to meet the stormwater infrastructure needs of municipalities.

"(c) Report.—Not later than 18 months after the date of enactment of this Act, the Administrator shall submit to Congress a report that describes the results of the study conducted, and the recommendations developed, under subsection (a).

"(d) State defined.—In this section, the term 'State' has the meaning given that term in section 502 of the Federal Water Pollution Control Act (33 U.S.C. 1362)."

Stormwater Permit Requirements

Pub. L. No. 102–240, Title I, § 1068, 105 Stat. 2007 (Dec. 18, 1991), provided that:

"(a) General rule.—Notwithstanding the requirements of sections 402(p)(2)(B), (C), and (D) of the Federal Water Pollution Control Act [subsec. (p)(2)(B), (C), and (D) of this section], permit application deadlines for stormwater discharges associated with industrial activities from facilities that are owned or operated by a municipality shall be established by the Administrator of the Environmental Protection Agency (hereinafter in this section referred to as the 'Administrator') pursuant to the requirements of this section.

"(b) Permit applications.—

"(1) Individual applications.—The Administrator shall require individual permit applications for discharges described in subsection (a) on or before October 1, 1992; except that any municipality that has participated in a timely part I group application for an industrial activity discharging stormwater that is denied such participation in a group application or for which a group application is denied shall not be required to submit an individual application until the 180th day following the date on which the denial is made.

"(2) Group applications.—With respect to group applications for permits for discharges described in subsection (a), the Administrator shall require—

"(A) part I applications on or before September 30, 1991, except that any municipality with a population of less than 250,000 shall not be required to submit a part I application before May 18, 1992; and

"(B) part II applications on or before October 1, 1992, except that any municipality with a population of less than 250,000 shall not be required to submit a part II application before May 17, 1993.

"(c) Municipalities with less than 100,000 population.—The Administrator shall not require any municipality with a population of less than 100,000 to apply for or obtain a permit for any stormwater discharge associated with an industrial activity other than an airport, powerplant, or uncontrolled sanitary landfill owned or operated by such municipality before October 1, 1992, unless such permit is required by section 402(p)(2)(A) or (E) of the Federal Water Pollution Control Act [subsec. (p)(2)(A) or (E) of this section].

"(d) Uncontrolled sanitary landfill defined.—For the purposes of this section, the term 'uncontrolled sanitary landfill' means a landfill or open dump, whether in operation or closed, that does not meet the requirements for run-on and run-off controls established pursuant to subtitle D of the Solid Waste Disposal Act [section 6941 et seq. of Title 42, The Public Health and Welfare].

"(e) Limitation on statutory construction.—Nothing in this section shall be construed to affect any application or permit requirement, including any deadline, to apply for or obtain a permit for stormwater discharges subject to section 402(p)(2)(A) or (E) of the Federal Water Pollution Control Act [subsec. (p)(2)(A) or (E) of this section].

"(f) Regulations.—The Administrator shall issue final regulations with respect to general permits for stormwater discharges associated with industrial activity on or before February 1, 1992."

Phosphate Fertilizer Effluent Limitation

Pub. L. No. 100–4, Title III, § 306(c), 101 Stat. 36 (Feb. 4, 1987), provided that:

"(1) Issuance of permit.—As soon as possible after the date of the enactment of this Act [Feb. 4, 1987], but not later than 180 days after such date of enactment [Feb. 4, 1987], the Administrator shall issue permits under section 402(a)(1)(B) of the Federal Water Pollution Control Act [subsec. (a)(1)(B) of this section] with respect to facilities—

"(A) which were under construction on or before April 8, 1974, and

"(B) for which the Administrator is proposing to revise the applicability of the effluent limitation established under section 301(b) of such Act [section 1311(b) of this title] for phosphate subcategory of the fertilizer manufacturing point source category to exclude such facilities.

"(2) Limitations on statutory construction.—Nothing in this section shall be construed—

"(A) to require the Administrator to permit the discharge of gypsum or gypsum waste into the navigable waters,

"(B) to affect the procedures and standards applicable to the Administrator in issuing permits under section 402(a)(1)(B) of the Federal Water Pollution Control Act [subsec. (a)(1)(B) of this section], and

"(C) to affect the authority of any State to deny or condition certification under section 401 of such Act [section 1341 of this title] with respect to the issuance of permits under section 402(a)(1)(B) of such Act [subsec. (a)(1)(B) of this section]."

Log Transfer Facilities

Pub. L. No. 100–4, Title IV, § 407, 101 Stat. 74 (Feb. 4, 1987), provided that:

"(a) Agreement.—The Administrator and Secretary of the Army shall enter into an agreement regarding coordination of permitting for log transfer facilities to designate a lead agency and to process permits required under sections 402 and 404 of the Federal Water Pollution Control Act [this section and section 1344 of this title], where both such sections apply, for discharges associated with the construction and operation of log transfer facilities. The Administrator and Secretary are authorized to act in accordance with the terms of such agreement to assure that, to the maximum extent practicable, duplication, needless paperwork and delay in the issuance of permits, and inequitable enforcement between and among facilities in different States, shall be eliminated.

"(b) Applications and permits before October 22, 1985.—Where both of sections 402 and 404 of the Federal Water Pollution Control Act [this section and section 1344 of this title] apply, log transfer facilities which have received a permit under section 404 of such Act [section 1344 of this title] before October 22, 1985, shall not be required to submit a new application for a permit under section 402 of such Act [this section]. If the Administrator determines that the terms of a permit issued on or before October 22, 1985, under section 404 of such Act [section 1344 of this title] satisfies the applicable requirements of sections 301, 302, 306, 307, 308, and 403 of such Act [sections 1311, 1312, 1316, 1317, 1318, and 1343 of this title] a separate application for a permit under section 402 of such Act [this section] shall not thereafter be required. In any case where the Administrator demonstrates, after an opportunity for a hearing, that the terms of a permit issued on or before October 22, 1985, under section 404 of such Act [section 1344 of this title] do not satisfy the applicable requirements of sections 301, 302, 306, 307, 308, and 403 of such Act [sections 1311, 1312, 1316, 1317, 1318, and 1343 of this title], modifications to the existing permit under section 404 of such Act [section 1344 of this title] to incorporate such applicable requirements shall be issued by the Administrator as an alternative to issuance of a separate new permit under section 402 of such Act [this section].

"(c) Log transfer facility defined.—For the purposes of this section, the term 'log transfer facility' means a facility which is constructed in whole or in part in waters of the United States and which is utilized for the purpose of transferring commercially harvested logs to or from a vessel or log raft, including the formation of a log raft."

Allowable Delay in Modifying Existing Approved State Permit Programs to Conform to 1977 Amendment

Pub. L. No. 95–217, § 54(c)(2), 91 Stat. 1591 (Dec. 27, 1977), provided that any State permit program approved under this section before Dec. 27, 1977, which required modification to conform to the amendment made by section 54(c)(1) of Pub. L. No. 95–217, which amended subsec. (b)(8) of this section, not be required to be modified before the end of the one year period which began on Dec. 27, 1977, unless in order to make the required modification a State must amend or enact a law in which case such modification not be required for such State before the end of the two year period which began on Dec. 27, 1977.

§ 1343. Ocean discharge criteria

[FWPCA § 403]

(a) Issuance of permits

No permit under section 1342 of this title for a discharge into the territorial sea, the waters of the contiguous zone, or the oceans shall be issued, after promulgation of guidelines established under subsection (c) of this section, except in compliance with such guidelines. Prior to the promulgation of such guidelines, a permit may be issued under such section 1342 of this title if the Administrator determines it to be in the public interest.

(b) Waiver

The requirements of subsection (d) of section 1342 of this title may not be waived in the case of permits for discharges into the territorial sea.

(c) Guidelines for determining degradation of waters

(1) The Administrator shall, within one hundred and eighty days after October 18, 1972 (and from time to time thereafter), promulgate guidelines for determining the degradation of the waters of the territorial seas, the contiguous zone, and the oceans, which shall include:

(A) the effect of disposal of pollutants on human health or welfare, including but not limited to plankton, fish, shellfish, wildlife, shorelines, and beaches;

(B) the effect of disposal of pollutants on marine life including the transfer, concentration, and dispersal of pollutants or their byproducts through biological, physical, and chemical processes; changes in marine ecosystem diversity, productivity, and stability; and species and community population changes;

(C) the effect of disposal, of pollutants on esthetic, recreation, and economic values;

(D) the persistence and permanence of the effects of disposal of pollutants;

(E) the effect of the disposal at varying rates, of particular volumes and concentrations of pollutants;

(F) other possible locations and methods of disposal or recycling of pollutants including land-based alternatives; and

(G) the effect on alternate uses of the oceans, such as mineral exploitation and scientific study.

(2) In any event where insufficient information exists on any proposed discharge to make a reasonable judgment on any of the guidelines established pursuant to this subsection no permit shall be issued under section 1342 of this title.

(June 30, 1948, c. 758, Title IV, § 403, as added by Pub. L. No. 92–500, § 2, 86 Stat. 883 (Oct. 18, 1972).)

HISTORICAL AND STATUTORY NOTES

Territorial Sea and Contiguous Zone of United States

For extension of territorial sea and contiguous zone of United States, see Proc. No. 5928 and Proc. No. 7219, respectively, set out as notes under 43 U.S.C.A. § 1331.

Discharges from Point Sources in United States Virgin Islands Attributable to Manufacture of Rum; Exemption; Conditions

Discharges from point sources in the United States Virgin Islands in existence on Aug. 5, 1983, attributable to the manufacture of rum not to be subject to the requirements of this section under certain conditions, see section 214(g) of Pub. L. No. 98–67, set out as a note under section 1311 of this title.

§ 1344. Permits for dredged or fill material
[FWPCA § 404]

(a) Discharge into navigable waters at specified disposal sites

The Secretary may issue permits, after notice and opportunity for public hearings for the discharge of dredged or fill material into the navigable waters at specified disposal sites. Not later than the fifteenth day after the date an applicant submits all the information required to complete an application for a permit under this subsection, the Secretary shall publish the notice required by this subsection.

(b) Specification for disposal sites

Subject to subsection (c) of this section, each such disposal site shall be specified for each such permit by the Secretary (1) through the application of guidelines developed by the Administrator, in conjunction with the Secretary, which guidelines shall be based upon criteria comparable to the criteria applicable to the territorial seas, the contiguous zone, and the ocean under section 1343(c) of this title, and (2) in any case where such guidelines under clause (1) alone would prohibit the specification of a site, through the application additionally of the economic impact of the site on navigation and anchorage.

(c) Denial or restriction of use of defined areas as disposal sites

The Administrator is authorized to prohibit the specification (including the withdrawal of specification) of any defined area as a disposal site, and he is authorized to deny or restrict the use of any defined area for specification (including the withdrawal of specification) as a disposal site, whenever he determines, after notice and opportunity for public hearings, that the discharge of such materials into such area will have an unacceptable adverse effect on municipal water supplies, shellfish beds and fishery areas (including spawning and breeding areas), wildlife, or recreational areas. Before making such determination, the Administrator shall consult with the Secretary. The Administrator shall set forth in writing and make public his findings and his reasons for making any determination under this subsection.

(d) "Secretary" defined

The term "Secretary" as used in this section means the Secretary of the Army, acting through the Chief of Engineers.

(e) General permits on State, regional, or nationwide basis

(1) In carrying out his functions relating to the discharge of dredged or fill material under this section, the Secretary may, after notice and opportunity for public hearing, issue general permits on a State, regional, or nationwide basis for any category of activities involving discharges of dredged or fill material if the Secretary determines that the activities in such category are similar in nature, will cause only minimal adverse environmental effects when performed separately, and will have only minimal cumulative adverse effect on the environment. Any general permit issued under this subsection shall (A) be based on the guidelines described in subsection (b)(1) of this section, and (B) set forth the requirements and standards which shall apply to any activity authorized by such general permit.

(2) No general permit issued under this subsection shall be for a period of more than five years after the date of its issuance and such general permit may be revoked or modified by the Secretary if, after opportunity for public hearing, the Secretary determines that the activities authorized by such general permit have an adverse impact on the environment or such activities are more appropriately authorized by individual permits.

(f) Non-prohibited discharge of dredged or fill material

(1) Except as provided in paragraph (2) of this subsection, the discharge of dredged or fill material—

(A) from normal farming, silviculture, and ranching activities such as plowing, seeding, cultivating, minor drainage, harvesting for the production of food, fiber, and forest products, or upland soil and water conservation practices;

(B) for the purpose of maintenance, including emergency reconstruction of recently damaged parts, of currently serviceable structures such as dikes, dams, levees, groins, riprap, breakwaters, causeways, and bridge abutments or approaches, and transportation structures;

(C) for the purpose of construction or maintenance of farm or stock ponds or irrigation ditches, or the maintenance of drainage ditches;

(D) for the purpose of construction of temporary sedimentation basins on a construction site which does not include placement of fill material into the navigable waters;

(E) for the purpose of construction or maintenance of farm roads or forest roads, or temporary roads for moving mining equipment, where such roads are constructed and maintained, in accordance with best management practices, to assure that flow and circulation patterns and chemical and biological characteristics of the navigable waters are not impaired, that the reach of the navigable waters is not reduced, and that any adverse effect on the aquatic environment will be otherwise minimized;

(F) resulting from any activity with respect to which a State has an approved program under section 1288(b)(4) of this title which meets the requirements of subparagraphs (B) and (C) of such section,

is not prohibited by or otherwise subject to regulation under this section or section 1311(a) or 1342 of this title (except for effluent standards or prohibitions under section 1317 of this title).

(2) Any discharge of dredged or fill material into the navigable waters incidental to any activity having as its purpose bringing an area of the navigable waters into a use to which it was not previously subject, where the flow or circulation of navigable waters may be impaired or the reach of such waters be reduced, shall be required to have a permit under this section.

(g) State administration

(1) The Governor of any State desiring to administer its own individual and general permit program for the discharge of dredged or fill material into the navigable waters (other than those waters which are presently used, or are susceptible to use in their natural condition or by reasonable improvement as a means to transport interstate or foreign commerce shoreward to their ordinary high water mark, including all waters which are subject to the ebb and flow of the tide shoreward to their mean high water mark, or mean higher high water mark on the west coast, including wetlands adjacent thereto) within its jurisdiction may submit to the Administrator a full and complete description of the program it proposes to establish and administer under State law or under an interstate compact. In addition, such State shall submit a statement from the attorney general (or the attorney for those State agencies which have independent legal counsel), or from the chief legal officer in the case of an interstate agency, that the laws of such State, or the interstate compact, as the case may be, provide adequate authority to carry out the described program.

(2) Not later than the tenth day after the date of the receipt of the program and statement submitted by any State under paragraph (1) of this subsection, the Administrator shall provide copies of such program and statement to the Secretary and the Secretary of the Interior, acting through the Director of the United States Fish and Wildlife Service.

(3) Not later than the ninetieth day after the date of the receipt by the Administrator of the program and statement submitted by any State, under paragraph (1) of this subsection, the Secretary and the Secretary of the Interior, acting through the Director of the United States Fish and Wildlife Service, shall submit any comments with respect to such program and statement to the Administrator in writing.

(h) Determination of State's authority to issue permits under State program; approval; notification; transfers to State program

(1) Not later than the one-hundred-twentieth day after the date of the receipt by the Administrator of a program and statement submitted by any State under paragraph (1) of this subsection, the Administrator shall determine, taking into account any comments submitted by the Secretary and the Secretary of the Interior, acting through the Director of the United States Fish and Wildlife Service, pursuant to subsection (g) of this section, whether such State has the following authority with respect to the issuance of permits pursuant to such program:

(A) To issue permits which—

(i) apply, and assure compliance with, any applicable requirements of this section, including, but not limited to, the guidelines established under subsection (b)(1) of this section, and sections 1317 and 1343 of this title;

(ii) are for fixed terms not exceeding five years; and

(iii) can be terminated or modified for cause including, but not limited to, the following:

(I) violation of any condition of the permit;

(II) obtaining a permit by misrepresentation, or failure to disclose fully all relevant facts;

(III) change in any condition that requires either a temporary or permanent reduction or elimination of the permitted discharge.

(B) To issue permits which apply, and assure compliance with, all applicable requirements of section 1318 of this title, or to inspect, monitor, enter, and require reports to at least the same extent as required in section 1318 of this title.

(C) To assure that the public, and any other State the waters of which may be affected, receive notice of each application for a permit and to provide an opportunity for public hearing before a ruling on each such application.

(D) To assure that the Administrator receives notice of each application (including a copy thereof) for a permit.

(E) To assure that any State (other than the permitting State), whose waters may be affected by the issuance of a permit may submit written recommendations to the permitting State (and the Administrator) with respect to any permit application and, if any part of such written recommendations are not accepted by the permitting State, that the permitting State will notify such affected State (and the Administrator) in writing of its failure to so accept such recommendations together with its reasons for so doing.

(F) To assure that no permit will be issued if, in the judgment of the Secretary, after consultation with the Secretary of the department in which the Coast Guard is operating, anchorage and navigation of any of the navigable waters would be substantially impaired thereby.

(G) To abate violations of the permit or the permit program, including civil and criminal penalties and other ways and means of enforcement.

(H) To assure continued coordination with Federal and Federal-State water-related planning and review processes.

(2) If, with respect to a State program submitted under subsection (g)(1) of this section, the Administrator determines that such State—

(A) has the authority set forth in paragraph (1) of this subsection, the Administrator shall approve the program and so notify (i) such State and (ii) the Secretary, who upon subsequent notification from such State that it is administering such program, shall suspend the issuance of permits under subsections (a) and (e) of this section for activities with respect to which a permit may be issued pursuant to such State program; or

(B) does not have the authority set forth in paragraph (1) of this subsection, the Administrator shall so notify such State, which notification shall also describe the revisions or modifications necessary so that such State may resubmit such program for a determination by the Administrator under this subsection.

(3) If the Administrator fails to make a determination with respect to any program submitted by a State under subsection (g)(1) of this section within one-hundred-twenty days after the date of the receipt of such program, such program shall be deemed approved pursuant to paragraph (2)(A) of this subsection and the Administrator shall so notify such State and the Secretary who, upon subsequent notification from such State that it is administering such program, shall suspend the issuance of permits under subsection (a) and (e) of this section for activities with respect to which a permit may be issued by such State.

(4) After the Secretary receives notification from the Administrator under paragraph (2) or (3) of this subsection that a State permit program has been approved, the Secretary shall transfer any applications for permits pending before the Secretary for activities with respect to which a permit may be issued pursuant to such State program to such State for appropriate action.

(5) Upon notification from a State with a permit program approved under this subsection that such State intends to administer and enforce the terms and conditions of a general permit issued by the Secretary under subsection (e) of this section with respect to activities in such State to which such general permit applies, the Secretary shall suspend the administration and enforcement of such general permit with respect to such activities.

(i) Withdrawal of approval

Whenever the Administrator determines after public hearing that a State is not administering a program approved under subsection (h)(2)(A) of this section, in accordance with this section, including, but not limited to, the guidelines established under subsection (b)(1) of this section, the Administrator shall so notify the State, and, if appropriate corrective action is not taken within a reasonable time, not to exceed ninety days after the date of the receipt of such notification, the Administrator shall (1) withdraw approval of such program until the Administrator determines such corrective action has been taken, and (2) notify the Secretary that the Secretary shall resume the program for the issuance of permits under subsections (a) and (e) of this section for activities with respect to which the State was issuing permits and that such authority of the Secretary shall continue in effect until such time as the Administrator makes the determination described in clause (1) of this subsection and such State again has an approved program.

(j) Copies of applications for State permits and proposed general permits to be transmitted to Administrator

Each State which is administering a permit program pursuant to this section shall transmit to the Administrator (1) a copy of each permit application received by such State and provide notice to the Administrator of every action related to the consideration of such permit application, including each permit proposed to be issued by such State, and (2) a copy of each proposed general permit which such State intends to issue. Not later than the tenth day after the date of the receipt of such permit application or such proposed general permit, the Administrator shall provide copies of such permit application or such proposed general permit to the Secretary and the Secretary of the Interior, acting through the Director of the United States Fish and Wildlife Service. If the Administrator intends to provide written comments to such State with respect to such permit application or such proposed general permit, he shall so notify such State not later than the thirtieth day after the date of the receipt of such application or such proposed general permit and provide such written comments to such State, after consideration of any comments made in writing with respect to such application or such proposed general permit by the Secretary and the Secretary of the Interior, acting through the Director of the United States Fish and Wildlife Service, not later than the ninetieth day after the date of such receipt. If such State is so notified by the Administrator, it shall not issue the proposed permit until after the receipt of such comments from the Administrator, or after such ninetieth day, whichever first occurs. Such State shall not issue such proposed permit after such ninetieth day if it has received such written comments in which the Administrator objects (A) to the issuance of such proposed permit and such proposed permit is one that has been submitted to the Administrator pursuant to subsection (h)(1)(E) of this section, or (B) to the issuance of such proposed permit as being outside the requirements of this section, including, but not limited to, the guidelines developed under subsection (b)(1) of this section unless it modifies such proposed permit in accordance with such comments. Whenever the Administrator objects to the issuance of a permit under the preceding sentence such written objection shall contain a statement of the reasons for such objection and the conditions which such permit would include if it were issued by the Administrator. In any case where the Administrator objects to the issuance of a permit, on request of the State, a public hearing shall be held by the Administrator on such objection. If the State does not resubmit such permit revised to meet such objection within 30 days after completion of the hearing or, if no hearing is requested within 90 days after the date of such objection, the Secretary may issue the permit pursuant to subsection (a) or (e) of this section, as the case may be, for such source in accordance with the guidelines and requirements of this chapter.

(k) Waiver

In accordance with guidelines promulgated pursuant to subsection (i)(2) of section 1314 of this title, the Administrator is authorized to waive the requirements of subsection (j) of this section at the time of the approval of a program pursuant to subsection (h)(2)(A) of this section for any category (including any class, type, or size within such category) of discharge within the State submitting such program.

(*l*) Categories of discharges not subject to requirements

The Administrator shall promulgate regulations establishing categories of discharges which he determines shall not be subject to the requirements of subsection (j) of this section in any State with a program approved pursuant to subsection (h)(2)(A) of this section. The Administrator may distinguish among classes, types, and sizes within any category of discharges.

(m) Comments on permit applications or proposed general permits by Secretary of the Interior acting through Director of United States Fish and Wildlife Service

Not later than the ninetieth day after the date on which the Secretary notifies the Secretary of the Interior, acting through the Director of the United States Fish and Wildlife Service that (1) an application for a permit under subsection (a) of this section has been received by the Secretary, or (2) the Secretary proposes to issue a general permit under subsection (e) of this section, the Secretary of the Interior, acting through the Director of the United States Fish and Wildlife Service, shall submit any comments with respect to such application or such proposed general permit in writing to the Secretary.

(n) Enforcement authority not limited

Nothing in this section shall be construed to limit the authority of the Administrator to take action pursuant to section 1319 of this title.

(*o*) Public availability of permits and permit applications

A copy of each permit application and each permit issued under this section shall be available to the public. Such permit application or portion thereof, shall further be available on request for the purpose of reproduction.

(p) Compliance

Compliance with a permit issued pursuant to this section, including any activity carried out pursuant to a general permit issued under this section, shall be deemed compliance, for purposes of sections 1319 and 1365 of this title, with sections 1311, 1317, and 1343 of this title.

(q) Minimization of duplication, needless paperwork, and delays in issuance; agreements

Not later than the one-hundred-eightieth day after December 27, 1977, the Secretary shall enter into agreements with the Administrator, the Secretaries of the Departments of Agriculture, Commerce, Interior, and Transportation, and the heads of other appropriate Federal agencies to minimize, to the maximum extent practicable, duplication, needless paperwork, and delays in the issuance of permits under this section. Such agreements shall be developed to assure that, to the maximum extent practicable, a decision with respect to an application for a permit under subsection (a) of this section will be made not later than the ninetieth day after the date the notice for such application is published under subsection (a) of this section.

(r) Federal projects specifically authorized by Congress

The discharge of dredged or fill material as part of the construction of a Federal project specifically authorized by Congress, whether prior to or on or after December 27, 1977, is not prohibited by or otherwise subject to regulation under this section, or a State program approved under this section, or section 1311(a) or 1342 of this title (except for effluent standards or prohibitions under section 1317 of this title), if information on the effects of such discharge, including consideration of the guidelines developed under subsection (b)(1) of this section, is included in an environmental impact statement for such project pursuant to the National Environmental Policy Act of 1969 [42 U.S.C.A. § 4321 et seq.] and such environmental impact statement has been submitted to Congress before the actual discharge of dredged or fill material in connection with the construction of such project and prior to either authorization of such project or an appropriation of funds for such construction.

(s) Violation of permits

(1) Whenever on the basis of any information available to him the Secretary finds that any person is in violation of any condition or limitation set forth in a permit issued by the Secretary under this section, the Secretary shall issue an order requiring such person to comply with such condition or limitation, or the Secretary shall bring a civil action in accordance with paragraph (3) of this subsection.

(2) A copy of any order issued under this subsection shall be sent immediately by the Secretary to the State in which the violation occurs and other affected States. Any order issued under this subsection shall be by personal service and shall state with reasonable specificity the nature of the violation, specify a time for compliance, not to exceed thirty days, which the Secretary determines is reasonable, taking into account the seriousness of the violation and any good faith efforts to comply with applicable requirements. In any case in which an order under this subsection is issued to a corporation, a copy of such order shall be served on any appropriate corporate officers.

(3) The Secretary is authorized to commence a civil action for appropriate relief, including a permanent or temporary injunction for any violation for which he is authorized to issue a compliance order under paragraph (1) of this subsection. Any action under this paragraph may be brought in the district court of the United States for the district in which the defendant is located or resides or is doing business, and such court shall have jurisdiction to restrain such violation and to require compliance. Notice of the commencement of such acton[1] shall be given immediately to the appropriate State.

(4) Any person who violates any condition or limitation in a permit issued by the Secretary under this section, and any person who violates any order issued by the Secretary under paragraph (1) of this subsection, shall be subject to a civil penalty not to exceed $25,000 per day for each violation. In determining the amount of a civil penalty the court shall consider the seriousness of the violation or violations, the economic benefit (if any) resulting from the violation, any history of such violations, any good-faith efforts to comply with the applicable requirements, the economic impact of the penalty on the violator, and such other matters as justice may require.

(t) Navigable waters within State jurisdiction

Nothing in this section shall preclude or deny the right of any State or interstate agency to control the discharge of dredged or fill material in any portion of the navigable waters within the jurisdiction of such State, including any activity of any Federal agency, and each such agency shall comply with such State or interstate requirements both substantive and procedural to control the discharge of dredged or fill material to the same extent that any person is subject to such requirements. This section shall not be construed as affecting or impairing the authority of the Secretary to maintain navigation.

(June 30, 1948, c. 758, Title IV, § 404, as added by Pub. L. No. 92–500, § 2, 86 Stat. 884 (Oct. 18, 1972); and amended by Pub. L. No. 95–217, § 67(a), (b), 91 Stat. 1600 (Dec. 27, 1977); Pub. L. No. 100–4, Title III, § 313(d), 101 Stat. 45 (Feb. 4, 1987).)

[1] So in original. Probably should be "action."

HISTORICAL AND STATUTORY NOTES

References in Text

The National Environmental Policy Act of 1969, referred to in subsec. (r), is Pub. L. No. 91–190, 83 Stat. 852 (Jan. 1, 1970), as amended, which is codified generally as chapter 55 (section 4321 et seq.) of Title 42, Public Health and Welfare. For complete classification of this Act to the Code, see Short Title note set out under section 4321 of Title 42 and Tables.

Termination of Reporting Requirements

For termination of reporting provisions of subsec. (r) of this section, effective May 15, 2000, see Pub. L. No. 104–66, § 3003, as amended, set out as a note under 31 U.S.C.A. § 1113, and the 2nd item on page 68 of House Document No. 103–7.

Transfer of Functions

Enforcement functions of Administrator or other official of the Environmental Protection Agency and of Secretary or other official in Department of Interior relating to review of the Corps of Engineers' dredged and fill material permits and such functions of Secretary of the Army, Chief of Engineers, or other official in Corps of Engineers of the United States Army relating to compliance with dredged and fill material permits issued under this section with respect to pre-construction, construction, and initial operation of transportation system for Canadian and Alaskan natural gas were transferred to the Federal Inspector, Office of Federal Inspector for the Alaska Natural Gas Transportation System, until the first anniversary of the date of initial operation of the Alaska Natural Gas Transportation System, see Reorg. Plan No. 1 of 1979, §§ 102(a), (b), (e), 203(a), 44 Fed. Reg. 33663, 33666, 93 Stat. 1373, 1376, effective July 1, 1979, set out in Appendix 1 to Title 5, Government Organization and Employees.

Dredged Material Disposal

The Water Infrastructure Improvements for the Nation Act, Pub. L. No. 114–322, § 1189, 130 Stat 1681 (Dec. 16, 2016), provided that:

> "Disposal of dredged material shall not be considered environmentally acceptable for the purposes of identifying the Federal standard (as defined in section 335.7 of title 33, Code of Federal Regulations (or successor regulations)) if the disposal violates applicable State water quality standards approved by the Administrator of the Environmental Protection Agency under section 303 of the Federal Water Pollution Control Act (33 U.S.C. 1313)."

Interpretive Rule Withdrawal Ordered

Pub. L. No. 113–235, § 112, 128 Stat. 2308 (Dec. 16, 2014), provided that:

> "The U.S. Environmental Protection Agency and the U.S. Department of the Army shall withdraw the interpretive rule, 'U.S. Environmental Protection Agency and the U.S. Department of the Army Interpretive Rule Regarding the Applicability of the Clean Water Act Section 404(f)(1)(A),' signed on March 25, 2014."

The referenced interpretive rule governed the applicability of Section 404 to agriculture.

Limitations on Uses of Funding

Pub. L. No. 116–6, § 431, 133 Stat. 13, 266 (Feb. 15, 2019), provided that: "None of the funds made available in this Act may be used to require a permit for the discharge of dredged or fill material under the Federal Water Pollution Control Act (33 U.S.C. 1251 et seq.) for the activities identified in subparagraphs (A) and (C) of section 404(f)(1) of the Act (33 U.S.C. 1344(f)(1)(A), (C))."

Pub. L. No. 115–244, § 108, 132 Stat. 2897, 2903 (Sept. 21, 2018), provided that: "None of the funds made available by this Act may be used to require a permit for the discharge of dredged or fill material under the Federal Water Pollution Control Act (33 U.S.C. 1251 et seq.) for the activities identified in subparagraphs (A) and (C) of section 404(f)(1) of the Act (33 U.S.C. 1344(f)(1)(A), (C))."

Pub. L. No. 115–141, § 108, 132 Stat. 348, 515 (Mar. 23, 2018), provided that: "None of the funds made available by this Act may be used to require a permit for the discharge of dredged or fill material under the Federal Water Pollution Control Act (33 U.S.C. 1251 et seq.) for the activities identified in subparagraphs (A) and (C) of section 404(f)(1) of the Act (33 U.S.C. 1344(f)(1)(A), (C))." Section 432 of the same public law, 132 Stat. 695, provided that: "None of the funds made available in this Act may be used to require a permit for the discharge of dredged or fill material under the Federal Water Pollution Control Act (33 U.S.C. 1251 et seq.) for the activities identified in subparagraphs (A) and (C) of section 404(f)(1) of the Act (33 U.S.C. 1344(f)(1)(A), (C))."

Pub. L. No. 115–31, 131 Stat. 134 (May 5, 2017) imposed several restrictions on the uses of funding in implementing Section 404. Section 105, 131 Stat. 306, provided:

> None of the funds in this Act shall be used for an open lake placement alternative for dredged material, after evaluating the least costly, environmentally acceptable manner for the disposal or management of dredged material originating from Lake Erie or tributaries thereto, unless it is approved under a State water quality certification pursuant to section 401 of the Federal Water Pollution Control Act (33 U.S.C. 1341); Provided

further, That until an open lake placement alternative for dredged material is approved under a State water quality certification, the Corps of Engineers shall continue upland placement of such dredged material consistent with the requirements of section 101 of the Water Resources Development Act of 1986 (33 U.S.C. 2211).

Section 108, 131 Stat. 306, provided:

None of the funds made available in this or any other Act making appropriations for Energy and Water Development for any fiscal year may be used by the Corps of Engineers during the fiscal year ending September 30, 2017, to develop, adopt, implement, administer, or enforce any change to the regulations in effect on October 1, 2012, pertaining to the definitions of the terms "fill material" or "discharge of fill material" for the purposes of the Federal Water Pollution Control Act (33 U.S.C. 1251 et seq.).

Section 109, 131 Stat. 306–307, provided: "None of the funds made available by this Act may be used to require a permit for the discharge of dredged or fill material under the Federal Water Pollution Control Act (33 U.S.C. 1251 et seq.) for the activities identified in subparagraphs (A) and (C) of section 404(f)(1) of the Act (33 U.S.C. 1344(f)(1)(A), (C))." Section 424, 131 Stat. 499, provided: "None of the funds made available in this Act may be used to require a permit for the discharge of dredged or fill material under the Federal Water Pollution Control Act (33 U.S.C. 1251, et seq.) for the activities identified in subparagraphs (A) and (C) of section 404(f)(1) of the Act (33 U.S.C. 1344(f)(1)(A), (C))."

Pub. L. No. 113–76, § 115, 128 Stat. 158–59 (Jan. 17, 2014), provided that:

"None of the funds made available in this or any other Act making appropriations for Energy and Water Development for any fiscal year may be used by the Corps of Engineers during the fiscal year ending September 30, 2014, to develop, adopt, implement, administer, or enforce any change to the regulations in effect on October 1, 2012, pertaining to the definitions of the terms 'fill material' or 'discharge of fill material' for the purposes of the Federal Water Pollution Control Act (33 U.S.C. 1251 et seq.)."

Similarly, Pub. L. No. 113–235, § 109, 128 Stat. 2308 (Dec. 16, 2014), provided that:

"None of the funds made available in this or any other Act making appropriations for Energy and Water Development for any fiscal year may be used by the Corps of Engineers during the fiscal year ending September 30, 2015, to develop, adopt, implement, administer, or enforce any change to the regulations in effect on October 1, 2012, pertaining to the definitions of the terms 'fill material' or 'discharge of fill material' for the purposes of the Federal Water Pollution Control Act (33 U.S.C. 1251 et seq.)."

Section 111 of the same Public Law provided that:

"None of the funds made available by this Act may be used to require a permit for the discharge of dredged or fill material under the Federal Water Pollution Control Act (33 U.S.C. 1251, et seq.) for the activities identified in subparagraphs (A) and (C) of section 404(f)(1) of the Act (33 U.S.C. 1344(f)(1)(A), (C)).

Mitigation and Mitigation Banking Regulations

Pub. L. No. 108–136, Div. A, Title III, § 314(b), 117 Stat. 1431 (Nov. 24, 2003), provided that:

"(1) To ensure opportunities for Federal agency participation in mitigation banking, the Secretary of the Army, acting through the Chief of Engineers, shall issue regulations establishing performance standards and criteria for the use, consistent with section 404 of the Federal Water Pollution Control Act (33 U.S.C. 1344) [this section], of on-site, off-site, and in-lieu fee mitigation and mitigation banking as compensation for lost wetlands functions in permits issued by the Secretary of the Army under such section. To the maximum extent practicable, the regulatory standards and criteria shall maximize available credits and opportunities for mitigation, provide flexibility for regional variations in wetland conditions, functions and values, and apply equivalent standards and criteria to each type of compensatory mitigation.

"(2) Final regulations shall be issued not later than two years after the date of the enactment of this Act [Nov. 24, 2003]."

Contiguous Zone of United States

For extension of contiguous zone of United States, see Proc. No. 7219, set out as a note under 43 U.S.C.A. § 1331.

Regulatory Program

Pub. L. No. 106–377, § 1(a)(2) [Title I], 114 Stat. 1441, 1441A–63 (Oct. 27, 2000), provided in part that: "For expenses necessary for administration of laws pertaining to regulation of navigable waters and wetlands, $125,000,000, to remain available until expended: *Provided,* That the Secretary of the Army, acting through the Chief of Engineers, is directed to use funds appropriated herein to: (1) by March 1, 2001, supplement the report, Cost Analysis For the 1999 Proposal to Issue and Modify Nationwide Permits, to reflect the Nationwide Permits actually issued on March 9, 2000, including changes in the acreage limits, preconstruction notification requirements and general conditions between the rule proposed on July 21, 1999, and the rule promulgated and published in the Federal Register; (2) after consideration of the cost analysis for the 1999 proposal to issue and modify nationwide permits and the supplement prepared pursuant to this Act [Pub. L. No. 106–377, 114 Stat. 1441 (Oct. 27, 2000)] and by September 30, 2001, prepare, submit to Congress and publish in the Federal Register a Permit Processing Management Plan by which the Corps of Engineers will handle the additional work associated with all projected increases in the number of individual permit applications and preconstruction notifications related to the new and replacement permits and general conditions. The Permit Processing Management Plan shall include specific objective goals and criteria by which the Corps of Engineers' progress towards reducing any permit backlog can be measured; (3) beginning on December 31, 2001, and on a biannual basis thereafter, report to Congress and publish in the Federal Register, an analysis of the performance of its program as measured against the criteria set out in the Permit Processing Management Plan; (4) implement a 1-year pilot program to publish quarterly on the U.S. Army Corps of Engineer's Regulatory Program website all Regulatory Analysis and Management Systems (RAMS) data for the South Pacific Division and North Atlantic Division beginning within 30 days of the enactment of this Act [Oct. 27, 2000]; and (5) publish in Division Office websites all findings, rulings, and decisions rendered under the administrative appeals process for the Corps of Engineers Regulatory Program as established in Public Law 106–60: *Provided further,* That, through the period ending on September 30, 2003, the Corps of Engineers shall allow any appellant to keep a verbatim record of the proceedings of the appeals conference under the aforementioned administrative appeals process: *Provided further,* That within 30 days of the enactment of this Act [Oct. 27, 2000], the Secretary of the Army, acting through the Chief of Engineers, shall require all U.S. Army Corps of Engineers Divisions and Districts to record the date on which a section 404 individual permit application or nationwide permit notification is filed with the Corps of Engineers: *Provided further,* That the Corps of Engineers, when reporting permit processing times, shall track both the date a permit application is first received and the date the application is considered complete, as well as the reason that the application is not considered complete upon first submission."

Authority to Delegate to State of Washington Functions of the Secretary Relating to Lake Chelan, Washington

Section 76 of Pub. L. No. 95–217 provided that: "The Secretary of the Army, acting through the Chief of Engineers, is authorized to delegate to the State of Washington upon its request all or any part of those functions vested in such Secretary by section 404 of the Federal Water Pollution Control Act [this section] and by sections 9, 10, and 13 of the Act of March 3, 1899 [sections 401, 403, and 407 of this title], relating to Lake Chelan, Washington, if the Secretary determines (1) that such State has the authority, responsibility, and capability to carry out such functions, and (2) that such delegation is in the public interest. Such delegation shall be subject to such terms and conditions as the Secretary deems necessary, including, but not limited to, suspension and revocation for cause of such delegation."

§ 1345. Disposal or use of sewage sludge

[FWPCA § 405]

(a) Permit

Notwithstanding any other provision of this chapter or of any other law, in any case where the disposal of sewage sludge resulting from the operation of a treatment works as defined in section 1292 of this title (including the removal of in-place sewage sludge from one location and its deposit at another location) would result in any pollutant from such sewage sludge entering the navigable waters, such disposal is prohibited except in accordance with a permit issued by the Administrator under section 1342 of this title.

(b) Issuance of permit; regulations

The Administrator shall issue regulations governing the issuance of permits for the disposal of sewage sludge subject to subsection (a) of this section and section 1342 of this title. Such regulations shall require the application to such disposal of each criterion, factor, procedure, and requirement applicable to a permit issued under section 1342 of this title.

(c) State permit program

Each State desiring to administer its own permit program for disposal of sewage sludge subject to subsection (a) of this section within its jurisdiction may do so in accordance with section 1342 of this title.

(d) Regulations

(1) Regulations

The Administrator, after consultation with appropriate Federal and State agencies and other interested persons, shall develop and publish, within one year after December 27, 1977, and from time to time thereafter, regulations providing guidelines for the disposal of sludge and the utilization of sludge for various purposes. Such regulations shall—

(A) identify uses for sludge, including disposal;

(B) specify factors to be taken into account in determining the measures and practices applicable to each such use or disposal (including publication of information on costs);

(C) identify concentrations of pollutants which interfere with each such use or disposal.

The Administrator is authorized to revise any regulation issued under this subsection.

(2) Identification and regulation of toxic pollutants

(A) On basis of available information

(i) Proposed regulations

Not later than November 30, 1986,[1] the Administrator shall identify those toxic pollutants which, on the basis of available information on their toxicity, persistence, concentration, mobility, or potential for exposure, may be present in sewage sludge in concentrations which may adversely affect public health or the environment, and propose regulations specifying acceptable management practices for sewage sludge containing each such toxic pollutant and establishing numerical limitations for each such pollutant for each use identified under paragraph (1)(A).

(ii) Final regulations

Not later than August 31, 1987, and after opportunity for public hearing, the Administrator shall promulgate the regulations required by subparagraph (A)(i).

(B) Others

(i) Proposed regulations

Not later than July 31, 1987, the Administrator shall identify those toxic pollutants not identified under subparagraph (A)(i) which may be present in sewage sludge in concentrations which may adversely affect public health or the environment, and propose regulations specifying acceptable management practices for sewage sludge containing each such toxic pollutant and establishing numerical limitations for each pollutant for each such use identified under paragraph (1)(A).

(ii) Final regulations

Not later than June 15, 1988, the Administrator shall promulgate the regulations required by subparagraph (B)(i).

(C) Review

From time to time, but not less often than every 2 years, the Administrator shall review the regulations promulgated under this paragraph for the purpose of identifying additional toxic pollutants and promulgating regulations for such pollutants consistent with the requirements of this paragraph.

(D) Minimum standards; compliance date

The management practices and numerical criteria established under subparagraphs (A), (B), and (C) shall be adequate to protect public health and the environment from any reasonably anticipated adverse effects of each pollutant. Such regulations shall require compliance as expeditiously as practicable but in no case later than 12 months after their publication, unless such regulations require the construction of new pollution control facilities, in which case the regulations shall require compliance as expeditiously as practicable but in no case later than two years from the date of their publication.

(3) Alternative standards

For purposes of this subsection, if, in the judgment of the Administrator, it is not feasible to prescribe or enforce a numerical limitation for a pollutant identified under paragraph (2), the Administrator may instead promulgate a design, equipment, management practice, or operational standard, or combination thereof, which in the Administrator's judgment is adequate to protect public health and the environment from any reasonably anticipated adverse effects of such pollutant. In the event the Administrator promulgates a design or equipment standard under this subsection, the Administrator shall include as part of such standard such requirements as will assure the proper operation and maintenance of any such element of design or equipment.

(4) Conditions on permits

Prior to the promulgation of the regulations required by paragraph (2), the Administrator shall impose conditions in permits issued to publicly owned treatment works under section 1342 of this title or take such other measures as the Administrator deems appropriate to protect public health and the environment from any adverse effects which may occur from toxic pollutants in sewage sludge.

(5) Limitation on statutory construction

Nothing in this section is intended to waive more stringent requirements established by this chapter or any other law.

(e) Manner of sludge disposal

The determination of the manner of disposal or use of sludge is a local determination, except that it shall be unlawful for any person to dispose of sludge from a publicly owned treatment works or any other treatment works treating domestic sewage for any use for which regulations have been established pursuant to subsection (d) of this section, except in accordance with such regulations.

(f) Implementation of regulations

(1) Through section 1342 permits

Any permit issued under section 1342 of this title to a publicly owned treatment works or any other treatment works treating domestic sewage shall include requirements for the use and disposal of sludge that implement the regulations established pursuant to subsection (d) of this section, unless such requirements have been included in a permit issued under the appropriate provisions of subtitle C of the Solid Waste Disposal Act [42 U.S.C.A. § 6921 et seq.], part C of the Safe Drinking Water Act [42 U.S.C.A. § 300h et seq.], the Marine Protection, Research, and Sanctuaries Act of 1972 [33 U.S.C.A. § 1401 et seq.], or the Clean Air Act [42 U.S.C.A. § 7401 et seq.], or under State permit programs approved by the Administrator, where the Administrator determines that such programs assure compliance with any applicable requirements of this section. Not later than December 15, 1986,[2] the Administrator shall promulgate procedures for approval of State programs pursuant to this paragraph.

(2) Through other permits

In the case of a treatment works described in paragraph (1) that is not subject to section 1342 of this title and to which none of the other above listed permit programs nor approved State permit authority apply, the Administrator may issue a permit to such treatment works solely to impose requirements for the use and disposal of sludge that implement the regulations established pursuant to subsection (d) of this section. The Administrator shall include in the permit appropriate requirements to assure compliance with the regulations established pursuant to subsection (d) of this section. The Administrator shall establish procedures for issuing permits pursuant to this paragraph.

(g) Studies and projects

(1) Grant program; information gathering

The Administrator is authorized to conduct or initiate scientific studies, demonstration projects, and public information and education projects which are designed to promote the safe and beneficial management or use of sewage sludge for such purposes as aiding the restoration of abandoned mine sites, conditioning soil for parks and recreation areas, agricultural and horticultural uses, and other beneficial purposes. For the purposes of carrying out this subsection, the Administrator may make grants to State water pollution control agencies, other public or nonprofit agencies, institutions, organizations, and individuals. In cooperation with other Federal departments and agencies, other public and private agencies, institutions, and organizations, the Administrator is authorized to collect and disseminate information pertaining to the safe and beneficial use of sewage sludge.

(2) Authorization of appropriations

For the purposes of carrying out the scientific studies, demonstration projects, and public information and education projects authorized in this section, there is authorized to be appropriated for fiscal years beginning after September 30, 1986, not to exceed $5,000,000.

(June 30, 1948, c. 758, Title IV, § 405, as added by Pub. L. No. 92–500, § 2, 86 Stat. 884 (Oct. 18, 1972); and amended by Pub. L. No. 95–217, §§ 54(d), 68, 91 Stat. 1591, 1606 (Dec. 27, 1977); Pub. L. No. 100–4, Title IV, § 406(a)–(c), (f), 101 Stat. 71, 72, 74 (Feb. 4, 1987).)

[1] So in original. Subsec. (d)(2) was enacted by Pub. L. No. 100–4, which was approved Feb. 4, 1987.

[2] So in original. Subsec. (f) was enacted by Pub. L. No. 100–4, which was approved Feb. 4, 1987.

HISTORICAL AND STATUTORY NOTES

References in Text

The Solid Waste Disposal Act, referred to in subsec. (f)(1), is Title II of Pub. L. No. 89–272, Oct. 20, 1965, 79 Stat. 997, as amended generally by Pub. L. No. 94–580, § 2, Oct. 21, 1976, 90 Stat. 2795. Subtitle C of the Solid Waste Disposal Act is codified generally to subchapter III (section 6921 et seq.) of chapter 82 of Title 42, The Public Health and Welfare. For complete classification of this Act to the Code, see Short Title note set out under section 6901 of Title 42 and Tables.

The Safe Drinking Water Act, referred to in subsec. (f)(1), is Pub. L. No. 93–523, Dec. 16, 1974, 88 Stat. 1660, as amended. Part C of the Safe Drinking Water Act is codified generally to part C (section 300h et seq.) of subchapter XII of chapter 6A of Title 42, The Public Health and Welfare. For complete classification of this Act to the Code, see Short Title of 1974 Amendments note set out under section 201 of Title 42 and Tables.

The Marine Protection, Research, and Sanctuaries Act of 1972, referred to in subsec. (f)(1), is Pub. L. No. 92–532, Oct. 23, 1972, 86 Stat. 1052, as amended, which is codified principally to chapter 27 (section 1401 et seq.) of this title. For complete classification of this Act to the Code, see Short Title note set out under section 1401 of this title and Tables.

The Clean Air Act, referred to in subsec. (f)(1), is Act of July 14, 1955, c. 360, as amended generally by Pub. L. No. 88–206, Dec. 17, 1963, 77 Stat. 392, and later by Pub. L. No. 95–95, Aug. 7, 1977, 91 Stat. 685. The Clean Air Act was originally codified as chapter 15B (section 1857 et seq.) of Title 42, The Public Health and Welfare. On enactment of Pub. L. No. 95–95, the Act was recodified as chapter 85 (section 7401 et seq.) of Title 42. For complete classification of this Act to the Code, see short Title note set out under section 7401 of Title 42 and Tables.

Removal Credits

Pub. L. No. 100–4, § 406(e), 101 Stat. 7 (Feb. 4, 1987), provided that:

"The part of the decision of Natural Resources Defense Council, Inc. v. U.S. Environmental Protection Agency, No. 84–3530 (3d Cir.1986), which addresses section 405(d) of the Federal Water Pollution Control Act [subsec. (d) of this section] is stayed until August 31, 1987, with respect to—

"(1) those publicly owned treatment works the owner or operator of which received authority to revise pretreatment requirements under section 307(b)(1) of such Act [section 1317(b)(1) of this title] before the date of the enactment of this section [Feb. 4, 1987], and

"(2) those publicly owned treatment works the owner or operator of which has submitted an application for authority to revise pretreatment requirements under such section 307(b)(1) [section 1317(b)(1) of this title] which application is pending on such date of enactment [Feb. 4, 1987] and is approved before August 31, 1987.

The Administrator shall not authorize any other removal credits under such Act [this chapter] until the Administrator issues the regulations required by paragraph (2)(A)(ii) of section 405(d) of such Act, as amended by subsection (a) of this section [subsec. (d)(2)(A)(ii) of this section]."

§ 1346. Coastal recreation water quality monitoring and notification [FWPCA § 406]

(a) Monitoring and notification

(1) In general

Not later than 18 months after October 10, 2000, after consultation and in cooperation with appropriate Federal, State, tribal, and local officials (including local health officials), and after providing public notice and an opportunity for comment, the Administrator shall publish performance criteria for—

(A) monitoring and assessment (including specifying available methods for monitoring) of coastal recreation waters adjacent to beaches or similar points of access that are used by the public for attainment of applicable water quality standards for pathogens and pathogen indicators; and

(B) the prompt notification of the public, local governments, and the Administrator of any exceeding of or likelihood of exceeding applicable water quality standards for coastal recreation waters described in subparagraph (A).

(2) Level of protection

The performance criteria referred to in paragraph (1) shall provide that the activities described in subparagraphs (A) and (B) of that paragraph shall be carried out as necessary for the protection of public health and safety.

(b) Program development and implementation grants

(1) In general

The Administrator may make grants to States and local governments to develop and implement programs for monitoring and notification for coastal recreation waters adjacent to beaches or similar points of access that are used by the public.

(2) Limitations

(A) In general

The Administrator may award a grant to a State or a local government to implement a monitoring and notification program if—

(i) the program is consistent with the performance criteria published by the Administrator under subsection (a) of this section;

(ii) the State or local government prioritizes the use of grant funds for particular coastal recreation waters based on the use of the water and the risk to human health presented by pathogens or pathogen indicators;

(iii) the State or local government makes available to the Administrator the factors used to prioritize the use of funds under clause (ii);

(iv) the State or local government provides a list of discrete areas of coastal recreation waters that are subject to the program for monitoring and notification for which the grant is provided that specifies any coastal recreation waters for which fiscal constraints will prevent consistency with the performance criteria under subsection (a) of this section; and

(v) the public is provided an opportunity to review the program through a process that provides for public notice and an opportunity for comment.

(B) Grants to local governments

The Administrator may make a grant to a local government under this subsection for implementation of a monitoring and notification program only if, after the 1-year period beginning on the date of publication of performance criteria under subsection (a)(1) of this section, the Administrator determines that the State is not implementing a program that meets the requirements of this subsection, regardless of whether the State has received a grant under this subsection.

(3) Other requirements

(A) Report

A State recipient of a grant under this subsection shall submit to the Administrator, in such format and at such intervals as the Administrator determines to be appropriate, a report that describes—

(i) data collected as part of the program for monitoring and notification as described in subsection (c) of this section; and

(ii) actions taken to notify the public when water quality standards are exceeded.

(B) Delegation

A State recipient of a grant under this subsection shall identify each local government to which the State has delegated or intends to delegate responsibility for implementing a monitoring and notification program consistent with the performance criteria published under subsection (a) of this section (including any coastal recreation waters for which the authority to implement a monitoring and notification program would be subject to the delegation).

(4) Federal share

(A) In general

The Administrator, through grants awarded under this section, may pay up to 100 percent of the costs of developing and implementing a program for monitoring and notification under this subsection.

(B) Non-Federal share

The non-Federal share of the costs of developing and implementing a monitoring and notification program may be—

(i) in an amount not to exceed 50 percent, as determined by the Administrator in consultation with State, tribal, and local government representatives; and

(ii) provided in cash or in kind.

(c) Content of State and local government programs

As a condition of receipt of a grant under subsection (b) of this section, a State or local government program for monitoring and notification under this section shall identify—

(1) lists of coastal recreation waters in the State, including coastal recreation waters adjacent to beaches or similar points of access that are used by the public;

(2) in the case of a State program for monitoring and notification, the process by which the State may delegate to local governments responsibility for implementing the monitoring and notification program;

(3) the frequency and location of monitoring and assessment of coastal recreation waters based on—

(A) the periods of recreational use of the waters;

(B) the nature and extent of use during certain periods;

(C) the proximity of the waters to known point sources and nonpoint sources of pollution; and

(D) any effect of storm events on the waters;

(4) **(A)** the methods to be used for detecting levels of pathogens and pathogen indicators that are harmful to human health; and

(B) the assessment procedures for identifying short-term increases in pathogens and pathogen indicators that are harmful to human health in coastal recreation waters (including increases in relation to storm events);

(5) measures for prompt communication of the occurrence, nature, location, pollutants involved, and extent of any exceeding of, or likelihood of exceeding, applicable water quality standards for pathogens and pathogen indicators to—

(A) the Administrator, in such form as the Administrator determines to be appropriate; and

(B) a designated official of a local government having jurisdiction over land adjoining the coastal recreation waters for which the failure to meet applicable standards is identified;

(6) measures for the posting of signs at beaches or similar points of access, or functionally equivalent communication measures that are sufficient to give notice to the public that the coastal recreation waters are not meeting or are not expected to meet applicable water quality standards for pathogens and pathogen indicators; and

(7) measures that inform the public of the potential risks associated with water contact activities in the coastal recreation waters that do not meet applicable water quality standards.

(d) Federal agency programs

Not later than 3 years after October 10, 2000, each Federal agency that has jurisdiction over coastal recreation waters adjacent to beaches or similar points of access that are used by the public shall develop and implement, through a process that provides for public notice and an opportunity for comment, a monitoring and notification program for the coastal recreation waters that—

(1) protects the public health and safety;

(2) is consistent with the performance criteria published under subsection (a) of this section;

(3) includes a completed report on the information specified in subsection (b)(3)(A) of this section, to be submitted to the Administrator; and

(4) addresses the matters specified in subsection (c) of this section.

(e) Database

The Administrator shall establish, maintain, and make available to the public by electronic and other means a national coastal recreation water pollution occurrence database that provides—

(1) the data reported to the Administrator under subsections (b)(3)(A)(i) and (d)(3) of this section; and

(2) other information concerning pathogens and pathogen indicators in coastal recreation waters that—

(A) is made available to the Administrator by a State or local government, from a coastal water quality monitoring program of the State or local government; and

(B) the Administrator determines should be included.

(f) Technical assistance for monitoring floatable material

The Administrator shall provide technical assistance to States and local governments for the development of assessment and monitoring procedures for floatable material to protect public health and safety in coastal recreation waters.

(g) List of waters

(1) In general

Beginning not later than 18 months after the date of publication of performance criteria under subsection (a) of this section, based on information made available to the Administrator, the Administrator shall identify, and maintain a list of, discrete coastal recreation waters adjacent to beaches or similar points of access that are used by the public that—

(A) specifies any waters described in this paragraph that are subject to a monitoring and notification program consistent with the performance criteria established under subsection (a) of this section; and

(B) specifies any waters described in this paragraph for which there is no monitoring and notification program (including waters for which fiscal constraints will prevent the State or the Administrator from performing monitoring and notification consistent with the performance criteria established under subsection (a) of this section).

(2) Availability

The Administrator shall make the list described in paragraph (1) available to the public through—

(A) publication in the Federal Register; and

(B) electronic media.

(3) Updates

The Administrator shall update the list described in paragraph (1) periodically as new information becomes available.

(h) EPA implementation

In the case of a State that has no program for monitoring and notification that is consistent with the performance criteria published under subsection (a) of this section after the last day of the 3-year period beginning on the date on which the Administrator lists waters in the State under subsection (g)(1)(B) of this section, the Administrator shall conduct a monitoring and notification program for the listed waters based on a priority ranking established by the Administrator using funds appropriated for grants under subsection (i) of this section—

(1) to conduct monitoring and notification; and

(2) for related salaries, expenses, and travel.

(i) Authorization of appropriations

There is authorized to be appropriated for making grants under subsection (b) of this section, including implementation of monitoring and notification programs by the Administrator under subsection (h), $30,000,000 for each of fiscal years 2001 through 2005.

(June 30, 1948, c. 758, Title IV, § 406, as added by Pub. L. No. 106–284, § 4, 114 Stat. 872 (Oct. 10, 2000).)

SUBCHAPTER V—GENERAL PROVISIONS

§ 1361. Administration

[FWPCA § 501]

(a) Authority of Administrator to prescribe regulations

The Administrator is authorized to prescribe such regulations as are necessary to carry out his functions under this chapter.

(b) Utilization of other agency officers and employees

The Administrator, with the consent of the head of any other agency of the United States, may utilize such officers and employees of such agency as may be found necessary to assist in carrying out the purposes of this chapter.

(c) Recordkeeping

Each recipient of financial assistance under this chapter shall keep such records as the Administrator shall prescribe, including records which fully disclose the amount and disposition by such recipient of the proceeds of such assistance, the total cost of the project or undertaking in connection with which such assistance is given or used, and the amount of that portion of the cost of the project or undertaking supplied by other sources, and such other records as will facilitate effective audit.

(d) Audit

The Administrator and the Comptroller General of the United States, or any of their duly authorized representatives, shall have access, for the purpose of audit and examination, to any books, documents, papers, and records of the recipients that are pertinent to the grants received under this chapter. For the purpose of carrying out audits and examinations with respect to recipients of Federal assistance under this chapter, the Administrator is authorized to enter into noncompetitive procurement contracts with independent State audit organizations, consistent with chapter 75 of Title 31. Such contracts may only be entered into to the extent and in such amounts as may be provided in advance in appropriation Acts.

(e) Awards for outstanding technological achievement or innovative processes, methods, or devices in waste treatment and pollution abatement programs

(1) It is the purpose of this subsection to authorize a program which will provide official recognition by the United States Government to those industrial organizations and political subdivisions of States which during the preceding year demonstrated an outstanding technological achievement or an innovative process, method, or device in their waste treatment and pollution abatement programs. The Administrator shall, in consultation with the appropriate State water pollution control agencies, establish regulations under which such recognition may be applied for and granted, except that no applicant shall be eligible for an award under this subsection if such applicant is not in total compliance with all applicable water quality requirements under this chapter, or otherwise does not have a satisfactory record with respect to environmental quality.

(2) The Administrator shall award a certificate or plaque of suitable design to each industrial organization or political subdivision which qualifies for such recognition under regulations established under this subsection.

(3) The President of the United States, the Governor of the appropriate State, the Speaker of the House of Representatives, and the President pro tempore of the Senate shall be notified of the award by the Administrator and the awarding of such recognition shall be published in the Federal Register.

(f) Detail of Environmental Protection Agency personnel to State water pollution control agencies

Upon the request of a State water pollution control agency, personnel of the Environmental Protection Agency may be detailed to such agency for the purpose of carrying out the provisions of this chapter.

(June 30, 1948, c. 758, Title V, § 501, as added by Pub. L. No. 92–500, § 2, 86 Stat. 885 (Oct. 18, 1972); and amended by Pub. L. No. 100–4, Title V, § 501, 101 Stat. 75 (Feb. 4, 1987).)

HISTORICAL AND STATUTORY NOTES

Environmental Court Feasibility Study

Pub. L. No. 92–500, § 9, 86 Stat. 816 (Oct. 18, 1972), authorized the President, acting through the Attorney General, to study the feasibility of establishing a separate court or court system with jurisdiction over environmental matters and required him to report the results of his study, together with his recommendations, to Congress not later than one year after Oct. 18, 1972.

Transfer of Public Health Service Officers

Pub. L. No. 89–234, § 2(b) to (k), 79 Stat. 903 (Oct. 2, 1965), authorized the transfer of certain commissioned officers of the Public Health Service to codified positions in the Federal Water Pollution Control Administration, now the Environmental Protection Agency, where such transfer was requested within six months after the establishment of the Administration and made certain administrative provisions relating to pension and retirement rights of the transferees, sick leave benefits, group life insurance, and certain other miscellaneous provisions.

Applicability of Spill Prevention, Control, and Countermeasure Rule

Pub. L. No. 113–121, § 1049, 128 Stat. 1257–58 (June 10, 2014), as amended by Pub. L. No. 114–322, § 5011, 130 Stat 1902 (Dec. 16, 2016), provided that:

"(a) **Definitions.**—In this section:

"(1) **Administrator.**—The term "Administrator" means the Administrator of the Environmental Protection Agency.

"(2) **Farm.**—The term "farm" has the meaning given the term in section 112.2 of title 40, Code of Federal Regulations (or successor regulations).

"(3) **Gallon.**—The term "gallon" means a United States gallon.

"(4) **Oil.**—The term "oil" has the meaning given the term in section 112.2 of title 40, Code of Federal Regulations (or successor regulations).

"(5) **Oil Discharge.**—The term "oil discharge" has the meaning given the term "discharge" in section 112.2 of title 40, Code of Federal Regulations (or successor regulations).

"(6) **Reportable Oil Discharge History.**—

"(A) **In General.**—Subject to subparagraph (B), the term "reportable oil discharge history" means a single oil discharge, as described in section 112.1(b) of title 40, Code of Federal Regulations (including successor regulations), that exceeds 1,000 gallons or 2 oil discharges, as described in section 112.1(b) of title 40, Code of Federal Regulations (including successor regulations), that each exceed 42 gallons within any 12-month period—

"(i) in the 3 years prior to the certification date of the Spill Prevention, Control, and Countermeasure plan (as described in section 112.3 of title 40, Code of Federal Regulations (including successor regulations); or

"(ii) since becoming subject to part 112 of title 40, Code of Federal Regulations, if the facility has been in operation for less than 3 years.

"(B) **Exclusions.**—The term "reportable oil discharge history" does not include an oil discharge, as described in section 112.1(b) of title 40, Code of Federal Regulations (including successor regulations), that is the result of a natural disaster, an act of war, or terrorism.

"(7) **Spill Prevention, Control, and Countermeasure Rule.**—The term "Spill Prevention, Control, and Countermeasure rule" means the regulation, including amendments, promulgated by the Administrator under part 112 of title 40, Code of Federal Regulations (or successor regulations).

"(b) **Certification.**—In implementing the Spill Prevention, Control, and Countermeasure rule with respect to any farm, the Administrator shall—

"(1) require certification by a professional engineer for a farm with—

"(A) an individual tank with an aboveground storage capacity greater than 10,000 gallons;

"(B) an aggregate aboveground storage capacity greater than or equal to 20,000 gallons; or

"(C) a reportable oil discharge history; or

"(2) allow certification by the owner or operator of the farm (via self-certification) for a farm with—

"(A) an aggregate aboveground storage capacity less than 20,000 gallons and greater than the lesser of—

"(i) 6,000 gallons; and

"(ii) the adjustment quantity established under subsection (d)(2); and

"(B) no reportable oil discharge history; and

"(3) not require compliance with the rule by any farm—

"(A) with an aggregate aboveground storage capacity greater than 2,500 gallons and less than the lesser of—

"(i) 6,000 gallons; and

"(ii) the adjustment quantity established under subsection (d)(2); and

"(B) no reportable oil discharge history; and

"(4) not require compliance with the rule by any farm with an aggregate aboveground storage capacity of less than 2,500 gallons.

"(c) Regulation of aboveground storage at farms.—

"(1) **Calculation of aggregate aboveground storage capacity.**—For purposes of subsection (b), the aggregate aboveground storage capacity of a farm excludes—

"(A) all containers on separate parcels that have a capacity that is 1,000 gallons or less; and

"(B) all containers holding animal feed ingredients approved for use in livestock feed by the Commissioner of Food and Drugs.

"(2) **Certain farm containers.**—Part 112 of title 40, Code of Federal Regulations (or successor regulations), shall not apply to the following containers located at a farm:

"(A) Containers on a separate parcel that have—

"(i) an individual capacity of not greater than 1,000 gallons; and

"(ii) an aggregate capacity of not greater than 2,500 gallons.

"(B) A container holding animal feed ingredients approved for use in livestock feed by the Food and Drug Administration."

"(d) Study.—

"(1) **In General.**—Not later than 1 year after the date of enactment of this Act, the Administrator, in consultation with the Secretary of Agriculture, shall conduct a study to determine the appropriate exemption under paragraphs (2) and (3) of subsection (b), which shall be not more than 6,000 gallons and not less than 2,500 gallons, based on a significant risk of discharge to water.

"(2) **Adjustment.**—Not later than 18 months after the date on which the study described in paragraph (1) is complete, the Administrator, in consultation with the Secretary of Agriculture, shall promulgate a rule to adjust the exemption levels described in paragraphs (2) and (3) of subsection (b) in accordance with the study."

§ 1362. Definitions

[FWPCA § 502]

Except as otherwise specifically provided, when used in this chapter:

(1) The term "State water pollution control agency" means the State agency designated by the Governor having responsibility for enforcing State laws relating to the abatement of pollution.

(2) The term "interstate agency" means an agency of two or more States established by or pursuant to an agreement or compact approved by the Congress, or any other agency of two or more States, having substantial powers or duties pertaining to the control of pollution as determined and approved by the Administrator.

(3) The term "State" means a State, the District of Columbia, the Commonwealth of Puerto Rico, the Virgin Islands, Guam, American Samoa, the Commonwealth of the Northern Mariana Islands, and the Trust Territory of the Pacific Islands.

(4) The term "municipality" means a city, town, borough, county, parish, district, association, or other public body created by or pursuant to State law and having jurisdiction over disposal of sewage, industrial wastes, or other wastes, or an Indian tribe or an authorized Indian tribal organization, or a designated and approved management agency under section 1288 of this title.

(5) The term "person" means an individual, corporation, partnership, association, State, municipality, commission, or political subdivision of a State, or any interstate body.

(6) The term "pollutant" means dredged spoil, solid waste, incinerator residue, sewage, garbage, sewage sludge, munitions, chemical wastes, biological materials, radioactive materials, heat, wrecked or discarded equipment, rock, sand, cellar dirt and industrial, municipal, and agricultural waste discharged into water. This term does not mean (A) "sewage from vessels or a discharge incidental to the normal operation of a vessel of the Armed Forces" within the meaning of section 1322 of this title; or (B) water, gas, or other material which is injected into a well to facilitate production of oil or gas, or water derived in association with oil or gas production and disposed of in a well, if the well used either to facilitate production or for disposal purposes is approved by authority of the State in which the well is located, and if such State determines that such injection or disposal will not result in the degradation of ground or surface water resources.

(7) The term "navigable waters" means the waters of the United States, including the territorial seas.

(8) The term "territorial seas" means the belt of the seas measured from the line of ordinary low water along that portion of the coast which is in direct contact with the open sea and the line marking the seaward limit of inland waters, and extending seaward a distance of three miles.

(9) The term "contiguous zone" means the entire zone established or to be established by the United States under article 24 of the Convention of the Territorial Sea and the Contiguous Zone.

(10) The term "ocean" means any portion of the high seas beyond the contiguous zone.

(11) The term "effluent limitation" means any restriction established by a State or the Administrator on quantities, rates, and concentrations of chemical, physical, biological, and other constituents which are discharged from point sources into navigable waters, the waters of the contiguous zone, or the ocean, including schedules of compliance.

(12) The term "discharge of a pollutant" and the term "discharge of pollutants" each means (A) any addition of any pollutant to navigable waters from any point source, (B) any addition of any pollutant to the waters of the contiguous zone or the ocean from any point source other than a vessel or other floating craft.

(13) The term "toxic pollutant" means those pollutants, or combinations of pollutants, including disease-causing agents, which after discharge and upon exposure, ingestion, inhalation or assimilation into any organism, either directly from the environment or indirectly by ingestion through food chains, will, on the basis of information available to the Administrator, cause death, disease, behavioral abnormalities, cancer, genetic mutations, physiological malfunctions (including malfunctions in reproduction) or physical deformations, in such organisms or their offspring.

(14) The term "point source" means any discernible, confined and discrete conveyance, including but not limited to any pipe, ditch, channel, tunnel, conduit, well, discrete fissure, container, rolling stock, concentrated animal feeding operation, or vessel or other floating craft, from which pollutants are or may be discharged. This term does not include agricultural stormwater discharges and return flows from irrigated agriculture.

(15) The term "biological monitoring" shall mean the determination of the effects on aquatic life, including accumulation of pollutants in tissue, in receiving waters due to the discharge of pollutants (A) by techniques and procedures, including sampling of organisms representative of appropriate levels of the food chain appropriate to the volume and the physical, chemical, and biological characteristics of the effluent, and (B) at appropriate frequencies and locations.

(16) The term "discharge" when used without qualification includes a discharge of a pollutant, and a discharge of pollutants.

(17) The term "schedule of compliance" means a schedule of remedial measures including an enforceable sequence of actions or operations leading to compliance with an effluent limitation, other limitation, prohibition, or standard.

(18) The term "industrial user" means those industries identified in the Standard Industrial Classification Manual, Bureau of the Budget, 1967, as amended and supplemented, under the category of "Division D—Manufacturing" and such other classes of significant waste producers as, by regulation, the Administrator deems appropriate.

(19) The term "pollution" means the man-made or man-induced alteration of the chemical, physical, biological, and radiological integrity of water.

(20) The term "medical waste" means isolation wastes; infectious agents; human blood and blood products; pathological wastes; sharps; body parts; contaminated bedding; surgical wastes and potentially contaminated laboratory wastes; dialysis wastes; and such additional medical items as the Administrator shall prescribe by regulation.

(21) Coastal recreation waters

(A) In general

The term "coastal recreation waters" means—

(i) the Great Lakes; and

(ii) marine coastal waters (including coastal estuaries) that are designated under section 1313(c) of this title by a State for use for swimming, bathing, surfing, or similar water contact activities.

(B) Exclusions

The term "coastal recreation waters" does not include—

(i) inland waters; or

(ii) waters upstream of the mouth of a river or stream having an unimpaired natural connection with the open sea.

(22) Floatable material

(A) In general

The term "floatable material" means any foreign matter that may float or remain suspended in the water column.

(B) Inclusions

The term "floatable material" includes—

(i) plastic;

(ii) aluminum cans;

(iii) wood products;

(iv) bottles; and

(v) paper products.

(23) Pathogen indicator

The term "pathogen indicator" means a substance that indicates the potential for human infectious disease.

(24) Oil and gas exploration and production

The term "oil and gas exploration, production, processing, or treatment operations or transmission facilities" means all field activities or operations associated with exploration, production, processing, or treatment operations, or transmission facilities, including activities necessary to prepare a site for drilling and for the movement and placement of drilling equipment, whether or not such field activities or operations may be considered to be construction activities.

(25) Recreational vessel

(A) In general

The term "recreational vessel" means any vessel that is—

(i) manufactured or used primarily for pleasure; or

(ii) leased, rented, or chartered to a person for the pleasure of that person.

(B) Exclusion

The term "recreational vessel" does not include a vessel that is subject to Coast Guard inspection and that—

(i) is engaged in commercial use; or

(ii) carries paying passengers.

(26) Treatment works

The term "treatment works" has the meaning given the term in section 212.

(27) Green infrastructure.—The term 'green infrastructure' means the range of measures that use plant or soil systems, permeable pavement or other permeable surfaces or substrates, stormwater harvest and reuse, or landscaping to store, infiltrate, or evapotranspirate stormwater and reduce flows to sewer systems or to surface waters.

(June 30, 1948, c. 758, Title V, § 502, as added by Pub. L. No. 92–500, § 2, 86 Stat. 886 (Oct. 18, 1972); and amended by Pub. L. No. 95–217, § 33(b), 91 Stat. 1577 (Dec. 27, 1977); Pub. L. No. 100–4, Title V, §§ 502(a), 503, 101 Stat. 75 (Feb. 4, 1987); Pub. L. No. 100–688, Title III, § 3202(a), 102 Stat. 4154 (Nov. 18, 1988); Pub. L. No. 104–106, Div. A, Title III, § 325(c)(3), 110 Stat. 259 (Feb. 10, 1996); Pub. L. No. 106–284, § 5, 114 Stat. 875 (Oct. 10, 2000); Pub. L. No. 109–58, Title III, § 323, 119 Stat. 694 (Aug. 8, 2005); Pub. L. No. 110–288, § 3, 122 Stat. 2650 (July 29, 2008); Pub. L. No. 113–121, § 5012(b), 128 Stat. 1328 (June 10, 2014); Pub. L. No. 115–436, § 5(a), 132 Stat. 5558, 5561 (Jan. 14, 2019).)

HISTORICAL AND STATUTORY NOTES

Termination of Trust Territory of the Pacific Islands

For termination of Trust Territory of the Pacific Islands, see note set out preceding 48 U.S.C.A. § 1681.

Territorial Sea and Contiguous Zone of United States

For extension of territorial sea and contiguous zone of United States, see Proc. No. 5928 and Proc. No. 7219, respectively, set out as notes under 43 U.S.C.A. § 1331.

Term "Point Source" to Include Landfill Leachate Collection System

Pub. L. No. 100–4, § 507, 101 Stat. 7 (Feb. 4, 1987), provided that: "For purposes of the Federal Water Pollution Control Act [this chapter], the term 'point source' includes a landfill leachate collection system."

§ 1363. Water Pollution Control Advisory Board

[FWPCA § 503]

(a) Establishment; composition; terms of office

(1) There is hereby established in the Environmental Protection Agency a Water Pollution Control Advisory Board, composed of the Administrator or his designee, who shall be Chairman, and nine members appointed by the President, none of whom shall be Federal officers or employees. The appointed members, having due regard for the purposes of this chapter, shall be selected from among representatives of various State, interstate, and local governmental agencies, of public or private interests contributing to, affected by, or concerned with pollution, and of other public and private agencies, organizations, or groups demonstrating an active interest in the field of pollution prevention and control, as well as other individuals who are expert in this field.

(2) (A) Each member appointed by the President shall hold office for a term of three years, except that (i) any member appointed to fill a vacancy occurring prior to the expiration of the term for which his predecessor was appointed shall be appointed for the remainder of such term, and (ii) the terms of office of the members first taking office after June 30, 1956, shall expire as follows: three at the end of one year after such date, three at the end of two years after such date, and three at the end of three years after such date, as designated by the President at the time of appointment, and (iii) the term of any member under the preceding provisions shall be extended until the date on which his successor's appointment is effective. None of the members appointed by the President shall be eligible for reappointment within one year after the end of his preceding term.

(B) The members of the Board who are not officers or employees of the United States, while attending conferences or meetings of the Board or while serving at the request of the Administrator, shall be entitled to receive compensation at a rate to be fixed by the Administrator, but not exceeding $100 per diem, including travel-time, and while away from their homes or regular places of business they may be allowed travel expenses, including per diem in lieu of subsistence, as authorized by law for persons in the Government service employed intermittently.

(b) Functions

The Board shall advise, consult with, and make recommendations to the Administrator on matters of policy relating to the activities and functions of the Administrator under this chapter.

(c) Clerical and technical assistance

Such clerical and technical assistance as may be necessary to discharge the duties of the Board shall be provided from the personnel of the Environmental Protection Agency.

(June 30, 1948, c. 758, Title V, § 503, as added by Pub. L. No. 92–500, § 2, 86 Stat. 887 (Oct. 18, 1972).)

HISTORICAL AND STATUTORY NOTES

References in Text

Travel expenses, including per diem in lieu of subsistence as authorized by law, referred to in subsec. (a)(2)(B), probably means the allowances authorized by section 5703 of Title 5, Government Organization and Employees.

Continuation of Term of Office

Pub. L. No. 87–88, § 6(c), 75 Stat. 207 (July 20, 1961), provided that members of the Water Pollution Control Advisory Board holding office immediately preceding July 20, 1961 were to remain in office as members of the Board as established by section 6(a) of Pub. L. No. 87–88 until the expiration of the terms of office for which they were originally appointed.

Terms of Office of Members of Water Pollution Control Advisory Board

Act of July 9, 1956, c. 518, § 3, 70 Stat. 507, provided that the terms of office of members of the Water Pollution Control Advisory Board, holding office on July 9, 1956, were to terminate at the close of business on that date.

Termination of Advisory Boards

Advisory Boards in existence on Jan. 5, 1973, to terminate not later than the expiration of the two-year period following Jan. 5, 1973, unless, in the case of a board established by the President or an officer of the Federal Government, such board is renewed by appropriate action prior to the expiration of such two-year period, or in the case of a Board established by the Congress, its duration is otherwise provided for by law, see sections 3(2) and 14 of Pub. L. No. 92–463, 86 Stat. 770, 776 (Oct. 6, 1972), set out in Appendix 2 to Title 5, Government Organization and Employees.

§ 1364. Emergency powers

[FWPCA § 504]

(a) Emergency powers

Notwithstanding any other provision of this chapter, the Administrator upon receipt of evidence that a pollution source or combination of sources is presenting an imminent and substantial endangerment to the health of persons or to the welfare of persons where such endangerment is to the livelihood of such persons, such as inability to market shellfish, may bring suit on behalf of the United States in the appropriate district court to immediately restrain any person causing or contributing to the alleged pollution to stop the discharge of pollutants causing or contributing to such pollution or to take such other action as may be necessary.

(b) Repealed. Pub. L. No. 96–510, Title III, § 304(a), 94 Stat. 2809 (Dec. 11, 1980)

(June 30, 1948, c. 758, Title V, § 504, as added by Pub. L. No. 92–500, § 2, 86 Stat. 888 (Oct. 18, 1972); and amended by Pub. L. No. 95–217, § 69, 91 Stat. 1607 (Dec. 27, 1977); Pub. L. No. 96–510, Title III, § 304(a), 94 Stat. 2809 (Dec. 11, 1980).)

HISTORICAL AND STATUTORY NOTES

Effective and Applicability Provisions

1980 Acts. Amendment by Pub. L. No. 96–510 effective Dec. 11, 1980, see section 9652 of Title 42, The Public Health and Welfare.

§ 1365. Citizen suits

[FWPCA § 505]

(a) Authorization; jurisdiction

Except as provided in subsection (b) of this section and section 1319(g)(6) of this title, any citizen may commence a civil action on his own behalf—

(1) against any person (including (i) the United States, and (ii) any other governmental instrumentality or agency to the extent permitted by the eleventh amendment to the Constitution) who is alleged to be in violation of (A) an effluent standard or limitation under this chapter or (B) an order issued by the Administrator or a State with respect to such a standard or limitation, or

(2) against the Administrator where there is alleged a failure of the Administrator to perform any act or duty under this chapter which is not discretionary with the Administrator.

The district courts shall have jurisdiction, without regard to the amount in controversy or the citizenship of the parties, to enforce such an effluent standard or limitation, or such an order, or to order the Administrator to perform such act or duty, as the case may be, and to apply any appropriate civil penalties under section 1319(d) of this title.

(b) Notice

No action may be commenced—

(1) under subsection (a)(1) of this section—

(A) prior to sixty days after the plaintiff has given notice of the alleged violation (i) to the Administrator, (ii) to the State in which the alleged violation occurs, and (iii) to any alleged violator of the standard, limitation, or order, or

(B) if the Administrator or State has commenced and is diligently prosecuting a civil or criminal action in a court of the United States, or a State to require compliance with the standard, limitation, or order, but in any such action in a court of the United States any citizen may intervene as a matter of right.

(2) under subsection (a)(2) of this section prior to sixty days after the plaintiff has given notice of such action to the Administrator, except that such action may be brought immediately after such notification in the case of an action under this section respecting a violation of sections 1316 and 1317(a) of this title. Notice under this subsection shall be given in such manner as the Administrator shall prescribe by regulation.

(c) Venue; intervention by Administrator; United States interests protected

(1) Any action respecting a violation by a discharge source of an effluent standard or limitation or an order respecting such standard or limitation may be brought under this section only in the judicial district in which such source is located.

(2) In such action under this section, the Administrator, if not a party, may intervene as a matter of right.

(3) Protection of interests of United States

Whenever any action is brought under this section in a court of the United States, the plaintiff shall serve a copy of the complaint on the Attorney General and the Administrator. No consent judgment shall be entered in an action in which the United States is not a party prior to 45 days following the receipt of a copy of the proposed consent judgment by the Attorney General and the Administrator.

(d) Litigation costs

The court, in issuing any final order in any action brought pursuant to this section, may award costs of litigation (including reasonable attorney and expert witness fees) to any prevailing or substantially prevailing party, whenever the court determines such award is appropriate. The court may, if a temporary restraining order or preliminary injunction is sought, require the filing of a bond or equivalent security in accordance with the Federal Rules of Civil Procedure.

(e) Statutory or common law rights not restricted

Nothing in this section shall restrict any right which any person (or class of persons) may have under any statute or common law to seek enforcement of any effluent standard or limitation or to seek any other relief (including relief against the Administrator or a State agency).

(f) Effluent standard or limitation

For purposes of this section, the term "effluent standard or limitation under this chapter" means (1) effective July 1, 1973, an unlawful act under subsection (a) of section 1311 of this title; (2) an effluent limitation or other limitation under section 1311 or 1312 of this title; (3) standard of performance under section 1316 of this title; (4) prohibition, effluent standard or pretreatment standards under section 1317 of this title; (5) a standard of performance or requirement under section 1322(p); (6) a certification under section 1341; (7) a permit or condition of a permit issued under section 1342 that is in effect under this Act (including a requirement applicable by reason of section 1323); or (8) a regulation under section 1345(d).

(g) "Citizen" defined

For the purposes of this section the term "citizen" means a person or persons having an interest which is or may be adversely affected.

(h) Civil action by State Governors

A Governor of a State may commence a civil action under subsection (a) of this section, without regard to the limitations of subsection (b) of this section, against the Administrator where there is alleged a failure of the Administrator to enforce an effluent standard or limitation under this chapter the violation of which is occurring in another State and is causing an adverse effect on the public health or welfare in his State, or is causing a violation of any water quality requirement in his State.

(June 30, 1948, c. 758, Title V, § 505, as added by Pub. L. No. 92–500, § 2, 86 Stat. 888 (Oct. 18, 1972); and amended by Pub. L. No. 100–4, Title III, § 314(c), Title IV, § 406(d)(2), Title V, §§ 504, 505(c), 101 Stat. 49, 73, 75, 76 (Feb. 4, 1987); Pub. L. No. 115–282, § 903(c)(2)(D), 132 Stat. 4192, 4356 (Dec. 4, 2018).)

HISTORICAL AND STATUTORY NOTES

References in Text

The Federal Rules of Civil Procedure, referred to in subsec. (d), are codified generally to Title 28, Judiciary and Judicial Procedure.

§ 1366. Appearance

[FWPCA § 506]

The Administrator shall request the Attorney General to appear and represent the United States in any civil or criminal action instituted under this chapter to which the Administrator is a party. Unless the Attorney General notifies the Administrator within a reasonable time, that he will appear in a civil action, attorneys who are officers or employees of the Environmental Protection Agency shall appear and represent the United States in such action.

(June 30, 1948, c. 758, Title V, § 506, as added by Pub. L. No. 92–500, § 2, 86 Stat. 889 (Oct. 18, 1972).)

§ 1367. Employee protection

[FWPCA § 507]

(a) Discrimination against persons filing, instituting, or testifying in proceedings under this chapter prohibited

No person shall fire, or in any other way discriminate against, or cause to be fired or discriminated against, any employee or any authorized representative of employees by reason of the fact that such employee or representative has filed, instituted, or caused to be filed or instituted any proceeding under this chapter, or has testified or is about to testify in any proceeding resulting from the administration or enforcement of the provisions of this chapter.

(b) Application for review; investigation; hearing; review

Any employee or a representative of employees who believes that he has been fired or otherwise discriminated against by any person in violation of subsection (a) of this section may, within thirty days after such alleged violation occurs, apply to the Secretary of Labor for a review of such firing or alleged discrimination. A copy of the application shall be sent to such person who shall be the respondent. Upon receipt of such application, the Secretary of Labor shall cause such investigation to be made as he deems appropriate. Such investigation shall provide an opportunity for a public hearing at the request of any party to such review to enable the parties to present information relating to such alleged violation. The parties shall be given written notice of the time and place of the hearing at least five days prior to the hearing. Any such hearing shall be of record and shall be subject to section 554 of Title 5. Upon receiving the report of such investigation, the Secretary of Labor shall make findings of fact. If he finds that such violation did occur, he shall issue a decision, incorporating an order therein and his findings, requiring the party committing such violation to take such affirmative action to abate the violation as the Secretary of Labor deems appropriate, including, but not limited to, the rehiring or reinstatement of the employee or representative of employees to his former position with compensation. If he finds that there was no such violation, he shall issue an order denying the application. Such order issued by the Secretary of Labor under this subparagraph shall be subject to judicial review in the same manner as orders and decisions of the Administrator are subject to judicial review under this chapter.

(c) Costs and expenses

Whenever an order is issued under this section to abate such violation, at the request of the applicant, a sum equal to the aggregate amount of all costs and expenses (including the attorney's fees), as determined by the Secretary of Labor, to have been reasonably incurred by the applicant for, or in connection with, the institution and prosecution of such proceedings, shall be assessed against the person committing such violation.

(d) Deliberate violations by employee acting without direction from his employer or his agent

This section shall have no application to any employee who, acting without direction from his employer (or his agent) deliberately violates any prohibition of effluent limitation or other limitation under section 1311 or 1312 of this title, standards of performance under section 1316 of this title, effluent standard, prohibition or pretreatment standard under section 1317 of this title, or any other prohibition or limitation established under this chapter.

(e) Investigations of employment reductions

The Administrator shall conduct continuing evaluations of potential loss or shifts of employment which may result from the issuance of any effluent limitation or order under this chapter, including, where appropriate, investigating threatened plant closures or reductions in employment allegedly resulting from such limitation or order. Any employee who is discharged or laid-off, threatened with discharge or lay-off, or otherwise discriminated against by any person because of the alleged results of any effluent limitation or order issued under this chapter, or any representative of such employee, may request the Administrator to conduct a full investigation of the matter. The Administrator shall thereupon investigate the matter and, at the request of any party, shall hold public hearings on not less than five days notice, and shall at such hearings require the parties, including the employer involved, to present information relating to the actual or potential effect of such limitation or order on employment and on any alleged discharge, lay-off, or other discrimination and the detailed reasons or justification therefor. Any such hearing shall be of record and shall be subject to section 554 of Title 5. Upon receiving the report of such investigation, the Administrator shall make findings of fact as to the effect of such effluent limitation or order on employment and on the alleged discharge, lay-off, or discrimination and shall make such recommendations as he deems appropriate. Such report, findings, and recommendations shall be available to the public. Nothing in this subsection shall be construed to require or authorize the Administrator to modify or withdraw any effluent limitation or order issued under this chapter.

(June 30, 1948, c. 758, Title V, § 507, as added by Pub. L. No. 92–500, § 2, 86 Stat. 890 (Oct. 18, 1972).)

§ 1368. Federal procurement

[FWPCA § 508]

(a) Contracts with violators prohibited

No Federal agency may enter into any contract with any person, who has been convicted of any offense under section 1319(c) of this title, for the procurement of goods, materials, and services if such contract is to be performed at any facility at which the violation which gave rise to such conviction occurred, and if such facility is owned, leased, or supervised by such person. The prohibition in the preceding sentence shall continue until the Administrator certifies that the condition giving rise to such conviction has been corrected.

(b) Notification of agencies

The Administrator shall establish procedures to provide all Federal agencies with the notification necessary for the purposes of subsection (a) of this section.

(c) Omitted

(d) Exemptions

The President may exempt any contract, loan, or grant from all or part of the provisions of this section where he determines such exemption is necessary in the paramount interest of the United States and he shall notify the Congress of such exemption.

(e) Annual report to Congress

The President shall annually report to the Congress on measures taken in compliance with the purpose and intent of this section, including, but not limited to, the progress and problems associated with such compliance.

(f) Contractor certification or contract clause in acquisition of commercial items

(1) No certification by a contractor, and no contract clause, may be required in the case of a contract for the acquisition of commercial products or commercial services in order to implement a prohibition or requirement of this section or a prohibition or requirement issued in the implementation of this section.

(2) In paragraph (1), the terms "commercial product" and "commercial service" have the meanings given those terms in sections 103 and 103a, respectively, of title 41, United States Code.

(June 30, 1948, c. 758, Title V, § 508, as added by Pub. L. No. 92–500, § 2, 86 Stat. 891 (Oct. 18, 1972); and amended by Pub. L. No. 103–355, Title VIII, § 8301(a), 108 Stat. 3396 (Oct. 13, 1994); Pub. L. No. 115–232, § 836(g)(5), 132 Stat. 1636, 1872–1873 (Aug. 13. 2018).)

HISTORICAL AND STATUTORY NOTES

Codifications

Subsec. (c) authorized the President to cause to be issued, not more than 180 days after October 18, 1972, an order (1) requiring each Federal agency authorized to enter into contracts or to extend Federal assistance by way of grant, loan, or contract, to effectuate the purpose and policy of this chapter, and (2) setting forth procedures, sanctions and penalties as the President determines necessary to carry out such requirement.

In subsec. (f)(2), "section 103 of Title 41" substituted for "section 4(12) of the Office of Federal Procurement Policy Act (41 U.S.C. 403(12))" on authority of Pub. L. No. 111–350, § 6(c), 124 Stat. 3854 (Jan. 4, 2011), which Act enacted Title 41, Public Contracts.

Effective and Applicability Provisions

1994 Acts. Amendment by section 8301(a) of Pub. L. No. 103–355 effective Oct. 13, 1994, except as otherwise provided, see section 10001 of Pub. L. No. 103–355, set out as a note under section 10 U.S.C.A. § 2302.

Termination of Reporting Requirements

Reporting requirement of subsec. (e) of this section excepted from termination under Pub. L. No. 104–66, § 3003(a)(1), as amended, set out as a note under 31 U.S.C.A. § 1113, and page 20 of House Document No. 103–7, see Pub. L. No. 107–303, § 302(a).

Administration of Chapter With Respect to Federal Contracts, Grants, or Loans

For provisions concerning the administration of this chapter with respect to Federal contracts, grants, or loans, see Ex. Ord. No. 11738, Sept. 10, 1973, 38 Fed. Reg. 25161, set out as a note under section 7606 of Title 42, The Public Health and Welfare.

§ 1369. Administrative procedure and judicial review

[FWPCA § 509]

(a) Subpenas

(1) For purposes of obtaining information under section 1315 of this title, or carrying out section 1367(e) of this title, the Administrator may issue subpenas for the attendance and testimony of witnesses and the production of relevant papers, books, and documents, and he may administer oaths. Except for effluent data, upon a showing satisfactory to the Administrator that such papers, books, documents, or information or particular part thereof, if made public, would divulge trade secrets or secret processes, the Administrator shall consider such record, report, or information or particular portion thereof confidential in accordance with the purposes of section 1905 of Title 18, except that such paper, book, document, or information may be disclosed to other officers, employees, or authorized representatives of the United States concerned with carrying out this chapter, or when relevant in any proceeding under this chapter. Witnesses summoned shall be paid the same fees and mileage that are paid witnesses in the courts of the United States. In case of contumacy or refusal to obey a subpena served upon any person under this subsection, the district court of the United States for any district in which such person is found or resides or transacts business, upon application by the United States and after notice to such person, shall have jurisdiction to issue an order requiring such person to appear and give testimony before the Administrator, to appear and produce papers, books, and documents before the Administrator, or both, and any failure to obey such order of the court may be punished by such court as a contempt thereof.

(2) The district courts of the United States are authorized, upon application by the Administrator, to issue subpenas for attendance and testimony of witnesses and the production of relevant papers, books, and documents, for purposes of obtaining information under sections 1314(b) and (c) of this title. Any papers, books, documents, or other information or part thereof, obtained by reason of such a subpena shall be subject to the same requirements as are provided in paragraph (1) of this subsection.

(b) Review of Administrator's actions; selection of court; fees

(1) Review of the Administrator's action (A) in promulgating any standard of performance under section 1316 of this title, (B) in making any determination pursuant to section 1316(b)(1)(C) of this title, (C) in promulgating any effluent standard, prohibition, or pretreatment standard under section 1317 of this title, (D) in making any determination as to a State permit program submitted under section 1342(b) of this title, (E) in approving or promulgating any effluent limitation or other limitation under section 1311, 1312, 1316, or 1345 of this title, (F) in issuing or denying any permit under section 1342 of this title, and (G) in promulgating any individual control strategy under section 1314(*l*) of this title, may be had by any interested person in the Circuit Court of Appeals of the United States for the Federal judicial district in which such person resides or transacts business which is directly affected by such action upon application by such person. Any such application shall be made within 120 days from the date of such determination, approval, promulgation, issuance or denial, or after such date only if such application is based solely on grounds which arose after such 120th day.

(2) Action of the Administrator with respect to which review could have been obtained under paragraph (1) of this subsection shall not be subject to judicial review in any civil or criminal proceeding for enforcement.

(3) Award of fees

In any judicial proceeding under this subsection, the court may award costs of litigation (including reasonable attorney and expert witness fees) to any prevailing or substantially prevailing party whenever it determines that such award is appropriate.

(4) Discharges incidental to normal operation of vessels.—

(A) In general.—Except as provided in subparagraph (B), any interested person may file a petition for review of a final agency action under section 312(p) of the Administrator or the Secretary of the department in which the Coast Guard is operating in accordance with the requirements of this subsection.

(B) Venue exception.—Subject to section 312(p)(7)(C)(v), a petition for review of a final agency action under section 1322(p) of the Administrator or the Secretary of the department in which the Coast Guard is operating may be filed only in the United States Court of Appeals for the District of Columbia Circuit.

(c) Additional evidence

In any judicial proceeding brought under subsection (b) of this section in which review is sought of a determination under this chapter required to be made on the record after notice and opportunity for hearing, if any party applies to the court for leave to adduce additional evidence, and shows to the satisfaction of the court that such additional evidence is material and that there were reasonable grounds for the failure to adduce such evidence in the proceeding before the Administrator, the court may order such additional evidence (and evidence in rebuttal thereof) to be taken before the Administrator, in such manner and upon such terms and conditions as the court may deem proper. The Administrator may modify his findings as to the facts, or make new findings, by reason of the additional evidence so taken and he shall file such modified or new findings, and his recommendation, if any, for the modification or setting aside of his original determination, with the return of such additional evidence.

(June 30, 1948, c. 758, Title V, § 509, as added by Pub. L. No. 92–500, § 2, 86 Stat. 891 (Oct. 18, 1972); and amended by Pub. L. No. 93–207, § 1(6), 87 Stat. 906 (Dec. 28, 1973); Pub. L. No. 100–4, Title III, § 308(b), Title IV, § 406(d)(3), Title V, § 505(a), (b), 101 Stat. 39, 73, 75 (Feb. 4, 1987); Pub. L. No. 100–236, § 2, 101 Stat. 1732 (Jan. 8, 1988); Pub. L. No. 115–282, § 903(c)(4), 132 Stat. 4192, 4356–4357 (Dec. 4, 2018).)

HISTORICAL AND STATUTORY NOTES

Effective and Applicability Provisions

1988 Acts. Amendment to subsec. (b) of this section by Pub. L. No. 100–236 to take effect 180 days after Jan. 8, 1988, see section 3 of Pub. L. No. 100–236, set out as a note under section 2112 of Title 28, Judiciary and Judicial Procedure.

§ 1370. State authority

[FWPCA § 510]

Except as expressly provided in this chapter, nothing in this chapter shall (1) preclude or deny the right of any State or political subdivision thereof or interstate agency to adopt or enforce (A) any standard or limitation respecting discharges of pollutants, or (B) any requirement respecting control or abatement of pollution; except that if an effluent limitation, or other limitation, effluent standard, prohibition, pretreatment standard, or standard of performance is in effect under this chapter, such State or political subdivision or interstate agency may not adopt or enforce any effluent limitation, or other limitation, effluent standard, prohibition, pretreatment standard, or standard of performance which is less stringent than the effluent limitation, or other limitation, effluent standard, prohibition, pretreatment standard, or standard of performance under this chapter; or (2) be construed as impairing or in any manner affecting any right or jurisdiction of the States with respect to the waters (including boundary waters) of such States.

(June 30, 1948, c. 758, Title V, § 510, as added by Pub. L. No. 92–500, § 2, 86 Stat. 893 (Oct. 18, 1972).)

§ 1371. Authority under other laws and regulations

[FWPCA § 511]

(a) Impairment of authority or functions of officials and agencies; treaty provisions

This chapter shall not be construed as (1) limiting the authority or functions of any officer or agency of the United States under any other law or regulation not inconsistent with this chapter; (2) affecting or impairing the authority of the Secretary of the Army (A) to maintain navigation or (B) under the Act of March 3, 1899 (30 Stat. 1112); except that any permit issued under section 1344 of this title shall be conclusive as to the effect on water quality of any discharge resulting from any activity subject to section 403 of this title, or (3) affecting or impairing the provisions of any treaty of the United States.

(b) Discharges of pollutants into navigable waters

Discharges of pollutants into the navigable waters subject to the Rivers and Harbors Act of 1910 (36 Stat. 593; 33 U.S.C. 421) and the Supervisory Harbors Act of 1888 (25 Stat. 209; 33 U.S.C. 441–451b) shall be regulated pursuant to this chapter, and not subject to such Act of 1910 and the Act of 1888 except as to effect on navigation and anchorage.

(c) Action of the Administrator deemed major Federal action; construction of the National Environmental Policy Act of 1969

(1) Except for the provision of Federal financial assistance for the purpose of assisting the construction of publicly owned treatment works as authorized by section 1281 of this title, and the issuance of a permit under section 1342 of this title for the discharge of any pollutant by a new source as defined in section 1316 of this title, no action of the Administrator taken pursuant to this chapter shall be deemed a major Federal action significantly affecting the quality of the human environment within the meaning of the National Environmental Policy Act of 1969 (83 Stat. 852) [42 U.S.C.A. § 4321 et seq.]; and

(2) Nothing in the National Environmental Policy Act of 1969 (83 Stat. 852) shall be deemed to—

(A) authorize any Federal agency authorized to license or permit the conduct of any activity which may result in the discharge of a pollutant into the navigable waters to review any effluent limitation or other requirement established pursuant to this chapter or the adequacy of any certification under section 1341 of this title; or

(B) authorize any such agency to impose, as a condition precedent to the issuance of any license or permit, any effluent limitation other than any such limitation established pursuant to this chapter.

(d) Consideration of international water pollution control agreements

Notwithstanding this chapter or any other provision of law, the Administrator (1) shall not require any State to consider in the development of the ranking in order of priority of needs for the construction of treatment works (as defined in subchapter II of this chapter), any water pollution control agreement which may have been entered into between the United States and any other nation, and (2) shall not consider any such agreement in the approval of any such priority ranking.

(June 30, 1948, c. 758, Title V, § 511, as added by Pub. L. No. 92–500, § 2, 86 Stat. 893 (Oct. 18, 1972); and amended by Pub. L. No. 93–243, § 3, 87 Stat. 1069 (Jan. 2, 1974).)

HISTORICAL AND STATUTORY NOTES

References in Text

The Act of March 3, 1899, referred to in subsec. (a), is Act of Mar. 3, 1899, c. 425, 30 Stat. 1121, as amended, which enacted sections 401, 403, 404, 406, 407, 408, 409, 411 to 416, 418, 502, 549, and 687 of this title and amended section 686 of this title. For complete classification of this Act to the Code, see Tables.

The Rivers and Harbors Act of 1910, referred to in subsec. (b), probably means Act of June 23, 1910, c. 359, 36 Stat. 593.

The Supervisory Harbors Act of 1888, referred to in subsec. (b), probably means Act of June 29, 1888, c. 496, 25 Stat. 209, as amended, which is codified generally as subchapter III (section 441 et seq.) of chapter 9 of this title. For complete classification of this Act to the Code, see Tables.

The National Environmental Policy Act of 1969, referred to in subsec. (c), is Pub. L. No. 91–190, 83 Stat. 852 (Jan. 1, 1970), as amended, which is codified generally as chapter 55 (section 4321 et seq.) of Title 42, Public Health and Welfare. For complete classification of this Act to the Code, see Short Title note set out under section 4321 of Title 42 and Tables.

§ 1372. Labor standards

[FWPCA § 513]

The Administrator shall take such action as may be necessary to insure that all laborers and mechanics employed by contractors or subcontractors on treatment works for which grants are made under this chapter shall be paid wages at rates not less than those prevailing for the same type of work on similar construction in the immediate locality, as determined by the Secretary of Labor, in accordance with sections 3141–3144, 3146, and 3147 of Title 40. The Secretary of Labor shall have, with respect to the labor standards specified in this subsection[1], the authority and functions set forth in Reorganization Plan Numbered 14 of 1950 (15 Fed. Reg. 3176) and section 3145 of Title 40.

(June 30, 1948, c. 758, Title V, § 513, as added by Pub. L. No. 92–500, § 2, 86 Stat. 894 (Oct. 18, 1972).)

[1] So in original. Probably should be "section".

HISTORICAL AND STATUTORY NOTES

References in Text

Reorganization Plan Numbered 14 of 1950, referred to in text, is Reorg. Plan No. 14 of 1950, eff. May 24, 1950, 15 Fed. Reg. 3176, 64 Stat. 1267, which is set out in Appendix 1 of Title 5, Government Organization and Employees.

Codifications

In text, "sections 3141–3144, 3146, and 3147 of Title 40" substituted for "the Davis-Bacon Act of March 3, 1931 (46 Stat. 1494; 40 U.S.C. 276a through 276a–5)" on authority of Pub. L. No. 107–217, § 5(c), 116 Stat. 1301 (Aug. 21, 2002), which is set out as a note preceding 40 U.S.C.A. § 101. Pub. L. No. 107–217, § 1, enacted Title 40 into positive law. The Davis-Bacon Act is Act of Mar. 3, 1931, c. 411, 46 Stat. 1494, which was codified as former

40 U.S.C.A. §§ 276a, 276a–1 to 276a–6, prior to being repealed by Pub. L. No. 107–217, § 6(b), 116 Stat. 1308 (Aug. 21, 2002), and its substance reenacted as 40 U.S.C.A. §§ 3141–3144, 3146, and 3147.

In text, "section 3145 of Title 40" substituted for "section 276c of Title 40", which originally read "section 2 of the Act of June 13, 1934, as amended (48 Stat. 948; 40 U.S.C. 276c)", on authority of Pub. L. No. 107–217, § 5(c), 116 Stat. 1301 (Aug. 21, 2002), which is set out as a note preceding 40 U.S.C.A. § 101. Pub. L. No. 107–217, § 1, enacted Title 40 into positive law. Section 2 of the Act of June 13, 1934, as amended, is Act of June 13, 1934, c. 482, § 2, 48 Stat. 948, which was codified as former 40 U.S.C.A. § 276c prior to being repealed by Pub. L. No. 107–217, § 6(b), 116 Stat. 1309 (Aug. 21, 2002), and its substance reenacted as 40 U.S.C.A. § 3145.

Construction of Treatment Works

Pub. L. No. 112–74, Div. E, Title II, 125 Stat. 1020 (Dec. 23, 2011), provided that: "For fiscal year 2012 and each fiscal year thereafter, the requirements of section 513 of the Federal Water Pollution Control Act (33 U.S.C. 1372) shall apply to the construction of treatment works carried out in whole or in part with assistance made available by a State water pollution control revolving fund as authorized by title VI of that Act (33 U.S.C. 1381 et seq.), or with assistance made available under section 205(m) of that Act (33 U.S.C. 1285(m)), or both."

§ 1373. Public health agency coordination [FWPCA § 514]

The permitting agency under section 1342 of this title shall assist the applicant for a permit under such section in coordinating the requirements of this chapter with those of the appropriate public health agencies.

(June 30, 1948, c. 758, Title V, § 514, as added by Pub. L. No. 92–500, § 2, 86 Stat. 894 (Oct. 18, 1972).)

§ 1374. Effluent Standards and Water Quality Information Advisory Committee [FWPCA § 515]

(a) Establishment; membership; term

(1) There is established an Effluent Standards and Water Quality Information Advisory Committee, which shall be composed of a Chairman and eight members who shall be appointed by the Administrator within sixty days after October 18, 1972.

(2) All members of the Committee shall be selected from the scientific community, qualified by education, training, and experience to provide, assess, and evaluate scientific and technical information on effluent standards and limitations.

(3) Members of the Committee shall serve for a term of four years, and may be reappointed.

(b) Action on proposed regulations

(1) No later than one hundred and eighty days prior to the date on which the Administrator is required to publish any proposed regulations required by section 1314(b) of this title, any proposed standard of performance for new sources required by section 1316 of this title, or any proposed toxic effluent standard required by section 1317 of this title, he shall transmit to the Committee a notice of intent to propose such regulations. The Chairman of the Committee within ten days after receipt of such notice may publish a notice of a public hearing by the Committee, to be held within thirty days.

(2) No later than one hundred and twenty days after receipt of such notice, the Committee shall transmit to the Administrator such scientific and technical information as is in its possession, including that presented at any public hearing, related to the subject matter contained in such notice.

(3) Information so transmitted to the Administrator shall constitute a part of the administrative record and comments on any proposed regulations or standards as information to be considered with other comments and information in making any final determinations.

(4) In preparing information for transmittal, the Committee shall avail itself of the technical and scientific services of any Federal agency, including the United States Geological Survey and any national environmental laboratories which may be established.

(c) Secretary; legal counsel; compensation

(1) The Committee shall appoint and prescribe the duties of a Secretary, and such legal counsel as it deems necessary. The Committee shall appoint such other employees as it deems necessary to exercise and fulfill its powers and responsibilities. The compensation of all employees appointed by the Committee shall be fixed in accordance with chapter 51 and subchapter III of chapter 53 of Title 5.

(2) Members of the Committee shall be entitled to receive compensation at a rate to be fixed by the President but not in excess of the maximum rate of pay for grade GS–18, as provided in the General Schedule under section 5332 of Title 5.

(d) Quorum; special panel

Five members of the Committee shall constitute a quorum, and official actions of the Committee shall be taken only on the affirmative vote of at least five members. A special panel composed of one or more members upon order of the Committee shall conduct any hearing authorized by this section and submit the transcript of such hearing to the entire Committee for its action thereon.

(e) Rules

The Committee is authorized to make such rules as are necessary for the orderly transaction of its business.

(June 30, 1948, c. 758, Title V, § 515, as added by Pub. L. No. 92–500, § 2, 86 Stat. 894 (Oct. 18, 1972).)

HISTORICAL AND STATUTORY NOTES

Termination of Advisory Committees

Advisory Committees in existence on Jan. 5, 1973, to terminate not later than the expiration of the two-year period following Jan. 5, 1973, unless, in the case of a committee established by the President or an officer of the Federal Government, such committee is renewed by appropriate action prior to the expiration of such two-year period, or in the case of a committee established by the Congress, its duration is otherwise provided by law, see section 14 of Pub. L. No. 92–463, 86 Stat. 770 (Oct. 6, 1972), set out in Appendix 2 to Title 5, Government Organization and Employees.

References in Other Laws to GS–16, 17, or 18 Pay Rates

References in laws to the rates of pay for GS–16, 17, or 18, or to maximum rates of pay under the General Schedule, to be considered references to rates payable under specified sections of Title 5, see section 529 [Title I, § 101(c)(1)] of Pub. L. No. 101–509, set out in a note under 5 U.S.C.A. § 5376.

§ 1375. Reports to Congress; detailed estimates and comprehensive study on costs; State estimates

[FWPCA § 516]

(a) Implementation of chapter objectives; status and progress of programs

Within ninety days following the convening of each session of Congress, the Administrator shall submit to the Congress a report, in addition to any other report required by this chapter, on measures taken toward implementing the objective of this chapter, including, but not limited to, (1) the progress and problems associated with developing comprehensive plans under section 1252 of this title, areawide plans under section 1288 of this title, basin plans under section 1289 of this title, and plans under section 1313(e) of this title; (2) a summary of actions taken and results achieved in the field of water pollution control research, experiments, studies, and related matters by the Administrator and other Federal agencies and by other persons and agencies under Federal grants or contracts; (3) the progress and problems associated with the development of effluent limitations and recommended control techniques; (4) the status of State programs, including a detailed summary of the progress obtained as compared to that planned under State program plans for development and enforcement of water quality requirements; (5) the identification and status of enforcement actions pending or completed under this chapter during the preceding year; (6) the status of State, interstate, and local pollution control programs established pursuant to, and assisted by, this chapter; (7) a summary of the results of the survey required to be taken under section 1290 of this title; (8) his activities including recommendations under sections 1259 through 1261 of this title; and (9) all reports and recommendations made by the Water Pollution Control Advisory Board.

(b) Detailed estimates and comprehensive study on costs; State estimates, survey form

(1) The Administrator, in cooperation with the States, including water pollution control agencies and other water pollution control planning agencies, shall make (A) a detailed estimate of the cost of carrying out the provisions of this chapter; (B) a detailed estimate, biennially revised, of the cost of construction of all needed publicly owned treatment works in all of the States and of the cost of construction of all needed publicly owned treatment works in each of the States; (C) a comprehensive study of the economic impact on affected units of government of the cost of installation of treatment facilities; and (D) a comprehensive analysis of the national requirements for and the cost of treating municipal, industrial, and other effluent to attain the water quality objectives as established by this chapter or applicable State law. The Administrator shall submit such detailed estimate and such comprehensive study of such cost to the Congress no later than February 10 of each odd-numbered year. Whenever the Administrator, pursuant to this subsection, requests and receives an estimate of cost from a State, he shall furnish copies of such estimate together with such detailed estimate to Congress.

(2) Notwithstanding the second sentence of paragraph (1) of this subsection, the Administrator shall make a preliminary detailed estimate called for by subparagraph (B) of such paragraph and shall submit such preliminary detailed estimate to the Congress no later than September 3, 1974. The Administrator shall require each State to prepare an estimate of cost for such State, and shall utilize the survey form EPA-1, O.M.B. No. 158–R0017, prepared for the 1973 detailed estimate, except that such estimate shall include all costs of compliance with section 1281(g)(2)(A) of this title and water quality standards established pursuant to section 1313 of this title, and all costs of treatment works as defined in section 1292(2) of this title, including all eligible costs of constructing sewage collection systems and correcting excessive infiltration or inflow and all eligible costs of correcting combined storm and sanitary sewer problems and treating storm water flows. The survey form shall be distributed by the Administrator to each State no later than January 31, 1974.

(c) Status of combined sewer overflows in municipal treatment works operations

The Administrator shall submit to the Congress by October 1, 1978, a report on the status of combined sewer overflows in municipal treatment works operations. The report shall include (1) the status of any projects funded under this chapter to address combined sewer overflows (2) a listing by State of combined sewer overflow needs identified in the 1977 State priority listings, (3) an estimate for each applicable municipality of the number of years necessary, assuming an annual authorization and appropriation for the construction grants program of $5,000,000,000, to correct combined sewer overflow problems, (4) an analysis using representative municipalities faced with major combined sewer overflow needs, of the annual discharges of pollutants from overflows in comparison to treated effluent discharges, (5) an analysis of the technological alternatives available to municipalities to correct major combined sewer overflow problems, and (6) any recommendations of the Administrator for legislation to address the problem of combined sewer overflows, including whether a separate authorization and grant program should be established by the Congress to address combined sewer overflows.

(d) Legislative recommendations on program requiring coordination between water supply and wastewater control plans as condition for construction grants; public hearing

The Administrator, in cooperation with the States, including water pollution control agencies, and other water pollution control planning agencies, and water supply and water resources agencies of the States and the United States shall submit to Congress, within two years of December 27, 1977, a report with recommendations for legislation on a program to require coordination between water supply and wastewater control plans as a condition to grants for construction of treatment works under this chapter. No such report shall be submitted except after opportunity for public hearings on such proposed report.

(e) State revolving fund report

(1) In general

Not later than February 10, 1990, the Administrator shall submit to Congress a report on the financial status and operations of water pollution control revolving funds established by the States under subchapter VI of this chapter. The Administrator shall prepare such report in cooperation with the States, including water pollution control agencies and other water pollution control planning and financing agencies.

(2) Contents

The report under this subsection shall also include the following:

(A) an inventory of the facilities that are in significant noncompliance with the enforceable requirements of this chapter

(B) an estimate of the cost of construction necessary to bring such facilities into compliance with such requirements;

(C) an assessment of the availability of sources of funds for financing such needed construction, including an estimate of the amount of funds available for providing assistance for such construction through September 30, 1999, from the water pollution control revolving funds established by the States under subchapter VI of this chapter;

(D) an assessment of the operations, loan portfolio, and loan conditions of such revolving funds;

(E) an assessment of the effect on user charges of the assistance provided by such revolving funds compared to the assistance provided with funds appropriated pursuant to section 1287 of this title; and

(F) an assessment of the efficiency of the operation and maintenance of treatment works constructed with assistance provided by such revolving funds compared to the efficiency of the operation and maintenance of treatment works constructed with assistance provided under section 1281 of this title.

(June 30, 1948, c. 758, Title V, § 516, as added by Pub. L. No. 92–500, § 2, 86 Stat. 895 (Oct. 18, 1972); and amended by Pub. L. No. 93–243, § 4, 87 Stat. 1069 (Jan. 2, 1974); Pub. L. No. 95–217, §§ 70–72, 91 Stat. 1608, 1609 (Dec. 27, 1977); Pub. L. No. 100–4, Title II, § 212(c), 101 Stat. 27 (Feb. 4, 1987); Pub. L. No. 104–66, Title II, § 2021(d), 109 Stat. 727 (Dec. 21, 1995); Pub. L. No. 105–362, Title V, § 501(d)(1), 112 Stat. 3283 (Nov. 10, 1998); Pub. L. No. 107–303, Title III, § 302(b)(1), 116 Stat. 2361 (Nov. 27, 2002).)

HISTORICAL AND STATUTORY NOTES

Effective and Applicability Provisions

2002 Acts. Effective November 10, 1998, section 501 of the Federal Reports Elimination Act of 1998 [Pub. L. No. 105–362, Title V, § 501, 112 Stat. 3283 (Nov. 10, 1998)] is amended by striking subsections (a), (b), (c), and (d) [amending this section and others, see Tables for complete classification]. The Federal Water Pollution Control Act (33 U.S.C.A. § 1254(n)(3)) shall be applied and administered on and after Nov. 27, 2002 as if the amendments made by subsections (a), (b), (c), and (d) of Pub. L. No. 105–362, § 501, had not been enacted, see Pub. L. No. 107–303, § 302(b)(2), set out as a note under 33 U.S.C.A. § 1254.

Termination of Reporting Requirements

Reporting requirements of this section excepted from termination under Pub. L. No. 104–66, § 3003, as amended, set out as a note under 31 U.S.C.A. § 1113, and pages 163 and 165 of House Document No. 103–7, see Pub. L. No. 107–303, § 302(a), set out as a note under 31 U.S.C.A. § 1113.

Studies and Reports

Pub. L. No. 100–4, Title III, § 308(g), 101 Stat. 40 (Feb. 4, 1987), directed the Administrator to conduct a water quality improvement study and report the results of such study to specified Congressional committees not later than 2 years after Feb. 4, 1987.

Pub. L. No. 100–4, Title III, § 314(b), 101 Stat. 49 (Feb. 4, 1987), directed that the Secretary of the Army and the Administrator each prepare a report on enforcement mechanisms and submit the reports to Congress not later than Dec. 1, 1988.

Pub. L. No. 100–4, Title IV, § 404(c), 101 Stat. 69 (Feb. 4, 1987), which directed the Administrator to study the extent to which States have adopted water quality standards in accordance with section 1313a of this title and the extent to which modifications of permits issued under section 1342(a)(1)(B) of this title for the purpose of reflecting revisions of water quality standards be encouraged and to submit a report on such study to Congress not later than 2 years after Feb. 4, 1987, was repealed by Pub. L. No. 104–66, Title II, § 2021(e)(1), 109 Stat. 727 (Dec. 21, 1995).

Pub. L. No. 100–4, Title V, § 516, 101 Stat. 86 (Feb. 4, 1987), directed the Administrator to conduct a study of de minimis discharges and report the results of such study to specified Congressional committees not later than 1 year after Feb. 4, 1987.

Pub. L. No. 100–4, Title V, § 517, 100 Stat. 86 (Feb. 4, 1987), directed the Administrator to conduct a study of effectiveness of innovative and alternative processes and techniques and report the results of such study to specified Congressional committees not later than 1 year after Feb. 4, 1987.

Pub. L. No. 100–4, Title V, § 518, 101 Stat. 86 (Feb. 4, 1987), directed the Administrator to conduct a study of testing procedures and report the results of such study to specified Congressional committees not later than 1 year after Feb. 4, 1987.

Pub. L. No. 100–4, Title V, § 519, 100 Stat. 87 (Feb. 4, 1987), directed the Administrator to conduct a study of pretreatment of toxic pollutants and report the results of such study to specified Congressional committees not later than 4 years after Feb. 4, 1987.

Pub. L. No. 100–4, Title V, § 520, 101 Stat. 87 (Feb. 4, 1987), directed the Administrator, in conjunction with State and local agencies, to conduct studies of water pollution problems in aquifers and report the result of such studies to Congress not later than 2 years after Feb. 4, 1987.

Pub. L. No. 100–4, Title V, § 522, 101 Stat. 88 (Feb. 4, 1987), directed the Administrator to conduct a study on sulfide corrosion and report the results of such study to specified Congressional committees not later than 1 year after Feb. 4, 1987.

Pub. L. No. 100–4, Title V, § 523, 101 Stat. 89 (Feb. 4, 1987), directed the Administrator to conduct a study of rainfall induced infiltration into sewer systems and report the results of such study to Congress not later than 1 year after Feb. 4, 1987.

Pub. L. No. 100–4, Title V, § 524, 101 Stat. 89 (Feb. 4, 1987), directed the Administrator to conduct a study of dam water quality and report the results of such study to Congress not later than Dec. 31, 1987.

Pub. L. No. 100–4, Title V, § 525, 101 Stat. 89 (Feb. 4, 1987), directed the Administrator to conduct a study of pollution in Lake Pend Oreille, Idaho, and the Clark Fork River and its tributaries, Idaho, Montana, and Washington, and to report to Congress the findings and recommendations. For termination of reporting provisions pertaining to sources of pollution in Lake Pend Oreille, Idaho, the Clark Fork River and its tributaries, effective May 15, 2000, see Pub. L. No. 104–66, § 3003, as amended, set out as a note under 31 U.S.C.A. § 1113, and the 18th item on page 163 of House Document No. 103–7, which references 33 U.S.C. § 1375 note.

Detailed Estimates, Comprehensive Study, and Comprehensive Analysis; Report to Congress not Later Than December 31, 1982

Pub. L. No. 97–117, § 25, 95 Stat. 1633 (Dec. 29, 1981), provided that the Administrator of the Environmental Protection Agency submit to the Congress, not later than December 31, 1982, a report containing the detailed estimates, comprehensive study, and comprehensive analysis required by section 1375(b) of this title, including an estimate of the total cost and the amount of Federal funds necessary for the construction of needed publicly owned treatment facilities, such report to reflect the changes made in the Federal water pollution control program by Pub. L. No. 97–117 [see Short Title of 1981 Amendment note set out under section 1251 of this title]. The Administrator was to give emphasis to the effects of the amendment made by section 2(a) of Pub. L. No. 97–117 [amending section 1281(g)(1) of this title] in addressing water quality needs adequately and appropriately.

Study and Report to Congress by Secretary of Interior of Financing Water Pollution Prevention, Control, and Abatement Programs

Pub. L. No. 91–224, Title I, § 109, 34 Stat. 113 (Apr. 3, 1970), directed the Secretary of the Interior to conduct a full and complete investigation and study of the feasibility of all methods of financing the cost of preventing, controlling, and abating water pollution, other than methods authorized by existing law, with results of such investigation and study to be reported to Congress no later than Dec. 31, 1970, together with the recommendations of the Secretary for financing the programs for preventing, controlling, and abating water pollution for the fiscal years beginning after fiscal year 1971, including any necessary legislation.

Termination of Advisory Boards

Advisory Boards in existence on Jan. 5, 1973, to terminate not later than the expiration of the two-year period following Jan. 5, 1973, unless, in the case of a board established by the President or an officer of the Federal Government, such board is renewed by appropriate action prior to the expiration of such two-year period, or in the case of a board established by the Congress, its duration is otherwise provided by law, see sections 3(2) and 14 of Pub. L. No. 92–463, 86 Stat. 770, 776 (Oct. 6, 1972), set out in Appendix 2 to Title 5, Government Organization and Employees.

§ 1375a. Report on coastal recreation waters

(a) In general

Not later than 4 years after October 10, 2000, and every 4 years thereafter, the Administrator of the Environmental Protection Agency shall submit to Congress a report that includes—

(1) recommendations concerning the need for additional water quality criteria for pathogens and pathogen indicators and other actions that should be taken to improve the quality of coastal recreation waters;

(2) an evaluation of Federal, State, and local efforts to implement this Act, including the amendments made by this Act; and

(3) recommendations on improvements to methodologies and techniques for monitoring of coastal recreation waters.

(b) Coordination

The Administrator of the Environmental Protection Agency may coordinate the report under this section with other reporting requirements under the Federal Water Pollution Control Act (33 U.S.C. 1251 et seq.).

(Pub. L. No. 106–284, § 7, 114 Stat. 876 (Oct. 10, 2000).)

HISTORICAL AND STATUTORY NOTES

References in Text

This Act, referred to in subsec. (a)(2), is Pub. L. No. 106–284, 114 Stat. 870 (Oct. 10, 2000), which enacted this section and section 1346 of this title, amended sections 1254, 1313, 1314, 1362, and 1377 of this title, and enacted provisions set out as a note under section 1251 of this title.

The Federal Water Pollution Control Act, referred to in subsec. (b), is Act of June 30, 1948, c. 758, as amended generally by Pub. L. No. 92–500, § 2, 86 Stat. 816 (Oct. 18, 1972), which is codified principally as this chapter. For complete classification of this Act to the Code, see Short Title note set out under 33 U.S.C.A. § 1251 and Tables.

Codifications

This section was enacted as part of the Beaches Environmental Assessment and Coastal Health Act of 2000 and not as part of the Federal Water Pollution Control Act, which comprises this chapter.

§ 1376. Authorization of appropriations

[FWPCA § 517]

There are authorized to be appropriated to carry out this chapter, other than sections 1254, 1255, 1256(a), 1257, 1258, 1262, 1263, 1264, 1265, 1286, 1287, 1288(f) and (h), 1289, 1314, 1321(c), (d), (i), (*l*), and (k), 1324, 1325, and 1327 of this title, $250,000,000 for the fiscal year ending June 30, 1973, $300,000,000 for the fiscal year ending June 30, 1974, $350,000,000 for the fiscal year ending June 30, 1975, $100,000,000 for the fiscal year ending September 30, 1977, $150,000,000 for the fiscal year ending September 30, 1978, $150,000,000 for the fiscal year ending September 30, 1979, $150,000,000 for the fiscal year ending September 30, 1980, $150,000,000 for the fiscal year ending September 30, 1981, $161,000,000 for the fiscal year ending September 30, 1982, such sums as may be necessary for fiscal years 1983 through 1985, and $135,000,000 per fiscal year for each of the fiscal years 1986 through 1990.

(June 30, 1948, c. 758, Title V, § 517, as added by Pub. L. No. 92–500, § 2, 86 Stat. 896 (Oct. 18, 1972); and amended by Pub. L. No. 95–217, § 4(g), 91 Stat. 1567 (Dec. 27, 1977); Pub. L. No. 96–483, § 1(g), 94 Stat. 2360 (Oct. 21, 1980); Pub. L. No. 100–4, Title I, § 101(h), 101 Stat. 9 (Feb. 4, 1987).)

HISTORICAL AND STATUTORY NOTES

References in Text

Section 1264 of this title, referred to in text, was omitted from the Code as executed.

Section 1321(k) of this title, referred to in text, was repealed by Pub. L. No. 101–380, Title II, § 2002(b)(2), 104 Stat. 507 (Aug. 18, 1990).

Authorization Approval for Funds Appropriated Before December 27, 1977, for Expenditures Through Fiscal Year Ending September 30, 1977

Pub. L. No. 95–217, § 3, 91 Stat. 1566 (Dec. 27, 1977), provided that funds appropriated before Dec. 27, 1977 for expenditure during the fiscal year ending June 30, 1976, the transition quarter ending September 30, 1976, and the fiscal year ending September 30, 1977, under authority of this chapter were authorized for those purposes for which appropriated.

§ 1377. Indian tribes

[FWPCA § 518]

(a) Policy

Nothing in this section shall be construed to affect the application of section 1251(g) of this title, and all of the provisions of this section shall be carried out in accordance with the provisions of such section 1251(g) of this title. Indian tribes shall be treated as States for purposes of such section 1251(g) of this title.

(b) Assessment of sewage treatment needs; report

The Administrator, in cooperation with the Director of the Indian Health Service, shall assess the need for sewage treatment works to serve Indian tribes, the degree to which such needs will be met through funds allotted to States under section 1285 of this title and priority lists under section 1296 of this title, and any obstacles which prevent such needs from being met. Not later than one year after February 4, 1987, the Administrator shall submit a report to Congress on the assessment under this subsection, along with recommendations specifying (1) how the Administrator intends to provide assistance to Indian tribes to develop waste treatment management plans and to construct treatment works under this chapter, and (2) methods by which the participation in and administration of programs under this chapter by Indian tribes can be maximized.

(c) Reservation of funds

(1) Fiscal years 1987–2014.—The Administrator shall reserve each of fiscal years 1987 through 2014, before allotments to the States under section 1285(e) of this title, one-half of one percent of the sums appropriated under section 1287 of this title.

(2) Fiscal year 2015 and thereafter.—For fiscal year 2015 and each fiscal year thereafter, the Administrator shall reserve, before allotments to the States under section 604(a), not less than 0.5 percent and not more than 2.0 percent of the funds made available to carry out title VI.

(3) Use of funds.—Funds reserved under this subsection shall be available only for grants for projects and activities eligible for assistance under section 603(c) to serve—

(A) Indian tribes (as defined in subsection (h));

(B) former Indian reservations in Oklahoma (as determined by the Secretary of the Interior); and

(C) Native villages (as defined in section 3 of the Alaska Native Claims Settlement Act (43 U.S.C. 1602)).

(d) Cooperative agreements

In order to ensure the consistent implementation of the requirements of this chapter, an Indian tribe and the State or States in which the lands of such tribe are located may enter into a cooperative agreement, subject to the review and approval of the Administrator, to jointly plan and administer the requirements of this chapter.

(e) Treatment as States

The Administrator is authorized to treat an Indian tribe as a State for purposes of subchapter II of this chapter and sections 1254, 1256, 1313, 1315, 1318, 1319, 1324, 1329, 1341, 1342, 1344, and 1346 of this title to the degree necessary to carry out the objectives of this section, but only if—

(1) the Indian tribe has a governing body carrying out substantial governmental duties and powers;

(2) the functions to be exercised by the Indian tribe pertain to the management and protection of water resources which are held by an Indian tribe, held by the United States in trust for Indians, held by a member of an Indian tribe if such property interest is subject to a trust restriction on alienation, or otherwise within the borders of an Indian reservation; and

(3) the Indian tribe is reasonably expected to be capable, in the Administrator's judgment, of carrying out the functions to be exercised in a manner consistent with the terms and purposes of this chapter and of all applicable regulations.

Such treatment as a State may include the direct provision of funds reserved under subsection (c) of this section to the governing bodies of Indian tribes, and the determination of priorities by Indian tribes, where not determined by the Administrator in cooperation with the Director of the Indian Health Service. The Administrator, in cooperation with the Director of the Indian Health Service, is authorized to make grants under subchapter II of this chapter in an amount not to exceed 100 percent of the cost of a project. Not later than 18 months after February 4, 1987, the Administrator shall, in consultation with Indian tribes, promulgate final regulations which specify how Indian tribes shall be treated as States for purposes of this chapter. The Administrator shall, in promulgating such regulations, consult affected States sharing common water bodies and provide a mechanism for the resolution of any unreasonable consequences that may arise as a result of differing water quality standards that may be set by States and Indian tribes located on common bodies of water. Such mechanism shall provide for explicit consideration of relevant factors including, but not limited to, the effects of differing water quality permit requirements on upstream and downstream dischargers, economic impacts, and present and historical uses and quality of the waters subject to such standards. Such mechanism should provide for the avoidance of such unreasonable consequences in a manner consistent with the objective of this chapter.

(f) Grants for nonpoint source programs

The Administrator shall make grants to an Indian tribe under section 1329 of this title as though such tribe was a State. Not more than one-third of one percent of the amount appropriated for any fiscal year under section 1329 of this title may be used to make grants under this subsection. In addition to the requirements of section 1329 of this title, an Indian tribe shall be required to meet the requirements of paragraphs (1), (2), and (3) of subsection (d)[1] of this section in order to receive such a grant.

(g) Alaska Native organizations

No provision of this chapter shall be construed to—

(1) grant, enlarge, or diminish, or in any way affect the scope of the governmental authority, if any, of any Alaska Native organization, including any federally-recognized tribe, traditional Alaska Native council, or Native council organized pursuant to the Act of June 18, 1934 (48 Stat. 987), over lands or persons in Alaska;

(2) create or validate any assertion by such organization or any form of governmental authority over lands or persons in Alaska; or

(3) in any way affect any assertion that Indian country, as defined in section 1151 of Title 18, exists or does not exist in Alaska.

(h) Definitions

For purposes of this section, the term—

(1) "Federal Indian reservation" means all land within the limits of any Indian reservation under the jurisdiction of the United States Government, notwithstanding the issuance of any patent, and including rights-of-way running through the reservation; and

(2) "Indian tribe" means any Indian tribe, band, group, or community recognized by the Secretary of the Interior and exercising governmental authority over a Federal Indian reservation.

(June 30, 1948, c. 758, Title V, § 518, as added by Pub. L. No. 100–4, Title V, § 506, 101 Stat. 76 (Feb. 4, 1987); and amended by Pub. L. No. 100–581, Title II, § 207, 102 Stat. 2940 (Nov. 1, 1988); Pub. L. No. 106–284, § 6, 114 Stat. 876 (Oct. 10, 2000); Pub. L. No. 113–121, § 5013, 128 Stat. 1328–29 (June 10, 2014).)

[1] So in original. Probably should be subsection "(e)."

HISTORICAL AND STATUTORY NOTES

References in Text

Pub. L. No. 92–203, referred to in subsec. (c), is Pub. L. No. 92–203, 85 Stat. 688 (Dec. 18, 1971), as amended, popularly known as the "Alaska Native Claims Settlement Act", which is codified generally as chapter 33 (section 1601 et seq.) of Title 43, Public Lands. "Alaska Native Villages", also so referred, are defined in section 1602(c) of Title 43, defining "Native village". For complete classification of this Act to the Code, see Short Title note set out under section 1601 of Title 43 and Tables.

Act of June 18, 1934, referred to in subsec. (g)(1), is Act of June 18, 1934, c. 576, 48 Stat. 984, as amended, popularly known as the Indian Reorganization Act, which enacted sections 461, 462, 463, 464, 465, 466 to 470, 471 to 473, 474, 475, 476 to 478, and 479 of Title 25, Indians. For complete classification of this Act to the Code, see Short Title note set out under section 461 of Title 25 and Tables.

Codifications

In original enactment, subsec. (f) contained a reference to "paragraphs (1), (2), and (3) of subsection (d)", which reference has been editorially changed to "subsection (e)" as the probable intent of Congress as such subsec. (e) and not subsec. (d) contains pars. (1), (2), and (3).

Prior Provisions

A prior section 518 of Act of June 30, 1948, was renumbered as section 519 of Act of June 30, 1948, and is set out as a note under section 1251 of this title.

Tribal Assistance Grants

Pub. L. No. 109–54, Title II, 119 Stat. 530 (Aug. 2, 2005), provided in part: "That, notwithstanding this or any other appropriations Act, heretofore and hereafter, after consultation with the House and Senate Committees on Appropriations and for the purpose of making technical corrections, the Administrator is authorized to award grants under this heading to entities and for purposes other than those listed in the joint explanatory statements of the managers accompanying the Agency's appropriations Acts for the construction of drinking water, wastewater and stormwater infrastructure and for water quality protection."

Grants to Indian Tribes

Pub. L. No. 109–54, Title II, 119 Stat. 530 (Aug. 2, 2005), provided in part that for fiscal year 2006, and notwithstanding section 518(f) of the Act (section 518(f) of the Federal Water Pollution Control Act which is subsec. (f) of this section), the Administrator was authorized to use the amounts appropriated for any fiscal year under section 319 of that Act (33 U.S.C.A. § 1329) to make grants to Indian tribes pursuant to sections 319(h) (33 U.S.C.A. § 1329(h)) and 518(e) of that Act (subsec. (e) of this section), was from the Department of the Interior, Environment, and Related Agencies Appropriations Act, 2006, and was repeated in subsequent Appropriations Acts but not set out in the Code.

Similar provisions were contained in the following prior appropriations Acts:

Pub. L. No. 108–447, Div. I, Title III, 118 Stat. 3330 (Dec. 8, 2004).

Pub. L. No. 108–199, Div. G, Title III, 118 Stat. 406 (Jan. 23, 2004).

Pub. L. No. 108–7, Div. K, Title III, 117 Stat. 511 (Feb. 20, 2003).

Pub. L. No. 107–73, Title III, 115 Stat. 685 (Nov. 26, 2001).

Pub. L. No. 106–377, § 1(a)(1) [Title III], 114 Stat. 1441, 1441A–43 (Oct. 27, 2000).

Pub. L. No. 106–74, Title III, 113 Stat. 1083 (Oct. 20, 1999).

§ 1377a. Green infrastructure promotion

[FWPCA § 519]

(a) In general.—The Administrator shall promote the use of green infrastructure in, and coordinate the integration of green infrastructure into, permitting and enforcement under this Act, planning efforts, research, technical assistance, and funding guidance of the Environmental Protection Agency.

(b) Coordination of efforts.—The Administrator shall ensure that the Office of Water coordinates efforts to increase the use of green infrastructure with—

(1) other Federal departments and agencies;

(2) State, tribal, and local governments; and

(3) the private sector.

(c) Regional green infrastructure promotion.—The Administrator shall direct each regional office of the Environmental Protection Agency, as appropriate based on local factors, and consistent with the requirements of this Act, to promote and integrate the use of green infrastructure within the region, including through—

(1) outreach and training regarding green infrastructure implementation for State, tribal, and local governments, tribal communities, and the private sector; and

(2) the incorporation of green infrastructure into permitting and other regulatory programs, codes, and ordinance development, including the requirements under consent decrees and settlement agreements in enforcement actions.

(d) Green infrastructure information sharing.—The Administrator shall promote green infrastructure information-sharing, including through an internet website, to share information with, and provide technical assistance to, State, tribal, and local governments, tribal communities, the private sector, and the public, regarding green infrastructure approaches for—

(1) reducing water pollution;

(2) protecting water resources;

(3) complying with regulatory requirements; and

(4) achieving other environmental, public health, and community goals.".

(June 30, 1948, c. 758, Title V, § 518, as added by Pub. L. No. 115–436, § 5(b)(2), 132 Stat. 5558, 5561–5562 (Jan. 14, 2019).)

SUBCHAPTER VI—STATE WATER POLLUTION CONTROL REVOLVING FUNDS

§ 1381. Grants to States for establishment of revolving funds

[FWPCA § 601]

(a) General authority

Subject to the provisions of this subchapter, the Administrator shall make capitalization grants to each State for the purpose of establishing a water pollution control revolving fund to accomplish the objectives, goals, and policies of this Act by providing assistance for projects and activities identified in section 603(c).

(b) Schedule of grant payments

The Administrator and each State shall jointly establish a schedule of payments under which the Administrator will pay to the State the amount of each grant to be made to the State under this subchapter. Such schedule shall be based on the State's intended use plan under section 1386(c) of this title, except that—

(1) such payments shall be made in quarterly installments, and

(2) such payments shall be made as expeditiously as possible, but in no event later than the earlier of—

(A) 8 quarters after the date such funds were obligated by the State, or

(B) 12 quarters after the date such funds were allotted to the State.

(June 30, 1948, c. 758, Title VI, § 601, as added by Pub. L. No. 100–4, Title II, § 212(a), 101 Stat. 22 (Feb. 4, 1987); Pub. L. No. 113–121, § 5001, 128 Stat. 1322 (June 10, 2014).)

Effective Date

Pub. L. No. 113–121, § 5006, 128 Stat. 1327 (June 10, 2014), provided that the amendments to Title VI in that statute "shall take effect on October 1, 2014."

EPA Review and Report

Pub. L. No. 113–121, § 5005, 128 Stat. 1327 (June 10, 2014), provided that:

"(a) Review.—The Administrator of the Environmental Protection Agency shall conduct a review of the allotment formula in effect on the date of enactment of this Act for allocation of funds authorized under title VI of the Federal Water Pollution Control Act (33 U.S.C. 1381 et seq.) to determine whether that formula adequately addresses the water quality needs of eligible States, territories, and Indian tribes, based on—

"(1) the most recent survey of needs developed by the Administrator under section 516(b) of that Act (33 U.S.C. 1375(b)); and

"(2) any other information the Administrator considers appropriate.

"(b) Report.—Not later than 18 months after the date of enactment of this Act, the Administrator shall submit to the Committee on Environment and Public Works of the Senate and the Committee on Transportation and Infrastructure of the House of Representatives and make publicly available a report on the results of the review under subsection (a), including any recommendations for changing the allotment formula."

§ 1382. Capitalization grant agreements

[FWPCA § 602]

(a) General rule

To receive a capitalization grant with funds made available under this subchapter and section 1285(m) of this title, a State shall enter into an agreement with the Administrator which shall include but not be limited to the specifications set forth in subsection (b) of this section.

(b) Specific requirements

The Administrator shall enter into an agreement under this section with a State only after the State has established to the satisfaction of the Administrator that—

(1) the State will accept grant payments with funds to be made available under this subchapter and section 1285(m) of this title in accordance with a payment schedule established jointly by the Administrator under section 1381(b) of this title and will deposit all such payments in the water pollution control revolving fund established by the State in accordance with this subchapter;

(2) the State will deposit in the fund from State moneys an amount equal to at least 20 percent of the total amount of all capitalization grants which will be made to the State with funds to be made available under this subchapter and section 1285(m) of this title on or before the date on which each quarterly grant payment will be made to the State under this subchapter;

(3) the State will enter into binding commitments to provide assistance in accordance with the requirements of this subchapter in an amount equal to 120 percent of the amount of each such grant payment within 1 year after the receipt of such grant payment;

(4) all funds in the fund will be expended in an expeditious and timely manner;

(5) all funds in the fund as a result of capitalization grants under this subchapter and section 1285(m) of this title will first be used to assure maintenance of progress, as determined by the Governor of the State, toward compliance with enforceable deadlines, goals, and requirements of this chapter, including the municipal compliance deadline;

(6) treatment works eligible under this title which will be constructed in whole or in part with assistance made available by a state water pollution control revolving fund authorized under this title or, section 205(m) of this Act, or both, will meet the requirements of, or otherwise be treated (as determined by the Governor of the State) under sections 501(c)(1) and 502 of this title in the same manner as treatment works constructed with assistance under subchapter II of this chapter;

(7) in addition to complying with the requirements of this subchapter, the State will commit or expend each quarterly grant payment which it will receive under this subchapter in accordance with laws and procedures applicable to the commitment or expenditure of revenues of the State;

(8) in carrying out the requirements of section 1386 of this title, the State will use accounting, audit, and fiscal procedures conforming to generally accepted government accounting standards;

(9) the State will require as a condition of making a loan or providing other assistance, as described in section 1383(d) of this title, from the fund that the recipient of such assistance will maintain project accounts in accordance with generally accepted government accounting standards, including standards relating to the reporting of infrastructure assets; and

(10) the State will make annual reports to the Administrator on the actual use of funds in accordance with section 1386(d) of this title;

(11) the State will establish, maintain, invest, and credit the fund with repayments, such that the fund balance will be available in perpetuity for activities under this Act;

(12) any fees charged by the State to recipients of assistance that are considered program income will be used for the purpose of financing the cost of administering the fund or financing projects or activities eligible for assistance from the fund;

(13) beginning in fiscal year 2016, the State will require as a condition of providing assistance to a municipality or intermunicipal, interstate, or State agency that the recipient of such assistance certify, in a manner determined by the Governor of the State, that the recipient—

(A) has studied and evaluated the cost and effectiveness of the processes, materials, techniques, and technologies for carrying out the proposed project or activity for which assistance is sought under this title; and

(B) has selected, to the maximum extent practicable, a project or activity that maximizes the potential for efficient water use, reuse, recapture, and conservation, and energy conservation, taking into account—

(i) the cost of constructing the project or activity;

(ii) the cost of operating and maintaining the project or activity over the life of the project or activity; and

(iii) the cost of replacing the project or activity; and

(14) a contract to be carried out using funds directly made available by a capitalization grant under this title for program management, construction management, feasibility studies, preliminary engineering, design, engineering, surveying, mapping, or architectural related services shall be negotiated in the same manner as a contract for architectural and engineering services is negotiated under chapter 11 of title 40, United States Code, or an equivalent State qualifications-based requirement (as determined by the Governor of the State).

(June 30, 1948, c. 758, Title VI, § 602, as added by Pub. L. No. 100–4, Title II, § 212(a), 101 Stat. 22 (Feb. 4, 1987); and amended by Pub. L. No. 113–121, § 5002, 128 Stat. 1322–23 (June 10, 2014).)

§ 1383. Water pollution control revolving loan funds [FWPCA § 603]

(a) Requirements for obligation of grant funds

Before a State may receive a capitalization grant with funds made available under this subchapter and section 1285(m) of this title, the State shall first establish a water pollution control revolving fund which complies with the requirements of this section.

(b) Administration

Each State water pollution control revolving fund shall be administered by an instrumentality of the State with such powers and limitations as may be required to operate such fund in accordance with the requirements and objectives of this chapter.

(c) Projects and activities eligible for assistance

The amounts of funds available to each State water pollution control revolving fund shall be used only for providing financial assistance—

(1) to any municipality or intermunicipal, interstate, or State agency for construction of publicly owned treatment works (as defined in section 212);

(2) for the implementation of a management program established under section 319;

(3) for development and implementation of a conservation and management plan under section 320;

(4) for the construction, repair, or replacement of decentralized wastewater treatment systems that treat municipal wastewater or domestic sewage;

(5) for measures to manage, reduce, treat, or recapture stormwater or subsurface drainage water;

(6) to any municipality or intermunicipal, interstate, or State agency for measures to reduce the demand for publicly owned treatment works capacity through water conservation, efficiency, or reuse;

(7) for the development and implementation of watershed projects meeting the criteria set forth in section 122;

(8) to any municipality or intermunicipal, interstate, or State agency for measures to reduce the energy consumption needs for publicly owned treatment works;

(9) for reusing or recycling wastewater, stormwater, or subsurface drainage water;

(10) for measures to increase the security of publicly owned treatment works;

(11) to any qualified nonprofit entity, as determined by the Administrator, to provide assistance to owners and operators of small and medium publicly owned treatment works—

(A) to plan, develop, and obtain financing for eligible projects under this subsection, including planning, design, and associated preconstruction activities; and

(B) to assist such treatment works in achieving compliance with this Act; and

(12) to any qualified nonprofit entity, as determined by the Administrator, to provide assistance to an eligible individual (as defined in subsection (j))—

(A) for the repair or replacement of existing individual household decentralized wastewater treatment systems; or

(B) in a case in which an eligible individual resides in a household that could be cost-effectively connected to an available publicly owned treatment works, for the connection of the applicable household to such treatment works.

(d) Types of assistance

Except as otherwise limited by State law, a water pollution control revolving fund of a State under this section may be used only—

(1) to make loans, on the condition that—

(A) such loans are made at or below market interest rates, including interest free loans, at terms not to exceed the lesser of 30 years and the projected useful life (as determined by the state) of the project to be financed with the proceeds of the loans;

(B) annual principal and interest payments will commence not later than 1 year after completion of any project and all loans will be fully amortized upon expiration of the term of the loan;

(C) the recipient of a loan will establish a dedicated source of revenue for repayment of loans;

(D) the fund will be credited with all payments of principal and interest on all loans; and

(E) for a treatment works proposed for repair, replacement, or expansion, and eligible for assistance under subsection (c)(1), the recipient of a loan shall—

(i) develop and implement a fiscal sustainability plan that includes—

(I) an inventory of critical assets that are a part of the treatment works;

(II) an evaluation of the condition and performance of inventoried assets or asset groupings;

(III) a certification that the recipient has evaluated and will be implementing water and energy conservation efforts as part of the plan; and

(IV) a plan for maintaining, repairing, and, as necessary, replacing the treatment works and a plan for funding such activities; or

(ii) certify that the recipient has developed and implemented a plan that meets the requirements under clause (i);

(2) to buy or refinance the debt obligation of municipalities and intermunicipal and interstate agencies within the State at or below market rates, where such debt obligations were incurred after March 7, 1985;

(3) to guarantee, or purchase insurance for, local obligations where such action would improve credit market access or reduce interest rates;

(4) as a source of revenue or security for the payment of principal and interest on revenue or general obligation bonds issued by the State if the proceeds of the sale of such bonds will be deposited in the fund;

(5) to provide loan guarantees for similar revolving funds established by municipalities or intermunicipal agencies;

(6) to earn interest on fund accounts; and

(7) for the reasonable costs of administering the fund and conducting activities under this subchapter, except that such amounts shall not exceed 4 percent of all grant awards to such fund under this subchapter, $400,000 per year, or 1/5 percent per year of the current valuation of the fund, whichever is greatest, plus the amount of any fees collected by the State for such purposes regardless of the source.

(e) Limitation to prevent double benefits

If a State makes, from its water pollution revolving fund, a loan which will finance the cost of facility planning and the preparation of plans, specifications, and estimates for construction of publicly owned treatment works, the State shall ensure that if the recipient of such loan receives a grant under section 1281(g) of this title for construction of such treatment works and an allowance under section 1281(*l*)(1) of this title for non-Federal funds expended for such planning and preparation, such recipient will promptly repay such loan to the extent of such allowance.

(f) Consistency with planning requirements

A State may provide financial assistance from its water pollution control revolving fund only with respect to a project which is consistent with plans, if any, developed under sections 1285(j), 1288, 1313(e), 1329, and 1330 of this title.

(g) Priority list requirement

The State may provide financial assistance from its water pollution control revolving fund only with respect to a project for construction of a treatment works described in subsection (c)(1) of this section if such project is on the State's priority list under section 1296 of this title. Such assistance may be provided regardless of the rank of such project on such list.

(h) Eligibility of non-Federal share of construction grant projects

A State water pollution control revolving fund may provide assistance (other than under subsection (d)(1) of this section) to a municipality or intermunicipal or interstate agency with respect to the non-Federal share of the costs of a treatment works project for which such municipality or agency is receiving assistance from the Administrator under any other authority only if such assistance is necessary to allow such project to proceed.

(i) Additional Subsidization

(1) In General.—In any case in which a State provides assistance to an eligible recipient under subsection (d), the State may provide additional subsidization, including forgiveness of principal and negative interest loans—

(A) in assistance to a municipality or intermunicipal, interstate, or State agency to benefit a municipality that—

(i) meets the affordability criteria of the State established under paragraph (2); or

(ii) does not meet the affordability criteria of the State if the recipient—

(I) seeks additional subsidization to benefit individual ratepayers in the residential user rate class;

(II) demonstrates to the State that such ratepayers will experience a significant hardship from the increase in rates necessary to finance the project or activity for which assistance is sought; and

(III) ensures, as part of an assistance agreement between the State and the recipient, that the additional subsidization provided under this paragraph is directed through a user charge rate system (or other appropriate method) to such ratepayers; or

(B) to implement a process, material, technique, or technology—

(i) to address water-efficiency goals;

(ii) to address energy-efficiency goals;

(iii) to mitigate stormwater runoff; or

(iv) to encourage sustainable project planning, design, and construction.

(2) Affordability Criteria.—

(A) Establishment.—

(i) In General.—Not later than September 30, 2015, and after providing notice and an opportunity for public comment, a State shall establish affordability criteria to assist in identifying municipalities that would experience a significant hardship raising the revenue necessary to finance a project or activity eligible for assistance under subsection (c)(1) if additional subsidization is not provided.

(ii) Contents.—The criteria under clause (i) shall be based on income and unemployment data, population trends, and other data determined relevant by the State, including whether the project or activity is to be carried out in an economically distressed area, as described in section 301 of the Public Works and Economic Development Act of 1965 (42 U.S.C. 3161).

(B) Existing Criteria.—If a State has previously established, after providing notice and an opportunity for public comment, affordability criteria that meet the requirements of subparagraph (A)—

(i) the State may use the criteria for the purposes of this subsection; and

(ii) those criteria shall be treated as affordability criteria established under this paragraph.

(C) Information to Assist States.—The Administrator may publish information to assist States in establishing affordability criteria under subparagraph (A).

(3) Limitations.—

(A) In General.—A State may provide additional subsidization in a fiscal year under this subsection only if the total amount appropriated for making capitalization grants to all States under this title for the fiscal year exceeds $1,000,000,000.

(B) Additional Limitation.—

(i) General Rule.—Subject to clause (ii), a State may use not more than 30 percent of the total amount received by the State in capitalization grants under this title for a fiscal year for providing additional subsidization under this subsection.

(ii) Exception.—If, in a fiscal year, the amount appropriated for making capitalization grants to all States under this title exceeds $1,000,000,000 by a percentage that is less than 30 percent, clause (i) shall be applied by substituting that percentage for 30 percent.

(C) Applicability.—The authority of a State to provide additional subsidization under this subsection shall apply to amounts received by the State in capitalization grants under this title for fiscal years beginning after September 30, 2014.

(D) Consideration.—If the State provides additional subsidization to a municipality or intermunicipal, interstate, or State agency under this subsection that meets the criteria under paragraph (1)(A), the State shall take the criteria set forth in section 602(b)(5) into consideration.

(j) Definition of eligible individual.—In subsection (c)(12), the term "eligible individual" means a member of a household, the members of which have a combined income (for the most recent 12-month period for which information is available) equal to not more than 50 percent of the median nonmetropolitan household income for the State in which the household is located, according to the most recent decennial census.

(June 30, 1948, c. 758, Title VI, § 603, as added by Pub. L. No. 100–4, Title II, § 212(a), 101 Stat. 23 (Feb. 4, 1987); and amended by Pub. L. No. 113–121 Title V, § 5003, 128 Stat. 1323–26 (June 10, 2014); Pub. L. No. 114–322, § 5012, 130 Stat 1628 (Dec. 16, 2016); Pub. L. No. 115–270, § 4107(a), 132 Stat. 3765, 3876–3877 (Oct. 23, 2018).)

Report on New Municipal Grants

Pub. L. No. 115–270, § 4107(b), 132 Stat. 3877 (Oct. 23, 2018), provided that: "Not later than 2 years after the date of enactment of this section, the Administrator of the Environmental Protection Agency shall submit to the Committee on Environment and Public Works of the Senate and the Committee on Transportation and Infrastructure of the House of Representatives a report describing—

"(1) the prevalence throughout the United States of low- and moderate-income households without access to a treatment works; and

"(2) the use by States of assistance under section 603(c)(12) of the Federal Water Pollution Control Act."

§ 1384. Allotment of funds

[FWPCA § 604]

(a) Formula

Sums authorized to be appropriated to carry out this section for each of fiscal years 1989 and 1990 shall be allotted by the Administrator in accordance with section 1285(c) of this title.

(b) Reservation of funds for planning

Each State shall reserve each fiscal year 1 percent of the sums allotted to such State under this section for such fiscal year, or $100,000, whichever amount is greater, to carry out planning under sections 1285(j) and 1313(e) of this title.

(c) Allotment period

(1) Period of availability for grant award

Sums allotted to a State under this section for a fiscal year shall be available for obligation by the State during the fiscal year for which sums are authorized and during the following fiscal year.

(2) Reallotment of unobligated funds

The amount of any allotment not obligated by the State by the last day of the 2-year period of availability established by paragraph (1) shall be immediately reallotted by the Administrator on the basis of the same ratio as is applicable to sums allotted under subchapter II of this chapter for the second fiscal year of such 2-year period. None of the funds reallotted by the Administrator shall be reallotted to any State which has not obligated all sums allotted to such State in the first fiscal year of such 2-year period.

(June 30, 1948, c. 758, Title VI, § 604, as added by Pub. L. No. 100–4, Title II, § 212(a), 101 Stat. 25 (Feb. 4, 1987).)

HISTORICAL AND STATUTORY NOTES

Use of Capitalization Grant Funds for Construction Grants

Pub. L. No. 101–144, Title III, 103 Stat. 858 (Nov. 9, 1989), as amended by Pub. L. No. 101–302, Title II, 104 Stat. 238 (May 25, 1990), provided in part: "That, notwithstanding any other provision of law, sums heretofore, herein or hereafter appropriated under this heading allotted for title VI capitalization grants to American Samoa, Commonwealth of the Northern Mariana Islands, Guam, the Republic of Palau (or its successor entity), Virgin Islands and the District of Columbia, may be used for title II construction grants at the request of the chief executive of each of the above named entities, and sums appropriated in fiscal year 1989 shall remain available for obligation until September 30, 1992."

§ 1385. Corrective action

[FWPCA § 605]

(a) Notification of noncompliance

If the Administrator determines that a State has not complied with its agreement with the Administrator under section 1382 of this title or any other requirement of this subchapter, the Administrator shall notify the State of such noncompliance and the necessary corrective action.

(b) Withholding of payments

If a State does not take corrective action within 60 days after the date a State receives notification of such action under subsection (a) of this section, the Administrator shall withhold additional payments to the State until the Administrator is satisfied that the State has taken the necessary corrective action.

(c) Reallotment of withheld payments

If the Administrator is not satisfied that adequate corrective actions have been taken by the State within 12 months after the State is notified of such actions under subsection (a) of this section, the payments withheld from the State by the Administrator under subsection (b) of this section shall be made available for reallotment in accordance with the most recent formula for allotment of funds under this subchapter.

(June 30, 1948, c. 758, Title VI, § 605, as added by Pub. L. No. 100–4, Title II, § 212(a), 101 Stat. 25 (Feb. 4, 1987).)

§ 1386. Audits, reports, and fiscal controls; intended use plan

[FWPCA § 606]

(a) Fiscal control and auditing procedures

Each State electing to establish a water pollution control revolving fund under this subchapter shall establish fiscal controls and accounting procedures sufficient to assure proper accounting during appropriate accounting periods for—

(1) payments received by the fund;

(2) disbursements made by the fund; and

(3) fund balances at the beginning and end of the accounting period.

(b) Annual Federal audits

The Administrator shall, at least on an annual basis, conduct or require each State to have independently conducted reviews and audits as may be deemed necessary or appropriate by the Administrator to carry out the objectives of this section. Audits of the use of funds deposited in the water pollution revolving fund established by such State shall be conducted in accordance with the auditing procedures of the Government Accountability Office, including chapter 75 of Title 31.

(c) Intended use plan

After providing for public comment and review, each State shall annually prepare a plan identifying the intended uses of the amounts available to its water pollution control revolving fund. Such intended use plan shall include, but not be limited to—

(1) a list of those projects for construction of publicly owned treatment works on the State's priority list developed pursuant to section 1296 of this title and a list of activities eligible for assistance under sections 1329 and 1330 of this title;

(2) a description of the short- and long-term goals and objectives of its water pollution control revolving fund;

(3) information on the activities to be supported, including a description of project categories, discharge requirements under subchapters III and IV of this chapter, terms of financial assistance, and communities served;

(4) assurances and specific proposals for meeting the requirements of paragraphs (3), (4), (5), and (6) of section 1382(b) of this title; and

(5) the criteria and method established for the distribution of funds.

(d) Annual report

Beginning the first fiscal year after the receipt of payments under this subchapter, the State shall provide an annual report to the Administrator describing how the State has met the goals and objectives for the previous fiscal year as identified in the plan prepared for the previous fiscal year pursuant to subsection (c) of this section, including identification of loan recipients, loan amounts, and loan terms and similar details on other forms of financial assistance provided from the water pollution control revolving fund.

(e) Annual Federal oversight review

The Administrator shall conduct an annual oversight review of each State plan prepared under subsection (c) of this section, each State report prepared under subsection (d) of this section, and other such materials as are considered necessary and appropriate in carrying out the purposes of this subchapter. After reasonable notice by the Administrator to the State or the recipient of a loan from a water pollution control revolving fund, the State or loan recipient shall make available to the Administrator such records as the Administrator reasonably requires to review and determine compliance with this subchapter.

(f) Applicability of subchapter II provisions

Except to the extent provided in this subchapter, the provisions of subchapter II of this chapter shall not apply to grants under this subchapter.

(June 30, 1948, c. 758, Title VI, § 606, as added by Pub. L. No. 100–4, Title II, § 212(a), 101 Stat. 25 (Feb. 4, 1987); and amended by Pub. L. No. 108–271, § 8(b), 118 Stat. 814 (July 7, 2004).)

HISTORICAL AND STATUTORY NOTES

Change of Name

"Government Accountability Office" substituted for "General Accounting Office" in subsec. (b) on authority of Pub. L. No. 108–271, § 8(b), 118 Stat. 811 (July 7, 2004), cited in the credit to this section and set out as a note under 31 U.S.C.A. § 702, which provided that any reference to the General Accounting Office in any law, rule, regulation, certificate, directive, instruction, or other official paper in force on July 17, 2004, to refer and apply to the Government Accountability Office.

§ 1387. Authorization of appropriations

[FWPCA § 607]

There is authorized to be appropriated to carry out the purposes of this subchapter the following sums:

(1) $1,200,000,000 per fiscal year for each of fiscal years 1989 and 1990;

(2) $2,400,000,000 for fiscal year 1991;

(3) $1,800,000,000 for fiscal year 1992;

(4) $1,200,000,000 for fiscal year 1993; and

(5) $600,000,000 for fiscal year 1994.

(June 30, 1948, c. 758, Title VI, § 607, as added by Pub. L. No. 100–4, Title II, § 212(a), 101 Stat. 26 (Feb. 4, 1987).)

§ 1388. Requirements

[FWPCA § 608]

(a) In General.—Funds made available from a State water pollution control revolving fund established under this title may not be used for a project for the construction, alteration, maintenance, or repair of treatment works unless all of the iron and steel products used in the project are produced in the United States.

(b) Definition of Iron and Steel Products.—In this section, the term 'iron and steel products' means the following products made primarily of iron or steel: lined or unlined pipes and fittings, manhole covers and other municipal castings, hydrants, tanks, flanges, pipe clamps and restraints, valves, structural steel, reinforced precast concrete, construction materials.

(c) Application.—Subsection (a) shall not apply in any case or category of cases in which the Administrator finds that—

(1) applying subsection (a) would be inconsistent with the public interest;

(2) iron and steel products are not produced in the United States in sufficient and reasonably available quantities and of a satisfactory quality; or

(3) inclusion of iron and steel products produced in the United States will increase the cost of the overall project by more than 25 percent.

(d) Waiver.—If the Administrator receives a request for a waiver under this section, the Administrator shall make available to the public, on an informal basis, a copy of the request and information available to the Administrator concerning the request, and shall allow for informal public input on the request for at least 15 days prior to making a finding based on the request. The Administrator shall make the request and accompanying information available by electronic means, including on the official public Internet site of the Environmental Protection Agency.

(e) International Agreements.—This section shall be applied in a manner consistent with United States obligations under international agreements.

(f) Management and Oversight.—The Administrator may retain up to 0.25 percent of the funds appropriated for this title for management and oversight of the requirements of this section.

(g) Effective Date.—This section does not apply with respect to a project if a State agency approves the engineering plans and specifications for the project, in that agency's capacity to approve such plans and specifications prior to a project requesting bids, prior to the date of enactment of the Water Resources Reform and Development Act of 2014.

(As added by Pub. L. No. 113–121, Title V, § 5004, 128 Stat. 1326–27 (June 10, 2014).)

OCEAN DUMPING

MARINE PROTECTION, RESEARCH, AND SANCTUARIES ACT OF 1972 [MPRSA § ____]

(33 U.S.C.A. §§ 1401 to 1445)

CHAPTER 27—OCEAN DUMPING

§ 1401. Congressional finding, policy, and declaration of purpose

[MPRSA § 2]

(a) Dangers of unregulated dumping

Unregulated dumping of material into ocean waters endangers human health, welfare, and amenities, and the marine environment, ecological systems, and economic potentialities.

(b) Policy of regulation and prevention or limitation

The Congress declares that it is the policy of the United States to regulate the dumping of all types of materials into ocean waters and to prevent or strictly limit the dumping into ocean waters of any material which would adversely affect human health, welfare, or amenities, or the marine environment, ecological systems, or economic potentialities.

(c) Regulation of dumping and transportation for dumping purposes

It is the purpose of this Act to regulate (1) the transportation by any person of material from the United States and, in the case of United States vessels, aircraft, or agencies, the transportation of material from a location outside the United States, when in either case the transportation is for the purpose of dumping the material into ocean waters, and (2) the dumping of material transported by any person from a location outside the United States, if the dumping occurs in the territorial sea or the contiguous zone of the United States.

(Pub. L. No. 92–532, § 2, 86 Stat. 1052 (Oct. 23, 1972); as amended by Pub. L. No. 93–254, § 1(1), 88 Stat. 50 (Mar. 22, 1974).)

HISTORICAL AND STATUTORY NOTES

References in Text

This Act, referred to in subsec. (c), means Pub. L. 92–532, which is codified principally in this chapter, chapter 41 of this title [33 U.S.C.A. § 2801 et seq.], and chapters 32 [16 U.S.C.A. § 1431 et seq.] and 32A [16 U.S.C.A. § 1447 et seq.] of Title 16.

Effective and Applicability Provisions

1974 Acts. Pub. L. No. 93–254, § 2, 88 Stat. 50 (Mar. 22, 1974), provided in part that amendment of subsecs. (b) and (c) of this section and sections 1402, 1411, and 1412(a), other than last sentence of subsec. (a), of this title, by Pub. L. No. 93–254 shall become effective Mar. 22, 1974.

Short Title

1988 Amendments. Pub. L. No. 100–688, Title I, § 1001, 102 Stat. 4139 (Nov. 18, 1988), provided that: "This title [enacting sections 1414b and 1414c of this title, amending sections 1268 and 1412a of this title, repealing provisions formerly codified as section 1414a of this title, and amending provisions set out as a note under section 2267 of this title] may be cited as the 'Ocean Dumping Ban Act of 1988'."

1972 Acts. Pub. L. No. 92–532, § 1, 86 Stat. 1052 (Oct. 23, 1972), provided "[t]hat this Act [enacting this chapter and sections 1431 to 1434 of Title 16, Conservation] may be cited as the 'Marine Protection, Research, and Sanctuaries Act of 1972'."

Territorial Sea and Contiguous Zone of United States

For extension of territorial sea and contiguous zone of United States, see Proc. No. 5928 and Proc. No. 7219, respectively, set out as notes under 43 U.S.C.A. § 1331.

Environmental Effects Abroad of Major Federal Actions

For provisions relating to environmental effects abroad of major federal actions, see Ex. Ord. No. 12114, Jan. 4, 1979, 44 Fed. Reg. 1957, set out as a note under section 4321 of Title 42, The Public Health and Welfare.

Federal Compliance with Pollution Control Standards

For provisions relating to the responsibility of the head of each Executive agency for compliance with applicable pollution control standards, see Ex. Ord. No. 12088, Oct. 13, 1978, 43 Fed. Reg. 47707, set out as a note under section 4321 of Title 42, The Public Health and Welfare.

§ 1402. Definitions

[MPRSA § 3]

For the purposes of this Act the term—

(a) "Administrator" means the Administrator of the Environmental Protection Agency.

(b) "Ocean waters" means those waters of the open seas lying seaward of the base line from which the territorial sea is measured, as provided for in the Convention on the Territorial Sea and the Contiguous Zone (15 UST 1606; TIAS 5639).

(c) "Material" means matter of any kind or description, including, but not limited to, dredged material, solid waste, incinerator residue, garbage, sewage, sewage sludge, munitions, radiological, chemical, and biological warfare agents, radioactive materials, chemicals, biological and laboratory waste, wreck or discarded equipment, rock, sand, excavation debris, and industrial, municipal, agricultural, and other waste; but such term does not mean sewage from vessels within the meaning of section 1322 of this title. Oil within the meaning of section 1321 of this title shall be included only to the extent that such oil is taken on board a vessel or aircraft for the purpose of dumping.

(d) "United States" includes the several States, the District of Columbia, the Commonwealth of Puerto Rico, the Canal Zone, the territories and possessions of the United States, and the Trust Territory of the Pacific Islands.

(e) "Person" means any private person or entity, or any officer, employee, agent, department, agency, or instrumentality of the Federal Government, of any State or local unit of government, or of any foreign government.

(f) "Dumping" means a disposition of material: *Provided,* That it does not mean a disposition of any effluent from any outfall structure to the extent that such disposition is regulated under the provisions of the Federal Water Pollution Control Act, as amended [33 U.S.C.A. § 1251 et seq.] under the provisions of section 407 of this title, or under the provisions of the Atomic Energy Act of 1954, as amended [42 U.S.C.A. § 2011 et seq.], nor does it mean a routine discharge of effluent incidental to the propulsion of, or operation of motor-driven equipment on, vessels: *Provided, further,* That it does not mean the construction of any fixed structure or artificial island nor the intentional placement of any device in ocean waters or on or in the submerged land beneath such waters, for a purpose other than disposal, when such construction or such placement is otherwise regulated by Federal or State law or occurs pursuant to an authorized Federal or State program: *And provided further,* That it does not include the deposit of oyster shells, or other materials when such deposit is made for the purpose of developing, maintaining, or harvesting fisheries resources and is otherwise regulated by Federal or State law or occurs pursuant to an authorized Federal or State program.

(g) "District court of the United States" includes the District Court of Guam, the District Court of the Virgin Islands, the District Court of Puerto Rico, the District Court of the Canal Zone, and in the case of American Samoa and the Trust Territory of the Pacific Islands, the District Court of the United States for the District of Hawaii, which court shall have jurisdiction over actions arising therein.

(h) "Secretary" means the Secretary of the Army.

(i) "Dredged material" means any material excavated or dredged from the navigable waters of the United States.

(j) "High-level radioactive waste" means the aqueous waste resulting from the operation of the first cycle solvent extraction system, or equivalent and the concentrated waste from subsequent extraction cycles, or equivalent, in a facility for reprocessing irradiated reactor fuels, or irradiated fuel from nuclear power reactors.

(k) "Medical waste" means isolation wastes; infectious agents; human blood and blood products; pathological wastes; sharps; body parts; contaminated bedding; surgical wastes and potentially contaminated laboratory wastes; dialysis wastes; and such additional medical items as the Administrator shall prescribe by regulation.

(*l*) "Transport" or "transportation" refers to the carriage and related handling of any material by a vessel, or by any other vehicle, including aircraft.

(m) "Convention" means the Convention on the Prevention of Marine Pollution by Dumping of Wastes and Other Matter.

(Pub. L. No. 92–532, § 3, 86 Stat. 1052 (Oct. 23, 1972); and amended by Pub. L. No. 93–254, § 1(2), 88 Stat. 50 (Mar. 22, 1974); Pub. L. No. 100–688, Title III, § 3201(a), 102 Stat. 4153 (Nov. 18, 1988).)

HISTORICAL AND STATUTORY NOTES

References in Text

This Act, referred to in text, means Pub. L. 92–532, which is codified principally as this chapter, chapter 41 of this title [33 U.S.C.A. § 2801 et seq.], and chapters 32 [16 U.S.C.A. § 1431 et seq.] and 32A [16 U.S.C.A. § 1447 et seq.] of Title 16.

For definition of Canal Zone, referred to in subsec. (d), see section 3602(b) of Title 22, Foreign Relations and Intercourse.

The Federal Water Pollution Control Act, as amended, referred to in subsec. (f), is Act of June 30, 1948, c. 758, as amended generally by Pub. L. No. 92–500, § 2, 86 Stat. 816 (Oct. 18, 1972), which is codified generally as chapter 26 (section 1251 et seq.) of this title. For complete classification of this Act to the Code, see Short Title note set out under section 1251 of this title and Tables.

The Atomic Energy Act of 1954, as amended, referred to in subsec. (f), is Act of Aug. 30, 1954, c. 1073, § 1, 68 Stat. 919, as amended, which is codified principally as chapter 23 (section 2011 et seq.) of Title 42, Public Health and Welfare. For complete classification of this Act to the Code, see Short Title note set out under section 2011 of Title 42 and Tables.

Effective and Applicability Provisions

1974 Acts. Amendment by Pub. L. No. 93–254 effective Mar. 22, 1974, see section 2 of Pub. L. No. 93–254, set out in part as a note under section 1401 of this title.

Termination of Trust Territory of the Pacific Islands

For termination of Trust Territory of the Pacific Islands, see note set out preceding 48 U.S.C.A. § 1681.

Termination of United States District Court for the District of the Canal Zone

For termination of the United States District Court for the District of the Canal Zone at end of the "transition period", being the 30-month period beginning Oct. 1, 1979, and ending midnight Mar. 31, 1982, see Paragraph 5 of Article XI of the Panama Canal Treaty of 1977 and sections 2101 and 2201 to 2203 of Pub. L. No. 96–70, Title II, 93 Stat. 493 (Sept. 27, 1979), formerly codified as 22 U.S.C.A. §§ 3831 and 3841 to 3843, respectively.

Territorial Sea and Contiguous Zone of United States

For extension of territorial sea and contiguous zone of United States, see Proc. No. 5928 and Proc. No. 7219, respectively, set out as notes under 43 U.S.C.A. § 1331.

SUBCHAPTER I—REGULATION

§ 1411. Prohibited acts

[MPRSA § 101]

(a) Except as may be authorized by a permit issued pursuant to section 1412 or section 1413 of this title, and subject to regulations issued pursuant to section 1418 of this title,

(1) no person shall transport from the United States, and

(2) in the case of a vessel or aircraft registered in the United States or flying the United States flag or in the case of a United States department, agency, or instrumentality, no person shall transport from any location

any material for the purpose of dumping it into ocean waters.

(b) Except as may be authorized by a permit issued pursuant to section 1412 of this title, and subject to regulations issued pursuant to section 1418 of this title, no person shall dump any material transported from a location outside the United States (1) into the territorial sea of the United States, or (2) into a zone contiguous to the territorial sea of the United States, extending to a line twelve nautical miles seaward from the base line from which the breadth of the territorial sea is measured, to the extent that it may affect the territorial sea or the territory of the United States.

(Pub. L. No. 92–532, Title I, § 101, 86 Stat. 1053 (Oct. 23, 1972); and amended by Pub. L. No. 93–254, § 1(3), 88 Stat. 51 (Mar. 22, 1974).)

HISTORICAL AND STATUTORY NOTES

Effective and Applicability Provisions

1974 Acts. Amendment by Pub. L. No. 93–254 effective Mar. 22, 1974, see section 2 of Pub. L. No. 93–254, set out in part as a note under section 1401 of this title.

1972 Acts. Pub. L. No. 92–532, § 110(a), 86 Stat. 1054 (Oct. 23, 1972), provided that: "This title [this subchapter] shall take effect six months after the date of the enactment of this Act [Oct. 23, 1972]."

Savings Provisions

Pub. L. No. 92–532, § 110(b), 86 Stat. 1054 (Oct. 23, 1972), provided that: "No legal action begun, or right of action accrued, prior to the effective date of this title [this subchapter] shall be affected by any provision of this title [this subchapter]."

Territorial Sea and Contiguous Zone of United States

For extension of territorial sea and contiguous zone of United States, see Proc. No. 5928 and Proc. No. 7219, respectively, set out as notes under 43 U.S.C.A. § 1331.

§ 1412. Dumping permit program

[MPRSA § 102]

(a) Environmental Protection Agency permits

Except in relation to dredged material, as provided for in section 1413 of this title, and in relation to radiological, chemical, and biological warfare agents, high-level radioactive waste, and medical waste, for which no permit may be issued, the Administrator may issue permits, after notice and opportunity for public hearings, for the transportation from the United States or, in the case of an agency or instrumentality of the United States, or in the case of a vessel or aircraft registered in the United States or flying the United States flag, for the transportation from a location outside the United States, of material for the purpose of dumping it into ocean waters, or for the dumping of material into the waters described in section 1411(b) of this title, where the Administrator determines that such dumping will not unreasonably degrade or endanger human health, welfare, or amenities, or the marine environment, ecological systems, or economic potentialities. The Administrator shall establish and apply criteria for reviewing and evaluating such permit applications, and, in establishing or revising such criteria, shall consider, but not be limited in his consideration to, the following:

(A) The need for the proposed dumping.

(B) The effect of such dumping on human health and welfare, including economic, esthetic, and recreational values.

(C) The effect of such dumping on fisheries resources, plankton, fish, shellfish, wildlife, shore lines and beaches.

(D) The effect of such dumping on marine ecosystems, particularly with respect to—

(i) the transfer, concentration, and dispersion of such material and its byproducts through biological, physical, and chemical processes,

(ii) potential changes in marine ecosystem diversity, productivity, and stability, and

(iii) species and community population dynamics.

(E) The persistence and permanence of the effects of the dumping.

(F) The effect of dumping particular volumes and concentrations of such materials.

(G) Appropriate locations and methods of disposal or recycling, including land-based alternatives and the probable impact of requiring use of such alternate locations or methods upon considerations affecting the public interest.

(H) The effect on alternate uses of oceans, such as scientific study, fishing, and other living resource exploitation, and non-living resource exploitation.

(I) In designating recommended sites, the Administrator shall utilize wherever feasible locations beyond the edge of the Continental Shelf.

In establishing or revising such criteria, the Administrator shall consult with Federal, State, and local officials, and interested members of the general public, as may appear appropriate to the Administrator.

With respect to such criteria as may affect the civil works program of the Department of the Army, the Administrator shall also consult with the Secretary. In reviewing applications for permits, the Administrator shall make such provision for consultation with interested Federal and State agencies as he deems useful or necessary. No permit shall be issued for a dumping of material which will violate applicable water quality standards. To the extent that he may do so without relaxing the requirements of this subchapter, the Administrator, in establishing or revising such criteria, shall apply the standards and criteria binding upon the United States under the Convention, including its Annexes.

(b) Permit categories

The Administrator may establish and issue various categories of permits, including the general permits described in section 1414(c) of this title.

(c) Designation of sites

(1) In general

The Administrator shall, in a manner consistent with the criteria established pursuant to subsection (a) of this section, designate sites or time periods for dumping. The Administrator shall designate sites or time periods for dumping that will mitigate adverse impact on the environment to the greatest extent practicable.

(2) Prohibitions regarding site or time period

In any case where the Administrator determines that, with respect to certain materials, it is necessary to prohibit dumping at a site or during a time period, the Administrator shall prohibit the dumping of such materials in such site or during such time period. This prohibition shall apply to any dumping at the site or during such time period. This prohibition shall apply to any dumping at the site or during the time period, including any dumping under section 1413(e) of this title.

(3) Dredged material disposal sites

In the case of dredged material disposal sites, the Administrator, in conjunction with the Secretary, shall develop a site management plan for each site designated pursuant to this section. In developing such plans, the Administrator and the Secretary shall provide opportunity for public comment. Such plans shall include, but not be limited to—

(A) a baseline assessment of conditions at the site;

(B) a program for monitoring the site;

(C) special management conditions or practices to be implemented at each site that are necessary for protection of the environment;

(D) consideration of the quantity of the material to be disposed of at the site, and the presence, nature, and bioavailability of the contaminants in the material;

(E) consideration of the anticipated use of the site over the long term, including the anticipated closure date for the site, if applicable, and any need for management of the site after the closure of the site; and

(F) a schedule for review and revision of the plan (which shall not be reviewed and revised less frequently than 10 years after adoption of the plan, and every 10 years thereafter).

(4) General site management plan requirement; prohibitions

After January 1, 1995, no site shall receive a final designation unless a management plan has been developed pursuant to this section. Beginning on January 1, 1997, no permit for dumping pursuant to this Act or authorization for dumping under section 1413(e) of this title shall be issued for a site (other than the site located off the coast of Newport Beach, California, which is known as "LA-3") unless such site has received a final designation pursuant to this subsection or an alternative site has been selected pursuant to section 1413(b) of this title. Beginning January 1, 2011, no permit for dumping pursuant to this Act or authorization for dumping under section 1413(e) of this title shall be issued for the site located off the coast of Newport Beach, California, which is known as "LA-3", unless such site has received a final designation pursuant to this subsection or an alternative site has been selected pursuant to section 1413(b) of this title.

(5) Management plans for previously designated sites

The Administrator shall develop a site management plan for any site designated prior to January 1, 1995, as expeditiously as practicable, but not later than January 1, 1997, giving priority consideration to management plans for designated sites that are considered to have the greatest impact on the environment.

(d) Fish wastes

No permit is required under this subchapter for the transportation for dumping or the dumping of fish wastes, except when deposited in harbors or other protected or enclosed coastal waters, or where the Administrator finds that such deposits could endanger health, the environment, or ecological systems in a specific location. Where the Administrator makes such a finding, such material may be deposited only as authorized by a permit issued by the Administrator under this section.

(e) Foreign State permits; acceptance

In the case of transportation of material, by an agency or instrumentality of the United States or by a vessel or aircraft registered in the United States or flying the United States flag, from a location in a foreign State Party to the Convention, a permit issued pursuant to the authority of that foreign State Party, in accordance with Convention requirements, and which otherwise could have been issued pursuant to subsection (a) of this section, shall be accepted, for the purposes of this subchapter, as if it were issued by the Administrator under the authority of this section: *Provided,* That in the case of an agency or instrumentality of the United States, no application shall be made for a permit to be issued pursuant to the authority of a foreign State Party to the Convention unless the Administrator concurs in the filing of such application.

(Pub. L. No. 92–532, Title I, § 102, 86 Stat. 1054 (Oct. 23, 1972); and amended by Pub. L. No. 93–254, § 1(4), 88 Stat. 51 (Mar. 22, 1974); Pub. L. No. 96–572, § 3, 94 Stat. 3345 (Dec. 22, 1980); Pub. L. No. 100–688, Title III, § 3201(b), 102 Stat. 4153 (Nov. 18, 1988); Pub. L. No. 102–580, Title V, § 506(a), 106 Stat. 4868 (Oct. 31, 1992); Pub. L. No. 104–303, Title V, § 582, 110 Stat. 3791 (Oct. 12, 1996); Pub. L. No. 106–53, Title V, § 562, 113 Stat. 355 (Aug. 17, 1999); Pub. L. No. 110–114, Title V, § 5046, 121 Stat. 1209 (Nov. 8, 2007).)

HISTORICAL AND STATUTORY NOTES

References in Text

This Act, referred to in subsec. (c)(4), means Pub. L. 92–532, which is codified principally in this chapter, chapter 41 of this title [33 U.S.C.A. § 2801 et seq.], and chapters 32 [16 U.S.C.A. § 1431 et seq.] and 32A [16 U.S.C.A. § 1447 et seq.] of Title 16.

Effective and Applicability Provisions

1974 Acts. Pub. L. No. 93–254, § 2, 88 Stat. 51 (Mar. 22, 1974), provided in part that: "The amendments made by subparagraph 1(4)(A)(iii) and paragraph 1(4)(B) of this Act [enacting provision of subsec. (a) respecting application of standards by Administrator and subsec. (e) of this section] shall become effective on the date that the Convention on the Prevention of Marine Pollution by Dumping of Wastes and Other Matters enters into force for the United States." [The Convention entered into force for the United States Aug. 30, 1975.]

Amendment of subsec. (a) of this section, other than last sentence, by Pub. L. No. 93–254 effective Mar. 22, 1974, see section 2 of Pub. L. No. 93–254, set out in part as a note under section 1401 of this title.

1972 Acts. Section effective six months after Oct. 23, 1972, see section 110(a) of Pub. L. No. 92–532, set out as a note under section 1411 of this title.

§ 1412a. Emergency dumping of industrial waste

(a) Emergency permits for dumping of industrial waste; issuance, etc.

Notwithstanding section 104B of the Marine Protection, Research, and Sanctuaries Act of 1972 [33 U.S.C.A. § 1414b], after December 31, 1981, the Administrator may issue emergency permits under Title I of such Act [33 U.S.C.A. § 1411 et seq.] for the dumping of industrial waste into ocean waters, or into waters described in such section 101(b) [33 U.S.C.A. § 1411(b)], if the Administrator determines that there has been demonstrated to exist an emergency, requiring the dumping of such waste, which poses an unacceptable risk relating to human health and admits of no other feasible solution. As used herein, "emergency" refers to situations requiring action with a marked degree of urgency.

(b) "Industrial waste" defined

For purposes of this section, the term "industrial waste" means any solid, semisolid, or liquid waste generated by a manufacturing or processing plant.

(Pub. L. No. 95–153, § 4, 91 Stat. 1255 (Nov. 4, 1977); and amended by Pub. L. No. 96–572, § 2, 94 Stat. 3344 (Dec. 22, 1980); Pub. L. No. 100–688, Title I, § 1003(a), 102 Stat. 4149 (Nov. 18, 1988).)

HISTORICAL AND STATUTORY NOTES

References in Text

The Marine Protection, Research, and Sanctuaries Act of 1972, referred to in subsec. (a), is Pub. L. No. 92–532, 86 Stat. 1052 (Oct. 23, 1972), as amended. Title I of such Act of 1972 is codified generally as subchapter I (section 1411 et seq.) of this chapter. For complete classification of this Act to the Code, see Short Title note set out under section 1401 of this title and Tables.

Such section 101(b), referred to in subsec. (a), means section 101(b) of the Marine Protection, Research, and Sanctuaries Act of 1972, which is codified as 33 U.S.C.A. § 1411(b).

Codifications

Section was not enacted as part of the Marine Protection, Research, and Sanctuaries Act of 1972, which comprises this chapter.

§ 1413. Dumping permit program for dredged material

[MPRSA § 103]

(a) Issuance by Secretary of the Army

Subject to the provisions of subsections (b), (c), and (d) of this section, the Secretary may issue permits, after notice and opportunity for public hearings, for the transportation of dredged material for the purpose of dumping it into ocean waters, where the Secretary determines that the dumping will not unreasonably degrade or endanger human health, welfare, or amenities, or the marine environment, ecological systems, or economic potentialities.

(b) Independent determination of need for dumping, other methods of disposal, and appropriate locations; alternative sites

In making the determination required by subsection (a) of this section, the Secretary shall apply those criteria, established pursuant to section 1412(a) of this title, relating to the effects of the dumping. Based upon an evaluation of the potential effect of a permit denial on navigation, economic and industrial development, and foreign and domestic commerce of the United States, the Secretary shall make an independent determination as to the need for the dumping. The Secretary shall also make an independent determination as to other possible methods of disposal and as to appropriate locations for the dumping. In considering appropriate locations, he shall, to the maximum extent feasible, utilize the recommended sites designated by the Administrator pursuant to section 1412(c) of this title. In any case in which the use of a designated site is not feasible, the Secretary may, with the concurrence of the Administrator, select an alternative site. The criteria and factors established in section 1412(a) of this title relating to site selection shall be used in selecting the alternative site in a manner consistent with the application of such factors and criteria pursuant to section 1412(c) of this title. Disposal at or in the vicinity of an alternative site shall be limited to a period of not greater than 5 years unless the site is subsequently designated pursuant to section 1412(c) of this title; except that an alternative site may continue to be used for an additional period of time that shall not exceed 5 years if—

(1) no feasible disposal site has been designated by the Administrator;

(2) the continued use of the alternative site is necessary to maintain navigation and facilitate interstate or international commerce; and

(3) the Administrator determines that the continued use of the site does not pose an unacceptable risk to human health, aquatic resources, or the environment.

(c) Concurrence by Administrator

(1) Notification

Prior to issuing a permit to any person under this section, the Secretary shall first notify the Administrator of the Secretary's intention to do so and provide necessary and appropriate information concerning the permit to the Administrator. Within 30 days of receiving such information, the Administrator shall review the information and request any additional information the Administrator deems necessary to evaluate the proposed permit.

(2) Concurrence by Administrator

Within 45 days after receiving from the Secretary all information the Administrator considers to be necessary to evaluate the proposed permit, the Administrator shall, in writing, concur with (either entirely or with conditions) or decline to concur with the determination of the Secretary as to compliance with the criteria, conditions, and restrictions established pursuant to sections 1412(a) and 1412(c) of this title relating to the environmental impact of the permit. The Administrator may request one 45-day extension in writing and the Secretary shall grant such request on receipt of the request.

(3) Effect of concurrence

In any case where the Administrator makes a determination to concur (with or without conditions) or to decline to concur within the time period specified in paragraph (2) the determination shall prevail. If the Administrator declines to concur in the determination of the Secretary no permit shall be issued. If the Administrator concurs with conditions the permit shall include such conditions. The Administrator shall state in writing the reasons for declining to concur or for the conditions of the concurrence.

(4) Failure to act

If no written documentation is made by the Administrator within the time period provided for in paragraph (2), the Secretary may issue the permit.

(5) Compliance with criteria and restrictions

Unless the Administrator grants a waiver pursuant to subsection (d) of this section, any permit issued by the Secretary shall require compliance with such criteria and restrictions.

(d) Waiver of requirements

If, in any case, the Secretary finds that, in the disposition of dredged material, there is no economically feasible method or site available other than a dumping site the utilization of which would result in non-compliance with the criteria established pursuant to section 1412(a) of this title relating to the effects of dumping or with the restrictions established pursuant to section 1412(c) of this title relating to critical areas, he shall so certify and request a waiver from the Administrator of the specific requirements involved. Within thirty days of the receipt of the waiver request, unless the Administrator finds that the dumping of the material will result in an unacceptably adverse impact on municipal water supplies, shell-fish beds, wildlife, fisheries (including spawning and breeding areas), or recreational areas, he shall grant the waiver.

(e) Federal projects involving dredged material

In connection with Federal projects involving dredged material, the Secretary may, in lieu of the permit procedure, issue regulations which will require the application to such projects of the same criteria, other factors to be evaluated, the same procedures, and the same requirements which apply to the issuance of permits under subsections (a), (b), (c), and (d) of this section and section 1414(a) and (d) of this title.

(Pub. L. No. 92–532, Title I, § 103, 86 Stat. 1055 (Oct. 23, 1972); and amended by Pub. L. No. 102–580, Title V, §§ 504, 506(b), 106 Stat. 4866, 4869 (Oct. 31, 1992).)

HISTORICAL AND STATUTORY NOTES

Effective and Applicability Provisions

1972 Acts. Section effective six months after Oct. 23, 1972, see section 110(a) of Pub. L. No. 92–532, set out as a note under section 1411 of this title.

§ 1414. Permit conditions

[MPRSA § 104]

(a) Designated and included conditions

Permits issued under this subchapter shall designate and include (1) the type of material authorized to be transported for dumping or to be dumped; (2) the amount of material authorized to be transported for dumping or to be dumped; (3) the location where such transport for dumping will be terminated or where such dumping will occur; (4) such requirements, limitations, or conditions as are necessary to assure consistency with any site management plan approved pursuant to section 1412(c) of this title; (5) any special provisions deemed necessary by the Administrator or the Secretary, as the case may be, after consultation with the Secretary of the Department in which the Coast Guard is operating, for the monitoring and surveillance of the transportation or dumping; and (6) such other matters as the Administrator or the Secretary, as the case may be, deems appropriate. Permits issued under this subchapter shall be issued for a period of not to exceed 7 years.

(b) Permit processing fees; reporting requirements

The Administrator or the Secretary, as the case may be, may prescribe such processing fees for permits and such reporting requirements for actions taken pursuant to permits issued by him under this subchapter as he deems appropriate.

(c) General permits

Consistent with the requirements of sections 1412 and 1413 of this title, but in lieu of a requirement for specific permits in such case, the Administrator or the Secretary, as the case may be, may issue general permits for the transportation for dumping, or dumping, or both, of specified materials or classes of materials for which he may issue permits, which he determines will have a minimal adverse environmental impact.

(d) Review

Any permit issued under this subchapter shall be reviewed periodically and, if appropriate, revised. The Administrator or the Secretary, as the case may be, may limit or deny the issuance of permits, or he may alter or revoke partially or entirely the terms of permits issued by him under this subchapter, for the transportation for dumping, or for the dumping, or both, of specified materials or classes of materials, where he finds, based upon monitoring data from the dump site and surrounding area, that such materials cannot be dumped consistently with the criteria and other factors required to be applied in evaluating the permit application. No action shall be taken under this subsection unless the affected person or permittee shall have been given notice and opportunity for a hearing on such action as proposed.

(e) Information for review and evaluation of applications

The Administrator or the Secretary, as the case may be, shall require an applicant for a permit under this subchapter to provide such information as he may consider necessary to review and evaluate such application.

(f) Public information

Information received by the Administrator or the Secretary, as the case may be, as a part of any application or in connection with any permit granted under this subchapter shall be available to the public as a matter of public record, at every stage of the proceeding. The final determination of the Administrator or the Secretary, as the case may be, shall be likewise available.

(g) Display of issued permits

A copy of any permit issued under this subchapter shall be placed in a conspicuous place in the vessel which will be used for the transportation or dumping authorized by such permit, and an additional copy shall be furnished by the issuing official to the Secretary of the department in which the Coast Guard is operating, or its designee.

(h) Low-level radioactive waste; research purposes

Notwithstanding any provision of this subchapter to the contrary, during the two-year period beginning on January 6, 1983, no permit may be issued under this subchapter that authorizes the dumping of any low-level radioactive waste unless the Administrator of the Environmental Protection Agency determines—

(1) that the proposed dumping is necessary to conduct research—

(A) on new technology related to ocean dumping, or

(B) to determine the degree to which the dumping of such substance will degrade the marine environment;

(2) that the scale of the proposed dumping is limited to the smallest amount of such material and the shortest duration of time that is necessary to fulfill the purposes of the research, such that the dumping will have minimal adverse impact upon human health, welfare, and amenities, and the marine environment, ecological systems, economic potentialities, and other legitimate uses;

(3) after consultation with the Secretary of Commerce, that the potential benefits of such research will outweigh any such adverse impact; and

(4) that the proposed dumping will be preceded by appropriate baseline monitoring studies of the proposed dump site and its surrounding environment.

Each permit issued pursuant to this subsection shall be subject to such conditions and restrictions as the Administrator determines to be necessary to minimize possible adverse impacts of such dumping.

(i) Radioactive Material Disposal Impact Assessment; Congressional approval

(1) Two years after January 6, 1983, the Administrator may not issue a permit under this subchapter for the disposal of radioactive waste material until the applicant, in addition to complying with all other requirements of this subchapter, prepares, with respect to the site at which the disposal is proposed, a Radioactive Material Disposal Impact Assessment which shall include—

(A) a listing of all radioactive materials in each container to be disposed, the number of containers to be dumped, the structural diagrams of each container, the number of curies of each material in each container, and the exposure levels in rems at the inside and outside of each container;

(B) an analysis of the environmental impact of the proposed action, at the site at which the applicant desires to dispose of the material, upon human health and welfare and marine life;

(C) any adverse environmental effects at the site which cannot be avoided should the proposal be implemented;

(D) an analysis of the resulting environmental and economic conditions if the containers fail to contain the radioactive waste material when initially deposited at the specific site;

(E) a plan for the removal or containment of the disposed nuclear material if the container leaks or decomposes;

(F) a determination by each affected State whether the proposed action is consistent with its approved Coastal Zone Management Program;

(G) an analysis of the economic impact upon other users of marine resources;

(H) alternatives to the proposed action;

(I) comments and results of consultation with State officials and public hearings held in the coastal States that are nearest to the affected areas;

(J) a comprehensive monitoring plan to be carried out by the applicant to determine the full effect of the disposal on the marine environment, living resources, or human health, which plan shall include, but not be limited to, the monitoring of exterior container radiation samples, the taking of water and sediment samples, and fish and benthic animal samples, adjacent to the containers, and the acquisition of such other information as the Administrator may require; and

(K) such other information which the Administrator may require in order to determine the full effects of such disposal.

(2) The Administrator shall include, in any permit to which paragraph (1) applies, such terms and conditions as may be necessary to ensure that the monitoring plan required under paragraph (1)(J) is fully implemented, including the analysis by the Administrator of the samples required to be taken under the plan.

(3) The Administrator shall submit a copy of the assessment prepared under paragraph (1) with respect to any permit to the Committee on Merchant Marine and Fisheries of the House of Representatives and the Committee on Environment and Public Works of the Senate.

(4) **(A)** Upon a determination by the Administrator that a permit to which this subsection applies should be issued, the Administrator shall transmit such a recommendation to the House of Representatives and the Senate.

(B) No permit may be issued by the Administrator under this Act for the disposal of radioactive materials in the ocean unless the Congress, by approval of a resolution described in paragraph (D) within 90 days of continuous session of the Congress beginning on the date after the date of receipt by the Senate and the House of Representatives of such recommendation, authorizes the Administrator to grant a permit to dispose of radioactive material under this Act.

(C) For purposes of this subsection—

(1) continuity of session of the Congress is broken only by an adjournment sine die;

(2) the days on which either House is not in session because of an adjournment of more than three days to a day certain are excluded in the computation of the 90 day calendar period.

(D) For the purposes of this subsection, the term "resolution" means a joint resolution, the resolving clause of which is as follows: "That the House of Representatives and the Senate approve and authorize the Administrator of the Environmental Protection Agency to grant a permit to ________ under the Marine Protection, Research, and Sanctuaries Act of 1972 to dispose of radioactive materials in the ocean as recommended by the Administrator to the Congress on _______, 19____."; the first blank space therein to be filled with the appropriate applicant to dispose of nuclear material and the second blank therein to be filled with the date on which the Administrator submits the recommendation to the House of Representatives and the Senate.

(Pub. L. No. 92–532, Title I, § 104, 86 Stat. 1056 (Oct. 23, 1972); as amended by Pub. L. No. 97–424, Title IV, § 424(a), 96 Stat. 2165 (Jan. 6, 1983); Pub. L. No. 100–17, Title I, § 133(c)(1), 101 Stat. 172 (Apr. 2, 1987); Pub. L. No. 102–580, Title V, § 507, 106 Stat. 4869 (Oct. 31, 1992).)

HISTORICAL AND STATUTORY NOTES

References in Text

This Act and the Marine Protection, Research, and Sanctuaries Act of 1972, referred to in subsec. (i)(4)(B), (D), is Pub. L. No. 92–532, 86 Stat. 1052 (Oct. 23, 1972), as amended, which is codified generally as this chapter, chapter 41 of this title [33 U.S.C.A. § 2801 et seq.], and chapters 32 [16 U.S.C.A. § 1431 et seq.] and 32A [16 U.S.C.A. § 1447 et seq.] of Title 16. For complete classification of this Act to the Code, see Short Title note set out under 33 U.S.C.A. § 1401 and Tables.

Effective and Applicability Provisions

1972 Acts. Section effective six months after Oct. 23, 1972, see section 110(a) of Pub. L. No. 92–532, set out as a note under section 1411 of this title.

Abolition of House Committee on Merchant Marine and Fisheries

Committee on Merchant Marine and Fisheries of House of Representatives abolished and its jurisdiction transferred by House Resolution No. 6, One Hundred Fourth Congress, Jan. 4, 1995. For treatment of references to Committee on Merchant Marine and Fisheries, see section 1(b)(3) of Pub. L. No. 104–14, set out as a note preceding section 21 of Title 2.

§ 1414a. Special provisions regarding certain dumping sites

[MPRSA § 104A]

(a) New York Bight Apex

(1) For purposes of this subsection—

(A) The term "Apex" means the New York Bight Apex consisting of the ocean waters of the Atlantic Ocean westward of 73 degrees 30 minutes west longitude and northward of 40 degrees 10 minutes north latitude.

(B) The term "Apex site" means that site within the Apex at which the dumping of municipal sludge occurred before October 1, 1983.

(C) The term "eligible authority" means any sewerage authority or other unit of State or local government that on November 2, 1983, was authorized under court order to dump municipal sludge at the Apex site.

(2) No person may apply for a permit under this subchapter in relation to the dumping of, or the transportation for purposes of dumping, municipal sludge within the Apex unless that person is an eligible authority.

(3) The Administrator may not issue, or renew, any permit under this subchapter that authorizes the dumping of, or the transportation for purposes of dumping, municipal sludge within the Apex after the earlier of—

(A) December 15, 1987; or

(B) the day determined by the Administrator to be the first day on which municipal sludge generated by eligible authorities can reasonably be dumped at a site designated under section 1412 of this title other than a site within the Apex.

(b) Restriction on use of the 106-mile site

The Administrator may not issue or renew any permit under this subchapter which authorizes any person, other than a person that is an eligible authority within the meaning of subsection (a)(1)(C) of this section, to dump, or to transport for the purposes of dumping, municipal sludge within the site designated under section 1412(c) of this title by the Administrator and known as the "106-Mile Ocean Waste Dump Site" (as described in 49 FED. REG. 19005).

(Pub. L. No. 92–532, Title I, § 104A, as added by Pub. L. No. 99–662, Title XI, § 1172(b), 100 Stat. 4259 (Nov. 17, 1986).)

HISTORICAL AND STATUTORY NOTES

Prior Provisions

An identical section 104A, which was added to Pub. L. No. 92–532 by Pub. L. No. 100–4, Title V, § 508(b), 101 Stat. 79 (Feb. 4, 1987,), and also codified as this section, was repealed by Pub. L. No. 100–688, Title I, § 1002, 102 Stat. 4139 (Nov. 18, 1988).

Congressional Finding

Section 1172(a) of Pub. L. No. 99–662 provided that: "The Congress finds that the New York Bight Apex is no longer a suitable location for the ocean dumping of municipal sludge."

[An identical provision was enacted by Pub. L. No. 100–4, Title V, § 508(a), 101 Stat. 79 (Feb. 4, 1987).]

§ 1414b. Ocean dumping of sewage sludge and industrial waste

[MPRSA § 104B]

(a) Termination of dumping

(1) Prohibitions on dumping

Notwithstanding any other provision of law—

(A) on and after the 270th day after November 18, 1988, no person (including a person described in section 1414a(a)(1)(C) of this title) shall dump into ocean waters, or transport for the purpose of dumping into ocean waters, sewage sludge or industrial waste, unless such person—

(i) has entered into a compliance agreement or enforcement agreement which meets the requirements of subsection (c)(2) or (3) of this section, as applicable; and

(ii) has obtained a permit issued under section 1412 of this title which authorizes such transportation and dumping; and

(B) after December 31, 1991, it shall be unlawful for any person to dump into ocean waters, or to transport for the purposes of dumping into ocean waters, sewage sludge or industrial waste.

(2) Prohibition on new entrants

The Administrator shall not issue any permit under this Act which authorizes a person to dump into ocean waters, or to transport for the purposes of dumping into ocean waters, sewage sludge or industrial waste, unless that person was authorized by a permit issued under section 1412 of this title or by a court order to dump into ocean waters, or to transport for the purpose of dumping into ocean waters, sewage sludge or industrial waste on September 1, 1988.

(b) Special dumping fees

(1) In general

Subject to paragraph (4), any person who dumps into ocean waters, or transports for the purpose of dumping into ocean waters, sewage sludge or industrial waste shall be liable for a fee equal to—

(A) $100 for each dry ton (or equivalent) of sewage sludge or industrial waste transported or dumped by the person on or after the 270th day after November 18, 1988, and before January 1, 1990;

(B) $150 for each dry ton (or equivalent) of sewage sludge or industrial waste transported or dumped by the person on or after January 1, 1990, and before January 1, 1991; and

(C) $200 for each dry ton (or equivalent) of sewage sludge or industrial waste transported or dumped by the person on or after January 1, 1991, and before January 1, 1992.

(2) Payment of fees

Of the amount of fees under paragraph (1) for which a person is liable, such person—

(A) shall pay into a trust account established by the person in accordance with subsection (e) of this section a sum equal to 85 percent of such amount;

(B) shall pay to the Administrator a sum equal to $15 per dry ton (or equivalent) of sewage sludge and industrial waste transported or dumped by such person, for use for agency activities as provided in subsection (f)(1) of this section;

(C) subject to paragraph (5), shall pay into the Clean Oceans Fund established by the State in which the person is located a sum equal to 50 percent of the balance of such amount after application of subparagraphs (A) and (B); and

(D) subject to paragraph (5), shall pay to the State in which the person is located a sum equal to the balance of such amount after application of subparagraphs (A), (B), and (C), for deposit into the water pollution control revolving fund established by the State under title VI of the Federal Water Pollution Control Act [33 U.S.C.A. § 1381 et seq.], as provided in subsection (f)(2) of this section.

(3) Schedule for payment

Fees under this subsection shall be paid on a quarterly basis.

(4) Waiver of fees

(A) The Administrator shall waive all fees under this subsection, other than the portion of fees required to be paid to the Administrator under paragraph (2)(B) for agency activities, for any person who has entered into a compliance agreement which meets the requirements of subsection (c)(2) of this section.

(B) The Administrator shall reimpose fees under this subsection for a person for whom such fees are waived under subparagraph (A) if the Administrator determines that—

(i) the person has failed to comply with the terms of a compliance agreement which the person entered into under subsection (c)(2) of this section; and

(ii) such failure is likely to result in the person not being able to terminate by December 31, 1991, dumping of sewage sludge or industrial waste into ocean waters.

(C) The Administrator may waive fees reimposed for a person under subparagraph (B) if the Administrator determines that the person has returned to compliance with a compliance agreement which the person entered into under subsection (c)(2) of this section.

(5) Payments prior to establishment of account

(A) In any case in which a State has not established a Clean Oceans Fund or a water pollution control revolving fund under title VI of the Federal Water Pollution Control Act [33 U.S.C.A. § 1381 et seq.], fees required to be paid by a person in that State under paragraph (2)(C) or (D), as applicable, shall be paid to the Administrator.

(B) Amounts paid to the Administrator pursuant to this paragraph shall be held by the Administrator in escrow until the establishment of the fund into which such amounts are required to be paid under paragraph (2), or until the last day of the 1-year period beginning on the date of such payment, whichever is earlier, and thereafter—

(i) if such fund has been established, shall be paid by the Administrator into the fund; or

(ii) if such fund has not been established, shall revert to the general fund of the Treasury.

(c) Compliance agreements and enforcement agreements

(1) In general

As a condition of issuing a permit under section 1412 of this title which authorizes a person to transport or dump sewage sludge or industrial waste, the Administrator shall require that, before the issuance of such permit, the person and the State in which the person is located enter into with the Administrator—

(A) a compliance agreement which meets the requirements of paragraph (2); or

(B) an enforcement agreement which meets the requirements of paragraph (3).

(2) Compliance agreements

An agreement shall be a compliance agreement for purposes of this section only if—

(A) it includes a plan negotiated by the person, the State in which the person is located, and the Administrator that will, in the opinion of the Administrator, if adhered to by the person in good faith, result in the phasing out and termination of ocean dumping, and transportation for the purpose of ocean dumping, of sewage sludge and industrial waste by such person by not later than December 31, 1991, through the design, construction, and full implementation of an alternative system for the management of sewage sludge and industrial waste transported or dumped by the person;

(B) it includes a schedule which—

(i) in the opinion of the Administrator, specifies reasonable dates by which the person shall complete the various activities that are necessary for the timely implementation of the alternative system referred to in subparagraph (A); and

(ii) meets the requirements of paragraph (4);

(C) it requires the person to notify in a timely manner the Administrator and the Governor of the State of any problems the person has in complying with the schedule referred to in subparagraph (B);

(D) it requires the Administrator and the Governor of the State to evaluate on an ongoing basis the compliance of the person with the schedule referred to in subparagraph (B);

(E) it requires the person to pay in accordance with this section all fees and penalties the person is liable for under this section; and

(F) it authorizes the person to use interim measures before completion of the alternative system referred to in subparagraph (A).

(3) Enforcement agreements

An agreement shall be an enforcement agreement for purposes of this section only if—

(A) it includes a plan negotiated by the person, the State in which the person is located, and the Administrator that will, in the opinion of the Administrator, if adhered to by the person in good faith, result in the phasing out and termination of ocean dumping, and transportation for the purpose of ocean dumping, of sewage sludge and industrial waste by such person through the design, construction, and full implementation of an alternative system for the management of sewage sludge and industrial waste transported or dumped by the person;

(B) it includes a schedule which—

(i) in the opinion of the Administrator, specifies reasonable dates by which the person shall complete the various activities that are necessary for the timely implementation of the alternative system referred to in subparagraph (A); and

(ii) meets the requirements of paragraph (4);

(C) it requires the person to notify in a timely manner the Administrator and the Governor of the State of any problems the person has in complying with the schedule referred to in subparagraph (B);

(D) it requires the Administrator and the Governor of the State to evaluate on an ongoing basis the compliance of the person with the schedule referred to in subparagraph (B);

(E) it requires the person to pay in accordance with this section all fees and penalties the person is liable for under this section; and

(F) it authorizes the person to use interim measures before completion of the alternative system referred to in subparagraph (A).

(4) Schedules

A schedule included in a compliance agreement pursuant to paragraph (2)(B) or an enforcement agreement pursuant to paragraph (3)(B) shall establish deadlines for—

(A) preparation of engineering designs and related specifications for the alternative system referred to in paragraph (2)(A) or paragraph (3)(A), as applicable;

(B) compliance with appropriate Federal, State, and local statutes, regulations, and ordinances;

(C) site and equipment acquisitions for such alternative system;

(D) construction and testing of such alternative system;

(E) operation of such alternative system at full capacity; and

(F) any other activities, including interim measures, that the Administrator considers necessary or appropriate.

(5) Clean oceans funds

(A) Each State that is a party to a compliance agreement or an enforcement agreement under this subsection shall establish an interest bearing account, to be known as a Clean Oceans Fund, into which a person shall pay fees and penalties in accordance with subsections (b)(2)(C) and (d)(2)(C)(i) of this section, respectively.

(B) A State which establishes a Clean Oceans Fund pursuant to this paragraph shall allocate and pay from the fund each year, to each person in the State which has entered into a compliance agreement or enforcement agreement under this subsection, a portion of amounts in the fund on the last day of that year which is equal to the sum of—

(i) amounts paid by the person into the fund in that year as fees pursuant to subsection (b)(2)(C) of this section and as penalties pursuant to subsection (d)(2)(C)(i) of this section;

(ii) amounts paid by the Administrator into the fund in that year as fees held in escrow for the person pursuant to subsection (b)(5)(B) of this section; and

(iii) interest on such amounts.

(C) Amounts allocated and paid to a person pursuant to subparagraph (B)—

(i) shall be used for the purposes described in subsection (e)(2)(B) of this section; and

(ii) may be used for matching Federal grants.

(D) A Clean Oceans Fund established by a State pursuant to this paragraph shall be subject to such accounting, reporting, and other requirements as may be established by the Administrator to assure accountability of payments into and out of the fund.

(6) Public participation

The Administrator shall provide an opportunity for public comment regarding the establishment and implementation of compliance agreements and enforcement agreements entered into pursuant to this section.

(d) Penalties

(1) In general

In lieu of any other civil penalty under this Act, any person who has entered into a compliance agreement or enforcement agreement under subsection (c) of this section and who dumps or transports sewage sludge or industrial waste in violation of subsection (a)(1)(B) of this section shall be liable for a civil penalty, to be assessed by the Administrator, as follows:

(A) For each dry ton (or equivalent) of sewage sludge or industrial waste dumped or transported by the person in violation of this subsection in calendar year 1992, $600.

(B) For each dry ton (or equivalent) of sewage sludge or industrial waste dumped or transported by the person in violation of this subsection in any year after calendar year 1992, a sum equal to—

(i) the amount of penalty per dry ton (or equivalent) for a violation occurring in the preceding calendar year, plus

(ii) a percentage of such amount equal to 10 percent of such amount, plus an additional 1 percent of such amount for each full calendar year since December 31, 1991.

(2) Payment of penalty

Of the amount of penalties under paragraph (1) for which a person is liable, such person—

(A) shall pay into a trust account established by the person in accordance with subsection (e) of this section a sum which is a percentage of such amount equal to—

(i) 90 percent of such amount, reduced by

(ii) 5 percent of such amount for each full calendar year since December 31, 1991;

(B) shall pay to the Administrator a sum equal to $15 per dry ton (or equivalent) of sewage sludge and industrial waste transported or dumped by such person in that year, for use for agency activities as provided in subsection (f)(1) of this section;

(C) for violations in any year before calendar year 1995—

(i) subject to paragraph (4), shall pay into the Clean Oceans Fund established by the State in which the person is located a sum equal to 50 percent of the balance of such amount; and

(ii) subject to paragraph (4), shall pay to the State in which the person is located a sum equal to the portion of such amount which is not paid as provided in subparagraphs (A), (B), and (C), for deposit into the water pollution control revolving fund established by the State under title VI of the Federal Water Pollution Control Act [33 U.S.C.A. § 1381 et seq.]; as provided in subsection (f)(2) of this section; and

(D) for violations in any year after calendar year 1994, shall pay to the State in which the person is located a sum equal to the balance of such amount, for use by the State for providing assistance under subsection (f)(3) of this section.

(3) Schedule for payment

Penalties under this subsection shall be paid on a quarterly basis.

(4) Payments prior to establishment of account

In any case in which a State has not established a Clean Oceans Fund or a water pollution control revolving fund under title VI of the Federal Water Pollution Control Act, penalties required to be paid by a person in that State under paragraph (2)(C)(i) or (ii), as applicable, shall be paid to the Administrator for holding and payment or reversion, as applicable, in the same manner as fees are held and paid or revert under subsection (b)(5) of this section.

(e) Trust account

(1) In general

A person who enters into a compliance agreement or an enforcement agreement under subsection (c) of this section shall establish a trust account for the payment and use of fees and penalties under this section.

(2) Trust account requirements

An account shall be a trust account for purposes of this subsection only if it meets, to the satisfaction of the Administrator, the following requirements:

(A) Amounts in the account may be used only with the concurrence of the person who establishes the account and the Administrator; except that the person may use amounts in the account for a purpose authorized by subparagraph (B) after 60 days after notification of the Administrator if the Administrator does not disapprove such use before the end of such 60-day period.

(B) Amounts in the account may be used only for projects which will identify, develop, and implement—

(i) an alternative system, and any interim measures, for the management of sewage sludge and industrial waste, including but not limited to any such system or measures utilizing resource recovery, recycling, thermal reduction, or composting techniques; or

(ii) improvements in pretreatment, treatment, and storage techniques for sewage sludge and industrial waste to facilitate the implementation of such alternative system or interim measures.

(C) Upon a finding by the Administrator that a person did not pay fees or penalties into an account as required by this section, or did not use amounts in the account in accordance with this subsection, the balance of the amounts in the account shall be paid to the State in which the person is located, for deposit into the water pollution control revolving fund established by the State under title VI of the Federal Water Pollution Control Act [33 U.S.C.A. § 1381 et seq.], as provided in subsection (f)(2) of this section.

(3) Use of unexpended amounts

Upon a determination by the Administrator that a person has terminated ocean dumping of sewage sludge or industrial waste, the balance of amounts in an account established by the person under this subsection shall be paid to the person for use—

(A) for debts incurred by the person in complying with this Act or the Federal Water Pollution Control Act [33 U.S.C.A. § 1251 et seq.];

(B) in meeting the requirements of the Federal Water Pollution Control Act (33 U.S.C. 1251 et seq.) which apply to the person, including operations and maintenance; and

(C) for matching Federal grants.

(4) Use for matching Federal grants

Amounts in a trust account under this subsection may be used for matching Federal grants.

(f) Use of fees and penalties

(1) Agency activities

Of the total amount of fees and penalties paid to the Administrator in a fiscal year pursuant to subsections (b)(2)(B) and (d)(2)(B) of this section, respectively—

(A) not to exceed one-third of such total amount shall be used by the Administrator for—

(i) costs incurred or expected to be incurred in undertaking activities directly associated with the issuance under this Act of permits for the transportation or dumping of sewage sludge and industrial waste, including the costs of any environmental assessment of the direct effects of dumping under the permits;

(ii) preparation of reports under subsection (i) of this section; and

(iii) such other research, studies, and projects the Administrator considers necessary for, and consistent with, the development and implementation of alternative systems for the management of sewage sludge and industrial waste;

(B) not to exceed one-third of such total amount shall be transferred to the Secretary of the department in which the Coast Guard is operating for use for—

(i) Coast Guard surveillance of transportation and dumping of sewage sludge and industrial waste subject to this Act; and

(ii) such enforcement activities conducted by the Coast Guard with respect to such transportation and dumping as may be necessary to ensure to the maximum extent practicable complete compliance with the requirements of this Act; and

(C) not to exceed one-third of such total amount shall be transferred to the Under Secretary of Commerce for Oceans and Atmosphere for use for—

(i) monitoring, research, and related activities consistent with the program developed pursuant to subsection (j)(1) of this section; and

(ii) preparing annual reports to the Congress pursuant to subsection (j)(4) which describe the results of such monitoring, research, and activities.

(2) Deposits into State water pollution control revolving fund

(A) Amounts paid to a State pursuant to subsection (b)(2)(D), (d)(2)(C)(ii), or (e)(2)(C) of this section shall be deposited into the water pollution control revolving fund established by the State pursuant to title VI of the Federal Water Pollution Control Act [33 U.S.C.A. § 1381 et seq.].

(B) Amounts deposited into a State water pollution control revolving fund pursuant to this paragraph—

(i) shall not be used by the State to provide assistance to the person who paid such amounts for development or implementation of any alternative system;

(ii) shall not be considered to be State matching amounts under title VI of the Federal Water Pollution Control Act; and

(iii) shall not be subject to State matching requirements under such title.

(3) Penalty payments to States after 1994

(A) Amounts paid to a State as penalties pursuant to subsection (d)(2)(D) of this section may be used by the State—

(i) for providing assistance to any person in the State—

(I) for implementing a management program under section 319 of the Federal Water Pollution Control Act [33 U.S.C.A. § 1329];

(II) for developing and implementing a conservation and management plan under section 320 of such [33 U.S.C.A. § 1330]; or

(III) for implementing technologies and management practices necessary for controlling pollutant inputs adversely affecting the New York Bight, as such inputs are identified in the New York Bight Restoration Plan prepared under section 2301 of the Marine Plastic Pollution Research and Control Act of 1987; and

(ii) for providing assistance to any person in the State who was not required to pay such penalties for construction of treatment works (as defined in section 212 of the Federal Water Pollution Control Act [33 U.S.C.A. § 1292]) which are publicly owned.

(B) Amounts paid to a State as penalties pursuant to subsection (d)(2)(D) of this section which are not used in accordance with subparagraph (A) shall be deposited into the water pollution control revolving fund established by the State under title VI of the Federal Water Pollution Control Act [33 U.S.C.A. § 1381 et seq.]. Amounts deposited into such a fund pursuant to this subparagraph—

(i) shall not be used by the State to provide assistance to the person who paid such amounts;

(ii) shall not be considered to be State matching amounts under title VI of the Federal Water Pollution Control Act [33 U.S.C.A. § 1381 et seq.]; and

(iii) shall not be subject to State matching requirements under such title.

(4) Deposits into Treasury as offsetting collections

Amounts of fees and penalties paid to the Administrator pursuant to subsection (b)(2)(B) or (d)(2)(B) of this section which are used by an agency in accordance with paragraph (1) shall be deposited into the Treasury as offsetting collections of the agency.

(g) Enforcement

(1) In general

Whenever, on the basis of any information available, the Administrator finds that a person is dumping or transporting sewage sludge or industrial waste in violation of subsection (a)(1) of this section, the Administrator shall issue an order requiring such person to terminate such dumping or transporting (as applicable) until such person—

(A) enters into a compliance agreement or an enforcement agreement under subsection (c) of this section; and

(B) obtains a permit under section 1412 of this title which authorizes such dumping or transporting.

(2) Requirements of order

Any order issued by the Administrator under this subsection—

(A) shall be delivered by personal service to the person named in the order;

(B) shall state with reasonable specificity the nature of the violation for which the order is issued; and

(C) shall require that the person named in the order, as a condition of dumping into ocean waters, or transporting for the purpose of dumping into ocean waters, sewage sludge or industrial waste—

(i) shall enter into a compliance agreement or an enforcement agreement under subsection (c) of this section; and

(ii) shall obtain a permit under section 1412 of this title which authorizes such dumping or transporting.

(3) Actions

The Administrator may request the Attorney General to commence a civil action for appropriate relief, including a temporary or permanent injunction and the imposition of civil penalties authorized by subsection (d)(1) of this section, for any violation of subsection (a)(1) of this section or of an order issued by the Administrator under this section. Such an action may be brought in the district court of the United States for the district in which the defendant is located, resides, or is doing business, and such court shall have jurisdiction to restrain such violation and require compliance with subsection (a)(1) of this section and any such order.

(h) State progress reports

(1) In general

The Governor of each State that is a party to a compliance agreement or an enforcement agreement under subsection (c) of this section shall submit to the Administrator on September 30 of 1989 and of every year thereafter until the Administrator determines that ocean dumping of sewage sludge and industrial waste by persons located in that State has terminated, a report which describes—

(A) the efforts of each person located in the State to comply with a compliance agreement or enforcement agreement entered into by the person pursuant to subsection (c) of this section, including the extent to which such person has complied with deadlines established by the schedule included in such agreement;

(B) activity of the State regarding permits for the construction and operation of each alternative system; and

(C) an accounting of amounts paid into and withdrawn from a Clean Oceans Fund established by the State.

(2) Failure to submit report

If a State fails to submit a report in accordance with this subsection, the Administrator shall withhold funds reserved for such State under section 205(g) of the Federal Water Pollution Control Act (33 U.S.C. 1285(g)). Funds withheld pursuant to this paragraph may, at the discretion of the Administrator, be restored to a State upon compliance with this subsection.

(i) EPA progress reports

(1) In general

Not later than December 31 of 1989 and of each year thereafter until the Administrator determines that ocean dumping of sewage sludge and industrial waste has terminated, the Administrator shall prepare and submit to the Congress a report on—

(A) progress being made by persons issued permits under section 1412 of this title for transportation or dumping of sewage sludge or industrial waste in developing alternative systems for managing sewage sludge and industrial waste;

(B) the efforts of each such person to comply with a compliance agreement or enforcement agreement entered into by the person pursuant to subsection (c) of this section, including the extent to which such person has complied with deadlines established by the schedule included in such agreement;

(C) progress being made by the Administrator and others in identifying and implementing alternative systems for the management of sewage sludge and industrial waste; and

(D) progress being made toward the termination of ocean dumping of sewage sludge and industrial waste.

(2) Referral to Congressional committees

Each report submitted to the Congress under this subsection shall be referred to each standing committee of the House of Representatives and of the Senate having jurisdiction over any part of the subject matter of the report.

(j) Environmental monitoring

(1) In general

The Administrator, in cooperation with the Under Secretary of Commerce for Oceans and Atmosphere, shall design a program for monitoring environmental conditions—

(A) at the Apex site (as that term is defined in section 1414a of this title);

(B) at the site designated by the Administrator under section 1412(c) of this title and known as the "106-Mile Ocean Waste Dump Site" (as described in 49 Fed. Reg. 19005);

(C) at the site at which industrial waste is dumped; and

(D) within the potential area of influence of the sewage sludge and industrial waste dumped at those sites.

(2) Program requirements

The program designed under paragraph (1) shall include, but is not limited to—

(A) sampling of an appropriate number of fish and shellfish species and other organisms to assess the effects of environmental conditions on living marine organisms in these areas; and

(B) use of satellite and other advanced technologies in conducting the program.

(3) Monitoring activities

The Administrator and the Under Secretary of Commerce for Oceans and Atmosphere shall each conduct monitoring activities consistent with the program designed under paragraph (1).

(4) Omitted

(k) Definitions

For purposes of this section—

(1) the term "alternative system" means any method for the management of sewage sludge or industrial waste which does not require a permit under this Act;

(2) the term "Clean Oceans Fund" means such a fund established by a State in accordance with subsection (c)(5);

(3) the term "excluded material" means—

(A) any dredged material discharged by the United States Army Corps of Engineers or discharged pursuant to a permit issued by the Secretary in accordance with section 1413 of this title; and

(B) any waste from a tuna cannery operation located in American Samoa or Puerto Rico discharged pursuant to a permit issued by the Administrator under section 1412 of this title;

(4) the term "industrial waste" means any solid, semisolid, or liquid waste generated by a manufacturing or processing plant, other than an excluded material;

(5) the term "interim measure" means any short-term method for the management of sewage sludge or industrial waste, which—

(A) is used before implementation of an alternative system; and

(B) does not require a permit under this Act; and

(6) the term "sewage sludge" means any solid, semisolid, or liquid waste generated by a wastewater treatment plant, other than an excluded material.

(Pub. L. No. 92–532, Title I, § 104B, as added by Pub. L. No. 100–688, Title I, § 1002, 102 Stat. 4139 (Nov. 18, 1988).)

HISTORICAL AND STATUTORY NOTES

References in Text

This Act, referred to in subsecs. (a)(2), (d)(1), (e)(3)(A), (f)(1)(A)(i), (B), and (k)(1), (5)(B), means Pub. L. No. 92–532, which is codified principally as this chapter, chapter 41 [33 U.S.C.A. § 2801 et seq.] of this title, and chapters 32 [16 U.S.C.A. § 1431 et seq.] and 32A [16 U.S.C.A. § 1447 et seq.] of Title 16.

The Federal Water Pollution Control Act, referred to in text, is Act of June 30, 1948, c. 758, as amended generally by Pub. L. No. 92–500, § 2, 86 Stat. 816 (Oct. 18, 1972), which is codified generally as chapter 26 (section 1251 et seq.) of this title. Title VI of that Act is codified as subchapter VI (Section 1381 et seq.) of chapter 26 of this title. For complete classification of this Act to the Code, see Short Title note set out under section 1251 of this title and Tables.

Subsection (j)(4) of this section, referred to in subsec. (f)(1)(C)(ii), was omitted from the Code. See Codifications note under this section.

Section 2301 of the Marine Plastic Pollution Research and Control Act of 1987, referred to in subsec. (f)(3)(A)(i)(III), is section 2301 of Pub. L. No. 100–220, Title II, 101 Stat. 1467 (Dec. 29, 1987), set out as a note under section 2267 of this title.

Codifications

Subsec. (j)(4)(A) of this section, shown as omitted, directed the Administrator, in cooperation with the Under Secretary of Commerce for Oceans and Atmosphere, to submit to Congress a report describing the program designed pursuant to subsec. (j)(1) of this section not later than one year after Nov. 18, 1988.

Subsec. (j)(4)(B) of this section, shown as omitted, which required the Administrator and the Under Secretary of Commerce for Oceans and Atmosphere to report annually to Congress on monitoring activities conducted under the program designed pursuant to subsec. (j)(1) of this section, terminated, effective May 15, 2000, pursuant to Pub. L. No. 104–66, § 3003, as amended, set out as a note under 31 U.S.C.A. § 1113. See, also, page 148 of House Document No. 103–7.

§ 1414c. Prohibition on disposal of sewage sludge at landfills on Staten Island

[MPRSA § 104C]

(a) In general

No person shall dispose of sewage sludge at any landfill located on Staten Island, New York.

(b) Exclusion from penalties

(1) In general

Subject to paragraph (2), a person who violates this section shall not be subject to any penalty under this Act.

(2) Injunction

Paragraph (1) shall not prohibit the bringing of an action for, or the granting of, an injunction under section 1415 of this title with respect to a violation of this section.

(c) "Sewage sludge" defined

For purposes of this section, the term "sewage sludge" has the meaning such term has in section 1414b of this title.

(Pub. L. No. 92–532, Title I, § 104C, as added by Pub. L. No. 100–688, Title I, § 1005, 102 Stat. 4150 (Nov. 18, 1988).)

HISTORICAL AND STATUTORY NOTES

References in Text

This Act, referred to in subsec. (b)(1), means Pub. L. No. 92–532, which is codified principally as this chapter, chapter 41 [33 U.S.C.A. § 2801 et seq.] of this title, and chapters 32 [16 U.S.C.A. § 1431 et seq.] and 32A [16 U.S.C.A. § 1447 et seq.] of Title 16.

§ 1415. Penalties

[MPRSA § 105]

(a) Assessment of civil penalty by Administrator; remission or mitigation; court action for appropriate relief

Any person who violates any provision of this subchapter, or of the regulations promulgated under this subchapter, or a permit issued under this subchapter shall be liable to a civil penalty of not more than $50,000 for each violation to be assessed by the Administrator. In addition, any person who violates this subchapter or any regulation issued under this subchapter by engaging in activity involving the dumping of medical waste shall be liable for a civil penalty of not more than $125,000 for each violation, to be assessed by the Administrator after written notice and an opportunity for a hearing. No penalty shall be assessed until the person charged shall have been given notice and an opportunity for a hearing of such violation. In determining the amount of the penalty, the gravity of the violation, prior violations, and the demonstrated good faith of the person charged in attempting to achieve rapid compliance after notification of a violation shall be considered by said Administrator. For good cause shown, the Administrator may remit or mitigate such penalty. Upon failure of the offending party to pay the penalty, the Administrator may request the Attorney General to commence an action in the appropriate district court of the United States for such relief as may be appropriate.

(b) Criminal penalties

In addition to any action that may be brought under subsection (a) of this section—

(1) any person who knowingly violates any provision of this subchapter, any regulation promulgated under this subchapter, or a permit issued under this subchapter, shall be fined under Title 18 or imprisoned for not more than 5 years, or both; and

(2) any person who is convicted of such a violation pursuant to paragraph (1) shall forfeit to the United States—

(A) any property constituting or derived from any proceeds that the person obtained, directly or indirectly, as a result of such violation; and

(B) any of the property of the person which was used, or intended to be used in any manner or part, to commit or to facilitate the commission of the violation.

(c) Separate offenses

For the purpose of imposing civil penalties and criminal fines under this section, each day of a continuing violation shall constitute a separate offense as shall the dumping from each of several vessels, or other sources.

(d) Injunctive relief

The Attorney General or his delegate may bring actions for equitable relief to enjoin an imminent or continuing violation of this subchapter, of regulations promulgated under this subchapter, or of permits issued under this subchapter, and the district courts of the United States shall have jurisdiction to grant such relief as the equities of the case may require.

(e) Liability of vessels in rem

A vessel, except a public vessel within the meaning of section 13 of the Federal Water Pollution Control Act, as amended, used in a violation, shall be liable in rem for any civil penalty assessed or criminal fine imposed and may be proceeded against in any district court of the United States having jurisdiction thereof; but no vessel shall be liable unless it shall appear that one or more of the owners, or bareboat charterers, was at the time of the violation a consenting party or privy to such violation.

(f) Revocation and suspension of permits

If the provisions of any permit issued under section 1412 or 1413 of this title are violated, the Administrator or the Secretary, as the case may be, may revoke the permit or may suspend the permit for a specified period of time. No permit shall be revoked or suspended unless the permittee shall have been given notice and opportunity for a hearing on such violation and proposed suspension or revocation.

(g) Civil suits by private persons

(1) Except as provided in paragraph (2) of this subsection any person may commence a civil suit on his own behalf to enjoin any person, including the United States and any other governmental instrumentality or agency (to the extent permitted by the eleventh amendment to the Constitution), who is alleged to be in violation of any prohibition, limitation, criterion, or permit established or issued by or under this subchapter. The district courts shall have jurisdiction, without regard to the amount in controversy or the citizenship of the parties, to enforce such prohibition, limitation, criterion, or permit, as the case may be.

(2) No action may be commenced—

(A) prior to sixty days after notice of the violation has been given to the Administrator or to the Secretary, and to any alleged violator of the prohibition, limitation, criterion, or permit; or

(B) if the Attorney General has commenced and is diligently prosecuting a civil action in a court of the United States to require compliance with the prohibition, limitation, criterion, or permit; or

(C) if the Administrator has commenced action to impose a penalty pursuant to subsection (a) of this section, or if the Administrator, or the Secretary, has initiated permit revocation or suspension proceedings under subsection (f) of this section; or

(D) if the United States has commenced and is diligently prosecuting a criminal action in a court of the United States or a State to redress a violation of this subchapter.

(3) **(A)** Any suit under this subsection may be brought in the judicial district in which the violation occurs.

(B) In any such suit under this subsection in which the United States is not a party, the Attorney General, at the request of the Administrator or Secretary, may intervene on behalf of the United States as a matter of right.

(4) The court, in issuing any final order in any suit brought pursuant to paragraph (1) of this subsection may award costs of litigation (including reasonable attorney and expert witness fees) to any party, whenever the court determines such award is appropriate.

(5) The injunctive relief provided by this subsection shall not restrict any right which any person (or class of persons) may have under any statute or common law to seek enforcement of any standard or limitation or to seek any other relief (including relief against the Administrator, the Secretary, or a State agency).

(h) Emergencies

No person shall be subject to a civil penalty or to a criminal fine or imprisonment for dumping materials from a vessel if such materials are dumped in an emergency to safeguard life at sea. Any such emergency dumping shall be reported to the Administrator under such conditions as he may prescribe.

(i) Seizure and forfeiture

(1) In general

Any vessel used to commit an act for which a penalty is imposed under subsection (b) of this section shall be subject to seizure and forfeiture to the United States under procedures established for seizure and forfeiture of conveyances under sections 853 and 881 of Title 21.

(2) Limitation on application

This subsection does not apply to an act committed substantially in accordance with a compliance agreement or enforcement agreement entered into by the Administrator under section 1414b(c) of this title.

(Pub. L. No. 92–532, Title I, § 105, 86 Stat. 1057 (Oct. 23, 1972); as amended by Pub. L. No. 100–688, Title III, § 3201(c), (d), 102 Stat. 4153 (Nov. 18, 1988); Pub. L. No. 102–580, Title V, § 508, 106 Stat. 4869 (Oct. 31, 1992).)

HISTORICAL AND STATUTORY NOTES

References in Text

Section 13 of the Federal Water Pollution Control Act, referred to in subsec. (e), is section 13 of Act of June 30, 1948, c. 758, as added by Pub. L. No. 91–224, Title I, § 102, 84 Stat. 100 (Apr. 3, 1970), which was codified as section 1163 of this title and was superseded by Pub. L. No. 92–500, 86 Stat. 816 (Oct. 18, 1972). See section 1322 of this title.

Effective and Applicability Provisions

1972 Acts. Section effective six months after Oct. 23, 1972, see section 110(a) of Pub. L. No. 92–532, set out as a note under section 1411 of this title.

§ 1416. Relationship to other laws

[MPRSA § 106]

(a) Voiding of preexisting licenses

After the effective date of this subchapter, all licenses, permits, and authorizations other than those issued pursuant to this subchapter shall be void and of no legal effect, to the extent that they purport to authorize any activity regulated by this subchapter, and whether issued before or after the effective date of this subchapter.

(b) Actions under authority of Rivers and Harbors Act

The provisions of subsection (a) of this section shall not apply to actions taken before the effective date of this subchapter under the authority of the Rivers and Harbors Act of 1899 (30 Stat. 1151), as amended (33 U.S.C. 401 et seq.).

(c) Impairment of navigation

Prior to issuing any permit under this subchapter, if it appears to the Administrator that the disposition of material, other than dredged material, may adversely affect navigation in the territorial sea of the United States, or in the approaches to any harbor of the United States, or may create an artificial island on the Outer Continental Shelf, the Administrator shall consult with the Secretary and no permit shall be issued if the Secretary determines that navigation will be unreasonably impaired.

(d) State programs

(1) State rights preserved

Except as expressly provided in this subsection, nothing in this subchapter shall preclude or deny the right of any State to adopt or enforce any requirements respecting dumping of materials into ocean waters within the jurisdiction of the State.

(2) Federal projects

In the case of a Federal project, a State may not adopt or enforce a requirement that is more stringent than a requirement under this subchapter if the Administrator finds that such requirement—

(A) is not supported by relevant scientific evidence showing the requirement to be protective of human health, aquatic resources, or the environment;

(B) is arbitrary or capricious; or

(C) is not applicable or is not being applied to all projects without regard to Federal, State, or private participation and the Secretary of the Army concurs in such finding.

(3) Exemption from State requirements

The President may exempt a Federal project from any State requirement respecting dumping of materials into ocean waters if it is in the paramount interest of the United States to do so.

(4) Consideration of site of origin prohibited

Any requirement respecting dumping of materials into ocean waters applied by a State shall be applied without regard to the site of origin of the material to be dumped.

(e) Existing conservation programs not affected

Nothing in this subchapter shall be deemed to affect in any manner or to any extent any provision of the Fish and Wildlife Coordination Act as amended (16 U.S.C. 661–666c).

(f) Dumping of dredged material in Long Island Sound from any Federal, etc., project

In addition to other provisions of law and not withstanding the specific exclusion relating to dredged material in the first sentence in section 1412(a) of this title, the dumping of dredged material in Long Island Sound from any Federal project (or pursuant to Federal authorization) or from a dredging project by a non-Federal applicant exceeding 25,000 cubic yards shall comply with the requirements of this subchapter.

(g) Savings clause

Nothing in this Act shall restrict, affect or modify the rights of any person (1) to seek damages or enforcement of any standard or limitation under State law, including State common law, or (2) to seek damages under other Federal law, including maritime tort law, resulting from noncompliance with any requirement of this Act or any permit under this Act.

(Pub. L. No. 92–532, Title I, § 106, 86 Stat. 1058 (Oct. 23, 1972); as amended by Pub. L. No. 96–572, § 4, 94 Stat. 3345 (Dec. 22, 1980); Pub. L. No. 99–499, Title I, § 127(d), 100 Stat. 1693 (Oct. 17, 1986); Pub. L. No. 101–596, Title II, § 203, 104 Stat. 3006 (Nov. 16, 1990); Pub. L. No. 102–580, Title V, § 505, 106 Stat. 4867 (Oct. 31, 1992).)

HISTORICAL AND STATUTORY NOTES

References in Text

The effective date of this subchapter, referred to in subsecs. (a) and (b), means the effective date of Title I of Pub. L. No. 92–532 which is six months after Oct. 23, 1972. See section 110(a) of Pub. L. No. 92–532, set out as a note under section 1411 of this title.

The Rivers and Harbors Act of 1899, referred to in subsec. (b), is Act Mar. 3, 1899, c. 425, 30 Stat. 1151, as amended, which enacted sections 401, 403, 404, 406 to 409, 411 to 416, 418, 502, 549, 686, and 687 of this title. For complete classification of this Act to the Code, see Tables volume.

The Fish and Wildlife Coordination Act, referred to in subsec. (e), is Act of Mar. 10, 1934, c. 55, 48 Stat. 401, as amended, which is codified generally as sections 661 to 666c of Title 16, Conservation. For complete classification of this Act to the Code, see Short Title note set out under section 661 of Title 16 and Tables volume.

This Act, referred to in subsec. (g), means Pub. L. No. 92–532, which is codified principally as this chapter, chapter 41 [33 U.S.C.A. § 2801 et seq.] of this title, and chapters 32 [16 U.S.C.A. § 1431 et seq.] and 32A [16 U.S.C.A. § 1447 et seq.] of Title 16.

Codifications

Direction in Pub. L. No. 101–596, § 203, for substitution, in subsec. (g), of "the requirements of this subchapter" for all that follows "shall comply with" has been executed in subsec. (f) as reflecting Congressional intent by such substitution for "the criteria established pursuant to the second sentence of section 1412(a) of this title relating to the effects of dumping. Subsection (d) of this section shall not apply to this subsection."

Effective and Applicability Provisions

1986 Acts. Amendment by Pub. L. No. 99–499 effective Oct. 17, 1986, see section 4 of Pub. L. No. 99–499, set out as a note under section 9601 of Title 42, Public Health and Welfare.

1972 Acts. Section effective six months after Oct. 23, 1972, see section 110(a) of Pub. L. No. 92–532, set out as a note under section 1411 of this title.

Territorial Sea of United States

For extension of territorial sea of United States, see Proc. No. 5928, set out as a note under 43 U.S.C.A. § 1331.

§ 1417. Enforcement

[MPRSA § 107]

(a) Utilization of other departments, agencies, and instrumentalities

The Administrator or the Secretary, as the case may be, may, whenever appropriate, utilize by agreement, the personnel, services and facilities of other Federal departments, agencies, and instrumentalities, or State agencies or instrumentalities, whether on a reimbursable or a nonreimbursable basis, in carrying out his responsibilities under this subchapter.

(b) Delegation of review and evaluation authority

The Administrator or the Secretary may delegate responsibility and authority for reviewing and evaluating permit applications, including the decision as to whether a permit will be issued, to an officer of his agency, or he may delegate, by agreement, such responsibility and authority to the heads of other Federal departments or agencies, whether on a reimbursable or nonreimbursable basis.

(c) Surveillance and other enforcement activity

The Secretary of the department in which the Coast Guard is operating shall conduct surveillance and other appropriate enforcement activity to prevent unlawful transportation of material for dumping, or unlawful dumping. Such enforcement activity shall include, but not be limited to, enforcement of regulations issued by him pursuant to section 1418 of this title, relating to safe transportation, handling, carriage, storage, and stowage. The Secretary of the Department in which the Coast Guard is operating shall supply to the Administrator and to the Attorney General, as appropriate, such information of enforcement activities and such evidentiary material assembled as they may require in carrying out their duties relative to penalty assessments, criminal prosecutions, or other actions involving litigation pursuant to the provisions of this subchapter.

(Pub. L. No. 92–532, Title I, § 107, 86 Stat. 1059 (Oct. 23, 1972).)

HISTORICAL AND STATUTORY NOTES

Effective and Applicability Provisions

1972 Acts. Section effective six months after Oct. 23, 1972, see section 110(a) of Pub. L. No. 92–532, set out as a note under section 1411 of this title.

§ 1418. Regulations

[MPRSA § 108]

In carrying out the responsibilities and authority conferred by this subchapter, the Administrator, the Secretary, and the Secretary of the department in which the Coast Guard is operating are authorized to issue such regulations as they may deem appropriate.

(Pub. L. No. 92–532, Title I, § 108, 86 Stat. 1059 (Oct. 23, 1972).)

HISTORICAL AND STATUTORY NOTES

Effective and Applicability Provisions

1972 Acts. Section effective six months after Oct. 23, 1972, see section 110(a) of Pub. L. No. 92–532, set out as a note under section 1411 of this title.

§ 1419. International cooperation

[MPRSA § 109]

The Secretary of State, in consultation with the Administrator, shall seek effective international action and cooperation to insure protection of the marine environment, and may, for this purpose, formulate, present, or support specific proposals in the United Nations and other component international organizations for the development of appropriate international rules and regulations in support of the policy of this Act.

(Pub. L. No. 92–532, Title I, § 109, 86 Stat. 1060 (Oct. 23, 1972).)

HISTORICAL AND STATUTORY NOTES

References in Text

This Act, referred to in text, means Pub. L. No. 92–532, which is codified principally as this chapter, chapter 41 [33 U.S.C.A. § 2801 et seq.] of this title, and chapters 32 [16 U.S.C.A. § 1431 et seq.] and 32A [16 U.S.C.A. § 1447 et seq.] of Title 16.

Effective and Applicability Provisions

1972 Acts. Section effective six months after Oct. 23, 1972, see section 110(a) of Pub. L. No. 92–532, set out as a note under section 1411 of this title.

§ 1420. Authorization of appropriations

[MPRSA § 111]

There are authorized to be appropriated, for purposes of carrying out this subchapter, not to exceed $12,000,000 for fiscal year 1993 and not to exceed $14,000,000 for each of the fiscal years 1994, 1995, 1996, and 1997, to remain available until expended.

(Pub. L. No. 92–532, Title I, § 111, 86 Stat. 1060 (Oct. 23, 1972); as amended by Pub. L. No. 93–472, 88 Stat. 1430 (Oct. 26, 1974); Pub. L. No. 94–62, § 1, 89 Stat. 303 (July 25, 1975); Pub. L. No. 94–326, § 1, 90 Stat. 725 (June 30, 1976); Pub. L. No. 95–153, § 1, 91 Stat. 1255 (Nov. 4, 1977); Pub. L. No. 96–572, § 1, 94 Stat. 3344 (Dec. 22, 1980);

Pub. L. No. 97–16, 95 Stat. 100 (June 23, 1981); Pub. L. No. 100–536, 102 Stat. 2710 (Oct. 28, 1988); Pub. L. No. 102–580, Title V, § 509(a), 106 Stat. 4870 (Oct. 31, 1992).)

HISTORICAL AND STATUTORY NOTES

Effective and Applicability Provisions

1972 Acts. Section effective six months after Oct. 23, 1972, see section 110(a) of Pub. L. No. 92–532, set out as a note under section 1411 of this title.

§ 1421. Omitted

[MPRSA § 112]

HISTORICAL AND STATUTORY NOTES

This section was Pub. L. No. 92–532, Title I, § 112, 86 Stat. 1060 (Oct. 23, 1972); as amended by Pub. L. No. 94–326, § 2, 90 Stat. 725 (June 30, 1976); Pub. L. No. 96–470, Title II, § 209(f), 94 Stat. 2245 (Oct. 19, 1980); Pub. L. No. 102–580, Title V, § 510, 106 Stat. 4870 (Oct. 31, 1992), and required the Administrator of the Environmental Protection Agency to report annually to Congress on the administration of this subchapter, terminated, effective May 15, 2000, pursuant to Pub. L. No. 104–66, § 3003, as amended, set out as a note under 31 U.S.C.A. § 1113. See, also, page 163 of House Document No. 103–7.

SUBCHAPTER II—RESEARCH

§ 1441. Monitoring and research program

[MPRSA § 201]

The Secretary of Commerce, in coordination with the Secretary of the Department in which the Coast Guard is operating and with the Administrator shall, within six months of October 23, 1972, initiate a comprehensive and continuing program of monitoring and research regarding the effects of the dumping of material into ocean waters or other coastal waters where the tide ebbs and flows or into the Great Lakes or their connecting waters.

(Pub. L. No. 92–532, Title II, § 201, 86 Stat. 1060 (Oct. 23, 1972); as amended by Pub. L. No. 99–272, Title VI, § 6061, 100 Stat. 131 (Apr. 7, 1986).)

§ 1442. Research program respecting possible long-range effects of pollution, overfishing, and man-induced changes of ocean ecosystems

[MPRSA § 202]

(a) Secretary of Commerce

(1) The Secretary of Commerce, in close consultation with other appropriate Federal departments, agencies, and instrumentalities shall, within six months of October 23, 1972, initiate a comprehensive and continuing program of research with respect to the possible long-range effects of pollution, overfishing, and man-induced changes of ocean ecosystems. These responsibilities shall include the scientific assessment of damages to the natural resources from spills of petroleum or petroleum products. In carrying out such research, the Secretary of Commerce shall take into account such factors as existing and proposed international policies affecting oceanic problems, economic considerations involved in both the protection and the use of the oceans, possible alternatives to existing programs, and ways in which the health of the oceans may best be preserved for the benefit of succeeding generations of mankind.

(2) The Secretary of Commerce shall ensure that the program under this section complements, when appropriate, the activities undertaken by other Federal agencies pursuant to subchapter I of this chapter and section 1443 of this title. That program shall include but not be limited to—

(A) the development and assessment of scientific techniques to define and quantify the degradation of the marine environment;

(B) the assessment of the capacity of the marine environment to receive materials without degradation;

(C) continuing monitoring programs to assess the health of the marine environment, including but not limited to the monitoring of bottom oxygen concentrations, contaminant levels in biota, sediments, and the water column, diseases in fish and shellfish, and changes in types and abundance of indicator species;

(D) the development of methodologies, techniques, and equipment for disposal of waste materials to minimize degradation of the marine environment.

(3) The Secretary of Commerce shall ensure that the comprehensive and continuing research program conducted under this subsection is consistent with the comprehensive plan for ocean pollution research and development and monitoring prepared under section 1703 of this title.

(b) Action with other nations

In carrying out his responsibilities under this section, the Secretary of Commerce, under the foreign policy guidance of the President and pursuant to international agreements and treaties made by the President with the advice and consent of the Senate, may act alone or in conjunction with any other nation or group of nations, and shall make known the results of his activities by such channels of communication as may appear appropriate.

(c) Cooperation of other departments, agencies, and independent instrumentalities

Each department, agency, and independent instrumentality of the Federal Government is authorized and directed to cooperate with the Secretary of Commerce in carrying out the purposes of this section and, to the extent permitted by law, to furnish such information as may be requested.

(d) Utilization of personnel, services, and facilities; inter-agency agreements

The Secretary of Commerce, in carrying out his responsibilities under this section, shall, to the extent feasible utilize the personnel, services, and facilities of other Federal departments, agencies, and instrumentalities (including those of the Coast Guard for monitoring purposes), and is authorized to enter into appropriate inter-agency agreements to accomplish this action.

(Pub. L. No. 92–532, Title II, § 202, 86 Stat. 1060 (Oct. 23, 1972); as amended by Pub. L. No. 94–62, § 2, 89 Stat. 303 (July 25, 1975); Pub. L. No. 96–381, § 3, 94 Stat. 1524 (Oct. 6, 1980); Pub. L. No. 96–470, Title II, § 201(f), 94 Stat. 2242 (Oct. 19, 1980); Pub. L. No. 99–272, Title VI, § 6062, 100 Stat. 131 (Apr. 7, 1986); Pub. L. No. 100–627, Title I, § 101, 102 Stat. 3213 (Nov. 7, 1988).)

HISTORICAL AND STATUTORY NOTES

References in Text

Section 1703 of this title, referred to in subsec. (a)(3), was repealed by Pub. L. No. 102–567, Title II, § 204, 106 Stat. 4282 (Oct. 29, 1992).

§ 1443. Research program respecting ocean dumping and other methods of waste disposal

[MPRSA § 203]

(a) Cooperation with public authorities, agencies, and institutions, private agencies and institutions, and individuals

The Administrator of the Environmental Protection Agency shall—

(1) conduct research, investigations, experiments, training, demonstrations, surveys, and studies for the purpose of—

(A) determining means of minimizing or ending, as soon as possible after October 6, 1980, the dumping into ocean waters, or waters described in section 1411(b) of this title, of material which may unreasonably degrade or endanger human health, welfare, or amenities, or the marine environment, ecological systems, or economic potentialities, and

(B) developing disposal methods as alternatives to the dumping described in subparagraph (A); and

(2) encourage, cooperate with, promote the coordination of, and render financial and other assistance to appropriate public authorities, agencies, and institutions (whether Federal, State, interstate, or local) and appropriate private agencies, institutions, and individuals in the conduct of research and other activities described in paragraph (1).

(b) Termination date for ocean dumping of sewage sludge not affected

Nothing in this section shall be construed to affect in any way the December 31, 1981, termination date, established in section 1412a of this title, for the ocean dumping of sewage sludge.

(c) Regional management plans for waste disposal

The Administrator, in cooperation with the Secretary, the Secretary of Commerce, and other officials of appropriate Federal, State, and local agencies, shall assess the feasibility in coastal areas of regional management plans for the disposal of waste materials. Such plans should integrate where appropriate Federal, State, regional, and local waste disposal activities into a comprehensive regional disposal strategy. These plans should address, among other things—

(1) the sources, quantities, and types of materials that require and will require disposal;

(2) the environmental, economic, social, and human health factors (and the methods used to assess these factors) associated with disposal alternatives;

(3) the improvements in production processes, methods of disposal, and recycling to reduce the adverse effects associated with such disposal alternatives;

(4) the applicable laws and regulations governing waste disposal; and

(5) improvements in permitting processes to reduce administrative burdens.

(d) Report on sewage disposal in New York metropolitan area

The Administrator, in cooperation with the Secretary of Commerce, shall submit to the Congress and the President, not later than one year after April 7, 1986, a report on sewage sludge disposal in the New York City metropolitan region. The report shall—

(1) consider the factors listed in subsection (c) of this section as they relate to landfilling, incineration, ocean dumping, or any other feasible disposal or reuse/recycling option;

(2) include an assessment of the cost of these alternatives; and

(3) recommend such regulatory or legislative changes as may be necessary to reduce the adverse impacts associated with sewage sludge disposal.

(Pub. L. No. 92–532, Title II, § 203, 86 Stat. 1061 (Oct. 23, 1972); Pub. L. No. 96–381, § 1, 94 Stat. 1523 (Oct. 6, 1980); Pub. L. No. 99–272, Title VI, § 6063, 100 Stat. 131 (Apr. 7, 1986).)

HISTORICAL AND STATUTORY NOTES

Codifications

In subsec. (a)(1)(A), October 6, 1980, was substituted for "the date of the enactment of this section", which has been translated to reflect the probable intent of Congress as meaning the date of enactment of Pub. L. No. 96–381 which amended this section generally and which was approved Oct. 6, 1980.

§ 1444. Annual reports

[MPRSA § 204]

(a) Report by Secretary of Commerce

In March of each year, the Secretary of Commerce shall report to the Congress on his activities under this subchapter during the previous fiscal year. The report shall include—

(1) the Secretary's findings made under section 1441 of this title, including an evaluation of the short-term ecological effects and the social and economic factors involved with the dumping;

(2) the results of activities undertaken pursuant to section 1442 of this title;

(3) with the concurrence of the Administrator and after consulting with officials of other appropriate Federal agencies, an identification of the short- and long-term research requirements associated with activities under subchapter I of this chapter, and a description of how Federal research under this subchapter and subchapter I of this chapter will meet those requirements; and

(4) activities of the Department of Commerce under section 665 of Title 16.

(b) Report by Administrator

In March of each year, the Administrator shall report to the Congress on his activities during the previous fiscal year under section 1443 of this title.

(c) Report by Under Secretary

On October 31 of each year, the Under Secretary shall report to the Congress the specific programs that the National Oceanic and Atmospheric Administration and the Environmental Protection Agency carried out pursuant to this subchapter in the previous fiscal year, specifically listing the amount of funds allocated to those specific programs in the previous fiscal year.

(Pub. L. No. 92–532, Title II, § 204, 86 Stat. 1061 (Oct. 23, 1972); Pub. L. No. 94–62, § 3, 89 Stat. 303 (July 25, 1975); Pub. L. No. 94–326, § 3, 90 Stat. 725 (June 30, 1976); Pub. L. No. 95–153, § 2, 91 Stat. 1255 (Nov. 4, 1977); Pub. L. No. 96–381, § 2, 94 Stat. 1523 (Oct. 6, 1980); Pub. L. No. 92–532, Title II, § 204, formerly § 205, as added by Pub. L. No. 96–572, § 5, 94 Stat. 3345 (Dec. 22, 1980); renumbered and amended by Pub. L. No. 99–272, Title VI, § 6065, 100 Stat. 132 (Apr. 7, 1986); and amended by Pub. L. No. 100–627, Title I, § 102, 102 Stat. 3213 (Nov. 7, 1988).)

HISTORICAL AND STATUTORY NOTES

Prior Provisions

A prior section 204 of Pub. L. No. 92–532, which was codified as this section, was renumbered section 205 and is codified as 33 U.S.C.A. § 1445.

§ 1445. Authorization of appropriations

[MPRSA § 205]

There are authorized to be appropriated for the first fiscal year after October 23, 1972, and for the next two fiscal years thereafter such sums as may be necessary to carry out this subchapter, but the sums appropriated for any such fiscal year may not exceed $6,000,000. There are authorized to be appropriated not to exceed $1,500,000 for the transition period (July 1 through September 30, 1976), not to exceed $5,600,000 for fiscal year 1977, and not to exceed $6,500,000 for fiscal year 1978, not to exceed $11,396,000 for fiscal year 1981, not to exceed $12,000,000 for fiscal year 1982, not to exceed $10,635,000 for fiscal year 1986, not to exceed $11,114,000 for fiscal year 1987, not to exceed $13,500,000 for fiscal year 1989, and not to exceed $14,500,000 for fiscal year 1990.

(Pub. L. No. 92–532, Title II, § 205, as added by Pub. L. No. 96–572, § 5, 94 Stat. 3345 (Dec. 22, 1980); formerly § 204, 86 Stat. 1061 (Oct. 23, 1972); and amended by Pub. L. No. 94–62, § 3, 89 Stat. 303 (July 25, 1975); Pub. L. No. 94–326, § 3, 90 Stat. 725 (June 30, 1976); Pub. L. No. 95–153, § 2, 91 Stat. 1255 (Nov. 4, 1977); Pub. L. No. 96–381, § 2, 94 Stat. 1523 (Oct. 6, 1980); renumbered and amended by Pub. L. No. 99–272, Title VI, § 6064, 100 Stat. 132 (Apr. 7, 1986); and amended by Pub. L. No. 100–627, Title I, § 103, 102 Stat. 3213 (Nov. 7, 1988).)

HISTORICAL AND STATUTORY NOTES

Prior Provisions

A prior section 205 of Pub. L. No. 92–532, which was codified as this section, was renumbered section 204 and is codified as 33 U.S.C.A. § 1444.

OIL POLLUTION

OIL POLLUTION ACT OF 1990
[OPA § ______]

(33 U.S.C.A. §§ 2701 to 2762)

CHAPTER 40—OIL POLLUTION

SUBCHAPTER I—OIL POLLUTION LIABILITY AND COMPENSATION

SUBCHAPTER II—PRINCE WILLIAM SOUND PROVISIONS

SUBCHAPTER III—MISCELLANEOUS

SUBCHAPTER IV—OIL POLLUTION RESEARCH AND DEVELOPMENT PROGRAM

SUBCHAPTER I—OIL POLLUTION LIABILITY AND COMPENSATION

§ 2701. Definitions

[OPA § 1001]

For the purposes of this Act, the term—

(1) "act of God" means an unanticipated grave natural disaster or other natural phenomenon of an exceptional, inevitable, and irresistible character the effects of which could not have been prevented or avoided by the exercise of due care or foresight;

(2) "barrel" means 42 United States gallons at 60 degrees fahrenheit;

(3) "claim" means a request, made in writing for a sum certain, for compensation for damages or removal costs resulting from an incident;

(4) "claimant" means any person or government who presents a claim for compensation under this subchapter;

(5) "damages" means damages specified in section 2702(b) of this title, and includes the cost of assessing these damages;

(6) "deepwater port" is a facility licensed under the Deepwater Port Act of 1974 (33 U.S.C. 1501–1524);

(7) "discharge" means any emission (other than natural seepage), intentional or unintentional, and includes, but is not limited to, spilling, leaking, pumping, pouring, emitting, emptying, or dumping;

(8) "exclusive economic zone" means the zone established by Presidential Proclamation Numbered 5030, dated March 10, 1983, including the ocean waters of the areas referred to as "eastern special areas" in Article 3(1) of the Agreement between the United States of America and the Union of Soviet Socialist Republics on the Maritime Boundary, signed June 1, 1990;

(9) "facility" means any structure, group of structures, equipment, or device (other than a vessel) which is used for one or more of the following purposes: exploring for, drilling for, producing, storing, handling, transferring, processing, or transporting oil. This term includes any motor vehicle, rolling stock, or pipeline used for one or more of these purposes;

(10) "foreign offshore unit" means a facility which is located, in whole or in part, in the territorial sea or on the continental shelf of a foreign country and which is or was used for one or more of the following purposes: exploring for, drilling for, producing, storing, handling, transferring, processing, or transporting oil produced from the seabed beneath the foreign country's territorial sea or from the foreign country's continental shelf;

(11) "Fund" means the Oil Spill Liability Trust Fund, established by section 9509 of Title 26;

(12) "gross ton" has the meaning given that term by the Secretary under part J of Title 46;

(13) "guarantor" means any person, other than the responsible party, who provides evidence of financial responsibility for a responsible party under this Act;

(14) "incident" means any occurrence or series of occurrences having the same origin, involving one or more vessels, facilities, or any combination thereof, resulting in the discharge or substantial threat of discharge of oil;

(15) "Indian tribe" means any Indian tribe, band, nation, or other organized group or community, but not including any Alaska Native regional or village corporation, which is recognized as eligible for the special programs and services provided by the United States to Indians because of their status as Indians and has governmental authority over lands belonging to or controlled by the tribe;

(16) "lessee" means a person holding a leasehold interest in an oil or gas lease on lands beneath navigable waters (as that term is defined in section 1301(a) of Title 43) or on submerged lands of the Outer Continental Shelf, granted or maintained under applicable State law or the Outer Continental Shelf Lands Act (43 U.S.C. 1331 et seq.);

(17) "liable" or "liability" shall be construed to be the standard of liability which obtains under section 1321 of this title;

(18) "mobile offshore drilling unit" means a vessel (other than a self-elevating lift vessel) capable of use as an offshore facility;

(19) "National Contingency Plan" means the National Contingency Plan prepared and published under section 1321(d) of this title or revised under section 105 of the Comprehensive Environmental Response, Compensation, and Liability Act (42 U.S.C. 9605);

(20) "natural resources" includes land, fish, wildlife, biota, air, water, ground water, drinking water supplies, and other such resources belonging to, managed by, held in trust by, appertaining to, or otherwise controlled by the United States (including the resources of the exclusive economic zone), any State or local government or Indian tribe, or any foreign government;

(21) "navigable waters" means the waters of the United States, including the territorial sea;

(22) "offshore facility" means any facility of any kind located in, on, or under any of the navigable waters of the United States, and any facility of any kind which is subject to the jurisdiction of the United States and is located in, on, or under any other waters, other than a vessel or a public vessel;

(23) "oil" means oil of any kind or in any form, including petroleum, fuel oil, sludge, oil refuse, and oil mixed with wastes other than dredged spoil, but does not include any substance which is specifically listed or designated as a hazardous substance under subparagraphs (A) through (F) of section 101(14) of the Comprehensive Environmental Response, Compensation, and Liability Act (42 U.S.C. 9601) and which is subject to the provisions of that Act [42 U.S.C.A. § 9601 et seq.];

(24) "onshore facility" means any facility (including, but not limited to, motor vehicles and rolling stock) of any kind located in, on, or under, any land within the United States other than submerged land;

(25) the term "Outer Continental Shelf facility" means an offshore facility which is located, in whole or in part, on the Outer Continental Shelf and is or was used for one or more of the following purposes: exploring for, drilling for, producing, storing, handling, transferring, processing, or transporting oil produced from the Outer Continental Shelf;

(26) "owner or operator"—

(A) means—

(i) in the case of a vessel, any person owning, operating, or chartering by demise, the vessel;

(ii) in the case of an onshore facility, offshore facility, or foreign offshore unit or other facility located seaward of the exclusive economic zone, any person or entity owning or operating such facility;

(iii) in the case of any abandoned offshore facility or foreign offshore unit or other facility located seaward of the exclusive economic zone, the person or entity that owned or operated such facility immediately prior to such abandonment;

(iv) in the case of any facility, title or control of which was conveyed due to bankruptcy, foreclosure, tax delinquency, abandonment, or similar means to a unit of State or local government, any person who owned, operated, or otherwise controlled activities at such facility immediately beforehand;

(v) notwithstanding subparagraph (B)(i), and in the same manner and to the same extent, both procedurally and substantively, as any nongovernmental entity, including for purposes of liability under section 2702 of this title, any State or local government that has caused or contributed to a discharge or substantial threat of a discharge of oil from a vessel or facility ownership or control of which was acquired involuntarily through—

(I) seizure or otherwise in connection with law enforcement activity;

(II) bankruptcy;

(III) tax delinquency;

(IV) abandonment; or

(V) other circumstances in which the government involuntarily acquires title by virtue of its function as sovereign;

(vi) notwithstanding subparagraph (B)(ii), a person that is a lender and that holds indicia of ownership primarily to protect a security interest in a vessel or facility if, while the borrower is still in possession of the vessel or facility encumbered by the security interest, the person—

(I) exercises decision making control over the environmental compliance related to the vessel or facility, such that the person has undertaken responsibility for oil handling or disposal practices related to the vessel or facility; or

(II) exercises control at a level comparable to that of a manager of the vessel or facility, such that the person has assumed or manifested responsibility—

(aa) for the overall management of the vessel or facility encompassing day-to-day decision making with respect to environmental compliance; or

(bb) over all or substantially all of the operational functions (as distinguished from financial or administrative functions) of the vessel or facility other than the function of environmental compliance; and

(B) does not include—

(i) A unit of state or local government that acquired ownership or control of a vessel or facility involuntarily through—

(I) seizure or otherwise in connection with law enforcement activity;

(II) bankruptcy;

(III) tax delinquency;

(IV) abandonment; or

(V) other circumstances in which the government involuntarily acquires title by virtue of its function as sovereign;

(ii) a person that is a lender that does not participate in management of a vessel or facility, but holds indicia of ownership primarily to protect the security interest of the person in the vessel or facility; or

(iii) a person that is a lender that did not participate in management of a vessel or facility prior to foreclosure, notwithstanding that the person—

(I) forecloses on the vessel or facility; and

(II) after foreclosure, sells, re-leases (in the case of a lease finance transaction), or liquidates the vessel or facility, maintains business activities, winds up operations, undertakes a removal action under section 1321(c) of this title or under the direction of an on-scene coordinator appointed under the National Contingency Plan, with respect to the vessel or facility, or takes any other measure to preserve, protect, or prepare the vessel or facility prior to sale or disposition,

if the person seeks to sell, re-lease (in the case of a lease finance transaction), or otherwise divest the person of the vessel or facility at the earliest practicable, commercially reasonable time, on commercially reasonable terms, taking into account market conditions and legal and regulatory requirements;

(27) "person" means an individual, corporation, partnership, association, State, municipality, commission, or political subdivision of a State, or any interstate body;

(28) "permittee" means a person holding an authorization, license, or permit for geological exploration issued under section 11 of the Outer Continental Shelf Lands Act (43 U.S.C. 1340) or applicable State law;

(29) "public vessel" means a vessel owned or bareboat chartered and operated by the United States, or by a State or political subdivision thereof, or by a foreign nation, except when the vessel is engaged in commerce;

(30) "remove" or "removal" means containment and removal of oil or a hazardous substance from water and shorelines or the taking of other actions as may be necessary to minimize or mitigate damage to the public health or welfare, including, but not limited to, fish, shellfish, wildlife, and public and private property, shorelines, and beaches;

(31) "removal costs" means the costs of removal that are incurred after a discharge of oil has occurred or, in any case in which there is a substantial threat of a discharge of oil, the costs to prevent, minimize, or mitigate oil pollution from such an incident;

(32) "responsible party" means the following:

(A) Vessels

In the case of a vessel, any person owning, operating, or demise chartering the vessel. In the case of a vessel, the term "responsible party" also includes the owner of oil being transported in a tank vessel with a single hull after December 31, 2010.

(B) Onshore facilities

In the case of an onshore facility (other than a pipeline), any person owning or operating the facility, except a Federal agency, State, municipality, commission, or political subdivision of a State, or any interstate body, that as the owner transfers possession and right to use the property to another person by lease, assignment, or permit.

(C) Offshore facilities

In the case of an offshore facility (other than a pipeline or a deepwater port licensed under the Deepwater Port Act of 1974 (33 U.S.C. 1501 et seq.)), the lessee or permittee of the area in which the facility is located or the holder of a right of use and easement granted under applicable State law or the Outer Continental Shelf Lands Act (43 U.S.C. 1301–1356) for the area in which the facility is located (if the holder is a different person than the lessee or permittee), except a Federal agency, State, municipality, commission, or political subdivision of a State, or any interstate body, that as owner transfers possession and right to use the property to another person by lease, assignment, or permit.

(D) Foreign facilities.—In the case of a foreign offshore unit or other facility located seaward of the exclusive economic zone, any person or other entity owning or operating the facility, and any leaseholder, permit holder, assignee, or holder of a right of use and easement granted under applicable foreign law for the area in which the facility is located.

(E) Deepwater ports

In the case of a deepwater port licensed under the Deepwater Port Act of 1974 (33 U.S.C. 1501–1524), the licensee.

(F) Pipelines

In the case of a pipeline, any person owning or operating the pipeline.

(G) Abandonment

In the case of an abandoned vessel, onshore facility, deepwater port, pipeline, offshore facility, or foreign offshore unit or other facility located seaward of the exclusive economic zone, the persons or entities that would have been responsible parties immediately prior to the abandonment of the vessel or facility.

(33) "Secretary" means the Secretary of the department in which the Coast Guard is operating;

(34) "tank vessel" means a vessel that is constructed or adapted to carry, or that carries, oil or hazardous material in bulk as cargo or cargo residue, and that—

(A) is a vessel of the United States;

(B) operates on the navigable waters; or

(C) transfers oil or hazardous material in a place subject to the jurisdiction of the United States;

(35) "territorial seas" means the belt of the seas measured from the line of ordinary low water along that portion of the coast which is in direct contact with the open sea and the line marking the seaward limit of inland waters, and extending seaward a distance of 3 miles;

(36) "United States" and "State" mean the several States of the United States, the District of Columbia, the Commonwealth of Puerto Rico, Guam, American Samoa, the United States Virgin Islands, the Commonwealth of the Northern Marianas, and any other territory or possession of the United States;

(37) "vessel" means every description of watercraft or other artificial contrivance used, or capable of being used, as a means of transportation on water, other than a public vessel;

(38) "participate in management"—

(A)(i) means actually participating in the management or operational affairs of a vessel or facility; and

(ii) does not include merely having the capacity to influence, or the unexercised right to control, vessel or facility operations; and

(B) does not include—

(i) performing an act or failing to act prior to the time at which a security interest is created in a vessel or facility;

(ii) holding a security interest or abandoning or releasing a security interest;

(iii) including in the terms of an extension of credit, or in a contract or security agreement relating to the extension, a covenant, warranty, or other term or condition that relates to environmental compliance;

(iv) monitoring or enforcing the terms and conditions of the extension of credit or security interest;

(v) monitoring or undertaking one or more inspections of the vessel or facility;

(vi) requiring a removal action or other lawful means of addressing a discharge or substantial threat of a discharge of oil in connection with the vessel or facility prior to, during, or on the expiration of the term of the extension of credit;

(vii) providing financial or other advice or counseling in an effort to mitigate, prevent, or cure default or diminution in the value of the vessel or facility;

(viii) restructuring, renegotiating, or otherwise agreeing to alter the terms and conditions of the extension of credit or security interest, exercising forbearance;

(ix) exercising other remedies that may be available under applicable law for the breach of a term or condition of the extension of credit or security agreement; or

(x) conducting a removal action under section 1321(c) of this title or under the direction of an on-scene coordinator appointed under the National Contingency Plan,

if such actions do not rise to the level of participating in management under subparagraph (A) of this paragraph and paragraph (26)(A)(vi);

(39) "extension of credit" has the meaning provided in section 9601(20)(G)(i) of Title 42;

(40) "financial or administrative function" has the meaning provided in section 9601(20)(G)(ii) of Title 42;

(41) "foreclosure" and "foreclose" each has the meaning provided in section 9601(20)(G)(iii) of Title 42;

(42) "lender" has the meaning provided in section 9601(20)(G)(iv) of Title 42;

(43) "operational function" has the meaning provided in section 9601(20)(G)(v) of Title 42; and

(44) "security interest" has the meaning provided in section 9601(20)(G)(vi) of Title 42.

(Pub. L. No. 101–380, Title I, § 1001, 104 Stat. 486 (Aug. 18, 1990); as amended by Pub. L. No. 105–383, Title III, § 307(a), 112 Stat. 3421 (Nov. 13, 1998); Pub. L. No. 108–293, Title VII, § 703(a), (b), 118 Stat. 1069, 1071 (Aug. 9, 2004); Pub. L. No. 111–281, Title VII, § 713, 124 Stat. 2988 (Oct. 15, 2010); Pub. L. No. 115–91, § 3508(b), 131 Stat. 1915–1916 (Dec. 12, 2017); Pub. L. No. 115–232, § 3544(d), 132 Stat. 1636, 2325–2326 (Aug. 13, 2018).)

HISTORICAL AND STATUTORY NOTES

References in Text

This Act, referred to in text, is Pub. L. No. 101–380, 104 Stat. 484 (Aug. 18, 1990), as amended, known as the Oil Pollution Act of 1990, which is codified principally as this chapter. For complete classification to the Code, see Short Title note under this section and Tables.

This subchapter, referred to in par. (4), was in the original "this title", meaning Title I of the Oil Pollution Act of 1990, Pub. L. No. 101–380, Title I, 104 Stat. 486 (Aug. 18, 1990), as amended, which is codified principally as this subchapter. For complete classification, see Short Title note set out under 33 U.S.C.A. § 2701 and Tables.

The Deepwater Port Act of 1974, referred to in pars. (6) and (32), is Pub. L. No. 93–627, 88 Stat. 2126 (Jan. 3, 1975), as amended, which is codified generally as chapter 29 (§ 1501 et seq.) of this title. For complete classification of this Act to the Code, see Short Title note set out under section 1501 of this title and Tables.

The Outer Continental Shelf Lands Act, referred to in pars. (16), (28), and (32), is Act of Aug. 7, 1953, c. 345, 67 Stat. 462, as amended, which is codified generally as subchapter III (§ 1331 et seq.) of chapter 29 of Title 43, Public Lands. For complete classification of this Act to the Code, see Short Title note set out under section 1331 of Title 43 and Tables.

Reference in par. (19) to the amendment of section 1321(d) of this title "by this Act" refers to the amendment by Pub. L. No. 101–380, 104 Stat. 484 (Aug. 18, 1990).

The Comprehensive Environmental Response, Compensation, and Liability Act of 1980, referred to in pars. (19) and (23), is Pub. L. No. 96–510, 94 Stat. 2767 (Dec. 11, 1980), as amended, which is codified principally as chapter 103 (§ 9601 et seq.) of Title 42, Public Health and Welfare. section 101(14) of that Act, also referred to in par. (23), is section 101(14) of Pub. L. No. 96–510, Title I, 94 Stat. 2767 (Dec. 11, 1980), as amended, which is codified as section 9601(14) of Title 42.

Effective and Applicability Provisions

1990 Acts. Section 1020 of Pub. L. No. 101–380 provided that: "This Act [probably refers to title I of Pub. L. No. 101–380 which enacted this subchapter] shall apply to an incident occurring after the date of the enactment of this Act [Aug. 18, 1990]."

Short Title

2017 Amendments. Pub. L. No. 115–31, § 3508(a), 131 Stat. 1915 (Dec. 12, 2017), provided: "This section may be cited as the 'Foreign Spill Protection Act of 2017.' "

2006 Amendments. Pub. L. No. 109–241, Title VI, § 601, 120 Stat. 553 (July 11, 2006), provided that: "This title [enacting 33 U.S.C.A. §§ 1232b and 2762, amending 33 U.S.C.A. §§ 1321, 2704, and 2761, and enacting provisions set out as notes under 33 U.S.C.A. § 2704] may be cited as the 'Delaware River Protection Act of 2006'."

1995 Amendments. Pub. L. No. 104–55, § 1, 109 Stat. 546 (Nov. 20, 1995), provided that: "This Act [enacting section 2720 of this title, and amending sections 2704 and 2716 of this title] may be cited as the 'Edible Oil Regulatory Reform Act'."

1990 Amendments. Pub. L. No. 101–646, Title IV, § 4001, 104 Stat. 4788 (Nov. 29, 1990), as amended by Pub. L. No. 104–332, § 2(h)(1), 110 Stat. 4091 (Oct. 26, 1996), provided that: "This title [amending section 2761 of this title] may be cited as the 'Great Lakes Oil Pollution Research and Development Act'."

Pub. L. No. 101–537, Title II, § 2001, 104 Stat. 2375 (Nov. 8, 1990), provided that: "This title [amending section 2761 of this title] may be cited as the 'Great Lakes Oil Pollution Research and Development Act'."

1990 Acts. Section 1 of Pub. L. No. 101–380 provided that: "This Act [enacting this chapter and sections 1642 and 1656 of Title 43, Public Lands, section 3703a of Title 46, Shipping, and section 1274a of the Appendix to Title 46 (repealed by Pub. L. No. 109–304, § 19, 120 Stat. 1710 (Oct. 6, 2006)); amending sections 1223, 1228, 1232, 1236, 1319, 1321, 1481, 1486, 1503, 1514, and 1908 of this title, section 3145 of Title 16, Conservation, section 401 note of Title 23, Highways, sections 4612 and 9509 of Title 26, Internal Revenue Code, sections 1334, 1350, and 1653 of Title 43, sections 2101, 2302, 3318, 3715, 3718, 5116, 6101, 7101, 7106, 7107, 7109, 7302, 7502, 7503, 7505, 7701, 7702, 7703, 8101, 8104, 8502, 8503, 8702, 9101, 9302, 9308, and 12106 of Title 46, and section 1274 of the Appendix to Title 46 (repealed by Pub. L. No. 109–304, § 19, Oct. 6, 2006, 120 Stat. 1710); repealing section 1517 of this title and sections 1811, 1811 note, and 1812 to 1824 of Title 43; and enacting provisions set out as notes under sections 1203, 1223, and 1321 of this title, section 92 of Title 14, Coast Guard, section 9509 of Title 26, sections 1334, 1651, and 1653 of Title 43, sections 3703, 3703a, and 7106 of Title 46, and section 1295 of the Appendix to Title 46] may be cited as the 'Oil Pollution Act of 1990'."

§ 2702. Elements of liability

[OPA § 1002]

(a) In general

Notwithstanding any other provision or rule of law, and subject to the provisions of this Act, each responsible party for a vessel or a facility from which oil is discharged, or which poses the substantial threat of a discharge of oil, into or upon the navigable waters or adjoining shorelines or the exclusive economic zone is liable for the removal costs and damages specified in subsection (b) of this section that result from such incident.

(b) Covered removal costs and damages

(1) Removal costs

The removal costs referred to in subsection (a) of this section are—

(A) all removal costs incurred by the United States, a State, or an Indian tribe under subsection (c), (d), (e), or (*l*) of section 1321 of this title under the Intervention on the High Seas Act (33 U.S.C. 1471 et seq.), or under State law; and

(B) any removal costs incurred by any person for acts taken by the person which are consistent with the National Contingency Plan.

(2) Damages

The damages referred to in subsection (a) of this section are the following:

(A) Natural resources

Damages for injury to, destruction of, loss of, or loss of use of, natural resources, including the reasonable costs of assessing the damage, which shall be recoverable by a United States trustee, a State trustee, an Indian tribe trustee, or a foreign trustee.

(B) Real or personal property

Damages for injury to, or economic losses resulting from destruction of, real or personal property, which shall be recoverable by a claimant who owns or leases that property.

(C) Subsistence use

Damages for loss of subsistence use of natural resources, which shall be recoverable by any claimant who so uses natural resources which have been injured, destroyed, or lost, without regard to the ownership or management of the resources.

(D) Revenues

Damages equal to the net loss of taxes, royalties, rents, fees, or net profit shares due to the injury, destruction, or loss of real property, personal property, or natural resources, which shall be recoverable by the Government of the United States, a State, or a political subdivision thereof.

(E) **Profits and earning capacity**

Damages equal to the loss of profits or impairment of earning capacity due to the injury, destruction, or loss of real property, personal property, or natural resources, which shall be recoverable by any claimant.

(F) **Public services**

Damages for net costs of providing increased or additional public services during or after removal activities, including protection from fire, safety, or health hazards, caused by a discharge of oil, which shall be recoverable by a State, or a political subdivision of a State.

(c) Excluded discharges

This subchapter does not apply to any discharge—

(1) permitted by a permit issued under Federal, State, or local law;

(2) from a public vessel; or

(3) from an onshore facility which is subject to the Trans-Alaska Pipeline Authorization Act (43 U.S.C. 1651 et seq.).

(d) Liability of third parties

(1) In general

(A) Third party treated as responsible party

Except as provided in subparagraph (B), in any case in which a responsible party establishes that a discharge or threat of a discharge and the resulting removal costs and damages were caused solely by an act or omission of one or more third parties described in section 2703(a)(3) of this title (or solely by such an act or omission in combination with an act of God or an act of war), the third party or parties shall be treated as the responsible party or parties for purposes of determining liability under this subchapter.

(B) Subrogation of responsible party

If the responsible party alleges that the discharge or threat of a discharge was caused solely by an act or omission of a third party, the responsible party—

(i) in accordance with section 2713 of this title, shall pay removal costs and damages to any claimant; and

(ii) shall be entitled by subrogation to all rights of the United States Government and the claimant to recover removal costs or damages from the third party or the Fund paid under this subsection.

(2) Limitation applied

(A) Owner or operator of vessel or facility

If the act or omission of a third party that causes an incident occurs in connection with a vessel or facility owned or operated by the third party, the liability of the third party shall be subject to the limits provided in section 2704 of this title as applied with respect to the vessel or facility.

(B) Other cases

In any other case, the liability of a third party or parties shall not exceed the limitation which would have been applicable to the responsible party of the vessel or facility from which the discharge actually occurred if the responsible party were liable.

(Pub. L. No. 101–380, Title I, § 1002, 104 Stat. 489 (Aug. 18, 1990).)

HISTORICAL AND STATUTORY NOTES

References in Text

This Act, referred to in subsec. (a), is Pub. L. No. 101–380, 104 Stat. 484 (Aug. 18, 1990), as amended, known as the Oil Pollution Act of 1990, which is codified principally as this chapter. For complete classification to the Code, see Short Title note under 33 U.S.C.A. § 2701 and Tables.

Reference in subsec. (b)(1)(A) to the amendment of section 1321 of this title "by this Act" refers to amendment by Pub. L. No. 101–380, 104 Stat. 484 (Aug. 18, 1990).

The Intervention on the High Seas Act, referred to in subsec. (b)(1)(A), is Pub. L. No. 93–248, 88 Stat. 8 (Feb. 5, 1974), as amended, which is codified generally as chapter 28 (§ 1471 et seq.) of this title. For complete classification of this Act to the Code, see Short Title note set out under section 1471 of this title and Tables.

This subchapter, referred to in subsec. (c), was in the original "this title", meaning Title I of the Oil Pollution Act of 1990, Pub. L. No. 101–380, Title I, 104 Stat. 486 (Aug. 18, 1990), as amended, which is codified principally as this subchapter. For complete classification, see Short Title note set out under 33 U.S.C.A. § 2701 and Tables.

The Trans-Alaska Pipeline Authorization Act, referred to in subsec. (c)(3), is title II of Pub. L. No. 93–153, 87 Stat. 584 (Nov. 16, 1973), which is codified as chapter 34 (§ 1651 et seq.) of Title 43, Public Lands. For complete classification of this Act to the Code, see Short Title note set out under section 1651 of Title 43 and Tables.

Effective and Applicability Provisions

1990 Acts. Section applicable to incidents occurring after Aug. 18, 1990, see section 1020 of Pub. L. No. 101–380, set out as a note under section 2701 of this title.

§ 2703. Defenses to liability

[OPA § 1003]

(a) Complete defenses

A responsible party is not liable for removal costs or damages under section 2702 of this title if the responsible party establishes, by a preponderance of the evidence, that the discharge or substantial threat of a discharge of oil and the resulting damages or removal costs were caused solely by—

(1) an act of God;

(2) an act of war;

(3) an act or omission of a third party, other than an employee or agent of the responsible party or a third party whose act or omission occurs in connection with any contractual relationship with the responsible party (except where the sole contractual arrangement arises in connection with carriage by a common carrier by rail), if the responsible party establishes, by a preponderance of the evidence, that the responsible party—

(A) exercised due care with respect to the oil concerned, taking into consideration the characteristics of the oil and in light of all relevant facts and circumstances; and

(B) took precautions against foreseeable acts or omissions of any such third party and the foreseeable consequences of those acts or omissions; or

(4) any combination of paragraphs (1), (2), and (3).

(b) Defenses as to particular claimants

A responsible party is not liable under section 2702 of this title to a claimant, to the extent that the incident is caused by the gross negligence or willful misconduct of the claimant.

(c) Limitation on complete defense

Subsection (a) of this section does not apply with respect to a responsible party who fails or refuses—

(1) to report the incident as required by law if the responsible party knows or has reason to know of the incident;

(2) to provide all reasonable cooperation and assistance requested by a responsible official in connection with removal activities; or

(3) without sufficient cause, to comply with an order issued under subsection (c) or (e) of section 1321 of this title or the Intervention on the High Seas Act (33 U.S.C. 1471 et seq.).

(d) Definition of contractual relationship

(1) In general

For purposes of subsection (a)(3) of this section the term "contractual relationship" includes, but is not limited to, land contracts, deeds, easements, leases, or other instruments transferring title or possession, unless—

(A) the real property on which the facility concerned is located was acquired by the responsible party after the placement of the oil on, in, or at the real property on which the facility concerned is located;

(B) one or more of the circumstances described in subparagraph (A), (B), or (C) of paragraph (2) is established by the responsible party by a preponderance of the evidence; and

(C) the responsible party complies with paragraph (3).

(2) Required circumstance

The circumstances referred to in paragraph (1)(B) are the following:

(A) At the time the responsible party acquired the real property on which the facility is located the responsible party did not know and had no reason to know that oil that is the subject of the discharge or substantial threat of discharge was located on, in, or at the facility.

(B) The responsible party is a government entity that acquired the facility—

(i) by escheat;

(ii) through any other involuntary transfer or acquisition; or

(iii) through the exercise of eminent domain authority by purchase or condemnation.

(C) The responsible party acquired the facility by inheritance or bequest.

(3) Additional requirements

For purposes of paragraph (1)(C), the responsible party must establish by a preponderance of the evidence that the responsible party—

(A) has satisfied the requirements of subsection (a)(3)(A) and (B) of this section;

(B) has provided full cooperation, assistance, and facility access to the persons that are authorized to conduct removal actions, including the cooperation and access necessary for the installation, integrity, operation, and maintenance of any complete or partial removal action;

(C) is in compliance with any land use restrictions established or relied on in connection with the removal action; and

(D) has not impeded the effectiveness or integrity of any institutional control employed in connection with the removal action.

(4) Reason to know

(A) Appropriate inquiries

To establish that the responsible party had no reason to know of the matter described in paragraph (2)(A), the responsible party must demonstrate to a court that—

(i) on or before the date on which the responsible party acquired the real property on which the facility is located, the responsible party carried out all appropriate inquiries, as provided in subparagraphs (B) and (D), into the previous ownership and uses of the real property on which the facility is located in accordance with generally accepted good commercial and customary standards and practices; and

(ii) the responsible party took reasonable steps to—

(I) stop any continuing discharge;

(II) prevent any substantial threat of discharge; and

(III) prevent or limit any human, environmental, or natural resource exposure to any previously discharged oil.

(B) Regulations establishing standards and practices

Not later than 2 years after August 9, 2004, the Secretary, in consultation with the Administrator of the Environmental Protection Agency, shall by regulation establish standards and practices for the purpose of satisfying the requirement to carry out all appropriate inquiries under subparagraph (A).

(C) Criteria

In promulgating regulations that establish the standards and practices referred to in subparagraph (B), the Secretary shall include in such standards and practices provisions regarding each of the following:

(i) The results of an inquiry by an environmental professional.

(ii) Interviews with past and present owners, operators, and occupants of the facility and the real property on which the facility is located for the purpose of gathering information regarding the potential for oil at the facility and on the real property on which the facility is located.

(iii) Reviews of historical sources, such as chain of title documents, aerial photographs, building department records, and land use records, to determine previous uses and occupancies of the real property on which the facility is located since the property was first developed.

(iv) Searches for recorded environmental cleanup liens against the facility and the real property on which the facility is located that are filed under Federal, State, or local law.

(v) Reviews of Federal, State, and local government records, waste disposal records, underground storage tank records, and waste handling, generation, treatment, disposal, and spill records, concerning oil at or near the facility and on the real property on which the facility is located.

(vi) Visual inspections of the facility, the real property on which the facility is located, and adjoining properties.

(vii) Specialized knowledge or experience on the part of the responsible party.

(viii) The relationship of the purchase price to the value of the facility and the real property on which the facility is located, if oil was not at the facility or on the real property.

(ix) Commonly known or reasonably ascertainable information about the facility and the real property on which the facility is located.

(x) The degree of obviousness of the presence or likely presence of oil at the facility and on the real property on which the facility is located, and the ability to detect the oil by appropriate investigation.

(D) Interim standards and practices

(i) Real property purchased before May 31, 1997

With respect to real property purchased before May 31, 1997, in making a determination with respect to a responsible party described in subparagraph (A), a court shall take into account—

(I) any specialized knowledge or experience on the part of the responsible party;

(II) the relationship of the purchase price to the value of the facility and the real property on which the facility is located, if the oil was not at the facility or on the real property;

(III) commonly known or reasonably ascertainable information about the facility and the real property on which the facility is located;

(IV) the obviousness of the presence or likely presence of oil at the facility and on the real property on which the facility is located; and

(V) the ability of the responsible party to detect oil by appropriate inspection.

(ii) Real property purchased on or after May 31, 1997

With respect to real property purchased on or after May 31, 1997, until the Secretary promulgates the regulations described in clause (ii), the procedures of the American Society for Testing and Materials, including the document known as "Standard E1527–97", entitled "Standard Practice for Environmental Site Assessment: Phase I Environmental Site Assessment Process", shall satisfy the requirements in subparagraph (A).

(E) Site inspection and title search

In the case of real property for residential use or other similar use purchased by a nongovernmental or noncommercial entity, inspection and title search of the facility and the real property on which the facility is located that reveal no basis for further investigation shall be considered to satisfy the requirements of this paragraph.

(5) Previous owner or operator

Nothing in this paragraph or in subsection (a)(3) of this section shall diminish the liability of any previous owner or operator of such facility who would otherwise be liable under this Act. Notwithstanding this paragraph, if a responsible party obtained actual knowledge of the discharge or substantial threat of discharge of oil at such facility when the responsible party owned the facility and then subsequently transferred ownership of the facility or the real property on which the facility is located to another person without disclosing such knowledge, the responsible party shall be treated as liable under section 2702(a) of this title and no defense under subsection (a) of this section shall be available to such responsible party.

(6) Limitation on defense

Nothing in this paragraph shall affect the liability under this Act of a responsible party who, by any act or omission, caused or contributed to the discharge or substantial threat of discharge of oil which is the subject of the action relating to the facility.

(Pub. L. No. 101–380, Title I, § 1003, 104 Stat. 491 (Aug. 18, 1990); as amended by Pub. L. No. 108–293, Title VII, § 703(c), 118 Stat. 1072 (Aug. 9, 2004); Pub. L. No. 115–232, § 3547(b), 132 Stat. 1636, 2328 (Aug. 13, 2018).)

HISTORICAL AND STATUTORY NOTES

References in Text

Reference in subsec. (c)(3), to the amendment of section 1321 of this title "by this Act" refers to amendment by Pub. L. No. 101–380, 104 Stat. 484 (Aug. 18, 1990).

The Intervention on the High Seas Act, referred to in subsec. (c)(3), is Pub. L. No. 93–248, 88 Stat. 8 (Feb. 5, 1974), as amended, which is codified generally as chapter 28 (§ 1471 et seq.) of this title. For complete classification of this Act to the Code, see Short Title note set out under section 1471 of this title and Tables.

August 9, 2004, referred to in subsec. (d)(4)(B), originally read "the date of enactment of this paragraph", meaning August 9, 2004, the approval date of Pub. L. No. 108–293, Title VII, § 703(c), 118 Stat. 1072, which enacted paragraph (4) of subsec. (d).

This Act, referred to in subsec. (d)(5), (6), is Pub. L. No. 101–380, 104 Stat. 484 (Aug. 18, 1990, as amended, known as the Oil Pollution Act of 1990, which is codified principally as this chapter. For complete classification, see Short Title note set out under 33 U.S.C.A. § 2701 and Tables.

Effective and Applicability Provisions

1990 Acts. Section applicable to incidents occurring after Aug. 18, 1990, see section 1020 of Pub. L. No. 101–380, set out as a note under section 2701 of this title.

§ 2704. Limits on liability

[OPA § 1004]

(a) General rule

Except as otherwise provided in this section, the total of the liability of a responsible party under section 2702 of this title and any removal costs incurred by, or on behalf of, the responsible party, with respect to each incident shall not exceed—

(1) for a tank vessel, the greater of—

(A) with respect to a single-hull vessel, including a single-hull vessel fitted with double sides only or a double bottom only, $3,000 per gross ton;

(B) with respect to a vessel other than a vessel referred to in subparagraph (A), $1,900 per gross ton; or

(C) (i) with respect to a vessel greater than 3,000 gross tons that is—

(I) a vessel described in subparagraph (A), $22,000,000; or

(II) a vessel described in subparagraph (B), $16,000,000; or

(ii) with respect to a vessel of 3,000 gross tons or less that is—

(I) a vessel described in subparagraph (A), $6,000,000; or

(II) a vessel described in subparagraph (B), $4,000,000;

(2) for any other vessel, $950 per gross ton or $800,000, whichever is greater;

(3) for an offshore facility except a deepwater port, the total of all removal costs plus $75,000,000; and

(4) for any onshore facility and a deepwater port, $350,000,000.

(b) Division of liability for mobile offshore drilling units

(1) Treated first as tank vessel

For purposes of determining the responsible party and applying this Act and except as provided in paragraph (2), a mobile offshore drilling unit which is being used as an offshore facility is deemed to be a tank vessel with respect to the discharge, or the substantial threat of a discharge, of oil on or above the surface of the water.

(2) Treated as facility for excess liability

To the extent that removal costs and damages from any incident described in paragraph (1) exceed the amount for which a responsible party is liable (as that amount may be limited under subsection (a)(1) of this section), the mobile offshore drilling unit is deemed to be an offshore facility. For purposes of applying subsection (a)(3) of this section, the amount specified in that subsection shall be reduced by the amount for which the responsible party is liable under paragraph (1).

(c) Exceptions

(1) Acts of responsible party

Subsection (a) of this section does not apply if the incident was proximately caused by—

(A) gross negligence or willful misconduct of, or

(B) the violation of an applicable Federal safety, construction, or operating regulation by, the responsible party, an agent or employee of the responsible party, or a person acting pursuant to a contractual relationship with the responsible party (except where the sole contractual arrangement arises in connection with carriage by a common carrier by rail).

(2) Failure or refusal of responsible party

Subsection (a) of this section does not apply if the responsible party fails or refuses—

(A) to report the incident as required by law and the responsible party knows or has reason to know of the incident;

(B) to provide all reasonable cooperation and assistance requested by a responsible official in connection with removal activities; or

(C) without sufficient cause, to comply with an order issued under subsection (c) or (e) of section 1321 of this title or the Intervention on the High Seas Act (33 U.S.C. 1471 et seq.).

(3) OCS facility or vessel

Notwithstanding the limitations established under subsection (a) of this section and the defenses of section 2703 of this title, all removal costs incurred by the United States Government or any State or local official or agency in connection with a discharge or substantial threat of a discharge of oil from any Outer Continental Shelf facility or a vessel carrying oil as cargo from such a facility shall be borne by the owner or operator of such facility or vessel.

(4) Certain tank vessels

Subsection (a)(1) of this section shall not apply to—

(A) a tank vessel on which the only oil carried as cargo is an animal fat or vegetable oil, as those terms are used in section 2720 of this title; and

(B) a tank vessel that is designated in its certificate of inspection as an oil spill response vessel (as that term is defined in section 2101 of Title 46) and that is used solely for removal.

(d) Adjusting limits of liability

(1) Onshore facilities

Subject to paragraph (2), the President may establish by regulation, with respect to any class or category of onshore facility, a limit of liability under this section of less than $350,000,000, but not less than $8,000,000, taking into account size, storage capacity, oil throughput, proximity to sensitive areas, type of oil handled, history of discharges, and other factors relevant to risks posed by the class or category of facility.

(2) Deepwater ports and associated vessels

(A) Study

The Secretary shall conduct a study of the relative operational and environmental risks posed by the transportation of oil by vessel to deepwater ports (as defined in section 1502 of this title) versus the transportation of oil by vessel to other ports. The study shall include a review and analysis of offshore lightering practices used in connection with that transportation, an analysis of the volume of oil transported by vessel using those practices, and an analysis of the frequency and volume of oil discharges which occur in connection with the use of those practices.

(B) Report

Not later than 1 year after August 18, 1990, the Secretary shall submit to the Congress a report on the results of the study conducted under subparagraph (A).

(C) Rulemaking proceeding

If the Secretary determines, based on the results of the study conducted under subparagraph (A), that the use of deepwater ports in connection with the transportation of oil by vessel results in a lower operational or environmental risk than the use of other ports, the Secretary shall initiate, not later than the 180th day following the date of submission of the report to the Congress under subparagraph (B), a rulemaking proceeding to lower the limits of liability under this section for deepwater ports as the Secretary determines appropriate. The Secretary may establish a limit of liability of less than $350,000,000, but not less than $50,000,000, in accordance with paragraph (1).

(3) Periodic reports

The President shall, within 6 months after August 18, 1990, and from time to time thereafter, report to the Congress on the desirability of adjusting the limits of liability specified in subsection (a) of this section.

(4) Adjustment to reflect consumer price index

The President, by regulations issued not later than 3 years after July 11, 2006, and not less than every 3 years thereafter, shall adjust the limits on liability specified in subsection (a) of this section to reflect significant increases in the Consumer Price Index.

(Pub. L. No. 101–380, Title I, § 1004, 104 Stat. 491 (Aug. 18, 1990); as amended by Pub. L. No. 104–55, § 2(d)(1), 109 Stat. 546 (Nov. 20, 1995); Pub. L. No. 105–383, Title IV, § 406, 112 Stat. 3429 (Nov. 13, 1998); Pub. L. No. 109–241, Title VI, § 603(a)(1), (2), (b), 120 Stat. 553, 554 (July 11, 2006); Pub. L. No. 111–281, Title IX, § 903(a)(2), (e)(1), 124 Stat. 3010, 3011 (Oct. 15, 2010); Pub. L. No. 115–232, § 3547(c), 132 Stat. 1636, 2328 (Aug. 13, 2018).)

HISTORICAL AND STATUTORY NOTES

References in Text

This Act, referred to in subsec. (b)(1), is Pub. L. No. 101–380, 104 Stat. 484 (Aug. 18, 1990), as amended, known as the Oil Pollution Act of 1990, which is codified principally as this chapter. For complete classification to the Code, see Short Title note under 33 U.S.C.A. § 2701 and Tables.

Reference in subsec. (c)(2)(C) to the amendment of section 1321 of this title "by this Act" refers to amendment by Pub. L. No. 101–380, 104 Stat. 484 (Aug. 18, 1990).

The Intervention on the High Seas Act, referred to in subsec. (c)(2)(C), is Pub. L. No. 93–248, 88 Stat. 8 (Feb. 5, 1974), as amended, which is codified generally as chapter 28 (§ 1471 et seq.) of this title. For complete classification of this Act to the Code, see Short Title note set out under section 1471 of this title and Tables.

The Deepwater Port Act of 1974, referred to in subsec. (d)(2)(A), is Pub. L. No. 93–627, 88 Stat. 2126 (Jan. 3, 1975), as amended, which is codified generally as chapter 29 (§ 1501 et seq.) of this title. For complete classification of this Act to the Code, see Short Title note set out under section 1501 of this title and Tables.

Effective and Applicability Provisions

2010 Acts. Amendments by Pub. L. No. 111–281, § 903(a) to Pub. L. No. 109–241 are effective with enactment of Pub. L. No. 109–241, July 11, 2006, see Pub. L. No. 111–281, § 903(a), set out in part as a note under 16 U.S.C.A. § 460kkk.

1990 Acts. Section applicable to incidents occurring after Aug. 18, 1990, see section 1020 of Pub. L. No. 101–380, set out as a note under section 2701 of this title.

Termination of Reporting Requirements

For termination of reporting provisions of subsec. (d)(3) of this section, effective May 15, 2000, see Pub. L. No. 104–66, § 3003, as amended, set out as a note under 31 U.S.C.A. § 1113, and the 10th item on page 36 of House Document No. 103–7, which references subsec. (d)(3) of Pub. L. No. 101–380, § 1004, which enacted this section.

Delegation of Functions

The functions vested in the President by subsec. (d) of this section respecting the establishment of limits of liability, with respect to classes or categories of non-transportation-related onshore facilities, the reporting to Congress on the desirability of adjusting limits of liability with respect to non-transportation-related onshore facilities, and the adjustment of limits of liability to reflect significant increases in the Consumer Price Index with respect to non-transportation-related onshore facilities, are delegated to the Administrator of the Environmental Protection Agency, acting in consultation with the Secretary of Transportation, the Secretary of Energy, and the Attorney General, see Ex. Ord. No. 12777, 56 Fed. Reg. 54757 (Oct. 18, 1991), set out as a note under section 1321 of this title.

The functions vested in the President by subsec. (d) of this section respecting the establishment of limits of liability, with respect to classes or categories of transportation-related onshore facilities, the reporting to Congress on the desirability of adjusting limits of liability, with respect to vessels or transportation-related onshore facilities and deepwater ports subject to chapter 29 [section 1501 et seq.] of this title, and the adjustment of limits of liability to reflect significant increases in the Consumer Price Index with respect to vessels or transportation-related onshore facilities and deepwater ports subject to chapter 29 of this title, are delegated to the Secretary of Transportation, see Ex. Ord. No. 12777, 56 Fed. Reg. 54757 (Oct. 18, 1991), set out as a note under section 1321 of this title.

The functions vested in the President by subsec. (d) of this section, respecting the reporting to Congress on the desirability of adjusting limits of liability with respect to offshore facilities, including associated pipelines, other than deepwater ports subject to chapter 29 [section 1501 et seq.] of this title, and the adjustment of limits of liability to reflect significant increases in the Consumer Price Index with respect to offshore facilities, including associated pipelines, other than deepwater ports subject to chapter 29 of this title, are delegated to the Secretary of the Interior, see Ex. Ord. No. 122777, 56 Fed. Reg. 54757 (Oct. 18, 1991), set out as a note under section 1321 of this title.

Limitation on Application

Pub. L. No. 109–241, Title VI, § 603(a)(3), 120 Stat. 554 (July 11, 2006), provided that: "In the case of an incident occurring before the 90th day following the date of enactment of this Act [July 11, 2006], section 1004(a)(1) of the Oil Pollution Act of 1990 (33 U.S.C. 2704(a)(1)) shall apply as in effect immediately before the effective date of this subsection [which probably means July 11, 2006, the approval date of Pub. L. No. 109–241, which enacted this note]."

Report Requirements

Section 8246 of Pub. L. No. 116–283, 134 Stat 4671 (Jan. 1, 2021), provided that:

"Not later than 180 days after the date of the enactment of this Act, the Commandant shall submit to the Committee on Commerce, Science, and Transportation of the Senate and the Committee on Transportation and Infrastructure of the House of Representatives a report setting forth the following:

"(1) Each liability limit set under section 1004 of the Oil Pollution Act of 1990 (33 U.S.C. 2704), including the statutory or regulatory authority establishing such limit.

"(2) If the Commandant determines that any liability limit listed in such section should be modified—

"(A) a description of the modification;

"(B) a justification for such modification; and

"(C) a recommendation for legislative or regulatory action to achieve such modification."

Section 603(c) of Pub. L. No. 109–241, Title VI, 120 Stat. 516, 554 (July 11, 2006), as amended by Pub. L. No. 114–120, § 601(b), 130 Stat. 79 (Feb. 8, 2016), provided that:

"(1) Initial report.—Not later than 45 days after the date of enactment of this Act [July 11, 2006], the Secretary of the department in which the Coast Guard is operating shall submit a report on liability limits described in paragraph (2) to the Committee on Commerce, Science, and Transportation of the Senate and the Committee on Transportation and Infrastructure of the House of Representatives.

"(2) Contents.—The report shall include, at a minimum, the following:

"(A) An analysis of the extent to which oil discharges from vessels and nonvessel sources have or are likely to result in removal costs and damages (as defined in section 1001 of the Oil Pollution Act of 1990 (33 U.S.C. 2701)) for which no defense to liability exists under section 1003 of such Act [33 U.S.C.A. § 2703] and that exceed the liability limits established in section 1004 of such Act [this section], as amended by this section.

"(B) An analysis of the impacts that claims against the Oil Spill Liability Trust Fund for amounts exceeding such liability limits will have on the Fund.

"(C) Based on analyses under this paragraph and taking into account other factors impacting the Fund, recommendations on whether the liability limits need to be adjusted in order to prevent the principal of the Fund from declining to levels that are likely to be insufficient to cover expected claims.

"(3) **Annual updates.**—The Secretary shall provide an update of the report to the Committees referred to in paragraph (1) not later than January 30 of the year following each year in which occurs an oil discharge from a vessel or nonvessel source that results or is likely to result in removal costs and damages (as those terms are defined in section 1001 of the Oil Pollution Act of 1990 (33 U.S.C. 2701)) that exceed liability limits established under section 1004 of the Oil Pollution Act of 1990 (33 U.S.C. 2704)."

§ 2705. Interest; partial payment of claims

[OPA § 1005]

(a) General rule

The responsible party or the responsible party's guarantor is liable to a claimant for interest on the amount paid in satisfaction of a claim under this Act for the period described in subsection (b) of this section. The responsible party shall establish a procedure for the payment or settlement of claims for interim, short-term damages. Payment or settlement of a claim for interim, short-term damages representing less than the full amount of damages to which the claimant ultimately may be entitled shall not preclude recovery by the claimant for damages not reflected in the paid or settled partial claim.

(b) Period

(1) In general

Except as provided in paragraph (2), the period for which interest shall be paid is the period beginning on the 30th day following the date on which the claim is presented to the responsible party or guarantor and ending on the date on which the claim is paid.

(2) Exclusion of period due to offer by guarantor

If the guarantor offers to the claimant an amount equal to or greater than that finally paid in satisfaction of the claim, the period described in paragraph (1) does not include the period beginning on the date the offer is made and ending on the date the offer is accepted. If the offer is made within 60 days after the date on which the claim is presented under section 2713(a) of this title, the period described in paragraph (1) does not include any period before the offer is accepted.

(3) Exclusion of periods in interests of justice

If in any period a claimant is not paid due to reasons beyond the control of the responsible party or because it would not serve the interests of justice, no interest shall accrue under this section during that period.

(4) Calculation of interest

The interest paid under this section shall be calculated at the average of the highest rate for commercial and finance company paper of maturities of 180 days or less obtaining on each of the days included within the period for which interest must be paid to the claimant, as published in the Federal Reserve Bulletin.

(5) Interest not subject to liability limits

(A) In general

Interest (including prejudgment interest) under this paragraph is in addition to damages and removal costs for which claims may be asserted under section 2702 of this title and shall be paid without regard to any limitation of liability under section 2704 of this title.

(B) Payment by guarantor

The payment of interest under this subsection by a guarantor is subject to section 2716(g) of this title.

(Pub. L. No. 101–380, Title I, § 1005, 104 Stat. 493 (Aug. 18, 1990); as amended by Pub. L. No. 104–324, Title XI, § 1142(a), 110 Stat. 3991 (Oct. 19, 1996).)

HISTORICAL AND STATUTORY NOTES

References in Text

This Act, referred to in subsec. (a), is Pub. L. No. 101–380, 104 Stat. 484 (Aug. 18, 1990), as amended, known as the Oil Pollution Act of 1990, which is codified principally as this chapter. For complete classification to the Code, see Short Title note under 33 U.S.C.A. § 2701 and Tables.

Effective and Applicability Provisions

1990 Acts. Section applicable to incidents occurring after Aug. 18, 1990, see section 1020 of Pub. L. No. 101–380, set out as a note under section 2701 of this title.

§ 2706. Natural resources

[OPA § 1006]

(a) Liability

In the case of natural resource damages under section 2702(b)(2)(A) of this title, liability shall be—

(1) to the United States Government for natural resources belonging to, managed by, controlled by, or appertaining to the United States;

(2) to any State for natural resources belonging to, managed by, controlled by, or appertaining to such State or political subdivision thereof;

(3) to any Indian tribe for natural resources belonging to, managed by, controlled by, or appertaining to such Indian tribe; and

(4) in any case in which section 2707 of this title applies, to the government of a foreign country for natural resources belonging to, managed by, controlled by, or appertaining to such country.

(b) Designation of trustees

(1) In general

The President, or the authorized representative of any State, Indian tribe, or foreign government, shall act on behalf of the public, Indian tribe, or foreign country as trustee of natural resources to present a claim for and to recover damages to the natural resources.

(2) Federal trustees

The President shall designate the Federal officials who shall act on behalf of the public as trustees for natural resources under this Act.

(3) State trustees

The Governor of each State shall designate State and local officials who may act on behalf of the public as trustee for natural resources under this Act and shall notify the President of the designation.

(4) Indian tribe trustees

The governing body of any Indian tribe shall designate tribal officials who may act on behalf of the tribe or its members as trustee for natural resources under this Act and shall notify the President of the designation.

(5) Foreign trustees

The head of any foreign government may designate the trustee who shall act on behalf of that government as trustee for natural resources under this Act.

(c) Functions of trustees

(1) Federal trustees

The Federal officials designated under subsection (b)(2) of this section—

(A) shall assess natural resource damages under section 2702(b)(2)(A) of this title for the natural resources under their trusteeship;

(B) may, upon request of and reimbursement from a State or Indian tribe and at the Federal officials' discretion, assess damages for the natural resources under the State's or tribe's trusteeship; and

(C) shall develop and implement a plan for the restoration, rehabilitation, replacement, or acquisition of the equivalent, of the natural resources under their trusteeship.

(2) State trustees

The State and local officials designated under subsection (b)(3) of this section—

(A) shall assess natural resource damages under section 2702(b)(2)(A) of this title for the purposes of this Act for the natural resources under their trusteeship; and

(B) shall develop and implement a plan for the restoration, rehabilitation, replacement, or acquisition of the equivalent, of the natural resources under their trusteeship.

(3) Indian tribe trustees

The tribal officials designated under subsection (b)(4) of this section—

(A) shall assess natural resource damages under section 2702(b)(2)(A) of this title for the purposes of this Act for the natural resources under their trusteeship; and

(B) shall develop and implement a plan for the restoration, rehabilitation, replacement, or acquisition of the equivalent, of the natural resources under their trusteeship.

(4) Foreign trustees

The trustees designated under subsection (b)(5) of this section—

(A) shall assess natural resource damages under section 2702(b)(2)(A) of this title for the purposes of this Act for the natural resources under their trusteeship; and

(B) shall develop and implement a plan for the restoration, rehabilitation, replacement, or acquisition of the equivalent, of the natural resources under their trusteeship.

(5) Notice and opportunity to be heard

Plans shall be developed and implemented under this section only after adequate public notice, opportunity for a hearing, and consideration of all public comment.

(d) Measure of damages

(1) In general

The measure of natural resource damages under section 2702(b)(2)(A) of this title is—

(A) the cost of restoring, rehabilitating, replacing, or acquiring the equivalent of, the damaged natural resources;

(B) the diminution in value of those natural resources pending restoration; plus

(C) the reasonable cost of assessing those damages.

(2) Determine costs with respect to plans

Costs shall be determined under paragraph (1) with respect to plans adopted under subsection (c) of this section.

(3) No double recovery

There shall be no double recovery under this Act for natural resource damages, including with respect to the costs of damage assessment or restoration, rehabilitation, replacement, or acquisition for the same incident and natural resource.

(e) Damage assessment regulations

(1) Regulations

The President, acting through the Under Secretary of Commerce for Oceans and Atmosphere and in consultation with the Administrator of the Environmental Protection Agency, the Director of the United States Fish and Wildlife Service, and the heads of other affected agencies, not later than 2 years after August 18, 1990, shall promulgate regulations for the assessment of natural resource damages under section 2702(b)(2)(A) of this title resulting from a discharge of oil for the purpose of this Act.

(2) Rebuttable presumption

Any determination or assessment of damages to natural resources for the purposes of this Act made under subsection (d) of this section by a Federal, State, or Indian trustee in accordance with the regulations promulgated under paragraph (1) shall have the force and effect of a rebuttable presumption on behalf of the trustee in any administrative or judicial proceeding under this Act.

(f) Use of recovered sums

Sums recovered under this Act by a Federal, State, Indian, or foreign trustee for natural resource damages under section 2702(b)(2)(A) of this title shall be retained by the trustee in a revolving trust account, without further appropriation, for use only to reimburse or pay costs incurred by the trustee under subsection (c) of this section with respect to the damaged natural resources. Any amounts in excess of those required for these reimbursements and costs shall be deposited in the Fund.

(g) Compliance

Review of actions by any Federal official where there is alleged to be a failure of that official to perform a duty under this section that is not discretionary with that official may be had by any person in the district court in which the person resides or in which the alleged damage to natural resources occurred. The court may award costs of litigation (including reasonable attorney and expert witness fees) to any prevailing or substantially prevailing party. Nothing in this subsection shall restrict any right which any person may have to seek relief under any other provision of law.

(Pub. L. No. 101–380, Title I, § 1006, 104 Stat. 494 (Aug. 18, 1990).)

HISTORICAL AND STATUTORY NOTES

References in Text

This Act, referred to in text, is Pub. L. No. 101–380, 104 Stat. 484 (Aug. 18, 1990), as amended, known as the Oil Pollution Act of 1990, which is codified principally as this chapter. For complete classification to the Code, see Short Title note under 33 U.S.C.A. § 2701 and Tables.

Effective and Applicability Provisions

1990 Acts. Section applicable to incidents occurring after Aug. 18, 1990, see section 1020 of Pub. L. No. 101–380, set out as a note under section 2701 of this title.

Delegation of Functions

The functions vested in the President by section 2752 (b) of this title respecting making amounts, not to exceed $50,000,000 and subject to normal budget controls, in any fiscal year, available from the Fund (i) to carry out section 1321(c) of this title, and (ii) to initiate the assessment of natural resources damages required under this section are delegated to the Secretary of the Department in which the Coast Guard is operating, with such Secretary required to make amounts available from the Fund to initiate the assessment of natural resources damages exclusively to the Federal trustees designated in the NCP [National Contingency Plan], who are in turn directed to allocate such amounts among all trustees required to assess natural resources damages under this section, see Ex. Ord. No. 12777, 56 Fed. Reg. 54757 (Oct. 18, 1991), set out as a note under section 1321 of this title.

The functions vested in the President by subsec. (b)(3),(4) of this section respecting the receipt of designations of State and Indian tribe trustees for natural resources are delegated to the Administrator of the Environmental Protection Agency, see Ex. Ord. No. 12777, 56 Fed. Reg. 54757 (Oct. 18, 1991), set out as a note under section 1321 of this title.

NOAA Oil and Hazardous Substance Spill Cost Reimbursement

Pub. L. No. 102–567, Title II, § 205, 106 Stat. 4282 (Oct. 29, 1992), provided that:

"(a) Treatment of amounts received as reimbursement of expenses.—Notwithstanding any other provision of law, amounts received by the United States as reimbursement of expenses related to oil or hazardous substance spill response activities, or natural resource damage assessment, restoration, rehabilitation, replacement, or acquisition activities, conducted (or to be conducted) by the National Oceanic and Atmospheric Administration—

"(1) shall be deposited into the Fund;

"(2) shall be available, without fiscal year limitation and without apportionment, for use in accordance with the law under which the activities are conducted; and

"(3) shall not be considered to be an augmentation of appropriations.

"(b) Application.—Subsection (a) shall apply to amounts described in subsection (a) that are received—

"(1) after the date of the enactment of this Act [Oct. 29, 1992]; or

"(2) with respect to the oil spill associated with the grounding of the EXXON VALDEZ.

"(c) Definitions.—For purposes of this section—

"(1) the term 'Fund' means the Damage Assessment and Restoration Revolving Fund of the National Oceanic and Atmospheric Administration referred to in title I of Public Law 101–515 under the heading 'National Oceanic and Atmospheric Administration' (104 Stat. 2105) [Pub. L. No. 101–515, Title I (part), Nov. 5, 1990, 104 Stat. 2105, which is not codified as the Code]; and

"(2) the term 'expenses' includes incremental and base salaries, ships, aircraft, and associated indirect costs, except the term does not include base salaries and benefits of National Oceanic and Atmospheric Administration Support Coordinators."

Damage Assessment and Restoration Revolving Fund; Deposits; Availability; Transfer

Pub. L. No. 101–515, Title I, 104 Stat. 2105 (Nov. 5, 1990), provided in part that: "Notwithstanding any other provision of law, in fiscal year 1991 and thereafter, sums provided by any party or governmental entity for natural resource damage assessment, response or restoration activities conducted or to be conducted by the National Oceanic and Atmospheric Administration as a result of any injury to the marine environment and/or resources for which the National Oceanic and Atmospheric Administration acts as trustee of said marine environment and/or resources, shall be deposited in the Damage Assessment and Restoration Revolving Fund and said funds so deposited shall remain available until expended: *Provided further,* That for purposes of obligation and expenditure in fiscal year 1991 and thereafter, sums available in the Damage Assessment and Restoration Revolving Fund may be transferred, upon the approval of the Secretary of Commerce or his delegate, to the Operations, Research, and Facilities appropriation of the National Oceanic and Atmospheric Administration."

Designation of Federal Trustees for Natural Resources

For designation by the President, in accordance with subsec. (b)(1),(2) of this section, of the Secretaries of Defense, Interior, Agriculture, Commerce and Energy as among those to be designated in the National Contingency Plan as Federal trustees for natural resources, with additional provisions for the designation of Lead Administrative Trustees, see section 1(c) of Ex. Ord. No. 12580, 52 Fed. Reg. 2923 (Jan. 23, 1987), as amended, set out as a note under section 9615 of Title 42, Public Health and Welfare.

§ 2707. Recovery by foreign claimants

[OPA § 1007]

(a) Required showing by foreign claimants

(1) In general

In addition to satisfying the other requirements of this Act, to recover removal costs or damages resulting from an incident a foreign claimant shall demonstrate that—

(A) the claimant has not been otherwise compensated for the removal costs or damages; and

(B) recovery is authorized by a treaty or executive agreement between the United States and the claimant's country, or the Secretary of State, in consultation with the Attorney General and other appropriate officials, has certified that the claimant's country provides a comparable remedy for United States claimants.

(2) Exceptions

Paragraph (1)(B) shall not apply with respect to recovery by a resident of Canada in the case of an incident described in subsection (b)(4) of this section.

(b) Discharges in foreign countries

A foreign claimant may make a claim for removal costs and damages resulting from a discharge, or substantial threat of a discharge, of oil in or on the territorial sea, internal waters, or adjacent shoreline of a foreign country, only if the discharge is from—

(1) an Outer Continental Shelf facility or a deepwater port;

(2) a vessel in the navigable waters;

(3) a vessel carrying oil as cargo between 2 places in the United States; or

(4) a tanker that received the oil at the terminal of the pipeline constructed under the Trans-Alaska Pipeline Authorization Act (43 U.S.C. 1651 et seq.), for transportation to a place in the United States, and the discharge or threat occurs prior to delivery of the oil to that place.

(c) "Foreign claimant" defined

In this section, the term "foreign claimant" means—

(1) a person residing in a foreign country;

(2) the government of a foreign country; and

(3) an agency or political subdivision of a foreign country.

(Pub. L. No. 101–380, Title I, § 1007, 104 Stat. 496 (Aug. 18, 1990).)

HISTORICAL AND STATUTORY NOTES

References in Text

This Act, referred to in subsec. (a)(1), is Pub. L. No. 101–380, 104 Stat. 484 (Aug. 18, 1990), as amended, known as the Oil Pollution Act of 1990, which is codified principally as this chapter. For complete classification to the Code, see Short Title note under 33 U.S.C.A. § 2701 and Tables.

The Trans-Alaska Pipeline Authorization Act, referred to in subsec. (b)(4), is title II of Pub. L. No. 93–153, 87 Stat. 584 (Nov. 16, 1973), which is codified as chapter 34 (§ 1651 et seq.) of Title 43, Public Lands. For complete classification of this Act to the Code, see Short Title note set out under section 1651 of Title 43 and Tables.

Effective and Applicability Provisions

1990 Acts. Section applicable to incidents occurring after Aug. 18, 1990, see section 1020 of Pub. L. No. 101–380, set out as a note under section 2701 of this title.

§ 2708. Recovery by responsible party

[OPA § 1008]

(a) In general

The responsible party for a vessel or facility from which oil is discharged, or which poses the substantial threat of a discharge of oil, may assert a claim for removal costs and damages under section 2713 of this title only if the responsible party demonstrates that—

(1) the responsible party is entitled to a defense to liability under section 2703 of this title; or

(2) the responsible party is entitled to a limitation of liability under section 2704 of this title.

(b) Extent of recovery

A responsible party who is entitled to a limitation of liability may assert a claim under section 2713 of this title only to the extent that the sum of the removal costs and damages incurred by the responsible party plus the amounts paid by the responsible party, or by the guarantor on behalf of the responsible party, for claims asserted under section 2713 of this title exceeds the amount to which the total of the liability under section 2702 of this title and removal costs and damages incurred by, or on behalf of, the responsible party is limited under section 2704 of this title.

(Pub. L. No. 101–380, Title I, § 1008, 104 Stat. 497 (Aug. 18, 1990).)

HISTORICAL AND STATUTORY NOTES

Effective and Applicability Provisions

1990 Acts. Section applicable to incidents occurring after Aug. 18, 1990, see section 1020 of Pub. L. No. 101–380, set out as a note under section 2701 of this title.

§ 2709. Contribution

[OPA § 1009]

A person may bring a civil action for contribution against any other person who is liable or potentially liable under this Act or another law. The action shall be brought in accordance with section 2717 of this title.

(Pub. L. No. 101–380, Title I, § 1009, 104 Stat. 497 (Aug. 18, 1990).)

HISTORICAL AND STATUTORY NOTES

References in Text

This Act, referred to in text, is Pub. L. No. 101–380, 104 Stat. 484 (Aug. 18, 1990), as amended, known as the Oil Pollution Act of 1990, which is codified principally as this chapter. For complete classification to the Code, see Short Title note under 33 U.S.C.A. § 2701 and Tables.

Effective and Applicability Provisions

1990 Acts. Section applicable to incidents occurring after Aug. 18, 1990, see section 1020 of Pub. L. No. 101–380, set out as a note under section 2701 of this title.

§ 2710. Indemnification agreements

[OPA § 1010]

(a) Agreements not prohibited

Nothing in this Act prohibits any agreement to insure, hold harmless, or indemnify a party to such agreement for any liability under this Act.

(b) Liability not transferred

No indemnification, hold harmless, or similar agreement or conveyance shall be effective to transfer liability imposed under this Act from a responsible party or from any person who may be liable for an incident under this Act to any other person.

(c) Relationship to other causes of action

Nothing in this Act, including the provisions of subsection (b) of this section, bars a cause of action that a responsible party subject to liability under this Act, or a guarantor, has or would have, by reason of subrogation or otherwise, against any person.

(Pub. L. No. 101–380, Title I, § 1010, 104 Stat. 498 (Aug. 18, 1990).)

HISTORICAL AND STATUTORY NOTES

References in Text

This Act, referred to in text, is Pub. L. No. 101–380, 104 Stat. 484 (Aug. 18, 1990), as amended, known as the Oil Pollution Act of 1990, which is codified principally as this chapter. For complete classification to the Code, see Short Title note under 33 U.S.C.A. § 2701 and Tables.

Effective and Applicability Provisions

1990 Acts. Section applicable to incidents occurring after Aug. 18, 1990, see section 1020 of Pub. L. No. 101–380, set out as a note under section 2701 of this title.

§ 2711. Consultation on removal actions

[OPA § 1011]

The President shall consult with the affected trustees designated under section 2706 of this title on the appropriate removal action to be taken in connection with any discharge of oil. For the purposes of the National Contingency Plan, removal with respect to any discharge shall be considered completed when so determined by the President in consultation with the Governor or Governors of the affected States. However, this determination shall not preclude additional removal actions under applicable State law.

(Pub. L. No. 101–380, Title I, § 1011, 104 Stat. 498 (Aug. 18, 1990).)

HISTORICAL AND STATUTORY NOTES

Effective and Applicability Provisions

1990 Acts. Section applicable to incidents occurring after Aug. 18, 1990, see section 1020 of Pub. L. No. 101–380, set out as a note under section 2701 of this title.

Delegation of Functions

The functions vested in the President by this section, respecting an effective and immediate removal or arrangement for removal of a discharge and mitigation or prevention of a substantial threat of a discharge of oil or a hazardous substance, the direction and monitoring of all Federal, State and private actions, the removal and destruction of a vessel the issuance of directions consulting with affected trustees, and removal completion determinations, are delegated to the Administrator of the Environmental Protection Agency for the inland zone and to the Secretary of the Department in which the Coast Guard is operating for the coastal zone, see Ex. Ord. No. 12777, 56 Fed. Reg. 54757 (Oct. 18, 1991), set out as a note under section 1321 of this title.

§ 2712. Uses of Fund

[OPA § 1012]

(a) Uses generally

The Fund shall be available to the President for—

(1) the payment of removal costs, including the costs of monitoring removal actions, determined by the President to be consistent with the National Contingency Plan—

(A) by Federal authorities; or

(B) by a Governor or designated State official under subsection (d) of this section;

(2) the payment of costs incurred by Federal, State, or Indian tribe trustees in carrying out their functions under section 2706 of this title for assessing natural resource damages and for developing and implementing plans for the restoration, rehabilitation, replacement, or acquisition of the equivalent of damaged resources determined by the President to be consistent with the National Contingency Plan;

(3) the payment of removal costs determined by the President to be consistent with the National Contingency Plan as a result of, and damages resulting from, a discharge, or a substantial threat of a discharge, of oil from a foreign offshore unit;

(4) the payment of claims in accordance with section 2713 of this title for uncompensated removal costs determined by the President to be consistent with the National Contingency Plan or uncompensated damages; and

(5) the payment of Federal administrative, operational, and personnel costs and expenses reasonably necessary for and incidental to the implementation, administration, and enforcement of this Act (including, but not limited to, sections 1004(d)(2), 1006(e), 4107, 4110, 4111, 4112, 4117, 5006, 8103, and Title IV) and subsections (b), (c), (d), (j), and (*l*) of section 1321 of this title, with respect to prevention, removal, and enforcement related to oil discharges, provided that—

(A) not more than $25,000,000 in each fiscal year shall be available to the Secretary for operations and support incurred by the Coast Guard;

(B) not more than $15,000,000 in each fiscal year shall be available to the Under Secretary of Commerce for Oceans and Atmosphere for expenses incurred by, and activities related to, response and damage assessment capabilities of the National Oceanic and Atmospheric Administration;

(C) not more than $30,000,000 each year through the end of fiscal year 1992 shall be available to establish the National Response System under section 1321(j) of this title including the purchase and prepositioning of oil spill removal equipment; and

(D) not more than $27,250,000 in each fiscal year shall be available to carry out subchapter IV of this chapter.

(b) Defense to liability for Fund

(1) In General—The Fund shall not be available to pay any claim for removal costs or damages to a particular claimant, to the extent that the incident, removal costs, or damages are caused by the gross negligence or willful misconduct of that claimant.

(2) Subrogated Rights.—Except for a guarantor claim pursuant to a defense under section 1016(f)(1), Fund compensation of any claim by an insurer or other indemnifier of a responsible party or injured third party is subject to the subrogated rights of that responsible party or injured third party to such compensation.

(c) Obligation of Fund by Federal officials

The President may promulgate regulations designating one or more Federal officials who may obligate money in accordance with subsection (a) of this section.

(d) Access to Fund by State officials

(1) Immediate removal

In accordance with regulations promulgated under this section, the President, upon the request of the Governor of a State or pursuant to an agreement with a State under paragraph (2), may obligate the Fund for payment in an amount not to exceed $250,000 for removal costs consistent with the National Contingency Plan required for the immediate removal of a discharge, or the mitigation or prevention of a substantial threat of a discharge, of oil.

(2) Agreements

(A) In general

The President shall enter into an agreement with the Governor of any interested State to establish procedures under which the Governor or a designated State official may receive payments from the Fund for removal costs pursuant to paragraph (1).

(B) Terms

Agreements under this paragraph—

(i) may include such terms and conditions as may be agreed upon by the President and the Governor of a State;

(ii) shall provide for political subdivisions of the State to receive payments for reasonable removal costs; and

(iii) may authorize advance payments from the Fund to facilitate removal efforts.

(e) Regulations

The President shall—

(1) not later than 6 months after August 18, 1990, publish proposed regulations detailing the manner in which the authority to obligate the Fund and to enter into agreements under this subsection shall be exercised; and

(2) not later than 3 months after the close of the comment period for such proposed regulations, promulgate final regulations for that purpose.

(f) Rights of subrogation

Payment of any claim or obligation by the Fund under this Act shall be subject to the United States Government acquiring by subrogation all rights of the claimant or State to recover from the responsible party.

(g) Repealed.

(h) Period of limitations for claims

(1) Removal costs

No claim may be presented under this subchapter for recovery of removal costs for an incident unless the claim is presented within 6 years after the date of completion of all removal actions for that incident.

(2) Damages

No claim may be presented under this section for recovery of damages unless the claim is presented within 3 years after the date on which the injury and its connection with the discharge in question were reasonably discoverable with the exercise of due care, or in the case of natural resource damages under section 2702(b)(2)(A) of this title, if later, the date of completion of the natural resources damage assessment under section 2706(e) of this title.

(3) Minors and incompetents

The time limitations contained in this subsection shall not begin to run—

(A) against a minor until the earlier of the date when such minor reaches 18 years of age or the date on which a legal representative is duly appointed for the minor, or

(B) against an incompetent person until the earlier of the date on which such incompetent's incompetency ends or the date on which a legal representative is duly appointed for the incompetent.

(i) Limitation on payment for same costs

In any case in which the President has paid an amount from the Fund for any removal costs or damages specified under subsection (a) of this section, no other claim may be paid from the Fund for the same removal costs or damages.

(j) Obligation in accordance with plan

(1) In general

Except as provided in paragraph (2), amounts may be obligated from the Fund for the restoration, rehabilitation, replacement, or acquisition of natural resources only in accordance with a plan adopted under section 2706(c) of this title.

(2) Exception

Paragraph (1) shall not apply in a situation requiring action to avoid irreversible loss of natural resources or to prevent or reduce any continuing danger to natural resources or similar need for emergency action.

(k) Preference for private persons in area affected by discharge

(1) In general

In the expenditure of Federal funds for removal of oil, including for distribution of supplies, construction, and other reasonable and appropriate activities, under a contract or agreement with a private person, preference shall be given, to the extent feasible and practicable, to private persons residing or doing business primarily in the area affected by the discharge of oil.

(2) Limitation

This subsection shall not be considered to restrict the use of Department of Defense resources.

(*l*) Reports

(1) In general

Each year, on the date on which the President submits to Congress a budget under section 1105 of title 31, United States Code, the President, through the Secretary of the Department in which the Coast Guard is operating, shall—

(A) provide a report on disbursements for the preceding fiscal year from the Fund, regardless of whether those disbursements were subject to annual appropriations, to—

(i) the Senate Committee on Commerce, Science, and Transportation; and

(ii) the House of Representatives Committee on Transportation and Infrastructure; and

(B) make the report available to the public on the National Pollution Funds Center Internet website.

(2) Contents.—The report shall include—

(A) a list of each incident that—

(i) occurred in the preceding fiscal year; and

(ii) resulted in disbursements from the Fund, for removal costs and damages, totaling $500,000 or more;

(B) a list of each incident that—

(i) occurred in the fiscal year preceding the preceding fiscal year; and

(ii) resulted in disbursements from the Fund, for removal costs and damages, totaling $500,000 or more; and

(C) an accounting of any amounts reimbursed to the Fund in the preceding fiscal year that were recovered from a responsible party for an incident that resulted in disbursements from the Fund, for removal costs and damages, totaling $500,000 or more.

(3) Agency recordkeeping

Each Federal agency that receives amounts from the Fund shall maintain records describing the purposes for which such funds were obligated or expended in such detail as the Secretary may require for purposes of the report required under paragraph (1).

(Pub. L. No. 101–380, Title I, § 1012, 104 Stat. 498 (Aug. 18, 1990); as amended by Pub. L. No. 108–293, Title VII, § 708(b), 118 Stat. 1077 (Aug. 9, 2004); Pub. L. No. 111–281, Title VII, § 708, 124 Stat. 2984 (Oct. 15, 2010); Pub. L. No. 115–282, § 816, 132 Stat. 4192, 4305–4306 (Dec. 4, 2018); Pub. L. No. 116–283, §§ 8302–8303, 8513)c), 134 Stat. 3388, 4692 (Jan. 1, 2021).)

HISTORICAL AND STATUTORY NOTES

References in Text

This Act, referred to in subsecs. (a)(5) and (f), is Pub. L. No. 101–380, 104 Stat. 484 (Aug. 18, 1990), known as the Oil Pollution Act of 1990, which is codified principally as this chapter. Sections 1004(d)(2) and 1006(e) are codified as 33 U.S.C.A. §§ 2704(d)(2) and 2706(e), respectively. Section 4107 amended 33 U.S.C.A. § 1223 and enacted provisions set out as a note under 33 U.S.C.A. § 1223. Sections 4110 and 4111 enacted provisions set out as notes under 46 U.S.C.A. § 3703. Section 4112 is not codified into the Code. Section 4117 enacted provisions set out as a note under 46 U.S.C.A. § 1295, Appendix. Section 5006 is codified as 33 U.S.C.A. § 2736. Section 8103 enacted provisions set out as a note under 43 U.S.C.A. § 1651. Title VII is codified as subchapter IV of this chapter [33 U.S.C.A. § 2761 et seq.]. For complete classification of this Act to the Code, see Short Title note set out under 33 U.S.C.A. § 2701 and Tables.

References in subsec. (a)(5) to the amendment of section 1321 of this title "by this Act" refer to amendment by Pub. L. No. 101–380, 104 Stat. 484 (Aug. 18, 1990).

This subchapter, referred to in subsec. (h), was in the original "this title", meaning Title I of the Oil Pollution Act of 1990, Pub. L. No. 101–380, Title I, 104 Stat. 486 (Aug. 18, 1990), as amended, which is codified principally as this subchapter. For complete classification, see Short Title note set out under 33 U.S.C.A. § 2701 and Tables.

Effective and Applicability Provisions

1990 Acts. Section applicable to incidents occurring after Aug. 18, 1990, see section 1020 of Pub. L. No. 101–380, set out as a note under section 2701 of this title.

Delegation of Functions

Memorandum of the President of Aug. 24, 1990, 55 Fed. Reg. 35291, delegating certain authorities of the President under this section and section 2752 of this title, was revoked by Ex. Ord. No. 12777, 56 Fed. Reg. 54757 (Oct. 18, 1991), set out as a note under section 1321 of this title.

The functions vested in the President by subsec. (a)(1), (3), and (4) of this section respecting payment of removal costs and claims and determining consistency with the National Contingency Plan (NCP) are delegated to the Secretary or the Department in which the Coast Guard is operating, see Ex. Ord. No. 12777, 56 Fed. Reg. 54757 (Oct. 18, 1991), set out as a note under section 1321 of this title.

[The functions vested in the President by subsec. (a) of this section, respecting the payment of costs, damages, and claims, delegated by Ex. Ord. No. 12777 to the Secretary of the Department in which the Coast Guard is operating, include, *inter alia,* the authority to process, settle, and administratively adjudicate such costs, damages, and claims, regardless of amount.]

The functions vested in the President by subsec. (a)(2) of this section, respecting the payment of costs and determining consistency with the NCP, are delegated to the Federal trustees designated in the NCP [National Contingency Plan], see Ex. Ord. No. 12777, 56 Fed. Reg. 54757 (Oct. 18, 1991), set out as a note under section 1321 of this title.

The functions vested in the President by subsec. (a)(5) of this section, respecting the payment of costs and expenses of departments and agencies having responsibility for the implementation, administration, and enforcement of the Oil Pollution Act of 1990 [Pub. L. No. 101–380, 104 Stat. 484 (Aug. 18, 1990). See Tables for classification] are delegated to each head of such department and agency, see Ex. Ord. No. 12777, 56 Fed. Reg. 54757 (Oct. 18, 1991), set out as a note under section 1321 of this title.

The functions vested in the President by subsec. (c) of this section, respecting designation of Federal officials who may obligate money, are delegated to each head of the departments and agencies to whom functions have been delegated under section 7(a) of this order for the purpose of carrying out such functions, see Ex. Ord. No. 12777, 56 Fed. Reg. 54757 (Oct. 18, 1991), set out as a note under section 1321 of this title.

The functions vested in the President by subsecs. (d) and (e) of this section, respecting the obligation of the Trust Fund on the request of a Governor or pursuant to an agreement with a State, entrance into agreements with States, agreement upon terms and conditions, and the promulgation of regulations concerning such obligation and entrance into such agreement, are delegated to the Secretary of the Department in which the Coast Guard is operating, in consultation with the Administrator of the Environmental Protection Agency, see Ex. Ord. No. 12777, 56 Fed. Reg. 54757 (Oct. 18, 1991), set out as a note under section 1321 of this title.

Spill of National Significance; Payment to Coast Guard

Pub. L. No. 112–74, Div. D, Title V, § 563, 125 Stat. 981 (Dec. 23, 2011), provided that: "For fiscal year 2012 and thereafter, notwithstanding section 1012(a)(5) of the Oil Pollution Act of 1990 (33 U.S.C. 2712(a)(5)) and 31 U.S.C. 3302, in the event that a spill of national significance occurs, any payment of amounts from the Oil Spill Liability Trust Fund pursuant to section 1012(a) (1) of the Oil Pollution Act of 1990 (33 U.S.C. 2712(a)(1)) for the removal costs incurred by the Coast Guard for such spill, shall be credited directly to the accounts of the Coast Guard current at the time such removal costs were incurred or when reimbursement is received: *Provided*, That such amounts shall be merged with and, without further appropriations, made available for the same time period and the same purpose as the appropriation to which it is credited."

§ 2713. Claims procedure

[OPA § 1013]

(a) Presentation

Except as provided in subsection (b) of this section, all claims for removal costs or damages shall be presented first to the responsible party or guarantor of the source designated under section 2714(a) of this title.

(b) Presentation to Fund

(1) In general

Claims for removal costs or damages may be presented first to the Fund—

(A) if the President has advertised or otherwise notified claimants in accordance with section 2714(c) of this title;

(B) by a responsible party who may assert a claim under section 2708 of this title;

(C) by the Governor of a State for removal costs incurred by that State; or

(D) by a United States claimant in a case where a foreign offshore unit has discharged oil causing damage for which the Fund is liable under section 2712(a) of this title.

(2) Limitation on presenting claim

No claim of a person against the Fund may be approved or certified during the pendency of an action by the person in court to recover costs which are the subject of the claim.

(c) Election

If a claim is presented in accordance with subsection (a) of this section and—

(1) each person to whom the claim is presented denies all liability for the claim, or

(2) the claim is not settled by any person by payment within 90 days after the date upon which (A) the claim was presented, or (B) advertising was begun pursuant to section 2714(b) of this title, whichever is later,

the claimant may elect to commence an action in court against the responsible party or guarantor or to present the claim to the Fund.

(d) Uncompensated damages

If a claim is presented in accordance with this section, including a claim for interim, short-term damages representing less than the full amount of damages to which the claimant ultimately may be entitled, and full and adequate compensation is unavailable, a claim for the uncompensated damages and removal costs may be presented to the Fund.

(e) Procedure for claims against Fund

The President shall promulgate, and may from time to time amend, regulations for the presentation, filing, processing, settlement, and adjudication of claims under this Act against the Fund.

(f) REMOVED BY PUB. L. NO. 116–283 (Jan. 1, 2021).

(Pub. L. No. 101–380, Title I, § 1013, 104 Stat. 501 (Aug. 18, 1990); as amended by Pub. L. No. 104–324, Title XI, § 1142(b), 110 Stat. 3991 (Oct. 19, 1996); Pub. L. No. 108–293, Title VII, § 708(a), 118 Stat. 1077 (Aug. 9, 2004); Pub. L. No. 116–283, § 8303(a), 134 Stat. 3388, 4692 (Jan. 1, 2021).)

HISTORICAL AND STATUTORY NOTES

References in Text

This Act, referred to in subsec. (e), is Pub. L. No. 101–380, 104 Stat. 484 (Aug. 18, 1990), as amended, known as the Oil Pollution Act of 1990, which is codified principally as this chapter. For complete classification to the Code, see Short Title note under 33 U.S.C.A. § 2701 and Tables.

Effective and Applicability Provisions

1990 Acts. Section applicable to incidents occurring after Aug. 18, 1990, see section 1020 of Pub. L. No. 101–380, set out as a note under section 2701 of this title.

Delegation of Functions

The functions vested in the President by subsec. (e) of this section, respecting the promulgation and amendment of regulations for the presentation, filing, processing, settlement, and adjudication of claims under this subchapter against the Trust Fund, are delegated to the Secretary of the Department in which the Coast Guard is operating, in consultation with the Attorney General, see Ex. Ord. No. 12777, 56 Fed. Reg. 54757 (Oct. 18, 1991), set out as a note under section 1321 of this title.

§ 2714. Designation of source and advertisement

[OPA § 1014]

(a) Designation of source and notification

When the President receives information of an incident, the President shall, where possible and appropriate, designate the source or sources of the discharge or threat. If a designated source is a vessel or a facility, the President shall immediately notify the responsible party and the guarantor, if known, of that designation.

(b) Advertisement by responsible party or guarantor

(1) If a responsible party or guarantor fails to inform the President, within 5 days after receiving notification of a designation under subsection (a) of this section, of the party's or the guarantor's denial of the designation, such party or guarantor shall advertise the designation and the procedures by which claims may be presented, in accordance with regulations promulgated by the President. Advertisement under the preceding sentence shall begin no later than 15 days after the date of the designation made under subsection (a) of this section. If advertisement is not otherwise made in accordance with this subsection, the President shall promptly and at the expense of the responsible party or the guarantor involved, advertise the designation and the procedures by which claims may be presented to the responsible party or guarantor. Advertisement under this subsection shall continue for a period of no less than 30 days.

(2) An advertisement under paragraph (1) shall state that a claimant may present a claim for interim, short-term damages representing less than the full amount of damages to which the claimant ultimately may be entitled and that payment of such a claim shall not preclude recovery for damages not reflected in the paid or settled partial claim.

(c) Advertisement by President

If

(1) the responsible party and the guarantor both deny a designation within 5 days after receiving notification of a designation under subsection (a) of this section,

(2) the source of the discharge or threat was a public vessel, or

(3) the President is unable to designate the source or sources of the discharge or threat under subsection (a) of this section,

the President shall advertise or otherwise notify potential claimants of the procedures by which claims may be presented to the Fund.

(Pub. L. No. 101–380, Title I, § 1014, 104 Stat. 501 (Aug. 18, 1990); as amended by Pub. L. No. 104–324, Title XI, § 1142(c), 110 Stat. 3991 (Oct. 19, 1996).)

HISTORICAL AND STATUTORY NOTES

Effective and Applicability Provisions

1990 Acts. Section applicable to incidents occurring after Aug. 18, 1990, see section 1020 of Pub. L. No. 101–380, set out as a note under section 2701 of this title.

Delegation of Functions

The functions vested in the President by this section, respecting designation of sources of discharges or threats, notification to responsible parties, promulgation of regulations respecting advertisements, the advertisement of designation, and notification of claims procedures, are delegated to the Secretary of the Department in which the Coast Guard is operating, see Ex. Ord. No. 12777, 56 Fed. Reg. 54757 (Oct. 18, 1991), set out as a note under section 1321 of this title.

§ 2715. Subrogation

[OPA § 1015]

(a) In general

Any person, including the Fund, who pays compensation pursuant to this Act to any claimant for removal costs or damages shall be subrogated to all rights, claims, and causes of action that the claimant has under any other law.

(b) Interim damages

(1) In general

If a responsible party, a guarantor, or the Fund has made payment to a claimant for interim, short-term damages representing less than the full amount of damages to which the claimant ultimately may be entitled, subrogation under subsection (a) of this section shall apply only with respect to the portion of the claim reflected in the paid interim claim.

(2) Final damages

Payment of such a claim shall not foreclose a claimant's right to recovery of all damages to which the claimant otherwise is entitled under this Act or under any other law.

(c) Actions on behalf of Fund

At the request of the Secretary, the Attorney General shall commence an action on behalf of the Fund to recover any compensation paid by the Fund to any claimant pursuant to this Act, and all costs incurred by the Fund by reason of the claim, including interest (including prejudgment interest), administrative and adjudicative costs, and attorney's fees. Such an action may be commenced against any responsible party or (subject to section 2716 of this title) guarantor, or against any other person who is liable, pursuant to any law, to the compensated claimant or to the Fund, for the cost or damages for which the compensation was paid. Such an action shall be commenced against the responsible foreign government or other responsible party to recover any removal costs or damages paid from the Fund as the result of the discharge, or substantial threat of discharge, of oil from a foreign offshore unit or other facility located seaward of the exclusive economic zone.

(d) Authority to settle

The head of any department or agency responsible for recovering amounts for which a person is liable under this subchapter may consider, compromise, and settle a claim for such amounts, including such costs paid from the Fund, if the claim has not been referred to the Attorney General. In any case in which the total amount to be recovered may exceed $500,000 (excluding interest), a claim may be compromised and settled under the preceding sentence only with the prior written approval of the Attorney General.

(Pub. L. No. 101–380, Title I, § 1015, 104 Stat. 502 (Aug. 18, 1990); as amended by Pub. L. No. 104–324, Title XI, § 1142(d), 110 Stat. 3991 (Oct. 19, 1996); Pub. L. No. 108–293, Title VII, § 706, 118 Stat. 1076 (Aug. 9, 2004); Pub. L. No. 115–91, § 3508(b), 131 Stat. 1916 (Dec. 12, 2017).)

HISTORICAL AND STATUTORY NOTES

References in Text

This Act, referred to in text, is Pub. L. No. 101–380, 104 Stat. 484 (Aug. 18, 1990), as amended, known as the Oil Pollution Act of 1990, which is codified principally as this chapter. For complete classification to the Code, see Short Title note under 33 U.S.C.A. § 2701 and Tables.

This subchapter, referred to in subsec. (d), was in the original "this title", meaning Title I of the Oil Pollution Act of 1990, Pub. L. No. 101–380, Title I, 104 Stat. 486 (Aug. 18, 1990), as amended, which is codified principally as this subchapter. For complete classification, see Short Title note set out under 33 U.S.C.A. § 2701 and Tables.

Effective and Applicability Provisions

1990 Acts. Section applicable to incidents occurring after Aug. 18, 1990, see section 1020 of Pub. L. No. 101–380, set out as a note under section 2701 of this title.

§ 2716. Financial responsibility

[OPA § 1016]

(a) Requirement

The responsible party for—

(1) any vessel over 300 gross tons (except a non-self-propelled vessel that does not carry oil as cargo or fuel) using any place subject to the jurisdiction of the United States;

(2) any vessel using the waters of the exclusive economic zone to transship or lighter oil destined for a place subject to the jurisdiction of the United States; or

(3) any tank vessel over 100 gross tons using any place subject to the jurisdiction of the United States;

shall establish and maintain, in accordance with regulations promulgated by the Secretary, evidence of financial responsibility sufficient to meet the maximum amount of liability to which the responsible party could be subjected under section 2704(a) or (d) of this title, in a case where the responsible party would be entitled to limit liability under that section. If the responsible party owns or operates more than one vessel, evidence of financial responsibility need be established only to meet the amount of the maximum liability applicable to the vessel having the greatest maximum liability.

(b) Sanctions

(1) Withholding clearance

The Secretary of the Treasury shall withhold or revoke the clearance required by section 60105 of Title 46 of any vessel subject to this section that does not have the evidence of financial responsibility required for the vessel under this section.

(2) Denying entry to or detaining vessels

The Secretary may—

(A) deny entry to any vessel to any place in the United States, or to the navigable waters, or

(B) detain at the place,

any vessel that, upon request, does not produce the evidence of financial responsibility required for the vessel under this section.

(3) Seizure of vessel

Any vessel subject to the requirements of this section which is found in the navigable waters without the necessary evidence of financial responsibility for the vessel shall be subject to seizure by and forfeiture to the United States.

(c) Offshore facilities

(1) In general

(A) Evidence of financial responsibility required

Except as provided in paragraph (2), a responsible party with respect to an offshore facility that—

(i) **(I)** is located seaward of the line of ordinary low water along that portion of the coast that is in direct contact with the open sea and the line marking the seaward limit of inland waters; or

(II) is located in coastal inland waters, such as bays or estuaries, seaward of the line of ordinary low water along that portion of the coast that is not in direct contact with the open sea;

(ii) is used for exploring for, drilling for, producing, or transporting oil from facilities engaged in oil exploration, drilling, or production; and

(iii) has a worst-case oil spill discharge potential of more than 1,000 barrels of oil (or a lesser amount if the President determines that the risks posed by such facility justify it),

shall establish and maintain evidence of financial responsibility in the amount required under subparagraph (B) or (C), as applicable.

(B) Amount required generally

Except as provided in subparagraph (C), the amount of financial responsibility for offshore facilities that meet the criteria of subparagraph (A) is—

(i) $35,000,000 for an offshore facility located seaward of the seaward boundary of a State; or

(ii) $10,000,000 for an offshore facility located landward of the seaward boundary of a State.

(C) Greater amount

If the President determines that an amount of financial responsibility for a responsible party greater than the amount required by subparagraph (B) is justified based on the relative operational, environmental, human health, and other risks posed by the quantity or quality of oil that is explored for, drilled for, produced, or transported by the responsible party, the evidence of financial responsibility required shall be for an amount determined by the President not exceeding $150,000,000.

(D) Multiple facilities

In a case in which a person is a responsible party for more than one facility subject to this subsection, evidence of financial responsibility need be established only to meet the amount applicable to the facility having the greatest financial responsibility requirement under this subsection.

(E) Definition

For the purpose of this paragraph, the seaward boundary of a State shall be determined in accordance with section 1301(b) of Title 43.

(2) Deepwater ports

Each responsible party with respect to a deepwater port shall establish and maintain evidence of financial responsibility sufficient to meet the maximum amount of liability to which the responsible party could be subjected under section 2704(a) of this title in a case where the responsible party would be entitled to limit liability under that section. If the Secretary exercises the authority under section 2704(d)(2) of this title to lower the limit of liability for deepwater ports, the responsible party shall establish and maintain evidence of financial responsibility sufficient to meet the maximum amount of liability so established. In a case in which a person is the responsible party for more than one deepwater port, evidence of financial responsibility need be established only to meet the maximum liability applicable to the deepwater port having the greatest maximum liability.

(e)[1] Methods of financial responsibility

Financial responsibility under this section may be established by any one, or by any combination, of the following methods which the Secretary (in the case of a vessel) or the President (in the case of a facility) determines to be acceptable: evidence of insurance, surety bond, guarantee, letter of credit, qualification as a self-insurer, or other evidence of financial responsibility. Any bond filed shall be issued by a bonding company authorized to do business in the United States. In promulgating requirements under this section, the Secretary or the President, as appropriate, may specify policy or other contractual terms, conditions, or defenses which are necessary, or which are unacceptable, in establishing evidence of financial responsibility to effectuate the purposes of this Act.

(f) Claims against guarantor

(1) In general

Subject to paragraph (2), a claim for which liability may be established under section 2702 of this title may be asserted directly against any guarantor providing evidence of financial responsibility for a responsible party liable under that section for removal costs and damages to which the claim pertains. In defending against such a claim, the guarantor may invoke—

(A) all rights and defenses which would be available to the responsible party under this Act;

(B) any defense authorized under subsection (e) of this section; and

(C) the defense that the incident was caused by the willful misconduct of the responsible party.

The guarantor may not invoke any other defense that might be available in proceedings brought by the responsible party against the guarantor.

(2) Further requirement

A claim may be asserted pursuant to paragraph (1) directly against a guarantor providing evidence of financial responsibility under subsection (c)(1) of this section with respect to an offshore facility only if—

(A) the responsible party for whom evidence of financial responsibility has been provided has denied or failed to pay a claim under this Act on the basis of being insolvent, as defined under section 101(32) of Title 11, and applying generally accepted accounting principles;

(B) the responsible party for whom evidence of financial responsibility has been provided has filed a petition for bankruptcy under Title 11; or

(C) the claim is asserted by the United States for removal costs and damages or for compensation paid by the Fund under this Act, including costs incurred by the Fund for processing compensation claims.

(3) Rulemaking authority

Not later than 1 year after October 19, 1996, the President shall promulgate regulations to establish a process for implementing paragraph (2) in a manner that will allow for the orderly and expeditious presentation and resolution of claims and effectuate the purposes of this Act.

(g) Limitation on guarantor's liability

Nothing in this Act shall impose liability with respect to an incident on any guarantor for damages or removal costs which exceed, in the aggregate, the amount of financial responsibility which that guarantor has provided for a responsible party pursuant to this section. The total liability of the guarantor on direct action for claims brought under this Act with respect to an incident shall be limited to that amount.

(h) Continuation of regulations

Any regulation relating to financial responsibility, which has been issued pursuant to any provision of law repealed or superseded by this Act, and which is in effect on the date immediately preceding the effective date of this Act, is deemed and shall be construed to be a regulation issued pursuant to this section. Such a regulation shall remain in full force and effect unless and until superseded by a new regulation issued under this section.

(i) Unified certificate

The Secretary may issue a single unified certificate of financial responsibility for purposes of this Act and any other law.

(Pub. L. No. 101–380, Title I, § 1016, 104 Stat. 502 (Aug. 18, 1990); as amended by Pub. L. No. 104–55, § 2(d)(2), 109 Stat. 547; (Nov. 20, 1995,) Pub. L. No. 104–324, Title XI, § 1125(a), 110 Stat. 3981 (Oct. 19, 1996); Pub. L. No. 111–281, Title VII, § 712, 124 Stat. 2988 (Oct. 15, 2010).)

[1] So in original. No subsec. (d) was enacted.

HISTORICAL AND STATUTORY NOTES

References in Text

This Act, referred to in text, is Pub. L. No. 101–380, 104 Stat. 484 (Aug. 18, 1990), as amended, known as the Oil Pollution Act of 1990, which is codified principally as this chapter. For complete classification to the Code, see Short Title note under 33 U.S.C.A. § 2701 and Tables.

Reference in subsec. (h) to the "effective date of this Act" probably refers to the date of enactment of Pub. L. No. 101–380 which was approved on Aug. 18, 1990.

Codifications

"Section 60105 of Title 46" substituted in subsec. (b)(1) for "section 91 of the Appendix to Title 46" on authority of Pub. L. No. 109–304, § 18(c), 120 Stat. 1709 (Oct. 6, 2006), which completed the codification of T. 46, Shipping, as positive law.

Effective and Applicability Provisions

1996 Acts. Section 1125(b) of Pub. L. No. 104–324 provided that: "The amendment made by subsection (a)(2) [amending subsec. (f) of this section] shall not apply to any final rule issued before the date of enactment of this section [Oct. 19, 1996].

1990 Acts. Section applicable to incidents occurring after Aug. 18, 1990, see section 1020 of Pub. L. No. 101–380, set out as a note under section 2701 of this title.

Delegation of Functions

The functions vested in the President by subsec. (e) of this section, respecting (in the case of offshore facilities other than deepwater ports) the issuance of regulations concerning financial responsibility, the determination of acceptable methods of financial responsibility, and the specification of necessary or unacceptable terms, conditions, or defenses, are delegated to the Secretary of the Interior, see Ex. Ord. No. 12777, 56 Fed. Reg. 54757 (Oct. 18, 1991), set out as a note under section 1321 of this title.

The functions vested in the President by subsec. (e) of this section, respecting (in the case of deepwater ports) the issuance of regulations concerning financial responsibility, the determination of acceptable methods of financial responsibility, and the specification of necessary or unacceptable terms, conditions, or defenses, are delegated to the Secretary of Transportation, see Ex. Ord. No. 12777, 56 Fed. Reg. 54757 (Oct. 18, 1991), set out as a note under section 1321 of this title.

§ 2716a. Financial responsibility civil penalties

[OPA § 4303]

(a) Administrative

Any person who, after notice and an opportunity for a hearing, is found to have failed to comply with the requirements of section 2716 of this title or the regulations issued under that section, or with a denial or detention order issued under subsection (b)(2) of that section[1], shall be liable to the United States for a civil penalty, not to exceed $25,000 per day of violation. The amount of the civil penalty shall be assessed by the President by written notice. In determining the amount of the penalty, the President shall take into account the nature, circumstances, extent, and gravity of the violation, the degree of culpability, any history of prior violation, ability to pay, and such other matters as justice may require. The President may compromise, modify, or remit, with or without conditions, any civil penalty which is subject to imposition or which had been imposed under this paragraph. If any person fails to pay an assessed civil penalty after it has become final, the President may refer the matter to the Attorney General for collection.

(b) Judicial

In addition to, or in lieu of, assessing a penalty under subsection (a) of this section, the President may request the Attorney General to secure such relief as necessary to compel compliance with section 2716 of this title, including a judicial order terminating operations. The district courts of the United States shall have jurisdiction to grant any relief as the public interest and the equities of the case may require.

(Pub. L. No. 101–380, Title IV, § 4303, 104 Stat. 539 (Aug. 18, 1990); and amended by Pub. L. No. 115–232, § 3547(d), 132 Stat. 1636, 2328 (Aug. 13, 2018).)

[1] So in original. Probably should read "under subsection (b)(2) of that section".

HISTORICAL AND STATUTORY NOTES

Codifications

This section was not enacted as part of title I of Pub. L. No. 101–380 which comprises this subchapter.

Effective and Applicability Provisions

1990 Acts. Incidents occurring after Aug. 18, 1990, as constituting the basis for violations of section 2716 of this title for which penalties are assessed under this section, see section 1020 of Pub. L. No. 101–380, set out as a note under section 2701 of this title.

Delegation of Functions

The functions vested in the President by this section, respecting (in cases involving vessels) the assessment of civil penalties, the compromising, modification or remission, with or without condition, and the referral for collection of such imposed penalties, and requests to the Attorney General to secure necessary judicial relief, are delegated to the Secretary of the Department in which the Coast Guard is operating, see Ex. Ord. No. 12777, 56 Fed. Reg. 54757 (Oct. 18, 1991), set out as a note under section 1321 of this title.

The functions vested in the President by this section, respecting (in cases involving offshore facilities other than deepwater ports) the assessment of civil penalties, the compromising, modification or remission, with or without condition, and the referral for collection of such imposed penalties, and requests to the Attorney General to secure necessary judicial relief, are delegated to the Secretary of the Interior, see Ex. Ord. No. 12777, 56 Fed. Reg. 54757 (Oct. 18, 1991), set out as a note under section 1321 of this title.

The functions vested in the President by this section, respecting (in cases involving deepwater ports) the assessment of civil penalties, the compromising, modification or remission, with or without condition, and the referral for collection of such imposed penalties, and requests to the Attorney General to secure necessary judicial relief, are delegated to the Secretary of Transportation, see Ex. Ord. No. 12777, 56 Fed. Reg. 54757 (Oct. 18, 1991), set out as a note under section 1321 of this title.

§ 2717. Litigation, jurisdiction, and venue

[OPA § 1017]

(a) Review of regulations

Review of any regulation promulgated under this Act may be had upon application by any interested person only in the Circuit Court of Appeals of the United States for the District of Columbia. Any such application shall be made within 90 days from the date of promulgation of such regulations. Any matter with respect to which review could have been obtained under this subsection shall not be subject to judicial review in any civil or criminal proceeding for enforcement or to obtain damages or recovery of response costs.

(b) Jurisdiction

Except as provided in subsections (a) and (c) of this section, the United States district courts shall have exclusive original jurisdiction over all controversies arising under this Act, without regard to the citizenship of the parties or the amount in controversy. Venue shall lie in any district in which the discharge or injury or damages occurred, or in which the defendant resides, may be found, has its principal office, or has appointed an agent for service of process. For the purposes of this section, the Fund shall reside in the District of Columbia.

(c) State court jurisdiction

A State trial court of competent jurisdiction over claims for removal costs or damages, as defined under this Act, may consider claims under this Act or State law and any final judgment of such court (when no longer subject to ordinary forms of review) shall be recognized, valid, and enforceable for all purposes of this Act.

(d) Assessment and collection of tax

The provisions of subsections (a), (b), and (c) of this section shall not apply to any controversy or other matter resulting from the assessment or collection of any tax, or to the review of any regulation promulgated under Title 26.

(e) Savings provision

Nothing in this subchapter shall apply to any cause of action or right of recovery arising from any incident which occurred prior to August 18, 1990. Such claims shall be adjudicated pursuant to the law applicable on the date of the incident.

(f) Period of limitations

(1) Damages

Except as provided in paragraphs (3) and (4), an action for damages under this Act shall be barred unless the action is brought within 3 years after—

(A) the date on which the loss and the connection of the loss with the discharge in question are reasonably discoverable with the exercise of due care, or

(B) in the case of natural resource damages under section 2702(b)(2)(A) of this title, the date of completion of the natural resources damage assessment under section 2706(c) of this title.

(2) Removal costs

An action for recovery of removal costs referred to in section 2702(b)(1) of this title must be commenced within 3 years after completion of the removal action. In any such action described in this subsection, the court shall enter a declaratory judgment on liability for removal costs or damages that will be binding on any subsequent action or actions to recover further removal costs or damages. Except as otherwise provided in this paragraph, an action may be commenced under this subchapter for recovery of removal costs at any time after such costs have been incurred.

(3) Contribution

No action for contribution for any removal costs or damages may be commenced more than 3 years after—

(A) the date of judgment in any action under this Act for recovery of such costs or damages, or

(B) the date of entry of a judicially approved settlement with respect to such costs or damages.

(4) Subrogation

No action based on rights subrogated pursuant to this Act by reason of payment of a claim may be commenced under this Act more than 3 years after the date of payment of such claim.

(5) Commencement

The time limitations contained herein shall not begin to run—

(A) against a minor until the earlier of the date when such minor reaches 18 years of age or the date on which a legal representative is duly appointed for such minor, or

(B) against an incompetent person until the earlier of the date on which such incompetent's incompetency ends or the date on which a legal representative is duly appointed for such incompetent.

(Pub. L. No. 101–380, Title I, § 1017, 104 Stat. 504 (Aug. 18, 1990).)

HISTORICAL AND STATUTORY NOTES

References in Text

This Act, referred to in text, is Pub. L. No. 101–380, 104 Stat. 484 (Aug. 18, 1990), as amended, known as the Oil Pollution Act of 1990, which is codified principally as this chapter. For complete classification to the Code, see Short Title note under 33 U.S.C.A. § 2701 and Tables.

This subchapter, referred to in subsecs. (e), (f), was in the original "this title", meaning Title I of the Oil Pollution Act of 1990, Pub. L. No. 101–380, Title I, 104 Stat. 486 (Aug. 18, 1990), as amended, which is codified principally as this subchapter. For complete classification, see Short Title note set out under 33 U.S.C.A. § 2701 and Tables.

Effective and Applicability Provisions

1990 Acts. Section applicable to incidents occurring after Aug. 18, 1990, see section 1020 of Pub. L. No. 101–380, set out as a note under section 2701 of this title.

§ 2718. Relationship to other law

[OPA § 1018]

(a) Preservation of State authorities; Solid Waste Disposal Act

Nothing in this Act or the Act of March 3, 1851 shall—

(1) affect, or be construed or interpreted as preempting, the authority of any State or political subdivision thereof from imposing any additional liability or requirements with respect to—

(A) the discharge of oil or other pollution by oil within such State; or

(B) any removal activities in connection with such a discharge; or

(2) affect, or be construed or interpreted to affect or modify in any way the obligations or liabilities of any person under the Solid Waste Disposal Act (42 U.S.C. 6901 et seq.) or State law, including common law.

(b) Preservation of State funds

Nothing in this Act or in section 9509 of Title 26 shall in any way affect, or be construed to affect, the authority of any State—

(1) to establish, or to continue in effect, a fund any purpose of which is to pay for costs or damages arising out of, or directly resulting from, oil pollution or the substantial threat of oil pollution; or

(2) to require any person to contribute to such a fund.

(c) Additional requirements and liabilities; penalties

Nothing in this Act, the Act of March 3, 1851 (46 U.S.C. 183 et seq.), or section 9509 of Title 26, shall in any way affect, or be construed to affect, the authority of the United States or any State or political subdivision thereof—

(1) to impose additional liability or additional requirements; or

(2) to impose, or to determine the amount of, any fine or penalty (whether criminal or civil in nature) for any violation of law;

relating to the discharge, or substantial threat of a discharge, of oil.

(d) Federal employee liability

For purposes of section 2679(b)(2)(B) of Title 28, nothing in this Act shall be construed to authorize or create a cause of action against a Federal officer or employee in the officer's or employee's personal or individual capacity for any act or omission while acting within the scope of the officer's or employee's office or employment.

(Pub. L. No. 101–380, Title I, § 1018, 104 Stat. 505 (Aug. 18, 1990).)

HISTORICAL AND STATUTORY NOTES

References in Text

This Act, referred to in text, is Pub. L. No. 101–380, 104 Stat. 484 (Aug. 18, 1990), as amended, known as the Oil Pollution Act of 1990, which is codified principally as this chapter. For complete classification to the Code, see Short Title note under 33 U.S.C.A. § 2701 and Tables.

Reference in subsecs. (a) and (c) to "the Act of March 3, 1851" probably is a reference to Act of March 3, 1851, c. 43, 9 Stat. 635, entitled "An Act to limit the liability of ship-owners, and for other purposes", which is now covered by section 181 et seq. of the Appendix to Title 46, Shipping (repealed by Pub. L. No. 109–304, § 19, 120 Stat. 1710 (Oct. 6, 2006)).

The Solid Waste Disposal Act, referred to in subsec. (a)(2), is title II of Pub. L. No. 89–272, 79 Stat. 997 (Oct. 20, 1965), as amended generally by Pub. L. No. 94–580, § 2, 90 Stat. 2795 (Oct. 21, 1976), which is codified generally as chapter 82 (§ 6901 et seq.) of Title 42, Public Health and Welfare. For complete classification of this Act to the Code, see Short Title note set out under section 6901 of Title 42 and Tables.

Effective and Applicability Provisions

1990 Acts. Section applicable to incidents occurring after Aug. 18, 1990, see section 1020 of Pub. L. No. 101–380, set out as a note under section 2701 of this title.

Report on Vessel Safety and Ability to Meet Legal Obligations

Pub. L. No. 102–241, § 32, 105 Stat. 2222 (Dec. 19, 1991), which provided for the Secretary of Transportation to report to Congress not later than one year after Dec. 19, 1991, on the effect of this section on the safety of vessels being used to transport oil and the capability of owners and operators to meet their legal obligations in the event of an oil spill, terminated, effective May 15, 2000, pursuant to Pub. L. No. 104–66, § 3003, as amended, set out as a note under 31 U.S.C.A. § 1113, and the 13th item on page 134 of House Document No. 103–7.

§ 2719. State financial responsibility

[OPA § 1019]

A State may enforce, on the navigable waters of the State, the requirements for evidence of financial responsibility under section 2716 of this title.

(Pub. L. No. 101–380, Title I, § 1019, 104 Stat. 506 (Aug. 18, 1990).)

HISTORICAL AND STATUTORY NOTES

Effective and Applicability Provisions

1990 Acts. Section applicable to incidents occurring after Aug. 18, 1990, see section 1020 of Pub. L. No. 101–380, set out as a note under section 2701 of this title.

§ 2720. Differentiation among fats, oils, and greases

(a) In general

Except as provided in subsection (c) of this section, in issuing or enforcing any regulation or establishing any interpretation or guideline relating to the transportation, storage, discharge, release, emission, or disposal of a fat, oil, or grease under any Federal law, the head of that Federal agency shall—

(1) differentiate between and establish separate classes for—

(A) animal fats and oils and greases, and fish and marine mammal oils, within the meaning of paragraph (2) of section 61(a) of Title 13, and oils of vegetable origin, including oils from the seeds, nuts, and kernels referred to in paragraph (1)(A) of that section; and

(B) other oils and greases, including petroleum; and

(2) apply standards to different classes of fats and oils based on considerations in subsection (b) of this section.

(b) Considerations

In differentiating between the class of fats, oils, and greases described in subsection (a)(1)(A) of this section and the class of oils and greases described in subsection (a)(1)(B) of this section, the head of the Federal agency shall consider differences in the physical, chemical, biological, and other properties, and in the environmental effects, of the classes.

(c) Exception

The requirements of this Act shall not apply to the Food and Drug Administration and the Food Safety and Inspection Service.

(d) Omitted

(Pub. L. No. 104–55, § 2, 109 Stat. 546 (Nov. 20, 1995).)

HISTORICAL AND STATUTORY NOTES

References in Text

This Act, referred to in subsec. (c), is Pub. L. No. 104–55, 109 Stat. 546 (Nov. 20, 1995), which enacted this section, amended sections 2704 and 2716 of this title, and enacted provisions set out as a note under section 2701 of this title. For complete classification of this Act to the Code, see Short Title note set out under section 2701 of this title and Tables.

Codifications

This section was enacted as part of the Edible Oil Regulatory Reform Act [Pub. L. No. 104–55] and not as part of the Oil Pollution Act of 1990 [Pub. L. No. 101–380] which enacted this chapter.

Section 2 of Pub. L. No. 104–55, which enacted this section, consisted in the original of subsecs. (a) to (d). Section 2(d) of Pub. L. No. 104–55, which has been omitted from the text of this section, amended sections 2704(a)(1) and 2716(a) of this title.

Interpretations or Guidelines under the Edible Oil Regulatory Reform Act

Pub. L. No. 105–277, Div. A, § 101(g) [Title III, § 343], 112 Stat. 2681–473, (Oct. 21, 1998,) provided that:

"(a) None of the funds made available by this Act or subsequent Acts may be used by the Coast Guard to issue, implement, or enforce a regulation or to establish an interpretation or guideline under the Edible Oil Regulatory Reform Act (Public Law 104–55), or the amendments made by that Act [Pub. L. No. 104–55, 109 Stat. 546 (Nov. 20, 1995), enacting this section and amending sections 2704 and 2716 of this title], that does not recognize and provide for, with respect to fats, oils, and greases (as described in that Act, or the amendments made by that Act) differences in—

"(1) physical, chemical, biological and other relevant properties; and

"(2) environmental effects.

"(b) Not later than March 31, 1999, the Secretary of Transportation shall issue regulations amending 33 C.F.R. 154 to comply with the requirements of Public Law 104–55 [Edible Oil Regulatory Reform Act, Pub. L. No. 104–55, 109 Stat. 546 (Nov. 20, 1995), enacting this section and amending sections 2704 and 2716 of this title]."

Administrative Provision

Pub. L. No. 105–276, Title III, 112 Stat. 2499 (Oct. 21, 1998), provided in part that: "Not later than March 31, 1999, the Administrator of the Environmental Protection Agency shall issue regulations amending 40 C.F.R. 112 to comply with the requirements of the Edible Oil Regulatory Reform Act (Public Law 104–55). Such regulations shall differentiate between and establish separate classes for animal fats and oils and greases, and fish and marine mammal oils (as described in that Act), and other oils and greases, and shall apply standards to such different classes of fats and oils based on differences in the physical, chemical, biological, and other properties, and in the environmental effects, of the classes. None of the funds made available by this Act [Pub. L. No. 105–276, 112 Stat. 2461 (Oct. 21, 1998), for classification of which, see Tables] or in subsequent Acts may be used by the Environmental Protection Agency to issue or to establish an interpretation or guidance relating to fats, oils, and greases (as described in Public Law 104–55) that does not comply with the requirements of the Edible Oil Regulatory Reform Act."

Sense of Congress on the Implementation of Regulations Regarding Animal Fats and Vegetable Oils

Pub. L. No. 104–324, Title XI, § 1130, 110 Stat. 3985 (Oct. 19, 1996), as amended by Pub. L. No. 111–207, § 4(a)(1), 124 Stat. 2251 (July 27, 2010), provided that regulations or guidelines issued pursuant to Pub. L. No. 104–55 should take into account the differences among classes of fats, oils, and greases described under that law.

SUBCHAPTER II—PRINCE WILLIAM SOUND PROVISIONS

§ 2731. Oil Spill Recovery Institute

[OPA § 5001]

(a) Establishment of Institute

The Secretary of Commerce shall provide for the establishment of a Prince William Sound Oil Spill Recovery Institute (hereinafter in this section referred to as the "Institute") through the Prince William Sound Science and Technology Institute located in Cordova, Alaska.

(b) Functions

The Institute shall conduct research and carry out educational and demonstration projects designed to—

(1) identify and develop the best available techniques, equipment, and materials for dealing with oil spills in the arctic and subarctic marine environment; and

(2) complement Federal and State damage assessment efforts and determine, document, assess, and understand the long-range effects of Arctic or Subarctic oil spills on the natural resources of Prince William Sound and its adjacent waters (as generally depicted on the map entitled "EXXON VALDEZ oil spill dated March 1990"), and the environment, the economy, and the lifestyle and well-being of the people who are dependent on them, except that the Institute shall not conduct studies or make recommendations on any matter which is not directly related to Arctic or Subarctic oil spills or the effects thereof.

(c) Advisory board

(1) In general

The policies of the Institute shall be determined by an advisory board, composed of 16 members appointed as follows:

(A) One representative appointed by each of the Commissioners of Fish and Game, Environmental Conservation, and Natural Resources of the State of Alaska, all of whom shall be State employees.

(B) One representative appointed by each of the Secretaries of Commerce and the Interior and the Commandant of the Coast Guard, who shall be Federal employees.

(C) Two representatives from the fishing industry appointed by the Governor of the State of Alaska from among residents of communities in Alaska that were affected by the EXXON

VALDEZ oil spill, who shall serve terms of 2 years each. Interested organizations from within the fishing industry may submit the names of qualified individuals for consideration by the Governor.

(D) Two Alaska Natives who represent Native entities affected by the EXXON VALDEZ oil spill, at least one of whom represents an entity located in Prince William Sound, appointed by the Governor of Alaska from a list of 4 qualified individuals submitted by the Alaska Federation of Natives, who shall serve terms of 2 years each.

(E) Two representatives from the oil and gas industry to be appointed by the Governor of the State of Alaska who shall serve terms of 2 years each. Interested organizations from within the oil and gas industry may submit the names of qualified individuals for consideration by the Governor.

(F) Two at-large representatives from among residents of communities in Alaska that were affected by the EXXON VALDEZ oil spill who are knowledgeable about the marine environment and wildlife within Prince William Sound, and who shall serve terms of 2 years each, appointed by the remaining members of the Advisory Board. Interested parties may submit the names of qualified individuals for consideration by the Advisory Board.

(G) One nonvoting representative of the Institute of Marine Science.

(H) One nonvoting representative appointed by the Prince William Sound Science and Technology Institute.

(2) Chairman

The representative of the Secretary of Commerce shall serve as Chairman of the Advisory Board.

(3) Policies

Policies determined by the Advisory Board under this subsection shall include policies for the conduct and support, through contracts and grants awarded on a nationally competitive basis, of research, projects, and studies to be supported by the Institute in accordance with the purposes of this section.

(4) Scientific review

The Advisory Board may request a scientific review of the research program every five years by the National Academy of Sciences which shall perform the review, if requested, as part of its responsibilities under section 2761(b)(2) of this title.

(d) Scientific and technical committee

(1) In general

The Advisory Board shall establish a scientific and technical committee, composed of specialists in matters relating to oil spill containment and cleanup technology, arctic and subarctic marine ecology, and the living resources and socioeconomics of Prince William Sound and its adjacent waters, from the University of Alaska, the Institute of Marine Science, the Prince William Sound Science and Technology Institute, and elsewhere in the academic community.

(2) Functions

The Scientific and Technical Committee shall provide such advice to the Advisory Board as the Advisory Board shall request, including recommendations regarding the conduct and support of research, projects, and studies in accordance with the purposes of this section. The Advisory Board shall not request, and the Committee shall not provide, any advice which is not directly related to Arctic or Subarctic oil spills or the effects thereof.

(e) Director

The Institute shall be administered by a Director appointed by the Advisory Board. The Prince William Sound Science and Technology Institute and the Scientific and Technical Committee may each submit independent recommendations for the Advisory Board's consideration for appointment as Director. The

Director may hire such staff and incur such expenses on behalf of the Institute as are authorized by the Advisory Board.

(f) Evaluation

The Secretary of Commerce may conduct an ongoing evaluation of the activities of the Institute to ensure that funds received by the Institute are used in a manner consistent with this section.

(g) Audit

The Comptroller General of the United States, and any of his or her duly authorized representatives, shall have access, for purposes of audit and examination, to any books, documents, papers, and records of the Institute and its administering agency that are pertinent to the funds received and expended by the Institute and its administering agency.

(h) Status of employees

Employees of the Institute shall not, by reason of such employment, be considered to be employees of the Federal Government for any purpose.

(i) Termination

The authorization in section 2736(b) of this title providing funding for the Institute shall terminate 1 year after the date on which the Secretary, in consultation with the Secretary of the Interior, determines that oil and gas exploration, development, and production in the State of Alaska have ceased.

(j) Use of funds

No funds made available to carry out this section may be used to initiate litigation. No funds made available to carry out this section may be used for the acquisition of real property (including buildings) or construction of any building. No more than 20 percent of funds made available to carry out this section may be used to lease necessary facilities and to administer the Institute. The Advisory Board may compensate its Federal representatives for their reasonable travel costs. None of the funds authorized by this section shall be used for any purpose other than the functions specified in subsection (b) of this section.

(k) Research

The Institute shall publish and make available to any person upon request the results of all research, educational, and demonstration projects conducted by the Institute. The Administrator shall provide a copy of all research, educational, and demonstration projects conducted by the Institute to the National Oceanic and Atmospheric Administration.

(*l*) "Prince William Sound and its adjacent waters" defined

In this section, the term "Prince William Sound and its adjacent waters" means such sound and waters as generally depicted on the map entitled "EXXON VALDEZ oil spill dated March 1990".

(Pub. L. No. 101–380, Title V, § 5001, 104 Stat. 542 (Aug. 18, 1990); as amended by Pub. L. No. 104–324, Title XI, § 1102(a), 110 Stat. 3964 (Oct. 19, 1996); Pub. L. No. 107–295, Title IV, § 427, 116 Stat. 2127 (Nov. 25, 2002); Pub. L. No. 109–58, Title III, § 389(1), 119 Stat. 747 (Aug. 8, 2005); Pub. L. No. 109–241, Title IX, § 902(*l*)(1), 120 Stat. 568 (July 11, 2006).)

HISTORICAL AND STATUTORY NOTES

Termination of Advisory Boards

Advisory boards established after Jan. 5, 1973, to terminate not later than the expiration of the 2-year period beginning on the date of their establishment, unless, in the case of a board established by the President or an officer of the Federal Government, such board is renewed by appropriate action prior to the expiration of such 2-year period, or in the case of a board established by Congress, its duration is otherwise provided for by law. See sections 3(2) and 14 of Pub. L. No. 92–463, 86 Stat. 770, 776 (Oct. 6, 1972), set out in the Appendix to Title 5.

§ 2732. Terminal and tanker oversight and monitoring [OPA § 5002]

(a) Short title and findings

(1) Short title

This section may be cited as the "Oil Terminal and Oil Tanker Environmental Oversight and Monitoring Act of 1990".

(2) Findings

The Congress finds that—

(A) the March 24, 1989, grounding and rupture of the fully loaded oil tanker, the EXXON VALDEZ, spilled 11 million gallons of crude oil in Prince William Sound, an environmentally sensitive area;

(B) many people believe that complacency on the part of the industry and government personnel responsible for monitoring the operation of the Valdez terminal and vessel traffic in Prince William Sound was one of the contributing factors to the EXXON VALDEZ oil spill;

(C) one way to combat this complacency is to involve local citizens in the process of preparing, adopting, and revising oil spill contingency plans;

(D) a mechanism should be established which fosters the long-term partnership of industry, government, and local communities in overseeing compliance with environmental concerns in the operation of crude oil terminals;

(E) such a mechanism presently exists at the Sullom Voe terminal in the Shetland Islands and this terminal should serve as a model for others;

(F) because of the effective partnership that has developed at Sullom Voe, Sullom Voe is considered the safest terminal in Europe;

(G) the present system of regulation and oversight of crude oil terminals in the United States has degenerated into a process of continual mistrust and confrontation;

(H) only when local citizens are involved in the process will the trust develop that is necessary to change the present system from confrontation to consensus;

(I) a pilot program patterned after Sullom Voe should be established in Alaska to further refine the concepts and relationships involved; and

(J) similar programs should eventually be established in other major crude oil terminals in the United States because the recent oil spills in Texas, Delaware, and Rhode Island indicate that the safe transportation of crude oil is a national problem.

(b) Demonstration programs

(1) Establishment

There are established 2 Oil Terminal and Oil Tanker Environmental Oversight and Monitoring Demonstration Programs (hereinafter referred to as "Programs") to be carried out in the State of Alaska.

(2) Advisory function

The function of these Programs shall be advisory only.

(3) Purpose

The Prince William Sound Program shall be responsible for environmental monitoring of the terminal facilities in Prince William Sound and the crude oil tankers operating in Prince William Sound. The Cook Inlet Program shall be responsible for environmental monitoring of the terminal facilities and crude oil tankers operating in Cook Inlet located South of the latitude at Point Possession and North of the latitude at Amatuli Island, including offshore facilities in Cook Inlet.

(4) Suits barred

No program, association, council, committee or other organization created by this section may sue any person or entity, public or private, concerning any matter arising under this section except for the performance of contracts.

(c) Oil Terminal Facilities and Oil Tanker Operations Association

(1) Establishment

There is established an Oil Terminal Facilities and Oil Tanker Operations Association (hereinafter in this section referred to as the "Association") for each of the Programs established under subsection (b) of this section.

(2) Membership

Each Association shall be comprised of 4 individuals as follows:

(A) One individual shall be designated by the owners and operators of the terminal facilities and shall represent those owners and operators.

(B) One individual shall be designated by the owners and operators of the crude oil tankers calling at the terminal facilities and shall represent those owners and operators.

(C) One individual shall be an employee of the State of Alaska, shall be designated by the Governor of the State of Alaska, and shall represent the State government.

(D) One individual shall be an employee of the Federal Government, shall be designated by the President, and shall represent the Federal Government.

(3) Responsibilities

Each Association shall be responsible for reviewing policies relating to the operation and maintenance of the oil terminal facilities and crude oil tankers which affect or may affect the environment in the vicinity of their respective terminals. Each Association shall provide a forum among the owners and operators of the terminal facilities, the owners and operators of crude oil tankers calling at those facilities, the United States, and the State of Alaska to discuss and to make recommendations concerning all permits, plans, and site-specific regulations governing the activities and actions of the terminal facilities which affect or may affect the environment in the vicinity of the terminal facilities and of crude oil tankers calling at those facilities.

(4) Designation of existing organization

The Secretary may designate an existing nonprofit organization as an Association under this subsection if the organization is organized to meet the purposes of this section and consists of at least the individuals listed in paragraph (2).

(d) Regional Citizens' Advisory Councils

(1) Membership

There is established a Regional Citizens' Advisory Council (hereinafter in this section referred to as the "Council") for each of the programs established by subsection (b) of this section.

(2) Membership

Each Council shall be composed of voting members and nonvoting members, as follows:

(A) Voting members

Voting members shall be Alaska residents and, except as provided in clause (vii) of this paragraph, shall be appointed by the Governor of the State of Alaska from a list of nominees provided by each of the following interests, with one representative appointed to represent each of the following interests, taking into consideration the need for regional balance on the Council:

(i) Local commercial fishing industry organizations, the members of which depend on the fisheries resources of the waters in the vicinity of the terminal facilities.

(ii) Aquaculture associations in the vicinity of the terminal facilities.

(iii) Alaska Native Corporations and other Alaska Native organizations the members of which reside in the vicinity of the terminal facilities.

(iv) Environmental organizations the members of which reside in the vicinity of the terminal facilities.

(v) Recreational organizations the members of which reside in or use the vicinity of the terminal facilities.

(vi) The Alaska State Chamber of Commerce, to represent the locally based tourist industry.

(vii)(I) For the Prince William Sound Terminal Facilities Council, one representative selected by each of the following municipalities: Cordova, Whittier, Seward, Valdez, Kodiak, the Kodiak Island Borough, and the Kenai Peninsula Borough.

(II) For the Cook Inlet Terminal Facilities Council, one representative selected by each of the following municipalities: Homer, Seldovia, Anchorage, Kenai, Kodiak, the Kodiak Island Borough, and the Kenai Peninsula Borough.

(B) Nonvoting members

One ex-officio, nonvoting representative shall be designated by, and represent, each of the following:

(i) The Environmental Protection Agency.

(ii) The Coast Guard.

(iii) The National Oceanic and Atmospheric Administration.

(iv) The United States Forest Service.

(v) The Bureau of Land Management.

(vi) The Alaska Department of Environmental Conservation.

(vii) The Alaska Department of Fish and Game.

(viii) The Alaska Department of Natural Resources.

(ix) The Division of Emergency Services, Alaska Department of Military and Veterans Affairs.

(3) Terms

(A) Duration of Councils

The term of the Councils shall continue throughout the life of the operation of the Trans-Alaska Pipeline System and so long as oil is transported to or from Cook Inlet.

(B) Three years

The voting members of each Council shall be appointed for a term of 3 years except as provided for in subparagraph (C).

(C) Initial appointments

The terms of the first appointments shall be as follows:

(i) For the appointments by the Governor of the State of Alaska, one-third shall serve for 3 years, one-third shall serve for 2 years, and one-third shall serve for one year.

(ii) For the representatives of municipalities required by subsection (d)(2)(A)(vii) of this section, a drawing of lots among the appointees shall determine that one-third of that group serves for 3 years, one-third serves for 2 years, and the remainder serves for 1 year.

(4) Self-governing

Each Council shall elect its own chairperson, select its own staff, and make policies with regard to its internal operating procedures. After the initial organizational meeting called by the Secretary under subsection (i) of this section, each Council shall be self-governing.

(5) Dual membership and conflicts of interest prohibited

(A) No individual selected as a member of the Council shall serve on the Association.

(B) No individual selected as a voting member of the Council shall be engaged in any activity which might conflict with such individual carrying out his functions as a member thereof.

(6) Duties

Each Council shall—

(A) provide advice and recommendations to the Association on policies, permits, and site-specific regulations relating to the operation and maintenance of terminal facilities and crude oil tankers which affect or may affect the environment in the vicinity of the terminal facilities;

(B) monitor through the committee established under subsection (e) of this section, the environmental impacts of the operation of the terminal facilities and crude oil tankers;

(C) monitor those aspects of terminal facilities' and crude oil tankers' operations and maintenance which affect or may affect the environment in the vicinity of the terminal facilities;

(D) review through the committee established under subsection (f) of this section, the adequacy of oil spill prevention and contingency plans for the terminal facilities and the adequacy of oil spill prevention and contingency plans for crude oil tankers, operating in Prince William Sound or in Cook Inlet;

(E) provide advice and recommendations to the Association on port operations, policies and practices;

(F) recommend to the Association—

(i) standards and stipulations for permits and site-specific regulations intended to minimize the impact of the terminal facilities' and crude oil tankers' operations in the vicinity of the terminal facilities;

(ii) modifications of terminal facility operations and maintenance intended to minimize the risk and mitigate the impact of terminal facilities, operations in the vicinity of the terminal facilities and to minimize the risk of oil spills;

(iii) modifications of crude oil tanker operations and maintenance in Prince William Sound and Cook Inlet intended to minimize the risk and mitigate the impact of oil spills; and

(iv) modifications to the oil spill prevention and contingency plans for terminal facilities and for crude oil tankers in Prince William Sound and Cook Inlet intended to enhance the ability to prevent and respond to an oil spill; and

(G) create additional committees of the Council as necessary to carry out the above functions, including a scientific and technical advisory committee to the Prince William Sound Council.

(7) No estoppel

No Council shall be held liable under State or Federal law for costs or damages as a result of rendering advice under this section. Nor shall any advice given by a voting member of a Council, or program representative or agent, be grounds for estopping the interests represented by the voting Council members from seeking damages or other appropriate relief.

(8) Scientific work

In carrying out its research, development and monitoring functions, each Council is authorized to conduct its own scientific research and shall review the scientific work undertaken by or on behalf of the terminal operators or crude oil tanker operators as a result of a legal requirement to undertake that work. Each Council shall also review the relevant scientific work undertaken by or on behalf of any government entity relating to the terminal facilities or crude oil tankers. To the extent possible, to avoid unnecessary duplication, each Council shall coordinate its independent scientific work with the scientific work performed by or on behalf of the terminal operators and with the scientific work performed by or on behalf of the operators of the crude oil tankers.

(e) Committee for Terminal and Oil Tanker Operations and Environmental Monitoring

(1) Monitoring Committee

Each Council shall establish standing Terminal and Oil Tanker Operations and Environmental Monitoring Committee (hereinafter in this section referred to as the "Monitoring Committee") to devise and manage a comprehensive program of monitoring the environmental impacts of the operations of terminal facilities and of crude oil tankers while operating in Prince William Sound and Cook Inlet. The membership of the Monitoring Committee shall be made up of members of the Council, citizens, and recognized scientific experts selected by the Council.

(2) Duties

In fulfilling its responsibilities, the Monitoring Committee shall—

(A) advise the Council on a monitoring strategy that will permit early detection of environmental impacts of terminal facility operations and crude oil tanker operations while in Prince William Sound and Cook Inlet;

(B) develop monitoring programs and make recommendations to the Council on the implementation of those programs;

(C) at its discretion, select and contract with universities and other scientific institutions to carry out specific monitoring projects authorized by the Council pursuant to an approved monitoring strategy;

(D) complete any other tasks assigned by the Council; and

(E) provide written reports to the Council which interpret and assess the results of all monitoring programs.

(f) Committee for Oil Spill Prevention, Safety, and Emergency Response

(1) Technical Oil Spill Committee

Each Council shall establish a standing technical committee (hereinafter referred to as "Oil Spill Committee") to review and assess measures designed to prevent oil spills and the planning and preparedness for responding to, containing, cleaning up, and mitigating impacts of oil spills. The membership of the Oil Spill Committee shall be made up of members of the Council, citizens, and recognized technical experts selected by the Council.

(2) Duties

In fulfilling its responsibilities, the Oil Spill Committee shall—

(A) periodically review the respective oil spill prevention and contingency plans for the terminal facilities and for the crude oil tankers while in Prince William Sound or Cook Inlet, in light of new technological developments and changed circumstances;

(B) monitor periodic drills and testing of the oil spill contingency plans for the terminal facilities and for crude oil tankers while in Prince William Sound and Cook Inlet;

(C) study wind and water currents and other environmental factors in the vicinity of the terminal facilities which may affect the ability to prevent, respond to, contain, and clean up an oil spill;

(D) identify highly sensitive areas which may require specific protective measures in the event of a spill in Prince William Sound or Cook Inlet;

(E) monitor developments in oil spill prevention, containment, response, and cleanup technology;

(F) periodically review port organization, operations, incidents, and the adequacy and maintenance of vessel traffic service systems designed to assure safe transit of crude oil tankers pertinent to terminal operations;

(G) periodically review the standards for tankers bound for, loading at, exiting from, or otherwise using the terminal facilities;

(H) complete any other tasks assigned by the Council; and

(I) provide written reports to the Council outlining its findings and recommendations.

(g) Agency cooperation

On and after the expiration of the 180-day period following August 18, 1990, each Federal department, agency, or other instrumentality shall, with respect to all permits, site-specific regulations, and other matters governing the activities and actions of the terminal facilities which affect or may affect the vicinity of the terminal facilities, consult with the appropriate Council prior to taking substantive action with respect to the permit, site-specific regulation, or other matter. This consultation shall be carried out with a view to enabling the appropriate Association and Council to review the permit, site-specific regulation, or other matters and make appropriate recommendations regarding operations, policy or agency actions. Prior consultation shall not be required if an authorized Federal agency representative reasonably believes that an emergency exists requiring action without delay.

(h) Recommendations of Council

In the event that the Association does not adopt, or significantly modifies before adoption, any recommendation of the Council made pursuant to the authority granted to the Council in subsection (d) of this section, the Association shall provide to the Council, in writing, within 5 days of its decision, notice of its decision and a written statement of reasons for its rejection or significant modification of the recommendation.

(i) Administrative actions

Appointments, designations, and selections of individuals to serve as members of the Associations and Councils under this section shall be submitted to the Secretary prior to the expiration of the 120-day period following August 18, 1990. On or before the expiration of the 180-day period following August 18, 1990, the Secretary shall call an initial meeting of each Association and Council for organizational purposes.

(j) Location and compensation

(1) Location

Each Association and Council established by this section shall be located in the State of Alaska.

(2) Compensation

No member of an Association or Council shall be compensated for the member's services as a member of the Association or Council, but shall be allowed travel expenses, including per diem in lieu of subsistence, at a rate established by the Association or Council not to exceed the rates authorized for employees of agencies under sections 5702 and 5703 of Title 5. However, each Council may enter into contracts to provide compensation and expenses to members of the committees created under subsections (d), (e), and (f) of this section.

(k) Funding

(1) Requirement

Approval of the contingency plans required of owners and operators of the Cook Inlet and Prince William Sound terminal facilities and crude oil tankers while operating in Alaskan waters in commerce with those terminal facilities shall be effective only so long as the respective Association and Council for a facility are funded pursuant to paragraph (2).

(2) Prince William Sound program

The owners or operators of terminal facilities or crude oil tankers operating in Prince William Sound shall provide, on an annual basis, an aggregate amount of not more than $2,000,000, as determined by the Secretary. Such amount—

(A) shall provide for the establishment and operation on the environmental oversight and monitoring program in Prince William Sound;

(B) shall be adjusted annually by the Anchorage Consumer Price Index; and

(C) may be adjusted periodically upon the mutual consent of the owners or operators of terminal facilities or crude oil tankers operating in Prince William Sound and the Prince William Sound terminal facilities Council.

(3) Cook Inlet program

The owners or operators of terminal facilities, offshore facilities, or crude oil tankers operating in Cook Inlet shall provide, on an annual basis, an aggregate amount of not less than $1,400,000, as determined by the Secretary. Such amount—

(A) shall provide for the establishment and operation of the environmental oversight and monitoring program in Cook Inlet;

(B) shall be adjusted annually by the Anchorage Consumer Price Index; and

(C) may be adjusted periodically upon the mutual consent of the owners or operators of terminal facilities, offshore facilities, or crude oil tankers operating in Cook Inlet and the Cook Inlet Council.

(*l*) Reports

(1) Associations and Councils

Prior to the expiration of the 36-month period following August 18, 1990, each Association and Council established by this section shall report to the President and the Congress concerning its activities under this section, together with its recommendations.

(2) GAO

Prior to the expiration of the 36-month period following August 18, 1990, the Government Accountability Office shall report to the President and the Congress as to the handling of funds, including donated funds, by the entities carrying out the programs under this section, and the effectiveness of the demonstration programs carried out under this section, together with its recommendations.

(m) Definitions

As used in this section, the term—

(1) "terminal facilities" means—

(A) in the case of the Prince William Sound Program, the entire oil terminal complex located in Valdez, Alaska, consisting of approximately 1,000 acres including all buildings, docks (except docks owned by the City of Valdez if those docks are not used for loading of crude oil), pipes, piping, roads, ponds, tanks, crude oil tankers only while at the terminal dock, tanker escorts owned or operated by the operator of the terminal, vehicles, and other facilities associated with, and necessary for, assisting tanker movement of crude oil into and out of the oil terminal complex; and

(B) in the case of the Cook Inlet Program, the entire oil terminal complex including all buildings, docks, pipes, piping, roads, ponds, tanks, vessels, vehicles, crude oil tankers only while at the terminal dock, tanker escorts owned or operated by the operator of the terminal, emergency spill response vessels owned or operated by the operator of the terminal, and other facilities associated with, and necessary for, assisting tanker movement of crude oil into and out of the oil terminal complex;

(2) "crude oil tanker" means a tanker (as that term is defined under section 2101 of Title 46)—

(A) in the case of the Prince William Sound Program, calling at the terminal facilities for the purpose of receiving and transporting oil to refineries, operating north of Middleston Island and bound for or exiting from Prince William Sound; and

(B) in the case of the Cook Inlet Program, calling at the terminal facilities for the purpose of receiving and transporting oil to refineries and operating in Cook Inlet and the Gulf of Alaska north of Amatuli Island, including tankers transiting to Cook Inlet from Prince William Sound;

(3) "vicinity of the terminal facilities" means that geographical area surrounding the environment of terminal facilities which is directly affected or may be directly affected by the operation of the terminal facilities; and

(4) "Secretary" means the Secretary of the department in which the Coast Guard is operating.

(n) Savings clause

(1) Regulatory authority

Nothing in this section shall be construed as modifying, repealing, superseding, or preempting any municipal, State or Federal law or regulation, or in any way affecting litigation arising from oil spills or the rights and responsibilities of the United States or the State of Alaska, or municipalities thereof, to preserve and protect the environment through regulation of land, air, and water uses, of safety, and of related development. The monitoring provided for by this section shall be designed to help assure compliance with applicable laws and regulations and shall only extend to activities—

(A) that would affect or have the potential to affect the vicinity of the terminal facilities and the area of crude oil tanker operations included in the Programs; and

(B) are subject to the United States or State of Alaska, or municipality thereof, law, regulation, or other legal requirement.

(2) Recommendations

This subsection is not intended to prevent the Association or Council from recommending to appropriate authorities that existing legal requirements should be modified or that new legal requirements should be adopted.

(*o*) Alternative voluntary advisory group in lieu of Council

The requirements of subsections (c) through (*l*) of this section, as such subsections apply respectively to the Prince William Sound Program and the Cook Inlet Program, are deemed to have been satisfied so long as the following conditions are met:

(1) Prince William Sound

With respect to the Prince William Sound Program, the Alyeska Pipeline Service Company or any of its owner companies enters into a contract for the duration of the operation of the Trans-Alaska Pipeline System with the Alyeska Citizens Advisory Committee in existence on August 18, 1990, or a successor organization, to fund that Committee or organization on an annual basis in the amount provided for by subsection (k)(2)(A) of this section and the President annually certifies that the Committee or organization fosters the general goals and purposes of this section and is broadly representative of the communities and interests in the vicinity of the terminal facilities and Prince William Sound.

(2) Cook Inlet

With respect to the Cook Inlet Program, the terminal facilities, offshore facilities, or crude oil tanker owners and operators enter into a contract with a voluntary advisory organization to fund that organization on an annual basis and the President annually certifies that the organization fosters the general goals and purposes of this section and is broadly representative of the communities and interests in the vicinity of the terminal facilities and Cook Inlet.

(Pub. L. No. 101–380, Title V, § 5002, 104 Stat. 544 (Aug. 18, 1990); as amended by Pub. L. No. 109–241, Title IX, § 902(*l*)(2), 120 Stat. 568 (July 11, 2006); Pub. L. No. 113–281, § 318, 128 Stat. 3051 (Dec. 18, 2014); Pub. L. No. 115–232, § 3547(e), 132 Stat. 1636, 2328 (Aug. 13, 2018).)

HISTORICAL AND STATUTORY NOTES

Change of Name

"General Accounting Office" was changed to "Government Accountability Office" by Pub. L. No. 108–271, § 8(b), set out as a note under 31 U.S.C.A. § 702, which provided that any reference to the General Accounting Office in any law, rule, regulation, certificate, directive, instruction, or other official paper in force on July 17, 2004, was considered to refer and apply to the Government Accountability Office.

Delegation of Functions

The function vested in the President by subsec. (c)(2)(D) of this section, respecting the designating of an employee of the Federal Government who shall represent the Federal Government on the Oil Terminal Facilities and Oil Tanker Operations Associations, is delegated to the Secretary of Transportation, see Ex. Ord. No. 12777, 56 Fed. Reg. 54757 (Oct. 18, 1991), set out as a note under section 1321 of this title.

The functions vested in the President by subsec. (*o*) of this section, respecting the annual certification of alternative voluntary advisory groups, are delegated to the Secretary of Transportation, see Ex. Ord. No. 12777, 56 Fed. Reg. 54757 (Oct. 18, 1991), set out as a note under section 1321 of this title.

MESSAGE OF PRESIDENT

Mar. 21, 1991, 56 Fed. Reg. 12439

PRINCE WILLIAM SOUND REGIONAL CITIZENS ADVISORY COMMITTEE

By the authority vested in me as President by the Constitution and the laws of the United States of America, including section 5002(*o*)(1) of the Oil Pollution Act of 1990 (Public Law 101–380, 104 Stat. 552) [subsec. (*o*)(1) of this section], I hereby certify for the year 1991 the following:

(1) that the Prince William Sound Regional Citizens Advisory Committee fosters the general goals and purposes of section 5002 of the Oil Pollution Act of 1990 [this section] for the year 1991; and

(2) that the Prince William Sound Regional Citizens Advisory Committee is broadly representative of the communities and interests in the vicinity of the terminal facilities and Prince William Sound.

This certification shall be published in the **Federal Register**.

GEORGE BUSH

Aug. 6, 1991, 56 Fed. Reg. 37819

By the authority vested in me as President by the Constitution and the laws of the United States of America, including section 5002(*o*)(2) of the Oil Pollution Act of 1990 [subsec. (*o*)(2) of this section], I hereby certify for the year 1991 the following:

(1) that the Cook Inlet Regional Citizens Advisory Council has met the general goals and purposes of section 5002 of the Oil Pollution Act of 1990 [this section] for the year 1991; and

(2) that the Cook Inlet Regional Citizens Advisory Council is broadly representative of the communities and interests in the vicinity of the terminal facilities and offshore facilities in Cook Inlet.

This certification shall be published in the **Federal Register**.

§ 2733. Bligh Reef light

[OPA § 5003]

The Secretary of Transportation shall within one year after August 18, 1990, install and ensure operation of an automated navigation light on or adjacent to Bligh Reef in Prince William Sound, Alaska, of sufficient power and height to provide long-range warning of the location of Bligh Reef.

(Pub. L. No. 101–380, Title V, § 5003, 104 Stat. 553 (Aug. 18, 1990).)

§ 2734. Vessel traffic service system

[OPA § 5004]

The Secretary of Transportation shall within one year after August 18, 1990—

(1) acquire, install, and operate such additional equipment (which may consist of radar, closed circuit television, satellite tracking systems, or other shipboard dependent surveillance), train and locate such personnel, and issue such final regulations as are necessary to increase the range of the existing VTS system in the Port of Valdez, Alaska, sufficiently to track the locations and movements of tank vessels carrying oil from the Trans-Alaska Pipeline when such vessels are transiting Prince William Sound, Alaska, and to sound an audible alarm when such tankers depart from designated navigation routes; and

(2) submit to the Committee on Commerce, Science, and Transportation of the Senate and the Committee on Transportation and Infrastructure of the House of Representatives a report on the feasibility and desirability of instituting positive control of tank vessel movements in Prince William Sound by Coast Guard personnel using the Port of Valdez, Alaska, VTS system, as modified pursuant to paragraph (1).

(Pub. L. No. 101–380, Title V, § 5004, 104 Stat. 553 (Aug. 18, 1990); as amended by Pub. L. No. 107–295, Title IV, § 408(b)(2), 116 Stat. 2117 (Nov. 25, 2002).)

HISTORICAL AND STATUTORY NOTES

Abolition of House Committee on Merchant Marine and Fisheries

Committee on Merchant Marine and Fisheries of House of Representatives abolished and its jurisdiction transferred by House Resolution No. 6, One Hundred Fourth Congress, Jan. 4, 1995. Committee on Merchant Marine and Fisheries of the House of Representatives treated as referring to the Committee on Resources of the House of Representatives, in the case of a provision of law relating to fisheries, wildlife, international fishing agreements, marine affairs (including coastal zone management) except for measures relating to oil and other pollution of navigable waters, or oceanography by section 1(b)(3) of Pub. L. No. 104–14, set out as a note preceding 2 U.S.C.A. § 21. Committee on Resources of the House of Representatives, changed to Committee on Natural Resources of the House of Representatives by House Resolution No. 6, One Hundred Tenth Congress, Jan. 5, 2007.

§ 2735. Equipment and personnel requirements under tank vessel and facility response plans

[OPA § 5005]

(a) In general

In addition to the requirements for response plans for vessels established by section 1321(j) of this title a response plan for a tanker loading cargo at a facility permitted under the Trans-Alaska Pipeline Authorization Act (43 U.S.C. 1651 et seq.), and a response plan for such a facility, shall provide for—

(1) prepositioned oil spill containment and removal equipment in communities and other strategic locations within the geographic boundaries of Prince William Sound, including escort vessels with skimming capability; barges to receive recovered oil; heavy duty sea boom, pumping, transferring, and lightering equipment; and other appropriate removal equipment for the protection of the environment, including fish hatcheries;

(2) the establishment of an oil spill removal organization at appropriate locations in Prince William Sound, consisting of trained personnel in sufficient numbers to immediately remove, to the maximum extent practicable, a worst case discharge or a discharge of 200,000 barrels of oil, whichever is greater;

(3) training in oil removal techniques for local residents and individuals engaged in the cultivation or production of fish or fish products in Prince William Sound;

(4) practice exercises not less than 2 times per year which test the capacity of the equipment and personnel required under this paragraph; and

(5) periodic testing and certification of equipment required under this paragraph, as required by the Secretary.

(b) Definitions

In this section—

(1) the term "Prince William Sound" means all State and Federal waters within Prince William Sound, Alaska, including the approach to Hinchenbrook Entrance out to and encompassing Seal Rocks; and

(2) the term "worst case discharge" means—

(A) in the case of a vessel, a discharge in adverse weather conditions of its entire cargo; and

(B) in the case of a facility, the largest foreseeable discharge in adverse weather conditions.

(Pub. L. No. 101–380, Title V, § 5005, 104 Stat. 553 (Aug. 18, 1990); as amended by Pub. L. No. 102–388, Title III, § 354, 106 Stat. 1555 (Oct. 6, 1992).)

HISTORICAL AND STATUTORY NOTES

References in Text

Reference in subsec. (a) to the amendment of section 1321(j) of this title "by this Act" refers to the amendment by Pub. L. No. 101–380, 104 Stat. 484 (Aug. 18, 1990).

The Trans-Alaska Pipeline Authorization Act, referred to in subsec. (a), is title II of Pub. L. No. 93–153, 87 Stat. 584 (Nov. 16, 1973), which is codified as chapter 34 (§ 1651 et seq.) of Title 43, Public Lands. For complete classification of this Act to the Code, see Short Title note set out under section 1651 of Title 43 and Tables.

§ 2736. Funding

[OPA § 5006]

(a) Sections 2731, 2733, and 2734

Amounts in the Fund shall be available, without further appropriations and without fiscal year limitation, to carry out section 2731 of this title in the amount as determined in subsection (b) of this section, and to carry out sections 2733 and 2734 of this title, in an amount not to exceed $5,000,000.

(b) Use of interest only

The amount of funding to be made available annually to carry out section 2731 of this title shall be the interest produced by the Fund's investment of the $22,500,000 remaining funding authorized for the Prince William Sound Oil Spill Recovery Institute and currently deposited in the Fund and invested by the Secretary of the Treasury in income producing securities along with other funds comprising the Fund. The National Pollution Funds Center shall transfer all such accrued interest, including the interest earned from the date funds in the Trans-Alaska Liability Pipeline Fund were transferred into the Oil Spill Liability Trust Fund pursuant to section 8102(a)(2)(B)(ii), to the Prince William Sound Oil Spill Recovery Institute annually, beginning 60 days after October 19, 1996.

(c) Use for section 2712

Beginning 1 year after the date on which the Secretary, in consultation with the Secretary of the Interior, determines that oil and gas exploration, development, and production in the State of Alaska have ceased, the funding authorized for the Prince William Sound Oil Spill Recovery Institute and deposited in the Fund shall thereafter be made available for purposes of section 2712 of this title in Alaska.

(d) Section 2738

Amounts in the Fund shall be available, without further appropriation and without fiscal year limitation, to carry out section 2738(b) of this title, in an annual amount not to exceed $5,000,000 of which up to $3,000,000 may be used for the lease payment to the Alaska SeaLife Center under section 2738(b)(2) of this title: *Provided,* That the entire amount is designated by the Congress as an emergency requirement pursuant to section 251(b)(2)(A) of the Balanced Budget and Emergency Deficit Control Act of 1985, as amended [2 U.S.C.A. § 901(b)(2)(A)]: *Provided further,* That the entire amount shall be available only to the extent an official budget request that includes designation of the entire amount of the request as an emergency requirement as defined in the Balanced Budget and Emergency Deficit Control Act of 1985, as amended, is transmitted by the President to the Congress.

(Pub. L. No. 101–380, Title V, § 5006, 104 Stat. 554 (Aug. 18, 1990); as amended by Pub. L. No. 104–324, Title XI, § 1102(b), 110 Stat. 3965 (Oct. 19, 1996); Pub. L. No. 106–246, Div. B, Title II, § 2204(2), 114 Stat. 547 (July 13, 2000); Pub. L. No. 106–554, § 1(a)(4) [Div. B, Title I, § 144(c)(1)(C)], 114 Stat. 2763, 2763A–239 (Dec. 21, 2000); Pub. L. No. 108–293, Title VII, § 704, 118 Stat. 1075 (Aug. 9, 2004); Pub. L. No. 109–58, Title III, § 389(2), 119 Stat. 747 (Aug. 8, 2005); Pub. L. No. 109–59, Title IV, § 4413, 119 Stat. 1779 (Aug. 10, 2005); Pub. L. No. 109–241, Title IX, § 901(j), 120 Stat. 564 (July 11, 2006).)

HISTORICAL AND STATUTORY NOTES

References in Text

Section 8102(a)(2)(B)(ii), referred to in subsec. (b), is section 8102(a)(2)(B)(ii) of Pub. L. No. 101–380, 104 Stat. 565 (Aug. 18, 1990), which is set out as a note under section 1653 of Title 43, Public Lands.

The Balanced Budget and Emergency Deficit Control Act of 1985, referred to in subsec. (c), also known as the BBEDCA and the Gramm-Rudman-Hollings Act, is Pub. L. No. 99–177, Title II, 99 Stat. 1038 (Dec. 12, 1985), as amended, which is codified generally as subchapter I of chapter 20 of Title 2 (2 U.S.C.A. § 901 et seq.). For complete classification of this Act to the Code, see Tables.

Codifications

Amendment by Pub. L. No. 109–241, § 901(j), which directed that subsec. (c) of this section be amended by inserting a comma after "October 1, 2012", was not capable of execution due to prior amendment by Pub. L. No. 109–58, § 389(2), which struck out "October 1, 2012" and inserted "1 year after the date on which the Secretary, in consultation with the Secretary of the Interior, determines that oil and gas exploration, development, and production in the State of Alaska have ceased, ..." See 2006 and 2005 Amendments notes under this section.

Amendment by Pub. L. No. 109–59, Title IV, § 4413, 119 Stat. 1779 (Aug. 10, 2005), which directed the insertion of "annual" before "amount", was executed by inserting "annual" before the first occurrence of "amount", as the probable intent of Congress.

Investment Amount

Pub. L. No. 112–213, Title VII, § 710, 126 Stat. 1581 (Dec. 20, 2012), provided that: "Not later than 30 days after the date of enactment of this Act [Dec. 20, 2012], the Secretary of the Treasury shall increase the $22,500,000 invested in income-producing securities for purposes of section 5006(b) of the Oil Pollution Act of 1990 (33 U.S.C. 2736(b)) by $12,851,340."

§ 2737. Limitation

[OPA § 5007]

Notwithstanding any other law, tank vessels that have spilled more than 1,000,000 gallons of oil into the marine environment after March 22, 1989, are prohibited from operating on the navigable waters of Prince William Sound, Alaska.

(Pub. L. No. 101–380, Title V, § 5007, 104 Stat. 554 (Aug. 18, 1990_.)

§ 2738. North Pacific Marine Research Institute

[OPA § 5008]

(a) Institute established

The Secretary of Commerce shall establish a North Pacific Marine Research Institute (hereafter in this section referred to as the "Institute") to be administered at the Alaska SeaLife Center by the North Pacific Research Board.

(b) Functions

The Institute shall—

(1) conduct research and carry out education and demonstration projects on or relating to the North Pacific marine ecosystem with particular emphasis on marine mammal, sea bird, fish, and shellfish populations in the Bering Sea and Gulf of Alaska including populations located in or near Kenai Fjords National Park and the Alaska Maritime National Wildlife Refuge; and

(2) lease, maintain, operate, and upgrade the necessary research equipment and related facilities necessary to conduct such research at the Alaska SeaLife Center.

(c) Evaluation and audit

The Secretary of Commerce may periodically evaluate the activities of the Institute to ensure that funds received by the Institute are used in a manner consistent with this section. The Federal Advisory Committee Act (5 U.S.C. App. 2) shall not apply to the Institute.

(d) Status of employees

Employees of the Institute shall not, by reason of such employment, be considered to be employees of the Federal Government for any purpose.

(e) Use of funds

No funds made available to carry out this section may be used to initiate litigation, or for the acquisition of real property (other than facilities leased at the Alaska SeaLife Center). No more than 10 percent of the funds made available to carry out subsection (b)(1) of this section may be used to administer the Institute. The administrative funds of the Institute and the administrative funds of the North Pacific Research Board created under Public Law 105–83 may be used to jointly administer such programs at the discretion of the North Pacific Research Board.

(f) Availability of research

The Institute shall publish and make available to any person on request the results of all research, educational, and demonstration projects conducted by the Institute. The Institute shall provide a copy of all research, educational, and demonstration projects conducted by the Institute to the National Park Service, the United States Fish and Wildlife Service, and the National Oceanic and Atmospheric Administration.

(Pub. L. No. 101–380, Title V, § 5008, as added by Pub. L. No. 106–246, Div. B, Title II, § 2204(1), 114 Stat. 546 (July 13, 2000); and amended by Pub. L. No. 106–554, § 1(a)(4) [Div. B, Title I, § 144(c)(1)(A), (B)], 114 Stat. 2763, 2763A–239 (Dec. 21, 2000).)

HISTORICAL AND STATUTORY NOTES

References in Text

The Federal Advisory Committee Act, referred to in subsec. (c), is Pub. L. No. 92–463, 86 Stat. 770 (Oct. 6, 1972), as amended, which is set out as Appendix 2 to Title 5.

Pub. L. No. 105–83, referred to in subsec. (e), is Department of the Interior and Related Agencies Appropriations Act, 1998, Pub. L. No. 105–83, 111 Stat. 1543 (Nov. 14, 1997). See Tables for complete classification.

SUBCHAPTER III—MISCELLANEOUS

§ 2751. Savings provisions

[OPA § 6001]

(a) Cross-references

A reference to a law replaced by this Act, including a reference in a regulation, order, or other law, is deemed to refer to the corresponding provision of this Act.

(b) Continuation of regulations

An order, rule, or regulation in effect under a law replaced by this Act continues in effect under the corresponding provision of this Act until repealed, amended, or superseded.

(c) Rule of construction

An inference of legislative construction shall not be drawn by reason of the caption or catch line of a provision enacted by this Act.

(d) Actions and rights

Nothing in this Act shall apply to any rights and duties that matured, penalties that were incurred, and proceedings that were begun before August 18, 1990, except as provided by this section, and shall be adjudicated pursuant to the law applicable on the date prior to August 18, 1990.

(e) Admiralty and maritime law

Except as otherwise provided in this Act, this Act does not affect—

(1) admiralty and maritime law; or

(2) the jurisdiction of the district courts of the United States with respect to civil actions under admiralty and maritime jurisdiction, saving to suitors in all cases all other remedies to which they are otherwise entitled.

(Pub. L. No. 101–380, Title VI, § 6001, 104 Stat. 554 (Aug. 18, 1990).)

HISTORICAL AND STATUTORY NOTES

References in Text

This Act, referred to in text, is Pub. L. No. 101–380, 104 Stat. 484 (Aug. 18, 1990), as amended, known as the Oil Pollution Act of 1990, which is codified principally as this chapter. For complete classification to the Code, see Short Title note under 33 U.S.C.A. § 2701 and Tables.

§ 2752. Annual appropriations

[OPA § 6002]

(a) Required

Except as provided in subsection (b) of this section, amounts in the Fund shall be available only as provided in annual appropriation Acts.

(b) Exceptions

Subsection (a) of this section shall not apply to sections[1] 2706(f), 2712(a)(4), or 2736 of this title, and shall not apply to an amount not to exceed $50,000,000 in any fiscal year which the President may make available from the Fund to carry out section 1321(c) of this title and to initiate the assessment of natural resources damages required under section 2706 of this title. To the extent that such amount is not adequate, the Coast Guard (1) may obtain an advance from the Fund of such sums as may be necessary, up to a maximum of $100,000,000, and within 30 days shall notify Congress of the amount advanced and the facts and circumstances necessitating the advance and (2) in the case of the discharge of oil that began in 2010 in connection with the explosion on, and sinking of, the mobile offshore drilling unit Deepwater Horizon, may, without further appropriation, obtain 1 or more advances from the Fund as needed, up to a maximum of $100,000,000 for each advance, with the total amount of all advances not to exceed the amounts available under section 9509(c)(2) of Title 26, and within 7 days of each advance, shall notify Congress of the amount advanced and the facts and circumstances necessitating the advance. Amounts advanced shall be repaid to the Fund when, and to the extent that, removal costs are recovered by the Coast Guard from responsible parties for the discharge or substantial threat of discharge. Sums to which this subsection applies shall remain available until expended.

(Pub. L. No. 101–380, Title VI, § 6002, 104 Stat. 555 (Aug. 18, 1990); as amended by Pub. L. No. 104–324, Title XI, § 1102(c)(1), 110 Stat. 3966 (Oct. 19, 1996); Pub. L. No. 107–295, Title III, § 323, 116 Stat. 2104 (Nov. 25, 2002); Pub. L. No. 111–191, § 1, 124 Stat. 1278 (June 15, 2010); Pub. L. No. 111–212, Title II, § 2001, 124 Stat. 2337 (July 29, 2010).)

[1] So in original. Probably should be "section".

HISTORICAL AND STATUTORY NOTES

References in Text

Reference in subsec. (b) to the amendment of section 1321(c) of this title "by this Act" refers to the amendment by Pub. L. No. 101–380, 104 Stat. 484 (Aug. 18, 1990).

Codifications

Amendment by Pub. L. No. 111–212, Title II, § 2001, 124 Stat. 2337 (July 29, 2010), in the second sentence of subsec. (b) of this section, which directed insertion of ": (1)" before "may obtain an advance" and after "the Coast Guard", striking of "advance. Amounts" and insertion of "advance; (2) in the case of discharge of oil that began in 2010 in connection with the explosion on, and sinking of, the mobile offshore drilling unit Deepwater Horizon, may, without further appropriation, obtain one or more advances from the Oil Spill Liability Trust Fund as needed, up to a maximum of $100,000,000 for each advance, the total amount of all advances not to exceed the amounts available under section 9509(c)(2) of the Internal Revenue Code of 1986 (26 U.S.C. 9509(c)(2)), and within 7 days of each advance, shall notify Congress of the amount advanced and the facts and circumstances necessitating the advance; and (3) amounts", was incapable of execution due to previous amendment by Pub. L. No. 111–191, § 1, which inserted similar but conflicting text. See 2010 Amendments notes set out under this section.

Transfer of Functions

For transfer of authorities, functions, personnel, and assets of the Coast Guard, including the authorities and functions of the Secretary of Transportation relating thereto, to the Department of Homeland Security, and for treatment of related references, see 6 U.S.C.A. §§ 468(b), 551(d), 552(d), and 557 and the Department of Homeland Security Reorganization Plan of November 25, 2002, as modified, set out as a note under 6 U.S.C.A. § 542.

Delegation of Functions

The functions vested in the President by subsec. (b) of this section respecting making amounts, not to exceed $50,000,000 and subject to normal budget controls, in any fiscal year, available from the Fund (i) to carry out section 1321(c) of this title, and (ii) to initiate the assessment of natural resources damages required under section 2706 of this title are delegated to the Secretary of the Department in which the Coast Guard is operating, with such Secretary required to make amounts available from the Fund to initiate the assessment of natural resources damages exclusively to the Federal trustees designated in the NCP [National Contingency Plan], who are in turn directed to allocate such amounts among all trustees required to assess natural resources damages under section 2706 of this title, see Ex. Ord. No. 12777, 56 Fed. Reg. 54757 (Oct. 18, 1991), set out as a note under section 1321 of this title.

§ 2753. Repealed. Pub. L. No. 104–134, Title I, § 101(c) [Title I, § 109], 110 Stat. 1321–177 (Apr. 26, 1996); renumbered Title I by Pub. L. No. 104–140, § 1(a), 110 Stat. 1327 (May 2, 1996).

HISTORICAL AND STATUTORY NOTES

Section, Pub. L. No. 101–380, Title VI, § 6003, 104 Stat. 555 (Aug. 18, 1990), related to protection of the Outer Banks of North Carolina.

SUBCHAPTER IV—OIL POLLUTION RESEARCH AND DEVELOPMENT PROGRAM

§ 2761. Oil pollution research and development program

[OPA § 7001]

(a) Definitions.—In this section—

(1) the term 'Chair' means the Chairperson of the Interagency Committee designated under subsection (c)(2);

(2) the term 'Commandant' means the Commandant of the Coast Guard;

(3) the term 'institution of higher education' means an institution of higher education, as defined in section 101(a) of the Higher Education Act of 1965 (20 U.S.C. 1001(a));

(4) the term 'Interagency Committee' means the Interagency Coordinating Committee on Oil Pollution Research established under subsection (b);

(5) the term 'Under Secretary' means the Under Secretary of Commerce for Oceans and Atmosphere; and

(6) the term 'Vice Chair' means the Vice Chairperson of the Interagency Committee designated under subsection (c)(3).

(b) Establishment of Interagency Coordinating Committee on Oil Pollution Research.—

(1) Establishment.—There is established an Interagency Coordinating Committee on Oil Pollution Research.

(2) Purpose.—The Interagency Committee shall coordinate a comprehensive program of oil pollution research, technology development, and demonstration among the Federal agencies, in cooperation and coordination with industry, 4-year institutions of higher education and research institutions, State governments, and other nations, as appropriate, and shall foster cost-effective research mechanisms, including the joint funding of research.

(c) Membership.—

(1) Composition.—The Interagency Committee shall be composed of—

(A) at least 1 representative of the Coast Guard;

(B) at least 1 representative of the National Oceanic and Atmospheric Administration;

(C) at least 1 representative of the Environmental Protection Agency;

(D) at least 1 representative of the Department of the Interior;

(E) at least 1 representative of the Bureau of Safety and Environmental Enforcement;

(F) at least 1 representative of the Bureau of Ocean Energy Management;

(G) at least 1 representative of the United States Fish and Wildlife Service;

(H) at least 1 representative of the Department of Energy;

(I) at least 1 representative of the Pipeline and Hazardous Materials Safety Administration;

(J) at least 1 representative of the Federal Emergency Management Agency;

(K) at least 1 representative of the Navy;

(L) at least 1 representative of the Corps of Engineers;

(M) at least 1 representative of the United States Arctic Research Commission; and

(N) at least 1 representative of each of such other Federal agencies as the President considers to be appropriate.

(2) Chairperson.—The Commandant shall designate a Chairperson from among the members of the Interagency Committee selected under paragraph (1)(A).

(3) Vice Chairperson.—The Under Secretary shall designate a Vice Chairperson from among the members of the Interagency Committee selected under paragraph (1)(B).

(4) Meetings.—

(A) Quarterly Meetings.—At a minimum, the members of the Interagency Committee shall meet once each quarter.

(B) Public Summaries.—After each meeting, a summary shall be made available by the Chair or Vice Chair, as appropriate.

(d) Duties of the Interagency Committee.—

(1) Research.—The Interagency Committee shall—

(A) coordinate a comprehensive program of oil pollution research, technology development, and demonstration among the Federal agencies, in cooperation and coordination with industry, 4-year institutions of higher education and research institutions, States, Indian tribes, and other countries, as appropriate; and

(B) foster cost-effective research mechanisms, including the joint funding of research and the development of public-private partnerships for the purpose of expanding research.

(2) Oil Pollution Research and Technology Plan.—

(A) Implementation Plan.—Not later than 180 days after the date of enactment of the Elijah E. Cummings Coast Guard Authorization Act of 2020, the Interagency Committee shall submit to Congress a research plan to report on the state of oil discharge prevention and response capabilities that—

(i) identifies current research programs conducted by Federal agencies, States, Indian tribes, 4-year institutions of higher education, and corporate entities;

(ii) assesses the current status of knowledge on oil pollution prevention, response, and mitigation technologies and effects of oil pollution on the environment;

(iii) identifies significant oil pollution research gaps, including an assessment of major technological deficiencies in responses to past oil discharges;

(iv) establishes national research priorities and goals for oil pollution technology development related to prevention, response, mitigation, and environmental effects;

(v) assesses the research on the applicability and effectiveness of the prevention, response, and mitigation technologies to each class of oil;

(vi) estimates the resources needed to conduct the oil pollution research and development program established pursuant to subsection (e), and timetables for completing research tasks;

(vii) summarizes research on response equipment in varying environmental conditions, such as in currents, ice cover, and ice floes; and

(viii) includes such other information or recommendations as the Interagency Committee determines to be appropriate.

(B) Advice and Guidance.—

(i) National Academy of Sciences Contract.—The Chair, through the department in which the Coast Guard is operating, shall contract with the National Academy of Sciences to

(I) provide advice and guidance in the preparation and development of the research plan;

(II) assess the adequacy of the plan as submitted, and submit a report to Congress on the conclusions of such assessment; and

(III) provide organization guidance regarding the implementation of the research plan, including delegation of topics and research among Federal agencies represented on the Interagency Committee.

(ii) NIST Advice and Guidance. The National Institute of Standards and Technology shall provide the Interagency Committee with advice and guidance on issues relating to quality assurance and standards measurements relating to its activities under this section.

(C) 10-Year Updates.—Not later than 10 years after the date of enactment of the Elijah E. Cummings Coast Guard Authorization Act of 2020, and every 10 years thereafter, the

Interagency Committee shall submit to Congress a research plan that updates the information contained in the previous research plan submitted under this subsection.

(e) Oil pollution research and development program

(1) Establishment

The Interagency Committee shall coordinate the establishment, by the agencies represented on the Interagency Committee, of a program for conducting oil pollution research, technology, and development, as provided in this subsection.

(2) Innovative oil pollution technology

The program established under paragraph (1) shall provide for research, development, and demonstration of new or improved technologies and methods that are effective in preventing, mitigating, or restoring damage from oil discharges and that protect the environment, including—

(A) development of improved designs for vessels and facilities, and improved operational practices;

(B) research, development, and demonstration of improved technologies to measure the ullage of a vessel tank, prevent discharges from tank vents, prevent discharges during lightering and bunkering operations, contain discharges on the deck of a vessel, prevent discharges through the use of vacuums in tanks, and otherwise contain discharges of oil from vessels and facilities;

(C) research, development, and demonstration of new or improved systems of mechanical, chemical, biological, and other methods (including the use of dispersants, solvents, and bioremediation) for the recovery, removal, and disposal of oil, including evaluation of the environmental effects of the use of such systems;

(D) research and training, in consultation with the National Response Team, to improve industry's and Government's ability to quickly and effectively remove an oil discharge, including the long-term use, as appropriate, of the National Spill Control School in Corpus Christi, Texas, and the Center for Marine Training and Safety in Galveston, Texas;

(E) research to improve information systems for decisionmaking, including the use of data from coastal mapping, baseline data, and other data related to the environmental effects of oil discharges, and cleanup technologies;

(F) development of technologies and methods to protect public health and safety from oil discharges, including the population directly exposed to an oil discharge;

(G) development of technologies, methods, and standards for protecting removal personnel, including training, adequate supervision, protective equipment, maximum exposure limits, and decontamination procedures;

(H) research and development of methods to restore and rehabilitate natural resources damaged by oil discharges;

(I) research to evaluate the relative effectiveness and environmental impacts of bioremediation technologies; and

(J) the demonstration of a satellite-based, dependent surveillance vessel traffic system in Narragansett Bay to evaluate the utility of such system in reducing the risk of oil discharges from vessel collisions and groundings in confined waters.

(3) Oil pollution technology evaluation

The program established under paragraph (1) shall provide for oil pollution prevention and mitigation technology evaluation including—

(A) the evaluation and testing of technologies developed independently of the research and development program established under paragraph (1);

(B) the establishment, where appropriate, of standards and testing protocols traceable to national standards to measure the performance of oil pollution prevention or mitigation technologies; and

(C) the use, where appropriate, of controlled field testing to evaluate real-world application of oil discharge prevention or mitigation technologies.

(4) Oil pollution effects research

(A) The Committee shall establish a research program to monitor and evaluate the environmental effects of acute and chronic oil discharges on coastal and marine resources (including impacts on protected areas such as sanctuaries) and protected species, and such program shall include the following elements:

(i) The development of improved models and capabilities for predicting the environmental fate, transport, and effects of oil discharges.

(ii) The development of methods, including economic methods, to assess damages to natural resources resulting from oil discharges.

(iii) Research to understand and quantify the effects of sublethal impacts of oil discharge on living natural marine resources, including impacts on pelagic fish species, marine mammals, and commercially and recreationally targeted fish and shellfish species.

(iv) The identification of types of ecologically sensitive areas at particular risk to oil discharges and the preparation of scientific monitoring and evaluation plans, one for each of several types of ecological conditions, to be implemented in the event of major oil discharges in such areas.

(v) The collection of environmental baseline data in ecologically sensitive areas at particular risk to oil discharges where such data are insufficient.

(vi) Research to understand the long-term effects of major oil discharges and the long-term effects of smaller endemic oil discharges.

(vii) The identification of potential impacts on ecosystems, habitat, and wildlife from the additional toxicity, heavy metal concentrations, and increased corrosiveness of mixed crude, such as diluted bitumen crude.

(viii) The development of methods to restore and rehabilitate natural resources and ecosystem functions damaged by oil discharges.";

(B) The Department of Commerce in consultation with the Environmental Protection Agency shall monitor and scientifically evaluate the long-term environmental effects of oil discharges if—

(i) the amount of oil discharged exceeds 250,000 gallons;

(ii) the oil discharge has occurred on or after January 1, 1989; and

(iii) the Interagency Committee determines that a study of the long-term environmental effects of the discharge would be of significant scientific value, especially for preventing or responding to future oil discharges.

Areas for study may include the following sites where oil discharges have occurred: the New York/New Jersey Harbor area, where oil was discharged by an Exxon underwater pipeline, the T/B CIBRO SAVANNAH, and the M/V BT NAUTILUS; Narragansett Bay where oil was discharged by the WORLD PRODIGY; the Houston Ship Channel where oil was discharged by the RACHEL B; the Delaware River, where oil was discharged by the PRESIDENTE RIVERA and the T/V ATHOS I, and Huntington Beach, California, where oil was discharged by the AMERICAN TRADER.

(C) Research conducted under this paragraph by, or through, the United States Fish and Wildlife Service shall be directed and coordinated by the National Wetland Research Center.

(5) Marine Simulation Research

The program established under paragraph (1) shall include research on the greater use and application of geographic and vessel response simulation models, including the development of additional data bases and updating of existing data bases using, among others, the resources of the National Maritime Research Center. It shall include research and vessel simulations for—

(A) contingency plan evaluation and amendment;

(B) removal and strike team training;

(C) tank vessel personnel training; and

(D) those geographic areas where there is a significant likelihood of a major oil discharge.

(6) Demonstration Projects

The United States Coast Guard, in conjunction with such agencies as the President may designate, shall conduct 4 port oil pollution minimization demonstration projects, one each with (A) the Port Authority of New York and New Jersey, (B) the Ports of Los Angeles and Long Beach, California, (C) the Port of New Orleans, Louisiana, and (D) ports on the Great Lakes, for the purpose of developing and demonstrating integrated port oil pollution prevention and cleanup systems which utilize the information and implement the improved practices and technologies developed from the research, development, and demonstration program established in this section. Such systems shall utilize improved technologies and management practices for reducing the risk of oil discharges, including, as appropriate, improved data access, computerized tracking of oil shipments, improved vessel tracking and navigation systems, advanced technology to monitor pipeline and tank conditions, improved oil spill response capability, improved capability to predict the flow and effects of oil discharges in both the inner and outer harbor areas for the purposes of making infrastructure decisions, and such other activities necessary to achieve the purposes of this section.

(7) Simulated Environmental Testing

(A) In General.—Agencies represented on the Interagency Committee shall ensure the long-term use and operation of the Oil and Hazardous Materials Simulated Environmental Test Tank (OHMSETT) Research Center in New Jersey for oil pollution technology testing and evaluations.

(B) Other Testing Facilities.—Nothing in subparagraph (A) shall be construed as limiting the ability of the Interagency Committee to contract or partner with a facility or facilities other than the Center described in subparagraph (A) for the purpose of oil pollution technology testing and evaluations, provided such a facility or facilities have testing and evaluation capabilities equal to or greater than those of such Center.

(C) In-Kind Contributions.—

(i) In General.—The Secretary of the department in which the Coast Guard is operating and the Administrator of the Environmental Protection Agency may accept donations of crude oil and crude oil product samples in the form of in-kind contributions for use by the Federal Government for product testing, research and development, and for other purposes as the Secretary and the Administrator determine appropriate.

(ii) Use of Donated Oil.—Oil accepted under clause (i) may be used directly by the Secretary and shall be provided to other Federal agencies or departments through interagency agreements to carry out the purposes of this Act.

(8) Regional research program

(A) Consistent with the research plan in subsection (d) of this section, the Interagency Committee shall coordinate a program of competitive grants to universities or other research institutions, or groups of universities or research institutions, for the purposes of conducting a coordinated research program related to the regional aspects of oil pollution, such as prevention, removal, mitigation, and the effects of discharged oil on regional environments. For the purposes of this paragraph, a region means a Coast Guard district as set out in part 3 of title 33, Code of Federal Regulations (2010).

(B) The Interagency Committee shall coordinate the publication by the agencies represented on the Interagency Committee of a solicitation for grants under this subsection. The application shall be in such form and contain such information as may be required in the published solicitation. The applications shall be reviewed by the Interagency Committee, which shall make recommendations to the appropriate granting agency represented on the Interagency Committee for awarding the grant. The granting agency shall award the grants recommended by the Interagency Committee unless the agency decides not to award the grant due to budgetary or other compelling considerations and publishes its reasons for such a determination in the Federal Register. No grants may be made by any agency from any funds authorized for this paragraph unless such grant award has first been recommended by the Interagency Committee.

(C) Any university or other research institution, or group of universities or research institutions, may apply for a grant for the regional research program established by this paragraph. The applicant must be located in the region, or in a State a part of which is in the region, for which the project is proposed as part of the regional research program. With respect to a group application, the entity or entities which will carry out the substantial portion of the proposed research must be located in the region, or in a State a part of which is in the region, for which the project is proposed as part of the regional research program.

(D) The Interagency Committee shall make recommendations on grants in such a manner as to ensure an appropriate balance within a region among the various aspects of oil pollution research, including prevention, removal, mitigation, and the effects of discharged oil on regional environments. In addition, the Interagency Committee shall make recommendations for grants based on the following criteria:

(i) There is available to the applicant for carrying out this paragraph demonstrated research resources.

(ii) The applicant demonstrates the capability of making a significant contribution to regional research needs.

(iii) The projects which the applicant proposes to carry out under the grant are consistent with the research plan under subsection (d) of this section and would further the objectives of the research and development program established in this section.

(E) Grants provided under this paragraph shall be for a period up to 3 years, subject to annual review by the granting agency, and provide not more than 80 percent of the costs of the research activities carried out in connection with the grant.

(F) No funds made available to carry out this subsection may be used for the acquisition of real property (including buildings) or construction of any building.

(G) Nothing in this paragraph is intended to alter or abridge the authority under existing law of any Federal agency to make grants, or enter into contracts or cooperative agreements, using funds other than those authorized in this Act for the purposes of carrying out this paragraph.

(9) Funding

For each of the fiscal years 1991, 1992, 1993, 1994, and 1995, $6,000,000 of amounts in the Fund shall be available to carry out the regional research program in paragraph (8), such amounts to be available in equal amounts for the regional research program in each region; except that if the agencies represented on the Interagency Committee determine that regional research needs exist which cannot be addressed within such funding limits, such agencies may use their authority under paragraph (10) to make additional grants to meet such needs. For the purposes of this paragraph, the research program carried out by the Prince William Sound Oil Spill Recovery Institute established under section 2731 of this title, shall not be eligible to receive grants under this paragraph until the authorization for funding under section 2736(b) of this title expires.

(10) Grants

In carrying out the research and development program established under paragraph (1), the Under Secretary may enter into contracts and cooperative agreements and make grants to universities, research institutions, and other persons, ad States and Indian tribes. Such contracts, cooperative agreements, and grants shall address research and technology priorities set forth in the oil pollution research plan under subsection (d) of this section.

(11) In carrying out research under this section, the Department of Transportation shall continue to utilize the resources of the Pipeline and Hazardous Materials Safety Administration of the Department of Transportation, to the maximum extent practicable.

(f) International cooperation

In accordance with the research plan submitted under subsection (d) of this section, the Interagency Committee shall coordinate and cooperate with other nations and foreign research entities in conducting oil pollution research, development, and demonstration activities, including controlled field tests of oil discharges.

(g) Biennial reports

The Chair shall submit to Congress every 2 years on October 30 a report on the activities carried out under this section in the preceding 2 fiscal years, and on activities proposed to be carried out under this section in the current 2 fiscal year period.

(h) Funding

Not to exceed $22,000,000 of amounts in the Fund shall be available annually to carry out this section except for subsection (e)(8) of this section. Of such sums—

(1) funds authorized to be appropriated to carry out the activities under subsection (c)(4) of this section shall not exceed $5,000,000 for fiscal year 1991 or $3,500,000 for any subsequent fiscal year; and

(2) not less than $3,000,000 shall be available for carrying out the activities in subsection (c)(6) of this section for fiscal years 1992, 1993, 1994, and 1995.

All activities authorized in this section, including subsection (e)(8) of this section, are subject to appropriations.

(Pub. L. No. 101–380, Title VII, § 7001, 104 Stat. 559 (Aug. 18, 1990); as amended by Pub. L. No. 101–537, Title II, § 2002, 104 Stat. 2375 (Nov. 18, 1990); Pub. L. No. 101–646, Title IV, § 4002, 104 Stat. 4788 (Nov. 29, 1990); Pub. L. No. 104–324, Title XI, §§ 1102(c)(2), 1108, 110 Stat. 3966, 3968 (Oct. 19, 1996); Pub. L. No. 104–332, § 2(h)(1), (2), 110 Stat. 4091 (Oct. 26, 1996); Pub. L. No. 108–426, § 2(c)(5), 118 Stat. 2424 (Nov. 30, 2004); Pub. L. No. 109–241, Title VI, § 605(a)(1), Title IX, § 902(*l*)(3), (4), 120 Stat. 555, 568 (July 11, 2006); Pub. L. No. 114–120, § 319, 130 Stat. 66 (Feb. 8, 2016); Pub. L. No. 116–283, § 8304, 134 Stat. 3388, 4693–97 (Jan. 1, 2021).)

HISTORICAL AND STATUTORY NOTES

References in Text

This Act, referred to in subsec. (c)(8)(G), is Pub. L. No. 101–380, 104 Stat. 484 (Aug. 18, 1990), as amended, known as the Oil Pollution Act of 1990, which is codified principally as this chapter. For complete classification to the Code, see Short Title note under 33 U.S.C.A. § 2701 and Tables.

Codifications

Identical amendments were made by Pub. L. No. 101–537 and Pub. L. No. 101–646 to subsecs. (c)(6), (f) and (f)(2).

Termination of Reporting Requirements

For termination of reporting provisions of subsec. (b)(2)(B) of this section, effective May 15, 2000, see Pub. L. No. 104–66, § 3003, as amended, set out as a note under 31 U.S.C.A. § 1113, and the 5th item on page 136 of House Document No. 103–7.

Reporting requirement of subsec. (e) of this section excepted from termination under Pub. L. No. 104–66, § 3003(a)(1), as amended, set out as a note under 31 U.S.C.A. § 1113, see Pub. L. No. 107–295, § 322(b), set out as a note under 31 U.S.C.A. § 1113.

Transfer of Functions

For transfer of functions of the Federal Emergency Management Agency, including existing responsibilities for emergency alert systems and continuity of operations and continuity of government plans and programs as constituted on June 1, 2006, including all of its personnel, assets, components, authorities, grant programs, and liabilities, and including the functions of the Under Secretary for Federal Emergency Management relating thereto, see 6 U.S.C.A. § 315.

Delegation of Functions

The function vested in the President by subsec. (a)(3) of this section, respecting the appointment of Federal agencies to membership on the Interagency Coordinating Committee on Oil Pollution Research, is delegated to the Secretary of Transportation, see Ex. Ord. No. 12777, 56 Fed. Reg. 54757 (Oct. 18, 1991), set out as a note under section 1321 of this title.

§ 2762. Submerged oil program

[OPA § 7002]

(a) Program

(1) Establishment

The Under Secretary of Commerce for Oceans and Atmosphere, in conjunction with the Commandant of the Coast Guard, shall establish a program to detect, monitor, and evaluate the environmental effects of submerged oil in the Delaware River and Bay region. The program shall include the following elements:

(A) The development of methods to remove, disperse, or otherwise diminish the persistence of submerged oil.

(B) The development of improved models and capacities for predicting the environmental fate, transport, and effects of submerged oil.

(C) The development of techniques to detect and monitor submerged oil.

(2) Report

Not later than 3 years after July 11, 2006, the Secretary of Commerce shall submit to the Committee on Commerce, Science, and Transportation of the Senate and the Committee on Transportation and Infrastructure of the House of Representatives a report on the activities carried out under this subsection and activities proposed to be carried out under this subsection.

(b) Demonstration project

(1) Removal of submerged oil

The Commandant of the Coast Guard, in conjunction with the Under Secretary of Commerce for Oceans and Atmosphere, shall conduct a demonstration project for the purpose of developing and demonstrating technologies and management practices to remove submerged oil from the Delaware River and other navigable waters.

(2) Funding

There is authorized to be appropriated to the Commandant of the Coast Guard $2,000,000 for each of fiscal years 2006 through 2010 to carry out this subsection.

(Pub. L. No. 101–380, Title VII, § 7002, as added by Pub. L. No. 109–241, Title VI, § 605(a)(2), 120 Stat. 555 (July 11, 2006).)

TITLE 42

THE PUBLIC HEALTH AND WELFARE

SAFETY OF PUBLIC WATER SYSTEMS

PUBLIC HEALTH SERVICE ACT (TITLE XIV) [PHSA § ______]

(42 U.S.C.A. §§ 300f to 300j–27)

CHAPTER 6A—PUBLIC HEALTH SERVICE

SUBCHAPTER XII—SAFETY OF PUBLIC WATER SYSTEMS

PART A—DEFINITIONS

SUBCHAPTER XII—SAFETY OF PUBLIC WATER SYSTEMS

PART A—DEFINITIONS

§ 300f. Definitions

[PHSA § 1401]

For purposes of this subchapter:

(1) The term "primary drinking water regulation" means a regulation which—

(A) applies to public water systems;

(B) specifies contaminants which, in the judgment of the Administrator, may have any adverse effect on the health of persons;

(C) specifies for each such contaminant either—

(i) a maximum contaminant level, if, in the judgment of the Administrator, it is economically and technologically feasible to ascertain the level of such contaminant in water in public water systems, or

(ii) if, in the judgment of the Administrator, it is not economically or technologically feasible to so ascertain the level of such contaminant, each treatment technique known to the Administrator which leads to a reduction in the level of such contaminant sufficient to satisfy the requirements of section 300g–1 of this title; and

(D) contains criteria and procedures to assure a supply of drinking water which dependably complies with such maximum contaminant levels; including accepted methods for quality control and testing procedures to insure compliance with such levels and to insure proper operation and maintenance of the system, and requirements as to (i) the minimum quality of water which may be taken into the system and (ii) siting for new facilities for public water systems.

At any time after promulgation of a regulation referred to in this paragraph, the Administrator may add equally effective quality control and testing procedures by guidance published in the Federal Register. Such procedures shall be treated as an alternative for public water systems to the quality control and testing procedures listed in the regulation.

(2) The term "secondary drinking water regulation" means a regulation which applies to public water systems and which specifies the maximum contaminant levels which, in the judgment of the Administrator, are requisite to protect the public welfare. Such regulations may apply to any contaminant in drinking water (A) which may adversely affect the odor or appearance of such water and consequently may cause a substantial number of the persons served by the public water system providing such water to discontinue its use, or (B) which may otherwise adversely affect the public welfare. Such regulations may vary according to geographic and other circumstances.

(3) The term "maximum contaminant level" means the maximum permissible level of a contaminant in water which is delivered to any user of a public water system.

(4) Public water system.—

(A) In general.—The term "public water system" means a system for the provision to the public of water for human consumption through pipes or other constructed conveyances, if such system has at least fifteen service connections or regularly serves at least twenty-five individuals. Such term includes (i) any collection, treatment, storage, and distribution facilities under control of the operator of such system and used primarily in connection with such system, and (ii) any collection or pretreatment storage facilities not under such control which are used primarily in connection with such system.

(B) Connections.—

(i) In general.—For purposes of subparagraph (A), a connection to a system that delivers water by a constructed conveyance other than a pipe shall not be considered a connection, if—

(I) the water is used exclusively for purposes other than residential uses (consisting of drinking, bathing, and cooking, or other similar uses);

(II) the Administrator or the State (in the case of a State exercising primary enforcement responsibility for public water systems) determines that alternative water to achieve the equivalent level of public health protection provided by the applicable national primary drinking water regulation is provided for residential or similar uses for drinking and cooking; or

(III) the Administrator or the State (in the case of a State exercising primary enforcement responsibility for public water systems) determines that the water provided for residential or similar uses for drinking, cooking, and bathing is centrally treated or treated at the point of entry by the provider, a pass-through entity, or the user to achieve the equivalent level of protection provided by the applicable national primary drinking water regulations.

(ii) Irrigation districts.—An irrigation district in existence prior to May 18, 1994, that provides primarily agricultural service through a piped water system with only incidental residential or similar use shall not be considered to be a public water system if the system or the residential or similar users of the system comply with subclause (II) or (III) of clause (i).

(C) Transition period.—A water supplier that would be a public water system only as a result of modifications made to this paragraph by the Safe Drinking Water Act Amendments of 1996 shall not be considered a public water system for purposes of the Act until the date that is two years after August 6, 1996. If a water supplier does not serve 15 service connections (as defined in subparagraphs (A) and (B)) or 25 people at any time after the conclusion of the 2-year period, the water supplier shall not be considered a public water system.

(5) The term "supplier of water" means any person who owns or operates a public water system.

(6) The term "contaminant" means any physical, chemical, biological, or radiological substance or matter in water.

(7) The term "Administrator" means the Administrator of the Environmental Protection Agency.

(8) The term "Agency" means the Environmental Protection Agency.

(9) The term "Council" means the National Drinking Water Advisory Council established under section 300j–5 of this title.

(10) The term "municipality" means a city, town, or other public body created by or pursuant to State law, or an Indian Tribe.

(11) The term "Federal agency" means any department, agency, or instrumentality of the United States.

(12) The term "person" means an individual, corporation, company, association, partnership, State, municipality, or Federal agency (and includes officers, employees, and agents of any corporation, company, association, State, municipality, or Federal agency).

(13) (A) Except as provided in subparagraph (B), the term "State" includes, in addition to the several States, only the District of Columbia, Guam, the Commonwealth of Puerto Rico, the Northern Mariana Islands, the Virgin Islands, American Samoa, and the Trust Territory of the Pacific Islands.

(B) For purposes of section 300j–12 of this title, the term "State" means each of the 50 States, the District of Columbia, and the Commonwealth of Puerto Rico.

(14) The term "Indian Tribe" means any Indian tribe having a Federally recognized governing body carrying out substantial governmental duties and powers over any area. For purposes of sections 1452, 1459A, and 1459B of this title, the term includes any Native village (as defined in section 1602(c) of Title 43).

(15) Community water system.—The term "community water system" means a public water system that—

(A) serves at least 15 service connections used by year-round residents of the area served by the system; or

(B) regularly serves at least 25 year-round residents.

(16) Noncommunity water system.—The term "noncommunity water system" means a public water system that is not a community water system.

(July 1, 1944, c. 373, Title XIV, § 1401, as added by Pub. L. No. 93–523, § 2(a), 88 Stat. 1661 (Dec. 16, 1974); and amended by Pub. L. No. 94–317, Title III, § 301(b)(2), 90 Stat. 707 (June 23, 1976); Pub. L. No. 94–484, Title IX, § 905(b)(1), 90 Stat. 2325 (Oct. 12, 1976); Pub. L. No. 95–190, § 8(b), 91 Stat. 1397 (Nov. 16, 1977); Pub. L. No. 99–339, Title III, § 302(b), 100 Stat. 666 (June 19, 1986); Pub. L. No. 104–182, Title I, § 101(a), (b)(1), 110 Stat. 1615, 1616 (Aug. 6, 1996); Pub. L. No. 114–322, § 2111, 130 Stat. 1729 (Dec. 16, 2016).)

HISTORICAL AND STATUTORY NOTES

References in Text

The Safe Drinking Water Act Amendments of 1996, referred to in par. (4)(C), is Pub. L. No. 104–182, 110 Stat. 1613 (Aug. 6, 1996). The modifications made by such Act to par. (4) are the amendments made by Pub. L.

No. 104–182, Title I, § 101(b)(1), 110 Stat. 1616 (Aug. 6, 1996); see 1996 Amendments note set out under this section. For complete classification of this Act to the Code, see Short Title note set out under section 201 of this title and Tables.

Effective and Applicability Provisions

1996 Acts. Section 2(b) of Pub. L. No. 104–182 provided that: "Except as otherwise specified in this Act [Pub. L. No. 104–182, 110 Stat. 1613 (Aug. 6, 1996), for classification of which to the Code, see Short Title of 1996 Amendments note, set out under section 201 of this title] or in the amendments made by this Act, this Act and the amendments made by this Act shall take effect on the date of enactment of this Act [Aug. 6, 1996]".

Short Title

1996 Amendments. For short title of Pub. L. No. 104–182, which amended this subchapter, as the "Safe Drinking Water Act Amendments of 1996", see section 1(a) of Pub. L. No. 104–182, set out as a note under section 201 of this title.

1986 Amendments. For short title of Pub. L. No. 99–339, which amended this subchapter, as the "Safe Drinking Water Act Amendments of 1986", see section 1 of Pub. L. No. 99–339, set out as a note under section 201 of this title.

1977 Amendments. For Short Title of Pub. L. No. 95–190, which amended this subchapter, see Short Title of 1977 Amendments note set out under section 201 of this title.

1974 Acts. For Short Title of Pub. L. No. 93–523, which enacted this subchapter, as the "Safe Drinking Water Act of 1974", see section 1 of Pub. L. No. 93–523, as amended, set out as a Short Title of 1974 Amendments note under section 201 of this title.

Termination of Trust Territory of the Pacific Islands

For termination of Trust Territory of the Pacific Islands, see note set out preceding 48 U.S.C.A. § 1681.

Effect of Public Law 104–182 on Federal Water Pollution Control Act

Section 2(c) of Pub. L. No. 104–182 provided that: "Except for the provisions of section 302 (relating to transfers of funds) [section 302 of Pub. L. No. 104–182, set out as a note under section 300j–12 of this title], nothing in this Act [Pub. L. No. 104–182, 110 Stat. 1613 (Aug. 6, 1996), for classification of which to the Code, see Short Title of 1996 Amendments note, set out under section 201 of this title] or in any amendments made by this Act to title XIV of the Public Health Service Act (commonly known as the 'Safe Drinking Water Act') [this subchapter] or any other law shall be construed by the Administrator of the Environmental Protection Agency or the courts as affecting, modifying, expanding, changing, or altering—

"(1) the provisions of the Federal Water Pollution Control Act [Act of June 30, 1948, c. 758, as amended generally by Pub. L. No. 92–500, § 2, 86 Stat. 816 (Oct. 18, 1972), also known as the Clean Water Act, which is codified generally to chapter 26 (section 1251 et seq.) of Title 33, Navigation and Navigable Waters];

"(2) the duties and responsibilities of the Administrator under that Act; or

"(3) the regulation or control of point or nonpoint sources of pollution discharged into waters covered by that Act.

The Administrator shall identify in the agency's annual budget all funding and full-time equivalents administering such title XIV [this subchapter] separately from funding and staffing for the Federal Water Pollution Control Act."

Congressional Findings

Section 3 of Pub. L. No. 104–182 provided that: "The Congress finds that—

"(1) safe drinking water is essential to the protection of public health;

"(2) because the requirements of the Safe Drinking Water Act (42 U.S.C. 300f et seq.) [this subchapter] now exceed the financial and technical capacity of some public water systems, especially many small public water systems, the Federal Government needs to provide assistance to communities to help the communities meet Federal drinking water requirements;

"(3) the Federal Government commits to maintaining and improving its partnership with the States in the administration and implementation of the Safe Drinking Water Act [this subchapter];

"(4) States play a central role in the implementation of safe drinking water programs, and States need increased financial resources and appropriate flexibility to ensure the prompt and effective development and implementation of drinking water programs;

"(5) the existing process for the assessment and selection of additional drinking water contaminants needs to be revised and improved to ensure that there is a sound scientific basis for setting priorities in establishing drinking water regulations;

"(6) procedures for assessing the health effects of contaminants establishing drinking water standards should be revised to provide greater opportunity for public education and participation;

"(7) in considering the appropriate level of regulation for contaminants in drinking water, risk assessment, based on sound and objective science, and benefit-cost analysis are important analytical tools for improving the efficiency and effectiveness of drinking water regulations to protect human health;

"(8) more effective protection of public health requires—

"(A) a Federal commitment to set priorities that will allow scarce Federal, State, and local resources to be targeted toward the drinking water problems of greatest public health concern;

"(B) maximizing the value of the different and complementary strengths and responsibilities of the Federal and State governments in those States that have primary enforcement responsibility for the Safe Drinking Water Act [this subchapter]; and

"(C) prevention of drinking water contamination through well-trained system operators, water systems with adequate managerial, technical, and financial capacity, and enhanced protection of source waters of public water systems;

"(9) compliance with the requirements of the Safe Drinking Water Act [this subchapter] continues to be a concern at public water systems experiencing technical and financial limitations, and Federal, State, and local governments need more resources and more effective authority to attain the objectives of the Safe Drinking Water Act; and

"(10) consumers served by public water systems should be provided with information on the source of the water they are drinking and its quality and safety, as well as prompt notification of any violation of drinking water regulations."

GAO Study

Section 101(b)(2) of Pub. L. No. 104–182 provided that: "The Comptroller General of the United States shall undertake a study to—

"(A) ascertain the numbers and locations of individuals and households relying for their residential water needs, including drinking, bathing, and cooking (or other similar uses) on irrigation water systems, mining water systems, industrial water systems, or other water systems covered by section 1401(4)(B) of the Safe Drinking Water Act [par. (4)(B) of this section] that are not public water systems subject to the Safe Drinking Water Act [this subchapter];

"(B) determine the sources and costs and affordability (to users and systems) of water used by such populations for their residential water needs; and

"(C) review State and water system compliance with the exclusion provisions of section 1401(4)(B) of such Act [par. (4)(B) of this section]. The Comptroller General shall submit a report to the Congress within 3 years after the date of enactment of this Act [Aug. 6, 1996] containing the results of such study."

Federal Compliance With Pollution Control Standards

For provisions relating to the responsibility of the head of each Executive agency for compliance with applicable pollution control standards, see Ex. Ord. No. 12088, 43 Fed. Reg. 47707 (Oct. 13, 1978), set out as a note under § 4321 of this title.

Safe Drinking Water Amendments of 1977 as Not Affecting Authority of Administrator With Respect to Contaminants

Section 3(e)(2) of Pub. L. No. 95–190 provided that: "Nothing in this Act [see Short Title of 1977 Amendment note set out under section 201 of this title] shall be construed to alter or affect the Administrator's authority or duty under title 14 of the Public Health Service Act [this subchapter] to promulgate regulations or take other action with respect to any contaminant."

Safe Drinking Water Amendments of 1977 Restrictions on Appropriations for Research

Section 2(e) of Pub. L. No. 95–190 provided that: "Nothing in this Act [see Short Title of 1977 Amendment note set out under section 201 of this title] shall be construed to authorize the appropriation of any amount for research under title XIV of the Public Health Service Act [this subchapter] (relating to safe drinking water)."

Rural Water Survey; Report to President and Congress; Authorization of Appropriations

Section 3 of Pub. L. No. 93–523, as amended by Pub. L. No. 95–190, §§ 2(d), 3(d), 91 Stat. 1393, 1394 (Nov. 16, 1977), directed the Administrator of the Environmental Protection Agency, after consultation with the Secretary of Agriculture and the several States, to enter into arrangements with public or private entities to conduct a survey of the quantity, quality, and availability of rural drinking water supplies, which survey was to include, but not be limited to, the consideration of the number of residents in each rural area who presently are being inadequately served by a public or private drinking water supply system, or by an individual home drinking water supply system, or who presently have limited or otherwise inadequate access to drinking water, or who, due to the absence or inadequacy of a drinking water supply system, are exposed to an increased health hazard, and who have experienced incidents or chronic or acute illness, which may be attributed to the inadequacy of a drinking water supply system. Since the survey was to be completed within eighteen months of Dec. 16, 1974 and a final report thereon submitted, not later than six months after the completion of the survey, to the President and to the Congress, the provision was omitted from the Code as executed.

Termination of Advisory Committees

Pub. L. No. 93–641, § 6, 88 Stat. 2275 (Jan. 4, 1975), set out as a note under section 217a of this title, provided that an advisory committee established pursuant to the Public Health Service Act [this chapter] shall terminate at such time as may be specifically prescribed by an Act of Congress enacted after Jan. 4, 1975.

PART B—PUBLIC WATER SYSTEMS

§ 300g. Coverage

[PHSA § 1411]

Subject to sections 300g–4 and 300g–5 of this title, national primary drinking water regulations under this part shall apply to each public water system in each State; except that such regulations shall not apply to a public water system—

(1) which consists only of distribution and storage facilities (and does not have any collection and treatment facilities);

(2) which obtains all of its water from, but is not owned or operated by, a public water system to which such regulations apply;

(3) which does not sell water to any person; and

(4) which is not a carrier which conveys passengers in interstate commerce.

(July 1, 1944, c. 373, Title XIV, § 1411, as added by Pub. L. No. 93–523, § 2(a), 88 Stat. 1662 (Dec. 16, 1974).)

§ 300g–1. National drinking water regulations

[PHSA § 1412]

(a) National primary drinking water regulations; maximum contaminant level goals; simultaneous publication of regulations and goals

(1) Effective on June 19, 1986, each national interim or revised primary drinking water regulation promulgated under this section before June 19, 1986, shall be deemed to be a national primary drinking water regulation under subsection (b) of this section. No such regulation shall be required to comply with the standards set forth in subsection (b)(4) of this section unless such regulation is amended to establish a different maximum contaminant level after June 19, 1986.

(2) After June 19, 1986, each recommended maximum contaminant level published before June 19, 1986, shall be treated as a maximum contaminant level goal.

(3) Whenever a national primary drinking water regulation is proposed under subsection (b) of this section for any contaminant, the maximum contaminant level goal for such contaminant shall be proposed simultaneously. Whenever a national primary drinking water regulation is promulgated under subsection (b) of this section for any contaminant, the maximum contaminant level goal for such contaminant shall be published simultaneously.

(4) Paragraph (3) shall not apply to any recommended maximum contaminant level published before June 19, 1986.

(b) Standards

(1) Identification of contaminants for listing

(A) General authority

The Administrator shall, in accordance with the procedures established by this subsection, publish a maximum contaminant level goal and promulgate a national primary drinking water regulation for a contaminant (other than a contaminant referred to in paragraph (2) for which a national primary drinking water regulation has been promulgated as of August 6, 1996) if the Administrator determines that—

(i) the contaminant may have an adverse effect on the health of persons;

(ii) the contaminant is known to occur or there is a substantial likelihood that the contaminant will occur in public water systems with a frequency and at levels of public health concern; and

(iii) in the sole judgment of the Administrator, regulation of such contaminant presents a meaningful opportunity for health risk reduction for persons served by public water systems.

(B) Regulation of unregulated contaminants

(i) Listing of contaminants for consideration

(I) Not later than 18 months after August 6, 1996, and every 5 years thereafter, the Administrator, after consultation with the scientific community, including the Science Advisory Board, after notice and opportunity for public comment, and after considering the occurrence data base established under section 300j–4(g) of this title, shall publish a list of contaminants which, at the time of publication, are not subject to any proposed or promulgated national primary drinking water regulation, which are known or anticipated to occur in public water systems, and which may require regulation under this subchapter.

(II) The unregulated contaminants considered under subclause (I) shall include, but not be limited to, substances referred to in section 9601(14) of this title, and substances registered as pesticides under the Federal Insecticide, Fungicide, and Rodenticide Act [7 U.S.C.A. § 136 et seq.].

(III) The Administrator's decision whether or not to select an unregulated contaminant for a list under this clause shall not be subject to judicial review.

(ii) Determination to regulate

(I) Not later than 5 years after August 6, 1996, and every 5 years thereafter, the Administrator shall, after notice of the preliminary determination and opportunity for public comment, for not fewer than 5 contaminants included on the list published under clause (i), make determinations of whether or not to regulate such contaminants.

(II) A determination to regulate a contaminant shall be based on findings that the criteria of clauses (i), (ii), and (iii) of subparagraph (A) are satisfied. Such findings shall be based on the best available public health information, including the occurrence data base established under section 300j–4(g) of this title.

(III) The Administrator may make a determination to regulate a contaminant that does not appear on a list under clause (i) if the determination to regulate is made pursuant to subclause (II).

(IV) A determination under this clause not to regulate a contaminant shall be considered final agency action and subject to judicial review.

(iii) Review

Each document setting forth the determination for a contaminant under clause (ii) shall be available for public comment at such time as the determination is published.

(C) Priorities

In selecting unregulated contaminants for consideration under subparagraph (B), the Administrator shall select contaminants that present the greatest public health concern. The Administrator, in making such selection, shall take into consideration, among other factors of public health concern, the effect of such contaminants upon subgroups that comprise a meaningful portion of the general population (such as infants, children, pregnant women, the elderly, individuals with a history of serious illness, or other subpopulations) that are identifiable as being at greater risk of adverse health effects due to exposure to contaminants in drinking water than the general population.

(D) Urgent threats to public health

The administrator may promulgate an interim national primary drinking water regulation for a contaminant without making a determination for the contaminant under paragraph (4)(C), or completing the analysis under paragraph (3)(C), to address an urgent threat to public health as determined by the Administrator after consultation with and written response to any comments provided by the Secretary of Health and Human Services, acting through the director of the Centers for Disease Control and Prevention or the director of the National Institutes of Health. A determination for any contaminant in accordance with paragraph (4)(C) subject to an interim regulation under this subparagraph shall be issued, and a completed analysis meeting the requirements of paragraph (3)(C) shall be published, not later than 3 years after the date on which the regulation is promulgated and the regulation shall be repromulgated, or revised if appropriate, not later than 5 years after that date.

(E) Regulation

For each contaminant that the Administrator determines to regulate under subparagraph (B), the Administrator shall publish maximum contaminant level goals and promulgate, by rule, national primary drinking water regulations under this subsection. The Administrator shall propose the maximum contaminant level goal and national primary drinking water regulation for a contaminant not later than 24 months after the determination to regulate under subparagraph (B), and may publish such proposed regulation concurrent with the determination to regulate. The Administrator shall publish a maximum contaminant level goal and promulgate a national primary drinking water regulation within 18 months after the proposal thereof. The Administrator, by notice in the Federal Register, may extend the deadline for such promulgation for up to 9 months.

(F) Health advisories and other actions

The Administrator may publish health advisories (which are not regulations) or take other appropriate actions for contaminants not subject to any national primary drinking water regulation.

(2) Schedules and deadlines

(A) In general

In the case of the contaminants listed in the Advance Notice of Proposed Rulemaking published in volume 47, Federal Register, page 9352, and in volume 48, Federal Register, page

45502, the Administrator shall publish maximum contaminant level goals and promulgate national primary drinking water regulations—

(i) not later than 1 year after June 19, 1986, for not fewer than 9 of the listed contaminants;

(ii) not later than 2 years after June 19, 1986, for not fewer than 40 of the listed contaminants; and

(iii) not later than 3 years after June 19, 1986, for the remainder of the listed contaminants.

(B) Substitution of contaminants

If the Administrator identifies a drinking water contaminant the regulation of which, in the judgment of the Administrator, is more likely to be protective of public health (taking into account the schedule for regulation under subparagraph (A)) than a contaminant referred to in subparagraph (A), the Administrator may publish a maximum contaminant level goal and promulgate a national primary drinking water regulation for the identified contaminant in lieu of regulating the contaminant referred to in subparagraph (A). Substitutions may be made for not more than 7 contaminants referred to in subparagraph (A). Regulation of a contaminant identified under this subparagraph shall be in accordance with the schedule applicable to the contaminant for which the substitution is made.

(C) Disinfectants and disinfection byproducts

The Administrator shall promulgate an Interim Enhanced Surface Water Treatment Rule, a Final Enhanced Surface Water Treatment Rule, a Stage I Disinfectants and Disinfection Byproducts Rule, and a Stage II Disinfectants and Disinfection Byproducts Rule in accordance with the schedule published in volume 59, Federal Register, page 6361 (February 10, 1994), in table III.13 of the proposed Information Collection Rule. If a delay occurs with respect to the promulgation of any rule in the schedule referred to in this subparagraph, all subsequent rules shall be completed as expeditiously as practicable but no later than a revised date that reflects the interval or intervals for the rules in the schedule.

(3) Risk assessment, management, and communication

(A) Use of science in decisionmaking

In carrying out this section, and, to the degree that an Agency action is based on science, the Administrator shall use—

(i) the best available, peer-reviewed science and supporting studies conducted in accordance with sound and objective scientific practices; and

(ii) data collected by accepted methods or best available methods (if the reliability of the method and the nature of the decision justifies use of the data).

(B) Public information

In carrying out this section, the Administrator shall ensure that the presentation of information on public health effects is comprehensive, informative, and understandable. The Administrator shall, in a document made available to the public in support of a regulation promulgated under this section, specify, to the extent practicable—

(i) each population addressed by any estimate of public health effects;

(ii) the expected risk or central estimate of risk for the specific populations;

(iii) each appropriate upper-bound or lower-bound estimate of risk;

(iv) each significant uncertainty identified in the process of the assessment of public health effects and studies that would assist in resolving the uncertainty; and

(v) peer-reviewed studies known to the Administrator that support, are directly relevant to, or fail to support any estimate of public health effects and the methodology used to reconcile inconsistencies in the scientific data.

(C) Health risk reduction and cost analysis

(i) Maximum contaminant levels

When proposing any national primary drinking water regulation that includes a maximum contaminant level, the Administrator shall, with respect to a maximum contaminant level that is being considered in accordance with paragraph (4) and each alternative maximum contaminant level that is being considered pursuant to paragraph (5) or (6)(A), publish, seek public comment on, and use for the purposes of paragraphs (4), (5), and (6) an analysis of each of the following:

(I) Quantifiable and nonquantifiable health risk reduction benefits for which there is a factual basis in the rulemaking record to conclude that such benefits are likely to occur as the result of treatment to comply with each level.

(II) Quantifiable and nonquantifiable health risk reduction benefits for which there is a factual basis in the rulemaking record to conclude that such benefits are likely to occur from reductions in co-occurring contaminants that may be attributed solely to compliance with the maximum contaminant level, excluding benefits resulting from compliance with other proposed or promulgated regulations.

(III) Quantifiable and nonquantifiable costs for which there is a factual basis in the rulemaking record to conclude that such costs are likely to occur solely as a result of compliance with the maximum contaminant level, including monitoring, treatment, and other costs and excluding costs resulting from compliance with other proposed or promulgated regulations.

(IV) The incremental costs and benefits associated with each alternative maximum contaminant level considered.

(V) The effects of the contaminant on the general population and on groups within the general population such as infants, children, pregnant women, the elderly, individuals with a history of serious illness, or other subpopulations that are identified as likely to be at greater risk of adverse health effects due to exposure to contaminants in drinking water than the general population.

(VI) Any increased health risk that may occur as the result of compliance, including risks associated with co-occurring contaminants.

(VII) Other relevant factors, including the quality and extent of the information, the uncertainties in the analysis supporting subclauses (I) through (VI), and factors with respect to the degree and nature of the risk.

(ii) Treatment techniques

When proposing a national primary drinking water regulation that includes a treatment technique in accordance with paragraph (7)(A), the Administrator shall publish and seek public comment on an analysis of the health risk reduction benefits and costs likely to be experienced as the result of compliance with the treatment technique and alternative treatment techniques that are being considered, taking into account, as appropriate, the factors described in clause (i).

(iii) Approaches to measure and value benefits

The Administrator may identify valid approaches for the measurement and valuation of benefits under this subparagraph, including approaches to identify consumer willingness to pay for reductions in health risks from drinking water contaminants.

(iv) Authorization

There are authorized to be appropriated to the Administrator, acting through the Office of Ground Water and Drinking Water, to conduct studies, assessments, and analyses in support of regulations or the development of methods, $35,000,000 for each of fiscal years 1996 through 2003.

(4) Goals and standards

(A) Maximum contaminant level goals

Each maximum contaminant level goal established under this subsection shall be set at the level at which no known or anticipated adverse effects on the health of persons occur and which allows an adequate margin of safety.

(B) Maximum contaminant levels

Except as provided in paragraphs (5) and (6), each national primary drinking water regulation for a contaminant for which a maximum contaminant level goal is established under this subsection shall specify a maximum contaminant level for such contaminant which is as close to the maximum contaminant level goal as is feasible.

(C) Determination

At the time the Administrator proposes a national primary drinking water regulation under this paragraph, the Administrator shall publish a determination as to whether the benefits of the maximum contaminant level justify, or do not justify, the costs based on the analysis conducted under paragraph (3)(C).

(D) Definition of feasible

For the purposes of this subsection, the term "feasible" means feasible with the use of the best technology, treatment techniques and other means which the Administrator finds, after examination for efficacy under field conditions and not solely under laboratory conditions, are available (taking cost into consideration). For the purpose of this paragraph, granular activated carbon is feasible for the control of synthetic organic chemicals, and any technology, treatment technique, or other means found to be the best available for the control of synthetic organic chemicals must be at least as effective in controlling synthetic organic chemicals as granular activated carbon.

(E) Feasible technologies

(i) In general

Each national primary drinking water regulation which establishes a maximum contaminant level shall list the technology, treatment techniques, and other means which the Administrator finds to be feasible for purposes of meeting such maximum contaminant level, but a regulation under this subsection shall not require that any specified technology, treatment technique, or other means be used for purposes of meeting such maximum contaminant level.

(ii) List of technologies for small systems

The Administrator shall include in the list any technology, treatment technique, or other means that is affordable, as determined by the Administrator in consultation with the States, for small public water systems serving—

(I) a population of 10,000 or fewer but more than 3,300;

(II) a population of 3,300 or fewer but more than 500; and

(III) a population of 500 or fewer but more than 25;

and that achieves compliance with the maximum contaminant level or treatment technique, including packaged or modular systems and point-of-entry or point-of-use treatment units. Point-of-entry and point-of-use treatment units shall be owned, controlled and maintained by the public water system or by a person under contract with the public water system to ensure proper operation and maintenance and compliance with the maximum contaminant level or treatment technique and equipped with mechanical warnings to ensure that customers are automatically notified of operational problems. The Administrator shall not include in the list any point-of-use treatment technology, treatment technique, or other means to achieve compliance with a maximum contaminant level or treatment technique requirement for a microbial contaminant (or an indicator of a microbial contaminant). If the American National Standards Institute has issued product standards applicable to a specific type of point-of-entry or point-of-use treatment unit, individual units of that type shall not be accepted for compliance with a maximum contaminant level or treatment technique requirement unless they are independently certified in accordance with such standards. In listing any technology, treatment technique, or other means pursuant to this clause, the Administrator shall consider the quality of the source water to be treated.

(iii) List of technologies that achieve compliance

Except as provided in clause (v), not later than 2 years after August 6, 1996, and after consultation with the States, the Administrator shall issue a list of technologies that achieve compliance with the maximum contaminant level or treatment technique for each category of public water systems described in subclauses (I), (II), and (III) of clause (ii) for each national primary drinking water regulation promulgated prior to June 19, 1986.

(iv) Additional technologies

The Administrator may, at any time after a national primary drinking water regulation has been promulgated, supplement the list of technologies describing additional or new or innovative treatment technologies that meet the requirements of this paragraph for categories of small public water systems described in subclauses (I), (II), and (III) of clause (ii) that are subject to the regulation.

(v) Technologies that meet surface water treatment rules

Within one year after August 6, 1996, the Administrator shall list technologies that meet the Surface Water Treatment Rule for each category of public water systems described in subclauses (I), (II), and (III) of clause (ii).

(5) Additional health risk considerations

(A) In general

Notwithstanding paragraph (4), the Administrator may establish a maximum contaminant level for a contaminant at a level other than the feasible level, if the technology, treatment techniques, and other means used to determine the feasible level would result in an increase in the health risk from drinking water by—

(i) increasing the concentration of other contaminants in drinking water; or

(ii) interfering with the efficacy of drinking water treatment techniques or processes that are used to comply with other national primary drinking water regulations.

(B) Establishment of level

If the Administrator establishes a maximum contaminant level or levels or requires the use of treatment techniques for any contaminant or contaminants pursuant to the authority of this paragraph—

(i) the level or levels or treatment techniques shall minimize the overall risk of adverse health effects by balancing the risk from the contaminant and the risk from other contaminants the concentrations of which may be affected by the use of a treatment technique or process that would be employed to attain the maximum contaminant level or levels; and

(ii) the combination of technology, treatment techniques, or other means required to meet the level or levels shall not be more stringent than is feasible (as defined in paragraph (4)(D)).

(6) Additional health risk reduction and cost considerations

(A) In general

Notwithstanding paragraph (4), if the Administrator determines based on an analysis conducted under paragraph (3)(C) that the benefits of a maximum contaminant level promulgated in accordance with paragraph (4) would not justify the costs of complying with the level, the Administrator may, after notice and opportunity for public comment, promulgate a maximum contaminant level for the contaminant that maximizes health risk reduction benefits at a cost that is justified by the benefits.

(B) Exception

The Administrator shall not use the authority of this paragraph to promulgate a maximum contaminant level for a contaminant, if the benefits of compliance with a national primary drinking water regulation for the contaminant that would be promulgated in accordance with paragraph (4) experienced by—

(i) persons served by large public water systems; and

(ii) persons served by such other systems as are unlikely, based on information provided by the States, to receive a variance under section 300g–4(e) of this title (relating to small system variances);

would justify the costs to the systems of complying with the regulation. This subparagraph shall not apply if the contaminant is found almost exclusively in small systems eligible under section 300g–4(e) of this title for a small system variance.

(C) Disinfectants and disinfection byproducts

The Administrator may not use the authority of this paragraph to establish a maximum contaminant level in a Stage I or Stage II national primary drinking water regulation (as described in paragraph (2)(C)) for contaminants that are disinfectants or disinfection byproducts, or to establish a maximum contaminant level or treatment technique requirement for the control of cryptosporidium. The authority of this paragraph may be used to establish regulations for the use of disinfection by systems relying on ground water sources as required by paragraph (8).

(D) Judicial review

A determination by the Administrator that the benefits of a maximum contaminant level or treatment requirement justify or do not justify the costs of complying with the level shall be reviewed by the court pursuant to section 300j–7 of this title only as part of a review of a final national primary drinking water regulation that has been promulgated based on the determination and shall not be set aside by the court under that section unless the court finds that the determination is arbitrary and capricious.

(7) (A) The Administrator is authorized to promulgate a national primary drinking water regulation that requires the use of a treatment technique in lieu of establishing a maximum contaminant level, if the Administrator makes a finding that it is not economically or technologically feasible to ascertain the level of the contaminant. In such case, the Administrator shall identify those treatment techniques which, in the Administrator's judgment, would prevent known or anticipated adverse effects on the health of persons to the extent feasible. Such regulations shall specify each treatment technique known to the Administrator which meets the requirements of this paragraph, but the Administrator may grant a variance from any specified treatment technique in accordance with section 300g–4(a)(3) of this title.

(B) Any schedule referred to in this subsection for the promulgation of a national primary drinking water regulation for any contaminant shall apply in the same manner if the regulation requires a treatment technique in lieu of establishing a maximum contaminant level.

(C) (i) Not later than 18 months after June 19, 1986, the Administrator shall propose and promulgate national primary drinking water regulations specifying criteria under which filtration (including coagulation and sedimentation, as appropriate) is required as a treatment technique for public water systems supplied by surface water sources. In promulgating such rules, the Administrator shall consider the quality of source waters, protection afforded by watershed management, treatment practices (such as disinfection and length of water storage) and other factors relevant to protection of health.

(ii) In lieu of the provisions of section 300g–4 of this title the Administrator shall specify procedures by which the State determines which public water systems within its jurisdiction shall adopt filtration under the criteria of clause (i). The State may require the public water system to provide studies or other information to assist in this determination. The procedures shall provide notice and opportunity for public hearing on this determination. If the State determines that filtration is required, the State shall prescribe a schedule for compliance by the public water system with the filtration requirement. A schedule shall require compliance within 18 months of a determination made under clause (iii).

(iii) Within 18 months from the time that the Administrator establishes the criteria and procedures under this subparagraph, a State with primary enforcement responsibility shall adopt any necessary regulations to implement this subparagraph. Within 12 months of adoption of such regulations the State shall make determinations regarding filtration for all the public water systems within its jurisdiction supplied by surface waters.

(iv) If a State does not have primary enforcement responsibility for public water systems, the Administrator shall have the same authority to make the determination in clause (ii) in such State as the State would have under that clause. Any filtration requirement or schedule under this subparagraph shall be treated as if it were a requirement of a national primary drinking water regulation.

(v) As an additional alternative to the regulations promulgated pursuant to clauses (i) and (iii), including the criteria for avoiding filtration contained in 40 CF.R. 141.71, a State exercising primary enforcement responsibility for public water systems may, on a case-by-case basis, and after notice and opportunity for public comment, establish treatment requirements as an alternative to filtration in the case of systems having uninhabited, undeveloped watersheds in consolidated ownership, and having control over access to, and activities in, those watersheds, if the State determines (and the Administrator concurs) that the quality of the source water and the alternative treatment requirements established by the State ensure greater removal or inactivation efficiencies of pathogenic organisms for which national primary drinking water regulations have been promulgated or that are of public health concern than would be achieved by the combination of filtration and chlorine disinfection (in compliance with this section).

(8) Disinfection

At any time after the end of the 3-year period that begins on August 6, 1996, but not later than the date on which the Administrator promulgates a Stage II rulemaking for disinfectants and disinfection byproducts (as described in paragraph (2)(C)), the Administrator shall also promulgate national primary drinking water regulations requiring disinfection as a treatment technique for all public water systems, including surface water systems and, as necessary, ground water systems. After consultation with the States, the Administrator shall (as part of the regulations) promulgate criteria that the Administrator, or a State that has primary enforcement responsibility under section 300g–2 of this title, shall apply to determine whether disinfection shall be required as a treatment technique for any public water system served by ground water. The Administrator shall simultaneously promulgate a rule specifying criteria that will be used by the Administrator (or delegated State authorities) to grant variances from this requirement according to the provisions of sections 300g–4(a)(1)(B) and 300g–4(a)(3) of this title. In implementing section 300j–1(e) of this title the Administrator or the delegated State authority shall, where appropriate, give special consideration to providing technical assistance to small public water systems in complying with the regulations promulgated under this paragraph.

(9) Review and revision

The Administrator shall, not less often than every 6 years, review and revise, as appropriate, each national primary drinking water regulation promulgated under this subchapter. Any revision of a national primary drinking water regulation shall be promulgated in accordance with this section, except that each revision shall maintain, or provide for greater, protection of the health of persons.

(10) Effective date

A national primary drinking water regulation promulgated under this section (and any amendment thereto) shall take effect on the date that is 3 years after the date on which the regulation is promulgated unless the Administrator determines that an earlier date is practicable, except that the Administrator, or a State (in the case of an individual system), may allow up to 2 additional years to comply with a maximum contaminant level or treatment technique if the Administrator or State (in the case of an individual system) determines that additional time is necessary for capital improvements.

(11) No national primary drinking water regulation may require the addition of any substance for preventive health care purposes unrelated to contamination of drinking water.

(12) Certain contaminants

(A) Arsenic

(i) Schedule and standard

Notwithstanding the deadlines set forth in paragraph (1), the Administrator shall promulgate a national primary drinking water regulation for arsenic pursuant to this subsection, in accordance with the schedule established by this paragraph.

(ii) Study plan

Not later than 180 days after August 6, 1996, the Administrator shall develop a comprehensive plan for study in support of drinking water rulemaking to reduce the uncertainty in assessing health risks associated with exposure to low levels of arsenic. In conducting such study, the Administrator shall consult with the National Academy of Sciences, other Federal agencies, and interested public and private entities.

(iii) Cooperative agreements

In carrying out the study plan, the Administrator may enter into cooperative agreements with other Federal agencies, State and local governments, and other interested public and private entities.

(iv) Proposed regulations

The Administrator shall propose a national primary drinking water regulation for arsenic not later than January 1, 2000.

(v) Final regulations

Not later than January 1, 2001, after notice and opportunity for public comment, the Administrator shall promulgate a national primary drinking water regulation for arsenic.

(vi) Authorization

There are authorized to be appropriated $2,500,000 for each of fiscal years 1997 through 2000 for the studies required by this paragraph.

(B) Sulfate

(i) Additional study

Prior to promulgating a national primary drinking water regulation for sulfate, the Administrator and the Director of the Centers for Disease Control and Prevention shall jointly conduct an additional study to establish a reliable dose-response relationship for the adverse human health effects that may result from exposure to sulfate in drinking water, including the health effects that may be experienced by groups within the general population (including infants and travelers) that are potentially at greater risk of adverse health effects as the result of such exposure. The study shall be conducted in consultation with interested States, shall be based on the best available, peer-reviewed science and supporting studies conducted in accordance with sound and objective scientific practices, and shall be completed not later than 30 months after August 6, 1996.

(ii) Determination

The Administrator shall include sulfate among the 5 or more contaminants for which a determination is made pursuant to paragraph (3)(B) not later than 5 years after August 6, 1996.

(iii) Proposed and final rule

Notwithstanding the deadlines set forth in paragraph (2), the Administrator may, pursuant to the authorities of this subsection and after notice and opportunity for public comment, promulgate a final national primary drinking water regulation for sulfate. Any such regulation shall include requirements for public notification and options for the provision of alternative water supplies to populations at risk as a means of complying with the regulation in lieu of a best available treatment technology or other means.

(13) Radon in drinking water

(A) National primary drinking water regulation

Notwithstanding paragraph (2), the Administrator shall withdraw any national primary drinking water regulation for radon proposed prior to August 6, 1996, and shall propose and promulgate a regulation for radon under this section, as amended by the Safe Drinking Water Act Amendments of 1996.

(B) Risk assessment and studies

(i) Assessment by NAS

Prior to proposing a national primary drinking water regulation for radon, the Administrator shall arrange for the National Academy of Sciences to prepare a risk assessment for radon in drinking water using the best available science in accordance with the requirements of paragraph (3). The risk assessment shall consider each of the risks associated with exposure to radon from drinking water and consider studies on the health effects of radon at levels and under conditions likely to be experienced through residential exposure. The risk assessment shall be peer-reviewed.

(ii) Study of other measures

The Administrator shall arrange for the National Academy of Sciences to prepare an assessment of the health risk reduction benefits associated with various mitigation measures to reduce radon levels in indoor air. The assessment may be conducted as part of the risk assessment authorized by clause (i) and shall be used by the Administrator to prepare the guidance and approve State programs under subparagraph (G).

(iii) Other organization

If the National Academy of Sciences declines to prepare the risk assessment or studies required by this subparagraph, the Administrator shall enter into a contract or cooperative agreement with another independent, scientific organization to prepare such assessments or studies.

(C) Health risk reduction and cost analysis

Not later than 30 months after August 6, 1996, the Administrator shall publish, and seek public comment on, a health risk reduction and cost analysis meeting the requirements of paragraph (3)(C) for potential maximum contaminant levels that are being considered for radon in drinking water. The Administrator shall include a response to all significant public comments received on the analysis with the preamble for the proposed rule published under subparagraph (D).

(D) Proposed regulation

Not later than 36 months after August 6, 1996, the Administrator shall propose a maximum contaminant level goal and a national primary drinking water regulation for radon pursuant to this section.

(E) Final regulation

Not later than 12 months after the date of the proposal under subparagraph (D), the Administrator shall publish a maximum contaminant level goal and promulgate a national primary drinking water regulation for radon pursuant to this section based on the risk assessment prepared pursuant to subparagraph (B) and the health risk reduction and cost analysis published pursuant to subparagraph (C). In considering the risk assessment and the health risk reduction and cost analysis in connection with the promulgation of such a standard, the Administrator shall take into account the costs and benefits of control programs for radon from other sources.

(F) Alternative maximum contaminant level

If the maximum contaminant level for radon in drinking water promulgated pursuant to subparagraph (E) is more stringent than necessary to reduce the contribution to radon in indoor air from drinking water to a concentration that is equivalent to the national average concentration of radon in outdoor air, the Administrator shall, simultaneously with the promulgation of such level, promulgate an alternative maximum contaminant level for radon that would result in a contribution of radon from drinking water to radon levels in indoor air equivalent to the national average concentration of radon in outdoor air. If the Administrator promulgates an alternative maximum contaminant level under this subparagraph, the Administrator shall, after notice and opportunity for public comment and in consultation with the States, publish guidelines for State programs, including criteria for multimedia measures to mitigate radon levels in indoor air, to be used by the States in preparing programs under subparagraph (G). The guidelines shall take into account data from existing radon mitigation programs and the assessment of mitigation measures prepared under subparagraph (B).

(G) Multimedia radon mitigation programs

(i) In general

A State may develop and submit a multimedia program to mitigate radon levels in indoor air for approval by the Administrator under this subparagraph. If, after notice and the opportunity for public comment, such program is approved by the Administrator, public water systems in the State may comply with the alternative maximum contaminant level promulgated under subparagraph (F) in lieu of the maximum contaminant level in the national primary drinking water regulation promulgated under subparagraph (E).

(ii) Elements of programs

State programs may rely on a variety of mitigation measures including public education, testing, training, technical assistance, remediation grant and loan or incentive programs, or other regulatory or nonregulatory measures. The effectiveness of elements in State programs shall be evaluated by the Administrator based on the assessment prepared by the National Academy of Sciences under subparagraph (B) and the guidelines published by the Administrator under subparagraph (F).

(iii) Approval

The Administrator shall approve a State program submitted under this paragraph if the health risk reduction benefits expected to be achieved by the program are equal to or greater than the health risk reduction benefits that would be achieved if each public water system in the State complied with the maximum contaminant level promulgated under subparagraph (E). The Administrator shall approve or disapprove a program submitted under this paragraph within 180 days of receipt. A program that is not disapproved during such period shall be deemed approved. A program that is disapproved may be modified to address the objections of the Administrator and be resubmitted for approval.

(iv) Review

The Administrator shall periodically, but not less often than every 5 years, review each multimedia mitigation program approved under this subparagraph to determine whether it continues to meet the requirements of clause (iii) and shall, after written notice to the State and an opportunity for the State to correct any deficiency in the program, withdraw approval of programs that no longer comply with such requirements.

(v) Extension

If, within 90 days after the promulgation of an alternative maximum contaminant level under subparagraph (F), the Governor of a State submits a letter to the Administrator committing to develop a multimedia mitigation program under this subparagraph, the effective date of the national primary drinking water regulation for radon in the State that would be applicable under paragraph (10) shall be extended for a period of 18 months.

(vi) Local programs

In the event that a State chooses not to submit a multimedia mitigation program for approval under this subparagraph or has submitted a program that has been disapproved, any public water system in the State may submit a program for approval by the Administrator according to the same criteria, conditions, and approval process that would apply to a State program. The Administrator shall approve a multimedia mitigation program if the health risk reduction benefits expected to be achieved by the program are equal to or greater than the health risk reduction benefits that would result from compliance by the public water system with the maximum contaminant level for radon promulgated under subparagraph (E).

(14) Recycling of filter backwash

The Administrator shall promulgate a regulation to govern the recycling of filter backwash water within the treatment process of a public water system. The Administrator shall promulgate such regulation not later than 4 years after August 6, 1996, unless such recycling has been addressed by the Administrator's Enhanced Surface Water Treatment Rule prior to such date.

(15) Variance technologies

(A) In general

At the same time as the Administrator promulgates a national primary drinking water regulation for a contaminant pursuant to this section, the Administrator shall issue guidance or regulations describing the best treatment technologies, treatment techniques, or other means (referred to in this paragraph as "variance technology") for the contaminant that the Administrator finds, after examination for efficacy under field conditions and not solely under laboratory conditions, are available and affordable, as determined by the Administrator in consultation with the States, for public water systems of varying size, considering the quality of the source water to be treated. The Administrator shall identify such variance technologies for public water systems serving—

(i) a population of 10,000 or fewer but more than 3,300;

(ii) a population of 3,300 or fewer but more than 500; and

(iii) a population of 500 or fewer but more than 25,

if, considering the quality of the source water to be treated, no treatment technology is listed for public water systems of that size under paragraph (4)(E). Variance technologies identified by the Administrator pursuant to this paragraph may not achieve compliance with the maximum contaminant level or treatment technique requirement of such regulation, but shall achieve the maximum reduction or inactivation efficiency that is affordable considering the size of the system and the quality of the source water. The guidance or regulations shall not require the use of a technology from a specific manufacturer or brand.

(B) Limitation

The Administrator shall not identify any variance technology under this paragraph, unless the Administrator has determined, considering the quality of the source water to be treated and the expected useful life of the technology, that the variance technology is protective of public health.

(C) Additional information

The Administrator shall include in the guidance or regulations identifying variance technologies under this paragraph any assumptions supporting the public health determination referred to in subparagraph (B), where such assumptions concern the public water system to which the technology may be applied, or its source waters. The Administrator shall provide any assumptions used in determining affordability, taking into consideration the number of persons served by such systems. The Administrator shall provide as much reliable information as practicable on performance, effectiveness, limitations, costs, and other relevant factors including the applicability of variance technology to waters from surface and underground sources.

(D) Regulations and guidance

Not later than 2 years after August 6, 1996, and after consultation with the States, the Administrator shall issue guidance or regulations under subparagraph (A) for each national primary drinking water regulation promulgated prior to August 6, 1996, for which a variance may be granted under section 300g–4(e) of this title. The Administrator may, at any time after a national primary drinking water regulation has been promulgated, issue guidance or regulations describing additional variance technologies. The Administrator shall, not less often than every 7 years, or upon receipt of a petition supported by substantial information, review variance technologies identified under this paragraph. The Administrator shall issue revised guidance or regulations if new or innovative variance technologies become available that meet the requirements of this paragraph and achieve an equal or greater reduction or inactivation efficiency than the variance technologies previously identified under this subparagraph. No public water system shall be required to replace a variance technology during the useful life of the technology for the sole reason that a more efficient variance technology has been listed under this subparagraph.

(c) Secondary regulations; publication of proposed regulations; promulgation; amendments

The Administrator shall publish proposed national secondary drinking water regulations within 270 days after December 16, 1974. Within 90 days after publication of any such regulation, he shall promulgate such regulation with such modifications as he deems appropriate. Regulations under this subsection may be amended from time to time.

(d) Regulations; public hearings; administrative consultations

Regulations under this section shall be prescribed in accordance with section 553 of Title 5 (relating to rulemaking), except that the Administrator shall provide opportunity for public hearing prior to promulgation of such regulations. In proposing and promulgating regulations under this section, the Administrator shall consult with the Secretary and the National Drinking Water Advisory Council.

(e) Science Advisory Board comments

The Administrator shall request comments from the Science Advisory Board (established under the Environmental Research, Development, and Demonstration Act of 1978) prior to proposal of a maximum contaminant level goal and national primary drinking water regulation. The Board shall respond, as it deems appropriate, within the time period applicable for promulgation of the national primary drinking water standard concerned. This subsection shall, under no circumstances, be used to delay final promulgation of any national primary drinking water standard.

(July 1, 1944, c. 373, Title XIV, § 1412, as added by Pub. L. No. 93–523, § 2(a), 88 Stat. 1662 (Dec. 16, 1974); and amended by Pub. L. No. 95–190, §§ 3(c), 12(a), 91 Stat. 1394, 1398 (Nov. 16, 1977); Pub. L. No. 99–339, Title I,

§ 101(a) to (c)(1), (d), (e), 100 Stat. 642 to 646 (June 19, 1986); Pub. L. No. 104–182, Title I, §§ 102(a), (c)(2), 103, 104(a), (c), 105 to 111(a), Title V, § 501(a)(1), (2), 110 Stat. 1617, 1621, 1623, 1625 to 1631, 1691 (Aug. 6, 1996).)

HISTORICAL AND STATUTORY NOTES

References in Text

The Federal Insecticide, Fungicide, and Rodenticide Act, referred to in subsec. (b)(1)(B)(i)(II), is Act of June 25, 1947, c. 125, as amended generally by Pub. L. No. 92–516, 86 Stat. 973 (Oct. 21, 1972), which is codified generally as subchapter II (section 136 et seq.) of chapter 6 of Title 7, Agriculture. For complete classification of this Act to the Code, see Short Title note set out under section 136 of Title 7 and Tables.

The Safe Drinking Water Act Amendments of 1996, referred to in subsec. (b)(13)(A), is Pub. L. No. 104–182, 110 Stat. 1613 (Aug. 6, 1996), which is codified principally as this subchapter. For complete classification of such Act to the Code, see Short Title of 1996 Amendments note set out under section 201 of this title and Tables.

The Environmental Research, Development, and Demonstration Act of 1978, referred to in subsec. (e), is Pub. L. No. 95–155, 91 Stat. 1257 (Nov. 8, 1977), which enacted sections 300j–3a, 4361a, 4361b, 4363, 4364, 4365, 4366, and 4367 of this title. Section 4365 of this title established the Science Advisory Board. For complete classification of this Act to the Code, see Tables.

Effective and Applicability Provisions

1996 Acts. Amendment by Pub. L. No. 104–182 effective Aug. 6, 1996, except as otherwise specifically provided, see section 2(b) of Pub. L. No. 104–182, set out as a note under section 300f of this title.

National Regulation For Arsenic In Primary Drinking Water

Pub. L. No. 106–377, § 1(a)(1) [Title III], 114 Stat. 1441, 1441A–41 (Oct. 27, 2000), provided in part: "That notwithstanding section 1412(b)(12)(A)(v) of the Safe Drinking Water Act [subsec. (b)(12)(A)(v) of this section], as amended, the Administrator shall promulgate a national primary drinking water regulation for arsenic not later than June 22, 2001."

Applicability of Prior Requirements

Section 102(b) of Pub. L. No. 104–182 provided that: "The requirements of subparagraphs (C) and (D) of section 1412(b)(3) of the Safe Drinking Water Act as in effect before the date of enactment of this Act [former subsec. (b)(3)(C) and (D) of this section, as in effect prior to Aug. 6, 1996], and any obligation to promulgate regulations pursuant to such subparagraphs not promulgated as of the date of enactment of this Act [Aug. 6, 1996], are superseded by the amendments made by subsection (a) [amending subsec. (b) of this section]."

Disinfectants and Disinfection Byproducts

Section 104(b) of Pub. L. No. 104–182 provided that: "The Administrator of the Environmental Protection Agency may use the authority of section 1412(b)(5) of the Safe Drinking Water Act (as amended by this Act) [subsec. (b)(5) of this section] to promulgate the Stage I and Stage II Disinfectants and Disinfection Byproducts Rules as proposed in volume 59, Federal Register, page 38668 (July 29, 1994). The considerations used in the development of the July 29, 1994, proposed national primary drinking water regulation on disinfectants and disinfection byproducts shall be treated as consistent with such section 1412(b)(5) [subsec. (b)(5) of this section] for purposes of such Stage I and Stage II rules."

§ 300g–2. State primary enforcement responsibility

[PHSA § 1413]

(a) In general

For purposes of this subchapter, a State has primary enforcement responsibility for public water systems during any period for which the Administrator determines (pursuant to regulations prescribed under subsection (b) of this section) that such State—

(1) has adopted drinking water regulations that are no less stringent than the national primary drinking water regulations promulgated by the Administrator under subsections (a) and (b) of section 300g–1 of this title not later than 2 years after the date on which the regulations are promulgated by the Administrator, except that the Administrator may provide for an extension of not more than 2 years if, after submission and review of appropriate, adequate documentation from the State, the Administrator determines that the extension is necessary and justified;

(2) has adopted and is implementing adequate procedures for the enforcement of such State regulations, including conducting such monitoring and making such inspections as the Administrator may require by regulation;

(3) will keep such records and make such reports with respect to its activities under paragraphs (1) and (2) as the Administrator may require by regulation;

(4) if it permits variances or exemptions, or both, from the requirements of its drinking water regulations which meet the requirements of paragraph (1), permits such variances and exemptions under conditions and in a manner which is not less stringent than the conditions under, and the manner in which variances and exemptions may be granted under sections 300g–4 and 300g–5 of this title;

(5) has adopted and can implement an adequate plan for the provision of safe drinking water under emergency circumstances including earthquakes, floods, hurricanes, and other natural disasters, as appropriate;

(6) has adopted and is implementing procedures for requiring public water systems to assess options for consolidation or transfer of ownership or other actions in accordance with the regulations issued by the Administrator under section 1414(h)(6); and

(7) has adopted authority for administrative penalties (unless the constitution of the State prohibits the adoption of the authority) in a maximum amount—

(A) in the case of a system serving a population of more than 10,000, that is not less than $1,000 per day per violation; and

(B) in the case of any other system, that is adequate to ensure compliance (as determined by the State);

except that a State may establish a maximum limitation on the total amount of administrative penalties that may be imposed on a public water system per violation.

(b) Regulations

(1) The Administrator shall, by regulation (proposed within 180 days of December 16, 1974), prescribe the manner in which a State may apply to the Administrator for a determination that the requirements of subsection (a) of this section are satisfied with respect to the State, the manner in which the determination is made, the period for which the determination will be effective, and the manner in which the Administrator may determine that such requirements are no longer met. Such regulations shall require that before a determination of the Administrator that such requirements are met or are no longer met with respect to a State may become effective, the Administrator shall notify such State of the determination and the reasons therefor and shall provide an opportunity for public hearing on the determination. Such regulations shall be promulgated (with such modifications as the Administrator deems appropriate) within 90 days of the publication of the proposed regulations in the Federal Register. The Administrator shall promptly notify in writing the chief executive officer of each State of the promulgation of regulations under this paragraph. Such notice shall contain a copy of the regulations and shall specify a State's authority under this subchapter when it is determined to have primary enforcement responsibility for public water systems.

(2) When an application is submitted in accordance with the Administrator's regulations under paragraph (1), the Administrator shall within 90 days of the date on which such application is submitted (A) make the determination applied for, or (B) deny the application and notify the applicant in writing of the reasons for his denial.

(c) Interim primary enforcement authority

A State that has primary enforcement authority under this section with respect to each existing national primary drinking water regulation shall be considered to have primary enforcement authority with respect to each new or revised national primary drinking water regulation during the period beginning on the effective date of a regulation adopted and submitted by the State with respect to the new or revised national primary drinking water regulation in accordance with subsection (b)(1) of this section and ending at such time as the Administrator makes a determination under subsection (b)(2)(B) of this section with respect to the regulation.

(July 1, 1944, c. 373, Title XIV, § 1413, as added by Pub. L. No. 93–523, § 2(a), 88 Stat. 1665 (Dec. 16, 1974); and amended by Pub. L. No. 99–339, Title I, § 101(c)(2), 100 Stat. 646 (June 19, 1986); Pub. L. No. 104–182, Title I, §§ 112, 113(b), 110 Stat. 1633, 1635 (Aug. 6, 1996); Pub. L. No. 115–270, § 2020(b), 132 Stat. 3765, 3848 (Oct. 23, 2018).)

HISTORICAL AND STATUTORY NOTES

Effective and Applicability Provisions

1996 Acts. Amendment by Pub. L. No. 104–182 effective Aug. 6, 1996, except as otherwise specifically provided, see section 2(b) of Pub. L. No. 104–182, set out as a note under section 300f of this title.

§ 300g–3. Enforcement of drinking water regulations

[PHSA § 1414]

(a) Notice to State and public water system; issuance of administrative order; civil action

(1) (A) Whenever the Administrator finds during a period during which a State has primary enforcement responsibility for public water systems (within the meaning of section 300g–2(a) of this title) that any public water system—

(i) for which a variance under section 300g–4 or an exemption under section 300g–5 of this title is not in effect, does not comply with any applicable requirement, or

(ii) for which a variance under section 300g–4 or an exemption under section 300g–5 of this title is in effect, does not comply with any schedule or other requirement imposed pursuant thereto,

he shall so notify the State and such public water system and provide such advice and technical assistance to such State and public water system as may be appropriate to bring the system into compliance with the requirement by the earliest feasible time.

(B) If, beyond the thirtieth day after the Administrator's notification under subparagraph (A), the State has not commenced appropriate enforcement action, the Administrator shall issue an order under subsection (g) of this section requiring the public water system to comply with such applicable requirement or the Administrator shall commence a civil action under subsection (b) of this section.

(2) Enforcement in nonprimacy States

(A) In general

If, on the basis of information available to the Administrator, the Administrator finds, with respect to a period in which a State does not have primary enforcement responsibility for public water systems, that a public water system in the State—

(i) for which a variance under section 300g–4 of this title or an exemption under section 300g–5 of this title is not in effect, does not comply with any applicable requirement; or

(ii) for which a variance under section 300g–4 of this title or an exemption under section 300g–5 of this title is in effect, does not comply with any schedule or other requirement imposed pursuant to the variance or exemption;

the Administrator shall issue an order under subsection (g) of this section requiring the public water system to comply with the requirement, or commence a civil action under subsection (b) of this section.

(B) Notice

If the Administrator takes any action pursuant to this paragraph, the Administrator shall notify an appropriate local elected official, if any, with jurisdiction over the public water system of the action prior to the time that the action is taken.

(b) Judicial determinations in appropriate Federal district courts; civil penalties; separate violations

The Administrator may bring a civil action in the appropriate United States district court to require compliance with any applicable requirement, with an order issued under subsection (g) of this section, or with any schedule or other requirement imposed pursuant to a variance or exemption granted under section 300g–4 or 300g–5 of this title if—

(1) authorized under paragraph (1) or (2) of subsection (a) of this section, or

(2) if requested by (A) the chief executive officer of the State in which is located the public water system which is not in compliance with such regulation or requirement, or (B) the agency of such State which has jurisdiction over compliance by public water systems in the State with national primary drinking water regulations or State drinking water regulations.

The court may enter, in an action brought under this subsection, such judgment as protection of public health may require, taking into consideration the time necessary to comply and the availability of alternative water supplies; and, if the court determines that there has been a violation of the regulation or schedule or other requirement with respect to which the action was brought, the court may, taking into account the seriousness of the violation, the population at risk, and other appropriate factors, impose on the violator a civil penalty of not to exceed $25,000 for each day in which such violation occurs.

(c) Notice to States, the Administrator, and persons served

(1) In general

Each owner or operator of a public water system shall give notice of each of the following to the persons served by the system:

(A) Notice of any failure on the part of the public water system to—

(i) comply with an applicable maximum contaminant level or treatment technique requirement of, or a testing procedure prescribed by, a national primary drinking water regulation; or

(ii) perform monitoring required by section 300j–4(a) of this title.

(B) If the public water system is subject to a variance granted under subsection (a)(1)(A), (a)(2), or (e) of section 300g–4 of this title for an inability to meet a maximum contaminant level requirement or is subject to an exemption granted under section 300g–5 of this title, notice of—

(i) the existence of the variance or exemption; and

(ii) any failure to comply with the requirements of any schedule prescribed pursuant to the variance or exemption.

(C) Notice of the concentration level of any unregulated contaminant for which the Administrator has required public notice pursuant to paragraph (2)(F).

(D) Notice that the public water system exceeded the lead action level under section 141.80(c) of title 40, Code of Federal Regulations (or a prescribed level of lead that the Administrator establishes for public education or notification in a successor regulation promulgated pursuant to section 1412).

(2) Form, manner, and frequency of notice

(A) In general

The Administrator shall, by regulation, and after consultation with the States, prescribe the manner, frequency, form, and content for giving notice under this subsection. The regulations shall—

(i) provide for different frequencies of notice based on the differences between violations that are intermittent or infrequent and violations that are continuous or frequent; and

(ii) take into account the seriousness of any potential adverse health effects that may be involved.

(B) State requirements

(i) In general

A State may, by rule, establish alternative notification requirements—

(I) with respect to the form and content of notice given under and in a manner in accordance with subparagraph (C); and

(II) with respect to the form and content of notice given under subparagraph (E).

(ii) Contents

The alternative requirements shall provide the same type and amount of information as required pursuant to this subsection and regulations issued under subparagraph (A).

(iii) Relationship to section 300g–2

Nothing in this subparagraph shall be construed or applied to modify the requirements of section 300g–2 of this title.

(C) Notice of violations or exceedances with potential to have serious adverse effects on human health

Regulations issued under subparagraph (A) shall specify notification procedures for each violation, and each exceedance described in paragraph (1)(D), by a public water system that has the potential to have serious adverse effects on human health as a result of short-term exposure. Each notice of violation or exceedance provided under this subparagraph shall—

(i) be distributed as soon as practicable, but not later than 24 hours, after the public water system learns of the violation or exceedance;

(ii) provide a clear and readily understandable explanation of—

(I) the violation or exceedance;

(II) the potential adverse effects on human health;

(III) the steps that the public water system is taking to correct the violation or exceedance; and

(IV) the necessity of seeking alternative water supplies until the violation or exceedance is corrected;

(iii) be provided to the Administrator and the head of the State agency that has primary enforcement responsibility under section 1413, as applicable, as soon as practicable, but not later than 24 hours after the public water system learns of the violation or exceedance; and

(iv) as required by the State agency in general regulations of the State agency, or on a case-by-case basis after the consultation referred to in clause (iii), considering the health risks involved—

(I) be provided to appropriate media, including broadcast media;

(II) be prominently published in a newspaper of general circulation serving the area not later than 1 day after distribution of a notice pursuant to clause (i) or the date of publication of the next issue of the newspaper; or

(III) be provided by posting or door-to-door notification.

(D) Notice by the Administrator.—If the State with primary enforcement responsibility or the owner or operator of a public water system has not issued a notice under subparagraph (C) for an exceedance of the lead action level under section 141.80(c) of title 40, Code of Federal

Regulations (or a prescribed level of lead that the Administrator establishes for public education or notification in a successor regulation promulgated pursuant to section 1412) that has the potential to have serious adverse effects on human health as a result of short-term exposure, not later than 24 hours after the Administrator is notified of the exceedance, the Administrator shall issue the required notice under that subparagraph.

(E) Written notice

(i) In general

Regulations issued under subparagraph (A) shall specify notification procedures for violations other than the violations covered by subparagraph (C). The procedures shall specify that a public water system shall provide written notice to each person served by the system by notice (I) in the first bill (if any) prepared after the date of occurrence of the violation, (II) in an annual report issued not later than 1 year after the date of occurrence of the violation, or (III) by mail or direct delivery as soon as practicable, but not later than 1 year after the date of occurrence of the violation.

(ii) Form and manner of notice

The Administrator shall prescribe the form and manner of the notice to provide a clear and readily understandable explanation of the violation, any potential adverse health effects, and the steps that the system is taking to seek alternative water supplies, if any, until the violation is corrected.

(F) Unregulated contaminants

The Administrator may require the owner or operator of a public water system to give notice to the persons served by the system of the concentration levels of an unregulated contaminant required to be monitored under section 300j–4(a) of this title.

(3) Reports

(A) Annual report by State

(i) In general

Not later than January 1, 1998, and annually thereafter, each State that has primary enforcement responsibility under section 300g–2 of this title shall prepare, make readily available to the public, and submit to the Administrator an annual report on violations of national primary drinking water regulations by public water systems in the State, including violations with respect to (I) maximum contaminant levels, (II) treatment requirements, (III) variances and exemptions, and (IV) monitoring requirements determined to be significant by the Administrator after consultation with the States.

(ii) Distribution

The State shall publish and distribute summaries of the report and indicate where the full report is available for review.

(B) Annual report by Administrator

Not later than July 1, 1998, and annually thereafter, the Administrator shall prepare and make available to the public an annual report summarizing and evaluating reports submitted by States pursuant to subparagraph (A), notices submitted by public water systems serving Indian Tribes provided to the Administrator pursuant to subparagraph (C) or (E) of paragraph (2), and notices issued by the Administrator with respect to public water systems serving Indian Tribes under subparagraph (D) of that paragraph and making recommendations concerning the resources needed to improve compliance with this subchapter. The report shall include information about public water system compliance on Indian reservations and about enforcement activities undertaken and financial assistance provided by the Administrator on Indian reservations, and shall make specific recommendations concerning the resources needed to improve compliance with this subchapter on Indian reservations.

(4) Consumer confidence reports by community water systems

(A) Reports to consumers

The Administrator, in consultation with public water systems, environmental groups, public interest groups, risk communication experts, and the States, and other interested parties, shall issue regulations within 24 months after August 6, 1996, to require each community water system to mail, or provide by electronic means, to each customer of the system at least once annually a report on the level of contaminants in the drinking water purveyed by that system (referred to in this paragraph as a "consumer confidence report"). Such regulations shall provide a brief and plainly worded definition of the terms "maximum contaminant level goal", "maximum contaminant level", "variances", and "exemptions" and brief statements in plain language regarding the health concerns that resulted in regulation of each regulated contaminant. The regulations shall also include a brief and plainly worded explanation regarding contaminants that may reasonably be expected to be present in drinking water, including bottled water. The regulations shall also provide for an Environmental Protection Agency toll-free hotline that consumers can call for more information and explanation.

(B) Contents of report

The consumer confidence reports under this paragraph shall include, but not be limited to, each of the following:

(i) Information on the source of the water purveyed.

(ii) A brief and plainly worded definition of the terms "action level", "maximum contaminant level goal", "maximum contaminant level", "variances", and "exemptions" as provided in the regulations of the Administrator.

(iii) If any regulated contaminant is detected in the water purveyed by the public water system, a statement describing, as applicable—

(I) the maximum contaminant level goal;

(II) the maximum contaminant level;

(III) the level of the contaminant in the water system;

(IV) the action level for the contaminant; and

(V) for any contaminant for which there has been a violation of the maximum contaminant level during the year concerned, a brief statement in plain language regarding the health concerns that resulted in regulation of the contaminant, as provided by the Administrator in regulations under subparagraph (A).

(iv) Information on compliance with national primary drinking water regulations, as required by the Administrator, including corrosion control efforts, and notice if the system is operating under a variance or exemption and the basis on which the variance or exemption was granted.

(v) Information on the levels of unregulated contaminants for which monitoring is required under section 300j–4(a)(2) of this title (including levels of cryptosporidium and radon where States determine they may be found).

(vi) A statement that the presence of contaminants in drinking water does not necessarily indicate that the drinking water poses a health risk and that more information about contaminants and potential health effects can be obtained by calling the Environmental Protection Agency hotline.

(vii) Identification of, if any—

(I) exceedances described in paragraph (1)(D) for which corrective action has been required by the Administrator or the State (in the case of a State exercising primary enforcement responsibility for public water systems) during the monitoring period covered by the consumer confidence report; and

(II) violations that occurred during the monitoring period covered by the consumer confidence report.

A public water system may include such additional information as it deems appropriate for public education. The Administrator may, for not more than 3 regulated contaminants other than those referred to in clause (iii)(V) require a consumer confidence report under this paragraph to include the brief statement in plain language regarding the health concerns that resulted in regulation of the contaminant or contaminants concerned, as provided by the Administrator in regulations under subparagraph (A).

(C) Coverage

The Governor of a State may determine not to apply the mailing requirement of subparagraph (A) to a community water system serving fewer than 10,000 persons. Any such system shall—

(i) inform, in the newspaper notice required by clause (iii) or by other means, its customers that the system will not be mailing the report as required by subparagraph (A);

(ii) make the consumer confidence report available upon request to the public; and

(iii) publish the report referred to in subparagraph (A) annually in one or more local newspapers serving the area in which customers of the system are located.

(D) Alternative to publication

For any community water system which, pursuant to subparagraph (C), is not required to meet the mailing requirement of subparagraph (A) and which serves 500 persons or fewer, the community water system may elect not to comply with clause (i) or (iii) of subparagraph (C). If the community water system so elects, the system shall, at a minimum—

(i) prepare an annual consumer confidence report pursuant to subparagraph (B); and

(ii) provide notice at least once per year to each of its customers by mail, by door-to-door delivery, by posting or by other means authorized by the regulations of the Administrator that the consumer confidence report is available upon request.

(E) Alternative form and content

A State exercising primary enforcement responsibility may establish, by rule, after notice and public comment, alternative requirements with respect to the form and content of consumer confidence reports under this paragraph.

(F) Revisions.—

(i) Understandability and frequency.—Not later than 24 months after the date of enactment of America's Water Infrastructure Act of 2018, the Administrator, in consultation with the parties identified in subparagraph (A), shall issue revisions to the regulations issued under subparagraph (A)—

(I) to increase—

(aa) the readability, clarity, and understandability of the information presented in consumer confidence reports; and

(bb) the accuracy of information presented, and risk communication, in consumer confidence reports; and

(II) with respect to community water systems that serve 10,000 or more persons, to require each such community water system to provide, by mail, electronic means, or other methods described in clause (ii), a consumer confidence report to each customer of the system at least biannually.

(ii) Electronic delivery.—Any revision of regulations pursuant to clause (i) shall allow delivery of consumer confidence reports by methods consistent with methods described in the memorandum 'Safe Drinking Water Act—Consumer Confidence Report Rule Delivery Options' issued by the Environmental Protection Agency on January 3, 2013.

(5) Exceedance of lead level at households.—

(A) Strategic plan.—Not later than 180 days after the date of enactment of this paragraph, the Administrator shall, in collaboration with owners and operators of public water systems and States, establish a strategic plan for how the Administrator, a State with primary enforcement responsibility, and owners and operators of public water systems shall provide targeted outreach, education, technical assistance, and risk communication to populations affected by the concentration of lead in a public water system, including dissemination of information described in subparagraph (C).

(B) EPA initiation of notice.—

(i) Forwarding of data by employee of the Agency.—If the Agency develops, or receives from a source other than a State or a public water system, data that meets the requirements of section 1412(b)(3)(A)(ii) that indicates that the drinking water of a household served by a public water system contains a level of lead that exceeds the lead action level under section 141.80(c) of title 40, Code of Federal Regulations (or a prescribed level of lead that the Administrator establishes for public education or notification in a successor regulation promulgated pursuant to section 1412) (referred to in this paragraph as an 'affected household'), the Administrator shall require an appropriate employee of the Agency to forward the data, and information on the sampling techniques used to obtain the data, to the owner or operator of the public water system and the State in which the affected household is located within a time period determined by the Administrator.

(ii) Dissemination of information by owner or operator.—The owner or operator of a public water system shall disseminate to affected households the information described in subparagraph (C) within a time period established by the Administrator, if the owner or operator—

(I) receives data and information under clause (i); and

(II) has not, since the date of the test that developed the data, notified the affected households—

(aa) with respect to the concentration of lead in the drinking water of the affected households; and

(bb) that the concentration of lead in the drinking water of the affected households exceeds the lead action level under section 141.80(c) of title 40, Code of Federal Regulations (or a prescribed level of lead that the Administrator establishes for public education or notification in a successor regulation promulgated pursuant to section 1412).

(iii) Consultation.—

(I) Deadline.—If the owner or operator of the public water system does not disseminate to the affected households the information described in subparagraph (C) as required under clause (ii) within the time period established by the Administrator, not later than 24 hours after the Administrator becomes aware of the failure by the owner or operator of the public water system to disseminate the information, the Administrator shall consult, within a period not to exceed 24 hours, with the applicable Governor to develop a plan, in accordance with the strategic plan, to disseminate the information to the affected households not later than 24 hours after the end of the consultation period.

(II) Delegation.—The Administrator may only delegate the duty to consult under subclause (I) to an employee of the Agency who, as of the date of the delegation, works in the Office of Water at the headquarters of the Agency.

(iv) Dissemination by Administrator.—The Administrator shall, as soon as practicable, disseminate to affected households the information described in subparagraph (C) if—

(I) the owner or operator of the public water system does not disseminate the information to the affected households within the time period determined by the Administrator, as required by clause (ii); and

(II) (aa) the Administrator and the applicable Governor do not agree on a plan described in clause (iii)(I) during the consultation period under that clause; or

(bb) the applicable Governor does not disseminate the information within 24 hours after the end of the consultation period.

(C) Information required.—The information described in this subparagraph includes—

(i) a clear explanation of the potential adverse effects on human health of drinking water that contains a concentration of lead that exceeds the lead action level under section 141.80(c) of title 40, Code of Federal Regulations (or a prescribed level of lead that the Administrator establishes for public education or notification in a successor regulation promulgated pursuant to section 1412);

(ii) the steps that the owner or operator of the public water system is taking to mitigate the concentration of lead; and

(iii) the necessity of seeking alternative water supplies until the date on which the concentration of lead is mitigated.

(6) Privacy.—Any notice to the public or an affected household under this subsection shall protect the privacy of individual customer information.".

(d) Notice of noncompliance with secondary drinking water regulations

Whenever, on the basis of information available to him, the Administrator finds that within a reasonable time after national secondary drinking water regulations have been promulgated, one or more public water systems in a State do not comply with such secondary regulations, and that such noncompliance appears to result from a failure of such State to take reasonable action to assure that public water systems throughout such State meet such secondary regulations, he shall so notify the State.

(e) State authority to adopt or enforce laws or regulations respecting drinking water regulations or public water systems unaffected

Nothing in this subchapter shall diminish any authority of a State or political subdivision to adopt or enforce any law or regulation respecting drinking water regulations or public water systems, but no such law or regulation shall relieve any person of any requirement otherwise applicable under this subchapter.

(f) Notice and public hearing; availability of recommendations transmitted to State and public water system

If the Administrator makes a finding of noncompliance (described in subparagraph (A) or (B) of subsection (a)(1) of this section) with respect to a public water system in a State which has primary enforcement responsibility, the Administrator may, for the purpose of assisting that State in carrying out such responsibility and upon the petition of such State or public water system or persons served by such system, hold, after appropriate notice, public hearings for the purpose of gathering information from technical or other experts, Federal, State, or other public officials, representatives of such public water system, persons served by such system, and other interested persons on—

(1) the ways in which such system can within the earliest feasible time be brought into compliance with the regulation or requirement with respect to which such finding was made, and

(2) the means for the maximum feasible protection of the public health during any period in which such system is not in compliance with a national primary drinking water regulation or requirement applicable to a variance or exemption.

On the basis of such hearings the Administrator shall issue recommendations which shall be sent to such State and public water system and shall be made available to the public and communications media.

(g) Administrative order requiring compliance; notice and hearing; civil penalty; civil actions

(1) In any case in which the Administrator is authorized to bring a civil action under this section or under section 300j–4 of this title with respect to any applicable requirement, the Administrator also may issue an order to require compliance with such applicable requirement.

(2) An order issued under this subsection shall not take effect, in the case of a State having primary enforcement responsibility for public water systems in that State, until after the Administrator has provided the State with an opportunity to confer with the Administrator regarding the order. A copy of any order issued under this subsection shall be sent to the appropriate State agency of the State involved if the State has primary enforcement responsibility for public water systems in that State. Any order issued under this subsection shall state with reasonable specificity the nature of the violation. In any case in which an order under this subsection is issued to a corporation, a copy of such order shall be issued to appropriate corporate officers.

(3) **(A)** Any person who violates, or fails or refuses to comply with, an order under this subsection shall be liable to the United States for a civil penalty of not more than $25,000 per day of violation.

(B) In a case in which a civil penalty sought by the Administrator under this paragraph does not exceed $5,000, the penalty shall be assessed by the Administrator after notice and opportunity for a public hearing (unless the person against whom the penalty is assessed requests a hearing on the record in accordance with section 554 of Title 5). In a case in which a civil penalty sought by the Administrator under this paragraph exceeds $5,000, but does not exceed $25,000, the penalty shall be assessed by the Administrator after notice and opportunity for a hearing on the record in accordance with section 554 of Title 5.

(C) Whenever any civil penalty sought by the Administrator under this subsection for a violation of an applicable requirement exceeds $25,000, the penalty shall be assessed by a civil action brought by the Administrator in the appropriate United States district court (as determined under the provisions of Title 28).

(D) If any person fails to pay an assessment of a civil penalty after it has become a final and unappealable order, or after the appropriate court of appeals has entered final judgment in favor of the Administrator, the Attorney General shall recover the amount for which such person is liable in any appropriate district court of the United States. In any such action, the validity and appropriateness of the final order imposing the civil penalty shall not be subject to review.

(h) Consolidation incentive

(1) In general

An owner or operator of a public water system may submit to the State in which the system is located (if the State has primary enforcement responsibility under section 300g–2 of this title) or to the Administrator (if the State does not have primary enforcement responsibility) a plan (including specific measures and schedules) for—

(A) the physical consolidation of the system with 1 or more other systems;

(B) the consolidation of significant management and administrative functions of the system with 1 or more other systems;

(C) the transfer of ownership of the system that may reasonably be expected to improve drinking water quality; or

(D) entering into a contractual agreement for significant management or administrative functions of the system to correct violations identified in the plan.

(2) Consequences of approval

If the state or the administrator approves a plan pursuant to paragraph (1), no enforcement action shall be taken pursuant to this part with respect to a specific violation identified in the approved plan prior to the date that is the earlier of the date on which consolidation is completed according to the plan or the date that is 2 years after the plan is approved.

(3) Authority for mandatory assessment.—

(A) Authority.—A State with primary enforcement responsibility or the Administrator (if the State does not have primary enforcement responsibility) may require the owner or operator of a public water system to assess options for consolidation, or transfer of ownership of the system, as described in paragraph (1), or other actions expected to achieve compliance with national primary drinking water regulations described in clause (i)(I), if—

(i) the public water system—

(I) has repeatedly violated one or more national primary drinking water regulations and such repeated violations are likely to adversely affect human health; and

(II) (aa) is unable or unwilling to take feasible and affordable actions, as determined by the State with primary enforcement responsibility or the Administrator (if the State does not have primary enforcement responsibility), that will result in the public water system complying with the national primary drinking water regulations described in subclause (I), including accessing technical assistance and financial assistance through the State loan fund pursuant to section 1452; or

(bb) has already undertaken actions described in item (aa) without achieving compliance;

(ii) such consolidation, transfer, or other action is feasible; and

(iii) such consolidation, transfer, or other action could result in greater compliance with national primary drinking water regulations.

(B) Tailoring of assessments.—Requirements for any assessment to be conducted pursuant to subparagraph (A) shall be tailored with respect to the size, type, and characteristics, of the public water system to be assessed.

(C) Approved entities.—An assessment conducted pursuant to subparagraph (A) may be conducted by an entity approved by the State requiring such assessment (or the Administrator, if the State does not have primary enforcement responsibility), which may include such State (or the Administrator, as applicable), the public water system, or a third party.

(D) Burden of assessments.—It is the sense of Congress that any assessment required pursuant to subparagraph (A) should not be overly burdensome on the public water system that is assessed.

(4) Financial assistance.—Notwithstanding section 1452(a)(3), a public water system undertaking consolidation or transfer of ownership or other actions pursuant to an assessment completed under paragraph (3) may receive a loan described in section 1452(a)(2)(A) to carry out such consolidation, transfer, or other action.

(5) Protection of nonresponsible system.—

(A) Identification of liabilities.—

(i) In general.—An owner or operator of a public water system that submits a plan pursuant to paragraph (1) based on an assessment conducted with respect to such public water system under paragraph (3) shall identify as part of such plan—

(I) any potential and existing liability for penalties and damages arising from each specific violation identified in the plan of which the owner or operator is aware; and

(II) any funds or other assets that are available to satisfy such liability, as of the date of submission of such plan, to the public water system that committed such violation.

(ii) Inclusion.—In carrying out clause (i), the owner or operator shall take reasonable steps to ensure that all potential and existing liabilities for penalties and damages arising from each specific violation identified in the plan are identified.

(B) Reservation of funds.—A public water system that, consistent with the findings of an assessment conducted pursuant to paragraph (3), has completed the actions under a plan submitted and approved pursuant to this subsection shall not be liable under this title for a violation of this title identified in the plan, except to the extent to which funds or other assets are identified pursuant to subparagraph (A)(i)(II) as available to satisfy such liability.

(6) Regulations.—Not later than 2 years after the date of enactment of America's Water Infrastructure Act of 2018, the Administrator shall promulgate regulations to implement paragraphs (3), (4), and (5).

(i) "Applicable requirement" defined

In this section, the term "applicable requirement" means—

(1) a requirement of section 300g–1, 300g–3, 300g–4, 300g–5, 300g–6, 300i–2, 300j, or 300j–4 of this title;

(2) a regulation promulgated pursuant to a section referred to in paragraph (1);

(3) a schedule or requirement imposed pursuant to a section referred to in paragraph (1); and

(4) a requirement of, or permit issued under, an applicable State program for which the Administrator has made a determination that the requirements of section 300g–2 of this title have been satisfied, or an applicable State program approved pursuant to this part.

(j) Improved accuracy and availability of compliance monitoring data.—

(1) Strategic plan.—Not later than 1 year after the date of enactment of this subsection, the Administrator, in coordination with States (including States without primary enforcement responsibility under section 1413), public water systems, and other interested stakeholders, shall develop and provide to Congress a strategic plan for improving the accuracy and availability of monitoring data collected to demonstrate compliance with national primary drinking water regulations and submitted—

(A) by public water systems to States; or

(B) by States to the Administrator.

(2) Evaluation.—In developing the strategic plan under paragraph (1), the Administrator shall evaluate any challenges faced—

(A) in ensuring the accuracy and integrity of submitted data described in paragraph (1);

(B) by States and public water systems in implementing an electronic system for submitting such data, including the technical and economic feasibility of implementing such a system; and

(C) by users of such electronic systems in being able to access such data.

(3) Findings and recommendations.—The Administrator shall include in the strategic plan provided to Congress under paragraph (1)—

(A) a summary of the findings of the evaluation under paragraph (2); and

(B) recommendations on practicable, cost-effective methods and means that can be employed to improve the accuracy and availability of submitted data described in paragraph (1).

(4) Consultation.—In developing the strategic plan under paragraph (1), the Administrator may, as appropriate, consult with States or other Federal agencies that have experience using practicable methods and means to improve the accuracy and availability of submitted data described in such paragraph.

(July 1, 1944, c. 373, Title XIV, § 1414, as added by Pub. L. No. 93–523, § 2(a), 88 Stat. 1666 (Dec. 16, 1974); and amended by Pub. L. No. 95–190, § 12(b), 91 Stat. 1398 (Nov. 16, 1977); Pub. L. No. 99–339, Title I, §§ 102, 103, 100 Stat. 647, 648 (June 19, 1986); Pub. L. No. 104–182, Title I, §§ 113(a), 114(a), 110 Stat. 1634, 1636 (Aug. 6, 1996); Pub. L. No. 107–188, Title IV, § 403(1), 116 Stat. 687 (June 12, 2002); Pub. L. No. 114–322. § 2106(a), 130 Stat. 1722–26 (Dec. 16, 2016); Pub. L. No. 115–270, §§ 2008–2010(a), 2011 132 Stat. 3765, 3846–3848, 3849 (Oct. 23, 2018).)

HISTORICAL AND STATUTORY NOTES

Effective and Applicability Provisions

1996 Acts. Amendment by Pub. L. No. 104–182 effective Aug. 6, 1996, except as otherwise specifically provided, see section 2(b) of Pub. L. No. 104–182, set out as a note under section 300f of this title.

§ 300g–4. Variances

[PHSA § 1415]

(a) Characteristics of raw water sources; specific treatment technique; notice to Administrator, reasons for variance; compliance, enforcement; approval or revision of schedules and revocation of variances; review of variances and schedules; publication in Federal Register, notice and results of review; notice to State; considerations respecting abuse of discretion in granting variances or failing to prescribe schedules; State corrective action; authority of Administrator in a State without primary enforcement responsibility; alternative treatment techniques

Notwithstanding any other provision of this part, variances from national primary drinking water regulations may be granted as follows:

(1) (A) A State which has primary enforcement responsibility for public water systems may grant one or more variances from an applicable national primary drinking water regulation to one or more public water systems within its jurisdiction which, because of characteristics of the raw water sources which are reasonably available to the systems, cannot meet the requirements respecting the maximum contaminant levels of such drinking water regulation. A variance may be issued to a system on condition that the system install the best technology, treatment techniques, or other means, which the Administrator finds are available (taking costs into consideration), and based upon an evaluation satisfactory to the State that indicates that alternative sources of water are not reasonably available to the system. The Administrator shall propose and promulgate his finding of the best available technology, treatment techniques or other means available for each contaminant for purposes of this subsection at the time he proposes and promulgates a maximum contaminant level for each such contaminant. The Administrator's finding of best available technology, treatment techniques or other means for purposes of this subsection may vary depending on the number of persons served by the system or for other physical conditions related to engineering feasibility and costs of compliance with maximum contaminant levels as considered appropriate by the Administrator. Before a State may grant a variance under this subparagraph, the State must find that the variance will not result in an unreasonable risk to health. If a State grants a public water system a variance under this subparagraph, the State shall prescribe at the the[1] time the variance is granted, a schedule for—

(i) compliance (including increments of progress) by the public water system with each contaminant level requirement with respect to which the variance was granted, and

(ii) implementation by the public water system of such additional control measures as the State may require for each contaminant, subject to such contaminant level requirement, during the period ending on the date compliance with such requirement is required.

Before a schedule prescribed by a State pursuant to this subparagraph may take effect, the State shall provide notice and opportunity for a public hearing on the schedule. A notice given pursuant to the preceding sentence may cover the prescribing of more than one such schedule and a hearing held pursuant to such notice shall include each of the schedules covered by the notice. A schedule prescribed pursuant to this subparagraph for a public water system granted a variance shall require compliance by the system with each contaminant level requirement with respect to which the variance was granted as expeditiously as practicable (as the State may reasonably determine).

(B) A State which has primary enforcement responsibility for public water systems may grant to one or more public water systems within its jurisdiction one or more variances from any provision of a national primary drinking water regulation which requires the use of a specified treatment technique with respect to a contaminant if the public water system applying for the variance demonstrates to the satisfaction of the State that such treatment technique is not necessary to protect the health of persons because of the nature of the raw water source of such system. A variance granted under this subparagraph shall be conditioned on such monitoring and other requirements as the Administrator may prescribe.

(C) Before a variance proposed to be granted by a State under subparagraph (A) or (B) may take effect, such State shall provide notice and opportunity for public hearing on the proposed variance. A notice given pursuant to the preceding sentence may cover the granting of more than one variance and a hearing held pursuant to such notice shall include each of the variances covered by the notice. The State shall promptly notify the Administrator of all variances granted by it. Such notification shall contain the reason for the variance (and in the case of a variance under subparagraph (A), the basis for the finding required by that subparagraph before the granting of the variance) and documentation of the need for the variance.

(D) Each public water system's variance granted by a State under subparagraph (A) shall be conditioned by the State upon compliance by the public water system with the schedule prescribed by the State pursuant to that subparagraph. The requirements of each schedule prescribed by a State pursuant to that subparagraph shall be enforceable by the State under its laws. Any requirement of a schedule on which a variance granted under that subparagraph is conditioned may be enforced under section 300g–3 of this title as if such requirement was part of a national primary drinking water regulation.

(E) Each schedule prescribed by a State pursuant to subparagraph (A) shall be deemed approved by the Administrator unless the variance for which it was prescribed is revoked by the Administrator under subparagraph (G) or the schedule is revised by the Administrator under such subparagraph.

(F) Not later than 18 months after the effective date of the interim national primary drinking water regulations the Administrator shall complete a comprehensive review of the variances granted under subparagraph (A) (and schedules prescribed pursuant thereto) and under subparagraph (B) by the States during the one-year period beginning on such effective date. The Administrator shall conduct such subsequent reviews of variances and schedules as he deems necessary to carry out the purposes of this subchapter, but each subsequent review shall be completed within each 3-year period following the completion of the first review under this subparagraph. Before conducting any review under this subparagraph, the Administrator shall publish notice of the proposed review in the Federal Register. Such notice shall (i) provide information respecting the location of data and other information respecting the variances to be reviewed (including data and other information concerning new scientific matters bearing on such variances), and (ii) advise of the opportunity to submit comments on the variances reviewed and on the need for continuing them. Upon completion of any such review, the Administrator shall publish in the Federal Register the results of his review together with findings responsive to comments submitted in connection with such review.

(G) **(i)** If the Administrator finds that a State has, in a substantial number of instances, abused its discretion in granting variances under subparagraph (A) or (B) or that in a substantial number of cases the State has failed to prescribe schedules in accordance with subparagraph (A), the Administrator shall notify the State of his findings. In determining if a State has abused its discretion in granting variances in a substantial number of instances, the Administrator shall consider the number of persons who are affected by the variances and if the requirements applicable to the granting of the variances were complied with. A notice under this clause shall—

(I) identify each public water system with respect to which the finding was made,

(II) specify the reasons for the finding, and

(III) as appropriate, propose revocations of specific variances or propose revised schedules or other requirements for specific public water systems granted variances, or both.

(ii) The Administrator shall provide reasonable notice and public hearing on the provisions of each notice given pursuant to clause (i) of this subparagraph. After a hearing on a notice pursuant to such clause, the Administrator shall (I) rescind the finding for which the notice was given and promptly notify the State of such rescission, or (II) promulgate (with such modifications as he deems appropriate) such variance revocations and revised schedules or other requirements proposed in such notice as he deems appropriate. Not later than 180 days after the date a notice is given pursuant to clause (i) of this subparagraph, the Administrator shall complete the hearing on the notice and take the action required by the preceding sentence.

(iii) If a State is notified under clause (i) of this subparagraph of a finding of the Administrator made with respect to a variance granted a public water system within that State or to a schedule or other requirement for a variance and if, before a revocation of such variance or a revision of such schedule or other requirement promulgated by the Administrator takes effect, the State takes corrective action with respect to such variance or schedule or other requirement which the Administrator determines makes his finding inapplicable to such variance or schedule or other requirement, the Administrator shall rescind the application of his finding to that variance or schedule or other requirement. No variance revocation or revised schedule or other requirement may take effect before the expiration of 90 days following the date of the notice in which the revocation or revised schedule or other requirement was proposed.

(2) If a State does not have primary enforcement responsibility for public water systems, the Administrator shall have the same authority to grant variances in such State as the State would have under paragraph (1) if it had primary enforcement responsibility.

(3) The Administrator may grant a variance from any treatment technique requirement of a national primary drinking water regulation upon a showing by any person that an alternative treatment technique not included in such requirement is at least as efficient in lowering the level of the contaminant with respect to which such requirement was prescribed. A variance under this paragraph shall be conditioned on the use of the alternative treatment technique which is the basis of the variance.

(b) Enforcement of schedule or other requirement

Any schedule or other requirement on which a variance granted under paragraph (1)(B) or (2) of subsection (a) of this section is conditioned may be enforced under section 300g–3 of this title as if such schedule or other requirement was part of a national primary drinking water regulation.

(c) Applications for variances; regulations: reasonable time for acting

If an application for a variance under subsection (a) of this section is made, the State receiving the application or the Administrator, as the case may be, shall act upon such application within a reasonable period (as determined under regulations prescribed by the Administrator) after the date of its submission.

(d) "Treatment technique requirement" defined

For purposes of this section, the term "treatment technique requirement" means a requirement in a national primary drinking water regulation which specifies for a contaminant (in accordance with section 300f(1)(C)(ii) of this title) each treatment technique known to the Administrator which leads to a reduction in the level of such contaminant sufficient to satisfy the requirements of section 300g–1(b) of this title.

(e) Small system variances

(1) In general

A State exercising primary enforcement responsibility for public water systems under section 300g–2 of this title (or the Administrator in nonprimacy States) may grant a variance under this subsection for compliance with a requirement specifying a maximum contaminant level or treatment technique contained in a national primary drinking water regulation to—

(A) public water systems serving 3,300 or fewer persons; and

(B) with the approval of the Administrator pursuant to paragraph (9), public water systems serving more than 3,300 persons but fewer than 10,000 persons,

if the variance meets each requirement of this subsection.

(2) Availability of variances

A public water system may receive a variance pursuant to paragraph (1), if—

(A) the Administrator has identified a variance technology under section 300g–1(b)(15) of this title that is applicable to the size and source water quality conditions of the public water system;

(B) the public water system installs, operates, and maintains, in accordance with guidance or regulations issued by the Administrator, such treatment technology, treatment technique, or other means; and

(C) the State in which the system is located determines that the conditions of paragraph (3) are met.

(3) Conditions for granting variances

A variance under this subsection shall be available only to a system—

(A) that cannot afford to comply, in accordance with affordability criteria established by the Administrator (or the State in the case of a State that has primary enforcement responsibility under section 300g–2 of this title), with a national primary drinking water regulation, including compliance through—

(i) treatment;

(ii) alternative source of water supply; or

(iii) restructuring or consolidation (unless the Administrator (or the State in the case of a State that has primary enforcement responsibility under section 300g–2 of this title) makes a written determination that restructuring or consolidation is not practicable); and

(B) for which the Administrator (or the State in the case of a State that has primary enforcement responsibility under section 300g–2 of this title) determines that the terms of the variance ensure adequate protection of human health, considering the quality of the source water for the system and the removal efficiencies and expected useful life of the treatment technology required by the variance.

(4) Compliance schedules

A variance granted under this subsection shall require compliance with the conditions of the variance not later than 3 years after the date on which the variance is granted, except that the Administrator (or the State in the case of a State that has primary enforcement responsibility under section 300g–2 of this title) may allow up to 2 additional years to comply with a variance technology, secure an alternative source of water, restructure or consolidate if the Administrator (or the State) determines that additional time is necessary for capital improvements, or to allow for financial assistance provided pursuant to section 300j–12 of this title or any other Federal or State program.

(5) Duration of variances

The Administrator (or the State in the case of a State that has primary enforcement responsibility under section 300g–2 of this title) shall review each variance granted under this subsection not less often than every 5 years after the compliance date established in the variance to determine whether the system remains eligible for the variance and is conforming to each condition of the variance.

(6) Ineligibility for variances

A variance shall not be available under this subsection for—

(A) any maximum contaminant level or treatment technique for a contaminant with respect to which a national primary drinking water regulation was promulgated prior to January 1, 1986; or

(B) a national primary drinking water regulation for a microbial contaminant (including a bacterium, virus, or other organism) or an indicator or treatment technique for a microbial contaminant.

(7) Regulations and guidance

(A) In general

Not later than 2 years after August 6, 1996, and in consultation with the States, the Administrator shall promulgate regulations for variances to be granted under this subsection. The regulations shall, at a minimum, specify—

(i) procedures to be used by the Administrator or a State to grant or deny variances, including requirements for notifying the Administrator and consumers of the public water system that a variance is proposed to be granted (including information regarding the contaminant and variance) and requirements for a public hearing on the variance before the variance is granted;

(ii) requirements for the installation and proper operation of variance technology that is identified (pursuant to section 300g–1(b)(15) of this title) for small systems and the financial and technical capability to operate the treatment system, including operator training and certification;

(iii) eligibility criteria for a variance for each national primary drinking water regulation, including requirements for the quality of the source water (pursuant to section 300g–1(b)(15)(A) of this title); and

(iv) information requirements for variance applications.

(B) Affordability criteria

Not later than 18 months after August 6, 1996, the Administrator, in consultation with the States and the Rural Utilities Service of the Department of Agriculture, shall publish information to assist the States in developing affordability criteria. The affordability criteria shall be reviewed by the States not less often than every 5 years to determine if changes are needed to the criteria.

(8) Review by the Administrator

(A) In general

The Administrator shall periodically review the program of each State that has primary enforcement responsibility for public water systems under section 300g–2 of this title with respect to variances to determine whether the variances granted by the State comply with the requirements of this subsection. With respect to affordability, the determination of the Administrator shall be limited to whether the variances granted by the State comply with the affordability criteria developed by the State.

(B) Notice and publication

If the Administrator determines that variances granted by a State are not in compliance with affordability criteria developed by the State and the requirements of this subsection, the Administrator shall notify the State in writing of the deficiencies and make public the determination.

(9) Approval of variances

A State proposing to grant a variance under this subsection to a public water system serving more than 3,300 and fewer than 10,000 persons shall submit the variance to the Administrator for review and approval prior to the issuance of the variance. The Administrator shall approve the variance if it meets each of the requirements of this subsection. The Administrator shall approve or disapprove the variance within 90 days. If the Administrator disapproves a variance under this paragraph, the Administrator shall notify the State in writing of the reasons for disapproval and the variance may be resubmitted with modifications to address the objections stated by the Administrator.

(10) Objections to variances

(A) By the Administrator

The Administrator may review and object to any variance proposed to be granted by a State, if the objection is communicated to the State not later than 90 days after the State proposes to grant the variance. If the Administrator objects to the granting of a variance, the Administrator shall notify the State in writing of each basis for the objection and propose a modification to the variance to resolve the concerns of the Administrator. The State shall make the recommended modification or respond in writing to each objection. If the State issues the variance without resolving the concerns of the Administrator, the Administrator may overturn the State decision to grant the variance if the Administrator determines that the State decision does not comply with this subsection.

(B) Petition by consumers

Not later than 30 days after a State exercising primary enforcement responsibility for public water systems under section 300g–2 of this title proposes to grant a variance for a public water system, any person served by the system may petition the Administrator to object to the granting of a variance. The Administrator shall respond to the petition and determine whether to object to the variance under subparagraph (A) not later than 60 days after the receipt of the petition.

(C) Timing

No variance shall be granted by a State until the later of the following:

(i) 90 days after the State proposes to grant a variance.

(ii) If the Administrator objects to the variance, the date on which the State makes the recommended modifications or responds in writing to each objection.

(July 1, 1944, c. 373, Title XIV, § 1415, as added by Pub. L. No. 93–523, § 2(a), 88 Stat. 1669 (Dec. 16, 1974); and amended by Pub. L. No. 99–339, Title I, § 104, 100 Stat. 649 (June 19, 1986); Pub. L. No. 104–182, Title I, §§ 102(c)(1), 115, 116, Title V, § 501(a)(3), 110 Stat. 1621, 1641, 1691 (Aug. 6, 1996).)

[1] So in original.

HISTORICAL AND STATUTORY NOTES

Effective and Applicability Provisions

1996 Acts. Amendment by Pub. L. No. 104–182 effective Aug. 6, 1996, except as otherwise specifically provided, see section 2(b) of Pub. L. No. 104–182, set out as a note under section 300f of this title.

§ 300g–5. Exemptions

[PHSA § 1416]

(a) Requisite findings

A State which has primary enforcement responsibility may exempt any public water system within the State's jurisdiction from any requirement respecting a maximum contaminant level or any treatment technique requirement, or from both, of an applicable national primary drinking water regulation upon a finding that—

(1) due to compelling factors (which may include economic factors, including qualification of the public water system as a system serving a disadvantaged community pursuant to section 300j–12(d) of this title), the public water system is unable to comply with such contaminant level or treatment technique requirement, or to implement measures to develop an alternative source of water supply,

(2) the public water system was in operation on the effective date of such contaminant level or treatment technique requirement, or, for a system that was not in operation by that date, only if no reasonable alternative source of drinking water is available to such new system,

(3) the granting of the exemption will not result in an unreasonable risk to health;[1] and

(4) management or restructuring changes (or both) cannot reasonably be made that will result in compliance with this subchapter or, if compliance cannot be achieved, improve the quality of the drinking water.

(b) Compliance schedule and implementation of control measures; notice and hearing; dates for compliance with schedule; compliance, enforcement; approval or revision of schedules and revocation of exemptions

(1) If a State grants a public water system an exemption under subsection (a) of this section, the State shall prescribe, at the time the exemption is granted, a schedule for—

(A) compliance (including increments of progress or measures to develop an alternative source of water supply) by the public water system with each contaminant level requirement or treatment technique requirement with respect to which the exemption was granted, and

(B) implementation by the public water system of such control measures as the State may require for each contaminant, subject to such contaminant level requirement or treatment technique requirement, during the period ending on the date compliance with such requirement is required.

Before a schedule prescribed by a State pursuant to this subsection may take effect, the State shall provide notice and opportunity for a public hearing on the schedule. A notice given pursuant to the preceding sentence may cover the prescribing of more than one such schedule and a hearing held pursuant to such notice shall include each of the schedules covered by the notice.

(2) **(A)** A schedule prescribed pursuant to this subsection for a public water system granted an exemption under subsection (a) of this section shall require compliance by the system with each contaminant level and treatment technique requirement with respect to which the exemption was granted as expeditiously as practicable (as the State may reasonably determine) but not later than 3 years after the otherwise applicable compliance date established in section 300g–1(b)(10) of this title.

(B) No exemption shall be granted unless the public water system establishes that—

(i) the system cannot meet the standard without capital improvements which cannot be completed prior to the date established pursuant to section 300g–1(b)(10) of this title;

(ii) in the case of a system which needs financial assistance for the necessary improvements, the system has entered into an agreement to obtain such financial assistance or assistance pursuant to section 300j–12 of this title, or any other Federal or State program is reasonably likely to be available within the period of the exemption; or

(iii) the system has entered into an enforceable agreement to become a part of a regional public water system; and

the system is taking all practicable steps to meet the standard.

(C) In the case of a system which does not serve more than a population of 3,300 and which needs financial assistance for the necessary improvements, an exemption granted under clause (i) or (ii) of subparagraph (B) may be renewed for one or more additional 2-year periods, but not to exceed a total of 6 years, if the system establishes that it is taking all practicable steps to meet the requirements of subparagraph (B).

(D) Limitation

A public water system may not receive an exemption under this section if the system was granted a variance under section 300g–4(e) of this title.

(3) Each public water system's exemption granted by a State under subsection (a) of this section shall be conditioned by the State upon compliance by the public water system with the schedule prescribed by the State pursuant to this subsection. The requirements of each schedule prescribed by a State pursuant to this subsection shall be enforceable by the State under its laws. Any requirement of a schedule on which an exemption granted under this section is conditioned may be enforced under section 300g–3 of this title as if such requirement was part of a national primary drinking water regulation.

(4) Each schedule prescribed by a State pursuant to this subsection shall be deemed approved by the Administrator unless the exemption for which it was prescribed is revoked by the Administrator under subsection (d)(2) of this section or the schedule is revised by the Administrator under such subsection.

(c) Notice to Administrator; reasons for exemption

Each State which grants an exemption under subsection (a) of this section shall promptly notify the Administrator of the granting of such exemption. Such notification shall contain the reasons for the exemption (including the basis for the finding required by subsection (a)(3) of this section before the exemption may be granted) and document the need for the exemption.

(d) Review of exemptions and schedules; publication in Federal Register, notice and results of review; notice to State; considerations respecting abuse of discretion in granting exemptions or failing to prescribe schedules; State corrective action

(1) Not later than 18 months after the effective date of the interim national primary drinking water regulations the Administrator shall complete a comprehensive review of the exemptions granted (and schedules prescribed pursuant thereto) by the States during the one-year period beginning on such effective date. The Administrator shall conduct such subsequent reviews of exemptions and schedules as he deems necessary to carry out the purposes of this subchapter, but each subsequent review shall be completed within each 3-year period following the completion of the first review under this subparagraph. Before conducting any review under this subparagraph, the Administrator shall publish notice of the proposed review in the Federal Register. Such notice shall (A) provide information respecting the location of data and other information respecting the exemptions to be reviewed (including data and other information concerning new scientific matters bearing on such exemptions), and (B) advise of the opportunity to submit comments on the exemptions reviewed and on the need for continuing them. Upon completion of any such review, the Administrator shall publish in the Federal Register the results of his review, together with findings responsive to comments submitted in connection with such review.

(2) (A) If the Administrator finds that a State has, in a substantial number of instances, abused its discretion in granting exemptions under subsection (a) of this section or failed to prescribe schedules in accordance with subsection (b) of this section, the Administrator shall notify the State of his findings. In determining if a State has abused its discretion in granting exemptions in a substantial number of instances, the Administrator shall consider the number of persons who are affected by the exemptions and if the requirements applicable to the granting of the exemptions were complied with. A notice under this subparagraph shall—

(i) identify each exempt public water system with respect to which the finding was made,

(ii) specify the reasons for the finding, and

(iii) as appropriate, propose revocations of specific exemptions or propose revised schedules for specific exempt public water systems, or both.

(B) The Administrator shall provide reasonable notice and public hearing on the provisions of each notice given pursuant to subparagraph (A). After a hearing on notice pursuant to subparagraph (A), the Administrator shall (i) rescind the finding for which the notice was given and promptly notify the State of such rescission, or (ii) promulgate (with such modifications as he deems appropriate) such exemption revocations and revised schedules proposed in such notice as he deems appropriate. Not later than 180 days after the date a notice is given pursuant to subparagraph (A), the Administrator shall complete the hearing on the notice and take the action required by the preceding sentence.

(C) If a State is notified under subparagraph (A) of a finding of the Administrator made with respect to an exemption granted a public water system within that State or to a schedule prescribed pursuant to such an exemption and if before a revocation of such exemption or a revision of such schedule promulgated by the Administrator takes effect the State takes corrective action with respect to such exemption or schedule which the Administrator determines makes his finding inapplicable to such exemption or schedule, the Administrator shall rescind the application of his finding to that exemption or schedule. No exemption revocation or revised schedule may take effect before the expiration of 90 days following the date of the notice in which the revocation or revised schedule was proposed.

(e) "Treatment technique requirement" defined

For purposes of this section, the term "treatment technique requirement" means a requirement in a national primary drinking water regulation which specifies for a contaminant (in accordance with section 300f(1)(C)(ii) of this title) each treatment technique known to the Administrator which leads to a reduction in the level of such contaminant sufficient to satisfy the requirements of section 300g–1(b) of this title.

(f) Authority of Administrator in a State without primary enforcement responsibility

If a State does not have primary enforcement responsibility for public water systems, the Administrator shall have the same authority to exempt public water systems in such State from maximum contaminant level requirements and treatment technique requirements under the same conditions and in the same manner as the State would be authorized to grant exemptions under this section if it had primary enforcement responsibility.

(g) Applications for exemptions; regulations; reasonable time for acting

If an application for an exemption under this section is made, the State receiving the application or the Administrator, as the case may be, shall act upon such application within a reasonable period (as determined under regulations prescribed by the Administrator) after the date of its submission.

(July 1, 1944, c. 373, Title XIV, § 1416, as added by Pub. L. No. 93–523, § 2(a), 88 Stat. 1672 (Dec. 16, 1974); and amended by Pub. L. No. 95–190, § 10(a), 91 Stat. 1398 (Nov. 16, 1977); Pub. L. No. 96–502, §§ 1, 4(b), 94 Stat. 2737, 2738 (Dec. 5, 1980); Pub. L. No. 99–339, Title I, §§ 101(c)(4), 105, 100 Stat. 646, 649 (June 19, 1986); Pub. L. No. 104–182, Title I, § 117(a), 110 Stat. 1644 (Aug. 6, 1996).)

[1] So in original. Semicolon probably should be a comma.

HISTORICAL AND STATUTORY NOTES

Effective and Applicability Provisions

1996 Acts. Amendment by Pub. L. No. 104–182 effective Aug. 6, 1996, except as otherwise specifically provided, see section 2(b) of Pub. L. No. 104–182, set out as a note under section 300f of this title.

§ 300g–6. Prohibition on use of lead pipes, solder, and flux

[PHSA § 1417]

(a) In general

(1) Prohibitions

(A) In general

No person may use any pipe, any pipe or plumbing fitting or fixture, any solder, or any flux, after June 19, 1986, in the installation or repair of—

(i) any public water system; or

(ii) any plumbing in a residential or nonresidential facility providing water for human consumption,

that is not lead free (within the meaning of subsection (d) of this section).

(B) Leaded joints

Subparagraph (A) shall not apply to leaded joints necessary for the repair of cast iron pipes.

(2) Public notice requirements

(A) In general

Each owner or operator of a public water system shall identify and provide notice to persons that may be affected by lead contamination of their drinking water where such contamination results from either or both of the following:

(i) The lead content in the construction materials of the public water distribution system.

(ii) Corrosivity of the water supply sufficient to cause leaching of lead.

The notice shall be provided in such manner and form as may be reasonably required by the Administrator. Notice under this paragraph shall be provided notwithstanding the absence of a violation of any national drinking water standard.

(B) Contents of notice

Notice under this paragraph shall provide a clear and readily understandable explanation of—

(i) the potential sources of lead in the drinking water,

(ii) potential adverse health effects,

(iii) reasonably available methods of mitigating known or potential lead content in drinking water,

(iv) any steps the system is taking to mitigate lead content in drinking water, and

(v) the necessity for seeking alternative water supplies, if any.

(3) Unlawful acts

Effective 2 years after August 6, 1996, it shall be unlawful—

(A) for any person to introduce into commerce any pipe, or any pipe or plumbing fitting or fixture, that is not lead free, except for a pipe that is used in manufacturing or industrial processing;

(B) for any person engaged in the business of selling plumbing supplies, except manufacturers, to sell solder or flux that is not lead free; or

(C) for any person to introduce into commerce any solder or flux that is not lead free unless the solder or flux bears a prominent label stating that it is illegal to use the solder or flux in the installation or repair of any plumbing providing water for human consumption.

(4) Exemptions

The prohibitions in paragraphs (1) and (3) shall not apply to—

(A) pipes, pipe fittings, plumbing fittings, or fixtures, including backflow preventers, that are used exclusively for nonpotable services such as manufacturing, industrial processing, irrigation, outdoor watering, or any other uses where the water is not anticipated to be used for human consumption; or

(B) toilets, bidets, urinals, fill valves, flushometer valves, tub fillers, shower valves, fire hydrants, service saddles, or water distribution main gate valves that are 2 inches in diameter or larger.

(b) State enforcement

(1) Enforcement of prohibition

The requirements of subsection (a)(1) of this section shall be enforced in all States effective 24 months after June 19, 1986. States shall enforce such requirements through State or local plumbing codes, or such other means of enforcement as the State may determine to be appropriate.

(2) Enforcement of public notice requirements

The requirements of subsection (a)(2) of this section shall apply in all States effective 24 months after June 19, 1986.

(c) Penalties

If the Administrator determines that a State is not enforcing the requirements of subsection (a) of this section as required pursuant to subsection (b) of this section, the Administrator may withhold up to 5 percent of Federal funds available to that State for State program grants under section 300j–2(a) of this title.

(d) Definition of lead free

(1) In general

For the purposes of this section, the term "lead free" means—

(A) not containing more than 0.2 percent lead when used with respect to solder and flux; and

(B) not more than a weighted average of 0.25 percent lead when used with respect to the wetted surfaces of pipes, pipe fittings, plumbing fittings, and fixtures.

(2) Calculation

The weighted average lead content of a pipe, pipe fitting, plumbing fitting, or fixture shall be calculated by using the following formula: For each wetted component, the percentage of lead in the component shall be multiplied by the ratio of the wetted surface area of that component to the total wetted surface area of the entire product to arrive at the weighted percentage of lead of the component. The weighted percentage of lead of each wetted component shall be added together, and the sum of these weighted percentages shall constitute the weighted average lead content of the product. The lead content of the material used to produce wetted components shall be used to determine compliance with paragraph (1)(B). For lead content of materials that are provided as a range, the maximum content of the range shall be used.

(e) Plumbing fittings and fixtures

(1) In general

The Administrator shall provide accurate and timely technical information and assistance to qualified third-party certifiers in the development of voluntary standards and testing protocols for the leaching of lead from new plumbing fittings and fixtures that are intended by the manufacturer to dispense water for human ingestion.

(2) Standards

(A) In general

If a voluntary standard for the leaching of lead is not established by the date that is 1 year after August 6, 1996, the Administrator shall, not later than 2 years after August 6, 1996, promulgate regulations setting a health-effects-based performance standard establishing maximum leaching levels from new plumbing fittings and fixtures that are intended by the manufacturer to dispense water for human ingestion. The standard shall become effective on the date that is 5 years after the date of promulgation of the standard.

(B) Alternative requirement

If regulations are required to be promulgated under subparagraph (A) and have not been promulgated by the date that is 5 years after August 6, 1996, no person may import, manufacture, process, or distribute in commerce a new plumbing fitting or fixture, intended by the manufacturer to dispense water for human ingestion, that contains more than 4 percent lead by dry weight.

(f) Public education.—

(1) In general.—The Administrator shall make information available to the public regarding lead in drinking water, including information regarding—

(A) risks associated with lead in drinking water;

(B) the conditions that contribute to drinking water containing lead in a residence;

(C) steps that States, public water systems, and consumers can take to reduce the risks of lead in drinking water; and

(D) the availability of additional resources that consumers can use to minimize lead exposure, including information on sampling for lead in drinking water.

(2) Vulnerable populations.—In making information available to the public under this subsection, the Administrator shall, subject to the availability of appropriations, carry out targeted outreach strategies that focus on educating groups within the general population that may be at greater risk than the general population of adverse health effects from exposure to lead in drinking water.

(July 1, 1944, c. 373, Title XIV, § 1417, as added by Pub. L. No. 99–339, Title I, § 109(a)(1), 100 Stat. 651 (June 19, 1986); and amended by Pub. L. No. 104–182, Title I, § 118, Title V, § 501(f)(1), 110 Stat. 1645, 1691 (Aug. 6, 1996); Pub. L. No. 111–380, § 2(a), 124 Stat. 4131 (Jan. 4, 2011); Pub. L. No. 113–64, § 2, 127 Stat. 668 (Dec. 20, 2013); Pub. L. No. 114–322, § 2106(b), 130 Stat. 1726 (Dec. 16, 2016).)

HISTORICAL AND STATUTORY NOTES

Effective and Applicability Provisions

2011 Acts. Pub. L. No. 111–380, § 2(b), 124 Stat. 4132 (Jan. 4, 2011), provided that: "The provisions of subsections (a)(4) and (d) of section 1417 of the Safe Drinking Water Act, as added by this section [subsec. (a)(4) and (d) of this section, respectively, as added by subsec. (a) of section 2 of Pub. L. No. 111–380, Jan. 4, 2011, 124 Stat. 4131], apply beginning on the day that is 36 months after the date of the enactment of this Act [Jan. 4, 2011]."

1996 Acts. Amendment by Pub. L. No. 104–182 effective Aug. 6, 1996, except as otherwise specifically provided, see section 2(b) of Pub. L. No. 104–182, set out as a note under section 300f of this title.

Evaluation of Source of Lead in Water Distribution Systems and Alternative Routing Systems

Pub. L. 113–64, § 3, 127 Stat. 668 (Dec. 20, 2013), provided that:

"The Administrator of the Environmental Protection Agency shall—

"(1) consult with and seek the advice of the National Drinking Water Advisory Council on potential changes to the regulations pertaining to lead under the Safe Drinking Water Act (42 U.S.C. 300f et seq.); and

"(2) request the Council to consider sources of lead throughout drinking water distribution systems, including through components used to reroute drinking water during distribution system repairs."

Ban on Lead Water Pipes, Solder and Flux in Department of Veterans Affairs and HUD Insured or Assisted Property

Section 109(c) of Pub. L. No. 99–339, as amended by Pub. L. No. 102–54, § 13(q)(2), 105 Stat. 279 (June 13, 1991), provided that:

"(1) Prohibition.—The Secretary of Housing and Urban Development and the Secretary of Veterans Affairs may not insure or guarantee a mortgage or furnish assistance with respect to newly constructed residential property which contains a potable water system unless such system uses only lead free pipe, solder, and flux.

"(2) Definition of Lead Free.—For purposes of paragraph (1) the term 'lead free'—

"(A) when used with respect to solders and flux refers to solders and flux containing not more than 0.2 percent lead, and

"(B) when used with respect to pipes and pipe fittings refers to pipes and pipe fittings containing not more than 8.0 percent lead.

"(3) Effective Date.—Paragraph (1) shall become effective 24 months after the enactment of this Act [June 19, 1986]."

Notification to States

Section 109(b) of Pub. L. No. 99–339 provided that: "The Administrator of the Environmental Protection Agency shall notify all States with respect to the requirements of section 1417 of the Public Health Service Act [this section] within 90 days after the enactment of this Act [June 19, 1986]."

§ 300g–7. Monitoring of contaminants

[PHSA § 1418]

(a) Interim monitoring relief authority

(1) In general

A State exercising primary enforcement responsibility for public water systems may modify the monitoring requirements for any regulated or unregulated contaminants for which monitoring is required other than microbial contaminants (or indicators thereof), disinfectants and disinfection byproducts or corrosion byproducts for an interim period to provide that any public water system serving 10,000 persons or fewer shall not be required to conduct additional quarterly monitoring during an interim relief period for such contaminants if—

(A) monitoring, conducted at the beginning of the period for the contaminant concerned and certified to the State by the public water system, fails to detect the presence of the contaminant in the ground or surface water supplying the public water system; and

(B) the State, considering the hydrogeology of the area and other relevant factors, determines in writing that the contaminant is unlikely to be detected by further monitoring during such period.

(2) Termination; timing of monitoring

The interim relief period referred to in paragraph (1) shall terminate when permanent monitoring relief is adopted and approved for such State, or at the end of 36 months after August 6, 1996, whichever comes first. In order to serve as a basis for interim relief, the monitoring conducted at the beginning of the period must occur at the time determined by the State to be the time of the public water system's greatest vulnerability to the contaminant concerned in the relevant ground or surface water, taking into account in the case of pesticides the time of application of the pesticide for the source water area and the travel time for the pesticide to reach such waters and taking into account, in the case of other contaminants, seasonality of precipitation and contaminant travel time.

(b) Permanent monitoring relief authority

(1) In general

Each State exercising primary enforcement responsibility for public water systems under this subchapter and having an approved source water assessment program may adopt, in accordance with guidance published by the Administrator, tailored alternative monitoring requirements for public water systems in such State (as an alternative to the monitoring requirements for chemical contaminants set forth in the applicable national primary drinking water regulations) where the State concludes that (based on data available at the time of adoption concerning susceptibility, use, occurrence, or wellhead protection, or from the State's drinking water source water assessment program) such alternative monitoring would provide assurance that it complies with the Administrator's guidelines. The State program must be adequate to assure compliance with, and enforcement of, applicable national primary drinking water regulations. Alternative monitoring shall not apply to regulated microbiological contaminants (or indicators thereof), disinfectants and disinfection byproducts, or corrosion byproducts. The preceding sentence is not intended to limit other authority of the Administrator under other provisions of this subchapter to grant monitoring flexibility.

(2) Guidelines

(A) In general

The Administrator shall issue, after notice and comment and at the same time as guidelines are issued for source water assessment under section 300j–13 of this title, guidelines for States to follow in proposing alternative monitoring requirements under paragraph (1) for chemical contaminants. The Administrator shall publish such guidelines in the Federal Register. The guidelines shall assure that the public health will be protected from drinking water contamination. The guidelines shall require that a State alternative monitoring program apply on a contaminant-by-contaminant basis and that, to be eligible for such alternative monitoring program, a public water system must show the State that the contaminant is not present in the drinking water supply or, if present, it is reliably and consistently below the maximum contaminant level.

(B) Definition

For purposes of subparagraph (A), the phrase "reliably and consistently below the maximum contaminant level" means that, although contaminants have been detected in a water supply, the State has sufficient knowledge of the contamination source and extent of contamination to predict that the maximum contaminant level will not be exceeded. In determining that a contaminant is reliably and consistently below the maximum contaminant level, States shall consider the quality and completeness of data, the length of time covered and the volatility or stability of monitoring results during that time, and the proximity of such results to the maximum contaminant level. Wide variations in the analytical results, or analytical results close to the maximum contaminant level, shall not be considered to be reliably and consistently below the maximum contaminant level.

(3) Effect of detection of contaminants

The guidelines issued by the Administrator under paragraph (2) shall require that if, after the monitoring program is in effect and operating, a contaminant covered by the alternative monitoring program is detected at levels at or above the maximum contaminant level or is no longer reliably or consistently below the maximum contaminant level, the public water system must either—

(A) demonstrate that the contamination source has been removed or that other action has been taken to eliminate the contamination problem; or

(B) test for the detected contaminant pursuant to the applicable national primary drinking water regulation.

(4) States not exercising primary enforcement responsibility

The Governor of any State not exercising primary enforcement responsibility under section 300g–2 of this title on August 6, 1996, may submit to the Administrator a request that the Administrator modify the monitoring requirements established by the Administrator and applicable to public water systems in that State. After consultation with the Governor, the Administrator shall modify the requirements for public water systems in that State if the request of the Governor is in accordance with each of the requirements of this subsection that apply to alternative monitoring requirements established by States that have primary enforcement responsibility. A decision by the Administrator to approve a request under this clause shall be for a period of 3 years and may subsequently be extended for periods of 5 years.

(c) Treatment as NPDWR

All monitoring relief granted by a State to a public water system for a regulated contaminant under subsection (a) or (b) of this section shall be treated as part of the national primary drinking water regulation for that contaminant.

(d) Other monitoring relief

Nothing in this section shall be construed to affect the authority of the States under applicable national primary drinking water regulations to alter monitoring requirements through waivers or other existing authorities. The Administrator shall periodically review and, as appropriate, revise such authorities.

(July 1, 1944, c. 373, Title XIV, § 1418, as added by Pub. L. No. 104–182, Title I, § 125(b), 110 Stat. 1654 (Aug. 6, 1996).)

HISTORICAL AND STATUTORY NOTES

Effective and Applicability Provisions

1996 Acts. Section effective Aug. 6, 1996, except as otherwise specifically provided, see section 2(b) of Pub. L. No. 104–182, set out as a note under section 300f of this title.

§ 300g–8. Operator certification

[PHSA § 1419]

(a) Guidelines

Not later than 30 months after August 6, 1996, and in cooperation with the States, the Administrator shall publish guidelines in the Federal Register, after notice and opportunity for comment from interested persons, including States and public water systems, specifying minimum standards for certification (and recertification) of the operators of community and nontransient noncommunity public water systems. Such guidelines shall take into account existing State programs, the complexity of the system, and other factors aimed at providing an effective program at reasonable cost to States and public water systems, taking into account the size of the system.

(b) State programs

Beginning 2 years after the date on which the Administrator publishes guidelines under subsection (a) of this section, the Administrator shall withhold 20 percent of the funds a State is otherwise entitled to receive under section 300j–12 of this title unless the State has adopted and is implementing a program for the certification of operators of community and nontransient noncommunity public water systems that meets the requirements of the guidelines published pursuant to subsection (a) of this section or that has been submitted in compliance with subsection (c) of this section and that has not been disapproved.

(c) Existing programs

For any State exercising primary enforcement responsibility for public water systems or any other State which has an operator certification program, the guidelines under subsection (a) of this section shall allow the State to enforce such program in lieu of the guidelines under subsection (a) of this section if the State submits the program to the Administrator within 18 months after the publication of the guidelines unless the Administrator determines (within 9 months after the State submits the program to the Administrator) that such program is not substantially equivalent to such guidelines. In making this determination, an existing State program shall be presumed to be substantially equivalent to the guidelines, notwithstanding program differences, based on the size of systems or the quality of source water, providing the State program meets the overall public health objectives of the guidelines. If disapproved, the program may be resubmitted within 6 months after receipt of notice of disapproval.

(d) Expense reimbursement

(1) In general

The Administrator shall provide reimbursement for the costs of training, including an appropriate per diem for unsalaried operators, and certification for persons operating systems serving 3,300 persons or fewer that are required to undergo training pursuant to this section.

(2) State grants

The reimbursement shall be provided through grants to States with each State receiving an amount sufficient to cover the reasonable costs for training all such operators in the State, as determined by the Administrator, to the extent required by this section. Grants received by a State pursuant to this paragraph shall first be used to provide reimbursement for training and certification costs of persons operating systems serving 3,300 persons or fewer. If a State has reimbursed all such costs, the State may, after notice to the Administrator, use any remaining funds from the grant for any of the other purposes authorized for grants under section 300j–12 of this title.

(3) Authorization

There are authorized to be appropriated to the Administrator to provide grants for reimbursement under this section $30,000,000 for each of fiscal years 1997 through 2003.

(4) Reservation

If the appropriation made pursuant to paragraph (3) for any fiscal year is not sufficient to satisfy the requirements of paragraph (1), the Administrator shall, prior to any other allocation or reservation, reserve such sums as necessary from the funds appropriated pursuant to section 300j–12(m) of this title to provide reimbursement for the training and certification costs mandated by this subsection.

(July 1, 1944, c. 373, Title XIV, § 1419, as added by Pub. L. No. 104–182, Title I, § 123, 110 Stat. 1652 (Aug. 6, 1996).)

HISTORICAL AND STATUTORY NOTES

Effective and Applicability Provisions

1996 Acts. Section effective Aug. 6, 1996, except as otherwise specifically provided, see section 2(b) of Pub. L. No. 104–182, set out as a note under section 300f of this title.

§ 300g–9. Capacity development

[PHSA § 1420]

(a) State authority for new systems

A State shall receive only 80 percent of the allotment that the State is otherwise entitled to receive under section 300j–12 of this title (relating to State loan funds) unless the State has obtained the legal authority or other means to ensure that all new community water systems and new nontransient, noncommunity water systems commencing operation after October 1, 1999, demonstrate technical, managerial, and financial capacity with respect to each national primary drinking water regulation in effect, or likely to be in effect, on the date of commencement of operations.

(b) Systems in significant noncompliance

(1) List

Beginning not later than 1 year after August 6, 1996, each State shall prepare, periodically update, and submit to the Administrator a list of community water systems and nontransient, noncommunity water systems that have a history of significant noncompliance with this subchapter (as defined in guidelines issued prior to August 6, 1996, or any revisions of the guidelines that have been made in consultation with the States) and, to the extent practicable, the reasons for noncompliance.

(2) Report

Not later than 5 years after August 6, 1996, and as part of the capacity development strategy of the State, each State shall report to the Administrator on the success of enforcement mechanisms and initial capacity development efforts in assisting the public water systems listed under paragraph (1) to improve technical, managerial, and financial capacity.

(3) Withholding

The list and report under this subsection shall be considered part of the capacity development strategy of the State required under subsection (c) of this section for purposes of the withholding requirements of section 300j–12(a)(1)(G)(i) of this title (relating to State loan funds).

(c) Capacity development strategy

(1) In general

Beginning 4 years after August 6, 1996, a State shall receive only—

(A) 90 percent in fiscal year 2001;

(B) 85 percent in fiscal year 2002; and

(C) 80 percent in each subsequent fiscal year,

of the allotment that the State is otherwise entitled to receive under section 300j–12 of this title (relating to State loan funds), unless the State is developing and implementing a strategy to assist public water systems in acquiring and maintaining technical, managerial, and financial capacity.

(2) Content

In preparing the capacity development strategy, the State shall consider, solicit public comment on, and include as appropriate—

(A) the methods or criteria that the State will use to identify and prioritize the public water systems most in need of improving technical, managerial, and financial capacity;

(B) a description of the institutional, regulatory, financial, tax, or legal factors at the Federal, State, or local level that encourage or impair capacity development;

(C) a description of how the State will use the authorities and resources of this subchapter or other means to—

(i) assist public water systems in complying with national primary drinking water regulations;

(ii) encourage the development of partnerships between public water systems to enhance the technical, managerial, and financial capacity of the systems; and

(iii) assist public water systems in the training and certification of operators;

(D) a description of how the State will establish a baseline and measure improvements in capacity with respect to national primary drinking water regulations and State drinking water law;

(E) an identification of the persons that have an interest in and are involved in the development and implementation of the capacity development strategy (including all appropriate agencies of Federal, State, and local governments, private and nonprofit public water systems, and public water system customers); and

(F) a description of how the State will, as appropriate—

(i) encourage development by public water systems of asset management plans that include best practices for asset management; and

(ii) assist, including through the provision of technical assistance, public water systems in training operators or other relevant and appropriate persons in implementing such asset management plans.

(3) Report

Not later than 2 years after the date on which a State first adopts a capacity development strategy under this subsection, and every 3 years thereafter, the head of the State agency that has primary responsibility to carry out this subchapter in the State shall submit to the Governor a report that shall also be available to the public on the efficacy of the strategy and progress made toward improving the technical, managerial, and financial capacity of public water systems in the State, including efforts of the State to encourage development by public water systems of asset management plans and to assist public water systems in training relevant and appropriate persons in implementing such asset management plans.

(4) **Review**

The decisions of the State under this section regarding any particular public water system are not subject to review by the Administrator and may not serve as the basis for withholding funds under section 300j–12 of this title.

(d) **Federal assistance**

(1) **In general**

The Administrator shall support the States in developing capacity development strategies.

(2) **Informational assistance**

(A) **In general**

Not later than 180 days after August 6, 1996, the Administrator shall—

(i) conduct a review of State capacity development efforts in existence on August 6, 1996, and publish information to assist States and public water systems in capacity development efforts; and

(ii) initiate a partnership with States, public water systems, and the public to develop information for States on recommended operator certification requirements.

(B) **Publication of information**

The Administrator shall publish the information developed through the partnership under subparagraph (A)(ii) not later than 18 months after August 6, 1996.

(3) **Promulgation of drinking water regulations**

In promulgating a national primary drinking water regulation, the Administrator shall include an analysis of the likely effect of compliance with the regulation on the technical, financial, and managerial capacity of public water systems.

(4) **Guidance for new systems**

Not later than 2 years after August 6, 1996, the Administrator shall publish guidance developed in consultation with the States describing legal authorities and other means to ensure that all new community water systems and new nontransient, noncommunity water systems demonstrate technical, managerial, and financial capacity with respect to national primary drinking water regulations.

(5) **Information on asset management practices.**—Not later than 5 years after the date of enactment of this paragraph, and not less often than every 5 years thereafter, the Administrator shall review and, if appropriate, update educational materials, including handbooks, training materials, and technical information, made available by the Administrator to owners, managers, and operators of public water systems, local officials, technical assistance providers (including nonprofit water associations), and State personnel concerning best practices for asset management strategies that may be used by public water systems.

(e) **Variances and exemptions**

Based on information obtained under subsection (c)(3) of this section, the Administrator shall, as appropriate, modify regulations concerning variances and exemptions for small public water systems to ensure flexibility in the use of the variances and exemptions. Nothing in this subsection shall be interpreted, construed, or applied to affect or alter the requirements of section 300g–4 or 300g–5 of this title.

(f) **Small public water systems technology assistance centers**

(1) **Grant program**

The Administrator is authorized to make grants to institutions of higher learning to establish and operate small public water system technology assistance centers in the United States.

(2) Responsibilities of the centers

The responsibilities of the small public water system technology assistance centers established under this subsection shall include the conduct of training and technical assistance relating to the information, performance, and technical needs of small public water systems or public water systems that serve Indian Tribes.

(3) Applications

Any institution of higher learning interested in receiving a grant under this subsection shall submit to the Administrator an application in such form and containing such information as the Administrator may require by regulation.

(4) Selection criteria

The Administrator shall select recipients of grants under this subsection on the basis of the following criteria:

(A) The small public water system technology assistance center shall be located in a State that is representative of the needs of the region in which the State is located for addressing the drinking water needs of small and rural communities or Indian Tribes.

(B) The grant recipient shall be located in a region that has experienced problems, or may reasonably be foreseen to experience problems, with small and rural public water systems.

(C) The grant recipient shall have access to expertise in small public water system technology management.

(D) The grant recipient shall have the capability to disseminate the results of small public water system technology and training programs.

(E) The projects that the grant recipient proposes to carry out under the grant are necessary and appropriate.

(F) The grant recipient has regional support beyond the host institution.

(5) Consortia of States

At least 2 of the grants under this subsection shall be made to consortia of States with low population densities.

(6) Authorization of appropriations

There are authorized to be appropriated to make grants under this subsection $2,000,000 for each of the fiscal years 1997 through 1999, and $5,000,000 for each of the fiscal years 2000 through 2003.

(g) Environmental finance centers

(1) In general

The Administrator shall provide initial funding for one or more university-based environmental finance centers for activities that provide technical assistance to State and local officials in developing the capacity of public water systems. Any such funds shall be used only for activities that are directly related to this subchapter.

(2) National capacity development clearinghouse

The Administrator shall establish a national public water system capacity development clearinghouse to receive and disseminate information with respect to developing, improving, and maintaining financial and managerial capacity at public water systems. The Administrator shall ensure that the clearinghouse does not duplicate other federally supported clearinghouse activities.

(3) Capacity development techniques

The Administrator may request an environmental finance center funded under paragraph (1) to develop and test managerial, financial, and institutional techniques for capacity development. The techniques may include capacity assessment methodologies, manual and computer based public water system rate models and capital planning models, public water system consolidation procedures, and regionalization models.

(4) Authorization of appropriations

There are authorized to be appropriated to carry out this subsection $1,500,000 for each of the fiscal years 1997 through 2003.

(5) Limitation

No portion of any funds made available under this subsection may be used for lobbying expenses.

(July 1, 1944, c. 373, Title XIV, § 1420, as added by Pub. L. No. 104–182, Title I, § 119, 110 Stat. 1647 (Aug. 6, 1996); and amended by Pub. L. No. 115–270, § 2012, 132 Stat. 3765, 3849–3850 (Oct. 23, 2018).)

HISTORICAL AND STATUTORY NOTES

References in Text

This subchapter, referred to in subsec. (b)(1), originally read "this title", meaning Title XIV of Act of July 1, 1944, c. 373, Title XIV, § 1401 et seq., as added Dec. 16, 1974, Pub. L. No. 93–523, § 2(a), 88 Stat. 1661, and amended, which enacted this subchapter.

Effective and Applicability Provisions

1996 Acts. Section effective Aug. 6, 1996, except as otherwise specifically provided, see section 2(b) of Pub. L. No. 104–182, set out as a note under section 300f of this title.

PART C—PROTECTION OF UNDERGROUND SOURCES OF DRINKING WATER

§ 300h. Regulations for State programs

[PHSA § 1421]

(a) Publication of proposed regulations; promulgation; amendments; public hearings; administrative consultations

(1) The Administrator shall publish proposed regulations for State underground injection control programs within 180 days after December 16, 1974. Within 180 days after publication of such proposed regulations, he shall promulgate such regulations with such modifications as he deems appropriate. Any regulation under this subsection may be amended from time to time.

(2) Any regulation under this section shall be proposed and promulgated in accordance with section 553 of Title 5 (relating to rulemaking), except that the Administrator shall provide opportunity for public hearing prior to promulgation of such regulations. In proposing and promulgating regulations under this section, the Administrator shall consult with the Secretary, the National Drinking Water Advisory Council, and other appropriate Federal entities and with interested State entities.

(b) Minimum requirements; restrictions

(1) Regulations under subsection (a) of this section for State underground injection programs shall contain minimum requirements for effective programs to prevent underground injection which endangers drinking water sources within the meaning of subsection (d)(2) of this section. Such regulations shall require that a State program, in order to be approved under section 300h–1 of this title—

(A) shall prohibit, effective on the date on which the applicable underground injection control program takes effect, any underground injection in such State which is not authorized by a permit issued by the State (except that the regulations may permit a State to authorize underground injection by rule);

(B) shall require (i) in the case of a program which provides for authorization of underground injection by permit, that the applicant for the permit to inject must satisfy the State that the underground injection will not endanger drinking water sources, and (ii) in the case of a program which provides for such an authorization by rule, that no rule may be promulgated which authorizes any underground injection which endangers drinking water sources;

(C) shall include inspection, monitoring, recordkeeping, and reporting requirements; and

(D) shall apply (i) as prescribed by section 300j–6(b) of this title, to underground injections by Federal agencies, and (ii) to underground injections by any other person whether or not occurring on property owned or leased by the United States.

(2) Regulations of the Administrator under this section for State underground injection control programs may not prescribe requirements which interfere with or impede—

(A) the underground injection of brine or other fluids which are brought to the surface in connection with oil or natural gas production or natural gas storage operations, or

(B) any underground injection for the secondary or tertiary recovery of oil or natural gas,

unless such requirements are essential to assure that underground sources of drinking water will not be endangered by such injection.

(3) (A) The regulations of the Administrator under this section shall permit or provide for consideration of varying geologic, hydrological, or historical conditions in different States and in different areas within a State.

(B) (i) In prescribing regulations under this section the Administrator shall, to the extent feasible, avoid promulgation of requirements which would unnecessarily disrupt State underground injection control programs which are in effect and being enforced in a substantial number of States.

(ii) For the purpose of this subparagraph, a regulation prescribed by the Administrator under this section shall be deemed to disrupt a State underground injection control program only if it would be infeasible to comply with both such regulation and the State underground injection control program.

(iii) For the purpose of this subparagraph, a regulation prescribed by the Administrator under this section shall be deemed unnecessary only if, without such regulation, underground sources of drinking water will not be endangered by an underground injection.

(C) Nothing in this section shall be construed to alter or affect the duty to assure that underground sources of drinking water will not be endangered by any underground injection.

(c) Temporary permits; notice and hearing

(1) The Administrator may, upon application of the Governor of a State which authorizes underground injection by means of permits, authorize such State to issue (without regard to subsection (b)(1)(B)(i) of this section) temporary permits for underground injection which may be effective until the expiration of four years after December 16, 1974, if—

(A) the Administrator finds that the State has demonstrated that it is unable and could not reasonably have been able to process all permit applications within the time available;

(B) the Administrator determines the adverse effect on the environment of such temporary permits is not unwarranted;

(C) such temporary permits will be issued only with respect to injection wells in operation on the date on which such State's permit program approved under this part first takes effect and for which there was inadequate time to process its permit application; and

(D) the Administrator determines the temporary permits require the use of adequate safeguards established by rules adopted by him.

(2) The Administrator may, upon application of the Governor of a State which authorizes underground injection by means of permits, authorize such State to issue (without regard to subsection (b)(1)(B)(i) of this section), but after reasonable notice and hearing, one or more temporary permits each of which is applicable to a particular injection well and to the underground injection of a particular fluid and which may be effective until the expiration of four years after December 16, 1974, if the State finds, on the record of such hearing—

(A) that technology (or other means) to permit safe injection of the fluid in accordance with the applicable underground injection control program is not generally available (taking costs into consideration);

(B) that injection of the fluid would be less harmful to health than the use of other available means of disposing of waste or producing the desired product; and

(C) that available technology or other means have been employed (and will be employed) to reduce the volume and toxicity of the fluid and to minimize the potentially adverse effect of the injection on the public health.

(d) "Underground injection" defined; underground injection endangerment of drinking water sources

For purposes of this part:

(1) Underground injection

The term "underground injection"—

(A) means the subsurface emplacement of fluids by well injection; and

(B) excludes—

(i) the underground injection of natural gas for purposes of storage; and

(ii) the underground injection of fluids or propping agents (other than diesel fuels) pursuant to hydraulic fracturing operations related to oil, gas, or geothermal production activities.

(2) Underground injection endangers drinking water sources if such injection may result in the presence in underground water which supplies or can reasonably be expected to supply any public water system of any contaminant, and if the presence of such contaminant may result in such system's not complying with any national primary drinking water regulation or may otherwise adversely affect the health of persons.

(July 1, 1944, c. 373, Title XIV, § 1421, as added by Pub. L. No. 93–523, § 2(a), 88 Stat. 1674 (Dec. 16, 1974); and amended by Pub. L. No. 95–190, § 6(b), 91 Stat. 1396 (Nov. 16, 1977); Pub. L. No. 96–502, §§ 3, 4(c), 94 Stat. 2738 (Dec. 5, 1980); Pub. L. No. 99–339, Title II, § 201(a), 100 Stat. 653 (June 19, 1986); Pub. L. No. 104–182, Title V, § 501(b)(1), 110 Stat. 1691 (Aug. 6, 1996); Pub. L. No. 109–58, Title III, § 322, 119 Stat. 694 (Aug. 8, 2005).)

HISTORICAL AND STATUTORY NOTES

References in Text

Section 300j–6(b) of this title, referred to in subsec. (b)(1)(D), was repealed, and a new section 300j–6(b) relating to administrative penalty orders was added by Pub. L. No. 104–182, title I, § 129(a), 110 Stat. 1660 (Aug. 6, 1996).

Effective and Applicability Provisions

1996 Acts. Amendment by Pub. L. No. 104–182 effective Aug. 6, 1996, except as otherwise specifically provided, see section 2(b) of Pub. L. No. 104–182, set out as a note under section 300f of this title.

§ 300h–1. State primary enforcement responsibility

[PHSA § 1422]

(a) List of States in need of a control program; amendment of list

Within 180 days after December 16, 1974, the Administrator shall list in the Federal Register each State for which in his judgment a State underground injection control program may be necessary to assure that underground injection will not endanger drinking water sources. Such list may be amended from time to time.

(b) State applications; notice to Administrator of compliance with revised or added requirements; approval or disapproval by Administrator; duration of State primary enforcement responsibility; public hearing

(1) (A) Each State listed under subsection (a) of this section shall within 270 days after the date of promulgation of any regulation under section 300h of this title (or, if later, within 270 days after such State is first listed under subsection (a)of this section) submit to the Administrator an application which contains a showing satisfactory to the Administrator that the State—

(i) has adopted after reasonable notice and public hearings, and will implement, an underground injection control program which meets the requirements of regulations in effect under section 300h of this title; and

(ii) will keep such records and make such reports with respect to its activities under its underground injection control program as the Administrator may require by regulation.

The Administrator may, for good cause, extend the date for submission of an application by any State under this subparagraph for a period not to exceed an additional 270 days.

(B) Within 270 days of any amendment of a regulation under section 300h of this title revising or adding any requirement respecting State underground injection control programs, each State listed under subsection (a) of this section shall submit (in such form and manner as the Administrator may require) a notice to the Administrator containing a showing satisfactory to him that the State underground injection control program meets the revised or added requirement.

(2) Within ninety days after the State's application under paragraph (1)(A) or notice under paragraph (1)(B) and after reasonable opportunity for presentation of views, the Administrator shall by rule either approve, disapprove, or approve in part and disapprove in part, the State's underground injection control program.

(3) If the Administrator approves the State's program under paragraph (2), the State shall have primary enforcement responsibility for underground water sources until such time as the Administrator determines, by rule, that such State no longer meets the requirements of clause (i) or (ii) of paragraph (1)(A) of this subsection.

(4) Before promulgating any rule under paragraph (2) or (3) of this subsection, the Administrator shall provide opportunity for public hearing respecting such rule.

(c) Program by Administrator for State without primary enforcement responsibility; restrictions

If the Administrator disapproves a State's program (or part thereof) under subsection (b)(2) of this section, if the Administrator determines under subsection (b)(3) of this section that a State no longer meets the requirements of clause (i) or (ii) of subsection (b)(1)(A) of this section, or if a State fails to submit an application or notice before the date of expiration of the period specified in subsection (b)(1) of this section, the Administrator shall by regulation within 90 days after the date of such disapproval, determination, or expiration (as the case may be) prescribe (and may from time to time by regulation revise) a program applicable to such State meeting the requirements of section 300h(b) of this title. Such program may not include requirements which interfere with or impede—

(1) the underground injection of brine or other fluids which are brought to the surface in connection with oil or natural gas production or natural gas storage operations, or

(2) any underground injection for the secondary or tertiary recovery of oil or natural gas,

unless such requirements are essential to assure that underground sources of drinking water will not be endangered by such injection. Such program shall apply in such State to the extent that a program adopted by such State which the Administrator determines meets such requirements is not in effect. Before promulgating any regulation under this section, the Administrator shall provide opportunity for public hearing respecting such regulation.

(d) "Applicable underground injection control program" defined

For purposes of this subchapter, the term "applicable underground injection control program" with respect to a State means the program (or most recent amendment thereof) (1) which has been adopted by the State and which has been approved under subsection (b) of this section, or (2) which has been prescribed by the Administrator under subsection (c) of this section.

(e) Primary enforcement responsibility by Indian Tribe

An Indian Tribe may assume primary enforcement responsibility for underground injection control under this section consistent with such regulations as the Administrator has prescribed pursuant to this part and section 300j–11 of this title. The area over which such Indian Tribe exercises governmental jurisdiction need not have been listed under subsection (a) of this section, and such Tribe need not submit an application to assume primary enforcement responsibility within the 270-day deadline noted in subsection (b)(1)(A) of this section. Until an Indian Tribe assumes primary enforcement responsibility, the currently applicable underground injection control program shall continue to apply. If an applicable underground injection control program does not exist for an Indian Tribe, the Administrator shall prescribe such a program pursuant to subsection (c) of this section, and consistent with section 300h(b) of this title, within 270 days after June 19, 1986, unless an Indian Tribe first obtains approval to assume primary enforcement responsibility for underground injection control.

(July 1, 1944, c. 373, Title XIV, § 1422, as added by Pub. L. No. 93–523, § 2(a), 88 Stat. 1676 (Dec. 16, 1974); and amended by Pub. L. No. 95–190, § 6(a), 91 Stat. 1396 (Nov. 16, 1977); Pub. L. No. 99–339, Title II, § 201(a), Title III, § 302(c), 100 Stat. 653, 666 (June 19, 1986).)

§ 300h–2. Enforcement of program

[PHSA § 1423]

(a) Notice to State and violator; issuance of administrative order; civil action

(1) Whenever the Administrator finds during a period during which a State has primary enforcement responsibility for underground water sources (within the meaning of section 300h–1(b)(3) of this title or section 300h–4(c) of this title) that any person who is subject to a requirement of an applicable underground injection control program in such State is violating such requirement, he shall so notify the State and the person violating such requirement. If beyond the thirtieth day after the Administrator's notification the State has not commenced appropriate enforcement action, the Administrator shall issue an order under subsection (c) of this section requiring the person to comply with such requirement or the Administrator shall commence a civil action under subsection (b) of this section.

(2) Whenever the Administrator finds during a period during which a State does not have primary enforcement responsibility for underground water sources that any person subject to any requirement of any applicable underground injection control program in such State is violating such requirement, the Administrator shall issue an order under subsection (c) of this section requiring the person to comply with such requirement or the Administrator shall commence a civil action under subsection (b) of this section.

(b) Civil and criminal actions

Civil actions referred to in paragraphs (1) and (2) of subsection (a) of this section shall be brought in the appropriate United States district court. Such court shall have jurisdiction to require compliance with any requirement of an applicable underground injection program or with an order issued under subsection (c) of this section. The court may enter such judgment as protection of public health may require. Any person who violates any requirement of an applicable underground injection control program or an order requiring compliance under subsection (c) of this section—

(1) shall be subject to a civil penalty of not more than $25,000 for each day of such violation, and

(2) if such violation is willful, such person may, in addition to or in lieu of the civil penalty authorized by paragraph (1), be imprisoned for not more than 3 years, or fined in accordance with Title 18, or both.

(c) Administrative orders

(1) In any case in which the Administrator is authorized to bring a civil action under this section with respect to any regulation or other requirement of this part other than those relating to—

(A) the underground injection of brine or other fluids which are brought to the surface in connection with oil or natural gas production, or

(B) any underground injection for the secondary or tertiary recovery of oil or natural gas,

the Administrator may also issue an order under this subsection either assessing a civil penalty of not more than $10,000 for each day of violation for any past or current violation, up to a maximum administrative penalty of $125,000, or requiring compliance with such regulation or other requirement, or both.

(2) In any case in which the Administrator is authorized to bring a civil action under this section with respect to any regulation, or other requirement of this part relating to—

(A) the underground injection of brine or other fluids which are brought to the surface in connection with oil or natural gas production, or

(B) any underground injection for the secondary or tertiary recovery of oil or natural gas,

the Administrator may also issue an order under this subsection either assessing a civil penalty of not more than $5,000 for each day of violation for any past or current violation, up to a maximum administrative penalty of $125,000, or requiring compliance with such regulation or other requirement, or both.

(3) (A) An order under this subsection shall be issued by the Administrator after opportunity (provided in accordance with this subparagraph) for a hearing. Before issuing the order, the Administrator shall give to the person to whom it is directed written notice of the Administrator's proposal to issue such order and the opportunity to request, within 30 days of the date the notice is received by such person, a hearing on the order. Such hearing shall not be subject to section 554 or 556 of Title 5, but shall provide a reasonable opportunity to be heard and to present evidence.

(B) The Administrator shall provide public notice of, and reasonable opportunity to comment on, any proposed order.

(C) Any citizen who comments on any proposed order under subparagraph (B) shall be given notice of any hearing under this subsection and of any order. In any hearing held under subparagraph (A), such citizen shall have a reasonable opportunity to be heard and to present evidence.

(D) Any order issued under this subsection shall become effective 30 days following its issuance unless an appeal is taken pursuant to paragraph (6).

(4) (A) Any order issued under this subsection shall state with reasonable specificity the nature of the violation and may specify a reasonable time for compliance.

(B) In assessing any civil penalty under this subsection, the Administrator shall take into account appropriate factors, including (i) the seriousness of the violation; (ii) the economic benefit (if any) resulting from the violation; (iii) any history of such violations; (iv) any good-faith efforts to comply with the applicable requirements; (v) the economic impact of the penalty on the violator; and (vi) such other matters as justice may require.

(5) Any violation with respect to which the Administrator has commenced and is diligently prosecuting an action, or has issued an order under this subsection assessing a penalty, shall not be subject to an action under subsection (b) of this section or section 300h–3(c) or 300j–8 of this title, except that the foregoing limitation on civil actions under section 300j–8 of this title shall not apply with respect to any violation for which—

(A) a civil action under section 300j–8(a)(1) of this title has been filed prior to commencement of an action under this subsection, or

(B) a notice of violation under section 300j–8(b)(1) of this title has been given before commencement of an action under this subsection and an action under section 300j–8(a)(1) of this title is filed before 120 days after such notice is given.

(6) Any person against whom an order is issued or who commented on a proposed order pursuant to paragraph (3) may file an appeal of such order with the United States District Court for the District of Columbia or the district in which the violation is alleged to have occurred. Such an appeal may only be filed within the 30-day period beginning on the date the order is issued. Appellant shall simultaneously send a copy of the appeal by certified mail to the Administrator and to the Attorney General. The Administrator shall promptly file in such court a certified copy of the record on which such order was imposed. The district court shall not set aside or remand such order unless there is not substantial evidence on the record, taken as a whole, to support the finding of a violation or, unless the Administrator's assessment of penalty or requirement for compliance constitutes an abuse of discretion. The district court shall not impose additional civil penalties for the same violation unless the Administrator's assessment of a penalty constitutes an abuse of discretion. Notwithstanding section 300j–7(a)(2) of this title, any order issued under paragraph (3) shall be subject to judicial review exclusively under this paragraph.

(7) If any person fails to pay an assessment of a civil penalty—

(A) after the order becomes effective under paragraph (3), or

(B) after a court, in an action brought under paragraph (6), has entered a final judgment in favor of the Administrator,

the Administrator may request the Attorney General to bring a civil action in an appropriate district court to recover the amount assessed (plus costs, attorneys' fees, and interest at currently prevailing rates from the date the order is effective or the date of such final judgment, as the case may be). In such an action, the validity, amount, and appropriateness of such penalty shall not be subject to review.

(8) The Administrator may, in connection with administrative proceedings under this subsection, issue subpoenas compelling the attendance and testimony of witnesses and subpoenas duces tecum, and may request the Attorney General to bring an action to enforce any subpoena under this section. The district courts shall have jurisdiction to enforce such subpoenas and impose sanction.

(d) State authority to adopt or enforce laws or regulations respecting underground injection unaffected

Nothing in this subchapter shall diminish any authority of a State or political subdivision to adopt or enforce any law or regulation respecting underground injection but no such law or regulation shall relieve any person of any requirement otherwise applicable under this subchapter.

(July 1, 1944, c. 373, Title XIV, § 1423, as added by Pub. L. No. 93–523, § 2(a), 88 Stat. 1677 (Dec. 16, 1974); and amended by Pub. L. No. 96–502, § 2(b), 94 Stat. 2738 (Dec. 5, 1980); Pub. L. No. 99–339, Title II, § 202, 100 Stat. 654 (June 19, 1986).)

§ 300h–3. Interim regulation of underground injections

[PHSA § 1424]

(a) Necessity for well operation permit; designation of one aquifer areas

(1) Any person may petition the Administrator to have an area of a State (or States) designated as an area in which no new underground injection well may be operated during the period beginning on the date of the designation and ending on the date on which the applicable underground injection control program covering such area takes effect unless a permit for the operation of such well has been issued by the Administrator under subsection (b) of this section. The Administrator may so designate an area within a State if he finds that the area has one aquifer which is the sole or principal drinking water source for the area and which, if contaminated, would create a significant hazard to public health.

(2) Upon receipt of a petition under paragraph (1) of this subsection, the Administrator shall publish it in the Federal Register and shall provide an opportunity to interested persons to submit written data, views, or arguments thereon. Not later than the 30th day following the date of the publication of a petition under this paragraph in the Federal Register, the Administrator shall either make the designation for which the petition is submitted or deny the petition.

(b) Well operation permits; publication in Federal Register; notice and hearing; issuance or denial; conditions for issuance

(1) During the period beginning on the date an area is designated under subsection (a) of this section and ending on the date the applicable underground injection control program covering such area takes effect, no new underground injection well may be operated in such area unless the Administrator has issued a permit for such operation.

(2) Any person may petition the Administrator for the issuance of a permit for the operation of such a well in such an area. A petition submitted under this paragraph shall be submitted in such manner and contain such information as the Administrator may require by regulation. Upon receipt of such a petition, the Administrator shall publish it in the Federal Register. The Administrator shall give notice of any proceeding on a petition and shall provide opportunity for agency hearing. The Administrator shall act upon such petition on the record of any hearing held pursuant to the preceding sentence respecting such petition. Within 120 days of the publication in the Federal Register of a petition submitted under this paragraph, the Administrator shall either issue the permit for which the petition was submitted or shall deny its issuance.

(3) The Administrator may issue a permit for the operation of a new underground injection well in an area designated under subsection (a) of this section only if he finds that the operation of such well will not cause contamination of the aquifer of such area so as to create a significant hazard to public health. The Administrator may condition the issuance of such a permit upon the use of such control measures in connection with the operation of such well, for which the permit is to be issued, as he deems necessary to assure that the operation of the well will not contaminate the aquifer of the designated area in which the well is located so as to create a significant hazard to public health.

(c) Civil penalties; separate violations; penalties for willful violations; temporary restraining order or injunction

Any person who operates a new underground injection well in violation of subsection (b) of this section, (1) shall be subject to a civil penalty of not more than $5,000 for each day in which such violation occurs, or (2) if such violation is willful, such person may, in lieu of the civil penalty authorized by clause (1), be fined not more than $10,000 for each day in which such violation occurs. If the Administrator has reason to believe that any person is violating or will violate subsection (b) of this section, he may petition the United States district court to issue a temporary restraining order or injunction (including a mandatory injunction) to enforce such subsection.

(d) "New underground injection well" defined

For purposes of this section, the term "new underground injection well" means an underground injection well whose operation was not approved by appropriate State and Federal agencies before December 16, 1974.

(e) Areas with one aquifer; publication in Federal Register; commitments for Federal financial assistance

If the Administrator determines, on his own initiative or upon petition, that an area has an aquifer which is the sole or principal drinking water source for the area and which, if contaminated, would create a significant hazard to public health, he shall publish notice of that determination in the Federal Register. After the publication of any such notice, no commitment for Federal financial assistance (through a grant, contract, loan guarantee, or otherwise) may be entered into for any project which the Administrator determines may contaminate such aquifer through a recharge zone so as to create a significant hazard to public health, but a commitment for Federal financial assistance may, if authorized under another provision of law, be entered into to plan or design the project to assure that it will not so contaminate the aquifer.

(July 1, 1944, c. 373, Title XIV, § 1424, as added by Pub. L. No. 93–523, § 2(a), 88 Stat. 1678 (Dec. 16, 1974).)

§ 300h–4. Optional demonstration by States relating to oil or natural gas

[PHSA § 1425]

(a) Approval of State underground injection control program; alternative showing of effectiveness of program by State

For purposes of the Administrator's approval or disapproval under section 300h–1 of this title of that portion of any State underground injection control program which relates to—

(1) the underground injection of brine or other fluids which are brought to the surface in connection with oil or natural gas production or natural gas storage operations, or

(2) any underground injection for the secondary or tertiary recovery of oil or natural gas,

in lieu of the showing required under subparagraph (A) of section 300h–1(b)(1) of this title the State may demonstrate that such portion of the State program meets the requirements of subparagraphs (A) through (D) of section 300h(b)(1) of this title and represents an effective program (including adequate recordkeeping and reporting) to prevent underground injection which endangers drinking water sources.

(b) Revision or amendment of requirements of regulation; showing of effectiveness of program by State

If the Administrator revises or amends any requirement of a regulation under section 300h of this title relating to any aspect of the underground injection referred to in subsection (a) of this section, in the case of that portion of a State underground injection control program for which the demonstration referred to in subsection (a) of this section has been made, in lieu of the showing required under section 300h–1(b)(1)(B) of this title the State may demonstrate that, with respect to that aspect of such underground injection, the State program meets the requirements of subparagraphs (A) through (D) of section 300h(b)(1) of this title and represents an effective program (including adequate recordkeeping and reporting) to prevent underground injection which endangers drinking water sources.

(c) Primary enforcement responsibility of State; voiding by Administrator under duly promulgated rule

(1) Section 300h–1(b)(3) of this title shall not apply to that portion of any State underground injection control program approved by the Administrator pursuant to a demonstration under subsection (a) of this section (and under subsection (b) of this section where applicable).

(2) If pursuant to such a demonstration, the Administrator approves such portion of the State program, the State shall have primary enforcement responsibility with respect to that portion until such time as the Administrator determines, by rule, that such demonstration is no longer valid. Following such a determination, the Administrator may exercise the authority of subsection (c) of section 300h–1 of this title in the same manner as provided in such subsection with respect to a determination described in such subsection.

(3) Before promulgating any rule under paragraph (2), the Administrator shall provide opportunity for public hearing respecting such rule.

(July 1, 1944, c. 373, Title XIV, § 1425, as added by Pub. L. No. 96–502, § 2(a), 94 Stat. 2737 (Dec. 5, 1980); and amended by Pub. L. No. 99–339, Title II, § 201(a), 100 Stat. 653 (June 19, 1986).)

§ 300h–5. Regulation of State programs

[PHSA § 1426]

Not later than 18 months after June 19, 1986, the Administrator shall modify regulations issued under this chapter for Class I injection wells to identify monitoring methods, in addition to those in effect on November 1, 1985, including groundwater monitoring. In accordance with such regulations, the Administrator, or delegated State authority, shall determine the applicability of such monitoring methods, wherever appropriate, at locations and in such a manner as to provide the earliest possible detection of fluid migration into, or in the direction of, underground sources of drinking water from such wells, based on its assessment of the potential for fluid migration from the injection zone that may be harmful to human health or the environment. For purposes of this subsection, a class I injection well is defined in accordance with 40 C.F.R. 146.05 as in effect on November 1, 1985.

(July 1, 1944, c. 373, Title XIV, § 1426, as added by Pub. L. No. 99–339, Title II, § 201(b), 100 Stat. 653 (June 19, 1986); and amended by Pub. L. No. 104–66, Title II, § 2021(f), 109 Stat. 727 (Dec. 21, 1995); Pub. L. No. 104–182, Title V, § 501(f)(2), 110 Stat. 1691 (Aug. 6, 1996).)

HISTORICAL AND STATUTORY NOTES

Effective and Applicability Provisions

1996 Acts. Amendment by Pub. L. No. 104–182 effective Aug. 6, 1996, except as otherwise specifically provided, see section 2(b) of Pub. L. No. 104–182, set out as a note under section 300f of this title.

§ 300h–6. Sole source aquifer demonstration program

[PHSA § 1427]

(a) Purpose

The purpose of this section is to establish procedures for development, implementation, and assessment of demonstration programs designed to protect critical aquifer protection areas located within areas designated as sole or principal source aquifers under section 300h–3(e) of this title.

(b) "Critical aquifer protection area" defined

For purposes of this section, the term "critical aquifer protection area" means either of the following:

(1) All or part of an area located within an area for which an application or designation as a sole or principal source aquifer pursuant to section 300h–3(e) of this title, has been submitted and approved by the Administrator and which satisfies the criteria established by the Administrator under subsection (d) of this section.

(2) All or part of an area which is within an aquifer designated as a sole source aquifer as of June 19, 1986, and for which an areawide ground water quality protection plan has been approved under section 208 of the Clean Water Act [33 U.S.C.A. § 1288] prior to June 19, 1986.

(c) Application

Any State, municipal or local government or political subdivision thereof or any planning entity (including any interstate regional planning entity) that identifies a critical aquifer protection area over which it has authority or jurisdiction may apply to the Administrator for the selection of such area for a demonstration program under this section. Any applicant shall consult with other government or planning entities with authority or jurisdiction in such area prior to application. Applicants, other than the Governor, shall submit the application for a demonstration program jointly with the Governor.

(d) Criteria

Not later than 1 year after June 19, 1986, the Administrator shall, by rule, establish criteria for identifying critical aquifer protection areas under this section. In establishing such criteria, the Administrator shall consider each of the following:

(1) The vulnerability of the aquifer to contamination due to hydrogeologic characteristics.

(2) The number of persons or the proportion of population using the ground water as a drinking water source.

(3) The economic, social and environmental benefits that would result to the area from maintenance of ground water of high quality.

(4) The economic, social and environmental costs that would result from degradation of the quality of the ground water.

(e) Contents of application

An application submitted to the Administrator by any applicant for a demonstration program under this section shall meet each of the following requirements:

(1) The application shall propose boundaries for the critical aquifer protection area within its jurisdiction.

(2) The application shall designate or, if necessary, establish a planning entity (which shall be a public agency and which shall include representation of elected local and State governmental officials) to develop a comprehensive management plan (hereinafter in this section referred to as the "plan") for the critical protection area. Where a local government planning agency exists with adequate authority to carry out this section with respect to any proposed critical protection area, such agency shall be designated as the planning entity.

(3) The application shall establish procedures for public participation in the development of the plan, for review, approval, and adoption of the plan, and for assistance to municipalities and other public agencies with authority under State law to implement the plan.

(4) The application shall include a hydrogeologic assessment of surface and ground water resources within the critical protection area.

(5) The application shall include a comprehensive management plan for the proposed protection area.

(6) The application shall include the measures and schedule proposed for implementation of such plan.

(f) Comprehensive plan

(1) The objective of a comprehensive management plan submitted by an applicant under this section shall be to maintain the quality of the ground water in the critical protection area in a manner reasonably expected to protect human health, the environment and ground water resources. In order to achieve such objective, the plan may be designed to maintain, to the maximum extent possible, the natural vegetative and hydrogeological conditions. Each of the following elements shall be included in such a protection plan:

(A) A map showing the detailed boundary of the critical protection area.

(B) An identification of existing and potential point and nonpoint sources of ground water degradation.

(C) An assessment of the relationship between activities on the land surface and ground water quality.

(D) Specific actions and management practices to be implemented in the critical protection area to prevent adverse impacts on ground water quality.

(E) Identification of authority adequate to implement the plan, estimates of program costs, and sources of State matching funds.

(2) Such plan may also include the following:

(A) A determination of the quality of the existing ground water recharged through the special protection area and the natural recharge capabilities of the special protection area watershed.

(B) Requirements designed to maintain existing underground drinking water quality or improve underground drinking water quality if prevailing conditions fail to meet drinking water standards, pursuant to this chapter and State law.

(C) Limits on Federal, State, and local government, financially assisted activities and projects which may contribute to degradation of such ground water or any loss of natural surface and subsurface infiltration of purification capability of the special protection watershed.

(D) A comprehensive statement of land use management including emergency contingency planning as it pertains to the maintenance of the quality of underground sources of drinking water or to the improvement of such sources if necessary to meet drinking water standards pursuant to this chapter and State law.

(E) Actions in the special protection area which would avoid adverse impacts on water quality, recharge capabilities, or both.

(F) Consideration of specific techniques, which may include clustering, transfer of development rights, and other innovative measures sufficient to achieve the objectives of this section.

(G) Consideration of the establishment of a State institution to facilitate and assist funding a development transfer credit system.

(H) A program for State and local implementation of the plan described in this subsection in a manner that will insure the continued, uniform, consistent protection of the critical protection area in accord with the purposes of this section.

(I) Pollution abatement measures, if appropriate.

(g) Plans under section 208 of Clean Water Act

A plan approved before June 19, 1986, under section 208 of the Clean Water Act [33 U.S.C.A. § 1288] to protect a sole source aquifer designated under section 300h–3(e) of this title shall be considered a comprehensive management plan for the purposes of this section.

(h) Consultation and hearings

During the development of a comprehensive management plan under this section, the planning entity shall consult with, and consider the comments of, appropriate officials of any municipality and State or Federal agency which has jurisdiction over lands and waters within the special protection area, other concerned organizations and technical and citizen advisory committees. The planning entity shall conduct public hearings at places within the special protection area for the purpose of providing the opportunity to comment on any aspect of the plan.

(i) Approval or disapproval

Within 120 days after receipt of an application under this section, the Administrator shall approve or disapprove the application. The approval or disapproval shall be based on a determination that the critical protection area satisfies the criteria established under subsection (d) of this section and that a demonstration program for the area would provide protection for ground water quality consistent with the objectives stated in subsection (f) of this section. The Administrator shall provide to the Governor a written explanation of the reasons for the disapproval of any such application. Any petitioner may modify and resubmit any application which is not approved. Upon approval of an application, the Administrator may enter into a cooperative agreement with the applicant to establish a demonstration program under this section.

(j) Grants and reimbursement

Upon entering a cooperative agreement under subsection (i) of this section, the Administrator may provide to the applicant, on a matching basis, a grant of 50 per centum of the costs of implementing the plan established under this section. The Administrator may also reimburse the applicant of an approved plan up to 50 per centum of the costs of developing such plan, except for plans approved under section 208 of the Clean Water Act [33 U.S.C.A. § 1288]. The total amount of grants under this section for any one aquifer, designated under section 300h–3(e) of this title, shall not exceed $4,000,000 in any one fiscal year.

(k) Activities funded under other law

No funds authorized under this section may be used to fund activities funded under other sections of this chapter or the Clean Water Act [33 U.S.C.A. § 1251 et seq.], the Solid Waste Disposal Act [42 U.S.C.A. § 6901 et seq.], the Comprehensive Environmental Response, Compensation, and Liability Act of 1980 [42 U.S.C.A. § 9601 et seq.] or other environmental laws.

(*l*) Savings provision

Nothing under this section shall be construed to amend, supersede or abrogate rights to quantities of water which have been established by interstate water compacts, Supreme Court decrees, or State water laws; or any requirement imposed or right provided under any Federal or State environmental or public health statute.

(m) Authorization of appropriations

There are authorized to be appropriated to carry out this section not more than the following amounts:

Fiscal year:	*Amount*
1987	$10,000,000
1988	15,000,000
1989	17,500,000
1990	17,500,000
1991	17,500,000
1992–2003	15,000,000.

Matching grants under this section may also be used to implement or update any water quality management plan for a sole or principal source aquifer approved (before June 19, 1986) by the Administrator under section 208 of the Federal Water Pollution Control Act [33 U.S.C.A. § 1288].

(July 1, 1944, c. 373, Title XIV, § 1427, as added and amended by Pub. L. No. 99–339, Title II, § 203, Title III, § 301(f), 100 Stat. 657, 664 (June 19, 1986); Pub. L. No. 104–66, Title II, § 2021(g), 109 Stat. 727 (Dec. 21, 1995); Pub. L. No. 104–182, Title I, § 120(a), Title V, § 501(b)(2), (f)(3), 110 Stat. 1650, 1691 (Aug. 6, 1996).)

HISTORICAL AND STATUTORY NOTES

References in Text

The Clean Water Act, referred to in subsec. (k), is Act of June 30, 1948, c. 758, as amended generally by Pub. L. No. 92–500, § 2, 86 Stat. 816 (Oct. 18, 1972), also known as the Federal Water Pollution Control Act, which is codified generally as chapter 26 (section 1251 et seq.) of Title 33, Navigation and Navigable Waters. For complete classification of this Act to the Code, see Short Title note set out under section 1251 of Title 33 and Tables.

The Solid Waste Disposal Act, referred to in subsec. (k) is Title II of Pub. L. No. 89–272, 79 Stat. 997 (Oct. 20, 1965), as amended generally by Pub. L. No. 94–580, § 2, 90 Stat. 2795 (Oct. 21, 1976), which is codified generally as chapter 82 (section 6901 et seq.) of this title. For complete classification of this Act to the Code, see Short Title note set out under section 6901 of this title and Tables.

The Comprehensive Environmental Response, Compensation, and Liability Act of 1980, referred to in subsec. (k), is Pub. L. No. 96–510, 94 Stat. 2767 (Dec. 11, 1980), as amended, which is codified principally as chapter 103 (section 9601 et seq.) of this title. For complete classification of this Act to the Code, see Short Title note set out under section 9601 of this title and Tables.

Effective and Applicability Provisions

1996 Acts. Amendment by Pub. L. No. 104–182 effective Aug. 6, 1996, except as otherwise specifically provided, see section 2(b) of Pub. L. No. 104–182, set out as a note under section 300f of this title.

§ 300h–7. State programs to establish wellhead protection areas

[PHSA § 1428]

(a) State programs

The Governor or Governor's designee of each State shall, within 3 years of June 19, 1986, adopt and submit to the Administrator a State program to protect wellhead areas within their jurisdiction from contaminants which may have any adverse effect on the health of persons. Each State program under this section shall, at a minimum—

(1) specify the duties of State agencies, local governmental entities, and public water supply systems with respect to the development and implementation of programs required by this section;

(2) for each wellhead, determine the wellhead protection area as defined in subsection (e) of this section based on all reasonably available hydrogeologic information on ground water flow, recharge and discharge and other information the State deems necessary to adequately determine the wellhead protection area;

(3) identify within each wellhead protection area all potential anthropogenic sources of contaminants which may have any adverse effect on the health of persons;

(4) describe a program that contains, as appropriate, technical assistance, financial assistance, implementation of control measures, education, training, and demonstration projects to protect the water supply within wellhead protection areas from such contaminants;

(5) include contingency plans for the location and provision of alternate drinking water supplies for each public water system in the event of well or wellfield contamination by such contaminants; and

(6) include a requirement that consideration be given to all potential sources of such contaminants within the expected wellhead area of a new water well which serves a public water supply system.

(b) Public participation

To the maximum extent possible, each State shall establish procedures, including but not limited to the establishment of technical and citizens' advisory committees, to encourage the public to participate in developing the protection program for wellhead areas and source water assessment programs under section 300j-13 of this title. Such procedures shall include notice and opportunity for public hearing on the State program before it is submitted to the Administrator.

(c) Disapproval

(1) In general

If, in the judgment of the Administrator, a State program or portion thereof under subsection (a) of this section is not adequate to protect public water systems as required by subsection (a) of this section or a State program under section 300j-13 of this title or section 300g-7(b) of this title does not meet the applicable requirements of section 300j-13 of this title or section 300g-7(b) of this title, the Administrator shall disapprove such program or portion thereof. A State program developed pursuant to subsection (a) of this section shall be deemed to be adequate unless the Administrator determines, within 9 months of the receipt of a State program, that such program (or portion thereof) is inadequate for the purpose of protecting public water systems as required by this section from contaminants that may have any adverse effect on the health of persons. A State program developed pursuant to section 300j-13 of this title or section 300g-7(b) of this title shall be deemed to meet the applicable requirements of section 300j-13 of this title or section 300g-7(b) of this title unless the Administrator determines within 9 months of the receipt of the program that such program (or portion thereof) does not meet such requirements. If the Administrator determines that a proposed State program (or any portion thereof) is disapproved, the Administrator shall submit a written statement of the reasons for such determination to the Governor of the State.

(2) Modification and resubmission

Within 6 months after receipt of the Administrator's written notice under paragraph (1) that any proposed State program (or portion thereof) is disapproved, the Governor or Governor's designee, shall modify the program based upon the recommendations of the Administrator and resubmit the modified program to the Administrator.

(d) Federal assistance

After the date 3 years after June 19, 1986, no State shall receive funds authorized to be appropriated under this section except for the purpose of implementing the program and requirements of paragraphs (4) and (6) of subsection (a) of this section.

(e) "Wellhead protection area" defined

As used in this section, the term "wellhead protection area" means the surface and subsurface area surrounding a water well or wellfield, supplying a public water system, through which contaminants are reasonably likely to move toward and reach such water well or wellfield. The extent of a wellhead protection area, within a State, necessary to provide protection from contaminants which may have any adverse effect on the health of persons is to be determined by the State in the program submitted under subsection (a) of this section. Not later than one year after June 19, 1986, the Administrator shall issue technical guidance which States may use in making such determinations. Such guidance may reflect such factors as the radius of influence around a well or wellfield, the depth of drawdown of the water table by such well or wellfield at any given point, the time or rate of travel of various contaminants in various hydrologic conditions, distance from the well or wellfield, or other factors affecting the likelihood of contaminants reaching the well or wellfield, taking into account available engineering pump tests or comparable data, field reconnaissance, topographic information, and the geology of the formation in which the well or wellfield is located.

(f) Prohibitions

(1) Activities under other laws

No funds authorized to be appropriated under this section may be used to support activities authorized by the Federal Water Pollution Control Act [33 U.S.C.A. § 1251 et seq.], the Solid Waste Disposal Act [42 U.S.C.A. § 6901 et seq.], the Comprehensive Environmental Response, Compensation, and Liability Act of 1980 [42 U.S.C.A. § 9601 et seq.], or other sections of this chapter.

(2) Individual sources

No funds authorized to be appropriated under this section may be used to bring individual sources of contamination into compliance.

(g) Implementation

Each State shall make every reasonable effort to implement the State wellhead area protection program under this section within 2 years of submitting the program to the Administrator. Each State shall submit to the Administrator a biennial status report describing the State's progress in implementing the program. Such report shall include amendments to the State program for water wells sited during the biennial period.

(h) Federal agencies

Each department, agency, and instrumentality of the executive, legislative, and judicial branches of the Federal Government having jurisdiction over any potential source of contaminants identified by a State program pursuant to the provisions of subsection (a)(3) of this section shall be subject to and comply with all requirements of the State program developed according to subsection (a)(4) of this section applicable to such potential source of contaminants, both substantive and procedural, in the same manner, and to the same extent, as any other person is subject to such requirements, including payment of reasonable charges and fees. The President may exempt any potential source under the jurisdiction of any department, agency, or instrumentality in the executive branch if the President determines it to be in the paramount interest of the United States to do so. No such exemption shall be granted due to the lack of an appropriation unless the President shall have specifically requested such appropriation as part of the budgetary process and the Congress shall have failed to make available such requested appropriations.

(i) Additional requirement

(1) In general

In addition to the provisions of subsection (a) of this section, States in which there are more than 2,500 active wells at which annular injection is used as of January 1, 1986, shall include in their State program a certification that a State program exists and is being adequately enforced that provides protection from contaminants which may have any adverse effect on the health of persons and which are associated with the annular injection or surface disposal of brines associated with oil and gas production.

(2) "Annular injection" defined

For purposes of this subsection, the term "annular injection" means the reinjection of brines associated with the production of oil or gas between the production and surface casings of a conventional oil or gas producing well.

(3) Review

The Administrator shall conduct a review of each program certified under this subsection.

(4) Disapproval

If a State fails to include the certification required by this subsection or if in the judgment of the Administrator the State program certified under this subsection is not being adequately enforced, the Administrator shall disapprove the State program submitted under subsection (a) of this section.

(j) Coordination with other laws

Nothing in this section shall authorize or require any department, agency, or other instrumentality of the Federal Government or State or local government to apportion, allocate or otherwise regulate the withdrawal or beneficial use of ground or surface waters, so as to abrogate or modify any existing rights to water established pursuant to State or Federal law, including interstate compacts.

(k) Authorization of appropriations

Unless the State program is disapproved under this section, the Administrator shall make grants to the State for not less than 50 or more than 90 percent of the costs incurred by a State (as determined by the Administrator) in developing and implementing each State program under this section. For purposes of making such grants there is authorized to be appropriated not more than the following amounts:

Fiscal year:	*Amount*
1987	$20,000,000
1988	20,000,000
1989	35,000,000
1990	35,000,000
1991	35,000,000
1992–2003	30,000,000.

(July 1, 1944, c. 373, Title XIV, § 1428, as added and amended by Pub. L. No. 99–339, Title II, § 205, Title III, § 301(e), 100 Stat. 660, 664 (June 19, 1986); and amended by Pub. L. No. 104–182, Title I, §§ 120(b), 132(b), Title V, § 501(f)(4), 110 Stat. 1650, 1674, 1692 (Aug. 6, 1996).

HISTORICAL AND STATUTORY NOTES

References in Text

The Federal Water Pollution Control Act, referred to in subsec. (f)(1), is Act of June 30, 1948, c. 758, as amended generally by Pub. L. No. 92–500, § 2, 86 Stat. 816 (Oct. 18, 1972), which is codified generally as chapter 26 (section 1251 et seq.) of Title 33, Navigation and Navigable Waters. For complete classification of this Act to the Code, see Short Title note set out under section 1251 of Title 33 and Tables.

The Solid Waste Disposal Act, referred to in subsec. (f)(1), is Title II of Pub. L. No. 89–272, as amended generally by Pub. L. No. 94–580, § 2, 90 Stat. 2795 (Oct. 21, 1976), which is codified generally as chapter 82 (section 6901 et seq.) of this title. For complete classification of this Act to the Code, see Short Title note set out under section 6901 of this title and Tables.

The Comprehensive Environmental Response, Compensation, and Liability Act of 1980, referred to in subsec. (f)(1), is Pub. L. No. 96–510, 94 Stat. 2767 (Dec. 11, 1980), as amended, which is codified principally as chapter 103 (section 9601 et seq.) of this title. For complete classification of this Act to the Code, see Short Title note set out under section 9601 of this title and Tables.

Effective and Applicability Provisions

1996 Acts. Amendment by Pub. L. No. 104–182 effective Aug. 6, 1996, except as otherwise specifically provided, see section 2(b) of Pub. L. No. 104–182, set out as a note under section 300f of this title.

§ 300h–8. State ground water protection grants

[PHSA § 1429]

(a) In general

The Administrator may make a grant to a State for the development and implementation of a State program to ensure the coordinated and comprehensive protection of ground water resources within the State.

(b) Guidance

Not later than 1 year after August 6, 1996, and annually thereafter, the Administrator shall publish guidance that establishes procedures for application for State ground water protection program assistance and that identifies key elements of State ground water protection programs.

(c) Conditions of grants

(1) In general

The Administrator shall award grants to States that submit an application that is approved by the Administrator. The Administrator shall determine the amount of a grant awarded pursuant to this paragraph on the basis of an assessment of the extent of ground water resources in the State and the likelihood that awarding the grant will result in sustained and reliable protection of ground water quality.

(2) Innovative program grants

The Administrator may also award a grant pursuant to this subsection for innovative programs proposed by a State for the prevention of ground water contamination.

(3) Allocation of funds

The Administrator shall, at a minimum, ensure that, for each fiscal year, not less than 1 percent of funds made available to the Administrator by appropriations to carry out this section are allocated to each State that submits an application that is approved by the Administrator pursuant to this section.

(4) Limitation on grants

No grant awarded by the Administrator may be used for a project to remediate ground water contamination.

(d) Amount of grants

The amount of a grant awarded pursuant to paragraph (1) shall not exceed 50 percent of the eligible costs of carrying out the ground water protection program that is the subject of the grant (as determined by the Administrator) for the 1-year period beginning on the date that the grant is awarded. The State shall pay a State share to cover the costs of the ground water protection program from State funds in an amount that is not less than 50 percent of the cost of conducting the program.

(e) Evaluations and reports

Not later than 3 years after August 6, 1996, and every 3 years thereafter, the Administrator shall evaluate the State ground water protection programs that are the subject of grants awarded pursuant to this section and report to the Congress on the status of ground water quality in the United States and the effectiveness of State programs for ground water protection.

(f) Authorization of appropriations

There are authorized to be appropriated to carry out this section $15,000,000 for each of fiscal years 1997 through 2003.

(July 1, 1944, c. 373, Title XIV, § 1429, as added by Pub. L. No. 104–182, Title I, § 131, 110 Stat. 1672 (Aug. 6, 1996).)

HISTORICAL AND STATUTORY NOTES

Effective and Applicability Provisions

1996 Acts. Section effective Aug. 6, 1996, except as otherwise specifically provided, see section 2(b) of Pub. L. No. 104–182, set out as a note under section 300f of this title.

PART D—EMERGENCY POWERS

§ 300i. Emergency powers

[PHSA § 1431]

(a) Actions authorized against imminent and substantial endangerment to health

Notwithstanding any other provision of this subchapter, the Administrator, upon receipt of information that a contaminant which is present in or is likely to enter a public water system or an underground source of drinking water, or that there is a threatened or potential terrorist attack (or other intentional act designed to disrupt the provision of safe drinking water or to impact adversely the safety of drinking water supplied to communities and individuals), which may present an imminent and substantial endangerment to the health of persons, and that appropriate State and local authorities have not acted to protect the health of such persons, may take such actions as he may deem necessary in order to protect the health of such persons. To the extent he determines it to be practicable in light of such imminent endangerment, he shall consult with the State and local authorities in order to confirm the correctness of the information on which action proposed to be taken under this subsection is based and to ascertain the action which such authorities are or will be taking. The action which the Administrator may take may include (but shall not be limited to) (1) issuing such orders as may be necessary to protect the health of persons who are or may be users of such system (including travelers), including orders requiring the provision of alternative water supplies by persons who caused or contributed to the endangerment, and (2) commencing a civil action for appropriate relief, including a restraining order or permanent or temporary injunction.

(b) Penalties for violations; separate offenses

Any person who violates or fails or refuses to comply with any order issued by the Administrator under subsection (a)(1) of this section may, in an action brought in the appropriate United States district court to enforce such order, be subject to a civil penalty of not to exceed $15,000 for each day in which such violation occurs or failure to comply continues.

(July 1, 1944, c. 373, Title XIV, § 1431, as added by Pub. L. No. 93–523, § 2(a), 88 Stat. 1680 (Dec. 16, 1974); and amended by Pub. L. No. 99–339, Title II, § 204, 100 Stat. 660 (June 19, 1986); Pub. L. No. 104–182, Title I, § 113(d), 110 Stat. 1636 (Aug. 6, 1996); Pub. L. No. 107–188, Title IV, § 403(2), 116 Stat. 687 (June 12, 2002).)

HISTORICAL AND STATUTORY NOTES

Effective and Applicability Provisions

1996 Acts. Amendment by Pub. L. No. 104–182 effective Aug. 6, 1996, except as otherwise specifically provided, see section 2(b) of Pub. L. No. 104–182, set out as a note under section 300f of this title.

§ 300i–1. Tampering with public water systems

[PHSA § 1432]

(a) Tampering

Any person who tampers with a public water system shall be imprisoned for not more than 20 years, or fined in accordance with Title 18, or both.

(b) Attempt or threat

Any person who attempts to tamper, or makes a threat to tamper, with a public drinking water system be imprisoned for not more than 10 years, or fined in accordance with Title 18, or both.

(c) Civil penalty

The Administrator may bring a civil action in the appropriate United States district court (as determined under the provisions of Title 28) against any person who tampers, attempts to tamper, or makes a threat to tamper with a public water system. The court may impose on such person a civil penalty of not more than $1,000,000 for such tampering or not more than $100,000 for such attempt or threat.

(d) "Tamper" defined

For purposes of this section, the term "tamper" means—

(1) to introduce a contaminant into a public water system with the intention of harming persons; or

(2) to otherwise interfere with the operation of a public water system with the intention of harming persons.

(July 1, 1944, c. 373, Title XIV, § 1432, as added by Pub. L. No. 99–339, Title I, § 108, 100 Stat. 651 (June 19, 1986); and amended by Pub. L. No. 104–182, Title V, § 501(f)(5), 110 Stat. 1692 (Aug. 6, 1996); Pub. L. No. 107–188, Title IV, § 403(3), 116 Stat. 687 (June 12, 2002).)

HISTORICAL AND STATUTORY NOTES

Effective and Applicability Provisions

1996 Acts. Amendment by Pub. L. No. 104–182 effective Aug. 6, 1996, except as otherwise specifically provided, see section 2(b) of Pub. L. No. 104–182, set out as a note under section 300f of this title.

§ 300i–2. Community water system risk and resilience

[PHSA § 1433]

(a) Risk and resilience assessments.—

(1) In general.—Each community water system serving a population of greater than 3,300 persons shall conduct an assessment of the risks to, and resilience of, its system. Such an assessment—

(A) shall include an assessment of—

(i) the risk to the system from malevolent acts and natural hazards;

(ii) the resilience of the pipes and constructed conveyances, physical barriers, source water, water collection and intake, pretreatment, treatment, storage and distribution facilities, electronic, computer, or other automated systems (including the security of such systems) which are utilized by the system;

(iii) the monitoring practices of the system;

(iv) the financial infrastructure of the system;

(v) the use, storage, or handling of various chemicals by the system; and

(vi) the operation and maintenance of the system; and

(B) may include an evaluation of capital and operational needs for risk and resilience management for the system.

(2) Baseline information.—The Administrator, not later than August 1, 2019, after consultation with appropriate departments and agencies of the Federal Government and with State and local governments, shall provide baseline information on malevolent acts of relevance to community water systems, which shall include consideration of acts that may—

(A) substantially disrupt the ability of the system to provide a safe and reliable supply of drinking water; or

(B) otherwise present significant public health or economic concerns to the community served by the system.

(3) Certification.—

(A) Certification.—Each community water system described in paragraph (1) shall submit to the Administrator a certification that the system has conducted an assessment complying with paragraph (1). Such certification shall be made prior to—

(i) March 31, 2020, in the case of systems serving a population of 100,000 or more;

(ii) December 31, 2020, in the case of systems serving a population of 50,000 or more but less than 100,000; and

(iii) June 30, 2021, in the case of systems serving a population greater than 3,300 but less than 50,000.

(B) Review and revision.—Each community water system described in paragraph (1) shall review the assessment of such system conducted under such paragraph at least once every 5 years after the applicable deadline for submission of its certification under subparagraph (A) to determine whether such assessment should be revised. Upon completion of such a review, the community water system shall submit to the Administrator a certification that the system has reviewed its assessment and, if applicable, revised such assessment.

(4) Contents of certifications.—A certification required under paragraph (3) shall contain only—

(A) information that identifies the community water system submitting the certification;

(B) the date of the certification; and

(C) a statement that the community water system has conducted, reviewed, or revised the assessment, as applicable.

(5) Provision to other entities.—No community water system shall be required under State or local law to provide an assessment described in this section (or revision thereof) to any State, regional, or local governmental entity solely by reason of the requirement set forth in paragraph (3) that the system submit a certification to the Administrator.

(b) Emergency response plan.—Each community water system serving a population greater than 3,300 shall prepare or revise, where necessary, an emergency response plan that incorporates findings of the assessment conducted under subsection (a) for such system (and any revisions thereto). Each community water system shall certify to the Administrator, as soon as reasonably possible after the date of enactment of America's Water Infrastructure Act of 2018, but not later than 6 months after **completion** of the assessment under subsection (a), that the system has completed such plan. The emergency response plan shall include—

(1) strategies and resources to improve the resilience of the system, including the physical security and cybersecurity of the system;

(2) plans and procedures that can be implemented, and identification of equipment that can be utilized, in the event of a malevolent act or natural hazard that threatens the ability of the community water system to deliver safe drinking water;

(3) actions, procedures, and equipment which can obviate or significantly lessen the impact of a malevolent act or natural hazard on the public health and the safety and supply of drinking water provided to communities and individuals, including the development of alternative source water options, relocation of water intakes, and construction of flood protection barriers; and

(4) strategies that can be used to aid in the detection of malevolent acts or natural hazards that threaten the security or resilience of the system.

(c) Coordination.—Community water systems shall, to the extent possible, coordinate with existing local emergency planning committees established pursuant to the Emergency Planning and Community Right-To-Know Act of 1986 (42 U.S.C. 11001 et seq.) when preparing or revising an assessment or emergency response plan under this section.

(d) Record maintenance.—Each community water system shall maintain a copy of the assessment conducted under subsection (a) and the emergency response plan prepared under subsection (b) (including any revised assessment or plan) for 5 years after the date on which a certification of such assessment or plan is submitted to the Administrator under this section.

(e) Guidance to small public water systems.—The Administrator shall provide guidance and technical assistance to community water systems serving a population of less than 3,300 persons on how to conduct resilience assessments, prepare emergency response plans, and address threats from malevolent acts and natural hazards that threaten to disrupt the provision of safe drinking water or significantly affect the public health or significantly affect the safety or supply of drinking water provided to communities and individuals.

(f) Alternative preparedness and operational resilience programs.—

(1) Satisfaction of requirement.—A community water system that is required to comply with the requirements of subsections (a) and (b) may satisfy such requirements by—

(A) using and complying with technical standards that the Administrator has recognized under paragraph (2); and

(B) submitting to the Administrator a certification that the community water system is complying with subparagraph (A).

(2) Authority to recognize.—Consistent with section 12(d) of the National Technology Transfer and Advancement Act of 1995, the Administrator shall recognize technical standards that are developed or adopted by third-party organizations or voluntary consensus standards bodies that carry out the objectives or activities required by this section as a means of satisfying the requirements under subsection (a) or (b).

(g) Technical assistance and grants.—

(1) In general.—The Administrator shall establish and implement a program, to be known as the Drinking Water Infrastructure Risk and Resilience Program, under which the Administrator may award grants in each of fiscal years 2020 and 2021 to owners or operators of community water systems for the purpose of increasing the resilience of such community water systems.

(2) Use of funds.—As a condition on receipt of a grant under this section, an owner or operator of a community water system shall agree to use the grant funds exclusively to assist in the planning, design, construction, or implementation of a program or project consistent with an emergency response plan prepared pursuant to subsection (b), which may include—

(A) the purchase and installation of equipment for detection of drinking water contaminants or malevolent acts;

(B) the purchase and installation of fencing, gating, lighting, or security cameras;

(C) the tamper-proofing of manhole covers, fire hydrants, and valve boxes;

(D) the purchase and installation of improved treatment technologies and equipment to improve the resilience of the system;

(E) improvements to electronic, computer, financial, or other automated systems and remote systems;

(F) participation in training programs, and the purchase of training manuals and guidance materials, relating to security and resilience;

(G) improvements in the use, storage, or handling of chemicals by the community water system;

(H) security screening of employees or contractor support services;

(I) equipment necessary to support emergency power or water supply, including standby and mobile sources; and

(J) the development of alternative source water options, relocation of water intakes, and construction of flood protection barriers.

(3) Exclusions.—A grant under this subsection may not be used for personnel costs, or for monitoring, operation, or maintenance of facilities, equipment, or systems.

(4) Technical assistance.—For each fiscal year, the Administrator may use not more than $5,000,000 from the funds made available to carry out this subsection to provide technical assistance to community water systems to assist in responding to and alleviating a vulnerability that would substantially disrupt the ability of the system to provide a safe and reliable supply of drinking water (including sources of water for such systems) which the Administrator determines to present an immediate and urgent need.

(5) Grants for small systems.—For each fiscal year, the Administrator may use not more than $10,000,000 from the funds made available to carry out this subsection to make grants to community water systems serving a population of less than 3,300 persons, or nonprofit organizations receiving assistance under section 1442(e), **for activities and projects** undertaken in accordance with the guidance provided to such systems under subsection (e) of this section.

(6) Authorization of appropriations.—To carry out this subsection, there are authorized to be appropriated $25,000,000 for each of fiscal years 2020 and 2021.

(h) Definitions.—In this section—

(1) the term 'resilience' means the ability of a community water system or an asset of a community water system to adapt to or withstand the effects of a malevolent act or natural hazard without interruption to the asset's or system's function, or if the function is interrupted, to rapidly return to a normal operating condition; and

(2) the term 'natural hazard' means a natural event that threatens the functioning of a community water system, including an earthquake, tornado, flood, hurricane, wildfire, and hydrologic changes.

(July 1, 1944, c. 373, Title XIV, § 1433, as added by Pub. L. No. 107–188, Title IV, § 401, 116 Stat. 682 (June 12, 2002); and amended by Pub. L. No. 115–270, § 2013(a), 132 Stat. 3765, 3850–3854 (Oct. 23, 2018).)

HISTORICAL AND STATUTORY NOTES

References in Text

Chapter 227 of Title 18, referred to in subsec. (a)(6)(A), is 18 U.S.C.A. § 3551 et seq.

The Emergency Planning and Community Right-to-Know Act, referred to in subsec. (b), probably means the Emergency Planning and Community Right-to-Know Act of 1986, Title III of Pub. L. No. 99–499, 100 Stat. 1728 (Oct. 17, 1986), which is codified principally as chapter 116 of this title, 42 U.S.C.A. § 11001 et seq. For complete classification of this Act to the Code, see Short Title of 1986 Amendments note set out under 42 U.S.C.A. § 11001 and Tables.

Sensitive Information

Pub. L. No. 115–270, § 2013(b), 132 Stat. 3854 (Oct. 23, 2018), provided that:

"**(1) Protection from disclosure.**—Information submitted to the Administrator of the Environmental Protection Agency pursuant to section 1433 of the Safe Drinking Water Act, as in effect on the day before the date of enactment of America's Water Infrastructure Act of 2018, shall be protected from disclosure in accordance with the provisions of such section as in effect on such day.

"**(2) Disposal.**—The Administrator, in partnership with community water systems (as defined in section 1401 of the Safe Drinking Water Act), shall develop a strategy to, in a timeframe determined appropriate by the Administrator, securely and permanently dispose of, or return to the applicable community water system, any information described in paragraph (1)."

§ 300i–3. Contaminant prevention, detection and response

[PHSA § 1434]

(a) In general

The Administrator, in consultation with the Centers for Disease Control and, after consultation with appropriate departments and agencies of the Federal Government and with State and local governments, shall review (or enter into contracts or cooperative agreements to provide for a review of) current and future methods to prevent, detect and respond to the intentional introduction of chemical, biological or radiological contaminants into community water systems and source water for community water systems, including each of the following:

(1) Methods, means and equipment, including real time monitoring systems, designed to monitor and detect various levels of chemical, biological, and radiological contaminants or indicators of contaminants and reduce the likelihood that such contaminants can be successfully introduced into public water systems and source water intended to be used for drinking water.

(2) Methods and means to provide sufficient notice to operators of public water systems, and individuals served by such systems, of the introduction of chemical, biological or radiological contaminants and the possible effect of such introduction on public health and the safety and supply of drinking water.

(3) Methods and means for developing educational and awareness programs for community water systems.

(4) Procedures and equipment necessary to prevent the flow of contaminated drinking water to individuals served by public water systems.

(5) Methods, means, and equipment which could negate or mitigate deleterious effects on public health and the safety and supply caused by the introduction of contaminants into water intended to be used for drinking water, including an examination of the effectiveness of various drinking water technologies in removing, inactivating, or neutralizing biological, chemical, and radiological contaminants.

(6) Biomedical research into the short-term and long-term impact on public health of various chemical, biological and radiological contaminants that may be introduced into public water systems through terrorist or other intentional acts.

(b) Funding

For the authorization of appropriations to carry out this section, see section 300i–4(e) of this title.

(July 1, 1944, c. 373, Title XIV, § 1434, as added by Pub. L. No. 107–188, Title IV, § 402, 116 Stat. 685 (June 12, 2002).)

HISTORICAL AND STATUTORY NOTES

Change of Name

Centers for Disease Control changed to Centers for Disease Control and Prevention by Pub. L. No. 102–531, Title III, § 312, 106 Stat. 3504 (Oct. 27, 1992).

§ 300i–4. Supply disruption prevention, detection and response [PHSA § 1435]

(a) Disruption of supply or safety

The Administrator, in coordination with the appropriate departments and agencies of the Federal Government, shall review (or enter into contracts or cooperative agreements to provide for a review of) methods and means by which terrorists or other individuals or groups could disrupt the supply of safe drinking water or take other actions against water collection, pretreatment, treatment, storage and distribution facilities which could render such water significantly less safe for human consumption, including each of the following:

(1) Methods and means by which pipes and other constructed conveyances utilized in public water systems could be destroyed or otherwise prevented from providing adequate supplies of drinking water meeting applicable public health standards.

(2) Methods and means by which collection, pretreatment, treatment, storage and distribution facilities utilized or used in connection with public water systems and collection and pretreatment storage facilities used in connection with public water systems could be destroyed or otherwise prevented from providing adequate supplies of drinking water meeting applicable public health standards.

(3) Methods and means by which pipes, constructed conveyances, collection, pretreatment, treatment, storage and distribution systems that are utilized in connection with public water systems could be altered or affected so as to be subject to cross-contamination of drinking water supplies.

(4) Methods and means by which pipes, constructed conveyances, collection, pretreatment, treatment, storage and distribution systems that are utilized in connection with public water systems

could be reasonably protected from terrorist attacks or other acts intended to disrupt the supply or affect the safety of drinking water.

(5) Methods and means by which information systems, including process controls and supervisory control and data acquisition and cyber systems at community water systems could be disrupted by terrorists or other groups.

(b) Alternative sources

The review under this section shall also include a review of the methods and means by which alternative supplies of drinking water could be provided in the event of the destruction, impairment or contamination of public water systems.

(c) Requirements and considerations

In carrying out this section and section 300i–3 of this title—

(1) the Administrator shall ensure that reviews carried out under this section reflect the needs of community water systems of various sizes and various geographic areas of the United States; and

(2) the Administrator may consider the vulnerability of, or potential for forced interruption of service for, a region or service area, including community water systems that provide service to the National Capital area.

(d) Information sharing

As soon as practicable after reviews carried out under this section or section 300i–3 of this title have been evaluated, the Administrator shall disseminate, as appropriate as determined by the Administrator, to community water systems information on the results of the project through the Information Sharing and Analysis Center, or other appropriate means.

(e) Funding

There are authorized to be appropriated to carry out this section and section 300i–3 of this title not more than $15,000,000 for the fiscal year 2002 and such sums as may be necessary for the fiscal years 2003 through 2005.

(July 1, 1944, c. 373, Title XIV, § 1435, as added by Pub. L. No. 107–188, Title IV, § 402, 116 Stat. 686 (June 12, 2002).)

PART E—GENERAL PROVISIONS

§ 300j. Assurances of availability of adequate supplies of chemicals necessary for treatment of water

[PHSA § 1441]

(a) Certification of need application

If any person who uses chlorine, activated carbon, lime, ammonia, soda ash, potassium permanganate, caustic soda, or other chemical or substance for the purpose of treating water in any public water system or in any public treatment works determines that the amount of such chemical or substance necessary to effectively treat such water is not reasonably available to him or will not be so available to him when required for the effective treatment of such water, such person may apply to the Administrator for a certification (hereinafter in this section referred to as a "certification of need") that the amount of such chemical or substance which such person requires to effectively treat such water is not reasonably available to him or will not be so available when required for the effective treatment of such water.

(b) Application requirements; publication in Federal Register; waiver; certification, issuance or denial

(1) An application for a certification of need shall be in such form and submitted in such manner as the Administrator may require and shall (A) specify the persons the applicant determines are able to provide the chemical or substance with respect to which the application is submitted, (B) specify the persons from whom the applicant has sought such chemical or substance, and (C) contain such other information as the Administrator may require.

(2) Upon receipt of an application under this section, the Administrator shall (A) publish in the Federal Register a notice of the receipt of the application and a brief summary of it, (B) notify in writing each person whom the President or his delegate (after consultation with the Administrator) determines could be made subject to an order required to be issued upon the issuance of the certification of need applied for in such application, and (C) provide an opportunity for the submission of written comments on such application. The requirements of the preceding sentence of this paragraph shall not apply when the Administrator for good cause finds (and incorporates the finding with a brief statement of reasons therefor in the order issued) that waiver of such requirements is necessary in order to protect the public health.

(3) Within 30 days after—

(A) the date a notice is published under paragraph (2) in the Federal Register with respect to an application submitted under this section for the issuance of a certification of need, or

(B) the date on which such application is received if as authorized by the second sentence of such paragraph no notice is published with respect to such application,

the Administrator shall take action either to issue or deny the issuance of a certification of need.

(c) Certification of need; issuance; executive orders; implementation of orders; equitable apportionment of orders; factors considered

(1) If the Administrator finds that the amount of a chemical or substance necessary for an applicant under an application submitted under this section to effectively treat water in a public water system or in a public treatment works is not reasonably available to the applicant or will not be so available to him when required for the effective treatment of such water, the Administrator shall issue a certification of need. Not later than seven days following the issuance of such certification, the President or his delegate shall issue an order requiring the provision to such person of such amounts of such chemical or substance as the Administrator deems necessary in the certification of need issued for such person. Such order shall apply to such manufacturers, producers, processors, distributors, and repackagers of such chemical or substance as the President or his delegate deems necessary and appropriate, except that such order may not apply to any manufacturer, producer, or processor of such chemical or substance who manufactures, produces, or processes (as the case may be) such chemical or substance solely for its own use. Persons subject to an order issued under this section shall be given a reasonable opportunity to consult with the President or his delegate with respect to the implementation of the order.

(2) Orders which are to be issued under paragraph (1) to manufacturers, producers, and processors of a chemical or substance shall be equitably apportioned, as far as practicable, among all manufacturers, producers, and processors of such chemical or substance; and orders which are to be issued under paragraph (1) to distributors and repackagers of a chemical or substance shall be equitably apportioned, as far as practicable, among all distributors and repackagers of such chemical or substance. In apportioning orders issued under paragraph (1) to manufacturers, producers, processors, distributors, and repackagers of chlorine, the President or his delegate shall, in carrying out the requirements of the preceding sentence, consider—

(A) the geographical relationships and established commercial relationships between such manufacturers, producers, processors, distributors, and repackagers and the persons for whom the orders are issued;

(B) in the case of orders to be issued to producers of chlorine, the (i) amount of chlorine historically supplied by each such producer to treat water in public water systems and public treatment works, and (ii) share of each such producer of the total annual production of chlorine in the United States; and

(C) such other factors as the President or his delegate may determine are relevant to the apportionment of orders in accordance with the requirements of the preceding sentence.

(3) Subject to subsection (f) of this section, any person for whom a certification of need has been issued under this subsection may upon the expiration of the order issued under paragraph (1) upon such certification apply under this section for additional certifications.

(d) Breach of contracts; defense

There shall be available as a defense to any action brought for breach of contract in a Federal or State court arising out of delay or failure to provide, sell, or offer for sale or exchange a chemical or substance subject to an order issued pursuant to subsection (c)(1) of this section, that such delay or failure was caused solely by compliance with such order.

(e) Penalties for noncompliance with orders; temporary restraining orders and preliminary or permanent injunctions

(1) Whoever knowingly fails to comply with any order issued pursuant to subsection (c)(1) of this section shall be fined not more than $5,000 for each such failure to comply.

(2) Whoever fails to comply with any order issued pursuant to subsection (c)(1) of this section shall be subject to a civil penalty of not more than $2,500 for each such failure to comply.

(3) Whenever the Administrator or the President or his delegate has reason to believe that any person is violating or will violate any order issued pursuant to subsection (c)(1) of this section, he may petition a United States district court to issue a temporary restraining order or preliminary or permanent injunction (including a mandatory injunction) to enforce the provision of such order.

(f) Termination date

No certification of need or order issued under this section may remain in effect for more than one year.

(July 1, 1944, c. 373, Title XIV, § 1441, as added by Pub. L. No. 93–523, § 2(a), 88 Stat. 1680 (Dec. 16, 1974); and amended by Pub. L. No. 95–190, § 7, 91 Stat. 1396 (Nov. 16, 1977); Pub. L. No. 96–63, § 3, 93 Stat. 411 (Sept. 6, 1979); Pub. L. No. 99–339, Title III, § 301(d), 100 Stat. 664 (June 19, 1986); Pub. L. No. 104–182, Title V, § 501(c), 110 Stat. 1691 (Aug. 6, 1996).)

HISTORICAL AND STATUTORY NOTES

Effective and Applicability Provisions

1996 Acts. Amendment by Pub. L. No. 104–182 effective Aug. 6, 1996, except as otherwise specifically provided, see section 2(b) of Pub. L. No. 104–182, set out as a note under section 300f of this title.

Definition of Administrator

The Waste and Water Act of 2016, Pub. L. No. 114–322, § 2002, 130 Stat. 1716 (Dec. 16, 2016), stated that "[i]n this title, the term 'Administrator' means the Administrator of the Environmental Protection Agency."

§ 300j–1. Research, technical assistance, information, training of personnel

[PHSA § 1442]

(a) Specific powers and duties of Administrator

(1) The Administrator may conduct research, studies, and demonstrations relating to the causes, diagnosis, treatment, control, and prevention of physical and mental diseases and other impairments of man resulting directly or indirectly from contaminants in water, or to the provision of a dependably safe supply of drinking water, including—

(A) improved methods (i) to identify and measure the existence of contaminants in drinking water (including methods which may be used by State and local health and water officials), and (ii) to identify the source of such contaminants;

(B) improved methods to identify and measure the health effects of contaminants in drinking water;

(C) new methods of treating raw water to prepare it for drinking, so as to improve the efficiency of water treatment and to remove contaminants from water;

(D) improved methods for providing a dependably safe supply of drinking water, including improvements in water purification and distribution, and methods of assessing the health related hazards of drinking water;

(E) improved methods of protecting underground water sources of public water systems from contamination; and

(F) innovative water technologies (including technologies to improve water treatment to ensure compliance with this title and technologies to identify and mitigate sources of drinking water contamination, including lead contamination).".

(2) Information and research facilities—

In carrying out this subchapter, the Administrator is authorized to—

(A) collect and make available information pertaining to research, investigations, and demonstrations with respect to providing a dependably safe supply of drinking water, together with appropriate recommendations in connection with the information; and

(B) make available research facilities of the Agency to appropriate public authorities, institutions, and individuals engaged in studies and research relating to this subchapter.

(3) The Administrator shall carry out a study of polychlorinated biphenyl contamination of actual or potential sources of drinking water, contamination of such sources by other substances known or suspected to be harmful to public health, the effects of such contamination, and means of removing, treating, or otherwise controlling such contamination. To assist in carrying out this paragraph, the Administrator is authorized to make grants to public agencies and private nonprofit institutions.

(4) The Administrator shall conduct a survey and study of—

(A) disposal of waste (including residential waste) which may endanger underground water which supplies, or can reasonably be expected to supply, any public water systems, and

(B) means of control of such waste disposal.

Not later than one year after December 16, 1974, he shall transmit to the Congress the results of such survey and study, together with such recommendations as he deems appropriate.

(5) The Administrator shall carry out a study of methods of underground injection which do not result in the degradation of underground drinking water sources.

(6) The Administrator shall carry out a study of methods of preventing, detecting, and dealing with surface spills of contaminants which may degrade underground water sources for public water systems.

(7) The Administrator shall carry out a study of virus contamination of drinking water sources and means of control of such contamination.

(8) The Administrator shall carry out a study of the nature and extent of the impact on underground water which supplies or can reasonably be expected to supply public water systems of (A) abandoned injection or extraction wells; (B) intensive application of pesticides and fertilizers in underground water recharge areas; and (C) ponds, pools, lagoons, pits, or other surface disposal of contaminants in underground water recharge areas.

(9) The Administrator shall conduct a comprehensive study of public water supplies and drinking water sources to determine the nature, extent, sources of and means of control of contamination by chemicals or other substances suspected of being carcinogenic. Not later than six months after December 16, 1974, he shall transmit to the Congress the initial results of such study, together with such recommendations for further review and corrective action as he deems appropriate.

(10) The Administrator shall carry out a study of the reaction of chlorine and humic acids and the effects of the contaminants which result from such reaction on public health and on the safety of drinking water, including any carcinogenic effect.

(b) Emergency situations

The Administrator is authorized to provide technical assistance and to make grants to States, or publicly owned water systems to assist in responding to and alleviating any emergency situation affecting public water systems (including sources of water for such systems) which the Administrator determines to present substantial danger to the public health. Grants provided under this subsection shall be used only to support those actions which (i) are necessary for preventing, limiting or mitigating danger to the public health in such emergency situation and (ii) would not, in the judgment of the Administrator, be taken without such emergency assistance. The Administrator may carry out the program authorized under this subsection as part of, and in accordance with the terms and conditions of, any other program of assistance for environmental emergencies which the Administrator is authorized to carry out under any other provision of law. No limitation on appropriations for any such other program shall apply to amounts appropriated under this subsection.

(c) Establishment of training programs and grants for training; training fees

The Administrator shall—

(1) provide training for, and make grants for training (including postgraduate training) of (A) personnel of State agencies which have primary enforcement responsibility and of agencies or units of local government to which enforcement responsibilities have been delegated by the State, and (B) personnel who manage or operate public water systems, and

(2) make grants for postgraduate training of individuals (including grants to educational institutions for traineeships) for purposes of qualifying such individuals to work as personnel referred to in paragraph (1).

(3) make grants to, and enter into contracts with, any public agency, educational institution, and any other organization, in accordance with procedures prescribed by the Administrator, under which he may pay all or part of the costs (as may be determined by the Administrator) of any project or activity which is designed—

(A) to develop, expand, or carry out a program (which may combine training education and employment) for training persons for occupations involving the public health aspects of providing safe drinking water;

(B) to train inspectors and supervisory personnel to train or supervise persons in occupations involving the public health aspects of providing safe drinking water; or

(C) to develop and expand the capability of programs of States and municipalities to carry out the purposes of this subchapter (other than by carrying out State programs of public water system supervision or underground water source protection (as defined in section 300j–2(c) of this title)).

Reasonable fees may be charged for training provided under paragraph (1)(B) to persons other than personnel of State or local agencies but such training shall be provided to personnel of State or local agencies without charge.

(d) Authorization of appropriations

There are authorized to be appropriated to carry out subsection (b) of this section not more than $35,000,000 for the fiscal year 2002 and such sums as may be necessary for each fiscal year thereafter.

(e) Technical assistance to small public water systems

(1) The Administrator may provide technical assistance to small public water systems to enable such systems to achieve and maintain compliance with applicable national primary drinking water regulations.

(2) Such assistance may include circuit-rider and multi-State regional technical assistance programs, training, and preliminary engineering evaluations.

(3) The Administrator shall ensure that technical assistance pursuant to this subsection is available in each State.

(4) Each nonprofit organization receiving assistance under this subsection shall consult with the State in which the assistance is to be expended or otherwise made available before using assistance to undertake activities to carry out this subsection.

(5) There are authorized to be appropriated to the Administrator to be used for such technical assistance $15,000,000 for each of the fiscal years 2015 through 2020.

(6) No portion of any State loan fund established under section 300j–12 of this title (relating to State loan funds) and no portion of any funds made available under this subsection may be used for lobbying expenses.

(7) Of the total amount appropriated under this subsection, 3 percent shall be used for technical assistance to public water systems owned or operated by Indian Tribes, including grants to provide training and operator certification services under section 1452(i)(5).

(8) **Nonprofit Organizations.**—

(A) **In General.**—The Administrator may use amounts made available to carry out this section to provide grants or cooperative agreements to nonprofit organizations that provide to small public water systems onsite technical assistance, circuit-rider technical assistance programs, multistate, regional technical assistance programs, onsite and regional training, assistance with implementing source water protection plans, and assistance with implementing monitoring plans, rules, regulations, and water security enhancements.

(B) **Preference.**—To ensure that technical assistance funding is used in a manner that is most beneficial to the small and rural communities of a State, the Administrator shall give preference under this paragraph to nonprofit organizations that, as determined by the Administrator, are the most qualified and experienced in providing training and technical assistance to small public water systems and that the small community water systems in that State find to be the most beneficial and effective.

(C) **Limitation.**—No grant or cooperative agreement provided or otherwise made available under this section may be used for litigation pursuant to section 1449.

(f) **Technical assistance for innovative water technologies.**—

(1) The Administrator may provide technical assistance to public water systems to facilitate use of innovative water technologies.

(2) There are authorized to be appropriated to the Administrator for use in providing technical assistance under paragraph (1) $10,000,000 for each of fiscal years 2017 through 2021.".

(July 1, 1944, c. 373, Title XIV, § 1442, as added by Pub. L. No. 93–523, § 2(a), 88 Stat. 1682 (Dec. 16, 1974); and amended by Pub. L. No. 95–190, §§ 2(a), 3(a), (b), (e)(1), 4, 9, 10(b), 13, 91 Stat. 1393–1395, 1397–1399 (Nov. 16, 1977); Pub. L. No. 96–63, § 1, 93 Stat. 411 (Sept. 6, 1979); Pub. L. No. 96–502, § 5, 94 Stat. 2738 (Dec. 5, 1980); Pub. L. No. 99–339, Title I, § 107, Title III, §§ 301(a), (g), 304(a), 100 Stat. 651, 663, 665, 667 (June 19, 1986); Pub. L. No. 104–66, Title II, § 2021(h), 109 Stat. 727 (Dec. 21, 1995); Pub. L. No. 104–182, Title I, §§ 121, 122, 110 Stat. 1651 (Aug. 6, 1996); Pub. L. No. 107–188, Title IV, § 403(4), 116 Stat. 687 (June 12, 2002); Pub. L. No. 114–98, § 4, 129 Stat. 2199, 2200 (Dec. 11, 2015); Pub. L. No. 114–322, §§ 2109(a), (b), 2111, 130 Stat. 1729–30 (Dec. 16, 2016).)

HISTORICAL AND STATUTORY NOTES

Codifications

Section 121(1) of Pub. L. No. 104–182, which directed that this section be amended by redesignating subsec. (b)(3) as subsec. (d)(3), was executed, as the probable intent of Congress, by redesignating such subsec. (b)(3) as subsec. (c)(3). Former subsec. (d) was redesignated as subsec. (c) by section 2021(h) of Pub. L. No. 104–66. See 1996 Amendments notes set out under this section.

Effective and Applicability Provisions

1996 Acts. Amendment by Pub. L. No. 104–182 effective Aug. 6, 1996, except as otherwise specifically provided, see section 2(b) of Pub. L. No. 104–182, set out as a note under section 300f of this title.

Report

Pub. L. No. 114–322, § 2109(c), 130 Stat. 1729 (Dec. 16, 2016), provided that:

"(c) Report.—Not later than 1 year after the date of enactment of the Water and Waste Act of 2016, and not less frequently than every 5 years thereafter, the Administrator shall report to Congress on—

"(1) the amount of funding used to provide technical assistance under section 1442(f) of the Safe Drinking Water Act to deploy innovative water technologies;

"(2) the barriers impacting greater use of innovative water technologies; and

"(3) the cost-saving potential to cities and future infrastructure investments from innovative water technologies."

Innovative Water Technology Grant Program

Pub. L. No. 115–270, § 2007, 132 Stat. 3845 (Oct. 23, 2018), provided:

"(a) Definitions.—In this section:

"(1) Administrator.—The term "Administrator" means the Administrator of the Environmental Protection Agency.

"(2) Eligible entity.—The term "eligible entity" means—

"(A) a public water system (as defined under section 1401(4) of the Safe Drinking Water Act (42 U.S.C. 300f(4)));

"(B) an institution of higher education;

"(C) a research institution or foundation;

"(D) a regional water organization; or

"(E) a nonprofit organization described in section 1442(e)(8) of the Safe Drinking Water Act (42 U.S.C. 300j–1(e)(8)).

"(b) Grant program authorized.—The Administrator shall carry out a grant program for the purpose of accelerating the development and deployment of innovative water technologies that address pressing drinking water supply, quality, treatment, or security challenges of public water systems, areas served by private wells, or source waters.

"(c) Grants.—In carrying out the program under subsection (b), the Administrator shall make grants to eligible entities—

"(1) to develop, test, and deploy innovative water technologies; or

"(2) to provide technical assistance to deploy demonstrated innovative water technologies.

"(d) Selection criteria.—In making grants under this section, the Administrator shall—

"(1) award grants through a competitive process to eligible entities the Administrator determines are best able to carry out the purpose of the program; and

"(2) give priority to projects that have the potential—

"(A) to reduce ratepayer or community costs or costs of future capital investments;

"(B) to significantly improve human health or the environment; or

"(C) to provide additional drinking water supplies with minimal environmental impact.

"(e) Cost-sharing.—The Federal share of the cost of activities carried out using a grant under this section shall be not more than 65 percent.

"(f) Limitation.—The maximum amount of a grant under this section shall be $5,000,000.

"(g) Report.—Each year, the Administrator shall submit to Congress and make publicly available on the website of the Administrator a report that describes any advancements during the previous year in development of innovative water technologies made as a result of funding provided under this section.

"(h) Partnerships.—Grants awarded under this program may include projects that are carried out by an eligible entity in cooperation with a private entity, including a farmer, farmer cooperative, or manufacturer of water technologies.

"(i) Authorization of appropriations.—There is authorized to be appropriated to carry out this section $10,000,000 for each of fiscal years 2019 and 2020."

Comparative Health Effects Assessment

Section 304(b) of Pub. L. No. 99–339, provided that: "The Administrator of the Environmental Protection Agency shall conduct a comparative health effects assessment, using available data, to compare the public health effects (both positive and negative) associated with water treatment chemicals and their byproducts to the public health effects associated with contaminants found in public water supplies. Not later than 18 months after the date of the enactment of this Act [June 19, 1986], the Administrator shall submit a report to the Congress setting forth the results of such assessment."

National Center for Ground Water Research

Section 203 of Pub. L. No. 104–182 provided that: "The Administrator of the Environmental Protection Agency, acting through the Robert S. Kerr Environmental Research Laboratory, is authorized to reestablish a partnership between the Laboratory and the National Center for Ground Water Research, a university consortium, to conduct research, training, and technology transfer for ground water quality protection and restoration. No funds are authorized by this section."

Scientific Research Review

Pub. L. No. 104–182, Title II, § 202, 110 Stat. 1682 (Aug. 6, 1996), provided that:

"(a) In general.—The Administrator shall—

"(1) develop a strategic plan for drinking water research activities throughout the Environmental Protection Agency (in this section referred to as the 'Agency');

"(2) integrate that strategic plan into ongoing Agency planning activities; and

"(3) review all Agency drinking water research to ensure the research—

"(A) is of high quality; and

"(B) does not duplicate any other research being conducted by the Agency.

"(b) Plan.—The Administrator shall transmit the plan to the Committees on Commerce [now Energy and Commerce] and Science [now Science, Space, and Technology] of the House of Representatives and the Committee on Environment and Public Works of the Senate and the plan shall be made available to the public."

Grassroots Rural and Small Community Water Systems Assistance Act

Pub. L. No. 114–98, §§ 2, 3, 129 Stat. 2199 (Dec. 11, 2015), provided that:

"Sec. 2 Findings.

"Congress finds that—

"(1) the Safe Drinking Water Act Amendments of 1996 (Public Law 104–182) authorized technical assistance for small and rural communities to assist those communities in complying with regulations promulgated pursuant to the Safe Drinking Water Act (42 U.S.C. 300f et seq.);

"(2) technical assistance and compliance training—

"(A) ensures that Federal regulations do not overwhelm the resources of small and rural communities; and

"(B) provides small and rural communities lacking technical resources with the necessary skills to improve and protect water resources;

"(3) across the United States, more than 90 percent of the community water systems serve a population of less than 10,000 individuals;

"(4) small and rural communities have the greatest difficulty providing safe, affordable public drinking water and wastewater services due to limited economies of scale and lack of technical expertise; and

"(5) in addition to being the main source of compliance assistance, small and rural water technical assistance has been the main source of emergency response assistance in small and rural communities.

"Sec. 3 Sense of Congress.

"It is the sense of Congress that—

"(1) to assist small and rural communities most effectively, the Administrator of the Environmental Protection Agency should prioritize the types of technical assistance that are most beneficial to those communities, based on input from those communities; and

"(2) local support is the key to making Federal assistance initiatives work in small and rural communities to the maximum benefit."

§ 300j-2. Grants for State programs

[PHSA § 1443]

(a) Public water systems supervision programs; applications for grants; allotment of sums; waiver of grant restrictions; notice of approval or disapproval of application; authorization of appropriations

(1) From allotments made pursuant to paragraph (4), the Administrator may make grants to States to carry out public water system supervision programs.

(2) No grant may be made under paragraph (1) unless an application therefor has been submitted to the Administrator in such form and manner as he may require. The Administrator may not approve an application of a State for its first grant under paragraph (1) unless he determines that the State—

(A) has established or will establish within one year from the date of such grant a public water system supervision program, and

(B) will, within that one year, assume primary enforcement responsibility for public water systems within the State.

No grant may be made to a State under paragraph (1) for any period beginning more than one year after the date of the State's first grant unless the State has assumed and maintains primary enforcement responsibility for public water systems within the State. The prohibitions contained in the preceding two sentences shall not apply to such grants when made to Indian Tribes.

(3) A grant under paragraph (1) shall be made to cover not more than 75 per centum of the grant recipient's costs (as determined under regulations of the Administrator) in carrying out, during the one-year period beginning on the date the grant is made, a public water system supervision program.

(4) In each fiscal year the Administrator shall, in accordance, with regulations, allot the sums appropriated for such year under paragraph (5) among the States on the basis of population, geographical area, number of public water systems, and other relevant factors. No State shall receive less than 1 per centum of the annual appropriation for grants under paragraph (1): *Provided*, That the Administrator may, by regulation, reduce such percentage in accordance with the criteria specified in this paragraph: *And provided further*, That such percentage shall not apply to grants allotted to Guam, American Samoa, or the Virgin Islands.

(5) The prohibition contained in the last sentence of paragraph (2) may be waived by the Administrator with respect to a grant to a State through fiscal year 1979 but such prohibition may only be waived if, in the judgment of the Administrator—

(A) the State is making a diligent effort to assume and maintain primary enforcement responsibility for public water systems within the State;

(B) the State has made significant progress toward assuming and maintaining such primary enforcement responsibility; and

(C) there is reason to believe the State will assume such primary enforcement responsibility by October 1, 1979.

The amount of any grant awarded for the fiscal years 1978 and 1979 pursuant to a waiver under this paragraph may not exceed 75 per centum of the allotment which the State would have received for such fiscal year if it had assumed and maintained such primary enforcement responsibility. The remaining 25 per centum of the amount allotted to such State for such fiscal year shall be retained by the Administrator, and the Administrator may award such amount to such State at such time as the State assumes such responsibility before the beginning of fiscal year 1980. At the beginning of each fiscal years[1] 1979 and 1980 the amounts retained by the Administrator for any preceding fiscal year and not awarded by the beginning of fiscal year 1979 or 1980 to the States to which such amounts were originally allotted may be removed from the original allotment and reallotted for fiscal year 1979 or 1980 (as the case may be) to States which have assumed primary enforcement responsibility by the beginning of such fiscal year.

(6) The Administrator shall notify the State of the approval or disapproval of any application for a grant under this section—

(A) within ninety days after receipt of such application, or

(B) not later than the first day of the fiscal year for which the grant application is made,

whichever is later.

(7) Authorization

For the purpose of making grants under paragraph (1), there are authorized to be appropriated $125,000,000 for each of fiscal years 2020 and 2021.

(8) Reservation of funds by the Administrator

If the Administrator assumes the primary enforcement responsibility of a State public water system supervision program, the Administrator may reserve from funds made available pursuant to this subsection an amount equal to the amount that would otherwise have been provided to the State pursuant to this subsection. The Administrator shall use the funds reserved pursuant to this paragraph to ensure the full and effective administration of a public water system supervision program in the State.

(9) State loan funds

(A) Reservation of funds

For any fiscal year for which the amount made available to the Administrator by appropriations to carry out this subsection is less than the amount that the Administrator determines is necessary to supplement funds made available pursuant to paragraph (8) to ensure the full and effective administration of a public water system supervision program in a State, the Administrator may reserve from the funds made available to the State under section 300j–12 of this title (relating to State loan funds) an amount that is equal to the amount of the shortfall. This paragraph shall not apply to any State not exercising primary enforcement responsibility for public water systems as of August 6, 1996.

(B) Duty of Administrator

If the Administrator reserves funds from the allocation of a State under subparagraph (A), the Administrator shall carry out in the State each of the activities that would be required of the State if the State had primary enforcement authority under section 300g–2 of this title.

(b) Underground water source protection programs; applications for grants; allotment of sums; authorization of appropriations

(1) From allotments made pursuant to paragraph (4), the Administrator may make grants to States to carry out underground water source protection programs.

(2) No grant may be made under paragraph (1) unless an application therefor has been submitted to the Administrator in such form and manner as he may require. No grant may be made to any State

under paragraph (1) unless the State has assumed primary enforcement responsibility within two years after the date the Administrator promulgates regulations for State underground injection control programs under section 300h of this title. The prohibition contained in the preceding sentence shall not apply to such grants when made to Indian Tribes.

(3) A grant under paragraph (1) shall be made to cover not more than 75 per centum of the grant recipient's costs (as determined under regulations of the Administrator) in carrying out, during the one-year period beginning on the date the grant is made, an underground water source protection program.

(4) In each fiscal year the Administrator shall, in accordance with regulations, allot the sums appropriated for such year under paragraph (5) among the States on the basis of population, geographical area, and other relevant factors.

(5) For purposes of making grants under paragraph (1) there are authorized to be appropriated $5,000,000 for the fiscal year ending June 30, 1976, $7,500,000 for the fiscal year ending June 30, 1977, $10,000,000 for each of the fiscal years 1978 and 1979, $7,795,000 for the fiscal year ending September 30, 1980, $18,000,000 for the fiscal year ending September 30, 1981, and $21,000,000 for the fiscal year ending September 30, 1982. For the purpose of making grants under paragraph (1) there are authorized to be appropriated not more than the following amounts:

Fiscal year:	*Amount*
1987	$19,700,000
1988	19,700,000
1989	20,850,000
1990	20,850,000
1991	20,850,000
1992–2003	15,000,000

(c) Definitions

For purposes of this section:

(1) The term "public water system supervision program" means a program for the adoption and enforcement of drinking water regulations (with such variances and exemptions from such regulations under conditions and in a manner which is not less stringent than the conditions under, and the manner in, which variances and exemptions may be granted under sections 300g–4 and 300g–5 of this title) which are no less stringent than the national primary drinking water regulations under section 300g–1 of this title, and for keeping records and making reports required by section 300g–2(a)(3) of this title.

(2) The term "underground water source protection program" means a program for the adoption and enforcement of a program which meets the requirements of regulations under section 300h of this title, and for keeping records and making reports required by section 300h–1(b)(1)(A)(ii) of this title. Such term includes, where applicable, a program which meets the requirements of section 300h–4 of this title.

(d) New York City watershed protection program

(1) In general

The Administrator is authorized to provide financial assistance to the State of New York for demonstration projects implemented as part of the watershed program for the protection and enhancement of the quality of source waters of the New York City water supply system, including projects that demonstrate, assess, or provide for comprehensive monitoring and surveillance and projects necessary to comply with the criteria for avoiding filtration contained in 40 C.F.R. 141.71. Demonstration projects which shall be eligible for financial assistance shall be certified to the Administrator by the State of New York as satisfying the purposes of this subsection. In certifying projects to the Administrator, the State of New York shall give priority to monitoring projects that have undergone peer review.

(2) Report

Not later than 5 years after the date on which the Administrator first provides assistance pursuant to this paragraph, the Governor of the State of New York shall submit a report to the Administrator on the results of projects assisted.

(3) Matching requirements

Federal assistance provided under this subsection shall not exceed 50 percent of the total cost of the protection program being carried out for any particular watershed or ground water recharge area.

(4) Authorization

There are authorized to be appropriated to the Administrator to carry out this subsection for each of fiscal years 2003 through 2010, $15,000,000 for the purpose of providing assistance to the State of New York to carry out paragraph (1).

(July 1, 1944, c. 373, Title XIV, § 1443, as added by Pub. L. No. 93–523, § 2(a), 88 Stat. 1684 (Dec. 16, 1974); and amended by Pub. L. No. 95–190, §§ 2(b), (c), 5(a), 91 Stat. 1393, 1395 (Nov. 16, 1977); Pub. L. No. 96–63, § 2, 93 Stat. 411 (Sept. 6, 1979); Pub. L. No. 96–502, §§ 2(c), 4(d), 94 Stat. 2738 (Dec. 5, 1980); Pub. L. No. 99–339, Title III, §§ 301(b), (c), 302(d), 100 Stat. 664, 666 (June 19, 1986); Pub. L. No. 104–182, Title I, §§ 120(c), 124, 128, 110 Stat. 1651, 1653, 1659 (Aug. 6, 1996); Pub. L. No. 108–328, § 1, 118 Stat. 1273 (Oct. 16, 2004); Pub. L. No. 115–270, § 2014, 132 Stat. 3765, 3854 (Oct. 23, 2018).)

[1] So in original. Probably should be "year".

HISTORICAL AND STATUTORY NOTES

Effective and Applicability Provisions

1996 Acts. Amendment by Pub. L. No. 104–182 effective Aug. 6, 1996, except as otherwise specifically provided, see section 2(b) of Pub. L. No. 104–182, set out as a note under section 300f of this title.

§ 300j–3. Special project grants and guaranteed loans

[PHSA § 1444]

(a) Special study and demonstration project grants

The Administrator may make grants to any person for the purposes of—

(1) assisting in the development and demonstration (including construction) of any project which will demonstrate a new or improved method, approach, or technology, for providing a dependably safe supply of drinking water to the public; and

(2) assisting in the development and demonstration (including construction) of any project which will investigate and demonstrate health implications involved in the reclamation, recycling, and reuse of waste waters for drinking and the processes and methods for the preparation of safe and acceptable drinking water.

(b) Limitations

Grants made by the Administrator under this section shall be subject to the following limitations:

(1) Grants under this section shall not exceed $66^2/_3$ per centum of the total cost of construction of any facility and 75 per centum of any other costs, as determined by the Administrator.

(2) Grants under this section shall not be made for any project involving the construction or modification of any facilities for any public water system in a State unless such project has been approved by the State agency charged with the responsibility for safety of drinking water (or if there is no such agency in a State, by the State health authority).

(3) Grants under this section shall not be made for any project unless the Administrator determines, after consulting the National Drinking Water Advisory Council, that such project will serve a useful purpose relating to the development and demonstration of new or improved techniques, methods, or technologies for the provision of safe water to the public for drinking.

(4) Priority for grants under this section shall be given where there are known or potential public health hazards which require advanced technology for the removal of particles which are too small to be removed by ordinary treatment technology.

(c) Authorization of appropriations

For the purposes of making grants under subsections (a) and (b) of this section there are authorized to be appropriated $7,500,000 for the fiscal year ending June 30, 1975; and $7,500,000 for the fiscal year ending June 30, 1976; and $10,000,000 for the fiscal year ending June 30, 1977.

(d) Loan guarantees to public water systems; conditions; indebtedness limitation; regulations

The Administrator during the fiscal years ending June 30, 1975, and June 30, 1976, shall carry out a program of guaranteeing loans made by private lenders to small public water systems for the purpose of enabling such systems to meet national primary drinking water regulations prescribed under section 300g–1 of this title. No such guarantee may be made with respect to a system unless (1) such system cannot reasonably obtain financial assistance necessary to comply with such regulations from any other source, and (2) the Administrator determines that any facilities constructed with a loan guaranteed under this subsection is not likely to be made obsolete by subsequent changes in primary regulations. The aggregate amount of indebtedness guaranteed with respect to any system may not exceed $50,000. The aggregate amount of indebtedness guaranteed under this subsection may not exceed $50,000,000. The Administrator shall prescribe regulations to carry out this subsection.

(July 1, 1944, c. 373, Title XIV, § 1444, as added by Pub. L. No. 93–523, § 2(a), 88 Stat. 1685 (Dec. 16, 1974); and amended by Pub. L. No. 99–339, Title I, § 101(c)(3), 100 Stat. 646 (June 19, 1986).)

§ 300j–3a. Grants to public sector agencies

(a) Assistance for development and demonstration projects

The Administrator of the Environmental Protection Agency shall offer grants to public sector agencies for the purposes of—

(1) assisting in the development and demonstration (including construction) of any project which will demonstrate a new or improved method, approach, or technology for providing a dependably safe supply of drinking water to the public; and

(2) assisting in the development and demonstration (including construction) of any project which will investigate and demonstrate health and conservation implications involved in the reclamation, recycling, and reuse of wastewaters for drinking and agricultural use or the processes and methods for the preparation of safe and acceptable drinking water.

(b) Limitations

Grants made by the Administrator under this section shall be subject to the following limitations:

(1) Grants under this section shall not exceed 66⅔ per centum of the total cost of construction of any facility and 75 per centum of any other costs, as determined by the Administrator.

(2) Grants under this section shall not be made for any project involving the construction or modification of any facilities for any public water system in a State unless such project has been approved by the State agency charged with the responsibility for safety of drinking water (or if there is no such agency in a State, by the State health authority).

(3) Grants under this section shall not be made for any project unless the Administrator determines, after consultation, that such project will serve a useful purpose relating to the development and demonstration of new or improved techniques, methods, or technologies for the provision of safe water to the public for drinking.

(c) Authorization of appropriations

There are authorized to be appropriated for the purposes of this section $25,000,000 for fiscal year 1978.

(Pub. L. No. 95–155, § 5, 91 Stat. 1258 (Nov. 8, 1977); as amended by Pub. L. No. 95–477, § 7(a)(1), 92 Stat. 1511 (Oct. 18, 1978).)

HISTORICAL AND STATUTORY NOTES

Codifications

Section was enacted as part of the Environmental Research, Development, and Demonstration Authorization Act of 1978, and not as part of the Public Health Service Act, which comprises this chapter.

Effective and Applicability Provisions

1978 Acts. Section 7(a)(2) of Pub. L. No. 95–477 provided that: "This subsection [amending this section] shall become effective October 1, 1978."

§ 300j–3b. Contaminant standards or treatment technique guidelines

(1) Not later than nine months after October 18, 1978, the Administrator shall promulgate guidelines establishing supplemental standards or treatment technique requirements for microbiological, viral, radiological, organic, and inorganic contaminants, which guidelines shall be conditions, as provided in paragraph (2), of any grant for a demonstration project for water reclamation, recycling, and reuse funded under section 300j–3a of this title or under section 300j–3(a)(2) of this title, where such project involves direct human consumption of treated wastewater. Such guidelines shall provide for sufficient control of each such contaminant, such that in the Administrator's judgment, no adverse effects on the health of persons may reasonably be anticipated to occur, allowing an adequate margin of safety.

(2) A grant referred to in paragraph (1) for a project which involves direct human consumption of treated wastewater may be awarded on or after the date of promulgation of guidelines under this section only if the applicant demonstrates to the satisfaction of the Administrator that the project—

(A) will comply with all national primary drinking water regulations under section 300g–1 of this title;

(B) will comply with all guidelines under this section; and

(C) will in other respects provide safe drinking water.

Any such grant awarded before the date of promulgation of such guidelines shall be conditioned on the applicant's agreement to comply to the maximum feasible extent with such guidelines as expeditiously as practicable following the date of promulgation thereof.

(3) Guidelines under this section may, in the discretion of the Administrator—

(A) be nationally and uniformly applicable to all projects funded under section 300j–3a of this title or section 300j–1(a)(2) of this title;

(B) vary for different classes or categories of such projects (as determined by the Administrator);

(C) be established and applicable on a project-by-project basis; or

(D) any combination of the above.

(4) Nothing in this section shall be construed to prohibit or delay the award of any grant referred to in paragraph (1) prior to the date of promulgation of such guidelines.

(Pub. L. No. 95–477, § 7(b), 92 Stat. 1511 (Oct. 18, 1978).)

HISTORICAL AND STATUTORY NOTES

References in Text

Section 300j–1(a)(2) of this title, referred to in par. (3)(A), was amended by Pub. L. No. 104–182, title I, § 121(3), (4)(A), Aug. 6, 1996, 110 Stat. 1651, to redesignate par. (2)(B) as subsec. (b) of section 300j–1, strike par. (2)(A), and add a new par. (2) relating to information and research facilities.

Codifications

Section was enacted as part of the Environmental Research, Development, and Demonstration Authorization Act of 1979, and not as part of the Public Health Service Act which comprises this chapter.

§ 300j–3c. National assistance program for water infrastructure and watersheds

(a) Technical and financial assistance

The Administrator of the Environmental Protection Agency may provide technical and financial assistance in the form of grants to States (1) for the construction, rehabilitation, and improvement of water supply systems, and (2) consistent with nonpoint source management programs established under section 1329 of Title 33, for source water quality protection programs to address pollutants in navigable waters for the purpose of making such waters usable by water supply systems.

(b) Limitation

Not more than 30 percent of the amounts appropriated to carry out this section in a fiscal year may be used for source water quality protection programs described in subsection (a)(2) of this section.

(c) Condition

As a condition to receiving assistance under this section, a State shall ensure that such assistance is carried out in the most cost-effective manner, as determined by the State.

(d) Authorization of appropriations

(1) Unconditional authorization

There are authorized to be appropriated to carry out this section $25,000,000 for each of fiscal years 1997 through 2003. Such sums shall remain available until expended.

(2) Conditional authorization

In addition to amounts authorized under paragraph (1), there are authorized to be appropriated to carry out this section $25,000,000 for each of fiscal years 1997 through 2003, provided that such authorization shall be in effect for a fiscal year only if at least 75 percent of the total amount of funds authorized to be appropriated for such fiscal year by section 300j–12(m) of this title are appropriated.

(e) Acquisition of lands

Assistance provided with funds made available under this section may be used for the acquisition of lands and other interests in lands; however, nothing in this section authorizes the acquisition of lands or other interests in lands from other than willing sellers.

(f) Federal share

The Federal share of the cost of activities for which grants are made under this section shall be 50 percent.

(g) Definitions

In this section, the following definitions apply:

(1) State

The term "State" means a State, the District of Columbia, the Commonwealth of Puerto Rico, the Virgin Islands, Guam, American Samoa, and the Commonwealth of the Northern Mariana Islands.

(2) Water supply system

The term "water supply system" means a system for the provision to the public of piped water for human consumption if such system has at least 15 service connections or regularly serves at least 25 individuals and a draw and fill system for the provision to the public of water for human consumption. Such term does not include a system owned by a Federal agency. Such term includes (A) any collection, treatment, storage, and distribution facilities under control of the operator of such system and used primarily in connection with such system, and (B) any collection or pretreatment facilities not under such control that are used primarily in connection with such system.

(Pub. L. No. 104–182, Title IV, § 401, 110 Stat. 1690 (Aug. 6, 1996).)

HISTORICAL AND STATUTORY NOTES

Codifications

Section was enacted as part of the Safe Drinking Water Act Amendments of 1996, and not as part of the Safe Drinking Water Act, which comprises this subchapter, nor as part of the Public Health Service Act, which comprises this chapter.

Effective and Applicability Provisions

1996 Acts. Section effective Aug. 6, 1996, except as otherwise specifically provided, see section 2(b) of Pub. L. No. 104–182, set out as a note under section 300f of this title.

§ 300j–3d. Water supply cost savings

(a) Drinking water technology clearinghouse.—The Administrator, in consultation with the Secretary of Agriculture, shall—

(1) develop a technology clearinghouse for information on the cost-effectiveness of innovative and alternative drinking water delivery systems, including wells and well systems; and

(2) disseminate such information to the public and to communities and not-for-profit organizations seeking Federal funding for drinking water delivery systems serving 500 or fewer persons.

(b) Water system assessment.—In any application for a grant or loan for the purpose of construction, replacement, or rehabilitation of a drinking water delivery system serving 500 or fewer persons, the funding for which would come from the Federal Government (either directly or through a State), a unit of local government or not-for-profit organization shall self-certify that the unit of local government or organization has considered, as an alternative drinking water supply, drinking water delivery systems sourced by publicly owned—

(1) individual wells;

(2) shared wells; and

(3) community wells.

(c) Report to Congress.—Not later than 3 years after the date of enactment of this Act, the Comptroller General of the United States shall submit to Congress a report that describes—

(1) the use of innovative and alternative drinking water delivery systems described in this section;

(2) the range of cost savings for communities using innovative and alternative drinking water delivery systems described in this section; and

(3) the use of drinking water technical assistance programs operated by the Administrator and the Secretary of Agriculture."

(Pub. L. No. 114–322, § 2108, 130 Stat. 1728–39 (Dec. 16, 2016).)

HISTORICAL AND STATUTORY NOTES

Codifications

This section was enacted as part of the Water Infrastructure Improvement for the Nation Act of 2016 and not as part of the Public Health Service Act, which comprises this chapter, or of the Safe Drinking Water Act, which comprises this subchapter.

§ 300j–4. Records and inspections

[PHSA § 1445]

(a) Provision of information to Administrator; monitoring program for unregulated contaminants

(1) (A) Every person who is subject to any requirement of this subchapter or who is a grantee, shall establish and maintain such records, make such reports, conduct such monitoring, and provide such information as the Administrator may reasonably require by regulation to assist the Administrator in establishing regulations under this subchapter, in determining whether such person has acted or is acting in compliance with this subchapter, in administering any program of financial assistance under this subchapter, in evaluating the health risks of unregulated contaminants, or in advising the public of such risks. In requiring a public water system to monitor under this subsection, the Administrator may take into consideration the system size and the contaminants likely to be found in the system's drinking water.

(B) Every person who is subject to a national primary drinking water regulation under section 300g–1 of this title shall provide such information as the Administrator may reasonably require, after consultation with the State in which such person is located if such State has primary enforcement responsibility for public water systems, on a case-by-case basis, to determine whether such person has acted or is acting in compliance with this subchapter.

(C) Every person who is subject to a national primary drinking water regulation under section 300g–1 of this title shall provide such information as the Administrator may reasonably require to assist the Administrator in establishing regulations under section 300g–1 of this title, after consultation with States and suppliers of water. The Administrator may not require under this subparagraph the installation of treatment equipment or process changes, the testing of treatment technology, or the analysis or processing of monitoring samples, except where the Administrator provides the funding for such activities. Before exercising this authority, the Administrator shall first seek to obtain the information by voluntary submission.

(D) The Administrator shall not later than 2 years after August 6, 1996, after consultation with public health experts, representatives of the general public, and officials of State and local governments, review the monitoring requirements for not fewer than 12 contaminants identified by the Administrator, and promulgate any necessary modifications.

(2) Monitoring program for unregulated contaminants

(A) Establishment

The Administrator shall promulgate regulations establishing the criteria for a monitoring program for unregulated contaminants. The regulations shall require monitoring of drinking water supplied by public water systems and shall vary the frequency and schedule for monitoring requirements for systems based on the number of persons served by the system, the source of supply, and the contaminants likely to be found, ensuring that only a representative sample of systems serving 10,000 persons or fewer are required to monitor.

(B) Monitoring program for certain unregulated contaminants

(i) Initial list

Not later than 3 years after August 6, 1996, and every 5 years thereafter, the Administrator shall issue a list pursuant to subparagraph (A) of not more than 30 unregulated contaminants to be monitored by public water systems and to be included in the national drinking water occurrence data base maintained pursuant to subsection (g) of this section.

(ii) Governors' petition

The Administrator shall include among the list of contaminants for which monitoring is required under this paragraph each contaminant recommended in a petition signed by the Governor of each of 7 or more States, unless the Administrator determines that the action would prevent the listing of other contaminants of a higher public health concern.

(C) Monitoring plan for small and medium systems

(i) In general

Based on the regulations promulgated by the Administrator, each State may develop a representative monitoring plan to assess the occurrence of unregulated contaminants in public water systems that serve a population of 10,000 or fewer in that State. The plan shall require monitoring for systems representative of different sizes, types, and geographic locations in the State.

(ii) Grants for small system costs

From funds reserved under section 300j–12(*o*) of this title or appropriated under subparagraph (H), the Administrator shall pay the reasonable cost of such testing and laboratory analysis as are necessary to carry out monitoring under the plan.

(D) Monitoring results

Each public water system that conducts monitoring of unregulated contaminants pursuant to this paragraph shall provide the results of the monitoring to the primary enforcement authority for the system.

(E) Notification

Notification of the availability of the results of monitoring programs required under paragraph (2)(A) shall be given to the persons served by the system.

(F) Waiver of monitoring requirement

The Administrator shall waive the requirement for monitoring for a contaminant under this paragraph in a State, if the State demonstrates that the criteria for listing the contaminant do not apply in that State.

(G) Analytical methods

The State may use screening methods approved by the Administrator under subsection (i) of this section in lieu of monitoring for particular contaminants under this paragraph.

(H) Authorization of appropriations

There are authorized to be appropriated to carry out this paragraph $10,000,000 for each of the fiscal years 2019 through 2021.

(b) Entry of establishments, facilities, or other property; inspections; conduct of certain tests; audit and examination of records; entry restrictions; prohibition against informing of a proposed entry

(1) Except as provided in paragraph (2), the Administrator, or representatives of the Administrator duly designated by him, upon presenting appropriate credentials and a written notice to any supplier of water or other person subject to (A) a national primary drinking water regulation prescribed under section 300g–1 of this title, (B) an applicable underground injection control program, or (C) any requirement to monitor an unregulated contaminant pursuant to subsection (a) of this section, or person in charge of any of the property of such supplier or other person referred to in clause (A), (B), or (C), is authorized to enter any establishment, facility, or other property of such supplier or other person in order to determine whether such supplier or other person has acted or is acting in compliance with this subchapter, including for this purpose, inspection, at reasonable times, of records, files, papers, processes, controls, and facilities, or in order to test any feature of a public water system, including its raw water source. The Administrator or the Comptroller General (or any representative designated by either) shall have access for the purpose of audit and examination to any records, reports, or information of a grantee which are required to be maintained under subsection (a) of this section or which are pertinent to any financial assistance under this subchapter.

(2) No entry may be made under the first sentence of paragraph (1) in an establishment, facility, or other property of a supplier of water or other person subject to a national primary drinking water regulation if the establishment, facility, or other property is located in a State which has primary enforcement responsibility for public water systems unless, before written notice of such entry is made, the Administrator (or his representative) notifies the State agency charged with responsibility for safe drinking water of the reasons for such entry. The Administrator shall, upon a showing by the State agency that such an entry will be detrimental to the administration of the State's program of primary enforcement responsibility, take such showing into consideration in determining whether to make such entry. No State agency which receives notice under this paragraph of an entry proposed to be made under paragraph (1) may use the information contained in the notice to inform the person whose property is proposed to be entered of the proposed entry; and if a State agency so uses such information, notice to the agency under this paragraph is not required until such time as the Administrator determines the agency has provided him satisfactory assurances that it will no longer so use information contained in a notice under this paragraph.

(c) Penalty

Whoever fails or refuses to comply with any requirement of subsection (a) of this section or to allow the Administrator, the Comptroller General, or representatives of either, to enter and conduct any audit or inspection authorized by subsection (b) of this section shall be subject to a civil penalty of not to exceed $25,000.

(d) Confidential information; trade secrets and secret processes; information disclosure; "information required under this section" defined

(1) Subject to paragraph (2), upon a showing satisfactory to the Administrator by any person that any information required under this section from such person, if made public, would divulge trade secrets or secret processes of such person, the Administrator shall consider such information confidential in accordance with the purposes of section 1905 of Title 18. If the applicant fails to make a showing satisfactory to the Administrator, the Administrator shall give such applicant thirty days' notice before releasing the information to which the application relates (unless the public health or safety requires an earlier release of such information).

(2) Any information required under this section (A) may be disclosed to other officers, employees, or authorized representatives of the United States concerned with carrying out this subchapter or to committees of the Congress, or when relevant in any proceeding under this subchapter, and (B) shall be disclosed to the extent it deals with the level of contaminants in drinking water. For purposes of this subsection the term "information required under this section" means any papers, books, documents, or information, or any particular part thereof, reported to or otherwise obtained by the Administrator under this section.

(e) "Grantee" and "person" defined

For purposes of this section, (1) the term "grantee" means any person who applies for or receives financial assistance, by grant, contract, or loan guarantee under this subchapter, and (2) the term "person" includes a Federal agency.

(f) Information regarding drinking water coolers

The Administrator may utilize the authorities of this section for purposes of part F of this subchapter. Any person who manufactures, imports, sells, or distributes drinking water coolers in interstate commerce shall be treated as a supplier of water for purposes of applying the provisions of this section in the case of persons subject to part F of this subchapter.

(g) Occurrence data base

(1) In general

Not later than 3 years after August 6, 1996, the Administrator shall assemble and maintain a national drinking water contaminant occurrence data base, using information on the occurrence of both regulated and unregulated contaminants in public water systems obtained under subsection (a)(1)(A) of this section or subsection (a)(2) of this section and reliable information from other public and private sources.

(2) Public input

In establishing the occurrence data base, the Administrator shall solicit recommendations from the Science Advisory Board, the States, and other interested parties concerning the development and maintenance of a national drinking water contaminant occurrence data base, including such issues as the structure and design of the data base, data input parameters and requirements, and the use and interpretation of data.

(3) Use

The data shall be used by the Administrator in making determinations under section 300g–1(b)(1) of this title with respect to the occurrence of a contaminant in drinking water at a level of public health concern.

(4) Public recommendations

The Administrator shall periodically solicit recommendations from the appropriate officials of the National Academy of Sciences and the States, and any person may submit recommendations to the Administrator, with respect to contaminants that should be included in the national drinking water contaminant occurrence data base, including recommendations with respect to additional unregulated contaminants that should be listed under subsection (a)(2) of this section. Any recommendation submitted under this clause shall be accompanied by reasonable documentation that—

(A) the contaminant occurs or is likely to occur in drinking water; and

(B) the contaminant poses a risk to public health.

(5) Public availability

The information from the data base shall be available to the public in readily accessible form.

(6) Regulated contaminants

With respect to each contaminant for which a national primary drinking water regulation has been established, the data base shall include information on the detection of the contaminant at a quantifiable level in public water systems (including detection of the contaminant at levels not constituting a violation of the maximum contaminant level for the contaminant).

(7) Unregulated contaminants

With respect to contaminants for which a national primary drinking water regulation has not been established, the data base shall include—

(A) monitoring information collected by public water systems that serve a population of more than 10,000, as required by the Administrator under subsection (a) of this section;

(B) monitoring information collected from a representative sampling of public water systems that serve a population of 10,000 or fewer;

(C) if applicable, monitoring information collected by public water systems pursuant to subsection (j) that is not duplicative of monitoring information included in the data base under subparagraph (B) or (D); and

(D) other reliable and appropriate monitoring information on the occurrence of the contaminants in public water systems that is available to the Administrator.

(h) Availability of information on small system technologies

For purposes of sections 300g–1(b)(4)(E) and 300g–4(e) of this title (relating to small system variance program), the Administrator may request information on the characteristics of commercially available treatment systems and technologies, including the effectiveness and performance of the systems and technologies under various operating conditions. The Administrator may specify the form, content, and submission date of information to be submitted by manufacturers, States, and other interested persons for the purpose of considering the systems and technologies in the development of regulations or guidance under sections 300g–1(b)(4)(E) and 300g–4(e) of this title.

(i) Screening methods

The Administrator shall review new analytical methods to screen for regulated contaminants and may approve such methods as are more accurate or cost-effective than established reference methods for use in compliance monitoring.

(j) Monitoring by certain systems.—

(1) In general.—Notwithstanding subsection (a)(2)(A), the Administrator shall, subject to the availability of appropriations for such purpose—

(A) require public water systems serving between 3,300 and 10,000 persons to monitor for unregulated contaminants in accordance with this section; and

(B) ensure that only a representative sample of public water systems serving fewer than 3,300 persons are required to monitor.

(2) Effective date.—Paragraph (1) shall take effect 3 years after the date of enactment of this subsection.

(3) Limitation.—Paragraph (1) shall take effect unless the Administrator determines that there is not sufficient laboratory capacity to accommodate the analysis necessary to carry out monitoring required under such paragraph.

(4) Limitation on enforcement.—The Administrator may not enforce a requirement to monitor pursuant to paragraph (1) with respect to any public water system serving fewer than 3,300 persons, including by subjecting such a public water system to any civil penalty.

(5) Authorization of appropriations.—There are authorized to be appropriated $15,000,000 in each fiscal year for which monitoring is required to be carried out under this subsection for the Administrator to pay the reasonable cost of such testing and laboratory analysis as are necessary to carry out monitoring required under this subsection.

(July 1, 1944, c. 373, Title XIV, § 1445, as added by Pub. L. No. 93–523, § 2(a), 88 Stat. 1686 (Dec. 16, 1974); and amended by Pub. L. No. 95–190, § 12(c), (d), 91 Stat. 1398 (Nov. 16, 1977); Pub. L. No. 99–339, Title I, § 106, Title III, § 301(h), 100 Stat. 650, 665 (June 19, 1986); Pub. L. No. 100–572, § 5, 102 Stat. 2889 (Oct. 31, 1988); Pub. L. No. 104–182, Title I, §§ 111(b), 125(a), (c), (d), 126, 110 Stat. 1633, 1653, 1656, 1658 (Aug. 6, 1996); Pub. L. No. 115–270, § 2021, 132 Stat. 3765, 3861 (Oct. 23, 2018).)

HISTORICAL AND STATUTORY NOTES

Effective and Applicability Provisions

1996 Acts. Amendment by Pub. L. No. 104–182 effective Aug. 6, 1996, except as otherwise specifically provided, see section 2(b) of Pub. L. No. 104–182, set out as a note under section 300f of this title.

§ 300j–5. National Drinking Water Advisory Council [PHSA § 1446]

(a) Establishment; membership; representation of interests; term of office, vacancies; reappointment

There is established a National Drinking Water Advisory Council which shall consist of fifteen members appointed by the Administrator after consultation with the Secretary. Five members shall be appointed from the general public; five members shall be appointed from appropriate State and local agencies concerned with water hygiene and public water supply; and five members shall be appointed from representatives of private organizations or groups demonstrating an active interest in the field of water hygiene and public water supply, of which two such members shall be associated with small, rural public water systems. Each member of the Council shall hold office for a term of three years, except that—

(1) any member appointed to fill a vacancy occurring prior to the expiration of the term for which his predecessor was appointed shall be appointed for the remainder of such term; and

(2) the terms of the members first taking office shall expire as follows: Five shall expire three years after December 16, 1974, five shall expire two years after such date, and five shall expire one year after such date, as designated by the Administrator at the time of appointment.

The members of the Council shall be eligible for reappointment.

(b) Functions

The Council shall advise, consult with, and make recommendations to, the Administrator on matters relating to activities, functions, and policies of the Agency under this subchapter.

(c) Compensation and allowances; travel expenses

Members of the Council appointed under this section shall, while attending meetings or conferences of the Council or otherwise engaged in business of the Council, receive compensation and allowances at a rate to be fixed by the Administrator, but not exceeding the daily equivalent of the annual rate of basic pay in effect for grade GS–18 of the General Schedule for each day (including traveltime) during which they are engaged in the actual performance of duties vested in the Council. While away from their homes or regular places of business in the performance of services for the Council, members of the Council shall be allowed travel expenses, including per diem in lieu of subsistence, in the same manner as persons employed intermittently in the Government service are allowed expenses under section 5703(b) of Title 5.

(d) Advisory committee termination provision inapplicable

Section 14(a) of the Federal Advisory Committee Act (relating to termination) shall not apply to the Council.

(July 1, 1944, c. 373, Title XIV, § 1446, as added by Pub. L. No. 93–523, § 2(a), 88 Stat. 1688 (Dec. 16, 1974); and amended by Pub. L. No. 104–182, Title I, § 127, 110 Stat. 1659 (Aug. 6, 1996).)

HISTORICAL AND STATUTORY NOTES

References in Text

The General Schedule, referred to in subsec. (c), is set out under section 5332 of Title 5, Government Organization and Employees.

Section 5703 of Title 5, referred to in subsec. (c), was amended generally by Pub. L. No. 94–22, § 4, 89 Stat. 85 (May 19, 1975), and as so amended does not contain a subsec. (b).

Section 14(a) of the Federal Advisory Committee Act, referred to in subsec. (d), is § 14(a) of Pub. L. No.92–463, 86 Stat. 776 (Oct. 6, 1972), which is set out in Appendix 2 to Title 5, Government Organization and Employees.

Codifications

Section 127 of Pub. L. No. 104–182, which directed that section 1446(a) of the Public Health Service Act (subsec. (a) of this section) be amended by inserting ", of which two such members shall be associated with small, rural public water systems" before the period at the end of the second sentence, was executed to subsec. (a) of this section, despite parenthetical reference to "42 U.S.C. 300j–6(a)", as the probable intent of Congress. See 1996 Amendments note set out under this section.

Effective and Applicability Provisions

1996 Acts. Amendment by Pub. L. No. 104–182 effective Aug. 6, 1996, except as otherwise specifically provided, see section 2(b) of Pub. L. No. 104–182, set out as a note under section 300f of this title.

Termination of Advisory Committees

Pub. L. No. 93–641, § 6, 88 Stat. 2275 (Jan. 4, 1975), set out as a note under § 217a of this title, provided that an advisory committee established pursuant to the Public Health Service Act [this chapter] shall terminate at such time as may be specifically prescribed by an Act of Congress enacted after Jan. 4, 1975.

§ 300j–6. Federal agencies

[PHSA § 1447]

(a) In general

Each department, agency, and instrumentality of the executive, legislative, and judicial branches of the Federal Government—

(1) owning or operating any facility in a wellhead protection area;

(2) engaged in any activity at such facility resulting, or which may result, in the contamination of water supplies in any such area;

(3) owning or operating any public water system; or

(4) engaged in any activity resulting, or which may result in, underground injection which endangers drinking water (within the meaning of section 300h(d)(2) of this title),

shall be subject to, and comply with, all Federal, State, interstate, and local requirements, both substantive and procedural (including any requirement for permits or reporting or any provisions for injunctive relief and such sanctions as may be imposed by a court to enforce such relief), respecting the protection of such wellhead areas, respecting such public water systems, and respecting any underground injection in the same manner and to the same extent as any person is subject to such requirements, including the payment of reasonable service charges. The Federal, State, interstate, and local substantive and procedural requirements referred to in this subsection include, but are not limited to, all administrative orders and all civil and administrative penalties and fines, regardless of whether such penalties or fines are punitive or coercive in nature or are imposed for isolated, intermittent, or continuing violations. The United States hereby expressly waives any immunity otherwise applicable to the United States with respect to any such substantive or procedural requirement (including, but not limited to, any injunctive relief, administrative order or civil or administrative penalty or fine referred to in the preceding sentence, or reasonable service charge). The reasonable service charges referred to in this subsection include, but are not limited to, fees or charges assessed in connection with the processing and issuance of permits, renewal of permits, amendments to permits, review of plans, studies, and other documents, and inspection and monitoring of facilities, as well as any other nondiscriminatory charges that are assessed in connection with a Federal, State, interstate, or local regulatory program respecting the protection of wellhead areas or public water systems or respecting any underground injection. Neither the United States, nor any agent, employee, or officer thereof, shall be immune or exempt from any process or sanction of any State or Federal Court[1] with respect to the enforcement of any such injunctive relief. No agent, employee, or officer of the United States shall be personally liable for any civil penalty under any Federal, State, interstate, or local law concerning the protection of wellhead areas or public water systems or concerning underground injection with respect to any act or omission within the scope of the official duties of the agent, employee, or officer. An agent, employee, or officer of the United States shall be subject to any criminal sanction (including, but not limited to, any fine or imprisonment) under any Federal or State requirement adopted pursuant to this subchapter, but no department, agency, or instrumentality of the executive, legislative, or judicial branch of the Federal Government shall be subject to any such sanction. The President may exempt any facility of any department, agency, or instrumentality in the executive branch from compliance with such a requirement if he determines it to be in the paramount interest of the United States to do so. No such exemption shall be granted due to lack of appropriation unless the President shall have specifically requested such appropriation as a part of the budgetary process and the Congress shall have failed to make available such requested appropriation. Any exemption shall be for a period not in excess of 1 year, but additional exemptions may be granted for periods not to exceed 1 year upon the President's making a new determination. The President shall report each January to the Congress all exemptions from the requirements of this section granted during the preceding calendar year, together with his reason for granting each such exemption.

(b) Administrative penalty orders

(1) In general

If the Administrator finds that a Federal agency has violated an applicable requirement under this subchapter, the Administrator may issue a penalty order assessing a penalty against the Federal agency.

(2) Penalties

The Administrator may, after notice to the agency, assess a civil penalty against the agency in an amount not to exceed $25,000 per day per violation.

(3) Procedure

Before an administrative penalty order issued under this subsection becomes final, the Administrator shall provide the agency an opportunity to confer with the Administrator and shall provide the agency notice and an opportunity for a hearing on the record in accordance with chapters 5 and 7 of Title 5.

(4) Public review

(A) In general

Any interested person may obtain review of an administrative penalty order issued under this subsection. The review may be obtained in the United States District Court for the District of Columbia or in the United States District Court for the district in which the violation is alleged to have occurred by the filing of a complaint with the court within the 30-day period beginning on the date the penalty order becomes final. The person filing the complaint shall simultaneously send a copy of the complaint by certified mail to the Administrator and the Attorney General.

(B) Record

The Administrator shall promptly file in the court a certified copy of the record on which the order was issued.

(C) Standard of review

The court shall not set aside or remand the order unless the court finds that there is not substantial evidence in the record, taken as a whole, to support the finding of a violation or that the assessment of the penalty by the Administrator constitutes an abuse of discretion.

(D) Prohibition on additional penalties

The court may not impose an additional civil penalty for a violation that is subject to the order unless the court finds that the assessment constitutes an abuse of discretion by the Administrator.

(c) Limitation on State use of funds collected from Federal Government

Unless a State law in effect on August 6, 1996, or a State constitution requires the funds to be used in a different manner, all funds collected by a State from the Federal Government from penalties and fines imposed for violation of any substantive or procedural requirement referred to in subsection (a) of this section shall be used by the State only for projects designed to improve or protect the environment or to defray the costs of environmental protection or enforcement.

(d) Indian rights and sovereignty as unaffected; "Federal agency" defined

(1) Nothing in the Safe Drinking Water Amendments of 1977 shall be construed to alter or affect the status of American Indian lands or water rights nor to waive any sovereignty over Indian lands guaranteed by treaty or statute.

(2) For the purposes of this chapter, the term "Federal agency" shall not be construed to refer to or include any American Indian tribe, nor to the Secretary of the Interior in his capacity as trustee of Indian lands.

(e) Washington Aqueduct

The Secretary of the Army shall not pass the cost of any penalty assessed under this subchapter on to any customer, user, or other purchaser of drinking water from the Washington Aqueduct system, including finished water from the Dalecarlia or McMillan treatment plant.

(July 1, 1944, c. 373, Title XIV, § 1447, as added by Pub. L. No. 93–523, § 2(a), 88 Stat. 1688 (Dec. 16, 1974); and amended by Pub. L. No. 95–190, § 8(a), (d), 91 Stat. 1396, 1397 (Nov. 16, 1977); Pub. L. No. 104–182, Title I, § 129(a), (c), 110 Stat. 1660, 1662 (Aug. 6, 1996).)

[1] So in original. Probably should not be capitalized.

HISTORICAL AND STATUTORY NOTES

References in Text

The Safe Drinking Water Amendments of 1977, referred to in subsec. (d)(1), is Pub. L. No. 95–190, 91 Stat. 1393 (Nov. 16, 1977). For complete classification of this Act to the Code, see Short Title of 1977 Amendment note set out under section 201 of this title and Tables.

Effective and Applicability Provisions

1996 Acts. Amendment by Pub. L. No. 104–182 effective Aug. 6, 1996, except as otherwise specifically provided, see section 2(b) of Pub. L. No. 104–182, set out as a note under section 300f of this title.

§ 300j–7. Judicial review

[PHSA § 1448]

(a) Courts of appeals; petition for review; actions respecting regulations; filing period; grounds arising after expiration of filing period; exclusiveness of remedy

A petition for review of—

(1) actions pertaining to the establishment of national primary drinking water regulations (including maximum contaminant level goals) may be filed only in the United States Court of Appeals for the District of Columbia circuit; and

(2) any other final action of the Administrator under this chapter may be filed in the circuit in which the petitioner resides or transacts business which is directly affected by the action.

Any such petition shall be filed within the 45-day period beginning on the date of the promulgation of the regulation or any other final Agency action with respect to which review is sought or on the date of the determination with respect to which review is sought, and may be filed after the expiration of such 45-day period if the petition is based solely on grounds arising after the expiration of such period. Action of the Administrator with respect to which review could have been obtained under this subsection shall not be subject to judicial review in any civil or criminal proceeding for enforcement or in any civil action to enjoin enforcement. In any petition concerning the assessment of a civil penalty pursuant to section 300g–3(g)(3)(B) of this title, the petitioner shall simultaneously send a copy of the complaint by certified mail to the Administrator and the Attorney General. The court shall set aside and remand the penalty order if the court finds that there is not substantial evidence in the record to support the finding of a violation or that the assessment of the penalty by the Administrator constitutes an abuse of discretion.

(b) District courts; petition for review; actions respecting variances or exemptions; filing period; grounds arising after expiration of filing period; exclusiveness of remedy

The United States district courts shall have jurisdiction of actions brought to review (1) the granting of, or the refusing to grant, a variance or exemption under section 300g–4 or 300g–5 of this title or (2) the requirements of any schedule prescribed for a variance or exemption under such section or the failure to prescribe such a schedule. Such an action may only be brought upon a petition for review filed with the court within the 45-day period beginning on the date the action sought to be reviewed is taken or, in the case of a petition to review the refusal to grant a variance or exemption or the failure to prescribe a schedule, within the 45-day period beginning on the date action is required to be taken on the variance, exemption, or schedule, as the case may be. A petition for such review may be filed after the expiration of such period if the petition is based solely on grounds arising after the expiration of such period. Action with respect to which review could have been obtained under this subsection shall not be subject to judicial review in any civil or criminal proceeding for enforcement or in any civil action to enjoin enforcement.

(c) Judicial order for additional evidence before Administrator; modified or new findings; recommendation for modification or setting aside of original determination

In any judicial proceeding in which review is sought of a determination under this subchapter required to be made on the record after notice and opportunity for hearing, if any party applies to the court for leave to adduce additional evidence and shows to the satisfaction of the court that such additional evidence is material and that there were reasonable grounds for the failure to adduce such evidence in the proceeding before the Administrator, the court may order such additional evidence (and evidence in rebuttal thereof) to be taken before the Administrator, in such manner and upon such terms and conditions as the court may deem proper. The Administrator may modify his findings as to the facts, or make new findings, by reason of the additional evidence so taken, and he shall file such modified or new findings, and his recommendation, if any, for the modification or setting aside of his original determination, with the return of such additional evidence.

(July 1, 1944, c. 373, Title XIV, § 1448, as added by Pub. L. No. 93–523, § 2(a), 88 Stat. 1689 (Dec. 16, 1974); and amended by Pub. L. No. 99–339, Title III, § 303, 100 Stat. 667 (June 19, 1986); Pub. L. No. 104–182, Title I, § 113(c), 110 Stat. 1636 (Aug. 6, 1996).)

HISTORICAL AND STATUTORY NOTES

Effective and Applicability Provisions

1996 Acts. Amendment by Pub. L. No. 104–182 effective Aug. 6, 1996, except as otherwise specifically provided, see section 2(b) of Pub. L. No. 104–182, set out as a note under section 300f of this title.

§ 300j–8. Citizen's civil action

[PHSA § 1449]

(a) Persons subject to civil action; jurisdiction of enforcement proceedings

Except as provided in subsection (b) of this section, any person may commence a civil action on his own behalf—

(1) against any person (including (A) the United States, and (B) any other governmental instrumentality or agency to the extent permitted by the eleventh amendment to the Constitution) who is alleged to be in violation of any requirement prescribed by or under this subchapter;

(2) against the Administrator where there is alleged a failure of the Administrator to perform any act or duty under this subchapter which is not discretionary with the Administrator; or

(3) for the collection of a penalty by the United States Government (and associated costs and interest) against any Federal agency that fails, by the date that is 18 months after the effective date of a final order to pay a penalty assessed by the Administrator under section 300h–8(b)[1] of this title, to pay the penalty.

No action may be brought under paragraph (1) against a public water system for a violation of a requirement prescribed by or under this subchapter which occurred within the 27-month period beginning on the first day of the month in which this subchapter is enacted. The United States district courts shall have jurisdiction, without regard to the amount in controversy or the citizenship of the parties, to enforce in an action brought under this subsection any requirement prescribed by or under this subchapter or to order the Administrator to perform an act or duty described in paragraph (2), as the case may be.

(b) Conditions for commencement of civil action; notice

No civil action may be commenced—

(1) under subsection (a)(1) of this section respecting violation of a requirement prescribed by or under this subchapter—

(A) prior to sixty days after the plaintiff has given notice of such violation (i) to the Administrator, (ii) to any alleged violator of such requirement and (iii) to the State in which the violation occurs, or

(B) if the Administrator, the Attorney General, or the State has commenced and is diligently prosecuting a civil action in a court of the United States to require compliance with such requirement, but in any such action in a court of the United States any person may intervene as a matter of right; or

(2) under subsection (a)(2) of this section prior to sixty days after the plaintiff has given notice of such action to the Administrator; or

(3) under subsection (a)(3) of this section prior to 60 days after the plaintiff has given notice of such action to the Attorney General and to the Federal agency.

Notice required by this subsection shall be given in such manner as the Administrator shall prescribe by regulation. No person may commence a civil action under subsection (a) of this section to require a State to prescribe a schedule under section 300g–4 or 300g–5 of this title for a variance or exemption, unless such person shows to the satisfaction of the court that the State has in a substantial number of cases failed to prescribe such schedules.

(c) Intervention of right

In any action under this section, the Administrator or the Attorney General, if not a party, may intervene as a matter of right.

(d) Costs; attorney fees; expert witness fees; filing of bond

The court, in issuing any final order in any action brought under subsection (a) of this section, may award costs of litigation (including reasonable attorney and expert witness fees) to any party whenever the court determines such an award is appropriate. The court may, if a temporary restraining order or preliminary injunction is sought, require the filing of a bond or equivalent security in accordance with the Federal Rules of Civil Procedure.

(e) Availability of other relief

Nothing in this section shall restrict any right which any person (or class of persons) may have under any statute or common law to seek enforcement of any requirement prescribed by or under this subchapter or to seek any other relief. Nothing in this section or in any other law of the United States shall be construed to prohibit, exclude, or restrict any State or local government from—

(1) bringing any action or obtaining any remedy or sanction in any State or local court, or

(2) bringing any administrative action or obtaining any administrative remedy or sanction,

against any agency of the United States under State or local law to enforce any requirement respecting the provision of safe drinking water or respecting any underground injection control program. Nothing in this section shall be construed to authorize judicial review of regulations or orders of the Administrator under this subchapter, except as provided in section 300j–7 of this title. For provisions providing for application of certain requirements to such agencies in the same manner as to nongovernmental entities, see section 300j–6 of this title.

(July 1, 1944, c. 373, Title XIV, § 1449, as added by Pub. L. No. 93–523, § 2(a), 88 Stat. 1690 (Dec. 16, 1974); and amended by Pub. L. No. 95–190, § 8(c), 91 Stat. 1397 (Nov. 16, 1977); Pub. L. No. 104–182, Title I, § 129(b), 110 Stat. 1662 (Aug. 6, 1996).)

[1] So in original. Probably should be "300j–6(b)".

HISTORICAL AND STATUTORY NOTES

References in Text

The Federal Rules of Civil Procedure, referred to in subsec. (d), are set out in Title 28, Judiciary and Judicial Procedure.

Effective and Applicability Provisions

1996 Acts. Amendment by Pub. L. No. 104–182 effective Aug. 6, 1996, except as otherwise specifically provided, see section 2(b) of Pub. L. No. 104–182, set out as a note under section 300f of this title.

§ 300j–9. General provisions

[PHSA § 1450]

(a) Regulations; delegation of functions

(1) The Administrator is authorized to prescribe such regulations as are necessary or appropriate to carry out his functions under this subchapter.

(2) The Administrator may delegate any of his functions under this subchapter (other than prescribing regulations) to any officer or employee of the Agency.

(b) Utilization of officers and employees of Federal agencies

The Administrator, with the consent of the head of any other agency of the United States, may utilize such officers and employees of such agency as he deems necessary to assist him in carrying out the purposes of this subchapter.

(c) Assignment of Agency personnel to State or interstate agencies

Upon the request of a State or interstate agency, the Administrator may assign personnel of the Agency to such State or interstate agency for the purposes of carrying out the provisions of this subchapter.

(d) Payments of grants; adjustments; advances; reimbursement; installments; conditions; eligibility for grants; "nonprofit agency or institution" defined

(1) The Administrator may make payments of grants under this subchapter (after necessary adjustment on account of previously made underpayments or overpayments) in advance or by way of reimbursement, and in such installments and on such conditions as he may determine.

(2) Financial assistance may be made available in the form of grants only to individuals and nonprofit agencies or institutions. For purposes of this paragraph, the term "nonprofit agency or institution" means an agency or institution no part of the net earnings of which inure, or may lawfully inure, to the benefit of any private shareholder or individual.

(e) Labor standards

The Administrator shall take such action as may be necessary to assure compliance with provisions of sections 3141–3144, 3146, and 3147 of Title 40. The Secretary of Labor shall have, with respect to the labor standards specified in this subsection, the authority and functions set forth in Reorganization Plan Numbered 14 of 1950 (15 F.R. 3176; 64 Stat. 1267) and section 3145 of Title 40.

(f) Appearance and representation of Administrator through Attorney General or attorney appointees

The Administrator shall request the Attorney General to appear and represent him in any civil action instituted under this subchapter to which the Administrator is a party. Unless, within a reasonable time, the Attorney General notifies the Administrator that he will appear in such action, attorneys appointed by the Administrator shall appear and represent him.

(g) Authority of Administrator under other provisions unaffected

The provisions of this subchapter shall not be construed as affecting any authority of the Administrator under part G of subchapter II of this chapter.

(h) Reports to Congressional committees; review by Office of Management and Budget: submittal of comments to Congressional committees

Not later than April 1 of each year, the Administrator shall submit to the Committee on Commerce, Science, and Transportation of the Senate and the Committee on Energy and Commerce of the House of Representatives a report respecting the activities of the Agency under this subchapter and containing such recommendations for legislation as he considers necessary. The report of the Administrator under this subsection which is due not later than April 1, 1975, and each subsequent report of the Administrator under this subsection shall include a statement on the actual and anticipated cost to public water systems in each State of compliance with the requirements of this subchapter. The Office of Management and Budget may review any report required by this subsection before its submission to such committees of Congress, but the Office may not revise any such report, require any revision in any such report, or delay its submission beyond the day prescribed for its submission, and may submit to such committees of Congress its comments respecting any such report.

(i) Discrimination prohibition; filing of complaint; investigation; orders of Secretary; notice and hearing; settlements; attorneys' fees; judicial review; filing of petition; procedural requirements; stay of orders; exclusiveness of remedy; civil actions for enforcement of orders; appropriate relief; mandamus proceedings; prohibition inapplicable to undirected but deliberate violations

(1) No employer may discharge any employee or otherwise discriminate against any employee with respect to his compensation, terms, conditions, or privileges of employment because the employee (or any person acting pursuant to a request of the employee) has—

(A) commenced, caused to be commenced, or is about to commence or cause to be commenced a proceeding under this subchapter or a proceeding for the administration or enforcement of drinking water regulations or underground injection control programs of a State,

(B) testified or is about to testify in any such proceeding, or

(C) assisted or participated or is about to assist or participate in any manner in such a proceeding or in any other action to carry out the purposes of this subchapter.

(2) **(A)** Any employee who believes that he has been discharged or otherwise discriminated against by any person in violation of paragraph (1) may, within 30 days after such violation occurs, file (or have any person file on his behalf) a complaint with the Secretary of Labor (hereinafter in this subsection referred to as the "Secretary") alleging such discharge or discrimination. Upon receipt of such a complaint, the Secretary shall notify the person named in the complaint of the filing of the complaint.

(B) **(i)** Upon receipt of a complaint filed under subparagraph (A), the Secretary shall conduct an investigation of the violation alleged in the complaint. Within 30 days of the receipt of such complaint, the Secretary shall complete such investigation and shall notify in writing the complainant (and any person acting in his behalf) and the person alleged to have committed such violation of the results of the investigation conducted pursuant to this subparagraph. Within 90 days of the receipt of such complaint the Secretary shall, unless the proceeding on the complaint is terminated by the Secretary on the basis of a settlement entered into by the Secretary and the person alleged to have committed such violation, issue an order either providing the relief prescribed by clause (ii) or denying the complaint. An order of the Secretary shall be made on the record after notice and opportunity for agency hearing. The Secretary may not enter into a settlement terminating a proceeding on a complaint without the participation and consent of the complainant.

(ii) If in response to a complaint filed under subparagraph (A) the Secretary determines that a violation of paragraph (1) has occurred, the Secretary shall order (I) the person who committed such violation to take affirmative action to abate the violation, (II) such person to reinstate the complainant to his former position together with the compensation (including back pay), terms, conditions, and privileges of his employment, (III) compensatory damages, and (IV) where appropriate, exemplary damages. If such an order is issued, the Secretary, at the request of the complainant, shall assess against the person against whom the order is issued a sum equal to the aggregate amount of all costs and expenses (including attorneys' fees) reasonably incurred, as determined by the Secretary, by the complainant for, or in connection with, the bringing of the complaint upon which the order was issued.

(3) **(A)** Any person adversely affected or aggrieved by an order issued under paragraph (2) may obtain review of the order in the United States Court of Appeals for the circuit in which the violation, with respect to which the order was issued, allegedly occurred. The petition for review must be filed within sixty days from the issuance of the Secretary's order. Review shall conform to chapter 7 of Title 5. The commencement of proceedings under this subparagraph shall not, unless ordered by the court, operate as a stay of the Secretary's order.

(B) An order of the Secretary with respect to which review could have been obtained under subparagraph (A) shall not be subject to judicial review in any criminal or other civil proceeding.

(4) Whenever a person has failed to comply with an order issued under paragraph (2)(B), the Secretary shall file a civil action in the United States District Court for the district in which the violation was found to occur to enforce such order. In actions brought under this paragraph, the district courts shall have jurisdiction to grant all appropriate relief including, but not limited to, injunctive relief, compensatory, and exemplary damages.

(5) Any nondiscretionary duty imposed by this section is enforceable in mandamus proceeding brought under section 1361 of Title 28.

(6) Paragraph (1) shall not apply with respect to any employee who, acting without direction from his employer (or the employer's agent), deliberately causes a violation of any requirement of this subchapter.

(July 1, 1944, c. 373, Title XIV, § 1450, as added by Pub. L. No. 93–523, § 2(a), 88 Stat. 1691 (Dec. 16, 1974); and amended by S.Res. 4 (Feb. 4, 1977); H.Res. 549 (Mar. 25, 1980); Pub. L. No. 98–620, Title IV, § 402(38), 98 Stat. 3360 (Nov. 8, 1984); Pub. L. No. 103–437, § 15(a)(2), 108 Stat. 4591 (Nov. 2, 1994).)

HISTORICAL AND STATUTORY NOTES

References in Text

Reorganization Plan Numbered 14 of 1950 (15 Fed. Red. 3176; 64 Stat. 1267), referred to in subsec. (e), is set out in Appendix 1 to Title 5, Government Organization and Employees.

Part G of subchapter II of this chapter, referred to in subsec. (g), is codified as section 264 et seq. of this title.

Codifications

In subsec. (e), "sections 3141–3144, 3146, and 3147 of Title 40" substituted for "the Act of March 3, 1931 (known as the Davis-Bacon Act; 40 U.S.C. 276a—276a–5)" on authority of Pub. L. No. 107–217, § 5(c), 116 Stat. 1301 (Aug. 21, 2002), which is set out as a note preceding 40 U.S.C.A. § 101. Pub. L. No. 107–217, § 1, enacted Title 40 into positive law. The Davis-Bacon Act is Act of Mar. 3, 1931, c. 411, 46 Stat. 1494, which was codified as former 40 U.S.C.A. §§ 276a, 276a–1 to 276a–6, prior to being repealed by Pub. L. No. 107–217, § 6(b), 116 Stat. 1308 (Aug. 21, 2002), and its substance reenacted as 40 U.S.C.A. §§ 3141 to 3144, 3146, and 3147.

In subsec. (e), "section 3145 of Title 40" substituted for "section 276c of Title 40", which originally read "section 2 of the Act of June 13, 1934 (40 U.S.C. 276c)", on authority of Pub. L. No. 107–217, § 5(c), 116 Stat. 1301 (Aug. 21, 2002), which is set out as a note preceding 40 U.S.C.A. § 101. Pub. L. No. 107–217, § 1, enacted Title 40 into positive law. Section 2 of the Act of June 13, 1934, as amended, is Act of June 13, 1934, c. 482, § 2, 48 Stat. 948, which was codified as former 40 U.S.C.A. § 276c prior to being repealed by Pub. L. No. 107–217, § 6(b), 116 Stat. 1309 (Aug. 21, 2002), and its substance reenacted as 40 U.S.C.A. § 3145.

Effective and Applicability Provisions

1984 Acts. Amendment by Pub. L. No. 98–620 not to apply to cases pending on Nov. 8, 1984, see section 403 of Pub. L. No. 98–620, set out as a note under section 1657 of Title 28, Judiciary and Judicial Procedure.

Change of Name

Any reference in any provision of law enacted before Jan. 4, 1995, to the Committee on Energy and Commerce of the House of Representatives treated as referring to the Committee on Commerce of the House of Representatives, except that any reference in any provision of law enacted before Jan. 4, 1995, to the Committee on Energy and Commerce of the House of Representatives treated as referring to the Committee on Agriculture of the House of Representatives, in the case of a provision of law relating to inspection of seafood or seafood products, the Committee on Banking and Financial Services of the House of Representatives, in the case of a provision of law relating to bank capital markets activities generally or to depository institution securities activities generally, and the Committee on Transportation and Infrastructure of the House of Representatives, in the case of a provision of law relating to railroads, railway labor, or railroad retirement and unemployment (except revenue measures related thereto), see section 1(a)(4) and (c)(1) of Pub. L. No. 104–14, set out as a note preceding section 21 of Title 2, The Congress.

The Committee on Commerce of the Senate was abolished and replaced by the Committee on Commerce, Science, and Transportation of the Senate, effective Feb. 11, 1977. See Rule XXV of the Standing Rules of the Senate, as amended by Senate Resolution 4 (popularly cited as the "Committee System Reorganization Amendments of 1977"), approved Feb. 4, 1977.

The name of the Committee on Interstate and Foreign Commerce of the House of Representatives was changed to Committee on Energy and Commerce immediately prior to noon on Jan. 3, 1981, by House Resolution 549, Ninety-sixth Congress, Mar. 25, 1980.

Construction Projects

Pub. L. No. 112–74, Div. E, Title II, 125 Stat. 1020 (Dec. 23, 2011), provided that: "For fiscal year 2012 and each fiscal year thereafter, the requirements of section 1450(e) of the Safe Drinking Water Act (42 U.S.C. 300j–9(e)) shall apply to any construction project carried out in whole or in part with assistance made available by a drinking water treatment revolving loan fund as authorized by section 1452 of that Act (42 U.S.C. 300j–12)."

§ 300j–10. Appointment of scientific, etc., personnel by Administrator of Environmental Protection Agency for implementation of responsibilities; compensation

To the extent that the Administrator of the Environmental Protection Agency deems such action necessary to the discharge of his functions under Title XIV of the Public Health Service Act [42 U.S.C.A. § 300f et seq.] (relating to safe drinking water) and under other provisions of law, he may appoint personnel to fill not more than thirty scientific, engineering, professional, legal, and administrative positions within the Environmental Protection Agency without regard to the civil service laws and may fix the compensation of such personnel not in excess of the maximum rate payable for GS–18 of the General Schedule under section 5332 of Title 5.

(Pub. L. No. 95–190, § 11(b), 91 Stat. 1398 (Nov. 16, 1977).)

HISTORICAL AND STATUTORY NOTES

References in Text

The Public Health Service Act, referred to in text, is Act of July 1, 1944, c. 373, 58 Stat. 682, as amended. Title XIV of the Public Health Service Act is codified generally as this subchapter (section 300f et seq.). For complete classification of this Act to the Code, see Short Title note set out under section 201 of this title and Tables.

The civil service laws, referred to in text, are set out in Title 5, Government Organization and Employees. See, particularly, section 3301 et seq. of Title 5.

Codifications

Section was enacted as part of the Safe Drinking Water Amendments of 1977 and not as part of the Public Health Service Act, which comprises this chapter.

§ 300j–11. Indian Tribes

[PHSA § 1451]

(a) In general

Subject to the provisions of subsection (b) of this section, the Administrator—

(1) is authorized to treat Indian Tribes as States under this subchapter,

(2) may delegate to such Tribes primary enforcement responsibility for public water systems and for underground injection control, and

(3) may provide such Tribes grant and contract assistance to carry out functions provided by this subchapter.

(b) EPA regulations

(1) Specific provisions

The Administrator shall, within 18 months after June 19, 1986, promulgate final regulations specifying those provisions of this subchapter for which it is appropriate to treat Indian Tribes as States. Such treatment shall be authorized only if:

(A) the Indian Tribe is recognized by the Secretary of the Interior and has a governing body carrying out substantial governmental duties and powers;

(B) the functions to be exercised by the Indian Tribe are within the area of the Tribal Government's jurisdiction; and

(C) the Indian Tribe is reasonably expected to be capable, in the Administrator's judgment, of carrying out the functions to be exercised in a manner consistent with the terms and purposes of this subchapter and of all applicable regulations.

(2) Provisions where treatment as State inappropriate

For any provision of this subchapter where treatment of Indian Tribes as identical to States is inappropriate, administratively infeasible or otherwise inconsistent with the purposes of this subchapter, the Administrator may include in the regulations promulgated under this section, other means for administering such provision in a manner that will achieve the purpose of the provision. Nothing in this section shall be construed to allow Indian Tribes to assume or maintain primary enforcement responsibility for public water systems or for underground injection control in a manner less protective of the health of persons than such responsibility may be assumed or maintained by a State. An Indian tribe[1] shall not be required to exercise criminal enforcement jurisdiction for purposes of complying with the preceding sentence.

(July 1, 1944, c. 373, Title XIV, § 1451, as added by Pub. L. No. 99–339, Title III, § 302(a), 100 Stat. 665 (June 19, 1986); and amended by Pub. L. No. 104–182, Title V, § 501(f)(6), 110 Stat. 1692 (Aug. 6, 1996).)

[1] So in original. Probably should be "Tribe".

HISTORICAL AND STATUTORY NOTES

Effective and Applicability Provisions

1996 Acts. Amendment by Pub. L. No. 104–182 effective Aug. 6, 1996, except as otherwise specifically provided, see section 2(b) of Pub. L. No. 104–182, set out as a note under section 300f of this title.

§ 300j–12. State revolving loan funds

[PHSA § 1452]

(a) General authority

(1) Grants to States to establish State loan funds

(A) In general

The Administrator shall offer to enter into agreements with eligible States to make capitalization grants, including letters of credit, to the States under this subsection to further the health protection objectives of this subchapter, promote the efficient use of fund resources, and for other purposes as are specified in this subchapter.

(B) Establishment of fund

To be eligible to receive a capitalization grant under this section, a State shall establish a drinking water treatment revolving loan fund (referred to in this section as a "State loan fund") and comply with the other requirements of this section. Each grant to a State under this section shall be deposited in the State loan fund established by the State, except as otherwise provided in this section and in other provisions of this subchapter. No funds authorized by other provisions of this subchapter to be used for other purposes specified in this subchapter shall be deposited in any State loan fund.

(C) Extended period

The grant to a State shall be available to the State for obligation during the fiscal year for which the funds are authorized and during the following fiscal year, except that grants made available from funds provided prior to fiscal year 1997 shall be available for obligation during each of the fiscal years 1997 and 1998.

(D) Allotment formula

Except as otherwise provided in this section, funds made available to carry out this section shall be allotted to States that have entered into an agreement pursuant to this section (other than the District of Columbia) in accordance with—

(i) for each of fiscal years 1995 through 1997, a formula that is the same as the formula used to distribute public water system supervision grant funds under section 300j–2 of this title in fiscal year 1995, except that the minimum proportionate share established in the formula shall be 1 percent of available funds and the formula shall be adjusted to include a minimum proportionate share for the State of Wyoming and the District of Columbia; and

(ii) for fiscal year 1998 and each subsequent fiscal year, a formula that allocates to each State the proportional share of the State needs identified in the most recent survey conducted pursuant to subsection (h) of this section, except that the minimum proportionate share provided to each State shall be the same as the minimum proportionate share provided under clause (i).

(E) Reallotment

The grants not obligated by the last day of the period for which the grants are available shall be reallotted according to the appropriate criteria set forth in subparagraph (D), except that the Administrator may reserve and allocate 10 percent of the remaining amount for financial assistance to Indian Tribes in addition to the amount allotted under subsection (i) of this section and none of the funds reallotted by the Administrator shall be reallotted to any State that has not obligated all sums allotted to the State pursuant to this section during the period in which the sums were available for obligation.

(F) Nonprimacy States

The State allotment for a State not exercising primary enforcement responsibility for public water systems shall not be deposited in any such fund but shall be allotted by the Administrator under this subparagraph. Pursuant to section 300j–2(a)(9)(A) of this title such sums allotted under this subparagraph shall be reserved as needed by the Administrator to exercise primary enforcement responsibility under this subchapter in such State and the remainder shall be reallotted to States exercising primary enforcement responsibility for public water systems for deposit in such funds. Whenever the Administrator makes a final determination pursuant to section 300g–2(b) of this title that the requirements of section 300g–2(a) of this title are no longer being met by a State, additional grants for such State under this subchapter shall be immediately terminated by the Administrator. This subparagraph shall not apply to any State not exercising primary enforcement responsibility for public water systems as of August 6, 1996.

(G) Other programs

(i) New system capacity

Beginning in fiscal year 1999, the Administrator shall withhold 20 percent of each capitalization grant made pursuant to this section to a State unless the State has met the requirements of section 300g–9(a) of this title (relating to capacity development) and shall withhold 10 percent for fiscal year 2001, 15 percent for fiscal year 2002, and 20 percent for fiscal year 2003 if the State has not complied with the provisions of section 300g–9(c) of this title (relating to capacity development strategies). Not more than a total of 20 percent of the capitalization grants made to a State in any fiscal year may be withheld under the preceding provisions of this clause. All funds withheld by the Administrator pursuant to this clause shall be reallotted by the Administrator on the basis of the same ratio as is applicable to funds allotted under subparagraph (D). None of the funds reallotted by the Administrator pursuant to this paragraph shall be allotted to a State unless the State has met the requirements of section 300g–9 of this title (relating to capacity development).

(ii) Operator certification

The Administrator shall withhold 20 percent of each capitalization grant made pursuant to this section unless the State has met the requirements of 300g–8[1] of this title (relating to operator certification). All funds withheld by the Administrator pursuant to this clause shall be reallotted by the Administrator on the basis of the same ratio as applicable to funds allotted under subparagraph (D). None of the funds reallotted by the Administrator pursuant to this paragraph shall be allotted to a State unless the State has met the requirements of section 300g–8 of this title (relating to operator certification).

(2) Use of funds

(A) In general.—Except otherwise authorized by this subchapter, amounts deposited in a State loan fund, including loan repayments and interest earned on such amounts, shall be used only for providing loans or loan guarantees, or as a source of reserve and security for leveraged loans, the proceeds of which are deposited in a State loan fund established under paragraph (1), or other financial assistance authorized under this section to community water systems and nonprofit noncommunity water systems, other than systems owned by Federal agencies.

(B) Limitation.—Financial assistance under this section may be used by a public water system only for expenditures "(including expenditures for planning, design, siting, and associated preconstruction activities, or for replacing or rehabilitating aging treatment, storage, or distribution facilities of public water systems, but not including monitoring, operation, and maintenance expenditures) of a type or category which the Administrator has determined, through guidance, will facilitate compliance with national primary drinking water regulations applicable to the system under section 300g–1 of this title or otherwise significantly further the health protection objectives of this subchapter.

(C) Sale of bonds.—Funds may also be used by a public water system as a source of revenue (restricted solely to interest earnings of the applicable State loan fund) or security for payment of the principal and interest on revenue or general obligation bonds issued by the State to provide matching funds under subsection (e), if the proceeds of the sale of the bonds will be deposited in the State loan fund.

(D) Water treatment loans.—The funds under this section may also be used to provide loans to a system referred to in section 300f(4)(B) of this title for the purpose of providing the treatment described in section 300f(4)(B)(i)(III) of this title.

(E) Acquisition of real property.—The funds under this section shall not be used for the acquisition of real property or interests therein, unless the acquisition is integral to a project authorized by this paragraph and the purchase is from a willing seller.

(F) Loan assistance.—Of the amount credited to any State loan fund established under this section in any fiscal year, 15 percent shall be available solely for providing loan assistance to public water systems which regularly serve fewer than 10,000 persons to the extent such funds can be obligated for eligible projects of public water systems.

(G) Emerging Contaminants.—

(i) In General.—Notwithstanding any other provision of law and subject to clause (ii), amounts deposited under subsection (t) in a State loan fund established under this section may only be used to provide grants for the purpose of addressing emerging contaminants, with a focus on perfluoroalkyl and polyfluoroalkyl substances.

(ii) Requirements.—

(I) Small and Disadvantaged Communities.—Not less than 25 percent of the amounts described in clause (i) shall be used to provide grants to—

(aa) disadvantaged communities (as defined in subsection (d)(3)); or

(bb) public water systems serving fewer than 25,000 persons.

(II) Priorities.—In selecting the recipient of a grant using amounts described in clause (i), a State shall use the priorities described in subsection (b)(3)(A).

(iii) No Increased Bonding Authority.—The amounts deposited in the State loan fund of a State under subsection (t) may not be used as a source of payment of, or security for (directly or indirectly), in whole or in part, any obligation the interest on which is exempt from the tax imposed under chapter 1 of the Internal Revenue Code of 1986.

(3) Limitation

(A) In general

Except as provided in subparagraph (B), no assistance under this section shall be provided to a public water system that—

(i) does not have the technical, managerial, and financial capability to ensure compliance with the requirements of this subchapter; or

(ii) is in significant noncompliance with any requirement of a national primary drinking water regulation or variance.

(B) Restructuring

A public water system described in subparagraph (A) may receive assistance under this section if—

(i) the use of the assistance will ensure compliance; and

(ii) if subparagraph (A)(i) applies to the system, the owner or operator of the system agrees to undertake feasible and appropriate changes in operations (including ownership, management, accounting, rates, maintenance, consolidation, alternative water supply, or other procedures) if the State determines that the measures are necessary to ensure that the system has the technical, managerial, and financial capability to comply with the requirements of this subchapter over the long term.

(C) Review

Prior to providing assistance under this section to a public water system that is in significant noncompliance with any requirement of a national primary drinking water regulation or variance, the State shall conduct a review to determine whether subparagraph (A)(i) applies to the system.

(4) American iron and steel products.—

(A) In general.—During fiscal years 2019 through 2021, funds made available from a State loan fund established pursuant to this section may not be used for a project for the construction, alteration, or repair of a public water system unless all of the iron and steel products used in the project are produced in the United States.

(B) Definition of iron and steel products.—In this paragraph, the term 'iron and steel products' means the following products made primarily of iron or steel:

(i) Lined or unlined pipes and fittings.

(ii) Manhole covers and other municipal castings.

(iii) Hydrants.

(iv) Tanks.

(v) Flanges.

(vi) Pipe clamps and restraints.

(vii) Valves.

(viii) Structural steel.

(ix) Reinforced precast concrete.

(x) Construction materials.

(C) Application.—Subparagraph (A) shall be waived in any case or category of cases in which the Administrator finds that—

(i) applying subparagraph (A) would be inconsistent with the public interest;

(ii) iron and steel products are not produced in the United States in sufficient and reasonably available quantities and of a satisfactory quality; or

(iii) inclusion of iron and steel products produced in the United States will increase the cost of the overall project by more than 25 percent.

(D) Waiver.—If the Administrator receives a request for a waiver under this paragraph, the Administrator shall make available to the public, on an informal basis, a copy of the request and information available to the Administrator concerning the request, and shall allow for informal public input on the request for at least 15 days prior to making a finding based on the request. The Administrator shall make the request and accompanying information available by electronic means, including on the official public Internet site of the Agency.

(E) International agreements.—This paragraph shall be applied in a manner consistent with United States obligations under international agreements.

(F) Management and oversight.—The Administrator may retain up to 0.25 percent of the funds appropriated for this section for management and oversight of the requirements of this paragraph.

(G) Effective date.—This paragraph does not apply with respect to a project if a State agency approves the engineering plans and specifications for the project, in that agency's capacity to approve such plans and specifications prior to a project requesting bids, prior to the date of enactment of this paragraph.

(5) Prevailing wages.—The requirements of section 1450(e) shall apply to any construction project carried out in whole or in part with assistance made available by a State loan fund.

(b) Intended use plans

(1) In general

After providing for public review and comment, each State that has entered into a capitalization agreement pursuant to this section shall annually prepare a plan that identifies the intended uses of the amounts available to the State loan fund of the State.

(2) Contents

An intended use plan shall include—

(A) a list of the projects to be assisted in the first fiscal year that begins after the date of the plan, including a description of the project, the expected terms of financial assistance, and the size of the community served;

(B) the criteria and methods established for the distribution of funds; and

(C) a description of the financial status of the State loan fund and the short-term and long-term goals of the State loan fund.

(3) Use of funds

(A) In general

An intended use plan shall provide, to the maximum extent practicable, that priority for the use of funds be given to projects that—

(i) address the most serious risk to human health;

(ii) are necessary to ensure compliance with the requirements of this subchapter (including requirements for filtration); and

(iii) assist systems most in need on a per household basis according to State affordability criteria.

(B) List of projects

Each State shall, after notice and opportunity for public comment, publish and periodically update a list of projects in the State that are eligible for assistance under this section, including the priority assigned to each project and, to the extent known, the expected funding schedule for each project.

(c) Fund management

Each State loan fund under this section shall be established, maintained, and credited with repayments and interest. The fund corpus shall be available in perpetuity for providing financial assistance under this section. To the extent amounts in the fund are not required for current obligation or expenditure, such amounts shall be invested in interest bearing obligations.

(d) Assistance for disadvantaged communities

(1) Loan subsidy

Notwithstanding any other provision of this section, in any case in which the State makes a loan pursuant to subsection (a)(2) of this section to a disadvantaged community or to a community that the State expects to become a disadvantaged community as the result of a proposed project, the State may provide additional subsidization (including forgiveness of principal).

(2) Total amount of subsidies.—For each fiscal year, of the amount of the capitalization grant received by the State for the year, the total amount of loan subsidies made by a State pursuant to paragraph (1)—

(A) may not exceed 35 percent; and

(B) to the extent that there are sufficient applications for loans to communities described in paragraph (1), may not be less than 6 percent.

(3) "Disadvantaged community" defined

In this subsection, the term "disadvantaged community" means the service area of a public water system that meets affordability criteria established after public review and comment by the State in which the public water system is located. The Administrator may publish information to assist States in establishing affordability criteria.

(e) State contribution

Each agreement under subsection (a) of this section shall require that the State deposit in the State loan fund from State moneys an amount equal to at least 20 percent of the total amount of the grant to be made to the State on or before the date on which the grant payment is made to the State, except that a State shall not be required to deposit such amount into the fund prior to the date on which each grant payment is made for fiscal years 1994, 1995, 1996, and 1997 if the State deposits the State contribution amount into the State loan fund prior to September 30, 1999.

(f) Types of assistance

Except as otherwise limited by State law, the amounts deposited into a State loan fund under this section may be used only—

(1) to make loans, on the condition that—

(A) the interest rate for each loan is less than or equal to the market interest rate, including an interest free loan;

(B) principal and interest payments on each loan will commence not later than 18 months after completion of the project for which the loan was made;

(C) each loan will be fully amortized not later than 30 years after the completion of the project, except that in the case of a disadvantaged community (as defined in subsection (d)(3)) a State may provide an extended term for a loan, if the extended term—

(i) terminates not later than the date that is 40 years after the date of project completion; and

(ii) does not exceed the expected design life of the project;

(D) the recipient of each loan will establish a dedicated source of revenue (or, in the case of a privately owned system, demonstrate that there is adequate security) for the repayment of the loan; and

(E) the State loan fund will be credited with all payments of principal and interest on each loan;

(2) to buy or refinance the debt obligation of a municipality or an intermunicipal or interstate agency within the State at an interest rate that is less than or equal to the market interest rate in any case in which a debt obligation is incurred after July 1, 1993;

(3) to guarantee, or purchase insurance for, a local obligation (all of the proceeds of which finance a project eligible for assistance under this section) if the guarantee or purchase would improve credit market access or reduce the interest rate applicable to the obligation;

(4) as a source of revenue or security for the payment of principal and interest on revenue or general obligation bonds issued by the State if the proceeds of the sale of the bonds will be deposited into the State loan fund; and

(5) to earn interest on the amounts deposited into the State loan fund.

(g) Administration of State loan funds

(1) Combined financial administration

Notwithstanding subsection (c) of this section, a State may (as a convenience and to avoid unnecessary administrative costs) combine, in accordance with State law, the financial administration of a State loan fund established under this section with the financial administration of any other revolving fund established by the State if otherwise not prohibited by the law under which the State loan fund was established and if the Administrator determines that—

(A) the grants under this section, together with loan repayments and interest, will be separately accounted for and used solely for the purposes specified in subsection (a) of this section; and

(B) the authority to establish assistance priorities and carry out oversight and related activities (other than financial administration) with respect to assistance remains with the State agency having primary responsibility for administration of the State program under section 300g–2 of this title, after consultation with other appropriate State agencies (as determined by the State): *Provided,* That in nonprimacy States eligible to receive assistance under this section, the Governor shall determine which State agency will have authority to establish priorities for financial assistance from the State loan fund.

(2) Cost of administering fund

(A) Authorization.—

(i) In general.—For each fiscal year, a State may use the amount described in clause (ii)—

(I) to cover the reasonable costs of administration of the programs under this section, including the recovery of reasonable costs expended to establish a State loan fund that are incurred after the date of enactment of this section; and

(II) to provide technical assistance to public water systems within the State.

(ii) Description of amount.—The amount referred to in clause (i) is an amount equal to the sum of—

(I) the amount of any fees collected by the State for use in accordance with clause (i)(I), regardless of the source; and

(II) the greatest of—

(aa) $400,000;

(bb) 1/5 percent of the current valuation of the fund; and

(cc) an amount equal to 4 percent of all grant awards to the fund under this section for the fiscal year."; and

(B) Additional use of funds.—For fiscal year 1995 and each fiscal year thereafter, each State may use up to an additional 10 percent of the funds allotted to the State under this section—

(i) for public water system supervision programs under section 300j–2(a) of this title;

(ii) to administer or provide technical assistance through source water protection programs;

(iii) to develop and implement a capacity development strategy under section 300g–9(c) of this title; and

(iv) for an operator certification program for purposes of meeting the requirements of section 1419.

At least half of the match must be additional to the amount expended by the State for public water supervision in fiscal year 1993.

(C) Technical assistance.—An additional 2 percent of the funds annually allotted to each State under this section may be used by the State to provide technical assistance to public water systems serving 10,000 or fewer persons in the State.

(D) Enforcement actions.—Funds used under subparagraph (B)(ii) shall not be used for enforcement actions.

(3) Guidance and regulations

The Administrator shall publish guidance and promulgate regulations as may be necessary to carry out the provisions of this section, including—

(A) provisions to ensure that each State commits and expends funds allotted to the State under this section as efficiently as possible in accordance with this subchapter and applicable State laws;

(B) guidance to prevent waste, fraud, and abuse; and

(C) guidance to avoid the use of funds made available under this section to finance the expansion of any public water system in anticipation of future population growth.

The guidance and regulations shall also ensure that the States, and public water systems receiving assistance under this section, use accounting, audit, and fiscal procedures that conform to generally accepted accounting standards.

(4) State report

Each State administering a loan fund and assistance program under this subsection shall publish and submit to the Administrator a report every 2 years on its activities under this section, including the findings of the most recent audit of the fund and the entire State allotment. The Administrator shall periodically audit all State loan funds established by, and all other amounts allotted to, the States pursuant to this section in accordance with procedures established by the Comptroller General.

(h) Needs survey

(1) The Administrator shall conduct an assessment of water system capital improvement needs of all eligible public water systems in the United States and submit a report to the Congress containing the results of the assessment within 180 days after August 6, 1996, and every 4 years thereafter.

(2) Any assessment conducted under paragraph (1) after the date of enactment of America's Water Infrastructure Act of 2018 shall include an assessment of costs to replace all lead service lines (as defined in section 1459B(a)(4)) of all eligible public water systems in the United States, and such assessment shall describe separately the costs associated with replacing the portions of such lead service lines that are owned by an eligible public water system and the costs associated with replacing any remaining portions of such lead service lines, to the extent practicable.

(i) Indian Tribes

(1) In general

$1^1/_2$ percent of the amounts appropriated annually to carry out this section may be used by the Administrator to make grants to Indian Tribes, Alaska Native villages, and, for the purpose of carrying out paragraph (5), intertribal consortia or tribal organizations that have not otherwise received either grants from the Administrator under this section or assistance from State loan funds established under this section. Except as otherwise provided, the grants may only be used for expenditures by tribes and villages for public water system expenditures referred to in subsection (a)(2) of this section.

(2) Use of funds

Funds reserved pursuant to paragraph (1) shall be used to address the most significant threats to public health associated with public water systems that serve Indian Tribes, as determined by the Administrator in consultation with the Director of the Indian Health Service and Indian Tribes.

(3) Alaska Native villages

In the case of a grant for a project under this subsection in an Alaska Native village, the Administrator is also authorized to make grants to the State of Alaska for the benefit of Native villages. An amount not to exceed 4 percent of the grant amount may be used by the State of Alaska for project management.

(4) Needs assessment

The Administrator, in consultation with the Director of the Indian Health Service and Indian Tribes, shall, in accordance with a schedule that is consistent with the needs surveys conducted pursuant to subsection (h) of this section, prepare surveys and assess the needs of drinking water treatment facilities to serve Indian Tribes, including an evaluation of the public water systems that pose the most significant threats to public health.

(5) Training and operator certification.—

(A) In general.—The Administrator may use funds made available under this subsection and section 1442(e)(7) to make grants to intertribal consortia or tribal organizations for the purpose of providing operations and maintenance training and operator certification services to Indian Tribes to enable public water systems that serve Indian Tribes to achieve and maintain compliance with applicable national primary drinking water regulations.

(B) Eligible Tribal organizations.—Intertribal consortia or tribal organizations eligible for a grant under subparagraph (A) are intertribal consortia or tribal organizations that—

(i) as determined by the Administrator, are the most qualified and experienced to provide training and technical assistance to Indian Tribes; and

(ii) the Indian Tribes find to be the most beneficial and effective.".

(j) Other areas

Of the funds annually available under this section for grants to States, the Administrator shall make allotments in accordance with section 300j–2(a)(4) of this title for the Virgin Islands, the Commonwealth of the Northern Mariana Islands, American Samoa, and Guam. The grants allotted as provided in this subsection may be provided by the Administrator to the governments of such areas, to public water systems in such areas, or to both, to be used for the public water system expenditures referred to in subsection (a)(2) of this section. The grants, and grants for the District of Columbia, shall not be deposited in State loan funds. The total allotment of grants under this section for all areas described in this subsection in any fiscal year shall not exceed 0.33 percent of the aggregate amount made available to carry out this section in that fiscal year.

(k) Other authorized activities

(1) In general

Notwithstanding subsection (a)(2) of this section, a State may take each of the following actions:

(A) Provide assistance, only in the form of a loan, to one or more of the following:

(i) Any public water system described in subsection (a)(2) of this section to acquire land or a conservation easement from a willing seller or grantor, if the purpose of the acquisition is to protect the source water of the system from contamination and to ensure compliance with national primary drinking water regulations.

(ii) Any community water system to implement local, voluntary source water protection measures to protect source water in areas delineated pursuant to section 300j–13 of this title, in order to facilitate compliance with national primary drinking water regulations applicable to the system under section 300g–1 of this title or otherwise significantly further the health protection objectives of this subchapter. Funds authorized under this clause may be used to fund only voluntary, incentive-based mechanisms.

(iii) Any community water system to provide funding in accordance with section 300j–14(a)(1)(B)(i) of this title.

(B) Provide assistance, including technical and financial assistance, to any public water system as part of a capacity development strategy developed and implemented in accordance with section 300g–9(c) of this title.

(C) Make expenditures from the capitalization grant of the State for to delineate, assess, and update assessments for source water protection areas in accordance with section 300j–13 of this title, except that funds set aside for such expenditure shall be obligated within 4 fiscal years.

(D) Make expenditures from the fund for the establishment and implementation of wellhead protection programs under section 300h–7 of this title and for the implementation of efforts (other than actions authorized under subparagraph (A)) to protect source water in areas delineated pursuant to section 1453.

(2) Limitation

For each fiscal year, the total amount of assistance provided and expenditures made by a State under this subsection may not exceed 15 percent of the amount of the capitalization grant received by the State for that year and may not exceed 10 percent of that amount for any one of the following activities:

(A) To acquire land or conservation easements pursuant to paragraph (1)(A)(i).

(B) To provide funding to implement voluntary, incentive-based source water quality protection measures pursuant to clauses (ii) and (iii) of paragraph (1)(A).

(C) To provide assistance through a capacity development strategy pursuant to paragraph (1)(B).

(D) To make expenditures to delineate or assess source water protection areas pursuant to paragraph (1)(C).

(E) To make expenditures to establish and implement wellhead protection programs, and to implement efforts to protect source water, pursuant to paragraph (1)(D).

(3) Statutory construction

Nothing in this section creates or conveys any new authority to a State, political subdivision of a State, or community water system for any new regulatory measure, or limits any authority of a State, political subdivision of a State or community water system.

(*l*) Savings

The failure or inability of any public water system to receive funds under this section or any other loan or grant program, or any delay in obtaining the funds, shall not alter the obligation of the system to comply in a timely manner with all applicable drinking water standards and requirements of this subchapter.

(m) Authorization of appropriations

(1) There are authorized to be appropriated to carry out the purposes of this section, except for subsections (a)(2)(G) and (t)—

(A) $1,174,000,000 for fiscal year 2019;

(B) $1,300,000,000 for fiscal year 2020; and

(C) $1,950,000,000 for fiscal year 2021.";

(2) To the extent amounts authorized to be appropriated under this subsection in any fiscal year are not appropriated in that fiscal year, such amounts are authorized to be appropriated in a subsequent fiscal year. Such sums shall remain available until expended.

(n) Health effects studies

From funds appropriated pursuant to this section for each fiscal year, the Administrator shall reserve $10,000,000 for health effects studies on drinking water contaminants authorized by the Safe Drinking Water Act Amendments of 1996. In allocating funds made available under this subsection, the Administrator shall give priority to studies concerning the health effects of cryptosporidium (as authorized by section 300j–18(c) of this title), disinfection byproducts (as authorized by section 300j–18(c) of this title), and arsenic (as authorized by section 300g–1(b)(12)(A) of this title), and the implementation of a plan for studies of subpopulations at greater risk of adverse effects (as authorized by section 300j–18(a) of this title).

(*o*) Monitoring for unregulated contaminants

From funds appropriated pursuant to this section for each fiscal year beginning with fiscal year 1998, the Administrator shall reserve $2,000,000 to pay the costs of monitoring for unregulated contaminants under section 300j–4(a)(2)(C) of this title.

(p) Demonstration project for State of Virginia

Notwithstanding the other provisions of this section limiting the use of funds deposited in a State loan fund from any State allotment, the State of Virginia may, as a single demonstration and with the approval of the Virginia General Assembly and the Administrator, conduct a program to demonstrate alternative approaches to intergovernmental coordination to assist in the financing of new drinking water facilities in the following rural communities in southwestern Virginia where none exists on August 6, 1996, and where such communities are experiencing economic hardship: Lee County, Wise County, Scott County, Dickenson County, Russell County, Buchanan County, Tazewell County, and the city of Norton, Virginia. The funds allotted to that State and deposited in the State loan fund may be loaned to a regional endowment fund for the purpose set forth in this subsection under a plan to be approved by the Administrator. The plan may include an advisory group that includes representatives of such counties.

(q) Small system technical assistance

The Administrator may reserve up to 2 percent of the total funds made available to carry out this section for each of fiscal years 2016 through 2021 to carry out the provisions of section 300j–1(e) of this title (relating to technical assistance for small systems), except that the total amount of funds made available for such purpose in any fiscal year through appropriations (as authorized by section 300j–1(e) of this title) and reservations made pursuant to this subsection shall not exceed the amount authorized by section 300j–1(e) of this title.

(r) Evaluation

The Administrator shall conduct an evaluation of the effectiveness of the State loan funds through fiscal year 2001. The evaluation shall be submitted to the Congress at the same time as the President submits to the Congress, pursuant to section 1108 of Title 31, an appropriations request for fiscal year 2003 relating to the budget of the Environmental Protection Agency.

(s) Best practices for State loan fund administration.—The Administrator shall—

(1) collect information from States on administration of State loan funds established pursuant to subsection (a)(1), including—

(A) efforts to streamline the process for applying for assistance through such State loan funds;

(B) programs in place to assist with the completion of applications for assistance through such State loan funds;

(C) incentives provided to public water systems that partner with small public water systems to assist with the application process for assistance through such State loan funds;

(D) practices to ensure that amounts in such State loan funds are used to provide loans, loan guarantees, or other authorized assistance in a timely fashion;

(E) practices that support effective management of such State loan funds;

(F) practices and tools to enhance financial management of such State loan funds; and

(G) key financial measures for use in evaluating State loan fund operations, including—

(i) measures of lending capacity, such as current assets and current liabilities or undisbursed loan assistance liability; and

(ii) measures of growth or sustainability, such as return on net interest;

(2) not later than 3 years after the date of enactment of America's Water Infrastructure Act of 2018, disseminate to the States best practices for administration of such State loan funds, based on the information collected pursuant to this subsection; and

(3) periodically update such best practices, as appropriate.

(t) Emerging Contaminants.—

(1) In General.—Amounts made available under this subsection shall be allotted to a State as if allotted under subsection (a)(1)(D) as a capitalization grant, for deposit into the State loan fund of the State, for the purposes described in subsection (a)(2)(G).

(2) Authorization of Appropriations.—There is authorized to be appropriated to carry out this subsection $100,000,000 for each of fiscal years 2020 through 2024, to remain available until expended.

(July 1, 1944, c. 373, Title XIV, § 1452, as added by Pub. L. No. 104–182, Title I, § 130, 110 Stat. 1662 (Aug. 6, 1996), and amended by Pub. L. No. 114–322, §§ 2102, 2103, 2110, 2112(b), 2113 130 Stat. 1717–18, 1729, 1730–31 (Dec. 16, 2016); Pub. L. No. 115–270, §§ 2002, 2015, 2022, 2023, 132 Stat. 3765, 3840–3841, 3855–3856, 3862 (Oct. 23, 2018); Pub. L. No. 116–92, § 7312, 133 Stat. 2277 (Dec. 20, 2019).)

[1] So in original. Probably should be preceded by "section".

HISTORICAL AND STATUTORY NOTES

References in Text

The Safe Drinking Water Act Amendments of 1996, referred to in subsec. (n), is Pub. L. No. 104–182, 110 Stat. 1613 (Aug. 6, 1996). For complete classification of this Act to the Code, see Short Title note set out under section 201 of this title and Tables.

Effective and Applicability Provisions

1996 Acts. Section effective Aug. 6, 1996, except as otherwise specifically provided, see section 2(b) of Pub. L. No. 104–182, set out as a note under section 300f of this title.

Drinking Water Infrastructure

Pub. L. No. 114–322, § 2114, 130 Stat. 1731–33 (Dec. 16, 2016), provided that:

"(a) Definitions.—In this section:

"(1) Eligible State.—The term 'eligible State' means a State for which the President has declared an emergency under the Robert T. Stafford Disaster Relief and Emergency Assistance Act (42 U.S.C. 5121 et seq.) relating to the public health threats associated with the presence of lead or other contaminants in drinking water provided by a public water system.

"(2) Eligible system.—The term 'eligible system' means a public water system that has been the subject of an emergency declaration referred to in paragraph (1).

"(3) Lead service line.—The term "lead service line" means a pipe and its fittings, which are not lead free (as defined under section 1417 of the Safe Drinking Water Act (42 U.S.C. 300g–6)), that connect the drinking water main to the building inlet.

"(4) Public water system.—The term "public water system" has the meaning given such term in section 1401(4) of the Safe Drinking Water Act (42 U.S.C. 300f(4)).

"(b) State revolving loan fund assistance.—

"(1) In general.—An eligible system shall be—

"(A) considered to be a disadvantaged community under section 1452(d) of the Safe Drinking Water Act (42 U.S.C. 300j–12(d)); and

"(B) eligible to receive loans with additional subsidization under section 1452(d)(1) of that Act (42 U.S.C. 300j–12(d)(1)), including forgiveness of principal under that section.

"(2) Authorization.—

"(A) In general.—Using funds provided pursuant to subsection (d), an eligible State may provide assistance to an eligible system within the eligible State for the purpose of addressing lead or other contaminants in drinking water, including repair and replacement of lead service lines and public water system infrastructure.

"(B) Inclusion.—Assistance provided under subparagraph (A) may include additional subsidization under section 1452(d)(1) of the Safe Drinking Water Act (42 U.S.C. 300j–12(d)(1)), as described in paragraph (1)(B).

"(C) Exclusion.—Assistance provided under subparagraph (A) shall not include assistance for a project that is financed (directly or indirectly), in whole or in part, with proceeds of any obligation issued after the date of enactment of this Act—

"(i) the interest of which is exempt from the tax imposed under chapter 1 of the Internal Revenue Code of 1986; or

"(ii) with respect to which credit is allowable under subpart I or J of part IV of subchapter A of chapter 1 of such Code.

"(3) Inapplicability of limitation.—Section 1452(d)(2) of the Safe Drinking Water Act (42 U.S.C. 300j–12(d)(2)) shall not apply to—

"(A) any funds provided pursuant to subsection (d) of this section;

"(B) any other assistance provided to an eligible system; or

"(C) any funds required to match the funds provided under subsection (d).

"(c) Nonduplication of work.—An activity carried out pursuant to this section shall not duplicate the work or activity of any other Federal or State department or agency.

"(d) Additional drinking water State revolving fund capitalization grants.—

"(1) In general.—There is authorized to be appropriated to the Administrator a total of $100,000,000 to provide additional capitalization grants to eligible States pursuant to section 1452 of the Safe Drinking Water Act (42 U.S.C. 300j–12), to be available for a period of 18 months beginning on the date on which the funds are made available, for the purposes described in subsection (b)(2), and after the end of the 18-month period, until expended for the purposes described in paragraph (3).

"(2) Supplemented intended use plans.—From funds made available under paragraph (1), the Administrator shall obligate to an eligible State such amounts as are necessary to meet the needs identified in a supplemented intended use plan for the purposes described in subsection (b)(2) by not later than 30 days after the date on which the eligible State submits to the Administrator a supplemented intended use plan under section 1452(b) of the Safe Drinking Water Act (42 U.S.C. 300j–

12(b)) that includes preapplication information regarding projects to be funded using the additional assistance, including, with respect to each such project—

"(A) a description of the project;

"(B) an explanation of the means by which the project will address a situation causing a declared emergency in the eligible State;

"(C) the estimated cost of the project; and

"(D) the projected start date for construction of the project.

"(3) Unobligated amounts.—Any amounts made available to the Administrator under paragraph (1) that are unobligated on the date that is 18 months after the date on which the amounts are made available shall be available to provide additional grants to States to capitalize State loan funds as provided under section 1452 of the Safe Drinking Water Act (42 U.S.C. 300j–12).

"(4) Applicability.—

"(A) Section 1452(b)(1) of the Safe Drinking Water Act (42 U.S.C. 300j–12(b)(1)) shall not apply to a supplement to an intended use plan under paragraph (2).

"(B) Unless explicitly waived, all requirements under the Safe Drinking Water Act (42 U.S.C. 300f et seq.) shall apply to funding provided under this subsection.

"(e) Health effects evaluation.—

"(1) In general.—Pursuant to section 104(i)(1)(E) of the Comprehensive Environmental Response, Compensation, and Liability Act of 1980 (42 U.S.C. 9604(i)(1)(E)), and on receipt of a request of an appropriate State or local health official of an eligible State, the Director of the Agency for Toxic Substances and Disease Registry of the National Center for Environmental Health shall in coordination with other agencies, as appropriate, conduct voluntary surveillance activities to evaluate any adverse health effects on individuals exposed to lead from drinking water in the affected communities.

"(2) Consultations.—Pursuant to section 104(i)(4) of the Comprehensive Environmental Response, Compensation, and Liability Act of 1980 (42 U.S.C. 9604(i)(4)), and on receipt of a request of an appropriate State or local health official of an eligible State, the Director of the Agency for Toxic Substances and Disease Registry of the National Center for Environmental Health shall provide consultations regarding health issues described in paragraph (1).

"(f) No effect on other projects.—This section shall not affect the application of any provision of the Water Infrastructure Finance and Innovation Act of 2014 (33 U.S.C. 3901 et seq.) or the Safe Drinking Water Act (42 U.S.C. 300f et seq.) to any project that does not receive assistance pursuant to this subtitle.

Sense of Congress

Pub. L. No. 114–322, § 2101, 130 Stat. 1717 (Dec. 16, 2016), provided that:

"It is the sense of Congress that Congress should provide robust funding of capitalization grants to States to fund those States' drinking water treatment revolving loan funds established under section 1452 of the Safe Drinking Water Act (42 U.S.C. 300j–12) and the State water pollution control revolving funds established under title VI of the Federal Water Pollution Control Act (33 U.S.C. 1381 et seq.)."

In addition, Section 2202 of the same law, 130 Stat. 1734, provided that:

"It is the sense of Congress that secured loans under the Water Infrastructure Finance and Innovation Act of 2014 (33 U.S.C. 3901 et seq.) shall be—

"(1) initially appropriated at $20,000,000; and

"(2) used for eligible projects, including those to address lead and other contaminants in drinking water systems."

Use of American Iron and Steel

Section 421 of Pub.L. No. 116–260, 134 Stat. 1182, 1540–41 (Dec. 27, 2020), provided:

"(a) (1) None of the funds made available by a State water pollution control revolving fund as authorized by section 1452 of the Safe Drinking Water Act (42 U.S.C. 300j–12) shall be used for a project for the construction, alteration, maintenance, or repair of a public water system or treatment works unless all of the iron and steel products used in the project are produced in the United States.

"(2) In this section, the term "iron and steel" products means the following products made primarily of iron or steel: lined or unlined pipes and fittings, manhole covers and other municipal castings, hydrants, tanks, flanges, pipe clamps and restraints, valves, structural steel, reinforced precast concrete, and construction materials.

"(b) Subsection (a) shall not apply in any case or category of cases in which the Administrator of the Environmental Protection Agency (in this section referred to as the "Administrator") finds that—

"(1) applying subsection (a) would be inconsistent with the public interest;

"(2) iron and steel products are not produced in the United States in sufficient and reasonably available quantities and of a satisfactory quality; or

"(3) inclusion of iron and steel products produced in the United States will increase the cost of the overall project by more than 25 percent.

"(c) If the Administrator receives a request for a waiver under this section, the Administrator shall make available to the public on an informal basis a copy of the request and information available to the Administrator concerning the request, and shall allow for *1541 informal public input on the request for at least 15 days prior to making a finding based on the request. The Administrator shall make the request and accompanying information available by electronic means, including on the official public Internet Web site of the Environmental Protection Agency.

"(d) This section shall be applied in a manner consistent with United States obligations under international agreements.

"(e) The Administrator may retain up to 0.25 percent of the funds appropriated in this Act for the Clean and Drinking Water State Revolving Funds for carrying out the provisions described in subsection (a)(1) for management and oversight of the requirements of this section."

Section 421 of Pub. L. No. 116094, 133 Stat. 2747–48 (Dec. 20, 2019), provided:

"(a) (1) None of the funds made available by a State water pollution control revolving fund as authorized by section 1452 of the Safe Drinking Water Act (42 U.S.C. 300j–12) shall be used for a project for the construction, alteration, maintenance, or repair of a public water system or treatment works unless all of the iron and steel products used in the project are produced in the United States.

"(2) In this section, the term "iron and steel" products means the following products made primarily of iron or steel: lined or unlined pipes and fittings, manhole covers and other municipal castings, hydrants, tanks, flanges, pipe clamps and restraints, valves, structural steel, reinforced precast concrete, and construction materials.

"(b) Subsection (a) shall not apply in any case or category of cases in which the Administrator of the Environmental Protection Agency (in this section referred to as the "Administrator") finds that—

"(1) applying subsection (a) would be inconsistent with the public interest;

"(2) iron and steel products are not produced in the United States in sufficient and reasonably available quantities and of a satisfactory quality; or

"(3) inclusion of iron and steel products produced in the United States will increase the cost of the overall project by more than 25 percent.

"(c) If the Administrator receives a request for a waiver under this section, the Administrator shall make available to the public on an informal basis a copy of the request and information available to the Administrator concerning the request, and shall allow for informal public input on the request for at least 15 days prior to making a finding based on the request. The Administrator shall make the request and accompanying information available by electronic means, including on the official public Internet Web site of the Environmental Protection Agency.

"(d) This section shall be applied in a manner consistent with United States obligations under international agreements.

"(e) The Administrator may retain up to 0.25 percent of the funds appropriated in this Act for the Clean and Drinking Water State Revolving Funds for carrying out the provisions described in subsection (a)(1) for management and oversight of the requirements of this section."

Section 423 of Pub. L. No. 116–6, 133 Stat. 263–64 (Feb. 15, 2019), provided:

"(a) (1) None of the funds made available by a State water pollution control revolving fund as authorized by section 1452 of the Safe Drinking Water Act (42 U.S.C. 300j–12) shall be used for a project for the construction, alteration, maintenance, or repair of a public water system or treatment works unless all of the iron and steel products used in the project are produced in the United States.

"(2) In this section, the term "iron and steel" products means the following products made primarily of iron or steel: lined or unlined pipes and fittings, manhole covers and other municipal castings, hydrants, tanks, flanges, pipe clamps and restraints, valves, structural steel, reinforced precast concrete, and construction materials.

"(b) Subsection (a) shall not apply in any case or category of cases in which the Administrator of the Environmental Protection Agency (in this section referred to as the "Administrator") finds that—

"(1) applying subsection (a) would be inconsistent with the public interest;

"(2) iron and steel products are not produced in the United States in sufficient and reasonably available quantities and of a satisfactory quality; or

"(3) inclusion of iron and steel products produced in the United States will increase the cost of the overall project by more than 25 percent.

"(c) If the Administrator receives a request for a waiver under this section, the Administrator shall make available to the public on an informal basis a copy of the request and information available to the Administrator concerning the request, and shall allow for informal public input on the request for at least 15 days prior to making a finding based on the request. The Administrator shall make the request and accompanying information available by electronic means, including on the official public Internet Web site of the Environmental Protection Agency.

"(d) This section shall be applied in a manner consistent with United States obligations under international agreements.

"(e) The Administrator may retain up to 0.25 percent of the funds appropriated in this Act for the Clean and Drinking Water State Revolving Funds for carrying out the provisions described in subsection (a)(1) for management and oversight of the requirements of this section."

Pub. L. No. 115–141, § 424, 132 Stat. 692 (Mar. 23, 2018), provided:

"(a) (1) None of the funds made available by a State water pollution control revolving fund as authorized by section 1452 of the Safe Drinking Water Act (42 U.S.C. 300j–12) shall be used for a project for the construction, alteration, maintenance, or repair of a public water system or treatment works unless all of the iron and steel products used in the project are produced in the United States.

"(2) In this section, the term "iron and steel" products means the following products made primarily of iron or steel: lined or unlined pipes and fittings, manhole covers and other municipal castings, hydrants, tanks, flanges, pipe clamps and restraints, valves, structural steel, reinforced precast concrete, and construction materials.

"(b) Subsection (a) shall not apply in any case or category of cases in which the Administrator of the Environmental Protection Agency (in this section referred to as the "Administrator") finds that—

"(1) applying subsection (a) would be inconsistent with the public interest;

"(2) iron and steel products are not produced in the United States in sufficient and reasonably available quantities and of a satisfactory quality; or

"(3) inclusion of iron and steel products produced in the United States will increase the cost of the overall project by more than 25 percent.

"(c) If the Administrator receives a request for a waiver under this section, the Administrator shall make available to the public on an informal basis a copy of the request and information available to the Administrator concerning the request, and shall allow for informal public input on the request for at least 15 days prior to making a finding based on the request. The Administrator shall make the request and accompanying information available by electronic means, including on the official public Internet Web site of the Environmental Protection Agency.

"(d) This section shall be applied in a manner consistent with United States obligations under international agreements.

Pub. L. No. 115–31, § 425, 131 Stat. 499–500 (May 5, 2017), provided:

"(a) (1) None of the funds made available by a State water pollution control revolving fund as authorized by section 1452 of the Safe Drinking Water Act (42 U.S.C. 300j–12) shall be used for a project for the construction, alteration, maintenance, or repair of a public water system or treatment works unless all of the iron and steel products used in the project are produced in the United States.

"(2) In this section, the term "iron and steel" products means the following products made primarily of iron or steel: lined or unlined pipes and fittings, manhole covers and other municipal castings, hydrants, tanks, flanges, pipe clamps and restraints, valves, structural steel, reinforced precast concrete, and construction materials.

"(b) Subsection (a) shall not apply in any case or category of cases in which the Administrator of the Environmental Protection Agency (in this section referred to as the "Administrator") finds that—

"(1) applying subsection (a) would be inconsistent with the public interest;

"(2) iron and steel products are not produced in the United States in sufficient and reasonably available quantities and of a satisfactory quality; or

"(3) inclusion of iron and steel products produced in the United States will increase the cost of the overall project by more than 25 percent.

"(c) If the Administrator receives a request for a waiver under this section, the Administrator shall make available to the public on an informal basis a copy of the request and information available to the Administrator concerning the request, and shall allow for informal public input on the request for at least 15 days prior to making a finding based on the request. The Administrator shall make the request and accompanying information available by electronic means, including on the official public Internet Web site of the Environmental Protection Agency.

"(d) This section shall be applied in a manner consistent with United States obligations under international agreements.

"(e) The Administrator may retain up to 0.25 percent of the funds appropriated in this Act for the Clean and Drinking Water State Revolving Funds for carrying out the provisions described in subsection (a)(1) for management and oversight of the requirements of this section."

Both Pub. L. No. 113–76, § 436, 128 Stat. 346–347 (Jan. 17, 2014), and Pub. L. 113–235, § 424, 128 Stat. 2449–2450 (Dec. 16, 2014), provided that:

"(a) (1) None of the funds made available by a State water pollution control revolving fund as authorized by section 1452 of the Safe Drinking Water Act (42 U.S.C. 300j–12) shall be used for a project for the construction, alteration, maintenance, or repair of a public water system or treatment works unless all of the iron and steel products used in the project are produced in the United States.

"(2) In this section, the term 'iron and steel products' means the following products made primarily of iron or steel: lined or unlined pipes and fittings, manhole covers and other municipal castings, hydrants, tanks, flanges, pipe clamps and restraints, valves, structural steel, reinforced precast concrete, and construction materials.

"(b) Subsection (a) shall not apply in any case or category of cases in which the Administrator of the Environmental Protection Agency (in this section referred to as the "Administrator") finds that—

"(1) applying subsection (a) would be inconsistent with the public interest;

"(2) iron and steel products are not produced in the United States in sufficient and reasonably available quantities and of a satisfactory quality; or

"(3) inclusion of iron and steel products produced in the United States will increase the cost of the overall project by more than 25 percent.

"(c) If the Administrator receives a request for a waiver under this section, the Administrator shall make available to the public on an informal basis a copy of the request and information available to the Administrator concerning the request, and shall allow for informal public input on the request for at least 15 days prior to making a finding based on the request. The Administrator shall make the request and accompanying information available by electronic means, including on the official public Internet Web site of the Environmental Protection Agency.

"(d) This section shall be applied in a manner consistent with United States obligations under international agreements.

"(e) The Administrator may retain up to 0.25 percent of the funds appropriated in this Act for the Clean and Drinking Water State Revolving Funds for carrying out the provisions described in subsection (a)(1) for management and oversight of the requirements of this section.

"(f) This section does not apply with respect to a project if a State agency approves the engineering plans and specifications for the project, in that agency's capacity to approve such plans and specifications prior to a project requesting bids, prior to the date of the enactment of this Act."

State and Tribal Assistance Grants

Pub. L. No. 112–74, Div. E, Title II, 125 Stat. 1018 (Dec. 23, 2011), provided in part: "That for fiscal year 2006 and thereafter, State authority under section 302(a) of Public Law 104–182 [Pub. L. No. 104–182, Title III, § 302(a), Aug. 6, 1996, 110 Stat. 1683, which is set out as a note under this section] shall remain in effect."

Similar provisions were contained in the following prior appropriations Acts:

Pub. L. No. 109–54, Title II, 119 Stat. 530 (Aug. 2, 2005).

Pub. L. No. 108–447, Div. I, Title III, 118 Stat. 3330 (Dec. 8, 2005).

Pub. L. No. 108–199, Div. G, Title III, 118 Stat. 406 (Jan. 23, 2004).

Pub. L. No. 108–7, Div. K, Title III, 117 Stat. 512 (Feb. 20, 2003).

Pub. L. No. 107–73, Title III, 115 Stat. 685 (Nov. 26, 2001).

Combining Fund Assets For Enhancement of Lending Capacity

Pub. L. No. 105–276, Title III, 112 Stat. 2498 (Oct. 21, 1998), provided in part: "That, consistent with section 1452(g) of the Safe Drinking Water Act (42 U.S.C.A. § 300j–12(g)), section 302 of the Safe Drinking Water Act Amendments of 1996 (Public Law 104–182) (set out as a note below) and the accompanying joint explanatory statement of the committee of conference (H. Rept. No. 104–741 to accompany S. 1316, the Safe Drinking Water Act Amendments of 1996), and notwithstanding any other provision of law, beginning in fiscal year 1999 and thereafter, States may combine the assets of State Revolving Funds (SRFs) established under section 1452 of the Safe Drinking Water Act, as amended, and title VI of the Federal Water Pollution Control Act (33 U.S.C.A. § 381 et seq.), as amended, as security for bond issues to enhance the lending capacity of one or both SRFs, but not to acquire the state match for either program, provided that revenues from the bonds are allocated to the purposes of the Safe Drinking Water Act (this subchapter) and the Federal Water Pollution Control Act (33 U.S.C.A. § 1251 et seq.) in the same portion as the funds are used as security for the bonds."

Transfer of Funds

Pub. L. No. 104–182, Title III, § 302, 110 Stat. 1683 (Aug. 6, 1996), provided that:

"(a) In general.—Notwithstanding any other provision of law, at any time after the date 1 year after a State establishes a State loan fund pursuant to section 1452 of the Safe Drinking Water Act [this section] but prior to fiscal year 2002, a Governor of the State may—

"(1) reserve up to 33 percent of a capitalization grant made pursuant to such section 1452 [this section] and add the funds reserved to any funds provided to the State pursuant to section 601 of the Federal Water Pollution Control Act (33 U.S.C. 1381) [section 1381 of Title 33, Navigation and Navigable Waters]; and

"(2) reserve in any year a dollar amount up to the dollar amount that may be reserved under paragraph (1) for that year from capitalization grants made pursuant to section 601 of such Act (33 U.S.C. 1381) [section 1381 of Title 33] and add the reserved funds to any funds provided to the State pursuant to section 1452 of the Safe Drinking Water Act [this section].

"(b) Report.—Not later than 4 years after the date of enactment of this Act [Aug. 6, 1996], the Administrator shall submit a report to the Congress regarding the implementation of this section, together with the Administrator's recommendations, if any, for modifications or improvement.

"(c) State match.—Funds reserved pursuant to this section shall not be considered to be a State match of a capitalization grant required pursuant to section 1452 of the Safe Drinking Water Act [this section] or the Federal Water Pollution Control Act (33 U.S.C. 1251 et seq.) [section 1251 et seq. of Title 33]."

§ 300j–13. Source water quality assessment

[PHSA § 1453]

(a) Source water assessment

(1) Guidance

Within 12 months after August 6, 1996, after notice and comment, the Administrator shall publish guidance for States exercising primary enforcement responsibility for public water systems to carry out directly or through delegation (for the protection and benefit of public water systems and for the support of monitoring flexibility) a source water assessment program within the State's boundaries. Each State adopting modifications to monitoring requirements pursuant to section 300g–7(b) of this title shall, prior to adopting such modifications, have an approved source water assessment program under this section and shall carry out the program either directly or through delegation.

(2) Program requirements

A source water assessment program under this subsection shall—

(A) delineate the boundaries of the assessment areas in such State from which one or more public water systems in the State receive supplies of drinking water, using all reasonably available hydrogeologic information on the sources of the supply of drinking water in the State and the water flow, recharge, and discharge and any other reliable information as the State deems necessary to adequately determine such areas; and

(B) identify for contaminants regulated under this subchapter for which monitoring is required under this subchapter (or any unregulated contaminants selected by the State, in its discretion, which the State, for the purposes of this subsection, has determined may present a threat to public health), to the extent practical, the origins within each delineated area of such contaminants to determine the susceptibility of the public water systems in the delineated area to such contaminants.

(3) Approval, implementation, and monitoring relief

A State source water assessment program under this subsection shall be submitted to the Administrator within 18 months after the Administrator's guidance is issued under this subsection and shall be deemed approved 9 months after the date of such submittal unless the Administrator disapproves the program as provided in section 300h–7(c) of this title. States shall begin implementation of the program immediately after its approval. The Administrator's approval of a State program under this subsection shall include a timetable, established in consultation with the State, allowing not more than 2 years for completion after approval of the program. Public water systems seeking monitoring relief in addition to the interim relief provided under section 300g–7(a) of this title shall be eligible for monitoring relief, consistent with section 300g–7(b) of this title, upon completion of the assessment in the delineated source water assessment area or areas concerned.

(4) Timetable

The timetable referred to in paragraph (3) shall take into consideration the availability to the State of funds under section 300j–12 of this title (relating to State loan funds) for assessments and other relevant factors. The Administrator may extend any timetable included in a State program approved under paragraph (3) to extend the period for completion by an additional 18 months.

(5) Demonstration project

The Administrator shall, as soon as practicable, conduct a demonstration project, in consultation with other Federal agencies, to demonstrate the most effective and protective means of assessing and protecting source waters serving large metropolitan areas and located on Federal lands.

(6) Use of other programs

To avoid duplication and to encourage efficiency, the program under this section may make use of any of the following:

(A) Vulnerability assessments, sanitary surveys, and monitoring programs.

(B) Delineations or assessments of ground water sources under a State wellhead protection program developed pursuant to this section.

(C) Delineations or assessments of surface or ground water sources under a State pesticide management plan developed pursuant to the Pesticide and Ground Water State Management Plan Regulation (subparts I and J of part 152 of title 40, Code of Federal Regulations), promulgated under section 136a(d) of Title 7.

(D) Delineations or assessments of surface water sources under a State watershed initiative or to satisfy the watershed criterion for determining if filtration is required under the Surface Water Treatment Rule (section 141.70 of title 40, Code of Federal Regulations).

(E) Delineations or assessments of surface or ground water sources under programs or plans pursuant to the Federal Water Pollution Control Act [33 U.S.C.A. § 1251 et seq.].

(7) Public availability

The State shall make the results of the source water assessments conducted under this subsection available to the public.

(b) Approval and disapproval

For provisions relating to program approval and disapproval, see section 300h–7(c) of this title.

(July 1, 1944, c. 373, Title XIV, § 1453, as added by Pub. L. No. 104–182, Title I, § 132(a), 110 Stat. 1673 (Aug. 6, 1996).)

HISTORICAL AND STATUTORY NOTES

References in Text

The Federal Water Pollution Control Act, referred to in subsec. (a)(6)(E), is Act of June 30, 1948, c. 758, 62 Stat. 155, as amended, also known as the Clean Water Act, which is codified generally as chapter 26 (section 1251 et seq.) of Title 33, Navigation and Navigable Waters. For complete classification of this Act to the Code, see Short Title note set out under section 1251 of Title 33 and Tables.

Effective and Applicability Provisions

1996 Acts. Section effective Aug. 6, 1996, except as otherwise specifically provided, see section 2(b) of Pub. L. No. 104–182, set out as a note under section 300f of this title.

§ 300j–14. Source water petition program

[PHSA § 1454]

(a) Petition program

(1) In general

(A) Establishment

A State may establish a program under which an owner or operator of a community water system in the State, or a municipal or local government or political subdivision of a State, may submit a source water quality protection partnership petition to the State requesting that the State assist in the local development of a voluntary, incentive-based partnership, among the owner, operator, or government and other persons likely to be affected by the recommendations of the partnership, to—

(i) reduce the presence in drinking water of contaminants that may be addressed by a petition by considering the origins of the contaminants, including to the maximum extent practicable the specific activities that affect the drinking water supply of a community;

(ii) obtain financial or technical assistance necessary to facilitate establishment of a partnership, or to develop and implement recommendations of a partnership for the protection of source water to assist in the provision of drinking water that complies with national primary drinking water regulations with respect to contaminants addressed by a petition; and

(iii) develop recommendations regarding voluntary and incentive-based strategies for the long-term protection of the source water of community water systems.

(B) Funding

Each State may—

(i) use funds set aside pursuant to section 300j–12(k)(1)(A)(iii) of this title by the State to carry out a program described in subparagraph (A), including assistance to voluntary local partnerships for the development and implementation of partnership recommendations for the protection of source water such as source water quality assessment, contingency plans, and demonstration projects for partners within a source water area delineated under section 300j–13(a)of this title; and

(ii) provide assistance in response to a petition submitted under this subsection using funds referred to in subsection (b)(2)(B) of this section.

(2) Objectives

The objectives of a petition submitted under this subsection shall be to—

(A) facilitate the local development of voluntary, incentive-based partnerships among owners and operators of community water systems, governments, and other persons in source water areas; and

(B) obtain assistance from the State in identifying resources which are available to implement the recommendations of the partnerships to address the origins of drinking water contaminants that may be addressed by a petition (including to the maximum extent practicable the specific activities contributing to the presence of the contaminants) that affect the drinking water supply of a community.

(3) Contaminants addressed by a petition

A petition submitted to a State under this subsection may address only those contaminants—

(A) that are pathogenic organisms for which a national primary drinking water regulation has been established or is required under section 300g–1 of this title; or

(B) for which a national primary drinking water regulation has been promulgated or proposed and that are detected by adequate monitoring methods in the source water at the intake structure or in any collection, treatment, storage, or distribution facilities by the community water systems at levels—

(i) above the maximum contaminant level; or

(ii) that are not reliably and consistently below the maximum contaminant level.

(4) Contents

A petition submitted under this subsection shall, at a minimum—

(A) include a delineation of the source water area in the State that is the subject of the petition;

(B) identify, to the maximum extent practicable, the origins of the drinking water contaminants that may be addressed by a petition (including to the maximum extent practicable the specific activities contributing to the presence of the contaminants) in the source water area delineated under section 300j–13 of this title;

(C) identify any deficiencies in information that will impair the development of recommendations by the voluntary local partnership to address drinking water contaminants that may be addressed by a petition;

(D) specify the efforts made to establish the voluntary local partnership and obtain the participation of—

(i) the municipal or local government or other political subdivision of the State with jurisdiction over the source water area delineated under section 300j–13 of this title; and

(ii) each person in the source water area delineated under section 300j–13 of this title—

(I) who is likely to be affected by recommendations of the voluntary local partnership; and

(II) whose participation is essential to the success of the partnership;

(E) outline how the voluntary local partnership has or will, during development and implementation of recommendations of the voluntary local partnership, identify, recognize and take into account any voluntary or other activities already being undertaken by persons in the source water area delineated under section 300j–13 of this title under Federal or State law to reduce the likelihood that contaminants will occur in drinking water at levels of public health concern; and

(F) specify the technical, financial, or other assistance that the voluntary local partnership requests of the State to develop the partnership or to implement recommendations of the partnership.

(b) Approval or disapproval of petitions

(1) In general

After providing notice and an opportunity for public comment on a petition submitted under subsection (a) of this section, the State shall approve or disapprove the petition, in whole or in part, not later than 120 days after the date of submission of the petition.

(2) Approval

The State may approve a petition if the petition meets the requirements established under subsection (a) of this section. The notice of approval shall, at a minimum, include for informational purposes—

(A) an identification of technical, financial, or other assistance that the State will provide to assist in addressing the drinking water contaminants that may be addressed by a petition based on—

(i) the relative priority of the public health concern identified in the petition with respect to the other water quality needs identified by the State;

(ii) any necessary coordination that the State will perform of the program established under this section with programs implemented or planned by other States under this section; and

(iii) funds available (including funds available from a State revolving loan fund established under title VI of the Federal Water Pollution Control Act (33 U.S.C. 1381 et seq.)) or section 300j–12 of this title;

(B) a description of technical or financial assistance pursuant to Federal and State programs that is available to assist in implementing recommendations of the partnership in the petition, including—

(i) any program established under the Federal Water Pollution Control Act (33 U.S.C. 1251 et seq.);

(ii) the program established under section 1455b of Title 16;

(iii) the agricultural water quality protection program established under chapter 2 of subtitle D of title XII of the Food Security Act of 1985 (16 U.S.C. 3838 et seq.);

(iv) the sole source aquifer protection program established under section 300h–6 of this title;

(v) the community wellhead protection program established under section 300h–7 of this title;

(vi) any pesticide or ground water management plan;

(vii) any voluntary agricultural resource management plan or voluntary whole farm or whole ranch management plan developed and implemented under a process established by the Secretary of Agriculture; and

(viii) any abandoned well closure program; and

(C) a description of activities that will be undertaken to coordinate Federal and State programs to respond to the petition.

(3) Disapproval

If the State disapproves a petition submitted under subsection (a) of this section, the State shall notify the entity submitting the petition in writing of the reasons for disapproval. A petition may be resubmitted at any time if—

(A) new information becomes available;

(B) conditions affecting the source water that is the subject of the petition change; or

(C) modifications are made in the type of assistance being requested.

(c) Grants to support State programs

(1) In general

The Administrator may make a grant to each State that establishes a program under this section that is approved under paragraph (2). The amount of each grant shall not exceed 50 percent of the cost of administering the program for the year in which the grant is available.

(2) Approval

In order to receive grant assistance under this subsection, a State shall submit to the Administrator for approval a plan for a source water quality protection partnership program that is consistent with the guidance published under subsection (d) of this section. The Administrator shall approve the plan if the plan is consistent with the guidance published under subsection (d) of this section.

(d) Guidance

(1) In general

Not later than 1 year after August 6, 1996, the Administrator, in consultation with the States, shall publish guidance to assist—

(A) States in the development of a source water quality protection partnership program; and

(B) municipal or local governments or political subdivisions of a State and community water systems in the development of source water quality protection partnerships and in the assessment of source water quality.

(2) Contents of the guidance

The guidance shall, at a minimum—

(A) recommend procedures for the approval or disapproval by a State of a petition submitted under subsection (a) of this section;

(B) recommend procedures for the submission of petitions developed under subsection (a) of this section;

(C) recommend criteria for the assessment of source water areas within a State; and

(D) describe technical or financial assistance pursuant to Federal and State programs that is available to address the contamination of sources of drinking water and to develop and respond to petitions submitted under subsection (a) of this section.

(e) Authorization of appropriations

There are authorized to be appropriated to carry out this section $5,000,000 for each of the fiscal years 2020 through 2021. Each State with a plan for a program approved under subsection (b) of this section shall receive an equitable portion of the funds available for any fiscal year.

(f) Statutory construction

Nothing in this section—

(1) (A) creates or conveys new authority to a State, political subdivision of a State, or community water system for any new regulatory measure; or

(B) limits any authority of a State, political subdivision, or community water system; or

(2) precludes a community water system, municipal or local government, or political subdivision of a government from locally developing and carrying out a voluntary, incentive-based, source water quality protection partnership to address the origins of drinking water contaminants of public health concern.

(July 1, 1944, c. 373, Title XIV, § 1454, as added by Pub. L. No. 104–182, Title I, § 133(a), 110 Stat. 1675 (Aug. 6, 1996); and amended by Pub. L. No. 115–270, § 2016, 132 Stat. 3765, 3856 (Oct. 23, 2018).)

HISTORICAL AND STATUTORY NOTES

References in Text

The Federal Water Pollution Control Act, referred to in subsec. (b)(2)(A)(iii) and (B)(i), is Act of June 30, 1948, c. 758, 62 Stat. 1155, as amended, also known as the Clean Water Act, which is codified generally as chapter 26 (section 1251 et seq.) of Title 33, Navigation and Navigable Waters. Title VI of such Act is codified as subchapter VI (section 1381 et seq.) of chapter 26 of Title 33. For complete classification of this Act to the Code, see Short Title note set out under section 1251 of Title 33 and Tables.

Chapter 2 of Subtitle D of Title XII of the Food Security Act of 1985, referred to in subsec. (b)(2)(B)(iii), is section 1238 et seq. of Title XII of Pub. L. No. 99–198, as added, which is codified generally as part II (section 3838 et seq.) of subchapter IV of chapter 58 of Title 16, Conservation.

Effective and Applicability Provisions

1996 Acts. Section effective Aug. 6, 1996, except as otherwise specifically provided, see section 2(b) of Pub. L. No. 104–182, set out as a note under section 300f of this title.

§ 300j–15. Water conservation plan

[PHSA § 1455]

(a) Guidelines

Not later than 2 years after August 6, 1996, the Administrator shall publish in the Federal Register guidelines for water conservation plans for public water systems serving fewer than 3,300 persons, public water systems serving between 3,300 and 10,000 persons, and public water systems serving more than 10,000 persons, taking into consideration such factors as water availability and climate.

(b) Loans or grants

Within 1 year after publication of the guidelines under subsection (a) of this section, a State exercising primary enforcement responsibility for public water systems may require a public water system, as a condition of receiving a loan or grant from a State loan fund under section 300j–12 of this title, to submit with its application for such loan or grant a water conservation plan consistent with such guidelines.

(July 1, 1944, c. 373, Title XIV, § 1455, as added by Pub. L. No. 104–182, Title I, § 134, 110 Stat. 1679 (Aug. 6, 1996).)

HISTORICAL AND STATUTORY NOTES

Effective and Applicability Provisions

1996 Acts. Section effective Aug. 6, 1996, except as otherwise specifically provided, see section 2(b) of Pub. L. No. 104–182, set out as a note under section 300f of this title.

§ 300j–16. Assistance to colonias

[PHSA § 1456]

(a) Definitions

As used in this section:

(1) Border State

The term "border State" means Arizona, California, New Mexico, and Texas.

(2) Eligible community

The term "eligible community" means a low-income community with economic hardship that—

(A) is commonly referred to as a colonia;

(B) is located along the United States-Mexico border (generally in an unincorporated area); and

(C) lacks a safe drinking water supply or adequate facilities for the provision of safe drinking water for human consumption.

(b) Grants to alleviate health risks

The Administrator of the Environmental Protection Agency and the heads of other appropriate Federal agencies are authorized to award grants to a border State to provide assistance to eligible communities to facilitate compliance with national primary drinking water regulations or otherwise significantly further the health protection objectives of this subchapter.

(c) Use of funds

Each grant awarded pursuant to subsection (b) of this section shall be used to provide assistance to one or more eligible communities with respect to which the residents are subject to a significant health risk (as determined by the Administrator or the head of the Federal agency making the grant) attributable to the lack of access to an adequate and affordable drinking water supply system.

(d) Cost sharing

The amount of a grant awarded pursuant to this section shall not exceed 50 percent of the costs of carrying out the project that is the subject of the grant.

(e) Authorization of appropriations

There are authorized to be appropriated to carry out this section $25,000,000 for each of the fiscal years 1997 through 1999.

(July 1, 1944, c. 373, Title XIV, § 1456, as added by Pub. L. No. 104–182, Title I, § 135, 110 Stat. 1679 (Aug. 6, 1996).)

HISTORICAL AND STATUTORY NOTES

Effective and Applicability Provisions

1996 Acts. Section effective Aug. 6, 1996, except as otherwise specifically provided, see section 2(b) of Pub. L. No. 104–182, set out as a note under section 300f of this title.

§ 300j–17. Estrogenic substances screening program

[PHSA § 1457]

In addition to the substances referred to in section 346a(p)(3)(B) of Title 21 the Administrator may provide for testing under the screening program authorized by section 346a(p) of Title 21, in accordance with the provisions of section 346a(p) of Title 21, of any other substance that may be found in sources of drinking water if the Administrator determines that a substantial population may be exposed to such substance.

(July 1, 1994, c. 373, Title XIV, § 1457, as added by Pub. L. No. 104–182, Title I, § 136, 110 Stat. 1680 (Aug. 6, 1996).)

HISTORICAL AND STATUTORY NOTES

Effective and Applicability Provisions

1996 Acts. Section effective Aug. 6, 1996, except as otherwise specifically provided, see section 2(b) of Pub. L. No. 104–182, set out as a note under section 300f of this title.

§ 300j–18. Drinking water studies

[PHSA § 1458]

(a) Subpopulations at greater risk

(1) In general

The Administrator shall conduct a continuing program of studies to identify groups within the general population that may be at greater risk than the general population of adverse health effects from exposure to contaminants in drinking water. The study shall examine whether and to what degree infants, children, pregnant women, the elderly, individuals with a history of serious illness, or other subpopulations that can be identified and characterized are likely to experience elevated health risks, including risks of cancer, from contaminants in drinking water.

(2) Report

Not later than 4 years after August 6, 1996, and periodically thereafter as new and significant information becomes available, the Administrator shall report to the Congress on the results of the studies.

(b) Biological mechanisms

The Administrator shall conduct biomedical studies to—

(1) understand the mechanisms by which chemical contaminants are absorbed, distributed, metabolized, and eliminated from the human body, so as to develop more accurate physiologically based models of the phenomena;

(2) understand the effects of contaminants and the mechanisms by which the contaminants cause adverse effects (especially noncancer and infectious effects) and the variations in the effects among humans, especially subpopulations at greater risk of adverse effects, and between test animals and humans; and

(3) develop new approaches to the study of complex mixtures, such as mixtures found in drinking water, especially to determine the prospects for synergistic or antagonistic interactions that may affect the shape of the dose-response relationship of the individual chemicals and microbes, and to examine noncancer endpoints and infectious diseases, and susceptible individuals and subpopulations.

(c) Studies on harmful substances in drinking water

(1) Development of studies

The Administrator shall, not later than 180 days after August 6, 1996, and after consultation with the Secretary of Health and Human Services, the Secretary of Agriculture, and, as appropriate, the heads of other Federal agencies, conduct the studies described in paragraph (2) to support the development and implementation of the most current version of each of the following:

(A) Enhanced Surface Water Treatment Rule (59 Fed. Reg. 38832 (July 29, 1994)).

(B) Disinfectant and Disinfection Byproducts Rule (59 Fed. Reg. 38668 (July 29, 1994)).

(C) Ground Water Disinfection Rule (availability of draft summary announced at (57 Fed. Reg. 33960; July 31, 1992)).

(2) Contents of studies

The studies required by paragraph (1) shall include, at a minimum, each of the following:

(A) Toxicological studies and, if warranted, epidemiological studies to determine what levels of exposure from disinfectants and disinfection byproducts, if any, may be associated with developmental and birth defects and other potential toxic end points.

(B) Toxicological studies and, if warranted, epidemiological studies to quantify the carcinogenic potential from exposure to disinfection byproducts resulting from different disinfectants.

(C) The development of dose-response curves for pathogens, including cryptosporidium and the Norwalk virus.

(3) Authorization of appropriations

There are authorized to be appropriated to carry out this subsection $12,500,000 for each of fiscal years 1997 through 2003.

(d) Waterborne disease occurrence study

(1) System

The Director of the Centers for Disease Control and Prevention, and the Administrator shall jointly—

(A) within 2 years after August 6, 1996, conduct pilot waterborne disease occurrence studies for at least 5 major United States communities or public water systems; and

(B) within 5 years after August 6, 1996, prepare a report on the findings of the pilot studies, and a national estimate of waterborne disease occurrence.

(2) Training and education

The Director and Administrator shall jointly establish a national health care provider training and public education campaign to inform both the professional health care provider community and the general public about waterborne disease and the symptoms that may be caused by infectious agents, including microbial contaminants. In developing such a campaign, they shall seek comment from interested groups and individuals, including scientists, physicians, State and local governments, environmental groups, public water systems, and vulnerable populations.

(3) Funding

There are authorized to be appropriated for each of the fiscal years 1997 through 2001, $3,000,000 to carry out this subsection. To the extent funds under this subsection are not fully appropriated, the Administrator may use not more than $2,000,000 of the funds from amounts reserved under section 300j–12(n) of this title for health effects studies for purposes of this subsection. The Administrator may transfer a portion of such funds to the Centers for Disease Control and Prevention for such purposes.

(July 1, 1944, c. 373, Title XIV, § 1458, as added by Pub. L. No. 104–182, Title I, § 137, 110 Stat. 1680 (Aug. 6, 1996).)

HISTORICAL AND STATUTORY NOTES

Effective and Applicability Provisions

1996 Acts. Section effective Aug. 6, 1996, except as otherwise specifically provided, see section 2(b) of Pub. L. No. 104–182, set out as a note under section 300f of this title.

Public Health Assessment of Exposure to Perchlorate

Pub. L. No. 108–136, Div. A, Title III, § 323, 117 Stat. 1440 (Nov. 24, 2003), provided that:

"(a) Epidemiological study of exposure to perchlorate.—The Secretary of Defense shall provide for an independent epidemiological study of exposure to perchlorate in drinking water. The entity conducting the study shall—

"(1) assess the incidence of thyroid disease and measurable effects of thyroid function in relation to exposure to perchlorate;

"(2) ensure that the study is of sufficient scope and scale to permit the making of meaningful conclusions of the measurable public health threat associated with exposure to perchlorate, especially the threat to sensitive subpopulations; and

"(3) examine thyroid function, including measurements of urinary iodine and thyroid hormone levels, in a sufficient number of pregnant women, neonates, and infants exposed to perchlorate in drinking water and match measurements of perchlorate levels in the drinking water of each study participant in order to permit the development of meaningful conclusions on the public health threat to individuals exposed to perchlorate.

"(b) Review of effects of perchlorate on endocrine system.—The Secretary shall provide for an independent review of the effects of perchlorate on the human endocrine system. The entity conducting the review shall assess—

"(1) available data on human exposure to perchlorate, including clinical data and data on exposure of sensitive subpopulations, and the levels at which health effects were observed; and

"(2) available data on other substances that have endocrine effects similar to perchlorate to which the public is frequently exposed.

"(c) Performance of study and review.—(1) The Secretary shall provide for the performance of the study under subsection (a) [of this note] through the Centers for Disease Control and Prevention, the National Institutes of Health, or another Federal entity with experience in environmental toxicology selected by the Secretary.

"(2) The Secretary shall provide for the performance of the review under subsection (b) [of this note] through the Centers for Disease Control and Prevention, the National Institutes of Health, or another appropriate Federal research entity with experience in human endocrinology selected by the Secretary. The Secretary shall ensure that the panel conducting the review is composed of individuals with expertise in human endocrinology.

"(d) Reporting requirements.—Not later than June 1, 2005, the Federal entities conducting the study and review under this section [this note] shall submit to the Secretary reports containing the results of the study and review."

§ 300j–19. Algal toxin risk assessment and management [DWPA § 1459]

(a) Strategic plan.—

(1) Development.—Not later than 90 days after the date of enactment of this section, the Administrator shall develop and submit to Congress a strategic plan for assessing and managing risks associated with algal toxins in drinking water provided by public water systems. The strategic plan shall include steps and timelines to—

(A) evaluate the risk to human health from drinking water provided by public water systems contaminated with algal toxins;

(B) establish, publish, and update a comprehensive list of algal toxins which the Administrator determines may have an adverse effect on human health when present in drinking water provided by public water systems, taking into account likely exposure levels;

(C) summarize—

(i) the known adverse human health effects of algal toxins included on the list published under subparagraph (B) when present in drinking water provided by public water systems; and

(ii) factors that cause toxin-producing cyanobacteria and algae to proliferate and express toxins;

(D) with respect to algal toxins included on the list published under subparagraph (B), determine whether to—

(i) publish health advisories pursuant to section 1412(b)(1)(F) for such algal toxins in drinking water provided by public water systems;

(ii) establish guidance regarding feasible analytical methods to quantify the presence of algal toxins; and

(iii) establish guidance regarding the frequency of monitoring necessary to determine if such algal toxins are present in drinking water provided by public water systems;

(E) recommend feasible treatment options, including procedures, equipment, and source water protection practices, to mitigate any adverse public health effects of algal toxins included on the list published under subparagraph (B); and

(F) enter into cooperative agreements with, and provide technical assistance to, affected States and public water systems, as identified by the Administrator, for the purpose of managing risks associated with algal toxins included on the list published under subparagraph (B).

(2) Updates.—The Administrator shall, as appropriate, update and submit to Congress the strategic plan developed under paragraph (1).

(b) Information coordination.—In carrying out this section the Administrator shall—

(1) identify gaps in the Agency's understanding of algal toxins, including—

(A) the human health effects of algal toxins included on the list published under subsection (a)(1)(B); and

(B) methods and means of testing and monitoring for the presence of harmful algal toxins in source water of, or drinking water provided by, public water systems;

(2) as appropriate, consult with—

(A) other Federal agencies that—

(i) examine or analyze cyanobacteria or algal toxins; or

(ii) address public health concerns related to harmful algal blooms;

(B) States;

(C) operators of public water systems;

(D) multinational agencies;

(E) foreign governments;

(F) research and academic institutions; and

(G) companies that provide relevant drinking water treatment options; and

(3) assemble and publish information from each Federal agency that has—

(A) examined or analyzed cyanobacteria or algal toxins; or

(B) addressed public health concerns related to harmful algal blooms.

(c) Use of science.—The Administrator shall carry out this section in accordance with the requirements described in section 1412(b)(3)(A), as applicable.

(d) Feasible.—For purposes of this section, the term 'feasible' has the meaning given such term in section 1412(b)(4)(D).

(July 1, 1944, c. 373, Title XIV, § 1459, as added by the Drinking Water Protection Act, Pub. L. No. 114–45, § 2(a), 129 Stat. 473 (Aug. 7, 2015).)

HISTORICAL AND STATUTORY NOTES

Effective and Applicability Provisions

2015 Act. This section of the Drinking Water Protection Act became effective Aug. 7. 2015.

Report to Congress

The Drinking Water Protection Act, Public Law No. 114–45, § 2(b), 129 Stat. 473 (Aug. 7., 2015), provided that:

"(b) Report to Congress.—Not later than 90 days after the date of enactment of this Act, the Comptroller General of the United States shall prepare and submit to Congress a report that includes—

"(1) an inventory of funds—

"(A) expended by the United States, for each of fiscal years 2010 through 2014, to examine or analyze toxin-producing cyanobacteria and algae or address public health concerns related to harmful algal blooms; and

"(B) that includes the specific purpose for which the funds were made available, the law under which the funds were authorized, and the Federal agency that received or spent the funds; and

"(2) recommended steps to reduce any duplication, and improve interagency coordination, of such expenditures.

§ 300j–19a. Assistance for small and disadvantaged communities [DWPA § 1459A]

(a) Definition of underserved community.—In this section:

(1) In general.—The term 'underserved community' means a political subdivision of a State that, as determined by the Administrator, has an inadequate system for obtaining drinking water.

(2) Inclusions.—The term 'underserved community' includes a political subdivision of a State that either, as determined by the Administrator—

(A) does not have household drinking water or wastewater services; or

(B) is served by a public water system that violates, or exceeds, as applicable, a requirement of a national primary drinking water regulation issued under section 1412, including—

(i) a maximum contaminant level;

(ii) a treatment technique; and

(iii) an action level.

(b) Establishment.—

(1) In general.—The Administrator shall establish a program under which grants are provided to eligible entities for use in carrying out projects and activities the primary purposes of which are to assist public water systems in meeting the requirements of this title.

(2) Inclusions.—Projects and activities under paragraph (1) include—

(A) investments necessary for the public water system to comply with the requirements of this title;

(B) assistance that directly and primarily benefits the disadvantaged community on a per-household basis; and

(C) programs to provide household water quality testing, including testing for unregulated contaminants.

(c) **Eligible entities.**—An eligible entity under this section—

(1) is—

(A) a public water system;

(B) a water system that is located in an area governed by an Indian Tribe; or

(C) a State, on behalf of an underserved community; and

(2) serves a community—

(A) that, under affordability criteria established by the State under section 1452(d)(3), is determined by the State—

(i) to be a disadvantaged community; or

(ii) to be a community that may become a disadvantaged community as a result of carrying out a project or activity under subsection (b); or

(B) with a population of less than 10,000 individuals that the Administrator determines does not have the capacity to incur debt sufficient to finance a project or activity under subsection (b).

(d) **Priority.**—In prioritizing projects and activities for implementation under this section, the Administrator shall give priority to projects and activities that benefit underserved communities.

(e) **Local participation.**—In prioritizing projects and activities for implementation under this section, the Administrator shall consult with and consider the priorities of States, Indian Tribes, and local governments in which communities described in subsection (c)(2) are located.

(f) **Technical, managerial, and financial capability.**—The Administrator may provide assistance to increase the technical, managerial, and financial capability of an eligible entity receiving a grant under this section if the Administrator determines that the eligible entity lacks appropriate technical, managerial, or financial capability and is not receiving such assistance under another Federal program.

(g) **Cost sharing.**—Before providing a grant to an eligible entity under this section, the Administrator shall enter into a binding agreement with the eligible entity to require the eligible entity—

(1) to pay not less than 45 percent of the total costs of the project or activity, which may include services, materials, supplies, or other in-kind contributions;

(2) to provide any land, easements, rights-of-way, and relocations necessary to carry out the project or activity; and

(3) to pay 100 percent of any operation and maintenance costs associated with the project or activity.

(h) **Waiver.**—The Administrator may waive, in whole or in part, the requirement under subsection (g)(1) if the Administrator determines that an eligible entity is unable to pay, or would experience significant financial hardship if required to pay, the non-Federal share.

(i) **Limitation on use of funds.**—Not more than 4 percent of funds made available for grants under this section may be used to pay the administrative costs of the Administrator.

(j) **State response to contaminants.**—

(1) **In general.**—The Administrator may, subject to the terms and conditions of this section, issue a grant to a requesting State, on behalf of an underserved community, so the State may assist in, or otherwise carry out, necessary and appropriate activities related to a contaminant—

(A) that is determined by the State to—

(i) be present in, or likely to enter into, a public water system serving, or an underground source of drinking water for, such underserved community; and

(ii) potentially present an imminent and substantial endangerment to the health of persons; and

(B) with respect to which the State determines appropriate authorities have not acted sufficiently to protect the health of such persons.

(2) **Recovery of funds.**—If, subsequent to the Administrator's award of a grant to a State under this subsection, any person or entity (including an eligible entity), is found by the Administrator or a court of competent jurisdiction to have caused or contributed to contamination that was detected as a result of testing conducted, or treated, with funds provided under this subsection, and such contamination violated a law administered by the Administrator, such person or entity shall, upon issuance of a final judgment or settlement and the exhaustion of all appellate and administrative remedies—

(A) notify the Administrator in writing not later than 30 days after such issuance of a final judgment or settlement and the exhaustion of all appellate and administrative remedies; and

(B) promptly pay the Administrator an amount equal to the amount of such funds.

(k) **Authorization of appropriations.**—There are authorized to be appropriated to carry out this section, $60,000,000 for each of fiscal years 2017 through 2021.

(*l*) **Drinking water infrastructure resilience and sustainability.**—

(1) **Resilience and natural hazard.**—The terms 'resilience' and 'natural hazard' have the meaning given such terms in section 1433(h).

(2) **In general.**—The Administrator may establish and carry out a program, to be known as the Drinking Water System Infrastructure Resilience and Sustainability Program, under which the Administrator, subject to the availability of appropriations for such purpose, shall award grants in each of fiscal years 2019 and 2020 to eligible entities for the purpose of increasing resilience to natural hazards.

(3) **Use of funds.**—An eligible entity may only use grant funds received under this subsection to assist in the planning, design, construction, implementation, operation, or maintenance of a program or project that increases resilience to natural hazards through—

(A) the conservation of water or the enhancement of water use efficiency;

(B) the modification or relocation of existing drinking water system infrastructure made, or that is at risk of being, significantly impaired by natural hazards, including risks to drinking water from flooding;

(C) the design or construction of desalination facilities to serve existing communities;

(D) the enhancement of water supply through the use of watershed management and source water protection;

(E) the enhancement of energy efficiency or the use and generation of renewable energy in the conveyance or treatment of drinking water; or

(F) the development and implementation of measures to increase the resilience of the eligible entity to natural hazards.

(4) **Application.**—To seek a grant under this subsection, the eligible entity shall submit to the Administrator an application that—

(A) includes a proposal of the program or project to be planned, designed, constructed, implemented, operated, or maintained by the eligible entity;

(B) identifies the natural hazard risk to be addressed by the proposed program or project;

(C) provides documentation prepared by a Federal, State, regional, or local government agency of the natural hazard risk to the area where the proposed program or project is to be located;

(D) includes a description of any recent natural hazard events that have affected the applicable water system;

(E) includes a description of how the proposed program or project would improve the performance of the system under the anticipated natural hazards; and

(F) explains how the proposed program or project is expected to enhance the resilience of the system to the anticipated natural hazards.

(5) Authorization of appropriations.—There is authorized to be appropriated to carry out this subsection $4,000,000 for each of fiscal years 2019 and 2020.

(July 1, 1944, c. 373, Title XIV, § 1459A, as added by Pub. L. No. 114–322, § 2104, 130 Stat. 1718–20 (Dec. 16, 2016; and amended by Pub. L. No. 115–270, § 2005, 132 Stat. 3765, 3842–3843 (Oct. 23, 2018).)

§ 300j–19b. Reducing lead in drinking water

[DWPA § 1459B]

(a) Definitions.—In this section:

(1) Eligible entity.—The term 'eligible entity' means—

(A) a community water system;

(B) a water system located in an area governed by an Indian Tribe;

(C) a nontransient noncommunity water system;

(D) a qualified nonprofit organization, as determined by the Administrator, servicing a public water system; and

(E) a municipality or State, interstate, or intermunicipal agency.

(2) Lead reduction project.—

(A) In general.—The term 'lead reduction project' means a project or activity the primary purpose of which is to reduce the concentration of lead in water for human consumption by—

(i) replacement of publicly owned lead service lines;

(ii) testing, planning, or other relevant activities, as determined by the Administrator, to identify and address conditions (including corrosion control) that contribute to increased concentration of lead in water for human consumption; and

(iii) providing assistance to low-income homeowners to replace lead service lines.

(B) Limitation.—The term 'lead reduction project' does not include a partial lead service line replacement if, at the conclusion of the service line replacement, drinking water is delivered to a household through a publicly or privately owned portion of a lead service line.

(3) Low-income.—The term 'low-income', with respect to an individual provided assistance under this section, has such meaning as may be given the term by the Governor of the State in which the eligible entity is located, based upon the affordability criteria established by the State under section 1452(d)(3).

(4) Lead service line.—The term 'lead service line' means a pipe and its fittings, which are not lead free (as defined in section 1417(d)), that connect the drinking water main to the building inlet.

(5) Nontransient noncommunity water system.—The term 'nontransient noncommunity water system' means a public water system that is not a community water system and that regularly serves at least 25 of the same persons over 6 months per year.

(b) Grant program.—

(1) Establishment.—The Administrator shall establish a grant program to provide assistance to eligible entities for lead reduction projects in the United States.

(2) Precondition.—As a condition of receipt of assistance under this section, an eligible entity shall take steps to identify—

(A) the source of lead in the public water system that is subject to human consumption; and

(B) the means by which the proposed lead reduction project would meaningfully reduce the concentration of lead in water provided for human consumption by the applicable public water system.

(3) **Priority application.**—In providing grants under this subsection, the Administrator shall give priority to an eligible entity that—

(A) the Administrator determines, based on affordability criteria established by the State under section 1452(d)(3), to be a disadvantaged community; and

(B) proposes to—

(i) carry out a lead reduction project at a public water system or nontransient noncommunity water system that has exceeded the lead action level established by the Administrator under section 1412 at any time during the 3-year period preceding the date of submission of the application of the eligible entity; or

(ii) address lead levels in water for human consumption at a school, daycare, or other facility that primarily serves children or other vulnerable human subpopulation described in section 1458(a)(1).

(4) **Cost sharing.**—

(A) **In general.**—Subject to subparagraph (B), the non-Federal share of the total cost of a project funded by a grant under this subsection shall be not less than 20 percent.

(B) **Waiver.**—The Administrator may reduce or eliminate the non-Federal share under subparagraph (A) for reasons of affordability, as the Administrator determines to be appropriate.

(5) **Low-income assistance.**—

(A) **In general.**—Subject to subparagraph (B), an eligible entity may use a grant provided under this subsection to provide assistance to low-income homeowners to replace the lead service lines of such homeowners.

(B) **Limitation.**—The amount of a grant provided to a low-income homeowner under this paragraph shall not exceed the standard cost of replacement of the privately owned portion of the lead service line.

(6) **Special consideration for lead service line replacement.**—In carrying out lead service line replacement using a grant under this subsection, an eligible entity—

(A) shall notify customers of the replacement of any publicly owned portion of the lead service line;

(B) may, in the case of a homeowner who is not low-income, offer to replace the privately owned portion of the lead service line at the cost of replacement for that homeowner's property;

(C) may, in the case of a low-income homeowner, offer to replace the privately owned portion of the lead service line at a cost that is equal to the difference between—

(i) the cost of replacement; and

(ii) the amount of assistance available to the low-income homeowner under paragraph (5);

(D) shall notify each customer that a planned replacement of any publicly owned portion of a lead service line that is funded by a grant made under this subsection will not be carried out unless the customer agrees to the simultaneous replacement of the privately owned portion of the lead service line; and

(E) shall demonstrate that the eligible entity has considered other options for reducing the concentration of lead in its drinking water, including an evaluation of options for corrosion control.

(c) Limitation on use of funds.—Not more than 4 percent of funds made available for grants under this section may be used to pay the administrative costs of the Administrator.

(d) Authorization of appropriations.—There is authorized to be appropriated to carry out this section $60,000,000 for each of fiscal years 2017 through 2021.

(e) Savings clause.—Nothing in this section affects whether a public water system is responsible for the replacement of a lead service line that is—

(1) subject to the control of the public water system; and

(2) located on private property.

(July 1, 1944, c. 373, Title XIV, § 1459A, as added by Pub. L. No. 114–322, § 2105, 130 Stat. 1720–22 (Dec. 16, 2016.).

§ 300j–19c. Study on intractable water systems

[DWPA § 1459C]

(a) Definition of intractable water system.—In this section, the term "intractable water system" means a community water system or a noncommunity water system—

(1) that serves fewer than 1,000 individuals;

(2) the owner or operator of which—

(A) is unable or unwilling to provide safe and adequate service to those individuals;

(B) has abandoned or effectively abandoned the community water system or noncommunity water system, as applicable;

(C) has defaulted on a financial obligation relating to the community water system or noncommunity water system, as applicable; or

(D) fails to maintain the facilities of the community water system or noncommunity water system, as applicable, in a manner so as to prevent a potential public health hazard; and

(3) that is, as of the date of enactment of America's Water Infrastructure Act of 2018—

(A) in significant noncompliance with this Act or any regulation promulgated pursuant to this Act; or

(B) listed as having a history of significant noncompliance with this title pursuant to section 1420(b)(1).

(b) Study required.—

(1) In general.—Not later than 2 years after the date of enactment of this section, the Administrator, in consultation with the Secretary of Agriculture and the Secretary of Health and Human Services, shall complete a study that—

(A) identifies intractable water systems; and

(B) describes barriers to delivery of potable water to individuals served by an intractable water system.

(2) Report to Congress.—Not later than 2 years after the date of enactment of this section, the Administrator shall submit to Congress a report describing findings and recommendations based on the study under this subsection.

(July 1, 1944, c. 373, Title XIV, § 1459A, as added by Pub. L. No. 115–270, § 2003, 132 Stat. 3765, 3841 (Oct. 23, 2018).

§ 300j–19d. Review of technologies

[DWPA § 1459D]

(a) Review.—The Administrator, after consultation with appropriate departments and agencies of the Federal Government and with State and local governments, shall review (or enter into contracts or cooperative agreements to provide for a review of) existing and potential methods, means, equipment, and technologies (including review of cost, availability, and efficacy of such methods, means, equipment, and technologies) that—

(1) ensure the physical integrity of community water systems;

(2) prevent, detect, and respond to any contaminant for which a national primary drinking water regulation has been promulgated in community water systems and source water for community water systems;

(3) allow for use of alternate drinking water supplies from nontraditional sources; and

(4) facilitate source water assessment and protection.

(b) Inclusions.—The review under subsection (a) shall include review of methods, means, equipment, and technologies—

(1) that are used for corrosion protection, metering, leak detection, or protection against water loss;

(2) that are intelligent systems, including hardware, software, or other technology, used to assist in protection and detection described in paragraph (1);

(3) that are point-of-use devices or point-of-entry devices;

(4) that are physical or electronic systems that monitor, or assist in monitoring, contaminants in drinking water in real-time; and

(5) that allow for the use of nontraditional sources for drinking water, including physical separation and chemical and biological transformation technologies.

(c) Availability.—The Administrator shall make the results of the review under subsection (a) available to the public.

(d) Authorization of appropriations.—There is authorized to be appropriated to the Administrator to carry out this section $10,000,000 for fiscal year 2019, which shall remain available until expended.

(July 1, 1944, c. 373, Title XIV, § 1459A, as added by Pub. L. No. 115–270, § 2017, 132 Stat. 3765, 3856–57 (Oct. 23, 2018).

PART F—ADDITIONAL REQUIREMENTS TO REGULATE SAFETY OF DRINKING WATER

§ 300j–21. Definitions

[PHSA § 1461]

As used in this part—

(1) Drinking water cooler

The term "drinking water cooler" means any mechanical device affixed to drinking water supply plumbing which actively cools water for human consumption.

(2) Lead Free

The term "lead free" means, with respect to a drinking water cooler, that each part or component of the cooler which may come in contact with drinking water contains not more than 8 percent lead, except that no drinking water cooler which contains any solder, flux, or storage tank interior surface which may come in contact with drinking water shall be considered lead free if the solder, flux, or storage tank interior surface contains more than 0.2 percent lead. The Administrator may establish more stringent requirements for treating any part or component of a drinking water cooler as lead free for purposes of this part whenever he determines that any such part may constitute an important source of lead in drinking water.

(3) Local educational agency

The term "local educational agency" means—

(A) any local educational agency as defined in section 7801 of Title 20,

(B) the owner of any private, nonprofit elementary or secondary school building, and

(C) the governing authority of any school operating under the defense dependent's education system provided for under the Defense Dependent's Education Act of 1978 (20 U.S.C. 921 and following).

(4) Repair

The term "repair" means, with respect to a drinking water cooler, to take such corrective action as is necessary to ensure that water cooler is lead free.

(5) Replacement

The term "replacement", when used with respect to a drinking water cooler or drinking water fountain, means the permanent removal of the water cooler or drinking water fountain and the installation of a lead free water cooler or drinking water fountains.

(6) School

The term "school" means any elementary school or secondary school as defined in section 7801 of Title 20 and any kindergarten or day care facility.

(7) Lead-lined tank

The term "lead-lined tank" means a water reservoir container in a drinking water cooler which container is constructed of lead or which has an interior surface which is not lead free.

(July 1, 1944, c. 373, Title XIV, § 1461, as added by Pub. L. No. 100–572, § 2(a), 102 Stat. 2884 (Oct. 31, 1988); and amended by Pub. L. No. 103–382, Title III, § 391(p), 108 Stat. 4024 (Oct. 20, 1994); Pub. L. No. 104–182, Title V, § 501(f)(7), 110 Stat. 1692 (Aug. 6, 1996); Pub. L. No. 107–110, Title X, § 1076(x), 115 Stat. 2093 (Jan. 8, 2002); Pub. L. No. 115–270, § 2006(b)(2), 132 Stat. 3765, 3844–3845 (Oct. 23, 2018).)

HISTORICAL AND STATUTORY NOTES

References in Text

The Defense Dependent's Education Act of 1978, referred to in par. (3)(C), probably means the Defense Dependents' Education Act of 1978, Title XIV of Pub. L. No. 95–561, 92 Stat. 2365 (Nov. 1, 1978), as amended, which is codified principally as chapter 25A (§ 921 et seq.) of Title 20. For complete classification of this Act to the Code, see Short Title note set out under section 921 of Title 20 and Tables.

Codifications

Section 391(p) of Pub. L. No. 103–382 directed amendment of "section 1461 of the Safe Water Drinking Act (42 U.S.C. 300j–21(6))", section 1461 is codified as this section, section 1461(6) is codified as par. (6) of this section. Par. (1) of section 391(p) of Pub. L. No. 103–382 directed amendment of subpar. (A) of par. (3), which was executed to subpar. (A) of par. (3) of this section as the probable intent of Congress.

Effective and Applicability Provisions

2002 Acts. Except as otherwise provided, amendments by Pub. L. No. 107–110 effective Jan. 8, 2002, see Pub. L. No. 107–110, § 5, set out as a note under 20 U.S.C.A. § 6301.

1996 Acts. Amendment by Pub. L. No. 104–182 effective Aug. 6, 1996, except as otherwise specifically provided, see section 2(b) of Pub. L. No. 104–182, set out as a note under section 300f of this title.

§ 300j–22. Recall of drinking water coolers with lead-lined tanks

[PHSA § 1462]

For purposes of the Consumer Product Safety Act [15 U.S.C.A. § 2051 et seq.], all drinking water coolers identified by the Administrator on the list under section 300j–23 of this title as having a lead-lined tank shall be considered to be imminently hazardous consumer products within the meaning of section 12 of such Act [15 U.S.C.A. § 2061]. After notice and opportunity for comment, including a public hearing, the Consumer Product Safety Commission shall issue an order requiring the manufacturers and importers of such coolers to repair, replace, or recall and provide a refund for such coolers within 1 year after October 31, 1988. For purposes of enforcement, such order shall be treated as an order under section 15(d) of that Act) [15 U.S.C.A. § 2064(d)].

(July 1, 1944, c. 373, Title XIV, § 1462, as added by Pub. L. No. 100–572, § 2(a), 102 Stat. 2885 (Oct. 31, 1988); and amended by Pub. L. No. 104–182, Title V, § 501(f)(8), 110 Stat. 1692 (Aug. 6, 1996).)

HISTORICAL AND STATUTORY NOTES

References in Text

The Consumer Product Safety Act, referred to in text, is Pub. L. No. 92–573, 86 Stat. 1207 (Oct. 27, 1972), as amended, which is codified generally to chapter 47 (section 2051 et seq.) of Title 15, Commerce and Trade. For complete classification of this Act to the Code, see Short Title note set out under section 2051 of Title 15 and Tables.

Effective and Applicability Provisions

1996 Acts. Amendment by Pub. L. No. 104–182 effective Aug. 6, 1996, except as otherwise specifically provided, see section 2(b) of Pub. L. No. 104–182, set out as a note under section 300f of this title.

§ 300j–23. Drinking water coolers containing lead

[PHSA § 1463]

(a) Publication of lists

The Administrator shall, after notice and opportunity for public comment, identify each brand and model of drinking water cooler which is not lead free, including each brand and model of drinking water cooler which has a lead-lined tank. For purposes of identifying the brand and model of drinking water coolers under this subsection, the Administrator shall use the best information available to the Environmental Protection Agency. Within 100 days after October 31, 1988, the Administrator shall publish a list of each brand and model of drinking water cooler identified under this subsection. Such list shall separately identify each brand and model of cooler which has a lead-lined tank. The Administrator shall continue to gather information regarding lead in drinking water coolers and shall revise and republish the list from time to time as may be appropriate as new information or analysis becomes available regarding lead contamination in drinking water coolers.

(b) Prohibition

No person may sell in interstate commerce, or manufacture for sale in interstate commerce, any drinking water cooler listed under subsection (a) of this section or any other drinking water cooler which is not lead free, including a lead-lined drinking water cooler.

(c) Criminal penalty

Any person who knowingly violates the prohibition contained in subsection (b) of this section shall be imprisoned for not more than 5 years, or fined in accordance with Title 18, or both.

(d) Civil penalty

The Administrator may bring a civil action in the appropriate United States District Court (as determined under the provisions of Title 28) to impose a civil penalty on any person who violates subsection (b) of this section. In any such action the court may impose on such person a civil penalty of not more than $5,000 ($50,000 in the case of a second or subsequent violation).

(July 1, 1944, c. 373, Title XIV, § 1463, as added by Pub. L. No. 100–572, § 2(a), 102 Stat. 2885 (Oct. 31, 1988); and amended by Pub. L. No. 104–182, Title V, § 501(f)(9), 110 Stat. 1692 (Aug. 6, 1996).)

HISTORICAL AND STATUTORY NOTES

Effective and Applicability Provisions

1996 Acts. Amendment by Pub. L. No. 104–182 effective Aug. 6, 1996, except as otherwise specifically provided, see section 2(b) of Pub. L. No. 104–182, set out as a note under section 300f of this title.

§ 300j–24. Lead contamination in school drinking water [PHSA § 1464]

(a) Distribution of drinking water cooler list

Within 100 days after October 31, 1988, the Administrator shall distribute to the States a list of each brand and model of drinking water cooler identified and listed by the Administrator under section 300j–23(a) of this title.

(b) Guidance document and testing protocol

The Administrator shall publish a guidance document and a testing protocol to assist schools in determining the source and degree of lead contamination in school drinking water supplies and in remedying such contamination. The guidance document shall include guidelines for sample preservation. The guidance document shall also include guidance to assist States, schools, and the general public in ascertaining the levels of lead contamination in drinking water coolers and in taking appropriate action to reduce or eliminate such contamination. The guidance document shall contain a testing protocol for the identification of drinking water coolers which contribute to lead contamination in drinking water. Such document and protocol may be revised, republished and redistributed as the Administrator deems necessary. The Administrator shall distribute the guidance document and testing protocol to the States within 100 days after October 31, 1988.

(c) Dissemination to schools, etc.

Each State shall provide for the dissemination to local educational agencies, private nonprofit elementary or secondary schools and to day care centers of the guidance document and testing protocol published under subsection (b) of this section, together with the list of drinking water coolers published under section 300j–23(a) of this title.

(d) Voluntary school and child care program lead testing grant program.—

(1) Definitions.—In this subsection:

(A) Child care program.—The term 'child care program' has the meaning given the term 'early childhood education program' in section 103(8) of the Higher Education Act of 1965 (20 U.S.C. 1003(8)).

(B) Local educational agency.—The term 'local educational agency' means—

(i) a local educational agency (as defined in section 8101 of the Elementary and Secondary Education Act of 1965 (20 U.S.C. 7801));

(ii) a tribal education agency (as defined in section 3 of the National Environmental Education Act (20 U.S.C. 5502)); and

(iii) a person that owns or operates a child care program facility.

(2) Establishment.—

(A) In general.—Not later than 180 days after the date of enactment of the Water and Waste Act of 2016, the Administrator shall establish a voluntary school and child care program lead testing grant program to make grants available to States to assist local educational agencies in voluntary testing for lead contamination in drinking water at schools and child care programs under the jurisdiction of the local educational agencies.

(B) Direct grants to local educational agencies.—The Administrator may make a grant for the voluntary testing described in subparagraph (A) directly available to—

(i) any local educational agency described in clause (i) or (iii) of paragraph (1)(B) located in a State that does not participate in the voluntary grant program established under subparagraph (A); or

(ii) any local educational agency described in clause (ii) of paragraph (1)(B).

(C) Technical assistance.—In carrying out the grant program under subparagraph (A), beginning not later than 1 year after the date of enactment of America's Water Infrastructure Act of 2018, the Administrator shall provide technical assistance to recipients of grants under this subsection—

(i) to assist in identifying the source of lead contamination in drinking water at schools and child care programs under the jurisdiction of the grant recipient;

(ii) to assist in identifying and applying for other Federal and State grant programs that may assist the grant recipient in eliminating lead contamination described in clause (i);

(iii) to provide information on other financing options in eliminating lead contamination described in clause (i); and

(iv) to connect grant recipients with nonprofit and other organizations that may be able to assist with the elimination of lead contamination described in clause (i)

(3) Application.—To be eligible to receive a grant under this subsection, a State or local educational agency shall submit to the Administrator an application at such time, in such manner, and containing such information as the Administrator may require.

(4) Priority.—In making grants under this subsection, the Administrator shall give priority to States and local educational agencies that will assist in voluntary testing for lead contamination in drinking water at schools and child care programs that are in low-income areas.

(5) Limitation on use of funds.—Not more than 4 percent of grant funds accepted by a State or local educational agency for a fiscal year under this subsection shall be used to pay the administrative costs of carrying out this subsection.

(6) Guidance; public availability.—As a condition of receiving a grant under this subsection, the recipient State or local educational agency shall ensure that each local educational agency to which grant funds are distributed shall—

(A) expend grant funds in accordance with—

(i) the guidance of the Environmental Protection Agency entitled '3Ts for Reducing Lead in Drinking Water in Schools: Revised Technical Guidance' and dated October 2006 (or any successor guidance); or

(ii) applicable State regulations or guidance regarding reducing lead in drinking water in schools and child care programs that are not less stringent than the guidance referred to in clause (i); and

(B) (i) make available, if applicable, in the administrative offices and, to the extent practicable, on the Internet website of the local educational agency for inspection by the public (including teachers, other school personnel, and parents) a copy of the results of any voluntary testing for lead contamination in school and child care program drinking water carried out using grant funds under this subsection; and

(ii) notify parent, teacher, and employee organizations of the availability of the results described in clause (i).

(7) Maintenance of effort.—If resources are available to a State or local educational agency from any other Federal agency, a State, or a private foundation for testing for lead contamination in drinking water, the State or local educational agency shall demonstrate that the funds provided under this subsection will not displace those resources.

(8) **Authorization of appropriations.**—There are authorized to be appropriated to carry out this subsection $20,000,000 for each of fiscal years 2017 through 2019, and $25,000,000 for each of fiscal years 2020 and 2021.

(July 1, 1944, c. 373, Title XIV, § 1464, as added by Pub. L. No. 100–572, § 2(a), 102 Stat. 2886 (Oct. 31, 1988); and amended by Pub. L. No. 104–182, Title V, § 501(f)(10), 110 Stat. 1692 (Aug. 6, 1996); Pub. L. No. 114–322, § 2107(a), 130 Stat. 1727–28 (Dec. 16, 2016); Pub. L. No. 115–270, § 2006(a), 132 Stat. 3765, 3843–3844 (Oct. 23, 2018).)

HISTORICAL AND STATUTORY NOTES

Effective and Applicability Provisions

1996 Acts. Amendment by Pub. L. No. 104–182 effective Aug. 6, 1996, except as otherwise specifically provided, see section 2(b) of Pub. L. No. 104–182, set out as a note under section 300f of this title.

§ 300j–25. Drinking water fountain replacement for schools

[PHSA § 1465]

(a) Establishment.—Not later than 1 year after the date of enactment of this section, the Administrator shall establish a grant program to provide assistance to local educational agencies for the replacement of drinking water fountains manufactured prior to 1988.

(b) Use of funds.—Funds awarded under the grant program—

(1) shall be used to pay the costs of replacement of drinking water fountains in schools; and

(2) may be used to pay the costs of monitoring and reporting of lead levels in the drinking water of schools of a local educational agency receiving such funds, as determined appropriate by the Administrator.

(c) Priority.—In awarding funds under the grant program, the Administrator shall give priority to local educational agencies based on economic need.

(d) Authorization of appropriations.—There are authorized to be appropriated to carry out this section $5,000,000 for each of fiscal years 2019 through 2021.

(July 1, 1944, c. 373, Title XIV, § 1465, as added by Pub. L. No. 100–572, § 2(a), 102 Stat. 2887 (Oct. 31, 1988); and amended by Pub. L. No. 104–182, Title V, § 501(d), (f)(11), 110 Stat. 1691, 1692 (Aug. 6, 1996); and repealed by Pub. L. No. 114–322, § 2107(a), 130 Stat. 1728 (Dec. 16, 2016); and re-added by Pub. L. No. 115–270, § 2006(b)(1), 132 Stat. 3765, 3844 (Oct. 23, 2018).)

HISTORICAL AND STATUTORY NOTES

Effective and Applicability Provisions

1996 Acts. Amendment by Pub. L. No. 104–182 effective Aug. 6, 1996, except as otherwise specifically provided, see section 2(b) of Pub. L. No. 104–182, set out as a note under section 300f of this title.

Repeal and replacement

Congress repealed the original version of § 300j–25 in Pub. L. No. 114–322, § 2107(b), 130 Stat. 1728 (Dec. 16, 2016) before replacing it with the current version in 2018.

§ 300j–26. Certification of testing laboratories

The Administrator of the Environmental Protection Agency shall assure that programs for the certification of testing laboratories which test drinking water supplies for lead contamination certify only those laboratories which provide reliable accurate testing. The Administrator (or the State in the case of a State to which certification authority is delegated under this subsection[1]) shall publish and make available to the public upon request the list of laboratories certified under this subsection[1].

(Pub. L. No. 100–572, § 4, 102 Stat. 2889 (Oct. 31, 1988).)

[1] So in original. Probably should be "section".

HISTORICAL AND STATUTORY NOTES

Codifications

This section was enacted as part of the Lead Contamination Control Act of 1988 and not as part of the Public Health Service Act, which comprises this chapter, or of the Safe Drinking Water Act, which comprises this subchapter.

§ 300j–27. Registry for lead exposure and advisory committee

(a) Definitions.—In this section:

(1) City.—The term "City" means a city exposed to lead contamination in the local drinking water system.

(2) Committee.—The term "Committee" means the Advisory Committee established under subsection (c).

(3) Secretary.—The term "Secretary" means the Secretary of Health and Human Services.

(b) Lead exposure registry.—The Secretary shall establish within the Agency for Toxic Substances and Disease Registry or the Centers for Disease Control and Prevention at the discretion of the Secretary, or establish through a grant award or contract, a lead exposure registry to collect data on the lead exposure of residents of a City on a voluntary basis.

(c) Advisory Committee.—

(1) Membership.—

(A) In general.—The Secretary shall establish, within the Agency for Toxic Substances and Disease Registry an Advisory Committee in coordination with the Director of the Centers for Disease Control and Prevention and other relevant agencies as determined by the Secretary consisting of Federal members and non-Federal members, and which shall include—

(i) an epidemiologist;

(ii) a toxicologist;

(iii) a mental health professional;

(iv) a pediatrician;

(v) an early childhood education expert;

(vi) a special education expert;

(vii) a dietician; and

(viii) an environmental health expert.

(B) Requirements.—Membership in the Committee shall not exceed 15 members and not less than ½ of the members shall be Federal members.

(2) Chair.—The Secretary shall designate a chair from among the Federal members appointed to the Committee.

(3) Terms.—Members of the Committee shall serve for a term of not more than 3 years and the Secretary may reappoint members for consecutive terms.

(4) Application of FACA.—The Committee shall be subject to the Federal Advisory Committee Act (5 U.S.C. App.).

(5) Responsibilities.—The Committee shall, at a minimum—

(A) review the Federal programs and services available to individuals and communities exposed to lead;

(B) review current research on lead poisoning to identify additional research needs;

(C) review and identify best practices, or the need for best practices, regarding lead screening and the prevention of lead poisoning;

(D) identify effective services, including services relating to healthcare, education, and nutrition for individuals and communities affected by lead exposure and lead poisoning, including in consultation with, as appropriate, the lead exposure registry as established in subsection (b); and

(E) undertake any other review or activities that the Secretary determines to be appropriate.

(6) Report.—Annually for 5 years and thereafter as determined necessary by the Secretary or as required by Congress, the Committee shall submit to the Secretary, the Committees on Finance, Health, Education, Labor, and Pensions, and Agriculture, Nutrition, and Forestry of the Senate and the Committees on Education and the Workforce, Energy and Commerce, and Agriculture of the House of Representatives a report that includes—

(A) an evaluation of the effectiveness of the Federal programs and services available to individuals and communities exposed to lead;

(B) an evaluation of additional lead poisoning research needs;

(C) an assessment of any effective screening methods or best practices used or developed to prevent or screen for lead poisoning;

(D) input and recommendations for improved access to effective services relating to health care, education, or nutrition for individuals and communities impacted by lead exposure; and

(E) any other recommendations for communities affected by lead exposure, as appropriate.

(d) Authorization of appropriations.—There are authorized to be appropriated for the period of fiscal years 2017 through 2021—

(1) $17,500,000 to carry out subsection (b); and

(2) $2,500,000 to carry out subsection (c).

(Pub. L. No. 114–322, § 2203, 130 Stat. 1734–35 (Dec. 16, 2016).)

HISTORICAL AND STATUTORY NOTES

Codifications

This section was enacted as part of the Water Infrastructure Improvement for the Nation Act of 2016 and not as part of the Public Health Service Act, which comprises this chapter, or of the Safe Drinking Water Act, which comprises this subchapter.

NATIONAL ENVIRONMENTAL POLICY

NATIONAL ENVIRONMENTAL POLICY ACT OF 1969 [NEPA § ____]

(42 U.S.C.A. §§ 4321 to 4370h)

CHAPTER 55—NATIONAL ENVIRONMENTAL POLICY

§ 4321. Congressional declaration of purpose

[NEPA § 2]

The purposes of this chapter are: To declare a national policy which will encourage productive and enjoyable harmony between man and his environment; to promote efforts which will prevent or eliminate damage to the environment and biosphere and stimulate the health and welfare of man; to enrich the understanding of the ecological systems and natural resources important to the Nation; and to establish a Council on Environmental Quality.

(Pub. L. No. 91–190, § 2, 83 Stat. 852 (Jan. 1, 1970).)

HISTORICAL AND STATUTORY NOTES

Transfer of Functions

Enforcement functions of Secretary or other official in Department of Interior related to compliance with system activities requiring coordination and approval under this chapter, and enforcement functions of Secretary or other official in Department of Agriculture, insofar as they involve lands and programs under jurisdiction of that Department, related to compliance with this chapter with respect to pre-construction, construction, and initial operation of transportation system for Canadian and Alaskan natural gas transferred to Federal Inspector, Office of Federal Inspector for Alaska Natural Gas Transportation System, until first anniversary of date of initial operation of Alaska Natural Gas Transportation System, see Reorg. Plan No. 1 of 1979, §§ 102(e), (f), 203(a), 44 Fed. Reg. 33663, 33666, 93 Stat. 1373, 1376, effective July 1, 1979, set out in Appendix 1 to Title 5, Government Organization and Employees. Office of Federal Inspector for the Alaska Natural Gas Transportation System abolished and functions and authority vested in Inspector transferred to Secretary of Energy by section 3012(b) of Pub. L. No. 102–486, set out as an Abolition of Office of Federal Inspector note under section 719e of Title 15, Commerce and Trade.

Short Title

1970 Acts. Section 1 of Pub. L. No. 91–190 provided: "That this Act [enacting this chapter] may be cited as the 'National Environmental Policy Act of 1969'."

Redesignation of Ariel Rios Building as William Jefferson Clinton Federal Building

Pub. L. No. 112–237, § 2, 126 Stat. 1628 (Dec. 28, 2012), provided that:

"**(a) Redesignation.**—The Environmental Protection Agency Headquarters located at 1200 Pennsylvania Avenue N.W. in Washington, D.C., known as the Ariel Rios Building, shall be known and redesignated as the 'William Jefferson Clinton Federal Building'.

"**(b) References.**—Any reference in a law, map, regulation, document, paper, or other record of the United States to the Environmental Protection Agency Headquarters referred to in subsection (a) shall be deemed to be a reference to the 'William Jefferson Clinton Federal Building'."

Necessity of Military Low-Level Flight Training to Protect National Security and Enhance Military Readiness.

Pub. L. No. 106–398, § 1 [Div. A, Title III, § 317], 114 Stat. 1654, 1654A–57 (Oct. 30, 2000), provided that: "Nothing in the National Environmental Policy Act of 1969 (42 U.S.C. 4321 et seq.) [Pub. L. No. 91–190, 83 Stat. 852 (Jan. 1, 1970), which is codified principally as this chapter; see Tables for complete classification] or the regulations implementing such law shall require the Secretary of Defense or the Secretary of a military department to prepare a programmatic, nation-wide environmental impact statement for low-level flight training as a precondition to the use by the Armed Forces of an airspace for the performance of low-level training flights."

Emergency Preparedness Functions

For assignment of certain emergency preparedness functions to the Administrator of the Environmental Protection Agency, see Parts 1, 2, and 16 of Ex. Ord. No. 12656, 53 Fed. Reg. 47491 (Nov. 18, 1988), set out as a note under section 2251 of Appendix to Title 50, War and National Defense.

Pollution Prosecution

Pub. L. No. 101–593, Title II, 104 Stat. 2962 (Nov. 16, 1990), provided that:

"Sec. 201. Short Title

"This title [this note] may be cited as the 'Pollution Prosecution Act of 1990'.

"Sec. 202. EPA Office of Criminal Investigation

"(a) The Administrator of the Environmental Protection Agency (hereinafter referred to as the 'Administrator') shall increase the number of criminal investigators assigned to the Office of Criminal Investigations by such numbers as may be necessary to assure that the number of criminal investigators assigned to the office—

"(1) for the period October 1, 1991, through September 30, 1992, is not less than 72;

"(2) for the period October 1, 1992, through September 30, 1993, is not less than 110;

"(3) for the period October 1, 1993, through September 30, 1994, is not less than 123;

"(4) for the period October 1, 1994, through September 30, 1995, is not less than 160;

"(5) beginning October 1, 1995, is not less than 200.

"(b) For fiscal year 1991 and in each of the following 4 fiscal years, the Administrator shall, during each such fiscal year, provide increasing numbers of additional support staff to the Office of Criminal Investigations.

"(c) The head of the Office of Criminal Investigations shall be a position in the competitive service as defined in 2102 of title 5 U.S.C. [section 2102 of Title 5, Government Organization and Employees] or a career reserve position as defined in 3132(A) of title 5 U.S.C. [section 3132(A) of Title 5] and the head of such office shall report directly, without intervening review or approval, to the Assistant Administrator for Enforcement.

"Sec. 203. Civil Investigators

"The Administrator, as soon as practicable following the date of the enactment of this Act [Nov. 16, 1990], but no later than September 30, 1991, shall increase by fifty the number of civil investigators assigned to assist the Office of Enforcement in developing and prosecuting civil and administrative actions and carrying out its other functions.

"Sec. 204. National Training Institute

"The Administrator shall, as soon as practicable but no later than September 30, 1991 establish within the Office of Enforcement the National Enforcement Training Institute. It shall be the function of the Institute, among others, to train Federal, State, and local lawyers, inspectors, civil and criminal investigators, and technical experts in the enforcement of the Nation's environmental laws.

"Sec. 205. Authorization

"For the purposes of carrying out the provisions of this Act, there is authorized to be appropriated to the Environmental Protection Agency $13,000,000 for fiscal year 1991, $18,000,000 for fiscal year 1992, $20,000,000 for fiscal year 1993, $26,000,000 for fiscal year 1994, and $33,000,000 for fiscal year 1995."

SUBCHAPTER I—POLICIES AND GOALS

§ 4331. Congressional declaration of national environmental policy

[NEPA § 101]

(a) The Congress, recognizing the profound impact of man's activity on the interrelations of all components of the natural environment, particularly the profound influences of population growth, high-density urbanization, industrial expansion, resource exploitation, and new and expanding technological advances and recognizing further the critical importance of restoring and maintaining environmental quality to the overall welfare and development of man, declares that it is the continuing policy of the Federal Government, in cooperation with State and local governments, and other concerned public and private organizations, to use all practicable means and measures, including financial and technical assistance, in a manner calculated to foster and promote the general welfare, to create and maintain conditions under which man and nature can exist in productive harmony, and fulfill the social, economic, and other requirements of present and future generations of Americans.

(b) In order to carry out the policy set forth in this chapter, it is the continuing responsibility of the Federal Government to use all practicable means, consistent with other essential considerations of national policy, to improve and coordinate Federal plans, functions, programs, and resources to the end that the Nation may—

(1) fulfill the responsibilities of each generation as trustee of the environment for succeeding generations;

(2) assure for all Americans safe, healthful, productive, and esthetically and culturally pleasing surroundings;

(3) attain the widest range of beneficial uses of the environment without degradation, risk to health or safety, or other undesirable and unintended consequences;

(4) preserve important historic, cultural, and natural aspects of our national heritage, and maintain, wherever possible, an environment which supports diversity and variety of individual choice;

(5) achieve a balance between population and resource use which will permit high standards of living and a wide sharing of life's amenities; and

(6) enhance the quality of renewable resources and approach the maximum attainable recycling of depletable resources.

(c) The Congress recognizes that each person should enjoy a healthful environment and that each person has a responsibility to contribute to the preservation and enhancement of the environment.

(Pub. L. No. 91–190, Title I, § 101, 83 Stat. 852 (Jan. 1, 1970).)

HISTORICAL AND STATUTORY NOTES

Commission on Population Growth and the American Future

Pub. L. No. 91–213, §§ 1 to 9, 84 Stat. 67–69 (Mar. 16, 1970), established the Commission on Population Growth and the American Future to conduct and sponsor such studies and research and make such recommendations as might be necessary to provide information and education to all levels of government in the United States, and to our people regarding a broad range of problems associated with population growth and their implications for America's future; prescribed the composition of the Commission; provided for the appointment of its members, and the designation of a Chairman and Vice Chairman; required a majority of the members of the Commission to constitute a quorum, but allowed a lesser number to conduct hearings; prescribed the compensation of members of the Commission; required the Commission to conduct an inquiry into certain prescribed aspects of population growth in the United States and its foreseeable social consequences; provided for the appointment of an Executive Director and other personnel and prescribed their compensation; authorized the Commission to enter into contracts with public agencies, private firms, institutions, and individuals for the conduct of research and surveys, the preparation of reports, and other activities necessary to the discharge of its duties, and to request from any Federal department or agency any information and assistance it deems necessary to carry out its functions; required the General Services Administration to provide administrative services for the Commission on a reimbursable basis; required the Commission to submit an interim report to the President and the Congress one year after it was established and to submit its final report two years after Mar. 16, 1970; terminated the Commission sixty days after the date of the submission of its final report; and authorized to be appropriated, out of any money in the Treasury not otherwise appropriated, such amounts as might be necessary to carry out the provisions of Pub. L. No. 91–213.

§ 4332. Cooperation of agencies; reports; availability of information; recommendations; international and national coordination of efforts

[NEPA § 102]

The Congress authorizes and directs that, to the fullest extent possible: (1) the policies, regulations, and public laws of the United States shall be interpreted and administered in accordance with the policies set forth in this chapter, and (2) all agencies of the Federal Government shall—

(A) utilize a systematic, interdisciplinary approach which will insure the integrated use of the natural and social sciences and the environmental design arts in planning and in decisionmaking which may have an impact on man's environment;

(B) identify and develop methods and procedures, in consultation with the Council on Environmental Quality established by subchapter II of this chapter, which will insure that presently unquantified environmental amenities and values may be given appropriate consideration in decisionmaking along with economic and technical considerations;

(C) include in every recommendation or report on proposals for legislation and other major Federal actions significantly affecting the quality of the human environment, a detailed statement by the responsible official on—

(i) the environmental impact of the proposed action,

(ii) any adverse environmental effects which cannot be avoided should the proposal be implemented,

(iii) alternatives to the proposed action,

(iv) the relationship between local short-term uses of man's environment and the maintenance and enhancement of long-term productivity, and

(v) any irreversible and irretrievable commitments of resources which would be involved in the proposed action should it be implemented.

Prior to making any detailed statement, the responsible Federal official shall consult with and obtain the comments of any Federal agency which has jurisdiction by law or special expertise with respect to any environmental impact involved. Copies of such statement and the comments and views of the appropriate Federal, State, and local agencies, which are authorized to develop and enforce environmental standards, shall be made available to the President, the Council on Environmental Quality and to the public as provided by section 552 of Title 5, and shall accompany the proposal through the existing agency review processes;

(D) Any detailed statement required under subparagraph (C) after January 1, 1970, for any major Federal action funded under a program of grants to States shall not be deemed to be legally insufficient solely by reason of having been prepared by a State agency or official, if:

(i) the State agency or official has statewide jurisdiction and has the responsibility for such action,

(ii) the responsible Federal official furnishes guidance and participates in such preparation,

(iii) the responsible Federal official independently evaluates such statement prior to its approval and adoption, and

(iv) after January 1, 1976, the responsible Federal official provides early notification to, and solicits the views of, any other State or any Federal land management entity of any action or any alternative thereto which may have significant impacts upon such State or affected Federal land management entity and, if there is any disagreement on such impacts, prepares a written assessment of such impacts and views for incorporation into such detailed statement.

The procedures in this subparagraph shall not relieve the Federal official of his responsibilities for the scope, objectivity, and content of the entire statement or of any other responsibility under this chapter; and further, this subparagraph does not affect the legal sufficiency of statements prepared by State agencies with less than statewide jurisdiction.[1]

(E) study, develop, and describe appropriate alternatives to recommended courses of action in any proposal which involves unresolved conflicts concerning alternative uses of available resources;

(F) recognize the worldwide and long-range character of environmental problems and, where consistent with the foreign policy of the United States, lend appropriate support to initiatives, resolutions, and programs designed to maximize international cooperation in anticipating and preventing a decline in the quality of mankind's world environment;

(G) make available to States, counties, municipalities, institutions, and individuals, advice and information useful in restoring, maintaining, and enhancing the quality of the environment;

(H) initiate and utilize ecological information in the planning and development of resource-oriented projects; and

(I) assist the Council on Environmental Quality established by subchapter II of this chapter.

(Pub. L. No. 91–190, Title I, § 102, 83 Stat. 853 (Jan. 1, 1970); as amended by Pub. L. No. 94–83, 89 Stat. 424 (Aug. 9, 1975).)

[1] So in original. The period probably should be a semicolon.

HISTORICAL AND STATUTORY NOTES

Certain Commercial Space Launch Activities

Pub. L. No. 104–88, Title IV, § 401, 109 Stat. 955 (Dec. 29, 1995), provided that: "The licensing of a launch vehicle or launch site operator (including any amendment, extension, or renewal of the license) under chapter 701 of title 49, United States Code [section 70101 et seq. of Title 49, Transportation], shall not be considered a major Federal action for purposes of section 102(C) of the National Environmental Policy Act of 1969 (42 U.S.C. 4332(C)) if—

"(1) the Department of the Army has issued a permit for the activity; and

"(2) the Army Corps of Engineers has found that the activity has no significant impact."

[Section 401 of Pub. L. No. 104–88 effective Jan. 1, 1996, see section 2 of Pub. L. No. 104–88, set out as a note under section 701 of Title 49, Transportation.]

§ 4332a. Accelerated decisionmaking in environmental reviews

(a) In general

In preparing a final environmental impact statement under the National Environmental Policy Act of 1969 (42 U.S.C. 4321 et seq.), if the lead agency modifies the statement in response to comments that are minor and are confined to factual corrections or explanations of why the comments do not warrant additional agency response, the lead agency may write on errata sheets attached to the statement instead of rewriting the draft statement, subject to the condition that the errata sheets—

(1) cite the sources, authorities, or reasons that support the position of the agency; and

(2) if appropriate, indicate the circumstances that would trigger agency reappraisal or further response.

(b) Incorporation

To the maximum extent practicable, the lead agency shall expeditiously develop a single document that consists of a final environmental impact statement and a record of decision, unless—

(1) the final environmental impact statement makes substantial changes to the proposed action that are relevant to environmental or safety concerns; or

(2) there are significant new circumstances or information relevant to environmental concerns and that bear on the proposed action or the impacts of the proposed action.

(Pub. L. No. 112–141, Div. A, Title I, § 1319, 126 Stat. 551 (July 6, 2012).)

HISTORICAL AND STATUTORY NOTES

References in Text

The National Environmental Policy Act of 1969, referred to in subsec. (a), also known as NEPA, is Pub. L. No. 91–190, 83 Stat. 852 (Jan. 1, 1970), as amended, which is codified principally to this chapter, 42 U.S.C.A. § 4321 et seq. For complete classification, see Short Title note set out under 42 U.S.C.A. § 4321 and Tables.

Codifications

This section was enacted as part of the Moving Ahead for Progress in the 21st Century Act, also known as MAP-21, and not as part of the National Environmental Policy Act of 1969, which otherwise comprises this chapter.

Effective and Applicability Provisions

2012 Acts. Except as otherwise provided, Divisions A, B, C (other than amendments to 16 U.S.C.A. § 777c and 49 U.S.C.A. § 31104, and provisions set out as notes under 49 U.S.C.A. §§ 31100 and 31301), and E of Pub. L. No. 112–141, take effect on Oct. 1, 2012, see Pub. L. No. 112–141, § 3(a), set out as a note under 23 U.S.C.A. § 101.

§ 4333. Conformity of administrative procedures to national environmental policy

[NEPA § 103]

All agencies of the Federal Government shall review their present statutory authority, administrative regulations, and current policies and procedures for the purpose of determining whether there are any deficiencies or inconsistencies therein which prohibit full compliance with the purposes and provisions of this chapter and shall propose to the President not later than July 1, 1971, such measures as may be necessary to bring their authority and policies into conformity with the intent, purposes, and procedures set forth in this chapter.

(Pub. L. No. 91–190, Title I, § 103, 83 Stat. 854 (Jan. 1, 1970).)

§ 4334. Other statutory obligations of agencies

[NEPA § 104]

Nothing in section 4332 or 4333 of this title shall in any way affect the specific statutory obligations of any Federal agency (1) to comply with criteria or standards of environmental quality, (2) to coordinate or consult with any other Federal or State agency, or (3) to act, or refrain from acting contingent upon the recommendations or certification of any other Federal or State agency.

(Pub. L. No. 91–190, Title I, § 104, 83 Stat. 854 (Jan. 1, 1970).)

§ 4335. Efforts supplemental to existing authorizations

[NEPA § 105]

The policies and goals set forth in this chapter are supplementary to those set forth in existing authorizations of Federal agencies.

(Pub. L. No. 91–190, Title I, § 105, 83 Stat. 854 (Jan. 1, 1970).)

SUBCHAPTER II—COUNCIL ON ENVIRONMENTAL QUALITY

§ 4341. Omitted

HISTORICAL AND STATUTORY NOTES

Codifications

Section, Pub. L. No. 91–190, Title II, § 201, 83 Stat. 854 (Jan. 1, 1970), which required the President to transmit to Congress annually an Environmental Quality Report, terminated, effective May 15, 2000, pursuant to Pub. L. No. 104–66, § 3003, as amended, set out as a note under 31 U.S.C.A. § 1113. See, also, item 1 on page 41 of House Document No. 103–7.

§ 4342. Establishment; membership; Chairman; appointments

[NEPA § 202]

There is created in the Executive Office of the President a Council on Environmental Quality (hereinafter referred to as the "Council"). The Council shall be composed of three members who shall be appointed by the President to serve at his pleasure, by and with the advice and consent of the Senate. The President shall designate one of the members of the Council to serve as Chairman. Each member shall be a person who, as a result of his training, experience, and attainments, is exceptionally well qualified to analyze and interpret environmental trends and information of all kinds; to appraise programs and activities of the Federal Government in the light of the policy set forth in subchapter I of this chapter; to be conscious of and responsive to the scientific, economic, social, esthetic, and cultural needs and interests of the Nation; and to formulate and recommend national policies to promote the improvement of the quality of the environment.

(Pub. L. No. 91–190, Title II, § 202, 83 Stat. 854 (Jan. 1, 1970).)

HISTORICAL AND STATUTORY NOTES

Council on Environmental Quality

Provisions stating that notwithstanding this section, the Council was to consist of one member, appointed by the President, by and with the advice and consent of the Senate, serving as chairman and exercising all powers, functions, and duties of the Council, were contained in the Department of the Interior, Environment, and Related Agencies Appropriations Act, 2006, Pub. L. No. 109–54, Title III, 119 Stat. 543 (Aug. 2, 2005), and were repeated in provisions of subsequent appropriations acts which are not set out in the Code. Similar provisions were also contained in the following prior appropriations acts:

Similar provisions were contained in the following prior appropriations Acts:

Pub. L. No. 108–447, Div. I, Title III, 118 Stat. 3332 (Dec. 8, 2004).

Pub. L. No. 108–199, Div. G, Title III, 118 Stat. 408 (Jan. 23, 2004).

Pub. L. No. 108–7, Div. K, Title I, 117 Stat. 514 (Feb. 20, 2003).

Pub. L. No. 107–73, Title III, 115 Stat. 686 (Nov. 26, 2001).

Pub. L. No. 106–377, § 1(a)(1) [Title III], 114 Stat. 1441, 1441A–45 (Oct. 27, 2000).

Pub. L. No. 106–74, Title III, 113 Stat. 1084 (Oct. 20, 1999).

Pub. L. No. 105–276, Title III, 112 Stat. 2500 (Oct. 21, 1998).

Pub. L. No. 105–65, Title III, 111 Stat. 1375 (Oct. 27, 1997).

§ 4343. Employment of personnel, experts and consultants

[NEPA § 203]

(a) The Council may employ such officers and employees as may be necessary to carry out its functions under this chapter. In addition, the Council may employ and fix the compensation of such experts and consultants as may be necessary for the carrying out of its functions under this chapter, in accordance with section 3109 of Title 5 (but without regard to the last sentence thereof).

(b) Notwithstanding section 1342 of Title 31, the Council may accept and employ voluntary and uncompensated services in furtherance of the purposes of the Council.

(Pub. L. No. 91–190, Title II, § 203, 83 Stat. 855 (Jan. 1, 1970); as amended by Pub. L. No. 94–52, § 2, 89 Stat. 258 (July 3, 1975).)

HISTORICAL AND STATUTORY NOTES

Codifications

In subsec. (b), "section 1342 of Title 31" was substituted for "section 3679(b) of the Revised Statutes (31 U.S.C. 665(b))" on authority of Pub. L. No. 97–258, § 4(b), 96 Stat. 1067 (Sept. 13, 1982), the first section of which enacted Title 31, Money and Finance.

§ 4344. Duties and functions

[NEPA § 204]

It shall be the duty and function of the Council—

(1) to assist and advise the President in the preparation of the Environmental Quality Report required by section 4341 of this title;

(2) to gather timely and authoritative information concerning the conditions and trends in the quality of the environment both current and prospective, to analyze and interpret such information for the purpose of determining whether such conditions and trends are interfering, or are likely to interfere, with the achievement of the policy set forth in subchapter I of this chapter, and to compile and submit to the President studies relating to such conditions and trends;

(3) to review and appraise the various programs and activities of the Federal Government in the light of the policy set forth in subchapter I of this chapter for the purpose of determining the extent to which such programs and activities are contributing to the achievement of such policy, and to make recommendations to the President with respect thereto;

(4) to develop and recommend to the President national policies to foster and promote the improvement of environmental quality to meet the conservation, social, economic, health, and other requirements and goals of the Nation;

(5) to conduct investigations, studies, surveys, research, and analyses relating to ecological systems and environmental quality;

(6) to document and define changes in the natural environment, including the plant and animal systems, and to accumulate necessary data and other information for a continuing analysis of these changes or trends and an interpretation of their underlying causes;

(7) to report at least once each year to the President on the state and condition of the environment; and

(8) to make and furnish such studies, reports thereon, and recommendations with respect to matters of policy and legislation as the President may request.

(Pub. L. No. 91–190, Title II, § 204, 83 Stat. 855 (Jan. 1, 1970).)

HISTORICAL AND STATUTORY NOTES

References in Text

Section 4341 of this title, referred to in par. (1), was omitted from the Code.

Termination of Reporting Requirements

For termination, effective May 15, 2000, of reporting provisions in this section, see Pub. L. No. 104–66, § 3003, as amended, set out as a note under 31 U.S.C.A. § 1113, and the 1st item on page 41 of House Document No. 103–7.

Transfer of Functions

So much of the functions of the Council on Environmental Quality under par. (4) of this section as pertains to ecological systems was transferred to the Administrator of the Environmental Protection Agency by 1970 Reorg. Plan No. 3, Section 2(a)(5), eff. Dec. 2, 1970, 35 Fed. Reg. 15623, 84 Stat. 2086, set out under section 4321 of this title.

§ 4345. Consultation with Citizens' Advisory Committee on Environmental Quality and other representatives

[NEPA § 205]

In exercising its powers, functions, and duties under this chapter, the Council shall—

(1) consult with the Citizens' Advisory Committee on Environmental Quality established by Executive Order numbered 11472, dated May 29, 1969, and with such representatives of science, industry, agriculture, labor, conservation organizations, State and local governments and other groups, as it deems advisable; and

(2) utilize, to the fullest extent possible, the services, facilities, and information (including statistical information) of public and private agencies and organizations, and individuals, in order that duplication of effort and expense may be avoided, thus assuring that the Council's activities will not unnecessarily overlap or conflict with similar activities authorized by law and performed by established agencies.

(Pub. L. No. 91–190, Title II, § 205, 83 Stat. 855 (Jan. 1, 1970).)

HISTORICAL AND STATUTORY NOTES

References in Text

Executive Order numbered 11472, dated May 29, 1969, referred to in par. (1), is set out as a note under section 4321 of this title.

Citizens' Advisory Committee on Environmental Quality

For provisions relating to termination of Citizens' Advisory Committee on Environmental Quality, see Ex. Ord. No. 12007, 42 Fed. Reg. 42839 (Aug. 22, 1977), set out as a note under section 14 of the Federal Advisory Committee Act in Appendix 2 to Title 5, Government Organization and Employees.

§ 4346. Tenure and compensation of members

[NEPA § 206]

Members of the Council shall serve full time and the Chairman of the Council shall be compensated at the rate provided for Level II of the Executive Schedule Pay Rates (5 U.S.C. 5313). The other members of the Council shall be compensated at the rate provided for Level IV or[1] the Executive Schedule Pay Rates (5 U.S.C. 5315).

(Pub. L. No. 91–190, Title II, § 206, 83 Stat. 856 (Jan. 1, 1970).)

[1] So in original. Probably should be "of".

§ 4346a. Travel reimbursement by private organizations and Federal, State, and local governments

[NEPA § 207]

The Council may accept reimbursements from any private nonprofit organization or from any department, agency, or instrumentality of the Federal Government, any State, or local government, for the reasonable travel expenses incurred by an officer or employee of the Council in connection with his attendance at any conference, seminar, or similar meeting conducted for the benefit of the Council.

(Pub. L. No. 91–190, Title II, § 207, as added by Pub. L. No. 94–52, § 3, 89 Stat. 258 (July 3, 1975).)

§ 4346b. Expenditures in support of international activities

[NEPA § 208]

The Council may make expenditures in support of its international activities, including expenditures for: (1) international travel; (2) activities in implementation of international agreements; and (3) the support of international exchange programs in the United States and in foreign countries.

(Pub. L. No. 91–190, Title II, § 208, as added by Pub. L. No. 94–52, § 3, 89 Stat. 258 (July 3, 1975).)

§ 4347. Authorization of appropriations

[NEPA § 209]

There are authorized to be appropriated to carry out the provisions of this chapter not to exceed $300,000 for fiscal year 1970, $700,000 for fiscal year 1971, and $1,000,000 for each fiscal year thereafter.

(Pub. L. No. 91–190, Title II, § 209, formerly § 207, 83 Stat. 856 (Jan. 1, 1970); renumbered § 209 by Pub. L. No. 94–52, § 3, 89 Stat. 258 (July 3, 1975).)

SUBCHAPTER III—MISCELLANEOUS PROVISIONS

§ 4361. Repealed. Pub. L. No. 104–66, Title II, § 2021(k)(1), 109 Stat. 728 (Dec. 21, 1995).

HISTORICAL AND STATUTORY NOTES

This section, Pub. L. No. 94–475, § 5, 90 Stat. 2071 (Oct. 11, 1976), related to a plan for research, development, and demonstration.

§ 4361a. Repealed. Pub. L. No. 104–66, Title II, § 2021(k)(2), 109 Stat. 728 (Dec. 21, 1995).

HISTORICAL AND STATUTORY NOTES

Section, Pub. L. No. 95–155, § 4, Nov. 8, 1977, 91 Stat. 1258, related to budget projections in annual revisions of the plan for research, development, and demonstration.

§ 4361b. Implementation by Administrator of Environmental Protection Agency of recommendations of "CHESS" Investigative Report; waiver; inclusion of status of implementation requirements in annual revisions of plan for research, development, and demonstration

The Administrator of the Environmental Protection Agency shall implement the recommendations of the report prepared for the House Committee on Science and Technology entitled "The Environmental Protection Agency Research Program with primary emphasis on the Community Health and Environmental Surveillance System (CHESS): An Investigative Report", unless for any specific recommendation he determines (1) that such recommendation has been implemented, (2) that implementation of such recommendation would not enhance the quality of the research, or (3) that implementation of such recommendation will require funding which is not available. Where such funding is not available, the Administrator shall request the required authorization or appropriation for such implementation. The Administrator shall report the status of such implementation in each annual revision of the five-year plan transmitted to the Congress under section 4361 of this title.

(Pub. L. No. 95–155, § 10, 91 Stat. 1262 (Nov. 8, 1977).)

HISTORICAL AND STATUTORY NOTES

References in Text

Section 4361 of this title, referred to in text, was repealed by Pub. L. No. 104–66, Title II, § 2021(k)(1), Dec. 21, 1995, 109 Stat. 728.

Codifications

This section was enacted as part of the Environmental Research, Development, and Demonstration Authorization Act of 1978, and not as part of the National Environmental Policy Act of 1969, which comprises this chapter.

Change of Name

Committee on Science and Technology of House of Representatives changed to Committee on Science, Space, and Technology of House of Representatives by House Resolution No. 5, One Hundred Twelfth Congress, Jan. 5, 2011.

§ 4361c. Staff management

(a) Appointments for educational programs

(1) The Administrator is authorized to select and appoint up to 75 full-time permanent staff members in the Office of Research and Development to pursue full-time educational programs for the purpose of (A) securing an advanced degree or (B) securing academic training, for the purpose of making a career change in order to better carry out the Agency's research mission.

(2) The Administrator shall select and appoint staff members for these assignments according to rules and criteria promulgated by him. The Agency may continue to pay the salary and benefits of the appointees as well as reasonable and appropriate relocation expenses and tuition.

(3) The term of each appointment shall be for up to one year, with a single renewal of up to one year in appropriate cases at the discretion of the Administrator.

(4) Staff members appointed to this program shall not count against any Agency personnel ceiling during the term of their appointment.

(b) Post-doctoral research fellows

(1) The Administrator is authorized to appoint up to 25 Post-doctoral Research Fellows in accordance with the provisions of section 213.3102(aa) of title 5 of the Code of Federal Regulations.

(2) Persons holding these appointments shall not count against any personnel ceiling of the Agency.

(c) Non-Government research associates

(1) The Administrator is authorized and encouraged to utilize research associates from outside the Federal Government in conducting the research, development, and demonstration programs of the Agency.

(2) These persons shall be selected and shall serve according to rules and criteria promulgated by the Administrator.

(d) Women and minority groups

For all programs in this section, the Administrator shall place special emphasis on providing opportunities for education and training of women and minority groups.

(Pub. L. No. 95–477, § 6, 92 Stat. 1510 (Oct. 18, 1978).)

HISTORICAL AND STATUTORY NOTES

Codifications

Section was enacted as part of the Environmental Research, Development, and Demonstration Authorization Act of 1969, and not as part of the National Environmental Policy Act of 1969, which comprises this chapter.

Environmental Protection Agency

Pub. L. No. 108–7, Div. K, Title III, 117 Stat. 509 (Feb. 20, 2003), provided in part that: "The Office of Research and Development of the Environmental Protection Agency may hereafter [on or after Feb. 20, 2003] contract directly with individuals or indirectly with institutions or nonprofit organizations, without regard to 41 U.S.C. 5 [see, now, 41 U.S.C.A. § 6101], for the temporary or intermittent personal services of students or recent graduates, who shall be considered employees for the purposes of chapters 57 and 81 of title 5, United States Code

[5 U.S.C.A. §§ 5701 et seq. and 8101 et seq.], relating to compensation for travel and work injuries, and chapter 171 of title 28, United States Code [28 U.S.C.A. § 2671 et seq.], relating to tort claims, but shall not be considered to be Federal employees for any other purposes."

§ 4362. Interagency cooperation on prevention of environmental cancer and heart and lung disease

(a) Not later than three months after August 7, 1977, there shall be established a Task Force on Environmental Cancer and Heart and Lung Disease (hereinafter referred to as the "Task Force"). The Task Force shall include representatives of the Environmental Protection Agency, the National Cancer Institute, the National Heart, Lung, and Blood Institute, the National Institute of Occupational Safety and Health, and the National Institute on Environmental Health Sciences, and shall be chaired by the Administrator (or his delegate).

(b) The Task Force shall—

(1) recommend a comprehensive research program to determine and quantify the relationship between environmental pollution and human cancer and heart and lung disease;

(2) recommend comprehensive strategies to reduce or eliminate the risks of cancer or such other diseases associated with environmental pollution;

(3) recommend research and such other measures as may be appropriate to prevent or reduce the incidence of environmentally related cancer and heart and lung diseases;

(4) coordinate research by, and stimulate cooperation between, the Environmental Protection Agency, the Department of Health and Human Services, and such other agencies as may be appropriate to prevent environmentally related cancer and heart and lung diseases; and

(5) report to Congress, not later than one year after August 7, 1977, and annually thereafter, on the problems and progress in carrying out this section.

(Pub. L. No. 95–95, Title IV, § 402, 91 Stat. 791 (Aug. 7, 1977); as amended by Pub. L. No. 96–88, Title V, § 509(b), 93 Stat. 695 (Oct. 17, 1979).)

HISTORICAL AND STATUTORY NOTES

Codifications

Section was enacted as part of the Clean Air Act Amendments of 1977 and not as part of the National Environmental Policy Act of 1969, which comprises this chapter.

Effective and Applicability Provisions

1977 Acts. Section effective Aug. 7, 1977, except as otherwise expressly provided, see section 406(d) of Pub. L. No. 95–95, set out as a note under section 7401 of this title.

Change of Name

"Department of Health and Human Services" was substituted for "Department of Health, Education, and Welfare" in subsec. (b)(4), pursuant to section 509(b) of Pub. L. No. 96–88, which is codified as section 3508(b) of Title 20, Education.

Termination of Reporting Requirements

For termination, effective May 15, 2000, of provisions in subsec. (b)(5) of this section relating to annual report to Congress, see Pub. L. No. 104–66, § 3003, as amended, set out as a note under 31 U.S.C.A. § 1113, and item 18 on page 164 of House Document No. 103–7.

§ 4362a. Membership of Task Force on Environmental Cancer and Heart and Lung Disease

The Director of the National Center for Health Statistics and the head of the Center for Disease Control (or the successor to such entity) shall each serve as members of the Task Force on Environmental Cancer and Heart and Lung Disease established under section 4362 of this title.

(Pub. L. No. 95–623, § 9, 92 Stat. 3455 (Nov. 9, 1978).)

HISTORICAL AND STATUTORY NOTES

Codifications

This section was enacted as part of the Health Services Research, Health Statistics, and Health Care Technology Act of 1978 and not as part of the National Environmental Policy Act of 1969, which comprises this chapter.

Change of Name

Centers for Disease Control changed to Centers for Disease Control and Prevention by Pub. L. No. 102–531, Title III, § 312, 106 Stat. 3504 (Oct. 27, 1992).

§ 4363. Continuing and long-term environmental research and development

The Administrator of the Environmental Protection Agency shall establish a separately identified program of continuing, long-term environmental research and development for each activity listed in section 2(a) of this Act. Unless otherwise specified by law, at least 15 per centum of funds appropriated to the Administrator for environmental research and development for each activity listed in section 2(a) of this Act shall be obligated and expended for such long-term environmental research and development under this section.

(Pub. L. No. 96–569, § 2(f), 94 Stat. 3337 (Dec. 22, 1980).)

HISTORICAL AND STATUTORY NOTES

References in Text

Section 2(a) of this Act, referred to in text, is section 2(a) of Pub. L. No. 96–569, 94 Stat. 3335 (Dec. 22, 1980), which was not codified into the Code.

Codifications

Section was enacted as part of the Environmental Research, Development and Demonstration Authorization Act of 1981, and not as part of the National Environmental Policy Act of 1969, which comprises this chapter.

Similar Provisions

Provisions similar to this section were contained in the following prior authorization acts:

Pub. L. No. 96–229, § 2(e), 94 Stat. 327 (Apr. 7, 1980).

Pub. L. No. 95–155, § 6, 91 Stat. 1259 (Nov. 8, 1977).

§ 4363a. Pollution control technologies demonstrations

(1) The Administrator shall continue to be responsible for conducting and shall continue to conduct full-scale demonstrations of energy-related pollution control technologies as necessary in his judgment to fulfill the provisions of the Clean Air Act as amended [42 U.S.C.A. § 7401 et seq.], the Federal Water Pollution Control Act as amended [33 U.S.C.A. § 1251 et seq.], and other pertinent pollution control statutes.

(2) Energy-related environmental protection projects authorized to be administered by the Environmental Protection Agency under this Act shall not be transferred administratively to the Department of Energy or reduced through budget amendment. No action shall be taken through administrative or budgetary means to diminish the ability of the Environmental Protection Agency to initiate such projects.

(Pub. L. No. 96–229, § 2(d), 94 Stat. 327 (Apr. 7, 1980).)

HISTORICAL AND STATUTORY NOTES

References in Text

The Clean Air Act as amended, referred to in par. (1), is Act of July 14, 1955, c. 360, as amended generally by Pub. L. No. 88–206, 77 Stat. 392 (Dec. 17, 1963), and later by Pub. L. No. 95–95, 91 Stat. 685 (Aug. 7, 1977). The Clean Air Act was originally codified as chapter 15B (section 1857 et seq.) of this title. On enactment of Pub.

L. No. 95–95, the Act was recodified as chapter 85 (section 7401 et seq.) of this title. For complete classification of this Act to the Code, see Short Title note set out under section 7401 of this title and Tables.

The Federal Water Pollution Control Act as amended, referred to in par. (1), is Act of June 30, 1948, c. 758, as amended generally by Pub. L. No. 92–500, § 2, 86 Stat. 816 (Oct. 18, 1972), which is codified generally as chapter 26 (section 1251 et seq.) of Title 33, Navigation and Navigable Waters. For complete classification of this Act to the Code, see Short Title note set out under section 1251 of Title 33 and Tables.

This Act, referred to in par. (2), is Pub. L. No. 96–229, 94 Stat. 325 (Apr. 7, 1980), known as the Environmental Research, Development, and Demonstration Authorization Act of 1980, which enacted sections 4363, 4363a, 4369a, and 4370 of this title. For complete classification of this Act to the Code, see Tables.

Codifications

This section was enacted as part of the Environmental Research, Development, and Demonstration Authorization Act of 1980, and not as part of the National Environmental Policy Act of 1969, which comprises this chapter.

Similar Provisions

Provisions similar to this section were contained in the following prior authorization act:

Pub. L. No. 95–477, § 2(d), 92 Stat. 1508 (Oct. 18, 1978).

§ 4364. Expenditure of funds for research and development related to regulatory program activities

(a) Coordination, etc., with research needs and priorities of program offices and Environmental Protection Agency

The Administrator of the Environmental Protection Agency shall assure that the expenditure of any funds appropriated pursuant to this Act or any other provision of law for environmental research and development related to regulatory program activities shall be coordinated with and reflect the research needs and priorities of the program offices, as well as the overall research needs and priorities of the Agency, including those defined in the five-year research plan.

(b) Program offices subject to coverage

For purposes of subsection (a) of this section, the appropriate program offices are—

(1) the Office of Air and Waste Management, for air quality activities;

(2) the Office of Water and Hazardous Materials, for water quality activities and water supply activities;

(3) the Office of Pesticides, for environmental effects of pesticides;

(4) the Office of Solid Waste, for solid waste activities;

(5) the Office of Toxic Substances, for toxic substance activities;

(6) the Office of Radiation Programs, for radiation activities; and

(7) the Office of Noise Abatement and Control, for noise activities.

(c) Report to Congress; contents

The Administrator shall submit to the President and the Congress a report concerning the most appropriate means of assuring, on a continuing basis, that the research efforts of the Agency reflect the needs and priorities of the regulatory program offices, while maintaining a high level of scientific quality. Such report shall be submitted on or before March 31, 1978.

(Pub. L. No. 95–155, § 7, 91 Stat. 1259 (Nov. 8, 1977).)

HISTORICAL AND STATUTORY NOTES

References in Text

This Act, referred to in subsec. (a), is the Environmental Research, Development, and Demonstration Authorization Act of 1978, Pub. L. No. 95–155, 91 Stat. 1257 (Nov. 8, 1977). For distribution in the Code of such Act see Tables.

Codifications

This section was enacted as part of the Environmental Research, Development, and Demonstration Authorization Act of 1978, and not as part of the National Environmental Policy Act of 1969, which comprises this chapter.

§ 4365. Science Advisory Board

(a) Establishment; requests for advice by Administrator of Environmental Protection Agency and Congressional committees

The Administrator of the Environmental Protection Agency shall establish a Science Advisory Board which shall provide such scientific advice as may be requested by the Administrator, the Committee on Environment and Public Works of the United States Senate, or the Committee on Science, Space, and Technology, on Energy and Commerce, or on Public Works and Transportation of the House of Representatives.

(b) Membership; Chairman; meetings; qualifications of members

Such Board shall be composed of at least nine members, one of whom shall be designated Chairman, and shall meet at such times and places as may be designated by the Chairman of the Board in consultation with the Administrator. Each member of the Board shall be qualified by education, training, and experience to evaluate scientific and technical information on matters referred to the Board under this section.

(c) Proposed environmental criteria document, standard, limitation, or regulation; functions respecting in conjunction with Administrator

(1) The Administrator, at the time any proposed criteria document, standard, limitation, or regulation under the Clean Air Act [42 U.S.C.A. § 7401 et seq.], the Federal Water Pollution Control Act [33 U.S.C.A. § 1251 et seq.], the Resource Conservation and Recovery Act of 1976 [42 U.S.C.A. § 6901 et seq.], the Noise Control Act [42 U.S.C.A. § 4901 et seq.], the Toxic Substances Control Act [15 U.S.C.A. § 2601 et seq.], or the Safe Drinking Water Act [42 U.S.C.A. § 300f et seq.], or under any other authority of the Administrator, is provided to any other Federal agency for formal review and comment, shall make available to the Board such proposed criteria document, standard, limitation, or regulation, together with relevant scientific and technical information in the possession of the Environmental Protection Agency on which the proposed action is based.

(2) The Board may make available to the Administrator, within the time specified by the Administrator, its advice and comments on the adequacy of the scientific and technical basis of the proposed criteria document, standard, limitation, or regulation, together with any pertinent information in the Board's possession.

(d) Utilization of technical and scientific capabilities of Federal agencies and national environmental laboratories for determining adequacy of scientific and technical basis of proposed criteria document, etc.

In preparing such advice and comments, the Board shall avail itself of the technical and scientific capabilities of any Federal agency, including the Environmental Protection Agency and any national environmental laboratories.

(e) Committees

(1) Member committees.—

(A) In general.—The Board is authorized to establish such member committees and investigative panels as the Administrator and the Board determine to be necessary to carry out this section.

(B) Chairmanship.—Each member committee or investigative panel established under this subsection shall be chaired by a member of the Board.

(2) Agriculture-related committees.—

(A) In general.—The Administrator and the Board—

(i) shall establish a standing agriculture-related committee; and

(ii) may establish such additional agriculture-related committees and investigative panels as the Administrator and the Board determines to be necessary to carry out the duties under subparagraph (C).

(B) Membership.—The standing committee and each agriculture-related committee or investigative panel established under subparagraph (A) shall be—

(i) composed of—

(I) such quantity of members as the Administrator and the Board determines to be necessary; and

(II) individuals who are not members of the Board on the date of appointment to the committee or investigative panel; and

(ii) appointed by the Administrator and the Board, in consultation with the Secretary of Agriculture.

(C) Duties.—The agriculture-related standing committee and each additional committee and investigative panel established under subparagraph (A) shall provide scientific and technical advice to the Board relating to matters referred to the Board that the Administrator and the Board determines, in consultation with the Secretary of Agriculture, to have a significant direct impact on enterprises that are engaged in the business of the production of food and fiber, ranching and raising livestock, aquaculture, and all other farming- and agriculture-related industries.

(f) Appointment and compensation of secretary and other personnel; compensation of members

(1) Upon the recommendation of the Board, the Administrator shall appoint a secretary, and such other employees as deemed necessary to exercise and fulfill the Board's powers and responsibilities. The compensation of all employees appointed under this paragraph shall be fixed in accordance with chapter 51 and subchapter III of chapter 53 of Title 5.

(2) Members of the Board may be compensated at a rate to be fixed by the President but not in excess of the maximum rate of pay for grade GS–18, as provided in the General Schedule under section 5332 of Title 5.

(g) Consultation and coordination with Scientific Advisory Panel

In carrying out the functions assigned by this section, the Board shall consult and coordinate its activities with the Scientific Advisory Panel established by the Administrator pursuant to section 136w(d) of Title 7.

(h) Public Participation and Transparency.—The Board shall make every effort, consistent with applicable law, including section 552 of Title 5 (commonly known as the "Freedom of Information Act") and section 552a of Title 5 (commonly known as the "Privacy Act"), to maximize public participation and transparency, including making the scientific and technical advice of the Board and any committees or investigative panels of the Board publically available in electronic form on the website of the Environmental Protection Agency.

(i) Report to Congress.—The Administrator shall annually report to the Committees on Environment and Public Works and Agriculture of the Senate and the Committees on Transportation and Infrastructure, Energy and Commerce, and Agriculture of the House of Representatives regarding the membership and activities of the standing agriculture-related committee established pursuant to subsection (e)(2)(A)(i).

(Pub. L. No. 95–155, § 8, 91 Stat. 1260 (Nov. 8, 1977); as amended by Pub. L. No. 96–569, § 3, 94 Stat. 3337 (Dec. 22, 1980); Pub. L. No. 103–437, § 15(*o*), 108 Stat. 4593 (Nov. 2, 1994); Pub. L. No. 104–66, Title II, § 2021(k)(3), 109 Stat. 728 (Dec. 21, 1995); Pub. L. No. 113–79, Title XII, § 12307, 128 Stat. 989–990 (Feb. 7, 2014).)

HISTORICAL AND STATUTORY NOTES

References in Text

The Clean Air Act, referred to in subsec. (c)(1), is Act of July 14, 1955, c. 360, as amended generally by Pub. L. No. 88–206, 77 Stat. 392 (Dec. 17, 1963), and later by Pub. L. No. 95–95, 91 Stat. 685 (Aug. 7, 1977). The Clean Air Act was originally codified as chapter 15B (section 1857 et seq.) of this title. On enactment of Pub. L. No. 95–95, the Act was recodified as chapter 85 (section 7401 et seq.) of this title. For complete classification of this Act to the Code, see Short Title note set out under section 7401 of this title and Tables.

The Federal Water Pollution Control Act, referred to in subsec. (c)(1), is Act of June 30, 1948, c. 758, as amended generally by Pub. L. No. 92–500, § 2, 86 Stat. 816 (Oct. 18, 1972), which is codified generally as chapter 26 (section 1251 et seq.) of Title 33, Navigation and Navigable Waters. For complete classification of this Act to the Code, see Short Title note set out under section 1251 of Title 33 and Tables.

The Resource Conservation and Recovery Act of 1976, referred to in subsec. (c)(1), is Pub. L. No. 94–580, 90 Stat. 2796 (Oct. 21, 1976), as amended, which is codified generally as chapter 82 (section 6901 et seq.) of this title. For complete classification of this Act to the Code, see Short Title note set out under section 6901 of this title and Tables.

The Noise Control Act, referred to in subsec. (c)(1), probably means the Noise Control Act of 1972, Pub. L. No. 92–574, 86 Stat. 1234 (Oct. 27, 1972), as amended, which is codified principally as chapter 65 (section 4901 et seq.) of this title. For complete classification of this Act to the Code, see Short Title note set out under section 4901 of this title and Tables.

The Toxic Substances Control Act, referred to in subsec. (c)(1), is Pub. L. No. 94–469, 90 Stat. 2003 (Oct. 11, 1976), as amended, which is codified generally as chapter 53 (section 2601 et seq.) of Title 15, Commerce and Trade. For complete classification of this Act to the Code, see Short Title note set out under section 2601 of Title 15 and Tables.

The Safe Drinking Water Act, referred to in subsec. (c)(1), is Pub. L. No. 93–523, 88 Stat. 1660 (Dec. 16, 1974), as amended, which is codified principally as subchapter XII (section 300f et seq.) of chapter 6A of this title. For complete classification of this Act to the Code, see Short Title of 1974 Amendments note set out under section 201 of this title and Tables.

Codifications

This section was enacted as part of the Environmental Research, Development, and Demonstration Authorization Act of 1978, and not as part of the National Environmental Policy Act of 1969, which comprises this chapter.

Change of Name

Committee on Energy and Commerce of House of Representatives treated as referring to Committee on Commerce of House of Representatives by section 1(a) of Pub. L. 104–14, set out as a note preceding section 21 of Title 2. Committee on Commerce of House of Representatives changed to Committee on Energy and Commerce of House of Representatives, and jurisdiction over matters relating to securities and exchanges and insurance generally transferred to Committee on Financial Services of House of Representatives by House Resolution No. 5, One Hundred Seventh Congress, Jan. 3, 2001.

Any reference in any provision of law enacted before Jan. 4, 1995, to the Committee on Public Works and Transportation of the House of Representatives treated as referring to the Committee on Transportation and Infrastructure of the House of Representatives, see section 1(a)(9) of Pub. L. No. 104–14, set out as a note preceding section 21 of Title 2.

References in Other Laws to GS–16, 17, or 18 Pay Rates

References in laws to the rates of pay for GS–16, 17, or 18, or to maximum rates of pay under the General Schedule, to be considered references to rates payable under specified sections of Title 5, see section 529 [Title I, § 101(c)(1)] of Pub. L. No. 101–509, set out in a note under 5 U.S.C.A. § 5376.

Termination of Advisory Boards

Advisory boards established after Jan. 5, 1973, to terminate not later than the expiration of the 2-year period beginning on the date of their establishment, unless, in the case of a board established by the President or an officer of the Federal Government, such board is renewed by appropriate action prior to the expiration of such 2-year period, or in the case of a board established by the Congress, its duration is otherwise provided for by law. See sections 3(2) and 14 of Pub. L. No. 92–463, 86 Stat. 770, 776 (Oct. 6, 1972), set out in Appendix 2 to Title 5, Government Organization and Employees.

§ 4366. Identification and coordination of research, development, and demonstration activities

(a) Consultation and cooperation of Administrator of Environmental Protection Agency with heads of Federal agencies; inclusion of activities in annual revisions of plan for research, etc.

The Administrator of the Environmental Protection Agency, in consultation and cooperation with the heads of other Federal agencies, shall take such actions on a continuing basis as may be necessary or appropriate—

(1) to identify environmental research, development, and demonstration activities, within and outside the Federal Government, which may need to be more effectively coordinated in order to minimize unnecessary duplication of programs, projects, and research facilities;

(2) to determine the steps which might be taken under existing law, by him and by the heads of such other agencies, to accomplish or promote such coordination, and to provide for or encourage the taking of such steps; and

(3) to determine the additional legislative actions which would be needed to assure such coordination to the maximum extent possible.

The Administrator shall include in each annual revision of the five-year plan provided for by section 4361 of this title a full and complete report on the actions taken and determinations made during the preceding year under this subsection, and may submit interim reports on such actions and determinations at such other times as he deems appropriate.

(b) Coordination of programs by Administrator

The Administrator of the Environmental Protection Agency shall coordinate environmental research, development, and demonstration programs of such Agency with the heads of other Federal agencies in order to minimize unnecessary duplication of programs, projects, and research facilities.

(c) Joint study by Council on Environmental Quality in consultation with Office of Science and Technology Policy for coordination of activities; report to President and Congress; report by President to Congress on implementation of joint study and report

(1) In order to promote the coordination of environmental research and development activities, and to assure that the action taken and methods used (under subsection (a) of this section and otherwise) to bring about such coordination will be as effective as possible for that purpose, the Council on Environmental Quality in consultation with the Office of Science and Technology Policy shall promptly undertake and carry out a joint study of all aspects of the coordination of environmental research and development. The Chairman of the Council shall prepare a report on the results of such study, together with such recommendations (including legislative recommendations) as he deems appropriate, and shall submit such report to the President and the Congress not later than May 31, 1978.

(2) Not later than September 30, 1978, the President shall report to the Congress on steps he has taken to implement the recommendations included in the report under paragraph (1), including any recommendations he may have for legislation.

(Pub. L. No. 95–155, § 9, 91 Stat. 1261 (Nov. 8, 1977).)

HISTORICAL AND STATUTORY NOTES

References in Text

Section 4361 of this title, referred to in subsec. (a), was repealed by Pub. L. No. 104–66, title II, § 2021(k)(1), 109 Stat. 728 (Dec. 21, 1995).

Codifications

This section was enacted as part of the Environmental Research, Development, and Demonstration Authorization Act of 1978, and not as part of the National Environmental Policy Act of 1969, which comprises this chapter.

Coordination of Environmental Research, Development, and Demonstration Efforts; Study and Report

Pub. L. No. 95–477, § 3(c), 92 Stat. 1509 (Oct. 18, 1978), authorized to be appropriated to the Environmental Protection Agency for the fiscal year 1979, $1,000,000, and for the fiscal year 1980, $1,000,000, for a study and report, under a contract let by the Administrator, to be conducted outside the Federal Government, on coordination of the Federal Government's efforts in environmental research, development, and demonstration, and the application of the results of such efforts to environmental problems, with the report on the study submitted to the President, the Administrator, and the Congress within two years after Oct. 18, 1978, accompanied by recommendations for action by the President, the Administrator, other agencies, or the Congress, as may be appropriate.

§ 4366a. Omitted

HISTORICAL AND STATUTORY NOTES

Codifications

This section, Pub. L. No. 101–617, § 4, 104 Stat. 3287 (Nov. 16, 1990), which related to development of a data base of environmental research articles indexed by geographic location, expired 10 years after Nov. 16, 1990, pursuant to section 6 of Pub. L. No. 101–617, formerly set out as a note under this section.

Termination Date

Pub. L. No. 101–617, § 6, 104 Stat. 3287 (Nov. 16, 1990), provided that Pub. L. No. 101–617, which enacted this section and provisions formerly set out under this section, was to expire 10 years after Nov. 16, 1990.

Short Title; Findings; Purpose; Authorization

Pub. L. No. 101–617, §§ 1 to 3, 104 Stat. 3287 (Nov. 16, 1990), which provided that Pub. L. No. 101–617, which enacted this section and provisions formerly set out under this section, could be cited as the "Environmental Research Geographic Location Information Act", and further provided for findings, purpose to develop a data base of environmental research articles indexed by geographic location, and authorization of appropriations, expired 10 years after Nov. 16, 1990, pursuant to section 6 of Pub. L. No. 101–617, formerly set out as a note under this section.

§ 4367. Reporting requirements of financial interests of officers and employees of Environmental Protection Agency

(a) Covered officers and employees

Each officer or employee of the Environmental Protection Agency who—

(1) performs any function or duty under this Act; and

(2) has any known financial interest in any person who applies for or receives grants, contracts, or other forms of financial assistance under this Act,

shall, beginning on February 1, 1978, annually file with the Administrator a written statement concerning all such interests held by such officer or employee during the preceding calendar year. Such statement shall be available to the public.

(b) Implementation of requirements by Administrator

The Administrator shall—

(1) act within ninety days after November 8, 1977—

(A) to define the term "known financial interest" for purposes of subsection (a) of this section; and

(B) to establish the methods by which the requirement to file written statements specified in subsection (a) of this section will be monitored and enforced, including appropriate provision for the filing by such officers and employees of such statements and the review by the Administrator of such statements; and

(2) Omitted.

(c) Exemption of positions by Administrator

In the rules prescribed under subsection (b) of this section, the Administrator may identify specific positions of a nonpolicymaking nature within the Administration and provide that officers or employees occupying such positions shall be exempt from the requirements of this section.

(d) Violations; penalties

Any officer or employee who is subject to, and knowingly violates, this section, shall be fined not more than $2,500 or imprisoned not more than one year, or both.

(Pub. L. No. 95–155, § 12, 91 Stat. 1263 (Nov. 8, 1977).)

HISTORICAL AND STATUTORY NOTES

References in Text

This Act, referred to in subsec. (a)(1), (2), is Pub. L. No. 95–155, 91 Stat. 1257 (Nov. 8, 1977), as amended, known as the Environmental Research, Development, and Demonstration Authorization Act of 1978, which to the extent codified as the Code enacted sections 300j–3a, 4361a, 4361b, and 4363 to 4367 of this title. For complete classification of this Act to the Code, see Tables.

Codifications

This section was enacted as part of the Environmental Research, Development, and Demonstration Authorization Act of 1978, and not as part of the National Environmental Policy Act of 1969, which comprises this chapter.

Subsec. (b)(2) of this section, shown as omitted, which required the Administrator to report to Congress on June 1 of each calendar year with respect to such disclosures and the actions taken in regard thereto during the preceding calendar year, terminated, effective May 15, 2000, pursuant to Pub. L. No. 104–66, § 3003, as amended, set out as a note under 31 U.S.C.A. § 1113. See, also, item 9 on page 164 of House Document No. 103–7.

§ 4368. Grants to qualified citizens groups

(1) There is authorized to be appropriated to the Environmental Protection Agency, for grants to qualified citizens groups in States and regions, $3,000,000.

(2) Grants under this section may be made for the purpose of supporting and encouraging participation by qualified citizens groups in determining how scientific, technological, and social trends and changes affect the future environment and quality of life of an area, and for setting goals and identifying measures for improvement.

(3) The term "qualified citizens group" shall mean a nonprofit organization of citizens having an area based focus, which is not single-issue oriented and which can demonstrate a prior record of interest and involvement in goal-setting and research concerned with improving the quality of life, including plans to identify, protect and enhance significant natural and cultural resources and the environment.

(4) A citizens group shall be eligible for assistance only if certified by the Governor in consultation with the State legislature as a bonafide organization entitled to receive Federal assistance to pursue the aims of this program. The group shall further demonstrate its capacity to employ usefully the funds for the purposes of this program and its broad-based representative nature.

(5) After an initial application for assistance under this section has been approved, the Administrator may make grants on an annual basis, on condition that the Governor recertify the group and that the applicant submits to the Administrator annually—

(A) an evaluation of the progress made during the previous year in meeting the objectives for which the grant was made;

(B) a description of any changes in the objectives of the activities; and

(C) a description of the proposed activities for the succeeding one year period.

(6) A grant made under this program shall not exceed 75 per centum of the estimated cost of the project or program for which the grant is made, and no group shall receive more than $50,000 in any one year.

(7) No financial assistance provided under this section shall be used to support lobbying or litigation by any recipient group.

(Pub. L. No. 95–477, § 3(d), 92 Stat. 1509 (Oct. 18, 1978).)

HISTORICAL AND STATUTORY NOTES

References in Text

This section, referred to in par. (5), means section 3 of Pub. L. No. 95–477, in its entirety, subsec. (d) of which enacted this section, subsecs. (a) and (b) of which were not codified into the Code, and subsec. (c) of which is set out as a note under section 4366 of this title.

Codifications

This section was enacted as part of the Environmental Research, Development, and Demonstration Authorization Act of 1979, and not as part of the National Environmental Policy Act of 1969, which comprises this chapter.

§ 4368a. Utilization of talents of older Americans in projects of pollution prevention, abatement, and control

(a) Technical assistance to environmental agencies

Notwithstanding any other provision of law relating to Federal grants and cooperative agreements, the Administrator of the Environmental Protection Agency is authorized to make grants to, or enter into cooperative agreements with, private nonprofit organizations designated by the Secretary of Labor under title V of the Older Americans Act of 1965 [42 U.S.C.A. § 3056 et seq.] to utilize the talents of older Americans in programs authorized by other provisions of law administered by the Administrator (and consistent with such provisions of law) in providing technical assistance to Federal, State, and local environmental agencies for projects of pollution prevention, abatement, and control. Funding for such grants or agreements may be made available from such programs or through title V of the Older Americans Act of 1965 [42 U.S.C.A. § 3056 et seq.] and subtitle D of title I of the Workforce Innovation and Opportunity Act [29 U.S.C.A. § 3221 et seq.].

(b) Pre-award certifications

Prior to awarding any grant or agreement under subsection (a) of this section, the applicable Federal, State, or local environmental agency shall certify to the Administrator that such grants or agreements will not—

(1) result in the displacement of individuals currently employed by the environmental agency concerned (including partial displacement through reduction of nonovertime hours, wages, or employment benefits);

(2) result in the employment of any individual when any other person is in a layoff status from the same or substantially equivalent job within the jurisdiction of the environmental agency concerned; or

(3) affect existing contracts for services.

(c) Prior appropriation Acts

Grants or agreements awarded under this section shall be subject to prior appropriation Acts.

(Pub. L. No. 98–313, § 2, 98 Stat. 235 (June 12, 1984); as amended by Pub. L. No. 105–277, Div. A, § 101(f) [Title VIII, § 405(d)(35), (f)(27)], 112 Stat. 2681–426, 2681–434 (Oct. 21, 1998); Pub. L. No. 113–128, § 512(g), 128 Stat. 1709 (July 22, 2014).)

HISTORICAL AND STATUTORY NOTES

References in Text

Title V of the Older Americans Act of 1965, referred to in subsec. (a), is Title V of Pub. L. No. 89–73, 79 Stat. 218 (July 14, 1965), as amended, which is known as the "Older Americans Community Service Employment Act" and which is codified as subchapter IX (section 3056 et seq.) of chapter 35 of this title. For complete classification of the Act to the Code, see Short Title note set out under section 3001 of this title and Tables.

Subtitle D of title I of the Workforce Investment Act of 1998, is Subtitle D (sections 166 to 174) of title I of Pub. L. No. 105–220, 112 Stat. 1021 (Aug. 7, 1998), which is codified generally as subchapter IV (section 2911 et seq.) of chapter 30 of Title 29. For complete classification of this Act to the Code, see Tables.

Codifications

This section was enacted as part of the Environmental Programs Assistance Act of 1984 and not as part of the National Environmental Policy Act of 1969, which comprises this chapter.

Effective and Applicability Provisions

1998 Acts. Amendment by section 101(f) [Title VIII, § 405(f)(27)] of Pub. L. No. 105–277 shall take effect July 1, 2000, see section 101(f) [Title VIII, § 405(g)(2)(B)] of Pub. L. No. 105–277, set out as a note under section 3502 of Title 5.

Amendment by section 101(f) [Title VIII, § 405(d)(35)] of Pub. L. No. 105–277 effective Oct. 21, 1998, see section 101(f) [Title VIII, § 405(g)(1)] of Pub. L. No. 105–277, set out as a note under section 3502 of Title 5.

Change of Name

Effective August 7, 1998, all references in any provision of law (other than 18 U.S.C.A. § 665) to the Comprehensive Employment and Training Act, or the Job Training Partnership Act, deemed to refer to the Workforce Investment Act of 1998 (Pub. L. No. 105–220, 112 Stat. 936 (Aug. 7, 1998)), see section 2940 of Title 29.

All references in any other provision of law to a provision of the Comprehensive Employment and Training Act, or of the Job Training Partnership Act, deemed to refer to the corresponding provision of Title I of the Workforce Investment Act of 1998 (Pub. L. No. 105–220, Title I, §§ 101 to 199A, 112 Stat. 936 (Aug. 7, 1998,) [29 U.S.C.A. § 2801 et seq.]), see section 199A(c) of Pub. L. No. 105–220, set out as a note under section 2940 of Title 29.

Short Title

1984 Acts. Section 1 of Pub. L. No. 98–313 provided that: "This Act [enacting this section] may be cited as the 'Environmental Programs Assistance Act of 1984'."

§ 4368b. General assistance program

(a) Short title

This section may be cited as the "Indian Environmental General Assistance Program Act of 1992".

(b) Purposes

The purposes of this section are to—

(1) provide general assistance grants to Indian tribal governments and intertribal consortia to build capacity to administer environmental regulatory programs that may be delegated by the Environmental Protection Agency on Indian lands; and

(2) provide technical assistance from the Environmental Protection Agency to Indian tribal governments and intertribal consortia in the development of multimedia programs to address environmental issues on Indian lands.

(c) Definitions

For purposes of this section:

(1) The term "Indian tribal government" means any Indian tribe, band, nation, or other organized group or community, including any Alaska Native village or regional or village corporation (as defined in, or established pursuant to, the Alaska Native Claims Settlement Act (43 U.S.C.A. § 1601, et seq.)), which is recognized as eligible for the special services provided by the United States to Indians because of their status as Indians.

(2) The term "intertribal consortia" or "intertribal consortium" means a partnership between two or more Indian tribal governments authorized by the governing bodies of those tribes to apply for and receive assistance pursuant to this section.

(3) The term "Administrator" means the Administrator of the Environmental Protection Agency.

(d) General assistance program

(1) The Administrator of the Environmental Protection Agency shall establish an Indian Environmental General Assistance Program that provides grants to eligible Indian tribal governments or intertribal consortia to cover the costs of planning, developing, and establishing environmental protection programs consistent with other applicable provisions of law providing for enforcement of such laws by Indian tribes on Indian lands.

(2) Each grant awarded for general assistance under this subsection for a fiscal year shall be no less than $75,000, and no single grant may be awarded to an Indian tribal government or intertribal consortium for more than 10 percent of the funds appropriated under subsection (h) of this section.

(3) The term of any general assistance award made under this subsection may exceed one year. Any awards made pursuant to this section shall remain available until expended. An Indian tribal government or intertribal consortium may receive a general assistance grant for a period of up to four years in each specific media area.

(e) No reduction in amounts

In no case shall the award of a general assistance grant to an Indian tribal government or intertribal consortium under this section result in a reduction of Environmental Protection Agency grants for environmental programs to that tribal government or consortium. Nothing in this section shall preclude an Indian tribal government or intertribal consortium from receiving individual media grants or cooperative agreements. Funds provided by the Environmental Protection Agency through the general assistance program shall be used by an Indian tribal government or intertribal consortium to supplement other funds provided by the Environmental Protection Agency through individual media grants or cooperative agreements.

(f) Expenditure of general assistance

Any general assistance under this section shall be expended for the purpose of planning, developing, and establishing the capability to implement programs administered by the Environmental Protection Agency and specified in the assistance agreement. Purposes and programs authorized under this section shall include the development and implementation of solid and hazardous waste programs for Indian lands. An Indian tribal government or intertribal consortium receiving general assistance pursuant to this section shall utilize such funds for programs and purposes to be carried out in accordance with the terms of the assistance agreement. Such programs and general assistance shall be carried out in accordance with the purposes and requirements of applicable provisions of law, including the Solid Waste Disposal Act (42 U.S.C. 6901 et seq.).

(g) Procedures

(1) Within 12 months following October 24, 1992, the Administrator shall promulgate regulations establishing procedures under which an Indian tribal government or intertribal consortium may apply for general assistance grants under this section.

(2) The Administrator shall publish regulations issued pursuant to this section in the Federal Register.

(3) The Administrator shall establish procedures for accounting, auditing, evaluating, and reviewing any programs or activities funded in whole or in part for a general assistance grant under this section.

(h) Authorization

There are authorized to be appropriated to carry out the provisions of this section, such sums as may be necessary for each of the fiscal years 1993, 1994, 1995, 1996, 1997, and 1998.

(i) Report to Congress

The Administrator shall transmit an annual report to the appropriate Committees of the Congress with jurisdiction over the applicable environmental laws and Indian tribes describing which Indian tribes or intertribal consortia have been granted approval by the Administrator pursuant to law to enforce certain environmental laws and the effectiveness of any such enforcement.

(Pub. L. No. 95–134, Title V, § 502, as added by Pub. L. No. 102–497, § 11, 106 Stat. 3258 (Oct. 24, 1992); and amended by Pub. L. No. 103–155, 107 Stat. 1523 (Nov. 24, 1993); Pub. L. No. 104–233, § 1, 110 Stat. 3057 (Oct. 2, 1996).)

HISTORICAL AND STATUTORY NOTES

References in Text

The Alaska Native Claims Settlement Act, referred to in subsec. (c)(1), is Pub. L. No. 92–203, 85 Stat. 688 (Dec. 18, 1971), as amended, which is codified generally as chapter 33 (section 1601 et seq.) of Title 43, Public Lands. For complete classification of this Act to the Code, see Short Title note set out under section 1601 of Title 43 and Tables.

The Solid Waste Disposal Act, referred to in subsec. (f), is Title II of Pub. L. No. 89–272, 79 Stat. 997 (Oct. 20, 1965), as amended generally by Pub. L. No. 94–580, § 2, 90 Stat. 2795 (Oct. 21, 1976), which is codified generally as chapter 82 (section 6901 et seq.) of this title. For complete classification of this Act to the Code, see Short Title note set out under section 6901 of this title and Tables.

Codifications

Section was enacted as part of the Indian Environmental General Assistance Program Act of 1992 and as part of the Omnibus Territories Act of 1977, and not as part of the National Environmental Policy Act of 1969, which comprises this chapter.

§ 4369. Miscellaneous reports

(a) Availability to Congressional committees

All reports to or by the Administrator relevant to the Agency's program of research, development, and demonstration shall promptly be made available to the Committee on Science, Space, and Technology of the House of Representatives and the Committee on Environment and Public Works of the Senate, unless otherwise prohibited by law.

(b) Transmittal of jurisdictional information

The Administrator shall keep the Committee on Science, Space, and Technology of the House of Representatives and the Committee on Environment and Public Works of the Senate fully and currently informed with respect to matters falling within or related to the jurisdiction of the committees.

(c) Comment by Government agencies and the public

The reports provided for in section 5910 of this title shall be made available to the public for comment, and to the heads of affected agencies for comment and, in the case of recommendations for action, for response.

(d) Transmittal of research information to the Department of Energy

For the purpose of assisting the Department of Energy in planning and assigning priorities in research development and demonstration activities related to environmental control technologies, the Administrator shall actively make available to the Department all information on research activities and results of research programs of the Environmental Protection Agency.

(Pub. L. No. 95–477, § 5, 92 Stat. 1510 (Oct. 18, 1978); Pub. L. No. 103–437, § 15(c)(6), 108 Stat. 4592 (Nov. 2, 1994).)

HISTORICAL AND STATUTORY NOTES

References in Text

Section 5910 of this title, referred to in subsec. (c), was repealed by Pub. L. No. 104–66, title II, § 2021(i), 109 Stat. 727 (Dec. 21, 1995).

Codifications

Section was enacted as part of the Environmental Research, Development, and Demonstration Authorization Act of 1979, and not as part of the National Environmental Policy Act of 1969, which comprises this chapter.

§ 4369a. Reports on environmental research and development activities of Agency

(a) Reports to keep Congressional committees fully and currently informed

The Administrator shall keep the appropriate committees of the House and the Senate fully and currently informed about all aspects of the environmental research and development activities of the Environmental Protection Agency.

(b) Omitted

(Pub. L. No. 96–229, § 4, 94 Stat. 328 (Apr. 7, 1980).)

HISTORICAL AND STATUTORY NOTES

Codifications

Section was enacted as part of the Environmental Research, Development, and Demonstration Authorization Act of 1980, and not as part of the National Environmental Policy Act of 1969, which comprises this chapter.

Subsec. (b) of this section, shown as omitted, which required the Administrator to annually make available to the appropriate committees of Congress sufficient copies of a report fully describing funds requested and the environmental research and development activities to be carried out with these funds, terminated, effective May 15, 2000, pursuant to Pub. L. No. 104–66, § 3003, as amended, set out as a note under 31 U.S.C.A. § 1113. See also, item 24 on page 163 of House Document No. 103–7.

§ 4370. Reimbursement for use of facilities

(a) Authority to allow outside groups or individuals to use research and test facilities; reimbursement

The Administrator is authorized to allow appropriate use of special Environmental Protection Agency research and test facilities by outside groups or individuals and to receive reimbursement or fees for costs incurred thereby when he finds this to be in the public interest. Such reimbursement or fees are to be used by the Agency to defray the costs of use by outside groups or individuals.

(b) Rules and regulations

The Administrator may promulgate regulations to cover such use of Agency facilities in accordance with generally accepted accounting, safety, and laboratory practices.

(c) Waiver of reimbursement by Administrator

When he finds it is in the public interest the Administrator may waive reimbursement or fees for outside use of Agency facilities by nonprofit private or public entities.

(Pub. L. No. 96–229, § 5, 94 Stat. 328 (Apr. 7, 1980).)

HISTORICAL AND STATUTORY NOTES

Codifications

Section was enacted as part of the Environmental Research, Development, and Demonstration Authorization Act of 1980, and not as part of the National Environmental Policy Act of 1969, which comprises this chapter.

§ 4370a. Assistant Administrators of Environmental Protection Agency; appointment; duties

(a) The President, by and with the advice and consent of the Senate, may appoint three Assistant Administrators of the Environmental Protection Agency in addition to—

(1) the five Assistant Administrators provided for in section 1(d) of Reorganization Plan Numbered 3 of 1970 (5 U.S.C. Appendix);

(2) the Assistant Administrator provided by section 2625(g) of Title 15; and

(3) the Assistant Administrator provided by section 6911a of this title.

(b) Each Assistant Administrator appointed under subsection (a) of this section shall perform such duties as the Administrator of the Environmental Protection Agency may prescribe.

(Pub. L. No. 98–80, § 1, 97 Stat. 485 (Aug. 23, 1983).)

HISTORICAL AND STATUTORY NOTES

References in Text

Reorganization Plan Numbered 3 of 1970, referred to in subsec. (a)(1), is set out in Appendix 1 to Title 5, Government Organization and Employees, and also as a note under section 4321 of this title.

Codifications

This section was not enacted as part of the National Environmental Policy Act of 1969, which comprises this chapter.

§ 4370b. Availability of fees and charges to carry out Agency programs

Notwithstanding any other provision of law, after September 30, 1990, amounts deposited in the Licensing and Other Services Fund from fees and charges assessed and collected by the Administrator for services and activities carried out pursuant to the statutes administered by the Environmental Protection Agency shall thereafter be available to carry out the Agency's activities in the programs for which the fees or charges are made.

(Pub. L. No. 101–144, Title III, 103 Stat. 858 (Nov. 9, 1989).)

HISTORICAL AND STATUTORY NOTES

Codifications

This section was enacted as part of the Departments of Veterans Affairs and Housing and Urban Development, and Independent Agencies Appropriations Act, 1990, and not as part of the National Environmental Policy Act of 1969, which comprises this chapter.

§ 4370c. Environmental Protection Agency fees

(a) Assessment and collection

The Administrator of the Environmental Protection Agency shall, by regulation, assess and collect fees and charges for services and activities carried out pursuant to laws administered by the Environmental Protection Agency.

(b) Amount of fees and charges

Fees and charges assessed pursuant to this section shall be in such amounts as may be necessary to ensure that the aggregate amount of fees and charges collected pursuant to this section, in excess of the amount of fees and charges collected under current law—

(1) in fiscal year 1991, is not less than $28,000,000; and

(2) in each of fiscal years 1992, 1993, 1994, and 1995, is not less than $38,000,000.

(c) Limitation on fees and charges

(1) The maximum aggregate amount of fees and charges in excess of the amounts being collected under current law which may be assessed and collected pursuant to this section in a fiscal year—

(A) for services and activities carried out pursuant to[1] the Federal Water Pollution Control Act [33 U.S.C.A. § 1251 et seq.] is $10,000,000; and

(B) for services and activities in programs within the jurisdiction of the House Committee on Energy and Commerce and administered by the Environmental Protection Agency through the Administrator, shall be limited to such sums collected as of November 5, 1990, pursuant to sections 2625(b) and 2665(e)(2) of Title 15, and such sums specifically authorized by the Clean Air Act Amendments of 1990.

(2) Any remaining amounts required to be collected under this section shall be collected from services and programs administered by the Environmental Protection Agency other than those specified in subparagraphs (A) and (B) of paragraph (1).

(d) Rule of construction

Nothing in this section increases or diminishes the authority of the Administrator to promulgate regulations pursuant to section 9701 of Title 31.

(e) Uses of fees

Fees and charges collected pursuant to this section shall be deposited into a special account for environmental services in the Treasury of the United States. Subject to appropriation Acts, such funds shall be available to the Environmental Protection Agency to carry out the activities for which such fees and charges are collected. Such funds shall remain available until expended.

(Pub. L. No. 101–508, Title VI, § 6501, 104 Stat. 1388–320 (Nov. 5, 1990).)

[1] So in original. Probably should be "to".

HISTORICAL AND STATUTORY NOTES

References in Text

The Federal Water Pollution Control Act, referred to in subsec. (c)(1)(A), is Act of June 30, 1948, c. 758, 62 Stat. 1155, as amended generally by Pub. L. No. 92–500, § 2, 86 Stat. 816 (Oct. 18, 1972), which is codified generally as chapter 26 (section 1251 et seq.) of Title 33. For complete classification of this Act to the Code, see Short Title note set out under section 1251 of Title 33 and Tables.

The Clean Air Act Amendments of 1990, referred to in subsec. (c)(1)(B), is Pub. L. No. 101–549, 104 Stat. 2399 (Nov. 15, 1990), which is codified principally as chapter 85 (section 7401 et seq.) of this title. For complete classification of this Act to the Code, see Tables.

Section 2665(e)(2) of Title 15, referred to in subsec. (c)(1)(B), was redesignated section 2655(d)(2) of Title 15, by Pub. L. No. 104–66, title II, § 2021(*l*)(2), 109 Stat. 728 (Dec. 21, 1995).

Codifications

In subsec. (d), "section 9701 of Title 31" was in the original "the Independent Office Appropriations Act (31 U.S.C. 9701)" and substitution was made as if it read for "title V of the Independent Offices Appropriation Act of 1952" on authority of Pub. L. No. 97–258, § 4(b), Dec. 21, 1995, 96 Stat. 1067 (Dec. 21, 1995), the first section of which enacted Title 31, Money and Finance.

Section was enacted as part of the Omnibus Budget Reconciliation Act of 1990, and not as part of the National Environmental Policy Act of 1969, which comprises this chapter.

Change of Name

Any reference in any provision of law enacted before Jan. 4, 1995, to the Committee on Energy and Commerce of the House of Representatives treated as referring to the Committee on Commerce of the House of Representatives, except that any reference in any provision of law enacted before Jan. 4, 1995, to the Committee on Energy and Commerce of the House of Representatives treated as referring to the Committee on Agriculture of the House of Representatives, in the case of a provision of law relating to inspection of seafood or seafood products, the Committee on Banking and Financial Services of the House of Representatives, in the case of a provision of law relating to bank capital markets activities generally or to depository institution securities activities generally, and the Committee on Transportation and Infrastructure of the House of Representatives, in the case of a provision of law relating to railroads, railway labor, or railroad retirement and unemployment (except revenue measures related thereto), see section 1(a)(4) and (c)(1) of Pub. L. No. 104–14, set out as a note preceding section 21 of Title 2, The Congress.

§ 4370d. Percentage of Federal funding for organizations owned by socially and economically disadvantaged individuals

The Administrator of the Environmental Protection Agency shall, on and after October 6, 1992, to the fullest extent possible, ensure that at least 8 per centum of Federal funding for prime and subcontracts awarded in support of authorized programs, including grants, loans, and contracts for wastewater treatment and leaking underground storage tanks grants, be made available to business concerns or other organizations owned or controlled by socially and economically disadvantaged individuals (within the meaning of section 637(a)(5) and (6) of Title 15), including historically black colleges and universities. For purposes of this section, economically and socially disadvantaged individuals shall be deemed to include women.

(Pub. L. No. 102–389, Title III, 106 Stat. 1602 (Oct. 6, 1992).)

HISTORICAL AND STATUTORY NOTES

Codifications

This section was enacted as part of the Departments of Veterans Affairs and Housing and Urban Development, and Independent Agencies Appropriations Act, 1993, and not as part of the National Environmental Policy Act of 1969, which comprises this chapter.

§ 4370e. Working capital fund in Treasury

There is hereby established in the Treasury a "Working capital fund", to be available without fiscal year limitation for expenses and equipment necessary for the maintenance and operation of such administrative services as the Administrator determines may be performed more advantageously as central services: *Provided,* That any inventories, equipment, and other assets pertaining to the services to be provided by such fund, either on hand or on order, less the related liabilities or unpaid obligations, and any appropriations made hereafter for the purpose of providing capital, shall be used to capitalize such fund: *Provided further,* That such fund shall be paid in advance or reimbursed from funds available to the Agency and other Federal agencies for which such centralized services are performed, at rates which will return in full all expenses of operation, including accrued leave, depreciation of fund plant and equipment, amortization of automated data processing (ADP) software and systems (either acquired or donated), and an amount necessary to maintain a reasonable operating reserve, as determined by the Administrator: *Provided further,* That such fund shall provide services on a competitive basis: *Provided further,* That an amount not to exceed four percent of the total annual income to such fund may be retained in the fund for fiscal year 1997 and each fiscal year thereafter, to remain available until expended, to be used for the acquisition of capital equipment and for the improvement and implementation of Agency financial management, ADP, and other support systems: *Provided further,* That no later than thirty days after the end of each fiscal year amounts in excess of this reserve limitation shall be transferred to the Treasury.

(Pub. L. No. 104–204, Title III, 110 Stat. 2912 (Sept. 26, 1996); as amended by Pub. L. No. 105–65, Title III, 111 Stat. 1374 (Oct. 27, 1997); Pub. L. No. 105–276, Title III, 112 Stat. 2499 (Oct. 21, 1998).)

HISTORICAL AND STATUTORY NOTES

Codifications

This section was enacted as part of the Departments of Veterans Affairs and Housing and Urban Development, and Independent Agencies Appropriations Act, 1997, and not as part of the National Environmental Policy Act of 1969, which comprises this chapter.

This section was formerly set out as a note under section 501 of Title 31.

Pub. L. No. 105–276, Title III, 112 Stat. 2499 (Oct. 21, 1998), instructed that "or reimbursed" be inserted after the phrase "that such fund shall be paid in advance". This instruction was executed by inserting the language after the phrase "That such fund shall be paid in advance" as the probable intent of Congress.

§ 4370f. Availability of funds after expiration of period for liquidating obligations

For fiscal year 2001 and thereafter, the obligated balances of sums available in multiple-year appropriations accounts shall remain available through the seventh fiscal year after their period of availability has expired for liquidating obligations made during the period of availability.

(Pub. L. No. 106–377, § 1(a)(1)[Title III], 114 Stat. 1441, 1441A–44 (Oct. 27, 2000).)

§ 4370g. Availability of funds for uniforms and certain services

For fiscal year 2009 and thereafter, the Science and Technology and Environmental Programs and Management Accounts are available for uniforms, or allowances therefore, as authorized by sections 5901 and 5902 of Title 5 and for services as authorized by section 3109 of Title 5, but at rates for individuals not to exceed the daily equivalent of the rate paid for level IV of the Executive Schedule.

(Pub. L. No. 111–8, Div. E, Title II, 123 Stat. 728 (Mar. 11, 2009).)

HISTORICAL AND STATUTORY NOTES

References in Text

Level IV of the Executive Schedule, referred to in text, is set out in 5 U.S.C.A. § 5315.

Codifications

This section was enacted as part of the Department of the Interior, Environment, and Related Agencies Appropriations Act, 2009 and also as part of the Omnibus Appropriations Act, 2009, and not as part of the National Environmental Policy Act of 1969, which comprises this chapter.

§ 4370h. Availability of funds for facilities

For fiscal year 2009 and thereafter, the Science and Technology, Environmental Programs and Management, Office of Inspector General, Hazardous Substance Superfund, and Leaking Underground Storage Tank Trust Fund Program Accounts, are available for the construction, alteration, repair, rehabilitation, and renovation of facilities provided that the cost does not exceed $85,000 per project.

(Pub. L. No. 111–8, Div. E, Title II, 123 Stat. 729 (Mar. 11, 2009).)

HISTORICAL AND STATUTORY NOTES

Codifications

Section was enacted as part of the Department of the Interior, Environment, and Related Agencies Appropriations Act, 2009 and also as part of the Omnibus Appropriations Act, 2009, and not as part of the National Environmental Policy Act of 1969, which comprises this chapter.

NOISE CONTROL

NOISE CONTROL ACT OF 1972
[NCA § ______]

(42 U.S.C.A. §§ 4901 to 4918)

CHAPTER 65—NOISE CONTROL

Sec.

§ 4901. Congressional findings and statement of policy

[NCA § 2]

(a) The Congress finds—

(1) that inadequately controlled noise presents a growing danger to the health and welfare of the Nation's population, particularly in urban areas;

(2) that the major sources of noise include transportation vehicles and equipment, machinery, appliances, and other products in commerce; and

(3) that, while primary responsibility for control of noise rests with State and local governments, Federal action is essential to deal with major noise sources in commerce control of which require national uniformity of treatment.

(b) The Congress declares that it is the policy of the United States to promote an environment for all Americans free from noise that jeopardizes their health or welfare. To that end, it is the purpose of this chapter to establish a means for effective coordination of Federal research and activities in noise control, to authorize the establishment of Federal noise emission standards for products distributed in commerce, and to provide information to the public respecting the noise emission and noise reduction characteristics of such products.

(Pub. L. No. 92–574, § 2, 86 Stat. 1234 (Oct. 27, 1972).)

HISTORICAL AND STATUTORY NOTES

Short Title

1978 Amendments. Pub. L. No. 95–609, § 1, 92 Stat. 3079 (Nov. 8, 1978), provided: "That this Act [amending sections 4905, 4910, 4913, 4918, 6901, 6903, 6907, 6913, 6922, 6923, 6925 to 6928, 6947, 6961, 6962, 6964, 6972, 6973, 6977, and 6981 to 6984 of this title] may be cited as the 'Quiet Communities Act of 1978'."

1972 Acts. Section 1 of Pub. L. No. 92–574 provided that: "This Act [which enacted this chapter, and enacted provisions set out as notes under this section] may be cited as the 'Noise Control Act of 1972'."

Federal Compliance With Pollution Control Standards

For provisions relating to the responsibility of the head of each Executive agency for compliance with applicable pollution control standards, see Ex. Ord. No. 12088, 43 Fed. Reg. 47707 (Oct. 13, 1978), set out as a note under section 4321 of this title.

§ 4902. Definitions

[NCA § 3]

For purposes of this chapter:

(1) The term "Administrator" means the Administrator of the Environmental Protection Agency.

(2) The term "person" means an individual, corporation, partnership, or association, and (except as provided in sections 4910(e) and 4911(a) of this title) includes any officer, employee, department, agency, or instrumentality of the United States, a State, or any political subdivision of a State.

(3) The term "product" means any manufactured article or goods or component thereof; except that such term does not include—

(A) any aircraft, aircraft engine, propeller, or appliance, as such terms are defined in section 40102(a) of Title 49; or

(B) (i) any military weapons or equipment which are designed for combat use; (ii) any rockets or equipment which are designed for research, experimental, or developmental work to be performed by the National Aeronautics and Space Administration; or (iii) to the extent provided by regulations of the Administrator, any other machinery or equipment designed for use in experimental work done by or for the Federal Government.

(4) The term "ultimate purchaser" means the first person who in good faith purchases a product for purposes other than resale.

(5) The term "new product" means (A) a product the equitable or legal title of which has never been transferred to an ultimate purchaser, or (B) a product which is imported or offered for importation into the United States and which is manufactured after the effective date of a regulation under section 4905 or 4907 of this title which would have been applicable to such product had it been manufactured in the United States.

(6) The term "manufacturer" means any person engaged in the manufacturing or assembling of new products, or the importing of new products for resale, or who acts for, and is controlled by, any such person in connection with the distribution of such products.

(7) The term "commerce" means trade, traffic, commerce, or transportation—

(A) between a place in a State and any place outside thereof, or

(B) which affects trade, traffic, commerce, or transportation described in subparagraph (A).

(8) The term "distribute in commerce" means sell in, offer for sale in, or introduce or deliver for introduction into, commerce.

(9) The term "State" includes the District of Columbia, the Commonwealth of Puerto Rico, the Virgin Islands, American Samoa, Guam, and the Trust Territory of the Pacific Islands.

(10) The term "Federal agency" means an executive agency (as defined in section 105 of Title 5) and includes the United States Postal Service.

(11) The term "environmental noise" means the intensity, duration, and the character of sounds from all sources.

(Pub. L. No. 92–574, § 3, 86 Stat. 1234 (Oct. 27, 1972).)

HISTORICAL AND STATUTORY NOTES

Termination of Trust Territory of the Pacific Islands

For termination of Trust Territory of the Pacific Islands, see note set out preceding 48 U.S.C.A. § 1681.

§ 4903. Federal programs

[NCA § 4]

(a) Furtherance of Congressional policy

The Congress authorizes and directs that Federal agencies shall, to the fullest extent consistent with their authority under Federal laws administered by them, carry out the programs within their control in such a manner as to further the policy declared in section 4901(b) of this title.

(b) Presidential authority to exempt activities or facilities from compliance requirements

Each department, agency, or instrumentality of the executive, legislative, and judicial branches of the Federal Government—

(1) having jurisdiction over any property or facility, or

(2) engaged in any activity resulting, or which may result, in the emission of noise,

shall comply with Federal, State, interstate, and local requirements respecting control and abatement of environmental noise to the same extent that any person is subject to such requirements. The President may exempt any single activity or facility, including noise emission sources or classes thereof, of any department, agency, or instrumentality in the executive branch from compliance with any such requirement if he determines it to be in the paramount interest of the United States to do so; except that no exemption, other than for those products referred to in section 4902(3)(B) of this title, may be granted from the requirements of sections 4905, 4916, and 4917 of this title. No such exemption shall be granted due to lack of appropriation unless the President shall have specifically requested such appropriation as a part of the budgetary process and the Congress shall have failed to make available such requested appropriation. Any exemption shall be for a period not in excess of one year, but additional exemptions may be granted for periods of not to exceed one year upon the President's making a new determination. The President shall report each January to the Congress all exemptions from the requirements of this section granted during the preceding calendar year, together with his reason for granting such exemption.

(c) Coordination of programs of Federal agencies; standards and regulations; status reports

(1) The Administrator shall coordinate the programs of all Federal agencies relating to noise research and noise control. Each Federal agency shall, upon request, furnish to the Administrator such information as he may reasonably require to determine the nature, scope, and results of the noise-research and noise-control programs of the agency.

(2) Each Federal agency shall consult with the Administrator in prescribing standards or regulations respecting noise. If at any time the Administrator has reason to believe that a standard or regulation, or any proposed standard or regulation, of any Federal agency respecting noise does not protect the public health and welfare to the extent he believes to be required and feasible, he may request such agency to review and report to him on the advisability of revising such standard or regulation to provide such protection. Any such request may be published in the Federal Register and shall be accompanied by a detailed statement of the information on which it is based. Such agency shall complete the requested review and report to the Administrator within such time as the Administrator specifies in the request, but such time specified may not be less than ninety days from the date the request was made. The report shall be published in the Federal Register and shall be accompanied by a detailed statement of the findings and conclusions of the agency respecting the revision of its standard or regulation. With respect to the Federal Aviation Administration, section 44715 of Title 49 shall apply in lieu of this paragraph.

(3) On the basis of regular consultation with appropriate Federal agencies, the Administrator shall compile and publish, from time to time, a report on the status and progress of Federal activities relating to noise research and noise control. This report shall describe the noise-control programs of each Federal agency and assess the contributions of those programs to the Federal Government's overall efforts to control noise.

(Pub. L. No. 92–574, § 4, 86 Stat. 1235 (Oct. 27, 1972).)

HISTORICAL AND STATUTORY NOTES

Termination of Reporting Requirements

For termination, effective May 15, 2000, of provisions in subsec. (b) of this section relating to annual report to Congress, see Pub. L. No. 104–66, § 3003, as amended, set out as a note under 31 U.S.C.A. § 1113, and item 7 on page 20 of House Document No. 103–7.

§ 4904. Identification of major noise sources

[NCA § 5]

(a) Development and publication of criteria

(1) The Administrator shall, after consultation with appropriate Federal agencies and within nine months of October 27, 1972, develop and publish criteria with respect to noise. Such criteria shall reflect the scientific knowledge most useful in indicating the kind and extent of all identifiable effects on the public health or welfare which may be expected from differing quantities and qualities of noise.

(2) The Administrator shall, after consultation with appropriate Federal agencies and within twelve months of October 27, 1972, publish information on the levels of environmental noise the attainment and maintenance of which in defined areas under various conditions are requisite to protect the public health and welfare with an adequate margin of safety.

(b) Compilation and publication of reports on noise sources and control technology

The Administrator shall, after consultation with appropriate Federal agencies, compile and publish a report or series of reports (1) identifying products (or classes of products) which in his judgment are major sources of noise, and (2) giving information on techniques for control of noise from such products, including available data on the technology, costs, and alternative methods of noise control. The first such report shall be published not later than eighteen months after October 27, 1972.

(c) Supplemental criteria and reports

The Administrator shall from time to time review and, as appropriate, revise or supplement any criteria or reports published under this section.

(d) Publication in Federal Register

Any report (or revision thereof) under subsection (b)(1) of this section identifying major noise sources shall be published in the Federal Register. The publication or revision under this section of any criteria or information on control techniques shall be announced in the Federal Register, and copies shall be made available to the general public.

(Pub. L. No. 92–574, § 5, 86 Stat. 1236 (Oct. 27, 1972).)

§ 4905. Noise emission standards for products distributed in commerce

[NCA § 6]

(a) Proposed regulations

(1) The Administrator shall publish proposed regulations, meeting the requirements of subsection (c) of this section, for each product—

(A) which is identified (or is part of a class identified) in any report published under section 4904(b)(1) of this title as a major source of noise,

(B) for which, in his judgment, noise emission standards are feasible, and

(C) which falls in one of the following categories:

(i) Construction equipment.

(ii) Transportation equipment (including recreational vehicles and related equipment).

(iii) Any motor or engine (including any equipment of which an engine or motor is an integral part).

(iv) Electrical or electronic equipment.

(2) **(A)** Initial proposed regulations under paragraph (1) shall be published not later than eighteen months after October 27, 1972, and shall apply to any product described in paragraph (1) which is identified (or is a part of a class identified) as a major source of noise in any report published under section 4904(b)(1) of this title on or before the date of publication of such initial proposed regulations.

(B) In the case of any product described in paragraph (1) which is identified (or is part of a class identified) as a major source of noise in a report published under section 4904(b)(1) of this title after publication of the initial proposed regulations under subparagraph (A) of this paragraph, regulations under paragraph (1) for such product shall be proposed and published by the Administrator not later than eighteen months after such report is published.

(3) After proposed regulations respecting a product have been published under paragraph (2), the Administrator shall, unless in his judgment noise emission standards are not feasible for such product, prescribe regulations, meeting the requirements of subsection (c) of this section, for such product—

(A) not earlier than six months after publication of such proposed regulations, and

(B) not later than—

(i) twenty-four months after October 27, 1972, in the case of a product subject to proposed regulations published under paragraph (2)(A), or

(ii) in the case of any other product, twenty-four months after the publication of the report under section 4904(b)(1) of this title identifying it (or a class of products of which it is a part) as a major source of noise.

(b) Authority to publish regulations not otherwise required

The Administrator may publish proposed regulations, meeting the requirements of subsection (c) of this section, for any product for which he is not required by subsection (a) of this section to prescribe regulations but for which, in his judgment, noise emission standards are feasible and are requisite to protect the public health and welfare. Not earlier than six months after the date of publication of such proposed regulations respecting such product, he may prescribe regulations, meeting the requirements of subsection (c) of this section, for such product.

(c) Contents of regulations; appropriate consideration of other standards; participation by interested persons; revision

(1) Any regulation prescribed under subsection (a) or (b) of this section (and any revision thereof) respecting a product shall include a noise emission standard which shall set limits on noise emissions from such product and shall be a standard which in the Administrator's judgment, based on criteria published under section 4904 of this title, is requisite to protect the public health and welfare, taking into account the magnitude and conditions of use of such product (alone or in combination with other noise sources), the degree of noise reduction achievable through the application of the best available technology, and the cost of compliance. In establishing such a standard for any product, the Administrator shall give appropriate consideration to standards under other laws designed to safeguard the health and welfare of persons, including any standards under chapter 301 of title 49, the Clean Air Act [42 U.S.C.A. § 7401 et seq.], and the Federal Water Pollution Control Act [33 U.S.C.A. § 1251 et seq.]. Any such noise emission standards shall be a performance standard. In addition, any regulation under subsection (a) or (b) of this section (and any revision thereof) may contain testing procedures necessary to assure compliance with the emission standard in such regulation, and may contain provisions respecting instructions of the manufacturer for the maintenance, use, or repair of the product.

(2) After publication of any proposed regulations under this section, the Administrator shall allow interested persons an opportunity to participate in rulemaking in accordance with the first sentence of section 553(c) of Title 5.

(3) The Administrator may revise any regulation prescribed by him under this section by (A) publication of proposed revised regulations, and (B) the promulgation, not earlier than six months after the date of such publication, of regulations making the revision; except that a revision which makes only technical or clerical corrections in a regulation under this section may be promulgated earlier than six months after such date if the Administrator finds that such earlier promulgation is in the public interest.

(d) Warranty by manufacturer of conformity of product with regulations; transfer of cost obligation from manufacturer to dealer prohibited

(1) On and after the effective date of any regulation prescribed under subsection (a) or (b) of this section, the manufacturer of each new product to which such regulation applies shall warrant to the ultimate purchaser and each subsequent purchaser that such product is designed, built, and equipped so as to conform at the time of sale with such regulation.

(2) Any cost obligation of any dealer incurred as a result of any requirement imposed by paragraph (1) of this subsection shall be borne by the manufacturer. The transfer of any such cost obligation from a manufacturer to any dealer through franchise or other agreement is prohibited.

(3) If a manufacturer includes in any advertisement a statement respecting the cost or value of noise emission control devices or systems, such manufacturer shall set forth in such statement the cost or value attributed to such devices or systems by the Secretary of Labor (through the Bureau of Labor Statistics). The Secretary of Labor, and his representatives, shall have the same access for this purpose to the books, documents, papers, and records of a manufacturer as the Comptroller General has to those of a recipient of assistance for purposes of section 311 of the Clean Air Act [42 U.S.C.A. § 7611].

(e) State and local regulations

(1) No State or political subdivision thereof may adopt or enforce—

(A) with respect to any new product for which a regulation has been prescribed by the Administrator under this section, any law or regulation which sets a limit on noise emissions from such new product and which is not identical to such regulation of the Administrator; or

(B) with respect to any component incorporated into such new product by the manufacturer of such product, any law or regulation setting a limit on noise emissions from such component when so incorporated.

(2) Subject to sections 4916 and 4917 of this title, nothing in this section precludes or denies the right of any State or political subdivision thereof to establish and enforce controls on environmental noise (or one or more sources thereof) through the licensing, regulation, or restriction of the use, operation, or movement of any product or combination of products.

(f) Publication of notice of receipt of revision petitions and proposed revised regulations

At any time after the promulgation of regulations respecting a product under this section, a State or political subdivision thereof may petition the Administrator to revise such standard on the grounds that a more stringent standard under subsection (c) of this section is necessary to protect the public health and welfare. The Administration shall publish notice of receipt of such petition in the Federal Register and shall within ninety days of receipt of such petition respond by (1) publication of proposed revised regulations in accordance with subsection (c)(3) of this section, or (2) publication in the Federal Register of a decision not to publish such proposed revised regulations at that time, together with a detailed explanation for such decision.

(Pub. L. No. 92–574, § 6, 86 Stat. 1237 (Oct. 27, 1972); as amended by Pub. L. No. 95–609, § 5, 92 Stat. 3081 (Nov. 8, 1978).)

HISTORICAL AND STATUTORY NOTES

References in Text

Chapter 301 of title 49, referred to in subsec. (c)(1), is 49 U.S.C.A. § 30101 et seq.

The Clean Air Act, referred to in subsec. (c)(1), is Act of July 14, 1955, c. 360, as amended generally by Pub. L. No. 88–206, 77 Stat. 392 (Dec. 17, 1963), and later by Pub. L. No. 95–95, 91 Stat. 685 (Aug. 7, 1977). The Clean Air Act was originally codified as chapter 15B (section 1857 et seq.) of this title. On enactment of Pub. L. No. 95–95, the Act was recodified as chapter 85 (section 7401 et seq.) of this title. For complete classification of this Act to the Code, see Short Title of 1955 Acts note set out under section 7401 of this title and Tables.

The Federal Water Pollution Control Act, referred to in subsec. (c)(1), is Act of June 30, 1948, c. 758, as amended generally by Pub. L. No. 92–500, § 2, 86 Stat. 816 (Oct. 18, 1972), which is codified generally as chapter 26 (section 1251 et seq.) of Title 33, Navigation and Navigable Waters. For complete classification of this Act to the Code, see Short Title note set out under section 1251 of Title 33 and Tables.

§ 4906. Omitted

HISTORICAL AND STATUTORY NOTES

Codifications

Section, Pub. L. No. 92–574, § 7(a), 86 Stat. 1239 (Oct. 27, 1972), related to a study by the Administrator of the adequacy of noise controls, noise emission standards, and measures available to control such noise, the results of such study to be reported to the appropriate committees of Congress within nine months after Oct. 27, 1972.

§ 4907. Labeling

[NCA § 8]

(a) Regulations

The Administrator shall by regulation designate any product (or class thereof)—

(1) which emits noise capable of adversely affecting the public health or welfare; or

(2) which is sold wholly or in part on the basis of its effectiveness in reducing noise.

(b) Manner of notice; form; methods and units of measurement

For each product (or class thereof) designated under subsection (a) of this section the Administrator shall by regulation require that notice be given to the prospective user of the level of the noise the product emits, or of its effectiveness in reducing noise, as the case may be. Such regulations shall specify (1) whether such notice shall be affixed to the product or to the outside of its container, or to both, at the time of its sale to the ultimate purchaser or whether such notice shall be given to the prospective user in some other manner, (2) the form of the notice, and (3) the methods and units of measurement to be used. Section 4905(c)(2) of this title shall apply to the prescribing of any regulation under this section.

(c) State regulation of product labeling

This section does not prevent any State or political subdivision thereof from regulating product labeling or information respecting products in any way not in conflict with regulations prescribed by the Administrator under this section.

(Pub. L. No. 92–574, § 8, 86 Stat. 1241 (Oct. 27, 1972).)

§ 4908. Imports

[NCA § 9]

The Secretary of the Treasury shall, in consultation with the Administrator, issue regulations to carry out the provisions of this chapter with respect to new products imported or offered for importation.

(Pub. L. No. 92–574, § 9, 86 Stat. 1242 (Oct. 27, 1972).)

§ 4909. Prohibited acts

[NCA § 10]

(a) Except as otherwise provided in subsection (b) of this section, the following acts or the causing thereof are prohibited:

(1) In the case of a manufacturer, to distribute in commerce any new product manufactured after the effective date of a regulation prescribed under section 4905 of this title which is applicable to such product, except in conformity with such regulation.

(2) (A) The removal or rendering inoperative by any person, other than for purposes of maintenance, repair, or replacement, of any device or element of design incorporated into any product in compliance with regulations under section 4905 of this title, prior to its sale or delivery to the ultimate purchaser or while it is in use, or (B) the use of a product after such device or element of design has been removed or rendered inoperative by any person.

(3) In the case of a manufacturer, to distribute in commerce any new product manufactured after the effective date of a regulation prescribed under section 4907(b) of this title (requiring information respecting noise) which is applicable to such product, except in conformity with such regulation.

(4) The removal by any person of any notice affixed to a product or container pursuant to regulations prescribed under section 4907(b) of this title, prior to sale of the product to the ultimate purchaser.

(5) The importation into the United States by any person of any new product in violation of a regulation prescribed under section 4908 of this title which is applicable to such product.

(6) The failure or refusal by any person to comply with any requirement of section 4910(d) or 4912(a) of this title or regulations prescribed under section 4912(a), 4916, or 4917 of this title.

(b) **(1)** For the purpose of research, investigations, studies, demonstrations, or training, or for reasons of national security, the Administrator may exempt for a specified period of time any product, or class thereof, from paragraphs (1), (2), (3), and (5) of subsection (a) of this section, upon such terms and conditions as he may find necessary to protect the public health or welfare.

(2) Paragraphs (1), (2), (3), and (4) of subsection (a) of this section shall not apply with respect to any product which is manufactured solely for use outside any State and which (and the container of which) is labeled or otherwise marked to show that it is manufactured solely for use outside any State; except that such paragraphs shall apply to such product if it is in fact distributed in commerce for use in any State.

(Pub. L. No. 92–574, § 10, 86 Stat. 1242 (Oct. 27, 1972).)

§ 4910. Enforcement

[NCA § 11]

(a) Criminal penalties

(1) Any person who willfully or knowingly violates paragraph (1), (3), (5), or (6) of subsection (a) of section 4909 of this title shall be punished by a fine of not more than $25,000 per day of violation, or by imprisonment for not more than one year, or by both. If the conviction is for a violation committed after a first conviction of such person under this subsection, punishment shall be by a fine of not more than $50,000 per day of violation, or by imprisonment for not more than two years, or by both.

(2) Any person who violates paragraph (1), (3), (5), or (6) of subsection (a) of section 4909 of this title shall be subject to a civil penalty not to exceed $10,000 per day of such violation.

(b) Separate violations

For the purpose of this section, each day of violation of any paragraph of section 4909(a) of this title shall constitute a separate violation of that section.

(c) Actions to restrain violations

The district courts of the United States shall have jurisdiction of actions brought by and in the name of the United States to restrain any violations of section 4909(a) of this title.

(d) Orders issued to protect public health and welfare; notice; opportunity for hearing

(1) Whenever any person is in violation of section 4909(a) of this title, the Administrator may issue an order specifying such relief as he determines is necessary to protect the public health and welfare.

(2) Any order under this subsection shall be issued only after notice and opportunity for a hearing in accordance with section 554 of Title 5.

(e) "Person" defined

The term "person," as used in this section, does not include a department, agency, or instrumentality of the United States.

(Pub. L. No. 92–574, § 11, 86 Stat. 1242 (Oct. 27, 1972); as amended by Pub. L. No. 95–609, § 4, 92 Stat. 3081 (Nov. 8, 1978).)

§ 4911. Citizen suits

[NCA § 12]

(a) Authority to commence suits

Except as provided in subsection (b) of this section, any person (other than the United States) may commence a civil action on his own behalf—

(1) against any person (including (A) the United States, and (B) any other governmental instrumentality or agency to the extent permitted by the eleventh amendment to the Constitution) who is alleged to be in violation of any noise control requirement (as defined in subsection (e)[1] of this section), or

(2) against—

(A) the Administrator of the Environmental Protection Agency where there is alleged a failure of such Administrator to perform any act or duty under this chapter which is not discretionary with such Administrator, or

(B) the Administrator of the Federal Aviation Administration where there is alleged a failure of such Administrator to perform any act or duty under section 44715 of Title 49 which is not discretionary with such Administrator.

The district courts of the United States shall have jurisdiction, without regard to the amount in controversy, to restrain such person from violating such noise control requirement or to order such Administrator to perform such act or duty, as the case may be.

(b) Notice

No action may be commenced—

(1) under subsection (a)(1) of this section—

(A) prior to sixty days after the plaintiff has given notice of the violation (i) to the Administrator of the Environmental Protection Agency (and to the Federal Aviation Administrator in the case of a violation of a noise control requirement under such section 44715 of Title 49) and (ii) to any alleged violator of such requirement, or

(B) if an Administrator has commenced and is diligently prosecuting a civil action to require compliance with the noise control requirement, but in any such action in a court of the United States any person may intervene as a matter of right, or

(2) under subsection (a)(2) of this section prior to sixty days after the plaintiff has given notice to the defendant that he will commence such action.

Notice under this subsection shall be given in such manner as the Administrator of the Environmental Protection Agency shall prescribe by regulation.

(c) Intervention

In an action under this section, the Administrator of the Environmental Protection Agency, if not a party, may intervene as a matter of right. In an action under this section respecting a noise control requirement under section 44715 of Title 49, the Administrator of the Federal Aviation Administration, if not a party, may also intervene as a matter of right.

(d) Litigation costs

The court, in issuing any final order in any action brought pursuant to subsection (a) of this section, may award costs of litigation (including reasonable attorney and expert witness fees) to any party, whenever the court determines such an award is appropriate.

(e) Other common law or statutory rights of action

Nothing in this section shall restrict any right which any person (or class of persons) may have under any statute or common law to seek enforcement of any noise control requirement or to seek any other relief (including relief against an Administrator).

(f) "Noise control requirement" defined

For purposes of this section, the term "noise control requirement" means paragraph (1), (2), (3), (4), or (5) of section 4909(a) of this title, or a standard, rule, or regulation issued under section 4916 or 4917 of this title or under section 44715 of Title 49.

(Pub. L. No. 92–574, § 12, 86 Stat. 1243 (Oct. 27, 1972).)

[1] So in original. Probably should be subsection "(f)".

§ 4912. Records, reports, and information

[NCA § 13]

(a) Duties of manufacturers of products

Each manufacturer of a product to which regulations under section 4905 or 4907 of this title apply shall—

(1) establish and maintain such records, make such reports, provide such information, and make such tests, as the Administrator may reasonably require to enable him to determine whether such manufacturer has acted or is acting in compliance with this chapter,

(2) upon request of an officer or employee duly designated by the Administrator, permit such officer or employee at reasonable times to have access to such information and the results of such tests and to copy such records, and

(3) to the extent required by regulations of the Administrator, make products coming off the assembly line or otherwise in the hands of the manufacturer available for testing by the Administrator.

(b) Confidential information; disclosure

(1) All information obtained by the Administrator or his representatives pursuant to subsection (a) of this section, which information contains or relates to a trade secret or other matter referred to in section 1905 of Title 18, shall be considered confidential for the purpose of that section, except that such information may be disclosed to other Federal officers or employees, in whose possession it shall remain confidential, or when relevant to the matter in controversy in any proceeding under this chapter.

(2) Nothing in this subsection shall authorize the withholding of information by the Administrator, or by any officers or employees under his control, from the duly authorized committees of the Congress.

(c) Violations and penalties

Any person who knowingly makes any false statement, representation, or certification in any application, record, report, plan, or other document filed or required to be maintained under this chapter or who falsifies, tampers with, or knowingly renders inaccurate any monitoring device or method required to be maintained under this chapter, shall upon conviction be punished by a fine of not more than $10,000, or by imprisonment for not more than six months, or by both.

(Pub. L. No. 92–574, § 13, 86 Stat. 1244 (Oct. 27, 1972).)

§ 4913. Quiet communities, research, and public information

[NCA § 14]

To promote the development of effective State and local noise control programs, to provide an adequate Federal noise control research program designed to meet the objectives of this chapter, and to otherwise carry out the policy of this chapter, the Administrator shall, in cooperation with other Federal agencies and through the use of grants, contracts, and direct Federal actions—

(a) develop and disseminate information and educational materials to all segments of the public on the public health and other effects of noise and the most effective means for noise control, through the use of materials for school curricula, volunteer organizations, radio and television programs, publication, and other means;

(b) conduct or finance research directly or with any public or private organization or any person on the effects, measurement, and control of noise, including but not limited to—

(1) investigation of the psychological and physiological effects of noise on humans and the effects of noise on domestic animals, wildlife, and property, and the determination of dose/response relationships suitable for use in decisionmaking, with special emphasis on the nonauditory effects of noise;

(2) investigation, development, and demonstration of noise control technology for products subject to possible regulation under sections 4905 and 4907 of this title and section 44715 of Title 49;

(3) investigation, development, and demonstration of monitoring equipment and other technology especially suited for use by State and local noise control programs;

(4) investigation of the economic impact of noise on property and human activities; and

(5) investigation and demonstration of the use of economic incentives (including emission charges) in the control of noise;

(c) administer a nationwide Quiet Communities Program which shall include, but not be limited to—

(1) grants to States, local governments, and authorized regional planning agencies for the purpose of—

(A) identifying and determining the nature and extent of the noise problem within the subject jurisdiction;

(B) planning, developing, and establishing a noise control capacity in such jurisdiction, including purchasing initial equipment;

(C) developing abatement plans for areas around major transportation facilities (including airports, highways, and rail yards) and other major stationary sources of noise, and, where appropriate, for the facility or source itself; and,

(D) evaluating techniques for controlling noise (including institutional arrangements) and demonstrating the best available techniques in such jurisdiction;

(2) purchase of monitoring and other equipment for loan to State and local noise control programs to meet special needs or assist in the beginning implementation of a noise control program or project;

(3) development and implementation of a quality assurance program for equipment and monitoring procedures of State and local noise control programs to help communities assure that their data collection activities are accurate;

(4) conduct of studies and demonstrations to determine the resource and personnel needs of States and local governments required for the establishment and implementation of effective noise abatement and control programs; and

(5) development of education and training materials and programs, including national and regional workshops, to support State and local noise abatement and control programs;

except that no actions, plans or programs hereunder shall be inconsistent with existing Federal authority under this chapter to regulate sources of noise in interstate commerce;

(d) develop and implement a national noise environmental assessment program to identify trends in noise exposure and response, ambient levels, and compliance data and to determine otherwise the effectiveness of noise abatement actions through the collection of physical, social, and human response data;

(e) establish regional technical assistance centers which use the capabilities of university and private organizations to assist State and local noise control programs;

(f) provide technical assistance to State and local governments to facilitate their development and enforcement of noise control, including direct onsite assistance of agency or other personnel with technical expertise, and preparation of model State or local legislation for noise control; and

(g) provide for the maximum use in programs assisted under this section of senior citizens and persons eligible for participation in programs under the Older Americans Act [42 U.S.C.A. § 3001 et seq.].

(Pub. L. No. 92–574, § 14, 86 Stat. 1244 (Oct. 27, 1972); as amended by Pub. L. No. 95–609, § 2, 92 Stat. 3079 (Nov. 8, 1978).)

HISTORICAL AND STATUTORY NOTES

References in Text

The Older Americans Act, referred to in subsec. (g), probably means the Older Americans Act of 1965, Pub. L. No. 89–73, 79 Stat. 218 (July 14, 1965), as amended, which is codified generally as chapter 35 (section 3001 et seq.) of this title. For complete classification of this Act to the Code, see Short Title of 1965 Acts note set out under section 3001 of this title and Tables.

§ 4914. Development of low-noise-emission products

[NCA § 15]

(a) Definitions

For the purpose of this section:

(1) The term "Committee" means the Low-Noise-Emission Product Advisory Committee.

(2) The term "Federal Government" includes the legislative, executive, and judicial branches of the Government of the United States, and the government of the District of Columbia.

(3) The term "low-noise-emission product" means any product which emits noise in amounts significantly below the levels specified in noise emission standards under regulations applicable under section 4905 of this title at the time of procurement to that type of product.

(4) The term "retail price" means (A) the maximum statutory price applicable to any type of product; or (B) in any case where there is no applicable maximum statutory price, the most recent procurement price paid for any type of product.

(b) Certification of products; Low-Noise-Emission Product Advisory Committee

(1) The Administrator shall determine which products qualify as low-noise-emission products in accordance with the provisions of this section.

(2) The Administrator shall certify any product—

(A) for which a certification application has been filed in accordance with paragraph (5)(A) of this subsection;

(B) which is a low-noise-emission product as determined by the Administrator; and

(C) which he determines is suitable for use as a substitute for a type of product at that time in use by agencies of the Federal Government.

(3) The Administrator may establish a Low-Noise-Emission Product Advisory Committee to assist him in determining which products qualify as low-noise-emission products for purposes of this section. The Committee shall include the Administrator or his designee, a representative of the National Institute of Standards and Technology, and representatives of such other Federal agencies and private individuals as the Administrator may deem necessary from time to time. Any member of the Committee not employed on a full-time basis by the United States may receive the daily equivalent of the annual rate of basic pay in effect for Grade GS–18 of the General Schedule for each day such member is engaged upon work of the Committee. Each member of the Committee shall be reimbursed for travel expenses, including per diem in lieu of subsistence as authorized by section 5703 of Title 5 for persons in the Government service employed intermittently.

(4) Certification under this section shall be effective for a period of one year from the date of issuance.

(5) (A) Any person seeking to have a class or model of product certified under this section shall file a certification application in accordance with regulations prescribed by the Administrator.

(B) The Administrator shall publish in the Federal Register a notice of each application received.

(C) The Administrator shall make determinations for the purpose of this section in accordance with procedures prescribed by him by regulation.

(D) The Administrator shall conduct whatever investigation is necessary, including actual inspection of the product at a place designated in regulations prescribed under subparagraph (A).

(E) The Administrator shall receive and evaluate written comments and documents from interested persons in support of, or in opposition to, certification of the class or model of product under consideration.

(F) Within ninety days after the receipt of a properly filed certification application the Administrator shall determine whether such product is a low-noise-emission product for purposes of this section. If the Administrator determines that such product is a low-noise-emission product, then within one hundred and eighty days of such determination the Administrator shall reach a decision as to whether such product is a suitable substitute for any class or classes of products presently being purchased by the Federal Government for use by its agencies.

(G) Immediately upon making any determination or decision under subparagraph (F), the Administrator shall publish in the Federal Register notice of such determination or decision, including reasons therefor.

(c) Federal procurement of low-noise-emission products

(1) Certified low-noise-emission products shall be acquired by purchase or lease by the Federal Government for use by the Federal Government in lieu of other products if the Administrator of General Services determines that such certified products have procurement costs which are no more than 125 per centum of the retail price of the least expensive type of product for which they are certified substitutes.

(2) Data relied upon by the Administrator in determining that a product is a certified low-noise-emission product shall be incorporated in any contract for the procurement of such product.

(d) Product selection

The procuring agency shall be required to purchase available certified low-noise-emission products which are eligible for purchase to the extent they are available before purchasing any other products for which any low-noise-emission product is a certified substitute. In making purchasing selections between competing eligible certified low-noise-emission products, the procuring agency shall give priority to any class or model which does not require extensive periodic maintenance to retain its low-noise-emission qualities or which does not involve operating costs significantly in excess of those products for which it is a certified substitute.

(e) Waiver of statutory price limitations

For the purpose of procuring certified low-noise-emission products any statutory price limitations shall be waived.

(f) Tests of noise emissions from products purchased by Federal Government

The Administrator shall, from time to time as he deems appropriate, test the emissions of noise from certified low-noise-emission products purchased by the Federal Government. If at any time he finds that the noise-emission levels exceed the levels on which certification under this section was based, the Administrator shall give the supplier of such product written notice of this finding, issue public notice of it, and give the supplier an opportunity to make necessary repairs, adjustments, or replacements. If no such repairs, adjustments, or replacements are made within a period to be set by the Administrator, he may order the supplier to show cause why the product involved should be eligible for recertification.

(g) Authorization of appropriations

There are authorized to be appropriated for paying additional amounts for products pursuant to, and for carrying out the provisions of, this section, $1,000,000 for the fiscal year ending June 30, 1973, and $2,000,000 for each of the two succeeding fiscal years, $2,200,000 for the fiscal year ending June 30, 1976, $550,000 for the transition period of July 1, 1976, through September 30, 1976, and $2,420,000 for the fiscal year ending September 30, 1977.

(h) Promulgation of procedures

The Administrator shall promulgate the procedures required to implement this section within one hundred and eighty days after October 27, 1972.

(Pub. L. No. 92–574, § 15, 86 Stat. 1245 (Oct. 27, 1972); as amended by Pub. L. No. 94–301, § 1, 90 Stat. 590 (May 31, 1976); Pub. L. No. 100–418, Title V, § 5115(c), 102 Stat. 1433 (Aug. 23, 1988).)

HISTORICAL AND STATUTORY NOTES

References in Text

The General Schedule, referred to in subsec. (b)(3), is set out under section 5332 of Title 5, Government Organization and Employees.

References in Other Laws to GS–16, 17, or 18 Pay Rates

References in laws to the rates of pay for GS–16, 17, or 18, or to maximum rates of pay under the General Schedule, to be considered references to rates payable under specified sections of Title 5, Government Organization and Employees, see section 529 [Title I, § 101(c)(1)] of Pub. L. No. 101–509, set out in a note under section 5376 of Title 5.

Termination of Advisory Committees

Advisory committees in existence on Jan. 5, 1973, to terminate not later than the expiration of the two-year period following Jan. 5, 1973, unless, in the case of a committee established by the President or an officer of the Federal Government, such committee is renewed by appropriate action prior to the expiration of such two-year period, or in the case of a committee established by the Congress, its duration is otherwise provided by law. A committee established after Jan. 5, 1973, to terminate not later than the expiration of the two-year period beginning on the date of its establishment unless in the case of a committee established by the President or an officer of the federal government, such committee is renewed by appropriate action prior to the end of such period, or in the case of a committee established by the Congress, its duration is otherwise provided by law, see section 14 of Pub. L. No. 92–463, 86 Stat. 776 (Oct. 6, 1972), set out in Appendix 2 to Title 5, Government Organization and Employees.

§ 4915. Judicial review

[NCA § 16]

(a) Petition for review

A petition for review of action of the Administrator of the Environmental Protection Agency in promulgating any standard or regulation under sections 4905, 4916, or 4917 of this title or any labeling regulation under section 4907 of this title may be filed only in the United States Court of Appeals for the District of Columbia Circuit, and a petition for review of action of the Administrator of the Federal Aviation Administration in promulgating any standard or regulation under section 44715 of Title 49 may be filed only in such court. Any such petition shall be filed within ninety days from the date of such promulgation, or after such date if such petition is based solely on grounds arising after such ninetieth day. Action of either Administrator with respect to which review could have been obtained under this subsection shall not be subject to judicial review in civil or criminal proceedings for enforcement.

(b) Additional evidence

If a party seeking review under this chapter applies to the court for leave to adduce additional evidence, and shows to the satisfaction of the court that the information is material and was not available at the time of the proceeding before the Administrator of such Agency or Administration (as the case may be), the court may order such additional evidence (and evidence in rebuttal thereof) to be taken before such Administrator, and to be adduced upon the hearing, in such manner and upon such terms and conditions as the court may deem proper. Such Administrator may modify his findings as to the facts, or make new findings, by reason of the additional evidence so taken, and he shall file with the court such modified or new findings, and his recommendation, if any, for the modification or setting aside of his original order, with the return of such additional evidence.

(c) Stay of agency action

With respect to relief pending review of an action by either Administrator, no stay of an agency action may be granted unless the reviewing court determines that the party seeking such stay is (1) likely to prevail on the merits in the review proceeding and (2) will suffer irreparable harm pending such proceeding.

(d) Subpenas

For the purpose of obtaining information to carry out this chapter, the Administrator of the Environmental Protection Agency may issue subpenas for the attendance and testimony of witnesses and the production of relevant papers, books, and documents, and he may administer oaths. Witnesses summoned shall be paid the same fees and mileage that are paid witnesses in the courts of the United States. In cases of contumacy or refusal to obey a subpena served upon any person under this subsection, the district court of the United States for any district in which such person is found or resides or transacts business, upon application by the United States and after notice to such person, shall have jurisdiction to issue an order requiring such person to appear and give testimony before the Administrator, to appear and produce papers, books, and documents before the Administrator, or both, and any failure to obey such order of the court may be punished by such court as a contempt thereof.

(Pub. L. No. 92–574, § 16, 86 Stat. 1247 (Oct. 27, 1972).)

§ 4916. Railroad noise emission standards

[NCA § 17]

(a) Regulations; standards; consultation with Secretary of Transportation

(1) Within nine months after October 27, 1972, the Administrator shall publish proposed noise emission regulations for surface carriers engaged in interstate commerce by railroad. Such proposed regulations shall include noise emission standards setting such limits on noise emissions resulting from operation of the equipment and facilities of surface carriers engaged in interstate commerce by railroad which reflect the degree of noise reduction achievable through the application of the best available technology, taking into account the cost of compliance. These regulations shall be in addition to any regulations that may be proposed under section 4905 of this title.

(2) Within ninety days after the publication of such regulations as may be proposed under paragraph (1) of this subsection, and subject to the provisions of section 4915 of this title, the Administrator shall promulgate final regulations. Such regulations may be revised, from time to time, in accordance with this subsection.

(3) Any standard or regulation, or revision thereof, proposed under this subsection shall be promulgated only after consultation with the Secretary of Transportation in order to assure appropriate consideration for safety and technological availability.

(4) Any regulation or revision thereof promulgated under this subsection shall take effect after such period as the Administrator finds necessary, after consultation with the Secretary of Transportation, to permit the development and application of the requisite technology, giving appropriate consideration to the cost of compliance within such period.

(b) Regulations to insure compliance with noise emission standards

The Secretary of Transportation, after consultation with the Administrator, shall promulgate regulations to insure compliance with all standards promulgated by the Administrator under this section. The Secretary of Transportation shall carry out such regulations through the use of his powers and duties of enforcement and inspection authorized by the Safety Appliance Acts [45 U.S.C.A. § 1 et seq.], subtitle IV of Title 49, and the Department of Transportation Act. Regulations promulgated under this section shall be subject to the provisions of sections 4909, 4910, 4911, and 4915 of this title.

(c) State and local standards and controls

(1) Subject to paragraph (2) but notwithstanding any other provision of this chapter, after the effective date of a regulation under this section applicable to noise emissions resulting from the operation of any equipment or facility of a surface carrier engaged in interstate commerce by railroad, no State or political subdivision thereof may adopt or enforce any standard applicable to noise emissions resulting from the operation of the same equipment or facility of such carrier unless such standard is identical to a standard applicable to noise emissions resulting from such operation prescribed by any regulation under this section.

(2) Nothing in this section shall diminish or enhance the rights of any State or political subdivision thereof to establish and enforce standards or controls on levels of environmental noise, or to control, license, regulate, or restrict the use, operation, or movement of any product if the Administrator, after consultation with the Secretary of Transportation, determines that such standard, control, license, regulation, or restriction is necessitated by special local conditions and is not in conflict with regulations promulgated under this section.

(d) "Carrier" and "railroad" defined

The terms "carrier" and "railroad" as used in this section shall have the same meaning as the term "railroad carrier" has in section 20102 of Title 49.

(Pub. L. No. 92–574, § 17, 86 Stat. 1248 (Oct. 27, 1972); as amended by Pub. L. No. 104–287, § 6(i), 110 Stat. 3399 (Oct. 11, 1996).)

HISTORICAL AND STATUTORY NOTES

References in Text

The Safety Appliance Acts, referred to in subsec. (b), are Act of Mar. 2, 1893, c. 196, 27 Stat. 531, which enacted former sections 1 to 7 of Title 45, Railroads, Act of Mar. 2, 1903, c. 976, 32 Stat. 943, which enacted former sections 8, 9, and 10 of Title 45, and Act of Apr. 14, 1910, c. 160, 36 Stat. 298, which enacted former sections 11 to 16 of Title 45.

The Department of Transportation Act, referred to in subsec. (b), is Pub. L. No. 89–670, 80 Stat. 931 (Oct. 15, 1966), as amended, which was codified principally as sections 1651 to 1660 of former Title 49, Transportation. The Act was substantially repealed and the provisions thereof reenacted in Title 49, Transportation, by Pub. L. No. 97–449, 96 Stat. 2413 (Jan. 12, 1983), and Pub. L. No. 103–272, 108 Stat. 745 (July 5, 1994). The Act was also repealed by Pub. L. No. 104–287, § 7(5), 110 Stat. 3400 (Oct. 11, 1996). For disposition of sections of former Title 49, see Table at the beginning of Title 49.

Codifications

"Subtitle IV of Title 49" was substituted in subsec. (b) for "the Interstate Commerce Act", on authority of Pub. L. No. 95–473, § 3(b), 92 Stat. 1466 (Oct. 17, 1978), the first section of which enacted subtitle IV of Title 49, Transportation.

§ 4917. Motor carrier noise emission standards

[NCA § 18]

(a) Regulations; standards; consultation with Secretary of Transportation

(1) Within nine months after October 27, 1972, the Administrator shall publish proposed noise emission regulations for motor carriers engaged in interstate commerce. Such proposed regulations shall include noise emission standards setting such limits on noise emissions resulting from operation of motor carriers engaged in interstate commerce which reflect the degree of noise reduction achievable through the application of the best available technology, taking into account the cost of compliance. These regulations shall be in addition to any regulations that may be proposed under section 4905 of this title.

(2) Within ninety days after the publication of such regulations as may be proposed under paragraph (1) of this subsection, and subject to the provisions of section 4915 of this title, the Administrator shall promulgate final regulations. Such regulations may be revised from time to time, in accordance with this subsection.

(3) Any standard or regulation, or revision thereof, proposed under this subsection shall be promulgated only after consultation with the Secretary of Transportation in order to assure appropriate consideration for safety and technological availability.

(4) Any regulation or revision thereof promulgated under this subsection shall take effect after such period as the Administrator finds necessary, after consultation with the Secretary of Transportation, to permit the development and application of the requisite technology, giving appropriate consideration to the cost of compliance within such period.

(b) Regulations to insure compliance with noise emission standards

The Secretary of Transportation, after consultation with the Administrator shall promulgate regulations to insure compliance with all standards promulgated by the Administrator under this section. The Secretary of Transportation shall carry out such regulations through the use of his powers and duties of enforcement and inspection authorized by subtitle IV of Title 49 and the Department of Transportation Act. Regulations promulgated under this section shall be subject to the provisions of sections 4909, 4910, 4911, and 4915 of this title.

(c) State and local standards and controls

(1) Subject to paragraph (2) of this subsection but notwithstanding any other provision of this chapter, after the effective date of a regulation under this section applicable to noise emissions resulting from the operation of any motor carrier engaged in interstate commerce, no State or political subdivision thereof may adopt or enforce any standard applicable to the same operation of such motor carrier, unless such standard is identical to a standard applicable to noise emissions resulting from such operation prescribed by any regulation under this section.

(2) Nothing in this section shall diminish or enhance the rights of any State or political subdivision thereof to establish and enforce standards or controls on levels of environmental noise, or to control, license, regulate, or restrict the use, operation, or movement of any product if the Administrator, after consultation with the Secretary of Transportation, determines that such standard, control, license, regulation, or restriction is necessitated by special local conditions and is not in conflict with regulations promulgated under this section.

(d) "Motor carrier" defined

For purposes of this section, the term "motor carrier" includes a motor carrier and motor private carrier as those terms are defined in section 13102 of Title 49.

(Pub. L. No. 92–574, § 18, 86 Stat. 1249 (Oct. 27, 1972); as amended by Pub. L. No. 104–88, Title III, § 339, 109 Stat. 955 (Dec. 29, 1995).)

HISTORICAL AND STATUTORY NOTES

References in Text

The Department of Transportation Act, referred to in subsec. (b), is Pub. L. No. 89–670, 80 Stat. 931 (Oct. 15, 1966), as amended, which was codified principally as sections 1651 to 1660 of former Title 49, Transportation. The Act was substantially repealed and the provisions thereof reenacted in Title 49, Transportation, by Pub. L. No. 97–449, 96 Stat. 2413 (Jan. 12, 1983), and Pub. L. No. 103–272, 108 Stat. 745 (July 5, 1994). The Act was also repealed by Pub. L. No. 104–287, § 7(5), 110 Stat. 3400 (Oct. 11, 1996). For disposition of sections of former Title 49, see Table at the beginning of Title 49.

Codifications

"Subtitle IV of Title 49" was substituted in subsec. (b) for "Interstate Commerce Act" and in subsec. (d) "section 10102 of Title 49" was substituted for "paragraphs (14), (15), and (17) of section 203(a) of the Interstate Commerce Act (49 U.S.C. 303(a))" on authority of Pub. L. No. 95–473, § 3(b), 92 Stat. 1466 (Oct. 17, 1978), the first section of which enacted subtitle IV of Title 49, Transportation.

Effective and Applicability Provisions

1995 Acts. Amendment of this section by Pub. L. No. 104–88 effective Jan. 1, 1996, see section 2 of Pub. L. No. 104–88, set out as a note under section 701 of Title 49, Transportation.

§ 4918. Authorization of appropriations

[NCA § 19]

There are authorized to be appropriated to carry out this chapter (other than for research and development) $15,000,000 for the fiscal year ending September 30, 1979.

(Pub. L. No. 92–574, § 19, 86 Stat. 1250 (Oct. 27, 1972); as amended by Pub. L. No. 94–301, § 2, 90 Stat. 590 (May 31, 1976); Pub. L. No. 95–609, § 6, 92 Stat. 3081 (Nov. 8, 1978).)

SOLID WASTE DISPOSAL

SOLID WASTE DISPOSAL ACT [SWDA § _____]

(42 U.S.C.A. §§ 6901 to 6992k)

CHAPTER 82—SOLID WASTE DISPOSAL

SUBCHAPTER I—GENERAL PROVISIONS

SUBCHAPTER II—OFFICE OF SOLID WASTE; AUTHORITIES OF THE ADMINISTRATOR

SUBCHAPTER III—HAZARDOUS WASTE MANAGEMENT

SUBCHAPTER IV—STATE OR REGIONAL SOLID WASTE PLANS

SUBCHAPTER V—DUTIES OF THE SECRETARY OF COMMERCE IN RESOURCE AND RECOVERY

SUBCHAPTER VI—FEDERAL RESPONSIBILITIES

SUBCHAPTER VII—MISCELLANEOUS PROVISIONS

SUBCHAPTER VIII—RESEARCH, DEVELOPMENT, DEMONSTRATION, AND INFORMATION

SUBCHAPTER IX—REGULATION OF UNDERGROUND STORAGE TANKS

SUBCHAPTER X—DEMONSTRATION MEDICAL WASTE TRACKING PROGRAM

SUBCHAPTER I—GENERAL PROVISIONS

§ 6901. Congressional findings

[SWDA § 1002]

(a) Solid waste

The Congress finds with respect to solid waste—

(1) that the continuing technological progress and improvement in methods of manufacture, packaging, and marketing of consumer products has resulted in an ever-mounting increase, and in a change in the characteristics, of the mass material discarded by the purchaser of such products;

(2) that the economic and population growth of our Nation, and the improvements in the standard of living enjoyed by our population, have required increased industrial production to meet our needs, and have made necessary the demolition of old buildings, the construction of new buildings, and the provision of highways and other avenues of transportation, which, together with related industrial, commercial, and agricultural operations, have resulted in a rising tide of scrap, discarded, and waste materials;

(3) that the continuing concentration of our population in expanding metropolitan and other urban areas has presented these communities with serious financial, management, intergovernmental, and technical problems in the disposal of solid wastes resulting from the industrial, commercial, domestic, and other activities carried on in such areas;

(4) that while the collection and disposal of solid wastes should continue to be primarily the function of State, regional, and local agencies, the problems of waste disposal as set forth above have become a matter national in scope and in concern and necessitate Federal action through financial and technical assistance and leadership in the development, demonstration, and application of new and improved methods and processes to reduce the amount of waste and unsalvageable materials and to provide for proper and economical solid waste disposal practices.

(b) Environment and health

The Congress finds with respect to the environment and health, that—

(1) although land is too valuable a national resource to be needlessly polluted by discarded materials, most solid waste is disposed of on land in open dumps and sanitary landfills;

(2) disposal of solid waste and hazardous waste in or on the land without careful planning and management can present a danger to human health and the environment;

(3) as a result of the Clean Air Act [42 U.S.C.A. § 7401 et seq.], the Water Pollution Control Act [33 U.S.C.A. § 1251 et seq.], and other Federal and State laws respecting public health and the environment, greater amounts of solid waste (in the form of sludge and other pollution treatment residues) have been created. Similarly, inadequate and environmentally unsound practices for the disposal or use of solid waste have created greater amounts of air and water pollution and other problems for the environment and for health;

(4) open dumping is particularly harmful to health, contaminates drinking water from underground and surface supplies, and pollutes the air and the land;

(5) the placement of inadequate controls on hazardous waste management will result in substantial risks to human health and the environment;

(6) if hazardous waste management is improperly performed in the first instance, corrective action is likely to be expensive, complex, and time consuming;

(7) certain classes of land disposal facilities are not capable of assuring long-term containment of certain hazardous wastes, and to avoid substantial risk to human health and the environment, reliance on land disposal should be minimized or eliminated, and land disposal, particularly landfill and surface impoundment, should be the least favored method for managing hazardous wastes; and

(8) alternatives to existing methods of land disposal must be developed since many of the cities in the United States will be running out of suitable solid waste disposal sites within five years unless immediate action is taken.

(c) Materials

The Congress finds with respect to materials, that—

(1) millions of tons of recoverable material which could be used are needlessly buried each year;

(2) methods are available to separate usable materials from solid waste; and

(3) the recovery and conservation of such materials can reduce the dependence of the United States on foreign resources and reduce the deficit in its balance of payments.

(d) Energy

The Congress finds with respect to energy, that—

(1) solid waste represents a potential source of solid fuel, oil, or gas that can be converted into energy;

(2) the need exists to develop alternative energy sources for public and private consumption in order to reduce our dependence on such sources as petroleum products, natural gas, nuclear and hydroelectric generation; and

(3) technology exists to produce usable energy from solid waste.

(Pub. L. No. 89–272, Title II, § 1002, as added by Pub. L. No. 94–580, § 2, 90 Stat. 2796 (Oct. 21, 1976); and amended by Pub. L. No. 95–609, § 7(a), 92 Stat. 3081 (Nov. 8, 1978); Pub. L. No. 98–616, Title I, § 101(a), 98 Stat. 3224 (Nov. 8, 1984).)

HISTORICAL AND STATUTORY NOTES

References in Text

The Clean Air Act, referred to in subsec. (b)(3), is Act of July 14, 1955, c. 360, as amended generally by Pub. L. No. 88–206, 77 Stat. 392 (Dec. 17, 1963), and later by Pub. L. No. 95–95, 91 Stat. 685 (Aug. 7, 1977). The Clean Air Act was originally codified as chapter 15B (section 1857 et seq.) of this title. On enactment of Pub. L. No. 95–95, the Act was recodified as chapter 85 (section 7401 et seq.) of this title. For complete classification of this Act to the Code, see Short Title of 1955 Acts note set out under section 7401 of this title and Tables.

The Water Pollution Control Act, referred to in subsec. (b)(3), is Act of June 30, 1948, c. 758, as amended generally by Pub. L. No. 92–500, § 2, 86 Stat. 816 (Oct. 18, 1972), which is codified generally as chapter 26 (section 1251 et seq.) of Title 33, Navigation and Navigable Waters. For complete classification of this Act to the Code, see Short Title note set out under section 1251 of Title 33 and Tables.

Codifications

The statutory system governing the disposal of solid wastes set out in this chapter is found in Pub. L. No. 89–272, Title II, as amended in its entirety and completely revised by section 2 of Pub. L. No. 94–580, 90 Stat. 2795 (Oct. 21, 1976). See Short Title of 1965 Acts note under this section.

The Act, as set out in this chapter, carries a statutory credit showing the sections as having been added by Pub. L. No. 94–580, without reference to amendments to the Act between its original enactment in 1965 and its complete revision in 1976. The Act, as originally enacted in 1965, was codified as section 3251 et seq. of this title. For a recapitulation of the provisions of the Act as originally enacted, see notes in chapter 39 of this title [section 3251 et seq. of this title] where the Act was originally set out.

Short Title

2012 Amendments. Pub. L. No. 112–195, § 1, 126 Stat. 1452 (Oct. 5, 2012), provided that: "This Act [enacting 42 U.S.C.A. § 6939g] may be cited as the 'Hazardous Waste Electronic Manifest Establishment Act'."

2005 Amendments. Pub. L. No. 109–58, Title XV, § 1521, 119 Stat. 1092 (Aug. 8, 2005), provided that: "This subtitle [enacting 42 U.S.C.A. §§ 6991j to 6991m, amending 42 U.S.C.A. §§ 6991, 6991a to 6991f, 6991h, and 6991i, and enacting provisions set out as notes under 42 U.S.C.A. § 6991b] may be cited as the 'Underground Storage Tank Compliance Act'."

1996 Amendments. Pub. L. No. 104–119, § 1, 110 Stat. 830 (Mar. 26, 1996), provided that: "This Act [amending sections 6921, 6924, 6925, 6947 and 6949a of this title, and enacting provisions set out as a note under section 6949a of this title] may be cited as the 'Land Disposal Program Flexibility Act of 1996'."

1992 Amendments. Pub. L. No. 102–386, Title I, § 101, 106 Stat. 1505 (Oct. 6, 1992), provided that: "This title [enacting sections 6908, 6939c, 6939d, 6939e, and 6965 of this title, amending sections 6903, 6924, 6927, and 6961 of this title, and enacting provisions set out as notes under sections 6939c and 6961 of this title] may be cited as the 'Federal Facility Compliance Act of 1992'."

1988 Amendments. Pub. L. No. 100–582, § 1, 102 Stat. 2950 (Nov. 1, 1988), provided that: "This Act [enacting section 6903(40) and sections 6992 to 6992k of this title (subchapter X of this chapter) and section 3063 of Title 18, Crimes and Criminal Procedure] may be cited as the 'Medical Waste Tracking Act of 1988'."

1984 Amendments. Section 1 of Pub. L. No. 98–616 provided that: "This Act [enacting sections 6917, 6936 to 6939a, 6949a, 6979a, 6979b, and 6991 to 6991i of this title, amending this section and sections 6902, 6905, 6912, 6915, 6916, 6921 to 6930, 6931, 6932, 6933, 6935, 6941 to 6945, 6948, 6956, 6962, 6972, 6973, 6976, 6982 and 6984 of this title and enacting provisions set out as notes under sections 6905, 6921 and 6926 of this title] may be cited as 'The Hazardous and Solid Waste Amendments of 1984'."

1980 Amendments. Pub. L. No. 96–482, § 1, 94 Stat. 2334 (Oct. 21, 1980), provided: "This Act [enacting sections 6933, 6934, 6941a, 6955, and 6956 of this title, amending sections 6903, 6905, 6911, 6912, 6916, 6921, 6922, 6924, 6925, 6927 to 6931, 6941 to 6943, 6945, 6946, 6948, 6949, 6952, 6953, 6962, 6963, 6964, 6971, 6973, 6974, 6976, 6979, and 6982 of this title; and enacting and repealing provisions set out as a note under section 6981 of this title] may be cited as the 'Solid Waste Disposal Act Amendments of 1980'."

Pub. L. No. 96–463, § 1, 94 Stat. 2055 (Oct. 15, 1980), provided: "This Act [enacting sections 6901a, 6914a and 6932 of this title, amending sections 6903, 6943 and 6948 of this title, and enacting provisions set out as notes under sections 6363 and 6932 of this title] may be cited as the 'Used Oil Recycling Act of 1980'."

1976 Amendments. Section 1 of Pub. L. No. 94–580 provided that: "This Act [enacting this chapter and provisions set out as notes under this section and section 6981 of this title] may be cited as the 'Resource Conservation and Recovery Act of 1976'." See Codification notes set out under this section.

1965 Acts. Section 1001 of Pub. L. No. 89–272, as added by Pub. L. No. 94–580, § 2, 90 Stat. 2795 (Oct. 21, 1976), provided in part that: "This title [Title II of Pub. L. No. 89–272, enacting this chapter] may be cited as the 'Solid Waste Disposal Act'."

Prior Provisions

Provisions similar to this section were contained in section 3251 of this title, prior to the complete revision of the Solid Waste Disposal Act by Pub. L. No. 94–580.

Federal Compliance with Pollution Control Standards

For provisions relating to the responsibility of the head of each Executive agency for compliance with applicable pollution control standards, see Ex. Ord. No. 12088, 43 Fed. Reg. 47707 (Oct. 13, 1978), set out as a note under section 4321 of this title.

National Commission on Materials Policy

Pub. L. No. 91–512, Title II, §§ 201 to 206, 84 Stat. 1234 (Oct. 26, 1970), known as the "National Materials Policy Act of 1970", provided for the establishment of the National Commission on Materials Policy to make a full investigation and study for the purpose of developing a national materials policy to utilize present resources and technology more efficiently and to anticipate the future materials requirements of the Nation and the world, the Commission to submit to the President and Congress a report on its findings and recommendations no later than June 30, 1973, ninety days after the submission of which it should cease to exist.

§ 6901a. Congressional findings: used oil recycling

The Congress finds and declares that—

(1) used oil is a valuable source of increasingly scarce energy and materials;

(2) technology exists to re-refine, reprocess, reclaim, and otherwise recycle used oil;

(3) used oil constitutes a threat to public health and the environment when reused or disposed of improperly; and that, therefore, it is in the national interest to recycle used oil in a manner which does not constitute a threat to public health and the environment and which conserves energy and materials.

(Pub. L. No. 96–463, § 2, 94 Stat. 2055 (Oct. 15, 1980).)

HISTORICAL AND STATUTORY NOTES

Codifications

This section was not enacted as part of the Solid Waste Disposal Act, which comprises this chapter, but was enacted as part of the Used Oil Recycling Act of 1980.

§ 6902. Objectives and national policy

[SWDA § 1003]

(a) Objectives

The objectives of this chapter are to promote the protection of health and the environment and to conserve valuable material and energy resources by—

(1) providing technical and financial assistance to State and local governments and interstate agencies for the development of solid waste management plans (including resource recovery and resource conservation systems) which will promote improved solid waste management techniques (including more effective organizational arrangements), new and improved methods of collection, separation, and recovery of solid waste, and the environmentally safe disposal of nonrecoverable residues;

(2) providing training grants in occupations involving the design, operation, and maintenance of solid waste disposal systems;

(3) prohibiting future open dumping on the land and requiring the conversion of existing open dumps to facilities which do not pose a danger to the environment or to health;

(4) assuring that hazardous waste management practices are conducted in a manner which protects human health and the environment;

(5) requiring that hazardous waste be properly managed in the first instance thereby reducing the need for corrective action at a future date;

(6) minimizing the generation of hazardous waste and the land disposal of hazardous waste by encouraging process substitution, materials recovery, properly conducted recycling and reuse, and treatment;

(7) establishing a viable Federal-State partnership to carry out the purposes of this chapter and insuring that the Administrator will, in carrying out the provisions of subchapter III of this chapter, give a high priority to assisting and cooperating with States in obtaining full authorization of State programs under subchapter III of this chapter;

(8) providing for the promulgation of guidelines for solid waste collection, transport, separation, recovery, and disposal practices and systems;

(9) promoting a national research and development program for improved solid waste management and resource conservation techniques, more effective organizational arrangements, and new and improved methods of collection, separation, and recovery, and recycling of solid wastes and environmentally safe disposal of nonrecoverable residues;

(10) promoting the demonstration, construction, and application of solid waste management, resource recovery, and resource conservation systems which preserve and enhance the quality of air, water, and land resources; and

(11) establishing a cooperative effort among the Federal, State, and local governments and private enterprise in order to recover valuable materials and energy from solid waste.

(b) National policy

The Congress hereby declares it to be the national policy of the United States that, wherever feasible, the generation of hazardous waste is to be reduced or eliminated as expeditiously as possible. Waste that is nevertheless generated should be treated, stored, or disposed of so as to minimize the present and future threat to human health and the environment.

(Pub. L. No. 89–272, Title II, § 1003, as added by Pub. L. No. 94–580, § 2, 90 Stat. 2798; (Oct. 21, 1976); and amended by Pub. L. No. 98–616, Title I, § 101(b), 98 Stat. 3224 (Nov. 8, 1984).)

HISTORICAL AND STATUTORY NOTES

Prior Provisions

Provisions similar to this section were contained in section 3251 of this title, prior to the complete revision of the Solid Waste Disposal Act by Pub. L. No. 94–580.

§ 6903. Definitions

[SWDA § 1004]

As used in this chapter:

(1) The term "Administrator" means the Administrator of the Environmental Protection Agency.

(2) The term "construction," with respect to any project of construction under this chapter, means (A) the erection or building of new structures and acquisition of lands or interests therein, or the acquisition, replacement, expansion, remodeling, alteration, modernization, or extension of existing structures, and (B) the acquisition and installation of initial equipment of, or required in connection with, new or newly acquired structures or the expanded, remodeled, altered, modernized or extended part of existing structures (including trucks and other motor vehicles, and tractors, cranes, and other machinery) necessary for the proper utilization and operation of the facility after completion of the project; and includes preliminary planning to determine the economic and engineering feasibility and the public health and safety aspects of the project, the engineering, architectural, legal, fiscal, and economic investigations and studies, and any surveys, designs, plans, working drawings, specifications, and other action necessary for the carrying out of the project, and (C) the inspection and supervision of the process of carrying out the project to completion.

(2A) The term "demonstration" means the initial exhibition of a new technology process or practice or a significantly new combination or use of technologies, processes or practices, subsequent to the development stage, for the purpose of proving technological feasibility and cost effectiveness.

(3) The term "disposal" means the discharge, deposit, injection, dumping, spilling, leaking, or placing of any solid waste or hazardous waste into or on any land or water so that such solid waste or hazardous waste or any constituent thereof may enter the environment or be emitted into the air or discharged into any waters, including ground waters.

(4) The term "Federal agency" means any department, agency, or other instrumentality of the Federal Government, any independent agency or establishment of the Federal Government including any Government corporation, and the Government Printing Office.

(5) The term "hazardous waste" means a solid waste, or combination of solid wastes, which because of its quantity, concentration, or physical, chemical, or infectious characteristics may—

(A) cause, or significantly contribute to an increase in mortality or an increase in serious irreversible, or incapacitating reversible, illness; or

(B) pose a substantial present or potential hazard to human health or the environment when improperly treated, stored, transported, or disposed of, or otherwise managed.

(6) The term "hazardous waste generation" means the act or process of producing hazardous waste.

(7) The term "hazardous waste management" means the systematic control of the collection, source separation, storage, transportation, processing, treatment, recovery, and disposal of hazardous wastes.

(8) For purposes of Federal financial assistance (other than rural communities assistance), the term "implementation" does not include the acquisition, leasing, construction, or modification of facilities or equipment or the acquisition, leasing, or improvement of land.

(9) The term "intermunicipal agency" means an agency established by two or more municipalities with responsibility for planning or administration of solid waste.

(10) The term "interstate agency" means an agency of two or more municipalities in different States, or an agency established by two or more States, with authority to provide for the management of solid wastes and serving two or more municipalities located in different States.

(11) The term "long-term contract" means, when used in relation to solid waste supply, a contract of sufficient duration to assure the viability of a resource recovery facility (to the extent that such viability depends upon solid waste supply).

(12) The term "manifest" means the form used for identifying the quantity, composition, and the origin, routing, and destination of hazardous waste during its transportation from the point of generation to the point of disposal, treatment, or storage.

(13) The term "municipality" (A) means a city, town, borough, county, parish, district, or other public body created by or pursuant to State law, with responsibility for the planning or administration of solid waste management, or an Indian tribe or authorized tribal organization or Alaska Native village or organization, and (B) includes any rural community or unincorporated town or village or any other public entity for which an application for assistance is made by a State or political subdivision thereof.

(14) The term "open dump" means any facility or site where solid waste is disposed of which is not a sanitary landfill which meets the criteria promulgated under section 6944 of this title and which is not a facility for disposal of hazardous waste.

(15) The term "person" means an individual, trust, firm, joint stock company, corporation (including a government corporation), partnership, association, State, municipality, commission, political subdivision of a State, or any interstate body and shall include each department, agency, and instrumentality of the United States.

(16) The term "procurement item" means any device, good, substance, material, product, or other item whether real or personal property which is the subject of any purchase, barter, or other exchange made to procure such item.

(17) The term "procuring agency" means any Federal agency, or any State agency or agency of a political subdivision of a State which is using appropriated Federal funds for such procurement, or any person contracting with any such agency with respect to work performed under such contract.

(18) The term "recoverable" refers to the capability and likelihood of being recovered from solid waste for a commercial or industrial use.

(19) The term "recovered material" means waste material and byproducts which have been recovered or diverted from solid waste, but such term does not include those materials and byproducts generated from, and commonly reused within, an original manufacturing process.

(20) The term "recovered resources" means material or energy recovered from solid waste.

(21) The term "resource conservation" means reduction of the amounts of solid waste that are generated, reduction of overall resource consumption, and utilization of recovered resources.

(22) The term "resource recovery" means the recovery of material or energy from solid waste.

(23) The term "resource recovery system" means a solid waste management system which provides for collection, separation, recycling, and recovery of solid wastes, including disposal of nonrecoverable waste residues.

(24) The term "resource recovery facility" means any facility at which solid waste is processed for the purpose of extracting, converting to energy, or otherwise separating and preparing solid waste for reuse.

(25) The term "regional authority" means the authority established or designated under section 6946 of this title.

(26) The term "sanitary landfill" means a facility for the disposal of solid waste which meets the criteria published under section 6944 of this title.

(26A) The term "sludge" means any solid, semisolid or liquid waste generated from a municipal, commercial, or industrial wastewater treatment plant, water supply treatment plant, or air pollution control facility or any other such waste having similar characteristics and effects.

(27) The term "solid waste" means any garbage, refuse, sludge from a waste treatment plant, water supply treatment plant, or air pollution control facility and other discarded material, including solid, liquid, semisolid, or contained gaseous material resulting from industrial, commercial, mining, and agricultural operations, and from community activities, but does not include solid or dissolved material in domestic sewage, or solid or dissolved materials in irrigation return flows or industrial discharges which are point sources subject to permits under section 1342 of Title 33, or source, special nuclear, or byproduct material as defined by the Atomic Energy Act of 1954, as amended (68 Stat. 923) [42 U.S.C.A. § 2011 et seq.].

(28) The term "solid waste management" means the systematic administration of activities which provide for the collection, source separation, storage, transportation, transfer, processing, treatment, and disposal of solid waste.

(29) The term "solid waste management facility" includes—

(A) any resource recovery system or component thereof,

(B) any system, program, or facility for resource conservation, and

(C) any facility for the collection, source separation, storage, transportation, transfer, processing, treatment or disposal of solid wastes, including hazardous wastes, whether such facility is associated with facilities generating such wastes or otherwise.

(30) The terms "solid waste planning", "solid waste management", and "comprehensive planning" include planning or management respecting resource recovery and resource conservation.

(31) The term "State" means any of the several States, the District of Columbia, the Commonwealth of Puerto Rico, the Virgin Islands, Guam, American Samoa, and the Commonwealth of the Northern Mariana Islands.

(32) The term "State authority" means the agency established or designated under section 6947 of this title.

(33) The term "storage", when used in connection with hazardous waste, means the containment of hazardous waste, either on a temporary basis or for a period of years, in such a manner as not to constitute disposal of such hazardous waste.

(34) The term "treatment", when used in connection with hazardous waste, means any method, technique, or process, including neutralization, designed to change the physical, chemical, or biological character or composition of any hazardous waste so as to neutralize such waste or so as to render such waste nonhazardous, safer for transport, amenable for recovery, amenable for storage, or reduced in volume. Such term includes any activity or processing designed to change the physical form or chemical composition of hazardous waste so as to render it nonhazardous.

(35) The term "virgin material" means a raw material, including previously unused copper, aluminum, lead, zinc, iron, or other metal or metal ore, any undeveloped resource that is, or with new technology will become, a source of raw materials.

(36) The term "used oil" means any oil which has been—

(A) refined from crude oil,

(B) used, and

(C) as a result of such use, contaminated by physical or chemical impurities.

(37) The term "recycled oil" means any used oil which is reused, following its original use, for any purpose (including the purpose for which the oil was originally used). Such term includes oil which is re-refined, reclaimed, burned, or reprocessed.

(38) The term "lubricating oil" means the fraction of crude oil which is sold for purposes of reducing friction in any industrial or mechanical device. Such term includes re-refined oil.

(39) The term "re-refined oil" means used oil from which the physical and chemical contaminants acquired through previous use have been removed through a refining process.

(40) Except as otherwise provided in this paragraph, the term "medical waste" means any solid waste which is generated in the diagnosis, treatment, or immunization of human beings or animals, in research pertaining thereto, or in the production or testing of biologicals. Such term does not include any hazardous waste identified or listed under subchapter III of this chapter or any household waste as defined in regulations under subchapter III of this chapter.

(41) The term "mixed waste" means waste that contains both hazardous waste and source, special nuclear, or by-product material subject to the Atomic Energy Act of 1954 (42 U.S.C. 2011 et seq.).

(Pub. L. No. 89–272, Title II, § 1004, as added by Pub. L. No. 94–580, § 2, 90 Stat. 2798 (Oct. 21, 1976); and amended by Pub. L. No. 95–609, § 7(b), 92 Stat. 3081 (Nov. 8, 1978); Pub. L. No. 96–463, § 3, 94 Stat. 2055 (Oct. 15, 1980); Pub. L. No. 96–482, § 2, 94 Stat. 2334 (Oct. 21, 1980); Pub. L. No. 100–582, § 3, 102 Stat. 2958 (Nov. 1, 1988); Pub. L. No. 102–386, Title I, §§ 103, 105(b), 106 Stat. 1507, 1512 (Oct. 6, 1992).)

HISTORICAL AND STATUTORY NOTES

References in Text

The Atomic Energy Act of 1954, as amended, referred to in pars. (27) and (41), is Act of Aug. 30, 1954, c. 1073, § 1, 68 Stat. 919, as amended, which is codified principally as chapter 23 (section 2011 et seq.) of this title. For complete classification of this Act to the Code, see Short Title note set out under section 2011 of this title and Tables.

Transfer of Functions

Enforcement functions of Administrator or other official of the Environmental Protection Agency related to compliance with resource conservation and recovery permits used under this chapter with respect to preconstruction, construction, and initial operation of transportation system for Canadian and Alaskan natural gas were transferred to the Federal inspector, Office of Federal Inspector for the Alaska Natural Gas Transportation System, until the first anniversary of date of initial operation of the Alaska Natural Gas Transportation System, see Reorg. Plan No. 1 of 1979, eff. July 1, 1979, §§ 102(a), 203(a), 44 Fed. Reg. 33663, 33666, 93 Stat. 1373, 1376, set out in Appendix 1 to Title 5, Government Organization and Employees. Office of Federal Inspector for the Alaska Natural Gas Transportation System abolished and functions and authority vested in Inspector transferred to Secretary of Energy by section 3012(b) of Pub. L. No. 102–486, set out as an Abolition of Office of Federal Inspector note under section 719e of Title 15, Commerce and Trade.

Prior Provisions

Provisions similar to this section were contained in section 3252 of this title, prior to the complete revision of the Solid Waste Disposal Act by Pub. L. No. 94–580.

§ 6904. Governmental cooperation

[SWDA § 1005]

(a) Interstate cooperation

The provisions of this chapter to be carried out by States may be carried out by interstate agencies and provisions applicable to States may apply to interstate regions where such agencies and regions have been established by the respective States and approved by the Administrator. In any such case, action required to be taken by the Governor of a State, respecting regional designation shall be required to be taken by the Governor of each of the respective States with respect to so much of the interstate region as is within the jurisdiction of that State.

(b) Consent of Congress to compacts

The consent of the Congress is hereby given to two or more States to negotiate and enter into agreements or compacts, not in conflict with any law or treaty of the United States, for—

(1) cooperative effort and mutual assistance for the management of solid waste or hazardous waste (or both) and the enforcement of their respective laws relating thereto, and

(2) the establishment of such agencies, joint or otherwise, as they may deem desirable for making effective such agreements or compacts.

No such agreement or compact shall be binding or obligatory upon any State a party thereto unless it is agreed upon by all parties to the agreement and until it has been approved by the Administrator and the Congress.

(Pub. L. No. 89–272, Title II, § 1005, as added by Pub. L. No. 94–580, § 2, 90 Stat. 2801 (Oct. 21, 1976).)

HISTORICAL AND STATUTORY NOTES

Transfer of Functions

For transfer of certain enforcement functions of Administrator or other official of the Environmental Protection Agency under this chapter to Federal Inspector, Office of Federal Inspector for the Alaska Natural Gas Transportation System, see note set out under section 6903 of this title.

§ 6905. Application of chapter and integration with other Acts

[SWDA § 1006]

(a) Application of chapter

Nothing in this chapter shall be construed to apply to (or to authorize any State, interstate, or local authority to regulate) any activity or substance which is subject to the Federal Water Pollution Control Act [33 U.S.C.A. § 1251 et seq.], the Safe Drinking Water Act [42 U.S.C.A. § 300f et seq.], the Marine Protection, Research and Sanctuaries Act of 1972 [16 U.S.C.A. §§ 1431 et seq., 1447 et seq., 33 U.S.C.A. §§ 1401 et seq., 2801 et seq.], or the Atomic Energy Act of 1954 [42 U.S.C.A. § 2011 et seq.] except to the extent that such application (or regulation) is not inconsistent with the requirements of such Acts.

(b) Integration with other Acts

(1) The Administrator shall integrate all provisions of this chapter for purposes of administration and enforcement and shall avoid duplication, to the maximum extent practicable, with the appropriate provisions of the Clean Air Act [42 U.S.C.A. § 7401 et seq.], the Federal Water Pollution Control Act [33 U.S.C.A. § 1251 et seq.], the Federal Insecticide, Fungicide, and Rodenticide Act [7 U.S.C.A. § 136 et seq.], the Safe Drinking Water Act [42 U.S.C.A. § 300f et seq.], the Marine Protection, Research and Sanctuaries Act of 1972 [16 U.S.C.A. §§ 1431 et seq., 1447 et seq., 33 U.S.C.A. §§ 1401 et seq., 2801 et seq.], and such other Acts of Congress as grant regulatory authority to the Administrator. Such integration shall be effected only to the extent that it can be done in a manner consistent with the goals and policies expressed in this chapter and in the other acts referred to in this subsection.

(2) **(A)** As promptly as practicable after November 8, 1984, the Administrator shall submit a report describing—

(i) the current data and information available on emissions of polychlorinated dibenzo-p-dioxins from resource recovery facilities burning municipal solid waste;

(ii) any significant risks to human health posed by these emissions; and

(iii) operating practices appropriate for controlling these emissions.

(B) Based on the report under subparagraph (A) and on any future information on such emissions, the Administrator may publish advisories or guidelines regarding the control of dioxin emissions from such facilities. Nothing in this paragraph shall be construed to preempt or otherwise affect the authority of the Administrator to promulgate any regulations under the

Clean Air Act [42 U.S.C.A. § 7401 et seq.] regarding emissions of polychlorinated dibenzo-p-dioxins.

(3) Notwithstanding any other provisions of law, in developing solid waste plans, it is the intention of this chapter that in determining the size of a waste-to-energy facility, adequate provisions shall be given to the present and reasonably anticipated future needs, including those needs created by thorough implementation of section 6962(h) of this title, of the recycling and resource recovery interests within the area encompassed by the solid waste plan.

(c) Integration with the Surface Mining Control and Reclamation Act of 1977

(1) No later than 90 days after October 21, 1980, the Administrator shall review any regulations applicable to the treatment, storage, or disposal of any coal mining wastes or overburden promulgated by the Secretary of the Interior under the Surface Mining and Reclamation Act of 1977 [30 U.S.C.A. § 1201 et seq.]. If the Administrator determines that any requirement of final regulations promulgated under any section of subchapter III of this chapter relating to mining wastes or overburden is not adequately addressed in such regulations promulgated by the Secretary, the Administrator shall promptly transmit such determination, together with suggested revisions and supporting documentation, to the Secretary.

(2) The Secretary of the Interior shall have exclusive responsibility for carrying out any requirement of subchapter III of this chapter with respect to coal mining wastes or overburden for which a surface coal mining and reclamation permit is issued or approved under the Surface Mining Control and Reclamation Act of 1977 [30 U.S.C.A. § 1201 et seq.]. The Secretary shall, with the concurrence of the Administrator, promulgate such regulations as may be necessary to carry out the purposes of this subsection and shall integrate such regulations with regulations promulgated under the Surface Mining Control and Reclamation Act of 1977.

(Pub. L. No. 89–272, Title II, § 1006, as added by Pub. L. No. 94–580, § 2, 90 Stat. 2802 (Oct. 21, 1976); and amended by Pub. L. No. 96–482, § 3, 94 Stat. 2334 (Oct. 21, 1980); Pub. L. No. 98–616, Title I, § 102, Title V, § 501(f)(2), 98 Stat. 3225, 3276 (Nov. 8, 1984).)

HISTORICAL AND STATUTORY NOTES

References in Text

The Federal Water Pollution Control Act, referred to in subsecs. (a) and (b), is Act of June 30, 1948, c. 758, as amended generally by Pub. L. No. 92–500, § 2, 86 Stat. 816 (Oct. 18, 1972), which is codified generally as chapter 26 (section 1251 et seq.) of Title 33, Navigation and Navigable Waters. For complete classification of this Act to the Code, see Short Title note set out under section 1251 of Title 33 and Tables.

The Safe Drinking Water Act, referred to in subsecs. (a) and (b), is Pub. L. No. 93–523, 88 Stat. 1660 (Dec. 16, 1974), as amended, which is codified principally as subchapter XII (section 300f et seq.) of chapter 6A of this title. For complete classification of this Act to the Code see Short Title note set out under section 201 of this title and Tables.

The Marine Protection, Research and Sanctuaries Act of 1972, referred to in subsecs. (a) and (b), is Pub. L. No. 92–532, 86 Stat. 1052 (Oct. 23, 1972), as amended, which enacted chapters 32 (section 1431 et seq.) and 32A (section 1447 et seq.) of Title 16, Conservation and chapters 27 (section 1401 et seq.) and 41 (section 2801 et seq.) of Title 33, Navigation and Navigable Waters. For complete classification of this Act to the Code, see Short Title note set out under section 1401 of Title 33 and Tables.

The Atomic Energy Act of 1954, as amended, referred to in subsec. (a), is Act of Aug. 30, 1954, c. 1073, § 1, 68 Stat. 919, which is codified principally as chapter 23 (section 2011 et seq.) of this title. For complete classification of this Act to the Code, see Short Title note set out under section 2011 of this title and Tables.

The Clean Air Act, as amended, referred to in subsec. (b)(1), (2)(B), is Act of July 14, 1955, c. 360, as amended generally by Pub. L. No. 88–206, 77 Stat. 392 (Dec. 17, 1963), and later by Pub. L. No. 95–95, 91 Stat. 685 (Aug. 7, 1977). The Clean Air Act was originally codified as chapter 15B (section 1857 et seq.) of this title. On enactment of Pub. L. No. 95–95, the Act was recodified as chapter 85 (section 7401 et seq.) of this title. For complete classification of this Act to the Code, see Short Title of 1955 Acts note set out under section 7401 of this title and Tables.

The Federal Insecticide, Fungicide, and Rodenticide Act, referred to in subsec. (b), is Act of June 25, 1947, c. 125, as amended generally by Pub. L. No. 92–516, 86 Stat. 973 (Oct. 21, 1972), which is codified generally as subchapter II (section 136 et seq.) of chapter 6 of Title 7, Agriculture. For complete classification of this Act to the Code, see Short Title note set out under section 136 of Title 7 and Tables.

The Surface Mining and Reclamation Act of 1977, referred to in subsec. (c)(1), is probably the Surface Mining Control and Reclamation Act of 1977, which is referred to in subsec. (c)(2), which is Pub. L. No. 95–87, 91 Stat. 448 (Aug. 3, 1977), as amended, which is codified generally as chapter 25 (section 1201 et seq.) of Title 30, Mineral Lands and Mining. For complete classification of this Act to the Code, see Short Title note set out under section 1201 of Title 30 and Tables.

Transfer of Functions

For transfer of certain enforcement functions of Administrator or other official of the Environmental Protection Agency under this chapter to Federal Inspector, Office of Federal Inspector for the Alaska Natural Gas Transportation System, see note set out under section 6903 of this title.

Prior Provisions

Provisions similar to this section were contained in section 3257 of this title, prior to the complete revision of the Solid Waste Disposal Act by Pub. L. No. 94–580.

Uranium Mill Tailings

Section 703 of Pub. L. No. 98–616 provided that: "Nothing in the Hazardous and Solid Waste Amendments of 1984 [see Short Title of 1984 Amendments note set out under section 6901 of this title] shall be construed to affect, modify, or amend the Uranium Mill Tailings Radiation Control Act of 1978 [Pub. L. No. 95–604, see Short Title of 1978 Acts note set out under section 7901 of this title]."

§ 6906. Financial disclosure

[SWDA § 1007]

(a) Statement

Each officer or employee of the Administrator who—

(1) performs any function or duty under this chapter; and

(2) has any known financial interest in any person who applies for or receives financial assistance under this chapter

shall, beginning on February 1, 1977, annually file with the Administrator a written statement concerning all such interests held by such officer or employee during the preceding calendar year. Such statement shall be available to the public.

(b) Action by Administrator

The Administrator shall—

(1) act within ninety days after October 21, 1976—

(A) to define the term "known financial interest" for purposes of subsection (a) of this section; and

(B) to establish the methods by which the requirement to file written statements specified in subsection (a) of this section will be monitored and enforced, including appropriate provision for the filing by such officers and employees of such statements and the review by the Administrator of such statements; and

(2) report to the Congress on June 1, 1978, and of each succeeding calendar year with respect to such disclosures and the actions taken in regard thereto during the preceding calendar year.

(c) Exemption

In the rules prescribed under subsection (b) of this section, the Administrator may identify specific positions within the Environmental Protection Agency which are of a nonpolicy-making nature and provide that officers or employees occupying such positions shall be exempt from the requirements of this section.

(d) Penalty

Any officer or employee who is subject to, and knowingly violates, this section shall be fined not more than $2,500 or imprisoned not more than one year, or both.

(Pub. L. No. 89–272, Title II, § 1007, as added by Pub. L. No. 94–580, § 2, 90 Stat. 2802 (Oct. 21, 1976).)

HISTORICAL AND STATUTORY NOTES

Transfer of Functions

For transfer of certain enforcement functions of Administrator or other official of the Environmental Protection Agency under this chapter to Federal Inspector, Office of Federal Inspector for the Alaska Natural Gas Transportation System, see note set out under section 6903 of this title.

Termination of Reporting Requirements

For termination, effective May 15, 2000, of reporting provisions in subsec. (b)(2) of this section, see Pub. L. No. 104–66, § 3003, as amended, set out as a note under 31 U.S.C.A. § 1113, and the 14th item on page 164 of House Document No. 103–7.

§ 6907. Solid waste management information and guidelines

[SWDA § 1008]

(a) Guidelines

Within one year of October 21, 1976, and from time to time thereafter, the Administrator shall, in cooperation with appropriate Federal, State, municipal, and intermunicipal agencies, and in consultation with other interested persons, and after public hearings, develop and publish suggested guidelines for solid waste management. Such suggested guidelines shall—

(1) provide a technical and economic description of the level of performance that can be attained by various available solid waste management practices (including operating practices) which provide for the protection of public health and the environment;

(2) not later than two years after October 21, 1976, describe levels of performance, including appropriate methods and degrees of control, that provide at a minimum for (A) protection of public health and welfare; (B) protection of the quality of ground waters and surface waters from leachates; (C) protection of the quality of surface waters from runoff through compliance with effluent limitations under the Federal Water Pollution Control Act, as amended [33 U.S.C.A. § 1251 et seq.]; (D) protection of ambient air quality through compliance with new source performance standards or requirements of air quality implementation plans under the Clean Air Act, as amended [42 U.S.C.A. § 7401 et seq.]; (E) disease and vector control; (F) safety; and (G) esthetics; and

(3) provide minimum criteria to be used by the States to define those solid waste management practices which constitute the open dumping of solid waste or hazardous waste and are to be prohibited under subchapter IV of this chapter.

Where appropriate, such suggested guidelines also shall include minimum information for use in deciding the adequate location, design, and construction of facilities associated with solid waste management practices, including the consideration of regional, geographic, demographic, and climatic factors.

(b) Notice

The Administrator shall notify the Committee on Environment and Public Works of the Senate and the Committee on Energy and Commerce of the House of Representatives a reasonable time before publishing any suggested guidelines or proposed regulations under this chapter of the content of such proposed suggested guidelines or proposed regulations under this chapter.

(Pub. L. No. 89–272, Title II, § 1008, as added by Pub. L. No. 94–580, § 2, 90 Stat. 2803 (Oct. 21, 1976); and amended by Pub. L. No. 95–609, § 7(c), (d), 92 Stat. 3081 (Nov. 8, 1978); Pub. L. No. 103–437, § 15(r), 108 Stat. 4594 (Nov. 2, 1994).)

HISTORICAL AND STATUTORY NOTES

References in Text

The Federal Water Pollution Control Act, referred to in subsec. (a)(2), is Act of June 30, 1948, c. 758, as amended generally by Pub. L. No. 92–500, § 2, 86 Stat. 816 (Oct. 18, 1972), which is codified generally as chapter 26 (section 1251 et seq.) of Title 33, Navigation and Navigable Waters. For complete classification of this Act to the Code, see Short Title note set out under section 1251 of Title 33 and Tables.

The Clean Air Act, as amended, referred to in subsec. (a)(2), is Act of July 14, 1955, c. 360, as amended generally by Pub. L. No. 88–206, 77 Stat. 392 (Dec. 17, 1963), and later by Pub. L. No. 95–95, 91 Stat. 685 (Aug. 7, 1977). The Clean Air Act was originally codified as chapter 15B (section 1857 et seq.) of this title. On enactment of Pub. L. No. 95–95, the Act was recodified as chapter 85 (section 7401 et seq.) of this title. For complete classification of this Act to the Code, see Short Title of 1955 Acts note set out under section 7401 of this title and Tables.

Codifications

Subchapter IV of this chapter, referred to in subsec. (a)(3), was in the original "subtitle D of this Act". Reference to subtitle D of this Act probably means subtitle D of Title II of this Act (Pub. L. No. 89–272), as added by Pub. L. No. 94–580, which is known as the Solid Waste Disposal Act and which is codified generally to subchapter IV (section 6941 et seq.) of this chapter.

Change of Name

The Committee on Public Works of the Senate, was abolished and replaced by the Committee on Environment and Public Works of the Senate, effective Feb. 11, 1977. See Rule XXV of the Standing Rules of the Senate, as amended by Senate Resolution 4 (popularly cited as the "Committee System Reorganization Amendments of 1977"), approved Feb. 4, 1977.

Any reference in any provision of law enacted before Jan. 4, 1995, to the Committee on Energy and Commerce of the House of Representatives treated as referring to the Committee on Commerce of the House of Representatives, except that any reference in any provision of law enacted before Jan. 4, 1995, to the Committee on Energy and Commerce of the House of Representatives treated as referring to the Committee on Agriculture of the House of Representatives, in the case of a provision of law relating to inspection of seafood or seafood products, the Committee on Banking and Financial Services of the House of Representatives, in the case of a provision of law relating to bank capital markets activities generally or to depository institution securities activities generally, and the Committee on Transportation and Infrastructure of the House of Representatives, in the case of a provision of law relating to railroads, railway labor, or railroad retirement and unemployment (except revenue measures related thereto), see section 1(a)(4) and (c)(1) of Pub. L. No. 104–14, set out as a note preceding section 21 of Title 2, The Congress.

The name of the Committee on Interstate and Foreign Commerce of the House of Representatives was changed, in subsec. (b), to Committee on Energy and Commerce immediately prior to noon on Jan. 3, 1981, by House Resolution 549, Ninety-sixth Congress, Mar. 25, 1980.

Transfer of Functions

For transfer of certain enforcement functions of Administrator or other official of the Environmental Protection Agency under this chapter to Federal Inspector, Office of Federal Inspector for the Alaska Natural Gas Transportation System, see note set out under section 6903 of this title.

Prior Provisions

Provisions similar to this section were contained in section 3254c of this title, prior to the complete revision of the Solid Waste Disposal Act by Pub. L. No. 94–580.

§ 6908. Small town environmental planning

[FFCA § 109]

(a) Establishment

The Administrator of the Environmental Protection Agency (hereafter referred to as the "Administrator") shall establish a program to assist small communities in planning and financing environmental facilities. The program shall be known as the "Small Town Environmental Planning Program".

(b) Small Town Environmental Planning Task Force

(1) The Administrator shall establish a Small Town Environmental Planning Task Force which shall be composed of representatives of small towns from different areas of the United States, Federal and State governmental agencies, and public interest groups. The Administrator shall terminate the Task Force not later than 2 years after the establishment of the Task Force.

(2) The Task Force shall—

(A) identify regulations developed pursuant to Federal environmental laws which pose significant compliance problems for small towns;

(B) identify means to improve the working relationship between the Environmental Protection Agency (hereafter referred to as the Agency) and small towns;

(C) review proposed regulations for the protection of the environmental and public health and suggest revisions that could improve the ability of small towns to comply with such regulations;

(D) identify means to promote regionalization of environmental treatment systems and infrastructure serving small towns to improve the economic condition of such systems and infrastructure; and

(E) provide such other assistance to the Administrator as the Administrator deems appropriate.

(c) Identification of environmental requirements

(1) Not later than 6 months after October 6, 1992, the Administrator shall publish a list of requirements under Federal environmental and public health statutes (and the regulations developed pursuant to such statutes) applicable to small towns. Not less than annually, the Administrator shall make such additions and deletions to and from the list as the Administrator deems appropriate.

(2) The Administrator shall, as part of the Small Town Environmental Planning Program under this section, implement a program to notify small communities of the regulations identified under paragraph (1) and of future regulations and requirements through methods that the Administrator determines to be effective to provide information to the greatest number of small communities, including any of the following:

(A) Newspapers and other periodicals.

(B) Other news media.

(C) Trade, municipal, and other associations that the Administrator determines to be appropriate.

(D) Direct mail.

(d) Small Town Ombudsman

The Administrator shall establish and staff an Office of the Small Town Ombudsman. The Office shall provide assistance to small towns in connection with the Small Town Environmental Planning Program and other business with the Agency. Each regional office shall identify a small town contact. The Small Town Ombudsman and the regional contacts also may assist larger communities, but only if first priority is given to providing assistance to small towns.

(e) Multi-media permits

(1) The Administrator shall conduct a study of establishing a multi-media permitting program for small towns. Such evaluation shall include an analysis of—

(A) environmental benefits and liabilities of a multi-media permitting program;

(B) the potential of using such a program to coordinate a small town's environmental and public health activities; and

(C) the legal barriers, if any, to the establishment of such a program.

(2) Within 3 years after October 6, 1992, the Administrator shall report to Congress on the results of the evaluation performed in accordance with paragraph (1). Included in this report shall be a description of the activities conducted pursuant to subsections (a) through (d) of this section.

(f) "Small town" defined

For purposes of this section, the term "small town" means an incorporated or unincorporated community (as defined by the Administrator) with a population of less than 2,500 individuals.

(g) Authorization

There is authorized to be appropriated the sum of $500,000 to implement this section.

(As added by the Federal Facility Compliance Act, Pub. L. No. 102–386, Title I, § 109, 106 Stat. 1515 (Oct. 6, 1992).)

HISTORICAL AND STATUTORY NOTES

Codifications

This section was enacted as part of the Federal Facility Compliance Act of 1992 and not as part of the Solid Waste Disposal Act.

§ 6908a. Agreements with Indian tribes

On and after October 21, 1998, the Administrator is authorized to enter into assistance agreements with Federally[1] recognized Indian tribes on such terms and conditions as the Administrator deems appropriate for the development and implementation of programs to manage hazardous waste, and underground storage tanks.

(As added by Pub. L. No. 105–276, Title III, 112 Stat. 2499 (Oct. 21, 1998).)

[1] So in original. Probably should not be capitalized.

SUBCHAPTER II—OFFICE OF SOLID WASTE; AUTHORITIES OF THE ADMINISTRATOR

§ 6911. Office of Solid Waste and Interagency Coordinating Committee

[SWDA § 2001]

(a) Office of Solid Waste

The Administrator shall establish within the Environmental Protection Agency an Office of Solid Waste (hereinafter referred to as the "Office") to be headed by an Assistant Administrator of the Environmental Protection Agency. The duties and responsibilities (other than duties and responsibilities relating to research and development) of the Administrator under this chapter (as modified by applicable reorganization plans) shall be carried out through the Office.

(b) Interagency Coordinating Committee

(1) There is hereby established an Interagency Coordinating Committee on Federal Resource Conservation and Recovery Activities which shall have the responsibility for coordinating all activities dealing with resource conservation and recovery from solid waste carried out by the Environmental Protection Agency, the Department of Energy, the Department of Commerce, and all other Federal agencies which conduct such activities pursuant to this chapter or any other Act. For purposes of this subsection, the term "resource conservation and recovery activities" shall include, but not be limited to, all research, development and demonstration projects on resource conservation or energy, or material, recovery from solid waste, and all technical or financial assistance for State or local planning for, or implementation of, projects related to resource conservation or energy or material, recovery from solid waste. The Committee shall be chaired by the Administrator of the Environmental Protection Agency or such person as the Administrator may designate. Members of the Committee shall include representatives of the Department of Energy, the Department of Commerce, the Department of the Treasury, and each other Federal agency which the Administrator determines to have programs or responsibilities affecting resource conservation or recovery.

(2) The Interagency Coordinating Committee shall include oversight of the implementation of—

(A) the May 1979 Memorandum of Understanding on Energy Recovery from Municipal Solid Waste between the Environmental Protection Agency and the Department of Energy;

(B) the May 30, 1978, Interagency Agreement between the Department of Commerce and the Environmental Protection Agency on the Implementation[1] of the Resource Conservation and Recovery Act [42 U.S.C.A. § 6901 et seq.]; and

(C) any subsequent agreements between these agencies or other Federal agencies which address Federal resource recovery or conservation activities.

(Pub. L. No. 89–272, Title II, § 2001, as added by Pub. L. No. 94–580, § 2, 90 Stat. 2804 (Oct. 21, 1976); and amended by Pub. L. No. 96–482, § 4(c), 94 Stat. 2335 (Oct. 21, 1980); Pub. L. No. 96–510, Title III, § 307(a), 94 Stat. 2810 (Dec. 11, 1980).)

[1] So in original. Probably should not be capitalized.

HISTORICAL AND STATUTORY NOTES

References in Text

The Resource Conservation and Recovery Act, referred to in subsec. (b)(2)(B), is Pub. L. No. 94–580, § 1, Oct. 21, 1976, 90 Stat. 2795, which is codified generally as this chapter. For complete classification of this Act to the Code, see Short Title of 1976 Acts note set out under section 6901 of this title and Tables.

Codifications

Subsection (b)(3) of this section, shown as omitted, which required the Interagency Coordinating Committee to submit to Congress on March 1 of each year, a five-year action plan for Federal resource conservation or recovery activities, terminated, effective May 15, 2000, pursuant to Pub. L. No. 104–66, § 3003, as amended, set out as a note under 31 U.S.C.A. § 1113. See, also, the 2nd item on page 175 of House Document No. 103–7.

Effective and Applicability Provisions

1980 Acts. Section 307(c) of Pub. L. No. 96–510 provided that: "The amendment made by subsection (a) [amending this section] shall become effective ninety days after the date of the enactment of this Act [Dec. 11, 1980]."

Transfer of Functions

For transfer of certain enforcement functions of Administrator or other official of the Environmental Protection Agency under this chapter to Federal Inspector, Office of Federal Inspector for the Alaska Natural Gas Transportation System, see note set out under section 6903 of this title.

§ 6911a. Assistant Administrator of Environmental Protection Agency; appointment, etc.

The Assistant Administrator of the Environmental Protection Agency appointed to head the Office of Solid Waste shall be in addition to the five Assistant Administrators of the Environmental Protection Agency provided for in section 1(d) of Reorganization Plan Numbered 3 of 1970 and the additional Assistant Administrator provided by the Toxic Substances Control Act [15 U.S.C.A. § 2601 et seq.], shall be appointed by the President by and with the advice and consent of the Senate.

(Pub. L. No. 96–510, Title III, § 307(b), 94 Stat. 2810 (Dec. 11, 1980); as amended by Pub. L. No. 98–80, § 2(c)(2)(B), 97 Stat. 485 (Aug. 23, 1983).)

HISTORICAL AND STATUTORY NOTES

References in Text

Reorganization Plan Numbered 3 of 1970, referred to in text, is set out in Appendix 1 to Title 5, Government Organization and Employees.

The Toxic Substances Control Act, referred to in text, is Pub. L. No. 94–469, 90 Stat. 2003 (Oct. 11, 1976), as amended, which is codified generally as chapter 53 (section 2601 et seq.) of Title 15, Commerce and Trade. For complete classification of this Act to the Code, see Short Title note set out under section 2601 of Title 15 and Tables.

Codifications

Section was enacted as part of the Comprehensive Environmental Response, Compensation, and Liability Act of 1980, and not as part of the Solid Waste Disposal Act which comprises this chapter.

Effective and Applicability Provisions

1980 Acts. Section effective Dec. 11, 1980, see section 9652 of this title.

§ 6912. Authorities of Administrator

[SWDA § 2002]

(a) Authorities

In carrying out this chapter, the Administrator is authorized to—

(1) prescribe, in consultation with Federal, State, and regional authorities, such regulations as are necessary to carry out his functions under this chapter;

(2) consult with or exchange information with other Federal agencies undertaking research, development, demonstration projects, studies, or investigations relating to solid waste;

(3) provide technical and financial assistance to States or regional agencies in the development and implementation of solid waste plans and hazardous waste management programs;

(4) consult with representatives of science, industry, agriculture, labor, environmental protection and consumer organizations, and other groups, as he deems advisable;

(5) utilize the information, facilities, personnel and other resources of Federal agencies, including the National Institute of Standards and Technology and the National Bureau of the Census, on a reimbursable basis, to perform research and analyses and conduct studies and investigations related to resource recovery and conservation and to otherwise carry out the Administrator's functions under this chapter; and

(6) to delegate to the Secretary of Transportation the performance of any inspection or enforcement function under this chapter relating to the transportation of hazardous waste where such delegation would avoid unnecessary duplication of activity and would carry out the objectives of this chapter and of chapter 51 of Title 49.

(b) Revision of regulations

Each regulation promulgated under this chapter shall be reviewed and, where necessary, revised not less frequently than every three years.

(c) Criminal investigations

In carrying out the provisions of this chapter, the Administrator, and duly-designated agents and employees of the Environmental Protection Agency, are authorized to initiate and conduct investigations under the criminal provisions of this chapter, and to refer the results of these investigations to the Attorney General for prosecution in appropriate cases.

(Pub. L. No. 89–272, Title II, § 2002, as added by Pub. L. No. 94–580, § 2, 90 Stat. 2804 (Oct. 21, 1976); as amended by Pub. L. No. 96–482, § 5, 94 Stat. 2335 (Oct. 21, 1980); Pub. L. No. 98–616, Title IV, § 403(d)(4), 98 Stat. 3272 (Nov. 8, 1984); Pub. L. No. 100–418, Title V, § 5115(c), 102 Stat. 1433 (Aug. 23, 1988).)

HISTORICAL AND STATUTORY NOTES

References in Text

Chapter 51 of Title 49, referred to in subsec. (a)(6), is 49 U.S.C.A. § 5101 et seq.

Transfer of Functions

For transfer of certain enforcement functions of Administrator or other official of the Environmental Protection Agency under this chapter to Federal Inspector, Office of Federal Inspector for the Alaska Natural Gas Transportation System, see note set out under section 6903 of this title.

§ 6913. Resource Recovery and Conservation Panels

[SWDA § 2003]

The Administrator shall provide teams of personnel, including Federal, State, and local employees or contractors (hereinafter referred to as "Resource Conservation and Recovery Panels") to provide Federal agencies, States and local governments upon request with technical assistance on solid waste management, resource recovery, and resource conservation. Such teams shall include technical, marketing, financial, and institutional specialists, and the services of such teams shall be provided without charge to States or local governments.

(Pub. L. No. 89–272, Title II, § 2003, as added by Pub. L. No. 94–580, § 2, 90 Stat. 2804 (Oct. 21, 1976); and amended by Pub. L. No. 95–609, § 7(e), 92 Stat. 3081 (Nov. 8, 1978).)

HISTORICAL AND STATUTORY NOTES

Transfer of Functions

For transfer of certain enforcement functions of Administrator or other official of the Environmental Protection Agency under this chapter to Federal Inspector, Office of Federal Inspector for the Alaska Natural Gas Transportation System, see note set out under section 6903 of this title.

§ 6914. Grants for discarded tire disposal

[SWDA § 2004]

(a) Grants

The Administrator shall make available grants equal to 5 percent of the purchase price of tire shredders (including portable shredders attached to tire collection trucks) to those eligible applicants best meeting criteria promulgated under this section. An eligible applicant may be any private purchaser, public body, or public-private joint venture. Criteria for receiving grants shall be promulgated under this section and shall include the policy to offer any private purchaser the first option to receive a grant, the policy to develop widespread geographic distribution of tire shredding facilities, the need for such facilities within a geographic area, and the projected risk and viability of any such venture. In the case of an application under this section from a public body, the Administrator shall first make a determination that there are no private purchasers interested in making an application before approving a grant to a public body.

(b) Authorization of appropriations

There is authorized to be appropriated $750,000 for each of the fiscal years 1978 and 1979 to carry out this section.

(Pub. L. No. 89–272, Title II, § 2004, as added by Pub. L. No. 94–580, § 2, 90 Stat. 2805 (Oct. 21, 1976).)

HISTORICAL AND STATUTORY NOTES

Transfer of Functions

For transfer of certain enforcement functions of Administrator or other official of the Environmental Protection Agency under this chapter to Federal Inspector, Office of Federal Inspector for the Alaska Natural Gas Transportation System, see note set out under section 6903 of this title.

§ 6914a. Labeling of lubricating oil

[SWDA § 2005]

For purposes of any provision of law which requires the labeling of commodities, lubricating oil shall be treated as lawfully labeled only if it bears the following statement, prominently displayed:

"DON'T POLLUTE—CONSERVE RESOURCES; RETURN USED OIL TO COLLECTION CENTERS".

(Pub. L. No. 89–272, Title II, § 2005, as added by Pub. L. No. 96–463, § 4(a), 94 Stat. 2056 (Oct. 15, 1980).)

HISTORICAL AND STATUTORY NOTES

Prior Provisions

A prior section 2005 of Pub. L. No. 89–272 was renumbered section 2006 and is codified as section 6915 of this title.

§ 6914b. Degradable plastic ring carriers; definitions

As used in this title—

(1) the term "regulated item" means any plastic ring carrier device that contains at least one hole greater than 1¾ inches in diameter which is made, used, or designed for the purpose of packaging, transporting, or carrying multipackaged cans or bottles, and which is of a size, shape, design, or type capable, when discarded, of becoming entangled with fish or wildlife; and

(2) the term "naturally degradable material" means a material which, when discarded, will be reduced to environmentally benign subunits under the action of normal environmental forces, such as, among others, biological decomposition, photodegradation, or hydrolysis.

(Pub. L. No. 100–556, Title I, § 102, 102 Stat. 2779 (Oct. 28, 1988).)

HISTORICAL AND STATUTORY NOTES

References in Text

This title, referred to in text, is Title I of Pub. L. No. 100–556, 102 Stat. 2779 (Oct. 28, 1988), which enacted sections 6914b and 6914b–1 of this title, and provisions set out as a note under section 6914b of this title. For complete classification of this title to the Code, see Tables.

Codifications

Section was not enacted as part of the Solid Waste Disposal Act which comprises this chapter.

Congressional Findings

Section 101 of Pub. L. No. 100–556 provided that: "The Congress finds that—

"(1) plastic ring carrier devices have been found in large quantities in the marine environment;

"(2) fish and wildlife have been known to have become entangled in plastic ring carriers;

"(3) nondegradable plastic ring carrier devices can remain intact in the marine environment for decades, posing a threat to fish and wildlife; and

"(4) 16 States have enacted laws requiring that plastic ring carrier devices be made from degradable material in order to reduce litter and to protect fish and wildlife."

§ 6914b–1. Regulation of plastic ring carriers

Not later than 24 months after October 28, 1988 (unless the Administrator of the Environmental Protection Agency determines that it is not feasible or that the byproducts of degradable regulated items present a greater threat to the environment than nondegradable regulated items), the Administrator of the Environmental Protection Agency shall require, by regulation, that any regulated item intended for use in the United States shall be made of naturally degradable material which, when discarded, decomposes within a period established by such regulation. The period within which decomposition must occur after being discarded shall be the shortest period of time consistent with the intended use of the item and the physical integrity required for such use. Such regulation shall allow a reasonable time for affected parties to come into compliance, including the use of existing inventories.

(As added by Pub. L. No. 100–556, Title I, § 103, 102 Stat. 2779 (Oct. 28, 1988).)

HISTORICAL AND STATUTORY NOTES

Codifications

This section was not enacted as part of the Solid Waste Disposal Act which comprises this chapter.

§ 6915. Annual report

[SWDA § 2006]

The Administrator shall transmit to the Congress and the President, not later than ninety days after the end of each fiscal year, a comprehensive and detailed report on all activities of the Office during the preceding fiscal year. Each such report shall include—

(1) a statement of specific and detailed objectives for the activities and programs conducted and assisted under this chapter;

(2) statements of the Administrator's conclusions as to the effectiveness of such activities and programs in meeting the stated objectives and the purposes of this chapter, measured through the end of such fiscal year;

(3) a summary of outstanding solid waste problems confronting the Administrator, in order of priority;

(4) recommendations with respect to such legislation which the Administrator deems necessary or desirable to assist in solving problems respecting solid waste;

(5) all other information required to be submitted to the Congress pursuant to any other provision of this chapter; and

(6) the Administrator's plans for activities and programs respecting solid waste during the next fiscal year.

(Pub. L. No. 89–272, Title II, § 2006, formerly § 2005, as added by Pub. L. No. 94–580, § 2, 90 Stat. 2805 (Oct. 21, 1976); and renumbered by Pub. L. No. 96–463, § 4(a), 94 Stat. 2056 (Oct. 15, 1980); and amended by Pub. L. No. 98–616, Title V, § 502(b), 98 Stat. 3276 (Nov. 8, 1984).)

HISTORICAL AND STATUTORY NOTES

Transfer of Functions

For transfer of certain enforcement functions of Administrator or other official of the Environmental Protection Agency under this chapter to Federal Inspector, Office of Federal Inspector for the Alaska Natural Gas Transportation System, see note set out under section 6903 of this title.

Prior Provisions

A prior section 2006 of Pub. L. No. 89–272 was renumbered section 2007 and is codified as section 6916 of this title.

Termination of Reporting Requirements

For termination, effective May 15, 2000, of provisions of this section relating to transmittal of annual report to Congress, see Pub. L. No. 104–66, § 3003, as amended, set out as a note under 31 U.S.C.A. § 1113, and the 19th item on page 164 of House Document No. 103–7.

§ 6916. General authorization

[SWDA § 2007]

(a) General administration

There are authorized to be appropriated to the Administrator for the purpose of carrying out the provisions of this chapter, $35,000,000 for the fiscal year ending September 30, 1977, $38,000,000 for the fiscal year ending September 30, 1978, $42,000,000 for the fiscal year ending September 30, 1979, $70,000,000 for the fiscal year ending September 30, 1980, $80,000,000 for the fiscal year ending September 30, 1981, $80,000,000 for the fiscal year ending September 30, 1982, $70,000,000 for the fiscal year ending September 30, 1985, $80,000,000 for the fiscal year ending September 30, 1986, $80,000,000 for the fiscal year ending September 30, 1987, and $80,000,000 for the fiscal year 1988.

(b) Resource Recovery and Conservation Panels

Not less than 20 percent of the amount appropriated under subsection (a) of this section, or $5,000,000 per fiscal year, whichever is less, shall be used only for purposes of Resource Recovery and Conservation Panels established under section 6913 of this title (including travel expenses incurred by such panels in carrying out their functions under this chapter).

(c) Hazardous waste

Not less than 30 percent of the amount appropriated under subsection (a) of this section shall be used only for purposes of carrying out subchapter III of this chapter (relating to hazardous waste) other than section 6931 of this title.

(d) State and local support

Not less than 25 per centum of the total amount appropriated under this chapter, up to the amount authorized in section 6948(a)(1) of this title, shall be used only for purposes of support to State, regional, local, and interstate agencies in accordance with subchapter IV of this chapter other than section 6948(a)(2) or 6949 of this title.

(e) Criminal investigators

There is authorized to be appropriated to the Administrator $3,246,000 for the fiscal year 1985, $2,408,300 for the fiscal year 1986, $2,529,000 for the fiscal year 1987, and $2,529,000 for the fiscal year 1988 to be used—

(1) for additional officers or employees of the Environmental Protection Agency authorized by the Administrator to conduct criminal investigations (to investigate, or supervise the investigation of, any activity for which a criminal penalty is provided) under this chapter; and

(2) for support costs for such additional officers or employees.

(f) Underground storage tanks

(1) There are authorized to be appropriated to the Administrator for the purpose of carrying out the provisions of subchapter IX of this chapter (relating to regulation of underground storage tanks), $10,000,000 for each of the fiscal years 1985 through 1988.

(2) There is authorized to be appropriated $25,000,000 for each of the fiscal years 1985 through 1988 to be used to make grants to the States for purposes of assisting the States in the development and implementation of approved State underground storage tank release detection, prevention, and correction programs under subchapter IX of this chapter.

(Pub. L. No. 89–272, Title II, § 2007, formerly § 2006, as added by Pub. L. No. 94–580, § 2, 90 Stat. 2805 (Oct. 21, 1976); and renumbered by Pub. L. No. 96–463, § 4(a), 94 Stat. 2055 (Oct. 15, 1980); and amended by Pub. L. No.

96–482, §§ 6, 31(a), 94 Stat. 2336, 2352 (Oct. 21, 1980); Pub. L. No. 98–616, § 2(a), (i), 98 Stat. 3222, 3223 (Nov. 8, 1984).)

HISTORICAL AND STATUTORY NOTES

Transfer of Functions

For transfer of certain enforcement functions of Administrator or other official of the Environmental Protection Agency under this chapter to Federal Inspector, Office of Federal Inspector for the Alaska Natural Gas Transportation System, see note set out under section 6903 of this title.

§ 6917. Office of Ombudsman

[SWDA § 2008]

(a) Establishment; functions

The Administrator shall establish an Office of Ombudsman, to be directed by an Ombudsman. It shall be the function of the Office of Ombudsman to receive individual complaints, grievances, requests for information submitted by any person with respect to any program or requirement under this chapter.

(b) Authority to render assistance

The Ombudsman shall render assistance with respect to the complaints, grievances, and requests submitted to the Office of Ombudsman, and shall make appropriate recommendations to the Administrator.

(c) Effect on procedures for grievances, appeals, or administrative matters

The establishment of the Office of Ombudsman shall not affect any procedures for grievances, appeals, or administrative matters in any other provision of this chapter, any other provision of law, or any Federal regulation.

(d) Termination

The Office of the Ombudsman shall cease to exist 4 years after November 8, 1984.

(Pub. L. No. 89–272, Title II, § 2008, as added by Pub. L. No. 98–616, Title I, § 103(a), 98 Stat. 3225 (Nov. 8, 1984).)

SUBCHAPTER III—HAZARDOUS WASTE MANAGEMENT

§ 6921. Identification and listing of hazardous waste

[SWDA § 3001]

(a) Criteria for identification or listing

Not later than eighteen months after October 21, 1976, the Administrator shall, after notice and opportunity for public hearing, and after consultation with appropriate Federal and State agencies, develop and promulgate criteria for identifying the characteristics of hazardous waste, and for listing hazardous waste, which should be subject to the provisions of this subchapter, taking into account toxicity, persistence, and degradability in nature, potential for accumulation in tissue, and other related factors such as flammability, corrosiveness, and other hazardous characteristics. Such criteria shall be revised from time to time as may be appropriate.

(b) Identification and listing

(1) Not later than eighteen months after October 21, 1976, and after notice and opportunity for public hearing, the Administrator shall promulgate regulations identifying the characteristics of hazardous waste, and listing particular hazardous wastes (within the meaning of section 6903(5) of this title), which shall be subject to the provisions of this subchapter. Such regulations shall be based on the criteria promulgated under subsection (a) of this section and shall be revised from time to time thereafter as may be appropriate. The Administrator, in cooperation with the Agency for Toxic Substances and Disease Registry and the National Toxicology Program, shall also identify or list those hazardous wastes which shall be subject to the provisions of this subchapter solely because of the presence in such wastes of certain constituents (such as identified carcinogens, mutagens, or teratagens[1]) at levels in excess of levels which endanger human health.

(2) (A) Notwithstanding the provisions of paragraph (1) of this subsection, drilling fluids, produced waters, and other wastes associated with the exploration, development, or production of crude oil or natural gas or geothermal energy shall be subject only to existing State or Federal regulatory programs in lieu of this subchapter until at least 24 months after October 21, 1980, and after promulgation of the regulations in accordance with subparagraphs (B) and (C) of this paragraph. It is the sense of the Congress that such State or Federal programs should include, for waste disposal sites which are to be closed, provisions requiring at least the following:

(i) The identification through surveying, platting, or other measures, together with recordation of such information on the public record, so as to assure that the location where such wastes are disposed of can be located in the future; except however, that no such surveying, platting, or other measure identifying the location of a disposal site for drilling fluids and associated wastes shall be required if the distance from the disposal site to the surveyed or platted location to the associated well is less than two hundred lineal feet; and

(ii) A chemical and physical analysis of a produced water and a composition of a drilling fluid suspected to contain a hazardous material, with such information to be acquired prior to closure and to be placed on the public record.

(B) Not later than six months after completion and submission of the study required by section 6982(m) of this title, the Administrator shall, after public hearings and opportunity for comment, determine either to promulgate regulations under this subchapter for drilling fluids, produced waters, and other wastes associated with the exploration, development, or production of crude oil or natural gas or geothermal energy or that such regulations are unwarranted. The Administrator shall publish his decision in the Federal Register accompanied by an explanation and justification of the reasons for it. In making the decision under this paragraph, the Administrator shall utilize the information developed or accumulated pursuant to the study required under section 6982(m) of this title.

(C) The Administrator shall transmit his decision, along with any regulations, if necessary, to both Houses of Congress. Such regulations shall take effect only when authorized by Act of Congress.

(3) (A) Notwithstanding the provisions of paragraph (1) of this subsection, each waste listed below shall, except as provided in subparagraph (B) of this paragraph, be subject only to regulation under other applicable provisions of Federal or State law in lieu of this subchapter until at least six months after the date of submission of the applicable study required to be conducted under subsection (f), (n), (*o*), or (p) of section 6982 of this title and after promulgation of regulations in accordance with subparagraph (C) of this paragraph:

(i) Fly ash waste, bottom ash waste, slag waste, and flue gas emission control waste generated primarily from the combustion of coal or other fossil fuels.

(ii) Solid waste from the extraction, beneficiation, and processing of ores and minerals, including phosphate rock and overburden from the mining of uranium ore.

(iii) Cement kiln dust waste.

(B) (i) Owners and operators of disposal sites for wastes listed in subparagraph (A) may be required by the Administrator, through regulations prescribed under authority of section 6912 of this title—

(I) as to disposal sites for such wastes which are to be closed, to identify the locations of such sites through surveying, platting, or other measures, together with recordation of such information on the public record, to assure that the locations where such wastes are disposed of are known and can be located in the future, and

(II) to provide chemical and physical analysis and composition of such wastes, based on available information, to be placed on the public record.

(ii) (I) In conducting any study under subsection (f), (n), (*o*), or (p), of section 6982 of this title, any officer, employee, or authorized representative of the Environmental Protection Agency, duly designated by the Administrator, is authorized, at reasonable times and as reasonably necessary for the purposes of such study, to enter any establishment where any waste subject to such study is generated, stored, treated, disposed of, or transported from; to inspect, take samples, and conduct monitoring and testing; and to have access to and copy records relating to such waste. Each such inspection shall be commenced and completed with reasonable promptness. If the officer, employee, or authorized representative obtains any samples prior to leaving the premises, he shall give to the owner, operator, or agent in charge a receipt describing the sample obtained and if requested a portion of each such sample equal in volume or weight to the portion retained. If any analysis is made of such samples, or monitoring and testing performed, a copy of the results shall be furnished promptly to the owner, operator, or agent in charge.

(II) Any records, reports, or information obtained from any person under subclause (I) shall be available to the public, except that upon a showing satisfactory to the Administrator by any person that records, reports, or information, or particular part thereof, to which the Administrator has access under this subparagraph if made public, would divulge information entitled to protection under section 1905 of Title 18, the Administrator shall consider such information or particular portion thereof confidential in accordance with the purposes of that section, except that such record, report, document, or information may be disclosed to other officers, employees, or authorized representatives of the United States concerned with carrying out this chapter. Any person not subject to the provisions of section 1905 of Title 18 who knowingly and willfully divulges or discloses any information entitled to protection under this subparagraph shall, upon conviction, be subject to a fine of not more than $5,000 or to imprisonment not to exceed one year, or both.

(iii) The Administrator may prescribe regulations, under the authority of this chapter, to prevent radiation exposure which presents an unreasonable risk to human health from the use in construction or land reclamation (with or without revegetation) of (I) solid waste from the extraction, beneficiation, and processing of phosphate rock or (II) overburden from the mining of uranium ore.

(iv) Whenever on the basis of any information the Administrator determines that any person is in violation of any requirement of this subparagraph, the Administrator shall give notice to the violator of his failure to comply with such requirement. If such violation extends beyond the thirtieth day after the Administrator's notification, the Administrator may issue an order requiring compliance within a specified time period or the Administrator may commence a civil action in the United States district court in the district in which the violation occurred for appropriate relief, including a temporary or permanent injunction.

(C) Not later than six months after the date of submission of the applicable study required to be conducted under subsection (f), (n), (*o*), or (p), of section 6982 of this title, the Administrator shall, after public hearings and opportunity for comment, either determine to promulgate regulations under this subchapter for each waste listed in subparagraph (A) of this paragraph or determine that such regulations are unwarranted. The Administrator shall publish his determination, which shall be based on information developed or accumulated pursuant to such study, public hearings, and comment, in the Federal Register accompanied by an explanation and justification of the reasons for it.

(c) Petition by State Governor

At any time after the date eighteen months after October 21, 1976, the Governor of any State may petition the Administrator to identify or list a material as a hazardous waste. The Administrator shall act upon such petition within ninety days following his receipt thereof and shall notify the Governor of such action. If the Administrator denies such petition because of financial considerations, in providing such notice to the Governor he shall include a statement concerning such considerations.

(d) Small quantity generator waste

(1) By March 31, 1986, the Administrator shall promulgate standards under sections 6922, 6923, and 6924 of this title for hazardous waste generated by a generator in a total quantity of hazardous waste greater than one hundred kilograms but less than one thousand kilograms during a calendar month.

(2) The standards referred to in paragraph (1), including standards applicable to the legitimate use, reuse, recycling, and reclamation of such wastes, may vary from the standards applicable to hazardous waste generated by larger quantity generators, but such standards shall be sufficient to protect human health and the environment.

(3) Not later than two hundred and seventy days after November 8, 1984, any hazardous waste which is part of a total quantity generated by a generator generating greater than one hundred kilograms but less than one thousand kilograms during one calendar month and which is shipped off the premises on which such waste is generated shall be accompanied by a copy of the Environmental Protection Agency Uniform Hazardous Waste Manifest form signed by the generator. This form shall contain the following information:

(A) the name and address of the generator of the waste;

(B) the United States Department of Transportation description of the waste, including the proper shipping name, hazard class, and identification number (UN/NA), if applicable;

(C) the number and type of containers;

(D) the quantity of waste being transported; and

(E) the name and address of the facility designated to receive the waste.

If subparagraph (B) is not applicable, in lieu of the description referred to in such subparagraph (B), the form shall contain the Environmental Protection Agency identification number, or a generic description of the waste, or a description of the waste by hazardous waste characteristic. Additional requirements related to the manifest form shall apply only if determined necessary by the Administrator to protect human health and the environment.

(4) The Administrator's responsibility under this subchapter to protect human health and the environment may require the promulgation of standards under this subchapter for hazardous wastes which are generated by any generator who does not generate more than one hundred kilograms of hazardous waste in a calendar month.

(5) Until the effective date of standards required to be promulgated under paragraph (1), any hazardous waste identified or listed under this section generated by any generator during any calendar month in a total quantity greater than one hundred kilograms but less than one thousand kilograms, which is not treated, stored, or disposed of at a hazardous waste treatment, storage, or disposal facility with a permit under section 6925 of this title, shall be disposed of only in a facility which is permitted, licensed, or registered by a State to manage municipal or industrial solid waste.

(6) Standards promulgated as provided in paragraph (1) shall, at a minimum, require that all treatment, storage, or disposal of hazardous wastes generated by generators referred to in paragraph (1) shall occur at a facility with interim status or a permit under this subchapter, except that onsite storage of hazardous waste generated by a generator generating a total quantity of hazardous waste greater than one hundred kilograms, but less than one thousand kilograms during a calendar month, may occur without the requirement of a permit for up to one hundred and eighty days. Such onsite storage may occur without the requirement of a permit for not more than six thousand kilograms for up to two hundred and seventy days if such generator must ship or haul such waste over two hundred miles.

(7) **(A)** Nothing in this subsection shall be construed to affect or impair the validity of regulations promulgated by the Secretary of Transportation pursuant to chapter 51 of Title 49.

(B) Nothing in this subsection shall be construed to affect, modify, or render invalid any requirements in regulations promulgated prior to January 1, 1983 applicable to any acutely hazardous waste identified or listed under this section which is generated by any generator during any calendar month in a total quantity less than one thousand kilograms.

(8) Effective March 31, 1986, unless the Administrator promulgates standards as provided in paragraph (1) of this subsection prior to such date, hazardous waste generated by any generator in a total quantity greater than one hundred kilograms but less than one thousand kilograms during a calendar month shall be subject to the following requirements until the standards referred to in paragraph (1) of this subsection have become effective:

(A) the notice requirements of paragraph (3) of this subsection shall apply and in addition, the information provided in the form shall include the name of the waste transporters and the name and address of the facility designated to receive the waste;

(B) except in the case of the onsite storage referred to in paragraph (6) of this subsection, the treatment, storage, or disposal of such waste shall occur at a facility with interim status or a permit under this subchapter;

(C) generators of such waste shall file manifest exception reports as required of generators producing greater amounts of hazardous waste per month except that such reports shall be filed by January 31, for any waste shipment occurring in the last half of the preceding calendar year, and by July 31, for any waste shipment occurring in the first half of the calendar year; and

(D) generators of such waste shall retain for three years a copy of the manifest signed by the designated facility that has received the waste.

Nothing in this paragraph shall be construed as a determination of the standards appropriate under paragraph (1).

(9) The last sentence of section 6930(b) of this title shall not apply to regulations promulgated under this subsection.

(e) Specified wastes

(1) Not later than 6 months after November 8, 1984, the Administrator shall, where appropriate, list under subsection (b)(1) of this section, additional wastes containing chlorinated dioxins or chlorinated-dibenzofurans. Not later than one year after November 8, 1984, the Administrator shall, where appropriate, list under subsection (b)(1) of this section wastes containing remaining halogenated dioxins and halogenated-dibenzofurans.

(2) Not later than fifteen months after November 8, 1984, the Administrator shall make a determination of whether or not to list under subsection (b)(1) of this section the following wastes: Chlorinated Aliphatics, Dioxin, Dimethyl Hydrazine, TDI (toluene diisocyanate), Carbamates, Bromacil, Linuron, Organo-bromines, solvents, refining wastes, chlorinated aromatics, dyes and pigments, inorganic chemical industry wastes, lithium batteries, coke byproducts, paint production wastes, and coal slurry pipeline effluent.

(f) Delisting procedures

(1) When evaluating a petition to exclude a waste generated at a particular facility from listing under this section, the Administrator shall consider factors (including additional constituents) other than those for which the waste was listed if the Administrator has a reasonable basis to believe that such additional factors could cause the waste to be a hazardous waste. The Administrator shall provide notice and opportunity for comment on these additional factors before granting or denying such petition.

(2) **(A)** To the maximum extent practicable the Administrator shall publish in the Federal Register a proposal to grant or deny a petition referred to in paragraph (1) within twelve months after receiving a complete application to exclude a waste generated at a particular facility from being regulated as a hazardous waste and shall grant or deny such a petition within twenty-four months after receiving a complete application.

(B) The temporary granting of such a petition prior to November 8, 1984, without the opportunity for public comment and the full consideration of such comments shall not continue for more than twenty-four months after November 8, 1984. If a final decision to grant or deny such a petition has not been promulgated after notice and opportunity for public comment within the time limit prescribed by the preceding sentence, any such temporary granting of such petition shall cease to be in effect.

(g) EP toxicity

Not later than twenty-eight months after November 8, 1984, the Administrator shall examine the deficiencies of the extraction procedure toxicity characteristic as a predictor of the leaching potential of wastes and make changes in the extraction procedure toxicity characteristic, including changes in the leaching media, as are necessary to insure that it accurately predicts the leaching potential of wastes which pose a threat to human health and the environment when mismanaged.

(h) Additional characteristics

Not later than two years after November 8, 1984, the Administrator shall promulgate regulations under this section identifying additional characteristics of hazardous waste, including measures or indicators of toxicity.

(i) Clarification of household waste exclusion

A resource recovery facility recovering energy from the mass burning of municipal solid waste shall not be deemed to be treating, storing, disposing of, or otherwise managing hazardous wastes for the purposes of regulation under this subchapter, if—

(1) such facility—

(A) receives and burns only—

(i) household waste (from single and multiple dwellings, hotels, motels, and other residential sources), and

(ii) solid waste from commercial or industrial sources that does not contain hazardous waste identified or listed under this section, and

(B) does not accept hazardous wastes identified or listed under this section, and

(2) the owner or operator of such facility has established contractual requirements or other appropriate notification or inspection procedures to assure that hazardous wastes are not received at or burned in such facility.

(j) Methamphetamine production

Not later than every 24 months, the Administrator shall submit to the Committee on Energy and Commerce of the House of Representatives and the Committee on Environment and Public Works of the Senate a report setting forth information collected by the Administrator from law enforcement agencies, States, and other relevant stakeholders that identifies the byproducts of the methamphetamine production process and whether the Administrator considers each of the byproducts to be a hazardous waste pursuant to this section and relevant regulations.

(Pub. L. No. 89–272, Title II, § 3001, as added by Pub. L. No. 94–580, § 2, 90 Stat. 2806 (Oct. 21, 1976); and amended by Pub. L. No. 96–482, § 7, 94 Stat. 2336 (Oct. 21, 1980); Pub. L. No. 98–616, Title II, §§ 221(a), 222, 223(a), 98 Stat. 3248, 3251, 3252 (Nov. 8, 1984); Pub. L. No. 104–119, § 4(1), 110 Stat. 833 (Mar. 26, 1996); Pub. L. No. 109–177, Title VII, § 742, 120 Stat. 272 (Mar. 9, 2006).)

[1] So in original. Probably should be "teratogens".

HISTORICAL AND STATUTORY NOTES

References in Text

Chapter 51 of Title 49, referred to in subsec. (d)(7)(A), is 49 U.S.C.A. § 5101 et seq.

Transfer of Functions

For transfer of certain enforcement functions of Administrator or other official of the Environmental Protection Agency under this chapter to Federal Inspector, Office of Federal Inspector for the Alaska Natural Gas Transportation System, see note set out under section 6903 of this title.

Educational Institutions; Accumulation, Storage and Disposal of Hazardous Wastes; Study

Section 221(f) of Pub. L. No. 98–616, as amended by Pub. L. No. 107–110, Title X, § 1076(aa), 115 Stat. 2093 (Jan. 8, 2002), provided that:

"(1) The Administrator of the Environmental Protection Agency shall, in consultation with the Secretary of Education, the States, and appropriate educational associations, conduct a comprehensive study of problems associated with the accumulation, storage and disposal of hazardous wastes from educational institutions. The study shall include an investigation of the feasibility and availability of environmentally sound methods for the treatment, storage or disposal of hazardous waste from such institutions, taking into account the types and quantities of such waste which are generated by these institutions, and the nonprofit nature of these institutions.

"(2) The Administrator shall submit a report to the Congress containing the findings of the study carried out under paragraph (1) not later than April 1, 1987.

"(3) For purposes of this subsection—

"(A) the term 'hazardous waste' means hazardous waste which is listed or identified under Section 3001 of the Solid Waste Disposal Act [this section];

"(B) the term 'educational institution' includes, but shall not be limited to,

"(i) secondary schools as defined in section 9101 of the Elementary and Secondary Education Act of 1965 [20 U.S.C.A. § 7801]; and

"(ii) institutions of higher education as defined in section 1201(a) of the Higher Education Act of 1965 [section 1141(a) of Title 20]."

[Except as otherwise provided, amendments by Pub. L. No. 107–110 effective Jan. 8, 2002, see Pub. L. No. 107–110, § 5, set out as a note under 20 U.S.C.A. § 6301.]

Ash Management and Disposal

Pub. L. No. 101–549, Title III, § 306, 104 Stat. 2584 (Nov. 15, 1990), provided that: "For a period of 2 years after the date of enactment of the Clean Air Act Amendments of 1990 [Nov. 15, 1990], ash from solid waste incineration units burning municipal waste shall not be regulated by the Administrator of the Environmental Protection Agency pursuant to section 3001 of the Solid Waste Disposal Act [this section]. Such reference and limitation shall not be construed to prejudice, endorse or otherwise affect any activity by the Administrator following the 2-year period from the date of enactment of the Clean Air Act Amendments of 1990 [Nov. 15, 1990]."

Regulation Under the Solid Waste Disposal Act

Pub. L. No. 99–499, Title I, § 124(b), 100 Stat. 1689 (Oct. 17, 1986), provided that: "Unless the Administrator of the Environmental Protection Agency promulgates regulations under subtitle C of the Solid Waste Disposal Act [this subchapter] addressing the extraction of wastes from landfills as part of the process of recovering methane from such landfills, the owner and operator of equipment used to recover methane from a landfill shall not be deemed to be managing, generating, transporting, treating, storing, or disposing of hazardous or liquid wastes within the meaning of that subtitle. If the aqueous or hydrocarbon phase of the condensate or any other waste material removed from the gas recovered from the landfill meets any of the characteristics identified under section 3001 of subtitle C of the Solid Waste Disposal Act [this section], the preceding sentence shall not apply and such condensate phase or other waste material shall be deemed a hazardous waste under that subtitle, and shall be regulated accordingly."

Small Quantity Generator Waste; Administrator of Environmental Protection Agency; Information and Education; Waste Generators

Section 221(b) of Pub. L. No. 98–616 provided that: "The Administrator of the Environmental Protection Agency shall undertake activities to inform and educate the waste generators of their responsibilities under the amendments made by this section [enacting subsec. (d) of this section] during the period within thirty months after the enactment of the Hazardous and Solid Waste Amendments of 1984 [Nov. 8, 1984] to help assure compliance."

Study of Existing Manifest System for Hazardous Wastes as Applicable to Small Quantity Generators; Submittal to Congress

Section 221(d) of Pub. L. No. 98–616 provided that: "The Administrator of the Environmental Protection Agency shall cause to be studied the existing manifest system for hazardous wastes as it applies to small quantity generators and recommend whether the current system shall be retained or whether a new system should be introduced. The study shall include an analysis of the cost versus the benefits of the system studied as well as an analysis of the ease of retrieving and collating information and identifying a given substance. Finally, any new proposal shall include a list of those standards that are necessary to protect human health and the environment. Such study shall be submitted to the Congress not later than April 1, 1987."

Administrative Burdens; Small Quantity Generators; Retention of Current System; Report to Congress

Section 221(e) of Pub. L. No. 98–616 provided that: "The Administrator of the Environmental Protection Agency, in conjunction with the Secretary of Transportation, shall prepare and submit to the Congress a report on the feasibility of easing the administrative burden on small quantity generators, increasing compliance with statutory and regulatory requirements, and simplifying enforcement efforts through a program of licensing hazardous waste transporters to assume the responsibilities of small quantity generators relating to the preparation of manifests and associated recordkeeping and reporting requirements. The report shall examine the appropriate licensing requirements under such a program including the need for financial assurances by licensed transporters and shall make recommendations on provisions and requirements for such a program including the appropriate division of responsibilities between the Department of Transportation and the Environmental Protection Administration. Such report shall be submitted to the Congress not later than April 1, 1987."

§ 6922. Standards applicable to generators of hazardous waste [SWDA § 3002]

(a) In general

Not later than eighteen months after October 21, 1976, and after notice and opportunity for public hearings and after consultation with appropriate Federal and State agencies, the Administrator shall promulgate regulations establishing such standards, applicable to generators of hazardous waste identified or listed under this subchapter, as may be necessary to protect human health and the environment. Such standards shall establish requirements respecting—

(1) recordkeeping practices that accurately identify the quantities of such hazardous waste generated, the constituents thereof which are significant in quantity or in potential harm to human health or the environment, and the disposition of such wastes;

(2) labeling practices for any containers used for the storage, transport, or disposal of such hazardous waste such as will identify accurately such waste;

(3) use of appropriate containers for such hazardous waste;

(4) furnishing of information on the general chemical composition of such hazardous waste to persons transporting, treating, storing, or disposing of such wastes;

(5) use of a manifest system and any other reasonable means necessary to assure that all such hazardous waste generated is designated for treatment, storage, or disposal in, and arrives at, treatment, storage, or disposal facilities (other than facilities on the premises where the waste is generated) for which a permit has been issued as provided in this subchapter, or pursuant to title I of the Marine Protection, Research, and Sanctuaries Act (86 Stat. 1052) [33 U.S.C.A. § 1411 et seq.]; and

(6) submission of reports to the Administrator (or the State agency in any case in which such agency carries out a permit program pursuant to this subchapter) at least once every two years, setting out—

(A) the quantities and nature of hazardous waste identified or listed under this subchapter that he has generated during the year;

(B) the disposition of all hazardous waste reported under subparagraph (A);

(C) the efforts undertaken during the year to reduce the volume and toxicity of waste generated; and

(D) the changes in volume and toxicity of waste actually achieved during the year in question in comparison with previous years, to the extent such information is available for years prior to November 8, 1984.

(b) Waste minimization

Effective September 1, 1985, the manifest required by subsection (a)(5) of this section shall contain a certification by the generator that—

(1) the generator of the hazardous waste has a program in place to reduce the volume or quantity and toxicity of such waste to the degree determined by the generator to be economically practicable; and

(2) the proposed method of treatment, storage, or disposal is that practicable method currently available to the generator which minimizes the present and future threat to human health and the environment.

(Pub. L. No. 89–272, Title II, § 3002, as added by Pub. L. No. 94–580, § 2, 90 Stat. 2806 (Oct. 21, 1976); and amended by Pub. L. No. 95–609, § 7(f), 92 Stat. 3082 (Nov. 8, 1978); Pub. L. No. 96–482, § 8, 94 Stat. 2338 (Oct. 21, 1980); Pub. L. No. 98–616, Title II, § 224(a), 98 Stat. 3252 (Nov. 8, 1984).)

HISTORICAL AND STATUTORY NOTES

References in Text

The Marine Protection, Research, and Sanctuaries Act, referred to in subsec. (a)(5), probably means the Marine Protection, Research, and Sanctuaries Act of 1972, Pub. L. No. 92–532, 86 Stat. 1052 (Oct. 23, 1972), as amended. Title I of the Marine Protection, Research, and Sanctuaries Act of 1972 is codified generally as subchapter I (section 1411 et seq.) of chapter 27 of Title 33, Navigation and Navigable Waters. For complete classification of this Act to the Code, see Short Title note set out under section 1401 of Title 33 and Tables.

Transfer of Functions

For transfer of certain enforcement functions of Administrator or other official of the Environmental Protection Agency under this chapter to Federal Inspector, Office of Federal Inspector for the Alaska Natural Gas Transportation System, see note set out under section 6903 of this title.

§ 6923. Standards applicable to transporters of hazardous waste

[SWDA § 3003]

(a) Standards

Not later than eighteen months after October 21, 1976, and after opportunity for public hearings, the Administrator, after consultation with the Secretary of Transportation and the States, shall promulgate regulations establishing such standards, applicable to transporters of hazardous waste identified or listed under this subchapter, as may be necessary to protect human health and the environment. Such standards shall include but need not be limited to requirements respecting—

(1) recordkeeping concerning such hazardous waste transported, and their source and delivery points;

(2) transportation of such waste only if properly labeled;

(3) compliance with the manifest system referred to in section 6922(5) of this title; and

(4) transportation of all such hazardous waste only to the hazardous waste treatment, storage, or disposal facilities which the shipper designates on the manifest form to be a facility holding a permit issued under this subchapter, or pursuant to title I of the Marine Protection, Research, and Sanctuaries Act (86 Stat. 1052) [33 U.S.C.A. § 1411 et seq.].

(b) Coordination with regulations of Secretary of Transportation

In case of any hazardous waste identified or listed under this subchapter which is subject to chapter 51 of Title 49, the regulations promulgated by the Administrator under this section shall be consistent with the requirements of such Act and the regulations thereunder. The Administrator is authorized to make recommendations to the Secretary of Transportation respecting the regulations of such hazardous waste under the Hazardous Materials Transportation Act and for addition of materials to be covered by such Act.

(c) Fuel from hazardous waste

Not later than two years after November 8, 1984, and after opportunity for public hearing, the Administrator shall promulgate regulations establishing standards, applicable to transporters of fuel produced (1) from any hazardous waste identified or listed under section 6921 of this title, or (2) from any hazardous waste identified or listed under section 6921 of this title and any other material, as may be necessary to protect human health and the environment. Such standards may include any of the requirements set forth in paragraphs (1) through (4) of subsection (a) of this section as may be appropriate.

(Pub. L. No. 89–272, Title II, § 3003, as added by Pub. L. No. 94–580, § 2, 90 Stat. 2807 (Oct. 21, 1976); and amended by Pub. L. No. 95–609, § 7(g), 92 Stat. 3082 (Nov. 8, 1978); Pub. L. No. 98–616, Title II, § 204(b)(2), 98 Stat. 3238 (Nov. 8, 1984).)

HISTORICAL AND STATUTORY NOTES

References in Text

Section 6922(5) of this title, referred to in subsec. (a)(3), was redesignated section 6922(a)(5) of this title, by Pub. L. No. 98–616, Title II, § 224(a)(1), 98 Stat. 3253 (Nov. 8, 1984).

The Marine Protection, Research, and Sanctuaries Act, referred to in subsec. (a)(4), probably means the Marine Protection, Research, and Sanctuaries Act of 1972, Pub. L. No. 92–532, 86 Stat. 1052 (Oct. 23, 1972), as amended. Title I of the Marine Protection, Research, and Sanctuaries Act of 1972 is codified generally as subchapter I (section 1411 et seq.) of chapter 27 of Title 33, Navigation and Navigable Waters. For complete classification of this Act to the Code, see Short Title note set out under section 1401 of Title 33 and Tables.

Chapter 51 of Title 49, referred to in subsec. (b), is 49 U.S.C.A. § 5101 et seq.

Transfer of Functions

For transfer of certain enforcement functions of Administrator or other official of the Environmental Protection Agency under this chapter to Federal Inspector, Office of Federal Inspector for the Alaska Natural Gas Transportation System, see note set out under section 6903 of this title.

§ 6924. Standards applicable to owners and operators of hazardous waste treatment, storage, and disposal facilities

[SWDA § 3004]

(a) In general

Not later than eighteen months after October 21, 1976, and after opportunity for public hearings and after consultation with appropriate Federal and State agencies, the Administrator shall promulgate regulations establishing such performance standards, applicable to owners and operators of facilities for the treatment, storage, or disposal of hazardous waste identified or listed under this subchapter, as may be necessary to protect human health and the environment. In establishing such standards the Administrator shall, where appropriate, distinguish in such standards between requirements appropriate for new facilities and for facilities in existence on the date of promulgation of such regulations. Such standards shall include, but need not be limited to, requirements respecting—

(1) maintaining records of all hazardous wastes identified or listed under this chapter which is treated, stored, or disposed of, as the case may be, and the manner in which such wastes were treated, stored, or disposed of;

(2) satisfactory reporting, monitoring, and inspection and compliance with the manifest system referred to in section 6922(5) of this title;

(3) treatment, storage, or disposal of all such waste received by the facility pursuant to such operating methods, techniques, and practices as may be satisfactory to the Administrator;

(4) the location, design, and construction of such hazardous waste treatment, disposal, or storage facilities;

(5) contingency plans for effective action to minimize unanticipated damage from any treatment, storage, or disposal of any such hazardous waste;

(6) the maintenance of operation of such facilities and requiring such additional qualifications as to ownership, continuity of operation, training for personnel, and financial responsibility (including financial responsibility for corrective action) as may be necessary or desirable; and

(7) compliance with the requirements of section 6925 of this title respecting permits for treatment, storage, or disposal.

No private entity shall be precluded by reason of criteria established under paragraph (6) from the ownership or operation of facilities providing hazardous waste treatment, storage, or disposal services where such entity can provide assurances of financial responsibility and continuity of operation consistent with the degree and duration of risks associated with the treatment, storage, or disposal of specified hazardous waste.

(b) Salt dome formations, salt bed formations, underground mines and caves

(1) Effective on November 8, 1984, the placement of any noncontainerized or bulk liquid hazardous waste in any salt dome formation, salt bed formation, underground mine, or cave is prohibited until such time as—

(A) the Administrator has determined, after notice and opportunity for hearings on the record in the affected areas, that such placement is protective of human health and the environment;

(B) the Administrator has promulgated performance and permitting standards for such facilities under this subchapter, and;

(C) a permit has been issued under section 6925(c) of this title for the facility concerned.

(2) Effective on November 8, 1984, the placement of any hazardous waste other than a hazardous waste referred to in paragraph (1) in a salt dome formation, salt bed formation, underground mine, or cave is prohibited until such time as a permit has been issued under section 6925(c) of this title for the facility concerned.

(3) No determination made by the Administrator under subsection (d), (e), or (g) of this section regarding any hazardous waste to which such subsection (d), (e), or (g) of this section applies shall affect the prohibition contained in paragraph (1) or (2) of this subsection.

(4) Nothing in this subsection shall apply to the Department of Energy Waste Isolation Pilot Project in New Mexico.

(c) Liquids in landfills

(1) Effective 6 months after November 8, 1984, the placement of bulk or noncontainerized liquid hazardous waste or free liquids contained in hazardous waste (whether or not absorbents have been added) in any landfill is prohibited. Prior to such date the requirements (as in effect on April 30, 1983) promulgated under this section by the Administrator regarding liquid hazardous waste shall remain in force and effect to the extent such requirements are applicable to the placement of bulk or noncontainerized liquid hazardous waste, or free liquids contained in hazardous waste, in landfills.

(2) Not later than fifteen months after November 8, 1984, the Administrator shall promulgate final regulations which—

(A) minimize the disposal of containerized liquid hazardous waste in landfills, and

(B) minimize the presence of free liquids in containerized hazardous waste to be disposed of in landfills.

Such regulations shall also prohibit the disposal in landfills of liquids that have been absorbed in materials that biodegrade or that release liquids when compressed as might occur during routine landfill operations. Prior to the date on which such final regulations take effect, the requirements (as in effect on April 30, 1983) promulgated under this section by the Administrator shall remain in force and effect to the extent such requirements are applicable to the disposal of containerized liquid hazardous waste, or free liquids contained in hazardous waste, in landfills.

(3) Effective twelve months after November 8, 1984, the placement of any liquid which is not a hazardous waste in a landfill for which a permit is required under section 6925(c) of this title or which is operating pursuant to interim status granted under section 6925(e) of this title is prohibited unless the owner or operator of such landfill demonstrates to the Administrator, or the Administrator determines, that—

(A) the only reasonably available alternative to the placement in such landfill is placement in a landfill or unlined surface impoundment, whether or not permitted under section 6925(c) of this title or operating pursuant to interim status under section 6925(e) of this title, which contains, or may reasonably be anticipated to contain, hazardous waste; and

(B) placement in such owner or operator's landfill will not present a risk of contamination of any underground source of drinking water.

As used in subparagraph (B), the term "underground source of drinking water" has the same meaning as provided in regulations under the Safe Drinking Water Act (title XIV of the Public Health Service Act) [42 U.S.C.A. § 300f et seq.].

(4) No determination made by the Administrator under subsection (d), (e), or (g) of this section regarding any hazardous waste to which such subsection (d), (e), or (g) of this section applies shall affect the prohibition contained in paragraph (1) of this subsection.

(d) Prohibitions on land disposal of specified wastes

(1) Effective 32 months after November 8, 1984 (except as provided in subsection (f) of this section with respect to underground injection into deep injection wells), the land disposal of the hazardous wastes referred to in paragraph (2) is prohibited unless the Administrator determines the prohibition on one or more methods of land disposal of such waste is not required in order to protect human health and the environment for as long as the waste remains hazardous, taking into account—

(A) the long-term uncertainties associated with land disposal,

(B) the goal of managing hazardous waste in an appropriate manner in the first instance, and

(C) the persistence, toxicity, mobility, and propensity to bioaccumulate of such hazardous wastes and their hazardous constituents.

For the purposes of this paragraph, a method of land disposal may not be determined to be protective of human health and the environment for a hazardous waste referred to in paragraph (2) (other than a hazardous waste which has complied with the pretreatment regulations promulgated under subsection (m) of this section), unless, upon application by an interested person, it has been demonstrated to the Administrator, to a reasonable degree of certainty, that there will be no migration of hazardous constituents from the disposal unit or injection zone for as long as the wastes remain hazardous.

(2) Paragraph (1) applies to the following hazardous wastes listed or identified under section 6921 of this title:

(A) Liquid hazardous wastes, including free liquids associated with any solid or sludge, containing free cyanides at concentrations greater than or equal to 1,000 mg/l.

(B) Liquid hazardous wastes, including free liquids associated with any solid or sludge, containing the following metals (or elements) or compounds of these metals (or elements) at concentrations greater than or equal to those specified below:

(i) arsenic and/or compounds (as As) 500 mg/l;

(ii) cadmium and/or compounds (as Cd) 100 mg/l;

(iii) chromium (VI and/or compounds (as Cr VI)) 500 mg/l;

(iv) lead and/or compounds (as Pb) 500 mg/l;

(v) mercury and/or compounds (as Hg) 20 mg/l;

(vi) nickel and/or compounds (as Ni) 134 mg/l;

(vii) selenium and/or compounds (as Se) 100 mg/l; and

(viii) thallium and/or compounds (as Th) 130 mg/l.

(C) Liquid hazardous waste having a pH less than or equal to two (2.0).

(D) Liquid hazardous wastes containing polychlorinated biphenyls at concentrations greater than or equal to 50 ppm.

(E) Hazardous wastes containing halogenated organic compounds in total concentration greater than or equal to 1,000 mg/kg.

When necessary to protect human health and the environment, the Administrator shall substitute more stringent concentration levels than the levels specified in subparagraphs (A) through (E).

(3) During the period ending forty-eight months after November 8, 1984, this subsection shall not apply to any disposal of contaminated soil or debris resulting from a response action taken under section 9604 or 9606 of this title or a corrective action required under this subchapter.

(e) Solvents and dioxins

(1) Effective twenty-four months after November 8, 1984 (except as provided in subsection (f)of this section with respect to underground injection into deep injection wells), the land disposal of the hazardous wastes referred to in paragraph (2) is prohibited unless the Administrator determines the prohibition of one or more methods of land disposal of such waste is not required in order to protect human health and the environment for as long as the waste remains hazardous, taking into account the factors referred to in subparagraph (A) through (C) of subsection (d)(1) of this section. For the purposes of this paragraph, a method of land disposal may not be determined to be protective of human health and the environment for a hazardous waste referred to in paragraph (2) (other than a hazardous waste which has complied with the pretreatment regulations promulgated under subsection (m) of this section), unless upon application by an interested person it has been demonstrated to the Administrator, to a reasonable degree of certainty, that there will be no migration of hazardous constituents from the disposal unit or injection zone for as long as the wastes remain hazardous.

(2) The hazardous wastes to which the prohibition under paragraph (1) applies are as follows—

(A) dioxin-containing hazardous wastes numbered F020, F021, F022, and F023 (as referred to in the proposed rule published by the Administrator in the Federal Register for April 4, 1983), and

(B) those hazardous wastes numbered F001, F002, F003, F004, and F005 in regulations promulgated by the Administrator under section 6921 of this title (40 C.FED. REG. 261.31 (July 1, 1983)), as those regulations are in effect on July 1, 1983.

(3) During the period ending forty-eight months after November 8, 1984, this subsection shall not apply to any disposal of contaminated soil or debris resulting from a response action taken under section 9604 or 9606 of this title or a corrective action required under this subchapter.

(f) Disposal into deep injection wells; specified subsection (d) wastes; solvents and dioxins

(1) Not later than forty-five months after November 8, 1984, the Administrator shall complete a review of the disposal of all hazardous wastes referred to in paragraph (2) of subsection (d) of this section and in paragraph (2) of subsection (e) of this section by underground injection into deep injection wells.

(2) Within forty-five months after November 8, 1984, the Administrator shall make a determination regarding the disposal by underground injection into deep injection wells of the hazardous wastes referred to in paragraph (2) of subsection (d) of this section and the hazardous wastes referred to in paragraph (2) of subsection (e) of this section. The Administrator shall promulgate final regulations prohibiting the disposal of such wastes into such wells if it may reasonably be determined that such disposal may not be protective of human health and the environment for as long as the waste remains hazardous, taking into account the factors referred to in subparagraphs (A) through (C) of subsection (d)(1) of this section. In promulgating such regulations, the Administrator shall consider each hazardous waste referred to in paragraph (2) of subsection (d) of this section or in paragraph (2) of subsection (e) of this section which is prohibited from disposal into such wells by any State.

(3) If the Administrator fails to make a determination under paragraph (2) for any hazardous waste referred to in paragraph (2) of subsection (d) of this section or in paragraph (2) of subsection (e) of this section within forty-five months after November 8, 1984, such hazardous waste shall be prohibited from disposal into any deep injection well.

(4) As used in this subsection, the term "deep injection well" means a well used for the underground injection of hazardous waste other than a well to which section 6979a(a) of this title applies.

(g) Additional land disposal prohibition determinations

(1) Not later than twenty-four months after November 8, 1984, the Administrator shall submit a schedule to Congress for—

(A) reviewing all hazardous wastes listed (as of November 8, 1984) under section 6921 of this title other than those wastes which are referred to in subsection (d) or (e) of this section; and

(B) taking action under paragraph (5) of this subsection with respect to each such hazardous waste.

(2) The Administrator shall base the schedule on a ranking of such listed wastes considering their intrinsic hazard and their volume such that decisions regarding the land disposal of high volume hazardous wastes with high intrinsic hazard shall, to the maximum extent possible, be made by the date forty-five months after November 8, 1984. Decisions regarding low volume hazardous wastes with lower intrinsic hazard shall be made by the date sixty-six months after November 8, 1984.

(3) The preparation and submission of the schedule under this subsection shall not be subject to the Paperwork Reduction Act of 1980. No hearing on the record shall be required for purposes of preparation or submission of the schedule. The schedule shall not be subject to judicial review.

(4) The schedule under this subsection shall require that the Administrator shall promulgate regulations in accordance with paragraph (5) or make a determination under paragraph (5)—

(A) for at least one-third of all hazardous wastes referred to in paragraph (1) by the date forty-five months after November 8, 1984;

(B) for at least two-thirds of all such listed wastes by the date fifty-five months after November 8, 1984; and

(C) for all such listed wastes and for all hazardous wastes identified under section 6921 of this title by the date sixty-six months after November 8, 1984.

In the case of any hazardous waste identified or listed under section 6921 of this title after November 8, 1984, the Administrator shall determine whether such waste shall be prohibited from one or more methods of land disposal in accordance with paragraph (5) within six months after the date of such identification or listing.

(5) Not later than the date specified in the schedule published under this subsection, the Administrator shall promulgate final regulations prohibiting one or more methods of land disposal of the hazardous wastes listed on such schedule except for methods of land disposal which the Administrator determines will be protective of human health and the environment for as long as the waste remains hazardous, taking into account the factors referred to in subparagraphs (A) through (C) of subsection (d)(1) of this section. For the purposes of this paragraph, a method of land disposal may not be determined to be protective of human health and the environment (except with respect to a hazardous waste which has complied with the pretreatment regulations promulgated under subsection (m) of this section) unless, upon application by an interested person, it has been demonstrated to the

Administrator, to a reasonable degree of certainty, that there will be no migration of hazardous constituents from the disposal unit or injection zone for as long as the wastes remain hazardous.

(6) **(A)** If the Administrator fails (by the date forty-five months after November 8, 1984) to promulgate regulations or make a determination under paragraph (5) for any hazardous waste which is included in the first one-third of the schedule published under this subsection, such hazardous waste may be disposed of in a landfill or surface impoundment only if—

(i) such facility is in compliance with the requirements of subsection (*o*) of this section which are applicable to new facilities (relating to minimum technological requirements); and

(ii) prior to such disposal, the generator has certified to the Administrator that such generator has investigated the availability of treatment capacity and has determined that the use of such landfill or surface impoundment is the only practical alternative to treatment currently available to the generator.

The prohibition contained in this subparagraph shall continue to apply until the Administrator promulgates regulations or makes a determination under paragraph (5) for the waste concerned.

(B) If the Administrator fails (by the date 55 months after November 8, 1984) to promulgate regulations or make a determination under paragraph (5) for any hazardous waste which is included in the first two-thirds of the schedule published under this subsection, such hazardous waste may be disposed of in a landfill or surface impoundment only if—

(i) such facility is in compliance with the requirements of subsection (*o*) of this section which are applicable to new facilities (relating to minimum technological requirements); and

(ii) prior to such disposal, the generator has certified to the Administrator that such generator has investigated the availability of treatment capacity and has determined that the use of such landfill or surface impoundment is the only practical alternative to treatment currently available to the generator.

The prohibition contained in this subparagraph shall continue to apply until the Administrator promulgates regulations or makes a determination under paragraph (5) for the waste concerned.

(C) If the Administrator fails to promulgate regulations, or make a determination under paragraph (5) for any hazardous waste referred to in paragraph (1) within 66 months after November 8, 1984, such hazardous waste shall be prohibited from land disposal.

(7) Solid waste identified as hazardous based solely on one or more characteristics shall not be subject to this subsection, any prohibitions under subsection (d), (e), or (f) of this section, or any requirement promulgated under subsection (m) of this section (other than any applicable specific methods of treatment, as provided in paragraph (8)) if the waste—

(A) is treated in a treatment system that subsequently discharges to waters of the United States pursuant to a permit issued under section 1342 of Title 33, treated for the purposes of the pretreatment requirements of section 1317 of Title 33, or treated in a zero discharge system that, prior to any permanent land disposal, engages in treatment that is equivalent to treatment required under section 1342 of Title 33 for discharges to waters of the United States, as determined by the Administrator; and

(B) no longer exhibits a hazardous characteristic prior to management in any land-based solid waste management unit.

(8) Solid waste that otherwise qualifies under paragraph (7) shall nevertheless be required to meet any applicable specific methods of treatment specified for such waste by the Administrator under subsection (m) of this section, including those specified in the rule promulgated by the Administrator June 1, 1990, prior to management in a land-based unit as part of a treatment system specified in paragraph (7)(A). No solid waste may qualify under paragraph (7) that would generate toxic gases, vapors, or fumes due to the presence of cyanide when exposed to pH conditions between 2.0 and 12.5.

(9) Solid waste identified as hazardous based on one or more characteristics alone shall not be subject to this subsection, any prohibitions under subsection (d), (e), or (f) of this section, or any requirement promulgated under subsection (m) of this section if the waste no longer exhibits a hazardous characteristic at the point of injection in any Class I injection well permitted under section 300h–1 of this title.

(10) Not later than five years after March 26, 1996, the Administrator shall complete a study of hazardous waste managed pursuant to paragraph (7) or (9) to characterize the risks to human health or the environment associated with such management. In conducting this study, the Administrator shall evaluate the extent to which risks are adequately addressed under existing State or Federal programs and whether unaddressed risks could be better addressed under such laws or programs. Upon receipt of additional information or upon completion of such study and as necessary to protect human health and the environment, the Administrator may impose additional requirements under existing Federal laws, including subsection (m)(1) of this section, or rely on other State or Federal programs or authorities to address such risks. In promulgating any treatment standards pursuant to subsection (m)(1) of this section under the previous sentence, the Administrator shall take into account the extent to which treatment is occurring in land-based units as part of a treatment system specified in paragraph (7)(A).

(11) Nothing in paragraph (7) or (9) shall be interpreted or applied to restrict any inspection or enforcement authority under the provisions of this chapter.

(h) Variance from land disposal prohibitions

(1) A prohibition in regulations under subsection (d), (e), (f), or (g) of this section shall be effective immediately upon promulgation.

(2) The Administrator may establish an effective date different from the effective date which would otherwise apply under subsection (d), (e), (f), or (g) of this section with respect to a specific hazardous waste which is subject to a prohibition under subsection (d), (e), (f), or (g) of this section or under regulations under subsection (d), (e), (f), or (g) of this section. Any such other effective date shall be established on the basis of the earliest date on which adequate alternative treatment, recovery, or disposal capacity which protects human health and the environment will be available. Any such other effective date shall in no event be later than 2 years after the effective date of the prohibition which would otherwise apply under subsection (d), (e), (f), or (g) of this section.

(3) The Administrator, after notice and opportunity for comment and after consultation with appropriate State agencies in all affected States, may on a case-by-case basis grant an extension of the effective date which would otherwise apply under subsection (d), (e), (f), or (g) of this section or under paragraph (2) for up to one year, where the applicant demonstrates that there is a binding contractual commitment to construct or otherwise provide such alternative capacity but due to circumstances beyond the control of such applicant such alternative capacity cannot reasonably be made available by such effective date. Such extension shall be renewable once for no more than one additional year.

(4) Whenever another effective date (hereinafter referred to as a "variance") is established under paragraph (2), or an extension is granted under paragraph (3), with respect to any hazardous waste, during the period for which such variance or extension is in effect, such hazardous waste may be disposed of in a landfill or surface impoundment only if such facility is in compliance with the requirements of subsection (*o*) of this section.

(i) Publication of determination

If the Administrator determines that a method of land disposal will be protective of human health and the environment, he shall promptly publish in the Federal Register notice of such determination, together with an explanation of the basis for such determination.

(j) Storage of hazardous waste prohibited from land disposal

In the case of any hazardous waste which is prohibited from one or more methods of land disposal under this section (or under regulations promulgated by the Administrator under any provision of this section) the storage of such hazardous waste is prohibited unless such storage is solely for the purpose of the accumulation of such quantities of hazardous waste as are necessary to facilitate proper recovery, treatment or disposal.

(k) "Land disposal" defined

For the purposes of this section, the term "land disposal", when used with respect to a specified hazardous waste, shall be deemed to include, but not be limited to, any placement of such hazardous waste in a landfill, surface impoundment, waste pile, injection well, land treatment facility, salt dome formation, salt bed formation, or underground mine or cave.

(*l*) Ban on dust suppression

The use of waste or used oil or other material, which is contaminated or mixed with dioxin or any other hazardous waste identified or listed under section 6921 of this title (other than a waste identified solely on the basis of ignitability), for dust suppression or road treatment is prohibited.

(m) Treatment standards for wastes subject to land disposal prohibition

(1) Simultaneously with the promulgation of regulations under subsection (d), (e), (f), or (g) of this section prohibiting one or more methods of land disposal of a particular hazardous waste, and as appropriate thereafter, the Administrator shall, after notice and an opportunity for hearings and after consultation with appropriate Federal and State agencies, promulgate regulations specifying those levels or methods of treatment, if any, which substantially diminish the toxicity of the waste or substantially reduce the likelihood of migration of hazardous constituents from the waste so that short-term and long-term threats to human health and the environment are minimized.

(2) If such hazardous waste has been treated to the level or by a method specified in regulations promulgated under this subsection, such waste or residue thereof shall not be subject to any prohibition promulgated under subsection (d), (e), (f), or (g) of this section and may be disposed of in a land disposal facility which meets the requirements of this subchapter. Any regulation promulgated under this subsection for a particular hazardous waste shall become effective on the same date as any applicable prohibition promulgated under subsection (d), (e), (f), or (g) of this section.

(n) Air emissions

Not later than thirty months after November 8, 1984, the Administrator shall promulgate such regulations for the monitoring and control of air emissions at hazardous waste treatment, storage, and disposal facilities, including but not limited to open tanks, surface impoundments, and landfills, as may be necessary to protect human health and the environment.

(*o*) Minimum technological requirements

(1) The regulations under subsection (a) of this section shall be revised from time to time to take into account improvements in the technology of control and measurement. At a minimum, such regulations shall require, and a permit issued pursuant to section 6925(c) of this title after November 8, 1984, by the Administrator or a State shall require—

(A) for each new landfill or surface impoundment, each new landfill or surface impoundment unit at an existing facility, each replacement of an existing landfill or surface impoundment unit, and each lateral expansion of an existing landfill or surface impoundment unit, for which an application for a final determination regarding issuance of a permit under section 6925(c) of this title is received after November 8, 1984—

(i) the installation of two or more liners and a leachate collection system above (in the case of a landfill) and between such liners; and

(ii) ground water monitoring; and

(B) for each incinerator which receives a permit under section 6925(c) of this title after November 8, 1984, the attainment of the minimum destruction and removal efficiency required by regulations in effect on June 24, 1982.

The requirements of this paragraph shall apply with respect to all waste received after the issuance of the permit.

(2) Paragraph (1)(A)(i) shall not apply if the owner or operator demonstrates to the Administrator, and the Administrator finds for such landfill or surface impoundment, that alternative design and operating practices, together with location characteristics, will prevent the migration of any hazardous constituents into the ground water or surface water at least as effectively as such liners and leachate collection systems.

(3) The double-liner requirement set forth in paragraph (1)(A)(i) may be waived by the Administrator for any monofill, if—

(A) such monofill contains only hazardous wastes from foundry furnace emission controls or metal casting molding sand,

(B) such wastes do not contain constituents which would render the wastes hazardous for reasons other than the Extraction Procedure ("EP") toxicity characteristics set forth in regulations under this subchapter, and

(C) such monofill meets the same requirements as are applicable in the case of a waiver under section 6925(j)(2) or (4) of this title.

(4) **(A)** Not later than thirty months after November 8, 1984, the Administrator shall promulgate standards requiring that new landfill units, surface impoundment units, waste piles, underground tanks and land treatment units for the storage, treatment, or disposal of hazardous waste identified or listed under section 6921 of this title shall be required to utilize approved leak detection systems.

(B) For the purposes of subparagraph (A)—

(i) the term "approved leak detection system" means a system or technology which the Administrator determines to be capable of detecting leaks of hazardous constituents at the earliest practicable time; and

(ii) the term "new units" means units on which construction commences after the date of promulgation of regulations under this paragraph.

(5) **(A)** The Administrator shall promulgate regulations or issue guidance documents implementing the requirements of paragraph (1)(A) within two years after November 8, 1984.

(B) Until the effective date of such regulations or guidance documents, the requirement for the installation of two or more liners may be satisfied by the installation of a top liner designed, operated, and constructed of materials to prevent the migration of any constituent into such liner during the period such facility remains in operation (including any post-closure monitoring period), and a lower liner designed, operated[1] and constructed to prevent the migration of any constituent through such liner during such period. For the purpose of the preceding sentence, a lower liner shall be deemed to satisfy such requirement if it is constructed of at least a 3-foot thick layer of recompacted clay or other natural material with a permeability of no more than 1 $\times 10^{-7}$ centimeter per second.

(6) Any permit under section 6925 of this title which is issued for a landfill located within the State of Alabama shall require the installation of two or more liners and a leachate collection system above and between such liners, notwithstanding any other provision of this chapter.

(7) In addition to the requirements set forth in this subsection, the regulations referred to in paragraph (1) shall specify criteria for the acceptable location of new and existing treatment, storage, or disposal facilities as necessary to protect human health and the environment. Within 18 months after November 8, 1984, the Administrator shall publish guidance criteria identifying areas of vulnerable hydrogeology.

(p) Ground water monitoring

The standards under this section concerning ground water monitoring which are applicable to surface impoundments, waste piles, land treatment units, and landfills shall apply to such a facility whether or not—

(1) the facility is located above the seasonal high water table;

(2) two liners and a leachate collection system have been installed at the facility; or

(3) the owner or operator inspects the liner (or liners) which has been installed at the facility.

This subsection shall not be construed to affect other exemptions or waivers from such standards provided in regulations in effect on November 8, 1984, or as may be provided in revisions to those regulations, to the extent consistent with this subsection. The Administrator is authorized on a case-by-case basis to exempt from ground water monitoring requirements under this section (including subsection (*o*) of this section) any engineered structure which the Administrator finds does not receive or contain liquid waste (nor waste containing free liquids), is designed and operated to exclude liquid from precipitation or other runoff, utilizes multiple leak detection systems within the outer layer of containment, and provides for continuing operation and maintenance of these leak detection systems during the operating period, closure, and the period required for post-closure monitoring and for which the Administrator concludes on the basis of such findings that there is a reasonable certainty hazardous constituents will not migrate beyond the outer layer of containment prior to the end of the period required for post-closure monitoring.

(q) Hazardous waste used as fuel

(1) Not later than two years after November 8, 1984, and after notice and opportunity for public hearing, the Administrator shall promulgate regulations establishing such—

(A) standards applicable to the owners and operators of facilities which produce a fuel—

(i) from any hazardous waste identified or listed under section 6921 of this title, or

(ii) from any hazardous waste identified or listed under section 6921 of this title and any other material;

(B) standards applicable to the owners and operators of facilities which burn, for purposes of energy recovery, any fuel produced as provided in subparagraph (A) or any fuel which otherwise contains any hazardous waste identified or listed under section 6921 of this title; and

(C) standards applicable to any person who distributes or markets any fuel which is produced as provided in subparagraph (A) or any fuel which otherwise contains any hazardous waste identified or listed under section 6921 of this title;

as may be necessary to protect human health and the environment. Such standards may include any of the requirements set forth in paragraphs (1) through (7) of subsection (a) of this section as may be appropriate. Nothing in this subsection shall be construed to affect or impair the provisions of section 6921(b)(3) of this title. For purposes of this subsection, the term "hazardous waste listed under section 6921 of this title" includes any commercial chemical product which is listed under section 6921 of this title and which, in lieu of its original intended use, is (i) produced for use as (or as a component of) a fuel, (ii) distributed for use as a fuel, or (iii) burned as a fuel.

(2) **(A)** This subsection, subsection (r) of this section, and subsection (s) of this section shall not apply to petroleum refinery wastes containing oil which are converted into petroleum coke at the same facility at which such wastes were generated, unless the resulting coke product would exceed one or more characteristics by which a substance would be identified as a hazardous waste under section 6921 of this title.

(B) The Administrator may exempt from the requirements of this subsection, subsection (r) of this section, or subsection (s) of this section facilities which burn de minimis quantities of hazardous waste as fuel, as defined by the Administrator, if the wastes are burned at the same facility at which such wastes are generated; the waste is burned to recover useful energy, as determined by the Administrator on the basis of the design and operating characteristics of the facility and the heating value and other characteristics of the waste; and the waste is burned in a type of device determined by the Administrator to be designed and operated at a destruction and removal efficiency sufficient such that protection of human health and environment is assured.

(C) **(i)** After November 8, 1984, and until standards are promulgated and in effect under paragraph (2) of this subsection, no fuel which contains any hazardous waste may be burned in any cement kiln which is located within the boundaries of any incorporated municipality with a population greater than five hundred thousand (based on the most recent census statistics) unless such kiln fully complies with regulations (as in effect on November 8, 1984) under this subchapter which are applicable to incinerators.

(ii) Any person who knowingly violates the prohibition contained in clause (i) shall be deemed to have violated section 6928(d)(2) of this title.

(r) Labeling

(1) Notwithstanding any other provision of law, until such time as the Administrator promulgates standards under subsection (q) of this section specifically superceding[2] this requirement, it shall be unlawful for any person who is required to file a notification in accordance with paragraph (1) or (3) of section 6930 of this title to distribute or market any fuel which is produced from any hazardous waste identified or listed under section 6921 of this title, or any fuel which otherwise contains any hazardous waste identified or listed under section 6921 of this title if the invoice or the bill of sale fails—

(A) to bear the following statement: "WARNING: THIS FUEL CONTAINS HAZARDOUS WASTES", and

(B) to list the hazardous wastes contained therein.

Beginning ninety days after November 8, 1984, such statement shall be located in a conspicuous place on every such invoice or bill of sale and shall appear in conspicuous and legible type in contrast by typography, layouts, or color with other printed matter on the invoice or bill of sale.

(2) Unless the Administrator determines otherwise as may be necessary to protect human health and the environment, this subsection shall not apply to fuels produced from petroleum refining waste containing oil if—

(A) such materials are generated and reinserted onsite into the refining process;

(B) contaminants are removed; and

(C) such refining waste containing oil is converted along with normal process streams into petroleum-derived fuel products at a facility at which crude oil is refined into petroleum products and which is classified as a number SIC 2911 facility under the Office of Management and Budget Standard Industrial Classification Manual.

(3) Unless the Administrator determines otherwise as may be necessary to protect human health and the environment, this subsection shall not apply to fuels produced from oily materials, resulting from normal petroleum refining, production and transportation practices, if (A) contaminants are removed; and (B) such oily materials are converted along with normal process streams into petroleum-derived fuel products at a facility at which crude oil is refined into petroleum products and which is classified as a number SIC 2911 facility under the Office of Management and Budget Standard Industrial Classification Manual.

(s) Recordkeeping

Not later than fifteen months after November 8, 1984, the Administrator shall promulgate regulations requiring that any person who is required to file a notification in accordance with subparagraph (1), (2), or (3), of section 6930(a) of this title shall maintain such records regarding fuel blending, distribution, or use as may be necessary to protect human health and the environment.

(t) Financial responsibility provisions

(1) Financial responsibility required by subsection (a) of this section may be established in accordance with regulations promulgated by the Administrator by any one, or any combination, of the following: insurance, guarantee, surety bond, letter of credit, or qualification as a self-insurer. In promulgating requirements under this section, the Administrator is authorized to specify policy or other contractual terms, conditions, or defenses which are necessary or are unacceptable in establishing such evidence of financial responsibility in order to effectuate the purposes of this chapter.

(2) In any case where the owner or operator is in bankruptcy, reorganization, or arrangement pursuant to the Federal Bankruptcy Code or where (with reasonable diligence) jurisdiction in any State court or any Federal Court cannot be obtained over an owner or operator likely to be solvent at the time of judgment, any claim arising from conduct for which evidence of financial responsibility must be provided under this section may be asserted directly against the guarantor providing such evidence of financial responsibility. In the case of any action pursuant to this subsection, such guarantor shall be entitled to invoke all rights and defenses which would have been available to the owner or operator if any action had been brought against the owner or operator by the claimant and which would have been available to the guarantor if an action had been brought against the guarantor by the owner or operator.

(3) The total liability of any guarantor shall be limited to the aggregate amount which the guarantor has provided as evidence of financial responsibility to the owner or operator under this chapter. Nothing in this subsection shall be construed to limit any other State or Federal statutory, contractual or common law liability of a guarantor to its owner or operator including, but not limited to, the liability of such guarantor for bad faith either in negotiating or in failing to negotiate the settlement of any claim. Nothing in this subsection shall be construed to diminish the liability of any person under section 9607 or 9611 of this title or other applicable law.

(4) For the purpose of this subsection, the term "guarantor" means any person, other than the owner or operator, who provides evidence of financial responsibility for an owner or operator under this section.

(u) Continuing releases at permitted facilities

Standards promulgated under this section shall require, and a permit issued after November 8, 1984, by the Administrator or a State shall require, corrective action for all releases of hazardous waste or constituents from any solid waste management unit at a treatment, storage, or disposal facility seeking a permit under this subchapter, regardless of the time at which waste was placed in such unit. Permits issued under section 6925 of this title shall contain schedules of compliance for such corrective action (where such corrective action cannot be completed prior to issuance of the permit) and assurances of financial responsibility for completing such corrective action.

(v) Corrective action beyond facility boundary

As promptly as practicable after November 8, 1984, the Administrator shall amend the standards under this section regarding corrective action required at facilities for the treatment, storage, or disposal, of hazardous waste listed or identified under section 6921 of this title to require that corrective action be taken beyond the facility boundary where necessary to protect human health and the environment unless the owner or operator of the facility concerned demonstrates to the satisfaction of the Administrator that, despite the owner or operator's best efforts, the owner or operator was unable to obtain the necessary permission to undertake such action. Such regulations shall take effect immediately upon promulgation, notwithstanding section 6930(b) of this title, and shall apply to—

(1) all facilities operating under permits issued under subsection (c) of this section, and

(2) all landfills, surface impoundments, and waste pile units (including any new units, replacements of existing units, or lateral expansions of existing units) which receive hazardous waste after July 26, 1982.

Pending promulgation of such regulations, the Administrator shall issue corrective action orders for facilities referred to in paragraphs (1) and (2), on a case-by-case basis, consistent with the purposes of this subsection.

(w) Underground tanks

Not later than March 1, 1985, the Administrator shall promulgate final permitting standards under this section for underground tanks that cannot be entered for inspection. Within forty-eight months after November 8, 1984, such standards shall be modified, if necessary, to cover at a minimum all requirements and standards described in section 6991b of this title.

(x) Mining and other special wastes

If (1) solid waste from the extraction, beneficiation or processing of ores and minerals, including phosphate rock and overburden from the mining of uranium, (2) fly ash waste, bottom ash waste, slag waste, and flue gas emission control waste generated primarily from the combustion of coal or other fossil fuels, or (3) cement kiln dust waste, is subject to regulation under this subchapter, the Administrator is authorized to modify the requirements of subsections (c), (d), (e), (f), (g), (*o*), and (u) of this section and section 6925(j) of this title, in the case of landfills or surface impoundments receiving such solid waste, to take into account the special characteristics of such wastes, the practical difficulties associated with implementation of such requirements, and site-specific characteristics, including but not limited to the climate, geology, hydrology and soil chemistry at the site, so long as such modified requirements assure protection of human health and the environment.

(y) Munitions

(1) Not later than 6 months after October 6, 1992, the Administrator shall propose, after consulting with the Secretary of Defense and appropriate State officials, regulations identifying when military munitions become hazardous waste for purposes of this subchapter and providing for the safe transportation and storage of such waste. Not later than 24 months after October 6, 1992, and after notice and opportunity for comment, the Administrator shall promulgate such regulations. Any such regulations shall assure protection of human health and the environment.

(2) For purposes of this subsection, the term "military munitions" includes chemical and conventional munitions.

(Pub. L. No. 89–272, Title II, § 3004, as added by Pub. L. No. 94–580, § 2, 90 Stat. 2807 (Oct. 21, 1976); and amended by Pub. L. No. 96–482, § 9, 94 Stat. 2338 (Oct. 21, 1980); Pub. L. No. 98–616, Title II, §§ 201(a), 202(a), 203, 204(b)(1), 205 to 209, 98 Stat. 3226, 3233, 3234, 3236, 3238 to 3240 (Nov. 8, 1984); Pub. L. No. 102–386, Title I, § 107, 106 Stat. 1513 (Oct. 6, 1992); Pub. L. No. 104–119, §§ 2, 4(2) to (5), 110 Stat. 830, 833 (Mar. 26, 1996).)

[1] So in original. Probably should be followed by a comma.

[2] So spelled in original.

HISTORICAL AND STATUTORY NOTES

References in Text

Section 6922(5) of this title, referred to in subsec. (a)(2), was redesignated section 6922(a)(5) of this title, by Pub. L. No. 98–616, Title II, § 224(a)(1), 98 Stat. 3253 (Nov. 8, 1984).

The Safe Drinking Water Act, referred to in subsec. (c)(3), is Pub. L. No. 93–523, 88 Stat. 1660 (Dec. 16, 1974), as amended, which is codified principally as subchapter XII (section 300f et seq.) of chapter 6A of this title. For complete classification of this Act to the Code, see Short Title of 1974 Amendments note set out under section 201 of this title and Tables.

Section 6979a of this title, referred to in subsec. (f)(4), was in the original a reference to section 7010 of Pub. L. No. 89–272, which was renumbered section 3020 of Pub. L. No. 89–272 by Pub. L. No. 99–339, Title II, § 201(c), 100 Stat. 654 (June 19, 1986), and transferred to section 6939b of this title.

The Paperwork Reduction Act of 1980, referred to in subsec. (g)(3), is Pub. L. 96–511, 94 Stat. 2812 (Dec. 11, 1980), as amended, which was codified principally as chapter 35 of Title 44, 44 U.S.C.A. § 3501 et seq., prior to the general amendment of that chapter by Pub. L. No. 104–13, § 2, 109 Stat. 163 (May 22, 1995). For complete classification, see Short Title of 1980 Amendment note set out under 44 U.S.C.A. § 101 and Tables.

The Federal Bankruptcy Code, referred to in subsec. (t)(2), probably means a reference to Title 11, Bankruptcy.

Transfer of Functions

For transfer of certain enforcement functions of Administrator or other official of the Environmental Protection Agency under this chapter to Federal Inspector, Office of Federal Inspector for the Alaska Natural Gas Transportation System, see note set out under section 6903 of this title.

§ 6925. Permits for treatment, storage, or disposal of hazardous waste

[SWDA § 3005]

(a) Permit requirements

Not later than eighteen months after October 21, 1976, the Administrator shall promulgate regulations requiring each person owning or operating an existing facility or planning to construct a new facility for the treatment, storage, or disposal of hazardous waste identified or listed under this subchapter to have a permit issued pursuant to this section. Such regulations shall take effect on the date provided in section 6930 of this title and upon and after such date the treatment, storage, or disposal of any such hazardous waste and the construction of any new facility for the treatment, storage, or disposal of any such hazardous waste is prohibited except in accordance with such a permit. No permit shall be required under this section in order to construct a facility if such facility is constructed pursuant to an approval issued by the Administrator under section 2605(e) of Title 15 for the incineration of polychlorinated biphenyls and any person owning or operating such a facility may, at any time after operation or construction of such facility has begun, file an application for a permit pursuant to this section authorizing such facility to incinerate hazardous waste identified or listed under this subchapter.

(b) Requirements of permit application

Each application for a permit under this section shall contain such information as may be required under regulations promulgated by the Administrator, including information respecting—

(1) estimates with respect to the composition, quantities, and concentrations of any hazardous waste identified or listed under this subchapter, or combinations of any such hazardous waste and any other solid waste, proposed to be disposed of, treated, transported, or stored, and the time, frequency, or rate of which such waste is proposed to be disposed of, treated, transported, or stored; and

(2) the site at which such hazardous waste or the products of treatment of such hazardous waste will be disposed of, treated, transported to, or stored.

(c) Permit issuance

(1) Upon a determination by the Administrator (or a State, if applicable), of compliance by a facility for which a permit is applied for under this section with the requirements of this section and section 6924 of this title, the Administrator (or the State) shall issue a permit for such facilities. In the event permit applicants propose modification of their facilities, or in the event the Administrator (or the State) determines that modifications are necessary to conform to the requirements under this section and section 6924 of this title, the permit shall specify the time allowed to complete the modifications.

(2) (A) (i) Not later than the date four years after November 8, 1984, in the case of each application under this subsection for a permit for a land disposal facility which was submitted before such date, the Administrator shall issue a final permit pursuant to such application or issue a final denial of such application.

(ii) Not later than the date five years after November 8, 1984, in the case of each application for a permit under this subsection for an incinerator facility which was submitted before such date, the Administrator shall issue a final permit pursuant to such application or issue a final denial of such application.

(B) Not later than the date eight years after November 8, 1984, in the case of each application for a permit under this subsection for any facility (other than a facility referred to in subparagraph (A)) which was submitted before such date, the Administrator shall issue a final permit pursuant to such application or issue a final denial of such application.

(C) The time periods specified in this paragraph shall also apply in the case of any State which is administering an authorized hazardous waste program under section 6926 of this title. Interim status under subsection (e) of this section shall terminate for each facility referred to in subparagraph (A)(ii) or (B) on the expiration of the five- or eight-year period referred to in subparagraph (A) or (B), whichever is applicable, unless the owner or operator of the facility applies for a final determination regarding the issuance of a permit under this subsection within—

(i) two years after November 8, 1984 (in the case of a facility referred to in subparagraph (A)(ii)), or

(ii) four years after November 8, 1984 (in the case of a facility referred to in subparagraph (B)).

(3) Any permit under this section shall be for a fixed term, not to exceed 10 years in the case of any land disposal facility, storage facility, or incinerator or other treatment facility. Each permit for a land disposal facility shall be reviewed five years after date of issuance or reissuance and shall be modified as necessary to assure that the facility continues to comply with the currently applicable requirements of this section and section 6924 of this title. Nothing in this subsection shall preclude the Administrator from reviewing and modifying a permit at any time during its term. Review of any application for a permit renewal shall consider improvements in the state of control and measurement technology as well as changes in applicable regulations. Each permit issued under this section shall contain such terms and conditions as the Administrator (or the State) determines necessary to protect human health and the environment.

(d) Permit revocation

Upon a determination by the Administrator (or by a State, in the case of a State having an authorized hazardous waste program under section 6926 of this title) of noncompliance by a facility having a permit under this chapter with the requirements of this section or section 6924 of this title, the Administrator (or State, in the case of a State having an authorized hazardous waste program under section 6926 of this title) shall revoke such permit.

(e) Interim status

(1) Any person who—

(A) owns or operates a facility required to have a permit under this section which facility—

(i) was in existence on November 19, 1980, or

(ii) is in existence on the effective date of statutory or regulatory changes under this chapter that render the facility subject to the requirement to have a permit under this section,

(B) has complied with the requirements of section 6930(a) of this title, and

(C) has made an application for a permit under this section,

shall be treated as having been issued such permit until such time as final administrative disposition of such application is made, unless the Administrator or other plaintiff proves that final administrative disposition of such application has not been made because of the failure of the applicant to furnish information reasonably required or requested in order to process the application. This paragraph shall not apply to any facility which has been previously denied a permit under this section or if authority to operate the facility under this section has been previously terminated.

(2) In the case of each land disposal facility which has been granted interim status under this subsection before November 8, 1984, interim status shall terminate on the date twelve months after November 8, 1984, unless the owner or operator of such facility—

(A) applies for a final determination regarding the issuance of a permit under subsection (c) of this section for such facility before the date twelve months after November 8, 1984; and

(B) certifies that such facility is in compliance with all applicable groundwater monitoring and financial responsibility requirements.

(3) In the case of each land disposal facility which is in existence on the effective date of statutory or regulatory changes under this chapter that render the facility subject to the requirement to have a permit under this section and which is granted interim status under this subsection, interim status shall terminate on the date twelve months after the date on which the facility first becomes subject to such permit requirement unless the owner or operator of such facility—

(A) applies for a final determination regarding the issuance of a permit under subsection (c) of this section for such facility before the date twelve months after the date on which the facility first becomes subject to such permit requirement; and

(B) certifies that such facility is in compliance with all applicable groundwater monitoring and financial responsibility requirements.

(f) Coal mining wastes and reclamation permits

Notwithstanding subsection (a) through (e) of this section, any surface coal mining and reclamation permit covering any coal mining wastes or overburden which has been issued or approved under the Surface Mining Control and Reclamation Act of 1977 [30 U.S.C.A. § 1201 et seq.] shall be deemed to be a permit issued pursuant to this section with respect to the treatment, storage, or disposal of such wastes or overburden. Regulations promulgated by the Administrator under this subchapter shall not be applicable to treatment, storage, or disposal of coal mining wastes and overburden which are covered by such a permit.

(g) Research, development, and demonstration permits

(1) The Administrator may issue a research, development, and demonstration permit for any hazardous waste treatment facility which proposes to utilize an innovative and experimental hazardous waste treatment technology or process for which permit standards for such experimental activity have not been promulgated under this subchapter. Any such permit shall include such terms and conditions as will assure protection of human health and the environment. Such permits—

(A) shall provide for the construction of such facilities, as necessary, and for operation of the facility for not longer than one year (unless renewed as provided in paragraph (4)), and

(B) shall provide for the receipt and treatment by the facility of only those types and quantities of hazardous waste which the Administrator deems necessary for purposes of determining the efficacy and performance capabilities of the technology or process and the effects of such technology or process on human health and the environment, and

(C) shall include such requirements as the Administrator deems necessary to protect human health and the environment (including, but not limited to, requirements regarding monitoring, operation, insurance or bonding, financial reponsibility,[1] closure, and remedial action), and such requirements as the Administrator deems necessary regarding testing and providing of information to the Administrator with respect to the operation of the facility.

The Administrator may apply the criteria set forth in this paragraph in establishing the conditions of each permit without separate establishment of regulations implementing such criteria.

(2) For the purpose of expediting review and issuance of permits under this subsection, the Administrator may, consistent with the protection of human health and the environment, modify or waive permit application and permit issuance requirements established in the Administrator's general permit regulations except that there may be no modification or waiver of regulations regarding financial responsibility (including insurance) or of procedures established under section 6974(b)(2) of this title regarding public participation.

(3) The Administrator may order an immediate termination of all operations at the facility at any time he determines that termination is necessary to protect human health and the environment.

(4) Any permit issued under this subsection may be renewed not more than three times. Each such renewal shall be for a period of not more than 1 year.

(h) Waste minimization

Effective September 1, 1985, it shall be a condition of any permit issued under this section for the treatment, storage, or disposal of hazardous waste on the premises where such waste was generated that the permittee certify, no less often than annually, that—

(1) the generator of the hazardous waste has a program in place to reduce the volume or quantity and toxicity of such waste to the degree determined by the generator to be economically practicable; and

(2) the proposed method of treatment, storage, or disposal is that practicable method currently available to the generator which minimizes the present and future threat to human health and the environment.

(i) Interim status facilities receiving wastes after July 26, 1982

The standards concerning ground water monitoring, unsaturated zone monitoring, and corrective action, which are applicable under section 6924 of this title to new landfills, surface impoundments, land treatment units, and waste-pile units required to be permitted under subsection (c) of this section shall also apply to any landfill, surface impoundment, land treatment unit, or waste-pile unit qualifying for the authorization to operate under subsection (e) of this section which receives hazardous waste after July 26, 1982.

(j) Interim status surface impoundments

(1) Except as provided in paragraph (2), (3), or (4), each surface impoundment in existence on November 8, 1984, and qualifying for the authorization to operate under subsection (e) of this section shall not receive, store, or treat hazardous waste after the date four years after November 8, 1984, unless such surface impoundment is in compliance with the requirements of section 6924(*o*)(1)(A) of this title which would apply to such impoundment if it were new.

(2) Paragraph (1) of this subsection shall not apply to any surface impoundment which (A) has at least one liner, for which there is no evidence that such liner is leaking; (B) is located more than one-quarter mile from an underground source of drinking water; and (C) is in compliance with generally applicable ground water monitoring requirements for facilities with permits under subsection (c) of this section.

(3) Paragraph (1) of this subsection shall not apply to any surface impoundment which (A) contains treated waste water during the secondary or subsequent phases of an aggressive biological treatment facility subject to a permit issued under section 1342 of Title 33 (or which holds such treated waste water after treatment and prior to discharge); (B) is in compliance with generally applicable ground water monitoring requirements for facilities with permits under subsection (c) of this section; and (C)(i) is part of a facility in compliance with section 1311(b)(2) of Title 33, or (ii) in the case of a facility for which no effluent guidelines required under section 1314(b)(2) of Title 33 are in effect and no permit under section 1342(a)(1) of Title 33 implementing section 1311(b)(2) of Title 33 has been issued, is part of a facility in compliance with a permit under section 1342 of Title 33, which is achieving significant degradation of toxic pollutants and hazardous constituents contained in the untreated waste stream and which has identified those toxic pollutants and hazardous constituents in the untreated waste stream to the appropriate permitting authority.

(4) The Administrator (or the State, in the case of a State with an authorized program), after notice and opportunity for comment, may modify the requirements of paragraph (1) for any surface impoundment if the owner or operator demonstrates that such surface impoundment is located, designed and operated so as to assure that there will be no migration of any hazardous constitutent[2] into ground water or surface water at any future time. The Administrator or the State shall take into account locational criteria established under section 6924(*o*)(7) of this title.

(5) The owner or operator of any surface impoundment potentially subject to paragraph (1) who has reason to believe that on the basis of paragraph (2), (3), or (4) such surface impoundment is not required to comply with the requirements of paragraph (1), shall apply to the Administrator (or the State, in the case of a State with an authorized program) not later than twenty-four months after November 8, 1984, for a determination of the applicability of paragraph (1) (in the case of paragraph (2) or (3)) or for a modification of the requirements of paragraph (1) (in the case of paragraph (4)), with respect to such surface impoundment. Such owner or operator shall provide, with such application, evidence pertinent to such decision, including:

(A) an application for a final determination regarding the issuance of a permit under subsection (c) of this section for such facility, if not previously submitted;

(B) evidence as to compliance with all applicable ground water monitoring requirements and the information and analysis from such monitoring;

(C) all reasonably ascertainable evidence as to whether such surface impoundment is leaking; and

(D) in the case of applications under paragraph (2) or (3), a certification by a registered professional engineer with academic training and experience in ground water hydrology that—

(i) under paragraph (2), the liner of such surface impoundment is designed, constructed, and operated in accordance with applicable requirements, such surface impoundment is more than one-quarter mile from an underground source of drinking water and there is no evidence such liner is leaking; or

(ii) under paragraph (3), based on analysis of those toxic pollutants and hazardous constituents that are likely to be present in the untreated waste stream, such impoundment satisfies the conditions of paragraph (3).

In the case of any surface impoundment for which the owner or operator fails to apply under this paragraph within the time provided by this paragraph or paragraph (6), such surface impoundment shall comply with paragraph (1) notwithstanding paragraph (2), (3), or (4). Within twelve months after receipt of such application and evidence and not later than thirty-six months after November 8, 1984, and after notice and opportunity to comment, the Administrator (or, if appropriate, the State) shall advise such owner or operator on the applicability of paragraph (1) to such surface impoundment or as to whether and how the requirements of paragraph (1) shall be modified and applied to such surface impoundment.

(6) **(A)** In any case in which a surface impoundment becomes subject to paragraph (1) after November 8, 1984, due to the promulgation of additional listings or characteristics for the identification of hazardous waste under section 6921 of this title, the period for compliance in paragraph (1) shall be four years after the date of such promulgation, the period for demonstrations under paragraph (4) and for submission of evidence under paragraph (5) shall be not later than twenty-four months after the date of such promulgation, and the period for the Administrator (or if appropriate, the State) to advise such owners or operators under paragraph (5) shall be not later than thirty-six months after the date of promulgation.

(B) In any case in which a surface impoundment is initially determined to be excluded from the requirements of paragraph (1) but due to a change in condition (including the existence of a leak) no longer satisfies the provisions of paragraph (2), (3), or (4) and therefore becomes subject to paragraph (1), the period for compliance in paragraph (1) shall be two years after the date of discovery of such change of condition, or in the case of a surface impoundment excluded under paragraph (3) three years after such date of discovery.

(7) **(A)** The Administrator shall study and report to the Congress on the number, range of size, construction, likelihood of hazardous constituents migrating into ground water, and potential threat to human health and the environment of existing surface impoundments excluded by paragraph (3) from the requirements of paragraph (1). Such report shall address the need, feasibility, and estimated costs of subjecting such existing surface impoundments to the requirements of paragraph (1).

(B) In the case of any existing surface impoundment or class of surface impoundments from which the Administrator (or the State, in the case of a State with an authorized program) determines hazardous constituents are likely to migrate into ground water, the Administrator (or if appropriate, the State) is authorized to impose such requirements as may be necessary to protect human health and the environment, including the requirements of section 6924(*o*) of this title which would apply to such impoundments if they were new.

(C) In the case of any surface impoundment excluded by paragraph (3) from the requirements of paragraph (1) which is subsequently determined to be leaking, the Administrator (or, if appropriate, the State) shall require compliance with paragraph (1), unless the Administrator (or, if appropriate, the State) determines that such compliance is not necessary to protect human health and the environment.

(8) In the case of any surface impoundment in which the liners and leak detection system have been installed pursuant to the requirements of paragraph (1) and in good faith compliance with section 6924(*o*) of this title and the Administrator's regulations and guidance documents governing liners and leak detection systems, no liner or leak detection system which is different from that which was so installed pursuant to paragraph (1) shall be required for such unit by the Administrator when issuing the first permit under this section to such facility. Nothing in this paragraph shall preclude the Administrator from requiring installation of a new liner when the Administrator has reason to believe that any liner installed pursuant to the requirements of this subsection is leaking.

(9) In the case of any surface impoundment which has been excluded by paragraph (2) on the basis of a liner meeting the definition under paragraph (12)(A)(ii), at the closure of such impoundment the Administrator shall require the owner or operator of such impoundment to remove or decontaminate all waste residues, all contaminated liner material, and contaminated soil to the extent practicable. If all contaminated soil is not removed or decontaminated, the owner or operator of such impoundment shall be required to comply with appropriate post-closure requirements, including but not limited to ground water monitoring and corrective action.

(10) Any incremental cost attributable to the requirements of this subsection or section 6924(*o*) of this title shall not be considered by the Administrator (or the State, in the case of a State with an authorized program under section 1342 of Title 33)—

(A) in establishing effluent limitations and standards under section 1311, 1314, 1316, 1317, or 1342 of Title 33 based on effluent limitations guidelines and standards promulgated any time before twelve months after November 8, 1984; or

(B) in establishing any other effluent limitations to carry out the provisions of section 1311, 1317, or 1342 of Title 33 on or before October 1, 1986.

(11) (A) If the Administrator allows a hazardous waste which is prohibited from one or more methods of land disposal under subsection (d), (e), or (g) of section 6924 of this title (or under regulations promulgated by the Administrator under such subsections) to be placed in a surface impoundment (which is operating pursuant to interim status) for storage or treatment, such impoundment shall meet the requirements that are applicable to new surface impoundments under section 6924(*o*)(1) of this title, unless such impoundment meets the requirements of paragraph (2) or (4).

(B) In the case of any hazardous waste which is prohibited from one or more methods of land disposal under subsection (d), (e), or (g) of section 6924 of this title (or under regulations promulgated by the Administrator under such subsection) the placement or maintenance of such hazardous waste in a surface impoundment for treatment is prohibited as of the effective date of such prohibition unless the treatment residues which are hazardous are, at a minimum, removed for subsequent management within one year of the entry of the waste into the surface impoundment.

(12) (A) For the purposes of paragraph (2)(A) of this subsection, the term "liner" means—

(i) a liner designed, constructed, installed, and operated to prevent hazardous waste from passing into the liner at any time during the active life of the facility; or

(ii) a liner designed, constructed, installed, and operated to prevent hazardous waste from migrating beyond the liner to adjacent subsurface soil, ground water, or surface water at any time during the active life of the facility.

(B) For the purposes of this subsection, the term "aggressive biological treatment facility" means a system of surface impoundments in which the initial impoundment of the secondary treatment segment of the facility utilizes intense mechanical aeration to enhance biological activity to degrade waste water pollutants and

(i) the hydraulic retention time in such initial impoundment is no longer than 5 days under normal operating conditions, on an annual average basis;

(ii) the hydraulic retention time in such initial impoundment is no longer than thirty days under normal operating conditions, on an annual average basis: *Provided,* That the sludge in such impoundment does not constitute a hazardous waste as identified by the extraction procedure toxicity characteristic in effect on November 8, 1984; or

(iii) such system utilizes activated sludge treatment in the first portion of secondary treatment.

(C) For the purposes of this subsection, the term "underground source or[3] drinking water" has the same meaning as provided in regulations under the Safe Drinking Water Act (title XIV of the Public Health Service Act) [42 U.S.C.A. § 300f et seq.].

(13) The Administrator may modify the requirements of paragraph (1) in the case of a surface impoundment for which the owner or operator, prior to October 1, 1984, has entered into, and is in compliance with, a consent order, decree, or agreement with the Administrator or a State with an authorized program mandating corrective action with respect to such surface impoundment that provides a degree of protection of human health and the environment which is at a minimum equivalent to that provided by paragraph (1).

(Pub. L. No. 89–272, Title II, § 3005, as added by Pub. L. No. 94–580, § 2, 90 Stat. 2808 (Oct. 21, 1976); and amended by Pub. L. No. 95–609, § 7(h), 92 Stat. 3082 (Nov. 8, 1978); Pub. L. No. 96–482, §§ 10, 11, 94 Stat. 2338 (Oct. 21, 1980); Pub. L. No. 98–616, Title II, §§ 211 to 213(a), (c), 214(a), 215, 224(b), 243(c), 98 Stat. 3240 to 3243, 3253, 3261 (Nov. 8, 1984); Pub. L. No. 104–119, § 4(6), (7), 110 Stat. 833 (Mar. 26, 1996).)

[1] So in original. Probably should be "responsibility".

[2] So in original. Probably should be "constituent".

[3] So in original. Probably should be "of".

HISTORICAL AND STATUTORY NOTES

References in Text

The Surface Mining Control and Reclamation Act of 1977, referred to in subsec. (f), is Pub. L. No. 95–87, 91 Stat. 445 (Aug. 3, 1977), as amended, which is codified generally as chapter 25 (section 1201 et seq.) of Title 30, Mineral Lands and Mining. For complete classification of this Act to the Code, see Short Title note set out under section 1201 of Title 30 and Tables.

The Safe Drinking Water Act, referred to in subsec. (j)(12)(C), is Pub. L. No. 93–523, 88 Stat. 1660 (Dec. 16, 1974), as amended, which is codified generally as subchapter XII (section 300f et seq.) of chapter 6A of this title. For complete classification of this Act to the Code, see Short Title of 1974 Amendments note set out under section 201 of this title and Tables.

Transfer of Functions

For transfer of certain enforcement functions of Administrator or other official of the Environmental Protection Agency under this chapter to Federal Inspector, Office of Federal Inspector for the Alaska Natural Gas Transportation System, see note set out under section 6903 of this title.

§ 6926. Authorized State hazardous waste programs

[SWDA § 3006]

(a) Federal guidelines

Not later than eighteen months after October 21, 1976, the Administrator, after consultation with State authorities, shall promulgate guidelines to assist States in the Development of State hazardous waste programs.

(b) Authorization of State program

Any State which seeks to administer and enforce a hazardous waste program pursuant to this subchapter may develop and, after notice and opportunity for public hearing, submit to the Administrator an application, in such form as he shall require, for authorization of such program. Within ninety days following submission of an application under this subsection, the Administrator shall issue a notice as to whether or not he expects such program to be authorized, and within ninety days following such notice (and after opportunity for public hearing) he shall publish his findings as to whether or not the conditions listed in items (1), (2), and (3) below have been met. Such State is authorized to carry out such program in lieu of the Federal program under this subchapter in such State and to issue and enforce permits for the storage, treatment, or disposal of hazardous waste (and to enforce permits deemed to have been issued under section 6935(d)(1) of this title) unless, within ninety days following submission of the application the Administrator notifies such State that such program may not be authorized and, within ninety days following such notice and after opportunity for public hearing, he finds that (1) such State program is not equivalent to the Federal program under this subchapter, (2) such program is not consistent with the Federal or State programs applicable in other States, or (3) such program does not provide adequate enforcement of compliance with the requirements of this subchapter. In authorizing a State program, the Administrator may base his findings on the Federal program in effect one year prior to submission of a State's application or in effect on January 26, 1983, whichever is later.

(c) Interim authorization

(1) Any State which has in existence a hazardous waste program pursuant to State law before the date ninety days after the date of promulgation of regulations under sections 6922, 6923, 6924, and 6925 of this title, may submit to the Administrator evidence of such existing program and may request a temporary authorization to carry out such program under this subchapter. The Administrator shall, if the evidence submitted shows the existing State program to be substantially equivalent to the Federal program under this subchapter, grant an interim authorization to the State to carry out such program in lieu of the Federal program pursuant to this subchapter for a period ending no later than January 31, 1986.

(2) The Administrator shall, by rule, establish a date for the expiration of interim authorization under this subsection.

(3) Pending interim or final authorization of a State program for any State which reflects the amendments made by the Hazardous and Solid Waste Amendments of 1984, the State may enter into an agreement with the Administrator under which the State may assist in the administration of the requirements and prohibitions which take effect pursuant to such Amendments.

(4) In the case of a State permit program for any State which is authorized under subsection (b) of this section or under this subsection, until such program is amended to reflect the amendments made by the Hazardous and Solid Waste Amendments of 1984 and such program amendments receive interim or final authorization, the Administrator shall have the authority in such State to issue or deny permits or those portions of permits affected by the requirements and prohibitions established by the Hazardous and Solid Waste Amendments of 1984. The Administrator shall coordinate with States the procedures for issuing such permits.

(d) Effect of State permit

Any action taken by a State under a hazardous waste program authorized under this section shall have the same force and effect as action taken by the Administrator under this subchapter.

(e) Withdrawal of authorization

Whenever the Administrator determines after public hearing that a State is not administering and enforcing a program authorized under this section in accordance with requirements of this section, he shall so notify the State and, if appropriate corrective action is not taken within a reasonable time, not to exceed ninety days, the Administrator shall withdraw authorization of such program and establish a Federal program pursuant to this subchapter. The Administrator shall not withdraw authorization of any such program unless he shall first have notified the State, and made public, in writing, the reasons for such withdrawal.

(f) Availability of information

No State program may be authorized by the Administrator under this section unless—

(1) such program provides for the public availability of information obtained by the State regarding facilities and sites for the treatment, storage, and disposal of hazardous waste; and

(2) such information is available to the public in substantially the same manner, and to the same degree, as would be the case if the Administrator was carrying out the provisions of this subchapter in such State.

(g) Amendments made by 1984 act

(1) Any requirement or prohibition which is applicable to the generation, transportation, treatment, storage, or disposal of hazardous waste and which is imposed under this subchapter pursuant to the amendments made by the Hazardous and Solid Waste Amendments of 1984 shall take effect in each State having an interim or finally authorized State program on the same date as such requirement takes effect in other States. The Administrator shall carry out such requirement directly in each such State unless the State program is finally authorized (or is granted interim authorization as provided in paragraph (2)) with respect to such requirement.

(2) Any State which, before November 8, 1984, has an existing hazardous waste program which has been granted interim or final authorization under this section may submit to the Administrator evidence that such existing program contains (or has been amended to include) any requirement which is substantially equivalent to a requirement referred to in paragraph (1) and may request interim authorization to carry out that requirement under this subchapter. The Administrator shall, if the evidence submitted shows the State requirement to be substantially equivalent to the requirement referred to in paragraph (1), grant an interim authorization to the State to carry out such requirement in lieu of direct administration in the State by the Administrator of such requirement.

(h) State programs for used oil

In the case of used oil which is not listed or identified under this subchapter as a hazardous waste but which is regulated under section 6935 of this title, the provisions of this section regarding State programs shall apply in the same manner and to the same extent as such provisions apply to hazardous waste identified or listed under this subchapter.

(Pub. L. No. 89–272, Title II, § 3006, as added by Pub. L. No. 94–580, § 2, 90 Stat. 2809 (Oct. 21, 1976); and amended by Pub. L. No. 95–609, § 7(i), 92 Stat. 3082 (Nov. 8, 1978); Pub. L. No. 98–616, Title II, §§ 225, 226(a), 227, 228, 241(b)(2), 98 Stat. 3254, 3255, 3260 (Nov. 8, 1984); Pub. L. No. 99–499, Title II, § 205(j), 100 Stat. 1703 (Oct. 17, 1986).)

HISTORICAL AND STATUTORY NOTES

References in Text

Section 6935(d)(1) of this title, referred to in subsec. (b), was in the original a reference to section 3012(d)(1) of Pub. L. No. 89–272, which was renumbered section 3014(d)(1) of Pub. L. No. 89–272 by Pub. L. No. 98–616 and is codified as section 6935(d)(1) of this title.

The Hazardous and Solid Waste Amendments of 1984, referred to in subsecs. (c)(3), (4), and (g), is Pub. L. No. 98–616, 98 Stat. 3221 (Nov. 8, 1984), which amended this chapter. For complete classification of this Act to the Code, see Short Title of 1984 Amendments note set out under section 6901 of this title and Tables.

Effective and Applicability Provisions

1986 Acts. Amendment by Pub. L. No. 99–499 effective Oct. 17, 1986, see section 4 of Pub. L. No. 99–499, set out as a note under section 9601 of this title.

1984 Acts. Section 226(b) of Pub. L. No. 98–616 provided that: "The amendment made by subsection (a) [enacting subsec. (f) of this section] shall apply with respect to State programs authorized under section 3006 [this section] before, on, or after the date of the enactment of the Hazardous and Solid Waste Amendments of 1984 [Nov. 8, 1984]."

Transfer of Functions

For transfer of certain enforcement functions of Administrator or other official of the Environmental Protection Agency under this chapter to Federal Inspector, Office of Federal Inspector for the Alaska Natural Gas Transportation System, see note set out under section 6903 of this title.

§ 6927. Inspections

[SWDA § 3007]

(a) Access entry

For purposes of developing or assisting in the development of any regulation or enforcing the provisions of this chapter, any person who generates, stores, treats, transports, disposes of, or otherwise handles or has handled hazardous wastes shall, upon request of any officer, employee or representative of the Environmental Protection Agency, duly designated by the Administrator, or upon request of any duly designated officer, employee or representative of a State having an authorized hazardous waste program, furnish information relating to such wastes and permit such person at all reasonable times to have access to, and to copy all records relating to such wastes. For the purposes of developing or assisting in the development of any regulation or enforcing the provisions of this chapter, such officers, employees or representatives are authorized—

(1) to enter at reasonable times any establishment or other place where hazardous wastes are or have been generated, stored, treated, disposed of, or transported from;

(2) to inspect and obtain samples from any person of any such wastes and samples of any containers or labeling for such wastes.

Each such inspection shall be commenced and completed with reasonable promptness. If the officer, employee or representative obtains any samples, prior to leaving the premises, he shall give to the owner, operator, or agent in charge a receipt describing the sample obtained and if requested a portion of each such sample equal in volume or weight to the portion retained. If any analysis is made of such samples, a copy of the results of such analysis shall be furnished promptly to the owner, operator, or agent in charge.

(b) Availability to public

(1) Any records, reports, or information (including records, reports, or information obtained by representatives of the Environmental Protection Agency) obtained from any person under this section shall be available to the public, except that upon a showing satisfactory to the Administrator (or the State, as the case may be) by any person that records, reports, or information, or particular part thereof, to which the Administrator (or the State, as the case may be) or any officer, employee or representative thereof has access under this section if made public, would divulge information entitled to protection under section 1905 of Title 18, such information or particular portion thereof shall be considered confidential in accordance with the purposes of that section, except that such record, report, document, or information may be disclosed to other officers, employees, or authorized representatives of the United States concerned with carrying out this chapter, or when relevant in any proceeding under this chapter.

(2) Any person not subject to the provisions of section 1905 of Title 18 who knowingly and willfully divulges or discloses any information entitled to protection under this subsection shall, upon conviction, be subject to a fine of not more than $5,000 or to imprisonment not to exceed one year, or both.

(3) In submitting data under this chapter, a person required to provide such data may—

(A) designate the data which such person believes is entitled to protection under this subsection, and

(B) submit such designated data separately from other data submitted under this chapter.

A designation under this paragraph shall be made in writing and in such manner as the Administrator may prescribe.

(4) Notwithstanding any limitation contained in this section or any other provision of law, all information reported to, or otherwise obtained by, the Administrator (or any representative of the Administrator) under this chapter shall be made available, upon written request of any duly authorized committee of the Congress, to such committee.

(c) Federal facility inspections

The Administrator shall undertake on an annual basis a thorough inspection of each facility for the treatment, storage, or disposal of hazardous waste which is owned or operated by a department, agency, or instrumentality of the United States to enforce its compliance with this subchapter and the regulations promulgated thereunder. Any State with an authorized hazardous waste program also may conduct an inspection of any such facility for purposes of enforcing the facility's compliance with the State hazardous waste program. The records of such inspections shall be available to the public as provided in subsection (b) of this section. The department, agency, or instrumentality owning or operating each such facility shall reimburse the Environmental Protection Agency for the costs of the inspection of the facility. With respect to the first inspection of each such facility occurring after October 6, 1992, the Administrator shall conduct a comprehensive ground water monitoring evaluation at the facility, unless such an evaluation was conducted during the 12-month period preceding October 6, 1992.

(d) State-operated facilities

The Administrator shall annually undertake a thorough inspection of every facility for the treatment, storage, or disposal of hazardous waste which is operated by a State or local government for which a permit is required under section 6925 of this title. The records of such inspection shall be available to the public as provided in subsection (b) of this section.

(e) Mandatory inspections

(1) The Administrator (or the State in the case of a State having an authorized hazardous waste program under this subchapter) shall commence a program to thoroughly inspect every facility for the treatment, storage, or disposal of hazardous waste for which a permit is required under section 6925 of this title no less often than every two years as to its compliance with this subchapter (and the regulations promulgated under this subchapter). Such inspections shall commence not later than twelve months after November 8, 1984. The Administrator shall, after notice and opportunity for public comment, promulgate regulations governing the minimum frequency and manner of such inspections, including the manner in which records of such inspections shall be maintained and the manner in which reports of such inspections shall be filed. The Administrator may distinguish between classes and categories of facilities commensurate with the risks posed by each class or category.

(2) Not later than six months after November 8, 1984, the Administrator shall submit to the Congress a report on the potential for inspections of hazardous waste treatment, storage, or disposal facilities by nongovernmental inspectors as a supplement to inspections conducted by officers, employees, or representatives of the Environmental Protection Agency or States having authorized hazardous waste programs or operating under a cooperative agreement with the Administrator. Such report shall be prepared in cooperation with the States, insurance companies offering environmental impairment insurance, independent companies providing inspection services, and other such groups as appropriate. Such report shall contain recommendations on provisions and requirements for a program of private inspections to supplement governmental inspections.

(Pub. L. No. 89–272, Title II, § 3007, as added by Pub. L. No. 94–580, § 2, 90 Stat. 2810 (Oct. 21, 1976); as amended by Pub. L. No. 95–609, § 7(j), 92 Stat. 3082 (Nov. 8, 1978); Pub. L. No. 96–482, § 12, 94 Stat. 2339 (Oct. 21, 1980); Pub. L. No. 98–616, Title II, §§ 229 to 231, Title V, § 502(a), 98 Stat. 3255, 3256, 3276 (Nov. 8, 1984); Pub. L. No. 102–386, Title I, § 104, 106 Stat. 1507 (Oct. 6, 1992).)

HISTORICAL AND STATUTORY NOTES

Codifications

Amendment by section 12(b)(4) of Pub. L. No. 96–482, directing that subsec. (b) of this section be amended by inserting "(including records, reports, or information obtained by representatives of the Environmental Protection Agency)", without specifying where in text such phrase be inserted, could not be executed.

Transfer of Functions

For transfer of certain enforcement functions of Administrator or other official of the Environmental Protection Agency under this chapter to Federal Inspector, Office of Federal Inspector for the Alaska Natural Gas Transportation System, see note set out under section 6903 of this title.

§ 6928. Federal enforcement

[SWDA § 3008]

(a) Compliance orders

(1) Except as provided in paragraph (2), whenever on the basis of any information the Administrator determines that any person has violated or is in violation of any requirement of this subchapter, the Administrator may issue an order assessing a civil penalty for any past or current violation, requiring compliance immediately or within a specified time period, or both, or the Administrator may commence a civil action in the United States district court in the district in which the violation occurred for appropriate relief, including a temporary or permanent injunction.

(2) In the case of a violation of any requirement of this subchapter where such violation occurs in a State which is authorized to carry out a hazardous waste program under section 6926 of this title, the Administrator shall give notice to the State in which such violation has occurred prior to issuing an order or commencing a civil action under this section.

(3) Any order issued pursuant to this subsection may include a suspension or revocation of any permit issued by the Administrator or a State under this subchapter and shall state with reasonable specificity the nature of the violation. Any penalty assessed in the order shall not exceed $25,000 per day of noncompliance for each violation of a requirement of this subchapter. In assessing such a penalty, the Administrator shall take into account the seriousness of the violation and any good faith efforts to comply with applicable requirements.

(b) Public hearing

Any order issued under this section shall become final unless, no later than thirty days after the order is served, the person or persons named therein request a public hearing. Upon such request the Administrator shall promptly conduct a public hearing. In connection with any proceeding under this section the Administrator may issue subpenas for the attendance and testimony of witnesses and the production of relevant papers, books, and documents, and may promulgate rules for discovery procedures.

(c) Violation of compliance orders

If a violator fails to take corrective action within the time specified in a compliance order, the Administrator may assess a civil penalty of not more than $25,000 for each day of continued noncompliance with the order and the Administrator may suspend or revoke any permit issued to the violator (whether issued by the Administrator or the State).

(d) Criminal penalties

Any person who—

(1) knowingly transports or causes to be transported any hazardous waste identified or listed under this subchapter to a facility which does not have a permit under this subchapter, or pursuant to title I of the Marine Protection, Research, and Sanctuaries Act (86 Stat. 1052) [33 U.S.C.A. § 1411 et seq.],

(2) knowingly treats, stores, or disposes of any hazardous waste identified or listed under this subchapter—

(A) without a permit under this subchapter or pursuant to title I of the Marine Protection, Research, and Sanctuaries Act (86 Stat. 1052) [33 U.S.C.A. § 1411 et seq.]; or

(B) in knowing violation of any material condition or requirement of such permit; or

(C) in knowing violation of any material condition or requirement of any applicable interim status regulations or standards;

(3) knowingly omits material information or makes any false material statement or representation in any application, label, manifest, record, report, permit, or other document filed, maintained, or used for purposes of compliance with regulations promulgated by the Administrator (or by a State in the case of an authorized State program) under this subchapter;

(4) knowingly generates, stores, treats, transports, disposes of, exports, or otherwise handles any hazardous waste or any used oil not identified or listed as a hazardous waste under this subchapter (whether such activity took place before or takes place after November 8, 1984) and who knowingly destroys, alters, conceals, or fails to file any record, application, manifest, report, or other document required to be maintained or filed for purposes of compliance with regulations promulgated by the Administrator (or by a State in the case of an authorized State program) under this subchapter;

(5) knowingly transports without a manifest, or causes to be transported without a manifest, any hazardous waste or any used oil not identified or listed as a hazardous waste under this subchapter required by regulations promulgated under this subchapter (or by a State in the case of a State program authorized under this subchapter) to be accompanied by a manifest;

(6) knowingly exports a hazardous waste identified or listed under this subchapter (A) without the consent of the receiving country or, (B) where there exists an international agreement between the United States and the government of the receiving country establishing notice, export, and enforcement procedures for the transportation, treatment, storage, and disposal of hazardous wastes, in a manner which is not in conformance with such agreement; or

(7) knowingly stores, treats, transports, or causes to be transported, disposes of, or otherwise handles any used oil not identified or listed as a hazardous waste under this subchapter—

(A) in knowing violation of any material condition or requirement of a permit under this subchapter; or

(B) in knowing violation of any material condition or requirement of any applicable regulations or standards under this chapter;

shall, upon conviction, be subject to a fine of not more than $50,000 for each day of violation, or imprisonment not to exceed two years (five years in the case of a violation of paragraph (1) or (2)), or both. If the conviction is for a violation committed after a first conviction of such person under this paragraph, the maximum punishment under the respective paragraph shall be doubled with respect to both fine and imprisonment.

(e) Knowing endangerment

Any person who knowingly transports, treats, stores, disposes of, or exports any hazardous waste identified or listed under this subchapter or used oil not identified or listed as a hazardous waste under this subchapter in violation of paragraph (1), (2), (3), (4), (5), (6), or (7) of subsection (d) of this section who knows at that time that he thereby places another person in imminent danger of death or serious bodily injury, shall, upon conviction, be subject to a fine of not more than $250,000 or imprisonment for not more than fifteen years, or both. A defendant that is an organization shall, upon conviction of violating this subsection, be subject to a fine of not more than $1,000,000.

(f) Special rules

For the purposes of subsection (e) of this section—

(1) A person's state of mind is knowing with respect to—

(A) his conduct, if he is aware of the nature of his conduct;

(B) an existing circumstance, if he is aware or believes that the circumstance exists; or

(C) a result of his conduct, if he is aware or believes that his conduct is substantially certain to cause danger of death or serious bodily injury.

(2) In determining whether a defendant who is a natural person knew that his conduct placed another person in imminent danger of death or serious bodily injury—

(A) the person is responsible only for actual awareness or actual belief that he possessed; and

(B) knowledge possessed by a person other than the defendant but not by the defendant himself may not be attributed to the defendant;

Provided, That in proving the defendant's possession of actual knowledge, circumstantial evidence may be used, including evidence that the defendant took affirmative steps to shield himself from relevant information.

(3) It is an affirmative defense to a prosecution that the conduct charged was consented to by the person endangered and that the danger and conduct charged were reasonably foreseeable hazards of—

(A) an occupation, a business, or a profession; or

(B) medical treatment or medical or scientific experimentation conducted by professionally approved methods and such other person had been made aware of the risks involved prior to giving consent.

The defendant may establish an affirmative defense under this subsection by a preponderance of the evidence.

(4) All general defenses, affirmative defenses, and bars to prosecution that may apply with respect to other Federal criminal offenses may apply under subsection (e) of this section and shall be determined by the courts of the United States according to the principles of common law as they may be interpreted in the light of reason and experience. Concepts of justification and excuse applicable under this section may be developed in the light of reason and experience.

(5) The term "organization" means a legal entity, other than a government, established or organized for any purpose, and such term includes a corporation, company, association, firm, partnership, joint stock company, foundation, institution, trust, society, union, or any other association of persons.

(6) The term "serious bodily injury" means—

(A) bodily injury which involves a substantial risk of death;

(B) unconsciousness;

(C) extreme physical pain;

(D) protracted and obvious disfigurement; or

(E) protracted loss or impairment of the function of a bodily member, organ, or mental faculty.

(g) Civil penalty

Any person who violates any requirement of this subchapter shall be liable to the United States for a civil penalty in an amount not to exceed $25,000 for each such violation. Each day of such violation shall, for purposes of this subsection, constitute a separate violation.

(h) Interim status corrective action orders

(1) Whenever on the basis of any information the Administrator determines that there is or has been a release of hazardous waste into the environment from a facility authorized to operate under section 6925(e) of this title, the Administrator may issue an order requiring corrective action or such other response measure as he deems necessary to protect human health or the environment or the Administrator may commence a civil action in the United States district court in the district in which the facility is located for appropriate relief, including a temporary or permanent injunction.

(2) Any order issued under this subsection may include a suspension or revocation of authorization to operate under section 6925(e) of this title, shall state with reasonable specificity the nature of the required corrective action or other response measure, and shall specify a time for compliance. If any person named in an order fails to comply with the order, the Administrator may assess, and such person shall be liable to the United States for, a civil penalty in an amount not to exceed $25,000 for each day of noncompliance with the order.

(Pub. L. No. 89–272, Title II, § 3008, as added by Pub. L. No. 94–580, § 2, 90 Stat. 2811 (Oct. 21, 1976); and amended by Pub. L. No. 95–609, § 7(k), 92 Stat. 3082 (Nov. 8, 1978); Pub. L. No. 96–482, § 13, 94 Stat. 2339 (Oct. 21, 1980); Pub. L. No. 98–616, Title II, §§ 232, 233, 245(c), Title IV, § 403(d)(1) to (3), 98 Stat. 3256, 3257, 3264, 3272 (Nov. 8, 1984); Pub. L. No. 99–499, Title II, § 205(i), 100 Stat. 1703 (Oct. 17, 1986).)

HISTORICAL AND STATUTORY NOTES

References in Text

The Marine Protection, Research, and Sanctuaries Act, referred to in subsec. (d)(1) and (2)(A), probably means the Marine Protection, Research, and Sanctuaries Act of 1972, Pub. L. No. 92–532, 86 Stat. 1052 (Oct. 23, 1972), as amended. Title I of the Marine Protection, Research, and Sanctuaries Act of 1972 is codified generally as subchapter I (section 1411 et seq.) of chapter 27 of Title 33, Navigation and Navigable Waters. For complete classification of this Act to the Code, see Short Title note set out under section 1401 of Title 33 and Tables.

Effective and Applicability Provisions

1986 Acts. Amendment by Pub. L. No. 99–499 effective Oct. 17, 1986, see section 4 of Pub. L. No. 99–499, set out as a note under section 9601 of this title.

Transfer of Functions

For transfer of certain enforcement functions of Administrator or other official of the Environmental Protection Agency under this chapter to Federal Inspector, Office of Federal Inspector for the Alaska Natural Gas Transportation System, see note set out under section 6903 of this title.

§ 6929. Retention of State authority

Upon the effective date of regulations under this subchapter no State or political subdivision may impose any requirements less stringent than those authorized under this subchapter respecting the same matter as governed by such regulations, except that if application of a regulation with respect to any matter under this subchapter is postponed or enjoined by the action of any court, no State or political subdivision shall be prohibited from acting with respect to the same aspect of such matter until such time as such regulation takes effect. Nothing in this chapter shall be construed to prohibit any State or political subdivision thereof from imposing any requirements, including those for site selection, which are more stringent than those imposed by such regulations. Nothing in this chapter (or in any regulation adopted under this chapter) shall be construed to prohibit any State from requiring that the State be provided with a copy of each manifest used in connection with hazardous waste which is generated within that State or transported to a treatment, storage, or disposal facility within that State.

(Pub. L. No. 89–272, Title II, § 3009, as added by Pub. L. No. 94–580, § 2, 90 Stat. 2812 (Oct. 21, 1976); and amended by Pub. L. No. 96–482, § 14, 94 Stat. 2342 (Oct. 21, 1980); Pub. L. No. 98–616, Title II, § 213(b), 98 Stat. 3242 (Nov. 8, 1984).)

§ 6930. Effective date

[SWDA § 3010]

(a) Preliminary notification

Not later than ninety days after promulgation of regulations under section 6921 of this title identifying by its characteristics or listing any substance as hazardous waste subject to this subchapter, any person generating or transporting such substance or owning or operating a facility for treatment, storage, or disposal of such substance shall file with the Administrator (or with States having authorized hazardous waste permit programs under section 6926 of this title) a notification stating the location and general description of such activity and the identified or listed hazardous wastes handled by such person. Not later than fifteen months after November 8, 1984—

(1) the owner or operator of any facility which produces a fuel (A) from any hazardous waste identified or listed under section 6921 of this title, (B) from such hazardous waste identified or listed under section 6921 of this title and any other material, (C) from used oil, or (D) from used oil and any other material;

(2) the owner or operator of any facility (other than a single- or two-family residence) which burns for purposes of energy recovery any fuel produced as provided in paragraph (1) or any fuel which otherwise contains used oil or any hazardous waste identified or listed under section 6921 of this title; and

(3) any person who distributes or markets any fuel which is produced as provided in paragraph (1) or any fuel which otherwise contains used oil or any hazardous waste identified or listed under section 6921 of this title[1]

shall file with the Administrator (and with the State in the case of a State with an authorized hazardous waste program) a notification stating the location and general description of the facility, together with a description of the identified or listed hazardous waste involved and, in the case of a facility referred to in paragraph (1) or (2), a description of the production or energy recovery activity carried out at the facility and such other information as the Administrator deems necessary. For purposes of the preceding provisions, the term "hazardous waste listed under section 6921 of this title" also includes any commercial chemical product which is listed under section 6921 of this title and which, in lieu of its original intended use, is (i) produced for use as (or as a component of) a fuel, (ii) distributed for use as a fuel, or (iii) burned as a fuel.

Notification shall not be required under the second sentence of this subsection in the case of facilities (such as residential boilers) where the Administrator determines that such notification is not necessary in order for the Administrator to obtain sufficient information respecting current practices of facilities using hazardous waste for energy recovery. Nothing in this subsection shall be construed to affect or impair the provisions of section 6921(b)(3) of this title. Nothing in this subsection shall affect regulatory determinations under section 6935 of this title. In revising any regulation under section 6921 of this title identifying additional characteristics of hazardous waste or listing any additional substance as hazardous waste subject to this subchapter, the Administrator may require any person referred to in the preceding provisions to file with the Administrator (or with States having authorized hazardous waste permit programs under section 6926 of this title) the notification described in the preceding provisions. Not more than one such notification shall be required to be filed with respect to the same substance. No identified or listed hazardous waste subject to this subchapter may be transported, treated, stored, or disposed of unless notification has been given as required under this subsection.

(b) Effective date of regulation

The regulations under this subchapter respecting requirements applicable to the generation, transportation, treatment, storage, or disposal of hazardous waste (including requirements respecting permits for such treatment, storage, or disposal) shall take effect on the date six months after the date of promulgation thereof (or six months after the date of revision in the case of any regulation which is revised after the date required for promulgation thereof). At the time a regulation is promulgated, the Administrator may provide for a shorter period prior to the effective date, or an immediate effective date for:

(1) a regulation with which the Administrator finds the regulated community does not need six months to come into compliance;

(2) a regulation which responds to an emergency situation; or

(3) other good cause found and published with the regulation.

(Pub. L. No. 89–272, Title II, § 3010, as added by Pub. L. No. 94–580, § 2, 90 Stat. 2812 (Oct. 21, 1976); and amended by Pub. L. No. 96–482, § 15, 94 Stat. 2342 (Oct. 21, 1980); Pub. L. No. 98–616, Title II, §§ 204(a), 234, 98 Stat. 3235, 3258 (Nov. 8, 1984).)

[1] So in original. Probably should be followed by a semicolon.

HISTORICAL AND STATUTORY NOTES

Transfer of Functions

For transfer of certain enforcement functions of Administrator or other official of the Environmental Protection Agency under this chapter to Federal Inspector, Office of Federal Inspector for the Alaska Natural Gas Transportation System, see note set out under section 6903 of this title.

§ 6931. Authorization of assistance to States

[SWDA § 3011]

(a) Authorization of appropriations

There is authorized to be appropriated $25,000,000 for each of the fiscal years 1978 and 1979[1] $20,000,000 for fiscal year 1980, $35,000,000 for fiscal year 1981, $40,000,000 for the fiscal year 1982, $55,000,000 for the fiscal year 1985, $60,000,000 for the fiscal year 1986, $60,000,000 for the fiscal year 1987, and $60,000,000 for the fiscal year 1988 to be used to make grants to the States for purposes of assisting the States in the development and implementation of authorized State hazardous waste programs.

(b) Allocation

Amounts authorized to be appropriated under subsection (a) of this section shall be allocated among the States on the basis of regulations promulgated by the Administrator, after consultation with the States, which take into account, the extent to which hazardous waste is generated, transported, treated, stored, and disposed of within such State, the extent of exposure of human beings and the environment within such State to such waste, and such other factors as the Administrator deems appropriate.

(c) Activities included

State hazardous waste programs for which grants may be made under subsection (a) of this section may include (but shall not be limited to) planning for hazardous waste treatment, storage and disposal facilities, and the development and execution of programs to protect health and the environment from inactive facilities which may contain hazardous waste.

(Pub. L. No. 89–272, Title II, § 3011, as added by Pub. L. No. 94–580, § 2, 90 Stat. 2812 (Oct. 21, 1976); and amended by Pub. L. No. 96–482, §§ 16, 31(b), 94 Stat. 2342, 2352 (Oct. 21, 1980); Pub. L. No. 98–616, § 2(b), 98 Stat. 3222 (Nov. 8, 1984).)

[1] So in original. Probably should be followed by a comma.

HISTORICAL AND STATUTORY NOTES

Transfer of Functions

For transfer of certain enforcement functions of Administrator or other official of the Environmental Protection Agency under this chapter to Federal Inspector, Office of Federal Inspector for the Alaska Natural Gas Transportation System, see note set out under section 6903 of this title.

§ 6932. Transferred

HISTORICAL AND STATUTORY NOTES

Codifications

Section 6932, Pub. L. No. 89–272, Title II, § 3012, as added by Pub. L. No. 96–463, § 7(a), 94 Stat. 2057 (Oct. 15, 1980), was redesignated section 3014 of Pub. L. No. 89–272, by Pub. L. No. 98–616, Title V, § 502(g)(1), 98 Stat. 3277 (Nov. 8, 1984), and was transferred to section 6935 of this title.

§ 6933. Hazardous waste site inventory

[SWDA § 3012]

(a) State inventory programs

Each State shall, as expeditiously as practicable, undertake a continuing program to compile, publish, and submit to the Administrator an inventory describing the location of each site within such State at which hazardous waste has at any time been stored or disposed of. Such inventory shall contain—

(1) a description of the location of the sites at which any such storage or disposal has taken place before the date on which permits are required under section 6925 of this title for such storage or disposal;

(2) such information relating to the amount, nature, and toxicity of the hazardous waste at each such site as may be practicable to obtain and as may be necessary to determine the extent of any health hazard which may be associated with such site;

(3) the name and address, or corporate headquarters of, the owner of each such site, determined as of the date of preparation of the inventory;

(4) an identification of the types or techniques of waste treatment or disposal which have been used at each such site; and

(5) information concerning the current status of the site, including information respecting whether or not hazardous waste is currently being treated or disposed of at such site (and if not, the date on which such activity ceased) and information respecting the nature of any other activity currently carried out at such site.

For purposes of assisting the States in compiling information under this section, the Administrator shall make available to each State undertaking a program under this section such information as is available to him concerning the items specified in paragraphs (1) through (5) with respect to the sites within such State, including such information as the Administrator is able to obtain from other agencies or departments of the United States and from surveys and studies carried out by any committee or subcommittee of the Congress.

Any State may exercise the authority of section 6927 of this title for purposes of this section in the same manner and to the same extent as provided in such section in the case of States having an authorized hazardous waste program, and any State may by order require any person to submit such information as may be necessary to compile the data referred to in paragraphs (1) through (5).

(b) Environmental Protection Agency program

If the Administrator determines that any State program under subsection (a) of this section is not adequately providing information respecting the sites in such State referred to in subsection (a) of this section, the Administrator shall notify the State. If within ninety days following such notification, the State program has not been revised or amended in such manner as will adequately provide such information, the Administrator shall carry out the inventory program in such State. In any such case—

(1) the Administrator shall have the authorities provided with respect to State programs under subsection (a) of this section;

(2) the funds allocated under subsection (c) of this section for grants to States under this section may be used by the Administrator for carrying out such program in such State; and

(3) no further expenditure may be made for grants to such State under this section until such time as the Administrator determines that such State is carrying out, or will carry out, an inventory program which meets the requirements of this section.

(c) Grants

(1) Upon receipt of an application submitted by any State to carry out a program under this section, the Administrator may make grants to the States for purposes of carrying out such a program. Grants under this section shall be allocated among the several States by the Administrator based upon such regulations as he prescribes to carry out the purposes of this section. The Administrator may make grants to any State which has conducted an inventory program which effectively carried out the purposes of this section before October 21, 1980, to reimburse such State for all, or any portion of, the costs incurred by such State in conducting such program.

(2) There are authorized to be appropriated to carry out this section $25,000,000 for each of the fiscal years 1985 through 1988.

(d) No impediment to immediate remedial action

Nothing in this section shall be construed to provide that the Administrator or any State should, pending completion of the inventory required under this section, postpone undertaking any enforcement or remedial action with respect to any site at which hazardous waste has been treated, stored, or disposed of.

(Pub. L. No. 89–272, Title II, § 3012, as added by Pub. L. No. 96–482, § 17(a), 94 Stat. 2342 (Oct. 21, 1980); and amended by Pub. L. No. 98–616, § 2(c), 98 Stat. 3222 (Nov. 8, 1984).)

HISTORICAL AND STATUTORY NOTES

Codifications

Another section 3012 of Pub. L. No. 89–272, providing for restrictions on recycled oil, was enacted by Pub. L. No. 96–463, § 7(a), 94 Stat. 2057 (Oct. 15, 1980), was redesignated section 3014 of Pub. L. No. 89–272, and is codified as section 6935 of this title.

Transfer of Functions

For transfer of certain enforcement functions of Administrator or other official of the Environmental Protection Agency under this chapter to Federal Inspector, Office of Federal Inspector for the Alaska Natural Gas Transportation System, see note set out under section 6903 of this title.

§ 6934. Monitoring, analysis, and testing

[SWDA § 3013]

(a) Authority of Administrator

If the Administrator determines, upon receipt of any information, that—

(1) the presence of any hazardous waste at a facility or site at which hazardous waste is, or has been, stored, treated, or disposed of, or

(2) the release of any such waste from such facility or site

may present a substantial hazard to human health or the environment, he may issue an order requiring the owner or operator of such facility or site to conduct such monitoring, testing, analysis, and reporting with respect to such facility or site as the Administrator deems reasonable to ascertain the nature and extent of such hazard.

(b) Previous owners and operators

In the case of any facility or site not in operation at the time a determination is made under subsection (a) of this section with respect to the facility or site, if the Administrator finds that the owner of such facility or site could not reasonably be expected to have actual knowledge of the presence of hazardous waste at such facility or site and of its potential for release, he may issue an order requiring the most recent previous owner or operator of such facility or site who could reasonably be expected to have such actual knowledge to carry out the actions referred to in subsection (a) of this section.

(c) Proposal

An order under subsection (a) or (b) of this section shall require the person to whom such order is issued to submit to the Administrator within 30 days from the issuance of such order a proposal for carrying out the required monitoring, testing, analysis, and reporting. The Administrator may, after providing such person with an opportunity to confer with the Administrator respecting such proposal, require such person to carry out such monitoring, testing, analysis, and reporting in accordance with such proposal, and such modifications in such proposal as the Administrator deems reasonable to ascertain the nature and extent of the hazard.

(d) Monitoring, etc., carried out by Administrator

(1) If the Administrator determines that no owner or operator referred to in subsection (a) or (b) of this section is able to conduct monitoring, testing, analysis, or reporting satisfactory to the Administrator, if the Administrator deems any such action carried out by an owner or operator to be unsatisfactory, or if the Administrator cannot initially determine that there is an owner or operator referred to in subsection (a) or (b) of this section who is able to conduct such monitoring, testing, analysis, or reporting, he may—

(A) conduct monitoring, testing, or analysis (or any combination thereof) which he deems reasonable to ascertain the nature and extent of the hazard associated with the site concerned, or

(B) authorize a State or local authority or other person to carry out any such action,

and require, by order, the owner or operator referred to in subsection (a) or (b) of this section to reimburse the Administrator or other authority or person for the costs of such activity.

(2) No order may be issued under this subsection requiring reimbursement of the costs of any action carried out by the Administrator which confirms the results of an order issued under subsection (a) or (b) of this section.

(3) For purposes of carrying out this subsection, the Administrator or any authority or other person authorized under paragraph (1), may exercise the authorities set forth in section 6927 of this title.

(e) Enforcement

The Administrator may commence a civil action against any person who fails or refuses to comply with any order issued under this section. Such action shall be brought in the United States district court in which the defendant is located, resides, or is doing business. Such court shall have jurisdiction to require compliance with such order and to assess a civil penalty of not to exceed $5,000 for each day during which such failure or refusal occurs.

(Pub. L. No. 89–272, Title II, § 3013, as added by Pub. L. No. 96–482, § 17(a), 94 Stat. 2344 (Oct. 21, 1980).)

HISTORICAL AND STATUTORY NOTES

Transfer of Functions

For transfer of certain enforcement functions of Administrator or other official of the Environmental Protection Agency under this chapter to Federal Inspector, Office of Federal Inspector for the Alaska Natural Gas Transportation System, see note set out under section 6903 of this title.

§ 6935. Restrictions on recycled oil

[SWDA § 3014]

(a) In general

Not later than one year after October 15, 1980, the Administrator shall promulgate regulations establishing such performance standards and other requirements as may be necessary to protect the public health and the environment from hazards associated with recycled oil. In developing such regulations, the Administrator shall conduct an analysis of the economic impact of the regulations on the oil recycling industry. The Administrator shall ensure that such regulations do not discourage the recovery or recycling of used oil, consistent with the protection of human health and the environment.

(b) Identification or listing of used oil as hazardous waste

Not later than twelve months after November 8, 1984, the Administrator shall propose whether to list or identify used automobile and truck crankcase oil as hazardous waste under section 6921 of this title. Not later than twenty-four months after November 8, 1984, the Administrator shall make a final determination whether to list or identify used automobile and truck crankcase oil and other used oil as hazardous wastes under section 6921 of this title.

(c) Used oil which is recycled

(1) With respect to generators and transporters of used oil identified or listed as a hazardous waste under section 6921 of this title, the standards promulgated under section[1] 6921(d), 6922, and 6923 of this title shall not apply to such used oil if such used oil is recycled.

(2) (A) In the case of used oil which is exempt under paragraph (1), not later than twenty-four months after November 8, 1984, the Administrator shall promulgate such standards under this subsection regarding the generation and transportation of used oil which is recycled as may be necessary to protect human health and the environment. In promulgating such regulations with respect to generators, the Administrator shall take into account the effect of such regulations on environmentally acceptable types of used oil recycling and the effect of such regulations on small quantity generators and generators which are small businesses (as defined by the Administrator).

(B) The regulations promulgated under this subsection shall provide that no generator of used oil which is exempt under paragraph (1) from the standards promulgated under section[1] 6921(d), 6922, and 6923 of this title shall be subject to any manifest requirement or any associated recordkeeping and reporting requirement with respect to such used oil if such generator—

(i) either—

(I) enters into an agreement or other arrangement (including an agreement or arrangement with an independent transporter or with an agent of the recycler) for delivery of such used oil to a recycling facility which has a permit under section 6925(c) of this title (or for which a valid permit is deemed to be in effect under subsection (d) of this section), or

(II) recycles such used oil at one or more facilities of the generator which has such a permit under section 6925 of this title (or for which a valid permit is deemed to have been issued under subsection (d) of this section);

(ii) such used oil is not mixed by the generator with other types of hazardous wastes; and

(iii) the generator maintains such records relating to such used oil, including records of agreements or other arrangements for delivery of such used oil to any recycling facility referred to in clause (i)(I), as the Administrator deems necessary to protect human health and the environment.

(3) The regulations under this subsection regarding the transportation of used oil which is exempt from the standards promulgated under section[1] 6921(d), 6922, and 6923 of this title under paragraph (1) shall require the transporters of such used oil to deliver such used oil to a facility which has a valid permit under section 6925 of this title or which is deemed to have a valid permit under subsection (d) of this section. The Administrator shall also establish other standards for such transporters as may be necessary to protect human health and the environment.

(d) Permits

(1) The owner or operator of a facility which recycles used oil which is exempt under subsection (c)(1) of this section, shall be deemed to have a permit under this subsection for all such treatment or recycling (and any associated tank or container storage) if such owner and operator comply with standards promulgated by the Administrator under section 6924 of this title; except that the Administrator may require such owners and operators to obtain an individual permit under section 6925(c) of this title if he determines that an individual permit is necessary to protect human health and the environment.

(2) Notwithstanding any other provision of law, any generator who recycles used oil which is exempt under subsection (c)(1) of this section shall not be required to obtain a permit under section 6925(c) of this title with respect to such used oil until the Administrator has promulgated standards under section 6924 of this title regarding the recycling of such used oil.

(Pub. L. No. 89–272, Title II, § 3014, formerly § 3012, as added by Pub. L. No. 96–463, § 7(a), 94 Stat. 2057 (Oct. 15, 1980); and renumbered and amended by Pub. L. No. 98–616, Title II, §§ 241(a), 242, Title V, § 502(g)(1), 98 Stat. 3258, 3260, 3277 (Nov. 8, 1984).)

[1] So in original. Probably should be "sections".

HISTORICAL AND STATUTORY NOTES

Codifications

Section was formerly codified as section 6932 of this title.

Transfer of Functions

For transfer of certain enforcement functions of Administrator or other official of the Environmental Protection Agency under this chapter to Federal Inspector, Office of Federal Inspector for the Alaska Natural Gas Transportation System, see note set out under section 6903 of this title.

§ 6936. Expansion during interim status

[SWDA § 3015]

(a) Waste piles

The owner or operator of a waste pile qualifying for the authorization to operate under section 6925(e) of this title shall be subject to the same requirements for liners and leachate collection systems or equivalent protection provided in regulations promulgated by the Administrator under section 6924 of this title before October 1, 1982, or revised under section 6924(*o*) of this title (relating to minimum technological requirements), for new facilities receiving individual permits under subsection (c) of section 6925 of this title, with respect to each new unit, replacement of an existing unit, or lateral expansion of an existing unit that is within the waste management area identified in the permit application submitted under section 6925 of this title, and with respect to waste received beginning six months after November 8, 1984.

(b) Landfills and surface impoundments

(1) The owner or operator of a landfill or surface impoundment qualifying for the authorization to operate under section 6925(e) of this title shall be subject to the requirements of section 6924(*o*) of this title (relating to minimum technological requirements), with respect to each new unit, replacement of an existing unit, or lateral expansion of an existing unit that is within the waste management area identified in the permit application submitted under this section, and with respect to waste received beginning 6 months after November 8, 1984.

(2) The owner or operator of each unit referred to in paragraph (1) shall notify the Administrator (or the State, if appropriate) at least sixty days prior to receiving waste. The Administrator (or the State) shall require the filing, within six months of receipt of such notice, of an application for a final determination regarding the issuance of a permit for each facility submitting such notice.

(3) In the case of any unit in which the liner and leachate collection system has been installed pursuant to the requirements of this section and in good faith compliance with the Administrator's regulations and guidance documents governing liners and leachate collection systems, no liner or leachate collection system which is different from that which was so installed pursuant to this section shall be required for such unit by the Administrator when issuing the first permit under section 6925 of this title to such facility, except that the Administrator shall not be precluded from requiring installation of a new liner when the Administrator has reason to believe that any liner installed pursuant to the requirements of this section is leaking. The Administrator may, under section 6924 of this title, amend the requirements for liners and leachate collection systems required under this section as may be necessary to provide additional protection for human health and the environment.

(Pub. L. No. 89–272, Title II, § 3015, as added by Pub. L. No. 98–616, Title II, § 243(a), 98 Stat. 3260 (Nov. 8, 1984).)

§ 6937. Inventory of Federal agency hazardous waste facilities [SWDA § 3016]

(a) Program requirement; submission; availability; contents

Each Federal agency shall undertake a continuing program to compile, publish, and submit to the Administrator (and to the State in the case of sites in States having an authorized hazardous waste program) an inventory of each site which the Federal agency owns or operates or has owned or operated at which hazardous waste is stored, treated, or disposed of or has been disposed of at any time. The inventory shall be submitted every two years beginning January 31, 1986. Such inventory shall be available to the public as provided in section 6927(b) of this title. Information previously submitted by a Federal agency under section 9603 of this title, or under section 6925 or 6930 of this title, or under this section need not be resubmitted except that the agency shall update any previous submission to reflect the latest available data and information. The inventory shall include each of the following:

(1) A description of the location of each site at which any such treatment, storage, or disposal has taken place before the date on which permits are required under section 6925 of this title for such storage, treatment, or disposal, and where hazardous waste has been disposed, a description of hydrogeology of the site and the location of withdrawal wells and surface water within one mile of the site.

(2) Such information relating to the amount, nature, and toxicity of the hazardous waste in each site as may be necessary to determine the extent of any health hazard which may be associated with any site.

(3) Information on the known nature and extent of environmental contamination at each site, including a description of the monitoring data obtained.

(4) Information concerning the current status of the site, including information respecting whether or not hazardous waste is currently being treated, stored, or disposed of at such site (and if not, the date on which such activity ceased) and information respecting the nature of any other activity currently carried out at such site.

(5) A list of sites at which hazardous waste has been disposed and environmental monitoring data has not been obtained, and the reasons for the lack of monitoring data at each site.

(6) A description of response actions undertaken or contemplated at contaminated sites.

(7) An identification of the types of techniques of waste treatment, storage, or disposal which have been used at each site.

(8) The name and address and responsible Federal agency for each site, determined as of the date of preparation of the inventory.

(b) Environmental Protection Agency program

If the Administrator determines that any Federal agency under subsection (a) of this section is not adequately providing information respecting the sites referred to in subsection (a) of this section, the Administrator shall notify the chief official of such agency. If within ninety days following such notification, the Federal agency has not undertaken a program to adequately provide such information, the Administrator shall carry out the inventory program for such agency.

(Pub. L. No. 89–272, Title II, § 3016, as added by Pub. L. No. 98–616, Title II, § 244, 98 Stat. 3261 (Nov. 8, 1984).)

§ 6938. Export of hazardous wastes [SWDA § 3017]

(a) In general

Beginning twenty-four months after November 8, 1984, no person shall export any hazardous waste identified or listed under this subchapter unless[1]

(1) (A) such person has provided the notification required in subsection (c) of this section,

(B) the government of the receiving country has consented to accept such hazardous waste,

(C) a copy of the receiving country's written consent is attached to the manifest accompanying each waste shipment, and

(D) the shipment conforms with the terms of the consent of the government of the receiving country required pursuant to subsection (e) of this section, or

(2) the United States and the government of the receiving country have entered into an agreement as provided for in subsection (f) of this section and the shipment conforms with the terms of such agreement.

(b) Regulations

Not later than twelve months after November 8, 1984, the Administrator shall promulgate the regulations necessary to implement this section. Such regulations shall become effective one hundred and eighty days after promulgation.

(c) Notification

Any person who intends to export a hazardous waste identified or listed under this subchapter beginning twelve months after November 8, 1984, shall, before such hazardous waste is scheduled to leave the United States, provide notification to the Administrator. Such notification shall contain the following information:

(1) the name and address of the exporter;

(2) the types and estimated quantities of hazardous waste to be exported;

(3) the estimated frequency or rate at which such waste is to be exported; and the period of time over which such waste is to be exported;

(4) the ports of entry;

(5) a description of the manner in which such hazardous waste will be transported to and treated, stored, or disposed in the receiving country; and

(6) the name and address of the ultimate treatment, storage or disposal facility.

(d) Procedures for requesting consent of receiving country

Within thirty days of the Administrator's receipt of a complete notification under this section, the Secretary of State, acting on behalf of the Administrator, shall—

(1) forward a copy of the notification to the government of the receiving country;

(2) advise the government that United States law prohibits the export of hazardous waste unless the receiving country consents to accept the hazardous waste;

(3) request the government to provide the Secretary with a written consent or objection to the terms of the notification; and

(4) forward to the government of the receiving country a description of the Federal regulations which would apply to the treatment, storage, and disposal of the hazardous waste in the United States.

(e) Conveyance of written consent to exporter

Within thirty days of receipt by the Secretary of State of the receiving country's written consent or objection (or any subsequent communication withdrawing a prior consent or objection), the Administrator shall forward such a consent, objection, or other communication to the exporter.

(f) International agreements

Where there exists an international agreement between the United States and the government of the receiving country establishing notice, export, and enforcement procedures for the transportation, treatment, storage, and disposal of hazardous wastes, only the requirements of subsections (a)(2) and (g) of this section shall apply.

(g) Reports

After November 8, 1984, any person who exports any hazardous waste identified or listed under section 6921 of this title shall file with the Administrator no later than March 1 of each year, a report summarizing the types, quantities, frequency, and ultimate destination of all such hazardous waste exported during the previous calendar year.

(h) Other standards

Nothing in this section shall preclude the Administrator from establishing other standards for the export of hazardous wastes under section 6922 of this title or section 6923 of this title.

(Pub. L. No. 89–272, Title II, § 3017, as added by Pub. L. No. 98–616, Title II, § 245(a), 98 Stat. 3262 (Nov. 8, 1984).)

[1] So in original.

§ 6939. Domestic sewage

[SWDA § 3018]

(a) Report

The Administrator shall, not later than 15 months after November 8, 1984, submit a report to the Congress concerning those substances identified or listed under section 6921 of this title which are not regulated under this subchapter by reason of the exclusion for mixtures of domestic sewage and other wastes that pass through a sewer system to a publicly owned treatment works. Such report shall include the types, size and number of generators which dispose of such substances in this manner, the types and quantities disposed of in this manner, and the identification of significant generators, wastes, and waste constituents not regulated under existing Federal law or regulated in a manner sufficient to protect human health and the environment.

(b) Revisions of regulations

Within eighteen months after submitting the report specified in subsection (a) of this section, the Administrator shall revise existing regulations and promulgate such additional regulations pursuant to this subchapter (or any other authority of the Administrator, including section 1317 of Title 33) as are necessary to assure that substances identified or listed under section 6921 of this title which pass through a sewer system to a publicly owned treatment works are adequately controlled to protect human health and the environment.

(c) Report on wastewater lagoons

The Administrator shall, within thirty-six months after November 8, 1984, submit a report to Congress concerning wastewater lagoons at publicly owned treatment works and their effect on groundwater quality. Such report shall include—

(1) the number and size of such lagoons;

(2) the types and quantities of waste contained in such lagoons;

(3) the extent to which such waste has been or may be released from such lagoons and contaminate ground water; and

(4) available alternatives for preventing or controlling such releases.

The Administrator may utilize the authority of sections 6927 and 6934 of this title for the purpose of completing such report.

(d) Application of sections 6927 and 6930

The provisions of sections 6927 and 6930 of this title shall apply to solid or dissolved materials in domestic sewage to the same extent and in the same manner as such provisions apply to hazardous waste.

(Pub. L. No. 89–272, Title II, § 3018, as added by Pub. L. No. 98–616, Title II, § 246(a), 98 Stat. 3264 (Nov. 8, 1984).)

§ 6939a. Exposure information and health assessments

[SWDA § 3019]

(a) Exposure information

Beginning on the date nine months after November 8, 1984, each application for a final determination regarding a permit under section 6925(c) of this title for a landfill or surface impoundment shall be accompanied by information reasonably ascertainable by the owner or operator on the potential for the public to be exposed to hazardous wastes or hazardous constituents through releases related to the unit. At a minimum, such information must address:

(1) reasonably foreseeable potential releases from both normal operations and accidents at the unit, including releases associated with transportation to or from the unit;

(2) the potential pathways of human exposure to hazardous wastes or constituents resulting from the releases described under paragraph (1); and

(3) the potential magnitude and nature of the human exposure resulting from such releases.

The owner or operator of a landfill or surface impoundment for which an application for such a final determination under section 6925(c) of this title has been submitted prior to November 8, 1984, shall submit the information required by this subsection to the Administrator (or the State, in the case of a State with an authorized program) no later than the date nine months after November 8, 1984.

(b) Health assessments

(1) The Administrator (or the State, in the case of a State with an authorized program) shall make the information required by subsection (a) of this section, together with other relevant information, available to the Agency for Toxic Substances and Disease Registry established by section 9604(i) of this title.

(2) Whenever in the judgment of the Administrator, or the State (in the case of a State with an authorized program), a landfill or a surface impoundment poses a substantial potential risk to human health, due to the existence of releases of hazardous constituents, the magnitude of contamination with hazardous constituents which may be the result of a release, or the magnitude of the population exposed to such release or contamination, the Administrator or the State (with the concurrence of the Administrator) may request the Administrator of the Agency for Toxic Substances and Disease Registry to conduct a health assessment in connection with such facility and take other appropriate action with respect to such risks as authorized by section 9604(b) and (i) of this title. If funds are provided in connection with such request the Administrator of such Agency shall conduct such health assessment.

(c) Members of the public

Any member of the public may submit evidence of releases of or exposure to hazardous constituents from such a facility, or as to the risks or health effects associated with such releases or exposure, to the Administrator of the Agency for Toxic Substances and Disease Registry, the Administrator, or the State (in the case of a State with an authorized program).

(d) Priority

In determining the order in which to conduct health assessments under this subsection, the Administrator of the Agency for Toxic Substances and Disease Registry shall give priority to those facilities or sites at which there is documented evidence of release of hazardous constituents, at which the potential risk to human health appears highest, and for which in the judgment of the Administrator of such Agency existing health assessment data is inadequate to assess the potential risk to human health as provided in subsection (f) of this section.

(e) Periodic reports

The Administrator of such Agency shall issue periodic reports which include the results of all the assessments carried out under this section. Such assessments or other activities shall be reported after appropriate peer review.

(f) "Health assessments" defined

For the purposes of this section, the term "health assessments" shall include preliminary assessments of the potential risk to human health posed by individual sites and facilities subject to this section, based on such factors as the nature and extent of contamination, the existence of potential for pathways of human exposure (including ground or surface water contamination, air emissions, and food chain contamination), the size and potential susceptibility of the community within the likely pathways of exposure, the comparison of expected human exposure levels to the short-term and long-term health effects associated with identified contaminants and any available recommended exposure or tolerance limits for such contaminants, and the comparison of existing morbidity and mortality data on diseases that may be associated with the observed levels of exposure. The assessment shall include an evaluation of the risks to the potentially affected population from all sources of such contaminants, including known point or nonpoint sources other than the site or facility in question. A purpose of such preliminary assessments shall be to help determine whether full-scale health or epidemiological studies and medical evaluations of exposed populations shall be undertaken.

(g) Cost recovery

In any case in which a health assessment performed under this section discloses the exposure of a population to the release of a hazardous substance, the costs of such health assessment may be recovered as a cost of response under section 9607 of this title from persons causing or contributing to such release of such hazardous substance or, in the case of multiple releases contributing to such exposure, to all such release.

(Pub. L. No. 89–272, Title II, § 3019, as added by Pub. L. No. 98–616, Title II, § 247(a), 98 Stat. 3265 (Nov. 8, 1984).)

§ 6939b. Interim control of hazardous waste injection

[SWDA § 3020]

(a) Underground source of drinking water

No hazardous waste may be disposed of by underground injection—

(1) into a formation which contains (within one-quarter mile of the well used for such underground injection) an underground source of drinking water; or

(2) above such a formation.

The prohibitions established under this section shall take effect 6 months after November 8, 1984, except in the case of any State in which identical or more stringent prohibitions are in effect before such date under the Safe Drinking Water Act [42 U.S.C.A. § 300f et seq.].

(b) Actions under Comprehensive Environmental Response, Compensation, and Liability Act

Subsection (a) of this section shall not apply to the injection of contaminated ground water into the aquifer from which it was withdrawn, if—

(1) such injection is—

(A) a response action taken under section 9604 or 9606 of this title, or

(B) part of corrective action required under this chapter[1]

intended to clean up such contamination;

(2) such contaminated ground water is treated to substantially reduce hazardous constituents prior to such injection; and

(3) such response action or corrective action will, upon completion, be sufficient to protect human health and the environment.

(c) Enforcement

In addition to enforcement under the provisions of this chapter, the prohibitions established under paragraphs (1) and (2) of subsection (a) of this section shall be enforceable under the Safe Drinking Water Act [42 U.S.C.A. § 300f et seq.] in any State—

(1) which has adopted identical or more stringent prohibitions under part C of the Safe Drinking Water Act [42 U.S.C.A. § 300h et seq.] and which has assumed primary enforcement responsibility under that Act for enforcement of such prohibitions; or

(2) in which the Administrator has adopted identical or more stringent prohibitions under the Safe Drinking Water Act [42 U.S.C.A. § 300f et seq.] and is exercising primary enforcement responsibility under that Act for enforcement of such prohibitions.

(d) Definitions

The terms "primary enforcement responsibility", "underground source of drinking water", "formation" and "well" have the same meanings as provided in regulations of the Administrator under the Safe Drinking Water Act [42 U.S.C.A. § 300f et seq.]. The term "Safe Drinking Water Act" means title XIV of the Public Health Service Act.

(Pub. L. No. 89–272, Title II, § 3020, formerly § 7010, as added by Pub. L. No. 98–616, Title IV, § 405(a), 98 Stat. 3273 (Nov. 8, 1984); and renumbered § 3020, and amended by Pub. L. No. 99–339, Title II, § 201(c), 100 Stat. 654 (June 19, 1986).)

[1] So in original. Probably should be followed by a comma.

HISTORICAL AND STATUTORY NOTES

References in Text

Title XIV of the Public Health Service Act, referred to in subsec. (d), is Title XIV of Act of July 1, 1944, as added by Pub. L. 93–523, 2(a), 88 Stat. 1660 (Dec. 16, 1974), as amended, known as the Safe Drinking Water Act, which is codified principally as subchapter XII of chapter 6A of this title, 42 U.S.C.A. § 300f et seq. Part C of the Act is codified generally as part C of subchapter XII of chapter 6A of this title, 42 U.S.C.A. § 300h et seq. For complete classification, see Short Title note set out under 42 U.S.C.A. § 201 of this title and Tables.

Codifications

Section was formerly codified as section 6979a of this title, prior to renumbering by section 201(c)(2) of Pub. L. No. 99–339.

§ 6939c. Mixed waste inventory reports and plan

[SWDA § 3021]

(a) Mixed waste inventory reports

(1) Requirement

Not later than 180 days after October 6, 1992, the Secretary of Energy shall submit to the Administrator and to the Governor of each State in which the Department of Energy stores or generates mixed wastes the following reports:

(A) A report containing a national inventory of all such mixed wastes, regardless of the time they were generated, on a State-by-State basis.

(B) A report containing a national inventory of mixed waste treatment capacities and technologies.

(2) Inventory of wastes

The report required by paragraph (1)(A) shall include the following:

(A) A description of each type of mixed waste at each Department of Energy facility in each State, including, at a minimum, the name of the waste stream.

(B) The amount of each type of mixed waste currently stored at each Department of Energy facility in each State, set forth separately by mixed waste that is subject to the land disposal prohibition requirements of section 6924 of this title and mixed waste that is not subject to such prohibition requirements.

(C) An estimate of the amount of each type of mixed waste the Department expects to generate in the next 5 years at each Department of Energy facility in each State.

(D) A description of any waste minimization actions the Department has implemented at each Department of Energy facility in each State for each mixed waste stream.

(E) The EPA hazardous waste code for each type of mixed waste containing waste that has been characterized at each Department of Energy facility in each State.

(F) An inventory of each type of waste that has not been characterized by sampling and analysis at each Department of Energy facility in each State.

(G) The basis for the Department's determination of the applicable hazardous waste code for each type of mixed waste at each Department of Energy facility and a description of whether the determination is based on sampling and analysis conducted on the waste or on the basis of process knowledge.

(H) A description of the source of each type of mixed waste at each Department of Energy facility in each State.

(I) The land disposal prohibition treatment technology or technologies specified for the hazardous waste component of each type of mixed waste at each Department of Energy facility in each State.

(J) A statement of whether and how the radionuclide content of the waste alters or affects use of the technologies described in subparagraph (I).

(3) Inventory of treatment capacities and technologies

The report required by paragraph (1)(B) shall include the following:

(A) An estimate of the available treatment capacity for each waste described in the report required by paragraph (1)(A) for which treatment technologies exist.

(B) A description, including the capacity, number and location, of each treatment unit considered in calculating the estimate under subparagraph (A).

(C) A description, including the capacity, number and location, of any existing treatment unit that was not considered in calculating the estimate under subparagraph (A) but that could, alone or in conjunction with other treatment units, be used to treat any of the wastes described in the report required by paragraph (1)(A) to meet the requirements of regulations promulgated pursuant to section 6924(m) of this title.

(D) For each unit listed in subparagraph (C), a statement of the reasons why the unit was not included in calculating the estimate under subparagraph (A).

(E) A description, including the capacity, number, location, and estimated date of availability, of each treatment unit currently proposed to increase the treatment capacities estimated under subparagraph (A).

(F) For each waste described in the report required by paragraph (1)(A) for which the Department has determined no treatment technology exists, information sufficient to support such determination and a description of the technological approaches the Department anticipates will need to be developed to treat the waste.

(4) Comments and revisions

Not later than 90 days after the date of the submission of the reports by the Secretary of Energy under paragraph (1), the Administrator and each State which received the reports shall submit any comments they may have concerning the reports to the Department of Energy. The Secretary of Energy shall consider and publish the comments prior to publication of the final report.

(5) Requests for additional information

Nothing in this subsection limits or restricts the authority of States or the Administrator to request additional information from the Secretary of Energy.

(b) Plan for development of treatment capacities and technologies

(1) Plan requirement

(A) (i) For each facility at which the Department of Energy generates or stores mixed wastes, except any facility subject to a permit, agreement, or order described in clause (ii), the Secretary of Energy shall develop and submit, as provided in paragraph (2), a plan for developing treatment capacities and technologies to treat all of the facility's mixed wastes, regardless of the time they were generated, to the standards promulgated pursuant to section 6924(m) of this title.

(ii) Clause (i) shall not apply with respect to any facility subject to any permit establishing a schedule for treatment of such wastes, or any existing agreement or administrative or judicial order governing the treatment of such wastes, to which the State is a party.

(B) Each plan shall contain the following:

(i) For mixed wastes for which treatment technologies exist, a schedule for submitting all applicable permit applications, entering into contracts, initiating construction, conducting systems testing, commencing operations, and processing backlogged and currently generated mixed wastes.

(ii) For mixed wastes for which no treatment technologies exist, a schedule for identifying and developing such technologies, identifying the funding requirements for the identification and development of such technologies, submitting treatability study exemptions, and submitting research and development permit applications.

(iii) For all cases where the Department proposes radionuclide separation of mixed wastes, or materials derived from mixed wastes, it shall provide an estimate of the volume of waste generated by each case of radionuclide separation, the volume of waste that would exist or be generated without radionuclide separation, the estimated costs of waste treatment and disposal if radionuclide separation is used compared to the estimated costs if it is not used, and the assumptions underlying such waste volume and cost estimates.

(C) A plan required under this subsection may provide for centralized, regional, or on-site treatment of mixed wastes, or any combination thereof.

(2) Review and approval of plan

(A) For each facility that is located in a State (i) with authority under State law to prohibit land disposal of mixed waste until the waste has been treated and (ii) with both authority under State law to regulate the hazardous components of mixed waste and authorization from the Environmental Protection Agency under section 6926 of this title to regulate the hazardous components of mixed waste, the Secretary of Energy shall submit the plan required under paragraph (1) to the appropriate State regulatory officials for their review and approval, modification, or disapproval. In reviewing the plan, the State shall consider the need for regional treatment facilities. The State shall consult with the Administrator and any other State in which a facility affected by the plan is located and consider public comments in making its determination on the plan. The State shall approve, approve with modifications, or disapprove the plan within 6 months after receipt of the plan.

(B) For each facility located in a State that does not have the authority described in subparagraph (A), the Secretary shall submit the plan required under paragraph (1) to the Administrator of the Environmental Protection Agency for review and approval, modification, or disapproval. A copy of the plan also shall be provided by the Secretary to the State in which such facility is located. In reviewing the plan, the Administrator shall consider the need for regional treatment facilities. The Administrator shall consult with the State or States in which any facility affected by the plan is located and consider public comments in making a determination on the plan. The Administrator shall approve, approve with modifications, or disapprove the plan within 6 months after receipt of the plan.

(C) Upon the approval of a plan under this paragraph by the Administrator or a State, the Administrator shall issue an order under section 6928(a) of this title, or the State shall issue an order under appropriate State authority, requiring compliance with the approved plan.

(3) Public participation

Upon submission of a plan by the Secretary of Energy to the Administrator or a State, and before approval of the plan by the Administrator or a State, the Administrator or State shall publish a notice of the availability of the submitted plan and make such submitted plan available to the public on request.

(4) Revisions of plan

If any revisions of an approved plan are proposed by the Secretary of Energy or required by the Administrator or a State, the provisions of paragraphs (2) and (3) shall apply to the revisions in the same manner as they apply to the original plan.

(5) Waiver of plan requirement

(A) A State may waive the requirement for the Secretary of Energy to develop and submit a plan under this subsection for a facility located in the State if the State (i) enters into an agreement with the Secretary of Energy that addresses compliance at that facility with section 6924(j) of this title with respect to mixed waste, and (ii) issues an order requiring compliance with such agreement and which is in effect.

(B) Any violation of an agreement or order referred to in subparagraph (A) is subject to the waiver of sovereign immunity contained in section 6961(a) of this title.

(c) Schedule and progress reports

(1) Schedule

Not later than 6 months after October 6, 1992, the Secretary of Energy shall publish in the Federal Register a schedule for submitting the plans required under subsection (b) of this section.

(2) Progress reports

(A) Not later than the deadlines specified in subparagraph (B), the Secretary of Energy shall submit to the Committee on Environment and Public Works of the Senate and the Committee on Energy and Commerce of the House of Representatives a progress report containing the following:

(i) An identification, by facility, of the plans that have been submitted to States or the Administrator of the Environmental Protection Agency pursuant to subsection (b) of this section.

(ii) The status of State and Environmental Protection Agency review and approval of each such plan.

(iii) The number of orders requiring compliance with such plans that are in effect.

(iv) For the first 2 reports required under this paragraph, an identification of the plans required under such subsection (b) of this section that the Secretary expects to submit in the 12-month period following submission of the report.

(B) The Secretary of Energy shall submit a report under subparagraph (A) not later than 12 months after October 6, 1992, 24 months after October 6, 1992, and 36 months after October 6, 1992.

(Pub. L. No. 89–272, Title II, § 3021, as added by Pub. L. No. 102–386, Title I, § 105(a)(1), 106 Stat. 1508 (Oct. 6, 1992).)

HISTORICAL AND STATUTORY NOTES

Change of Name

Any reference in any provision of law enacted before Jan. 4, 1995, to the Committee on Energy and Commerce of the House of Representatives treated as referring to the Committee on Commerce of the House of Representatives, except that any reference in any provision of law enacted before Jan. 4, 1995, to the Committee on Energy and Commerce of the House of Representatives treated as referring to the Committee on Agriculture of the House of Representatives, in the case of a provision of law relating to inspection of seafood or seafood products, the Committee on Banking and Financial Services of the House of Representatives, in the case of a provision of law relating to bank capital markets activities generally or to depository institution securities activities generally, and the Committee on Transportation and Infrastructure of the House of Representatives, in the case of a provision of law relating to railroads, railway labor, or railroad retirement and unemployment (except revenue measures related thereto), see section 1(a)(4) and (c)(1) of Pub. L. No. 104–14, set out as a note preceding section 21 of Title 2, The Congress.

GAO Report

Section 105(c) of Pub. L. No. 102–386 provided that:

"**(1) Requirement.**—Not later than 18 months after the date of the enactment of this Act [Oct. 6, 1992], the Comptroller General shall submit to Congress a report on the Department of Energy's progress in complying with section 3021(b) of the Solid Waste Disposal Act [subsec. (b) of this section].

"**(2) Matters to be included.**—The report required under paragraph (1) shall contain, at a minimum, the following:

"(A) The Department of Energy's progress in submitting to the States or the Administrator of the Environmental Protection Agency a plan for each facility for which a plan is required under section 3021(b) of the Solid Waste Disposal Act [subsec. (b) of this section] and the status of State or Environmental Protection Agency review and approval of each such plan.

"(B) The Department of Energy's progress in entering into orders requiring compliance with any such plans that have been approved.

"(C) An evaluation of the completeness and adequacy of each such plan as of the date of submission of the report required under paragraph (1).

"(D) An identification of any recurring problems among the Department of Energy's submitted plans.

"(E) A description of treatment technologies and capacity that have been developed by the Department of Energy since the date of the enactment of this Act [Oct. 6, 1992] and a list of the wastes that are expected to be treated by such technologies and the facilities at which the wastes are generated or stored.

"(F) The progress made by the Department of Energy in characterizing its mixed waste streams at each such facility by sampling and analysis.

"(G) An identification and analysis of additional actions that the Department of Energy must take to—

"(i) complete submission of all plans required under such section 3021(b) [subsec. (b) of this section] for all such facilities;

"(ii) obtain the adoption of orders requiring compliance with all such plans; and

"(iii) develop mixed waste treatment capacity and technologies."

[For termination, effective May 15, 2000, of reporting provisions of above note, see Pub. L. No. 104–66, § 3003, as amended, set out as a note under 31 U.S.C.A. § 1113, and the 8th item on page 6 of House Document No. 103–7.]

§ 6939d. Public vessels

[SWDA § 3022]

(a) Waste generated on public vessels

Any hazardous waste generated on a public vessel shall not be subject to the storage, manifest, inspection, or recordkeeping requirements of this chapter until such waste is transferred to a shore facility, unless—

(1) the waste is stored on the public vessel for more than 90 days after the public vessel is placed in reserve or is otherwise no longer in service; or

(2) the waste is transferred to another public vessel within the territorial waters of the United States and is stored on such vessel or another public vessel for more than 90 days after the date of transfer.

(b) Computation of storage period

For purposes of subsection (a) of this section, the 90-day period begins on the earlier of—

(1) the date on which the public vessel on which the waste was generated is placed in reserve or is otherwise no longer in service; or

(2) the date on which the waste is transferred from the public vessel on which the waste was generated to another public vessel within the territorial waters of the United States;

and continues, without interruption, as long as the waste is stored on the original public vessel (if in reserve or not in service) or another public vessel.

(c) Definitions

For purposes of this section:

(1) The term "public vessel" means a vessel owned or bareboat chartered and operated by the United States, or by a foreign nation, except when the vessel is engaged in commerce.

(2) The terms "in reserve" and "in service" have the meanings applicable to those terms under section 8663 and sections 8674 through 8678 of title 10, United States Code and regulations prescribed under those sections.

(d) Relationship to other law

Nothing in this section shall be construed as altering or otherwise affecting the provisions of section 8681 of title 10, United States Code.

(Pub. L. No. 89–272, Title II, § 3022, as added by Pub. L. No. 102–386, Title I, § 106(a), 106 Stat. 1513 (Oct. 6, 1992); and amended by Pub. L. No. 115–232, § 809(n)(2), 132 Stat. 1636, 1844 (Aug. 13, 2018).)

§ 6939e. Federally owned treatment works

[SWDA § 3023]

(a) In general

For purposes of section 6903(27) of this title, the phrase "but does not include solid or dissolved material in domestic sewage" shall apply to any solid or dissolved material introduced by a source into a federally owned treatment works if—

(1) such solid or dissolved material is subject to a pretreatment standard under section 1317 of Title 33, and the source is in compliance with such standard;

(2) for a solid or dissolved material for which a pretreatment standard has not been promulgated pursuant to section 1317 of Title 33, the Administrator has promulgated a schedule for establishing such a pretreatment standard which would be applicable to such solid or dissolved material not later than 7 years after October 6, 1992, such standard is promulgated on or before the date established in the schedule, and after the effective date of such standard the source is in compliance with such standard;

(3) such solid or dissolved material is not covered by paragraph (1) or (2) and is not prohibited from land disposal under subsections[1] (d), (e), (f), or (g) of section 6924 of this title because such material has been treated in accordance with section 6924(m) of this title; or

(4) notwithstanding paragraphs[1] (1), (2), or (3), such solid or dissolved material is generated by a household or person which generates less than 100 kilograms of hazardous waste per month unless such solid or dissolved material would otherwise be an acutely hazardous waste and subject to standards, regulations, or other requirements under this chapter notwithstanding the quantity generated.

(b) Prohibition

It is unlawful to introduce into a federally owned treatment works any pollutant that is a hazardous waste.

(c) Enforcement

(1) Actions taken to enforce this section shall not require closure of a treatment works if the hazardous waste is removed or decontaminated and such removal or decontamination is adequate, in the discretion of the Administrator or, in the case of an authorized State, of the State, to protect human health and the environment.

(2) Nothing in this subsection shall be construed to prevent the Administrator or an authorized State from ordering the closure of a treatment works if the Administrator or State determines such closure is necessary for protection of human health and the environment.

(3) Nothing in this subsection shall be construed to affect any other enforcement authorities available to the Administrator or a State under this subchapter.

(d) "Federally owned treatment works" defined

For purposes of this section, the term "federally owned treatment works" means a facility that is owned and operated by a department, agency, or instrumentality of the Federal Government treating wastewater, a majority of which is domestic sewage, prior to discharge in accordance with a permit issued under section 1342 of Title 33.

(e) Savings clause

Nothing in this section shall be construed as affecting any agreement, permit, or administrative or judicial order, or any condition or requirement contained in such an agreement, permit, or order, that is in existence on October 6, 1992, and that requires corrective action or closure at a federally owned treatment works or solid waste management unit or facility related to such a treatment works.

(Pub. L. No. 89–272, Title II, § 3023, as added by Pub. L. No. 102–386, Title I, § 108(a), 106 Stat. 1514 (Oct. 6, 1992).)

[1] So in original. Probably should be singular.

§ 6939f. Long-term storage

(a) Designation of facility

(1) In general

Not later than January 1, 2010, the Secretary of Energy (referred to in this section as the "Secretary") shall designate a facility or facilities of the Department of Energy, which shall not include the Y–12 National Security Complex or any other portion or facility of the Oak Ridge Reservation of the Department of Energy, for the purpose of long-term management and storage of elemental mercury generated within the United States.

(2) Operation of facility

Not later than January 1, 2019, the facility designated in paragraph (1) shall be operational and shall accept custody, for the purpose of long-term management and storage, of elemental mercury generated within the United States and delivered to such facility.

(b) Fees

(1) In general

(A) Assessment and collection.—After consultation with persons who are likely to deliver elemental mercury to a designated facility for long-term management and storage under the program prescribed in subsection (a), and with other interested persons, the Secretary shall assess and collect a fee at the time of delivery for providing such management and storage, based on the pro rata cost of long-term management and storage of elemental mercury delivered to the facility.

(B) Amount.—The amount of the fees described in subparagraph (A)—

(i) shall be made publicly available not later than October 1, 2018;

(ii) may be adjusted annually;

(iii) shall be set in an amount sufficient to cover the costs described in paragraph (2), subject to clause (iv); and

(iv) for generators temporarily accumulating elemental mercury in a facility subject to subparagraphs (B) and (D)(iv) of subsection (g)(2) if the facility designated in subsection (a) is not operational by January 1, 2019, shall be adjusted to subtract the cost of the temporary accumulation during the period in which the facility designated under subsection (a) is not operational.

(C) Conveyance of title and permitting.—If the facility designated in subsection (a) is not operational by January 1, 2020, the Secretary—

(i) shall immediately accept the conveyance of title to all elemental mercury that has accumulated in facilities in accordance with subsection (g)(2)(D), before January 1, 2020, and deliver the accumulated mercury to the facility designated under subsection (a) on the date on which the facility becomes operational;

(ii) shall pay any applicable Federal permitting costs, including the costs for permits issued under section 3005(c) of the Solid Waste Disposal Act (42 U.S.C. 6925(c)); and

(iii) shall store, or pay the cost of storage of, until the time at which a facility designated in subsection (a) is operational, accumulated mercury to which the Secretary has title under this subparagraph in a facility that has been issued a permit under section 3005(c) of the Solid Waste Disposal Act (42 U.S.C. 6925(c)).

(2) Costs

The costs referred to in paragraph (1)(B)(iii) are the costs to the Department of Energy of providing such management and storage, including facility operation and maintenance, security, monitoring, reporting, personnel, administration, inspections, training, fire suppression, closure, and other costs required for compliance with applicable law. Such costs shall not include costs associated with land acquisition or permitting of a designated facility under the Solid Waste Disposal Act or other applicable law. Building design and building construction costs shall only be included to the extent that the Secretary finds that the management and storage of elemental mercury accepted under the program under this section cannot be accomplished without construction of a new building or buildings.

(c) Report

Not later than 60 days after the end of each Federal fiscal year, the Secretary shall transmit to the Committee on Energy and Commerce of the House of Representatives and the Committee on Environment and Public Works of the Senate a report on all of the costs incurred in the previous fiscal year associated with the long-term management and storage of elemental mercury. Such report shall set forth separately the costs associated with activities taken under this section.

(d) Management standards for a facility

(1) Guidance

Not later than October 1, 2009, the Secretary, after consultation with the Administrator of the Environmental Protection Agency and all appropriate State agencies in affected States, shall make available, including to potential users of the long-term management and storage program established under subsection (a), guidance that establishes procedures and standards for the receipt, management, and long-term storage of elemental mercury at a designated facility or facilities, including requirements to ensure appropriate use of flasks or other suitable shipping containers. Such procedures and standards shall be protective of human health and the environment and shall ensure that the elemental mercury is stored in a safe, secure, and effective manner. In addition to such procedures and standards, elemental mercury managed and stored under this section at a designated facility shall be subject to the requirements of the Solid Waste Disposal Act, including the requirements of subtitle C of that Act, except as provided in subsection (g)(2) of this section. A designated facility is authorized to operate under interim status pursuant to section 3005(e) of the Solid Waste Disposal Act [42 U.S.C. 6925(e)] until a final decision on a permit application is made pursuant to section 3005(e) of the Solid Waste Disposal Act. Not later than January 1, 2020, the Administrator of the Environmental Protection Agency (or an authorized State) shall issue a final decision on the permit application.

(2) Training

The Secretary shall conduct operational training and emergency training for all staff that have responsibilities related to elemental mercury management, transfer, storage, monitoring, or response.

(3) Equipment

The Secretary shall ensure that each designated facility has all equipment necessary for routine operations, emergencies, monitoring, checking inventory, loading, and storing elemental mercury at the facility.

(4) Fire detection and suppression systems

The Secretary shall—

(A) ensure the installation of fire detection systems at each designated facility, including smoke detectors and heat detectors; and

(B) ensure the installation of a permanent fire suppression system, unless the Secretary determines that a permanent fire suppression system is not necessary to protect human health and the environment.

(e) Indemnification of persons delivering elemental mercury

(1) In general

(A) Except as provided in subparagraph (B) and subject to paragraph (2), the Secretary shall hold harmless, defend, and indemnify in full any person who delivers elemental mercury to a designated facility under the program established under subsection (a) from and against any suit, claim, demand or action, liability, judgment, cost, or other fee arising out of any claim for personal injury or property damage (including death, illness, or loss of or damage to property or economic loss) that results from, or is in any manner predicated upon, the release or threatened release of elemental mercury as a result of acts or omissions occurring after such mercury is delivered to a designated facility described in subsection (a).

(B) To the extent that a person described in subparagraph (A) contributed to any such release or threatened release, subparagraph (A) shall not apply.

(2) Conditions

No indemnification may be afforded under this subsection unless the person seeking indemnification—

(A) notifies the Secretary in writing within 30 days after receiving written notice of the claim for which indemnification is sought;

(B) furnishes to the Secretary copies of pertinent papers the person receives;

(C) furnishes evidence or proof of any claim, loss, or damage covered by this subsection; and

(D) provides, upon request by the Secretary, access to the records and personnel of the person for purposes of defending or settling the claim or action.

(3) Authority of Secretary

(A) In any case in which the Secretary determines that the Department of Energy may be required to make indemnification payments to a person under this subsection for any suit, claim, demand or action, liability, judgment, cost, or other fee arising out of any claim for personal injury or property damage referred to in paragraph (1)(A), the Secretary may settle or defend, on behalf of that person, the claim for personal injury or property damage.

(B) In any case described in subparagraph (A), if the person to whom the Department of Energy may be required to make indemnification payments does not allow the Secretary to settle or defend the claim, the person may not be afforded indemnification with respect to that claim under this subsection.

(f) Terms, conditions, and procedures

The Secretary is authorized to establish such terms, conditions, and procedures as are necessary to carry out this section.

(g) Effect on other law

(1) In general

Except as provided in paragraph (2), nothing in this section changes or affects any Federal, State, or local law or the obligation of any person to comply with such law.

(2) Exception

(A) Elemental mercury that the Secretary is storing on a long-term basis shall not be subject to the storage prohibition of section 3004(j) of the Solid Waste Disposal Act (42 U.S.C. 6924(j)). For the purposes of section 3004(j) of the Solid Waste Disposal Act, a generator accumulating elemental mercury destined for a facility designated by the Secretary under subsection (a) for 90 days or less shall be deemed to be accumulating the mercury to facilitate proper treatment, recovery, or disposal.

(B) Elemental mercury may be stored at a facility with respect to which any permit has been issued under section 3005(c) of the Solid Waste Disposal Act (42 U.S.C. 6925(c)), and shall not be subject to the storage prohibition of section 3004(j) of the Solid Waste Disposal Act (42 U.S.C. 6924(j)) if—

(i) the Secretary is unable to accept the mercury at a facility designated by the Secretary under subsection (a) for reasons beyond the control of the owner or operator of the permitted facility;

(ii) the owner or operator of the permitted facility certifies in writing to the Secretary that it will ship the mercury to the designated facility when the Secretary is able to accept the mercury; and

(iii) the owner or operator of the permitted facility certifies in writing to the Secretary that it will not sell, or otherwise place into commerce, the mercury.

(C) Subparagraph (B) shall not apply to mercury with respect to which the owner or operator of the permitted facility fails to comply with a certification provided under clause (ii) or (iii) of that subparagraph.

(D) A generator producing elemental mercury incidentally from the beneficiation or processing of ore or related pollution control activities may accumulate the mercury produced onsite that is destined for a facility designated by the Secretary under subsection (a) for more than 90 days without a permit issued under section 3005(c) of the Solid Waste Disposal Act (42 U.S.C. 6925(c)), and shall not be subject to the storage prohibition of section 3004(j) of that Act (42 U.S.C. 6924(j)), if—

(i) the Secretary is unable to accept the mercury at a facility designated by the Secretary under subsection (a) for reasons beyond the control of the generator;

(ii) the generator certifies in writing to the Secretary that the generator will ship the mercury to a designated facility when the Secretary is able to accept the mercury;

(iii) the generator certifies in writing to the Secretary that the generator is storing only mercury the generator has produced or recovered onsite and will not sell, or otherwise place into commerce, the mercury; and

(iv) the generator has obtained an identification number under section 262.12 of title 40, Code of Federal Regulations, and complies with the requirements described in paragraphs (1) through (4) of section 262.34(a) of title 40, Code of Federal Regulations (as in effect on the date of enactment of this subparagraph).

(E) Management standards for temporary storage.—Not later than January 1, 2017, the Secretary, after consultation with the Administrator of the Environmental Protection Agency and State agencies in affected States, shall develop and make available guidance that establishes procedures and standards for the management and short-term storage of elemental mercury at a generator covered under subparagraph (D), including requirements to ensure appropriate use of flasks or other suitable containers. Such procedures and standards shall be protective of health and the environment and shall ensure that the elemental mercury is stored in a safe, secure, and effective manner. A generator may accumulate mercury in accordance with subparagraph (D) immediately upon enactment of this subparagraph, and notwithstanding that guidance called for by this paragraph has not been developed or made available

(h) Study

Not later than July 1, 2014, the Secretary shall transmit to the Congress the results of a study, conducted in consultation with the Administrator of the Environmental Protection Agency, that—

(1) determines the impact of the long-term storage program under this section on mercury recycling; and

(2) includes proposals, if necessary, to mitigate any negative impact identified under paragraph (1).

(Pub. L. No. 110–414, § 5, 122 Stat. 4344 (Oct. 14, 2008), as amended by Pub. L. No. 114–182, § 10(c), 130 Stat. 478–81 (Oct. 14, 2008).)

HISTORICAL AND STATUTORY NOTES

References in Text

The Solid Waste Disposal Act, referred to in subsecs. (b)(2) and (d)(1), is Pub. L. No. 89–272, Title II, 79 Stat. 997 (Oct. 20, 1965), which is principally codified as this chapter. "Subtitle C of that Act", means subtitle C of Pub. L. No. 89–272, as added by Pub. L. No. 94–580, which is codified as this subchapter, 42 U.S.C.A. § 6921 et seq. For complete classification, see Short Title note set out under 42 U.S.C.A. § 6901 and Tables.

Codifications

This section was enacted as part of the Mercury Export Ban Act of 2008 and not as part of the Solid Waste Disposal Act, which otherwise comprises this chapter.

§ 6939g. Hazardous Waste Electronic Manifest System

[SWDA § 3024]

(a) Definitions

In this section:

(1) Board

The term "Board" means the Hazardous Waste Electronic Manifest System Advisory Board established under subsection (f).

(2) Fund

The term "Fund" means the Hazardous Waste Electronic Manifest System Fund established by subsection (d).

(3) Person

The term "person" includes an individual, corporation (including a Government corporation), company, association, firm, partnership, society, joint stock company, trust, municipality, commission, Federal agency, State, political subdivision of a State, or interstate body.

(4) System

The term "system" means the hazardous waste electronic manifest system established under subsection (b).

(5) User

The term "user" means a hazardous waste generator, a hazardous waste transporter, an owner or operator of a hazardous waste treatment, storage, recycling, or disposal facility, or any other person that—

(A) is required to use a manifest to comply with any Federal or State requirement to track the shipment, transportation, and receipt of hazardous waste or other material that is shipped from the site of generation to an off-site facility for treatment, storage, disposal, or recycling; and

(B) **(i)** elects to use the system to complete and transmit an electronic manifest format; or

(ii) submits to the system for data processing purposes a paper copy of the manifest (or data from such a paper copy), in accordance with such regulations as the Administrator may promulgate to require such a submission.

(b) Establishment

Not later than 3 years after October 5, 2012, the Administrator shall establish a hazardous waste electronic manifest system that may be used by any user.

(c) User fees

(1) In general

In accordance with paragraph (4), the Administrator may impose on users such reasonable service fees as the Administrator determines to be necessary to pay costs incurred in developing, operating, maintaining, and upgrading the system, including any costs incurred in collecting and processing data from any paper manifest submitted to the system after the date on which the system enters operation.

(2) Collection of fees

The Administrator shall—

(A) collect the fees described in paragraph (1) from the users in advance of, or as reimbursement for, the provision by the Administrator of system-related services; and

(B) deposit the fees in the Fund.

(3) Fee structure

(A) In general

The Administrator, in consultation with information technology vendors, shall determine through the contract award process described in subsection (e) the fee structure that is necessary to recover the full cost to the Administrator of providing system-related services, including—

(i) contractor costs relating to—

(I) materials and supplies;

(II) contracting and consulting;

(III) overhead;

(IV) information technology (including costs of hardware, software, and related services);

(V) information management;

(VI) collection of service fees;

(VII) reporting and accounting; and

(VIII) project management; and

(ii) costs of employment of direct and indirect Government personnel dedicated to establishing, managing, and maintaining the system.

(B) Adjustments in fee amount

(i) In general

The Administrator, in consultation with the Board, shall increase or decrease the amount of a service fee determined under the fee structure described in subparagraph (A) to a level that will—

(I) result in the collection of an aggregate amount for deposit in the Fund that is sufficient and not more than reasonably necessary to cover current and projected system-related costs (including any necessary system upgrades); and

(II) minimize, to the maximum extent practicable, the accumulation of unused amounts in the Fund.

(ii) Exception for initial period of operation

The requirement described in clause (i)(II) shall not apply to any additional fees that accumulate in the Fund, in an amount that does not exceed $2,000, 000, during the 3-year period beginning on the date on which the system enters operation.

(iii) Timing of adjustments

Adjustments to service fees described in clause (i) shall be made—

(I) initially, at the time at which initial development costs of the system have been recovered by the Administrator such that the service fee may be reduced to reflect the elimination of the system development component of the fee; and

(II) periodically thereafter, upon receipt and acceptance of the findings of any annual accounting or auditing report under subsection (d)(3), if the report discloses a significant disparity for a fiscal year between the funds collected from service fees under this subsection for the fiscal year and expenditures made for the fiscal year to provide system-related services.

(4) Crediting and availability of fees

Fees authorized under this section shall be collected and available for obligation only to the extent and in the amount provided in advance in appropriations Acts.

(d) Hazardous Waste Electronic Manifest System Fund

(1) Establishment

There is established in the Treasury of the United States a revolving fund, to be known as the 'Hazardous Waste Electronic Manifest System Fund', consisting of such amounts as are deposited in the Fund under subsection (c)(2)(B).

(2) Expenditures from Fund

(A) In general

Only to the extent provided in advance in appropriations Acts, on request by the Administrator, the Secretary of the Treasury shall transfer from the Fund to the Administrator amounts appropriated to pay costs incurred in developing, operating, maintaining, and upgrading the system under subsection (c).

(B) Use of Funds by Administrator

Fees collected by the Administrator and deposited in the Fund under this section shall be available to the Administrator subject to appropriations Acts for use in accordance with this section without fiscal year limitation.

(C) Oversight of Funds

The Administrator shall carry out all necessary measures to ensure that amounts in the Fund are used only to carry out the goals of establishing, operating, maintaining, upgrading, managing, supporting, and overseeing the system.

(3) Accounting and auditing

(A) Accounting

For each 2-fiscal-year period, the Administrator shall prepare and submit to the Committee on Environment and Public Works and the Committee on Appropriations of the Senate and the Committee on Energy and Commerce and the Committee on Appropriations of the House of Representatives a report that includes—

(i) an accounting of the fees paid to the Administrator under subsection (c) and disbursed from the Fund for the period covered by the report, as reflected by financial statements provided in accordance with—

(I) the Chief Financial Officers Act of 1990 (Public Law 101–576; 104 Stat. 2838) and amendments made by that Act; and

(II) the Government Management Reform Act of 1994 (Public Law 103–356; 108 Stat. 3410) and amendments made by that Act; and

(ii) an accounting describing actual expenditures from the Fund for the period covered by the report for costs described in subsection (c)(1).

(B) Auditing

(i) In general

For the purpose of section 3515(c) of Title 31, the Fund shall be considered a component of an Executive agency.

(ii) Components of audit

The annual audit required in accordance with sections 3515(b) and 3521 of Title 31, of the financial statements of activities carried out using amounts from the Fund shall include an analysis of—

(I) the fees collected and disbursed under this section;

(II) the reasonableness of the fee structure in place as of the date of the audit to meet current and projected costs of the system;

(III) the level of use of the system by users; and

(IV) the success to date of the system in operating on a self-sustaining basis and improving the efficiency of tracking waste shipments and transmitting waste shipment data.

(iii) Federal responsibility

The Inspector General of the Environmental Protection Agency shall—

(I) conduct the annual audit described in clause (ii); and

(II) submit to the Administrator a report that describes the findings and recommendations of the Inspector General resulting from the audit.

(e) Contracts

(1) Authority to enter into contracts funded by service fees

After consultation with the Secretary of Transportation, the Administrator may enter into 1 or more information technology contracts with entities determined to be appropriate by the Administrator (referred to in this subsection as 'contractors') for the provision of system-related services.

(2) Term of contract

A contract awarded under this subsection shall have a term of not more than 10 years.

(3) Achievement of goals

The Administrator shall ensure, to the maximum extent practicable, that a contract awarded under this subsection—

(A) is performance-based;

(B) identifies objective outcomes; and

(C) contains performance standards that may be used to measure achievement and goals to evaluate the success of a contractor in performing under the contract and the right of the contractor to payment for services under the contract, taking into consideration that a primary measure of successful performance shall be the development of a hazardous waste electronic manifest system that—

(i) meets the needs of the user community (including States that rely on data contained in manifests);

(ii) attracts sufficient user participation and service fee revenues to ensure the viability of the system;

(iii) decreases the administrative burden on the user community; and

(iv) provides the waste receipt data applicable to the biennial reports required by section 6922(a)(6) of this title.

(4) Payment structure

Each contract awarded under this subsection shall include a provision that specifies—

(A) the service fee structure of the contractor that will form the basis for payments to the contractor; and

(B) the fixed-share ratio of monthly service fee revenues from which the Administrator shall reimburse the contractor for system-related development, operation, and maintenance costs.

(5) Cancellation and termination

(A) In general

If the Administrator determines that sufficient funds are not made available for the continuation in a subsequent fiscal year of a contract entered into under this subsection, the Administrator may cancel or terminate the contract.

(B) Negotiation of amounts

The amount payable in the event of cancellation or termination of a contract entered into under this subsection shall be negotiated with the contractor at the time at which the contract is awarded.

(6) No effect on ownership

Regardless of whether the Administrator enters into a contract under this subsection, the system shall be owned by the Federal Government.

(f) Hazardous Waste Electronic Manifest System Advisory Board

(1) Establishment

Not later than 3 years after October 5, 2012, the Administrator shall establish a board to be known as the "Hazardous Waste Electronic Manifest System Advisory Board".

(2) Composition

The Board shall be composed of 9 members, of which—

(A) 1 member shall be the Administrator (or a designee), who shall serve as Chairperson of the Board; and

(B) 8 members shall be individuals appointed by the Administrator—

(i) at least 2 of whom shall have expertise in information technology;

(ii) at least 3 of whom shall have experience in using or represent users of the manifest system to track the transportation of hazardous waste under this subchapter (or an equivalent State program); and

(iii) at least 3 of whom shall be a State representative responsible for processing those manifests.

(3) Duties

The Board shall meet annually to discuss, evaluate the effectiveness of, and provide recommendations to the Administrator relating to, the system.

(g) Regulations

(1) Promulgation

(A) In general

Not later than 1 year after October 5, 2012, after consultation with the Secretary of Transportation, the Administrator shall promulgate regulations to carry out this section.

(B) Inclusions

The regulations promulgated pursuant to subparagraph (A) may include such requirements as the Administrator determines to be necessary to facilitate the transition from the use of paper manifests to the use of electronic manifests, or to accommodate the processing of data from paper manifests in the electronic manifest system, including a requirement that users of paper manifests submit to the system copies of the paper manifests for data processing purposes.

(C) Requirements

The regulations promulgated pursuant to subparagraph (A) shall ensure that each electronic manifest provides, to the same extent as paper manifests under applicable Federal and State law, for—

(i) the ability to track and maintain legal accountability of—

(I) the person that certifies that the information provided in the manifest is accurately described; and

(II) the person that acknowledges receipt of the manifest;

(ii) if the manifest is electronically submitted, State authority to access paper printout copies of the manifest from the system; and

(iii) access to all publicly available information contained in the manifest.

(2) Effective date of regulations

Any regulation promulgated by the Administrator under paragraph (1) and in accordance with section 6923 of this title relating to electronic manifesting of hazardous waste shall take effect in each State as of the effective date specified in the regulation.

(3) Administration

The Administrator shall carry out regulations promulgated under this subsection in each State unless the State program is fully authorized to carry out such regulations in lieu of the Administrator.

(h) Requirement of compliance with respect to certain States

In any case in which the State in which waste is generated, or the State in which waste will be transported to a designated facility, requires that the waste be tracked through a hazardous waste manifest, the designated facility that receives the waste shall, regardless of the State in which the facility is located—

(1) complete the facility portion of the applicable manifest;

(2) sign and date the facility certification; and

(3) submit to the system a final copy of the manifest for data processing purposes.

(i) Authorization for start-up activities

There are authorized to be appropriated $2,000,000 for each of fiscal years 2013 through 2015 for start-up activities to carry out this section, to be offset by collection of user fees under subsection (c) such that all such appropriated funds are offset by fees as provided in subsection (c).

(Pub. L. No. 89–272, Title II, § 3024, as added by Pub. L. No. 112–195, § 2(a), 126 Stat. 1452 (Oct. 5, 2012).)

HISTORICAL AND STATUTORY NOTES

References in Text

This subchapter, referred to in text, originally read "this subtitle", meaning Subtitle C of the Solid Waste Disposal Act, Pub. L. No. 89–272, Title II, § 3001 et seq., as added and amended, which is codified as this subchapter.

The Chief Financial Officers Act of 1990, referred to in subsec. (d)(3)(A)(i)(I), is Pub. L. No. 101–576, 104 Stat. 2838 (Nov. 15, 1990). For classification of this Act to the Code, see Short Title note set out under 31 U.S.C.A. § 501 and Tables.

The Government Management Reform Act of 1994, referred to in subsec. (d)(3)(A)(i)(II), is Pub. L. No. 103–356, 108 Stat. 3410 (Oct. 13, 1994). For complete classification, see Short Title note set out under 31 U.S.C.A. § 3301 and Tables.

SUBCHAPTER IV—STATE OR REGIONAL SOLID WASTE PLANS

§ 6941. Objectives of subchapter

[SWDA § 4001]

The objectives of this subchapter are to assist in developing and encouraging methods for the disposal of solid waste which are environmentally sound and which maximize the utilization of valuable resources including energy and materials which are recoverable from solid waste and to encourage resource conservation. Such objectives are to be accomplished through Federal technical and financial assistance to States or regional authorities for comprehensive planning pursuant to Federal guidelines designed to foster cooperation among Federal, State, and local governments and private industry. In developing such comprehensive plans, it is the intention of this chapter that in determining the size of the waste-to-energy facility, adequate provision shall be given to the present and reasonably anticipated future needs, including those needs created by thorough implementation of section 6962(h) of this title, of the recycling and resource recovery interest within the area encompassed by the planning process.

(Pub. L. No. 89–272, Title II, § 4001, as added by Pub. L. No. 94–580, § 2, 90 Stat. 2813 (Oct. 21, 1976); and amended by Pub. L. No. 96–482, § 32(b), 94 Stat. 2353 (Oct. 21, 1980); Pub. L. No. 98–616, Title III, § 301(a), Title V, § 501(f)(1), 98 Stat. 3267, 3276 (Nov. 8, 1984).)

HISTORICAL AND STATUTORY NOTES

Prior Provisions

Provisions similar to this section were contained in section 3254 of this title, prior to the complete revision of the Solid Waste Disposal Act by Pub. L. No. 94–580.

§ 6941a. Energy and materials conservation and recovery; Congressional findings

The Congress finds that—

(1) significant savings could be realized by conserving materials in order to reduce the volume or quantity of material which ultimately becomes waste;

(2) solid waste contains valuable energy and material resources which can be recovered and used thereby conserving increasingly scarce and expensive fossil fuels and virgin materials;

(3) the recovery of energy and materials from municipal waste, and the conservation of energy and materials contributing to such waste streams, can have the effect of reducing the volume of the municipal waste stream and the burden of disposing of increasing volumes of solid waste;

(4) the technology to conserve resources exists and is commercially feasible to apply;

(5) the technology to recover energy and materials from solid waste is of demonstrated commercial feasibility; and

(6) various communities throughout the nation have different needs and different potentials for conserving resources and for utilizing techniques for the recovery of energy and materials from waste, and Federal assistance in planning and implementing such energy and materials conservation and recovery programs should be available to all such communities on an equitable basis in relation to their needs and potential.

(Pub. L. No. 96–482, § 32(a), 94 Stat. 2353 (Oct. 21, 1980).)

HISTORICAL AND STATUTORY NOTES

Codifications

Section was enacted as part of the Solid Waste Disposal Act Amendments of 1980, and not as part of the Solid Waste Disposal Act which comprises this chapter.

§ 6942. Federal guidelines for plans

[SWDA § 4002]

(a) Guidelines for identification of regions

For purposes of encouraging and facilitating the development of regional planning for solid waste management, the Administrator, within one hundred and eighty days after October 21, 1976, and after consultation with appropriate Federal, State, and local authorities, shall by regulation publish guidelines for the identification of those areas which have common solid waste management problems and are appropriate units for planning regional solid waste management services. Such guidelines shall consider—

(1) the size and location of areas which should be included,

(2) the volume of solid waste which should be included, and

(3) the available means of coordinating regional planning with other related regional planning and for coordination of such regional planning into the State plan.

(b) Guidelines for State plans

Not later than eighteen months after October 21, 1976, and after notice and hearing, the Administrator shall, after consultation with appropriate Federal, State, and local authorities, promulgate regulations containing guidelines to assist in the development and implementation of State solid waste management plans (hereinafter in this chapter referred to as "State plans"). The guidelines shall contain methods for achieving the objectives specified in section 6941 of this title. Such guidelines shall be reviewed from time to time, but not less frequently than every three years, and revised as may be appropriate.

(c) Considerations for State plan guidelines

The guidelines promulgated under subsection (b) of this section shall consider—

(1) the varying regional, geologic, hydrologic, climatic, and other circumstances under which different solid waste practices are required in order to insure the reasonable protection of the quality of the ground and surface waters from leachate contamination, the reasonable protection of the quality of the surface waters from surface runoff contamination, and the reasonable protection of ambient air quality;

(2) characteristics and conditions of collection, storage, processing, and disposal operating methods, techniques and practices, and location of facilities where such operating methods, techniques, and practices are conducted, taking into account the nature of the material to be disposed;

(3) methods for closing or upgrading open dumps for purposes of eliminating potential health hazards;

(4) population density, distribution, and projected growth;

(5) geographic, geologic, climatic, and hydrologic characteristics;

(6) the type and location of transportation;

(7) the profile of industries;

(8) the constituents and generation rates of waste;

(9) the political, economic, organizational, financial, and management problems affecting comprehensive solid waste management;

(10) types of resource recovery facilities and resource conservation systems which are appropriate; and

(11) available new and additional markets for recovered material and energy and energy resources recovered from solid waste as well as methods for conserving such materials and energy.

(Pub. L. No. 89–272, Title II, § 4002, as added by Pub. L. No. 94–580, § 2, 90 Stat. 2813 (Oct. 21, 1976); and amended by Pub. L. No. 96–482, § 32(c), 94 Stat. 2353 (Oct. 21, 1980).)

HISTORICAL AND STATUTORY NOTES

Transfer of Functions

For transfer of certain enforcement functions of Administrator or other official of the Environmental Protection Agency under this chapter to Federal Inspector, Office of Federal Inspector for the Alaska Natural Gas Transportation System, see note set out under section 6903 of this title.

§ 6943. Requirements for approval of plans

[SWDA § 4003]

(a) Minimum requirements

In order to be approved under section 6947 of this title, each State plan must comply with the following minimum requirements—

(1) The plan shall identify (in accordance with section 6946(b) of this title) (A) the responsibilities of State, local, and regional authorities in the implementation of the State plan, (B) the distribution of Federal funds to the authorities responsible for development and implementation of the State plan, and (C) the means for coordinating regional planning and implementation under the State plan.

(2) The plan shall, in accordance with sections 6944(b) and 6945(a) of this title, prohibit the establishment of new open dumps within the State, and contain requirements that all solid waste (including solid waste originating in other States, but not including hazardous waste) shall be (A) utilized for resource recovery or (B) disposed of in sanitary landfills (within the meaning of section 6944(a) of this title) or otherwise disposed of in an environmentally sound manner.

(3) The plan shall provide for the closing or upgrading of all existing open dumps within the State pursuant to the requirements of section 6945 of this title.

(4) The plan shall provide for the establishment of such State regulatory powers as may be necessary to implement the plan.

(5) The plan shall provide that no State or local government within the State shall be prohibited under State or local law from negotiating and entering into long-term contracts for the supply of solid waste to resource recovery facilities, from entering into long-term contracts for the operation of such facilities, or from securing long-term markets for material and energy recovered from such facilities or for conserving materials or energy by reducing the volume of waste.

(6) The plan shall provide for such resource conservation or recovery and for the disposal of solid waste in sanitary landfills or any combination of practices so as may be necessary to use or dispose of such waste in a manner that is environmentally sound.

(b) Discretionary plan provisions relating to recycled oil

Any State plan submitted under this subchapter may include, at the option of the State, provisions to carry out each of the following:

(1) Encouragement, to the maximum extent feasible and consistent with the protection of the public health and the environment, of the use of recycled oil in all appropriate areas of State and local government.

(2) Encouragement of persons contracting with the State to use recycled oil to the maximum extent feasible, consistent with protection of the public health and the environment.

(3) Informing the public of the uses of recycled oil.

(4) Establishment and implementation of a program (including any necessary licensing of persons and including the use, where appropriate, of manifests) to assure that used oil is collected, transported, treated, stored, reused, and disposed of, in a manner which does not present a hazard to the public health or the environment.

Any plan submitted under this chapter before October 15, 1980, may be amended, at the option of the State, at any time after such date to include any provision referred to in this subsection.

(c) Energy and materials conservation and recovery feasibility planning and assistance

(1) A State which has a plan approved under this subchapter or which has submitted a plan for such approval shall be eligible for assistance under section 6948(a)(3) of this title if the Administrator determines that under such plan the State will—

(A) analyze and determine the economic and technical feasibility of facilities and programs to conserve resources which contribute to the waste stream or to recover energy and materials from municipal waste;

(B) analyze the legal, institutional, and economic impediments to the development of systems and facilities for conservation of energy or materials which contribute to the waste stream or for the recovery of energy and materials from municipal waste and make recommendations to appropriate governmental authorities for overcoming such impediments;

(C) assist municipalities within the State in developing plans, programs, and projects to conserve resources or recover energy and materials from municipal waste; and

(D) coordinate the resource conservation and recovery planning under subparagraph (C).

(2) The analysis referred to in paragraph (1)(A) shall include—

(A) the evaluation of, and establishment of priorities among, market opportunities for industrial and commercial users of all types (including public utilities and industrial parks) to utilize energy and materials recovered from municipal waste;

(B) comparisons of the relative costs of energy recovered from municipal waste in relation to the costs of energy derived from fossil fuels and other sources;

(C) studies of the transportation and storage problems and other problems associated with the development of energy and materials recovery technology, including curbside source separation;

(D) the evaluation and establishment of priorities among ways of conserving energy or materials which contribute to the waste stream;

(E) comparison of the relative total costs between conserving resources and disposing of or recovering such waste; and

(F) studies of impediments to resource conservation or recovery, including business practices, transportation requirements, or storage difficulties.

Such studies and analyses shall also include studies of other sources of solid waste from which energy and materials may be recovered or minimized.

(d) Size of waste-to-energy facilities

Notwithstanding any of the above requirements, it is the intention of this chapter and the planning process developed pursuant to this chapter that in determining the size of the waste-to-energy facility, adequate provision shall be given to the present and reasonably anticipated future needs of the recycling and resource recovery interest within the area encompassed by the planning process.

(Pub. L. No. 89–272, Title II, § 4003, as added by Pub. L. No. 94–580, § 2, 90 Stat. 2814 (Oct. 21, 1976); and amended by Pub. L. No. 96–463, § 5(a), (b), 94 Stat. 2056 (Oct. 15, 1980); Pub. L. No. 96–482, §§ 18, 32(d), 94 Stat.

2345, 2353 (Oct. 21, 1980); Pub. L. No. 98–616, Title III, § 301(b), Title V, § 502(h), 98 Stat. 3267, 3277 (Nov. 8, 1984).)

HISTORICAL AND STATUTORY NOTES

Codifications

Another section 5(b) of Pub. L. No. 96–463 amended section 6948 of this title.

§ 6944. Criteria for sanitary landfills; sanitary landfills required for all disposal [SWDA § 4004]

(a) Criteria for sanitary landfills

Not later than one year after October 21, 1976, after consultation with the States, and after notice and public hearings, the Administrator shall promulgate regulations containing criteria for determining which facilities shall be classified as sanitary landfills and which shall be classified as open dumps within the meaning of this chapter. At a minimum, such criteria shall provide that a facility may be classified as a sanitary landfill and not an open dump only if there is no reasonable probability of adverse effects on health or the environment from disposal of solid waste at such facility. Such regulations may provide for the classification of the types of sanitary landfills.

(b) Disposal required to be in sanitary landfills, etc.

For purposes of complying with section 6943(2) of this title each State plan shall prohibit the establishment of open dumps and contain a requirement that disposal of all solid waste within the State shall be in compliance with such section 6943(2) of this title.

(c) Effective date

The prohibition contained in subsection (b) of this section shall take effect on the date six months after the date of promulgation of regulations under subsection (a) of this section.

(Pub. L. No. 89–272, Title II, § 4004, as added by Pub. L. No. 94–580, § 2, 90 Stat. 2815 (Oct. 21, 1976); and amended by Pub. L. No. 98–616, Title III, § 302(b), 98 Stat. 3268 (Nov. 8, 1984).)

HISTORICAL AND STATUTORY NOTES

References in Text

Section 6943(2) of this title, referred to in subsec. (b), was redesignated section 6943(a)(2) of this title by Pub. L. No. 96–463, § 5(b), 94 Stat. 2056 (Oct. 15, 1980), and Pub. L. No. 96–482, § 32(d)(2), 94 Stat. 2353 (Oct. 21, 1980).

Transfer of Functions

For transfer of certain enforcement functions of Administrator or other official of the Environmental Protection Agency under this chapter to Federal Inspector, Office of Federal Inspector for the Alaska Natural Gas Transportation System, see note set out under section 6903 of this title.

§ 6945. Upgrading of open dumps [SWDA § 4005]

(a) Closing or upgrading of existing open dumps

Upon promulgation of criteria under section 6907(a)(3) of this title, any solid waste management practice or disposal of solid waste or hazardous waste which constitutes the open dumping of solid waste or hazardous waste is prohibited, except in the case of any practice or disposal of solid waste under a timetable or schedule for compliance established under this section. The prohibition contained in the preceding sentence shall be enforceable under section 6972 of this title against persons engaged in the act of open dumping. For purposes of complying with section 6943(a)(2) and 6943(a)(3) of this title, each State plan shall contain a requirement that all existing disposal facilities or sites for solid waste in such State which are open dumps listed in the inventory under subsection (b) of this section shall comply with such measures as may be promulgated by the Administrator to eliminate health hazards and minimize potential health hazards. Each such plan shall establish, for any entity which demonstrates that it has considered other public or private alternatives for solid waste management to comply with the prohibition on open dumping and is unable to utilize such alternatives to so comply, a timetable or schedule for compliance for such practice or disposal of solid waste which specifies a schedule of remedial measures, including an enforceable sequence of actions or operations, leading to compliance with the prohibition on open dumping of solid waste within a reasonable time (not to exceed 5 years from the date of publication of criteria under section 6907(a)(3) of this title).

(b) Inventory

To assist the States in complying with section 6943(a)(3) of this title, not later than one year after promulgation of regulations under section 6944 of this title, the Administrator, with the cooperation of the Bureau of the Census shall publish an inventory of all disposal facilities or sites in the United States which are open dumps within the meaning of this chapter.

(c) Control of hazardous disposal

(1) (A) Not later than 36 months after November 8, 1984, each State shall adopt and implement a permit program or other system of prior approval and conditions to assure that each solid waste management facility within such State which may receive hazardous household waste or hazardous waste due to the provision of section 6921(d) of this title for small quantity generators (otherwise not subject to the requirement for a permit under section 6925 of this title) will comply with the applicable criteria promulgated under section 6944(a) and 6907(a)(3) of this title.

(B) Not later than eighteen months after the promulgation of revised criteria under subsection[1] 6944(a) of this title (as required by section 6949a(c) of this title), each State shall adopt and implement a permit program or other system or[2] prior approval and conditions, to assure that each solid waste management facility within such State which may receive hazardous household waste or hazardous waste due to the provision of section 6921(d) of this title for small quantity generators (otherwise not subject to the requirement for a permit under section 6925 of this title) will comply with the criteria revised under section 6944(a) of this title.

(C) The Administrator shall determine whether each State has developed an adequate program under this paragraph. The Administrator may make such a determination in conjunction with approval, disapproval or partial approval of a State plan under section 6947 of this title.

(2) (A) In any State that the Administrator determines has not adopted an adequate program for such facilities under paragraph (1)(B) by the date provided in such paragraph, the Administrator may use the authorities available under sections 6927 and 6928 of this title to enforce the prohibition contained in subsection (a) of this section with respect to such facilities.

(B) For purposes of this paragraph, the term "requirement of this subchapter" in section 6928 of this title shall be deemed to include criteria promulgated by the Administrator under sections 6907(a)(3) and 6944(a) of this title, and the term "hazardous wastes" in section 6927 of this title shall be deemed to include solid waste at facilities that may handle hazardous household wastes or hazardous wastes from small quantity generators.

(d) State programs for control of coal combustion residuals.—

(1) Approval by Administrator.—

(A) In general.—Each State may submit to the Administrator, in such form as the Administrator may establish, evidence of a permit program or other system of prior approval and conditions under State law for regulation by the State of coal combustion residuals units that are located in the State that, after approval by the Administrator, will operate in lieu of regulation of coal combustion residuals units in the State by—

(i) application of part 257 of title 40, Code of Federal Regulations (or successor regulations promulgated pursuant to sections 1008(a)(3) and 4004(a)); or

(ii) implementation by the Administrator of a permit program under paragraph (2)(B).

(B) Requirement.—Not later than 180 days after the date on which a State submits the evidence described in subparagraph (A), the Administrator, after public notice and an opportunity for public comment, shall approve, in whole or in part, a permit program or other system of prior approval and conditions submitted under subparagraph (A) if the Administrator determines that the program or other system requires each coal combustion residuals unit located in the State to achieve compliance with—

(i) the applicable criteria for coal combustion residuals units under part 257 of title 40, Code of Federal Regulations (or successor regulations promulgated pursuant to sections 1008(a)(3) and 4004(a)); or

(ii) such other State criteria that the Administrator, after consultation with the State, determines to be at least as protective as the criteria described in clause (i).

(C) Permit requirements.—The Administrator shall approve under subparagraph (B)(ii) a State permit program or other system of prior approval and conditions that allows a State to include technical standards for individual permits or conditions of approval that differ from the criteria under part 257 of title 40, Code of Federal Regulations (or successor regulations promulgated pursuant to sections 1008(a)(3) and 4004(a)) if, based on site-specific conditions, the Administrator determines that the technical standards established pursuant to a State permit program or other system are at least as protective as the criteria under that part.

(D) Program review and notification.—

(i) Program review.—The Administrator shall review a State permit program or other system of prior approval and conditions that is approved under subparagraph (B)—

(I) from time to time, as the Administrator determines necessary, but not less frequently than once every 12 years;

(II) not later than 3 years after the date on which the Administrator revises the applicable criteria for coal combustion residuals units under part 257 of title 40, Code of Federal Regulations (or successor regulations promulgated pursuant to sections 1008(a)(3) and 4004(a));

(III) not later than 1 year after the date of a significant release (as defined by the Administrator), that was not authorized at the time the release occurred, from a coal combustion residuals unit located in the State; and

(IV) on request of any other State that asserts that the soil, groundwater, or surface water of the State is or is likely to be adversely affected by a release or potential release from a coal combustion residuals unit located in the State for which the program or other system was approved.

(ii) Notification and opportunity for a public hearing.—The Administrator shall provide to a State notice of deficiencies with respect to the permit program or other system of prior approval and conditions of the State that is approved under subparagraph (B), and an opportunity for a public hearing, if the Administrator determines that—

(I) a revision or correction to the permit program or other system of prior approval and conditions of the State is necessary to ensure that the permit program or other system of prior approval and conditions continues to ensure that each coal combustion residuals unit located in the State achieves compliance with the criteria described in clauses (i) and (ii) of subparagraph (B);

(II) the State has not implemented an adequate permit program or other system of prior approval and conditions that requires each coal combustion residuals unit located in the State to achieve compliance with the criteria described in subparagraph (B); or

(III) the State has, at any time, approved or failed to revoke a permit for a coal combustion residuals unit, a release from which adversely affects or is likely to adversely affect the soil, groundwater, or surface water of another State.

(E) Withdrawal.—

(i) In general.—The Administrator shall withdraw approval of a State permit program or other system of prior approval and conditions if, after the Administrator provides notice and an opportunity for a public hearing to the relevant State under subparagraph (D)(ii), the Administrator determines that the State has not corrected the deficiencies identified by the Administrator under subparagraph (D)(ii).

(ii) Reinstatement of State approval.—Any withdrawal of approval under clause (i) shall cease to be effective on the date on which the Administrator makes a determination that the State has corrected the deficiencies identified by the Administrator under subparagraph (D)(ii).

(2) Nonparticipating States.—

(A) Definition of nonparticipating State.—In this paragraph, the term 'nonparticipating State' means a State—

(i) for which the Administrator has not approved a State permit program or other system of prior approval and conditions under paragraph (1)(B);

(ii) the Governor of which has not submitted to the Administrator for approval evidence to operate a State permit program or other system of prior approval and conditions under paragraph (1)(A);

(iii) the Governor of which provides notice to the Administrator that, not fewer than 90 days after the date on which the Governor provides the notice to the Administrator, the State will relinquish an approval under paragraph (1)(B) to operate a permit program or other system of prior approval and conditions; or

(iv) for which the Administrator has withdrawn approval for a permit program or other system of prior approval and conditions under paragraph (1)(E).

(B) Implementation of permit program.—In the case of a nonparticipating State and subject to the availability of appropriations specifically provided in an appropriations Act to carry out a program in a nonparticipating State, the Administrator shall implement a permit program to require each coal combustion residuals unit located in the nonparticipating State to achieve compliance with applicable criteria established by the Administrator under part 257 of title 40, Code of Federal Regulations (or successor regulations promulgated pursuant to sections 1008(a)(3) and 4004(a)).

(3) Applicability of criteria.—The applicable criteria for coal combustion residuals units under part 257 of title 40, Code of Federal Regulations (or successor regulations promulgated pursuant to sections 1008(a)(3) and 4004(a)), shall apply to each coal combustion residuals unit in a State unless—

(A) a permit under a State permit program or other system of prior approval and conditions approved by the Administrator under paragraph (1)(B) is in effect for the coal combustion residuals unit; or

(B) a permit issued by the Administrator in a State in which the Administrator is implementing a permit program under paragraph (2)(B) is in effect for the coal combustion residuals unit.

(4) Prohibition on open dumping.—

(A) In general.—The Administrator may use the authority provided by sections 3007 and 3008 to enforce the prohibition on open dumping under subsection (a) with respect to a coal combustion residuals unit—

(i) in a nonparticipating State (as defined in paragraph (2)); and

(ii) located in a State that is approved to operate a permit program or other system of prior approval and conditions under paragraph (1)(B), in accordance with subparagraph (B) of this paragraph.

(B) Federal enforcement in an approved State.—

(i) In general.—In the case of a coal combustion residuals unit located in a State that is approved to operate a permit program or other system of prior approval and conditions under paragraph (1)(B), the Administrator may commence an administrative or judicial enforcement action under section 3008 if—

(I) the State requests that the Administrator provide assistance in the performance of an enforcement action; or

(II) after consideration of any other administrative or judicial enforcement action involving the coal combustion residuals unit, the Administrator determines that an enforcement action is likely to be necessary to ensure that the coal combustion residuals unit is operating in accordance with the criteria established under the permit program or other system of prior approval and conditions.

(ii) Notification.—In the case of an enforcement action by the Administrator under clause (i)(II), before issuing an order or commencing a civil action, the Administrator shall notify the State in which the coal combustion residuals unit is located.

(iii) Annual report to Congress.—

(I) In general.—Subject to subclause (II), not later than December 31, 2017, and December 31 of each year thereafter, the Administrator shall submit to the Committee on Environment and Public Works of the Senate and the Committee on Energy and Commerce of the House of Representatives a report that describes any enforcement action commenced under clause (i), including a description of the basis for the enforcement action.

(II) Applicability.—Subclause (I) shall not apply for any calendar year during which the Administrator does not commence an enforcement action under clause (i).

(5) Indian Country.—The Administrator shall establish and carry out a permit program, in accordance with this subsection, for coal combustion residuals units in Indian country (as defined in section 1151 of title 18, United States Code) to require each coal combustion residuals unit located in Indian country to achieve compliance with the applicable criteria established by the Administrator under part 257 of title 40, Code of Federal Regulations (or successor regulations promulgated pursuant to sections 1008(a)(3) and 4004(a)).

(6) Treatment of coal combustion residuals units.—A coal combustion residuals unit shall be considered to be a sanitary landfill for purposes of this Act, including subsection (a), only if the coal combustion residuals unit is operating in accordance with—

(A) the requirements of a permit issued by—

(i) the State in accordance with a program or system approved under paragraph (1)(B); or

(ii) the Administrator pursuant to paragraph (2)(B) or paragraph (5); or

(B) the applicable criteria for coal combustion residuals units under part 257 of title 40, Code of Federal Regulations (or successor regulations promulgated pursuant to sections 1008(a)(3) and 4004(a)).

(7) Effect of subsection.—Nothing in this subsection affects any authority, regulatory determination, other law, or legal obligation in effect on the day before the date of enactment of the Water and Waste Act of 2016.

(Pub. L. No. 89–272, Title II, § 4005, as added by Pub. L. No. 94–580, § 2, 90 Stat. 2815 (Oct. 21, 1976); and amended by Pub. L. No. 96–482, § 19(a), (b), 94 Stat. 2345 (Oct. 21, 1980); Pub. L. No. 98–616, Title III, § 302(c), Title IV, § 403(c), Title V, § 502(c), 98 Stat. 3268, 3272, 3276 (Nov. 8, 1984); Pub. L. No. 114–322, § 2301, 130 Stat. 1736–40 (Dec. 16, 2016).)

[1] So in original. Probably should be "section".

[2] So in original. Probably should be "of".

HISTORICAL AND STATUTORY NOTES

Codifications

Another section 19(b) of Pub. L. No. 96–482 amended section 6946 of this title.

Transfer of Functions

For transfer of certain enforcement functions of Administrator or other official of the Environmental Protection Agency under this chapter to Federal Inspector, Office of Federal Inspector for the Alaska Natural Gas Transportation System, see note set out under section 6903 of this title.

§ 6946. Procedure for development and implementation of State plan

[SWDA § 4006]

(a) Identification of regions

Within one hundred and eighty days after publication of guidelines under section 6942(a) of this title (relating to identification of regions), the Governor of each State, after consultation with local elected officials, shall promulgate regulations based on such guidelines identifying the boundaries of each area within the State which, as a result of urban concentrations, geographic conditions, markets, and other factors, is appropriate for carrying out regional solid waste management. Such regulations may be modified from time to time (identifying additional or different regions) pursuant to such guidelines.

(b) Identification of State and local agencies and responsibilities

(1) Within one hundred and eighty days after the Governor promulgates regulations under subsection (a) of this section, for purposes of facilitating the development and implementation of a State plan which will meet the minimum requirements of section 6943 of this title, the State, together with appropriate elected officials of general purpose units of local government, shall jointly (A) identify an agency to develop the State plan and identify one or more agencies to implement such plan, and (B) identify which solid waste management activities will, under such State plan, be planned for and carried out by the State and which such management activities will, under such State plan, be planned for and carried out by a regional or local authority or a combination of regional or local and State authorities. If a multi-functional regional agency authorized by State law to conduct solid waste planning and management (the members of which are appointed by the Governor) is in existence on October 21, 1976, the Governor shall identify such authority for purposes of carrying out within such region clause (A) of this paragraph. Where feasible, designation of the agency for the affected area designated under section 1288 of Title 33 shall be considered. A State agency identified under this paragraph shall be established or designated by the Governor of such State. Local or regional agencies identified under this paragraph shall be composed of individuals at least a majority of whom are elected local officials.

(2) If planning and implementation agencies are not identified and designated or established as required under paragraph (1) for any affected area, the governor shall, before the date two hundred and seventy days after promulgation of regulations under subsection (a) of this section, establish or designate a State agency to develop and implement the State plan for such area.

(c) Interstate regions

(1) In the case of any region which, pursuant to the guidelines published by the Administrator under section 6942(a) of this title (relating to identification of regions), would be located in two or more States, the Governors of the respective States, after consultation with local elected officials, shall consult, cooperate, and enter into agreements identifying the boundaries of such region pursuant to subsection (a) of this section.

(2) Within one hundred and eighty days after an interstate region is identified by agreement under paragraph (1), appropriate elected officials of general purpose units of local government within such region shall jointly establish or designate an agency to develop a plan for such region. If no such agency is established or designated within such period by such officials, the Governors of the respective States may, by agreement, establish or designate for such purpose a single representative organization including elected officials of general purpose units of local government within such region.

(3) Implementation of interstate regional solid waste management plans shall be conducted by units of local government for any portion of a region within their jurisdiction, or by multijurisdictional agencies or authorities designated in accordance with State law, including those designated by agreement by such units of local government for such purpose. If no such unit, agency, or authority is so designated, the respective Governors shall designate or establish a single interstate agency to implement such plan.

(4) For purposes of this subchapter, so much of an interstate regional plan as is carried out within a particular State shall be deemed part of the State plan for such State.

(Pub. L. No. 89–272, Title II, § 4006, as added by Pub. L. No. 94–580, § 2, 90 Stat. 2816 (Oct. 21, 1976); and amended by Pub. L. No. 96–482, § 19(b), 94 Stat. 2345 (Oct. 21, 1980).)

HISTORICAL AND STATUTORY NOTES

Codifications

Another section 19(b) of Pub. L. No. 96–482 amended section 6945 of this title.

Transfer of Functions

For transfer of certain enforcement functions of Administrator or other official of the Environmental Protection Agency under this chapter to Federal Inspector, Office of Federal Inspector for the Alaska Natural Gas Transportation System, see note set out under section 6903 of this title.

§ 6947. Approval of State plan; Federal assistance

[SWDA § 4007]

(a) Plan approval

The Administrator shall, within six months after a State plan has been submitted for approval, approve or disapprove the plan. The Administrator shall approve a plan if he determines that—

(1) it meets the requirements of paragraphs (1), (2), (3), and (5) of section 6943(a) of this title; and

(2) it contains provision for revision of such plan, after notice and public hearing, whenever the Administrator, by regulation, determines—

(A) that revised regulations respecting minimum requirements have been promulgated under paragraphs (1), (2), (3), and (5) of section 6943(a) of this title with which the State plan is not in compliance;

(B) that information has become available which demonstrates the inadequacy of the plan to effectuate the purposes of this subchapter; or

(C) that such revision is otherwise necessary.

The Administrator shall review approved plans from time to time and if he determines that revision or corrections are necessary to bring such plan into compliance with the minimum requirements promulgated under section 6943 of this title (including new or revised requirements), he shall, after notice and opportunity for public hearing, withdraw his approval of such plan. Such withdrawal of approval shall cease to be effective upon the Administrator's determination that such complies with such minimum requirements.

(b) Eligibility of States for Federal financial assistance

(1) The Administrator shall approve a State application for financial assistance under this subchapter, and make grants to such State, if such State and local and regional authorities within such State have complied with the requirements of section 6946 of this title within the period required under such section and if such State has a State plan which has been approved by the Administrator under this subchapter.

(2) The Administrator shall approve a State application for financial assistance under this subchapter, and make grants to such State, for fiscal years 1978 and 1979 if the Administrator determines that the State plan continues to be eligible for approval under subsection (a) of this section and is being implemented by the State.

(3) Upon withdrawal of approval of a State plan under subsection (a) of this section, the Administrator shall withhold Federal financial and technical assistance under this subchapter (other than such technical assistance as may be necessary to assist in obtaining the reinstatement of approval) until such time as such approval is reinstated.

(c) Existing activities

Nothing in this subchapter shall be construed to prevent or affect any activities respecting solid waste planning or management which are carried out by State, regional, or local authorities unless such activities are inconsistent with a State plan approved by the Administrator under this subchapter.

(Pub. L. No. 89–272, Title II, § 4007, as added by Pub. L. No. 94–580, § 2, 90 Stat. 2817 (Oct. 21, 1976); and amended by Pub. L. No. 95–609, § 7(*l*), 92 Stat. 3082 (Nov. 8, 1978); Pub. L. No. 104–119, § 4(8), 110 Stat. 833 (Mar. 26, 1996).)

HISTORICAL AND STATUTORY NOTES

Transfer of Functions

For transfer of certain enforcement functions of Administrator or other official of the Environmental Protection Agency under this chapter to Federal Inspector, Office of Federal Inspector for the Alaska Natural Gas Transportation System, see note set out under section 6903 of this title.

§ 6948. Federal assistance

[SWDA § 4008]

(a) Authorization of Federal financial assistance

(1) There are authorized to be appropriated $30,000,000 for fiscal year 1978, $40,000,000 for fiscal year 1979, $20,000,000 for fiscal year 1980, $15,000,000 for fiscal year 1981, $20,000,000 for the fiscal year 1982, and $10,000,000 for each of the fiscal years 1985 through 1988 for purposes of financial assistance to States and local, regional, and interstate authorities for the development and implementation of plans approved by the Administrator under this subchapter (other than the provisions of such plans referred to in section 6943(b) of this title, relating to feasibility planning for municipal waste energy and materials conservation and recovery).

(2) (A) The Administrator is authorized to provide financial assistance to States, counties, municipalities, and intermunicipal agencies and State and local public solid waste management authorities for implementation of programs to provide solid waste management, resource recovery, and resource conservation services and hazardous waste management. Such assistance shall include assistance for facility planning and feasibility studies; expert consultation; surveys and analyses of market needs; marketing of recovered resources; technology assessments; legal expenses; construction feasibility studies; source separation projects; and fiscal or economic investigations or studies; but such assistance shall not include any other element of construction, or any acquisition of land or interest in land, or any subsidy for the price of recovered resources. Agencies assisted under this subsection shall consider existing solid waste management and hazardous waste management services and facilities as well as facilities proposed for construction.

(B) An applicant for financial assistance under this paragraph must agree to comply with respect to the project or program assisted with the applicable requirements of section 6945 of this title and subchapter III of this chapter and apply applicable solid waste management practices, methods, and levels of control consistent with any guidelines published pursuant to section 6907 of this title. Assistance under this paragraph shall be available only for programs certified by the State to be consistent with any applicable State or areawide solid waste management plan or program. Applicants for technical and financial assistance under this section shall not preclude or foreclose consideration of programs for the recovery of recyclable materials through source separation or other resource recovery techniques.

(C) There are authorized to be appropriated $15,000,000 for each of the fiscal years 1978 and 1979 for purposes of this section. There are authorized to be appropriated $10,000,000 for fiscal year 1980, $10,000,000 for fiscal year 1981, $10,000,000 for fiscal year 1982, and $10,000,000 for each of the fiscal years 1985 through 1988 for purposes of this paragraph.

(D) There are authorized—

(i) to be made available $15,000,000 out of funds appropriated for fiscal year 1985, and

(ii) to be appropriated for each of the fiscal years 1986 though[1] 1988, $20,000,000[2]

for grants to States (and where appropriate to regional, local, and interstate agencies) to implement programs requiring compliance by solid waste management facilities with the criteria promulgated under section 6944(a) of this title and section 6907(a)(3) of this title and with the provisions of section 6945 of this title. To the extent practicable, such programs shall require such compliance not later than thirty-six months after November 8, 1984.

(3) (A) There is authorized to be appropriated for the fiscal year beginning October 1, 1981, and for each fiscal year thereafter before October 1, 1986, $4,000,000 for purposes of making grants to States to carry out section 6943(b) of this title. No amount may be appropriated for such purposes for the fiscal year beginning on October 1, 1986, or for any fiscal year thereafter.

(B) Assistance provided by the Administrator under this paragraph shall be used only for the purposes specified in section 6943(b) of this title. Such assistance may not be used for purposes of land acquisition, final facility design, equipment purchase, construction, startup or operation activities.

(C) Where appropriate, any State receiving assistance under this paragraph may make all or any part of such assistance available to municipalities within the State to carry out the activities specified in section 6943(b)(1)(A) and (B) of this title.

(b) State allotment

The sums appropriated in any fiscal year under subsection (a)(1) of this section shall be allotted by the Administrator among all States, in the ratio that the population in each State bears to the population in all of the States, except that no State shall receive less than one-half of 1 per centum of the sums so allotted in any fiscal year. No State shall receive any grant under this section during any fiscal year when its expenditures of non-Federal funds for other than non-recurrent expenditures for solid waste management control programs will be less than its expenditures were for such programs during fiscal year 1975, except that such funds may be reduced by an amount equal to their proportionate share of any general reduction of State spending ordered by the Governor or legislature of such State. No State shall receive any grant for solid waste management programs unless the Administrator is satisfied that such grant will be so used as to supplement and, to the extent practicable, increase the level of State, local, regional, or other non-Federal funds that would in the absence of such grant be made available for the maintenance of such programs.

(c) Distribution of Federal financial assistance within the State

The Federal assistance allotted to the States under subsection (b) of this section shall be allocated by the State receiving such funds to State, local, regional, and interstate authorities carrying out planning and implementation of the State plan. Such allocation shall be based upon the responsibilities of the respective parties as determined pursuant to section 6946(b) of this title.

(d) Technical assistance

(1) The Administrator may provide technical assistance to State and local governments for purposes of developing and implementing State plans. Technical assistance respecting resource recovery and conservation may be provided through resource recovery and conservation panels, established in the Environmental Protection Agency under subchapter II of this chapter, to assist the State and local governments with respect to particular resource recovery and conservation projects under consideration and to evaluate their effect on the State plan.

(2) In carrying out this subsection, the Administrator may, upon request, provide technical assistance to States to assist in the removal or modification of legal, institutional, economic, and other impediments to the recycling of used oil. Such impediments may include laws, regulations, and policies, including State procurement policies, which are not favorable to the recycling of used oil.

(3) In carrying out this subsection, the Administrator is authorized to provide technical assistance to States, municipalities, regional authorities, and intermunicipal agencies upon request, to assist in the removal or modification of legal, institutional, and economic impediments which have the effect of impeding the development of systems and facilities to recover energy and materials from municipal waste or to conserve energy or materials which contribute to the waste stream. Such impediments may include—

(A) laws, regulations, and policies, including State and local procurement policies, which are not favorable to resource conservation and recovery policies, systems, and facilities;

(B) impediments to the financing of facilities to conserve or recover energy and materials from municipal waste through the exercise of State and local authority to issue revenue bonds and the use of State and local credit assistance; and

(C) impediments to institutional arrangements necessary to undertake projects for the conservation or recovery of energy and materials from municipal waste, including the creation of special districts, authorities, or corporations where necessary having the power to secure the supply of waste of a project, to conserve resources, to implement the project, and to undertake related activities.

(e) Special communities

(1) The Administrator, in cooperation with State and local officials, shall identify local governments within the United States (A) having a solid waste disposal facility (i) which is owned by the unit of local government, (ii) for which an order has been issued by the State to cease receiving solid waste for treatment, storage, or disposal, and (iii) which is subject to a State-approved end-use recreation plan, and (B) which are located over an aquifer which is the source of drinking water for any person or public water system and which has serious environmental problems resulting from the disposal of such solid waste, including possible methane migration.

(2) There is authorized to be appropriated to the Administrator $2,500,000 for the fiscal year 1980 and $1,500,000 for each of the fiscal years 1981 and 1982 to make grants to be used for containment and stabilization of solid waste located at the disposal sites referred to in paragraph (1). Not more than one community in any State shall be eligible for grants under this paragraph and not more than one project in any State shall be eligible for such grants. No unit of local government shall be eligible for grants under this paragraph with respect to any site which exceeds 65 acres in size.

(f) Assistance to States for discretionary program for recycled oil

(1) The Administrator may make grants to States, which have a State plan approved under section 6947 of this title, or which have submitted a State plan for approval under such section, if such plan includes the discretionary provisions described in section 6943(b) of this title. Grants under this subsection shall be for purposes of assisting the State in carrying out such discretionary provisions. No grant under this subsection may be used for construction or for the acquisition of land or equipment.

(2) Grants under this subsection shall be allotted among the States in the same manner as provided in the first sentence of subsection (b) of this section.

(3) No grant may be made under this subsection unless an application therefor is submitted to, and approved by, the Administrator. The application shall be in such form, be submitted in such manner, and contain such information as the Administrator may require.

(4) For purposes of making grants under this subsection, there are authorized to be appropriated $5,000,000 for fiscal year 1982, $5,000,000 for fiscal year 1983, and $5,000,000 for each of the fiscal years 1985 through 1988.

(g) Assistance to municipalities for energy and materials conservation and recovery planning activities

(1) The Administrator is authorized to make grants to municipalities, regional authorities, and intermunicipal agencies to carry out activities described in subparagraphs (A) and (B) of section 6943(b)(1) of this title. Such grants may be made only pursuant to an application submitted to the Administrator by the municipality which application has been approved by the State and determined by the State to be consistent with any State plan approved or submitted under this subchapter or any other appropriate planning carried out by the State.

(2) There is authorized to be appropriated for the fiscal year beginning October 1, 1981, and for each fiscal year thereafter before October 1, 1986, $8,000,000 for purposes of making grants to municipalities under this subsection. No amount may be appropriated for such purposes for the fiscal year beginning on October 1, 1986, or for any fiscal year thereafter.

(3) Assistance provided by the Administrator under this subsection shall be used only for the purposes specified in paragraph (1). Such assistance may not be used for purposes of land acquisition, final facility design, equipment purchase, construction, startup or operation activities.

(Pub. L. No. 89–272, Title II, § 4008, as added by Pub. L. No. 94–580, § 2, 90 Stat. 2818 (Oct. 21, 1976); and amended by Pub. L. No. 96–463, §§ 5(b), 6, 94 Stat. 2057 (Oct. 15, 1980); Pub. L. No. 96–482, §§ 20, 31(c), (d), 32(e), (f), 94 Stat. 2345, 2352, 2354, 2355 (Oct. 21, 1980); Pub. L. No. 98–616, § 2(d) to (g), (k), Title V, § 502(d), (e), 98 Stat. 3222, 3223, 3276 (Nov. 8, 1984).)

[1] So in original. Probably should be "through."

[2] So in original. Probably should be followed by a comma.

HISTORICAL AND STATUTORY NOTES

References in Text

Section 6943(b) of this title, referred to in subsecs. (a)(1), (3), and (g)(1), was redesignated section 6943(c) of this title by Pub. L. No. 98–616, Title V, § 502(h), 98 Stat. 3277 (Nov. 8, 1984).

Codifications

Section 2(d) to (g) of Pub. L. No. 98–616, cited in the credit to this section, appears to contain a typographical error in that the text of subsec. "(f)(1)" of such section 2 is also shown as the text of subsec. (f)(1) of section 2007 of the Solid Waste Disposal Act (as added by section 2(i) of Pub. L. No. 98–616). Subsec. (f) of section 2, as set out in the Conference Report (H.Rept. 98–1133) to accompany H.R. 2867 (which became Pub. L. No. 98–616) read:

"(f) Section 4008(e)(2) of the Solid Waste Disposal Act (relating to special communities) is amended by striking out 'and $1,500,000 for each of the fiscal years 1981 and 1982' and substituting ', $1,500,000 for each of the fiscal years 1981 and 1982, and $500,000 for each of the fiscal years 1985 through 1988'."

Another section 5(b) of Pub. L. No. 96–463 amended section 6943 of this title.

Transfer of Functions

For transfer of certain enforcement functions of Administrator or other official of the Environmental Protection Agency under this chapter to Federal Inspector, Office of Federal Inspector for the Alaska Natural Gas Transportation System, see note set out under section 6903 of this title.

§ 6949. Rural communities assistance

[SWDA § 4009]

(a) In general

The Administrator shall make grants to States to provide assistance to municipalities with a population of five thousand or less, or counties with a population of ten thousand or less or less than twenty persons per square mile and not within a metropolitan area, for solid waste management facilities (including equipment) necessary to meet the requirements of section 6945 of this title or restrictions on open burning or other requirements arising under the Clean Air Act [42 U.S.C.A. § 7401 et seq.] or the Federal Water Pollution Control Act [33 U.S.C.A. § 1251 et seq.]. Such assistance shall only be available—

(1) to any municipality or county which could not feasibly be included in a solid waste management system or facility serving an urbanized, multijurisdictional area because of its distance from such systems;

(2) where existing or planned solid waste management services or facilities are unavailable or insufficient to comply with the requirements of section 6945 of this title; and

(3) for systems which are certified by the State to be consistent with any plans or programs established under any State or areawide planning process.

(b) Allotment

The Administrator shall allot the sums appropriated to carry out this section in any fiscal year among the States in accordance with regulations promulgated by him on the basis of the average of the ratio which the population of rural areas of each State bears to the total population of rural areas of all the States, the ratio which the population of counties in each State having less than twenty persons per square mile bears to the total population of such counties in all the States, and the ratio which the population of such low-density counties in each State having 33 per centum or more of all families with incomes not in excess of 125 per centum of the poverty level bears to the total population of such counties in all the States.

(c) Limit

The amount of any grant under this section shall not exceed 75 per centum of the costs of the project. No assistance under this section shall be available for the acquisition of land or interests in land.

(d) Authorization of appropriations

There are authorized to be appropriated $25,000,000 for each of the fiscal years 1978 and 1979 to carry out this section. There are authorized to be appropriated $10,000,000 for the fiscal year 1980 and $15,000,000 for each of the fiscal years 1981 and 1982 to carry out this section.

(e) Additional appropriations

(1) In general

There are authorized to be appropriated to carry out this section for the Denali Commission to provide assistance to municipalities in the State of Alaska $1,500,000 for each of fiscal years 2008 through 2012.

(2) Administration

For the purpose of carrying out this subsection, the Denali Commission shall—

(A) be considered a State; and

(B) comply with all other requirements and limitations of this section.

(Pub. L. No. 89–272, Title II, § 4009, as added by Pub. L. No. 94–580, § 2, 90 Stat. 2819 (Oct. 21, 1976); and amended by Pub. L. No. 96–482, § 31(e), 94 Stat. 2353 (Oct. 21, 1980); Pub. L. No. 110–234, Title VI, § 6009(b), 122 Stat. 1163 (May 22, 2008); Pub. L. No. 110–246, § 4(a), Title VI, § 6009(b), 122 Stat. 1664, 1924 (June 18, 2008).)

HISTORICAL AND STATUTORY NOTES

References in Text

The Clean Air Act, referred to in subsec. (a), is Act of July 14, 1955, c. 360, as amended generally by Pub. L. No. 88–206, 77 Stat. 392 (Dec. 17, 1963), and later by Pub. L. No. 95–95, 91 Stat. 685 (Aug. 7, 1977). The Clean Air Act was originally codified as chapter 15B (section 1857 et seq.) of this title. On enactment of Pub. L. No. 95–95, the Act was recodified as chapter 85 (section 7401 et seq.) of this title. For complete classification of this Act to the Code, see Short Title of 1955 Acts note set out under section 7401 of this title and Tables.

The Federal Water Pollution Control Act, referred to in subsec. (a), is Act of June 30, 1948, c. 758, as amended generally by Pub. L. No. 92–500, § 2, 86 Stat. 816 (Oct. 18, 1972), which is codified generally as chapter 26 (section 1251 et seq.) of Title 33, Navigation and Navigable Waters. For complete classification of this Act to the Code, see Short Title note set out under section 1251 of Title 33 and Tables.

Codifications

The authorities provided by each provision of, and each amendment made by, Pub. L. No. 110–246, as in effect on Sept. 30, 2012, to continue, and the Secretary of Agriculture to carry out the authorities, until the later of Sept. 30, 2013, or the date specified in the provision of, or amendment made by, Pub. L. No. 110–246, see section 701(a) of Pub. L. No. 112–240, set out in a note under 7 U.S.C.A. § 8701.

Effective and Applicability Provisions

2008 Acts. Amendments by Pub. L. No. 110–246, except as otherwise provided, shall take effect on the earlier of June 18, 2008, or May 22, 2008, see Pub. L. No. 110–246, § 4(b), set out in a Repeal of Duplicative Enactment note under 7 U.S.C.A. § 8701.

Transfer of Functions

For transfer of certain enforcement functions of Administrator or other official of the Environmental Protection Agency under this chapter to Federal Inspector, Office of Federal Inspector for the Alaska Natural Gas Transportation System, see note set out under section 6903 of this title.

Repeals

Pub. L. No. 110–234 repealed effective May 22, 2008, see Repeal of Duplicative Enactment by Pub. L. No. 110–246, § 4(a), set out in a note under 7 U.S.C.A. § 8701.

§ 6949a. Adequacy of certain guidelines and criteria

[SWDA § 4010]

(a) Study

The Administrator shall conduct a study of the extent to which the guidelines and criteria under this chapter (other than guidelines and criteria for facilities to which subchapter III of this chapter applies) which are applicable to solid waste management and disposal facilities, including, but not limited to landfills and surface impoundments, are adequate to protect human health and the environment from ground water contamination. Such study shall include a detailed assessment of the degree to which the criteria under section 6907(a) of this title and the criteria under section 6944 of this title regarding monitoring, prevention of contamination, and remedial action are adequate to protect ground water and shall also include recommendation with respect to any additional enforcement authorities which the Administrator, in consultation with the Attorney General, deems necessary for such purposes.

(b) Report

Not later than thirty-six months after November 8, 1984, the Administrator shall submit a report to the Congress setting forth the results of the study required under this section, together with any recommendations made by the Administrator on the basis of such study.

(c) Revisions of guidelines and criteria

(1) In general

Not later than March 31, 1988, the Administrator shall promulgate revisions of the criteria promulgated under paragraph (1) of section 6944(a) of this title and under section 6907(a)(3) of this title for facilities that may receive hazardous household wastes or hazardous wastes from small quantity generators under section 6921(d) of this title. The criteria shall be those necessary to protect human health and the environment and may take into account the practicable capability of such facilities. At a minimum such revisions for facilities potentially receiving such wastes should require ground water monitoring as necessary to detect contamination, establish criteria for the acceptable location of new or existing facilities, and provide for corrective action as appropriate.

(2) Additional revisions

Subject to paragraph (3), the requirements of the criteria described in paragraph (1) relating to ground water monitoring shall not apply to an owner or operator of a new municipal solid waste landfill unit, an existing municipal solid waste landfill unit, or a lateral expansion of a municipal solid waste landfill unit, that disposes of less than 20 tons of municipal solid waste daily, based on an annual average, if—

(A) there is no evidence of ground water contamination from the municipal solid waste landfill unit or expansion; and

(B) the municipal solid waste landfill unit or expansion serves—

(i) a community that experiences an annual interruption of at least 3 consecutive months of surface transportation that prevents access to a regional waste management facility; or

(ii) a community that has no practicable waste management alternative and the landfill unit is located in an area that annually receives less than or equal to 25 inches of precipitation.

(3) Protection of ground water resources

(A) Monitoring requirement

A State may require ground water monitoring of a solid waste landfill unit that would otherwise be exempt under paragraph (2) if necessary to protect ground water resources and ensure compliance with a State ground water protection plan, where applicable.

(B) Methods

If a State requires ground water monitoring of a solid waste landfill unit under subparagraph (A), the State may allow the use of a method other than the use of ground water monitoring wells to detect a release of contamination from the unit.

(C) Corrective action

If a State finds a release from a solid waste landfill unit, the State shall require corrective action as appropriate.

(4) No-migration exemption

(A) In general

Ground water monitoring requirements may be suspended by the Director of an approved State for a landfill operator if the operator demonstrates that there is no potential for migration of hazardous constituents from the unit to the uppermost aquifer during the active life of the unit and the post-closure care period.

(B) Certification

A demonstration under subparagraph (A) shall be certified by a qualified ground-water scientist and approved by the Director of an approved State.

(C) Guidance

Not later than 6 months after March 26, 1996, the Administrator shall issue a guidance document to facilitate small community use of the no migration[1] exemption under this paragraph.

(5) Alaska Native villages

Upon certification by the Governor of the State of Alaska that application of the requirements described in paragraph (1) to a solid waste landfill unit of a Native village (as defined in section 1602 of Title 43) or unit that is located in or near a small, remote Alaska village would be infeasible, or would not be cost-effective, or is otherwise inappropriate because of the remote location of the unit, the State may exempt the unit from some or all of those requirements. This paragraph shall apply only to solid waste landfill units that dispose of less than 20 tons of municipal solid waste daily, based on an annual average.

(6) Further revisions of guidelines and criteria

Recognizing the unique circumstances of small communities, the Administrator shall, not later than two years after March 26, 1996, promulgate revisions to the guidelines and criteria promulgated under this subchapter to provide additional flexibility to approved States to allow landfills that receive

20 tons or less of municipal solid waste per day, based on an annual average, to use alternative frequencies of daily cover application, frequencies of methane gas monitoring, infiltration layers for final cover, and means for demonstrating financial assurance: Provided, That such alternative requirements take into account climatic and hydrogeologic conditions and are protective of human health and environment.

(Pub. L. No. 89–272, Title II, § 4010, as added by Pub. L. No. 98–616, Title III, § 302(a)(1), 98 Stat. 3267 (Nov. 8, 1984); and amended by Pub. L. No. 104–119, § 3(a), 110 Stat. 831 (Mar. 26, 1996).)

[1] So in original. Probably should be "no-migration".

HISTORICAL AND STATUTORY NOTES

Codifications

Section 1602 of Title 43, appearing in subsec. (c)(5), was in the original section 3 of the Alaska Native Claims Settlement Act (16 U.S.C. 1602), which is section 3 of Pub. L. No. 92–203, 85 Stat. 688 (Dec. 18, 1971), as amended, and is codified as section 1602 of Title 43, Public Lands. Translation was made to section 1602 of Title 43 as the probable intent of Congress.

Not later than two years after March 26, 1996, appearing in subsec. (c)(6), was in the original not later than two years after enactment of this provision. Such provision was enacted by Pub. L. No. 104–119, 110 Stat. 830, which was approved Mar. 26, 1996; translation to this date was made as the probable intent of Congress.

Reinstatement of Regulatory Exemption

Section 3(b) of Pub. L. No. 104–119 provided that: "It is the intent of section 4010(c)(2) of the Solid Waste Disposal Act, as added by subsection (a) [subsec. (c)(2) of this section], to immediately reinstate subpart E of part 258 of title 40, Code of Federal Regulations, as added by the final rule published at 56 Federal Register 50798 on October 9, 1991."

SUBCHAPTER V—DUTIES OF THE SECRETARY OF COMMERCE IN RESOURCE AND RECOVERY

§ 6951. Functions

[SWDA § 5001]

The Secretary of Commerce shall encourage greater commercialization of proven resource recovery technology by providing—

(1) accurate specifications for recovered materials;

(2) stimulation of development of markets for recovered materials;

(3) promotion of proven technology; and

(4) a forum for the exchange of technical and economic data relating to resource recovery facilities.

(Pub. L. No. 89–272, Title II, § 5001, as added by Pub. L. No. 94–580, § 2, 90 Stat. 2820 (Oct. 21, 1976).)

§ 6952. Development of specifications for secondary materials

[SWDA § 5002]

The Secretary of Commerce, acting through the National Institute of Standards and Technology, and in conjunction with national standards-setting organizations in resource recovery, shall, after public hearings, and not later than two years after September 1, 1979, publish guidelines for the development of specifications for the classification of materials recovered from waste which were destined for disposal. The specifications shall pertain to the physical and chemical properties and characteristics of such materials with regard to their use in replacing virgin materials in various industrial, commercial, and governmental uses. In establishing such guidelines the Secretary shall also, to the extent feasible, provide such information as may be necessary to assist Federal agencies with procurement of items containing recovered materials. The Secretary shall continue to cooperate with national standards-setting organizations, as may be necessary, to encourage the publication, promulgation and updating of standards for recovered materials and for the use of recovered materials in various industrial, commercial, and governmental uses.

(Pub. L. No. 89–272, Title II, § 5002, as added by Pub. L. No. 94–580, § 2, 90 Stat. 2820 (Oct. 21, 1976); and amended by Pub. L. No. 96–482, § 21(a), 94 Stat. 2346 (Oct. 21, 1980); Pub. L. No. 100–418, Title V, § 5115(c), 102 Stat. 1433 (Aug. 23, 1988).)

§ 6953. Development of markets for recovered materials

[SWDA § 5003]

The Secretary of Commerce shall within two years after September 1, 1979, take such actions as may be necessary to—

(1) identify the geographical location of existing or potential markets for recovered materials;

(2) identify the economic and technical barriers to the use of recovered materials; and

(3) encourage the development of new uses for recovered materials.

(Pub. L. No. 89–272, Title II, § 5003, as added by Pub. L. No. 94–580, § 2, 90 Stat. 2821 (Oct. 21, 1976); and amended by Pub. L. No. 96–482, § 21(b), 94 Stat. 2346 (Oct. 21, 1980).)

§ 6954. Technology promotion

[SWDA § 5004]

The Secretary of Commerce is authorized to evaluate the commercial feasibility of resource recovery facilities and to publish the results of such evaluation, and to develop a data base for purposes of assisting persons in choosing such a system.

(Pub. L. No. 89–272, Title II, § 5004, as added by Pub. L. No. 94–580, § 2, 90 Stat. 2821 (Oct. 21, 1976).)

§ 6955. Marketing policies, establishment; nondiscrimination requirement

[SWDA § 5005]

In establishing any policies which may affect the development of new markets for recovered materials and in making any determination concerning whether or not to impose monitoring or other controls on any marketing or transfer of recovered materials, the Secretary of Commerce may consider whether to establish the same or similar policies or impose the same or similar monitoring or other controls on virgin materials.

(Pub. L. No. 89–272, Title II, § 5005, as added by Pub. L. No. 96–482, § 21(c)(1), 94 Stat. 2346 (Oct. 21, 1980).)

§ 6956. Authorization of appropriations

[SWDA § 5006]

There are authorized to be appropriated to the Secretary of Commerce $5,000,000 for each of fiscal years 1980, 1981, and 1982 and $1,500,000 for each of the fiscal years 1985 through 1988 to carry out the purposes of this subchapter.

(Pub. L. No. 89–272, Title II, § 5006, as added by Pub. L. No. 96–482, § 31(f)(1), 94 Stat. 2353 (Oct. 21, 1980); and amended by Pub. L. No. 98–616, § 2(h), 98 Stat. 3223 (Nov. 8, 1984).)

SUBCHAPTER VI—FEDERAL RESPONSIBILITIES

§ 6961. Application of Federal, State, and local law to Federal facilities [SWDA § 6001]

(a) In general

Each department, agency, and instrumentality of the executive, legislative, and judicial branches of the Federal Government (1) having jurisdiction over any solid waste management facility or disposal site, or (2) engaged in any activity resulting, or which may result, in the disposal or management of solid waste or hazardous waste shall be subject to, and comply with, all Federal, State, interstate, and local requirements, both substantive and procedural (including any requirement for permits or reporting or any provisions for injunctive relief and such sanctions as may be imposed by a court to enforce such relief), respecting control and abatement of solid waste or hazardous waste disposal and management in the same manner, and to the same extent, as any person is subject to such requirements, including the payment of reasonable service charges. The Federal, State, interstate, and local substantive and procedural requirements referred to in this subsection include, but are not limited to, all administrative orders and all civil and administrative penalties and fines, regardless of whether such penalties or fines are punitive or coercive in nature or are imposed for isolated, intermittent, or continuing violations. The United States hereby expressly waives any immunity otherwise applicable to the United States with respect to any such substantive or procedural requirement (including, but not limited to, any injunctive relief, administrative order or civil or administrative penalty or fine referred to in the preceding sentence, or reasonable service charge). The reasonable service charges referred to in this subsection include, but are not limited to, fees or charges assessed in connection with the processing and issuance of permits, renewal of permits, amendments to permits, review of plans, studies, and other documents, and inspection and monitoring of facilities, as well as any other nondiscriminatory charges that are assessed in connection with a Federal, State, interstate, or local solid waste or hazardous waste regulatory program. Neither the United States, nor any agent, employee, or officer thereof, shall be immune or exempt from any process or sanction of any State or Federal Court with respect to the enforcement of any such injunctive relief. No agent, employee, or officer of the United States shall be personally liable for any civil penalty under any Federal, State, interstate, or local solid or hazardous waste law with respect to any act or omission within the scope of the official duties of the agent, employee, or officer. An agent, employee, or officer of the United States shall be subject to any criminal sanction (including, but not limited to, any fine or imprisonment) under any Federal or State solid or hazardous waste law, but no department, agency, or instrumentality of the executive, legislative, or judicial branch of the Federal Government shall be subject to any such sanction. The President may exempt any solid waste management facility of any department, agency, or instrumentality in the executive branch from compliance with such a requirement if he determines it to be in the paramount interest of the United States to do so. No such exemption shall be granted due to lack of appropriation unless the President shall have specifically requested such appropriation as a part of the budgetary process and the Congress shall have failed to make available such requested appropriation. Any exemption shall be for a period not in excess of one year, but additional exemptions may be granted for periods not to exceed one year upon the President's making a new determination. The President shall report each January to the Congress all exemptions from the requirements of this section granted during the preceding calendar year, together with his reason for granting each such exemption.

(b) Administrative enforcement actions

(1) The Administrator may commence an administrative enforcement action against any department, agency, or instrumentality of the executive, legislative, or judicial branch of the Federal Government pursuant to the enforcement authorities contained in this chapter. The Administrator shall initiate an administrative enforcement action against such a department, agency, or instrumentality in the same manner and under the same circumstances as an action would be initiated against another person. Any voluntary resolution or settlement of such an action shall be set forth in a consent order.

(2) No administrative order issued to such a department, agency, or instrumentality shall become final until such department, agency, or instrumentality has had the opportunity to confer with the Administrator.

(c) Limitation on State use of funds collected from Federal Government

Unless a State law in effect on October 6, 1992, or a State constitution requires the funds to be used in a different manner, all funds collected by a State from the Federal Government from penalties and fines imposed for violation of any substantive or procedural requirement referred to in subsection (a) of this section shall be used by the State only for projects designed to improve or protect the environment or to defray the costs of environmental protection or enforcement.

(Pub. L. No. 89–272, Title II, § 6001, as added by Pub. L. No. 94–580, § 2, 90 Stat. 2821 (Oct. 21, 1976); and amended by Pub. L. No. 95–609, § 7(m), 92 Stat. 3082 (Nov. 8, 1978); Pub. L. No. 102–386, Title I, § 102(a), (b), 106 Stat. 1505, 1506 (Oct. 6, 1992).)

HISTORICAL AND STATUTORY NOTES

Effective and Applicability Provisions

1992 Acts. Section 102(c) of Pub. L. No. 102–386 provided that:

"(1) In general.—Except as otherwise provided in paragraphs (2) and (3), the amendments made by subsection (a) [amending subsec. (a) of this section] shall take effect upon the date of the enactment of this Act [Oct. 6, 1992].

"(2) Delayed effective date for certain mixed waste.—Until the date that is 3 years after the date of the enactment of this Act [Oct. 6, 1992], the waiver of sovereign immunity contained in section 6001(a) of the Solid Waste Disposal Act with respect to civil, criminal, and administrative penalties and fines (as added by the amendments made by subsection (a) [subsec. (a) of this section]) shall not apply to departments, agencies, and instrumentalities of the executive branch of the Federal Government for violations of section 3004(j) of the Solid Waste Disposal Act [section 6924(j) of this title] involving storage of mixed waste that is not subject to an existing agreement, permit, or administrative or judicial order, so long as such waste is managed in compliance with all other applicable requirements.

"(3) Effective date for certain mixed waste.—(A) Except as provided in subparagraph (B), after the date that is 3 years after the date of the enactment of this Act [Oct. 6, 1992], the waiver of sovereign immunity contained in section 6001(a) of the Solid Waste Disposal Act with respect to civil, criminal, and administrative penalties and fines (as added by the amendments made by subsection (a) [subsec. (a) of this section]) shall apply to departments, agencies, and instrumentalities of the executive branch of the Federal Government for violations of section 3004(j) of the Solid Waste Disposal Act [section 6924(j) of this title] involving storage of mixed waste.

"(B) With respect to the Department of Energy, the waiver of sovereign immunity referred to in subparagraph (A) shall not apply after the date that is 3 years after the date of the enactment of this Act [Oct. 6, 1992] for violations of section 3004(j) of such Act [section 6924(j) of this title] involving storage of mixed waste, so long as the Department of Energy is in compliance with both—

"(i) a plan that has been submitted and approved pursuant to section 3021(b) of the Solid Waste Disposal Act [section 6939c(b) of this title] and which is in effect; and

"(ii) an order requiring compliance with such plan which has been issued pursuant to such section 3021(b) [section 6939c(b) of this title] and which is in effect.

"(4) Application of waiver to agreements and orders.—The waiver of sovereign immunity contained in section 6001(a) of the Solid Waste Disposal Act (as added by the amendments made by subsection (a) [subsec. (a) of this section]) shall take effect on the date of the enactment of this Act [Oct. 6, 1992] with respect to any agreement, permit, or administrative or judicial order existing on such date of enactment [Oct. 6, 1992] (and any subsequent modifications to such an agreement, permit, or order), including, without limitation, any provision of an agreement, permit, or order that addresses compliance with section 3004(j) of such Act [section 6924(j) of this title] with respect to mixed waste.

"(5) Agreement or order.—Except as provided in paragraph (4), nothing in this Act [see Short Title of 1992 Amendments note set out under section 6901 of this title] shall be construed to alter, modify, or change in any manner any agreement, permit, or administrative or judicial order, including, without limitation, any provision of an agreement, permit, or order—

"(i) that addresses compliance with section 3004(j) of the Solid Waste Disposal Act [section 6924(j) of this title] with respect to mixed waste;

"(ii) that is in effect on the date of enactment of this Act [Oct. 6, 1992]; and

"(iii) to which a department, agency, or instrumentality of the executive branch of the Federal Governmental is a party."

Termination of Reporting Requirements

For termination, effective May 15, 2000, of provisions in subsec. (a) of this section requiring the President to report annually to Congress, see Pub. L. No. 104–66, § 3003, as amended, set out as a note under 31 U.S.C.A. § 1113 and the 8th item on page 20 of House Document No. 103–7.

§ 6962. Federal procurement

[SWDA § 6002]

(a) Application of section

Except as provided in subsection (b) of this section, a procuring agency shall comply with the requirements set forth in this section and any regulations issued under this section, with respect to any purchase or acquisition of a procurement item where the purchase price of the item exceeds $10,000 or where the quantity of such items or of functionally equivalent items purchased or acquired in the course of the preceding fiscal year was $10,000 or more.

(b) Procurement subject to other law

Any procurement, by any procuring agency, which is subject to regulations of the Administrator under section 6964 of this title (as promulgated before October 21, 1976, under comparable provisions of prior law) shall not be subject to the requirements of this section to the extent that such requirements are inconsistent with such regulations.

(c) Requirements

(1) After the date specified in applicable guidelines prepared pursuant to subsection (e) of this section, each procuring agency which procures any items designated in such guidelines shall procure such items composed of the highest percentage of recovered materials practicable (and in the case of paper, the highest percentage of the postconsumer recovered materials referred to in subsection (h)(1) of this section practicable), consistent with maintaining a satisfactory level of competition, considering such guidelines. The decision not to procure such items shall be based on a determination that such procurement items—

(A) are not reasonably available within a reasonable period of time;

(B) fail to meet the performance standards set forth in the applicable specifications or fail to meet the reasonable performance standards of the procuring agencies; or

(C) are only available at an unreasonable price. Any determination under subparagraph (B) shall be made on the basis of the guidelines of the National Institute of Standards and Technology in any case in which such material is covered by such guidelines.

(2) Agencies that generate heat, mechanical, or electrical energy from fossil fuel in systems that have the technical capability of using energy or fuels derived from solid waste as a primary or supplementary fuel shall use such capability to the maximum extent practicable.

(3) **(A)** After the date specified in any applicable guidelines prepared pursuant to subsection (e) of this section, contracting officers shall require that vendors:

(i) certify that the percentage of recovered materials to be used in the performance of the contract will be at least the amount required by applicable specifications or other contractual requirements and

(ii) estimate the percentage of the total material utilized for the performance of the contract which is recovered materials.

(B) Clause (ii) of subparagraph (A) applies only to a contract in an amount greater than $100,000.

(d) Specifications

All Federal agencies that have the responsibility for drafting or reviewing specifications for procurement items procured by Federal agencies shall—

(1) as expeditiously as possible but in any event no later than eighteen months after November 8, 1984, eliminate from such specifications—

(A) any exclusion of recovered materials and

(B) any requirement that items be manufactured from virgin materials; and

(2) within one year after the date of publication of applicable guidelines under subsection (e) of this section, or as otherwise specified in such guidelines, assure that such specifications require the use of recovered materials to the maximum extent possible without jeopardizing the intended end use of the item.

(e) Guidelines

The Administrator, after consultation with the Administrator of General Services, the Secretary of Commerce (acting through the National Institute of Standards and Technology), and the Public Printer, shall prepare, and from time to time revise, guidelines for the use of procuring agencies in complying with the requirements of this section. Such guidelines shall—

(1) designate those items which are or can be produced with recovered materials and whose procurement by procuring agencies will carry out the objectives of this section, and in the case of paper, provide for maximizing the use of post consumer recovered materials referred to in subsection (h)(1) of this section; and

(2) set forth recommended practices with respect to the procurement of recovered materials and items containing such materials and with respect to certification by vendors of the percentage of recovered materials used,

and shall provide information as to the availability, relative price, and performance of such materials and items and where appropriate shall recommend the level of recovered material to be contained in the procured product. The Administrator shall prepare final guidelines for paper within one hundred and eighty days after November 8, 1984, and for three additional product categories (including tires) by October 1, 1985. In making the designation under paragraph (1), the Administrator shall consider, but is not limited in his considerations, to—

(A) the availability of such items;

(B) the impact of the procurement of such items by procuring agencies on the volume of solid waste which must be treated, stored or disposed of;

(C) the economic and technological feasibility of producing and using such items; and

(D) other uses for such recovered materials.

(f) Procurement of services

A procuring agency shall, to the maximum extent practicable, manage or arrange for the procurement of solid waste management services in a manner which maximizes energy and resource recovery.

(g) Executive Office

The Office of Procurement Policy in the Executive Office of the President, in cooperation with the Administrator, shall implement the requirements of this section. It shall be the responsibility of the Office of Procurement Policy to coordinate this policy with other policies for Federal procurement, in such a way as to maximize the use of recovered resources, and to, every two years beginning in 1984, report to the Congress on actions taken by Federal agencies and the progress made in the implementation of this section, including agency compliance with subsection (d) of this section.

(h) "Recovered materials" defined

As used in this section, in the case of paper products, the term "recovered materials" includes—

(1) postconsumer materials such as—

(A) paper, paperboard, and fibrous wastes from retail stores, office buildings, homes, and so forth, after they have passed through their end-usage as a consumer item, including: used corrugated boxes; old newspapers; old magazines; mixed waste paper; tabulating cards; and used cordage; and

(B) all paper, paperboard, and fibrous wastes that enter and are collected from municipal solid waste, and

(2) manufacturing, forest residues, and other wastes such as—

(A) dry paper and paperboard waste generated after completion of the papermaking process (that is, those manufacturing operations up to and including the cutting and trimming of the paper machine reel into smaller rolls or rough sheets) including: envelope cuttings, bindery trimmings, and other paper and paperboard waste, resulting from printing, cutting, forming, and other converting operations; bag, box, and carton manufacturing wastes; and butt rolls, mill wrappers, and rejected unused stock; and

(B) finished paper and paperboard from obsolete inventories of paper and paperboard manufacturers, merchants, wholesalers, dealers, printers, converters, or others;

(C) fibrous byproducts of harvesting, manufacturing, extractive, or wood-cutting processes, flax, straw, linters, bagasse, slash, and other forest residues;

(D) wastes generated by the conversion of goods made from fibrous material (that is, waste rope from cordage manufacture, textile mill waste, and cuttings); and

(E) fibers recovered from waste water which otherwise would enter the waste stream.

(i) Procurement program

(1) Within one year after the date of publication of applicable guidelines under subsection (e) of this section, each procuring agency shall develop an affirmative procurement program which will assure that items composed of recovered materials will be purchased to the maximum extent practicable and which is consistent with applicable provisions of Federal procurement law.

(2) Each affirmative procurement program required under this subsection shall, at a minimum, contain—

(A) a recovered materials preference program;

(B) an agency promotion program to promote the preference program adopted under subparagraph (A);

(C) a program for requiring estimates of the total percentage of recovered material utilized in the performance of a contract; certification of minimum recovered material content actually utilized, where appropriate; and reasonable verification procedures for estimates and certifications; and

(D) annual review and monitoring of the effectiveness of an agency's affirmative procurement program.

In the case of paper, the recovered materials preference program required under subparagraph (A) shall provide for the maximum use of the post consumer recovered materials referred to in subsection (h)(1) of this section.

(3) In developing the preference program, the following options shall be considered for adoption:

(A) Case-by-Case Policy Development: Subject to the limitations of subsection (c)(1) (A) through (C) of this section, a policy of awarding contracts to the vendor offering an item composed of the highest percentage of recovered materials practicable (and in the case of paper, the highest percentage of the post consumer recovered materials referred to in subsection (h)(1) of this section). Subject to such limitations, agencies may make an award to a vendor offering items with less than the maximum recovered materials content.

(B) Minimum Content Standards: Minimum recovered materials content specifications which are set in such a way as to assure that the recovered materials content (and in the case of paper, the content of post consumer materials referred to in subsection (h)(1) of this section) required is the maximum available without jeopardizing the intended end use of the item, or violating the limitations of subsection (c)(1) (A) through (C) of this section.

Procuring agencies shall adopt one of the options set forth in subparagraphs (A) and (B) or a substantially equivalent alternative, for inclusion in the affirmative procurement program.

(Pub. L. No. 89–272, Title II, § 6002, as added by Pub. L. No. 94–580, § 2, 90 Stat. 2822 (Oct. 21, 1976); and amended by Pub. L. No. 95–609, § 7(n), 92 Stat. 3082 (Nov. 8, 1978); Pub. L. No. 96–482, § 22, 94 Stat. 2346 (Oct. 21, 1980); Pub. L. No. 97–375, Title I, § 102, 96 Stat. 1819 (Dec. 21, 1982); Pub. L. No. 98–616, Title V, § 501(a)–(e), 98 Stat. 3274–3276 (Nov. 8, 1984); Pub. L. No. 100–418, Title V, § 5115(c), 102 Stat. 1433 (Aug. 23, 1988); Pub. L. No. 102–393, Title VI, § 630, 106 Stat. 1773 (Oct. 6, 1992); Pub. L. No. 103–355, Title I, § 1554(1), Title IV, § 4104(e), 108 Stat. 3300, 3342 (Oct. 13, 1994).)

HISTORICAL AND STATUTORY NOTES

Effective and Applicability Provisions

1994 Acts. Amendment by section 1554(1) of Pub. L. No. 103–355 effective Oct. 13, 1994, and applicable on and after such date; amendment by section 4104(e) of Pub. L. No. 103–355 effective Oct. 13, 1994, except as otherwise provided, see section 10001 of Pub. L. No. 103–355, set out as a note under 10 U.S.C.A. § 2302.

Transfer of Functions

For transfer of certain enforcement functions of Administrator or other official of the Environmental Protection Agency under this chapter to Federal Inspector, Office of Federal Inspector for the Alaska Natural Gas Transportation System, see note set out under section 6903 of this title.

Federal Acquisition, Recycling, and Waste Prevention

Executive agency heads to develop and implement affirmative procurement programs in accordance with this section and Ex. Ord. No. 12873, and specifications, standards, and product descriptions inconsistent with this section or Ex. Ord. No. 12873 to be revised, see Ex. Ord. No. 12873, §§ 402, 501(a), 58 Fed. Reg. 54914, 54915 (Oct. 20, 1993), set out as a note under section 6961 of this title.

Procurement Preference for U.S. Made Remanufactured or Recycled Toner Cartridges

Pub. L. No. 103–123, Title IV, § 401, 107 Stat. 1238 (Oct. 28, 1993), which provided in part that a Federal agency, when purchasing toner cartridges, give preference to remanufactured toner cartridges made in the U.S. by small businesses and to recycled toner cartridges, unless such cartridges do not exist, the cost is greater than new cartridges, or sufficient quantities are not available, but authorizing the purchase of one or more new cartridges as a part of an initial printer or copier acquisition, and providing that such purchasing preference directives shall not affect current law with respect to Organizations for the Blind or Other Severely Handicapped, was repealed by Pub. L. No. 103–355, Title I, § 1554(2), Title X, § 10001, 108 Stat. 3300, 3404 (Oct. 13, 1994), effective Oct. 13, 1994, and applicable on and after such date.

§ 6963. Cooperation with Environmental Protection Agency

[SWDA § 6003]

(a) General rule

All Federal agencies shall assist the Administrator in carrying out his functions under this chapter and shall promptly make available all requested information concerning past or present Agency waste management practices and past or present Agency owned, leased, or operated solid or hazardous waste facilities. This information shall be provided in such format as may be determined by the Administrator.

(b) Information relating to energy and materials conservation and recovery

The Administrator shall collect, maintain, and disseminate information concerning the market potential of energy and materials recovered from solid waste, including materials obtained through source separation, and information concerning the savings potential of conserving resources contributing to the waste stream. The Administrator shall identify the regions in which the increased substitution of such energy for energy derived from fossil fuels and other sources is most likely to be feasible, and provide information on the technical and economic aspects of developing integrated resource conservation or recovery systems which provide for the recovery of source-separated materials to be recycled or the conservation of resources. The Administrator shall utilize the authorities of subsection (a) of this section in carrying out this subsection.

(Pub. L. No. 89–272, Title II, § 6003, as added by Pub. L. No. 94–580, § 2, 90 Stat. 2823 (Oct. 21, 1976); and amended by Pub. L. No. 96–482, § 32(g), 94 Stat. 2355 (Oct. 21, 1980).)

HISTORICAL AND STATUTORY NOTES

Transfer of Functions

For transfer of certain enforcement functions of Administrator or other official of the Environmental Protection Agency under this chapter to Federal Inspector, Office of Federal Inspector for the Alaska Natural Gas Transportation System, see note set out under section 6903 of this title.

§ 6964. Applicability of solid waste disposal guidelines to Executive agencies

[SWDA § 6004]

(a) Compliance

(1) If—

(A) an Executive agency (as defined in section 105 of Title 5) or any unit of the legislative branch of the Federal Government has jurisdiction over any real property or facility the operation or administration of which involves such agency in solid waste management activities, or

(B) such an agency enters into a contract with any person for the operation by such person of any Federal property or facility, and the performance of such contract involves such person in solid waste management activities,

then such agency shall insure compliance with the guidelines recommended under section 6907 of this title and the purposes of this chapter in the operation or administration of such property or facility, or the performance of such contract, as the case may be.

(2) Each Executive agency or any unit of the legislative branch of the Federal Government which conducts any activity—

(A) which generates solid waste, and

(B) which, if conducted by a person other than such agency, would require a permit or license from such agency in order to dispose of such solid waste,

shall insure compliance with such guidelines and the purposes of this chapter in conducting such activity.

(3) Each Executive agency which permits the use of Federal property for purposes of disposal of solid waste shall insure compliance with such guidelines and the purposes of this chapter in the disposal of such waste.

(4) The President or the Committee on House Oversight of the House of Representatives and the Committee on Rules and Administration of the Senate with regard to any unit of the legislative branch of the Federal Government shall prescribe regulations to carry out this subsection.

(b) Licenses and permits

Each Executive agency which issues any license or permit for disposal of solid waste shall, prior to the issuance of such license or permit, consult with the Administrator to insure compliance with guidelines recommended under section 6907 of this title and the purposes of this chapter.

(Pub. L. No. 89–272, Title II, § 6004, as added by Pub. L. No. 94–580, § 2, 90 Stat. 2823 (Oct. 21, 1976); and amended by Pub. L. No. 95–609, § 7(*o*), 92 Stat. 3083 (Nov. 8, 1978); Pub. L. No. 96–482, § 23, 94 Stat. 2347 (Oct. 21, 1980); Pub. L. No. 104–186, Title II, § 222(2), 110 Stat. 1751 (Aug. 20, 1996).)

HISTORICAL AND STATUTORY NOTES

Transfer of Functions

For transfer of certain enforcement functions of Administrator or other official of the Environmental Protection Agency under this chapter to Federal Inspector, Office of Federal Inspector for the Alaska Natural Gas Transportation System, see note set out under section 6903 of this title.

Prior Provisions

Prior to the complete revision of the Solid Waste Disposal Act by Pub. L. No. 94–580, provisions similar to this section were contained in section 211 of that Act, which was codified as section 3254e of this title. See note thereunder.

§ 6965. Chief Financial Officer report

The Chief Financial Officer of each affected agency shall submit to Congress an annual report containing, to the extent practicable, a detailed description of the compliance activities undertaken by the agency for mixed waste streams, and an accounting of the fines and penalties imposed on the agency for violations involving mixed waste.

(Pub. L. No. 102–386, Title I, § 110, 106 Stat. 1516 (Oct. 6, 1992).)

HISTORICAL AND STATUTORY NOTES

Codifications

Section was enacted as part of the Federal Facility Compliance Act of 1992 and not as part of the Solid Waste Disposal Act, which comprises this chapter.

§ 6966. Increased use of recovered mineral component in federally funded projects involving procurement of cement or concrete.

[SWDA § 6005]

(a) Definitions

In this section:

(1) Agency head

The term "agency head" means—

(A) the Secretary of Transportation; and

(B) the head of any other Federal agency that, on a regular basis, procures, or provides Federal funds to pay or assist in paying the cost of procuring, material for cement or concrete projects.

(2) Cement or concrete project

The term "cement or concrete project" means a project for the construction or maintenance of a highway or other transportation facility or a Federal, State, or local government building or other public facility that—

(A) involves the procurement of cement or concrete; and

(B) is carried out, in whole or in part, using Federal funds.

(3) Recovered mineral component

The term "recovered mineral component" means—

(A) ground granulated blast furnace slag, excluding lead slag;

(B) coal combustion fly ash; and

(C) any other waste material or byproduct recovered or diverted from solid waste that the Administrator, in consultation with an agency head, determines should be treated as recovered mineral component under this section for use in cement or concrete projects paid for, in whole or in part, by the agency head.

(b) Implementation of requirements

(1) In general

Not later than 1 year after August 8, 2005, the Administrator and each agency head shall take such actions as are necessary to implement fully all procurement requirements and incentives in effect as of August 8, 2005 (including guidelines under section 6962 of this title) that provide for the use of cement and concrete incorporating recovered mineral component in cement or concrete projects.

(2) Priority

In carrying out paragraph (1), an agency head shall give priority to achieving greater use of recovered mineral component in cement or concrete projects for which recovered mineral components historically have not been used or have been used only minimally.

(3) Federal procurement requirements

The Administrator and each agency head shall carry out this subsection in accordance with section 6962 of this title.

(c) Full implementation study

(1) In general

The Administrator, in cooperation with the Secretary of Transportation and the Secretary of Energy, shall conduct a study to determine the extent to which procurement requirements, when fully implemented in accordance with subsection (b) of this section, may realize energy savings and environmental benefits attainable with substitution of recovered mineral component in cement used in cement or concrete projects.

(2) Matters to be addressed

The study shall—

(A) quantify—

(i) the extent to which recovered mineral components are being substituted for Portland cement, particularly as a result of procurement requirements; and

(ii) the energy savings and environmental benefits associated with the substitution;

(B) identify all barriers in procurement requirements to greater realization of energy savings and environmental benefits, including barriers resulting from exceptions from the law; and

(C) (i) identify potential mechanisms to achieve greater substitution of recovered mineral component in types of cement or concrete projects for which recovered mineral components historically have not been used or have been used only minimally;

(ii) evaluate the feasibility of establishing guidelines or standards for optimized substitution rates of recovered mineral component in those cement or concrete projects; and

(iii) identify any potential environmental or economic effects that may result from greater substitution of recovered mineral component in those cement or concrete projects.

(3) Report

Not later than 30 months after August 8, 2005, the Administrator shall submit to Congress a report on the study.

(d) Additional procurement requirements

Unless the study conducted under subsection (c) of this section identifies any effects or other problems described in subsection (c)(2)(C)(iii) of this section that warrant further review or delay, the Administrator and each agency head shall, not later than 1 year after the date on which the report under subsection (c)(3) of this section is submitted, take additional actions under this chapter to establish procurement requirements and incentives that provide for the use of cement and concrete with increased substitution of recovered mineral component in the construction and maintenance of cement or concrete projects—

(1) to realize more fully the energy savings and environmental benefits associated with increased substitution; and

(2) to eliminate barriers identified under subsection (c)(2)(B) of this section.

(e) Effect of section

Nothing in this section affects the requirements of section 6962 of this title (including the guidelines and specifications for implementing those requirements).

(Pub. L. No. 89–272, Title II, § 6005, as added by Pub. L. No. 109–58, Title I, § 108(a), 119 Stat. 612 (Aug. 8, 2005).)

HISTORICAL AND STATUTORY NOTES

References in Text

August 8, 2005, referred to in subsecs. (b)(1) and (c)(3), originally read "the date of enactment of this section", meaning the date of enactment of Pub. L. No. 109–58, 119 Stat. 594 (Aug. 8, 2005), which enacted this section on Aug. 8, 2005.

This chapter, referred to in subsec. (d), originally read "this Act", meaning Solid Waste Disposal Act, Pub. L. No. 89–272, Title II, 79 Stat. 997 (Oct. 20, 1965), as amended, which is codified principally as this chapter.

Codifications

Another section 6005 of Pub. L. No. 89–272 was enacted by Pub. L. No. 109–59, § 6017(a), and is codified as 42 U.S.C.A. § 6966a.

§ 6966a. Increased use of recovered mineral component in federally funded projects involving procurement of cement or concrete

[SWDA § 6005]

(a) Definitions

In this section:

(1) Agency head

The term "agency head" means—

(A) the Secretary of Transportation; and

(B) the head of each other Federal agency that on a regular basis procures, or provides Federal funds to pay or assist in paying the cost of procuring, material for cement or concrete projects.

(2) Cement or concrete project

The term "cement or concrete project" means a project for the construction or maintenance of a highway or other transportation facility or a Federal, State, or local government building or other public facility that—

(A) involves the procurement of cement or concrete; and

(B) is carried out in whole or in part using Federal funds.

(3) Recovered mineral component

The term "recovered mineral component" means—

(A) ground granulated blast furnace slag other than lead slag;

(B) coal combustion fly ash;

(C) blast furnace slag aggregate other than lead slag aggregate;

(D) silica fume; and

(E) any other waste material or byproduct recovered or diverted from solid waste that the Administrator, in consultation with an agency head, determines should be treated as recovered mineral component under this section for use in cement or concrete projects paid for, in whole or in part, by the agency head.

(b) Implementation of requirements

(1) In general

Not later than 1 year after August 10, 2005, the Administrator and each agency head shall take such actions as are necessary to implement fully all procurement requirements and incentives in effect as of August 10, 2005 (including guidelines under section 6962 of this title) that provide for the use of cement and concrete incorporating recovered mineral component in cement or concrete projects.

(2) Priority

In carrying out paragraph (1) an agency head shall give priority to achieving greater use of recovered mineral component in cement or concrete projects for which recovered mineral components historically have not been used or have been used only minimally.

(3) Conformance

The Administrator and each agency head shall carry out this subsection in accordance with section 6962 of this title.

(c) Full implementation study

(1) In general

The Administrator, in cooperation with the Secretary of Transportation and the Secretary of Energy, shall conduct a study to determine the extent to which current procurement requirements, when fully implemented in accordance with subsection (b) of this section, may realize energy savings and environmental benefits attainable with substitution of recovered mineral component in cement used in cement or concrete projects.

(2) Matters to be addressed

The study shall—

(A) quantify the extent to which recovered mineral components are being substituted for Portland cement, particularly as a result of current procurement requirements, and the energy savings and environmental benefits associated with that substitution;

(B) identify all barriers in procurement requirements to greater realization of energy savings and environmental benefits, including barriers resulting from exceptions from current law; and

(C) (i) identify potential mechanisms to achieve greater substitution of recovered mineral component in types of cement or concrete projects for which recovered mineral components historically have not been used or have been used only minimally;

(ii) evaluate the feasibility of establishing guidelines or standards for optimized substitution rates of recovered mineral component in those cement or concrete projects; and

(iii) identify any potential environmental or economic effects that may result from greater substitution of recovered mineral component in those cement or concrete projects.

(3) Report

Not later than 30 months after August 10, 2005, the Administrator shall submit to Congress a report on the study.

(d) Additional procurement requirements

Unless the study conducted under subsection (c) of this section identifies any effects or other problems described in subsection (c)(2)(C)(iii) of this section that warrant further review or delay, the Administrator and each agency head shall, not later than 1 year after the release of the report in accordance with subsection (c)(3) of this section, take additional actions authorized under this chapter to establish procurement requirements and incentives that provide for the use of cement and concrete with increased substitution of recovered mineral component in the construction and maintenance of cement or concrete projects, so as to—

(1) realize more fully the energy savings and environmental benefits associated with increased substitution; and

(2) eliminate barriers identified under subsection (c) of this section.

(e) Effect of section

Nothing in this section affects the requirements of section 6962 of this title (including the guidelines and specifications for implementing those requirements).

(Pub. L. No. 89–272, Title II, § 6005, as added by Pub. L. No. 109–59, Title VI, § 6017(a), 119 Stat. 1888 (Aug. 10, 2005).)

HISTORICAL AND STATUTORY NOTES

References in Text

August 10, 2005, referred to in text, originally read "the date of enactment of this section", meaning the date of enactment of Pub. L. No. 109–59, 119 Stat. 1144 (Aug. 10, 2005), which enacted this section on Aug. 10, 2005.

This chapter, referred to in subsec. (d), originally read "this Act", meaning Solid Waste Disposal Act, Pub. L. No. 89–272, Title II, 79 Stat. 997 (Oct. 20, 1965), as amended, which is codified principally as this chapter.

Codifications

Another section 6005 of Pub. L. No. 89–272 was enacted by Pub. L. No. 109–58, § 108(a), and is codified as 42 U.S.C.A. § 6966.

§ 6966b. Use of granular mine tailings

[SWDA § 6006]

(a) Mine tailings

(1) In general

Not later than 180 days after August 10, 2005, the Administrator, in consultation with the Secretary of Transportation and heads of other Federal agencies, shall establish criteria (including an evaluation of whether to establish a numerical standard for concentration of lead and other hazardous substances) for the safe and environmentally protective use of granular mine tailings from the Tar Creek, Oklahoma Mining District, known as "chat", for—

(A) cement or concrete projects; and

(B) transportation construction projects (including transportation construction projects involving the use of asphalt) that are carried out, in whole or in part, using Federal funds.

(2) Requirements

In establishing criteria under paragraph (1), the Administrator shall consider—

(A) the current and previous uses of granular mine tailings as an aggregate for asphalt; and

(B) any environmental and public health risks and benefits derived from the removal, transportation, and use in transportation projects of granular mine tailings.

(3) Public participation

In establishing the criteria under paragraph (1), the Administrator shall solicit and consider comments from the public.

(4) Applicability of criteria

On the establishment of the criteria under paragraph (1), any use of the granular mine tailings described in paragraph (1) in a transportation project that is carried out, in whole or in part, using Federal funds, shall meet the criteria established under paragraph (1).

(b) Effect of sections

Nothing in this section or section 6966a of this title affects any requirement of any law (including a regulation) in effect on August 10, 2005.

(Pub. L. No. 89–272, Title II, § 6006, as added by Pub. L. No. 109–59, Title VI, § 6018(a), 119 Stat. 1890 (Aug. 10, 2005).)

HISTORICAL AND STATUTORY NOTES

References in Text

Section 6966a of this title, referred to in subsec. (b), and which originally read "section 6005", meaning Pub. L. No. 89–272, Title II, § 6005, was translated as meaning the section 6005 of Pub. L. No. 89–272 as added by Pub. L. No. 108–59, § 6017(a) and not the section 6005 of Pub. L. No. 89–272 as added by Pub. L. No. 109–58, § 108(a), which is codified as 42 U.S.C.A. § 6966, because of the proximity of the reference to the section 6005 as added by Pub. L. No. 109–59.

SUBCHAPTER VII—MISCELLANEOUS PROVISIONS

§ 6971. Employee protection

[SWDA § 7001]

(a) General

No person shall fire, or in any other way discriminate against, or cause to be fired or discriminated against, any employee or any authorized representative of employees by reason of the fact that such employee or representative has filed, instituted, or caused to be filed or instituted any proceeding under this chapter or under any applicable implementation plan, or has testified or is about to testify in any proceeding resulting from the administration or enforcement of the provisions of this chapter or of any applicable implementation plan.

(b) Remedy

Any employee or a representative of employees who believes that he has been fired or otherwise discriminated against by any person in violation of subsection (a) of this section may, within thirty days after such alleged violation occurs, apply to the Secretary of Labor for a review of such firing or alleged discrimination. A copy of the application shall be sent to such person who shall be the respondent. Upon receipt of such application, the Secretary of Labor shall cause such investigation to be made as he deems appropriate. Such investigation shall provide an opportunity for a public hearing at the request of any party to such review to enable the parties to present information relating to such alleged violation. The parties shall be given written notice of the time and place of the hearing at least five days prior to the hearing. Any such hearing shall be of record and shall be subject to section 554 of Title 5. Upon receiving the report of such investigation, the Secretary of Labor shall make findings of fact. If he finds that such violation did occur, he shall issue a decision, incorporating an order therein and his findings, requiring the party committing such violation to take such affirmative action to abate the violation as the Secretary of Labor deems appropriate, including, but not limited to, the rehiring or reinstatement of the employee or representative of employees to his former position with compensation. If he finds that there was no such violation, he shall issue an order denying the application. Such order issued by the Secretary of Labor under this subparagraph shall be subject to judicial review in the same manner as orders and decisions of the Administrator or subject to judicial review under this chapter.

(c) Costs

Whenever an order is issued under this section to abate such violation, at the request of the applicant, a sum equal to the aggregate amount of all costs and expenses (including the attorney's fees) as determined by the Secretary of Labor, to have been reasonably incurred by the applicant for, or in connection with, the institution and prosecution of such proceedings, shall be assessed against the person committing such violation.

(d) Exception

This section shall have no application to any employee who, acting without direction from his employer (or his agent) deliberately violates any requirement of this chapter.

(e) Employment shifts and loss

The Administrator shall conduct continuing evaluations of potential loss or shifts of employment which may result from the administration or enforcement of the provisions of this chapter and applicable implementation plans, including, where appropriate, investigating threatened plant closures or reductions in employment allegedly resulting from such administration or enforcement. Any employee who is discharged, or laid off, threatened with discharge or layoff, or otherwise discriminated against by any person because of the alleged results of such administration or enforcement, or any representative of such employee, may request the Administrator to conduct a full investigation of the matter. The Administrator shall thereupon investigate the matter and, at the request of any party, shall hold public hearings on not less than five days' notice, and shall at such hearings require the parties, including the employer involved, to present information relating to the actual or potential effect of such administration or enforcement on employment and on any alleged discharge, layoff, or other discrimination and the detailed reasons or justification therefor. Any such hearing shall be of record and shall be subject to section 554 of Title 5. Upon receiving the report of such investigation, the Administrator shall make findings of fact as to the effect of such administration or enforcement on employment and on the alleged discharge, layoff, or discrimination and shall make such recommendations as he deems appropriate. Such report, findings, and recommendations shall be available to the public. Nothing in this subsection shall be construed to require or authorize the Administrator or any State to modify or withdraw any standard, limitation, or any other requirement of this chapter or any applicable implementation plan.

(f) Occupational safety and health

In order to assist the Secretary of Labor and the Director of the National Institute for Occupational Safety and Health in carrying out their duties under the Occupational Safety and Health Act of 1970 [29 U.S.C.A. § 651 et seq.], the Administrator shall—

(1) provide the following information, as such information becomes available, to the Secretary and the Director:

(A) the identity of any hazardous waste generation, treatment, storage, disposal facility or site where cleanup is planned or underway;

(B) information identifying the hazards to which persons working at a hazardous waste generation, treatment, storage, disposal facility or site or otherwise handling hazardous waste may be exposed, the nature and extent of the exposure, and methods to protect workers from such hazards; and

(C) incidents of worker injury or harm at a hazardous waste generation, treatment, storage or disposal facility or site; and

(2) notify the Secretary and the Director of the Administrator's receipt of notifications under section 6930 or reports under sections 6922, 6923, and 6924 of this title and make such notifications and reports available to the Secretary and the Director.

(Pub. L. No. 89–272, Title II, § 7001, as added by Pub. L. No. 94–580, § 2, 90 Stat. 2824 (Oct. 21, 1976); and amended by Pub. L. No. 96–482, § 24, 94 Stat. 2347 (Oct. 21, 1980).)

HISTORICAL AND STATUTORY NOTES

References in Text

The Occupational Safety and Health Act of 1970, referred to in subsec. (f), is Pub. L. No. 91–596, 84 Stat. 1590 (Dec. 29, 1970), as amended, which is codified principally as chapter 15 (section 651 et seq.) of Title 29, Labor.

For complete classification of this Act to the Code, see Short Title note set out under section 651 of Title 29 and Tables.

Transfer of Functions

For transfer of certain enforcement functions of Administrator or other official of the Environmental Protection Agency under this chapter to Federal Inspector, Office of Federal Inspector for the Alaska Natural Gas Transportation System, see note set out under section 6903 of this title.

§ 6972. Citizen suits

[SWDA § 7002]

(a) In general

Except as provided in subsection (b) or (c) of this section, any person may commence a civil action on his own behalf—

(1) **(A)** against any person (including (a) the United States, and (b) any other governmental instrumentality or agency, to the extent permitted by the eleventh amendment to the Constitution) who is alleged to be in violation of any permit, standard, regulation, condition, requirement, prohibition, or order which has become effective pursuant to this chapter; or

(B) against any person, including the United States and any other governmental instrumentality or agency, to the extent permitted by the eleventh amendment to the Constitution, and including any past or present generator, past or present transporter, or past or present owner or operator of a treatment, storage, or disposal facility, who has contributed or who is contributing to the past or present handling, storage, treatment, transportation, or disposal of any solid or hazardous waste which may present an imminent and substantial endangerment to health or the environment; or

(2) against the Administrator where there is alleged a failure of the Administrator to perform any act or duty under this chapter which is not discretionary with the Administrator.

Any action under paragraph (a)(1) of this subsection shall be brought in the district court for the district in which the alleged violation occurred or the alleged endangerment may occur. Any action brought under paragraph (a)(2) of this subsection may be brought in the district court for the district in which the alleged violation occurred or in the District Court of the District of Columbia. The district court shall have jurisdiction, without regard to the amount in controversy or the citizenship of the parties, to enforce the permit, standard, regulation, condition, requirement, prohibition, or order, referred to in paragraph (1)(A), to restrain any person who has contributed or who is contributing to the past or present handling, storage, treatment, transportation, or disposal of any solid or hazardous waste referred to in paragraph (1)(B), to order such person to take such other action as may be necessary, or both, or to order the Administrator to perform the act or duty referred to in paragraph (2), as the case may be, and to apply any appropriate civil penalties under section 6928(a) and (g) of this title.

(b) Actions prohibited

(1) No action may be commenced under subsection (a)(1)(A) of this section—

(A) prior to 60 days after the plaintiff has given notice of the violation to—

(i) the Administrator;

(ii) the State in which the alleged violation occurs; and

(iii) to any alleged violator of such permit, standard, regulation, condition, requirement, prohibition, or order,

except that such action may be brought immediately after such notification in the case of an action under this section respecting a violation of subchapter III of this chapter; or

(B) if the Administrator or State has commenced and is diligently prosecuting a civil or criminal action in a court of the United States or a State to require compliance with such permit, standard, regulation, condition, requirement, prohibition, or order.

In any action under subsection (a)(1)(A) of this section in a court of the United States, any person may intervene as a matter of right.

(2) (A) No action may be commenced under subsection (a)(1)(B) of this section prior to ninety days after the plaintiff has given notice of the endangerment to—

(i) the Administrator;

(ii) the State in which the alleged endangerment may occur;

(iii) any person alleged to have contributed or to be contributing to the past or present handling, storage, treatment, transportation, or disposal of any solid or hazardous waste referred to in subsection (a)(1)(B) of this section,

except that such action may be brought immediately after such notification in the case of an action under this section respecting a violation of subchapter III of this chapter.

(B) No action may be commenced under subsection (a)(1)(B) of this section if the Administrator, in order to restrain or abate acts or conditions which may have contributed or are contributing to the activities which may present the alleged endangerment—

(i) has commenced and is diligently prosecuting an action under section 6973 of this title or under section 106 of the Comprehensive Environmental Response, Compensation and Liability Act of 1980 [42 U.S.C.A. § 9606],[1]

(ii) is actually engaging in a removal action under section 104 of the Comprehensive Environmental Response, Compensation and Liability Act of 1980 [42 U.S.C.A. § 9604];

(iii) has incurred costs to initiate a Remedial Investigation and Feasibility Study under section 104 of the Comprehensive Environmental Response, Compensation and Liability Act of 1980 [42 U.S.C.A. § 9604] and is diligently proceeding with a remedial action under that Act [42 U.S.C.A. § 9601 et seq.]; or

(iv) has obtained a court order (including a consent decree) or issued an administrative order under section 106 of the Comprehensive Environmental Response, Compensation and Liability Act of 980[2] [42 U.S.C.A. § 9606] or section 6973 of this title pursuant to which a responsible party is diligently conducting a removal action, Remedial Investigation and Feasibility Study (RIFS), or proceeding with a remedial action.

In the case of an administrative order referred to in clause (iv), actions under subsection (a)(1)(B) of this section are prohibited only as to the scope and duration of the administrative order referred to in clause (iv).

(C) No action may be commenced under subsection (a)(1)(B) of this section if the State, in order to restrain or abate acts or conditions which may have contributed or are contributing to the activities which may present the alleged endangerment—

(i) has commenced and is diligently prosecuting an action under subsection (a)(1)(B) of this section;

(ii) is actually engaging in a removal action under section 104 of the Comprehensive Environmental Response, Compensation and Liability Act of 1980 [42 U.S.C.A. § 9604]; or

(iii) has incurred costs to initiate a Remedial Investigation and Feasibility Study under section 104 of the Comprehensive Environmental Response, Compensation and Liability Act of 1980 [42 U.S.C.A. § 9604] and is diligently proceeding with a remedial action under that Act [42 U.S.C.A. § 9601 et seq.].

(D) No action may be commenced under subsection (a)(1)(B) of this section by any person (other than a State or local government) with respect to the siting of a hazardous waste treatment, storage, or a disposal facility, nor to restrain or enjoin the issuance of a permit for such facility.

(E) In any action under subsection (a)(1)(B) of this section in a court of the United States, any person may intervene as a matter of right when the applicant claims an interest relating to the subject of the action and he is so situated that the disposition of the action may, as a practical matter, impair or impede his ability to protect that interest, unless the Administrator or the State shows that the applicant's interest is adequately represented by existing parties.

(F) Whenever any action is brought under subsection (a)(1)(B) of this section in a court of the United States, the plaintiff shall serve a copy of the complaint on the Attorney General of the United States and with the Administrator.

(c) Notice

No action may be commenced under paragraph (a)(2) of this section prior to sixty days after the plaintiff has given notice to the Administrator that he will commence such action, except that such action may be brought immediately after such notification in the case of an action under this section respecting a violation of subchapter III of this chapter. Notice under this subsection shall be given in such manner as the Administrator shall prescribe by regulation. Any action respecting a violation under this chapter may be brought under this section only in the judicial district in which such alleged violation occurs.

(d) Intervention

In any action under this section the Administrator, if not a party, may intervene as a matter of right.

(e) Costs

The court, in issuing any final order in any action brought pursuant to this section or section 6976 of this title, may award costs of litigation (including reasonable attorney and expert witness fees) to the prevailing or substantially prevailing party, whenever the court determines such an award is appropriate. The court may, if a temporary restraining order or preliminary injunction is sought, require the filing of a bond or equivalent security in accordance with the Federal Rules of Civil Procedure.

(f) Other rights preserved

Nothing in this section shall restrict any right which any person (or class of persons) may have under any statute or common law to seek enforcement of any standard or requirement relating to the management of solid waste or hazardous waste, or to seek any other relief (including relief against the Administrator or a State agency).

(g) Transporters

A transporter shall not be deemed to have contributed or to be contributing to the handling, storage, treatment, or disposal, referred to in subsection (a)(1)(B) of this section taking place after such solid waste or hazardous waste has left the possession or control of such transporter, if the transportation of such waste was under a sole contractual arrangement arising from a published tariff and acceptance for carriage by common carrier by rail and such transporter has exercised due care in the past or present handling, storage, treatment, transportation and disposal of such waste.

(Pub. L. No. 89–272, Title II, § 7002, as added by Pub. L. No. 94–580, § 2, 90 Stat. 2825 (Oct. 21, 1976); and amended by Pub. L. No. 95–609, § 7(p), 92 Stat. 3083 (Nov. 8, 1978); Pub. L. No. 98–616, Title IV, § 401, 98 Stat. 3268 (Nov. 8, 1984).)

[1] So in original. The comma probably should be a semicolon.

[2] So in original. Probably should be "1980."

HISTORICAL AND STATUTORY NOTES

References in Text

That Act, referred to in subsec. (b)(2)(B)(iii), (C)(iii), means Pub. L. No. 96–510, 94 Stat. 2767 (Dec. 11, 1980), as amended, known as the Comprehensive Environmental Response, Compensation, and Liability Act of 1980, which is codified principally to chapter 103 (section 9601 et seq.) of this title. For complete classification of this Act to the Code, see Short Title of 1980 Acts note set out under section 9601 of this title and Tables.

The Federal Rules of Civil Procedure, referred to in subsec. (e), are set out in the Appendix to Title 28, Judiciary and Judicial Procedure.

Transfer of Functions

For transfer of certain enforcement functions of Administrator or other official of the Environmental Protection Agency under this chapter to Federal Inspector, Office of Federal Inspector for the Alaska Natural Gas Transportation System, see note set out under section 6903 of this title.

§ 6973. Imminent hazard

[SWDA § 7003]

(a) Authority of Administrator

Notwithstanding any other provision of this chapter, upon receipt of evidence that the past or present handling, storage, treatment, transportation or disposal of any solid waste or hazardous waste may present an imminent and substantial endangerment to health or the environment, the Administrator may bring suit on behalf of the United States in the appropriate district court against any person (including any past or present generator, past or present transporter, or past or present owner or operator of a treatment, storage, or disposal facility) who has contributed or who is contributing to such handling, storage, treatment, transportation or disposal to restrain such person from such handling, storage, treatment, transportation, or disposal, to order such person to take such other action as may be necessary, or both. A transporter shall not be deemed to have contributed or to be contributing to such handling, storage, treatment, or disposal taking place after such solid waste or hazardous waste has left the possession or control of such transporter if the transportation of such waste was under a sole contractural[1] arrangement arising from a published tariff and acceptance for carriage by common carrier by rail and such transporter has exercised due care in the past or present handling, storage, treatment, transportation and disposal of such waste. The Administrator shall provide notice to the affected State of any such suit. The Administrator may also, after notice to the affected State, take other action under this section including, but not limited to, issuing such orders as may be necessary to protect public health and the environment.

(b) Violations

Any person who willfully violates, or fails or refuses to comply with, any order of the Administrator under subsection (a) of this section may, in an action brought in the appropriate United States district court to enforce such order, be fined not more than $5,000 for each day in which such violation occurs or such failure to comply continues.

(c) Immediate notice

Upon receipt of information that there is hazardous waste at any site which has presented an imminent and substantial endangerment to human health or the environment, the Administrator shall provide immediate notice to the appropriate local government agencies. In addition, the Administrator shall require notice of such endangerment to be promptly posted at the site where the waste is located.

(d) Public participation in settlements

Whenever the United States or the Administrator proposes to covenant not to sue or to forbear from suit or to settle any claim arising under this section, notice, and opportunity for a public meeting in the affected area, and a reasonable opportunity to comment on the proposed settlement prior to its final entry shall be afforded to the public. The decision of the United States or the Administrator to enter into or not to enter into such Consent Decree, covenant or agreement shall not constitute a final agency action subject to judicial review under this chapter or chapter 7 of Title 5.

(Pub. L. No. 89–272, Title II, § 7003, as added by Pub. L. No. 94–580, § 2, 90 Stat. 2826 (Oct. 21, 1976); and amended by Pub. L. No. 95–609, § 7(q), 92 Stat. 3083 (Nov. 8, 1978); Pub. L. No. 96–482, § 25, 94 Stat. 2348 (Oct. 21, 1980); Pub. L. No. 98–616, Title IV, §§ 402, 403(a), 404, 98 Stat. 3271, 3273 (Nov. 8, 1984).)

[1] So in original. Probably should be "contractual".

HISTORICAL AND STATUTORY NOTES

Codifications

In subsec. (d), "chapter 7 of Title 5" was substituted for "the Administrative Procedure Act" on authority of Pub. L. No. 89–554, § 7(b), 80 Stat. 631 (Sept. 6, 1966), the first section of which enacted Title 5, Government Organization and Employees.

Transfer of Functions

For transfer of certain enforcement functions of Administrator or other official of the Environmental Protection Agency under this chapter to Federal Inspector, Office of Federal Inspector for the Alaska Natural Gas Transportation System, see note set out under section 6903 of this title.

§ 6974. Petition for regulations; public participation [SWDA § 7004]

(a) Petition

Any person may petition the Administrator for the promulgation, amendment, or repeal of any regulation under this chapter. Within a reasonable time following receipt of such petition, the Administrator shall take action with respect to such petition and shall publish notice of such action in the Federal Register, together with the reasons therefor.

(b) Public participation

(1) Public participation in the development, revision, implementation, and enforcement of any regulation, guideline, information, or program under this chapter shall be provided for, encouraged, and assisted by the Administrator and the States. The Administrator, in cooperation with the States, shall develop and publish minimum guidelines for public participation in such processes.

(2) Before the issuing of a permit to any person with any respect to any facility for the treatment, storage, or disposal of hazardous wastes under section 6925 of this title, the Administrator shall—

(A) cause to be published in major local newspapers of general circulation and broadcast over local radio stations notice of the agency's intention to issue such permit, and

(B) transmit in writing notice of the agency's intention to issue such permit to each unit of local government having jurisdiction over the area in which such facility is proposed to be located and to each State agency having any authority under State law with respect to the construction or operation of such facility.

If within 45 days the Administrator receives written notice of opposition to the agency's intention to issue such permit and a request for a hearing, or if the Administrator determines on his own initiative, he shall hold an informal public hearing (including an opportunity for presentation of written and oral views) on whether he should issue a permit for the proposed facility. Whenever possible the Administrator shall schedule such hearing at a location convenient to the nearest population center to such proposed facility and give notice in the aforementioned manner of the date, time, and subject matter of such hearing. No State program which provides for the issuance of permits referred to in this paragraph may be authorized by the Administrator under section 6926 of this title unless such program provides for the notice and hearing required by the paragraph.

(Pub. L. No. 89–272, Title II, § 7004, as added by Pub. L. No. 94–580, § 2, 90 Stat. 2826 (Oct. 21, 1976); and amended by Pub. L. No. 96–482, § 26, 94 Stat. 2348 (Oct. 21, 1980).)

HISTORICAL AND STATUTORY NOTES

Transfer of Functions

For transfer of certain enforcement functions of Administrator or other official of the Environmental Protection Agency under this chapter to Federal Inspector, Office of Federal Inspector for the Alaska Natural Gas Transportation System, see note set out under section 6903 of this title.

§ 6975. Separability

[SWDA § 7005]

If any provision of this chapter, or the application of any provision of this chapter to any person or circumstance, is held invalid, the application of such provision to other persons or circumstances, and the remainder of this chapter, shall not be affected thereby.

(Pub. L. No. 89–272, Title II, § 7005, as added by Pub. L. No. 94–580, § 2, 90 Stat. 2827 (Oct. 21, 1976).)

§ 6976. Judicial review

[SWDA § 7006]

(a) Review of final regulations and certain petitions

Any judicial review of final regulations promulgated pursuant to this chapter and the Administrator's denial of any petition for the promulgation, amendment, or repeal of any regulation under this chapter shall be in accordance with sections 701 through 706 of Title 5, except that—

(1) a petition for review of action of the Administrator in promulgating any regulation, or requirement under this chapter or denying any petition for the promulgation, amendment or repeal of any regulation under this chapter may be filed only in the United States Court of Appeals for the District of Columbia, and such petition shall be filed within ninety days from the date of such promulgation or denial, or after such date if such petition for review is based solely on grounds arising after such ninetieth day; action of the Administrator with respect to which review could have been obtained under this subsection shall not be subject to judicial review in civil or criminal proceedings for enforcement; and

(2) in any judicial proceeding brought under this section in which review is sought of a determination under this chapter required to be made on the record after notice and opportunity for hearing, if a party seeking review under this chapter applies to the court for leave to adduce additional evidence, and shows to the satisfaction of the court that the information is material and that there were reasonable grounds for the failure to adduce such evidence in the proceeding before the Administrator, the court may order such additional evidence (and evidence in rebuttal thereof) to be taken before the Administrator, and to be adduced upon the hearing in such manner and upon such terms and conditions as the court may deem proper; the Administrator may modify his findings as to the facts, or make new findings, by reason of the additional evidence so taken, and he shall file with the court such modified or new findings and his recommendation, if any, for the modification or setting aside of his original order, with the return of such additional evidence.

(b) Review of certain actions under sections 6925 and 6926 of this title

Review of the Administrator's action (1) in issuing, denying, modifying, or revoking any permit under section 6925 of this title (or in modifying or revoking any permit which is deemed to have been issued under section 6935(d)(1) of this title), or (2) in granting, denying, or withdrawing authorization or interim authorization under section 6926 of this title, may be had by any interested person in the Circuit Court of Appeals of the United States for the Federal judicial district in which such person resides or transacts such business upon application by such person. Any such application shall be made within ninety days from the date of such issuance, denial, modification, revocation, grant, or withdrawal, or after such date only if such application is based solely on grounds which arose after such ninetieth day. Action of the Administrator with respect to which review could have been obtained under this subsection shall not be subject to judicial review in civil or criminal proceedings for enforcement. Such review shall be in accordance with sections 701 through 706 of Title 5.

(Pub. L. No. 89–272, Title II, § 7006, as added by Pub. L. No. 94–580, § 2, 90 Stat. 2827 (Oct. 21, 1976); and amended by Pub. L. No. 96–482, § 27, 94 Stat. 2349 (Oct. 21, 1980); Pub. L. No. 98–616, Title II, § 241(b)(1), Title IV, § 403(d)(5), 98 Stat. 3259, 3273 (Nov. 8, 1984).)

HISTORICAL AND STATUTORY NOTES

References in Text

Section 6935(d)(1) of this title, referred to in subsec. (b), was in the original a reference to section 3012(d)(1) of Pub. L. No. 89–272, which was renumbered section 3014(d)(1) of Pub. L. No. 89–272 by Pub. L. No. 98–616 and is codified as section 6935(d)(1) of this title.

Transfer of Functions

For transfer of certain enforcement functions of Administrator or other official of the Environmental Protection Agency under this chapter to Federal Inspector, Office of Federal Inspector for the Alaska Natural Gas Transportation System, see note set out under section 6903 of this title.

§ 6977. Grants or contracts for training projects

[SWDA § 7007]

(a) General authority

The Administrator is authorized to make grants to, and contracts with any eligible organization. For purposes of this section the term "eligible organization" means a State or interstate agency, a municipality, educational institution, and any other organization which is capable of effectively carrying out a project which may be funded by grant under subsection (b) of this section.

(b) Purposes

(1) Subject to the provisions of paragraph (2), grants or contracts may be made to pay all or a part of the costs, as may be determined by the Administrator, of any project operated or to be operated by an eligible organization, which is designed—

(A) to develop, expand, or carry out a program (which may combine training, education, and employment) for training persons for occupations involving the management, supervision, design, operation, or maintenance of solid waste management and resource recovery equipment and facilities; or

(B) to train instructors and supervisory personnel to train or supervise persons in occupations involving the design, operation, and maintenance of solid waste management and resource recovery equipment and facilities.

(2) A grant or contract authorized by paragraph (1) of this subsection may be made only upon application to the Administrator at such time or times and containing such information as he may prescribe, except that no such application shall be approved unless it provides for the same procedures and reports (and access to such reports and to other records) as required by section 3254a(b)(4) and (5) of this title (as in effect before October 21, 1976) with respect to applications made under such section (as in effect before October 21, 1976).

(Pub. L. No. 89–272, Title II, § 7007, as added by Pub. L. No. 94–580, § 2, 90 Stat. 2827 (Oct. 21, 1976); and amended by Pub. L. No. 95–609, § 7(r), 92 Stat. 3083 (Nov. 8, 1978); Pub. L. No. 105–362, § 501(f), Title V, 112 Stat. 3284 (Nov. 10, 1998).)

HISTORICAL AND STATUTORY NOTES

References in Text

Section 3254a(b)(4) and (5) of this title, referred to in subsec. (b)(2), was in the original, "section 207(b)(4) and (5)", meaning section 207(b)(4) and (5) of the Solid Waste Disposal Act, which was omitted in the general revision of the Solid Waste Disposal Act by Pub. L. No. 94–580 on Oct. 21, 1976.

Transfer of Functions

For transfer of certain enforcement functions of Administrator or other official of the Environmental Protection Agency under this chapter to Federal Inspector, Office of Federal Inspector for the Alaska Natural Gas Transportation System, see note set out under section 6903 of this title.

Prior Provisions

Provisions similar to this section were contained in section 3254d of this title, prior to the complete revision of the Solid Waste Disposal Act by Pub. L. No. 94–580.

§ 6978. Payments

[SWDA § 7008]

(a) General rule

Payments of grants under this chapter may be made (after necessary adjustment on account of previously made underpayments or overpayments) in advance or by way of reimbursement, and in such installments and on such conditions as the Administrator may determine.

(b) Prohibition

No grant may be made under this chapter to any private profitmaking organization.

(Pub. L. No. 89–272, Title II, § 7008, as added by Pub. L. No. 94–580, § 2, 90 Stat. 2828 (Oct. 21, 1976).)

HISTORICAL AND STATUTORY NOTES

Transfer of Functions

For transfer of certain enforcement functions of Administrator or other official of the Environmental Protection Agency under this chapter to Federal Inspector, Office of Federal Inspector for the Alaska Natural Gas Transportation System, see note set out under section 6903 of this title.

Prior Provisions

Provisions similar to this section were contained in section 3258 of this title, prior to the complete revision of the Solid Waste Disposal Act by Pub. L. No. 94–580.

§ 6979. Labor standards

[SWDA § 7009]

No grant for a project of construction under this chapter shall be made unless the Administrator finds that the application contains or is supported by reasonable assurance that all laborers and mechanics employed by contractors or subcontractors on projects of the type covered by sections 3141–3144, 3146, and 3147 of Title 40, will be paid wages at rates not less than those prevailing on similar work in the locality as determined by the Secretary of Labor in accordance with those sections; and the Secretary of Labor shall have with respect to the labor standards specified in this section the authority and functions set forth in Reorganization Plan Numbered 14 of 1950 (15 Fed. Reg. 3176) and section 3145 of Title 40.

(Pub. L. No. 89–272, Title II, § 7009, as added by Pub. L. No. 94–580, § 2, 90 Stat. 2828 (Oct. 21, 1976); and amended by Pub. L. No. 96–482, § 28, 94 Stat. 2349 (Oct. 21, 1980).)

HISTORICAL AND STATUTORY NOTES

References in Text

Reorganization Plan No. 14 of 1950, referred to in text, is set out in Appendix 1 to Title 5, Government Organization and Employees.

Codifications

In text, "sections 3141–3144, 3146, and 3147 of Title 40" substituted for "the Davis-Bacon Act, as amended (40 U.S.C. 276a to 276a–5)" on authority of Pub. L. No. 107–217, § 5(c), 116 Stat. 1301 (Aug. 21, 2002), which is set out as a note preceding 40 U.S.C.A. § 101. Pub. L. No. 107–217, § 1, enacted Title 40 into positive law. The Davis-Bacon Act is Act of Mar. 3, 1931, c. 411, 46 Stat. 1494, which was codified as former 40 U.S.C.A. §§ 276a, 276a–1 to 276a–6, prior to being repealed by Pub. L. No. 107–217, § 6(b), 116 Stat. 1308 (Aug. 21, 2002), and its substance reenacted as 40 U.S.C.A. §§ 3141–3144, 3146, and 3147.

In text, "section 3145 of Title 40" substituted for "section 276c of Title 40", which originally read "section 2 of the Act of June 1, 1934, as amended (40 U.S.C. 276c)", on authority of Pub. L. No. 107–217, § 5(c), 116 Stat. 1301

(Aug. 21, 2002), which is set out as a note preceding 40 U.S.C.A. § 101. Pub. L. No. 107–217, § 1, enacted Title 40 into positive law. Act of June 13, 1934, c. 482, 48 Stat. 948, was codified as former 40 U.S.C.A. § 276c prior to being repealed by Pub. L. No. 107–217, § 6(b), 116 Stat. 1309 (Aug. 21, 2002), and its substance reenacted as 40 U.S.C.A. § 3145.

Prior Provisions

Provisions similar to this section were contained in section 3256 of this title, prior to the complete revision of the Solid Waste Disposal Act by Pub. L. No. 94–580.

§ 6979a. Transferred

HISTORICAL AND STATUTORY NOTES

Codifications

Section, Pub. L. No. 89–272, Title II, § 7010, as added by Pub. L. No. 98–616, Title IV, § 405(a), 98 Stat. 3273 (Nov. 8, 1984), and amended by Pub. L. No. 99–339, Title II, § 201(c)(1), 100 Stat. 654 (June 19, 1986), was renumbered section 3020 of Pub. L. No. 89–272 by Pub. L. No. 99–339 Title II, § 201(c)(2), 100 Stat. 654 (June 19, 1986), and transferred to section 6939b of this title.

§ 6979b. Law enforcement authority

[SWDA § 7010]

The Attorney General of the United States shall, at the request of the Administrator and on the basis of a showing of need, deputize qualified employees of the Environmental Protection Agency to serve as special deputy United States marshals in criminal investigations with respect to violations of the criminal provisions of this chapter.

(Pub. L. No. 89–272, Title II, § 7010, formerly § 7012, as added by Pub. L. No. 98–616, Title IV, § 403(b)(1), 98 Stat. 3272 (Nov. 8, 1984); and renumbered § 7010 by Pub. L. No. 99–339, Title II, § 201(c)(2), 100 Stat. 654 (June 19, 1986).)

HISTORICAL AND STATUTORY NOTES

Prior Provisions

A prior section 7010 of Pub. L. No. 89–272, which was codified as section 6979a of this title, was redesignated as section 3020 of Pub. L. No. 89–272 by section 201(c)(2) of Pub. L. No. 99–339, and transferred to section 6939b of this title.

SUBCHAPTER VIII—RESEARCH, DEVELOPMENT, DEMONSTRATION, AND INFORMATION

§ 6981. Research, demonstration, training, and other activities

[SWDA § 8001]

(a) General authority

The Administrator, alone or after consultation with the Secretary of Energy, shall conduct, and encourage, cooperate with, and render financial and other assistance to appropriate public (whether Federal, State, interstate, or local) authorities, agencies, and institutions, private agencies and institutions, and individuals in the conduct of, and promote the coordination of, research, investigations, experiments, training, demonstrations, surveys, public education programs, and studies relating to—

(1) any adverse health and welfare effects of the release into the environment of material present in solid waste, and methods to eliminate such effects;

(2) the operation and financing of solid waste management programs;

(3) the planning, implementation, and operation of resource recovery and resource conservation systems and hazardous waste management systems, including the marketing of recovered resources;

(4) the production of usable forms of recovered resources, including fuel, from solid waste;

(5) the reduction of the amount of such waste and unsalvageable waste materials;

(6) the development and application of new and improved methods of collecting and disposing of solid waste and processing and recovering materials and energy from solid wastes;

(7) the identification of solid waste components and potential materials and energy recoverable from such waste components;

(8) small scale and low technology solid waste management systems, including but not limited to, resource recovery source separation systems;

(9) methods to improve the performance characteristics of resources recovered from solid waste and the relationship of such performance characteristics to available and potentially available markets for such resources;

(10) improvements in land disposal practices for solid waste (including sludge) which may reduce the adverse environmental effects of such disposal and other aspects of solid waste disposal on land, including means for reducing the harmful environmental effects of earlier and existing landfills, means for restoring areas damaged by such earlier or existing landfills, means for rendering landfills safe for purposes of construction and other uses, and techniques of recovering materials and energy from landfills;

(11) methods for the sound disposal of, or recovery of resources, including energy, from, sludge (including sludge from pollution control and treatment facilities, coal slurry pipelines, and other sources);

(12) methods of hazardous waste management, including methods of rendering such waste environmentally safe; and

(13) any adverse effects on air quality (particularly with regard to the emission of heavy metals) which result from solid waste which is burned (either alone or in conjunction with other substances) for purposes of treatment, disposal or energy recovery.

(b) Management program

(1) (A) In carrying out his functions pursuant to this chapter, and any other Federal legislation respecting solid waste or discarded material research, development, and demonstrations, the Administrator shall establish a management program or system to insure the coordination of all such activities and to facilitate and accelerate the process of development of sound new technology (or other discoveries) from the research phase, through development, and into the demonstration phase.

(B) The Administrator shall (i) assist, on the basis of any research projects which are developed with assistance under this chapter or without Federal assistance, the construction of pilot plant facilities for the purpose of investigating or testing the technological feasibility of any promising new fuel, energy, or resource recovery or resource conservation method or technology; and (ii) demonstrate each such method and technology that appears justified by an evaluation at such pilot plant stage or at a pilot plant stage developed without Federal assistance. Each such demonstration shall incorporate new or innovative technical advances or shall apply such advances to different circumstances and conditions, for the purpose of evaluating design concepts or to test the performance, efficiency, and economic feasibility of a particular method or technology under actual operating conditions. Each such demonstration shall be so planned and designed that, if successful, it can be expanded or utilized directly as a full-scale operational fuel, energy, or resource recovery or resource conservation facility.

(2) Any energy-related research, development, or demonstration project for the conversion including bioconversion, of solid waste carried out by the Environmental Protection Agency or by the Secretary of Energy pursuant to this chapter or any other Act shall be administered in accordance with the May 7, 1976, Interagency Agreement between the Environmental Protection Agency and the Energy Research and Development Administration on the Development of Energy from Solid Wastes and specifically, that in accordance with this agreement, (A) for those energy-related projects of mutual interest, planning will be conducted jointly by the Environmental Protection Agency and the Secretary

of Energy, following which project responsibility will be assigned to one agency; (B) energy-related portions of projects for recovery of synthetic fuels or other forms of energy from solid waste shall be the responsibility of the Secretary of Energy; (C) the Environmental Protection Agency shall retain responsibility for the environmental, economic, and institutional aspects of solid waste projects and for assurance that such projects are consistent with any applicable suggested guidelines published pursuant to section 6907 of this title, and any applicable State or regional solid waste management plan; and (D) any activities undertaken under provisions of sections 6982 and 6983 of this title as related to energy; as related to energy or synthetic fuels recovery from waste; or as related to energy conservation shall be accomplished through coordination and consultation with the Secretary of Energy.

(c) Authorities

(1) In carrying out subsection (a) of this section respecting solid waste research, studies, development, and demonstration, except as otherwise specifically provided in section 6984(d) of this title, the Administrator may make grants to or enter into contracts (including contracts for construction) with, public agencies and authorities or private persons.

(2) Contracts for research, development, or demonstrations or for both (including contracts for construction) shall be made in accordance with and subject to the limitations provided with respect to research contracts of the military departments in section 2353 of Title 10, except that the determination, approval, and certification required thereby shall be made by the Administrator.

(3) Any invention made or conceived in the course of, or under, any contract under this chapter shall be subject to section 9 of the Federal Nonnuclear Energy Research and Development Act of 1974 [42 U.S.C.A. § 5908] to the same extent and in the same manner as inventions made or conceived in the course of contracts under such Act [42 U.S.C.A. § 5901 et seq.], except that in applying such section, the Environmental Protection Agency shall be substituted for the Secretary of Energy and the words "solid waste" shall be substituted for the word "energy" where appropriate.

(4) For carrying out the purpose of this chapter the Administrator may detail personnel of the Environmental Protection Agency to agencies eligible for assistance under this section.

(Pub. L. No. 89–272, Title II, § 8001, as added by Pub. L. No. 94–580, § 2, 90 Stat. 2829 (Oct. 21, 1976); and amended by Pub. L. No. 95–91, Title III, § 301, Title VII, §§ 703, 707, 91 Stat. 577, 606, 607 (Aug. 4, 1977); Pub. L. No. 95–609, § 7(s), 92 Stat. 3083 (Nov. 8, 1978).)

HISTORICAL AND STATUTORY NOTES

References in Text

Such Act, referred to in subsec. (c)(3), means the Federal Nonnuclear Energy Research and Development Act of 1974, which is Pub. L. No. 93–577, 88 Stat. 1878 (Dec. 31, 1974), as amended, and which is codified generally as chapter 74 (section 5901 et seq.) of this title. For complete classification of this Act to the Code, see Short Title of 1974 Acts note set out under section 5901 of this title and Tables.

Transfer of Functions

For transfer of certain enforcement functions of Administrator or other official of the Environmental Protection Agency under this chapter to Federal Inspector, Office of Federal Inspector for the Alaska Natural Gas Transportation System, see note set out under section 6903 of this title.

"Secretary of Energy" was substituted for "Administrator of the Federal Energy Administration, the Administrator of the Energy Research and Development Administration, or the Chairman of the Federal Power Commission" in subsec. (a) and for "Energy Research and Development Administration" in subsecs. (b)(2) and (c)(3) pursuant to sections 301, 703, and 707 of Pub. L. No. 95–91, which are codified as sections 7151, 7293, and 7297 of this title and which terminated the Federal Energy Administration and the Energy Research and Development Administration and transferred their functions and the functions of the Administrators thereof (with certain exceptions) to the Secretary of Energy and terminated the Federal Power Commission and transferred its functions and the functions of the Chairman thereof (with certain exceptions) to the Secretary of Energy.

Prior Provisions

Provisions similar to this section were contained in section 3253 of this title, prior to the complete revision of the Solid Waste Disposal Act by Pub. L. No. 94–580.

EPA Study of Methods to Reduce Plastic Pollution

Pub. L. No. 100–220, Title II, § 2202, 101 Stat. 1465 (Dec. 29, 1987), authorized the Administrator of the Environmental Agency, in consultation with the Secretary of Commerce, to conduct a study of the adverse effects of the improper disposal of plastic articles on the environment and waste disposal, and various methods to reduce or eliminate such adverse effects, and directed the Administrator, within 18 months after Dec. 29, 1987, to report the results of this study to Congress.

Plastic Pollution Public Education Program

Pub. L. No. 100–220, Title II, § 2204, 101 Stat. 1466 (Dec. 29, 1987), formerly set out as a note under this section was transferred and, as amended by Pub. L. No. 104–324, is now set out as section 1915 of Title 33, Navigation and Navigable Waters.

National Advisory Commission on Resource Conservation and Recovery

Pub. L. No. 96–482, § 33, 94 Stat. 2356 (Oct. 21, 1980), as amended by Pub. L. No. 105–362, Title V, § 501(g), 112 Stat. 3284 (Nov. 10, 1998), provided for the establishment, membership, functions, etc., of a National Advisory Commission on Resource Conservation and Recovery, directed the Commission to submit an interim report for legislative and administrative actions relating to this chapter on Feb. 15, 1982, and upon the expiration of the two-year period beginning on the date when all initial members of the Commission have been appointed or the date initial funds become available, whichever is later, to transmit a final report to the President and Congress containing a detailed statement of the findings and conclusions of the Commission, and terminated the Commission 30 days after the submission of its final report.

Leachate Control Research Program in Delaware

Section 4 of Pub. L. No. 94–580 directed the Administrator of the Environmental Protection Agency, in order to demonstrate effective means of dealing with contamination of public water supplies by leachate from abandoned or other landfills, to provide technical and financial assistance for a research program, designed by the New Castle County areawide waste treatment management program, to control leachate from Llangollen Landfill in New Castle County, Delaware, and provided up to $200,000 in each of the fiscal years 1978 and 1979 for the operating costs of a counter-pumping program to contain the leachate from the Llangollen Landfill during the period of this study.

Solid Waste Cleanup on Federal Lands in Alaska; Study and Report to Congressional Committees

Pub. L. No. 94–580, § 3, 90 Stat. 2829 (Oct. 21, 1976), providing for study of procedures for removal of solid waste from Federal lands in Alaska and submission of a Presidential Report to Senate Committee on Public Lands and House Committee on Interstate and Foreign Commerce no later than one year after Oct. 21, 1976, and implementing recommendations to such committees within six months thereafter, was repealed by Pub. L. No. 96–482, § 30, Oct. 21, 1980, 94 Stat. 2352.

§ 6982. Special studies; plans for research, development, and demonstrations

[SWDA § 8002]

(a) Glass and plastic

The Administrator shall undertake a study and publish a report on resource recovery from glass and plastic waste, including a scientific, technological, and economic investigation of potential solutions to implement such recovery.

(b) Composition of waste stream

The Administrator shall undertake a systematic study of the composition of the solid waste stream and of anticipated future changes in the composition of such stream and shall publish a report containing the results of such study and quantitatively evaluating the potential utility of such components.

(c) Priorities study

For purposes of determining priorities for research on recovery of materials and energy from solid waste and developing materials and energy recovery research, development, and demonstration strategies, the Administrator shall review, and make a study of, the various existing and promising techniques of energy recovery from solid waste (including, but not limited to, waterwall furnace incinerators, dry shredded fuel systems, pyrolysis, densified refuse-derived fuel systems, anerobic digestion, and fuel and feedstock preparation systems). In carrying out such study the Administrator shall investigate with respect to each such technique—

(1) the degree of public need for the potential results of such research, development, or demonstration,

(2) the potential for research, development, and demonstration without Federal action, including the degree of restraint on such potential posed by the risks involved, and

(3) the magnitude of effort and period of time necessary to develop the technology to the point where Federal assistance can be ended.

(d) Small-scale and low technology study

The Administrator shall undertake a comprehensive study and analysis of, and publish a report on, systems of small-scale and low technology solid waste management, including household resource recovery and resource recovery systems which have special application to multiple dwelling units and high density housing and office complexes. Such study and analysis shall include an investigation of the degree to which such systems could contribute to energy conservation.

(e) Front-end source separation

The Administrator shall undertake research and studies concerning the compatibility of front-end source separation systems with high technology resource recovery systems and shall publish a report containing the results of such research and studies.

(f) Mining waste

The Administrator, in consultation with the Secretary of the Interior, shall conduct a detailed and comprehensive study on the adverse effects of solid wastes from active and abandoned surface and underground mines on the environment, including, but not limited to, the effects of such wastes on humans, water, air, health, welfare, and natural resources, and on the adequacy of means and measures currently employed by the mining industry, Government agencies, and others to dispose of and utilize such solid wastes and to prevent or substantially mitigate such adverse effects. Such study shall include an analysis of—

(1) the sources and volume of discarded material generated per year from mining;

(2) present disposal practices;

(3) potential dangers to human health and the environment from surface runoff of leachate and air pollution by dust;

(4) alternatives to current disposal methods;

(5) the cost of those alternatives in terms of the impact on mine product costs; and

(6) potential for use of discarded material as a secondary source of the mine product.

In furtherance of this study, the Administrator shall, as he deems appropriate, review studies and other actions of other Federal agencies concerning such wastes with a view toward avoiding duplication of effort and the need to expedite such study. Not later than thirty-six months after October 21, 1980, the Administrator shall publish a report of such study and shall include appropriate findings and recommendations for Federal and non-Federal actions concerning such effects. Such report shall be submitted to the Committee on Environment and Public Works of the United States Senate and the Committee on Energy and Commerce of the United States House of Representatives.

(g) Sludge

The Administrator shall undertake a comprehensive study and publish a report on sludge. Such study shall include an analysis of—

(1) what types of solid waste (including but not limited to sewage and pollution treatment residues and other residues from industrial operations such as extraction of oil from shale, liquefaction and gasification of coal and coal slurry pipeline operations) shall be codified as sludge;

(2) the effects of air and water pollution legislation on the creation of large volumes of sludge;

(3) the amounts of sludge originating in each State and in each industry producing sludge;

(4) methods of disposal of such sludge, including the cost, efficiency, and effectiveness of such methods;

(5) alternative methods for the use of sludge, including agricultural applications of sludge and energy recovery from sludge; and

(6) methods to reclaim areas which have been used for the disposal of sludge or which have been damaged by sludge.

(h) Tires

The Administrator shall undertake a study and publish a report respecting discarded motor vehicle tires which shall include an analysis of the problems involved in the collection, recovery of resources including energy, and use of such tires.

(i) Resource recovery facilities

The Administrator shall conduct research and report on the economics of, and impediments, to the effective functioning of resource recovery facilities.

(j) Resource Conservation Committee

(1) The Administrator shall serve as Chairman of a Committee composed of himself, the Secretary of Commerce, the Secretary of Labor, the Chairman of the Council on Environmental Quality, the Secretary of Treasury, the Secretary of the Interior, the Secretary of Energy, the Chairman of the Council of Economic Advisors, and a representative of the Office of Management and Budget, which shall conduct a full and complete investigation and study of all aspects of the economic, social, and environmental consequences of resource conservation with respect to—

(A) the appropriateness of recommended incentives and disincentives to foster resource conservation;

(B) the effect of existing public policies (including subsidies and economic incentives and disincentives, percentage depletion allowances, capital gains treatment and other tax incentives and disincentives) upon resource conservation, and the likely effect of the modification or elimination of such incentives and disincentives upon resource conservation;

(C) the appropriateness and feasibility of restricting the manufacture or use of categories of consumer products as a resource conservation strategy;

(D) the appropriateness and feasibility of employing as a resource conservation strategy the imposition of solid waste management charges on consumer products, which charges would reflect the costs of solid waste management services, litter pickup, the value of recoverable components of such product, final disposal, and any social value associated with the nonrecycling or uncontrolled disposal of such product; and

(E) the need for further research, development, and demonstration in the area of resource conservation.

(2) The study required in paragraph (1)(D) may include pilot scale projects, and shall consider and evaluate alternative strategies with respect to—

(A) the product categories on which such charges would be imposed;

(B) the appropriate state in the production of such consumer product at which to levy such charge;

(C) appropriate criteria for establishing such charges for each consumer product category;

(D) methods for the adjustment of such charges to reflect actions such as recycling which would reduce the overall quantities of solid waste requiring disposal; and

(E) procedures for amending, modifying, or revising such charges to reflect changing conditions.

(3) The design for the study required in paragraph (1) of this subsection shall include timetables for the completion of the study. A preliminary report putting forth the study design shall be sent to the President and the Congress within six months following October 21, 1976, and followup reports shall be sent six months thereafter. Each recommendation resulting from the study shall include at least two alternatives to the proposed recommendation.

(4) The results of such investigation and study, including recommendations, shall be reported to the President and the Congress not later than two years after October 21, 1976.

(5) There are authorized to be appropriated not to exceed $2,000,000 to carry out this subsection.

(k) Airport landfills

The Administrator shall undertake a comprehensive study and analysis of and publish a report on systems to alleviate the hazards to aviation from birds congregating and feeding on landfills in the vicinity of airports.

(*l*) Completion of research and studies

The Administrator shall complete the research and studies, and submit the reports, required under subsections (b), (c), (d), (e), (f), (g), and (k) of this section not later than October 1, 1978. The Administrator shall complete the research and studies, and submit the reports, required under subsections (a), (h), and (i) of this section not later than October 1, 1979. Upon completion, each study specified in subsections (a) through (k) of this section, the Administrator shall prepare a plan for research, development, and demonstration respecting the findings of the study and shall submit any legislative recommendations resulting from such study to appropriate committees of Congress.

(m) Drilling fluids, produced waters, and other wastes associated with the exploration, development, or production of crude oil or natural gas or geothermal energy

(1) The Administrator shall conduct a detailed and comprehensive study and submit a report on the adverse effects, if any, of drilling fluids, produced waters, and other wastes associated with the exploration, development, or production of crude oil or natural gas or geothermal energy on human health and the environment, including, but not limited to, the effects of such wastes on humans, water, air, health, welfare, and natural resources and on the adequacy of means and measures currently employed by the oil and gas and geothermal drilling and production industry, Government agencies, and others to dispose of and utilize such wastes and to prevent or substantially mitigate such adverse effects. Such study shall include an analysis of—

(A) the sources and volume of discarded material generated per year from such wastes;

(B) present disposal practices;

(C) potential danger to human health and the environment from the surface runoff or leachate;

(D) documented cases which prove or have caused danger to human health and the environment from surface runoff or leachate;

(E) alternatives to current disposal methods;

(F) the cost of such alternatives; and

(G) the impact of those alternatives on the exploration for, and development and production of, crude oil and natural gas or geothermal energy.

In furtherance of this study, the Administrator shall, as he deems appropriate, review studies and other actions of other Federal agencies concerning such wastes with a view toward avoiding duplication of effort and the need to expedite such study. The Administrator shall publish a report of such study and shall include appropriate findings and recommendations for Federal and non-Federal actions concerning such effects.

(2) The Administrator shall complete the research and study and submit the report required under paragraph (1) not later than twenty-four months from October 21, 1980. Upon completion of the study, the Administrator shall prepare a summary of the findings of the study, a plan for research, development, and demonstration respecting the findings of the study, and shall submit the findings and the study, along with any recommendations resulting from such study, to the Committee on Environment and Public Works of the United States Senate and the Committee on Energy and Commerce of the United States House of Representatives.

(3) There are authorized to be appropriated not to exceed $1,000,000 to carry out the provisions of this subsection.

(n) Materials generated from the combustion of coal and other fossil fuels

The Administrator shall conduct a detailed and comprehensive study and submit a report on the adverse effects on human health and the environment, if any, of the disposal and utilization of fly ash waste, bottom ash waste, slag waste, flue gas emission control waste, and other byproduct materials generated primarily from the combustion of coal or other fossil fuels. Such study shall include an analysis of—

(1) the source and volumes of such material generated per year;

(2) present disposal and utilization practices;

(3) potential danger, if any, to human health and the environment from the disposal and reuse of such materials;

(4) documented cases in which danger to human health or the environment from surface runoff or leachate has been proved;

(5) alternatives to current disposal methods;

(6) the costs of such alternatives;

(7) the impact of those alternatives on the use of coal and other natural resources; and

(8) the current and potential utilization of such materials.

In furtherance of this study, the Administrator shall, as he deems appropriate, review studies and other actions of other Federal and State agencies concerning such material and invite participation by other concerned parties, including industry and other Federal and State agencies, with a view toward avoiding duplication of effort. The Administrator shall publish a report on such study, which shall include appropriate findings, not later than twenty-four months after October 21, 1980. Such study and findings shall be submitted to the Committee on Environment and Public Works of the United States Senate and the Committee on Energy and Commerce of the United States House of Representatives.

(*o*) Cement kiln dust waste

The Administrator shall conduct a detailed and comprehensive study of the adverse effects on human health and the environment, if any, of the disposal of cement kiln dust waste. Such study shall include an analysis of—

(1) the source and volumes of such materials generated per year;

(2) present disposal practices;

(3) potential danger, if any, to human health and the environment from the disposal of such materials;

(4) documented cases in which danger to human health or the environment has been proved;

(5) alternatives to current disposal methods;

(6) the costs of such alternatives;

(7) the impact of those alternatives on the use of natural resources; and

(8) the current and potential utilization of such materials.

In furtherance of this study, the Administrator shall, as he deems appropriate, review studies and other actions of other Federal and State agencies concerning such waste or materials and invite participation by other concerned parties, including industry and other Federal and State agencies, with a view toward avoiding duplication of effort. The Administrator shall publish a report of such study, which shall include appropriate findings, not later than thirty-six months after October 21, 1980. Such report shall be submitted to the Committee on Environment and Public Works of the United States Senate and the Committee on Energy and Commerce of the United States House of Representatives.

(p) Materials generated from extraction, beneficiation, and processing of ores and minerals, including phosphate rock and overburden from uranium mining

The Administrator shall conduct a detailed and comprehensive study on the adverse effects on human health and the environment, if any, of the disposal and utilization of solid waste from the extraction, beneficiation, and processing of ores and minerals, including phosphate rock and overburden from uranium mining. Such study shall be conducted in conjunction with the study of mining wastes required by subsection (f) of this section and shall include an analysis of—

(1) the source and volumes of such materials generated per year;

(2) present disposal and utilization practices;

(3) potential danger, if any, to human health and the environment from the disposal and reuse of such materials;

(4) documented cases in which danger to human health or the environment has been proved;

(5) alternatives to current disposal methods;

(6) the costs of such alternatives;

(7) the impact of those alternatives on the use of phosphate rock and uranium ore, and other natural resources; and

(8) the current and potential utilization of such materials.

In furtherance of this study, the Administrator shall, as he deems appropriate, review studies and other actions of other Federal and State agencies concerning such waste or materials and invite participation by other concerned parties, including industry and other Federal and State agencies, with a view toward avoiding duplication of effort. The Administrator shall publish a report of such study, which shall include appropriate findings, in conjunction with the publication of the report of the study of mining wastes required to be conducted under subsection (f) of this section. Such report and findings shall be submitted to the Committee on Environment and Public Works of the United States Senate and the Committee on Energy and Commerce of the United States House of Representatives.

(q) Authorization of appropriations

There are authorized to be appropriated not to exceed $8,000,000 for the fiscal years 1978 and 1979 to carry out this section other than subsection (j) of this section.

(r) Minimization of hazardous waste

The Administrator shall compile, and not later than October 1, 1986, submit to the Congress, a report on the feasibility and desirability of establishing standards of performance or of taking other additional actions under this chapter to require the generators of hazardous waste to reduce the volume or quantity and toxicity of the hazardous waste they generate, and of establishing with respect to hazardous wastes required management practices or other requirements to assure such wastes are managed in ways that minimize present and future risks to human health and the environment. Such report shall include any recommendations for legislative changes which the Administrator determines are feasible and desirable to implement the national policy established by section 6902 of this title.

(s) Extending landfill life and reusing landfilled areas

The Administrator shall conduct detailed, comprehensive studies of methods to extend the useful life of sanitary landfills and to better use sites in which filled or closed landfills are located. Such studies shall address—

(1) methods to reduce the volume of materials before placement in landfills;

(2) more efficient systems for depositing waste in landfills;

(3) methods to enhance the rate of decomposition of solid waste in landfills, in a safe and environmentally acceptable manner;

(4) methane production from closed landfill units;

(5) innovative uses of closed landfill sites, including use for energy production such as solar or wind energy and use for metals recovery;

(6) potential for use of sewage treatment sludge in reclaiming landfilled areas; and

(7) methods to coordinate use of a landfill owned by one municipality by nearby municipalities, and to establish equitable rates for such use, taking into account the need to provide future landfill capacity to replace that so used.

The Administrator is authorized to conduct demonstrations in the areas of study provided in this subsection. The Administrator shall periodically report on the results of such studies, with the first such report not later than October 1, 1986. In carrying out this subsection, the Administrator need not duplicate other studies which have been completed and may rely upon information which has previously been compiled.

(Pub. L. No. 89–272, Title II, § 8002, as added by Pub. L. No. 94–580, § 2, 90 Stat. 2831 (Oct. 21, 1976); and amended by Pub. L. No. 95–609, § 7(t), 92 Stat. 3083 (Nov. 8, 1978); H.Res. 549 (Mar. 25, 1980); Pub. L. No. 96–482, § 29, 94 Stat. 2349 (Oct. 21, 1980); Pub. L. No. 98–616, Title II, § 224(c), Title VII, § 702, 98 Stat. 3253, 3289 (Nov. 8, 1984).)

HISTORICAL AND STATUTORY NOTES

Change of Name

The name of the Committee on Interstate and Foreign Commerce of the House of Representatives was changed to Committee on Energy and Commerce immediately prior to noon on Jan. 3, 1981, by House Resolution 549, Ninety-sixth Congress, Mar. 25, 1980.

Any reference in any provision of law enacted before Jan. 4, 1995, to the Committee on Energy and Commerce of the House of Representatives treated as referring to the Committee on Commerce of the House of Representatives, except that any reference in any provision of law enacted before Jan. 4, 1995, to the Committee on Energy and Commerce of the House of Representatives treated as referring to the Committee on Agriculture of the House of Representatives, in the case of a provision of law relating to inspection of seafood or seafood products, the Committee on Banking and Financial Services of the House of Representatives, in the case of a provision of law relating to bank capital markets activities generally or to depository institution securities activities generally, and the Committee on Transportation and Infrastructure of the House of Representatives, in the case of a provision of law relating to railroads, railway labor, or railroad retirement and unemployment (except revenue measures related thereto), see section 1(a)(4) and (c)(1) of Pub. L. No. 104–14, set out as a note preceding section 21 of Title 2, The Congress.

Transfer of Functions

For transfer of certain enforcement functions of Administrator or other official of the Environmental Protection Agency under this chapter to Federal Inspector, Office of Federal Inspector for the Alaska Natural Gas Transportation System, see note set out under section 6903 of this title.

§ 6983. Coordination, collection, and dissemination of information

[SWDA § 8003]

(a) Information

The Administrator shall develop, collect, evaluate, and coordinate information on—

(1) methods and costs of the collection of solid waste;

(2) solid waste management practices, including data on the different management methods and the cost, operation, and maintenance of such methods;

(3) the amounts and percentages of resources (including energy) that can be recovered from solid waste by use of various solid waste management practices and various technologies;

(4) methods available to reduce the amount of solid waste that is generated;

(5) existing and developing technologies for the recovery of energy or materials from solid waste and the costs, reliability, and risks associated with such technologies;

(6) hazardous solid waste, including incidents of damage resulting from the disposal of hazardous solid wastes; inherently and potentially hazardous solid wastes; methods of neutralizing or properly disposing of hazardous solid wastes; facilities that properly dispose of hazardous wastes;

(7) methods of financing resource recovery facilities or, sanitary landfills, or hazardous solid waste treatment facilities, whichever is appropriate for the entity developing such facility or landfill (taking into account the amount of solid waste reasonably expected to be available to such entity);

(8) the availability of markets for the purchase of resources, either materials or energy, recovered from solid waste; and

(9) research and development projects respecting solid waste management.

(b) Library

(1) The Administrator shall establish and maintain a central reference library for (A) the materials collected pursuant to subsection (a) of this section and (B) the actual performance and cost effectiveness records and other data and information with respect to—

(i) the various methods of energy and resource recovery from solid waste,

(ii) the various systems and means of resource conservation,

(iii) the various systems and technologies for collection, transport, storage, treatment, and final disposition of solid waste, and

(iv) other aspects of solid waste and hazardous solid waste management.

Such central reference library shall also contain, but not be limited to, the model codes and model accounting systems developed under this section, the information collected under subsection (d) of this section, and, subject to any applicable requirements of confidentiality, information respecting any aspect of solid waste provided by officers and employees of the Environmental Protection Agency which has been acquired by them in the conduct of their functions under this chapter and which may be of value to Federal, State, and local authorities and other persons.

(2) Information in the central reference library shall, to the extent practicable, be collated, analyzed, verified, and published and shall be made available to State and local governments and other persons at reasonable times and subject to such reasonable charges as may be necessary to defray expenses of making such information available.

(c) Model accounting system

In order to assist State and local governments in determining the cost and revenues associated with the collection and disposal of solid waste and with resource recovery operations, the Administrator shall develop and publish a recommended model cost and revenue accounting system applicable to the solid waste management functions of State and local governments. Such system shall be in accordance with generally accepted accounting principles. The Administrator shall periodically, but not less frequently than once every five years, review such accounting system and revise it as necessary.

(d) Model codes

The Administrator is authorized, in cooperation with appropriate State and local agencies, to recommend model codes, ordinances, and statutes, providing for sound solid waste management.

(e) Information programs

(1) The Administrator shall implement a program for the rapid dissemination of information on solid waste management, hazardous waste management, resource conservation, and methods of resource recovery from solid waste, including the results of any relevant research, investigations, experiments, surveys, studies, or other information which may be useful in the implementation of new or improved solid waste management practices and methods and information on any other technical, managerial, financial, or market aspect of resource conservation and recovery facilities.

(2) The Administrator shall develop and implement educational programs to promote citizen understanding of the need for environmentally sound solid waste management practices.

(f) Coordination

In collecting and disseminating information under this section, the Administrator shall coordinate his actions and cooperate to the maximum extent possible with State and local authorities.

(g) Special restriction

Upon request, the full range of alternative technologies, programs or processes deemed feasible to meet the resource recovery or resource conservation needs of a jurisdiction shall be described in such a manner as to provide a sufficient evaluative basis from which the jurisdiction can make its decisions, but no officer or employee of the Environmental Protection Agency shall, in an official capacity, lobby for or otherwise represent an agency position in favor of resource recovery or resource conservation, as a policy alternative for adoption into ordinances, codes, regulations, or law by any State or political subdivision thereof.

(Pub. L. No. 89–272, Title II, § 8003, as added by Pub. L. No. 94–580, § 2, 90 Stat. 2834 (Oct. 21, 1976); and amended by Pub. L. No. 95–609, § 7(u), 92 Stat. 3083 (Nov. 8, 1978).)

HISTORICAL AND STATUTORY NOTES

Transfer of Functions

For transfer of certain enforcement functions of Administrator or other official of the Environmental Protection Agency under this chapter to Federal Inspector, Office of Federal Inspector for the Alaska Natural Gas Transportation System, see note set out under section 6903 of this title.

§ 6984. Full-scale demonstration facilities

[SWDA § 8004]

(a) Authority

The Administrator may enter into contracts with public agencies or authorities or private persons for the construction and operation of a full-scale demonstration facility under this chapter, or provide financial assistance in the form of grants to a full-scale demonstration facility under this chapter only if the Administrator finds that—

(1) such facility or proposed facility will demonstrate at full scale a new or significantly improved technology or process, a practical and significant improvement in solid waste management practice, or the technological feasibility and cost effectiveness of an existing, but unproven technology, process, or practice, and will not duplicate any other Federal, State, local, or commercial facility which has been constructed or with respect to which construction has begun (determined as of the date action is taken by the Administrator under this chapter),

(2) such contract or assistance meets the requirements of section 6981 of this title and meets other applicable requirements of this chapter,

(3) such facility will be able to comply with the guidelines published under section 6907 of this title and with other laws and regulations for the protection of health and the environment,

(4) in the case of a contract for construction or operation, such facility is not likely to be constructed or operated by State, local, or private persons or in the case of an application for financial assistance, such facility is not likely to receive adequate financial assistance from other sources, and

(5) any Federal interest in, or assistance to, such facility will be disposed of or terminated, with appropriate compensation, within such period of time as may be necessary to carry out the basic objectives of this chapter.

(b) Time limitation

No obligation may be made by the Administrator for financial assistance under this subchapter for any full-scale demonstration facility after the date ten years after October 21, 1976. No expenditure of funds for any such full-scale demonstration facility under this subchapter may be made by the Administrator after the date fourteen years after October 21, 1976.

(c) Cost sharing

(1) Wherever practicable, in constructing, operating, or providing financial assistance under this subchapter to a full-scale demonstration facility, the Administrator shall endeavor to enter into agreements and make other arrangements for maximum practicable cost sharing with other Federal, State, and local agencies, private persons, or any combination thereof.

(2) The Administrator shall enter into arrangements, wherever practicable and desirable, to provide monitoring of full-scale solid waste facilities (whether or not constructed or operated under this chapter) for purposes of obtaining information concerning the performance, and other aspects, of such facilities. Where the Administrator provides only monitoring and evaluation instruments or personnel (or both) or funds for such instruments or personnel and provides no other financial assistance to a facility, notwithstanding section 6981(c)(3) of this title, title to any invention made or conceived of in the course of developing, constructing, or operating such facility shall not be required to vest in the United States and patents respecting such invention shall not be required to be issued to the United States.

(d) Prohibition

After October 21, 1976, the Administrator shall not construct or operate any full-scale facility (except by contract with public agencies or authorities or private persons).

(Pub. L. No. 89–272, Title II, § 8004, as added by Pub. L. No. 94–580, § 2, 90 Stat. 2836 (Oct. 21, 1976); and amended by Pub. L. No. 95–609, § 7(v), 92 Stat. 3084 (Nov. 8, 1978); Pub. L. No. 98–616, Title V, § 502(f), 98 Stat. 3276 (Nov. 8, 1984).)

HISTORICAL AND STATUTORY NOTES

Transfer of Functions

For transfer of certain enforcement functions of Administrator or other official of the Environmental Protection Agency under this chapter to Federal Inspector, Office of Federal Inspector for the Alaska Natural Gas Transportation System, see note set out under section 6903 of this title.

§ 6985. Special study and demonstration projects on recovery of useful energy and materials

[SWDA § 8005]

(a) Studies

The Administrator shall conduct studies and develop recommendations for administrative or legislative action on—

(1) means of recovering materials and energy from solid waste, recommended uses of such materials and energy for national or international welfare, including identification of potential markets for such recovered resources, the impact of distribution of such resources on existing markets, and potentials for energy conservation through resource conservation and resource recovery;

(2) actions to reduce waste generation which have been taken voluntarily or in response to governmental action, and those which practically could be taken in the future, and the economic, social, and environmental consequences of such actions;

(3) methods of collection, separation, and containerization which will encourage efficient utilization of facilities and contribute to more effective programs of reduction, reuse, or disposal of wastes;

(4) the use of Federal procurement to develop market demand for recovered resources;

(5) recommended incentives (including Federal grants, loans, and other assistance) and disincentives to accelerate the reclamation or recycling of materials from solid wastes, with special emphasis on motor vehicle hulks;

(6) the effect of existing public policies, including subsidies and economic incentives and disincentives, percentage depletion allowances, capital gains treatment and other tax incentives and disincentives, upon the recycling and reuse of materials, and the likely effect of the modification or elimination of such incentives and disincentives upon the reuse, recycling and conservation of such materials;

(7) the necessity and method of imposing disposal or other charges on packaging, containers, vehicles, and other manufactured goods, which charges would reflect the cost of final disposal, the value of recoverable components of the item, and any social costs associated with nonrecycling or uncontrolled disposal of such items; and

(8) the legal constraints and institutional barriers to the acquisition of land needed for solid waste management, including land for facilities and disposal sites;

(9) in consultation with the Secretary of Agriculture, agricultural waste management problems and practices, the extent of reuse and recovery of resources in such wastes, the prospects for improvement, Federal, State, and local regulations governing such practices, and the economic, social, and environmental consequences of such practices; and

(10) in consultation with the Secretary of the Interior, mining waste management problems, and practices, including an assessment of existing authorities, technologies, and economics, and the environmental and public health consequences of such practices.

(b) Demonstration

The Administrator is also authorized to carry out demonstration projects to test and demonstrate methods and techniques developed pursuant to subsection (a) of this section.

(c) Application of other sections

Section 6981(b) and (c) of this title shall be applicable to investigations, studies, and projects carried out under this section.

(Pub. L. No. 89–272, Title II, § 8005, as added by Pub. L. No. 94–580, § 2, 90 Stat. 2837 (Oct. 21, 1976).)

HISTORICAL AND STATUTORY NOTES

Transfer of Functions

For transfer of certain enforcement functions of Administrator or other official of the Environmental Protection Agency under this chapter to Federal Inspector, Office of Federal Inspector for the Alaska Natural Gas Transportation System, see note set out under section 6903 of this title.

Prior Provisions

Provisions similar to this section were contained in section 3253a of this title, prior to the complete revision of the Solid Waste Disposal Act by Pub. L. No. 94–580.

§ 6986. Grants for resource recovery systems and improved solid waste disposal facilities

[SWDA § 8006]

(a) Authority

The Administrator is authorized to make grants pursuant to this section to any State, municipal, or interstate or intermunicipal agency for the demonstration of resource recovery systems or for the construction of new or improved solid waste disposal facilities.

(b) Conditions

(1) Any grant under this section for the demonstration of a resource recovery system may be made only if it (A) is consistent with any plans which meet the requirements of subchapter IV of this chapter; (B) is consistent with the guidelines recommended pursuant to section 6907 of this title; (C) is designed to provide area-wide resource recovery systems consistent with the purposes of this chapter, as determined by the Administrator, pursuant to regulations promulgated under subsection (d) of this section; and (D) provides an equitable system for distributing the costs associated with construction, operation, and maintenance of any resource recovery system among the users of such system.

(2) The Federal share for any project to which paragraph (1) applies shall not be more than 75 percent.

(c) Limitations

(1) A grant under this section for the construction of a new or improved solid waste disposal facility may be made only if—

(A) a State or interstate plan for solid waste disposal has been adopted which applies to the area involved, and the facility to be constructed (i) is consistent with such plan, (ii) is included in a comprehensive plan for the area involved which is satisfactory to the Administrator for the purposes of this chapter, and (iii) is consistent with the guidelines recommended under section 6907 of this title, and

(B) the project advances the state of the art by applying new and improved techniques in reducing the environmental impact of solid waste disposal, in achieving recovery of energy or resources, or in recycling useful materials.

(2) The Federal share for any project to which paragraph (1) applies shall be not more than 50 percent in the case of a project serving an area which includes only one municipality, and not more than 75 percent in any other case.

(d) Regulations

(1) The Administrator shall promulgate regulations establishing a procedure for awarding grants under this section which—

(A) provides that projects will be carried out in communities of varying sizes, under such conditions as will assist in solving the community waste problems of urban-industrial centers, metropolitan regions, and rural areas, under representative geographic and environmental conditions; and

(B) provides deadlines for submission of, and action on, grant requests.

(2) In taking action on applications for grants under this section, consideration shall be given by the Administrator (A) to the public benefits to be derived by the construction and the propriety of Federal aid in making such grant; (B) to the extent applicable, to the economic and commercial viability of the project (including contractual arrangements with the private sector to market any resources recovered); (C) to the potential of such project for general application to community solid waste disposal problems; and (D) to the use by the applicant of comprehensive regional or metropolitan area planning.

(e) Additional limitations

A grant under this section—

(1) may be made only in the amount of the Federal share of (A) the estimated total design and construction costs, plus (B) in the case of a grant to which subsection (b)(1) of this section applies, the first-year operation and maintenance costs;

(2) may not be provided for land acquisition or (except as otherwise provided in paragraph (1)(B)) for operating or maintenance costs;

(3) may not be made until the applicant has made provision satisfactory to the Administrator for proper and efficient operation and maintenance of the project (subject to paragraph (1)(B)); and

(4) may be made subject to such conditions and requirements, in addition to those provided in this section, as the Administrator may require to properly carry out his functions pursuant to this chapter.

For purposes of paragraph (1), the non-Federal share may be in any form, including, but not limited to, lands or interests therein needed for the project or personal property or services, the value of which shall be determined by the Administrator.

(f) Single State

(1) Not more than 15 percent of the total of funds authorized to be appropriated for any fiscal year to carry out this section shall be granted under this section for projects in any one State.

(2) The Administrator shall prescribe by regulation the manner in which this subsection shall apply to a grant under this section for a project in an area which includes all or part of more than one State.

(Pub. L. No. 89–272, Title II, § 8006, as added by Pub. L. No. 94–580, § 2, 90 Stat. 2838 (Oct. 21, 1976).)

HISTORICAL AND STATUTORY NOTES

Transfer of Functions

For transfer of certain enforcement functions of Administrator or other official of the Environmental Protection Agency under this chapter to Federal Inspector, Office of Federal Inspector for the Alaska Natural Gas Transportation System, see note set out under section 6903 of this title.

Prior Provisions

Provisions similar to this section were contained in section 3254b of this title, prior to the complete revision of the Solid Waste Disposal Act by Pub. L. No. 94–580.

§ 6987. Authorization of appropriations

[SWDA § 8007]

There are authorized to be appropriated not to exceed $35,000,000 for the fiscal year 1978 to carry out the purposes of this subchapter (except for section 6982 of this title).

(Pub. L. No. 89–272, Title II, § 8007, as added by Pub. L. No. 94–580, § 2, 90 Stat. 2839 (Oct. 21, 1976).)

HISTORICAL AND STATUTORY NOTES

Prior Provisions

Provisions similar to this section were contained in section 3259 of this title, prior to the complete revision of the Solid Waste Disposal Act by Pub. L. No. 94–580.

SUBCHAPTER IX—REGULATION OF UNDERGROUND STORAGE TANKS

§ 6991. Definitions and exemptions

[SWDA § 9001]

In this subchapter:

(1) Indian tribe

(A) In general

The term "Indian tribe" means any Indian tribe, band, nation, or other organized group or community that is recognized as being eligible for special programs and services provided by the United States to Indians because of their status as Indians.

(B) Inclusions

The term "Indian tribe" includes an Alaska Native village, as defined in or established under the Alaska Native Claims Settlement Act (43 U.S.C. 1601 et seq.); and[1]

(2) The term "nonoperational storage tank" means any underground storage tank in which regulated substances will not be deposited or from which regulated substances will not be dispensed after November 8, 1984.

(3) The term "operator" means any person in control of, or having responsibility for, the daily operation of the underground storage tank.

(4) The term "owner" means—

(A) in the case of an underground storage tank in use on November 8, 1984, or brought into use after that date, any person who owns an underground storage tank used for the storage, use, or dispensing of regulated substances and

(B) in the case of any underground storage tank in use before November 8, 1984, but no longer in use on November 8, 1984, any person who owned such tank immediately before the discontinuation of its use.

(5) The term "person" has the same meaning as provided in section 6903(15) of this title, except that such term includes a consortium, a joint venture, and a commercial entity, and the United States Government.

(6) The term "petroleum" means petroleum, including crude oil or any fraction thereof which is liquid at standard conditions of temperature and pressure (60 degrees Fahrenheit and 14.7 pounds per square inch absolute).

(7) The term "regulated substance" means—

(A) any substance defined in section 9601(14) of this title (but not including any substance regulated as a hazardous waste under subchapter III of this chapter), and

(B) petroleum.

(8) The term "release" means any spilling, leaking, emitting, discharging, escaping, leaching, or disposing from an underground storage tank into ground water, surface water or subsurface soils.

(9) Trust fund

The term "Trust Fund" means the Leaking Underground Storage Tank Trust Fund established by section 9508 of Title 26.

(10) The term "underground storage tank" means any one or combination of tanks (including underground pipes connected thereto) which is used to contain an accumulation of regulated substances, and the volume of which (including the volume of the underground pipes connected thereto) is 10 per centum or more beneath the surface of the ground. Such term does not include any—

(A) farm or residential tank of 1,100 gallons or less capacity used for storing motor fuel for noncommercial purposes,

(B) tank used for storing heating oil for consumptive use on the premises where stored,

(C) septic tank,

(D) pipeline facility (including gathering lines)—

(i) which is regulated under chapter 601 of Title 49, or

(ii) which is an intrastate pipeline facility regulated under State laws as provided in chapter 601 of Title 49,

and which is determined by the Secretary to be connected to a pipeline or to be operated or intended to be capable of operating at pipeline pressure or as an integral part of a pipeline,

(E) surface impoundment, pit, pond, or lagoon,

(F) storm water or waste water collection system,

(G) flow-through process tank,

(H) liquid trap or associated gathering lines directly related to oil or gas production and gathering operations, or

(I) storage tank situated in an underground area (such as a basement, cellar, mineworking, drift, shaft, or tunnel) if the storage tank is situated upon or above the surface of the floor.

The term "underground storage tank" shall not include any pipes connected to any tank which is described in subparagraphs (A) through (I).

(Pub. L. No. 89–272, Title II, § 9001, as added by Pub. L. No. 98–616, Title VI, § 601(a), 98 Stat. 3277 (Nov. 8, 1984); and amended by Pub. L. No. 99–499, Title II, § 205(a), 100 Stat. 1696 (Oct. 17, 1986); Pub. L. No. 102–508, Title III, § 302, 106 Stat. 3307 (Oct. 24, 1992); Pub. L. No. 103–429, § 7(d), 108 Stat. 4389 (Oct. 31, 1994); Pub. L. No. 109–58, Title XV, §§ 1532(a), 1533(1), 119 Stat. 1104, 1105 (Aug. 8, 2005).)

[1] So in original. The semicolon and "and" should probably be a period.

HISTORICAL AND STATUTORY NOTES

References in Text

This subchapter, referred to in text, originally read "this subtitle", meaning subtitle I of the Solid Waste Disposal Act, Pub. L. No. 89–272, Title II, § 9001 et seq., as added Pub. L. No. 98–616, Title VI, § 601(a), 98 Stat. 3277 (Nov. 8, 1984), and amended, which is codified principally as this subchapter.

The Alaska Native Claims Settlement Act, referred to in par. (1)(B), is Pub. L. No. 92–203, 85 Stat. 688 (Dec. 18, 1971), as amended, which is codified principally as chapter 33 of Title 43, 43 U.S.C.A. § 1601 et seq. For complete classification, see Short Title note set out under 43 U.S.C.A. § 1601 and Tables.

Effective and Applicability Provisions

1986 Acts. Amendment by Pub. L. No. 99–499 effective Oct. 17, 1986, see section 4 of Pub. L. No. 99–499, set out as a note under section 9601 of this title.

Aboveground Storage Tank Grant Program

Pub. L. No. 106–554, § 1(a)(4) [Div. B, Title XII, § 1201], 114 Stat. 2763, 2763A–313 (Dec. 21, 2000), provided that:

"**(a) Definitions.**—In this provision:

"**(1) Aboveground storage tank.**—The term 'aboveground storage tank' means any tank or combination of tanks (including any connected pipe)—

"**(A)** that is used to contain an accumulation of regulated substances; and

"**(B)** the volume of which (including the volume of any connected pipe) is located wholly above the surface of the ground.

"**(2) Administrator.**—The term 'Administrator' means the Administrator of the Environmental Protection Agency.

"**(3) Denali Commission.**—The term 'Denali Commission' means the commission established by section 303(a) of the Denali Commission Act of 1998 (42 U.S.C. 3121 note).

"**(4) Federal environmental law.**—The term 'Federal environmental law' means—

"**(A)** the Oil Pollution Control Act of 1990 [Oil Pollution Act of 1990, Pub. L. No. 101–380, Aug. 18, 1990, 104 Stat. 484] (33 U.S.C. 2701 et seq.);

"**(B)** the Comprehensive Environmental Response, Compensation, and Liability Act of 1980 [Pub. L. No. 96–510, 94 Stat. 2767 (Dec. 11, 1980)] (42 U.S.C. 9601 et seq.);

"**(C)** the Solid Waste Disposal Act [Pub. L. No. 89–272, Title II, 79 Stat. 997 (Oct. 20, 1965)] (42 U.S.C. 6901 et seq.);

"**(D)** the Federal Water Pollution Control Act [Act of June 30, 1948, ch. 758, 62 Stat. 1155] (33 U.S.C. 1251 et seq.); or

"**(E)** any other Federal law that is applicable to the release into the environment of a regulated substance, as determined by the Administrator.

"**(5) Native village.**—The term 'Native village' has the meaning given the term in section 11(b) in Public Law 92–203 (85 Stat. 688) [43 U.S.C.A. § 1601(b)].

"**(6) Program.**—The term 'program' means the Aboveground Storage Tank Grant Program established by subsection (b)(1).

"**(7) Regulated substance.**—The term 'regulated substance' has the meaning given the term in section 9001 of the Solid Waste Disposal Act (42 U.S.C. 6991).

"**(8) State.**—The term 'State' means the State of Alaska.

"**(b) Establishment.**—

"**(1) In general.**—There is established a grant program to be known as the 'Aboveground Storage Tank Grant Program'.

"(2) Grants.—Under the program, the Administrator shall award a grant to—

"(A) the State, on behalf of a Native village; or

"(B) the Denali Commission.

"(c) Use of grants.—The State or the Denali Commission shall use the funds of a grant under subsection (b) to repair, upgrade, or replace one or more aboveground storage tanks that—

"(1) leaks or poses an imminent threat of leaking, as certified by the Administrator, the Commandant of the Coast Guard, or any other appropriate Federal or State agency (as determined by the Administrator); and

"(2) Is located in a native village—

"(A) the median household income of which is less than 80 percent of the median household income in the State;

"(B) That is located—

"(i) Within the boundaries of—

"(I) a unit of the National Park System;

"(II) a unit of the National Wildlife Refuge System; or

"(III) a National Forest; or

"(ii) on public land under the administrative jurisdiction of the Bureau of Land Management; or

"(C) that receives payments from the Federal Government under chapter 69 of title 31, United States Code (commonly known as 'payments in lieu of taxes').

"(d) Reports.—Not later than 1 year after the date on which the State or the Denali Commission receives a grant under subsection (c), and annually thereafter, the State or the Denali Commission, as the case may be, shall submit a report describing each project completed with grant funds and any projects planned for the following year, to—

"(1) the Administrator;

"(2) the Committee on Resources [now Committee on Natural Resources] of the House of Representatives;

"(3) the Committee on Environment and Public Works of the Senate;

"(4) the Committee on Appropriations of the House of Representatives; and

"(5) the Committee on Appropriations of the Senate.

"(e) Authorization of appropriations.—There are authorized to be appropriated to carry out this Act [Pub. L. No. 106–554, § 1(a)(4), 114 Stat. 2763, 2763A–313 (Dec. 21, 2000)], to remain available until expended—

"(1) $20,000,000 for fiscal year 2001; and

"(2) such sums as are necessary for each fiscal year thereafter."

[For transfer of authorities, functions, personnel, and assets of the Coast Guard, including the authorities and functions of the Secretary of Transportation relating thereto, to the Department of Homeland Security, and for treatment of related references, see 6 U.S.C.A. §§ 468(b), 551(d), 552(d) and 557, and the Department of Homeland Security Reorganization Plan of November 25, 2002, as modified, set out as a note under 6 U.S.C.A. § 542.]

§ 6991a. Notification

[SWDA § 9002]

(a) Underground storage tanks

(1) Within 18 months after November 8, 1984, each owner of an underground storage tank shall notify the State or local agency or department designated pursuant to subsection (b)(1) of this section of the existence of such tank, specifying the age, size, type, location, and uses of such tank.

(2) (A) For each underground storage tank taken out of operation after January 1, 1974, the owner of such tank shall, within eighteen months after November 8, 1984, notify the State or local agency, or department designated pursuant to subsection (b)(1) of this section of the existence of such tanks (unless the owner knows the tank subsequently was removed from the ground). The owner of a tank taken out of operation on or before January 1, 1974, shall not be required to notify the State or local agency under this subsection.

(B) Notice under subparagraph (A) shall specify, to the extent known to the owner—

(i) the date the tank was taken out of operation,

(ii) the age of the tank on the date taken out of operation,

(iii) the size, type and location of the tank, and

(iv) the type and quantity of substances left stored in such tank on the date taken out of operation.

(3) Any owner which brings into use an underground storage tank after the initial notification period specified under paragraph (1), shall notify the designated State or local agency or department within thirty days of the existence of such tank, specifying the age, size, type, location and uses of such tank.

(4) Paragraphs (1) through (3) of this subsection shall not apply to tanks for which notice was given pursuant to section 9603(c) of this title.

(5) Beginning thirty days after the Administrator prescribes the form of notice pursuant to subsection (b)(2) of this section and for eighteen months thereafter, any person who deposits regulated substances in an underground storage tank shall reasonably notify the owner or operator of such tank of the owner's notification requirements pursuant to this subsection.

(6) Beginning thirty days after the Administrator issues new tank performance standards pursuant to section 6991b(c) of this title, any person who sells a tank intended to be used as an underground storage tank shall notify the purchaser of such tank of the owner's notification requirements pursuant to this subsection.

(b) Agency designation

(1) Within one hundred and eighty days after November 8, 1984, the Governors of each State shall designate the appropriate State agency or department or local agencies or departments to receive the notifications under subsection (a)(1), (2), or (3) of this section.

(2) Within twelve months after November 8, 1984, the Administrator, in consultation with State and local officials designated pursuant to subsection (b)(1) of this section, and after notice and opportunity for public comment, shall prescribe the form of the notice and the information to be included in the notifications under subsection (a)(1), (2), or (3) of this section. In prescribing the form of such notice, the Administrator shall take into account the effect on small businesses and other owners and operators.

(c) State inventories

Each State shall make 2 separate inventories of all underground storage tanks in such State containing regulated substances. One inventory shall be made with respect to petroleum and one with respect to other regulated substances. In making such inventories, the State shall utilize and aggregate the data in the notification forms submitted pursuant to subsections (a) and (b) of this section. Each State shall submit such aggregated data to the Administrator not later than 270 days after October 17, 1986.

(d) Public record

(1) In general

The Administrator shall require each State that receives Federal funds to carry out this subchapter to maintain, update at least annually, and make available to the public, in such manner and form as the Administrator shall prescribe (after consultation with States), a record of underground storage tanks regulated under this subchapter.

(2) Considerations

To the maximum extent practicable, the public record of a State, respectively, shall include, for each year—

(A) the number, sources, and causes of underground storage tank releases in the State;

(B) the record of compliance by underground storage tanks in the State with—

(i) this subchapter; or

(ii) an applicable State program approved under section 6991c of this title; and

(C) data on the number of underground storage tank equipment failures in the State.

(Pub. L. No. 89–272, Title II, § 9002, as added by Pub. L. No. 98–616, Title VI, § 601(a), 98 Stat. 3278 (Nov. 8, 1984); and amended by Pub. L. No. 99–499, Title II, § 205(b), 100 Stat. 1696 (Oct. 17, 1986); Pub. L. No. 109–58, Title XV, § 1526(c), 119 Stat. 1098 (Aug. 8, 2005).)

HISTORICAL AND STATUTORY NOTES

References in Text

This subchapter, referred to in subsec. (d), originally read "this subtitle", meaning subtitle I of the Solid Waste Disposal Act, Pub. L. No. 89–272, Title II, § 9001 et seq., as added Pub. L. No. 98–616, Title VI, § 601(a), 98 Stat. 3277 (Nov. 8, 1984), and amended, which is codified principally to this subchapter.

Effective and Applicability Provisions

1986 Acts. Amendment by Pub. L. No. 99–499, effective Oct. 17, 1986, see section 4 of Pub. L. No. 99–499, set out as a note under section 9601 of this title.

§ 6991b. Release detection, prevention, and correction regulations [SWDA § 9003]

(a) Regulations

The Administrator, after notice and opportunity for public comment, and at least three months before the effective dates specified in subsection (f) of this section, shall promulgate release detection, prevention, and correction regulations applicable to all owners and operators of underground storage tanks, as may be necessary to protect human health and the environment.

(b) Distinctions in regulations

In promulgating regulations under this section, the Administrator may distinguish between types, classes, and ages of underground storage tanks. In making such distinctions, the Administrator may take into consideration factors, including, but not limited to: location of the tanks, soil and climate conditions, uses of the tanks, history of maintenance, age of the tanks, current industry recommended practices, national consensus codes, hydrogeology, water table, size of the tanks, quantity of regulated substances periodically deposited in or dispensed from the tank, the technical capability of the owners and operators, and the compatibility of the regulated substance and the materials of which the tank is fabricated.

(c) Requirements

The regulations promulgated pursuant to this section shall include, but need not be limited to, the following requirements respecting all underground storage tanks—

(1) requirements for maintaining a leak detection system, an inventory control system together with tank testing, or a comparable system or method designed to identify releases in a manner consistent with the protection of human health and the environment;

(2) requirements for maintaining records of any monitoring or leak detection system or inventory control system or tank testing or comparable system;

(3) requirements for reporting of releases and corrective action taken in response to a release from an underground storage tank;

(4) requirements for taking corrective action in response to a release from an underground storage tank;

(5) requirements for the closure of tanks to prevent future releases of regulated substances into the environment; and

(6) requirements for maintaining evidence of financial responsibility for taking corrective action and compensating third parties for bodily injury and property damage caused by sudden and nonsudden accidental releases arising from operating an underground storage tank.

(d) Financial responsibility

(1) Financial responsibility required by this subsection may be established in accordance with regulations promulgated by the Administrator by any one, or any combination, of the following: insurance, guarantee, surety bond, letter of credit, qualification as a self-insurer or any other method satisfactory to the Administrator. In promulgating requirements under this subsection, the Administrator is authorized to specify policy or other contractual terms, conditions, or defenses which are necessary or are unacceptable in establishing such evidence of financial responsibility in order to effectuate the purposes of this subchapter.

(2) In any case where the owner or operator is in bankruptcy, reorganization, or arrangement pursuant to the Federal Bankruptcy Code or where with reasonable diligence jurisdiction in any State court of the Federal courts cannot be obtained over an owner or operator likely to be solvent at the time of judgment, any claim arising from conduct for which evidence of financial responsibility must be provided under this subsection may be asserted directly against the guarantor providing such evidence of financial responsibility. In the case of any action pursuant to this paragraph such guarantor shall be entitled to invoke all rights and defenses which would have been available to the owner or operator if any action had been brought against the owner or operator by the claimant and which would have been available to the guarantor if an action had been brought against the guarantor by the owner or operator.

(3) The total liability of any guarantor shall be limited to the aggregate amount which the guarantor has provided as evidence of financial responsibility to the owner or operator under this section. Nothing in this subsection shall be construed to limit any other State or Federal statutory, contractual or common law liability of a guarantor to its owner or operator including, but not limited to, the liability of such guarantor for bad faith either in negotiating or in failing to negotiate the settlement of any claim. Nothing in this subsection shall be construed to diminish the liability of any person under section 9607 or 9611 of this title or other applicable law.

(4) For the purpose of this subsection, the term "guarantor" means any person, other than the owner or operator, who provides evidence of financial responsibility for an owner or operator under this subsection.

(5) (A) The Administrator, in promulgating financial responsibility regulations under this section, may establish an amount of coverage for particular classes or categories of underground storage tanks containing petroleum which shall satisfy such regulations and which shall not be less than $1,000,000 for each occurrence with an appropriate aggregate requirement.

(B) The Administrator may set amounts lower than the amounts required by subparagraph (A) of this paragraph for underground storage tanks containing petroleum which are at facilities not engaged in petroleum production, refining, or marketing and which are not used to handle substantial quantities of petroleum.

(C) In establishing classes and categories for purposes of this paragraph, the Administrator may consider the following factors:

(i) The size, type, location, storage, and handling capacity of underground storage tanks in the class or category and the volume of petroleum handled by such tanks.

(ii) The likelihood of release and the potential extent of damage from any release from underground storage tanks in the class or category.

(iii) The economic impact of the limits on the owners and operators of each such class or category, particularly relating to the small business segment of the petroleum marketing industry.

(iv) The availability of methods of financial responsibility in amounts greater than the amount established by this paragraph.

(v) Such other factors as the Administrator deems pertinent.

(D) The Administrator may suspend enforcement of the financial responsibility requirements for a particular class or category of underground storage tanks or in a particular State, if the Administrator makes a determination that methods of financial responsibility satisfying the requirements of this subsection are not generally available for underground storage tanks in that class or category, and—

(i) steps are being taken to form a risk retention group for such class of tanks; or

(ii) such State is taking steps to establish a fund pursuant to section 6991c(c)(1) of this title to be submitted as evidence of financial responsibility.

A suspension by the Administrator pursuant to this paragraph shall extend for a period not to exceed 180 days. A determination to suspend may be made with respect to the same class or category or for the same State at the end of such period, but only if substantial progress has been made in establishing a risk retention group, or the owners or operators in the class or category demonstrate, and the Administrator finds, that the formation of such a group is not possible and that the State is unable or unwilling to establish such a fund pursuant to clause (ii).

(e) New tank performance standards

The Administrator shall, not later than three months prior to the effective date specified in subsection (f) of this section, issue performance standards for underground storage tanks brought into use on or after the effective date of such standards. The performance standards for new underground storage tanks shall include, but need not be limited to, design, construction, installation, release detection, and compatibility standards.

(f) Effective dates

(1) Regulations issued pursuant to subsections (c) and (d) of this section, and standards issued pursuant to subsection (e) of this section, for underground storage tanks containing regulated substances defined in section 6991(7)(B) of this title (petroleum, including crude oil or any fraction thereof which is liquid at standard conditions of temperature and pressure) shall be effective not later than thirty months after November 8, 1984.

(2) Standards issued pursuant to subsection (e) of this section (entitled "New Tank Performance Standards") for underground storage tanks containing regulated substances defined in section 6991(7)(A) of this title shall be effective not later than thirty-six months after November 8, 1984.

(3) Regulations issued pursuant to subsection (c) of this section (entitled "Requirements") and standards issued pursuant to subsection (d) of this section (entitled "Financial Responsibility") for underground storage tanks containing regulated substances defined in section 6991(7)(A) of this title shall be effective not later than forty-eight months after November 8, 1984.

(g) Interim prohibition

(1) Until the effective date of the standards promulgated by the Administrator under subsection (e) of this section and after one hundred and eighty days after November 8, 1984, no person may install an underground storage tank for the purpose of storing regulated substances unless such tank (whether of single or double wall construction)—

(A) will prevent releases due to corrosion or structural failure for the operational life of the tank;

(B) is cathodically protected against corrosion, constructed of noncorrosive material, steel clad with a noncorrosive material, or designed in a manner to prevent the release or threatened release of any stored substance; and

(C) the material used in the construction or lining of the tank is compatible with the substance to be stored.

(2) Notwithstanding paragraph (1), if soil tests conducted in accordance with ASTM Standard G57–78, or another standard approved by the Administrator, show that soil resistivity in an installation location is 12,000 ohm/cm or more (unless a more stringent standard is prescribed by the Administrator by rule), a storage tank without corrosion protection may be installed in that location during the period referred to in paragraph (1).

(h) EPA response program for petroleum

(1) Before regulations

Before the effective date of regulations under subsection (c) of this section, the Administrator (or a State pursuant to paragraph (7)) is authorized to—

(A) require the owner or operator of an underground storage tank to undertake corrective action with respect to any release of petroleum when the Administrator (or the State) determines that such corrective action will be done properly and promptly by the owner or operator of the underground storage tank from which the release occurs; or

(B) undertake corrective action with respect to any release of petroleum into the environment from an underground storage tank if such action is necessary, in the judgment of the Administrator (or the State), to protect human health and the environment.

The corrective action undertaken or required under this paragraph shall be such as may be necessary to protect human health and the environment. The Administrator shall use funds in the Trust Fund for payment of costs incurred for corrective action under subparagraph (B), enforcement action under subparagraph (A), and cost recovery under paragraph (6) of this subsection. Subject to the priority requirements of paragraph (3), the Administrator (or the State) shall give priority in undertaking such actions under subparagraph (B) to cases where the Administrator (or the State) cannot identify a solvent owner or operator of the tank who will undertake action properly.

(2) After regulations

Following the effective date of regulations under subsection (c) of this section, all actions or orders of the Administrator (or a State pursuant to paragraph (7)) described in paragraph (1) of this subsection shall be in conformity with such regulations. Following such effective date, the Administrator (or the State) may undertake corrective action with respect to any release of petroleum into the environment from an underground storage tank only if such action is necessary, in the judgment of the Administrator (or the State), to protect human health and the environment and one or more of the following situations exists:

(A) No person can be found, within 90 days or such shorter period as may be necessary to protect human health and the environment, who is—

(i) an owner or operator of the tank concerned,

(ii) subject to such corrective action regulations, and

(iii) capable of carrying out such corrective action properly.

(B) A situation exists which requires prompt action by the Administrator (or the State) under this paragraph to protect human health and the environment.

(C) Corrective action costs at a facility exceed the amount of coverage required by the Administrator pursuant to the provisions of subsections (c) and (d)(5) of this section and, considering the class or category of underground storage tank from which the release occurred, expenditures from the Trust Fund are necessary to assure an effective corrective action.

(D) The owner or operator of the tank has failed or refused to comply with an order of the Administrator under this subsection or section 6991e of this title or with the order of a State under this subsection to comply with the corrective action regulations.

(3) Priority of corrective actions

The Administrator (or a State pursuant to paragraph (7)) shall give priority in undertaking corrective actions under this subsection, and in issuing orders requiring owners or operators to undertake such actions, to releases of petroleum from underground storage tanks which pose the greatest threat to human health and the environment.

(4) Corrective action orders

The Administrator is authorized to issue orders to the owner or operator of an underground storage tank to carry out subparagraph (A) of paragraph (1) or to carry out regulations issued under subsection (c)(4) of this section. A State acting pursuant to paragraph (7) of this subsection is authorized to carry out subparagraph (A) of paragraph (1) only until the State's program is approved by the Administrator under section 6991c of this title. Such orders shall be issued and enforced in the same manner and subject to the same requirements as orders under section 6991e of this title.

(5) Allowable corrective actions

The corrective actions undertaken by the Administrator (or a State pursuant to paragraph (7)) under paragraph (1) or (2) may include temporary or permanent relocation of residents and alternative household water supplies. In connection with the performance of any corrective action under paragraph (1) or (2), the Administrator may undertake an exposure assessment as defined in paragraph (10) of this subsection or provide for such an assessment in a cooperative agreement with a State pursuant to paragraph (7) of this subsection. The costs of any such assessment may be treated as corrective action for purposes of paragraph (6), relating to cost recovery.

(6) Recovery of costs

(A) In general

Whenever costs have been incurred by the Administrator, or by a State pursuant to paragraph (7), for undertaking corrective action or enforcement action with respect to the release of petroleum from an underground storage tank, the owner or operator of such tank shall be liable to the Administrator or the State for such costs. The liability under this paragraph shall be construed to be the standard of liability which obtains under section 1321 of Title 33.

(B) Recovery

In determining the equities for seeking the recovery of costs under subparagraph (A), the Administrator (or a State pursuant to paragraph (7) of this subsection) may consider the amount of financial responsibility required to be maintained under subsections (c) and (d)(5) of this section and the factors considered in establishing such amount under subsection (d)(5) of this section.

(C) Effect on liability

(i) No transfers of liability

No indemnification, hold harmless, or similar agreement or conveyance shall be effective to transfer from the owner or operator of any underground storage tank or from any person who may be liable for a release or threat of release under this subsection, to any other person the liability imposed under this subsection. Nothing in this subsection shall bar any agreement to insure, hold harmless, or indemnify a party to such agreement for any liability under this section.

(ii) No bar to cause of action

Nothing in this subsection, including the provisions of clause (i) of this subparagraph, shall bar a cause of action that an owner or operator or any other person subject to liability under this section, or a guarantor, has or would have, by reason of subrogation or otherwise against any person.

(D) Facility

For purposes of this paragraph, the term "facility" means, with respect to any owner or operator, all underground storage tanks used for the storage of petroleum which are owned or operated by such owner or operator and located on a single parcel of property (or on any contiguous or adjacent property).

(E) Inability or limited ability to pay

(i) In general

In determining the level of recovery effort, or amount that should be recovered, the Administrator (or the State pursuant to paragraph (7)) shall consider the owner or operator's ability to pay. An inability or limited ability to pay corrective action costs must be demonstrated to the Administrator (or the State pursuant to paragraph (7)) by the owner or operator.

(ii) Considerations

In determining whether or not a demonstration is made under clause (i), the Administrator (or the State pursuant to paragraph (7)) shall take into consideration the ability of the owner or operator to pay corrective action costs and still maintain its basic business operations, including consideration of the overall financial condition of the owner or operator and demonstrable constraints on the ability of the owner or operator to raise revenues.

(iii) Information

An owner or operator requesting consideration under this subparagraph shall promptly provide the Administrator (or the State pursuant to paragraph (7)) with all relevant information needed to determine the ability of the owner or operator to pay corrective action costs.

(iv) Alternative payment methods

The Administrator (or the State pursuant to paragraph (7)) shall consider alternative payment methods as may be necessary or appropriate if the Administrator (or the State pursuant to paragraph (7)) determines that an owner or operator cannot pay all or a portion of the costs in a lump sum payment.

(v) Misrepresentation

If an owner or operator provides false information or otherwise misrepresents their financial situation under clause (ii), the Administrator (or the State pursuant to paragraph (7)) shall seek full recovery of the costs of all such actions pursuant to the provisions of subparagraph (A) without consideration of the factors in subparagraph (B).

(7) State authorities

(A) General

A State may exercise the authorities in paragraphs (1), (2), and (12), subject to the terms and conditions of paragraphs (3), (5), (9), (10), and (11), and the authority under sections 6991j and 6991k of this title and paragraphs (4), (6), and (8), if—

(i) the Administrator determines that the State has the capabilities to carry out effective corrective actions and enforcement activities; and

(ii) the Administrator enters into a cooperative agreement with the State setting out the actions to be undertaken by the State.

The Administrator may provide funds from the Trust Fund for the reasonable costs of the State's actions under the cooperative agreement.

(B) Cost share

Following the effective date of the regulations under subsection (c) of this section, the State shall pay 10 per centum of the cost of corrective actions undertaken either by the Administrator or by the State under a cooperative agreement, except that the Administrator may take corrective action at a facility where immediate action is necessary to respond to an imminent and substantial endangerment to human health or the environment if the State fails to pay the cost share.

(8) Emergency procurement powers

Notwithstanding any other provision of law, the Administrator may authorize the use of such emergency procurement powers as he deems necessary.

(9) Definition of owner or operator

(A) In general

As used in this subchapter, the terms "owner" and "operator" do not include a person that, without participating in the management of an underground storage tank and otherwise not engaged in petroleum production, refining, or marketing, holds indicia of ownership primarily to protect the person's security interest.

(B) Security interest holders

The provisions regarding holders of security interests in subparagraphs (E) through (G) of section 9601(20) of this title and the provisions regarding fiduciaries at section 9607(n) of this title shall apply in determining a person's liability as an owner or operator of an underground storage tank for the purposes of this subchapter.

(C) Effect on rule

Nothing in subparagraph (B) shall be construed as modifying or affecting the final rule issued by the Administrator on September 7, 1995 (60 F.R. 46,692), or as limiting the authority of the Administrator to amend the final rule, in accordance with applicable law. The final rule in effect on September 30, 1996, shall prevail over any inconsistent provision regarding holders of security interests in subparagraphs (E) through (G) of section 9601(20) of this title or any inconsistent provision regarding fiduciaries in section 9607(n) of this title. Any amendment to the final rule shall be consistent with the provisions regarding holders of security interests in subparagraphs (E) through (G) of section 9601(20) of this title and the provisions regarding fiduciaries in section 9607(n) of this title. This subparagraph does not preclude judicial review of any amendment of the final rule made after September 30, 1996.

(10) Definition of exposure assessment

As used in this subsection, the term "exposure assessment" means an assessment to determine the extent of exposure of, or potential for exposure of, individuals to petroleum from a release from an underground storage tank based on such factors as the nature and extent of contamination and the existence of or potential for pathways of human exposure (including ground or surface water contamination, air emissions, and food chain contamination), the size of the community within the likely pathways of exposure, and the comparison of expected human exposure levels to the short-term and long-term health effects associated with identified contaminants and any available recommended exposure or tolerance limits for such contaminants. Such assessment shall not delay corrective action to abate immediate hazards or reduce exposure.

(11) Facilities without financial responsibility

At any facility where the owner or operator has failed to maintain evidence of financial responsibility in amounts at least equal to the amounts established by subsection (d)(5)(A) of this section (or a lesser amount if such amount is applicable to such facility as a result of subsection (d)(5)(B) of this section) for whatever reason the Administrator shall expend no monies from the Trust Fund to clean up releases at such facility pursuant to the provisions of paragraph (1) or (2) of this subsection. At such facilities the Administrator shall use the authorities provided in subparagraph (A) of paragraph (1) and paragraph (4) of this subsection and section 6991e of this title to order corrective action to clean up such releases. States acting pursuant to paragraph (7) of this subsection shall use the authorities provided in subparagraph (A) of paragraph (1) and paragraph (4) of this subsection to order corrective action to clean up such releases. Notwithstanding the provisions of this paragraph, the Administrator may use monies from the fund to take the corrective actions authorized by paragraph (5) of this subsection to protect human health at such facilities and shall seek full recovery of the costs of all such actions pursuant to the provisions of paragraph (6)(A) of this subsection and without consideration of the factors in paragraph (6)(B) of this subsection. Nothing in this paragraph shall prevent the Administrator (or a State pursuant to paragraph (7) of this subsection) from taking corrective action at a facility where there is no solvent owner or operator or where immediate action is necessary to respond to an imminent and substantial endangerment of human health or the environment.

(12) Remediation of oxygenated fuel contamination

(A) In general

The Administrator and the States may use funds made available under section 6991m(2)(B) of this title to carry out corrective actions with respect to a release of a fuel containing an oxygenated fuel additive that presents a threat to human health or welfare or the environment.

(B) Applicable authority

The Administrator or a State shall carry out subparagraph (A) in accordance with paragraph (2), and in the case of a State, in accordance with a cooperative agreement entered into by the Administrator and the State under paragraph (7).

(i) Additional measures to protect groundwater from contamination

The Administrator shall require each State that receives funding under this subchapter to require one of the following:

(1) Tank and piping secondary containment

(A) Each new underground storage tank, or piping connected to any such new tank, installed after the effective date of this subsection, or any existing underground storage tank, or existing piping connected to such existing tank, that is replaced after the effective date of this subsection, shall be secondarily contained and monitored for leaks if the new or replaced underground storage tank or piping is within 1,000 feet of any existing community water system or any existing potable drinking water well.

(B) In the case of a new underground storage tank system consisting of one or more underground storage tanks and connected by piping, subparagraph (A) shall apply to all underground storage tanks and connected pipes comprising such system.

(C) In the case of a replacement of an existing underground storage tank or existing piping connected to the underground storage tank, subparagraph (A) shall apply only to the specific underground storage tank or piping being replaced, not to other underground storage tanks and connected pipes comprising such system.

(D) Each installation of a new motor fuel dispenser system, after the effective date of this subsection, shall include under-dispenser spill containment if the new dispenser is within 1,000 feet of any existing community water system or any existing potable drinking water well.

(E) This paragraph shall not apply to repairs to an underground storage tank, piping, or dispenser that are meant to restore a tank, pipe, or dispenser to operating condition.

(F) As used in this subsection:

(i) The term "secondarily contained" means a release detection and prevention system that meets the requirements of 40 C.F.R. 280.43(g), but shall not include under-dispenser spill containment or control systems.

(ii) The term "underground storage tank" has the meaning given to it in section 6991 of this title, except that such term does not include tank combinations or more than a single underground pipe connected to a tank.

(iii) The term "installation of a new motor fuel dispenser system" means the installation of a new motor fuel dispenser and the equipment necessary to connect the dispenser to the underground storage tank system, but does not mean the installation of a motor fuel dispenser installed separately from the equipment need to connect the dispenser to the underground storage tank system.

(2) Evidence of financial responsibility and certification

(A) Manufacturer and installer financial responsibility

A person that manufactures an underground storage tank or piping for an underground storage tank system or that installs an underground storage tank system is required to maintain evidence of financial responsibility under subsection (d) of this section in order to provide for the costs of corrective actions directly related to releases caused by improper manufacture or installation unless the person can demonstrate themselves to be already covered as an owner or operator of an underground storage tank under this section.

(B) Installer certification

The Administrator and each State that receives funding under this subchapter, as appropriate, shall require that a person that installs an underground storage tank system is—

(i) certified or licensed by the tank and piping manufacturer;

(ii) certified or licensed by the Administrator or a State, as appropriate;

(iii) has their underground storage tank system installation certified by a registered professional engineer with education and experience in underground storage tank system installation;

(iv) has had their installation of the underground storage tank inspected and approved by the Administrator or the State, as appropriate;

(v) compliant with a code of practice developed by a nationally recognized association or independent testing laboratory and in accordance with the manufacturer's instructions; or

(vi) compliant with another method that is determined by the Administrator or a State, as appropriate, to be no less protective of human health and the environment.

(C) Savings clause

Nothing in subparagraph (A) alters or affects the liability of any owner or operator of an underground storage tank.

(j) Government-owned tanks

(1) State compliance report

(A) Not later than 2 years after August 8, 2005, each State that receives funding under this subchapter shall submit to the Administrator a State compliance report that—

(i) lists the location and owner of each underground storage tank described in subparagraph (B) in the State that, as of the date of submission of the report, is not in compliance with this section; and

(ii) specifies the date of the last inspection and describes the actions that have been and will be taken to ensure compliance of the underground storage tank listed under clause (i) with this subchapter.

(B) An underground storage tank described in this subparagraph is an underground storage tank that is—

(i) regulated under this subchapter; and

(ii) owned or operated by the Federal, State, or local government.

(C) The Administrator shall make each report, received under subparagraph (A), available to the public through an appropriate media[1].

(2) Financial incentive

The Administrator may award to a State that develops a report described in paragraph (1), in addition to any other funds that the State is entitled to receive under this subchapter, not more than $50,000, to be used to carry out the report.

(3) Not a safe harbor

This subsection does not relieve any person from any obligation or requirement under this subchapter.

(Pub. L. No. 89–272, Title II, § 9003, as added by Pub. L. No. 98–616, Title VI, § 601(a), 98 Stat. 3279 (Nov. 8, 1984); and amended by Pub. L. No. 99–499, Title II, § 205(c), (d), 100 Stat. 1697, 1698 (Oct. 17, 1986); Pub. L. No. 104–208, Div. A, Title II, § 2503, 110 Stat. 3009–468 (Sept. 30, 1996); Pub. L. No. 109–58, Title XV, §§ 1522(c), 1525, 1526(b), 1530(a), 1532(b)(1), (2), 1533(2), 119 Stat. 1093, 1096, 1097, 1102, 1105 (Aug. 8, 2005); Pub. L. No. 109–168, § 1(a)(2), 119 Stat. 3580 (Jan. 10, 2006).)

[1] So in original. Probably should be "medium".

HISTORICAL AND STATUTORY NOTES

References in Text

This subchapter, referred to in text, originally read "this subtitle", meaning subtitle I of the Solid Waste Disposal Act, Pub. L. No. 89–272, Title II, § 9001 et seq., as added Pub. L. No. 98–616, Title VI, § 601(a), 98 Stat. 3277 (Nov. 8, 1984), and amended, which is codified principally as this subchapter.

The Federal Bankruptcy Code, referred to in subsec. (d)(2), probably means a reference to Title 11, Bankruptcy.

The effective date of this subsection, referred to in subsec. (i)(1)(A), (D), probably means 18 months after Aug. 8, 2005; see Pub. L. No. 109–58, § 1530(b), set out as a note under this section.

August 8, 2005, referred to in subsec. (j), originally read "the date of enactment of this subsection", meaning Aug. 8, 2005, the date of enactment of the Underground Storage Tank Compliance Act, Pub. L. No. 109–58, Title XV, §§ 1521 to 1533, 119 Stat. 1092, which enacted subsec. (j) of this section.

Codifications

Amendment by Pub. L. No. 109–58, Title XV, § 1530(a), (b), which directed the addition of subsec. (i) at the end of this section, effective 18 months after the date of enactment of this subsection [Aug. 8, 2005], was executed by adding the second subsec. (i), relating to groundwater protection from contamination, after the first subsec. (i), relating to government-owned tanks.

Effective and Applicability Provisions

2005 Acts. Pub. L. No. 109–58, Title XV, § 1530(b), 119 Stat. 1104 (Aug. 8, 2005), provided that: "This subsection [sic; probably means 'this section', which enacted subsec. (i) of this section (as added by Pub. L. No. 109–58, § 1530(a)) and amended 42 U.S.C.A. § 6991e] shall take effect 18 months after the date of enactment of this subsection [Aug. 8, 2005]."

1996 Acts. Pub. L. No. 104–208, Div. A, Title II, § 2505, 110 Stat. 3009–469 (Sept. 30, 1996), provided that: "The amendments made by this subtitle [Pub. L. No. 104–208, Div. A, Title II, Subtitle E, § 2501 et seq., Sept. 30, 1996, 110 Stat. 3009–462, amending this section and sections 9601 and 9607 of this title] shall be applicable with respect to any claim that has not been finally adjudicated as of the date of enactment of this Act [Sept. 30, 1996]."

1986 Acts. Amendment by Pub. L. No. 99–499 effective Oct. 17, 1986, see section 4 of Pub. L. No. 99–499, set out as a note under section 9601 of this title.

Promulgation of Regulations or Guidelines

Pub. L. No. 109–58, Title XV, § 1530(c), 119 Stat. 1104 (Aug. 8, 2005), provided that: "The Administrator shall issue regulations or guidelines implementing the requirements of this subsection [sic; probably should read 'section'], including guidance to differentiate between the terms 'repair' and 'replace' for the purposes of section 9003(i)(1) of the Solid Waste Disposal Act [subsec. (i)(1) of this section (as added by Pub. L. No. 109–58, § 1530(a)]."

Leaking Underground Storage Tank Program

Pub. L. No. 105–276, Title III, 112 Stat. 2497 (Oct. 21, 1998), provided in part: "That hereafter, the Administrator is authorized to enter into assistance agreements with Federally recognized Indian tribes on such terms and conditions as the Administrator deems appropriate for the same purposes as are set forth in section 9003(h)(7) of the Resource Conservation and Recovery Act [subsec. (h)(7) of this section]."

Pollution Liability Insurance

Section 205(h) of Pub. L. No. 99–499 provided that:

"**(1) Study.**—The Comptroller General shall conduct a study of the availability of pollution liability insurance, leak insurance, and contamination insurance for owners and operators of petroleum storage and distribution facilities. The study shall assess the current and projected extent to which private insurance can contribute to the financial responsibility of owners and operators of underground storage tanks and the ability of owners and operators of underground storage tanks to maintain financial responsibility through other methods. The study shall consider the experience of owners and operators of marine vessels in getting insurance for their liabilities under the Federal Water Pollution Control Act [33 U.S.C.A. § 1251 et seq.] and the operation of the Water Quality Insurance Syndicate.

"**(2) Report.**—The Comptroller General shall report the findings under this subsection to the Congress within 15 months after the enactment of this subsection [eff. Oct. 17, 1986]. Such report shall include recommendations for legislative or administrative changes that will enable owners and operators of underground storage tanks to maintain financial responsibility sufficient to provide all clean-up costs and damages that may result from reasonably foreseeable releases and events."

§ 6991c. Approval of State programs

[SWDA § 9004]

(a) Elements of State program

Beginning 30 months after November 8, 1984, any State may,[1] submit an underground storage tank release detection, prevention, and correction program for review and approval by the Administrator. The program may cover tanks used to store regulated substances referred to in subparagraph (A) or (B) of section 6991(7) of this title. A State program may be approved by the Administrator under this section only if the State demonstrates that the State program includes the following requirements and standards and provides for adequate enforcement of compliance with such requirements and standards—

(1) requirements for maintaining a leak detection system, an inventory control system together with tank testing, or a comparable system or method designed to identify releases in a manner consistent with the protection of human health and the environment;

(2) requirements for maintaining records of any monitoring or leak detection system or inventory control system or tank testing system;

(3) requirements for reporting of any releases and corrective action taken in response to a release from an underground storage tank;

(4) requirements for taking corrective action in response to a release from an underground storage tank;

(5) requirements for the closure of tanks to prevent future releases of regulated substances into the environment;

(6) requirements for maintaining evidence of financial responsibility for taking corrective action and compensating third parties for bodily injury and property damage caused by sudden and nonsudden accidental releases arising from operating an underground storage tank;

(7) standards of performance for new underground storage tanks;

(8) requirements—

(A) for notifying the appropriate State agency or department (or local agency or department) designated according to section 6991a(b)(1) of this title of the existence of any operational or non-operational underground storage tank; and

(B) for providing the information required on the form issued pursuant to section 6991a(b)(2) of this title; and

(9) State-specific training requirements as required by section 6991i of this title.

(b) Federal standards

(1) A State program submitted under this section may be approved only if the requirements under paragraphs (1) through (7) of subsection (a) of this section are no less stringent than the corresponding requirements standards promulgated by the Administrator pursuant to section 6991b(a) of this title.

(2) (A) A State program may be approved without regard to whether or not the requirements referred to in paragraphs (1), (2), (3), and (5) of subsection (a) of this section are less stringent than the corresponding standards under section 6991b(a) of this title during the one-year period commencing on the date of promulgation of regulations under section 6991b(a) of this title if State regulatory action but no State legislative action is required in order to adopt a State program.

(B) If such State legislative action is required, the State program may be approved without regard to whether or not the requirements referred to in paragraphs (1), (2), (3), and (5) of subsection (a) of this section are less stringent than the corresponding standards under section 6991b(a) of this title during the two-year period commencing on the date of promulgation of regulations under section 6991b(a) of this title (and during an additional one-year period after such legislative action if regulations are required to be promulgated by the State pursuant to such legislative action).

(c) Financial responsibility

(1) Corrective action and compensation programs administered by State or local agencies or departments may be submitted for approval under subsection (a)(6) of this section as evidence of financial responsibility.

(2) Financial responsibility required by this subsection may be established in accordance with regulations promulgated by the Administrator by any one, or any combination, of the following: insurance, guarantee, surety bond, letter of credit, qualification as a self-insurer or any other method satisfactory to the Administrator. In promulgating requirements under this subsection, the Administrator is authorized to specify policy or other contractual terms including the amount of coverage required for various classes and categories of underground storage tanks pursuant to section 6991b(d)(5) of this title, conditions, or defenses which are necessary or are unacceptable in establishing such evidence of financial responsibility in order to effectuate the purposes of this subchapter.

(3) In any case where the owner or operator is in bankruptcy, reorganization, or arrangement pursuant to the Federal Bankruptcy Code or where with reasonable diligence jurisdiction in any State court of the Federal courts cannot be obtained over an owner or operator likely to be solvent at the time of judgment, any claim arising from conduct for which evidence of financial responsibility must be provided under this subsection may be asserted directly against the guarantor providing such evidence of financial responsibility. In the case of any action pursuant to this paragraph such guarantor shall be entitled to invoke all rights and defenses which would have been available to the owner or operator if any action had been brought against the owner or operator by the claimant and which would have been available to the guarantor if an action had been brought against the guarantor by the owner or operator.

(4) The total liability of any guarantor shall be limited to the aggregate amount which the guarantor has provided as evidence of financial responsibility to the owner or operator under this section. Nothing in this subsection shall be construed to limit any other State or Federal statutory, contractual or common law liability of a guarantor to its owner or operator including, but not limited to, the liability of such guarantor for bad faith either in negotiating or in failing to negotiate the settlement of any claim. Nothing in this subsection shall be construed to diminish the liability of any person under section 9607 or 9611 of this title or other applicable law.

(5) For the purpose of this subsection, the term "guarantor" means any person, other than the owner or operator, who provides evidence of financial responsibility for an owner or operator under this subsection.

(6) Withdrawal of approval

After an opportunity for good faith, collaborative efforts to correct financial deficiencies with a State fund, the Administrator may withdraw approval of any State fund or State assurance program to be used as a financial responsibility mechanism without withdrawing approval of a State underground storage tank program under subsection (a) of this section.

(d) EPA determination

(1) Within one hundred and eighty days of the date of receipt of a proposed State program, the Administrator shall, after notice and opportunity for public comment, make a determination whether the State's program complies with the provisions of this section and provides for adequate enforcement of compliance with the requirements and standards adopted pursuant to this section.

(2) If the Administrator determines that a State program complies with the provisions of this section and provides for adequate enforcement of compliance with the requirements and standards adopted pursuant to this section, he shall approve the State program in lieu of the Federal program and the State shall have primary enforcement responsibility with respect to requirements of its program.

(e) Withdrawal of authorization

Whenever the Administrator determines after public hearing that a State is not administering and enforcing a program authorized under this subchapter in accordance with the provisions of this section, he shall so notify the State. If appropriate action is not taken within a reasonable time, not to exceed one hundred and twenty days after such notification, the Administrator shall withdraw approval of such program and reestablish the Federal program pursuant to this subchapter.

(f) Trust Fund distribution

(1) In general

(A) Amount and permitted uses of distribution

The Administrator shall distribute to States not less than 80 percent of the funds from the Trust Fund that are made available to the Administrator under section 6991m(2)(A) of this title for each fiscal year for use in paying the reasonable costs, incurred under a cooperative agreement with any State for—

(i) corrective actions taken by the State under section 6991b(h)(7)(A) of this title;

(ii) necessary administrative expenses, as determined by the Administrator, that are directly related to State fund or State assurance programs under subsection (c)(1) of this section; or

(iii) enforcement, by a State or a local government, of State or local regulations pertaining to underground storage tanks regulated under this subchapter.

(B) Use of funds for enforcement

In addition to the uses of funds authorized under subparagraph (A), the Administrator may use funds from the Trust Fund that are not distributed to States under subparagraph (A) for enforcement of any regulation promulgated by the Administrator under this subchapter.

(C) Prohibited uses

Funds provided to a State by the Administrator under subparagraph (A) shall not be used by the State to provide financial assistance to an owner or operator to meet any requirement relating to underground storage tanks under subparts B, C, D, H, and G of part 280 of title 40, Code of Federal Regulations (as in effect on August 8, 2005).

(2) Allocation

(A) Process

Subject to subparagraphs (B) and (C), in the case of a State with which the Administrator has entered into a cooperative agreement under section 6991b(h)(7)(A) of this title, the Administrator shall distribute funds from the Trust Fund to the State using an allocation process developed by the Administrator.

(B) Diversion of State funds

The Administrator shall not distribute funds under subparagraph (A)(iii) of subsection (f)(1) of this section to any State that has diverted funds from a State fund or State assurance program for purposes other than those related to the regulation of underground storage tanks covered by this subchapter, with the exception of those transfers that had been completed earlier than August 8, 2005.

(C) Revisions to process

The Administrator may revise the allocation process referred to in subparagraph (A) after—

(i) consulting with State agencies responsible for overseeing corrective action for releases from underground storage tanks; and

(ii) taking into consideration, at a minimum, each of the following:

(I) The number of confirmed releases from federally regulated leaking underground storage tanks in the States.

(II) The number of federally regulated underground storage tanks in the States.

(III) The performance of the States in implementing and enforcing the program.

(IV) The financial needs of the States.

(V) The ability of the States to use the funds referred to in subparagraph (A) in any year.

(3) Distributions to State agencies

Distributions from the Trust Fund under this subsection shall be made directly to a State agency that—

(A) enters into a cooperative agreement referred to in paragraph (2)(A); or

(B) is enforcing a State program approved under this section.

(Pub. L. No. 89–272, Title II, § 9004, as added by Pub. L. No. 98–616, Title VI, § 601(a), 98 Stat. 3282 (Nov. 8, 1984); and amended by Pub. L. No. 99–499, Title II, § 205(e), 100 Stat. 1702 (Oct. 17, 1986); Pub. L. No. 109–58, Title XV, §§ 1522(a), (b), 1524(b), 1533(3), 119 Stat. 1092, 1093, 1096, 1105 (Aug. 8, 2005).)

[1] So in original.

HISTORICAL AND STATUTORY NOTES

References in Text

This subchapter, referred to in text, originally read "this subtitle", meaning subtitle I of the Solid Waste Disposal Act, Pub. L. No. 89–272, Title II, § 9001 et seq., as added Pub. L. No. 98–616, Title VI, § 601(a), 98 Stat. 3277 (Nov. 8, 1984), and amended, which is codified principally to this subchapter.

The Federal Bankruptcy Code, referred to in subsec. (c)(3), probably means a reference to Title 11, Bankruptcy.

August 8, 2005, referred to in subsec. (f)(1)(C), originally read "the date of enactment of this subsection", meaning Aug. 8, 2005, the date of enactment of the Underground Storage Tank Compliance Act, Pub. L. No. 109–58, Title XV, §§ 1521 to 1533, 119 Stat. 1092, which enacted subsec. (f) of this section.

Effective and Applicability Provisions

1986 Acts. Amendment by Pub. L. No. 99–499 effective Oct. 17, 1986, see section 4 of Pub. L. No. 99–499, set out as a note under section 9601 of this title.

§ 6991d. Inspections, monitoring, testing, and corrective action

[SWDA § 9005]

(a) Furnishing information

For the purposes of developing or assisting in the development of any regulation, conducting any study, taking any corrective action, or enforcing the provisions of this subchapter, any owner or operator of an underground storage tank (or any tank subject to study under section 6991h of this title that is used for storing regulated substances) shall, upon request of any officer, employee or representative of the Environmental Protection Agency, duly designated by the Administrator, or upon request of any duly designated officer, employee, or representative of a State acting pursuant to subsection (h)(7) of section 6991b of this title or with an approved program, furnish information relating to such tanks, their associated equipment, their contents, conduct monitoring or testing, permit such officer at all reasonable times to have access to, and to copy all records relating to such tanks and permit such officer to have access for corrective action. For the purposes of developing or assisting in the development of any regulation, conducting any study, taking corrective action, or enforcing the provisions of this subchapter, such officers, employees, or representatives are authorized—

(1) to enter at reasonable times any establishment or other place where an underground storage tank is located;

(2) to inspect and obtain samples from any person of any regulated substances contained in such tank;

(3) to conduct monitoring or testing of the tanks, associated equipment, contents, or surrounding soils, air, surface water or ground water; and

(4) to take corrective action.

Each such inspection shall be commenced and completed with reasonable promptness.

(b) Confidentiality

(1) Any records, reports, or information obtained from any persons under this section shall be available to the public, except that upon a showing satisfactory to the Administrator (or the State, as the case may be) by any person that records, reports, or information, or a particular part thereof, to which the Administrator (or the State, as the case may be) or any officer, employee, or representative thereof has access under this section if made public, would divulge information entitled to protection under section 1905 of Title 18, such information or particular portion thereof shall be considered confidential in accordance with the purposes of that section, except that such record, report, document, or information may be disclosed to other officers, employees, or authorized representatives of the United States concerned with carrying out this chapter, or when relevant in any proceeding under this chapter.

(2) Any person not subject to the provisions of section 1905 of Title 18 who knowingly and willfully divulges or discloses any information entitled to protection under this subsection shall, upon conviction, be subject to a fine of not more than $5,000 or to imprisonment not to exceed one year, or both.

(3) In submitting data under this subchapter, a person required to provide such data may—

(A) designate the data which such person believes is entitled to protection under this subsection, and

(B) submit such designated data separately from other data submitted under this subchapter.

A designation under this paragraph shall be made in writing and in such manner as the Administrator may prescribe.

(4) Notwithstanding any limitation contained in this section or any other provision of law, all information reported to, or otherwise obtained, by the Administrator (or any representative of the Administrator) under this chapter shall be made available, upon written request of any duly authorized committee of the Congress, to such committee (including records, reports, or information obtained by representatives of the Environmental Protection Agency).

(c) Inspection requirements

(1) Uninspected tanks

In the case of underground storage tanks regulated under this subchapter that have not undergone an inspection since December 22, 1998, not later than 2 years after August 8, 2005, the Administrator or a State that receives funding under this subchapter, as appropriate, shall conduct on-site inspections of all such tanks to determine compliance with this subchapter and the regulations under this subchapter (40 C.F.R. 280) or a requirement or standard of a State program developed under section 6991c of this title.

(2) Periodic inspections

After completion of all inspections required under paragraph (1), the Administrator or a State that receives funding under this subchapter, as appropriate, shall conduct on-site inspections of each underground storage tank regulated under this subchapter at least once every 3 years to determine compliance with this subchapter and the regulations under this subchapter (40 C.F.R. 280) or a requirement or standard of a State program developed under section 6991c of this title. The Administrator may extend for up to one additional year the first 3-year inspection interval under this paragraph if the State demonstrates that it has insufficient resources to complete all such inspections within the first 3-year period.

(3) Inspection authority

Nothing in this section shall be construed to diminish the Administrator's or a State's authorities under subsection (a) of this section.

(Pub. L. No. 89–272, Title II, § 9005, as added by Pub. L. No. 98–616, Title VI, § 601(a), 98 Stat. 3284 (Nov. 8, 1984); and amended by Pub. L. No. 99–499, Title II, § 205(f), 100 Stat. 1702 (Oct. 17, 1986); Pub. L. No. 109–58, Title XV, §§ 1523(a), 1533(4), 119 Stat. 1094, 1105 (Aug. 8, 2005).)

HISTORICAL AND STATUTORY NOTES

References in Text

This subchapter, referred to in text, originally read "this subtitle", meaning subtitle I of the Solid Waste Disposal Act, Pub. L. No. 89–272, Title II, § 9001 et seq., as added Pub. L. No. 98–616, Title VI, § 601(a), 98 Stat. 3277 (Nov. 8, 1984), and amended, which is codified principally to this subchapter.

Effective and Applicability Provisions

1986 Acts. Amendment by Pub. L. No. 99–499 effective Oct. 17, 1986, see section 4 of Pub. L. No. 99–499, set out as a note under section 9601 of this title.

§ 6991e. Federal enforcement

[SWDA § 9006]

(a) Compliance orders

(1) Except as provided in paragraph (2), whenever on the basis of any information, the Administrator determines that any person is in violation of any requirement of this subchapter, the Administrator may issue an order requiring compliance within a reasonable specified time period or the

Administrator may commence a civil action in the United States district court in which the violation occurred for appropriate relief, including a temporary or permanent injunction.

(2) In the case of a violation of any requirement of this subchapter where such violation occurs in a State with a program approved under section 6991c of this title, the Administrator shall give notice to the State in which such violation has occurred prior to issuing an order or commencing a civil action under this section.

(3) If a violator fails to comply with an order under this subsection within the time specified in the order, he shall be liable for a civil penalty of not more than $25,000 for each day of continued noncompliance.

(b) Procedure

Any order issued under this section shall become final unless, no later than thirty days after the order is served, the person or persons named therein request a public hearing. Upon such request the Administrator shall promptly conduct a public hearing. In connection with any proceeding under this section the Administrator may issue subpoenas for the attendance and testimony of witnesses and the production of relevant papers, books, and documents, and may promulgate rules for discovery procedures.

(c) Contents of order

Any order issued under this section shall state with reasonable specificity the nature of the violation, specify a reasonable time for compliance, and assess a penalty, if any, which the Administrator determines is reasonable taking into account the seriousness of the violation and any good faith efforts to comply with the applicable requirements.

(d) Civil penalties

(1) Any owner who knowingly fails to notify or submits false information pursuant to section 6991a(a) of this title shall be subject to a civil penalty not to exceed $10,000 for each tank for which notification is not given or false information is submitted.

(2) Any owner or operator of an underground storage tank who fails to comply with—

(A) any requirement or standard promulgated by the Administrator under section 6991b of this title;

(B) any requirement or standard of a State program approved pursuant to section 6991c of this title;

(C) the provisions of section 6991b(g) of this title (entitled "Interim Prohibition"); or

(D)[1] the requirements established in section 6991b(i) of this title,

(D)[1] the training requirements established by States pursuant to section 6991i of this title (relating to operator training); or

(E) the delivery prohibition requirement established by section 6991k of this title,

shall be subject to a civil penalty not to exceed $10,000 for each tank for each day of violation. Any person making or accepting a delivery or deposit of a regulated substance to an underground storage tank at an ineligible facility in violation of section 6991k of this title shall also be subject to the same civil penalty for each day of such violation.

(e) Incentive for performance

Both of the following may be taken into account in determining the terms of a civil penalty under subsection (d) of this section:

(1) The compliance history of an owner or operator in accordance with this subchapter or a program approved under section 6991c of this title.

(2) Any other factor the Administrator considers appropriate.

(Pub. L. No. 89–272, Title II, § 9006, as added by Pub. L. No. 98–616, Title VI, § 601(a), 98 Stat. 3285 (Nov. 8, 1984); and amended by Pub. L. No. 109–58, Title XV, §§ 1524(c), 1526(d), 1527(b), 1530(d), 119 Stat. 1096, 1098, 1099, 1104 (Aug. 8, 2005).)

[1] So in original. Two subparagraphs (D) have been enacted.

HISTORICAL AND STATUTORY NOTES

References in Text

This subchapter, referred to in text, originally read "this subtitle", meaning subtitle I of the Solid Waste Disposal Act, Pub. L. No. 89–272, Title II, § 9001 et seq., as added by Pub. L. No. 98–616, Title VI, § 601(a), 98 Stat. 3277 (Nov. 8, 1984), and amended, which is codified principally to this subchapter.

Codifications

Amendment by Pub. L. No. 109–58, Title XV, § 1530(d), effective 18 months after August 8, 2005 (see, also, Pub. L. No. 109–58, Title XV, § 1530(b), set out as a note under 42 U.S.C.A. § 6991b, regarding the applicability of this effective date to this section), directed that subsec. (d)(2) be amended in part by striking "or" at the end of subpar. (B) and adding a new subpar. (D), relating to requirements established in section 6991b(i) of this title. Subsec. (d)(2) had previously been amended by Pub. L. No. 109–58, § 1524(c), which directed that subsec. (d)(2) be amended in part by striking "or" at the end of subpar. (B) and adding a new subpar. (D), relating to training requirements established by States pursuant to section 6991i of this title.

Effective and Applicability Provisions

2005 Acts. Amendments made by Pub. L. No. 109–58, § 1530, effective 18 months after Aug. 8, 2005, see Pub. L. No. 109–58, § 1530(b), set out as a note under 42 U.S.C.A. § 6991b.

§ 6991f. Federal facilities

[SWDA § 9007]

(a) In general

Each department, agency, and instrumentality of the executive, legislative, and judicial branches of the Federal Government (1) having jurisdiction over any underground storage tank or underground storage tank system, or (2) engaged in any activity resulting, or which may result, in the installation, operation, management, or closure of any underground storage tank, release response activities related thereto, or in the delivery, acceptance, or deposit of any regulated substance to an underground storage tank or underground storage tank system shall be subject to, and comply with, all Federal, State, interstate, and local requirements, both substantive and procedural (including any requirement for permits or reporting or any provisions for injunctive relief and such sanctions as may be imposed by a court to enforce such relief), respecting underground storage tanks in the same manner, and to the same extent, as any person is subject to such requirements, including the payment of reasonable service charges. The Federal, State, interstate, and local substantive and procedural requirements referred to in this subsection include, but are not limited to, all administrative orders and all civil and administrative penalties and fines, regardless of whether such penalties or fines are punitive or coercive in nature or are imposed for isolated, intermittent, or continuing violations. The United States hereby expressly waives any immunity otherwise applicable to the United States with respect to any such substantive or procedural requirement (including, but not limited to, any injunctive relief, administrative order or civil or administrative penalty or fine referred to in the preceding sentence, or reasonable service charge). The reasonable service charges referred to in this subsection include, but are not limited to, fees or charges assessed in connection with the processing and issuance of permits, renewal of permits, amendments to permits, review of plans, studies, and other documents, and inspection and monitoring of facilities, as well as any other nondiscriminatory charges that are assessed in connection with a Federal, State, interstate, or local underground storage tank regulatory program. Neither the United States, nor any agent, employee, or officer thereof, shall be immune or exempt from any process or sanction of any State or Federal Court with respect to the enforcement of any such injunctive relief. No agent, employee, or officer of the United States shall be personally liable for any civil penalty under any Federal, State, interstate, or local law concerning underground storage tanks with respect to any act or omission within the scope of the official duties of the agent, employee, or officer. An agent, employee, or officer of the United States shall be subject to any criminal sanction (including, but not limited to, any fine or imprisonment) under any Federal or State law concerning underground storage tanks, but no department, agency, or instrumentality of the executive, legislative, or judicial branch of the Federal Government shall be subject to any such sanction. The President may exempt any underground storage tank of any department, agency, or instrumentality in the executive branch from compliance with such a requirement if he determines it to be in the paramount interest of the United States to do so. No such exemption shall be granted due to lack of appropriation unless the President shall have specifically requested such appropriation as a part of the budgetary process and the Congress shall have failed to make available such requested appropriation. Any exemption shall be for a period not in excess of 1 year, but additional exemptions may be granted for periods not to exceed 1 year upon the President's making a new determination. The President shall report each January to the Congress all exemptions from the requirements of this section granted during the preceding calendar year, together with his reason for granting each such exemption.

(b) Review of and report on Federal underground storage tanks

(1) Review

Not later than 12 months after August 8, 2005, each Federal agency that owns or operates one or more underground storage tanks, or that manages land on which one or more underground storage tanks are located, shall submit to the Administrator, the Committee on Energy and Commerce of the United States House of Representatives, and the Committee on the Environment and Public Works of the Senate a compliance strategy report that—

(A) lists the location and owner of each underground storage tank described in this paragraph;

(B) lists all tanks that are not in compliance with this subchapter that are owned or operated by the Federal agency;

(C) specifies the date of the last inspection by a State or Federal inspector of each underground storage tank owned or operated by the agency;

(D) lists each violation of this subchapter respecting any underground storage tank owned or operated by the agency;

(E) describes the operator training that has been provided to the operator and other persons having primary daily on-site management responsibility for the operation and maintenance of underground storage tanks owned or operated by the agency; and

(F) describes the actions that have been and will be taken to ensure compliance for each underground storage tank identified under subparagraph (B).

(2) Not a safe harbor

This subsection does not relieve any person from any obligation or requirement under this subchapter.

(Pub. L. No. 89–272, Title II, § 9007, as added by Pub. L. No. 98–616, Title VI, § 601(a), 98 Stat. 3286 (Nov. 8, 1984); and amended by Pub. L. No. 109–58, Title XV, § 1528, 119 Stat. 1100 (Aug. 8, 2005).)

HISTORICAL AND STATUTORY NOTES

References in Text

August 8, 2005, referred to in subsec. (b)(1), originally read "the date of enactment of the Underground Storage Tank Compliance Act", meaning Aug. 8, 2005, the date of enactment of the Underground Storage Tank Compliance Act, Pub. L. No. 109–58, Title XV, §§ 1521 to 1533, 119 Stat. 1092, which enacted this section.

This subchapter, referred to in subsec. (b)(1)(B), (2), originally read "this subtitle", meaning subtitle I of the Solid Waste Disposal Act, Pub. L. No. 89–272, Title II, § 9001 et seq., as added by Pub. L. No. 98–616, Title VI, § 601(a), 98 Stat. 3277 (Nov. 8, 1984), and amended, which is codified principally as this subchapter.

Termination of Reporting Requirements

For termination, effective May 15, 2000, of provisions in subsec. (b) of this section requiring the President to report annually to Congress, see Pub. L. No. 104–66, § 3003, as amended, set out as a note under 31 U.S.C.A. § 1113, and the 9th item on page 20 of House Document No. 103–7.

§ 6991g. State authority

[SWDA § 9008]

Nothing in this subchapter shall preclude or deny any right of any State or political subdivision thereof to adopt or enforce any regulation, requirement, or standard of performance respecting underground storage tanks that is more stringent than a regulation, requirement, or standard of performance in effect under this subchapter or to impose any additional liability with respect to the release of regulated substances within such State or political subdivision.

(Pub. L. No. 89–272, Title II, § 9008, as added by Pub. L. No. 98–616, Title VI, § 601(a), 98 Stat. 3286 (Nov. 8, 1984); and amended by Pub. L. No. 99–499, Title II, § 205(g), 100 Stat. 1702 (Oct. 17, 1986).)

HISTORICAL AND STATUTORY NOTES

Effective and Applicability Provisions

1986 Acts. Amendment by Pub. L. No. 99–499 effective Oct. 17, 1986, see section 4 of Pub. L. No. 99–499, set out as a note under section 9601 of this title.

§ 6991h. Study of underground storage tanks

[SWDA § 9009]

(a) Petroleum tanks

Not later than twelve months after November 8, 1984, the Administrator shall complete a study of underground storage tanks used for the storage of regulated substances defined in section 6991(7)(B) of this title.

(b) Other tanks

Not later than thirty-six months after November 8, 1984, the Administrator shall complete a study of all other underground storage tanks.

(c) Elements of studies

The studies under subsections (a) and (b) of this section shall include an assessment of the ages, types (including methods of manufacture, coatings, protection systems, the compatibility of the construction materials and the installation methods) and locations (including the climate of the locations) of such tanks; soil conditions, water tables, and the hydrogeology of tank locations; the relationship between the foregoing factors and the likelihood of releases from underground storage tanks; the effectiveness and costs of inventory systems, tank testing, and leak detection systems; and such other factors as the Administrator deems appropriate.

(d) Farm and heating oil tanks

Not later than thirty-six months after November 8, 1984, the Administrator shall conduct a study regarding the tanks referred to in subparagraphs (A) and (B) of section 6991(10) of this title. Such study shall include estimates of the number and location of such tanks and an analysis of the extent to which there may be releases or threatened releases from such tanks into the environment.

(e) Reports

Upon completion of the studies authorized by this section, the Administrator shall submit reports to the President and to the Congress containing the results of the studies and recommendations respecting whether or not such tanks should be subject to the preceding provisions of this subchapter.

(f) Reimbursement

(1) If any owner or operator (excepting an agency, department, or instrumentality of the United States Government, a State or a political subdivision thereof) shall incur costs, including the loss of business opportunity, due to the closure or interruption of operation of an underground storage tank solely for the purpose of conducting studies authorized by this section, the Administrator shall provide such person fair and equitable reimbursement for such costs.

(2) All claims for reimbursement shall be filed with the Administrator not later than ninety days after the closure or interruption which gives rise to the claim.

(3) Reimbursements made under this section shall be from funds appropriated by the Congress pursuant to the authorization contained in section 6916(g) of this title.

(4) For purposes of judicial review, a determination by the Administrator under this subsection shall be considered final agency action.

(Pub. L. No. 89–272, Title II, § 9009, as added by Pub. L. No. 98–616, Title VI, § 601(a), 98 Stat. 3287 (Nov. 8, 1984); and amended by Pub. L. No. 109–58, Title XV, § 1532(b)(3), 119 Stat. 1105 (Aug. 8, 2005).)

HISTORICAL AND STATUTORY NOTES

References in Text

Section 6916(g) of this title, referred to in subsec. (f)(3), probably means section 6916(f) of this title, which authorizes appropriations for this subchapter. There is no subsec. (g) of that section.

§ 6991i. Operator training

[SWDA § 9010]

(a) Guidelines

(1) In general

Not later than 2 years after August 8, 2005, in consultation and cooperation with States and after public notice and opportunity for comment, the Administrator shall publish guidelines that specify training requirements for—

(A) persons having primary responsibility for on-site operation and maintenance of underground storage tank systems;

(B) persons having daily on-site responsibility for the operation and maintenance of underground storage tanks systems; and

(C) daily, on-site employees having primary responsibility for addressing emergencies presented by a spill or release from an underground storage tank system.

(2) Considerations

The guidelines described in paragraph (1) shall take into account—

(A) State training programs in existence as of the date of publication of the guidelines;

(B) training programs that are being employed by tank owners and tank operators as of August 8, 2005;

(C) the high turnover rate of tank operators and other personnel;

(D) the frequency of improvement in underground storage tank equipment technology;

(E) the nature of the businesses in which the tank operators are engaged;

(F) the substantial differences in the scope and length of training needed for the different classes of persons described in subparagraphs (A), (B), and (C) of paragraph (1); and

(G) such other factors as the Administrator determines to be necessary to carry out this section.

(b) State programs

(1) In general

Not later than 2 years after the date on which the Administrator publishes the guidelines under subsection (a)(1) of this section, each State that receives funding under this subchapter shall develop State-specific training requirements that are consistent with the guidelines developed under subsection (a)(1) of this section.

(2) Requirements

State requirements described in paragraph (1) shall—

(A) be consistent with subsection (a) of this section;

(B) be developed in cooperation with tank owners and tank operators;

(C) take into consideration training programs implemented by tank owners and tank operators as of August 8, 2005; and

(D) be appropriately communicated to tank owners and operators.

(3) Financial incentive

The Administrator may award to a State that develops and implements requirements described in paragraph (1), in addition to any funds that the State is entitled to receive under this subchapter, not more than $200,000, to be used to carry out the requirements.

(c) Training

All persons that are subject to the operator training requirements of subsection (a) of this section shall—

(1) meet the training requirements developed under subsection (b) of this section; and

(2) repeat the applicable requirements developed under subsection (b) of this section, if the tank for which they have primary daily on-site management responsibilities is determined to be out of compliance with—

(A) a requirement or standard promulgated by the Administrator under section 6991b of this title; or

(B) a requirement or standard of a State program approved under section 6991c of this title.

(Pub. L. No. 89–272, Title II, § 9010, as added by Pub. L. No. 98–616, Title VI, § 601(a), 98 Stat. 3287 (Nov. 8, 1984); and amended by Pub. L. No. 109–58, Title XV, § 1524(a), 119 Stat. 1095 (Aug. 8, 2005).)

HISTORICAL AND STATUTORY NOTES

References in Text

August 8, 2005, referred to in subsec. (a)(1), (2)(B), originally read "the date of enactment of the Underground Storage Tank Compliance Act", meaning Aug. 8, 2005, the date of enactment of the Underground Storage Tank Compliance Act, Pub. L. No. 109–58, Title XV, §§ 1521 to 1533, 119 Stat. 1092, which rewrote this section.

This subchapter, referred to in subsec. (b)(1), originally read "this subtitle", meaning subtitle I of the Solid Waste Disposal Act, Pub. L. No. 89–272, Title II, § 9001 et seq., as added Pub. L. No. 98–616, Title VI, § 601(a), 98 Stat. 3277 (Nov. 8, 1984), and amended, which is codified principally as this subchapter.

August 8, 2005, referred to in subsec. (b)(2)(C), originally read "the date of enactment of this section", meaning Aug. 8, 2005, the date of enactment of the Underground Storage Tank Compliance Act, Pub. L. No. 109–58, Title XV, §§ 1521 to 1533, 119 Stat. 1092, which rewrote this section.

§ 6991j. Use of funds for release prevention and compliance

[SWDA § 9011]

Funds made available under section 6991m(2)(D) of this title from the Trust Fund may be used to conduct inspections, issue orders, or bring actions under this subchapter—

(1) by a State, in accordance with a grant or cooperative agreement with the Administrator, of[1] State regulations pertaining to underground storage tanks regulated under this subchapter; and

(2) by the Administrator, for tanks regulated under this subchapter (including under a State program approved under section 6991c of this title).

(Pub. L. No. 89–272, Title II, § 9011, as added by Pub. L. No. 109–58, Title XV, § 1526(a), 119 Stat. 1097 (Aug. 8, 2005).)

[1] So in original.

HISTORICAL AND STATUTORY NOTES

References in Text

This subchapter, referred to in text, originally read "this subtitle", meaning subtitle I of the Solid Waste Disposal Act, Pub. L. No. 89–272, Title II, § 9001 et seq., as added Pub. L. No. 98–616, Title VI, § 601(a), 98 Stat. 3277 (Nov. 8, 1984), and amended, which is codified principally as this subchapter.

§ 6991k. Delivery prohibition

[SWDA § 9012]

(a) Requirements

(1) Prohibition of delivery or deposit

Beginning 2 years after August 8, 2005, it shall be unlawful to deliver to, deposit into, or accept a regulated substance into an underground storage tank at a facility which has been identified by the Administrator or a State implementing agency to be ineligible for such delivery, deposit, or acceptance.

(2) Guidance

Within 1 year after August 8, 2005, the Administrator shall, in consultation with the States, underground storage tank owners, and product delivery industries, publish guidelines detailing the specific processes and procedures they will use to implement the provisions of this section. The processes and procedures include, at a minimum—

(A) the criteria for determining which underground storage tank facilities are ineligible for delivery, deposit, or acceptance of a regulated substance;

(B) the mechanisms for identifying which facilities are ineligible for delivery, deposit, or acceptance of a regulated substance to the underground storage tank owning and fuel delivery industries;

(C) the process for reclassifying ineligible facilities as eligible for delivery, deposit, or acceptance of a regulated substance;

(D) one or more processes for providing adequate notice to underground storage tank owners and operators and supplier industries that an underground storage tank has been determined to be ineligible for delivery, deposit, or acceptance of a regulated substance; and

(E) a delineation of, or a process for determining, the specified geographic areas subject to paragraph (4).

(3) Compliance

States that receive funding under this subchapter shall, at a minimum, comply with the processes and procedures published under paragraph (2).

(4) Consideration

(A) Rural and remote areas

Subject to subparagraph (B), the Administrator or a State may consider not treating an underground storage tank as ineligible for delivery, deposit, or acceptance of a regulated substance if such treatment would jeopardize the availability of, or access to, fuel in any rural and remote areas unless an urgent threat to public health, as determined by the Administrator, exists.

(B) Applicability

Subparagraph (A) shall apply only during the 180-day period following the date of a determination by the Administrator or the appropriate State under subparagraph (A).

(b) Effect on State authority

Nothing in this section shall affect or preempt the authority of a State to prohibit the delivery, deposit, or acceptance of a regulated substance to an underground storage tank.

(c) Defense to violation

A person shall not be in violation of subsection (a)(1) of this section if the person has not been provided with notice pursuant to subsection (a)(2)(D) of this section of the ineligibility of a facility for delivery, deposit, or acceptance of a regulated substance as determined by the Administrator or a State, as appropriate, under this section.

(Pub. L. No. 89–272, Title II, § 9012, as added by Pub. L. No. 109–58, Title XV, § 1527(a), 119 Stat. 1098 (Aug. 8, 2005); and amended by Pub. L. No. 109–168, § 1(a)(1), 119 Stat. 3580 (Jan. 10, 2006).)

HISTORICAL AND STATUTORY NOTES

References in Text

August 8, 2005, referred to in subsec. (a)(1), (2), originally read "the date of enactment of this section", meaning Aug. 8, 2005, the date of enactment of the Underground Storage Tank Compliance Act, Pub. L. No. 109–58, Title XV, §§ 1521 to 1533, 119 Stat. 1092, which enacted this section.

This subchapter, referred to in subsec. (a)(3), originally read "this subtitle", meaning subtitle I of the Solid Waste Disposal Act, Pub. L. No. 89–272, Title II, § 9001 et seq., as added Pub. L. No. 98–616, Title VI, § 601(a), 98 Stat. 3277 (Nov. 8, 1984), and amended, which is codified principally to this subchapter.

§ 6991*l*. Tanks on tribal lands

[SWDA § 9013]

(a) Strategy

The Administrator, in coordination with Indian tribes, shall, not later than 1 year after August 8, 2005, develop and implement a strategy—

(1) giving priority to releases that present the greatest threat to human health or the environment, to take necessary corrective action in response to releases from leaking underground storage tanks located wholly within the boundaries of—

(A) an Indian reservation; or

(B) any other area under the jurisdiction of an Indian tribe; and

(2) to implement and enforce requirements concerning underground storage tanks located wholly within the boundaries of—

(A) an Indian reservation; or

(B) any other area under the jurisdiction of an Indian tribe.

(b) Report

Not later than 2 years after August 8, 2005, the Administrator shall submit to Congress a report that summarizes the status of implementation and enforcement of this subchapter in areas located wholly within—

(1) the boundaries of Indian reservations; and

(2) any other areas under the jurisdiction of an Indian tribe.

The Administrator shall make the report under this subsection available to the public.

(c) Not a safe harbor

This section does not relieve any person from any obligation or requirement under this subchapter.

(d) State authority

Nothing in this section applies to any underground storage tank that is located in an area under the jurisdiction of a State, or that is subject to regulation by a State, as of August 8, 2005.

(Pub. L. No. 89–272, Title II, § 9013, as added by Pub. L. No. 109–58, Title XV, § 1529(a), 119 Stat. 1101 (Aug. 8, 2005).)

HISTORICAL AND STATUTORY NOTES

References in Text

August 8, 2005, referred to in subsecs. (a), (b), and (d), originally read "the date of enactment of this section", meaning Aug. 8, 2005, the date of enactment of the Underground Storage Tank Compliance Act, Pub. L. No. 109–58, Title XV, §§ 1521 to 1533, 119 Stat. 1092, which enacted this section.

This subchapter, referred to in subsecs. (b) and (c), originally read "this subtitle", meaning subtitle I of the Solid Waste Disposal Act, Pub. L. No. 89–272, Title II, § 9001 et seq., as added Pub. L. No. 98–616, Title VI, § 601(a), 98 Stat. 3277 (Nov. 8, 1984), and amended, which is codified principally as this subchapter.

§ 6991m. Authorization of appropriations

[SWDA § 9014]

There are authorized to be appropriated to the Administrator the following amounts:

(1) To carry out this subchapter (except sections 6991b(h), 6991d(c), 6991j and 6991k of this title) $50,000,000 for each of fiscal years 2006 through 2011.

(2) From the Trust Fund—

(A) to carry out section 6991b(h) of this title (except section 6991b(h)(12) of this title) $200,000,000 for each of fiscal years 2006 through 2011;

(B) to carry out section 6991b(h)(12) of this title, $200,000,000 for each of fiscal years 2006 through 2011;

(C) to carry out sections 6991b(i), 6991c(f), and 6991d(c) of this title $100,000,000 for each of fiscal years 2006 through 2011; and

(D) to carry out sections 6991i, 6991j, 6991k, and 6991*l* of this title $55,000,000 for each of fiscal years 2006 through 2011.

(Pub. L. No. 89–272, Title II, § 9014, as added by Pub. L. No. 109–58, Title XV, § 1531(a), 119 Stat. 1104 (Aug. 8, 2005); and amended by Pub. L. No. 109–168, § 1(a)(3), 119 Stat. 3580 (Jan. 10, 2006); Pub. L. No. 109–432, Div. A, Title II, § 210(b), 120 Stat. 2947 (Dec. 20, 2006); Pub. L. No. 109–433, § 1(b), 120 Stat. 3196 (Dec. 20, 2006).)

HISTORICAL AND STATUTORY NOTES

References in Text

This subchapter, referred to in par. (1), originally read "subtitle I", meaning subtitle I of the Solid Waste Disposal Act, Pub. L. No. 89–272, Title II, § 9001 et seq., as added Pub. L. No. 98–616, Title VI, § 601(a), 98 Stat. 3277 (Nov. 8, 1984), and amended, which is codified principally to this subchapter.

Codifications

Pub. L. No. 109–432, Div. A, Title II, § 210(b) and Pub. L. No. 109–433, § 1(b), made identical amendments to par. (2) of this section. See 2006 Amendments note set out under this section.

Effective and Applicability Provisions

2006 Acts. Amendments made by Pub. L. No. 109–433 effective Dec. 20, 2006, see Pub. L. No. 109–433, § 1(c), set out as a note under 26 U.S.C.A. § 9508.

Amendment to this section by Pub. L. No. 109–432, Div. A, Title II, § 210(b), effective Dec. 20, 2006, see Pub. L. No. 109–432, Div. A, Title II, § 210(c), set out as an Effective and Applicability Provisions note under 26 U.S.C.A. § 9508.

SUBCHAPTER X—DEMONSTRATION MEDICAL WASTE TRACKING PROGRAM

§ 6992. Scope of demonstration program for medical waste

[SWDA § 11001]

(a) Covered States

The States within the demonstration program established under this subchapter for tracking medical wastes shall be New York, New Jersey, Connecticut, the States contiguous to the Great Lakes and any State included in the program through the petition procedure described in subsection (c) of this section, except for any of such States in which the Governor notifies the Administrator under subsection (b) of this section that such State shall not be covered by the program.

(b) Opt out

(1) If the Governor of any State covered under subsection (a) of this section which is not contiguous to the Atlantic Ocean notifies the Administrator that such State elects not to participate in the demonstration program, the Administrator shall remove such State from the program.

(2) If the Governor of any other State covered under subsection (a) of this section notifies the Administrator that such State has implemented a medical waste tracking program that is no less stringent than the demonstration program under this subchapter and that such State elects not to participate in the demonstration program, the Administrator shall, if the Administrator determines that such State program is no less stringent than the demonstration program under this subchapter, remove such State from the demonstration program.

(3) Notifications under paragraphs (1) or (2) shall be submitted to the Administrator no later than 30 days after the promulgation of regulations implementing the demonstration program under this subchapter.

(c) Petition in

The Governor of any State may petition the Administrator to be included in the demonstration program and the Administrator may, in his discretion, include any such State. Such petition may not be made later than 30 days after promulgation of regulations establishing the demonstration program under this subchapter, and the Administrator shall determine whether to include the State within 30 days after receipt of the State's petition.

(d) Expiration of demonstration program

The demonstration program shall expire on the date 24 months after the effective date of the regulations under this subchapter.

(Pub. L. No. 89–272, Title II, § 11001, as added by Pub. L. No. 100–582, § 2(a), 102 Stat. 2950 (Nov. 1, 1988).)

§ 6992a. Listing of medical wastes

[SWDA § 11002]

(a) List

Not later than 6 months after November 1, 1988, the Administrator shall promulgate regulations listing the types of medical waste to be tracked under the demonstration program. Except as provided in subsection (b) of this section, such list shall include, but need not be limited to, each of the following types of solid waste:

(1) Cultures and stocks of infectious agents and associated biologicals, including cultures from medical and pathological laboratories, cultures and stocks of infectious agents from research and industrial laboratories, wastes from the production of biologicals, discarded live and attenuated vaccines, and culture dishes and devices used to transfer, inoculate, and mix cultures.

(2) Pathological wastes, including tissues, organs, and body parts that are removed during surgery or autopsy.

(3) Waste human blood and products of blood, including serum, plasma, and other blood components.

(4) Sharps that have been used in patient care or in medical, research, or industrial laboratories, including hypodermic needles, syringes, pasteur pipettes, broken glass, and scalpel blades.

(5) Contaminated animal carcasses, body parts, and bedding of animals that were exposed to infectious agents during research, production of biologicals, or testing of pharmaceuticals.

(6) Wastes from surgery or autopsy that were in contact with infectious agents, including soiled dressings, sponges, drapes, lavage tubes, drainage sets, underpads, and surgical gloves.

(7) Laboratory wastes from medical, pathological, pharmaceutical, or other research, commercial, or industrial laboratories that were in contact with infectious agents, including slides and cover slips, disposable gloves, laboratory coats, and aprons.

(8) Dialysis wastes that were in contact with the blood of patients undergoing hemodialysis, including contaminated disposable equipment and supplies such as tubing, filters, disposable sheets, towels, gloves, aprons, and laboratory coats.

(9) Discarded medical equipment and parts that were in contact with infectious agents.

(10) Biological waste and discarded materials contaminated with blood, excretion, excudates[1] or secretion from human beings or animals who are isolated to protect others from communicable diseases.

(11) Such other waste material that results from the administration of medical care to a patient by a health care provider and is found by the Administrator to pose a threat to human health or the environment.

(b) Exclusions from list

The Administrator may exclude from the list under this section any categories or items described in paragraphs (6) through (10) of subsection (a) of this section which he determines do not pose a substantial present or potential hazard to human health or the environment when improperly treated, stored, transported, disposed of, or otherwise managed.

(Pub. L. No. 89–272, Title II, § 11002, as added by Pub. L. No. 100–582, § 2(a), 102 Stat. 2951 (Nov. 1, 1988).)

[1] So in original. Probably should be "exudates".

§ 6992b. Tracking of medical waste

[SWDA § 11003]

(a) Demonstration program

Not later than 6 months after November 1, 1988, the Administrator shall promulgate regulations establishing a program for the tracking of the medical waste listed in section 6992a of this title which is generated in a State subject to the demonstration program. The program shall (1) provide for tracking of the transportation of the waste from the generator to the disposal facility, except that waste that is incinerated need not be tracked after incineration, (2) include a system for providing the generator of the waste with assurance that the waste is received by the disposal facility, (3) use a uniform form for tracking in each of the demonstration States, and (4) include the following requirements:

(A) A requirement for segregation of the waste at the point of generation where practicable.

(B) A requirement for placement of the waste in containers that will protect waste handlers and the public from exposure.

(C) A requirement for appropriate labeling of containers of the waste.

(b) Small quantities

In the program under subsection (a) of this section, the Administrator may establish an exemption for generators of small quantities of medical waste listed under section 6992a of this title, except that the Administrator may not exempt from the program any person who, or facility that, generates 50 pounds or more of such waste in any calendar month.

(c) On-site incinerators

Concurrently with the promulgation of regulations under subsection (a) of this section, the Administrator shall promulgate a recordkeeping and reporting requirement for any generator in a demonstration State of medical waste listed in section 6992a of this title that (1) incinerates medical waste listed in section 6992a of this title on site and (2) does not track such waste under the regulations promulgated under subsection (a) of this section. Such requirement shall require the generator to report to the Administrator on the volume and types of medical waste listed in section 6992a of this title that the generator incinerated on site during the 6 months following the effective date of the requirements of this subsection.

(d) Type of medical waste and types of generators

For each of the requirements of this section, the regulations may vary for different types of medical waste and for different types of medical waste generators.

(Pub. L. No. 89–272, Title II, § 11003, as added by Pub. L. No. 100–582, § 2(a), 102 Stat. 2952 (Nov. 1, 1988).)

§ 6992c. Inspections

[SWDA § 11004]

(a) Requirements for access

For purposes of developing or assisting in the development of any regulation or report under this subchapter or enforcing any provision of this subchapter, any person who generates, stores, treats, transports, disposes of, or otherwise handles or has handled medical waste shall, upon request of any officer, employee, or representative of the Environmental Protection Agency duly designated by the Administrator, furnish information relating to such waste, including any tracking forms required to be maintained under section 6992b of this title, conduct monitoring or testing, and permit such person at all reasonable times to have access to, and to copy, all records relating to such waste. For such purposes, such officers, employees, or representatives are authorized to—

(1) enter at reasonable times any establishment or other place where medical wastes are or have been generated, stored, treated, disposed of, or transported from;

(2) conduct monitoring or testing; and

(3) inspect and obtain samples from any person of any such wastes and samples of any containers or labeling for such wastes.

(b) Procedures

Each inspection under this section shall be commenced and completed with reasonable promptness. If the officer, employee, or representative obtains any samples, prior to leaving the premises he shall give to the owner, operator, or agent in charge a receipt describing the sample obtained and, if requested, a portion of each such sample equal in volume or weight to the portion retained if giving such an equal portion is feasible. If any analysis is made of such samples, a copy of the results of such analysis shall be furnished promptly to the owner, operator, or agent in charge of the premises concerned.

(c) Availability to public

The provisions of section 6927(b) of this title shall apply to records, reports, and information obtained under this section in the same manner and to the same extent as such provisions apply to records, reports, and information obtained under section 6927 of this title.

(Pub. L. No. 89–272, Title II, § 11004, as added by Pub. L. No. 100–582, § 2(a), 102 Stat. 2952 (Nov. 1, 1988).)

§ 6992d. Enforcement

[SWDA § 11005]

(a) Compliance orders

(1) Violations

Whenever on the basis of any information the Administrator determines that any person has violated, or is in violation of, any requirement or prohibition in effect under this subchapter (including any requirement or prohibition in effect under regulations under this subchapter) (A) the Administrator may issue an order (i) assessing a civil penalty for any past or current violation, (ii) requiring compliance immediately or within a specified time period, or (iii) both, or (B) the Administrator may commence a civil action in the United States district court in the district in which the violation occurred for appropriate relief, including a temporary or permanent injunction. Any order issued pursuant to this subsection shall state with reasonable specificity the nature of the violation.

(2) Orders assessing penalties

Any penalty assessed in an order under this subsection shall not exceed $25,000 per day of noncompliance for each violation of a requirement or prohibition in effect under this subchapter. In assessing such a penalty, the Administrator shall take into account the seriousness of the violation and any good faith efforts to comply with applicable requirements.

(3) Public hearing

Any order issued under this subsection shall become final unless, not later than 30 days after issuance of the order, the persons named therein request a public hearing. Upon such request, the Administrator shall promptly conduct a public hearing. In connection with any proceeding under this section, the Administrator may issue subpoenas for the production of relevant papers, books, and documents, and may promulgate rules for discovery procedures.

(4) Violation of compliance orders

In the case of an order under this subsection requiring compliance with any requirement of or regulation under this subchapter, if a violator fails to take corrective action within the time specified in an order, the Administrator may assess a civil penalty of not more than $25,000 for each day of continued noncompliance with the order.

(b) Criminal penalties

Any person who—

(1) knowingly violates the requirements of or regulations under this subchapter;

(2) knowingly omits material information or makes any false material statement or representation in any label, record, report, or other document filed, maintained, or used for purposes of compliance with this subchapter or regulations thereunder; or

(3) knowingly generates, stores, treats, transports, disposes of, or otherwise handles any medical waste (whether such activity took place before or takes place after November 1, 1988) and who knowingly destroys, alters, conceals, or fails to file any record, report, or other document required to be maintained or filed for purposes of compliance with this subchapter or regulations thereunder

shall, upon conviction, be subject to a fine of not more than $50,000 for each day of violation, or imprisonment not to exceed 2 years (5 years in the case of a violation of paragraph (1)). If the conviction is for a violation committed after a first conviction of such person under this paragraph, the maximum punishment under the respective paragraph shall be doubled with respect to both fine and imprisonment.

(c) Knowing endangerment

Any person who knowingly violates any provision of subsection (b) of this section who knows at that time that he thereby places another person in imminent danger of death or serious bodily injury, shall upon conviction be subject to a fine of not more than $250,000 or imprisonment for not more than 15 years, or both. A defendant that is an organization shall, upon conviction under this subsection, be subject to a fine of not more than $1,000,000. The terms of this paragraph shall be interpreted in accordance with the rules provided under section 6928(f) of this title.

(d) Civil penalties

Any person who violates any requirement of or regulation under this subchapter shall be liable to the United States for a civil penalty in an amount not to exceed $25,000 for each such violation. Each day of such violation shall, for purposes of this section, constitute a separate violation.

(e) Civil penalty policy

Civil penalties assessed by the United States or by the States under this subchapter shall be assessed in accordance with the Administrator's "RCRA Civil Penalty Policy", as such policy may be amended from time to time.

(Pub. L. No. 89–272, Title II, § 11005, as added by Pub. L. No. 100–582, § 2(a), 102 Stat. 2953 (Nov. 1, 1988).)

§ 6992e. Federal facilities

[SWDA § 11006]

(a) In general

Each department, agency, and instrumentality of the executive, legislative, and judicial branches of the Federal Government in a demonstration State (1) having jurisdiction over any solid waste management facility or disposal site at which medical waste is disposed of or otherwise handled, or (2) engaged in any activity resulting, or which may result, in the disposal, management, or handling of medical waste shall be subject to, and comply with, all Federal, State, interstate, and local requirements, both substantive and procedural (including any requirement for permits or reporting or any provisions for injunctive relief and such sanctions as may be imposed by a court to enforce such relief), respecting control and abatement of medical waste disposal and management in the same manner, and to the same extent, as any person is subject to such requirements, including the payment of reasonable service charges. The Federal, State, interstate, and local substantive and procedural requirements referred to in this subsection include, but are not limited to, all administrative orders, civil, criminal, and administrative penalties, and other sanctions, including injunctive relief, fines, and imprisonment. Neither the United States, nor any agent, employee, or officer thereof, shall be immune or exempt from any process or sanction of any State or Federal court with respect to the enforcement of any such order, penalty, or other sanction. For purposes of enforcing any such substantive or procedural requirement (including, but not limited to, any injunctive relief, administrative order, or civil, criminal, administrative penalty, or other sanction), against any such department, agency, or instrumentality, the United States hereby expressly waives any immunity otherwise applicable to the United States. The President may exempt any department, agency, or instrumentality in the executive branch from compliance with such a requirement if he determines it to be in the paramount interest of the United States to do so. No such exemption shall be granted due to lack of appropriation unless the President shall have specifically requested such appropriation as a part of the budgetary process and the Congress shall have failed to make available such requested appropriation. Any exemption shall be for a period not in excess of one year, but additional exemptions may be granted for periods not to exceed one year upon the President's making a new determination. The President shall report each January to the Congress all exemptions from the requirements of this section granted during the preceding calendar year, together with his reason for granting each such exemption.

(b) "Person" defined

For purposes of this chapter, the term "person" shall be treated as including each department, agency, and instrumentality of the United States.

(Pub. L. No. 89–272, Title II, § 11006, as added by Pub. L. No. 100–582, § 2(a), 102 Stat. 2954 (Nov. 1, 1988).)

HISTORICAL AND STATUTORY NOTES

Termination of Reporting Requirements

For termination, effective May 15, 2000, of provisions in subsec. (a) of this section requiring the President to report annually to Congress, see Pub. L. No. 104–66, § 3003, as amended, set out as a note under 31 U.S.C.A. § 1113, and the 10th item on page 20 of House Document No. 103–7.

§ 6992f. Relationship to State law

[SWDA § 11007]

(a) State inspections and enforcement

A State may conduct inspections under 6992c of this title[1] and take enforcement actions under section 6992d of this title against any person, including any person who has imported medical waste into a State in violation of the requirements of, or regulations under, this subchapter, to the same extent as the Administrator. At the time a State initiates an enforcement action under section 6992d of this title against any person, the State shall notify the Administrator in writing.

(b) Retention of State authority

Nothing in this subchapter shall—

(1) preempt any State or local law; or

(2) except as provided in subsection (c) of this section, otherwise affect any State or local law or the authority of any State or local government to adopt or enforce any State or local law.

(c) State forms

Any State or local law which requires submission of a tracking form from any person subject to this subchapter shall require that the form be identical in content and format to the form required under section 6992b of this title, except that a State may require the submission of other tracking information which is supplemental to the information required on the form required under section 6992b of this title through additional sheets or such other means as the State deems appropriate.

(Pub. L. No. 89–272, Title II, § 11007, as added by Pub. L. No. 100–582, § 2(a), 102 Stat. 2955 (Nov. 1, 1988).)

[1] The phrase "under 6992c" should read "under section 6992c".

§ 6992g. Repealed. Pub. L. No. 105–362, Title V, § 501(h)(1)(A), 112 Stat. 3284 (Nov. 10, 1998).

HISTORICAL AND STATUTORY NOTES

Section Pub. L. No. 89–272, Title II, § 11008, as added by Pub. L. No. 100–582, § 2(a), 102 Stat. 2956 (Nov. 1, 1988), repealed by Pub. L. No. 105–362, Title V, § 501(h)(1)(A), 112 Stat. 3284 (Nov. 10, 1998), related to reports to Congress.

§ 6992h. Health impacts report

[SWDA § 11008]

Within 24 months after November 1, 1988, the Administrator of the Agency for Toxic Substances and Disease Registry shall prepare for Congress a report on the health effects of medical waste, including each of the following—

(1) A description of the potential for infection or injury from the segregation, handling, storage, treatment, or disposal of medical wastes.

(2) An estimate of the number of people injured or infected annually by sharps, and the nature and seriousness of those injuries or infections.

(3) An estimate of the number of people infected annually by other means related to waste segregation, handling, storage, treatment, or disposal, and the nature and seriousness of those infections.

(4) For diseases possibly spread by medical waste, including Acquired Immune Deficiency Syndrome and hepatitis B, an estimate of what percentage of the total number of cases nationally may be traceable to medical wastes.

(Pub. L. No. 89–272, Title II, § 11008, formerly § 11009, as added by Pub. L. No. 100–582, § 2(a), 102 Stat. 2957 (Nov. 1, 1988); and renumbered § 11008 by Pub. L. No. 105–362, Title V, § 501(h)(1)(B), 112 Stat. 3284 (Nov. 10, 1998).)

§ 6992i. General provisions

[SWDA § 11009]

(a) Consultation

(1) In promulgating regulations under this subchapter, the Administrator shall consult with the affected States and may consult with other interested parties.

(2) The Administrator shall also consult with the International Joint Commission to determine how to monitor the disposal of medical waste emanating from Canada.

(b) Public comment

In the case of the regulations required by this subchapter to be promulgated within 9 months after November 1, 1988, the Administrator may promulgate such regulations in interim final form without prior opportunity for public comment, but the Administrator shall provide an opportunity for public comment on the interim final rule. The promulgation of such regulations shall not be subject to the Paperwork Reduction Act of 1980.

(c) Relationship to subchapter III

Nothing in this subchapter shall affect the authority of the Administrator to regulate medical waste, including medical waste listed under section 6992a of this title, under subchapter III of this chapter.

(Pub. L. No. 89–272, Title II, § 11009, formerly § 11010, as added by Pub. L. No. 100–582, § 2(a), 102 Stat. 2957 (Nov. 1, 1988); and renumbered § 11009 by Pub. L. No. 105–362, Title V, § 501(h)(1)(B), 112 Stat. 3284 (Nov. 10, 1998).)

HISTORICAL AND STATUTORY NOTES

References in Text

The Paperwork Reduction Act of 1980, referred to in subsec. (b), is Pub. L. 96–511, 94 Stat. 2812 (Dec. 11, 1980), as amended, which was codified principally as chapter 35 of Title 44, 44 U.S.C.A. § 3501 et seq., prior to the general amendment of that chapter by Pub. L. 104–13, § 2, May 22, 1995, 109 Stat. 163. For complete classification, see Short Title of 1980 Amendment note set out under 44 U.S.C.A. § 101 and Tables.

§ 6992j. Effective date

[SWDA § 11010]

The regulations promulgated under this subchapter shall take effect within 90 days after promulgation, except that, at the time of promulgation, the Administrator may provide for a shorter period prior to the effective date if he finds the regulated community does not need 90 days to come into compliance.

(Pub. L. No. 89–272, Title II, § 11010, formerly § 11011, as added by Pub. L. No. 100–582, § 2(a), 102 Stat. 2958 (Nov. 1, 1988); and renumbered § 11010 by Pub. L. No. 105–362, Title V, § 501(h)(1)(B), 112 Stat. 3284 (Nov. 10, 1998).)

§ 6992k. Authorization of appropriations

[SWDA § 11011]

There are authorized to be appropriated to the Administrator such sums as may be necessary for each of the fiscal years 1989 through 1991 for purposes of carrying out activities under this subchapter.

(Pub. L. No. 89–272, Title II, § 11011, formerly § 11012, as added by Pub. L. No. 100–582, § 2(a), 102 Stat. 2958 (Nov. 1, 1988); and renumbered § 11011 by Pub. L. No. 105–362, Title V, § 501(h)(1)(B), 112 Stat. 3284 (Nov. 10, 1998).)

AIR POLLUTION PREVENTION AND CONTROL

CLEAN AIR ACT [CAA § ______]

(42 U.S.C.A. §§ 7401 to 7671q)

CHAPTER 85—AIR POLLUTION PREVENTION AND CONTROL

SUBCHAPTER I—PROGRAMS AND ACTIVITIES

PART A—AIR QUALITY AND EMISSIONS LIMITATIONS

PART B—OZONE PROTECTION

PART C—PREVENTION OF SIGNIFICANT DETERIORATION OF AIR QUALITY

Subpart I—Clean Air

SUBCHAPTER I—PROGRAMS AND ACTIVITIES

PART A—AIR QUALITY AND EMISSIONS LIMITATIONS

HISTORICAL AND STATUTORY NOTES

Codifications

Act of July 14, 1955, c. 360, 69 Stat. 322, as amended, known as the Clean Air Act, which was formerly codified as chapter 15B (section 1857 et seq.) of this title, was completely revised by Pub. L. No. 95–95, 91 Stat. 685 (Aug. 7, 1977), and was recodified as this chapter.

§ 7401. Congressional findings and declaration of purpose

[CAA § 101]

(a) Findings

The Congress finds—

(1) that the predominant part of the Nation's population is located in its rapidly expanding metropolitan and other urban areas, which generally cross the boundary lines of local jurisdictions and often extend into two or more States;

(2) that the growth in the amount and complexity of air pollution brought about by urbanization, industrial development, and the increasing use of motor vehicles, has resulted in mounting dangers to the public health and welfare, including injury to agricultural crops and livestock, damage to and the deterioration of property, and hazards to air and ground transportation;

(3) that air pollution prevention (that is, the reduction or elimination, through any measures, of the amount of pollutants produced or created at the source) and air pollution control at its source is the primary responsibility of States and local governments; and

(4) that Federal financial assistance and leadership is essential for the development of cooperative Federal, State, regional, and local programs to prevent and control air pollution.

(b) Declaration

The purposes of this subchapter are—

(1) to protect and enhance the quality of the Nation's air resources so as to promote the public health and welfare and the productive capacity of its population;

(2) to initiate and accelerate a national research and development program to achieve the prevention and control of air pollution;

(3) to provide technical and financial assistance to State and local governments in connection with the development and execution of their air pollution prevention and control programs; and

(4) to encourage and assist the development and operation of regional air pollution prevention and control programs.

(c) Pollution prevention

A primary goal of this chapter is to encourage or otherwise promote reasonable Federal, State, and local governmental actions, consistent with the provisions of this chapter, for pollution prevention.

(July 14, 1955, c. 360, Title I, § 101, formerly § 1, as added by Pub. L. No. 88–206, § 1, 77 Stat. 392 (Dec. 17, 1963); and renumbered § 101 and amended by Pub. L. No. 89–272, Title I, § 101(2), (3), 79 Stat. 992 (Oct. 20, 1965); and amended by Pub. L. No. 90–148, § 2, 81 Stat. 485 (Nov. 21, 1967); Pub. L. No. 101–549, Title I, § 108(k), 104 Stat. 2468 (Nov. 15, 1990).)

HISTORICAL AND STATUTORY NOTES

Codifications

Section was formerly codified as section 1857 of this title.

Effective and Applicability Provisions

1990 Acts. Section 711(b) of Pub. L. No. 101–549 provided that:

"(1) Except as otherwise expressly provided, the amendments made by this Act [Pub. L. No. 101–549, Nov. 15, 1990, 104 Stat. 2399, popularly known as the Clean Air Act Amendments of 1990, for distribution of this Act to the Code see Tables] shall be effective on the date of enactment of this Act [Nov. 15, 1990].

"(2) The Administrator's authority to assess civil penalties under section 205(c) of the Clean Air Act, as amended by this Act, [section 7524(c) of this title], shall apply to violations that occur or continue on or after the date of enactment of this Act [Nov. 15, 1990]. Civil penalties for violations that occur prior to such date and do not continue after such date shall be assessed in accordance with the provisions of the Clean Air Act [this chapter] in effect immediately prior to the date of enactment of this Act.

"(3) The civil penalties prescribed under sections 205(a) and 211(d)(1) of the Clean Air Act, as amended by this Act [sections 7524(a) and 7545(d)(1) of this title], shall apply to violations that occur on or after the date of enactment of this Act [Nov. 15, 1990]. Violations that occur prior to such date shall be subject to the civil penalty provisions prescribed in sections 205(a) and 211(d) of the Clean Air Act in effect immediately prior to the enactment of this Act. The injunctive authority prescribed under section 211(d)(2) of the Clean Air Act, as amended by this Act [section 7545(d)(2) of this title], shall apply to violations that occur or continue on or after the date of enactment of this Act [Nov. 15, 1990].

"(4) For purposes of paragraphs (2) and (3), where the date of a violation cannot be determined it will be assumed to be the date on which the violation is discovered."

1977 Acts. Section 406 of Pub. L. No. 95–95, as amended by Pub. L. No. 95–190, § 14(b)(6), 91 Stat. 1405 (Nov. 16, 1977), provided that:

"(a) No suit, action, or other proceeding lawfully commenced by or against the Administrator or any other officer or employee of the United States in his official capacity or in relation to the discharge of his official duties under the Clean Air Act [this chapter], as in effect immediately prior to the date of enactment of this Act [Aug. 7, 1977] shall abate by reason of the taking effect of the amendments made by this Act [see Short Title of 1977 Acts note under this section]. The court may, on its own motion or that of any party made at any time within twelve months after such taking effect, allow the same to be maintained by or against the Administrator or such officer or employee.

"**(b)** All rules, regulations, orders, determinations, contracts, certifications, authorizations, delegations or other actions duly issued, made, or taken by or pursuant to the Clean Air Act [this chapter], as in effect immediately prior to the date of enactment of this Act [Aug. 7, 1977], and pertaining to any functions, powers, requirements, and duties under the Clean Air Act, as in effect immediately prior to the date of enactment of this Act, and not suspended by the Administrator or the courts, shall continue in full force and effect after the date of enactment of this Act until modified or rescinded in accordance with the Clean Air Act as amended by this Act [see Short Title of 1977 Acts note under this section].

"**(c)** Nothing in this Act [see Short Title of 1977 Acts note under this section] nor any action taken pursuant to this Act shall in any way affect any requirement of an approved implementation plan in effect under section 110 of the Clean Air Act [section 7410 of this title] or any other provision of the Act in effect under the Clean Air Act before the date of enactment of this section [Aug. 7, 1977] until modified or rescinded in accordance with the Clean Air Act [this chapter] as amended by this Act [see Short Title of 1977 Acts note under this section].

"**(d) (1)** Except as otherwise expressly provided, the amendments made by this Act [see Short Title of 1977 Acts note under this section] shall be effective on date of enactment [Aug. 7, 1977].

"**(2)** Except as otherwise expressly provided, each State required to revise its applicable implementation plan by reason of any amendment made by this Act [see Short Title of 1977 Acts note under this section] shall adopt and submit to the Administrator of the Environmental Protection Administration such plan revision before the later of the date—

"**(A)** one year after the date of enactment of this Act [Aug. 7, 1977], or

"**(B)** nine months after the date of promulgation by the Administrator of the Environmental Protection Administration of any regulations under an amendment made by this Act [see Short Title of 1977 Acts note under this section] which are necessary for the approval of such plan revision".

Transfer of Functions

Reorg. Plan No. 3 of 1970, § 2(a)(3), eff. Dec. 2, 1970, 35 Fed. Reg. 15623, 84 Stat. 2086, transferred to the Administrator of the Environmental Protection Agency the functions vested by law in the Secretary of Health, Education, and Welfare or in the Department of Health, Education, and Welfare which are administered through the Environmental Health Service, including the functions exercised by the National Air Pollution Control Administration, and the Environmental Control Administration's Bureau of Solid Waste Management, Bureau of Water Hygiene, and Bureau of Radiological Health, except insofar as the functions carried out by the Bureau of Radiological Health pertain to regulation of radiation from consumer products, including electronic product radiation, radiation as used in the healing arts, occupational exposure to radiation, and research, technical assistance, and training related to radiation from consumer products, radiation as used in the healing arts, and occupational exposure to radiation.

Savings Provisions

Section 711(a) of Pub. L. No. 101–549 provided that: "Except as otherwise expressly provided in this Act [Pub. L. No. 101–549, 104 Stat. 2399 (Nov. 15, 1990), popularly known as the Clean Air Act Amendments of 1990, for distribution of this Act to the Code see Tables], no suit, action, or other proceeding lawfully commenced by the Administrator or any other officer or employee of the United States in his official capacity or in relation to the discharge of his official duties under the Clean Air Act [this chapter], as in effect immediately prior to the date of enactment of this Act, [Nov. 15, 1990], shall abate by reason of the taking effect of the amendments made by this Act."

Prior Provisions

Provisions similar to those comprising this section were contained in a prior section 1857 of this title, Act of July 14, 1955, c. 360, § 1, 69 Stat. 322, prior to the general amendment of this chapter by Pub. L. No. 88–206.

Short Title

1999 Amendments. Pub. L. No. 106–40, § 1, 113 Stat. 207 (Aug. 5, 1999), provided that: "This Act [amending section 7412 of this title, and enacting provisions set out as notes under section 7412 of this title] may be cited as the 'Chemical Safety Information, Site Security and Fuels Regulatory Relief Act'."

1998 Amendments. Pub. L. No. 105–286, § 1, 112 Stat. 2773 (Oct. 27, 1998), provided that: "This Act [amending section 7511b of this title, and enacting provisions set out as notes under section 7511b of this title] may be cited as the 'Border Smog Reduction Act of 1998'."

1990 Amendments. Pub. L. No. 101–549, 104 Stat. 2399 (Nov. 15, 1990), is popularly known as the "Clean Air Act Amendments of 1990". See Tables for classification.

1981 Amendments. Pub. L. No. 97–23, § 1, 95 Stat. 139 (July 17, 1981), provided: "That this Act [amending sections 7410 and 7413 of this title] may be cited as the 'Steel Industry Compliance Extension Act of 1981'."

1977 Amendments. Pub. L. No. 95–95, § 1, 91 Stat. 685 (Aug. 7, 1977), provided that: "This Act [enacting sections 4362, 7419 to 7428, 7450 to 7459, 7470 to 7479, 7491, 7501 to 7508, 7548, 7549, 7551, 7617 to 7625, and 7626 of this title, amending sections 7403, 7405, 7407 to 7415, 7417, 7418, 7521 to 7525, 7541, 7543, 7544, 7545, 7550, 7571, 7601 to 7605, 7607, 7612, 7613, and 7616 of this title, repealing section 1857c–10 of this title and enacting provisions set out as notes under this section and sections 7403, 7422, 7470, 7479, 7502, 7521, 7548, and 7621 of this title and section 792 of Title 15, Commerce and Trade] may be cited as the 'Clean Air Act Amendments of 1977'."

1970 Amendments. Pub. L. No. 91–604, § 1, 84 Stat. 1676 (Dec. 31, 1970), provided: "That this Act [amending this chapter generally] may be cited as the 'Clean Air Amendments of 1970'."

Section 401 of Act of July 14, 1955, as added by Pub. L. No. 91–604, § 14, 84 Stat. 1709 (Dec. 31, 1970), provided that: "This title [subchapter IV of this chapter] may be cited as the 'Noise Pollution and Abatement Act of 1970'."

1967 Amendments. Section 1 of Pub. L. No. 90–148 provided: "That this Act [amending this chapter generally] may be cited as the 'Air Quality Act of 1967'."

1966 Amendments. Pub. L. No. 89–675, § 1, 80 Stat. 954 (Oct. 15, 1966), provided: "That this Act [amending sections 7405 and 7616 of this title and repealing section 1857f–8 of this title] may be cited as the 'Clean Air Act Amendments of 1966'."

1965 Amendments. Section 201 of Act of July 14, 1955, as added by Pub. L. No. 89–272, Title I, § 101(8), 79 Stat. 992 (Oct. 20, 1965), and amended by Pub. L. No. 90–148, § 2, 81 Stat. 499 (Nov. 2, 1967), provided that: "This title [subchapter II of this chapter] may be cited as the 'National Emission Standards Act'." Prior to its amendment by Pub. L. No. 90–148, Title II of Act of July 14, 1955, was known as the "Motor Vehicle Air Pollution Control Act".

1963 Acts. Section 317, formerly section 14, of Act of July 14, 1955, as added by section 1 of Pub. L. No. 88–206, renumbered section 307 by section 101(4) of Pub. L. No. 89–272, renumbered section 310 by section 2 of Pub. L. No. 90–148, and renumbered section 317 by Pub. L. No. 91–604, § 12(a), 84 Stat. 1705 (Dec. 31, 1970), provided that: "This Act [this chapter] may be cited as the 'Clean Air Act'." The Act is also commonly known as CAA and the Air Pollution Control Act. The Clean Air Act was originally codified as chapter 15B of this title, 42 U.S.C.A. § 1857 et seq., and was amended generally by Pub. L. No. 88–206, 77 Stat. 392 (Dec. 17, 1963), and later by Pub. L. No. 95–95, 91 Stat. 685 (Aug. 7, 1977). On enactment of Pub. L. No. 95–95, the Act was recodified as this chapter.

Federal Compliance with Pollution Control Standards

For provisions relating to the responsibility of the head of each Executive agency for compliance with applicable pollution control standards, see Ex. Ord. No. 12088, 43 Fed. Reg. 47707 (Oct. 13, 1978), as amended, set out as a note under section 4321 of this title.

Greenhouse Gases and Regulating Farms

Pub. L. No. 115–31, § 117, 131 Stat. 498 (May 5, 2017), provided: "Notwithstanding any other provision of law, none of the funds made available in this Act or any other Act may be used to promulgate or implement any regulation requiring the issuance of permits under title V of the Clean Air Act (42 U.S.C. 7661 et seq.) for carbon dioxide, nitrous oxide, water vapor, or methane emissions resulting from biological processes associated with livestock production." In addition, Section 118 of the same statute provided: "Notwithstanding any other provision of law, none of the funds made available in this or any other Act may be used to implement any provision in a rule, if that provision requires mandatory reporting of greenhouse gas emissions from manure management systems."

National Industrial Pollution Control Council

For provisions relating to the establishment of the National Industrial Pollution Control Council, see Ex. Ord. No. 11523, 35 Fed. Reg. 5993 (Apr. 9, 1970), set out as a note under section 4321 of this title.

Radon Assessment and Mitigation

Pub. L. No. 99–499, Title I, § 118(k), 100 Stat. 1659 (Oct. 17, 1986), as amended by Pub. L. No. 105–362, Title V, § 501(i), 112 Stat. 3284 (Nov. 10, 1998), provided that:

"**(1) National assessment of radon gas.**—No later than one year after the enactment of this Act [Oct. 17, 1986], the Administrator shall submit to the Congress a report which shall, to the extent possible—

"**(A)** identify the locations in the United States where radon is found in structures where people normally live or work, including educational institutions;

"**(B)** assess the levels of radon gas that are present in such structures;

"**(C)** determine the level of radon gas and radon daughters which poses a threat to human health and assess for each location identified under subparagraph (A) the extent of the threat to human health;

"**(D)** determine methods of reducing or eliminating the threat to human health of radon gas and radon daughters; and

"**(E)** include guidance and public information materials based on the findings or research of mitigating radon.

"**(2) Radon mitigation demonstration program.**—

"**(A) Demonstration program.**—The Administrator shall conduct a demonstration program to test methods and technologies of reducing or eliminating radon gas and radon daughters where it poses a threat to human health. The Administrator shall take into consideration any demonstration program underway in the Reading Prong of Pennsylvania, New Jersey, and New York and at other sites prior to enactment. The demonstration program under this section shall be conducted in the Reading Prong, and at such other sites as the Administrator considers appropriate.

"**(B) Liability.**—Liability, if any, for persons undertaking activities pursuant to the radon mitigation demonstration program authorized under this subsection shall be determined under principles of existing law.

"**(3) Construction of section.**—Nothing in this subsection shall be construed to authorize the Administrator to carry out any regulatory program or any activity other than research, development, and related reporting, information dissemination, and coordination activities specified in this subsection. Nothing in paragraph (1) or (2) shall be construed to limit the authority of the Administrator or of any other agency or instrumentality of the United States under any other authority of law."

[For termination, effective May 15, 2000, of reporting provisions pertaining to a demonstration program to test methods and technologies of reducing or eliminating radon gas and radon daughters where it poses a threat to human health, set out above, see Pub. L. No. 104–66, § 3003, as amended, set out as a note under 31 U.S.C.A. § 1113, and item 26 on page 163 of House Document No. 103–7.]

Impact on Small Communities

Section 810 of Pub. L. No. 101–549 provided that: "Before implementing a provision of this Act [Pub. L. No. 101–549, 104 Stat. 2399 (Nov. 15, 1990), popularly known as the Clean Air Act Amendments of 1990, for distribution of this Act to the Code, see Tables], the Administrator of the Environmental Protection Agency shall consult with the Small Communities Coordinator of the Environmental Protection Agency to determine the impact of such provision on small communities, including the estimated cost of compliance with such provision."

Spill Control Technology

Pub. L. No. 99–499, Title I, § 118(n), 100 Stat. 1660 (Oct. 17, 1986), provided that:

"**(1) Establishment of program.**—Within 180 days of enactment of this subsection [Oct. 17, 1986], the Secretary of the United States Department of Energy is directed to carry out a program of testing and evaluation of technologies which may be utilized in responding to liquefied gaseous and other hazardous substance spills at the Liquefied Gaseous Fuels Spill Test Facility that threaten public health or the environment.

"**(2) Technology transfer.**—In carrying out the program established under this subsection, the Secretary shall conduct a technology transfer program that, at a minimum—

"**(A)** documents and archives spill control technology;

"(B) investigates and analyzes significant hazardous spill incidents;

"(C) develops and provides generic emergency action plans;

"(D) documents and archives spill test results;

"(E) develops emergency action plans to respond to spills;

"(F) conducts training of spill response personnel; and

"(G) establishes safety standards for personnel engaged in spill response activities.

"(3) **Contracts and grants.**—The Secretary is directed to enter into contracts and grants with a nonprofit organization in Albany County, Wyoming, that is capable of providing the necessary technical support and which is involved in environmental activities related to such hazardous substance related emergencies.

"(4) **Use of site.**—The Secretary shall arrange for the use of the Liquefied Gaseous Fuels Spill Test Facility to carry out the provisions of this subsection."

Radon Gas and Indoor Air Quality Research

Pub. L. No. 99–499, Title IV, §§ 401 to 405, 100 Stat. 1758 (Oct. 17, 1986), provided that:

"Sec. 401. Short title.

"This title may be cited as the 'Radon Gas and Indoor Air Quality Research Act of 1986'.

"Sec. 402. Findings.

"The Congress finds that:

"(1) High levels of radon gas pose a serious health threat in structures in certain areas of the country.

"(2) Various scientific studies have suggested that exposure to radon, including exposure to naturally occurring radon and indoor air pollutants, poses a public health risk.

"(3) Existing Federal radon and indoor air pollutant research programs are fragmented and underfunded.

"(4) An adequate information base concerning exposure to radon and indoor air pollutants should be developed by the appropriate Federal agencies.

"Sec. 403. Radon gas and indoor air quality research program.

"(a) **Design of program.**—The Administrator of the Environmental Protection Agency shall establish a research program with respect to radon gas and indoor air quality. Such program shall be designed to—

"(1) gather data and information on all aspects of indoor air quality in order to contribute to the understanding of health problems associated with the existence of air pollutants in the indoor environment;

"(2) coordinate Federal, State, local, and private research and development efforts relating to the improvement of indoor air quality; and

"(3) assess appropriate Federal Government actions to mitigate the environmental and health risks associated with indoor air quality problems.

"(b) **Program requirements.**—The research program required under this section shall include—

"(1) research and development concerning the identification, characterization, and monitoring of the sources and levels of indoor air pollution, including radon, which includes research and development relating to—

"(A) the measurement of various pollutant concentrations and their strengths and sources,

"(B) high-risk building types, and

"(C) instruments for indoor air quality data collection;

"(2) research relating to the effects of indoor air pollution and radon on human health;

"(3) research and development relating to control technologies or other mitigation measures to prevent or abate indoor air pollution (including the development, evaluation, and testing of individual and generic control devices and systems);

"(4) demonstration of methods for reducing or eliminating indoor air pollution and radon, including sealing, venting, and other methods that the Administrator determines may be effective;

"(5) research, to be carried out in conjunction with the Secretary of Housing and Urban Development, for the purpose of developing—

"(A) methods for assessing the potential for radon contamination of new construction, including (but not limited to) consideration of the moisture content of soil, porosity of soil, and radon content of soil; and

"(B) design measures to avoid indoor air pollution; and

"(6) the dissemination of information to assure the public availability of the findings of the activities under this section.

"(c) **Advisory committees.**—The Administrator shall establish a committee comprised of individuals representing Federal agencies concerned with various aspects of indoor air quality and an advisory group comprised of individuals representing the States, the scientific community, industry, and public interest organizations to assist him in carrying out the research program for radon gas and indoor air quality.

"(d) **Implementation plan.**—Not later than 90 days after the enactment of this Act [Oct. 17, 1986], the Administrator shall submit to the Congress a plan for implementation of the research program under this section. Such plan shall also be submitted to the EPA Science Advisory Board, which shall, within a reasonable period of time, submit its comments on such plan to Congress.

"(e) **Report.**—Not later than 2 years after the enactment of this Act [Oct. 17, 1986], the Administrator shall submit to Congress a report respecting his activities under this section and making such recommendations as appropriate.

"Sec. 404. Construction of title.

"Nothing in this title shall be construed to authorize the Administrator to carry out any regulatory program or any activity other than research, development, and related reporting, information dissemination, and coordination activities specified in this title. Nothing in this title shall be construed to limit the authority of the Administrator or of any other agency or instrumentality of the United States under any other authority of law.

"Sec. 405. Authorizations.

"There are authorized to be appropriated to carry out the activities under this title and under section 118(k) of the Superfund Amendments and Reauthorization Act of 1986 (relating to radon gas assessment and demonstration program) not to exceed $5,000,000 for each of the fiscal years 1987, 1988, and 1989. Of such sums appropriated in fiscal years 1987 and 1988, two-fifths shall be reserved for the implementation of section 118(k)(2)."

List of Chemical Contaminants from Environmental Pollution Found in Human Tissue

Pub. L. No. 95–95, Title IV, § 403(c), 91 Stat. 792 (Aug. 7, 1977), provided that, not later than twelve months after Aug. 7, 1977, the Administrator of the Environmental Protection Agency was to publish throughout the United States a list of all known chemical contaminants resulting from environmental pollution which had been found in human tissue including blood, urine, breast milk, and all other human tissue, and that, not later than eighteen months after Aug. 7, 1977, the Administrator was to publish in the same manner an explanation of what was known about the manner in which the chemicals had entered the environment and thereafter human tissue, and, further, that the Administrator, in consultation with National Institutes of Health, the National Center for Health Statistics, and the National Center for Health Services Research and Development, if feasible, was to conduct an epidemiological study to demonstrate the relationship between levels of chemicals in the environment and in human tissue.

Railroad Emission Study

Pub. L. No. 95–95, Title IV, § 404, 91 Stat. 793 (Aug. 7, 1977), as amended by H.Res. 549, Mar. 25, 1980, directed the Administrator of the Environmental Protection Agency to conduct a study and investigation of emissions of air pollutants from railroad locomotives, locomotive engines, and secondary power sources on railroad rolling stock in order to determine the extent to which such emissions affect air quality in air quality control regions throughout the United States, the technological feasibility and the current state of technology for controlling such emissions, and the status and effect of current and proposed State and local regulations affecting such emissions, and, within one hundred and eighty days after commencing such study and investigation, to submit a report of such study and investigation, together with recommendations for appropriate legislation, to the Senate Committee on Environment and Public Works and the House Committee on Energy and Commerce.

[Any reference in any provision of law enacted before Jan. 4, 1995, to the Committee on Energy and Commerce of the House of Representatives treated as referring to the Committee on Commerce of the House of Representatives, except that any reference in any provision of law enacted before Jan. 4, 1995, to the Committee on Energy and Commerce of the House of Representatives treated as referring to the Committee on Agriculture of the House of Representatives, in the case of a provision of law relating to inspection of seafood or seafood products, the Committee on Banking and Financial Services of the House of Representatives, in the case of a provision of law relating to bank capital markets activities generally or to depository institution securities activities generally, and the Committee on Transportation and Infrastructure of the House of Representatives, in the case of a provision of law relating to railroads, railway labor, or railroad retirement and unemployment (except revenue measures related thereto), see section 1(a)(4) and (c)(1) of Pub. L. No. 104–14, set out as a note preceding section 21 of Title 2, The Congress.]

Study and Report Concerning Economic Approaches to Controlling Air Pollution

Pub. L. No. 95–95, Title IV, § 405, 91 Stat. 794 (Aug. 7, 1977), directed the Administrator of the Environmental Protection Agency, in conjunction with the Council of Economic Advisors, to undertake a study and assessment of economic measures for the control of air pollution which could strengthen the effectiveness of existing methods of controlling air pollution, provide incentives to abate air pollution to a greater degree than was required by existing provisions of the Clean Air Act, and serve as the primary incentive for controlling air pollution problems not addressed by any provision of the Clean Air Act, and, not later than two years after Aug. 7, 1977, to conclude the study and assessment and submit a report containing the results thereof to the President and to the Congress.

Study of Odors and Odorous Emissions

Pub. L. No. 95–95, Title IV, § 403(b), 91 Stat. 792 (Aug. 7, 1977), provided that the Administrator of the Environmental Protection Agency conduct a study and report to the Congress not later than Jan. 1, 1979, on the effects on public health and welfare of odors or odorous emissions, the sources of such emissions, the technology or other measures available for control of such emissions and the costs of such technology or measures, and the costs and benefits of alternative measures or strategies to abate such emissions.

Study on Regional Air Quality

Pub. L. No. 95–95, Title IV, § 403(d), 91 Stat. 793 (Aug. 7, 1977), directed the Administrator of the Environmental Protection Agency to conduct a study of air quality in various areas throughout the country including the gulf coast region, with such study to include analysis of liquid and solid aerosols and other fine particulate matter and the contribution of such substances to visibility and public health problems in such areas."

§ 7402. Cooperative activities

[CAA § 102]

(a) Interstate cooperation; uniform State laws; State compacts

The Administrator shall encourage cooperative activities by the States and local governments for the prevention and control of air pollution; encourage the enactment of improved and, so far as practicable in the light of varying conditions and needs, uniform State and local laws relating to the prevention and control of air pollution; and encourage the making of agreements and compacts between States for the prevention and control of air pollution.

(b) Federal cooperation

The Administrator shall cooperate with and encourage cooperative activities by all Federal departments and agencies having functions relating to the prevention and control of air pollution, so as to assure the utilization in the Federal air pollution control program of all appropriate and available facilities and resources within the Federal Government.

(c) Consent of Congress to compacts

The consent of the Congress is hereby given to two or more States to negotiate and enter into agreements or compacts, not in conflict with any law or treaty of the United States, for (1) cooperative effort and mutual assistance for the prevention and control of air pollution and the enforcement of their respective laws relating thereto, and (2) the establishment of such agencies, joint or otherwise, as they may deem desirable for making effective such agreements or compacts. No such agreement or compact shall be binding or obligatory upon any State a party thereto unless and until it has been approved by Congress. It is the intent of Congress that no agreement or compact entered into between States after November 21, 1967, which relates to the control and abatement of air pollution in an air quality control region, shall provide for participation by a State which is not included (in whole or in part) in such air quality control region.

(July 14, 1955, c. 360, Title I, § 102, formerly § 2, as added by Pub. L. No. 88–206, § 1, 77 Stat. 393 (Dec. 17, 1963); and renumbered § 102 by Pub. L. No. 89–272, Title I, § 101(3), 79 Stat. 992 (Oct. 20, 1965); and amended by Pub. L. No. 90–148, § 2, 81 Stat. 485 (Nov. 21, 1967); Pub. L. No. 91–604, § 15(c)(2), 84 Stat. 1713 (Dec. 31, 1970).)

HISTORICAL AND STATUTORY NOTES

Codifications

Section was formerly codified as section 1857a of this title.

Prior Provisions

Provisions similar to those comprising the first clause of subsec. (a) of this section were contained in subsec. (b)(1) of a prior section 1857a of this title, Act of July 14, 1955, c. 360, § 2, 69 Stat. 322, prior to the general amendment of this chapter by Pub. L. No. 88–206.

§ 7403. Research, investigation, training, and other activities

[CAA § 103]

(a) Research and development program for prevention and control of air pollution

The Administrator shall establish a national research and development program for the prevention and control of air pollution and as part of such program shall—

(1) conduct, and promote the coordination and acceleration of, research, investigations, experiments, demonstrations, surveys, and studies relating to the causes, effects (including health and welfare effects), extent, prevention, and control of air pollution;

(2) encourage, cooperate with, and render technical services and provide financial assistance to air pollution control agencies and other appropriate public or private agencies, institutions, and organizations, and individuals in the conduct of such activities;

(3) conduct investigations and research and make surveys concerning any specific problem of air pollution in cooperation with any air pollution control agency with a view to recommending a solution of such problem, if he is requested to do so by such agency or if, in his judgment, such problem may affect any community or communities in a State other than that in which the source of the matter causing or contributing to the pollution is located;

(4) establish technical advisory committees composed of recognized experts in various aspects of air pollution to assist in the examination and evaluation of research progress and proposals and to avoid duplication of research; and

(5) conduct and promote coordination and acceleration of training for individuals relating to the causes, effects, extent, prevention, and control of air pollution.

(b) Authorized activities of Administrator in establishing research and development program

In carrying out the provisions of the preceding subsection the Administrator is authorized to—

(1) collect and make available, through publications and other appropriate means, the results of and other information, including appropriate recommendations by him in connection therewith, pertaining to such research and other activities;

(2) cooperate with other Federal departments and agencies, with air pollution control agencies, with other public and private agencies, institutions, and organizations, and with any industries involved, in the preparation and conduct of such research and other activities;

(3) make grants to air pollution control agencies, to other public or nonprofit private agencies, institutions, and organizations, and to individuals, for purposes stated in subsection (a)(1) of this section;

(4) contract with public or private agencies, institutions, and organizations, and with individuals, without regard to section 3324(a) and (b) of Title 31 and section 6101 of Title 41;

(5) establish and maintain research fellowships, in the Environmental Protection Agency and at public or nonprofit private educational institutions or research organizations;

(6) collect and disseminate, in cooperation with other Federal departments and agencies, and with other public or private agencies, institutions, and organizations having related responsibilities, basic data on chemical, physical, and biological effects of varying air quality and other information pertaining to air pollution and the prevention and control thereof;

(7) develop effective and practical processes, methods, and prototype devices for the prevention or control of air pollution; and

(8) construct facilities, provide equipment, and employ staff as necessary to carry out this chapter.

In carrying out the provisions of subsection (a) of this section, the Administrator shall provide training for, and make training grants to, personnel of air pollution control agencies and other persons with suitable qualifications and make grants to such agencies, to other public or nonprofit private agencies, institutions, and organizations for the purposes stated in subsection (a)(5) of this section. Reasonable fees may be charged for such training provided to persons other than personnel of air pollution control agencies but such training shall be provided to such personnel of air pollution control agencies without charge.

(c) Air pollutant monitoring, analysis, modeling, and inventory research

In carrying out subsection (a) of this section, the Administrator shall conduct a program of research, testing, and development of methods for sampling, measurement, monitoring, analysis, and modeling of air pollutants. Such program shall include the following elements:

(1) Consideration of individual, as well as complex mixtures of, air pollutants and their chemical transformations in the atmosphere.

(2) Establishment of a national network to monitor, collect, and compile data with quantification of certainty in the status and trends of air emissions, deposition, air quality, surface water quality, forest condition, and visibility impairment, and to ensure the comparability of air quality data collected in different States and obtained from different nations.

(3) Development of improved methods and technologies for sampling, measurement, monitoring, analysis, and modeling to increase understanding of the sources of ozone precursors[1], ozone formation, ozone transport, regional influences on urban ozone, regional ozone trends, and interactions of ozone with other pollutants. Emphasis shall be placed on those techniques which—

(A) improve the ability to inventory emissions of volatile organic compounds and nitrogen oxides that contribute to urban air pollution, including anthropogenic and natural sources;

(B) improve the understanding of the mechanism through which anthropogenic and biogenic volatile organic compounds react to form ozone and other oxidants; and

(C) improve the ability to identify and evaluate region-specific prevention and control options for ozone pollution.

(4) Submission of periodic reports to the Congress, not less than once every 5 years, which evaluate and assess the effectiveness of air pollution control regulations and programs using monitoring and modeling data obtained pursuant to this subsection.

(d) Environmental health effects research

(1) The Administrator, in consultation with the Secretary of Health and Human Services, shall conduct a research program on the short-term and long-term effects of air pollutants, including wood smoke, on human health. In conducting such research program the Administrator—

(A) shall conduct studies, including epidemiological, clinical, and laboratory and field studies, as necessary to identify and evaluate exposure to and effects of air pollutants on human health;

(B) may utilize, on a reimbursable basis, the facilities of existing Federal scientific laboratories and research centers; and

(C) shall consult with other Federal agencies to ensure that similar research being conducted in other agencies is coordinated to avoid duplication.

(2) In conducting the research program under this subsection, the Administrator shall develop methods and techniques necessary to identify and assess the risks to human health from both routine and accidental exposures to individual air pollutants and combinations thereof. Such research program shall include the following elements:

(A) The creation of an Interagency Task Force to coordinate such program. The Task Force shall include representatives of the National Institute for Environmental Health Sciences, the Environmental Protection Agency, the Agency for Toxic Substances and Disease Registry, the National Toxicology Program, the National Institute of Standards and Technology, the National Science Foundation, the Surgeon General, and the Department of Energy. This Interagency Task Force shall be chaired by a representative of the Environmental Protection Agency and shall convene its first meeting within 60 days after November 15, 1990.

(B) An evaluation, within 12 months after November 15, 1990, of each of the hazardous air pollutants listed under section 7412(b) of this title, to decide, on the basis of available information, their relative priority for preparation of environmental health assessments pursuant to subparagraph (C). The evaluation shall be based on reasonably anticipated toxicity to humans and exposure factors such as frequency of occurrence as an air pollutant and volume of emissions in populated areas. Such evaluation shall be reviewed by the Interagency Task Force established pursuant to subparagraph (A).

(C) Preparation of environmental health assessments for each of the hazardous air pollutants referred to in subparagraph (B), beginning 6 months after the first meeting of the Interagency Task Force and to be completed within 96 months thereafter. No fewer than 24 assessments shall be completed and published annually. The assessments shall be prepared in accordance with guidelines developed by the Administrator in consultation with the Interagency Task Force and the Science Advisory Board of the Environmental Protection Agency. Each such assessment shall include—

(i) an examination, summary, and evaluation of available toxicological and epidemiological information for the pollutant to ascertain the levels of human exposure which pose a significant threat to human health and the associated acute, subacute, and chronic adverse health effects;

(ii) a determination of gaps in available information related to human health effects and exposure levels; and

(iii) where appropriate, an identification of additional activities, including toxicological and inhalation testing, needed to identify the types or levels of exposure which may present significant risk of adverse health effects in humans.

(e) Ecosystem research

In carrying out subsection (a) of this section, the Administrator, in cooperation, where appropriate, with the Under Secretary of Commerce for Oceans and Atmosphere, the Director of the Fish and Wildlife Service, and the Secretary of Agriculture, shall conduct a research program to improve understanding of the short-term and long-term causes, effects, and trends of ecosystems damage from air pollutants on ecosystems. Such program shall include the following elements:

(1) Identification of regionally representative and critical ecosystems for research.

(2) Evaluation of risks to ecosystems exposed to air pollutants, including characterization of the causes and effects of chronic and episodic exposures to air pollutants and determination of the reversibility of those effects.

(3) Development of improved atmospheric dispersion models and monitoring systems and networks for evaluating and quantifying exposure to and effects of multiple environmental stresses associated with air pollution.

(4) Evaluation of the effects of air pollution on water quality, including assessments of the short-term and long-term ecological effects of acid deposition and other atmospherically derived pollutants on surface water (including wetlands and estuaries) and groundwater.

(5) Evaluation of the effects of air pollution on forests, materials, crops, biological diversity, soils, and other terrestrial and aquatic systems exposed to air pollutants.

(6) Estimation of the associated economic costs of ecological damage which have occurred as a result of exposure to air pollutants.

Consistent with the purpose of this program, the Administrator may use the estuarine research reserves established pursuant to section 1461 of Title 16 to carry out this research.

(f) Liquefied Gaseous Fuels Spill Test Facility

(1) The Administrator, in consultation with the Secretary of Energy and the Federal Coordinating Council for Science, Engineering, and Technology, shall oversee an experimental and analytical research effort, with the experimental research to be carried out at the Liquefied Gaseous Fuels Spill Test Facility. In consultation with the Secretary of Energy, the Administrator shall develop a list of chemicals and a schedule for field testing at the Facility. Analysis of a minimum of 10 chemicals per year shall be carried out, with the selection of a minimum of 2 chemicals for field testing each year. Highest priority shall be given to those chemicals that would present the greatest potential risk to human health as a result of an accidental release—

(A) from a fixed site; or

(B) related to the transport of such chemicals.

(2) The purpose of such research shall be to—

(A) develop improved predictive models for atmospheric dispersion which at a minimum—

(i) describe dense gas releases in complex terrain including man-made structures or obstacles with variable winds;

(ii) improve understanding of the effects of turbulence on dispersion patterns; and

(iii) consider realistic behavior of aerosols by including physicochemical reactions with water vapor, ground deposition, and removal by water spray;

(B) evaluate existing and future atmospheric dispersion models by—

(i) the development of a rigorous, standardized methodology for dense gas models; and

(ii) the application of such methodology to current dense gas dispersion models using data generated from field experiments; and

(C) evaluate the effectiveness of hazard mitigation and emergency response technology for fixed site and transportation related accidental releases of toxic chemicals.

Models pertaining to accidental release shall be evaluated and improved periodically for their utility in planning and implementing evacuation procedures and other mitigative strategies designed to minimize human exposure to hazardous air pollutants released accidentally.

(3) The Secretary of Energy shall make available to interested persons (including other Federal agencies and businesses) the use of the Liquefied Gaseous Fuels Spill Test Facility to conduct research and other activities in connection with the activities described in this subsection.

(g) Pollution prevention and emissions control

(1) In General.—In carrying out subsection (a) of this section, the Administrator shall conduct a basic engineering research and technology program to develop, evaluate, and demonstrate nonregulatory strategies and technologies for air pollution prevention.

(2) Participation Requirement.—Such strategies and technologies described in paragraph (1) shall be development with priority on those pollutants which pose a significant risk to human health and the environment, and with opportunities for participation by industry, public interest groups, scientists, States, institutions of higher education, and other interested persons in the development of such strategies and technologies.

(3) Program Inclusions.—The program under this subsection shall include the following elements:

(A) Improvements in nonregulatory strategies and technologies for preventing or reducing multiple air pollutants, including sulfur oxides, nitrogen oxides, heavy metals, PM-10 (particulate matter), carbon monoxide, and carbon dioxide, from stationary sources, including fossil fuel power plants. Such strategies and technologies shall include improvements in the relative cost effectiveness and long-range implications of various air pollutant reduction and nonregulatory control strategies such as energy conservation, including end-use efficiency, and fuel-switching to cleaner fuels. Such strategies and technologies shall be considered for existing and new facilities.

(B) Improvements in nonregulatory strategies and technologies for reducing air emissions from area sources.

(C) Improvements in nonregulatory strategies and technologies for preventing, detecting, and correcting accidental releases of hazardous air pollutants.

(D) Improvements in nonregulatory strategies and technologies that dispose of tires in ways that avoid adverse air quality impacts.

(4) Effect of Subsection.—Nothing in this subsection shall be construed to authorize the imposition on any person of air pollution control requirements.

(5) Coordination and Avoidance of Duplication.—The Administrator shall consult with other appropriate Federal agencies to ensure coordination and to avoid duplication of activities authorized under this subsection.

(6) Certain Carbon Dioxide Activities.—

(A) In General.—In carrying out paragraph (3)(A) with respect to carbon dioxide, the Administrator—

(i) is authorized to carry out the activities described in subparagraph (B); and

(ii) shall carry out the activities described in subparagraph (C).

(B) Direct Air Capture Research.—

(i) Definitions.—In this subparagraph:

(I) Board.—The term 'Board' means the Direct Air Capture Technology Advisory Board established by clause (iii)(I).

(II) Dilute.—The term 'dilute' means a concentration of less than 1 percent by volume.

(III) Direct Air Capture.—

(aa) In General.—The term 'direct air capture', with respect to a facility, technology, or system, means that the facility, technology, or system uses carbon capture equipment to capture carbon dioxide directly from the air.

(bb) Exclusion.—The term 'direct air capture' does not include any facility, technology, or system that captures carbon dioxide—

(AA) that is deliberately released from a naturally occurring subsurface spring; or

(BB) using natural photosynthesis.

(IV) Intellectual Property.—The term 'intellectual property' means—

(aa) an invention that is patentable under title 35, United States Code; and

(bb) any patent on an invention described in item (aa).

(ii) Technology Prizes.—

(I) In General.—Not later than 1 year after the date of enactment of the Utilizing Significant Emissions with Innovative Technologies Act, the Administrator, in consultation with the Secretary of Energy, is authorized to establish a program to provide financial awards on a competitive basis for direct air capture from media in which the concentration of carbon dioxide is dilute.

(II) Duties.—In carrying out this clause, the Administrator shall—

(aa) subject to subclause (III), develop specific requirements for—

(AA) the competition process; and

(BB) the demonstration of performance of approved projects;

(bb) offer financial awards for a project designed—

(AA) to the maximum extent practicable, to capture more than 10,000 tons of carbon dioxide per year;

(BB) to operate in a manner that would be commercially viable in the foreseeable future (as determined by the Board); and

(CC) to improve the technologies or information systems that enable monitoring and verification methods for direct air capture projects; and

(cc) to the maximum extent practicable, make financial awards to geographically diverse projects, including at least—

(AA) 1 project in a coastal State; and

(BB) 1 project in a rural State.

(III) Public Participation.—In carrying out subclause (II)(aa), the Administrator shall—

(aa) provide notice of and, for a period of not less than 60 days, an opportunity for public comment on, any draft or proposed version of the requirements described in subclause (II)(aa); and

(bb) take into account public comments received in developing the final version of those requirements.

(iii) Direct Air Capture Technology Advisory Board.—

(I) Establishment.—The Administrator may establish an advisory board to be known as the 'Direct Air Capture Technology Advisory Board'.

(II) Composition.—The Board, on the establishment of the Board, shall be composed of 9 members appointed by the Administrator, who shall provide expertise in—

(aa) climate science;

(bb) physics;

(cc) chemistry;

(dd) biology;

(ee) engineering;

(ff) economics;

(gg) business management; and

(hh) such other disciplines as the Administrator determines to be necessary to achieve the purposes of this subparagraph.

(III) Term; Vacancies.—

(aa) Term.—A member of the Board shall serve for a term of 6 years.

(bb) Vacancies.—A vacancy on the Board—

(AA) shall not affect the powers of the Board; and

(BB) shall be filled in the same manner as the original appointment was made.

(IV) Initial Meeting.—Not later than 30 days after the date on which all members of the Board have been appointed, the Board shall hold the initial meeting of the Board.

(V) Meetings.—The Board shall meet at the call of the Chairperson or on the request of the Administrator.

(VI) Quorum.—A majority of the members of the Board shall constitute a quorum, but a lesser number of members may hold hearings.

(VII) Chairperson and Vice Chairperson.—The Board shall select a Chairperson and Vice Chairperson from among the members of the Board.

(VIII) Compensation.—Each member of the Board may be compensated at not to exceed the daily equivalent of the annual rate of basic pay in effect for a position at level V of the Executive Schedule under section 5316 of title 5, United States Code, for each day during which the member is engaged in the actual performance of the duties of the Board.

(IX) Duties.—The Board shall—

(aa) advise the Administrator on carrying out the duties of the Administrator under this subparagraph; and

(bb) provide other assistance and advice as requested by the Administrator.

(iv) Intellectual Property.—

(I) In General.—As a condition of receiving a financial award under this subparagraph, an applicant shall agree to vest the intellectual property of the applicant derived from the technology in 1 or more entities that are incorporated in the United States.

(II) Reservation of License.—The United States—

(aa) may reserve a nonexclusive, nontransferable, irrevocable, paid-up license, to have practiced for or on behalf of the United States, in connection with any intellectual property described in subclause (I); but

(bb) shall not, in the exercise of a license reserved under item (aa), publicly disclose proprietary information relating to the license.

(III) Transfer of Title.—Title to any intellectual property described in subclause (I) shall not be transferred or passed, except to an entity that is incorporated in the United States, until the expiration of the first patent obtained in connection with the intellectual property.

(v) Authorization of Appropriations.—There is authorized to be appropriated to carry out this subparagraph $35,000,000, to remain available until expended.

(vi) Termination of Authority.—Notwithstanding section 14 of the Federal Advisory Committee Act (5 U.S.C. App.), the Board and all authority provided under this subparagraph shall terminate not later than 12 years after the date of enactment of the Utilizing Significant Emissions with Innovative Technologies Act.

(C) Deep Saline Formation Report.—

(i) Defiition of Deep Saline Formation.—

(I) In General.—In this subparagraph, the term 'deep saline formation' means a formation of subsurface geographically extensive sedimentary rock layers saturated with waters or brines that have a high total dissolved solids content and that are below the depth where carbon dioxide can exist in the formation as a supercritical fluid.

(II) Clarification.—In this subparagraph, the term 'deep saline formation' does not include oil and gas reservoirs.

(ii) Report.—In consultation with the Secretary of Energy, and, as appropriate, with the head of any other relevant Federal agency and relevant stakeholders, not later than 1 year after the date of enactment of the Utilizing Significant Emissions with Innovative Technologies Act, the Administrator shall prepare, submit to Congress, and make publicly available a report that includes—

(I) a comprehensive identification of potential risks and benefits to project developers associated with increased storage of carbon dioxide captured from stationary sources in deep saline formations, using existing research;

(II) recommendations for managing the potential risks identified under subclause (I), including potential risks unique to public land; and

(III) recommendations for Federal legislation or other policy changes to mitigate any potential risks identified under subclause (I).

(D) GAO Report.—Not later than 5 years after the date of enactment of the Utilizing Significant Emissions with Innovative Technologies Act, the Comptroller General of the United States shall submit to Congress a report that—

(i) identifies all Federal grant programs in which a purpose of a grant under the program is to perform research on carbon capture and utilization technologies, including direct air capture technologies; and

(ii) examines the extent to which the Federal grant programs identified pursuant to clause (i) overlap or are duplicative.

(h) NIEHS studies

(1) The Director of the National Institute of Environmental Health Sciences may conduct a program of basic research to identify, characterize, and quantify risks to human health from air pollutants. Such research shall be conducted primarily through a combination of university and medical school-based grants, as well as through intramural studies and contracts.

(2) The Director of the National Institute of Environmental Health Sciences shall conduct a program for the education and training of physicians in environmental health.

(3) The Director shall assure that such programs shall not conflict with research undertaken by the Administrator.

(4) There are authorized to be appropriated to the National Institute of Environmental Health Sciences such sums as may be necessary to carry out the purposes of this subsection.

(i) Coordination of research

The Administrator shall develop and implement a plan for identifying areas in which activities authorized under this section can be carried out in conjunction with other Federal ecological and air pollution research efforts. The plan, which shall be submitted to Congress within 6 months after November 15, 1990, shall include—

(1) an assessment of ambient monitoring stations and networks to determine cost effective ways to expand monitoring capabilities in both urban and rural environments;

(2) a consideration of the extent of the feasibility and scientific value of conducting the research program under subsection (e) of this section to include consideration of the effects of atmospheric processes and air pollution effects; and

(3) a methodology for evaluating and ranking pollution prevention technologies, such as those developed under subsection (g) of this section, in terms of their ability to reduce cost effectively the emissions of air pollutants and other airborne chemicals of concern.

Not later than 2 years after November 15, 1990, and every 4 years thereafter, the Administrator shall report to Congress on the progress made in implementing the plan developed under this subsection, and shall include in such report any revisions of the plan.

(j) Continuation of national acid precipitation assessment program

(1) The acid precipitation research program set forth in the Acid Precipitation Act of 1980 [42 U.S.C.A. § 8901 et seq.] shall be continued with modifications pursuant to this subsection.

(2) The Acid Precipitation Task Force shall consist of the Administrator of the Environmental Protection Agency, the Secretary of Energy, the Secretary of the Interior, the Secretary of Agriculture, the Administrator of the National Oceanic and Atmospheric Administration, the Administrator of the National Aeronautics and Space Administration, and such additional members as the President may select. The President shall appoint a chairman for the Task Force from among its members within 30 days after November 15, 1990.

(3) The responsibilities of the Task Force shall include the following:

(A) Review of the status of research activities conducted to date under the comprehensive research plan developed pursuant to the Acid Precipitation Act of 1980 [42 U.S.C.A. § 8901 et seq.], and development of a revised plan that identifies significant research gaps and establishes a coordinated program to address current and future research priorities. A draft of the revised plan shall be submitted by the Task Force to Congress within 6 months after November 15, 1990. The plan shall be available for public comment during the 60 day period after its submission, and a final plan shall be submitted by the President to the Congress within 45 days after the close of the comment period.

(B) Coordination with participating Federal agencies, augmenting the agencies' research and monitoring efforts and sponsoring additional research in the scientific community as necessary to ensure the availability and quality of data and methodologies needed to evaluate the status and effectiveness of the acid deposition control program. Such research and monitoring efforts shall include, but not be limited to—

(i) continuous monitoring of emissions of precursors of acid deposition;

(ii) maintenance, upgrading, and application of models, such as the Regional Acid Deposition Model, that describe the interactions of emissions with the atmosphere, and models that describe the response of ecosystems to acid deposition; and

(iii) analysis of the costs, benefits, and effectiveness of the acid deposition control program.

(C) Publication and maintenance of a National Acid Lakes Registry that tracks the condition and change over time of a statistically representative sample of lakes in regions that are known to be sensitive to surface water acidification.

(D) Submission every two years of a unified budget recommendation to the President for activities of the Federal Government in connection with the research program described in this subsection.

(E) Beginning in 1992 and biennially thereafter, submission of a report to Congress describing the results of its investigations and analyses. The reporting of technical information about acid deposition shall be provided in a format that facilitates communication with policymakers and the public. The report shall include—

(i) actual and projected emissions and acid deposition trends;

(ii) average ambient concentrations of acid deposition percursors[1] and their transformation products;

(iii) the status of ecosystems (including forests and surface waters), materials, and visibility affected by acid deposition;

(iv) the causes and effects of such deposition, including changes in surface water quality and forest and soil conditions;

(v) the occurrence and effects of episodic acidification, particularly with respect to high elevation watersheds; and

(vi) the confidence level associated with each conclusion to aid policymakers in use of the information.

(F) Beginning in 1996, and every 4 years thereafter, the report under subparagraph (E) shall include—

(i) the reduction in deposition rates that must be achieved in order to prevent adverse ecological effects; and

(ii) the costs and benefits of the acid deposition control program created by subchapter IV-A of this chapter.

(k) Air pollution conferences

If, in the judgment of the Administrator, an air pollution problem of substantial significance may result from discharge or discharges into the atmosphere, the Administrator may call a conference concerning this potential air pollution problem to be held in or near one or more of the places where such discharge or discharges are occurring or will occur. All interested persons shall be given an opportunity to be heard at such conference, either orally or in writing, and shall be permitted to appear in person or by representative in accordance with procedures prescribed by the Administrator. If the Administrator finds, on the basis of the evidence presented at such conference, that the discharge or discharges if permitted to take place or continue are likely to cause or contribute to air pollution subject to abatement under this part, the Administrator shall send such findings, together with recommendations concerning the measures which the Administrator finds reasonable and suitable to prevent such pollution, to the person or persons whose actions will result in the discharge or discharges involved; to air pollution agencies of the State or States and of the municipality or municipalities where such discharge or discharges will originate; and to the interstate air pollution control agency, if any, in the jurisdictional area of which any such municipality is located. Such findings and recommendations shall be advisory only, but shall be admitted together with the record of the conference, as part of the proceedings under subsections (b), (c), (d), (e), and (f) of section 7408 of this title.

(July 14, 1955, c. 360, Title I, § 103, formerly § 3, as added by Pub. L. No. 88–206, § 1, 77 Stat. 394 (Dec. 17, 1963); and renumbered § 103 and amended by Pub. L. No. 89–272, Title I, §§ 101(3), 103, 79 Stat. 992, 996 (Oct. 20, 1965); and amended by Pub. L. No. 90–148, § 2, 81 Stat. 486 (Nov. 21, 1967); Pub. L. No. 91–604, §§ 2(a), 4(b)(2), 15(a)(2), (c)(2), 84 Stat. 1676, 1689, 1710, 1713 (Dec. 31, 1970); Pub. L. No. 95–95, Title I, § 101(a), (b), 91 Stat. 686, 687 (Aug. 7, 1977); Pub. L. No. 101–549, Title IX, § 901(a) to (c), 104 Stat. 2700 to 2703 (Nov. 15, 1990); Pub. L. No 116–260, § 102(b), 134 Stat. 2243–47 (Dec. 27, 2020).)

[1] So in original. Probably should be "precursors".

HISTORICAL AND STATUTORY NOTES

References in Text

The Acid Precipitation Act of 1980, referred to in subsec. (j)(1) and (3)(A), is Title VII of Pub. L. No. 96–294, 94 Stat. 770 (June 30, 1980), which is codified generally as chapter 97 (section 8901 et seq.) of this title. For complete classification of this Act to the Code, see Short Title of 1980 Acts note set out under 42 U.S.C.A. § 8901 and Tables.

Codifications

Section was formerly codified as 42 U.S.C.A. § 1857b.

In subsec. (b)(4), "section 3324(a) and (b) of Title 31 and section 6101 of Title 41" substituted for "sections 3648 and 3709 of the Revised Statutes (31 U.S.C. 529; 41 U.S.C. 5)" on authority of Pub. L. No. 97–258, § 4(b), 96 Stat. 1067 (Sept. 13, 1982), which Act enacted Title 31, Money and Finance, and Pub. L. No. 111–350, § 6(c), Jan. 4, 2011, 124 Stat. 3854, which Act enacted Title 41, Public Contracts.

Short Title.

2020 Amendments. Section 102(a) of Pub. L. No. 116–260, 134 Stat. 2243 (Dec. 27, 2020), provided that "[t]his section may be cited as the 'Utilizing Significant Emissions with Innovative Technologies Act' or the "USE IT Act.' "

Effective and Applicability Provisions

1990 Acts. Amendment by Pub. L. No. 101–549 effective Nov. 15, 1990, except as otherwise provided, see section 711(b) of Pub. L. No. 101–549, set out as a note under 42 U.S.C.A. § 7401.

1977 Acts. Amendment by Pub. L. No. 95–95 effective Aug. 7, 1977, except as otherwise expressly provided, see section 406(d) of Pub. L. No. 95–95, set out as a note under 42 U.S.C.A. § 7401.

Savings Provisions

Suits, actions or proceedings commenced under this chapter as in effect prior to Nov. 15, 1990, not to abate by reason of the taking effect of amendments by Pub. L. No. 101–549, except as otherwise provided for, see section 711(a) of Pub. L. No. 101–549, set out as a note under 42 U.S.C.A. § 7401.

Prior Provisions

Provisions similar to those comprising subsec. (a)(3) of this section were contained in subsec. (a) of a prior section 1857b of this title, Act of July 14, 1955, c. 360, § 3, 69 Stat. 322, as amended Oct. 9, 1962, Pub. L. No. 87–761, § 2, 76 Stat. 760, prior to the general amendment of this chapter by Pub. L. No. 88–206.

Provisions similar to those comprising this section were contained in prior sections 1857a to 1857d of this title, Act of July 14, 1955, c. 360, §§ 2 to 5, 69 Stat. 322 (section 1857b as amended Oct. 9, 1962, Pub. L. No. 87–761, § 2, 76 Stat. 760; section 1857d as amended Sept. 22, 1959, Pub. L. No. 86–365, § 1, 73 Stat. 646 and Oct. 9, 1962, Pub. L. No. 87–761, § 1, 76 Stat. 760), prior to the general amendment of this chapter by Pub. L. No. 88–206.

Termination of Reporting Requirements

For termination, effective May 15, 2000, of provisions in subsec. (i) of this section requiring quadrennial reports to Congress and of reporting provisions in subsec. (j)(3)(E) and (F) of this section, see Pub. L. No. 104–66, § 3003, as amended, set out as a note under 31 U.S.C.A. § 1113 and the 7th and 8th items on page 163 of House Document No. 103–7.

Pilot Design Program

Pub. L. No. 106–246, Div. B, Title II, § 2603, 114 Stat. 558 (July 13, 2000), provided that:

"(a) The Administrator of the Environmental Protection Agency shall make a grant for the purpose of carrying out the first year of a 2-year program to implement in five metropolitan areas pilot design programs developed under section 365(a)(2) of the Department of Transportation and Related Agencies Appropriations Act, 2000 (113 Stat. 1028–1029) [Pub. L. No. 106–69, Title III, § 365(a)(2), 113 Stat. 1028 (Oct. 9, 1999), which is not codified into the Code].

"(b) The Administrator shall ensure that each pilot design program is implemented in accordance with recommendations developed by the National Telecommuting and Air Quality Steering Committee, in consultation with the local design teams.

"(c) Grants received under subsection (a) may be used for—

"(1) protocol development in the five metropolitan areas;

"(2) marketing of the telecommute, emissions reduction, pollution credits strategy and recruitment of participating employers; and

"(3) data gathering on emissions reductions.

"(d) In addition to the grant under subsection (a), for the purpose of carrying out the second year of the 2-year program referred to in subsection (a), the administrator shall—

"(1) make a grant of $750,000 to the National Environmental Policy Institute (a nonprofit private entity incorporated under the laws of and located in the District of Columbia); and

"(2) make grants totaling $1,250,000 to local agencies within the five metropolitan areas referred to in subsection (a).

"(e) Not later than 360 days from first day of the second year of the 2-year program referred to in subsection (a), the Administrator shall transmit to Congress a report on the results of the program.

"(f) The Administrator shall carry out this section in collaboration with the Secretary of Transportation.

"(g) There is appropriated to the Department of Transportation, 'Office of the Assistant Secretary for Policy', $2,000,000 to carry out this section . Such amounts shall be transferred to and administered by the Environmental Protection Agency and shall remain available until expended: *Provided,* That the entire amount is designated by the Congress as an emergency requirement pursuant to section 251(b)(2)(A) of the Balanced Budget and Emergency Deficit Control Act of 1985 [2 U.S.C.A. § 901(b)(2)(A)], as amended: *Provided further,* That the entire amount shall be available only to the extent an official budget request for a specific dollar amount, that includes designation of the entire amount of the request as an emergency requirement as defined by such Act, is transmitted by the President to the Congress."

National Acid Lakes Registry

Section 405 of Pub. L. No. 101–549 provided that: "The Administrator of the Environmental Protection Agency shall create a National Acid Lakes Registry that shall list, to the extent practical, all lakes that are known to be acidified due to acid deposition, and shall publish such list within one year of the enactment of this Act [Nov. 15, 1990]. Lakes shall be added to the registry as they become acidic or as data becomes available to show they are acidic. Lakes shall be deleted from the registry as they become nonacidic."

Assessment of International Air Pollution Control Technologies

Pub. L. No. 101–549, § 901(e), directed Administrator of the Environmental Protection Agency to conduct a study that compares international air pollution control technologies of selected industrialized countries to determine if there exist air pollution control technologies in countries outside the United States that may have beneficial applications to this Nation's air pollution control efforts, including, with respect to each country studied, the topics of urban air quality, motor vehicle emissions, toxic air emissions, and acid deposition, and within 2 years after Nov. 15, 1990, submit to Congress a report detailing the results of such study. For termination of reporting provisions of Pub. L. No. 101–549, § 901(e), set out above, effective May 15, 2000, see Pub. L. No. 104–66, § 3003, as amended, set out as a note under 31 U.S.C.A. § 1113, and the 9th item on page 163 of House Document No. 103–7.

Western States Acid Deposition Research

Section 901(g) of Pub. L. No. 101–549 provided that:

"(1) The Administrator of the Environmental Protection Agency shall sponsor monitoring and research and submit to Congress annual and periodic assessment reports on—

"(A) the occurrence and effects of acid deposition on surface waters located in that part of the United States west of the Mississippi River;

"(B) the occurrence and effects of acid deposition on high elevation ecosystems (including forests, and surface waters); and

"(C) the occurrence and effects of episodic acidification, particularly with respect to high elevation watersheds.

"(2) The Administrator of the Environmental Protection Agency shall analyze data generated from the studies conducted under paragraph (1), data from the Western Lakes Survey, and other appropriate research and utilize predictive modeling techniques that take into account the unique geographic, climatological, and atmospheric conditions which exist in the western United States to determine the potential occurrence and effects of acid deposition due to any projected increases in the emission of sulfur dioxide and nitrogen oxides in that part of the United States located west of the Mississippi River. The Administrator shall include the results of the project conducted under this paragraph in the reports issued to Congress under paragraph (1)."

Consultation With Committee on Science and Technology of House of Representatives

Section 101(c) of Pub. L. No. 95–95 provided that: "The Administrator of the Environmental Protection Agency shall consult with the House Committee on Science and Technology [now Committee on Science, Space, and Technology] on the environmental and atmospheric research, development, and demonstration aspects of this Act [see Short Title of 1977 Acts note set out under section 7401 of this title]. In addition, the reports and studies required by this Act that relate to research, development, and demonstration issues shall be transmitted to the Committee on Science and Technology [now Committee on Science, Space, and Technology] at the same time they are made available to other committees of the Congress."

Modification or Rescission of Rules, Regulations, Orders, Determinations, Contracts, Certifications, Authorizations, Delegations, and Other Actions

All rules, regulations, orders, determinations, contracts, certifications, authorizations, delegations, or other actions duly issued, made, or taken by or pursuant to Act of July 14, 1955, the Clean Air Act, as in effect immediately prior to the date of enactment of Pub. L. No. 95–95 [Aug. 7, 1977] to continue in full force and effect until modified or rescinded in accordance with Act of July 14, 1955, as amended by Pub. L. No. 95–95 [this chapter], see section 406(b) of Pub. L. No. 95–95, set out as an Effective and Applicability Provisions note under 42 U.S.C.A. § 7401.

Study of Substances Discharged from Exhausts of Motor Vehicles

Pub. L. No. 86–493, 74 Stat. 162 (June 8, 1960), directed the Surgeon General of the Public Health Service to conduct a thorough study for the purposes of determining, with respect to the various substances discharged from the exhausts of motor vehicles, the amounts and kinds of such substances which, from the standpoint of human health, it is safe for motor vehicles to discharge into the atmosphere under the various conditions under which such vehicles may operate. Not later than two years after June 8, 1960, the Surgeon General was required to submit to Congress a report on the results of the study, together with such recommendations, if any, based upon the findings made in such study, as he deemed necessary for the protection of the public health.

Termination of Advisory Committees

Advisory Committees in existence on Jan. 5, 1973, to terminate not later than the expiration of the two-year period following Jan. 5, 1973, unless, in the case of a committee established by the President or an officer of the Federal Government, such committee is renewed by appropriate action prior to the expiration of such two-year period, or in the case of a committee established by the Congress, its duration is otherwise provided by law, see section 14 of Pub. L. No. 92–463, 86 Stat. 776 (Oct. 6, 1972), set out in Appendix 2 to Title 5, Government Organization and Employees.

§ 7404. Research relating to fuels and vehicles

[CAA § 104]

(a) Research programs; grants; contracts; pilot and demonstration plants; byproducts research

The Administrator shall give special emphasis to research and development into new and improved methods, having industry-wide application, for the prevention and control of air pollution resulting from the combustion of fuels. In furtherance of such research and development he shall—

(1) conduct and accelerate research programs directed toward development of improved, cost-effective techniques for—

(A) control of combustion byproducts of fuels,

(B) removal of potential air pollutants from fuels prior to combustion,

(C) control of emissions from the evaporation of fuels,

(D) improving the efficiency of fuels combustion so as to decrease atmospheric emissions, and

(E) producing synthetic or new fuels which, when used, result in decreased atmospheric emissions.

(2) provide for Federal grants to public or nonprofit agencies, institutions, and organizations and to individuals, and contracts with public or private agencies, institutions, or persons, for payment of (A) part of the cost of acquiring, constructing, or otherwise securing for research and development purposes, new or improved devices or methods having industrywide application of preventing or controlling discharges into the air of various types of pollutants; (B) part of the cost of programs to develop low emission alternatives to the present internal combustion engine; (C) the cost to purchase vehicles and vehicle engines, or portions thereof, for research, development, and testing purposes; and (D) carrying out the other provisions of this section, without regard to section 3324(a) and (b) of Title 31 and section 6101 of Title 41: *Provided,* That research or demonstration contracts awarded pursuant to this subsection (including contracts for construction) may be made in accordance with, and subject to the limitations provided with respect to research contracts of the military departments in, section 2353 of Title 10, except that the determination, approval, and certification required thereby shall be made by the Administrator; *Provided further,* That no grant may be made under this paragraph in excess of $1,500,000;

(3) determine, by laboratory and pilot plant testing, the results of air pollution research and studies in order to develop new or improved processes and plant designs to the point where they can be demonstrated on a large and practical scale;

(4) construct, operate, and maintain, or assist in meeting the cost of the construction, operation, and maintenance of new or improved demonstration plants or processes which have promise of accomplishing the purposes of this chapter;

(5) study new or improved methods for the recovery and marketing of commercially valuable byproducts resulting from the removal of pollutants.

(b) Powers of Administrator in establishing research and development programs

In carrying out the provisions of this section, the Administrator may—

(1) conduct and accelerate research and development of cost-effective instrumentation techniques to facilitate determination of quantity and quality of air pollutant emissions, including, but not limited to, automotive emissions;

(2) utilize, on a reimbursable basis, the facilities of existing Federal scientific laboratories;

(3) establish and operate necessary facilities and test sites at which to carry on the research, testing, development, and programming necessary to effectuate the purposes of this section;

(4) acquire secret processes, technical data, inventions, patent applications, patents, licenses, and an interest in lands, plants, and facilities, and other property or rights by purchase, license, lease, or donation; and

(5) cause on-site inspections to be made of promising domestic and foreign projects, and cooperate and participate in their development in instances in which the purposes of the chapter will be served thereby.

(c) Clean alternative fuels

The Administrator shall conduct a research program to identify, characterize, and predict air emissions related to the production, distribution, storage, and use of clean alternative fuels to determine the risks and benefits to human health and the environment relative to those from using conventional gasoline and diesel fuels. The Administrator shall consult with other Federal agencies to ensure coordination and to avoid duplication of activities authorized under this subsection.

(July 14, 1955, c. 360, Title I, § 104, as added by Pub. L. No. 90–148, § 2, 81 Stat. 487 (Nov. 21, 1967); and amended by Pub. L. No. 91–137, 83 Stat. 283 (Dec. 5, 1969); Pub. L. No. 91–604, §§ 2(b), (c), 13(a), 15(c)(2), 84 Stat. 1676, 1677, 1709, 1713 (Dec. 31, 1970); Pub. L. No. 93–15, § 1(a), 87 Stat. 11 (Apr. 9, 1973); Pub. L. No. 93–319, § 13(a), 88 Stat. 265 (June 22, 1974); Pub. L. No. 97–258, § 4(b), 96 Stat. 1067 (Sept. 13, 1982); Pub. L. No. 101–549, Title IX, § 901(d), 104 Stat. 2706 (Nov. 15, 1990).)

HISTORICAL AND STATUTORY NOTES

Codifications

Section was formerly codified as section 1857b–1 of this title.

In subsec. (a)(2)(D), "section 3324(a) and (b) of Title 31 and section 6101 of Title 41" substituted for "sections 3648 and 3709 of the Revised Statutes (31 U.S.C. 529; 41 U.S.C. 5)" on authority of Pub. L. No. 97–258, § 4(b), 96 Stat. 1067 (Sept. 13, 1982), which Act enacted Title 31, Money and Finance, and Pub. L. No. 111–350, § 6(c), 124 Stat. 3854 (Jan. 4, 2011), which Act enacted Title 41, Public Contracts.

Effective and Applicability Provisions

1990 Acts. Amendment by Pub. L. No. 101–549 effective Nov. 15, 1990, except as otherwise provided, see section 711(b) of Pub. L. No. 101–549, set out as a note under section 7401 of this title.

Savings Provisions

Suits, actions or proceedings commenced under this chapter as in effect prior to Nov. 15, 1990, not to abate by reason of the taking effect of amendments by Pub. L. No. 101–549, except as otherwise provided for, see section 711(a) of Pub. L. No. 101–549, set out as a note under section 7401 of this title.

Prior Provisions

A prior section 104 of Act of July 14, 1955, was renumbered section 105 by Pub. L. No. 90–148 and is set out as section 7405 of this title.

Hydrogen Fuel Cell Vehicle Study and Test Program

Section 807 of Pub. L. No. 101–549 provided that: "The Administrator of the Environmental Protection Agency, in conjunction with the National Aeronautics and Space Administration and the Department of Energy, shall conduct a study and test program on the development of a hydrogen fuel cell electric vehicle. The study and test program shall determine how best to transfer existing NASA hydrogen fuel cell technology into the form of a mass-producible, cost effective hydrogen fuel cell vehicle. Such study and test program shall include at a minimum a feasibility-design study, the construction of a prototype, and a demonstration. This study and test program should be completed and a report submitted to Congress within 3 years after the enactment of the Clean Air Act Amendments of 1990 [Nov. 15, 1990]. This study and test program should be performed in the university or universities which are best exhibiting the facilities and expertise to develop such a fuel cell vehicle."

Combustion of Contaminated Used Oil in Ships

Section 813 of Pub. L. No. 101–549 provided that: "Within 2 years after the enactment of the Clean Air Act Amendments of 1990 [Nov. 15, 1990], the Administrator of the Environmental Protection Agency shall complete a study and submit a report to Congress evaluating the health and environmental impacts of the combustion of contaminated used oil in ships, the reasons for using such oil for such purposes, the alternatives to such use, the costs of such alternatives, and other relevant factors and impacts. In preparing such study, the Administrator shall obtain the view and comments of all interested persons and shall consult with the Secretary of Transportation and the Secretary of the department in which the Coast Guard is operating."

[For termination, effective May 15, 2000, of reporting provisions of Pub. L. No. 101–549, § 813, set out above, see Pub. L. No. 104–66, § 3003, as amended, set out as a note under 31 U.S.C.A. § 1113, and the 5th item on page 163 of House Document No. 103–7.]

Extension to Aug. 31, 1970 of Authorization Period for Fiscal Year 1970

Pub. L. No. 91–316, 84 Stat. 416 (July 10, 1970), provided in part that the authorization contained in section 104(c) of the Clean Air Act [subsec. (c) of this section] for the fiscal year ending June 30, 1970, should remain available through Aug. 31, 1970, notwithstanding any provisions of this section.

§ 7405. Grants for support of air pollution planning and control programs

[CAA § 105]

(a) Amounts; limitations; assurances of plan development capability

(1) (A) The Administrator may make grants to air pollution control agencies, within the meaning of paragraph (1), (2), (3), (4), or (5) of section 7602 of this title, in an amount up to three-fifths of the cost of implementing programs for the prevention and control of air pollution or implementation of national primary and secondary ambient air quality standards. For the purpose of this section, "implementing" means any activity related to the planning, developing, establishing, carrying-out, improving, or maintaining of such programs.

(B) Subject to subsections (b) and (c) of this section, an air pollution control agency which receives a grant under subparagraph (A) and which contributes less than the required two-fifths minimum shall have 3 years following November 15, 1990, in which to contribute such amount. If such an agency fails to meet and maintain this required level, the Administrator shall reduce the amount of the Federal contribution accordingly.

(C) With respect to any air quality control region or portion thereof for which there is an applicable implementation plan under section 7410 of this title, grants under subparagraph (A) may be made only to air pollution control agencies which have substantial responsibilities for carrying out such applicable implementation plan.

(2) Before approving any grant under this subsection to any air pollution control agency within the meaning of sections 7602(b)(2) and 7602(b)(4) of this title, the Administrator shall receive assurances that such agency provides for adequate representation of appropriate State, interstate, local, and (when appropriate) international, interests in the air quality control region.

(3) Before approving any planning grant under this subsection to any air pollution control agency within the meaning of sections 7602(b)(2) and 7602(b)(4) of this title, the Administrator shall receive assurances that such agency has the capability of developing a comprehensive air quality plan for the air quality control region, which plan shall include (when appropriate) a recommended system of alerts to avert and reduce the risk of situations in which there may be imminent and serious danger to the public health or welfare from air pollutants and the various aspects relevant to the establishment of air quality standards for such air quality control region, including the concentration of industries, other commercial establishments, population and naturally occurring factors which shall affect such standards.

(b) Terms and conditions; regulations; factors for consideration; State expenditure limitations

(1) From the sums available for the purposes of subsection (a) of this section for any fiscal year, the Administrator shall from time to time make grants to air pollution control agencies upon such terms and conditions as the Administrator may find necessary to carry out the purpose of this section. In establishing regulations for the granting of such funds the Administrator shall, so far as practicable, give due consideration to (A) the population, (B) the extent of the actual or potential air pollution problem, and (C) the financial need of the respective agencies.

(2) Not more than 10 per centum of the total of funds appropriated or allocated for the purposes of subsection (a) of this section shall be granted for air pollution control programs in any one State. In the case of a grant for a program in an area crossing State boundaries, the Administrator shall determine the portion of such grant that is chargeable to the percentage limitation under this subsection for each State into which such area extends. Subject to the provisions of paragraph (1) of this subsection, no State shall have made available to it for application less than one-half of 1 per centum of the annual appropriation for grants under this section for grants to agencies within such State.

(c) Maintenance of effort

(1) No agency shall receive any grant under this section during any fiscal year when its expenditures of non-Federal funds for recurrent expenditures for air pollution control programs will be less than its expenditures were for such programs during the preceding fiscal year. In order for the Administrator to award grants under this section in a timely manner each fiscal year, the Administrator shall compare an agency's prospective expenditure level to that of its second preceding fiscal year. The Administrator shall revise the current regulations which define applicable nonrecurrent and recurrent expenditures, and in so doing, give due consideration to exempting an agency from the limitations of this paragraph and subsection (a) of this section due to periodic increases experienced by that agency from time to time in its annual expenditures for purposes acceptable to the Administrator for that fiscal year.

(2) The Administrator may still award a grant to an agency not meeting the requirements of paragraph (*l*)[1] of this subsection if the Administrator, after notice and opportunity for public hearing, determines that a reduction in expenditures is attributable to a non-selective reduction in the expenditures in the programs of all Executive branch agencies of the applicable unit of Government. No agency shall receive any grant under this section with respect to the maintenance of a program for the prevention and control of air pollution unless the Administrator is satisfied that such a grant will be so used to supplement and, to the extent practicable, increase the level of State, local, or other non-Federal funds. No grants shall be made under this section until the Administrator has consulted with the appropriate official as designated by the Governor or Governors of the State or States affected.

(d) Reduction of payments; availability of reduced amounts; reduced amount as deemed paid to agency for purpose of determining amount of grant

The Administrator, with the concurrence of any recipient of a grant under this section, may reduce the payments to such recipient by the amount of the pay, allowances, traveling expenses, and any other costs in connection with the detail of any officer or employee to the recipient under section 7601 of this title, when such detail is for the convenience of, and at the request of, such recipient and for the purpose of carrying out the provisions of this chapter. The amount by which such payments have been reduced shall be available for payment of such costs by the Administrator, but shall, for the purpose of determining the amount of any grant to a recipient under subsection (a) of this section, be deemed to have been paid to such agency.

(e) Notice and opportunity for hearing when affected by adverse action

No application by a State for a grant under this section may be disapproved by the Administrator without prior notice and opportunity for a public hearing in the affected State, and no commitment or obligation of any funds under any such grant may be revoked or reduced without prior notice and opportunity for a public hearing in the affected State (or in one of the affected States if more than one State is affected).

(July 14, 1955, c. 360, Title I, § 105, formerly § 4, as added by Pub. L. No. 88–206, § 1, 77 Stat. 395 (Dec. 17, 1963); and renumbered § 104 and amended by Pub. L. No. 89–272, Title I, § 101(2)–(4), 79 Stat. 992 (Oct. 20, 1965); and amended by Pub. L. No. 89–675, § 3, 80 Stat. 954 (Oct. 15, 1966); and renumbered § 105 and amended by Pub. L. No. 90–148, § 2, 81 Stat. 489 (Nov. 21, 1967); and amended by Pub. L. No. 91–604, §§ 3(a), (b)(1), 15(c)(2), 84 Stat. 1677, 1713 (Dec. 31, 1970); Pub. L. No. 95–95, Title I, § 102, Title III, § 305(b), 91 Stat. 687, 776 (Aug. 7, 1977); Pub. L. No. 101–549, Title VIII, § 802(a)–(e), 104 Stat. 2687, 2688 (Nov. 15, 1990).)

[1] So in original. Probably should be paragraph "(1)."

HISTORICAL AND STATUTORY NOTES

Codifications

Section was formerly codified as section 1857c of this title.

Effective and Applicability Provisions

1990 Acts. Amendment by Pub. L. No. 101–549 effective Nov. 15, 1990, except as otherwise provided, see section 711(b) of Pub. L. No. 101–549, set out as a note under section 7401 of this title.

1977 Acts. Amendment by Pub. L. No. 95–95 effective Aug. 7, 1977, except as otherwise expressly provided, see section 406(d) of Pub. L. No. 95–95, set out as a note under section 7401 of this title.

Savings Provisions

Suits, actions or proceedings commenced under this chapter as in effect prior to Nov. 15, 1990, not to abate by reason of the taking effect of amendments by Pub. L. No. 101–549, except as otherwise provided for, see section 711(a) of Pub. L. No. 101–549, set out as a note under section 7401 of this title.

Prior Provisions

A prior section 105 of Act of July 14, 1955 was renumbered section 108 by Pub. L. No. 90–148, and is set out as section 7415 of this title.

A prior section 4 of Act of July 14, 1955, c. 360, 69 Stat. 322, which was codified as a prior section 1857c of this title, related to the preparation of reports and recommendations prior to the general amendment by Pub. L. No. 88–206. See section 7403 of this title.

Provisions similar to those comprising subsecs. (a) and (b) of this section were contained in a prior section 1857d of this title, Act of July 14, 1955, c. 360, § 5, 69 Stat. 322, as amended by Pub. L. No. 86–365, § 1, 73 Stat. 646 (Sept. 22, 1959); Pub. L. No. 87–761, § 1, 76 Stat. 760 (Oct. 9, 1962), prior to the general amendment by Pub. L. No. 88–206.

Modification or Rescission of Rules, Regulations, Orders, Determinations, Contracts, Certifications, Authorizations, Delegations, and Other Actions

All rules, regulations, orders, determinations, contracts, certifications, authorizations, delegations, or other actions duly issued, made, or taken by or pursuant to Act of July 14, 1955, the Clean Air Act, as in effect immediately prior to the date of enactment of Pub. L. No. 95–95 [Aug. 7, 1977] to continue in full force and effect until modified or rescinded in accordance with Act of July 14, 1955, as amended by Pub. L. No. 95–95 [this chapter], see section 406(b) of Pub. L. No. 95–95, set out as an Effective Date of 1977 Acts note under section 7401 of this title.

§ 7406. Interstate air quality agencies; program cost limitations

[CAA § 106]

For the purpose of developing implementation plans for any interstate air quality control region designated pursuant to section 7407 of this title or of implementing section 7506a of this title (relating to control of interstate air pollution) or section 7511c of this title (relating to control of interstate ozone pollution), the Administrator is authorized to pay, for two years, up to 100 per centum of the air quality planning program costs of any commission established under section 7506a of this title (relating to control of interstate air pollution) or section 7511c of this title (relating to control of interstate ozone pollution) or any agency designated by the Governors of the affected States, which agency shall be capable of recommending to the Governors plans for implementation of national primary and secondary ambient air quality standards and shall include representation from the States and appropriate political subdivisions within the air quality control region. After the initial two-year period the Administrator is authorized to make grants to such agency or such commission in an amount up to three-fifths of the air quality implementation program costs of such agency or commission.

(July 14, 1955, c. 360, Title I, § 106, as added by Pub. L. No. 90–148, § 2, 81 Stat. 490 (Nov. 21, 1967); and amended by Pub. L. No. 91–604, § 3(c), 84 Stat. 1677 (Dec. 31, 1970); Pub. L. No. 101–549, Title I, § 102(f)(2), Title VIII, § 802(f), 104 Stat. 2420, 2688 (Nov. 15, 1990).)

HISTORICAL AND STATUTORY NOTES

Codifications

Section was formerly codified as section 1857c–1 of this title.

Effective and Applicability Provisions

1990 Acts. Amendment by Pub. L. No. 101–549 effective Nov. 15, 1990, except as otherwise provided, see section 711(b) of Pub. L. No. 101–549, set out as a note under section 7401 of this title.

Savings Provisions

Suits, actions or proceedings commenced under this chapter as in effect prior to Nov. 15, 1990, not to abate by reason of the taking effect of amendments by Pub. L. No. 101–549, except as otherwise provided for, see section 711(a) of Pub. L. No. 101–549, set out as a note under section 7401 of this title.

Prior Provisions

A prior section 106 of Act of July 14, 1955, was renumbered section 117 by Pub. L. No. 91–604 and is set out as section 7417 of this title.

§ 7407. Air quality control regions

[CAA § 107]

(a) Responsibility of each State for air quality; submission of implementation plan

Each State shall have the primary responsibility for assuring air quality within the entire geographic area comprising such State by submitting an implementation plan for such State which will specify the manner in which national primary and secondary ambient air quality standards will be achieved and maintained within each air quality control region in such State.

(b) Designated regions

For purposes of developing and carrying out implementation plans under section 7410 of this title—

(1) an air quality control region designated under this section before December 31, 1970, or a region designated after such date under subsection (c) of this section, shall be an air quality control region; and

(2) the portion of such State which is not part of any such designated region shall be an air quality control region, but such portion may be subdivided by the State into two or more air quality control regions with the approval of the Administrator.

(c) Authority of Administrator to designate regions; notification of Governors of affected States

The Administrator shall, within 90 days after December 31, 1970, after consultation with appropriate State and local authorities, designate as an air quality control region any interstate area or major intrastate area which he deems necessary or appropriate for the attainment and maintenance of ambient air quality standards. The Administrator shall immediately notify the Governors of the affected States of any designation made under this subsection.

(d) Designations

(1) Designations generally

(A) Submission by Governors of initial designations following promulgation of new or revised standards

By such date as the Administrator may reasonably require, but not later than 1 year after promulgation of a new or revised national ambient air quality standard for any pollutant under section 7409 of this title, the Governor of each State shall (and at any other time the Governor of a State deems appropriate the Governor may) submit to the Administrator a list of all areas (or portions thereof) in the State, designating as—

(i) nonattainment, any area that does not meet (or that contributes to ambient air quality in a nearby area that does not meet) the national primary or secondary ambient air quality standard for the pollutant,

(ii) attainment, any area (other than an area identified in clause (i)) that meets the national primary or secondary ambient air quality standard for the pollutant, or

(iii) unclassifiable, any area that cannot be codified on the basis of available information as meeting or not meeting the national primary or secondary ambient air quality standard for the pollutant.

The Administrator may not require the Governor to submit the required list sooner than 120 days after promulgating a new or revised national ambient air quality standard.

(B) Promulgation by EPA of designations

(i) Upon promulgation or revision of a national ambient air quality standard, the Administrator shall promulgate the designations of all areas (or portions thereof) submitted under subparagraph (A) as expeditiously as practicable, but in no case later than 2 years from the date of promulgation of the new or revised national ambient air quality standard. Such period may be extended for up to one year in the event the Administrator has insufficient information to promulgate the designations.

(ii) In making the promulgations required under clause (i), the Administrator may make such modifications as the Administrator deems necessary to the designations of the areas (or portions thereof) submitted under subparagraph (A) (including to the boundaries of such areas or portions thereof). Whenever the Administrator intends to make a modification, the Administrator shall notify the State and provide such State with an opportunity to demonstrate why any proposed modification is inappropriate. The Administrator shall give such notification no later than 120 days before the date the Administrator promulgates the designation, including any modification thereto. If the Governor fails to submit the list in whole or in part, as required under subparagraph (A), the Administrator shall promulgate the designation that the Administrator deems appropriate for any area (or portion thereof) not designated by the State.

(iii) If the Governor of any State, on the Governor's own motion, under subparagraph (A), submits a list of areas (or portions thereof) in the State designated as nonattainment, attainment, or unclassifiable, the Administrator shall act on such designations in accordance with the procedures under paragraph (3) (relating to redesignation).

(iv) A designation for an area (or portion thereof) made pursuant to this subsection shall remain in effect until the area (or portion thereof) is redesignated pursuant to paragraph (3) or (4).

(C) Designations by operation of law

(i) Any area designated with respect to any air pollutant under the provisions of paragraph (1)(A), (B), or (C) of this subsection (as in effect immediately before November 15, 1990) is designated, by operation of law, as a nonattainment area for such pollutant within the meaning of subparagraph (A)(i).

(ii) Any area designated with respect to any air pollutant under the provisions of paragraph (1)(E) (as in effect immediately before November 15, 1990) is designated by operation of law, as an attainment area for such pollutant within the meaning of subparagraph (A)(ii).

(iii) Any area designated with respect to any air pollutant under the provisions of paragraph (1)(D) (as in effect immediately before November 15, 1990) is designated, by operation of law, as an unclassifiable area for such pollutant within the meaning of subparagraph (A)(iii).

(2) Publication of designations and redesignations

(A) The Administrator shall publish a notice in the Federal Register promulgating any designation under paragraph (1) or (5), or announcing any designation under paragraph (4), or promulgating any redesignation under paragraph (3).

(B) Promulgation or announcement of a designation under paragraph (1), (4) or (5) shall not be subject to the provisions of sections 553 through 557 of Title 5 (relating to notice and comment), except nothing herein shall be construed as precluding such public notice and comment whenever possible.

(3) Redesignation

(A) Subject to the requirements of subparagraph (E), and on the basis of air quality data, planning and control considerations, or any other air quality-related considerations the Administrator deems appropriate, the Administrator may at any time notify the Governor of any State that available information indicates that the designation of any area or portion of an area within the State or interstate area should be revised. In issuing such notification, which shall be public, to the Governor, the Administrator shall provide such information as the Administrator may have available explaining the basis for the notice.

(B) No later than 120 days after receiving a notification under subparagraph (A), the Governor shall submit to the Administrator such redesignation, if any, of the appropriate area (or areas) or portion thereof within the State or interstate area, as the Governor considers appropriate.

(C) No later than 120 days after the date described in subparagraph (B) (or paragraph (1)(B)(iii)), the Administrator shall promulgate the redesignation, if any, of the area or portion thereof, submitted by the Governor in accordance with subparagraph (B), making such modifications as the Administrator may deem necessary, in the same manner and under the same procedure as is applicable under clause (ii) of paragraph (1)(B), except that the phrase "60 days" shall be substituted for the phrase "120 days" in that clause. If the Governor does not submit, in accordance with subparagraph (B), a redesignation for an area (or portion thereof) identified by the Administrator under subparagraph (A), the Administrator shall promulgate such redesignation, if any, that the Administrator deems appropriate.

(D) The Governor of any State may, on the Governor's own motion, submit to the Administrator a revised designation of any area or portion thereof within the State. Within 18 months of receipt of a complete State redesignation submittal, the Administrator shall approve or deny such redesignation. The submission of a redesignation by a Governor shall not affect the effectiveness or enforceability of the applicable implementation plan for the State.

(E) The Administrator may not promulgate a redesignation of a nonattainment area (or portion thereof) to attainment unless—

(i) the Administrator determines that the area has attained the national ambient air quality standard;

(ii) the Administrator has fully approved the applicable implementation plan for the area under section 7410(k) of this title;

(iii) the Administrator determines that the improvement in air quality is due to permanent and enforceable reductions in emissions resulting from implementation of the applicable implementation plan and applicable Federal air pollutant control regulations and other permanent and enforceable reductions;

(iv) the Administrator has fully approved a maintenance plan for the area as meeting the requirements of section 7505a of this title; and

(v) the State containing such area has met all requirements applicable to the area under section 7410 of this title and part D of this subchapter.

(F) The Administrator shall not promulgate any redesignation of any area (or portion thereof) from nonattainment to unclassifiable.

(4) Nonattainment designations for ozone, carbon monoxide and particulate matter (PM-10)

(A) Ozone and carbon monoxide

(i) Within 120 days after November 15, 1990, each Governor of each State shall submit to the Administrator a list that designates, affirms or reaffirms the designation of, or redesignates (as the case may be), all areas (or portions thereof) of the Governor's State as attainment, nonattainment, or unclassifiable with respect to the national ambient air quality standards for ozone and carbon monoxide.

(ii) No later than 120 days after the date the Governor is required to submit the list of areas (or portions thereof) required under clause (i) of this subparagraph, the Administrator shall promulgate such designations, making such modifications as the Administrator may deem necessary, in the same manner, and under the same procedure, as is applicable under clause (ii) of paragraph (1)(B), except that the phrase "60 days" shall be substituted for the phrase "120 days" in that clause. If the Governor does not submit, in accordance with clause (i) of this subparagraph, a designation for an area (or portion thereof), the Administrator shall promulgate the designation that the Administrator deems appropriate.

(iii) No nonattainment area may be redesignated as an attainment area under this subparagraph.

(iv) Notwithstanding paragraph (1)(C)(ii) of this subsection, if an ozone or carbon monoxide nonattainment area located within a metropolitan statistical area or consolidated metropolitan statistical area (as established by the Bureau of the Census) is classified under part D of this subchapter as a Serious, Severe, or Extreme Area, the boundaries of such area are hereby revised (on the date 45 days after such classification) by operation of law to include the entire metropolitan statistical area or consolidated metropolitan statistical area, as the case may be, unless within such 45-day period the Governor (in consultation with State and local air pollution control agencies) notifies the Administrator that additional time is necessary to evaluate the application of clause (v). Whenever a Governor has submitted such a notice to the Administrator, such boundary revision shall occur on the later of the date 8 months after such classification or 14 months after November 15, 1990, unless the Governor makes the finding referred to in clause (v), and the Administrator concurs in such finding, within such period. Except as otherwise provided in this paragraph, a boundary revision under this clause or clause (v) shall apply for purposes of any State implementation plan revision required to be submitted after November 15, 1990.

(v) Whenever the Governor of a State has submitted a notice under clause (iv), the Governor, in consultation with State and local air pollution control agencies, shall undertake a study to evaluate whether the entire metropolitan statistical area or consolidated metropolitan statistical area should be included within the nonattainment area. Whenever a Governor finds and demonstrates to the satisfaction of the Administrator, and the Administrator concurs in such finding, that with respect to a portion of a metropolitan statistical area or consolidated metropolitan statistical area, sources in the portion do not contribute significantly to violation of the national ambient air quality standard, the Administrator shall approve the Governor's request to exclude such portion from the nonattainment area. In making such finding, the Governor and the Administrator shall consider factors such as population density, traffic congestion, commercial development, industrial development, meteorological conditions, and pollution transport.

(B) PM-10 designations

By operation of law, until redesignation by the Administrator pursuant to paragraph (3)—

(i) each area identified in 52 Federal Register 29383 (Aug. 7, 1987) as a Group I area (except to the extent that such identification was modified by the Administrator before November 15, 1990) is designated nonattainment for PM-10;

(ii) any area containing a site for which air quality monitoring data show a violation of the national ambient air quality standard for PM-10 before January 1, 1989 (as determined under part 50, appendix K of title 40 of the Code of Federal Regulations) is hereby designated nonattainment for PM-10; and

(iii) each area not described in clause (i) or (ii) is hereby designated unclassifiable for PM-10.

Any designation for particulate matter (measured in terms of total suspended particulates) that the Administrator promulgated pursuant to this subsection (as in effect immediately before November 15, 1990) shall remain in effect for purposes of implementing the maximum allowable increases in concentrations of particulate matter (measured in terms of total suspended particulates) pursuant to section 7473(b) of this title, until the Administrator determines that such designation is no longer necessary for that purpose.

(5) Designations for lead

The Administrator may, in the Administrator's discretion at any time the Administrator deems appropriate, require a State to designate areas (or portions thereof) with respect to the national ambient air quality standard for lead in effect as of November 15, 1990, in accordance with the procedures under subparagraphs (A) and (B) of paragraph (1), except that in applying subparagraph (B)(i) of paragraph (1) the phrase "2 years from the date of promulgation of the new or revised national ambient air quality standard" shall be replaced by the phrase "1 year from the date the Administrator notifies the State of the requirement to designate areas with respect to the standard for lead".

(6) **Designations**

(A) **Submission**

Notwithstanding any other provision of law, not later than February 15, 2004, the Governor of each State shall submit designations referred to in paragraph (1) for the July 1997 $PM_{2.5}$ national ambient air quality standards for each area within the State, based on air quality monitoring data collected in accordance with any applicable Federal reference methods for the relevant areas.

(B) **Promulgation**

Notwithstanding any other provision of law, not later than December 31, 2004, the Administrator shall, consistent with paragraph (1), promulgate the designations referred to in subparagraph (A) for each area of each State for the July 1997 $PM_{2.5}$ national ambient air quality standards.

(7) **Implementation plan for regional haze**

(A) **In general**

Notwithstanding any other provision of law, not later than 3 years after the date on which the Administrator promulgates the designations referred to in paragraph (6)(B) for a State, the State shall submit, for the entire State, the State implementation plan revisions to meet the requirements promulgated by the Administrator under section 7492(e)(1) of this title (referred to in this paragraph as "regional haze requirements").

(B) **No preclusion of other provisions**

Nothing in this paragraph precludes the implementation of the agreements and recommendations stemming from the Grand Canyon Visibility Transport Commission Report dated June 1996, including the submission of State implementation plan revisions by the States of Arizona, California, Colorado, Idaho, Nevada, New Mexico, Oregon, Utah, or Wyoming by December 31, 2003, for implementation of regional haze requirements applicable to those States.

(e) **Redesignation of air quality control regions**

(1) Except as otherwise provided in paragraph (2), the Governor of each State is authorized, with the approval of the Administrator, to redesignate from time to time the air quality control regions within such State for purposes of efficient and effective air quality management. Upon such redesignation, the list under subsection (d) of this section shall be modified accordingly.

(2) In the case of an air quality control region in a State, or part of such region, which the Administrator finds may significantly affect air pollution concentrations in another State, the Governor of the State in which such region, or part of a region, is located may redesignate from time to time the boundaries of so much of such air quality control region as is located within such State only with the approval of the Administrator and with the consent of all Governors of all States which the Administrator determines may be significantly affected.

(3) No compliance date extension granted under section 7413(d)(5) of this title (relating to coal conversion) shall cease to be effective by reason of the regional limitation provided in section 7413(d)(5) of this title if the violation of such limitation is due solely to a redesignation of a region under this subsection.

(July 14, 1955, c. 360, Title I, § 107, as added by Pub. L. No. 91–604, § 4(a), 84 Stat. 1678 (Dec. 31, 1970); and amended by Pub. L. No. 95–95, Title I, § 103, 91 Stat. 687 (Aug. 7, 1977); Pub. L. No. 101–549, Title I, § 101(a), 104 Stat. 2399 (Nov. 15, 1990); Pub. L. No. 108–199, Div. G, Title IV, § 425(a), 118 Stat. 417 (Jan. 23, 2004).)

HISTORICAL AND STATUTORY NOTES

References in Text

Section 7413 of this title, referred to in subsec. (e)(3), was amended generally by Pub. L. No. 101–549, Title VII, § 701, 104 Stat. 2672 (Nov. 15, 1990), and, as so amended, subsec. (d) of section 7413 no longer relates to final compliance orders.

Codifications

Section was formerly codified as section 1857c–2 of this title.

Effective and Applicability Provisions

1990 Acts. Amendment by Pub. L. No. 101–549 effective Nov. 15, 1990, except as otherwise provided, see section 711(b) of Pub. L. No. 101–549, set out as a note under section 7401 of this title.

1977 Acts. Amendment by Pub. L. No. 95–95 effective Aug. 7, 1977, except as otherwise expressly provided, see section 406(d) of Pub. L. No. 95–95, set out as a note under section 7401 of this title.

Savings Provisions

Suits, actions or proceedings commenced under this chapter as in effect prior to Nov. 15, 1990, not to abate by reason of the taking effect of amendments by Pub. L. No. 101–549, except as otherwise provided for, see section 711(a) of Pub. L. No. 101–549, set out as a note under section 7401 of this title.

Suits, actions, and other proceedings lawfully commenced by or against the Administrator or any other officer or employee of the United States in his official capacity or in relation to the discharge of his official duties under Act of July 14, 1955, the Clean Air Act, as in effect immediately prior to the enactment of Pub. L. No. 95–95 [Aug. 7, 1977], not to abate by reason of the taking effect of Pub. L. No. 95–95, see section 406(a) of Pub. L. No. 95–95, set out as an Effective and Applicability Provisions of 1977 Acts note under section 7401 of this title.

Prior Provisions

A prior section 107 of Act of July 14, 1955, as added Nov. 21, 1967, Pub. L. No. 90–148, § 2, 81 Stat. 490, which was codified as section 1857c–2 of this title, related to air quality control regions and was repealed by Pub. L. No. 91–604.

Another prior section 107 of Act of July 14, 1955, as added by Pub. L. No. 88–206, § 1, 77 Stat. 399 (Dec. 17, 1963); renumbered § 107 by Pub. L. No. 89–272, Title I, § 101(3), 79 Stat. 992 (Oct. 25, 1965); renumbered § 111 and amended by Pub. L. No. 90–148, § 2, 81 Stat. 499 (Nov. 21, 1967); renumbered § 118 and amended by Pub. L. No. 91–604, §§ 4(a), 5, 84 Stat. 1678, 1689 (Dec. 31, 1970); and amended by Pub. L. No. 95–95, Title I, § 116, 91 Stat. 711 (Aug. 7, 1977); Pub. L. No. 101–549, Title I, § 101(e), Title II, § 235, Title III, § 302(d), 104 Stat. 2409, 2530, 2574 (Nov. 15, 1990), is codified as section 7418 of this title.

Relationship to Transportation Equity Act for the 21st Century

Pub. L. No. 108–199, Div. G, Title IV, § 425(b), 118 Stat. 417 (Jan. 23, 2004), provided that: "Except as provided in paragraphs (6) and (7) of section 107(d) of the Clean Air Act (as added by subsection (a) [subsec. (d)(6), (7) of this section]), section 6101, subsections (a) and (b) of section 6102, and section 6103 of the Transportation Equity Act for the 21st Century (42 U.S.C. 7407 note; 112 Stat. 463), as in effect on the day before the date of enactment of this Act [Departments of Veterans Affairs and Housing and Urban Development, and Independent Agencies Appropriations Act, 2004, Pub. L. No. 108–199, Div.G, 118 Stat. § 363 (Jan. 23, 2004), was enacted on Jan. 23, 2004, see Tables for complete classification], shall remain in effect."

Ozone and Particulate Matter Standards

Pub. L. No. 105–178, Title VI, 112 Stat. 463 (June 9, 1998), as amended by Pub. L. No. 109–59, Title VI, § 6012, June 9, 1998, 119 Stat. 1882 (June 9, 1998), provided that:

"Sec. 6101. Findings and purpose.

"(a) The Congress finds that—

"(1) there is a lack of air quality monitoring data for fine particle levels, measured as $PM_{2.5}$ in the United States and the States should receive full funding for the monitoring efforts;

"(2) such data would provide a basis for designating areas as attainment or nonattainment for any $PM_{2.5}$ national ambient air quality standards pursuant to the standards promulgated in July 1997;

"(3) the President of the United States directed the Administrator of the Environmental Protection Agency (referred to in this title [this note] as the 'Administrator') in a memorandum dated July 16, 1997, to complete the next periodic review of the particulate matter national ambient air quality standards by July 2002 in order to determine 'whether to revise or maintain the standards';

"(4) the Administrator has stated that 3 years of air quality monitoring data for fine particle levels, measured as $PM_{2.5}$ and performed in accordance with any applicable Federal reference methods, is appropriate for designating areas as attainment or nonattainment pursuant to the July 1997 promulgated standards; and

"(5) the Administrator has acknowledged that in drawing boundaries for attainment and nonattainment areas for the July 1997 ozone national air quality standards, Governors would benefit from considering implementation guidance from EPA on drawing area boundaries.

"(b) The purposes of this title are—

"(1) to ensure that 3 years of air quality monitoring data regarding fine particle levels are gathered for use in the determination of area attainment or nonattainment designations respecting any $PM_{2.5}$ national ambient air quality standards;

"(2) to ensure that the Governors have adequate time to consider implementation guidance from EPA on drawing area boundaries prior to submitting area designations respecting the July 1997 ozone national ambient air quality standards;

"(3) to ensure that the schedule for implementation of the July 1997 revisions of the ambient air quality standards for particulate matter and the schedule for the Environmental Protection Agency's visibility regulations related to regional haze are consistent with the timetable for implementation of such particulate matter standards as set forth in the President's Implementation Memorandum dated July 16, 1997.

"Sec. 6102. Particulate matter monitoring program.

"(a) Through grants under section 103 of the Clean Air Act [section 7403 of this title] the Administrator of the Environmental Protection Agency shall use appropriated funds no later than fiscal year 2000 to fund 100 percent of the cost of the establishment, purchase, operation and maintenance of a $PM_{2.5}$ monitoring network necessary to implement the national ambient air quality standards for $PM_{2.5}$ under section 109 of the Clean Air Act. This implementation shall not result in a diversion or reprogramming of funds from other Federal, State or local Clean Air Act activities. Any funds previously diverted or reprogrammed from section 105 Clean Air Act [section 7405 of this title] grants for $PM_{2.5}$ monitors must be restored to State or local air programs in fiscal year 1999.

"(b) EPA and the States, consistent with their respective authorities under the Clean Air Act [Act of July 14, 1955, ch. 360, 69 Stat. 322, which is codified generally to section 7401 et seq. of this title], shall ensure that the national network (designated in subsection (a)) which consists of the $PM_{2.5}$ monitors necessary to implement the national ambient air quality standards is established by December 31, 1999.

"(c) (1) The Governors shall be required to submit designations referred to in section 107(d)(1) of the Clean Air Act [subsec. (d)(1) of this section] for each area following promulgation of the July 1997 $PM_{2.5}$ national ambient air quality standard within 1 year after receipt of 3 years of air quality monitoring data performed in accordance with any applicable Federal reference methods for the relevant areas. Only data from the monitoring network designated in subsection (a) and other Federal reference method $PM_{2.5}$ monitors shall be considered for such designations. Nothing in the previous sentence shall be construed as affecting the Governor's authority to designate an area initially as nonattainment, and the Administrator's authority to promulgate the designation of an area as nonattainment, under section 107(d)(1) of the Clean Air Act [subsec. (d)(1) of this section], based on its contribution to ambient air quality in a nearby nonattainment area.

"(2) For any area designated as nonattainment for the July 1997 $PM_{2.5}$ national ambient air quality standard in accordance with the schedule set forth in this section, notwithstanding the time limit prescribed in paragraph (2) of section 169B(e) of the Clean Air Act [section 7492(e)(2) of this title], the Administrator shall require State implementation plan revisions referred to in such paragraph (2) to be submitted at the same time as State implementation plan revisions referred to in section 172 of the Clean Air Act [section 7502 of this title] implementing the revised national ambient air quality standard for fine particulate matter are required to be submitted. For any area designated as attainment or unclassifiable for such standard, the Administrator shall require the State implementation plan revisions referred to in such paragraph (2) to be submitted 1 year after the area has been so designated. The preceding provisions of this paragraph shall not preclude the implementation of the agreements and recommendations set forth in the Grand Canyon Visibility Transport Commission Report dated June 1996.

"(d) The Administrator shall promulgate the designations referred to in section 107(d)(1) of the Clean Air Act [subsec. (d)(1) of this section] for each area following promulgation of the July 1997 $PM_{2.5}$ national ambient air quality standard by the earlier of 1 year after the initial designations required under subsection (c)(1) are required to be submitted or December 31, 2005.

"(e) **Field study.**—Not later than 2 years after the date of enactment of the SAFETEA-LU [Aug. 10, 2005], the Administrator shall—

"(1) conduct a field study of the ability of the $PM_{2.5}$ Federal Reference Method to differentiate those particles that are larger than 2.5 micrometers in diameter;

"(2) develop a Federal reference method to measure directly particles that are larger than 2.5 micrometers in diameter without reliance on subtracting from coarse particle measurements those particles that are equal to or smaller than 2.5 micrometers in diameter;

"(3) develop a method of measuring the composition of coarse particles; and

"(4) Submit a report on the study and responsibilities of the administrator under paragraphs (1) through (3) to—

"(A) the Committee on Energy and Commerce of the House of Representatives; and

"(B) the Committee on Environment and Public Works of the Senate.

"Sec. 6103. Ozone designation requirements.

"(a) The Governors shall be required to submit the designations referred to in section 107(d)(1) of the Clean Air Act [subsec. (d)(1) of this section] within 2 years following the promulgation of the July 1997 ozone national ambient air quality standards.

"(b) The Administrator shall promulgate final designations no later than 1 year after the designations required under subsection (a) are required to be submitted.

"Sec. 6104. Additional provisions.

"Nothing in sections 6101 through 6103 [set out above in this note] shall be construed by the Administrator of Environmental Protection Agency or any court, State, or person to affect any pending litigation or to be a ratification of the ozone or $PM_{2.5}$ standards."

Modification or Rescission of Rules, Regulations, Orders, Determinations, Contracts, Certifications, Authorizations, Delegations, and Other Actions

All rules, regulations, orders, determinations, contracts, certifications, authorizations, delegations, or other actions duly issued, made, or taken by or pursuant to Act of July 14, 1955, the Clean Air Act, as in effect immediately prior to the date of enactment of Pub. L. No. 95–95 [Aug. 7, 1977] to continue in full force and effect until modified or rescinded in accordance with Act of July 14, 1955, as amended by Pub. L. No. 95–95 [this chapter], see section 406(b) of Pub. L. No. 95–95, set out as an Effective and Applicability Provisions of 1977 Acts note under section 7401 of this title.

§ 7408. Air quality criteria and control techniques

[CAA § 108]

(a) Air pollutant list; publication and revision by Administrator; issuance of air quality criteria for air pollutants

(1) For the purpose of establishing national primary and secondary ambient air quality standards, the Administrator shall within 30 days after December 31, 1970, publish, and shall from time to time thereafter revise, a list which includes each air pollutant—

(A) emissions of which, in his judgment, cause or contribute to air pollution which may reasonably be anticipated to endanger public health or welfare;

(B) the presence of which in the ambient air results from numerous or diverse mobile or stationary sources; and

(C) for which air quality criteria had not been issued before December 31, 1970 but for which he plans to issue air quality criteria under this section.

(2) The Administrator shall issue air quality criteria for an air pollutant within 12 months after he has included such pollutant in a list under paragraph (1). Air quality criteria for an air pollutant shall accurately reflect the latest scientific knowledge useful in indicating the kind and extent of all identifiable effects on public health or welfare which may be expected from the presence of such pollutant in the ambient air, in varying quantities. The criteria for an air pollutant, to the extent practicable, shall include information on—

(A) those variable factors (including atmospheric conditions) which of themselves or in combination with other factors may alter the effects on public health or welfare of such air pollutant;

(B) the types of air pollutants which, when present in the atmosphere, may interact with such pollutant to produce an adverse effect on public health or welfare; and

(C) any known or anticipated adverse effects on welfare.

(b) Issuance by Administrator of information on air pollution control techniques; standing consulting committees for air pollutants; establishment; membership

(1) Simultaneously with the issuance of criteria under subsection (a) of this section, the Administrator shall, after consultation with appropriate advisory committees and Federal departments and agencies, issue to the States and appropriate air pollution control agencies information on air pollution control techniques, which information shall include data relating to the cost of installation and operation, energy requirements, emission reduction benefits, and environmental impact of the emission control technology. Such information shall include such data as are available on available technology and alternative methods of prevention and control of air pollution. Such information shall also include data on alternative fuels, processes, and operating methods which will result in elimination or significant reduction of emissions.

(2) In order to assist in the development of information on pollution control techniques, the Administrator may establish a standing consulting committee for each air pollutant included in a list published pursuant to subsection (a)(1) of this section, which shall be comprised of technically qualified individuals representative of State and local governments, industry, and the academic community. Each such committee shall submit, as appropriate, to the Administrator information related to that required by paragraph (1).

(c) Review, modification, and reissuance of criteria or information

The Administrator shall from time to time review, and, as appropriate, modify, and reissue any criteria or information on control techniques issued pursuant to this section. Not later than six months after August 7, 1977, the Administrator shall revise and reissue criteria relating to concentrations of NO_2 over such period (not more than three hours) as he deems appropriate. Such criteria shall include a discussion of nitric and nitrous acids, nitrites, nitrates, nitrosamines, and other carcinogenic and potentially carcinogenic derivatives of oxides of nitrogen.

(d) Publication in Federal Register; availability of copies for general public

The issuance of air quality criteria and information on air pollution control techniques shall be announced in the Federal Register and copies shall be made available to the general public.

(e) Transportation planning and guidelines

The Administrator shall, after consultation with the Secretary of Transportation, and after providing public notice and opportunity for comment, and with State and local officials, within nine months after November 15, 1990, and periodically thereafter as necessary to maintain a continuous transportation-air quality planning process, update the June 1978 Transportation-Air Quality Planning Guidelines and publish guidance on the development and implementation of transportation and other measures necessary to demonstrate and maintain attainment of national ambient air quality standards. Such guidelines shall include information on—

(1) methods to identify and evaluate alternative planning and control activities;

(2) methods of reviewing plans on a regular basis as conditions change or new information is presented;

(3) identification of funds and other resources necessary to implement the plan, including interagency agreements on providing such funds and resources;

(4) methods to assure participation by the public in all phases of the planning process; and

(5) such other methods as the Administrator determines necessary to carry out a continuous planning process.

(f) Information regarding processes, procedures, and methods to reduce or control pollutants in transportation; reduction of mobile source related pollutants; reduction of impact on public health

(1) The Administrator shall publish and make available to appropriate Federal, State, and local environmental and transportation agencies not later than one year after November 15, 1990, and from time to time thereafter—

(A) information prepared, as appropriate, in consultation with the Secretary of Transportation, and after providing public notice and opportunity for comment, regarding the formulation and emission reduction potential of transportation control measures related to criteria pollutants and their precursors, including, but not limited to—

(i) programs for improved public transit;

(ii) restriction of certain roads or lanes to, or construction of such roads or lanes for use by, passenger buses or high occupancy vehicles;

(iii) employer-based transportation management plans, including incentives;

(iv) trip-reduction ordinances;

(v) traffic flow improvement programs that achieve emission reductions;

(vi) fringe and transportation corridor parking facilities serving multiple occupancy vehicle programs or transit service;

(vii) programs to limit or restrict vehicle use in downtown areas or other areas of emission concentration particularly during periods of peak use;

(viii) programs for the provision of all forms of high-occupancy, shared-ride services;

(ix) programs to limit portions of road surfaces or certain sections of the metropolitan area to the use of non-motorized vehicles or pedestrian use, both as to time and place;

(x) programs for secure bicycle storage facilities and other facilities, including bicycle lanes, for the convenience and protection of bicyclists, in both public and private areas;

(xi) programs to control extended idling of vehicles;

(xii) programs to reduce motor vehicle emissions, consistent with subchapter II of this chapter, which are caused by extreme cold start conditions;

(xiii) employer-sponsored programs to permit flexible work schedules;

(xiv) programs and ordinances to facilitate non-automobile travel, provision and utilization of mass transit, and to generally reduce the need for single-occupant vehicle travel, as part of transportation planning and development efforts of a locality, including programs and ordinances applicable to new shopping centers, special events, and other centers of vehicle activity;

(xv) programs for new construction and major reconstructions of paths, tracks or areas solely for the use by pedestrian or other non-motorized means of transportation when economically feasible and in the public interest. For purposes of this clause, the Administrator shall also consult with the Secretary of the Interior; and

(xvi) program to encourage the voluntary removal from use and the marketplace of pre-1980 model year light duty vehicles and pre-1980 model light duty trucks.

(B) information on additional methods or strategies that will contribute to the reduction of mobile source related pollutants during periods in which any primary ambient air quality standard will be exceeded and during episodes for which an air pollution alert, warning, or emergency has been declared;

(C) information on other measures which may be employed to reduce the impact on public health or protect the health of sensitive or susceptible individuals or groups; and

(D) information on the extent to which any process, procedure, or method to reduce or control such air pollutant may cause an increase in the emissions or formation of any other pollutant.

(2) In publishing such information the Administrator shall also include an assessment of—

(A) the relative effectiveness of such processes, procedures, and methods;

(B) the potential effect of such processes, procedures, and methods on transportation systems and the provision of transportation services; and

(C) the environmental, energy, and economic impact of such processes, procedures, and methods.

(g) Assessment of risks to ecosystems

The Administrator may assess the risks to ecosystems from exposure to criteria air pollutants (as identified by the Administrator in the Administrator's sole discretion).

(h) RACT/BACT/LAER clearinghouse

The Administrator shall make information regarding emission control technology available to the States and to the general public through a central database. Such information shall include all control technology information received pursuant to State plan provisions requiring permits for sources, including operating permits for existing sources.

(July 14, 1955, c. 360, Title I, § 108, as added by Pub. L. No. 91–604, § 4(a), 84 Stat. 1678 (Dec. 31, 1970); and amended by Pub. L. No. 95–95, Title I, §§ 104, 105, Title IV, § 401(a), 91 Stat. 689, 790 (Aug. 7, 1977); Pub. L. No. 101–549, Title I, §§ 108(a) to (c), (*o*), 111, 104 Stat. 2465, 2466, 2469, 2470 (Nov. 15, 1990); Pub. L. No. 105–362, Title XV, § 1501(b), 112 Stat. 3294 (Nov. 10, 1998).)

HISTORICAL AND STATUTORY NOTES

Codifications

This section was formerly codified as section 1857c–3 of this title.

Reference in subsec. (e) in the original to "enactment of the Clean Air Act Amendments of 1989" has been codified as "November 15, 1990" as manifesting Congressional intent in the date of the enactment of Pub. L. No. 101–549, 104 Stat. 2399 (Nov. 15, 1990), popularly known as the Clean Air Act Amendments of 1990.

Effective and Applicability Provisions

1990 Acts. Amendment by Pub. L. No. 101–549 effective Nov. 15, 1990, except as otherwise provided, see section 711(b) of Pub. L. No. 101–549, set out as a note under section 7401 of this title.

1977 Acts. Amendment by Pub. L. No. 95–95 effective Aug. 7, 1977, except as otherwise expressly provided, see section 406(d) of Pub. L. No. 95–95, set out as a note under section 7401 of this title.

Savings Provisions

Suits, actions or proceedings commenced under this chapter as in effect prior to Nov. 15, 1990, not to abate by reason of the taking effect of amendments by Pub. L. No. 101–549, except as otherwise provided for, see section 711(a) of Pub. L. No. 101–549, set out as a note under section 7401 of this title.

Prior Provisions

A prior section 108 of Act of July 14, 1955, was renumbered section 115 by Pub. L. No. 91–604 and is set out as section 7415 of this title.

Modification or Rescission of Rules, Regulations, Orders, Determinations, Contracts, Certifications, Authorizations, Delegations, and Other Actions

All rules, regulations, orders, determinations, contracts, certifications, authorizations, delegations, or other actions duly issued, made, or taken by or pursuant to Act of July 14, 1955, the Clean Air Act, as in effect immediately prior to the date of enactment of Pub. L. No. 95–95 [Aug. 7, 1977] to continue in full force and effect until modified or rescinded in accordance with Act of July 14, 1955, as amended by Pub. L. No. 95–95 [this chapter], see section 406(b) of Pub. L. No. 95–95, set out as an Effective and Applicability Provisions of 1977 Acts note under section 7401 of this title.

§ 7409. National primary and secondary ambient air quality standards

[CAA § 109]

(a) Promulgation

(1) The Administrator—

(A) within 30 days after December 31, 1970, shall publish proposed regulations prescribing a national primary ambient air quality standard and a national secondary ambient air quality standard for each air pollutant for which air quality criteria have been issued prior to such date; and

(B) after a reasonable time for interested persons to submit written comments thereon (but no later than 90 days after the initial publication of such proposed standards) shall by regulation promulgate such proposed national primary and secondary ambient air quality standards with such modifications as he deems appropriate.

(2) With respect to any air pollutant for which air quality criteria are issued after December 31, 1970, the Administrator shall publish, simultaneously with the issuance of such criteria and information, proposed national primary and secondary ambient air quality standards for any such pollutant. The procedure provided for in paragraph (1)(B) of this subsection shall apply to the promulgation of such standards.

(b) Protection of public health and welfare

(1) National primary ambient air quality standards, prescribed under subsection (a) of this section shall be ambient air quality standards the attainment and maintenance of which in the judgment of the Administrator, based on such criteria and allowing an adequate margin of safety, are requisite to protect the public health. Such primary standards may be revised in the same manner as promulgated.

(2) Any national secondary ambient air quality standard prescribed under subsection (a) of this section shall specify a level of air quality the attainment and maintenance of which in the judgment of the Administrator, based on such criteria, is requisite to protect the public welfare from any known or anticipated adverse effects associated with the presence of such air pollutant in the ambient air. Such secondary standards may be revised in the same manner as promulgated.

(c) National primary ambient air quality standard for nitrogen dioxide

The Administrator shall, not later than one year after August 7, 1977, promulgate a national primary ambient air quality standard for NO_2 concentrations over a period of not more than 3 hours unless, based on the criteria issued under section 7408(c) of this title, he finds that there is no significant evidence that such a standard for such a period is requisite to protect public health.

(d) Review and revision of criteria and standards; independent scientific review committee; appointment; advisory functions

(1) Not later than December 31, 1980, and at five-year intervals thereafter, the Administrator shall complete a thorough review of the criteria published under section 7408 of this title and the national ambient air quality standards promulgated under this section and shall make such revisions in such criteria and standards and promulgate such new standards as may be appropriate in accordance with section 7408 of this title and subsection (b) of this section. The Administrator may review and revise criteria or promulgate new standards earlier or more frequently than required under this paragraph.

(2) (A) The Administrator shall appoint an independent scientific review committee composed of seven members including at least one member of the National Academy of Sciences, one physician, and one person representing State air pollution control agencies.

(B) Not later than January 1, 1980, and at five-year intervals thereafter, the committee referred to in subparagraph (A) shall complete a review of the criteria published under section 7408 of this title and the national primary and secondary ambient air quality standards promulgated under this section and shall recommend to the Administrator any new national ambient air quality standards and revisions of existing criteria and standards as may be appropriate under section 7408 of this title and subsection (b) of this section.

(C) Such committee shall also (i) advise the Administrator of areas in which additional knowledge is required to appraise the adequacy and basis of existing, new, or revised national ambient air quality standards, (ii) describe the research efforts necessary to provide the required information, (iii) advise the Administrator on the relative contribution to air pollution concentrations of natural as well as anthropogenic activity, and (iv) advise the Administrator of any adverse public health, welfare, social, economic, or energy effects which may result from various strategies for attainment and maintenance of such national ambient air quality standards.

(July 14, 1955, c. 360, Title I, § 109, as added by Pub. L. No. 91–604, § 4(a), 84 Stat. 1679 (Dec. 31, 1970); and amended by Pub. L. No. 95–95, Title I, § 106, 91 Stat. 691 (Aug. 7, 1977).)

HISTORICAL AND STATUTORY NOTES

Codifications

This section was formerly codified as section 1857c–4 of this title.

Effective and Applicability Provisions

1977 Acts. Amendment by Pub. L. No. 95–95 effective Aug. 7, 1977, except as otherwise expressly provided, see section 406(d) of Pub. L. No. 95–95, set out as a note under section 7401 of this title.

Prior Provisions

A prior section 109 of Act of July 14, 1955, was renumbered section 116 by Pub. L. No. 91–604 and is set out as section 7416 of this title.

Modification or Rescission of Rules, Regulations, Orders, Determinations, Contracts, Certifications, Authorizations, Delegations, and Other Actions

All rules, regulations, orders, determinations, contracts, certifications, authorizations, delegations, or other actions duly issued, made, or taken by or pursuant to Act of July 14, 1955, the Clean Air Act, as in effect immediately prior to the date of enactment of Pub. L. No. 95–95 [Aug. 7, 1977] to continue in full force and effect until modified or rescinded in accordance with Act of July 14, 1955, as amended by Pub. L. No. 95–95 [this chapter], see section 406(b) of Pub. L. No. 95–95, set out as an Effective and Applicability Provisions of 1977 Acts note under section 7401 of this title.

Role of Secondary Standards

Pub. L. No. 101–549, Title VIII, § 817, 104 Stat. 2697 (Nov. 15, 1990), which provided for a report to Congress to be prepared by the National Academy of Sciences, relating to the role of national secondary ambient air quality standards in protecting welfare and the environment, and to be transmitted not later than 3 years after the date of enactment of the Clean Air Act Amendments of 1990 [Nov. 15, 1990], terminated, effective May 15, 2000, pursuant to Pub. L. No. 104–66, § 3003, as amended, set out as a note under 31 U.S.C.A. § 1113, and the 6th item on page 163 of House Document No. 103–7.

Termination of Advisory Committees

Advisory committees established after Jan. 5, 1973, to terminate not later than the expiration of the two-year period beginning on the date of their establishment, unless, in the case of a committee established by the President or an officer of the Federal Government, such committee is renewed by appropriate action prior to the expiration of such two-year period, or in the case of a committee established by the Congress, its duration is otherwise provided for by law, see section 14 of Pub. L. No. 92–463, 86 Stat. 776 (Oct. 6, 1972), set out in Appendix 2 to Title 5, Government Organization and Employees.

§ 7410. State implementation plans for national primary and secondary ambient air quality standards

[CAA § 110]

(a) Adoption of plan by State; submission to Administrator; content of plan; revision; new sources; indirect source review program; supplemental or intermittent control systems

(1) Each State shall, after reasonable notice and public hearings, adopt and submit to the Administrator, within 3 years (or such shorter period as the Administrator may prescribe) after the promulgation of a national primary ambient air quality standard (or any revision thereof) under section 7409 of this title for any air pollutant, a plan which provides for implementation, maintenance, and enforcement of such primary standard in each air quality control region (or portion thereof) within such State. In addition, such State shall adopt and submit to the Administrator (either as a part of a plan submitted under the preceding sentence or separately) within 3 years (or such shorter period as the Administrator may prescribe) after the promulgation of a national ambient air quality secondary standard (or revision thereof), a plan which provides for implementation, maintenance, and enforcement of such secondary standard in each air quality control region (or portion thereof) within such State. Unless a separate public hearing is provided, each State shall consider its plan implementing such secondary standard at the hearing required by the first sentence of this paragraph.

(2) Each implementation plan submitted by a State under this chapter shall be adopted by the State after reasonable notice and public hearing. Each such plan shall—

(A) include enforceable emission limitations and other control measures, means, or techniques (including economic incentives such as fees, marketable permits, and auctions of emissions rights), as well as schedules and timetables for compliance, as may be necessary or appropriate to meet the applicable requirements of this chapter;

(B) provide for establishment and operation of appropriate devices, methods, systems, and procedures necessary to—

(i) monitor, compile, and analyze data on ambient air quality, and

(ii) upon request, make such data available to the Administrator;

(C) include a program to provide for the enforcement of the measures described in subparagraph (A), and regulation of the modification and construction of any stationary source within the areas covered by the plan as necessary to assure that national ambient air quality standards are achieved, including a permit program as required in parts C and D of this subchapter;

(D) contain adequate provisions—

(i) prohibiting, consistent with the provisions of this subchapter, any source or other type of emissions activity within the State from emitting any air pollutant in amounts which will—

(I) contribute significantly to nonattainment in, or interfere with maintenance by, any other State with respect to any such national primary or secondary ambient air quality standard, or

(II) interfere with measures required to be included in the applicable implementation plan for any other State under part C of this subchapter to prevent significant deterioration of air quality or to protect visibility,

(ii) insuring compliance with the applicable requirements of sections 7426 and 7415 of this title (relating to interstate and international pollution abatement);

(E) provide (i) necessary assurances that the State (or, except where the Administrator deems inappropriate, the general purpose local government or governments, or a regional agency designated by the State or general purpose local governments for such purpose) will have adequate personnel, funding, and authority under State (and, as appropriate, local) law to carry out such implementation plan (and is not prohibited by any provision of Federal or State law from carrying out such implementation plan or portion thereof), (ii) requirements that the State comply with the requirements respecting State boards under section 7428 of this title, and (iii) necessary assurances that, where the State has relied on a local or regional government, agency, or instrumentality for the implementation of any plan provision, the State has responsibility for ensuring adequate implementation of such plan provision;

(F) require, as may be prescribed by the Administrator—

(i) the installation, maintenance, and replacement of equipment, and the implementation of other necessary steps, by owners or operators of stationary sources to monitor emissions from such sources,

(ii) periodic reports on the nature and amounts of emissions and emissions-related data from such sources, and

(iii) correlation of such reports by the State agency with any emission limitations or standards established pursuant to this chapter, which reports shall be available at reasonable times for public inspection;

(G) provide for authority comparable to that in section 7603 of this title and adequate contingency plans to implement such authority;

(H) provide for revision of such plan—

(i) from time to time as may be necessary to take account of revisions of such national primary or secondary ambient air quality standard or the availability of improved or more expeditious methods of attaining such standard, and

(ii) except as provided in paragraph (3)(C), whenever the Administrator finds on the basis of information available to the Administrator that the plan is substantially inadequate to attain the national ambient air quality standard which it implements or to otherwise comply with any additional requirements established under this chapter;

(I) in the case of a plan or plan revision for an area designated as a nonattainment area, meet the applicable requirements of part D of this subchapter (relating to nonattainment areas);

(J) meet the applicable requirements of section 7421 of this title (relating to consultation), section 7427 of this title (relating to public notification), and part C of this subchapter (relating to prevention of significant deterioration of air quality and visibility protection);

(K) provide for—

(i) the performance of such air quality modeling as the Administrator may prescribe for the purpose of predicting the effect on ambient air quality of any emissions of any air pollutant for which the Administrator has established a national ambient air quality standard, and

(ii) the submission, upon request, of data related to such air quality modeling to the Administrator;

(L) require the owner or operator of each major stationary source to pay to the permitting authority, as a condition of any permit required under this chapter, a fee sufficient to cover—

(i) the reasonable costs of reviewing and acting upon any application for such a permit, and

(ii) if the owner or operator receives a permit for such source, the reasonable costs of implementing and enforcing the terms and conditions of any such permit (not including any court costs or other costs associated with any enforcement action),

until such fee requirement is superseded with respect to such sources by the Administrator's approval of a fee program under subchapter V of this chapter; and

(M) provide for consultation and participation by local political subdivisions affected by the plan.

(3) (A) Repealed. Pub. L. No. 101–549, Title I, § 101(d)(1), 104 Stat. 2409 (Nov. 15, 1990).

(B) As soon as practicable, the Administrator shall, consistent with the purposes of this chapter and the Energy Supply and Environmental Coordination Act of 1974 [15 U.S.C.A. § 791 et seq.], review each State's applicable implementation plans and report to the State on whether such plans can be revised in relation to fuel burning stationary sources (or persons supplying fuel to such sources) without interfering with the attainment and maintenance of any national ambient air quality standard within the period permitted in this section. If the Administrator determines that any such plan can be revised, he shall notify the State that a plan revision may be submitted by the State. Any plan revision which is submitted by the State shall, after public notice and opportunity for public hearing, be approved by the Administrator if the revision relates only to fuel burning stationary sources (or persons supplying fuel to such sources), and the plan as revised complies with paragraph (2) of this subsection. The Administrator shall approve or disapprove any revision no later than three months after its submission.

(C) Neither the State, in the case of a plan (or portion thereof) approved under this subsection, nor the Administrator, in the case of a plan (or portion thereof) promulgated under subsection (c) of this section, shall be required to revise an applicable implementation plan because one or more exemptions under section 7418 of this title (relating to Federal facilities), enforcement orders under section 7413(d) of this title, suspensions under subsection (f) or (g) of this section (relating to temporary energy or economic authority), orders under section 7419 of this title (relating to primary nonferrous smelters), or extensions of compliance in decrees entered under section 7413(e) of this title (relating to iron- and steel-producing operations) have been granted, if such plan would have met the requirements of this section if no such exemptions, orders, or extensions had been granted.

(4) Repealed. Pub. L. No. 101–549, Title I, § 101(d)(2), 104 Stat. 2409 (Nov. 15, 1990).

(5) (A) (i) Any State may include in a State implementation plan, but the Administrator may not require as a condition of approval of such plan under this section, any indirect source review program. The Administrator may approve and enforce, as part of an applicable implementation plan, an indirect source review program which the State chooses to adopt and submit as part of its plan.

(ii) Except as provided in subparagraph (B), no plan promulgated by the Administrator shall include any indirect source review program for any air quality control region, or portion thereof.

(iii) Any State may revise an applicable implementation plan approved under this subsection to suspend or revoke any such program included in such plan, provided that such plan meets the requirements of this section.

(B) The Administrator shall have the authority to promulgate, implement and enforce regulations under subsection (c) of this section respecting indirect source review programs which apply only to federally assisted highways, airports, and other major federally assisted indirect sources and federally owned or operated indirect sources.

(C) For purposes of this paragraph, the term "indirect source" means a facility, building, structure, installation, real property, road, or highway which attracts, or may attract, mobile sources of pollution. Such term includes parking lots, parking garages, and other facilities subject to any measure for management of parking supply (within the meaning of subsection (c)(2)(D)(ii) of this section), including regulation of existing off-street parking but such term does not include new or existing on-street parking. Direct emissions sources or facilities at, within, or associated with, any indirect source shall not be deemed indirect sources for the purpose of this paragraph.

(D) For purposes of this paragraph the term "indirect source review program" means the facility-by-facility review of indirect sources of air pollution, including such measures as are necessary to assure, or assist in assuring, that a new or modified indirect source will not attract mobile sources of air pollution, the emissions from which would cause or contribute to air pollution concentrations—

(i) exceeding any national primary ambient air quality standard for a mobile source-related air pollutant after the primary standard attainment date, or

(ii) preventing maintenance of any such standard after such date.

(E) For purposes of this paragraph and paragraph (2)(B), the term "transportation control measure" does not include any measure which is an "indirect source review program".

(6) No State plan shall be treated as meeting the requirements of this section unless such plan provides that in the case of any source which uses a supplemental, or intermittent control system for purposes of meeting the requirements of an order under section 7413(d) of this title or section 7419 of this title (relating to primary nonferrous smelter orders), the owner or operator of such source may not temporarily reduce the pay of any employee by reason of the use of such supplemental or intermittent or other dispersion dependent control system.

(b) Extension of period for submission of plans

The Administrator may, wherever he determines necessary, extend the period for submission of any plan or portion thereof which implements a national secondary ambient air quality standard for a period not to exceed 18 months from the date otherwise required for submission of such plan.

(c) Preparation and publication by Administrator of proposed regulations setting forth implementation plan; transportation regulations study and report; parking surcharge; suspension authority; plan implementation

(1) The Administrator shall promulgate a Federal implementation plan at any time within 2 years after the Administrator—

(A) finds that a State has failed to make a required submission or finds that the plan or plan revision submitted by the State does not satisfy the minimum criteria established under subsection (k)(1)(A) of this section, or

(B) disapproves a State implementation plan submission in whole or in part,

unless the State corrects the deficiency, and the Administrator approves the plan or plan revision, before the Administrator promulgates such Federal implementation plan.

(2) (A) **Repealed. Pub. L. No. 101–549, Title I, § 101(d)(3)(A), 104 Stat. 2409 (Nov. 15, 1990).**

(B) No parking surcharge regulation may be required by the Administrator under paragraph (1) of this subsection as a part of an applicable implementation plan. All parking surcharge regulations previously required by the Administrator shall be void upon June 22, 1974. This subparagraph shall not prevent the Administrator from approving parking surcharges if they are adopted and submitted by a State as part of an applicable implementation plan. The Administrator may not condition approval of any implementation plan submitted by a State on such plan's including a parking surcharge regulation.

(C) **Repealed. Pub. L. No. 101–549, Title I, § 101(d)(3)(B), 104 Stat. 2409 (Nov. 15, 1990).**

(D) For purposes of this paragraph—

(i) The term "parking surcharge regulation" means a regulation imposing or requiring the imposition of any tax, surcharge, fee, or other charge on parking spaces, or any other area used for the temporary storage of motor vehicles.

(ii) The term "management of parking supply" shall include any requirement providing that any new facility containing a given number of parking spaces shall receive a permit or other prior approval, issuance of which is to be conditioned on air quality considerations.

(iii) The term "preferential bus/carpool lane" shall include any requirement for the setting aside of one or more lanes of a street or highway on a permanent or temporary basis for the exclusive use of buses or carpools, or both.

(E) No standard, plan, or requirement, relating to management of parking supply or preferential bus/carpool lanes shall be promulgated after June 22, 1974, by the Administrator pursuant to this section, unless such promulgation has been subjected to at least one public hearing which has been held in the area affected and for which reasonable notice has been given in such area. If substantial changes are made following public hearings, one or more additional hearings shall be held in such area after such notice.

(3) Upon application of the chief executive officer of any general purpose unit of local government, if the Administrator determines that such unit has adequate authority under State or local law, the Administrator may delegate to such unit the authority to implement and enforce within the jurisdiction of such unit any part of a plan promulgated under this subsection. Nothing in this paragraph shall prevent the Administrator from implementing or enforcing any applicable provision of a plan promulgated under this subsection.

(4) Repealed. Pub. L. No. 101–549, Title I, § 101(d)(3)(C), 104 Stat. 2409 (Nov. 15, 1990).

(5) **(A)** Any measure in an applicable implementation plan which requires a toll or other charge for the use of a bridge located entirely within one city shall be eliminated from such plan by the Administrator upon application by the Governor of the State, which application shall include a certification by the Governor that he will revise such plan in accordance with subparagraph (B).

(B) In the case of any applicable implementation plan with respect to which a measure has been eliminated under subparagraph (A), such plan shall, not later than one year after August 7, 1977, be revised to include comprehensive measures to:

(i) establish, expand, or improve public transportation measures to meet basic transportation needs, as expeditiously as is practicable; and

(ii) implement transportation control measures necessary to attain and maintain national ambient air quality standards,

and such revised plan shall, for the purpose of implementing such comprehensive public transportation measures, include requirements to use (insofar as is necessary) Federal grants, State or local funds, or any combination of such grants and funds as may be consistent with the terms of the legislation providing such grants and funds. Such measures shall, as a substitute for the tolls or charges eliminated under subparagraph (A), provide for emissions reductions equivalent to the reductions which may reasonably be expected to be achieved through the use of the tolls or charges eliminated.

(C) Any revision of an implementation plan for purposes of meeting the requirements of subparagraph (B) shall be submitted in coordination with any plan revision required under part D of this subchapter.

(d), (e) Repealed. Pub. L. No. 101–549, Title I, § 101(d)(4), (5), 104 Stat. 2409 (Nov. 15, 1990).

(f) National or regional energy emergencies; determination by President

(1) Upon application by the owner or operator of a fuel burning stationary source, and after notice and opportunity for public hearing, the Governor of the State in which such source is located may petition the President to determine that a national or regional energy emergency exists of such severity that—

(A) a temporary suspension of any part of the applicable implementation plan or of any requirement under section 7651j of this title (concerning excess emissions penalties or offsets) may be necessary, and

(B) other means of responding to the energy emergency may be inadequate.

Such determination shall not be delegable by the President to any other person. If the President determines that a national or regional energy emergency of such severity exists, a temporary emergency suspension of any part of an applicable implementation plan or of any requirement under section 7651j of this title (concerning excess emissions penalties or offsets) adopted by the State may be issued by the Governor of any State covered by the President's determination under the condition specified in paragraph (2) and may take effect immediately.

(2) A temporary emergency suspension under this subsection shall be issued to a source only if the Governor of such State finds that—

(A) there exists in the vicinity of such source a temporary energy emergency involving high levels of unemployment or loss of necessary energy supplies for residential dwellings; and

(B) such unemployment or loss can be totally or partially alleviated by such emergency suspension.

Not more than one such suspension may be issued for any source on the basis of the same set of circumstances or on the basis of the same emergency.

(3) A temporary emergency suspension issued by a Governor under this subsection shall remain in effect for a maximum of four months or such lesser period as may be specified in a disapproval order of the Administrator, if any. The Administrator may disapprove such suspension if he determines that it does not meet the requirements of paragraph (2).

(4) This subsection shall not apply in the case of a plan provision or requirement promulgated by the Administrator under subsection (c) of this section, but in any such case the President may grant a temporary emergency suspension for a four month period of any such provision or requirement if he makes the determinations and findings specified in paragraphs (1) and (2).

(5) The Governor may include in any temporary emergency suspension issued under this subsection a provision delaying for a period identical to the period of such suspension any compliance schedule (or increment of progress) to which such source is subject under section 1857c–10 of this title, as in effect before August 7, 1977, or section 7413(d) of this title, upon a finding that such source is unable to comply with such schedule (or increment) solely because of the conditions on the basis of which a suspension was issued under this subsection.

(g) Governor's authority to issue temporary emergency suspensions

(1) In the case of any State which has adopted and submitted to the Administrator a proposed plan revision which the State determines—

(A) meets the requirements of this section, and

(B) is necessary (i) to prevent the closing for one year or more of any source of air pollution, and (ii) to prevent substantial increases in unemployment which would result from such closing, and

which the Administrator has not approved or disapproved under this section within 12 months of submission of the proposed plan revision, the Governor may issue a temporary emergency suspension of the part of the applicable implementation plan for such State which is proposed to be revised with respect to such source. The determination under subparagraph (B) may not be made with respect to a source which would close without regard to whether or not the proposed plan revision is approved.

(2) A temporary emergency suspension issued by a Governor under this subsection shall remain in effect for a maximum of four months or such lesser period as may be specified in a disapproval order of the Administrator. The Administrator may disapprove such suspension if he determines that it does not meet the requirements of this subsection.

(3) The Governor may include in any temporary emergency suspension issued under this subsection a provision delaying for a period identical to the period of such suspension any compliance schedule (or increment of progress) to which such source is subject under section 1857c–10 of this title as in effect before August 7, 1977, or under section 7413(d) of this title upon a finding that such source is unable to comply with such schedule (or increment) solely because of the conditions on the basis of which a suspension was issued under this subsection.

(h) Publication of comprehensive document for each State setting forth requirements of applicable implementation plan

(1) Not later than 5 years after November 15, 1990, and every 3 years thereafter, the Administrator shall assemble and publish a comprehensive document for each State setting forth all requirements of the applicable implementation plan for such State and shall publish notice in the Federal Register of the availability of such documents.

(2) The Administrator may promulgate such regulations as may be reasonably necessary to carry out the purpose of this subsection.

(i) Modification of requirements prohibited

Except for a primary nonferrous smelter order under section 7419 of this title, a suspension under subsection (f) or (g) of this section (relating to emergency suspensions), an exemption under section 7418 of this title (relating to certain Federal facilities), an order under section 7413(d) of this title (relating to compliance orders), a plan promulgation under subsection (c) of this section, or a plan revision under subsection (a)(3) of this section, no order, suspension, plan revision, or other action modifying any requirement of an applicable implementation plan may be taken with respect to any stationary source by the State or by the Administrator.

(j) Technological systems of continuous emission reduction on new or modified stationary sources; compliance with performance standards

As a condition for issuance of any permit required under this subchapter, the owner or operator of each new or modified stationary source which is required to obtain such a permit must show to the satisfaction of the permitting authority that the technological system of continuous emission reduction which is to be used at such source will enable it to comply with the standards of performance which are to apply to such source and that the construction or modification and operation of such source will be in compliance with all other requirements of this chapter.

(k) Environmental Protection Agency action on plan submissions

(1) Completeness of plan submissions

(A) Completeness criteria

Within 9 months after November 15, 1990, the Administrator shall promulgate minimum criteria that any plan submission must meet before the Administrator is required to act on such submission under this subsection. The criteria shall be limited to the information necessary to enable the Administrator to determine whether the plan submission complies with the provisions of this chapter.

(B) Completeness finding

Within 60 days of the Administrator's receipt of a plan or plan revision, but no later than 6 months after the date, if any, by which a State is required to submit the plan or revision, the Administrator shall determine whether the minimum criteria established pursuant to subparagraph (A) have been met. Any plan or plan revision that a State submits to the Administrator, and that has not been determined by the Administrator (by the date 6 months after receipt of the submission) to have failed to meet the minimum criteria established pursuant to subparagraph (A), shall on that date be deemed by operation of law to meet such minimum criteria.

(C) Effect of finding of incompleteness

Where the Administrator determines that a plan submission (or part thereof) does not meet the minimum criteria established pursuant to subparagraph (A), the State shall be treated as not having made the submission (or, in the Administrator's discretion, part thereof).

(2) Deadline for action

Within 12 months of a determination by the Administrator (or a determination deemed by operation of law) under paragraph (1) that a State has submitted a plan or plan revision (or, in the Administrator's discretion, part thereof) that meets the minimum criteria established pursuant to paragraph (1), if applicable (or, if those criteria are not applicable, within 12 months of submission of the plan or revision), the Administrator shall act on the submission in accordance with paragraph (3).

(3) Full and partial approval and disapproval

In the case of any submittal on which the Administrator is required to act under paragraph (2), the Administrator shall approve such submittal as a whole if it meets all of the applicable requirements of this chapter. If a portion of the plan revision meets all the applicable requirements of this chapter, the Administrator may approve the plan revision in part and disapprove the plan revision in part. The plan revision shall not be treated as meeting the requirements of this chapter until the Administrator approves the entire plan revision as complying with the applicable requirements of this chapter.

(4) Conditional approval

The Administrator may approve a plan revision based on a commitment of the State to adopt specific enforceable measures by a date certain, but not later than 1 year after the date of approval of the plan revision. Any such conditional approval shall be treated as a disapproval if the State fails to comply with such commitment.

(5) Calls for plan revisions

Whenever the Administrator finds that the applicable implementation plan for any area is substantially inadequate to attain or maintain the relevant national ambient air quality standard, to mitigate adequately the interstate pollutant transport described in section 7506a of this title or section 7511c of this title, or to otherwise comply with any requirement of this chapter, the Administrator shall require the State to revise the plan as necessary to correct such inadequacies. The Administrator shall notify the State of the inadequacies, and may establish reasonable deadlines (not to exceed 18 months after the date of such notice) for the submission of such plan revisions. Such findings and notice shall be public. Any finding under this paragraph shall, to the extent the Administrator deems appropriate, subject the State to the requirements of this chapter to which the State was subject when it developed and submitted the plan for which such finding was made, except that the Administrator may adjust any dates applicable under such requirements as appropriate (except that the Administrator may not adjust any attainment date prescribed under part D of this subchapter, unless such date has elapsed).

(6) Corrections

Whenever the Administrator determines that the Administrator's action approving, disapproving, or promulgating any plan or plan revision (or part thereof), area designation, redesignation, classification, or reclassification was in error, the Administrator may in the same manner as the approval, disapproval, or promulgation revise such action as appropriate without requiring any further submission from the State. Such determination and the basis thereof shall be provided to the State and public.

(*l*) Plan revisions

Each revision to an implementation plan submitted by a State under this chapter shall be adopted by such State after reasonable notice and public hearing. The Administrator shall not approve a revision of a plan if the revision would interfere with any applicable requirement concerning attainment and reasonable further progress (as defined in section 7501 of this title), or any other applicable requirement of this chapter.

(m) Sanctions

The Administrator may apply any of the sanctions listed in section 7509(b) of this title at any time (or at any time after) the Administrator makes a finding, disapproval, or determination under paragraphs (1) through (4), respectively, of section 7509(a) of this title in relation to any plan or plan item (as that term is defined by the Administrator) required under this chapter, with respect to any portion of the State the Administrator determines reasonable and appropriate, for the purpose of ensuring that the requirements of this chapter relating to such plan or plan item are met. The Administrator shall, by rule, establish criteria for exercising his authority under the previous sentence with respect to any deficiency referred to in section 7509(a) of this title to ensure that, during the 24-month period following the finding, disapproval, or determination referred to in section 7509(a) of this title, such sanctions are not applied on a statewide basis where one or more political subdivisions covered by the applicable implementation plan are principally responsible for such deficiency.

(n) Savings clauses

(1) Existing plan provisions

Any provision of any applicable implementation plan that was approved or promulgated by the Administrator pursuant to this section as in effect before November 15, 1990, shall remain in effect as part of such applicable implementation plan, except to the extent that a revision to such provision is approved or promulgated by the Administrator pursuant to this chapter.

(2) **Attainment dates**

For any area not designated nonattainment, any plan or plan revision submitted or required to be submitted by a State—

(A) in response to the promulgation or revision of a national primary ambient air quality standard in effect on November 15, 1990, or

(B) in response to a finding of substantial inadequacy under subsection (a)(2) of this section (as in effect immediately before November 15, 1990),

shall provide for attainment of the national primary ambient air quality standards within 3 years of November 15, 1990, or within 5 years of issuance of such finding of substantial inadequacy, whichever is later.

(3) **Retention of construction moratorium in certain areas**

In the case of an area to which, immediately before November 15, 1990, the prohibition on construction or modification of major stationary sources prescribed in subsection (a)(2)(I) of this section (as in effect immediately before November 15, 1990) applied by virtue of a finding of the Administrator that the State containing such area had not submitted an implementation plan meeting the requirements of section 7502(b)(6) of this title (relating to establishment of a permit program) (as in effect immediately before November 15, 1990) or 7502(a)(1) of this title (to the extent such requirements relate to provision for attainment of the primary national ambient air quality standard for sulfur oxides by December 31, 1982) as in effect immediately before November 15, 1990, no major stationary source of the relevant air pollutant or pollutants shall be constructed or modified in such area until the Administrator finds that the plan for such area meets the applicable requirements of section 7502(c)(5) of this title (relating to permit programs) or subpart 5 of part D of this subchapter (relating to attainment of the primary national ambient air quality standard for sulfur dioxide), respectively.

(*o*) Indian tribes

If an Indian tribe submits an implementation plan to the Administrator pursuant to section 7601(d) of this title, the plan shall be reviewed in accordance with the provisions for review set forth in this section for State plans, except as otherwise provided by regulation promulgated pursuant to section 7601(d)(2) of this title. When such plan becomes effective in accordance with the regulations promulgated under section 7601(d) of this title, the plan shall become applicable to all areas (except as expressly provided otherwise in the plan) located within the exterior boundaries of the reservation, notwithstanding the issuance of any patent and including rights-of-way running through the reservation.

(p) Reports

Any State shall submit, according to such schedule as the Administrator may prescribe, such reports as the Administrator may require relating to emission reductions, vehicle miles traveled, congestion levels, and any other information the Administrator may deem necessary to assess the development effectiveness, need for revision, or implementation of any plan or plan revision required under this chapter.

(July 14, 1955, c. 360, Title I, § 110, as added by Pub. L. No. 91–604, § 4(a), 84 Stat. 1680 (Dec. 31, 1970); and amended by Pub. L. No. 93–319, § 4, 88 Stat. 256 (June 22, 1974); S.Res. 4 (Feb. 4, 1977); Pub. L. No. 95–95, Title I, §§ 107, 108, 91 Stat. 691, 693 (Aug. 7, 1977); Pub. L. No. 95–190, § 14(a)(1)–(6), 91 Stat. 1399 (Nov. 16, 1977); Pub. L. No. 97–23, § 3, 95 Stat. 142 (July 17, 1981); Pub. L. No. 101–549, Title I, §§ 101(b)–(d), 102(h), 107(c), 108(d), Title IV, § 412, 104 Stat. 2404–2408, 2422, 2464, 2466, 2634 (Nov. 15, 1990).)

HISTORICAL AND STATUTORY NOTES

References in Text

The Energy Supply and Environmental Coordination Act of 1974, referred to in subsec. (a)(3)(B), is Pub. L. No. 93–319, 88 Stat. 246 (June 22, 1974), as amended, which is codified principally as chapter 16C (section 791 et seq.) of Title 15, Commerce and Trade. For complete classification of this Act to the Code, see Short Title note set out under section 791 of Title 15 and Tables.

Section 7413 of this title, referred to in subsecs. (a)(3)(C), (6), (f)(5), (g)(3), and (i), was amended generally by Pub. L. No. 101–549, Title VII, § 701, 104 Stat. 2672 (Nov. 15, 1990), and, as so amended, subsecs. (d) and (e) of section 7413 no longer relate to final compliance orders and steel industry compliance extension, respectively.

Section 1857c–10 of this title, as in effect before August 7, 1977, referred to in subsecs. (f)(5) and (g)(3), was in the original "section 119, as in effect before the date of the enactment of this paragraph", meaning section 119 of Act of July 14, 1955, c. 360, Title I, as added by Pub. L. No. 93–319, § 3, 88 Stat. 248 (June 22, 1974), (which was codified as section 1857c–10 of this title) as in effect prior to the enactment of subsecs. (f)(5) and (g)(3) of this section by Pub. L. No. 95–95, § 107, 91 Stat. 691 (Aug. 7, 1977), effective Aug. 7, 1977. Section 112(b)(1) of Pub. L. No. 95–95 repealed section 119 of Act of July 14, 1955, c. 360, Title I, as added by Pub. L. No. 93–319, and provided that all references to such section 119 in any subsequent enactment which supersedes Pub. L. No. 93–319 shall be construed to refer to section 113(d) of the Clean Air Act and to paragraph (5) thereof in particular which is codified as section 7413(d)(5) of this title. Section 7413 of this title was subsequently amended generally by Pub. L. No. 101–549, Title VII, § 701, 104 Stat. 2672 (Nov. 15, 1990), see note above. Section 117(b) of Pub. L. No. 95–95 added a new section 119 of Act of July 14, 1955, which is codified as section 7419 of this title.

Codifications

This section was formerly codified as section 1857c–5 of this title.

Effective and Applicability Provisions

1990 Acts. Amendment by Pub. L. No. 101–549 effective Nov. 15, 1990, except as otherwise provided, see section 711(b) of Pub. L. No. 101–549, set out as a note under section 7401 of this title.

1977 Acts. Amendment by Pub. L. No. 95–95 effective Aug. 7, 1977, except as otherwise expressly provided, see section 406(d) of Pub. L. No. 95–95, set out as a note under section 7401 of this title.

Change of Name

The Committee on Public Works of the Senate was abolished and replaced by the Committee on Environment and Public Works of the Senate, effective Feb. 11, 1977. See Rule XXV of the Standing Rules of the Senate, as amended by Senate Resolution 4 (popularly cited as the "Committee System Reorganization Amendments of 1977"), approved Feb. 4, 1977.

Transfer of Functions

The 'Federal Energy Administrator', for purposes of this chapter, to mean the Administrator of the Federal Energy Administration established by Pub. L. No. 93–2175, 88 Stat. 97 (May 7, 1974), which is codified as section 761 et seq. of Title 15. Commerce and Trade, but with the term to mean any officer of the United States designated as such by the President until the Federal Energy Administrator takes office and after the Federal Energy Administration ceases to exist, see section 798 of Title 15. The Federal Energy Administration was terminated and functions vested by law in the Administrator thereof were transferred to the Secretary of Energy (unless otherwise specifically provided) by sections 7151(a) and 7293 of this title.

Savings Provisions

Suits, actions or proceedings commenced under this chapter as in effect prior to Nov. 15, 1990, not to abate by reason of the taking effect of amendments by Pub. L. No. 101–549, except as otherwise provided for, see section 711(a) of Pub. L. No. 101–549, set out as a note under section 7401 of this title.

Suits, actions and other proceedings lawfully commenced by or against the Administrator or any other officer or employee of the United States in his official capacity or in relation to the discharge of his official duties under Act of July 14, 1955, the Clean Air Act, as in effect immediately prior to the enactment of Pub. L. No. 95–95 [Aug. 7, 1977], not to abate by reason of the taking effect of Pub. L. No. 95–95, see section 406(a) of Pub. L. No. 95–95, set out as an Effective and Applicability Provisions of 1977 Acts note under section 7401 of this title.

Section 16 of Pub. L. No. 91–604 provided that:

"(a)(1) Any implementation plan adopted by any State and submitted to the Secretary of Health, Education, and Welfare, or to the Administrator pursuant to the Clean Air Act [this chapter] prior to enactment of this Act [Dec. 31, 1970] may be approved under section 110 of the Clean Air Act [this section] (as amended by this Act) [Pub. L. No. 91–604] and shall remain in effect, unless the Administrator determines that such implementation plan, or any portion thereof, is not consistent with the applicable requirements of the Clean Air Act [this chapter] (as amended by this Act) and will not provide for the attainment of national primary ambient air quality standards in the time required by such Act. If the Administrator so determines, he shall, within 90 days after promulgation of any national ambient air quality standards pursuant to section 109(a) of the Clean Air Act [section 7409(a) of this title], notify the State and specify in what respects changes are needed to meet the additional requirements of such Act, including requirements to implement national secondary ambient air quality standards. If such changes are not adopted by the State after public hearings and within six months after such notification, the Administrator shall promulgate such changes pursuant to section 110(c) of such Act [subsec. (c) of this section].

"(2) The amendments made by section 4(b) [amending sections 7403 and 7415 of this title] shall not be construed as repealing or modifying the powers of the Administrator with respect to any conference convened under section 108(d) of the Clean Air Act [section 7415 of this title] before the date of enactment of this Act [Dec. 31, 1970].

"(b) Regulations or standards issued under title II of the Clean Air Act [subchapter II of this chapter] prior to the enactment of this Act [Dec. 31, 1970] shall continue in effect until revised by the Administrator consistent with the purposes of such Act [this chapter]."

Prior Provisions

A prior section 110 of Act of July 14, 1955, was renumbered section 117 by Pub. L. No. 91–604 and is set out as section 7417 of this title.

Modification or Rescission of Implementation Plans Approved and In Effect Prior to Aug. 7, 1977

Nothing in the Clean Air Act Amendments of 1977 [Pub. L. No. 95–95] to affect any requirement of an approved implementation plan under this section or any other provision in effect under this chapter before Aug. 7, 1977, until modified or rescinded in accordance with this chapter as amended by the Clean Air Act Amendments of 1977, see section 406(c) of Pub. L. No. 95–95, set out as an Effective and Applicability Provisions of 1977 Acts note under section 7401 of this title.

Modification or Rescission of Rules, Regulations, Orders, Determinations, Contracts, Certifications, Authorizations, Delegations, and Other Actions

All rules, regulations, orders, determinations, contracts, certifications, authorizations, delegations or other actions duly issued, made, or taken by or pursuant to Act of July 14, 1955, the Clean Air Act, as in effect immediately prior to the date of enactment of Pub. L. No. 95–95 [Aug. 7, 1977] to continue in full force and effect until modified or rescinded in accordance with Act of July 14, 1955, as amended by Pub. L. No. 95–95 [this chapter], see section 406(b) of Pub. L. No. 95–95, set out as an Effective and Applicability Provisions of 1977 Acts note under section 7401 of this title.

§ 7411. Standards of performance for new stationary sources

[CAA § 111]

(a) Definitions

For purposes of this section:

(1) The term "standard of performance" means a standard for emissions of air pollutants which reflects the degree of emission limitation achievable through the application of the best system of emission reduction which (taking into account the cost of achieving such reduction and any nonair quality health and environmental impact and energy requirements) the Administrator determines has been adequately demonstrated.

(2) The term "new source" means any stationary source, the construction or modification of which is commenced after the publication of regulations (or, if earlier, proposed regulations) prescribing a standard of performance under this section which will be applicable to such source.

(3) The term "stationary source" means any building, structure, facility, or installation which emits or may emit any air pollutant. Nothing in subchapter II of this chapter relating to nonroad engines shall be construed to apply to stationary internal combustion engines.

(4) The term "modification" means any physical change in, or change in the method of operation of, a stationary source which increases the amount of any air pollutant emitted by such source or which results in the emission of any air pollutant not previously emitted.

(5) The term "owner or operator" means any person who owns, leases, operates, controls, or supervises a stationary source.

(6) The term "existing source" means any stationary source other than a new source.

(7) The term "technological system of continuous emission reduction" means—

(A) a technological process for production or operation by any source which is inherently low-polluting or nonpolluting, or

(B) a technological system for continuous reduction of the pollution generated by a source before such pollution is emitted into the ambient air, including precombustion cleaning or treatment of fuels.

(8) A conversion to coal (A) by reason of an order under section 2(a) of the Energy Supply and Environmental Coordination Act of 1974 [15 U.S.C.A. § 792(a)] or any amendment thereto, or any subsequent enactment which supersedes such Act [15 U.S.C.A. § 791 et seq.], or (B) which qualifies under section 7413(d)(5)(A)(ii) of this title, shall not be deemed to be a modification for purposes of paragraphs (2) and (4) of this subsection.

(b) List of categories of stationary sources; standards of performance; information on pollution control techniques; sources owned or operated by United States; particular systems; revised standards

(1) **(A)** The Administrator shall, within 90 days after December 31, 1970, publish (and from time to time thereafter shall revise) a list of categories of stationary sources. He shall include a category of sources in such list if in his judgment it causes, or contributes significantly to, air pollution which may reasonably be anticipated to endanger public health or welfare.

(B) Within one year after the inclusion of a category of stationary sources in a list under subparagraph (A), the Administrator shall publish proposed regulations, establishing Federal standards of performance for new sources within such category. The Administrator shall afford interested persons an opportunity for written comment on such proposed regulations. After considering such comments, he shall promulgate, within one year after such publication, such standards with such modifications as he deems appropriate. The Administrator shall, at least every 8 years, review and, if appropriate, revise such standards following the procedure required by this subsection for promulgation of such standards. Notwithstanding the requirements of the previous sentence, the Administrator need not review any such standard if the Administrator determines that such review is not appropriate in light of readily available information on the efficacy of such standard. Standards of performance or revisions thereof shall become effective upon promulgation. When implementation and enforcement of any requirement of this chapter indicate that emission limitations and percent reductions beyond those required by the standards promulgated under this section are achieved in practice, the Administrator shall, when revising standards promulgated under this section, consider the emission limitations and percent reductions achieved in practice.

(2) The Administrator may distinguish among classes, types, and sizes within categories of new sources for the purpose of establishing such standards.

(3) The Administrator shall, from time to time, issue information on pollution control techniques for categories of new sources and air pollutants subject to the provisions of this section.

(4) The provisions of this section shall apply to any new source owned or operated by the United States.

(5) Except as otherwise authorized under subsection (h) of this section, nothing in this section shall be construed to require, or to authorize the Administrator to require, any new or modified source to install and operate any particular technological system of continuous emission reduction to comply with any new source standard of performance.

(6) The revised standards of performance required by enactment of subsection (a)(1)(A)(i) and (ii) of this section shall be promulgated not later than one year after August 7, 1977. Any new or modified fossil fuel fired stationary source which commences construction prior to the date of publication of the proposed revised standards shall not be required to comply with such revised standards.

(c) State implementation and enforcement of standards of performance

(1) Each State may develop and submit to the Administrator a procedure for implementing and enforcing standards of performance for new sources located in such State. If the Administrator finds the State procedure is adequate, he shall delegate to such State any authority he has under this chapter to implement and enforce such standards.

(2) Nothing in this subsection shall prohibit the Administrator from enforcing any applicable standard of performance under this section.

(d) Standards of performance for existing sources; remaining useful life of source

(1) The Administrator shall prescribe regulations which shall establish a procedure similar to that provided by section 7410 of this title under which each State shall submit to the Administrator a plan which (A) establishes standards of performance for any existing source for any air pollutant (i) for which air quality criteria have not been issued or which is not included on a list published under section 7408(a) of this title or emitted from a source category which is regulated under section 7412 of this title but (ii) to which a standard of performance under this section would apply if such existing source were a new source, and (B) provides for the implementation and enforcement of such standards of performance. Regulations of the Administrator under this paragraph shall permit the State in applying a standard of performance to any particular source under a plan submitted under this paragraph to take into consideration, among other factors, the remaining useful life of the existing source to which such standard applies.

(2) The Administrator shall have the same authority—

(A) to prescribe a plan for a State in cases where the State fails to submit a satisfactory plan as he would have under section 7410(c) of this title in the case of failure to submit an implementation plan, and

(B) to enforce the provisions of such plan in cases where the State fails to enforce them as he would have under sections 7413 and 7414 of this title with respect to an implementation plan.

In promulgating a standard of performance under a plan prescribed under this paragraph, the Administrator shall take into consideration, among other factors, remaining useful lives of the sources in the category of sources to which such standard applies.

(e) Prohibited acts

After the effective date of standards of performance promulgated under this section, it shall be unlawful for any owner or operator of any new source to operate such source in violation of any standard of performance applicable to such source.

(f) New source standards of performance

(1) For those categories of major stationary sources that the Administrator listed under subsection (b)(1)(A) of this section before November 15, 1990, and for which regulations had not been proposed by the Administrator by November 15, 1990, the Administrator shall—

(A) propose regulations establishing standards of performance for at least 25 percent of such categories of sources within 2 years after November 15, 1990;

(B) propose regulations establishing standards of performance for at least 50 percent of such categories of sources within 4 years after November 15, 1990; and

(C) propose regulations for the remaining categories of sources within 6 years after November 15, 1990.

(2) In determining priorities for promulgating standards for categories of major stationary sources for the purpose of paragraph (1), the Administrator shall consider—

(A) the quantity of air pollutant emissions which each such category will emit, or will be designed to emit;

(B) the extent to which each such pollutant may reasonably be anticipated to endanger public health or welfare; and

(C) the mobility and competitive nature of each such category of sources and the consequent need for nationally applicable new source standards of performance.

(3) Before promulgating any regulations under this subsection or listing any category of major stationary sources as required under this subsection, the Administrator shall consult with appropriate representatives of the Governors and of State air pollution control agencies.

(g) Revision of regulations

(1) Upon application by the Governor of a State showing that the Administrator has failed to specify in regulations under subsection (f)(1) of this section any category of major stationary sources required to be specified under such regulations, the Administrator shall revise such regulations to specify any such category.

(2) Upon application of the Governor of a State, showing that any category of stationary sources which is not included in the list under subsection (b)(1)(A) of this section contributes significantly to air pollution which may reasonably be anticipated to endanger public health or welfare (notwithstanding that such category is not a category of major stationary sources), the Administrator shall revise such regulations to specify such category of stationary sources.

(3) Upon application of the Governor of a State showing that the Administrator has failed to apply properly the criteria required to be considered under subsection (f)(2) of this section, the Administrator shall revise the list under subsection (b)(1)(A) of this section to apply properly such criteria.

(4) Upon application of the Governor of a State showing that—

(A) a new, innovative, or improved technology or process which achieves greater continuous emission reduction has been adequately demonstrated for any category of stationary sources, and

(B) as a result of such technology or process, the new source standard of performance in effect under this section for such category no longer reflects the greatest degree of emission limitation achievable through application of the best technological system of continuous emission reduction which (taking into consideration the cost of achieving such emission reduction, and any non-air quality health and environmental impact and energy requirements) has been adequately demonstrated,

the Administrator shall revise such standard of performance for such category accordingly.

(5) Unless later deadlines for action of the Administrator are otherwise prescribed under this section, the Administrator shall, not later than three months following the date of receipt of any application by a Governor of a State, either—

(A) find that such application does not contain the requisite showing and deny such application, or

(B) grant such application and take the action required under this subsection.

(6) Before taking any action required by subsection (f) of this section or by this subsection, the Administrator shall provide notice and opportunity for public hearing.

(h) Design, equipment, work practice, or operational standard; alternative emission limitation

(1) For purposes of this section, if in the judgment of the Administrator, it is not feasible to prescribe or enforce a standard of performance, he may instead promulgate a design, equipment, work practice, or operational standard, or combination thereof, which reflects the best technological system of continuous emission reduction which (taking into consideration the cost of achieving such emission reduction, and any non-air quality health and environmental impact and energy requirements) the Administrator determines has been adequately demonstrated. In the event the Administrator promulgates a design or equipment standard under this subsection, he shall include as part of such standard such requirements as will assure the proper operation and maintenance of any such element of design or equipment.

(2) For the purpose of this subsection, the phrase "not feasible to prescribe or enforce a standard of performance" means any situation in which the Administrator determines that (A) a pollutant or pollutants cannot be emitted through a conveyance designed and constructed to emit or capture such pollutant, or that any requirement for, or use of, such a conveyance would be inconsistent with any Federal, State, or local law, or (B) the application of measurement methodology to a particular class of sources is not practicable due to technological or economic limitations.

(3) If after notice and opportunity for public hearing, any person establishes to the satisfaction of the Administrator that an alternative means of emission limitation will achieve a reduction in emissions of any air pollutant at least equivalent to the reduction in emissions of such air pollutant achieved under the requirements of paragraph (1), the Administrator shall permit the use of such alternative by the source for purposes of compliance with this section with respect to such pollutant.

(4) Any standard promulgated under paragraph (1) shall be promulgated in terms of standard of performance whenever it becomes feasible to promulgate and enforce such standard in such terms.

(5) Any design, equipment, work practice, or operational standard, or any combination thereof, described in this subsection shall be treated as a standard of performance for purposes of the provisions of this chapter (other than the provisions of subsection (a) of this section and this subsection).

(i) Country elevators

Any regulations promulgated by the Administrator under this section applicable to grain elevators shall not apply to country elevators (as defined by the Administrator) which have a storage capacity of less than two million five hundred thousand bushels.

(j) Innovative technological systems of continuous emission reduction

(1) (A) Any person proposing to own or operate a new source may request the Administrator for one or more waivers from the requirements of this section for such source or any portion thereof with respect to any air pollutant to encourage the use of an innovative technological system or systems of continuous emission reduction. The Administrator may, with the consent of the Governor of the State in which the source is to be located, grant a waiver under this paragraph, if the Administrator determines after notice and opportunity for public hearing, that—

(i) the proposed system or systems have not been adequately demonstrated,

(ii) the proposed system or systems will operate effectively and there is a substantial likelihood that such system or systems will achieve greater continuous emission reduction than that required to be achieved under the standards of performance which would otherwise apply, or achieve at least an equivalent reduction at lower cost in terms of energy, economic, or nonair quality environmental impact,

(iii) the owner or operator of the proposed source has demonstrated to the satisfaction of the Administrator that the proposed system will not cause or contribute to an unreasonable risk to public health, welfare, or safety in its operation, function, or malfunction, and

(iv) the granting of such waiver is consistent with the requirements of subparagraph (C).

In making any determination under clause (ii), the Administrator shall take into account any previous failure of such system or systems to operate effectively or to meet any requirement of the new source performance standards. In determining whether an unreasonable risk exists under clause (iii), the Administrator shall consider, among other factors, whether and to what extent the use of the proposed technological system will cause, increase, reduce, or eliminate emissions of any unregulated pollutants; available methods for reducing or eliminating any risk to public health, welfare, or safety which may be associated with the use of such system; and the availability of other technological systems which may be used to conform to standards under this section without causing or contributing to such unreasonable risk. The Administrator may conduct such tests and may require the owner or operator of the proposed source to conduct such tests and provide such information as is necessary to carry out clause (iii) of this subparagraph. Such requirements shall include a requirement for prompt reporting of the emission of any unregulated pollutant from a system if such pollutant was not emitted, or was emitted in significantly lesser amounts without use of such system.

(B) A waiver under this paragraph shall be granted on such terms and conditions as the Administrator determines to be necessary to assure—

(i) emissions from the source will not prevent attainment and maintenance of any national ambient air quality standards, and

(ii) proper functioning of the technological system or systems authorized.

Any such term or condition shall be treated as a standard of performance for the purposes of subsection (e) of this section and section 7413 of this title.

(C) The number of waivers granted under this paragraph with respect to a proposed technological system of continuous emission reduction shall not exceed such number as the Administrator finds necessary to ascertain whether or not such system will achieve the conditions specified in clauses (ii) and (iii) of subparagraph (A).

(D) A waiver under this paragraph shall extend to the sooner of—

(i) the date determined by the Administrator, after consultation with the owner or operator of the source, taking into consideration the design, installation, and capital cost of the technological system or systems being used, or

(ii) the date on which the Administrator determines that such system has failed to—

(I) achieve at least an equivalent continuous emission reduction to that required to be achieved under the standards of performance which would otherwise apply, or

(II) comply with the condition specified in paragraph (1)(A)(iii),

and that such failure cannot be corrected.

(E) In carrying out subparagraph (D)(i), the Administrator shall not permit any waiver for a source or portion thereof to extend beyond the date—

(i) seven years after the date on which any waiver is granted to such source or portion thereof, or

(ii) four years after the date on which such source or portion thereof commences operation, whichever is earlier.

(F) No waiver under this subsection shall apply to any portion of a source other than the portion on which the innovative technological system or systems of continuous emission reduction is used.

(2) **(A)** If a waiver under paragraph (1) is terminated under clause (ii) of paragraph (1)(D), the Administrator shall grant an extension of the requirements of this section for such source for such minimum period as may be necessary to comply with the applicable standard of performance under this section. Such period shall not extend beyond the date three years from the time such waiver is terminated.

(B) An extension granted under this paragraph shall set forth emission limits and a compliance schedule containing increments of progress which require compliance with the applicable standards of performance as expeditiously as practicable and include such measures as are necessary and practicable in the interim to minimize emissions. Such schedule shall be treated as a standard of performance for purposes of subsection (e) of this section and section 7413 of this title.

(July 14, 1955, c. 360, Title I, § 111, as added by Pub. L. No. 91–604, § 4(a), 84 Stat. 1683 (Dec. 31, 1970); and amended by Pub. L. No. 92–157, Title III, § 302(f), 85 Stat. 464 (Nov. 18, 1971); Pub. L. No. 95–95, Title I, § 109(a)–(d)(1), (e), (f), Title IV, § 401(b), 91 Stat. 697 to 703, 791 (Aug. 7, 1977); Pub. L. No. 95–190, § 14(a)(7) to (9), 91 Stat. 1399 (Nov. 16, 1977); Pub. L. No. 95–623, § 13(a), 92 Stat. 3457 (Nov. 9, 1978); Pub. L. No. 101–549, Title I, § 108(e) to (g), Title III, § 302(a), (b), Title IV, § 403(a), 104 Stat. 2467, 2574, 2631 (Nov. 15, 1990).)

HISTORICAL AND STATUTORY NOTES

References in Text

Such Act, referred to in subsec. (a)(8), means Pub. L. No. 93–319, 88 Stat. 246 (June 22, 1974), as amended, known as the Energy Supply and Environmental Coordination Act of 1974, which is codified principally as chapter 16C (section 791 et seq.) of Title 15, Commerce and Trade. For complete classification of this Act to the Code, see Short Title note set out under section 791 of Title 15 and Tables.

Section 7413 of this title, referred to in subsec. (a)(8), was amended generally by Pub. L. No. 101–549, Title VII, § 701, 104 Stat. 2672 (Nov. 15, 1990), and, as so amended, subsec. (d) of section 7413 no longer relates to final compliance orders.

Subsec. (a)(1) of this section, referred to in subsec. (b)(6), was amended generally by Pub. L. No. 101–549, Title IV, § 403(a), 104 Stat. 2631 (Nov. 15, 1990), and, as so amended, no longer contains subpars.

Codifications

This section was formerly codified as section 1857c–6 of this title.

Effective and Applicability Provisions

1990 Acts. Amendment by Pub. L. No. 101–549 effective Nov. 15, 1990, except as otherwise provided, see section 711(b) of Pub. L. No. 101–549, set out as a note under section 7401 of this title.

1977 Acts. Amendment by Pub. L. No. 95–95 effective Aug. 7, 1977, except as otherwise expressly provided, see section 406(d) of Pub. L. No. 95–95, set out as a note under section 7401 of this title.

Transfer of Functions

Enforcement functions of Administrator or other official in Environmental Protection Agency related to compliance with new source performance standards under this section with respect to pre-construction, construction, and initial operation of transportation system for Canadian and Alaskan natural gas transferred to Federal Inspector, Office of Federal Inspector for the Alaska Natural Gas Transportation System, until first anniversary of date of initial operation of Alaska Natural Gas Transportation System, see Reorg. Plan No. 1 of 1979, eff. July 1, 1979, §§ 102(a), 203(a), 44 Fed. Reg. 33663, 33666, 93 Stat. 1373, 1376, set out in Appendix 1 to Title 5, Government Organization and Employees Office of Federal Inspector for the Alaska Natural Gas Transportation System abolished and functions and authority vested in Inspector transferred to Secretary of Energy by section 3012(b) of Pub. L. No. 102–486, set out as an Abolition of Office of Federal Inspector note under section 719e of Title 15, Commerce and Trade.

Savings Provisions

Suits, actions or proceedings commenced under this chapter as in effect prior to Nov. 15, 1990, not to abate by reason of the taking effect of amendments by Pub. L. No. 101–549, except as otherwise provided for, see section 711(a) of Pub. L. No. 101–549, set out as a note under section 7401 of this title.

Suits, actions, and other proceedings lawfully commenced by or against the Administrator or any other officer or employee of the United States in his official capacity or in relation to the discharge of his official duties under Act of July 14, 1955, the Clean Air Act, as in effect immediately prior to the enactment of Pub. L. No. 95–95 [Aug. 7, 1977], not to abate by reason of the taking effect of Pub. L. No. 95–95, see section 406(a) of Pub. L. No. 95–95, set out as an Effective and Applicability Provisions note under section 7401 of this title.

Prior Provisions

A prior section 111 of Act of July 14, 1955, was renumbered section 118 by Pub. L. No. 91–604, and is set out as section 7418 of this title.

Modification or Rescission of Rules, Regulations, Orders, Determinations, Contracts, Certifications, Authorizations, Delegations, and Other Actions

All rules, regulations, orders, determinations, contracts, certifications, authorizations, delegations, or other actions duly issued, made, or taken by or pursuant to Act of July 14, 1955, the Clean Air Act, as in effect immediately prior to the date of enactment of Pub. L. No. 95–95 [Aug. 7, 1977] to continue in full force and effect until modified or rescinded in accordance with Act of July 14, 1955, as amended by Pub. L. No. 95–95 [this chapter], see section 406(b) of Pub. L. No. 95–95, set out as an Effective Date note under section 7401 of this title.

Revised Regulations; Applicability

Section 403(b), (c) of Pub. L. No. 101–549 provided that:

"(b) Revised regulations.—Not later than three years after the date of enactment of the Clean Air Act Amendments of 1990 [Nov. 15, 1990], the Administrator shall promulgate revised regulations for standards of performance for new fossil fuel fired electric utility units commencing construction after the date on which such regulations are proposed that, at a minimum, require any source subject to such revised standards to emit sulfur dioxide at a rate not greater than would have resulted from compliance by such source with the applicable standards of performance under this section [amending sections 9411 and 7479 of this title] prior to such revision.

"(c) Applicability.—The provisions of subsections (a) [amending subsec. (a)(1) of this section] and (b) [subsec. (b) of this note] apply only so long as the provisions of section 403(e) of the Clean Air Act [section 7651b(e) of this title] remain in effect."

§ 7412. Hazardous air pollutants

[CAA § 112]

(a) Definitions

For purposes of this section, except subsection (r) of this section—

(1) Major source

The term "major source" means any stationary source or group of stationary sources located within a contiguous area and under common control that emits or has the potential to emit considering controls, in the aggregate, 10 tons per year or more of any hazardous air pollutant or 25 tons per year or more of any combination of hazardous air pollutants. The Administrator may establish a lesser quantity, or in the case of radionuclides different criteria, for a major source than that specified in the previous sentence, on the basis of the potency of the air pollutant, persistence, potential for bioaccumulation, other characteristics of the air pollutant, or other relevant factors.

(2) Area source

The term "area source" means any stationary source of hazardous air pollutants that is not a major source. For purposes of this section, the term "area source" shall not include motor vehicles or nonroad vehicles subject to regulation under subchapter II of this chapter.

(3) Stationary source

The term "stationary source" shall have the same meaning as such term has under section 7411(a) of this title.

(4) New source

The term "new source" means a stationary source the construction or reconstruction of which is commenced after the Administrator first proposes regulations under this section establishing an emission standard applicable to such source.

(5) Modification

The term "modification" means any physical change in, or change in the method of operation of, a major source which increases the actual emissions of any hazardous air pollutant emitted by such source by more than a de minimis amount or which results in the emission of any hazardous air pollutant not previously emitted by more than a de minimis amount.

(6) Hazardous air pollutant

The term "hazardous air pollutant" means any air pollutant listed pursuant to subsection (b) of this section.

(7) Adverse environmental effect

The term "adverse environmental effect" means any significant and widespread adverse effect, which may reasonably be anticipated, to wildlife, aquatic life, or other natural resources, including adverse impacts on populations of endangered or threatened species or significant degradation of environmental quality over broad areas.

(8) Electric utility steam generating unit

The term "electric utility steam generating unit" means any fossil fuel fired combustion unit of more than 25 megawatts that serves a generator that produces electricity for sale. A unit that cogenerates steam and electricity and supplies more than one-third of its potential electric output capacity and more than 25 megawatts electrical output to any utility power distribution system for sale shall be considered an electric utility steam generating unit.

(9) Owner or operator

The term "owner or operator" means any person who owns, leases, operates, controls, or supervises a stationary source.

(10) Existing source

The term "existing source" means any stationary source other than a new source.

(11) Carcinogenic effect

Unless revised, the term "carcinogenic effect" shall have the meaning provided by the Administrator under Guidelines for Carcinogenic Risk Assessment as of the date of enactment. Any revisions in the existing Guidelines shall be subject to notice and opportunity for comment.

(b) List of pollutants

(1) Initial list

The Congress establishes for purposes of this section a list of hazardous air pollutants as follows:

CAS number	Chemical name
75070	Acetaldehyde
60355	Acetamide
75058	Acetonitrile
98862	Acetophenone
53963	2–Acetylaminofluorene
107028	Acrolein
79061	Acrylamide
79107	Acrylic acid
107131	Acrylonitrile
107051	Allyl chloride
92671	4–Aminobiphenyl
62533	Aniline
90040	o-Anisidine
1332214	Asbestos
71432	Benzene (including benzene from gasoline)
92875	Benzidine
98077	Benzotrichloride
100447	Benzyl chloride
92524	Biphenyl
117817	Bis(2–ethylhexyl)phthalate (DEHP)
542881	Bis(chloromethyl)ether
75252	Bromoform

CAS number	Chemical name
106990	1,3–Butadiene
156627	Calcium cyanamide
105602	Caprolactam
133062	Captan
63252	Carbaryl
75150	Carbon disulfide
56235	Carbon tetrachloride
463581	Carbonyl sulfide
120809	Catechol
133904	Chloramben
57749	Chlordane
7782505	Chlorine
79118	Chloroacetic acid
532274	2–Chloroacetophenone
108907	Chlorobenzene
510156	Chlorobenzilate
67663	Chloroform
107302	Chloromethyl methyl ether
126998	Chloroprene
1319773	Cresols/Cresylic acid (isomers and mixture)
95487	o-Cresol
108394	m-Cresol
106445	p-Cresol
98828	Cumene
94757	2,4–D, salts and esters
3547044	DDE
334883	Diazomethane
132649	Dibenzofurans
96128	1,2–Dibromo–3–chloropropane
84742	Dibutylphthalate
106467	1,4–Dichlorobenzene(p)
91941	3,3–Dichlorobenzidene
111444	Dichloroethyl ether (Bis(2–chloroethyl)ether)
542756	1,3–Dichloropropene
62737	Dichlorvos
111422	Diethanolamine
121697	N,N–Diethyl aniline (N,N–Dimethylaniline)
64675	Diethyl sulfate
119904	3,3–Dimethoxybenzidine
60117	Dimethyl aminoazobenzene
119937	3,3′–Dimethyl benzidine
79447	Dimethyl carbamoyl chloride
68122	Dimethyl formamide
57147	1,1–Dimethyl hydrazine
131113	Dimethyl phthalate
77781	Dimethyl sulfate
534521	4,6–Dinitro-o-cresol, and salts
51285	2,4–Dinitrophenol
121142	2,4–Dinitrotoluene

CAS number	Chemical name
123911	1,4–Dioxane (1,4–Diethyleneoxide)
122667	1,2–Diphenylhydrazine
106898	Epichlorohydrin (1–Chloro–2,3–epoxypropane)
106887	1,2–Epoxybutane
140885	Ethyl acrylate
100414	Ethyl benzene
51796	Ethyl carbamate (Urethane)
75003	Ethyl chloride (Chloroethane)
106934	Ethylene dibromide (Dibromoethane)
107062	Ethylene dichloride (1,2–Dichloroethane)
107211	Ethylene glycol
151564	Ethylene imine (Aziridine)
75218	Ethylene oxide
96457	Ethylene thiourea
75343	Ethylidene dichloride (1,1–Dichloroethane)
50000	Formaldehyde
76448	Heptachlor
118741	Hexachlorobenzene
87683	Hexachlorobutadiene
77474	Hexachlorocyclopentadiene
67721	Hexachloroethane
822060	Hexamethylene–1,6–diisocyanate
680319	Hexamethylphosphoramide
110543	Hexane
302012	Hydrazine
7647010	Hydrochloric acid
7664393	Hydrogen fluoride (Hydrofluoric acid)
123319	Hydroquinone
78591	Isophorone
58899	Lindane (all isomers)
108316	Maleic anhydride
67561	Methanol
72435	Methoxychlor
74839	Methyl bromide (Bromomethane)
74873	Methyl chloride (Chloromethane)
71556	Methyl chloroform (1,1,1–Trichloroethane)
78933	Methyl ethyl ketone (2–Butanone)
60344	Methyl hydrazine
74884	Methyl iodide (Iodomethane)
108101	Methyl isobutyl ketone (Hexone)
624839	Methyl isocyanate
80626	Methyl methacrylate
1634044	Methyl tert butyl ether
101144	4,4–Methylene bis(2–chloroaniline)
75092	Methylene chloride (Dichloromethane)
101688	Methylene diphenyl diisocyanate (MDI)
101779	4,4′–Methylenedianiline
91203	Naphthalene
98953	Nitrobenzene

CAS number	Chemical name
92933	4–Nitrobiphenyl
100027	4–Nitrophenol
79469	2–Nitropropane
684935	N–Nitroso–N–methylurea
62759	N–Nitrosodimethylamine
59892	N–Nitrosomorpholine
56382	Parathion
82688	Pentachloronitrobenzene (Quintobenzene)
87865	Pentachlorophenol
108952	Phenol
106503	p-Phenylenediamine
75445	Phosgene
7803512	Phosphine
7723140	Phosphorus
85449	Phthalic anhydride
1336363	Polychlorinated biphenyls (Aroclors)
1120714	1,3–Propane sultone
57578	beta-Propiolactone
123386	Propionaldehyde
114261	Propoxur (Baygon)
78875	Propylene dichloride (1,2–Dichloropropane)
75569	Propylene oxide
75558	1,2–Propylenimine (2–Methyl aziridine)
91225	Quinoline
106514	Quinone
100425	Styrene
96093	Styrene oxide
1746016	2,3,7,8–Tetrachlorodibenzo-p-dioxin
79345	1,1,2,2–Tetrachloroethane
127184	Tetrachloroethylene (Perchloroethylene)
7550450	Titanium tetrachloride
108883	Toluene
95807	2,4–Toluene diamine
584849	2,4–Toluene diisocyanate
95534	o-Toluidine
8001352	Toxaphene (chlorinated camphene)
120821	1,2,4–Trichlorobenzene
79005	1,1,2–Trichloroethane
79016	Trichloroethylene
95954	2,4,5–Trichlorophenol
88062	2,4,6–Trichlorophenol
121448	Triethylamine
1582098	Trifluralin
540841	2,2,4–Trimethylpentane
108054	Vinyl acetate
593602	Vinyl bromide
75014	Vinyl chloride
75354	Vinylidene chloride (1,1–Dichloroethylene)
1330207	Xylenes (isomers and mixture)

CAS number	Chemical name
95476	o-Xylenes
108383	m-Xylenes
106423	p-Xylenes
0	Antimony Compounds
0	Arsenic Compounds (inorganic including arsine)
0	Beryllium Compounds
0	Cadmium Compounds
0	Chromium Compounds
0	Cobalt Compounds
0	Coke Oven Emissions
0	Cyanide Compounds[1]
0	Glycol ethers[2]
0	Lead Compounds
0	Manganese Compounds
0	Mercury Compounds
0	Fine mineral fibers[3]
0	Nickel Compounds
0	Polycylic Organic Matter[4]
0	Radionuclides (including radon)[5]
0	Selenium Compounds

NOTE: For all listings above which contain the word "compounds" and for glycol ethers, the following applies: Unless otherwise specified, these listings are defined as including any unique chemical substance that contains the named chemical (i.e., antimony, arsenic, etc.) as part of that chemical's infrastructure.

[1] X′CN where X = H′ or any other group where a formal dissociation may occur. For example KCN or $Ca(CN)_2$

[2] Includes mono- and di-ethers of ethylene glycol, diethylene glycol, and triethylene glycol $R\text{–}(OCH_2CH_2)_n\text{–}OR'$ where

n = 1, 2, or 3

R = alkyl or aryl groups

R′ = R, H, or groups which, when removed, yield glycol ethers with the structure: $R\text{–}(OCH_2CH)_n\text{–}OH$. Polymers are excluded from the glycol category.

[3] Includes mineral fiber emissions from facilities manufacturing or processing glass, rock, or slag fibers (or other mineral derived fibers) of average diameter 1 micrometer or less.

[4] Includes organic compounds with more than one benzene ring, and which have a boiling point greater than or equal to 100°C.

[5] A type of atom which spontaneously undergoes radioactive decay.

(2) Revision of the list

The Administrator shall periodically review the list established by this subsection and publish the results thereof and, where appropriate, revise such list by rule, adding pollutants which present, or may present, through inhalation or other routes of exposure, a threat of adverse human health effects (including, but not limited to, substances which are known to be, or may reasonably be anticipated to be, carcinogenic, mutagenic, teratogenic, neurotoxic, which cause reproductive dysfunction, or which are acutely or chronically toxic) or adverse environmental effects whether through ambient concentrations, bioaccumulation, deposition, or otherwise, but not including releases subject to regulation under subsection (r) of this section as a result of emissions to the air. No air pollutant which is listed under section 7408(a) of this title may be added to the list under this section, except that the prohibition of this sentence shall not apply to any pollutant which independently meets the listing criteria of this paragraph and is a precursor to a pollutant which is listed under section

7408(a) of this title or to any pollutant which is in a class of pollutants listed under such section. No substance, practice, process or activity regulated under subchapter VI of this chapter shall be subject to regulation under this section solely due to its adverse effects on the environment.

(3) Petitions to modify the list

(A) Beginning at any time after 6 months after November 15, 1990, any person may petition the Administrator to modify the list of hazardous air pollutants under this subsection by adding or deleting a substance or, in case of listed pollutants without CAS numbers (other than coke oven emissions, mineral fibers, or polycyclic organic matter) removing certain unique substances. Within 18 months after receipt of a petition, the Administrator shall either grant or deny the petition by publishing a written explanation of the reasons for the Administrator's decision. Any such petition shall include a showing by the petitioner that there is adequate data on the health or environmental defects[1] of the pollutant or other evidence adequate to support the petition. The Administrator may not deny a petition solely on the basis of inadequate resources or time for review.

(B) The Administrator shall add a substance to the list upon a showing by the petitioner or on the Administrator's own determination that the substance is an air pollutant and that emissions, ambient concentrations, bioaccumulation or deposition of the substance are known to cause or may reasonably be anticipated to cause adverse effects to human health or adverse environmental effects.

(C) The Administrator shall delete a substance from the list upon a showing by the petitioner or on the Administrator's own determination that there is adequate data on the health and environmental effects of the substance to determine that emissions, ambient concentrations, bioaccumulation or deposition of the substance may not reasonably be anticipated to cause any adverse effects to the human health or adverse environmental effects.

(D) The Administrator shall delete one or more unique chemical substances that contain a listed hazardous air pollutant not having a CAS number (other than coke oven emissions, mineral fibers, or polycyclic organic matter) upon a showing by the petitioner or on the Administrator's own determination that such unique chemical substances that contain the named chemical of such listed hazardous air pollutant meet the deletion requirements of subparagraph (C). The Administrator must grant or deny a deletion petition prior to promulgating any emission standards pursuant to subsection (d) of this section applicable to any source category or subcategory of a listed hazardous air pollutant without a CAS number listed under subsection (b) of this section for which a deletion petition has been filed within 12 months of November 15, 1990.

(4) Further information

If the Administrator determines that information on the health or environmental effects of a substance is not sufficient to make a determination required by this subsection, the Administrator may use any authority available to the Administrator to acquire such information.

(5) Test methods

The Administrator may establish, by rule, test measures and other analytic procedures for monitoring and measuring emissions, ambient concentrations, deposition, and bioaccumulation of hazardous air pollutants.

(6) Prevention of significant deterioration

The provisions of part C of this subchapter (prevention of significant deterioration) shall not apply to pollutants listed under this section.

(7) Lead

The Administrator may not list elemental lead as a hazardous air pollutant under this subsection.

(c) List of source categories

(1) In general

Not later than 12 months after November 15, 1990, the Administrator shall publish, and shall from time to time, but no less often than every 8 years, revise, if appropriate, in response to public comment or new information, a list of all categories and subcategories of major sources and area sources (listed under paragraph (3)) of the air pollutants listed pursuant to subsection (b) of this section. To the extent practicable, the categories and subcategories listed under this subsection shall be consistent with the list of source categories established pursuant to section 7411 of this title and part C of this subchapter. Nothing in the preceding sentence limits the Administrator's authority to establish subcategories under this section, as appropriate.

(2) Requirement for emissions standards

For the categories and subcategories the Administrator lists, the Administrator shall establish emissions standards under subsection (d) of this section, according to the schedule in this subsection and subsection (e) of this section.

(3) Area sources

The Administrator shall list under this subsection each category or subcategory of area sources which the Administrator finds presents a threat of adverse effects to human health or the environment (by such sources individually or in the aggregate) warranting regulation under this section. The Administrator shall, not later than 5 years after November 15, 1990, and pursuant to subsection (k)(3)(B) of this section, list, based on actual or estimated aggregate emissions of a listed pollutant or pollutants, sufficient categories or subcategories of area sources to ensure that area sources representing 90 percent of the area source emissions of the 30 hazardous air pollutants that present the greatest threat to public health in the largest number of urban areas are subject to regulation under this section. Such regulations shall be promulgated not later than 10 years after November 15, 1990.

(4) Previously regulated categories

The Administrator may, in the Administrator's discretion, list any category or subcategory of sources previously regulated under this section as in effect before November 15, 1990.

(5) Additional categories

In addition to those categories and subcategories of sources listed for regulation pursuant to paragraphs (1) and (3), the Administrator may at any time list additional categories and subcategories of sources of hazardous air pollutants according to the same criteria for listing applicable under such paragraphs. In the case of source categories and subcategories listed after publication of the initial list required under paragraph (1) or (3), emission standards under subsection (d) of this section for the category or subcategory shall be promulgated within 10 years after November 15, 1990, or within 2 years after the date on which such category or subcategory is listed, whichever is later.

(6) Specific pollutants

With respect to alkylated lead compounds, polycyclic organic matter, hexachlorobenzene, mercury, polychlorinated biphenyls, 2,3,7,8–tetrachlorodibenzofurans and 2,3,7,8–tetrachlorodibenzo-p-dioxin, the Administrator shall, not later than 5 years after November 15, 1990, list categories and subcategories of sources assuring that sources accounting for not less than 90 per centum of the aggregate emissions of each such pollutant are subject to standards under subsection (d)(2) or (d)(4) of this section. Such standards shall be promulgated not later than 10 years after November 15, 1990. This paragraph shall not be construed to require the Administrator to promulgate standards for such pollutants emitted by electric utility steam generating units.

(7) Research facilities

The Administrator shall establish a separate category covering research or laboratory facilities, as necessary to assure the equitable treatment of such facilities. For purposes of this section, "research or laboratory facility" means any stationary source whose primary purpose is to conduct research and development into new processes and products, where such source is operated under the close supervision of technically trained personnel and is not engaged in the manufacture of products for commercial sale in commerce, except in a de minimis manner.

(8) Boat manufacturing

When establishing emissions standards for styrene, the Administrator shall list boat manufacturing as a separate subcategory unless the Administrator finds that such listing would be inconsistent with the goals and requirements of this chapter.

(9) Deletions from the list

(A) Where the sole reason for the inclusion of a source category on the list required under this subsection is the emission of a unique chemical substance, the Administrator shall delete the source category from the list if it is appropriate because of action taken under either subparagraphs (C) or (D) of subsection (b)(3) of this section.

(B) The Administrator may delete any source category from the list under this subsection, on petition of any person or on the Administrator's own motion, whenever the Administrator makes the following determination or determinations, as applicable:

(i) In the case of hazardous air pollutants emitted by sources in the category that may result in cancer in humans, a determination that no source in the category (or group of sources in the case of area sources) emits such hazardous air pollutants in quantities which may cause a lifetime risk of cancer greater than one in one million to the individual in the population who is most exposed to emissions of such pollutants from the source (or group of sources in the case of area sources).

(ii) In the case of hazardous air pollutants that may result in adverse health effects in humans other than cancer or adverse environmental effects, a determination that emissions from no source in the category or subcategory concerned (or group of sources in the case of area sources) exceed a level which is adequate to protect public health with an ample margin of safety and no adverse environmental effect will result from emissions from any source (or from a group of sources in the case of area sources).

The Administrator shall grant or deny a petition under this paragraph within 1 year after the petition is filed.

(d) Emission standards

(1) In general

The Administrator shall promulgate regulations establishing emission standards for each category or subcategory of major sources and area sources of hazardous air pollutants listed for regulation pursuant to subsection (c) of this section in accordance with the schedules provided in subsections (c) and (e) of this section. The Administrator may distinguish among classes, types, and sizes of sources within a category or subcategory in establishing such standards except that, there shall be no delay in the compliance date for any standard applicable to any source under subsection (i) of this section as the result of the authority provided by this sentence.

(2) Standards and methods

Emissions standards promulgated under this subsection and applicable to new or existing sources of hazardous air pollutants shall require the maximum degree of reduction in emissions of the hazardous air pollutants subject to this section (including a prohibition on such emissions, where achievable) that the Administrator, taking into consideration the cost of achieving such emission reduction, and any non-air quality health and environmental impacts and energy requirements, determines is achievable for new or existing sources in the category or subcategory to which such emission standard applies, through application of measures, processes, methods, systems or techniques including, but not limited to, measures which—

(A) reduce the volume of, or eliminate emissions of, such pollutants through process changes, substitution of materials or other modifications,

(B) enclose systems or processes to eliminate emissions,

(C) collect, capture or treat such pollutants when released from a process, stack, storage or fugitive emissions point,

(D) are design, equipment, work practice, or operational standards (including requirements for operator training or certification) as provided in subsection (h) of this section, or

(E) are a combination of the above.

None of the measures described in subparagraphs (A) through (D) shall, consistent with the provisions of section 7414(c) of this title, in any way compromise any United States patent or United States trademark right, or any confidential business information, or any trade secret or any other intellectual property right.

(3) New and existing sources

The maximum degree of reduction in emissions that is deemed achievable for new sources in a category or subcategory shall not be less stringent than the emission control that is achieved in practice by the best controlled similar source, as determined by the Administrator. Emission standards promulgated under this subsection for existing sources in a category or subcategory may be less stringent than standards for new sources in the same category or subcategory but shall not be less stringent, and may be more stringent than—

(A) the average emission limitation achieved by the best performing 12 percent of the existing sources (for which the Administrator has emissions information), excluding those sources that have, within 18 months before the emission standard is proposed or within 30 months before such standard is promulgated, whichever is later, first achieved a level of emission rate or emission reduction which complies, or would comply if the source is not subject to such standard, with the lowest achievable emission rate (as defined by section 7501 of this title) applicable to the source category and prevailing at the time, in the category or subcategory for categories and subcategories with 30 or more sources, or

(B) the average emission limitation achieved by the best performing 5 sources (for which the Administrator has or could reasonably obtain emissions information) in the category or subcategory for categories or subcategories with fewer than 30 sources.

(4) Health threshold

With respect to pollutants for which a health threshold has been established, the Administrator may consider such threshold level, with an ample margin of safety, when establishing emission standards under this subsection.

(5) Alternative standard for area sources

With respect only to categories and subcategories of area sources listed pursuant to subsection (c) of this section, the Administrator may, in lieu of the authorities provided in paragraph (2) and subsection (f) of this section, elect to promulgate standards or requirements applicable to sources in such categories or subcategories which provide for the use of generally available control technologies or management practices by such sources to reduce emissions of hazardous air pollutants.

(6) Review and revision

The Administrator shall review, and revise as necessary (taking into account developments in practices, processes, and control technologies), emission standards promulgated under this section no less often than every 8 years.

(7) Other requirements preserved

No emission standard or other requirement promulgated under this section shall be interpreted, construed or applied to diminish or replace the requirements of a more stringent emission limitation or other applicable requirement established pursuant to section 7411 of this title, part C or D of this subchapter, or other authority of this chapter or a standard issued under State authority.

(8) Coke ovens

(A) Not later than December 31, 1992, the Administrator shall promulgate regulations establishing emission standards under paragraphs (2) and (3) of this subsection for coke oven batteries. In establishing such standards, the Administrator shall evaluate—

(i) the use of sodium silicate (or equivalent) luting compounds to prevent door leaks, and other operating practices and technologies for their effectiveness in reducing coke oven emissions, and their suitability for use on new and existing coke oven batteries, taking into account costs and reasonable commercial door warranties; and

(ii) as a basis for emission standards under this subsection for new coke oven batteries that begin construction after the date of proposal of such standards, the Jewell design Thompson non-recovery coke oven batteries and other non-recovery coke oven technologies, and other appropriate emission control and coke production technologies, as to their effectiveness in reducing coke oven emissions and their capability for production of steel quality coke.

Such regulations shall require at a minimum that coke oven batteries will not exceed 8 per centum leaking doors, 1 per centum leaking lids, 5 per centum leaking offtakes, and 16 seconds visible emissions per charge, with no exclusion for emissions during the period after the closing of self-sealing oven doors. Notwithstanding subsection (i) of this section, the compliance date for such emission standards for existing coke oven batteries shall be December 31, 1995.

(B) The Administrator shall promulgate work practice regulations under this subsection for coke oven batteries requiring, as appropriate—

(i) the use of sodium silicate (or equivalent) luting compounds, if the Administrator determines that use of sodium silicate is an effective means of emissions control and is achievable, taking into account costs and reasonable commercial warranties for doors and related equipment; and

(ii) door and jam cleaning practices.

Notwithstanding subsection (i) of this section, the compliance date for such work practice regulations for coke oven batteries shall be not later than the date 3 years after November 15, 1990.

(C) For coke oven batteries electing to qualify for an extension of the compliance date for standards promulgated under subsection (f) of this section in accordance with subsection (i)(8) of this section, the emission standards under this subsection for coke oven batteries shall require that coke oven batteries not exceed 8 per centum leaking doors, 1 per centum leaking lids, 5 per centum leaking offtakes, and 16 seconds visible emissions per charge, with no exclusion for emissions during the period after the closing of self-sealing doors. Notwithstanding subsection (i) of this section, the compliance date for such emission standards for existing coke oven batteries seeking an extension shall be not later than the date 3 years after November 15, 1990.

(9) Sources licensed by the Nuclear Regulatory Commission

No standard for radionuclide emissions from any category or subcategory of facilities licensed by the Nuclear Regulatory Commission (or an Agreement State) is required to be promulgated under this section if the Administrator determines, by rule, and after consultation with the Nuclear Regulatory Commission, that the regulatory program established by the Nuclear Regulatory Commission pursuant to the Atomic Energy Act [42 U.S.C.A. § 2011 et seq.] for such category or subcategory provides an ample margin of safety to protect the public health. Nothing in this subsection shall preclude or deny the right of any State or political subdivision thereof to adopt or enforce any standard or limitation respecting emissions of radionuclides which is more stringent than the standard or limitation in effect under section 7411 of this title or this section.

(10) Effective date

Emission standards or other regulations promulgated under this subsection shall be effective upon promulgation.

(e) Schedule for standards and review

(1) In general

The Administrator shall promulgate regulations establishing emission standards for categories and subcategories of sources initially listed for regulation pursuant to subsection (c)(1) of this section as expeditiously as practicable, assuring that—

(A) emission standards for not less than 40 categories and subcategories (not counting coke oven batteries) shall be promulgated not later than 2 years after November 15, 1990;

(B) emission standards for coke oven batteries shall be promulgated not later than December 31, 1992;

(C) emission standards for 25 per centum of the listed categories and subcategories shall be promulgated not later than 4 years after November 15, 1990;

(D) emission standards for an additional 25 per centum of the listed categories and subcategories shall be promulgated not later than 7 years after November 15, 1990; and

(E) emission standards for all categories and subcategories shall be promulgated not later than 10 years after November 15, 1990.

(2) Priorities

In determining priorities for promulgating standards under subsection (d) of this section, the Administrator shall consider—

(A) the known or anticipated adverse effects of such pollutants on public health and the environment;

(B) the quantity and location of emissions or reasonably anticipated emissions of hazardous air pollutants that each category or subcategory will emit; and

(C) the efficiency of grouping categories or subcategories according to the pollutants emitted, or the processes or technologies used.

(3) Published schedule

Not later than 24 months after November 15, 1990, and after opportunity for comment, the Administrator shall publish a schedule establishing a date for the promulgation of emission standards for each category and subcategory of sources listed pursuant to subsection (c)(1) and (3) of this section which shall be consistent with the requirements of paragraphs (1) and (2). The determination of priorities for the promulgation of standards pursuant to this paragraph is not a rulemaking and shall not be subject to judicial review, except that, failure to promulgate any standard pursuant to the schedule established by this paragraph shall be subject to review under section 7604 of this title.

(4) Judicial review

Notwithstanding section 7607 of this title, no action of the Administrator adding a pollutant to the list under subsection (b) of this section or listing a source category or subcategory under subsection (c) of this section shall be a final agency action subject to judicial review, except that any such action may be reviewed under such section 7607 of this title when the Administrator issues emission standards for such pollutant or category.

(5) Publicly owned treatment works

The Administrator shall promulgate standards pursuant to subsection (d) of this section applicable to publicly owned treatment works (as defined in title II of the Federal Water Pollution Control Act [33 U.S.C.A. § 1281 et seq.]) not later than 5 years after November 15, 1990.

(f) Standard to protect health and environment

(1) Report

Not later than 6 years after November 15, 1990, the Administrator shall investigate and report, after consultation with the Surgeon General and after opportunity for public comment, to Congress on—

(A) methods of calculating the risk to public health remaining, or likely to remain, from sources subject to regulation under this section after the application of standards under subsection (d) of this section;

(B) the public health significance of such estimated remaining risk and the technologically and commercially available methods and costs of reducing such risks;

(C) the actual health effects with respect to persons living in the vicinity of sources, any available epidemiological or other health studies, risks presented by background concentrations of hazardous air pollutants, any uncertainties in risk assessment methodology or other health assessment technique, and any negative health or environmental consequences to the community of efforts to reduce such risks; and

(D) recommendations as to legislation regarding such remaining risk.

(2) Emission standards

(A) If Congress does not act on any recommendation submitted under paragraph (1), the Administrator shall, within 8 years after promulgation of standards for each category or subcategory of sources pursuant to subsection (d) of this section, promulgate standards for such category or subcategory if promulgation of such standards is required in order to provide an ample margin of safety to protect public health in accordance with this section (as in effect before November 15, 1990) or to prevent, taking into consideration costs, energy, safety, and other relevant factors, an adverse environmental effect. Emission standards promulgated under this subsection shall provide an ample margin of safety to protect public health in accordance with this section (as in effect before November 15, 1990), unless the Administrator determines that a more stringent standard is necessary to prevent, taking into consideration costs, energy, safety, and other relevant factors, an adverse environmental effect. If standards promulgated pursuant to subsection (d) of this section and applicable to a category or subcategory of sources emitting a pollutant (or pollutants) codified as a known, probable or possible human carcinogen do not reduce lifetime excess cancer risks to the individual most exposed to emissions from a source in the category or subcategory to less than one in one million, the Administrator shall promulgate standards under this subsection for such source category.

(B) Nothing in subparagraph (A) or in any other provision of this section shall be construed as affecting, or applying to the Administrator's interpretation of this section, as in effect before November 15, 1990, and set forth in the Federal Register of September 14, 1989 (54 Federal Register 38044).

(C) The Administrator shall determine whether or not to promulgate such standards and, if the Administrator decides to promulgate such standards, shall promulgate the standards 8 years after promulgation of the standards under subsection (d) of this section for each source category or subcategory concerned. In the case of categories or subcategories for which standards under subsection (d) of this section are required to be promulgated within 2 years after November 15, 1990, the Administrator shall have 9 years after promulgation of the standards under subsection (d) of this section to make the determination under the preceding sentence and, if required, to promulgate the standards under this paragraph.

(3) Effective date

Any emission standard established pursuant to this subsection shall become effective upon promulgation.

(4) Prohibition

No air pollutant to which a standard under this subsection applies may be emitted from any stationary source in violation of such standard, except that in the case of an existing source—

(A) such standard shall not apply until 90 days after its effective date, and

(B) the Administrator may grant a waiver permitting such source a period of up to 2 years after the effective date of a standard to comply with the standard if the Administrator finds that such period is necessary for the installation of controls and that steps will be taken during the period of the waiver to assure that the health of persons will be protected from imminent endangerment.

(5) Area sources

The Administrator shall not be required to conduct any review under this subsection or promulgate emission limitations under this subsection for any category or subcategory of area sources that is listed pursuant to subsection (c)(3) of this section and for which an emission standard is promulgated pursuant to subsection (d)(5) of this section.

(6) Unique chemical substances

In establishing standards for the control of unique chemical substances of listed pollutants without CAS numbers under this subsection, the Administrator shall establish such standards with respect to the health and environmental effects of the substances actually emitted by sources and direct transformation byproducts of such emissions in the categories and subcategories.

(g) Modifications

(1) Offsets

(A) A physical change in, or change in the method of operation of, a major source which results in a greater than de minimis increase in actual emissions of a hazardous air pollutant shall not be considered a modification, if such increase in the quantity of actual emissions of any hazardous air pollutant from such source will be offset by an equal or greater decrease in the quantity of emissions of another hazardous air pollutant (or pollutants) from such source which is deemed more hazardous, pursuant to guidance issued by the Administrator under subparagraph (B). The owner or operator of such source shall submit a showing to the Administrator (or the State) that such increase has been offset under the preceding sentence.

(B) The Administrator shall, after notice and opportunity for comment and not later than 18 months after November 15, 1990, publish guidance with respect to implementation of this subsection. Such guidance shall include an identification, to the extent practicable, of the relative hazard to human health resulting from emissions to the ambient air of each of the pollutants listed under subsection (b) of this section sufficient to facilitate the offset showing authorized by subparagraph (A). Such guidance shall not authorize offsets between pollutants where the increased pollutant (or more than one pollutant in a stream of pollutants) causes adverse effects to human health for which no safety threshold for exposure can be determined unless there are corresponding decreases in such types of pollutant(s).

(2) Construction, reconstruction and modifications

(A) After the effective date of a permit program under subchapter V of this chapter in any State, no person may modify a major source of hazardous air pollutants in such State, unless the Administrator (or the State) determines that the maximum achievable control technology emission limitation under this section for existing sources will be met. Such determination shall be made on a case-by-case basis where no applicable emissions limitations have been established by the Administrator.

(B) After the effective date of a permit program under subchapter V of this chapter in any State, no person may construct or reconstruct any major source of hazardous air pollutants, unless the Administrator (or the State) determines that the maximum achievable control technology emission limitation under this section for new sources will be met. Such determination shall be made on a case-by-case basis where no applicable emission limitations have been established by the Administrator.

(3) Procedures for modifications

The Administrator (or the State) shall establish reasonable procedures for assuring that the requirements applying to modifications under this section are reflected in the permit.

(h) Work practice standards and other requirements

(1) In general

For purposes of this section, if it is not feasible in the judgment of the Administrator to prescribe or enforce an emission standard for control of a hazardous air pollutant or pollutants, the Administrator may, in lieu thereof, promulgate a design, equipment, work practice, or operational standard, or combination thereof, which in the Administrator's judgment is consistent with the provisions of subsection (d) or (f) of this section. In the event the Administrator promulgates a design or equipment standard under this subsection, the Administrator shall include as part of such standard such requirements as will assure the proper operation and maintenance of any such element of design or equipment.

(2) Definition

For the purpose of this subsection, the phrase "not feasible to prescribe or enforce an emission standard" means any situation in which the Administrator determines that—

(A) a hazardous air pollutant or pollutants cannot be emitted through a conveyance designed and constructed to emit or capture such pollutant, or that any requirement for, or use of, such a conveyance would be inconsistent with any Federal, State or local law, or

(B) the application of measurement methodology to a particular class of sources is not practicable due to technological and economic limitations.

(3) Alternative standard

If after notice and opportunity for comment, the owner or operator of any source establishes to the satisfaction of the Administrator that an alternative means of emission limitation will achieve a reduction in emissions of any air pollutant at least equivalent to the reduction in emissions of such pollutant achieved under the requirements of paragraph (1), the Administrator shall permit the use of such alternative by the source for purposes of compliance with this section with respect to such pollutant.

(4) Numerical standard required

Any standard promulgated under paragraph (1) shall be promulgated in terms of an emission standard whenever it is feasible to promulgate and enforce a standard in such terms.

(i) Schedule for compliance

(1) Preconstruction and operating requirements

After the effective date of any emission standard, limitation, or regulation under subsection (d), (f) or (h) of this section, no person may construct any new major source or reconstruct any existing major source subject to such emission standard, regulation or limitation unless the Administrator (or a State with a permit program approved under subchapter V of this chapter) determines that such source, if properly constructed, reconstructed and operated, will comply with the standard, regulation or limitation.

(2) Special rule

Notwithstanding the requirements of paragraph (1), a new source which commences construction or reconstruction after a standard, limitation or regulation applicable to such source is proposed and before such standard, limitation or regulation is promulgated shall not be required to comply with such promulgated standard until the date 3 years after the date of promulgation if—

(A) the promulgated standard, limitation or regulation is more stringent than the standard, limitation or regulation proposed; and

(B) the source complies with the standard, limitation, or regulation as proposed during the 3-year period immediately after promulgation.

(3) Compliance schedule for existing sources

(A) After the effective date of any emissions standard, limitation or regulation promulgated under this section and applicable to a source, no person may operate such source in violation of such standard, limitation or regulation except, in the case of an existing source, the Administrator shall establish a compliance date or dates for each category or subcategory of existing sources, which shall provide for compliance as expeditiously as practicable, but in no event later than 3 years after the effective date of such standard, except as provided in subparagraph (B) and paragraphs (4) through (8).

(B) The Administrator (or a State with a program approved under subchapter V of this chapter) may issue a permit that grants an extension permitting an existing source up to 1 additional year to comply with standards under subsection (d) of this section if such additional period is necessary for the installation of controls. An additional extension of up to 3 years may be added for mining waste operations, if the 4-year compliance time is insufficient to dry and cover mining waste in order to reduce emissions of any pollutant listed under subsection (b) of this section.

(4) Presidential exemption

The President may exempt any stationary source from compliance with any standard or limitation under this section for a period of not more than 2 years if the President determines that the technology to implement such standard is not available and that it is in the national security interests of the United States to do so. An exemption under this paragraph may be extended for 1 or more additional periods, each period not to exceed 2 years. The President shall report to Congress with respect to each exemption (or extension thereof) made under this paragraph.

(5) Early reduction

(A) The Administrator (or a State acting pursuant to a permit program approved under subchapter V of this chapter) shall issue a permit allowing an existing source, for which the owner or operator demonstrates that the source has achieved a reduction of 90 per centum or more in emissions of hazardous air pollutants (95 per centum in the case of hazardous air pollutants which are particulates) from the source, to meet an alternative emission limitation reflecting such reduction in lieu of an emission limitation promulgated under subsection (d) of this section for a period of 6 years from the compliance date for the otherwise applicable standard, provided that such reduction is achieved before the otherwise applicable standard under subsection (d) of this section is first proposed. Nothing in this paragraph shall preclude a State from requiring reductions in excess of those specified in this subparagraph as a condition of granting the extension authorized by the previous sentence.

(B) An existing source which achieves the reduction referred to in subparagraph (A) after the proposal of an applicable standard but before January 1, 1994, may qualify under subparagraph (A), if the source makes an enforceable commitment to achieve such reduction before the proposal of the standard. Such commitment shall be enforceable to the same extent as a regulation under this section.

(C) The reduction shall be determined with respect to verifiable and actual emissions in a base year not earlier than calendar year 1987, provided that, there is no evidence that emissions in the base year are artificially or substantially greater than emissions in other years prior to implementation of emissions reduction measures. The Administrator may allow a source to use a baseline year of 1985 or 1986 provided that the source can demonstrate to the satisfaction of the Administrator that emissions data for the source reflects verifiable data based on information for such source, received by the Administrator prior to November 15, 1990, pursuant to an information request issued under section 7414 of this title.

(D) For each source granted an alternative emission limitation under this paragraph there shall be established by a permit issued pursuant to subchapter V of this chapter an enforceable emission limitation for hazardous air pollutants reflecting the reduction which qualifies the source for an alternative emission limitation under this paragraph. An alternative emission limitation under this paragraph shall not be available with respect to standards or requirements promulgated pursuant to subsection (f) of this section and the Administrator shall, for the purpose of determining whether a standard under subsection (f) of this section is necessary, review emissions from sources granted an alternative emission limitation under this paragraph at the same time that other sources in the category or subcategory are reviewed.

(E) With respect to pollutants for which high risks of adverse public health effects may be associated with exposure to small quantities including, but not limited to, chlorinated dioxins and furans, the Administrator shall by regulation limit the use of offsetting reductions in emissions of other hazardous air pollutants from the source as counting toward the 90 per centum reduction in such high-risk pollutants qualifying for an alternative emissions limitation under this paragraph.

(6) Other reductions

Notwithstanding the requirements of this section, no existing source that has installed—

(A) best available control technology (as defined in section 7479(3) of this title), or

(B) technology required to meet a lowest achievable emission rate (as defined in section 7501 of this title),

prior to the promulgation of a standard under this section applicable to such source and the same pollutant (or stream of pollutants) controlled pursuant to an action described in subparagraph (A) or (B) shall be required to comply with such standard under this section until the date 5 years after the date on which such installation or reduction has been achieved, as determined by the Administrator. The Administrator may issue such rules and guidance as are necessary to implement this paragraph.

(7) Extension for new sources

A source for which construction or reconstruction is commenced after the date an emission standard applicable to such source is proposed pursuant to subsection (d) of this section but before the date an emission standard applicable to such source is proposed pursuant to subsection (f) of this section shall not be required to comply with the emission standard under subsection (f) of this section until the date 10 years after the date construction or reconstruction is commenced.

(8) Coke ovens

(A) Any coke oven battery that complies with the emission limitations established under subsection (d)(8)(C) of this section, subparagraph (B), and subparagraph (C), and complies with the provisions of subparagraph (E), shall not be required to achieve emission limitations promulgated under subsection (f) of this section until January 1, 2020.

(B) **(i)** Not later than December 31, 1992, the Administrator shall promulgate emission limitations for coke oven emissions from coke oven batteries. Notwithstanding paragraph (3) of this subsection, the compliance date for such emission limitations for existing coke oven batteries shall be January 1, 1998. Such emission limitations shall reflect the lowest achievable emission rate as defined in section 7501 of this title for a coke oven battery that is rebuilt or a replacement at a coke oven plant for an existing battery. Such emission limitations shall be no less stringent than—

(I) 3 per centum leaking doors (5 per centum leaking doors for six meter batteries);

(II) 1 per centum leaking lids;

(III) 4 per centum leaking offtakes; and

(IV) 16 seconds visible emissions per charge,

with an exclusion for emissions during the period after the closing of self-sealing oven doors (or the total mass emissions equivalent). The rulemaking in which such emission limitations are promulgated shall also establish an appropriate measurement methodology for determining compliance with such emission limitations, and shall establish such emission limitations in terms of an equivalent level of mass emissions reduction from a coke oven battery, unless the Administrator finds that such a mass emissions standard would not be practicable or enforceable. Such measurement methodology, to the extent it measures leaking doors, shall take into consideration alternative test methods that reflect the best technology and practices actually applied in the affected industries, and shall assure that the final test methods are consistent with the performance of such best technology and practices.

(ii) If the Administrator fails to promulgate such emission limitations under this subparagraph prior to the effective date of such emission limitations, the emission limitations applicable to coke oven batteries under this subparagraph shall be—

(I) 3 per centum leaking doors (5 per centum leaking doors for six meter batteries);

(II) 1 per centum leaking lids;

(III) 4 per centum leaking offtakes; and

(IV) 16 seconds visible emissions per charge,

or the total mass emissions equivalent (if the total mass emissions equivalent is determined to be practicable and enforceable), with no exclusion for emissions during the period after the closing of self-sealing oven doors.

(C) Not later than January 1, 2007, the Administrator shall review the emission limitations promulgated under subparagraph (B) and revise, as necessary, such emission limitations to reflect the lowest achievable emission rate as defined in section 7501 of this title at the time for a coke oven battery that is rebuilt or a replacement at a coke oven plant for an existing battery. Such emission limitations shall be no less stringent than the emission limitation promulgated under subparagraph (B). Notwithstanding paragraph (2) of this subsection, the compliance date for such emission limitations for existing coke oven batteries shall be January 1, 2010.

(D) At any time prior to January 1, 1998, the owner or operator of any coke oven battery may elect to comply with emission limitations promulgated under subsection (f) of this section by the date such emission limitations would otherwise apply to such coke oven battery, in lieu of the emission limitations and the compliance dates provided under subparagraphs (B) and (C) of this paragraph. Any such owner or operator shall be legally bound to comply with such emission limitations promulgated under subsection (f) of this section with respect to such coke oven battery as of January 1, 2003. If no such emission limitations have been promulgated for such coke oven battery, the Administrator shall promulgate such emission limitations in accordance with subsection (f) of this section for such coke oven battery.

(E) Coke oven batteries qualifying for an extension under subparagraph (A) shall make available not later than January 1, 2000, to the surrounding communities the results of any risk assessment performed by the Administrator to determine the appropriate level of any emission standard established by the Administrator pursuant to subsection (f) of this section.

(F) Notwithstanding the provisions of this section, reconstruction of any source of coke oven emissions qualifying for an extension under this paragraph shall not subject such source to emission limitations under subsection (f) of this section more stringent than those established under subparagraphs (B) and (C) until January 1, 2020. For the purposes of this subparagraph, the term "reconstruction" includes the replacement of existing coke oven battery capacity with new coke oven batteries of comparable or lower capacity and lower potential emissions.

(j) Equivalent emission limitation by permit

(1) Effective date

The requirements of this subsection shall apply in each State beginning on the effective date of a permit program established pursuant to subchapter V of this chapter in such State, but not prior to the date 42 months after November 15, 1990.

(2) Failure to promulgate a standard

In the event that the Administrator fails to promulgate a standard for a category or subcategory of major sources by the date established pursuant to subsection (e)(1) and (3) of this section, and beginning 18 months after such date (but not prior to the effective date of a permit program under subchapter V of this chapter), the owner or operator of any major source in such category or subcategory shall submit a permit application under paragraph (3) and such owner or operator shall also comply with paragraphs (5) and (6).

(3) Applications

By the date established by paragraph (2), the owner or operator of a major source subject to this subsection shall file an application for a permit. If the owner or operator of a source has submitted a timely and complete application for a permit required by this subsection, any failure to have a permit shall not be a violation of paragraph (2), unless the delay in final action is due to the failure of the applicant to timely submit information required or requested to process the application. The Administrator shall not later than 18 months after November 15, 1990, and after notice and opportunity for comment, establish requirements for applications under this subsection including a standard application form and criteria for determining in a timely manner the completeness of applications.

(4) Review and approval

Permit applications submitted under this subsection shall be reviewed and approved or disapproved according to the provisions of section 7661d of this title. In the event that the Administrator (or the State) disapproves a permit application submitted under this subsection or determines that the application is incomplete, the applicant shall have up to 6 months to revise the application to meet the objections of the Administrator (or the State).

(5) Emission limitation

The permit shall be issued pursuant to subchapter V of this chapter and shall contain emission limitations for the hazardous air pollutants subject to regulation under this section and emitted by the source that the Administrator (or the State) determines, on a case-by-case basis, to be equivalent to the limitation that would apply to such source if an emission standard had been promulgated in a timely manner under subsection (d) of this section. In the alternative, if the applicable criteria are met, the permit may contain an emissions limitation established according to the provisions of subsection (i)(5) of this section. For purposes of the preceding sentence, the reduction required by subsection (i)(5)(A) of this section shall be achieved by the date on which the relevant standard should have been promulgated under subsection (d) of this section. No such pollutant may be emitted in amounts exceeding an emission limitation contained in a permit immediately for new sources and, as expeditiously as practicable, but not later than the date 3 years after the permit is issued for existing sources or such other compliance date as would apply under subsection (i) of this section.

(6) Applicability of subsequent standards

If the Administrator promulgates an emission standard that is applicable to the major source prior to the date on which a permit application is approved, the emission limitation in the permit shall reflect the promulgated standard rather than the emission limitation determined pursuant to paragraph (5), provided that the source shall have the compliance period provided under subsection (i) of this section. If the Administrator promulgates a standard under subsection (d) of this section that would be applicable to the source in lieu of the emission limitation established by permit under this subsection after the date on which the permit has been issued, the Administrator (or the State) shall revise such permit upon the next renewal to reflect the standard promulgated by the Administrator providing such source a reasonable time to comply, but no longer than 8 years after such standard is promulgated or 8 years after the date on which the source is first required to comply with the emissions limitation established by paragraph (5), whichever is earlier.

(k) Area source program

(1) Findings and purpose

The Congress finds that emissions of hazardous air pollutants from area sources may individually, or in the aggregate, present significant risks to public health in urban areas. Considering the large number of persons exposed and the risks of carcinogenic and other adverse health effects from hazardous air pollutants, ambient concentrations characteristic of large urban areas should be reduced to levels substantially below those currently experienced. It is the purpose of this subsection to achieve a substantial reduction in emissions of hazardous air pollutants from area sources and an equivalent reduction in the public health risks associated with such sources including a reduction of not less than 75 per centum in the incidence of cancer attributable to emissions from such sources.

(2) Research program

The Administrator shall, after consultation with State and local air pollution control officials, conduct a program of research with respect to sources of hazardous air pollutants in urban areas and shall include within such program—

(A) ambient monitoring for a broad range of hazardous air pollutants (including, but not limited to, volatile organic compounds, metals, pesticides and products of incomplete combustion) in a representative number of urban locations;

(B) analysis to characterize the sources of such pollution with a focus on area sources and the contribution that such sources make to public health risks from hazardous air pollutants; and

(C) consideration of atmospheric transformation and other factors which can elevate public health risks from such pollutants.

Health effects considered under this program shall include, but not be limited to, carcinogenicity, mutagenicity, teratogenicity, neurotoxicity, reproductive dysfunction and other acute and chronic effects including the role of such pollutants as precursors of ozone or acid aerosol formation. The Administrator shall report the preliminary results of such research not later than 3 years after November 15, 1990.

(3) National strategy

(A) Considering information collected pursuant to the monitoring program authorized by paragraph (2), the Administrator shall, not later than 5 years after November 15, 1990, and after notice and opportunity for public comment, prepare and transmit to the Congress a comprehensive strategy to control emissions of hazardous air pollutants from area sources in urban areas.

(B) The strategy shall—

(i) identify not less than 30 hazardous air pollutants which, as the result of emissions from area sources, present the greatest threat to public health in the largest number of urban areas and that are or will be listed pursuant to subsection (b) of this section, and

(ii) identify the source categories or subcategories emitting such pollutants that are or will be listed pursuant to subsection (c) of this section. When identifying categories and subcategories of sources under this subparagraph, the Administrator shall assure that sources accounting for 90 per centum or more of the aggregate emissions of each of the 30 identified hazardous air pollutants are subject to standards pursuant to subsection (d) of this section.

(C) The strategy shall include a schedule of specific actions to substantially reduce the public health risks posed by the release of hazardous air pollutants from area sources that will be implemented by the Administrator under the authority of this or other laws (including, but not limited to, the Toxic Substances Control Act [15 U.S.C.A. § 2601 et seq.], the Federal Insecticide,

Fungicide and Rodenticide Act [7 U.S.C.A. § 136 et seq.] and the Resource Conservation and Recovery Act [42 U.S.C.A. § 6901 et seq.]) or by the States. The strategy shall achieve a reduction in the incidence of cancer attributable to exposure to hazardous air pollutants emitted by stationary sources of not less than 75 per centum, considering control of emissions of hazardous air pollutants from all stationary sources and resulting from measures implemented by the Administrator or by the States under this or other laws.

(D) The strategy may also identify research needs in monitoring, analytical methodology, modeling or pollution control techniques and recommendations for changes in law that would further the goals and objectives of this subsection.

(E) Nothing in this subsection shall be interpreted to preclude or delay implementation of actions with respect to area sources of hazardous air pollutants under consideration pursuant to this or any other law and that may be promulgated before the strategy is prepared.

(F) The Administrator shall implement the strategy as expeditiously as practicable assuring that all sources are in compliance with all requirements not later than 9 years after November 15, 1990.

(G) As part of such strategy the Administrator shall provide for ambient monitoring and emissions modeling in urban areas as appropriate to demonstrate that the goals and objectives of the strategy are being met.

(4) Areawide activities

In addition to the national urban air toxics strategy authorized by paragraph (3), the Administrator shall also encourage and support areawide strategies developed by State or local air pollution control agencies that are intended to reduce risks from emissions by area sources within a particular urban area. from the funds available for grants under this section, the Administrator shall set aside not less than 10 per centum to support areawide strategies addressing hazardous air pollutants emitted by area sources and shall award such funds on a demonstration basis to those States with innovative and effective strategies. At the request of State or local air pollution control officials, the Administrator shall prepare guidelines for control technologies or management practices which may be applicable to various categories or subcategories of area sources.

(5) Report

The Administrator shall report to the Congress at intervals not later than 8 and 12 years after November 15, 1990, on actions taken under this subsection and other parts of this chapter to reduce the risk to public health posed by the release of hazardous air pollutants from area sources. The reports shall also identify specific metropolitan areas that continue to experience high risks to public health as the result of emissions from area sources.

(*l*) State programs

(1) In general

Each State may develop and submit to the Administrator for approval a program for the implementation and enforcement (including a review of enforcement delegations previously granted) of emission standards and other requirements for air pollutants subject to this section or requirements for the prevention and mitigation of accidental releases pursuant to subsection (r) of this section. A program submitted by a State under this subsection may provide for partial or complete delegation of the Administrator's authorities and responsibilities to implement and enforce emissions standards and prevention requirements but shall not include authority to set standards less stringent than those promulgated by the Administrator under this chapter.

(2) Guidance

Not later than 12 months after November 15, 1990, the Administrator shall publish guidance that would be useful to the States in developing programs for submittal under this subsection. The guidance shall also provide for the registration of all facilities producing, processing, handling or storing any substance listed pursuant to subsection (r) of this section in amounts greater than the threshold quantity. The Administrator shall include as an element in such guidance an optional program begun in 1986 for the review of high-risk point sources of air pollutants including, but not limited to, hazardous air pollutants listed pursuant to subsection (b) of this section.

(3) Technical assistance

The Administrator shall establish and maintain an air toxics clearinghouse and center to provide technical information and assistance to State and local agencies and, on a cost recovery basis, to others on control technology, health and ecological risk assessment, risk analysis, ambient monitoring and modeling, and emissions measurement and monitoring. The Administrator shall use the authority of section 7403 of this title to examine methods for preventing, measuring, and controlling emissions and evaluating associated health and ecological risks. Where appropriate, such activity shall be conducted with not-for-profit organizations. The Administrator may conduct research on methods for preventing, measuring and controlling emissions and evaluating associated health and environment risks. All information collected under this paragraph shall be available to the public.

(4) Grants

Upon application of a State, the Administrator may make grants, subject to such terms and conditions as the Administrator deems appropriate, to such State for the purpose of assisting the State in developing and implementing a program for submittal and approval under this subsection. Programs assisted under this paragraph may include program elements addressing air pollutants or extremely hazardous substances other than those specifically subject to this section. Grants under this paragraph may include support for high-risk point source review as provided in paragraph (2) and support for the development and implementation of areawide area source programs pursuant to subsection (k) of this section.

(5) Approval or disapproval

Not later than 180 days after receiving a program submitted by a State, and after notice and opportunity for public comment, the Administrator shall either approve or disapprove such program. The Administrator shall disapprove any program submitted by a State, if the Administrator determines that—

(A) the authorities contained in the program are not adequate to assure compliance by all sources within the State with each applicable standard, regulation or requirement established by the Administrator under this section;

(B) adequate authority does not exist, or adequate resources are not available, to implement the program;

(C) the schedule for implementing the program and assuring compliance by affected sources is not sufficiently expeditious; or

(D) the program is otherwise not in compliance with the guidance issued by the Administrator under paragraph (2) or is not likely to satisfy, in whole or in part, the objectives of this chapter.

If the Administrator disapproves a State program, the Administrator shall notify the State of any revisions or modifications necessary to obtain approval. The State may revise and resubmit the proposed program for review and approval pursuant to the provisions of this subsection.

(6) Withdrawal

Whenever the Administrator determines, after public hearing, that a State is not administering and enforcing a program approved pursuant to this subsection in accordance with the guidance published pursuant to paragraph (2) or the requirements of paragraph (5), the Administrator shall so notify the State and, if action which will assure prompt compliance is not taken within 90 days, the Administrator shall withdraw approval of the program. The Administrator shall not withdraw approval of any program unless the State shall have been notified and the reasons for withdrawal shall have been stated in writing and made public.

(7) Authority to enforce

Nothing in this subsection shall prohibit the Administrator from enforcing any applicable emission standard or requirement under this section.

(8) Local program

The Administrator may, after notice and opportunity for public comment, approve a program developed and submitted by a local air pollution control agency (after consultation with the State) pursuant to this subsection and any such agency implementing an approved program may take any action authorized to be taken by a State under this section.

(9) Permit authority

Nothing in this subsection shall affect the authorities and obligations of the Administrator or the State under subchapter V of this chapter.

(m) Atmospheric deposition to Great Lakes and coastal waters

(1) Deposition assessment

The Administrator, in cooperation with the Under Secretary of Commerce for Oceans and Atmosphere, shall conduct a program to identify and assess the extent of atmospheric deposition of hazardous air pollutants (and in the discretion of the Administrator, other air pollutants) to the Great Lakes, the Chesapeake Bay, Lake Champlain and coastal waters. As part of such program, the Administrator shall—

(A) monitor the Great Lakes, the Chesapeake Bay, Lake Champlain and coastal waters, including monitoring of the Great Lakes through the monitoring network established pursuant to paragraph (2) of this subsection and designing and deploying an atmospheric monitoring network for coastal waters pursuant to paragraph (4);

(B) investigate the sources and deposition rates of atmospheric deposition of air pollutants (and their atmospheric transformation precursors);

(C) conduct research to develop and improve monitoring methods and to determine the relative contribution of atmospheric pollutants to total pollution loadings to the Great Lakes, the Chesapeake Bay, Lake Champlain, and coastal waters;

(D) evaluate any adverse effects to public health or the environment caused by such deposition (including effects resulting from indirect exposure pathways) and assess the contribution of such deposition to violations of water quality standards established pursuant to the Federal Water Pollution Control Act [33 U.S.C.A. § 1251 et seq.] and drinking water standards established pursuant to the Safe Drinking Water Act [42 U.S.C.A. § 300f et seq.]; and

(E) sample for such pollutants in biota, fish, and wildlife of the Great Lakes, the Chesapeake Bay, Lake Champlain and coastal waters and characterize the sources of such pollutants.

(2) Great Lakes monitoring network

The Administrator shall oversee, in accordance with Annex 15 of the Great Lakes Water Quality Agreement, the establishment and operation of a Great Lakes atmospheric deposition network to monitor atmospheric deposition of hazardous air pollutants (and in the Administrator's discretion, other air pollutants) to the Great Lakes.

(A) As part of the network provided for in this paragraph, and not later than December 31, 1991, the Administrator shall establish in each of the 5 Great Lakes at least 1 facility capable of monitoring the atmospheric deposition of hazardous air pollutants in both dry and wet conditions.

(B) The Administrator shall use the data provided by the network to identify and track the movement of hazardous air pollutants through the Great Lakes, to determine the portion of water pollution loadings attributable to atmospheric deposition of such pollutants, and to support development of remedial action plans and other management plans as required by the Great Lakes Water Quality Agreement.

(C) The Administrator shall assure that the data collected by the Great Lakes atmospheric deposition monitoring network is in a format compatible with databases sponsored by the International Joint Commission, Canada, and the several States of the Great Lakes region.

(3) Monitoring for the Chesapeake Bay and Lake Champlain

The Administrator shall establish at the Chesapeake Bay and Lake Champlain atmospheric deposition stations to monitor deposition of hazardous air pollutants (and in the Administrator's discretion, other air pollutants) within the Chesapeake Bay and Lake Champlain watersheds. The Administrator shall determine the role of air deposition in the pollutant loadings of the Chesapeake Bay and Lake Champlain, investigate the sources of air pollutants deposited in the watersheds, evaluate the health and environmental effects of such pollutant loadings, and shall sample such pollutants in biota, fish and wildlife within the watersheds, as necessary to characterize such effects.

(4) Monitoring for coastal waters

The Administrator shall design and deploy atmospheric deposition monitoring networks for coastal waters and their watersheds and shall make any information collected through such networks available to the public. As part of this effort, the Administrator shall conduct research to develop and improve deposition monitoring methods, and to determine the relative contribution of atmospheric pollutants to pollutant loadings. For purposes of this subsection, "coastal waters" shall mean estuaries selected pursuant to section 320(a)(2)(A) of the Federal Water Pollution Control Act [33 U.S.C.A. § 1330(a)(2)(A)] or listed pursuant to section 320(a)(2)(B) of such Act [33 U.S.C.A. § 1330(a)(2)(B)] or estuarine research reserves designated pursuant to section 1461 of Title 16.

(5) Report

Within 3 years of November 15, 1990, and biennially thereafter, the Administrator, in cooperation with the Under Secretary of Commerce for Oceans and Atmosphere, shall submit to the Congress a report on the results of any monitoring, studies, and investigations conducted pursuant to this subsection. Such report shall include, at a minimum, an assessment of—

(A) the contribution of atmospheric deposition to pollution loadings in the Great Lakes, the Chesapeake Bay, Lake Champlain and coastal waters;

(B) the environmental and public health effects of any pollution which is attributable to atmospheric deposition to the Great Lakes, the Chesapeake Bay, Lake Champlain and coastal waters;

(C) the source or sources of any pollution to the Great Lakes, the Chesapeake Bay, Lake Champlain and coastal waters which is attributable to atmospheric deposition;

(D) whether pollution loadings in the Great Lakes, the Chesapeake Bay, Lake Champlain or coastal waters cause or contribute to exceedances[2] of drinking water standards pursuant to the Safe Drinking Water Act [42 U.S.C.A. § 300f et seq.] or water quality standards pursuant to the Federal Water Pollution Control Act [33 U.S.C.A. § 1251 et seq.] or, with respect to the Great Lakes, exceedances[2] of the specific objectives of the Great Lakes Water Quality Agreement; and

(E) a description of any revisions of the requirements, standards, and limitations pursuant to this chapter and other applicable Federal laws as are necessary to assure protection of human health and the environment.

(6) Additional regulation

As part of the report to Congress, the Administrator shall determine whether the other provisions of this section are adequate to prevent serious adverse effects to public health and serious or widespread environmental effects, including such effects resulting from indirect exposure pathways, associated with atmospheric deposition to the Great Lakes, the Chesapeake Bay, Lake Champlain and coastal waters of hazardous air pollutants (and their atmospheric transformation products). The Administrator shall take into consideration the tendency of such pollutants to bioaccumulate. Within 5 years after November 15, 1990, the Administrator shall, based on such report and determination, promulgate, in accordance with this section, such further emission standards or control measures as may be necessary and appropriate to prevent such effects, including effects due to bioaccumulation and indirect exposure pathways. Any requirements promulgated pursuant to this paragraph with respect to coastal waters shall only apply to the coastal waters of the States which are subject to section 7627(a) of this title.

(n) Other provisions

(1) Electric utility steam generating units

(A) The Administrator shall perform a study of the hazards to public health reasonably anticipated to occur as a result of emissions by electric utility steam generating units of pollutants listed under subsection (b) of this section after imposition of the requirements of this chapter. The Administrator shall report the results of this study to the Congress within 3 years after November 15, 1990. The Administrator shall develop and describe in the Administrator's report to Congress alternative control strategies for emissions which may warrant regulation under this section. The Administrator shall regulate electric utility steam generating units under this section, if the Administrator finds such regulation is appropriate and necessary after considering the results of the study required by this subparagraph.

(B) The Administrator shall conduct, and transmit to the Congress not later than 4 years after November 15, 1990, a study of mercury emissions from electric utility steam generating units, municipal waste combustion units, and other sources, including area sources. Such study shall consider the rate and mass of such emissions, the health and environmental effects of such emissions, technologies which are available to control such emissions, and the costs of such technologies.

(C) The National Institute of Environmental Health Sciences shall conduct, and transmit to the Congress not later than 3 years after November 15, 1990, a study to determine the threshold level of mercury exposure below which adverse human health effects are not expected to occur. Such study shall include a threshold for mercury concentrations in the tissue of fish which may be consumed (including consumption by sensitive populations) without adverse effects to public health.

(2) Coke oven production technology study

(A) The Secretary of the Department of Energy and the Administrator shall jointly undertake a 6-year study to assess coke oven production emission control technologies and to assist in the development and commercialization of technically practicable and economically viable control technologies which have the potential to significantly reduce emissions of hazardous air pollutants from coke oven production facilities. In identifying control technologies, the Secretary and the Administrator shall consider the range of existing coke oven operations and battery design and the availability of sources of materials for such coke ovens as well as alternatives to existing coke oven production design.

(B) The Secretary and the Administrator are authorized to enter into agreements with persons who propose to develop, install and operate coke production emission control technologies which have the potential for significant emissions reductions of hazardous air pollutants provided that Federal funds shall not exceed 50 per centum of the cost of any project assisted pursuant to this paragraph.

(C) On completion of the study, the Secretary shall submit to Congress a report on the results of the study and shall make recommendations to the Administrator identifying practicable and economically viable control technologies for coke oven production facilities to reduce residual risks remaining after implementation of the standard under subsection (d) of this section.

(D) There are authorized to be appropriated $5,000,000 for each of the fiscal years 1992 through 1997 to carry out the program authorized by this paragraph.

(3) Publicly owned treatment works

The Administrator may conduct, in cooperation with the owners and operators of publicly owned treatment works, studies to characterize emissions of hazardous air pollutants emitted by such facilities, to identify industrial, commercial and residential discharges that contribute to such emissions and to demonstrate control measures for such emissions. When promulgating any standard under this section applicable to publicly owned treatment works, the Administrator may provide for control measures that include pretreatment of discharges causing emissions of hazardous air pollutants and process or product substitutions or limitations that may be effective in reducing such emissions. The Administrator may prescribe uniform sampling, modeling and risk assessment methods for use in implementing this subsection.

(4) Oil and gas wells; pipeline facilities

(A) Notwithstanding the provisions of subsection (a) of this section, emissions from any oil or gas exploration or production well (with its associated equipment) and emissions from any pipeline compressor or pump station shall not be aggregated with emissions from other similar units, whether or not such units are in a contiguous area or under common control, to determine whether such units or stations are major sources, and in the case of any oil or gas exploration or production well (with its associated equipment), such emissions shall not be aggregated for any purpose under this section.

(B) The Administrator shall not list oil and gas production wells (with its associated equipment) as an area source category under subsection (c) of this section, except that the Administrator may establish an area source category for oil and gas production wells located in any metropolitan statistical area or consolidated metropolitan statistical area with a population in excess of 1 million, if the Administrator determines that emissions of hazardous air pollutants from such wells present more than a negligible risk of adverse effects to public health.

(5) Hydrogen sulfide

The Administrator is directed to assess the hazards to public health and the environment resulting from the emission of hydrogen sulfide associated with the extraction of oil and natural gas resources. To the extent practicable, the assessment shall build upon and not duplicate work conducted for an assessment pursuant to section 8002(m) of the Solid Waste Disposal Act [42 U.S.C.A. § 6982(m)] and shall reflect consultation with the States. The assessment shall include a review of existing State and industry control standards, techniques and enforcement. The Administrator shall report to the Congress within 24 months after November 15, 1990, with the findings of such assessment, together with any recommendations, and shall, as appropriate, develop and implement a control strategy for emissions of hydrogen sulfide to protect human health and the environment, based on the findings of such assessment, using authorities under this chapter including sections[3] 7411 of this title and this section.

(6) Hydrofluoric acid

Not later than 2 years after November 15, 1990, the Administrator shall, for those regions of the country which do not have comprehensive health and safety regulations with respect to hydrofluoric acid, complete a study of the potential hazards of hydrofluoric acid and the uses of hydrofluoric acid in industrial and commercial applications to public health and the environment considering a range of events including worst-case accidental releases and shall make recommendations to the Congress for the reduction of such hazards, if appropriate.

(7) RCRA facilities

In the case of any category or subcategory of sources the air emissions of which are regulated under subtitle C of the Solid Waste Disposal Act [42 U.S.C.A. § 6921 et seq.], the Administrator shall take into account any regulations of such emissions which are promulgated under such subtitle and shall, to the maximum extent practicable and consistent with the provisions of this section, ensure that the requirements of such subtitle and this section are consistent.

(*o*) National Academy of Sciences study

(1) Request of the Academy

Within 3 months of November 15, 1990, the Administrator shall enter into appropriate arrangements with the National Academy of Sciences to conduct a review of—

(A) risk assessment methodology used by the Environmental Protection Agency to determine the carcinogenic risk associated with exposure to hazardous air pollutants from source categories and subcategories subject to the requirements of this section; and

(B) improvements in such methodology.

(2) Elements to be studied

In conducting such review, the National Academy of Sciences should consider, but not be limited to, the following—

(A) the techniques used for estimating and describing the carcinogenic potency to humans of hazardous air pollutants; and

(B) the techniques used for estimating exposure to hazardous air pollutants (for hypothetical and actual maximally exposed individuals as well as other exposed individuals).

(3) Other health effects of concern

To the extent practicable, the Academy shall evaluate and report on the methodology for assessing the risk of adverse human health effects other than cancer for which safe thresholds of exposure may not exist, including, but not limited to, inheritable genetic mutations, birth defects, and reproductive dysfunctions.

(4) Report

A report on the results of such review shall be submitted to the Senate Committee on Environment and Public Works, the House Committee on Energy and Commerce, the Risk Assessment and Management Commission established by section 303 of the Clean Air Act Amendments of 1990 and the Administrator not later than 30 months after November 15, 1990.

(5) Assistance

The Administrator shall assist the Academy in gathering any information the Academy deems necessary to carry out this subsection. The Administrator may use any authority under this chapter to obtain information from any person, and to require any person to conduct tests, keep and produce records, and make reports respecting research or other activities conducted by such person as necessary to carry out this subsection.

(6) Authorization

Of the funds authorized to be appropriated to the Administrator by this chapter, such amounts as are required shall be available to carry out this subsection.

(7) Guidelines for carcinogenic risk assessment

The Administrator shall consider, but need not adopt, the recommendations contained in the report of the National Academy of Sciences prepared pursuant to this subsection and the views of the Science Advisory Board, with respect to such report. Prior to the promulgation of any standard under subsection (f) of this section, and after notice and opportunity for comment, the Administrator shall publish revised Guidelines for Carcinogenic Risk Assessment or a detailed explanation of the reasons that any recommendations contained in the report of the National Academy of Sciences will not be implemented. The publication of such revised Guidelines shall be a final Agency action for purposes of section 7607 of this title.

(p) Mickey Leland National Urban Air Toxics Research Center

(1) Establishment

The Administrator shall oversee the establishment of a National Urban Air Toxics Research Center, to be located at a university, a hospital, or other facility capable of undertaking and maintaining similar research capabilities in the areas of epidemiology, oncology, toxicology, pulmonary medicine, pathology, and biostatistics. The center shall be known as the Mickey Leland National Urban Air Toxics Research Center. The geographic site of the National Urban Air Toxics Research Center should be further directed to Harris County, Texas, in order to take full advantage of the well developed scientific community presence on-site at the Texas Medical Center as well as the extensive data previously compiled for the comprehensive monitoring system currently in place.

(2) Board of Directors

The National Urban Air Toxics Research Center shall be governed by a Board of Directors to be comprised of 9 members, the appointment of which shall be allocated pro rata among the Speaker of the House, the Majority Leader of the Senate and the President. The members of the Board of Directors shall be selected based on their respective academic and professional backgrounds and expertise in matters relating to public health, environmental pollution and industrial hygiene. The duties of the Board of Directors shall be to determine policy and research guidelines, submit views from center sponsors and the public and issue periodic reports of center findings and activities.

(3) Scientific Advisory Panel

The Board of Directors shall be advised by a Scientific Advisory Panel, the 13 members of which shall be appointed by the Board, and to include eminent members of the scientific and medical communities. The Panel membership may include scientists with relevant experience from the National Institute of Environmental Health Sciences, the Center for Disease Control, the Environmental Protection Agency, the National Cancer Institute, and others, and the Panel shall conduct peer review and evaluate research results. The Panel shall assist the Board in developing the research agenda, reviewing proposals and applications, and advise on the awarding of research grants.

(4) Funding

The center shall be established and funded with both Federal and private source funds.

(q) Savings provision

(1) Standards previously promulgated

Any standard under this section in effect before the date of enactment of the Clean Air Act Amendments of 1990 [November 15, 1990] shall remain in force and effect after such date unless modified as provided in this section before the date of enactment of such Amendments or under such Amendments. Except as provided in paragraph (4), any standard under this section which has been promulgated, but has not taken effect, before such date shall not be affected by such Amendments unless modified as provided in this section before such date or under such Amendments. Each such standard shall be reviewed and, if appropriate, revised, to comply with the requirements of subsection (d) of this section within 10 years after the date of enactment of the Clean Air Act Amendments of 1990. If a timely petition for review of any such standard under section 7607 of this title is pending on such date of enactment, the standard shall be upheld if it complies with this section as in effect before that date. If any such standard is remanded to the Administrator, the Administrator may in the Administrator's discretion apply either the requirements of this section, or those of this section as in effect before the date of enactment of the Clean Air Act Amendments of 1990.

(2) Special rule

Notwithstanding paragraph (1), no standard shall be established under this section, as amended by the Clean Air Act Amendments of 1990, for radionuclide emissions from (A) elemental phosphorous plants, (B) grate calcination elemental phosphorous plants, (C) phosphogypsum stacks, or (D) any subcategory of the foregoing. This section, as in effect prior to the date of enactment of the Clean Air Act Amendments of 1990 [November 15, 1990], shall remain in effect for radionuclide emissions from such plants and stacks.

(3) Other categories

Notwithstanding paragraph (1), this section, as in effect prior to the date of enactment of the Clean Air Act Amendments of 1990 [November 15, 1990], shall remain in effect for radionuclide emissions from non-Department of Energy Federal facilities that are not licensed by the Nuclear Regulatory Commission, coal-fired utility and industrial boilers, underground uranium mines, surface uranium mines, and disposal of uranium mill tailings piles, unless the Administrator, in the Administrator's discretion, applies the requirements of this section as modified by the Clean Air Act Amendments of 1990 to such sources of radionuclides.

(4) **Medical facilities**

Notwithstanding paragraph (1), no standard promulgated under this section prior to November 15, 1990, with respect to medical research or treatment facilities shall take effect for two years following November 15, 1990, unless the Administrator makes a determination pursuant to a rulemaking under subsection (d)(9) of this section. If the Administrator determines that the regulatory program established by the Nuclear Regulatory Commission for such facilities does not provide an ample margin of safety to protect public health, the requirements of this section shall fully apply to such facilities. If the Administrator determines that such regulatory program does provide an ample margin of safety to protect the public health, the Administrator is not required to promulgate a standard under this section for such facilities, as provided in subsection (d)(9) of this section.

(r) **Prevention of accidental releases**

(1) **Purpose and general duty**

It shall be the objective of the regulations and programs authorized under this subsection to prevent the accidental release and to minimize the consequences of any such release of any substance listed pursuant to paragraph (3) or any other extremely hazardous substance. The owners and operators of stationary sources producing, processing, handling or storing such substances have a general duty in the same manner and to the same extent as section 654 of Title 29 to identify hazards which may result from such releases using appropriate hazard assessment techniques, to design and maintain a safe facility taking such steps as are necessary to prevent releases, and to minimize the consequences of accidental releases which do occur. For purposes of this paragraph, the provisions of section 7604 of this title shall not be available to any person or otherwise be construed to be applicable to this paragraph. Nothing in this section shall be interpreted, construed, implied or applied to create any liability or basis for suit for compensation for bodily injury or any other injury or property damages to any person which may result from accidental releases of such substances.

(2) **Definitions**

(A) The term "accidental release" means an unanticipated emission of a regulated substance or other extremely hazardous substance into the ambient air from a stationary source.

(B) The term "regulated substance" means a substance listed under paragraph (3).

(C) The term "stationary source" means any buildings, structures, equipment, installations or substance emitting stationary activities (i) which belong to the same industrial group, (ii) which are located on one or more contiguous properties, (iii) which are under the control of the same person (or persons under common control), and (iv) from which an accidental release may occur.

(D) The term "retail facility" means a stationary source at which more than one-half of the income is obtained from direct sales to end users or at which more than one-half of the fuel sold, by volume, is sold through a cylinder exchange program.

(3) **List of substances**

The Administrator shall promulgate not later than 24 months after November 15, 1990, an initial list of 100 substances which, in the case of an accidental release, are known to cause or may reasonably be anticipated to cause death, injury, or serious adverse effects to human health or the environment. For purposes of promulgating such list, the Administrator shall use, but is not limited to, the list of extremely hazardous substances published under the Emergency Planning and Community Right-to-Know Act of 1986 [42 U.S.C.A. § 11001 et seq.], with such modifications as the Administrator deems appropriate. The initial list shall include chlorine, anhydrous ammonia, methyl chloride, ethylene oxide, vinyl chloride, methyl isocyanate, hydrogen cyanide, ammonia, hydrogen sulfide, toluene diisocyanate, phosgene, bromine, anhydrous hydrogen chloride, hydrogen fluoride, anhydrous sulfur dioxide, and sulfur trioxide. The initial list shall include at least 100 substances which pose the greatest risk of causing death, injury, or serious adverse effects to human health or the environment from accidental releases. Regulations establishing the list shall include an explanation of the basis for establishing the list. The list may be revised from time to time by the Administrator on the Administrator's own motion or by petition and shall be reviewed at least every 5 years. No air pollutant for which a national primary ambient air quality standard has been established shall be included on any such list. No substance, practice, process, or activity regulated under subchapter VI of this chapter shall be subject to regulations under this subsection. The Administrator shall establish procedures for the addition and deletion of substances from the list established under this paragraph consistent with those applicable to the list in subsection (b) of this section.

(4) Factors to be considered

In listing substances under paragraph (3), the Administrator—

(A) shall consider—

(i) the severity of any acute adverse health effects associated with accidental releases of the substance;

(ii) the likelihood of accidental releases of the substance; and

(iii) the potential magnitude of human exposure to accidental releases of the substance; and

(B) shall not list a flammable substance when used as a fuel or held for sale as a fuel at a retail facility under this subsection solely because of the explosive or flammable properties of the substance, unless a fire or explosion caused by the substance will result in acute adverse health effects from human exposure to the substance, including the unburned fuel or its combustion byproducts, other than those caused by the heat of the fire or impact of the explosion.

(5) Threshold quantity

At the time any substance is listed pursuant to paragraph (3), the Administrator shall establish by rule, a threshold quantity for the substance, taking into account the toxicity, reactivity, volatility, dispersibility, combustibility, or flammability of the substance and the amount of the substance which, as a result of an accidental release, is known to cause or may reasonably be anticipated to cause death, injury or serious adverse effects to human health for which the substance was listed. The Administrator is authorized to establish a greater threshold quantity for, or to exempt entirely, any substance that is a nutrient used in agriculture when held by a farmer.

(6) Chemical Safety Board

(A) There is hereby established an independent safety board to be known as the Chemical Safety and Hazard Investigation Board.

(B) The Board shall consist of 5 members, including a Chairperson, who shall be appointed by the President, by and with the advice and consent of the Senate. Members of the Board shall be appointed on the basis of technical qualification, professional standing, and demonstrated knowledge in the fields of accident reconstruction, safety engineering, human factors, toxicology, or air pollution regulation. The terms of office of members of the Board shall be 5 years. Any member of the Board, including the Chairperson, may be removed for inefficiency, neglect of duty, or malfeasance in office. The Chairperson shall be the Chief Executive Officer of the Board and shall exercise the executive and administrative functions of the Board.

(C) The Board shall—

(i) investigate (or cause to be investigated), determine and report to the public in writing the facts, conditions, and circumstances and the cause or probable cause of any accidental release resulting in a fatality, serious injury or substantial property damages;

(ii) issue periodic reports to the Congress, Federal, State and local agencies, including the Environmental Protection Agency and the Occupational Safety and Health Administration, concerned with the safety of chemical production, processing, handling and storage, and other interested persons recommending measures to reduce the likelihood or the consequences of accidental releases and proposing corrective steps to make chemical production, processing, handling and storage as safe and free from risk of injury as is possible and may include in such reports proposed rules or orders which should be issued by the Administrator under the authority of this section or the Secretary of Labor under the Occupational Safety and Health Act [29 U.S.C.A. § 651 et seq.] to prevent or minimize the consequences of any release of substances that may cause death, injury or other serious adverse effects on human health or substantial property damage as the result of an accidental release; and

(iii) establish by regulation requirements binding on persons for reporting accidental releases into the ambient air subject to the Board's investigatory jurisdiction. Reporting releases to the National Response Center, in lieu of the Board directly, shall satisfy such regulations. The National Response Center shall promptly notify the Board of any releases which are within the Board's jurisdiction.

(D) The Board may utilize the expertise and experience of other agencies.

(E) The Board shall coordinate its activities with investigations and studies conducted by other agencies of the United States having a responsibility to protect public health and safety. The Board shall enter into a memorandum of understanding with the National Transportation Safety Board to assure coordination of functions and to limit duplication of activities which shall designate the National Transportation Safety Board as the lead agency for the investigation of releases which are transportation related. The Board shall not be authorized to investigate marine oil spills, which the National Transportation Safety Board is authorized to investigate. The Board shall enter into a memorandum of understanding with the Occupational Safety and Health Administration so as to limit duplication of activities. In no event shall the Board forego an investigation where an accidental release causes a fatality or serious injury among the general public, or had the potential to cause substantial property damage or a number of deaths or injuries among the general public.

(F) The Board is authorized to conduct research and studies with respect to the potential for accidental releases, whether or not an accidental release has occurred, where there is evidence which indicates the presence of a potential hazard or hazards. To the extent practicable, the Board shall conduct such studies in cooperation with other Federal agencies having emergency response authorities, State and local governmental agencies and associations and organizations from the industrial, commercial, and nonprofit sectors.

(G) No part of the conclusions, findings, or recommendations of the Board relating to any accidental release or the investigation thereof shall be admitted as evidence or used in any action or suit for damages arising out of any matter mentioned in such report.

(H) Not later than 18 months after November 15, 1990, the Board shall publish a report accompanied by recommendations to the Administrator on the use of hazard assessments in preventing the occurrence and minimizing the consequences of accidental releases of extremely hazardous substances. The recommendations shall include a list of extremely hazardous substances which are not regulated substances (including threshold quantities for such substances) and categories of stationary sources for which hazard assessments would be an appropriate measure to aid in the prevention of accidental releases and to minimize the consequences of those releases that do occur. The recommendations shall also include a description of the information and analysis which would be appropriate to include in any hazard assessment. The Board shall also make recommendations with respect to the role of risk management plans as required by paragraph (8)(B)[4] in preventing accidental releases. The Board may from time to time review and revise its recommendations under this subparagraph.

(I) Whenever the Board submits a recommendation with respect to accidental releases to the Administrator, the Administrator shall respond to such recommendation formally and in writing not later than 180 days after receipt thereof. The response to the Board's recommendation by the Administrator shall indicate whether the Administrator will—

(i) initiate a rulemaking or issue such orders as are necessary to implement the recommendation in full or in part, pursuant to any timetable contained in the recommendation;

(ii) decline to initiate a rulemaking or issue orders as recommended.

Any determination by the Administrator not to implement a recommendation of the Board or to implement a recommendation only in part, including any variation from the schedule contained in the recommendation, shall be accompanied by a statement from the Administrator setting forth the reasons for such determination.

(J) The Board may make recommendations with respect to accidental releases to the Secretary of Labor. Whenever the Board submits such recommendation, the Secretary shall respond to such recommendation formally and in writing not later than 180 days after receipt thereof. The response to the Board's recommendation by the Administrator shall indicate whether the Secretary will—

(i) initiate a rulemaking or issue such orders as are necessary to implement the recommendation in full or in part, pursuant to any timetable contained in the recommendation;

(ii) decline to initiate a rulemaking or issue orders as recommended.

Any determination by the Secretary not to implement a recommendation or to implement a recommendation only in part, including any variation from the schedule contained in the recommendation, shall be accompanied by a statement from the Secretary setting forth the reasons for such determination.

(K) Within 2 years after November 15, 1990, the Board shall issue a report to the Administrator of the Environmental Protection Agency and to the Administrator of the Occupational Safety and Health Administration recommending the adoption of regulations for the preparation of risk management plans and general requirements for the prevention of accidental releases of regulated substances into the ambient air (including recommendations for listing substances under paragraph (3)) and for the mitigation of the potential adverse effect on human health or the environment as a result of accidental releases which should be applicable to any stationary source handling any regulated substance in more than threshold amounts. The Board may include proposed rules or orders which should be issued by the Administrator under authority of this subsection or by the Secretary of Labor under the Occupational Safety and Health Act [29 U.S.C.A. § 651 et seq.]. Any such recommendations shall be specific and shall identify the regulated substance or class of regulated substances (or other substances) to which the recommendations apply. The Administrator shall consider such recommendations before promulgating regulations required by paragraph (7)(B).

(L) The Board, or upon authority of the Board, any member thereof, any administrative law judge employed by or assigned to the Board, or any officer or employee duly designated by the Board, may for the purpose of carrying out duties authorized by subparagraph (C)—

(i) hold such hearings, sit and act at such times and places, administer such oaths, and require by subpoena or otherwise attendance and testimony of such witnesses and the production of evidence and may require by order that any person engaged in the production, processing, handling, or storage of extremely hazardous substances submit written reports and responses to requests and questions within such time and in such form as the Board may require; and

(ii) upon presenting appropriate credentials and a written notice of inspection authority, enter any property where an accidental release causing a fatality, serious injury or substantial property damage has occurred and do all things therein necessary for a proper investigation pursuant to subparagraph (C) and inspect at reasonable times records, files, papers, processes, controls, and facilities and take such samples as are relevant to such investigation.

Whenever the Administrator or the Board conducts an inspection of a facility pursuant to this subsection, employees and their representatives shall have the same rights to participate in such inspections as provided in the Occupational Safety and Health Act [29 U.S.C.A. § 651 et seq.].

(M) In addition to that described in subparagraph (L), the Board may use any information gathering authority of the Administrator under this chapter, including the subpoena power provided in section 7607(a)(1) of this title.

(N) The Board is authorized to establish such procedural and administrative rules as are necessary to the exercise of its functions and duties. The Board is authorized without regard to section 6101 of Title 41 to enter into contracts, leases, cooperative agreements or other transactions as may be necessary in the conduct of the duties and functions of the Board with any other agency, institution, or person.

(O) After the effective date of any reporting requirement promulgated pursuant to subparagraph (C)(iii) it shall be unlawful for any person to fail to report any release of any extremely hazardous substance as required by such subparagraph. The Administrator is authorized to enforce any regulation or requirements established by the Board pursuant to subparagraph (C)(iii) using the authorities of sections 7413 and 7414 of this title. Any request for information from the owner or operator of a stationary source made by the Board or by the Administrator under this section shall be treated, for purposes of sections 7413, 7414, 7416, 7420, 7603, 7604 and 7607 of this title and any other enforcement provisions of this chapter, as a request made by the Administrator under section 7414 of this title and may be enforced by the Chairperson of the Board or by the Administrator as provided in such section.

(P) The Administrator shall provide to the Board such support and facilities as may be necessary for operation of the Board.

(Q) Consistent with subsection (G)[5] and section 7414(c) of this title any records, reports or information obtained by the Board shall be available to the Administrator, the Secretary of Labor, the Congress and the public, except that upon a showing satisfactory to the Board by any person that records, reports, or information, or particular part thereof (other than release or emissions data) to which the Board has access, if made public, is likely to cause substantial harm to the person's competitive position, the Board shall consider such record, report, or information or particular portion thereof confidential in accordance with section 1905 of Title 18, except that such record, report, or information may be disclosed to other officers, employees, and authorized representatives of the United States concerned with carrying out this chapter or when relevant under any proceeding under this chapter. This subparagraph does not constitute authority to withhold records, reports, or information from the Congress.

(R) Whenever the Board submits or transmits any budget estimate, budget request, supplemental budget request, or other budget information, legislative recommendation, prepared testimony for congressional hearings, recommendation or study to the President, the Secretary of Labor, the Administrator, or the Director of the Office of Management and Budget, it shall concurrently transmit a copy thereof to the Congress. No report of the Board shall be subject to review by the Administrator or any Federal agency or to judicial review in any court. No officer or agency of the United States shall have authority to require the Board to submit its budget requests or estimates, legislative recommendations, prepared testimony, comments, recommendations or reports to any officer or agency of the United States for approval or review prior to the submission of such recommendations, testimony, comments or reports to the Congress. In the performance of their functions as established by this chapter, the members, officers and employees of the Board shall not be responsible to or subject to supervision or direction, in carrying out any duties under this subsection, of any officer or employee or agent of the Environmental Protection Agency, the Department of Labor or any other agency of the United States except that the President may remove any member, officer or employee of the Board for inefficiency, neglect of duty or malfeasance in office. Nothing in this section shall affect the application of Title 5 to officers or employees of the Board.

(S) The Board shall submit an annual report to the President and to the Congress which shall include, but not be limited to, information on accidental releases which have been investigated by or reported to the Board during the previous year, recommendations for legislative or administrative action which the Board has made, the actions which have been taken by the Administrator or the Secretary of Labor or the heads of other agencies to implement such recommendations, an identification of priorities for study and investigation in the succeeding year, progress in the development of risk-reduction technologies and the response to and implementation of significant research findings on chemical safety in the public and private sector.

(7) Accident prevention

(A) In order to prevent accidental releases of regulated substances, the Administrator is authorized to promulgate release prevention, detection, and correction requirements which may include monitoring, record-keeping, reporting, training, vapor recovery, secondary containment, and other design, equipment, work practice, and operational requirements. Regulations promulgated under this paragraph may make distinctions between various types, classes, and kinds of facilities, devices and systems taking into consideration factors including, but not limited to, the size, location, process, process controls, quantity of substances handled, potency of substances, and response capabilities present at any stationary source. Regulations promulgated pursuant to this subparagraph shall have an effective date, as determined by the Administrator, assuring compliance as expeditiously as practicable.

(B) (i) Within 3 years after November 15, 1990, the Administrator shall promulgate reasonable regulations and appropriate guidance to provide, to the greatest extent practicable, for the prevention and detection of accidental releases of regulated substances and for response to such releases by the owners or operators of the sources of such releases. The Administrator shall utilize the expertise of the Secretaries of Transportation and Labor in promulgating such regulations. As appropriate, such regulations shall cover the use, operation, repair, replacement, and maintenance of equipment to monitor, detect, inspect, and control such releases, including training of persons in the use and maintenance of such equipment and in the conduct of periodic inspections. The regulations shall include procedures and measures for emergency response after an accidental release of a regulated substance in order to protect human health and the environment. The regulations shall cover storage, as well as operations. The regulations shall, as appropriate, recognize differences in size, operations, processes, class and categories of sources and the voluntary actions of such sources to prevent such releases and respond to such releases. The regulations shall be applicable to a stationary source 3 years after the date of promulgation, or 3 years after the date on which a regulated substance present at the source in more than threshold amounts is first listed under paragraph (3), whichever is later.

(ii) The regulations under this subparagraph shall require the owner or operator of stationary sources at which a regulated substance is present in more than a threshold quantity to prepare and implement a risk management plan to detect and prevent or minimize accidental releases of such substances from the stationary source, and to provide a prompt emergency response to any such releases in order to protect human health and the environment. Such plan shall provide for compliance with the requirements of this subsection and shall also include each of the following:

(I) a hazard assessment to assess the potential effects of an accidental release of any regulated substance. This assessment shall include an estimate of potential release quantities and a determination of downwind effects, including potential exposures to affected populations. Such assessment shall include a previous release history of the past 5 years, including the size, concentration, and duration of releases, and shall include an evaluation of worst case accidental releases;

(II) a program for preventing accidental releases of regulated substances, including safety precautions and maintenance, monitoring and employee training measures to be used at the source; and

(III) a response program providing for specific actions to be taken in response to an accidental release of a regulated substance so as to protect human health and the environment, including procedures for informing the public and local agencies responsible for responding to accidental releases, emergency health care, and employee training measures.

At the time regulations are promulgated under this subparagraph, the Administrator shall promulgate guidelines to assist stationary sources in the preparation of risk management plans. The guidelines shall, to the extent practicable, include model risk management plans.

(iii) The owner or operator of each stationary source covered by clause (ii) shall register a risk management plan prepared under this subparagraph with the Administrator before the effective date of regulations under clause (i) in such form and manner as the Administrator shall, by rule, require. Plans prepared pursuant to this subparagraph shall also be submitted to the Chemical Safety and Hazard Investigation Board, to the State in which the stationary source is located, and to any local agency or entity having responsibility for planning for or responding to accidental releases which may occur at such source, and shall be available to the public under section 7414(c) of this title. The Administrator shall establish, by rule, an auditing system to regularly review and, if necessary, require revision in risk management plans to assure that the plans comply with this subparagraph. Each such plan shall be updated periodically as required by the Administrator, by rule.

(C) Any regulations promulgated pursuant to this subsection shall to the maximum extent practicable, consistent with this subsection, be consistent with the recommendations and standards established by the American Society of Mechanical Engineers (ASME), the American National Standards Institute (ANSI) or the American Society of Testing Materials (ASTM). The Administrator shall take into consideration the concerns of small business in promulgating regulations under this subsection.

(D) In carrying out the authority of this paragraph, the Administrator shall consult with the Secretary of Labor and the Secretary of Transportation and shall coordinate any requirements under this paragraph with any requirements established for comparable purposes by the Occupational Safety and Health Administration or the Department of Transportation. Nothing in this subsection shall be interpreted, construed or applied to impose requirements affecting, or to grant the Administrator, the Chemical Safety and Hazard Investigation Board, or any other agency any authority to regulate (including requirements for hazard assessment), the accidental release of radionuclides arising from the construction and operation of facilities licensed by the Nuclear Regulatory Commission.

(E) After the effective date of any regulation or requirement imposed under this subsection, it shall be unlawful for any person to operate any stationary source subject to such regulation or requirement in violation of such regulation or requirement. Each regulation or requirement under this subsection shall for purposes of sections 7413, 7414, 7416, 7420, 7604, and 7607 of this title and other enforcement provisions of this chapter, be treated as a standard in effect under subsection (d) of this section.

(F) Notwithstanding the provisions of subchapter V of this chapter or this section, no stationary source shall be required to apply for, or operate pursuant to, a permit issued under such subchapter solely because such source is subject to regulations or requirements under this subsection.

(G) In exercising any authority under this subsection, the Administrator shall not, for purposes of section 653(b)(1) of Title 29, be deemed to be exercising statutory authority to prescribe or enforce standards or regulations affecting occupational safety and health.

(H) Public access to off-site consequence analysis information

(i) Definitions

In this subparagraph:

(I) Covered person

The term "covered person" means—

(aa) an officer or employee of the United States;

(bb) an officer or employee of an agent or contractor of the Federal Government;

(cc) an officer or employee of a State or local government;

(dd) an officer or employee of an agent or contractor of a State or local government;

(ee) an individual affiliated with an entity that has been given, by a State or local government, responsibility for preventing, planning for, or responding to accidental releases;

(ff) an officer or employee or an agent or contractor of an entity described in item (ee); and

(gg) a qualified researcher under clause (vii).

(II) Official use

The term "official use" means an action of a Federal, State, or local government agency or an entity referred to in subclause (I)(ee) intended to carry out a function relevant to preventing, planning for, or responding to accidental releases.

(III) Off-site consequence analysis information

The term "off-site consequence analysis information" means those portions of a risk management plan, excluding the executive summary of the plan, consisting of an evaluation of 1 or more worst-case release scenarios or alternative release scenarios, and any electronic data base created by the Administrator from those portions.

(IV) Risk management plan

The term "risk management plan" means a risk management plan submitted to the Administrator by an owner or operator of a stationary source under subparagraph (B)(iii).

(ii) Regulations

Not later than 1 year after August 5, 1999, the President shall—

(I) assess—

(aa) the increased risk of terrorist and other criminal activity associated with the posting of off-site consequence analysis information on the Internet; and

(bb) the incentives created by public disclosure of off-site consequence analysis information for reduction in the risk of accidental releases; and

(II) based on the assessment under subclause (I), promulgate regulations governing the distribution of off-site consequence analysis information in a manner that, in the opinion of the President, minimizes the likelihood of accidental releases and the risk described in subclause (I)(aa) and the likelihood of harm to public health and welfare, and—

(aa) allows access by any member of the public to paper copies of off-site consequence analysis information for a limited number of stationary sources located anywhere in the United States, without any geographical restriction;

(bb) allows other public access to off-site consequence analysis information as appropriate;

(cc) allows access for official use by a covered person described in any of items (cc) through (ff) of clause (i)(I) (referred to in this subclause as a "State or local covered person") to off-site consequence analysis information relating to stationary sources located in the person's State;

(dd) allows a State or local covered person to provide, for official use, off-site consequence analysis information relating to stationary sources located in the person's State to a State or local covered person in a contiguous State; and

(ee) allows a State or local covered person to obtain for official use, by request to the Administrator, off-site consequence analysis information that is not available to the person under item (cc).

(iii) Availability under Freedom of information act

(I) First year

Off-site consequence analysis information, and any ranking of stationary sources derived from the information, shall not be made available under section 552 of Title 5, during the 1-year period beginning on August 5, 1999.

(II) After first year

If the regulations under clause (ii) are promulgated on or before the end of the period described in subclause (I), off-site consequence analysis information covered by the regulations, and any ranking of stationary sources derived from the information, shall not be made available under section 552 of Title 5, after the end of that period.

(III) Applicability

Subclauses (I) and (II) apply to off-site consequence analysis information submitted to the Administrator before, on, or after August 5, 1999.

(iv) Availability of information during transition period

The Administrator shall make off-site consequence analysis information available to covered persons for official use in a manner that meets the requirements of items (cc)through (ee) of clause (ii)(II), and to the public in a form that does not make available any information concerning the identity or location of stationary sources, during the period—

(I) beginning on August 5, 1999; and

(II) ending on the earlier of the date of promulgation of the regulations under clause (ii) or the date that is 1 year after August 5, 1999.

(v) Prohibition on unauthorized disclosure of information by covered persons

(I) In general

Beginning on August 5, 1999, a covered person shall not disclose to the public off-site consequence analysis information in any form, or any statewide or national ranking of identified stationary sources derived from such information, except as authorized by this subparagraph (including the regulations promulgated under clause (ii)). After the end of the 1-year period beginning on August 5, 1999, if regulations have not been promulgated under clause (ii), the preceding sentence shall not apply.

(II) Criminal penalties

Notwithstanding section 7413 of this title, a covered person that willfully violates a restriction or prohibition established by this subparagraph (including the regulations promulgated under clause (ii)) shall, upon conviction, be fined for an infraction under section 3571 of Title 18 (but shall not be subject to imprisonment) for each unauthorized disclosure of off-site consequence analysis information, except that subsection (d) of such section 3571 shall not apply to a case in which the offense results in pecuniary loss unless the defendant knew that such loss would occur. The disclosure of off-site consequence analysis information for each specific stationary source shall be considered a separate offense. The total of all penalties that may be imposed on a single person or organization under this item shall not exceed $1,000,000 for violations committed during any 1 calendar year.

(III) Applicability

If the owner or operator of a stationary source makes off-site consequence analysis information relating to that stationary source available to the public without restriction—

(aa) subclauses (I) and (II) shall not apply with respect to the information; and

(bb) the owner or operator shall notify the Administrator of the public availability of the information.

(IV) List

The Administrator shall maintain and make publicly available a list of all stationary sources that have provided notification under subclause (III)(bb).

(vi) Notice

The Administrator shall provide notice of the definition of official use as provided in clause (i)(III) and examples of actions that would and would not meet that definition, and notice of the restrictions on further dissemination and the penalties established by this chapter to each covered person who receives off-site consequence analysis information under clause (iv) and each covered person who receives off-site consequence analysis information for an official use under the regulations promulgated under clause (ii).

(vii) Qualified researchers

(I) In general

Not later than 180 days after August 5, 1999, the Administrator, in consultation with the Attorney General, shall develop and implement a system for providing off-site consequence analysis information, including facility identification, to any qualified researcher, including a qualified researcher from industry or any public interest group.

(II) Limitation on dissemination

The system shall not allow the researcher to disseminate, or make available on the Internet, the off-site consequence analysis information, or any portion of the off-site consequence analysis information, received under this clause.

(viii) Read-only information technology system

In consultation with the Attorney General and the heads of other appropriate Federal agencies, the Administrator shall establish an information technology system that provides for the availability to the public of off-site consequence analysis information by means of a central data base under the control of the Federal Government that contains information that users may read, but that provides no means by which an electronic or mechanical copy of the information may be made.

(ix) Voluntary industry accident prevention standards

The Environmental Protection Agency, the Department of Justice, and other appropriate agencies may provide technical assistance to owners and operators of stationary sources and participate in the development of voluntary industry standards that will help achieve the objectives set forth in paragraph (1).

(x) Effect on State or local law

(I) In general

Subject to subclause (II), this subparagraph (including the regulations promulgated under this subparagraph) shall supersede any provision of State or local law that is inconsistent with this subparagraph (including the regulations).

(II) Availability of information under State law

Nothing in this subparagraph precludes a State from making available data on the off-site consequences of chemical releases collected in accordance with State law.

(xi) Report

(I) In general

Not later than 3 years after August 5, 1999, the Attorney General, in consultation with appropriate State, local, and Federal Government agencies, affected industry, and the public, shall submit to Congress a report that describes the extent to which regulations promulgated under this paragraph have resulted in actions, including the design and maintenance of safe facilities, that are effective in detecting, preventing, and minimizing the consequences of releases of regulated substances that may be caused by criminal activity. As part of this report, the Attorney General, using available data to the extent possible, and a sampling of covered stationary sources selected at the discretion of the Attorney General, and in consultation with appropriate State, local, and Federal governmental agencies, affected industry, and the public, shall review the vulnerability of covered stationary sources to criminal and terrorist activity, current industry practices regarding site security, and security of transportation of regulated substances. The Attorney General shall submit this report, containing the results of the review, together with recommendations, if any, for reducing vulnerability of covered stationary sources to criminal and terrorist activity, to the Committee on Commerce of the United States House of Representatives and the Committee on Environment and Public Works of the United States Senate and other relevant committees of Congress.

(II) Interim report

Not later than 12 months after August 5, 1999, the Attorney General shall submit to the Committee on Commerce of the United States House of Representatives and the Committee on Environment and Public Works of the United States Senate, and other relevant committees of Congress, an interim report that includes, at a minimum—

(aa) the preliminary findings under subclause (I);

(bb) the methods used to develop the findings; and

(cc) an explanation of the activities expected to occur that could cause the findings of the report under subclause (I) to be different than the preliminary findings.

(III) Availability of information

Information that is developed by the Attorney General or requested by the Attorney General and received from a covered stationary source for the purpose of conducting the review under subclauses(I) and (II) shall be exempt from disclosure under section 552 of Title 5 if such information would pose a threat to national security.

(xii) Scope

This subparagraph—

(I) applies only to covered persons; and

(II) does not restrict the dissemination of off-site consequence analysis information by any covered person in any manner or form except in the form of a risk management plan or an electronic data base created by the Administrator from off-site consequence analysis information.

(xiii) Authorization of appropriations

There are authorized to be appropriated to the Administrator and the Attorney General such sums as are necessary to carry out this subparagraph (including the regulations promulgated under clause (ii)), to remain available until expended.

(8) Research on hazard assessments

The Administrator may collect and publish information on accident scenarios and consequences covering a range of possible events for substances listed under paragraph (3). The Administrator shall establish a program of long-term research to develop and disseminate information on methods and techniques for hazard assessment which may be useful in improving and validating the procedures employed in the preparation of hazard assessments under this subsection.

(9) Order authority

(A) In addition to any other action taken, when the Administrator determines that there may be an imminent and substantial endangerment to the human health or welfare or the environment because of an actual or threatened accidental release of a regulated substance, the Administrator may secure such relief as may be necessary to abate such danger or threat, and the district court of the United States in the district in which the threat occurs shall have jurisdiction to grant such relief as the public interest and the equities of the case may require. The Administrator may also, after notice to the State in which the stationary source is located, take other action under this paragraph including, but not limited to, issuing such orders as may be necessary to protect human health. The Administrator shall take action under section 7603 of this title rather than this paragraph whenever the authority of such section is adequate to protect human health and the environment.

(B) Orders issued pursuant to this paragraph may be enforced in an action brought in the appropriate United States district court as if the order were issued under section 7603 of this title.

(C) Within 180 days after November 15, 1990, the Administrator shall publish guidance for using the order authorities established by this paragraph. Such guidance shall provide for the coordinated use of the authorities of this paragraph with other emergency powers authorized by section 9606 of this title, sections 311(c), 308, 309 and 504(a) of the Federal Water Pollution Control Act [33 U.S.C.A. §§ 1321(c), 1318, 1319, 1364(a)], sections 3007, 3008, 3013, and 7003 of the Solid Waste Disposal Act [42 U.S.C.A. §§ 6927, 6928, 6934, 6973], sections 1445 and 1431 of the Safe Drinking Water Act [42 U.S.C.A. §§ 300j–4, 300i], sections 5 and 7 of the Toxic Substances Control Act [15 U.S.C.A. §§ 2604, 2606], and sections 7413, 7414, and 7603 of this title.

(10) Presidential review

The President shall conduct a review of release prevention, mitigation and response authorities of the various Federal agencies and shall clarify and coordinate agency responsibilities to assure the most effective and efficient implementation of such authorities and to identify any deficiencies in authority or resources which may exist. The President may utilize the resources and solicit the recommendations of the Chemical Safety and Hazard Investigation Board in conducting such review. At the conclusion of such review, but not later than 24 months after November 15, 1990, the President shall transmit a message to the Congress on the release prevention, mitigation and response activities of the Federal Government making such recommendations for change in law as the President may deem appropriate. Nothing in this paragraph shall be interpreted, construed or applied to authorize the President to modify or reassign release prevention, mitigation or response authorities otherwise established by law.

(11) State authority

Nothing in this subsection shall preclude, deny or limit any right of a State or political subdivision thereof to adopt or enforce any regulation, requirement, limitation or standard (including any procedural requirement) that is more stringent than a regulation, requirement, limitation or standard in effect under this subsection or that applies to a substance not subject to this subsection.

(s) Periodic report

Not later than January 15, 1993 and every 3 years thereafter, the Administrator shall prepare and transmit to the Congress a comprehensive report on the measures taken by the Agency and by the States to implement the provisions of this section. The Administrator shall maintain a database on pollutants and sources subject to the provisions of this section and shall include aggregate information from the database in each annual report. The report shall include, but not be limited to—

(1) a status report on standard-setting under subsections (d) and (f) of this section;

(2) information with respect to compliance with such standards including the costs of compliance experienced by sources in various categories and subcategories;

(3) development and implementation of the national urban air toxics program; and

(4) recommendations of the Chemical Safety and Hazard Investigation Board with respect to the prevention and mitigation of accidental releases.

(July 14, 1955, c. 360, Title I, § 112, as added by Pub. L. No. 91–604, § 4(a), 84 Stat. 1685 (Dec. 31, 1970); and amended by Pub. L. No. 95–95, Title I, §§ 109(d)(2), 110, Title IV, § 401(c), 91 Stat. 701, 703, 791 (Aug. 7, 1977); Pub. L. No. 95–623, § 13(b), 92 Stat. 3458 (Nov. 9, 1978); Pub. L. No. 101–549, Title III, § 301, 104 Stat. 2531 (Nov. 15, 1990); Pub. L. No. 102–187, 105 Stat. 1285 (Dec. 4, 1991); Pub. L. No. 105–362, Title IV, § 402(b), 112 Stat. 3283 (Nov. 10, 1998); Pub. L. No. 106–40, §§ 2, 3(a), 113 Stat. 207 (Aug. 5, 1999).)

[1] So in original. Probably should be "effects."

[2] So in original.

[3] So in original. Probably should be "section."

[4] So in original. Probably should be paragraph "(7)(B)."

[5] So in original. Probably should be "subparagraph."

HISTORICAL AND STATUTORY NOTES

References in Text

The date of enactment, referred to in subsec. (a)(11), probably means the date of enactment of Pub. L. No. 101–549, which amended this section generally and was approved Nov. 15, 1990.

The Atomic Energy Act of 1954, referred to in subsec. (d)(9), is Act of Aug. 30, 1954, c. 1073, 68 Stat. 919, as amended, which is codified generally as chapter 23 of this title (42 U.S.C.A. § 2011 et seq.). For complete classification of this Act to the Code, see Short Title of 1954 Acts note set out under 42 U.S.C.A. § 2011 and Tables.

The Federal Water Pollution Control Act, referred to in subsecs. (e)(5), (m)(1)(D), (m)(4), (m)(5)(D) and (r)(9)(C), is Act of June 30, 1948, c. 758, as amended generally by Pub. L. No. 92–500, § 2, 86 Stat. 816 (Oct. 18, 1972), which is codified generally as chapter 26 (section 1251 et seq.) of Title 33, Navigation and Navigable Waters. Title II of the Federal Water Pollution Control Act, referred to in subsec. (e)(5), is codified generally to subchapter II (section 1281 et seq.) of Title 33. Section 320 of such Act, referred to in subsec. (m)(4), is codified as 33 U.S.C.A. § 1330. Sections 308, 309, 311(c) and 504(a) of such Act, referred to in subsec. (r)(9)(C), are codified as 33 U.S.C.A. §§ 1318, 1319, 1321(c), and 1364(a), respectively. For complete classification of this Act to the Code, see Short Title note set out under 33 U.S.C.A. § 1251 and Tables.

The Toxic Substances Control Act, referred to in subsecs. (k)(3)(C) and (r)(9)(C), is Pub. L. No. 94–469, 90 Stat. 2003 (Oct. 11, 1976), as amended, which is codified generally to chapter 53 (section 2601 et seq.) of Title 15, Commerce and Trade. Sections 5 and 7 of such Act, referred to in subsec. (r)(9)(C), are codified as 15 U.S.C.A. §§ 2604 and 2606, respectively. For complete classification of this Act to the Code, see Short Title note set out under 15 U.S.C.A. § 2601 and Tables.

The Federal Insecticide, Fungicide, and Rodenticide Act, referred to in subsec. (k)(3)(C), is Act of June 25, 1947, c. 125, as amended generally by Pub. L. No. 92–516, 86 Stat. 973 (Oct. 21, 1972), which is codified generally as subchapter II (section 136 et seq.) of chapter 6 of Title 7, Agriculture. For complete classification of this Act to the Code, see Short Title note set out under 7 U.S.C.A. § 136 and Tables.

The Resource Conservation and Recovery Act of 1976, referred to in subsec. (k)(3)(C), is Pub. L. No. 94–580, 90 Stat. 2796 (Oct. 21, 1976), as amended, which is codified generally as chapter 82 of this title (42 U.S.C.A. § 6901 et seq.). For complete classification of this Act to the Code, see Short Title of 1976 Acts note set out under 42 U.S.C.A. § 6901 and Tables.

The Safe Drinking Water Act, referred to in subsecs. (m)(1)(D), (m)(5)(D), and (r)(9)(C), is Pub. L. No. 93–523, 88 Stat. 1660 (Dec. 16, 1974), as amended, which is codified principally as subchapter XII (section 300f et seq.) of chapter 6A of this title. Sections 1431 and 1445 of such Act, referred to in subsec. (r)(9)(C), are codified as 42 U.S.C.A. §§ 300i and 300j–4, respectively. For complete classification of this Act to the Code see Short Title of 1974 Amendments note set out under 42 U.S.C.A. § 201 and Tables.

The Solid Waste Disposal Act, referred to in subsecs. (n)(5), (n)(7), and (r)(9)(C), is Title II of Pub. L. No. 89–272, 79 Stat. 997 (Oct. 20, 1965), as amended generally by Pub. L. No. 94–580, § 2, 90 Stat. 2795 (Oct. 21, 1976), which is codified generally as chapter 82 of this title (42 U.S.C.A. § 6901 et seq.). Section 8002(m) of the Solid Waste Disposal Act, referred to in subsec. (n)(5), is codified as 42 U.S.C.A. § 6982(m). Subtitle C of such Act, referred to in subsec. (n)(7), is codified generally to subchapter III (section 6921 et seq.) of chapter 82 of this title. Sections 3007, 3008, 3013 and 7003 of such Act, referred to in subsec. (r)(9)(C), are codified as 42 U.S.C.A. §§ 6927, 6928, 6934, and 6973, respectively. For complete classification of this Act to the Code, see Short Title of 1976 Acts note set out under 42 U.S.C.A. § 6901 and Tables.

The Clean Air Act Amendments of 1990, referred to in subsecs. (*o*)(4), (q)(1), (q)(2) and (q)(3), is Pub. L. No. 101–549, 104 Stat. 2399 (Nov. 15, 1990). Section 303 of such Act, referred to in subsec. (*o*)(4), is set out as a note under this section. For complete classification of this Act to the Code, see Tables.

The date of enactment of the Clean Air Act Amendments of 1990, referred to in subsec. (q)(1) to (3), is the date of enactment of Pub. L. No. 101–549, Nov. 15, 1990, 104 Stat. 2399, which was approved Nov. 15, 1990.

The Emergency Planning and Community Right-to-Know Act of 1986, referred to in subsec. (r)(3), is Title III of Pub. L. No. 99–499, 100 Stat. 1728 (Oct. 17, 1986), which is codified generally to chapter 116 of this title (42 U.S.C.A. § 11001 et seq.). For complete classification of this Act to the Code, see Short Title of 1986 Amendments note set out under 42 U.S.C.A. § 11001 and Tables.

The Occupational Safety and Health Act of 1970, referred to in subsecs. (r)(6)(C)(ii), (r)(6)(K), and (L) is Pub. L. No. 91–596, 84 Stat. 1590 (Dec. 29, 1970), as amended, which is codified principally to chapter 15 of Title 29, Labor (29 U.S.C.A. § 651 et seq.). For complete classification of this Act to the Code, see Short Title note set out under 29 U.S.C.A. § 651 and Tables.

Codifications

This section was formerly codified as section 1857c–7 of this title.

In subsec. (r)(6)(N), "section 6101 of Title 41" substituted for "section 5 of title 41 of the United States Code" on authority of Pub. L. No. 111–350, § 6(c), 124 Stat. 3854 (Jan. 4, 2011), which Act enacted Title 41, Public Contracts.

Effective and Applicability Provisions

1990 Acts. Amendment by Pub. L. No. 101–549 effective Nov. 15, 1990, except as otherwise provided, see section 711(b) of Pub. L. No. 101–549, set out as a note under section 7401 of this title.

1977 Acts. Amendment by Pub. L. No. 95–95 effective Aug. 7, 1977, except as otherwise expressly provided, see section 406(d) of Pub. L. No. 95–95, set out as a note under section 7401 of this title.

Termination of Reporting Requirements

For termination, effective May 15, 2000, of reporting provisions of subsec. (n)(2)(C) of this section, pertaining to the coke oven production technology study, see Pub. L. No. 104–66, § 3003, as amended, set out as a note under 31 U.S.C.A. § 1113, and the 10th item on page 87 of House Document No. 103–7, referencing Pub. L. No. 101–549, § 301 (104 Stat. 2559), on which page the report pertaining to the coke oven production technology study is found.

For termination, effective May 15, 2000, of provisions of law requiring submittal to Congress of any annual, semiannual, or other regular periodic report listed in House Document No. 103–7 (in which reports required under subsecs. (f), (m)(5), (r)(6)(C)(ii), and (s) of this section are listed, respectively, as the 16th item on p. 164, the 8th item on page 162, the 9th item on page 198, and the 9th item on page 162), see Pub. L. No. 104–66, § 3003, as amended, set out as a note under 31 U.S.C.A. § 1113.

Change of Name

Any reference in any provision of law enacted before Jan. 4, 1995, to the Committee on Energy and Commerce of the House of Representatives treated as referring to the Committee on Commerce of the House of Representatives, except that any reference in any provision of law enacted before Jan. 4, 1995, to the Committee on Energy and Commerce of the House of Representatives treated as referring to the Committee on Agriculture of the House of Representatives, in the case of a provision of law relating to inspection of seafood or seafood products, the Committee on Banking and Financial Services of the House of Representatives, in the case of a provision of law relating to bank capital markets activities generally or to depository institution securities activities generally, and the Committee on Transportation and Infrastructure of the House of Representatives, in the case of a provision of law relating to railroads, railway labor, or railroad retirement and unemployment (except revenue measures related thereto), see section 1(a)(4) and (c)(1) of Pub. L. No. 104–14, set out as a note preceding 2 U.S.C.A. § 21.

Savings Provisions

Suits, actions or proceedings commenced under this chapter as in effect prior to Nov. 15, 1990, not to abate by reason of the taking effect of amendments by Pub. L. No. 101–549, except as otherwise provided for, see section 711(a) of Pub. L. No. 101–549, set out as a note under 42 U.S.C.A. § 7401.

Suits, actions, and other proceedings lawfully commenced by or against the Administrator or any other officer or employee of the United States in his official capacity or in relation to the discharge of his official duties under Act of July 14, 1955, the Clean Air Act, as in effect immediately prior to the enactment of Pub. L. No. 95–95 [Aug. 7, 1977], not to abate by reason of the taking effect of Pub. L. No. 95–95, see section 406(a) of Pub. L. No. 95–95, set out as an Effective and Applicability Provisions of 1977 Acts note under 42 U.S.C.A. § 7401.

Modification or Rescission of Rules, Regulations, Orders, Determinations, Contracts, Certifications, Authorizations, Delegations, and Other Actions

All rules, regulations, orders, determinations, contracts, certifications, authorizations, delegations, or other actions duly issued, made, or taken by or pursuant to Act of July 14, 1955, the Clean Air Act, as in effect immediately prior to the date of enactment of Pub. L. No. 95–95 [Aug. 7, 1977] to continue in full force and effect until modified or rescinded in accordance with Act of July 14, 1955, as amended by Pub. L. No. 95–95 [this chapter], see section 406(b) of Pub. L. No. 95–95, set out as an Effective and Applicability Provisions of 1977 Acts note under section 7401 of this title.

Public Meeting During Moratorium Period

Pub. L. No. 106–40, § 4, 113 Stat. 214 (Aug. 5, 1999), provided that:

"(a) In general.—Not later than 180 days after the date of enactment of this Act [August 5, 1999], each owner or operator of a stationary source covered by section 112(r)(7)(B)(ii) of the Clean Air Act [42 U.S.C.A. § 7412(r)(7)(B)(ii)] shall convene a public meeting, after reasonable public notice, in order to describe and discuss the local implications of the risk management plan submitted by the stationary source pursuant to section 112(r)(7)(B)(iii) of the Clean Air Act [42 U.S.C.A. § 7412(r)(7)(B)(iii)], including a summary of the off-site consequence analysis portion of the plan. Two or more stationary sources may conduct a joint meeting. In lieu of conducting such a meeting, small business stationary sources as defined in section 507(c)(1) of the Clean Air Act [42 U.S.C.A. § 7661f(c)(1)] may comply with this section by publicly posting a summary of the off-site consequence analysis information for their facility not later than 180 days after the enactment of this Act [August 5, 1999]. Not later than 10 months after the date of enactment of this Act [August 5, 1999], each such owner or operator shall send a certification to the director of the Federal Bureau of Investigation stating that such meeting has been held, or that such summary has been posted, within 1 year prior to, or within 6 months after, the date of the enactment of this Act [August 5, 1999]. This section shall not apply to sources that employ only Program 1 processes within the meaning of regulations promulgated under section 112(r)(7)(B)(i) of the Clean Air Act [42 U.S.C.A. § 7412(r)(7)(B)(i)].

"(b) Enforcement.—The Administrator of the Environmental Protection Agency may bring an action in the appropriate United States district court against any person who fails or refuses to comply with the requirements of this section, and such court may issue such orders, and take such other actions, as may be necessary to require compliance with such requirements."

Reevaluation of Regulations

Pub. L. No. 106–40, § 3(c), 113 Stat. 213 (Aug. 5, 1999), provided that: "The President shall reevaluate the regulations promulgated under this section within 6 years after the enactment of this Act [Chemical Safety Information, Site Security and Fuels Regulatory Relief Act, Pub. L. No. 106–40, Aug. 5, 1999, 113 Stat. 207]. If the President determines not to modify such regulations, the President shall publish a notice in the Federal Register stating that such reevaluation has been completed and that a determination has been made not to modify the regulations. Such notice shall include an explanation of the basis of such decision."

Reports

Pub. L. No. 106–40, § 3(b), 113 Stat. 213 (Aug. 5, 1999), provided that:

"(1) Definition of accidental release.—In this subsection, the term 'accidental release' has the meaning given the term in section 112(r)(2) of the Clean Air Act (42 U.S.C. 7412(r)(2)).

"(2) Report on status of certain amendments.—Not later than 2 years after the date of enactment of this Act [Aug. 5, 1999], the Comptroller General of the United States shall submit to Congress a report on the status of the development of amendments to the National Fire Protection Association Code for Liquefied Petroleum Gas that will result in the provision of information to local emergency response personnel concerning the off-site effects of accidental releases of substances exempted from listing under section 112(r)(4)(B) of the Clean Air Act [42 U.S.C.A. § 7412(r)(4)(B)] (as added by section 3) [sic; probably should be section 2 of Pub. L. No. 106–40, 113 Stat. 207 (Aug. 5, 1999), which added subsec. (r)(4)(B)].

"(3) Report on compliance with certain information submission requirements.—Not later than 3 years after the date of enactment of this Act [Aug. 5, 1999], the Comptroller General of the United States shall submit to Congress a report that—

"(A) describes the level of compliance with Federal and State requirements relating to the submission to local emergency response personnel of information intended to help the local emergency response personnel respond to chemical accidents or related environmental or public health threats; and

"(B) contains an analysis of the adequacy of the information required to be submitted and the efficacy of the methods for delivering the information to local emergency response personnel."

Risk Assessment and Management Commission

Pub. L. No. 101–549, § 303, 104 Stat. 2574 (Nov. 15, 1990), provided that:

"(a) Establishment.—There is hereby established a Risk Assessment and Management Commission (hereafter referred to in this section as the "Commission"), which shall commence proceedings not later than 18 months after the date of enactment of the Clean Air Act Amendments of 1990 [Nov. 15, 1990] and which shall make a full investigation of the policy implications and appropriate uses of risk assessment and risk management in regulatory programs under various Federal laws to prevent cancer and other chronic human health effects which may result from exposure to hazardous substances.

"(b) Charge.—The Commission shall consider—

"(1) the report of the National Academy of Sciences authorized by section 112(*o*) of the Clean Air Act [subsec. (*o*) of this section], the use and limitations of risk assessment in establishing emission or effluent standards, ambient standards, exposure standards, acceptable concentration levels, tolerances or other environmental criteria for hazardous substances that present a risk of carcinogenic effects or other chronic health effects and the suitability of risk assessment for such purposes;

"(2) the most appropriate methods for measuring and describing cancer risks or risks of other chronic health effects from exposure to hazardous substances considering such alternative approaches as the lifetime risk of cancer or other effects to the individual or individuals most exposed to emissions from a source or sources on both an actual and worst case basis, the range of such risks, the total number of health effects avoided by exposure reductions, effluent standards, ambient standards, exposures standards, acceptable concentration levels, tolerances and other environmental criteria, reductions in the number of persons exposed at various levels of risk, the incidence of cancer, and other public health factors;

"(3) methods to reflect uncertainties in measurement and estimation techniques, the existence of synergistic or antagonistic effects among hazardous substances, the accuracy of extrapolating human health risks from animal exposure data, and the existence of unquantified direct or indirect effects on human health in risk assessment studies;

"(4) risk management policy issues including the use of lifetime cancer risks to individuals most exposed, incidence of cancer, the cost and technical feasibility of exposure reduction measures and the use of site-specific actual exposure information in setting emissions standards and other limitations applicable to sources of exposure to hazardous substances; and

"(5) and comment on the degree to which it is possible or desirable to develop a consistent risk assessment methodology, or a consistent standard of acceptable risk, among various Federal programs.

"(c) Membership.—Such Commission shall be composed of ten members who shall have knowledge or experience in fields of risk assessment or risk management, including three members to be appointed by the President, two members to be appointed by the Speaker of the House of Representatives, one member to be appointed by the Minority Leader of the House of Representatives, two members to be appointed by the Majority Leader of the Senate, one member to be appointed by the Minority Leader of the Senate, and one member to be appointed by the President of the National Academy of Sciences. Appointments shall be made not later than 18 months after the date of enactment of the Clean Air Act Amendments of 1990 [Nov. 15, 1990].

"(d) Assistance from agencies.—The Administrator of the Environmental Protection Agency and the heads of all other departments, agencies, and instrumentalities of the executive branch of the Federal Government shall, to the maximum extent practicable, assist the Commission in gathering such information as the Commission deems necessary to carry out this section subject to other provisions of law.

"(e) Staff and contracts.—

"(1) In the conduct of the study required by this section, the Commission is authorized to contract (in accordance with Federal contract law) with nongovernmental entities that are competent to perform research or investigations within the Commission's mandate, and to hold public hearings, forums, and workshops to enable full public participation.

"(2) The Commission may appoint and fix the pay of such staff as it deems necessary in accordance with the provisions of title 5, United States Code [Title 5, Government Organization and Employees]. The Commission may request the temporary assignment of personnel from the Environmental Protection Agency or other Federal agencies.

"(3) The members of the Commission who are not officers or employees of the United States, while attending conferences or meetings of the Commission or while otherwise serving at the request of the Chair, shall be entitled to receive compensation at a rate not in excess of the maximum rate of pay for Grade GS–18, as provided in the General Schedule under section 5332 of title 5 of the United States Code [section 5332 of Title 5], including travel time, and while away from their homes or regular places of business they may be allowed travel expenses, including per diem in lieu of subsistence as authorized by law for persons in the Government service employed intermittently.

"(f) Report.—A report containing the results of all Commission studies and investigations under this section, together with any appropriate legislative recommendations or administrative recommendations, shall be made available to the public for comment not later than 42 months after the date of enactment of the Clean Air Act Amendments of 1990 [Nov. 15, 1990] and shall be submitted to the President and to the Congress not later than 48 months after such date of enactment. In the report, the Commission shall make recommendations with respect to the appropriate use of risk assessment and risk management in Federal regulatory programs to prevent cancer or other chronic health effects which may result from exposure to hazardous substances. The Commission shall cease to exist upon the date determined by the Commission, but not later than 9 months after the submission of such report.

"(g) Authorization.—There are authorized to be appropriated such sums as are necessary to carry out the activities of the Commission established by this section."

[For termination, effective May 15, 2000, of reporting provisions pertaining to the activities of the Commission of Pub. L. No. 101–549, § 303(f) set out above, see Pub. L. No. 104–66, § 3003, as amended, set out as a note under 31 U.S.C.A. § 1113, and the 13th item on page 190 of House Document No. 103–7.]

§ 7413. Federal enforcement

[CAA § 113]

(a) In general

(1) Order to comply with SIP

Whenever, on the basis of any information available to the Administrator, the Administrator finds that any person has violated or is in violation of any requirement or prohibition of an applicable implementation plan or permit, the Administrator shall notify the person and the State in which the plan applies of such finding. At any time after the expiration of 30 days following the date on which such notice of a violation is issued, the Administrator may, without regard to the period of violation (subject to section 2462 of Title 28)—

(A) issue an order requiring such person to comply with the requirements or prohibitions of such plan or permit,

(B) issue an administrative penalty order in accordance with subsection (d) of this section, or

(C) bring a civil action in accordance with subsection (b) of this section.

(2) State failure to enforce SIP or permit program

Whenever, on the basis of information available to the Administrator, the Administrator finds that violations of an applicable implementation plan or an approved permit program under subchapter V of this chapter are so widespread that such violations appear to result from a failure of the State in which the plan or permit program applies to enforce the plan or permit program effectively, the Administrator shall so notify the State. In the case of a permit program, the notice shall be made in accordance with subchapter V of this chapter. If the Administrator finds such failure extends beyond the 30th day after such notice (90 days in the case of such permit program), the Administrator shall give public notice of such finding. During the period beginning with such public notice and ending when such State satisfies the Administrator that it will enforce such plan or permit program (hereafter referred to in this section as "period of federally assumed enforcement"), the Administrator may enforce any requirement or prohibition of such plan or permit program with respect to any person by—

(A) issuing an order requiring such person to comply with such requirement or prohibition,

(B) issuing an administrative penalty order in accordance with subsection (d) of this section, or

(C) bringing a civil action in accordance with subsection (b) of this section.

(3) EPA enforcement of other requirements

Except for a requirement or prohibition enforceable under the preceding provisions of this subsection, whenever, on the basis of any information available to the Administrator, the Administrator finds that any person has violated, or is in violation of, any other requirement or prohibition of this subchapter, section 7603 of this title, subchapter IV-A, subchapter V, or subchapter VI of this chapter, including, but not limited to, a requirement or prohibition of any rule, plan, order, waiver, or permit promulgated, issued, or approved under those provisions or subchapters, or for the payment of any fee owed to the United States under this chapter (other than subchapter II of this chapter), the Administrator may—

(A) issue an administrative penalty order in accordance with subsection (d) of this section,

(B) issue an order requiring such person to comply with such requirement or prohibition,

(C) bring a civil action in accordance with subsection (b) of this section or section 7605 of this title, or

(D) request the Attorney General to commence a criminal action in accordance with subsection (c) of this section.

(4) Requirements for orders

An order issued under this subsection (other than an order relating to a violation of section 7412 of this title) shall not take effect until the person to whom it is issued has had an opportunity to confer with the Administrator concerning the alleged violation. A copy of any order issued under this subsection shall be sent to the State air pollution control agency of any State in which the violation occurs. Any order issued under this subsection shall state with reasonable specificity the nature of the violation and specify a time for compliance which the Administrator determines is reasonable, taking into account the seriousness of the violation and any good faith efforts to comply with applicable requirements. In any case in which an order under this subsection (or notice to a violator under paragraph (1)) is issued to a corporation, a copy of such order (or notice) shall be issued to appropriate corporate officers. An order issued under this subsection shall require the person to whom it was issued to comply with the requirement as expeditiously as practicable, but in no event longer than one year after the date the order was issued, and shall be nonrenewable. No order issued under this subsection shall prevent the State or the Administrator from assessing any penalties nor otherwise affect or limit the State's or the United States authority to enforce under other provisions of this chapter, nor affect any person's obligations to comply with any section of this chapter or with a term or condition of any permit or applicable implementation plan promulgated or approved under this chapter.

(5) Failure to comply with new source requirements

Whenever, on the basis of any available information, the Administrator finds that a State is not acting in compliance with any requirement or prohibition of the chapter relating to the construction of new sources or the modification of existing sources, the Administrator may—

(A) issue an order prohibiting the construction or modification of any major stationary source in any area to which such requirement applies;[1]

(B) issue an administrative penalty order in accordance with subsection (d) of this section, or

(C) bring a civil action under subsection (b) of this section.

Nothing in this subsection shall preclude the United States from commencing a criminal action under subsection (c) of this section at any time for any such violation.

(b) Civil judicial enforcement

The Administrator shall, as appropriate, in the case of any person that is the owner or operator of an affected source, a major emitting facility, or a major stationary source, and may, in the case of any other person, commence a civil action for a permanent or temporary injunction, or to assess and recover a civil penalty of not more than $25,000 per day for each violation, or both, in any of the following instances:

(1) Whenever such person has violated, or is in violation of, any requirement or prohibition of an applicable implementation plan or permit. Such an action shall be commenced (A) during any period of federally assumed enforcement, or (B) more than 30 days following the date of the Administrator's notification under subsection (a)(1) of this section that such person has violated, or is in violation of, such requirement or prohibition.

(2) Whenever such person has violated, or is in violation of, any other requirement or prohibition of this subchapter, section 7603 of this title, subchapter IV-A, subchapter V, or subchapter VI of this chapter, including, but not limited to, a requirement or prohibition of any rule, order, waiver or permit promulgated, issued, or approved under this chapter, or for the payment of any fee owed the United States under this chapter (other than subchapter II of this chapter).

(3) Whenever such person attempts to construct or modify a major stationary source in any area with respect to which a finding under subsection (a)(5) of this section has been made.

Any action under this subsection may be brought in the district court of the United States for the district in which the violation is alleged to have occurred, or is occurring, or in which the defendant resides, or where the defendant's principal place of business is located, and such court shall have jurisdiction to restrain such violation, to require compliance, to assess such civil penalty, to collect any fees owed the United States under this chapter (other than subchapter II of this chapter) and any noncompliance assessment and nonpayment penalty owed under section 7420 of this title, and to award any other appropriate relief. Notice of the commencement of such action shall be given to the appropriate State air pollution control agency. In the case of any action brought by the Administrator under this subsection, the court may award costs of litigation (including reasonable attorney and expert witness fees) to the party or parties against whom such action was brought if the court finds that such action was unreasonable.

(c) Criminal penalties

(1) Any person who knowingly violates any requirement or prohibition of an applicable implementation plan (during any period of federally assumed enforcement or more than 30 days after having been notified under subsection (a)(1) of this section by the Administrator that such person is violating such requirement or prohibition), any order under subsection (a) of this section, requirement or prohibition of section 7411(e) of this title (relating to new source performance standards), section 7412 of this title, section 7414 of this title (relating to inspections, etc.), section 7429 of this title (relating to solid waste combustion), section 7475(a) of this title (relating to preconstruction requirements), an order under section 7477 of this title (relating to preconstruction requirements), an order under section 7603 of this title (relating to emergency orders), section 7661a(a) or 7661b(c) of this title (relating to permits), or any requirement or prohibition of subchapter IV-A of this chapter (relating to acid deposition control), or subchapter VI of this chapter (relating to stratospheric ozone control), including a requirement of any rule, order, waiver, or permit promulgated or approved under such sections or subchapters, and including any requirement for the payment of any fee owed the United States under this chapter (other than subchapter II of this chapter) shall, upon conviction, be punished by a fine pursuant to Title 18 or by imprisonment for not to exceed 5 years, or both. If a conviction of any person under this paragraph is for a violation committed after a first conviction of such person under this paragraph, the maximum punishment shall be doubled with respect to both the fine and imprisonment.

(2) Any person who knowingly—

(A) makes any false material statement, representation, or certification in, or omits material information from, or knowingly alters, conceals, or fails to file or maintain any notice, application, record, report, plan, or other document required pursuant to this chapter to be either filed or maintained (whether with respect to the requirements imposed by the Administrator or by a State);

(B) fails to notify or report as required under this chapter; or

(C) falsifies, tampers with, renders inaccurate, or fails to install any monitoring device or method required to be maintained or followed under this chapter[2]

shall, upon conviction, be punished by a fine pursuant to Title 18 or by imprisonment for not more than 2 years, or both. If a conviction of any person under this paragraph is for a violation committed after a first conviction of such person under this paragraph, the maximum punishment shall be doubled with respect to both the fine and imprisonment.

(3) Any person who knowingly fails to pay any fee owed the United States under this subchapter, subchapter III, IV-A, V, or VI of this chapter shall, upon conviction, be punished by a fine pursuant to Title 18 or by imprisonment for not more than 1 year, or both. If a conviction of any person under this paragraph is for a violation committed after a first conviction of such person under this paragraph, the maximum punishment shall be doubled with respect to both the fine and imprisonment.

(4) Any person who negligently releases into the ambient air any hazardous air pollutant listed pursuant to section 7412 of this title or any extremely hazardous substance listed pursuant to section 11002(a)(2) of this title that is not listed in section 7412 of this title, and who at the time negligently places another person in imminent danger of death or serious bodily injury shall, upon conviction, be punished by a fine under Title 18 or by imprisonment for not more than 1 year, or both. If a conviction of any person under this paragraph is for a violation committed after a first conviction of such person under this paragraph, the maximum punishment shall be doubled with respect to both the fine and imprisonment.

(5) (A) Any person who knowingly releases into the ambient air any hazardous air pollutant listed pursuant to section 7412 of this title or any extremely hazardous substance listed pursuant to section

11002(a)(2) of this title that is not listed in section 7412 of this title, and who knows at the time that he thereby places another person in imminent danger of death or serious bodily injury shall, upon conviction, be punished by a fine under Title 18 or by imprisonment of not more than 15 years, or both. Any person committing such violation which is an organization shall, upon conviction under this paragraph, be subject to a fine of not more than $1,000,000 for each violation. If a conviction of any person under this paragraph is for a violation committed after a first conviction of such person under this paragraph, the maximum punishment shall be doubled with respect to both the fine and imprisonment. For any air pollutant for which the Administrator has set an emissions standard or for any source for which a permit has been issued under subchapter V of this chapter, a release of such pollutant in accordance with that standard or permit shall not constitute a violation of this paragraph or paragraph (4).

(B) In determining whether a defendant who is an individual knew that the violation placed another person in imminent danger of death or serious bodily injury—

(i) the defendant is responsible only for actual awareness or actual belief possessed; and

(ii) knowledge possessed by a person other than the defendant, but not by the defendant, may not be attributed to the defendant;

except that in proving a defendant's possession of actual knowledge, circumstantial evidence may be used, including evidence that the defendant took affirmative steps to be shielded from relevant information.

(C) It is an affirmative defense to a prosecution that the conduct charged was freely consented to by the person endangered and that the danger and conduct charged were reasonably foreseeable hazards of—

(i) an occupation, a business, or a profession; or

(ii) medical treatment or medical or scientific experimentation conducted by professionally approved methods and such other person had been made aware of the risks involved prior to giving consent.

The defendant may establish an affirmative defense under this subparagraph by a preponderance of the evidence.

(D) All general defenses, affirmative defenses, and bars to prosecution that may apply with respect to other Federal criminal offenses may apply under subparagraph (A) of this paragraph and shall be determined by the courts of the United States according to the principles of common law as they may be interpreted in the light of reason and experience. Concepts of justification and excuse applicable under this section may be developed in the light of reason and experience.

(E) The term "organization" means a legal entity, other than a government, established or organized for any purpose, and such term includes a corporation, company, association, firm, partnership, joint stock company, foundation, institution, trust, society, union, or any other association of persons.

(F) The term "serious bodily injury" means bodily injury which involves a substantial risk of death, unconsciousness, extreme physical pain, protracted and obvious disfigurement or protracted loss or impairment of the function of a bodily member, organ, or mental faculty.

(6) For the purpose of this subsection, the term "person" includes, in addition to the entities referred to in section 7602(e) of this title, any responsible corporate officer.

(d) Administrative assessment of civil penalties

(1) The Administrator may issue an administrative order against any person assessing a civil administrative penalty of up to $25,000, per day of violation, whenever, on the basis of any available information, the Administrator finds that such person—

(A) has violated or is violating any requirement or prohibition of an applicable implementation plan (such order shall be issued (i) during any period of federally assumed enforcement, or (ii) more than thirty days following the date of the Administrator's notification under subsection (a)(1) of this section of a finding that such person has violated or is violating such requirement or prohibition); or

(B) has violated or is violating any other requirement or prohibition of this subchapter or subchapter III, IV-A, V, or VI of this chapter, including, but not limited to, a requirement or prohibition of any rule, order, waiver, permit, or plan promulgated, issued, or approved under this chapter, or for the payment of any fee owed the United States under this chapter (other than subchapter II of this chapter); or

(C) attempts to construct or modify a major stationary source in any area with respect to which a finding under subsection (a)(5) of this section has been made.

The Administrator's authority under this paragraph shall be limited to matters where the total penalty sought does not exceed $200,000 and the first alleged date of violation occurred no more than 12 months prior to the initiation of the administrative action, except where the Administrator and the Attorney General jointly determine that a matter involving a larger penalty amount or longer period of violation is appropriate for administrative penalty action. Any such determination by the Administrator and the Attorney General shall not be subject to judicial review.

(2) **(A)** An administrative penalty assessed under paragraph (1) shall be assessed by the Administrator by an order made after opportunity for a hearing on the record in accordance with sections 554 and 556 of Title 5. The Administrator shall issue reasonable rules for discovery and other procedures for hearings under this paragraph. Before issuing such an order, the Administrator shall give written notice to the person to be assessed an administrative penalty of the Administrator's proposal to issue such order and provide such person an opportunity to request such a hearing on the order, within 30 days of the date the notice is received by such person.

(B) The Administrator may compromise, modify, or remit, with or without conditions, any administrative penalty which may be imposed under this subsection.

(3) The Administrator may implement, after consultation with the Attorney General and the States, a field citation program through regulations establishing appropriate minor violations for which field citations assessing civil penalties not to exceed $5,000 per day of violation may be issued by officers or employees designated by the Administrator. Any person to whom a field citation is assessed may, within a reasonable time as prescribed by the Administrator through regulation, elect to pay the penalty assessment or to request a hearing on the field citation. If a request for a hearing is not made within the time specified in the regulation, the penalty assessment in the field citation shall be final. Such hearing shall not be subject to section 554 or 556 of Title 5, but shall provide a reasonable opportunity to be heard and to present evidence. Payment of a civil penalty required by a field citation shall not be a defense to further enforcement by the United States or a State to correct a violation, or to assess the statutory maximum penalty pursuant to other authorities in the chapter, if the violation continues.

(4) Any person against whom a civil penalty is assessed under paragraph (3) of this subsection or to whom an administrative penalty order is issued under paragraph (1) of this subsection may seek review of such assessment in the United States District Court for the District of Columbia or for the district in which the violation is alleged to have occurred, in which such person resides, or where such person's principal place of business is located, by filing in such court within 30 days following the date the administrative penalty order becomes final under paragraph (2), the assessment becomes final under paragraph (3), or a final decision following a hearing under paragraph (3) is rendered, and by simultaneously sending a copy of the filing by certified mail to the Administrator and the Attorney General. Within 30 days thereafter, the Administrator shall file in such court a certified copy, or certified index, as appropriate, of the record on which the administrative penalty order or assessment was issued. Such court shall not set aside or remand such order or assessment unless there is not substantial evidence in the record, taken as a whole, to support the finding of a violation or unless the order or penalty assessment constitutes an abuse of discretion. Such order or penalty assessment shall not be subject to review by any court except as provided in this paragraph. In any such proceedings, the United States may seek to recover civil penalties ordered or assessed under this section.

(5) If any person fails to pay an assessment of a civil penalty or fails to comply with an administrative penalty order—

(A) after the order or assessment has become final, or

(B) after a court in an action brought under paragraph (4) has entered a final judgment in favor of the Administrator,

the Administrator shall request the Attorney General to bring a civil action in an appropriate district court to enforce the order or to recover the amount ordered or assessed (plus interest at rates established pursuant to section 6621(a)(2) of Title 26 from the date of the final order or decision or the date of the final judgment, as the case may be). In such an action, the validity, amount, and appropriateness of such order or assessment shall not be subject to review. Any person who fails to pay on a timely basis a civil penalty ordered or assessed under this section shall be required to pay, in addition to such penalty and interest, the United States enforcement expenses, including but not limited to attorneys fees and costs incurred by the United States for collection proceedings and a quarterly nonpayment penalty for each quarter during which such failure to pay persists. Such nonpayment penalty shall be 10 percent of the aggregate amount of such person's outstanding penalties and nonpayment penalties accrued as of the beginning of such quarter.

(e) Penalty assessment criteria

(1) In determining the amount of any penalty to be assessed under this section or section 7604(a) of this title, the Administrator or the court, as appropriate, shall take into consideration (in addition to such other factors as justice may require) the size of the business, the economic impact of the penalty on the business, the violator's full compliance history and good faith efforts to comply, the duration of the violation as established by any credible evidence (including evidence other than the applicable test method), payment by the violator of penalties previously assessed for the same violation, the economic benefit of noncompliance, and the seriousness of the violation. The court shall not assess penalties for noncompliance with administrative subpoenas under section 7607(a) of this title, or actions under section 7414 of this title, where the violator had sufficient cause to violate or fail or refuse to comply with such subpoena or action.

(2) A penalty may be assessed for each day of violation. For purposes of determining the number of days of violation for which a penalty may be assessed under subsection (b) or (d)(1) of this section, or section 7604(a) of this title, or an assessment may be made under section 7420 of this title, where the Administrator or an air pollution control agency has notified the source of the violation, and the plaintiff makes a prima facie showing that the conduct or events giving rise to the violation are likely to have continued or recurred past the date of notice, the days of violation shall be presumed to include the date of such notice and each and every day thereafter until the violator establishes that continuous compliance has been achieved, except to the extent that the violator can prove by a preponderance of the evidence that there were intervening days during which no violation occurred or that the violation was not continuing in nature.

(f) Awards

The Administrator may pay an award, not to exceed $10,000, to any person who furnishes information or services which lead to a criminal conviction or a judicial or administrative civil penalty for any violation of this subchapter or subchapter III, IV-A, V, or VI of this chapter enforced under this section. Such payment is subject to available appropriations for such purposes as provided in annual appropriation Acts. Any officer, or employee of the United States or any State or local government who furnishes information or renders service in the performance of an official duty is ineligible for payment under this subsection. The Administrator may, by regulation, prescribe additional criteria for eligibility for such an award.

(g) Settlements; public participation

At least 30 days before a consent order or settlement agreement of any kind under this chapter to which the United States is a party (other than enforcement actions under this section, section 7420 of this title, or subchapter II of this chapter, whether or not involving civil or criminal penalties, or judgments subject to Department of Justice policy on public participation) is final or filed with a court, the Administrator shall provide a reasonable opportunity by notice in the Federal Register to persons who are not named as parties or intervenors to the action or matter to comment in writing. The Administrator or the Attorney General, as appropriate, shall promptly consider any such written comments and may withdraw or withhold his consent to the proposed order or agreement if the comments disclose facts or considerations which indicate that such consent is inappropriate, improper, inadequate, or inconsistent with the requirements of this chapter. Nothing in this subsection shall apply to civil or criminal penalties under this chapter.

(h) Operator

For purposes of the provisions of this section and section 7420 of this title, the term "operator", as used in such provisions, shall include any person who is senior management personnel or a corporate officer. Except in the case of knowing and willful violations, such term shall not include any person who is a stationary engineer or technician responsible for the operation, maintenance, repair, or monitoring of equipment and facilities and who often has supervisory and training duties but who is not senior management personnel or a corporate officer. Except in the case of knowing and willful violations, for purposes of subsection (c)(4) of this section, the term "a person" shall not include an employee who is carrying out his normal activities and who is not a part of senior management personnel or a corporate officer. Except in the case of knowing and willful violations, for purposes of paragraphs (1), (2), (3), and (5) of subsection (c) of this section the term "a person" shall not include an employee who is carrying out his normal activities and who is acting under orders from the employer.

(July 14, 1955, c. 360, Title I, § 113, as added by Pub. L. No. 91–604, § 4(a), 84 Stat. 1686 (Dec. 31, 1970); and amended by Pub. L. No. 92–157, Title III, § 302(b), (c), 85 Stat. 464 (Nov. 18, 1971); Pub. L. No. 93–319, § 6(a)(1) to (3), 88 Stat. 259 (June 22, 1974); Pub. L. No. 95–95, Title I, §§ 111, 112(a), 91 Stat. 704, 705 (Aug. 7, 1977); Pub. L. No. 95–190, § 14(a)(10) to (21), (b)(1), 91 Stat. 1400, 1404 (Nov. 16, 1977); Pub. L. No. 97–23, § 2, 95 Stat. 139 (July 17, 1981); Pub. L. No. 101–549, Title VII, § 701, 104 Stat. 2672 (Nov. 15, 1990).)

[1] So in original. The semicolon probably should be a comma.

[2] So in original. Probably should be followed by a comma.

HISTORICAL AND STATUTORY NOTES

Codifications

This section was formerly codified as section 1857c–8 of this title.

Effective and Applicability Provisions

1990 Acts. Amendment by Pub. L. No. 101–549 effective Nov. 15, 1990, except as otherwise provided, see section 711(b) of Pub. L. No. 101–549, set out as a note under section 7401 of this title.

1977 Acts. Amendment by Pub. L. No. 95–95 effective Aug. 7, 1977, except as otherwise expressly provided, see section 406(d) of Pub. L. No. 95–95, set out as a note under section 7401 of this title.

Transfer of Functions

The Federal Power Commission was terminated and its functions, personnel, property, funds, etc. were transferred to the Secretary of Energy (except for certain functions which were transferred to the Federal Energy Regulatory Commission) by sections 7151(b), 7171(a), 7172(a), 7291, and 7293 of this title.

Savings Provisions

Suits, actions or proceedings commenced under this chapter as in effect prior to Nov. 15, 1990, not to abate by reason of the taking effect of amendments by Pub. L. No. 101–549, except as otherwise provided for, see section 711(a) of Pub. L. No. 101–549, set out as a note under section 7401 of this title.

Suits, actions, and other proceedings lawfully commenced by or against the Administrator or any other officer or employee of the United States in his official capacity or in relation to the discharge of his official duties under Act of July 14, 1955, the Clean Air Act, as in effect immediately prior to the enactment of Pub. L. No. 95–95 [Aug. 7, 1977], not to abate by reason of the taking effect of Pub. L. No. 95–95, see section 406(a) of Pub. L. No. 95–95, set out as an Effective Date of 1977 Acts note under section 7401 of this title.

Short Title

1981 Amendments. Citation of Pub. L. No. 97–23, which enacted subsec. (e) of this section, as the "Steel Industry Compliance Extension Act of 1981", see section 1 of Pub. L. No. 97–23, set out as a note under section 7401 of this title.

Modification or Rescission of Rules, Regulations, Orders, Determinations, Contracts, Certifications, Authorizations, Delegations, and Other Actions

All rules, regulations, orders, determinations, contracts, certifications, authorizations, delegations, or other actions duly issued, made, or taken by or pursuant to Act of July 14, 1955, the Clean Air Act, as in effect immediately prior to the date of enactment of Pub. L. No. 95–95 [Aug. 7, 1977] to continue in full force and effect until modified or rescinded in accordance with Act of July 14, 1955, as amended by Pub. L. No. 95–95 [this chapter], see section 406(b) of Pub. L. No. 95–95, set out as an Effective Date of 1977 Acts note under section 7401 of this title.

§ 7414. Recordkeeping, inspections, monitoring, and entry

[CAA § 114]

(a) Authority of Administrator or authorized representative

For the purpose (i) of developing or assisting in the development of any implementation plan under section 7410 or section 7411(d) of this title, any standard of performance under section 7411 of this title, any emission standard under section 7412 of this title,[1] or any regulation of solid waste combustion under section 7429 of this title, or any regulation under section 7429 of this title (relating to solid waste combustion), (ii) of determining whether any person is in violation of any such standard or any requirement of such a plan, or (iii) carrying out any provision of this chapter (except a provision of subchapter II of this chapter with respect to a manufacturer of new motor vehicles or new motor vehicle engines)—

(1) the Administrator may require any person who owns or operates any emission source, who manufactures emission control equipment or process equipment, who the Administrator believes may have information necessary for the purposes set forth in this subsection, or who is subject to any requirement of this chapter (other than a manufacturer subject to the provisions of section 7525(c) or 7542 of this title with respect to a provision of subchapter II of this chapter) on a one-time, periodic or continuous basis to—

(A) establish and maintain such records;

(B) make such reports;

(C) install, use, and maintain such monitoring equipment, and use such audit procedures, or methods;

(D) sample such emissions (in accordance with such procedures or methods, at such locations, at such intervals, during such periods and in such manner as the Administrator shall prescribe);

(E) keep records on control equipment parameters, production variables or other indirect data when direct monitoring of emissions is impractical;

(F) submit compliance certifications in accordance with subsection (a)(3) of this section; and

(G) provide such other information as the Administrator may reasonably require; and

(2) the Administrator or his authorized representative, upon presentation of his credentials—

(A) shall have a right of entry to, upon, or through any premises of such person or in which any records required to be maintained under paragraph (1) of this section are located, and

(B) may at reasonable times have access to and copy any records, inspect any monitoring equipment or method required under paragraph (1), and sample any emissions which such person is required to sample under paragraph (1).[2]

(3) The[3] Administrator shall in the case of any person which is the owner or operator of a major stationary source, and may, in the case of any other person, require enhanced monitoring and submission of compliance certifications. Compliance certifications shall include (A) identification of the applicable requirement that is the basis of the certification, (B) the method used for determining the compliance status of the source, (C) the compliance status, (D) whether compliance is continuous or intermittent, (E) such other facts as the Administrator may require. Compliance certifications and monitoring data shall be subject to subsection (c) of this section. Submission of a compliance certification shall in no way limit the Administrator's authorities to investigate or otherwise implement this chapter. The Administrator shall promulgate rules to provide guidance and to implement this paragraph within 2 years after November 15, 1990.

(b) State enforcement

(1) Each State may develop and submit to the Administrator a procedure for carrying out this section in such State. If the Administrator finds the State procedure is adequate, he may delegate to such State any authority he has to carry out this section.

(2) Nothing in this subsection shall prohibit the Administrator from carrying out this section in a State.

(c) Availability of records, reports, and information to public; disclosure of trade secrets

Any records, reports or information obtained under subsection (a) of this section shall be available to the public, except that upon a showing satisfactory to the Administrator by any person that records, reports, or information, or particular part thereof, (other than emission data) to which the Administrator has access under this section if made public, would divulge methods or processes entitled to protection as trade secrets of such person, the Administrator shall consider such record, report, or information or particular portion thereof confidential in accordance with the purposes of section 1905 of Title 18, except that such record, report, or information may be disclosed to other officers, employees, or authorized representatives of the United States concerned with carrying out this chapter or when relevant in any proceeding under this chapter.

(d) Notice of proposed entry, inspection, or monitoring

(1) In the case of any emission standard or limitation or other requirement which is adopted by a State, as part of an applicable implementation plan or as part of an order under section 7413(d) of this title, before carrying out an entry, inspection, or monitoring under paragraph (2) of subsection (a) of this section with respect to such standard, limitation, or other requirement, the Administrator (or his representatives) shall provide the State air pollution control agency with reasonable prior notice of such action, indicating the purpose of such action. No State agency which receives notice under this paragraph of an action proposed to be taken may use the information contained in the notice to inform the person whose property is proposed to be affected of the proposed action. If the Administrator has reasonable basis for believing that a State agency is so using or will so use such information, notice to the agency under this paragraph is not required until such time as the Administrator determines the agency will no longer so use information contained in a notice under this paragraph. Nothing in this section shall be construed to require notification to any State agency of any action taken by the Administrator with respect to any standard, limitation, or other requirement which is not part of an applicable implementation plan or which was promulgated by the Administrator under section 7410(c) of this title.

(2) Nothing in paragraph (1) shall be construed to provide that any failure of the Administrator to comply with the requirements of such paragraph shall be a defense in any enforcement action brought by the Administrator or shall make inadmissible as evidence in any such action any information or material obtained notwithstanding such failure to comply with such requirements.

(July 14, 1955, c. 360, Title I, § 114, as added by Pub. L. No. 91–604, § 4(a), 84 Stat. 1687 (Dec. 31, 1970); and amended by Pub. L. No. 93–319, § 6(a)(4), 88 Stat. 259 (June 22, 1974); Pub. L. No. 95–95, Title I, §§ 109(d)(3), 113, Title III, § 305(d), 91 Stat. 701, 709, 776 (Aug. 7, 1977); Pub. L. No. 95–190, § 14(a)(22), (23), 91 Stat. 1400 (Nov. 16, 1977); Pub. L. No. 101–549, Title III, § 302(c), Title VII, § 702(a), (b), 104 Stat. 2574, 2680, 2681 (Nov. 15, 1990).)

[1] So in original.

[2] The period probably should be "; and."

[3] So in original. Probably should not be capitalized.

HISTORICAL AND STATUTORY NOTES

References in Text

Section 7413(d) of this title, referred to in subsec. (d)(1), was amended generally by Pub. L. No. 101–549, Title VII, § 701, 104 Stat. 2672 (Nov. 15, 1990), and, as so amended, no longer relates to final compliance orders.

Codifications

This section was formerly codified as section 1857c–9 of this title.

Effective and Applicability Provisions

1990 Acts. Amendment by Pub. L. No. 101–549 effective Nov. 15, 1990, except as otherwise provided, see section 711(b) of Pub. L. No. 101–549, set out as a note under section 7401 of this title.

1977 Acts. Amendment by Pub. L. No. 95–95 effective Aug. 7, 1977, except as otherwise expressly provided, see section 406(d) of Pub. L. No. 95–95, set out as a note under section 7401 of this title.

Savings Provisions

Suits, actions or proceedings commenced under this chapter as in effect prior to Nov. 15, 1990, not to abate by reason of the taking effect of amendments by Pub. L. No. 101–549, except as otherwise provided for, see section 711(a) of Pub. L. No. 101–549, set out as a note under section 7401 of this title.

Modification or Rescission of Rules, Regulations, Orders, Determinations, Contracts, Certifications, Authorizations, Delegations, and Other Actions

All rules, regulations, orders, determinations, contracts, certifications, authorizations, delegations, or other actions duly issued, made, or taken by or pursuant to Act of July 14, 1955, the Clean Air Act, as in effect immediately prior to the date of enactment of Pub. L. No. 95–95 [Aug. 7, 1977] to continue in full force and effect until modified or rescinded in accordance with Act of July 14, 1955, as amended by Pub. L. No. 95–95 [this chapter], see section 406(b) of Pub. L. No. 95–95, set out as an Effective Date of 1977 Acts note under section 7401 of this title.

Pending Actions and Proceedings

Suits, actions, and other proceedings lawfully commenced by or against the Administrator or any other officer or employee of the United States in his official capacity or in relation to the discharge of his official duties under Act of July 14, 1955, the Clean Air Act, as in effect immediately prior to the enactment of Pub. L. No. 95–95 [Aug. 7, 1977], not to abate by reason of the taking effect of Pub. L. No. 95–95, see section 406(a) of Pub. L. No. 95–95, set out as an Effective and Applicability Provisions of 1977 Acts note under section 7401 of this title.

§ 7415. International air pollution

[CAA § 115]

(a) Endangerment of public health or welfare in foreign countries from pollution emitted in United States

Whenever the Administrator, upon receipt of reports, surveys or studies from any duly constituted international agency has reason to believe that any air pollutant or pollutants emitted in the United States cause or contribute to air pollution which may reasonably be anticipated to endanger public health or welfare in a foreign country or whenever the Secretary of State requests him to do so with respect to such pollution which the Secretary of State alleges is of such a nature, the Administrator shall give formal notification thereof to the Governor of the State in which such emissions originate.

(b) Prevention or elimination of endangerment

The notice of the Administrator shall be deemed to be a finding under section 7410(a)(2)(H)(ii) of this title which requires a plan revision with respect to so much of the applicable implementation plan as is inadequate to prevent or eliminate the endangerment referred to in subsection (a) of this section. Any foreign country so affected by such emission of pollutant or pollutants shall be invited to appear at any public hearing associated with any revision of the appropriate portion of the applicable implementation plan.

(c) Reciprocity

This section shall apply only to a foreign country which the Administrator determines has given the United States essentially the same rights with respect to the prevention or control of air pollution occurring in that country as is given that country by this section.

(d) Recommendations

Recommendations issued following any abatement conference conducted prior to August 7, 1977, shall remain in effect with respect to any pollutant for which no national ambient air quality standard has been established under section 7409 of this title unless the Administrator, after consultation with all agencies which were party to the conference, rescinds any such recommendation on grounds of obsolescence.

(July 14, 1955, c. 360, Title I, § 115, formerly § 5, as added by Pub. L. No. 88–206, § 1, 77 Stat. 396 (Dec. 17, 1963); and renumbered § 105 and amended by Pub. L. No. 89–272, Title I, §§ 101(2), (3), 102, 79 Stat. 992, 995 (Oct. 20, 1965); and renumbered § 108 and amended by Pub. L. No. 90–148, § 2, 81 Stat. 491 (Nov. 21, 1967); and renumbered § 115 and amended by Pub. L. No. 91–604, §§ 4(a), (b)(2) to (10), 15(c)(2), 84 Stat. 1678, 1688, 1689, 1713 (Dec. 31, 1970); and amended by Pub. L. No. 95–95, Title I, § 114, 91 Stat. 710 (Aug. 7, 1977).)

HISTORICAL AND STATUTORY NOTES

Codifications

This section was formerly codified as section 1857d of this title.

Effective and Applicability Provisions

1977 Acts. Amendment by Pub. L. No. 95–95 effective Aug. 7, 1977, except as otherwise expressly provided, see section 406(d) of Pub. L. No. 95–95, set out as a note under section 7401 of this title.

Prior Provisions

A prior section 5 of Act of July 14, 1955, c. 360, 69 Stat. 322, as amended by Pub. L. No. 86–365, § 1, 73 Stat. 646 (Sept. 22, 1959); Pub. L. No. 87–761, § 1, 76 Stat. 760 (Oct. 9, 1962), which was codified as a prior section 1857d of this title prior to the general amendment of this chapter by Pub. L. No. 88–206, related to appropriations, grants-in-aid, and contracts.

Modification or Rescission of Rules, Regulations, Orders, Determinations, Contracts, Certifications, Authorizations, Delegations, and Other Actions

All rules, regulations, orders, determinations, contracts, certifications, authorizations, delegations, or other actions duly issued, made, or taken by or pursuant to Act of July 14, 1955, the Clean Air Act, as in effect immediately prior to the date of enactment of Pub. L. No. 95–95 [Aug. 7, 1977] to continue in full force and effect until modified or rescinded in accordance with Act of July 14, 1955, as amended by Pub. L. No. 95–95 [this chapter], see section 406(b) of Pub. L. No. 95–95, set out as an Effective and Applicability Provisions of 1977 Acts note under section 7401 of this title.

United States—Canadian Negotiations on Air Quality

Pub. L. No. 95–426, Title VI, § 612, 92 Stat. 990 (Oct. 7, 1978), provided that:

"(a) The Congress finds that—

"(1) the United States and Canada share a common environment along a 5,500 mile border;

"(2) the United States and Canada are both becoming increasingly concerned about the effects of pollution, particularly that resulting from power generation facilities, since the facilities of each country affect the environment of the other;

"(3) the United States and Canada have subscribed to international conventions; have joined in the environmental work of the United Nations, the Organization for Economic Cooperation and Development, and other international environmental forums; and have entered into and implemented effectively the provisions of the historic Boundary Waters Treaty of 1909; and

"(4) the United States and Canada have a tradition of cooperative resolution of issues of mutual concern which is nowhere more evident than in the environmental area.

"(b) It is the sense of the Congress that the President should make every effort to negotiate a cooperative agreement with the Government of Canada aimed at preserving the mutual airshed of the United States and Canada so as to protect and enhance air resources and insure the attainment and maintenance of air quality protective of public health and welfare.

"(c) It is further the sense of the Congress that the President, through the Secretary of State working in concert with interested Federal agencies and the affected States, should take whatever diplomatic actions appear necessary to reduce or eliminate any undesirable impact upon the United States and Canada resulting from air pollution from any source."

§ 7416. Retention of State authority

[CAA § 116]

Except as otherwise provided in sections 1857c–10(c), (e), and (f) (as in effect before August 7, 1977), 7543, 7545(c)(4), and 7573 of this title (preempting certain State regulation of moving sources) nothing in this chapter shall preclude or deny the right of any State or political subdivision thereof to adopt or enforce (1) any standard or limitation respecting emissions of air pollutants or (2) any requirement respecting control or abatement of air pollution; except that if an emission standard or limitation is in effect under an applicable implementation plan or under section 7411 or section 7412 of this title, such State or political subdivision may not adopt or enforce any emission standard or limitation which is less stringent than the standard or limitation under such plan or section.

(July 14, 1955, c. 360, Title I, § 116, formerly § 109, as added by Pub. L. No. 90–148, § 2, 81 Stat. 497 (Nov. 21, 1967); and renumbered and amended by Pub. L. No. 91–604, § 4(a), (c), 84 Stat. 1678, 1689 (Dec. 31, 1970); and amended by Pub. L. No. 93–319, § 6(b), 88 Stat. 259 (June 22, 1974); Pub. L. No. 95–190, § 14(a)(24), 91 Stat. 1400 (Nov. 16, 1977).)

HISTORICAL AND STATUTORY NOTES

References in Text

"1857c–10(c), (e), and (f) (as in effect before August 7, 1977)", referred to in text, was in the original "119(c), (e), and (f) (as in effect before the date of the enactment of the Clean Air Act Amendments of 1977)" meaning section 119 of Act of July 14, 1955, c. 360, Title I, as added by Pub. L. No. 93–319, § 3, 88 Stat. 248 (June 22, 1974), (which was codified as section 1857c–10 of this title) as in effect prior to the enactment of Pub. L. No. 95–95, 91 Stat. 691 (Aug. 7, 1977), effective Aug. 7, 1977. Section 112(b)(1) of Pub. L. No. 95–95 repealed section 119 of Act of July 14, 1955, c. 360, Title I, as added by Pub. L. No. 93–319, and provided that all references to such section 119 in any subsequent enactment which supersedes Pub. L. No. 93–319 shall be construed to refer to section 113(d) of the Clean Air Act and to paragraph (5) thereof in particular which is codified as subsec. (d)(5) of section 7413 of this title. Section 7413 of this title was subsequently amended generally by Pub. L. No. 101–549, Title VII, § 701, Nov. 15, 1990, 104 Stat. 2672, and as so amended, no longer relates to final compliance orders. Section 117(b) of Pub. L. No. 95–95 added a new section 119 of Act of July 14, 1955, which is codified as section 7419 of this title.

Codifications

This section was formerly codified as section 1857d–1 of this title.

Modification or Rescission of Rules, Regulations, Orders, Determinations, Contracts, Certifications, Authorizations, Delegations, and Other Actions

All rules, regulations, orders, determinations, contracts, certifications, authorizations, delegations, or other actions duly issued, made, or taken by or pursuant to Act of July 14, 1955, the Clean Air Act, as in effect immediately prior to the date of enactment of Pub. L. No. 95–95 [Aug. 7, 1977] to continue in full force and effect until modified or rescinded in accordance with Act of July 14, 1955, as amended by Pub. L. No. 95–95 [this chapter], see section 406(b) of Pub. L. No. 95–95, set out as an Effective and Applicability Provisions of 1977 Acts note under section 7401 of this title.

§ 7417. Advisory committees

[CAA § 117]

(a) Establishment; membership

In order to obtain assistance in the development and implementation of the purposes of this chapter including air quality criteria, recommended control techniques, standards, research and development, and to encourage the continued efforts on the part of industry to improve air quality and to develop economically feasible methods for the control and abatement of air pollution, the Administrator shall from time to time establish advisory committees. Committee members shall include, but not be limited to, persons who are knowledgeable concerning air quality from the standpoint of health, welfare, economics or technology.

(b) Compensation

The members of any other advisory committees appointed pursuant to this chapter who are not officers or employees of the United States while attending conferences or meetings or while otherwise serving at the request of the Administrator, shall be entitled to receive compensation at a rate to be fixed by the Administrator, but not exceeding $100 per diem, including traveltime, and while away from their homes or regular places of business they may be allowed travel expenses, including per diem in lieu of subsistence, as authorized by section 5703 of Title 5 for persons in the Government service employed intermittently.

(c) Consultations by Administrator

Prior to—

(1) issuing criteria for an air pollutant under section 7408(a)(2) of this title,

(2) publishing any list under section 7411(b)(1)(A) or section 7412(b)(1)(A) of this title,

(3) publishing any standard under section 7411 or section 7412 of this title, or

(4) publishing any regulation under section 7521(a) of this title,

the Administrator shall, to the maximum extent practicable within the time provided, consult with appropriate advisory committees, independent experts, and Federal departments and agencies.

(July 14, 1955, c. 360, Title I, § 117, formerly § 6, as added by Pub. L. No. 88–206, § 1, 77 Stat. 399 (Dec. 17, 1963); and renumbered § 106 by Pub. L. No. 89–272, Title I, § 101(3), 79 Stat. 992 (Oct. 20, 1965); and renumbered § 110 and amended by Pub. L. No. 90–148, § 2, 81 Stat. 498 (Nov. 21, 1967); and renumbered § 117 and amended by Pub. L. No. 91–604, §§ 4(a), (d), 15(c)(2), 84 Stat. 1678, 1689, 1713 (Dec. 31, 1970); and amended by Pub. L. No. 95–95, Title I, § 115, 91 Stat. 711 (Aug. 7, 1977); Pub. L. No. 95–623, § 13(c), 92 Stat. 3458 (Nov. 9, 1978).)

HISTORICAL AND STATUTORY NOTES

References in Text

Section 7412(b)(1), referred to in subsec. (c)(2), was amended generally by Pub. L. No. 101–549, Title III, § 301, 104 Stat. 2531 (Nov. 15, 1990), and, as so amended, no longer contains a subpar. (A).

Codifications

Subsec. (c) was originally enacted as subsec. (f) but has been redesignated (c) for purposes of codification in view of the omission by Pub. L. No. 95–95 to redesignate subsec. (f) as (c) after repealing former subsecs. (a) and (b) and redesignating former subsecs. (d) and (e) as (a) and (b).

This section was formerly codified as section 1857e of this title.

Effective and Applicability Provisions

1977 Acts. Amendment by Pub. L. No. 95–95 effective Aug. 7, 1977, except as otherwise expressly provided, see section 406(d) of Pub. L. No. 95–95, set out as a note under section 7401 of this title.

Prior Provisions

A prior section 6 of Act of July 14, 1955, c. 360, 69 Stat. 323, which was codified as a prior section 1857e of this title, prior to the general amendment of this chapter by Pub. L. No. 88–206, defined "State air pollution control agency", "local government air pollution control agency" and "State". See section 7602 of this title.

Modification or Rescission of Rules, Regulations, Orders, Determinations, Contracts, Certifications, Authorizations, Delegations, and Other Actions

All rules, regulations, orders, determinations, contracts, certifications, authorizations, delegations, or other actions duly issued, made, or taken by or pursuant to Act of July 14, 1955, the Clean Air Act, as in effect immediately prior to the date of enactment of Pub. L. No. 95–95 [Aug. 7, 1977] to continue in full force and effect until modified or rescinded in accordance with Act of July 14, 1955, as amended by Pub. L. No. 95–95 [this chapter], see section 406(b) of Pub. L. No. 95–95, set out as an Effective and Applicability Provisions of 1977 Acts note under section 7401 of this title.

Termination of Advisory Committees

Advisory committees in existence on Jan. 5, 1973, to terminate not later than the expiration of the two-year period following Jan. 5, 1973, unless, in the case of a committee established by the President or an officer of the Federal Government, such committee is renewed by appropriate action prior to the expiration of such two-year period, or in the case of a committee established by the Congress, its duration is otherwise provided by law. Advisory committees established after Jan. 5, 1973, to terminate not later than the expiration of the two-year period beginning on the date of their establishment, unless, in the case of a committee established by the President or an officer of the Federal Government, such committee is renewed by appropriate action prior to the expiration of such two-year period, or in the case of a committee established by the Congress, its duration is otherwise provided by law. See section 14 of Pub. L. No. 92–463, 86 Stat. 776 (Oct. 6, 1972), set out in Appendix 2 to Title 5, Government Organization and Employees.

§ 7418. Control of pollution from Federal facilities

[CAA § 118]

(a) General compliance

Each department, agency, and instrumentality of the executive, legislative, and judicial branches of the Federal Government (1) having jurisdiction over any property or facility, or (2) engaged in any activity resulting, or which may result, in the discharge of air pollutants, and each officer, agent, or employee thereof, shall be subject to, and comply with, all Federal, State, interstate, and local requirements, administrative authority, and process and sanctions respecting the control and abatement of air pollution in the same manner, and to the same extent as any nongovernmental entity. The preceding sentence shall apply (A) to any requirement whether substantive or procedural (including any recordkeeping or reporting requirement, any requirement respecting permits and any other requirement whatsoever), (B) to any requirement to pay a fee or charge imposed by any State or local agency to defray the costs of its air pollution regulatory program, (C) to the exercise of any Federal, State, or local administrative authority, and (D) to any process and sanction, whether enforced in Federal, State, or local courts, or in any other manner. This subsection shall apply notwithstanding any immunity of such agencies, officers, agents, or employees under any law or rule of law. No officer, agent, or employee of the United States shall be personally liable for any civil penalty for which he is not otherwise liable.

(b) Exemption

The President may exempt any emission source of any department, agency, or instrumentality in the executive branch from compliance with such a requirement if he determines it to be in the paramount interest of the United States to do so, except that no exemption may be granted from section 7411 of this title, and an exemption from section 7412 of this title may be granted only in accordance with section 7412(i)(4) of this title. No such exemption shall be granted due to lack of appropriation unless the President shall have specifically requested such appropriation as a part of the budgetary process and the Congress shall have failed to make available such requested appropriation. Any exemption shall be for a period not in excess of one year, but additional exemptions may be granted for periods of not to exceed one year upon the President's making a new determination. In addition to any such exemption of a particular emission source, the President may, if he determines it to be in the paramount interest of the United States to do so, issue regulations exempting from compliance with the requirements of this section any weaponry, equipment, aircraft, vehicles, or other classes or categories of property which are owned or operated by the Armed Forces of the United States (including the Coast Guard) or by the National Guard of any State and which are uniquely military in nature. The President shall reconsider the need for such regulations at three-year intervals. The President shall report each January to the Congress all exemptions from the requirements of this section granted during the preceding calendar year, together with his reason for granting each such exemption.

(c) Government vehicles

Each department, agency, and instrumentality of executive, legislative, and judicial branches of the Federal Government shall comply with all applicable provisions of a valid inspection and maintenance program established under the provisions of subpart 2 of part D of this subchapter or subpart 3 of part D of this subchapter except for such vehicles that are considered military tactical vehicles.

(d) Vehicles operated on Federal installations

Each department, agency, and instrumentality of executive, legislative, and judicial branches of the Federal Government having jurisdiction over any property or facility shall require all employees which operate motor vehicles on the property or facility to furnish proof of compliance with the applicable requirements of any vehicle inspection and maintenance program established under the provisions of subpart 2 of part D of this subchapter or subpart 3 of part D of this subchapter for the State in which such property or facility is located (without regard to whether such vehicles are registered in the State). The installation shall use one of the following methods to establish proof of compliance—

(1) presentation by the vehicle owner of a valid certificate of compliance from the vehicle inspection and maintenance program;

(2) presentation by the vehicle owner of proof of vehicle registration within the geographic area covered by the vehicle inspection and maintenance program (except for any program whose enforcement mechanism is not through the denial of vehicle registration);

(3) another method approved by the vehicle inspection and maintenance program administrator.

(July 14, 1955, c. 360, Title I, § 118, formerly § 7, as added by Pub. L. No. 88–206, § 1, 77 Stat. 399 (Dec. 17, 1963); and renumbered § 107 by Pub. L. No. 89–272, Title I, § 101(3), 79 Stat. 992 (Oct. 20, 1965); and renumbered § 111 and amended by Pub. L. No. 90–148, § 2, 81 Stat. 499 (Nov. 21, 1967); and renumbered § 118 and amended by Pub. L. No. 91–604, §§ 4(a), 5, 84 Stat. 1678, 1689 (Dec. 31, 1970); and amended by Pub. L. No. 95–95, Title I, § 116, 91 Stat. 711 (Aug. 7, 1977); Pub. L. No. 101–549, Title I, § 101(e), Title II, § 235, Title III, § 302(d), 104 Stat. 2409, 2530, 2574 (Nov. 15, 1990).)

HISTORICAL AND STATUTORY NOTES

Codifications

This section was formerly codified as section 1857f of this title.

Effective and Applicability Provisions

1990 Acts. Amendment by Pub. L. No. 101–549 effective Nov. 15, 1990, except as otherwise provided, see section 711(b) of Pub. L. No. 101–549, set out as a note under section 7401 of this title.

1977 Acts. Amendment by Pub. L. No. 95–95 effective Aug. 7, 1977, except as otherwise expressly provided, see section 406(d) of Pub. L. No. 95–95, set out as a note under section 7401 of this title.

Transfer of Functions

For transfer of authorities, functions, personnel, and assets of the Coast Guard, including the authorities and functions of the Secretary of Transportation relating thereto, to the Department of Homeland Security, and for treatment of related references, see 6 U.S.C.A. §§ 468(b), 551(d), 552(d) and 557, and the Department of Homeland Security Reorganization Plan of November 25, 2002, as modified, set out as a note under 6 U.S.C.A. § 542.

Savings Provisions

Suits, actions or proceedings commenced under this chapter as in effect prior to Nov. 15, 1990, not to abate by reason of the taking effect of amendments by Pub. L. No. 101–549, except as otherwise provided for, see section 711(a) of Pub. L. No. 101–549, set out as a note under section 7401 of this title.

Prior Provisions

A prior section 7 of Act of July 14, 1955, c. 360, 69 Stat. 323, which was codified as a prior section 1857f of this title, related to research and experiments under other laws.

Termination of Reporting Requirements

For termination, effective May 15, 2000, of provisions in subsec. (b) of this section relating to annual reports to Congress, see Pub. L. No. 104–66, § 3003, as amended, set out as a note under 31 U.S.C.A. § 1113, and the 12th item on page 20 of House Document No. 103–7.

Exemption for Fort Allen in Puerto Rico

For provisions relating to the exemption for Fort Allen in Puerto Rico, in its use as temporary housing for Haitian refugees, from compliance with provisions of this chapter relating to emission sources located at Fort Allen, with exceptions, see sections 1–102 and 1–105 of Ex. Ord. No. 12327, 46 Fed. Reg. 48893 (Oct. 1, 1981), set out as a note under section 2601 of Title 22, Foreign Relations and Intercourse.

Modification or Rescission of Rules, Regulations, Orders, Determinations, Contracts, Certifications, Authorizations, Delegations, and Other Actions

All rules, regulations, orders, determinations, contracts, certifications, authorizations, delegations, or other actions duly issued, made, or taken by or pursuant to Act of July 14, 1955, the Clean Air Act, as in effect immediately prior to the date of enactment of Pub. L. No. 95–95 [Aug. 7, 1977] to continue in full force and effect until modified or rescinded in accordance with Act of July 14, 1955, as amended by Pub. L. No. 95–95 [this chapter], see section 406(b) of Pub. L. No. 95–95, set out as an Effective and Applicability Provisions of 1977 Acts note under section 7401 of this title.

Pending Actions and Proceedings

Suits, actions, and other proceedings lawfully commenced by or against the Administrator or any other officer or employee of the United States in his official capacity or in relation to the discharge of his official duties under Act of July 14, 1955, the Clean Air Act, as in effect immediately prior to the enactment of Pub. L. No. 95–95 [Aug. 7, 1977], not to abate by reason of the taking effect of Pub. L. No. 95–95, see section 406(a) of Pub. L. No. 95–95, set out as an Effective Date of 1977 Acts note under section 7401 of this title.

§ 7419. Primary nonferrous smelter orders

[CAA § 119]

(a) Issuance; hearing; enforcement orders; statement of grounds for application; findings

(1) Upon application by the owner or operator of a primary nonferrous smelter, a primary nonferrous smelter order under subsection (b) of this section may be issued—

(A) by the Administrator, after thirty days' notice to the State, or

(B) by the State in which such source is located, but no such order issued by the State shall take effect until the Administrator determines that such order has been issued in accordance with the requirements of this chapter.

Not later than ninety days after submission by the State to the Administrator of notice of the issuance of a primary nonferrous smelter order under this section, the Administrator shall determine whether or not such order has been issued by the State in accordance with the requirements of this chapter. If the Administrator determines that such order has not been issued in accordance with such requirements, he shall conduct a hearing respecting the reasonably available control technology for primary nonferrous smelters.

(2) **(A)** An order issued under this section to a primary nonferrous smelter shall be referred to as a "primary nonferrous smelter order". No primary nonferrous smelter may receive both an enforcement order under section 7413(d) of this title and a primary nonferrous smelter order under this section.

(B) Before any hearing conducted under this section, in the case of an application made by the owner or operator of a primary nonferrous smelter for a second order under this section, the applicant shall furnish the Administrator (or the State as the case may be) with a statement of the grounds on which such application is based (including all supporting documents and information). The statement of the grounds for the proposed order shall be provided by the Administrator or the State in any case in which such State or Administrator is acting on its own initiative. Such statement (including such documents and information) shall be made available to the public for a thirty-day period before such hearing and shall be considered as part of such hearing. No primary nonferrous smelter order may be granted unless the applicant establishes that he meets the conditions required for the issuance of such order (or the Administrator or State establishes the meeting of such conditions when acting on their own initiative).

(C) Any decision with respect to the issuance of a primary nonferrous smelter order shall be accompanied by a concise statement of the findings and of the basis of such findings.

(3) For the purposes of sections 7410, 7604, and 7607 of this title, any order issued by the State and in effect pursuant to this subsection shall become part of the applicable implementation plan.

(b) Prerequisites to issuance of orders

A primary nonferrous smelter order under this section may be issued to a primary nonferrous smelter if—

(1) such smelter is in existence on August 7, 1977;

(2) the requirement of the applicable implementation plan with respect to which the order is issued is an emission limitation or standard for sulfur oxides which is necessary and intended to be itself sufficient to enable attainment and maintenance of national primary and secondary ambient air quality standards for sulfur oxides; and

(3) such smelter is unable to comply with such requirement by the applicable date for compliance because no means of emission limitation applicable to such smelter which will enable it to achieve compliance with such requirement has been adequately demonstrated to be reasonably available (as determined by the Administrator, taking into account the cost of compliance, non-air quality health and environmental impact, and energy consideration).

(c) Second orders

(1) A second order issued to a smelter under this section shall set forth compliance schedules containing increments of progress which require compliance with the requirement postponed as expeditiously as practicable. The increments of progress shall be limited to requiring compliance with subsection (d) of this section and, in the case of a second order, to procuring, installing, and operating the necessary means of emission limitation as expeditiously as practicable after the Administrator determines such means have been adequately demonstrated to be reasonably available within the meaning of subsection (b)(3) of this section.

(2) Not in excess of two primary nonferrous smelter orders may be issued under this section to any primary nonferrous smelter. The first such order issued to a smelter shall not result in the postponement of the requirement with respect to which such order is issued beyond January 1, 1983. The second such order shall not result in the postponement of such requirement beyond January 1, 1988.

(d) Interim measures; continuous emission reduction technology

(1) (A) Each primary nonferrous smelter to which an order is issued under this section shall be required to use such interim measures for the period during which such order is in effect as may be necessary in the judgment of the Administrator to assure attainment and maintenance of the national primary and secondary ambient air quality standards during such period, taking into account the aggregate effect on air quality of such order together with all variances, extensions, waivers, enforcement orders, delayed compliance orders and primary nonferrous smelter orders previously issued under this chapter.

(B) Such interim requirements shall include—

(i) a requirement that the source to which the order applies comply with such reporting requirements and conduct such monitoring as the Administrator determines may be necessary, and

(ii) such measures as the Administrator determines are necessary to avoid an imminent and substantial endangerment to health of persons.

(C) Such interim measures shall also, except as provided in paragraph (2), include continuous emission reduction technology. The Administrator shall condition the use of any such interim measures upon the agreement of the owner or operator of the smelter—

(i) to comply with such conditions as the Administrator determines are necessary to maximize the reliability and enforceability of such interim measures, as applied to the smelter, in attaining and maintaining the national ambient air quality standards to which the order relates, and

(ii) to commit reasonable resources to research and development of appropriate emission control technology.

(2) The requirement of paragraph (1) for the use of continuous emission reduction technology may be waived with respect to a particular smelter by the State or the Administrator, after notice and a hearing on the record, and upon a showing by the owner or operator of the smelter that such requirement would be so costly as to necessitate permanent or prolonged temporary cessation of operations of the smelter. Upon application for such waiver, the Administrator shall be notified and shall, within ninety days, hold a hearing on the record in accordance with section 554 of Title 5. At such hearing the Administrator shall require the smelter involved to present information relating to any alleged cessation of operations and the detailed reasons or justifications therefor. On the basis of such hearing the Administrator shall make findings of fact as to the effect of such requirement and on the alleged cessation of operations and shall make such recommendations as he deems appropriate. Such report, findings, and recommendations shall be available to the public, and shall be taken into account by the State or the Administrator in making the decision whether or not to grant such waiver.

(3) In order to obtain information for purposes of a waiver under paragraph (2), the Administrator may, on his own motion, conduct an investigation and use the authority of section 7621 of this title.

(4) In the case of any smelter which on August 7, 1977, uses continuous emission reduction technology and supplemental controls and which receives an initial primary nonferrous smelter order under this section, no additional continuous emission reduction technology shall be required as a condition of such order unless the Administrator determines, at any time, after notice and public hearing, that such additional continuous emission reduction technology is adequately demonstrated to be reasonably available for the primary nonferrous smelter industry.

(e) Termination of orders

At any time during which an order under this section applies, the Administrator may enter upon a public hearing respecting the availability of technology. Any order under this section shall be terminated if the Administrator determines on the record, after notice and public hearing, that the conditions upon which the order was based no longer exist. If the owner or operator of the smelter to which the order is issued demonstrates that prompt termination of such order would result in undue hardship, the termination shall become effective at the earliest practicable date on which such undue hardship would not result, but in no event later than the date required under subsection (c) of this section.

(f) Violation of requirements

If the Administrator determines that a smelter to which an order is issued under this section is in violation of any requirement of subsection (c) or (d) of this section, he shall—

(1) enforce such requirement under section 7413 of this title,

(2) (after notice and opportunity for public hearing) revoke such order and enforce compliance with the requirement with respect to which such order was granted,

(3) give notice of noncompliance and commence action under section 7420 of this title, or

(4) take any appropriate combination of such actions.

(July 14, 1955, c. 360, Title I, § 119, as added by Pub. L. No. 95–95, Title I, § 117(b), 91 Stat. 712 (Aug. 7, 1977); and amended by Pub. L. No. 95–190, § 14(a)(25) to (27), 91 Stat. 1401 (Nov. 16, 1977).)

HISTORICAL AND STATUTORY NOTES

References in Text

Section 7413(d) of this title, referred to in subsec. (a)(2)(A), was amended generally by Pub. L. No. 101–549, Title VII, § 701, 104 Stat. 2672 (Nov. 15, 1990), and, as so amended, no longer relates to final compliance orders.

Effective and Applicability Provisions

1977 Acts. Section effective Aug. 7, 1977, except as otherwise expressly provided, see section 406(d) of Pub. L. No. 95–95, set out as a note under section 7401 of this title.

Prior Provisions

A prior section 119 of Act of July 14, 1955, c. 360, Title I, as added by Pub. L. No. 93–319, § 3, 88 Stat. 248 (June 22, 1974), which was codified as section 1857c–10 of this title, provided for the authority to deal with energy shortages. Such section 119 was repealed by Pub. L. No. 95–95, Title I, § 112(b)(1), 91 Stat. 709 (Aug. 7, 1977), which provided that all references to such section 119 in any subsequent enactment which supersedes Pub. L. No. 93–319 shall be construed to refer to section 113(d) of the Clean Air Act and to paragraph (5) thereof in particular which is codified as section 7413(d)(5) of this title.

Modification or Rescission of Rules, Regulations, Orders, Determinations, Contracts, Certifications, Authorizations, Delegations, and Other Actions

All rules, regulations, orders, determinations, contracts, certifications, authorizations, delegations, or other actions duly issued, made, or taken by or pursuant to Act of July 14, 1955, the Clean Air Act, as in effect immediately prior to the date of enactment of Pub. L. No. 95–95 [Aug. 7, 1977] to continue in full force and effect until modified or rescinded in accordance with Act of July 14, 1955, as amended by Pub. L. No. 95–95 [this chapter], see section 406(b) of Pub. L. No. 95–95, set out as an Effective and Applicability Provisions of 1977 Acts note under section 7401 of this title.

§ 7420. Noncompliance penalty

[CAA § 120]

(a) Assessment and collection

(1) (A) Not later than 6 months after August 7, 1977, and after notice and opportunity for a public hearing, the Administrator shall promulgate regulations requiring the assessment and collection of a noncompliance penalty against persons referred to in paragraph (2)(A).

(B) (i) Each State may develop and submit to the Administrator a plan for carrying out this section in such State. If the Administrator finds that the State plan meets the requirements of this section, he may delegate to such State any authority he has to carry out this section.

(ii) Notwithstanding a delegation to a State under clause (i), the Administrator may carry out this section in such State under the circumstances described in subsection (b)(2)(B) of this section.

(2) (A) Except as provided in subparagraph (B) or (C) of this paragraph, the State or the Administrator shall assess and collect a noncompliance penalty against every person who owns or operates—

(i) a major stationary source (other than a primary nonferrous smelter which has received a primary nonferrous smelter order under section 7419 of this title), which is not in compliance with any emission limitation, emission standard or compliance schedule under any applicable implementation plan (whether or not such source is subject to a Federal or State consent decree), or

(ii) a stationary source which is not in compliance with an emission limitation, emission standard, standard of performance, or other requirement established under section 7411, 7477, 7603, or 7412 of this title, or

(iii) a stationary source which is not in compliance with any requirement of subchapter IV-A, V, or VI of this chapter, or

(iv) any source referred to in clause (i), (ii), or (iii) (for which an extension, order, or suspension referred to in subparagraph (B), or Federal or State consent decree is in effect), or a primary nonferrous smelter which has received a primary nonferrous smelter order under section 7419 of this title which is not in compliance with any interim emission control requirement or schedule of compliance under such extension, order, suspension, or consent decree.

For purposes of subsection (d)(2) of this section, in the case of a penalty assessed with respect to a source referred to in clause (iii) of this subparagraph, the costs referred to in such subsection (d)(2) shall be the economic value of noncompliance with the interim emission control requirement or the remaining steps in the schedule of compliance referred to in such clause.

(B) Notwithstanding the requirements of subparagraph (A)(i) and (ii), the owner or operator of any source shall be exempted from the duty to pay a noncompliance penalty under such requirements with respect to that source if, in accordance with the procedures in subsection (b)(5) of this section, the owner or operator demonstrates that the failure of such source to comply with any such requirement is due solely to—

(i) a conversion by such source from the burning of petroleum products or natural gas, or both, as the permanent primary energy source to the burning of coal pursuant to an order under section 7413(d)(5) of this title or section 1857c–10 of this title (as in effect before August 7, 1977);

(ii) in the case of a coal-burning source granted an extension under the second sentence of section 1857c–10(c)(1) of this title (as in effect before August 7, 1977), a prohibition from using petroleum products or natural gas or both, by reason of an order under the provisions of section 792(a) and (b) of Title 15 or under any legislation which amends or supersedes such provisions;

(iii) the use of innovative technology sanctioned by an enforcement order under section 7413(d)(4) of this title;

(iv) an inability to comply with any such requirement, for which inability the source has received an order under section 7413(d) of this title (or an order under section 7413 of this title issued before August 7, 1977) which has the effect of permitting a delay or violation of any requirement of this chapter (including a requirement of an applicable implementation plan) which inability results from reasons entirely beyond the control of the owner or operator of such source or of any entity controlling, controlled by, or under common control with the owner or operator of such source; or

(v) the conditions by reason of which a temporary emergency suspension is authorized under section 7410(f) or (g) of this title.

An exemption under this subparagraph shall cease to be effective if the source fails to comply with the interim emission control requirements or schedules of compliance (including increments of progress) under any such extension, order, or suspension.

(C) The Administrator may, after notice and opportunity for public hearing, exempt any source from the requirements of this section with respect to a particular instance of noncompliance if he finds that such instance of noncompliance is de minimis in nature and in duration.

(b) Regulations

Regulations under subsection (a) of this section shall—

(1) permit the assessment and collection of such penalty by the State if the State has a delegation of authority in effect under subsection (a)(1)(B)(i) of this section;

(2) provide for the assessment and collection of such penalty by the Administrator, if—

(A) the State does not have a delegation of authority in effect under subsection (a)(1)(B)(i) of this section, or

(B) the State has such a delegation in effect but fails with respect to any particular person or source to assess or collect the penalty in accordance with the requirements of this section;

(3) require the States, or in the event the States fail to do so, the Administrator, to give a brief but reasonably specific notice of noncompliance under this section to each person referred to in subsection (a)(2)(A) of this section with respect to each source owned or operated by such person which is not in compliance as provided in such subsection, not later than July 1, 1979, or thirty days after the discovery of such noncompliance, whichever is later;

(4) require each person to whom notice is given under paragraph (3) to—

(A) calculate the amount of the penalty owed (determined in accordance with subsection (d)(2) of this section) and the schedule of payments (determined in accordance with subsection (d)(3) of this section) for each such source and, within forty-five days after the issuance of such notice or after the denial of a petition under subparagraph (B), to submit that calculation and proposed schedule, together with the information necessary for an independent verification thereof, to the State and to the Administrator, or

(B) submit a petition, within forty-five days after the issuance of such notice, challenging such notice of noncompliance or alleging entitlement to an exemption under subsection (a)(2)(B) of this section with respect to a particular source;

(5) require the Administrator to provide a hearing on the record (within the meaning of subchapter II of chapter 5 of Title 5) and to make a decision on such petition (including findings of fact and conclusions of law) not later than ninety days after the receipt of any petition under paragraph (4)(B), unless the State agrees to provide a hearing which is substantially similar to such a hearing on the record and to make a decision on such petition (including such findings and conclusions) within such ninety-day period;

(6) **(A)** authorize the Administrator on his own initiative to review the decision of the State under paragraph (5) and disapprove it if it is not in accordance with the requirements of this section, and

(B) require the Administrator to do so not later than sixty days after receipt of a petition under this subparagraph, notice, and public hearing and a showing by such petitioner that the State decision under paragraph (5) is not in accordance with the requirements of this section;

(7) require payment, in accordance with subsection (d) of this section, of the penalty by each person to whom notice of noncompliance is given under paragraph (3) with respect to each noncomplying source for which such notice is given unless there has been a final determination granting a petition under paragraph (4)(B) with respect to such source;

(8) authorize the State or the Administrator to adjust (and from time to time to readjust) the amount of the penalty assessment calculated or the payment schedule proposed by such owner or operator under paragraph (4), if the Administrator finds after notice and opportunity for a hearing on the record that the penalty or schedule does not meet the requirements of this section; and

(9) require a final adjustment of the penalty within 180 days after such source comes into compliance in accordance with subsection (d)(4) of this section.

In any case in which the State establishes a noncompliance penalty under this section, the State shall provide notice thereof to the Administrator. A noncompliance penalty established by a State under this section shall apply unless the Administrator, within ninety days after the date of receipt of notice of the State penalty assessment under this section, objects in writing to the amount of the penalty as less than would be required to comply with guidelines established by the Administrator. If the Administrator objects, he shall immediately establish a substitute noncompliance penalty applicable to such source.

(c) Contract to assist in determining amount of penalty assessment or payment schedule

If the owner or operator of any stationary source to whom a notice is issued under subsection (b)(3) of this section—

(1) does not submit a timely petition under subsection (b)(4)(B) of this section, or

(2) submits a petition under subsection (b)(4)(B) of this section which is denied, and

fails to submit a calculation of the penalty assessment, a schedule for payment, and the information necessary for independent verification thereof, the State (or the Administrator, as the case may be) may enter into a contract with any person who has no financial interest in the owner or operator of the source (or in any person controlling, controlled by or under common control with such source) to assist in determining the amount of the penalty assessment or payment schedule with respect to such source. The cost of carrying out such contract may be added to the penalty to be assessed against the owner or operator of such source.

(d) Payment

(1) All penalties assessed by the Administrator under this section shall be paid to the United States Treasury. All penalties assessed by the State under this section shall be paid to such State.

(2) The amount of the penalty which shall be assessed and collected with respect to any source under this section shall be equal to—

(A) the amount determined in accordance with regulations promulgated by the Administrator under subsection (a) of this section, which is no less than the economic value which a delay in compliance beyond July 1, 1979, may have for the owner of such source, including the quarterly equivalent of the capital costs of compliance and debt service over a normal amortization period, not to exceed ten years, operation and maintenance costs foregone as a result of noncompliance, and any additional economic value which such a delay may have for the owner or operator of such source, minus

(B) the amount of any expenditure made by the owner or operator of that source during any such quarter for the purpose of bringing that source into, and maintaining compliance with, such requirement, to the extent that such expenditures have not been taken into account in the calculation of the penalty under subparagraph (A).

To the extent that any expenditure under subparagraph (B) made during any quarter is not subtracted for such quarter from the costs under subparagraph (A), such expenditure may be subtracted for any subsequent quarter from such costs. In no event shall the amount paid be less than the quarterly payment minus the amount attributed to actual cost of construction.

(3) **(A)** The assessed penalty required under this section shall be paid in quarterly installments for the period of covered noncompliance. All quarterly payments (determined without regard to any adjustment or any subtraction under paragraph (2)(B)) after the first payment shall be equal.

(B) The first payment shall be due on the date six months after the date of issuance of the notice of noncompliance under subsection (b)(3) of this section with respect to any source or on January 1, 1980, whichever is later. Such first payment shall be in the amount of the quarterly installment for the upcoming quarter, plus the amount owed for any preceding period within the period of covered noncompliance for such source.

(C) For the purpose of this section, the term "period of covered noncompliance" means the period which begins—

(i) two years after August 7, 1977, in the case of a source for which notice of noncompliance under subsection (b)(3) of this section is issued on or before the date two years after August 7, 1977, or

(ii) on the date of issuance of the notice of noncompliance under subsection (b)(3) of this section, in the case of a source for which such notice is issued after July 1, 1979,

and ending on the date on which such source comes into (or for the purpose of establishing the schedule of payments, is estimated to come into) compliance with such requirement.

(4) Upon making a determination that a source with respect to which a penalty has been paid under this section is in compliance and is maintaining compliance with the applicable requirement, the State (or the Administrator as the case may be) shall review the actual expenditures made by the owner or operator of such source for the purpose of attaining and maintaining compliance, and shall within 180 days after such source comes into compliance—

(A) provide reimbursement with interest (to be paid by the State or Secretary of the Treasury, as the case may be) at appropriate prevailing rates (as determined by the Secretary of the Treasury) for any overpayment by such person, or

(B) assess and collect an additional payment with interest at appropriate prevailing rates (as determined by the Secretary of the Treasury) for any underpayment by such person.

(5) Any person who fails to pay the amount of any penalty with respect to any source under this section on a timely basis shall be required to pay in addition a quarterly nonpayment penalty for each quarter during which such failure to pay persists. Such nonpayment penalty shall be in an amount equal to 20 percent of the aggregate amount of such person's penalties and nonpayment penalties with respect to such source which are unpaid as of the beginning of such quarter.

(e) Judicial review

Any action pursuant to this section, including any objection of the Administrator under the last sentence of subsection (b) of this section, shall be considered a final action for purposes of judicial review of any penalty under section 7607 of this title.

(f) Other orders, payments, sanctions, or requirements

Any orders, payments, sanctions, or other requirements under this section shall be in addition to any other permits, orders, payments, sanctions, or other requirements established under this chapter, and shall in no way affect any civil or criminal enforcement proceedings brought under any provision of this chapter or State or local law.

(g) More stringent emission limitations or other requirements

In the case of any emission limitation or other requirement approved or promulgated by the Administrator under this chapter after August 7, 1977, which is more stringent than the emission limitation or requirement for the source in effect prior to such approval or promulgation, if any, or where there was no emission limitation or requirement approved or promulgated before August 7, 1977, the date for imposition of the non-compliance penalty under this section, shall be either July 1, 1979, or the date on which the source is required to be in full compliance with such emission limitation or requirement, whichever is later, but in no event later than three years after the approval or promulgation of such emission limitation or requirement.

(July 14, 1955, c. 360, Title I, § 120, as added by Pub. L. No. 95–95, Title I, § 118, 91 Stat. 714 (Aug. 7, 1977); and amended by Pub. L. No. 95–190, § 14(a)(28) to (38), 91 Stat. 1401 (Nov. 16, 1977); Pub. L. No. 101–549, Title VII, § 710(a), 104 Stat. 2684 (Nov. 15, 1990).)

HISTORICAL AND STATUTORY NOTES

References in Text

Section 7413(d) of this title, referred to in subsec. (a)(2)(B), was amended generally by Pub. L. No. 101–549, Title VII, § 701, 104 Stat. 2672 (Nov. 15, 1990), and, as so amended, no longer relates to final compliance orders.

Section 1857c–10 of this title (as in effect before August 7, 1977), referred to in subsec. (a)(2)(B)(i), was in the original "section 119 (as in effect before the date of the enactment of the Clean Air Act Amendments of 1977)", meaning section 119 of Act of July 14, 1955, c. 360, Title I, as added by Pub. L. No. 93–319, § 3, 88 Stat. 248 (June 22, 1974), (which was codified as section 1857c–10 of this title) as in effect prior to the enactment of Pub. L. No. 95–95, 91 Stat. 691 (Aug. 7, 1977), effective Aug. 7, 1977. Section 112(b)(1) of Pub. L. No. 95–95 repealed section 119 of Act of July 14, 1955, c. 360, Title I, as added by Pub. L. No. 93–319, and provided that all references to such section 119 in any subsequent enactment which supersedes Pub. L. No. 93–319 shall be construed to refer to section 113(d) of the Clean Air Act and to paragraph (5) thereof in particular which is codified as subsec. (d)(5) of section 7413 of this title. Section 7413(d) of this title was subsequently amended generally by Pub. L. No. 101–549, Title VII, § 701, 104 Stat. 2672 (Nov. 15, 1990), and, as so amended, no longer relates to final compliance orders. Section 117(b) of Pub. L. No. 95–95 added a new section 119 of Act of July 14, 1955, which is codified as section 7419 of this title.

Section 1857c–10(c)(1) of this title (as in effect before August 7, 1977), referred to in subsec. (a)(2)(B)(ii), was in the original "section 119(c)(1) (as in effect before the date of the enactment of the Clean Air Act Amendments of 1977)."

Effective and Applicability Provisions

1990 Acts. Amendment by Pub. L. No. 101–549 effective Nov. 15, 1990, except as otherwise provided, see section 711(b) of Pub. L. No. 101–549, set out as a note under section 7401 of this title.

1977 Acts. Section effective Aug. 7, 1977, except as otherwise expressly provided, see section 406(d) of Pub. L. No. 95–95, set out as a note under section 7401 of this title.

Savings Provisions

Suits, actions or proceedings commenced under this chapter as in effect prior to Nov. 15, 1990, not to abate by reason of the taking effect of amendments by Pub. L. No. 101–549, except as otherwise provided for, see section 711(a) of Pub. L. No. 101–549, set out as a note under section 7401 of this title.

§ 7421. Consultation

[CAA § 121]

In carrying out the requirements of this chapter requiring applicable implementation plans to contain—

(1) any transportation controls, air quality maintenance plan requirements or preconstruction review of direct sources of air pollution, or

(2) any measure referred to—

(A) in part D of this subchapter (pertaining to nonattainment requirements), or

(B) in part C of this subchapter (pertaining to prevention of significant deterioration),

and in carrying out the requirements of section 7413(d) of this title (relating to certain enforcement orders), the State shall provide a satisfactory process of consultation with general purpose local governments, designated organizations of elected officials of local governments and any Federal land manager having authority over Federal land to which the State plan applies, effective with respect to any such requirement which is adopted more than one year after August 7, 1977, as part of such plan. Such process shall be in accordance with regulations promulgated by the Administrator to assure adequate consultation. The Administrator shall update as necessary the original regulations required and promulgated under this section (as in effect immediately before November 15, 1990) to ensure adequate consultation. Only a general purpose unit of local government, regional agency, or council of governments adversely affected by action of the Administrator approving any portion of a plan referred to in this subsection[1] may petition for judicial review of such action on the basis of a violation of the requirements of this section.

(July 14, 1955, c. 360, Title I, § 121, as added by Pub. L. No. 95–95, Title I, § 119, 91 Stat. 719 (Aug. 7, 1977); and amended by Pub. L. No. 101–549, Title I, § 108(h), 104 Stat. 2467 (Nov. 15, 1990).)

[1] So in original. Probably should be "section".

HISTORICAL AND STATUTORY NOTES

References in Text

Section 7413(d) of this title, referred to in text, was amended generally by Pub. L. No. 101–549, Title VII, § 701, Nov. 15, 1990, 104 Stat. 2672, and, as so amended, no longer relates to final compliance orders.

Effective and Applicability Provisions

1990 Acts. Amendment by Pub. L. No. 101–549 effective Nov. 15, 1990, except as otherwise provided, see section 711(b) of Pub. L. No. 101–549, set out as a note under section 7401 of this title.

1977 Acts. Section effective Aug. 7, 1977, except as otherwise expressly provided, see section 406(d) of Pub. L. No. 95–95, set out as a note under section 7401 of this title.

Savings Provisions

Suits, actions or proceedings commenced under this chapter as in effect prior to Nov. 15, 1990, not to abate by reason of the taking effect of amendments by Pub. L. No. 101–549, except as otherwise provided for, see section 711(a) of Pub. L. No. 101–549, set out as a note under section 7401 of this title.

§ 7422. Listing of certain unregulated pollutants

[CAA § 122]

(a) Radioactive pollutants, cadmium, arsenic, and polycyclic organic matter

Not later than one year after August 7, 1977 (two years for radioactive pollutants) and after notice and opportunity for public hearing, the Administrator shall review all available relevant information and determine whether or not emissions of radioactive pollutants (including source material, special nuclear material, and byproduct material), cadmium, arsenic and polycyclic organic matter into the ambient air will cause, or contribute to, air pollution which may reasonably be anticipated to endanger public health. If the Administrator makes an affirmative determination with respect to any such substance, he shall simultaneously with such determination include such substance in the list published under section 7408(a)(1) or 7412(b)(1)(A) of this title (in the case of a substance which, in the judgment of the Administrator, causes, or contributes to, air pollution which may reasonably be anticipated to result in an increase in mortality or an increase in serious irreversible, or incapacitating reversible, illness), or shall include each category of stationary sources emitting such substance in significant amounts in the list published under section 7411(b)(1)(A) of this title, or take any combination of such actions.

(b) Revision authority

Nothing in subsection (a) of this section shall be construed to affect the authority of the Administrator to revise any list referred to in subsection (a) of this section with respect to any substance (whether or not enumerated in subsection (a) of this section).

(c) Consultation with Nuclear Regulatory Commission; interagency agreement; notice and hearing

(1) Before listing any source material, special nuclear, or byproduct material (or component or derivative thereof) as provided in subsection (a) of this section, the Administrator shall consult with the Nuclear Regulatory Commission.

(2) Not later than six months after listing any such material (or component or derivative thereof) the Administrator and the Nuclear Regulatory Commission shall enter into an interagency agreement with respect to those sources or facilities which are under the jurisdiction of the Commission. This agreement shall, to the maximum extent practicable consistent with this chapter, minimize duplication of effort and conserve administrative resources in the establishment, implementation, and enforcement of emission limitations, standards of performance, and other requirements and authorities (substantive and procedural) under this chapter respecting the emission of such material (or component or derivative thereof) from such sources or facilities.

(3) In case of any standard or emission limitation promulgated by the Administrator, under this chapter or by any State (or the Administrator) under any applicable implementation plan under this chapter, if the Nuclear Regulatory Commission determines, after notice and opportunity for public hearing that the application of such standard or limitation to a source or facility within the jurisdiction of the Commission would endanger public health or safety, such standard or limitation shall not apply to such facilities or sources unless the President determines otherwise within ninety days from the date of such finding.

(July 14, 1955, c. 360, Title I, § 122, as added by Pub. L. No. 95–95, Title I, § 120(a), 91 Stat. 720 (Aug. 7, 1977).)

HISTORICAL AND STATUTORY NOTES

References in Text

Section 7412(b)(1), referred to in subsec. (a), was amended generally by Pub. L. No. 101–549, Title III, § 301, 104 Stat. 2531 (Nov. 15, 1990), and, as so amended, no longer contains a subpar. (A).

Effective and Applicability Provisions

1977 Acts. Section effective Aug. 7, 1977, except as otherwise expressly provided, see section 406(d) of Pub. L. No. 95–95, set out as a note under section 7401 of this title.

Transfer of Functions

For transfer of certain functions from the Nuclear Regulatory Commission to the Chairman thereof, see Reorg. Plan No. 1 of 1980, 45 Fed. Reg. 40561, 94 Stat. 3585, set out as a note under section 5841 of this title.

Study by Administrator of Environmental Protection Agency

Section 120(b) of Pub. L. No. 95–95 provided that: "The Administrator of the Environmental Protection Agency shall conduct a study, in conjunction with other appropriate agencies, concerning the effect on the public health and welfare of sulfates, radioactive pollutants, cadmium, arsenic, and polycyclic organic matter which are present or may reasonably be anticipated to occur in the ambient air. Such study shall include a thorough investigation of how sulfates are formed and how to protect public health and welfare from the injurious effects, if any, of sulfates, cadmium, arsenic, and polycyclic organic matter."

§ 7423. Stack heights

[CAA § 123]

(a) Heights in excess of good engineering practice; other dispersion techniques

The degree of emission limitation required for control of any air pollutant under an applicable implementation plan under this subchapter shall not be affected in any manner by—

(1) so much of the stack height of any source as exceeds good engineering practice (as determined under regulations promulgated by the Administrator), or

(2) any other dispersion technique.

The preceding sentence shall not apply with respect to stack heights in existence before December 31, 1970, or dispersion techniques implemented before such date. In establishing an emission limitation for coal-fired steam electric generating units which are subject to the provisions of section 7418 of this title and which commenced operation before July 1, 1957, the effect of the entire stack height of stacks for which a construction contract was awarded before February 8, 1974, may be taken into account.

(b) Dispersion technique

For the purpose of this section, the term "dispersion technique" includes any intermittent or supplemental control of air pollutants varying with atmospheric conditions.

(c) Regulations; good engineering practice

Not later than six months after August 7, 1977, the Administrator, shall after notice and opportunity for public hearing, promulgate regulations to carry out this section. For purposes of this section, good engineering practice means, with respect to stack heights, the height necessary to insure that emissions from the stack do not result in excessive concentrations of any air pollutant in the immediate vicinity of the source as a result of atmospheric downwash, eddies and wakes which may be created by the source itself, nearby structures or nearby terrain obstacles (as determined by the Administrator). For purposes of this section such height shall not exceed two and a half times the height of such source unless the owner or operator of the source demonstrates, after notice and opportunity for public hearing, to the satisfaction of the Administrator, that a greater height is necessary as provided under the preceding sentence. In no event may the Administrator prohibit any increase in any stack height or restrict in any manner the stack height of any source.

(July 14, 1955, c. 360, Title I, § 123, as added by Pub. L. No. 95–95, Title I, § 121, 91 Stat. 721 (Aug. 7, 1977).)

HISTORICAL AND STATUTORY NOTES

Effective and Applicability Provisions

1977 Acts. Section effective Aug. 7, 1977, except as otherwise expressly provided, see section 406(d) of Pub. L. No. 95–95, set out as a note under section 7401 of this title.

§ 7424. Assurance of adequacy of State plans

[CAA § 124]

(a) State review of implementation plans which relate to major fuel burning sources

As expeditiously as practicable but not later than one year after August 7, 1977, each State shall review the provisions of its implementation plan which relate to major fuel burning sources and shall determine—

(1) the extent to which compliance with requirements of such plan is dependent upon the use by major fuel burning stationary sources of petroleum products or natural gas,

(2) the extent to which such plan may reasonably be anticipated to be inadequate to meet the requirements of this chapter in such State on a reliable and long-term basis by reason of its dependence upon the use of such fuels, and

(3) the extent to which compliance with the requirements of such plan is dependent upon use of coal or coal derivatives which is not locally or regionally available.

Each State shall submit the results of its review and its determination under this paragraph to the Administrator promptly upon completion thereof.

(b) Plan revision

(1) Not later than eighteen months after August 7, 1977, the Administrator shall review the submissions of the States under subsection (a) of this section and shall require each State to revise its plan if, in the judgment of the Administrator, such plan revision is necessary to assure that such plan will be adequate to assure compliance with the requirements of this chapter in such State on a reliable and long-term basis, taking into account the actual or potential prohibitions on use of petroleum products or natural gas, or both, under any other authority of law.

(2) Before requiring a plan revision under this subsection, with respect to any State the Administrator shall take into account the report of the review conducted by such State under paragraph (1) and shall consult with the Governor of the State respecting such required revision.

(July 14, 1955, c. 360, Title I, § 124, as added by Pub. L. No. 95–95, Title I, § 122, 91 Stat. 722 (Aug. 7, 1977).)

HISTORICAL AND STATUTORY NOTES

Effective and Applicability Provisions

1977 Acts. Section effective Aug. 7, 1977, except as otherwise expressly provided, see section 406(d) of Pub. L. No. 95–95, set out as a note under section 7401 of this title.

§ 7425. Measures to prevent economic disruption or unemployment

[CAA § 125]

(a) Determination that action is necessary

After notice and opportunity for a public hearing—

(1) the Governor of any State in which a major fuel burning stationary source referred to in this subsection (or class or category thereof) is located,

(2) the Administrator, or

(3) the President (or his designee),

may determine that action under subsection (b) of this section is necessary to prevent or minimize significant local or regional economic disruption or unemployment which would otherwise result from use by such source (or class or category) of—

(A) coal or coal derivatives other than locally or regionally available coal,

(B) petroleum products,

(C) natural gas, or

(D) any combination of fuels referred to in subparagraphs (A) through (C),

to comply with the requirements of a State implementation plan.

(b) Use of locally or regionally available coal or coal derivatives to comply with implementation plan requirements

Upon a determination under subsection (a) of this section—

(1) such Governor, with the written consent of the President or his designee,

(2) the President's designee with the written consent of such Governor, or

(3) the President

may by rule or order prohibit any such major fuel burning stationary source (or class or category thereof) from using fuels other than locally or regionally available coal or coal derivatives to comply with implementation plan requirements. In taking any action under this subsection, the Governor, the President, or the President's designee as the case may be, shall take into account, the final cost to the consumer of such an action.

(c) Contracts; schedules

The Governor, in the case of action under subsection (b)(1) of this section, or the Administrator, in the case of an action under subsection (b)(2) or (3) of this section shall, by rule or order, require each source to which such action applies to—

(1) enter into long-term contracts of at least ten years in duration (except as the President or his designee may otherwise permit or require by rule or order for good cause) for supplies of regionally available coal or coal derivatives,

(2) enter into contracts to acquire any additional means of emission limitation which the Administrator or the State determines may be necessary to comply with the requirements of this chapter while using such coal or coal derivatives as fuel, and

(3) comply with such schedules (including increments of progress), timetables and other requirements as may be necessary to assure compliance with the requirements of this chapter.

Requirements under this subsection shall be established simultaneously with, and as a condition of, any action under subsection (b) of this section.

(d) Existing or new major fuel burning stationary sources

This section applies only to existing or new major fuel burning stationary sources—

(1) which have the design capacity to produce 250,000,000 Btu's per hour (or its equivalent), as determined by the Administrator, and

(2) which are not in compliance with the requirements of an applicable implementation plan or which are prohibited from burning oil or natural gas, or both, under any other authority of law.

(e) Actions not to be deemed modifications of major fuel burning stationary sources

Except as may otherwise be provided by rule by the State or the Administrator for good cause, any action required to be taken by a major fuel burning stationary source under this section shall not be deemed to constitute a modification for purposes of section 7411(a)(2) and (4) of this title.

(f) Treatment of prohibitions, rules, or orders as requirements or parts of plans under other provisions

For purposes of sections 7413 and 7420 of this title a prohibition under subsection (b) of this section, and a corresponding rule or order under subsection (c) of this section, shall be treated as a requirement of section 7413 of this title. For purposes of any plan (or portion thereof) promulgated under section 7410(c) of this title, any rule or order under subsection (c) of this section corresponding to a prohibition under subsection (b) of this section, shall be treated as a part of such plan. For purposes of section 7413 of this title, a prohibition under subsection (b) of this section, applicable to any source, and a corresponding rule or order under subsection (c) of this section, shall be treated as part of the applicable implementation plan for the State in which subject source is located.

(g) Delegation of Presidential authority

The President may delegate his authority under this section to an officer or employee of the United States designated by him on a case-by-case basis or in any other manner he deems suitable.

(h) "Locally or regionally available coal or coal derivatives" defined

For the purpose of this section the term "locally or regionally available coal or coal derivatives" means coal or coal derivatives which is, or can in the judgment of the State or the Administrator feasibly be, mined or produced in the local or regional area (as determined by the Administrator) in which the major fuel burning stationary source is located.

(July 14, 1955, c. 360, Title I, § 125, as added by Pub. L. No. 95–95, Title I, § 122, 91 Stat. 722 (Aug. 7, 1977).)

HISTORICAL AND STATUTORY NOTES

Effective and Applicability Provisions

1977 Acts. Section effective Aug. 7, 1977, except as otherwise expressly provided, see section 406(d) of Pub. L. No. 95–95, set out as a note under section 7401 of this title.

§ 7426. Interstate pollution abatement

[CAA § 126]

(a) Written notice to all nearby States

Each applicable implementation plan shall—

(1) require each major proposed new (or modified) source—

(A) subject to part C of this subchapter (relating to significant deterioration of air quality) or

(B) which may significantly contribute to levels of air pollution in excess of the national ambient air quality standards in any air quality control region outside the State in which such source intends to locate (or make such modification),

to provide written notice to all nearby States the air pollution levels of which may be affected by such source at least sixty days prior to the date on which commencement of construction is to be permitted by the State providing notice, and

(2) identify all major existing stationary sources which may have the impact described in paragraph (1) with respect to new or modified sources and provide notice to all nearby States of the identity of such sources not later than three months after August 7, 1977.

(b) Petition for finding that major sources emit or would emit prohibited air pollutants

Any State or political subdivision may petition the Administrator for a finding that any major source or group of stationary sources emits or would emit any air pollutant in violation of the prohibition of section 7410(a)(2)(D)(ii) of this title or this section. Within 60 days after receipt of any petition under this subsection and after public hearing, the Administrator shall make such a finding or deny the petition.

(c) Violations; allowable continued operation

Notwithstanding any permit which may have been granted by the State in which the source is located (or intends to locate), it shall be a violation of this section and the applicable implementation plan in such State—

(1) for any major proposed new (or modified) source with respect to which a finding has been made under subsection (b) of this section to be constructed or to operate in violation of the prohibition of section 7410(a)(2)(D)(ii) of this title or this section, or

(2) for any major existing source to operate more than three months after such finding has been made with respect to it.

The Administrator may permit the continued operation of a source referred to in paragraph (2) beyond the expiration of such three-month period if such source complies with such emission limitations and compliance schedules (containing increments of progress) as may be provided by the Administrator to bring about compliance with the requirements contained in section 7410(a)(2)(D)(ii) of this title or this section as expeditiously as practicable, but in no case later than three years after the date of such finding. Nothing in the preceding sentence shall be construed to preclude any such source from being eligible for an enforcement order under section 7413(d) of this title after the expiration of such period during which the Administrator has permitted continuous operation.

(July 14, 1955, c. 360, Title I, § 126, as added by Pub. L. No. 95–95, Title I, § 123, 91 Stat. 724 (Aug. 7, 1977); and amended by Pub. L. No. 95–190, § 14(a)(39), 91 Stat. 1401 (Nov. 16, 1977); Pub. L. No. 101–549, Title I, § 109(a), 104 Stat. 2469 (Nov. 15, 1990).)

HISTORICAL AND STATUTORY NOTES

References in Text

Section 7413(d) of this title, referred to in subsec. (c), was amended generally by Pub. L. No. 101–549, Title VII, § 701, 104 Stat. 2672 (Nov. 15, 1990), and, as so amended, no longer relates to final compliance orders.

Effective and Applicability Provisions

1990 Acts. Amendment by Pub. L. No. 101–549 effective Nov. 15, 1990, except as otherwise provided, see section 711(b) of Pub. L. No. 101–549, set out as a note under section 7401 of this title.

1977 Acts. Section effective Aug. 7, 1977, except as otherwise expressly provided, see section 406(d) of Pub. L. No. 95–95, set out as a note under section 7401 of this title.

Savings Provisions

Suits, actions or proceedings commenced under this chapter as in effect prior to Nov. 15, 1990, not to abate by reason of the taking effect of amendments by Pub. L. No. 101–549, except as otherwise provided for, see section 711(a) of Pub. L. No. 101–549, set out as a note under section 7401 of this title.

§ 7427. Public notification

[CAA § 127]

(a) Warning signs; television, radio, or press notices or information

Each State plan shall contain measures which will be effective to notify the public during any calendar[1] on a regular basis of instances or areas in which any national primary ambient air quality standard is exceeded or was exceeded during any portion of the preceding calendar year to advise the public of the health hazards associated with such pollution, and to enhance public awareness of the measures which can be taken to prevent such standards from being exceeded and the ways in which the public can participate in regulatory and other efforts to improve air quality. Such measures may include the posting of warning signs on interstate highway access points to metropolitan areas or television, radio, or press notices or information.

(b) Grants

The Administrator is authorized to make grants to States to assist in carrying out the requirements of subsection (a) of this section.

(July 14, 1955, c. 360, Title I, § 127, as added by Pub. L. No. 95–95, Title I, § 124, 91 Stat. 725 (Aug. 7, 1977).)

[1] So in original. Probably should be "calendar year".

HISTORICAL AND STATUTORY NOTES

Effective and Applicability Provisions

1977 Acts. Section effective Aug. 7, 1977, except as otherwise expressly provided, see section 406(d) of Pub. L. No. 95–95, set out as a note under section 7401 of this title.

§ 7428. State boards

[CAA § 128]

(a)[1] Not later than the date one year after August 7, 1977, each applicable implementation plan shall contain requirements that—

(1) any board or body which approves permits or enforcement orders under this chapter shall have at least a majority of members who represent the public interest and do not derive any significant portion of their income from persons subject to permits or enforcement orders under this chapter, and

(2) any potential conflicts of interest by members of such board or body or the head of an executive agency with similar powers be adequately disclosed.

A State may adopt any requirements respecting conflicts of interest for such boards or bodies or heads of executive agencies, or any other entities which are more stringent than the requirements of paragraph (1) and (2), and the Administrator shall approve any such more stringent requirements submitted as part of an implementation plan.

(July 14, 1955, c. 360, Title I, § 128, as added by Pub. L. No. 95–95, Title I, § 125, 91 Stat. 725 (Aug. 7, 1977).)

[1] So in original. Section enacted without a subsec. (b).

HISTORICAL AND STATUTORY NOTES

Effective and Applicability Provisions

1977 Acts. Section effective Aug. 7, 1977, except as otherwise expressly provided, see section 406(d) of Pub. L. No. 95–95, set out as a note under section 7401 of this title.

§ 7429. Solid waste combustion

[CAA § 129]

(a) New source performance standards

(1) In general

(A) The Administrator shall establish performance standards and other requirements pursuant to section 7411 of this title and this section for each category of solid waste incineration units. Such standards shall include emissions limitations and other requirements applicable to new units and guidelines (under section 7411(d) of this title and this section) and other requirements applicable to existing units.

(B) Standards under section 7411 of this title and this section applicable to solid waste incineration units with capacity greater than 250 tons per day combusting municipal waste shall be promulgated not later than 12 months after November 15, 1990. Nothing in this subparagraph shall alter any schedule for the promulgation of standards applicable to such units under section 7411 of this title pursuant to any settlement and consent decree entered by the Administrator before November 15, 1990: *Provided,* That, such standards are subsequently modified pursuant to the schedule established in this subparagraph to include each of the requirements of this section.

(C) Standards under section 7411 of this title and this section applicable to solid waste incineration units with capacity equal to or less than 250 tons per day combusting municipal waste and units combusting hospital waste, medical waste and infectious waste shall be promulgated not later than 24 months after November 15, 1990.

(D) Standards under section 7411 of this title and this section applicable to solid waste incineration units combusting commercial or industrial waste shall be proposed not later than 36 months after November 15, 1990, and promulgated not later than 48 months after November 15, 1990.

(E) Not later than 18 months after November 15, 1990, the Administrator shall publish a schedule for the promulgation of standards under section 7411 of this title and this section applicable to other categories of solid waste incineration units.

(2) Emissions standard

Standards applicable to solid waste incineration units promulgated under section 7411 of this title and this section shall reflect the maximum degree of reduction in emissions of air pollutants listed under section[1] (a)(4) that the Administrator, taking into consideration the cost of achieving such emission reduction, and any non-air quality health and environmental impacts and energy requirements, determines is achievable for new or existing units in each category. The Administrator may distinguish among classes, types (including mass-burn, refuse-derived fuel, modular and other types of units), and sizes of units within a category in establishing such standards. The degree of reduction in emissions that is deemed achievable for new units in a category shall not be less stringent than the emissions control that is achieved in practice by the best controlled similar unit, as determined by the Administrator. Emissions standards for existing units in a category may be less stringent than standards for new units in the same category but shall not be less stringent than the average emissions limitation achieved by the best performing 12 percent of units in the category (excluding units which first met lowest achievable emissions rates 18 months before the date such standards are proposed or 30 months before the date such standards are promulgated, whichever is later).

(3) Control methods and technologies

Standards under section 7411 of this title and this section applicable to solid waste incineration units shall be based on methods and technologies for removal or destruction of pollutants before, during, or after combustion, and shall incorporate for new units siting requirements that minimize, on a site specific basis, to the maximum extent practicable, potential risks to public health or the environment.

(4) Numerical emissions limitations

The performance standards promulgated under section 7411 of this title and this section and applicable to solid waste incineration units shall specify numerical emission limitations for the following substances or mixtures: particulate matter (total and fine), opacity (as appropriate), sulfur dioxide, hydrogen chloride, oxides of nitrogen, carbon monoxide, lead, cadmium, mercury, and dioxins and dibenzofurans. The Administrator may promulgate numerical emissions limitations or provide for the monitoring of postcombustion concentrations of surrogate substances, parameters or periods of residence time in excess of stated temperatures with respect to pollutants other than those listed in this paragraph.

(5) Review and revision

Not later than 5 years following the initial promulgation of any performance standards and other requirements under this section and section 7411 of this title applicable to a category of solid waste incineration units, and at 5 year intervals thereafter, the Administrator shall review, and in accordance with this section and section 7411 of this title, revise such standards and requirements.

(b) Existing units

(1) Guidelines

Performance standards under this section and section 7411 of this title for solid waste incineration units shall include guidelines promulgated pursuant to section 7411(d) of this title and this section applicable to existing units. Such guidelines shall include, as provided in this section, each of the elements required by subsection (a) of this section (emissions limitations, notwithstanding any restriction in section 7411(d) of this title regarding issuance of such limitations), subsection (c) of this section (monitoring), subsection (d) of this section (operator training), subsection (e) of this section (permits), and subsection (h)(4)[2] of this section (residual risk).

(2) State plans

Not later than 1 year after the Administrator promulgates guidelines for a category of solid waste incineration units, each State in which units in the category are operating shall submit to the Administrator a plan to implement and enforce the guidelines with respect to such units. The State plan shall be at least as protective as the guidelines promulgated by the Administrator and shall provide that each unit subject to the guidelines shall be in compliance with all requirements of this section not later than 3 years after the State plan is approved by the Administrator but not later than 5 years after the guidelines were promulgated. The Administrator shall approve or disapprove any State plan within 180 days of the submission, and if a plan is disapproved, the Administrator shall state the reasons for disapproval in writing. Any State may modify and resubmit a plan which has been disapproved by the Administrator.

(3) Federal plan

The Administrator shall develop, implement and enforce a plan for existing solid waste incineration units within any category located in any State which has not submitted an approvable plan under this subsection with respect to units in such category within 2 years after the date on which the Administrator promulgated the relevant guidelines. Such plan shall assure that each unit subject to the plan is in compliance with all provisions of the guidelines not later than 5 years after the date the relevant guidelines are promulgated.

(c) Monitoring

The Administrator shall, as part of each performance standard promulgated pursuant to subsection (a) of this section and section 7411 of this title, promulgate regulations requiring the owner or operator of each solid waste incineration unit—

(1) to monitor emissions from the unit at the point at which such emissions are emitted into the ambient air (or within the stack, combustion chamber or pollution control equipment, as appropriate) and at such other points as necessary to protect public health and the environment;

(2) to monitor such other parameters relating to the operation of the unit and its pollution control technology as the Administrator determines are appropriate; and

(3) to report the results of such monitoring.

Such regulations shall contain provisions regarding the frequency of monitoring, test methods and procedures validated on solid waste incineration units, and the form and frequency of reports containing the results of monitoring and shall require that any monitoring reports or test results indicating an exceedance of any standard under this section shall be reported separately and in a manner that facilitates review for purposes of enforcement actions. Such regulations shall require that copies of the results of such monitoring be maintained on file at the facility concerned and that copies shall be made available for inspection and copying by interested members of the public during business hours.

(d) Operator training

Not later than 24 months after November 15, 1990, the Administrator shall develop and promote a model State program for the training and certification of solid waste incineration unit operators and high-capacity fossil fuel fired plant operators. The Administrator may authorize any State to implement a model program for the training of solid waste incineration unit operators and high-capacity fossil fuel fired plant operators, if the State has adopted a program which is at least as effective as the model program developed by the Administrator. Beginning on the date 36 months after the date on which performance standards and guidelines are promulgated under subsection (a) of this section and section 7411 of this title for any category of solid waste incineration units it shall be unlawful to operate any unit in the category unless each person with control over processes affecting emissions from such unit has satisfactorily completed a training program meeting the requirements established by the Administrator under this subsection.

(e) Permits

Beginning (1) 36 months after the promulgation of a performance standard under subsection (a) of this section and section 7411 of this title applicable to a category of solid waste incineration units, or (2) the effective date of a permit program under subchapter V of this chapter in the State in which the unit is located, whichever is later, each unit in the category shall operate pursuant to a permit issued under this subsection and subchapter V of this chapter. Permits required by this subsection may be renewed according to the provisions of subchapter V of this chapter. Notwithstanding any other provision of this chapter, each permit for a solid waste incineration unit combusting municipal waste issued under this chapter shall be issued for a period of up to 12 years and shall be reviewed every 5 years after date of issuance or reissuance. Each permit shall continue in effect after the date of issuance until the date of termination, unless the Administrator or State determines that the unit is not in compliance with all standards and conditions contained in the permit. Such determination shall be made at regular intervals during the term of the permit, such intervals not to exceed 5 years, and only after public comment and public hearing. No permit for a solid waste incineration unit may be issued under this chapter by an agency, instrumentality or person that is also responsible, in whole or part, for the design and construction or operation of the unit. Notwithstanding any other provision of this subsection, the Administrator or the State shall require the owner or operator of any unit to comply with emissions limitations or implement any other measures, if the Administrator or the State determines that emissions in the absence of such limitations or measures may reasonably be anticipated to endanger public health or the environment. The Administrator's determination under the preceding sentence is a discretionary decision.

(f) Effective date and enforcement

(1) New units

Performance standards and other requirements promulgated pursuant to this section and section 7411 of this title and applicable to new solid waste incineration units shall be effective as of the date 6 months after the date of promulgation.

(2) Existing units

Performance standards and other requirements promulgated pursuant to this section and section 7411 of this title and applicable to existing solid waste incineration units shall be effective as expeditiously as practicable after approval of a State plan under subsection (b)(2) of this section (or promulgation of a plan by the Administrator under subsection (b)(3) of this section) but in no event later than 3 years after the State plan is approved or 5 years after the date such standards or requirements are promulgated, whichever is earlier.

(3) Prohibition

After the effective date of any performance standard, emission limitation or other requirement promulgated pursuant to this section and section 7411 of this title, it shall be unlawful for any owner or operator of any solid waste incineration unit to which such standard, limitation or requirement applies to operate such unit in violation of such limitation, standard or requirement or for any other person to violate an applicable requirement of this section.

(4) Coordination with other authorities

For purposes of sections 7411(e), 7413, 7414, 7416, 7420, 7603, 7604, 7607 of this title and other provisions for the enforcement of this chapter, each performance standard, emission limitation or other requirement established pursuant to this section by the Administrator or a State or local government, shall be treated in the same manner as a standard of performance under section 7411 of this title which is an emission limitation.

(g) Definitions

For purposes of section 306 of the Clean Air Act Amendments of 1990 and this section only—

(1) Solid waste incineration unit

The term "solid waste incineration unit" means a distinct operating unit of any facility which combusts any solid waste material from commercial or industrial establishments or the general public (including single and multiple residences, hotels, and motels). Such term does not include incinerators or other units required to have a permit under section 3005 of the Solid Waste Disposal Act [42 U.S.C.A. § 6925]. The term "solid waste incineration unit" does not include (A) materials recovery facilities (including primary or secondary smelters) which combust waste for the primary purpose of recovering metals, (B) qualifying small power production facilities, as defined in section 796(17)(C) of Title 16, or qualifying cogeneration facilities, as defined in section 796(18)(B) of Title 16, which burn homogeneous waste (such as units which burn tires or used oil, but not including refuse-derived fuel) for the production of electric energy or in the case of qualifying cogeneration facilities which burn homogeneous waste for the production of electric energy and steam or forms of useful energy (such as heat) which are used for industrial, commercial, heating or cooling purposes, or (C) air curtain incinerators provided that such incinerators only burn wood wastes, yard wastes and clean lumber and that such air curtain incinerators comply with opacity limitations to be established by the Administrator by rule.

(2) New solid waste incineration unit

The term "new solid waste incineration unit" means a solid waste incineration unit the construction of which is commenced after the Administrator proposes requirements under this section establishing emissions standards or other requirements which would be applicable to such unit or a modified solid waste incineration unit.

(3) Modified solid waste incineration unit

The term "modified solid waste incineration unit" means a solid waste incineration unit at which modifications have occurred after the effective date of a standard under subsection (a) of this section if (A) the cumulative cost of the modifications, over the life of the unit, exceed 50 per centum of the original cost of construction and installation of the unit (not including the cost of any land purchased in connection with such construction or installation) updated to current costs, or (B) the modification is a physical change in or change in the method of operation of the unit which increases the amount of any air pollutant emitted by the unit for which standards have been established under this section or section 7411 of this title.

(4) Existing solid waste incineration unit

The term "existing solid waste incineration unit" means a solid waste unit which is not a new or modified solid waste incineration unit.

(5) Municipal waste

The term "municipal waste" means refuse (and refuse-derived fuel) collected from the general public and from residential, commercial, institutional, and industrial sources consisting of paper, wood, yard wastes, food wastes, plastics, leather, rubber, and other combustible materials and non-combustible materials such as metal, glass and rock, provided that: (A) the term does not include industrial process wastes or medical wastes that are segregated from such other wastes; and (B) an incineration unit shall not be considered to be combusting municipal waste for purposes of section 7411 of this title or this section if it combusts a fuel feed stream, 30 percent or less of the weight of which is comprised, in aggregate, of municipal waste.

(6) Other terms

The terms "solid waste" and "medical waste" shall have the meanings established by the Administrator pursuant to the Solid Waste Disposal Act [42 U.S.C.A. § 6901 et seq.].

(h) Other authority

(1) State authority

Nothing in this section shall preclude or deny the right of any State or political subdivision thereof to adopt or enforce any regulation, requirement, limitation or standard relating to solid waste incineration units that is more stringent than a regulation, requirement, limitation or standard in effect under this section or under any other provision of this chapter.

(2) Other authority under this chapter

Nothing in this section shall diminish the authority of the Administrator or a State to establish any other requirements applicable to solid waste incineration units under any other authority of law, including the authority to establish for any air pollutant a national ambient air quality standard, except that no solid waste incineration unit subject to performance standards under this section and section 7411 of this title shall be subject to standards under section 7412(d) of this title.

(3) Residual risk

The Administrator shall promulgate standards under section 7412(f) of this title for a category of solid waste incineration units, if promulgation of such standards is required under section 7412(f) of this title. For purposes of this[3] preceding sentence only—

(A) the performance standards under subsection (a) of this section and section 7411 of this title applicable to a category of solid waste incineration units shall be deemed standards under section 7412(d)(2) of this title, and

(B) the Administrator shall consider and regulate, if required, the pollutants listed under subsection (a)(4) of this section and no others.

(4) Acid rain

A solid waste incineration unit shall not be a utility unit as defined in subchapter IV-A of this chapter: *Provided,* That, more than 80 per centum of its annual average fuel consumption measured on a Btu basis, during a period or periods to be determined by the Administrator, is from a fuel (including any waste burned as a fuel) other than a fossil fuel.

(5) Requirements of parts C and D

No requirement of an applicable implementation plan under section 7475 of this title (relating to construction of facilities in regions identified pursuant to section 7407(d)(1)(A)(ii) or (iii) of this title) or under section 7502(c)(5) of this title (relating to permits for construction and operation in nonattainment areas) may be used to weaken the standards in effect under this section.

(July 14, 1955, c. 360, Title I, § 129, as added by Pub. L. No. 101–549, Title III, § 305(a), 104 Stat. 2577 (Nov. 15, 1990).)

[1] So in original. Probably should be "subsection."

[2] So in original. Probably should be subsection "(h)(3)."

[3] So in original. Probably should be "the."

HISTORICAL AND STATUTORY NOTES

References in Text

Section 306 of the Clean Air Act Amendments of 1990, referred to in subsec. (g), probably means section 306 of Pub. L. No. 101–549, which is set out as a note under section 6921 of this title.

The Solid Waste Disposal Act, referred to in subsecs. (g)(1) and (6), is Title II of Pub. L. No. 89–272, 79 Stat. 997 (Oct. 20, 1965), as amended generally by Pub. L. No. 94–580, § 2, 90 Stat. 2795 (Oct. 21, 1976), which is codified generally as chapter 82 (section 6901 et seq.) of this title. Section 3005 of the Solid Waste Disposal Act, referred to in subsec. (g)(1), is codified as section 6925 of this title. For complete classification of this Act to the Code, see Short Title of 1965 Acts note set out under section 6901 of this title and Tables.

Effective and Applicability Provisions

1990 Acts. Section to take effect Nov. 15, 1990, except as otherwise provided, see section 711(b) of Pub. L. No. 101–549, set out as a note under section 7401 of this title.

Savings Provisions

Suits, actions or proceedings commenced under this chapter as in effect prior to Nov. 15, 1990, not to abate by reason of the taking effect of amendments by Pub. L. No. 101–549, except as otherwise provided for, see section 711(a) of Pub. L. No. 101–549, set out as a note under section 7401 of this title.

Review of Acid Gas Scrubbing Requirements

Section 305(c) of Pub. L. No. 101–549 provided that: "Prior to the promulgation of any performance standard for solid waste incineration units combusting municipal waste under section 111 [section 7411 of this title] or section 129 of the Clean Air Act [this section], the Administrator shall review the availability of acid gas scrubbers as a pollution control technology for small new units and for existing units (as defined in 54 Federal Register 52190

(December 20, 1989)[)], taking into account the provisions of subsection (a)(2) of section 129 of the Clean Air Act [subsec. (a)(2) of this section]."

§ 7430. Emission factors

[CAA § 130]

Within 6 months after November 15, 1990, and at least every 3 years thereafter, the Administrator shall review and, if necessary, revise, the methods ("emission factors") used for purposes of this chapter to estimate the quantity of emissions of carbon monoxide, volatile organic compounds, and oxides of nitrogen from sources of such air pollutants (including area sources and mobile sources). In addition, the Administrator shall establish emission factors for sources for which no such methods have previously been established by the Administrator. The Administrator shall permit any person to demonstrate improved emissions estimating techniques, and following approval of such techniques, the Administrator shall authorize the use of such techniques. Any such technique may be approved only after appropriate public participation. Until the Administrator has completed the revision required by this section, nothing in this section shall be construed to affect the validity of emission factors established by the Administrator before November 15, 1990.

(July 14, 1955, c. 360, Title I, § 130, as added by Pub. L. No. 101–549, Title VIII, § 804, 104 Stat. 2689 (Nov. 15, 1990).)

HISTORICAL AND STATUTORY NOTES

Effective and Applicability Provisions

1990 Acts. Section to take effect Nov. 15, 1990, except as otherwise provided, see section 711(b) of Pub. L. No. 101–549, set out as a note under section 7401 of this title.

Savings Provisions

Suits, actions or proceedings commenced under this chapter as in effect prior to Nov. 15, 1990, not to abate by reason of the taking effect of amendments by Pub. L. No. 101–549, except as otherwise provided for, see section 711(a) of Pub. L. No. 101–549, set out as a note under section 7401 of this title.

§ 7431. Land use authority

[CAA § 131]

Nothing in this chapter constitutes an infringement on the existing authority of counties and cities to plan or control land use, and nothing in this chapter provides or transfers authority over such land use.

(July 14, 1955, c. 360, Title I, § 131, as added Pub. L. No. 101–549, Title VIII, § 805, 104 Stat. 2689 (Nov. 15, 1990).)

HISTORICAL AND STATUTORY NOTES

Effective and Applicability Provisions

1990 Acts. Section to take effect Nov. 15, 1990, except as otherwise provided, see section 711(b) of Pub. L. No. 101–549, set out as a note under section 7401 of this title.

Savings Provisions

Suits, actions or proceedings commenced under this chapter as in effect prior to Nov. 15, 1990, not to abate by reason of the taking effect of amendments by Pub. L. No. 101–549, except as otherwise provided for, see section 711(a) of Pub. L. No. 101–549, set out as a note under section 7401 of this title.

PART B—OZONE PROTECTION

§§ 7450 to 7459. Repealed. Pub. L. No. 101–549, Title VI, § 601, 104 Stat. 2648 (Nov. 15, 1990).

HISTORICAL AND STATUTORY NOTES

Section 7450, Act of July 14, 1955, c. 360, Title I, § 150, as added by Pub. L. No. 95–95, Title I, § 126, 91 Stat. 725 (Aug. 7, 1977), set forth the Congressional declaration of purpose.

Section 7451, Act of July 14, 1955, c. 360, Title I, § 151, as added by Pub. L. No. 95–95, Title I, § 126, 91 Stat. 726 (Aug. 7, 1977), set forth Congressional findings.

Section 7452, Act of July 14, 1955, c. 360, Title I, § 152, as added by, Pub. L. No. 95–95, Title I, § 126, 91 Stat. 726 (Aug. 7, 1977), set forth definitions applicable to this part.

Section 7453, Act of July 14, 1955, c. 360, Title I, § 153, as added by Pub. L. No. 95–95, Title I, § 126, 91 Stat. 726 (Aug. 7, 1977), related to studies by the Environmental Protection Agency.

Section 7454, Act of July 14, 1955, c. 360, Title I, § 154, as added by Pub. L. No. 95–95, Title I, § 126, 91 Stat. 728 (Aug. 7, 1977), and amended by Pub. L. No. 96–88, Title V, § 509(b), 93 Stat. 695 (Oct. 17, 1979), related to research and monitoring activities by Federal agencies.

Section 7455, Act of July 14, 1955, c. 360, Title I, § 155, as added by Pub. L. No. 95–95, Title I, § 126, 91 Stat. 726 (Aug. 7, 1977), related to reports on the progress of regulation.

Section 7456, Act of July 14, 1955, c. 360, Title I, § 156, as added by Pub. L. No. 95–95, Title I, § 126, 91 Stat. 729 (Aug. 7, 1977), authorized the President to enter into international agreements to foster cooperative research.

Section 7457, Act of July 14, 1955, c. 360, Title I, § 157, as added by Pub. L. No. 95–95, Title I, § 126, 91 Stat. 729 (Aug. 7, 1977), related to promulgation of regulations.

Section 7458, Act of July 14, 1955, c. 360, Title I, § 158, as added by Pub. L. No. 95–95, Title I, § 126, 91 Stat. 730 (Aug. 7, 1977), set forth other provisions of law that would be unaffected by the provisions of this part.

Section 7459, Act of July 14, 1955, c. 360, Title I, § 159, as added by Pub. L. No. 95–95, Title I, § 126, 91 Stat. 730 (Aug. 7, 1977), related to the authority of the State to protect the stratosphere.

Effective Date of Repeal

Repeal of sections 7450 to 7459 effective Nov. 15, 1990, except as otherwise provided, see section 711(b) of Pub. L. No. 101–549, set out as a note under section 7401 of this title.

Savings Provisions

Suits, actions or proceedings commenced under this chapter as in effect prior to Nov. 15, 1990, not to abate by reason of the taking effect of amendments by Pub. L. No. 101–549, except as otherwise provided for, see section 711(a) of Pub. L. No. 101–549, set out as a note under section 7401 of this title.

Similar Provisions

For provisions relating to stratospheric ozone protection, see section 7671 et seq. of this title.

PART C—PREVENTION OF SIGNIFICANT DETERIORATION OF AIR QUALITY

Subpart I—Clean Air

§ 7470. Congressional declaration of purpose

[CAA § 160]

The purposes of this part are as follows:

(1) to protect public health and welfare from any actual or potential adverse effect which in the Administrator's judgment may reasonably be anticipate[1] to occur from air pollution or from exposures to pollutants in other media, which pollutants originate as emissions to the ambient air)[2], notwithstanding attainment and maintenance of all national ambient air quality standards;

(2) to preserve, protect, and enhance the air quality in national parks, national wilderness areas, national monuments, national seashores, and other areas of special national or regional natural, recreational, scenic, or historic value;

(3) to insure that economic growth will occur in a manner consistent with the preservation of existing clean air resources;

(4) to assure that emissions from any source in any State will not interfere with any portion of the applicable implementation plan to prevent significant deterioration of air quality for any other State; and

(5) to assure that any decision to permit increased air pollution in any area to which this section applies is made only after careful evaluation of all the consequences of such a decision and after adequate procedural opportunities for informed public participation in the decisionmaking process.

(July 14, 1955, c. 360, Title I, § 160, as added by Pub. L. No. 95–95, Title I, § 127(a), 91 Stat. 731 (Aug. 7, 1977).)

[1] So in original. Probably should be "anticipated."

[2] So in original. Section was enacted without an opening parenthesis.

HISTORICAL AND STATUTORY NOTES

Effective and Applicability Provisions

1977 Acts. Section effective Aug. 7, 1977, except as otherwise expressly provided, see section 406(d) of Pub. L. No. 95–95, set out as a note under section 7401 of this title.

Guidance Document

Section 127(c) of Pub. L. No. 95–95 provided that not later than 1 year after Aug. 7, 1977, the Administrator publish a guidance document to assist the States in carrying out their functions under part C of Title I of the Clean Air Act [this part] with respect to pollutants for which national ambient air quality standards are promulgated.

Study and Report on Progress Made in Program Relating to Significant Deterioration of Air Quality

Section 127(d) of Pub. L. No. 95–95 provided that not later than 2 years after Aug. 7, 1977, the Administrator shall complete a study and report to the Congress on the progress made in carrying out part C of Title I of the Clean Air Act [this part] and the problems associated with carrying out such section.

§ 7471. Plan requirements

[CAA § 161]

In accordance with the policy of section 7401(b)(1) of this title, each applicable implementation plan shall contain emission limitations and such other measures as may be necessary, as determined under regulations promulgated under this part, to prevent significant deterioration of air quality in each region (or portion thereof) designated pursuant to section 7407 of this title as attainment or unclassifiable.

(July 14, 1955, c. 360, Title I, § 161, as added by Pub. L. No. 95–95, Title I, § 127(a), 91 Stat. 731 (Aug. 7, 1977); and amended by Pub. L. No. 101–549, Title I, § 110(1), 104 Stat. 2470 (Nov. 15, 1990).)

HISTORICAL AND STATUTORY NOTES

Effective and Applicability Provisions

1990 Acts. Amendment by Pub. L. No. 101–549 effective Nov. 15, 1990, except as otherwise provided, see section 711(b) of Pub. L. No. 101–549, set out as a note under section 7401 of this title.

1977 Acts. Section effective Aug. 7, 1977, except as otherwise expressly provided, see section 406(d) of Pub. L. No. 95–95, set out as a note under section 7401 of this title.

Savings Provisions

Suits, actions or proceedings commenced under this chapter as in effect prior to Nov. 15, 1990, not to abate by reason of the taking effect of amendments by Pub. L. No. 101–549, except as otherwise provided for, see section 711(a) of Pub. L. No. 101–549, set out as a note under section 7401 of this title.

§ 7472. Initial classifications

[CAA § 162]

(a) Areas designated as class I

Upon the enactment of this part, all—

(1) international parks,

(2) national wilderness areas which exceed 5,000 acres in size,

(3) national memorial parks which exceed 5,000 acres in size, and

(4) national parks which exceed six thousand acres in size,

and which are in existence on August 7, 1977, shall be class I areas and may not be redesignated. All areas which were redesignated as class I under regulations promulgated before August 7, 1977, shall be class I areas which may be redesignated as provided in this part. The extent of the areas designated as Class I under this section shall conform to any changes in the boundaries of such areas which have occurred subsequent to August 7, 1977, or which may occur subsequent to November 15, 1990.

(b) Areas designated as class II

All areas in such State designated pursuant to section 7407(d) of this title as attainment or unclassifiable which are not established as class I under subsection (a) of this section shall be class II areas unless redesignated under section 7474 of this title.

(July 14, 1955, c. 360, Title I, § 162, as added by Pub. L. No. 95–95, Title I, § 127(a), 91 Stat. 731 (Aug. 7, 1977); and amended by Pub. L. No. 95–190, § 14(a)(40), 91 Stat. 1401 (Nov. 16, 1977); Pub. L. No. 101–549, Title I, §§ 108(m), 110(2), 104 Stat. 2469, 2470 (Nov. 15, 1990).)

HISTORICAL AND STATUTORY NOTES

Effective and Applicability Provisions

1990 Acts. Amendment by Pub. L. No. 101–549 effective Nov. 15, 1990, except as otherwise provided, see section 711(b) of Pub. L. No. 101–549, set out as a note under section 7401 of this title.

1977 Acts. Section effective Aug. 7, 1977, except as otherwise expressly provided, see section 406(d) of Pub. L. No. 95–95, set out as a note under section 7401 of this title.

Savings Provisions

Suits, actions or proceedings commenced under this chapter as in effect prior to Nov. 15, 1990, not to abate by reason of the taking effect of amendments by Pub. L. No. 101–549, except as otherwise provided for, see section 711(a) of Pub. L. No. 101–549, set out as a note under section 7401 of this title.

§ 7473. Increments and ceilings

[CAA § 163]

(a) Sulfur oxide and particulate matter; requirement that maximum allowable increases and maximum allowable concentrations not be exceeded

In the case of sulfur oxide and particulate matter, each applicable implementation plan shall contain measures assuring that maximum allowable increases over baseline concentrations of, and maximum allowable concentrations of, such pollutant shall not be exceeded. In the case of any maximum allowable increase (except an allowable increase specified under section 7475(d)(2)(C)(iv) of this title) for a pollutant based on concentrations permitted under national ambient air quality standards for any period other than an annual period, such regulations shall permit such maximum allowable increase to be exceeded during one such period per year.

(b) Maximum allowable increases in concentrations over baseline concentrations

(1) For any class I area, the maximum allowable increase in concentrations of sulfur dioxide and particulate matter over the baseline concentration of such pollutants shall not exceed the following amounts:

Pollutant	Maximum allowable increase (in micrograms per cubic meter)
Particulate matter:	
Annual geometric mean	5
Twenty-four-hour maximum	10
Sulfur dioxide:	
Annual arithmetic mean	2
Twenty-four-hour maximum	5
Three-hour maximum	25

(2) For any class II area, the maximum allowable increase in concentrations of sulfur dioxide and particulate matter over the baseline concentration of such pollutants shall not exceed the following amounts:

Pollutant	Maximum allowable increase (in micrograms per cubic meter)
Particulate matter:	
Annual geometric mean	19
Twenty-four-hour maximum	37
Sulfur dioxide:	
Annual arithmetic mean	20
Twenty-four-hour maximum	91
Three-hour maximum	512

(3) For any class III area, the maximum allowable increase in concentrations of sulfur dioxide and particulate matter over the baseline concentration of such pollutants shall not exceed the following amounts:

Pollutant	Maximum allowable increase (in micrograms per cubic meter)
Particulate matter:	
Annual geometric mean	37
Twenty-four-hour maximum	75
Sulfur dioxide:	
Annual arithmetic mean	40
Twenty-four-hour maximum	182
Three-hour maximum	700

(4) The maximum allowable concentration of any air pollutant in any area to which this part applies shall not exceed a concentration for such pollutant for each period of exposure equal to—

(A) the concentration permitted under the national secondary ambient air quality standard, or

(B) the concentration permitted under the national primary ambient air quality standard,

whichever concentration is lowest for such pollutant for such period of exposure.

(c) Orders or rules for determining compliance with maximum allowable increases in ambient concentrations of air pollutants

(1) In the case of any State which has a plan approved by the Administrator for purposes of carrying out this part, the Governor of such State may, after notice and opportunity for public hearing, issue orders or promulgate rules providing that for purposes of determining compliance with the maximum allowable increases in ambient concentrations of an air pollutant, the following concentrations of such pollutant shall not be taken into account:

(A) concentrations of such pollutant attributable to the increase in emissions from stationary sources which have converted from the use of petroleum products, or natural gas, or both, by reason of an order which is in effect under the provisions of sections 792(a) and (b) of Title 15 (or any subsequent legislation which supersedes such provisions) over the emissions from such sources before the effective date of such order.[1]

(B) the concentrations of such pollutant attributable to the increase in emissions from stationary sources which have converted from using natural gas by reason of a natural gas curtailment pursuant to a natural gas curtailment plan in effect pursuant to the Federal Power Act [16 U.S.C.A. § 791a et seq.] over the emissions from such sources before the effective date of such plan,

(C) concentrations of particulate matter attributable to the increase in emissions from construction or other temporary emission-related activities, and

(D) the increase in concentrations attributable to new sources outside the United States over the concentrations attributable to existing sources which are included in the baseline concentration determined in accordance with section 7479(4) of this title.

(2) No action taken with respect to a source under paragraph (1)(A) or (1)(B) shall apply more than five years after the effective date of the order referred to in paragraph (1)(A) or the plan referred to in paragraph (1)(B), whichever is applicable. If both such order and plan are applicable, no such action shall apply more than five years after the later of such effective dates.

(3) No action under this subsection shall take effect unless the Governor submits the order or rule providing for such exclusion to the Administrator and the Administrator determines that such order or rule is in compliance with the provisions of this subsection.

(July 14, 1955, c. 360, Title I, § 163, as added by Pub. L. No. 95–95, Title I, § 127(a), 91 Stat. 732 (Aug. 7, 1977); and amended by Pub. L. No. 95–190, § 14(a)(41), 91 Stat. 1401 (Nov. 16, 1977).)

[1] So in original. The period probably should be a comma.

HISTORICAL AND STATUTORY NOTES

References in Text

The Federal Power Act, referred to in subsec. (c)(1)(B), is Act of June 10, 1920, c. 285, 41 Stat. 1063, as amended, which is codified generally as chapter 12 (section 791a et seq.) of Title 16, Conservation. For complete classification of this Act to the Code, see section 791a of Title 16 and Tables.

Effective and Applicability Provisions

1977 Acts. Section effective Aug. 7, 1977, except as otherwise expressly provided, see section 406(d) of Pub. L. No. 95–95, set out as a note under section 7401 of this title.

§ 7474. Area redesignation

[CAA § 164]

(a) Authority of States to redesignate areas

Except as otherwise provided under subsection (c) of this section, a State may redesignate such areas as it deems appropriate as class I areas. The following areas may be redesignated only as class I or II:

(1) an area which exceeds ten thousand acres in size and is a national monument, a national primitive area, a national preserve, a national recreation area, a national wild and scenic river, a national wildlife refuge, a national lakeshore or seashore, and

(2) a national park or national wilderness area established after August 7, 1977, which exceeds ten thousand acres in size.

The extent of the areas referred to in paragraph[1] (1) and (2) shall conform to any changes in the boundaries of such areas which have occurred subsequent to August 7, 1977, or which may occur subsequent to November 15, 1990. Any area (other than an area referred to in paragraph (1) or (2) or an area established as class I under the first sentence of section 7472(a) of this title) may be redesignated by the State as class III if—

(A) such redesignation has been specifically approved by the Governor of the State, after consultation with the appropriate Committees of the legislature if it is in session or with the leadership of the legislature if it is not in session (unless State law provides that such redesignation must be specifically approved by State legislation) and if general purpose units of local government representing a majority of the residents of the area so redesignated enact legislation (including for such units of local government resolutions where appropriate) concurring in the State's redesignation;

(B) such redesignation will not cause, or contribute to, concentrations of any air pollutant which exceed any maximum allowable increase or maximum allowable concentration permitted under the classification of any other area; and

(C) such redesignation otherwise meets the requirements of this part.

Subparagraph (A) of this paragraph shall not apply to area redesignations by Indian tribes.

(b) Notice and hearing; notice to Federal land manager; written comments and recommendations; regulations; disapproval of redesignation

(1) (A) Prior to redesignation of any area under this part, notice shall be afforded and public hearings shall be conducted in areas proposed to be redesignated and in areas which may be affected by the proposed redesignation. Prior to any such public hearing a satisfactory description and analysis of the health, environmental, economic, social, and energy effects of the proposed redesignation shall be prepared and made available for public inspection and prior to any such redesignation, the description and analysis of such effects shall be reviewed and examined by the redesignating authorities.

(B) Prior to the issuance of notice under subparagraph (A) respecting the redesignation of any area under this subsection, if such area includes any Federal lands, the State shall provide written notice to the appropriate Federal land manager and afford adequate opportunity (but not in excess of 60 days) to confer with the State respecting the intended notice of redesignation and to submit written comments and recommendations with respect to such intended notice of redesignation. In redesignating any area under this section with respect to which any Federal land manager has submitted written comments and recommendations, the State shall publish a list of any inconsistency between such redesignation and such recommendations and an explanation of such inconsistency (together with the reasons for making such redesignation against the recommendation of the Federal land manager).

(C) The Administrator shall promulgate regulations not later than six months after August 7, 1977, to assure, insofar as practicable, that prior to any public hearing on redesignation of any area, there shall be available for public inspection any specific plans for any new or modified major emitting facility which may be permitted to be constructed and operated only if the area in question is designated or redesignated as class III.

(2) The Administrator may disapprove the redesignation of any area only if he finds, after notice and opportunity for public hearing, that such redesignation does not meet the procedural requirements of this section or is inconsistent with the requirements of section 7472(a) of this title or of subsection (a) of this section. If any such disapproval occurs, the classification of the area shall be that which was in effect prior to the redesignation which was disapproved.

(c) Indian reservations

Lands within the exterior boundaries of reservations of federally recognized Indian tribes may be redesignated only by the appropriate Indian governing body. Such Indian governing body shall be subject in all respect to the provisions of subsection (e) of this section.

(d) Review of national monuments, primitive areas, and national preserves

The Federal Land Manager shall review all national monuments, primitive areas, and national preserves, and shall recommend any appropriate areas for redesignation as class I where air quality related values are important attributes of the area. The Federal Land Manager shall report such recommendations, within[2] supporting analysis, to the Congress and the affected States within one year after August 7, 1977. The Federal Land Manager shall consult with the appropriate States before making such recommendations.

(e) Resolution of disputes between State and Indian tribes

If any State affected by the redesignation of an area by an Indian tribe or any Indian tribe affected by the redesignation of an area by a State disagrees with such redesignation of any area, or if a permit is proposed to be issued for any new major emitting facility proposed for construction in any State which the Governor of an affected State or governing body of an affected Indian tribe determines will cause or contribute to a cumulative change in air quality in excess of that allowed in this part within the affected State or tribal reservation, the Governor or Indian ruling body may request the Administrator to enter into negotiations with the parties involved to resolve such dispute. If requested by any State or Indian tribe involved, the Administrator shall make a recommendation to resolve the dispute and protect the air quality related values of the lands involved. If the parties involved do not reach agreement, the Administrator shall resolve the dispute and his determination, or the results of agreements reached through other means, shall become part of the applicable plan and shall be enforceable as part of such plan. In resolving such disputes relating to area redesignation, the Administrator shall consider the extent to which the lands involved are of sufficient size to allow effective air quality management or have air quality related values of such an area.

(July 14, 1955, c. 360, Title I, § 164, as added by Pub. L. No. 95–95, Title I, § 127(a), 91 Stat. 733 (Aug. 7, 1977); and amended by Pub. L. No. 95–190, § 14(a)(42), (43), 91 Stat. 1402 (Nov. 16, 1977); Pub. L. No. 101–549, Title I, § 108(n), 104 Stat. 2469 (Nov. 15, 1990).)

[1] So in original. Probably should be "paragraphs."

[2] So in original. Probably should be "with."

HISTORICAL AND STATUTORY NOTES

Effective and Applicability Provisions

1990 Acts. Amendment by Pub. L. No. 101–549 effective Nov. 15, 1990, except as otherwise provided, see section 711(b) of Pub. L. No. 101–549, set out as a note under section 7401 of this title.

1977 Acts. Section effective Aug. 7, 1977, except as otherwise expressly provided, see section 406(d) of Pub. L. No. 95–95, set out as a note under section 7401 of this title.

Savings Provisions

Suits, actions or proceedings commenced under this chapter as in effect prior to Nov. 15, 1990, not to abate by reason of the taking effect of amendments by Pub. L. No. 101–549, except as otherwise provided for, see section 711(a) of Pub. L. No. 101–549, set out as a note under section 7401 of this title.

§ 7475. Preconstruction requirements

[CAA § 165]

(a) Major emitting facilities on which construction is commenced

No major emitting facility on which construction is commenced after August 7, 1977, may be constructed in any area to which this part applies unless—

(1) a permit has been issued for such proposed facility in accordance with this part setting forth emission limitations for such facility which conform to the requirements of this part;

(2) the proposed permit has been subject to a review in accordance with this section, the required analysis has been conducted in accordance with regulations promulgated by the Administrator, and a public hearing has been held with opportunity for interested persons including representatives of the Administrator to appear and submit written or oral presentations on the air quality impact of such source, alternatives thereto, control technology requirements, and other appropriate considerations;

(3) the owner or operator of such facility demonstrates, as required pursuant to section 7410(j) of this title, that emissions from construction or operation of such facility will not cause, or contribute to, air pollution in excess of any (A) maximum allowable increase or maximum allowable concentration for any pollutant in any area to which this part applies more than one time per year, (B) national ambient air quality standard in any air quality control region, or (C) any other applicable emission standard or standard of performance under this chapter;

(4) the proposed facility is subject to the best available control technology for each pollutant subject to regulation under this chapter emitted from, or which results from, such facility;

(5) the provisions of subsection (d) of this section with respect to protection of class I areas have been complied with for such facility;

(6) there has been an analysis of any air quality impacts projected for the area as a result of growth associated with such facility;

(7) the person who owns or operates, or proposes to own or operate, a major emitting facility for which a permit is required under this part agrees to conduct such monitoring as may be necessary to determine the effect which emissions from any such facility may have, or is having, on air quality in any area which may be affected by emissions from such source; and

(8) in the case of a source which proposes to construct in a class III area, emissions from which would cause or contribute to exceeding the maximum allowable increments applicable in a class II area and where no standard under section 7411 of this title has been promulgated subsequent to August 7, 1977, for such source category, the Administrator has approved the determination of best available technology as set forth in the permit.

(b) Exception

The demonstration pertaining to maximum allowable increases required under subsection (a)(3) of this section shall not apply to maximum allowable increases for class II areas in the case of an expansion or modification of a major emitting facility which is in existence on August 7, 1977, whose allowable emissions of air pollutants, after compliance with subsection (a)(4) of this section, will be less than fifty tons per year and for which the owner or operator of such facility demonstrates that emissions of particulate matter and sulfur oxides will not cause or contribute to ambient air quality levels in excess of the national secondary ambient air quality standard for either of such pollutants.

(c) Permit applications

Any completed permit application under section 7410 of this title for a major emitting facility in any area to which this part applies shall be granted or denied not later than one year after the date of filing of such completed application.

(d) Action taken on permit applications; notice; adverse impact on air quality related values; variance; emission limitations

(1) Each State shall transmit to the Administrator a copy of each permit application relating to a major emitting facility received by such State and provide notice to the Administrator of every action related to the consideration of such permit.

(2) **(A)** The Administrator shall provide notice of the permit application to the Federal Land Manager and the Federal official charged with direct responsibility for management of any lands within a class I area which may be affected by emissions from the proposed facility.

(B) The Federal Land Manager and the Federal official charged with direct responsibility for management of such lands shall have an affirmative responsibility to protect the air quality related values (including visibility) of any such lands within a class I area and to consider, in consultation with the Administrator, whether a proposed major emitting facility will have an adverse impact on such values.

(C) (i) In any case where the Federal official charged with direct responsibility for management of any lands within a class I area or the Federal Land Manager of such lands, or the Administrator, or the Governor of an adjacent State containing such a class I area files a notice alleging that emissions from a proposed major emitting facility may cause or contribute to a change in the air quality in such area and identifying the potential adverse impact of such change, a permit shall not be issued unless the owner or operator of such facility demonstrates that emissions of particulate matter and sulfur dioxide will not cause or contribute to concentrations which exceed the maximum allowable increases for a class I area.

(ii) In any case where the Federal Land Manager demonstrates to the satisfaction of the State that the emissions from such facility will have an adverse impact on the air quality-related values (including visibility) of such lands, notwithstanding the fact that the change in air quality resulting from emissions from such facility will not cause or contribute to concentrations which exceed the maximum allowable increases for a class I area, a permit shall not be issued.

(iii) In any case where the owner or operator of such facility demonstrates to the satisfaction of the Federal Land Manager, and the Federal Land Manager so certifies, that the emissions from such facility will have no adverse impact on the air quality-related values of such lands (including visibility), notwithstanding the fact that the change in air quality resulting from emissions from such facility will cause or contribute to concentrations which exceed the maximum allowable increases for class I areas, the State may issue a permit.

(iv) In the case of a permit issued pursuant to clause (iii), such facility shall comply with such emission limitations under such permit as may be necessary to assure that emissions of sulfur oxides and particulates from such facility will not cause or contribute to concentrations of such pollutant which exceed the following maximum allowable increases over the baseline concentration for such pollutants:

	Maximum allowable increase (in micrograms per cubic meter)
Particulate matter:	
Annual geometric mean	19
Twenty-four-hour maximum	37
Sulfur dioxide:	
Annual arithmetic mean	20
Twenty-four-hour maximum	91
Three-hour maximum	325

(D) (i) In any case where the owner or operator of a proposed major emitting facility who has been denied a certification under subparagraph (C)(iii) demonstrates to the satisfaction of the Governor, after notice and public hearing, and the Governor finds, that the facility cannot be constructed by reason of any maximum allowable increase for sulfur dioxide for periods of twenty-four hours or less applicable to any class I area and, in the case of Federal mandatory class I areas, that a variance under this clause will not adversely affect the air quality related values of the area (including visibility), the Governor, after consideration of the Federal Land Manager's recommendation (if any) and subject to his concurrence, may grant a variance from such maximum allowable increase. If such variance is granted, a permit may be issued to such source pursuant to the requirements of this subparagraph.

(ii) In any case in which the Governor recommends a variance under this subparagraph in which the Federal Land Manager does not concur, the recommendations of the Governor and the Federal Land Manager shall be transmitted to the President. The President may approve the Governor's recommendation if he finds that such variance is in the national interest. No Presidential finding shall be reviewable in any court. The variance shall take effect if the President approves the Governor's recommendations. The President shall approve or disapprove such recommendation within ninety days after his receipt of the recommendations of the Governor and the Federal Land Manager.

(iii) In the case of a permit issued pursuant to this subparagraph, such facility shall comply with such emission limitations under such permit as may be necessary to assure that emissions of sulfur oxides from such facility will not (during any day on which the otherwise applicable maximum allowable increases are exceeded) cause or contribute to concentrations which exceed the following maximum allowable increases for such areas over the baseline concentration for such pollutant and to assure that such emissions will not cause or contribute to concentrations which exceed the otherwise applicable maximum allowable increases for periods of exposure of 24 hours or less on more than 18 days during any annual period:

MAXIMUM ALLOWABLE INCREASE
[In micrograms per cubic meter]

Period of exposure	Low terrain areas	High terrain areas
24-hr maximum	36	62
3-hr maximum	130	221

(iv) For purposes of clause (iii), the term "high terrain area" means with respect to any facility, any area having an elevation of 900 feet or more above the base of the stack of such facility, and the term "low terrain area" means any area other than a high terrain area.

(e) Analysis; continuous air quality monitoring data; regulations; model adjustments

(1) The review provided for in subsection (a) of this section shall be preceded by an analysis in accordance with regulations of the Administrator, promulgated under this subsection, which may be conducted by the State (or any general purpose unit of local government) or by the major emitting facility applying for such permit, of the ambient air quality at the proposed site and in areas which may be affected by emissions from such facility for each pollutant subject to regulation under this chapter which will be emitted from such facility.

(2) Effective one year after August 7, 1977, the analysis required by this subsection shall include continuous air quality monitoring data gathered for purposes of determining whether emissions from such facility will exceed the maximum allowable increases or the maximum allowable concentration permitted under this part. Such data shall be gathered over a period of one calendar year preceding the date of application for a permit under this part unless the State, in accordance with regulations promulgated by the Administrator, determines that a complete and adequate analysis for such purposes may be accomplished in a shorter period. The results of such analysis shall be available at the time of the public hearing on the application for such permit.

(3) The Administrator shall within six months after August 7, 1977, promulgate regulations respecting the analysis required under this subsection which regulations—

(A) shall not require the use of any automatic or uniform buffer zone or zones,

(B) shall require an analysis of the ambient air quality, climate and meteorology, terrain, soils and vegetation, and visibility at the site of the proposed major emitting facility and in the area potentially affected by the emissions from such facility for each pollutant regulated under this chapter which will be emitted from, or which results from the construction or operation of, such facility, the size and nature of the proposed facility, the degree of continuous emission reduction which could be achieved by such facility, and such other factors as may be relevant in determining the effect of emissions from a proposed facility on any air quality control region,

(C) shall require the results of such analysis shall be available at the time of the public hearing on the application for such permit, and

(D) shall specify with reasonable particularity each air quality model or models to be used under specified sets of conditions for purposes of this part.

Any model or models designated under such regulations may be adjusted upon a determination, after notice and opportunity for public hearing, by the Administrator that such adjustment is necessary to take into account unique terrain or meteorological characteristics of an area potentially affected by emissions from a source applying for a permit required under this part.

(July 14, 1955, c. 360, Title I, § 165, as added by Pub. L. No. 95–95, Title I, § 127(a), 91 Stat. 735 (Aug. 7, 1977); and amended by Pub. L. No. 95–190, § 14(a)(44)–(51), 91 Stat. 1402 (Nov. 16, 1977).)

HISTORICAL AND STATUTORY NOTES

Effective and Applicability Provisions

1977 Acts. Section effective Aug. 7, 1977, except as otherwise expressly provided, see section 406(d) of Pub. L. No. 95–95, set out as a note under section 7401 of this title.

§ 7476. Other pollutants

[CAA § 166]

(a) Hydrocarbons, carbon monoxide, photochemical oxidants, and nitrogen oxides

In the case of the pollutants hydrocarbons, carbon monoxide, photochemical oxidants, and nitrogen oxides, the Administrator shall conduct a study and not later than two years after August 7, 1977, promulgate regulations to prevent the significant deterioration of air quality which would result from the emissions of such pollutants. In the case of pollutants for which national ambient air quality standards are promulgated after August 7, 1977, he shall promulgate such regulations not more than 2 years after the date of promulgation of such standards.

(b) Effective date of regulations

Regulations referred to in subsection (a) of this section shall become effective one year after the date of promulgation. Within 21 months after such date of promulgation such plan revision shall be submitted to the Administrator who shall approve or disapprove the plan within 25 months after such date or promulgation in the same manner as required under section 7410 of this title.

(c) Contents of regulations

Such regulations shall provide specific numerical measures against which permit applications may be evaluated, a framework for stimulating improved control technology, protection of air quality values, and fulfill the goals and purposes set forth in section 7401 and section 7470 of this title.

(d) Specific measures to fulfill goals and purposes

The regulations of the Administrator under subsection (a) of this section shall provide specific measures at least as effective as the increments established in section 7473 of this title to fulfill such goals and purposes, and may contain air quality increments, emission density requirements, or other measures.

(e) Area classification plan not required

With respect to any air pollutant for which a national ambient air quality standard is established other than sulfur oxides or particulate matter, an area classification plan shall not be required under this section if the implementation plan adopted by the State and submitted for the Administrator's approval or promulgated by the Administrator under section 7410(c) of this title contains other provisions which when considered as a whole, the Administrator finds will carry out the purposes in section 7470 of this title at least as effectively as an area classification plan for such pollutant. Such other provisions referred to in the preceding sentence need not require the establishment of maximum allowable increases with respect to such pollutant for any area to which this section applies.

(f) PM-10 increments

The Administrator is authorized to substitute, for the maximum allowable increases in particulate matter specified in section 7473(b) of this title and section 7475(d)(2)(C)(iv) of this title, maximum allowable increases in particulate matter with an aerodynamic diameter smaller than or equal to 10 micrometers. Such substituted maximum allowable increases shall be of equal stringency in effect as those specified in the provisions for which they are substituted. Until the Administrator promulgates regulations under the authority of this subsection, the current maximum allowable increases in concentrations of particulate matter shall remain in effect.

(July 14, 1955, c. 360, Title I, § 166, as added by Pub. L. No. 95–95, Title I, § 127(a), 91 Stat. 739 (Aug. 7, 1977); and amended by Pub. L. No. 101–549, Title I, § 105(b), 104 Stat. 2462 (Nov. 15, 1990).)

HISTORICAL AND STATUTORY NOTES

Effective and Applicability Provisions

1990 Acts. Amendment by Pub. L. No. 101–549 effective Nov. 15, 1990, except as otherwise provided, see section 711(b) of Pub. L. No. 101–549, set out as a note under section 7401 of this title.

1977 Acts. Section effective Aug. 7, 1977, except as otherwise expressly provided, see section 406(d) of Pub. L. No. 95–95, set out as a note under section 7401 of this title.

Savings Provisions

Suits, actions or proceedings commenced under this chapter as in effect prior to Nov. 15, 1990, not to abate by reason of the taking effect of amendments by Pub. L. No. 101–549, except as otherwise provided for, see section 711(a) of Pub. L. No. 101–549, set out as a note under section 7401 of this title.

§ 7477. Enforcement

[CAA § 167]

The Administrator shall, and a State may, take such measures, including issuance of an order, or seeking injunctive relief, as necessary to prevent the construction or modification of a major emitting facility which does not conform to the requirements of this part, or which is proposed to be constructed in any area designated pursuant to section 7407(d) of this title as attainment or unclassifiable and which is not subject to an implementation plan which meets the requirements of this part.

(July 14, 1955, c. 360, Title I, § 167, as added by Pub. L. No. 95–95, Title I, § 127(a), 91 Stat. 740 (Aug. 7, 1977); and amended by Pub. L. No. 101–549, Title I, § 110(3), Title VII, § 708, 104 Stat. 2470, 2684 (Nov. 15, 1990).)

HISTORICAL AND STATUTORY NOTES

Effective and Applicability Provisions

1990 Acts. Amendment by Pub. L. No. 101–549 effective Nov. 15, 1990, except as otherwise provided, see section 711(b) of Pub. L. No. 101–549, set out as a note under section 7401 of this title.

1977 Acts. Section effective Aug. 7, 1977, except as otherwise expressly provided, see section 406(d) of Pub. L. No. 95–95, set out as a note under section 7401 of this title.

Savings Provisions

Suits, actions or proceedings commenced under this chapter as in effect prior to Nov. 15, 1990, not to abate by reason of the taking effect of amendments by Pub. L. No. 101–549, except as otherwise provided for, see section 711(a) of Pub. L. No. 101–549, set out as a note under section 7401 of this title.

§ 7478. Period before plan approval

[CAA § 168]

(a) Existing regulations to remain in effect

Until such time as an applicable implementation plan is in effect for any area, which plan meets the requirements of this part to prevent significant deterioration of air quality with respect to any air pollutant, applicable regulations under this chapter prior to August 7, 1977, shall remain in effect to prevent significant deterioration of air quality in any such area for any such pollutant except as otherwise provided in subsection (b) of this section.

(b) Regulations deemed amended; construction commenced after June 1, 1975

If any regulation in effect prior to August 7, 1977, to prevent significant deterioration of air quality would be inconsistent with the requirements of section 7472(a), section 7473(b) or section 7474(a) of this

title, then such regulations shall be deemed amended so as to conform with such requirements. In the case of a facility on which construction was commenced (in accordance with the definition of "commenced" in section 7479(2) of this title) after June 1, 1975, and prior to August 7, 1977, the review and permitting of such facility shall be in accordance with the regulations for the prevention of significant deterioration in effect prior to August 7, 1977.

(July 14, 1955, c. 360, Title I, § 168, as added by Pub. L. No. 95–95, Title I, § 127(a), 91 Stat. 740 (Aug. 7, 1977); and amended by Pub. L. No. 95–190, § 14(a)(52), 91 Stat. 1402 (Nov. 16, 1977).)

HISTORICAL AND STATUTORY NOTES

Effective and Applicability Provisions

1977 Acts. Section effective Aug. 7, 1977, except as otherwise expressly provided, see section 406(d) of Pub. L. No. 95–95, set out as a note under section 7401 of this title.

§ 7479. Definitions

[CAA § 169]

For purposes of this part—

(1) The term "major emitting facility" means any of the following stationary sources of air pollutants which emit, or have the potential to emit, one hundred tons per year or more of any air pollutant from the following types of stationary sources: fossil-fuel fired steam electric plants of more than two hundred and fifty million British thermal units per hour heat input, coal cleaning plants (thermal dryers), kraft pulp mills, Portland Cement plants, primary zinc smelters, iron and steel mill plants, primary aluminum ore reduction plants, primary copper smelters, municipal incinerators capable of charging more than fifty tons of refuse per day, hydrofluoric, sulfuric, and nitric acid plants, petroleum refineries, lime plants, phosphate rock processing plants, coke oven batteries, sulfur recovery plants, carbon black plants (furnace process), primary lead smelters, fuel conversion plants, sintering plants, secondary metal production facilities, chemical process plants, fossil-fuel boilers of more than two hundred and fifty million British thermal units per hour heat input, petroleum storage and transfer facilities with a capacity exceeding three hundred thousand barrels, taconite ore processing facilities, glass fiber processing plants, charcoal production facilities. Such term also includes any other source with the potential to emit two hundred and fifty tons per year or more of any air pollutant. This term shall not include new or modified facilities which are nonprofit health or education institutions which have been exempted by the State.

(2) **(A)** The term "commenced" as applied to construction of a major emitting facility means that the owner or operator has obtained all necessary preconstruction approvals or permits required by Federal, State, or local air pollution emissions and air quality laws or regulations and either has (i) begun, or caused to begin, a continuous program of physical on-site construction of the facility or (ii) entered into binding agreements or contractual obligations, which cannot be canceled or modified without substantial loss to the owner or operator, to undertake a program of construction of the facility to be completed within a reasonable time.

(B) The term "necessary preconstruction approvals or permits" means those permits or approvals, required by the permitting authority as a precondition to undertaking any activity under clauses (i) or (ii) of subparagraph (A) of this paragraph.

(C) The term "construction" when used in connection with any source or facility, includes the modification (as defined in section 7411(a) of this title) of any source or facility.

(3) The term "best available control technology" means an emission limitation based on the maximum degree of reduction of each pollutant subject to regulation under this chapter emitted from or which results from any major emitting facility, which the permitting authority, on a case-by-case basis, taking into account energy, environmental, and economic impacts and other costs, determines is achievable for such facility through application of production processes and available methods, systems, and techniques, including fuel cleaning, clean fuels, or treatment or innovative fuel combustion techniques for control of each such pollutant. In no event shall application of "best available control technology" result in emissions of any pollutants which will exceed the emissions allowed by any applicable standard established pursuant to section 7411 or 7412 of this title. Emissions from any source utilizing clean fuels, or any other means, to comply with this paragraph shall not be allowed to increase above levels that would have been required under this paragraph as it existed prior to November 15, 1990.

(4) The term "baseline concentration" means, with respect to a pollutant, the ambient concentration levels which exist at the time of the first application for a permit in an area subject to this part, based on air quality data available in the Environmental Protection Agency or a State air pollution control agency and on such monitoring data as the permit applicant is required to submit. Such ambient concentration levels shall take into account all projected emissions in, or which may affect, such area from any major emitting facility on which construction commenced prior to January 6, 1975, but which has not begun operation by the date of the baseline air quality concentration determination. Emissions of sulfur oxides and particulate matter from any major emitting facility on which construction commenced after January 6, 1975, shall not be included in the baseline and shall be counted against the maximum allowable increases in pollutant concentrations established under this part.

(July 14, 1955, c. 360, Title I, § 169, as added by Pub. L. No. 95–95, Title I, § 127(a), 91 Stat. 740 (Aug. 7, 1977); and amended by Pub. L. No. 95–190, § 14(a)(54), 91 Stat. 1402 (Nov. 16, 1977); Pub. L. No. 101–549, Title III, § 305(b), Title IV, § 403(d), 104 Stat. 2583, 2631 (Nov. 15, 1990).)

HISTORICAL AND STATUTORY NOTES

Effective and Applicability Provisions

1990 Acts. Amendment by Pub. L. No. 101–549 effective Nov. 15, 1990, except as otherwise provided, see section 711(b) of Pub. L. No. 101–549, set out as a note under section 7401 of this title.

1977 Acts. Section effective Aug. 7, 1977, except as otherwise expressly provided, see section 406(d) of Pub. L. No. 95–95, set out as a note under section 7401 of this title.

Savings Provisions

Suits, actions or proceedings commenced under this chapter as in effect prior to Nov. 15, 1990, not to abate by reason of the taking effect of amendments by Pub. L. No. 101–549, except as otherwise provided for, see section 711(a) of Pub. L. No. 101–549, set out as a note under section 7401 of this title.

Study of Major Emitting Facilities With Potential of Emitting 250 Tons Per Year

Section 127(b) of Pub. L. No. 95–95 provided that within 1 year after Aug. 7, 1977, the Administrator report to the Congress on the consequences of that portion of the definition of "major emitting facility" under this subpart which applies to facilities with the potential to emit 250 hundred tons per year or more.

Subpart II—Visibility Protection

HISTORICAL AND STATUTORY NOTES

Codifications

As originally enacted, subpart II of part C of subchapter I of this chapter was added following section 7478 of this title. Pub. L. No. 95–190, § 14(a)(53), 91 Stat. 1402 (Nov. 16, 1977), struck out subpart II and inserted such subpart following section 7479 of this title.

§ 7491. Visibility protection for Federal class I areas

[CAA § 169A]

(a) Impairment of visibility; list of areas; study and report

(1) Congress hereby declares as a national goal the prevention of any future, and the remedying of any existing, impairment of visibility in mandatory class I Federal areas which impairment results from manmade air pollution.

(2) Not later than six months after August 7, 1977, the Secretary of the Interior in consultation with other Federal land managers shall review all mandatory class I Federal areas and identify those where visibility is an important value of the area. from time to time the Secretary of the Interior may revise such identifications. Not later than one year after August 7, 1977, the Administrator shall, after consultation with the Secretary of the Interior, promulgate a list of mandatory class I Federal areas in which he determines visibility is an important value.

(3) Not later than eighteen months after August 7, 1977, the Administrator shall complete a study and report to Congress on available methods for implementing the national goal set forth in paragraph (1). Such report shall include recommendations for—

(A) methods for identifying, characterizing, determining, quantifying, and measuring visibility impairment in Federal areas referred to in paragraph (1), and

(B) modeling techniques (or other methods) for determining the extent to which manmade air pollution may reasonably be anticipated to cause or contribute to such impairment, and

(C) methods for preventing and remedying such manmade air pollution and resulting visibility impairment.

Such report shall also identify the classes or categories of sources and the types of air pollutants which, alone or in conjunction with other sources or pollutants, may reasonably be anticipated to cause or contribute significantly to impairment of visibility.

(4) Not later than twenty-four months after August 7, 1977, and after notice and public hearing, the Administrator shall promulgate regulations to assure (A) reasonable progress toward meeting the national goal specified in paragraph (1), and (B) compliance with the requirements of this section.

(b) Regulations

Regulations under subsection (a)(4) of this section shall—

(1) provide guidelines to the States, taking into account the recommendations under subsection (a)(3) of this section on appropriate techniques and methods for implementing this section (as provided in subparagraphs (A) through (C) of such subsection (a)(3)), and

(2) require each applicable implementation plan for a State in which any area listed by the Administrator under subsection (a)(2) of this section is located (or for a State the emissions from which may reasonably be anticipated to cause or contribute to any impairment of visibility in any such area) to contain such emission limits, schedules of compliance and other measures as may be necessary to make reasonable progress toward meeting the national goal specified in subsection (a) of this section, including—

(A) except as otherwise provided pursuant to subsection (c) of this section, a requirement that each major stationary source which is in existence on August 7, 1977, but which has not been in operation for more than fifteen years as of such date, and which, as determined by the State (or the Administrator in the case of a plan promulgated under section 7410(c) of this title) emits any air pollutant which may reasonably be anticipated to cause or contribute to any impairment of visibility in any such area, shall procure, install, and operate, as expeditiously as practicable (and maintain thereafter) the best available retrofit technology, as determined by the State (or the Administrator in the case of a plan promulgated under section 7410(c) of this title) for controlling emissions from such source for the purpose of eliminating or reducing any such impairment, and

(B) a long-term (ten to fifteen years) strategy for making reasonable progress toward meeting the national goal specified in subsection (a) of this section.

In the case of a fossil-fuel fired generating powerplant having a total generating capacity in excess of 750 megawatts, the emission limitations required under this paragraph shall be determined pursuant to guidelines, promulgated by the Administrator under paragraph (1).

(c) Exemptions

(1) The Administrator may, by rule, after notice and opportunity for public hearing, exempt any major stationary source from the requirement of subsection (b)(2)(A) of this section, upon his determination that such source does not or will not, by itself or in combination with other sources, emit any air pollutant which may reasonably be anticipated to cause or contribute to a significant impairment of visibility in any mandatory class I Federal area.

(2) Paragraph (1) of this subsection shall not be applicable to any fossil-fuel fired powerplant with total design capacity of 750 megawatts or more, unless the owner or operator of any such plant demonstrates to the satisfaction of the Administrator that such powerplant is located at such distance from all areas listed by the Administrator under subsection (a)(2) of this section that such powerplant does not or will not, by itself or in combination with other sources, emit any air pollutant which may reasonably be anticipated to cause or contribute to significant impairment of visibility in any such area.

(3) An exemption under this subsection shall be effective only upon concurrence by the appropriate Federal land manager or managers with the Administrator's determination under this subsection.

(d) Consultations with appropriate Federal land managers

Before holding the public hearing on the proposed revision of an applicable implementation plan to meet the requirements of this section, the State (or the Administrator, in the case of a plan promulgated under section 7410(c) of this title) shall consult in person with the appropriate Federal land manager or managers and shall include a summary of the conclusions and recommendations of the Federal land managers in the notice to the public.

(e) Buffer zones

In promulgating regulations under this section, the Administrator shall not require the use of any automatic or uniform buffer zone or zones.

(f) Nondiscretionary duty

For purposes of section 7604(a)(2) of this title, the meeting of the national goal specified in subsection (a)(1) of this section by any specific date or dates shall not be considered a "nondiscretionary duty" of the Administrator.

(g) Definitions

For the purpose of this section—

(1) in determining reasonable progress there shall be taken into consideration the costs of compliance, the time necessary for compliance, and the energy and nonair quality environmental impacts of compliance, and the remaining useful life of any existing source subject to such requirements;

(2) in determining best available retrofit technology the State (or the Administrator in determining emission limitations which reflect such technology) shall take into consideration the costs of compliance, the energy and nonair quality environmental impacts of compliance, any existing pollution control technology in use at the source, the remaining useful life of the source, and the degree of improvement in visibility which may reasonably be anticipated to result from the use of such technology;

(3) the term "manmade air pollution" means air pollution which results directly or indirectly from human activities;

(4) the term "as expeditiously as practicable" means as expeditiously as practicable but in no event later than five years after the date of approval of a plan revision under this section (or the date of promulgation of such a plan revision in the case of action by the Administrator under section 7410(c) of this title for purposes of this section);

(5) the term "mandatory class I Federal areas" means Federal areas which may not be designated as other than class I under this part;

(6) the terms "visibility impairment" and "impairment of visibility" shall include reduction in visual range and atmospheric discoloration; and

(7) the term "major stationary source" means the following types of stationary sources with the potential to emit 250 tons or more of any pollutant: fossil-fuel fired steam electric plants of more than

250 million British thermal units per hour heat input, coal cleaning plants (thermal dryers), kraft pulp mills, Portland Cement plants, primary zinc smelters, iron and steel mill plants, primary aluminum ore reduction plants, primary copper smelters, municipal incinerators capable of charging more than 250 tons of refuse per day, hydrofluoric, sulfuric, and nitric acid plants, petroleum refineries, lime plants, phosphate rock processing plants, coke oven batteries, sulfur recovery plants, carbon black plants (furnace process), primary lead smelters, fuel conversion plants, sintering plants, secondary metal production facilities, chemical process plants, fossil-fuel boilers of more than 250 million British thermal units per hour heat input, petroleum storage and transfer facilities with a capacity exceeding 300,000 barrels, taconite ore processing facilities, glass fiber processing plants, charcoal production facilities.

(July 14, 1955, c. 360, Title I, § 169A, as added by Pub. L. No. 95–95, Title I, § 128, 91 Stat. 742 (Aug. 7, 1977).)

HISTORICAL AND STATUTORY NOTES

Effective and Applicability Provisions

1977 Acts. Section effective Aug. 7, 1977, except as otherwise expressly provided, see section 406(d) of Pub. L. No. 95–95, set out as a note under section 7401 of this title.

§ 7492. Visibility

[CAA § 169B]

(a) Studies

(1) The Administrator, in conjunction with the National Park Service and other appropriate Federal agencies, shall conduct research to identify and evaluate sources and source regions of both visibility impairment and regions that provide predominantly clean air in class I areas. A total of $8,000,000 per year for 5 years is authorized to be appropriated for the Environmental Protection Agency and the other Federal agencies to conduct this research. The research shall include—

(A) expansion of current visibility related monitoring in class I areas;

(B) assessment of current sources of visibility impairing pollution and clean air corridors;

(C) adaptation of regional air quality models for the assessment of visibility;

(D) studies of atmospheric chemistry and physics of visibility.

(2) Based on the findings available from the research required in subsection (a)(1) of this section as well as other available scientific and technical data, studies, and other available information pertaining to visibility source-receptor relationships, the Administrator shall conduct an assessment and evaluation that identifies, to the extent possible, sources and source regions of visibility impairment including natural sources as well as source regions of clear air for class I areas. The Administrator shall produce interim findings from this study within 3 years after November 15, 1990.

(b) Impacts of other provisions

Within 24 months after November 15, 1990, the Administrator shall conduct an assessment of the progress and improvements in visibility in class I areas that are likely to result from the implementation of the provisions of the Clean Air Act Amendments of 1990 other than the provisions of this section. Every 5 years thereafter the Administrator shall conduct an assessment of actual progress and improvement in visibility in class I areas. The Administrator shall prepare a written report on each assessment and transmit copies of these reports to the appropriate committees of Congress.

(c) Establishment of visibility transport regions and commissions

(1) Authority to establish visibility transport regions

Whenever, upon the Administrator's motion or by petition from the Governors of at least two affected States, the Administrator has reason to believe that the current or projected interstate transport of air pollutants from one or more States contributes significantly to visibility impairment in class I areas located in the affected States, the Administrator may establish a transport region for such pollutants that includes such States. The Administrator, upon the Administrator's own motion or upon petition from the Governor of any affected State, or upon the recommendations of a transport commission established under subsection (b) of this section[1] may—

(A) add any State or portion of a State to a visibility transport region when the Administrator determines that the interstate transport of air pollutants from such State significantly contributes to visibility impairment in a class I area located within the transport region, or

(B) remove any State or portion of a State from the region whenever the Administrator has reason to believe that the control of emissions in that State or portion of the State pursuant to this section will not significantly contribute to the protection or enhancement of visibility in any class I area in the region.

(2) Visibility transport commissions

Whenever the Administrator establishes a transport region under subsection (c)(1) of this section, the Administrator shall establish a transport commission comprised of (as a minimum) each of the following members:

(A) the Governor of each State in the Visibility Transport Region, or the Governor's designee;

(B) The[2] Administrator or the Administrator's designee; and

(C) A[2] representative of each Federal agency charged with the direct management of each class I area or areas within the Visibility Transport Region.

(3) Ex officio members

All representatives of the Federal Government shall be ex officio members.

(4) Federal Advisory Committee Act

The visibility transport commissions shall be exempt from the requirements of the Federal Advisory Committee Act [5 U.S.C.A. App.].

(d) Duties of visibility transport commissions

A Visibility Transport Commission—

(1) shall assess the scientific and technical data, studies, and other currently available information, including studies conducted pursuant to subsection (a)(1) of this section, pertaining to adverse impacts on visibility from potential or projected growth in emissions from sources located in the Visibility Transport Region; and

(2) shall, within 4 years of establishment, issue a report to the Administrator recommending what measures, if any, should be taken under this chapter to remedy such adverse impacts. The report required by this subsection shall address at least the following measures:

(A) the establishment of clean air corridors, in which additional restrictions on increases in emissions may be appropriate to protect visibility in affected class I areas;

(B) the imposition of the requirements of part D of this subchapter affecting the construction of new major stationary sources or major modifications to existing sources in such clean air corridors specifically including the alternative siting analysis provisions of section 7503(a)(5) of this title; and

(C) the promulgation of regulations under section 7491 of this title to address long range strategies for addressing regional haze which impairs visibility in affected class I areas.

(e) Duties of Administrator

(1) The Administrator shall, taking into account the studies pursuant to subsection (a)(1) of this section and the reports pursuant to subsection (d)(2) of this section and any other relevant information, within eighteen months of receipt of the report referred to in subsection (d)(2) of this section, carry out the Administrator's regulatory responsibilities under section 7491 of this title, including criteria for measuring "reasonable progress" toward the national goal.

(2) Any regulations promulgated under section 7491 of this title pursuant to this subsection shall require affected States to revise within 12 months their implementation plans under section 7410 of this title to contain such emission limits, schedules of compliance, and other measures as may be necessary to carry out regulations promulgated pursuant to this subsection.

(f) Grand Canyon visibility transport commission

The Administrator pursuant to subsection (c)(1) of this section shall, within 12 months, establish a visibility transport commission for the region affecting the visibility of the Grand Canyon National Park.

(July 14, 1955, c. 360, Title I, § 169B, as added by Pub. L. No. 101–549, Title VIII, § 816, 104 Stat. 2695 (Nov. 15, 1990).)

[1] So in original. Words "subsection (b) of this section" probably should be "paragraph (2)."

[2] So in original. Probably should not be capitalized.

HISTORICAL AND STATUTORY NOTES

References in Text

The Clean Air Act Amendments of 1990, referred to in subsec. (b), probably means Pub. L. No. 101–549, 104 Stat. 2399 (Nov. 15, 1990). For complete classification of this Act to the Code, see Short Title of 1990 Amendments note set out under section 7401 of this title and Tables.

The Federal Advisory Committee Act, referred to in subsec. (c)(4), is Pub. L. No. 92–463, 86 Stat. 770 (Oct. 6, 1972), as amended, which is set out in Appendix 2 to Title 5, Government Organization and Employees.

Effective and Applicability Provisions

1990 Acts. Section to take effect Nov. 15, 1990, except as otherwise provided, see section 711(b) of Pub. L. No. 101–549, set out as a note under section 7401 of this title.

Savings Provisions

Suits, actions or proceedings commenced under this chapter as in effect prior to Nov. 15, 1990, not to abate by reason of the taking effect of amendments by Pub. L. No. 101–549, except as otherwise provided for, see section 711(a) of Pub. L. No. 101–549, set out as a note under section 7401 of this title.

PART D—PLAN REQUIREMENTS FOR NONATTAINMENT AREAS

Subpart 1—Nonattainment Areas in General

§ 7501. Definitions

[CAA § 171]

For the purpose of this part—

(1) Reasonable further progress

The term "reasonable further progress" means such annual incremental reductions in emissions of the relevant air pollutant as are required by this part or may reasonably be required by the Administrator for the purpose of ensuring attainment of the applicable national ambient air quality standard by the applicable date.

(2) Nonattainment area

The term "nonattainment area" means, for any air pollutant, an area which is designated "nonattainment" with respect to that pollutant within the meaning of section 7407(d) of this title.

(3) The term "lowest achievable emission rate" means for any source, that rate of emissions which reflects—

(A) the most stringent emission limitation which is contained in the implementation plan of any State for such class or category of source, unless the owner or operator of the proposed source demonstrates that such limitations are not achievable, or

(B) the most stringent emission limitation which is achieved in practice by such class or category of source, whichever is more stringent.

In no event shall the application of this term permit a proposed new or modified source to emit any pollutant in excess of the amount allowable under applicable new source standards of performance.

(4) The terms "modifications" and "modified" mean the same as the term "modification" as used in section 7411(a)(4) of this title.

(July 14, 1955, c. 360, Title I, § 171, as added by Pub. L. No. 95–95, Title I, § 129(b), 91 Stat. 746 (Aug. 7, 1977); and amended by Pub. L. No. 101–549, Title I, § 102(a)(2), 104 Stat. 2412 (Nov. 15, 1990).)

HISTORICAL AND STATUTORY NOTES

Effective and Applicability Provisions

1990 Acts. Amendment by Pub. L. No. 101–549 effective Nov. 15, 1990, except as otherwise provided, see section 711(b) of Pub. L. No. 101–549, set out as a note under section 7401 of this title.

1977 Acts. Section effective Aug. 7, 1977, except as otherwise expressly provided, see section 406(d) of Pub. L. No. 95–95, set out as a note under section 7401 of this title.

Savings Provisions

Suits, actions or proceedings commenced under this chapter as in effect prior to Nov. 15, 1990, not to abate by reason of the taking effect of amendments by Pub. L. No. 101–549, except as otherwise provided for, see section 711(a) of Pub. L. No. 101–549, set out as a note under section 7401 of this title.

§ 7502. Nonattainment plan provisions in general [CAA § 172]

(a) Classifications and attainment dates

(1) Classifications

(A) On or after the date the Administrator promulgates the designation of an area as a nonattainment area pursuant to section 7407(d) of this title with respect to any national ambient air quality standard (or any revised standard, including a revision of any standard in effect on November 15, 1990), the Administrator may classify the area for the purpose of applying an attainment date pursuant to paragraph (2), and for other purposes. In determining the appropriate classification, if any, for a nonattainment area, the Administrator may consider such factors as the severity of nonattainment in such area and the availability and feasibility of the pollution control measures that the Administrator believes may be necessary to provide for attainment of such standard in such area.

(B) The Administrator shall publish a notice in the Federal Register announcing each classification under subparagraph (A), except the Administrator shall provide an opportunity for at least 30 days for written comment. Such classification shall not be subject to the provisions of sections 553 through 557 of Title 5 (concerning notice and comment) and shall not be subject to judicial review until the Administrator takes final action under subsection (k) or (*l*) of section 7410 of this title (concerning action on plan submissions) or section 7509 of this title (concerning sanctions) with respect to any plan submissions required by virtue of such classification.

(C) This paragraph shall not apply with respect to nonattainment areas for which classifications are specifically provided under other provisions of this part.

(2) Attainment dates for nonattainment areas

(A) The attainment date for an area designated nonattainment with respect to a national primary ambient air quality standard shall be the date by which attainment can be achieved as expeditiously as practicable, but no later than 5 years from the date such area was designated nonattainment under section 7407(d) of this title, except that the Administrator may extend the attainment date to the extent the Administrator determines appropriate, for a period no greater than 10 years from the date of designation as nonattainment, considering the severity of nonattainment and the availability and feasibility of pollution control measures.

(B) The attainment date for an area designated nonattainment with respect to a secondary national ambient air quality standard shall be the date by which attainment can be achieved as expeditiously as practicable after the date such area was designated nonattainment under section 7407(d) of this title.

(C) Upon application by any State, the Administrator may extend for 1 additional year (hereinafter referred to as the "Extension Year") the attainment date determined by the Administrator under subparagraph (A) or (B) if—

(i) the State has complied with all requirements and commitments pertaining to the area in the applicable implementation plan, and

(ii) in accordance with guidance published by the Administrator, no more than a minimal number of exceedances of the relevant national ambient air quality standard has occurred in the area in the year preceding the Extension Year.

No more than 2 one-year extensions may be issued under this subparagraph for a single nonattainment area.

(D) This paragraph shall not apply with respect to nonattainment areas for which attainment dates are specifically provided under other provisions of this part.

(b) Schedule for plan submissions

At the time the Administrator promulgates the designation of an area as nonattainment with respect to a national ambient air quality standard under section 7407(d) of this title, the Administrator shall establish a schedule according to which the State containing such area shall submit a plan or plan revision (including the plan items) meeting the applicable requirements of subsection (c) of this section and section 7410(a)(2) of this title. Such schedule shall at a minimum, include a date or dates, extending no later than 3 years from the date of the nonattainment designation, for the submission of a plan or plan revision (including the plan items) meeting the applicable requirements of subsection (c) of this section and section 7410(a)(2) of this title.

(c) Nonattainment plan provisions

The plan provisions (including plan items) required to be submitted under this part shall comply with each of the following:

(1) In general

Such plan provisions shall provide for the implementation of all reasonably available control measures as expeditiously as practicable (including such reductions in emissions from existing sources in the area as may be obtained through the adoption, at a minimum, of reasonably available control technology) and shall provide for attainment of the national primary ambient air quality standards.

(2) RFP

Such plan provisions shall require reasonable further progress.

(3) Inventory

Such plan provisions shall include a comprehensive, accurate, current inventory of actual emissions from all sources of the relevant pollutant or pollutants in such area, including such periodic revisions as the Administrator may determine necessary to assure that the requirements of this part are met.

(4) Identification and quantification

Such plan provisions shall expressly identify and quantify the emissions, if any, of any such pollutant or pollutants which will be allowed, in accordance with section 7503(a)(1)(B) of this title, from the construction and operation of major new or modified stationary sources in each such area. The plan shall demonstrate to the satisfaction of the Administrator that the emissions quantified for this purpose will be consistent with the achievement of reasonable further progress and will not interfere with attainment of the applicable national ambient air quality standard by the applicable attainment date.

(5) Permits for new and modified major stationary sources

Such plan provisions shall require permits for the construction and operation of new or modified major stationary sources anywhere in the nonattainment area, in accordance with section 7503 of this title.

(6) Other measures

Such plan provisions shall include enforceable emission limitations, and such other control measures, means or techniques (including economic incentives such as fees, marketable permits, and auctions of emission rights), as well as schedules and timetables for compliance, as may be necessary or appropriate to provide for attainment of such standard in such area by the applicable attainment date specified in this part.

(7) Compliance with section 7410(a)(2)

Such plan provisions shall also meet the applicable provisions of section 7410(a)(2) of this title.

(8) Equivalent techniques

Upon application by any State, the Administrator may allow the use of equivalent modeling, emission inventory, and planning procedures, unless the Administrator determines that the proposed techniques are, in the aggregate, less effective than the methods specified by the Administrator.

(9) Contingency measures

Such plan shall provide for the implementation of specific measures to be undertaken if the area fails to make reasonable further progress, or to attain the national primary ambient air quality standard by the attainment date applicable under this part. Such measures shall be included in the plan revision as contingency measures to take effect in any such case without further action by the State or the Administrator.

(d) Plan revisions required in response to finding of plan inadequacy

Any plan revision for a nonattainment area which is required to be submitted in response to a finding by the Administrator pursuant to section 7410(k)(5) of this title (relating to calls for plan revisions) must correct the plan deficiency (or deficiencies) specified by the Administrator and meet all other applicable plan requirements of section 7410 of this title and this part. The Administrator may reasonably adjust the dates otherwise applicable under such requirements to such revision (except for attainment dates that have not yet elapsed), to the extent necessary to achieve a consistent application of such requirements. In order to facilitate submittal by the States of adequate and approvable plans consistent with the applicable requirements of this chapter, the Administrator shall, as appropriate and from time to time, issue written guidelines, interpretations, and information to the States which shall be available to the public, taking into consideration any such guidelines, interpretations, or information provided before November 15, 1990.

(e) Future modification of standard

If the Administrator relaxes a national primary ambient air quality standard after November 15, 1990, the Administrator shall, within 12 months after the relaxation, promulgate requirements applicable to all areas which have not attained that standard as of the date of such relaxation. Such requirements shall provide for controls which are not less stringent than the controls applicable to areas designated nonattainment before such relaxation.

(July 14, 1955, c. 360, Title I, § 172, as added by Pub. L. No. 95–95, Title I, § 129(b), 91 Stat. 746 (Aug. 7, 1977); and amended by Pub. L. No. 95–190, § 14(a)(55), (56), 91 Stat. 1402 (Nov. 16, 1977); Pub. L. No. 101–549, Title I, § 102(b), 104 Stat. 2412 (Nov. 15, 1990).)

HISTORICAL AND STATUTORY NOTES

Effective and Applicability Provisions

1990 Acts. Amendment by Pub. L. No. 101–549 effective Nov. 15, 1990, except as otherwise provided, see section 711(b) of Pub. L. No. 101–549, set out as a note under section 7401 of this title.

1977 Acts. Section effective Aug. 7, 1977, except as otherwise expressly provided, see section 406(d) of Pub. L. No. 95–95, set out as a note under section 7401 of this title.

Savings Provisions

Suits, actions or proceedings commenced under this chapter as in effect prior to Nov. 15, 1990, not to abate by reason of the taking effect of amendments by Pub. L. No. 101–549, except as otherwise provided for, see section 711(a) of Pub. L. No. 101–549, set out as a note under section 7401 of this title.

Nonattainment Areas

Section 129(a) of Pub. L. No. 95–95, as amended by Pub. L. No. 95–190, § 14(b)(2), (3), 91 Stat. 1404 (Nov. 16, 1977), provided that:

"(1) Before July 1, 1979, the interpretative regulation of the Administrator of the Environmental Protection Agency published in 41 Federal Register 55524–30, December 21, 1976, as may be modified by rule of the Administrator, shall apply except that the baseline to be used for determination of appropriate emission offsets under such regulation shall be the applicable implementation plan of the State in effect at the time of application for a permit by a proposed major stationary source (within the meaning of section 302 of the Clean Air Act) [section 7602 of this title].

"(2) Before July 1, 1979, the requirements of the regulation referred to in paragraph (1) shall be waived by the Administrator with respect to any pollutant if he determines that the State has—

"(A) an inventory of emissions of the applicable pollutant for each nonattainment area (as defined in section 171 of the Clean Air Act) [section 7501 of this title] that identifies the type, quantity, and source of such pollutant so as to provide information sufficient to demonstrate that the requirements of subparagraph (C) are being met;

"(B) an enforceable permit program which—

"(i) requires new or modified major stationary sources to meet emission limitations at least as stringent as required under the permit requirements referred to in paragraphs (2) and (3) of section 173 of the Clean Air Act [section 7503 of this title] (relating to lowest achievable emission rate and compliance by other sources) and which assures compliance with the annual reduction requirements of subparagraph (C); and

"(ii) requires existing sources to achieve such reduction in emissions in the area as may be obtained through the adoption, at a minimum of reasonably available control technology, and

"(C) a program which requires reductions in total allowable emissions in the area prior to July 1, 1979, so as to provide for the same level of emission reduction as would result from the application of the regulation referred to in paragraph (1).

"The Administrator shall terminate such waiver if in his judgment the reduction in emissions actually being attained is less than the reduction on which the waiver was conditioned pursuant to subparagraph (C), or if the Administrator determines that the State is no longer in compliance with any requirement of this paragraph. Upon application by the State, the Administrator may reinstate a waiver terminated under the preceding sentence if he is satisfied that such State is in compliance with all requirements of this subsection.

"(3) Operating permits may be issued to those applicants who were properly granted construction permits, in accordance with the law and applicable regulations in effect at the time granted, for construction of a new or modified source in areas exceeding national primary air quality standards on or before the date of the enactment of this Act [Aug. 7, 1977] if such construction permits were granted prior to the date of the enactment of this Act and the person issued any such permit is able to demonstrate that the emissions from the source will be within the limitations set forth in such construction permit."

State Implementation Plan Revision

Section 129(c) of Pub. L. No. 95–95, as amended by Pub. L. No. 95–190, § 14(b)(4), 91 Stat. 1405 (Nov. 16, 1977), provided that: "Notwithstanding the requirements of section 406(d)(2) [set out as an Effective and Applicability

Provisions of 1977 Amendments note under section 7401 of this title] (relating to date required for submission of certain implementation plan revisions), for purposes of section 110(a)(2) of the Clean Air Act [section 7410(a)(2) of this title] each State in which there is any nonattainment area (as defined in part D of Title I of the Clean Air Act) [this part] shall adopt and submit an implementation plan revision which meets the requirements of section 110(a)(2)(I) [section 7410(a)(2)(I) of this title] and part D of Title I of the Clean Air Act [this part] not later than January 1, 1979. In the case of any State for which a plan revision adopted and submitted before such date has made the demonstration required under section 172(a)(2) of the Clean Air Act [subsec. (a)(2) of this section] (respecting impossibility of attainment before 1983), such State shall adopt and submit to the Administrator a plan revision before July 1, 1982, which meets the requirements of section 172(b) and (c) of such Act [subsecs. (b) and (c) of this section]."

§ 7503. Permit requirements

[CAA § 173]

(a) In general

The permit program required by section 7502(b)(6) of this title shall provide that permits to construct and operate may be issued if—

(1) in accordance with regulations issued by the Administrator for the determination of baseline emissions in a manner consistent with the assumptions underlying the applicable implementation plan approved under section 7410 of this title and this part, the permitting agency determines that—

(A) by the time the source is to commence operation, sufficient offsetting emissions reductions have been obtained, such that total allowable emissions from existing sources in the region, from new or modified sources which are not major emitting facilities, and from the proposed source will be sufficiently less than total emissions from existing sources (as determined in accordance with the regulations under this paragraph) prior to the application for such permit to construct or modify so as to represent (when considered together with the plan provisions required under section 7502 of this title) reasonable further progress (as defined in section 7501 of this title); or

(B) in the case of a new or modified major stationary source which is located in a zone (within the nonattainment area) identified by the Administrator, in consultation with the Secretary of Housing and Urban Development, as a zone to which economic development should be targeted, that emissions of such pollutant resulting from the proposed new or modified major stationary source will not cause or contribute to emissions levels which exceed the allowance permitted for such pollutant for such area from new or modified major stationary sources under section 7502(c) of this title;

(2) the proposed source is required to comply with the lowest achievable emission rate;

(3) the owner or operator of the proposed new or modified source has demonstrated that all major stationary sources owned or operated by such person (or by any entity controlling, controlled by, or under common control with such person) in such State are subject to emission limitations and are in compliance, or on a schedule for compliance, with all applicable emission limitations and standards under this chapter; and[1]

(4) the Administrator has not determined that the applicable implementation plan is not being adequately implemented for the nonattainment area in which the proposed source is to be constructed or modified in accordance with the requirements of this part; and

(5) an analysis of alternative sites, sizes, production processes, and environmental control techniques for such proposed source demonstrates that benefits of the proposed source significantly outweigh the environmental and social costs imposed as a result of its location, construction, or modification.

Any emission reductions required as a precondition of the issuance of a permit under paragraph (1) shall be federally enforceable before such permit may be issued.

(b) Prohibition on use of old growth allowances

Any growth allowance included in an applicable implementation plan to meet the requirements of section 7502(b)(5) of this title (as in effect immediately before November 15, 1990) shall not be valid for use in any area that received or receives a notice under section 7410(a)(2)(H)(ii) of this title (as in effect immediately before November 15, 1990) or under section 7410(k)(1) of this title that its applicable implementation plan containing such allowance is substantially inadequate.

(c) Offsets

(1) The owner or operator of a new or modified major stationary source may comply with any offset requirement in effect under this part for increased emissions of any air pollutant only by obtaining emission reductions of such air pollutant from the same source or other sources in the same nonattainment area, except that the State may allow the owner or operator of a source to obtain such emission reductions in another nonattainment area if (A) the other area has an equal or higher nonattainment classification than the area in which the source is located and (B) emissions from such other area contribute to a violation of the national ambient air quality standard in the nonattainment area in which the source is located. Such emission reductions shall be, by the time a new or modified source commences operation, in effect and enforceable and shall assure that the total tonnage of increased emissions of the air pollutant from the new or modified source shall be offset by an equal or greater reduction, as applicable, in the actual emissions of such air pollutant from the same or other sources in the area.

(2) Emission reductions otherwise required by this chapter shall not be creditable as emissions reductions for purposes of any such offset requirement. Incidental emission reductions which are not otherwise required by this chapter shall be creditable as emission reductions for such purposes if such emission reductions meet the requirements of paragraph (1).

(d) Control technology information

The State shall provide that control technology information from permits issued under this section will be promptly submitted to the Administrator for purposes of making such information available through the RACT/BACT/LAER clearinghouse to other States and to the general public.

(e) Rocket engines or motors

The permitting authority of a State shall allow a source to offset by alternative or innovative means emission increases from rocket engine and motor firing, and cleaning related to such firing, at an existing or modified major source that tests rocket engines or motors under the following conditions:

(1) Any modification proposed is solely for the purpose of expanding the testing of rocket engines or motors at an existing source that is permitted to test such engines on November 15, 1990.

(2) The source demonstrates to the satisfaction of the permitting authority of the State that it has used all reasonable means to obtain and utilize offsets, as determined on an annual basis, for the emissions increases beyond allowable levels, that all available offsets are being used, and that sufficient offsets are not available to the source.

(3) The source has obtained a written finding from the Department of Defense, Department of Transportation, National Aeronautics and Space Administration or other appropriate Federal agency, that the testing of rocket motors or engines at the facility is required for a program essential to the national security.

(4) The source will comply with an alternative measure, imposed by the permitting authority, designed to offset any emission increases beyond permitted levels not directly offset by the source. In lieu of imposing any alternative offset measures, the permitting authority may impose an emissions fee to be paid to such authority of a State which shall be an amount no greater than 1.5 times the average cost of stationary source control measures adopted in that area during the previous 3 years. The permitting authority shall utilize the fees in a manner that maximizes the emissions reductions in that area.

(July 14, 1955, c. 360, Title I, § 173, as added by Pub. L. No. 95–95, Title I, § 129(b), 91 Stat. 748 (Aug. 7, 1977); and amended by Pub. L. No. 95–190, § 14(a)(57), (58), 91 Stat. 1403 (Nov. 16, 1977); Pub. L. No. 101–549, Title I, § 102(c), 104 Stat. 2415 (Nov. 15, 1990).)

[1] So in original. The word "and" probably should not appear.

HISTORICAL AND STATUTORY NOTES

References in Text

Section 7502(b) of this title, referred to in subsec. (a), was amended generally by Pub. L. No. 101–549, Title I, § 102(b), 104 Stat. 2412 (Nov. 15, 1990), and, as so amended, does not contain a par. (6). See section 7502(c)(5) of this title.

Effective and Applicability Provisions

1990 Acts. Amendment by Pub. L. No. 101–549 effective Nov. 15, 1990, except as otherwise provided, see section 711(b) of Pub. L. No. 101–549, set out as a note under section 7401 of this title.

1977 Acts. Section effective Aug. 7, 1977, except as otherwise expressly provided, see section 406(d) of Pub. L. No. 95–95, set out as a note under section 7401 of this title.

Savings Provisions

Suits, actions or proceedings commenced under this chapter as in effect prior to Nov. 15, 1990, not to abate by reason of the taking effect of amendments by Pub. L. No. 101–549, except as otherwise provided for, see section 711(a) of Pub. L. No. 101–549, set out as a note under section 7401 of this title.

Failure to Attain National Primary Ambient Air Quality Standards Under the Clean Air Act

Pub. L. No. 100–202, § 101(f), [Title II], 101 Stat. 1329–199 (Dec. 22, 1987), provided that: "No restriction or prohibition on construction, permitting, or funding under sections 110(a)(2)(I) [section 7410(a)(2)(I) of this title], 173(4) [par. (4) of this section], 176(a) [former section 7506(a) of this title], 176(b) [former section 7506(b) of this title], or 316 [section 7616 of this title] of the Clean Air Act shall be imposed or take effect during the period prior to August 31, 1988, by reason of (1) the failure of any nonattainment area to attain the national primary ambient air quality standard under the Clean Air Act [this chapter] for photochemical oxidants (ozone) or carbon monoxide (or both) by December 31, 1987, (2) the failure of any State to adopt and submit to the Administrator of the Environmental Protection Agency an implementation plan that meets the requirements of part D of Title I of such Act [this part] and provides for attainment of such standards by December 31, 1987, (3) the failure of any State or designated local government to implement the applicable implementation plan, or (4) any combination of the foregoing. During such period and consistent with the preceding sentence, the issuance of a permit (including required offsets) under section 173 of such Act [this section] for the construction or modification of a source in a nonattainment area shall not be denied solely or partially by reason of the reference contained in section 171(*l*) of such Act [section 7501(1) of this title] to the applicable date established in section 172(a) [section 7502(a) of this title]. This subsection [probably means the first 3 sentences of this note] shall not apply to any restriction or prohibition in effect under sections 110(a)(2)(I), 173(4), 176(a), 176(b), or 316 of such Act prior to the enactment of this section [Dec. 22, 1987]. Prior to August 31, 1988, the Administrator of the Environmental Protection Agency shall evaluate air quality data and make determinations with respect to which areas throughout the nation have attained, or failed to attain, either or both of the national primary ambient air quality standards referred to in subsection (a) [probably means the first 3 sentences of this note] and shall take appropriate steps to designate those areas failing to attain either or both of such standards as nonattainment areas within the meaning of part D of Title I of the Clean Air Act."

§ 7504. Planning procedures

[CAA § 174]

(a) In general

For any ozone, carbon monoxide, or PM-10 nonattainment area, the State containing such area and elected officials of affected local governments shall, before the date required for submittal of the inventory described under sections 7511a(a)(1) and 7512a(a)(1) of this title, jointly review and update as necessary the planning procedures adopted pursuant to this subsection as in effect immediately before November 15, 1990, or develop new planning procedures pursuant to this subsection, as appropriate. In preparing such procedures the State and local elected officials shall determine which elements of a revised implementation plan will be developed, adopted, and implemented (through means including enforcement) by the State and which by local governments or regional agencies, or any combination of local governments, regional agencies, or the State. The implementation plan required by this part shall be prepared by an organization certified by the State, in consultation with elected officials of local governments and in accordance with the determination under the second sentence of this subsection. Such organization shall include elected officials of local governments in the affected area, and representatives of the State air quality planning agency, the State transportation planning agency, the metropolitan planning organization designated to conduct the continuing, cooperative and comprehensive transportation planning process for the area under section 134 of Title 23, the organization responsible for the air quality maintenance planning process under regulations implementing this chapter, and any other organization with responsibilities for developing, submitting, or implementing the plan required by this part. Such organization may be one that carried out these functions before November 15, 1990.

(b) Coordination

The preparation of implementation plan provisions and subsequent plan revisions under the continuing transportation-air quality planning process described in section 7408(e) of this title shall be coordinated with the continuing, cooperative and comprehensive transportation planning process required under section 134 of Title 23, and such planning processes shall take into account the requirements of this part.

(c) Joint planning

In the case of a nonattainment area that is included within more than one State, the affected States may jointly, through interstate compact or otherwise, undertake and implement all or part of the planning procedures described in this section.

(July 14, 1955, c. 360, Title I, § 174, as added by Pub. L. No. 95–95, Title I, § 129(b), 91 Stat. 748 (Aug. 7, 1977); and amended by Pub. L. No. 101–549, Title 1, § 102(d), 104 Stat. 2417 (Nov. 15, 1990).)

HISTORICAL AND STATUTORY NOTES

Effective and Applicability Provisions

1990 Acts. Amendment by Pub. L. No. 101–549 effective Nov. 15, 1990, except as otherwise provided, see section 711(b) of Pub. L. No. 101–549, set out as a note under section 7401 of this title.

1977 Acts. Section effective Aug. 7, 1977, except as otherwise expressly provided, see section 406(d) of Pub. L. No. 95–95, set out as a note under section 7401 of this title.

Savings Provisions

Suits, actions or proceedings commenced under this chapter as in effect prior to Nov. 15, 1990, not to abate by reason of the taking effect of amendments by Pub. L. No. 101–549, except as otherwise provided for, see section 711(a) of Pub. L. No. 101–549, set out as a note under section 7401 of this title.

§ 7505. Environmental Protection Agency grants

[CAA § 175]

(a) Plan revision development costs

The Administrator shall make grants to any organization of local elected officials with transportation or air quality maintenance planning responsibilities recognized by the State under section 7504(a) of this title for payment of the reasonable costs of developing a plan revision under this part.

(b) Uses of grant funds

The amount granted to any organization under subsection (a) of this section shall be 100 percent of any additional costs of developing a plan revision under this part for the first two fiscal years following receipt of the grant under this paragraph, and shall supplement any funds available under Federal law to such organization for transportation or air quality maintenance planning. Grants under this section shall not be used for construction.

(July 14, 1955, c. 360, Title I, § 175, as added by Pub. L. No. 95–95, Title I, § 129(b), 91 Stat. 749 (Aug. 7, 1977).)

HISTORICAL AND STATUTORY NOTES

Effective and Applicability Provisions

1977 Acts. Section effective Aug. 7, 1977, except as otherwise expressly provided, see section 406(d) of Pub. L. No. 95–95, set out as a note under section 7401 of this title.

§ 7505a. Maintenance plans

[CAA § 175A]

(a) Plan revision

Each State which submits a request under section 7407(d) of this title for redesignation of a nonattainment area for any air pollutant as an area which has attained the national primary ambient air quality standard for that air pollutant shall also submit a revision of the applicable State implementation plan to provide for the maintenance of the national primary ambient air quality standard for such air pollutant in the area concerned for at least 10 years after the redesignation. The plan shall contain such additional measures, if any, as may be necessary to ensure such maintenance.

(b) Subsequent plan revisions

8 years after redesignation of any area as an attainment area under section 7407(d) of this title, the State shall submit to the Administrator an additional revision of the applicable State implementation plan for maintaining the national primary ambient air quality standard for 10 years after the expiration of the 10-year period referred to in subsection (a) of this section.

(c) Nonattainment requirements applicable pending plan approval

Until such plan revision is approved and an area is redesignated as attainment for any area designated as a nonattainment area, the requirements of this part shall continue in force and effect with respect to such area.

(d) Contingency provisions

Each plan revision submitted under this section shall contain such contingency provisions as the Administrator deems necessary to assure that the State will promptly correct any violation of the standard which occurs after the redesignation of the area as an attainment area. Such provisions shall include a requirement that the State will implement all measures with respect to the control of the air pollutant concerned which were contained in the State implementation plan for the area before redesignation of the area as an attainment area. The failure of any area redesignated as an attainment area to maintain the national ambient air quality standard concerned shall not result in a requirement that the State revise its State implementation plan unless the Administrator, in the Administrator's discretion, requires the State to submit a revised State implementation plan.

(July 14, 1955, c. 360, Title I, § 175A, as added by Pub. L. No. 101–549, Title I, § 102(e), 104 Stat. 2418 (Nov. 15, 1990).)

HISTORICAL AND STATUTORY NOTES

Effective and Applicability Provisions

1990 Acts. Section to take effect Nov. 15, 1990, except as otherwise provided, see section 711(b) of Pub. L. No. 101–549, set out as a note under section 7401 of this title.

Savings Provisions

Suits, actions or proceedings commenced under this chapter as in effect prior to Nov. 15, 1990, not to abate by reason of the taking effect of amendments by Pub. L. No. 101–549, except as otherwise provided for, see section 711(a) of Pub. L. No. 101–549, set out as a note under section 7401 of this title.

§ 7506. Limitations on certain Federal assistance

[CAA § 176]

(a), (b) Repealed. Pub. L. No. 101–549, Title I, § 110(4), 104 Stat. 2470 (Nov. 15, 1990).

(c) Activities not conforming to approved or promulgated plans

(1) No department, agency, or instrumentality of the Federal Government shall engage in, support in any way or provide financial assistance for, license or permit, or approve, any activity which does not conform to an implementation plan after it has been approved or promulgated under section 7410 of this title. No metropolitan planning organization designated under section 134 of Title 23, shall give its approval to any project, program, or plan which does not conform to an implementation plan approved or promulgated under section 7410 of this title. The assurance of conformity to such an implementation plan shall be an affirmative responsibility of the head of such department, agency, or instrumentality. Conformity to an implementation plan means—

(A) conformity to an implementation plan's purpose of eliminating or reducing the severity and number of violations of the national ambient air quality standards and achieving expeditious attainment of such standards; and

(B) that such activities will not—

(i) cause or contribute to any new violation of any standard in any area;

(ii) increase the frequency or severity of any existing violation of any standard in any area; or

(iii) delay timely attainment of any standard or any required interim emission reductions or other milestones in any area.

The determination of conformity shall be based on the most recent estimates of emissions, and such estimates shall be determined from the most recent population, employment, travel and congestion estimates as determined by the metropolitan planning organization or other agency authorized to make such estimates.

(2) Any transportation plan or program developed pursuant to Title 23 or chapter 53 of Title 49 shall implement the transportation provisions of any applicable implementation plan approved under this chapter applicable to all or part of the area covered by such transportation plan or program. No Federal agency may approve, accept or fund any transportation plan, program or project unless such plan, program or project has been found to conform to any applicable implementation plan in effect under this chapter. In particular—

(A) no transportation plan or transportation improvement program may be adopted by a metropolitan planning organization designated under Title 23 or chapter 53 of Title 49, or be found to be in conformity by a metropolitan planning organization until a final determination has been made that emissions expected from implementation of such plans and programs are consistent with estimates of emissions from motor vehicles and necessary emissions reductions contained in the applicable implementation plan, and that the plan or program will conform to the requirements of paragraph (1)(B);

(B) no metropolitan planning organization or other recipient of funds under Title 23 or chapter 53 of Title 49 shall adopt or approve a transportation improvement program of projects until it determines that such program provides for timely implementation of transportation control measures consistent with schedules included in the applicable implementation plan;

(C) a transportation project may be adopted or approved by a metropolitan planning organization or any recipient of funds designated under Title 23 or chapter 53 of Title 49, or found in conformity by a metropolitan planning organization or approved, accepted, or funded by the Department of Transportation only if it meets either the requirements of subparagraph (D) or the following requirements—

(i) such a project comes from a conforming plan and program;

(ii) the design concept and scope of such project have not changed significantly since the conformity finding regarding the plan and program from which the project derived; and

(iii) the design concept and scope of such project at the time of the conformity determination for the program was adequate to determine emissions.

(D) Any project not referred to in subparagraph (C) shall be treated as conforming to the applicable implementation plan only if it is demonstrated that the projected emissions from such project, when considered together with emissions projected for the conforming transportation plans and programs within the nonattainment area, do not cause such plans and programs to exceed the emission reduction projections and schedules assigned to such plans and programs in the applicable implementation plan.

(E) The appropriate metropolitan planning organization shall redetermine conformity of existing transportation plans and programs not later than 2 years after the date on which the Administrator—

(i) finds a motor vehicle emissions budget to be adequate in accordance with section 93.118(e)(4) of title 40, Code of Federal Regulations (as in effect on October 1, 2004);

(ii) approves an implementation plan that establishes a motor vehicle emissions budget if that budget has not yet been determined to be adequate in accordance with clause (i); or

(iii) promulgates an implementation plan that establishes or revises a motor vehicle emissions budget.

(3) Until such time as the implementation plan revision referred to in paragraph (4)(C) is approved, conformity of such plans, programs, and projects will be demonstrated if—

(A) the transportation plans and programs—

(i) are consistent with the most recent estimates of mobile source emissions;

(ii) provide for the expeditious implementation of transportation control measures in the applicable implementation plan; and

(iii) with respect to ozone and carbon monoxide nonattainment areas, contribute to annual emissions reductions consistent with sections 7511a(b)(1) and 7512a(a)(7) of this title; and

(B) the transportation projects—

(i) come from a conforming transportation plan and program as defined in subparagraph (A) or for 12 months after November 15, 1990, from a transportation program found to conform within 3 years prior to November 15, 1990; and

(ii) in carbon monoxide nonattainment areas, eliminate or reduce the severity and number of violations of the carbon monoxide standards in the area substantially affected by the project.

With regard to subparagraph (B)(ii), such determination may be made as part of either the conformity determination for the transportation program or for the individual project taken as a whole during the environmental review phase of project development.

(4) Criteria and procedures for determining conformity

(A) In general

The Administrator shall promulgate, and periodically update, criteria and procedures for determining conformity (except in the case of transportation plans, programs, and projects) of, and for keeping the Administrator informed about, the activities referred to in paragraph (1).

(B) Transportation plans, programs, and projects

The Administrator, with the concurrence of the Secretary of Transportation, shall promulgate, and periodically update, criteria and procedures for demonstrating and assuring conformity in the case of transportation plans, programs, and projects.

(C) Civil action to compel promulgation

A civil action may be brought against the Administrator and the Secretary of Transportation under section 7604 of this title to compel promulgation of such criteria and procedures and the Federal district court shall have jurisdiction to order such promulgation.

(D) The procedures and criteria shall, at a minimum—

(i) address the consultation procedures to be undertaken by metropolitan planning organizations and the Secretary of Transportation with State and local air quality agencies and State departments of transportation before such organizations and the Secretary make conformity determinations;

(ii) address the appropriate frequency for making conformity determinations, but the frequency for making conformity determinations on updated transportation plans and programs shall be every 4 years, except in a case in which—

(I) the metropolitan planning organization elects to update a transportation plan or program more frequently; or

(II) the metropolitan planning organization is required to determine conformity in accordance with paragraph (2)(E); and

(iii) address how conformity determinations will be made with respect to maintenance plans.

(E) Inclusion of criteria and procedures in SIP

Not later than 2 years after August 10, 2005, the procedures under subparagraph (A) shall include a requirement that each State include in the State implementation plan criteria and procedures for consultation required by subparagraph (D)(i), and enforcement and enforceability (pursuant to sections 93.125(c) and 93.122(a)(4)(ii) of title 40, Code of Federal Regulations) in accordance with the Administrator's criteria and procedures for consultation, enforcement and enforceability.

(F) Compliance with the rules of the Administrator for determining the conformity of transportation plans, programs, and projects funded or approved under Title 23 or chapter 53 of Title 49 to State or Federal implementation plans shall not be required for traffic signal synchronization projects prior to the funding, approval or implementation of such projects. The supporting regional emissions analysis for any conformity determination made with respect to a transportation plan, program, or project shall consider the effect on emissions of any such project funded, approved, or implemented prior to the conformity determination.

(5) Applicability

This subsection shall apply only with respect to—

(A) a nonattainment area and each pollutant for which the area is designated as a nonattainment area; and

(B) an area that was designated as a nonattainment area but that was later redesignated by the Administrator as an attainment area and that is required to develop a maintenance plan under section 7505a of this title with respect to the specific pollutant for which the area was designated nonattainment.

(6) Notwithstanding paragraph 5,[1] this subsection shall not apply with respect to an area designated nonattainment under section 7407(d)(1) of this title until 1 year after that area is first designated nonattainment for a specific national ambient air quality standard. This paragraph only applies with respect to the national ambient air quality standard for which an area is newly designated nonattainment and does not affect the area's requirements with respect to all other national ambient air quality standards for which the area is designated nonattainment or has been redesignated from nonattainment to attainment with a maintenance plan pursuant to section 7505a of this title (including any pre-existing national ambient air quality standard for a pollutant for which a new or revised standard has been issued).

(7) Conformity horizon for transportation plans

(A) In general

Each conformity determination required under this section for a transportation plan under section 134(i) of Title 23 or section 5303(i) of Title 49 shall require a demonstration of conformity for the period ending on either the final year of the transportation plan, or at the election of the metropolitan planning organization, after consultation with the air pollution control agency and solicitation of public comments and consideration of such comments, the longest of the following periods:

(i) The first 10-year period of any such transportation plan.

(ii) The latest year in the implementation plan applicable to the area that contains a motor vehicle emission budget.

(iii) The year after the completion date of a regionally significant project if the project is included in the transportation improvement program or the project requires approval before the subsequent conformity determination.

(B) Regional emissions analysis

The conformity determination shall be accompanied by a regional emissions analysis for the last year of the transportation plan and for any year shown to exceed emission budgets by a prior analysis, if such year extends beyond the applicable period as determined under subparagraph (A).

(C) Exception

In any case in which an area has a revision to an implementation plan under section 7505a(b) of this title and the Administrator has found the motor vehicles emissions budgets from that revision to be adequate in accordance with section 93.118(e)(4) of title 40, Code of Federal Regulations (as in effect on October 1, 2004), or has approved the revision, the demonstration of conformity at the election of the metropolitan planning organization, after consultation with the air pollution control agency and solicitation of public comments and consideration of such comments, shall be required to extend only through the last year of the implementation plan required under section 7505a(b) of this title.

(D) Effect of election

Any election by a metropolitan planning organization under this paragraph shall continue in effect until the metropolitan planning organization elects otherwise.

(E) Air pollution control agency defined

In this paragraph, the term "air pollution control agency" means an air pollution control agency (as defined in section 7602(b) of this title) that is responsible for developing plans or controlling air pollution within the area covered by a transportation plan.

(8) Substitution of transportation control measures

(A) In general

Transportation control measures that are specified in an implementation plan may be replaced or added to the implementation plan with alternate or additional transportation control measures—

(i) if the substitute measures achieve equivalent or greater emissions reductions than the control measure to be replaced, as demonstrated with an emissions impact analysis that is consistent with the current methodology used for evaluating the replaced control measure in the implementation plan;

(ii) if the substitute control measures are implemented—

(I) in accordance with a schedule that is consistent with the schedule provided for control measures in the implementation plan; or

(II) if the implementation plan date for implementation of the control measure to be replaced has passed, as soon as practicable after the implementation plan date but not later than the date on which emission reductions are necessary to achieve the purpose of the implementation plan;

(iii) if the substitute and additional control measures are accompanied with evidence of adequate personnel and funding and authority under State or local law to implement, monitor, and enforce the control measures;

(iv) if the substitute and additional control measures were developed through a collaborative process that included—

(I) participation by representatives of all affected jurisdictions (including local air pollution control agencies, the State air pollution control agency, and State and local transportation agencies);

(II) consultation with the Administrator; and

(III) reasonable public notice and opportunity for comment; and

(v) if the metropolitan planning organization, State air pollution control agency, and the Administrator concur with the equivalency of the substitute or additional control measures.

(B) Adoption

(i) Concurrence by the metropolitan planning organization, State air pollution control agency and the Administrator as required by subparagraph (A)(v) shall constitute adoption of the substitute or additional control measures so long as the requirements of subparagraphs (A)(i), (A)(ii), (A)(iii) and (A)(iv) are met.

(ii) Once adopted, the substitute or additional control measures become, by operation of law, part of the State implementation plan and become federally enforceable.

(iii) Within 90 days of its concurrence under subparagraph (A)(v), the State air pollution control agency shall submit the substitute or additional control measure to the Administrator for incorporation in the codification of the applicable implementation plan. Nothwithstanding[2] any other provision of this chapter, no additional State process shall be necessary to support such revision to the applicable plan.

(C) No requirement for express permission

The substitution or addition of a transportation control measure in accordance with this paragraph and the funding or approval of such a control measure shall not be contingent on the existence of any provision in the applicable implementation plan that expressly permits such a substitution or addition.

(D) No requirement for new conformity determination

The substitution or addition of a transportation control measure in accordance with this paragraph shall not require—

(i) a new conformity determination for the transportation plan; or

(ii) a revision of the implementation plan.

(E) Continuation of control measure being replaced

A control measure that is being replaced by a substitute control measure under this paragraph shall remain in effect until the substitute control measure is adopted by the State pursuant to subparagraph (B).

(F) Effect of adoption

Adoption of a substitute control measure shall constitute rescission of the previously applicable control measure.

(9) Lapse of conformity

If a conformity determination required under this subsection for a transportation plan under section 134(i) of Title 23 or section 5303(i) of Title 49 or a transportation improvement program under section 134(j) of such Title 23 or under section 5303(j) of such Title 49 is not made by the applicable deadline and such failure is not corrected by additional measures to either reduce motor vehicle emissions sufficient to demonstrate compliance with the requirements of this subsection within 12 months after such deadline or other measures sufficient to correct such failures, the transportation plan shall lapse.

(10) Lapse

In this subsection, the term "lapse" means that the conformity determination for a transportation plan or transportation improvement program has expired, and thus there is no currently conforming transportation plan or transportation improvement program.

(d) Priority of achieving and maintaining national primary ambient air quality standards

Each department, agency, or instrumentality of the Federal Government having authority to conduct or support any program with air-quality related transportation consequences shall give priority in the exercise of such authority, consistent with statutory requirements for allocation among States or other jurisdictions, to the implementation of those portions of plans prepared under this section to achieve and maintain the national primary ambient air-quality standard. This paragraph extends to, but is not limited to, authority exercised under chapter 53 of Title 49, Title 23, and the Housing and Urban Development Act.

(July 14, 1955, c. 360, Title I, § 176, as added by Pub. L. No. 95–95, Title I, § 129(b), 91 Stat. 749 (Aug. 7, 1977); and amended by Pub. L. No. 95–190, § 14(a)(59), 91 Stat. 1403 (Nov. 16, 1977); Pub. L. No. 101–549, Title I, §§ 101(f), 110(4), 104 Stat. 2409, 2470 (Nov. 15, 1990); Pub. L. No. 104–59, Title III, § 305(b), 109 Stat. 580 (Nov. 28, 1995); Pub. L. No. 104–260, § 1, 110 Stat. 3175 (Oct. 9, 1996); Pub. L. No. 106–377, § 1(a)(1) [Title III], 114 Stat. 1441, 1441A–44 (Oct. 27, 2000); Pub. L. No. 109–59, Title VI, § 6011(a) to (f), 119 Stat. 1878 (Aug. 10, 2005).)

[1] So in original. Probably should be "paragraph (5),".

[2] So in original. Probably should be "Notwithstanding."

HISTORICAL AND STATUTORY NOTES

References in Text

Title 23, referred to in subsecs. (c) and (d), is Title 23, Highways.

This chapter, referred to in subsec. (c)(8)(B)(iii), originally read "this Act", meaning the Clean Air Act, Act of July 14, 1955, c. 360, 69 Stat. 322, as amended, also known as CAA and the Air Pollution Control Act, which is codified principally as this chapter. For complete classification, see Short Title note set out under 42 U.S.C.A. § 7401 and Tables.

The Housing and Urban Development Act, referred to in subsec. (d), may be the name for a series of Acts sharing the same name but enacted in different years by Pub. L. No. 89–117, 79 Stat. 451 (Aug. 10, 1965), Pub. L. No. 90–448, 82 Stat. 476 (Aug. 1, 1968), Pub. L. No. 91–152, 83 Stat. 379 (Dec. 24, 1969), and Pub. L. No. 91–609, 84 Stat. 1770 (Dec. 31, 1970), respectively. For complete classification of these Acts to the Code, see Short Title notes set out under section 1701 of Title 12 and Tables.

Codifications

In subsecs. (c)(2) and (d), "chapter 53 of title 49" was substituted for "the Urban Mass Transportation Act [49 App. USCA 1601 et seq.]" and in subsec. (c)(4)(D), same was substituted for the "Federal Transit Act" on authority of Pub. L. No. 103–272, § 6(b), 108 Stat. 1378 (July 5, 1994) (the first section of which enacted subtitles II, III, and V to X of Title 49, Transportation) and Pub. L. No. 102–240, Title III, § 3003(b), 105 Stat. 2088 (Dec. 18, 1991) (which provided that references in laws to the "Urban Mass Transportation Act of 1964" be deemed to be references to the "Federal Transit Act").

Effective and Applicability Provisions

1990 Acts. Amendment by Pub. L. No. 101–549 effective Nov. 15, 1990, except as otherwise provided, see section 711(b) of Pub. L. No. 101–549, set out as a note under section 7401 of this title.

1977 Acts. Section effective Aug. 7, 1977, except as otherwise expressly provided, see section 406(d) of Pub. L. No. 95–95, set out as a note under section 7401 of this title.

Savings Provisions

Suits, actions or proceedings commenced under this chapter as in effect prior to Nov. 15, 1990, not to abate by reason of the taking effect of amendments by Pub. L. No. 101–549, except as otherwise provided for, see section 711(a) of Pub. L. No. 101–549, set out as a note under section 7401 of this title.

Promulgation of Regulations

Pub. L. No. 109–59, Title VI, § 6011(g), 119 Stat. 1882 (Aug. 10, 2005), provided that: "Not later than 2 years after the date of enactment of this Act [Aug. 10, 2005], the Administrator of the Environmental Protection Agency shall promulgate revised regulations to implement the changes made by this section [amending this section]."

§ 7506a. Interstate transport commissions

[CAA § 176A]

(a) Authority to establish interstate transport regions

Whenever, on the Administrator's own motion or by petition from the Governor of any State, the Administrator has reason to believe that the interstate transport of air pollutants from one or more States contributes significantly to a violation of a national ambient air quality standard in one or more other States, the Administrator may establish, by rule, a transport region for such pollutant that includes such States. The Administrator, on the Administrator's own motion or upon petition from the Governor of any State, or upon the recommendation of a transport commission established under subsection (b) of this section, may—

(1) add any State or portion of a State to any region established under this subsection whenever the Administrator has reason to believe that the interstate transport of air pollutants from such State significantly contributes to a violation of the standard in the transport region, or

(2) remove any State or portion of a State from the region whenever the Administrator has reason to believe that the control of emissions in that State or portion of the State pursuant to this section will not significantly contribute to the attainment of the standard in any area in the region.

The Administrator shall approve or disapprove any such petition or recommendation within 18 months of its receipt. The Administrator shall establish appropriate proceedings for public participation regarding such petitions and motions, including notice and comment.

(b) Transport commissions

(1) Establishment

Whenever the Administrator establishes a transport region under subsection (a) of this section, the Administrator shall establish a transport commission comprised of (at a minimum) each of the following members:

(A) The Governor of each State in the region or the designee of each such Governor.

(B) The Administrator or the Administrator's designee.

(C) The Regional Administrator (or the Administrator's designee) for each Regional Office for each Environmental Protection Agency Region affected by the transport region concerned.

(D) An air pollution control official representing each State in the region, appointed by the Governor.

Decisions of, and recommendations and requests to, the Administrator by each transport commission may be made only by a majority vote of all members other than the Administrator and the Regional Administrators (or designees thereof).

(2) Recommendations

The transport commission shall assess the degree of interstate transport of the pollutant or precursors to the pollutant throughout the transport region, assess strategies for mitigating the interstate pollution, and recommend to the Administrator such measures as the Commission determines to be necessary to ensure that the plans for the relevant States meet the requirements of section 7410(a)(2)(D) of this title. Such commission shall not be subject to the provisions of the Federal Advisory Committee Act (5 U.S.C. App.).

(c) Commission requests

A transport commission established under subsection (b) of this section may request the Administrator to issue a finding under section 7410(k)(5) of this title that the implementation plan for one or more of the States in the transport region is substantially inadequate to meet the requirements of section 7410(a)(2)(D) of this title. The Administrator shall approve, disapprove, or partially approve and partially disapprove such a request within 18 months of its receipt and, to the extent the Administrator approves such request, issue the finding under section 7410(k)(5) of this title at the time of such approval. In acting on such request, the Administrator shall provide an opportunity for public participation and shall address each specific recommendation made by the commission. Approval or disapproval of such a request shall constitute final agency action within the meaning of section 7607(b) of this title.

(July 14, 1955, c. 360, Title I, § 176A, as added by Pub. L. No. 101–549, Title I, § 102(f)(1), 104 Stat. 2419 (Nov. 15, 1990).)

HISTORICAL AND STATUTORY NOTES

References in Text

The Federal Advisory Committee Act, referred to in subsec. (b)(2), is Pub. L. No. 92–463, 86 Stat. 770 (Oct. 6, 1972), as amended, which is set out in Appendix 2 to Title 5, Government Organization and Employees.

Effective and Applicability Provisions

1990 Acts. Section to take effect Nov. 15, 1990, except as otherwise provided, see section 711(b) of Pub. L. No. 101–549, set out as a note under section 7401 of this title.

Savings Provisions

Suits, actions or proceedings commenced under this chapter as in effect prior to Nov. 15, 1990, not to abate by reason of the taking effect of amendments by Pub. L. No. 101–549, except as otherwise provided for, see section 711(a) of Pub. L. No. 101–549, set out as a note under section 7401 of this title.

§ 7507. New motor vehicle emission standards in nonattainment areas

[CAA § 177]

Notwithstanding section 7543(a) of this title, any State which has plan provisions approved under this part may adopt and enforce for any model year standards relating to control of emissions from new motor vehicles or new motor vehicle engines and take such other actions as are referred to in section 7543(a) of this title respecting such vehicles if—

(1) such standards are identical to the California standards for which a waiver has been granted for such model year, and

(2) California and such State adopt such standards at least two years before commencement of such model year (as determined by regulations of the Administrator).

Nothing in this section or in subchapter II of this chapter shall be construed as authorizing any such State to prohibit or limit, directly or indirectly, the manufacture or sale of a new motor vehicle or motor vehicle engine that is certified in California as meeting California standards, or to take any action of any kind to create, or have the effect of creating, a motor vehicle or motor vehicle engine different than a motor vehicle or engine certified in California under California standards (a "third vehicle") or otherwise create such a "third vehicle".

(July 14, 1955, c. 360, Title I, § 177, as added by Pub. L. No. 95–95, Title I, § 129(b), 91 Stat. 750 (Aug. 7, 1977); and amended by Pub. L. No. 101–549, Title II, § 232, 104 Stat. 2529 (Nov. 15, 1990).)

HISTORICAL AND STATUTORY NOTES

Effective and Applicability Provisions

1990 Acts. Amendment by Pub. L. No. 101–549 effective Nov. 15, 1990, except as otherwise provided, see section 711(b) of Pub. L. No. 101–549, set out as a note under section 7401 of this title.

1977 Acts. Section effective Aug. 7, 1977, except as otherwise expressly provided, see section 406(d) of Pub. L. No. 95–95, set out as a note under section 7401 of this title.

Savings Provisions

Suits, actions or proceedings commenced under this chapter as in effect prior to Nov. 15, 1990, not to abate by reason of the taking effect of amendments by Pub. L. No. 101–549, except as otherwise provided for, see section 711(a) of Pub. L. No. 101–549, set out as a note under section 7401 of this title.

§ 7508. Guidance documents

[CAA § 178]

The Administrator shall issue guidance documents under section 7408 of this title for purposes of assisting States in implementing requirements of this part respecting the lowest achievable emission rate. Such a document shall be published not later than nine months after August 7, 1977, and shall be revised at least every two years thereafter.

(July 14, 1955, c. 360, Title I, § 178, as added by Pub. L. No. 95–95, Title I, § 129(b), 91 Stat. 750 (Aug. 7, 1977).)

HISTORICAL AND STATUTORY NOTES

Effective and Applicability Provisions

1977 Acts. Section effective Aug. 7, 1977, except as otherwise expressly provided, see section 406(d) of Pub. L. No. 95–95, set out as a note under section 7401 of this title.

§ 7509. Sanctions and consequences of failure to attain

[CAA § 179]

(a) State failure

For any implementation plan or plan revision required under this part (or required in response to a finding of substantial inadequacy as described in section 7410(k)(5) of this title), if the Administrator—

(1) finds that a State has failed, for an area designated nonattainment under section 7407(d) of this title, to submit a plan, or to submit 1 or more of the elements (as determined by the Administrator) required by the provisions of this chapter applicable to such an area, or has failed to make a submission for such an area that satisfies the minimum criteria established in relation to any such element under section 7410(k) of this title,

(2) disapproves a submission under section 7410(k) of this title, for an area designated nonattainment under section 7407 of this title, based on the submission's failure to meet one or more of the elements required by the provisions of this chapter applicable to such an area,

(3) (A) determines that a State has failed to make any submission as may be required under this chapter, other than one described under paragraph (1) or (2), including an adequate maintenance plan, or has failed to make any submission, as may be required under this chapter, other than one described under paragraph (1) or (2), that satisfies the minimum criteria established in relation to such submission under section 7410(k)(1)(A) of this title, or

(B) disapproves in whole or in part a submission described under subparagraph (A), or

(4) finds that any requirement of an approved plan (or approved part of a plan) is not being implemented,

unless such deficiency has been corrected within 18 months after the finding, disapproval, or determination referred to in paragraphs (1), (2), (3), and (4), one of the sanctions referred to in subsection (b) of this section

shall apply, as selected by the Administrator, until the Administrator determines that the State has come into compliance, except that if the Administrator finds a lack of good faith, sanctions under both paragraph (1) and paragraph (2) of subsection (b) of this section shall apply until the Administrator determines that the State has come into compliance. If the Administrator has selected one of such sanctions and the deficiency has not been corrected within 6 months thereafter, sanctions under both paragraph (1) and paragraph (2) of subsection (b) of this section shall apply until the Administrator determines that the State has come into compliance. In addition to any other sanction applicable as provided in this section, the Administrator may withhold all or part of the grants for support of air pollution planning and control programs that the Administrator may award under section 7405 of this title.

(b) Sanctions

The sanctions available to the Administrator as provided in subsection (a) of this section are as follows:

(1) Highway sanctions

(A) The Administrator may impose a prohibition, applicable to a nonattainment area, on the approval by the Secretary of Transportation of any projects or the awarding by the Secretary of any grants, under Title 23 other than projects or grants for safety where the Secretary determines, based on accident or other appropriate data submitted by the State, that the principal purpose of the project is an improvement in safety to resolve a demonstrated safety problem and likely will result in a significant reduction in, or avoidance of, accidents. Such prohibition shall become effective upon the selection by the Administrator of this sanction.

(B) In addition to safety, projects or grants that may be approved by the Secretary, notwithstanding the prohibition in subparagraph (A), are the following—

(i) capital programs for public transit;

(ii) construction or restriction of certain roads or lanes solely for the use of passenger buses or high occupancy vehicles;

(iii) planning for requirements for employers to reduce employee work-trip-related vehicle emissions;

(iv) highway ramp metering, traffic signalization, and related programs that improve traffic flow and achieve a net emission reduction;

(v) fringe and transportation corridor parking facilities serving multiple occupancy vehicle programs or transit operations;

(vi) programs to limit or restrict vehicle use in downtown areas or other areas of emission concentration particularly during periods of peak use, through road use charges, tolls, parking surcharges, or other pricing mechanisms, vehicle restricted zones or periods, or vehicle registration programs;

(vii) programs for breakdown and accident scene management, nonrecurring congestion, and vehicle information systems, to reduce congestion and emissions; and

(viii) such other transportation-related programs as the Administrator, in consultation with the Secretary of Transportation, finds would improve air quality and would not encourage single occupancy vehicle capacity.

In considering such measures, the State should seek to ensure adequate access to downtown, other commercial, and residential areas, and avoid increasing or relocating emissions and congestion rather than reducing them.

(2) Offsets

In applying the emissions offset requirements of section 7503 of this title to new or modified sources or emissions units for which a permit is required under this part, the ratio of emission reductions to increased emissions shall be at least 2 to 1.

(c) Notice of failure to attain

(1) As expeditiously as practicable after the applicable attainment date for any nonattainment area, but not later than 6 months after such date, the Administrator shall determine, based on the area's air quality as of the attainment date, whether the area attained the standard by that date.

(2) Upon making the determination under paragraph (1), the Administrator shall publish a notice in the Federal Register containing such determination and identifying each area that the Administrator has determined to have failed to attain. The Administrator may revise or supplement such determination at any time based on more complete information or analysis concerning the area's air quality as of the attainment date.

(d) Consequences for failure to attain

(1) Within 1 year after the Administrator publishes the notice under subsection (c)(2) of this section (relating to notice of failure to attain), each State containing a nonattainment area shall submit a revision to the applicable implementation plan meeting the requirements of paragraph (2) of this subsection.

(2) The revision required under paragraph (1) shall meet the requirements of section 7410 of this title and section 7502 of this title. In addition, the revision shall include such additional measures as the Administrator may reasonably prescribe, including all measures that can be feasibly implemented in the area in light of technological achievability, costs, and any nonair quality and other air quality-related health and environmental impacts.

(3) The attainment date applicable to the revision required under paragraph (1) shall be the same as provided in the provisions of section 7502(a)(2) of this title, except that in applying such provisions the phrase "from the date of the notice under section 7509(c)(2) of this title" shall be substituted for the phrase "from the date such area was designated nonattainment under section 7407(d) of this title" and for the phrase "from the date of designation as nonattainment".

(July 14, 1955, c. 360, Title I, § 179, as added by Pub. L. No. 101–549, Title I, § 102(g), 104 Stat. 2420 (Nov. 15, 1990).)

HISTORICAL AND STATUTORY NOTES

References in Text

Title 23, referred to in subsec. (b)(1)(A), is Title 23, Highways.

Effective and Applicability Provisions

1990 Acts. Section to take effect Nov. 15, 1990, except as otherwise provided, see section 711(b) of Pub. L. No. 101–549, set out as a note under section 7401 of this title.

Savings Provisions

Suits, actions or proceedings commenced under this chapter as in effect prior to Nov. 15, 1990, not to abate by reason of the taking effect of amendments by Pub. L. No. 101–549, except as otherwise provided for, see section 711(a) of Pub. L. No. 101–549, set out as a note under section 7401 of this title.

§ 7509a. International border areas

[CAA § 179B]

(a) Implementation plans and revisions

Notwithstanding any other provision of law, an implementation plan or plan revision required under this chapter shall be approved by the Administrator if—

(1) such plan or revision meets all the requirements applicable to it under the[1] chapter other than a requirement that such plan or revision demonstrate attainment and maintenance of the relevant national ambient air quality standards by the attainment date specified under the applicable provision of this chapter, or in a regulation promulgated under such provision, and

(2) the submitting State establishes to the satisfaction of the Administrator that the implementation plan of such State would be adequate to attain and maintain the relevant national ambient air quality standards by the attainment date specified under the applicable provision of this chapter, or in a regulation promulgated under such provision, but for emissions emanating from outside of the United States.

(b) Attainment of ozone levels

Notwithstanding any other provision of law, any State that establishes to the satisfaction of the Administrator that, with respect to an ozone nonattainment area in such State, such State would have attained the national ambient air quality standard for ozone by the applicable attainment date, but for emissions emanating from outside of the United States, shall not be subject to the provisions of section 7511(a)(2) or (5) of this title or section 7511d of this title.

(c) Attainment of carbon monoxide levels

Notwithstanding any other provision of law, any State that establishes to the satisfaction of the Administrator, with respect to a carbon monoxide nonattainment area in such State, that such State has attained the national ambient air quality standard for carbon monoxide by the applicable attainment date, but for emissions emanating from outside of the United States, shall not be subject to the provisions of section 7512(b)(2) or (9)[2] of this title.

(d) Attainment of PM-10 levels

Notwithstanding any other provision of law, any State that establishes to the satisfaction of the Administrator that, with respect to a PM-10 nonattainment area in such State, such State would have attained the national ambient air quality standard for carbon monoxide by the applicable attainment date, but for emissions emanating from outside the United States, shall not be subject to the provisions of section 7513(b)(2) of this title.

(July 14, 1955, c. 360, Title I, § 179B, as added by Pub. L. No. 101–549, Title VIII, § 818, 104 Stat. 2697 (Nov. 15, 1990).)

[1] So in original. Probably should be "this."

[2] So in original. Section 7512(b) of this title does not contain a par. (9).

HISTORICAL AND STATUTORY NOTES

Effective and Applicability Provisions

1990 Acts. Section effective Nov. 15, 1990, except as otherwise provided, see section 711(b) of Pub. L. No. 101–549, set out as a note under section 7401 of this title.

Savings Provisions

Suits, actions or proceedings commenced under this chapter as in effect prior to Nov. 15, 1990, not to abate by reason of the taking effect of amendments by Pub. L. No. 101–549, except as otherwise provided for, see section 711(a) of Pub. L. No. 101–549, set out as a note under section 7401 of this title.

Establishment of Program to Monitor and Improve Air Quality in Regions Along the Border Between the United States and Mexico

Section 815 of Pub. L. No. 101–549 provided that:

"(a) In general.—The Administrator of the Environmental Protection Agency (hereinafter referred to as the 'Administrator') is authorized, in cooperation with the Department of State and the affected States, to negotiate with representatives of Mexico to authorize a program to monitor and improve air quality in regions along the border between the United States and Mexico. The program established under this section shall not extend beyond July 1, 1995.

"(b) Monitoring and remediation.—

"(1) Monitoring.—The monitoring component of the program conducted under this section shall identify and determine sources of pollutants for which national ambient air quality standards (hereinafter referred to as 'NAAQS') and other air quality goals have been established in regions along the border between the United States and Mexico. Any such monitoring component of the program shall include, but not be limited to, the collection of meteorological data, the measurement of air quality, the compilation of an emissions inventory, and shall be sufficient to the extent necessary to successfully support the use of a state-of-the-art mathematical air modeling analysis. Any such monitoring component of the program shall collect and produce data projecting the level of emission reductions necessary in both Mexico and the United States to bring about attainment of both primary and secondary NAAQS, and other air quality goals, in regions along the border in the United States. Any such monitoring component of the program shall include to the extent possible, data from monitoring programs undertaken by other parties.

"(2) **Remediation.**—The Administrator is authorized to negotiate with appropriate representatives of Mexico to develop joint remediation measures to reduce the level of airborne pollutants to achieve and maintain primary and secondary NAAQS, and other air quality goals, in regions along the border between the United States and Mexico. Such joint remediation measures may include, but not be limited to measures included in the Environmental Protection Agency's Control Techniques and Control Technology documents. Any such remediation program shall also identify those control measures implementation of which in Mexico would be expedited by the use of material and financial assistance of the United States.

"(c) **Annual reports.**—The Administrator shall, each year the program authorized in this section is in operation, report to Congress on the progress of the program in bringing nonattainment areas along the border of the United States into attainment with primary and secondary NAAQS. The report issued by the Administrator under this paragraph shall include recommendations on funding mechanisms to assist in implementation of monitoring and remediation efforts.

"(d) **Funding and personnel.**—The Administrator may, where appropriate, make available, subject to the appropriations, such funds, personnel, and equipment as may be necessary to implement the provisions of this section. In those cases where direct financial assistance of the United States is provided to implement monitoring and remediation programs in Mexico, the Administrator shall develop grant agreements with appropriate representatives of Mexico to assure the accuracy and completeness of monitoring data and the performance of remediation measures which are financed by the United States. With respect to any control measures within Mexico funded by the United States, the Administrator shall, to the maximum extent practicable, utilize resources of Mexico where such utilization would reduce costs to the United States. Such funding agreements shall include authorization for the Administrator to—

"(1) review and agree to plans for monitoring and remediation;

"(2) inspect premises, equipment and records to insure compliance with the agreements established under and the purposes set forth in this section; and

"(3) where necessary, develop grant agreements with affected States to carry out the provisions of this section."

Subpart 2—Additional Provisions for Ozone Nonattainment Areas

§ 7511. Classifications and attainment dates

[CAA § 181]

(a) Classification and attainment dates for 1989 nonattainment areas

(1) Each area designated nonattainment for ozone pursuant to section 7407(d) of this title shall be classified at the time of such designation, under table 1, by operation of law, as a Marginal Area, a Moderate Area, a Serious Area, a Severe Area, or an Extreme Area based on the design value for the area. The design value shall be calculated according to the interpretation methodology issued by the Administrator most recently before November 15, 1990. For each area classified under this subsection, the primary standard attainment date for ozone shall be as expeditiously as practicable but not later than the date provided in table 1.

TABLE 1

Area class	*Design value**	*Primary standard attainment date***
Marginal	0.121 up to 0.138	3 years after November 15, 1990
Moderate	0.138 up to 0.160	6 years after November 15, 1990
Serious	0.160 up to 0.180	9 years after November 15, 1990
Severe	0.180 up to 0.280	15 years after November 15, 1990
Extreme	0.280 and above	20 years after November 15, 1990

* The design value is measured in parts per million (ppm).

** The primary standard attainment date is measured from November 15, 1990.

(2) Notwithstanding table 1, in the case of a severe area with a 1988 ozone design value between 0.190 and 0.280 ppm, the attainment date shall be 17 years (in lieu of 15 years) after November 15, 1990.

(3) At the time of publication of the notice under section 7407(d)(4) of this title (relating to area designations) for each ozone nonattainment area, the Administrator shall publish a notice announcing the classification of such ozone nonattainment area. The provisions of section 7502(a)(1)(B) of this title (relating to lack of notice and comment and judicial review) shall apply to such classification.

(4) If an area classified under paragraph (1) (Table 1) would have been classified in another category if the design value in the area were 5 percent greater or 5 percent less than the level on which such classification was based, the Administrator may, in the Administrator's discretion, within 90 days after the initial classification, by the procedure required under paragraph (3), adjust the classification to place the area in such other category. In making such adjustment, the Administrator may consider the number of exceedances of the national primary ambient air quality standard for ozone in the area, the level of pollution transport between the area and other affected areas, including both intrastate and interstate transport, and the mix of sources and air pollutants in the area.

(5) Upon application by any State, the Administrator may extend for 1 additional year (hereinafter referred to as the "Extension Year") the date specified in table 1 of paragraph (1) of this subsection if—

(A) the State has complied with all requirements and commitments pertaining to the area in the applicable implementation plan, and

(B) no more than 1 exceedance of the national ambient air quality standard level for ozone has occurred in the area in the year preceding the Extension Year.

No more than 2 one-year extensions may be issued under this paragraph for a single nonattainment area.

(b) New designations and reclassifications

(1) New designations to nonattainment

Any area that is designated attainment or unclassifiable for ozone under section 7407(d)(4) of this title, and that is subsequently redesignated to nonattainment for ozone under section 7407(d)(3) of this title, shall, at the time of the redesignation, be classified by operation of law in accordance with table 1 under subsection (a) of this section. Upon its classification, the area shall be subject to the same requirements under section 7410 of this title, subpart 1 of this part, and this subpart that would have applied had the area been so classified at the time of the notice under subsection (a)(3) of this section, except that any absolute, fixed date applicable in connection with any such requirement is extended by operation of law by a period equal to the length of time between November 15, 1990, and the date the area is classified under this paragraph.

(2) Reclassification upon failure to attain

(A) Within 6 months following the applicable attainment date (including any extension thereof) for an ozone nonattainment area, the Administrator shall determine, based on the area's design value (as of the attainment date), whether the area attained the standard by that date. Except for any Severe or Extreme area, any area that the Administrator finds has not attained the standard by that date shall be reclassified by operation of law in accordance with table 1 of subsection (a) of this section to the higher of—

(i) the next higher classification for the area, or

(ii) the classification applicable to the area's design value as determined at the time of the notice required under subparagraph (B).

No area shall be reclassified as Extreme under clause (ii).

(B) The Administrator shall publish a notice in the Federal Register, no later than 6 months following the attainment date, identifying each area that the Administrator has determined under subparagraph (A) as having failed to attain and identifying the reclassification, if any, described under subparagraph (A).

(3) Voluntary reclassification

The Administrator shall grant the request of any State to reclassify a nonattainment area in that State in accordance with table 1 of subsection (a) of this section to a higher classification. The Administrator shall publish a notice in the Federal Register of any such request and of action by the Administrator granting the request.

(4) Failure of Severe Areas to attain standard

(A) If any Severe Area fails to achieve the national primary ambient air quality standard for ozone by the applicable attainment date (including any extension thereof), the fee provisions under section 7511d of this title shall apply within the area, the percent reduction requirements of section 7511a(c)(2)(B) and (C) of this title (relating to reasonable further progress demonstration and NO_x control) shall continue to apply to the area, and the State shall demonstrate that such percent reduction has been achieved in each 3-year interval after such failure until the standard is attained. Any failure to make such a demonstration shall be subject to the sanctions provided under this part.

(B) In addition to the requirements of subparagraph (A), if the ozone design value for a Severe Area referred to in subparagraph (A) is above 0.140 ppm for the year of the applicable attainment date, or if the area has failed to achieve its most recent milestone under section 7511a(g) of this title, the new source review requirements applicable under this subpart in Extreme Areas shall apply in the area and the term[1] "major source" and "major stationary source" shall have the same meaning as in Extreme Areas.

(C) In addition to the requirements of subparagraph (A) for those areas referred to in subparagraph (A) and not covered by subparagraph (B), the provisions referred to in subparagraph (B) shall apply after 3 years from the applicable attainment date unless the area has attained the standard by the end of such 3-year period.

(D) If, after November 15, 1990, the Administrator modifies the method of determining compliance with the national primary ambient air quality standard, a design value or other indicator comparable to 0.140 in terms of its relationship to the standard shall be used in lieu of 0.140 for purposes of applying the provisions of subparagraphs (B) and (C).

(c) References to terms

(1) Any reference in this subpart to a "Marginal Area", a "Moderate Area", a "Serious Area", a "Severe Area", or an "Extreme Area" shall be considered a reference to a Marginal Area, a Moderate Area, a Serious Area, a Severe Area, or an Extreme Area as respectively classified under this section.

(2) Any reference in this subpart to "next higher classification" or comparable terms shall be considered a reference to the classification related to the next higher set of design values in table 1.

(July 14, 1955, c. 360, Title I, § 181, as added by Pub. L. No. 101–549, Title I, § 103, 104 Stat. 2423 (Nov. 15, 1990).)

[1] So in original. Probably should be "terms."

HISTORICAL AND STATUTORY NOTES

Effective and Applicability Provisions

1990 Acts. Section effective Nov. 15, 1990, except as otherwise provided, see section 711(b) of Pub. L. No. 101–549, set out as a note under section 7401 of this title.

Savings Provisions

Suits, actions or proceedings commenced under this chapter as in effect prior to Nov. 15, 1990, not to abate by reason of the taking effect of amendments by Pub. L. No. 101–549, except as otherwise provided for, see section 711(a) of Pub. L. No. 101–549, set out as a note under section 7401 of this title.

Exemptions for Stripper Wells

Section 819 of Pub. L. No. 101–549 provided that: "Notwithstanding any other provision of law, the amendments to the Clean Air Act [this chapter] made by section 103 of the Clean Air Act Amendments of 1990 [enacting sections 7511 to 7511f of this title] (relating to additional provisions for ozone nonattainment areas), by section 104 of such amendments [enacting sections 7512 and 7512a of this title] (relating to additional provisions for carbon monoxide nonattainment areas), by section 105 of such amendments [enacting sections 7513 to 7513b of this title and amending section 7476 of this title] (relating to additional provisions for PM-10 nonattainment areas), and by section 106 of such amendments [enacting sections 7514 and 7514a of this title] (relating to additional provisions for areas designated as nonattainment for sulfur oxides, nitrogen dioxide, and lead) shall not apply with respect to the production of and equipment used in the exploration, production, development, storage or processing of—

"**(1)** oil from a stripper well property, within the meaning of the June 1979 energy regulations (within the meaning of section 4996(b)(7) of the Internal Revenue Code of 1986 [26 U.S.C.A. § 4996(b)(7)], as in effect before the repeal of such section); and

"**(2)** stripper well natural gas, as defined in section 108(b) of the Natural Gas Policy Act of 1978 (15 U.S.C. 3318(b)) [section 3318(b) of Title 15, Commerce and Trade].[,]

except to the extent that provisions of such amendments cover areas designated as Serious pursuant to part D of title I of the Clean Air Act [this part] and having a population of 350,000 or more, or areas designated as Severe or Extreme pursuant to such part D."

§ 7511a. Plan submissions and requirements

[CAA § 182]

(a) Marginal Areas

Each State in which all or part of a Marginal Area is located shall, with respect to the Marginal Area (or portion thereof, to the extent specified in this subsection), submit to the Administrator the State implementation plan revisions (including the plan items) described under this subsection except to the extent the State has made such submissions as of November 15, 1990.

(1) Inventory

Within 2 years after November 15, 1990, the State shall submit a comprehensive, accurate, current inventory of actual emissions from all sources, as described in section 7502(c)(3) of this title, in accordance with guidance provided by the Administrator.

(2) Corrections to the State implementation plan

Within the periods prescribed in this paragraph, the State shall submit a revision to the State implementation plan that meets the following requirements—

(A) Reasonably available control technology corrections

For any Marginal Area (or, within the Administrator's discretion, portion thereof) the State shall submit, within 6 months of the date of classification under section 7511(a) of this title, a revision that includes such provisions to correct requirements in (or add requirements to) the plan concerning reasonably available control technology as were required under section 7502(b) of this title (as in effect immediately before November 15, 1990), as interpreted in guidance issued by the Administrator under section 7408 of this title before November 15, 1990.

(B) Savings clause for vehicle inspection and maintenance

(i) For any Marginal Area (or, within the Administrator's discretion, portion thereof), the plan for which already includes, or was required by section 7502(b)(11)(B) of this title (as in effect immediately before November 15, 1990) to have included, a specific schedule for implementation of a vehicle emission control inspection and maintenance program, the State shall submit, immediately after November 15, 1990, a revision that includes any provisions necessary to provide for a vehicle inspection and maintenance program of no less stringency than that of either the program defined in House Report Numbered 95–294, 95th Congress, 1st Session, 281–291 (1977) as interpreted in guidance of the Administrator issued pursuant to section 7502(b)(11)(B) of this title (as in effect immediately before November 15, 1990) or the program already included in the plan, whichever is more stringent.

(ii) Within 12 months after November 15, 1990, the Administrator shall review, revise, update, and republish in the Federal Register the guidance for the States for motor vehicle inspection and maintenance programs required by this chapter, taking into consideration the Administrator's investigations and audits of such program. The guidance shall, at a minimum, cover the frequency of inspections, the types of vehicles to be inspected (which shall include leased vehicles that are registered in the nonattainment area), vehicle maintenance by owners and operators, audits by the State, the test method and measures, including whether centralized or decentralized, inspection methods and procedures, quality of inspection, components covered, assurance that a vehicle subject to a recall notice from a manufacturer has complied with that notice, and effective implementation and enforcement, including ensuring that any retesting of a vehicle after a failure shall include proof of corrective action and providing for denial of vehicle registration in the case of tampering or misfueling. The guidance which shall be incorporated in the applicable State implementation plans by the States shall provide the States with continued reasonable flexibility to fashion effective, reasonable, and fair programs for the affected consumer. No later than 2 years after the Administrator promulgates regulations under section 7521(m)(3) of this title (relating to emission control diagnostics), the State shall submit a revision to such program to meet any requirements that the Administrator may prescribe under that section.

(C) Permit programs

Within 2 years after November 15, 1990, the State shall submit a revision that includes each of the following:

(i) Provisions to require permits, in accordance with sections 7502(c)(5) and 7503 of this title, for the construction and operation of each new or modified major stationary source (with respect to ozone) to be located in the area.

(ii) Provisions to correct requirements in (or add requirements to) the plan concerning permit programs as were required under section 7502(b)(6) of this title (as in effect immediately before November 15, 1990), as interpreted in regulations of the Administrator promulgated as of November 15, 1990.

(3) Periodic inventory

(A) General requirement

No later than the end of each 3-year period after submission of the inventory under paragraph (1) until the area is redesignated to attainment, the State shall submit a revised inventory meeting the requirements of subsection (a)(1) of this section.

(B) Emissions statements

(i) Within 2 years after November 15, 1990, the State shall submit a revision to the State implementation plan to require that the owner or operator of each stationary source of oxides of nitrogen or volatile organic compounds provide the State with a statement, in such form as the Administrator may prescribe (or accept an equivalent alternative developed by the State), for classes or categories of sources, showing the actual emissions of oxides of nitrogen and volatile organic compounds from that source. The first such statement shall be submitted within 3 years after November 15, 1990. Subsequent statements shall be submitted at least every year thereafter. The statement shall contain a certification that the information contained in the statement is accurate to the best knowledge of the individual certifying the statement.

(ii) The State may waive the application of clause (i) to any class or category of stationary sources which emit less than 25 tons per year of volatile organic compounds or oxides of nitrogen if the State, in its submissions under subparagraphs[1] (1) or (3)(A), provides an inventory of emissions from such class or category of sources, based on the use of the emission factors established by the Administrator or other methods acceptable to the Administrator.

(4) General offset requirement

For purposes of satisfying the emission offset requirements of this part, the ratio of total emission reductions of volatile organic compounds to total increased emissions of such air pollutant shall be at least 1.1 to 1.

The Administrator may, in the Administrator's discretion, require States to submit a schedule for submitting any of the revisions or other items required under this subsection. The requirements of this subsection shall apply in lieu of any requirement that the State submit a demonstration that the applicable implementation plan provides for attainment of the ozone standard by the applicable attainment date in any Marginal Area. Section 7502(c)(9) of this title (relating to contingency measures) shall not apply to Marginal Areas.

(b) Moderate Areas

Each State in which all or part of a Moderate Area is located shall, with respect to the Moderate Area, make the submissions described under subsection (a) of this section (relating to Marginal Areas), and shall also submit the revisions to the applicable implementation plan described under this subsection.

(1) Plan provisions for reasonable further progress

(A) General rule

(i) By no later than 3 years after November 15, 1990, the State shall submit a revision to the applicable implementation plan to provide for volatile organic compound emission reductions, within 6 years after November 15, 1990, of at least 15 percent from baseline emissions, accounting for any growth in emissions after 1990. Such plan shall provide for such specific annual reductions in emissions of volatile organic compounds and oxides of nitrogen as necessary to attain the national primary ambient air quality standard for ozone by the attainment date applicable under this chapter. This subparagraph shall not apply in the case of oxides of nitrogen for those areas for which the Administrator determines (when the Administrator approves the plan or plan revision) that additional reductions of oxides of nitrogen would not contribute to attainment.

(ii) A percentage less than 15 percent may be used for purposes of clause (i) in the case of any State which demonstrates to the satisfaction of the Administrator that—

(I) new source review provisions are applicable in the nonattainment areas in the same manner and to the same extent as required under subsection (e) of this section in the case of Extreme Areas (with the exception that, in applying such provisions, the terms "major source" and "major stationary source" shall include (in addition to the sources described in section 7602 of this title) any stationary source or group of sources located within a contiguous area and under common control that emits, or has the potential to emit, at least 5 tons per year of volatile organic compounds);

(II) reasonably available control technology is required for all existing major sources (as defined in subclause (I)); and

(III) the plan reflecting a lesser percentage than 15 percent includes all measures that can feasibly be implemented in the area, in light of technological achievability.

To qualify for a lesser percentage under this clause, a State must demonstrate to the satisfaction of the Administrator that the plan for the area includes the measures that are achieved in practice by sources in the same source category in nonattainment areas of the next higher category.

(B) Baseline emissions

For purposes of subparagraph (A), the term "baseline emissions" means the total amount of actual VOC or NO_x emissions from all anthropogenic sources in the area during the calendar year 1990, excluding emissions that would be eliminated under the regulations described in clauses (i) and (ii) of subparagraph (D).

(C) General rule for creditability of reductions

Except as provided under subparagraph (D), emissions reductions are creditable toward the 15 percent required under subparagraph (A) to the extent they have actually occurred, as of 6 years after November 15, 1990, from the implementation of measures required under the applicable implementation plan, rules promulgated by the Administrator, or a permit under subchapter V of this chapter.

(D) Limits on creditability of reductions

Emission reductions from the following measures are not creditable toward the 15 percent reductions required under subparagraph (A):

(i) Any measure relating to motor vehicle exhaust or evaporative emissions promulgated by the Administrator by January 1, 1990.

(ii) Regulations concerning Reid Vapor Pressure promulgated by the Administrator by November 15, 1990, or required to be promulgated under section 7545(h) of this title.

(iii) Measures required under subsection (a)(2)(A) of this section (concerning corrections to implementation plans prescribed under guidance by the Administrator).

(iv) Measures required under subsection (a)(2)(B) of this section to be submitted immediately after November 15, 1990 (concerning corrections to motor vehicle inspection and maintenance programs).

(2) Reasonably available control technology

The State shall submit a revision to the applicable implementation plan to include provisions to require the implementation of reasonably available control technology under section 7502(c)(1) of this title with respect to each of the following:

(A) Each category of VOC sources in the area covered by a CTG document issued by the Administrator between November 15, 1990, and the date of attainment.

(B) All VOC sources in the area covered by any CTG issued before November 15, 1990.

(C) All other major stationary sources of VOCs that are located in the area.

Each revision described in subparagraph (A) shall be submitted within the period set forth by the Administrator in issuing the relevant CTG document. The revisions with respect to sources described in subparagraphs (B) and (C) shall be submitted by 2 years after November 15, 1990, and shall provide for the implementation of the required measures as expeditiously as practicable but no later than May 31, 1995.

(3) Gasoline vapor recovery

(A) General rule

Not later than 2 years after November 15, 1990, the State shall submit a revision to the applicable implementation plan to require all owners or operators of gasoline dispensing systems to install and operate, by the date prescribed under subparagraph (B), a system for gasoline vapor recovery of emissions from the fueling of motor vehicles. The Administrator shall issue guidance as appropriate as to the effectiveness of such system. This subparagraph shall apply only to facilities which sell more than 10,000 gallons of gasoline per month (50,000 gallons per month in the case of an independent small business marketer of gasoline as defined in section 7625–1[2] of this title).

(B) Effective date

The date required under subparagraph (A) shall be—

(i) 6 months after the adoption date, in the case of gasoline dispensing facilities for which construction commenced after November 15, 1990;

(ii) one year after the adoption date, in the case of gasoline dispensing facilities which dispense at least 100,000 gallons of gasoline per month, based on average monthly sales for the 2-year period before the adoption date; or

(iii) 2 years after the adoption date, in the case of all other gasoline dispensing facilities.

Any gasoline dispensing facility described under both clause (i) and clause (ii) shall meet the requirements of clause (i).

(C) Reference to terms

For purposes of this paragraph, any reference to the term "adoption date" shall be considered a reference to the date of adoption by the State of requirements for the installation and operation of a system for gasoline vapor recovery of emissions from the fueling of motor vehicles.

(4) Motor vehicle inspection and maintenance

For all Moderate Areas, the State shall submit, immediately after November 15, 1990, a revision to the applicable implementation plan that includes provisions necessary to provide for a vehicle inspection and maintenance program as described in subsection (a)(2)(B) of this section (without regard to whether or not the area was required by section 7502(b)(11)(B) of this title (as in effect immediately before November 15, 1990) to have included a specific schedule for implementation of such a program).

(5) General offset requirement

For purposes of satisfying the emission offset requirements of this part, the ratio of total emission reductions of volatile organic compounds to total increase emissions of such air pollutant shall be at least 1.15 to 1.

(c) Serious Areas

Except as otherwise specified in paragraph (4), each State in which all or part of a Serious Area is located shall, with respect to the Serious Area (or portion thereof, to the extent specified in this subsection), make the submissions described under subsection (b) of this section (relating to Moderate Areas), and shall also submit the revisions to the applicable implementation plan (including the plan items) described under this subsection. For any Serious Area, the terms "major source" and "major stationary source" include (in addition to the sources described in section 7602 of this title) any stationary source or group of sources located within a contiguous area and under common control that emits, or has the potential to emit, at least 50 tons per year of volatile organic compounds.

(1) Enhanced monitoring

In order to obtain more comprehensive and representative data on ozone air pollution, not later than 18 months after November 15, 1990, the Administrator shall promulgate rules, after notice and public comment, for enhanced monitoring of ozone, oxides of nitrogen, and volatile organic compounds.

The rules shall, among other things, cover the location and maintenance of monitors. Immediately following the promulgation of rules by the Administrator relating to enhanced monitoring, the State shall commence such actions as may be necessary to adopt and implement a program based on such rules, to improve monitoring for ambient concentrations of ozone, oxides of nitrogen and volatile organic compounds and to improve monitoring of emissions of oxides of nitrogen and volatile organic compounds. Each State implementation plan for the area shall contain measures to improve the ambient monitoring of such air pollutants.

(2) Attainment and reasonable further progress demonstrations

Within 4 years after November 15, 1990, the State shall submit a revision to the applicable implementation plan that includes each of the following:

(A) Attainment demonstration

A demonstration that the plan, as revised, will provide for attainment of the ozone national ambient air quality standard by the applicable attainment date. This attainment demonstration must be based on photochemical grid modeling or any other analytical method determined by the Administrator, in the Administrator's discretion, to be at least as effective.

(B) Reasonable further progress demonstration

A demonstration that the plan, as revised, will result in VOC emissions reductions from the baseline emissions described in subsection (b)(1)(B) of this section equal to the following amount averaged over each consecutive 3-year period beginning 6 years after November 15, 1990, until the attainment date:

(i) at least 3 percent of baseline emissions each year; or

(ii) an amount less than 3 percent of such baseline emissions each year, if the State demonstrates to the satisfaction of the Administrator that the plan reflecting such lesser amount includes all measures that can feasibly be implemented in the area, in light of technological achievability.

To lessen the 3 percent requirement under clause (ii), a State must demonstrate to the satisfaction of the Administrator that the plan for the area includes the measures that are achieved in practice by sources in the same source category in nonattainment areas of the next higher classification. Any determination to lessen the 3 percent requirement shall be reviewed at each milestone under subsection (g) of this section and revised to reflect such new measures (if any) achieved in practice by sources in the same category in any State, allowing a reasonable time to implement such measures. The emission reductions described in this subparagraph shall be calculated in accordance with subsection (b)(1)(C) and (D) of this section (concerning creditability of reductions). The reductions creditable for the period beginning 6 years after November 15, 1990, shall include reductions that occurred before such period, computed in accordance with subsection (b)(1) of this section, that exceed the 15-percent amount of reductions required under subsection (b)(1)(A) of this section.

(C) NO_x control

The revision may contain, in lieu of the demonstration required under subparagraph (B), a demonstration to the satisfaction of the Administrator that the applicable implementation plan, as revised, provides for reductions of emissions of VOC's and oxides of nitrogen (calculated according to the creditability provisions of subsection (b)(1)(C) and (D) of this section), that would result in a reduction in ozone concentrations at least equivalent to that which would result from the amount of VOC emission reductions required under subparagraph (B). Within 1 year after November 15, 1990, the Administrator shall issue guidance concerning the conditions under which NO_x control may be substituted for VOC control or may be combined with VOC control in order to maximize the reduction in ozone air pollution. In accord with such guidance, a lesser percentage of VOCs may be accepted as an adequate demonstration for purposes of this subsection.

(3) Enhanced vehicle inspection and maintenance program

(A) Requirement for submission

Within 2 years after November 15, 1990, the State shall submit a revision to the applicable implementation plan to provide for an enhanced program to reduce hydrocarbon emissions and NO_x emissions from in-use motor vehicles registered in each urbanized area (in the nonattainment area), as defined by the Bureau of the Census, with a 1980 population of 200,000 or more.

(B) Effective date of State programs; guidance

The State program required under subparagraph (A) shall take effect no later than 2 years from November 15, 1990, and shall comply in all respects with guidance published in the Federal Register (and from time to time revised) by the Administrator for enhanced vehicle inspection and maintenance programs. Such guidance shall include—

(i) a performance standard achievable by a program combining emission testing, including on-road emission testing, with inspection to detect tampering with emission control devices and misfueling for all light-duty vehicles and all light-duty trucks subject to standards under section 7521 of this title; and

(ii) program administration features necessary to reasonably assure that adequate management resources, tools, and practices are in place to attain and maintain the performance standard.

Compliance with the performance standard under clause (i) shall be determined using a method to be established by the Administrator.

(C) State program

The State program required under subparagraph (A) shall include, at a minimum, each of the following elements—

(i) Computerized emission analyzers, including on-road testing devices.

(ii) No waivers for vehicles and parts covered by the emission control performance warranty as provided for in section 7541(b) of this title unless a warranty remedy has been denied in writing, or for tampering-related repairs.

(iii) In view of the air quality purpose of the program, if, for any vehicle, waivers are permitted for emissions-related repairs not covered by warranty, an expenditure to qualify for the waiver of an amount of $450 or more for such repairs (adjusted annually as determined by the Administrator on the basis of the Consumer Price Index in the same manner as provided in subchapter V of this chapter).

(iv) Enforcement through denial of vehicle registration (except for any program in operation before November 15, 1990, whose enforcement mechanism is demonstrated to the Administrator to be more effective than the applicable vehicle registration program in assuring that noncomplying vehicles are not operated on public roads).

(v) Annual emission testing and necessary adjustment, repair, and maintenance, unless the State demonstrates to the satisfaction of the Administrator that a biennial inspection, in combination with other features of the program which exceed the requirements of this chapter, will result in emission reductions which equal or exceed the reductions which can be obtained through such annual inspections.

(vi) Operation of the program on a centralized basis, unless the State demonstrates to the satisfaction of the Administrator that a decentralized program will be equally effective. An electronically connected testing system, a licensing system, or other measures (or any combination thereof) may be considered, in accordance with criteria established by the Administrator, as equally effective for such purposes.

(vii) Inspection of emission control diagnostic systems and the maintenance or repair of malfunctions or system deterioration identified by or affecting such diagnostics systems.

Each State shall biennially prepare a report to the Administrator which assesses the emission reductions achieved by the program required under this paragraph based on data collected during inspection and repair of vehicles. The methods used to assess the emission reductions shall be those established by the Administrator.

(4) Clean-fuel vehicle programs

(A) Except to the extent that substitute provisions have been approved by the Administrator under subparagraph (B), the State shall submit to the Administrator, within 42 months of November 15, 1990, a revision to the applicable implementation plan for each area described under part C of subchapter II of this chapter to include such measures as may be necessary to ensure the effectiveness of the applicable provisions of the clean-fuel vehicle program prescribed under part C of subchapter II of this chapter, including all measures necessary to make the use of clean alternative fuels in clean-fuel vehicles (as defined in part C of subchapter II of this chapter) economic from the standpoint of vehicle owners. Such a revision shall also be submitted for each area that opts into the clean fuel-vehicle program as provided in part C of subchapter II of this chapter.

(B) The Administrator shall approve, as a substitute for all or a portion of the clean-fuel vehicle program prescribed under part C of subchapter II of this chapter, any revision to the relevant applicable implementation plan that in the Administrator's judgment will achieve long-term reductions in ozone-producing and toxic air emissions equal to those achieved under part C of subchapter II of this chapter, or the percentage thereof attributable to the portion of the clean-fuel vehicle program for which the revision is to substitute. The Administrator may approve such revision only if it consists exclusively of provisions other than those required under this chapter for the area. Any State seeking approval of such revision must submit the revision to the Administrator within 24 months of November 15, 1990. The Administrator shall approve or disapprove any such revision within 30 months of November 15, 1990. The Administrator shall publish the revision submitted by a State in the Federal Register upon receipt. Such notice shall constitute a notice of proposed rulemaking on whether or not to approve such revision and shall be deemed to comply with the requirements concerning notices of proposed rulemaking contained in sections 553 through 557 of Title 5 (related to notice and comment). Where the Administrator approves such revision for any area, the State need not submit the revision required by subparagraph (A) for the area with respect to the portions of the Federal clean-fuel vehicle program for which the Administrator has approved the revision as a substitute.

(C) If the Administrator determines, under section 7509 of this title, that the State has failed to submit any portion of the program required under subparagraph (A), then, in addition to any sanctions available under section 7509 of this title, the State may not receive credit, in any demonstration of attainment or reasonable further progress for the area, for any emission reductions from implementation of the corresponding aspects of the Federal clean-fuel vehicle requirements established in part C of subchapter II of this chapter.

(5) Transportation control

(A)[3] Beginning 6 years after November 15, 1990, and each third year thereafter, the State shall submit a demonstration as to whether current aggregate vehicle mileage, aggregate vehicle emissions, congestion levels, and other relevant parameters are consistent with those used for the area's demonstration of attainment. Where such parameters and emissions levels exceed the levels projected for purposes of the area's attainment demonstration, the State shall within 18 months develop and submit a revision of the applicable implementation plan that includes a transportation control measures program consisting of measures from, but not limited to, section 7408(f) of this title that will reduce emissions to levels that are consistent with emission levels projected in such demonstration. In considering such measures, the State should ensure adequate access to downtown, other commercial, and residential areas and should avoid measures that increase or relocate emissions and congestion rather than reduce them. Such revision shall be developed in accordance with guidance issued by the Administrator pursuant to section 7408(e) of this title and with the requirements of section 7504(b) of this title and shall include implementation and funding schedules that achieve expeditious emissions reductions in accordance with implementation plan projections.

(6) De minimis rule

The new source review provisions under this part shall ensure that increased emissions of volatile organic compounds resulting from any physical change in, or change in the method of operation of, a stationary source located in the area shall not be considered de minimis for purposes of determining the applicability of the permit requirements established by this chapter unless the increase in net emissions of such air pollutant from such source does not exceed 25 tons when aggregated with all other net increases in emissions from the source over any period of 5 consecutive calendar years which includes the calendar year in which such increase occurred.

(7) Special rule for modifications of sources emitting less than 100 tons

In the case of any major stationary source of volatile organic compounds located in the area (other than a source which emits or has the potential to emit 100 tons or more of volatile organic compounds per year), whenever any change (as described in section 7411(a)(4) of this title) at that source results in any increase (other than a de minimis increase) in emissions of volatile organic compounds from any discrete operation, unit, or other pollutant emitting activity at the source, such increase shall be considered a modification for purposes of section 7502(c)(5) of this title and section 7503(a) of this title, except that such increase shall not be considered a modification for such purposes if the owner or operator of the source elects to offset the increase by a greater reduction in emissions of volatile organic compounds concerned from other operations, units, or activities within the source at an internal offset ratio of at least 1.3 to 1. If the owner or operator does not make such election, such change shall be considered a modification for such purposes, but in applying section 7503(a)(2) of this title in the case of any such modification, the best available control technology (BACT), as defined in section 7479 of this title, shall be substituted for the lowest achievable emission rate (LAER). The Administrator shall establish and publish policies and procedures for implementing the provisions of this paragraph.

(8) Special rule for modifications of sources emitting 100 tons or more

In the case of any major stationary source of volatile organic compounds located in the area which emits or has the potential to emit 100 tons or more of volatile organic compounds per year, whenever any change (as described in section 7411(a)(4) of this title) at that source results in any increase (other than a de minimis increase) in emissions of volatile organic compounds from any discrete operation, unit, or other pollutant emitting activity at the source, such increase shall be considered a modification for purposes of section 7502(c)(5) of this title and section 7503(a) of this title, except that if the owner or operator of the source elects to offset the increase by a greater reduction in emissions of volatile organic compounds from other operations, units, or activities within the source at an internal offset ratio of at least 1.3 to 1, the requirements of section 7503(a)(2) of this title (concerning the lowest achievable emission rate (LAER)) shall not apply.

(9) Contingency provisions

In addition to the contingency provisions required under section 7502(c)(9) of this title, the plan revision shall provide for the implementation of specific measures to be undertaken if the area fails to meet any applicable milestone. Such measures shall be included in the plan revision as contingency measures to take effect without further action by the State or the Administrator upon a failure by the State to meet the applicable milestone.

(10) General offset requirement

For purposes of satisfying the emission offset requirements of this part, the ratio of total emission reductions of volatile organic compounds to total increase emissions of such air pollutant shall be at least 1.2 to 1.

Any reference to "attainment date" in subsection (b) of this section, which is incorporated by reference into this subsection, shall refer to the attainment date for serious areas.

(d) Severe Areas

Each State in which all or part of a Severe Area is located shall, with respect to the Severe Area, make the submissions described under subsection (c) of this section (relating to Serious Areas), and shall also submit the revisions to the applicable implementation plan (including the plan items) described under this subsection. For any Severe Area, the terms "major source" and "major stationary source" include (in addition to the sources described in section 7602 of this title) any stationary source or group of sources located within a contiguous area and under common control that emits, or has the potential to emit, at least 25 tons per year of volatile organic compounds.

(1) Vehicle miles traveled

(A) Within 2 years after November 15, 1990, the State shall submit a revision that identifies and adopts specific enforceable transportation control strategies and transportation control measures to offset any growth in emissions from growth in vehicle miles traveled or numbers of vehicle trips in such area and to attain reduction in motor vehicle emissions as necessary, in combination with other emission reduction requirements of this subpart, to comply with the requirements of subsection[4] (b)(2)(B) and (c)(2)(B) of this section (pertaining to periodic emissions reduction requirements). The State shall consider measures specified in section 7408(f) of this title, and choose from among and implement such measures as necessary to demonstrate attainment with the national ambient air quality standards; in considering such measures, the State should ensure adequate access to downtown, other commercial, and residential areas and should avoid measures that increase or relocate emissions and congestion rather than reduce them.

(B) The State may also, in its discretion, submit a revision at any time requiring employers in such area to implement programs to reduce work-related vehicle trips and miles travelled by employees. Such revision shall be developed in accordance with guidance issued by the Administrator pursuant to section 7408(f) of this title and may require that employers in such area increase average passenger occupancy per vehicle in commuting trips between home and the workplace during peak travel periods. The guidance of the Administrator may specify average vehicle occupancy rates which vary for locations within a nonattainment area (suburban, center city, business district) or among nonattainment areas reflecting existing occupancy rates and the availability of high occupancy modes. Any State required to submit a revision under this subparagraph (as in effect before December 23, 1995) containing provisions requiring employers to reduce work-related vehicle trips and miles travelled by employees may, in accordance with State law, remove such provisions from the implementation plan, or withdraw its submission, if the State notifies the Administrator, in writing, that the State has undertaken, or will undertake, one or more alternative methods that will achieve emission reductions equivalent to those to be achieved by the removed or withdrawn provisions.

(2) Offset requirement

For purposes of satisfying the offset requirements pursuant to this part, the ratio of total emission reductions of VOCs to total increased emissions of such air pollutant shall be at least 1.3 to 1, except that if the State plan requires all existing major sources in the nonattainment area to use best available control technology (as defined in section 7479(3) of this title) for the control of volatile organic compounds, the ratio shall be at least 1.2 to 1.

(3) Enforcement under section 7511d

By December 31, 2000, the State shall submit a plan revision which includes the provisions required under section 7511d of this title.

Any reference to the term "attainment date" in subsection (b) or (c) of this section, which is incorporated by reference into this subsection (d), shall refer to the attainment date for Severe Areas.

(e) Extreme Areas

Each State in which all or part of an Extreme Area is located shall, with respect to the Extreme Area, make the submissions described under subsection (d) of this section (relating to Severe Areas), and shall also submit the revisions to the applicable implementation plan (including the plan items) described under this subsection. The provisions of clause (ii) of subsection (c)(2)(B) of this section (relating to reductions of less than 3 percent), the provisions of paragraphs[5] (6), (7) and (8) of subsection (c) of this section (relating to de minimus rule and modification of sources), and the provisions of clause (ii) of subsection (b)(1)(A) of this section (relating to reductions of less than 15 percent) shall not apply in the case of an Extreme Area. For any Extreme Area, the terms "major source" and "major stationary source" includes (in addition to the sources described in section 7602 of this title) any stationary source or group of sources located within a contiguous area and under common control that emits, or has the potential to emit, at least 10 tons per year of volatile organic compounds.

(1) Offset requirement

For purposes of satisfying the offset requirements pursuant to this part, the ratio of total emission reductions of VOCs to total increased emissions of such air pollutant shall be at least 1.5 to 1, except that if the State plan requires all existing major sources in the nonattainment area to use best available control technology (as defined in section 7479(3) of this title) for the control of volatile organic compounds, the ratio shall be at least 1.2 to 1.

(2) Modifications

Any change (as described in section 7411(a)(4) of this title) at a major stationary source which results in any increase in emissions from any discrete operation, unit, or other pollutant emitting activity at the source shall be considered a modification for purposes of section 7502(c)(5) of this title and section 7503(a) of this title, except that for purposes of complying with the offset requirement pursuant to section 7503(a)(1) of this title, any such increase shall not be considered a modification if the owner or operator of the source elects to offset the increase by a greater reduction in emissions of the air pollutant concerned from other discrete operations, units, or activities within the source at an internal offset ratio of at least 1.3 to 1. The offset requirements of this part shall not be applicable in Extreme Areas to a modification of an existing source if such modification consists of installation of equipment required to comply with the applicable implementation plan, permit, or this chapter.

(3) Use of clean fuels or advanced control technology

For Extreme Areas, a plan revision shall be submitted within 3 years after November 15, 1990, to require, effective 8 years after November 15, 1990, that each new, modified, and existing electric utility and industrial and commercial boiler which emits more than 25 tons per year of oxides of nitrogen—

(A) burn as its primary fuel natural gas, methanol, or ethanol (or a comparably low polluting fuel), or

(B) use advanced control technology (such as catalytic control technology or other comparably effective control methods) for reduction of emissions of oxides of nitrogen.

For purposes of this subsection, the term "primary fuel" means the fuel which is used 90 percent or more of the operating time. This paragraph shall not apply during any natural gas supply emergency (as defined in title III of the Natural Gas Policy Act of 1978 [15 U.S.C.A. § 3361 et seq.]).

(4) Traffic control measures during heavy traffic hours

For Extreme Areas, each implementation plan revision under this subsection may contain provisions establishing traffic control measures applicable during heavy traffic hours to reduce the use of high polluting vehicles or heavy-duty vehicles, notwithstanding any other provision of law.

(5) New technologies

The Administrator may, in accordance with section 7410 of this title, approve provisions of an implementation plan for an Extreme Area which anticipate development of new control techniques or improvement of existing control technologies, and an attainment demonstration based on such provisions, if the State demonstrates to the satisfaction of the Administrator that—

(A) such provisions are not necessary to achieve the incremental emission reductions required during the first 10 years after November 15, 1990; and

(B) the State has submitted enforceable commitments to develop and adopt contingency measures to be implemented as set forth herein if the anticipated technologies do not achieve planned reductions.

Such contingency measures shall be submitted to the Administrator no later than 3 years before proposed implementation of the plan provisions and approved or disapproved by the Administrator in accordance with section 7410 of this title. The contingency measures shall be adequate to produce emission reductions sufficient, in conjunction with other approved plan provisions, to achieve the periodic emission reductions required by subsection (b)(1) or (c)(2) of this section and attainment by the applicable dates. If the Administrator determines that an Extreme Area has failed to achieve an emission reduction requirement set forth in subsection (b)(1) or (c)(2) of this section, and that such failure is due in whole or part to an inability to fully implement provisions approved pursuant to this subsection, the Administrator shall require the State to implement the contingency measures to the extent necessary to assure compliance with subsections (b)(1) and (c)(2) of this section.

Any reference to the term "attainment date" in subsection (b), (c), or (d) of this section which is incorporated by reference into this subsection, shall refer to the attainment date for Extreme Areas.

(f) NO_x requirements

(1) The plan provisions required under this subpart for major stationary sources of volatile organic compounds shall also apply to major stationary sources (as defined in section 7602 of this title and subsections (c), (d), and (e) of this section) of oxides of nitrogen. This subsection shall not apply in the case of oxides of nitrogen for those sources for which the Administrator determines (when the Administrator approves a plan or plan revision) that net air quality benefits are greater in the absence of reductions of oxides of nitrogen from the sources concerned. This subsection shall also not apply in the case of oxides of nitrogen for—

(A) nonattainment areas not within an ozone transport region under section 7511c of this title, if the Administrator determines (when the Administrator approves a plan or plan revision) that additional reductions of oxides of nitrogen would not contribute to attainment of the national ambient air quality standard for ozone in the area, or

(B) nonattainment areas within such an ozone transport region if the Administrator determines (when the Administrator approves a plan or plan revision) that additional reductions of oxides of nitrogen would not produce net ozone air quality benefits in such region.

The Administrator shall, in the Administrator's determinations, consider the study required under section 7511f of this title.

(2) (A) If the Administrator determines that excess reductions in emissions of NO_x would be achieved under paragraph (1), the Administrator may limit the application of paragraph (1) to the extent necessary to avoid achieving such excess reductions.

(B) For purposes of this paragraph, excess reductions in emissions of NO_x are emission reductions for which the Administrator determines that net air quality benefits are greater in the absence of such reductions. Alternatively, for purposes of this paragraph, excess reductions in emissions of NO_x are, for—

(i) nonattainment areas not within an ozone transport region under section 7511c of this title, emission reductions that the Administrator determines would not contribute to attainment of the national ambient air quality standard for ozone in the area, or

(ii) nonattainment areas within such ozone transport region, emission reductions that the Administrator determines would not produce net ozone air quality benefits in such region.

(3) At any time after the final report under section 7511f of this title is submitted to Congress, a person may petition the Administrator for a determination under paragraph (1) or (2) with respect to any nonattainment area or any ozone transport region under section 7511c of this title. The Administrator shall grant or deny such petition within 6 months after its filing with the Administrator.

(g) Milestones

(1) Reductions in emissions

6 years after November 15, 1990, and at intervals of every 3 years thereafter, the State shall determine whether each nonattainment area (other than an area classified as Marginal or Moderate) has achieved a reduction in emissions during the preceding intervals equivalent to the total emission reductions required to be achieved by the end of such interval pursuant to subsection (b)(1) of this section and the corresponding requirements of subsections (c)(2)(B) and (C), (d), and (e) of this section. Such reduction shall be referred to in this section as an applicable milestone.

(2) Compliance demonstration

For each nonattainment area referred to in paragraph (1), not later than 90 days after the date on which an applicable milestone occurs (not including an attainment date on which a milestone occurs in cases where the standard has been attained), each State in which all or part of such area is located shall submit to the Administrator a demonstration that the milestone has been met. A demonstration under this paragraph shall be submitted in such form and manner, and shall contain such information and analysis, as the Administrator shall require, by rule. The Administrator shall determine whether or not a State's demonstration is adequate within 90 days after the Administrator's receipt of a demonstration which contains the information and analysis required by the Administrator.

(3) Serious and Severe Areas; State election

If a State fails to submit a demonstration under paragraph (2) for any Serious or Severe Area within the required period or if the Administrator determines that the area has not met any applicable milestone, the State shall elect, within 90 days after such failure or determination—

(A) to have the area reclassified to the next higher classification,

(B) to implement specific additional measures adequate, as determined by the Administrator, to meet the next milestone as provided in the applicable contingency plan, or

(C) to adopt an economic incentive program as described in paragraph (4).

If the State makes an election under subparagraph (B), the Administrator shall, within 90 days after the election, review such plan and shall, if the Administrator finds the contingency plan inadequate, require further measures necessary to meet such milestone. Once the State makes an election, it shall be deemed accepted by the Administrator as meeting the election requirement. If the State fails to make an election required under this paragraph within the required 90-day period or within 6 months thereafter, the area shall be reclassified to the next higher classification by operation of law at the expiration of such 6-month period. Within 12 months after the date required for the State to make an election, the State shall submit a revision of the applicable implementation plan for the area that meets the requirements of this paragraph. The Administrator shall review such plan revision and approve or disapprove the revision within 9 months after the date of its submission.

(4) Economic incentive program

(A) An economic incentive program under this paragraph shall be consistent with rules published by the Administrator and sufficient, in combination with other elements of the State plan, to achieve the next milestone. The State program may include a nondiscriminatory system, consistent with applicable law regarding interstate commerce, of State established emissions fees or a system of marketable permits, or a system of State fees on sale or manufacture of products the use of which contributes to ozone formation, or any combination of the foregoing or other similar measures. The program may also include incentives and requirements to reduce vehicle emissions and vehicle miles traveled in the area, including any of the transportation control measures identified in section 7408(f) of this title.

(B) Within 2 years after November 15, 1990, the Administrator shall publish rules for the programs to be adopted pursuant to subparagraph (A). Such rules shall include model plan provisions which may be adopted for reducing emissions from permitted stationary sources, area sources, and mobile sources. The guidelines shall require that any revenues generated by the plan provisions adopted pursuant to subparagraph (A) shall be used by the State for any of the following:

(i) Providing incentives for achieving emission reductions.

(ii) Providing assistance for the development of innovative technologies for the control of ozone air pollution and for the development of lower-polluting solvents and surface coatings. Such assistance shall not provide for the payment of more than 75 percent of either the costs of any project to develop such a technology or the costs of development of a lower-polluting solvent or surface coating.

(iii) Funding the administrative costs of State programs under this chapter. Not more than 50 percent of such revenues may be used for purposes of this clause.

(5) Extreme Areas

If a State fails to submit a demonstration under paragraph (2) for any Extreme Area within the required period, or if the Administrator determines that the area has not met any applicable milestone, the State shall, within 9 months after such failure or determination, submit a plan revision to implement an economic incentive program which meets the requirements of paragraph (4). The Administrator shall review such plan revision and approve or disapprove the revision within 9 months after the date of its submission.

(h) Rural transport areas

(1) Notwithstanding any other provision of section 7511 of this title or this section, a State containing an ozone nonattainment area that does not include, and is not adjacent to, any part of a Metropolitan Statistical Area or, where one exists, a Consolidated Metropolitan Statistical Area (as defined by the United States Bureau of the Census), which area is treated by the Administrator, in the Administrator's discretion, as a rural transport area within the meaning of paragraph (2), shall be treated by operation of law as satisfying the requirements of this section if it makes the submissions required under subsection (a) of this section (relating to marginal areas).

(2) The Administrator may treat an ozone nonattainment area as a rural transport area if the Administrator finds that sources of VOC (and, where the Administrator determines relevant, NO_x) emissions within the area do not make a significant contribution to the ozone concentrations measured in the area or in other areas.

(i) Reclassified areas

Each State containing an ozone nonattainment area reclassified under section 7511(b)(2) of this title shall meet such requirements of subsections (b) through (d) of this section as may be applicable to the area as reclassified, according to the schedules prescribed in connection with such requirements, except that the Administrator may adjust any applicable deadlines (other than attainment dates) to the extent such adjustment is necessary or appropriate to assure consistency among the required submissions.

(j) Multi-State ozone nonattainment areas

(1) Coordination among States

Each State in which there is located a portion of a single ozone nonattainment area which covers more than one State (hereinafter in this section referred to as a "multi-State ozone nonattainment area") shall—

(A) take all reasonable steps to coordinate, substantively and procedurally, the revisions and implementation of State implementation plans applicable to the nonattainment area concerned; and

(B) use photochemical grid modeling or any other analytical method determined by the Administrator, in his discretion, to be at least as effective.

The Administrator may not approve any revision of a State implementation plan submitted under this part for a State in which part of a multi-State ozone nonattainment area is located if the plan revision for that State fails to comply with the requirements of this subsection.

(2) Failure to demonstrate attainment

If any State in which there is located a portion of a multi-State ozone nonattainment area fails to provide a demonstration of attainment of the national ambient air quality standard for ozone in that portion within the required period, the State may petition the Administrator to make a finding that the State would have been able to make such demonstration but for the failure of one or more other States in which other portions of the area are located to commit to the implementation of all measures required under this section (relating to plan submissions and requirements for ozone nonattainment areas). If the Administrator makes such finding, the provisions of section 7509 of this title (relating to sanctions) shall not apply, by reason of the failure to make such demonstration, in the portion of the multi-State ozone nonattainment area within the State submitting such petition.

(July 14, 1955, c. 360, Title I, § 182, as added by Pub. L. No. 101–549, Title I, § 103, 104 Stat. 2426 (Nov. 15, 1990); and amended by Pub. L. No. 104–70, § 1, 109 Stat. 773 (Dec. 23, 1995).)

[1] So in original. Probably should be "subparagraph."

[2] So in original. Probably should be section "7625."

[3] So in original. No subpar. (B) has been enacted.

[4] So in original. Probably should be "subsections."

[5] So in original. Probably should be "paragraphs."

HISTORICAL AND STATUTORY NOTES

References in Text

The Natural Gas Policy Act of 1978, referred to in subsec. (e)(3), is Pub. L. No. 95–621, 92 Stat. 3350 (Nov. 9, 1978), as amended. Title III of the Natural Gas Policy Act of 1978 is codified as subchapter III (section 3361 et seq.) of chapter 60 of Title 15, Commerce and Trade. For complete classification of this Act to the Code, see Short Title note set out under section 3301 of Title 15 and Tables.

Effective and Applicability Provisions

1990 Acts. Section effective Nov. 15, 1990, except as otherwise provided, see section 711(b) of Pub. L. No. 101–549, set out as a note under section 7401 of this title.

Savings Provisions

Suits, actions or proceedings commenced under this chapter as in effect prior to Nov. 15, 1990, not to abate by reason of the taking effect of amendments by Pub. L. No. 101–549, except as otherwise provided for, see section 711(a) of Pub. L. No. 101–549, set out as a note under section 7401 of this title.

Moratorium on Certain Emissions Testing Requirements

Pub. L. No. 104–59, Title III, § 348, 109 Stat. 617 (Nov. 28, 1995), provided that:

"(a) In general.—The Administrator of the Environmental Protection Agency (hereinafter in this section referred to as the 'Administrator') shall not require adoption or implementation by a State of a test-only I/M240 enhanced vehicle inspection and maintenance program as a means of compliance with section 182 or 187 of the Clean Air Act (42 U.S.C. 7511a; 7512a), but the Administrator may approve such a program if a State chooses to adopt the program as a means of compliance with such section.

"(b) Limitation on plan disapproval.—The Administrator shall not disapprove or apply an automatic discount to a State implementation plan revision under section 182 or 187 of the Clean Air Act (42 U.S.C. 7511a; 7512a) on the basis of a policy, regulation, or guidance providing for a discount of emissions credits because the inspection and maintenance program in such plan revision is decentralized or a test-and-repair program.

"(c) Emissions reduction credits.—

"(1) State plan revision; approval.—Within 120 days of the date of the enactment of this subsection [Nov. 28, 1995], a State may submit an implementation plan revision proposing an interim inspection and maintenance program under section 182 or 187 of the Clean Air Act (42 U.S.C. 7511a; 7512a). The Administrator shall approve the program based on the full amount of credits proposed by the State for each element of the program if the proposed credits reflect good faith estimates by the State and the revision is otherwise in compliance with such Act [this chapter]. If, within such 120-day period, the State submits to the Administrator proposed revisions to the implementation plan, has all of the statutory authority necessary to implement the revisions, and has proposed a regulation to make the revisions, the Administrator may approve the revisions without regard to whether or not such regulation has been issued as a final regulation by the State.

"(2) Expiration of interim approval.—The interim approval shall expire on the earlier of (A) the last day of the 18-month period beginning on the date of the interim approval, or (B) the date of final approval. The interim approval may not be extended.

"(3) Final approval.—The Administrator shall grant final approval of the revision based on the credits proposed by the State during or after the period of interim approval if data collected on the operation of the State program demonstrates that the credits are appropriate and the revision is otherwise in compliance with the Clean Air Act [this chapter].

"(4) Basis of approval; no automatic discount.—Any determination with respect to interim or full approval shall be based on the elements of the program and shall not apply any automatic discount because the program is decentralized or a test-and-repair program."

§ 7511b. Federal ozone measures

[CAA § 183]

(a) Control techniques guidelines for VOC sources

Within 3 years after November 15, 1990, the Administrator shall issue control techniques guidelines, in accordance with section 7408 of this title, for 11 categories of stationary sources of VOC emissions for which such guidelines have not been issued as of November 15, 1990, not including the categories referred to in paragraphs (3) and (4) of subsection (b) of this section. The Administrator may issue such additional control techniques guidelines as the Administrator deems necessary.

(b) Existing and new CTGS

(1) Within 36 months after November 15, 1990, and periodically thereafter, the Administrator shall review and, if necessary, update control technique guidance issued under section 7408 of this title before November 15, 1990.

(2) In issuing the guidelines the Administrator shall give priority to those categories which the Administrator considers to make the most significant contribution to the formation of ozone air pollution in ozone nonattainment areas, including hazardous waste treatment, storage, and disposal facilities which are permitted under subtitle C of the Solid Waste Disposal Act [42 U.S.C.A. § 6921 et seq.]. Thereafter the Administrator shall periodically review and, if necessary, revise such guidelines.

(3) Within 3 years after November 15, 1990, the Administrator shall issue control techniques guidelines in accordance with section 7408 of this title to reduce the aggregate emissions of volatile organic compounds into the ambient air from aerospace coatings and solvents. Such control techniques guidelines shall, at a minimum, be adequate to reduce aggregate emissions of volatile organic compounds into the ambient air from the application of such coatings and solvents to such level as the Administrator determines may be achieved through the adoption of best available control measures. Such control technology guidance shall provide for such reductions in such increments and on such schedules as the Administrator determines to be reasonable, but in no event later than 10 years after the final issuance of such control technology guidance. In developing control technology guidance under this subsection, the Administrator shall consult with the Secretary of Defense, the Secretary of Transportation, and the Administrator of the National Aeronautics and Space Administration with regard to the establishment of specifications for such coatings. In evaluating VOC reduction strategies, the guidance shall take into account the applicable requirements of section 7412 of this title and the need to protect stratospheric ozone.

(4) Within 3 years after November 15, 1990, the Administrator shall issue control techniques guidelines in accordance with section 7408 of this title to reduce the aggregate emissions of volatile organic compounds and PM-10 into the ambient air from paints, coatings, and solvents used in shipbuilding operations and ship repair. Such control techniques guidelines shall, at a minimum, be adequate to reduce aggregate emissions of volatile organic compounds and PM-10 into the ambient air from the removal or application of such paints, coatings, and solvents to such level as the Administrator determines may be achieved through the adoption of the best available control measures. Such control techniques guidelines shall provide for such reductions in such increments and on such schedules as the Administrator determines to be reasonable, but in no event later than 10 years after the final issuance of such control technology guidance. In developing control techniques guidelines under this subsection, the Administrator shall consult with the appropriate Federal agencies.

(c) Alternative control techniques

Within 3 years after November 15, 1990, the Administrator shall issue technical documents which identify alternative controls for all categories of stationary sources of volatile organic compounds and oxides of nitrogen which emit, or have the potential to emit 25 tons per year or more of such air pollutant. The Administrator shall revise and update such documents as the Administrator determines necessary.

(d) Guidance for evaluating cost-effectiveness

Within 1 year after November 15, 1990, the Administrator shall provide guidance to the States to be used in evaluating the relative cost-effectiveness of various options for the control of emissions from existing stationary sources of air pollutants which contribute to nonattainment of the national ambient air quality standards for ozone.

(e) Control of emissions from certain sources

(1) Definitions

For purposes of this subsection—

(A) Best available controls

The term "best available controls" means the degree of emissions reduction that the Administrator determines, on the basis of technological and economic feasibility, health, environmental, and energy impacts, is achievable through the application of the most effective equipment, measures, processes, methods, systems or techniques, including chemical reformulation, product or feedstock substitution, repackaging, and directions for use, consumption, storage, or disposal.

(B) Consumer or commercial product

The term "consumer or commercial product" means any substance, product (including paints, coatings, and solvents), or article (including any container or packaging) held by any person, the use, consumption, storage, disposal, destruction, or decomposition of which may result in the release of volatile organic compounds. The term does not include fuels or fuel additives regulated under section 7545 of this title, or motor vehicles, non-road vehicles, and non-road engines as defined under section 7550 of this title.

(C) Regulated entities

The term "regulated entities" means—

(i) manufacturers, processors, wholesale distributors, or importers of consumer or commercial products for sale or distribution in interstate commerce in the United States; or

(ii) manufacturers, processors, wholesale distributors, or importers that supply the entities listed under clause (i) with such products for sale or distribution in interstate commerce in the United States.

(2) Study and report

(A) Study

The Administrator shall conduct a study of the emissions of volatile organic compounds into the ambient air from consumer and commercial products (or any combination thereof) in order to—

(i) determine their potential to contribute to ozone levels which violate the national ambient air quality standard for ozone; and

(ii) establish criteria for regulating consumer and commercial products or classes or categories thereof which shall be subject to control under this subsection.

The study shall be completed and a report submitted to Congress not later than 3 years after November 15, 1990.

(B) Consideration of certain factors

In establishing the criteria under subparagraph (A)(ii), the Administrator shall take into consideration each of the following:

(i) The uses, benefits, and commercial demand of consumer and commercial products.

(ii) The health or safety functions (if any) served by such consumer and commercial products.

(iii) Those consumer and commercial products which emit highly reactive volatile organic compounds into the ambient air.

(iv) Those consumer and commercial products which are subject to the most cost-effective controls.

(v) The availability of alternatives (if any) to such consumer and commercial products which are of comparable costs, considering health, safety, and environmental impacts.

(3) Regulations to require emission reductions

(A) In general

Upon submission of the final report under paragraph (2), the Administrator shall list those categories of consumer or commercial products that the Administrator determines, based on the study, account for at least 80 percent of the VOC emissions, on a reactivity-adjusted basis, from consumer or commercial products in areas that violate the NAAQS for ozone. Credit toward the 80 percent emissions calculation shall be given for emission reductions from consumer or commercial products made after November 15, 1990. At such time, the Administrator shall divide the list into 4 groups establishing priorities for regulation based on the criteria established in paragraph (2). Every 2 years after promulgating such list, the Administrator shall regulate one group of categories until all 4 groups are regulated. The regulations shall require best available controls as defined in this section. Such regulations may exempt health use products for which the Administrator determines there is no suitable substitute. In order to carry out this section, the Administrator may, by regulation, control or prohibit any activity, including the manufacture or introduction into commerce, offering for sale, or sale of any consumer or commercial product which results in emission of volatile organic compounds into the ambient air.

(B) Regulated entities

Regulations under this subsection may be imposed only with respect to regulated entities.

(C) Use of CTGS

For any consumer or commercial product the Administrator may issue control techniques guidelines under this chapter in lieu of regulations required under subparagraph (A) if the Administrator determines that such guidance will be substantially as effective as regulations in reducing emissions of volatile organic compounds which contribute to ozone levels in areas which violate the national ambient air quality standard for ozone.

(4) Systems of regulation

The regulations under this subsection may include any system or systems of regulation as the Administrator may deem appropriate, including requirements for registration and labeling, self-monitoring and reporting, prohibitions, limitations, or economic incentives (including marketable permits and auctions of emissions rights) concerning the manufacture, processing, distribution, use, consumption, or disposal of the product.

(5) Special fund

Any amounts collected by the Administrator under such regulations shall be deposited in a special fund in the United States Treasury for licensing and other services, which thereafter shall be available until expended, subject to annual appropriation Acts, solely to carry out the activities of the Administrator for which such fees, charges, or collections are established or made.

(6) Enforcement

Any regulation established under this subsection shall be treated, for purposes of enforcement of this chapter, as a standard under section 7411 of this title and any violation of such regulation shall be treated as a violation of a requirement of section 7411(e) of this title.

(7) State administration

Each State may develop and submit to the Administrator a procedure under State law for implementing and enforcing regulations promulgated under this subsection. If the Administrator finds the State procedure is adequate, the Administrator shall approve such procedure. Nothing in this paragraph shall prohibit the Administrator from enforcing any applicable regulations under this subsection.

(8) Size, etc.

No regulations regarding the size, shape, or labeling of a product may be promulgated, unless the Administrator determines such regulations to be useful in meeting any national ambient air quality standard.

(9) State consultation

Any State which proposes regulations other than those adopted under this subsection shall consult with the Administrator regarding whether any other State or local subdivision has promulgated or is promulgating regulations on any products covered under this part. The Administrator shall establish a clearinghouse of information, studies, and regulations proposed and promulgated regarding products covered under this subsection and disseminate such information collected as requested by State or local subdivisions.

(f) Tank vessel standards

(1) Schedule for standards

(A) Within 2 years after November 15, 1990, the Administrator, in consultation with the Secretary of the Department in which the Coast Guard is operating, shall promulgate standards applicable to the emission of VOCs and any other air pollutant from loading and unloading of tank vessels (as that term is defined in section 2101 of Title 46) which the Administrator finds causes, or contributes to, air pollution that may be reasonably anticipated to endanger public health or welfare. Such standards shall require the application of reasonably available control technology, considering costs, any nonair-quality benefits, environmental impacts, energy requirements and safety factors associated with alternative control techniques. To the extent practicable such standards shall apply to loading and unloading facilities and not to tank vessels.

(B) Any regulation prescribed under this subsection (and any revision thereof) shall take effect after such period as the Administrator finds (after consultation with the Secretary of the department[1] in which the Coast Guard is operating) necessary to permit the development and application of the requisite technology, giving appropriate consideration to the cost of compliance within such period, except that the effective date shall not be more than 2 years after promulgation of such regulations.

(2) Regulations on equipment safety

Within 6 months after November 15, 1990, the Secretary of the Department in which the Coast Guard is operating shall issue regulations to ensure the safety of the equipment and operations which are to control emissions from the loading and unloading of tank vessels, under section 3703 of Title 46 and section 1225 of Title 33. The standards promulgated by the Administrator under paragraph (1) and the regulations issued by a State or political subdivision regarding emissions from the loading and unloading of tank vessels shall be consistent with the regulations regarding safety of the Department in which the Coast Guard is operating.

(3) Agency authority

(A) The Administrator shall ensure compliance with the tank vessel emission standards prescribed under paragraph (1)(A). The Secretary of the Department in which the Coast Guard is operating shall also ensure compliance with the tank vessel standards prescribed under paragraph (1)(A).

(B) The Secretary of the Department in which the Coast Guard is operating shall ensure compliance with the regulations issued under paragraph (2).

(4) State or local standards

After the Administrator promulgates standards under this section, no State or political subdivision thereof may adopt or attempt to enforce any standard respecting emissions from tank vessels subject to regulation under paragraph (1) unless such standard is no less stringent than the standards promulgated under paragraph (1).

(5) Enforcement

Any standard established under paragraph (1)(A) shall be treated, for purposes of enforcement of this chapter, as a standard under section 7411 of this title and any violation of such standard shall be treated as a violation of a requirement of section 7411(e) of this title.

(g) Ozone design value study

The Administrator shall conduct a study of whether the methodology in use by the Environmental Protection Agency as of November 15, 1990, for establishing a design value for ozone provides a reasonable indicator of the ozone air quality of ozone nonattainment areas. The Administrator shall obtain input from States, local subdivisions thereof, and others. The study shall be completed and a report submitted to Congress not later than 3 years after November 15, 1990. The results of the study shall be subject to peer and public review before submitting it to Congress.

(h) Vehicles entering ozone nonattainment areas

(1) Authority regarding ozone inspection and maintenance testing

(A) In general

No noncommercial motor vehicle registered in a foreign country and operated by a United States citizen or by an alien who is a permanent resident of the United States, or who holds a visa for the purposes of employment or educational study in the United States, may enter a covered ozone nonattainment area from a foreign country bordering the United States and contiguous to the nonattainment area more than twice in a single calendar-month period, if State law has requirements for the inspection and maintenance of such vehicles under the applicable implementation plan in the nonattainment area.

(B) Applicability

Subparagraph (A) shall not apply if the operator presents documentation at the United States border entry point establishing that the vehicle has complied with such inspection and maintenance requirements as are in effect and are applicable to motor vehicles of the same type and model year.

(2) Sanctions for violations

The President may impose and collect from the operator of any motor vehicle who violates, or attempts to violate, paragraph (1) a civil penalty of not more than $200 for the second violation or attempted violation and $400 for the third and each subsequent violation or attempted violation.

(3) State election

The prohibition set forth in paragraph (1) shall not apply in any State that elects to be exempt from the prohibition. Such an election shall take effect upon the President's receipt of written notice from the Governor of the State notifying the President of such election.

(4) Alternative approach

The prohibition set forth in paragraph (1) shall not apply in a State, and the President may implement an alternative approach, if—

(A) the Governor of the State submits to the President a written description of an alternative approach to facilitate the compliance, by some or all foreign-registered motor vehicles, with the motor vehicle inspection and maintenance requirements that are—

(i) related to emissions of air pollutants;

(ii) in effect under the applicable implementation plan in the covered ozone nonattainment area; and

(iii) applicable to motor vehicles of the same types and model years as the foreign-registered motor vehicles; and

(B) the President approves the alternative approach as facilitating compliance with the motor vehicle inspection and maintenance requirements referred to in subparagraph (A).

(5) Definition of covered ozone nonattainment area

In this section, the term "covered ozone nonattainment area" means a Serious Area, as codified under section 7511 of this title as of October 27, 1998.

(July 14, 1955, c. 360, Title I, § 183, as added by Pub. L. No. 101–549, Title I, § 103, 104 Stat. 2443 (Nov. 15, 1990); and amended by Pub. L. No. 105–286, § 2, 112 Stat. 2773 (Oct. 27, 1998).)

[1] So in original. Probably should be capitalized.

HISTORICAL AND STATUTORY NOTES

References in Text

The Solid Waste Disposal Act, referred to in subsec. (b)(2), is Title II of Pub. L. No. 89–272, 79 Stat. 997 (Oct. 20, 1965), as amended generally by Pub. L. No. 94–580, § 2, 90 Stat. 2795 (Oct. 21, 1976). Subtitle C of the Solid Waste Disposal Act is codified generally as subchapter III (section 6921 et seq.) of chapter 82 of this title. For complete classification of this Act to the Code, see Short Title of 1965 Acts note set out under section 6901 of this title and Tables.

Effective and Applicability Provisions

1998 Acts. Pub. L. No. 105–286, § 3, provided that:

"(a) In general.—The amendment made by section 2 [amending this section] takes effect 180 days after the date of the enactment of this Act [Oct. 27, 1998]. Nothing in that amendment shall require action that is inconsistent with the obligations of the United States under any international agreement.

"(b) Information.—As soon as practicable after the date of enactment of this Act [Oct. 27, 1998], the appropriate agency of the United States shall distribute information to publicize the prohibition set forth in the amendment made by section 2 [amending this section]."

1990 Acts. Section effective Nov. 15, 1990, except as otherwise provided, see section 711(b) of Pub. L. No. 101–549, set out as a note under section 7401 of this title.

Transfer of Functions

For transfer of authorities, functions, personnel, and assets of the Coast Guard, including the authorities and functions of the Secretary of Transportation relating thereto, to the Department of Homeland Security, and for treatment of related references, see 6 U.S.C.A. §§ 468(b), 551(d), 552(d) and 557, and the Department of Homeland Security Reorganization Plan of November 25, 2002, as modified, set out as a note under 6 U.S.C.A. § 542.

Savings Provisions

Suits, actions or proceedings commenced under this chapter as in effect prior to Nov. 15, 1990, not to abate by reason of the taking effect of amendments by Pub. L. No. 101–549, except as otherwise provided for, see section 711(a) of Pub. L. No. 101–549, set out as a note under section 7401 of this title.

§ 7511c. Control of interstate ozone air pollution

[CAA § 184]

(a) Ozone transport regions

A single transport region for ozone (within the meaning of section 7506a(a) of this title), comprised of the States of Connecticut, Delaware, Maine, Maryland, Massachusetts, New Hampshire, New Jersey, New York, Pennsylvania, Rhode Island, Vermont, and the Consolidated Metropolitan Statistical Area that includes the District of Columbia, is hereby established by operation of law. The provisions of section 7506a(a)(1) and (2) of this title shall apply with respect to the transport region established under this section and any other transport region established for ozone, except to the extent inconsistent with the provisions of this section. The Administrator shall convene the commission required (under section 7506a(b) of this title) as a result of the establishment of such region within 6 months of November 15, 1990.

(b) Plan provisions for States in ozone transport regions

(1) In accordance with section 7410 of this title, not later than 2 years after November 15, 1990 (or 9 months after the subsequent inclusion of a State in a transport region established for ozone), each State included within a transport region established for ozone shall submit a State implementation plan or revision thereof to the Administrator which requires the following—

(A) that each area in such State that is in an ozone transport region, and that is a metropolitan statistical area or part thereof with a population of 100,000 or more comply with the provisions of section 7511a(c)(2)(A) of this title (pertaining to enhanced vehicle inspection and maintenance programs); and

(B) implementation of reasonably available control technology with respect to all sources of volatile organic compounds in the State covered by a control techniques guideline issued before or after November 15, 1990.

(2) Within 3 years after November 15, 1990, the Administrator shall complete a study identifying control measures capable of achieving emission reductions comparable to those achievable through vehicle refueling controls contained in section 7511a(b)(3) of this title, and such measures or such vehicle refueling controls shall be implemented in accordance with the provisions of this section. Notwithstanding other deadlines in this section, the applicable implementation plan shall be revised to reflect such measures within 1 year of completion of the study. For purposes of this section any stationary source that emits or has the potential to emit at least 50 tons per year of volatile organic compounds shall be considered a major stationary source and subject to the requirements which would be applicable to major stationary sources if the area were codified as a Moderate nonattainment area.

(c) Additional control measures

(1) Recommendations

Upon petition of any State within a transport region established for ozone, and based on a majority vote of the Governors on the Commission[1] (or their designees), the Commission[1] may, after notice and opportunity for public comment, develop recommendations for additional control measures to be applied within all or a part of such transport region if the commission determines such measures are necessary to bring any area in such region into attainment by the dates provided by this subpart. The commission shall transmit such recommendations to the Administrator.

(2) Notice and review

Whenever the Administrator receives recommendations prepared by a commission pursuant to paragraph (1) (the date of receipt of which shall hereinafter in this section be referred to as the "receipt date"), the Administrator shall—

(A) immediately publish in the Federal Register a notice stating that the recommendations are available and provide an opportunity for public hearing within 90 days beginning on the receipt date; and

(B) commence a review of the recommendations to determine whether the control measures in the recommendations are necessary to bring any area in such region into attainment by the dates provided by this subpart and are otherwise consistent with this chapter.

(3) Consultation

In undertaking the review required under paragraph (2)(B), the Administrator shall consult with members of the commission of the affected States and shall take into account the data, views, and comments received pursuant to paragraph (2)(A).

(4) Approval and disapproval

Within 9 months after the receipt date, the Administrator shall (A) determine whether to approve, disapprove, or partially disapprove and partially approve the recommendations; (B) notify the commission in writing of such approval, disapproval, or partial disapproval; and (C) publish such determination in the Federal Register. If the Administrator disapproves or partially disapproves the recommendations, the Administrator shall specify—

(i) why any disapproved additional control measures are not necessary to bring any area in such region into attainment by the dates provided by this subpart or are otherwise not consistent with the[2] chapter; and

(ii) recommendations concerning equal or more effective actions that could be taken by the commission to conform the disapproved portion of the recommendations to the requirements of this section.

(5) Finding

Upon approval or partial approval of recommendations submitted by a commission, the Administrator shall issue to each State which is included in the transport region and to which a requirement of the approved plan applies, a finding under section 7410(k)(5) of this title that the implementation plan for such State is inadequate to meet the requirements of section 7410(a)(2)(D) of this title. Such finding shall require each such State to revise its implementation plan to include the approved additional control measures within one year after the finding is issued.

(d) Best available air quality monitoring and modeling

For purposes of this section, not later than 6 months after November 15, 1990, the Administrator shall promulgate criteria for purposes of determining the contribution of sources in one area to concentrations of ozone in another area which is a nonattainment area for ozone. Such criteria shall require that the best available air quality monitoring and modeling techniques be used for purposes of making such determinations.

(July 14, 1955, c. 360, Title I, § 184, as added by Pub. L. No. 101–549, Title I, § 103, 104 Stat. 2448 (Nov. 15, 1990).)

[1] So in original. Probably should not be capitalized.

[2] So in original. Probably should be "this."

HISTORICAL AND STATUTORY NOTES

Effective and Applicability Provisions

1990 Acts. Section effective Nov. 15, 1990, except as otherwise provided, see section 711(b) of Pub. L. No. 101–549, set out as a note under section 7401 of this title.

Savings Provisions

Suits, actions or proceedings commenced under this chapter as in effect prior to Nov. 15, 1990, not to abate by reason of the taking effect of amendments by Pub. L. No. 101–549, except as otherwise provided for, see section 711(a) of Pub. L. No. 101–549, set out as a note under section 7401 of this title.

§ 7511d. Enforcement for Severe and Extreme ozone nonattainment areas for failure to attain

[CAA § 185]

(a) General rule

Each implementation plan revision required under section 7511a(d) and (e) of this title (relating to the attainment plan for Severe and Extreme ozone nonattainment areas) shall provide that, if the area to which such plan revision applies has failed to attain the national primary ambient air quality standard for ozone by the applicable attainment date, each major stationary source of VOCs located in the area shall, except as otherwise provided under subsection (c) of this section, pay a fee to the State as a penalty for such failure, computed in accordance with subsection (b) of this section, for each calendar year beginning after the attainment date, until the area is redesignated as an attainment area for ozone. Each such plan revision should include procedures for assessment and collection of such fees.

(b) Computation of fee

(1) Fee amount

The fee shall equal $5,000, adjusted in accordance with paragraph (3), per ton of VOC emitted by the source during the calendar year in excess of 80 percent of the baseline amount, computed under paragraph (2).

(2) Baseline amount

For purposes of this section, the baseline amount shall be computed, in accordance with such guidance as the Administrator may provide, as the lower of the amount of actual VOC emissions ("actuals") or VOC emissions allowed under the permit applicable to the source (or, if no such permit has been issued for the attainment year, the amount of VOC emissions allowed under the applicable implementation plan ("allowables")) during the attainment year. Notwithstanding the preceding sentence, the Administrator may issue guidance authorizing the baseline amount to be determined in accordance with the lower of average actuals or average allowables, determined over a period of more than one calendar year. Such guidance may provide that such average calculation for a specific source may be used if that source's emissions are irregular, cyclical, or otherwise vary significantly from year to year.

(3) Annual adjustment

The fee amount under paragraph (1) shall be adjusted annually, beginning in the year beginning after 1990, in accordance with section 7661a(b)(3)(B)(v) of this title (relating to inflation adjustment).

(c) Exception

Notwithstanding any provision of this section, no source shall be required to pay any fee under subsection (a) of this section with respect to emissions during any year that is treated as an Extension Year under section 7511(a)(5) of this title.

(d) Fee collection by Administrator

If the Administrator has found that the fee provisions of the implementation plan do not meet the requirements of this section, or if the Administrator makes a finding that the State is not administering and enforcing the fee required under this section, the Administrator shall, in addition to any other action authorized under this subchapter, collect, in accordance with procedures promulgated by the Administrator, the unpaid fees required under subsection (a) of this section. If the Administrator makes such a finding under section 7509(a)(4) of this title, the Administrator may collect fees for periods before the determination, plus interest computed in accordance with section 6621(a)(2) of Title 26 (relating to computation of interest on underpayment of Federal taxes), to the extent the Administrator finds such fees have not been paid to the State. The provisions of clauses (ii) through (iii) of section 7661a(b)(3)(C) of this title (relating to penalties and use of the funds, respectively) shall apply with respect to fees collected under this subsection.

(e) Exemptions for certain small areas

For areas with a total population under 200,000 which fail to attain the standard by the applicable attainment date, no sanction under this section or under any other provision of this chapter shall apply if the area can demonstrate, consistent with guidance issued by the Administrator, that attainment in the area is prevented because of ozone or ozone precursors transported from other areas. The prohibition applies only in cases in which the area has met all requirements and implemented all measures applicable to the area under this chapter.

(July 14, 1955, c. 360, Title I, § 185, as added by Pub. L. No. 101–549, Title I, § 103, 104 Stat. 2450 (Nov. 15, 1990).)

HISTORICAL AND STATUTORY NOTES

Effective and Applicability Provisions

1990 Acts. Section effective Nov. 15, 1990, except as otherwise provided, see section 711(b) of Pub. L. No. 101–549, set out as a note under section 7401 of this title.

Savings Provisions

Suits, actions or proceedings commenced under this chapter as in effect prior to Nov. 15, 1990, not to abate by reason of the taking effect of amendments by Pub. L. No. 101–549, except as otherwise provided for, see section 711(a) of Pub. L. No. 101–549, set out as a note under section 7401 of this title.

§ 7511e. Transitional areas

[CAA § 185A]

If an area designated as an ozone nonattainment area as of November 15, 1990, has not violated the national primary ambient air quality standard for ozone for the 36-month period commencing on January 1, 1987, and ending on December 31, 1989, the Administrator shall suspend the application of the requirements of this subpart to such area until December 31, 1991. By June 30, 1992, the Administrator shall determine by order, based on the area's design value as of the attainment date, whether the area attained such standard by December 31, 1991. If the Administrator determines that the area attained the standard, the Administrator shall require, as part of the order, the State to submit a maintenance plan for the area within 12 months of such determination. If the Administrator determines that the area failed to attain the standard, the Administrator shall, by June 30, 1992, designate the area as nonattainment under section 7407(d)(4) of this title.

(July 14, 1955, c. 360, Title I, § 185A, as added by Pub. L. No. 101–549, Title I, § 103, 104 Stat. 2451 (Nov. 15, 1990).)

HISTORICAL AND STATUTORY NOTES

Effective and Applicability Provisions

1990 Acts. Section effective Nov. 15, 1990, except as otherwise provided, see section 711(b) of Pub. L. No. 101–549, set out as a note under section 7401 of this title.

Savings Provisions

Suits, actions or proceedings commenced under this chapter as in effect prior to Nov. 15, 1990, not to abate by reason of the taking effect of amendments by Pub. L. No. 101–549, except as otherwise provided for, see section 711(a) of Pub. L. No. 101–549, set out as a note under section 7401 of this title.

§ 7511f. NO_x and VOC study

[CAA § 185B]

The Administrator, in conjunction with the National Academy of Sciences, shall conduct a study on the role of ozone precursors in tropospheric ozone formation and control. The study shall examine the roles of NO_x and VOC emission reductions, the extent to which NO_x reductions may contribute (or be counterproductive) to achievement of attainment in different nonattainment areas, the sensitivity of ozone to the control of NO_x, the availability and extent of controls for NO_x, the role of biogenic VOC emissions, and the basic information required for air quality models. The study shall be completed and a proposed report made public for 30 days comment within 1 year of November 15, 1990, and a final report shall be submitted to Congress within 15 months after November 15, 1990. The Administrator shall utilize all available information and studies, as well as develop additional information, in conducting the study required by this section.

(July 14, 1955, c. 360, Title I, § 185B, as added by Pub. L. No. 101–549, Title I, § 103, 104 Stat. 2452 (Nov. 15, 1990).)

HISTORICAL AND STATUTORY NOTES

Effective and Applicability Provisions

1990 Acts. Section effective Nov. 15, 1990, except as otherwise provided, see section 711(b) of Pub. L. No. 101–549, set out as a note under section 7401 of this title.

Termination of Reporting Requirements

For termination of reporting provisions of this section, effective May 15, 2000, see Pub. L. No. 104–66, § 3003, as amended, set out as a note under 31 U.S.C.A. § 1113, and the 6th item on page 162 of House Document No. 103–7

Savings Provisions

Suits, actions or proceedings commenced under this chapter as in effect prior to Nov. 15, 1990, not to abate by reason of the taking effect of amendments by Pub. L. No. 101–549, except as otherwise provided for, see section 711(a) of Pub. L. No. 101–549, set out as a note under section 7401 of this title.

Subpart 3—Additional Provisions for Carbon Monoxide Nonattainment Areas

§ 7512. Classification and attainment dates

[CAA § 186]

(a) Classification by operation of law and attainment dates for nonattainment areas

(1) Each area designated nonattainment for carbon monoxide pursuant to section 7407(d) of this title shall be classified at the time of such designation under table 1, by operation of law, as a Moderate Area or a Serious Area based on the design value for the area. The design value shall be calculated according to the interpretation methodology issued by the Administrator most recently before November 15, 1990. For each area classified under this subsection, the primary standard attainment date for carbon monoxide shall be as expeditiously as practicable but not later than the date provided in table 1:

TABLE 3[1]

Area classification	Design value	Primary standard attainment date
Moderate	9.1–16.4 ppm	December 31, 1995
Serious	16.5 and above	December 31, 2000

(2) At the time of publication of the notice required under section 7407 of this title (designating carbon monoxide nonattainment areas), the Administrator shall publish a notice announcing the classification of each such carbon monoxide nonattainment area. The provisions of section 7502(a)(1)(B) of this title (relating to lack of notice-and-comment and judicial review) shall apply with respect to such classification.

(3) If an area classified under paragraph (1), table 1, would have been classified in another category if the design value in the area were 5 percent greater or 5 percent less than the level on which such classification was based, the Administrator may, in the Administrator's discretion, within 90 days after November 15, 1990, by the procedure required under paragraph (2), adjust the classification of the area. In making such adjustment, the Administrator may consider the number of exceedances of the national primary ambient air quality standard for carbon monoxide in the area, the level of pollution transport between the area and the other affected areas, and the mix of sources and air pollutants in the area. The Administrator may make the same adjustment for purposes of paragraphs (2), (3), (6), and (7) of section 7512a(a) of this title.

(4) Upon application by any State, the Administrator may extend for 1 additional year (hereinafter in this subpart referred to as the "Extension Year") the date specified in table 1 of subsection (a) of this section if—

(A) the State has complied with all requirements and commitments pertaining to the area in the applicable implementation plan, and

(B) no more than one exceedance of the national ambient air quality standard level for carbon monoxide has occurred in the area in the year preceding the Extension Year.

No more than 2 one-year extensions may be issued under this paragraph for a single nonattainment area.

(b) New designations and reclassifications

(1) New designations to nonattainment

Any area that is designated attainment or unclassifiable for carbon monoxide under section 7407(d)(4) of this title, and that is subsequently redesignated to nonattainment for carbon monoxide under section 7407(d)(3) of this title, shall, at the time of the redesignation, be classified by operation of law in accordance with table 1 under subsections (a)(1) and (a)(4) of this section. Upon its classification, the area shall be subject to the same requirements under section 7410 of this title, subpart 1 of this part, and this subpart that would have applied had the area been so classified at the time of the notice under subsection (a)(2) of this section, except that any absolute, fixed date applicable in connection with any such requirement is extended by operation of law by a period equal to the length of time between November 15, 1990, and the date the area is classified.

(2) Reclassification of Moderate Areas upon failure to attain

(A) General rule

Within 6 months following the applicable attainment date for a carbon monoxide nonattainment area, the Administrator shall determine, based on the area's design value as of the attainment date, whether the area has attained the standard by that date. Any Moderate Area that the Administrator finds has not attained the standard by that date shall be reclassified by operation of law in accordance with table 1 of subsection (a)(1) of this section as a Serious Area.

(B) Publication of notice

The Administrator shall publish a notice in the Federal Register, no later than 6 months following the attainment date, identifying each area that the Administrator has determined, under subparagraph (A), as having failed to attain and identifying the reclassification, if any, described under subparagraph (A).

(c) References to terms

Any reference in this subpart to a "Moderate Area" or a "Serious Area" shall be considered a reference to a Moderate Area or a Serious Area, respectively, as classified under this section.

(July 14, 1955, c. 360, Title I, § 186, as added by Pub. L. No. 101–549, Title I, § 104, 104 Stat. 2452 (Nov. 15, 1990).)

[1] So in original. Probably should be "TABLE 1."

HISTORICAL AND STATUTORY NOTES

Effective and Applicability Provisions

1990 Acts. Section to take effect Nov. 15, 1990, except as otherwise provided, see section 711(b) of Pub. L. No. 101–549, set out as a note under section 7401 of this title.

Savings Provisions

Suits, actions or proceedings commenced under this chapter as in effect prior to Nov. 15, 1990, not to abate by reason of the taking effect of amendments by Pub. L. No. 101–549, except as otherwise provided for, see section 711(a) of Pub. L. No. 101–549, set out as a note under section 7401 of this title.

§ 7512a. Plan submissions and requirements

[CAA § 187]

(a) Moderate Areas

Each State in which all or part of a Moderate Area is located shall, with respect to the Moderate Area (or portion thereof, to the extent specified in guidance of the Administrator issued before November 15, 1990), submit to the Administrator the State implementation plan revisions (including the plan items) described under this subsection, within such periods as are prescribed under this subsection, except to the extent the State has made such submissions as of November 15, 1990:

(1) Inventory

No later than 2 years from November 15, 1990, the State shall submit a comprehensive, accurate, current inventory of actual emissions from all sources, as described in section 7502(c)(3) of this title, in accordance with guidance provided by the Administrator.

(2) (A) Vehicle miles traveled

No later than 2 years after November 15, 1990, for areas with a design value above 12.7 ppm at the time of classification, the plan revision shall contain a forecast of vehicle miles traveled in the nonattainment area concerned for each year before the year in which the plan projects the national ambient air quality standard for carbon monoxide to be attained in the area. The forecast shall be based on guidance which shall be published by the Administrator, in consultation with the Secretary of Transportation, within 6 months after November 15, 1990. The plan revision shall provide for annual updates of the forecasts to be submitted to the Administrator together with annual reports regarding the extent to which such forecasts proved to be accurate. Such annual reports shall contain estimates of actual vehicle miles traveled in each year for which a forecast was required.

(B) Special rule for Denver

Within 2 years after November 15, 1990, in the case of Denver, the State shall submit a revision that includes the transportation control measures as required in section 7511a(d)(1)(A) of this title except that such revision shall be for the purpose of reducing CO emissions rather than volatile organic compound emissions. If the State fails to include any such measure, the implementation plan shall contain an explanation of why such measure was not adopted and what emissions reduction measure was adopted to provide a comparable reduction in emissions, or reasons why such reduction is not necessary to attain the national primary ambient air quality standard for carbon monoxide.

(3) Contingency provisions

No later than 2 years after November 15, 1990, for areas with a design value above 12.7 ppm at the time of classification, the plan revision shall provide for the implementation of specific measures to be undertaken if any estimate of vehicle miles traveled in the area which is submitted in an annual report under paragraph (2) exceeds the number predicted in the most recent prior forecast or if the area fails to attain the national primary ambient air quality standard for carbon monoxide by the primary standard attainment date. Such measures shall be included in the plan revision as contingency measures to take effect without further action by the State or the Administrator if the prior forecast has been exceeded by an updated forecast or if the national standard is not attained by such deadline.

(4) Savings clause for vehicle inspection and maintenance provisions of the State implementation plan

Immediately after November 15, 1990, for any Moderate Area (or, within the Administrator's discretion, portion thereof), the plan for which is of the type described in section 7511a(a)(2)(B) of this title any provisions necessary to ensure that the applicable implementation plan includes the vehicle inspection and maintenance program described in section 7511a(a)(2)(B) of this title.

(5) Periodic inventory

No later than September 30, 1995, and no later than the end of each 3 year period thereafter, until the area is redesignated to attainment, a revised inventory meeting the requirements of subsection (a)(1) of this section.

(6) Enhanced vehicle inspection and maintenance

No later than 2 years after November 15, 1990, in the case of Moderate Areas with a design value greater than 12.7 ppm at the time of classification, a revision that includes provisions for an enhanced vehicle inspection and maintenance program as required in section 7511a(c)(3) of this title (concerning serious ozone nonattainment areas), except that such program shall be for the purpose of reducing carbon monoxide rather than hydrocarbon emissions.

(7) Attainment demonstration and specific annual emission reductions

In the case of Moderate Areas with a design value greater than 12.7 ppm at the time of classification, no later than 2 years after November 15, 1990, a revision to provide, and a demonstration that the plan as revised will provide, for attainment of the carbon monoxide NAAQS by the applicable attainment date and provisions for such specific annual emission reductions as are necessary to attain the standard by that date.

The Administrator may, in the Administrator's discretion, require States to submit a schedule for submitting any of the revisions or other items required under this subsection. In the case of Moderate Areas with a design value of 12.7 ppm or lower at the time of classification, the requirements of this subsection shall apply in lieu of any requirement that the State submit a demonstration that the applicable implementation plan provides for attainment of the carbon monoxide standard by the applicable attainment date.

(b) Serious Areas

(1) In general

Each State in which all or part of a Serious Area is located shall, with respect to the Serious Area, make the submissions (other than those required under subsection (a)(1)(B)[1] of this section) applicable under subsection (a) of this section to Moderate Areas with a design value of 12.7 ppm or greater at the time of classification, and shall also submit the revision and other items described under this subsection.

(2) Vehicle miles traveled

Within 2 years after November 15, 1990, the State shall submit a revision that includes the transportation control measures as required in section 7511a(d)(1) of this title except that such revision shall be for the purpose of reducing CO emissions rather than volatile organic compound emissions. In the case of any such area (other than an area in New York State) which is a covered area (as defined in section 7586(a)(2)(B) of this title) for purposes of the Clean Fuel Fleet program under part C of subchapter II of this chapter, if the State fails to include any such measure, the implementation plan shall contain an explanation of why such measure was not adopted and what emissions reduction measure was adopted to provide a comparable reduction in emissions, or reasons why such reduction is not necessary to attain the national primary ambient air quality standard for carbon monoxide.

(3) Oxygenated gasoline

(A) Within 2 years after November 15, 1990, the State shall submit a revision to require that gasoline sold, supplied, offered for sale or supply, dispensed, transported or introduced into commerce in the larger of—

(i) the Consolidated Metropolitan Statistical Area (as defined by the United States Office of Management and Budget) (CMSA) in which the area is located, or

(ii) if the area is not located in a CMSA, the Metropolitan Statistical Area (as defined by the United States Office of Management and Budget) in which the area is located, be blended, during the portion of the year in which the area is prone to high ambient concentrations of carbon monoxide (as determined by the Administrator), with fuels containing such level of oxygen as is necessary, in combination with other measures, to provide for attainment of the carbon monoxide national ambient air quality standard by the applicable attainment date and maintenance of the national ambient air quality standard thereafter in the area. The revision shall provide that such requirement shall take effect no later than October 1, 1993, and shall include a program for implementation and enforcement of the requirement consistent with guidance to be issued by the Administrator.

(B) Notwithstanding subparagraph (A), the revision described in this paragraph shall not be required for an area if the State demonstrates to the satisfaction of the Administrator that the revision is not necessary to provide for attainment of the carbon monoxide national ambient air quality standard by the applicable attainment date and maintenance of the national ambient air quality standard thereafter in the area.

(c) Areas with significant stationary source emissions of CO

(1) Serious Areas

In the case of Serious Areas in which stationary sources contribute significantly to carbon monoxide levels (as determined under rules issued by the Administrator), the State shall submit a plan revision within 2 years after November 15, 1990, which provides that the term "major stationary source" includes (in addition to the sources described in section 7602 of this title) any stationary source which emits, or has the potential to emit, 50 tons per year or more of carbon monoxide.

(2) Waivers for certain areas

The Administrator may, on a case-by-case basis, waive any requirements that pertain to transportation controls, inspection and maintenance, or oxygenated fuels where the Administrator determines by rule that mobile sources of carbon monoxide do not contribute significantly to carbon monoxide levels in the area.

(3) Guidelines

Within 6 months after November 15, 1990, the Administrator shall issue guidelines for and rules determining whether stationary sources contribute significantly to carbon monoxide levels in an area.

(d) CO milestone

(1) Milestone demonstration

By March 31, 1996, each State in which all or part of a Serious Area is located shall submit to the Administrator a demonstration that the area has achieved a reduction in emissions of CO equivalent to the total of the specific annual emission reductions required by December 31, 1995. Such reductions shall be referred to in this subsection as the milestone.

(2) Adequacy of demonstration

A demonstration under this paragraph shall be submitted in such form and manner, and shall contain such information and analysis, as the Administrator shall require. The Administrator shall determine whether or not a State's demonstration is adequate within 90 days after the Administrator's receipt of a demonstration which contains the information and analysis required by the Administrator.

(3) Failure to meet emission reduction milestone

If a State fails to submit a demonstration under paragraph (1) within the required period, or if the Administrator notifies the State that the State has not met the milestone, the State shall, within 9 months after such a failure or notification, submit a plan revision to implement an economic incentive and transportation control program as described in section 7511a(g)(4) of this title. Such revision shall be sufficient to achieve the specific annual reductions in carbon monoxide emissions set forth in the plan by the attainment date.

(e) Multi-State CO nonattainment areas

(1) Coordination among States

Each State in which there is located a portion of a single nonattainment area for carbon monoxide which covers more than one State ("multi-State nonattainment area") shall take all reasonable steps to coordinate, substantively and procedurally, the revisions and implementation of State implementation plans applicable to the nonattainment area concerned. The Administrator may not approve any revision of a State implementation plan submitted under this part for a State in which part of a multi-State nonattainment area is located if the plan revision for that State fails to comply with the requirements of this subsection.

(2) Failure to demonstrate attainment

If any State in which there is located a portion of a multi-State nonattainment area fails to provide a demonstration of attainment of the national ambient air quality standard for carbon monoxide in that portion within the period required under this part the State may petition the Administrator to make a finding that the State would have been able to make such demonstration but for the failure of one or more other States in which other portions of the area are located to commit to the implementation of all measures required under this section (relating to plan submissions for carbon monoxide nonattainment areas). If the Administrator makes such finding, in the portion of the nonattainment area within the State submitting such petition, no sanction shall be imposed under section 7509 of this title or under any other provision of this chapter, by reason of the failure to make such demonstration.

(f) Reclassified areas

Each State containing a carbon monoxide nonattainment area reclassified under section 7512(b)(2) of this title shall meet the requirements of subsection (b) of this section, as may be applicable to the area as reclassified, according to the schedules prescribed in connection with such requirements, except that the Administrator may adjust any applicable deadlines (other than the attainment date) where such deadlines are shown to be infeasible.

(g) Failure of Serious Area to attain standard

If the Administrator determines under section 7512(b)(2) of this title that the national primary ambient air quality standard for carbon monoxide has not been attained in a Serious Area by the applicable attainment date, the State shall submit a plan revision for the area within 9 months after the date of such determination. The plan revision shall provide that a program of incentives and requirements as described in section 7511a(g)(4) of this title shall be applicable in the area, and such program, in combination with other elements of the revised plan, shall be adequate to reduce the total tonnage of emissions of carbon monoxide in the area by at least 5 percent per year in each year after approval of the plan revision and before attainment of the national primary ambient air quality standard for carbon monoxide.

(July 14, 1955, c. 360, Title I, § 187, as added by Pub. L. No. 101–549, Title I, § 104, 104 Stat. 2454 (Nov. 15, 1990).)

[1] So in original. Subsec. (a)(1) of this section does not contain a subpar. (B).

HISTORICAL AND STATUTORY NOTES

Effective and Applicability Provisions

1990 Acts. Section to take effect Nov. 15, 1990, except as otherwise provided, see section 711(b) of Pub. L. No. 101–549, set out as a note under section 7401 of this title.

Savings Provisions

Suits, actions or proceedings commenced under this chapter as in effect prior to Nov. 15, 1990, not to abate by reason of the taking effect of amendments by Pub. L. No. 101–549, except as otherwise provided for, see section 711(a) of Pub. L. No. 101–549, set out as a note under section 7401 of this title.

Moratorium on Certain Emissions Testing Requirements

For provisions directing that the Administrator shall not require the adoption or implementation by a State of a test-only I/M240 enhanced vehicle inspection and maintenance program as a mean of compliance with this section, see section 348 of Pub. L. No. 104–59, set out as a note under section 7511a of this title.

Subpart 4—Additional Provisions for Particulate Matter Nonattainment Areas

§ 7513. Classifications and attainment dates

[CAA § 188]

(a) Initial classifications

Every area designated nonattainment for PM-10 pursuant to section 7407(d) of this title shall be classified at the time of such designation, by operation of law, as a moderate PM-10 nonattainment area (also referred to in this subpart as a "Moderate Area") at the time of such designation. At the time of publication of the notice under section 7407(d)(4) of this title (relating to area designations) for each PM-10 nonattainment area, the Administrator shall publish a notice announcing the classification of such area. The provisions of section 7502(a)(1)(B) of this title (relating to lack of notice-and-comment and judicial review) shall apply with respect to such classification.

(b) Reclassification as Serious

(1) Reclassification before attainment date

The Administrator may reclassify as a Serious PM-10 nonattainment area (identified in this subpart also as a "Serious Area") any area that the Administrator determines cannot practicably attain the national ambient air quality standard for PM-10 by the attainment date (as prescribed in subsection (c) of this section) for Moderate Areas. The Administrator shall reclassify appropriate areas as Serious by the following dates:

(A) For areas designated nonattainment for PM-10 under section 7407(d)(4) of this title, the Administrator shall propose to reclassify appropriate areas by June 30, 1991, and take final action by December 31, 1991.

(B) For areas subsequently designated nonattainment, the Administrator shall reclassify appropriate areas within 18 months after the required date for the State's submission of a SIP for the Moderate Area.

(2) Reclassification upon failure to attain

Within 6 months following the applicable attainment date for a PM-10 nonattainment area, the Administrator shall determine whether the area attained the standard by that date. If the Administrator finds that any Moderate Area is not in attainment after the applicable attainment date—

(A) the area shall be reclassified by operation of law as a Serious Area; and

(B) the Administrator shall publish a notice in the Federal Register no later than 6 months following the attainment date, identifying the area as having failed to attain and identifying the reclassification described under subparagraph (A).

(c) Attainment dates

Except as provided under subsection (d) of this section, the attainment dates for PM-10 nonattainment areas shall be as follows:

(1) Moderate Areas

For a Moderate Area, the attainment date shall be as expeditiously as practicable but no later than the end of the sixth calendar year after the area's designation as nonattainment, except that, for areas designated nonattainment for PM-10 under section 7407(d)(4) of this title, the attainment date shall not extend beyond December 31, 1994.

(2) Serious Areas

For a Serious Area, the attainment date shall be as expeditiously as practicable but no later than the end of the tenth calendar year beginning after the area's designation as nonattainment, except that, for areas designated nonattainment for PM-10 under section 7407(d)(4) of this title, the date shall not extend beyond December 31, 2001.

(d) Extension of attainment date for Moderate Areas

Upon application by any State, the Administrator may extend for 1 additional year (hereinafter referred to as the "Extension Year") the date specified in paragraph[1] (c)(1) if—

(1) the State has complied with all requirements and commitments pertaining to the area in the applicable implementation plan; and

(2) no more than one exceedance of the 24-hour national ambient air quality standard level for PM-10 has occurred in the area in the year preceding the Extension Year, and the annual mean concentration of PM-10 in the area for such year is less than or equal to the standard level.

No more than 2 one-year extensions may be issued under the subsection for a single nonattainment area.

(e) Extension of attainment date for Serious Areas

Upon application by any State, the Administrator may extend the attainment date for a Serious Area beyond the date specified under subsection (c) of this section, if attainment by the date established under subsection (c) of this section would be impracticable, the State has complied with all requirements and commitments pertaining to that area in the implementation plan, and the State demonstrates to the satisfaction of the Administrator that the plan for that area includes the most stringent measures that are included in the implementation plan of any State or are achieved in practice in any State, and can feasibly be implemented in the area. At the time of such application, the State must submit a revision to the implementation plan that includes a demonstration of attainment by the most expeditious alternative date practicable. In determining whether to grant an extension, and the appropriate length of time for any such extension, the Administrator may consider the nature and extent of nonattainment, the types and numbers of sources or other emitting activities in the area (including the influence of uncontrollable natural sources and transboundary emissions from foreign countries), the population exposed to concentrations in excess of the standard, the presence and concentration of potentially toxic substances in the mix of particulate emissions in the area, and the technological and economic feasibility of various control measures. The Administrator may not approve an extension until the State submits an attainment demonstration for the area. The Administrator may grant at most one such extension for an area, of no more than 5 years.

(f) Waivers for certain areas

The Administrator may, on a case-by-case basis, waive any requirement applicable to any Serious Area under this subpart where the Administrator determines that anthropogenic sources of PM-10 do not contribute significantly to the violation of the PM-10 standard in the area. The Administrator may also waive a specific date for attainment of the standard where the Administrator determines that nonanthropogenic sources of PM-10 contribute significantly to the violation of the PM-10 standard in the area.

(July 14, 1955, c. 360, Title I, § 188, as added by Pub. L. No. 101–549, Title I, § 105(a), 104 Stat. 2458 (Nov. 15, 1990).)

[1] So in original. Probably should be "subsection."

HISTORICAL AND STATUTORY NOTES

Effective and Applicability Provisions

1990 Acts. Section to take effect Nov. 15, 1990, except as otherwise provided, see section 711(b) of Pub. L. No. 101–549, set out as a note under section 7401 of this title.

Savings Provisions

Suits, actions or proceedings commenced under this chapter as in effect prior to Nov. 15, 1990, not to abate by reason of the taking effect of amendments by Pub. L. No. 101–549, except as otherwise provided for, see section 711(a) of Pub. L. No. 101–549, set out as a note under section 7401 of this title.

§ 7513a. Plan provisions and schedules for plan submissions

[CAA § 189]

(a) Moderate Areas

(1) Plan provisions

Each State in which all or part of a Moderate Area is located shall submit, according to the applicable schedule under paragraph (2), an implementation plan that includes each of the following:

(A) For the purpose of meeting the requirements of section 7502(c)(5) of this title, a permit program providing that permits meeting the requirements of section 7503 of this title are required for the construction and operation of new and modified major stationary sources of PM-10.

(B) Either (i) a demonstration (including air quality modeling) that the plan will provide for attainment by the applicable attainment date; or (ii) a demonstration that attainment by such date is impracticable.

(C) Provisions to assure that reasonably available control measures for the control of PM-10 shall be implemented no later than December 10, 1993, or 4 years after designation in the case of an area classified as moderate after November 15, 1990.

(2) Schedule for plan submissions

A State shall submit the plan required under subparagraph (1) no later than the following:

(A) Within 1 year of November 15, 1990, for areas designated nonattainment under section 7407(d)(4) of this title, except that the provision required under subparagraph (1)(A) shall be submitted no later than June 30, 1992.

(B) 18 months after the designation as nonattainment, for those areas designated nonattainment after the designations prescribed under section 7407(d)(4) of this title.

(b) Serious Areas

(1) Plan provisions

In addition to the provisions submitted to meet the requirements of paragraph[1] (a)(1) (relating to Moderate Areas), each State in which all or part of a Serious Area is located shall submit an implementation plan for such area that includes each of the following:

(A) A demonstration (including air quality modeling)—

(i) that the plan provides for attainment of the PM-10 national ambient air quality standard by the applicable attainment date, or

(ii) for any area for which the State is seeking, pursuant to section 7513(e) of this title, an extension of the attainment date beyond the date set forth in section 7513(c) of this title, that attainment by that date would be impracticable, and that the plan provides for attainment by the most expeditious alternative date practicable.

(B) Provisions to assure that the best available control measures for the control of PM-10 shall be implemented no later than 4 years after the date the area is classified (or reclassified) as a Serious Area.

(2) Schedule for plan submissions

A State shall submit the demonstration required for an area under paragraph (1)(A) no later than 4 years after reclassification of the area to Serious, except that for areas reclassified under section 7513(b)(2) of this title, the State shall submit the attainment demonstration within 18 months after reclassification to Serious. A State shall submit the provisions described under paragraph (1)(B) no later than 18 months after reclassification of the area as a Serious Area.

(3) Major sources

For any Serious Area, the terms "major source" and "major stationary source" include any stationary source or group of stationary sources located within a contiguous area and under common control that emits, or has the potential to emit, at least 70 tons per year of PM-10.

(c) Milestones

(1) Plan revisions demonstrating attainment submitted to the Administrator for approval under this subpart shall contain quantitative milestones which are to be achieved every 3 years until the area is redesignated attainment and which demonstrate reasonable further progress, as defined in section 7501(1) of this title, toward attainment by the applicable date.

(2) Not later than 90 days after the date on which a milestone applicable to the area occurs, each State in which all or part of such area is located shall submit to the Administrator a demonstration that all measures in the plan approved under this section have been implemented and that the milestone has been met. A demonstration under this subsection shall be submitted in such form and manner, and shall contain such information and analysis, as the Administrator shall require. The Administrator shall determine whether or not a State's demonstration under this subsection is adequate within 90 days after the Administrator's receipt of a demonstration which contains the information and analysis required by the Administrator.

(3) If a State fails to submit a demonstration under paragraph (2) with respect to a milestone within the required period or if the Administrator determines that the area has not met any applicable milestone, the Administrator shall require the State, within 9 months after such failure or determination to submit a plan revision that assures that the State will achieve the next milestone (or attain the national ambient air quality standard for PM-10, if there is no next milestone) by the applicable date.

(d) Failure to attain

In the case of a Serious PM-10 nonattainment area in which the PM-10 standard is not attained by the applicable attainment date, the State in which such area is located shall, after notice and opportunity for public comment, submit within 12 months after the applicable attainment date, plan revisions which provide for attainment of the PM-10 air quality standard and, from the date of such submission until attainment, for an annual reduction in PM-10 or PM-10 precursor emissions within the area of not less than 5 percent of the amount of such emissions as reported in the most recent inventory prepared for such area.

(e) PM-10 precursors

The control requirements applicable under plans in effect under this part for major stationary sources of PM-10 shall also apply to major stationary sources of PM-10 precursors, except where the Administrator determines that such sources do not contribute significantly to PM-10 levels which exceed the standard in the area. The Administrator shall issue guidelines regarding the application of the preceding sentence.

(July 14, 1955, c. 360, Title I, § 189, as added by Pub. L. No. 101–549, Title I, § 105(a), 104 Stat. 2460 (Nov. 15, 1990).)

[1] So in original. Probably should be "subsection".

HISTORICAL AND STATUTORY NOTES

Effective and Applicability Provisions

1990 Acts. Section to take effect Nov. 15, 1990, except as otherwise provided, see section 711(b) of Pub. L. No. 101–549, set out as a note under section 7401 of this title.

Savings Provisions

Suits, actions or proceedings commenced under this chapter as in effect prior to Nov. 15, 1990, not to abate by reason of the taking effect of amendments by Pub. L. No. 101–549, except as otherwise provided for, see section 711(a) of Pub. L. No. 101–549, set out as a note under section 7401 of this title.

§ 7513b. Issuance of RACM and BACM guidance

[CAA § 190]

The Administrator shall issue, in the same manner and according to the same procedure as guidance is issued under section 7408(c) of this title, technical guidance on reasonably available control measures and best available control measures for urban fugitive dust, and emissions from residential wood combustion (including curtailments and exemptions from such curtailments) and prescribed silvicultural and agricultural burning, no later than 18 months following November 15, 1990. The Administrator shall also examine other categories of sources contributing to nonattainment of the PM-10 standard, and determine whether additional guidance on reasonably available control measures and best available control measures is needed, and issue any such guidance no later than 3 years after November 15, 1990. In issuing guidelines and making determinations under this section, the Administrator (in consultation with the State) shall take into account emission reductions achieved, or expected to be achieved, under subchapter IV-A of this chapter and other provisions of this chapter.

(July 14, 1955, c. 360, Title I, § 190, as added by Pub. L. No. 101–549, Title I, § 105(a), 104 Stat. 2462 (Nov. 15, 1990).)

HISTORICAL AND STATUTORY NOTES

References in Text

Subchapter IV-A of this chapter, referred to in text, originally read "title IV", meaning Title IV of the Clean Air Act, July 14, 1955, c. 360, Title IV, as added Nov. 15, 1990, Pub. L. No. 101–549, Title IV, 104 Stat. 2584, which is codified as Subchapter IV-A of this chapter, 42 U.S.C.A. § 7651 et seq.

Effective and Applicability Provisions

1990 Acts. Section to take effect Nov. 15, 1990, except as otherwise provided, see section 711(b) of Pub. L. No. 101–549, set out as a note under section 7401 of this title.

Savings Provisions

Suits, actions or proceedings commenced under this chapter as in effect prior to Nov. 15, 1990, not to abate by reason of the taking effect of amendments by Pub. L. No. 101–549, except as otherwise provided for, see section 711(a) of Pub. L. No. 101–549, set out as a note under section 7401 of this title.

Subpart 5—Additional Provisions for Areas Designated Nonattainment for Sulfur Oxides, Nitrogen Dioxide, or Lead

§ 7514. Plan submission deadlines

[CAA § 191]

(a) Submission

Any State containing an area designated or redesignated under section 7407(d) of this title as nonattainment with respect to the national primary ambient air quality standards for sulfur oxides, nitrogen dioxide, or lead subsequent to November 15, 1990, shall submit to the Administrator, within 18 months of the designation, an applicable implementation plan meeting the requirements of this part.

(b) States lacking fully approved State implementation plans

Any State containing an area designated nonattainment with respect to national primary ambient air quality standards for sulfur oxides or nitrogen dioxide under section 7407(d)(1)(C)(i) of this title, but lacking a fully approved implementation plan complying with the requirements of this chapter (including this part) as in effect immediately before November 15, 1990, shall submit to the Administrator, within 18 months of November 15, 1990, an implementation plan meeting the requirements of subpart 1 (except as otherwise prescribed by section 7514a of this title).

(July 14, 1955, c. 360, Title I, § 191, as added by Pub. L. No. 101–549, Title I, § 106, 104 Stat. 2463 (Nov. 15, 1990).)

HISTORICAL AND STATUTORY NOTES

Effective and Applicability Provisions

1990 Acts. Section to take effect Nov. 15, 1990, except as otherwise provided, see section 711(b) of Pub. L. No. 101–549, set out as a note under section 7401 of this title.

Savings Provisions

Suits, actions or proceedings commenced under this chapter as in effect prior to Nov. 15, 1990, not to abate by reason of the taking effect of amendments by Pub. L. No. 101–549, except as otherwise provided for, see section 711(a) of Pub. L. No. 101–549, set out as a note under section 7401 of this title.

§ 7514a. Attainment dates

[CAA § 192]

(a) Plans under section 7514(a)

Implementation plans required under section 7514(a) of this title shall provide for attainment of the relevant primary standard as expeditiously as practicable but no later than 5 years from the date of the nonattainment designation.

(b) Plans under section 7514(b)

Implementation plans required under section 7514(b) of this title shall provide for attainment of the relevant primary national ambient air quality standard within 5 years after November 15, 1990.

(c) Inadequate plans

Implementation plans for nonattainment areas for sulfur oxides or nitrogen dioxide with plans that were approved by the Administrator before November 15, 1990, but, subsequent to such approval, were found by the Administrator to be substantially inadequate, shall provide for attainment of the relevant primary standard within 5 years from the date of such finding.

(July 14, 1955, c. 360, Title I, § 192, as added by Pub. L. No. 101–549, Title I, § 106, 104 Stat. 2463 (Nov. 15, 1990).)

HISTORICAL AND STATUTORY NOTES

Effective and Applicability Provisions

1990 Acts. Section to take effect Nov. 15, 1990, except as otherwise provided, see section 711(b) of Pub. L. No. 101–549, set out as a note under section 7401 of this title.

Savings Provisions

Suits, actions or proceedings commenced under this chapter as in effect prior to Nov. 15, 1990, not to abate by reason of the taking effect of amendments by Pub. L. No. 101–549, except as otherwise provided for, see section 711(a) of Pub. L. No. 101–549, set out as a note under section 7401 of this title.

Subpart 6—Savings Provisions

§ 7515. General savings clause

[CAA § 193]

Each regulation, standard, rule, notice, order and guidance promulgated or issued by the Administrator under this chapter, as in effect before November 15, 1990, shall remain in effect according to its terms, except to the extent otherwise provided under this chapter, inconsistent with any provision of this chapter, or revised by the Administrator. No control requirement in effect, or required to be adopted by an order, settlement agreement, or plan in effect before November 15, 1990, in any area which is a nonattainment area for any air pollutant may be modified after November 15, 1990, in any manner unless the modification insures equivalent or greater emission reductions of such air pollutant.

(July 14, 1955, c. 360, Title I, § 193, as added by Pub. L. No. 101–549, Title I, § 108(*l*), 104 Stat. 2469 (Nov. 15, 1990).)

HISTORICAL AND STATUTORY NOTES

Effective and Applicability Provisions

1990 Acts. Section to take effect Nov. 15, 1990, except as otherwise provided, see section 711(b) of Pub. L. No. 101–549, set out as a note under section 7401 of this title.

Termination of Reporting Requirements

For termination of reporting provisions of this section pertaining to exemptions from national emission standards for hazardous air pollutants in the construction of stationary sources, effective May 15, 2000, see Pub. L. No. 104–66, § 3003, as amended, set out as a note under 31 U.S.C.A. § 1113, and the 11th item on page 20 of House Document No. 103–7.

Savings Provisions

Suits, actions or proceedings commenced under this chapter as in effect prior to Nov. 15, 1990, not to abate by reason of the taking effect of amendments by Pub. L. No. 101–549, except as otherwise provided for, see section 711(a) of Pub. L. No. 101–549, set out as a note under section 7401 of this title.

SUBCHAPTER II—EMISSION STANDARDS FOR MOVING SOURCES

PART A—MOTOR VEHICLE EMISSION AND FUEL STANDARDS

§ 7521. Emission standards for new motor vehicles or new motor vehicle engines [CAA § 202]

(a) Authority of Administrator to prescribe by regulation

Except as otherwise provided in subsection (b) of this section—

(1) The Administrator shall by regulation prescribe (and from time to time revise) in accordance with the provisions of this section, standards applicable to the emission of any air pollutant from any class or classes of new motor vehicles or new motor vehicle engines, which in his judgment cause, or contribute to, air pollution which may reasonably be anticipated to endanger public health or welfare. Such standards shall be applicable to such vehicles and engines for their useful life (as determined under subsection (d) of this section, relating to useful life of vehicles for purposes of certification), whether such vehicles and engines are designed as complete systems or incorporate devices to prevent or control such pollution.

(2) Any regulation prescribed under paragraph (1) of this subsection (and any revision thereof) shall take effect after such period as the Administrator finds necessary to permit the development and application of the requisite technology, giving appropriate consideration to the cost of compliance within such period.

(3) (A) In general

(i) Unless the standard is changed as provided in subparagraph (B), regulations under paragraph (1) of this subsection applicable to emissions of hydrocarbons, carbon monoxide, oxides of nitrogen, and particulate matter from classes or categories of heavy-duty vehicles or engines manufactured during or after model year 1983 shall contain standards which reflect the greatest degree of emission reduction achievable through the application of technology which the Administrator determines will be available for the model year to which such standards apply, giving appropriate consideration to cost, energy, and safety factors associated with the application of such technology.

(ii) In establishing classes or categories of vehicles or engines for purposes of regulations under this paragraph, the Administrator may base such classes or categories on gross vehicle weight, horsepower, type of fuel used, or other appropriate factors.

(B) Revised standards for heavy duty trucks

(i) On the basis of information available to the Administrator concerning the effects of air pollutants emitted from heavy-duty vehicles or engines and from other sources of mobile source related pollutants on the public health and welfare, and taking costs into account, the Administrator may promulgate regulations under paragraph (1) of this subsection revising any standard promulgated under, or before the date of, the enactment of the Clean

Air Act Amendments of 1990 (or previously revised under this subparagraph) and applicable to classes or categories of heavy-duty vehicles or engines.

(ii) Effective for the model year 1998 and thereafter, the regulations under paragraph (1) of this subsection applicable to emissions of oxides of nitrogen (NO_x) from gasoline and diesel-fueled heavy duty trucks shall contain standards which provide that such emissions may not exceed 4.0 grams per brake horsepower hour (gbh).

(C) Lead time and stability

Any standard promulgated or revised under this paragraph and applicable to classes or categories of heavy-duty vehicles or engines shall apply for a period of no less than 3 model years beginning no earlier than the model year commencing 4 years after such revised standard is promulgated.

(D) Rebuilding practices

The Administrator shall study the practice of rebuilding heavy-duty engines and the impact rebuilding has on engine emissions. On the basis of that study and other information available to the Administrator, the Administrator may prescribe requirements to control rebuilding practices, including standards applicable to emissions from any rebuilt heavy-duty engines (whether or not the engine is past its statutory useful life), which in the Administrator's judgment cause, or contribute to, air pollution which may reasonably be anticipated to endanger public health or welfare taking costs into account. Any regulation shall take effect after a period the Administrator finds necessary to permit the development and application of the requisite control measures, giving appropriate consideration to the cost of compliance within the period and energy and safety factors.

(E) Motorcycles

For purposes of this paragraph, motorcycles and motorcycle engines shall be treated in the same manner as heavy-duty vehicles and engines (except as otherwise permitted under section 7525(f)(1) of this title) unless the Administrator promulgates a rule reclassifying motorcycles as light-duty vehicles within the meaning of this section or unless the Administrator promulgates regulations under subsection (a) of this section applying standards applicable to the emission of air pollutants from motorcycles as a separate class or category. In any case in which such standards are promulgated for such emissions from motorcycles as a separate class or category, the Administrator, in promulgating such standards, shall consider the need to achieve equivalency of emission reductions between motorcycles and other motor vehicles to the maximum extent practicable.

(4) (A) Effective with respect to vehicles and engines manufactured after model year 1978, no emission control device, system, or element of design shall be used in a new motor vehicle or new motor vehicle engine for purposes of complying with requirements prescribed under this subchapter if such device, system, or element of design will cause or contribute to an unreasonable risk to public health, welfare, or safety in its operation or function.

(B) In determining whether an unreasonable risk exists under subparagraph (A), the Administrator shall consider, among other factors, (i) whether and to what extent the use of any device, system, or element of design causes, increases, reduces, or eliminates emissions of any unregulated pollutants; (ii) available methods for reducing or eliminating any risk to public health, welfare, or safety which may be associated with the use of such device, system, or element of design, and (iii) the availability of other devices, systems, or elements of design which may be used to conform to requirements prescribed under this subchapter without causing or contributing to such unreasonable risk. The Administrator shall include in the consideration required by this paragraph all relevant information developed pursuant to section 7548 of this title.

(5) (A) If the Administrator promulgates final regulations which define the degree of control required and the test procedures by which compliance could be determined for gasoline vapor recovery of uncontrolled emissions from the fueling of motor vehicles, the Administrator shall, after consultation with the Secretary of Transportation with respect to motor vehicle safety, prescribe, by regulation, fill pipe standards for new motor vehicles in order to insure effective connection between such fill pipe and any vapor recovery system which the Administrator determines may be required to comply with such vapor recovery regulations. In promulgating such standards the Administrator shall take into consideration limits on fill pipe diameter, minimum design criteria for nozzle retainer lips, limits on the location of the unleaded fuel restrictors, a minimum access zone surrounding a fill pipe, a minimum pipe or nozzle insertion angle, and such other factors as he deems pertinent.

(B) Regulations prescribing standards under subparagraph (A) shall not become effective until the introduction of the model year for which it would be feasible to implement such standards, taking into consideration the restraints of an adequate leadtime for design and production.

(C) Nothing in subparagraph (A) shall (i) prevent the Administrator from specifying different nozzle and fill neck sizes for gasoline with additives and gasoline without additives or (ii) permit the Administrator to require a specific location, configuration, modeling, or styling of the motor vehicle body with respect to the fuel tank fill neck or fill nozzle clearance envelope.

(D) For the purpose of this paragraph, the term "fill pipe" shall include the fuel tank fill pipe, fill neck, fill inlet, and closure.

(6) Onboard vapor recovery

Within 1 year after November 15, 1990, the Administrator shall, after consultation with the Secretary of Transportation regarding the safety of vehicle-based ("onboard") systems for the control of vehicle refueling emissions, promulgate standards under this section requiring that new light-duty vehicles manufactured beginning in the fourth model year after the model year in which the standards are promulgated and thereafter shall be equipped with such systems. The standards required under this paragraph shall apply to a percentage of each manufacturer's fleet of new light-duty vehicles beginning with the fourth model year after the model year in which the standards are promulgated. The percentage shall be as specified in the following table:

IMPLEMENTATION SCHEDULE FOR ONBOARD VAPOR RECOVERY REQUIREMENTS

Model year commencing after standards promulgated	Percentage*
Fourth	40
Fifth	80
After Fifth	100

*Percentages in the table refer to a percentage of the manufacturer's sales volume.

The standards shall require that such systems provide a minimum evaporative emission capture efficiency of 95 percent. The requirements of section 7511a(b)(3) of this title (relating to stage II gasoline vapor recovery) for areas classified under section 7511 of this title as moderate for ozone shall not apply after promulgation of such standards and the Administrator may, by rule, revise or waive the application of the requirements of such section 7511a(b)(3) of this title for areas classified under section 7511 of this title as Serious, Severe, or Extreme for ozone, as appropriate, after such time as the Administrator determines that onboard emissions control systems required under this paragraph are in widespread use throughout the motor vehicle fleet.

(b) Emissions of carbon monoxide, hydrocarbons, and oxides of nitrogen; annual report to Congress; waiver of emission standards; research objectives

(1) (A) The regulations under subsection (a) of this section applicable to emissions of carbon monoxide and hydrocarbons from light-duty vehicles and engines manufactured during model years 1977 through 1979 shall contain standards which provide that such emissions from such vehicles and engines may not exceed 1.5 grams per vehicle mile of hydrocarbons and 15.0 grams per vehicle mile of carbon monoxide. The regulations under subsection (a) of this section applicable to emissions of carbon monoxide from light-duty vehicles and engines manufactured during the model year 1980 shall contain standards which provide that such emissions may not exceed 7.0 grams per vehicle mile. The regulations under subsection (a) of this section applicable to emissions of hydrocarbons from light-duty vehicles and engines manufactured during or after model year 1980 shall contain standards which require a reduction of at least 90 percent from emissions of such pollutant allowable under the standards under this section applicable to light-duty vehicles and engines manufactured in model year 1970. Unless waived as provided in paragraph (5), regulations under subsection (a) of this section applicable to emissions of carbon monoxide from light-duty vehicles and engines manufactured during or after the model year 1981 shall contain standards which require a reduction of at least 90 percent from emissions of such pollutant allowable under the standards under this section applicable to light-duty vehicles and engines manufactured in model year 1970.

(B) The regulations under subsection (a) of this section applicable to emissions of oxides of nitrogen from light-duty vehicles and engines manufactured during model years 1977 through 1980 shall contain standards which provide that such emissions from such vehicles and engines may not exceed 2.0 grams per vehicle mile. The regulations under subsection (a) of this section applicable to emissions of oxides of nitrogen from light-duty vehicles and engines manufactured during the model year 1981 and thereafter shall contain standards which provide that such emissions from such vehicles and engines may not exceed 1.0 gram per vehicle mile. The Administrator shall prescribe standards in lieu of those required by the preceding sentence, which provide that emissions of oxides of nitrogen may not exceed 2.0 grams per vehicle mile for any light-duty vehicle manufactured during model years 1981 and 1982 by any manufacturer whose production, by corporate identity, for calendar year 1976 was less than three hundred thousand light-duty motor vehicles worldwide if the Administrator determines that—

(i) the ability of such manufacturer to meet emission standards in the 1975 and subsequent model years was, and is, primarily dependent upon technology developed by other manufacturers and purchased from such manufacturers; and

(ii) such manufacturer lacks the financial resources and technological ability to develop such technology.

(C) The Administrator may promulgate regulations under subsection (a)(1) of this section revising any standard prescribed or previously revised under this subsection, as needed to protect public health or welfare, taking costs, energy, and safety into account. Any revised standard shall require a reduction of emissions from the standard that was previously applicable. Any such revision under this subchapter may provide for a phase-in of the standard. It is the intent of Congress that the numerical emission standards specified in subsections (a)(3)(B)(ii), (g), (h), and (i) of this section shall not be modified by the Administrator after November 15, 1990, for any model year before the model year 2004.

(2) Emission standards under paragraph (1), and measurement techniques on which such standards are based (if not promulgated prior to November 15, 1990), shall be promulgated by regulation within 180 days after November 15, 1990.

(3) For purposes of this part—

(A) **(i)** The term "model year" with reference to any specific calendar year means the manufacturer's annual production period (as determined by the Administrator) which includes January 1 of such calendar year. If the manufacturer has no annual production period, the term "model year" shall mean the calendar year.

(ii) For the purpose of assuring that vehicles and engines manufactured before the beginning of a model year were not manufactured for purposes of circumventing the effective date of a standard required to be prescribed by subsection (b) of this section, the Administrator may prescribe regulations defining "model year" otherwise than as provided in clause (i).

(B) Repealed. Pub. L. No. 101–549, Title II, § 230(1), 104 Stat. 2529 (Nov. 15, 1990).

(C) The term "heavy duty vehicle" means a truck, bus, or other vehicle manufactured primarily for use on the public streets, roads, and highways (not including any vehicle operated exclusively on a rail or rails) which has a gross vehicle weight (as determined under regulations promulgated by the Administrator) in excess of six thousand pounds. Such term includes any such vehicle which has special features enabling off-street or off-highway operation and use.

(3)[1] Upon the petition of any manufacturer, the Administrator, after notice and opportunity for public hearing, may waive the standard required under subparagraph (B) of paragraph (1) to not exceed 1.5 grams of oxides of nitrogen per vehicle mile for any class or category of light-duty vehicles or engines manufactured by such manufacturer during any period of up to four model years beginning after the model year 1980 if the manufacturer demonstrates that such waiver is necessary to permit the use of an innovative power train technology, or innovative emission control device or system, in such class or category of vehicles or engines and that such technology or system was not utilized by more than 1 percent of the light-duty vehicles sold in the United States in the 1975 model year. Such waiver may be granted only if the Administrator determines—

(A) that such waiver would not endanger public health,

(B) that there is a substantial likelihood that the vehicles or engines will be able to comply with the applicable standard under this section at the expiration of the waiver, and

(C) that the technology or system has a potential for long-term air quality benefit and has the potential to meet or exceed the average fuel economy standard applicable under the Energy Policy and Conservation Act [42 U.S.C.A. § 6201 et seq.] upon the expiration of the waiver.

No waiver under this subparagraph[2] granted to any manufacturer shall apply to more than 5 percent of such manufacturer's production or more than fifty thousand vehicles or engines, whichever is greater.

(c) Feasibility study and investigation by National Academy of Sciences; reports to Administrator and Congress; availability of information

(1) The Administrator shall undertake to enter into appropriate arrangements with the National Academy of Sciences to conduct a comprehensive study and investigation of the technological feasibility of meeting the emissions standards required to be prescribed by the Administrator by subsection (b) of this section.

(2) Of the funds authorized to be appropriated to the Administrator by this chapter, such amounts as are required shall be available to carry out the study and investigation authorized by paragraph (1) of this subsection.

(3) In entering into any arrangement with the National Academy of Sciences for conducting the study and investigation authorized by paragraph (1) of this subsection, the Administrator shall request the National Academy of Sciences to submit semiannual reports on the progress of its study and investigation to the Administrator and the Congress, beginning not later than July 1, 1971, and continuing until such study and investigation is completed.

(4) The Administrator shall furnish to such Academy at its request any information which the Academy deems necessary for the purpose of conducting the investigation and study authorized by paragraph (1) of this subsection. For the purpose of furnishing such information, the Administrator may use any authority he has under this chapter (A) to obtain information from any person, and (B) to require such person to conduct such tests, keep such records, and make such reports respecting research or other activities conducted by such person as may be reasonably necessary to carry out this subsection.

(d) Useful life of vehicles

The Administrator shall prescribe regulations under which the useful life of vehicles and engines shall be determined for purposes of subsection (a)(1) of this section and section 7541 of this title. Such regulations shall provide that except where a different useful life period is specified in this subchapter useful life shall—

(1) in the case of light duty vehicles and light duty vehicle engines and light-duty trucks up to 3,750 lbs. LVW and up to 6,000 lbs. GVWR, be a period of use of five years or fifty thousand miles (or the equivalent), whichever first occurs, except that in the case of any requirement of this section which first becomes applicable after November 15, 1990, where the useful life period is not otherwise specified for such vehicles and engines, the period shall be 10 years or 100,000 miles (or the equivalent), whichever first occurs, with testing for purposes of in-use compliance under section 7541 of this title up to (but not beyond) 7 years or 75,000 miles (or the equivalent), whichever first occurs;

(2) in the case of any other motor vehicle or motor vehicle engine (other than motorcycles or motorcycle engines), be a period of use set forth in paragraph (1) unless the Administrator determines that a period of use of greater duration or mileage is appropriate; and

(3) in the case of any motorcycle or motorcycle engine, be a period of use the Administrator shall determine.

(e) New power sources or propulsion systems

In the event of a new power source or propulsion system for new motor vehicles or new motor vehicle engines is submitted for certification pursuant to section 7525(a) of this title, the Administrator may postpone certification until he has prescribed standards for any air pollutants emitted by such vehicle or engine which in his judgment cause, or contribute to, air pollution which may reasonably be anticipated to endanger the public health or welfare but for which standards have not been prescribed under subsection (a) of this section.

(f)[3] High altitude regulations

(1) The high altitude regulation in effect with respect to model year 1977 motor vehicles shall not apply to the manufacture, distribution, or sale of 1978 and later model year motor vehicles. Any future regulation affecting the sale or distribution of motor vehicles or engines manufactured before the model year 1984 in high altitude areas of the country shall take effect no earlier than model year 1981.

(2) Any such future regulation applicable to high altitude vehicles or engines shall not require a percentage of reduction in the emissions of such vehicles which is greater than the required percentage of reduction in emissions from motor vehicles as set forth in subsection (b) of this section. This percentage reduction shall be determined by comparing any proposed high altitude emission standards to high altitude emissions from vehicles manufactured during model year 1970. In no event shall regulations applicable to high altitude vehicles manufactured before the model year 1984 establish a numerical standard which is more stringent than that applicable to vehicles certified under non-high altitude conditions.

(3) Section 7607(d) of this title shall apply to any high altitude regulation referred to in paragraph (2) and before promulgating any such regulation, the Administrator shall consider and make a finding with respect to—

(A) the economic impact upon consumers, individual high altitude dealers, and the automobile industry of any such regulation, including the economic impact which was experienced as a result of the regulation imposed during model year 1977 with respect to high altitude certification requirements;

(B) the present and future availability of emission control technology capable of meeting the applicable vehicle and engine emission requirements without reducing model availability; and

(C) the likelihood that the adoption of such a high altitude regulation will result in any significant improvement in air quality in any area to which it shall apply.

(g) Light-duty trucks up to 6,000 lbs. GVWR and light-duty vehicles; standards for model years after 1993

(1) NMHC, CO, and NO_x

Effective with respect to the model year 1994 and thereafter, the regulations under subsection (a) of this section applicable to emissions of nonmethane hydrocarbons (NMHC), carbon monoxide (CO), and oxides of nitrogen (NO_x) from light-duty trucks (LDTs) of up to 6,000 lbs. gross vehicle weight rating (GVWR) and light-duty vehicles (LDVs) shall contain standards which provide that emissions from a percentage of each manufacturer's sales volume of such vehicles and trucks shall comply with the levels specified in table G. The percentage shall be as specified in the implementation schedule below:

TABLE G—EMISSION STANDARDS FOR NMHC, CO, AND NO_x FROM LIGHT-DUTY TRUCKS OF UP TO 6,000 LBS. GVWR AND LIGHT-DUTY VEHICLES

Vehicle type	Column A (5 yrs/50,000 mi)			Column B (10 yrs/100,000 mi)		
	NMHC	CO	NO_x	NMHC	CO	NO_x
LDTs (0–3,750 lbs. LVW) and light-duty vehicles	0.25	3.4	0.4*	0.31	4.2	0.6*
LDTs (3,751–5,750 lbs. LVW)	0.32	4.4	0.7**	0.40	5.5	0.97

Standards are expressed in grams per mile (gpm).

For standards under column A, for purposes of certification under section 7525 of this title, the applicable useful life shall be 5 years or 50,000 miles (or the equivalent), whichever first occurs.

For standards under column B, for purposes of certification under section 7525 of this title, the applicable useful life shall be 10 years or 100,000 miles (or the equivalent), whichever first occurs.

* In the case of diesel-fueled LDTs (0–3,750 lvw) and light-duty vehicles, before the model year 2004, in lieu of the 0.4 and 0.6 standards for NO_x, the applicable standards for NO_x shall be 1.0 gpm for a useful life of 5 years or 50,000 miles (or the equivalent), whichever first occurs, and 1.25 gpm for a useful life of 10 years or 100,000 miles (or the equivalent), whichever first occurs.

** This standard does not apply to diesel-fueled LDTs (3,751–5,750 lbs. LVW).

IMPLEMENTATION SCHEDULE FOR TABLE G STANDARDS

Model year	Percentage *
1994	40
1995	80
after 1995	100

* Percentages in the table refer to a percentage of each manufacturer's sales volume.

(2) PM Standard

Effective with respect to model year 1994 and thereafter in the case of light-duty vehicles, and effective with respect to the model year 1995 and thereafter in the case of light-duty trucks (LDTs) of up to 6,000 lbs. gross vehicle weight rating (GVWR), the regulations under subsection (a) of this section applicable to emissions of particulate matter (PM) from such vehicles and trucks shall contain standards which provide that such emissions from a percentage of each manufacturer's sales volume of such vehicles and trucks shall not exceed the levels specified in the table below. The percentage shall be as specified in the Implementation Schedule below.

PM STANDARD FOR LDTS OF UP TO 6,000 LBS. GVWR

Useful life period	Standard
5/50,000	0.80 gpm
10/100,000	0.10 gpm

The applicable useful life, for purposes of certification under section 7525 of this title and for purposes of in-use compliance under section 7541 of this title, shall be 5 years or 50,000 miles (or the equivalent), whichever first occurs, in the case of the 5/50,000 standard.

The applicable useful life, for purposes of certification under section 7525 of this title and for purposes of in-use compliance under section 7541 of this title, shall be 10 years or 100,000 miles (or the equivalent), whichever first occurs in the case of the 10/100,000 standard.

IMPLEMENTATION SCHEDULE FOR PM STANDARDS

Model year	Light-duty vehicles	LDTs
1994	40%*	......
1995	80%*	40%*
1996	100%*	80%*
after 1996	100%*	100%*

* Percentages in the table refer to a percentage of each manufacturer's sales volume.

(h) Light-duty trucks of more than 6,000 lbs. GVWR; standards for model years after 1995

Effective with respect to the model year 1996 and thereafter, the regulations under subsection (a) of this section applicable to emissions of nonmethane hydrocarbons (NMHC), carbon monoxide (CO), oxides of nitrogen (NO_x), and particulate matter (PM) from light-duty trucks (LDTs) of more than 6,000 lbs. gross vehicle weight rating (GVWR) shall contain standards which provide that emissions from a specified percentage of each manufacturer's sales volume of such trucks shall comply with the levels specified in table H. The specified percentage shall be 50 percent in model year 1996 and 100 percent thereafter.

TABLE H—EMISSION STANDARDS FOR NMHC AND CO FROM GASOLINE AND DIESEL FUELED LIGHT-DUTY TRUCKS OF MORE THAN 6,000 LBS. GVWR

LDT Test weight	Column A (5 yrs/50,000 mi)			Column B (11 yrs/120,000 mi)			
	NMHC	CO	NO_x	NMHC	CO	NO_x	PM
3,751–5,750 lbs. TW	0.32	4.4	0.7*	0.46	6.4	0.98	0.10
Over 5,750 lbs. TW	0.39	5.0	1.1*	0.56	7.3	1.53	0.12

Standards are expressed in grams per mile (GPM).

For standards under column A, for purposes of certification under section 7525 of this title, the applicable useful life shall be 5 years or 50,000 miles (or the equivalent) whichever first occurs.

For standards under column B, for purposes of certification under section 7525 of this title, the applicable useful life shall be 11 years or 120,000 miles (or the equivalent), whichever first occurs.

* Not applicable to diesel-fueled LDTs.

(i) Phase II study for certain light-duty vehicles and light-duty trucks

(1) The Administrator, with the participation of the Office of Technology Assessment, shall study whether or not further reductions in emissions from light-duty vehicles and light-duty trucks should be required pursuant to this subchapter. The study shall consider whether to establish with respect to model years commencing after January 1, 2003, the standards and useful life period for gasoline and diesel-fueled light-duty vehicles and light-duty trucks with a loaded vehicle weight (LVW) of 3,750 lbs. or less specified in the following table:

TABLE 3—PENDING EMISSION STANDARDS FOR GASOLINE AND DIESEL FUELED LIGHT-DUTY VEHICLES AND LIGHT-DUTY TRUCKS 3,750 LBS. LVW OR LESS

Pollutant	Emission level*
NMHC	0.125 GPM
NO_x	0.2 GPM
CO	1.7 GPM

* Emission levels are expressed in grams per mile (GPM). For vehicles and engines subject to this subsection for purposes of subsection (d) of this section and any reference thereto, the useful life of such vehicles and engines shall be a period of 10 years or 100,000 miles (or the equivalent), whichever first occurs.

Such study shall also consider other standards and useful life periods which are more stringent or less stringent than those set forth in table 3 (but more stringent than those referred to in subsections (g) and (h) of this section).

(2) **(A)** As part of the study under paragraph (1), the Administrator shall examine the need for further reductions in emissions in order to attain or maintain the national ambient air quality standards, taking into consideration the waiver provisions of section 7543(b) of this title. As part of such study, the Administrator shall also examine—

(i) the availability of technology (including the costs thereof), in the case of light-duty vehicles and light-duty trucks with a loaded vehicle weight (LVW) of 3,750 lbs. or less, for meeting more stringent emission standards than those provided in subsections (g) and (h) of this section for model years commencing not earlier than after January 1, 2003, and not later than model year 2006, including the lead time and safety and energy impacts of meeting more stringent emission standards; and

(ii) the need for, and cost effectiveness of, obtaining further reductions in emissions from such light-duty vehicles and light-duty trucks, taking into consideration alternative means of attaining or maintaining the national primary ambient air quality standards pursuant to State implementation plans and other requirements of this chapter, including their feasibility and cost effectiveness.

(B) The Administrator shall submit a report to Congress no later than June 1, 1997, containing the results of the study under this subsection, including the results of the examination conducted under subparagraph (A). Before submittal of such report the Administrator shall provide a reasonable opportunity for public comment and shall include a summary of such comments in the report to Congress.

(3) **(A)** Based on the study under paragraph (1) the Administrator shall determine, by rule, within 3 calendar years after the report is submitted to Congress, but not later than December 31, 1999, whether—

(i) there is a need for further reductions in emissions as provided in paragraph (2)(A);

(ii) the technology for meeting more stringent emission standards will be available, as provided in paragraph (2)(A)(i), in the case of light-duty vehicles and light-duty trucks with a loaded vehicle weight (LVW) of 3,750 lbs. or less, for model years commencing not earlier than January 1, 2003, and not later than model year 2006, considering the factors listed in paragraph (2)(A)(i); and

(iii) obtaining further reductions in emissions from such vehicles will be needed and cost effective, taking into consideration alternatives as provided in paragraph (2)(A)(ii).

The rulemaking under this paragraph shall commence within 3 months after submission of the report to Congress under paragraph (2)(B).

(B) If the Administrator determines under subparagraph (A) that—

(i) there is no need for further reductions in emissions as provided in paragraph (2)(A);

(ii) the technology for meeting more stringent emission standards will not be available as provided in paragraph (2)(A)(i), in the case of light-duty vehicles and light-duty trucks with a loaded vehicle weight (LVW) of 3,750 lbs. or less, for model years commencing not earlier than January 1, 2003, and not later than model year 2006, considering the factors listed in paragraph (2)(A)(i); or

(iii) obtaining further reductions in emissions from such vehicles will not be needed or cost effective, taking into consideration alternatives as provided in paragraph (2)(A)(ii),

the Administrator shall not promulgate more stringent standards than those in effect pursuant to subsections (g) and (h) of this section. Nothing in this paragraph shall prohibit the Administrator from exercising the Administrator's authority under subsection (a) of this section to promulgate more stringent standards for light-duty vehicles and light-duty trucks with a loaded vehicle weight (LVW) of 3,750 lbs. or less at any other time thereafter in accordance with subsection (a) of this section.

(C) If the Administrator determines under subparagraph (A) that—

(i) there is a need for further reductions in emissions as provided in paragraph (2)(A);

(ii) the technology for meeting more stringent emission standards will be available, as provided in paragraph (2)(A)(i), in the case of light-duty vehicles and light-duty trucks with a loaded vehicle weight (LVW) of 3,750 lbs. or less, for model years commencing not earlier than January 1, 2003, and not later than model year 2006, considering the factors listed in paragraph (2)(A)(i); and

(iii) obtaining further reductions in emissions from such vehicles will be needed and cost effective, taking into consideration alternatives as provided in paragraph (2)(A)(ii),

the Administrator shall either promulgate the standards (and useful life periods) set forth in Table 3 in paragraph (1) or promulgate alternative standards (and useful life periods) which are more stringent than those referred to in subsections (g) and (h) of this section. Any such standards (or useful life periods) promulgated by the Administrator shall take effect with respect to any such vehicles or engines no earlier than the model year 2003 but not later than model year 2006, as determined by the Administrator in the rule.

(D) Nothing in this paragraph shall be construed by the Administrator or by a court as a presumption that any standards (or useful life period) set forth in Table 3 shall be promulgated in the rulemaking required under this paragraph. The action required of the Administrator in accordance with this paragraph shall be treated as a nondiscretionary duty for purposes of section 7604(a)(2) of this title (relating to citizen suits).

(E) Unless the Administrator determines not to promulgate more stringent standards as provided in subparagraph (B) or to postpone the effective date of standards referred to in Table 3 in paragraph (1) or to establish alternative standards as provided in subparagraph (C), effective with respect to model years commencing after January 1, 2003, the regulations under subsection (a) of this section applicable to emissions of nonmethane hydrocarbons (NMHC), oxides of nitrogen (NO_x), and carbon monoxide (CO) from motor vehicles and motor vehicle engines in the classes specified in Table 3 in paragraph (1) above shall contain standards which provide that emissions may not exceed the pending emission levels specified in Table 3 in paragraph (1).

(j) Cold CO standard

(1) Phase I

Not later than 12 months after November 15, 1990, the Administrator shall promulgate regulations under subsection (a) of this section applicable to emissions of carbon monoxide from 1994 and later model year light-duty vehicles and light-duty trucks when operated at 20 degrees Fahrenheit. The regulations shall contain standards which provide that emissions of carbon monoxide from a manufacturer's vehicles when operated at 20 degrees Fahrenheit may not exceed, in the case of light-duty vehicles, 10.0 grams per mile, and in the case of light-duty trucks, a level comparable in stringency to the standard applicable to light-duty vehicles. The standards shall take effect after model year 1993 according to a phase-in schedule which requires a percentage of each manufacturer's sales volume of light-duty vehicles and light-duty trucks to comply with applicable standards after model year 1993. The percentage shall be as specified in the following table:

PHASE-IN SCHEDULE FOR COLD START STANDARDS

Model Year	Percentage
1994	40
1995	80
1996 and after	100

(2) Phase II

(A) Not later than June 1, 1997, the Administrator shall complete a study assessing the need for further reductions in emissions of carbon monoxide and the maximum reductions in such emissions achievable from model year 2001 and later model year light-duty vehicles and light-duty trucks when operated at 20 degrees Fahrenheit.

(B) (i) If as of June 1, 1997, 6 or more nonattainment areas have a carbon monoxide design value of 9.5 ppm or greater, the regulations under subsection (a)(1) of this section applicable to emissions of carbon monoxide from model year 2002 and later model year light-duty vehicles and light-duty trucks shall contain standards which provide that emissions of carbon monoxide from such vehicles and trucks when operated at 20 degrees Fahrenheit may not exceed 3.4 grams per mile (gpm) in the case of light-duty vehicles and 4.4 grams per mile (gpm) in the case of light-duty trucks up to 6,000 GVWR and a level comparable in stringency in the case of light-duty trucks 6,000 GVWR and above.

(ii) In determining for purposes of this subparagraph whether 6 or more nonattainment areas have a carbon monoxide design value of 9.5 ppm or greater, the Administrator shall exclude the areas of Steubenville, Ohio, and Oshkosh, Wisconsin.

(3) Useful-life for phase I and phase II standards

In the case of the standards referred to in paragraphs (1) and (2), for purposes of certification under section 7525 of this title and in-use compliance under section 7541 of this title, the applicable useful life period shall be 5 years or 50,000 miles, whichever first occurs, except that the Administrator may extend such useful life period (for purposes of section 7525 of this title, or section 7541 of this title, or both) if he determines that it is feasible for vehicles and engines subject to such standards to meet such standards for a longer useful life. If the Administrator extends such useful life period, the Administrator may make an appropriate adjustment of applicable standards for such extended useful life. No such extended useful life shall extend beyond the useful life period provided in regulations under subsection (d) of this section.

(4) Heavy-duty vehicles and engines

The Administrator may also promulgate regulations under subsection (a)(1) of this section applicable to emissions of carbon monoxide from heavy-duty vehicles and engines when operated at cold temperatures.

(k) Control of evaporative emissions

The Administrator shall promulgate (and from time to time revise) regulations applicable to evaporative emissions of hydrocarbons from all gasoline-fueled motor vehicles—

(1) during operation; and

(2) over 2 or more days of nonuse;

under ozone-prone summertime conditions (as determined by regulations of the Administrator). The regulations shall take effect as expeditiously as possible and shall require the greatest degree of emission reduction achievable by means reasonably expected to be available for production during any model year to which the regulations apply, giving appropriate consideration to fuel volatility, and to cost, energy, and safety factors associated with the application of the appropriate technology. The Administrator shall commence a rulemaking under this subsection within 12 months after November 15, 1990. If final regulations are not promulgated under this subsection within 18 months after November 15, 1990, the Administrator shall submit a statement to the Congress containing an explanation of the reasons for the delay and a date certain for promulgation of such final regulations in accordance with this chapter. Such date certain shall not be later than 15 months after the expiration of such 18 month deadline.

***(l)* Mobile source-related air toxics**

(1) Study

Not later than 18 months after November 15, 1990, the Administrator shall complete a study of the need for, and feasibility of, controlling emissions of toxic air pollutants which are unregulated under this chapter and associated with motor vehicles and motor vehicle fuels, and the need for, and feasibility of, controlling such emissions and the means and measures for such controls. The study shall focus on those categories of emissions that pose the greatest risk to human health or about which significant uncertainties remain, including emissions of benzene, formaldehyde, and 1, 3 butadiene. The proposed report shall be available for public review and comment and shall include a summary of all comments.

(2) Standards

Within 54 months after November 15, 1990, the Administrator shall, based on the study under paragraph (1), promulgate (and from time to time revise) regulations under subsection (a)(1) of this section or section 7545(c)(1) of this title containing reasonable requirements to control hazardous air pollutants from motor vehicles and motor vehicle fuels. The regulations shall contain standards for such fuels or vehicles, or both, which the Administrator determines reflect the greatest degree of emission reduction achievable through the application of technology which will be available, taking into consideration the standards established under subsection (a) of this section, the availability and costs of the technology, and noise, energy, and safety factors, and lead time. Such regulations shall not be inconsistent with standards under subsection (a) of this section. The regulations shall, at a minimum, apply to emissions of benzene and formaldehyde.

(m) Emissions control diagnostics

(1) Regulations

Within 18 months after November 15, 1990, the Administrator shall promulgate regulations under subsection (a) of this section requiring manufacturers to install on all new light duty vehicles and light duty trucks diagnostics systems capable of—

(A) accurately identifying for the vehicle's useful life as established under this section, emission-related systems deterioration or malfunction, including, at a minimum, the catalytic converter and oxygen sensor, which could cause or result in failure of the vehicles to comply with emission standards established under this section,

(B) alerting the vehicle's owner or operator to the likely need for emission-related components or systems maintenance or repair,

(C) storing and retrieving fault codes specified by the Administrator, and

(D) providing access to stored information in a manner specified by the Administrator.

The Administrator may, in the Administrator's discretion, promulgate regulations requiring manufacturers to install such onboard diagnostic systems on heavy-duty vehicles and engines.

(2) Effective date

The regulations required under paragraph (1) of this subsection shall take effect in model year 1994, except that the Administrator may waive the application of such regulations for model year 1994 or 1995 (or both) with respect to any class or category of motor vehicles if the Administrator determines that it would be infeasible to apply the regulations to that class or category in such model year or years, consistent with corresponding regulations or policies adopted by the California Air Resources Board for such systems.

(3) State inspection

The Administrator shall by regulation require States that have implementation plans containing motor vehicle inspection and maintenance programs to amend their plans within 2 years after promulgation of such regulations to provide for inspection of onboard diagnostics systems (as prescribed by regulations under paragraph (1) of this subsection) and for the maintenance or repair of malfunctions or system deterioration identified by or affecting such diagnostics systems. Such regulations shall not be inconsistent with the provisions for warranties promulgated under section 7541(a) and (b) of this title.

(4) **Specific requirements**

In promulgating regulations under this subsection, the Administrator shall require—

(A) that any connectors through which the emission control diagnostics system is accessed for inspection, diagnosis, service, or repair shall be standard and uniform on all motor vehicles and motor vehicle engines;

(B) that access to the emission control diagnostics system through such connectors shall be unrestricted and shall not require any access code or any device which is only available from a vehicle manufacturer; and

(C) that the output of the data from the emission control diagnostics system through such connectors shall be usable without the need for any unique decoding information or device.

(5) **Information availability**

The Administrator, by regulation, shall require (subject to the provisions of section 7542(c) of this title regarding the protection of methods or processes entitled to protection as trade secrets) manufacturers to provide promptly to any person engaged in the repairing or servicing of motor vehicles or motor vehicle engines, and the Administrator for use by any such persons, with any and all information needed to make use of the emission control diagnostics system prescribed under this subsection and such other information including instructions for making emission related diagnosis and repairs. No such information may be withheld under section 7542(c) of this title if that information is provided (directly or indirectly) by the manufacturer to franchised dealers or other persons engaged in the repair, diagnosing, or servicing of motor vehicles or motor vehicle engines. Such information shall also be available to the Administrator, subject to section 7542(c) of this title, in carrying out the Administrator's responsibilities under this section.

(f)[4] **Model years after 1990**

For model years prior to model year 1994, the regulations under subsection (a) of this section applicable to buses other than those subject to standards under section 7554 of this title shall contain a standard which provides that emissions of particulate matter (PM) from such buses may not exceed the standards set forth in the following table:

PM STANDARD FOR BUSES

Model year	Standard*
1991	0.25
1992	0.25
1993 and thereafter	0.10

* Standards are expressed in grams per brake horsepower hour (g/bhp/hr).

(July 14, 1955, c. 360, Title II, § 202, as added by Pub. L. No. 89–272, Title I, § 101(8), 79 Stat. 992 (Oct. 20, 1965); and amended by Pub. L. No. 90–148, § 2, 81 Stat. 499 (Nov. 21, 1967); Pub. L. No. 91–604, § 6(a), 84 Stat. 1690 (Dec. 31, 1970); Pub. L. No. 93–319, § 5, 88 Stat. 258 (June 22, 1974); Pub. L. No. 95–95, Title II, §§ 201, 202(b), 213(b), 214(a), 215 to 217, 224(a), (b), (g), Title IV, § 401(d), 91 Stat. 751 to 753, 758 to 761, 765, 767, 769, 791 (Aug. 7, 1977); Pub. L. No. 95–190, § 14(a)(60) to (65), (b)(5), 91 Stat. 1403, 1405 (Nov. 16, 1977); Pub. L. No. 101–549, Title II, §§ 201 to 207, 227(b), 230(1) to (5), 104 Stat. 2472 to 2481, 2507, 2529 (Nov. 15, 1990).)

[1] So in original. Probably should be "(4)."

[2] So in original. Probably should be "paragraph."

[3] Another subsec. (f) is set out following subsec. (m).

[4] So in original. Probably should be (n).

HISTORICAL AND STATUTORY NOTES

References in Text

The enactment of the Clean Air Act Amendments of 1990, referred to in subsec. (a)(3)(B), probably means the enactment of Pub. L. No. 101–549, 104 Stat. 2399 (Nov. 15, 1990), which was approved Nov. 15, 1990. For complete classification of this Act to the Code, see Short Title of 1990 Amendments note set out under section 7401 of this title and Tables.

Section 7525(f)(1) of this title, referred to in subsec. (a)(3)(E), was redesignated section 7525(f) of this title by Pub. L. No. 101–549, Title II, § 230(8), 104 Stat. 2529 (Nov. 15, 1990).

The Energy Policy and Conservation Act, referred to in subsec. (b)(3)(C), is Pub. L. No. 94–163, 89 Stat. 871 (Dec. 22, 1975), as amended, which is codified principally as chapter 77 (section 6201 et seq.) of this title. For complete classification of this Act to the Code, see Short Title of 1975 Acts note set out under section 6201 of this title and Tables.

Codifications

This section was formerly codified as section 1857f–1 of this title.

Effective and Applicability Provisions

1990 Acts. Amendment by Pub. L. No. 101–549 effective Nov. 15, 1990, except as otherwise provided, see section 711(b) of Pub. L. No. 101–549, set out as a note under section 7401 of this title.

1977 Acts. Amendment by Pub. L. No. 95–95 effective Aug. 7, 1977, except as otherwise expressly provided, see section 406(d) of Pub. L. No. 95–95, set out as a note under section 7401 of this title.

Termination of Reporting Requirements

For termination of reporting provisions of subsec. (c)(3) of this section, effective May 15, 2000, see Pub. L. No. 104–66, § 3003, as amended, set out as a note under 31 U.S.C.A. § 1113, and page 202 of House Document No. 103–7.

For termination, effective May 15, 2000, of reporting provisions of subsec. (i) of this section relating to emission standards for conventional motor vehicles, see Pub. L. No. 104–66, § 3003, as amended, set out as a note under 31 U.S.C.A. § 1113, and the 1st item on page 165 of House Document No. 103–7.

Savings Provisions

Suits, actions or proceedings commenced under this chapter as in effect prior to Nov. 15, 1990, not to abate by reason of the taking effect of amendments by Pub. L. No. 101–549, except as otherwise provided for, see section 711(a) of Pub. L. No. 101–549, set out as a note under section 7401 of this title.

Continuing Comprehensive Studies and Investigations by National Academy of Sciences

Section 403(f) of Pub. L. No. 95–95 provided that: "The Administrator of the Environmental Protection Agency shall undertake to enter into appropriate arrangements with the National Academy of Sciences to conduct continuing comprehensive studies and investigations of the effects on public health and welfare of emissions subject to section 202(a) of the Clean Air Act [subsec. (a) of this section] (including sulfur compounds) and the technological feasibility of meeting emission standards required to be prescribed by the Administrator by section 202(b) of such Act [subsec. (b) of this section]. The Administrator shall report to the Congress within six months of the date of enactment of this section [Aug. 7, 1977] and each year thereafter regarding the status of the contractual arrangements and conditions necessary to implement this paragraph."

[For termination, effective May 15, 2000, of provisions relating to annual report to Congress in section 403(f) of Pub. L. No. 95–95, set out as note above, see Pub. L. No. 104–66, § 3003, as amended, set out as a note under 31 U.S.C.A. § 1113 and the 2nd item on page 165 of House Document No. 103–7.]

Modification or Rescission of Rules, Regulations, Orders, Determinations, Contracts, Certifications, Authorizations, Delegations, and Other Actions

All rules, regulations, orders, determinations, contracts, certifications, authorizations, delegations, or other actions duly issued, made, or taken by or pursuant to Act of July 14, 1955, the Clean Air Act, as in effect immediately prior to the date of enactment of Pub. L. No. 95–95 [Aug. 7, 1977] to continue in full force and effect until modified or rescinded in accordance with Act of July 14, 1955, as amended by Pub. L. No. 95–95 [this chapter], see section 406(b) of Pub. L. No. 95–95, set out as an Effective Date note under section 7401 of this title.

Study of Carbon Monoxide Intrusion Into Sustained-Use Vehicles

Section 226 of Pub. L. No. 95–95 provided that the Administrator, in conjunction with the Secretary of Transportation, study the problem of carbon monoxide intrusion into the passenger area of sustained-use motor vehicles and that within one year the Administrator report to the Congress respecting the results of such study.

Study on Emission of Sulfur-Bearing Compounds from Motor Vehicles and Motor Vehicle and Aircraft Engines

Section 403(g) of Pub. L. No. 95–95 provided that the Administrator of the Environmental Protection Agency conduct a study and report to the Congress by the date one year after Aug. 7, 1977, on the emission of sulfur-bearing compounds from motor vehicles and motor vehicle engines and aircraft engines.

Study on Oxides of Nitrogen from Light Duty Vehicles

Section 202(a) of Pub. L. No. 95–95 provided that the Administrator of the Environmental Protection Agency conduct a study of the public health implications of attaining an emission standard on oxides of nitrogen from light duty vehicles of 0.4 gram per vehicle mile, the cost and technological capability of attaining such standard, and the need for such a standard to protect public health or welfare and that the Administrator submit a report of such study to the Congress, together with recommendations not later than July 1, 1980.

§ 7522. Prohibited acts

[CAA § 203]

(a) Enumerated prohibitions

The following acts and the causing thereof are prohibited—

(1) in the case of a manufacturer of new motor vehicles or new motor vehicle engines for distribution in commerce, the sale, or the offering for sale, or the introduction, or delivery for introduction, into commerce, or (in the case of any person, except as provided by regulation of the Administrator), the importation into the United States, of any new motor vehicle or new motor vehicle engine, manufactured after the effective date of regulations under this part which are applicable to such vehicle or engine unless such vehicle or engine is covered by a certificate of conformity issued (and in effect) under regulations prescribed under this part or part C in the case of clean-fuel vehicles (except as provided in subsection (b) of this section);

(2) **(A)** for any person to fail or refuse to permit access to or copying of records or to fail to make reports or provide information required under section 7542 of this title;

(B) for any person to fail or refuse to permit entry, testing or inspection authorized under section 7525(c) of this title or section 7542 of this title;

(C) for any person to fail or refuse to perform tests, or have tests performed as required under section 7542 of this title;

(D) for any manufacturer to fail to make information available as provided by regulation under section 7521(m)(5) of this title;

(3) **(A)** for any person to remove or render inoperative any device or element of design installed on or in a motor vehicle or motor vehicle engine in compliance with regulations under this subchapter prior to its sale and delivery to the ultimate purchaser, or for any person knowingly to remove or render inoperative any such device or element of design after such sale and delivery to the ultimate purchaser; or

(B) for any person to manufacture or sell, or offer to sell, or install, any part or component intended for use with, or as part of, any motor vehicle or motor vehicle engine, where a principal effect of the part or component is to bypass, defeat, or render inoperative any device or element of design installed on or in a motor vehicle or motor vehicle engine in compliance with regulations under this subchapter, and where the person knows or should know that such part or component is being offered for sale or installed for such use or put to such use; or

(4) for any manufacturer of a new motor vehicle or new motor vehicle engine subject to standards prescribed under section 7521 of this title or part C of this subchapter—

(A) to sell or lease any such vehicle or engine unless such manufacturer has complied with (i) the requirements of section 7541(a) and (b) of this title with respect to such vehicle or engine, and unless a label or tag is affixed to such vehicle or engine in accordance with section 7541(c)(3) of this title, or (ii) the corresponding requirements of part C of this subchapter in the case of clean fuel vehicles unless the manufacturer has complied with the corresponding requirements of part C of this subchapter[1]

(B) to fail or refuse to comply with the requirements of section 7541(c) or (e) of this title, or the corresponding requirements of part C of this subchapter in the case of clean fuel vehicles[1]

(C) except as provided in subsection (c)(3) of section 7541 of this title and the corresponding requirements of part C of this subchapter in the case of clean fuel vehicles, to provide directly or indirectly in any communication to the ultimate purchaser or any subsequent purchaser that the coverage of any warranty under this chapter is conditioned upon use of any part, component, or system manufactured by such manufacturer or any person acting for such manufacturer or under his control, or conditioned upon service performed by any such person, or

(D) to fail or refuse to comply with the terms and conditions of the warranty under section 7541(a) or (b) of this title or the corresponding requirements of part C of this subchapter in the case of clean fuel vehicles with respect to any vehicle; or

(5) for any person to violate section 7553 of this title, 7554 of this title, or part C of this subchapter or any regulations under section 7553 of this title, 7554 of this title, or part C of this subchapter.

No action with respect to any element of design referred to in paragraph (3) (including any adjustment or alteration of such element) shall be treated as a prohibited act under such paragraph (3) if such action is in accordance with section 7549 of this title. Nothing in paragraph (3) shall be construed to require the use of manufacturer parts in maintaining or repairing any motor vehicle or motor vehicle engine. For the purposes of the preceding sentence, the term "manufacturer parts" means, with respect to a motor vehicle engine, parts produced or sold by the manufacturer of the motor vehicle or motor vehicle engine. No action with respect to any device or element of design referred to in paragraph (3) shall be treated as a prohibited act under that paragraph if (i) the action is for the purpose of repair or replacement of the device or element, or is a necessary and temporary procedure to repair or replace any other item and the device or element is replaced upon completion of the procedure, and (ii) such action thereafter results in the proper functioning of the device or element referred to in paragraph (3). No action with respect to any device or element of design referred to in paragraph (3) shall be treated as a prohibited act under that paragraph if the action is for the purpose of a conversion of a motor vehicle for use of a clean alternative fuel (as defined in this subchapter) and if such vehicle complies with the applicable standard under section 7521 of this title when operating on such fuel, and if in the case of a clean alternative fuel vehicle (as defined by rule by the Administrator), the device or element is replaced upon completion of the conversion procedure and such action results in proper functioning of the device or element when the motor vehicle operates on conventional fuel.

(b) Exemptions; refusal to admit vehicle or engine into United States; vehicles or engines intended for export

(1) The Administrator may exempt any new motor vehicle or new motor vehicle engine, from subsection (a) of this section, upon such terms and conditions as he may find necessary for the purpose of research, investigations, studies, demonstrations, or training, or for reasons of national security.

(2) A new motor vehicle or new motor vehicle engine offered for importation or imported by any person in violation of subsection (a) of this section shall be refused admission into the United States, but the Secretary of the Treasury and the Administrator may, by joint regulation, provide for deferring final determination as to admission and authorizing the delivery of such a motor vehicle or engine offered for import to the owner or consignee thereof upon such terms and conditions (including the furnishing of a bond) as may appear to them appropriate to insure that any such motor vehicle or engine will be brought into conformity with the standards, requirements, and limitations applicable to it under this part. The Secretary of the Treasury shall, if a motor vehicle or engine is finally refused admission under this paragraph, cause disposition thereof in accordance with the customs laws unless it is exported, under regulations prescribed by such Secretary, within ninety days of the date of notice of such refusal or such additional time as may be permitted pursuant to such regulations, except that disposition in accordance with the customs laws may not be made in such manner as may result, directly or indirectly, in the sale, to the ultimate consumer, of a new motor vehicle or new motor vehicle engine that fails to comply with applicable standards of the Administrator under this part.

(3) A new motor vehicle or new motor vehicle engine intended solely for export, and so labeled or tagged on the outside of the container and on the vehicle or engine itself, shall be subject to the provisions of subsection (a) of this section, except that if the country which is to receive such vehicle or engine has emission standards which differ from the standards prescribed under section 7521 of this title, then such vehicle or engine shall comply with the standards of such country which is to receive such vehicle or engine.

(July 14, 1955, c. 360, Title II, § 203, as added by Pub. L. No. 89–272, Title I, § 101(8), 79 Stat. 993 (Oct. 20, 1965); and amended by Pub. L. No. 90–148, § 2, 81 Stat. 499 (Nov. 21, 1967); Pub. L. No. 91–604, §§ 7(a), 11(a)(2)(A), 15(c)(2), 84 Stat. 1693, 1705, 1713 (Dec. 31, 1970); Pub. L. No. 95–95, Title II, §§ 206, 211(a), 218(a), (d), 219(a), (b), 91 Stat. 755, 757, 761, 762 (Aug. 7, 1977); Pub. L. No. 95–190, § 14(a)(66)–(68), 91 Stat. 1403 (Nov. 16, 1977); Pub. L. No. 101–549, Title II, §§ 228(a), (b), (e), 230(6), 104 Stat. 2507, 2511, 2529 (Nov. 15, 1990).)

[1] So in original. Probably should be followed by a comma.

HISTORICAL AND STATUTORY NOTES

Codifications

This section was formerly codified as section 1857f–2 of this title.

Effective and Applicability Provisions

1990 Acts. Amendment by Pub. L. No. 101–549 effective Nov. 15, 1990, except as otherwise provided, see section 711(b) of Pub. L. No. 101–549, set out as a note under section 7401 of this title.

1977 Acts. Amendment by Pub. L. No. 95–95 effective Aug. 7, 1977, except as otherwise expressly provided, see section 406(d) of Pub. L. No. 95–95, set out as a note under section 7401 of this title.

Savings Provisions

Suits, actions or proceedings commenced under this chapter as in effect prior to Nov. 15, 1990, not to abate by reason of the taking effect of amendments by Pub. L. No. 101–549, except as otherwise provided for, see section 711(a) of Pub. L. No. 101–549, set out as a note under section 7401 of this title.

§ 7523. Actions to restrain violations

[CAA § 204]

(a) Jurisdiction

The district courts of the United States shall have jurisdiction to restrain violations of section 7522(a) of this title.

(b) Actions brought by or in name of United States; subpenas

Actions to restrain such violations shall be brought by and in the name of the United States. In any such action, subpenas for witnesses who are required to attend a district court in any district may run into any other district.

(July 14, 1955, c. 360, Title II, § 204, as added by Pub. L. No. 89–272, Title I, § 101(8), 79 Stat. 994 (Oct. 20, 1965); and amended by Pub. L. No. 90–148, § 2, 81 Stat. 500 (Nov. 21, 1967); Pub. L. No. 91–604, § 7(b), 84 Stat. 1694 (Dec. 31, 1970); Pub. L. No. 95–95, Title II, § 218(b), 91 Stat. 761 (Aug. 7, 1977).)

HISTORICAL AND STATUTORY NOTES

Codifications

This section was formerly codified as section 1857f–3 of this title.

Effective and Applicability Provisions

1977 Acts. Amendment by Pub. L. No. 95–95 effective Aug. 7, 1977, except as otherwise expressly provided, see section 406(d) of Pub. L. No. 95–95, set out as a note under section 7401 of this title.

Pending Actions and Proceedings

Suits, actions, and other proceedings lawfully commenced by or against the Administrator or any other officer or employee of the United States in his official capacity or in relation to the discharge of his official duties under

Act of July 14, 1955, the Clean Air Act, as in effect immediately prior to the enactment of Pub. L. No. 95–95 [Aug. 7, 1977], not to abate by reason of the taking effect of Pub. L. No. 95–95, see section 406(a) of Pub. L. No. 95–95, set out as an Effective Date of 1977 Acts note under section 7401 of this title.

§ 7524. Civil penalties

[CAA § 205]

(a) Violations

Any person who violates sections[1] 7522(a)(1), 7522(a)(4), or 7522(a)(5) of this title or any manufacturer or dealer who violates section 7522(a)(3)(A) of this title shall be subject to a civil penalty of not more than $25,000. Any person other than a manufacturer or dealer who violates section 7522(a)(3)(A) of this title or any person who violates section 7522(a)(3)(B) of this title shall be subject to a civil penalty of not more than $2,500. Any such violation with respect to paragraph (1), (3)(A), or (4) of section 7522(a) of this title shall constitute a separate offense with respect to each motor vehicle or motor vehicle engine. Any such violation with respect to section 7522(a)(3)(B) of this title shall constitute a separate offense with respect to each part or component. Any person who violates section 7522(a)(2) of this title shall be subject to a civil penalty of not more than $25,000 per day of violation.

(b) Civil actions

The Administrator may commence a civil action to assess and recover any civil penalty under subsection (a) of this section, section 7545(d) of this title, or section 7547(d) of this title. Any action under this subsection may be brought in the district court of the United States for the district in which the violation is alleged to have occurred or in which the defendant resides or has the Administrator's principal place of business, and the court shall have jurisdiction to assess a civil penalty. In determining the amount of any civil penalty to be assessed under this subsection, the court shall take into account the gravity of the violation, the economic benefit or savings (if any) resulting from the violation, the size of the violator's business, the violator's history of compliance with this subchapter, action taken to remedy the violation, the effect of the penalty on the violator's ability to continue in business, and such other matters as justice may require. In any such action, subpoenas for witnesses who are required to attend a district court in any district may run into any other district.

(c) Administrative assessment of certain penalties

(1) Administrative penalty authority

In lieu of commencing a civil action under subsection (b) of this section, the Administrator may assess any civil penalty prescribed in subsection (a) of this section, section 7545(d) of this title, or section 7547(d) of this title, except that the maximum amount of penalty sought against each violator in a penalty assessment proceeding shall not exceed $200,000, unless the Administrator and the Attorney General jointly determine that a matter involving a larger penalty amount is appropriate for administrative penalty assessment. Any such determination by the Administrator and the Attorney General shall not be subject to judicial review. Assessment of a civil penalty under this subsection shall be by an order made on the record after opportunity for a hearing in accordance with sections 554 and 556 of Title 5. The Administrator shall issue reasonable rules for discovery and other procedures for hearings under this paragraph. Before issuing such an order, the Administrator shall give written notice to the person to be assessed an administrative penalty of the Administrator's proposal to issue such order and provide such person an opportunity to request such a hearing on the order, within 30 days of the date the notice is received by such person. The Administrator may compromise, or remit, with or without conditions, any administrative penalty which may be imposed under this section.

(2) Determining amount

In determining the amount of any civil penalty assessed under this subsection, the Administrator shall take into account the gravity of the violation, the economic benefit or savings (if any) resulting from the violation, the size of the violator's business, the violator's history of compliance with this subchapter, action taken to remedy the violation, the effect of the penalty on the violator's ability to continue in business, and such other matters as justice may require.

(3) Effect of Administrator's action

(A) Action by the Administrator under this subsection shall not affect or limit the Administrator's authority to enforce any provision of this chapter; except that any violation,

(i) with respect to which the Administrator has commenced and is diligently prosecuting an action under this subsection, or

(ii) for which the Administrator has issued a final order not subject to further judicial review and the violator has paid a penalty assessment under this subsection,

shall not be the subject of civil penalty action under subsection (b) of this section.

(B) No action by the Administrator under this subsection shall affect any person's obligation to comply with any section of this chapter.

(4) Finality of order

An order issued under this subsection shall become final 30 days after its issuance unless a petition for judicial review is filed under paragraph (5).

(5) Judicial review

Any person against whom a civil penalty is assessed in accordance with this subsection may seek review of the assessment in the United States District Court for the District of Columbia, or for the district in which the violation is alleged to have occurred, in which such person resides, or where such person's principal place of business is located, within the 30-day period beginning on the date a civil penalty order is issued. Such person shall simultaneously send a copy of the filing by certified mail to the Administrator and the Attorney General. The Administrator shall file in the court a certified copy, or certified index, as appropriate, of the record on which the order was issued within 30 days. The court shall not set aside or remand any order issued in accordance with the requirements of this subsection unless there is not substantial evidence in the record, taken as a whole, to support the finding of a violation or unless the Administrator's assessment of the penalty constitutes an abuse of discretion, and the court shall not impose additional civil penalties unless the Administrator's assessment of the penalty constitutes an abuse of discretion. In any proceedings, the United States may seek to recover civil penalties assessed under this section.

(6) Collection

If any person fails to pay an assessment of a civil penalty imposed by the Administrator as provided in this subsection—

(A) after the order making the assessment has become final, or

(B) after a court in an action brought under paragraph (5) has entered a final judgment in favor of the Administrator,

the Administrator shall request the Attorney General to bring a civil action in an appropriate district court to recover the amount assessed (plus interest at rates established pursuant to section 6621(a)(2) of Title 26 from the date of the final order or the date of the final judgment, as the case may be). In such an action, the validity, amount, and appropriateness of the penalty shall not be subject to review. Any person who fails to pay on a timely basis the amount of an assessment of a civil penalty as described in the first sentence of this paragraph shall be required to pay, in addition to that amount and interest, the United States' enforcement expenses, including attorneys fees and costs for collection proceedings, and a quarterly nonpayment penalty for each quarter during which such failure to pay persists. The nonpayment penalty shall be in an amount equal to 10 percent of the aggregate amount of that person's penalties and nonpayment penalties which are unpaid as of the beginning of such quarter.

(July 14, 1955, c. 360, Title II, § 205, as added by Pub. L. No. 89–272, Title I, § 101(8), 79 Stat. 994 (Oct. 20, 1965); and amended by Pub. L. No. 90–148, § 2, 81 Stat. 500 (Nov. 21, 1967); Pub. L. No. 91–604, § 7(c), 84 Stat. 1694 (Dec. 31, 1970); Pub. L. No. 95–95, Title II, § 219(c), 91 Stat. 762 (Aug. 7, 1977); Pub. L. No. 101–549, Title II, § 228(c), 104 Stat. 2508 (Nov. 15, 1990).)

[1] So in original. Probably should be "section."

HISTORICAL AND STATUTORY NOTES

Codifications

This section was formerly codified as section 1857f–4 of this title.

Effective and Applicability Provisions

1990 Acts. Amendment by Pub. L. No. 101–549 effective Nov. 15, 1990, except as otherwise provided, see section 711(b) of Pub. L. No. 101–549, set out as a note under section 7401 of this title.

1977 Acts. Amendment by Pub. L. No. 95–95 effective Aug. 7, 1977, except as otherwise expressly provided, see section 406(d) of Pub. L. No. 95–95, set out as a note under section 7401 of this title.

Savings Provisions

Suits, actions or proceedings commenced under this chapter as in effect prior to Nov. 15, 1990, not to abate by reason of the taking effect of amendments by Pub. L. No. 101–549, except as otherwise provided for, see section 711(a) of Pub. L. No. 101–549, set out as a note under section 7401 of this title.

§ 7525. Motor vehicle and motor vehicle engine compliance testing and certification

[CAA § 206]

(a) Testing and issuance of certificate of conformity

(1) The Administrator shall test, or require to be tested in such manner as he deems appropriate, any new motor vehicle or new motor vehicle engine submitted by a manufacturer to determine whether such vehicle or engine conforms with the regulations prescribed under section 7521 of this title. If such vehicle or engine conforms to such regulations, the Administrator shall issue a certificate of conformity upon such terms, and for such period (not in excess of one year), as he may prescribe. In the case of any original equipment manufacturer (as defined by the Administrator in regulations promulgated before November 15, 1990) of vehicles or vehicle engines whose projected sales in the United States for any model year (as determined by the Administrator) will not exceed 300, the Administrator shall not require, for purposes of determining compliance with regulations under section 7521 of this title for the useful life of the vehicle or engine, operation of any vehicle or engine manufactured during such model year for more than 5,000 miles or 160 hours, respectively, unless the Administrator, by regulation, prescribes otherwise. The Administrator shall apply any adjustment factors that the Administrator deems appropriate to assure that each vehicle or engine will comply during its useful life (as determined under section 7521(d) of this title) with the regulations prescribed under section 7521 of this title.

(2) The Administrator shall test any emission control system incorporated in a motor vehicle or motor vehicle engine submitted to him by any person, in order to determine whether such system enables such vehicle or engine to conform to the standards required to be prescribed under section 7521(b) of this title. If the Administrator finds on the basis of such tests that such vehicle or engine conforms to such standards, the Administrator shall issue a verification of compliance with emission standards for such system when incorporated in vehicles of a class of which the tested vehicle is representative. He shall inform manufacturers and the National Academy of Sciences, and make available to the public, the results of such tests. Tests under this paragraph shall be conducted under such terms and conditions (including requirements for preliminary testing by qualified independent laboratories) as the Administrator may prescribe by regulations.

(3) **(A)** A certificate of conformity may be issued under this section only if the Administrator determines that the manufacturer (or in the case of a vehicle or engine for import, any person) has established to the satisfaction of the Administrator that any emission control device, system, or element of design installed on, or incorporated in, such vehicle or engine conforms to applicable requirements of section 7521(a)(4) of this title.

(B) The Administrator may conduct such tests and may require the manufacturer (or any such person) to conduct such tests and provide such information as is necessary to carry out subparagraph (A) of this paragraph. Such requirements shall include a requirement for prompt reporting of the emission of any unregulated pollutant from a system, device, or element of design if such pollutant was not emitted, or was emitted in significantly lesser amounts, from the vehicle or engine without use of the system, device, or element of design.

(4) **(A)** Not later than 12 months after November 15, 1990, the Administrator shall revise the regulations promulgated under this subsection to add test procedures capable of determining whether model year 1994 and later model year light-duty vehicles and light-duty trucks, when properly maintained and used, will pass the inspection methods and procedures established under section 7541(b) of this title for that model year, under conditions reasonably likely to be encountered in the conduct of inspection and maintenance programs, but which those programs cannot reasonably influence or control. The conditions shall include fuel characteristics, ambient temperature, and short (30 minutes or less) waiting periods before tests are conducted. The Administrator shall not grant a certificate of conformity under this subsection for any 1994 or later model year vehicle or engine that the Administrator concludes cannot pass the test procedures established under this paragraph.

(B) From time to time, the Administrator may revise the regulations promulgated under subparagraph (A), as the Administrator deems appropriate.

(b) Testing procedures; hearing; judicial review; additional evidence

(1) In order to determine whether new motor vehicles or new motor vehicle engines being manufactured by a manufacturer do in fact conform with the regulations with respect to which the certificate of conformity was issued, the Administrator is authorized to test such vehicles or engines. Such tests may be conducted by the Administrator directly or, in accordance with conditions specified by the Administrator, by the manufacturer.

(2) **(A)** **(i)** If, based on tests conducted under paragraph (1) on a sample of new vehicles or engines covered by a certificate of conformity, the Administrator determines that all or part of the vehicles or engines so covered do not conform with the regulations with respect to which the certificate of conformity was issued and with the requirements of section 7521(a)(4) of this title, he may suspend or revoke such certificate in whole or in part, and shall so notify the manufacturer. Such suspension or revocation shall apply in the case of any new motor vehicles or new motor vehicle engines manufactured after the date of such notification (or manufactured before such date if still in the hands of the manufacturer), and shall apply until such time as the Administrator finds that vehicles and engines manufactured by the manufacturer do conform to such regulations and requirements. If, during any period of suspension or revocation, the Administrator finds that a vehicle or engine actually conforms to such regulations and requirements, he shall issue a certificate of conformity applicable to such vehicle or engine.

(ii) If, based on tests conducted under paragraph (1) on any new vehicle or engine, the Administrator determines that such vehicle or engine does not conform with such regulations and requirements, he may suspend or revoke such certificate insofar as it applies to such vehicle or engine until such time as he finds such vehicle or engine actually so conforms with such regulations and requirements, and he shall so notify the manufacturer.

(B) **(i)** At the request of any manufacturer the Administrator shall grant such manufacturer a hearing as to whether the tests have been properly conducted or any sampling methods have been properly applied, and make a determination on the record with respect to any suspension or revocation under subparagraph (A); but suspension or revocation under subparagraph (A) shall not be stayed by reason of such hearing.

(ii) In any case of actual controversy as to the validity of any determination under clause (i), the manufacturer may at any time prior to the 60th day after such determination is made file a petition with the United States court of appeals for the circuit wherein such manufacturer resides or has his principal place of business for a judicial review of such determination. A copy of the petition shall be forthwith transmitted by the clerk of the court to the Administrator or other officer designated by him for that purpose. The Administrator thereupon shall file in the court the record of the proceedings on which the Administrator based his determination, as provided in section 2112 of Title 28.

(iii) If the petitioner applies to the court for leave to adduce additional evidence, and shows to the satisfaction of the court that such additional evidence is material and that there were reasonable grounds for the failure to adduce such evidence in the proceeding before the Administrator, the court may order such additional evidence (and evidence in rebuttal thereof) to be taken before the Administrator, in such manner and upon such terms and conditions as the court may deem proper. The Administrator may modify his findings as to the facts, or make new findings, by reason of the additional evidence so taken and he shall file such modified or new findings, and his recommendation, if any, for the modification or setting aside of his original determination, with the return of such additional evidence.

(iv) Upon the filing of the petition referred to in clause (ii), the court shall have jurisdiction to review the order in accordance with chapter 7 of Title 5 and to grant appropriate relief as provided in such chapter.

(c) Inspection

For purposes of enforcement of this section, officers or employees duly designated by the Administrator, upon presenting appropriate credentials to the manufacturer or person in charge, are authorized (1) to enter, at reasonable times, any plant or other establishment of such manufacturer, for the purpose of conducting tests of vehicles or engines in the hands of the manufacturer, or (2) to inspect, at reasonable times, records, files, papers, processes, controls, and facilities used by such manufacturer in conducting tests under regulations of the Administrator. Each such inspection shall be commenced and completed with reasonable promptness.

(d) Rules and regulations

The Administrator shall by regulation establish methods and procedures for making tests under this section.

(e) Publication of test results

The Administrator shall make available to the public the results of his tests of any motor vehicle or motor vehicle engine submitted by a manufacturer under subsection (a) of this section as promptly as possible after December 31, 1970, and at the beginning of each model year which begins thereafter. Such results shall be described in such nontechnical manner as will reasonably disclose to prospective ultimate purchasers of new motor vehicles and new motor vehicle engines the comparative performance of the vehicles and engines tested in meeting the standards prescribed under section 7521 of this title.

(f) High altitude regulations

All light duty[1] vehicles and engines manufactured during or after model year 1984 and all light-duty trucks manufactured during or after model year 1995 shall comply with the requirements of section 7521 of this title regardless of the altitude at which they are sold.

(g) Nonconformance penalty

(1) In the case of any class or category of heavy-duty vehicles or engines to which a standard promulgated under section 7521(a) of this title applies, except as provided in paragraph (2), a certificate of conformity shall be issued under subsection (a) of this section and shall not be suspended or revoked under subsection (b) of this section for such vehicles or engines manufactured by a manufacturer notwithstanding the failure of such vehicles or engines to meet such standard if such manufacturer pays a nonconformance penalty as provided under regulations promulgated by the Administrator after notice and opportunity for public hearing. In the case of motorcycles to which such a standard applies, such a certificate may be issued notwithstanding such failure if the manufacturer pays such a penalty.

(2) No certificate of conformity may be issued under paragraph (1) with respect to any class or category of vehicle or engine if the degree by which the manufacturer fails to meet any standard promulgated under section 7521(a) of this title with respect to such class or category exceeds the percentage determined under regulations promulgated by the Administrator to be practicable. Such regulations shall require such testing of vehicles or engines being produced as may be necessary to determine the percentage of the classes or categories of vehicles or engines which are not in compliance with the regulations with respect to which a certificate of conformity was issued and shall be promulgated not later than one year after August 7, 1977.

(3) The regulations promulgated under paragraph (1) shall, not later than one year after August 7, 1977, provide for nonconformance penalties in amounts determined under a formula established by the Administrator. Such penalties under such formula—

(A) may vary from pollutant-to-pollutant;

(B) may vary by class or category or vehicle or engine;

(C) shall take into account the extent to which actual emissions of any air pollutant exceed allowable emissions under the standards promulgated under section 7521 of this title;

(D) shall be increased periodically in order to create incentives for the development of production vehicles or engines which achieve the required degree of emission reduction; and

(E) shall remove any competitive disadvantage to manufacturers whose engines or vehicles achieve the required degree of emission reduction (including any such disadvantage arising from the application of paragraph (4)).

(4) In any case in which a certificate of conformity has been issued under this subsection, any warranty required under section 7541(b)(2) of this title and any action under section 7541(c) of this title shall be required to be effective only for the emission levels which the Administrator determines that such certificate was issued and not for the emission levels required under the applicable standard.

(5) The authorities of section 7542(a) of this title shall apply, subject to the conditions of section 7542(b) of this title, for purposes of this subsection.

(h) Review and revision of regulations

Within 18 months after November 15, 1990, the Administrator shall review and revise as necessary the regulations under subsection[2] (a) and (b) of this section regarding the testing of motor vehicles and motor vehicle engines to insure that vehicles are tested under circumstances which reflect the actual current driving conditions under which motor vehicles are used, including conditions relating to fuel, temperature, acceleration, and altitude.

(July 14, 1955, c. 360, Title II, § 206, as added by Pub. L. No. 91–604, § 8(a), 84 Stat. 1694 (Dec. 31, 1970); and amended by Pub. L. No. 95–95, Title II, §§ 213(a), 214(b), (c), 220, 224(e), 91 Stat. 758–760, 762, 768 (Aug. 7, 1977); Pub. L. No. 95–190, § 14(a)(69), 91 Stat. 1403 (Nov. 16, 1977); Pub. L. No. 101–549, Title II, §§ 208, 230(7), (8), 104 Stat. 2483, 2529 (Nov. 15, 1990).)

[1] So in original. Probably should be "light-duty."

[2] So in original. Probably should be "subsections."

HISTORICAL AND STATUTORY NOTES

References in Text

Section 7542 of this title, referred to in subsec. (g)(5), was amended generally by Pub. L. No. 101–549, Title II, § 211, 104 Stat. 2487 (Nov. 15, 1990), and provisions formerly contained in section 7542(b) of this title are contained in section 7542(c).

Codifications

This section was formerly codified as section 1857f–5 of this title.

Effective and Applicability Provisions

1990 Acts. Amendment by Pub. L. No. 101–549 effective Nov. 15, 1990, except as otherwise provided, see section 711(b) of Pub. L. No. 101–549, set out as a note under section 7401 of this title.

1977 Acts. Amendment by Pub. L. No. 95–95 effective Aug. 7, 1977, except as otherwise expressly provided, see section 406(d) of Pub. L. No. 95–95, set out as a note under section 7401 of this title.

1970 Acts. Section 8(b) of Pub. L. No. 91–604 provided that: "The amendments made by this section [enacting this section and section 7541 of this title] shall not apply to vehicles or engines imported into the United States before the sixtieth day after the date of enactment of this Act [Dec. 31, 1970]."

Savings Provisions

Suits, actions or proceedings commenced under this chapter as in effect prior to Nov. 15, 1990, not to abate by reason of the taking effect of amendments by Pub. L. No. 101–549, except as otherwise provided for, see section 711(a) of Pub. L. No. 101–549, set out as a note under section 7401 of this title.

Prior Provisions

A prior section 206 of Act of July 14, 1955, relating to the testing of motor vehicles and motor vehicle engines, was repealed by Pub. L. No. 91–604, § 8(a), Dec. 31, 1970, 84 Stat. 1694.

Modification or Rescission of Rules, Regulations, Orders, Determinations, Contracts, Certifications, Authorizations, Delegations, and Other Actions

All rules, regulations, orders, determinations, contracts, certifications, authorizations, delegations, or other actions duly issued, made, or taken by or pursuant to Act of July 14, 1955, the Clean Air Act, as in effect immediately prior to the date of enactment of Pub. L. No. 95–95 [Aug. 7, 1977] to continue in full force and effect until modified or rescinded in accordance with Act of July 14, 1955, as amended by Pub. L. No. 95–95 [this chapter], see section 406(b) of Pub. L. No. 95–95, set out as an Effective Date of 1977 Acts note under section 7401 of this title.

§ 7541. Compliance by vehicles and engines in actual use

[CAA § 207]

(a) Warranty; certification; payment of replacement costs of parts, devices, or components designed for emission control

(1) Effective with respect to vehicles and engines manufactured in model years beginning more than 60 days after December 31, 1970, the manufacturer of each new motor vehicle and new motor vehicle engine shall warrant to the ultimate purchaser and each subsequent purchaser that such vehicle or engine is (A) designed, built, and equipped so as to conform at the time of sale with applicable regulations under section 7521 of this title, and (B) free from defects in materials and workmanship which cause such vehicle or engine to fail to conform with applicable regulations for its useful life (as determined under section 7521(d) of this title). In the case of vehicles and engines manufactured in the model year 1995 and thereafter such warranty shall require that the vehicle or engine is free from any such defects for the warranty period provided under subsection (i) of this section.

(2) In the case of a motor vehicle part or motor vehicle engine part, the manufacturer or rebuilder of such part may certify that use of such part will not result in a failure of the vehicle or engine to comply with emission standards promulgated under section 7521 of this title. Such certification shall be made only under such regulations as may be promulgated by the Administrator to carry out the purposes of subsection (b) of this section. The Administrator shall promulgate such regulations no later than two years following August 7, 1977.

(3) The cost of any part, device, or component of any light-duty vehicle that is designed for emission control and which in the instructions issued pursuant to subsection (c)(3) of this section is scheduled for replacement during the useful life of the vehicle in order to maintain compliance with regulations under section 7521 of this title, the failure of which shall not interfere with the normal performance of the vehicle, and the expected retail price of which, including installation costs, is greater than 2 percent of the suggested retail price of such vehicle, shall be borne or reimbursed at the time of replacement by the vehicle manufacturer and such replacement shall be provided without cost to the ultimate purchaser, subsequent purchaser, or dealer. The term "designed for emission control" as used in the preceding sentence means a catalytic converter, thermal reactor, or other component installed on or in a vehicle for the sole or primary purpose of reducing vehicle emissions (not including those vehicle components which were in general use prior to model year 1968 and the primary function of which is not related to emission control).

(b) Testing methods and procedures

If the Administrator determines that (i) there are available testing methods and procedures to ascertain whether, when in actual use throughout its[1] the warranty period (as determined under subsection

(i) of this section), each vehicle and engine to which regulations under section 7521 of this title apply complies with the emission standards of such regulations, (ii) such methods and procedures are in accordance with good engineering practices, and (iii) such methods and procedures are reasonably capable of being correlated with tests conducted under section 7525(a)(1) of this title, then—

(1) he shall establish such methods and procedures by regulation, and

(2) at such time as he determines that inspection facilities or equipment are available for purposes of carrying out testing methods and procedures established under paragraph (1), he shall prescribe regulations which shall require manufacturers to warrant the emission control device or system of each new motor vehicle or new motor vehicle engine to which a regulation under section 7521 of this title applies and which is manufactured in a model year beginning after the Administrator first prescribes warranty regulations under this paragraph (2). The warranty under such regulations shall run to the ultimate purchaser and each subsequent purchaser and shall provide that if—

(A) the vehicle or engine is maintained and operated in accordance with instructions under subsection (c)(3) of this section,

(B) it fails to conform at any time during its[1] the warranty period (as determined under subsection (i) of this section) to the regulations prescribed under section 7521 of this title, and

(C) such nonconformity results in the ultimate purchaser (or any subsequent purchaser) of such vehicle or engine having to bear any penalty or other sanction (including the denial of the right to use such vehicle or engine) under State or Federal law,

then such manufacturer shall remedy such nonconformity under such warranty with the cost thereof to be borne by the manufacturer. No such warranty shall be invalid on the basis of any part used in the maintenance or repair of a vehicle or engine if such part was certified as provided under subsection (a)(2) of this section.

(c) Nonconforming vehicles; plan for remedying nonconformity; instructions for maintenance and use; label or tag

Effective with respect to vehicles and engines manufactured during model years beginning more than 60 days after December 31, 1970—

(1) If the Administrator determines that a substantial number of any class or category of vehicles or engines, although properly maintained and used, do not conform to the regulations prescribed under section 7521 of this title, when in actual use throughout their useful life (as determined under section 7521(d) of this title), he shall immediately notify the manufacturer thereof of such nonconformity, and he shall require the manufacturer to submit a plan for remedying the nonconformity of the vehicles or engines with respect to which such notification is given. The plan shall provide that the nonconformity of any such vehicles or engines which are properly used and maintained will be remedied at the expense of the manufacturer. If the manufacturer disagrees with such determination of nonconformity and so advises the Administrator, the Administrator shall afford the manufacturer and other interested persons an opportunity to present their views and evidence in support thereof at a public hearing. Unless, as a result of such hearing the Administrator withdraws such determination of nonconformity, he shall, within 60 days after the completion of such hearing, order the manufacturer to provide prompt notification of such nonconformity in accordance with paragraph (2).

(2) Any notification required by paragraph (1) with respect to any class or category of vehicles or engines shall be given to dealers, ultimate purchasers, and subsequent purchasers (if known) in such manner and containing such information as the Administrator may by regulations require.

(3) **(A)** The manufacturer shall furnish with each new motor vehicle or motor vehicle engine written instructions for the proper maintenance and use of the vehicle or engine by the ultimate purchaser and such instructions shall correspond to regulations which the Administrator shall promulgate. The manufacturer shall provide in boldface type on the first page of the written maintenance instructions notice that maintenance, replacement, or repair of the emission control devices and systems may be performed by any automotive repair establishment or individual using any automotive part which has been certified as provided in subsection (a)(2) of this section.

(B) The instruction under subparagraph (A) of this paragraph shall not include any condition on the ultimate purchaser's using, in connection with such vehicle or engine, any component or service (other than a component or service provided without charge under the terms of the purchase agreement) which is identified by brand, trade, or corporate name; or directly or indirectly distinguishing between service performed by the franchised dealers of such manufacturer or any other service establishments with which such manufacturer has a commercial relationship, and service performed by independent automotive repair facilities with which such manufacturer has no commercial relationship; except that the prohibition of this subsection may be waived by the Administrator if—

(i) the manufacturer satisfies the Administrator that the vehicle or engine will function properly only if the component or service so identified is used in connection with such vehicle or engine, and

(ii) the Administrator finds that such a waiver is in the public interest.

(C) In addition, the manufacturer shall indicate by means of a label or tag permanently affixed to such vehicle or engine that such vehicle or engine is covered by a certificate of conformity issued for the purpose of assuring achievement of emissions standards prescribed under section 7521 of this title. Such label or tag shall contain such other information relating to control of motor vehicle emissions as the Administrator shall prescribe by regulation.

(4) Intermediate in-use standards

(A) Model years 1994 and 1995

For light-duty trucks of up to 6,000 lbs. gross vehicle weight rating (GVWR) and light-duty vehicles which are subject to standards under table G of section 7521(g)(1) of this title in model years 1994 and 1995 (40 percent of the manufacturer's sales volume in model year 1994 and 80 percent in model year 1995), the standards applicable to NMHC, CO, and NO_x for purposes of this subsection shall be those set forth in table A below in lieu of the standards for such air pollutants otherwise applicable under this subchapter.

TABLE A—INTERMEDIATE IN-USE STANDARDS LDTs UP TO 6,000 LBS. GVWR AND LIGHT-DUTY VEHICLES

Vehicle type	NMHC	CO	NO_x
Light-duty vehicles	0.32	3.4	0.4*
LDT's (0–3,750 LVW)	0.32	5.2	0.4*
LDT's (3,751–5,750 LVW)	0.41	6.7	0.7*

* Not applicable to diesel-fueled vehicles.

(B) Model years 1996 and thereafter

(i) In the model years 1996 and 1997, light-duty trucks (LDTs) up to 6,000 lbs. gross vehicle weight rating (GVWR) and light-duty vehicles which are not subject to final in-use standards under paragraph (5) (60 percent of the manufacturer's sales volume in model year 1996 and 20 percent in model year 1997) shall be subject to the standards set forth in table A of subparagraph (A) for NMHC, CO, and NO_x for purposes of this subsection in lieu of those set forth in paragraph (5).

(ii) For LDTs of more than 6,000 lbs. GVWR—

(I) in model year 1996 which are subject to the standards set forth in Table H of section 7521(h) of this title (50%);

(II) in model year 1997 (100%); and

(III) in model year 1998 which are not subject to final in-use standards under paragraph (5) (50%);

the standards for NMHC, CO, and NO_x for purposes of this subsection shall be those set forth in Table B below in lieu of the standards for such air pollutants otherwise applicable under this subchapter.

TABLE B—INTERMEDIATE IN-USE STANDARDS LDTS MORE THAN 6,000 LBS. GVWR

Vehicle type	NMHC	CO	NO_x
LDTs (3,751–5,750 lbs. TW)	0.40	5.5	0.88*
LDTs (over 5,750 lbs. TW)	0.49	6.2	1.38*

* Not applicable to diesel-fueled vehicles.

(C) Useful life

In the case of the in-use standards applicable under this paragraph, for purposes of applying this subsection, the applicable useful life shall be 5 years or 50,000 miles or the equivalent (whichever first occurs).

(5) Final in-use standards

(A) After the model year 1995, for purposes of applying this subsection, in the case of the percentage specified in the implementation schedule below of each manufacturer's sales volume of light-duty trucks of up to 6,000 lbs. gross vehicle weight rating (GVWR) and light duty[2] vehicles, the standards for NMHC, CO, and NO_x shall be as provided in Table G in section 7521(g) of this title, except that in applying the standards set forth in Table G for purposes of determining compliance with this subsection, the applicable useful life shall be (i) 5 years or 50,000 miles (or the equivalent) whichever first occurs in the case of standards applicable for purposes of certification at 50,000 miles; and (ii) 10 years or 100,000 miles (or the equivalent), whichever first occurs in the case of standards applicable for purposes of certification at 100,000 miles, except that no testing shall be done beyond 7 years or 75,000 miles, or the equivalent whichever first occurs.

LDTS UP TO 6,000 LBS. GVWR AND LIGHT-DUTY VEHICLE SCHEDULE FOR IMPLEMENTATION OF FINAL IN-USE STANDARDS

Model year	Percent
1996	40
1997	80
1998	100

(B) After the model year 1997, for purposes of applying this subsection, in the case of the percentage specified in the implementation schedule below of each manufacturer's sales volume of light-duty trucks of more than 6,000 lbs. gross vehicle weight rating (GVWR), the standards for NMHC, CO, and NO_x shall be as provided in Table H in section 7521(h) of this title, except that in applying the standards set forth in Table H for purposes of determining compliance with this subsection, the applicable useful life shall be (i) 5 years or 50,000 miles (or the equivalent) whichever first occurs in the case of standards applicable for purposes of certification at 50,000 miles; and (ii) 11 years or 120,000 miles (or the equivalent), whichever first occurs in the case of standards applicable for purposes of certification at 120,000 miles, except that no testing shall be done beyond 7 years or 90,000 miles (or the equivalent) whichever first occurs.

LDTS OF MORE THAN 6,000 LBS. GVWR IMPLEMENTATION SCHEDULE FOR IMPLEMENTATION OF FINAL IN-USE STANDARDS

Model year	Percent
1998	50
1999	100

(6) Diesel vehicles; in-use useful life and testing

(A) In the case of diesel-fueled light-duty trucks up to 6,000 lbs. GVWR and light-duty vehicles, the useful life for purposes of determining in-use compliance with the standards under section 7521(g) of this title for NO_x shall be a period of 10 years or 100,000 miles (or the equivalent), whichever first occurs, in the case of standards applicable for purposes of certification at 100,000 miles, except that testing shall not be done for a period beyond 7 years or 75,000 miles (or the equivalent) whichever first occurs.

(B) In the case of diesel-fueled light-duty trucks of 6,000 lbs. GVWR or more, the useful life for purposes of determining in-use compliance with the standards under section 7521(h) of this title for NO_x shall be a period of 11 years or 120,000 miles (or the equivalent), whichever first occurs, in the case of standards applicable for purposes of certification at 120,000 miles, except that testing shall not be done for a period beyond 7 years or 90,000 miles (or the equivalent) whichever first occurs.

(d) Dealer costs borne by manufacturer

Any cost obligation of any dealer incurred as a result of any requirement imposed by subsection (a), (b), or (c) of this section shall be borne by the manufacturer. The transfer of any such cost obligation from a manufacturer to any dealer through franchise or other agreement is prohibited.

(e) Cost statement

If a manufacturer includes in any advertisement a statement respecting the cost or value of emission control devices or systems, such manufacturer shall set forth in such statement the cost or value attributed to such devices or systems by the Secretary of Labor (through the Bureau of Labor Statistics). The Secretary of Labor, and his representatives, shall have the same access for this purpose to the books, documents, papers, and records of a manufacturer as the Comptroller General has to those of a recipient of assistance for purposes of section 7611 of this title.

(f) Inspection after sale to ultimate purchaser

Any inspection of a motor vehicle or a motor vehicle engine for purposes of subsection (c)(1) of this section, after its sale to the ultimate purchaser, shall be made only if the owner of such vehicle or engine voluntarily permits such inspection to be made, except as may be provided by any State or local inspection program.

(g) Replacement and maintenance costs borne by owner

For the purposes of this section, the owner of any motor vehicle or motor vehicle engine warranted under this section is responsible in the proper maintenance of such vehicle or engine to replace and to maintain, at his expense at any service establishment or facility of his choosing, such items as spark plugs, points, condensers, and any other part, item, or device related to emission control (but not designed for emission control under the terms of the last sentence of subsection (a)(3) of this section)),[3] unless such part, item, or device is covered by any warranty not mandated by this chapter.

(h) Dealer certification

(1) If at any time during the period for which the warranty applies under subsection (b) of this section, a motor vehicle fails to conform to the applicable regulations under section 7521 of this title as determined under subsection (b) of this section such nonconformity shall be remedied by the manufacturer at the cost of the manufacturer pursuant to such warranty as provided in subsection (b)(2) of this section (without regard to subparagraph (C) thereof).

(2) Nothing in section 7543(a) of this title shall be construed to prohibit a State from testing, or requiring testing of, a motor vehicle after the date of sale of such vehicle to the ultimate purchaser (except that no new motor vehicle manufacturer or dealer may be required to conduct testing under this paragraph).

(i) Warranty period

(1) In general

For purposes of subsection (a)(1) of this section and subsection (b) of this section, the warranty period, effective with respect to new light-duty trucks and new light-duty vehicles and engines, manufactured in the model year 1995 and thereafter, shall be the first 2 years or 24,000 miles of use (whichever first occurs), except as provided in paragraph (2). For purposes of subsection (a)(1) of this section and subsection (b) of this section, for other vehicles and engines the warranty period shall be the period established by the Administrator by regulation (promulgated prior to November 15, 1990) for such purposes unless the Administrator subsequently modifies such regulation.

(2) Specified major emission control components

In the case of a specified major emission control component, the warranty period for new light-duty trucks and new light-duty vehicles and engines manufactured in the model year 1995 and thereafter for purposes of subsection (a)(1) of this section and subsection (b) of this section shall be 8 years or 80,000 miles of use (whichever first occurs). As used in this paragraph, the term "specified major emission control component" means only a catalytic converter, an electronic emissions control unit, and an onboard emissions diagnostic device, except that the Administrator may designate any other pollution control device or component as a specified major emission control component if—

(A) the device or component was not in general use on vehicles and engines manufactured prior to the model year 1990; and

(B) the Administrator determines that the retail cost (exclusive of installation costs) of such device or component exceeds $200 (in 1989 dollars), adjusted for inflation or deflation as calculated by the Administrator at the time of such determination.

For purposes of this paragraph, the term "onboard emissions diagnostic device" means any device installed for the purpose of storing or processing emissions related diagnostic information, but not including any parts or other systems which it monitors except specified major emissions control components. Nothing in this chapter shall be construed to provide that any part (other than a part referred to in the preceding sentence) shall be required to be warranted under this chapter for the period of 8 years or 80,000 miles referred to in this paragraph.

(3) Instructions

Subparagraph (A) of subsection (b)(2) of this section shall apply only where the Administrator has made a determination that the instructions concerned conform to the requirements of subsection (c)(3) of this section.

(July 14, 1955, c. 360, Title II, § 207, as added by Pub. L. No. 91–604, § 8(a), 84 Stat. 1696 (Dec. 31, 1970); and amended by Pub. L. No. 95–95, Title II, §§ 205, 208–210, 212, 91 Stat. 754–756, 758 (Aug. 7, 1977); Pub. L. No. 95–190, § 14(a)(70)–(72), 91 Stat. 1403 (Nov. 16, 1977); Pub. L. No. 101–549, Title II, §§ 209, 210, 230(9), 104 Stat. 2484, 2485, 2529 (Nov. 15, 1990); Pub. L. No. 113–109, § 1, 128 Stat. 1170 (June 9, 2014).)

[1] So in original. The word "its" probably should not appear.

[2] So in original. Probably should be "light-duty."

[3] So in original. The second closing parenthesis probably should not appear.

HISTORICAL AND STATUTORY NOTES

Codifications

This section was formerly codified as section 1857f–5a of this title.

Effective and Applicability Provisions

1990 Acts. Amendment by sections 210 and 230(a) of Pub. L. No. 101–549 effective Nov. 15, 1990, except as otherwise provided, see section 711(b) of Pub. L. No. 101–549, set out as a note under section 7401 of this title.

Section 209 of Pub. L. No. 101–549, provided in part that the amendments made by such section [enacting subsec. (i) of this section and amending subsecs. (a) and (b) of this section] shall be effective with respect to new motor vehicles and engines manufactured in the model year 1995 and thereafter.

1977 Acts. Amendment by Pub. L. No. 95–95 effective Aug. 7, 1977, except as otherwise expressly provided, see section 406(d) of Pub. L. No. 95–95, set out as a note under section 7401 of this title.

1970 Acts. Section not applicable to vehicles or engines imported into the United States before the sixtieth day after Dec. 31, 1970, see section 8(b) of Pub. L. No. 91–604, set out as a note under section 7525 of this title.

Savings Provisions

Suits, actions or proceedings commenced under this chapter as in effect prior to Nov. 15, 1990, not to abate by reason of the taking effect of amendments by Pub. L. No. 101–549, except as otherwise provided for, see section 711(a) of Pub. L. No. 101–549, set out as a note under section 7401 of this title.

Prior Provisions

A prior section 207 of Act of July 14, 1955, was renumbered section 208 by Pub. L. No. 91–604 and is set out as section 7542 of this title.

Modification or Rescission of Rules, Regulations, Orders, Determinations, Contracts, Certifications, Authorizations, Delegations, and Other Actions

All rules, regulations, orders, determinations, contracts, certifications, authorizations, delegations, or other actions duly issued, made, or taken by or pursuant to Act of July 14, 1955, the Clean Air Act, as in effect immediately prior to the date of enactment of Pub. L. No. 95–95 [Aug. 7, 1977] to continue in full force and effect until modified or rescinded in accordance with Act of July 14, 1955, as amended by Pub. L. No. 95–95 [this chapter], see section 406(b) of Pub. L. No. 95–95, set out as an Effective Date of 1977 Acts note under section 7401 of this title.

§ 7542. Information collection

[CAA § 208]

(a) Manufacturer's responsibility

Every manufacturer of new motor vehicles or new motor vehicle engines, and every manufacturer of new motor vehicle or engine parts or components, and other persons subject to the requirements of this part or part C of this subchapter, shall establish and maintain records, perform tests where such testing is not otherwise reasonably available under this part and part C of this subchapter (including fees for testing), make reports and provide information the Administrator may reasonably require to determine whether the manufacturer or other person has acted or is acting in compliance with this part and part C of this subchapter and regulations thereunder, or to otherwise carry out the provision of this part and part C of this subchapter, and shall, upon request of an officer or employee duly designated by the Administrator, permit such officer or employee at reasonable times to have access to and copy such records.

(b) Enforcement authority

For the purposes of enforcement of this section, officers or employees duly designated by the Administrator upon presenting appropriate credentials are authorized—

(1) to enter, at reasonable times, any establishment of the manufacturer, or of any person whom the manufacturer engages to perform any activity required by subsection (a) of this section, for the purposes of inspecting or observing any activity conducted pursuant to subsection (a) of this section, and

(2) to inspect records, files, papers, processes, controls, and facilities used in performing any activity required by subsection (a) of this section, by such manufacturer or by any person whom the manufacturer engages to perform any such activity.

(c) Availability to public; trade secrets

Any records, reports, or information obtained under this part or part C of this subchapter shall be available to the public, except that upon a showing satisfactory to the Administrator by any person that records, reports, or information, or a particular portion thereof (other than emission data), to which the Administrator has access under this section, if made public, would divulge methods or processes entitled to protection as trade secrets of that person, the Administrator shall consider the record, report, or information or particular portion thereof confidential in accordance with the purposes of section 1905 of Title 18. Any authorized representative of the Administrator shall be considered an employee of the United States for purposes of section 1905 of Title 18. Nothing in this section shall prohibit the Administrator or authorized representative of the Administrator from disclosing records, reports or information to other officers, employees or authorized representatives of the United States concerned with carrying out this chapter or when relevant in any proceeding under this chapter. Nothing in this section shall authorize the withholding of information by the Administrator or any officer or employee under the Administrator's control from the duly authorized committees of the Congress.

(July 14, 1955, c. 360, Title II, § 208, formerly § 207, as added by Pub. L. No. 89–272, Title I, § 101(8), 79 Stat. 994 (Oct. 20, 1965); and amended by Pub. L. No. 90–148, § 2, 81 Stat. 501 (Nov. 21, 1967); and renumbered and amended by Pub. L. No. 91–604, §§ 8(a), 10(a), 11(a)(2)(A), 15(c)(2), 84 Stat. 1694, 1700, 1705, 1713 (Dec. 31, 1970); and amended by Pub. L. No. 101–549, Title II, § 211, 104 Stat. 2487 (Nov. 15, 1990).)

HISTORICAL AND STATUTORY NOTES

Codifications

This section was formerly codified as section 1857f–6 of this title.

Effective and Applicability Provisions

1990 Acts. Amendment by Pub. L. No. 101–549 effective Nov. 15, 1990, except as otherwise provided, see section 711(b) of Pub. L. No. 101–549, set out as a note under section 7401 of this title.

Savings Provisions

Suits, actions or proceedings commenced under this chapter as in effect prior to Nov. 15, 1990, not to abate by reason of the taking effect of amendments by Pub. L. No. 101–549, except as otherwise provided for, see section 711(a) of Pub. L. No. 101–549, set out as a note under section 7401 of this title.

Prior Provisions

A prior section 208 of Act of July 14, 1955, as added by Pub. L. No. 90–148, § 2, 81 Stat. 501 (Nov. 21, 1967), was renumbered section 209 by Pub. L. No. 91–604, and is set out as section 7543 of this title.

Another prior section 208 of Act of July 14, 1955, forming a part of such Act as originally enacted, was renumbered section 212 by Pub. L. No. 90–148, renumbered section 213 by Pub. L. No. 91–604, renumbered section 214 by Pub. L. No. 93–319, section 10, June 22, 1974, 88 Stat. 261, and renumbered section 216 by Pub. L. No. 95–95, Title II, § 224(d), Aug. 7, 1977, 91 Stat. 767, and is set out as section 7550 of this title.

§ 7543. State standards

[CAA § 209]

(a) Prohibition

No State or any political subdivision thereof shall adopt or attempt to enforce any standard relating to the control of emissions from new motor vehicles or new motor vehicle engines subject to this part. No State shall require certification, inspection, or any other approval relating to the control of emissions from any new motor vehicle or new motor vehicle engine as condition precedent to the initial retail sale, titling (if any), or registration of such motor vehicle, motor vehicle engine, or equipment.

(b) Waiver

(1) The Administrator shall, after notice and opportunity for public hearing, waive application of this section to any State which has adopted standards (other than crankcase emission standards) for the control of emissions from new motor vehicles or new motor vehicle engines prior to March 30, 1966, if the State determines that the State standards will be, in the aggregate, at least as protective of public health and welfare as applicable Federal standards. No such waiver shall be granted if the Administrator finds that—

(A) the determination of the State is arbitrary and capricious,

(B) such State does not need such State standards to meet compelling and extraordinary conditions, or

(C) such State standards and accompanying enforcement procedures are not consistent with section 7521(a) of this title.

(2) If each State standard is at least as stringent as the comparable applicable Federal standard, such State standard shall be deemed to be at least as protective of health and welfare as such Federal standards for purposes of paragraph (1).

(3) In the case of any new motor vehicle or new motor vehicle engine to which State standards apply pursuant to a waiver granted under paragraph (1), compliance with such State standards shall be treated as compliance with applicable Federal standards for purposes of this subchapter.

(c) Certification of vehicle parts or engine parts

Whenever a regulation with respect to any motor vehicle part or motor vehicle engine part is in effect under section 7541(a)(2) of this title, no State or political subdivision thereof shall adopt or attempt to enforce any standard or any requirement of certification, inspection, or approval which relates to motor vehicle emissions and is applicable to the same aspect of such part. The preceding sentence shall not apply in the case of a State with respect to which a waiver is in effect under subsection (b) of this section.

(d) Control, regulation, or restrictions on registered or licensed motor vehicles

Nothing in this part shall preclude or deny to any State or political subdivision thereof the right otherwise to control, regulate, or restrict the use, operation, or movement of registered or licensed motor vehicles.

(e) Nonroad engines or vehicles

(1) Prohibition on certain State standards

No State or any political subdivision thereof shall adopt or attempt to enforce any standard or other requirement relating to the control of emissions from either of the following new nonroad engines or nonroad vehicles subject to regulation under this chapter—

(A) New engines which are used in construction equipment or vehicles or used in farm equipment or vehicles and which are smaller than 175 horsepower.

(B) New locomotives or new engines used in locomotives.

Subsection (b) of this section shall not apply for purposes of this paragraph.

(2) Other nonroad engines or vehicles

(A) In the case of any nonroad vehicles or engines other than those referred to in subparagraph (A) or (B) of paragraph (1), the Administrator shall, after notice and opportunity for public hearing, authorize California to adopt and enforce standards and other requirements relating to the control of emissions from such vehicles or engines if California determines that California standards will be, in the aggregate, at least as protective of public health and welfare as applicable Federal standards. No such authorization shall be granted if the Administrator finds that—

(i) the determination of California is arbitrary and capricious,

(ii) California does not need such California standards to meet compelling and extraordinary conditions, or

(iii) California standards and accompanying enforcement procedures are not consistent with this section.

(B) Any State other than California which has plan provisions approved under part D of subchapter I of this chapter may adopt and enforce, after notice to the Administrator, for any period, standards relating to control of emissions from nonroad vehicles or engines (other than those referred to in subparagraph (A) or (B) of paragraph (1)) and take such other actions as are referred to in subparagraph (A) of this paragraph respecting such vehicles or engines if—

(i) such standards and implementation and enforcement are identical, for the period concerned, to the California standards authorized by the Administrator under subparagraph (A), and

(ii) California and such State adopt such standards at least 2 years before commencement of the period for which the standards take effect.

The Administrator shall issue regulations to implement this subsection.

(July 14, 1955, c. 360, Title II, § 209, formerly § 208, as added by Pub. L. No. 90–148, § 2, 81 Stat. 501 (Nov. 21, 1967); and renumbered and amended by Pub. L. No. 91–604, §§ 8(a), 11(a)(2)(A), 15(c)(2), 84 Stat. 1694, 1705, 1713 (Dec. 31, 1970); and amended by Pub. L. No. 95–95, Title II, §§ 207, 221, 91 Stat. 755, 762 (Aug. 7, 1977); Pub. L. No. 101–549, Title II, § 222(b), 104 Stat. 2502 (Nov. 15, 1990).)

HISTORICAL AND STATUTORY NOTES

Codifications

This section was formerly codified as section 1857f–6a of this title.

Effective and Applicability Provisions

1990 Acts. Amendment by Pub. L. No. 101–549 effective Nov. 15, 1990, except as otherwise provided, see section 711(b) of Pub. L. No. 101–549, set out as a note under section 7401 of this title.

1977 Acts. Amendment by Pub. L. No. 95–95 effective Aug. 7, 1977, except as otherwise expressly provided, see section 406(d) of Pub. L. No. 95–95, set out as a note under section 7401 of this title.

Savings Provisions

Suits, actions or proceedings commenced under this chapter as in effect prior to Nov. 15, 1990, not to abate by reason of the taking effect of amendments by Pub. L. No. 101–549, except as otherwise provided for, see section 711(a) of Pub. L. No. 101–549, set out as a note under section 7401 of this title.

Prior Provisions

A prior section 209 of Act of July 14, 1955, as added by Pub. L. No. 90–148, § 2, 81 Stat. 502 (Nov. 21, 1967), was renumbered section 210 by Pub. L. No. 91–604 and is codified as section 7544 of this title.

Another prior section 209 of Act of July 14, 1955, c. 360, Title II, as added by Pub. L. No. 89–272, Title I, § 101(8), 79 Stat. 995 (Oct. 20, 1965), relating to appropriations for the fiscal years ending June 30, 1966, 1967, 1968, and 1969, was codified as prior section 1857f–8 of this title and was repealed by Pub. L. No. 89–675, § 2(b), 80 Stat. 954 (Oct. 15, 1966).

Modification or Rescission of Rules, Regulations, Orders, Determinations, Contracts, Certifications, Authorizations, Delegations, and Other Actions

All rules, regulations, orders, determinations, contracts, certifications, authorizations, delegations, or other actions duly issued, made, or taken by or pursuant to Act of July 14, 1955, the Clean Air Act, as in effect immediately prior to the date of enactment of Pub. L. No. 95–95 [Aug. 7, 1977] to continue in full force and effect until modified or rescinded in accordance with Act of July 14, 1955, as amended by Pub. L. No. 95–95 [this chapter], see section 406(b) of Pub. L. No. 95–95, set out as an Effective Date of 1977 Acts note under section 7401 of this title.

§ 7544. State grants

[CAA § 210]

The Administrator is authorized to make grants to appropriate State agencies in an amount up to two-thirds of the cost of developing and maintaining effective vehicle emission devices and systems inspection and emission testing and control programs, except that—

(1) no such grant shall be made for any part of any State vehicle inspection program which does not directly relate to the cost of the air pollution control aspects of such a program;

(2) no such grant shall be made unless the Secretary of Transportation has certified to the Administrator that such program is consistent with any highway safety program developed pursuant to section 402 of Title 23; and

(3) no such grant shall be made unless the program includes provisions designed to insure that emission control devices and systems on vehicles in actual use have not been discontinued or rendered inoperative.

Grants may be made under this section by way of reimbursement in any case in which amounts have been expended by the State before the date on which any such grant was made.

(July 14, 1955, c. 360, Title II, § 210, formerly § 209, as added by Pub. L. No. 90–148, § 2, 81 Stat. 502 (Nov. 21, 1967); and renumbered and amended by Pub. L. No. 91–604, §§ 8(a), 10(b), 84 Stat. 1694, 1700 (Dec. 31, 1970); and amended by Pub. L. No. 95–95, Title II, § 204, 91 Stat. 754 (Aug. 7, 1977).)

HISTORICAL AND STATUTORY NOTES

Codifications

This section was formerly codified as section 1857f–6b of this title.

Effective and Applicability Provisions

1977 Acts. Amendment by Pub. L. No. 95–95 effective Aug. 7, 1977, except as otherwise expressly provided, see section 406(d) of Pub. L. No. 95–95, set out as a note under section 7401 of this title.

Prior Provisions

A prior section 210 of Act of July 14, 1955, was renumbered section 211 by Pub. L. No. 91–604 and is set out as section 7545 of this title.

§ 7545. Regulation of fuels

[CAA § 211]

(a) Authority of Administrator to regulate

The Administrator may by regulation designate any fuel or fuel additive (including any fuel or fuel additive used exclusively in nonroad engines or nonroad vehicles) and, after such date or dates as may be prescribed by him, no manufacturer or processor of any such fuel or additive may sell, offer for sale, or introduce into commerce such fuel or additive unless the Administrator has registered such fuel or additive in accordance with subsection (b) of this section.

(b) Registration requirement

(1) For the purpose of registration of fuels and fuel additives, the Administrator shall require—

(A) the manufacturer of any fuel to notify him as to the commercial identifying name and manufacturer of any additive contained in such fuel; the range of concentration of any additive in the fuel; and the purpose-in-use of any such additive; and

(B) the manufacturer of any additive to notify him as to the chemical composition of such additive.

(2) For the purpose of registration of fuels and fuel additives, the Administrator shall, on a regular basis, require the manufacturer of any fuel or fuel additive—

(A) to conduct tests to determine potential public health and environmental effects of the fuel or additive (including carcinogenic, teratogenic, or mutagenic effects); and

(B) to furnish the description of any analytical technique that can be used to detect and measure any additive in such fuel, the recommended range of concentration of such additive, and the recommended purpose-in-use of such additive, and such other information as is reasonable and necessary to determine the emissions resulting from the use of the fuel or additive contained in such fuel, the effect of such fuel or additive on the emission control performance of any vehicle, vehicle engine, nonroad engine or nonroad vehicle, or the extent to which such emissions affect the public health or welfare.

Tests under subparagraph (A) shall be conducted in conformity with test procedures and protocols established by the Administrator. The result of such tests shall not be considered confidential.

(3) Upon compliance with the provision of this subsection, including assurances that the Administrator will receive changes in the information required, the Administrator shall register such fuel or fuel additive.

(4) Study on certain fuel additives and blendstocks

(A) In general

Not later than 2 years after August 8, 2005, the Administrator shall—

(i) conduct a study on the effects on public health (including the effects on children, pregnant women, minority or low-income communities, and other sensitive populations), air quality, and water resources of increased use of, and the feasibility of using as substitutes for methyl tertiary butyl ether in gasoline—

(I) ethyl tertiary butyl ether;

(II) tertiary amyl methyl ether;

(III) di-isopropyl ether;

(IV) tertiary butyl alcohol;

(V) other ethers and heavy alcohols, as determined by then[1] Administrator;

(VI) ethanol;

(VII) iso-octane; and

(VIII) alkylates; and

(ii) conduct a study on the effects on public health (including the effects on children, pregnant women, minority or low-income communities, and other sensitive populations), air quality, and water resources of the adjustment for ethanol-blended reformulated gasoline to the volatile organic compounds performance requirements that are applicable under paragraphs (1) and (3) of subsection (k) of this section; and

(iii) submit to the Committee on Environment and Public Works of the Senate and the Committee on Energy and Commerce of the House of Representatives a report describing the results of the studies under clauses (i) and (ii).

(B) Contracts for study

In carrying out this paragraph, the Administrator may enter into one or more contracts with nongovernmental entities such as—

(i) the national energy laboratories; and

(ii) institutions of higher education (as defined in section 1001 of Title 20).

(c) Offending fuels and fuel additives; control; prohibition

(1) The Administrator may, from time to time on the basis of information obtained under subsection (b) of this section or other information available to him, by regulation, control or prohibit the manufacture, introduction into commerce, offering for sale, or sale of any fuel or fuel additive for use in a motor vehicle, motor vehicle engine, or nonroad engine or nonroad vehicle if, in the judgment of the Administrator, any fuel or fuel additive or any emission product of such fuel or fuel additive causes, or contributes, to air pollution or water pollution (including any degradation in the quality of groundwater) that may reasonably be anticipated to endanger the public health or welfare, or (B)[2] if emission products of such fuel or fuel additive will impair to a significant degree the performance of any emission control device or system which is in general use, or which the Administrator finds has been developed to a point where in a reasonable time it would be in general use were such regulation to be promulgated.

(2) (A) No fuel, class of fuels, or fuel additive may be controlled or prohibited by the Administrator pursuant to clause (A) of paragraph (1)[3] except after consideration of all relevant medical and scientific evidence available to him, including consideration of other technologically or economically feasible means of achieving emission standards under section 7521 of this title.

(B) No fuel or fuel additive may be controlled or prohibited by the Administrator pursuant to clause (B) of paragraph (1) except after consideration of available scientific and economic data, including a cost benefit analysis comparing emission control devices or systems which are or will be in general use and require the proposed control or prohibition with emission control devices or systems which are or will be in general use and do not require the proposed control or prohibition. On request of a manufacturer of motor vehicles, motor vehicle engines, fuels, or fuel additives submitted within 10 days of notice of proposed rulemaking, the Administrator shall hold a public hearing and publish findings with respect to any matter he is required to consider under this subparagraph. Such findings shall be published at the time of promulgation of final regulations.

(C) No fuel or fuel additive may be prohibited by the Administrator under paragraph (1) unless he finds, and publishes such finding, that in his judgment such prohibition will not cause the use of any other fuel or fuel additive which will produce emissions which will endanger the public health or welfare to the same or greater degree than the use of the fuel or fuel additive proposed to be prohibited.

(3) **(A)** For the purpose of obtaining evidence and data to carry out paragraph (2), the Administrator may require the manufacturer of any motor vehicle or motor vehicle engine to furnish any information which has been developed concerning the emissions from motor vehicles resulting from the use of any fuel or fuel additive, or the effect of such use on the performance of any emission control device or system.

(B) In obtaining information under subparagraph (A), section 7607(a) of this title (relating to subpenas) shall be applicable.

(4) **(A)** Except as otherwise provided in subparagraph (B) or (C), no State (or political subdivision thereof) may prescribe or attempt to enforce, for purposes of motor vehicle emission control, any control or prohibition respecting any characteristic or component of a fuel or fuel additive in a motor vehicle or motor vehicle engine—

(i) if the Administrator has found that no control or prohibition of the characteristic or component of a fuel or fuel additive under paragraph (1) is necessary and has published his finding in the Federal Register, or

(ii) if the Administrator has prescribed under paragraph (1) a control or prohibition applicable to such characteristic or component of a fuel or fuel additive, unless State prohibition or control is identical to the prohibition or control prescribed by the Administrator.

(B) Any State for which application of section 7543(a) of this title has at any time been waived under section 7543(b) of this title may at any time prescribe and enforce, for the purpose of motor vehicle emission control, a control or prohibition respecting any fuel or fuel additive.

(C) **(i)** A State may prescribe and enforce, for purposes of motor vehicle emission control, a control or prohibition respecting the use of a fuel or fuel additive in a motor vehicle or motor vehicle engine if an applicable implementation plan for such State under section 7410 of this title so provides. The Administrator may approve such provision in an implementation plan, or promulgate an implementation plan containing such a provision, only if he finds that the State control or prohibition is necessary to achieve the national primary or secondary ambient air quality standard which the plan implements. The Administrator may find that a State control or prohibition is necessary to achieve that standard if no other measures that would bring about timely attainment exist, or if other measures exist and are technically possible to implement, but are unreasonable or impracticable. The Administrator may make a finding of necessity under this subparagraph even if the plan for the area does not contain an approved demonstration of timely attainment.

(ii) The Administrator may temporarily waive a control or prohibition respecting the use of a fuel or fuel additive required or regulated by the Administrator pursuant to subsection (c), (h), (i), (k), or (m) of this section or prescribed in an applicable implementation plan under section 7410 of this title approved by the Administrator under clause (i) of this subparagraph if, after consultation with, and concurrence by, the Secretary of Energy, the Administrator determines that—

(I) extreme and unusual fuel or fuel additive supply circumstances exist in a State or region of the Nation which prevent the distribution of an adequate supply of the fuel or fuel additive to consumers;

(II) such extreme and unusual fuel and fuel additive supply circumstances are the result of a natural disaster, an Act of God, a pipeline or refinery equipment failure, or another event that could not reasonably have been foreseen or prevented and not the lack of prudent planning on the part of the suppliers of the fuel or fuel additive to such State or region; and

(III) it is in the public interest to grant the waiver (for example, when a waiver is necessary to meet projected temporary shortfalls in the supply of the fuel or fuel additive in a State or region of the Nation which cannot otherwise be compensated for).

(iii) If the Administrator makes the determinations required under clause (ii), such a temporary extreme and unusual fuel and fuel additive supply circumstances waiver shall be permitted only if—

(I) the waiver applies to the smallest geographic area necessary to address the extreme and unusual fuel and fuel additive supply circumstances;

(II) the waiver is effective for a period of 20 calendar days or, if the Administrator determines that a shorter waiver period is adequate, for the shortest practicable time period necessary to permit the correction of the extreme and unusual fuel and fuel additive supply circumstances and to mitigate impact on air quality;

(III) the waiver permits a transitional period, the exact duration of which shall be determined by the Administrator (but which shall be for the shortest practicable period), after the termination of the temporary waiver to permit wholesalers and retailers to blend down their wholesale and retail inventory;

(IV) the waiver applies to all persons in the motor fuel distribution system; and

(V) the Administrator has given public notice to all parties in the motor fuel distribution system, and local and State regulators, in the State or region to be covered by the waiver.

The term "motor fuel distribution system" as used in this clause shall be defined by the Administrator through rulemaking.

(iv) Within 180 days of August 8, 2005, the Administrator shall promulgate regulations to implement clauses (ii) and (iii).

(v)[4] Nothing in this subparagraph shall—

(I) limit or otherwise affect the application of any other waiver authority of the Administrator pursuant to this section or pursuant to a regulation promulgated pursuant to this section; and

(II) subject any State or person to an enforcement action, penalties, or liability solely arising from actions taken pursuant to the issuance of a waiver under this subparagraph.

(v)[4] **(I)** The Administrator shall have no authority, when considering a State implementation plan or a State implementation plan revision, to approve under this paragraph any fuel included in such plan or revision if the effect of such approval increases the total number of fuels approved under this paragraph as of September 1, 2004, in all State implementation plans.

(II) The Administrator, in consultation with the Secretary of Energy, shall determine the total number of fuels approved under this paragraph as of September 1, 2004, in all State implementation plans and shall publish a list of such fuels, including the States and Petroleum Administration for Defense District in which they are used, in the Federal Register for public review and comment no later than 90 days after August 8, 2005.

(III) The Administrator shall remove a fuel from the list published under subclause (II) if a fuel ceases to be included in a State implementation plan or if a fuel in a State implementation plan is identical to a Federal fuel formulation implemented by the Administrator, but the Administrator shall not reduce the total number of fuels authorized under the list published under subclause (II).

(IV) Subclause (I) shall not limit the Administrator's authority to approve a control or prohibition respecting any new fuel under this paragraph in a State implementation plan or revision to a State implementation plan if such new fuel—

(aa) completely replaces a fuel on the list published under subclause (II); or

(bb) does not increase the total number of fuels on the list published under subclause (II) as of September 1, 2004.

In the event that the total number of fuels on the list published under subclause (II) at the time of the Administrator's consideration of a control or prohibition respecting a new fuel is lower than the total number of fuels on such list as of September 1, 2004, the Administrator may approve a control or prohibition respecting a new fuel under this subclause if the Administrator, after consultation with the Secretary of Energy, publishes in the Federal Register after notice and comment a finding that, in the Administrator's judgment, such control or prohibition respecting a new fuel will not cause fuel supply or distribution interruptions or have a significant adverse impact on fuel producibility in the affected area or contiguous areas.

(V) The Administrator shall have no authority under this paragraph, when considering any particular State's implementation plan or a revision to that State's implementation plan, to approve any fuel unless that fuel was, as of the date of such consideration, approved in at least one State implementation plan in the applicable Petroleum Administration for Defense District. However, the Administrator may approve as part of a State implementation plan or State implementation plan revision a fuel with a summertime Reid Vapor Pressure of 7.0 psi. In no event shall such approval by the Administrator cause an increase in the total number of fuels on the list published under subclause (II).

(VI) Nothing in this clause shall be construed to have any effect regarding any available authority of States to require the use of any fuel additive registered in accordance with subsection (b) of this section, including any fuel additive registered in accordance with subsection (b) of this section after August 8, 2005.

(d) Penalties and injunctions

(1) Civil penalties

Any person who violates subsection (a), (f), (g), (k), (*l*), (m), (n), or (*o*) of this section or the regulations prescribed under subsection (c), (h), (i), (k), (*l*), (m), (n), or (*o*) of this section or who fails to furnish any information or conduct any tests required by the Administrator under subsection (b) of this section shall be liable to the United States for a civil penalty of not more than the sum of $25,000 for every day of such violation and the amount of economic benefit or savings resulting from the violation. Any violation with respect to a regulation prescribed under subsection (c), (k), (*l*), (m), or (*o*) of this section which establishes a regulatory standard based upon a multiday averaging period shall constitute a separate day of violation for each and every day in the averaging period. Civil penalties shall be assessed in accordance with subsections (b) and (c) of section 7524 of this title.

(2) Injunctive authority

The district courts of the United States shall have jurisdiction to restrain violations of subsections (a), (f), (g), (k), (*l*), (m), (n), and (*o*) of this section and of the regulations prescribed under subsections (c), (h), (i), (k), (*l*), (m), (n), and (*o*) of this section, to award other appropriate relief, and to compel the furnishing of information and the conduct of tests required by the Administrator under subsection (b) of this section. Actions to restrain such violations and compel such actions shall be brought by and in the name of the United States. In any such action, subpoenas for witnesses who are required to attend a district court in any district may run into any other district.

(e) Testing of fuels and fuel additives

(1) Not later than one year after August 7, 1977, and after notice and opportunity for a public hearing, the Administrator shall promulgate regulations which implement the authority under subsection (b)(2)(A) and (B) of this section with respect to each fuel or fuel additive which is registered on the date of promulgation of such regulations and with respect to each fuel or fuel additive for which an application for registration is filed thereafter.

(2) Regulations under subsection (b) of this section to carry out this subsection shall require that the requisite information be provided to the Administrator by each such manufacturer—

(A) prior to registration, in the case of any fuel or fuel additive which is not registered on the date of promulgation of such regulations; or

(B) not later than three years after the date of promulgation of such regulations, in the case of any fuel or fuel additive which is registered on such date.

(3) In promulgating such regulations, the Administrator may—

(A) exempt any small business (as defined in such regulations) from or defer or modify the requirements of, such regulations with respect to any such small business;

(B) provide for cost-sharing with respect to the testing of any fuel or fuel additive which is manufactured or processed by two or more persons or otherwise provide for shared responsibility to meet the requirements of this section without duplication; or

(C) exempt any person from such regulations with respect to a particular fuel or fuel additive upon a finding that any additional testing of such fuel or fuel additive would be duplicative of adequate existing testing.

(f) New fuels and fuel additives

(1) (A) Effective upon March 31, 1977, it shall be unlawful for any manufacturer of any fuel or fuel additive to first introduce into commerce, or to increase the concentration in use of, any fuel or fuel additive for general use in light duty motor vehicles manufactured after model year 1974 which is not substantially similar to any fuel or fuel additive utilized in the certification of any model year 1975, or subsequent model year, vehicle or engine under section 7525 of this title.

(B) Effective upon November 15, 1990, it shall be unlawful for any manufacturer of any fuel or fuel additive to first introduce into commerce, or to increase the concentration in use of, any fuel or fuel additive for use by any person in motor vehicles manufactured after model year 1974 which is not substantially similar to any fuel or fuel additive utilized in the certification of any model year 1975, or subsequent model year, vehicle or engine under section 7525 of this title.

(2) Effective November 30, 1977, it shall be unlawful for any manufacturer of any fuel to introduce into commerce any gasoline which contains a concentration of manganese in excess of .0625 grams per gallon of fuel, except as otherwise provided pursuant to a waiver under paragraph (4).

(3) Any manufacturer of any fuel or fuel additive which prior to March 31, 1977, and after January 1, 1974, first introduced into commerce or increased the concentration in use of a fuel or fuel additive that would otherwise have been prohibited under paragraph (1)(A) if introduced on or after March 31, 1977 shall, not later than September 15, 1978, cease to distribute such fuel or fuel additive in commerce. During the period beginning 180 days after August 7, 1977, and before September 15, 1978, the Administrator shall prohibit, or restrict the concentration of any fuel additive which he determines will cause or contribute to the failure of an emission control device or system (over the useful life of any vehicle in which such device or system is used) to achieve compliance by the vehicle with the emission standards with respect to which it has been certified under section 7525 of this title.

(4) The Administrator, upon application of any manufacturer of any fuel or fuel additive, may waive the prohibitions established under paragraph (1) or (3) of this subsection or the limitation specified in paragraph (2) of this subsection, if he determines that the applicant has established that such fuel or fuel additive or a specified concentration thereof, and the emission products of such fuel or fuel additive or specified concentration thereof, will not cause or contribute to a failure of any emission control device or system (over the useful life of the motor vehicle, motor vehicle engine, nonroad engine or nonroad vehicle in which such device or system is used) to achieve compliance by the vehicle or engine with the emission standards with respect to which it has been certified pursuant to sections 7525 and 7547(a) of this title. The Administrator shall take final action to grant or deny an application submitted under this paragraph, after public notice and comment, within 270 days of the receipt of such an application.

(5) No action of the Administrator under this section may be stayed by any court pending judicial review of such action.

(g) Misfueling

(1) No person shall introduce, or cause or allow the introduction of, leaded gasoline into any motor vehicle which is labeled "unleaded gasoline only," which is equipped with a gasoline tank filler inlet designed for the introduction of unleaded gasoline, which is a 1990 or later model year motor vehicle, or which such person knows or should know is a vehicle designed solely for the use of unleaded gasoline.

(2) Beginning October 1, 1993, no person shall introduce or cause or allow the introduction into any motor vehicle of diesel fuel which such person knows or should know contains a concentration of sulfur in excess of 0.05 percent (by weight) or which fails to meet a cetane index minimum of 40 or such equivalent alternative aromatic level as prescribed by the Administrator under subsection (i)(2) of this section.

(h) Reid Vapor Pressure requirements

(1) Prohibition

Not later than 6 months after November 15, 1990, the Administrator shall promulgate regulations making it unlawful for any person during the high ozone season (as defined by the Administrator) to sell, offer for sale, dispense, supply, offer for supply, transport, or introduce into commerce gasoline with a Reid Vapor Pressure in excess of 9.0 pounds per square inch (psi). Such regulations shall also establish more stringent Reid Vapor Pressure standards in a nonattainment area as the Administrator finds necessary to generally achieve comparable evaporative emissions (on a per-vehicle basis) in nonattainment areas, taking into consideration the enforceability of such standards, the need of an area for emission control, and economic factors.

(2) Attainment areas

The regulations under this subsection shall not make it unlawful for any person to sell, offer for supply, transport, or introduce into commerce gasoline with a Reid Vapor Pressure of 9.0 pounds per square inch (psi) or lower in any area designated under section 7407 of this title as an attainment area. Notwithstanding the preceding sentence, the Administrator may impose a Reid vapor pressure requirement lower than 9.0 pounds per square inch (psi) in any area, formerly an ozone nonattainment area, which has been redesignated as an attainment area.

(3) Effective date; enforcement

The regulations under this subsection shall provide that the requirements of this subsection shall take effect not later than the high ozone season for 1992, and shall include such provisions as the Administrator determines are necessary to implement and enforce the requirements of this subsection.

(4) Ethanol waiver

For fuel blends containing gasoline and 10 percent denatured anhydrous ethanol, the Reid vapor pressure limitation under this subsection shall be one pound per square inch (psi) greater than the applicable Reid vapor pressure limitations established under paragraph (1); Provided, however, That a distributor, blender, marketer, reseller, carrier, retailer, or wholesale purchaser-consumer shall be deemed to be in full compliance with the provisions of this subsection and the regulations promulgated thereunder if it can demonstrate (by showing receipt of a certification or other evidence acceptable to the Administrator) that—

(A) the gasoline portion of the blend complies with the Reid vapor pressure limitations promulgated pursuant to this subsection;

(B) the ethanol portion of the blend does not exceed its waiver condition under subsection (f)(4) of this section; and

(C) no additional alcohol or other additive has been added to increase the Reid Vapor Pressure of the ethanol portion of the blend.

(5) Exclusion from ethanol waiver

(A) Promulgation of regulations

Upon notification, accompanied by supporting documentation, from the Governor of a State that the Reid vapor pressure limitation established by paragraph (4) will increase emissions that contribute to air pollution in any area in the State, the Administrator shall, by regulation, apply, in lieu of the Reid vapor pressure limitation established by paragraph (4), the Reid vapor pressure limitation established by paragraph (1) to all fuel blends containing gasoline and 10 percent denatured anhydrous ethanol that are sold, offered for sale, dispensed, supplied, offered for supply, transported, or introduced into commerce in the area during the high ozone season.

(B) Deadline for promulgation

The Administrator shall promulgate regulations under subparagraph (A) not later than 90 days after the date of receipt of a notification from a Governor under that subparagraph.

(C) Effective date

(i) In general

With respect to an area in a State for which the Governor submits a notification under subparagraph (A), the regulations under that subparagraph shall take effect on the later of—

(I) the first day of the first high ozone season for the area that begins after the date of receipt of the notification; or

(II) 1 year after the date of receipt of the notification.

(ii) Extension of effective date based on determination of insufficient supply

(I) In general

If, after receipt of a notification with respect to an area from a Governor of a State under subparagraph (A), the Administrator determines, on the Administrator's own motion or on petition of any person and after consultation with the Secretary of Energy, that the promulgation of regulations described in subparagraph (A) would result in an insufficient supply of gasoline in the State, the Administrator, by regulation—

(aa) shall extend the effective date of the regulations under clause (i) with respect to the area for not more than 1 year; and

(bb) may renew the extension under item (aa) for two additional periods, each of which shall not exceed 1 year.

(II) Deadline for action on petitions

The Administrator shall act on any petition submitted under subclause (I) not later than 180 days after the date of receipt of the petition.

(6) Areas covered

The provisions of this subsection shall apply only to the 48 contiguous States and the District of Columbia.

(i) Sulfur content requirements for diesel fuel

(1) Effective October 1, 1993, no person shall manufacture, sell, supply, offer for sale or supply, dispense, transport, or introduce into commerce motor vehicle diesel fuel which contains a concentration of sulfur in excess of 0.05 percent (by weight) or which fails to meet a cetane index minimum of 40.

(2) Not later than 12 months after November 15, 1990, the Administrator shall promulgate regulations to implement and enforce the requirements of paragraph (1). The Administrator may require manufacturers and importers of diesel fuel not intended for use in motor vehicles to dye such fuel in a particular manner in order to segregate it from motor vehicle diesel fuel. The Administrator may establish an equivalent alternative aromatic level to the cetane index specification in paragraph (1).

(3) The sulfur content of fuel required to be used in the certification of 1991 through 1993 model year heavy-duty diesel vehicles and engines shall be 0.10 percent (by weight). The sulfur content and cetane index minimum of fuel required to be used in the certification of 1994 and later model year heavy-duty diesel vehicles and engines shall comply with the regulations promulgated under paragraph (2).

(4) The States of Alaska and Hawaii may be exempted from the requirements of this subsection in the same manner as provided in section 7625[5] of this title. The Administrator shall take final action on any petition filed under section 7625[5] of this title or this paragraph for an exemption from the requirements of this subsection, within 12 months from the date of the petition.

(j) Lead substitute gasoline additives

(1) After November 15, 1990, any person proposing to register any gasoline additive under subsection (a) of this section or to use any previously registered additive as a lead substitute may also elect to register the additive as a lead substitute gasoline additive for reducing valve seat wear by providing the Administrator with such relevant information regarding product identity and composition as the Administrator deems necessary for carrying out the responsibilities of paragraph (2) of this subsection (in addition to other information which may be required under subsection (b) of this section).

(2) In addition to the other testing which may be required under subsection (b) of this section, in the case of the lead substitute gasoline additives referred to in paragraph (1), the Administrator shall develop and publish a test procedure to determine the additives' effectiveness in reducing valve seat wear and the additives' tendencies to produce engine deposits and other adverse side effects. The test procedures shall be developed in cooperation with the Secretary of Agriculture and with the input of additive manufacturers, engine and engine components manufacturers, and other interested persons. The Administrator shall enter into arrangements with an independent laboratory to conduct tests of each additive using the test procedures developed and published pursuant to this paragraph. The Administrator shall publish the results of the tests by company and additive name in the Federal Register along with, for comparison purposes, the results of applying the same test procedures to gasoline containing 0.1 gram of lead per gallon in lieu of the lead substitute gasoline additive. The Administrator shall not rank or otherwise rate the lead substitute additives. Test procedures shall be established within 1 year after November 15, 1990. Additives shall be tested within 18 months of November 15, 1990, or 6 months after the lead substitute additives are identified to the Administrator, whichever is later.

(3) The Administrator may impose a user fee to recover the costs of testing of any fuel additive referred to in this subsection. The fee shall be paid by the person proposing to register the fuel additive concerned. Such fee shall not exceed $20,000 for a single fuel additive.

(4) There are authorized to be appropriated to the Administrator not more than $1,000,000 for the second full fiscal year after November 15, 1990, to establish test procedures and conduct engine tests as provided in this subsection. Not more than $500,000 per year is authorized to be appropriated for each of the 5 subsequent fiscal years.

(5) Any fees collected under this subsection shall be deposited in a special fund in the United States Treasury for licensing and other services which thereafter shall be available for appropriation, to remain available until expended, to carry out the Agency's activities for which the fees were collected.

(k) Reformulated gasoline for conventional vehicles

(1) EPA regulations

(A) In general

Not later than November 15, 1991, the Administrator shall promulgate regulations under this section establishing requirements for reformulated gasoline to be used in gasoline-fueled vehicles in specified nonattainment areas. Such regulations shall require the greatest reduction in emissions of ozone forming volatile organic compounds (during the high ozone season) and emissions of toxic air pollutants (during the entire year) achievable through the reformulation of conventional gasoline, taking into consideration the cost of achieving such emission reductions, any nonair-quality and other air-quality related health and environmental impacts and energy requirements.

(B) Maintenance of toxic air pollutant emissions reductions from reformulated gasoline

(i) Definition of PADD

In this subparagraph the term "PADD" means a Petroleum Administration for Defense District.

(ii) Regulations concerning emissions of toxic air pollutants

Not later than 270 days after August 8, 2005, the Administrator shall establish by regulation, for each refinery or importer (other than a refiner or importer in a State that has received a waiver under section 7543(b) of this title with respect to gasoline produced for use in that State), standards for toxic air pollutants from use of the reformulated gasoline produced or distributed by the refiner or importer that maintain the reduction of the average annual aggregate emissions of toxic air pollutants for reformulated gasoline produced or distributed by the refiner or importer during calendar years 2001 and 2002 (as determined on the basis of data collected by the Administrator with respect to the refiner or importer).

(iii) Standards applicable to specific refineries or importers

(I) Applicability of standards

For any calendar year, the standards applicable to a refiner or importer under clause (ii) shall apply to the quantity of gasoline produced or distributed by the refiner or importer in the calendar year only to the extent that the quantity is less than or equal to the average annual quantity of reformulated gasoline produced or distributed by the refiner or importer during calendar years 2001 and 2002.

(II) Applicability of other standards

For any calendar year, the quantity of gasoline produced or distributed by a refiner or importer that is in excess of the quantity subject to subclause (I) shall be subject to standards for emissions of toxic air pollutants promulgated under subparagraph (A) and paragraph (3)(B).

(iv) Credit program

The Administrator shall provide for the granting and use of credits for emissions of toxic air pollutants in the same manner as provided in paragraph (7).

(v) Regional protection of toxics reduction baselines

(I) In general

Not later than 60 days after August 8, 2005, and not later than April 1 of each calendar year that begins after August 8, 2005, the Administrator shall publish in the Federal Register a report that specifies, with respect to the previous calendar year—

(aa) the quantity of reformulated gasoline produced that is in excess of the average annual quantity of reformulated gasoline produced in 2001 and 2002; and

(bb) the reduction of the average annual aggregate emissions of toxic air pollutants in each PADD, based on retail survey data or data from other appropriate sources.

(II) Effect of failure to maintain aggregate toxics reductions

If, in any calendar year, the reduction of the average annual aggregate emissions of toxic air pollutants in a PADD fails to meet or exceed the reduction of the average annual aggregate emissions of toxic air pollutants in the PADD in calendar years 2001 and 2002, the Administrator, not later than 90 days after the date of publication of the report for the calendar year under subclause (I), shall—

(aa) identify, to the maximum extent practicable, the reasons for the failure, including the sources, volumes, and characteristics of reformulated gasoline that contributed to the failure; and

(bb) promulgate revisions to the regulations promulgated under clause (ii), to take effect not earlier than 180 days but not later than 270 days after the date of promulgation, to provide that, notwithstanding clause (iii)(II), all reformulated gasoline produced or distributed at each refiner or importer shall meet the standards applicable under clause (iii)(I) beginning not later than April 1 of the calendar year following publication of the report under subclause (I) and in each calendar year thereafter.

(vi) Not later than July 1, 2007, the Administrator shall promulgate final regulations to control hazardous air pollutants from motor vehicles and motor vehicle fuels, as provided for in section 80.1045 of title 40, Code of Federal Regulations (as in effect on August 8, 2005), and as authorized under section 7521(1) of this title. If the Administrator promulgates by such date, final regulations to control hazardous air pollutants from motor vehicles and motor vehicle fuels that achieve and maintain greater overall reductions in emissions of air toxics from reformulated gasoline than the reductions that would be achieved under subsection (k)(1)(B) of this section as amended by this clause, then subsections (k)(1)(B)(i) through (k)(1)(B)(v) of this section shall be null and void and regulations promulgated thereunder shall be rescinded and have no further effect.

(2) General requirements

The regulations referred to in paragraph (1) shall require that reformulated gasoline comply with paragraph (3) and with each of the following requirements (subject to paragraph (7)):

(A) NO_x emissions

The emissions of oxides of nitrogen (NO_x) from baseline vehicles when using the reformulated gasoline shall be no greater than the level of such emissions from such vehicles when using baseline gasoline. If the Administrator determines that compliance with the limitation on emissions of oxides of nitrogen under the preceding sentence is technically infeasible, considering the other requirements applicable under this subsection to such gasoline, the Administrator may, as appropriate to ensure compliance with this subparagraph, adjust (or waive entirely), any other requirements of this paragraph or any requirements applicable under paragraph (3)(A).

(B) Benzene content

The benzene content of the gasoline shall not exceed 1.0 percent by volume.

(C) Heavy metals

The gasoline shall have no heavy metals, including lead or manganese. The Administrator may waive the prohibition contained in this subparagraph for a heavy metal (other than lead) if the Administrator determines that addition of the heavy metal to the gasoline will not increase, on an aggregate mass or cancer-risk basis, toxic air pollutant emissions from motor vehicles.

(3) More stringent of formula or performance standards

The regulations referred to in paragraph (1) shall require compliance with the more stringent of either the requirements set forth in subparagraph (A) or the requirements of subparagraph (B) of this paragraph. For purposes of determining the more stringent provision, clause (i) and clause (ii) of subparagraph (B) shall be considered independently.

(A) Formula

(i) Benzene

The benzene content of the reformulated gasoline shall not exceed 1.0 percent by volume.

(ii) Aromatics

The aromatic hydrocarbon content of the reformulated gasoline shall not exceed 25 percent by volume.

(iii) Lead

The reformulated gasoline shall have no lead content.

(iv) Detergents

The reformulated gasoline shall contain additives to prevent the accumulation of deposits in engines or vehicle fuel supply systems.

(B) Performance standard

(i) VOC emissions

During the high ozone season (as defined by the Administrator), the aggregate emissions of ozone forming volatile organic compounds from baseline vehicles when using the reformulated gasoline shall be 15 percent below the aggregate emissions of ozone forming volatile organic compounds from such vehicles when using baseline gasoline. Effective in calendar year 2000 and thereafter, 25 percent shall be substituted for 15 percent in applying this clause, except that the Administrator may adjust such 25 percent requirement to provide for a lesser or greater reduction based on technological feasibility, considering the cost of achieving such reductions in VOC emissions. No such adjustment shall provide for less than a 20 percent reduction below the aggregate emissions of such air pollutants from such vehicles when using baseline gasoline. The reductions required under this clause shall be on a mass basis.

(ii) Toxics

During the entire year, the aggregate emissions of toxic air pollutants from baseline vehicles when using the reformulated gasoline shall be 15 percent below the aggregate emissions of toxic air pollutants from such vehicles when using baseline gasoline. Effective in calendar year 2000 and thereafter, 25 percent shall be substituted for 15 percent in applying this clause, except that the Administrator may adjust such 25 percent requirement to provide for a lesser or greater reduction based on technological feasibility, considering the cost of achieving such reductions in toxic air pollutants. No such adjustment shall provide for less than a 20 percent reduction below the aggregate emissions of such air pollutants from such vehicles when using baseline gasoline. The reductions required under this clause shall be on a mass basis.

Any reduction greater than a specific percentage reduction required under this subparagraph shall be treated as satisfying such percentage reduction requirement.

(4) Certification procedures

(A) Regulations

The regulations under this subsection shall include procedures under which the Administrator shall certify reformulated gasoline as complying with the requirements established pursuant to this subsection. Under such regulations, the Administrator shall establish procedures for any person to petition the Administrator to certify a fuel formulation, or slate of fuel formulations. Such procedures shall further require that the Administrator shall approve or deny such petition within 180 days of receipt. If the Administrator fails to act within such 180-day period, the fuel shall be deemed certified until the Administrator completes action on the petition.

(B) Certification; equivalency

The Administrator shall certify a fuel formulation or slate of fuel formulations as complying with this subsection if such fuel or fuels—

(i) comply with the requirements of paragraph (2), and

(ii) achieve equivalent or greater reductions in emissions of ozone forming volatile organic compounds and emissions of toxic air pollutants than are achieved by a reformulated gasoline meeting the applicable requirements of paragraph (3).

(C) EPA determination of emissions level

Within 1 year after November 15, 1990, the Administrator shall determine the level of emissions of ozone forming volatile organic compounds and emissions of toxic air pollutants emitted by baseline vehicles when operating on baseline gasoline. For purposes of this subsection, within 1 year after November 15, 1990, the Administrator shall, by rule, determine appropriate measures of, and methodology for, ascertaining the emissions of air pollutants (including calculations, equipment, and testing tolerances).

(5) Prohibition

Effective beginning January 1, 1995, each of the following shall be a violation of this subsection:

(A) The sale or dispensing by any person of conventional gasoline to ultimate consumers in any covered area.

(B) The sale or dispensing by any refiner, blender, importer, or marketer of conventional gasoline for resale in any covered area, without (i) segregating such gasoline from reformulated gasoline, and (ii) clearly marking such conventional gasoline as "conventional gasoline, not for sale to ultimate consumer in a covered area".

Any refiner, blender, importer or marketer who purchases property[6] segregated and marked conventional gasoline, and thereafter labels, represents, or wholesales such gasoline as reformulated gasoline shall also be in violation of this subsection. The Administrator may impose sampling, testing, and record-keeping requirements upon any refiner, blender, importer, or marketer to prevent violations of this section.

(6) Opt-in areas

(A) Classified areas

(i) In general

Upon the application of the Governor of a State, the Administrator shall apply the prohibition set forth in paragraph (5) in any area in the State classified under subpart 2 of part D of subchapter I of this chapter as a Marginal, Moderate, Serious, or Severe Area (without regard to whether or not the 1980 population of the area exceeds 250,000). In any such case, the Administrator shall establish an effective date for such prohibition as he deems appropriate, not later than January 1, 1995, or 1 year after such application is received, whichever is later. The Administrator shall publish such application in the Federal Register upon receipt.

(ii) Effect of insufficient domestic capacity to produce reformulated gasoline

If the Administrator determines, on the Administrator's own motion or on petition of any person, after consultation with the Secretary of Energy, that there is insufficient domestic capacity to produce gasoline certified under this subsection, the Administrator shall, by rule, extend the effective date of such prohibition in Marginal, Moderate, Serious, or Severe Areas referred to in clause (i) for one additional year, and may, by rule, renew such extension for 2 additional one-year periods. The Administrator shall act on any petition submitted under this subparagraph within 6 months after receipt of the petition. The Administrator shall issue such extensions for areas with a lower ozone classification before issuing any such extension for areas with a higher classification.

(B) Ozone transport region

(i) Application of prohibition

(I) In general

On application of the Governor of a State in the ozone transport region established by section 7511c(a) of this title, the Administrator, not later than 180 days after the date of receipt of the application, shall apply the prohibition specified in paragraph (5) to any area in the State (other than an area codified as a marginal, moderate, serious, or severe ozone nonattainment area under subpart 2 of part D of subchapter I of this chapter) unless the Administrator determines under clause (iii) that there is insufficient capacity to supply reformulated gasoline.

(II) Publication of application

As soon as practicable after the date of receipt of an application under subclause (I), the Administrator shall publish the application in the Federal Register.

(ii) Period of applicability

Under clause (i), the prohibition specified in paragraph (5) shall apply in a State—

(I) commencing as soon as practicable but not later than 2 years after the date of approval by the Administrator of the application of the Governor of the State; and

(II) ending not earlier than 4 years after the commencement date determined under subclause (I).

(iii) Extension of commencement date based on insufficient capacity

(I) In general

If, after receipt of an application from a Governor of a State under clause (i), the Administrator determines, on the Administrator's own motion or on petition of any person, after consultation with the Secretary of Energy, that there is insufficient capacity to supply reformulated gasoline, the Administrator, by regulation—

(aa) shall extend the commencement date with respect to the State under clause (ii)(I) for not more than 1 year; and

(bb) may renew the extension under item (aa) for 2 additional periods, each of which shall not exceed 1 year.

(II) Deadline for action on petitions

The Administrator shall act on any petition submitted under subclause (I) not later than 180 days after the date of receipt of the petition.

(7) Credits

(A) The regulations promulgated under this subsection shall provide for the granting of an appropriate amount of credits to a person who refines, blends, or imports and certifies a gasoline or slate of gasoline that—

(i) has an aromatic hydrocarbon content (by volume) that is less than the maximum aromatic hydrocarbon content required to comply with paragraph (3); or

(ii) has a benzene content (by volume) that is less than the maximum benzene content specified in paragraph (2).

(B) The regulations described in subparagraph (A) shall also provide that a person who is granted credits may use such credits, or transfer all or a portion of such credits to another person for use within the same nonattainment area, for the purpose of complying with this subsection.

(C) The regulations promulgated under subparagraphs (A) and (B) shall ensure the enforcement of the requirements for the issuance, application, and transfer of the credits. Such regulations shall prohibit the granting or transfer of such credits for use with respect to any gasoline in a nonattainment area, to the extent the use of such credits would result in any of the following:

(i) An average gasoline aromatic hydrocarbon content (by volume) for the nonattainment (taking into account all gasoline sold for use in conventional gasoline-fueled vehicles in the nonattainment area) higher than the average fuel aromatic hydrocarbon content (by volume) that would occur in the absence of using any such credits.

(ii) An average benzene content (by volume) for the nonattainment area (taking into account all gasoline sold for use in conventional gasoline-fueled vehicles in the nonattainment area) higher than the average benzene content (by volume) that would occur in the absence of using any such credits.

(8) Anti-dumping rules

(A) In general

Within 1 year after November 15, 1990, the Administrator shall promulgate regulations applicable to each refiner, blender, or importer of gasoline ensuring that gasoline sold or introduced into commerce by such refiner, blender, or importer (other than reformulated gasoline subject to the requirements of paragraph (1)) does not result in average per gallon emissions (measured on a mass basis) of (i) volatile organic compounds, (ii) oxides of nitrogen, (iii) carbon monoxide, and (iv) toxic air pollutants in excess of such emissions of such pollutants attributable to gasoline sold or introduced into commerce in calendar year 1990 by that refiner, blender, or importer. Such regulations shall take effect beginning January 1, 1995.

(B) Adjustments

In evaluating compliance with the requirements of subparagraph (A), the Administrator shall make appropriate adjustments to insure that no credit is provided for improvement in motor vehicle emissions control in motor vehicles sold after the calendar year 1990.

(C) Compliance determined for each pollutant independently

In determining whether there is an increase in emissions in violation of the prohibition contained in subparagraph (A) the Administrator shall consider an increase in each air pollutant referred to in clauses (i) through (iv) as a separate violation of such prohibition, except that the Administrator shall promulgate regulations to provide that any increase in emissions of oxides of nitrogen resulting from adding oxygenates to gasoline may be offset by an equivalent or greater reduction (on a mass basis) in emissions of volatile organic compounds, carbon monoxide, or toxic air pollutants, or any combination of the foregoing.

(D) Compliance period

The Administrator shall promulgate an appropriate compliance period or appropriate compliance periods to be used for assessing compliance with the prohibition contained in subparagraph (A).

(E) Baseline for determining compliance

If the Administrator determines that no adequate and reliable data exists regarding the composition of gasoline sold or introduced into commerce by a refiner, blender, or importer in calendar year 1990, for such refiner, blender, or importer, baseline gasoline shall be substituted for such 1990 gasoline in determining compliance with subparagraph (A).

(9) Emissions from entire vehicle

In applying the requirements of this subsection, the Administrator shall take into account emissions from the entire motor vehicle, including evaporative, running, refueling, and exhaust emissions.

(10) Definitions

For purposes of this subsection—

(A) Baseline vehicles

The term "baseline vehicles" mean representative model year 1990 vehicles.

(B) Baseline gasoline

(i) Summertime

The term "baseline gasoline" means in the case of gasoline sold during the high ozone period (as defined by the Administrator) a gasoline which meets the following specifications:

BASELINE GASOLINE FUEL PROPERTIES	
API Gravity	57.4
Sulfur, ppm	339
Benzene, %	1.53
RVP, psi	8.7
Octane, R + M/2	87.3
BP, F	91
10%, F	128
50%, F	218
90%, F	330
End Point, F	415
Aromatics, %	32.0
Olefins, %	9.2
Saturates, %	58.8

(ii) Wintertime

The Administrator shall establish the specifications of "baseline gasoline" for gasoline sold at times other than the high ozone period (as defined by the Administrator). Such specifications shall be the specifications of 1990 industry average gasoline sold during such period.

(C) Toxic air pollutants

The term "toxic air pollutants" means the aggregate emissions of the following:

Benzene

1,3 Butadiene

Polycyclic organic matter (POM)

Acetaldehyde

Formaldehyde.

(D) Covered area

The 9 ozone nonattainment areas having a 1980 population in excess of 250,000 and having the highest ozone design value during the period 1987 through 1989 shall be "covered areas" for purposes of this subsection. Effective one year after the reclassification of any ozone nonattainment area as a Severe ozone nonattainment area under section 7511(b) of this title, such Severe area shall also be a "covered area" for purposes of this subsection.

(E) Reformulated gasoline

The term "reformulated gasoline" means any gasoline which is certified by the Administrator under this section as complying with this subsection.

(F) Conventional gasoline

The term "conventional gasoline" means any gasoline which does not meet specifications set by a certification under this subsection.

(*l*) Detergents

Effective beginning January 1, 1995, no person may sell or dispense to an ultimate consumer in the United States, and no refiner or marketer may directly or indirectly sell or dispense to persons who sell or dispense to ultimate consumers in the United States any gasoline which does not contain additives to prevent the accumulation of deposits in engines or fuel supply systems. Not later than 2 years after November 15, 1990, the Administrator shall promulgate a rule establishing specifications for such additives.

(m) Oxygenated fuels

(1) Plan revisions for CO nonattainment areas

(A) Each State in which there is located all or part of an area which is designated under subchapter I of this chapter as a nonattainment area for carbon monoxide and which has a carbon monoxide design value of 9.5 parts per million (ppm) or above based on data for the 2-year period of 1988 and 1989 and calculated according to the most recent interpretation methodology issued by the Administrator prior to November 15, 1990, shall submit to the Administrator a State implementation plan revision under section 7410 of this title and part D of subchapter I of this chapter for such area which shall contain the provisions specified under this subsection regarding oxygenated gasoline.

(B) A plan revision which contains such provisions shall also be submitted by each State in which there is located any area which, for any 2-year period after 1989 has a carbon monoxide design value of 9.5 ppm or above. The revision shall be submitted within 18 months after such 2-year period.

(2) Oxygenated gasoline in CO nonattainment areas

Each plan revision under this subsection shall contain provisions to require that any gasoline sold, or dispensed, to the ultimate consumer in the carbon monoxide nonattainment area or sold or dispensed directly or indirectly by fuel refiners or marketers to persons who sell or dispense to ultimate consumers, in the larger of—

(A) the Consolidated Metropolitan Statistical Area (CMSA) in which the area is located, or

(B) if the area is not located in a CMSA, the Metropolitan Statistical Area in which the area is located,

be blended, during the portion of the year in which the area is prone to high ambient concentrations of carbon monoxide to contain not less than 2.7 percent oxygen by weight (subject to a testing tolerance established by the Administrator). The portion of the year in which the area is prone to high ambient concentrations of carbon monoxide shall be as determined by the Administrator, but shall not be less than 4 months. At the request of a State with respect to any area designated as nonattainment for carbon monoxide, the Administrator may reduce the period specified in the preceding sentence if the State can demonstrate that because of meteorological conditions, a reduced period will assure that there will be no exceedances of the carbon monoxide standard outside of such reduced period. For areas with a carbon monoxide design value of 9.5 ppm or more of[7] November 15, 1990, the revision shall provide that such requirement shall take effect no later than November 1, 1992 (or at such other date during 1992 as the Administrator establishes under the preceding provisions of this paragraph). For other areas, the revision shall provide that such requirement shall take effect no later than November 1 of the third year after the last year of the applicable 2-year period referred to in paragraph (1) (or at such other date during such third year as the Administrator establishes under the preceding provisions of this paragraph) and shall include a program for implementation and enforcement of the requirement consistent with guidance to be issued by the Administrator.

(3) Waivers

(A) The Administrator shall waive, in whole or in part, the requirements of paragraph (2) upon a demonstration by the State to the satisfaction of the Administrator that the use of oxygenated gasoline would prevent or interfere with the attainment by the area of a national primary ambient air quality standard (or a State or local ambient air quality standard) for any air pollutant other than carbon monoxide.

(B) The Administrator shall, upon demonstration by the State satisfactory to the Administrator, waive the requirement of paragraph (2) where the Administrator determines that mobile sources of carbon monoxide do not contribute significantly to carbon monoxide levels in an area.

(C) **(i)** Any person may petition the Administrator to make a finding that there is, or is likely to be, for any area, an inadequate domestic supply of, or distribution capacity for, oxygenated gasoline meeting the requirements of paragraph (2) or fuel additives (oxygenates) necessary to meet such requirements. The Administrator shall act on such petition within 6 months after receipt of the petition.

(ii) If the Administrator determines, in response to a petition under clause (i), that there is an inadequate supply or capacity described in clause (i), the Administrator shall delay the effective date of paragraph (2) for 1 year. Upon petition, the Administrator may extend such effective date for one additional year. No partial delay or lesser waiver may be granted under this clause.

(iii) In granting waivers under this subparagraph the Administrator shall consider distribution capacity separately from the adequacy of domestic supply and shall grant such waivers in such manner as will assure that, if supplies of oxygenated gasoline are limited, areas having the highest design value for carbon monoxide will have a priority in obtaining oxygenated gasoline which meets the requirements of paragraph (2).

(iv) As used in this subparagraph, the term distribution capacity includes capacity for transportation, storage, and blending.

(4) Fuel dispensing systems

Any person selling oxygenated gasoline at retail pursuant to this subsection shall be required under regulations promulgated by the Administrator to label the fuel dispensing system with a notice that the gasoline is oxygenated and will reduce the carbon monoxide emissions from the motor vehicle.

(5) Guidelines for credit

The Administrator shall promulgate guidelines, within 9 months after November 15, 1990, allowing the use of marketable oxygen credits from gasolines during that portion of the year specified in paragraph (2) with higher oxygen content than required to offset the sale or use of gasoline with a lower oxygen content than required. No credits may be transferred between nonattainment areas.

(6) Attainment areas

Nothing in this subsection shall be interpreted as requiring an oxygenated gasoline program in an area which is in attainment for carbon monoxide, except that in a carbon monoxide nonattainment area which is redesignated as attainment for carbon monoxide, the requirements of this subsection shall remain in effect to the extent such program is necessary to maintain such standard thereafter in the area.

(7) Failure to attain CO standard

If the Administrator determines under section 7512(b)(2) of this title that the national primary ambient air quality standard for carbon monoxide has not been attained in a Serious Area by the applicable attainment date, the State shall submit a plan revision for the area within 9 months after the date of such determination. The plan revision shall provide that the minimum oxygen content of gasoline referred to in paragraph (2) shall be 3.1 percent by weight unless such requirement is waived in accordance with the provisions of this subsection.

(n) Prohibition on leaded gasoline for highway use

After December 31, 1995, it shall be unlawful for any person to sell, offer for sale, supply, offer for supply, dispense, transport, or introduce into commerce, for use as fuel in any motor vehicle (as defined in section 7554(2)[8] of this title) any gasoline which contains lead or lead additives.

(*o*) Renewable fuel program

(1) Definitions

In this section:

(A) Additional renewable fuel

The term "additional renewable fuel" means fuel that is produced from renewable biomass and that is used to replace or reduce the quantity of fossil fuel present in home heating oil or jet fuel.

(B) Advanced biofuel

(i) In general

The term "advanced biofuel" means renewable fuel, other than ethanol derived from corn starch, that has lifecycle greenhouse gas emissions, as determined by the Administrator, after notice and opportunity for comment, that are at least 50 percent less than baseline lifecycle greenhouse gas emissions.

(ii) Inclusions

The types of fuels eligible for consideration as "advanced biofuel" may include any of the following:

(I) Ethanol derived from cellulose, hemicellulose, or lignin.

(II) Ethanol derived from sugar or starch (other than corn starch).

(III) Ethanol derived from waste material, including crop residue, other vegetative waste material, animal waste, and food waste and yard waste.

(IV) Biomass-based diesel.

(V) Biogas (including landfill gas and sewage waste treatment gas) produced through the conversion of organic matter from renewable biomass.

(VI) Butanol or other alcohols produced through the conversion of organic matter from renewable biomass.

(VII) Other fuel derived from cellulosic biomass.

(C) Baseline lifecycle greenhouse gas emissions

The term "baseline lifecycle greenhouse gas emissions" means the average lifecycle greenhouse gas emissions, as determined by the Administrator, after notice and opportunity for comment, for gasoline or diesel (whichever is being replaced by the renewable fuel) sold or distributed as transportation fuel in 2005.

(D) Biomass-based diesel

The term "biomass-based diesel" means renewable fuel that is biodiesel as defined in section 13220(f) of this title and that has lifecycle greenhouse gas emissions, as determined by the

Administrator, after notice and opportunity for comment, that are at least 50 percent less than the baseline lifecycle greenhouse gas emissions. Notwithstanding the preceding sentence, renewable fuel derived from co-processing biomass with a petroleum feedstock shall be advanced biofuel if it meets the requirements of subparagraph (B), but is not biomass-based diesel.

(E) Cellulosic biofuel

The term "cellulosic biofuel" means renewable fuel derived from any cellulose, hemicellulose, or lignin that is derived from renewable biomass and that has lifecycle greenhouse gas emissions, as determined by the Administrator, that are at least 60 percent less than the baseline lifecycle greenhouse gas emissions.

(F) Conventional biofuel

The term "conventional biofuel" means renewable fuel that is ethanol derived from corn starch.

(G) Greenhouse gas

The term "greenhouse gas" means carbon dioxide, hydrofluorocarbons, methane, nitrous oxide, perfluorocarbons,[9] sulfur hexafluoride. The Administrator may include any other anthropogenically-emitted gas that is determined by the Administrator, after notice and comment, to contribute to global warming.

(H) Lifecycle greenhouse gas emissions

The term "lifecycle greenhouse gas emissions" means the aggregate quantity of greenhouse gas emissions (including direct emissions and significant indirect emissions such as significant emissions from land use changes), as determined by the Administrator, related to the full fuel lifecycle, including all stages of fuel and feedstock production and distribution, from feedstock generation or extraction through the distribution and delivery and use of the finished fuel to the ultimate consumer, where the mass values for all greenhouse gases are adjusted to account for their relative global warming potential.

(I) Renewable biomass

The term "renewable biomass" means each of the following:

(i) Planted crops and crop residue harvested from agricultural land cleared or cultivated at any time prior to December 19, 2007, that is either actively managed or fallow, and nonforested.

(ii) Planted trees and tree residue from actively managed tree plantations on non-federal[10] land cleared at any time prior to December 19, 2007, including land belonging to an Indian tribe or an Indian individual, that is held in trust by the United States or subject to a restriction against alienation imposed by the United States.

(iii) Animal waste material and animal byproducts.

(iv) Slash and pre-commercial thinnings that are from non-federal forestlands, including forestlands belonging to an Indian tribe or an Indian individual, that are held in trust by the United States or subject to a restriction against alienation imposed by the United States, but not forests or forestlands that are ecological communities with a global or State ranking of critically imperiled, imperiled, or rare pursuant to a State Natural Heritage Program, old growth forest, or late successional forest.

(v) Biomass obtained from the immediate vicinity of buildings and other areas regularly occupied by people, or of public infrastructure, at risk from wildfire.

(vi) Algae.

(vii) Separated yard waste or food waste, including recycled cooking and trap grease.

(J) Renewable fuel

The term "renewable fuel" means fuel that is produced from renewable biomass and that is used to replace or reduce the quantity of fossil fuel present in a transportation fuel.

(K) Small refinery

The term "small refinery" means a refinery for which the average aggregate daily crude oil throughput for a calendar year (as determined by dividing the aggregate throughput for the calendar year by the number of days in the calendar year) does not exceed 75,000 barrels.

(L) Transportation fuel

The term "transportation fuel" means fuel for use in motor vehicles, motor vehicle engines, nonroad vehicles, or nonroad engines (except for ocean-going vessels).

(2) Renewable fuel program

(A) Regulations

(i) In general

Not later than 1 year after August 8, 2005, the Administrator shall promulgate regulations to ensure that gasoline sold or introduced into commerce in the United States (except in noncontiguous States or territories), on an annual average basis, contains the applicable volume of renewable fuel determined in accordance with subparagraph (B). Not later than 1 year after December 19, 2007, the Administrator shall revise the regulations under this paragraph to ensure that transportation fuel sold or introduced into commerce in the United States (except in noncontiguous States or territories), on an annual average basis, contains at least the applicable volume of renewable fuel, advanced biofuel, cellulosic biofuel, and biomass-based diesel, determined in accordance with subparagraph (B) and, in the case of any such renewable fuel produced from new facilities that commence construction after December 19, 2007, achieves at least a 20 percent reduction in lifecycle greenhouse gas emissions compared to baseline lifecycle greenhouse gas emissions.

(ii) Noncontiguous State opt-in

(I) In general

On the petition of a noncontiguous State or territory, the Administrator may allow the renewable fuel program established under this subsection to apply in the noncontiguous State or territory at the same time or any time after the Administrator promulgates regulations under this subparagraph.

(II) Other actions

In carrying out this clause, the Administrator may—

(aa) issue or revise regulations under this paragraph;

(bb) establish applicable percentages under paragraph (3);

(cc) provide for the generation of credits under paragraph (5); and

(dd) take such other actions as are necessary to allow for the application of the renewable fuels program in a noncontiguous State or territory.

(iii) Provisions of regulations

Regardless of the date of promulgation, the regulations promulgated under clause (i)—

(I) shall contain compliance provisions applicable to refineries, blenders, distributors, and importers, as appropriate, to ensure that the requirements of this paragraph are met; but

(II) shall not—

(aa) restrict geographic areas in which renewable fuel may be used; or (bb) impose any per-gallon obligation for the use of renewable fuel.

(iv) Requirement in case of failure to promulgate regulations

If the Administrator does not promulgate regulations under clause (i), the percentage of renewable fuel in gasoline sold or dispensed to consumers in the United States, on a volume basis, shall be 2.78 percent for calendar year 2006.

(B) Applicable volumes

(i) Calendar years after 2005

(I) Renewable fuel

For the purpose of subparagraph (A), the applicable volume of renewable fuel for the calendar years 2006 through 2022 shall be determined in accordance with the following table:

Calendar year:	Applicable volume of renewable Fuel (in billions of gallons):
2006	4.0
2007	4.7
2008	9.0
2009	11.1
2010	12.95
2011	13.95
2012	15.2
2013	16.55
2014	18.15
2015	20.5
2016	22.25
2017	24.0
2018	6.0
2019	28.0
2020	30.0
2021	33.0
2022	36.0

(II) Advanced biofuel

For the purpose of subparagraph (A), of the volume of renewable fuel required under subclause (I), the applicable volume of advanced biofuel for the calendar years 2009 through 2022 shall be determined in accordance with the following table:

Calendar year:	Applicable volume of advanced biofuel (in billions of gallons):
2009	0.6
2010	0.95
2011	1.35
2012	2.0
2013	2.75
2014	3.75

2015	5.5
2016	7.25
2017	9.0
2018	11.0
2019	13.0
2020	15.0
2021	18.0
2022	21.0

(III) Cellulosic biofuel

For the purpose of subparagraph (A), of the volume of advanced biofuel required under subclause (II), the applicable volume of cellulosic biofuel for the calendar years 2010 through 2022 shall be determined in accordance with the following table:

Calendar year:	Applicable volume of cellulosic biofuel (in billions of gallons):
2010	0.1
2011	0.25
2012	0.5
2013	1.0
2014	1.75
2015	3.0
2016	4.25
2017	5.5
2018	7.0
2019	8.5
2020	10.5
2021	13.5
2022	16.0

(IV) Biomass-based diesel

For the purpose of subparagraph (A), of the volume of advanced biofuel required under subclause (II), the applicable volume of biomass-based diesel for the calendar years 2009 through 2012 shall be determined in accordance with the following table:

Calendar year:	Applicable volume of biomass-c based diesel (in billions of gallons):
2009	0.5
2010	0.65
2011	0.80
2012	1.0

(ii) Other calendar years

For the purposes of subparagraph (A), the applicable volumes of each fuel specified in the tables in clause (i) for calendar years after the calendar years specified in the tables shall be determined by the Administrator, in coordination with the Secretary of Energy and the

Secretary of Agriculture, based on a review of the implementation of the program during calendar years specified in the tables, and an analysis of—

(I) the impact of the production and use of renewable fuels on the environment, including on air quality, climate change, conversion of wetlands, ecosystems, wildlife habitat, water quality, and water supply;

(II) the impact of renewable fuels on the energy security of the United States;

(III) the expected annual rate of future commercial production of renewable fuels, including advanced biofuels in each category (cellulosic biofuel and biomass-based diesel);

(IV) the impact of renewable fuels on the infrastructure of the United States, including deliverability of materials, goods, and products other than renewable fuel, and the sufficiency of infrastructure to deliver and use renewable fuel;

(V) the impact of the use of renewable fuels on the cost to consumers of transportation fuel and on the cost to transport goods; and

(VI) the impact of the use of renewable fuels on other factors, including job creation, the price and supply of agricultural commodities, rural economic development, and food prices.

The Administrator shall promulgate rules establishing the applicable volumes under this clause no later than 14 months before the first year for which such applicable volume will apply.

(iii) Applicable volume of advanced biofuel

For the purpose of making the determinations in clause (ii), for each calendar year, the applicable volume of advanced biofuel shall be at least the same percentage of the applicable volume of renewable fuel as in calendar year 2022.

(iv) Applicable volume of cellulosic biofuel

For the purpose of making the determinations in clause (ii), for each calendar year, the applicable volume of cellulosic biofuel established by the Administrator shall be based on the assumption that the Administrator will not need to issue a waiver for such years under paragraph (7)(D).

(v) Minimum applicable volume of biomass-based diesel

For the purpose of making the determinations in clause (ii), the applicable volume of biomass-based diesel shall not be less than the applicable volume listed in clause (i)(IV) for calendar year 2012.

(3) Applicable percentages

(A) Provision of estimate of volumes of gasoline sales

Not later than October 31 of each of calendar years 2005 through 2021, the Administrator of the Energy Information Administration shall provide to the Administrator of the Environmental Protection Agency an estimate, with respect to the following calendar year, of the volumes of transportation fuel, biomass-based diesel, and cellulosic biofuel projected to be sold or introduced into commerce in the United States.

(B) Determination of applicable percentages

(i) In general

Not later than November 30 of each of calendar years 2005 through 2021, based on the estimate provided under subparagraph (A), the Administrator of the Environmental Protection Agency shall determine and publish in the Federal Register, with respect to the following calendar year, the renewable fuel obligation that ensures that the requirements of paragraph (2) are met.

(ii) Required elements

The renewable fuel obligation determined for a calendar year under clause (i) shall—

(I) be applicable to refineries, blenders, and importers, as appropriate;

(II) be expressed in terms of a volume percentage of transportation fuel sold or introduced into commerce in the United States; and

(III) subject to subparagraph (C)(i), consist of a single applicable percentage that applies to all categories of persons specified in subclause (I).

(C) Adjustments

In determining the applicable percentage for a calendar year, the Administrator shall make adjustments—

(i) to prevent the imposition of redundant obligations on any person specified in subparagraph (B)(ii)(I); and

(ii) to account for the use of renewable fuel during the previous calendar year by small refineries that are exempt under paragraph (9).

(4) Modification of greenhouse gas reduction percentages

(A) In general

The Administrator may, in the regulations under the last sentence of paragraph (2)(A)(i), adjust the 20 percent, 50 percent, and 60 percent reductions in lifecycle greenhouse gas emissions specified in paragraphs (2)(A)(i) (relating to renewable fuel), (1)(D) (relating to biomass-based diesel), (1)(B)(i) (relating to advanced biofuel), and (1)(E) (relating to cellulosic biofuel) to a lower percentage. For the 50 and 60 percent reductions, the Administrator may make such an adjustment only if he determines that generally such reduction is not commercially feasible for fuels made using a variety of feedstocks, technologies, and processes to meet the applicable reduction.

(B) Amount of adjustment

In promulgating regulations under this paragraph, the specified 50 percent reduction in greenhouse gas emissions from advanced biofuel and in biomass-based diesel may not be reduced below 40 percent. The specified 20 percent reduction in greenhouse gas emissions from renewable fuel may not be reduced below 10 percent, and the specified 60 percent reduction in greenhouse gas emissions from cellulosic biofuel may not be reduced below 50 percent.

(C) Adjusted reduction levels

An adjustment under this paragraph to a percent less than the specified 20 percent greenhouse gas reduction for renewable fuel shall be the minimum possible adjustment, and the adjusted greenhouse gas reduction shall be established by the Administrator at the maximum achievable level, taking cost in consideration, for natural gas fired corn-based ethanol plants, allowing for the use of a variety of technologies and processes. An adjustment in the 50 or 60 percent greenhouse gas levels shall be the minimum possible adjustment for the fuel or fuels concerned, and the adjusted greenhouse gas reduction shall be established at the maximum achievable level, taking cost in consideration, allowing for the use of a variety of feedstocks, technologies, and processes.

(D) 5-year review

Whenever the Administrator makes any adjustment under this paragraph, not later than 5 years thereafter he shall review and revise (based upon the same criteria and standards as required for the initial adjustment) the regulations establishing the adjusted level.

(E) Subsequent adjustments

After the Administrator has promulgated a final rule under the last sentence of paragraph (2)(A)(i) with respect to the method of determining lifecycle greenhouse gas emissions, except as provided in subparagraph (D), the Administrator may not adjust the percent greenhouse gas reduction levels unless he determines that there has been a significant change in the analytical methodology used for determining the lifecycle greenhouse gas emissions. If he makes such determination, he may adjust the 20, 50, or 60 percent reduction levels through rulemaking using the criteria and standards set forth in this paragraph.

(F) Limit on upward adjustments

If, under subparagraph (D) or (E), the Administrator revises a percent level adjusted as provided in subparagraphs (A), (B), and (C) to a higher percent, such higher percent may not exceed the applicable percent specified in paragraph (2)(A)(i), (1)(D), (1)(B)(i), or (1)(E).

(G) Applicability of adjustments

If the Administrator adjusts, or revises, a percent level referred to in this paragraph or makes a change in the analytical methodology used for determining the lifecycle greenhouse gas emissions, such adjustment, revision, or change (or any combination thereof) shall only apply to renewable fuel from new facilities that commence construction after the effective date of such adjustment, revision, or change.

(5) Credit program

(A) In general

The regulations promulgated under paragraph (2)(A) shall provide—

(i) for the generation of an appropriate amount of credits by any person that refines, blends, or imports gasoline that contains a quantity of renewable fuel that is greater than the quantity required under paragraph (2);

(ii) for the generation of an appropriate amount of credits for biodiesel; and

(iii) for the generation of credits by small refineries in accordance with paragraph (9)(C).

(B) Use of credits

A person that generates credits under subparagraph (A) may use the credits, or transfer all or a portion of the credits to another person, for the purpose of complying with paragraph (2).

(C) Duration of credits

A credit generated under this paragraph shall be valid to show compliance for the 12 months as of the date of generation.

(D) Inability to generate or purchase sufficient credits

The regulations promulgated under paragraph (2)(A) shall include provisions allowing any person that is unable to generate or purchase sufficient credits to meet the requirements of paragraph (2) to carry forward a renewable fuel deficit on condition that the person, in the calendar year following the year in which the renewable fuel deficit is created—

(i) achieves compliance with the renewable fuel requirement under paragraph (2); and

(ii) generates or purchases additional renewable fuel credits to offset the renewable fuel deficit of the previous year.

(E) Credits for additional renewable fuel

The Administrator may issue regulations providing: (i) for the generation of an appropriate amount of credits by any person that refines, blends, or imports additional renewable fuels specified by the Administrator; and (ii) for the use of such credits by the generator, or the transfer of all or a portion of the credits to another person, for the purpose of complying with paragraph (2).

(6) Seasonal variations in renewable fuel use

(A) Study

For each of calendar years 2006 through 2012, the Administrator of the Energy Information Administration shall conduct a study of renewable fuel blending to determine whether there are excessive seasonal variations in the use of renewable fuel.

(B) Regulation of excessive seasonal variations

If, for any calendar year, the Administrator of the Energy Information Administration, based on the study under subparagraph (A), makes the determinations specified in subparagraph (C), the Administrator of the Environmental Protection Agency shall promulgate regulations to ensure that 25 percent or more of the quantity of renewable fuel necessary to meet the requirements of paragraph (2) is used during each of the 2 periods specified in subparagraph (D) of each subsequent calendar year.

(C) Determinations

The determinations referred to in subparagraph (B) are that—

(i) less than 25 percent of the quantity of renewable fuel necessary to meet the requirements of paragraph (2) has been used during 1 of the 2 periods specified in subparagraph (D) of the calendar year;

(ii) a pattern of excessive seasonal variation described in clause (i) will continue in subsequent calendar years; and

(iii) promulgating regulations or other requirements to impose a 25 percent or more seasonal use of renewable fuels will not prevent or interfere with the attainment of national ambient air quality standards or significantly increase the price of motor fuels to the consumer.

(D) Periods

The 2 periods referred to in this paragraph are—

(i) April through September; and

(ii) January through March and October through December.

(E) Exclusion

Renewable fuel blended or consumed in calendar year 2006 in a State that has received a waiver under section 7543(b) of this title shall not be included in the study under subparagraph (A).

(F) State exemption from seasonality requirements

Notwithstanding any other provision of law, the seasonality requirement relating to renewable fuel use established by this paragraph shall not apply to any State that has received a waiver under section 7543(b) of this title or any State dependent on refineries in such State for gasoline supplies.

(7) Waivers

(A) In general

The Administrator, in consultation with the Secretary of Agriculture and the Secretary of Energy, may waive the requirements of paragraph (2) in whole or in part on petition by one or more States, by any person subject to the requirements of this subsection, or by the Administrator on his own motion by reducing the national quantity of renewable fuel required under paragraph (2)—

(i) based on a determination by the Administrator, after public notice and opportunity for comment, that implementation of the requirement would severely harm the economy or environment of a State, a region, or the United States; or

(ii) based on a determination by the Administrator, after public notice and opportunity for comment, that there is an inadequate domestic supply.

(B) Petitions for waivers

The Administrator, in consultation with the Secretary of Agriculture and the Secretary of Energy, shall approve or disapprove a petition for a waiver of the requirements of paragraph (2) within 90 days after the date on which the petition is received by the Administrator.

(C) Termination of waivers

A waiver granted under subparagraph (A) shall terminate after 1 year, but may be renewed by the Administrator after consultation with the Secretary of Agriculture and the Secretary of Energy.

(D) Cellulosic biofuel

(i) For any calendar year for which the projected volume of cellulosic biofuel production is less than the minimum applicable volume established under paragraph (2)(B), as determined by the Administrator based on the estimate provided under paragraph (3)(A), not later than November 30 of the preceding calendar year, the Administrator shall reduce the applicable volume of cellulosic biofuel required under paragraph (2)(B) to the projected volume available during that calendar year. For any calendar year in which the Administrator makes such a reduction, the Administrator may also reduce the applicable volume of renewable fuel and advanced biofuels requirement established under paragraph (2)(B) by the same or a lesser volume.

(ii) Whenever the Administrator reduces the minimum cellulosic biofuel volume under this subparagraph, the Administrator shall make available for sale cellulosic biofuel credits at the higher of $0.25 per gallon or the amount by which $3.00 per gallon exceeds the average wholesale price of a gallon of gasoline in the United States. Such amounts shall be adjusted for inflation by the Administrator for years after 2008.

(iii) Eighteen months after December 19, 2007, the Administrator shall promulgate regulations to govern the issuance of credits under this subparagraph. The regulations shall set forth the method for determining the exact price of credits in the event of a waiver. The price of such credits shall not be changed more frequently than once each quarter. These regulations shall include such provisions, including limiting the credits' uses and useful life, as the Administrator deems appropriate to assist market liquidity and transparency, to provide appropriate certainty for regulated entities and renewable fuel producers, and to limit any potential misuse of cellulosic biofuel credits to reduce the use of other renewable fuels, and for such other purposes as the Administrator determines will help achieve the goals of this subsection. The regulations shall limit the number of cellulosic biofuel credits for any calendar year to the minimum applicable volume (as reduced under this subparagraph) of cellulosic biofuel for that year.

(E) Biomass-based diesel

(i) Market evaluation

The Administrator, in consultation with the Secretary of Energy and the Secretary of Agriculture, shall periodically evaluate the impact of the biomass-based diesel requirements established under this paragraph on the price of diesel fuel.

(ii) Waiver

If the Administrator determines that there is a significant renewable feedstock disruption or other market circumstances that would make the price of biomass-based diesel fuel increase significantly, the Administrator, in consultation with the Secretary of Energy and the Secretary of Agriculture, shall issue an order to reduce, for up to a 60-day period, the quantity of biomass-based diesel required under subparagraph (A) by an appropriate quantity that does not exceed 15 percent of the applicable annual requirement for biomass-based diesel. For any calendar year in which the Administrator makes a reduction under this subparagraph, the Administrator may also reduce the applicable volume of renewable fuel and advanced biofuels requirement established under paragraph (2)(B) by the same or a lesser volume.

(iii) Extensions

If the Administrator determines that the feedstock disruption or circumstances described in clause (ii) is continuing beyond the 60-day period described in clause (ii) or this clause, the Administrator, in consultation with the Secretary of Energy and the Secretary of Agriculture, may issue an order to reduce, for up to an additional 60-day period, the quantity of biomass-based diesel required under subparagraph (A) by an appropriate quantity that does not exceed an additional 15 percent of the applicable annual requirement for biomass-based diesel.

(F) Modification of applicable volumes

For any of the tables in paragraph (2)(B), if the Administrator waives—

(i) at least 20 percent of the applicable volume requirement set forth in any such table for 2 consecutive years; or

(ii) at least 50 percent of such volume requirement for a single year,

the Administrator shall promulgate a rule (within 1 year after issuing such waiver) that modifies the applicable volumes set forth in the table concerned for all years following the final year to which the waiver applies, except that no such modification in applicable volumes shall be made for any year before 2016. In promulgating such a rule, the Administrator shall comply with the processes, criteria, and standards set forth in paragraph (2)(B)(ii).

(8) Study and waiver for initial year of program

(A) In general

Not later than 180 days after August 8, 2005, the Secretary of Energy shall conduct for the Administrator a study assessing whether the renewable fuel requirement under paragraph (2) will likely result in significant adverse impacts on consumers in 2006, on a national, regional, or State basis.

(B) Required evaluations

The study shall evaluate renewable fuel—

(i) supplies and prices;

(ii) blendstock supplies; and

(iii) supply and distribution system capabilities.

(C) Recommendations by the Secretary

Based on the results of the study, the Secretary of Energy shall make specific recommendations to the Administrator concerning waiver of the requirements of paragraph (2), in whole or in part, to prevent any adverse impacts described in subparagraph (A).

(D) Waiver

(i) In general

Not later than 270 days after August 8, 2005, the Administrator shall, if and to the extent recommended by the Secretary of Energy under subparagraph (C), waive, in whole or in part, the renewable fuel requirement under paragraph (2) by reducing the national quantity of renewable fuel required under paragraph (2) in calendar year 2006.

(ii) No effect on waiver authority

Clause (i) does not limit the authority of the Administrator to waive the requirements of paragraph (2) in whole, or in part, under paragraph (7).

(9) Small refineries

(A) Temporary exemption

(i) In general

The requirements of paragraph (2) shall not apply to small refineries until calendar year 2011.

(ii) Extension of exemption

(I) Study by Secretary of Energy

Not later than December 31, 2008, the Secretary of Energy shall conduct for the Administrator a study to determine whether compliance with the requirements of paragraph (2) would impose a disproportionate economic hardship on small refineries.

(II) Extension of exemption

In the case of a small refinery that the Secretary of Energy determines under subclause (I) would be subject to a disproportionate economic hardship if required to comply with paragraph (2), the Administrator shall extend the exemption under clause (i) for the small refinery for a period of not less than 2 additional years.

(B) Petitions based on disproportionate economic hardship

(i) Extension of exemption

A small refinery may at any time petition the Administrator for an extension of the exemption under subparagraph (A) for the reason of disproportionate economic hardship.

(ii) Evaluation of petitions

In evaluating a petition under clause (i), the Administrator, in consultation with the Secretary of Energy, shall consider the findings of the study under subparagraph (A)(ii) and other economic factors.

(iii) Deadline for action on petitions

The Administrator shall act on any petition submitted by a small refinery for a hardship exemption not later than 90 days after the date of receipt of the petition.

(C) Credit program

If a small refinery notifies the Administrator that the small refinery waives the exemption under subparagraph (A), the regulations promulgated under paragraph (2)(A) shall provide for the generation of credits by the small refinery under paragraph (5) beginning in the calendar year following the date of notification.

(D) Opt-in for small refineries

A small refinery shall be subject to the requirements of paragraph (2) if the small refinery notifies the Administrator that the small refinery waives the exemption under subparagraph (A).

(10) Ethanol market concentration analysis

(A) Analysis

(i) In general

Not later than 180 days after August 8, 2005, and annually thereafter, the Federal Trade Commission shall perform a market concentration analysis of the ethanol production industry using the Herfindahl-Hirschman Index to determine whether there is sufficient competition among industry participants to avoid price-setting and other anticompetitive behavior.

(ii) **Scoring**

For the purpose of scoring under clause (i) using the Herfindahl-Hirschman Index, all marketing arrangements among industry participants shall be considered.

(B) **Report**

Not later than December 1, 2005, and annually thereafter, the Federal Trade Commission shall submit to Congress and the Administrator a report on the results of the market concentration analysis performed under subparagraph (A)(i).

(11) **Periodic reviews**

To allow for the appropriate adjustment of the requirements described in subparagraph (B) of paragraph (2), the Administrator shall conduct periodic reviews of—

(A) existing technologies;

(B) the feasibility of achieving compliance with the requirements; and

(C) the impacts of the requirements described in subsection (a)(2)[11] on each individual and entity described in paragraph (2).

(12) **Effect on other provisions**

Nothing in this subsection, or regulations issued pursuant to this subsection, shall affect or be construed to affect the regulatory status of carbon dioxide or any other greenhouse gas, or to expand or limit regulatory authority regarding carbon dioxide or any other greenhouse gas, for purposes of other provisions (including section 7475) of this chapter. The previous sentence shall not affect implementation and enforcement of this subsection.

(q)[12] **Analyses of motor vehicle fuel changes and emissions model**

(1) **Anti-backsliding analysis**

(A) **Draft analysis**

Not later than 4 years after August 8, 2005, the Administrator shall publish for public comment a draft analysis of the changes in emissions of air pollutants and air quality due to the use of motor vehicle fuel and fuel additives resulting from implementation of the amendments made by the Energy Policy Act of 2005.

(B) **Final analysis**

After providing a reasonable opportunity for comment but not later than 5 years after August 8, 2005, the Administrator shall publish the analysis in final form.

(2) **Emissions model**

For the purposes of this section, not later than 4 years after August 8, 2005, the Administrator shall develop and finalize an emissions model that reflects, to the maximum extent practicable, the effects of gasoline characteristics or components on emissions from vehicles in the motor vehicle fleet during calendar year 2007.

(3) **Permeation effects study**

(A) **In general**

Not later than 1 year after August 8, 2005, the Administrator shall conduct a study, and report to Congress the results of the study, on the effects of ethanol content in gasoline on permeation, the process by which fuel molecules migrate through the elastomeric materials (rubber and plastic parts) that make up the fuel and fuel vapor systems of a motor vehicle.

(B) **Evaporative emissions**

The study shall include estimates of the increase in total evaporative emissions likely to result from the use of gasoline with ethanol content in a motor vehicle, and the fleet of motor vehicles, due to permeation.

(r) Fuel and fuel additive importers and importation

For the purposes of this section, the term "manufacturer" includes an importer and the term "manufacture" includes importation.

(s) Conversion assistance for cellulosic biomass, waste-derived ethanol, approved renewable fuels

(1) In general

The Secretary of Energy may provide grants to merchant producers of cellulosic biomass ethanol, waste-derived ethanol, and approved renewable fuels in the United States to assist the producers in building eligible production facilities described in paragraph (2) for the production of ethanol or approved renewable fuels.

(2) Eligible production facilities

A production facility shall be eligible to receive a grant under this subsection if the production facility—

(A) is located in the United States; and

(B) uses cellulosic or renewable biomass or waste-derived feedstocks derived from agricultural residues, wood residues, municipal solid waste, or agricultural byproducts.

(3) Authorization of appropriations

There are authorized to be appropriated the following amounts to carry out this subsection:

(A) $100,000,000 for fiscal year 2006.

(B) $250,000,000 for fiscal year 2007.

(C) $400,000,000 for fiscal year 2008.

(4) Definitions

For the purposes of this subsection:

(A) The term "approved renewable fuels" are fuels and components of fuels that have been approved by the Department of Energy, as defined in section 13211 of this title, which have been made from renewable biomass.

(B) The term "renewable biomass" is, as defined in Presidential Executive Order 13134, published in the Federal Register on August 16, 1999, any organic matter that is available on a renewable or recurring basis (excluding old-growth timber), including dedicated energy crops and trees, agricultural food and feed crop residues, aquatic plants, animal wastes, wood and wood residues, paper and paper residues, and other vegetative waste materials. Old-growth timber means timber of a forest from the late successional stage of forest development.

(t) Blending of compliant reformulated gasolines

(1) In general

Notwithstanding subsections (h) and (k) of this section and subject to the limitations in paragraph (2) of this subsection, it shall not be a violation of this part for a gasoline retailer, during any month of the year, to blend at a retail location batches of ethanol-blended and non-ethanol-blended reformulated gasoline, provided that—

(A) each batch of gasoline to be blended has been individually certified as in compliance with subsections (h) and (k) of this section prior to being blended;

(B) the retailer notifies the Administrator prior to such blending, and identifies the exact location of the retail station and the specific tank in which such blending will take place;

(C) the retailer retains and, as requested by the Administrator or the Administrator's designee, makes available for inspection such certifications accounting for all gasoline at the retail outlet; and

(D) the retailer does not, between June 1 and September 15 of each year, blend a batch of VOC-controlled, or "summer", gasoline with a batch of non-VOC-controlled, or "winter", gasoline (as these terms are defined under subsections (h) and (k) of this section).

(2) Limitations

(A) frequency limitation

A retailer shall only be permitted to blend batches of compliant reformulated gasoline under this subsection a maximum of two blending periods between May 1 and September 15 of each calendar year.

(B) Duration of blending period

Each blending period authorized under subparagraph (A) shall extend for a period of no more than 10 consecutive calendar days.

(3) Surveys

A sample of gasoline taken from a retail location that has blended gasoline within the past 30 days and is in compliance with subparagraphs (A), (B), (C), and (D) of paragraph (1) shall not be used in a VOC survey mandated by 40 C.F.R. Part 80.

(4) State implementation plans

A State shall be held harmless and shall not be required to revise its State implementation plan under section 7410 of this title to account for the emissions from blended gasoline authorized under paragraph (1).

(5) Preservation of State law

Nothing in this subsection shall—

(A) preempt existing State laws or regulations regulating the blending of compliant gasolines; or

(B) prohibit a State from adopting such restrictions in the future.

(6) Regulations

The Administrator shall promulgate, after notice and comment, regulations implementing this subsection within 1 year after August 8, 2005.

(7) Effective date

This subsection shall become effective 15 months after August 8, 2005, and shall apply to blended batches of reformulated gasoline on or after that date, regardless of whether the implementing regulations required by paragraph (6) have been promulgated by the Administrator by that date.

(8) Liability

No person other than the person responsible for blending under this subsection shall be subject to an enforcement action or penalties under subsection (d) of this section solely arising from the blending of compliant reformulated gasolines by the retailers.

(9) Formulation of gasoline

This subsection does not grant authority to the Administrator or any State (or any subdivision thereof) to require reformulation of gasoline at the refinery to adjust for potential or actual emissions increases due to the blending authorized by this subsection.

(u) Standard specifications for biodiesel

(1) Unless the American Society for Testing and Materials has adopted a standard for diesel fuel containing 20 percent biodiesel (commonly known as "B20") within 1 year after December 19, 2007, the Administrator shall initiate a rulemaking to establish a uniform per gallon fuel standard for such fuel and designate an identification number so that vehicle manufacturers are able to design engines to use fuel meeting such standard.

(2) Unless the American Society for Testing and Materials has adopted a standard for diesel fuel containing 5 percent biodiesel (commonly known as "B5") within 1 year after December 19, 2007, the Administrator shall initiate a rulemaking to establish a uniform per gallon fuel standard for such fuel and designate an identification so that vehicle manufacturers are able to design engines to use fuel meeting such standard.

(3) Whenever the Administrator is required to initiate a rulemaking under paragraph (1) or (2), the Administrator shall promulgate a final rule within 18 months after December 19, 2007.

(4) Not later than 180 days after December 19, 2007, the Administrator shall establish an annual inspection and enforcement program to ensure that diesel fuel containing biodiesel sold or distributed in interstate commerce meets the standards established under regulations under this section, including testing and certification for compliance with applicable standards of the American Society for Testing and Materials. There are authorized to be appropriated to carry out the inspection and enforcement program under this paragraph $3,000,000 for each of fiscal years 2008 through 2010.

(5) For purposes of this subsection, the term "biodiesel" has the meaning provided by section 13220(f) of this title.

(v) Prevention of air quality deterioration

(1) Study

(A) In general

Not later than 18 months after December 19, 2007, the Administrator shall complete a study to determine whether the renewable fuel volumes required by this section will adversely impact air quality as a result of changes in vehicle and engine emissions of air pollutants regulated under this chapter.

(B) Considerations

The study shall include consideration of—

(i) different blend levels, types of renewable fuels, and available vehicle technologies; and

(ii) appropriate national, regional, and local air quality control measures.

(2) Regulations

Not later than 3 years after December 19, 2007, the Administrator shall—

(A) promulgate fuel regulations to implement appropriate measures to mitigate, to the greatest extent achievable, considering the results of the study under paragraph (1), any adverse impacts on air quality, as the result of the renewable volumes required by this section; or

(B) make a determination that no such measures are necessary.

(July 14, 1955, c. 360, Title II, § 211, formerly § 210, as added by Pub. L. No. 90–148, § 2, 81 Stat. 502 (Nov. 21, 1967); and renumbered and amended by Pub. L. No. 91–604, §§ 8(a), 9(a), 84 Stat. 1694, 1698 (Dec. 31, 1970); and amended by Pub. L. No. 92–157, Title III, § 302(d), (e), 85 Stat. 464 (Nov. 18, 1971); Pub. L. No. 95–95, Title II, §§ 222, 223, Title IV, § 401(e), 91 Stat. 762, 764, 791 (Aug. 7, 1977); Pub. L. No. 95–190, § 14(a)(73), (74), 91 Stat. 1403, 1404 (Nov. 16, 1977); Pub. L. No. 101–549, Title II, §§ 212 to 221, 228(d), 104 Stat. 2488 to 2500, 2510 (Nov. 15, 1990); Pub. L. No. 109–58, Title XV, §§ 1501(a) to (c), 1504(a)(1), (b), 1505 to 1507, 1512, 1513, 1541(a), (b), 119 Stat. 1067, 1076, 1077, 1080, 1088, 1089, 1106 (Aug. 8, 2005); Pub. L. No. 110–140, Title II, §§ 201, 202, 203(f), 208, 209, 210(b), 247, 251, 121 Stat. 1519, 1529, 1531, 1532, 1547, 1548 (Dec. 19, 2007).)

1 So in original. Probably should be "the."

2 So in original. See Codifications and 2007 Amendments notes set out under this section.

3 So in original. See Codifications and 2007 Amendments notes set out under this section.

4 So in original. Two cls. (v) enacted.

5 So in original. Probably should be section "7625–1."

6 So in original. Probably should be "properly."

[7] So in original. Probably should be "as of."

[8] So in original. Probably should be section "7550(2)."

[9] So in original. The word "and" probably should appear.

[10] So in original. Probably should be non-Federal.

[11] So in original. Subsection (a) does not contain a par. (2).

[12] So in original. No subsec. (p) was enacted.

HISTORICAL AND STATUTORY NOTES

References in Text

August 8, 2005, referred to in subsecs. (b)(4), (*o*)(2), (8), (10), and (q), originally read "the date of enactment of this paragraph", meaning the date of enactment of the Energy Policy Act of 2005, Pub. L. No. 109–58, 119 Stat. 594, which enacted par. (4) of subsec. (b), pars. (1) to (3) of subsec. (q), and pars. (2), (8), and (10) of subsec. (*o*) of this section on Aug. 8, 2005.

August 8, 2005, referred to in subsec. (c)(4)(C)(iv), originally read "the date of enactment of this clause", meaning the date of enactment of Pub. L. No. 109–58, 119 Stat. 594 (Aug. 8, 2005), which enacted cl. (iv) of subsec. (c)(4)(C) of this section on Aug. 8, 2005.

The enactment of this subclause, referred to in subcl. (VI) of subsec. (c)(4)(C)(v), set out second, probably means the date of enactment of Pub. L. No. 109–58, 119 Stat. 594 (Aug. 8, 2005), which enacted subcl. (VI) of subsec. (c)(4)(C)(v) of this section on Aug. 8, 2005.

August 8, 2005, referred to in subsec. (k)(1)(B)(ii), (v)(I), (vi), originally read "the date of enactment of this subparagraph", meaning the date of enactment of the Energy Policy Act of 2005, Pub. L. No. 109–58, 119 Stat. 594, which enacted subpar. (B) of subsec. (k)(1) of this section on Aug. 8, 2005.

Subpart 2 of part D of subchapter I of this chapter, referred to in subsec. (k)(6)(B), originally read "subpart 2 of part D of title I", meaning subpart 2 of part D of title I of the Clean Air Act, July 14, 1955, c. 360, Title I, as added by Pub. L. No. 101–549, Title I, § 103, 104 Stat. 2423 (Nov. 15, 1990), which enacted subpart 2 of part D of subchapter I of this chapter, 42 U.S.C.A. § 7511 et seq.

December 19, 2007, referred to in subsec. (*o*)(2)(A)(i), originally read "the date of enactment of this sentence", meaning the date of enactment of the Energy Independence and Security Act of 2007, Pub. L. No. 110–140, 121 Stat. 1492 (Dec. 19, 2007), which enacted that sentence.

December 19, 2007, referred to in subsec. (*o*)(7)(D)(iii), originally read "the date of enactment of this subparagraph", meaning the date of enactment of the Energy Independence and Security Act of 2007, Pub. L. No. 110–140, 121 Stat. 1492 (Dec. 19, 2007), which enacted subsec. (*o*)(7)(D) of this section.

The Energy Policy Act of 2005, referred to in subsec. (q)(1)(A), is Pub. L. No. 109–58, 119 Stat. 594 (Aug. 8, 2005), which is principally codified as chapter 149 of Title 42, 42 U.S.C.A. § 15801 et seq. For complete classification, see Short Title note set out under 42 U.S.C.A. § 15801 and Tables.

Executive Order 13134, referred to in subsec. (s)(4)(B), which was set out as a note under 7 U.S.C.A. § 8601, was revoked by Ex. Ord. No. 13423, 11(a)(iii), 72 Fed. Reg. 3923 (Jan. 24, 2007).

This part, referred to in subsec. (t)(1), originally read "this subtitle" which was translated as "this part", meaning part A of Title II of Act of July 14, 1955, as the probable intent of Congress, because Title II of Act of July 14, 1955 does not contain subtitles.

August 8, 2005, referred to in subsec. (t)(6), (7), originally read "the date of enactment of this subsection" and "the date of its enactment", respectively, meaning Aug. 8, 2005, the date of enactment of the Energy Policy Act of 2005, Pub. L. No. 109–58, 119 Stat. 594, which enacted subsec. (t) of this section.

December 19, 2007, referred to in subsec. (u)(1) and (2), originally read "the date of enactment of this subsection", meaning the date of enactment of the Energy Independence and Security Act of 2007, Pub. L. No. 110–140, 121 Stat. 1492 (Dec. 19, 2007), which enacted subsection (u) of this section.

December 19, 2007, referred to in subsec. (u)(3), originally read "the date of the enactment of this subsection", meaning the date of enactment of the Energy Independence and Security Act of 2007, Pub. L. No. 110–140, 121 Stat. 1492 (Dec. 19, 2007), which enacted subsection (u) of this section.

December 19, 2007, referred to in subsec. (u)(4), originally read "the enactment of this subsection", meaning the date of enactment of the Energy Independence and Security Act of 2007, Pub. L. No. 110–140, 121 Stat. 1492 (Dec. 19, 2007), which was approved Dec. 19, 2007 and which enacted subsection (u) of this section.

This chapter, referred to in subsec. (v), originally read "this Act", meaning the Clean Air Act, Act of July 14, 1955, c. 360, 69 Stat. 322, as amended, also known as CAA and the Air Pollution Control Act, which is codified principally as this chapter. For complete classification, see Short Title note set out under 42 U.S.C.A. § 7401 and Tables.

December 19, 2007, referred to in subsec. (v)(1)(A) and (2), originally read "the date of enactment of this subsection", meaning the date of enactment of the Energy Independence and Security Act of 2007, Pub. L. No. 110–140, 121 Stat. 1492 (Dec. 19, 2007), which enacted subsection (v) of this section.

Codifications

This section was formerly codified as section 1857f–6c of this title.

Pub. L. No. 110–140, Title II, § 208(1), 121 Stat. 1531 (Dec. 19, 2007), which directed in par. (1) of subsec. (c) of this section, the striking of "nonroad vehicle (A) if in the judgment of the Administrator" and inserting "nonroad vehicle if, in the judgment of the Administrator, any fuel or fuel additive or" resulted in the deletion of the clause (A) designation without a corresponding change to the existing clause (B) designation in par. (1) or references in other subsections of this section to clause (A) of par. (1) of subsec. (c).

Effective and Applicability Provisions

2007 Acts. Pub. L. No. 110–140, Title II, § 210(c), 121 Stat. 1532 (Dec. 19, 2007), provided that: "The amendments made by this title to section 211(*o*) of the Clean Air Act [Pub. L. No. 110–140, Title II, §§ 201, 202, 203(f), and 210(b), 121 Stat. 1519, 1529, and 1532 (Dec. 19, 2007), amended subsec. (*o*) of this section] shall take effect January 1, 2009, except that the Administrator shall promulgate regulations to carry out such amendments not later than 1 year after the enactment of this Act [Dec. 19, 2007]."

Amendment by Pub. L. 110–140 effective on the date that is 1 day after December 19, 2007, see Pub. L. No. 110–140, § 1601, set out as a note under 2 U.S.C.A. § 1824.

2005 Acts. Pub. L. No. 109–58, Title XV, § 1504(a)(2), 119 Stat. 1077 (Aug. 8, 2005), provided that:

"The amendments made by paragraph (1) [amending subsec. (k) of this section] apply—

"(A) in the case of a State that has received a waiver under section 209(b) of the Clean Air Act (42 U.S.C. 7543(b)), beginning on the date of enactment of this Act [Aug. 8, 2005]; and

"(B) in the case of any other State, beginning 270 days after the date of enactment of this Act [Aug. 8, 2005]."

1990 Acts. Amendment by Pub. L. No. 101–549 effective Nov. 15, 1990, except as otherwise provided, see section 711(b) of Pub. L. No. 101–549, set out as a note under section 7401 of this title.

1977 Acts. Amendment by Pub. L. No. 95–95 effective Aug. 7, 1977, except as otherwise expressly provided, see section 406(d) of Pub. L. No. 95–95, set out as a note under section 7401 of this title.

Savings Provisions

Suits, actions or proceedings commenced under this chapter as in effect prior to Nov. 15, 1990, not to abate by reason of the taking effect of amendments by Pub. L. No. 101–549, except as otherwise provided for, see section 711(a) of Pub. L. No. 101–549, set out as a note under section 7401 of this title.

Prior Provisions

A prior section 211 of Act of July 14, 1955, as added by Pub. L. No. 90–148, § 2, 81 Stat. 503 (Nov. 21, 1967), providing for a national emissions standards study, was set out as section 1857f–6d of this title and was repealed by Pub. L. No. 91–604, § 8(a), 84 Stat. 1694 (Dec. 31, 1970).

Environmental and Resource Conservation Impacts

Pub. L. No. 110–140, Title II, § 204, 121 Stat. 1529 (Dec. 19, 2007), provided that:

"(a) In general.—Not later than 3 years after the enactment of this section [Dec. 19, 2007] and every 3 years thereafter, the Administrator of the Environmental Protection Agency, in consultation with the Secretary of Agriculture and the Secretary of Energy, shall assess and report to Congress on the impacts to date and likely future impacts of the requirements of section 211(*o*) of the Clean Air Act [subsec. (*o*) of this section] on the following:

"(1) Environmental issues, including air quality, effects on hypoxia, pesticides, sediment, nutrient and pathogen levels in waters, acreage and function of waters, and soil environmental quality.

"(2) Resource conservation issues, including soil conservation, water availability, and ecosystem health and biodiversity, including impacts on forests, grasslands, and wetlands.

"(3) The growth and use of cultivated invasive or noxious plants and their impacts on the environment and agriculture.

"In advance of preparing the report required by this subsection, the Administrator may seek the views of the National Academy of Sciences or another appropriate independent research institute. The report shall include the annual volume of imported renewable fuels and feedstocks for renewable fuels, and the environmental impacts outside the United States of producing such fuels and feedstocks. The report required by this subsection shall include recommendations for actions to address any adverse impacts found

"(b) Effect on air quality and other environmental requirements.—Except as provided in section 211(*o*)(12) of the Clean Air Act [subsec. (*o*)(12) of this section], nothing in the amendments made by this title to section 211(*o*) of the Clean Air Act [Pub. L. No. 110–140, Title II, §§ 201, 202, 203(f), and 210(b), Dec. 19, 2007, 121 Stat. 1519, 1529, and 1532, amending subsec. (*o*) of this section] shall be construed as superseding, or limiting, any more environmentally protective requirement under the Clean Air Act [Act of July 14, 1955, c. 360, 69 Stat. 322, as amended, also known as CAA and the Air Pollution Control Act, which is codified principally as this chapter. For complete classification, see Short Title note set out under 42 U.S.C.A. § 7401 and Tables], or under any other provision of State or Federal law or regulation, including any environmental law or regulation."

[Enactment by Pub. L. 110–140 effective on the date that is 1 day after December 19, 2007, see Pub. L. No. 110–140, § 1601, set out as a note under 2 U.S.C.A. § 1824.]

Transition Rules

Pub. L. No. 110–140, Title II, § 210(a), 121 Stat. 1532 (Dec. 19, 2007), provided that:

"(1) For calendar year 2008, transportation fuel sold or introduced into commerce in the United States (except in noncontiguous States or territories), that is produced from facilities that commence construction after the date of enactment of this Act [Dec. 19, 2007] shall be treated as renewable fuel within the meaning of section 211(*o*) of the Clean Air Act [subsec. (*o*) of this section] only if it achieves at least a 20 percent reduction in lifecycle greenhouse gas emissions compared to baseline lifecycle greenhouse gas emissions. For calendar years 2008 and 2009, any ethanol plant that is fired with natural gas, biomass, or any combination thereof is deemed to be in compliance with such 20 percent reduction requirement and with the 20 percent reduction requirement of section 211(*o*)(1) of the Clean Air Act [subsec. (*o*)(1) of this section]. The terms used in this subsection shall have the same meaning as provided in the amendment made by this Act to section 211(*o*) of the Clean Air Act [Pub. L. No. 110–140, Title II, §§ 201, 202, 203(f), and 210(b), 121 Stat. 1519, 1529, and 1532 (Dec. 19, 2007), amending subsec. (*o*) of this section].

"(2) Until January 1, 2009, the Administrator of the Environmental Protection Agency shall implement section 211(*o*) of the Clean Air Act [subsec. (*o*) of this section] and the rules promulgated under that section in accordance with the provisions of that section as in effect before the enactment of this Act [Energy Independence and Security Act of 2007, Pub. L. No. 110–140, 121 Stat. 1492 (Dec. 19, 2007), which was approved Dec. 19, 2007] and in accordance with the rules promulgated before the enactment of this Act, except that for calendar year 2008, the number '9.0' shall be substituted for the number '5.4' in the table in section 211(*o*)(2)(B) [subsec. (*o*)(2)(B) of this section] and in the corresponding rules promulgated to carry out those provisions. The Administrator is authorized to take such other actions as may be necessary to carry out this paragraph notwithstanding any other provision of law."

Survey of Renewable Fuel Market

Pub. L. No. 109–58, Title XV, § 1501(d), 119 Stat. 1075 (Aug. 8, 2005), provided that:

"(1) Survey and report.—Not later than December 1, 2006, and annually thereafter, the Administrator of the Environmental Protection Agency (in consultation with the Secretary acting through the Administrator of the Energy Information Administration) shall—

"(A) conduct, with respect to each conventional gasoline use area and each reformulated gasoline use area in each state, a survey to determine the market shares of—

"(i) conventional gasoline containing ethanol;

"(ii) reformulated gasoline containing ethanol;

"(iii) conventional gasoline containing renewable fuel; and

"(iv) reformulated gasoline containing renewable fuel; and

"(B) submit to Congress, and make publicly available, a report on the results of the survey under subparagraph (A).

"(2) Recordkeeping and reporting requirements.—The Administrator of the Environmental Protection Agency (hereinafter in this subsection [this note] referred to as the 'Administrator') may require any refiner, blender, or importer to keep such records and make such reports as are necessary to ensure that the survey conducted under paragraph (1) is accurate. The Administrator, to avoid duplicative requirements, shall rely, to the extent practicable, on existing reporting and recordkeeping requirements and other information available to the Administrator including gasoline distribution patterns that include multistate use areas.

"(3) Applicable law.—Activities carried out under this subsection [this note] shall be conducted in a manner designed to protect confidentiality of individual responses."

Findings

Pub. L. No. 109–58, Title XV, § 1502, 119 Stat. 1076 (Aug. 8, 2005), provided that:

"Congress finds that—

"(1) since 1979, methyl tertiary butyl ether (hereinafter in this section referred to as 'MTBE') has been used nationwide at low levels in gasoline to replace lead as an octane booster or anti-knocking agent;

"(2) Public Law 101–549 (commonly known as the 'Clean Air Act Amendments of 1990') (42 U.S.C. 7401 et seq.) established a fuel oxygenate standard under which reformulated gasoline must contain at least 2 percent oxygen by weight; and

"(3) The fuel industry responded to the fuel oxygenate standard established by Public Law 101–549 by making substantial investments in—

"(A) MTBE production capacity; and

"(B) systems to deliver MTBE-containing gasoline to the marketplace."

Claims Filed After Enactment

Pub. L. No. 109–58, Title XV, § 1503, 119 Stat. 1076 (Aug. 8, 2005), provided that: "Claims and legal actions filed after the date of enactment of this Act [Aug. 8, 2005] related to allegations involving actual or threatened contamination of methyl tertiary butyl ether (MTBE) may be removed to the appropriate United States district court."

Savings Clause

Pub. L. No. 109–58, Title XV, § 1504(d), 119 Stat. 1079 (Aug. 8, 2005), provided that:

"(1) In general.—Nothing in this section or any amendment made by this section [amending subsec. (k) of this section and enacting provisions set out as notes under this section] affects or prejudices any legal claim or action with respect to regulations promulgated by the Administrator before the date of enactment of this Act [Aug. 8, 2005] regarding—

"(A) emissions of toxic air pollutants from motor vehicles; or

"(B) the adjustment of standards applicable to a specific refinery or importer made under those regulations.

"(2) Adjustment of standards.—

"(A) Applicability.—The Administrator may apply any adjustments to the standards applicable to a refinery or importer under subparagraph (B)(iii)(I) of section 211(k)(1) of the Clean Air Act (as added by subsection (b)(2)) [subsec. (k)(1)(B)(iii)(I) of this section], except that—

"(i) the Administrator shall revise the adjustments to be based only on calendar years 1999 and 2000;

"(ii) any such adjustment shall not be made at a level below the average percentage of reductions of emissions of toxic air pollutants for reformulated gasoline supplied to PADD I during calendar years 1999 and 2000; and

"(iii) In the case of an adjustment based on toxic air pollutant emissions from reformulated gasoline significantly below the National annual average emissions of toxic air pollutants from all reformulated gasoline—

"(I) the Administrator may revise the adjustment to take account of the scope of the prohibition on methyl tertiary butyl ether imposed by a State; and

"(II) any such adjustment shall require the refiner or importer, to the maximum extent practicable, to maintain the reduction achieved during calendar years 1999 and 2000 in the average annual aggregate emissions of toxic air pollutants from reformulated gasoline produced or distributed by the refiner or importer."

Findings and Sense of Congress on Ethanol Usage

Pub. L. No. 100–203, Title I, § 1508, 101 Stat. 1330–29 (Dec. 22, 1987), provided that:

"(a) Findings.—Congress finds that—

"(1) the United States is dependent for a large and growing share of its energy needs on the Middle East at a time when world petroleum reserves are declining;

"(2) the burning of gasoline causes pollution;

"(3) ethanol can be blended with gasoline to produce a cleaner source of fuel;

"(4) ethanol can be produced from grain, a renewable resource that is in considerable surplus in the United States;

"(5) the conversion of grain into ethanol would reduce farm program costs and grain surpluses; and

"(6) increasing the quantity of motor fuels that contain at least 10 percent ethanol from current levels to 50 percent by 1992 would create thousands of new jobs in ethanol production facilities.

"(b) Sense of Congress.—It is the sense of Congress that the Administrator of the Environmental Protection Agency should use authority provided under the Clean Air Act (42 U.S.C. 7401 et seq.) [42 U.S.C.A. § 7401 et seq.] to require greater use of ethanol as motor fuel."

Agricultural Machinery: Study of Unleaded Fuel

Pub. L. No. 99–198, Title XVII, § 1765, 99 Stat. 1653 (Dec. 23, 1985), directed the Administrator of the Environmental Protection Agency and the Secretary of Agriculture to conduct jointly a study of the use of fuel containing lead additives and alternative lubricating additives in gasoline engines that are used in agricultural machinery and are designed to combust fuel containing such additives, with the results of the study to be published not later than January 1, 1987.

Modification or Rescission of Rules, Regulations, Orders, Determinations, Contracts, Certifications, Authorizations, Delegations, and Other Actions

All rules, regulations, orders, determinations, contracts, certifications, authorizations, delegations, or other actions duly issued, made, or taken by or pursuant to Act of July 14, 1955, the Clean Air Act, as in effect immediately prior to the date of enactment of Pub. L. No. 95–95 [Aug. 7, 1977] to continue in full force and effect until modified or rescinded in accordance with Act of July 14, 1955, as amended by Pub. L. No. 95–95 [this chapter], see section 406(b) of Pub. L. No. 95–95, set out as an Effective Date of 1977 Acts note under section 7401 of this title.

§ 7546. Renewable fuel

[CAA § 212]

(a) Definitions

In this section:

(1) Municipal solid waste

The term "municipal solid waste" has the meaning given the term "solid waste" in section 6903 of this title.

(2) RFG State

The term "RFG State" means a State in which is located one or more covered areas (as defined in section 7545(k)(10)(D) of this title).

(3) Secretary

The term "Secretary" means the Secretary of Energy.

(b) Cellulosic biomass ethanol and municipal solid waste loan guarantee program

(1) In general

Funds may be provided for the cost (as defined in the Federal Credit Reform Act of 1990 (2 U.S.C. 661 et seq.)) of loan guarantees issued under title XIV of the Energy Policy Act to carry out commercial demonstration projects for celluosic biomass and sucrose-derived ethanol.

(2) Demonstration projects

(A) In general

The Secretary shall issue loan guarantees under this section to carry out not more than 4 projects to commercially demonstrate the feasibility and viability of producing cellulosic biomass ethanol or sucrose-derived ethanol, including at least 1 project that uses cereal straw as a feedstock and 1 project that uses municipal solid waste as a feedstock.

(B) Design capacity

Each project shall have a design capacity to produce at least 30,000,000 gallons of cellulosic biomass ethanol each year.

(3) Applicant assurances

An applicant for a loan guarantee under this section shall provide assurances, satisfactory to the Secretary, that—

(A) the project design has been validated through the operation of a continuous process facility with a cumulative output of at least 50,000 gallons of ethanol;

(B) the project has been subject to a full technical review;

(C) the project is covered by adequate project performance guarantees;

(D) the project, with the loan guarantee, is economically viable; and

(E) there is a reasonable assurance of repayment of the guaranteed loan.

(4) Limitations

(A) Maximum guarantee

Except as provided in subparagraph (B), a loan guarantee under this section may be issued for up to 80 percent of the estimated cost of a project, but may not exceed $250,000,000 for a project.

(B) Additional guarantees

(i) In general

The Secretary may issue additional loan guarantees for a project to cover up to 80 percent of the excess of actual project cost over estimated project cost but not to exceed 15 percent of the amount of the original guarantee.

(ii) **Principal and interest**

Subject to subparagraph (A), the Secretary shall guarantee 100 percent of the principal and interest of a loan made under subparagraph (A).

(5) **Equity contributions**

To be eligible for a loan guarantee under this section, an applicant for the loan guarantee shall have binding commitments from equity investors to provide an initial equity contribution of at least 20 percent of the total project cost.

(6) **Insufficient amounts**

If the amount made available to carry out this section is insufficient to allow the Secretary to make loan guarantees for 3 projects described in subsection (b) of this section, the Secretary shall issue loan guarantees for one or more qualifying projects under this section in the order in which the applications for the projects are received by the Secretary.

(7) **Approval**

An application for a loan guarantee under this section shall be approved or disapproved by the Secretary not later than 90 days after the application is received by the Secretary.

(c) **Authorization of appropriations for resource center**

There is authorized to be appropriated, for a resource center to further develop bioconversion technology using low-cost biomass for the production of ethanol at the Center for Biomass-Based Energy at the Mississippi State University and the Oklahoma State University, $4,000,000 for each of fiscal years 2005 through 2007.

(d) **Renewable fuel production research and development grants**

(1) **In general**

The Administrator shall provide grants for the research into, and development and implementation of, renewable fuel production technologies in RFG States with low rates of ethanol production, including low rates of production of cellulosic biomass ethanol.

(2) **Eligibility**

(A) **In general**

The entities eligible to receive a grant under this subsection are academic institutions in RFG States, and consortia made up of combinations of academic institutions, industry, State government agencies, or local government agencies in RFG States, that have proven experience and capabilities with relevant technologies.

(B) **Application**

To be eligible to receive a grant under this subsection, an eligible entity shall submit to the Administrator an application in such manner and form, and accompanied by such information, as the Administrator may specify.

(3) **Authorization of appropriations**

There is authorized to be appropriated to carry out this subsection $25,000,000 for each of fiscal years 2006 through 2010.

(e) **Cellulosic biomass ethanol conversion assistance**

(1) **In general**

The Secretary may provide grants to merchant producers of cellulosic biomass ethanol in the United States to assist the producers in building eligible production facilities described in paragraph (2) for the production of cellulosic biomass ethanol.

(2) Eligible production facilities

A production facility shall be eligible to receive a grant under this subsection if the production facility—

(A) is located in the United States; and

(B) uses cellulosic biomass feedstocks derived from agricultural residues or municipal solid waste.

(3) Authorization of appropriations

There is authorized to be appropriated to carry out this subsection—

(A) $250,000,000 for fiscal year 2006; and

(B) $400,000,000 for fiscal year 2007.

(July 14, 1955, c. 360, Title II, § 212, as added by Pub. L. No. 109–58, Title XV, § 1511, 119 Stat. 1086 (Aug. 8, 2005).)

HISTORICAL AND STATUTORY NOTES

References in Text

The Federal Credit Reform Act of 1990, referred to in subsec. (b)(1), is Title V of Pub. L. 93–344, as added Pub. L. 101–508, Title XIII, § 13201(a), 104 Stat. 1388–609 (Nov. 5, 1990), and amended, which is codified principally as subchapter III of chapter 17A of Title 2, 2 U.S.C.A. § 661 et seq. For complete classification, see Short Title note set out under 2 U.S.C.A. § 621 and Tables.

Title XIV of the Energy Policy Act, referred to in subsec. (b)(1), probably means Title XIV of the Energy Policy Act of 2005, Pub. L. No. 109–58, Title XIV, § 1401 et seq., 119 Stat. 1061 (Aug. 8, 2005), which principally enacted subchapter XIII of chapter 149 of Title 42, 42 U.S.C.A. § 16491 et seq. For complete classification, see Short Title note set out under 42 U.S.C.A. § 15801 and Tables.

Prior Provisions

A prior section 7546, Act of July 14, 1955, c. 360, Title II, § 212, as added by Pub. L. No. 91–604, § 10(c), 84 Stat. 1700 (Dec. 31, 1970), and amended by Pub. L. No. 91–605, § 202(a), 84 Stat. 1739 (Dec. 31, 1970); Pub. L. No. 93–15, § 1(b), 87 Stat. 11 (Apr. 9, 1973); Pub. L. No. 93–319, § 13(b), 88 Stat. 265 (June 22, 1974), relating to low-emission vehicles, was repealed by Pub. L. No. 101–549, Title II, § 230(10), 104 Stat. 2529 (Nov. 15, 1990).

Repeal of section effective Nov. 15, 1990, except as otherwise provided, see section 711(b) of Pub. L. No. 101–549, set out as an Effective Date of 1977 Acts note under section 7401 of this title.

Another prior section 212 of Act of July 14, 1955, was renumbered section 213 by Pub. L. No. 91–604, renumbered section 214 by Pub. L. No. 93–319, and renumbered section 216 by Pub. L. No. 95–95, and is codified as section 7550 of this title.

§ 7547. Nonroad engines and vehicles

[CAA § 213]

(a) Emissions standards

(1) The Administrator shall conduct a study of emissions from nonroad engines and nonroad vehicles (other than locomotives or engines used in locomotives) to determine if such emissions cause, or significantly contribute to, air pollution which may reasonably be anticipated to endanger public health or welfare. Such study shall be completed within 12 months of November 15, 1990.

(2) After notice and opportunity for public hearing, the Administrator shall determine within 12 months after completion of the study under paragraph (1), based upon the results of such study, whether emissions of carbon monoxide, oxides of nitrogen, and volatile organic compounds from new and existing nonroad engines or nonroad vehicles (other than locomotives or engines used in locomotives) are significant contributors to ozone or carbon monoxide concentrations in more than 1 area which has failed to attain the national ambient air quality standards for ozone or carbon monoxide. Such determination shall be included in the regulations under paragraph (3).

(3) If the Administrator makes an affirmative determination under paragraph (2) the Administrator shall, within 12 months after completion of the study under paragraph (1), promulgate (and from time to time revise) regulations containing standards applicable to emissions from those classes or categories of new nonroad engines and new nonroad vehicles (other than locomotives or engines used in locomotives) which in the Administrator's judgment cause, or contribute to, such air pollution. Such standards shall achieve the greatest degree of emission reduction achievable through the application of technology which the Administrator determines will be available for the engines or vehicles to which such standards apply, giving appropriate consideration to the cost of applying such technology within the period of time available to manufacturers and to noise, energy, and safety factors associated with the application of such technology. In determining what degree of reduction will be available, the Administrator shall first consider standards equivalent in stringency to standards for comparable motor vehicles or engines (if any) regulated under section 7521 of this title, taking into account the technological feasibility, costs, safety, noise, and energy factors associated with achieving, as appropriate, standards of such stringency and lead time. The regulations shall apply to the useful life of the engines or vehicles (as determined by the Administrator).

(4) If the Administrator determines that any emissions not referred to in paragraph (2) from new nonroad engines or vehicles significantly contribute to air pollution which may reasonably be anticipated to endanger public health or welfare, the Administrator may promulgate (and from time to time revise) such regulations as the Administrator deems appropriate containing standards applicable to emissions from those classes or categories of new nonroad engines and new nonroad vehicles (other than locomotives or engines used in locomotives) which in the Administrator's judgment cause, or contribute to, such air pollution, taking into account costs, noise, safety, and energy factors associated with the application of technology which the Administrator determines will be available for the engines and vehicles to which such standards apply. The regulations shall apply to the useful life of the engines or vehicles (as determined by the Administrator).

(5) Within 5 years after November 15, 1990, the Administrator shall promulgate regulations containing standards applicable to emissions from new locomotives and new engines used in locomotives. Such standards shall achieve the greatest degree of emission reduction achievable through the application of technology which the Administrator determines will be available for the locomotives or engines to which such standards apply, giving appropriate consideration to the cost of applying such technology within the period of time available to manufacturers and to noise, energy, and safety factors associated with the application of such technology.

(b) Effective date

Standards under this section shall take effect at the earliest possible date considering the lead time necessary to permit the development and application of the requisite technology, giving appropriate consideration to the cost of compliance within such period and energy and safety.

(c) Safe controls

Effective with respect to new engines or vehicles to which standards under this section apply, no emission control device, system, or element of design shall be used in such a new nonroad engine or new nonroad vehicle for purposes of complying with such standards if such device, system, or element of design will cause or contribute to an unreasonable risk to public health, welfare, or safety in its operation or function. In determining whether an unreasonable risk exists, the Administrator shall consider factors including those described in section 7521(a)(4)(B) of this title.

(d) Enforcement

The standards under this section shall be subject to sections 7525, 7541, 7542, and 7543 of this title, with such modifications of the applicable regulations implementing such sections as the Administrator deems appropriate, and shall be enforced in the same manner as standards prescribed under section 7521 of this title. The Administrator shall revise or promulgate regulations as may be necessary to determine compliance with, and enforce, standards in effect under this section.

(July 14, 1955, c. 360, Title II, § 213, as added by Pub. L. No. 93–319, § 10, 88 Stat. 261 (June 22, 1974); and amended by Pub. L. No. 101–549, Title II, § 222(a), 104 Stat. 2500 (Nov. 15, 1990).)

HISTORICAL AND STATUTORY NOTES

Codifications

This section was formerly codified as section 1857f–6f of this title.

Effective and Applicability Provisions

1990 Acts. Amendment by Pub. L. No. 101–549 effective Nov. 15, 1990, except as otherwise provided, see section 711(b) of Pub. L. No. 101–549, set out as a note under section 7401 of this title.

Change of Name

The Committee on Public Works and the Committee on Commerce of the Senate were abolished and replaced by the Committee on Environment and Public Works and the Committee on Commerce, Science, and Transportation of the Senate, respectively, effective Feb. 11, 1977. See Rule XXV of the Standing Rules of the Senate, as amended by Senate Resolution 4 (popularly cited as the "Committee System Reorganization Amendments of 1977"), approved Feb. 4, 1977.

Savings Provisions

Suits, actions or proceedings commenced under this chapter as in effect prior to Nov. 15, 1990, not to abate by reason of the taking effect of amendments by Pub. L. No. 101–549, except as otherwise provided for, see section 711(a) of Pub. L. No. 101–549, set out as a note under section 7401 of this title.

Prior Provisions

A prior section 213 of Act of July 14, 1955, was renumbered section 214 by Pub. L. No. 93–319 and renumbered section 216 by Pub. L. No. 95–95, and is codified as section 7550 of this title.

Regulations Relating to Standards to Reduce Emissions

Pub. L. No. 108–199, Div. G., Title IV, § 428(b), 118 Stat. 418 (Jan. 23, 2004), provided that: "Not later than December 1, 2004, the Administrator of the Environmental Protection Agency shall propose regulations under the Clean Air Act [Act of July 14, 1955, c. 360, 69 Stat. 322; see Tables for classification] that shall contain standards to reduce emissions from new nonroad spark-ignition engines smaller than 50 horsepower. Not later than December 31, 2005, the Administrator shall publish in the Federal Register final regulations containing such standards."

Federal Energy Administrator

The "Federal Energy Administrator", for purposes of this chapter, to mean the Administrator of the Federal Energy Administration established by Pub. L. No. 93–275, 88 Stat. 97 (May 7, 1974) [section 761 et seq. of Title 15, Commerce and Trade], but with the term to mean any officer of the United States designated as such by the President until the Federal Energy Administration takes office and after it ceases to exist, see section 798(a) of Title 15, Commerce and Trade.

The Federal Energy Administration was terminated and functions vested by law in the Administrator thereof were transferred to the Secretary of Energy (unless otherwise specifically provided) by sections 7151(a) and 7293 of this title.

§ 7548. Study of particulate emissions from motor vehicles

[CAA § 214]

(a) Study and analysis

(1) The Administrator shall conduct a study concerning the effects on health and welfare of particulate emissions from motor vehicles or motor vehicle engines to which section 7521 of this title applies. Such study shall characterize and quantify such emissions and analyze the relationship of such emissions to various fuels and fuel additives.

(2) The study shall also include an analysis of particulate emissions from mobile sources which are not related to engine emissions (including, but not limited to tire debris, and asbestos from brake lining).

(b) Report to Congress

The Administrator shall report to the Congress the findings and results of the study conducted under subsection (a) of this section not later than two years after August 7, 1977. Such report shall also include recommendations for standards or methods to regulate particulate emissions described in paragraph (2) of subsection (a) of this section.

(July 14, 1955, c. 360, Title II, § 214, as added by Pub. L. No. 95–95, Title II, § 224(d), 91 Stat. 767 (Aug. 7, 1977).)

HISTORICAL AND STATUTORY NOTES

Effective and Applicability Provisions

1977 Acts. Section effective Aug. 7, 1977, except as otherwise expressly provided, see section 406(d) of Pub. L. No. 95–95, set out as a note under section 7401 of this title.

Prior Provisions

A prior section 214 of Act of July 14, 1955, was renumbered section 216 by Pub. L. No. 95–95, and is codified as section 7550 of this title.

Study on Suspended Particulate Matter

Section 403(a) of Pub. L. No. 95–95 provided that not later than 18 months after Aug. 7, 1977, the Administrator of the Environmental Protection Agency, in cooperation with the National Academy of Sciences, study and report to Congress on the relationship between the size, weight, and chemical composition of suspended particulate matter and the nature and degree of the endangerment to public health or welfare presented by such particulate matter and the availability of technology for controlling such particulate matter.

§ 7549. High altitude performance adjustments

[CAA § 215]

(a) Instruction of the manufacturer

(1) Any action taken with respect to any element of design installed on or in a motor vehicle or motor vehicle engine in compliance with regulations under this subchapter (including any alteration or adjustment of such element), shall be treated as not in violation of section 7522(a) of this title if such action is performed in accordance with high altitude adjustment instructions provided by the manufacturer under subsection (b) of this section and approved by the Administrator.

(2) If the Administrator finds that adjustments or modifications made pursuant to instructions of the manufacturer under paragraph (1) will not insure emission control performance with respect to each standard under section 7521 of this title at least equivalent to that which would result if no such adjustments or modifications were made, he shall disapprove such instructions. Such finding shall be based upon minimum engineering evaluations consistent with good engineering practice.

(b) Regulations

(1) Instructions respecting each class or category of vehicles or engines to which this subchapter applies providing for such vehicle and engine adjustments and modifications as may be necessary to insure emission control performance at different altitudes shall be submitted by the manufacturer to the Administrator pursuant to regulations promulgated by the Administrator.

(2) Any knowing violation by a manufacturer of requirements of the Administrator under paragraph (1) shall be treated as a violation by such manufacturer of section 7522(a)(3) of this title for purposes of the penalties contained in section 7524 of this title.

(3) Such instructions shall provide, in addition to other adjustments, for adjustments for vehicles moving from high altitude areas to low altitude areas after the initial registration of such vehicles.

(c) Manufacturer parts

No instructions under this section respecting adjustments or modifications may require the use of any manufacturer parts (as defined in section 7522(a) of this title) unless the manufacturer demonstrates to the satisfaction of the Administrator that the use of such manufacturer parts is necessary to insure emission control performance.

(d) State inspection and maintenance programs

Before January 1, 1981 the authority provided by this section shall be available in any high altitude State (as determined under regulations of the Administrator under regulations promulgated before August 7, 1977) but after December 31, 1980, such authority shall be available only in any such State in which an inspection and maintenance program for the testing of motor vehicle emissions has been instituted for the portions of the State where any national ambient air quality standard for auto-related pollutants has not been attained.

(e) High altitude testing

(1) The Administrator shall promptly establish at least one testing center (in addition to the testing centers existing on November 15, 1990) located at a site that represents high altitude conditions, to ascertain in a reasonable manner whether, when in actual use throughout their useful life (as determined under section 7521(d) of this title), each class or category of vehicle and engines to which regulations under section 7521 of this title apply conforms to the emissions standards established by such regulations. For purposes of this subsection, the term "high altitude conditions" refers to high altitude as defined in regulations of the Administrator in effect as of November 15, 1990.

(2) The Administrator, in cooperation with the Secretary of Energy and the Administrator of the Federal Transit Administration, and such other agencies as the Administrator deems appropriate, shall establish a research and technology assessment center to provide for the development and evaluation of less-polluting heavy-duty engines and fuels for use in buses, heavy-duty trucks, and non-road engines and vehicles, which shall be located at a high-altitude site that represents high-altitude conditions. In establishing and funding such a center, the Administrator shall give preference to proposals which provide for local cost-sharing of facilities and recovery of costs of operation through utilization of such facility for the purposes of this section.

(3) The Administrator shall designate at least one center at high-altitude conditions to provide research on after-market emission components, dual-fueled vehicles and conversion kits, the effects of tampering on emissions equipment, testing of alternate fuels and conversion kits, and the development of curricula, training courses, and materials to maximize the effectiveness of inspection and maintenance programs as they relate to promoting effective control of vehicle emissions at high-altitude elevations. Preference shall be given to existing vehicle emissions testing and research centers that have established reputations for vehicle emissions research and development and training, and that possess in-house Federal Test Procedure capacity.

(July 14, 1955, c. 360, Title II, § 215, as added by Pub. L. No. 95–95, Title II, § 211(b), 91 Stat. 757 (Aug. 7, 1977); and amended by Pub. L. No. 95–190, § 14(a)(75), 91 Stat. 1404 (Nov. 16, 1977); Pub. L. No. 101–549, Title II, § 224, 104 Stat. 2503 (Nov. 15, 1990); Pub. L. No. 102–240, Title III, § 3004(b), 105 Stat. 2088 (Dec. 18, 1991).)

HISTORICAL AND STATUTORY NOTES

Codifications

In subsec. (d), "August 7, 1977" was substituted for "the date of enactment of this Act" to reflect the probable intent of Congress that such date of enactment meant the date of enactment of Pub. L. No. 95–95.

Effective and Applicability Provisions

1990 Acts. Amendment by Pub. L. No. 101–549 effective Nov. 15, 1990, except as otherwise provided, see section 711(b) of Pub. L. No. 101–549, set out as a note under section 7401 of this title.

1977 Acts. Section effective Aug. 7, 1977, except as otherwise expressly provided, see section 406(d) of Pub. L. No. 95–95, set out as a note under section 7401 of this title.

Change of Name

Any reference in a law, map, regulation, document, paper, or other record of the United States to the Urban Mass Transportation Administration deemed a reference to the Federal Transit Administration, see section 3004(b) of Pub. L. No. 102–240, set out as a note under section 107 of Title 49, Transportation.

Savings Provisions

Suits, actions or proceedings commenced under this chapter as in effect prior to Nov. 15, 1990, not to abate by reason of the taking effect of amendments by Pub. L. No. 101–549, except as otherwise provided for, see section 711(a) of Pub. L. No. 101–549, set out as a note under section 7401 of this title.

§ 7550. Definitions

[CAA § 216]

As used in this part—

(1) The term "manufacturer" as used in sections 7521, 7522, 7525, 7541, and 7542 of this title means any person engaged in the manufacturing or assembling of new motor vehicles, new motor vehicle engines, new nonroad vehicles or new nonroad engines, or importing such vehicles or engines for resale, or who acts for and is under the control of any such person in connection with the distribution of new motor vehicles, new motor vehicle engines, new nonroad vehicles or new nonroad engines, but shall not include any dealer with respect to new motor vehicles, new motor vehicle engines, new nonroad vehicles or new nonroad engines received by him in commerce.

(2) The term "motor vehicle" means any self-propelled vehicle designed for transporting persons or property on a street or highway.

(3) Except with respect to vehicles or engines imported or offered for importation, the term "new motor vehicle" means a motor vehicle the equitable or legal title to which has never been transferred to an ultimate purchaser; and the term "new motor vehicle engine" means an engine in a new motor vehicle or a motor vehicle engine the equitable or legal title to which has never been transferred to the ultimate purchaser; and with respect to imported vehicles or engines, such terms mean a motor vehicle and engine, respectively, manufactured after the effective date of a regulation issued under section 7521 of this title which is applicable to such vehicle or engine (or which would be applicable to such vehicle or engine had it been manufactured for importation into the United States).

(4) The term "dealer" means any person who is engaged in the sale or the distribution of new motor vehicles or new motor vehicle engines to the ultimate purchaser.

(5) The term "ultimate purchaser" means, with respect to any new motor vehicle or new motor vehicle engine, the first person who in good faith purchases such new motor vehicle or new engine for purposes other than resale.

(6) The term "commerce" means (A) commerce between any place in any State and any place outside thereof; and (B) commerce wholly within the District of Columbia.

(7) Vehicle curb weight, gross vehicle weight rating, light-duty truck, light-duty vehicle, and loaded vehicle weight

The terms "vehicle curb weight", "gross vehicle weight rating" (GVWR), "light-duty truck" (LDT), light-duty vehicle,[1] and "loaded vehicle weight" (LVW) have the meaning provided in regulations promulgated by the Administrator and in effect as of November 15, 1990. The abbreviations in parentheses corresponding to any term referred to in this paragraph shall have the same meaning as the corresponding term.

(8) Test weight

The term "test weight" and the abbreviation "tw" mean the vehicle curb weight added to the gross vehicle weight rating (gvwr) and divided by 2.

(9) Motor vehicle or engine part manufacturer

The term "motor vehicle or engine part manufacturer" as used in sections 7541 and 7542 of this title means any person engaged in the manufacturing, assembling or rebuilding of any device, system, part, component or element of design which is installed in or on motor vehicles or motor vehicle engines.

(10) Nonroad engine

The term "nonroad engine" means an internal combustion engine (including the fuel system) that is not used in a motor vehicle or a vehicle used solely for competition, or that is not subject to standards promulgated under section 7411 of this title or section 7521 of this title.

(11) Nonroad vehicle

The term "nonroad vehicle" means a vehicle that is powered by a nonroad engine and that is not a motor vehicle or a vehicle used solely for competition.

(July 14, 1955, c. 360, Title II, § 216, formerly § 208, as added by Pub. L. No. 89–272, Title I, § 101(8), 79 Stat. 994 (Oct. 20, 1965); and renumbered § 212 and amended by Pub. L. No. 90–148, § 2, 81 Stat. 503 (Nov. 21, 1967); and renumbered § 213 and amended by Pub. L. No. 91–604, §§ 8(a), 10(d), 11(a)(2)(A), 84 Stat. 1694, 1703, 1705 (Dec. 31, 1970); and renumbered § 214 by Pub. L. No. 93–319, § 10, 88 Stat. 261 (June 22, 1974); and renumbered § 216 by Pub. L. No. 95–95, Title II, § 224(d), 91 Stat. 767 (Aug. 7, 1977); and amended by Pub. L. No. 101–549, Title II, § 223, 104 Stat. 2503 (Nov. 15, 1990).)

[1] So in original. Probably should be set off by quotation marks.

HISTORICAL AND STATUTORY NOTES

Codifications

This section was formerly codified as section 1857f–7 of this title.

Effective and Applicability Provisions

1990 Acts. Amendment by Pub. L. No. 101–549 effective Nov. 15, 1990, except as otherwise provided, see section 711(b) of Pub. L. No. 101–549, set out as a note under section 7401 of this title.

Savings Provisions

Suits, actions or proceedings commenced under this chapter as in effect prior to Nov. 15, 1990, not to abate by reason of the taking effect of amendments by Pub. L. No. 101–549, except as otherwise provided for, see section 711(a) of Pub. L. No. 101–549, set out as a note under section 7401 of this title.

§ 7551. Omitted

HISTORICAL AND STATUTORY NOTES

Codifications

Section, Pub. L. No. 95–95, Title II, § 203, 91 Stat. 754 (Aug. 7, 1977); as amended by Pub. L. No. 97–375, Title I, § 106(a), 96 Stat. 1820 (Dec. 21, 1982), which required the Administrator of the Environmental Protection Agency to report to Congress respecting the motor vehicle fuel consumption associated with the standards applicable for the immediately preceding model year, terminated, effective May 15, 2000, pursuant to Pub. L. No. 104–66, § 3003, as amended, set out as a note under 31 U.S.C.A. § 1113. See, also, the 5th item on page 165 of House Document No. 103–7.

This section was enacted as part of the Clean Air Act Amendments of 1977, and not as part of the Clean Air Act, which comprises this chapter.

§ 7552. Motor vehicle compliance program fees

[CAA § 217]

(a) Fee collection

Consistent with section 9701 of Title 31, the Administrator may promulgate (and from time to time revise) regulations establishing fees to recover all reasonable costs to the Administrator associated with—

(1) new vehicle or engine certification under section 7525(a) of this title or part C of this subchapter,

(2) new vehicle or engine compliance monitoring and testing under section 7525(b) of this title or part C of this subchapter, and

(3) in-use vehicle or engine compliance monitoring and testing under section 7541(c) of this title or part C of this subchapter.

The Administrator may establish for all foreign and domestic manufacturers a fee schedule based on such factors as the Administrator finds appropriate and equitable and nondiscriminatory, including the number of vehicles or engines produced under a certificate of conformity. In the case of heavy-duty engine and vehicle manufacturers, such fees shall not exceed a reasonable amount to recover an appropriate portion of such reasonable costs.

(b) Special Treasury fund

Any fees collected under this section shall be deposited in a special fund in the United States Treasury for licensing and other services which thereafter shall be available for appropriation, to remain available until expended, to carry out the Agency's activities for which the fees were collected.

(c) Limitation on fund use

Moneys in the special fund referred to in subsection (b) of this section shall not be used until after the first fiscal year commencing after the first July 1 when fees are paid into the fund.

(d) Administrator's testing authority

Nothing in this subsection shall be construed to limit the Administrator's authority to require manufacturer or confirmatory testing as provided in this part.

(July 14, 1955, c. 360, Title II, § 217, as added by Pub. L. No. 101–549, Title II, § 225, 104 Stat. 2504 (Nov. 15, 1990).)

HISTORICAL AND STATUTORY NOTES

Effective and Applicability Provisions

1990 Acts. Section effective Nov. 15, 1990, except as otherwise provided, see section 711(b) of Pub. L. No. 101–549, set out as a note under section 7401 of this title.

Savings Provisions

Suits, actions or proceedings commenced under this chapter as in effect prior to Nov. 15, 1990, not to abate by reason of the taking effect of amendments by Pub. L. No. 101–549, except as otherwise provided for, see section 711(a) of Pub. L. No. 101–549, set out as a note under section 7401 of this title.

§ 7553. Prohibition on production of engines requiring leaded gasoline

[CAA § 218]

The Administrator shall promulgate regulations applicable to motor vehicle engines and nonroad engines manufactured after model year 1992 that prohibit the manufacture, sale, or introduction into commerce of any engine that requires leaded gasoline.

(July 14, 1955, c. 360, Title II, § 218, as added by Pub. L. No. 101–549, Title II, § 226, 104 Stat. 2505 (Nov. 15, 1990).)

HISTORICAL AND STATUTORY NOTES

Effective and Applicability Provisions

1990 Acts. Section effective Nov. 15, 1990, except as otherwise provided, see section 711(b) of Pub. L. No. 101–549, set out as a note under section 7401 of this title.

Savings Provisions

Suits, actions or proceedings commenced under this chapter as in effect prior to Nov. 15, 1990, not to abate by reason of the taking effect of amendments by Pub. L. No. 101–549, except as otherwise provided for, see section 711(a) of Pub. L. No. 101–549, set out as a note under section 7401 of this title.

§ 7554. Urban bus standards

[CAA § 219]

(a) Standards for model years after 1993

Not later than January 1, 1992, the Administrator shall promulgate regulations under section 7521(a) of this title applicable to urban buses for the model year 1994 and thereafter. Such standards shall be based on the best technology that can reasonably be anticipated to be available at the time such measures are to be implemented, taking costs, safety, energy, lead time, and other relevant factors into account. Such regulations shall require that such urban buses comply with the provisions of subsection (b) of this section (and subsection (c) of this subsection,[1] if applicable) in addition to compliance with the standards applicable under section 7521(a) of this title for heavy-duty vehicles of the same type and model year.

(b) PM standard

(1) 50 percent reduction

The standards under section 7521(a) of this title applicable to urban buses shall require that, effective for the model year 1994 and thereafter, emissions of particulate matter (PM) from urban buses shall not exceed 50 percent of the emissions of particulate matter (PM) allowed under the emission standard applicable under section 7521(a) of this title as of November 15, 1990, for particulate matter (PM) in the case of heavy-duty diesel vehicles and engines manufactured in the model year 1994.

(2) Revised reduction

The Administrator shall increase the level of emissions of particulate matter allowed under the standard referred to in paragraph (1) if the Administrator determines that the 50 percent reduction referred to in paragraph (1) is not technologically achievable, taking into account durability, costs, lead time, safety, and other relevant factors. The Administrator may not increase such level of emissions above 70 percent of the emissions of particulate matter (PM) allowed under the emission standard applicable under section 7521(a) of this title as of November 15, 1990, for particulate matter (PM) in the case of heavy-duty diesel vehicles and engines manufactured in the model year 1994.

(3) Determination as part of rule

As part of the rulemaking under subsection (a) of this section, the Administrator shall make a determination as to whether the 50 percent reduction referred to in paragraph (1) is technologically achievable, taking into account durability, costs, lead time, safety, and other relevant factors.

(c) Low-polluting fuel requirement

(1) Annual testing

Beginning with model year 1994 buses, the Administrator shall conduct annual tests of a representative sample of operating urban buses subject to the particulate matter (PM) standard applicable pursuant to subsection (b) of this section to determine whether such buses comply with such standard in use over their full useful life.

(2) Promulgation of additional low-polluting fuel requirement

(A) If the Administrator determines, based on the testing under paragraph (1), that urban buses subject to the particulate matter (PM) standard applicable pursuant to subsection (b) of this section do not comply with such standard in use over their full useful life, he shall revise the standards applicable to such buses to require (in addition to compliance with the PM standard applicable pursuant to subsection (b) of this section) that all new urban buses purchased or placed into service by owners or operators of urban buses in all metropolitan statistical areas or consolidated metropolitan statistical areas with a 1980 population of 750,000 or more shall be capable of operating, and shall be exclusively operated, on low-polluting fuels. The Administrator shall establish the pass-fail rate for purposes of testing under this subparagraph.

(B) The Administrator shall promulgate a schedule phasing in any low-polluting fuel requirement established pursuant to this paragraph to an increasing percentage of new urban buses purchased or placed into service in each of the first 5 model years commencing 3 years after the determination under subparagraph (A). Under such schedule 100 percent of new urban buses placed into service in the fifth model year commencing 3 years after the determination under subparagraph (A) shall comply with the low-polluting fuel requirement established pursuant to this paragraph.

(C) The Administrator may extend the requirements of this paragraph to metropolitan statistical areas or consolidated metropolitan statistical areas with a 1980 population of less than 750,000, if the Administrator determines that a significant benefit to public health could be expected to result from such extension.

(d) Retrofit requirements

Not later than 12 months after November 15, 1990, the Administrator shall promulgate regulations under section 7521(a) of this title requiring that urban buses which—

(1) are operating in areas referred to in subparagraph (A) of subsection (c)(2) of this section (or subparagraph (C) of subsection (c)(2) of this section if the Administrator has taken action under that subparagraph);

(2) were not subject to standards in effect under the regulations under subsection (a) of this section; and

(3) have their engines replaced or rebuilt after January 1, 1995,

shall comply with an emissions standard or emissions control technology requirement established by the Administrator in such regulations. Such emissions standard or emissions control technology requirement shall reflect the best retrofit technology and maintenance practices reasonably achievable.

(e) Procedures for administration and enforcement

The Administrator shall establish, within 18 months after November 15, 1990, and in accordance with section 7525(h) of this title, procedures for the administration and enforcement of standards for buses subject to standards under this section, testing procedures, sampling protocols, in-use compliance requirements, and criteria governing evaluation of buses. Procedures for testing (including, but not limited to, certification testing) shall reflect actual operating conditions.

(f) Definitions

For purposes of this section—

(1) Urban bus

The term "urban bus" has the meaning provided under regulations of the Administrator promulgated under section 7521(a) of this title.

(2) Low-polluting fuel

The term "low-polluting fuel" means methanol, ethanol, propane, or natural gas, or any comparably low-polluting fuel. In determining whether a fuel is comparably low-polluting, the Administrator shall consider both the level of emissions of air pollutants from vehicles using the fuel and the contribution of such emissions to ambient levels of air pollutants. For purposes of this paragraph, the term "methanol" includes any fuel which contains at least 85 percent methanol unless the Administrator increases such percentage as he deems appropriate to protect public health and welfare.

(July 14, 1955, c. 360, Title II, § 219, as added by Pub. L. No. 101–549, Title II, § 227[(a)], 104 Stat. 2505 (Nov. 15, 1990).)

[1] So in original. Probably should be "section,".

HISTORICAL AND STATUTORY NOTES

Effective and Applicability Provisions

1990 Acts. Section effective Nov. 15, 1990, except as otherwise provided, see section 711(b) of Pub. L. No. 101–549, set out as a note under section 7401 of this title.

Savings Provisions

Suits, actions or proceedings commenced under this chapter as in effect prior to Nov. 15, 1990, not to abate by reason of the taking effect of amendments by Pub. L. No. 101–549, except as otherwise provided for, see section 711(a) of Pub. L. No. 101–549, set out as a note under section 7401 of this title.

PART B—AIRCRAFT EMISSION STANDARDS

§ 7571. Establishment of standards

[CAA § 231]

(a) Study; proposed standards; hearings; issuance of regulations

(1) Within 90 days after December 31, 1970, the Administrator shall commence a study and investigation of emissions of air pollutants from aircraft in order to determine—

(A) the extent to which such emissions affect air quality in air quality control regions throughout the United States, and

(B) the technological feasibility of controlling such emissions.

(2) (A) The Administrator shall, from time to time, issue proposed emission standards applicable to the emission of any air pollutant from any class or classes of aircraft engines which in his judgment causes, or contributes to, air pollution which may reasonably be anticipated to endanger public health or welfare.

(B) (i) The Administrator shall consult with the Administrator of the Federal Aviation Administration on aircraft engine emission standards.

(ii) The Administrator shall not change the aircraft engine emission standards if such change would significantly increase noise and adversely affect safety.

(3) The Administrator shall hold public hearings with respect to such proposed standards. Such hearings shall, to the extent practicable, be held in air quality control regions which are most seriously affected by aircraft emissions. Within 90 days after the issuance of such proposed regulations, he shall issue such regulations with such modifications as he deems appropriate. Such regulations may be revised from time to time.

(b) Effective date of regulations

Any regulation prescribed under this section (and any revision thereof) shall take effect after such period as the Administrator finds necessary (after consultation with the Secretary of Transportation) to permit the development and application of the requisite technology, giving appropriate consideration to the cost of compliance within such period.

(c) Regulations which create hazards to aircraft safety

Any regulations in effect under this section on August 7, 1977, or proposed or promulgated thereafter, or amendments thereto, with respect to aircraft shall not apply if disapproved by the President, after notice and opportunity for public hearing, on the basis of a finding by the Secretary of Transportation that any such regulation would create a hazard to aircraft safety. Any such finding shall include a reasonably specific statement of the basis upon which the finding was made.

(July 14, 1955, c. 360, Title II, § 231, as added by Pub. L. No. 91–604, § 11(a)(1), 84 Stat. 1703 (Dec. 31, 1970); and amended by Pub. L. No. 95–95, Title II, § 225, Title IV, § 401(f), 91 Stat. 769, 791 (Aug. 7, 1977); Pub. L. No. 104–264, Title IV, § 406(b), 110 Stat. 3257 (Oct. 9, 1996).)

HISTORICAL AND STATUTORY NOTES

Codifications

Section was formerly codified as section 1857f–9 of this title.

Effective and Applicability Provisions

1977 Acts. Amendment by Pub. L. No. 95–95 effective Aug. 7, 1977, except as otherwise expressly provided, see section 406(d) of Pub. L. No. 95–95, set out as a note under section 7401 of this title.

Applicability of Pub. L. No. 104–264

Except as otherwise specifically provided, Pub. L. No. 104–264 and the amendments made by Pub. L. No. 104–264 applicable only to fiscal years beginning after Sept. 30, 1996, and not to be construed as affecting funds made available for a fiscal year ending before Oct. 1, 1996, see section 3 of Pub. L. No. 104–264, set out as a note under section 106 of Title 49, Transportation.

Modification or Rescission of Rules, Regulations, Orders, Determinations, Contracts, Certifications, Authorizations, Delegations, and Other Actions

All rules, regulations, orders, determinations, contracts, certifications, authorizations, delegations, or other actions duly issued, made, or taken by or pursuant to Act of July 14, 1955, the Clean Air Act, as in effect immediately prior to the date of enactment of Pub. L. No. 95–95 [Aug. 7, 1977] to continue in full force and effect until modified or rescinded in accordance with Act of July 14, 1955, as amended by Pub. L. No. 95–95 [this chapter], see section 406(b) of Pub. L. No. 95–95, set out as an Effective Date of 1977 Acts note under section 7401 of this title.

Study And Investigation Of Uninstalled Aircraft Engines

Pub. L. No. 101–549, Title II, § 233, 104 Stat. 2529 (Nov. 15, 1990), provided that:

"(a) Study.—The Administrator of the Environmental Protection Agency and the Secretary of Transportation, in consultation with the Secretary of Defense, shall commence a study and investigation of the testing of uninstalled aircraft engines in enclosed test cells that shall address at a minimum the following issues and such other issues as they shall deem appropriate—

"(1) whether technologies exist to control some or all emissions of oxides of nitrogen from test cells;

"(2) the effectiveness of such technologies;

"(3) the cost of implementing such technologies;

"(4) whether such technologies affect the safety, design, structure, operation, or performance of aircraft engines;

"(5) whether such technologies impair the effectiveness and accuracy of aircraft engine safety design, and performance tests conducted in test cells; and

"(6) the impact of not controlling such oxides of nitrogen in the applicable nonattainment areas and on other sources, stationary and mobile, on oxides of nitrogen in such areas.

"(b) Report, authority to regulate.—Not later than 24 months after enactment of the Clean Air Act Amendments of 1990 [probably means the date of enactment of the Clean Air Act Amendments of 1990, Pub. L. No. 101–549, which was approved Nov. 15, 1990], the Administrator of the Environmental Protection Agency and the Secretary of Transportation shall submit to Congress a report of the study conducted under this section. Following the completion of such study, any of the States may adopt or enforce any standard for emissions of oxides of nitrogen from test cells only after issuing a public notice stating whether such standards are in accordance with the findings of the study."

[For termination, effective May 15, 2000, of reporting provisions of Pub. L. No. 101–549, Title II, § 233, set out above, see Pub. L. No. 104–66, § 3003, as amended, set out as a note under 31 U.S.C.A. § 1113, and the 6th item on page 148 of House Document No. 103–7.]

§ 7572. Enforcement of standards

[CAA § 232]

(a) Regulations to insure compliance with standards

The Secretary of Transportation, after consultation with the Administrator, shall prescribe regulations to insure compliance with all standards prescribed under section 7571 of this title by the Administrator. The regulations of the Secretary of Transportation shall include provisions making such standards applicable in the issuance, amendment, modification, suspension, or revocation of any certificate authorized by part A of subtitle VII of Title 49 or the Department of Transportation Act. Such Secretary shall insure that all necessary inspections are accomplished, and,[1] may execute any power or duty vested in him by any other provision of law in the execution of all powers and duties vested in him under this section.

(b) Notice and appeal rights

In any action to amend, modify, suspend, or revoke a certificate in which violation of an emission standard prescribed under section 7571 of this title or of a regulation prescribed under subsection (a) of this section is at issue, the certificate holder shall have the same notice and appeal rights as are prescribed for such holders in part A of subtitle VII of Title 49 or the Department of Transportation Act, except that in any appeal to the National Transportation Safety Board, the Board may amend, modify, or revoke the order of the Secretary of Transportation only if it finds no violation of such standard or regulation and that such amendment, modification, or revocation is consistent with safety in air transportation.

(July 14, 1955, c. 360, Title II, § 232, as added by Pub. L. No. 91–604, § 11(a)(1), 84 Stat. 1704 (Dec. 31, 1970).)

[1] So in original. The comma probably should not appear.

HISTORICAL AND STATUTORY NOTES

References in Text

The Department of Transportation Act, referred to in subsecs. (a) and (b), is Pub. L. No. 89–670, 80 Stat. 931 (Oct. 15, 1966), as amended, which was codified principally as sections 1651 to 1660 of former Title 49, Transportation. The Act was repealed and the provisions thereof reenacted in Title 49, by Pub. L. No. 103–272, 108 Stat. 745 (July 5, 1994). The Act was also repealed by Pub. L. No. 104–287, § 7(5), 110 Stat. 3400 (Oct. 11, 1996). For Disposition of section of former Title 49, see Table at the beginning of Title 49.

Codifications

This section was formerly codified as section 1857f–10 of this title.

In subsecs. (a) and (b), "part A of subtitle VII of Title 49" substituted for "the Federal Aviation Act [49 App. U.S.C.A. § 1301 et seq.]" and "the Federal Aviation Act of 1958 [49 App. U.S.C.A. § 1301 et seq.]" on authority of Pub. L. No. 103–272, § 6(b), 108 Stat. 1378 (July 5, 1994), the first section of which enacted subtitles II, III, and V to X of Title 49.

§ 7573. State standards and controls

[CAA § 233]

No State or political subdivision thereof may adopt or attempt to enforce any standard respecting emissions of any air pollutant from any aircraft or engine thereof unless such standard is identical to a standard applicable to such aircraft under this part.

(July 14, 1955, c. 360, Title II, § 233, as added by Pub. L. No. 91–604, § 11(a)(1), 84 Stat. 1704 (Dec. 31, 1970).)

HISTORICAL AND STATUTORY NOTES

Codifications

This section was formerly codified as section 1857f–11 of this title.

§ 7574. Definitions

[CAA § 234]

Terms used in this part (other than Administrator) shall have the same meaning as such terms have under section 40102(a) of Title 49.

(July 14, 1955, c. 360, Title II, § 234, as added by Pub. L. No. 91–604, § 11(a)(1), 84 Stat. 1705 (Dec. 31, 1970).)

HISTORICAL AND STATUTORY NOTES

Codifications

This section was formerly codified as section 1857f–12 of this title.

In text, "section 40102(a) of Title 49" substituted for "section 101 of the Federal Aviation Act of 1958" on authority of Pub. L. No. 103–272, § 6(b), 108 Stat. 1378 (July 5, 1994), the first section of which enacted subtitles II, III, and V to X of Title 49.

PART C—CLEAN FUEL VEHICLES

§ 7581. Definitions

[CAA § 241]

For purposes of this part—

(1) Terms defined in part A

The definitions applicable to part A under section 7550 of this title shall also apply for purposes of this part.

(2) Clean alternative fuel

The term "clean alternative fuel" means any fuel (including methanol, ethanol, or other alcohols (including any mixture thereof containing 85 percent or more by volume of such alcohol with gasoline or other fuels), reformulated gasoline, diesel, natural gas, liquefied petroleum gas, and hydrogen) or power source (including electricity) used in a clean-fuel vehicle that complies with the standards and requirements applicable to such vehicle under this subchapter when using such fuel or power source. In the case of any flexible fuel vehicle or dual fuel vehicle, the term "clean alternative fuel" means only a fuel with respect to which such vehicle was certified as a clean-fuel vehicle meeting the standards applicable to clean-fuel vehicles under section 7583(d)(2) of this title when operating on clean alternative fuel (or any CARB standards which replaces such standards pursuant to section 7583(e) of this title).

(3) NMOG

The term nonmethane organic gas ("NMOG") means the sum of nonoxygenated and oxygenated hydrocarbons contained in a gas sample, including, at a minimum, all oxygenated organic gases containing 5 or fewer carbon atoms (i.e., aldehydes, ketones, alcohols, ethers, etc.), and all known alkanes, alkenes, alkynes, and aromatics containing 12 or fewer carbon atoms. To demonstrate compliance with a NMOG standard, NMOG emissions shall be measured in accordance with the "California Non-Methane Organic Gas Test Procedures". In the case of vehicles using fuels other than base gasoline, the level of NMOG emissions shall be adjusted based on the reactivity of the emissions relative to vehicles using base gasoline.

(4) Base gasoline

The term "base gasoline" means gasoline which meets the following specifications:

Specifications of Base Gasoline Used as
Basis for Reactivity Readjustment:

API gravity	57.8
Sulfur, ppm	317
Color	Purple
Benzene, vol. %	1.35
Reid vapor pressure	8.7
Drivability	1195
Antiknock index	87.3
Distillation, D–86° F	
IBP	92
10%	126

50% 219
90% 327
EP 414

Hydrocarbon Type, Vol. % FIA:

Aromatics 30.9
Olefins 8.2
Saturates 60.9

The Administrator shall modify the definitions of NMOG, base gasoline, and the methods for making reactivity adjustments, to conform to the definitions and method used in California under the Low-Emission Vehicle and Clean Fuel Regulations of the California Air Resources Board, so long as the California definitions are, in the aggregate, at least as protective of public health and welfare as the definitions in this section.

(5) Covered fleet

The term "covered fleet" means 10 or more motor vehicles which are owned or operated by a single person. In determining the number of vehicles owned or operated by a single person for purposes of this paragraph, all motor vehicles owned or operated, leased or otherwise controlled by such person, by any person who controls such person, by any person controlled by such person, and by any person under common control with such person shall be treated as owned by such person. The term "covered fleet" shall not include motor vehicles held for lease or rental to the general public, motor vehicles held for sale by motor vehicle dealers (including demonstration vehicles), motor vehicles used for motor vehicle manufacturer product evaluations or tests, law enforcement and other emergency vehicles, or nonroad vehicles (including farm and construction vehicles).

(6) Covered fleet vehicle

The term "covered fleet vehicle" means only a motor vehicle which is—

(i) in a vehicle class for which standards are applicable under this part; and

(ii) in a covered fleet which is centrally fueled (or capable of being centrally fueled).

No vehicle which under normal operations is garaged at a personal residence at night shall be considered to be a vehicle which is capable of being centrally fueled within the meaning of this paragraph.

(7) Clean-fuel vehicle

The term "clean-fuel vehicle" means a vehicle in a class or category of vehicles which has been certified to meet for any model year the clean-fuel vehicle standards applicable under this part for that model year to clean-fuel vehicles in that class or category.

(July 14, 1955, c. 360, Title II, § 241, as added by Pub. L. No. 101–549, Title II, § 229(a), 104 Stat. 2511 (Nov. 15, 1990).)

HISTORICAL AND STATUTORY NOTES

Effective and Applicability Provisions

1990 Acts. Section effective Nov. 15, 1990, except as otherwise provided, see section 711(b) of Pub. L. No. 101–549, set out as a note under section 7401 of this title.

Savings Provisions

Suits, actions or proceedings commenced under this chapter as in effect prior to Nov. 15, 1990, not to abate by reason of the taking effect of amendments by Pub. L. No. 101–549, except as otherwise provided for, see section 711(a) of Pub. L. No. 101–549, set out as a note under section 7401 of this title.

§ 7582. Requirements applicable to clean-fuel vehicles

[CAA § 242]

(a) Promulgation of standards

Not later than 24 months after November 15, 1990, the Administrator shall promulgate regulations under this part containing clean-fuel vehicle standards for the clean-fuel vehicles specified in this part.

(b) Other requirements

Clean-fuel vehicles of up to 8,500 gvwr subject to standards set forth in this part shall comply with all motor vehicle requirements of this subchapter (such as requirements relating to on-board diagnostics, evaporative emissions, etc.) which are applicable to conventional gasoline-fueled vehicles of the same category and model year, except as provided in section 7584 of this title with respect to administration and enforcement, and except to the extent that any such requirement is in conflict with the provisions of this part. Clean-fuel vehicles of 8,500 gvwr or greater subject to standards set forth in this part shall comply with all requirements of this subchapter which are applicable in the case of conventional gasoline-fueled or diesel fueled vehicles of the same category and model year, except as provided in section 7584 of this title with respect to administration and enforcement, and except to the extent that any such requirement is in conflict with the provisions of this part.

(c) In-use useful life and testing

(1) In the case of light-duty vehicles and light-duty trucks up to 6,000 lbs gvwr, the useful life for purposes of determining in-use compliance with the standards under section 7583 of this title shall be—

(A) a period of 5 years or 50,000 miles (or the equivalent) whichever first occurs, in the case of standards applicable for purposes of certification at 50,000 miles; and

(B) a period of 10 years or 100,000 miles (or the equivalent) whichever first occurs, in the case of standards applicable for purposes of certification at 100,000 miles, except that in-use testing shall not be done for a period beyond 7 years or 75,000 miles (or the equivalent) whichever first occurs.

(2) In the case of light-duty trucks of more than 6,000 lbs gvwr, the useful life for purposes of determining in-use compliance with the standards under section 7583 of this title shall be—

(A) a period of 5 years or 50,000 miles (or the equivalent) whichever first occurs in the case of standards applicable for purposes of certification at 50,000 miles; and

(B) a period of 11 years or 120,000 miles (or the equivalent) whichever first occurs in the case of standards applicable for purposes of certification at 120,000 miles, except that in-use testing shall not be done for a period beyond 7 years or 90,000 miles (or the equivalent) whichever first occurs.

(July 14, 1955, c. 360, Title II, § 242, as added by Pub. L. No. 101–549, Title II, § 229(a), 104 Stat. 2513 (Nov. 15, 1990).)

HISTORICAL AND STATUTORY NOTES

Effective and Applicability Provisions

1990 Acts. Section effective Nov. 15, 1990, except as otherwise provided, see section 711(b) of Pub. L. No. 101–549, set out as a note under section 7401 of this title.

Savings Provisions

Suits, actions or proceedings commenced under this chapter as in effect prior to Nov. 15, 1990, not to abate by reason of the taking effect of amendments by Pub. L. No. 101–549, except as otherwise provided for, see section 711(a) of Pub. L. No. 101–549, set out as a note under section 7401 of this title.

§ 7583. Standards for light-duty clean-fuel vehicles

[CAA § 243]

(a) Exhaust standards for light-duty vehicles and certain light-duty trucks

The standards set forth in this subsection shall apply in the case of clean-fuel vehicles which are light-duty trucks of up to 6,000 lbs. gross vehicle weight rating (gvwr) (but not including light-duty trucks of more than 3,750 lbs. loaded vehicle weight (lvw)) or light-duty vehicles:

(1) Phase I

Beginning with model year 1996, for the air pollutants specified in the following table, the clean-fuel vehicle standards under this section shall provide that vehicle exhaust emissions shall not exceed the levels specified in the following table:

PHASE I CLEAN FUEL VEHICLE EMISSION STANDARDS FOR LIGHT-DUTY TRUCKS OF UP TO 3,750 LBS. LVW AND UP TO 6,000 LBS. GVWR AND LIGHT-DUTY VEHICLES

Pollutant	NMOG	CO	NO_x	PM	HCHO (formaldehyde)
50,000 mile standard	0.125	3.4	0.4	0.015	
100,000 mile standard	0.156	4.2	0.6	0.08*	0.018

Standards are expressed in grams per mile (gpm).

* Standards for particulates (PM) shall apply only to diesel-fueled vehicles.

In the case of the 50,000 mile standards and the 100,000 mile standards, for purposes of certification, the applicable useful life shall be 50,000 miles or 100,000 miles, respectively.

(2) Phase II

Beginning with model year 2001, for air pollutants specified in the following table, the clean-fuel vehicle standards under this section shall provide that vehicle exhaust emissions shall not exceed the levels specified in the following table.

PHASE II CLEAN FUEL VEHICLE EMISSION STANDARDS FOR LIGHT-DUTY TRUCKS OF UP TO 3,750 LBS. LVW AND UP TO 6,000 LBS. GVWR AND LIGHT-DUTY VEHICLES

Pollutant	NMOG	CO	NO_x	PM*	HCHO (formaldehyde)
50,000 mile standard	0.075	3.4	0.2	......	0.015
100,000 mile standard	0.090	4.2	0.3	0.08	0.018

Standards are expressed in grams per mile (gpm).

* Standards for particulates (PM) shall apply only to diesel-fueled vehicles.

In the case of the 50,000 mile standards and the 100,000 mile standards, for purposes of certification, the applicable useful life shall be 50,000 miles or 100,000 miles, respectively.

(b) Exhaust standards for light-duty trucks of more than 3,750 lbs. LVW and up to 5,750 lbs. LVW and up to 6,000 lbs. GVWR

The standards set forth in this paragraph shall apply in the case of clean-fuel vehicles which are light-duty trucks of more than 3,750 lbs. loaded vehicle weight (lvw) but not more than 5,750 lbs. lvw and not more than 6,000 lbs. gross weight rating (GVWR):

(1) Phase I

Beginning with model year 1996, for the air pollutants specified in the following table, the clean-fuel vehicle standards under this section shall provide that vehicle exhaust emissions shall not exceed the levels specified in the following table.

PHASE I CLEAN FUEL VEHICLE EMISSION STANDARDS FOR LIGHT-DUTY TRUCKS OF MORE THAN 3,750 LBS. AND UP TO 5,750 LBS. LVW AND UP TO 6,000 LBS. GVWR

Pollutant	NMOG	CO	NO_x	PM*	HCHO (formaldehyde)
50,000 mile standard	0.160	4.4	0.7	......	0.018
100,000 mile standard	0.200	5.5	0.9	0.08	0.023

Standards are expressed in grams per mile (gpm).

* Standards for particulates (PM) shall apply only to diesel-fueled vehicles.

In the case of the 50,000 mile standards and the 100,000 mile standards, for purposes of certification, the applicable useful life shall be 50,000 miles or 100,000 miles, respectively.

(2) Phase II

Beginning with model year 2001, for the air pollutants specified in the following table, the clean-fuel vehicle standards under this section shall provide that vehicle exhaust emissions shall not exceed the levels specified in the following table.

PHASE II CLEAN FUEL VEHICLE EMISSION STANDARDS FOR LIGHT-DUTY TRUCKS OF MORE THAN 3,750 LBS. LVW AND UP TO 5,750 LBS. LVW AND UP TO 6,000 LBS. GVWR

Pollutant	NMOG	CO	NO_x	PM*	HCHO (formaldehyde)
50,000 mile standard	0.100	4.4	0.4	....	0.018
100,000 mile standard	0.130	5.5	0.5	0.08	0.023

Standards are expressed in grams per mile (gpm).

* Standards for particulates (PM) shall apply only to diesel-fueled vehicles.

In the case of the 50,000 mile standards and the 100,000 mile standards, for purposes of certification, the applicable useful life shall be 50,000 miles or 100,000 miles, respectively.

(c) Exhaust standards for light-duty trucks greater than 6,000 lbs. GVWR

The standards set forth in this subsection shall apply in the case of clean-fuel vehicles which are light-duty trucks of more than 6,000 lbs. gross weight rating (GVWR) and less than or equal to 8,500 lbs. GVWR, beginning with model year 1998. For the air pollutants specified in the following table, the clean-fuel vehicle standards under this section shall provide that vehicle exhaust emissions of vehicles within the test weight categories specified in the following table shall not exceed the levels specified in such table.

CLEAN FUEL VEHICLE EMISSION STANDARDS FOR LIGHT DUTY TRUCKS GREATER THAN 6,000 LBS. GVWR

Test Weight Category: Up to 3,750 lbs. tw

Pollutant	NMOG	CO	NO_x	PM*	HCHO (formaldehyde)
50,000 mile standard	0.125	3.4	0.4**	....	0.015
120,000 mile standard	0.180	5.0	0.6	0.08	0.022

Test Weight Category: Above 3,750 but not above 5,750 lbs. tw

Pollutant	NMOG	CO	NO_x	PM*	HCHO (formaldehyde)
50,000 mile standard	0.160	4.4	0.7**	....	0.018
120,000 mile standard	0.230	6.4	1.0	0.10	0.027

Test Weight Category: Above 5,750 tw but not above 8,500 lbs. gvwr

Pollutant	NMOG	CO	NO_x	PM*	HCHO (formaldehyde)
50,000 mile standard	0.195	5.0	1.1**	....	0.022
120,000 mile standard	0.280	7.3	1.5	0.12	0.032

Standards are expressed in grams per mile (gpm).

* Standards for particulates (PM) shall apply only to diesel-fueled vehicles.

** Standard not applicable to diesel-fueled vehicles.

For the 50,000 mile standards and the 120,000 mile standards set forth in the table, the applicable useful life for purposes of certification shall be 50,000 miles or 120,000 miles, respectively.

(d) Flexible and dual-fuel vehicles

(1) In general

The Administrator shall establish standards and requirements under this section for the model year 1996 and thereafter for vehicles weighing not more than 8,500 lbs. gvwr which are capable of operating on more than one fuel. Such standards shall require that such vehicles meet the exhaust standards applicable under subsection[1] (a), (b), and (c) of this section for CO, NO_x, and HCHO, and if appropriate, PM for single-fuel vehicles of the same vehicle category and model year.

(2) Exhaust NMOG standard for operation on clean alternative fuel

In addition to standards for the pollutants referred to in paragraph (1), the standards established under paragraph (1) shall require that vehicle exhaust emissions of NMOG not exceed the levels (expressed in grams per mile) specified in the tables below when the vehicle is operated on the clean alternative fuel for which such vehicle is certified:

NMOG STANDARDS FOR FLEXIBLE- AND DUAL-FUELED VEHICLES
WHEN OPERATING ON CLEAN ALTERNATIVE FUEL

Light-duty Trucks up to 6,000 lbs. GVWR and Light-duty vehicles

Vehicle Type	Column A (50,000 mi.) Standard (gpm)	Column B (100,000 mi.) Standard (gpm)
Beginning MY 1996:		
LDT's (0–3,750 lbs. LVW) and light-duty vehicles	0.125	0.156
LDT's (3,751–5,750 lbs. LVW)	0.160	0.20
Beginning MY 2001:		
LDT's (0–3,750 lbs. LVW) and light-duty vehicles	0.075	0.090
LDT's (3,751–5,750 lbs. LVW)	0.100	0.130

For standards under column A, for purposes of certification under section 7525 of this title, the applicable useful life shall be 50,000 miles.

For standards under column B, for purposes of certification under section 7525 of this title, the applicable useful life shall be 100,000 miles.

Light-duty Trucks More than 6,000 lbs. GVWR

Vehicle Type	Column A (50,000 mi.) Standard	Column B (120,000 mi.) Standard
Beginning MY 1998:		
LDT's (0–3,750 lbs. TW)	0.125	0.180
LDT's (3,751–5,750 lbs. TW)	0.160	0.230
LDT's (above 5,750 lbs. TW)	0.195	0.280

For standards under column A, for purposes of certification under section 7525 of this title, the applicable useful life shall be 50,000 miles.

For standards under column B, for purposes of certification under section 7525 of this title, the applicable useful life shall be 120,000 miles.

(3) NMOG standard for operation on conventional fuel

In addition to the standards referred to in paragraph (1), the standards established under paragraph (1) shall require that vehicle exhaust emissions of NMOG not exceed the levels (expressed in grams per mile) specified in the tables below:

NMOG STANDARDS FOR FLEXIBLE- AND DUAL-FUELED VEHICLES
WHEN OPERATING ON CONVENTIONAL FUEL

Light-duty Trucks of up to 6,000 lbs. GVWR and Light-duty vehicles

Vehicle Type	Column A (50,000 mi.) Standard (gpm)	Column B (100,000 mi.) Standard (gpm)
Beginning MY 1996:		
LDT's (0–3,750 lbs. LVW) and light-duty vehicles	0.25	0.31
LDT's (3,751–5,750 lbs. LVW)	0.32	0.40
Beginning MY 2001:		
LDT's (0–3,750 lbs. LVW) and light-duty vehicles	0.125	0.156
LDT's (3,751–5,750 lbs. LVW)	0.160	0.200

For standards under column A, for purposes of certification under section 7525 of this title, the applicable useful life shall be 50,000 miles.

For standards under column B, for purposes of certification under section 7525 of this title, the applicable useful life shall be 100,000 miles.

Light-duty Trucks of up to 6,000 lbs. GVWR

Vehicle Type	Column A (50,000 mi.) Standard	Column B (120,000 mi.) Standard
Beginning MY 1998:		
LDT's (0–3,750 lbs. TW)	0.25	0.36
LDT's (3,751–5,750 lbs. TW)	0.32	0.46
LDT's (above 5,750 lbs. TW)	0.39	0.56

For standards under column A, for purposes of certification under section 7525 of this title, the applicable useful life shall be 50,000 miles.

For standards under column B, for purposes of certification under section 7525 of this title, the applicable useful life shall be 120,000 miles.

(e) Replacement by CARB standards

(1) Single set of CARB standards

If the State of California promulgates regulations establishing and implementing a single set of standards applicable in California pursuant to a waiver approved under section 7543 of this title to any category of vehicles referred to in subsection (a), (b), (c), or (d) of this section and such set of standards is, in the aggregate, at least as protective of public health and welfare as the otherwise applicable standards set forth in section 7582 of this title and subsection (a), (b), (c), or (d) of this section, such set of California standards shall apply to clean-fuel vehicles in such category in lieu of the standards otherwise applicable under section 7582 of this title and subsection (a), (b), (c), or (d) of this section, as the case may be.

(2) Multiple sets of CARB standards

If the State of California promulgates regulations establishing and implementing several different sets of standards applicable in California pursuant to a waiver approved under section 7543 of this title to any category of vehicles referred to in subsection (a), (b), (c), or (d) of this section and each of such sets of California standards is, in the aggregate, at least as protective of public health and welfare as the otherwise applicable standards set forth in section 7582 of this title and subsection (a), (b), (c), or (d) of this section, such standards shall be treated as "qualifying California standards" for purposes of this paragraph. Where more than one set of qualifying standards are established and administered by the State of California, the least stringent set of qualifying California standards shall apply to the clean-fuel vehicles concerned in lieu of the standards otherwise applicable to such vehicles under section 7582 of this title and this section.

(f) Less stringent CARB standards

If the Low-Emission Vehicle and Clean Fuels Regulations of the California Air Resources Board applicable to any category of vehicles referred to in subsection (a), (b), (c), or (d) of this section are modified after November 15, 1990, to provide an emissions standard which is less stringent than the otherwise applicable standard set forth in subsection (a), (b), (c), or (d) of this section, or if any effective date contained in such regulations is delayed, such modified standards or such delay (or both, as the case may be) shall apply, for an interim period, in lieu of the standard or effective date otherwise applicable under subsection (a), (b), (c), or (d) of this section to any vehicles covered by such modified standard or delayed effective date. The interim period shall be a period of not more than 2 model years from the effective date otherwise applicable under subsection (a), (b), (c), or (d) of this section. After such interim period, the otherwise applicable standard set forth in subsection (a), (b), (c), or (d) of this section shall take effect with respect to such vehicles (unless subsequently replaced under subsection (e) of this section).

(g) Not applicable to heavy-duty vehicles

Notwithstanding any provision of the Low-Emission Vehicle and Clean Fuels Regulations of the California Air Resources Board nothing in this section shall apply to heavy-duty engines in vehicles of more than 8,500 lbs. GVWR.

(July 14, 1955, c. 360, Title II, § 243, as added by Pub. L. No. 101–549, Title II, § 229(a), 104 Stat. 2514 (Nov. 15, 1990).)

[1] So in original. Probably should be "subsections."

HISTORICAL AND STATUTORY NOTES

Effective and Applicability Provisions

1990 Acts. Section effective Nov. 15, 1990, except as otherwise provided, see section 711(b) of Pub. L. No. 101–549, set out as a note under section 7401 of this title.

Savings Provisions

Suits, actions or proceedings commenced under this chapter as in effect prior to Nov. 15, 1990, not to abate by reason of the taking effect of amendments by Pub. L. No. 101–549, except as otherwise provided for, see section 711(a) of Pub. L. No. 101–549, set out as a note under section 7401 of this title.

§ 7584. Administration and enforcement as per California standards [CAA § 244]

Where the numerical clean-fuel vehicle standards applicable under this part to vehicles of not more than 8,500 lbs. GVWR are the same as numerical emission standards applicable in California under the Low-Emission Vehicle and Clean Fuels Regulations of the California Air Resources Board ("CARB"), such standards shall be administered and enforced by the Administrator—

(1) in the same manner and with the same flexibility as the State of California administers and enforces corresponding standards applicable under the Low-Emission Vehicle and Clean Fuels Regulations of the California Air Resources Board ("CARB"); and

(2) subject to the same requirements, and utilizing the same interpretations and policy judgments, as are applicable in the case of such CARB standards, including, but not limited to, requirements regarding certification, production-line testing, and in-use compliance,

unless the Administrator determines (in promulgating the rules establishing the clean fuel vehicle program under this section) that any such administration and enforcement would not meet the criteria for a waiver under section 7543 of this title. Nothing in this section shall apply in the case of standards under section 7585 of this title for heavy-duty vehicles.

(July 14, 1955, c. 360, Title II, § 244, as added by Pub. L. No. 101–549, Title II, § 229(a), 104 Stat. 2519 (Nov. 15, 1990).)

HISTORICAL AND STATUTORY NOTES

Effective and Applicability Provisions

1990 Acts. Section effective Nov. 15, 1990, except as otherwise provided, see section 711(b) of Pub. L. No. 101–549, set out as a note under section 7401 of this title.

Savings Provisions

Suits, actions or proceedings commenced under this chapter as in effect prior to Nov. 15, 1990, not to abate by reason of the taking effect of amendments by Pub. L. No. 101–549, except as otherwise provided for, see section 711(a) of Pub. L. No. 101–549, set out as a note under section 7401 of this title.

§ 7585. Standards for heavy-duty clean-fuel vehicles (GVWR above 8,500 up to 26,000 lbs.)

[CAA § 245]

(a) Model years after 1997; combined NO_x and NMHC standard

For classes or categories of heavy-duty vehicles or engines manufactured for the model year 1998 or thereafter and having a GVWR greater than 8,500 lbs. and up to 26,000 lbs. GVWR, the standards under this part for clean-fuel vehicles shall require that combined emissions of oxides of nitrogen (NO_x) and nonmethane hydrocarbons (NMHC) shall not exceed 3.15 grams per brake horsepower hour (equivalent to 50 percent of the combined emission standards applicable under section 7521 of this title for such air pollutants in the case of a conventional model year 1994 heavy-duty diesel-fueled vehicle or engine). No standard shall be promulgated as provided in this section for any heavy-duty vehicle of more than 26,000 lbs. GVWR.

(b) Revised standards that are less stringent

(1) The Administrator may promulgate a revised less stringent standard for the vehicles or engines referred to in subsection (a) of this section if the Administrator determines that the 50 percent reduction required under subsection (a) of this section is not technologically feasible for clean diesel-fueled vehicles and engines, taking into account durability, costs, lead time, safety, and other relevant factors. To provide adequate lead time the Administrator shall make a determination with regard to the technological feasibility of such 50 percent reduction before December 31, 1993.

(2) Any person may at any time petition the Administrator to make a determination under paragraph (1). The Administrator shall act on such a petition within 6 months after the petition is filed.

(3) Any revised less stringent standards promulgated as provided in this subsection shall require at least a 30 percent reduction in lieu of the 50 percent reduction referred to in paragraph (1).

(July 14, 1955, c. 360, Title II, § 245, as added by Pub. L. No. 101–549, Title II, § 229(a), 104 Stat. 2519 (Nov. 15, 1990).)

HISTORICAL AND STATUTORY NOTES

Effective and Applicability Provisions

1990 Acts. Section effective Nov. 15, 1990, except as otherwise provided, see section 711(b) of Pub. L. No. 101–549, set out as a note under section 7401 of this title.

Savings Provisions

Suits, actions or proceedings commenced under this chapter as in effect prior to Nov. 15, 1990, not to abate by reason of the taking effect of amendments by Pub. L. No. 101–549, except as otherwise provided for, see section 711(a) of Pub. L. No. 101–549, set out as a note under section 7401 of this title.

§ 7586. Centrally fueled fleets

[CAA § 246]

(a) Fleet program required for certain nonattainment areas

(1) SIP revision

Each State in which there is located all or part of a covered area (as defined in paragraph (2)) shall submit, within 42 months after November 15, 1990, a State implementation plan revision under section 7410 of this title and part D of subchapter I of this chapter to establish a clean-fuel vehicle program for fleets under this section.

(2) Covered areas

For purposes of this subsection, each of the following shall be a "covered area":

(A) Ozone nonattainment areas

Any ozone nonattainment area with a 1980 population of 250,000 or more classified under subpart 2 of part D of subchapter I of this chapter as Serious, Severe, or Extreme based on data for the calendar years 1987, 1988, and 1989. In determining the ozone nonattainment areas to be treated as covered areas pursuant to this subparagraph, the Administrator shall use the most recent interpretation methodology issued by the Administrator prior to November 15, 1990.

(B) Carbon monoxide nonattainment areas

Any carbon monoxide nonattainment area with a 1980 population of 250,000 or more and a carbon monoxide design value at or above 16.0 parts per million based on data for calendar years 1988 and 1989 (as calculated according to the most recent interpretation methodology issued prior to November 15, 1990, by the United States Environmental Protection Agency), excluding those carbon monoxide nonattainment areas in which mobile sources do not contribute significantly to carbon monoxide exceedances.

(3) Plan revisions for reclassified areas

In the case of ozone nonattainment areas reclassified as Serious, Severe, or Extreme under part D of subchapter I of this chapter with a 1980 population of 250,000 or more, the State shall submit a plan revision meeting the requirements of this subsection within 1 year after reclassification. Such plan revision shall implement the requirements applicable under this subsection at the time of reclassification and thereafter, except that the Administrator may adjust for a limited period the deadlines for compliance where compliance with such deadlines would be infeasible.

(4) Consultation; consideration of factors

Each State required to submit an implementation plan revision under this subsection shall develop such revision in consultation with fleet operators, vehicle manufacturers, fuel producers and distributors, motor vehicle fuel, and other interested parties, taking into consideration operational range, specialty uses, vehicle and fuel availability, costs, safety, resale values of vehicles and equipment and other relevant factors.

(b) Phase-in of requirements

The plan revision required under this section shall contain provisions requiring that at least a specified percentage of all new covered fleet vehicles in model year 1998 and thereafter purchased by each covered fleet operator in each covered area shall be clean-fuel vehicles and shall use clean alternative fuels when operating in the covered area. For the applicable model years (MY) specified in the following table and thereafter, the specified percentage shall be as provided in the table for the vehicle types set forth in the table:

Clean Fuel Vehicle Phase-In Requirements for Fleets

Vehicle Type	MY1998	MY1999	MY2000
Light-duty trucks up to 6,000 lbs. GVWR and light-duty vehicles	30%	50%	70%
Heavy-duty trucks above 8,500 lbs. GVWR	50%	50%	50%

The term MY refers to model year.

(c) Accelerated standard for light-duty trucks up to 6,000 lbs. GVWR and light-duty vehicles

Notwithstanding the model years for which clean-fuel vehicle standards are applicable as provided in section 7583 of this title, for purposes of this section, light duty[1] trucks of up to 6,000 lbs. GVWR and light-duty vehicles manufactured in model years 1998 through model year 2000 shall be treated as clean-fuel vehicles only if such vehicles comply with the standards applicable under section 7583 of this title for vehicles in the same class for the model year 2001. The requirements of subsection (b) of this section shall take effect on the earlier of the following:

(1) The first model year after model year 1997 in which new light-duty trucks up to 6,000 lbs. GVWR and light-duty vehicles which comply with the model year 2001 standards under section 7583 of this title are offered for sale in California.

(2) Model year 2001.

Whenever the effective date of subsection (b) of this section is delayed pursuant to paragraph (1) of this subsection, the phase-in schedule under subsection (b) of this section shall be modified to commence with the model year referred to in paragraph (1) in lieu of model year 1998.

(d) Choice of vehicles and fuel

The plan revision under this subsection shall provide that the choice of clean-fuel vehicles and clean alternative fuels shall be made by the covered fleet operator subject to the requirements of this subsection.

(e) Availability of clean alternative fuel

The plan revision shall require fuel providers to make clean alternative fuel available to covered fleet operators at locations at which covered fleet vehicles are centrally fueled.

(f) Credits

(1) Issuance of credits

The State plan revision required under this section shall provide for the issuance by the State of appropriate credits to a fleet operator for any of the following (or any combination thereof):

(A) The purchase of more clean-fuel vehicles than required under this section.

(B) The purchase of clean fuel[2] vehicles which meet more stringent standards established by the Administrator pursuant to paragraph (4).

(C) The purchase of vehicles in categories which are not covered by this section but which meet standards established for such vehicles under paragraph (4).

(2) Use of credits; limitations based on weight classes

(A) Use of credits

Credits under this subsection may be used by the person holding such credits to demonstrate compliance with this section or may be traded or sold for use by any other person to demonstrate compliance with other requirements applicable under this section in the same nonattainment area. Credits obtained at any time may be held or banked for use at any later time, and when so used, such credits shall maintain the same value as if used at an earlier date.

(B) Limitations based on weight classes

Credits issued with respect to the purchase of vehicles of up to 8,500 lbs. GVWR may not be used to demonstrate compliance by any person with the requirements applicable under this subsection to vehicles of more than 8,500 lbs. GVWR. Credits issued with respect to the purchase of vehicles of more than 8,500 lbs. GVWR may not be used to demonstrate compliance by any person with the requirements applicable under this subsection to vehicles weighing up to 8,500 lbs. GVWR.

(C) Weighting

Credits issued for purchase of a clean fuel[2] vehicle under this subsection shall be adjusted with appropriate weighting to reflect the level of emission reduction achieved by the vehicle.

(3) Regulations and administration

Within 12 months after November 15, 1990, the Administrator shall promulgate regulations for such credit program. The State shall administer the credit program established under this subsection.

(4) Standards for issuing credits for cleaner vehicles

Solely for purposes of issuing credits under paragraph (1)(B), the Administrator shall establish under this paragraph standards for Ultra-Low Emission Vehicles ("ULEV"s) and Zero Emissions Vehicles ("ZEV"s) which shall be more stringent than those otherwise applicable to clean-fuel vehicles under this part. The Administrator shall certify clean fuel[2] vehicles as complying with such more stringent standards, and administer and enforce such more stringent standards, in the same manner as in the case of the otherwise applicable clean-fuel vehicle standards established under this section. The standards established by the Administrator under this paragraph for vehicles under 8,500 lbs. GVWR or greater shall conform as closely as possible to standards which are established by the State of California for ULEV and ZEV vehicles in the same class. For vehicles of 8,500 lbs. GVWR or more, the Administrator shall promulgate comparable standards for purposes of this subsection.

(5) Early fleet credits

The State plan revision shall provide credits under this subsection to fleet operators that purchase vehicles certified to meet clean-fuel vehicle standards under this part during any period after approval of the plan revision and prior to the effective date of the fleet program under this section.

(g) Availability to public

At any facility owned or operated by a department, agency, or instrumentality of the United States where vehicles subject to this subsection are supplied with clean alternative fuel, such fuel shall be offered for sale to the public for use in other vehicles during reasonable business times and subject to national security concerns, unless such fuel is commercially available for vehicles in the vicinity of such Federal facilities.

(h) Transportation control measures

The Administrator shall by rule, within 1 year after November 15, 1990, ensure that certain transportation control measures including time-of-day or day-of-week restrictions, and other similar measures that restrict vehicle usage, do not apply to any clean-fuel vehicle that meets the requirements of this section. This subsection shall apply notwithstanding subchapter I of this chapter.

(July 14, 1955, c. 360, Title II, § 246, as added by Pub. L. No. 101–549, Title II, § 229(a), 104 Stat. 2520 (Nov. 15, 1990).)

[1] So in original. Probably should be "light-duty."

[2] So in original. Probably should be "clean-fuel."

HISTORICAL AND STATUTORY NOTES

Effective and Applicability Provisions

1990 Acts. Section effective Nov. 15, 1990, except as otherwise provided, see section 711(b) of Pub. L. No. 101–549, set out as a note under section 7401 of this title.

Savings Provisions

Suits, actions or proceedings commenced under this chapter as in effect prior to Nov. 15, 1990, not to abate by reason of the taking effect of amendments by Pub. L. No. 101–549, except as otherwise provided for, see section 711(a) of Pub. L. No. 101–549, set out as a note under section 7401 of this title.

§ 7587. Vehicle conversions

[CAA § 247]

(a) Conversion of existing and new conventional vehicles to clean-fuel vehicles

The requirements of section 7586 of this title may be met through the conversion of existing or new gasoline or diesel-powered vehicles to clean-fuel vehicles which comply with the applicable requirements of that section. For purposes of such provisions the conversion of a vehicle to clean fuel[1] vehicle shall be treated as the purchase of a clean fuel[1] vehicle. Nothing in this part shall be construed to provide that any covered fleet operator subject to fleet vehicle purchase requirements under section 7586 of this title shall be required to convert existing or new gasoline or diesel-powered vehicles to clean-fuel vehicles or to purchase converted vehicles.

(b) Regulations

The Administrator shall, within 24 months after November 15, 1990, consistent with the requirements of this subchapter applicable to new vehicles, promulgate regulations governing conversions of conventional vehicles to clean-fuel vehicles. Such regulations shall establish criteria for such conversions which will ensure that a converted vehicle will comply with the standards applicable under this part to clean-fuel vehicles. Such regulations shall provide for the application to such conversions of the same provisions of this subchapter (including provisions relating to administration enforcement) as are applicable to standards under section[2] 7582, 7583, 7584, and 7585 of this title, except that in the case of conversions the Administrator may modify the applicable regulations implementing such provisions as the Administrator deems necessary to implement this part.

(c) Enforcement

Any person who converts conventional vehicles to clean fuel[1] vehicles pursuant to subsection (b) of this section shall be considered a manufacturer for purposes of sections 7525 and 7541 of this title and related enforcement provisions. Nothing in the preceding sentence shall require a person who performs such conversions to warrant any part or operation of a vehicle other than as required under this part. Nothing in this paragraph shall limit the applicability of any other warranty to unrelated parts or operations.

(d) Tampering

The conversion from a vehicle capable of operating on gasoline or diesel fuel only to a clean-fuel vehicle shall not be considered a violation of section 7522(a)(3) of this title if such conversion complies with the regulations promulgated under subsection (b) of this section.

(e) Safety

The Secretary of Transportation shall, if necessary, promulgate rules under applicable motor vehicle laws regarding the safety of vehicles converted from existing and new vehicles to clean-fuel vehicles.

(July 14, 1955, c. 360, Title II, § 247, as added by Pub. L. No. 101–549, Title II, § 229(a), 104 Stat. 2523 (Nov. 15, 1990).)

[1] So in original. Probably should be "clean-fuel."

[2] So in original. Probably should be "sections."

HISTORICAL AND STATUTORY NOTES

Effective and Applicability Provisions

1990 Acts. Section effective Nov. 15, 1990, except as otherwise provided, see section 711(b) of Pub. L. No. 101–549, set out as a note under section 7401 of this title.

Savings Provisions

Suits, actions or proceedings commenced under this chapter as in effect prior to Nov. 15, 1990, not to abate by reason of the taking effect of amendments by Pub. L. No. 101–549, except as otherwise provided for, see section 711(a) of Pub. L. No. 101–549, set out as a note under section 7401 of this title.

§ 7588. Federal agency fleets

[CAA § 248]

(a) Additional provisions applicable

The provisions of this section shall apply, in addition to the other provisions of this part, in the case of covered fleet vehicles owned or operated by an agency, department, or instrumentality of the United States, except as otherwise provided in subsection (e) of this section.

(b) Cost of vehicles to Federal agency

Notwithstanding the provisions of sections 601 to 611 of Title 40, the Administrator of General Services shall not include the incremental costs of clean-fuel vehicles in the amount to be reimbursed by Federal agencies if the Administrator of General Services determines that appropriations provided pursuant to this paragraph are sufficient to provide for the incremental cost of such vehicles over the cost of comparable conventional vehicles.

(c) Limitations on appropriations

Funds appropriated pursuant to the authorization under this paragraph shall be applicable only—

(1) to the portion of the cost of acquisition, maintenance and operation of vehicles acquired under this subparagraph which exceeds the cost of acquisition, maintenance and operation of comparable conventional vehicles;

(2) to the portion of the costs of fuel storage and dispensing equipment attributable to such vehicles which exceeds the costs for such purposes required for conventional vehicles; and

(3) to the portion of the costs of acquisition of clean-fuel vehicles which represents a reduction in revenue from the disposal of such vehicles as compared to revenue resulting from the disposal of comparable conventional vehicles.

(d) Vehicle costs

The incremental cost of vehicles acquired under this part over the cost of comparable conventional vehicles shall not be applied to any calculation with respect to a limitation under law on the maximum cost of individual vehicles which may be required by the United States.

(e) Exemptions

The requirements of this part shall not apply to vehicles with respect to which the Secretary of Defense has certified to the Administrator that an exemption is needed based on national security consideration.

(f) Acquisition requirement

Federal agencies, to the extent practicable, shall obtain clean-fuel vehicles from original equipment manufacturers.

(g) Authorization of appropriations

There are authorized to be appropriated such sums as may be required to carry out the provisions of this section: *Provided,* That such sums as are appropriated for the Administrator of General Services pursuant to the authorization under this section shall be added to the General Supply Fund established in section 321 of Title 40.

(July 14, 1955, c. 360, Title II, § 248, as added by Pub. L. No. 101–549, Title II, § 229(a), 104 Stat. 2524 (Nov. 15, 1990).)

HISTORICAL AND STATUTORY NOTES

Codifications

In subsec. (b), "sections 601–611 of Title 40" substituted for "section 211 of the Federal Property and Administrative Services Act of 1949", and, in subsec. (g), "the General Supply Fund established in section 321 of title 40" substituted for "the General Supply Fund established in section 109 of the Federal Property and Administrative Services Act of 1949", on authority of Pub. L. No. 107–217, § 5(c), 116 Stat. 1303 (Aug. 21, 2002), the first section of which enacted Title 40, Public Buildings, Property, and Works.

Effective and Applicability Provisions

1990 Acts. Section effective Nov. 15, 1990, except as otherwise provided, see section 711(b) of Pub. L. No. 101–549, set out as a note under section 7401 of this title.

Savings Provisions

Suits, actions or proceedings commenced under this chapter as in effect prior to Nov. 15, 1990, not to abate by reason of the taking effect of amendments by Pub. L. No. 101–549, except as otherwise provided for, see section 711(a) of Pub. L. No. 101–549, set out as a note under section 7401 of this title.

§ 7589. California pilot test program

[CAA § 249]

(a) Establishment

The Administrator shall establish a pilot program in the State of California to demonstrate the effectiveness of clean-fuel vehicles in controlling air pollution in ozone nonattainment areas.

(b) Applicability

The provisions of this section shall only apply to light-duty trucks and light-duty vehicles, and such provisions shall apply only in the State of California, except as provided in subsection (f) of this section.

(c) Program requirements

Not later than 24 months after November 15, 1990, the Administrator shall promulgate regulations establishing requirements under this section applicable in the State of California. The regulations shall provide the following:

(1) Clean-fuel vehicles

Clean-fuel vehicles shall be produced, sold, and distributed (in accordance with normal business practices and applicable franchise agreements) to ultimate purchasers in California (including owners of covered fleets referred to in section 7586 of this title) in numbers that meet or exceed the following schedule:

Model Years	Number of Clean-Fuel Vehicles
1996, 1997, 1998	150,000 vehicles
1999 and thereafter	300,000 vehicles

(2) Clean alternative fuels

(A) Within 2 years after November 15, 1990, the State of California shall submit a revision of the applicable implementation plan under part D of subchapter I of this chapter and section 7410 of this title containing a clean fuel plan that requires that clean alternative fuels on which the clean-fuel vehicles required under this paragraph can operate shall be produced and distributed by fuel suppliers and made available in California. At a minimum, sufficient clean alternative fuels shall be produced, distributed and made available to assure that all clean-fuel vehicles required under this section can operate, to the maximum extent practicable, exclusively on such fuels in California. The State shall require that clean alternative fuels be made available and offered for sale at an adequate number of locations with sufficient geographic distribution to ensure convenient refueling with clean alternative fuels, considering the number of, and type of, such vehicles sold and the geographic distribution of such vehicles within the State. The State shall determine the clean alternative fuels to be produced, distributed, and made available based on motor vehicle manufacturers' projections of future sales of such vehicles and consultations with the affected local governments and fuel suppliers.

(B) The State may by regulation grant persons subject to the requirements prescribed under this paragraph an appropriate amount of credits for exceeding such requirements, and any person granted credits may transfer some or all of the credits for use by one or more persons in demonstrating compliance with such requirements. The State may make the credits available for use after consideration of enforceability, environmental, and economic factors and upon such terms and conditions as the State finds appropriate.

(C) The State may also by regulation establish specifications for any clean alternative fuel produced and made available under this paragraph as the State finds necessary to reduce or eliminate an unreasonable risk to public health, welfare, or safety associated with its use or to ensure acceptable vehicle maintenance and performance characteristics.

(D) If a retail gasoline dispensing facility would have to remove or replace one or more motor vehicle fuel underground storage tanks and accompanying piping in order to comply with the provisions of this section, and it had removed and replaced such tank or tanks and accompanying piping in order to comply with subtitle I of the Solid Waste Disposal Act [42 U.S.C.A. § 6901 et seq.] prior to November 15, 1990, it shall not be required to comply with this subsection until a period of 7 years has passed from the date of the removal and replacement of such tank or tanks.

(E) Nothing in this section authorizes any State other than California to adopt provisions regarding clean alternative fuels.

(F) If the State of California fails to adopt a clean fuel program that meets the requirements of this paragraph, the Administrator shall, within 4 years after November 15, 1990, establish a clean fuel program for the State of California under this paragraph and section 7410(c) of this title that meets the requirements of this paragraph.

(d) Credits for motor vehicle manufacturers

(1) The Administrator may (by regulation) grant a motor vehicle manufacturer an appropriate amount of credits toward fulfillment of such manufacturer's share of the requirements of subsection (c)(1) of this section for any of the following (or any combination thereof):

(A) The sale of more clean-fuel vehicles than required under subsection (c)(1) of this section.

(B) The sale of clean fuel[1] vehicles which meet standards established by the Administrator as provided in paragraph (3) which are more stringent than the clean-fuel vehicle standards otherwise applicable to such clean-fuel vehicle. A manufacturer granted credits under this paragraph may transfer some or all of the credits for use by one or more other manufacturers in demonstrating compliance with the requirements prescribed under this paragraph. The Administrator may make the credits available for use after consideration of enforceability, environmental, and economic factors and upon such terms and conditions as he finds appropriate. The Administrator shall grant credits in accordance with this paragraph, notwithstanding any requirements of State law or any credits granted with respect to the same vehicles under any State law, rule, or regulation.

(2) Regulations and administration

The Administrator shall administer the credit program established under this subsection. Within 12 months after November 15, 1990, the Administrator shall promulgate regulations for such credit program.

(3) Standards for issuing credits for cleaner vehicles

The more stringent standards and other requirements (including requirements relating to the weighting of credits) established by the Administrator for purposes of the credit program under section 7585(e)[2] of this title (relating to credits for clean fuel[1] vehicles in the fleets program) shall also apply for purposes of the credit program under this paragraph.

(e) Program evaluation

(1) Not later than June 30, 1994 and again in connection with the report under paragraph (2), the Administrator shall provide a report to the Congress on the status of the California Air Resources Board Low-Emissions Vehicles and Clean Fuels Program. Such report shall examine the capability, from a technological standpoint, of motor vehicle manufacturers and motor vehicle fuel suppliers to comply with the requirements of such program and with the requirements of the California Pilot Program under this section.

(2) Not later than June 30, 1998, the Administrator shall complete and submit a report to Congress on the effectiveness of the California pilot program under this section. The report shall evaluate the

level of emission reductions achieved under the program, the costs of the program, the advantages and disadvantages of extending the program to other nonattainment areas, and desirability of continuing or expanding the program in California.

(3) The program under this section cannot be extended or terminated by the Administrator except by Act of Congress enacted after November 15, 1990. Section 7507 of this title does not apply to the program under this section.

(f) Voluntary opt-in for other States

(1) EPA regulations

Not later than 2 years after November 15, 1990, the Administrator shall promulgate regulations establishing a voluntary opt-in program under this subsection pursuant to which—

(A) clean-fuel vehicles which are required to be produced, sold, and distributed in the State of California under this section, and

(B) clean alternative fuels required to be produced and distributed under this section by fuel suppliers and made available in California[3]

may also be sold and used in other States which submit plan revisions under paragraph (2).

(2) Plan revisions

Any State in which there is located all or part of an ozone nonattainment area classified under subpart D of subchapter I of this chapter as Serious, Severe, or Extreme may submit a revision of the applicable implementation plan under part D of subchapter I of this chapter and section 7410 of this title to provide incentives for the sale or use in such an area or State of clean-fuel vehicles which are required to be produced, sold, and distributed in the State of California, and for the use in such an area or State of clean alternative fuels required to be produced and distributed by fuel suppliers and made available in California. Such plan provisions shall not take effect until 1 year after the State has provided notice of such provisions to motor vehicle manufacturers and to fuel suppliers.

(3) Incentives

The incentives referred to in paragraph (2) may include any or all of the following:

(A) A State registration fee on new motor vehicles registered in the State which are not clean-fuel vehicles in the amount of at least 1 percent of the cost of the vehicle. The proceeds of such fee shall be used to provide financial incentives to purchasers of clean-fuel vehicles and to vehicle dealers who sell high volumes or high percentages of clean-fuel vehicles and to defray the administrative costs of the incentive program.

(B) Provisions to exempt clean-fuel vehicles from high occupancy vehicle or trip reduction requirements.

(C) Provisions to provide preference in the use of existing parking spaces for clean-fuel vehicles.

The incentives under this paragraph shall not apply in the case of covered fleet vehicles.

(4) No sales or production mandate

The regulations and plan revisions under paragraphs (1) and (2) shall not include any production or sales mandate for clean-fuel vehicles or clean alternative fuels. Such regulations and plan revisions shall also provide that vehicle manufacturers and fuel suppliers may not be subject to penalties or sanctions for failing to produce or sell clean-fuel vehicles or clean alternative fuels.

(July 14, 1955, c. 360, Title II, § 249, as added by Pub. L. No. 101–549, Title II, § 229(a), 104 Stat. 2525 (Nov. 15, 1990).)

[1] So in original. Probably should be "clean-fuel."

[2] So in original. Probably should be "section 7586(f)."

[3] So in original. Probably should be followed by a comma.

HISTORICAL AND STATUTORY NOTES

References in Text

The Solid Waste Disposal Act, referred to in subsec. (c)(2)(D), is title II of Pub. L. No. 89–272, 79 Stat. 997 (Oct. 20, 1965), as amended generally by Pub. L. No. 94–580, § 2, 90 Stat. 2795 (Oct. 21, 1976), which is codified generally as chapter 82 (section 6901 et seq.) of this title. For complete classification of this Act to the Code, see Short Title of 1965 Acts note set out under section 6901 of this title and Tables.

November 15, 1990 referred to in subsec. (e)(3), was in the original "the date of the Clean Air Act Amendments of 1990", which was translated as meaning the date of enactment of Pub. L. No. 101–549, which enacted this section, to reflect the probable intent of Congress.

Effective and Applicability Provisions

1990 Acts. Section effective Nov. 15, 1990, except as otherwise provided, see section 711(b) of Pub. L. No. 101–549, set out as a note under section 7401 of this title.

Termination of Reporting Requirements

For termination of reporting provisions of subsec. (e) of this section, effective May 15, 2000, see Pub. L. No. 104–66, § 3003, as amended, set out as a note under 31 U.S.C.A. § 1113, and the 7th item on page 162 of House Document No. 103–7

Savings Provisions

Suits, actions or proceedings commenced under this chapter as in effect prior to Nov. 15, 1990, not to abate by reason of the taking effect of amendments by Pub. L. No. 101–549, except as otherwise provided for, see section 711(a) of Pub. L. No. 101–549, set out as a note under section 7401 of this title.

§ 7590. General provisions

[CAA § 250]

(a) State refueling facilities

If any State adopts enforceable provisions in an implementation plan applicable to a nonattainment area which provides that existing State refueling facilities will be made available to the public for the purchase of clean alternative fuels or that State-operated refueling facilities for such fuels will be constructed and operated by the State and made available to the public at reasonable times, taking into consideration safety, costs, and other relevant factors, in approving such plan under section 7410 of this title and part D[1], the Administrator may credit a State with the emission reductions for purposes of part D[1] attributable to such actions.

(b) No production mandate

The Administrator shall have no authority under this part to mandate the production of clean-fuel vehicles except as provided in the California pilot test program or to specify as applicable the models, lines, or types of, or marketing or price practices, policies, or strategies for, vehicles subject to this part. Nothing in this part shall be construed to give the Administrator authority to mandate marketing or pricing practices, policies, or strategies for fuels.

(c) Tank and fuel system safety

The Secretary of Transportation shall, in accordance with chapter 301 of Title 49, promulgate applicable regulations regarding the safety and use of fuel storage cylinders and fuel systems, including appropriate testing and retesting, in conversions of motor vehicles.

(d) Consultation with Department of Energy and Department of Transportation

The Administrator shall coordinate with the Secretaries of the Department of Energy and the Department of Transportation in carrying out the Administrator's duties under this part.

(July 14, 1955, c. 360, Title II, § 250, as added by Pub. L. No. 101–549, Title II, § 229(a), 104 Stat. 2528 (Nov. 15, 1990).)

[1] So in original. Probably should be "part D of subchapter I of this chapter."

HISTORICAL AND STATUTORY NOTES

Codifications

In subsec. (c), "chapter 301 of Title 49" substituted for "the National Motor Vehicle Traffic Safety Act of 1966 [15 U.S.C.A. § 1381 et seq.]", meaning "the National Traffic and Motor Vehicle Safety Act of 1966 [15 U.S.C.A. § 1381 et seq.]", on authority of Pub. L. No. 103–272, § 6(b), 108 Stat. 1378 (July 5, 1994), the first section of which enacted subtitles II, III, and V to X of Title 49.

Effective and Applicability Provisions

1990 Acts. Section effective Nov. 15, 1990, except as otherwise provided, see section 711(b) of Pub. L. No. 101–549, set out as a note under section 7401 of this title.

Savings Provisions

Suits, actions or proceedings commenced under this chapter as in effect prior to Nov. 15, 1990, not to abate by reason of the taking effect of amendments by Pub. L. No. 101–549, except as otherwise provided for, see section 711(a) of Pub. L. No. 101–549, set out as a note under section 7401 of this title.

SUBCHAPTER III—GENERAL PROVISIONS

§ 7601. Administration

[CAA § 301]

(a) Regulations; delegation of powers and duties; regional officers and employees

(1) The Administrator is authorized to prescribe such regulations as are necessary to carry out his functions under this chapter. The Administrator may delegate to any officer or employee of the Environmental Protection Agency such of his powers and duties under this chapter, except the making of regulations subject to section 7607(d) of this title, as he may deem necessary or expedient.

(2) Not later than one year after August 7, 1977, the Administrator shall promulgate regulations establishing general applicable procedures and policies for regional officers and employees (including the Regional Administrator) to follow in carrying out a delegation under paragraph (1), if any. Such regulations shall be designed—

(A) to assure fairness and uniformity in the criteria, procedures, and policies applied by the various regions in implementing and enforcing the chapter;

(B) to assure at least an adequate quality audit of each State's performance and adherence to the requirements of this chapter in implementing and enforcing the chapter, particularly in the review of new sources and in enforcement of the chapter; and

(C) to provide a mechanism for identifying and standardizing inconsistent or varying criteria, procedures, and policies being employed by such officers and employees in implementing and enforcing the chapter.

(b) Detail of Environmental Protection Agency personnel to air pollution control agencies

Upon the request of an air pollution control agency, personnel of the Environmental Protection Agency may be detailed to such agency for the purpose of carrying out the provisions of this chapter.

(c) Payments under grants; installments; advances or reimbursements

Payments under grants made under this chapter may be made in installments, and in advance or by way of reimbursement, as may be determined by the Administrator.

(d) Tribal authority

(1) Subject to the provisions of paragraph (2), the Administrator—

(A) is authorized to treat Indian tribes as States under this chapter, except for purposes of the requirement that makes available for application by each State no less than one-half of 1 percent of annual appropriations under section 7405 of this title; and

(B) may provide any such Indian tribe grant and contract assistance to carry out functions provided by this chapter.

(2) The Administrator shall promulgate regulations within 18 months after November 15, 1990, specifying those provisions of this chapter for which it is appropriate to treat Indian tribes as States. Such treatment shall be authorized only if—

(A) the Indian tribe has a governing body carrying out substantial governmental duties and powers;

(B) the functions to be exercised by the Indian tribe pertain to the management and protection of air resources within the exterior boundaries of the reservation or other areas within the tribe's jurisdiction; and

(C) the Indian tribe is reasonably expected to be capable, in the judgment of the Administrator, of carrying out the functions to be exercised in a manner consistent with the terms and purposes of this chapter and all applicable regulations.

(3) The Administrator may promulgate regulations which establish the elements of tribal implementation plans and procedures for approval or disapproval of tribal implementation plans and portions thereof.

(4) In any case in which the Administrator determines that the treatment of Indian tribes as identical to States is inappropriate or administratively infeasible, the Administrator may provide, by regulation, other means by which the Administrator will directly administer such provisions so as to achieve the appropriate purpose.

(5) Until such time as the Administrator promulgates regulations pursuant to this subsection, the Administrator may continue to provide financial assistance to eligible Indian tribes under section 7405 of this title.

(July 14, 1955, c. 360, Title III, § 301, formerly § 8, as added by Pub. L. No. 88–206, § 1, 77 Stat. 400 (Dec. 17, 1963); and renumbered by Pub. L. No. 89–272, Title I, § 101(4), 79 Stat. 992 (Oct. 20, 1965); and amended by Pub. L. No. 90–148, § 2, 81 Stat. 504 (Nov. 21, 1967); Pub. L. No. 91–604, §§ 3(b)(2), 15(c)(2), 84 Stat. 1677, 1713 (Dec. 31, 1970); Pub. L. No. 95–95, Title III, § 305(e), 91 Stat. 776 (Aug. 7, 1977); Pub. L. No. 101–549, Title I, §§ 107(d), 108(i), 104 Stat. 2464, 2467 (Nov. 15, 1990).)

Historical and statutory notes

Codifications

This section was formerly codified as section 1857g of this title.

Effective and Applicability Provisions

1990 Acts. Amendment by Pub. L. No. 101–549 effective Nov. 15, 1990, except as otherwise provided, see section 711(b) of Pub. L. No. 101–549, set out as a note under section 7401 of this title.

1977 Acts. Amendment by Pub. L. No. 95–95 effective Aug. 7, 1977, except as otherwise expressly provided, see section 406(d) of Pub. L. No. 95–95, set out as a note under section 7401 of this title.

Savings Provisions

Suits, actions or proceedings commenced under this chapter as in effect prior to Nov. 15, 1990, not to abate by reason of the taking effect of amendments by Pub. L. No. 101–549, except as otherwise provided for, see section 711(a) of Pub. L. No. 101–549, set out as a note under section 7401 of this title.

Prior Provisions

A prior section 8 of Act of July 14, 1955, c. 360, as added by Pub. L. No. 86–365, § 2, 73 Stat. 646 (Sept. 22, 1959), which was codified as a prior section 1857g of this title prior to the general amendment of this chapter by Pub. L. No. 88–206, provided for cooperative effort.

Disadvantaged Business Concerns; Use of Quotas Prohibited

Pub. L. No. 101–549, Title X, §§ 1001, 1002, 104 Stat. 2708 (Nov. 15, 1990), provided that:

"Sec. 1001. Disadvantaged business concerns.

"(a) In general.—In providing for any research relating to the requirements of the amendments made by the Clean Air Act Amendments of 1990 [Pub. L. No. 101–549, 104 Stat. 2399 (Nov. 15, 1990), for distribution which Act to the Code, see Tables] which uses funds of the Environmental Protection Agency, the Administrator of the Environmental Protection Agency shall, to the extent practicable, require that not less than 10 percent of total Federal funding for such research will be made available to disadvantaged business concerns.

"(b) Definition.—

"(1) (A) For purposes of subsection (a), the term 'disadvantaged business concern' means a concern—

"(i) which is at least 51 percent owned by one or more socially and economically disadvantaged individuals or, in the case of a publicly traded company, at least 51 percent of the stock of which is owned by one or more socially and economically disadvantaged individuals; and

"(ii) the management and daily business operations of which are controlled by such individuals.

"(B) (i) A for-profit business concern is presumed to be a disadvantaged business concern for purposes of subsection (a) if it is at least 51 percent owned by, or in the case of a concern which is a publicly traded company at least 51 percent of the stock of the company is owned by, one or more individuals who are members of the following groups:

"(I) Black Americans.

"(II) Hispanic Americans.

"(III) Native Americans.

"(IV) Asian Americans.

"(V) Women.

"(VI) Disabled Americans.

"(ii) The presumption established by clause (i) may be rebutted with respect to a particular business concern if it is reasonably established that the individual or individuals referred to in that clause with respect to that business concern are not experiencing impediments to establishing or developing such concern as a result of the individual's identification as a member of a group specified in that clause.

"(C) The following institutions are presumed to be disadvantaged business concerns for purposes of subsection (a):

"(i) Historically black colleges and universities, and colleges and universities having a student body in which 40 percent of the students are Hispanic.

"(ii) Minority institutions (as that term is defined by the Secretary of Education pursuant to the General Education Provision Act (20 U.S.C. 1221 et seq.) [section 1221 et seq. of Title 20], Education).

"(iii) Private and voluntary organizations controlled by individuals who are socially and economically disadvantaged.

"(D) A joint venture may be considered to be a disadvantaged business concern under subsection (a), notwithstanding the size of such joint venture, if—

"(i) a party to the joint venture is a disadvantaged business concern; and

"(ii) that party owns at least 51 percent of the joint venture.

A person who is not an economically disadvantaged individual or a disadvantaged business concern, as a party to a joint venture, may not be a party to more than 2 awarded contracts in a fiscal year solely by reason of this subparagraph.

"(E) Nothing in this paragraph shall prohibit any member of a racial or ethnic group that is not listed in subparagraph (B)(i) from establishing that they have been impeded in establishing or developing a business concern as a result of racial or ethnic discrimination.

"**Sec. 1002.** Use of quotas prohibited. Nothing in this title [Title X of Pub. L. No. 101–594, 104 Stat. 2708 (Nov. 15, 1990), enacting this note] shall permit or require the use of quotas or a requirement that has the effect of a quota in determining eligibility under section 1001."

Modification or Rescission of Rules, Regulations, Orders, Determinations, Contracts, Certifications, Authorizations, Delegations, and Other Actions

All rules, regulations, orders, determinations, contracts, certifications, authorizations, delegations, or other actions duly issued, made, or taken by or pursuant to Act of July 14, 1955, the Clean Air Act, as in effect immediately prior to the date of enactment of Pub. L. No. 95–95 [Aug. 7, 1977] to continue in full force and effect until modified or rescinded in accordance with Act of July 14, 1955, as amended by Pub. L. No. 95–95 [this chapter], see section 406(b) of Pub. L. No. 95–95, set out as an Effective Date of 1977 Acts note under section 7401 of this title.

§ 7602. Definitions

[CAA § 302]

When used in this chapter—

(a) The term "Administrator" means the Administrator of the Environmental Protection Agency.

(b) The term "air pollution control agency" means any of the following:

(1) A single State agency designated by the Governor of that State as the official State air pollution control agency for purposes of this chapter.

(2) An agency established by two or more States and having substantial powers or duties pertaining to the prevention and control of air pollution.

(3) A city, county, or other local government health authority, or, in the case of any city, county, or other local government in which there is an agency other than the health authority charged with responsibility for enforcing ordinances or laws relating to the prevention and control of air pollution, such other agency.

(4) An agency of two or more municipalities located in the same State or in different States and having substantial powers or duties pertaining to the prevention and control of air pollution.

(5) An agency of an Indian tribe.

(c) The term "interstate air pollution control agency" means—

(1) an air pollution control agency established by two or more States, or

(2) an air pollution control agency of two or more municipalities located in different States.

(d) The term "State" means a State, the District of Columbia, the Commonwealth of Puerto Rico, the Virgin Islands, Guam, and American Samoa and includes the Commonwealth of the Northern Mariana Islands.

(e) The term "person" includes an individual, corporation, partnership, association, State, municipality, political subdivision of a State, and any agency, department, or instrumentality of the United States and any officer, agent, or employee thereof.

(f) The term "municipality" means a city, town, borough, county, parish, district, or other public body created by or pursuant to State law.

(g) The term "air pollutant" means any air pollution agent or combination of such agents, including any physical, chemical, biological, radioactive (including source material, special nuclear material, and byproduct material) substance or matter which is emitted into or otherwise enters the ambient air. Such term includes any precursors to the formation of any air pollutant, to the extent the Administrator has identified such precursor or precursors for the particular purpose for which the term "air pollutant" is used.

(h) All language referring to effects on welfare includes, but is not limited to, effects on soils, water, crops, vegetation, manmade materials, animals, wildlife, weather, visibility, and climate, damage to and deterioration of property, and hazards to transportation, as well as effects on economic values and on personal comfort and well-being, whether caused by transformation, conversion, or combination with other air pollutants.

(i) The term "Federal land manager" means, with respect to any lands in the United States, the Secretary of the department with authority over such lands.

(j) Except as otherwise expressly provided, the terms "major stationary source" and "major emitting facility" mean any stationary facility or source of air pollutants which directly emits, or has the potential to emit, one hundred tons per year or more of any air pollutant (including any major emitting facility or source of fugitive emissions of any such pollutant, as determined by rule by the Administrator).

(k) The terms "emission limitation" and "emission standard" mean a requirement established by the State or the Administrator which limits the quantity, rate, or concentration of emissions of air pollutants on a continuous basis, including any requirement relating to the operation or maintenance of a source to assure continuous emission reduction, and any design, equipment, work practice or operational standard promulgated under this chapter.[1]

(*l*) The term "standard of performance" means a requirement of continuous emission reduction, including any requirement relating to the operation or maintenance of a source to assure continuous emission reduction.

(m) The term "means of emission limitation" means a system of continuous emission reduction (including the use of specific technology or fuels with specified pollution characteristics).

(n) The term "primary standard attainment date" means the date specified in the applicable implementation plan for the attainment of a national primary ambient air quality standard for any air pollutant.

(*o*) The term "delayed compliance order" means an order issued by the State or by the Administrator to an existing stationary source, postponing the date required under an applicable implementation plan for compliance by such source with any requirement of such plan.

(p) The term "schedule and timetable of compliance" means a schedule of required measures including an enforceable sequence of actions or operations leading to compliance with an emission limitation, other limitation, prohibition, or standard.

(q) For purposes of this chapter, the term "applicable implementation plan" means the portion (or portions) of the implementation plan, or most recent revision thereof, which has been approved under section 7410 of this title, or promulgated under section 7410(c) of this title, or promulgated or approved pursuant to regulations promulgated under section 7601(d) of this title and which implements the relevant requirements of this chapter.

(r) **Indian tribe.**—The term "Indian tribe" means any Indian tribe, band, nation, or other organized group or community, including any Alaska Native village, which is Federally recognized as eligible for the special programs and services provided by the United States to Indians because of their status as Indians.

(s) **VOC.**—The term "VOC" means volatile organic compound, as defined by the Administrator.

(t) **PM-10.**—The term "PM-10" means particulate matter with an aerodynamic diameter less than or equal to a nominal ten micrometers, as measured by such method as the Administrator may determine.

(u) **NAAQS and CTG.**—The term "NAAQS" means national ambient air quality standard. The term "CTG" means a Control Technique Guideline published by the Administrator under section 7408 of this title.

(v) **NO_x.**—The term "NO_x" means oxides of nitrogen.

(w) **CO.**—The term "CO" means carbon monoxide.

(x) **Small source.**—The term "small source" means a source that emits less than 100 tons of regulated pollutants per year, or any class of persons that the Administrator determines, through regulation, generally lack technical ability or knowledge regarding control of air pollution.

(y) **Federal implementation plan.**—The term "Federal implementation plan" means a plan (or portion thereof) promulgated by the Administrator to fill all or a portion of a gap or otherwise correct all or a portion of an inadequacy in a State implementation plan, and which includes enforceable emission limitations or other control measures, means or techniques (including economic incentives, such as marketable permits or auctions of emissions allowances), and provides for attainment of the relevant national ambient air quality standard.

(z) Stationary source.—The term "stationary source" means generally any source of an air pollutant except those emissions resulting directly from an internal combustion engine for transportation purposes or from a nonroad engine or nonroad vehicle as defined in section 7550 of this title.

(July 14, 1955, c. 360, Title III, § 302, formerly § 9, as added by Pub. L. No. 88–206, § 1, 77 Stat. 400 (Dec. 17, 1963); and renumbered by Pub. L. No. 89–272, Title I, § 101(4), 79 Stat. 992 (Oct. 20, 1965); and amended by Pub. L. No. 90–148, § 2, 81 Stat. 504 (Nov. 21, 1967); Pub. L. No. 91–604, § 15(a)(1), (c)(1), 84 Stat. 1710, 1713 (Dec. 31, 1970); Pub. L. No. 95–95, Title II, § 218(c), Title III, § 301, 91 Stat. 761, 769 (Aug. 7, 1977); Pub. L. No. 95–190, § 14(a)(76), 91 Stat. 1404 (Nov. 16, 1977); Pub. L. No. 101–549, Title I, §§ 101(d)(4), 107(a), (b), 108(j), 109(b), Title III, § 302(e), Title VII, § 709, 104 Stat. 2409, 2464, 2468, 2470, 2574, 2684 (Nov. 15, 1990).)

[1] So in original.

HISTORICAL AND STATUTORY NOTES

Codifications

This section was formerly codified as section 1857h of this title.

Effective and Applicability Provisions

1990 Acts. Amendment by Pub. L. No. 101–549 effective Nov. 15, 1990, except as otherwise provided, see section 711(b) of Pub. L. No. 101–549, set out as a note under section 7401 of this title.

1977 Acts. Amendment by Pub. L. No. 95–95 effective Aug. 7, 1977, except as otherwise expressly provided, see section 406(d) of Pub. L. No. 95–95, set out as a note under section 7401 of this title.

Savings Provisions

Suits, actions or proceedings commenced under this chapter as in effect prior to Nov. 15, 1990, not to abate by reason of the taking effect of amendments by Pub. L. No. 101–549, except as otherwise provided for, see section 711(a) of Pub. L. No. 101–549, set out as a note under section 7401 of this title.

Prior Provisions

Provisions similar to subsecs. (b) and (d) of this section were contained in a prior section 1857e, Act of July 14, 1955, c. 360, § 6, 69 Stat. 323, prior to the general amendment of this chapter by Pub. L. No. 88–206.

§ 7603. Emergency powers

[CAA § 303]

Notwithstanding any other provision of this chapter, the Administrator, upon receipt of evidence that a pollution source or combination of sources (including moving sources) is presenting an imminent and substantial endangerment to public health or welfare, or the environment, may bring suit on behalf of the United States in the appropriate United States district court to immediately restrain any person causing or contributing to the alleged pollution to stop the emission of air pollutants causing or contributing to such pollution or to take such other action as may be necessary. If it is not practicable to assure prompt protection of public health or welfare or the environment by commencement of such a civil action, the Administrator may issue such orders as may be necessary to protect public health or welfare or the environment. Prior to taking any action under this section, the Administrator shall consult with appropriate State and local authorities and attempt to confirm the accuracy of the information on which the action proposed to be taken is based. Any order issued by the Administrator under this section shall be effective upon issuance and shall remain in effect for a period of not more than 60 days, unless the Administrator brings an action pursuant to the first sentence of this section before the expiration of that period. Whenever the Administrator brings such an action within the 60-day period, such order shall remain in effect for an additional 14 days or for such longer period as may be authorized by the court in which such action is brought.

(July 14, 1955, c. 360, Title III, § 303, as added by Pub. L. No. 91–604, § 12(a), 84 Stat. 1705 (Dec. 31, 1970); and amended by Pub. L. No. 95–95, Title III, § 302(a), 91 Stat. 770 (Aug. 7, 1977); Pub. L. No. 101–549, Title VII, § 704, 104 Stat. 2681 (Nov. 15, 1990).)

HISTORICAL AND STATUTORY NOTES

Codifications

This section was formerly codified as section 1857h–1 of this title.

Effective and Applicability Provisions

1990 Acts. Amendment by Pub. L. No. 101–549 effective Nov. 15, 1990, except as otherwise provided, see section 711(b) of Pub. L. No. 101–549, set out as a note under section 7401 of this title.

1977 Acts. Amendment by Pub. L. No. 95–95 effective Aug. 7, 1977, except as otherwise expressly provided, see section 406(d) of Pub. L. No. 95–95, set out as a note under section 7401 of this title.

Savings Provisions

Suits, actions or proceedings commenced under this chapter as in effect prior to Nov. 15, 1990, not to abate by reason of the taking effect of amendments by Pub. L. No. 101–549, except as otherwise provided for, see section 711(a) of Pub. L. No. 101–549, set out as a note under section 7401 of this title.

Prior Provisions

A prior section 303 of Act of July 14, 1955, was renumbered section 310 by Pub. L. No. 91–604, and is set out as section 7610 of this title.

Modification or Rescission of Rules, Regulations, Orders, Determinations, Contracts, Certifications, Authorizations, Delegations, and Other Actions

All rules, regulations, orders, determinations, contracts, certifications, authorizations, delegations, or other actions duly issued, made, or taken by or pursuant to Act of July 14, 1955, the Clean Air Act, as in effect immediately prior to the date of enactment of Pub. L. No. 95–95 [Aug. 7, 1977] to continue in full force and effect until modified or rescinded in accordance with Act of July 14, 1955, as amended by Pub. L. No. 95–95 [this chapter], see section 406(b) of Pub. L. No. 95–95, set out as an Effective Date of 1977 Acts note under section 7401 of this title.

Pending Actions and Proceedings

Suits, actions, and other proceedings lawfully commenced by or against the Administrator or any other officer or employee of the United States in his official capacity or in relation to the discharge of his official duties under Act of July 14, 1955, the Clean Air Act, as in effect immediately prior to the enactment of Pub. L. No. 95–95 [Aug. 7, 1977], not to abate by reason of the taking effect of Pub. L. No. 95–95, see section 406(a) of Pub. L. No. 95–95, set out as an Effective Date of 1977 Acts note under section 7401 of this title.

§ 7604. Citizen suits

[CAA § 304]

(a) Authority to bring civil action; jurisdiction

Except as provided in subsection (b) of this section, any person may commence a civil action on his own behalf—

(1) against any person (including (i) the United States, and (ii) any other governmental instrumentality or agency to the extent permitted by the Eleventh Amendment to the Constitution) who is alleged to have violated (if there is evidence that the alleged violation has been repeated) or to be in violation of (A) an emission standard or limitation under this chapter or (B) an order issued by the Administrator or a State with respect to such a standard or limitation,

(2) against the Administrator where there is alleged a failure of the Administrator to perform any act or duty under this chapter which is not discretionary with the Administrator, or

(3) against any person who proposes to construct or constructs any new or modified major emitting facility without a permit required under part C of subchapter I of this chapter (relating to significant deterioration of air quality) or part D of subchapter I of this chapter (relating to nonattainment) or who is alleged to have violated (if there is evidence that the alleged violation has been repeated) or to be in violation of any condition of such permit.

The district courts shall have jurisdiction, without regard to the amount in controversy or the citizenship of the parties, to enforce such an emission standard or limitation, or such an order, or to order the Administrator to perform such act or duty, as the case may be, and to apply any appropriate civil penalties (except for actions under paragraph (2)). The district courts of the United States shall have jurisdiction to compel (consistent with paragraph (2) of this subsection) agency action unreasonably delayed, except that an action to compel agency action referred to in section 7607(b) of this title which is unreasonably delayed may only be filed in a United States District Court within the circuit in which such action would be reviewable under section 7607(b) of this title. In any such action for unreasonable delay, notice to the entities referred to in subsection (b)(1)(A) of this section shall be provided 180 days before commencing such action.

(b) Notice

No action may be commenced—

(1) under subsection (a)(1) of this section—

(A) prior to 60 days after the plaintiff has given notice of the violation (i) to the Administrator, (ii) to the State in which the violation occurs, and (iii) to any alleged violator of the standard, limitation, or order, or

(B) if the Administrator or State has commenced and is diligently prosecuting a civil action in a court of the United States or a State to require compliance with the standard, limitation, or order, but in any such action in a court of the United States any person may intervene as a matter of right.

(2) under subsection (a)(2) of this section prior to 60 days after the plaintiff has given notice of such action to the Administrator,

except that such action may be brought immediately after such notification in the case of an action under this section respecting a violation of section 7412(i)(3)(A) or (f)(4) of this title or an order issued by the Administrator pursuant to section 7413(a) of this title. Notice under this subsection shall be given in such manner as the Administrator shall prescribe by regulation.

(c) Venue; intervention by Administrator; service of complaint; consent judgment

(1) Any action respecting a violation by a stationary source of an emission standard or limitation or an order respecting such standard or limitation may be brought only in the judicial district in which such source is located.

(2) In any action under this section, the Administrator, if not a party, may intervene as a matter of right at any time in the proceeding. A judgment in an action under this section to which the United States is not a party shall not, however, have any binding effect upon the United States.

(3) Whenever any action is brought under this section the plaintiff shall serve a copy of the complaint on the Attorney General of the United States and on the Administrator. No consent judgment shall be entered in an action brought under this section in which the United States is not a party prior to 45 days following the receipt of a copy of the proposed consent judgment by the Attorney General and the Administrator during which time the Government may submit its comments on the proposed consent judgment to the court and parties or may intervene as a matter of right.

(d) Award of costs; security

The court, in issuing any final order in any action brought pursuant to subsection (a) of this section, may award costs of litigation (including reasonable attorney and expert witness fees) to any party, whenever the court determines such award is appropriate. The court may, if a temporary restraining order or preliminary injunction is sought, require the filing of a bond or equivalent security in accordance with the Federal Rules of Civil Procedure.

(e) Nonrestriction of other rights

Nothing in this section shall restrict any right which any person (or class of persons) may have under any statute or common law to seek enforcement of any emission standard or limitation or to seek any other relief (including relief against the Administrator or a State agency). Nothing in this section or in any other law of the United States shall be construed to prohibit, exclude, or restrict any State, local, or interstate authority from—

(1) bringing any enforcement action or obtaining any judicial remedy or sanction in any State or local court, or

(2) bringing any administrative enforcement action or obtaining any administrative remedy or sanction in any State or local administrative agency, department or instrumentality,

against the United States, any department, agency, or instrumentality thereof, or any officer, agent, or employee thereof under State or local law respecting control and abatement of air pollution. For provisions requiring compliance by the United States, departments, agencies, instrumentalities, officers, agents, and employees in the same manner as nongovernmental entities, see section 7418 of this title.

(f) "Emission standard or limitation under this chapter" defined

For purposes of this section, the term "emission standard or limitation under this chapter" means—

(1) a schedule or timetable of compliance, emission limitation, standard of performance or emission standard,

(2) a control or prohibition respecting a motor vehicle fuel or fuel additive, or[1]

(3) any condition or requirement of a permit under part C of subchapter I of this chapter (relating to significant deterioration of air quality) or part D of subchapter I of this chapter (relating to nonattainment),[2] section 7419 of this title (relating to primary nonferrous smelter orders), any condition or requirement under an applicable implementation plan relating to transportation control measures, air quality maintenance plans, vehicle inspection and maintenance programs or vapor recovery requirements, section 7545(e) and (f) of this title (relating to fuels and fuel additives), section 7491 of this title (relating to visibility protection), any condition or requirement under subchapter VI of this chapter (relating to ozone protection), or any requirement under section 7411 or 7412 of this title (without regard to whether such requirement is expressed as an emission standard or otherwise);[3] or

(4) any other standard, limitation, or schedule established under any permit issued pursuant to subchapter V of this chapter or under any applicable State implementation plan approved by the Administrator, any permit term or condition, and any requirement to obtain a permit as a condition of operations.[4]

which is in effect under this chapter (including a requirement applicable by reason of section 7418 of this title) or under an applicable implementation plan.

(g) Penalty fund

(1) Penalties received under subsection (a) of this section shall be deposited in a special fund in the United States Treasury for licensing and other services. Amounts in such fund are authorized to be appropriated and shall remain available until expended, for use by the Administrator to finance air compliance and enforcement activities. The Administrator shall annually report to the Congress about the sums deposited into the fund, the sources thereof, and the actual and proposed uses thereof.

(2) Notwithstanding paragraph (1) the court in any action under this subsection to apply civil penalties shall have discretion to order that such civil penalties, in lieu of being deposited in the fund referred to in paragraph (1), be used in beneficial mitigation projects which are consistent with this chapter and enhance the public health or the environment. The court shall obtain the view of the Administrator in exercising such discretion and selecting any such projects. The amount of any such payment in any such action shall not exceed $100,000.

(July 14, 1955, c. 360, Title III, § 304, as added by Pub. L. No. 91–604, § 12(a), 84 Stat. 1706 (Dec. 31, 1970); and amended by Pub. L. No. 95–95, Title III, § 303(a)–(c), 91 Stat. 771, 772 (Aug. 7, 1977); Pub. L. No. 95–190, § 14(a)(77), (78), 91 Stat. 1404 (Nov. 16, 1977); Pub. L. No. 101–549, Title III, § 302(f), Title VII, § 707(a)–(g), 104 Stat. 2574, 2682, 2683 (Nov. 15, 1990).)

[1] So in original. The word "or" probably should not appear.

[2] So in original.

[3] So in original. The semicolon probably should be comma.

[4] So in original. The period probably should be a comma.

HISTORICAL AND STATUTORY NOTES

References in Text

The Federal Rules of Civil Procedure, referred to in subsec. (d), are set out in Title 28, Judiciary and Judicial Procedure.

Codifications

This section was formerly codified as section 1857h–2 of this title.

Effective and Applicability Provisions

1990 Acts. Amendment by section 302(f) of Pub. L. No. 101–549 effective Nov. 15, 1990, except as otherwise provided, see section 711(b) of Pub. L. No. 101–549, set out as a note under section 7401 of this title.

Section 707(g) of Pub. L. No. 101–549 provided in part that: "The amendment made by this subsection [amending this section] shall take effect with respect to actions brought after the date 2 years after the enactment of the Clean Air Act Amendments of 1990 [Nov. 15, 1990]."

1977 Acts. Amendment by Pub. L. No. 95–95 effective Aug. 7, 1977, except as otherwise expressly provided, see section 406(d) of Pub. L. No. 95–95, set out as a note under section 7401 of this title.

Savings Provisions

Suits, actions or proceedings commenced under this chapter as in effect prior to Nov. 15, 1990, not to abate by reason of the taking effect of amendments by Pub. L. No. 101–549, except as otherwise provided for, see section 711(a) of Pub. L. No. 101–549, set out as a note under section 7401 of this title.

Prior Provisions

A prior section 304 of Act of July 14, 1955, was renumbered section 311 by Pub. L. No. 91–604, and is set out as section 7611 of this title.

Termination of Reporting Requirements

For termination, effective May 15, 2000, of reporting provisions in subsec. (g)(1) of this section, see Pub. L. No. 104–66, § 3003, as amended, set out as a note under 31 U.S.C.A. § 1113, and the sixth item on page 165 of House Document No. 103–7.

Modification or Rescission of Rules, Regulations, Orders, Determinations, Contracts, Certifications, Authorizations, Delegations, and Other Actions

All rules, regulations, orders, determinations, contracts, certifications, authorizations, delegations, or other actions duly issued, made, or taken by or pursuant to Act of July 14, 1955, the Clean Air Act, as in effect immediately prior to the date of enactment of Pub. L. No. 95–95 [Aug. 7, 1977] to continue in full force and effect until modified or rescinded in accordance with Act of July 14, 1955, as amended by Pub. L. No. 95–95 [this chapter], see section 406(b) of Pub. L. No. 95–95, set out as an Effective Date of 1977 Acts note under section 7401 of this title.

Pending Actions and Proceedings

Suits, actions, and other proceedings lawfully commenced by or against the Administrator or any other officer or employee of the United States in his official capacity or in relation to the discharge of his official duties under Act of July 14, 1955, the Clean Air Act, as in effect immediately prior to the enactment of Pub. L. No. 95–95 [Aug. 7, 1977], not to abate by reason of the taking effect of Pub. L. No. 95–95, see section 406(a) of Pub. L. No. 95–95, set out as an Effective Date of 1977 Acts note under section 7401 of this title.

§ 7605. Representation in litigation

[CAA § 305]

(a) Attorney General; attorneys appointed by Administrator

The Administrator shall request the Attorney General to appear and represent him in any civil action instituted under this chapter to which the Administrator is a party. Unless the Attorney General notifies the Administrator that he will appear in such action, within a reasonable time, attorneys appointed by the Administrator shall appear and represent him.

(b) Memorandum of understanding regarding legal representation

In the event the Attorney General agrees to appear and represent the Administrator in any such action, such representation shall be conducted in accordance with, and shall include participation by, attorneys appointed by the Administrator to the extent authorized by, the memorandum of understanding between the Department of Justice and the Environmental Protection Agency, dated June 13, 1977, respecting representation of the agency by the department in civil litigation.

(July 14, 1955, c. 360, Title III, § 305, as added by Pub. L. No. 91–604, § 12(a), 84 Stat. 1707 (Dec. 31, 1970); and amended by Pub. L. No. 95–95, Title III, § 304(a), 91 Stat. 772 (Aug. 7, 1977).)

HISTORICAL AND STATUTORY NOTES

Codifications

This section was formerly codified as section 1857h–3 of this title.

Effective and Applicability Provisions

1977 Acts. Amendment by Pub. L. No. 95–95 effective Aug. 7, 1977, except as otherwise expressly provided, see section 406(d) of Pub. L. No. 95–95, set out as a note under section 7401 of this title.

Prior Provisions

A prior section 305 of Act of July 14, 1955, was renumbered section 312 by Pub. L. No. 91–604, and is set out as section 7612 of this title.

Another prior section 305 of Act of July 14, 1955, ch. 360, title III, formerly § 12, as added by Pub. L. No. 88–206, § 1, 77 Stat. 401 (Dec. 17, 1963), was renumbered section 305 by Pub. L. No. 89–272, renumbered section 308 by Pub. L. No. 90–148, and renumbered section 315 by Pub. L. No. 91–604, and is codified as section 7615 of this title.

Modification or Rescission of Rules, Regulations, Orders, Determinations, Contracts, Certifications, Authorizations, Delegations, and Other Actions

All rules, regulations, orders, determinations, contracts, certifications, authorizations, delegations, or other actions duly issued, made, or taken by or pursuant to Act of July 14, 1955, the Clean Air Act, as in effect immediately prior to the date of enactment of Pub. L. No. 95–95 [Aug. 7, 1977] to continue in full force and effect until modified or rescinded in accordance with Act of July 14, 1955, as amended by Pub. L. No. 95–95 [this chapter], see section 406(b) of Pub. L. No. 95–95, set out as an Effective Date of 1977 Acts note under section 7401 of this title.

Pending Actions and Proceedings

Suits, actions, and other proceedings lawfully commenced by or against the Administrator or any other officer or employee of the United States in his official capacity or in relation to the discharge of his official duties under Act of July 14, 1955, the Clean Air Act, as in effect immediately prior to the enactment of Pub. L. No. 95–95 [Aug. 7, 1977], not to abate by reason of the taking effect of Pub. L. No. 95–95, see section 406(a) of Pub. L. No. 95–95, set out as an Effective Date of 1977 Acts note under section 7401 of this title.

§ 7606. Federal procurement

[CAA § 306]

(a) Contracts with violators prohibited

No Federal agency may enter into any contract with any person who is convicted of any offense under section 7413(c) of this title for the procurement of goods, materials, and services to perform such contract at any facility at which the violation which gave rise to such conviction occurred if such facility is owned, leased, or supervised by such person. The prohibition in the preceding sentence shall continue until the Administrator certifies that the condition giving rise to such a conviction has been corrected. For convictions arising under section 7413(c)(2) of this title, the condition giving rise to the conviction also shall be considered to include any substantive violation of this chapter associated with the violation of 7413(c)(2) of this title. The Administrator may extend this prohibition to other facilities owned or operated by the convicted person.

(b) Notification procedures

The Administrator shall establish procedures to provide all Federal agencies with the notification necessary for the purposes of subsection (a) of this section.

(c) Federal agency contracts

In order to implement the purposes and policy of this chapter to protect and enhance the quality of the Nation's air, the President shall, not more than 180 days after December 31, 1970, cause to be issued an order (1) requiring each Federal agency authorized to enter into contracts and each Federal agency which is empowered to extend Federal assistance by way of grant, loan, or contract to effectuate the purpose and policy of this chapter in such contracting or assistance activities, and (2) setting forth procedures, sanctions, penalties, and such other provisions, as the President determines necessary to carry out such requirement.

(d) Exemptions; notification to Congress

The President may exempt any contract, loan, or grant from all or part of the provisions of this section where he determines such exemption is necessary in the paramount interest of the United States and he shall notify the Congress of such exemption.

(July 14, 1955, c. 360, Title III, § 306, as added by Pub. L. No. 91–604, § 12(a), 84 Stat. 1707 (Dec. 31, 1970); and amended by Pub. L. No. 101–549, Title VII, § 705, 104 Stat. 2682 (Nov. 15, 1990).)

HISTORICAL AND STATUTORY NOTES

Codifications

This section was formerly codified as section 1857h–4 of this title.

Subsec. (e) of this section, shown as omitted, which required the President to annually report to Congress on measures taken toward implementing the purpose and intent of this section, terminated, effective May 15, 2000, pursuant to section 3003 of Pub. L. No. 104–66, as amended, set out as a note under 31 U.S.C.A. § 1113. See, also, the 14th item on page 20 of House Document No. 103–7.

Effective and Applicability Provisions

1990 Acts. Amendment by Pub. L. No. 101–549 effective Nov. 15, 1990, except as otherwise provided, see section 711(b) of Pub. L. No. 101–549, set out as a note under section 7401 of this title.

Savings Provisions

Suits, actions or proceedings commenced under this chapter as in effect prior to Nov. 15, 1990, not to abate by reason of the taking effect of amendments by Pub. L. No. 101–549, except as otherwise provided for, see section 711(a) of Pub. L. No. 101–549, set out as a note under section 7401 of this title.

Prior Provisions

A prior § 306 of Act of July 14, 1955, c. 360, Title III, as added by Pub. L. No. 90–148, § 2, 81 Stat. 506 (Nov. 21, 1967), was renumbered section 313 by Pub. L. No. 91–604, and is codified as former section 7613 of this title.

Another prior section 306 of Act of July 14, 1955, c. 360, Title III, formerly § 13, as added by Pub. L. No. 88–206, § 1, 77 Stat. 401 (Dec. 17, 1963), and renumbered § 306 by Pub. L. No. 89–272, Title I, § 101(4), 79 Stat. 992 (Oct. 20, 1965), and renumbered § 309 by Pub. L. No. 90–148, § 2, 81 Stat. 506 (Nov. 21, 1967), and renumbered § 316by Pub. L. No. 91–604, § 12(a), 84 Stat. 1705 (Dec. 31, 1970), which related to appropriations, was codified as prior section 1857*l* of this title and was repealed by section 306 of Pub. L. No. 95–95. See section 7626 of this title.

Federal Acquisition Regulation: Contractor Certification or Contract Clause for Acquisition of Commercial Items

Pub. L. No. 103–355, Title VIII, § 8301(g), 108 Stat. 3397 (Oct. 13, 1994), as amended by Pub. L. No. 115–232, § 836(g)(8), 132 Stat 1636, 1874 (Aug. 13, 2018), provided that: "The Federal Acquisition Regulation may not contain a requirement for a certification by a contractor under a contract for the acquisition of commercial products or commercial services, or a requirement that such a contract include a contract clause, in order to implement a prohibition or requirement of section 306 of the Clean Air Act (42 U.S.C. 7606) [this section] or a prohibition or requirement issued in the implementation of that section [this section], since there is nothing in such section 306 [this section] that requires such a certification or contract clause."

§ 7607. Administrative proceedings and judicial review

[CAA § 307]

(a) Administrative subpenas; confidentiality; witnesses

In connection with any determination under section 7410(f) of this title, or for purposes of obtaining information under section 7521(b)(4) or 7545(c)(3) of this title, any investigation, monitoring, reporting requirement, entry, compliance inspection, or administrative enforcement proceeding under the[1] chapter (including but not limited to section 7413, section 7414, section 7420, section 7429, section 7477, section 7524, section 7525, section 7542, section 7603, or section 7606 of this title),[2] the Administrator may issue subpenas for the attendance and testimony of witnesses and the production of relevant papers, books, and documents, and he may administer oaths. Except for emission data, upon a showing satisfactory to the Administrator by such owner or operator that such papers, books, documents, or information or particular part thereof, if made public, would divulge trade secrets or secret processes of such owner or operator, the Administrator shall consider such record, report, or information or particular portion thereof confidential in accordance with the purposes of section 1905 of Title 18, except that such paper, book, document, or information may be disclosed to other officers, employees, or authorized representatives of the United States concerned with carrying out this chapter, to persons carrying out the National Academy of Sciences' study and investigation provided for in section 7521(c) of this title, or when relevant in any proceeding under this chapter. Witnesses summoned shall be paid the same fees and mileage that are paid witnesses in the courts of the United States. In case of contumacy or refusal to obey a subpena served upon any person under this subparagraph, the district court of the United States for any district in which such person is found or resides or transacts business, upon application by the United States and after notice to such person, shall have jurisdiction to issue an order requiring such person to appear and give testimony before the Administrator to appear and produce papers, books, and documents before the Administrator, or both, and any failure to obey such order of the court may be punished by such court as a contempt thereof.

(b) Judicial review

(1) A petition for review of action of the Administrator in promulgating any national primary or secondary ambient air quality standard, any emission standard or requirement under section 7412 of this title, any standard of performance or requirement under section 7411 of this title,[2] any standard under section 7521 of this title (other than a standard required to be prescribed under section 7521(b)(1) of this title), any determination under section 7521(b)(5) of this title, any control or prohibition under section 7545 of this title, any standard under section 7571 of this title, any rule issued under section 7413, 7419, or under section 7420 of this title, or any other nationally applicable regulations promulgated, or final action taken, by the Administrator under this chapter may be filed only in the United States Court of Appeals for the District of Columbia. A petition for review of the Administrator's action in approving or promulgating any implementation plan under section 7410 of this title or section 7411(d) of this title, any order under section 7411(j) of this title, under section 7412 of this title, under section 7419 of this title, or under section 7420 of this title, or his action under section 1857c–10(c)(2)(A), (B), or (C) of this title (as in effect before August 7, 1977) or under regulations thereunder, or revising regulations for enhanced monitoring and compliance certification programs under section 7414(a)(3) of this title, or any other final action of the Administrator under this chapter (including any denial or disapproval by the Administrator under subchapter I of this chapter) which is locally or regionally applicable may be filed only in the United States Court of Appeals for the appropriate circuit. Notwithstanding the preceding sentence a petition for review of any action referred to in such sentence may be filed only in the United States Court of Appeals for the District of Columbia if such action is based on a determination of nationwide scope or effect and if in taking such action the Administrator finds and publishes that such action is based on such a determination. Any petition for review under this subsection shall be filed within sixty days from the date notice of such promulgation, approval, or action appears in the Federal Register, except that if such petition is based solely on grounds arising after such sixtieth day, then any petition for review under this subsection shall be filed within sixty days after such grounds arise. The filing of a petition for reconsideration by the Administrator of any otherwise final rule or action shall not affect the finality of such rule or action for purposes of judicial review nor extend the time within which a petition for judicial review of such rule or action under this section may be filed, and shall not postpone the effectiveness of such rule or action.

(2) Action of the Administrator with respect to which review could have been obtained under paragraph (1) shall not be subject to judicial review in civil or criminal proceedings for enforcement. Where a final decision by the Administrator defers performance of any nondiscretionary statutory action to a later time, any person may challenge the deferral pursuant to paragraph (1).

(c) Additional evidence

In any judicial proceeding in which review is sought of a determination under this chapter required to be made on the record after notice and opportunity for hearing, if any party applies to the court for leave to adduce additional evidence, and shows to the satisfaction of the court that such additional evidence is material and that there were reasonable grounds for the failure to adduce such evidence in the proceeding before the Administrator, the court may order such additional evidence (and evidence in rebuttal thereof) to be taken before the Administrator, in such manner and upon such terms and conditions as to[3] the court may deem proper. The Administrator may modify his findings as to the facts, or make new findings, by reason of the additional evidence so taken and he shall file such modified or new findings, and his recommendation, if any, for the modification or setting aside of his original determination, with the return of such additional evidence.

(d) Rulemaking

(1) This subsection applies to—

(A) the promulgation or revision of any national ambient air quality standard under section 7409 of this title,

(B) the promulgation or revision of an implementation plan by the Administrator under section 7410(c) of this title,

(C) the promulgation or revision of any standard of performance under section 7411 of this title, or emission standard or limitation under section 7412(d) of this title, any standard under section 7412(f) of this title, or any regulation under section 7412(g)(1)(D) and (F) of this title, or any regulation under section 7412(m) or (n) of this title,

(D) the promulgation of any requirement for solid waste combustion under section 7429 of this title,

(E) the promulgation or revision of any regulation pertaining to any fuel or fuel additive under section 7545 of this title,

(F) the promulgation or revision of any aircraft emission standard under section 7571 of this title,

(G) the promulgation or revision of any regulation under subchapter IV-A of this chapter (relating to control of acid deposition),

(H) promulgation or revision of regulations pertaining to primary nonferrous smelter orders under section 7419 of this title (but not including the granting or denying of any such order),

(I) promulgation or revision of regulations under subchapter VI of this chapter (relating to stratosphere and ozone protection),

(J) promulgation or revision of regulations under part C of subchapter I of this chapter (relating to prevention of significant deterioration of air quality and protection of visibility),

(K) promulgation or revision of regulations under section 7521 of this title and test procedures for new motor vehicles or engines under section 7525 of this title, and the revision of a standard under section 7521(a)(3) of this title,

(L) promulgation or revision of regulations for noncompliance penalties under section 7420 of this title,

(M) promulgation or revision of any regulations promulgated under section 7541 of this title (relating to warranties and compliance by vehicles in actual use),

(N) action of the Administrator under section 7426 of this title (relating to interstate pollution abatement),

(O) the promulgation or revision of any regulation pertaining to consumer and commercial products under section 7511b(e) of this title,

(P) the promulgation or revision of any regulation pertaining to field citations under section 7413(d)(3) of this title,

(Q) the promulgation or revision of any regulation pertaining to urban buses or the clean-fuel vehicle, clean-fuel fleet, and clean fuel programs under part C of subchapter II of this chapter,

(R) the promulgation or revision of any regulation pertaining to nonroad engines or nonroad vehicles under section 7547 of this title,

(S) the promulgation or revision of any regulation relating to motor vehicle compliance program fees under section 7552 of this title,

(T) the promulgation or revision of any regulation under subchapter IV-A of this chapter (relating to acid deposition),

(U) the promulgation or revision of any regulation under section 7511b(f) of this title pertaining to marine vessels, and

(V) such other actions as the Administrator may determine.

The provisions of section 553 through 557 and section 706 of Title 5 shall not, except as expressly provided in this subsection, apply to actions to which this subsection applies. This subsection shall not apply in the case of any rule or circumstance referred to in subparagraphs (A) or (B) of subsection 553(b) of Title 5.

(2) Not later than the date of proposal of any action to which this subsection applies, the Administrator shall establish a rulemaking docket for such action (hereinafter in this subsection referred to as a "rule"). Whenever a rule applies only within a particular State, a second (identical) docket shall be simultaneously established in the appropriate regional office of the Environmental Protection Agency.

(3) In the case of any rule to which this subsection applies, notice of proposed rulemaking shall be published in the Federal Register, as provided under section 553(b) of Title 5, shall be accompanied by a statement of its basis and purpose and shall specify the period available for public comment (hereinafter referred to as the "comment period"). The notice of proposed rulemaking shall also state the docket number, the location or locations of the docket, and the times it will be open to public inspection. The statement of basis and purpose shall include a summary of—

(A) the factual data on which the proposed rule is based;

(B) the methodology used in obtaining the data and in analyzing the data; and

(C) the major legal interpretations and policy considerations underlying the proposed rule.

The statement shall also set forth or summarize and provide a reference to any pertinent findings, recommendations, and comments by the Scientific Review Committee established under section 7409(d) of this title and the National Academy of Sciences, and, if the proposal differs in any important respect from any of these recommendations, an explanation of the reasons for such differences. All data, information, and documents referred to in this paragraph on which the proposed rule relies shall be included in the docket on the date of publication of the proposed rule.

(4) **(A)** The rulemaking docket required under paragraph (2) shall be open for inspection by the public at reasonable times specified in the notice of proposed rulemaking. Any person may copy documents contained in the docket. The Administrator shall provide copying facilities which may be used at the expense of the person seeking copies, but the Administrator may waive or reduce such expenses in such instances as the public interest requires. Any person may request copies by mail if the person pays the expenses, including personnel costs to do the copying.

(B) **(i)** Promptly upon receipt by the agency, all written comments and documentary information on the proposed rule received from any person for inclusion in the docket during the comment period shall be placed in the docket. The transcript of public hearings, if any, on the proposed rule shall also be included in the docket promptly upon receipt from the person who transcribed such hearings. All documents which become available after the proposed rule has been published and which the Administrator determines are of central relevance to the rulemaking shall be placed in the docket as soon as possible after their availability.

(ii) The drafts of proposed rules submitted by the Administrator to the Office of Management and Budget for any interagency review process prior to proposal of any such rule, all documents accompanying such drafts, and all written comments thereon by other agencies and all written responses to such written comments by the Administrator shall be placed in the docket no later than the date of proposal of the rule. The drafts of the final rule submitted for such review process prior to promulgation and all such written comments thereon, all documents accompanying such drafts, and written responses thereto shall be placed in the docket no later than the date of promulgation.

(5) In promulgating a rule to which this subsection applies (i) the Administrator shall allow any person to submit written comments, data, or documentary information; (ii) the Administrator shall give interested persons an opportunity for the oral presentation of data, views, or arguments, in addition to an opportunity to make written submissions; (iii) a transcript shall be kept of any oral presentation; and (iv) the Administrator shall keep the record of such proceeding open for thirty days after completion of the proceeding to provide an opportunity for submission of rebuttal and supplementary information.

(6) **(A)** The promulgated rule shall be accompanied by (i) a statement of basis and purpose like that referred to in paragraph (3) with respect to a proposed rule and (ii) an explanation of the reasons for any major changes in the promulgated rule from the proposed rule.

(B) The promulgated rule shall also be accompanied by a response to each of the significant comments, criticisms, and new data submitted in written or oral presentations during the comment period.

(C) The promulgated rule may not be based (in part or whole) on any information or data which has not been placed in the docket as of the date of such promulgation.

(7) **(A)** The record for judicial review shall consist exclusively of the material referred to in paragraph (3), clause (i) of paragraph (4)(B), and subparagraphs (A) and (B) of paragraph (6).

(B) Only an objection to a rule or procedure which was raised with reasonable specificity during the period for public comment (including any public hearing) may be raised during judicial review. If the person raising an objection can demonstrate to the Administrator that it was impracticable to raise such objection within such time or if the grounds for such objection arose after the period for public comment (but within the time specified for judicial review) and if such objection is of central relevance to the outcome of the rule, the Administrator shall convene a proceeding for reconsideration of the rule and provide the same procedural rights as would have been afforded had the information been available at the time the rule was proposed. If the Administrator refuses to convene such a proceeding, such person may seek review of such refusal in the United States court of appeals for the appropriate circuit (as provided in subsection (b) of this section). Such reconsideration shall not postpone the effectiveness of the rule. The effectiveness of the rule may be stayed during such reconsideration, however, by the Administrator or the court for a period not to exceed three months.

(8) The sole forum for challenging procedural determinations made by the Administrator under this subsection shall be in the United States court of appeals for the appropriate circuit (as provided in subsection (b) of this section) at the time of the substantive review of the rule. No interlocutory appeals shall be permitted with respect to such procedural determinations. In reviewing alleged procedural errors, the court may invalidate the rule only if the errors were so serious and related to matters of such central relevance to the rule that there is a substantial likelihood that the rule would have been significantly changed if such errors had not been made.

(9) In the case of review of any action of the Administrator to which this subsection applies, the court may reverse any such action found to be—

(A) arbitrary, capricious, an abuse of discretion, or otherwise not in accordance with law;

(B) contrary to constitutional right, power, privilege, or immunity;

(C) in excess of statutory jurisdiction, authority, or limitations, or short of statutory right; or

(D) without observance of procedure required by law, if (i) such failure to observe such procedure is arbitrary or capricious, (ii) the requirement of paragraph (7)(B) has been met, and (iii) the condition of the last sentence of paragraph (8) is met.

(10) Each statutory deadline for promulgation of rules to which this subsection applies which requires promulgation less than six months after date of proposal may be extended to not more than six months after date of proposal by the Administrator upon a determination that such extension is necessary to afford the public, and the agency, adequate opportunity to carry out the purposes of this subsection.

(11) The requirements of this subsection shall take effect with respect to any rule the proposal of which occurs after ninety days after August 7, 1977.

(e) Other methods of judicial review not authorized

Nothing in this chapter shall be construed to authorize judicial review of regulations or orders of the Administrator under this chapter, except as provided in this section.

(f) Costs

In any judicial proceeding under this section, the court may award costs of litigation (including reasonable attorney and expert witness fees) whenever it determines that such award is appropriate.

(g) Stay, injunction, or similar relief in proceedings relating to noncompliance penalties

In any action respecting the promulgation of regulations under section 7420 of this title or the administration or enforcement of section 7420 of this title no court shall grant any stay, injunctive, or similar relief before final judgment by such court in such action.

(h) Public participation

It is the intent of Congress that, consistent with the policy of subchapter II of chapter 5 of Title 5, the Administrator in promulgating any regulation under this chapter, including a regulation subject to a deadline, shall ensure a reasonable period for public participation of at least 30 days, except as otherwise expressly provided in section[4] 7407(d), 7502(a), 7511(a) and (b), and 7512(a) and (b) of this title.

(July 14, 1955, c. 360, Title III, § 307, as added by Pub. L. No. 91–604, § 12(a), 84 Stat. 1707 (Dec. 31, 1970); and amended by Pub. L. No. 92–157, Title III, § 302(a), 85 Stat. 464 (Nov. 18, 1971); Pub. L. No. 93–319, § 6(c), 88 Stat. 259 (June 22, 1974); Pub. L. No. 95–95, Title III, §§ 303(d), 305(a), (c), (f)–(h), 91 Stat. 772, 776, 777 (Aug. 7, 1977); Pub. L. No. 95–190, § 14(a)(79), (80), 91 Stat. 1404 (Nov. 16, 1977); Pub. L. No. 101–549, Title I, §§ 108(p), 110(5), Title III, § 302(g), (h), Title VII, §§ 702(c), 703, 706, 707(h), 710(b), 104 Stat. 2469, 2470, 2574, 2681–2684 (Nov. 15, 1990).)

[1] So in original. Probably should be "this."

[2] So in original.

[3] So in original. The word "to" probably should not appear.

[4] So in original. Probably should be "sections."

HISTORICAL AND STATUTORY NOTES

References in Text

Section 7521(b)(5) of this title, referred to in subsec. (b)(1), was repealed by Pub. L. No. 101–549, Title II, § 203(3), 104 Stat. 2529 (Nov. 15, 1990).

Section 1857c–10(c)(2)(A), (B), or (C) of this title (as in effect before August 7, 1977), referred to in subsec. (b)(1), was in the original "section 119(c)(2)(A), (B), or (C) (as in effect before the date of enactment of the Clean Air Act Amendments of 1977)", meaning section 119 of Act of July 14, 1955, c. 360, Title I, as added by Pub. L. No. 93–319, § 3, 88 Stat. 248 (June 22, 1974) (which was codified as section 1857c–10 of this title) as in effect prior to the enactment of Pub. L. No. 95–95, 91 Stat. 691 (Aug. 7, 1977), effective Aug. 7, 1977. Section 112(b)(1) of Pub. L. No. 95–95 repealed section 119 of Act of July 14, 1955, c. 360, Title I, as added by Pub. L. No. 93–319, and provided that all references to such section 119 in any subsequent enactment which supersedes Pub. L. No. 93–319 shall be construed to refer to section 113(d) of the Clean Air Act and to paragraph (5) thereof in particular which is codified as subsec. (d)(5) of section 7413 of this title. Section 7413(d) of this title was subsequently amended generally by Pub. L. No. 101–549, Title VII, § 701, 104 Stat. 2672 (Nov. 15, 1990), and, as so amended, no longer relates to final compliance orders. Section 117(b) of Pub. L. No. 95–95 added a new section 119 of Act of July 14, 1955, which is codified as section 7419 of this title.

Part C of subchapter I of this chapter, referred to in subsec. (d)(1)(J), was in the original "subtitle C of Title I", and was translated as reading "part C of Title I" to reflect the probable intent of Congress, because Title I does not contain subtitles.

Codifications

This section was formerly codified as section 1857h–5 of this title.

In subsec. (h), "subchapter II of chapter 5 of Title 5" was substituted for "the Administrative Procedures Act" on authority of Pub. L. No. 89–554, § 7(b), 80 Stat. 631 (Sept. 6, 1966), the first section of which enacted Title 5, Government Organization and Employees.

Effective and Applicability Provisions

1990 Acts. Amendment by Pub. L. No. 101–549 effective Nov. 15, 1990, except as otherwise provided, see section 711(b) of Pub. L. No. 101–549, set out as a note under section 7401 of this title.

1977 Acts. Amendment by Pub. L. No. 95–95 effective Aug. 7, 1977, except as otherwise expressly provided, see section 406(d) of Pub. L. No. 95–95, set out as a note under section 7401 of this title.

Savings Provisions

Suits, actions or proceedings commenced under this chapter as in effect prior to Nov. 15, 1990, not to abate by reason of the taking effect of amendments by Pub. L. No. 101–549, except as otherwise provided for, see section 711(a) of Pub. L. No. 101–549, set out as a note under section 7401 of this title.

Prior Provisions

A prior section 307 of Act of July 14, 1955, c. 360, Title III, as added by Pub. L. No. 90–148, § 2, 81 Stat. 506 (Nov. 21, 1967), and renumbered section 314 by Pub. L. No. 91–604, § 12(a), 84 Stat. 1705 (Dec. 31, 1970), which related to labor standards, is set out as section 7614 of this title.

Another prior section 307 of Act of July 14, 1955, c. 360, Title III, formerly § 14, as added by Pub. L. No. 88–206, § 1, 77 Stat. 401 (Dec. 17, 1963), was renumbered section 307 by Pub. L. No. 89–272, renumbered section 310 by Pub. L. No. 90–148, and renumbered section 317 by Pub. L. No. 91–604, and is set out as a Short Title of 1963 Acts note under section 7401 of this title.

Modification or Rescission of Rules, Regulations, Orders, Determinations Contracts, Certifications, Authorizations, Delegations, and Other Actions

All rules, regulations, orders, determinations, contracts, certifications, authorizations, delegations, or other actions duly issued, made, or taken by or pursuant to Act of July 14, 1955, the Clean Air Act, as in effect immediately prior to the date of enactment of Pub. L. No. 95–95 [Aug. 7, 1977] to continue in full force and effect until modified or rescinded in accordance with Act of July 14, 1955, as amended by Pub. L. No. 95–95 [this chapter], see section 406(b) of Pub. L. No. 95–95, set out as an Effective Date of 1977 Acts note under section 7401 of this title.

Pending Actions and Proceedings

Suits, actions, and other proceedings lawfully commenced by or against the Administrator or any other officer or employee of the United States in his official capacity or in relation to the discharge of his official duties under Act of July 14, 1955, the Clean Air Act, as in effect immediately prior to the enactment of Pub. L. No. 95–95 [Aug. 7, 1977], not to abate by reason of the taking effect of Pub. L. No. 95–95, see section 406(a) of Pub. L. No. 95–95, set out as an Effective Date of 1977 Acts note under section 7401 of this title.

Termination of Advisory Committees

Advisory Committees established after Jan. 5, 1973, to terminate not later than the expiration of the two-year period beginning on the date of their establishment, unless, in the case of a committee established by the President or an officer of the Federal Government, such committee is renewed by appropriate action prior to the expiration of such two-year period, or in the case of a committee established by the Congress, its duration is otherwise provided for by law, see section 14 of Pub. L. No. 92–463, 86 Stat. 776 (Oct. 6, 1972), set out in Appendix 2 to Title 5, Government Organization and Employees.

§ 7608. Mandatory licensing

[CAA § 308]

Whenever the Attorney General determines, upon application of the Administrator—

(1) that—

(A) in the implementation of the requirements of section 7411, 7412, or 7521 of this title, a right under any United States letters patent, which is being used or intended for public or commercial use and not otherwise reasonably available, is necessary to enable any person required to comply with such limitation to so comply, and

(B) there are no reasonable alternative methods to accomplish such purpose, and

(2) that the unavailability of such right may result in a substantial lessening of competition or tendency to create a monopoly in any line of commerce in any section of the country,

the Attorney General may so certify to a district court of the United States, which may issue an order requiring the person who owns such patent to license it on such reasonable terms and conditions as the court, after hearing, may determine. Such certification may be made to the district court for the district in which the person owning the patent resides, does business, or is found.

(July 14, 1955, c. 360, Title III, § 308, as added by Pub. L. No. 91–604, § 12(a), 84 Stat. 1708 (Dec. 31, 1970).)

HISTORICAL AND STATUTORY NOTES

Codifications

This section was formerly codified as section 1857h–6 of this title.

Prior Provisions

A prior section 308 of Act of July 14, 1955, c. 360, Title III, formerly § 12, as added by Pub. L. No. 88–206, § 1, 77 Stat. 401 (Dec. 17, 1963), and renumbered § 305 by Pub. L. No. 89–272, Title I, § 101(4), 79 Stat. 992 (Oct. 20, 1965), and renumbered § 308 by Pub. L. No. 90–148, § 2, 81 Stat. 506 (Nov. 21, 1967), and renumbered § 315 by Pub. L. No. 91–604, § 12(a), 84 Stat. 1705 (Dec. 31, 1970), which related to separability of provisions, is set out as section 7615 of this title.

Modification or Rescission of Rules, Regulations, Orders, Determinations, Contracts, Certifications, Authorizations, Delegations, and Other Actions

All rules, regulations, orders, determinations, contracts, certifications, authorizations, delegations, or other actions duly issued, made, or taken by or pursuant to Act of July 14, 1955, the Clean Air Act, as in effect immediately prior to the date of enactment of Pub. L. No. 95–95 [Aug. 7, 1977] to continue in full force and effect until modified or rescinded in accordance with Act of July 14, 1955, as amended by Pub. L. No. 95–95 [this chapter], see section 406(b) of Pub. L. No. 95–95, set out as an Effective Date of 1977 Acts note under section 7401 of this title.

§ 7609. Policy review

[CAA § 309]

(a) Environmental impact

The Administrator shall review and comment in writing on the environmental impact of any matter relating to duties and responsibilities granted pursuant to this chapter or other provisions of the authority of the Administrator, contained in any (1) legislation proposed by any Federal department or agency, (2) newly authorized Federal projects for construction and any major Federal agency action (other than a project for construction) to which section 4332(2)(C) of this title applies, and (3) proposed regulations published by any department or agency of the Federal Government. Such written comment shall be made public at the conclusion of any such review.

(b) Unsatisfactory legislation, action, or regulation

In the event the Administrator determines that any such legislation, action, or regulation is unsatisfactory from the standpoint of public health or welfare or environmental quality, he shall publish his determination and the matter shall be referred to the Council on Environmental Quality.

(July 14, 1955, c. 360, Title III, § 309, as added by Pub. L. No. 91–604, § 12(a), 84 Stat. 1709 (Dec. 31, 1970).)

HISTORICAL AND STATUTORY NOTES

Codifications

This section was formerly codified as section 1857h–7 of this title.

Prior Provisions

A prior section 309 of Act of July 14, 1955, c. 360, Title III, formerly § 13, as added by Pub. L. No. 88–206, § 1, 77 Stat. 401 (Dec. 17, 1963), and renumbered § 306 by Pub. L. No. 89–272, Title I, § 101(4), 79 Stat. 992 (Oct. 20, 1965), and renumbered § 309 by Pub. L. No. 90–148, § 2, 81 Stat. 506 (Nov. 21, 1967), and renumbered § 316 by Pub. L. No. 91–604, § 12(a), 84 Stat. 1705 (Dec. 31, 1970), which related to appropriations, was codified as section 1857*l* of this title and was repealed by section 306 of Pub. L. No. 95–95. Similar appropriation provisions are now codified as section 7626 of this title.

Modification or Rescission of Rules, Regulations, Orders, Determinations, Contracts, Certifications, Authorizations, Delegations, and Other Actions

All rules, regulations, orders, determinations, contracts, certifications, authorizations, delegations, or other actions duly issued, made, or taken by or pursuant to Act of July 14, 1955, the Clean Air Act, as in effect immediately prior to the date of enactment of Pub. L. No. 95–95 [Aug. 7, 1977] to continue in full force and effect until modified or rescinded in accordance with Act of July 14, 1955, as amended by Pub. L. No. 95–95 [this chapter], see section 406(b) of Pub. L. No. 95–95, set out as an Effective Date of 1977 Acts note under section 7401 of this title.

§ 7610. Other authority

[CAA § 310]

(a) Authority and responsibilities under other laws not affected

Except as provided in subsection (b) of this section, this chapter shall not be construed as superseding or limiting the authorities and responsibilities, under any other provision of law, of the Administrator or any other Federal officer, department, or agency.

(b) Nonduplication of appropriations

No appropriation shall be authorized or made under section 241, 243, or 246 of this title for any fiscal year after the fiscal year ending June 30, 1964, for any purpose for which appropriations may be made under authority of this chapter.

(July 14, 1955, c. 360, Title III, § 310, formerly § 10, as added by Pub. L. No. 88–206, § 1, 77 Stat. 401 (Dec. 17, 1963); and renumbered § 303 by Pub. L. No. 89–272, Title I, § 101(4), 79 Stat. 992 (Oct. 20, 1965); and amended by Pub. L. No. 90–148, § 2, 81 Stat. 505 (Nov. 21, 1967); and renumbered § 310 and amended by Pub. L. No. 91–604, §§ 12(a), 15(c)(2), 84 Stat. 1705, 1713 (Dec. 31, 1970).)

HISTORICAL AND STATUTORY NOTES

Codifications

This section was formerly codified as section 1857i of this title.

Prior Provisions

A prior section 310 of Act of July 14, 1955, c. 360, Title III, formerly § 14, as added by Pub. L. No. 88–206, § 1, 77 Stat. 401 (Dec. 17, 1963), and renumbered § 307 by Pub. L. No. 89–272, Title I, § 101(4), 79 Stat. 992 (Oct. 20, 1965), and renumbered § 310 by Pub. L. No. 90–148, § 2, 81 Stat. 506 (Nov. 21, 1967), and renumbered § 317 by Pub. L. No. 91–604, § 12(a), 84 Stat. 1705 (Dec. 31, 1970), is set out as a Short Title of 1963 Acts note under section 7401 of this title.

Provisions similar to those contained in subsec. (a) of this section were contained in a prior section 1857f of this title, Act of July 14, 1955, c. 360, § 7, 69 Stat. 323, prior to the general amendment of this chapter by Pub. L. No. 88–206.

Modification or Rescission of Rules, Regulations, Orders, Determinations, Contracts, Certifications, Authorizations, Delegations, and Other Actions

All rules, regulations, orders, determinations, contracts, certifications, authorizations, delegations, or other actions duly issued, made, or taken by or pursuant to Act of July 14, 1955, the Clean Air Act, as in effect immediately prior to the date of enactment of Pub. L. No. 95–95 [Aug. 7, 1977] to continue in full force and effect until modified or rescinded in accordance with Act of July 14, 1955, as amended by Pub. L. No. 95–95 [this chapter], see section 406(b) of Pub. L. No. 95–95, set out as an Effective Date of 1977 Acts note under section 7401 of this title.

§ 7611. Records and audit

[CAA § 311]

(a) Recipients of assistance to keep prescribed records

Each recipient of assistance under this chapter shall keep such records as the Administrator shall prescribe, including records which fully disclose the amount and disposition by such recipient of the proceeds of such assistance, the total cost of the project or undertaking in connection with which such assistance is given or used, and the amount of that portion of the cost of the project or undertaking supplied by other sources, and such other records as will facilitate an effective audit.

(b) Audits

The Administrator and the Comptroller General of the United States, or any of their duly authorized representatives, shall have access for the purpose of audit and examinations to any books, documents, papers, and records of the recipients that are pertinent to the grants received under this chapter.

(July 14, 1955, c. 360, Title III, § 311, formerly § 11, as added by Pub. L. No. 88–206, § 1, 77 Stat. 401 (Dec. 17, 1963); and renumbered § 304 by Pub. L. No. 89–272, Title I, § 101(4), 79 Stat. 992 (Oct. 20, 1965); and amended by Pub. L. No. 90–148, § 2, 81 Stat. 505 (Nov. 21, 1967); and renumbered § 311 and amended by Pub. L. No. 91–604, §§ 12(a), 15(c)(2), 84 Stat. 1705, 1713 (Dec. 31, 1970).)

HISTORICAL AND STATUTORY NOTES

Codifications

This section was formerly codified as section 1857j of this title.

Modification or Rescission of Rules, Regulations, Orders, Determinations, Contracts, Certifications, Authorizations, Delegations, and Other Actions

All rules, regulations, orders, determinations, contracts, certifications, authorizations, delegations, or other actions duly issued, made, or taken by or pursuant to Act of July 14, 1955, the Clean Air Act, as in effect immediately prior to the date of enactment of Pub. L. No. 95–95 [Aug. 7, 1977] to continue in full force and effect until modified or rescinded in accordance with Act of July 14, 1955, as amended by Pub. L. No. 95–95 [this chapter], see section 406(b) of Pub. L. No. 95–95, set out as an Effective Date of 1977 Acts note under section 7401 of this title.

§ 7612. Economic impact analyses

[CAA § 312]

(a) Cost-benefit analysis

The Administrator, in consultation with the Secretary of Commerce, the Secretary of Labor, and the Council on Clean Air Compliance Analysis (as established under subsection (f) of this section), shall conduct a comprehensive analysis of the impact of this chapter on the public health, economy, and environment of the United States. In performing such analysis, the Administrator should consider the costs, benefits and other effects associated with compliance with each standard issued for—

(1) a criteria air pollutant subject to a standard issued under section 7409 of this title;

(2) a hazardous air pollutant listed under section 7412 of this title, including any technology-based standard and any risk-based standard for such pollutant;

(3) emissions from mobile sources regulated under subchapter II of this chapter;

(4) a limitation under this chapter for emissions of sulfur dioxide or nitrogen oxides;

(5) a limitation under subchapter VI of this chapter on the production of any ozone-depleting substance; and

(6) any other section of this chapter.

(b) Benefits

In describing the benefits of a standard described in subsection (a) of this section, the Administrator shall consider all of the economic, public health, and environmental benefits of efforts to comply with such standard. In any case where numerical values are assigned to such benefits, a default assumption of zero value shall not be assigned to such benefits unless supported by specific data. The Administrator shall assess how benefits are measured in order to assure that damage to human health and the environment is more accurately measured and taken into account.

(c) Costs

In describing the costs of a standard described in subsection (a) of this section, the Administrator shall consider the effects of such standard on employment, productivity, cost of living, economic growth, and the overall economy of the United States.

(d) Initial report

Not later than 12 months after November 15, 1990, the Administrator, in consultation with the Secretary of Commerce, the Secretary of Labor, and the Council on Clean Air Compliance Analysis, shall submit a report to the Congress that summarizes the results of the analysis described in subsection (a) of this section, which reports—

(1) all costs incurred previous to November 15, 1990, in the effort to comply with such standards; and

(2) all benefits that have accrued to the United States as a result of such costs.

(e) Omitted

(f) Appointment of Advisory Council on Clean Air Compliance Analysis

Not later than 6 months after November 15, 1990, the Administrator, in consultation with the Secretary of Commerce and the Secretary of Labor, shall appoint an Advisory Council on Clean Air Compliance Analysis of not less than nine members (hereafter in this section referred to as the "Council"). In appointing such members, the Administrator shall appoint recognized experts in the fields of the health and environmental effects of air pollution, economic analysis, environmental sciences, and such other fields that the Administrator determines to be appropriate.

(g) Duties of Advisory Council

The Council shall—

(1) review the data to be used for any analysis required under this section and make recommendations to the Administrator on the use of such data;

(2) review the methodology used to analyze such data and make recommendations to the Administrator on the use of such methodology; and

(3) prior to the issuance of a report required under subsection (d) or (e) of this section, review the findings of such report, and make recommendations to the Administrator concerning the validity and utility of such findings.

(July 14, 1955, c. 360, Title III, § 312, formerly § 305, as added by Pub. L. No. 90–148, § 2, 81 Stat. 505 (Nov. 21, 1967); and renumbered § 312 and amended by Pub. L. No. 91–604, §§ 12(a), 15(c)(2), 84 Stat. 1705, 1713 (Dec. 31, 1970); and amended by Pub. L. No. 95–95, Title II, § 224(c), 91 Stat. 767 (Aug. 7, 1977); Pub. L. No. 101–549, Title VIII, § 812(a), 104 Stat. 2691 (Nov. 15, 1990).)

HISTORICAL AND STATUTORY NOTES

Codifications

This section was formerly codified as section 1857j–1 of this title.

Subsec. (e) of this section, shown as omitted, which required the Administrator, in consultation with the Secretary of Commerce, the Secretary of Labor, and the Council on Clean Air Compliance Analysis, to submit a report to Congress that updates the report issued pursuant to subsec. (d) of this section, and which, in addition, makes projections into the future regarding expected costs, benefits, and other effects of compliance with standards pursuant to this chapter as listed in subsec. (a) of this section, terminated, effective May 15, 2000, pursuant to section 3003 of Pub. L. No. 104–66, as amended, set out as a note under 31 U.S.C.A. § 1113. See, also, the 4th item on page 163 of House Document No. 103–7.

Effective and Applicability Provisions

1990 Acts. Amendment by Pub. L. No. 101–549 effective Nov. 15, 1990, except as otherwise provided, see section 711(b) of Pub. L. No. 101–549, set out as a note under section 7401 of this title.

1977 Acts. Amendment by Pub. L. No. 95–95 effective Aug. 7, 1977, except as otherwise expressly provided, see section 406(d) of Pub. L. No. 95–95, set out as a note under section 7401 of this title.

Savings Provisions

Suits, actions or proceedings commenced under this chapter as in effect prior to Nov. 15, 1990, not to abate by reason of the taking effect of amendments by Pub. L. No. 101–549, except as otherwise provided for, see section 711(a) of Pub. L. No. 101–549, set out as a note under section 7401 of this title.

Equivalent Air Quality Controls Among Trading Nations

Section 811 of Pub. L. No. 101–549 provided that:

"(a) Findings.—The Congress finds that—

"(1) all nations have the responsibility to adopt and enforce effective air quality standards and requirements and the United States, in enacting this Act [Pub. L. No. 101–549, Nov. 15, 1990, 104 Stat. 2399, popularly known as the Clean Air Act Amendments of 1990, for distribution of which to the Code, see Tables], is carrying out its responsibility in this regard;

"(2) as a result of complying with this Act, businesses in the United States will make significant capital investments and incur incremental costs in implementing control technology standards;

"(3) such compliance may impair the competitiveness of certain United States jobs, production, processes, and products if foreign goods are produced under less costly environmental standards and requirements than are United States goods; and

"(4) mechanisms should be sought through which the United States and its trading partners can agree to eliminate or reduce competitive disadvantages.

"(b) Action by the President.—

"(1) In general.—Within 18 months after the date of the enactment of the Clean Air Act Amendments of 1990 [Nov. 15, 1990], the President shall submit to the Congress a report—

"(A) identifying and evaluating the economic effects of—

"(i) the significant air quality standards and controls required under this Act, [Pub. L. No. 101–549, Nov. 15, 1990, 104 Stat. 2399, popularly known as the Clean Air Act Amendments of 1990, for distribution of which to the Code, see Tables] and

"(ii) the differences between the significant standards and controls required under this Act and similar standards and controls adopted and enforced by the major trading partners of the United States,

on the international competitiveness of United States manufacturers; and

"(B) containing a strategy for addressing such economic effects through trade consultations and negotiations.

"(2) Additional reporting requirements.—(A) The evaluation required under paragraph (1)(A) shall examine the extent to which the significant air quality standards and controls required under this Act [Pub. L. No. 101–549, 104 Stat. 2399 (Nov. 15, 1990), popularly known as the Clean Air Act Amendments of 1990, for distribution of which to the Code, see Tables] are comparable to existing internationally-agreed norms.

"(B) The strategy required to be developed under paragraph (1)(B) shall include recommended options (such as the harmonization of standards and trade adjustment measures) for reducing or eliminating competitive disadvantages caused by differences in standards and controls between the United States and each of its major trading partners.

"(3) Public comment.—Interested parties shall be given an opportunity to submit comments regarding the evaluations and strategy required in the report under paragraph (1). The President shall take any such comment into account in preparing the report.

"(4) Interim report.—Within 9 months after the date of the enactment of the Clean Air Act Amendments of 1990 [Nov. 15, 1990], the President shall submit to the Congress an interim report on the progress being made in complying with paragraph (1)."

GAO Reports on Costs and Benefits

Section 812(b) of Pub. L. No. 101–549 which directed the Comptroller General of the General Accounting Office, commencing on the second year after Nov. 15, 1990, and annually thereafter, in consultation with other agencies, to report to Congress on pollution control strategies and employment effects of the Clean Air Act Amendments of 1990 [Pub. L. No. 101–549, for classification of which to the Code, see Tables], was repealed by Pub. L. No. 104–316, Title I, §§ 101(e), 122(r), Oct. 19, 1996, 110 Stat. 3827, 3838.

Termination of Advisory Councils

Advisory councils established after Jan. 5, 1973, to terminate not later than the expiration of the 2-year period beginning on the date of their establishment, unless, in the case of a council established by the President or an officer of the Federal Government, such council is renewed by appropriate action prior to the expiration of such 2-year period, or in the case of a council established by Congress, its duration is otherwise provided by law. See sections 3(2) and 14 of Pub. L. No. 92–463, 86 Stat. 770, 776 (Oct. 6, 1972), set out in Appendix 2 to Title 5, Government Organization and Employees.

§ 7613. Repealed. Pub. L. No. 101–549, Title VIII, § 803, 104 Stat. 2689 (Nov. 15, 1990).

HISTORICAL AND STATUTORY NOTES

Section, Act of July 14, 1955, c. 360, Title III, § 313, formerly § 306, as added by Pub. L. No. 90–148, § 2, 81 Stat. 506 (Nov. 21, 1967); renumbered § 313 and amended by Pub. L. No. 91–604, §§ 12(a), 15(c)(2), 84 Stat. 1705, 1713 (Dec. 31, 1970); and amended by Pub. L. No. 95–95, Title III, § 302(b), 91 Stat. 771 (Aug. 7, 1977), required annual report to Congress on progress of programs under this chapter.

Effective Date of Repeal

Repeal of section effective Nov. 15, 1990, except as otherwise provided, see section 711(b) of Pub. L. No. 101–549, set out as a note under section 7401 of this title.

Savings Provisions

Suits, actions or proceedings commenced under this chapter as in effect prior to Nov. 15, 1990, not to abate by reason of the taking effect of amendments by Pub. L. No. 101–549, except as otherwise provided for, see section 711(a) of Pub. L. No. 101–549, set out as a note under section 7401 of this title.

§ 7614. Labor standards

[CAA § 314]

The Administrator shall take such action as may be necessary to insure that all laborers and mechanics employed by contractors or subcontractors on projects assisted under this chapter shall be paid wages at rates not less than those prevailing for the same type of work on similar construction in the locality as determined by the Secretary of Labor, in accordance with sections 3141–3144, 3146, and 3147 of Title 40. The Secretary of Labor shall have, with respect to the labor standards specified in this subsection, the authority and functions set forth in Reorganization Plan Numbered 14 of 1950 (15 Fed. Reg. 3176; 64 Stat. 1267) and section 3145 of Title 40.

(July 14, 1955, c. 360, Title III, § 314, formerly § 307, as added Pub. L. No. 90–148, § 2, 81 Stat. 506 (Nov. 21, 1967); and renumbered § 314 and amended by Pub. L. No. 91–604, §§ 12(a), 15(c)(2), 84 Stat. 1705, 1713 (Dec. 31, 1970).)

HISTORICAL AND STATUTORY NOTES

References in Text

Reorganization Plan Numbered 14 of 1950, referred to in text, is set out in Appendix 1 to Title 5, Government Organization and Employees.

Codifications

This section was formerly codified as section 1857j–3 of this title.

In text, "sections 3141–3144, 3146, and 3147 of Title 40" substituted for "the Act of March 3, 1931, as amended, known as the Davis-Bacon Act (46 Stat. 1494; 40 U.S.C. 276a—276a–5)" on authority of Pub. L. No. 107–217, § 5(c), 116 Stat. 1301 (Aug. 21, 2002), which is set out as a note preceding 40 U.S.C.A. § 101. Pub. L. No. 107–217, § 1, enacted Title 40 into positive law. The Davis-Bacon Act is Act Mar. 3, 1931, c. 411, 46 Stat. 1494, which was codified as former 40 U.S.C.A. §§ 276a, 276a–1 to 276a–6, prior to being repealed by Pub. L. No. 107–217, § 6(b), 116 Stat. 1308 (Aug. 21, 2002), and its substance reenacted as 40 U.S.C.A. §§ 3141–3144, 3146, and 3147.

In text, "section 3145 of Title 40" substituted for "section 276c of Title 40", which originally read "section 2 of the Act of June 13, 1934 (48 Stat. 948; 40 U.S.C. 276c)", on authority of Pub. L. No. 107–217, § 5(c), 116 Stat. 1301 (Aug. 21, 2002), which is set out as a note preceding 40 U.S.C.A. § 101. Pub. L. No. 107–217, § 1, enacted Title 40 into positive law. Section 2 of the Act of June 13, 1934, as amended, is Act of June 13, 1934, c. 482, § 2, 48 Stat. 948, which was codified as former 40 U.S.C.A. § 276c prior to being repealed by Pub. L. No. 107–217, § 6(b), Aug. 21, 2002, 116 Stat. 1309, and its substance reenacted as 40 U.S.C.A. § 3145.

§ 7615. Separability

[CAA § 315]

If any provision of this chapter, or the application of any provision of this chapter to any person or circumstance, is held invalid, the application of such provision to other persons or circumstances, and the remainder of this chapter shall not be affected thereby.

(July 14, 1955, c. 360, Title III, § 315, formerly § 12, as added by Pub. L. No. 88–206, § 1, 77 Stat. 401 (Dec. 17, 1963); and renumbered § 305 by Pub. L. No. 89–272, Title I, § 101(4), 79 Stat. 992 (Oct. 20, 1965); and renumbered § 308 and amended by Pub. L. No. 90–148, § 2, 81 Stat. 506 (Nov. 21, 1967); and renumbered § 315 by Pub. L. No. 91–604, § 12(a), 84 Stat. 1705 (Dec. 31, 1970).)

HISTORICAL AND STATUTORY NOTES

Codifications

This section was formerly codified as section 1857k of this title.

§ 7616. Sewage treatment grants

[CAA § 316]

(a) Construction

No grant which the Administrator is authorized to make to any applicant for construction of sewage treatment works in any area in any State may be withheld, conditioned, or restricted by the Administrator on the basis of any requirement of this chapter except as provided in subsection (b) of this section.

(b) Withholding, conditioning, or restriction of construction grants

The Administrator may withhold, condition, or restrict the making of any grant for construction referred to in subsection (a) of this section only if he determines that—

(1) such treatment works will not comply with applicable standards under section 7411 or 7412 of this title,

(2) the State does not have in effect, or is not carrying out, a State implementation plan approved by the Administrator which expressly quantifies and provides for the increase in emissions of each air pollutant (from stationary and mobile sources in any area to which either part C or part D of subchapter I of this chapter applies for such pollutant) which increase may reasonably be anticipated to result directly or indirectly from the new sewage treatment capacity which would be created by such construction.

(3) the construction of such treatment works would create new sewage treatment capacity which—

(A) may reasonably be anticipated to cause or contribute to, directly or indirectly, an increase in emissions of any air pollutant in excess of the increase provided for under the provisions referred to in paragraph (2) for any such area, or

(B) would otherwise not be in conformity with the applicable implementation plan, or

(4) such increase in emissions would interfere with, or be inconsistent with, the applicable implementation plan for any other State.

In the case of construction of a treatment works which would result, directly or indirectly, in an increase in emissions of any air pollutant from stationary and mobile sources in an area to which part D of subchapter I of this chapter applies, the quantification of emissions referred to in paragraph (2) shall include the emissions of any such pollutant resulting directly or indirectly from areawide and nonmajor stationary source growth (mobile and stationary) for each such area.

(c) National Environmental Policy Act

Nothing in this section shall be construed to amend or alter any provision of the National Environmental Policy Act [42 U.S.C.A. § 4321 et seq.] or to affect any determination as to whether or not the requirements of such Act have been met in the case of the construction of any sewage treatment works.

(July 14, 1955, c. 360, Title III, § 316, as added by Pub. L. No. 95–95, Title III, § 306, 91 Stat. 777 (Aug. 7, 1977).)

HISTORICAL AND STATUTORY NOTES

References in Text

The National Environmental Policy Act, referred to in subsec. (c), probably means the National Environmental Policy Act of 1969, Pub. L. No. 91–190, 83 Stat. 852 (Jan. 1, 1970), as amended, which is codified generally to chapter 55 (section 4321 et seq.) of this title. For complete classification of this Act to the Code, see Short Title of 1970 Acts note set out under section 4321 of this title and Tables.

Effective and Applicability Provisions

1977 Acts. Section effective Aug. 7, 1977, except as otherwise expressly provided, see section 406(d) of Pub. L. No. 95–95, set out as a note under section 7401 of this title.

Prior Provisions

A prior section 316 of Act of July 14, 1955, c. 360, Title III, formerly § 13, as added by Pub. L. No. 88–206, § 1, 77 Stat. 401 (Dec. 17, 1963); and renumbered § 306 and amended by Pub. L. No. 89–272, Title I, § 101(4), (6), (7), 79 Stat. 992 (Oct. 20, 1965); and amended by Pub. L. No. 89–675, § 2(a), 80 Stat. 954 (Oct. 15, 1966); and renumbered § 309 and amended by Pub. L. No. 90–148, § 2, 81 Stat. 506 (Nov. 21, 1967); and renumbered § 316 and amended by Pub. L. No. 91–604, §§ 12(a), 13(b), 84 Stat. 1705, 1709 (Dec. 31, 1970); and amended by Pub. L. No. 93–15, § 1(c), 87 Stat. 11 (Apr. 9, 1973); Pub. L. No. 93–319, § 13(c), 88 Stat. 265 (June 22, 1974), which authorized appropriations for air pollution control, was repealed by section 306 of Pub. L. No. 95–95. See section 7626 of this title.

§ 7617. Economic impact assessment

[CAA § 317]

(a) Notice of proposed rulemaking; substantial revisions

This section applies to action of the Administrator in promulgating or revising—

(1) any new source standard of performance under section 7411 of this title,

(2) any regulation under section 7411(d) of this title,

(3) any regulation under part B of subchapter I of this chapter (relating to ozone and stratosphere protection),

(4) any regulation under part C of subchapter I of this chapter (relating to prevention of significant deterioration of air quality),

(5) any regulation establishing emission standards under section 7521 of this title and any other regulation promulgated under that section,

(6) any regulation controlling or prohibiting any fuel or fuel additive under section 7545(c) of this title, and

(7) any aircraft emission standard under section 7571 of this title.

Nothing in this section shall apply to any standard or regulation described in paragraphs (1) through (7) of this subsection unless the notice of proposed rulemaking in connection with such standard or regulation is published in the Federal Register after the date ninety days after August 7, 1977. In the case of revisions of such standards or regulations, this section shall apply only to revisions which the Administrator determines to be substantial revisions.

(b) Preparation of assessment by Administrator

Before publication of notice of proposed rulemaking with respect to any standard or regulation to which this section applies, the Administrator shall prepare an economic impact assessment respecting such standard or regulation. Such assessment shall be included in the docket required under section 7607(d)(2) of this title and shall be available to the public as provided in section 7607(d)(4) of this title. Notice of proposed rulemaking shall include notice of such availability together with an explanation of the extent and manner in which the Administrator has considered the analysis contained in such economic impact assessment in proposing the action. The Administrator shall also provide such an explanation in his notice of promulgation of any regulation or standard referred to in subsection (a) of this section. Each such explanation shall be part of the statements of basis and purpose required under sections 7607(d)(3) and 7607(d)(6) of this title.

(c) Analysis

Subject to subsection (d) of this section, the assessment required under this section with respect to any standard or regulation shall contain an analysis of—

(1) the costs of compliance with any such standard or regulation, including extent to which the costs of compliance will vary depending on (A) the effective date of the standard or regulation, and (B) the development of less expensive, more efficient means or methods of compliance with the standard or regulation;

(2) the potential inflationary or recessionary effects of the standard or regulation;

(3) the effects on competition of the standard or regulation with respect to small business;

(4) the effects of the standard or regulation on consumer costs; and

(5) the effects of the standard or regulation on energy use.

Nothing in this section shall be construed to provide that the analysis of the factors specified in this subsection affects or alters the factors which the Administrator is required to consider in taking any action referred to in subsection (a) of this section.

(d) Extensiveness of assessment

The assessment required under this section shall be as extensive as practicable, in the judgment of the Administrator taking into account the time and resources available to the Environmental Protection Agency and other duties and authorities which the Administrator is required to carry out under this chapter.

(e) Limitations on construction of section

Nothing in this section shall be construed—

(1) to alter the basis on which a standard or regulation is promulgated under this chapter;

(2) to preclude the Administrator from carrying out his responsibility under this chapter to protect public health and welfare; or

(3) to authorize or require any judicial review of any such standard or regulation, or any stay or injunction of the proposal, promulgation, or effectiveness of such standard or regulation on the basis of failure to comply with this section.

(f) Citizen suits

The requirements imposed on the Administrator under this section shall be treated as nondiscretionary duties for purposes of section 7604(a)(2) of this title, relating to citizen suits. The sole method for enforcement of the Administrator's duty under this section shall be by bringing a citizen suit under such section 7604(a)(2) for a court order to compel the Administrator to perform such duty. Violation of any such order shall subject the Administrator to penalties for contempt of court.

(g) Costs

In the case of any provision of this chapter in which costs are expressly required to be taken into account, the adequacy or inadequacy of any assessment required under this section may be taken into consideration, but shall not be treated for purposes of judicial review of any such provision as conclusive with respect to compliance or noncompliance with the requirement of such provision to take cost into account.

(July 14, 1955, c. 360, Title III, § 317, as added by Pub. L. No. 95–95, Title III, § 307, 91 Stat. 778 (Aug. 7, 1977); and amended by Pub. L. No. 95–623, § 13(d), 92 Stat. 3458 (Nov. 9, 1978).)

HISTORICAL AND STATUTORY NOTES

References in Text

Part B of subchapter I of this chapter, referred to in subsec. (a)(3), was repealed by Pub. L. No. 101–549, Title VI, § 601, 104 Stat. 2648 (Nov. 15, 1990). See subchapter VI (section 7671 et seq.) of this chapter.

Codifications

Another section 317 of Act of July 14, 1955, is set out as a Short Title of 1955 Acts note under section 7401 of this title.

Effective and Applicability Provisions

1977 Acts. Section effective Aug. 7, 1977, except as otherwise expressly provided, see section 406(d) of Pub. L. No. 95–95, set out as a note under section 7401 of this title.

§ 7618. Repealed. Pub. L. No. 101–549, Title I, § 108(q), 104 Stat. 2469 (Nov. 15, 1990).

HISTORICAL AND STATUTORY NOTES

Section, Act of July 14, 1955, c. 360, Title III, § 318, as added by Pub. L. No. 95–95, Title III, § 308, 91 Stat. 780 (Aug. 7, 1977), related to financial disclosure and conflicts of interest.

Effective Date of Repeal

Repeal of section effective Nov. 15, 1990, except as otherwise provided, see section 711(b) of Pub. L. No. 101–549, set out as a note under section 7401 of this title.

Savings Provisions

Suits, actions or proceedings commenced under this chapter as in effect prior to Nov. 15, 1990, not to abate by reason of the taking effect of amendments by Pub. L. No. 101–549, except as otherwise provided for, see section 711(a) of Pub. L. No. 101–549, set out as a note under section 7401 of this title.

§ 7619. Air quality monitoring

[CAA § 319]

(a) In general

After notice and opportunity for public hearing, the Administrator shall promulgate regulations establishing an air quality monitoring system throughout the United States which—

(1) utilizes uniform air quality monitoring criteria and methodology and measures such air quality according to a uniform air quality index,

(2) provides for air quality monitoring stations in major urban areas and other appropriate areas throughout the United States to provide monitoring such as will supplement (but not duplicate) air quality monitoring carried out by the States required under any applicable implementation plan,

(3) provides for daily analysis and reporting of air quality based upon such uniform air quality index, and

(4) provides for recordkeeping with respect to such monitoring data and for periodic analysis and reporting to the general public by the Administrator with respect to air quality based upon such data.

The operation of such air quality monitoring system may be carried out by the Administrator or by such other departments, agencies, or entities of the Federal Government (including the National Weather Service) as the President may deem appropriate. Any air quality monitoring system required under any applicable implementation plan under section 7410 of this title shall, as soon as practicable following promulgation of regulations under this section, utilize the standard criteria and methodology, and measure air quality according to the standard index, established under such regulations.

(b) Air quality monitoring data influenced by exceptional events

(1) Definition of exceptional event

In this section:

(A) In general

The term "exceptional event" means an event that—

(i) affects air quality;

(ii) is not reasonably controllable or preventable;

(iii) is an event caused by human activity that is unlikely to recur at a particular location or a natural event; and

(iv) is determined by the Administrator through the process established in the regulations promulgated under paragraph (2) to be an exceptional event.

(B) Exclusions

In this subsection, the term "exceptional event" does not include—

(i) stagnation of air masses or meteorological inversions;

(ii) a meteorological event involving high temperatures or lack of precipitation; or

(iii) air pollution relating to source noncompliance.

(2) Regulations

(A) Proposed regulations

Not later than March 1, 2006, after consultation with Federal land managers and State air pollution control agencies, the Administrator shall publish in the Federal Register proposed regulations governing the review and handling of air quality monitoring data influenced by exceptional events.

(B) Final regulations

Not later than 1 year after the date on which the Administrator publishes proposed regulations under subparagraph (A), and after providing an opportunity for interested persons to make oral presentations of views, data, and arguments regarding the proposed regulations, the Administrator shall promulgate final regulations governing the review and handling or air quality monitoring data influenced by an exceptional event that are consistent with paragraph (3).

(3) Principles and requirements

(A) Principles

In promulgating regulations under this section, the Administrator shall follow—

(i) the principle that protection of public health is the highest priority;

(ii) the principle that timely information should be provided to the public in any case in which the air quality is unhealthy;

(iii) the principle that all ambient air quality data should be included in a timely manner, an appropriate Federal air quality database that is accessible to the public;

(iv) the principle that each State must take necessary measures to safeguard public health regardless of the source of the air pollution; and

(v) the principle that air quality data should be carefully screened to ensure that events not likely to recur are represented accurately in all monitoring data and analyses.

(B) Requirements

Regulations promulgated under this section shall, at a minimum, provide that—

(i) the occurrence of an exceptional event must be demonstrated by reliable, accurate data that is promptly produced and provided by Federal, State, or local government agencies;

(ii) a clear causal relationship must exist between the measured exceedances of a national ambient air quality standard and the exceptional event to demonstrate that the exceptional event caused a specific air pollution concentration at a particular air quality monitoring location;

(iii) there is a public process for determining whether an event is exceptional; and

(iv) there are criteria and procedures for the Governor of a State to petition the Administrator to exclude air quality monitoring data that is directly due to exceptional events from use in determinations by the Administrator with respect to exceedances or violations of the national ambient air quality standards.

(4) Interim provision

Until the effective date of a regulation promulgated under paragraph (2), the following guidance issued by the Administrator shall continue to apply:

(A) Guidance on the identification and use of air quality data affected by exceptional events (July 1986).

(B) Areas affected by PM-10 natural events, May 30, 1996.

(C) Appendices I, K, and N to part 50 of title 40, Code of Federal Regulations.

(July 14, 1955, c. 360, Title III, § 319, as added by Pub. L. No. 95–95, Title III, § 309, 91 Stat. 781 (Aug. 7, 1977); and amended by Pub. L. No. 109–59, Title VI, § 6013(a), 119 Stat. 1882 (Aug. 10, 2005).)

HISTORICAL AND STATUTORY NOTES

Effective and Applicability Provisions

1977 Acts. Section effective Aug. 7, 1977, except as otherwise expressly provided, see section 406(d) of Pub. L. No. 95–95, set out as a note under section 7401 of this title.

§ 7620. Standardized air quality modeling

[CAA § 320]

(a) Conferences

Not later than six months after August 7, 1977, and at least every three years thereafter, the Administrator shall conduct a conference on air quality modeling. In conducting such conference, special attention shall be given to appropriate modeling necessary for carrying out part C of subchapter I of this chapter (relating to prevention of significant deterioration of air quality).

(b) Conferees

The conference conducted under this section shall provide for participation by the National Academy of Sciences, representatives of State and local air pollution control agencies, and appropriate Federal agencies, including the National Science Foundation;[1] the National Oceanic and Atmospheric Administration, and the National Institute of Standards and Technology.

(c) Comments; transcripts

Interested persons shall be permitted to submit written comments and a verbatim transcript of the conference proceedings shall be maintained.

(d) Promulgation and revision of regulations relating to air quality modeling

The comments submitted and the transcript maintained pursuant to subsection (c) of this section shall be included in the docket required to be established for purposes of promulgating or revising any regulation relating to air quality modeling under part C of subchapter I of this chapter.

(July 14, 1955, c. 360, Title III, § 320, as added by Pub. L. No. 95–95, Title III, § 310, 91 Stat. 782 (Aug. 7, 1977); and amended by Pub. L. No. 100–418, Title V, § 5115(c), 102 Stat. 1433 (Aug. 23, 1988).)

[1] So in original. Probably should be a comma.

HISTORICAL AND STATUTORY NOTES

Effective and Applicability Provisions

1977 Acts. Section effective Aug. 7, 1977, except as otherwise expressly provided, see section 406(d) of Pub. L. No. 95–95, set out as a note under section 7401 of this title.

§ 7621. Employment effects

[CAA § 321]

(a) Continuous evaluation of potential loss or shifts of employment

The Administrator shall conduct continuing evaluations of potential loss or shifts of employment which may result from the administration or enforcement of the provision of this chapter and applicable implementation plans, including where appropriate, investigating threatened plant closures or reductions in employment allegedly resulting from such administration or enforcement.

(b) Request for investigation; hearings; record; report

Any employee, or any representative of such employee, who is discharged or laid off, threatened with discharge or layoff, or whose employment is otherwise adversely affected or threatened to be adversely affected because of the alleged results of any requirement imposed or proposed to be imposed under this chapter, including any requirement applicable to Federal facilities and any requirement imposed by a State or political subdivision thereof, may request the Administrator to conduct a full investigation of the matter. Any such request shall be reduced to writing, shall set forth with reasonable particularity the grounds for the request, and shall be signed by the employee, or representative of such employee, making the request. The Administrator shall thereupon investigate the matter and, at the request of any party, shall hold public hearings on not less than five days' notice. At such hearings, the Administrator shall require the parties, including the employer involved, to present information relating to the actual or potential effect of such requirements on employment and the detailed reasons or justification therefor. If the Administrator determines that there are no reasonable grounds for conducting a public hearing he shall notify (in writing) the party requesting such hearing of such a determination and the reasons therefor. If the Administrator does convene such a hearing, the hearing shall be on the record. Upon receiving the report of such investigation, the Administrator shall make findings of fact as to the effect of such requirements on employment and on the alleged actual or potential discharge, layoff, or other adverse effect on employment, and shall make such recommendations as he deems appropriate. Such report, findings, and recommendations shall be available to the public.

(c) Subpenas; confidential information; witnesses; penalty

In connection with any investigation or public hearing conducted under subsection (b) of this section or as authorized in section 7419 of this title (relating to primary nonferrous smelter orders), the Administrator may issue subpenas for the attendance and testimony of witnesses and the production of relevant papers, books and documents, and he may administer oaths. Except for emission data, upon a showing satisfactory to the Administrator by such owner or operator that such papers, books, documents, or information or particular part thereof, if made public, would divulge trade secrets or secret processes of such owner, or operator, the Administrator shall consider such record, report, or information or particular portion thereof confidential in accordance with the purposes of section 1905 of Title 18, except that such paper, book, document, or information may be disclosed to other officers, employees, or authorized representatives of the United States concerned with carrying out this chapter, or when relevant in any proceeding under this chapter. Witnesses summoned shall be paid the same fees and mileage that are paid witnesses in the courts of the United States. In cases of contumacy or refusal to obey a subpena served upon any person under this subparagraph, the district court of the United States for any district in which such person is found or resides or transacts business, upon application by the United States and after notice to such person, shall have jurisdiction to issue an order requiring such person to appear and give testimony before the Administrator, to appear and produce papers, books, and documents before the Administrator, or both, and any failure to obey such order of the court may be punished by such court as a contempt thereof.

(d) Limitations on construction of section

Nothing in this section shall be construed to require or authorize the Administrator, the States, or political subdivisions thereof, to modify or withdraw any requirement imposed or proposed to be imposed under this chapter.

(July 14, 1955, c. 360, Title III, § 321, as added by Pub. L. No. 95–95, Title III, § 311, 91 Stat. 782 (Aug. 7, 1977).)

HISTORICAL AND STATUTORY NOTES

Effective and Applicability Provisions

1977 Acts. Section effective Aug. 7, 1977, except as otherwise expressly provided, see section 406(d) of Pub. L. No. 95–95, set out as a note under section 7401 of this title.

Study of Potential Dislocation of Employees

Section 403(e) of Pub. L. No. 95–95 provided that the Secretary of Labor, in consultation with the Administrator, conduct a study of potential dislocation of employees due to implementation of laws administered by the Administrator and that the Secretary submit to Congress the results of the study not more than one year after Aug. 7, 1977.

§ 7622. Employee protection

[CAA § 322]

(a) Discharge or discrimination prohibited

No employer may discharge any employee or otherwise discriminate against any employee with respect to his compensation, terms, conditions, or privileges of employment because the employee (or any person acting pursuant to a request of the employee)—

(1) commenced, caused to be commenced, or is about to commence or cause to be commenced a proceeding under this chapter or a proceeding for the administration or enforcement of any requirement imposed under this chapter or under any applicable implementation plan,

(2) testified or is about to testify in any such proceeding, or

(3) assisted or participated or is about to assist or participate in any manner in such a proceeding or in any other action to carry out the purposes of this chapter.

(b) Complaint charging unlawful discharge or discrimination; investigation; order

(1) Any employee who believes that he has been discharged or otherwise discriminated against by any person in violation of subsection (a) of this section may, within thirty days after such violation occurs, file (or have any person file on his behalf) a complaint with the Secretary of Labor (hereinafter in this subsection referred to as the "Secretary") alleging such discharge or discrimination. Upon receipt of such a complaint, the Secretary shall notify the person named in the complaint of the filing of the complaint.

(2) (A) Upon receipt of a complaint filed under paragraph (1), the Secretary shall conduct an investigation of the violation alleged in the complaint. Within thirty days of the receipt of such complaint, the Secretary shall complete such investigation and shall notify in writing the complainant (and any person acting in his behalf) and the person alleged to have committed such violation of the results of the investigation conducted pursuant to this subparagraph. Within ninety days of the receipt of such complaint the Secretary shall, unless the proceeding on the complaint is terminated by the Secretary on the basis of a settlement entered into by the Secretary and the person alleged to have committed such violation, issue an order either providing the relief prescribed by subparagraph (B) or denying the complaint. An order of the Secretary shall be made on the record after notice and opportunity for public hearing. The Secretary may not enter into a settlement terminating a proceeding on a complaint without the participation and consent of the complainant.

(B) If, in response to a complaint filed under paragraph (1), the Secretary determines that a violation of subsection (a) of this section has occurred, the Secretary shall order the person who committed such violation to (i) take affirmative action to abate the violation, and (ii) reinstate the complainant to his former position together with the compensation (including back pay), terms, conditions, and privileges of his employment, and the Secretary may order such person to provide compensatory damages to the complainant. If an order is issued under this paragraph, the Secretary, at the request of the complainant, shall assess against the person against whom the order is issued a sum equal to the aggregate amount of all costs and expenses (including attorneys' and expert witness fees) reasonably incurred, as determined by the Secretary, by the complainant for, or in connection with, the bringing of the complaint upon which the order was issued.

(c) Review

(1) Any person adversely affected or aggrieved by an order issued under subsection (b) of this section may obtain review of the order in the United States court of appeals for the circuit in which the violation, with respect to which the order was issued, allegedly occurred. The petition for review must be filed within sixty days from the issuance of the Secretary's order. Review shall conform to chapter 7 of Title 5. The commencement of proceedings under this subparagraph shall not, unless ordered by the court, operate as a stay of the Secretary's order.

(2) An order of the Secretary with respect to which review could have been obtained under paragraph (1) shall not be subject to judicial review in any criminal or other civil proceeding.

(d) Enforcement of order by Secretary

Whenever a person has failed to comply with an order issued under subsection (b)(2) of this section, the Secretary may file a civil action in the United States district court for the district in which the violation was found to occur to enforce such order. In actions brought under this subsection, the district courts shall have jurisdiction to grant all appropriate relief including, but not limited to, injunctive relief, compensatory, and exemplary damages.

(e) Enforcement of order by person on whose behalf order was issued

(1) Any person on whose behalf an order was issued under paragraph (2) of subsection (b) of this section may commence a civil action against the person to whom such order was issued to require compliance with such order. The appropriate United States district court shall have jurisdiction, without regard to the amount in controversy or the citizenship of the parties, to enforce such order.

(2) The court, in issuing any final order under this subsection, may award costs of litigation (including reasonable attorney and expert witness fees) to any party whenever the court determines such award is appropriate.

(f) Mandamus

Any nondiscretionary duty imposed by this section shall be enforceable in a mandamus proceeding brought under section 1361 of Title 28.

(g) Deliberate violation by employee

Subsection (a) of this section shall not apply with respect to any employee who, acting without direction from his employer (or the employer's agent), deliberately causes a violation of any requirement of this chapter.

(July 14, 1955, c. 360, Title III, § 322, as added by Pub. L. No. 95–95, Title III, § 312, 91 Stat. 783 (Aug. 7, 1977).)

HISTORICAL AND STATUTORY NOTES

Effective and Applicability Provisions

1977 Acts. Section effective Aug. 7, 1977, except as otherwise expressly provided, see section 406(d) of Pub. L. No. 95–95, set out as a note under section 7401 of this title.

§ 7623. Repealed. Pub. L. No. 96–300, § 1(c), 94 Stat. 831 (July 2, 1980).

HISTORICAL AND STATUTORY NOTES

Section, Act of July 14, 1955, c. 360, Title III, § 323, as added by Pub. L. No. 95–95, Title III, § 313, 91 Stat. 785 (Aug. 7, 1977), and amended by Pub. L. No. 95–190, § 14(a)(81), 91 Stat. 1404 (Nov. 16, 1977); S.Res. 4 (Feb. 4, 1977); H.Res. 549 (Mar. 25, 1980); Pub. L. No. 96–300, § 1(a), 94 Stat. 831 (July 2, 1980), established a National Commission on Air Quality, prescribed numerous subjects for study and report to Congress, enumerated specific questions for study and investigation, required specific identification of loss or irretrievable commitment of resources, and provided for appointment and confirmation of its membership, cooperation of Federal executive agencies, submission of a National Academy of Sciences study to Congress, compensation and travel expenses, termination of Commission, appointment and compensation of staff, and public participation.

Effective Date of Repeal

Section 1(c) of Pub. L. No. 96–300 provided that this section is repealed on the date on which the National Commission on Air Quality ceases to exist pursuant to provisions of former subsec. (g) of this section, which provided that not later than Mar. 1, 1981, a report be submitted containing the results of all Commission studies and investigations and that the Commission cease to exist on Mar. 1, 1981, if the report is not submitted on Mar. 1, 1981, or the Commission would cease to exist on such date, but not later than May 1, 1981, as determined and ordered by the Commission if the report is submitted on Mar. 1, 1981.

§ 7624. Cost of vapor recovery equipment

[CAA § 323]

(a) Costs to be borne by owner of retail outlet

The regulations under this chapter applicable to vapor recovery with respect to mobile source fuels at retail outlets of such fuels shall provide that the cost of procurement and installation of such vapor recovery shall be borne by the owner of such outlet (as determined under such regulations). Except as provided in subsection (b) of this section, such regulations shall provide that no lease of a retail outlet by the owner thereof which is entered into or renewed after August 7, 1977, may provide for a payment by the lessee of the cost of procurement and installation of vapor recovery equipment. Such regulations shall also provide that the cost of procurement and installation of vapor recovery equipment may be recovered by the owner of such outlet by means of price increases in the cost of any product sold by such owner, notwithstanding any provision of law.

(b) Payment by lessee

The regulations of the Administrator referred to in subsection (a) of this section shall permit a lease of a retail outlet to provide for payment by the lessee of the cost of procurement and installation of vapor recovery equipment over a reasonable period (as determined in accordance with such regulations), if the owner of such outlet does not sell, trade in, or otherwise dispense any product at wholesale or retail at such outlet.

(July 14, 1955, c. 360, Title III, § 323, formerly § 324, as added by Pub. L. No. 95–95, Title III, § 314(a), 91 Stat. 788 (Aug. 7, 1977,); and amended by Pub. L. No. 95–190, § 14(a)(82), 91 Stat. 1404 (Nov. 16, 1977); and renumbered § 323 and amended by Pub. L. No. 96–300, § 1(b), (c), 94 Stat. 831 (July 2, 1980).)

HISTORICAL AND STATUTORY NOTES

Effective and Applicability Provisions

1977 Acts. Section effective Aug. 7, 1977, except as otherwise expressly provided, see section 406(d) of Pub. L. No. 95–95, set out as a note under section 7401 of this title.

Prior Provisions

A prior section 323 of Act of July 14, 1955, was codified as section 7623 of this title and was repealed by Pub. L. No. 96–300, § 1(c), July 2, 1980, 94 Stat. 831.

§ 7625. Vapor recovery for small business marketers of petroleum products

[CAA § 324]

(a) Marketers of gasoline

The regulations under this chapter applicable to vapor recovery from fueling of motor vehicles at retail outlets of gasoline shall not apply to any outlet owned by an independent small business marketer of gasoline having monthly sales of less than 50,000 gallons. In the case of any other outlet owned by an independent small business marketer, such regulations shall provide, with respect to independent small business marketers of gasoline, for a three-year phase-in period for the installation of such vapor recovery equipment at such outlets under which such marketers shall have—

(1) 33 percent of such outlets in compliance at the end of the first year during which such regulations apply to such marketers,

(2) 66 percent at the end of such second year, and

(3) 100 percent at the end of the third year.

(b) State requirements

Nothing in subsection (a) of this section shall be construed to prohibit any State from adopting or enforcing, with respect to independent small business marketers of gasoline having monthly sales of less than 50,000 gallons, any vapor recovery requirements for mobile source fuels at retail outlets. Any vapor recovery requirement which is adopted by a State and submitted to the Administrator as part of its implementation plan may be approved and enforced by the Administrator as part of the applicable implementation plan for that State.

(c) Refiners

For purposes of this section, an independent small business marketer of gasoline is a person engaged in the marketing of gasoline who would be required to pay for procurement and installation of vapor recovery equipment under section 7624 of this title or under regulations of the Administrator, unless such person—

(1) (A) is a refiner, or

(B) controls, is controlled by, or is under common control with, a refiner,

(C) is otherwise directly or indirectly affiliated (as determined under the regulations of the Administrator) with a refiner or with a person who controls, is controlled by, or is under a common control with a refiner (unless the sole affiliation referred to herein is by means of a supply contract or an agreement or contract to use a trademark, trade name, service mark, or other identifying symbol or name owned by such refiner or any such person), or

(2) receives less than 50 percent of his annual income from refining or marketing of gasoline.

For the purpose of this section, the term "refiner" shall not include any refiner whose total refinery capacity (including the refinery capacity of any person who controls, is controlled by, or is under common control with, such refiner) does not exceed 65,000 barrels per day. For purposes of this section, "control" of a corporation means ownership of more than 50 percent of its stock.

(July 14, 1955, c. 360, Title III, § 324, formerly § 325, as added by Pub. L. No. 95–95, Title III, § 314(b), 91 Stat. 789 (Aug. 7, 1977); and renumbered § 324 by Pub. L. No. 96–300, § 1(c), 94 Stat. 831 (July 2, 1980).)

HISTORICAL AND STATUTORY NOTES

Effective and Applicability Provisions

1977 Acts. Section effective Aug. 7, 1977, except as otherwise expressly provided, see section 406(d) of Pub. L. No. 95–95, set out as a note under section 7401 of this title.

Prior Provisions

A prior section 324 of Act of July 14, 1955, was renumbered section 323 by Pub. L. No. 96–300, and is codified as section 7624 of this title.

§ 7625–1. Exemptions for certain territories

[CAA § 325]

(a) (1) Upon petition by the governor[1] of Guam, American Samoa, the Virgin Islands, or the Commonwealth of the Northern Mariana Islands, the Administrator is authorized to exempt any person or source or class of persons or sources in such territory from any requirement under this chapter other than section 7412 of this title or any requirement under section 7410 of this title or part D of subchapter I of this chapter necessary to attain or maintain a national primary ambient air quality standard. Such exemption may be granted if the Administrator finds that compliance with such requirement is not feasible or is unreasonable due to unique geographical, meteorological, or economic factors of such territory, or such other local factors as the Administrator deems significant. Any such petition shall be considered in accordance with section 7607(d) of this title and any exemption under this subsection shall be considered final action by the Administrator for the purposes of section 7607(b) of this title.

(2) The Administrator shall promptly notify the Committees on Energy and Commerce and on Natural Resources of the House of Representatives and the Committees on Environment and Public Works and on Energy and Natural Resources of the Senate upon receipt of any petition under this subsection and of the approval or rejection of such petition and the basis for such action.

(b) Notwithstanding any other provision of this chapter, any fossil fuel fired steam electric power plant operating within Guam as of December 8, 1983, is hereby exempted from:

(1) any requirement of the new source performance standards relating to sulfur dioxide promulgated under section 7411 of this title as of December 8, 1983; and

(2) any regulation relating to sulfur dioxide standards or limitations contained in a State implementation plan approved under section 7410 of this title as of December 8, 1983: *Provided,* That such exemption shall expire eighteen months after December 8, 1983, unless the Administrator determines that such plant is making all emissions reductions practicable to prevent exceedances of the national ambient air quality standards for sulfur dioxide.

(July 14, 1955, c. 360, Title III, § 325, as added by Pub. L. No. 98–213, § 11, 97 Stat. 1461 (Dec. 8, 1983); and amended by Pub. L. No. 101–549, Title VIII, § 806, 104 Stat. 2689 (Nov. 15, 1990); Pub. L. No. 103–437, § 15(s), 108 Stat. 4594 (Nov. 2, 1994).)

[1] So in original. Probably should be capitalized.

HISTORICAL AND STATUTORY NOTES

Effective and Applicability Provisions

1990 Acts. Amendment by Pub. L. No. 101–549 effective Nov. 15, 1990, except as otherwise provided, see section 711(b) of Pub. L. No. 101–549, set out as a note under section 7401 of this title.

Change of Name

Committee on Energy and Commerce of House of Representatives treated as referring to Committee on Commerce of House of Representatives by section 1(a) of Pub. L. No. 104–14, set out as a note preceding 2 U.S.C.A. 21. Committee on Commerce of House of Representatives changed to Committee on Energy and Commerce of House of Representatives, and jurisdiction over matters relating to securities and exchanges and insurance generally transferred to Committee on Financial Services of House of Representatives by House Resolution No. 5, 107th Congress, Jan. 3, 2001.

Prior Provisions

A prior section 325 of Act of July 14, 1955, was renumbered section 326 by Pub. L. No. 98–213 and is codified as section 7625a of this title.

Another prior section 325 of Act of July 14, 1955, was renumbered section 324 by Pub. L. No. 96–300 and is codified as section 7625 of this title.

§ 7625a. Statutory construction

[CAA § 326]

The parenthetical cross references in any provision of this chapter to other provisions of the chapter, or other provisions of law, where the words “relating to” or “pertaining to” are used, are made only for convenience, and shall be given no legal effect.

(July 14, 1955, c. 360, Title III, § 326, as added by Pub. L. No. 95–190, § 14(a)(84), 91 Stat. 1404 (Nov. 16, 1977); and renumbered § 325 by Pub. L. No. 96–300, § 1(c), 94 Stat. 831 (July 2, 1980); and renumbered § 326 by Pub. L. No. 98–213, § 11, 97 Stat. 1461 (Dec. 8, 1983).)

HISTORICAL AND STATUTORY NOTES

Prior Provisions

A prior section 326 of Act of July 14, 1955, was renumbered section 327 by Pub. L. No. 98–213 and is codified as section 7626 of this title.

§ 7626. Authorization of appropriations

[CAA § 327]

(a) In general

There are authorized to be appropriated to carry out this chapter such sums as may be necessary for the 7 fiscal years commencing after November 15, 1990.

(b) Grants for planning

There are authorized to be appropriated (1) not more than $50,000,000 to carry out section 7505 of this title beginning in fiscal year 1991, to be available until expended, to develop plan revisions required by subpart 2, 3, or 4 of part D of subchapter I of this chapter, and (2) not more than $15,000,000 for each of the 7 fiscal years commencing after November 15, 1990, to make grants to the States to prepare implementation plans as required by subpart 2, 3, or 4 of part D of subchapter I of this chapter.

(July 14, 1955, c. 360, Title III, § 327, formerly § 325, as added by Pub. L. No. 95–95, Title III, § 315, 91 Stat. 790 (Aug. 7, 1977); and renumbered § 327 and amended by Pub. L. No. 95–190, § 14(a)(83), 91 Stat. 1404 (Nov. 16, 1977); and renumbered § 326 by Pub. L. No. 96–300, § 1(c), 94 Stat. 831 (July 2, 1980); and renumbered § 327 by Pub. L. No. 98–213, § 11, 97 Stat. 1461 (Dec. 8, 1983); and amended by Pub. L. No. 101–549, Title VIII, § 822, 104 Stat. 2699 (Nov. 15, 1990).)

HISTORICAL AND STATUTORY NOTES

Effective and Applicability Provisions

1990 Acts. Amendment by Pub. L. No. 101–549 effective Nov. 15, 1990, except as otherwise provided, see section 711(b) of Pub. L. No. 101–549, set out as a note under section 7401 of this title.

1977 Acts. Section effective Aug. 7, 1977, except as otherwise expressly provided, see section 406(d) of Pub. L. No. 95–95, set out as a note under section 7401 of this title.

Savings Provisions

Suits, actions or proceedings commenced under this chapter as in effect prior to Nov. 15, 1990, not to abate by reason of the taking effect of amendments by Pub. L. No. 101–549, except as otherwise provided for, see section 711(a) of Pub. L. No. 101–549, set out as a note under section 7401 of this title.

Prior Provisions

Provisions similar to those comprising this section were contained in section 1857*l* of this title, Act of July 14, 1955, c. 360, Title III, § 316, formerly § 13, as added by Pub. L. No. 88–206, § 1, 77 Stat. 401 (Dec. 17, 1963); and renumbered § 306 and amended by Pub. L. No. 89–272, Title I, § 101(4), (6), (7), 79 Stat. 992 (Oct. 20, 1965); and amended by Pub. L. No. 89–675, § 2(a), 80 Stat. 954 (Oct. 15, 1966); and renumbered § 309 and amended by Pub. L. No. 90–148, § 2, 81 Stat. 506 (Nov. 21, 1967); and renumbered § 316 and amended by Pub. L. No. 91–604, §§ 12(a), 13(b), 84 Stat. 1705, 1709 (Dec. 31, 1970); and amended by Pub. L. No. 93–15, § 1(c), 87 Stat. 11 (Apr. 9, 1973); Pub. L. No. 93–319, § 13(c), 88 Stat. 265 (June 22, 1974), prior to its repeal by section 306 of Pub. L. No. 95–95.

§ 7627. Air pollution from Outer Continental Shelf activities

[CAA § 328]

(a) Applicable requirements for certain areas

(1) In general

Not later than 12 months after November 15, 1990, following consultation with the Secretary of the Interior and the Commandant of the United States Coast Guard, the Administrator, by rule, shall establish requirements to control air pollution from Outer Continental Shelf sources located offshore of the States along the Pacific, Arctic and Atlantic Coasts (other than Outer Continental Shelf sources located offshore of the North Slope Borough of the State of Alaska), and along the United States Gulf Coast off the State of Florida eastward of longitude 87 degrees and 30 minutes ("OCS sources") to attain and maintain Federal and State ambient air quality standards and to comply with the provisions of part C of subchapter I of this chapter. For such sources located within 25 miles of the seaward boundary of such States, such requirements shall be the same as would be applicable if the source were located in the corresponding onshore area, and shall include, but not be limited to, State and local requirements for emission controls, emission limitations, offsets, permitting, monitoring, testing, and reporting. New OCS sources shall comply with such requirements on the date of promulgation and existing OCS sources shall comply on the date 24 months thereafter. The Administrator shall update such requirements as necessary to maintain consistency with onshore regulations and this chapter. The authority of this subsection shall supersede section 5(a)(8) of the Outer Continental Shelf Lands Act [43 U.S.C.A. § 1334(a)(8)] but shall not repeal or modify any other Federal, State, or local authorities with respect to air quality. Each requirement established under this section shall be treated, for purposes of sections 7413, 7414, 7416, 7420, and 7604 of this title, as a standard under section 7411 of this title and a violation of any such requirement shall be considered a violation of section 7411(e) of this title.

(2) Exemptions

The Administrator may exempt an OCS source from a specific requirement in effect under regulations under this subsection if the Administrator finds that compliance with a pollution control technology requirement is technically infeasible or will cause an unreasonable threat to health and safety. The Administrator shall make written findings explaining the basis of any exemption issued pursuant to this subsection and shall impose another requirement equal to or as close in stringency to the original requirement as possible. The Administrator shall ensure that any increase in emissions due to the granting of an exemption is offset by reductions in actual emissions, not otherwise required by this chapter, from the same source or other sources in the area or in the corresponding onshore area. The Administrator shall establish procedures to provide for public notice and comment on exemptions proposed pursuant to this subsection.

(3) State procedures

Each State adjacent to an OCS source included under this subsection may promulgate and submit to the Administrator regulations for implementing and enforcing the requirements of this subsection. If the Administrator finds that the State regulations are adequate, the Administrator shall delegate to that State any authority the Administrator has under this chapter to implement and enforce such requirements. Nothing in this subsection shall prohibit the Administrator from enforcing any requirement of this section.

(4) Definitions

For purposes of subsections (a) and (b) of this section—

(A) Outer Continental Shelf

The term "Outer Continental Shelf" has the meaning provided by section 2 of the Outer Continental Shelf Lands Act (43 U.S.C. 1331).

(B) Corresponding onshore area

The term "corresponding onshore area" means, with respect to any OCS source, the onshore attainment or nonattainment area that is closest to the source, unless the Administrator determines that another area with more stringent requirements with respect to the control and abatement of air pollution may reasonably be expected to be affected by such emissions. Such determination shall be based on the potential for air pollutants from the OCS source to reach the other onshore area and the potential of such air pollutants to affect the efforts of the other onshore area to attain or maintain any Federal or State ambient air quality standard or to comply with the provisions of part C of subchapter I of this chapter.

(C) Outer Continental Shelf source

The terms "Outer Continental Shelf source" and "OCS source" include any equipment, activity, or facility which—

(i) emits or has the potential to emit any air pollutant,

(ii) is regulated or authorized under the Outer Continental Shelf Lands Act [43 U.S.C.A. § 1331 et seq.], and

(iii) is located on the Outer Continental Shelf or in or on waters above the Outer Continental Shelf.

Such activities include, but are not limited to, platform and drill ship exploration, construction, development, production, processing, and transportation. For purposes of this subsection, emissions from any vessel servicing or associated with an OCS source, including emissions while at the OCS source or en route to or from the OCS source within 25 miles of the OCS source, shall be considered direct emissions from the OCS source.

(D) New and existing OCS sources

The term "new OCS source" means an OCS source which is a new source within the meaning of section 7411(a) of this title. The term "existing OCS source" means any OCS source other than a new OCS source.

(b) Requirements for other offshore areas

For portions of the United States Outer Continental Shelf that are adjacent to the States not covered by subsection (a) of this section which are Texas, Louisiana, Mississippi, and Alabama or are adjacent to the North Slope Borough of the State of Alaska, the Secretary shall consult with the Administrator to assure coordination of air pollution control regulation for Outer Continental Shelf emissions and emissions in adjacent onshore areas. Concurrently with this obligation, the Secretary shall complete within 3 years of November 15, 1990, a research study examining the impacts of emissions from Outer Continental Shelf activities in such areas that fail to meet the national ambient air quality standards for either ozone or nitrogen dioxide. Based on the results of this study, the Secretary shall consult with the Administrator and determine if any additional actions are necessary. There are authorized to be appropriated such sums as may be necessary to provide funding for the study required under this section.

(c) Coastal waters

(1) The study report of section 7412(n)[1] of this title shall apply to the coastal waters of the United States to the same extent and in the same manner as such requirements apply to the Great Lakes, the Chesapeake Bay, and their tributary waters.

(2) The regulatory requirements of section 7412(n)[1] of this title shall apply to the coastal waters of the States which are subject to subsection (a) of this section, to the same extent and in the same manner as such requirements apply to the Great Lakes, the Chesapeake Bay, and their tributary waters.

(July 14, 1955, c. 360, Title III, § 328, as added by Pub. L. No. 101–549, Title VIII, § 801, 104 Stat. 2685 (Nov. 15, 1990); and amended by Pub. L. No. 112–74, Div. E, Title IV, § 432(b), (c), 125 Stat. 1048 (Dec. 23, 2011).)

[1] So in original. Probably should be section "7412(m)".

HISTORICAL AND STATUTORY NOTES

References in Text

This chapter, referred to in text, originally read "this Act", meaning the Clean Air Act, Act of July 14, 1955, c. 360, 69 Stat. 322, as amended, also known as CAA and the Air Pollution Control Act, which is codified principally as this chapter. For complete classification, see Short Title note set out under 42 U.S.C.A. § 7401 and Tables.

The Outer Continental Shelf Lands Act, referred to in subsecs. (a)(1), (a)(4)(A) and (a)(4)(C)(ii), is Act of Aug. 7, 1953, c. 345, 67 Stat. 462, as amended, which is codified generally as subchapter III (section 1331 et seq.) of chapter 29 of Title 43, Public Lands. Section 5(a)(8) of such Act, referred to in subsec. (a)(1), is codified as section 1334(a)(8) of Title 43. Section 2 of such Act, referred to in subsec. (a)(4)(A), is codified as section 1331 of Title 43. For complete classification of this Act to the Code, see Short Title note set out under section 1301 of Title 43 and Tables.

Effective and Applicability Provisions

1990 Acts. Section effective Nov. 15, 1990, except as otherwise provided, see section 711(b) of Pub. L. No. 101–549, set out as a note under section 7401 of this title.

Transfer of Functions

For transfer of authorities, functions, personnel, and assets of the Coast Guard, including the authorities and functions of the Secretary of Transportation relating thereto, to the Department of Homeland Security, and for treatment of related references, see 6 U.S.C.A. §§ 468(b), 551(d), 552(d) and 557, and the Department of Homeland Security Reorganization Plan of November 25, 2002, as modified, set out as a note under 6 U.S.C.A. § 542.

Transfer of Air Quality Permitting Authority

Pub. L. No. 112–74, Div. E, Title IV, § 432(d), 125 Stat. 1049 (Dec. 23, 2011), provided that:

"(d) The transfer of air quality permitting authority pursuant to this section [amending this section and enacting provisions set out as a note under this section] shall not invalidate or stay—

"(1) any air quality permit pending or existing as of the date of the enactment of this Act [Dec. 23, 2011]; or

"(2) any proceeding related thereto."

Development of Domestic Energy Resources

Pub. L. No. 112–74, Div. E, Title IV, § 432(a), 125 Stat. 1048 (Dec. 23, 2011), provided that:

"(a) It is the purpose of this section [amending this section and enacting provisions set out as a note under this section] to ensure that the energy policy of the United States focuses on the expeditious and orderly development of domestic energy resources in a manner that protects human health and the environment."

§ 7628. Demonstration grant program for local governments

[CAA § 329]

(a) Grant program

(1) In general

The Administrator shall establish a demonstration program under which the Administrator shall provide competitive grants to assist local governments (such as municipalities and counties), with respect to local government buildings—

(A) to deploy cost-effective technologies and practices; and

(B) to achieve operational cost savings, through the application of cost-effective technologies and practices, as verified by the Administrator.

(2) Cost sharing

(A) In general

The Federal share of the cost of an activity carried out using a grant provided under this section shall be 40 percent.

(B) Waiver of non-Federal share

The Administrator may waive up to 100 percent of the local share of the cost of any grant under this section should the Administrator determine that the community is economically distressed, pursuant to objective economic criteria established by the Administrator in published guidelines.

(3) Maximum amount

The amount of a grant provided under this subsection shall not exceed $1,000,000.

(b) Guidelines

(1) In general

Not later than 1 year after December 19, 2007, the Administrator shall issue guidelines to implement the grant program established under subsection (a).

(2) **Requirements**

The guidelines under paragraph (1) shall establish—

(A) standards for monitoring and verification of operational cost savings through the application of cost-effective technologies and practices reported by grantees under this section;

(B) standards for grantees to implement training programs, and to provide technical assistance and education, relating to the retrofit of buildings using cost-effective technologies and practices; and

(C) a requirement that each local government that receives a grant under this section shall achieve facility-wide cost savings, through renovation of existing local government buildings using cost-effective technologies and practices, of at least 40 percent as compared to the baseline operational costs of the buildings before the renovation (as calculated assuming a 3-year, weather-normalized average).

(c) Compliance with State and local law

Nothing in this section or any program carried out using a grant provided under this section supersedes or otherwise affects any State or local law, to the extent that the State or local law contains a requirement that is more stringent than the relevant requirement of this section.

(d) Authorization of appropriations

There is authorized to be appropriated to carry out this section $20,000,000 for each of fiscal years 2007 through 2012.

(e) Reports

(1) In general

The Administrator shall provide annual reports to Congress on cost savings achieved and actions taken and recommendations made under this section, and any recommendations for further action.

(2) Final report

The Administrator shall issue a final report at the conclusion of the program, including findings, a summary of total cost savings achieved, and recommendations for further action.

(f) Termination

The program under this section shall terminate on September 30, 2012.

(g) Definitions

In this section, the terms "cost-effective technologies and practices" and "operating[1] cost savings" shall have the meanings defined in section 17061 of this title.

(July 14, 1955, c. 360, Title III, § 329, as added by Pub. L. No. 110–140, Title IV, § 493, 121 Stat. 1652 (Dec. 19, 2007).)

[1] So in original. Probably should be "operational".

HISTORICAL AND STATUTORY NOTES

Effective and Applicability Provisions

2007 Acts. Enactment by Pub. L. 110–140 effective on the date that is 1 day after December 19, 2007, see Pub. L. No. 110–140, § 1601, set out as a note under 2 U.S.C.A. § 1824.

SUBCHAPTER IV—NOISE POLLUTION

HISTORICAL AND STATUTORY NOTES

Codifications

Another Title IV was enacted by Pub. L. No. 101–549, Title IV, § 401, 104 Stat. 2584 (Nov. 15, 1990), as added to Act of July 14, 1955, c. 360, and is set out as subchapter IV-A (sections 7651 to 7651*o*) of this chapter.

§ 7641. Noise abatement

[CAA § 402]

(a) Office of Noise Abatement and Control

The Administrator shall establish within the Environmental Protection Agency an Office of Noise Abatement and Control, and shall carry out through such Office a full and complete investigation and study of noise and its effect on the public health and welfare in order to (1) identify and classify causes and sources of noise, and (2) determine—

(A) effects at various levels;

(B) projected growth of noise levels in urban areas through the year 2000;

(C) the psychological and physiological effect on humans;

(D) effects of sporadic extreme noise (such as jet noise near airports) as compared with constant noise;

(E) effect on wildlife and property (including values);

(F) effect of sonic booms on property (including values); and

(G) such other matters as may be of interest in the public welfare.

(b) Investigation techniques; report and recommendations

In conducting such investigation, the Administrator shall hold public hearings, conduct research, experiments, demonstrations, and studies. The Administrator shall report the results of such investigation and study, together with his recommendations for legislation or other action, to the President and the Congress not later than one year after December 31, 1970.

(c) Abatement of noise from Federal activities

In any case where any Federal department or agency is carrying out or sponsoring any activity resulting in noise which the Administrator determines amounts to a public nuisance or is otherwise objectionable, such department or agency shall consult with the Administrator to determine possible means of abating such noise.

(July 14, 1955, c. 360, Title IV, § 402, as added by Pub. L. No. 91–604, § 14, 84 Stat. 1709 (Dec. 31, 1970).)

HISTORICAL AND STATUTORY NOTES

Codifications

Another section 402 of Act of July 14, 1955, as added by Pub. L. No. 101–549, Title IV, § 401, 104 Stat. 2585 (Nov. 15, 1990), is codified as section 7651a of this title.

This section was formerly codified as section 1858 of this title.

Short Title

1955 Acts. For provisions authorizing the citation of Title IV of Act of July 14, 1955 [this subchapter], as the "Noise Pollution and Abatement Act of 1970", see section 401 of Act of July 14, 1955, as added by Pub. L. No. 91–604, set out as a Short Title of 1970 Amendments note under section 7401 of this title.

§ 7642. Authorization of appropriations

[CAA § 403]

There is authorized to be appropriated such amount, not to exceed $30,000,000, as may be necessary for the purposes of this subchapter.

(July 14, 1955, c. 360, Title IV, § 403, as added by Pub. L. No. 91–604, § 14, 84 Stat. 1710 (Dec. 31, 1970).)

HISTORICAL AND STATUTORY NOTES

Codifications

There are two sections 403 of Act of July 14, 1955, c. 360, Title IV, as amended. Section 403, as added Pub. L. No. 91–604, is codified as this section. Section 403, as added Pub. L. No. 101–549, is codified as section 7651b of this title.

Section was formerly codified as section 1858a of this title.

SUBCHAPTER IV-A—ACID DEPOSITION CONTROL

HISTORICAL AND STATUTORY NOTES

Codifications

Another Title IV was enacted by Pub. L. No. 91–604, § 14, Dec. 31, 1970, 84 Stat. 1709, as added to Act of July 14, 1955, c. 360, and is set out as subchapter IV (sections 7641, 7642) of this chapter.

§ 7651. Findings and purposes

[CAA § 401]

(a) Findings

The Congress finds that—

(1) the presence of acidic compounds and their precursors in the atmosphere and in deposition from the atmosphere represents a threat to natural resources, ecosystems, materials, visibility, and public health;

(2) the principal sources of the acidic compounds and their precursors in the atmosphere are emissions of sulfur and nitrogen oxides from the combustion of fossil fuels;

(3) the problem of acid deposition is of national and international significance;

(4) strategies and technologies for the control of precursors to acid deposition exist now that are economically feasible, and improved methods are expected to become increasingly available over the next decade;

(5) current and future generations of Americans will be adversely affected by delaying measures to remedy the problem;

(6) reduction of total atmospheric loading of sulfur dioxide and nitrogen oxides will enhance protection of the public health and welfare and the environment; and

(7) control measures to reduce precursor emissions from steam-electric generating units should be initiated without delay.

(b) Purposes

The purpose of this subchapter is to reduce the adverse effects of acid deposition through reductions in annual emissions of sulfur dioxide of ten million tons from 1980 emission levels, and, in combination with other provisions of this chapter, of nitrogen oxides emissions of approximately two million tons from 1980 emission levels, in the forty-eight contiguous States and the District of Columbia. It is the intent of this subchapter to effectuate such reductions by requiring compliance by affected sources with prescribed emission limitations by specified deadlines, which limitations may be met through alternative methods of compliance provided by an emission allocation and transfer system. It is also the purpose of this subchapter to encourage energy conservation, use of renewable and clean alternative technologies, and pollution prevention as a long-range strategy, consistent with the provisions of this subchapter, for reducing air pollution and other adverse impacts of energy production and use.

(July 14, 1955, c. 360, Title IV, § 401, as added by Pub. L. No. 101–549, Title IV, § 401, 104 Stat. 2584 (Nov. 15, 1990).)

HISTORICAL AND STATUTORY NOTES

Codifications

Another section 401 of Act of July 14, 1955, as added by Pub. L. No. 91–604, § 14, 84 Stat. 1709 (Dec. 31, 1970), is set out as a Short Title note under section 7401 of this title.

Effective and Applicability Provisions

1990 Acts. Section effective Nov. 15, 1990, except as otherwise provided, see section 711(b) of Pub. L. No. 101–549, set out as a note under section 7401 of this title.

Savings Provisions

Suits, actions or proceedings commenced under this chapter as in effect prior to Nov. 15, 1990, not to abate by reason of the taking effect of amendments by Pub. L. No. 101–549, except as otherwise provided for, see section 711(a) of Pub. L. No. 101–549, set out as a note under section 7401 of this title.

Acid Deposition Standards

Section 404 of Pub. L. No. 101–549 provided that: "Not later than 36 months after the date of enactment of this Act [Nov. 15, 1990], the Administrator of the Environmental Protection Agency shall transmit to the Committee on Environment and Public Works of the Senate and the Committee on Energy and Commerce of the House of Representatives a report on the feasibility and effectiveness of an acid deposition standard or standards to protect sensitive and critically sensitive aquatic and terrestrial resources. The study required by this section shall include, but not be limited to, consideration of the following matters:

"(1) identification of the sensitive and critically sensitive aquatic and terrestrial resources in the United States and Canada which may be affected by the deposition of acidic compounds;

"(2) description of the nature and numerical value of a deposition standard or standards that would be sufficient to protect such resources;

"(3) description of the use of such standard or standards in other Nations or by any of the several States in acid deposition control programs;

"(4) description of the measures that would need to be taken to integrate such standard or standards with the control program required by Title IV of the Clean Air Act [this subchapter];

"(5) description of the state of knowledge with respect to source-receptor relationships necessary to develop a control program on such standard or standards and the additional research that is on-going or would be needed to make such a control program feasible; and

"(6) description of the impediments to implementation of such control program and the cost-effectiveness of deposition standards compared to other control strategies including ambient air quality standards, new source performance standards and the requirements of title IV of the Clean Air Act [this subchapter]."

[Any reference in any provision of law enacted before Jan. 4, 1995, to the Committee on Energy and Commerce of the House of Representatives treated as referring to the Committee on Commerce of the House of Representatives, except that any reference in any provision of law enacted before Jan. 4, 1995, to the Committee on Energy and Commerce of the House of Representatives treated as referring to the Committee on Agriculture of the House of Representatives, in the case of a provision of law relating to inspection of seafood or seafood products, the Committee on Banking and Financial Services of the House of Representatives, in the case of a provision of law relating to bank capital markets activities generally or to depository institution securities activities generally, and the Committee on Transportation and Infrastructure of the House of Representatives, in the case of a provision of law relating to railroads, railway labor, or railroad retirement and unemployment (except revenue measures related thereto), see section 1(a)(4) and (c)(1) of Pub. L. No. 104–14, set out as a note preceding section 21 of Title 2, The Congress.]

Industrial SO_2 Emissions

Pub. L. No. 101–549, Title IV, § 406, 104 Stat. 2632 (Nov. 15, 1990), provided that:

"(a) Report.—Not later than January 1, 1995 and every 5 years thereafter, the Administrator of the Environmental Protection Agency shall transmit to the Congress a report containing an inventory of national annual sulfur dioxide emissions from industrial sources (as defined in Title IV of the Act [this subchapter]), including units subject to section 405(g)(6) of the Clean Air Act [subsec. (g)(6) of section 7651d of this title], for all years for which data are available, as well as the likely trend in such emissions over the following twenty-year period. The reports shall also contain estimates of the actual emission reduction in each year resulting from promulgation of the diesel fuel desulfurization regulations under section 214 [section 7548 of this title].

"(b) 5.60 Million ton cap.—Whenever the inventory required by this section indicates that sulfur dioxide emissions from industrial sources, including units subject to section 405(g)(5) of the Clean Air Act [subsec. (g)(5) of section 7651d of this title], may reasonably be expected to reach levels greater than 5.60 million tons per year, the Administrator of the Environmental Protection Agency shall take such actions under the Clean Air Act [this chapter] as may be appropriate to ensure that such emissions do not exceed 5.60 million tons per year. Such actions may include the promulgation of new and revised standards of performance for new sources, including units subject to section 405(g)(5) of the Clean Air Act, under section 111(b) of the Clean Air Act [section 7411(b) of this title], as well as promulgation of standards of performance for existing sources, including units subject to section 405(g)(5) of the Clean Air Act, under authority of this section. For an existing source regulated under this section [this note], 'standard of performance' means a standard which the Administrator determines is applicable to that source and which reflects the degree of emission reduction achievable through the application of the best system of continuous emission reduction which (taking into consideration the cost of achieving such emission reduction, and any nonair quality health and environmental impact and energy requirements) the Administrator determines has been adequately demonstrated for that category of sources.

"(c) Election.—Regulations promulgated under section 405(b) of the Clean Air Act [subsec. (b) of section 7651d of this title] shall not prohibit a source from electing to become an affected unit under section 410 of the Clean Air Act [section 7651i of this title]."

[For termination, effective May 15, 2000, of reporting provisions in Pub. L. No. 101–549, § 406(a), see Pub. L. No. 104–66, § 3003, as amended, set out as a note under 31 U.S.C.A. § 1113, and the 10th item on page 162 of House Document No. 103–7.]

Monitoring of Acid Rain Program in Canada

Pub. L. No. 101–549, § 408, which provided for a report to Congress by the Administrator of the Environmental Protection Agency, in consultation with the Secretary of State, the Secretary of Energy, and other persons, to be submitted on January 1, 1994, January 1, 1999, and January 1, 2005, regarding monitoring of the Acid Rain Program in Canada, as well as assessing the degree to which each province complied with its stated emissions cap, terminated, effective May 15, 2000, pursuant to Pub. L. No. 104–66, § 3003, as amended, set out as a note under 31 U.S.C.A. § 1113, and the 11th item on page 162 of House Document No. 103–7.

Sense of Congress on Emission Reductions Costs

Section 407 of Pub. L. No. 101–549 provided that: "It is the sense of the Congress that the Clean Air Act Amendments of 1990 [Pub. L. No. 101–549, Nov. 15, 1990, 104 Stat. 2399, see Tables for classification], through the allowance program, allocates the costs of achieving the required reductions in emissions of sulfur dioxide and oxides of nitrogen among sources in the United States. Broad based taxes and emissions fees that would provide for payment of the costs of achieving required emissions reductions by any party or parties other than the sources required to achieve the reductions are undesirable."

§ 7651a. Definitions

[CAA § 402]

As used in this subchapter:

(1) The term "affected source" means a source that includes one or more affected units.

(2) The term "affected unit" means a unit that is subject to emission reduction requirements or limitations under this subchapter.

(3) The term "allowance" means an authorization, allocated to an affected unit by the Administrator under this subchapter, to emit, during or after a specified calendar year, one ton of sulfur dioxide.

(4) The term "baseline" means the annual quantity of fossil fuel consumed by an affected unit, measured in millions of British Thermal Units ("mmBtu's"), calculated as follows:

(A) For each utility unit that was in commercial operation prior to January 1, 1985, the baseline shall be the annual average quantity of mmBtu's consumed in fuel during calendar years 1985,

1986, and 1987, as recorded by the Department of Energy pursuant to Form 767. For any utility unit for which such form was not filed, the baseline shall be the level specified for such unit in the 1985 National Acid Precipitation Assessment Program (NAPAP) Emissions Inventory, Version 2, National Utility Reference File (NURF) or in a corrected data base as established by the Administrator pursuant to paragraph (3). For nonutility units, the baseline is the NAPAP Emissions Inventory, Version 2. The Administrator, in the Administrator's sole discretion, may exclude periods during which a unit is shutdown for a continuous period of four calendar months or longer, and make appropriate adjustments under this paragraph. Upon petition of the owner or operator of any unit, the Administrator may make appropriate baseline adjustments for accidents that caused prolonged outages.

(B) For any other nonutility unit that is not included in the NAPAP Emissions Inventory, Version 2, or a corrected data base as established by the Administrator pursuant to paragraph (3), the baseline shall be the annual average quantity, in mmBtu consumed in fuel by that unit, as calculated pursuant to a method which the administrator shall prescribe by regulation to be promulgated not later than eighteen months after November 15, 1990.

(C) The Administrator shall, upon application or on his own motion, by December 31, 1991, supplement data needed in support of this subchapter and correct any factual errors in data from which affected Phase II units' baselines or actual 1985 emission rates have been calculated. Corrected data shall be used for purposes of issuing allowances under the[1] subchapter. Such corrections shall not be subject to judicial review, nor shall the failure of the Administrator to correct an alleged factual error in such reports be subject to judicial review.

(5) The term "capacity factor" means the ratio between the actual electric output from a unit and the potential electric output from that unit.

(6) The term "compliance plan" means, for purposes of the requirements of this subchapter, either—

(A) a statement that the source will comply with all applicable requirements under this subchapter, or

(B) where applicable, a schedule and description of the method or methods for compliance and certification by the owner or operator that the source is in compliance with the requirements of this subchapter.

(7) The term "continuous emission monitoring system" (CEMS) means the equipment as required by section 7651k of this title, used to sample, analyze, measure, and provide on a continuous basis a permanent record of emissions and flow (expressed in pounds per million British thermal units (lbs/mmBtu), pounds per hour (lbs/hr) or such other form as the Administrator may prescribe by regulations under section 7651k of this title).

(8) The term "existing unit" means a unit (including units subject to section 7411 of this title) that commenced commercial operation before November 15, 1990. Any unit that commenced commercial operation before November 15, 1990, which is modified, reconstructed, or repowered after November 15, 1990, shall continue to be an existing unit for the purposes of this subchapter. For the purposes of this subchapter, existing units shall not include simple combustion turbines, or units which serve a generator with a nameplate capacity of 25MWe or less.

(9) The term "generator" means a device that produces electricity and which is reported as a generating unit pursuant to Department of Energy Form 860.

(10) The term "new unit" means a unit that commences commercial operation on or after November 15, 1990.

(11) The term "permitting authority" means the Administrator, or the State or local air pollution control agency, with an approved permitting program under part B of title III of the Act.

(12) The term "repowering" means replacement of an existing coal-fired boiler with one of the following clean coal technologies: atmospheric or pressurized fluidized bed combustion, integrated gasification combined cycle, magnetohydrodynamics, direct and indirect coal-fired turbines, integrated gasification fuel cells, or as determined by the Administrator, in consultation with the Secretary of Energy, a derivative of one or more of these technologies, and any other technology capable of controlling multiple combustion emissions simultaneously with improved boiler or generation efficiency and with significantly greater waste reduction relative to the performance of technology in widespread commercial use as of November 15, 1990. Notwithstanding the provisions of section 7651h(a) of this title, for the purpose of this subchapter, the term "repowering" shall also include any oil and/or gas-fired unit which has been awarded clean coal technology demonstration funding as of January 1, 1991, by the Department of Energy.

(13) The term "reserve" means any bank of allowances established by the Administrator under this subchapter.

(14) The term "State" means one of the 48 contiguous States and the District of Columbia.

(15) The term "unit" means a fossil fuel-fired combustion device.

(16) The term "actual 1985 emission rate", for electric utility units means the annual sulfur dioxide or nitrogen oxides emission rate in pounds per million Btu as reported in the NAPAP Emissions Inventory, Version 2, National Utility Reference File. For nonutility units, the term "actual 1985 emission rate" means the annual sulfur dioxide or nitrogen oxides emission rate in pounds per million Btu as reported in the NAPAP Emission Inventory, Version 2.

(17) **(A)** The term "utility unit" means—

(i) a unit that serves a generator in any State that produces electricity for sale, or

(ii) a unit that, during 1985, served a generator in any State that produced electricity for sale.

(B) Notwithstanding subparagraph (A), a unit described in subparagraph (A) that—

(i) was in commercial operation during 1985, but

(ii) did not, during 1985, serve a generator in any State that produced electricity for sale shall not be a utility unit for purposes of this subchapter.

(C) A unit that cogenerates steam and electricity is not a "utility unit" for purposes of this subchapter unless the unit is constructed for the purpose of supplying, or commences construction after November 15, 1990, and supplies, more than one-third of its potential electric output capacity and more than 25 megawatts electrical output to any utility power distribution system for sale.

(18) The term "allowable 1985 emissions rate" means a federally enforceable emissions limitation for sulfur dioxide or oxides of nitrogen, applicable to the unit in 1985 or the limitation applicable in such other subsequent year as determined by the Administrator if such a limitation for 1985 does not exist. Where the emissions limitation for a unit is not expressed in pounds of emissions per million Btu, or the averaging period of that emissions limitation is not expressed on an annual basis, the Administrator shall calculate the annual equivalent of that emissions limitation in pounds per million Btu to establish the allowable 1985 emissions rate.

(19) The term "qualifying phase I technology" means a technological system of continuous emission reduction which achieves a 90 percent reduction in emissions of sulfur dioxide from the emissions that would have resulted from the use of fuels which were not subject to treatment prior to combustion.

(20) The term "alternative method of compliance" means a method of compliance in accordance with one or more of the following authorities:

(A) a substitution plan submitted and approved in accordance with subsections[2] 7651c(b) and (c) of this title;

(B) a Phase I extension plan approved by the Administrator under section 7651c(d) of this title, using qualifying phase I technology as determined by the Administrator in accordance with that section; or

(C) repowering with a qualifying clean coal technology under section 7651h of this title.

(21) The term "commenced" as applied to construction of any new electric utility unit means that an owner or operator has undertaken a continuous program of construction or that an owner or operator has entered into a contractual obligation to undertake and complete, within a reasonable time, a continuous program of construction.

(22) The term "commenced commercial operation" means to have begun to generate electricity for sale.

(23) The term "construction" means fabrication, erection, or installation of an affected unit.

(24) The term "industrial source" means a unit that does not serve a generator that produces electricity, a "nonutility unit" as defined in this section, or a process source as defined in section 7651i(e)[3] of this title.

(25) The term "nonutility unit" means a unit other than a utility unit.

(26) The term "designated representative" means a responsible person or official authorized by the owner or operator of a unit to represent the owner or operator in matters pertaining to the holding, transfer, or disposition of allowances allocated to a unit, and the submission of and compliance with permits, permit applications, and compliance plans for the unit.

(27) The term "life-of-the-unit, firm power contractual arrangement" means a unit participation power sales agreement under which a utility or industrial customer reserves, or is entitled to receive, a specified amount or percentage of capacity and associated energy generated by a specified generating unit (or units) and pays its proportional amount of such unit's total costs, pursuant to a contract either—

(A) for the life of the unit;

(B) for a cumulative term of no less than 30 years, including contracts that permit an election for early termination; or

(C) for a period equal to or greater than 25 years or 70 percent of the economic useful life of the unit determined as of the time the unit was built, with option rights to purchase or re-lease some portion of the capacity and associated energy generated by the unit (or units) at the end of the period.

(28) The term "basic Phase II allowance allocations" means:

(A) For calendar years 2000 through 2009 inclusive, allocations of allowances made by the Administrator pursuant to section 7651b of this title and subsections (b)(1), (3), and (4); (c)(1), (2), (3), and (5); (d)(1), (2), (4), and (5); (e); (f); (g)(1), (2), (3), (4), and (5); (h)(1); (i) and (j) of section 7651d of this title.

(B) For each calendar year beginning in 2010, allocations of allowances made by the Administrator pursuant to section 7651b of this title and subsections (b)(1), (3), and (4); (c)(1), (2), (3), and (5); (d)(1), (2), (4) and (5); (e); (f); (g)(1), (2), (3), (4), and (5); (h)(1) and (3); (i) and (j) of section 7651d of this title.

(29) The term "Phase II bonus allowance allocations" means, for calendar year 2000 through 2009, inclusive, and only for such years, allocations made by the Administrator pursuant to section 7651b of this title, subsections (a)(2), (b)(2), (c)(4), (d)(3) (except as otherwise provided therein), and (h)(2) of section 7651d of this title, and section 7651e of this title.

(July 14, 1955, c. 360, Title IV, § 402, as added by Pub. L. No. 101–549, Title IV, § 401, 104 Stat. 2585 (Nov. 15, 1990).)

1 So in original. Probably should be "this."

2 So in original. Probably should be "section."

3 So in original. Probably should be section "7651i(d)."

HISTORICAL AND STATUTORY NOTES

References in Text

Part B of Title III of the Act, referred to in par. (11), means Title III of the Clean Air Act, Act of July 14, 1955, c. 360, as added. Title III is codified as subchapter III of this chapter, but Title III does not contain parts. For provisions of the Clean Air Act relating to permits, see subchapter V (section 7661 et seq.) of this chapter.

Codifications

Another section 402 of Act of July 14, 1955, as added by Pub. L. No. 91–604, § 14, 84 Stat. 1709 (Dec. 31, 1970), is codified as section 7641 of this title.

Effective and Applicability Provisions

1990 Acts. Section effective Nov. 15, 1990, except as otherwise provided, see section 711(b) of Pub. L. No. 101–549, set out as a note under section 7401 of this title.

Savings Provisions

Suits, actions or proceedings commenced under this chapter as in effect prior to Nov. 15, 1990, not to abate by reason of the taking effect of amendments by Pub. L. No. 101–549, except as otherwise provided for, see section 711(a) of Pub. L. No. 101–549, set out as a note under section 7401 of this title.

§ 7651b. Sulfur dioxide allowance program for existing and new units

[CAA § 403]

(a) Allocations of annual allowances for existing and new units

(1) For the emission limitation programs under this subchapter, the Administrator shall allocate annual allowances for the unit, to be held or distributed by the designated representative of the owner or operator of each affected unit at an affected source in accordance with this subchapter, in an amount equal to the annual tonnage emission limitation calculated under section 7651c, 7651d, 7651e, 7651h, or 7651i of this title except as otherwise specifically provided elsewhere in this subchapter. Except as provided in sections 7651d(a)(2), 7651d(a)(3), 7651h and 7651i of this title, beginning January 1, 2000, the Administrator shall not allocate annual allowances to emit sulfur dioxide pursuant to section 7651d of this title in such an amount as would result in total annual emissions of sulfur dioxide from utility units in excess of 8.90 million tons except that the Administrator shall not take into account unused allowances carried forward by owners and operators of affected units or by other persons holding such allowances, following the year for which they were allocated. If necessary to meeting the restrictions imposed in the preceding sentence, the Administrator shall reduce, pro rata, the basic Phase II allowance allocations for each unit subject to the requirements of section 7651d of this title. Subject to the provisions of section 7651*o* of this title, the Administrator shall allocate allowances for each affected unit at an affected source annually, as provided in paragraphs (2) and (3)[1] and section 7651g of this title. Except as provided in sections 7651h and 7651i of this title, the removal of an existing affected unit or source from commercial operation at any time after November 15, 1990 (whether before or after January 1, 1995, or January 1, 2000) shall not terminate or otherwise affect the allocation of allowances pursuant to section 7651c or 7651d of this title to which the unit is entitled. Allowances shall be allocated by the Administrator without cost to the recipient, except for allowances sold by the Administrator pursuant to section 7651*o* of this title. Not later than December 31, 1991, the Administrator shall publish a proposed list of the basic Phase II allowance allocations, the Phase II bonus allowance allocations and, if applicable, allocations pursuant to section 7651d(a)(3) of this title for each unit subject to the emissions limitation requirements of section 7651d of this title for the year 2000 and the year 2010. After notice and opportunity for public comment, but not later than December 31, 1992, the Administrator shall publish a final list of such allocations, subject to the provisions of section 7651d(a)(2) of this title. Any owner or operator of an existing unit subject to the requirements of section 7651d(b) or (c) of this title who is considering applying for an extension of the emission limitation requirement compliance deadline for that unit from January 1, 2000, until not later than December 31, 2000, pursuant to section 7651h of this title, shall notify the Administrator no later than March 31, 1991. Such notification shall be used as the basis for estimating the basic Phase II allowances under this subsection. Prior to June 1, 1998, the Administrator shall publish a revised final statement of allowance allocations, subject to the provisions of section 7651d(a)(2) of this title and taking into account the effect of any compliance date extensions granted pursuant to section 7651h of this title on such allocations. Any person who may make an election concerning the amount of allowances to be allocated to a unit or units shall make such election and so inform the Administrator not later than March 31, 1991, in the case of an election under section 7651d of this title (or June 30, 1991, in the case of an election under section 7651e of this title). If such person fails to make such election, the Administrator shall set forth for each unit owned or operated by such person, the amount of allowances reflecting the election that would, in the judgment of the Administrator, provide the greatest benefit for the owner or operator of the unit. If such person is a Governor who may make an election under section 7651e of this title and the Governor fails to make an election, the Administrator shall set forth for each unit in the State the amount of allowances reflecting the election that would, in the judgment of the Administrator, provide the greatest benefit for units in the State.

(b) Allowance transfer system

Allowances allocated under this subchapter may be transferred among designated representatives of the owners or operators of affected sources under this subchapter and any other person who holds such allowances, as provided by the allowance system regulations to be promulgated by the Administrator not later than eighteen months after November 15, 1990. Such regulations shall establish the allowance system prescribed under this section, including, but not limited to, requirements for the allocation, transfer, and use of allowances under this subchapter. Such regulations shall prohibit the use of any allowance prior to the calendar year for which the allowance was allocated, and shall provide, consistent with the purposes of this subchapter, for the identification of unused allowances, and for such unused allowances to be carried forward and added to allowances allocated in subsequent years, including allowances allocated to units subject to Phase I requirements (as described in section 7651c of this title) which are applied to emissions limitations requirements in Phase II (as described in section 7651d of this title). Transfers of allowances shall not be effective until written certification of the transfer, signed by a responsible official of each party to the transfer, is received and recorded by the Administrator. Such regulations shall permit the transfer of allowances prior to the issuance of such allowances. Recorded pre-allocation transfers shall be deducted by the Administrator from the number of allowances which would otherwise be allocated to the transferor, and added to those allowances allocated to the transferee. Pre-allocation transfers shall not affect the prohibition contained in this subsection against the use of allowances prior to the year for which they are allocated.

(c) Interpollutant trading

Not later than January 1, 1994, the Administrator shall furnish to the Congress a study evaluating the environmental and economic consequences of amending this subchapter to permit trading sulfur dioxide allowances for nitrogen oxides allowances.

(d) Allowance tracking system

(1) The Administrator shall promulgate, not later than 18 months after November 15, 1990, a system for issuing, recording, and tracking allowances, which shall specify all necessary procedures and requirements for an orderly and competitive functioning of the allowance system. All allowance allocations and transfers shall, upon recordation by the Administrator, be deemed a part of each unit's permit requirements pursuant to section 7651g of this title, without any further permit review and revision.

(2) In order to insure electric reliability, such regulations shall not prohibit or affect temporary increases and decreases in emissions within utility systems, power pools, or utilities entering into allowance pool agreements, that result from their operations, including emergencies and central dispatch, and such temporary emissions increases and decreases shall not require transfer of allowances among units nor shall it require recordation. The owners or operators of such units shall act through a designated representative. Notwithstanding the preceding sentence, the total tonnage of emissions in any calendar year (calculated at the end thereof) from all units in such a utility system, power pool, or allowance pool agreements shall not exceed the total allowances for such units for the calendar year concerned.

(e) New utility units

After January 1, 2000, it shall be unlawful for a new utility unit to emit an annual tonnage of sulfur dioxide in excess of the number of allowances to emit held for the unit by the unit's owner or operator. Such new utility units shall not be eligible for an allocation of sulfur dioxide allowances under subsection (a)(1) of this section, unless the unit is subject to the provisions of subsection (g)(2) or (3) of section 7651d of this title. New utility units may obtain allowances from any person, in accordance with this subchapter. The owner or operator of any new utility unit in violation of this subsection shall be liable for fulfilling the obligations specified in section 7651j of this title.

(f) Nature of allowances

An allowance allocated under this subchapter is a limited authorization to emit sulfur dioxide in accordance with the provisions of this subchapter. Such allowance does not constitute a property right. Nothing in this subchapter or in any other provision of law shall be construed to limit the authority of the United States to terminate or limit such authorization. Nothing in this section relating to allowances shall be construed as affecting the application of, or compliance with, any other provision of this chapter to an affected unit or source, including the provisions related to applicable National Ambient Air Quality Standards and State implementation plans. Nothing in this section shall be construed as requiring a change of any kind in any State law regulating electric utility rates and charges or affecting any State law regarding such State regulation or as limiting State regulation (including any prudency review) under such a State law. Nothing in this section shall be construed as modifying the Federal Power Act [16 U.S.C.A. § 791a et seq.] or as affecting the authority of the Federal Energy Regulatory Commission under that Act. Nothing in this subchapter shall be construed to interfere with or impair any program for competitive bidding for power supply in a State in which such program is established. Allowances, once allocated to a person by the Administrator, may be received, held, and temporarily or permanently transferred in accordance with this subchapter and the regulations of the Administrator without regard to whether or not a permit is in effect under subchapter V of this chapter or section 7651g of this title with respect to the unit for which such allowance was originally allocated and recorded. Each permit under this subchapter and each permit issued under subchapter V of this chapter for any affected unit shall provide that the affected unit may not emit an annual tonnage of sulfur dioxide in excess of the allowances held for that unit.

(g) Prohibition

It shall be unlawful for any person to hold, use, or transfer any allowance allocated under this subchapter, except in accordance with regulations promulgated by the Administrator. It shall be unlawful for any affected unit to emit sulfur dioxide in excess of the number of allowances held for that unit for that year by the owner or operator of the unit. Upon the allocation of allowances under this subchapter, the prohibition contained in the preceding sentence shall supersede any other emission limitation applicable under this subchapter to the units for which such allowances are allocated. Allowances may not be used prior to the calendar year for which they are allocated. Nothing in this section or in the allowance system regulations shall relieve the Administrator of the Administrator's permitting, monitoring and enforcement obligations under this chapter, nor relieve affected sources of their requirements and liabilities under this chapter.

(h) Competitive bidding for power supply

Nothing in this subchapter shall be construed to interfere with or impair any program for competitive bidding for power supply in a State in which such program is established.

(i) Applicability of antitrust laws

(1) Nothing in this section affects—

(A) the applicability of the antitrust laws to the transfer, use, or sale of allowances, or

(B) the authority of the Federal Energy Regulatory Commission under any provision of law respecting unfair methods of competition or anticompetitive acts or practices.

(2) As used in this section, "antitrust laws" means those Acts set forth in section 12 of Title 15.

(j) **Public Utility Holding Company Act**

The acquisition or disposition of allowances pursuant to this subchapter including the issuance of securities or the undertaking of any other financing transaction in connection with such allowances shall not be subject to the provisions of the Public Utility Holding Company Act of 1935 [15 U.S.C.A. § 79 et seq.].

(July 14, 1955, c. 360, Title IV, § 403, as added by Pub. L. No. 101–549, Title IV, § 401, 104 Stat. 2589 (Nov. 15, 1990).)

[1] So in original. No pars. (2) and (3) have been enacted.

HISTORICAL AND STATUTORY NOTES

References in Text

The Federal Power Act, referred to in subsec. (f), is Act of June 10, 1920, c. 285, 41 Stat. 1063, as amended, which is codified generally as chapter 12 (section 791a et seq.) of Title 16, Conservation. For complete classification of this Act to the Code, see section 791a of Title 16 and Tables.

The Public Utility Holding Company Act of 1935, referred to in subsec. (j), is Act of Aug. 26, 1935, c. 687, Title I, 49 Stat. 838, as amended, which was codified generally as chapter 2C of Title 15, 15 U.S.C.A. § 79 et seq., prior to repeal by Pub. L. No. 109–58, Title XII, § 1263, 119 Stat. 974 (Aug. 8, 2005). For complete classification, see Tables.

Codifications

Another section 403 of Act of July 14, 1955, as added by Pub. L. No. 91–604, § 14, 84 Stat. 1710 (Dec. 31, 1970), is codified as section 7642 of this title.

Effective and Applicability Provisions

1990 Acts. Section effective Nov. 15, 1990, except as otherwise provided, see section 711(b) of Pub. L. No. 101–549, set out as a note under section 7401 of this title.

Savings Provisions

Suits, actions or proceedings commenced under this chapter as in effect prior to Nov. 15, 1990, not to abate by reason of the taking effect of amendments by Pub. L. No. 101–549, except as otherwise provided for, see section 711(a) of Pub. L. No. 101–549, set out as a note under section 7401 of this title.

Fossil Fuel Use

Section 402 of Pub. L. No. 101–549 provided that:

"(a) Contracts for hydroelectric energy.—Any person who, after the date of the enactment of the Clean Air Act Amendments of 1990 [Nov. 15, 1990], enters into a contract under which such person receives hydroelectric energy in return for the provision of electric energy by such person shall use allowances held by such person as necessary to satisfy such person's obligations under such contract.

"(b) Federal Power Marketing Administration.—A Federal Power Marketing Administration shall not be subject to the provisions and requirements of this title [this subchapter] with respect to electric energy generated by hydroelectric facilities and marketed by such Power Marketing Administration. Any person who sells or provides electric energy to a Federal Power Marketing Administration shall comply with the provisions and requirements of this title [this subchapter]."

§ 7651c. Phase I sulfur dioxide requirements

[CAA § 404]

(a) **Emission limitations**

(1) After January 1, 1995, each source that includes one or more affected units listed in table A is an affected source under this section. After January 1, 1995, it shall be unlawful for any affected unit (other than an eligible phase I unit under subsection (d)(2) of this section) to emit sulfur dioxide in excess of the tonnage limitation stated as a total number of allowances in table A for phase I, unless (A) the emissions reduction requirements applicable to such unit have been achieved pursuant to subsection (b) or (d) of this section, or (B) the owner or operator of such unit holds allowances to emit not less than the unit's total annual emissions, except that, after January 1, 2000, the emissions limitations established in this section shall be superseded by those established in section 7651d of this title. The owner or operator of any unit in violation of this section shall be fully liable for such violation including, but not limited to, liability for fulfilling the obligations specified in section 7651j of this title.

(2) Not later than December 31, 1991, the Administrator shall determine the total tonnage of reductions in the emissions of sulfur dioxide from all utility units in calendar year 1995 that will occur as a result of compliance with the emissions limitation requirements of this section, and shall establish a reserve of allowances equal in amount to the number of tons determined thereby not to exceed a total of 3.50 million tons. In making such a determination, the Administrator shall compute for each unit subject to the emissions limitation requirements of this section the difference between:

(A) the product of its baseline multiplied by the lesser of each unit's allowable 1985 emissions rate and its actual 1985 emissions rate, divided by 2,000, and

(B) the product of each unit's baseline multiplied by 2.50 lbs/mmBtu divided by 2,000,

and sum the computations. The Administrator shall adjust the foregoing calculation to reflect projected calendar year 1995 utilization of the units subject to the emissions limitations of this subchapter that the Administrator finds would have occurred in the absence of the imposition of such requirements. Pursuant to subsection (d) of this section, the Administrator shall allocate allowances from the reserve established hereinunder until the earlier of such time as all such allowances in the reserve are allocated or December 31, 1999.

(3) In addition to allowances allocated pursuant to paragraph (1), in each calendar year beginning in 1995 and ending in 1999, inclusive, the Administrator shall allocate for each unit on Table A that is located in the States of Illinois, Indiana, or Ohio (other than units at Kyger Creek, Clifty Creek and Joppa Steam), allowances in an amount equal to 200,000 multiplied by the unit's pro rata share of the total number of allowances allocated for all units on Table A in the 3 States (other than units at Kyger Creek, Clifty Creek, and Joppa Steam) pursuant to paragraph (1). Such allowances shall be excluded from the calculation of the reserve under paragraph (2).

(b) Substitutions

The owner or operator of an affected unit under subsection (a) of this section may include in its section 7651g of this title permit application and proposed compliance plan a proposal to reassign, in whole or in part, the affected unit's sulfur dioxide reduction requirements to any other unit(s) under the control of such owner or operator. Such proposal shall specify—

(1) the designation of the substitute unit or units to which any part of the reduction obligations of subsection (a) of this section shall be required, in addition to, or in lieu of, any original affected units designated under such subsection;

(2) the original affected unit's baseline, the actual and allowable 1985 emissions rate for sulfur dioxide, and the authorized annual allowance allocation stated in table A;

(3) calculation of the annual average tonnage for calendar years 1985, 1986, and 1987, emitted by the substitute unit or units, based on the baseline for each unit, as defined in section 7651a(d)[1] of this title, multiplied by the lesser of the unit's actual or allowable 1985 emissions rate;

(4) the emissions rates and tonnage limitations that would be applicable to the original and substitute affected units under the substitution proposal;

(5) documentation, to the satisfaction of the Administrator, that the reassigned tonnage limits will, in total, achieve the same or greater emissions reduction than would have been achieved by the original affected unit and the substitute unit or units without such substitution; and

(6) such other information as the Administrator may require.

(c) Administrator's action on substitution proposals

(1) The Administrator shall take final action on such substitution proposal in accordance with section 7651g(c) of this title if the substitution proposal fulfills the requirements of this subsection. The Administrator may approve a substitution proposal in whole or in part and with such modifications or conditions as may be consistent with the orderly functioning of the allowance system and which will ensure the emissions reductions contemplated by this subchapter. If a proposal does not meet the requirements of subsection (b) of this section, the Administrator shall disapprove it. The owner or operator of a unit listed in table A shall not substitute another unit or units without the prior approval of the Administrator.

(2) Upon approval of a substitution proposal, each substitute unit, and each source with such unit, shall be deemed affected under this subchapter, and the Administrator shall issue a permit to the original and substitute affected source and unit in accordance with the approved substitution plan and section 7651g of this title. The Administrator shall allocate allowances for the original and substitute affected units in accordance with the approved substitution proposal pursuant to section 7651b of this title. It shall be unlawful for any source or unit that is allocated allowances pursuant to this section to emit sulfur dioxide in excess of the emissions limitation provided for in the approved substitution permit and plan unless the owner or operator of each unit governed by the permit and approved substitution plan holds allowances to emit not less than the units total annual emissions. The owner or operator of any original or substitute affected unit operated in violation of this subsection shall be fully liable for such violation, including liability for fulfilling the obligations specified in section 7651j of this title. If a substitution proposal is disapproved, the Administrator shall allocate allowances to the original affected unit or units in accordance with subsection (a) of this section.

(d) Eligible phase I extension units

(1) The owner or operator of any affected unit subject to an emissions limitation requirement under this section may petition the Administrator in its permit application under section 7651g of this title for an extension of 2 years of the deadline for meeting such requirement, provided that the owner or operator of any such unit holds allowances to emit not less than the unit's total annual emissions for each of the 2 years of the period of extension. To qualify for such an extension, the affected unit must either employ a qualifying phase I technology, or transfer its phase I emissions reduction obligation to a unit employing a qualifying phase I technology. Such transfer shall be accomplished in accordance with a compliance plan, submitted and approved under section 7651g of this title, that shall govern operations at all units included in the transfer, and that specifies the emissions reduction requirements imposed pursuant to this subchapter.

(2) Such extension proposal shall—

(A) specify the unit or units proposed for designation as an eligible phase I extension unit;

(B) provide a copy of an executed contract, which may be contingent upon the Administrator approving the proposal, for the design engineering, and construction of the qualifying phase I technology for the extension unit, or for the unit or units to which the extension unit's emission reduction obligation is to be transferred;

(C) specify the unit's or units' baseline, actual 1985 emissions rate, allowable 1985 emissions rate, and projected utilization for calendar years 1995 through 1999;

(D) require CEMS on both the eligible phase I extension unit or units and the transfer unit or units beginning no later than January 1, 1995; and

(E) specify the emission limitation and number of allowances expected to be necessary for annual operation after the qualifying phase I technology has been installed.

(3) The Administrator shall review and take final action on each extension proposal in order of receipt, consistent with section 7651g of this title, and for an approved proposal shall designate the unit or units as an eligible phase I extension unit. The Administrator may approve an extension proposal in whole or in part, and with such modifications or conditions as may be necessary, consistent with the orderly functioning of the allowance system, and to ensure the emissions reductions contemplated by the[2] subchapter.

(4) In order to determine the number of proposals eligible for allocations from the reserve under subsection (a)(2) of this section and the number of allowances remaining available after each proposal is acted upon, the Administrator shall reduce the total number of allowances remaining available in the reserve by the number of allowances calculated according to subparagraphs (A), (B) and (C) until either no allowances remain available in the reserve for further allocation or all approved proposals have been acted upon. If no allowances remain available in the reserve for further allocation before all proposals have been acted upon by the Administrator, any pending proposals shall be disapproved. The Administrator shall calculate allowances equal to—

(A) the difference between the lesser of the average annual emissions in calendar years 1988 and 1989 or the projected emissions tonnage for calendar year 1995 of each eligible phase I extension unit, as designated under paragraph (3), and the product of the unit's baseline multiplied by an emission rate of 2.50 lbs/mmBtu, divided by 2,000;

(B) the difference between the lesser of the average annual emissions in calendar years 1988 and 1989 or the projected emissions tonnage for calendar year 1996 of each eligible phase I extension unit, as designated under paragraph (3), and the product of the unit's baseline multiplied by an emission rate of 2.50 lbs/mmBtu, divided by 2,000; and

(C) the amount by which (i) the product of each unit's baseline multiplied by an emission rate of 1.20 lbs/mmBtu, divided by 2,000, exceeds (ii) the tonnage level specified under subparagraph (E) of paragraph (2) of this subsection multiplied by a factor of 3.

(5) Each eligible Phase I extension unit shall receive allowances determined under subsection (a)(1) or (c) of this section. In addition, for calendar year 1995, the Administrator shall allocate to each eligible Phase I extension unit, from the allowance reserve created pursuant to subsection (a)(2) of this section, allowances equal to the difference between the lesser of the average annual emissions in calendar years 1988 and 1989 or its projected emissions tonnage for calendar year 1995 and the product of the unit's baseline multiplied by an emission rate of 2.50 lbs/mmBtu, divided by 2,000. In calendar year 1996, the Administrator shall allocate for each eligible unit, from the allowance reserve created pursuant to subsection (a)(2) of this section, allowances equal to the difference between the lesser of the average annual emissions in calendar years 1988 and 1989 or its projected emissions tonnage for calendar year 1996 and the product of the unit's baseline multiplied by an emission rate of 2.50 lbs/mmBtu, divided by 2,000. It shall be unlawful for any source or unit subject to an approved extension plan under this subsection to emit sulfur dioxide in excess of the emissions limitations provided for in the permit and approved extension plan, unless the owner or operator of each unit governed by the permit and approved plan holds allowances to emit not less than the unit's total annual emissions.

(6) In addition to allowances specified in paragraph (5), the Administrator shall allocate for each eligible Phase I extension unit employing qualifying Phase I technology, for calendar years 1997, 1998, and 1999, additional allowances, from any remaining allowances in the reserve created pursuant to subsection (a)(2) of this section, following the reduction in the reserve provided for in paragraph (4), not to exceed the amount by which (A) the product of each eligible unit's baseline times an emission rate of 1.20 lbs/mmBtu, divided by 2,000, exceeds (B) the tonnage level specified under subparagraph (E) of paragraph (2) of this subsection.

(7) After January 1, 1997, in addition to any liability under this chapter, including under section 7651j of this title, if any eligible phase I extension unit employing qualifying phase I technology or any transfer unit under this subsection emits sulfur dioxide in excess of the annual tonnage limitation specified in the extension plan, as approved in paragraph (3) of this subsection, the Administrator shall, in the calendar year following such excess, deduct allowances equal to the amount of such excess from such unit's annual allowance allocation.

(e) Allocation of allowances

(1) In the case of a unit that receives authorization from the Governor of the State in which such unit is located to make reductions in the emissions of sulfur dioxide prior to calendar year 1995 and that is part of a utility system that meets the following requirements: (A) the total coal-fired generation within the utility system as a percentage of total system generation decreased by more than 20 percent between January 1, 1980, and December 31, 1985; and (B) the weighted capacity factor of all coal-fired units within the utility system averaged over the period from January 1, 1985, through December 31, 1987, was below 50 percent, the Administrator shall allocate allowances under this paragraph for the unit pursuant to this subsection. The Administrator shall allocate allowances for a unit that is an affected unit pursuant to section 7651d of this title (but is not also an affected unit under this section) and part of a utility system that includes 1 or more affected units under section 7651d of this title for reductions in the emissions of sulfur dioxide made during the period 1995–1999 if the unit meets the requirements of this subsection and the requirements of the preceding sentence, except that for the purposes of applying this subsection to any such unit, the prior year concerned as specified below, shall be any year after January 1, 1995 but prior to January 1, 2000.

(2) In the case of an affected unit under this section described in subparagraph (A), the allowances allocated under this subsection for early reductions in any prior year may not exceed the amount which (A) the product of the unit's baseline multiplied by the unit's 1985 actual sulfur dioxide emission rate (in lbs. per mmBtu), divided by 2,000, exceeds (B) the allowances specified for such unit in Table A. In the case of an affected unit under section 7651d of this title described in subparagraph (A), the allowances awarded under this subsection for early reductions in any prior year may not exceed the amount by which (i) the product of the quantity of fossil fuel consumed by the unit (in mmBtu) in the prior year multiplied by the lesser of 2.50 or the most stringent emission rate (in lbs. per mmBtu) applicable to the unit under the applicable implementation plan, divided by 2,000, exceeds (ii) the unit's actual tonnage of sulfur dioxide emission for the prior year concerned. Allowances allocated under this subsection for units referred to in subparagraph (A) may be allocated only for emission reductions achieved as a result of physical changes or changes in the method of operation made after November 15, 1990, including changes in the type or quality of fossil fuel consumed.

(3) In no event shall the provisions of this paragraph be interpreted as an event of force majeur or a commercial impractibility[3] or in any other way as a basis for excused nonperformance by a utility system under a coal sales contract in effect before November 15, 1990.

TABLE A. AFFECTED SOURCES AND UNITS IN PHASE I AND THEIR SULFUR DIOXIDE ALLOWANCES (TONS)

State	Plant Name	Generator	Phase I Allowances
Alabama	Colbert	1	13,570
		2	15,310
		3	15,400
		4	15,410
		5	37,180
	E.C. Gaston	1	18,100
		2	18,540
		3	18,310
		4	19,280
		5	59,840
Florida	Big Bend	1	28,410
		2	27,100
		3	26,740
	Crist	6	19,200
		7	31,680
Georgia	Bowen	1	56,320
		2	54,770
		3	71,750
		4	71,740
	Hammond	1	8,780
		2	9,220
		3	8,910
		4	37,640
	J. McDonough	1	19,910

		2	20,600
	Wansley	1	70,770
		2	65,430
	Yates	1	7,210
		2	7,040
		3	6,950
		4	8,910
		5	9,410
		6	24,760
		7	21,480
Illinois	Baldwin	1	42,010
		2	44,420
		3	42,550
	Coffeen	1	11,790
		2	35,670
	Grand Tower	4	5,910
	Hennepin	2	18,410
	Joppa Steam	1	12,590
		2	10,770
		3	12,270
		4	11,360
		5	11,420
		6	10,620
	Kincaid	1	31,530
		2	33,810
	Meredosia	3	13,890
	Vermilion	2	8,880
Indiana	Bailly	7	11,180
		8	15,630
	Breed	1	18,500
	Cayuga	1	33,370
		2	34,130
	Clifty Creek	1	20,150
		2	19,810
		3	20,410
		4	20,080
		5	19,360
		6	20,380
	E.W. Stout	5	3,880
		6	4,770
		7	23,610
	F.B. Culley	2	4,290
		3	16,970
	F.E. Ratts	1	8,330
		2	8,480
	Gibson	1	40,400
		2	41,010
		3	41,080
		4	40,320
	H.T. Pritchard	6	5,770
	Michigan City	12	23,310

	Petersburg	1	16,430
		2	32,380
	R. Gallagher	1	6,490
		2	7,280
		3	6,530
		4	7,650
	Tanners Creek	4	24,820
	Wabash River	1	4,000
		2	2,860
		3	3,750
		5	3,670
		6	12,280
	Warrick	4	26,980
Iowa	Burlington	1	10,710
	Des Moines	7	2,320
	George Neal	1	1,290
	M.L. Kapp	2	13,800
	Prairie Creek	4	8,180
	Riverside	5	3,990
Kansas	Quindaro	2	4,220
Kentucky	Coleman	1	11,250
		2	12,840
		3	12,340
	Cooper	1	7,450
		2	15,320
	E.W. Brown	1	7,110
		2	10,910
		3	26,100
	Elmer Smith	1	6,520
		2	14,410
	Ghent	1	28,410
	Green River	4	7,820
	H.L. Spurlock	1	22,780
	Henderson II	1	13,340
		2	12,310
	Paradise	3	59,170
	Shawnee	10	10,170
Maryland	Chalk Point	1	21,910
		2	24,330
	C.P. Crane	1	10,330
		2	9,230
	Morgantown	1	35,260
		2	38,480
Michigan	J.H. Campbell	1	19,280
		2	23,060
Minnesota	High Bridge	6	4,270
Mississippi	Jack Watson	4	17,910
		5	36,700
Missouri	Asbury	1	16,190
	James River	5	4,850
	Labadie	1	40,110

		2	37,710
		3	40,310
		4	35,940
	Montrose	1	7,390
		2	8,200
		3	10,090
	New Madrid	1	28,240
		2	32,480
	Sibley	3	15,580
	Sioux	1	22,570
		2	23,690
	Thomas Hill	1	10,250
		2	19,390
New Hampshire	Merrimack	1	10,190
		2	22,000
New Jersey	B.L. England	1	9,060
		2	11,720
New York	Dunkirk	3	12,600
		4	14,060
	Greenidge	4	7,540
	Milliken	1	11,170
		2	12,410
	Northport	1	19,810
		2	24,110
		3	26,480
	Port Jefferson	3	10,470
		4	12,330
Ohio	Ashtabula	5	16,740
	Avon Lake	8	11,650
		9	30,480
	Cardinal	1	34,270
		2	38,320
	Conesville	1	4,210
		2	4,890
		3	5,500
		4	48,770
	Eastlake	1	7,800
		2	8,640
		3	10,020
		4	14,510
		5	34,070
	Edgewater	4	5,050
	Gen. J.M. Gavin	1	79,080
		2	80,560
	Kyger Creek	1	19,280
		2	18,560
		3	17,910
		4	18,710
		5	18,740
	Miami Fort	5	760
		6	11,380

		7	38,510
	Muskingum River	1	14,880
		2	14,170
		3	13,950
		4	11,780
		5	40,470
	Niles	1	6,940
		2	9,100
	Picway	5	4,930
	R.E. Burger	3	6,150
		4	10,780
		5	12,430
	W.H. Sammis	5	24,170
		6	39,930
		7	43,220
	W.C. Beckjord	5	8,950
		6	23,020
Pennsylvania	Armstrong	1	14,410
		2	15,430
	Brunner Island	1	27,760
		2	31,100
		3	53,820
	Cheswick	1	39,170
	Conemaugh	1	59,790
		2	66,450
	Hatfield's Ferry	1	37,830
		2	37,320
		3	40,270
	Martins Creek	1	12,660
		2	12,820
	Portland	1	5,940
		2	10,230
	Shawville	1	10,320
		2	10,320
		3	14,220
		4	14,070
	Sunbury	3	8,760
		4	11,450
Tennessee	Allen	1	15,320
		2	16,770
		3	15,670
	Cumberland	1	86,700
		2	94,840
	Gallatin	1	17,870
		2	17,310
		3	20,020
		4	21,260
	Johnsonville	1	7,790
		2	8,040
		3	8,410
		4	7,990

		5	8,240
		6	7,890
		7	8,980
		8	8,700
		9	7,080
		10	7,550
West Virginia	Albright	3	12,000
	Fort Martin	1	41,590
		2	41,200
	Harrison	1	48,620
		2	46,150
		3	41,500
	Kammer	1	18,740
		2	19,460
		3	17,390
	Mitchell	1	43,980
		2	45,510
	Mount Storm	1	43,720
		2	35,580
		3	42,430
Wisconsin	Edgewater	4	24,750
	La Crosse/Genoa	3	22,700
	Nelson Dewey	1	6,010
		2	6,680
	N. Oak Creek	1	5,220
		2	5,140
		3	5,370
		4	6,320
	Pulliam	8	7,510
	S. Oak Creek	5	9,670
		6	12,040
		7	16,180
		8	15,790

(f) Energy conservation and renewable energy

(1) Definitions

As used in this subsection:

(A) Qualified energy conservation measure

The term "qualified energy conservation measure" means a cost effective measure, as identified by the Administrator in consultation with the Secretary of Energy, that increases the efficiency of the use of electricity provided by an electric utility to its customers.

(B) Qualified renewable energy

The term "qualified renewable energy" means energy derived from biomass, solar, geothermal, or wind as identified by the Administrator in consultation with the Secretary of Energy.

(C) Electric utility

The term "electric utility" means any person, State agency, or Federal agency, which sells electric energy.

(2) **Allowances for emissions avoided through energy conservation and renewable energy**

(A) **In general**

The regulations under paragraph (4) of this subsection shall provide that for each ton of sulfur dioxide emissions avoided by an electric utility, during the applicable period, through the use of qualified energy conservation measures or qualified renewable energy, the Administrator shall allocate a single allowance to such electric utility, on a first-come-first-served basis from the Conservation and Renewable Energy Reserve established under subsection (g) of this section, up to a total of 300,000 allowances for allocation from such Reserve.

(B) **Requirements for issuance**

The Administrator shall allocate allowances to an electric utility under this subsection only if all of the following requirements are met:

(i) Such electric utility is paying for the qualified energy conservation measures or qualified renewable energy directly or through purchase from another person.

(ii) The emissions of sulfur dioxide avoided through the use of qualified energy conservation measures or qualified renewable energy are quantified in accordance with regulations promulgated by the Administrator under this subsection.

(iii) (I) Such electric utility has adopted and is implementing a least cost energy conservation and electric power plan which evaluates a range of resources, including new power supplies, energy conservation, and renewable energy resources, in order to meet expected future demand at the lowest system cost.

(II) The qualified energy conservation measures or qualified renewable energy, or both, are consistent with that plan.

(III) Electric utilities subject to the jurisdiction of a State regulatory authority must have such plan approved by such authority. For electric utilities not subject to the jurisdiction of a State regulatory authority such plan shall be approved by the entity with rate-making authority for such utility.

(iv) In the case of qualified energy conservation measures undertaken by a State regulated electric utility, the Secretary of Energy certifies that the State regulatory authority with jurisdiction over the electric rates of such electric utility has established rates and charges which ensure that the net income of such electric utility after implementation of specific cost effective energy conservation measures is at least as high as such net income would have been if the energy conservation measures had not been implemented. Upon the date of any such certification by the Secretary of Energy, all allowances which, but for this paragraph, would have been allocated under subparagraph (A) before such date, shall be allocated to the electric utility. This clause is not a requirement for qualified renewable energy.

(v) Such utility or any subsidiary of the utility's holding company owns or operates at least one affected unit.

(C) **Period of applicability**

Allowances under this subsection shall be allocated only with respect to kilowatt hours of electric energy saved by qualified energy conservation measures or generated by qualified renewable energy after January 1, 1992 and before the earlier of (i) December 31, 2000, or (ii) the date on which any electric utility steam generating unit owned or operated by the electric utility to which the allowances are allocated becomes subject to this subchapter (including those sources that elect to become affected by this subchapter, pursuant to section 7651i of this title).

(D) **Determination of avoided emissions**

(i) **Application**

In order to receive allowances under this subsection, an electric utility shall make an application which—

(I) designates the qualified energy conservation measures implemented and the qualified renewable energy sources used for purposes of avoiding emissions,[4]

(II) calculates, in accordance with subparagraphs (F) and (G), the number of tons of emissions avoided by reason of the implementation of such measures or the use of such renewable energy sources; and

(III) demonstrates that the requirements of subparagraph (B) have been met.

Such application for allowances by a State-regulated electric utility shall require approval by the State regulatory authority with jurisdiction over such electric utility. The authority shall review the application for accuracy and compliance with this subsection and the rules under this subsection. Electric utilities whose retail rates are not subject to the jurisdiction of a State regulatory authority shall apply directly to the Administrator for such approval.

(E) Avoided emissions from qualified energy conservation measures

For the purposes of this subsection, the emission tonnage deemed avoided by reason of the implementation of qualified energy conservation measures for any calendar year shall be a tonnage equal to the product of multiplying—

(i) the kilowatt hours that would otherwise have been supplied by the utility during such year in the absence of such qualified energy conservation measures, by

(ii) 0.004,

and dividing by 2,000.

(F) Avoided emissions from the use of qualified renewable energy

The emissions tonnage deemed avoided by reason of the use of qualified renewable energy by an electric utility for any calendar year shall be a tonnage equal to the product of multiplying—

(i) the actual kilowatt hours generated by, or purchased from, qualified renewable energy, by

(ii) 0.004,

and dividing by 2,000.

(G) Prohibitions

(i) No allowances shall be allocated under this subsection for the implementation of programs that are exclusively informational or educational in nature.

(ii) No allowances shall be allocated for energy conservation measures or renewable energy that were operational before January 1, 1992.

(3) Savings provision

Nothing in this subsection precludes a State or State regulatory authority from providing additional incentives to utilities to encourage investment in demand-side resources.

(4) Regulations

Not later than 18 months after November 15, 1990, and in conjunction with the regulations required to be promulgated under subsections (b) and (c) of this section, the Administrator shall, in consultation with the Secretary of Energy, promulgate regulations under this subsection. Such regulations shall list energy conservation measures and renewable energy sources which may be treated as qualified energy conservation measures and qualified renewable energy for purposes of this subsection. Allowances shall only be allocated if all requirements of this subsection and the rules promulgated to implement this subsection are complied with. The Administrator shall review the determinations of each State regulatory authority under this subsection to encourage consistency from electric utility to electric utility and from State to State in accordance with the Administrator's rules. The Administrator shall publish the findings of this review no less than annually.

(g) Conservation and Renewable Energy Reserve

The Administrator shall establish a Conservation and Renewable Energy Reserve under this subsection. Beginning on January 1, 1995, the Administrator may allocate from the Conservation and Renewable Energy Reserve an amount equal to a total of 300,000 allowances for emissions of sulfur dioxide pursuant to section 7651b of this title. In order to provide 300,000 allowances for such reserve, in each year beginning in calendar year 2000 and until calendar year 2009, inclusive, the Administrator shall reduce each unit's basic Phase II allowance allocation on the basis of its pro rata share of 30,000 allowances. If allowances remain in the reserve after January 2, 2010, the Administrator shall allocate such allowances for affected units under section 7651d of this title on a pro rata basis. For purposes of this subsection, for any unit subject to the emissions limitation requirements of section 7651d of this title, the term "pro rata basis" refers to the ratio which the reductions made in such unit's allowances in order to establish the reserve under this subsection bears to the total of such reductions for all such units.

(h) Alternative allowance allocation for units in certain utility systems with optional baseline

(1) Optional baseline for units in certain systems

In the case of a unit subject to the emissions limitation requirements of this section which (as of November 15, 1990)—

(A) has an emission rate below 1.0 lbs/mmBtu,

(B) has decreased its sulfur dioxide emissions rate by 60 percent or greater since 1980, and

(C) is part of a utility system which has a weighted average sulfur dioxide emissions rate for all fossil fueled-fired units below 1.0 lbs/mmBtu,

at the election of the owner or operator of such unit, the unit's baseline may be calculated (i) as provided under section 7651a(d)[1] of this title, or (ii) by utilizing the unit's average annual fuel consumption at a 60 percent capacity factor. Such election shall be made no later than March 1, 1991.

(2) Allowance allocation

Whenever a unit referred to in paragraph (1) elects to calculate its baseline as provided in clause (ii) of paragraph (1), the Administrator shall allocate allowances for the unit pursuant to section 7651b(a)(1) of this title, this section, and section 7651d of this title (as basic Phase II allowance allocations) in an amount equal to the baseline selected multiplied by the lower of the average annual emission rate for such unit in 1989, or 1.0 lbs./mmBtu. Such allowance allocation shall be in lieu of any allocation of allowances under this section and section 7651d of this title.

(July 14, 1955, c. 360, Title IV, § 404, as added by Pub. L. No. 101–549, Title IV, § 401, 104 Stat. 2592 (Nov. 15, 1990).)

[1] So in original. Probably should be section "7651a(4)."

[2] So in original. Probably should be "this."

[3] So in original. Probably should be "impracticability."

[4] So in original. The comma probably should be a semicolon.

HISTORICAL AND STATUTORY NOTES

Effective and Applicability Provisions

1990 Acts. Section effective Nov. 15, 1990, except as otherwise provided, see section 711(b) of Pub. L. No. 101–549, set out as a note under section 7401 of this title.

Savings Provisions

Suits, actions or proceedings commenced under this chapter as in effect prior to Nov. 15, 1990, not to abate by reason of the taking effect of amendments by Pub. L. No. 101–549, except as otherwise provided for, see section 711(a) of Pub. L. No. 101–549, set out as a note under section 7401 of this title.

§ 7651d. Phase II sulfur dioxide requirements

[CAA § 405]

(a) Applicability

(1) After January 1, 2000, each existing utility unit as provided below is subject to the limitations or requirements of this section. Each utility unit subject to an annual sulfur dioxide tonnage emission limitation under this section is an affected unit under this subchapter. Each source that includes one or more affected units is an affected source. In the case of an existing unit that was not in operation during calendar year 1985, the emission rate for a calendar year after 1985, as determined by the Administrator, shall be used in lieu of the 1985 rate. The owner or operator of any unit operated in violation of this section shall be fully liable under this chapter for fulfilling the obligations specified in section 7651j of this title.

(2) In addition to basic Phase II allowance allocations, in each year beginning in calendar year 2000 and ending in calendar year 2009, inclusive, the Administrator shall allocate up to 530,000 Phase II bonus allowances pursuant to subsections (b)(2), (c)(4), (d)(3)(A) and (B), and (h)(2) of this section and section 7651e of this title. Not later than June 1, 1998, the Administrator shall calculate, for each unit granted an extension pursuant to section 7651h of this title the difference between (A) the number of allowances allocated for the unit in calendar year 2000, and (B) the product of the unit's baseline multiplied by 1.20 lbs/mmBtu, divided by 2000, and sum the computations. In each year, beginning in calendar year 2000 and ending in calendar year 2009, inclusive, the Administrator shall deduct from each unit's basic Phase II allowance allocation its pro rata share of 10 percent of the sum calculated pursuant to the preceding sentence.

(3) In addition to basic Phase II allowance allocations and Phase II bonus allowance allocations, beginning January 1, 2000, the Administrator shall allocate for each unit listed on Table A in section 7651c of this title (other than units at Kyger Creek, Clifty Creek, and Joppa Steam) and located in the States of Illinois, Indiana, Ohio, Georgia, Alabama, Missouri, Pennsylvania, West Virginia, Kentucky, or Tennessee allowances in an amount equal to 50,000 multiplied by the unit's pro rata share of the total number of basic allowances allocated for all units listed on Table A (other than units at Kyger Creek, Clifty Creek, and Joppa Steam). Allowances allocated pursuant to this paragraph shall not be subject to the 8,900,000 ton limitation in section 7651b(a) of this title.

(b) Units equal to, or above, 75 MWe and 1.20 lbs/mmBtu

(1) Except as otherwise provided in paragraph (3), after January 1, 2000, it shall be unlawful for any existing utility unit that serves a generator with nameplate capacity equal to, or greater, than 75 MWe and an actual 1985 emission rate equal to or greater than 1.20 lbs/mmBtu to exceed an annual sulfur dioxide tonnage emission limitation equal to the product of the unit's baseline multiplied by an emission rate equal to 1.20 lbs/mmBtu, divided by 2,000, unless the owner or operator of such unit holds allowances to emit not less than the unit's total annual emissions.

(2) In addition to allowances allocated pursuant to paragraph (1) and section 7651b(a)(1) of this title as basic Phase II allowance allocations, beginning January 1, 2000, and for each calendar year thereafter until and including 2009, the Administrator shall allocate annually for each unit subject to the emissions limitation requirements of paragraph (1) with an actual 1985 emissions rate greater than 1.20 lbs/mmBtu and less than 2.50 lbs/mmBtu and a baseline capacity factor of less than 60 percent, allowances from the reserve created pursuant to subsection (a)(2) of this section in an amount equal to 1.20 lbs/mmBtu multiplied by 50 percent of the difference, on a Btu basis, between the unit's baseline and the unit's fuel consumption at a 60 percent capacity factor.

(3) After January 1, 2000, it shall be unlawful for any existing utility unit with an actual 1985 emissions rate equal to or greater than 1.20 lbs/mmBtu whose annual average fuel consumption during 1985, 1986, and 1987 on a Btu basis exceeded 90 percent in the form of lignite coal which is located in a State in which, as of July 1, 1989, no county or portion of a county was designated nonattainment under section 7407 of this title for any pollutant subject to the requirements of section 7409 of this title to exceed an annual sulfur dioxide tonnage limitation equal to the product of the unit's baseline multiplied by the lesser of the unit's actual 1985 emissions rate or its allowable 1985 emissions rate, divided by 2,000, unless the owner or operator of such unit holds allowances to emit not less than the unit's total annual emissions.

(4) After January 1, 2000, the Administrator shall allocate annually for each unit, subject to the emissions limitation requirements of paragraph (1), which is located in a State with an installed electrical generating capacity of more than 30,000,000 kw in 1988 and for which was issued a prohibition order or a proposed prohibition order (from burning oil), which unit subsequently converted to coal between January 1, 1980 and December 31, 1985, allowances equal to the difference between (A) the product of the unit's annual fuel consumption, on a Btu basis, at a 65 percent capacity factor multiplied by the lesser of its actual or allowable emissions rate during the first full calendar year after conversion, divided by 2,000, and (B) the number of allowances allocated for the unit pursuant to paragraph (1): *Provided*, That the number of allowances allocated pursuant to this paragraph shall not exceed an annual total of five thousand. If necessary to meeting the restriction imposed in the preceding sentence the Administrator shall reduce, pro rata, the annual allowances allocated for each unit under this paragraph.

(c) Coal or oil-fired units below 75 MWe and above 1.20 lbs/mmBtu

(1) Except as otherwise provided in paragraph (3), after January 1, 2000, it shall be unlawful for a coal or oil-fired existing utility unit that serves a generator with nameplate capacity of less than 75 MWe and an actual 1985 emission rate equal to, or greater than, 1.20 lbs/mmBtu and which is a unit owned by a utility operating company whose aggregate nameplate fossil fuel steam-electric capacity is, as of December 31, 1989, equal to, or greater than, 250 MWe to exceed an annual sulfur dioxide emissions limitation equal to the product of the unit's baseline multiplied by an emission rate equal to 1.20 lbs/mmBtu, divided by 2,000, unless the owner or operator of such unit holds allowances to emit not less than the unit's total annual emissions.

(2) After January 1, 2000, it shall be unlawful for a coal or oil-fired existing utility unit that serves a generator with nameplate capacity of less than 75 MWe and an actual 1985 emission rate equal to, or greater than, 1.20 lbs/mmBtu (excluding units subject to section 7411 of this title or to a federally enforceable emissions limitation for sulfur dioxide equivalent to an annual rate of less than 1.20 lbs/mmBtu) and which is a unit owned by a utility operating company whose aggregate nameplate fossil fuel steam-electric capacity is, as of December 31, 1989, less than 250 MWe, to exceed an annual sulfur dioxide tonnage emissions limitation equal to the product of the unit's baseline multiplied by the lesser of its actual 1985 emissions rate or its allowable 1985 emissions rate, divided by 2,000, unless the owner or operator of such unit holds allowances to emit not less than the unit's total annual emissions.

(3) After January 1, 2000, it shall be unlawful for any existing utility unit with a nameplate capacity below 75 MWe and an actual 1985 emissions rate equal to, or greater than, 1.20 lbs/mmBtu which became operational on or before December 31, 1965, which is owned by a utility operating company with, as of December 31, 1989, a total fossil fuel steam-electric generating capacity greater than 250 MWe, and less than 450 MWe which serves fewer than 78,000 electrical customers as of November 15, 1990, to exceed an annual sulfur dioxide emissions tonnage limitation equal to the product of its baseline multiplied by the lesser of its actual or allowable 1985 emission rate, divided by 2,000, unless the owner or operator holds allowances to emit not less than the units[1] total annual emissions. After January 1, 2010, it shall be unlawful for each unit subject to the emissions limitation requirements of this paragraph to exceed an annual emissions tonnage limitation equal to the product of its baseline multiplied by an emissions rate of 1.20 lbs/mmBtu, divided by 2,000, unless the owner or operator holds allowances to emit not less than the unit's total annual emissions.

(4) In addition to allowances allocated pursuant to paragraph (1) and section 7651b(a)(1) of this title as basic Phase II allowance allocations, beginning January 1, 2000, and for each calendar year thereafter until and including 2009, inclusive, the Administrator shall allocate annually for each unit subject to the emissions limitation requirements of paragraph (1) with an actual 1985 emissions rate equal to, or greater than, 1.20 lbs/mmBtu and less than 2.50 lbs/mmBtu and a baseline capacity factor of less than 60 percent, allowances from the reserve created pursuant to subsection (a)(2) of this section in an amount equal to 1.20 lbs/mmBtu multiplied by 50 percent of the difference, on a Btu basis, between the unit's baseline and the unit's fuel consumption at a 60 percent capacity factor.

(5) After January 1, 2000, it shall be unlawful for any existing utility unit with a nameplate capacity below 75 MWe and an actual 1985 emissions rate equal to, or greater than, 1.20 lbs/mmBtu which is part of an electric utility system which, as of November 15, 1990, (A) has at least 20 percent of its fossil-fuel capacity controlled by flue gas desulfurization devices, (B) has more than 10 percent of its fossil-fuel capacity consisting of coal-fired units of less than 75 MWe, and (C) has large units (greater than 400 MWe) all of which have difficult or very difficult FGD Retrofit Cost Factors (according to the Emissions and the FGD Retrofit Feasibility at the 200 Top Emitting Generating Stations, prepared for the United States Environmental Protection Agency on January 10, 1986) to exceed an annual sulfur dioxide emissions tonnage limitation equal to the product of its baseline multiplied by an emissions rate of 2.5 lbs/mmBtu, divided by 2,000, unless the owner or operator holds allowances to emit not less than the unit's total annual emissions. After January 1, 2010, it shall be unlawful for each unit subject to the emissions limitation requirements of this paragraph to exceed an annual emissions tonnage limitation equal to the product of its baseline multiplied by an emissions rate of 1.20 lbs/mmBtu, divided by 2,000, unless the owner or operator holds for use allowances to emit not less than the unit's total annual emissions.

(d) Coal-fired units below 1.20 lbs/mmBtu

(1) After January 1, 2000, it shall be unlawful for any existing coal-fired utility unit the lesser of whose actual or allowable 1985 sulfur dioxide emissions rate is less than 0.60 lbs/mmBtu to exceed an annual sulfur dioxide tonnage emission limitation equal to the product of the unit's baseline multiplied by (A) the lesser of 0.60 lbs/mmBtu or the unit's allowable 1985 emissions rate, and (B) a numerical factor of 120 percent, divided by 2,000, unless the owner or operator of such unit holds allowances to emit not less than the unit's total annual emissions.

(2) After January 1, 2000, it shall be unlawful for any existing coal-fired utility unit the lesser of whose actual or allowable 1985 sulfur dioxide emissions rate is equal to, or greater than, 0.60 lbs/mmBtu and less than 1.20 lbs/mmBtu to exceed an annual sulfur dioxide tonnage emissions limitation equal to the product of the unit's baseline multiplied by (A) the lesser of its actual 1985 emissions rate or its allowable 1985 emissions rate, and (B) a numerical factor of 120 percent, divided by 2,000, unless the owner or operator of such unit holds allowances to emit not less than the unit's total annual emissions.

(3) **(A)** In addition to allowances allocated pursuant to paragraph (1) and section 7651b(a)(1) of this title as basic Phase II allowance allocations, at the election of the designated representative of the operating company, beginning January 1, 2000, and for each calendar year thereafter until and including 2009, the Administrator shall allocate annually for each unit subject to the emissions limitation requirements of paragraph (1) allowances from the reserve created pursuant to subsection (a)(2) of this section in an amount equal to the amount by which (i) the product of the lesser of 0.60 lbs/mmBtu or the unit's allowable 1985 emissions rate multiplied by the unit's baseline adjusted to reflect operation at a 60 percent capacity factor, divided by 2,000, exceeds (ii) the number of allowances allocated for the unit pursuant to paragraph (1) and section 7651b(a)(1) of this title as basic Phase II allowance allocations.

(B) In addition to allowances allocated pursuant to paragraph (2) and section 7651b(a)(1) of this title as basic Phase II allowance allocations, at the election of the designated representative of the operating company, beginning January 1, 2000, and for each calendar year thereafter until and including 2009, the Administrator shall allocate annually for each unit subject to the emissions limitation requirements of paragraph (2) allowances from the reserve created pursuant to subsection (a)(2) of this section in an amount equal to the amount by which (i) the product of the lesser of the unit's actual 1985 emissions rate or its allowable 1985 emissions rate multiplied by the unit's baseline adjusted to reflect operation at a 60 percent capacity factor, divided by 2,000, exceeds (ii) the number of allowances allocated for the unit pursuant to paragraph (2) and section 7651b(a)(1) of this title as basic Phase II allowance allocations.

(C) An operating company with units subject to the emissions limitation requirements of this subsection may elect the allocation of allowances as provided under subparagraphs (A) and (B). Such election shall apply to the annual allowance allocation for each and every unit in the operating company subject to the emissions limitation requirements of this subsection. The

Administrator shall allocate allowances pursuant to subparagraphs (A) and (B) only in accordance with this subparagraph.

(4) Notwithstanding any other provision of this section, at the election of the owner or operator, after January 1, 2000, the Administrator shall allocate in lieu of allocation, pursuant to paragraph (1), (2), (3), (5), or (6), allowances for a unit subject to the emissions limitation requirements of this subsection which commenced commercial operation on or after January 1, 1981 and before December 31, 1985, which was subject to, and in compliance with, section 7411 of this title in an amount equal to the unit's annual fuel consumption, on a Btu basis, at a 65 percent capacity factor multiplied by the unit's allowable 1985 emissions rate, divided by 2,000.

(5) For the purposes of this section, in the case of an oil- and gas-fired unit which has been awarded a clean coal technology demonstration grant as of January 1, 1991, by the United States Department of Energy, beginning January 1, 2000, the Administrator shall allocate for the unit allowances in an amount equal to the unit's baseline multiplied by 1.20 lbs/mmBtu, divided by 2,000.

(e) Oil and gas-fired units equal to or greater than 0.60 lbs/mmBtu and less than 1.20 lbs/mmBtu

After January 1, 2000, it shall be unlawful for any existing oil and gas-fired utility unit the lesser of whose actual or allowable 1985 sulfur dioxide emission rate is equal to, or greater than, 0.60 lbs/mmBtu, but less than 1.20 lbs/mmBtu to exceed an annual sulfur dioxide tonnage limitation equal to the product of the unit's baseline multiplied by (A) the lesser of the unit's allowable 1985 emissions rate or its actual 1985 emissions rate and (B) a numerical factor of 120 percent divided by 2,000, unless the owner or operator of such unit holds allowances to emit not less than the unit's total annual emissions.

(f) Oil and gas-fired units less than 0.60 lbs/mmBtu

(1) After January 1, 2000, it shall be unlawful for any oil and gas-fired existing utility unit the lesser of whose actual or allowable 1985 emission rate is less than 0.60 lbs/mmBtu and whose average annual fuel consumption during the period 1980 through 1989 on a Btu basis was 90 percent or less in the form of natural gas to exceed an annual sulfur dioxide tonnage emissions limitation equal to the product of the unit's baseline multiplied by (A) the lesser of 0.60 lbs/mmBtu or the unit's allowable 1985 emissions, and (B) a numerical factor of 120 percent, divided by 2,000, unless the owner or operator of such unit holds allowances to emit not less than the unit's total annual emissions.

(2) In addition to allowances allocated pursuant to paragraph (1) as basic Phase II allowance allocations and section 7651b(a)(1) of this title, beginning January 1, 2000, the Administrator shall, in the case of any unit operated by a utility that furnishes electricity, electric energy, steam, and natural gas within an area consisting of a city and 1 contiguous county, and in the case of any unit owned by a State authority, the output of which unit is furnished within that same area consisting of a city and 1 contiguous county, the Administrator shall allocate for each unit in the utility its pro rata share of 7,000 allowances and for each unit in the State authority its pro rata share of 2,000 allowances.

(g) Units that commence operation between 1986 and December 31, 1995

(1) After January 1, 2000, it shall be unlawful for any utility unit that has commenced commercial operation on or after January 1, 1986, but not later than September 30, 1990 to exceed an annual tonnage emission limitation equal to the product of the unit's annual fuel consumption, on a Btu basis, at a 65 percent capacity factor multiplied by the unit's allowable 1985 sulfur dioxide emission rate (converted, if necessary, to pounds per mmBtu), divided by 2,000 unless the owner or operator of such unit holds allowances to emit not less than the unit's total annual emissions.

(2) After January 1, 2000, the Administrator shall allocate allowances pursuant to section 7651b of this title to each unit which is listed in table B of this paragraph in an annual amount equal to the amount specified in table B.

TABLE B

Unit	Allowances
Brandon Shores	8,907
Miller 4	9,197
TNP One 2	4,000

Zimmer 1 18,458
Spruce 1 7,647
Clover 1 2,796
Clover 2 2,796
Twin Oak 2 1,760
Twin Oak 1 9,158
Cross 1 6,401
Malakoff 1 1,759

Notwithstanding any other paragraph of this subsection, for units subject to this paragraph, the Administrator shall not allocate allowances pursuant to any other paragraph of this subsection, Provided[2] that the owner or operator of a unit listed on Table B may elect an allocation of allowances under another paragraph of this subsection in lieu of an allocation under this paragraph.

(3) Beginning January 1, 2000, the Administrator shall allocate to the owner or operator of any utility unit that commences commercial operation, or has commenced commercial operation, on or after October 1, 1990, but not later than December 31, 1992 allowances in an amount equal to the product of the unit's annual fuel consumption, on a Btu basis, at a 65 percent capacity factor multiplied by the lesser of 0.30 lbs/mmBtu or the unit's allowable sulfur dioxide emission rate (converted, if necessary, to pounds per mmBtu), divided by 2,000.

(4) Beginning January 1, 2000, the Administrator shall allocate to the owner or operator of any utility unit that has commenced construction before December 31, 1990 and that commences commercial operation between January 1, 1993 and December 31, 1995, allowances in an amount equal to the product of the unit's annual fuel consumption, on a Btu basis, at a 65 percent capacity factor multiplied by the lesser of 0.30 lbs/mmBtu or the unit's allowable sulfur dioxide emission rate (converted, if necessary, to pounds per mmBtu), divided by 2,000.

(5) After January 1, 2000, it shall be unlawful for any existing utility unit that has completed conversion from predominantly gas fired existing operation to coal fired operation between January 1, 1985 and December 31, 1987, for which there has been allocated a proposed or final prohibition order pursuant to section 301(b) of the Powerplant and Industrial Fuel Use Act of 1978 (42 U.S.C. 8301 et seq., repealed 1987) to exceed an annual sulfur dioxide tonnage emissions limitation equal to the product of the unit's annual fuel consumption, on a Btu basis, at a 65 percent capacity factor multiplied by the lesser of 1.20 lbs/mmBtu or the unit's allowable 1987 sulfur dioxide emissions rate, divided by 2,000, unless the owner or operator of such unit has obtained allowances equal to its actual emissions.

(6) **(A)**[3] Unless the Administrator has approved a designation of such facility under section 7651i of this title, the provisions of this subchapter shall not apply to a "qualifying small power production facility" or "qualifying cogeneration facility" (within the meaning of section 796(17)(C) or 796(18)(B) of Title 16) or to a "new independent power production facility" as defined in section 7651o of this title except that clause (iii)[4] of such definition in section 7651o of this title shall not apply for purposes of this paragraph if, as of November 15, 1990,

(i) an applicable power sales agreement has been executed;

(ii) the facility is the subject of a State regulatory authority order requiring an electric utility to enter into a power sales agreement with, purchase capacity from, or (for purposes of establishing terms and conditions of the electric utility's purchase of power) enter into arbitration concerning, the facility;

(iii) an electric utility has issued a letter of intent or similar instrument committing to purchase power from the facility at a previously offered or lower price and a power sales agreement is executed within a reasonable period of time; or

(iv) the facility has been selected as a winning bidder in a utility competitive bid solicitation.

(h) Oil and gas-fired units less than 10 percent oil consumed

(1) After January 1, 2000, it shall be unlawful for any oil- and gas-fired utility unit whose average annual fuel consumption during the period 1980 through 1989 on a Btu basis exceeded 90 percent in the form of natural gas to exceed an annual sulfur dioxide tonnage limitation equal to the product of the unit's baseline multiplied by the unit's actual 1985 emissions rate divided by 2,000 unless the owner or operator of such unit holds allowances to emit not less than the unit's total annual emissions.

(2) In addition to allowances allocated pursuant to paragraph (1) and section 7651b(a)(1) of this title as basic Phase II allowance allocations, beginning January 1, 2000, and for each calendar year thereafter until and including 2009, the Administrator shall allocate annually for each unit subject to the emissions limitation requirements of paragraph (1) allowances from the reserve created pursuant to subsection (a)(2) of this section in an amount equal to the unit's baseline multiplied by 0.050 lbs/mmBtu, divided by 2,000.

(3) In addition to allowances allocated pursuant to paragraph (1) and section 7651b(a)(1) of this title, beginning January 1, 2010, the Administrator shall allocate annually for each unit subject to the emissions limitation requirements of paragraph (1) allowances in an amount equal to the unit's baseline multiplied by 0.050 lbs/mmBtu, divided by 2,000.

(i) Units in high growth States

(1) In addition to allowances allocated pursuant to this section and section 7651b(a)(1) of this title as basic Phase II allowance allocations, beginning January 1, 2000, the Administrator shall allocate annually allowances for each unit, subject to an emissions limitation requirement under this section, and located in a State that—

(A) has experienced a growth in population in excess of 25 percent between 1980 and 1988 according to State Population and Household Estimates, With Age, Sex, and Components of Change: 1981–1988 allocated by the United States Department of Commerce, and

(B) had an installed electrical generating capacity of more than 30,000,000 kw in 1988,

in an amount equal to the difference between (A) the number of allowances that would be allocated for the unit pursuant to the emissions limitation requirements of this section applicable to the unit adjusted to reflect the unit's annual average fuel consumption on a Btu basis of any three consecutive calendar years between 1980 and 1989 (inclusive) as elected by the owner or operator and (B) the number of allowances allocated for the unit pursuant to the emissions limitation requirements of this section: *Provided,* That the number of allowances allocated pursuant to this subsection shall not exceed an annual total of 40,000. If necessary to meeting the 40,000 allowance restriction imposed under this subsection the Administrator shall reduce, pro rata, the additional annual allowances allocated to each unit under this subsection.

(2) Beginning January 1, 2000, in addition to allowances allocated pursuant to this section and section 7651b(a)(1) of this title as basic Phase II allowance allocations, the Administrator shall allocate annually for each unit subject to the emissions limitation requirements of subsection (b)(1) of this section, (A) the lesser of whose actual or allowable 1980 emissions rate has declined by 50 percent or more as of November 15, 1990, (B) whose actual emissions rate is less than 1.2 lbs/mmBtu as of January 1, 2000, (C) which commenced operation after January 1, 1970, (D) which is owned by a utility company whose combined commercial and industrial kilowatt-hour sales have increased by more than 20 percent between calendar year 1980 and November 15, 1990, and (E) whose company-wide fossil-fuel sulfur dioxide emissions rate has declined 40 per centum or more from 1980 to 1988, allowances in an amount equal to the difference between (i) the number of allowances that would be allocated for the unit pursuant to the emissions limitation requirements of subsection (b)(1) of this section adjusted to reflect the unit's annual average fuel consumption on a Btu basis for any three consecutive years between 1980 and 1989 (inclusive) as elected by the owner or operator and (ii) the number of allowances allocated for the unit pursuant to the emissions limitation requirements of subsection (b)(1) of this section: *Provided,* That the number of allowances allocated pursuant to this paragraph shall not exceed an annual total of 5,000. If necessary to meeting the 5,000-allowance restriction imposed in the last clause of the preceding sentence the Administrator shall reduce, pro rata, the additional allowances allocated to each unit pursuant to this paragraph.

(j) Certain municipally owned power plants

Beginning January 1, 2000, in addition to allowances allocated pursuant to this section and section 7651b(a)(1) of this title as basic Phase II allowance allocations, the Administrator shall allocate annually for each existing municipally owned oil and gas-fired utility unit with nameplate capacity equal to, or less than, 40 MWe, the lesser of whose actual or allowable 1985 sulfur dioxide emission rate is less than 1.20 lbs/mmBtu, allowances in an amount equal to the product of the unit's annual fuel consumption on a Btu basis at a 60 percent capacity factor multiplied by the lesser of its allowable 1985 emission rate or its actual 1985 emission rate, divided by 2,000.

(July 14, 1955, c. 360, Title IV, § 405, as added by Pub. L. No. 101–549, Title IV, § 401, 104 Stat. 2605 (Nov. 15, 1990).)

[1] So in original. Probably should be "unit's."

[2] So in original. Probably should not be capitalized.

[3] So in original. No subpar. (B) has been enacted.

[4] So in original. Probably means clause "(C)."

HISTORICAL AND STATUTORY NOTES

References in Text

Section 301(b) of the Powerplant and Industrial Fuel Use Act of 1978, referred to in subsec. (g)(5), is section 301(b) of Pub. L. No. 95–620, which is codified as section 8341(b) of this title. A prior section 301(b) of Pub. L. No. 95–620, Title III, 92 Stat. 3305 (Nov. 9, 1978), which was formerly codified as section 8341(b) of this title, was repealed by Pub. L. No. 97–35, Title X, § 1021(a), 95 Stat. 614 (Aug. 13, 1981).

Effective and Applicability Provisions

1990 Acts. Section effective Nov. 15, 1990, except as otherwise provided, see section 711(b) of Pub. L. No. 101–549, set out as a note under section 7401 of this title.

Savings Provisions

Suits, actions or proceedings commenced under this chapter as in effect prior to Nov. 15, 1990, not to abate by reason of the taking effect of amendments by Pub. L. No. 101–549, except as otherwise provided for, see section 711(a) of Pub. L. No. 101–549, set out as a note under section 7401 of this title.

§ 7651e. Allowances for States with emissions rates at or below 0.80 lbs/mmBtu

[CAA § 406]

(a) Election of Governor

In addition to basic Phase II allowance allocations, upon the election of the Governor of any State, with a 1985 state-wide annual sulfur dioxide emissions rate equal to or less than, 0.80 lbs/mmBtu, averaged over all fossil fuel-fired utility steam generating units, beginning January 1, 2000, and for each calendar year thereafter until and including 2009, the Administrator shall allocate, in lieu of other Phase II bonus allowance allocations, allowances from the reserve created pursuant to section 7651d(a)(2) of this title to all such units in the State in an amount equal to 125,000 multiplied by the unit's pro rata share of electricity generated in calendar year 1985 at fossil fuel-fired utility steam units in all States eligible for the election.

(b) Notification of Administrator

Pursuant to section 7651b(a)(1) of this title, each Governor of a State eligible to make an election under paragraph[1] (a) shall notify the Administrator of such election. In the event that the Governor of any such State fails to notify the Administrator of the Governor's elections, the Administrator shall allocate allowances pursuant to section 7651d of this title.

(c) Allowances after January 1, 2010

After January 1, 2010, the Administrator shall allocate allowances to units subject to the provisions of this section pursuant to section 7651d of this title.

(July 14, 1955, c. 360, Title IV, § 406, as added by Pub. L. No. 101–549, Title IV, § 401, 104 Stat. 2613 (Nov. 15, 1990).)

[1] So in original. Probably should be "subsection."

HISTORICAL AND STATUTORY NOTES

Effective and Applicability Provisions

1990 Acts. Section effective Nov. 15, 1990, except as otherwise provided, see section 711(b) of Pub. L. No. 101–549, set out as a note under section 7401 of this title.

Savings Provisions

Suits, actions or proceedings commenced under this chapter as in effect prior to Nov. 15, 1990, not to abate by reason of the taking effect of amendments by Pub. L. No. 101–549, except as otherwise provided for, see section 711(a) of Pub. L. No. 101–549, set out as a note under section 7401 of this title.

§ 7651f. Nitrogen oxides emission reduction program

[CAA § 407]

(a) Applicability

On the date that a coal-fired utility unit becomes an affected unit pursuant to sections 7651c, 7651d,[1] 7651h of this title, or on the date a unit subject to the provisions of section 7651c(d) or 7651h(b) of this title, must meet the SO_2 reduction requirements, each such unit shall become an affected unit for purposes of this section and shall be subject to the emission limitations for nitrogen oxides set forth herein.

(b) Emission limitations

(1) Not later than eighteen months after November 15, 1990, the Administrator shall by regulation establish annual allowable emission limitations for nitrogen oxides for the types of utility boilers listed below, which limitations shall not exceed the rates listed below: *Provided,* That the Administrator may set a rate higher than that listed for any type of utility boiler if the Administrator finds that the maximum listed rate for that boiler type cannot be achieved using low NO_x burner technology. The maximum allowable emission rates are as follows:

(A) for tangentially fired boilers, 0.45 lb/mmBtu;

(B) for dry bottom wall-fired boilers (other than units applying cell burner technology), 0.50 lb/mmBtu.

After January 1, 1995, it shall be unlawful for any unit that is an affected unit on that date and is of the type listed in this paragraph to emit nitrogen oxides in excess of the emission rates set by the Administrator pursuant to this paragraph.

(2) Not later than January 1, 1997, the Administrator shall, by regulation, establish allowable emission limitations on a lb/mmBtu, annual average basis, for nitrogen oxides for the following types of utility boilers:

(A) wet bottom wall-fired boilers;

(B) cyclones;

(C) units applying cell burner technology;

(D) all other types of utility boilers.

The Administrator shall base such rates on the degree of reduction achievable through the retrofit application of the best system of continuous emission reduction, taking into account available technology, costs and energy and environmental impacts; and which is comparable to the costs of nitrogen oxides controls set pursuant to subsection (b)(1) of this section. Not later than January 1, 1997, the Administrator may revise the applicable emission limitations for tangentially fired and dry bottom, wall-fired boilers (other than cell burners) to be more stringent if the Administrator determines that more effective low NO_x burner technology is available: *Provided,* That, no unit that is an affected unit pursuant to section 7651c of this title and that is subject to the requirements of subsection (b)(1) of this section, shall be subject to the revised emission limitations, if any.

(c) Revised performance standards

(1) Not later than January 1, 1993, the Administrator shall propose revised standards of performance to section 7411 of this title for nitrogen oxides emissions from fossil-fuel fired steam generating units, including both electric utility and nonutility units. Not later than January 1, 1994, the Administrator shall promulgate such revised standards of performance. Such revised standards of performance shall reflect improvements in methods for the reduction of emissions of oxides of nitrogen.

(d) Alternative emission limitations

The permitting authority shall, upon request of an owner or operator of a unit subject to this section, authorize an emission limitation less stringent than the applicable limitation established under subsection (b)(1) or (b)(2) of this section upon a determination that—

(1) a unit subject to subsection (b)(1) of this section cannot meet the applicable limitation using low NO_x burner technology; or

(2) a unit subject to subsection (b)(2) of this section cannot meet the applicable rate using the technology on which the Administrator based the applicable emission limitation.

The permitting authority shall base such determination upon a showing satisfactory to the permitting authority, in accordance with regulations established by the Administrator not later than eighteen months after November 15, 1990, that the owner or operator—

(1) has properly installed appropriate control equipment designed to meet the applicable emission rate;

(2) has properly operated such equipment for a period of fifteen months (or such other period of time as the Administrator determines through the regulations), and provides operating and monitoring data for such period demonstrating that the unit cannot meet the applicable emission rate; and

(3) has specified an emission rate that such unit can meet on an annual average basis.

The permitting authority shall issue an operating permit for the unit in question, in accordance with section 7651g of this title and part B of title III—

(i) that permits the unit during the demonstration period referred to in subparagraph (2) above, to emit at a rate in excess of the applicable emission rate;

(ii) at the conclusion of the demonstration period to revise the operating permit to reflect the alternative emission rate demonstrated in paragraphs (2) and (3) above.

Units subject to subsection (b)(1) of this section for which an alternative emission limitation is established shall not be required to install any additional control technology beyond low NO_x burners. Nothing in this section shall preclude an owner or operator from installing and operating an alternative NO_x control technology capable of achieving the applicable emission limitation. If the owner or operator of a unit subject to the emissions limitation requirements of subsection (b)(1) of this section demonstrates to the satisfaction of the Administrator that the technology necessary to meet such requirements is not in adequate supply to enable its installation and operation at the unit, consistent with system reliability, by January 1, 1995, then the Administrator shall extend the deadline for compliance for the unit by a period of 15 months. Any owner or operator may petition the Administrator to make a determination under the previous sentence. The Administrator shall grant or deny such petition within 3 months of submittal.

(e) Emissions averaging

In lieu of complying with the applicable emission limitations under subsection (b)(1), (2), or (d) of this section, the owner or operator of two or more units subject to one or more of the applicable emission limitations set pursuant to these sections, may petition the permitting authority for alternative contemporaneous annual emission limitations for such units that ensure that (1) the actual annual emission rate in pounds of nitrogen oxides per million Btu averaged over the units in question is a rate that is less than or equal to (2) the Btu-weighted average annual emission rate for the same units if they had been operated, during the same period of time, in compliance with limitations set in accordance with the applicable emission rates set pursuant to subsections (b)(1) and (2) of this section.

If the permitting authority determines, in accordance with regulations issued by the Administrator not later than eighteen months after November 15, 1990;[2] that the conditions in the paragraph above can be met, the permitting authority shall issue operating permits for such units, in accordance with section 7651g of this title and part B of title III, that allow alternative contemporaneous annual emission limitations. Such emission limitations shall only remain in effect while both units continue operation under the conditions specified in their respective operating permits.

(July 14, 1955, c. 360, Title IV, § 407, as added by Pub. L. No. 101–549, Title IV, § 401, 104 Stat. 2613 (Nov. 15, 1990).)

[1] So in original. Probably should be followed by "or."

[2] So in original. The semicolon probably should be a comma.

HISTORICAL AND STATUTORY NOTES

References in Text

Part B of Title III, referred to in subsecs. (d) and (e), means Title III of the Clean Air Act, Act of July 14, 1955, c. 360, as added, which is codified as subchapter III of this chapter, but Title III does not contain parts. For provisions of the Clean Air Act relating to permits, see subchapter V (section 7661 et seq.) of this chapter.

Effective and Applicability Provisions

1990 Acts. Section effective Nov. 15, 1990, except as otherwise provided, see section 711(b) of Pub. L. No. 101–549, set out as a note under section 7401 of this title.

Savings Provisions

Suits, actions or proceedings commenced under this chapter as in effect prior to Nov. 15, 1990, not to abate by reason of the taking effect of amendments by Pub. L. No. 101–549, except as otherwise provided for, see section 711(a) of Pub. L. No. 101–549, set out as a note under section 7401 of this title.

§ 7651g. Permits and compliance plans

[CAA § 408]

(a) Permit program

The provisions of this subchapter shall be implemented, subject to section 7651b of this title, by permits issued to units subject to this subchapter (and enforced) in accordance with the provisions of subchapter V of this chapter, as modified by this subchapter. Any such permit issued by the Administrator, or by a State with an approved permit program, shall prohibit—

(1) annual emissions of sulfur dioxide in excess of the number of allowances to emit sulfur dioxide the owner or operator, or the designated representative of the owners or operators, of the unit hold for the unit,

(2) exceedances of applicable emissions rates,

(3) the use of any allowance prior to the year for which it was allocated, and

(4) contravention of any other provision of the permit.

Permits issued to implement this subchapter shall be issued for a period of 5 years, notwithstanding subchapter V of this chapter. No permit shall be issued that is inconsistent with the requirements of this subchapter, and subchapter V of this chapter as applicable.

(b) Compliance plan

Each initial permit application shall be accompanied by a compliance plan for the source to comply with its requirements under this subchapter. Where an affected source consists of more than one affected unit, such plan shall cover all such units, and for purposes of section 7661a(c) of this title, such source shall be considered a "facility". Nothing in this section regarding compliance plans or in subchapter V of this chapter shall be construed as affecting allowances. Except as provided under subsection (c)(1)(B) of this section, submission of a statement by the owner or operator, or the designated representative of the owners and operators, of a unit subject to the emissions limitation requirements of sections 7651c, 7651d, and 7651f of this title, that the unit will meet the applicable emissions limitation requirements of such sections in a timely manner or that, in the case of the emissions limitation requirements of sections 7651c and 7651d of this title, the owners and operators will hold allowances to emit not less than the total annual emissions of the unit, shall be deemed to meet the proposed and approved compliance planning requirements of this section and subchapter V of this chapter, except that, for any unit that will meet the requirements of this subchapter by means of an alternative method of compliance authorized under section 7651c(b), (c), (d), or (f) of this title[1] section 7651f(d) or (e) of this title, section 7651h of this title and section 7651i of this title, the proposed and approved compliance plan, permit application and permit shall include, pursuant to regulations promulgated by the Administrator, for each alternative method of compliance a comprehensive description of the schedule and means by which the unit will rely on one or more alternative methods of compliance in the manner and time authorized under this subchapter. Recordation by the Administrator of transfers of allowances shall amend automatically all applicable proposed or approved permit applications, compliance plans and permits. The Administrator may also require—

(1) for a source, a demonstration of attainment of national ambient air quality standards, and

(2) from the owner or operator of two or more affected sources, an integrated compliance plan providing an overall plan for achieving compliance at the affected sources.

(c) First phase permits

The Administrator shall issue permits to affected sources under sections 7651c and 7651f of this title.

(1) Permit application and compliance plan

(A) Not later than 27 months after November 15, 1990, the designated representative of the owners or operators, or the owner and operator, of each affected source under sections 7651c and 7651f of this title shall submit a permit application and compliance plan for that source in accordance with regulations issued by the Administrator under paragraph (3). The permit application and the compliance plan shall be binding on the owner or operator or the designated representative of owners and operators for purposes of this subchapter and section 7651a(a)[2] of this title, and shall be enforceable in lieu of a permit until a permit is issued by the Administrator for the source.

(B) In the case of a compliance plan for an affected source under sections 7651c and 7651f of this title for which the owner or operator proposes to meet the requirements of that section by reducing utilization of the unit as compared with its baseline or by shutting down the unit, the owner or operator shall include in the proposed compliance plan a specification of the unit or units that will provide electrical generation to compensate for the reduced output at the affected source, or a demonstration that such reduced utilization will be accomplished through energy conservation or improved unit efficiency. The unit to be used for such compensating generation, which is not otherwise an affected unit under sections 7651c and 7651f of this title, shall be deemed an affected unit under section 7651c of this title, subject to all of the requirements for such units under this subchapter, except that allowances shall be allocated to such compensating unit in the amount of an annual limitation equal to the product of the unit's baseline multiplied by the lesser of the unit's actual 1985 emissions rate or its allowable 1985 emissions rate, divided by 2,000.

(2) EPA action on compliance plans

The Administrator shall review each proposed compliance plan to determine whether it satisfies the requirements of this subchapter, and shall approve or disapprove such plan within 6 months after receipt of a complete submission. If a plan is disapproved, it may be resubmitted for approval with such changes as the Administrator shall require consistent with the requirements of this subchapter and within such period as the Administrator prescribes as part of such disapproval.

(3) Regulations; issuance of permits

Not later than 18 months after November 15, 1990, the Administrator shall promulgate regulations, in accordance with subchapter V of this chapter, to implement a Federal permit program to issue permits for affected sources under this subchapter. Following promulgation, the Administrator shall issue a permit to implement the requirements of section 7651c of this title and the allowances provided under section 7651b of this title to the owner or operator of each affected source under section 7651c of this title. Such a permit shall supersede any permit application and compliance plan submitted under paragraph (1).

(4) Fees

During the years 1995 through 1999 inclusive, no fee shall be required to be paid under section 7661a(b)(3) of this title or under section 7410(a)(2)(L) of this title with respect to emissions from any unit which is an affected unit under section 7651c of this title.

(d) Second phase permits

(1) To provide for permits for (A) new electric utility steam generating units required under section 7651b(e) of this title to have allowances, (B) affected units or sources under section 7651d of this title, and (C) existing units subject to nitrogen oxide emission reductions under section 7651f of this title, each State in which one or more such units or sources are located shall submit in accordance with subchapter V of this chapter, a permit program for approval as provided by that subchapter. Upon approval of such program, for the units or sources subject to such approved program the Administrator shall suspend the issuance of permits as provided in subchapter V of this chapter.

(2) The owner or operator or the designated representative of each affected source under section 7651d of this title shall submit a permit application and compliance plan for that source to the permitting authority, not later than January 1, 1996.

(3) Not later than December 31, 1997, each State with an approved permit program shall issue permits to the owner or operator, or the designated representative of the owners and operators, of affected sources under section 7651d of this title that satisfy the requirements of subchapter V of this chapter and this subchapter and that submitted to such State a permit application and compliance plan pursuant to paragraph (2). In the case of a State without an approved permit program by July 1, 1996, the Administrator shall, not later than January 1, 1998, issue a permit to the owner or operator or the designated representative of each such affected source. In the case of affected sources for which applications and plans are timely received under paragraph (2), the permit application and the compliance plan, including amendments thereto, shall be binding on the owner or operator or the designated representative of the owners or operators and shall be enforceable as a permit for purposes of this subchapter and subchapter V of this chapter until a permit is issued by the permitting authority for the affected source. The provisions of section 558(c) of Title 5 (relating to renewals) shall apply to permits issued by a permitting authority under this subchapter and subchapter V of this chapter.

(4) The permit issued in accordance with this subsection for an affected source shall provide that the affected units at the affected source may not emit an annual tonnage of sulfur dioxide in excess of the number of allowances to emit sulfur dioxide the owner or operator or designated representative hold for the unit.

(e) New units

The owner or operator of each source that includes a new electric utility steam generating unit shall submit a permit application and compliance plan to the permitting authority not later than 24 months before the later of (1) January 1, 2000, or (2) the date on which the unit commences operation. The permitting authority shall issue a permit to the owner or operator, or the designated representative thereof, of the unit that satisfies the requirements of subchapter V of this chapter and this subchapter.

(f) Units subject to certain other limits

The owner or operator, or designated representative thereof, of any unit subject to an emission rate requirement under section 7651f of this title shall submit a permit application and compliance plan for such unit to the permitting authority, not later than January 1, 1998. The permitting authority shall issue a permit to the owner or operator that satisfies the requirements of subchapter V of this chapter and this subchapter, including any appropriate monitoring and reporting requirements.

(g) Amendment of application and compliance plan

At any time after the submission of an application and compliance plan under this section, the applicant may submit a revised application and compliance plan, in accordance with the requirements of this section. In considering any permit application and compliance plan under this subchapter, the permitting authority shall ensure coordination with the applicable electric ratemaking authority, in the case of regulated utilities, and with unregulated public utilities.

(h) Prohibition

(1) It shall be unlawful for an owner or operator, or designated representative, required to submit a permit application or compliance plan under this subchapter to fail to submit such application or plan in accordance with the deadlines specified in this section or to otherwise fail to comply with regulations implementing this section.

(2) It shall be unlawful for any person to operate any source subject to this subchapter except in compliance with the terms and requirements of a permit application and compliance plan (including amendments thereto) or permit issued by the Administrator or a State with an approved permit program. For purposes of this subsection, compliance, as provided in section 7661c(f) of this title, with a permit issued under subchapter V of this chapter which complies with this subchapter for sources subject to this subchapter shall be deemed compliance with this subsection as well as section 7661a(a) of this title.

(3) In order to ensure reliability of electric power, nothing in this subchapter or subchapter V of this chapter shall be construed as requiring termination of operations of an electric utility steam generating unit for failure to have an approved permit or compliance plan, except that any such unit may be subject to the applicable enforcement provisions of section 7413 of this title.

(i) Multiple owners

No permit shall be issued under this section to an affected unit until the designated representative of the owners or operators has filed a certificate of representation with regard to matters under this subchapter, including the holding and distribution of allowances and the proceeds of transactions involving allowances. Where there are multiple holders of a legal or equitable title to, or a leasehold interest in, such a unit, or where a utility or industrial customer purchases power from an affected unit (or units) under life-of-the-unit, firm power contractual arrangements, the certificate shall state (1) that allowances and the proceeds of transactions involving allowances will be deemed to be held or distributed in proportion to each holder's legal, equitable, leasehold, or contractual reservation or entitlement, or (2) if such multiple holders have expressly provided for a different distribution of allowances by contract, that allowances and the proceeds of transactions involving allowances will be deemed to be held or distributed in accordance with the contract. A passive lessor, or a person who has an equitable interest through such lessor, whose rental payments are not based, either directly or indirectly, upon the revenues or income from the affected unit shall not be deemed to be a holder of a legal, equitable, leasehold, or contractual interest for the purpose of holding or distributing allowances as provided in this subsection, during either the term of such leasehold or thereafter, unless expressly provided for in the leasehold agreement. Except as otherwise provided in this subsection, where all legal or equitable title to or interest in an affected unit is held by a single person, the certification shall state that all allowances received by the unit are deemed to be held for that person.

(July 14, 1955, c. 360, Title IV, § 408, as added by Pub. L. No. 101–549, Title IV, § 401, 104 Stat. 2616 (Nov. 15, 1990).)

[1] So in original. Probably should be followed by a comma.

[2] So in original. Section 7651a of this title does not contain subsections.

HISTORICAL AND STATUTORY NOTES

Effective and Applicability Provisions

1990 Acts. Section effective Nov. 15, 1990, except as otherwise provided, see section 711(b) of Pub. L. No. 101–549, set out as a note under section 7401 of this title.

Savings Provisions

Suits, actions or proceedings commenced under this chapter as in effect prior to Nov. 15, 1990, not to abate by reason of the taking effect of amendments by Pub. L. No. 101–549, except as otherwise provided for, see section 711(a) of Pub. L. No. 101–549, set out as a note under section 7401 of this title.

§ 7651h. Repowered sources

[CAA § 409]

(a) Availability

Not later than December 31, 1997, the owner or operator of an existing unit subject to the emissions limitation requirements of section 7651d(b) and (c) of this title may demonstrate to the permitting authority that one or more units will be repowered with a qualifying clean coal technology to comply with the requirements under section 7651d of this title. The owner or operator shall, as part of any such demonstration, provide, not later than January 1, 2000, satisfactory documentation of a preliminary design and engineering effort for such repowering and an executed and binding contract for the majority of the equipment to repower such unit and such other information as the Administrator may require by regulation. The replacement of an existing utility unit with a new utility unit using a repowering technology referred to in section 7651a(2)[1] of this title which is located at a different site, shall be treated as repowering of the existing unit for purposes of this subchapter, if—

(1) the replacement unit is designated by the owner or operator to replace such existing unit, and

(2) the existing unit is retired from service on or before the date on which the designated replacement unit enters commercial operation.

(b) Extension

(1) An owner or operator satisfying the requirements of subsection (a) of this section shall be granted an extension of the emission limitation requirement compliance date for that unit from January 1, 2000, to December 31, 2003. The extension shall be specified in the permit issued to the source under section 7651g of this title, together with any compliance schedule and other requirements necessary to meet second phase requirements by the extended date. Any unit that is granted an extension under this section shall not be eligible for a waiver under section 7411(j) of this title, and shall continue to be subject to requirements under this subchapter as if it were a unit subject to section 7651d of this title.

(2) If (A) the owner or operator of an existing unit has been granted an extension under paragraph (1) in order to repower such unit with a clean coal unit, and (B) such owner or operator demonstrates to the satisfaction of the Administrator that the repowering technology to be utilized by such unit has been properly constructed and tested on such unit, but nevertheless has been unable to achieve the emission reduction limitations and is economically or technologically infeasible, such existing unit may be retrofitted or repowered with equipment or facilities utilizing another clean coal technology or other available control technology.

(c) Allowances

(1) For the period of the extension under this section, the Administrator shall allocate to the owner or operator of the affected unit, annual allowances for sulfur dioxide equal to the affected unit's baseline multiplied by the lesser of the unit's federally approved State Implementation Plan emissions limitation or its actual emission rate for 1995 in lieu of any other allocation. Such allowances may not be transferred or used by any other source to meet emission requirements under this subchapter. The source owner or operator shall notify the Administrator sixty days in advance of the date on which the affected unit for which the extension has been granted is to be removed from operation to install the repowering technology.

(2) Effective on that date, the unit shall be subject to the requirements of section 7651d of this title. Allowances for the year in which the unit is removed from operation to install the repowering technology shall be calculated as the product of the unit's baseline multiplied by 1.20 lbs/mmBtu, divided by 2,000, and prorated accordingly, and are transferable.

(3) Allowances for such existing utility units for calendar years after the year the repowering is complete shall be calculated as the product of the existing unit's baseline multiplied by 1.20 lbs/mmBtu, divided by 2,000.

(4) Notwithstanding the provisions of section 7651b(a) and (e) of this title, allowances shall be allocated under this section for a designated replacement unit which replaces an existing unit (as provided in the last sentence of subsection (a) of this section) in lieu of any further allocations of allowances for the existing unit.

(5) For the purpose of meeting the aggregate emissions limitation requirement set forth in section 7651b(a)(1) of this title, the units with an extension under this subsection shall be treated in each calendar year during the extension period as holding allowances allocated under paragraph (3).

(d) Control requirements

Any unit qualifying for an extension under this section that does not increase actual hourly emissions for any pollutant regulated under the[2] chapter shall not be subject to any standard of performance under section 7411 of this title. Notwithstanding the provisions of this subsection, no new unit (1) designated as a replacement for an existing unit, (2) qualifying for the extension under subsection (b) of this section, and (3) located at a different site than the existing unit shall receive an exemption from the requirements imposed under section 7411 of this title.

(e) Expedited permitting

State permitting authorities and, where applicable, the Administrator, are encouraged to give expedited consideration to permit applications under parts C and D of subchapter I of this chapter for any source qualifying for an extension under this section.

(f) Prohibition

It shall be unlawful for the owner or operator of a repowered source to fail to comply with the requirement of this section, or any regulations of permit requirements to implement this section, including the prohibition against emitting sulfur dioxide in excess of allowances held.

(July 14, 1955, c. 360, Title IV, § 409, as added by Pub. L. No. 101–549, Title IV, § 401, 104 Stat. 2619 (Nov. 15, 1990).)

[1] So in original. Probably should be "section 7651a(12)."

[2] So in original. Probably should be "this."

HISTORICAL AND STATUTORY NOTES

Effective and Applicability Provisions

1990 Acts. Section effective Nov. 15, 1990, except as otherwise provided, see section 711(b) of Pub. L. No. 101–549, set out as a note under section 7401 of this title.

Savings Provisions

Suits, actions or proceedings commenced under this chapter as in effect prior to Nov. 15, 1990, not to abate by reason of the taking effect of amendments by Pub. L. No. 101–549, except as otherwise provided for, see section 711(a) of Pub. L. No. 101–549, set out as a note under section 7401 of this title.

§ 7651i. Election for additional sources

[CAA § 410]

(a) Applicability

The owner or operator of any unit that is not, nor will become, an affected unit under section 7651b(e), 7651c, or 7651d of this title, or that is a process source under subsection (d) of this section, that emits sulfur dioxide, may elect to designate that unit or source to become an affected unit and to receive allowances under this subchapter. An election shall be submitted to the Administrator for approval, along with a permit application and proposed compliance plan in accordance with section 7651g of this title. The Administrator shall approve a designation that meets the requirements of this section, and such designated unit, or source, shall be allocated allowances, and be an affected unit for purposes of this subchapter.

(b) Establishment of baseline

The baseline for a unit designated under this section shall be established by the Administrator by regulation, based on fuel consumption and operating data for the unit for calendar years 1985, 1986, and 1987, or if such data is not available, the Administrator may prescribe a baseline based on alternative representative data.

(c) Emission limitations

Annual emissions limitations for sulfur dioxide shall be equal to the product of the baseline multiplied by the lesser of the unit's 1985 actual or allowable emission rate in lbs/mmBtu, or, if the unit did not operate in 1985, by the lesser of the unit's actual or allowable emission rate for a calendar year after 1985 (as determined by the Administrator), divided by 2,000.

(d) Process sources

Not later than 18 months after November 15, 1990, the Administrator shall establish a program under which the owner or operator of a process source that emits sulfur dioxide may elect to designate that source as an affected unit for the purpose of receiving allowances under this subchapter. The Administrator shall, by regulation, define the sources that may be designated; specify the emissions limitation; specify the operating, emission baseline, and other data requirements; prescribe CEMS or other monitoring requirements; and promulgate permit, reporting, and any other requirements necessary to implement such a program.

(e) Allowances and permits

The Administrator shall issue allowances to an affected unit under this section in an amount equal to the emissions limitation calculated under subsection (c) or (d) of this section, in accordance with section 7651b of this title. Such allowance may be used in accordance with, and shall be subject to, the provisions of section 7651b of this title. Affected sources under this section shall be subject to the requirements of sections 7651b, 7651g, 7651j, 7651k, 7651*l*, and 7651m of this title.

(f) Limitation

Any unit designated under this section shall not transfer or bank allowances produced as a result of reduced utilization or shutdown, except that, such allowances may be transferred or carried forward for use in subsequent years to the extent that the reduced utilization or shutdown results from the replacement of thermal energy from the unit designated under this section, with thermal energy generated by any other unit or units subject to the requirements of this subchapter, and the designated unit's allowances are transferred or carried forward for use at such other replacement unit or units. In no case may the Administrator allocate to a source designated under this section allowances in an amount greater than the emissions resulting from operation of the source in full compliance with the requirements of this chapter. No such allowances shall authorize operation of a unit in violation of any other requirements of this chapter.

(g) Implementation

The Administrator shall issue regulations to implement this section not later than eighteen months after November 15, 1990.

(h) Small diesel refineries

The Administrator shall issue allowances to owners or operators of small diesel refineries who produce diesel fuel after October 1, 1993, meeting the requirements of subsection[1] 7545(i) of this title.

(1) Allowance period

Allowances may be allocated under this subsection only for the period from October 1, 1993, through December 31, 1999.

(2) Allowance determination

The number of allowances allocated pursuant to this paragraph shall equal the annual number of pounds of sulfur dioxide reduction attributable to desulfurization by a small refinery divided by 2,000. For the purposes of this calculation, the concentration of sulfur removed from diesel fuel shall be the difference between 0.274 percent (by weight) and 0.050 percent (by weight).

(3) Refinery eligibility

As used in this subsection, the term "small refinery" shall mean a refinery or portion of a refinery—

(A) which, as of November 15, 1990, has bona fide crude oil throughput of less than 18,250,000 barrels per year, as reported to the Department of Energy, and

(B) which, as of November 15, 1990, is owned or controlled by a refiner with a total combined bona fide crude oil throughput of less than 50,187,500 barrels per year, as reported to the Department of Energy.

(4) Limitation per refinery

The maximum number of allowances that can be annually allocated to a small refinery pursuant to this subsection is one thousand and five hundred.

(5) Limitation on total

In any given year, the total number of allowances allocated pursuant to this subsection shall not exceed thirty-five thousand.

(6) Required certification

The Administrator shall not allocate any allowances pursuant to this subsection unless the owner or operator of a small diesel refinery shall have certified, at a time and in a manner prescribed by the Administrator, that all motor diesel fuel produced by the refinery for which allowances are claimed, including motor diesel fuel for off-highway use, shall have met the requirements of subsection[1] 7545(i) of this title.

(July 14, 1955, c. 360, Title IV, § 410, as added by Pub. L. No. 101–549, Title IV, § 401, 104 Stat. 2621 (Nov. 15, 1990).)

[1] So in original. Probably should be "section."

HISTORICAL AND STATUTORY NOTES

Effective and Applicability Provisions

1990 Acts. Section effective Nov. 15, 1990, except as otherwise provided, see section 711(b) of Pub. L. No. 101–549, set out as a note under section 7401 of this title.

Savings Provisions

Suits, actions or proceedings commenced under this chapter as in effect prior to Nov. 15, 1990, not to abate by reason of the taking effect of amendments by Pub. L. No. 101–549, except as otherwise provided for, see section 711(a) of Pub. L. No. 101–549, set out as a note under section 7401 of this title.

§ 7651j. Excess emissions penalty

[CAA § 411]

(a) Excess emissions penalty

The owner or operator of any unit or process source subject to the requirements of sections[1] 7651b, 7651c, 7651d, 7651e, 7651f or 7651h of this title, or designated under section 7651i of this title, that emits sulfur dioxide or nitrogen oxides for any calendar year in excess of the unit's emissions limitation requirement or, in the case of sulfur dioxide, of the allowances the owner or operator holds for use for the unit for that calendar year shall be liable for the payment of an excess emissions penalty, except where such emissions were authorized pursuant to section 7410(f) of this title. That penalty shall be calculated on the basis of the number of tons emitted in excess of the unit's emissions limitation requirement or, in the case of sulfur dioxide, of the allowances the operator holds for use for the unit for that year, multiplied by $2,000. Any such penalty shall be due and payable without demand to the Administrator as provided in regulations to be issued by the Administrator by no later than eighteen months after November 15, 1990. Any such payment shall be deposited in the United States Treasury pursuant to the Miscellaneous Receipts Act. Any penalty due and payable under this section shall not diminish the liability of the unit's owner or operator for any fine, penalty or assessment against the unit for the same violation under any other section of this chapter.

(b) Excess emissions offset

The owner or operator of any affected source that emits sulfur dioxide during any calendar year in excess of the unit's emissions limitation requirement or of the allowances held for the unit for the calendar year, shall be liable to offset the excess emissions by an equal tonnage amount in the following calendar year, or such longer period as the Administrator may prescribe. The owner or operator of the source shall, within sixty days after the end of the year in which the excess emissions occured[2], submit to the Administrator, and to the State in which the source is located, a proposed plan to achieve the required offsets. Upon approval of the proposed plan by the Administrator, as submitted, modified or conditioned, the plan shall be deemed at a condition of the operating permit for the unit without further review or revision of the permit. The Administrator shall also deduct allowances equal to the excess tonnage from those allocated for the source for the calendar year, or succeeding years during which offsets are required, following the year in which the excess emissions occurred.

(c) Penalty adjustment

The Administrator shall, by regulation, adjust the penalty specified in subsection (a) of this section for inflation, based on the Consumer Price Index, on November 15, 1990, and annually thereafter.

(d) Prohibition

It shall be unlawful for the owner or operator of any source liable for a penalty and offset under this section to fail (1) to pay the penalty under subsection (a) of this section, (2) to provide, and thereafter comply with, a compliance plan as required by subsection (b) of this section, or (3) to offset excess emissions as required by subsection (b) of this section.

(e) Savings provision

Nothing in this subchapter shall limit or otherwise affect the application of section 7413, 7414, 7420, or 7604 of this title except as otherwise explicitly provided in this subchapter.

(July 14, 1955, c. 360, Title IV, § 411, as added by Pub. L. No. 101–549, Title IV, § 401, 104 Stat. 2623 (Nov. 15, 1990).)

[1] So in original. Probably should be "section."

[2] So in original. Probably should be "occurred."

HISTORICAL AND STATUTORY NOTES

References in Text

The Miscellaneous Receipts Act, referred to in subsec. (a), is not a recognized popular name for an act. For provisions relating to deposit of monies, see section 3302 of Title 31, Money and Finance.

Effective and Applicability Provisions

1990 Acts. Section effective Nov. 15, 1990, except as otherwise provided, see section 711(b) of Pub. L. No. 101–549, set out as a note under section 7401 of this title.

Savings Provisions

Suits, actions or proceedings commenced under this chapter as in effect prior to Nov. 15, 1990, not to abate by reason of the taking effect of amendments by Pub. L. No. 101–549, except as otherwise provided for, see section 711(a) of Pub. L. No. 101–549, set out as a note under section 7401 of this title.

§ 7651k. Monitoring, reporting, and recordkeeping requirements

[CAA § 412]

(a) Applicability

The owner and operator of any source subject to this subchapter shall be required to install and operate CEMS on each affected unit at the source, and to quality assure the data for sulfur dioxide, nitrogen oxides, opacity and volumetric flow at each such unit. The Administrator shall, by regulations issued not later than eighteen months after November 15, 1990, specify the requirements for CEMS, for any alternative monitoring system that is demonstrated as providing information with the same precision, reliability, accessibility, and timeliness as that provided by CEMS, and for recordkeeping and reporting of information from such systems. Such regulations may include limitations or the use of alternative compliance methods by units equipped with an alternative monitoring system as may be necessary to preserve the orderly functioning of the allowance system, and which will ensure the emissions reductions contemplated by this subchapter. Where 2 or more units utilize a single stack, a separate CEMS shall not be required for each unit, and for such units the regulations shall require that the owner or operator collect sufficient information to permit reliable compliance determinations for each such unit.

(b) First phase requirements

Not later than thirty-six months after November 15, 1990, the owner or operator of each affected unit under section 7651c of this title, including, but not limited to, units that become affected units pursuant to subsections (b) and (c) and eligible units under subsection (d), shall install and operate CEMS, quality assure the data, and keep records and reports in accordance with the regulations issued under subsection (a).

(c) Second phase requirements

Not later than January 1, 1995, the owner or operator of each affected unit that has not previously met the requirements of subsections (a) and (b) shall install and operate CEMS, quality assure the data, and keep records and reports in accordance with the regulations issued under subsection (a). Upon commencement of commercial operation of each new utility unit, the unit shall comply with the requirements of subsection (a).

(d) Unavailability of emissions data

If CEMS data or data from an alternative monitoring system approved by the Administrator under subsection (a) is not available for any affected unit during any period of a calendar year in which such data is required under this subchapter, and the owner or operator cannot provide information, satisfactory to the Administrator, on emissions during that period, the Administrator shall deem the unit to be operating in an uncontrolled manner during the entire period for which the data was not available and shall, by regulation which shall be issued not later than eighteen months after November 15, 1990, prescribe means to calculate emissions for that period. The owner or operator shall be liable for excess emissions fees and offsets under section 7651j of this title in accordance with such regulations. Any fee due and payable under this subsection shall not diminish the liability of the unit's owner or operator for any fine, penalty, fee or assessment against the unit for the same violation under any other section of this chapter.

(e) Prohibition

It shall be unlawful for the owner or operator of any source subject to this subchapter to operate a source without complying with the requirements of this section, and any regulations implementing this section.

(July 14, 1955, c. 360, Title IV, § 412, as added by Pub. L. No. 101–549, Title IV, § 401, 104 Stat. 2624 (Nov. 15, 1990).)

HISTORICAL AND STATUTORY NOTES

Effective and Applicability Provisions

1990 Acts. Section effective Nov. 15, 1990, except as otherwise provided, see section 711(b) of Pub. L. No. 101–549, set out as a note under section 7401 of this title.

Savings Provisions

Suits, actions or proceedings commenced under this chapter as in effect prior to Nov. 15, 1990, not to abate by reason of the taking effect of amendments by Pub. L. No. 101–549, except as otherwise provided for, see section 711(a) of Pub. L. No. 101–549, set out as a note under section 7401 of this title.

Information Gathering on Greenhouse Gases Contributing to Global Climate Change

Section 821 of Pub. L. No. 101–549 provided that:

"(a) Monitoring.—The Administrator of the Environmental Protection Agency shall promulgate regulations within 18 months after the enactment of the Clean Air Act Amendments of 1990 [Nov. 15, 1990] to require that all affected sources subject to Title V of the Clean Air Act [probably means Title IV of the Clean Air Act as added by Pub. L. No. 101–549, which is codified as section 7651 et seq. of this title] shall also monitor carbon dioxide emissions according to the same timetable as in section 511(b) and (c) [probably means section 412(b) and (c) of the Clean Air Act, which is codified as section 7651k(b) and (c) of this title]. The regulations shall require that such data be reported to the Administrator. The provisions of section 511(e) of Title V of the Clean Air Act [probably means section 412(e) of Title IV of the Clean Air Act, which is codified as section 7651k(e) of this title] shall apply for purposes of this section in the same manner and to the same extent as such provision applies to the monitoring and data referred to in section 511 [probably means section 412 of the Clean Air Act, which is codified as section 7651k of this title].

"(b) Public availability of carbon dioxide information.—For each unit required to monitor and provide carbon dioxide data under subsection (a), the Administrator shall compute the unit's aggregate annual total carbon dioxide emissions, incorporate such data into a computer data base, and make such aggregate annual data available to the public."

§ 7651*l*. General compliance with other provisions

[CAA § 413]

Except as expressly provided, compliance with the requirements of this subchapter shall not exempt or exclude the owner or operator of any source subject to this subchapter from compliance with any other applicable requirements of this chapter.

(July 14, 1955, c. 360, Title IV, § 413, as added by Pub. L. No. 101–549, Title IV, § 401, 104 Stat. 2625 (Nov. 15, 1990).)

HISTORICAL AND STATUTORY NOTES

Effective and Applicability Provisions

1990 Acts. Section effective Nov. 15, 1990, except as otherwise provided, see section 711(b) of Pub. L. No. 101–549, set out as a note under section 7401 of this title.

Savings Provisions

Suits, actions or proceedings commenced under this chapter as in effect prior to Nov. 15, 1990, not to abate by reason of the taking effect of amendments by Pub. L. No. 101–549, except as otherwise provided for, see section 711(a) of Pub. L. No. 101–549, set out as a note under section 7401 of this title.

§ 7651m. Enforcement

[CAA § 414]

It shall be unlawful for any person subject to this subchapter to violate any prohibition of, requirement of, or regulation promulgated pursuant to this subchapter shall be a violation of this chapter. In addition to the other requirements and prohibitions provided for in this subchapter, the operation of any affected unit to emit sulfur dioxide in excess of allowances held for such unit shall be deemed a violation, with each ton emitted in excess of allowances held constituting a separate violation.

(July 14, 1955, c. 360, Title IV, § 414, as added by Pub. L. No. 101–549, Title IV, § 401, 104 Stat. 2625 (Nov. 15, 1990).)

HISTORICAL AND STATUTORY NOTES

Effective and Applicability Provisions

1990 Acts. Section effective Nov. 15, 1990, except as otherwise provided, see section 711(b) of Pub. L. No. 101–549, set out as a note under section 7401 of this title.

Savings Provisions

Suits, actions or proceedings commenced under this chapter as in effect prior to Nov. 15, 1990, not to abate by reason of the taking effect of amendments by Pub. L. No. 101–549, except as otherwise provided for, see section 711(a) of Pub. L. No. 101–549, set out as a note under section 7401 of this title.

§ 7651n. Clean coal technology regulatory incentives

[CAA § 415]

(a) "Clean coal technology" defined

For purposes of this section, "clean coal technology" means any technology, including technologies applied at the precombustion, combustion, or post combustion stage, at a new or existing facility which will achieve significant reductions in air emissions of sulfur dioxide or oxides of nitrogen associated with the utilization of coal in the generation of electricity, process steam, or industrial products, which is not in widespread use as of November 15, 1990.

(b) Revised regulations for clean coal technology demonstrations

(1) Applicability

This subsection applies to physical or operational changes to existing facilities for the sole purpose of installation, operation, cessation, or removal of a temporary or permanent clean coal technology demonstration project. For the purposes of this section, a clean coal technology demonstration project shall mean a project using funds appropriated under the heading "Department of Energy—Clean Coal Technology", up to a total amount of $2,500,000,000 for commercial demonstration of clean coal technology, or similar projects funded through appropriations for the Environmental Protection Agency. The Federal contribution for a qualifying project shall be at least 20 percent of the total cost of the demonstration project.

(2) Temporary projects

Installation, operation, cessation, or removal of a temporary clean coal technology demonstration project that is operated for a period of five years or less, and which complies with the State implementation plans for the State in which the project is located and other requirements necessary to attain and maintain the national ambient air quality standards during and after the project is terminated, shall not subject such facility to the requirements of section 7411 of this title or part C or D of subchapter I of this chapter.

(3) Permanent projects

For permanent clean coal technology demonstration projects that constitute repowering as defined in section 7651a(1)[1] of this title, any qualifying project shall not be subject to standards of performance under section 7411 of this title or to the review and permitting requirements of part C for any pollutant the potential emissions of which will not increase as a result of the demonstration project.

(4) EPA regulations

Not later than 12 months after November 15, 1990, the Administrator shall promulgate regulations or interpretive rulings to revise requirements under section 7411 of this title and parts C and D, as appropriate, to facilitate projects consistent in[2] this subsection. With respect to parts C and D, such regulations or rulings shall apply to all areas in which EPA is the permitting authority. In those instances in which the State is the permitting authority under part C or D, any State may adopt and submit to the Administrator for approval revisions to its implementation plan to apply the regulations or rulings promulgated under this subsection.

(c) Exemption for reactivation of very clean units

Physical changes or changes in the method of operation associated with the commencement of commercial operations by a coal-fired utility unit after a period of discontinued operation shall not subject the unit to the requirements of section 7411 of this title or part C of the Act where the unit (1) has not been in operation for the two-year period prior to the enactment of the Clean Air Act Amendments of 1990 [November 15, 1990], and the emissions from such unit continue to be carried in the permitting authority's emissions inventory at the time of enactment, (2) was equipped prior to shut-down with a continuous system of emissions control that achieves a removal efficiency for sulfur dioxide of no less than 85 percent and a removal efficiency for particulates of no less than 98 percent, (3) is equipped with low-NO_x burners prior to the time of commencement, and (4) is otherwise in compliance with the requirements of this chapter.

(July 14, 1955, c. 360, Title IV, § 415, as added by Pub. L. No. 101–549, Title IV, § 401, 104 Stat. 2625 (Nov. 15, 1990).)

[1] So in original. Probably should be section "7651a(12)."

[2] So in original. Probably should be "with."

HISTORICAL AND STATUTORY NOTES

References in Text

Parts C and D and part C of the Act, referred to in subsecs. (b)(3), (4) and (c), probably mean parts C and D of subchapter I of this chapter.

Effective and Applicability Provisions

1990 Acts. Section effective Nov. 15, 1990, except as otherwise provided, see section 711(b) of Pub. L. No. 101–549, set out as a note under section 7401 of this title.

Savings Provisions

Suits, actions or proceedings commenced under this chapter as in effect prior to Nov. 15, 1990, not to abate by reason of the taking effect of amendments by Pub. L. No. 101–549, except as otherwise provided for, see section 711(a) of Pub. L. No. 101–549, set out as a note under section 7401 of this title.

§ 7651*o*. Contingency guarantee, auctions, reserve

[CAA § 416]

(a) Definitions

For purposes of this section—

(1) The term "independent power producer" means any person who owns or operates, in whole or in part, one or more new independent power production facilities.

(2) The term "new independent power production facility" means a facility that—

(A) is used for the generation of electric energy, 80 percent or more of which is sold at wholesale;

(B) is nonrecourse project-financed (as such term is defined by the Secretary of Energy within 3 months of November 15, 1990);

(C) does not generate electric energy sold to any affiliate (as defined in section 79b(a)(11) of Title 15) of the facility's owner or operator unless the owner or operator of the facility demonstrates that it cannot obtain allowances from the affiliate; and

(D) is a new unit required to hold allowances under this subchapter.

(3) The term "required allowances" means the allowances required to operate such unit for so much of the unit's useful life as occurs after January 1, 2000.

(b) Special reserve of allowances

Within 36 months after November 15, 1990, the Administrator shall promulgate regulations establishing a Special Allowance Reserve containing allowances to be sold under this section. For purposes of establishing the Special Allowance Reserve, the Administrator shall withhold—

(1) 2.8 percent of the allocation of allowances for each year from 1995 through 1999 inclusive; and

(2) 2.8 percent of the basic Phase II allowance allocation of allowances for each year beginning in the year 2000

which would (but for this subsection) be issued for each affected unit at an affected source. The Administrator shall record such withholding for purposes of transferring the proceeds of the allowance sales under this subsection. The allowances so withheld shall be deposited in the Reserve under this section.

(c) Direct sale at $1,500 per ton

(1) Subaccount for direct sales

In accordance with regulations under this section, the Administrator shall establish a Direct Sale Subaccount in the Special Allowance Reserve established under this section. The Direct Sale Subaccount shall contain allowances in the amount of 50,000 tons per year for each year beginning in the year 2000.

(2) Sales

Allowances in the subaccount shall be offered for direct sale to any person at the times and in the amounts specified in table 1 at a price of $1,500 per allowance, adjusted by the Consumer Price Index in the same manner as provided in paragraph (3). Requests to purchase allowances from the Direct Sale Subaccount established under paragraph (1) shall be approved in the order of receipt until no allowances remain in such subaccount, except that an opportunity to purchase such allowances shall be provided to the independent power producers referred to in this subsection before such allowances are offered to any other person. Each applicant shall be required to pay 50 percent of the total purchase price of the allowances within 6 months after the approval of the request to purchase. The remainder shall be paid on or before the transfer of the allowances.

TABLE 1—NUMBER OF ALLOWANCES AVAILABLE FOR SALE AT $1,500 PER TON

Year of Sale	Spot Sale (same year)	Advance Sale
1993–1999	....	25,000
2000 and after	25,000	25,000

Allowances sold in the spot sale in any year are allowances which may only be used in that year (unless banked for use in a later year). Allowances sold in the advance sale in any year are allowances which may only be used in the 7th year after the year in which they are first offered for sale (unless banked for use in a later year).

(3) Entitlement to written guarantee

Any independent power producer that submits an application to the Administrator establishing that such independent power producer—

(A) proposes to construct a new independent power production facility for which allowances are required under this subchapter;

(B) will apply for financing to construct such facility after January 1, 1990, and before the date of the first auction under this section;

(C) has submitted to each owner or operator of an affected unit listed in table A (in section 7651c of this title) a written offer to purchase the required allowances for $750 per ton; and

(D) has not received (within 180 days after submitting offers to purchase under subparagraph (C)) an acceptance of the offer to purchase the required allowances, shall, within 30 days after submission of such application, be entitled to receive the Administrator's written guarantee (subject to the eligibility requirements set forth in paragraph (4)) that such required allowances will be made available for purchase from the Direct Sale Subaccount established under this subsection and at a guaranteed price. The guaranteed price at which such allowances shall be made available for purchase shall be $1,500 per ton, adjusted by the percentage, if any, by which the Consumer Price Index (as determined under section 7661a(b)(3)(B)(v) of this title) for the year in which the allowance is purchased exceeds the Consumer Price Index for the calendar year 1990.

(4) Eligibility requirements

The guarantee issued by the Administrator under paragraph (3) shall be subject to a demonstration by the independent power producer, satisfactory to the Administrator, that—

(A) the independent power producer has—

(i) made good faith efforts to purchase the required allowances from the owners or operators of affected units to which allowances will be allocated, including efforts to purchase at annual auctions under this section, and from industrial sources that have elected to become affected units pursuant to section 7651i of this title; and

(ii) such bids and efforts were unsuccessful in obtaining the required allowances; and

(B) the independent power producer will continue to make good faith efforts to purchase the required allowances from the owners or operators of affected units and from industrial sources.

(5) Issuance of guaranteed allowances from Direct Sale Subaccount under this section

From the allowances available in the Direct Sale Subaccount established under this subsection, upon payment of the guaranteed price, the Administrator shall issue to any person exercising the right to purchase allowances pursuant to a guarantee under this subsection the allowances covered by such guarantee. Persons to which guarantees under this subsection have been issued shall have the opportunity to purchase allowances pursuant to such guarantee from such subaccount before the allowances in such reserve are offered for sale to any other person.

(6) Proceeds

Notwithstanding section 3302 of Title 31 or any other provision of law, the Administrator shall require that the proceeds of any sale under this subsection be transferred, within 90 days after the sale, without charge, on a pro rata basis to the owners or operators of the affected units from whom the allowances were withheld under subsection (b) of this section and that any unsold allowances be transferred to the Subaccount for Auction Sales established under subsection (d) of this section. No proceeds of any sale under this subsection shall be held by any officer or employee of the United States or treated for any purpose as revenue to the United States or to the Administrator.

(7) Termination of subaccount

If the Administrator determines that, during any period of 2 consecutive calendar years, less than 20 percent of the allowances available in the subaccount for direct sales established under this subsection have been purchased under this paragraph, the Administrator shall terminate the subaccount and transfer such allowances to the Auction Subaccount under subsection (d) of this section.

(d) Auction sales

(1) Subaccount for auctions

The Administrator shall establish an Auction Subaccount in the Special Reserve established under this section. The Auction Subaccount shall contain allowances to be sold at auction under this section in the amount of 150,000 tons per year for each year from 1995 through 1999, inclusive and 250,000 tons per year for each year beginning in the calendar year 2000.

(2) Annual auctions

Commencing in 1993 and in each year thereafter, the Administrator shall conduct auctions at which the allowances referred to in paragraph (1) shall be offered for sale in accordance with regulations promulgated by the Administrator, in consultation with the Secretary of the Treasury, within 12 months of November 15, 1990. The allowances referred to in paragraph (1) shall be offered for sale at auction in the amounts specified in table 2. The auction shall be open to any person. A person wishing to bid for such allowances shall submit (by a date set by the Administrator) to the Administrator (on a sealed bid schedule provided by the Administrator) offers to purchase specified numbers of allowances at specified prices. Such regulations shall specify that the auctioned allowances shall be allocated and sold on the basis of bid price, starting with the highest-priced bid and continuing until all allowances for sale at such auction have been allocated. The regulations shall not permit that a minimum price be set for the purchase of withheld allowances. Allowances purchased at the auction may be used for any purpose and at any time after the auction, subject to the provisions of this subchapter.

TABLE 2—NUMBER OF ALLOWANCES AVAILABLE FOR AUCTION

Year of Sale	Spot Auction (same year)	Advance Auction
1993	50,000*	100,000
1994	50,000*	100,000
1995	50,000*	100,000
1996	150,000	100,000
1997	150,000	100,000
1998	150,000	100,000
1999	150,000	100,000
2000 and after	100,000	100,000

Allowances sold in the spot sale in any year are allowances which may only be used in that year (unless banked for use in a later year), except as otherwise noted. Allowances sold in the advance auction in any year are allowances which may only be used in the 7th year after the year in which they are first offered for sale (unless banked for use in a later year).

* Available for use only in 1995 (unless banked for use in a later year).

(3) Proceeds

(A) Notwithstanding section 3302 of Title 31 or any other provision of law, within 90 days of receipt, the Administrator shall transfer the proceeds from the auction under this section, on a pro rata basis, to the owners or operators of the affected units at an affected source from whom allowances were withheld under subsection (b) of this section. No funds transferred from a purchaser to a seller of allowances under this paragraph shall be held by any officer or employee of the United States or treated for any purpose as revenue to the United States or the Administrator.

(B) At the end of each year, any allowances offered for sale but not sold at the auction shall be returned without charge, on a pro rata basis, to the owner or operator of the affected units from whose allocation the allowances were withheld.

(4) Additional auction participants

Any person holding allowances or to whom allowances are allocated by the Administrator may submit those allowances to the Administrator to be offered for sale at auction under this subsection. The proceeds of any such sale shall be transferred at the time of sale by the purchaser to the person submitting such allowances for sale. The holder of allowances offered for sale under this paragraph may specify a minimum sale price. Any person may purchase allowances offered for auction under this paragraph. Such allowances shall be allocated and sold to purchasers on the basis of bid price after the auction under paragraph (2) is complete. No funds transferred from a purchaser to a seller of allowances under this paragraph shall be held by any officer or employee of the United States or treated for any purpose as revenue to the United States or the Administrator.

(5) Recording by EPA

The Administrator shall record and publicly report the nature, prices and results of each auction under this subsection, including the prices of successful bids, and shall record the transfers of allowances as a result of each auction in accordance with the requirements of this section. The transfer of allowances at such auction shall be recorded in accordance with the regulations promulgated by the Administrator under this subchapter.

(e) Changes in sales, auctions, and withholding

Pursuant to rulemaking after public notice and comment the Administrator may at any time after the year 1998 (in the case of advance sales or advance auctions) and 2005 (in the case of spot sales or spot auctions) decrease the number of allowances withheld and sold under this section.

(f) Termination of auctions

The Administrator may terminate the withholding of allowances and the auction sales under this section if the Administrator determines that, during any period of 3 consecutive calendar years after 2002, less than 20 percent of the allowances available in the auction subaccount have been purchased. Pursuant to regulations under this section, the Administrator may by delegation or contract provide for the conduct of sales or auctions under the Administrator's supervision by other departments or agencies of the United States Government or by nongovernmental agencies, groups, or organizations.

(July 14, 1955, c. 360, Title IV, § 416, as added by Pub. L. No. 101–549, Title IV, § 401, 104 Stat. 2626 (Nov. 15, 1990).)

HISTORICAL AND STATUTORY NOTES

Effective and Applicability Provisions

1990 Acts. Section effective Nov. 15, 1990, except as otherwise provided, see section 711(b) of Pub. L. No. 101–549, set out as a note under section 7401 of this title.

Savings Provisions

Suits, actions or proceedings commenced under this chapter as in effect prior to Nov. 15, 1990, not to abate by reason of the taking effect of amendments by Pub. L. No. 101–549, except as otherwise provided for, see section 711(a) of Pub. L. No. 101–549, set out as a note under section 7401 of this title.

SUBCHAPTER V—PERMITS

§ 7661. Definitions

[CAA § 501]

As used in this subchapter—

(1) Affected source

The term "affected source" shall have the meaning given such term in subchapter IV-A of this chapter.

(2) Major source

The term "major source" means any stationary source (or any group of stationary sources located within a contiguous area and under common control) that is either of the following:

(A) A major source as defined in section 7412 of this title.

(B) A major stationary source as defined in section 7602 of this title or part D of subchapter I of this chapter.

(3) Schedule of compliance

The term "schedule of compliance" means a schedule of remedial measures, including an enforceable sequence of actions or operations, leading to compliance with an applicable implementation plan, emission standard, emission limitation, or emission prohibition.

(4) Permitting authority

The term "permitting authority" means the Administrator or the air pollution control agency authorized by the Administrator to carry out a permit program under this subchapter.

(July 14, 1955, c. 360, Title V, § 501, as added by Pub. L. No. 101–549, Title V, § 501, 104 Stat. 2635 (Nov. 15, 1990).)

HISTORICAL AND STATUTORY NOTES

Effective and Applicability Provisions

1990 Acts. Section effective Nov. 15, 1990, except as otherwise provided, see section 711(b) of Pub. L. No. 101–549, set out as a note under section 7401 of this title.

Savings Provisions

Suits, actions or proceedings commenced under this chapter as in effect prior to Nov. 15, 1990, not to abate by reason of the taking effect of amendments by Pub. L. No. 101–549, except as otherwise provided for, see section 711(a) of Pub. L. No. 101–549, set out as a note under section 7401 of this title.

Prohibitions on Requiring Title V Permits for Greenhouse Gas Emissions from Agriculture

Section 436 of Pub. L. No. 116–260, 134 Stat. 1546 (Dec. 27, 2020), provided that: "Notwithstanding any other provision of law, none of the funds made available in this Act or any other Act may be used to promulgate or implement any regulation requiring the issuance of permits under title V of the Clean Air Act (42 U.S.C. 7661 et seq.) for carbon dioxide, nitrous oxide, water vapor, or methane emissions resulting from biological processes associated with livestock production." In addition, Section 437 of the same law provided that "[n]otwithstanding any other provision of law, none of the funds made available in this or any other Act may be used to implement any provision in a rule, if that provision requires mandatory reporting of greenhouse gas emissions from manure management systems."

Section 437 of Pub. L. No. 116–94, 133 Stat. 2751 (Dec. 20, 2019), provided:

> "Notwithstanding any other provision of law, none of the funds made available in this Act or any other Act may be used to promulgate or implement any regulation requiring the issuance of permits under title V of the Clean Air Act (42 U.S.C. 7661 et seq.) for carbon dioxide, nitrous oxide, water vapor, or methane emissions resulting from biological processes associated with livestock production."

In addition, Section 438 of the same law provided that "[n]otwithstanding any other provision of law, none of the funds made available in this or any other Act may be used to implement any provision in a rule, if that provision requires mandatory reporting of greenhouse gas emissions from manure management systems."

Section 416 of Pub. L. No. 116–6, 133 Stat. 262 (Feb. 15, 2019), provided:

> "Notwithstanding any other provision of law, none of the funds made available in this Act or any other Act may be used to promulgate or implement any regulation requiring the issuance of permits under title V of the Clean Air Act (42 U.S.C. 7661 et seq.) for carbon dioxide, nitrous oxide, water vapor, or methane emissions resulting from biological processes associated with livestock production."

In addition, Section 417 of the same law provided that "[n]otwithstanding any other provision of law, none of the funds made available in this or any other Act may be used to implement any provision in a rule, if that provision requires mandatory reporting of greenhouse gas emissions from manure management systems."

Section 117 of Pub. L. 115–31, 131 Stat. 498 (May 5, 2017), provided:

> "Notwithstanding any other provision of law, none of the funds made available in this Act or any other Act may be used to promulgate or implement any regulation requiring the issuance of permits under title V of the Clean Air Act (42 U.S.C. 7661 et seq.) for carbon dioxide, nitrous oxide, water vapor, or methane emissions resulting from biological processes associated with livestock production." Section 118 of the same Public Law provided in addition: "Notwithstanding any other provision of law, none of the funds made available in this or any other Act may be used to implement any provision in a rule, if that provision requires mandatory reporting of greenhouse gas emissions from manure management systems."

§ 7661a. Permit programs

[CAA § 502]

(a) Violations

After the effective date of any permit program approved or promulgated under this subchapter, it shall be unlawful for any person to violate any requirement of a permit issued under this subchapter, or to operate an affected source (as provided in subchapter IV-A of this chapter), a major source, any other source (including an area source) subject to standards or regulations under section 7411 or 7412 of this title, any other source required to have a permit under parts[1] C or D of subchapter I of this chapter, or any other stationary source in a category designated (in whole or in part) by regulations promulgated by the Administrator (after notice and public comment) which shall include a finding setting forth the basis for such designation, except in compliance with a permit issued by a permitting authority under this subchapter. (Nothing in this subsection shall be construed to alter the applicable requirements of this chapter that a permit be obtained before construction or modification.) The Administrator may, in the Administrator's discretion and consistent with the applicable provisions of this chapter, promulgate regulations to exempt one or more source categories (in whole or in part) from the requirements of this subsection if the Administrator finds that compliance with such requirements is impracticable, infeasible, or unnecessarily burdensome on such categories, except that the Administrator may not exempt any major source from such requirements.

(b) Regulations

The Administrator shall promulgate within 12 months after November 15, 1990, regulations establishing the minimum elements of a permit program to be administered by any air pollution control agency. These elements shall include each of the following:

(1) Requirements for permit applications, including a standard application form and criteria for determining in a timely fashion the completeness of applications.

(2) Monitoring and reporting requirements.

(3) **(A)** A requirement under State or local law or interstate compact that the owner or operator of all sources subject to the requirement to obtain a permit under this subchapter pay an annual fee, or the equivalent over some other period, sufficient to cover all reasonable (direct and indirect) costs required to develop and administer the permit program requirements of this subchapter, including section 7661f of this title, including the reasonable costs of—

(i) reviewing and acting upon any application for such a permit,

(ii) if the owner or operator receives a permit for such source, whether before or after November 15, 1990, implementing and enforcing the terms and conditions of any such permit (not including any court costs or other costs associated with any enforcement action),

(iii) emissions and ambient monitoring,

(iv) preparing generally applicable regulations, or guidance,

(v) modeling, analyses, and demonstrations, and

(vi) preparing inventories and tracking emissions.

(B) The total amount of fees collected by the permitting authority shall conform to the following requirements:

(i) The Administrator shall not approve a program as meeting the requirements of this paragraph unless the State demonstrates that, except as otherwise provided in subparagraphs (ii) through (v) of this subparagraph, the program will result in the collection, in the aggregate, from all sources subject to subparagraph (A), of an amount not less than $25 per ton of each regulated pollutant, or such other amount as the Administrator may determine adequately reflects the reasonable costs of the permit program.

(ii) As used in this subparagraph, the term "regulated pollutant" shall mean (I) a volatile organic compound; (II) each pollutant regulated under section 7411 or 7412 of this title; and (III) each pollutant for which a national primary ambient air quality standard has been promulgated (except that carbon monoxide shall be excluded from this reference).

(iii) In determining the amount under clause (i), the permitting authority is not required to include any amount of regulated pollutant emitted by any source in excess of 4,000 tons per year of that regulated pollutant.

(iv) The requirements of clause (i) shall not apply if the permitting authority demonstrates that collecting an amount less than the amount specified under clause (i) will meet the requirements of subparagraph (A).

(v) The fee calculated under clause (i) shall be increased (consistent with the need to cover the reasonable costs authorized by subparagraph (A)) in each year beginning after 1990, by the percentage, if any, by which the Consumer Price Index for the most recent calendar year ending before the beginning of such year exceeds the Consumer Price Index for the calendar year 1989. For purposes of this clause—

(I) the Consumer Price Index for any calendar year is the average of the Consumer Price Index for all-urban consumers published by the Department of Labor, as of the close of the 12-month period ending on August 31 of each calendar year, and

(II) the revision of the Consumer Price Index which is most consistent with the Consumer Price Index for calendar year 1989 shall be used.

(C) (i) If the Administrator determines, under subsection (d) of this section, that the fee provisions of the operating permit program do not meet the requirements of this paragraph, or if the Administrator makes a determination, under subsection (i) of this section, that the permitting authority is not adequately administering or enforcing an approved fee program, the Administrator may, in addition to taking any other action authorized under this subchapter, collect reasonable fees from the sources identified under subparagraph (A). Such fees shall be designed solely to cover the Administrator's costs of administering the provisions of the permit program promulgated by the Administrator.

(ii) Any source that fails to pay fees lawfully imposed by the Administrator under this subparagraph shall pay a penalty of 50 percent of the fee amount, plus interest on the fee amount computed in accordance with section 6621(a)(2) of Title 26 (relating to computation of interest on underpayment of Federal taxes).

(iii) Any fees, penalties, and interest collected under this subparagraph shall be deposited in a special fund in the United States Treasury for licensing and other services, which thereafter shall be available for appropriation, to remain available until expended, subject to appropriation, to carry out the Agency's activities for which the fees were collected. Any fee required to be collected by a State, local, or interstate agency under this subsection shall be utilized solely to cover all reasonable (direct and indirect) costs required to support the permit program as set forth in subparagraph (A).

(4) Requirements for adequate personnel and funding to administer the program.

(5) A requirement that the permitting authority have adequate authority to:

(A) issue permits and assure compliance by all sources required to have a permit under this subchapter with each applicable standard, regulation or requirement under this chapter;

(B) issue permits for a fixed term, not to exceed 5 years;

(C) assure that upon issuance or renewal permits incorporate emission limitations and other requirements in an applicable implementation plan;

(D) terminate, modify, or revoke and reissue permits for cause;

(E) enforce permits, permit fee requirements, and the requirement to obtain a permit, including authority to recover civil penalties in a maximum amount of not less than $10,000 per day for each violation, and provide appropriate criminal penalties; and

(F) assure that no permit will be issued if the Administrator objects to its issuance in a timely manner under this subchapter.

(6) Adequate, streamlined, and reasonable procedures for expeditiously determining when applications are complete, for processing such applications, for public notice, including offering an opportunity for public comment and a hearing, and for expeditious review of permit actions, including applications, renewals, or revisions, and including an opportunity for judicial review in State court of the final permit action by the applicant, any person who participated in the public comment process, and any other person who could obtain judicial review of that action under applicable law.

(7) To ensure against unreasonable delay by the permitting authority, adequate authority and procedures to provide that a failure of such permitting authority to act on a permit application or permit renewal application (in accordance with the time periods specified in section 7661b of this title or, as appropriate, subchapter IV-A of this chapter) shall be treated as a final permit action solely for purposes of obtaining judicial review in State court of an action brought by any person referred to in paragraph (6) to require that action be taken by the permitting authority on such application without additional delay.

(8) Authority, and reasonable procedures consistent with the need for expeditious action by the permitting authority on permit applications and related matters, to make available to the public any permit application, compliance plan, permit, and monitoring or compliance report under section 7661b(e) of this title, subject to the provisions of section 7414(c) of this title.

(9) A requirement that the permitting authority, in the case of permits with a term of 3 or more years for major sources, shall require revisions to the permit to incorporate applicable standards and regulations promulgated under this chapter after the issuance of such permit. Such revisions shall occur as expeditiously as practicable and consistent with the procedures established under paragraph (6) but not later than 18 months after the promulgation of such standards and regulations. No such revision shall be required if the effective date of the standards or regulations is a date after the expiration of the permit term. Such permit revision shall be treated as a permit renewal if it complies with the requirements of this subchapter regarding renewals.

(10) Provisions to allow changes within a permitted facility (or one operating pursuant to section 7661b(d) of this title) without requiring a permit revision, if the changes are not modifications under any provision of subchapter I of this chapter and the changes do not exceed the emissions allowable under the permit (whether expressed therein as a rate of emissions or in terms of total emissions:[2] *Provided,* That the facility provides the Administrator and the permitting authority with written notification in advance of the proposed changes which shall be a minimum of 7 days, unless the permitting authority provides in its regulations a different timeframe for emergencies.

(c) Single permit

A single permit may be issued for a facility with multiple sources.

(d) Submission and approval

(1) Not later than 3 years after November 15, 1990, the Governor of each State shall develop and submit to the Administrator a permit program under State or local law or under an interstate compact meeting the requirements of this subchapter. In addition, the Governor shall submit a legal opinion from the attorney general (or the attorney for those State air pollution control agencies that have independent legal counsel), or from the chief legal officer of an interstate agency, that the laws of the State, locality, or the interstate compact provide adequate authority to carry out the program. Not later than 1 year after receiving a program, and after notice and opportunity for public comment, the Administrator shall approve or disapprove such program, in whole or in part. The Administrator may approve a program to the extent that the program meets the requirements of this chapter, including the regulations issued under subsection (b) of this section. If the program is disapproved, in whole or in part, the Administrator shall notify the Governor of any revisions or modifications necessary to obtain approval. The Governor shall revise and resubmit the program for review under this section within 180 days after receiving notification.

(2) **(A)** If the Governor does not submit a program as required under paragraph (1) or if the Administrator disapproves a program submitted by the Governor under paragraph (1), in whole or in part, the Administrator may, prior to the expiration of the 18-month period referred to in subparagraph (B), in the Administrator's discretion, apply any of the sanctions specified in section 7509(b) of this title.

(B) If the Governor does not submit a program as required under paragraph (1), or if the Administrator disapproves any such program submitted by the Governor under paragraph (1), in whole or in part, 18 months after the date required for such submittal or the date of such disapproval, as the case may be, the Administrator shall apply sanctions under section 7509(b) of this title in the same manner and subject to the same deadlines and other conditions as are applicable in the case of a determination, disapproval, or finding under section 7509(a) of this title.

(C) The sanctions under section 7509(b)(2) of this title shall not apply pursuant to this paragraph in any area unless the failure to submit or the disapproval referred to in subparagraph (A) or (B) relates to an air pollutant for which such area has been designated a nonattainment area (as defined in part D of subchapter I of this chapter).

(3) If a program meeting the requirements of this subchapter has not been approved in whole for any State, the Administrator shall, 2 years after the date required for submission of such a program under paragraph (1), promulgate, administer, and enforce a program under this subchapter for that State.

(e) Suspension

The Administrator shall suspend the issuance of permits promptly upon publication of notice of approval of a permit program under this section, but may, in such notice, retain jurisdiction over permits that have been federally issued, but for which the administrative or judicial review process is not complete. The Administrator shall continue to administer and enforce federally issued permits under this subchapter until they are replaced by a permit issued by a permitting program. Nothing in this subsection should be construed to limit the Administrator's ability to enforce permits issued by a State.

(f) Prohibition

No partial permit program shall be approved unless, at a minimum, it applies, and ensures compliance with, this subchapter and each of the following:

(1) All requirements established under subchapter IV-A of this chapter applicable to "affected sources".

(2) All requirements established under section 7412 of this title applicable to "major sources", "area sources," and "new sources".

(3) All requirements of subchapter I of this chapter (other than section 7412 of this title) applicable to sources required to have a permit under this subchapter.

Approval of a partial program shall not relieve the State of its obligation to submit a complete program, nor from the application of any sanctions under this chapter for failure to submit an approvable permit program.

(g) Interim approval

If a program (including a partial permit program) submitted under this subchapter substantially meets the requirements of this subchapter, but is not fully approvable, the Administrator may by rule grant the program interim approval. In the notice of final rulemaking, the Administrator shall specify the changes that must be made before the program can receive full approval. An interim approval under this subsection shall expire on a date set by the Administrator not later than 2 years after such approval, and may not be renewed. For the period of any such interim approval, the provisions of subsection (d)(2) of this section, and the obligation of the Administrator to promulgate a program under this subchapter for the State pursuant to subsection (d)(3) of this section, shall be suspended. Such provisions and such obligation of the Administrator shall apply after the expiration of such interim approval.

(h) Effective date

The effective date of a permit program, or partial or interim program, approved under this subchapter, shall be the effective date of approval by the Administrator. The effective date of a permit program, or partial permit program, promulgated by the Administrator shall be the date of promulgation.

(i) Administration and enforcement

(1) Whenever the Administrator makes a determination that a permitting authority is not adequately administering and enforcing a program, or portion thereof, in accordance with the requirements of this subchapter, the Administrator shall provide notice to the State and may, prior to the expiration of the 18-month period referred to in paragraph (2), in the Administrator's discretion, apply any of the sanctions specified in section 7509(b) of this title.

(2) Whenever the Administrator makes a determination that a permitting authority is not adequately administering and enforcing a program, or portion thereof, in accordance with the requirements of this subchapter, 18 months after the date of the notice under paragraph (1), the Administrator shall apply the sanctions under section 7509(b) of this title in the same manner and subject to the same deadlines and other conditions as are applicable in the case of a determination, disapproval, or finding under section 7509(a) of this title.

(3) The sanctions under section 7509(b)(2) of this title shall not apply pursuant to this subsection in any area unless the failure to adequately enforce and administer the program relates to an air pollutant for which such area has been designated a nonattainment area.

(4) Whenever the Administrator has made a finding under paragraph (1) with respect to any State, unless the State has corrected such deficiency within 18 months after the date of such finding, the Administrator shall, 2 years after the date of such finding, promulgate, administer, and enforce a program under this subchapter for that State. Nothing in this paragraph shall be construed to affect the validity of a program which has been approved under this subchapter or the authority of any permitting authority acting under such program until such time as such program is promulgated by the Administrator under this paragraph.

(July 14, 1955, c. 360, Title V, § 502, as added by Pub. L. No. 101–549, Title V, § 501, 104 Stat. 2635 (Nov. 15, 1990).)

[1] So in original. Probably should be "part."

[2] So in original. A closing parenthesis probably should precede the colon.

HISTORICAL AND STATUTORY NOTES

Effective and Applicability Provisions

1990 Acts. Section effective Nov. 15, 1990, except as otherwise provided, see section 711(b) of Pub. L. No. 101–549, set out as a note under section 7401 of this title.

Savings Provisions

Suits, actions or proceedings commenced under this chapter as in effect prior to Nov. 15, 1990, not to abate by reason of the taking effect of amendments by Pub. L. No. 101–549, except as otherwise provided for, see section 711(a) of Pub. L. No. 101–549, set out as a note under section 7401 of this title.

Greenhouse Gas Permitting and Reporting

Pub. L. No. 113–76, § 419, 128 Stat. 342 (Jan. 17, 2014), provided that:

"Not later than 120 days after the date on which the President's fiscal year 2015 budget request is submitted to the Congress, the President shall submit a comprehensive report to the Committees on Appropriations of the House of Representatives and the Senate describing in detail all Federal agency funding, domestic and international, for climate change programs, projects, and activities in fiscal years 2013 and 2014, including an accounting of funding by agency with each agency identifying climate change programs, projects, and activities and associated costs by line item as presented in the President's Budget Appendix, and including citations and linkages where practicable to each strategic plan that is driving funding within each climate change program, project, and activity listed in the report."

Section 420 of the same law, 128 Stat. 343, provided that:

"Notwithstanding any other provision of law, none of the funds made available in this Act or any other Act may be used to promulgate or implement any regulation requiring the issuance of permits under title V of the Clean Air Act (42 U.S.C. 7661 et seq.) for carbon dioxide, nitrous oxide, water vapor, or methane emissions resulting from biological processes associated with livestock production."

Finally, Section 421 of the same law, 128 Stat. 343, provided that:

"Notwithstanding any other provision of law, none of the funds made available in this or any other Act may be used to implement any provision in a rule, if that provision requires mandatory reporting of greenhouse gas emissions from manure management systems."

Similarly, Pub. L. No. 113–235, § 418, 128 Stat. 2448 (Dec. 16, 2014), provided that:

"Not later than 120 days after the date on which the President's fiscal year 2016 budget request is submitted to the Congress, the President shall submit a comprehensive report to the Committees on Appropriations of the House of Representatives and the Senate describing in detail all Federal agency funding, domestic and international, for climate change programs, projects, and activities in fiscal years 2014 and 2015, including an accounting of funding by agency with each agency identifying climate change programs, projects, and activities and associated costs by line item as presented in the President's Budget Appendix, and including citations and linkages where practicable to each strategic plan that is driving funding within each climate change program, project, and activity listed in the report."

Section 419 of the same law, 128 Stat. 2448, provided that:

"Notwithstanding any other provision of law, none of the funds made available in this Act or any other Act may be used to promulgate or implement any regulation requiring the issuance of permits under title V of the Clean Air Act (42 U.S.C. 7661 et seq.) for carbon dioxide, nitrous oxide, water vapor, or methane emissions resulting from biological processes associated with livestock production."

Finally, section 420 of the same law, 128 Stat. 2448–2449, provided that:

"Notwithstanding any other provision of law, none of the funds made available in this or any other Act may be used to implement any provision in a rule, if that provision requires mandatory reporting of greenhouse gas emissions from manure management systems."

§ 7661b. Permit applications

[CAA § 503]

(a) Applicable date

Any source specified in section 7661a(a) of this title shall become subject to a permit program, and required to have a permit, on the later of the following dates—

(1) the effective date of a permit program or partial or interim permit program applicable to the source; or

(2) the date such source becomes subject to section 7661a(a) of this title.

(b) Compliance plan

(1) The regulations required by section 7661a(b) of this title shall include a requirement that the applicant submit with the permit application a compliance plan describing how the source will comply with all applicable requirements under this chapter. The compliance plan shall include a schedule of compliance, and a schedule under which the permittee will submit progress reports to the permitting authority no less frequently than every 6 months.

(2) The regulations shall further require the permittee to periodically (but no less frequently than annually) certify that the facility is in compliance with any applicable requirements of the permit, and to promptly report any deviations from permit requirements to the permitting authority.

(c) Deadline

Any person required to have a permit shall, not later than 12 months after the date on which the source becomes subject to a permit program approved or promulgated under this subchapter, or such earlier date as the permitting authority may establish, submit to the permitting authority a compliance plan and an application for a permit signed by a responsible official, who shall certify the accuracy of the information submitted. The permitting authority shall approve or disapprove a completed application (consistent with the procedures established under this subchapter for consideration of such applications), and shall issue or deny the permit, within 18 months after the date of receipt thereof, except that the permitting authority shall establish a phased schedule for acting on permit applications submitted within the first full year after the effective date of a permit program (or a partial or interim program). Any such schedule shall assure that at least one-third of such permits will be acted on by such authority annually over a period of not to exceed 3 years after such effective date. Such authority shall establish reasonable procedures to prioritize such approval or disapproval actions in the case of applications for construction or modification under the applicable requirements of this chapter.

(d) Timely and complete applications

Except for sources required to have a permit before construction or modification under the applicable requirements of this chapter, if an applicant has submitted a timely and complete application for a permit required by this subchapter (including renewals), but final action has not been taken on such application, the source's failure to have a permit shall not be a violation of this chapter, unless the delay in final action was due to the failure of the applicant timely to submit information required or requested to process the application. No source required to have a permit under this subchapter shall be in violation of section 7661a(a) of this title before the date on which the source is required to submit an application under subsection (c) of this section.

(e) Copies; availability

A copy of each permit application, compliance plan (including the schedule of compliance), emissions or compliance monitoring report, certification, and each permit issued under this subchapter, shall be available to the public. If an applicant or permittee is required to submit information entitled to protection from disclosure under section 7414(c) of this title, the applicant or permittee may submit such information separately. The requirements of section 7414(c) of this title shall apply to such information. The contents of a permit shall not be entitled to protection under section 7414(c) of this title.

(July 14, 1955, c. 360, Title V, § 503, as added by Pub. L. No. 101–549, Title V, § 501, 104 Stat. 2641 (Nov. 15, 1990).)

HISTORICAL AND STATUTORY NOTES

Effective and Applicability Provisions

1990 Acts. Section effective Nov. 15, 1990, except as otherwise provided, see section 711(b) of Pub. L. No. 101–549, set out as a note under section 7401 of this title.

Savings Provisions

Suits, actions or proceedings commenced under this chapter as in effect prior to Nov. 15, 1990, not to abate by reason of the taking effect of amendments by Pub. L. No. 101–549, except as otherwise provided for, see section 711(a) of Pub. L. No. 101–549, set out as a note under section 7401 of this title.

§ 7661c. Permit requirements and conditions

[CAA § 504]

(a) Conditions

Each permit issued under this subchapter shall include enforceable emission limitations and standards, a schedule of compliance, a requirement that the permittee submit to the permitting authority, no less often than every 6 months, the results of any required monitoring, and such other conditions as are necessary to assure compliance with applicable requirements of this chapter, including the requirements of the applicable implementation plan.

(b) Monitoring and analysis

The Administrator may by rule prescribe procedures and methods for determining compliance and for monitoring and analysis of pollutants regulated under this chapter, but continuous emissions monitoring need not be required if alternative methods are available that provide sufficiently reliable and timely information for determining compliance. Nothing in this subsection shall be construed to affect any continuous emissions monitoring requirement of subchapter IV-A of this chapter, or where required elsewhere in this chapter.

(c) Inspection, entry, monitoring, certification, and reporting

Each permit issued under this subchapter shall set forth inspection, entry, monitoring, compliance certification, and reporting requirements to assure compliance with the permit terms and conditions. Such monitoring and reporting requirements shall conform to any applicable regulation under subsection (b) of this section. Any report required to be submitted by a permit issued to a corporation under this subchapter shall be signed by a responsible corporate official, who shall certify its accuracy.

(d) General permits

The permitting authority may, after notice and opportunity for public hearing, issue a general permit covering numerous similar sources. Any general permit shall comply with all requirements applicable to permits under this subchapter. No source covered by a general permit shall thereby be relieved from the obligation to file an application under section 7661b of this title.

(e) Temporary sources

The permitting authority may issue a single permit authorizing emissions from similar operations at multiple temporary locations. No such permit shall be issued unless it includes conditions that will assure compliance with all the requirements of this chapter at all authorized locations, including, but not limited to, ambient standards and compliance with any applicable increment or visibility requirements under part C of subchapter I of this chapter. Any such permit shall in addition require the owner or operator to notify the permitting authority in advance of each change in location. The permitting authority may require a separate permit fee for operations at each location.

(f) Permit shield

Compliance with a permit issued in accordance with this subchapter shall be deemed compliance with section 7661a of this title. Except as otherwise provided by the Administrator by rule, the permit may also provide that compliance with the permit shall be deemed compliance with other applicable provisions of this chapter that relate to the permittee if—

(1) the permit includes the applicable requirements of such provisions, or

(2) the permitting authority in acting on the permit application makes a determination relating to the permittee that such other provisions (which shall be referred to in such determination) are not applicable and the permit includes the determination or a concise summary thereof.

Nothing in the preceding sentence shall alter or affect the provisions of section 7603 of this title, including the authority of the Administrator under that section.

(July 14, 1955, c. 360, Title V, § 504, as added by Pub. L. No. 101–549, Title V, § 501, 104 Stat. 2642 (Nov. 15, 1990).)

HISTORICAL AND STATUTORY NOTES

Effective and Applicability Provisions

1990 Acts. Section effective Nov. 15, 1990, except as otherwise provided, see section 711(b) of Pub. L. No. 101–549, set out as a note under section 7401 of this title.

Savings Provisions

Suits, actions or proceedings commenced under this chapter as in effect prior to Nov. 15, 1990, not to abate by reason of the taking effect of amendments by Pub. L. No. 101–549, except as otherwise provided for, see section 711(a) of Pub. L. No. 101–549, set out as a note under section 7401 of this title.

§ 7661d. Notification to Administrator and contiguous States

[CAA § 505]

(a) Transmission and notice

(1) Each permitting authority—

(A) shall transmit to the Administrator a copy of each permit application (and any application for a permit modification or renewal) or such portion thereof, including any compliance plan, as the Administrator may require to effectively review the application and otherwise to carry out the Administrator's responsibilities under this chapter, and

(B) shall provide to the Administrator a copy of each permit proposed to be issued and issued as a final permit.

(2) The permitting authority shall notify all States—

(A) whose air quality may be affected and that are contiguous to the State in which the emission originates, or

(B) that are within 50 miles of the source,

of each permit application or proposed permit forwarded to the Administrator under this section, and shall provide an opportunity for such States to submit written recommendations respecting the issuance of the permit and its terms and conditions. If any part of those recommendations are not accepted by the permitting authority, such authority shall notify the State submitting the recommendations and the Administrator in writing of its failure to accept those recommendations and the reasons therefor.

(b) Objection by EPA

(1) If any permit contains provisions that are determined by the Administrator as not in compliance with the applicable requirements of this chapter, including the requirements of an applicable implementation plan, the Administrator shall, in accordance with this subsection, object to its issuance. The permitting authority shall respond in writing if the Administrator (A) within 45 days after receiving a copy of the proposed permit under subsection (a)(1) of this section, or (B) within 45 days after receiving notification under subsection (a)(2) of this section, objects in writing to its issuance as not in compliance with such requirements. With the objection, the Administrator shall provide a statement of the reasons for the objection. A copy of the objection and statement shall be provided to the applicant.

(2) If the Administrator does not object in writing to the issuance of a permit pursuant to paragraph (1), any person may petition the Administrator within 60 days after the expiration of the 45-day review period specified in paragraph (1) to take such action. A copy of such petition shall be provided to the permitting authority and the applicant by the petitioner. The petition shall be based only on objections to the permit that were raised with reasonable specificity during the public comment period provided by the permitting agency (unless the petitioner demonstrates in the petition to the Administrator that it was impracticable to raise such objections within such period or unless the grounds for such objection arose after such period). The petition shall identify all such objections. If the permit has been issued by the permitting agency, such petition shall not postpone the effectiveness of the permit. The Administrator shall grant or deny such petition within 60 days after the petition is filed. The Administrator shall issue an objection within such period if the petitioner demonstrates to the Administrator that the permit is not in compliance with the requirements of this chapter, including the requirements of the applicable implementation plan. Any denial of such petition shall be subject to judicial review under section 7607 of this title. The Administrator shall include in regulations under this subchapter provisions to implement this paragraph. The Administrator may not delegate the requirements of this paragraph.

(3) Upon receipt of an objection by the Administrator under this subsection, the permitting authority may not issue the permit unless it is revised and issued in accordance with subsection (c) of this section. If the permitting authority has issued a permit prior to receipt of an objection by the Administrator under paragraph (2) of this subsection, the Administrator shall modify, terminate, or revoke such permit and the permitting authority may thereafter only issue a revised permit in accordance with subsection (c) of this section.

(c) Issuance or denial

If the permitting authority fails, within 90 days after the date of an objection under subsection (b) of this section, to submit a permit revised to meet the objection, the Administrator shall issue or deny the permit in accordance with the requirements of this subchapter. No objection shall be subject to judicial review until the Administrator takes final action to issue or deny a permit under this subsection.

(d) Waiver of notification requirements

(1) The Administrator may waive the requirements of subsections (a) and (b) of this section at the time of approval of a permit program under this subchapter for any category (including any class, type, or size within such category) of sources covered by the program other than major sources.

(2) The Administrator may, by regulation, establish categories of sources (including any class, type, or size within such category) to which the requirements of subsections (a) and (b) of this section shall not apply. The preceding sentence shall not apply to major sources.

(3) The Administrator may exclude from any waiver under this subsection notification under subsection (a)(2) of this section. Any waiver granted under this subsection may be revoked or modified by the Administrator by rule.

(e) Refusal of permitting authority to terminate, modify, or revoke and reissue

If the Administrator finds that cause exists to terminate, modify, or revoke and reissue a permit under this subchapter, the Administrator shall notify the permitting authority and the source of the Administrator's finding. The permitting authority shall, within 90 days after receipt of such notification, forward to the Administrator under this section a proposed determination of termination, modification, or revocation and reissuance, as appropriate. The Administrator may extend such 90 day period for an additional 90 days if the Administrator finds that a new or revised permit application is necessary, or that the permitting authority must require the permittee to submit additional information. The Administrator may review such proposed determination under the provisions of subsections (a) and (b) of this section. If the permitting authority fails to submit the required proposed determination, or if the Administrator objects and the permitting authority fails to resolve the objection within 90 days, the Administrator may, after notice and in accordance with fair and reasonable procedures, terminate, modify, or revoke and reissue the permit.

(July 14, 1955, c. 360, Title V, § 505, as added by Pub. L. No. 101–549, Title V, § 501, 104 Stat. 2643 (Nov. 15, 1990).)

HISTORICAL AND STATUTORY NOTES

Effective and Applicability Provisions

1990 Acts. Section effective Nov. 15, 1990, except as otherwise provided, see section 711(b) of Pub. L. No. 101–549, set out as a note under section 7401 of this title.

Savings Provisions

Suits, actions or proceedings commenced under this chapter as in effect prior to Nov. 15, 1990, not to abate by reason of the taking effect of amendments by Pub. L. No. 101–549, except as otherwise provided for, see section 711(a) of Pub. L. No. 101–549, set out as a note under section 7401 of this title.

§ 7661e. Other authorities

[CAA § 506]

(a) In general

Nothing in this subchapter shall prevent a State, or interstate permitting authority, from establishing additional permitting requirements not inconsistent with this chapter.

(b) Permits implementing acid rain provisions

The provisions of this subchapter, including provisions regarding schedules for submission and approval or disapproval of permit applications, shall apply to permits implementing the requirements of subchapter IV-A of this chapter except as modified by that subchapter.

(July 14, 1955, c. 360, Title V, § 506, as added by Pub. L. No. 101–549, Title V, § 501, 104 Stat. 2645 (Nov. 15, 1990).)

HISTORICAL AND STATUTORY NOTES

Effective and Applicability Provisions

1990 Acts. Section effective Nov. 15, 1990, except as otherwise provided, see section 711(b) of Pub. L. No. 101–549, set out as a note under section 7401 of this title.

Savings Provisions

Suits, actions or proceedings commenced under this chapter as in effect prior to Nov. 15, 1990, not to abate by reason of the taking effect of amendments by Pub. L. No. 101–549, except as otherwise provided for, see section 711(a) of Pub. L. No. 101–549, set out as a note under section 7401 of this title.

§ 7661f. Small business stationary source technical and environmental compliance assistance program

[CAA § 507]

(a) Plan revisions

Consistent with sections 7410 and 7412 of this title, each State shall, after reasonable notice and public hearings, adopt and submit to the Administrator as part of the State implementation plan for such State or as a revision to such State implementation plan under section 7410 of this title, plans for establishing a small business stationary source technical and environmental compliance assistance program. Such submission shall be made within 24 months after November 15, 1990. The Administrator shall approve such program if it includes each of the following:

(1) Adequate mechanisms for developing, collecting, and coordinating information concerning compliance methods and technologies for small business stationary sources, and programs to encourage lawful cooperation among such sources and other persons to further compliance with this chapter.

(2) Adequate mechanisms for assisting small business stationary sources with pollution prevention and accidental release detection and prevention, including providing information concerning alternative technologies, process changes, products, and methods of operation that help reduce air pollution.

(3) A designated State office within the relevant State agency to serve as ombudsman for small business stationary sources in connection with the implementation of this chapter.

(4) A compliance assistance program for small business stationary sources which assists small business stationary sources in determining applicable requirements and in receiving permits under this chapter in a timely and efficient manner.

(5) Adequate mechanisms to assure that small business stationary sources receive notice of their rights under this chapter in such manner and form as to assure reasonably adequate time for such sources to evaluate compliance methods and any relevant or applicable proposed or final regulation or standard issued under this chapter.

(6) Adequate mechanisms for informing small business stationary sources of their obligations under this chapter, including mechanisms for referring such sources to qualified auditors or, at the option of the State, for providing audits of the operations of such sources to determine compliance with this chapter.

(7) Procedures for consideration of requests from a small business stationary source for modification of—

(A) any work practice or technological method of compliance, or

(B) the schedule of milestones for implementing such work practice or method of compliance preceding any applicable compliance date,

based on the technological and financial capability of any such small business stationary source. No such modification may be granted unless it is in compliance with the applicable requirements of this chapter, including the requirements of the applicable implementation plan. Where such applicable requirements are set forth in Federal regulations, only modifications authorized in such regulations may be allowed.

(b) Program

The Administrator shall establish within 9 months after November 15, 1990, a small business stationary source technical and environmental compliance assistance program. Such program shall—

(1) assist the States in the development of the program required under subsection (a) of this section (relating to assistance for small business stationary sources);

(2) issue guidance for the use of the States in the implementation of these programs that includes alternative control technologies and pollution prevention methods applicable to small business stationary sources; and

(3) provide for implementation of the program provisions required under subsection (a)(4) of this section in any State that fails to submit such a program under that subsection.

(c) Eligibility

(1) Except as provided in paragraphs (2) and (3), for purposes of this section, the term "small business stationary source" means a stationary source that—

(A) is owned or operated by a person that employs 100 or fewer individuals,[1]

(B) is a small business concern as defined in the Small Business Act [15 U.S.C.A. § 631 et seq.];

(C) is not a major stationary source;

(D) does not emit 50 tons or more per year of any regulated pollutant; and

(E) emits less than 75 tons per year of all regulated pollutants.

(2) Upon petition by a source, the State may, after notice and opportunity for public comment, include as a small business stationary source for purposes of this section any stationary source which does not meet the criteria of subparagraphs[2] (C), (D), or (E) of paragraph (1) but which does not emit more than 100 tons per year of all regulated pollutants.

(3) (A) The Administrator, in consultation with the Administrator of the Small Business Administration and after providing notice and opportunity for public comment, may exclude from the small business stationary source definition under this section any category or subcategory of sources that the Administrator determines to have sufficient technical and financial capabilities to meet the requirements of this chapter without the application of this subsection.

(B) The State, in consultation with the Administrator and the Administrator of the Small Business Administration and after providing notice and opportunity for public hearing, may exclude from the small business stationary source definition under this section any category or subcategory of sources that the State determines to have sufficient technical and financial capabilities to meet the requirements of this chapter without the application of this subsection.

(d) Monitoring

The Administrator shall direct the Agency's Office of Small and Disadvantaged Business Utilization through the Small Business Ombudsman (hereinafter in this section referred to as the "Ombudsman") to monitor the small business stationary source technical and environmental compliance assistance program under this section. In carrying out such monitoring activities, the Ombudsman shall—

(1) render advisory opinions on the overall effectiveness of the Small Business Stationary Source Technical and Environmental Compliance Assistance Program, difficulties encountered, and degree and severity of enforcement;

(2) make periodic reports to the Congress on the compliance of the Small Business Stationary Source Technical and Environmental Compliance Assistance Program with the requirements of the Paperwork Reduction Act, the Regulatory Flexibility Act [5 U.S.C.A. § 601 et seq.], and the Equal Access to Justice Act;

(3) review information to be issued by the Small Business Stationary Source Technical and Environmental Compliance Assistance Program for small business stationary sources to ensure that the information is understandable by the layperson; and

(4) have the Small Business Stationary Source Technical and Environmental Compliance Assistance Program serve as the secretariat for the development and dissemination of such reports and advisory opinions.

(e) Compliance Advisory Panel

(1) There shall be created a Compliance Advisory Panel (hereinafter referred to as the "Panel") on the State level of not less than 7 individuals. This Panel shall—

(A) render advisory opinions concerning the effectiveness of the small business stationary source technical and environmental compliance assistance program, difficulties encountered, and degree and severity of enforcement;

(B) make periodic reports to the Administrator concerning the compliance of the State Small Business Stationary Source Technical and Environmental Compliance Assistance Program with the requirements of the Paperwork Reduction Act, the Regulatory Flexibility Act [5 U.S.C.A. § 601 et seq.], and the Equal Access to Justice Act;

(C) review information for small business stationary sources to assure such information is understandable by the layperson; and

(D) have the Small Business Stationary Source Technical and Environmental Compliance Assistance Program serve as the secretariat for the development and dissemination of such reports and advisory opinions.

(2) The Panel shall consist of—

(A) 2 members, who are not owners, or representatives of owners, of small business stationary sources, selected by the Governor to represent the general public;

(B) 2 members selected by the State legislature who are owners, or who represent owners, of small business stationary sources (1 member each by the majority and minority leadership of the lower house, or in the case of a unicameral State legislature, 2 members each shall be selected by the majority leadership and the minority leadership, respectively, of such legislature, and subparagraph (C) shall not apply);

(C) 2 members selected by the State legislature who are owners, or who represent owners, of small business stationary sources (1 member each by the majority and minority leadership of the upper house, or the equivalent State entity); and

(D) 1 member selected by the head of the department or agency of the State responsible for air pollution permit programs to represent that agency.

(f) Fees

The State (or the Administrator) may reduce any fee required under this chapter to take into account the financial resources of small business stationary sources.

(g) Continuous emission monitors

In developing regulations and CTGs under this chapter that contain continuous emission monitoring requirements, the Administrator, consistent with the requirements of this chapter, before applying such requirements to small business stationary sources, shall consider the necessity and appropriateness of such requirements for such sources. Nothing in this subsection shall affect the applicability of subchapter IV-A of this chapter provisions relating to continuous emissions monitoring.

(h) Control technique guidelines

The Administrator shall consider, consistent with the requirements of this chapter, the size, type, and technical capabilities of small business stationary sources (and sources which are eligible under subsection (c)(2) of this section to be treated as small business stationary sources) in developing CTGs applicable to such sources under this chapter.

(July 14, 1955, c. 360, Title V, § 507, as added by Pub. L. No. 101–549, Title V, § 501, 104 Stat. 2645 (Nov. 15, 1990).)

[1] So in original. The comma probably should be a semicolon.

[2] So in original. Probably should be "subparagraph."

HISTORICAL AND STATUTORY NOTES

References in Text

The Small Business Act, referred to in subsec. (c)(1)(B), is Pub. L. No. 85–536, 72 Stat. 384 (July 18, 1958), as amended, which is codified generally as chapter 14A (section 631 et seq.) of Title 15, Commerce and Trade. For complete classification of this Act to the Code, see Short Title note set out under section 631 of Title 15 and Tables.

The Paperwork Reduction Act, referred to in subsecs. (d)(2) and (e)(1)(B), probably means the Paperwork Reduction Act of 1980, Pub. L. No. 96–511, 94 Stat. 2812 (Dec. 11, 1980), as amended, which is codified principally as chapter 35 (section 3501 et seq.) of Title 44, Public Printing and Documents. For complete classification of this Act to the Code, see Short Title of 1980 Amendments note set out under section 101 of Title 44 and Tables.

The Regulatory Flexibility Act, referred to in subsecs. (d)(2) and (e)(1)(B), is Pub. L. No. 96–354, 94 Stat. 1164 (Sept. 19, 1980), which is codified generally as chapter 6 (section 601 et seq.) of Title 5, Government Organization and Employees. For complete classification of this Act to the Code, see Short Title note set out under section 601 of Title 5 and Tables.

The Equal Access to Justice Act, referred to in subsecs. (d)(2) and (e)(1)(B), is Title II of Pub. L. No. 96–481, 94 Stat. 2325 (Oct. 21, 1980). For complete classification of this Act to the Code, see Short Title note set out under section 504 of Title 5 and Tables.

Effective and Applicability Provisions

1990 Acts. Section effective Nov. 15, 1990, except as otherwise provided, see section 711(b) of Pub. L. No. 101–549, set out as a note under section 7401 of this title.

Savings Provisions

Suits, actions or proceedings commenced under this chapter as in effect prior to Nov. 15, 1990, not to abate by reason of the taking effect of amendments by Pub. L. No. 101–549, except as otherwise provided for, see section 711(a) of Pub. L. No. 101–549, set out as a note under section 7401 of this title.

SUBCHAPTER VI—STRATOSPHERIC OZONE PROTECTION

§ 7671. Definitions

[CAA § 601]

As used in this subchapter—

(1) Appliance

The term "appliance" means any device which contains and uses a class I or class II substance as a refrigerant and which is used for household or commercial purposes, including any air conditioner, refrigerator, chiller, or freezer.

(2) Baseline year

The term "baseline year" means—

(A) the calendar year 1986, in the case of any class I substance listed in Group I or II under section 7671a(a) of this title,

(B) the calendar year 1989, in the case of any class I substance listed in Group III, IV, or V under section 7671a(a) of this title, and

(C) a representative calendar year selected by the Administrator, in the case of—

(i) any substance added to the list of class I substances after the publication of the initial list under section 7671a(a) of this title, and

(ii) any class II substance.

(3) Class I substance

The term "class I substance" means each of the substances listed as provided in section 7671a(a) of this title.

(4) Class II substance

The term "class II substance" means each of the substances listed as provided in section 7671a(b) of this title.

(5) Commissioner

The term "Commissioner" means the Commissioner of the Food and Drug Administration.

(6) Consumption

The term "consumption" means, with respect to any substance, the amount of that substance produced in the United States, plus the amount imported, minus the amount exported to Parties to the Montreal Protocol. Such term shall be construed in a manner consistent with the Montreal Protocol.

(7) Import

The term "import" means to land on, bring into, or introduce into, or attempt to land on, bring into, or introduce into, any place subject to the jurisdiction of the United States, whether or not such landing, bringing, or introduction constitutes an importation within the meaning of the customs laws of the United States.

(8) Medical device

The term "medical device" means any device (as defined in the Federal Food, Drug, and Cosmetic Act (21 U.S.C. 321)), diagnostic product, drug (as defined in the Federal Food, Drug, and Cosmetic Act), and drug delivery system—

(A) if such device, product, drug, or drug delivery system utilizes a class I or class II substance for which no safe and effective alternative has been developed, and where necessary, approved by the Commissioner; and

(B) if such device, product, drug, or drug delivery system, has, after notice and opportunity for public comment, been approved and determined to be essential by the Commissioner in consultation with the Administrator.

(9) Montreal Protocol

The terms "Montreal Protocol" and "the Protocol" mean the Montreal Protocol on Substances that Deplete the Ozone Layer, a protocol to the Vienna Convention for the Protection of the Ozone Layer, including adjustments adopted by Parties thereto and amendments that have entered into force.

(10) Ozone-depletion potential

The term "ozone-depletion potential" means a factor established by the Administrator to reflect the ozone-depletion potential of a substance, on a mass per kilogram basis, as compared to chlorofluorocarbon-11 (CFC-11). Such factor shall be based upon the substance's atmospheric lifetime, the molecular weight of bromine and chlorine, and the substance's ability to be photolytically disassociated, and upon other factors determined to be an accurate measure of relative ozone-depletion potential.

(11) Produce, produced, and production

The terms "produce", "produced", and "production", refer to the manufacture of a substance from any raw material or feedstock chemical, but such terms do not include—

(A) the manufacture of a substance that is used and entirely consumed (except for trace quantities) in the manufacture of other chemicals, or

(B) the reuse or recycling of a substance.

(July 14, 1955, c. 360, Title VI, § 601, as added by Pub. L. No. 101–549, Title VI, § 602(a), 104 Stat. 2649 (Nov. 15, 1990).)

HISTORICAL AND STATUTORY NOTES

References in Text

The customs laws of the United States, referred to in par. (7), are codified generally to Title 19, Customs Duties.

The Federal Food, Drug, and Cosmetic Act, referred to in par. (8), is Act of June 25, 1938, c. 675, 52 Stat. 1040, as amended, which is codified generally as chapter 9 (section 301 et seq.) of Title 21, Food and Drugs. For complete classification of this Act to the Code, see section 301 of Title 21 and Tables.

Effective and Applicability Provisions

1990 Acts. Section effective Nov. 15, 1990, except as otherwise provided, see section 711(b) of Pub. L. No. 101–549, set out as a note under section 7401 of this title.

Savings Provisions

Suits, actions or proceedings commenced under this chapter as in effect prior to Nov. 15, 1990, not to abate by reason of the taking effect of amendments by Pub. L. No. 101–549, except as otherwise provided for, see section 711(a) of Pub. L. No. 101–549, set out as a note under section 7401 of this title.

§ 7671a. Listing of class I and class II substances

[CAA § 602]

(a) List of class I substances

Within 60 days after November 15, 1990, the Administrator shall publish an initial list of class I substances, which list shall contain the following substances:

Group I

chlorofluorocarbon-11 (CFC-11)

chlorofluorocarbon-12 (CFC-12)

chlorofluorocarbon-113 (CFC-113)

chlorofluorocarbon-114 (CFC-114)

chlorofluorocarbon-115 (CFC-115)

Group II

halon-1211

halon-1301

halon-2402

Group III

chlorofluorocarbon-13 (CFC-13)

chlorofluorocarbon-111 (CFC-111)

chlorofluorocarbon-112 (CFC-112)

chlorofluorocarbon-211 (CFC-211)

chlorofluorocarbon-212 (CFC-212)

chlorofluorocarbon-213 (CFC-213)

chlorofluorocarbon-214 (CFC-214)

chlorofluorocarbon-215 (CFC-215)

chlorofluorocarbon-216 (CFC-216)

chlorofluorocarbon-217 (CFC-217)

Group IV

carbon tetrachloride

Group V

methyl chloroform

The initial list under this subsection shall also include the isomers of the substances listed above, other than 1,1,2-trichloroethane (an isomer of methyl chloroform). Pursuant to subsection (c) of this section, the Administrator shall add to the list of class I substances any other substance that the Administrator finds causes or contributes significantly to harmful effects on the stratospheric ozone layer. The Administrator shall, pursuant to subsection (c) of this section, add to such list all substances that the Administrator determines have an ozone depletion potential of 0.2 or greater.

(b) List of class II substances

Simultaneously with publication of the initial list of class I substances, the Administrator shall publish an initial list of class II substances, which shall contain the following substances:

hydrochlorofluorocarbon-21 (HCFC-21)

hydrochlorofluorocarbon-22 (HCFC-22)

hydrochlorofluorocarbon-31 (HCFC-31)

hydrochlorofluorocarbon-121 (HCFC-121)

hydrochlorofluorocarbon-122 (HCFC-122)

hydrochlorofluorocarbon-123 (HCFC-123)

hydrochlorofluorocarbon-124 (HCFC-124)

hydrochlorofluorocarbon-131 (HCFC-131)

hydrochlorofluorocarbon-132 (HCFC-132)

hydrochlorofluorocarbon-133 (HCFC-133)

hydrochlorofluorocarbon-141 (HCFC-141)

hydrochlorofluorocarbon-142 (HCFC-142)

hydrochlorofluorocarbon-221 (HCFC-221)

hydrochlorofluorocarbon-222 (HCFC-222)

hydrochlorofluorocarbon-223 (HCFC-223)

hydrochlorofluorocarbon-224 (HCFC-224)

hydrochlorofluorocarbon-225 (HCFC-225)

hydrochlorofluorocarbon-226 (HCFC-226)

hydrochlorofluorocarbon-231 (HCFC-231)

hydrochlorofluorocarbon-232 (HCFC-232)

hydrochlorofluorocarbon-233 (HCFC-233)

hydrochlorofluorocarbon-234 (HCFC-234)

hydrochlorofluorocarbon-235 (HCFC-235)

hydrochlorofluorocarbon-241 (HCFC-241)

hydrochlorofluorocarbon-242 (HCFC-242)

hydrochlorofluorocarbon-243 (HCFC-243)

hydrochlorofluorocarbon-244 (HCFC-244)

hydrochlorofluorocarbon-251 (HCFC-251)

hydrochlorofluorocarbon-252 (HCFC-252)

hydrochlorofluorocarbon-253 (HCFC-253)

hydrochlorofluorocarbon-261 (HCFC-261)

hydrochlorofluorocarbon-262 (HCFC-262)

hydrochlorofluorocarbon-271 (HCFC-271)

The initial list under this subsection shall also include the isomers of the substances listed above. Pursuant to subsection (c) of this section, the Administrator shall add to the list of class II substances any other substance that the Administrator finds is known or may reasonably be anticipated to cause or contribute to harmful effects on the stratospheric ozone layer.

(c) Additions to the lists

(1) The Administrator may add, by rule, in accordance with the criteria set forth in subsection (a) or (b) of this section, as the case may be, any substance to the list of class I or class II substances under subsection (a) or (b) of this section. For purposes of exchanges under section 7661f[1] of this title, whenever a substance is added to the list of class I substances the Administrator shall, to the extent consistent with the Montreal Protocol, assign such substance to existing Group I, II, III, IV, or V or place such substance in a new Group.

(2) Periodically, but not less frequently than every 3 years after November 15, 1990, the Administrator shall list, by rule, as additional class I or class II substances those substances which the Administrator finds meet the criteria of subsection (a) or (b) of this section, as the case may be.

(3) At any time, any person may petition the Administrator to add a substance to the list of class I or class II substances. Pursuant to the criteria set forth in subsection (a) or (b) of this section as the case may be, within 180 days after receiving such a petition, the Administrator shall either propose to add the substance to such list or publish an explanation of the petition denial. In any case where the Administrator proposes to add a substance to such list, the Administrator shall add, by rule, (or make a final determination not to add) such substance to such list within 1 year after receiving such petition. Any petition under this paragraph shall include a showing by the petitioner that there are data on the substance adequate to support the petition. If the Administrator determines that information on the substance is not sufficient to make a determination under this paragraph, the Administrator shall use any authority available to the Administrator, under any law administered by the Administrator, to acquire such information.

(4) Only a class II substance which is added to the list of class I substances may be removed from the list of class II substances. No substance referred to in subsection (a) of this section, including methyl chloroform, may be removed from the list of class I substances.

(d) New listed substances

In the case of any substance added to the list of class I or class II substances after publication of the initial list of such substances under this section, the Administrator may extend any schedule or compliance deadline contained in section 7671c or 7671d of this title to a later date than specified in such sections if such schedule or deadline is unattainable, considering when such substance is added to the list. No extension under this subsection may extend the date for termination of production of any class I substance to a date more than 7 years after January 1 of the year after the year in which the substance is added to the list of class I substances. No extension under this subsection may extend the date for termination of production of any class II substance to a date more than 10 years after January 1 of the year after the year in which the substance is added to the list of class II substances.

(e) Ozone-depletion and global warming potential

Simultaneously with publication of the lists under this section and simultaneously with any addition to either of such lists, the Administrator shall assign to each listed substance a numerical value representing the substance's ozone-depletion potential. In addition, the Administrator shall publish the chlorine and bromine loading potential and the atmospheric lifetime of each listed substance. One year after November 15, 1990 (one year after the addition of a substance to either of such lists in the case of a substance added after the publication of the initial lists of such substances), and after notice and opportunity for public comment, the Administrator shall publish the global warming potential of each listed substance. The preceding sentence shall not be construed to be the basis of any additional regulation under this chapter. In the case of the substances referred to in table 1, the ozone-depletion potential shall be as specified in table 1, unless the Administrator adjusts the substance's ozone-depletion potential based on criteria referred to in section 7671(10) of this title:

Table 1

Substance	Ozone-depletion potential
chlorofluorocarbon-11 (CFC-11)	1.0
chlorofluorocarbon-12 (CFC-12)	1.0
chlorofluorocarbon-13 (CFC-13)	1.0
chlorofluorocarbon-111 (CFC-111)	1.0
chlorofluorocarbon-112 (CFC-112)	1.0
chlorofluorocarbon-113 (CFC-113)	0.8
chlorofluorocarbon-114 (CFC-114)	1.0
chlorofluorocarbon-115 (CFC-115)	0.6
chlorofluorocarbon-211 (CFC-211)	1.0
chlorofluorocarbon-212 (CFC-212)	1.0
chlorofluorocarbon-213 (CFC-213)	1.0
chlorofluorocarbon-214 (CFC-214)	1.0
chlorofluorocarbon-215 (CFC-215)	1.0
chlorofluorocarbon-216 (CFC-216)	1.0
chlorofluorocarbon-217 (CFC-217)	1.0
halon-1211	3.0
halon-1301	10.0
halon-2402	6.0
carbon tetrachloride	1.1
methyl chloroform	0.1
hydrochlorofluorocarbon-22 (HCFC-22)	0.05
hydrochlorofluorocarbon-123 (HCFC-123)	0.02
hydrochlorofluorocarbon-124 (HCFC-124)	0.02
hydrochlorofluorocarbon-141(b) (HCFC-141(b))	0.1
hydrochlorofluorocarbon-142(b) (HCFC-142(b))	0.06

Where the ozone-depletion potential of a substance is specified in the Montreal Protocol, the ozone-depletion potential specified for that substance under this section shall be consistent with the Montreal Protocol.

(July 14, 1955, c. 360, Title VI, § 602, as added by Pub. L. No. 101–549, Title VI, § 602(a), 104 Stat. 2650 (Nov. 15, 1990).)

[1] So in original. Probably should be section "7671f."

HISTORICAL AND STATUTORY NOTES

Effective and Applicability Provisions

1990 Acts. Section effective Nov. 15, 1990, except as otherwise provided, see section 711(b) of Pub. L. No. 101–549, set out as a note under section 7401 of this title.

Savings Provisions

Suits, actions or proceedings commenced under this chapter as in effect prior to Nov. 15, 1990, not to abate by reason of the taking effect of amendments by Pub. L. No. 101–549, except as otherwise provided for, see section 711(a) of Pub. L. No. 101–549, set out as a note under section 7401 of this title.

§ 7671b. Monitoring and reporting requirements

[CAA § 603]

(a) Regulations

Within 270 days after November 15, 1990, the Administrator shall amend the regulations of the Administrator in effect on such date regarding monitoring and reporting of class I and class II substances. Such amendments shall conform to the requirements of this section. The amended regulations shall include requirements with respect to the time and manner of monitoring and reporting as required under this section.

(b) Production, import, and export level reports

On a quarterly basis, or such other basis (not less than annually) as determined by the Administrator, each person who produced, imported, or exported a class I or class II substance shall file a report with the Administrator setting forth the amount of the substance that such person produced, imported, and exported during the preceding reporting period. Each such report shall be signed and attested by a responsible officer. No such report shall be required from a person after April 1 of the calendar year after such person permanently ceases production, importation, and exportation of the substance and so notifies the Administrator in writing.

(c) Baseline reports for class I substances

Unless such information has previously been reported to the Administrator, on the date on which the first report under subsection (b) of this section is required to be filed, each person who produced, imported, or exported a class I substance (other than a substance added to the list of class I substances after the publication of the initial list of such substances under this section) shall file a report with the Administrator setting forth the amount of such substance that such person produced, imported, and exported during the baseline year. In the case of a substance added to the list of class I substances after publication of the initial list of such substances under this section, the regulations shall require that each person who produced, imported, or exported such substance shall file a report with the Administrator within 180 days after the date on which such substance is added to the list, setting forth the amount of the substance that such person produced, imported, and exported in the baseline year.

(d) Monitoring and reports to Congress

(1) The Administrator shall monitor and, not less often than every 3 years following November 15, 1990, submit a report to Congress on the production, use and consumption of class I and class II substances. Such report shall include data on domestic production, use and consumption, and an estimate of worldwide production, use and consumption of such substances. Not less frequently than every 6 years the Administrator shall report to Congress on the environmental and economic effects of any stratospheric ozone depletion.

(2) The Administrators of the National Aeronautics and Space Administration and the National Oceanic and Atmospheric Administration shall monitor, and not less often than every 3 years following November 15, 1990, submit a report to Congress on the current average tropospheric concentration of chlorine and bromine and on the level of stratospheric ozone depletion. Such reports shall include updated projections of—

(A) peak chlorine loading;

(B) the rate at which the atmospheric abundance of chlorine is projected to decrease after the year 2000; and

(C) the date by which the atmospheric abundance of chlorine is projected to return to a level of two parts per billion.

Such updated projections shall be made on the basis of current international and domestic controls on substances covered by this subchapter as well as on the basis of such controls supplemented by a year 2000 global phase out of all halocarbon emissions (the base case). It is the purpose of the Congress through the provisions of this section to monitor closely the production and consumption of class II substances to assure that the production and consumption of such substances will not:

(i) increase significantly the peak chlorine loading that is projected to occur under the base case established for purposes of this section;

(ii) reduce significantly the rate at which the atmospheric abundance of chlorine is projected to decrease under the base case; or

(iii) delay the date by which the average atmospheric concentration of chlorine is projected under the base case to return to a level of two parts per billion.

(e) Technology status report in 2015

The Administrator shall review, on a periodic basis, the progress being made in the development of alternative systems or products necessary to manufacture and operate appliances without class II substances. If the Administrator finds, after notice and opportunity for public comment, that as a result of technological development problems, the development of such alternative systems or products will not occur within the time necessary to provide for the manufacture of such equipment without such substances prior to the applicable deadlines under section 7671d of this title, the Administrator shall, not later than January 1, 2015, so inform the Congress.

(f) Emergency report

If, in consultation with the Administrators of the National Aeronautics and Space Administration and the National Oceanic and Atmospheric Administration, and after notice and opportunity for public comment, the Administrator determines that the global production, consumption, and use of class II substances are projected to contribute to an atmospheric chlorine loading in excess of the base case projections by more than 5/10 ths parts per billion, the Administrator shall so inform the Congress immediately. The determination referred to in the preceding sentence shall be based on the monitoring under subsection (d) of this section and updated not less often than every 3 years.

(July 14, 1955, c. 360, Title VI, § 603, as added by Pub. L. No. 101–549, Title VI, § 602(a), 104 Stat. 2653 (Nov. 15, 1990).)

HISTORICAL AND STATUTORY NOTES

Effective and Applicability Provisions

1990 Acts. Section effective Nov. 15, 1990, except as otherwise provided, see section 711(b) of Pub. L. No. 101–549, set out as a note under section 7401 of this title.

Savings Provisions

Suits, actions or proceedings commenced under this chapter as in effect prior to Nov. 15, 1990, not to abate by reason of the taking effect of amendments by Pub. L. No. 101–549, except as otherwise provided for, see section 711(a) of Pub. L. No. 101–549, set out as a note under section 7401 of this title.

Termination of Reporting Requirements

For termination, effective May 15, 2000, of provisions in subsec. (d)(1) of this section relating to submittal of triennial report to Congress, see Pub. L. No. 104–66, § 3003, as amended, set out as a note under 31 U.S.C.A. § 1113, and the 12th item on page 162 of House Document No. 103–7.

Methane Studies

Section 603 of Pub. L. No. 101–549 provided that:

"(a) Economically justified actions.—Not later than 2 years after enactment of this Act [Nov. 15, 1990], the Administrator shall prepare and submit a report to the Congress that identifies activities, substances, processes, or combinations thereof that could reduce methane emissions and that are economically and technologically justified with and without consideration of environmental benefit.

"(b) Domestic methane source inventory and control.—Not later than 2 years after the enactment of this Act [Nov. 15, 1990], the Administrator, in consultation and coordination with the Secretary of Energy and the Secretary of Agriculture, shall prepare and submit to the Congress reports on each of the following:

"(1) Methane emissions associated with natural gas extraction, transportation, distribution, storage, and use. Such report shall include an inventory of methane emissions associated with such activities within the United States. Such emissions include, but are not limited to, accidental and intentional releases from natural gas and oil wells, pipelines, processing facilities, and gas burners. The report shall also include an inventory of methane generation with such activities.

"(2) Methane emissions associated with coal extraction, transportation, distribution, storage, and use. Such report shall include an inventory of methane emissions associated with such activities within the United States. Such emissions include, but are not limited to, accidental and intentional releases from mining shafts, degasification wells, gas recovery wells and equipment, and from the processing and use of coal. The report shall also include an inventory of methane generation with such activities.

"(3) Methane emissions associated with management of solid waste. Such report shall include an inventory of methane emissions associated with all forms of waste management in the United States, including storage, treatment, and disposal.

"(4) Methane emissions associated with agriculture. Such report shall include an inventory of methane emissions associated with rice and livestock production in the United States.

"(5) Methane emissions associated with biomass burning. Such report shall include an inventory of methane emissions associated with the intentional burning of agricultural wastes, wood, grasslands, and forests.

"(6) Other methane emissions associated with human activities. Such report shall identify and inventory other domestic sources of methane emissions that are deemed by the Administrator and other such agencies to be significant.

"(c) International studies.—

"(1) Methane emissions.—Not later than 2 years after the enactment of this Act [Nov. 15, 1990], the Administrator shall prepare and submit to the Congress a report on methane emissions from countries other than the United States. Such report shall include inventories of methane emissions associated with the activities listed in subsection (b).

"(2) Preventing increases in methane concentrations.—Not later than 2 years after the enactment of this Act [Nov. 15, 1990], the Administrator shall prepare and submit to the Congress a report that analyzes the potential for preventing an increase in atmospheric concentrations of methane from activities and sources in other countries. Such report shall identify and evaluate the technical options for reducing methane emission from each of the activities listed in subsection (b), as well as other activities or sources that are deemed by the Administrator in consultation with other relevant Federal agencies and departments to be significant and shall include an evaluation of costs. The report shall identify the emissions reductions that would need to be achieved to prevent increasing atmospheric concentrations of methane. The report shall also identify technology transfer programs that could promote methane emissions reductions in lesser developed countries.

"(d) Natural sources.—Not later than 2 years after the enactment of this Act [Nov. 15, 1990], the Administrator shall prepare and submit to the Congress a report on—

"(1) methane emissions from biogenic sources such as (A) tropical, temperate, and subarctic forests, (B) tundra, and (C) freshwater and saltwater wetlands; and

"(2) the changes in methane emissions from biogenic sources that may occur as a result of potential increases in temperatures and atmospheric concentrations of carbon dioxide.

"(e) Study of measures to limit growth in methane concentrations.—Not later than 2 years after the completion of the studies in subsections (b), (c), and (d), the Administrator shall prepare and submit to the Congress a report that presents options outlining measures that could be implemented to stop or reduce the growth in atmospheric concentrations of methane from sources within the United States referred to in paragraphs (1) through (6) of subsection (b). This study shall identify and evaluate the technical options for reducing methane emissions from each of the activities listed in subsection (b), as well as other activities or sources deemed by such agencies to be significant, and shall include an evaluation of costs, technology, safety, energy, and other factors. The study shall be based on the other studies under this section. The study shall also identify programs of the United States and international lending agencies that could be used to induce lesser developed countries to undertake measures that will reduce methane emissions and the resource needs of such programs.

"(f) Information gathering.—In carrying out the studies under this section, the provisions and requirements of section 114 of the Clean Air Act [section 7414 of this title] shall be available for purposes of obtaining information to carry out such studies.

"(g) Consultation and coordination.—In preparing the studies under this section the Administrator shall consult and coordinate with the Secretary of Energy, the Administrators of the National Aeronautics and Space Administration and the National Oceanic and Atmospheric Administration, and the heads of other relevant Federal agencies and departments. In the case of the studies under subsections (a), (b), and (e), such consultation and coordination shall include the Secretary of Agriculture."

[For termination, effective May 15, 2000, of reporting provisions of Pub. L. No. 101–549, § 603, set out above, see Pub. L. No. 104–66, § 3003, as amended, set out as a note under 31 U.S.C.A. § 1113, and items 13 through 20 on page 162 and items 1 through 3 on page 163 of House Document No. 103–7.]

§ 7671c. Phase-out of production and consumption of class I substances [CAA § 604]

(a) Production phase-out

Effective on January 1 of each year specified in Table 2, it shall be unlawful for any person to produce any class I substance in an annual quantity greater than the relevant percentage specified in Table 2. The percentages in Table 2 refer to a maximum allowable production as a percentage of the quantity of the substance produced by the person concerned in the baseline year.

Table 2

Date	Carbon tetrachloride	Methyl chloroform	Other class I substances
1991	100%	100%	85%
1992	90%	100%	80%
1993	80%	90%	75%
1994	70%	85%	65%
1995	15%	70%	50%
1996	15%	50%	40%
1997	15%	50%	15%
1998	15%	50%	15%
1999	15%	50%	15%
2000		20%	—
2001		20%	—

(b) Termination of production of class I substances

Effective January 1, 2000 (January 1, 2002 in the case of methyl chloroform), it shall be unlawful for any person to produce any amount of a class I substance.

(c) Regulations regarding production and consumption of class I substances

The Administrator shall promulgate regulations within 10 months after November 15, 1990, phasing out the production of class I substances in accordance with this section and other applicable provisions of this subchapter. The Administrator shall also promulgate regulations to insure that the consumption of class I substances in the United States is phased out and terminated in accordance with the same schedule (subject to the same exceptions and other provisions) as is applicable to the phase-out and termination of production of class I substances under this subchapter.

(d) Exceptions for essential uses of methyl chloroform, medical devices, and aviation safety

(1) Essential uses of methyl chloroform

Notwithstanding the termination of production required by subsection (b) of this section, during the period beginning on January 1, 2002, and ending on January 1, 2005, the Administrator, after notice and opportunity for public comment, may, to the extent such action is consistent with the Montreal Protocol, authorize the production of limited quantities of methyl chloroform solely for use in essential applications (such as nondestructive testing for metal fatigue and corrosion of existing airplane engines and airplane parts susceptible to metal fatigue) for which no safe and effective substitute is available. Notwithstanding this paragraph, the authority to produce methyl chloroform for use in medical devices shall be provided in accordance with paragraph (2).

(2) Medical devices

Notwithstanding the termination of production required by subsection (b) of this section, the Administrator, after notice and opportunity for public comment, shall, to the extent such action is consistent with the Montreal Protocol, authorize the production of limited quantities of class I substances solely for use in medical devices if such authorization is determined by the Commissioner, in consultation with the Administrator, to be necessary for use in medical devices.

(3) Aviation safety

(A) Notwithstanding the termination of production required by subsection (b) of this section, the Administrator, after notice and opportunity for public comment, may, to the extent such action is consistent with the Montreal Protocol, authorize the production of limited quantities of halon-1211 (bromochlorodifluoromethane), halon-1301 (bromotrifluoromethane), and halon-2402 (dibromotetrafluoroethane) solely for purposes of aviation safety if the Administrator of the Federal Aviation Administration, in consultation with the Administrator, determines that no safe and effective substitute has been developed and that such authorization is necessary for aviation safety purposes.

(B) The Administrator of the Federal Aviation Administration shall, in consultation with the Administrator, examine whether safe and effective substitutes for methyl chloroform or alternative techniques will be available for nondestructive testing for metal fatigue and corrosion of existing airplane engines and airplane parts susceptible to metal fatigue and whether an exception for such uses of methyl chloroform under this paragraph will be necessary for purposes of airline safety after January 1, 2005 and provide a report to Congress in 1998.

(4) Cap on certain exceptions

Under no circumstances may the authority set forth in paragraphs (1), (2), and (3) of subsection (d) of this section be applied to authorize any person to produce a class I substance in annual quantities greater than 10 percent of that produced by such person during the baseline year.

(5) Sanitation and food protection

To the extent consistent with the Montreal Protocol's quarantine and pre-shipment provisions, the Administrator shall exempt the production, importation, and consumption of methyl bromide to fumigate commodities entering or leaving the United States or any State (or political subdivision thereof) for purposes of compliance with Animal and Plant Health Inspection Service requirements or with any international, Federal, State, or local sanitation or food protection standard.

(6) Critical uses

To the extent consistent with the Montreal Protocol, the Administrator, after notice and the opportunity for public comment, and after consultation with other departments or instrumentalities of the Federal Government having regulatory authority related to methyl bromide, including the Secretary of Agriculture, may exempt the production, importation, and consumption of methyl bromide for critical uses.

(e) Developing countries

(1) Exception

Notwithstanding the phase-out and termination of production required under subsections (a) and (b) of this section, the Administrator, after notice and opportunity for public comment, may, consistent with the Montreal Protocol, authorize the production of limited quantities of a class I substance in excess of the amounts otherwise allowable under subsection (a) or (b) of this section, or both, solely for export to, and use in, developing countries that are Parties to the Montreal Protocol and are operating under article 5 of such Protocol. Any production authorized under this paragraph shall be solely for purposes of satisfying the basic domestic needs of such countries.

(2) Cap on exception

(A) Under no circumstances may the authority set forth in paragraph (1) be applied to authorize any person to produce a class I substance in any year for which a production percentage is specified in Table 2 of subsection (a) of this section in an annual quantity greater than the specified percentage, plus an amount equal to 10 percent of the amount produced by such person in the baseline year.

(B) Under no circumstances may the authority set forth in paragraph (1) be applied to authorize any person to produce a class I substance in the applicable termination year referred to in subsection (b) of this section, or in any year thereafter, in an annual quantity greater than 15 percent of the baseline quantity of such substance produced by such person.

(C) An exception authorized under this subsection shall terminate no later than January 1, 2010 (2012 in the case of methyl chloroform).

(3) Methyl bromide

Notwithstanding the phaseout and termination of production of methyl bromide pursuant to subsection (h) of this section, the Administrator may, consistent with the Montreal Protocol, authorize the production of limited quantities of methyl bromide, solely for use in developing countries that are Parties to the Copenhagen Amendments to the Montreal Protocol.

(f) National security

The President may, to the extent such action is consistent with the Montreal Protocol, issue such orders regarding production and use of CFC-114 (chlorofluorocarbon-114), halon-1211, halon-1301, and halon-2402, at any specified site or facility or on any vessel as may be necessary to protect the national security interests of the United States if the President finds that adequate substitutes are not available and that the production and use of such substance are necessary to protect such national security interest. Such orders may include, where necessary to protect such interests, an exemption from any prohibition or requirement contained in this subchapter. The President shall notify the Congress within 30 days of the issuance of an order under this paragraph providing for any such exemption. Such notification shall include a statement of the reasons for the granting of the exemption. An exemption under this paragraph shall be for a specified period which may not exceed one year. Additional exemptions may be granted, each upon the President's issuance of a new order under this paragraph. Each such additional exemption shall be for a specified period which may not exceed one year. No exemption shall be granted under this paragraph due to lack of appropriation unless the President shall have specifically requested such appropriation as a part of the budgetary process and the Congress shall have failed to make available such requested appropriation.

(g) Fire suppression and explosion prevention

(1) Notwithstanding the production phase-out set forth in subsection (a) of this section, the Administrator, after notice and opportunity for public comment, may, to the extent such action is consistent with the Montreal Protocol, authorize the production of limited quantities of halon-1211, halon-1301, and halon-2402 in excess of the amount otherwise permitted pursuant to the schedule under subsection (a) of this section solely for purposes of fire suppression or explosion prevention if the Administrator, in consultation with the Administrator of the United States Fire Administration, determines that no safe and effective substitute has been developed and that such authorization is necessary for fire suppression or explosion prevention purposes. The Administrator shall not authorize production under this paragraph for purposes of fire safety or explosion prevention training or testing of fire suppression or explosion prevention equipment. In no event shall the Administrator grant an exception under this paragraph that permits production after December 31, 1999.

(2) The Administrator shall periodically monitor and assess the status of efforts to obtain substitutes for the substances referred to in paragraph (1) for purposes of fire suppression or explosion prevention and the probability of such substitutes being available by December 31, 1999. The Administrator, as part of such assessment, shall consider any relevant assessments under the Montreal Protocol and the actions of the Parties pursuant to Article 2B of the Montreal Protocol in identifying essential uses and in permitting a level of production or consumption that is necessary to satisfy such uses for which no adequate alternatives are available after December 31, 1999. The Administrator shall report to Congress the results of such assessment in 1994 and again in 1998.

(3) Notwithstanding the termination of production set forth in subsection (b) of this section, the Administrator, after notice and opportunity for public comment, may, to the extent consistent with the Montreal Protocol, authorize the production of limited quantities of halon-1211, halon-1301, and halon-2402 in the period after December 31, 1999, and before December 31, 2004, solely for purposes of fire suppression or explosion prevention in association with domestic production of crude oil and natural gas energy supplies on the North Slope of Alaska, if the Administrator, in consultation with the Administrator of the United States Fire Administration, determines that no safe and effective substitute has been developed and that such authorization is necessary for fire suppression and explosion prevention purposes. The Administrator shall not authorize production under the paragraph for purposes of fire safety or explosion prevention training or testing of fire suppression or explosion prevention equipment. In no event shall the Administrator authorize under this paragraph any person to produce any such halon in an amount greater than 3 percent of that produced by such person during the baseline year.

(h) Methyl bromide

Notwithstanding subsections (b) and (d) of this section, the Administrator shall not terminate production of methyl bromide prior to January 1, 2005. The Administrator shall promulgate rules for reductions in, and terminate the production, importation, and consumption of, methyl bromide under a schedule that is in accordance with, but not more stringent than, the phaseout schedule of the Montreal Protocol Treaty as in effect on October 21, 1998.

(July 14, 1955, c. 360, Title VI, § 604, as added by Pub. L. No. 101–549, Title VI, § 602(a), 104 Stat. 2655 (Nov. 15, 1990); and amended by Pub. L. No. 105–277, § 101(a) [Title VII, § 764], 112 Stat. 2681–36 (Oct. 21, 1998).)

HISTORICAL AND STATUTORY NOTES

Effective and Applicability Provisions

1990 Acts. Section effective Nov. 15, 1990, except as otherwise provided, see section 711(b) of Pub. L. No. 101–549, set out as a note under section 7401 of this title.

Termination of Reporting Requirements

For termination, effective May 15, 2000, of reporting provisions of this section relating to fire suppression and explosion prevention, see Pub. L. No. 104–66, § 3003, as amended, set out as a note under 31 U.S.C.A. § 1113, and the 11th item on page 164 of House Document No. 103–7.

Savings Provisions

Suits, actions or proceedings commenced under this chapter as in effect prior to Nov. 15, 1990, not to abate by reason of the taking effect of amendments by Pub. L. No. 101–549, except as otherwise provided for, see section 711(a) of Pub. L. No. 101–549, set out as a note under section 7401 of this title.

§ 7671d. Phase-out of production and consumption of class II substances

[CAA § 605]

(a) Restriction of use of class II substances

Effective January 1, 2015, it shall be unlawful for any person to introduce into interstate commerce or use any class II substance unless such substance—

(1) has been used, recovered, and recycled;

(2) is used and entirely consumed (except for trace quantities) in the production of other chemicals;

(3) is used as a refrigerant in appliances manufactured prior to January 1, 2020; or

(4) is listed as acceptable for use as a fire suppression agent for nonresidential applications in accordance with section 7671k(c) of this title.

As used in this subsection, the term "refrigerant" means any class II substance used for heat transfer in a refrigerating system.

(b) Production phase-out

(1) Effective January 1, 2015, it shall be unlawful for any person to produce any class II substance in an annual quantity greater than the quantity of such substance produced by such person during the baseline year.

(2) Effective January 1, 2030, it shall be unlawful for any person to produce any class II substance.

(c) Regulations regarding production and consumption of class II substances

By December 31, 1999, the Administrator shall promulgate regulations phasing out the production, and restricting the use, of class II substances in accordance with this section, subject to any acceleration of the phase-out of production under section 7671e of this title. The Administrator shall also promulgate regulations to insure that the consumption of class II substances in the United States is phased out and terminated in accordance with the same schedule (subject to the same exceptions and other provisions) as is applicable to the phase-out and termination of production of class II substances under this subchapter.

(d) Exceptions

(1) Medical devices

(A) In general

Notwithstanding the termination of production required under subsection (b)(2) of this section and the restriction on use referred to in subsection (a) of this section, the Administrator, after notice and opportunity for public comment, shall, to the extent such action is consistent with the Montreal Protocol, authorize the production and use of limited quantities of class II substances solely for purposes of use in medical devices if such authorization is determined by the Commissioner, in consultation with the Administrator, to be necessary for use in medical devices.

(B) Cap on exception

Under no circumstances may the authority set forth in subparagraph (A) be applied to authorize any person to produce a class II substance in annual quantities greater than 10 percent of that produced by such person during the baseline year.

(2) Developing countries

(A) In general

Notwithstanding the provisions of subsection (a) or (b) of this section, the Administrator, after notice and opportunity for public comment, may authorize the production of limited quantities of a class II substance in excess of the quantities otherwise permitted under such provisions solely for export to and use in developing countries that are Parties to the Montreal Protocol, as determined by the Administrator. Any production authorized under this subsection shall be solely for purposes of satisfying the basic domestic needs of such countries.

(B) Cap on exception

(i) Under no circumstances may the authority set forth in subparagraph (A) be applied to authorize any person to produce a class II substance in any year following the effective date of subsection (b)(1) of this section and before the year 2030 in annual quantities greater than 110 percent of the quantity of such substance produced by such person during the baseline year.

(ii) Under no circumstances may the authority set forth in subparagraph (A) be applied to authorize any person to produce a class II substance in the year 2030, or any year thereafter, in an annual quantity greater than 15 percent of the quantity of such substance produced by such person during the baseline year.

(iii) Each exception authorized under this paragraph shall terminate no later than January 1, 2040.

(July 14, 1955, c. 360, Title VI, § 605, as added by Pub. L. No. 101–549, Title VI, § 602(a), 104 Stat. 2658 (Nov. 15, 1990); and amended by Pub. L. No. 112–81, Div. A, Title III, § 320, 125 Stat. 1361 (Dec. 31, 2011).)

HISTORICAL AND STATUTORY NOTES

Effective and Applicability Provisions

1990 Acts. Section effective Nov. 15, 1990, except as otherwise provided, see section 711(b) of Pub. L. No. 101–549, set out as a note under section 7401 of this title.

Savings Provisions

Suits, actions or proceedings commenced under this chapter as in effect prior to Nov. 15, 1990, not to abate by reason of the taking effect of amendments by Pub. L. No. 101–549, except as otherwise provided for, see section 711(a) of Pub. L. No. 101–549, set out as a note under section 7401 of this title.

§ 7671e. Accelerated schedule

[CAA § 606]

(a) In general

The Administrator shall promulgate regulations, after notice and opportunity for public comment, which establish a schedule for phasing out the production and consumption of class I and class II substances (or use of class II substances) that is more stringent than set forth in section 7671c or 7671d of this title, or both, if—

(1) based on an assessment of credible current scientific information (including any assessment under the Montreal Protocol) regarding harmful effects on the stratospheric ozone layer associated with a class I or class II substance, the Administrator determines that such more stringent schedule may be necessary to protect human health and the environment against such effects,

(2) based on the availability of substitutes for listed substances, the Administrator determines that such more stringent schedule is practicable, taking into account technological achievability, safety, and other relevant factors, or

(3) the Montreal Protocol is modified to include a schedule to control or reduce production, consumption, or use of any substance more rapidly than the applicable schedule under this subchapter.

In making any determination under paragraphs (1) and (2), the Administrator shall consider the status of the period remaining under the applicable schedule under this subchapter.

(b) Petition

Any person may petition the Administrator to promulgate regulations under this section. The Administrator shall grant or deny the petition within 180 days after receipt of any such petition. If the Administrator denies the petition, the Administrator shall publish an explanation of why the petition was denied. If the Administrator grants such petition, such final regulations shall be promulgated within 1 year. Any petition under this subsection shall include a showing by the petitioner that there are data adequate to support the petition. If the Administrator determines that information is not sufficient to make a determination under this subsection, the Administrator shall use any authority available to the Administrator, under any law administered by the Administrator, to acquire such information.

(July 14, 1955, c. 360, Title VI, § 606, as added by Pub. L. No. 101–549, Title VI, § 602(a), 104 Stat. 2660 (Nov. 15, 1990).)

HISTORICAL AND STATUTORY NOTES

Effective and Applicability Provisions

1990 Acts. Section effective Nov. 15, 1990, except as otherwise provided, see section 711(b) of Pub. L. No. 101–549, set out as a note under section 7401 of this title.

Savings Provisions

Suits, actions or proceedings commenced under this chapter as in effect prior to Nov. 15, 1990, not to abate by reason of the taking effect of amendments by Pub. L. No. 101–549, except as otherwise provided for, see section 711(a) of Pub. L. No. 101–549, set out as a note under section 7401 of this title.

§ 7671f. Exchange authority

[CAA § 607]

(a) Transfers

The Administrator shall, within 10 months after November 15, 1990, promulgate rules under this subchapter providing for the issuance of allowances for the production of class I and II substances in accordance with the requirements of this subchapter and governing the transfer of such allowances. Such rules shall insure that the transactions under the authority of this section will result in greater total reductions in the production in each year of class I and class II substances than would occur in that year in the absence of such transactions.

(b) Interpollutant transfers

(1) The rules under this section shall permit a production allowance for a substance for any year to be transferred for a production allowance for another substance for the same year on an ozone depletion weighted basis.

(2) Allowances for substances in each group of class I substances (as listed pursuant to section 7671a of this title) may only be transferred for allowances for other substances in the same Group.

(3) The Administrator shall, as appropriate, establish groups of class II substances for trading purposes and assign class II substances to such groups. In the case of class II substances, allowances may only be transferred for allowances for other class II substances that are in the same Group.

(c) Trades with other persons

The rules under this section shall permit 2 or more persons to transfer production allowances (including interpollutant transfers which meet the requirements of subsections (a) and (b) of this section) if the transferor of such allowances will be subject, under such rules, to an enforceable and quantifiable reduction in annual production which—

(1) exceeds the reduction otherwise applicable to the transferor under this subchapter,

(2) exceeds the production allowances transferred to the transferee, and

(3) would not have occurred in the absence of such transaction.

(d) Consumption

The rules under this section shall also provide for the issuance of consumption allowances in accordance with the requirements of this subchapter and for the trading of such allowances in the same manner as is applicable under this section to the trading of production allowances under this section.

(July 14, 1955, c. 360, Title VI, § 607, as added by Pub. L. No. 101–549, Title VI, § 602(a), 104 Stat. 2660 (Nov. 15, 1990).)

HISTORICAL AND STATUTORY NOTES

Effective and Applicability Provisions

1990 Acts. Section effective Nov. 15, 1990, except as otherwise provided, see section 711(b) of Pub. L. No. 101–549, set out as a note under section 7401 of this title.

Savings Provisions

Suits, actions or proceedings commenced under this chapter as in effect prior to Nov. 15, 1990, not to abate by reason of the taking effect of amendments by Pub. L. No. 101–549, except as otherwise provided for, see section 711(a) of Pub. L. No. 101–549, set out as a note under section 7401 of this title.

§ 7671g. National recycling and emission reduction program

[CAA § 608]

(a) In general

(1) The Administrator shall, by not later than January 1, 1992, promulgate regulations establishing standards and requirements regarding the use and disposal of class I substances during the service, repair, or disposal of appliances and industrial process refrigeration. Such standards and requirements shall become effective not later than July 1, 1992.

(2) The Administrator shall, within 4 years after November 15, 1990, promulgate regulations establishing standards and requirements regarding use and disposal of class I and II substances not covered by paragraph (1), including the use and disposal of class II substances during service, repair, or disposal of appliances and industrial process refrigeration. Such standards and requirements shall become effective not later than 12 months after promulgation of the regulations.

(3) The regulations under this subsection shall include requirements that—

(A) reduce the use and emission of such substances to the lowest achievable level, and

(B) maximize the recapture and recycling of such substances.

Such regulations may include requirements to use alternative substances (including substances which are not class I or class II substances) or to minimize use of class I or class II substances, or to promote the use of safe alternatives pursuant to section 7671k of this title or any combination of the foregoing.

(b) Safe disposal

The regulations under subsection (a) of this section shall establish standards and requirements for the safe disposal of class I and II substances. Such regulations shall include each of the following—

(1) Requirements that class I or class II substances contained in bulk in appliances, machines or other goods shall be removed from each such appliance, machine or other good prior to the disposal of such items or their delivery for recycling.

(2) Requirements that any appliance, machine or other good containing a class I or class II substance in bulk shall not be manufactured, sold, or distributed in interstate commerce or offered for sale or distribution in interstate commerce unless it is equipped with a servicing aperture or an equally effective design feature which will facilitate the recapture of such substance during service and repair or disposal of such item.

(3) Requirements that any product in which a class I or class II substance is incorporated so as to constitute an inherent element of such product shall be disposed of in a manner that reduces, to the maximum extent practicable, the release of such substance into the environment. If the Administrator determines that the application of this paragraph to any product would result in producing only insignificant environmental benefits, the Administrator shall include in such regulations an exception for such product.

(c) Prohibitions

(1) Effective July 1, 1992, it shall be unlawful for any person, in the course of maintaining, servicing, repairing, or disposing of an appliance or industrial process refrigeration, to knowingly vent or otherwise knowingly release or dispose of any class I or class II substance used as a refrigerant in such appliance (or industrial process refrigeration) in a manner which permits such substance to enter the environment. De minimis releases associated with good faith attempts to recapture and recycle or safely dispose of any such substance shall not be subject to the prohibition set forth in the preceding sentence.

(2) Effective 5 years after November 15, 1990, paragraph (1) shall also apply to the venting, release, or disposal of any substitute substance for a class I or class II substance by any person maintaining, servicing, repairing, or disposing of an appliance or industrial process refrigeration which contains and uses as a refrigerant any such substance, unless the Administrator determines that venting, releasing, or disposing of such substance does not pose a threat to the environment. For purposes of this paragraph, the term "appliance" includes any device which contains and uses as a refrigerant a substitute substance and which is used for household or commercial purposes, including any air conditioner, refrigerator, chiller, or freezer.

(July 14, 1955, c. 360, Title VI, § 608, as added by Pub. L. No. 101–549, Title VI, § 602(a), 104 Stat. 2661 (Nov. 15, 1990).)

HISTORICAL AND STATUTORY NOTES

Effective and Applicability Provisions

1990 Acts. Section effective Nov. 15, 1990, except as otherwise provided, see section 711(b) of Pub. L. No. 101–549, set out as a note under section 7401 of this title.

Savings Provisions

Suits, actions or proceedings commenced under this chapter as in effect prior to Nov. 15, 1990, not to abate by reason of the taking effect of amendments by Pub. L. No. 101–549, except as otherwise provided for, see section 711(a) of Pub. L. No. 101–549, set out as a note under section 7401 of this title.

§ 7671h. Servicing of motor vehicle air conditioners

[CAA § 609]

(a) Regulations

Within 1 year after November 15, 1990, the Administrator shall promulgate regulations in accordance with this section establishing standards and requirements regarding the servicing of motor vehicle air conditioners.

(b) Definitions

As used in this section—

(1) The term "refrigerant" means any class I or class II substance used in a motor vehicle air conditioner. Effective 5 years after November 15, 1990, the term "refrigerant" shall also include any substitute substance.

(2) (A) The term "approved refrigerant recycling equipment" means equipment certified by the Administrator (or an independent standards testing organization approved by the Administrator) to meet the standards established by the Administrator and applicable to equipment for the extraction and reclamation of refrigerant from motor vehicle air conditioners. Such standards shall, at a minimum, be at least as stringent as the standards of the Society of Automotive Engineers in effect as of November 15, 1990, and applicable to such equipment (SAE standard J–1990).

(B) Equipment purchased before the proposal of regulations under this section shall be considered certified if it is substantially identical to equipment certified as provided in subparagraph (A).

(3) The term "properly using" means, with respect to approved refrigerant recycling equipment, using such equipment in conformity with standards established by the Administrator and applicable to the use of such equipment. Such standards shall, at a minimum, be at least as stringent as the standards of the Society of Automotive Engineers in effect as of November 15, 1990, and applicable to the use of such equipment (SAE standard J–1989).

(4) The term "properly trained and certified" means training and certification in the proper use of approved refrigerant recycling equipment for motor vehicle air conditioners in conformity with standards established by the Administrator and applicable to the performance of service on motor vehicle air conditioners. Such standards shall, at a minimum, be at least as stringent as specified, as of November 15, 1990, in SAE standard J–1989 under the certification program of the National Institute for Automotive Service Excellence (ASE) or under a similar program such as the training and certification program of the Mobile Air Conditioning Society (MACS).

(c) Servicing motor vehicle air conditioners

Effective January 1, 1992, no person repairing or servicing motor vehicles for consideration may perform any service on a motor vehicle air conditioner involving the refrigerant for such air conditioner without properly using approved refrigerant recycling equipment and no such person may perform such service unless such person has been properly trained and certified. The requirements of the previous sentence shall not apply until January 1, 1993 in the case of a person repairing or servicing motor vehicles for consideration at an entity which performed service on fewer than 100 motor vehicle air conditioners during calendar year 1990 and if such person so certifies, pursuant to subsection (d)(2) of this section, to the Administrator by January 1, 1992.

(d) Certification

(1) Effective 2 years after November 15, 1990, each person performing service on motor vehicle air conditioners for consideration shall certify to the Administrator either—

(A) that such person has acquired, and is properly using, approved refrigerant recycling equipment in service on motor vehicle air conditioners involving refrigerant and that each individual authorized by such person to perform such service is properly trained and certified; or

(B) that such person is performing such service at an entity which serviced fewer than 100 motor vehicle air conditioners in 1991.

(2) Effective January 1, 1993, each person who certified under paragraph (1)(B) shall submit a certification under paragraph (1)(A).

(3) Each certification under this subsection shall contain the name and address of the person certifying under this subsection and the serial number of each unit of approved recycling equipment acquired by such person and shall be signed and attested by the owner or another responsible officer. Certifications under paragraph (1)(A) may be made by submitting the required information to the Administrator on a standard form provided by the manufacturer of certified refrigerant recycling equipment.

(e) Small containers of class I or class II substances

Effective 2 years after November 15, 1990, it shall be unlawful for any person to sell or distribute, or offer for sale or distribution, in interstate commerce to any person (other than a person performing service for consideration on motor vehicle air-conditioning systems in compliance with this section) any class I or class II substance that is suitable for use as a refrigerant in a motor vehicle air-conditioning system and that is in a container which contains less than 20 pounds of such refrigerant.

(July 14, 1955, c. 360, Title VI, § 609, as added by Pub. L. No. 101–549, Title VI, § 602(a), 104 Stat. 2662 (Nov. 15, 1990).)

HISTORICAL AND STATUTORY NOTES

Effective and Applicability Provisions

1990 Acts. Section effective Nov. 15, 1990, except as otherwise provided, see section 711(b) of Pub. L. No. 101–549, set out as a note under section 7401 of this title.

Savings Provisions

Suits, actions or proceedings commenced under this chapter as in effect prior to Nov. 15, 1990, not to abate by reason of the taking effect of amendments by Pub. L. No. 101–549, except as otherwise provided for, see section 711(a) of Pub. L. No. 101–549, set out as a note under section 7401 of this title.

§ 7671i. Nonessential products containing chlorofluorocarbons

[CAA § 610]

(a) Regulations

The Administrator shall promulgate regulations to carry out the requirements of this section within 1 year after November 15, 1990.

(b) Nonessential products

The regulations under this section shall identify nonessential products that release class I substances into the environment (including any release occurring during manufacture, use, storage, or disposal) and prohibit any person from selling or distributing any such product, or offering any such product for sale or distribution, in interstate commerce. At a minimum, such prohibition shall apply to—

(1) chlorofluorocarbon-propelled plastic party streamers and noise horns,

(2) chlorofluorocarbon-containing cleaning fluids for noncommercial electronic and photographic equipment, and

(3) other consumer products that are determined by the Administrator—

(A) to release class I substances into the environment (including any release occurring during manufacture, use, storage, or disposal), and

(B) to be nonessential.

In determining whether a product is nonessential, the Administrator shall consider the purpose or intended use of the product, the technological availability of substitutes for such product and for such class I substance, safety, health, and other relevant factors.

(c) Effective date

Effective 24 months after November 15, 1990, it shall be unlawful for any person to sell or distribute, or offer for sale or distribution, in interstate commerce any nonessential product to which regulations under subsection (a) of this section implementing subsection (b) of this section are applicable.

(d) Other products

(1) Effective January 1, 1994, it shall be unlawful for any person to sell or distribute, or offer for sale or distribution, in interstate commerce—

(A) any aerosol product or other pressurized dispenser which contains a class II substance; or

(B) any plastic foam product which contains, or is manufactured with, a class II substance.

(2) The Administrator is authorized to grant exceptions from the prohibition under subparagraph (A) of paragraph (1) where—

(A) the use of the aerosol product or pressurized dispenser is determined by the Administrator to be essential as a result of flammability or worker safety concerns, and

(B) the only available alternative to use of a class II substance is use of a class I substance which legally could be substituted for such class II substance.

(3) Subparagraph (B) of paragraph (1) shall not apply to—

(A) a foam insulation product, or

(B) an integral skin, rigid, or semi-rigid foam utilized to provide for motor vehicle safety in accordance with Federal Motor Vehicle Safety Standards where no adequate substitute substance (other than a class I or class II substance) is practicable for effectively meeting such Standards.

(e) Medical devices

Nothing in this section shall apply to any medical device as defined in section 7671(8) of this title.

(July 14, 1955, c. 360, Title VI, § 610, as added by Pub. L. No. 101–549, Title VI, § 602(a), 104 Stat. 2664 (Nov. 15, 1990).)

HISTORICAL AND STATUTORY NOTES

Effective and Applicability Provisions

1990 Acts. Section effective Nov. 15, 1990, except as otherwise provided, see section 711(b) of Pub. L. No. 101–549, set out as a note under section 7401 of this title.

Savings Provisions

Suits, actions or proceedings commenced under this chapter as in effect prior to Nov. 15, 1990, not to abate by reason of the taking effect of amendments by Pub. L. No. 101–549, except as otherwise provided for, see section 711(a) of Pub. L. No. 101–549, set out as a note under section 7401 of this title.

§ 7671j. Labeling

[CAA § 611]

(a) Regulations

The Administrator shall promulgate regulations to implement the labeling requirements of this section within 18 months after November 15, 1990, after notice and opportunity for public comment.

(b) Containers containing class I or class II substances and products containing class I substances

Effective 30 months after November 15, 1990, no container in which a class I or class II substance is stored or transported, and no product containing a class I substance, shall be introduced into interstate commerce unless it bears a clearly legible and conspicuous label stating:

"Warning: Contains [insert name of substance], a substance which harms public health and environment by destroying ozone in the upper atmosphere".

(c) Products containing class II substances

(1) After 30 months after November 15, 1990, and before January 1, 2015, no product containing a class II substance shall be introduced into interstate commerce unless it bears the label referred to in subsection (b) of this section if the Administrator determines, after notice and opportunity for public comment, that there are substitute products or manufacturing processes (A) that do not rely on the use of such class II substance, (B) that reduce the overall risk to human health and the environment, and (C) that are currently or potentially available.

(2) Effective January 1, 2015, the requirements of subsection (b) of this section shall apply to all products containing a class II substance.

(d) Products manufactured with class I and class II substances

(1) In the case of a class II substance, after 30 months after November 15, 1990, and before January 1, 2015, if the Administrator, after notice and opportunity for public comment, makes the determination referred to in subsection (c) of this section with respect to a product manufactured with a process that uses such class II substance, no such product shall be introduced into interstate commerce unless it bears a clearly legible and conspicuous label stating:

"Warning: Manufactured with [insert name of substance], a substance which harms public health and environment by destroying ozone in the upper atmosphere"[1]

(2) In the case of a class I substance, effective 30 months after November 15, 1990, and before January 1, 2015, the labeling requirements of this subsection shall apply to all products manufactured with a process that uses such class I substance unless the Administrator determines that there are no substitute products or manufacturing processes that (A) do not rely on the use of such class I substance, (B) reduce the overall risk to human health and the environment, and (C) are currently or potentially available.

(e) Petitions

(1) Any person may, at any time after 18 months after November 15, 1990, petition the Administrator to apply the requirements of this section to a product containing a class II substance or a product manufactured with a class I or II substance which is not otherwise subject to such requirements. Within 180 days after receiving such petition, the Administrator shall, pursuant to the criteria set forth in subsection (c) of this section, either propose to apply the requirements of this section to such product or publish an explanation of the petition denial. If the Administrator proposes to apply such requirements to such product, the Administrator shall, by rule, render a final determination pursuant to such criteria within 1 year after receiving such petition.

(2) Any petition under this paragraph[2] shall include a showing by the petitioner that there are data on the product adequate to support the petition.

(3) If the Administrator determines that information on the product is not sufficient to make the required determination the Administrator shall use any authority available to the Administrator under any law administered by the Administrator to acquire such information.

(4) In the case of a product determined by the Administrator, upon petition or on the Administrator's own motion, to be subject to the requirements of this section, the Administrator shall establish an effective date for such requirements. The effective date shall be 1 year after such determination or 30 months after November 15, 1990, whichever is later.

(5) Effective January 1, 2015, the labeling requirements of this subsection[3] shall apply to all products manufactured with a process that uses a class I or class II substance.

(f) Relationship to other law

(1) The labeling requirements of this section shall not constitute, in whole or part, a defense to liability or a cause for reduction in damages in any suit, whether civil or criminal, brought under any law, whether Federal or State, other than a suit for failure to comply with the labeling requirements of this section.

(2) No other approval of such label by the Administrator under any other law administered by the Administrator shall be required with respect to the labeling requirements of this section.

(July 14, 1955, c. 360, Title VI, § 611, as added by Pub. L. No. 101–549, Title VI, § 602(a), 104 Stat. 2665 (Nov. 15, 1990).)

[1] So in original. Probably should be followed by a period.

[2] So in original. Probably should be "paragraph."

[3] So in original. Probably should be "section."

HISTORICAL AND STATUTORY NOTES

Effective and Applicability Provisions

1990 Acts. Section effective Nov. 15, 1990, except as otherwise provided, see section 711(b) of Pub. L. No. 101–549, set out as a note under section 7401 of this title.

Savings Provisions

Suits, actions or proceedings commenced under this chapter as in effect prior to Nov. 15, 1990, not to abate by reason of the taking effect of amendments by Pub. L. No. 101–549, except as otherwise provided for, see section 711(a) of Pub. L. No. 101–549, set out as a note under section 7401 of this title.

§ 7671k. Safe alternatives policy

[CAA § 612]

(a) Policy

To the maximum extent practicable, class I and class II substances shall be replaced by chemicals, product substitutes, or alternative manufacturing processes that reduce overall risks to human health and the environment.

(b) Reviews and reports

The Administrator shall—

(1) in consultation and coordination with interested members of the public and the heads of relevant Federal agencies and departments, recommend Federal research programs and other activities to assist in identifying alternatives to the use of class I and class II substances as refrigerants, solvents, fire retardants, foam blowing agents, and other commercial applications and in achieving a transition to such alternatives, and, where appropriate, seek to maximize the use of Federal research facilities and resources to assist users of class I and class II substances in identifying and developing alternatives to the use of such substances as refrigerants, solvents, fire retardants, foam blowing agents, and other commercial applications;

(2) examine in consultation and coordination with the Secretary of Defense and the heads of other relevant Federal agencies and departments, including the General Services Administration, Federal procurement practices with respect to class I and class II substances and recommend measures to promote the transition by the Federal Government, as expeditiously as possible, to the use of safe substitutes;

(3) specify initiatives, including appropriate intergovernmental, international, and commercial information and technology transfers, to promote the development and use of safe substitutes for class I and class II substances, including alternative chemicals, product substitutes, and alternative manufacturing processes; and

(4) maintain a public clearinghouse of alternative chemicals, product substitutes, and alternative manufacturing processes that are available for products and manufacturing processes which use class I and class II substances.

(c) Alternatives for class I or II substances

Within 2 years after November 15, 1990, the Administrator shall promulgate rules under this section providing that it shall be unlawful to replace any class I or class II substance with any substitute substance which the Administrator determines may present adverse effects to human health or the environment, where the Administrator has identified an alternative to such replacement that—

(1) reduces the overall risk to human health and the environment; and

(2) is currently or potentially available.

The Administrator shall publish a list of (A) the substitutes prohibited under this subsection for specific uses and (B) the safe alternatives identified under this subsection for specific uses.

(d) Right to petition

Any person may petition the Administrator to add a substance to the lists under subsection (c) of this section or to remove a substance from either of such lists. The Administrator shall grant or deny the petition within 90 days after receipt of any such petition. If the Administrator denies the petition, the Administrator shall publish an explanation of why the petition was denied. If the Administrator grants such petition the Administrator shall publish such revised list within 6 months thereafter. Any petition under this subsection shall include a showing by the petitioner that there are data on the substance adequate to support the petition. If the Administrator determines that information on the substance is not sufficient to make a determination under this subsection, the Administrator shall use any authority available to the Administrator, under any law administered by the Administrator, to acquire such information.

(e) Studies and notification

The Administrator shall require any person who produces a chemical substitute for a class I substance to provide the Administrator with such person's unpublished health and safety studies on such substitute and require producers to notify the Administrator not less than 90 days before new or existing chemicals are introduced into interstate commerce for significant new uses as substitutes for a class I substance. This subsection shall be subject to section 7414(c) of this title.

(July 14, 1955, c. 360, Title VI, § 612, as added by Pub. L. No. 101–549, Title VI, § 602(a), 104 Stat. 2667 (Nov. 15, 1990).)

HISTORICAL AND STATUTORY NOTES

Effective and Applicability Provisions

1990 Acts. Section effective Nov. 15, 1990, except as otherwise provided, see section 711(b) of Pub. L. No. 101–549, set out as a note under section 7401 of this title.

Savings Provisions

Suits, actions or proceedings commenced under this chapter as in effect prior to Nov. 15, 1990, not to abate by reason of the taking effect of amendments by Pub. L. No. 101–549, except as otherwise provided for, see section 711(a) of Pub. L. No. 101–549, set out as a note under section 7401 of this title.

§ 7671*l*. Federal procurement

[CAA § 613]

Not later than 18 months after November 15, 1990, the Administrator, in consultation with the Administrator of the General Services Administration and the Secretary of Defense, shall promulgate regulations requiring each department, agency, and instrumentality of the United States to conform its procurement regulations to the policies and requirements of this subchapter and to maximize the substitution of safe alternatives identified under section 7671k of this title for class I and class II substances. Not later than 30 months after November 15, 1990, each department, agency, and instrumentality of the United States shall so conform its procurement regulations and certify to the President that its regulations have been modified in accordance with this section.

(July 14, 1955, c. 360, Title VI, § 613, as added by Pub. L. No. 101–549, Title VI, § 602(a), 104 Stat. 2668 (Nov. 15, 1990).)

HISTORICAL AND STATUTORY NOTES

Effective and Applicability Provisions

1990 Acts. Section effective Nov. 15, 1990, except as otherwise provided, see section 711(b) of Pub. L. No. 101–549, set out as a note under section 7401 of this title.

Savings Provisions

Suits, actions or proceedings commenced under this chapter as in effect prior to Nov. 15, 1990, not to abate by reason of the taking effect of amendments by Pub. L. No. 101–549, except as otherwise provided for, see section 711(a) of Pub. L. No. 101–549, set out as a note under section 7401 of this title.

§ 7671m. Relationship to other laws

[CAA § 614]

(a) State laws

Notwithstanding section 7416 of this title, during the 2-year period beginning on November 15, 1990, no State or local government may enforce any requirement concerning the design of any new or recalled appliance for the purpose of protecting the stratospheric ozone layer.

(b) Montreal Protocol

This subchapter as added by the Clean Air Act Amendments of 1990 shall be construed, interpreted, and applied as a supplement to the terms and conditions of the Montreal Protocol, as provided in Article 2, paragraph 11 thereof, and shall not be construed, interpreted, or applied to abrogate the responsibilities or obligations of the United States to implement fully the provisions of the Montreal Protocol. In the case of conflict between any provision of this subchapter and any provision of the Montreal Protocol, the more stringent provision shall govern. Nothing in this subchapter shall be construed, interpreted, or applied to affect the authority or responsibility of the Administrator to implement Article 4 of the Montreal Protocol with other appropriate agencies.

(c) Technology export and overseas investment

Upon November 15, 1990, the President shall—

(1) prohibit the export of technologies used to produce a class I substance;

(2) prohibit direct or indirect investments by any person in facilities designed to produce a class I or class II substance in nations that are not parties to the Montreal Protocol; and

(3) direct that no agency of the government provide bilateral or multilateral subsidies, aids, credits, guarantees, or insurance programs, for the purpose of producing any class I substance.

(July 14, 1955, c. 360, Title VI, § 614, as added by Pub. L. No. 101–549, Title VI, § 602(a), 104 Stat. 2668 (Nov. 15, 1990).)

HISTORICAL AND STATUTORY NOTES

References in Text

The Clean Air Act Amendments of 1990, referred to in subsec. (b), probably means Pub. L. No. 101–549, 104 Stat. 2399 (Nov. 15, 1990). For complete classification of this Act to the Code, see Short Title of 1990 Amendments note set out under section 7401 of this title and Tables.

Effective and Applicability Provisions

1990 Acts. Section effective Nov. 15, 1990, except as otherwise provided, see section 711(b) of Pub. L. No. 101–549, set out as a note under section 7401 of this title.

Savings Provisions

Suits, actions or proceedings commenced under this chapter as in effect prior to Nov. 15, 1990, not to abate by reason of the taking effect of amendments by Pub. L. No. 101–549, except as otherwise provided for, see section 711(a) of Pub. L. No. 101–549, set out as a note under section 7401 of this title.

§ 7671n. Authority of Administrator

[CAA § 615]

If, in the Administrator's judgment, any substance, practice, process, or activity may reasonably be anticipated to affect the stratosphere, especially ozone in the stratosphere, and such effect may reasonably be anticipated to endanger public health or welfare, the Administrator shall promptly promulgate regulations respecting the control of such substance, practice, process, or activity, and shall submit notice of the proposal and promulgation of such regulation to the Congress.

(July 14, 1955, c. 360, Title VI, § 615, as added by Pub. L. No. 101–549, Title VI, § 602(a), 104 Stat. 2669 (Nov. 15, 1990).)

HISTORICAL AND STATUTORY NOTES

Effective and Applicability Provisions

1990 Acts. Section effective Nov. 15, 1990, except as otherwise provided, see section 711(b) of Pub. L. No. 101–549, set out as a note under section 7401 of this title.

Savings Provisions

Suits, actions or proceedings commenced under this chapter as in effect prior to Nov. 15, 1990, not to abate by reason of the taking effect of amendments by Pub. L. No. 101–549, except as otherwise provided for, see section 711(a) of Pub. L. No. 101–549, set out as a note under section 7401 of this title.

§ 7671*o*. Transfers among Parties to Montreal Protocol

[CAA § 616]

(a) In general

Consistent with the Montreal Protocol, the United States may engage in transfers with other Parties to the Protocol under the following conditions:

(1) The United States may transfer production allowances to another Party if, at the time of such transfer, the Administrator establishes revised production limits for the United States such that the aggregate national United States production permitted under the revised production limits equals the lesser of (A) the maximum production level permitted for the substance or substances concerned in the transfer year under the Protocol minus the production allowances transferred, (B) the maximum production level permitted for the substance or substances concerned in the transfer year under applicable domestic law minus the production allowances transferred, or (C) the average of the actual national production level of the substance or substances concerned for the 3 years prior to the transfer minus the production allowances transferred.

(2) The United States may acquire production allowances from another Party if, at the time of such transfer, the Administrator finds that the other Party has revised its domestic production limits in the same manner as provided with respect to transfers by the United States in this subsection.

(b) Effect of transfers on production limits

The Administrator is authorized to reduce the production limits established under this chapter as required as a prerequisite to transfers under paragraph (1) of subsection (a) of this section or to increase production limits established under this chapter to reflect production allowances acquired under a transfer under paragraph (2) of subsection (a) of this section.

(c) Regulations

The Administrator shall promulgate, within 2 years after November 15, 1990, regulations to implement this section.

(d) "Applicable domestic law" defined

In the case of the United States, the term "applicable domestic law" means this chapter.

(July 14, 1955, c. 360, Title VI, § 616, as added by Pub. L. No. 101–549, Title VI, § 602(a), 104 Stat. 2669 (Nov. 15, 1990).)

HISTORICAL AND STATUTORY NOTES

Effective and Applicability Provisions

1990 Acts. Section effective Nov. 15, 1990, except as otherwise provided, see section 711(b) of Pub. L. No. 101–549, set out as a note under section 7401 of this title.

Savings Provisions

Suits, actions or proceedings commenced under this chapter as in effect prior to Nov. 15, 1990, not to abate by reason of the taking effect of amendments by Pub. L. No. 101–549, except as otherwise provided for, see section 711(a) of Pub. L. No. 101–549, set out as a note under section 7401 of this title.

§ 7671p. International cooperation

[CAA § 617]

(a) In general

The President shall undertake to enter into international agreements to foster cooperative research which complements studies and research authorized by this subchapter, and to develop standards and regulations which protect the stratosphere consistent with regulations applicable within the United States. For these purposes the President through the Secretary of State and the Assistant Secretary of State for Oceans and International Environmental and Scientific Affairs, shall negotiate multilateral treaties, conventions, resolutions, or other agreements, and formulate, present, or support proposals at the United Nations and other appropriate international forums and shall report to the Congress periodically on efforts to arrive at such agreements.

(b) Assistance to developing countries

The Administrator, in consultation with the Secretary of State, shall support global participation in the Montreal Protocol by providing technical and financial assistance to developing countries that are Parties to the Montreal Protocol and operating under article 5 of the Protocol. There are authorized to be appropriated not more than $30,000,000 to carry out this section in fiscal years 1991, 1992 and 1993 and such sums as may be necessary in fiscal years 1994 and 1995. If China and India become Parties to the Montreal Protocol, there are authorized to be appropriated not more than an additional $30,000,000 to carry out this section in fiscal years 1991, 1992, and 1993.

(July 14, 1955, c. 360, Title VI, § 617, as added by Pub. L. No. 101–549, Title VI, § 602(a), 104 Stat. 2669 (Nov. 15, 1990).)

HISTORICAL AND STATUTORY NOTES

Effective and Applicability Provisions

1990 Acts. Section effective effect Nov. 15, 1990, except as otherwise provided, see section 711(b) of Pub. L. No. 101–549, set out as a note under section 7401 of this title.

Savings Provisions

Suits, actions or proceedings commenced under this chapter as in effect prior to Nov. 15, 1990, not to abate by reason of the taking effect of amendments by Pub. L. No. 101–549, except as otherwise provided for, see section 711(a) of Pub. L. No. 101–549, set out as a note under section 7401 of this title.

§ 7671q. Miscellaneous provisions

[CAA § 618]

For purposes of section 7416 of this title, requirements concerning the areas addressed by this subchapter for the protection of the stratosphere against ozone layer depletion shall be treated as requirements for the control and abatement of air pollution. For purposes of section 7418 of this title, the requirements of this subchapter and corresponding State, interstate, and local requirements, administrative authority, and process, and sanctions respecting the protection of the stratospheric ozone layer shall be treated as requirements for the control and abatement of air pollution within the meaning of section 7418 of this title.

(July 14, 1955, c. 360, Title VI, § 618, as added by Pub. L. No. 101–549, Title VI, § 602(a), 104 Stat. 2670 (Nov. 15, 1990).)

HISTORICAL AND STATUTORY NOTES

Effective and Applicability Provisions

1990 Acts. Section effective Nov. 15, 1990, except as otherwise provided, see section 711(b) of Pub. L. No. 101–549, set out as a note under section 7401 of this title.

Savings Provisions

Suits, actions or proceedings commenced under this chapter as in effect prior to Nov. 15, 1990, not to abate by reason of the taking effect of amendments by Pub. L. No. 101–549, except as otherwise provided for, see section 711(a) of Pub. L. No. 101–549, set out as a note under section 7401 of this title.

COMPREHENSIVE ENVIRONMENTAL RESPONSE, COMPENSATION, AND LIABILITY ACT

COMPREHENSIVE ENVIRONMENTAL RESPONSE, COMPENSATION, AND LIABILITY ACT OF 1980 [CERCLA § ______]

(42 U.S.C.A. §§ 9601 to 9675)

CHAPTER 103—COMPREHENSIVE ENVIRONMENTAL RESPONSE, COMPENSATION, AND LIABILITY

SUBCHAPTER I—HAZARDOUS SUBSTANCES RELEASES, LIABILITY, COMPENSATION

SUBCHAPTER II—HAZARDOUS SUBSTANCE RESPONSE REVENUE

PART A—HAZARDOUS SUBSTANCE RESPONSE TRUST FUND

PART B—POST-CLOSURE LIABILITY TRUST FUND

SUBCHAPTER III—MISCELLANEOUS PROVISIONS

SUBCHAPTER IV—POLLUTION INSURANCE

SUBCHAPTER I—HAZARDOUS SUBSTANCES RELEASES, LIABILITY, COMPENSATION

§ 9601. Definitions

[CERCLA § 101]

For purpose of this subchapter—

(1) The term "act of God" means an unanticipated grave natural disaster or other natural phenomenon of an exceptional, inevitable, and irresistible character, the effects of which could not have been prevented or avoided by the exercise of due care or foresight.

(2) The term "Administrator" means the Administrator of the United States Environmental Protection Agency.

(3) The term "barrel" means forty-two United States gallons at sixty degrees Fahrenheit.

(4) The term "claim" means a demand in writing for a sum certain.

(5) The term "claimant" means any person who presents a claim for compensation under this chapter.

(6) The term "damages" means damages for injury or loss of natural resources as set forth in section 9607(a) or 9611(b) of this title.

(7) The term "drinking water supply" means any raw or finished water source that is or may be used by a public water system (as defined in the Safe Drinking Water Act [42 U.S.C.A. § 300f et seq.]) or as drinking water by one or more individuals.

(8) The term "environment" means (A) the navigable waters, the waters of the contiguous zone, and the ocean waters of which the natural resources are under the exclusive management authority of the United States under the Magnuson-Stevens Fishery Conservation and Management Act [16 U.S.C.A. § 1801 et seq.], and (B) any other surface water, ground water, drinking water supply, land surface or subsurface strata, or ambient air within the United States or under the jurisdiction of the United States.

(9) The term "facility" means (A) any building, structure, installation, equipment, pipe or pipeline (including any pipe into a sewer or publicly owned treatment works), well, pit, pond, lagoon, impoundment, ditch, landfill, storage container, motor vehicle, rolling stock, or aircraft, or (B) any site or area where a hazardous substance has been deposited, stored, disposed of, or placed, or otherwise come to be located; but does not include any consumer product in consumer use or any vessel.

(10) The term "federally permitted release" means (A) discharges in compliance with a permit under section 402 of the Federal Water Pollution Control Act [33 U.S.C.A. § 1342], (B) discharges resulting from circumstances identified and reviewed and made part of the public record with respect to a permit issued or modified under section 402 of the Federal Water Pollution Control Act and subject to a condition of such permit, (C) continuous or anticipated intermittent discharges from a point source, identified in a permit or permit application under section 402 of the Federal Water Pollution Control Act, which are caused by events occurring within the scope of relevant operating or treatment systems, (D) discharges in compliance with a legally enforceable permit under section 404 of the Federal Water Pollution Control Act [33 U.S.C.A. § 1344], (E) releases in compliance with a legally enforceable final permit issued pursuant to section 3005(a) through (d) of the Solid Waste Disposal Act [42 U.S.C.A. § 6925(a)–(d)] from a hazardous waste treatment, storage, or disposal facility when such permit specifically identifies the hazardous substances and makes such substances subject to a standard of practice, control procedure or bioassay limitation or condition, or other control on the hazardous substances in such releases, (F) any release in compliance with a legally enforceable permit issued under section 1412 of Title 33 of[1] section 1413 of Title 33, (G) any injection of fluids authorized under Federal underground injection control programs or State programs submitted for Federal approval (and not disapproved by the Administrator of the Environmental Protection Agency) pursuant to part C of the Safe Drinking Water Act [42 U.S.C.A. § 300h et seq.], (H) any emission into the air subject to a permit or control regulation under section 111 [42 U.S.C.A. § 7411], section 112 [42 U.S.C.A. § 7412], Title I part C [42 U.S.C.A. § 7470 et seq.], Title I part D [42 U.S.C.A. § 7501 et seq.], or State implementation plans submitted in accordance with section 110 of the Clean Air Act [42 U.S.C.A. § 7410] (and not disapproved by the Administrator of the Environmental Protection Agency), including any schedule or waiver granted, promulgated, or approved under these sections, (I) any injection of fluids or other materials authorized under applicable State law (i) for the purpose of stimulating or treating wells for the production of crude oil, natural gas, or water, (ii) for the purpose of secondary, tertiary, or other enhanced recovery of crude oil or natural gas, or (iii) which are brought to the surface in conjunction with the production of crude oil or natural gas and which are reinjected, (J) the introduction of any pollutant into a publicly owned treatment works when such pollutant is specified in and in compliance with applicable pretreatment standards of section 307(b) or (c) of the Clean Water Act [33 U.S.C.A. § 1317(b), (c)] and enforceable requirements in a pretreatment program submitted by a State or municipality for Federal approval under section 402 of such Act [33 U.S.C.A. § 1342], and (K) any release of source, special nuclear, or byproduct material, as those terms are defined in the Atomic Energy Act of 1954 [42 U.S.C.A. § 2011 et seq.], in compliance with a legally enforceable license, permit, regulation, or order issued pursuant to the Atomic Energy Act of 1954.

(11) The term "Fund" or "Trust Fund" means the Hazardous Substance Superfund established by section 9507 of Title 26.

(12) The term "ground water" means water in a saturated zone or stratum beneath the surface of land or water.

(13) The term "guarantor" means any person, other than the owner or operator, who provides evidence of financial responsibility for an owner or operator under this chapter.

(14) The term "hazardous substance" means (A) any substance designated pursuant to section 311(b)(2)(A) of the Federal Water Pollution Control Act [33 U.S.C.A. § 1321(b)(2)(A)], (B) any element, compound, mixture, solution, or substance designated pursuant to section 9602 of this title, (C) any hazardous waste having the characteristics identified under or listed pursuant to section 3001 of the Solid Waste Disposal Act [42 U.S.C.A. § 6921] (but not including any waste the regulation of which under the Solid Waste Disposal Act [42 U.S.C.A. § 6901 et seq.] has been suspended by Act of Congress), (D) any toxic pollutant listed under section 307(a) of the Federal Water Pollution Control Act [33 U.S.C.A. § 1317(a)], (E) any hazardous air pollutant listed under section 112 of the Clean Air Act [42 U.S.C.A. § 7412], and (F) any imminently hazardous chemical substance or mixture with respect to which the Administrator has taken action pursuant to section 7 of the Toxic Substances Control Act [15 U.S.C.A. § 2606]. The term does not include petroleum, including crude oil or any fraction thereof which is not otherwise specifically listed or designated as a hazardous substance under subparagraphs (A) through (F) of this paragraph, and the term does not include natural gas, natural gas liquids, liquefied natural gas, or synthetic gas usable for fuel (or mixtures of natural gas and such synthetic gas).

(15) The term "navigable waters" or "navigable waters of the United States" means the waters of the United States, including the territorial seas.

(16) The term "natural resources" means land, fish, wildlife, biota, air, water, ground water, drinking water supplies, and other such resources belonging to, managed by, held in trust by, appertaining to, or otherwise controlled by the United States (including the resources of the fishery conservation zone established by the Magnuson-Stevens Fishery Conservation and Management Act [16 U.S.C.A. § 1801 et seq.]), any State or local government, any foreign government, any Indian tribe, or, if such resources are subject to a trust restriction on alienation, any member of an Indian tribe.

(17) The term "offshore facility" means any facility of any kind located in, on, or under, any of the navigable waters of the United States, and any facility of any kind which is subject to the jurisdiction of the United States and is located in, on, or under any other waters, other than a vessel or a public vessel.

(18) The term "onshore facility" means any facility (including, but not limited to, motor vehicles and rolling stock) of any kind located in, on, or under, any land or nonnavigable waters within the United States.

(19) The term "otherwise subject to the jurisdiction of the United States" means subject to the jurisdiction of the United States by virtue of United States citizenship, United States vessel documentation or numbering, or as provided by international agreement to which the United States is a party.

(20) (A) The term "owner or operator" means (i) in the case of a vessel, any person owning, operating, or chartering by demise, such vessel, (ii) in the case of an onshore facility or an offshore facility, any person owning or operating such facility, and (iii) in the case of any facility, title or control of which was conveyed due to bankruptcy, foreclosure, tax delinquency, abandonment, or similar means to a unit of State or local government, any person who owned, operated, or otherwise controlled activities at such facility immediately beforehand. Such term does not include a person, who, without participating in the management of a vessel or facility, holds indicia of ownership primarily to protect his security interest in the vessel or facility.

(B) In the case of a hazardous substance which has been accepted for transportation by a common or contract carrier and except as provided in section 9607(a)(3) or (4) of this title, (i) the term "owner or operator" shall mean such common carrier or other bona fide for hire carrier acting as an independent contractor during such transportation, (ii) the shipper of such hazardous substance shall not be considered to have caused or contributed to any release during such transportation which resulted solely from circumstances or conditions beyond his control.

(C) In the case of a hazardous substance which has been delivered by a common or contract carrier to a disposal or treatment facility and except as provided in section 9607(a)(3) or (4) of this title, (i) the term "owner or operator" shall not include such common or contract carrier, and (ii) such common or contract carrier shall not be considered to have caused or contributed to any release at such disposal or treatment facility resulting from circumstances or conditions beyond its control.

(D) The term "owner or operator" does not include a unit of State or local government which acquired ownership or control through seizure or otherwise in connection with law enforcement activity, or through bankruptcy, tax delinquency, abandonment, or other circumstances in which the government acquires title by virtue of its function as sovereign. The exclusion provided under this paragraph shall not apply to any State or local government which has caused or contributed to the release or threatened release of a hazardous substance from the facility, and such a State or local government shall be subject to the provisions of this chapter in the same manner and to the same extent, both procedurally and substantively, as any nongovernmental entity, including liability under section 9607 of this title.

(E) Exclusion of certain Alaska Native villages and Native corporations.—

(i) In general.—The term "owner or operator" does not include, with respect to a facility conveyed to a Native village or Native Corporation (as those terms are defined in section 3 of the Alaska Native Claims Settlement Act) under the Alaska Native Claims Settlement Act—

(I) the Native village or Native Corporation that received the facility from the United States Government; or

(II) a successor in interest to which the facility was conveyed under section 14(c) of such Act.

(ii) Limitation.—The exclusion provided under this subparagraph shall not apply to any entity described in clause (i) that causes or contributes to a release or threatened release of a hazardous substance from the facility conveyed as described in such clause.

(F) Exclusion of lenders not participants in management

(i) Indicia of ownership to protect security

The term "owner or operator" does not include a person that is a lender that, without participating in the management of a vessel or facility, holds indicia of ownership primarily to protect the security interest of the person in the vessel or facility.

(ii) Foreclosure

The term "owner or operator" does not include a person that is a lender that did not participate in management of a vessel or facility prior to foreclosure, notwithstanding that the person—

(I) forecloses on the vessel or facility; and

(II) after foreclosure, sells, re-leases (in the case of a lease finance transaction), or liquidates the vessel or facility, maintains business activities, winds up operations, undertakes a response action under section 9607(d)(1) of this title or under the direction of an on-scene coordinator appointed under the National Contingency Plan, with respect to the vessel or facility, or takes any other measure to preserve, protect, or prepare the vessel or facility prior to sale or disposition,

if the person seeks to sell, re-lease (in the case of a lease finance transaction), or otherwise divest the person of the vessel or facility at the earliest practicable, commercially reasonable time, on commercially reasonable terms, taking into account market conditions and legal and regulatory requirements.

(G) Participation in management

For purposes of subparagraph (F)—

(i) the term "participate in management"—

(I) means actually participating in the management or operational affairs of a vessel or facility; and

(II) does not include merely having the capacity to influence, or the unexercised right to control, vessel or facility operations;

(ii) a person that is a lender and that holds indicia of ownership primarily to protect a security interest in a vessel or facility shall be considered to participate in management only if, while the borrower is still in possession of the vessel or facility encumbered by the security interest, the person—

(I) exercises decisionmaking control over the environmental compliance related to the vessel or facility, such that the person has undertaken responsibility for the hazardous substance handling or disposal practices related to the vessel or facility; or

(II) exercises control at a level comparable to that of a manager of the vessel or facility, such that the person has assumed or manifested responsibility—

(aa) for the overall management of the vessel or facility encompassing day-to-day decisionmaking with respect to environmental compliance; or

(bb) over all or substantially all of the operational functions (as distinguished from financial or administrative functions) of the vessel or facility other than the function of environmental compliance;

(iii) the term "participate in management" does not include performing an act or failing to act prior to the time at which a security interest is created in a vessel or facility; and

(iv) the term "participate in management" does not include—

(I) holding a security interest or abandoning or releasing a security interest;

(II) including in the terms of an extension of credit, or in a contract or security agreement relating to the extension, a covenant, warranty, or other term or condition that relates to environmental compliance;

(III) monitoring or enforcing the terms and conditions of the extension of credit or security interest;

(IV) monitoring or undertaking 1 or more inspections of the vessel or facility;

(V) requiring a response action or other lawful means of addressing the release or threatened release of a hazardous substance in connection with the vessel or facility prior to, during, or on the expiration of the term of the extension of credit;

(VI) providing financial or other advice or counseling in an effort to mitigate, prevent, or cure default or diminution in the value of the vessel or facility;

(VII) restructuring, renegotiating, or otherwise agreeing to alter the terms and conditions of the extension of credit or security interest, exercising forbearance;

(VIII) exercising other remedies that may be available under applicable law for the breach of a term or condition of the extension of credit or security agreement; or

(IX) conducting a response action under section 9607(d) of this title or under the direction of an on-scene coordinator appointed under the National Contingency Plan,

if the actions do not rise to the level of participating in management (within the meaning of clauses (i) and (ii)).

(H) Other terms

As used in this chapter:

(i) Extension of credit

The term "extension of credit" includes a lease finance transaction—

(I) in which the lessor does not initially select the leased vessel or facility and does not during the lease term control the daily operations or maintenance of the vessel or facility; or

(II) that conforms with regulations issued by the appropriate Federal banking agency or the appropriate State bank supervisor (as those terms are defined in section 1813))[2] or with regulations issued by the National Credit Union Administration Board, as appropriate.

(ii) Financial or administrative function

The term "financial or administrative function" includes a function such as that of a credit manager, accounts payable officer, accounts receivable officer, personnel manager, comptroller, or chief financial officer, or a similar function.

(iii) Foreclosure; foreclose

The terms "foreclosure" and "foreclose" mean, respectively, acquiring, and to acquire, a vessel or facility through—

(I) **(aa)** purchase at sale under a judgment or decree, power of sale, or nonjudicial foreclosure sale;

(bb) a deed in lieu of foreclosure, or similar conveyance from a trustee; or

(cc) repossession,

if the vessel or facility was security for an extension of credit previously contracted;

(II) conveyance pursuant to an extension of credit previously contracted, including the termination of a lease agreement; or

(III) any other formal or informal manner by which the person acquires, for subsequent disposition, title to or possession of a vessel or facility in order to protect the security interest of the person.

(iv) Lender

The term "lender" means—

(I) an insured depository institution (as defined in section 1813 of Title 12);

(II) an insured credit union (as defined in section 1752 of Title 12);

(III) a bank or association chartered under the Farm Credit Act of 1971 (12 U.S.C. 2001 et seq.);

(IV) a leasing or trust company that is an affiliate of an insured depository institution;

(V) any person (including a successor or assignee of any such person) that makes a bona fide extension of credit to or takes or acquires a security interest from a nonaffiliated person;

(VI) the Federal National Mortgage Association, the Federal Home Loan Mortgage Corporation, the Federal Agricultural Mortgage Corporation, or any other entity that in a bona fide manner buys or sells loans or interests in loans;

(VII) a person that insures or guarantees against a default in the repayment of an extension of credit, or acts as a surety with respect to an extension of credit, to a nonaffiliated person; and

(VIII) a person that provides title insurance and that acquires a vessel or facility as a result of assignment or conveyance in the course of underwriting claims and claims settlement.

(v) Operational function

The term "operational function" includes a function such as that of a facility or plant manager, operations manager, chief operating officer, or chief executive officer.

(vi) Security interest

The term "security interest" includes a right under a mortgage, deed of trust, assignment, judgment lien, pledge, security agreement, factoring agreement, or lease and any other right accruing to a person to secure the repayment of money, the performance of a duty, or any other obligation by a nonaffiliated person.

(21) The term "person" means an individual, firm, corporation, association, partnership, consortium, joint venture, commercial entity, United States Government, State, municipality, commission, political subdivision of a State, or any interstate body.

(22) The term "release" means any spilling, leaking, pumping, pouring, emitting, emptying, discharging, injecting, escaping, leaching, dumping, or disposing into the environment (including the abandonment or discarding of barrels, containers, and other closed receptacles containing any hazardous substance or pollutant or contaminant), but excludes (A) any release which results in exposure to persons solely within a workplace, with respect to a claim which such persons may assert against the employer of such persons, (B) emissions from the engine exhaust of a motor vehicle, rolling stock, aircraft, vessel, or pipeline pumping station engine, (C) release of source, byproduct, or special nuclear material from a nuclear incident, as those terms are defined in the Atomic Energy Act of 1954 [42 U.S.C.A. § 2011 et seq.], if such release is subject to requirements with respect to financial protection established by the Nuclear Regulatory Commission under section 170 of such Act [42 U.S.C.A. § 2210], or, for the purposes of section 9604 of this title or any other response action, any release of source byproduct, or special nuclear material from any processing site designated under section 7912(a)(1) or 7942(a) of this title, and (D) the normal application of fertilizer.

(23) The terms "remove" or "removal" means[3] the cleanup or removal of released hazardous substances from the environment, such actions as may be necessary taken in the event of the threat of release of hazardous substances into the environment, such actions as may be necessary to monitor, assess, and evaluate the release or threat of release of hazardous substances, the disposal of removed material, or the taking of such other actions as may be necessary to prevent, minimize, or mitigate damage to the public health or welfare or to the environment, which may otherwise result from a release or threat of release. The term includes, in addition, without being limited to, security fencing or other measures to limit access, provision of alternative water supplies, temporary evacuation and housing of threatened individuals not otherwise provided for, action taken under section 9604(b) of this title, and any emergency assistance which may be provided under the Disaster Relief and Emergency Assistance Act [42 U.S.C.A. § 5121 et seq.].

(24) The terms "remedy" or "remedial action" means[3] those actions consistent with permanent remedy taken instead of or in addition to removal actions in the event of a release or threatened release of a hazardous substance into the environment, to prevent or minimize the release of hazardous substances so that they do not migrate to cause substantial danger to present or future public health or welfare or the environment. The term includes, but is not limited to, such actions at the location of the release as storage, confinement, perimeter protection using dikes, trenches, or ditches, clay cover, neutralization, cleanup of released hazardous substances and associated contaminated materials, recycling or reuse, diversion, destruction, segregation of reactive wastes, dredging or excavations, repair or replacement of leaking containers, collection of leachate and runoff, onsite treatment or incineration, provision of alternative water supplies, and any monitoring reasonably required to assure that such actions protect the public health and welfare and the environment. The term includes the costs of permanent relocation of residents and businesses and community facilities where the President determines that, alone or in combination with other measures, such relocation is more cost-effective than and environmentally preferable to the transportation, storage, treatment, destruction, or secure disposition offsite of hazardous substances, or may otherwise be necessary to protect the public health or welfare; the term includes offsite transport and offsite storage, treatment, destruction, or secure disposition of hazardous substances and associated contaminated materials.

(25) The terms "respond" or "response" means[3] remove, removal, remedy, and remedial action,[4] all such terms (including the terms "removal" and "remedial action") include enforcement activities related thereto.

(26) The terms "transport" or "transportation" means[3] the movement of a hazardous substance by any mode, including a hazardous liquid pipeline facility (as defined in section 60101(a) f Title 49), and in the case of a hazardous substance which has been accepted for transportation by a common or contract carrier, the term "transport" or "transportation" shall include any stoppage in transit which is temporary, incidental to the transportation movement, and at the ordinary operating convenience of a common or contract carrier, and any such stoppage shall be considered as a continuity of movement and not as the storage of a hazardous substance.

(27) The terms "United States" and "State" include the several States of the United States, the District of Columbia, the Commonwealth of Puerto Rico, Guam, American Samoa, the United States Virgin Islands, the Commonwealth of the Northern Marianas, and any other territory or possession over which the United States has jurisdiction.

(28) The term "vessel" means every description of watercraft or other artificial contrivance used, or capable of being used, as a means of transportation on water.

(29) The terms "disposal", "hazardous waste", and "treatment" shall have the meaning provided in section 1004 of the Solid Waste Disposal Act [42 U.S.C.A. § 6903].

(30) The terms "territorial sea" and "contiguous zone" shall have the meaning provided in section 502 of the Federal Water Pollution Control Act [33 U.S.C.A. § 1362].

(31) The term "national contingency plan" means the national contingency plan published under section 311(c) of the Federal Water Pollution Control Act or revised pursuant to section 9605 of this title.

(32) The terms "liable" or "liability" under this subchapter shall be construed to be the standard of liability which obtains under section 311 of the Federal Water Pollution Control Act [33 U.S.C.A. § 1321].

(33) The term "pollutant or contaminant" shall include, but not be limited to, any element, substance, compound, or mixture, including disease-causing agents, which after release into the environment and upon exposure, ingestion, inhalation, or assimilation into any organism, either directly from the environment or indirectly by ingestion through food chains, will or may reasonably be anticipated to cause death, disease, behavioral abnormalities, cancer, genetic mutation, physiological malfunctions (including malfunctions in reproduction) or physical deformations, in such organisms or their offspring; except that the term "pollutant or contaminant" shall not include petroleum, including crude oil or any fraction thereof which is not otherwise specifically listed or designated as a hazardous substance under subparagraphs (A) through (F) of paragraph (14) and shall not include natural gas, liquefied natural gas, or synthetic gas of pipeline quality (or mixtures of natural gas and such synthetic gas).

(34) The term "alternative water supplies" includes, but is not limited to, drinking water and household water supplies.

(35) (A) The term "contractual relationship", for the purpose of section 9607(b)(3) of this title, includes, but is not limited to, land contracts, deeds, easements, leases, or other instruments transferring title or possession, unless the real property on which the facility concerned is located was acquired by the defendant after the disposal or placement of the hazardous substance on, in, or at the facility, and one or more of the circumstances described in clause (i), (ii), or (iii) is also established by the defendant by a preponderance of the evidence:

(i) At the time the defendant acquired the facility the defendant did not know and had no reason to know that any hazardous substance which is the subject of the release or threatened release was disposed of on, in, or at the facility.

(ii) The defendant is a government entity which acquired the facility by escheat, or through any other involuntary transfer or acquisition, or through the exercise of eminent domain authority by purchase or condemnation.

(iii) The defendant acquired the facility by inheritance or bequest.

In addition to establishing the foregoing, the defendant must establish that the defendant has satisfied the requirements of section 9607(b)(3)(a) and (b) of this title, provides full cooperation, assistance, and facility access to the persons that are authorized to conduct response actions at the facility (including the cooperation and access necessary for the installation, integrity, operation, and maintenance of any complete or partial response action at the facility), is in compliance with any land use restrictions established or relied on in connection with the response action at a facility, and does not impede the effectiveness or integrity of any institutional control employed at the facility in connection with a response action.

(B) Reason to know

(i) All appropriate inquiries

To establish that the defendant had no reason to know of the matter described in subparagraph (A)(i), the defendant must demonstrate to a court that—

(I) on or before the date on which the defendant acquired the facility, the defendant carried out all appropriate inquiries, as provided in clauses (ii) and (iv), into the previous ownership and uses of the facility in accordance with generally accepted good commercial and customary standards and practices; and

(II) the defendant took reasonable steps to—

(aa) stop any continuing release;

(bb) prevent any threatened future release; and

(cc) prevent or limit any human, environmental, or natural resource exposure to any previously released hazardous substance.

(ii) Standards and practices

Not later than 2 years after January 11, 2002, the Administrator shall by regulation establish standards and practices for the purpose of satisfying the requirement to carry out all appropriate inquiries under clause (i).

(iii) Criteria

In promulgating regulations that establish the standards and practices referred to in clause (ii), the Administrator shall include each of the following:

(I) The results of an inquiry by an environmental professional.

(II) Interviews with past and present owners, operators, and occupants of the facility for the purpose of gathering information regarding the potential for contamination at the facility.

(III) Reviews of historical sources, such as chain of title documents, aerial photographs, building department records, and land use records, to determine previous uses and occupancies of the real property since the property was first developed.

(IV) Searches for recorded environmental cleanup liens against the facility that are filed under Federal, State, or local law.

(V) Reviews of Federal, State, and local government records, waste disposal records, underground storage tank records, and hazardous waste handling, generation, treatment, disposal, and spill records, concerning contamination at or near the facility.

(VI) Visual inspections of the facility and of adjoining properties.

(VII) Specialized knowledge or experience on the part of the defendant.

(VIII) The relationship of the purchase price to the value of the property, if the property was not contaminated.

(IX) Commonly known or reasonably ascertainable information about the property.

(X) The degree of obviousness of the presence or likely presence of contamination at the property, and the ability to detect the contamination by appropriate investigation.

(iv) Interim standards and practices

(I) Property purchased before May 31, 1997

With respect to property purchased before May 31, 1997, in making a determination with respect to a defendant described in clause (i), a court shall take into account—

(aa) any specialized knowledge or experience on the part of the defendant;

(bb) the relationship of the purchase price to the value of the property, if the property was not contaminated;

(cc) commonly known or reasonably ascertainable information about the property;

(dd) the obviousness of the presence or likely presence of contamination at the property; and

(ee) the ability of the defendant to detect the contamination by appropriate inspection.

(II) Property purchased on or after May 31, 1997

With respect to property purchased on or after May 31, 1997, and until the Administrator promulgates the regulations described in clause (ii), the procedures of the American Society for Testing and Materials, including the document known as "Standard E1527–97", entitled "Standard Practice for Environmental Site Assessment: Phase 1 Environmental Site Assessment Process", shall satisfy the requirements in clause (i).

(v) Site inspection and title search

In the case of property for residential use or other similar use purchased by a nongovernmental or noncommercial entity, a facility inspection and title search that reveal no basis for further investigation shall be considered to satisfy the requirements of this subparagraph.

(C) Nothing in this paragraph or in section 9607(b)(3) of this title shall diminish the liability of any previous owner or operator of such facility who would otherwise be liable under this chapter. Notwithstanding this paragraph, if the defendant obtained actual knowledge of the release or threatened release of a hazardous substance at such facility when the defendant owned the real property and then subsequently transferred ownership of the property to another person without disclosing such knowledge, such defendant shall be treated as liable under section 9607(a)(1) of this title and no defense under section 9607(b)(3) of this title shall be available to such defendant.

(D) Nothing in this paragraph shall affect the liability under this chapter of a defendant who, by any act or omission, caused or contributed to the release or threatened release of a hazardous substance which is the subject of the action relating to the facility.

(36) The term "Indian tribe" means any Indian tribe, band, nation, or other organized group or community, including any Alaska Native village but not including any Alaska Native regional or village corporation, which is recognized as eligible for the special programs and services provided by the United States to Indians because of their status as Indians.

(37) (A) The term "service station dealer" means any person—

(i) who owns or operates a motor vehicle service station, filling station, garage, or similar retail establishment engaged in the business of selling, repairing, or servicing motor vehicles, where a significant percentage of the gross revenue of the establishment is derived from the fueling, repairing, or servicing of motor vehicles, and

(ii) who accepts for collection, accumulation, and delivery to an oil recycling facility, recycled oil that (I) has been removed from the engine of a light duty motor vehicle or household appliances by the owner of such vehicle or appliances, and (II) is presented, by such owner, to such person for collection, accumulation, and delivery to an oil recycling facility.

(B) For purposes of section 9614(c) of this title, the term "service station dealer" shall, notwithstanding the provisions of subparagraph (A), include any government agency that establishes a facility solely for the purpose of accepting recycled oil that satisfies the criteria set forth in subclauses (I) and (II) of subparagraph (A)(ii), and, with respect to recycled oil that satisfies the criteria set forth in subclauses (I) and (II), owners or operators of refuse collection services who are compelled by State law to collect, accumulate, and deliver such oil to an oil recycling facility.

(C) The President shall promulgate regulations regarding the determination of what constitutes a significant percentage of the gross revenues of an establishment for purposes of this paragraph.

(38) The term "incineration vessel" means any vessel which carries hazardous substances for the purpose of incineration of such substances, so long as such substances or residues of such substances are on board.

(39) Brownfield site

(A) In general

The term "brownfield site" means real property, the expansion, redevelopment, or reuse of which may be complicated by the presence or potential presence of a hazardous substance, pollutant, or contaminant.

(B) Exclusions

The term "brownfield site" does not include—

(i) a facility that is the subject of a planned or ongoing removal action under this subchapter;

(ii) a facility that is listed on the National Priorities List or is proposed for listing;

(iii) a facility that is the subject of a unilateral administrative order, a court order, an administrative order on consent or judicial consent decree that has been issued to or entered into by the parties under this chapter;

(iv) a facility that is the subject of a unilateral administrative order, a court order, an administrative order on consent or judicial consent decree that has been issued to or entered into by the parties, or a facility to which a permit has been issued by the United States or an authorized State under the Solid Waste Disposal Act (42 U.S.C. 6901 et seq.), the Federal Water Pollution Control Act (33 U.S.C. 1321), the Toxic Substances Control Act (15 U.S.C. 2601 et seq.), or the Safe Drinking Water Act (42 U.S.C. 300f et seq.);

(v) a facility that—

(I) is subject to corrective action under section 3004(u) or 3008(h) of the Solid Waste Disposal Act (42 U.S.C. 6924(u), 6928(h)); and

(II) to which a corrective action permit or order has been issued or modified to require the implementation of corrective measures;

(vi) a land disposal unit with respect to which—

(I) a closure notification under subtitle C of the Solid Waste Disposal Act (42 U.S.C. 6921 et seq.) has been submitted; and

(II) closure requirements have been specified in a closure plan or permit;

(vii) a facility that is subject to the jurisdiction, custody, or control of a department, agency, or instrumentality of the United States, except for land held in trust by the United States for an Indian tribe;

(viii) a portion of a facility—

(I) at which there has been a release of polychlorinated biphenyls; and

(II) that is subject to remediation under the Toxic Substances Control Act (15 U.S.C. 2601 et seq.); or

(ix) a portion of a facility, for which portion, assistance for response activity has been obtained under subtitle I of the Solid Waste Disposal Act (42 U.S.C. 6991 et seq.) from the Leaking Underground Storage Tank Trust Fund established under section 9508 of Title 26.

(C) Site-by-site determinations

Notwithstanding subparagraph (B) and on a site-by-site basis, the President may authorize financial assistance under section 9604(k) of this title to an eligible entity at a site included in clause (i), (iv), (v), (vi), (viii), or (ix) of subparagraph (B) if the President finds that financial assistance will protect human health and the environment, and either promote economic development or enable the creation of, preservation of, or addition to parks, greenways, undeveloped property, other recreational property, or other property used for nonprofit purposes.

(D) Additional areas

For the purposes of section 9604(k) of this title, the term "brownfield site" includes a site that—

(i) meets the definition of "brownfield site" under subparagraphs (A) through (C); and

(ii)(I) is contaminated by a controlled substance (as defined in section 802 of Title 21);

(II) (aa) is contaminated by petroleum or a petroleum product excluded from the definition of "hazardous substance" under this section; and

(bb) is a site for which there is no viable responsible party and that is determined by the Administrator or the State, as appropriate, to be a site that will be assessed, investigated, or cleaned up by a person that is not potentially liable for cleaning up the site under this Act or any other law pertaining to the cleanup of petroleum products; and

(III) is mine-scarred land.

(40) Bona fide prospective purchaser

(A) In general.—The term 'bona fide prospective purchaser' means, with respect to a facility—

(i) a person who—

(I) acquires ownership of the facility after January 11, 2002; and

(II) establishes by a preponderance of the evidence each of the criteria described in clauses (i) through (viii) of subparagraph (B); and

(ii) a person—

(I) who acquires a leasehold interest in the facility after January 11, 2002;

(II) who establishes by a preponderance of the evidence that the leasehold interest is not designed to avoid liability under this Act by any person; and

(III) with respect to whom any of the following conditions apply:

(aa) The owner of the facility that is subject to the leasehold interest is a person described in clause (i).

(bb) (AA) The owner of the facility that is subject to the leasehold interest was a person described in clause (i) at the time the leasehold interest was acquired, but can no longer establish by a preponderance of the evidence each of the criteria described in clauses (i) through (viii) of subparagraph (B) due to circumstances unrelated to any action of the person who holds the leasehold interest; and

(BB) the person who holds the leasehold interest establishes by a preponderance of the evidence each of the criteria described in clauses (i), (iii), (iv), (v), (vi), (vii), and (viii) of subparagraph (B).

(cc) The person who holds the leasehold interest establishes by a preponderance of the evidence each of the criteria described in clauses (i) through (viii) of subparagraph (B).

(B) Criteria.—The criteria described in this subparagraph are as follows:

(i) Disposal prior to acquisition.—All disposal of hazardous substances at the facility occurred before the person acquired the facility.

(ii) Inquiries

(I) In general

The person made all appropriate inquiries into the previous ownership and uses of the facility in accordance with generally accepted good commercial and customary standards and practices in accordance with clauses (II) and (III).

(II) Standards and practices

The standards and practices referred to in clauses (ii) and (iv) of paragraph (35)(B) shall be considered to satisfy the requirements of this clause.

(III) Residential use

In the case of property in residential or other similar use at the time of purchase by a nongovernmental or noncommercial entity, a facility inspection and title search that reveal no basis for further investigation shall be considered to satisfy the requirements of this clause.

(iii) Notices

The person provides all legally required notices with respect to the discovery or release of any hazardous substances at the facility.

(iv) Care

The person exercises appropriate care with respect to hazardous substances found at the facility by taking reasonable steps to—

(I) stop any continuing release;

(II) prevent any threatened future release; and

(III) prevent or limit human, environmental, or natural resource exposure to any previously released hazardous substance.

(v) Cooperation, assistance, and access

The person provides full cooperation, assistance, and access to persons that are authorized to conduct response actions or natural resource restoration at a vessel or facility (including the cooperation and access necessary for the installation, integrity, operation, and maintenance of any complete or partial response actions or natural resource restoration at the vessel or facility).

(vi) Institutional control

The person—

(I) is in compliance with any land use restrictions established or relied on in connection with the response action at a vessel or facility; and

(II) does not impede the effectiveness or integrity of any institutional control employed at the vessel or facility in connection with a response action.

(vii) Requests; subpoenas

The person complies with any request for information or administrative subpoena issued by the President under this chapter.

(viii) No affiliation

The person is not—

(I) potentially liable, or affiliated with any other person that is potentially liable, for response costs at a facility through—

(aa) any direct or indirect familial relationship; or

(bb) any contractual, corporate, or financial relationship (other than a contractual, corporate, or financial relationship that is created by the instruments by which title to the facility is conveyed or financed, by a tenancy, by the instruments by which a leasehold interest in the facility is created, or by a contract for the sale of goods or services); or

(II) the result of a reorganization of a business entity that was potentially liable.

(41) Eligible response site

(A) In general

The term "eligible response site" means a site that meets the definition of a brownfield site in subparagraphs (A) and (B) of paragraph (39), as modified by subparagraphs (B) and (C) of this paragraph.

(B) Inclusions

The term "eligible response site" includes—

(i) notwithstanding paragraph (39)(B)(ix), a portion of a facility, for which portion assistance for response activity has been obtained under subtitle I of the Solid Waste Disposal Act (42 U.S.C. 6991 et seq.) from the Leaking Underground Storage Tank Trust Fund established under section 9508 of Title 26; or

(ii) a site for which, notwithstanding the exclusions provided in subparagraph (C) or paragraph (39)(B), the President determines, on a site-by-site basis and after consultation with the State, that limitations on enforcement under section 9628 of this title at sites specified in clause (iv), (v), (vi) or (viii) of paragraph (39)(B) would be appropriate and will—

(I) protect human health and the environment; and

(II) promote economic development or facilitate the creation of, preservation of, or addition to a park, a greenway, undeveloped property, recreational property, or other property used for nonprofit purposes.

(C) Exclusions

The term "eligible response site" does not include—

(i) a facility for which the President—

(I) conducts or has conducted a preliminary assessment or site inspection; and

(II) after consultation with the State, determines or has determined that the site obtains a preliminary score sufficient for possible listing on the National Priorities List, or that the site otherwise qualifies for listing on the National Priorities List; unless the President has made a determination that no further Federal action will be taken; or

(ii) facilities that the President determines warrant particular consideration as identified by regulation, such as sites posing a threat to a sole-source drinking water aquifer or a sensitive ecosystem.

(Pub. L. No. 96–510, Title I, § 101, 94 Stat. 2767 (Dec. 11, 1980); as amended by Pub. L. No. 96–561, Title II, § 238(b), 94 Stat. 3300 (Dec. 22, 1980); Pub. L. No. 99–499, Title I, §§ 101, 114(b), 127(a), Title V, § 517(c)(2), 100 Stat. 1615, 1652, 1692, 1774 (Oct. 17, 1986); Pub. L. No. 100–707, Title I, § 109(v), 102 Stat. 4710 (Nov. 23, 1988); Pub. L. No. 103–429, § 7(e)(1), 108 Stat. 4390 (Oct. 31, 1994); Pub. L. No. 104–208, Div. A, Title I, § 101(a) [Title II, § 211(b)], Title II, § 2502(b), 110 Stat. 3009–41, 3009–464 (Sept. 30, 1996); Pub. L. No. 104–287, § 6(j)(1), 110 Stat. 3400 (Oct. 11, 1996); Pub. L. No. 106–74, Title IV, § 427, 113 Stat. 1095 (Oct. 20, 1999); Pub. L. No. 107–118, Title II, §§ 211(a), 222(a), 223, 231(a), 115 Stat. 2360, 2370, 2372, 2375 (Jan. 11, 2002); Pub. L. No. 115–141, tit. VII, §§ 2–4, 5(a), 132 Stat. 348, 1052–1054 (Mar. 23, 2018).)

[1] So in original. Probably should be "or."

[2] Congress explicitly amended this section to add the second right parens.

[3] So in original. Probably should be "mean."

[4] So in original.

HISTORICAL AND STATUTORY NOTES

References in Text

"This subchapter", referred to in text, originally read "this title", meaning Title I of Pub. L. No. 96–510, 94 Stat. 2767 (Dec. 11, 1980), as amended, known as the Comprehensive Environmental Response, Compensation, and Liability Act of 1980, which is principally codified as this subchapter [42 U.S.C.A. § 9601 et seq.]. See Tables for complete classification.

The Federal Water Pollution Control Act, referred to in text, is Act of June 30, 1948, c. 758, as amended generally by Pub. L. No. 92–500, § 2, 86 Stat. 816 (Oct. 18, 1972), also known as the Clean Water Act, which is codified principally as chapter 26 of Title 33 [33 U.S.C.A. § 1251 et seq.]. See Tables for complete classification.

This chapter, referred to in pars. (5), (13), (20)(D), (G), (35)(C), (D), (39)(B)(iii), and (40)(G), originally read "this Act", meaning Pub. L. No. 96–510, 94 Stat. 2767 (Dec. 11, 1980), as amended, known as the Comprehensive Environmental Response, Compensation, and Liability Act of 1980, which is codified principally as this chapter [42 U.S.C.A. § 9601 et seq.]; See Tables for complete classification.

The Safe Drinking Water Act, referred to in pars. (7), (10), and (39)(B)(iv) is Pub. L. No. 93–523, 88 Stat. 1660 (Dec. 16, 1974), as amended, which is codified principally as subchapter XII of chapter 6A of this title [42 U.S.C.A. § 300f et seq.]. Part C of the Safe Drinking Water Act is codified generally to part C of subchapter XII of chapter 6A of this title [42 U.S.C.A. § 300h et seq.]. See Tables for complete classification.

The Magnuson-Stevens Fishery Conservation and Management Act, referred to in pars. (8) and (16), is Pub. L. No. 94–265, 90 Stat. 331 (Apr. 13, 1976), as amended, which is codified principally as chapter 38 (section 1801 et seq.) of Title 16, Conservation. The fishery conservation zone established by this Act, referred to in par. (16) was established by section 101 of this Act (16 U.S.C. 1811), which as amended generally by Pub. L. No. 99–659, title I, § 101(b), 100 Stat. 3706 (Nov. 14, 1986), relating to U.S. sovereign rights and fishery management authority over fish within the exclusive economic zone as defined in section 1802 of Title 16. For complete classification of this Act to the Code, see Short Title note set out under section 1801 of Title 16 and Tables.

The Clean Air Act, referred to in par. (10), is Act of July 14, 1955, c. 360, as amended generally by Pub. L. No. 88–206, 77 Stat. 392 (Dec. 17, 1963), and later by Pub. L. No. 95–95, 91 Stat. 685 (Aug. 7, 1977). The Clean Air Act was originally codified as chapter 15B (section 1857 et seq.) of this title. On enactment of Pub. L. No. 95–95, the Act was recodified as chapter 85 (section 7401 et seq.) of this title. Parts C and D of Title I of the Clean Air Act are codified generally to parts C (section 7470 et seq.) and D (section 7501 et seq.), respectively, of subchapter I of chapter 85 of this title. For complete classification of this Act to the Code, see Short Title of 1955 Acts note set out under section 7401 of this title and Tables.

The Atomic Energy Act of 1954, referred to in pars. (10) and (22), is Act of Aug. 30, 1954, c. 1073, § 1, 68 Stat. 919, as amended, which is codified generally as chapter 23 (section 2011 et seq.) of this title. For complete classification of this Act to the Code, see Short Title of 1954 Acts note set out under section 2011 of this title and Tables.

The Solid Waste Disposal Act, referred to in par. (14) and (39)(B)(iv), (v)(I), (vi)(I), and (ix), is Title II of Pub. L. No. 89–272, 79 Stat. 997 (Oct. 20, 1965), as amended generally by Pub. L. No. 94–580, § 2, 90 Stat. 2795 (Oct. 21, 1976), which is codified principally as chapter 82 [42 U.S.C.A. § 6901 et seq.] of this title. See Tables for complete classification.

The Farm Credit Act of 1971, referred to in par. (20)(G)(iv)(III), is Pub. L. No. 92–181, 85 Stat. 583 (Dec. 10, 1971), as amended, which is codified generally to chapter 23 (section 2001 et seq.) of Title 12, Banks and Banking. For complete classification of this Act to the Code, see Short Title note set out under section 2001 of Title 12 and Tables.

The Disaster Relief and Emergency Assistance Act, referred to in par. (23), is Pub. L. No. 93–288, 88 Stat. 143 (May 22, 1974), as amended, which is codified principally as chapter 68 (section 5121 et seq.) of this title. For complete classification of this Act to the Code, see Short Title of 1974 Acts note set out under section 5121 of this title and Tables.

Section 311(c) of the Federal Water Pollution Control Act, referred to in par. (31), was amended generally by Pub. L. No. 101–380, Title IV, § 4201(a), 104 Stat. 523 (Aug. 18, 1990), and no longer contains provisions directing the publishing of a National Contingency Plan. However, such provisions are contained in section 1321(d) of Title 33, Navigation and Navigable Waters.

The Toxic Substances Control Act, referred to in par. (39)(B)(iv), (viii)(II), is Pub. L. No. 94–469, 90 Stat. 2003 (Oct. 11, 1976), as amended, which is codified principally as chapter 53 of Title 15 [15 U.S.C.A. § 2601 et seq.]. See Tables for complete classification.

Subtitle I of the Solid Waste Disposal Act, referred to in par. (41)(B)(i), is subtitle I of Title II of Pub. L. No. 89–272, 79 Stat. 997 (Oct. 20, 1965), as amended generally by Pub. L. No. 94–580, § 2, 90 Stat. 2795 (Oct. 21, 1976), which is codified principally as subchapter IX of chapter 82 of this title [42 U.S.C.A. § 6991 et seq.].

Codifications

The amendment to par. (20)(D) by Pub. L. No. 106–74, Title IV, § 427, 113 Stat. 1096 (Oct. 20, 1999), purporting to insert "through seizure or otherwise in connection with law enforcement activity" before "involuntary" the first place it appears, was incapable of execution. The word "involuntary" does not appear in subpar. (D).

Reference in the original text of par. (39)(D)(ii)(II)(aa) of this section to "under section 101" has been translated in the codified text as "under this section" to reflect the probable intent of Congress.

Effective and Applicability Provisions

1996 Acts. Amendment by section 101(a) of Title I [Title II, § 211(b)] of Div. A of Pub. L. No. 104–208 effective 15 days after Oct. 11, 1996, see section 101(a) of Title I [Title II, § 211(b)] of Div. A of Pub. L. No. 104–208, set out as a note under section 1801 of Title 16, Conservation.

Amendment by section 2502 of Div. A of Title II of Pub. L. No. 104–208 applicable with respect to claims not finally adjudicated as of Sept. 30, 1996, see section 2505 of Div. A of Title II of Pub. L. No. 104–208, set out as a note under section 6991b of this title.

1986 Acts. Section 4 of Pub. L. No. 99–499 provided that: "Except as otherwise specified in section 121(b) of this Act [set out as a note under section 9621 of this title] or in any other provision of Titles I, II, III, and IV of this Act [see Tables for classification], the amendments made by Titles I through IV of this Act [enacting subchapter IV of this chapter and sections 9616 to 9626, 9658 to 9660, and 9661 of this title and sections 2701 to 2707 and 2810 of Title 10, Armed Forces, amending sections 6926, 6928, 6991 to 6991d, 6991g, 9601 to 9609, 9611 to 9614, 9651, 9656, and 9657 of this title and section 1416 of Title 33, Navigation and Navigable Waters, repealing section 9631 of this title, and renumbering former section 2701 of Title 10 as section 2721 of Title 10] shall take effect on the enactment of this Act [Oct. 17, 1986]."

Amendment by section 517(c)(2) of Pub. L. No. 99–499 effective Jan. 1, 1987, see section 517(e) of Pub. L. No. 99–499, set out as a note under section 9507 of Title 26, Internal Revenue Code.

1980 Acts. Amendment by Pub. L. No. 96–561 effective 15 days after Dec. 22, 1980, see section 238 of Pub. L. No. 96–561, set out as a Short Title of 1980 Amendments note under section 1801 of Title 16, Conservation.

Transfer of Functions

For transfer of certain functions from the Nuclear Regulatory Commission to the Chairman thereof, see Reorg. Plan No. 1 of 1980, 45 Fed. Reg. 40561, 94 Stat. 3585, set out as a note under section 5841 of this title.

Delegation of Functions

Functions vested in the President by par. (24) of this section, subject to section 2(a) to (f) of Ex. Ord. No. 12580, delegated, with authority to redelegate, to the Administrator of the Environmental Protection Agency, see sections 2(g), 11(g) of Ex. Ord. No. 12580, 52 Fed. Reg. 2923 (Jan. 23, 1987), set out as a note under section 9615 of this title.

Functions vested in the President by par. (37) of this section delegated to the Administrator of the Environmental Protection Agency, see section 11(a) of Ex. Ord. No. 12580, 52 Fed. Reg. 2923 (Jan. 23, 1987), set out as a note under section 9615 of this title.

Short Title

2002 Amendments. Pub. L. No. 107–118, § 1, 115 Stat. 2356 (Jan. 11, 2002), provided that: "This Act [enacting 42 U.S.C.A. § 9628, amending this section, 42 U.S.C.A. § 9604, 42 U.S.C.A. § 9605, 42 U.S.C.A. § 9607, and 42 U.S.C.A. § 9622, and enacting provisions set out as notes under this section and 42 U.S.C.A. § 9607] may be cited as the 'Small Business Liability Relief and Brownfields Revitalization Act'."

Pub. L. No. 107–118, Title I, § 101, 115 Stat. 2356 (Jan. 11, 2002), provided that: "This title [Pub. L. No. 107–118, Title I, § 101 et seq., 115 Stat. 2356 (Jan. 11, 2002), amending 42 U.S.C.A. § 9607(*o*), (p), and 42 U.S.C.A. § 9622(g)(7) to (12), and enacting provisions set out as a note under 42 U.S.C.A. § 9607] may be cited as the 'Small Business Liability Protection Act'."

Pub. L. No. 107–118, Title II, § 201, 115 Stat. 2360 (Jan. 11, 2002), provided that: "This title [Pub. L. No. 107–118, Title II, § 201 et seq., 115 Stat. 2360 (Jan. 11, 2002), enacting 42 U.S.C.A. § 9628, and amending pars. (35)(A) and (B) and (39) to (41) of this section, 42 U.S.C.A. § 9604(k), 42 U.S.C.A. § 9605(h), and 42 U.S.C.A. § 9607(q) and (r)] may be cited as the 'Brownfields Revitalization and Environmental Restoration Act of 2001'."

1996 Amendments. Pub. L. No. 104–208, Div. A, Title II, § 2501, 110 Stat. 3009–462 (Sept. 30, 1996), provided that: "This [Pub. L. No. 104–208, Div. A, Title II, Subtitle E, § 2501 et seq., Sept. 30, 1996, 110 Stat. 3009–462, amending this section and sections 6991b and 9607 of this title and enacting provisions set out as a note under section 6991b of this title] subtitle may be cited as the 'Asset Conservation, Lender Liability, and Deposit Insurance Protection Act of 1996'."

1992 Amendments. Pub. L. No. 102–426, § 1, 106 Stat. 2174 (Oct. 19, 1992), provided that: "This Act [amending section 9620 of this title and enacting provisions set out as a note under section 9620 of this title] may be cited as the 'Community Environmental Response Facilitation Act'."

1986 Amendments. Section 1 of Pub. L. No. 99–499 provided that: "This Act [enacting subchapter IV of this chapter and sections 9616 to 9626, 9658 to 9662, 11001 to 11005, 11021 to 11023, and 11041 to 11050 of this title, sections 2701 to 2707 and 2810 of Title 10, Armed Forces, and sections 59A, 4671, 4672, 9507, and 9508 of Title 26, Internal Revenue Code, amending sections 6926, 6928, 6991 to 6991d, 6991g, 9601 to 9609, 9611 to 9614, 9631, 9651, 9656, and 9657 of this title, sections 26, 164, 275, 936, 1561, 4041, 4042, 4081, 4221, 4611, 4612, 4661, 4662, 6416, 6420, 6421, 6425, 6427, 6655, 9502, 9503, and 9506 of Title 26, former section 6154 of Title 26, and section 1416 of Title 33, Navigation and Navigable Waters, renumbering former section 2701 of Title 10 as section 2721 of Title 10, repealing sections 9631 to 9633, 9641, and 9653 of this title and sections 4681 and 4682 of Title 26, and enacting provisions set out as notes under sections 6921, 6991b, 7401, 9601, 9620, 9621, 9658, 9660, 9661, and 11001 of this title, section 2703 of Title 10, sections 1, 26, 4041, 4611, 4661, 4671, 4681, 9507, and 9508 of Title 26, and section 655 of Title 29, Labor] may be cited as the 'Superfund Amendments and Reauthorization Act of 1986'."

1980 Acts. Section 1 of Pub. L. No. 96–510 provided: "That this Act [enacting this chapter, section 6911a of this title, and sections 4611, 4612, 4661, 4662, 4681, and former section 4682 of Title 26, Internal Revenue Code, amending section 6911 of this title, section 1364 of Title 33, Navigation and Navigable Waters, and section 11901 of Title 49, Transportation, and enacting provisions set out as notes under section 6911 of this title and sections 1 and 4611 of Title 26] may be cited as the 'Comprehensive Environmental Response, Compensation, and Liability Act of 1980'." The Act is also known as CERCLA.

Definitions

Section 2 of Pub. L. No. 99–499 provided that: "As used in this Act [see Short Title of 1986 Amendments note set out under this section]—

"(1) CERCLA.—The term 'CERCLA' means the Comprehensive Environmental Response, Compensation, and Liability Act of 1980 (42 U.S.C. 9601 et seq.).

"(2) Administrator.—The term 'Administrator' means the Administrator of the Environmental Protection Agency."

Territorial Sea of United States

For extension of territorial sea of United States, see Proc. No. 5928, set out as a note under section 1331 of Title 43, Public Lands.

§ 9602. Designation of additional hazardous substances and establishment of reportable released quantities; regulations

[CERCLA § 102]

(a) The Administrator shall promulgate and revise as may be appropriate, regulations designating as hazardous substances, in addition to those referred to in section 9601(14) of this title, such elements, compounds, mixtures, solutions, and substances which, when released into the environment may present substantial danger to the public health or welfare or the environment, and shall promulgate regulations establishing that quantity of any hazardous substance the release of which shall be reported pursuant to section 9603 of this title. The Administrator may determine that one single quantity shall be the reportable quantity for any hazardous substance, regardless of the medium into which the hazardous substance is released. For all hazardous substances for which proposed regulations establishing reportable quantities were published in the Federal Register under this subsection on or before March 1, 1986, the Administrator shall promulgate under this subsection final regulations establishing reportable quantities not later than December 31, 1986. For all hazardous substances for which proposed regulations establishing reportable quantities were not published in the Federal Register under this subsection on or before March 1, 1986, the Administrator shall publish under this subsection proposed regulations establishing reportable quantities not later than December 31, 1986, and promulgate final regulations under this subsection establishing reportable quantities not later than April 30, 1988.

(b) Unless and until superseded by regulations establishing a reportable quantity under subsection (a) of this section for any hazardous substance as defined in section 9601(14) of this title, (1) a quantity of one pound, or (2) for those hazardous substances for which reportable quantities have been established pursuant to section 1321(b)(4) of Title 33, such reportable quantity, shall be deemed that quantity, the release of which requires notification pursuant to section 9603(a) or (b) of this title.

(Pub. L. No. 96–510, Title I, § 102, 94 Stat. 2772 (Dec. 11, 1980); as amended by Pub. L. No. 99–499, Title I, § 102, 100 Stat. 1617 (Oct. 17, 1986).)

HISTORICAL AND STATUTORY NOTES

Effective and Applicability Provisions

1986 Acts. Amendment by Pub. L. No. 99–499 effective Oct. 17, 1986, see section 4 of Pub. L. No. 99–499, set out as a note under section 9601 of this title.

§ 9603. Notification requirements respecting released substances

[CERCLA § 103]

(a) Notice to National Response Center upon release from vessel or offshore or onshore facility by person in charge; conveyance of notice by Center

Any person in charge of a vessel or an offshore or an onshore facility shall, as soon as he has knowledge of any release (other than a federally permitted release) of a hazardous substance from such vessel or facility in quantities equal to or greater than those determined pursuant to section 9602 of this title, immediately notify the National Response Center established under the Clean Water Act [33 U.S.C.A. § 1251 et seq.] of such release. The National Response Center shall convey the notification expeditiously to all appropriate Government agencies, including the Governor of any affected State.

(b) Penalties for failure to notify; use of notice or information pursuant to notice in criminal case

Any person—

(1) in charge of a vessel from which a hazardous substance is released, other than a federally permitted release, into or upon the navigable waters of the United States, adjoining shorelines, or into or upon the waters of the contiguous zone, or

(2) in charge of a vessel from which a hazardous substance is released, other than a federally permitted release, which may affect natural resources belonging to, appertaining to, or under the exclusive management authority of the United States (including resources under the Magnuson-Stevens Fishery Conservation and Management Act [16 U.S.C.A. § 1801 et seq.]), and who is otherwise subject to the jurisdiction of the United States at the time of the release, or

(3) in charge of a facility from which a hazardous substance is released, other than a federally permitted release,

in a quantity equal to or greater than that determined pursuant to section 9602 of this title who fails to notify immediately the appropriate agency of the United States Government as soon as he has knowledge of such release or who submits in such a notification any information which he knows to be false or misleading shall, upon conviction, be fined in accordance with the applicable provisions of Title 18 or imprisoned for not more than 3 years (or not more than 5 years in the case of a second or subsequent conviction), or both. Notification received pursuant to this subsection or information obtained by the exploitation of such notification shall not be used against any such person in any criminal case, except a prosecution for perjury or for giving a false statement.

(c) Notice to Administrator of EPA of existence of storage, etc., facility by owner or operator; exception; time, manner, and form of notice; penalties for failure to notify; use of notice or information pursuant to notice in criminal case

Within one hundred and eighty days after December 11, 1980, any person who owns or operates or who at the time of disposal owned or operated, or who accepted hazardous substances for transport and selected, a facility at which hazardous substances (as defined in section 9601(14)(C) of this title) are or have been stored, treated, or disposed of shall, unless such facility has a permit issued under, or has been accorded interim status under, subtitle C of the Solid Waste Disposal Act [42 U.S.C.A. § 6921 et seq.], notify the Administrator of the Environmental Protection Agency of the existence of such facility, specifying the amount and type of any hazardous substance to be found there, and any known, suspected, or likely releases of such substances from such facility. The Administrator may prescribe in greater detail the manner and form of the notice and the information included. The Administrator shall notify the affected State agency, or any department designated by the Governor to receive such notice, of the existence of such facility. Any person who knowingly fails to notify the Administrator of the existence of any such facility shall, upon conviction, be fined not more than $10,000, or imprisoned for not more than one year, or both. In addition, any such person who knowingly fails to provide the notice required by this subsection shall not be entitled to any limitation of liability or to any defenses to liability set out in section 9607 of this title: *Provided, however*, That notification under this subsection is not required for any facility which would be reportable hereunder solely as a result of any stoppage in transit which is temporary, incidental to the transportation movement, or at the ordinary operating convenience of a common or contract carrier, and such stoppage shall be considered as a continuity of movement and not as the storage of a hazardous substance. Notification received pursuant to this subsection or information obtained by the exploitation of such notification shall not be used against any such person in any criminal case, except a prosecution for perjury or for giving a false statement.

(d) Recordkeeping requirements; promulgation of rules and regulations by Administrator of EPA; penalties for violations; waiver of retention requirements

(1) The Administrator of the Environmental Protection Agency is authorized to promulgate rules and regulations specifying, with respect to—

(A) the location, title, or condition of a facility, and

(B) the identity, characteristics, quantity, origin, or condition (including containerization and previous treatment) of any hazardous substances contained or deposited in a facility;

the records which shall be retained by any person required to provide the notification of a facility set out in subsection (c) of this section. Such specification shall be in accordance with the provisions of this subsection.

(2) Beginning with December 11, 1980, for fifty years thereafter or for fifty years after the date of establishment of a record (whichever is later), or at any such earlier time as a waiver if obtained under paragraph (3) of this subsection, it shall be unlawful for any such person knowingly to destroy, mutilate, erase, dispose of, conceal, or otherwise render unavailable or unreadable or falsify any records identified in paragraph (1) of this subsection. Any person who violates this paragraph shall, upon conviction, be fined in accordance with the applicable provisions of Title 18 or imprisoned for not more than 3 years (or not more than 5 years in the case of a second or subsequent conviction), or both.

(3) At any time prior to the date which occurs fifty years after December 11, 1980, any person identified under paragraph (1) of this subsection may apply to the Administrator of the Environmental Protection Agency for a waiver of the provisions of the first sentence of paragraph (2) of this subsection. The Administrator is authorized to grant such waiver if, in his discretion, such waiver would not unreasonably interfere with the attainment of the purposes and provisions of this chapter. The Administrator shall promulgate rules and regulations regarding such a waiver so as to inform parties of the proper application procedure and conditions for approval of such a waiver.

(4) Notwithstanding the provisions of this subsection, the Administrator of the Environmental Protection Agency may in his discretion require any such person to retain any record identified pursuant to paragraph (1) of this subsection for such a time period in excess of the period specified in paragraph (2) of this subsection as the Administrator determines to be necessary to protect the public health or welfare.

(e) Applicability to registered pesticide products and air emissions from animal waste at farms.—

(1) In general.—This section shall not apply to—

(A) the application of a pesticide product registered under the Federal Insecticide, Fungicide, and Rodenticide Act (7 U.S.C. 136 et seq.) or the handling and storage of such a pesticide product by an agricultural producer; or

(B) air emissions from animal waste (including decomposing animal waste) at a farm.

(2) Definitions.—In this subsection:

(A) Animal waste.—

(i) In general.—The term "animal waste" means feces, urine, or other excrement, digestive emission, urea, or similar substances emitted by animals (including any form of livestock, poultry, or fish).

(ii) Inclusions.—The term "animal waste" includes animal waste that is mixed or commingled with bedding, compost, feed, soil, or any other material typically found with such waste.

(B) Farm.—The term "farm" means a site or area (including associated structures) that—

(i) is used for—

(I) the production of a crop; or

(II) the raising or selling of animals (including any form of livestock, poultry, or fish); and

(ii) under normal conditions, produces during a farm year any agricultural products with a total value equal to not less than $1,000.

(f) Exemptions from notice and penalty provisions for substances reported under other Federal law or is in continuous release, etc.

No notification shall be required under subsection (a) or (b) of this section for any release of a hazardous substance—

(1) which is required to be reported (or specifically exempted from a requirement for reporting) under subtitle C of the Solid Waste Disposal Act [42 U.S.C.A. § 6921 et seq.] or regulations thereunder and which has been reported to the National Response Center, or

(2) which is a continuous release, stable in quantity and rate, and is—

(A) from a facility for which notification has been given under subsection (c) of this section, or

(B) a release of which notification has been given under subsections (a) and (b) of this section for a period sufficient to establish the continuity, quantity, and regularity of such release:

Provided, That notification in accordance with subsections (a) and (b) of this paragraph shall be given for releases subject to this paragraph annually, or at such time as there is any statistically significant increase in the quantity of any hazardous substance or constituent thereof released, above that previously reported or occurring.

(Pub. L. No. 96–510, Title I, § 103, 94 Stat. 2772 (Dec. 11, 1980); as amended by Pub. L. No. 96–561, Title II, § 238(b), 94 Stat. 3300 (Dec. 22, 1980); Pub. L. No. 99–499, Title I, §§ 103, 109(a)(1), (2), 100 Stat. 1617, 1632, 1633 (Oct. 17, 1986); Pub. L. No. 104–208, Title I, § 101(a) [Title II, § 211(b)], 110 Stat. 3009–41 (Sept. 30, 1996); Pub. L. No. 115–141, § 1102, 132 Stat. 348, 1147–1148 (Mar. 23, 2018).)

HISTORICAL AND STATUTORY NOTES

References in Text

The Clean Water Act, referred to in subsec. (a), is Act of June 30, 1948, c. 758, as amended generally by Pub. L. No. 92–500, § 2, 86 Stat. 816 (Oct. 18, 1972), also known as the Federal Water Pollution Control Act, which is codified generally as chapter 26 (section 1251 et seq.) of Title 33, Navigation and Navigable Waters. For complete classification of this Act to the Code, see Short Title note set out under section 1251 of Title 33 and Tables.

The Magnuson-Stevens Fishery Conservation and Management Act, referred to in subsec. (b)(2), is Pub. L. No. 94–265, 90 Stat. 331 (Apr. 13, 1976), as amended, which is codified principally as chapter 38 (section 1801 et seq.) of Title 16, Conservation. For complete classification of this Act to the Code, see Short Title note set out under section 1801 of Title 16 and Tables.

The Solid Waste Disposal Act, referred to in subsecs. (c) and (f)(1), is Title II of Pub. L. No. 89–272, 79 Stat. 997 (Oct. 20, 1965), as amended generally by Pub. L. No. 94–580, § 2, 90 Stat. 2795 (Oct. 21, 1976). Subtitle C of the Solid Waste Disposal Act is codified generally as subchapter III (section 6921 et seq.) of chapter 82 of this title. For complete classification of this Act to the Code, see Short Title of 1965 Acts note set out under section 6901 of this title and Tables.

The Federal Insecticide, Fungicide, and Rodenticide Act, referred to in subsec. (e), is Act of June 25, 1947, c. 125, as amended generally by Pub. L. No. 92–516, 86 Stat. 973 (Oct. 21, 1972), which is codified generally as subchapter II (section 136 et seq.) of chapter 6 of Title 7, Agriculture. For complete classification of this Act to the Code, see Short Title note set out under section 136 of Title 7 and Tables.

Effective and Applicability Provisions

1996 Acts. Amendment by section 101(a) of Title I [Title II, § 211(b)] of Div. A of Pub. L. No. 104–208 effective 15 days after Oct. 11, 1996, see section 101(a) of Title I [Title II, § 211(b)] of Div. A of Pub. L. No. 104–208, set out as a note under section 1801 of Title 16, Conservation.

1986 Acts. Amendment by Pub. L. No. 99–499 effective Oct. 17, 1986, see section 4 of Pub. L. No. 99–499, set out as a note under section 9601 of this title.

1980 Acts. Amendment by Pub. L. No. 96–561 effective 15 days after Dec. 22, 1980, see section 238 of Pub. L. No. 96–561, set out as a Short Title of 1980 Amendments note under section 1801 of Title 16, Conservation.

Application of the 2018 Farm Waste Amendments

Pub. L. No. 115–141, § 1103, 132 Stat. 1148 (Mar. 23, 2018), provided that: "Nothing in this title or an amendment made by this title affects, or supersedes or modifies the responsibility or authority of any Federal official or employee to comply with or enforce, any requirement under the Comprehensive Environmental Response, Compensation, and Liability Act of 1980 (42 U.S.C. 9601 et seq.), other than the hazardous substance notification requirements under section 103 of that Act (42 U.S.C. 9603) with respect to air emissions from animal waste at farms."

§ 9604. Response authorities

[CERCLA § 104]

(a) Removal and other remedial action by President; applicability of national contingency plan; response by potentially responsible parties; public health threats; limitations on response; exception

(1) Whenever (A) any hazardous substance is released or there is a substantial threat of such a release into the environment, or (B) there is a release or substantial threat of release into the environment of any pollutant or contaminant which may present an imminent and substantial danger to the public health or welfare, the President is authorized to act, consistent with the national contingency plan, to remove or arrange for the removal of, and provide for remedial action relating to such hazardous substance, pollutant, or contaminant at any time (including its removal from any contaminated natural resource), or take any other response measure consistent with the national contingency plan which the President deems necessary to protect the public health or welfare or the environment. When the President determines that such action will be done properly and promptly by the owner or operator of the facility or vessel or by any other responsible party, the President may allow such person to carry out the action, conduct the remedial investigation, or conduct the feasibility study in accordance with section 9622 of this title. No remedial investigation or feasibility study (RI/FS) shall be authorized except on a determination by the President that the party is qualified to conduct the RI/FS and only if the President contracts with or arranges for a qualified person to assist the President in overseeing and reviewing the conduct of such RI/FS and if the responsible party agrees to reimburse the Fund for any cost incurred by the President under, or in connection with, the oversight contract or arrangement. In no event shall a potentially responsible party be subject to a lesser standard of liability, receive preferential treatment, or in any other way, whether direct or indirect, benefit from any such arrangements as a response action contractor, or as a person hired or retained by such a response action contractor, with respect to the release or facility in question. The President shall give primary attention to those releases which the President deems may present a public health threat.

(2) Removal action

Any removal action undertaken by the President under this subsection (or by any other person referred to in section 9622 of this title) should, to the extent the President deems practicable, contribute to the efficient performance of any long term remedial action with respect to the release or threatened release concerned.

(3) Limitations on response

The President shall not provide for a removal or remedial action under this section in response to a release or threat of release—

(A) of a naturally occurring substance in its unaltered form, or altered solely through naturally occurring processes or phenomena, from a location where it is naturally found;

(B) from products which are part of the structure of, and result in exposure within, residential buildings or business or community structures; or

(C) into public or private drinking water supplies due to deterioration of the system through ordinary use.

(4) Exception to limitations

Notwithstanding paragraph (3) of this subsection, to the extent authorized by this section, the President may respond to any release or threat of release if in the President's discretion, it constitutes a public health or environmental emergency and no other person with the authority and capability to respond to the emergency will do so in a timely manner.

(b) Investigations, monitoring, coordination, etc., by President

(1) Information; studies and investigations

Whenever the President is authorized to act pursuant to subsection (a) of this section, or whenever the President has reason to believe that a release has occurred or is about to occur, or that illness, disease, or complaints thereof may be attributable to exposure to a hazardous substance, pollutant, or contaminant and that a release may have occurred or be occurring, he may undertake such investigations, monitoring, surveys, testing, and other information gathering as he may deem necessary or appropriate to identify the existence and extent of the release or threat thereof, the source and nature of the hazardous substances, pollutants or contaminants involved, and the extent of danger to the public health or welfare or to the environment. In addition, the President may undertake such planning, legal, fiscal, economic, engineering, architectural, and other studies or investigations as he may deem necessary or appropriate to plan and direct response actions, to recover the costs thereof, and to enforce the provisions of this chapter.

(2) Coordination of investigations

The President shall promptly notify the appropriate Federal and State natural resource trustees of potential damages to natural resources resulting from releases under investigation pursuant to this section and shall seek to coordinate the assessments, investigations, and planning under this section with such Federal and State trustees.

(c) Criteria for continuance of obligations from Fund over specified amount for response actions; consultation by President with affected States; contracts or cooperative agreements by States with President prior to remedial actions; cost-sharing agreements; selection by President of remedial actions; State credits: granting of credit, expenses before listing or agreement, response actions between 1978 and 1980, State expenses after December 11, 1980, in excess of 10 percent of costs, item-by-item approval, use of credits; operation and maintenance; limitation on source of funds for O & M; recontracting; siting.

(1) Unless (A) the President finds that (i) continued response actions are immediately required to prevent, limit, or mitigate an emergency, (ii) there is an immediate risk to public health or welfare or the environment, and (iii) such assistance will not otherwise be provided on a timely basis, or (B) the President has determined the appropriate remedial actions pursuant to paragraph (2) of this subsection and the State or States in which the source of the release is located have complied with the requirements of paragraph (3) of this subsection, or (C) continued response action is otherwise appropriate and consistent with the remedial action to be taken[1] obligations from the Fund, other than those authorized by subsection (b) of this section, shall not continue after $2,000,000 has been obligated for response actions or 12 months has elapsed from the date of initial response to a release or threatened release of hazardous substances.

(2) The President shall consult with the affected State or States before determining any appropriate remedial action to be taken pursuant to the authority granted under subsection (a) of this section.

(3) The President shall not provide any remedial actions pursuant to this section unless the State in which the release occurs first enters into a contract or cooperative agreement with the President providing assurances deemed adequate by the President that (A) the State will assure all future maintenance of the removal and remedial actions provided for the expected life of such actions as determined by the President; (B) the State will assure the availability of a hazardous waste disposal facility acceptable to the President and in compliance with the requirements of subtitle C of the Solid Waste Disposal Act [42 U.S.C.A. § 6921 et seq.] for any necessary offsite storage, destruction, treatment, or secure disposition of the hazardous substances; and (C) the State will pay or assure payment of (i) 10 per centum of the costs of the remedial action, including all future maintenance, or (ii) 50 percent (or such greater amount as the President may determine appropriate, taking into account the degree of responsibility of the State or political subdivision for the release) of any sums expended in response to a release at a facility, that was operated by the State or a political subdivision thereof, either directly or through a contractual relationship or otherwise, at the time of any disposal of hazardous substances therein. For the purpose of clause (ii) of this subparagraph, the term "facility" does not include navigable waters or the beds underlying those waters. In the case of remedial action to be taken on land or water held by an Indian tribe, held by the United States in trust for Indians, held by a member of an Indian tribe (if such land or water is subject to a trust restriction on alienation), or otherwise within the borders of an Indian reservation, the requirements of this paragraph for assurances regarding future maintenance and cost-sharing shall not apply, and the President shall provide the assurance required by this paragraph regarding the availability of a hazardous waste disposal facility.

(4) Selection of remedial action

The President shall select remedial actions to carry out this section in accordance with section 9621 of this title (relating to cleanup standards).

(5) State credits

(A) Granting of credit

The President shall grant a State a credit against the share of the costs, for which it is responsible under paragraph (3) with respect to a facility listed on the National Priorities List under the National Contingency Plan, for amounts expended by a State for remedial action at such facility pursuant to a contract or cooperative agreement with the President. The credit under this paragraph shall be limited to those State expenses which the President determines to be reasonable, documented, direct out-of-pocket expenditures of non-Federal funds.

(B) Expenses before listing or agreement

The credit under this paragraph shall include expenses for remedial action at a facility incurred before the listing of the facility on the National Priorities List or before a contract or cooperative agreement is entered into under subsection (d) of this section for the facility if—

(i) after such expenses are incurred the facility is listed on such list and a contract or cooperative agreement is entered into for the facility, and

(ii) the President determines that such expenses would have been credited to the State under subparagraph (A) had the expenditures been made after listing of the facility on such list and after the date on which such contract or cooperative agreement is entered into.

(C) Response actions between 1978 and 1980

The credit under this paragraph shall include funds expended or obligated by the State or a political subdivision thereof after January 1, 1978, and before December 11, 1980, for cost-eligible response actions and claims for damages compensable under section 9611 of this title.

(D) State expenses after December 11, 1980, in excess of 10 percent of costs

The credit under this paragraph shall include 90 percent of State expenses incurred at a facility owned, but not operated, by such State or by a political subdivision thereof. Such credit applies only to expenses incurred pursuant to a contract or cooperative agreement under subsection (d) of this section and only to expenses incurred after December 11, 1980, but before October 17, 1986.

(E) Item-by-item approval

In the case of expenditures made after October 17, 1986, the President may require prior approval of each item of expenditure as a condition of granting a credit under this paragraph.

(F) Use of credits

Credits granted under this paragraph for funds expended with respect to a facility may be used by the State to reduce all or part of the share of costs otherwise required to be paid by the State under paragraph (3) in connection with remedial actions at such facility. If the amount of funds for which credit is allowed under this paragraph exceeds such share of costs for such facility, the State may use the amount of such excess to reduce all or part of the share of such costs at other facilities in that State. A credit shall not entitle the State to any direct payment.

(6) Operation and maintenance

For the purposes of paragraph (3) of this subsection, in the case of ground or surface water contamination, completed remedial action includes the completion of treatment or other measures, whether taken onsite or offsite, necessary to restore ground and surface water quality to a level that assures protection of human health and the environment. With respect to such measures, the operation of such measures for a period of up to 10 years after the construction or installation and commencement of operation shall be considered remedial action. Activities required to maintain the effectiveness of such measures following such period or the completion of remedial action, whichever is earlier, shall be considered operation or maintenance.

(7) Limitation on source of funds for O&M

During any period after the availability of funds received by the Hazardous Substance Superfund established under subchapter A of chapter 98 of Title 26 from tax revenues or appropriations from general revenues, the Federal share of the payment of the cost of operation or maintenance pursuant to paragraph (3)(C)(i) or paragraph (6) of this subsection (relating to operation and maintenance) shall be from funds received by the Hazardous Substance Superfund from amounts recovered on behalf of such fund under this chapter.

(8) Recontracting

The President is authorized to undertake or continue whatever interim remedial actions the President determines to be appropriate to reduce risks to public health or the environment where the performance of a complete remedial action requires recontracting because of the discovery of sources, types, or quantities of hazardous substances not known at the time of entry into the original contract. The total cost of interim actions undertaken at a facility pursuant to this paragraph shall not exceed $2,000,000.

(9) Siting

Effective 3 years after October 17, 1986, the President shall not provide any remedial actions pursuant to this section unless the State in which the release occurs first enters into a contract or cooperative agreement with the President providing assurances deemed adequate by the President that the State will assure the availability of hazardous waste treatment or disposal facilities which—

(A) have adequate capacity for the destruction, treatment, or secure disposition of all hazardous wastes that are reasonably expected to be generated within the State during the 20-year period following the date of such contract or cooperative agreement and to be disposed of, treated, or destroyed,

(B) are within the State or outside the State in accordance with an interstate agreement or regional agreement or authority,

(C) are acceptable to the President, and

(D) are in compliance with the requirements of subtitle C of the Solid Waste Disposal Act [42 U.S.C.A. § 6921 et seq.]

(d) Contracts or cooperative agreements by President with States or political subdivisions or Indian tribes; State applications, terms and conditions; reimbursements; cost-sharing provisions; enforcement requirements and procedures

(1) Cooperative agreements

(A) State applications

A State or political subdivision thereof or Indian tribe may apply to the President to carry out actions authorized in this section. If the President determines that the State or political subdivision or Indian tribe has the capability to carry out any or all of such actions in accordance with the criteria and priorities established pursuant to section 9605(a)(8) of this title and to carry out related enforcement actions, the President may enter into a contract or cooperative agreement with the State or political subdivision or Indian tribe to carry out such actions. The

President shall make a determination regarding such an application within 90 days after the President receives the application.

(B) Terms and conditions

A contract or cooperative agreement under this paragraph shall be subject to such terms and conditions as the President may prescribe. The contract or cooperative agreement may cover a specific facility or specific facilities.

(C) Reimbursements

Any State which expended funds during the period beginning September 30, 1985, and ending on October 17, 1986, for response actions at any site included on the National Priorities List and subject to a cooperative agreement under this chapter shall be reimbursed for the share of costs of such actions for which the Federal Government is responsible under this chapter.

(2) If the President enters into a cost-sharing agreement pursuant to subsection (c) of this section or a contract or cooperative agreement pursuant to this subsection, and the State or political subdivision thereof fails to comply with any requirements of the contract, the President may, after providing sixty days notice, seek in the appropriate Federal district court to enforce the contract or to recover any funds advanced or any costs incurred because of the breach of the contract by the State or political subdivision.

(3) Where a State or a political subdivision thereof is acting in behalf of the President, the President is authorized to provide technical and legal assistance in the administration and enforcement of any contract or subcontract in connection with response actions assisted under this subchapter, and to intervene in any civil action involving the enforcement of such contract or subcontract.

(4) Where two or more noncontiguous facilities are reasonably related on the basis of geography, or on the basis of the threat, or potential threat to the public health or welfare or the environment, the President may, in his discretion, treat these related facilities as one for purposes of this section.

(e) Information gathering and access

(1) Action authorized

Any officer, employee, or representative of the President, duly designated by the President, is authorized to take action under paragraph (2), (3), or (4) (or any combination thereof) at a vessel, facility, establishment, place, property, or location or, in the case of paragraph (3) or (4), at any vessel, facility, establishment, place, property, or location which is adjacent to the vessel, facility, establishment, place, property, or location referred to in such paragraph (3) or (4). Any duly designated officer, employee, or representative of a State or political subdivision under a contract or cooperative agreement under subsection (d)(1) of this section is also authorized to take such action. The authority of paragraphs (3) and (4) may be exercised only if there is a reasonable basis to believe there may be a release or threat of release of a hazardous substance or pollutant or contaminant. The authority of this subsection may be exercised only for the purposes of determining the need for response, or choosing or taking any response action under this subchapter, or otherwise enforcing the provisions of this subchapter.

(2) Access to information

Any officer, employee, or representative described in paragraph (1) may require any person who has or may have information relevant to any of the following to furnish, upon reasonable notice, information or documents relating to such matter:

(A) The identification, nature, and quantity of materials which have been or are generated, treated, stored, or disposed of at a vessel or facility or transported to a vessel or facility.

(B) The nature or extent of a release or threatened release of a hazardous substance or pollutant or contaminant at or from a vessel or facility.

(C) Information relating to the ability of a person to pay for or to perform a cleanup.

In addition, upon reasonable notice, such person either (i) shall grant any such officer, employee, or representative access at all reasonable times to any vessel, facility, establishment, place, property, or location to inspect and copy all documents or records relating to such matters or (ii) shall copy and furnish to the officer, employee, or representative all such documents or records, at the option and expense of such person.

(3) Entry

Any officer, employee, or representative described in paragraph (1) is authorized to enter at reasonable times any of the following:

(A) Any vessel, facility, establishment, or other place or property where any hazardous substance or pollutant or contaminant may be or has been generated, stored, treated, disposed of, or transported from.

(B) Any vessel, facility, establishment, or other place or property from which or to which a hazardous substance or pollutant or contaminant has been or may have been released.

(C) Any vessel, facility, establishment, or other place or property where such release is or may be threatened.

(D) Any vessel, facility, establishment, or other place or property where entry is needed to determine the need for response or the appropriate response or to effectuate a response action under this subchapter.

(4) Inspection and samples

(A) Authority

Any officer, employee or representative described in paragraph (1) is authorized to inspect and obtain samples from any vessel, facility, establishment, or other place or property referred to in paragraph (3) or from any location of any suspected hazardous substance or pollutant or contaminant. Any such officer, employee, or representative is authorized to inspect and obtain samples of any containers or labeling for suspected hazardous substances or pollutants or contaminants. Each such inspection shall be completed with reasonable promptness.

(B) Samples

If the officer, employee, or representative obtains any samples, before leaving the premises he shall give to the owner, operator, tenant, or other person in charge of the place from which the samples were obtained a receipt describing the sample obtained and, if requested, a portion of each such sample. A copy of the results of any analysis made of such samples shall be furnished promptly to the owner, operator, tenant, or other person in charge, if such person can be located.

(5) Compliance orders

(A) Issuance

If consent is not granted regarding any request made by an officer, employee, or representative under paragraph (2), (3), or (4), the President may issue an order directing compliance with the request. The order may be issued after such notice and opportunity for consultation as is reasonably appropriate under the circumstances.

(B) Compliance

The President may ask the Attorney General to commence a civil action to compel compliance with a request or order referred to in subparagraph (A). Where there is a reasonable basis to believe there may be a release or threat of a release of a hazardous substance or pollutant or contaminant, the court shall take the following actions:

(i) In the case of interference with entry or inspection, the court shall enjoin such interference or direct compliance with orders to prohibit interference with entry or inspection unless under the circumstances of the case the demand for entry or inspection is arbitrary and capricious, an abuse of discretion, or otherwise not in accordance with law.

(ii) In the case of information or document requests or orders, the court shall enjoin interference with such information or document requests or orders or direct compliance with the requests or orders to provide such information or documents unless under the circumstances of the case the demand for information or documents is arbitrary and capricious, an abuse of discretion, or otherwise not in accordance with law.

The court may assess a civil penalty not to exceed $25,000 for each day of noncompliance against any person who unreasonably fails to comply with the provisions of paragraph (2), (3), or (4) or an order issued pursuant to subparagraph (A) of this paragraph.

(6) Other authority

Nothing in this subsection shall preclude the President from securing access or obtaining information in any other lawful manner.

(7) Confidentiality of information

(A) Any records, reports, or information obtained from any person under this section (including records, reports, or information obtained by representatives of the President) shall be available to the public, except that upon a showing satisfactory to the President (or the State, as the case may be) by any person that records, reports, or information, or particular part thereof (other than health or safety effects data), to which the President (or the State, as the case may be) or any officer, employee, or representative has access under this section if made public would divulge information entitled to protection under section 1905 of Title 18, such information or particular portion thereof shall be considered confidential in accordance with the purposes of that section, except that such record, report, document or information may be disclosed to other officers, employees, or authorized representatives of the United States concerned with carrying out this chapter, or when relevant in any proceeding under this chapter.

(B) Any person not subject to the provisions of section 1905 of Title 18 who knowingly and willfully divulges or discloses any information entitled to protection under this subsection shall, upon conviction, be subject to a fine of not more than $5,000 or to imprisonment not to exceed one year, or both.

(C) In submitting data under this chapter, a person required to provide such data may (i) designate the data which such person believes is entitled to protection under this subsection and (ii) submit such designated data separately from other data submitted under this chapter. A designation under this paragraph shall be made in writing and in such manner as the President may prescribe by regulation.

(D) Notwithstanding any limitation contained in this section or any other provision of law, all information reported to or otherwise obtained by the President (or any representative of the President) under this chapter shall be made available, upon written request of any duly authorized committee of the Congress, to such committee.

(E) No person required to provide information under this chapter may claim that the information is entitled to protection under this paragraph unless such person shows each of the following:

(i) Such person has not disclosed the information to any other person, other than a member of a local emergency planning committee established under title III of the Amendments and Reauthorization Act of 1986 [42 U.S.C.A. § 11001 et seq.], an officer or employee of the United States or a State or local government, an employee of such person, or a person who is bound by a confidentiality agreement, and such person has taken reasonable measures to protect the confidentiality of such information and intends to continue to take such measures.

(ii) The information is not required to be disclosed, or otherwise made available, to the public under any other Federal or State law.

(iii) Disclosure of the information is likely to cause substantial harm to the competitive position of such person.

(iv) The specific chemical identity, if sought to be protected, is not readily discoverable through reverse engineering.

(F) The following information with respect to any hazardous substance at the facility or vessel shall not be entitled to protection under this paragraph:

(i) The trade name, common name, or generic class or category of the hazardous substance.

(ii) The physical properties of the substance, including its boiling point, melting point, flash point, specific gravity, vapor density, solubility in water, and vapor pressure at 20 degrees celsius.

(iii) The hazards to health and the environment posed by the substance, including physical hazards (such as explosion) and potential acute and chronic health hazards.

(iv) The potential routes of human exposure to the substance at the facility, establishment, place, or property being investigated, entered, or inspected under this subsection.

(v) The location of disposal of any waste stream.

(vi) Any monitoring data or analysis of monitoring data pertaining to disposal activities.

(vii) Any hydrogeologic or geologic data.

(viii) Any groundwater monitoring data.

(f) Contracts for response actions; compliance with Federal health and safety standards

In awarding contracts to any person engaged in response actions, the President or the State, in any case where it is awarding contracts pursuant to a contract entered into under subsection (d) of this section, shall require compliance with Federal health and safety standards established under section 9651(f) of this title by contractors and subcontractors as a condition of such contracts.

(g) Rates for wages and labor standards applicable to covered work

(1) All laborers and mechanics employed by contractors or subcontractors in the performance of construction, repair, or alteration work funded in whole or in part under this section or section 9628(a)(1)(B)(ii)(III) shall be paid wages at rates not less than those prevailing on projects of a character similar in the locality as determined by the Secretary of Labor in accordance with sections 3141–3144, 3146, and 3147 of Title 40. The President shall not approve any such funding without first obtaining adequate assurance that required labor standards will be maintained upon the construction work.

(2) The Secretary of Labor shall have, with respect to the labor standards specified in paragraph (1), the authority and functions set forth in Reorganization Plan Numbered 14 of 1950 (15 F.R. 3176; 64 Stat. 1267) and section 3145 of Title 40.

(h) Emergency procurement powers; exercise by President

Notwithstanding any other provision of law, subject to the provisions of section 9611 of this title, the President may authorize the use of such emergency procurement powers as he deems necessary to effect the purpose of this chapter. Upon determination that such procedures are necessary, the President shall promulgate regulations prescribing the circumstances under which such authority shall be used and the procedures governing the use of such authority.

(i) Agency for Toxic Substances and Disease Registry; establishment, functions, etc.

(1) There is hereby established within the Public Health Service an agency, to be known as the Agency for Toxic Substances and Disease Registry, which shall report directly to the Surgeon General of the United States. The Administrator of said Agency shall, with the cooperation of the Administrator of the Environmental Protection Agency, the Commissioner of the Food and Drug Administration, the Directors of the National Institute of Medicine, National Institute of Environmental Health Sciences, National Institute of Occupational Safety and Health, Centers for Disease Control and Prevention, the Administrator of the Occupational Safety and Health Administration, the Administrator of the Social

Security Administration, the Secretary of Transportation, and appropriate State and local health officials, effectuate and implement the health related authorities of this chapter. In addition, said Administrator shall—

(A) in cooperation with the States, establish and maintain a national registry of serious diseases and illnesses and a national registry of persons exposed to toxic substances;

(B) establish and maintain inventory of literature, research, and studies on the health effects of toxic substances;

(C) in cooperation with the States, and other agencies of the Federal Government, establish and maintain a complete listing of areas closed to the public or otherwise restricted in use because of toxic substance contamination;

(D) in cases of public health emergencies caused or believed to be caused by exposure to toxic substances, provide medical care and testing to exposed individuals, including but not limited to tissue sampling, chromosomal testing where appropriate, epidemiological studies, or any other assistance appropriate under the circumstances; and

(E) either independently or as part of other health status survey, conduct periodic survey and screening programs to determine relationships between exposure to toxic substances and illness. In cases of public health emergencies, exposed persons shall be eligible for admission to hospitals and other facilities and services operated or provided by the Public Health Service.

(2) **(A)** Within 6 months after October 17, 1986, the Administrator of the Agency for Toxic Substances and Disease Registry (ATSDR) and the Administrator of the Environmental Protection Agency (EPA) shall prepare a list, in order of priority, of at least 100 hazardous substances which are most commonly found at facilities on the National Priorities List and which, in their sole discretion, they determine are posing the most significant potential threat to human health due to their known or suspected toxicity to humans and the potential for human exposure to such substances at facilities on the National Priorities List or at facilities to which a response to a release or a threatened release under this section is under consideration.

(B) Within 24 months after October 17, 1986, the Administrator of ATSDR and the Administrator of EPA shall revise the list prepared under subparagraph (A). Such revision shall include, in order of priority, the addition of 100 or more such hazardous substances. In each of the 3 consecutive 12-month periods that follow, the Administrator of ATSDR and the Administrator of EPA shall revise, in the same manner as provided in the 2 preceding sentences, such list to include not fewer than 25 additional hazardous substances per revision. The Administrator of ATSDR and the Administrator of EPA shall not less often than once every year thereafter revise such list to include additional hazardous substances in accordance with the criteria in subparagraph (A).

(3) Based on all available information, including information maintained under paragraph (1)(B) and data developed and collected on the health effects of hazardous substances under this paragraph, the Administrator of ATSDR shall prepare toxicological profiles of each of the substances listed pursuant to paragraph (2). The toxicological profiles shall be prepared in accordance with guidelines developed by the Administrator of ATSDR and the Administrator of EPA. Such profiles shall include, but not be limited to each of the following:

(A) An examination, summary, and interpretation of available toxicological information and epidemiologic evaluations on a hazardous substance in order to ascertain the levels of significant human exposure for the substance and the associated acute, subacute, and chronic health effects.

(B) A determination of whether adequate information on the health effects of each substance is available or in the process of development to determine levels of exposure which present a significant risk to human health of acute, subacute, and chronic health effects.

(C) Where appropriate, an identification of toxicological testing needed to identify the types or levels of exposure that may present significant risk of adverse health effects in humans.

Any toxicological profile or revision thereof shall reflect the Administrator of ATSDR's assessment of all relevant toxicological testing which has been peer reviewed. The profiles required to be prepared under this paragraph for those hazardous substances listed under subparagraph (A) of paragraph (2) shall be completed, at a rate of no fewer than 25 per year, within 4 years after October 17, 1986. A profile required on a substance listed pursuant to subparagraph (B) of paragraph (2) shall be completed within 3 years after addition to the list. The profiles prepared under this paragraph shall be of those substances highest on the list of priorities under paragraph (2) for which profiles have not previously been prepared. Profiles required under this paragraph shall be revised and republished as necessary, but no less often than once every 3 years. Such profiles shall be provided to the States and made available to other interested parties.

(4) The Administrator of the ATSDR shall provide consultations upon request on health issues relating to exposure to hazardous or toxic substances, on the basis of available information, to the Administrator of EPA, State officials, and local officials. Such consultations to individuals may be provided by States under cooperative agreements established under this chapter.

(5) **(A)** For each hazardous substance listed pursuant to paragraph (2), the Administrator of ATSDR (in consultation with the Administrator of EPA and other agencies and programs of the Public Health Service) shall assess whether adequate information on the health effects of such substance is available. For any such substance for which adequate information is not available (or under development), the Administrator of ATSDR, in cooperation with the Director of the National Toxicology Program, shall assure the initiation of a program of research designed to determine the health effects (and techniques for development of methods to determine such health effects) of such substance. Where feasible, such program shall seek to develop methods to determine the health effects of such substance in combination with other substances with which it is commonly found. Before assuring the initiation of such program, the Administrator of ATSDR shall consider recommendations of the Interagency Testing Committee established under section 4(e) of the Toxic Substances Control Act [15 U.S.C.A. § 2603(e)] on the types of research that should be done. Such program shall include, to the extent necessary to supplement existing information, but shall not be limited to—

(i) laboratory and other studies to determine short, intermediate, and long-term health effects;

(ii) laboratory and other studies to determine organ-specific, site-specific, and system-specific acute and chronic toxicity;

(iii) laboratory and other studies to determine the manner in which such substances are metabolized or to otherwise develop an understanding of the biokinetics of such substances; and

(iv) where there is a possibility of obtaining human data, the collection of such information.

(B) In assessing the need to perform laboratory and other studies, as required by subparagraph (A), the Administrator of ATSDR shall consider—

(i) the availability and quality of existing test data concerning the substance on the suspected health effect in question;

(ii) the extent to which testing already in progress will, in a timely fashion, provide data that will be adequate to support the preparation of toxicological profiles as required by paragraph (3); and

(iii) such other scientific and technical factors as the Administrator of ATSDR may determine are necessary for the effective implementation of this subsection.

(C) In the development and implementation of any research program under this paragraph, the Administrator of ATSDR and the Administrator of EPA shall coordinate such research program implemented under this paragraph with the National Toxicology Program and with programs of toxicological testing established under the Toxic Substances Control Act [15 U.S.C.A. § 2601 et seq.] and the Federal Insecticide, Fungicide and Rodenticide Act [7 U.S.C.A. § 136 et seq.]. The purpose of such coordination shall be to avoid duplication of effort and to assure that the hazardous substances listed pursuant to this subsection are tested thoroughly at the earliest practicable date. Where appropriate, consistent with such purpose, a research program under this paragraph may be carried out using such programs of toxicological testing.

(D) It is the sense of the Congress that the costs of research programs under this paragraph be borne by the manufacturers and processors of the hazardous substance in question, as required in programs of toxicological testing under the Toxic Substances Control Act [15 U.S.C.A. § 2601 et seq.]. Within 1 year after October 17, 1986, the Administrator of EPA shall promulgate regulations which provide, where appropriate, for payment of such costs by manufacturers and processors under the Toxic Substances Control Act, and registrants under the Federal Insecticide, Fungicide, and Rodenticide Act [7 U.S.C.A. § 136 et seq.], and recovery of such costs from responsible parties under this chapter.

(6) **(A)** The Administrator of ATSDR shall perform a health assessment for each facility on the National Priorities List established under section 9605 of this title. Such health assessment shall be completed not later than December 10, 1988, for each facility proposed for inclusion on such list prior to October 17, 1986, or not later than one year after the date of proposal for inclusion on such list for each facility proposed for inclusion on such list after October 17, 1986.

(B) The Administrator of ATSDR may perform health assessments for releases or facilities where individual persons or licensed physicians provide information that individuals have been exposed to a hazardous substance, for which the probable source of such exposure is a release. In addition to other methods (formal or informal) of providing such information, such individual persons or licensed physicians may submit a petition to the Administrator of ATSDR providing such information and requesting a health assessment. If such a petition is submitted and the Administrator of ATSDR does not initiate a health assessment, the Administrator of ATSDR shall provide a written explanation of why a health assessment is not appropriate.

(C) In determining the priority in which to conduct health assessments under this subsection, the Administrator of ATSDR, in consultation with the Administrator of EPA, shall give priority to those facilities at which there is documented evidence of the release of hazardous substances, at which the potential risk to human health appears highest, and for which in the judgment of the Administrator of ATSDR existing health assessment data are inadequate to assess the potential risk to human health as provided in subparagraph (F). In determining the priorities for conducting health assessments under this subsection, the Administrator of ATSDR shall consider the National Priorities List schedules and the needs of the Environmental Protection Agency and other Federal agencies pursuant to schedules for remedial investigation and feasibility studies.

(D) Where a health assessment is done at a site on the National Priorities List, the Administrator of ATSDR shall complete such assessment promptly and, to the maximum extent practicable, before the completion of the remedial investigation and feasibility study at the facility concerned.

(E) Any State or political subdivision carrying out a health assessment for a facility shall report the results of the assessment to the Administrator of ATSDR and the Administrator of EPA and shall include recommendations with respect to further activities which need to be carried out under this section. The Administrator of ATSDR shall state such recommendation in any report on the results of any assessment carried out directly by the Administrator of ATSDR for such facility and shall issue periodic reports which include the results of all the assessments carried out under this subsection.

(F) For the purposes of this subsection and section 9611(c)(4) of this title, the term "health assessments" shall include preliminary assessments of the potential risk to human health posed by individual sites and facilities, based on such factors as the nature and extent of contamination, the existence of potential pathways of human exposure (including ground or surface water contamination, air emissions, and food chain contamination), the size and potential susceptibility of the community within the likely pathways of exposure, the comparison of expected human exposure levels to the short-term and long-term health effects associated with identified hazardous substances and any available recommended exposure or tolerance limits for such hazardous substances, and the comparison of existing morbidity and mortality data on diseases that may be associated with the observed levels of exposure. The Administrator of ATSDR shall use appropriate data, risk assessments, risk evaluations and studies available from the Administrator of EPA.

(G) The purpose of health assessments under this subsection shall be to assist in determining whether actions under paragraph (11) of this subsection should be taken to reduce human exposure to hazardous substances from a facility and whether additional information on human exposure and associated health risks is needed and should be acquired by conducting epidemiological studies under paragraph (7), establishing a registry under paragraph (8), establishing a health surveillance program under paragraph (9), or through other means. In using the results of health assessments for determining additional actions to be taken under this section, the Administrator of ATSDR may consider additional information on the risks to the potentially affected population from all sources of such hazardous substances including known point or nonpoint sources other than those from the facility in question.

(H) At the completion of each health assessment, the Administrator of ATSDR shall provide the Administrator of EPA and each affected State with the results of such assessment, together with any recommendations for further actions under this subsection or otherwise under this chapter. In addition, if the health assessment indicates that the release or threatened release concerned may pose a serious threat to human health or the environment, the Administrator of ATSDR shall so notify the Administrator of EPA who shall promptly evaluate such release or threatened release in accordance with the hazard ranking system referred to in section 9605(a)(8)(A) of this title to determine whether the site shall be placed on the National Priorities List or, if the site is already on the list, the Administrator of ATSDR may recommend to the Administrator of EPA that the site be accorded a higher priority.

(7) (A) Whenever in the judgment of the Administrator of ATSDR it is appropriate on the basis of the results of a health assessment, the Administrator of ATSDR shall conduct a pilot study of health effects for selected groups of exposed individuals in order to determine the desirability of conducting full scale epidemiological or other health studies of the entire exposed population.

(B) Whenever in the judgment of the Administrator of ATSDR it is appropriate on the basis of the results of such pilot study or other study or health assessment, the Administrator of ATSDR shall conduct such full scale epidemiological or other health studies as may be necessary to determine the health effects on the population exposed to hazardous substances from a release or threatened release. If a significant excess of disease in a population is identified, the letter of transmittal of such study shall include an assessment of other risk factors, other than a release, that may, in the judgment of the peer review group, be associated with such disease, if such risk factors were not taken into account in the design or conduct of the study.

(8) In any case in which the results of a health assessment indicate a potential significant risk to human health, the Administrator of ATSDR shall consider whether the establishment of a registry of exposed persons would contribute to accomplishing the purposes of this subsection, taking into account circumstances bearing on the usefulness of such a registry, including the seriousness or unique character of identified diseases or the likelihood of population migration from the affected area.

(9) Where the Administrator of ATSDR has determined that there is a significant increased risk of adverse health effects in humans from exposure to hazardous substances based on the results of a health assessment conducted under paragraph (6), an epidemiologic study conducted under paragraph (7), or an exposure registry that has been established under paragraph (8), and the Administrator of ATSDR has determined that such exposure is the result of a release from a facility, the Administrator of ATSDR shall initiate a health surveillance program for such population. This program shall include but not be limited to—

(A) periodic medical testing where appropriate of population subgroups to screen for diseases for which the population or subgroup is at significant increased risk; and

(B) a mechanism to refer for treatment those individuals within such population who are screened positive for such diseases.

(10) Two years after October 17, 1986, and every 2 years thereafter, the Administrator of ATSDR shall prepare and submit to the Administrator of EPA and to the Congress a report on the results of the activities of ATSDR regarding—

(A) health assessments and pilot health effects studies conducted;

(B) epidemiologic studies conducted;

(C) hazardous substances which have been listed under paragraph (2), toxicological profiles which have been developed, and toxicologic testing which has been conducted or which is being conducted under this subsection;

(D) registries established under paragraph (8); and

(E) an overall assessment, based on the results of activities conducted by the Administrator of ATSDR, of the linkage between human exposure to individual or combinations of hazardous substances due to releases from facilities covered by this chapter or the Solid Waste Disposal Act [42 U.S.C.A. § 6901 et seq.] and any increased incidence or prevalence of adverse health effects in humans.

(11) If a health assessment or other study carried out under this subsection contains a finding that the exposure concerned presents a significant risk to human health, the President shall take such steps as may be necessary to reduce such exposure and eliminate or substantially mitigate the significant risk to human health. Such steps may include the use of any authority under this chapter, including, but not limited to—

(A) provision of alternative water supplies, and

(B) permanent or temporary relocation of individuals.

In any case in which information is insufficient, in the judgment of the Administrator of ATSDR or the President to determine a significant human exposure level with respect to a hazardous substance, the President may take such steps as may be necessary to reduce the exposure of any person to such hazardous substance to such level as the President deems necessary to protect human health.

(12) In any case which is the subject of a petition, a health assessment or study, or a research program under this subsection, nothing in this subsection shall be construed to delay or otherwise affect or impair the authority of the President, the Administrator of ATSDR, or the Administrator of EPA to exercise any authority vested in the President, the Administrator of ATSDR or the Administrator of EPA under any other provision of law (including, but not limited to, the imminent hazard authority of section 7003 of the Solid Waste Disposal Act [42 U.S.C.A. § 6973]) or the response and abatement authorities of this chapter.

(13) All studies and results of research conducted under this subsection (other than health assessments) shall be reported or adopted only after appropriate peer review. Such peer review shall be completed, to the maximum extent practicable, within a period of 60 days. In the case of research conducted under the National Toxicology Program, such peer review may be conducted by the Board of Scientific Counselors. In the case of other research, such peer review shall be conducted by panels consisting of no less than three nor more than seven members, who shall be disinterested scientific experts selected for such purpose by the Administrator of ATSDR or the Administrator of EPA, as appropriate, on the basis of their reputation for scientific objectivity and the lack of institutional ties with any person involved in the conduct of the study or research under review. Support services for such panels shall be provided by the Agency for Toxic Substances and Disease Registry, or by the Environmental Protection Agency, as appropriate.

(14) In the implementation of this subsection and other health-related authorities of this chapter, the Administrator of ATSDR shall assemble, develop as necessary, and distribute to the States, and upon request to medical colleges, physicians, and other health professionals, appropriate educational materials (including short courses) on the medical surveillance, screening, and methods of diagnosis and treatment of injury or disease related to exposure to hazardous substances (giving priority to those listed in paragraph (2)), through such means as the Administrator of ATSDR deems appropriate.

(15) The activities of the Administrator of ATSDR described in this subsection and section 9611(c)(4) of this title shall be carried out by the Administrator of ATSDR, either directly or through cooperative agreements with States (or political subdivisions thereof) which the Administrator of ATSDR determines are capable of carrying out such activities. Such activities shall include provision of consultations on health information, the conduct of health assessments, including those required under section 3019(b) of the Solid Waste Disposal Act [42 U.S.C.A. § 6939a(b)], health studies, registries, and health surveillance.

(16) The President shall provide adequate personnel for ATSDR, which shall not be fewer than 100 employees. For purposes of determining the number of employees under this subsection, an employee employed by ATSDR on a part-time career employment basis shall be counted as a fraction which is determined by dividing 40 hours into the average number of hours of such employee's regularly scheduled workweek.

(17) In accordance with section 9620 of this title (relating to Federal facilities), the Administrator of ATSDR shall have the same authorities under this section with respect to facilities owned or operated by a department, agency, or instrumentality of the United States as the Administrator of ATSDR has with respect to any nongovernmental entity.

(18) If the Administrator of ATSDR determines that it is appropriate for purposes of this section to treat a pollutant or contaminant as a hazardous substance, such pollutant or contaminant shall be treated as a hazardous substance for such purpose.

(j) Acquisition of property

(1) Authority

The President is authorized to acquire, by purchase, lease, condemnation, donation, or otherwise, any real property or any interest in real property that the President in his discretion determines is needed to conduct a remedial action under this chapter. There shall be no cause of action to compel the President to acquire any interest in real property under this chapter.

(2) State assurance

The President may use the authority of paragraph (1) for a remedial action only if, before an interest in real estate is acquired under this subsection, the State in which the interest to be acquired is located assures the President, through a contract or cooperative agreement or otherwise, that the State will accept transfer of the interest following completion of the remedial action.

(3) Exemption

No Federal, State, or local government agency shall be liable under this chapter solely as a result of acquiring an interest in real estate under this subsection.

(k) Brownfields revitalization funding

(1) Definition of eligible entity

In this subsection, the term "eligible entity" means—

(A) a general purpose unit of local government;

(B) a land clearance authority or other quasi-governmental entity that operates under the supervision and control of or as an agent of a general purpose unit of local government;

(C) a government entity created by a State legislature;

(D) a regional council or group of general purpose units of local government;

(E) a redevelopment agency that is chartered or otherwise sanctioned by a State;

(F) a State;

(G) an Indian Tribe other than in Alaska;

(H) an Alaska Native Regional Corporation and an Alaska Native Village Corporation as those terms are defined in the Alaska Native Claims Settlement Act (43 U.S.C. 1601 and following) and the Metlakatla Indian community;

(I) an organization described in section 501(c)(3) of the Internal Revenue Code of 1986 and exempt from taxation under section 501(a) of that Code;

(J) a limited liability corporation in which all managing members are organizations described in subparagraph (I) or limited liability corporations whose sole members are organizations described in subparagraph (I);

(K) a limited partnership in which all general partners are organizations described in subparagraph (I) or limited liability corporations whose sole members are organizations described in subparagraph (I); or

(L) a qualified community development entity (as defined in section 45D(c)(1) of the Internal Revenue Code of 1986).

(2) Brownfield site characterization and assessment grant program

(A) Establishment of program

The Administrator shall establish a program to—

(i) provide grants to inventory, characterize, assess, and conduct planning related to brownfield sites under subparagraph (B); and

(ii) perform targeted site assessments at brownfield sites.

(B) Assistance for site characterization and assessment

(i) In general

On approval of an application made by an eligible entity, the Administrator may make a grant to the eligible entity to be used for programs to inventory, characterize, assess, and conduct planning related to one or more brownfield sites.

(ii) Site characterization and assessment

A site characterization and assessment carried out with the use of a grant under clause (i) shall be performed in accordance with section 9601(35)(B) of this title.

(C) Exemption for certain publicly owned brownfield sites.—Notwithstanding paragraph (5)(B)(iii), an eligible entity described in any of subparagraphs (A) through (H) of paragraph (1) may receive a grant under this paragraph for property acquired by that eligible entity prior to January 11, 2002, even if the eligible entity does not qualify as a bona fide prospective purchaser, so long as the eligible entity has not caused or contributed to a release or threatened release of a hazardous substance at the property.

(3) Grants and loans for brownfield remediation

(A) Grants provided by the President

Subject to paragraphs (5) and (6), the President shall establish a program to provide grants to—

(i) eligible entities, to be used for capitalization of revolving loan funds; and

(ii) eligible entities or nonprofit organizations, where warranted, as determined by the President based on considerations under subparagraph (C), to be used directly for remediation of one or more brownfield sites owned by the entity or organization that receives the grant and in amounts not to exceed $500,000 for each site to be remediated, which limit may be waived by the Administrator, but not to exceed a total of $650,000 for each site, based on the anticipated level of contamination, size, or ownership status of the site.

(B) Loans and grants provided by eligible entities

An eligible entity that receives a grant under subparagraph (A)(i) shall use the grant funds to provide assistance for the remediation of brownfield sites in the form of—

(i) one or more loans to an eligible entity, a site owner, a site developer, or another person; or

(ii) one or more grants to an eligible entity or other nonprofit organization, where warranted, as determined by the eligible entity that is providing the assistance, based on considerations under subparagraph (C), to remediate sites owned by the eligible entity or nonprofit organization that receives the grant.

(C) Considerations

In determining whether a grant under subparagraph (A)(ii) or (B)(ii) is warranted, the President or the eligible entity, as the case may be, shall take into consideration—

(i) the extent to which a grant will facilitate the creation of, preservation of, or addition to a park, a greenway, undeveloped property, recreational property, or other property used for nonprofit purposes;

(ii) the extent to which a grant will meet the needs of a community that has an inability to draw on other sources of funding for environmental remediation and subsequent redevelopment of the area in which a brownfield site is located because of the small population or low income of the community;

(iii) the extent to which a grant will facilitate the use or reuse of existing infrastructure;

(iv) the benefit of promoting the long-term availability of funds from a revolving loan fund for brownfield remediation; and

(v) such other similar factors as the Administrator considers appropriate to consider for the purposes of this subsection.

(D) Transition

Revolving loan funds that have been established before January 11, 2002, may be used in accordance with this paragraph.

(E) Exemption for certain publicly owned brownfield sites.—Notwithstanding paragraph (5)(B)(iii), an eligible entity described in any of subparagraphs (A) through (H) of paragraph (1) may receive a grant or loan under this paragraph for property acquired by that eligible entity prior to January 11, 2002, even if the eligible entity does not qualify as a bona fide prospective purchaser, so long as the eligible entity has not caused or contributed to a release or threatened release of a hazardous substance at the property.

(4) Multipurpose browfield grants.—

(A) In general.—Subject to subparagraph (D) and paragraphs (5) and (6), the Administrator shall establish a program to provide multipurpose grants to an eligible entity based on the criteria under subparagraph (C) and the considerations under paragraph (3)(C), to carry out inventory, characterization, assessment, planning, or remediation activities at 1 or more brownfield sites in an area proposed by the eligible entity.

(B) Grant amounts.—

(i) Individual grant amounts.—Each grant awarded under this paragraph shall not exceed $1,000,000.

(ii) Cumulative grant amounts.—The total amount of grants awarded for each fiscal year under this paragraph may not exceed 15 percent of the funds made available for the fiscal year to carry out this subsection.

(C) Criteria.—In awarding a grant under this paragraph, the Administrator shall consider the extent to which the eligible entity is able—

(i) to provide an overall plan for revitalization of the 1 or more brownfield sites in the proposed area in which the multipurpose grant will be used;

(ii) to demonstrate a capacity to conduct the range of eligible activities that will be funded by the multipurpose grant; and

(iii) to demonstrate that a multipurpose grant will meet the needs of the 1 or more brownfield sites in the proposed area.

(D) Condition.—As a condition of receiving a grant under this paragraph, each eligible entity shall expend the full amount of the grant by not later than the date that is 5 years after the date on which the grant is awarded to the eligible entity, unless the Administrator provides an extension.

(E) Ownership.—An eligible entity that receives a grant under this paragraph may not expend any of the grant funds for the remediation of a brownfield site unless the eligible entity owns the brownfield site.

(5) General provisions

(A) Maximum grant amount

(i) Brownfield site characterization and assessment

(I) In general

A grant under paragraph (2) may be awarded to an eligible entity on a community-wide or site-by-site basis, and shall not exceed, for any individual brownfield site covered by the grant, $200,000.

(II) Waiver

The Administrator may waive the $200,000 limitation under subclause (I) to permit the brownfield site to receive a grant of not to exceed $350,000, based on the anticipated level of contamination, size, or status of ownership of the site.

(ii) Brownfield remediation

A grant under paragraph (3)(A)(i) may be awarded to an eligible entity on a community-wide or site-by-site basis, not to exceed $1,000,000 per eligible entity. The Administrator may make an additional grant to an eligible entity described in the previous sentence for any year after the year for which the initial grant is made, taking into consideration—

(I) the number of sites and number of communities that are addressed by the revolving loan fund;

(II) the demand for funding by eligible entities that have not previously received a grant under this subsection;

(III) the demonstrated ability of the eligible entity to use the revolving loan fund to enhance remediation and provide funds on a continuing basis; and

(IV) such other similar factors as the Administrator considers appropriate to carry out this subsection.

(B) Prohibition.—No part of a grant or loan under this subsection may be used for the payment of—

(i) a penalty or fine;

(ii) a Federal cost-share requirement;

(iii) a response cost at a brownfield site for which the recipient of the grant or loan is potentially liable under section 107; or

(iv) a cost of compliance with any Federal law (including a Federal law specified in section 101(39)(B)), excluding the cost of compliance with laws applicable to the cleanup.

(C) Assistance for development of local government site remediation programs

A local government that receives a grant under this subsection may use not to exceed 10 percent of the grant funds to develop and implement a brownfields program that may include—

(i) monitoring the health of populations exposed to one or more hazardous substances from a brownfield site; and

(ii) monitoring and enforcement of any institutional control used to prevent human exposure to any hazardous substance from a brownfield site.

(D) Insurance

A recipient of a grant or loan awarded under paragraph (2), (3), or (4) that performs a characterization, assessment, or remediation of a brownfield site may use a portion of the grant or loan to purchase insurance for the characterization, assessment, or remediation of that site.

(E) Administrative Costs.—

(i) In general.—An eligible entity may use up to 5 percent of the amounts made available under a grant or loan under this subsection for administrative costs.

(ii) Restriction.—For purposes of clause (i), the term 'administrative costs' does not include—

(I) investigation and identification of the extent of contamination of a brownfield site;

(II) design and performance of a response action; or

(III) monitoring of a natural resource.

(6) Grant applications

(A) Submission

(i) In general

(I) Application

An eligible entity may submit to the Administrator, through a regional office of the Environmental Protection Agency and in such form as the Administrator may require, an application for a grant under this subsection for one or more brownfield sites (including information on the criteria used by the Administrator to rank applications under subparagraph (C), to the extent that the information is available).

(II) NCP requirements

The Administrator may include in any requirement for submission of an application under subclause (I) a requirement of the National Contingency Plan only to the extent that the requirement is relevant and appropriate to the program under this subsection.

(ii) Coordination

The Administrator shall coordinate with other Federal agencies to assist in making eligible entities aware of other available Federal resources.

(iii) Guidance

The Administrator shall publish guidance to assist eligible entities in applying for grants under this subsection.

(B) Approval

The Administrator shall—

(i) at least annually, complete a review of applications for grants that are received from eligible entities under this subsection; and

(ii) award grants under this subsection to eligible entities that the Administrator determines have the highest rankings under the ranking criteria established under subparagraph (C).

(C) Ranking criteria

The Administrator shall establish a system for ranking grant applications received under this paragraph that includes the following criteria:

(i) The extent to which a grant will stimulate the availability of other funds for environmental assessment or remediation, and subsequent reuse, of an area in which one or more brownfield sites are located.

(ii) The potential of the proposed project or the development plan for an area in which one or more brownfield sites are located to stimulate economic development of the area on completion of the cleanup.

(iii) The extent to which a grant would address or facilitate the identification and reduction of threats to human health and the environment, including threats in areas in which there is a greater-than-normal incidence of diseases or conditions (including cancer, asthma, or birth defects) that may be associated with exposure to hazardous substances, pollutants, or contaminants.

(iv) The extent to which a grant would facilitate the use or reuse of existing infrastructure.

(v) The extent to which a grant would facilitate the creation of, preservation of, or addition to a park, a greenway, undeveloped property, recreational property, or other property used for nonprofit purposes.

(vi) The extent to which a grant would meet the needs of a community that has an inability to draw on other sources of funding for environmental remediation and subsequent redevelopment of the area in which a brownfield site is located because of the small population or low income of the community.

(vii) The extent to which the applicant is eligible for funding from other sources.

(viii) The extent to which a grant will further the fair distribution of funding between urban and nonurban areas.

(ix) The extent to which the grant provides for involvement of the local community in the process of making decisions relating to cleanup and future use of a brownfield site.

(x) The extent to which a grant would address or facilitate the identification and reduction of threats to the health or welfare of children, pregnant women, minority or low-income communities, or other sensitive populations.

(xi) The extent to which a grant would address a site adjacent to a body of water or a federally designated flood plain.

(xii) The extent to which a grant would facilitate—

(I) the location at a brownfield site of a facility that generates renewable electricity from wind, solar, or geothermal energy; or

(II) any energy efficiency improvement project at a brownfield site, including a project for a combined heat and power system or a district energy system.

(D) Report on ranking criteria.—Not later than September 30, 2022, the Administrator shall submit to Congress a report regarding the Administrator's use of the ranking criteria described in subparagraph (C) in awarding grants under this subsection.

(7) Implementation of brownfields programs

(A) Establishment of program

The Administrator may provide, or fund eligible entities or nonprofit organizations to provide, training, research, and technical assistance to individuals and organizations, as appropriate, to facilitate the inventory of brownfield sites, site assessments, remediation of brownfield sites, community involvement, or site preparation.

(B) Funding restrictions

The total Federal funds to be expended by the Administrator under this paragraph shall not exceed 15 percent of the total amount appropriated to carry out this subsection in any fiscal year.

(8) Audits

(A) In general

The Inspector General of the Environmental Protection Agency shall conduct such reviews or audits of grants and loans under this subsection as the Inspector General considers necessary to carry out this subsection.

(B) Procedure

An audit under this subparagraph shall be conducted in accordance with the auditing procedures of the Government Accountability Office, including chapter 75 of Title 31.

(C) Violations

If the Administrator determines that a person that receives a grant or loan under this subsection has violated or is in violation of a condition of the grant, loan, or applicable Federal law, the Administrator may—

(i) terminate the grant or loan;

(ii) require the person to repay any funds received; and

(iii) seek any other legal remedies available to the Administrator.

(D) Report to Congress

Not later than September 30, 2022, the Inspector General of the Environmental Protection Agency shall submit to Congress a report that provides a description of the management of the program (including a description of the allocation of funds under this subsection).

(9) Leveraging

An eligible entity that receives a grant under this subsection may use the grant funds for a portion of a project at a brownfield site for which funding is received from other sources if the grant funds are used only for the purposes described in paragraph (2), (3), or (4).

(10) Agreements

Each grant or loan made under this subsection shall—

(A) include a requirement of the National Contingency Plan only to the extent that the requirement is relevant and appropriate to the program under this subsection, as determined by the Administrator; and

(B) be subject to an agreement that—

(i) requires the recipient to—

(I) comply with all applicable Federal and State laws; and

(II) ensure that the cleanup protects human health and the environment;

(ii) requires that the recipient use the grant or loan exclusively for purposes specified in paragraph (2), (3), or (4), as applicable;

(iii) in the case of an application by an eligible entity under paragraph (3)(A), requires the eligible entity to pay a matching share (which may be in the form of a contribution of labor, material, or services) of at least 20 percent, from non-Federal sources of funding, unless the Administrator determines that the matching share would place an undue hardship on the eligible entity; and

(iv) contains such other terms and conditions as the Administrator determines to be necessary to carry out this subsection.

(11) Facility other than brownfield site

The fact that a facility may not be a brownfield site within the meaning of section 9601(39)(A) of this title has no effect on the eligibility of the facility for assistance under any other provision of Federal law.

(12) Effect on Federal laws

Nothing in this subsection affects any liability or response authority under any Federal law, including—

(A) this chapter (including the last sentence of section 9601(14) of this title);

(B) the Solid Waste Disposal Act (42 U.S.C. 6901 et seq.);

(C) the Federal Water Pollution Control Act (33 U.S.C. 1251 et seq.);

(D) the Toxic Substances Control Act (15 U.S.C. 2601 et seq.); and

(E) the Safe Drinking Water Act (42 U.S.C. 300f et seq.).

(13) Authorization of appropriations.—There is authorized to be appropriated to carry out this subsection $200,000,000 for each of fiscal years 2019 through 2023.

(Pub. L. No. 96–510, Title I, § 104, 94 Stat. 2774 (Dec. 11, 1980); as amended by Pub. L. No. 99–499, Title I, §§ 104, 110, Title II, § 207(b), 100 Stat. 1617, 1636, 1705 (Oct. 17, 1986); Pub. L. No. 99–514, § 2, 100 Stat. 2095 (Oct. 22, 1986); Pub. L. No. 102–531, Title III, § 312(h), 106 Stat. 3506 (Oct. 27, 1992); Pub. L. No. 107–118, Title II, § 211(b), 115 Stat. 2362 (Jan. 11, 2002); Pub. L. No. 108–271, § 8(b), 118 Stat. 814 (July 7, 2004); Pub. L. No. 109–59, Title I, § 1956, 119 Stat. 1515 (Aug. 10, 2005); Pub. L. No. 115–141, tit. VII, §§ 6–13, 14(b), 132 Stat. 346, 1154–1157, 1158 (Mar. 23, 2018).)

[1] So in original. Probably should be followed by a comma.

HISTORICAL AND STATUTORY NOTES

References in Text

"This chapter", referred to in text, originally read "this Act", meaning Pub. L. No. 96–510, Dec. 11, 1980, 94 Stat. 2767, as amended, known as the Comprehensive Environmental Response, Compensation, and Liability Act of 1980, which is codified principally as this chapter [42 U.S.C.A. § 9601 et seq.]; see Tables for complete classification.

The Solid Waste Disposal Act, referred to in subsecs. (c)(3), (9)(D), (i)(10)(E), and (k)(11)(B), is Title II of Pub. L. No. 89–272, 79 Stat. 997 (Oct. 20, 1965), as amended generally by Pub. L. No. 94–580, § 2, 90 Stat. 2795 (Oct. 21, 1976), which is codified principally to chapter 82 of this title [42 U.S.C.A. § 6901 et seq.]. Subtitle C of the Solid Waste Disposal Act is codified generally to subchapter III (section 6921 et seq.) of chapter 82 of this title. See Tables for complete classification.

Title III of the Amendments and Reauthorization Act of 1986, referred to in subsec. (e)(7)(E)(i), probably means Title III (section 300 et seq.) of the Superfund Amendments and Reauthorization Act of 1986, Pub. L. No. 99–499, 100 Stat. 1728 (Oct. 17, 1986), known as the Emergency Planning and Community Right-To-Know Act of 1986, which is codified generally as chapter 116 (section 11001 et seq.) of this title. For complete classification of the Emergency Planning and Community Right-To-Know Act of 1986 to the Code, see Short Title of 1986 Acts note set out under section 11001 of this title and Tables.

Reorganization Plan Numbered 14 of 1950, referred to in subsec. (g)(2), is set out in Appendix 1 to Title 5, Government Organization and Employees.

The Toxic Substances Control Act, referred to in subsecs. (i)(5)(C), (D) and (k)(11)(D), is Pub. L. No. 94–469, 90 Stat. 2003 (Oct. 11, 1976), as amended, which is codified principally as chapter 53 of Title 15 [15 U.S.C.A. § 2601 et seq.]. See Tables for complete classification.

The Federal Insecticide, Fungicide, and Rodenticide Act, referred to in subsec. (i)(5)(C), (D), is Act of June 25, 1947, c. 125, as amended generally by Pub. L. No. 92–516, 86 Stat. 973 (Oct. 21, 1972), which is codified generally as subchapter II (section 136 et seq.) of chapter 6 of Title 7, Agriculture. For complete classification of this Act to the Code, see Short Title note set out under section 136 of Title 7 and Tables.

The Alaska Native Claims Settlement Act, referred to in subsec. (k)(1)(H), is Pub. L. No. 92–203, 85 Stat. 688 (Dec. 18, 1971), as amended, which is codified principally as chapter 33 of Title 43 [43 U.S.C.A. § 1601 et seq.]. See Tables for complete classification.

Chapter 75 of Title 31, referred to in subsec. (k)(7)(B), is codified as 31 U.S.C.A. § 7501 et seq.

The Federal Water Pollution Control Act, referred to in subsec. (k)(11)(C), is Act of June 30, 1948, c. 758, as amended generally by Pub. L. No. 92–500, § 2, 86 Stat. 816 (Oct. 18, 1972), also known as the Clean Water Act, which is codified principally as chapter 26 of Title 33 [33 U.S.C.A. § 1251 et seq.]. See Tables for complete classification.

The Safe Drinking Water Act, referred to in subsec. (k)(11)(E), is Pub. L. No. 93–523, 88 Stat. 1660 (Dec. 16, 1974), as amended, which is codified principally as subchapter XII of chapter 6A of this title [42 U.S.C.A. § 300f et seq.]. Part C of the Safe Drinking Water Act is codified generally to part C of subchapter XII of chapter 6A of this title [42 U.S.C.A. § 300h et seq.]. See Tables for complete classification.

Codifications

In subsec. (g)(1), "sections 3141–3144, 3146, and 3147 of Title 40" substituted for "the Davis-Bacon Act [40 U.S.C. 276a et seq.]" on authority of Pub. L. No. 107–217, § 5(c), 116 Stat. 1301 (Aug. 21, 2002), which is set out as a note preceding 40 U.S.C.A. § 101. Pub. L. No. 107–217, § 1, enacted Title 40 into positive law. The Davis-Bacon Act is Act of Mar. 3, 1931, c. 411, 46 Stat. 1494, which was codified as former 40 U.S.C.A. §§ 276a, 276a–1 to 276a–6, prior to being repealed by Pub. L. No. 107–217, § 6(b), 116 Stat. 1308 (Aug. 21, 2002), and its substance reenacted as 40 U.S.C.A. §§ 3141–3144, 3146, and 3147.

In subsec. (g)(2), "section 3145 of Title 40" substituted for "section 276c of Title 40", on authority of Pub. L. No. 107–217, § 5(c), 116 Stat. 1301 (Aug. 21, 2002), which is set out as a note preceding 40 U.S.C.A. § 101. Pub. L. No. 107–217, § 1, enacted Title 40 into positive law. Former 40 U.S.C.A. § 276c was Act of June 13, 1934, c. 482, § 2, 48 Stat. 948, prior to being repealed by Pub. L. No. 107–217, § 6(b), 116 Stat. 1309 (Aug. 21, 2002), and its substance reenacted as 40 U.S.C.A. § 3145.

Effective and Applicability Provisions

1986 Acts. Amendment by Pub. L. No. 99–499 effective Oct. 17, 1986, see section 4 of Pub. L. No. 99–499, set out as a note under section 9601 of this title.

Termination of Reporting Requirements

For termination of reporting provisions of this section relating to review of remedial action taken to assure that human health and environment are being protected at the selected facilities, effective May 15, 2000, see Pub. L. No. 104–66, § 3003, as amended, set out as a note under 31 U.S.C.A. § 1113, and the 15th item on page 20 of House Document No. 103–7.

For termination, effective May 15, 2000, of provisions in subsec. (i)(10) of this section relating to the requirement that the Administrator of ATSDR submit a biennial report to Congress, see Pub. L. No. 104–66, § 3003, as amended, set out as a note under 31 U.S.C.A. § 1113, and page 154 of House Document No. 103–7.

Change of Name

"Government Accountability Office" substituted for "General Accounting Office" in subsec. (k)(7)(B) on authority of Pub. L. No. 108–271, § 8(b), cited in the credit to this section and set out as a note under 31 U.S.C.A. § 702, which provided that any reference to the General Accounting Office in any law, rule, regulation, certificate, directive, instruction, or other official paper in force on July 17, 2004, to refer and apply to the Government Accountability Office.

Delegation of Functions

Functions of the President under the first sentence of subsec. (b)(1) of this section, relating to "illness, disease, or complaints thereof", delegated to the Secretary of Health and Human Services (with authority to redelegate), who shall, in accord with subsec. (i) of this section, perform those functions through the Public Health Service, see sections 2(a) and 11(g) of Ex. Ord. No. 12580, 52 Fed. Reg. 2923 (Jan. 23, 1987), set out as a note under section 9615 of this title.

Functions vested in the President by subsec. (e)(7)(C) of this section, relating to the promulgation of regulations and guidelines, delegated to the Administrator of the Environmental Protection Agency, to be exercised in consultation with the National Response Team, see section 2(b) of Ex. Ord. No. 12580, 52 Fed. Reg. 2923 (Jan. 23, 1987), set out as a note under section 9615 of this title.

Functions vested in the President by subsec. (a) of this section, to the extent they require permanent relocation of residents, businesses, and community facilities or temporary evacuation and housing of threatened individuals not otherwise provided for, delegated to the Director of the Federal Emergency Management Agency, with authority to redelegate, see sections 2(c)(1), 11(g) of Ex. Ord. No. 12580, 52 Fed. Reg. 2923 (Jan. 23, 1987), set out as a note under section 9615 of this title. Functions vested in the President by sections 9617(a), (c) and section 9619 of this title, to the extent such authority is needed to carry out the delegation of functions by section 2(c)(1) of Ex. Ord. No. 12580 (and subject to delegation of certain rulemaking authority to the Administrator of the Environmental Protection Agency), delegated to the Director, with authority to redelegate, see sections 2(b), (c)(2), 11(g) of Ex. Ord. No. 12580.

Functions vested in the President by subsecs. (a), (b) and (c)(4) this section delegated, with authority to redelegate, (and subject to section 2(a), (b) and (c) of Ex. Ord. No. 12580) to the Secretaries of Defense and Energy, with respect to releases or threatened releases where either the release is on or the sole source of the release is from any facility or vessel under the jurisdiction, custody or control of their departments, respectively, including vessels bare-boat chartered and operated, with such functions to be exercised consistent with the requirements of section 9620 of this title, see sections 2(d), 11(g) of Ex. Ord. No. 12580, 52 Fed. Reg. 2923 (Jan. 23, 1987), set out as a note under section 9615 of this title.

Functions vested in the President by subsecs. (a), (b) and (c)(4) of this section, subject to section 2(a) to (d) of Ex. Ord. No. 12580, delegated, with authority to redelegate, to the heads of Executive departments and agencies, with respect to remedial actions for releases or threatened releases which are not on the National Priorities List and removal actions other than emergencies, where either the release is on or the sole source of the release is from any facility or vessel under the jurisdiction, custody or control of those departments and agencies, including vessels bare-boat chartered and operated with the Administrator of the Environmental Protection Agency to define the term "emergency", solely for the purposes of section 2(e) of Ex. Ord. No. 12580, either by regulation or by a memorandum of understanding with the head of an Executive department or agency, see sections 2(e)(1), 11(g) of Ex. Ord. No. 12580, 52 Fed. Reg. 2923 (Jan. 23, 1987), set out as a note under section 9615 of this title.

Functions vested in the President by subsec. (b)(2) of this section, subject to section 2(b) to (d) of Ex. Ord. No. 12580, delegated, with authority to redelegate, to the heads of Executive departments and agencies, with respect to releases or threatened releases where either the release is on or the sole source of the release is from any facility or vessel under the jurisdiction, custody or control of those departments and agencies, including vessels bare-boat chartered and operated, see sections 2(e)(2), 11(g) of Ex. Ord. No. 12580, 52 Fed. Reg. 2923 (Jan. 23, 1987), set out as a note under section 9615 of this title.

Functions vested in the President by subsecs. (a), (b) and (c)(4) of this section, subject to section 2(a) to (e) of Ex. Ord. No. 12580, delegated, with authority to redelegate, to the Secretary of the Department in which the Coast Guard is operating ("the Coast Guard"), with respect to any release or threatened release involving the coastal zone, Great Lakes waters, ports, and harbors, see sections 2(f), 11(g) of Ex. Ord. No. 12580, 52 Fed. Reg. 2923 (Jan. 23, 1987), set out as a note under section 9615 of this title.

Functions vested in the President by subsec. (a), (b), (c)(4) and (c)(9) of this section, subject to section 2(a) to (f) of Ex. Ord. No. 12580, delegated, with authority to redelegate, to the Administrator of the Environmental Protection Agency, see sections 2(g), 11(g) of Ex. Ord. No. 12580, 52 Fed. Reg. 2923 (Jan. 23, 1987), set out as a note under section 9615 of this title.

Functions vested in the President by subsec. (c)(3) of this section delegated to the Administrator of the Environmental Protection Agency, with authority to redelegate, with respect to providing assurances for Indian tribes, with such functions to be exercised in consultation with the Secretary of the Interior, see sections 2(h), 11(g) of Ex. Ord. No. 12580, 52 Fed. Reg. 2923 (Jan. 23, 1987), set out as a note under section 9615 of this title.

Functions vested in the President by subsecs. (c) and (d) of this section, subject to section 2(d) to (h) of Ex. Ord. No. 12580, delegated, with authority to redelegate, to the Coast Guard, the Secretary of Health and Human Services, the Director of the Federal Emergency Management Agency, and the Administrator of the Environmental Protection Agency in order to carry out the functions delegated to them by section 2 of Ex. Ord. No. 12580, see sections 2(i), 11(g) of Ex. Ord. No. 12580, 52 Fed. Reg. 2923 (Jan. 23, 1987), set out as a note under section 9615 of this title.

Functions vested in the President by subsec. (e)(5)(A) of this section delegated, with authority to redelegate, to the heads of Executive departments and agencies, with respect to releases or threatened releases where either the release is on or the sole source of the release is from any facility or vessel under the jurisdiction, custody or control of those departments and agencies, with such functions to be exercised with the concurrence of the Attorney General, see sections 2(j)(1), 11(g) of Ex. Ord. No. 12580, 52 Fed. Reg. 2923 (Jan. 23, 1987), set out as a note under section 9615 of this title.

Functions vested in the President by subsec. (e) of this section, delegated, (subject to delegations by section 2(b), (j)(1) of Ex. Ord. No. 12580, and with authority to redelegate) to the heads of Executive departments and agencies in order to carry out their functions under Ex. Ord. No. 12580 or this chapter, see sections 2(j)(2), 11(g) of Ex. Ord. No. 12580, 52 Fed. Reg. 2923 (Jan. 23, 1987), set out as a note under section 9615 of this title.

Functions vested in the President by subsecs. (f), (g), (h), (i)(11), and (j) of this section delegated, with authority to redelegate, to the heads of Executive departments and agencies in order to carry out the functions delegated to them by section 2 of Ex. Ord. No. 12580, with exercise of authority under subsec. (h) of this section subject to the approval of the Administrator of the Office of Federal Procurement Policy, see sections 2(k), 11(g) of Ex. Ord. No. 12580, 52 Fed. Reg. 2923 (Jan. 23, 1987), set out as a note under section 9615 of this title.

Authority under subsec. (e)(5)(A) of this section to seek information, entry, inspection, samples, or response actions from Executive departments and agencies to be exercised only with the concurrence of the Attorney General, notwithstanding any other provisions of Ex. Ord. No. 12580, see section 4(e) of Ex. Ord. No. 12580, 52 Fed. Reg. 2923 (Jan. 23, 1987), set out as a note under section 9615 of this title.

Coordination of Titles I to IV of Pub. L. No. 99–499

Any provision of Titles I to IV of Pub. L. No. 99–499, imposing any tax, premium, or fee; establishing any trust fund; or authorizing expenditures from any trust fund, to have no force or effect, see section 531 of Pub. L. No. 99–499, set out as a note under section 1 of Title 26, Internal Revenue Code.

§ 9605. National contingency plan

[CERCLA § 105]

(a) Revision and republication

Within one hundred and eighty days after December 11, 1980, the President shall, after notice and opportunity for public comments, revise and republish the national contingency plan for the removal of oil and hazardous substances, originally prepared and published pursuant to section 1321 of Title 33, to reflect and effectuate the responsibilities and powers created by this chapter, in addition to those matters specified in section 1321(c)(2) of Title 33. Such revision shall include a section of the plan to be known as the national hazardous substance response plan which shall establish procedures and standards for responding to releases of hazardous substances, pollutants, and contaminants, which shall include at a minimum:

(1) methods for discovering and investigating facilities at which hazardous substances have been disposed of or otherwise come to be located;

(2) methods for evaluating, including analyses of relative cost, and remedying any releases or threats of releases from facilities which pose substantial danger to the public health or the environment;

(3) methods and criteria for determining the appropriate extent of removal, remedy, and other measures authorized by this chapter;

(4) appropriate roles and responsibilities for the Federal, State, and local governments and for interstate and nongovernmental entities in effectuating the plan;

(5) provision for identification, procurement, maintenance, and storage of response equipment and supplies;

(6) a method for and assignment of responsibility for reporting the existence of such facilities which may be located on federally owned or controlled properties and any releases of hazardous substances from such facilities;

(7) means of assuring that remedial action measures are cost-effective over the period of potential exposure to the hazardous substances or contaminated materials;

(8) (A) criteria for determining priorities among releases or threatened releases throughout the United States for the purpose of taking remedial action and, to the extent practicable taking into account the potential urgency of such action, for the purpose of taking removal action. Criteria and priorities under this paragraph shall be based upon relative risk or danger to public health or welfare or the environment, in the judgment of the President, taking into account to the extent possible the population at risk, the hazard potential of the hazardous substances at such facilities, the potential for contamination of drinking water supplies, the potential for direct human contact, the potential for destruction of sensitive ecosystems, the damage to natural resources which may affect the human food chain and which is associated with any release or threatened release, the contamination or potential contamination of the ambient air which is associated with the release or threatened release, State preparedness to assume State costs and responsibilities, and other appropriate factors;

(B) based upon the criteria set forth in subparagraph (A) of this paragraph, the President shall list as part of the plan national priorities among the known releases or threatened releases throughout the United States and shall revise the list no less often than annually. Within one year after December 11, 1980, and annually thereafter, each State shall establish and submit for consideration by the President priorities for remedial action among known releases and potential releases in that State based upon the criteria set forth in subparagraph (A) of this paragraph. In assembling or revising the national list, the President shall consider any priorities established by the States. To the extent practicable, the highest priority facilities shall be designated individually and shall be referred to as the "top priority among known response targets", and, to the extent practicable, shall include among the one hundred highest priority facilities one such facility from each State which shall be the facility designated by the State as presenting the greatest danger to public health or welfare or the environment among the known facilities in such State. A State shall be allowed to designate its highest priority facility only once. Other priority facilities or incidents may be listed singly or grouped for response priority purposes;

(9) specified roles for private organizations and entities in preparation for response and in responding to releases of hazardous substances, including identification of appropriate qualifications and capacity therefor and including consideration of minority firms in accordance with subsection (f) of this section; and

(10) standards and testing procedures by which alternative or innovative treatment technologies can be determined to be appropriate for utilization in response actions authorized by this chapter.

The plan shall specify procedures, techniques, materials, equipment, and methods to be employed in identifying, removing, or remedying releases of hazardous substances comparable to those required under section 1321(c)(2)(F) and (G) and (j)(1) of Title 33. Following publication of the revised national contingency plan, the response to and actions to minimize damage from hazardous substances releases shall, to the greatest extent possible, be in accordance with the provisions of the plan. The President may, from time to time, revise and republish the national contingency plan.

(b) Revision of plan

Not later than 18 months after the enactment of the Superfund Amendments and Reauthorization Act of 1986 [October 17, 1986], the President shall revise the National Contingency Plan to reflect the requirements of such amendments. The portion of such Plan known as "the National Hazardous Substance Response Plan" shall be revised to provide procedures and standards for remedial actions undertaken pursuant to this chapter which are consistent with amendments made by the Superfund Amendments and Reauthorization Act of 1986 relating to the selection of remedial action.

(c) Hazard ranking system

(1) Revision

Not later than 18 months after October 17, 1986, and after publication of notice and opportunity for submission of comments in accordance with section 553 of Title 5, the President shall by rule promulgate amendments to the hazard ranking system in effect on September 1, 1984. Such amendments shall assure, to the maximum extent feasible, that the hazard ranking system accurately assesses the relative degree of risk to human health and the environment posed by sites and facilities subject to review. The President shall establish an effective date for the amended hazard ranking system which is not later than 24 months after October 17, 1986. Such amended hazard ranking system shall be applied to any site or facility to be newly listed on the National Priorities List after the effective date established by the President. Until such effective date of the regulations, the hazard ranking system in effect on September 1, 1984, shall continue in full force and effect.

(2) Health assessment of water contamination risks

In carrying out this subsection, the President shall ensure that the human health risks associated with the contamination or potential contamination (either directly or as a result of the runoff of any hazardous substance or pollutant or contaminant from sites or facilities) of surface water are appropriately assessed where such surface water is, or can be, used for recreation or potable water consumption. In making the assessment required pursuant to the preceding sentence, the President shall take into account the potential migration of any hazardous substance or pollutant or contaminant through such surface water to downstream sources of drinking water.

(3) Reevaluation not required

The President shall not be required to reevaluate, after October 17, 1986, the hazard ranking of any facility which was evaluated in accordance with the criteria under this section before the effective date of the amendments to the hazard ranking system under this subsection and which was assigned a national priority under the National Contingency Plan.

(4) New information

Nothing in paragraph (3) shall preclude the President from taking new information into account in undertaking response actions under this chapter.

(d) Petition for assessment of release

Any person who is, or may be, affected by a release or threatened release of a hazardous substance or pollutant or contaminant, may petition the President to conduct a preliminary assessment of the hazards to public health and the environment which are associated with such release or threatened release. If the President has not previously conducted a preliminary assessment of such release, the President shall, within 12 months after the receipt of any such petition, complete such assessment or provide an explanation of why the assessment is not appropriate. If the preliminary assessment indicates that the release or threatened release concerned may pose a threat to human health or the environment, the President shall promptly evaluate such release or threatened release in accordance with the hazard ranking system referred to in paragraph (8)(A) of subsection (a) of this section to determine the national priority of such release or threatened release.

(e) Releases from earlier sites

Whenever there has been, after January 1, 1985, a significant release of hazardous substances or pollutants or contaminants from a site which is listed by the President as a "Site Cleaned Up To Date" on the National Priorities List (revised edition, December 1984) the site shall be restored to the National Priorities List, without application of the hazard ranking system.

(f) Minority contractors

In awarding contracts under this chapter, the President shall consider the availability of qualified minority firms. The President shall describe, as part of any annual report submitted to the Congress under this chapter, the participation of minority firms in contracts carried out under this chapter. Such report shall contain a brief description of the contracts which have been awarded to minority firms under this chapter and of the efforts made by the President to encourage the participation of such firms in programs carried out under this chapter.

(g) Special study wastes

(1) Application

This subsection applies to facilities—

(A) which as of October 17, 1986, were not included on, or proposed for inclusion on, the National Priorities List; and

(B) at which special study wastes described in paragraph (2), (3)(A)(ii) or (3)(A)(iii) of section 6921(b) of this title are present in significant quantities, including any such facility from which there has been a release of a special study waste.

(2) Considerations in adding facilities to NPL

Pending revision of the hazard ranking system under subsection (c) of this section, the President shall consider each of the following factors in adding facilities covered by this section to the National Priorities List:

(A) The extent to which hazard ranking system score for the facility is affected by the presence of any special study waste at, or any release from, such facility.

(B) Available information as to the quantity, toxicity, and concentration of hazardous substances that are constituents of any special study waste at, or released from such facility, the extent of or potential for release of such hazardous constituents, the exposure or potential exposure to human population and the environment, and the degree of hazard to human health or the environment posed by the release of such hazardous constituents at such facility. This subparagraph refers only to available information on actual concentrations of hazardous substances and not on the total quantity of special study waste at such facility.

(3) Savings provisions

Nothing in this subsection shall be construed to limit the authority of the President to remove any facility which as of October 17, 1986, is included on the National Priorities List from such List, or not to list any facility which as of such date is proposed for inclusion on such list.

(4) Information gathering and analysis

Nothing in this chapter shall be construed to preclude the expenditure of monies from the Fund for gathering and analysis of information which will enable the President to consider the specific factors required by paragraph (2).

(h) NPL deferral

(1) Deferral to State voluntary cleanups

At the request of a State and subject to paragraphs (2) and (3), the President generally shall defer final listing of an eligible response site on the National Priorities List if the President determines that—

(A) the State, or another party under an agreement with or order from the State, is conducting a response action at the eligible response site—

(i) in compliance with a State program that specifically governs response actions for the protection of public health and the environment; and

(ii) that will provide long-term protection of human health and the environment; or

(B) the State is actively pursuing an agreement to perform a response action described in subparagraph (A) at the site with a person that the State has reason to believe is capable of conducting a response action that meets the requirements of subparagraph (A).

(2) Progress toward cleanup

If, after the last day of the 1-year period beginning on the date on which the President proposes to list an eligible response site on the National Priorities List, the President determines that the State or other party is not making reasonable progress toward completing a response action at the eligible response site, the President may list the eligible response site on the National Priorities List.

(3) Cleanup agreements

With respect to an eligible response site under paragraph (1)(B), if, after the last day of the 1-year period beginning on the date on which the President proposes to list the eligible response site on the National Priorities List, an agreement described in paragraph (1)(B) has not been reached, the President may defer the listing of the eligible response site on the National Priorities List for an additional period of not to exceed 180 days if the President determines deferring the listing would be appropriate based on—

(A) the complexity of the site;

(B) substantial progress made in negotiations; and

(C) other appropriate factors, as determined by the President.

(4) Exceptions

The President may decline to defer, or elect to discontinue a deferral of, a listing of an eligible response site on the National Priorities List if the President determines that—

(A) deferral would not be appropriate because the State, as an owner or operator or a significant contributor of hazardous substances to the facility, is a potentially responsible party;

(B) the criteria under the National Contingency Plan for issuance of a health advisory have been met; or

(C) the conditions in paragraphs (1) through (3), as applicable, are no longer being met.

(Pub. L. No. 96–510, Title I, § 105, 94 Stat. 2779 (Dec. 11, 1980); Pub. L. No. 99–499, Title I, § 105, 100 Stat. 1625 (Oct. 17, 1986); Pub. L. No. 107–118, Title II, § 232, 115 Stat. 2379 (Jan. 11, 2002).)

HISTORICAL AND STATUTORY NOTES

References in Text

Section 1321(c)(2) of Title 33, referred to in subsec. (a), was amended generally by Pub. L. No. 101–380. Title IV, § 4201(a), 104 Stat. 523 (Aug. 18, 1990). Prior to general amendment, subsec. (c)(2) related to preparation of a National Contingency Plan. Provisions relating to a National Contingency Plan are contained in section 1321(d) of Title 33, Navigation and Navigable Waters.

Such amendments and the amendments made by the Superfund Amendments and Reauthorization Act of 1986, referred to in subsec. (b), are the amendments made by Pub. L. No. 99–499, 100 Stat. 1613 (Oct. 17, 1986). For complete classification of this Act to the Code, see Short Title of 1986 Amendments note set out under section 9601 of this title and Tables.

Effective and Applicability Provisions

1986 Acts. Amendment by Pub. L. No. 99–499 effective Oct. 17, 1986, see section 4 of Pub. L. No. 99–499, set out as a note under section 9601 of this title.

Delegation of Functions

Responsibility for the revision of the National Contingency Plan, and all other functions vested in the President by subsecs. (a), (b), (c) and (g) of this section, delegated to the Administrator of the Environmental Protection Agency, see section 1(b)(1) of Ex. Ord. No. 12580, 52 Fed. Reg. 2923 (Jan. 23, 1987), set out as a note under section 9615 of this title.

Functions vested in the President by subsec. (d) of this section delegated, with authority to redelegate, to the Administrator of the Environmental Protection Agency, except that functions vested in the President by the first two sentences thereof (relating to petitions for preliminary assessments of releases or threatened releases of hazardous substances or pollutants or contaminants) delegated, with authority to redelegate, to the heads of Executive departments and agencies with respect to facilities under the jurisdiction, custody or control of those departments and agencies, see sections 3, 11(g) of Ex. Ord. No. 12580, 52 Fed. Reg. 2923 (Jan. 23, 1987), set out as a note under section 9615 of this title.

Functions vested in the President by subsec. (f) of this section, relating to reporting on minority participation in contracts, delegated to the Administrator of the Environmental Protection Agency, see section 11(b)(1) of Ex. Ord. No. 12580, 52 Fed. Reg. 2923 (Jan. 23, 1987), set out as a note under section 9615 of this title.

Functions vested in the President by subsec. (f) of this section delegated, subject to section 11(b)(1) of Ex. Ord. No. 12580, to the heads of Executive departments and agencies in order to carry out the functions delegated to them by Ex. Ord. No. 12580, with each Executive department and agency to provide to the Administrator of the Environmental Protection Agency any requested information on minority contracting for inclusion in the annual report under subsec. (f), see section 11(b)(2) of Ex. Ord. No. 12580, 52 Fed. Reg. 2923 (Jan. 23, 1987), set out as a note under section 9615 of this title.

§ 9606. Abatement actions

[CERCLA § 106]

(a) Maintenance, jurisdiction, etc.

In addition to any other action taken by a State or local government, when the President determines that there may be an imminent and substantial endangerment to the public health or welfare or the environment because of an actual or threatened release of a hazardous substance from a facility, he may require the Attorney General of the United States to secure such relief as may be necessary to abate such danger or threat, and the district court of the United States in the district in which the threat occurs shall have jurisdiction to grant such relief as the public interest and the equities of the case may require. The President may also, after notice to the affected State, take other action under this section including, but not limited to, issuing such orders as may be necessary to protect public health and welfare and the environment.

(b) Fines; reimbursement

(1) Any person who, without sufficient cause, willfully violates, or fails or refuses to comply with, any order of the President under subsection (a) of this section may, in an action brought in the appropriate United States district court to enforce such order, be fined not more than $25,000 for each day in which such violation occurs or such failure to comply continues.

(2) (A) Any person who receives and complies with the terms of any order issued under subsection (a) of this section may, within 60 days after completion of the required action, petition the President for reimbursement from the Fund for the reasonable costs of such action, plus interest. Any interest payable under this paragraph shall accrue on the amounts expended from the date of expenditure at the same rate as specified for interest on investments of the Hazardous Substance Superfund established under subchapter A of chapter 98 of Title 26.

(B) If the President refuses to grant all or part of a petition made under this paragraph, the petitioner may within 30 days of receipt of such refusal file an action against the President in the appropriate United States district court seeking reimbursement from the Fund.

(C) Except as provided in subparagraph (D), to obtain reimbursement, the petitioner shall establish by a preponderance of the evidence that it is not liable for response costs under section 9607(a) of this title and that costs for which it seeks reimbursement are reasonable in light of the action required by the relevant order.

(D) A petitioner who is liable for response costs under section 9607(a) of this title may also recover its reasonable costs of response to the extent that it can demonstrate, on the administrative record, that the President's decision in selecting the response action ordered was arbitrary and capricious or was otherwise not in accordance with law. Reimbursement awarded under this subparagraph shall include all reasonable response costs incurred by the petitioner pursuant to the portions of the order found to be arbitrary and capricious or otherwise not in accordance with law.

(E) Reimbursement awarded by a court under subparagraph (C) or (D) may include appropriate costs, fees, and other expenses in accordance with subsections (a) and (d) of section 2412 of Title 28.

(c) Guidelines for using imminent hazard, enforcement, and emergency response authorities; promulgation by Administrator of EPA, scope, etc.

Within one hundred and eighty days after December 11, 1980, the Administrator of the Environmental Protection Agency shall, after consultation with the Attorney General, establish and publish guidelines for using the imminent hazard, enforcement, and emergency response authorities of this section and other existing statutes administered by the Administrator of the Environmental Protection Agency to effectuate the responsibilities and powers created by this chapter. Such guidelines shall to the extent practicable be consistent with the national hazardous substance response plan, and shall include, at a minimum, the assignment of responsibility for coordinating response actions with the issuance of administrative orders, enforcement of standards and permits, the gathering of information, and other imminent hazard and emergency powers authorized by (1) sections 1321(c)(2), 1318, 1319, and 1364(a) of Title 33, (2) sections 6927, 6928, 6934, and 6973 of this title, (3) sections 300j–4 and 300i of this title, (4) sections 7413, 7414, and 7603 of this title, and (5) section 2606 of Title 15.

(Pub. L. No. 96–510, Title I, § 106, 94 Stat. 2780 (Dec. 11, 1980); as amended by Pub. L. No. 99–499, Title I, §§ 106, 109(b), 100 Stat. 1628, 1633 (Oct. 17, 1986); Pub. L. No. 99–514, § 2, 100 Stat. 2095 (Oct. 22, 1986).)

HISTORICAL AND STATUTORY NOTES

References in Text

Section 1321(c)(2) of Title 33, referred to in subsec. (c), was amended generally by Pub. L. No. 101–380, Title IV, § 4201(a), 104 Stat. 523 (Aug. 18, 1990). Prior to general amendment, subsec. (c)(2) related to preparation of a National Contingency Plan. Provisions relating to a National Contingency Plan are contained in section 1321(d) of Title 33, Navigation and Navigable Waters.

Effective and Applicability Provisions

1986 Acts. Amendment by Pub. L. No. 99–499 effective Oct. 17, 1986, see section 4 of Pub. L. No. 99–499, set out as a note under section 9601 of this title.

Termination of Reporting Requirements

For termination of reporting provisions of this section pertaining to review of remedial action taken to assure that human health and environment are being protected at the selected facilities, effective May 15, 2000, see Pub. L. No. 104–66, § 3003, as amended, set out as a note under 31 U.S.C.A. § 1113, and the 15th item on page 20 of House Document No. 103–7.

Delegation of Functions

Functions vested in the President by subsec. (a) of this section delegated, subject to section 4(a), (b)(1) of Ex. Ord. No. 12580, and with authority to redelegate, to the Coast Guard with respect to any release or threatened release involving the coastal zone, Great Lakes waters, ports, and harbors, see sections 4(c)(1), 11(g) of Ex. Ord. No. 12580, 52 Fed. Reg. 2923 (Jan. 23, 1987), set out as a note under section 9615 of this title.

Functions vested in the President by this section delegated, subject to section 4(a), (b)(1) and (c)(1) of Ex. Ord. No. 12580, and with authority to redelegate, to the Administrator of the Environmental Protection Agency, see sections 4(d)(1), 11(g) of Ex. Ord. No. 12580, 52 Fed. Reg. 2923 (Jan. 23, 1987), set out as a note under section 9615 of this title.

Authority under subsec. (a) of this section to seek information, entry, inspection, samples, or response actions from Executive departments and agencies to be exercised only with the concurrence of the Attorney General, notwithstanding any other provisions of Ex. Ord. No. 12580, see section 4(e) of Ex. Ord. No. 12580, 52 Fed. Reg. 2923 (Jan. 23, 1987), set out as a note under section 9615 of this title.

Functions vested in the President by subsec. (a) of this section delegated, subject to section 4(a), (b)(1), of Ex. Ord. No. 12580, to the Secretary of the Interior, the Secretary of Commerce, the Secretary of Agriculture, the Secretary of Defense, and the Secretary of Energy, to be exercised only with the concurrence of the Coast Guard, with respect to any release or threatened release in the coastal zone, Great Lakes waters, ports, and harbors, affecting (1) natural resources under their trusteeship, or (2) a vessel or facility subject to their custody, jurisdiction, or control, and with other exceptions and stipulations, see section 4(c)(3) of Ex. Ord. No. 12580, 52 Fed. Reg. 2923 (Jan. 23, 1987), as amended, set out as a note under section 9615 of this title.

Functions vested in the President by subsec. (a) of this section delegated, subject to section 4(a), (b) and (c)(1) of Ex. Ord. No. 12580, to the Secretary of the Interior, the Secretary of Commerce, the Secretary of Agriculture, the Secretary of Defense, and the Department of Energy, to be exercised only with the concurrence of the Administrator, with respect to any release or threatened release affecting (1) natural resources under their trusteeship, or (2) a vessel or facility subject to their custody, jurisdiction, or control, and with other exceptions and stipulations, see section 4(d)(3) of Ex. Ord. No. 12580, 52 Fed. Reg. 2923 (Jan. 23, 1987), as amended, set out as a note under section 9615 of this title.

Coordination of Titles I to IV of Pub. L. No. 99–499

Any provision of Titles I to IV of Pub. L. No. 99–499, imposing any tax, premium, or fee; establishing any trust fund; or authorizing expenditures from any trust fund, to have no force or effect, see section 531 of Pub. L. No. 99–499, set out as a note under section 1 of Title 26, Internal Revenue Code.

§ 9607. Liability

[CERCLA § 107]

(a) Covered persons; scope; recoverable costs and damages; interest rate; "comparable maturity" date

Notwithstanding any other provision or rule of law, and subject only to the defenses set forth in subsection (b) of this section—

(1) the owner and operator of a vessel or a facility,

(2) any person who at the time of disposal of any hazardous substance owned or operated any facility at which such hazardous substances were disposed of,

(3) any person who by contract, agreement, or otherwise arranged for disposal or treatment, or arranged with a transporter for transport for disposal or treatment, of hazardous substances owned or possessed by such person, by any other party or entity, at any facility or incineration vessel owned or operated by another party or entity and containing such hazardous substances, and

(4) any person who accepts or accepted any hazardous substances for transport to disposal or treatment facilities, incineration vessels or sites selected by such person, from which there is a release, or a threatened release which causes the incurrence of response costs, of a hazardous substance, shall be liable for—

(A) all costs of removal or remedial action incurred by the United States Government or a State or an Indian tribe not inconsistent with the national contingency plan;

(B) any other necessary costs of response incurred by any other person consistent with the national contingency plan;

(C) damages for injury to, destruction of, or loss of natural resources, including the reasonable costs of assessing such injury, destruction, or loss resulting from such a release; and

(D) the costs of any health assessment or health effects study carried out under section 9604(i) of this title.

The amounts recoverable in an action under this section shall include interest on the amounts recoverable under subparagraphs (A) through (D). Such interest shall accrue from the later of (i) the date payment of a specified amount is demanded in writing, or (ii) the date of the expenditure concerned. The rate of interest on the outstanding unpaid balance of the amounts recoverable under this section shall be the same rate as is specified for interest on investments of the Hazardous Substance Superfund established under subchapter A of chapter 98 of Title 26. For purposes of applying such amendments to interest under this subsection, the term "comparable maturity" shall be determined with reference to the date on which interest accruing under this subsection commences.

(b) Defenses

There shall be no liability under subsection (a) of this section for a person otherwise liable who can establish by a preponderance of the evidence that the release or threat of release of a hazardous substance and the damages resulting therefrom were caused solely by—

(1) an act of God;

(2) an act of war;

(3) an act or omission of a third party other than an employee or agent of the defendant, or than one whose act or omission occurs in connection with a contractual relationship, existing directly or indirectly, with the defendant (except where the sole contractual arrangement arises from a published tariff and acceptance for carriage by a common carrier by rail), if the defendant establishes by a preponderance of the evidence that (a) he exercised due care with respect to the hazardous substance concerned, taking into consideration the characteristics of such hazardous substance, in light of all relevant facts and circumstances, and (b) he took precautions against foreseeable acts or omissions of any such third party and the consequences that could foreseeably result from such acts or omissions; or

(4) any combination of the foregoing paragraphs.

(c) Determination of amounts

(1) Except as provided in paragraph (2) of this subsection, the liability under this section of an owner or operator or other responsible person for each release of a hazardous substance or incident involving release of a hazardous substance shall not exceed—

(A) for any vessel, other than an incineration vessel, which carries any hazardous substance as cargo or residue, $300 per gross ton, or $5,000,000, whichever is greater;

(B) for any other vessel, other than an incineration vessel, $300 per gross ton, or $500,000, whichever is greater;

(C) for any motor vehicle, aircraft, hazardous liquid pipeline facility (as defined in section 60101(a) of Title 49), or rolling stock, $50,000,000 or such lesser amount as the President shall establish by regulation, but in no event less than $5,000,000 (or, for releases of hazardous substances as defined in section 9601(14)(A) of this title into the navigable waters, $8,000,000). Such regulations shall take into account the size, type, location, storage, and handling capacity and other matters relating to the likelihood of release in each such class and to the economic impact of such limits on each such class; or

(D) for any incineration vessel or any facility other than those specified in subparagraph (C) of this paragraph, the total of all costs of response plus $50,000,000 for any damages under this subchapter.

(2) Notwithstanding the limitations in paragraph (1) of this subsection, the liability of an owner or operator or other responsible person under this section shall be the full and total costs of response and damages, if (A)(i) the release or threat of release of a hazardous substance was the result of willful misconduct or willful negligence within the privity or knowledge of such person, or (ii) the primary cause of the release was a violation (within the privity or knowledge of such person) of applicable safety, construction, or operating standards or regulations; or (B) such person fails or refuses to provide all reasonable cooperation and assistance requested by a responsible public official in connection with response activities under the national contingency plan with respect to regulated carriers subject to the provisions of Title 49 or vessels subject to the provisions of Title 33 or 46, subparagraph (A)(ii) of this paragraph shall be deemed to refer to Federal standards or regulations.

(3) If any person who is liable for a release or threat of release of a hazardous substance fails without sufficient cause to properly provide removal or remedial action upon order of the President pursuant to section 9604 or 9606 of this title, such person may be liable to the United States for punitive damages in an amount at least equal to, and not more than three times, the amount of any costs incurred by the Fund as a result of such failure to take proper action. The President is authorized to commence a civil action against any such person to recover the punitive damages, which shall be in addition to any costs recovered from such person pursuant to section 9612(c) of this title. Any moneys received by the United States pursuant to this subsection shall be deposited in the Fund.

(d) Rendering care or advice

(1) In general

Except as provided in paragraph (2), no person shall be liable under this subchapter for costs or damages as a result of actions taken or omitted in the course of rendering care, assistance, or advice in accordance with the National Contingency Plan ("NCP") or at the direction of an onscene coordinator appointed under such plan, with respect to an incident creating a danger to public health or welfare or the environment as a result of any releases of a hazardous substance or the threat thereof. This paragraph shall not preclude liability for costs or damages as the result of negligence on the part of such person.

(2) State and local governments

No State or local government shall be liable under this subchapter for costs or damages as a result of actions taken in response to an emergency created by the release or threatened release of a hazardous substance generated by or from a facility owned by another person. This paragraph shall not preclude liability for costs or damages as a result of gross negligence or intentional misconduct by the State or local government. For the purpose of the preceding sentence, reckless, willful, or wanton misconduct shall constitute gross negligence.

(3) Savings provision

This subsection shall not alter the liability of any person covered by the provisions of paragraph (1), (2), (3), or (4) of subsection (a) of this section with respect to the release or threatened release concerned.

(e) Indemnification, hold harmless, etc., agreements or conveyances; subrogation rights

(1) No indemnification, hold harmless, or similar agreement or conveyance shall be effective to transfer from the owner or operator of any vessel or facility or from any person who may be liable for a release or threat of release under this section, to any other person the liability imposed under this section. Nothing in this subsection shall bar any agreement to insure, hold harmless, or indemnify a party to such agreement for any liability under this section.

(2) Nothing in this subchapter, including the provisions of paragraph (1) of this subsection, shall bar a cause of action that an owner or operator or any other person subject to liability under this section, or a guarantor, has or would have, by reason of subrogation or otherwise against any person.

(f) Natural resources liability; designation of public trustees of natural resources

(1) Natural resources liability

In the case of an injury to, destruction of, or loss of natural resources under subparagraph (C) of subsection (a) of this section liability shall be to the United States Government and to any State for natural resources within the State or belonging to, managed by, controlled by, or appertaining to such State and to any Indian tribe for natural resources belonging to, managed by, controlled by, or appertaining to such tribe, or held in trust for the benefit of such tribe, or belonging to a member of such tribe if such resources are subject to a trust restriction on alienation: *Provided, however,* That no liability to the United States or State or Indian tribe shall be imposed under subparagraph (C) of subsection (a) of this section, where the party sought to be charged has demonstrated that the damages to natural resources complained of were specifically identified as an irreversible and irretrievable commitment of natural resources in an environmental impact statement, or other comparable environment analysis, and the decision to grant a permit or license authorizes such commitment of natural resources, and the facility or project was otherwise operating within the terms of its permit or license, so long as, in the case of damages to an Indian tribe occurring pursuant to a Federal permit or license, the issuance of that permit or license was not inconsistent with the fiduciary duty of the United States with respect to such Indian tribe. The President, or the authorized representative of any State, shall act on behalf of the public as trustee of such natural resources to recover for such damages. Sums recovered by the United States Government as trustee under this subsection shall be retained by the trustee, without further appropriation, for use only to restore, replace, or acquire the equivalent of such natural resources. Sums recovered by a State as trustee under this subsection shall be available for use only to restore, replace, or acquire the equivalent of such natural resources by the State. The measure of damages in any action under subparagraph (C) of subsection (a) of this section shall not be limited by the sums which can be used to restore or replace such resources. There shall be no double recovery under this chapter for natural resource damages, including the costs of damage assessment or restoration, rehabilitation, or acquisition for the same release and natural resource. There shall be no recovery under the authority of subparagraph (C) of subsection (a) of this section where such damages and the release of a hazardous substance from which such damages resulted have occurred wholly before December 11, 1980.

(2) **Designation of Federal and State officials**

(A) **Federal**

The President shall designate in the National Contingency Plan published under section 9605 of this title the Federal officials who shall act on behalf of the public as trustees for natural resources under this chapter and section 1321 of Title 33. Such officials shall assess damages for injury to, destruction of, or loss of natural resources for purposes of this chapter and such section 1321 of Title 33 for those resources under their trusteeship and may, upon request of and reimbursement from a State and at the Federal officials' discretion, assess damages for those natural resources under the State's trusteeship.

(B) **State**

The Governor of each State shall designate State officials who may act on behalf of the public as trustees for natural resources under this chapter and section 1321 of Title 33 and shall notify the President of such designations. Such State officials shall assess damages to natural resources for the purposes of this chapter and such section 1321 of Title 33 for those natural resources under their trusteeship.

(C) **Rebuttable presumption**

Any determination or assessment of damages to natural resources for the purposes of this chapter and section 1321 of Title 33 made by a Federal or State trustee in accordance with the regulations promulgated under section 9651(c) of this title shall have the force and effect of a rebuttable presumption on behalf of the trustee in any administrative or judicial proceeding under this chapter or section 1321 of Title 33.

(g) **Federal agencies**

For provisions relating to Federal agencies, see section 9620 of this title.

(h) **Owner or operator of vessel**

The owner or operator of a vessel shall be liable in accordance with this section, under maritime tort law, and as provided under section 9614 of this title notwithstanding any provision of the Act of March 3, 1851 (46 U.S.C. 183ff) or the absence of any physical damage to the proprietary interest of the claimant.

(i) **Application of a registered pesticide product**

No person (including the United States or any State or Indian tribe) may recover under the authority of this section for any response costs or damages resulting from the application of a pesticide product registered under the Federal Insecticide, Fungicide, and Rodenticide Act [7 U.S.C.A. § 136 et seq.]. Nothing in this paragraph shall affect or modify in any way the obligations or liability of any person under any other provision of State or Federal law, including common law, for damages, injury, or loss resulting from a release of any hazardous substance or for removal or remedial action or the costs of removal or remedial action of such hazardous substance.

(j) **Obligations or liability pursuant to federally permitted release**

Recovery by any person (including the United States or any State or Indian tribe) for response costs or damages resulting from a federally permitted release shall be pursuant to existing law in lieu of this section. Nothing in this paragraph shall affect or modify in any way the obligations or liability of any person under any other provision of State or Federal law, including common law, for damages, injury, or loss resulting from a release of any hazardous substance or for removal or remedial action or the costs of removal or remedial action of such hazardous substance. In addition, costs of response incurred by the Federal Government in connection with a discharge specified in section 9601(10)(B) or (C) of this title shall be recoverable in an action brought under section 1319(b) of Title 33.

(k) Transfer to, and assumption by, Post-Closure Liability Fund of liability of owner or operator of hazardous waste disposal facility in receipt of permit under applicable solid waste disposal law; time, criteria applicable, procedures, etc.; monitoring costs; reports

(1) The liability established by this section or any other law for the owner or operator of a hazardous waste disposal facility which has received a permit under subtitle C of the Solid Waste Disposal Act [42 U.S.C.A. § 6921 et seq.], shall be transferred to and assumed by the Post-closure Liability Fund established by section 9641 of this title when—

(A) such facility and the owner and operator thereof has complied with the requirements of subtitle C of the Solid Waste Disposal Act [42 U.S.C.A. § 6921 et seq.] and regulations issued thereunder, which may affect the performance of such facility after closure; and

(B) such facility has been closed in accordance with such regulations and the conditions of such permit, and such facility and the surrounding area have been monitored as required by such regulations and permit conditions for a period not to exceed five years after closure to demonstrate that there is no substantial likelihood that any migration offsite or release from confinement of any hazardous substance or other risk to public health or welfare will occur.

(2) Such transfer of liability shall be effective ninety days after the owner or operator of such facility notifies the Administrator of the Environmental Protection Agency (and the State where it has an authorized program under section 3006(b) of the Solid Waste Disposal Act [42 U.S.C.A. § 6926(b)]) that the conditions imposed by this subsection have been satisfied. If within such ninety-day period the Administrator of the Environmental Protection Agency or such State determines that any such facility has not complied with all the conditions imposed by this subsection or that insufficient information has been provided to demonstrate such compliance, the Administrator or such State shall so notify the owner and operator of such facility and the administrator of the Fund established by section 9641 of this title, and the owner and operator of such facility shall continue to be liable with respect to such facility under this section and other law until such time as the Administrator and such State determines that such facility has complied with all conditions imposed by this subsection. A determination by the Administrator or such State that a facility has not complied with all conditions imposed by this subsection or that insufficient information has been supplied to demonstrate compliance, shall be a final administrative action for purposes of judicial review. A request for additional information shall state in specific terms the data required.

(3) In addition to the assumption of liability of owners and operators under paragraph (1) of this subsection, the Post-closure Liability Fund established by section 9641 of this title may be used to pay costs of monitoring and care and maintenance of a site incurred by other persons after the period of monitoring required by regulations under subtitle C of the Solid Waste Disposal Act [42 U.S.C.A. § 6921 et seq.] for hazardous waste disposal facilities meeting the conditions of paragraph (1) of this subsection.

(4) (A) Not later than one year after December 11, 1980, the Secretary of the Treasury shall conduct a study and shall submit a report thereon to the Congress on the feasibility of establishing or qualifying an optional system of private insurance for postclosure financial responsibility for hazardous waste disposal facilities to which this subsection applies. Such study shall include a specification of adequate and realistic minimum standards to assure that any such privately placed insurance will carry out the purposes of this subsection in a reliable, enforceable, and practical manner. Such a study shall include an examination of the public and private incentives, programs, and actions necessary to make privately placed insurance a practical and effective option to the financing system for the Post-closure Liability Fund provided in subchapter II of this chapter.

(B) Not later than eighteen months after December 11, 1980, and after a public hearing, the President shall by rule determine whether or not it is feasible to establish or qualify an optional system of private insurance for postclosure financial responsibility for hazardous waste disposal facilities to which this subsection applies. If the President determines the establishment or qualification of such a system would be infeasible, he shall promptly publish an explanation of the reasons for such a determination. If the President determines the establishment or qualification of such a system would be feasible, he shall promptly publish notice of such determination. Not later than six months after an affirmative determination under the preceding sentence and after a public hearing, the President shall by rule promulgate adequate and realistic minimum standards which must be met by any such privately placed insurance, taking into account the purposes of this chapter and this subsection. Such rules shall also specify reasonably expeditious procedures by which privately placed insurance plans can qualify as meeting such minimum standards.

(C) In the event any privately placed insurance plan qualifies under subparagraph (B), any person enrolled in, and complying with the terms of, such plan shall be excluded from the provisions of paragraphs (1), (2), and (3) of this subsection and exempt from the requirements to pay any tax or fee to the Post-closure Liability Fund under subchapter II of this chapter.

(D) The President may issue such rules and take such other actions as are necessary to effectuate the purposes of this paragraph.

(5) Suspension of liability transfer

Notwithstanding paragraphs (1), (2), (3), and (4) of this subsection and subsection (j) of section 9611 of this title, no liability shall be transferred to or assumed by the Post-Closure Liability Trust Fund established by section 9641 of this title prior to completion of the study required under paragraph (6) of this subsection, transmission of a report of such study to both Houses of Congress, and authorization of such a transfer or assumption by Act of Congress following receipt of such study and report.

(6) Study of options for post-closure program

(A) Study

The Comptroller General shall conduct a study of options for a program for the management of the liabilities associated with hazardous waste treatment, storage, and disposal sites after their closure which complements the policies set forth in the Hazardous and Solid Waste Amendments of 1984 and assures the protection of human health and the environment.

(B) Program elements

The program referred to in subparagraph (A) shall be designed to assure each of the following:

(i) Incentives are created and maintained for the safe management and disposal of hazardous wastes so as to assure protection of human health and the environment.

(ii) Members of the public will have reasonable confidence that hazardous wastes will be managed and disposed of safely and that resources will be available to address any problems that may arise and to cover costs of long-term monitoring, care, and maintenance of such sites.

(iii) Persons who are or seek to become owners and operators of hazardous waste disposal facilities will be able to manage their potential future liabilities and to attract the investment capital necessary to build, operate, and close such facilities in a manner which assures protection of human health and the environment.

(C) Assessments

The study under this paragraph shall include assessments of treatment, storage, and disposal facilities which have been or are likely to be issued a permit under section 3005 of the Solid Waste Disposal Act [42 U.S.C.A. § 6925] and the likelihood of future insolvency on the part of owners and operators of such facilities. Separate assessments shall be made for different classes of facilities and for different classes of land disposal facilities and shall include but not be limited to—

(i) the current and future financial capabilities of facility owners and operators;

(ii) the current and future costs associated with facilities, including the costs of routine monitoring and maintenance, compliance monitoring, corrective action, natural resource damages, and liability for damages to third parties; and

(iii) the availability of mechanisms by which owners and operators of such facilities can assure that current and future costs, including post-closure costs, will be financed.

(D) Procedures

In carrying out the responsibilities of this paragraph, the Comptroller General shall consult with the Administrator, the Secretary of Commerce, the Secretary of the Treasury, and the heads of other appropriate Federal agencies.

(E) Consideration of options

In conducting the study under this paragraph, the Comptroller General shall consider various mechanisms and combinations of mechanisms to complement the policies set forth in the Hazardous and Solid Waste Amendments of 1984 to serve the purposes set forth in subparagraph (B) and to assure that the current and future costs associated with hazardous waste facilities, including post-closure costs, will be adequately financed and, to the greatest extent possible, borne by the owners and operators of such facilities. Mechanisms to be considered include, but are not limited to—

(i) revisions to closure, post-closure, and financial responsibility requirements under subtitles C and I of the Solid Waste Disposal Act [42 U.S.C.A. §§ 6921 et seq. and 6991 et seq.];

(ii) voluntary risk pooling by owners and operators;

(iii) legislation to require risk pooling by owners and operators;

(iv) modification of the Post-Closure Liability Trust Fund previously established by section 9641 of this title, and the conditions for transfer of liability under this subsection, including limiting the transfer of some or all liability under this subsection only in the case of insolvency of owners and operators;

(v) private insurance;

(vi) insurance provided by the Federal Government;

(vii) coinsurance, reinsurance, or pooled-risk insurance, whether provided by the private sector or provided or assisted by the Federal Government; and

(viii) creation of a new program to be administered by a new or existing Federal agency or by a federally chartered corporation.

(F) Recommendations

The Comptroller General shall consider options for funding any program under this section and shall, to the extent necessary, make recommendations to the appropriate committees of Congress for additional authority to implement such program.

(*l*) Federal lien

(1) In general

All costs and damages for which a person is liable to the United States under subsection (a) of this section (other than the owner or operator of a vessel under paragraph (1) of subsection (a) of this section) shall constitute a lien in favor of the United States upon all real property and rights to such property which—

(A) belong to such person; and

(B) are subject to or affected by a removal or remedial action.

(2) Duration

The lien imposed by this subsection shall arise at the later of the following:

(A) The time costs are first incurred by the United States with respect to a response action under this chapter.

(B) The time that the person referred to in paragraph (1) is provided (by certified or registered mail) written notice of potential liability.

Such lien shall continue until the liability for the costs (or a judgment against the person arising out of such liability) is satisfied or becomes unenforceable through operation of the statute of limitations provided in section 9613 of this title.

(3) Notice and validity

The lien imposed by this subsection shall be subject to the rights of any purchaser, holder of a security interest, or judgment lien creditor whose interest is perfected under applicable State law before notice of the lien has been filed in the appropriate office within the State (or county or other governmental subdivision), as designated by State law, in which the real property subject to the lien is located. Any such purchaser, holder of a security interest, or judgment lien creditor shall be afforded the same protections against the lien imposed by this subsection as are afforded under State law against a judgment lien which arises out of an unsecured obligation and which arises as of the time of the filing of the notice of the lien imposed by this subsection. If the State has not by law designated one office for the receipt of such notices of liens, the notice shall be filed in the office of the clerk of the United States district court for the district in which the real property is located. For purposes of this subsection, the terms "purchaser" and "security interest" shall have the definitions provided under section 6323(h) of Title 26.

(4) Action in rem

The costs constituting the lien may be recovered in an action in rem in the United States district court for the district in which the removal or remedial action is occurring or has occurred. Nothing in this subsection shall affect the right of the United States to bring an action against any person to recover all costs and damages for which such person is liable under subsection (a) of this section.

(m) Maritime lien

All costs and damages for which the owner or operator of a vessel is liable under subsection (a)(1) of this section with respect to a release or threatened release from such vessel shall constitute a maritime lien in favor of the United States on such vessel. Such costs may be recovered in an action in rem in the district court of the United States for the district in which the vessel may be found. Nothing in this subsection shall affect the right of the United States to bring an action against the owner or operator of such vessel in any court of competent jurisdiction to recover such costs.

(n) Liability of fiduciaries

(1) In general

The liability of a fiduciary under any provision of this chapter for the release or threatened release of a hazardous substance at, from, or in connection with a vessel or facility held in a fiduciary capacity shall not exceed the assets held in the fiduciary capacity.

(2) Exclusion

Paragraph (1) does not apply to the extent that a person is liable under this chapter independently of the person's ownership of a vessel or facility as a fiduciary or actions taken in a fiduciary capacity.

(3) Limitation

Paragraphs (1) and (4) do not limit the liability pertaining to a release or threatened release of a hazardous substance if negligence of a fiduciary causes or contributes to the release or threatened release.

(4) Safe harbor

A fiduciary shall not be liable in its personal capacity under this chapter for—

(A) undertaking or directing another person to undertake a response action under subsection (d)(1) of this section or under the direction of an on scene coordinator designated under the National Contingency Plan;

(B) undertaking or directing another person to undertake any other lawful means of addressing a hazardous substance in connection with the vessel or facility;

(C) terminating the fiduciary relationship;

(D) including in the terms of the fiduciary agreement a covenant, warranty, or other term or condition that relates to compliance with an environmental law, or monitoring, modifying or enforcing the term or condition;

(E) monitoring or undertaking 1 or more inspections of the vessel or facility;

(F) providing financial or other advice or counseling to other parties to the fiduciary relationship, including the settlor or beneficiary;

(G) restructuring, renegotiating, or otherwise altering the terms and conditions of the fiduciary relationship;

(H) administering, as a fiduciary, a vessel or facility that was contaminated before the fiduciary relationship began; or

(I) declining to take any of the actions described in subparagraphs (B) through (H).

(5) Definitions

As used in this chapter:

(A) Fiduciary

The term "fiduciary"—

(i) means a person acting for the benefit of another party as a bona fide—

(I) trustee;

(II) executor;

(III) administrator;

(IV) custodian;

(V) guardian of estates or guardian ad litem;

(VI) receiver;

(VII) conservator;

(VIII) committee of estates of incapacitated persons;

(IX) personal representative;

(X) trustee (including a successor to a trustee) under an indenture agreement, trust agreement, lease, or similar financing agreement, for debt securities, certificates of interest or certificates of participation in debt securities, or other forms of indebtedness as to which the trustee is not, in the capacity of trustee, the lender; or

(XI) representative in any other capacity that the Administrator, after providing public notice, determines to be similar to the capacities described in subclauses (I) through (X); and

(ii) does not include—

(I) a person that is acting as a fiduciary with respect to a trust or other fiduciary estate that was organized for the primary purpose of, or is engaged in, actively carrying on a trade or business for profit, unless the trust or other fiduciary estate was created as part of, or to facilitate, 1 or more estate plans or because of the incapacity of a natural person; or

(II) a person that acquires ownership or control of a vessel or facility with the objective purpose of avoiding liability of the person or of any other person.

(B) **Fiduciary capacity**

The term "fiduciary capacity" means the capacity of a person in holding title to a vessel or facility, or otherwise having control of or an interest in the vessel or facility, pursuant to the exercise of the responsibilities of the person as a fiduciary.

(6) **Savings clause**

Nothing in this subsection—

(A) affects the rights or immunities or other defenses that are available under this chapter or other law that is applicable to a person subject to this subsection; or

(B) creates any liability for a person or a private right of action against a fiduciary or any other person.

(7) **No effect on certain persons**

Nothing in this subsection applies to a person if the person—

(A) (i) acts in a capacity other than that of a fiduciary or in a beneficiary capacity; and

(ii) in that capacity, directly or indirectly benefits from a trust or fiduciary relationship; or

(B) (i) is a beneficiary and a fiduciary with respect to the same fiduciary estate; and

(ii) as a fiduciary, receives benefits that exceed customary or reasonable compensation, and incidental benefits, permitted under other applicable law.

(8) **Limitation**

This subsection does not preclude a claim under this chapter against—

(A) the assets of the estate or trust administered by the fiduciary; or

(B) a nonemployee agent or independent contractor retained by a fiduciary.

(*o*) **De micromis exemption**

(1) **In general**

Except as provided in paragraph (2), a person shall not be liable, with respect to response costs at a facility on the National Priorities List, under this chapter if liability is based solely on paragraph (3) or (4) of subsection (a) of this section, and the person, except as provided in paragraph (4) of this subsection, can demonstrate that—

(A) the total amount of the material containing hazardous substances that the person arranged for disposal or treatment of, arranged with a transporter for transport for disposal or treatment of, or accepted for transport for disposal or treatment, at the facility was less than 110 gallons of liquid materials or less than 200 pounds of solid materials (or such greater or lesser amounts as the Administrator may determine by regulation); and

(B) all or part of the disposal, treatment, or transport concerned occurred before April 1, 2001.

(2) **Exceptions**

Paragraph (1) shall not apply in a case in which—

(A) the President determines that—

(i) the materials containing hazardous substances referred to in paragraph (1) have contributed significantly or could contribute significantly, either individually or in the aggregate, to the cost of the response action or natural resource restoration with respect to the facility; or

(ii) the person has failed to comply with an information request or administrative subpoena issued by the President under this chapter or has impeded or is impeding, through action or inaction, the performance of a response action or natural resource restoration with respect to the facility; or

(B) a person has been convicted of a criminal violation for the conduct to which the exemption would apply, and that conviction has not been vitiated on appeal or otherwise.

(3) No judicial review

A determination by the President under paragraph (2)(A) shall not be subject to judicial review.

(4) Nongovernmental third-party contribution actions

In the case of a contribution action, with respect to response costs at a facility on the National Priorities List, brought by a party, other than a Federal, State, or local government, under this chapter, the burden of proof shall be on the party bringing the action to demonstrate that the conditions described in paragraph (1)(A) and (B) of this subsection are not met.

(p) Municipal solid waste exemption

(1) In general

Except as provided in paragraph (2) of this subsection, a person shall not be liable, with respect to response costs at a facility on the National Priorities List, under paragraph (3) of subsection (a) of this section for municipal solid waste disposed of at a facility if the person, except as provided in paragraph (5) of this subsection, can demonstrate that the person is—

(A) an owner, operator, or lessee of residential property from which all of the person's municipal solid waste was generated with respect to the facility;

(B) a business entity (including a parent, subsidiary, or affiliate of the entity) that, during its 3 taxable years preceding the date of transmittal of written notification from the President of its potential liability under this section, employed on average not more than 100 full-time individuals, or the equivalent thereof, and that is a small business concern (within the meaning of the Small Business Act (15 U.S.C. 631 et seq.)) from which was generated all of the municipal solid waste attributable to the entity with respect to the facility; or

(C) an organization described in section 501(c)(3) of Title 26 and exempt from tax under section 501(a) of such title that, during its taxable year preceding the date of transmittal of written notification from the President of its potential liability under this section, employed not more than 100 paid individuals at the location from which was generated all of the municipal solid waste attributable to the organization with respect to the facility.

For purposes of this subsection, the term "affiliate" has the meaning of that term provided in the definition of "small business concern" in regulations promulgated by the Small Business Administration in accordance with the Small Business Act (15 U.S.C. 631 et seq.).

(2) Exception

Paragraph (1) shall not apply in a case in which the President determines that—

(A) the municipal solid waste referred to in paragraph (1) has contributed significantly or could contribute significantly, either individually or in the aggregate, to the cost of the response action or natural resource restoration with respect to the facility;

(B) the person has failed to comply with an information request or administrative subpoena issued by the President under this chapter; or

(C) the person has impeded or is impeding, through action or inaction, the performance of a response action or natural resource restoration with respect to the facility.

(3) No judicial review

A determination by the President under paragraph (2) shall not be subject to judicial review.

(4) Definition of municipal solid waste

(A) In general

For purposes of this subsection, the term "municipal solid waste" means waste material—

(i) generated by a household (including a single or multifamily residence); and

(ii) generated by a commercial, industrial, or institutional entity, to the extent that the waste material—

(I) is essentially the same as waste normally generated by a household;

(II) is collected and disposed of with other municipal solid waste as part of normal municipal solid waste collection services; and

(III) contains a relative quantity of hazardous substances no greater than the relative quantity of hazardous substances contained in waste material generated by a typical single-family household.

(B) Examples

Examples of municipal solid waste under subparagraph (A) include food and yard waste, paper, clothing, appliances, consumer product packaging, disposable diapers, office supplies, cosmetics, glass and metal food containers, elementary or secondary school science laboratory waste, and household hazardous waste.

(C) Exclusions

The term "municipal solid waste" does not include—

(i) combustion ash generated by resource recovery facilities or municipal incinerators; or

(ii) waste material from manufacturing or processing operations (including pollution control operations) that is not essentially the same as waste normally generated by households.

(5) Burden of proof

In the case of an action, with respect to response costs at a facility on the National Priorities List, brought under this section or section 9613 of this title by—

(A) a party, other than a Federal, State, or local government, with respect to municipal solid waste disposed of on or after April 1, 2001; or

(B) any party with respect to municipal solid waste disposed of before April 1, 2001, the burden of proof shall be on the party bringing the action to demonstrate that the conditions described in paragraphs (1) and (4) for exemption for entities and organizations described in paragraph (1)(B) and (C) are not met.

(6) Certain actions not permitted

No contribution action may be brought by a party, other than a Federal, State, or local government, under this chapter with respect to circumstances described in paragraph (1)(A).

(7) Costs and fees

A nongovernmental entity that commences, after January 11, 2002, a contribution action under this chapter shall be liable to the defendant for all reasonable costs of defending the action, including all reasonable attorney's fees and expert witness fees, if the defendant is not liable for contribution based on an exemption under this subsection or subsection (*o*) of this section.

(q) Contiguous properties

(1) Not considered to be an owner or operator

(A) In general

A person that owns real property that is contiguous to or otherwise similarly situated with respect to, and that is or may be contaminated by a release or threatened release of a hazardous substance from, real property that is not owned by that person shall not be considered to be an owner or operator of a vessel or facility under paragraph (1) or (2) of subsection (a) of this section solely by reason of the contamination if—

(i) the person did not cause, contribute, or consent to the release or threatened release;

(ii) the person is not—

(I) potentially liable, or affiliated with any other person that is potentially liable, for response costs at a facility through any direct or indirect familial relationship or any contractual, corporate, or financial relationship (other than a contractual, corporate, or financial relationship that is created by a contract for the sale of goods or services); or

(II) the result of a reorganization of a business entity that was potentially liable;

(iii) the person takes reasonable steps to—

(I) stop any continuing release;

(II) prevent any threatened future release; and

(III) prevent or limit human, environmental, or natural resource exposure to any hazardous substance released on or from property owned by that person;

(iv) the person provides full cooperation, assistance, and access to persons that are authorized to conduct response actions or natural resource restoration at the vessel or facility from which there has been a release or threatened release (including the cooperation and access necessary for the installation, integrity, operation, and maintenance of any complete or partial response action or natural resource restoration at the vessel or facility);

(v) the person—

(I) is in compliance with any land use restrictions established or relied on in connection with the response action at the facility; and

(II) does not impede the effectiveness or integrity of any institutional control employed in connection with a response action;

(vi) the person is in compliance with any request for information or administrative subpoena issued by the President under this chapter;

(vii) the person provides all legally required notices with respect to the discovery or release of any hazardous substances at the facility; and

(viii) at the time at which the person acquired the property, the person

(I) conducted all appropriate inquiry within the meaning of section 9601(35)(B) of this title with respect to the property; and

(II) did not know or have reason to know that the property was or could be contaminated by a release or threatened release of one or more hazardous substances from other real property not owned or operated by the person.

(B) Demonstration

To qualify as a person described in subparagraph (A), a person must establish by a preponderance of the evidence that the conditions in clauses (i) through (viii) of subparagraph (A) have been met.

(C) Bona fide prospective purchaser

Any person that does not qualify as a person described in this paragraph because the person had, or had reason to have, knowledge specified in subparagraph (A)(viii) at the time of acquisition of the real property may qualify as a bona fide prospective purchaser under section 9601(40) of this title if the person is otherwise described in that section.

(D) Ground water

With respect to a hazardous substance from one or more sources that are not on the property of a person that is a contiguous property owner that enters ground water beneath the property of the person solely as a result of subsurface migration in an aquifer, subparagraph (A)(iii) shall not require the person to conduct ground water investigations or to install ground water remediation systems, except in accordance with the policy of the Environmental Protection Agency concerning owners of property containing contaminated aquifers, dated May 24, 1995.

(2) Effect of law

With respect to a person described in this subsection, nothing in this subsection—

(A) limits any defense to liability that may be available to the person under any other provision of law; or

(B) imposes liability on the person that is not otherwise imposed by subsection (a) of this section.

(3) Assurances

The Administrator may—

(A) issue an assurance that no enforcement action under this chapter will be initiated against a person described in paragraph (1); and

(B) grant a person described in paragraph (1) protection against a cost recovery or contribution action under section 9613(f) of this title.

(r) Prospective purchaser and windfall lien

(1) Limitation on liability

Notwithstanding subsection (a)(1) of this section, a bona fide prospective purchaser whose potential liability for a release or threatened release is based solely on the bona fide prospective purchaser being considered to be an owner or operator of a facility shall not be liable as long as the bona fide prospective purchaser does not impede the performance of a response action or natural resource restoration.

(2) Lien

If there are unrecovered response costs incurred by the United States at a facility for which an owner of the facility is not liable by reason of paragraph (1), and if each of the conditions described in paragraph (3) is met, the United States shall have a lien on the facility, or may by agreement with the owner, obtain from the owner a lien on any other property or other assurance of payment satisfactory to the Administrator, for the unrecovered response costs.

(3) Conditions

The conditions referred to in paragraph (2) are the following:

(A) Response action

A response action for which there are unrecovered costs of the United States is carried out at the facility.

(B) Fair market value

The response action increases the fair market value of the facility above the fair market value of the facility that existed before the response action was initiated.

(4) Amount; duration

A lien under paragraph (2)—

(A) shall be in an amount not to exceed the increase in fair market value of the property attributable to the response action at the time of a sale or other disposition of the property;

(B) shall arise at the time at which costs are first incurred by the United States with respect to a response action at the facility;

(C) shall be subject to the requirements of subsection (*l*)(3) of this section; and

(D) shall continue until the earlier of—

(i) satisfaction of the lien by sale or other means; or

(ii) notwithstanding any statute of limitations under section 9613 of this title, recovery of all response costs incurred at the facility.

(Pub. L. No. 96–510, Title I, § 107, 94 Stat. 2781 (Dec. 11, 1980); as amended by Pub. L. No. 99–499, Title I, §§ 107(a) to (d)(2), (e), (f), 127(b), (e), Title II, §§ 201, 207(c), 100 Stat. 1628 to 1630, 1692, 1693, 1705 (Oct. 17, 1986); Pub. L. No. 99–514, § 2, 100 Stat. 2095 (Oct. 22, 1986); Pub. L. No. 103–429, § 7(e)(2), 108 Stat. 4390 (Oct. 31, 1994); Pub. L. No. 104–208, Div. A, Title II, § 2502(a), 110 Stat. 3009–462 (Sept. 30, 1996); Pub. L. No. 104–287, § 6(j)(2), 110 Stat. 3400 (Oct. 11, 1996); Pub. L. No. 107–118, Title I, § 102(a), Title II, §§ 221, 222(b), 115 Stat. 2356, 2368, 2371 (Jan. 11, 2002); Pub. L. No. 115–141, tit. VII, § 5(b), 132 Stat. 348, 1054 (Mar. 23, 2018).)

HISTORICAL AND STATUTORY NOTES

References in Text

This chapter, referred to in text, originally read "this Act", meaning Pub. L. No. 96–510, 94 Stat. 2767 (Dec. 11, 1980), as amended, known as the Comprehensive Environmental Response, Compensation, and Liability Act of 1980, which is codified principally as this chapter [42 U.S.C.A. § 9601 et seq.]; see Tables for complete classification.

Such amendments, referred to in subsec. (a) closing par., probably means the amendments made by Pub. L. No. 99–499, 100 Stat. 1613 (Oct. 17, 1986), known as the "Superfund Amendments and Reauthorization Act of 1986". For complete classification of that Act to the Code, see Short Title of 1986 Amendments note set out under section 9601 of this title and Tables.

Act of March 3, 1851 (46 U.S.C. 183ff), referred to in subsec. (h), was Act of Mar. 3, 1851, c. 43, 9 Stat. 635, which was incorporated into the Revised Statutes as R.S. sections 4282 to 4287 and 4289, and was codified as sections 182, 183, and 184 to 188 of Title 46, Appendix, Shipping, prior to repeal by Pub. L. No. 109–304, § 19, 120 Stat. 1710 (Oct. 6, 2006). See Disposition Table preceding Title 46, Shipping.

The Federal Insecticide, Fungicide, and Rodenticide Act, referred to in subsec. (i), is Act of June 25, 1947, c. 125, as amended generally by Pub. L. No. 92–516, 86 Stat. 973 (Oct. 21, 1972), which is codified generally as subchapter II (section 136 et seq.) of chapter 6 of Title 7, Agriculture. For complete classification of this Act to the Code, see Short Title note set out under section 136 of Title 7 and Tables.

The Solid Waste Disposal Act, referred to in subsec. (k)(1), (3), (6)(E)(i), is Title II of Pub. L. No. 89–272, Oct. 20, 1965, 79 Stat. 997, as amended generally by Pub. L. No. 94–580, § 2, 90 Stat. 2795 (Oct. 21, 1976). Subtitle C of the Solid Waste Disposal Act is codified generally as subchapter III (section 6921 et seq.) of chapter 82 of this title. Subtitle I of that Act is codified generally as subchapter IX (section 6991 et seq.) of chapter 82 of this title. For complete classification of this Act to the Code, see Short Title of 1965 Acts note set out under section 6901 of this title and Tables.

Section 9641 of this title, referred to in subsec. (k)(1) to (3), (5), (6)(E)(iv), was repealed by Pub. L. No. 99–499, Title V, § 514(b), 100 Stat. 1767 (Oct. 17, 1986).

Subchapter II of this chapter, referred to in subsec. (k)(4)(A) and (C), was in the original, "Title II of this Act", meaning Title II of Pub. L. No. 96–510, 94 Stat. 2796 (Dec. 11, 1980), known as the Hazardous Substance Response Revenue Act of 1980, which enacted subchapter II of this chapter and sections 4611, 4612, 4661, 4662, and former sections 4681, and 4682 of Title 26, Internal Revenue Code. Sections 221 to 223 and 232 of Pub. L. No. 96–510, which were codified as sections 9631 to 9633 and 9641 of this title, comprising subchapter II of this chapter, were repealed by Pub. L. No. 99–499, Title V, §§ 514(b), 517(c)(1), 100 Stat. 1767, 1774 (Oct. 17, 1986). For complete classification of Title II to the Code, see Short Title of 1980 Amendments note set out under section 1 of Title 26 and Tables.

The Hazardous and Solid Waste Amendments of 1984, referred to in subsec. (k)(6)(A), (E), is Pub. L. No. 98–616, 98 Stat. 3221 (Nov. 8, 1984). For complete classification of this Act to the Code, see Short Title of 1984 Amendments note set out under section 6901 of this title.

The Small Business Act, referred to in subsec. (p)(1), is Pub. L. No. 85–536, 72 Stat. 384 (July 18, 1958), as amended, which is codified generally as chapter 14A of Title 15 [42 U.S.C.A. § 631 et seq.] see Tables for complete classification.

Codifications

Reference in the original text of subsec. (p)(5) of this section to "section 107 or 113" has been translated in the codified text as "this section or section 9613 of this title" to reflect the probable intent of Congress.

Effective and Applicability Provisions

1996 Acts. Amendment by section 2502 of Title II of Div. A of Pub. L. No. 104–208 applicable with respect to claims not finally adjudicated as of Sept. 30, 1996, see section 2505 of Title II of Div. A of Pub. L. No. 104–208, set out as a note under section 6991b of this title.

1986 Acts. Amendment by Pub. L. No. 99–499 effective Oct. 17, 1986, see section 4 of Pub. L. No. 99–499, set out as a note under section 9601 of this title.

Delegation of Functions

Functions vested in the President by subsec. (c)(1)(C) of this section delegated to the Secretary of Transportation, see section 5(a) of Ex. Ord. No. 12580, 52 Fed. Reg. 2923 (Jan. 23, 1987), set out as a note under section 9615 of this title.

Functions vested in the President by subsec. (c)(3) of this section delegated, with authority to redelegate, to the Coast Guard with respect to any release or threatened release involving the coastal zone, Great Lakes waters, ports, and harbors, see sections 5(b), 11(g) of Ex. Ord. No. 12580, 52 Fed. Reg. 2923 (Jan. 23, 1987), set out as a note under section 9615 of this title.

Functions vested in the President by subsec. (c)(3) of this section delegated, subject to section 5(b) of Ex. Ord. No. 12580, and with authority to redelegate, to the Administrator of the Environmental Protection Agency, see sections 5(c), 11(g) of Ex. Ord. No. 12580, 52 Fed. Reg. 2923 (Jan. 23, 1987), set out as a note under section 9615 of this title.

Functions vested in the President by subsec. (f)(1) of this section delegated to each of the Federal trustees for natural resources designated in the National Contingency Plan for resources under their trusteeship, see section 5(d) of Ex. Ord. No. 12580, 52 Fed. Reg. 2923 (Jan. 23, 1987), set out as a note under section 9615 of this title.

Functions vested in the President by subsec. (f)(2)(B) of this section, to receive notification of the state natural resource trustee designations, delegated to the Administrator of the Environmental Protection Agency, see section 5(e) of Ex. Ord. No. 12580, 52 Fed. Reg. 2923 (Jan. 23, 1987), set out as a note under section 9615 of this title.

Functions vested in the President by subsec. (k)(4)(B) of this section delegated to the Secretary of the Treasury, with the Administrator of the Environmental Protection Agency to provide the Secretary with such technical information and assistance as the Administrator may have available, see section 7(a) of Ex. Ord. No. 12580, 52 Fed. Reg. 2923 (Jan. 23, 1987), set out as a note under section 9615 of this title.

Coordination of Titles I to IV of Pub. L. No. 99–499

Any provision of Titles I to IV of Pub. L. No. 99–499, imposing any tax, premium, or fee; establishing any trust fund; or authorizing expenditures from any trust fund, to have no force or effect, see section 531 of Pub. L. No. 99–499, set out as a note under section 1 of Title 26, Internal Revenue Code.

Central Hazardous Materials Fund

Pub. L. No. 110–161, Div. F, Title I, 121 Stat. 2116 (Dec. 26, 2007), as amended by Pub. L. No. 111–88, Div. A, Title I, 123 Stat. 2924 (Oct. 30, 2009), provided in part: "That hereafter [on or after Dec. 26, 2007], notwithstanding 31 U.S.C. 3302, sums recovered from or paid by a party including any fines or penalties, shall be credited to this account, to be available until expended without further appropriation: *Provided further*, That hereafter [on or after Dec. 26, 2007] such sums recovered from or paid by any party are not limited to monetary payments and may include stocks, bonds or other personal or real property, which may be retained, liquidated, or otherwise disposed of by the Secretary and which shall be credited to this account."

Similar provisions were contained in the following prior Appropriations Acts:

Pub. L. No. 109–54, Title I, 119 Stat. 518 (Aug. 2, 2005).

Pub. L. No. 108–447, Div. E, Title I, 118 Stat. 3041 (Dec. 8, 2004).

Pub. L. No. 108–108, Title I, 117 Stat. 1243 (Nov. 10, 2003).

Pub. L. No. 108–7, Div. F, Title I, 117 Stat. 218 (Feb. 20, 2003).

Pub. L. No. 107–63, Title I, 115 Stat. 416 (Nov. 5, 2001).

Pub. L. No. 106–291, Title I, 114 Stat. 922 (Oct. 11, 2000).

Pub. L. No. 106–113, Div. B, § 1000(a)(3) [Title I], 113 Stat. 1535, 1501A–136 (Nov. 29, 1999).

Pub. L. No. 105–277, Div. A, § 101(e) [Title I], 112 Stat. 2681–233 (Oct. 21, 1998).

Pub. L. No. 105–83, Title I, 111 Stat. 1544 (Nov. 14, 1997).

Pub. L. No. 104–208, Div. A, § 101(d) [Title I], 110 Stat. 3009–182 (Sept. 30, 1996).

Pub. L. No. 104–134, Title I, § 101(c) [Title I], 110 Stat. 1321–157 (Apr. 26, 1996).

Pub. L. No. 103–332, Title I, 108 Stat. 2500 (Sept. 30, 1994).

Effect on Concluded Actions

Pub. L. No. 107–118, Title I, § 103, 115 Stat. 2360 (Jan. 11, 2002), provided that: "The amendments made by this title [Pub. L. No. 107–118, Title I, § 101 et seq., 115 Stat. 2356 (Jan. 11, 2002), enacting provisions set out as a note under 42 U.S.C.A. § 9601 and amending subsecs. (*o*) and (p) of this section and 42 U.S.C.A. § 9622(g)(7) to (12)] shall not apply to or in any way affect any settlement lodged in, or judgment issued by, a United States District Court, or any administrative settlement or order entered into or issued by the United States or any State, before the date of the enactment of this Act [Jan. 11, 2002]."

Recovery of Costs

Pub. L. No. 104–303, Title II, § 209, 110 Stat. 3681 (Oct. 12, 1996), provided that: "Amounts recovered under section 107 of the Comprehensive Environmental Response, Compensation, and Liability Act of 1980 (42 U.S.C. 9607) [this section] for any response action taken by the Secretary in support of the civil works program of the Department of the Army and any other amounts recovered by the Secretary from a contractor, insurer, surety, or other person to reimburse the Department of the Army for any expenditure for environmental response activities in support of the Army civil works program shall be credited to the appropriate trust fund account from which the cost of such response action has been paid or will be charged."

§ 9608. Financial responsibility

[CERCLA § 108]

(a) Establishment and maintenance by owner or operator of vessel; amount; failure to obtain certification of compliance

(1) The owner or operator of each vessel (except a nonself-propelled barge that does not carry hazardous substances as cargo) over three hundred gross tons that uses any port or place in the United States or the navigable waters or any offshore facility, shall establish and maintain, in accordance with regulations promulgated by the President, evidence of financial responsibility of $300 per gross ton (or for a vessel carrying hazardous substances as cargo, or $5,000,000, whichever is greater) to cover the liability prescribed under paragraph (1) of section 9607(a) of this title. Financial responsibility may be established by any one, or any combination, of the following: insurance, guarantee, surety bond, or qualification as a self-insurer. Any bond filed shall be issued by a bonding company authorized to do business in the United States. In cases where an owner or operator owns, operates, or charters more than one vessel subject to this subsection, evidence of financial responsibility need be established only to meet the maximum liability applicable to the largest of such vessels.

(2) The Secretary of the Treasury shall withhold or revoke the clearance required by section 60105 of Title 46 of any vessel subject to this subsection that does not have certification furnished by the President that the financial responsibility provisions of paragraph (1) of this subsection have been complied with.

(3) The Secretary of Transportation, in accordance with regulations issued by him, shall (A) deny entry to any port or place in the United States or navigable waters to, and (B) detain at the port or place in the United States from which it is about to depart for any other port or place in the United States, any vessel subject to this subsection that, upon request, does not produce certification furnished by the President that the financial responsibility provisions of paragraph (1) of this subsection have been complied with.

(4) In addition to the financial responsibility provisions of paragraph (1) of this subsection, the President shall require additional evidence of financial responsibility for incineration vessels in such amounts, and to cover such liabilities recognized by law, as the President deems appropriate, taking into account the potential risks posed by incineration and transport for incineration, and any other factors deemed relevant.

(b) Establishment and maintenance by owner or operator of production, etc., facilities; amount; adjustment; consolidated form of responsibility; coverage of motor carriers

(1) Beginning not earlier than five years after December 11, 1980, the President shall promulgate requirements (for facilities in addition to those under subtitle C of the Solid Waste Disposal Act [42 U.S.C.A. § 6921 et seq.] and other Federal law) that classes of facilities establish and maintain evidence of financial responsibility consistent with the degree and duration of risk associated with the production, transportation, treatment, storage, or disposal of hazardous substances. Not later than three years after December 11, 1980, the President shall identify those classes for which requirements will be first developed and publish notice of such identification in the Federal Register. Priority in the development of such requirements shall be accorded to those classes of facilities, owners, and operators which the President determines present the highest level of risk of injury.

(2) The level of financial responsibility shall be initially established, and, when necessary, adjusted to protect against the level of risk which the President in his discretion believes is appropriate based on the payment experience of the Fund, commercial insurers, courts settlements and judgments, and voluntary claims satisfaction. To the maximum extent practicable, the President shall cooperate with and seek the advice of the commercial insurance industry in developing financial responsibility requirements. Financial responsibility may be established by any one, or any combination, of the following: insurance, guarantee, surety bond, letter of credit, or qualification as a self-insurer. In promulgating requirements under this section, the President is authorized to specify policy or other contractual terms, conditions, or defenses which are necessary, or which are unacceptable, in establishing such evidence of financial responsibility in order to effectuate the purposes of this chapter.

(3) Regulations promulgated under this subsection shall incrementally impose financial responsibility requirements as quickly as can reasonably be achieved but in no event more than 4 years after the date of promulgation. Where possible, the level of financial responsibility which the President believes appropriate as a final requirement shall be achieved through incremental, annual increases in the requirements.

(4) Where a facility is owned or operated by more than one person, evidence of financial responsibility covering the facility may be established and maintained by one of the owners or operators, or, in consolidated form, by or on behalf of two or more owners or operators. When evidence of financial responsibility is established in a consolidated form, the proportional share of each participant shall be shown. The evidence shall be accompanied by a statement authorizing the applicant to act for and in behalf of each participant in submitting and maintaining the evidence of financial responsibility.

(5) The requirements for evidence of financial responsibility for motor carriers covered by this chapter shall be determined under section 31139 of title 49.

(c) Direct action

(1) Releases from vessels

In the case of a release or threatened release from a vessel, any claim authorized by section 9607 or 9611 of this title may be asserted directly against any guarantor providing evidence of financial responsibility for such vessel under subsection (a) of this section. In defending such a claim, the guarantor may invoke all rights and defenses which would be available to the owner or operator under this subchapter. The guarantor may also invoke the defense that the incident was caused by the willful misconduct of the owner or operator, but the guarantor may not invoke any other defense that the guarantor might have been entitled to invoke in a proceeding brought by the owner or operator against him.

(2) **Releases from facilities**

In the case of a release or threatened release from a facility, any claim authorized by section 9607 or 9611 of this title may be asserted directly against any guarantor providing evidence of financial responsibility for such facility under subsection (b) of this section, if the person liable under section 9607 of this title is in bankruptcy, reorganization, or arrangement pursuant to the Federal Bankruptcy Code, or if, with reasonable diligence, jurisdiction in the Federal courts cannot be obtained over a person liable under section 9607 of this title who is likely to be solvent at the time of judgment. In the case of any action pursuant to this paragraph, the guarantor shall be entitled to invoke all rights and defenses which would have been available to the person liable under section 9607 of this title if any action had been brought against such person by the claimant and all rights and defenses which would have been available to the guarantor if an action had been brought against the guarantor by such person.

(d) **Limitation of guarantor liability**

(1) **Total liability**

The total liability of any guarantor in a direct action suit brought under this section shall be limited to the aggregate amount of the monetary limits of the policy of insurance, guarantee, surety bond, letter of credit, or similar instrument obtained from the guarantor by the person subject to liability under section 9607 of this title for the purpose of satisfying the requirement for evidence of financial responsibility.

(2) **Other liability**

Nothing in this subsection shall be construed to limit any other State or Federal statutory, contractual, or common law liability of a guarantor, including, but not limited to, the liability of such guarantor for bad faith either in negotiating or in failing to negotiate the settlement of any claim. Nothing in this subsection shall be construed, interpreted, or applied to diminish the liability of any person under section 9607 of this title or other applicable law.

(Pub. L. No. 96–510, Title I, § 108, 94 Stat. 2785 (Dec. 11, 1980); as amended by Pub. L. No. 99–499, Title I, §§ 108, 127(c), 100 Stat. 1631, 1692 (Oct. 17, 1986).)

HISTORICAL AND STATUTORY NOTES

References in Text

The Solid Waste Disposal Act, referred to in subsec. (b)(1), is Title II of Pub. L. No. 89–272, 79 Stat. 997 (Oct. 20, 1965), as amended generally by Pub. L. No. 94–580, § 2, 90 Stat. 2795 (Oct. 21, 1976). Subtitle C of the Solid Waste Disposal Act is codified generally as subchapter III (section 6921 et seq.) of chapter 82 of this title. For complete classification of this Act to the Code, see Short Title note set out under section 6901 of this title and Tables.

The Federal Bankruptcy Code, referred to in subsec. (c)(2), probably means a reference to Title 11, Bankruptcy.

Codifications

"Section 60105 of Title 46" substituted in subsec. (a)(2) for "section 91 of Title 46, Appendix" on authority of Pub. L. No. 109–304, § 18(c), 120 Stat. 1709 (Oct. 6, 2006), which completed the codification of T. 46, Shipping, as positive law.

In subsec. (b)(5), "section 31139 of title 49" was substituted for "section 30 of the Motor Carrier Act of 1980, Pub. Law 96–296" on authority of Pub. L. No. 103–272, § 6(b), 108 Stat. 1378 (July 5, 1994), the first section of which enacted subtitles II, III, and V to X of Title 49.

Effective and Applicability Provisions

1986 Acts. Amendment by Pub. L. No. 99–499 effective Oct. 17, 1986, see section 4 of Pub. L. No. 99–499, set out as a note under section 9601 of this title.

Delegation of Functions

Functions vested in the President by subsec. (a)(1) of this section delegated to the Coast Guard, see section 7(b)(1) of Ex. Ord. No. 12580, 52 Fed. Reg. 2923 (Jan. 23, 1987), set out as a note under section 9615 of this title.

Functions vested in the President by provisions of section 9609 of this title relating to violations of subsec. (a)(1) of this section delegated, subject to section 4(a) of Ex. Ord. No. 12580, to the Coast Guard, see section 7(b)(2) of Ex. Ord. No. 12580, 52 Fed. Reg. 2923 (Jan. 23, 1987), set out as a note under section 9615 of this title.

Functions vested in the President by subsec. (b) of this section delegated to the Secretary of Transportation with respect to all transportation related facilities, including any pipeline, motor vehicle, rolling stock, or aircraft, see section 7(c)(1) of Ex. Ord. No. 12580, 52 Fed. Reg. 2923 (Jan. 23, 1987), set out as a note under section 9615 of this title.

Functions vested in the President by provisions of section 9609 of this title relating to violations of subsec. (a)(3) of this section delegated, subject to section 4(a) of Ex. Ord. No. 12580, to the Secretary of Transportation, see section 7(c)(2) of Ex. Ord. No. 12580, 52 Fed. Reg. 2923 (Jan. 23, 1987), set out as a note under section 9615 of this title.

Functions vested in the President by provisions of section 9609 of this title relating to violations of subsec. (b) of this section delegated, subject to section 4(a) of Ex. Ord. No. 12580, to the Secretary of Transportation with respect to all transportation related facilities, including any pipeline, motor vehicle, rolling stock, or aircraft, see section 7(c)(3) of Ex. Ord. No. 12580, 52 Fed. Reg. 2923 (Jan. 23, 1987), set out as a note under section 9615 of this title.

Functions vested in the President by provisions of section 9609 of this title relating to violations of subsecs. (a)(4) and (b) of this section delegated, subject to sections 4(a) and 7(c)(3) of Ex. Ord. No. 12580, to the Administrator of the Environmental Protection Agency, see section 7(d)(2) of Ex. Ord. No. 12580, 52 Fed. Reg. 2923 (Jan. 23, 1987), set out as a note under section 9615 of this title.

Functions vested in the President by subsecs. (a)(4) and (b) of this section delegated, subject to section 7(c)(1) of Ex. Ord. No. 12580, to the Administrator of the Environmental Protection Agency, see section 7(d)(1) of Ex. Ord. No. 12580, 52 Fed. Reg. 2923 (Jan. 23, 1987), set out as a note under section 9615 of this title.

§ 9609. Civil penalties and awards

[CERCLA § 109]

(a) Class I administrative penalty

(1) Violations

A civil penalty of not more than $25,000 per violation may be assessed by the President in the case of any of the following—

(A) A violation of the requirements of section 9603(a) or (b) of this title (relating to notice).

(B) A violation of the requirements of section 9603(d)(2) of this title (relating to destruction of records, etc.).

(C) A violation of the requirements of section 9608 of this title (relating to financial responsibility, etc.), the regulations issued under section 9608 of this title, or with any denial or detention order under section 9608 of this title.

(D) A violation of an order under section 9622(d)(3) of this title (relating to settlement agreements for action under section 9604(b) of this title).

(E) Any failure or refusal referred to in section 9622(*l*) of this title (relating to violations of administrative orders, consent decrees, or agreements under section 9620 of this title).

(2) Notice and hearings

No civil penalty may be assessed under this subsection unless the person accused of the violation is given notice and opportunity for a hearing with respect to the violation.

(3) Determining amount

In determining the amount of any penalty assessed pursuant to this subsection, the President shall take into account the nature, circumstances, extent and gravity of the violation or violations and, with respect to the violator, ability to pay, any prior history of such violations, the degree of culpability, economic benefit or savings (if any) resulting from the violation, and such other matters as justice may require.

(4) Review

Any person against whom a civil penalty is assessed under this subsection may obtain review thereof in the appropriate district court of the United States by filing a notice of appeal in such court within 30 days from the date of such order and by simultaneously sending a copy of such notice by certified mail to the President. The President shall promptly file in such court a certified copy of the record upon which such violation was found or such penalty imposed. If any person fails to pay an assessment of a civil penalty after it has become a final and unappealable order or after the appropriate court has entered final judgment in favor of the United States, the President may request the Attorney General of the United States to institute a civil action in an appropriate district court of the United States to collect the penalty, and such court shall have jurisdiction to hear and decide any such action. In hearing such action, the court shall have authority to review the violation and the assessment of the civil penalty on the record.

(5) Subpoenas

The President may issue subpoenas for the attendance and testimony of witnesses and the production of relevant papers, books, or documents in connection with hearings under this subsection. In case of contumacy or refusal to obey a subpoena issued pursuant to this paragraph and served upon any person, the district court of the United States for any district in which such person is found, resides, or transacts business, upon application by the United States and after notice to such person, shall have jurisdiction to issue an order requiring such person to appear and give testimony before the administrative law judge or to appear and produce documents before the administrative law judge, or both, and any failure to obey such order of the court may be punished by such court as a contempt thereof.

(b) Class II administrative penalty

A civil penalty of not more than $25,000 per day for each day during which the violation continues may be assessed by the President in the case of any of the following—

(1) A violation of the notice requirements of section 9603(a) or (b) of this title.

(2) A violation of section 9603(d)(2) of this title (relating to destruction of records, etc.).

(3) A violation of the requirements of section 9608 of this title (relating to financial responsibility, etc.), the regulations issued under section 9608 of this title, or with any denial or detention order under section 9608 of this title.

(4) A violation of an order under section 9622(d)(3) of this title (relating to settlement agreements for action under section 9604(b) of this title).

(5) Any failure or refusal referred to in section 9622(*l*) of this title (relating to violations of administrative orders, consent decrees, or agreements under section 9620 of this title).

In the case of a second or subsequent violation the amount of such penalty may be not more than $75,000 for each day during which the violation continues. Any civil penalty under this subsection shall be assessed and collected in the same manner, and subject to the same provisions, as in the case of civil penalties assessed and collected after notice and opportunity for hearing on the record in accordance with section 554 of Title 5. In any proceeding for the assessment of a civil penalty under this subsection the President may issue subpoenas for the attendance and testimony of witnesses and the production of relevant papers, books, and documents and may promulgate rules for discovery procedures. Any person who requested a hearing with respect to a civil penalty under this subsection and who is aggrieved by an order assessing the civil penalty may file a petition for judicial review of such order with the United States Court of Appeals for the District of Columbia Circuit or for any other circuit in which such person resides or transacts business. Such a petition may only be filed within the 30-day period beginning on the date the order making such assessment was issued.

(c) Judicial assessment

The President may bring an action in the United States district court for the appropriate district to assess and collect a penalty of not more than $25,000 per day for each day during which the violation (or failure or refusal) continues in the case of any of the following—

(1) A violation of the notice requirements of section 9603(a) or (b) of this title.

(2) A violation of section 9603(d)(2) of this title (relating to destruction of records, etc.).

(3) A violation of the requirements of section 9608 of this title (relating to financial responsibility, etc.), the regulations issued under section 9608 of this title, or with any denial or detention order under section 9608 of this title.

(4) A violation of an order under section 9622(d)(3) of this title (relating to settlement agreements for action under section 9604(b) of this title).

(5) Any failure or refusal referred to in section 9622(*l*) of this title (relating to violations of administrative orders, consent decrees, or agreements under section 9620 of this title).

In the case of a second or subsequent violation (or failure or refusal), the amount of such penalty may be not more than $75,000 for each day during which the violation (or failure or refusal) continues. For additional provisions providing for judicial assessment of civil penalties for failure to comply with a request or order under section 9604(e)of this title (relating to information gathering and access authorities), see section 9604(e) of this title.

(d) Awards

The President may pay an award of up to $10,000 to any individual who provides information leading to the arrest and conviction of any person for a violation subject to a criminal penalty under this chapter, including any violation of section 9603 of this title and any other violation referred to in this section. The President shall, by regulation, prescribe criteria for such an award and may pay any award under this subsection from the Fund, as provided in section 9611 of this title.

(e) Procurement procedures

Notwithstanding any other provision of law, any executive agency may use competitive procedures or procedures other than competitive procedures to procure the services of experts for use in preparing or prosecuting a civil or criminal action under this chapter, whether or not the expert is expected to testify at trial. The executive agency need not provide any written justification for the use of procedures other than competitive procedures when procuring such expert services under this chapter and need not furnish for publication in the Commerce Business Daily or otherwise any notice of solicitation or synopsis with respect to such procurement.

(f) Savings clause

Action taken by the President pursuant to this section shall not affect or limit the President's authority to enforce any provisions of this chapter.

(Pub. L. No. 96–510, Title I, § 109, 94 Stat. 2787 (Dec. 11, 1980); as amended by Pub. L. No. 99–499, Title I, § 109(c), 100 Stat. 1633 (Oct. 17, 1986).)

HISTORICAL AND STATUTORY NOTES

Effective and Applicability Provisions

1986 Acts. Amendment by Pub. L. No. 99–499 effective Oct. 17, 1986, see section 4 of Pub. L. No. 99–499, set out as a note under section 9601 of this title.

Delegation of Functions

Functions vested in the President by subsec. (d) of this section, relating to development of regulations and guidelines, delegated to the Administrator of the Environmental Protection Agency, to be exercised in consultation with the Attorney General, see section 4(a) of Ex. Ord. No. 12580, 52 Fed. Reg. 2923 (Jan. 23, 1987), set out as a note under section 9615 of this title.

Functions vested in the President by provisions of this section relating to violations of section 9622 of this title delegated, subject to section 4(a) of Ex. Ord. No. 12580, and with authority to redelegate, to the heads of Executive departments and agencies, with respect to releases or threatened releases not on the National Priorities List, where either the release is on or the sole source of the release is from any facility under the jurisdiction, custody or control of those Executive departments and agencies, with such functions to be exercised only with the concurrence of the Attorney General see sections 4(b)(2), 11(g) of Ex. Ord. No. 12580, 52 Fed. Reg. 2923 (Jan. 23, 1987), set out as a note under section 9615 of this title.

Functions vested in the President by provisions of this section relating to violations of sections 9603(a) and (b) and 9622 of this title delegated, subject to section 4(a), (b)(2) of Ex. Ord. No. 12580, and with authority to redelegate, to the Coast Guard with respect to any release or threatened release involving the coastal zone, Great Lakes waters, ports, and harbors, see sections 4(c)(2), 11(g) of Ex. Ord. No. 12580, 52 Fed. Reg. 2923 (Jan. 23, 1987), set out as a note under section 9615 of this title.

Functions vested in the President by provisions of this section relating to violations of sections 9603 and 9622 of this title delegated, subject to section 4(a), (b)(2), (c)(2) of Ex. Ord. No. 12580, and with authority to redelegate, to the Administrator of the Environmental Protection Agency, see sections 4(d)(2), 11(g) of Ex. Ord. No. 12580, 52 Fed. Reg. 2923 (Jan. 23, 1987), set out as a note under section 9615 of this title.

Functions vested in the President by provisions of this section relating to violations of section 9608(a)(1) of this title delegated, subject to section 4(a) of Ex. Ord. No. 12580, to the Coast Guard, see section 7(b)(2) of Ex. Ord. No. 12580, 52 Fed. Reg. 2923 (Jan. 23, 1987), set out as a note under section 9615 of this title.

Functions vested in the President by provisions of this section relating to violations of section 9608(a)(3) of this title delegated, subject to section 4(a) of Ex. Ord. No. 12580, to the Secretary of Transportation, see section 7(c)(2) of Ex. Ord. No. 12580, 52 Fed. Reg. 2923 (Jan. 23, 1987), set out as a note under section 9615 of this title.

Functions vested in the President by provisions of this section relating to violations of section 9608(b) of this title delegated, subject to section 4(a) of Ex. Ord. No. 12580, to the Secretary of Transportation with respect to all transportation related facilities, including any pipeline, motor vehicle, rolling stock, or aircraft, see section 7(c)(3) of Ex. Ord. No. 12580, 52 Fed. Reg. 2923 (Jan. 23, 1987), set out as a note under section 9615 of this title.

Functions vested in the President by provisions of this section relating to violations of section 9608(a)(4) and (b) of this title delegated, subject to sections 4(a) and 7(c)(3) of Ex. Ord. No. 12580, to the Administrator of the Environmental Protection Agency, see section 7(d)(2) of Ex. Ord. No. 12580, 52 Fed. Reg. 2923 (Jan. 23, 1987), set out as a note under section 9615 of this title.

Coordination of Titles I to IV of Pub. L. No. 99–499

Any provision of Titles I to IV of Pub. L. No. 99–499, imposing any tax, premium, or fee; establishing any trust fund; or authorizing expenditures from any trust fund, to have no force or effect, see section 531 of Pub. L. No. 99–499, set out as a note under section 1 of Title 26, Internal Revenue Code.

§ 9610. Employee protection

[CERCLA § 110]

(a) Activities of employee subject to protection

No person shall fire or in any other way discriminate against, or cause to be fired or discriminated against, any employee or any authorized representative of employees by reason of the fact that such employee or representative has provided information to a State or to the Federal Government, filed, instituted, or caused to be filed or instituted any proceeding under this chapter, or has testified or is about to testify in any proceeding resulting from the administration or enforcement of the provisions of this chapter.

(b) Administrative grievance procedure in cases of alleged violations

Any employee or a representative of employees who believes that he has been fired or otherwise discriminated against by any person in violation of subsection (a) of this section may, within thirty days after such alleged violation occurs, apply to the Secretary of Labor for a review of such firing or alleged discrimination. A copy of the application shall be sent to such person, who shall be the respondent. Upon receipt of such application, the Secretary of Labor shall cause such investigation to be made as he deems appropriate. Such investigation shall provide an opportunity for a public hearing at the request of any party to such review to enable the parties to present information relating to such alleged violation. The parties shall be given written notice of the time and place of the hearing at least five days prior to the hearing. Any such hearing shall be of record and shall be subject to section 554 of Title 5. Upon receiving the report of such investigation, the Secretary of Labor shall make findings of fact. If he finds that such violation did occur, he shall issue a decision, incorporating an order therein and his findings, requiring the party committing such violation to take such affirmative action to abate the violation as the Secretary of Labor deems appropriate, including, but not limited to, the rehiring or reinstatement of the employee or representative of employees to his former position with compensation. If he finds that there was no such violation, he shall issue an order denying the application. Such order issued by the Secretary of Labor under this subparagraph shall be subject to judicial review in the same manner as orders and decisions are subject to judicial review under this chapter.

(c) Assessment of costs and expenses against violator subsequent to issuance of order of abatement

Whenever an order is issued under this section to abate such violation, at the request of the applicant a sum equal to the aggregate amount of all costs and expenses (including the attorney's fees) determined by the Secretary of Labor to have been reasonably incurred by the applicant for, or in connection with, the institution and prosecution of such proceedings, shall be assessed against the person committing such violation.

(d) Defenses

This section shall have no application to any employee who acting without discretion from his employer (or his agent) deliberately violates any requirement of this chapter.

(e) Presidential evaluations of potential loss of shifts of employment resulting from administration or enforcement of provisions; investigations; procedures applicable, etc.

The President shall conduct continuing evaluations of potential loss of shifts of employment which may result from the administration or enforcement of the provisions of this chapter, including, where appropriate, investigating threatened plant closures or reductions in employment allegedly resulting from such administration or enforcement. Any employee who is discharged, or laid off, threatened with discharge or layoff, or otherwise discriminated against by any person because of the alleged results of such administration or enforcement, or any representative of such employee, may request the President to conduct a full investigation of the matter and, at the request of any party, shall hold public hearings, require the parties, including the employer involved, to present information relating to the actual or potential effect of such administration or enforcement on employment and any alleged discharge, layoff, or other discrimination, and the detailed reasons or justification therefore.[1] Any such hearing shall be of record and shall be subject to section 554 of Title 5. Upon receiving the report of such investigation, the President shall make findings of fact as to the effect of such administration or enforcement on employment and on the alleged discharge, layoff, or discrimination and shall make such recommendations as he deems appropriate. Such report, findings, and recommendations shall be available to the public. Nothing in this subsection shall be construed to require or authorize the President or any State to modify or withdraw any action, standard, limitation, or any other requirement of this chapter.

(Pub. L. No. 96–510, Title I, § 110, 94 Stat. 2787 (Dec. 11, 1980).)

[1] So in original.

HISTORICAL AND STATUTORY NOTES

Delegation of Functions

Functions vested in the President by subsec. (e) of this section delegated to the Administrator of the Environmental Protection Agency, see section 8(a) of Ex. Ord. No. 12580, 52 Fed. Reg. 2923 (Jan. 23, 1987), set out as a note under section 9615 of this title.

§ 9611. Uses of Fund

[CERCLA § 111]

(a) In general

For the purposes specified in this section there is authorized to be appropriated from the Hazardous Substance Superfund established under subchapter A of chapter 98 of Title 26 not more than $8,500,000,000 for the 5-year period beginning on October 17, 1986, and not more than $5,100,000,000 for the period commencing October 1, 1991, and ending September 30, 1994, and such sums shall remain available until expended. The preceding sentence constitutes a specific authorization for the funds appropriated under title II of Public Law 99–160 (relating to payment to the Hazardous Substances Trust Fund). The President shall use the money in the Fund for the following purposes:

(1) Payment of governmental response costs incurred pursuant to section 9604 of this title, including costs incurred pursuant to the Intervention on the High Seas Act [33 U.S.C.A. § 1471 et seq.].

(2) Payment of any claim for necessary response costs incurred by any other person as a result of carrying out the national contingency plan established under section 1321(c) of Title 33 and amended by section 9605 of this title: *Provided, however,* That such costs must be approved under said plan and certified by the responsible Federal official.

(3) Payment of any claim authorized by subsection (b) of this section and finally decided pursuant to section 9612 of this title, including those costs set out in subsection 9612(c)(3) of this title.

(4) Payment of costs specified under subsection (c) of this section.

(5) Grants for technical assistance

The cost of grants under section 9617(e) of this title (relating to public participation grants for technical assistance).

(6) Lead contaminated soil

Payment of not to exceed $15,000,000 for the costs of a pilot program for removal, decontamination, or other action with respect to lead-contaminated soil in one to three different metropolitan areas.

The President shall not pay for any administrative costs or expenses out of the Fund unless such costs and expenses are reasonably necessary for and incidental to the implementation of this subchapter.

(b) Additional authorized purposes

(1) In general

Claims asserted and compensable but unsatisfied under provisions of section 1321 of Title 33, which are modified by section 304 of this Act may be asserted against the Fund under this subchapter; and other claims resulting from a release or threat of release of a hazardous substance from a vessel or a facility may be asserted against the Fund under this subchapter for injury to, or destruction or loss of, natural resources, including cost for damage assessment: *Provided, however,* That any such claim may be asserted only by the President, as trustee, for natural resources over which the United States has sovereign rights, or natural resources within the territory or the fishery conservation zone of the United States to the extent they are managed or protected by the United States, or by any State for natural resources within the boundary of that State belonging to, managed by, controlled by, or appertaining to the State, or by any Indian tribe or by the United States acting on behalf of any Indian tribe for natural resources belonging to, managed by, controlled by, or appertaining to such tribe, or held in trust for the benefit of such tribe, or belonging to a member of such tribe if such resources are subject to a trust restriction on alienation.

(2) Limitation on payment of natural resource claims

(A) General requirements

No natural resource claim may be paid from the Fund unless the President determines that the claimant has exhausted all administrative and judicial remedies to recover the amount of such claim from persons who may be liable under section 9607 of this title.

(B) Definition

As used in this paragraph, the term "natural resource claim" means any claim for injury to, or destruction or loss of, natural resources. The term does not include any claim for the costs of natural resource damage assessment.

(c) Peripheral matters and limitations

Uses of the Fund under subsection (a) of this section include—

(1) The costs of assessing both short-term and long-term injury to, destruction of, or loss of any natural resources resulting from a release of a hazardous substance.

(2) The costs of Federal or State or Indian tribe efforts in the restoration, rehabilitation, or replacement or acquiring the equivalent of any natural resources injured, destroyed, or lost as a result of a release of a hazardous substance.

(3) Subject to such amounts as are provided in appropriation Acts, the costs of a program to identify, investigate, and take enforcement and abatement action against releases of hazardous substances.

(4) Any costs incurred in accordance with subsection (m) of this section (relating to ATSDR) and section 9604(i) of this title, including the costs of epidemiologic and laboratory studies, health assessments, preparation of toxicologic profiles, development and maintenance of a registry of persons exposed to hazardous substances to allow long-term health effect studies, and diagnostic services not otherwise available to determine whether persons in populations exposed to hazardous substances in connection with a release or a suspected release are suffering from long-latency diseases.

(5) Subject to such amounts as are provided in appropriation Acts, the costs of providing equipment and similar overhead, related to the purposes of this chapter and section 1321 of Title 33, and needed to supplement equipment and services available through contractors or other non-Federal entities, and of establishing and maintaining damage assessment capability, for any Federal agency involved in strike forces, emergency task forces, or other response teams under the national contingency plan.

(6) Subject to such amounts as are provided in appropriation Acts, the costs of a program to protect the health and safety of employees involved in response to hazardous substance releases. Such program shall be developed jointly by the Environmental Protection Agency, the Occupational Safety and Health Administration, and the National Institute for Occupational Safety and Health and shall include, but not be limited to, measures for identifying and assessing hazards to which persons engaged in removal, remedy, or other response to hazardous substances may be exposed, methods to protect workers from such hazards, and necessary regulatory and enforcement measures to assure adequate protection of such employees.

(7) Evaluation costs under petition provisions of section 9605(d)

Costs incurred by the President in evaluating facilities pursuant to petitions under section 9605(d) of this title (relating to petitions for assessment of release).

(8) Contract costs under section 9604(a)(1)

The costs of contracts or arrangements entered into under section 9604(a)(1) of this title to oversee and review the conduct of remedial investigations and feasibility studies undertaken by persons other than the President and the costs of appropriate Federal and State oversight of remedial activities at National Priorities List sites resulting from consent orders or settlement agreements.

(9) Acquisition costs under section 9604(j)

The costs incurred by the President in acquiring real estate or interests in real estate under section 9604(j) of this title (relating to acquisition of property).

(10) Research, development, and demonstration costs under section 9660

The cost of carrying out section 9660 of this title (relating to research, development, and demonstration), except that the amounts available for such purposes shall not exceed the amounts specified in subsection (n) of this section.

(11) Local government reimbursement

Reimbursements to local governments under section 9623 of this title, except that during the 8-fiscal year period beginning October 1, 1986, not more than 0.1 percent of the total amount appropriated from the Fund may be used for such reimbursements.

(12) Worker training and education grants

The costs of grants under section 9660a of this title for training and education of workers to the extent that such costs do not exceed $20,000,000 for each of the fiscal years 1987, 1988, 1989, 1990, 1991, 1992, 1993, and 1994.

(13) Awards under section 9609

The costs of any awards granted under section 9609(d) of this title.

(14) Lead poisoning study

The cost of carrying out the study under subsection (f) of section 118 of the Superfund Amendments and Reauthorization Act of 1986 (relating to lead poisoning in children).

(d) Additional limitations

(1) No money in the Fund may be used under subsection (c)(1) and (2) of this section, nor for the payment of any claim under subsection (b) of this section, where the injury, destruction, or loss of natural resources and the release of a hazardous substance from which such damages resulted have occurred wholly before December 11, 1980.

(2) No money in the Fund may be used for the payment of any claim under subsection (b) of this section where such expenses are associated with injury or loss resulting from long-term exposure to ambient concentrations of air pollutants from multiple or diffuse sources.

(e) Funding requirements respecting moneys in Fund; limitation on certain claims; Fund use outside Federal property boundaries

(1) Claims against or presented to the Fund shall not be valid or paid in excess of the total money in the Fund at any one time. Such claims become valid only when additional money is collected, appropriated, or otherwise added to the Fund. Should the total claims outstanding at any time exceed the current balance of the Fund, the President shall pay such claims, to the extent authorized under this section, in full in the order in which they were finally determined.

(2) In any fiscal year, 85 percent of the money credited to the Fund under subchapter II of this chapter shall be available only for the purposes specified in paragraphs (1), (2), and (4) of subsection (a) of this section. No money in the Fund may be used for the payment of any claim under subsection (a)(3) or subsection (b) of this section in any fiscal year for which the President determines that all of the Fund is needed for response to threats to public health from releases or threatened releases of hazardous substances.

(3) No money in the Fund shall be available for remedial action, other than actions specified in subsection (c) of this section, with respect to federally owned facilities; except that money in the Fund shall be available for the provision of alternative water supplies (including the reimbursement of costs incurred by a municipality) in any case involving groundwater contamination outside the boundaries of a federally owned facility in which the federally owned facility is not the only potentially responsible party.

(4) Paragraphs (1) and (4) of subsection (a) of this section shall in the aggregate be subject to such amounts as are provided in appropriation Acts.

(f) Obligation of moneys by Federal officials; obligation of moneys or settlement of claims by State officials or Indian tribe

The President is authorized to promulgate regulations designating one or more Federal officials who may obligate money in the Fund in accordance with this section or portions thereof. The President is also authorized to delegate authority to obligate money in the Fund or to settle claims to officials of a State or Indian tribe operating under a contract or cooperative agreement with the Federal Government pursuant to section 9604(d) of this title.

(g) Notice to potential injured parties by owner and operator of vessel or facility causing release of substance; rules and regulations

The President shall provide for the promulgation of rules and regulations with respect to the notice to be provided to potential injured parties by an owner and operator of any vessel, or facility from which a hazardous substance has been released. Such rules and regulations shall consider the scope and form of the notice which would be appropriate to carry out the purposes of this subchapter. Upon promulgation of such rules and regulations, the owner and operator of any vessel or facility from which a hazardous substance has been released shall provide notice in accordance with such rules and regulations. With respect to releases from public vessels, the President shall provide such notification as is appropriate to potential injured parties. Until the promulgation of such rules and regulations, the owner and operator of any vessel or facility from which a hazardous substance has been released shall provide reasonable notice to potential injured parties by publication in local newspapers serving the affected area.

(h) Repealed. Pub. L. No. 99–499, Title I, § 111(c)(2), 100 Stat. 1643 (Oct. 17, 1986).

(i) Restoration, etc., of natural resources

Except in a situation requiring action to avoid an irreversible loss of natural resources or to prevent or reduce any continuing danger to natural resources or similar need for emergency action, funds may not be used under this chapter for the restoration, rehabilitation, or replacement or acquisition of the equivalent of any natural resources until a plan for the use of such funds for such purposes has been developed and adopted by affected Federal agencies and the Governor or Governors of any State having sustained damage to natural resources within its borders, belonging to, managed by or appertaining to such State, and by the governing body of any Indian tribe having sustained damage to natural resources belonging to, managed by, controlled by, or appertaining to such tribe, or held in trust for the benefit of such tribe, or belonging to a member of such tribe if such resources are subject to a trust restriction on alienation, after adequate public notice and opportunity for hearing and consideration of all public comment.

(j) Use of Post-closure Liability Fund

The President shall use the money in the Post-closure Liability Fund for any of the purposes specified in subsection (a) of this section with respect to a hazardous waste disposal facility for which liability has transferred to such fund under section 9607(k) of this title, and, in addition, for payment of any claim or appropriate request for costs of response, damages, or other compensation for injury or loss under section 9607 of this title or any other State or Federal law, resulting from a release of a hazardous substance from such a facility.

(k) Inspector General

In each fiscal year, the Inspector General of each department, agency, or instrumentality of the United States which is carrying out any authority of this chapter shall conduct an annual audit of all payments, obligations, reimbursements, or other uses of the Fund in the prior fiscal year, to assure that the Fund is being properly administered and that claims are being appropriately and expeditiously considered. The audit shall include an examination of a sample of agreements with States (in accordance with the provisions of the Single Audit Act [31 U.S.C.A. § 7501 et seq.]) carrying out response actions under this subchapter and an examination of remedial investigations and feasibility studies prepared for remedial actions. The Inspector General shall submit to the Congress an annual report regarding the audit report required under this subsection. The report shall contain such recommendations as the Inspector General deems appropriate. Each department, agency, or instrumentality of the United States shall cooperate with its inspector general in carrying out this subsection.

(*l*) Foreign claimants

To the extent that the provisions of this chapter permit, a foreign claimant may assert a claim to the same extent that a United States claimant may assert a claim if—

(1) the release of a hazardous substance occurred (A) in the navigable waters or (B) in or on the territorial sea or adjacent shoreline of a foreign country of which the claimant is a resident;

(2) the claimant is not otherwise compensated for his loss;

(3) the hazardous substance was released from a facility or from a vessel located adjacent to or within the navigable waters or was discharged in connection with activities conducted under the Outer Continental Shelf Lands Act, as amended (43 U.S.C. 1331 et seq.) or the Deepwater Port Act of 1974, as amended (33 U.S.C. 1501 et seq.); and

(4) recovery is authorized by a treaty or an executive agreement between the United States and foreign country involved, or if the Secretary of State, in consultation with the Attorney General and other appropriate officials, certifies that such country provides a comparable remedy for United States claimants.

(m) Agency for Toxic Substances and Disease Registry

There shall be directly available to the Agency for Toxic Substances and Disease Registry to be used for the purpose of carrying out activities described in subsection (c)(4) of this section and section 9604(i) of this title not less than $50,000,000 per fiscal year for each of fiscal years 1987 and 1988, not less than $55,000,000 for fiscal year 1989, and not less than $60,000,000 per fiscal year for each of fiscal years 1990, 1991, 1992, 1993, and 1994. Any funds so made available which are not obligated by the end of the fiscal year in which made available shall be returned to the Fund.

(n) Limitations on research, development, and demonstration program

(1) Section 9660(b)

For each of the fiscal years 1987, 1988, 1989, 1990, 1991, 1992, 1993, and 1994, not more than $20,000,000 of the amounts available in the Fund may be used for the purposes of carrying out the applied research, development, and demonstration program for alternative or innovative technologies and training program authorized under section 9660(b) of this title (relating to research, development, and demonstration) other than basic research. Such amounts shall remain available until expended.

(2) Section 9660(a)

from the amounts available in the Fund, not more than the following amounts may be used for the purposes of section 9660(a) of this title (relating to hazardous substance research, demonstration, and training activities):

(A) For the fiscal year 1987, $3,000,000.

(B) For the fiscal year 1988, $10,000,000.

(C) For the fiscal year 1989, $20,000,000.

(D) For the fiscal year 1990, $30,000,000.

(E) For each of the fiscal years 1991, 1992, 1993, and 1994, $35,000,000.

No more than 10 percent of such amounts shall be used for training under section 9660(a) of this title in any fiscal year.

(3) Section 9660(d)

For each of the fiscal years 1987, 1988, 1989, 1990, 1991, 1992, 1993, and 1994, not more than $5,000,000 of the amounts available in the Fund may be used for the purposes of section 9660(d) of this title (relating to university hazardous substance research centers).

(*o*) Notification procedures for limitations on certain payments

Not later than 90 days after October 17, 1986, the President shall develop and implement procedures to adequately notify, as soon as practicable after a site is included on the National Priorities List, concerned local and State officials and other concerned persons of the limitations, set forth in subsection (a)(2) of this section, on the payment of claims for necessary response costs incurred with respect to such site.

(p) General revenue share of Superfund

(1) In general

The following sums are authorized to be appropriated, out of any money in the Treasury not otherwise appropriated, to the Hazardous Substance Superfund:

(A) For fiscal year 1987, $212,500,000.

(B) For fiscal year 1988, $212,500,000.

(C) For fiscal year 1989, $212,500,000.

(D) For fiscal year 1990, $212,500,000.

(E) For fiscal year 1991, $212,500,000.

(F) For fiscal year 1992, $212,500,000.

(G) For fiscal year 1993, $212,500,000.

(H) For fiscal year 1994, $212,500,000.

In addition there is authorized to be appropriated to the Hazardous Substance Superfund for each fiscal year an amount equal to so much of the aggregate amount authorized to be appropriated under this subsection (and paragraph (2) of section 9631(b) of this title) as has not been appropriated before the beginning of the fiscal year involved.

(2) Computation

The amounts authorized to be appropriated under paragraph (1) of this subsection in a given fiscal year shall be available only to the extent that such amount exceeds the amount determined by the Secretary under section 9507(b)(2) of Title 26 for the prior fiscal year.

(Pub. L. No. 96–510, Title I, § 111, 94 Stat. 2788 (Dec. 11, 1980); as amended by Pub. L. No. 99–499, Title I, § 111, Title II, § 207(d), 100 Stat. 1642, 1706 (Oct. 17, 1986); Pub. L. No. 101–144, Title III, 103 Stat. 857 (Nov. 9, 1989); Pub. L. No. 101–508, Title VI, § 6301, 104 Stat. 1388–319 (Nov. 5, 1990).)

HISTORICAL AND STATUTORY NOTES

References in Text

Title II of Public Law 99–160, relating to payments to the Hazardous Substances Trust Fund, referred to in subsec. (a) in provisions preceding par. (1), probably means Pub. L. No. 99–160, Title II, § 201, 99 Stat. 914 (Nov. 25, 1985), which in relevant part related to the Hazardous Substance Response Trust Fund. Provisions relating to that Fund were not codified as the Code.

The Intervention on the High Seas Act, referred to in subsec. (a)(1), is Pub. L. No. 93–248, 88 Stat. 8 (Feb. 5, 1974), as amended, which is codified generally as chapter 28 (section 1471 et seq.) of Title 33, Navigation and Navigable Waters. For complete classification of this Act to the Code, see Short Title note set out under section 1471 of Title 33 and Tables.

Section 1321(c) of Title 33, referred to in subsec. (a)(2), was amended generally by Pub. L. No. 101–380, Title IV, § 4201(a), 104 Stat. 523 (Aug. 18, 1990), and no longer contains provisions establishing a National Contingency Plan. However, such provisions are contained in section 1321(d) of Title 33, Navigation and Navigable Waters.

Section 304 of this Act, referred to in subsec. (b), is section 304 of Pub. L. No. 96–510, Title III, 94 Stat. 2809 (Dec. 11, 1980), which enacted section 9654 of this title and amended section 1364 of Title 33.

Fishery conservation zone, referred to in subsec. (b), probably means the fishery conservation zone established by section 1811 of Title 16, Conservation, which as amended generally by Pub. L. No. 99–659, Title I,

§ 101(b), 100 Stat. 3706 (Nov. 14, 1986), relates to United States sovereign rights and fishery management authority over fish within the exclusive economic zone as defined in section 1802 of Title 16.

Subsection (f) of section 118 of the Superfund Amendments and Reauthorization Act of 1986, referred to in subsec. (c)(14), is section 118(f) of Pub. L. No. 99–499, Title I, 100 Stat. 1657 (Oct. 17, 1986), which is not codified into the Code.

Subchapter II of this chapter, referred to in subsec. (e)(2), was in the original, "Title II of this Act", meaning Title II of Pub. L. No. 96–510, 94 Stat. 2796 (Dec. 11, 1980), known as the Hazardous Substance Response Revenue Act of 1980, which enacted subchapter II of this chapter and sections 4611, 4612, 4661, 4662, and former sections 4681, and 4682 of Title 26, Internal Revenue Code. Sections 221 to 223 and 232 of Pub. L. No. 96–510, which were codified as sections 9631 to 9633 and 9641 of this title, comprising subchapter II of this chapter, were repealed by Pub. L. No. 99–499, Title V, §§ 514(b), 517(c)(1), 100 Stat. 1767, 1774 (Oct. 17, 1986). For complete classification of Title II to the Code, see Short Title of 1980 Amendments note set out under section 1 of Title 26 and Tables.

The Single Audit Act, referred to in subsec. (k), probably means Pub. L. No. 98–502, 98 Stat. 2327 (Oct. 19, 1984), known as the Single Audit Act of 1984, which is codified as chapter 75 (section 7501 et seq.) of Title 31, Money and Finance. For complete classification of this Act to the Code, see Short Title note set out under section 7501 of Title 31 and Tables.

The Outer Continental Shelf Lands Act, as amended, referred to in subsec. (*l*)(3), is Act of Aug. 7, 1953, c. 345, 67 Stat. 462, as amended, which is codified generally as subchapter III (section 1331 et seq.) of chapter 29 of Title 43, Public Lands. For complete classification of this Act to the Code, see Short Title note set out under section 1301 of Title 43 and Tables.

The Deepwater Port Act of 1974, as amended, referred to in subsec. (*l*)(3), is Pub. L. No. 93–627, 88 Stat. 2126 (Jan. 3, 1975), as amended, which is codified generally as chapter 29 (section 1501 et seq.) of Title 33, Navigation and Navigable Waters. For complete classification of this Act to the Code, see Short Title note set out under section 1501 of Title 33 and Tables.

Section 9631(b) of this title, referred to in subsec. (p)(1), was repealed by Pub. L. No. 99–499, Title V, § 517(c)(1), 100 Stat. 1774 (Oct. 17, 1986).

Effective and Applicability Provisions

1986 Acts. Amendment by Pub. L. No. 99–499 effective Oct. 17, 1986, see section 4 of Pub. L. No. 99–499, set out as a note under section 9601 of this title.

Termination of Reporting Requirements

For termination, effective May 15, 2000, of provisions in subsec. (k) of this section relating to the requirement that the Inspector General submit an annual report to Congress on the audit report required under subsec. (k), see Pub. L. No. 104–66, § 3003, as amended, set out as a note under 31 U.S.C.A. § 1113, and the 7th item on page 151 of House Document No. 103–7.

Delegation of Functions

Functions vested in the President by subsec. (g) of this section delegated to the Secretaries of Defense and Energy with respect to releases m facilities or vessels under the jurisdiction, custody or control of their departments, respectively, including vessels bare-boat chartered and operated, see section 8(b) of Ex. Ord. No. 12580, 52 Fed. Reg. 2923 (Jan. 23, 1987), set out as a note under section 9615 of this title.

Functions vested in the President by subsec. (g) of this section delegated, subject to section 8(b) of Ex. Ord. No. 12580, and with authority to redelegate, to the Administrator of the Environmental Protection Agency, see sections 8(c), 11(g) of Ex. Ord. No. 12580, 52 Fed. Reg. 2923 (Jan. 23, 1987), set out as a note under section 9615 of this title.

Functions vested in the President by subsec. (a) of this section delegated, subject to the provisions of section 9 of Ex. Ord. No. 12580, 52 Fed. Reg. 2923 (Jan. 23, 1987), and other applicable provisions of Ex. Ord. No. 12580, see section 9(a) of Ex. Ord. No. 12580, set out as a note under section 9615 of this title.

The Administrator of the Environmental Protection Agency and each department and agency head to whom funds are provided pursuant to section 9 of Ex. Ord. No. 12580, with respect to funds provided to them, authorized in accordance with subsec. (f) of this section to designate Federal officials who may obligate such funds, see section 9(d) of Ex. Ord. No. 12580, 52 Fed. Reg. 2923 (Jan. 23, 1987), set out as a note under section 9615 of this title.

Functions vested in the President by section 9612 of this title delegated to the Administrator of the Environmental Protection Agency for all claims presented pursuant to this section, see section 9(e) of Ex. Ord. No. 12580, Jan. 23, 1987, 52 FED. REG. 2923, set out as a note under section 9615 of this title.

Functions vested in the President by subsec. (*o*) of this section delegated to the Administrator of the Environmental Protection Agency, see section 9(f) of Ex. Ord. No. 12580, 52 Fed. Reg. 2923 (Jan. 23, 1987), set out as a note under section 9615 of this title.

Satisfaction of Superfund Audit Requirements by Inspector General of the Department of Defense

Pub. L. No. 108–375, Div. A, Title III, § 311, 118 Stat. 1842 (Oct. 28, 2004), provided that:

"(a) Satisfaction of requirements.—The Inspector General of the Department of Defense shall be deemed to be in compliance with the requirements of section 111(k) of the Comprehensive Environmental Response, Compensation, and Liability Act of 1980 (42 U.S.C. 9611(k) [subsec. k of this section]) if the Inspector General conducts periodic audits of the payments, obligations, reimbursements, and other uses of the Hazardous Substance Superfund by the Department of Defense, even if such audits do not occur on an annual basis.

"(b) Reports to Congress on audits.—The Inspector General shall submit to Congress a report on each audit conducted by the Inspector General as described in subsection (a) [of this note]."

Coordination of Titles I to IV of Pub. L. No. 99–499

Any provision of Titles I to IV of Pub. L. No. 99–499, imposing any tax, premium, or fee; establishing any trust fund; or authorizing expenditures m any trust fund, shall have no force or effect. See section 531 of Pub. L. No. 99–499, set out as a note under section 1 of Title 26, Internal Revenue Code.

Designation of Federal Trustees for National Resources

For designation by the President of the Secretaries of Defense, Interior, Agriculture, and Commerce, as among those to be designated in the national contingency plan as Federal trustees for natural resources, see section 1(d) of Ex. Ord. No. 12316, 46 Fed. Reg. 42237 (Aug. 14, 1981), which was set out as a note under section 9615 of this title, prior to its repeal by section 11(h) of Ex. Ord. No. 12580, 52 Fed. Reg. 2923 (Jan. 23, 1987).

§ 9612. Claims procedure

[CERCLA § 112]

(a) Claims against Fund for response costs

No claim may be asserted against the Fund pursuant to section 9611(a) of this title unless such claim is presented in the first instance to the owner, operator, or guarantor of the vessel or facility m which a hazardous substance has been released, if known to the claimant, and to any other person known to the claimant who may be liable under section 9607 of this title. In any case where the claim has not been satisfied within 60 days of presentation in accordance with this subsection, the claimant may present the claim to the Fund for payment. No claim against the Fund may be approved or certified during the pendency of an action by the claimant in court to recover costs which are the subject of the claim.

(b) Forms and procedures applicable

(1) Prescribing forms and procedures

The President shall prescribe appropriate forms and procedures for claims filed hereunder, which shall include a provision requiring the claimant to make a sworn verification of the claim to the best of his knowledge. Any person who knowingly gives or causes to be given any false information as a part of any such claim shall, upon conviction, be fined in accordance with the applicable provisions of Title 18 or imprisoned for not more than 3 years (or not more than 5 years in the case of a second or subsequent conviction), or both.

(2) Payment or request for hearing

The President may, if satisfied that the information developed during the processing of the claim warrants it, make and pay an award of the claim, except that no claim may be awarded to the extent that a judicial judgment has been made on the costs that are the subject of the claim. If the President declines to pay all or part of the claim, the claimant may, within 30 days after receiving notice of the President's decision, request an administrative hearing.

(3) Burden of proof

In any proceeding under this subsection, the claimant shall bear the burden of proving his claim.

(4) Decisions

All administrative decisions made hereunder shall be in writing, with notification to all appropriate parties, and shall be rendered within 90 days of submission of a claim to an administrative law judge, unless all the parties to the claim agree in writing to an extension or unless the President, in his discretion, extends the time limit for a period not to exceed sixty days.

(5) Finality and appeal

All administrative decisions hereunder shall be final, and any party to the proceeding may appeal a decision within 30 days of notification of the award or decision. Any such appeal shall be made to the Federal district court for the district where the release or threat of release took place. In any such appeal, the decision shall be considered binding and conclusive, and shall not be overturned except for arbitrary or capricious abuse of discretion.

(6) Payment

Within 20 days after the expiration of the appeal period for any administrative decision concerning an award, or within 20 days after the final judicial determination of any appeal taken pursuant to this subsection, the President shall pay any such award m the Fund. The President shall determine the method, terms, and time of payment.

(c) Subrogation rights; actions maintainable

(1) Payment of any claim by the Fund under this section shall be subject to the United States Government acquiring by subrogation the rights of the claimant to recover those costs of removal or damages for which it has compensated the claimant m the person responsible or liable for such release.

(2) Any person, including the Fund, who pays compensation pursuant to this chapter to any claimant for damages or costs resulting m a release of a hazardous substance shall be subrogated to all rights, claims, and causes of action for such damages and costs of removal that the claimant has under this chapter or any other law.

(3) Upon request of the President, the Attorney General shall commence an action on behalf of the Fund to recover any compensation paid by the Fund to any claimant pursuant to this subchapter, and, without regard to any limitation of liability, all interest, administrative and adjudicative costs, and attorney's fees incurred by the Fund by reason of the claim. Such an action may be commenced against any owner, operator, or guarantor, or against any other person who is liable, pursuant to any law, to the compensated claimant or to the Fund, for the damages or costs for which compensation was paid.

(d) Statute of limitations

(1) Claims for recovery of costs

No claim may be presented under this section for recovery of the costs referred to in section 9607(a) of this title after the date 6 years after the date of completion of all response action.

(2) Claims for recovery of damages

No claim may be presented under this section for recovery of the damages referred to in section 9607(a) of this title unless the claim is presented within 3 years after the later of the following:

(A) The date of the discovery of the loss and its connection with the release in question.

(B) The date on which final regulations are promulgated under section 9651(c) of this title.

(3) Minors and incompetents

The time limitations contained herein shall not begin to run—

(A) against a minor until the earlier of the date when such minor reaches 18 years of age or the date on which a legal representative is duly appointed for the minor, or

(B) against an incompetent person until the earlier of the date on which such person's incompetency ends or the date on which a legal representative is duly appointed for such incompetent person.

(e) Other statutory or common law claims not waived, etc.

Regardless of any State statutory or common law to the contrary, no person who asserts a claim against the Fund pursuant to this subchapter shall be deemed or held to have waived any other claim not covered or assertable against the Fund under this subchapter arising m the same incident, transaction, or set of circumstances, nor to have split a cause of action. Further, no person asserting a claim against the Fund pursuant to this subchapter shall as a result of any determination of a question of fact or law made in connection with that claim be deemed or held to be collaterally estopped m raising such question in connection with any other claim not covered or assertable against the Fund under this subchapter arising m the same incident, transaction, or set of circumstances.

(f) Double recovery prohibited

Where the President has paid out of the Fund for any response costs or any costs specified under section 9611(c)(1) or (2) of this title, no other claim may be paid out of the Fund for the same costs.

(Pub. L. No. 96–510, Title I, § 112, 94 Stat. 2792 (Dec. 11, 1980); as amended by Pub. L. No. 99–499, Title I, §§ 109(a)(3), 112, 100 Stat. 1633, 1646 (Oct. 17, 1986).)

HISTORICAL AND STATUTORY NOTES

Effective and Applicability Provisions

1986 Acts. Amendment by Pub. L. No. 99–499 effective Oct. 17, 1986, see section 4 of Pub. L. No. 99–499, set out as a note under section 9601 of this title.

Delegation of Functions

Representation of any government agency pursuant to or under Ex. Ord. No. 12580 in any judicial proceeding to be by or through the Attorney General, with the conduct and control of all litigation arising under the provisions of this chapter to be the responsibility of the Attorney General, see section 6(a) of Ex. Ord. No. 12580, 52 Fed. Reg. 2923 (Jan. 23, 1987), set out as a note under section 9615 of this title.

Authority under the provisions of this chapter to require the Attorney General to commence litigation retained by the President, notwithstanding any other provision of Ex. Ord. No. 12580, see section 6(b) of Ex. Ord. No. 12580, 52 Fed. Reg. 2923 (Jan. 23, 1987), set out as a note under section 9615 of this title.

Functions vested in the President by this section delegated to the Administrator of the Environmental Protection Agency for all claims presented pursuant to section 9611 of this title, see section 9(e) of Ex. Ord. No. 12580, 52 Fed. Reg. 2923 (Jan. 23, 1987), set out as a note under section 9615 of this title.

Coordination of Titles I to IV of Pub. L. No. 99–499

Any provision of Titles I to IV of Pub. L. No. 99–499, imposing any tax, premium, or fee; establishing any trust fund; or authorizing expenditures m any trust fund, shall have no force or effect. See section 531 of Pub. L. No. 99–499, set out as a note under section 1 of Title 26, Internal Revenue Code.

§ 9613. Civil proceedings

[CERCLA § 113]

(a) Review of regulations in Circuit Court of Appeals of the United States for the District of Columbia

Review of any regulation promulgated under this chapter may be had upon application by any interested person only in the Circuit Court of Appeals of the United States for the District of Columbia. Any such application shall be made within ninety days m the date of promulgation of such regulations. Any matter with respect to which review could have been obtained under this subsection shall not be subject to judicial review in any civil or criminal proceeding for enforcement or to obtain damages or recovery of response costs.

(b) Jurisdiction; venue

Except as provided in subsections (a) and (h) of this section, the United States district courts shall have exclusive original jurisdiction over all controversies arising under this chapter, without regard to the citizenship of the parties or the amount in controversy. Venue shall lie in any district in which the release or damages occurred, or in which the defendant resides, may be found, or has his principal office. For the purposes of this section, the Fund shall reside in the District of Columbia.

(c) Controversies or other matters resulting m tax collection or tax regulation review

The provisions of subsections (a) and (b) of this section shall not apply to any controversy or other matter resulting m the assessment of collection of any tax, as provided by subchapter II of this chapter, or to the review of any regulation promulgated under Title 26.

(d) Litigation commenced prior to December 11, 1980

No provision of this chapter shall be deemed or held to moot any litigation concerning any release of any hazardous substance, or any damages associated therewith, commenced prior to December 11, 1980.

(e) Nationwide service of process

In any action by the United States under this chapter, process may be served in any district where the defendant is found, resides, transacts business, or has appointed an agent for the service of process.

(f) Contribution

(1) Contribution

Any person may seek contribution m any other person who is liable or potentially liable under section 9607(a) of this title, during or following any civil action under section 9606 of this title or under section 9607(a) of this title. Such claims shall be brought in accordance with this section and the Federal Rules of Civil Procedure, and shall be governed by Federal law. In resolving contribution claims, the court may allocate response costs among liable parties using such equitable factors as the court determines are appropriate. Nothing in this subsection shall diminish the right of any person to bring an action for contribution in the absence of a civil action under section 9606 of this title or section 9607 of this title.

(2) Settlement

A person who has resolved its liability to the United States or a State in an administrative or judicially approved settlement shall not be liable for claims for contribution regarding matters addressed in the settlement. Such settlement does not discharge any of the other potentially liable persons unless its terms so provide, but it reduces the potential liability of the others by the amount of the settlement.

(3) Persons not party to settlement

(A) If the United States or a State has obtained less than complete relief m a person who has resolved its liability to the United States or the State in an administrative or judicially approved settlement, the United States or the State may bring an action against any person who has not so resolved its liability.

(B) A person who has resolved its liability to the United States or a State for some or all of a response action or for some or all of the costs of such action in an administrative or judicially approved settlement may seek contribution m any person who is not party to a settlement referred to in paragraph (2).

(C) In any action under this paragraph, the rights of any person who has resolved its liability to the United States or a State shall be subordinate to the rights of the United States or the State. Any contribution action brought under this paragraph shall be governed by Federal law.

(g) Period in which action may be brought

(1) Actions for natural resource damages

Except as provided in paragraphs (3) and (4), no action may be commenced for damages (as defined in section 9601(6) of this title) under this chapter, unless that action is commenced within 3 years after the later of the following:

(A) The date of the discovery of the loss and its connection with the release in question.

(B) The date on which regulations are promulgated under section 9651(c) of this title.

With respect to any facility listed on the National Priorities List (NPL), any Federal facility identified under section 9620 of this title (relating to Federal facilities), or any vessel or facility at which a remedial action under this chapter is otherwise scheduled, an action for damages under this chapter must be commenced within 3 years after the completion of the remedial action (excluding operation and maintenance activities) in lieu of the dates referred to in subparagraph (A) or (B). In no event may an action for damages under this chapter with respect to such a vessel or facility be commenced (i) prior to 60 days after the Federal or State natural resource trustee provides to the President and the potentially responsible party a notice of intent to file suit, or (ii) before selection of the remedial action if the President is diligently proceeding with a remedial investigation and feasibility study under section 9604(b) of this title or section 9620 of this title (relating to Federal facilities). The limitation in the preceding sentence on commencing an action before giving notice or before selection of the remedial action does not apply to actions filed on or before October 17, 1986.

(2) Actions for recovery of costs

An initial action for recovery of the costs referred to in section 9607 of this title must be commenced—

(A) for a removal action, within 3 years after completion of the removal action, except that such cost recovery action must be brought within 6 years after a determination to grant a waiver under section 9604(c)(1)(C) of this title for continued response action; and

(B) for a remedial action, within 6 years after initiation of physical on-site construction of the remedial action, except that, if the remedial action is initiated within 3 years after the completion of the removal action, costs incurred in the removal action may be recovered in the cost recovery action brought under this subparagraph.

In any such action described in this subsection, the court shall enter a declaratory judgment on liability for response costs or damages that will be binding on any subsequent action or actions to recover further response costs or damages. A subsequent action or actions under section 9607 of this title for further response costs at the vessel or facility may be maintained at any time during the response action, but must be commenced no later than 3 years after the date of completion of all response action. Except as otherwise provided in this paragraph, an action may be commenced under section 9607 of this title for recovery of costs at any time after such costs have been incurred.

(3) Contribution

No action for contribution for any response costs or damages may be commenced more than 3 years after—

(A) the date of judgment in any action under this chapter for recovery of such costs or damages, or

(B) the date of an administrative order under section 9622(g) of this title (relating to de minimis settlements) or 9622(h) of this title (relating to cost recovery settlements) or entry of a judicially approved settlement with respect to such costs or damages.

(4) Subrogation

No action based on rights subrogated pursuant to this section by reason of payment of a claim may be commenced under this subchapter more than 3 years after the date of payment of such claim.

(5) Actions to recover indemnification payments

Notwithstanding any other provision of this subsection, where a payment pursuant to an indemnification agreement with a response action contractor is made under section 9619 of this title, an action under section 9607 of this title for recovery of such indemnification payment m a potentially responsible party may be brought at any time before the expiration of 3 years m the date on which such payment is made.

(6) Minors and incompetents

The time limitations contained herein shall not begin to run—

(A) against a minor until the earlier of the date when such minor reaches 18 years of age or the date on which a legal representative is duly appointed for such minor, or

(B) against an incompetent person until the earlier of the date on which such incompetent's incompetency ends or the date on which a legal representative is duly appointed for such incompetent.

(h) Timing of review

No Federal court shall have jurisdiction under Federal law other than under section 1332 of Title 28 (relating to diversity of citizenship jurisdiction) or under State law which is applicable or relevant and appropriate under section 9621 of this title (relating to cleanup standards) to review any challenges to removal or remedial action selected under section 9604 of this title, or to review any order issued under section 9606(a) of this title, in any action except one of the following:

(1) An action under section 9607 of this title to recover response costs or damages or for contribution.

(2) An action to enforce an order issued under section 9606(a) of this title or to recover a penalty for violation of such order.

(3) An action for reimbursement under section 9606(b)(2) of this title.

(4) An action under section 9659 of this title (relating to citizens suits) alleging that the removal or remedial action taken under section 9604 of this title or secured under section 9606 of this title was in violation of any requirement of this chapter. Such an action may not be brought with regard to a removal where a remedial action is to be undertaken at the site.

(5) An action under section 9606 of this title in which the United States has moved to compel a remedial action.

(i) Intervention

In any action commenced under this chapter or under the Solid Waste Disposal Act [42 U.S.C.A. § 6901 et seq.] in a court of the United States, any person may intervene as a matter of right when such person claims an interest relating to the subject of the action and is so situated that the disposition of the action may, as a practical matter, impair or impede the person's ability to protect that interest, unless the President or the State shows that the person's interest is adequately represented by existing parties.

(j) Judicial review

(1) Limitation

In any judicial action under this chapter, judicial review of any issues concerning the adequacy of any response action taken or ordered by the President shall be limited to the administrative record. Otherwise applicable principles of administrative law shall govern whether any supplemental materials may be considered by the court.

(2) Standard

In considering objections raised in any judicial action under this chapter, the court shall uphold the President's decision in selecting the response action unless the objecting party can demonstrate, on the administrative record, that the decision was arbitrary and capricious or otherwise not in accordance with law.

(3) Remedy

If the court finds that the selection of the response action was arbitrary and capricious or otherwise not in accordance with law, the court shall award (A) only the response costs or damages that are not inconsistent with the national contingency plan, and (B) such other relief as is consistent with the National Contingency Plan.

(4) Procedural errors

In reviewing alleged procedural errors, the court may disallow costs or damages only if the errors were so serious and related to matters of such central relevance to the action that the action would have been significantly changed had such errors not been made.

(k) Administrative record and participation procedures

(1) Administrative record

The President shall establish an administrative record upon which the President shall base the selection of a response action. The administrative record shall be available to the public at or near the facility at issue. The President also may place duplicates of the administrative record at any other location.

(2) Participation procedures

(A) Removal action

The President shall promulgate regulations in accordance with chapter 5 of Title 5 establishing procedures for the appropriate participation of interested persons in the development of the administrative record on which the President will base the selection of removal actions and on which judicial review of removal actions will be based.

(B) Remedial action

The President shall provide for the participation of interested persons, including potentially responsible parties, in the development of the administrative record on which the President will base the selection of remedial actions and on which judicial review of remedial actions will be based. The procedures developed under this subparagraph shall include, at a minimum, each of the following:

(i) Notice to potentially affected persons and the public, which shall be accompanied by a brief analysis of the plan and alternative plans that were considered.

(ii) A reasonable opportunity to comment and provide information regarding the plan.

(iii) An opportunity for a public meeting in the affected area, in accordance with section 9617(a)(2) of this title (relating to public participation).

(iv) A response to each of the significant comments, criticisms, and new data submitted in written or oral presentations.

(v) A statement of the basis and purpose of the selected action.

For purposes of this subparagraph, the administrative record shall include all items developed and received under this subparagraph and all items described in the second sentence of section 9617(d) of this title. The President shall promulgate regulations in accordance with chapter 5 of Title 5 to carry out the requirements of this subparagraph.

(C) Interim record

Until such regulations under subparagraphs (A) and (B) are promulgated, the administrative record shall consist of all items developed and received pursuant to current procedures for selection of the response action, including procedures for the participation of interested parties and the public. The development of an administrative record and the selection of response action under this chapter shall not include an adjudicatory hearing.

(D) Potentially responsible parties

The President shall make reasonable efforts to identify and notify potentially responsible parties as early as possible before selection of a response action. Nothing in this paragraph shall be construed to be a defense to liability.

(*l*) Notice of actions

Whenever any action is brought under this chapter in a court of the United States by a plaintiff other than the United States, the plaintiff shall provide a copy of the complaint to the Attorney General of the United States and to the Administrator of the Environmental Protection Agency.

(Pub. L. No. 96–510, Title I, § 113, 94 Stat. 2795 (Dec. 11, 1980); as amended by Pub. L. No. 99–499, Title I, § 113, 100 Stat. 1647 (Oct. 17, 1986); Pub. L. No. 99–514, § 2, 100 Stat. 2095 (Oct. 22, 1986).)

HISTORICAL AND STATUTORY NOTES

References in Text

Subchapter II of this chapter, referred to in subsec. (c), was in the original, "Title II of this Act", meaning Title II of Pub. L. No. 96–510, 94 Stat. 2796 (Dec. 11, 1980), known as the Hazardous Substance Response Revenue Act of 1980, which enacted subchapter II of this chapter and sections 4611, 4612, 4661, 4662, and former sections 4681 and 4682 of Title 26, Internal Revenue Code. Sections 221 to 223 and 232 of Pub. L. No. 96–510, which were codified as sections 9631 to 9633 and 9641 of this title, comprising subchapter II of this chapter, were repealed by Pub. L. No. 99–499, Title V, §§ 514(b), 517(c)(1), 100 Stat. 1767, 1774 (Oct. 17, 1986). For complete classification of Title II to the Code, see Short Title of 1980 Amendments note set out under section 1 of Title 26 and Tables.

The Federal Rules of Civil Procedure, referred to in subsec. (f)(1), are set out in the Appendix to Title 28, Judiciary and Judicial Procedure.

The Solid Waste Disposal Act, referred to in subsec. (i), is Title II of Pub. L. No. 89–272, 79 Stat. 997 (Oct. 20, 1965), as amended generally by Pub. L. No. 94–580, § 2, 90 Stat. 2795 (Oct. 21, 1976), which is codified generally as chapter 82 (section 6901 et seq.) of this Title. For complete classification of this Act to the Code, see Short Title of 1965 Acts note set out under section 6901 of this title and Tables.

Effective and Applicability Provisions

1986 Acts. Amendment by Pub. L. No. 99–499 effective Oct. 17, 1986, see section 4 of Pub. L. No. 99–499, set out as a note under section 9601 of this title.

Delegation of Functions

Functions vested in the President by subsec. (k)(2) of this section, relating to the promulgation of regulations and guidelines, delegated to the Administrator of the Environmental Protection Agency, to be exercised in consultation with the National Response Team, see section 2(b) of Ex. Ord. No. 12580, 52 Fed. Reg. 2923 (Jan. 23, 1987), set out as a note under section 9615 of this title.

Functions vested in the President by subsec. (k) of this section delegated, with authority to redelegate, (and subject to section 2(a), (b) and (c) of Ex. Ord. No. 12580) to the Secretaries of Defense and Energy, with respect to releases or threatened releases where either the release is on or the sole source of the release is m any facility or vessel under the jurisdiction, custody or control of their departments, respectively, including vessels bare-boat chartered and operated, with such functions to be exercised consistent with the requirements of section 9620 of this title, see sections 2(d), 11(g) of Ex. Ord. No. 12580, 52 Fed. Reg. 2923 (Jan. 23, 1987), set out as a note under section 9615 of this title.

Functions vested in the President by subsec. (k) of this section, subject to section 2(b) to (d) of Ex. Ord. No. 12580, delegated, with authority to redelegate, to the heads of Executive departments and agencies, with respect to releases or threatened releases where either the release is on or the sole source of the release is m any facility or vessel under the jurisdiction, custody or control of those departments and agencies, including vessels bare-boat chartered and operated, see sections 2(e)(2), 11(g) of Ex. Ord. No. 12580, 52 Fed. Reg. 2923 (Jan. 23, 1987), set out as a note under section 9615 of this title.

Functions vested in the President by subsec. (k) of this section, subject to section 2(a) to (e) of Ex. Ord. No. 12580, delegated, with authority to redelegate, to the Secretary of the Department in which the Coast Guard is operating ("the Coast Guard"), with respect to any release or threatened release involving the coastal zone, Great

Lakes waters, ports, and harbors, see sections 2(f), 11(g) of Ex. Ord. No. 12580, 52 Fed. Reg. 2923 (Jan. 23, 1987), set out as a note under section 9615 of this title.

Functions vested in the President by subsec. (k) of this section, subject to section 2(a) to (f) of Ex. Ord. No. 12580, delegated, with authority to redelegate, to the Administrator of the Environmental Protection Agency, see sections 2(g), 11(g) of Ex. Ord. No. 12580, 52 Fed. Reg. 2923 (Jan. 23, 1987), set out as a note under section 9615 of this title.

Representation of any government agency pursuant to or under Ex. Ord. No. 12580 in any judicial proceeding to be by or through the Attorney General, with the conduct and control of all litigation arising under the provisions of this chapter to be the responsibility of the Attorney General, see section 6(a) of Ex. Ord. No. 12580, 52 Fed. Reg. 2923 (Jan. 23, 1987), set out as a note under section 9615 of this title.

Functions vested in the President by subsec. (g) of this section, to receive notification of a natural resource trustee's intent to file suit, delegated to the heads of Executive departments and agencies with respect to response actions for which they have been delegated authority under section 2 of Ex. Ord. No. 12580, with the Administrator of the Environmental Protection Agency to promulgate procedural regulations for providing such notification, see section 6(c) of Ex. Ord. No. 12580, 52 Fed. Reg. 2923 (Jan. 23, 1987), set out as a note under section 9615 of this title.

§ 9614. Relationship to other law

[CERCLA § 114]

(a) Additional State liability or requirements with respect to release of substances within State

Nothing in this chapter shall be construed or interpreted as preempting any State m imposing any additional liability or requirements with respect to the release of hazardous substances within such State.

(b) Recovery under other State or Federal law of compensation for removal costs or damages, or payment of claims

Any person who receives compensation for removal costs or damages or claims pursuant to this chapter shall be precluded m recovering compensation for the same removal costs or damages or claims pursuant to any other State or Federal law. Any person who receives compensation for removal costs or damages or claims pursuant to any other Federal or State law shall be precluded m receiving compensation for the same removal costs or damages or claims as provided in this chapter.

(c) Recycled oil

(1) Service station dealers, etc.

No person (including the United States or any State) may recover, under the authority of subsection (a)(3) or (a)(4) of section 9607 of this title, m a service station dealer for any response costs or damages resulting m a release or threatened release of recycled oil, or use the authority of section 9606 of this title against a service station dealer other than a person described in subsection (a)(1) or (a)(2) of section 9607 of this title, if such recycled oil—

(A) is not mixed with any other hazardous substance, and

(B) is stored, treated, transported, or otherwise managed in compliance with regulations or standards promulgated pursuant to section 3014 of the Solid Waste Disposal Act [42 U.S.C.A. § 6935] and other applicable authorities.

Nothing in this paragraph shall affect or modify in any way the obligations or liability of any person under any other provision of State or Federal law, including common law, for damages, injury, or loss resulting m a release or threatened release of any hazardous substance or for removal or remedial action or the costs of removal or remedial action.

(2) Presumption

Solely for the purposes of this subsection, a service station dealer may presume that a small quantity of used oil is not mixed with other hazardous substances if it—

(A) has been removed m the engine of a light duty motor vehicle or household appliances by the owner of such vehicle or appliances, and

(B) is presented, by such owner, to the dealer for collection, accumulation, and delivery to an oil recycling facility.

(3) Definition

For purposes of this subsection, the terms "used oil" and "recycled oil" have the same meanings as set forth in sections 1004(36) and 1004(37) of the Solid Waste Disposal Act [42 U.S.C.A. § 6903(36), (37)] and regulations promulgated pursuant to that Act [42 U.S.C.A. § 6901 et seq.].

(4) Effective date

The effective date of paragraphs (1) and (2) of this subsection shall be the effective date of regulations or standards promulgated under section 3014 of the Solid Waste Disposal Act [42 U.S.C.A. § 6935] that include, among other provisions, a requirement to conduct corrective action to respond to any releases of recycled oil under subtitle C or subtitle I of such Act [42 U.S.C.A. § 6921 et seq., 6991 et seq.].

(d) Financial responsibility of owner or operator of vessel or facility under State or local law, rule, or regulation

Except as provided in this subchapter, no owner or operator of a vessel or facility who establishes and maintains evidence of financial responsibility in accordance with this subchapter shall be required under any State or local law, rule, or regulation to establish or maintain any other evidence of financial responsibility in connection with liability for the release of a hazardous substance m such vessel or facility. Evidence of compliance with the financial responsibility requirements of this subchapter shall be accepted by a State in lieu of any other requirement of financial responsibility imposed by such State in connection with liability for the release of a hazardous substance m such vessel or facility.

(Pub. L. No. 96–510, Title I, § 114, 94 Stat. 2795 (Dec. 11, 1980); as amended by Pub. L. No. 99–499, Title I, § 114(a), 100 Stat. 1652 (Oct. 17, 1986).)

HISTORICAL AND STATUTORY NOTES

References in Text

The Solid Waste Disposal Act and that Act, referred to in subsec. (c)(3), (4), is Title II of Pub. L. No. 89–272, 79 Stat. 997 (Oct. 20, 1965), as amended generally by Pub. L. No. 94–580, § 2, 90 Stat. 2795 (Oct. 21, 1976), which is codified generally as chapter 82 (section 6901 et seq.) of this Title. Subtitle C of the Solid Waste Disposal Act is codified generally as subchapter III (section 6921 et seq.) of chapter 82 of this title. Subtitle I of that Act is codified generally as subchapter IX (section 6991 et seq.) of that chapter. For complete classification of this Act to the Code, see Short Title of 1965 Acts note set out under section 6901 of this title and Tables.

Effective and Applicability Provisions

1986 Acts. Amendment by Pub. L. No. 99–499 effective Oct. 17, 1986, see section 4 of Pub. L. No. 99–499, set out as a note under section 9601 of this title.

§ 9615. Presidential delegation and assignment of duties or powers and promulgation of regulations

[CERCLA § 115]

The President is authorized to delegate and assign any duties or powers imposed upon or assigned to him and to promulgate any regulations necessary to carry out the provisions of this subchapter.

(Pub. L. No. 96–510, Title I, § 115, 94 Stat. 2796 (Dec. 11, 1980).)

§ 9616. Schedules

[CERCLA § 116]

(a) Assessment and listing of facilities

It shall be a goal of this chapter that, to the maximum extent practicable—

(1) not later than January 1, 1988, the President shall complete preliminary assessments of all facilities that are contained (as of October 17, 1986) on the Comprehensive Environmental Response, Compensation, and Liability Information System (CERCLIS) including in each assessment a statement as to whether a site inspection is necessary and by whom it should be carried out; and

(2) not later than January 1, 1989, the President shall assure the completion of site inspections at all facilities for which the President has stated a site inspection is necessary pursuant to paragraph (1).

(b) Evaluation

Within 4 years after October 17, 1986, each facility listed (as of October 17, 1986) in the CERCLIS shall be evaluated if the President determines that such evaluation is warranted on the basis of a site inspection or preliminary assessment. The evaluation shall be in accordance with the criteria established in section 9605 of this title under the National Contingency Plan for determining priorities among release for inclusion on the National Priorities List. In the case of a facility listed in the CERCLIS after October 17, 1986, the facility shall be evaluated within 4 years after the date of such listing if the President determines that such evaluation is warranted on the basis of a site inspection or preliminary assessment.

(c) Explanations

If any of the goals established by subsection (a) or (b) of this section are not achieved, the President shall publish an explanation of why such action could not be completed by the specified date.

(d) Commencement of RI/FS

The President shall assure that remedial investigations and feasibility studies (RI/FS) are commenced for facilities listed on the National Priorities List, in addition to those commenced prior to October 17, 1986, in accordance with the following schedule:

(1) not fewer than 275 by the date 36 months after October 17, 1986, and

(2) if the requirement of paragraph (1) is not met, not fewer than an additional 175 by the date 4 years after October 17, 1986, an additional 200 by the date 5 years after October 17, 1986, and a total of 650 by the date 5 years after October 17, 1986.

(e) Commencement of remedial action

The President shall assure that substantial and continuous physical on-site remedial action commences at facilities on the National Priorities List, in addition to those facilities on which remedial action has commenced prior to October 17, 1986, at a rate not fewer than:

(1) 175 facilities during the first 36-month period after October 17, 1986; and

(2) 200 additional facilities during the following 24 months after such 36-month period.

(Pub. L. No. 96–510, Title I, § 116, as added by Pub. L. No. 99–499, Title I, § 116, 100 Stat. 1653 (Oct. 17, 1986).)

HISTORICAL AND STATUTORY NOTES

Effective and Applicability Provisions

1986 Acts. Section effective Oct. 17, 1986, see section 4 of Pub. L. No. 99–499, set out as a note under section 9601 of this title.

Delegation of Functions

Functions vested in the President by this section delegated, with authority to redelegate, to the Administrator of the Environmental Protection Agency, except that functions vested in the President by subsec. (a) of this section delegated, with authority to redelegate, to the heads of Executive departments and agencies with respect to facilities under the jurisdiction, custody or control of those departments and agencies, see sections 3, 11(g) of Ex. Ord. No. 12580, 52 Fed. Reg. 2923 (Jan. 23, 1987), set out as a note under section 9615 of this title.

§ 9617. Public participation

[CERCLA § 117]

(a) Proposed plan

Before adoption of any plan for remedial action to be undertaken by the President, by a State, or by any other person, under section 9604, 9606, 9620, or 9622 of this title, the President or State, as appropriate, shall take both of the following actions:

(1) Publish a notice and brief analysis of the proposed plan and make such plan available to the public.

(2) Provide a reasonable opportunity for submission of written and oral comments and an opportunity for a public meeting at or near the facility at issue regarding the proposed plan and regarding any proposed findings under section 9621(d)(4) of this title (relating to cleanup standards). The President or the State shall keep a transcript of the meeting and make such transcript available to the public.

The notice and analysis published under paragraph (1) shall include sufficient information as may be necessary to provide a reasonable explanation of the proposed plan and alternative proposals considered.

(b) Final plan

Notice of the final remedial action plan adopted shall be published and the plan shall be made available to the public before commencement of any remedial action. Such final plan shall be accompanied by a discussion of any significant changes (and the reasons for such changes) in the proposed plan and a response to each of the significant comments, criticisms, and new data submitted in written or oral presentations under subsection (a) of this section.

(c) Explanation of differences

After adoption of a final remedial action plan—

(1) if any remedial action is taken,

(2) if any enforcement action under section 9606 of this title is taken, or

(3) if any settlement or consent decree under section 9606 of this title or section 9622 of this title is entered into,

and if such action, settlement, or decree differs in any significant respects m the final plan, the President or the State shall publish an explanation of the significant differences and the reasons such changes were made.

(d) Publication

For the purposes of this section, publication shall include, at a minimum, publication in a major local newspaper of general circulation. In addition, each item developed, received, published, or made available to the public under this section shall be available for public inspection and copying at or near the facility at issue.

(e) Grants for technical assistance

(1) Authority

Subject to such amounts as are provided in appropriations Acts and in accordance with rules promulgated by the President, the President may make grants available to any group of individuals which may be affected by a release or threatened release at any facility which is listed on the National Priorities List under the National Contingency Plan. Such grants may be used to obtain technical assistance in interpreting information with regard to the nature of the hazard, remedial investigation and feasibility study, record of decision, remedial design, selection and construction of remedial action, operation and maintenance, or removal action at such facility.

(2) Amount

The amount of any grant under this subsection may not exceed $50,000 for a single grant recipient. The President may waive the $50,000 limitation in any case where such waiver is necessary to carry out the purposes of this subsection. Each grant recipient shall be required, as a condition of the grant, to contribute at least 20 percent of the total of costs of the technical assistance for which such grant is made. The President may waive the 20 percent contribution requirement if the grant recipient demonstrates financial need and such waiver is necessary to facilitate public participation in the selection of remedial action at the facility. Not more than one grant may be made under this subsection with respect to a single facility, but the grant may be renewed to facilitate public participation at all stages of remedial action.

(Pub. L. No. 96–510, Title I, § 117, as added by Pub. L. No. 99–499, Title I, § 117, 100 Stat. 1654 (Oct. 17, 1986).)

HISTORICAL AND STATUTORY NOTES

Effective and Applicability Provisions

1986 Acts. Section effective Oct. 17, 1986, see section 4 of Pub. L. No. 99–499, set out as a note under section 9601 of this title.

Delegation of Functions

Functions vested in the President by subsecs. (a) and (c) of this section delegated, with authority to redelegate, to the Director of the Federal Emergency Management Agency, to the extent such authority is needed to carry out certain other functions delegated to the Director by section 2(c)(1) of Ex. Ord. No. 12580, and subject to certain rulemaking authority of the Administrator of the Environmental Protection Agency, see sections 2(b), (c)(2), 11(g) of Ex. Ord. No. 12580, 52 Fed. Reg. 2923 (Jan. 23, 1987), set out as a note under section 9615 of this title.

Functions vested in the President by subsecs. (a) and (c) of this section delegated, with authority to redelegate, (and subject to section 2(a), (b) and (c) of Ex. Ord. No. 12580) to the Secretaries of Defense and Energy, with respect to releases or threatened releases where either the release is on or the sole source of the release is m any facility or vessel under the jurisdiction, custody or control of their departments, respectively, including vessels bare-boat chartered and operated, with such functions to be exercised consistent with the requirements of section 9620 of this title, see sections 2(d), 11(g) of Ex. Ord. No. 12580, 52 Fed. Reg. 2923 (Jan. 23, 1987), set out as a note under section 9615 of this title.

Functions vested in the President by subsecs. (a) and (c) of this section, subject to section 2(b) to (d) of Ex. Ord. No. 12580, delegated, with authority to redelegate, to the heads of Executive departments and agencies, with respect to releases or threatened releases where either the release is on or the sole source of the release is m any facility or vessel under the jurisdiction, custody or control of those departments and agencies, including vessels bare-boat chartered and operated, see sections 2(e)(2), 11(g) of Ex. Ord. No. 12580, 52 Fed. Reg. 2923 (Jan. 23, 1987), set out as a note under section 9615 of this title.

Functions vested in the President by subsecs. (a) and (c) of this section, subject to section 2(a) to (e) of Ex. Ord. No. 12580, delegated, with authority to redelegate, to the Secretary of the Department in which the Coast Guard is operating ("the Coast Guard"), with respect to any release or threatened release involving the coastal zone, Great Lakes waters, ports, and harbors, see sections 2(f), 11(g) of Ex. Ord. No. 12580, 52 Fed. Reg. 2923 (Jan. 23, 1987), set out as a note under section 9615 of this title.

Functions vested in the President by subsecs. (a) and (c) of this section, subject to section 2(a) to (f) of Ex. Ord. No. 12580, delegated, with authority to redelegate, to the Administrator of the Environmental Protection Agency, see sections 2(g), 11(g) of Ex. Ord. No. 12580, 52 Fed. Reg. 2923 (Jan. 23, 1987), set out as a note under section 9615 of this title.

Functions vested in the President by subsec. (e) of this section delegated to the Administrator of Environmental Protection Agency, to be exercised in consultation with the Attorney General, see section 9(g) of Ex. Ord. No. 12580, 52 Fed. Reg. 2923 (Jan. 23, 1987), set out as a note under section 9615 of this title.

§ 9618. High priority for drinking water supplies

[CERCLA § 118]

For purposes of taking action under section 9604 or 9606 of this title and listing facilities on the National Priorities List, the President shall give a high priority to facilities where the release of hazardous substances or pollutants or contaminants has resulted in the closing of drinking water wells or has contaminated a principal drinking water supply.

(Pub. L. No. 96–510, Title I, § 118, as added by Pub. L. No. 99–499, Title I, § 118(a), 100 Stat. 1655 (Oct. 17, 1986).)

HISTORICAL AND STATUTORY NOTES

Effective and Applicability Provisions

1986 Acts. Section effective Oct. 17, 1986, see section 4 of Pub. L. No. 99–499, set out as a note under section 9601 of this title.

§ 9619. Response action contractors

[CERCLA § 119]

(a) Liability of response action contractors

(1) Response action contractors

A person who is a response action contractor with respect to any release or threatened release of a hazardous substance or pollutant or contaminant m a vessel or facility shall not be liable under this subchapter or under any other Federal law to any person for injuries, costs, damages, expenses, or other liability (including but not limited to claims for indemnification or contribution and claims by third parties for death, personal injury, illness or loss of or damage to property or economic loss) which results m such release or threatened release.

(2) Negligence, etc.

Paragraph (1) shall not apply in the case of a release that is caused by conduct of the response action contractor which is negligent, grossly negligent, or which constitutes intentional misconduct.

(3) Effect on warranties; employer liability

Nothing in this subsection shall affect the liability of any person under any warranty under Federal, State, or common law. Nothing in this subsection shall affect the liability of an employer who is a response action contractor to any employee of such employer under any provision of law, including any provision of any law relating to worker's compensation.

(4) Governmental employees

A state employee or an employee of a political subdivision who provides services relating to response action while acting within the scope of his authority as a governmental employee shall have the same exemption m liability (subject to the other provisions of this section) as is provided to the response action contractor under this section.

(b) Savings provisions

(1) Liability of other persons

The defense provided by section 9607(b)(3) of this title shall not be available to any potentially responsible party with respect to any costs or damages caused by any act or omission of a response action contractor. Except as provided in subsection (a)(4) of this section and the preceding sentence, nothing in this section shall affect the liability under this chapter or under any other Federal or State law of any person, other than a response action contractor.

(2) Burden of plaintiff

Nothing in this section shall affect the plaintiff's burden of establishing liability under this subchapter.

(c) Indemnification

(1) In general

The President may agree to hold harmless and indemnify any response action contractor meeting the requirements of this subsection against any liability (including the expenses of litigation or settlement) for negligence arising out of the contractor's performance in carrying out response action activities under this subchapter, unless such liability was caused by conduct of the contractor which was grossly negligent or which constituted intentional misconduct.

(2) Applicability

This subsection shall apply only with respect to a response action carried out under written agreement with—

(A) the President;

(B) any Federal agency;

(C) a State or political subdivision which has entered into a contract or cooperative agreement in accordance with section 9604(d)(1) of this title; or

(D) any potentially responsible party carrying out any agreement under section 9622 of this title (relating to settlements) or section 9606 of this title (relating to abatement).

(3) Source of funding

This subsection shall not be subject to section 1301 or 1341 of Title 31 or section 6301(a) and (b) of Title 41 or to section 9662 of this title. For purposes of section 9611 of this title, amounts expended pursuant to this subsection for indemnification of any response action contractor (except with respect to federally owned or operated facilities) shall be considered governmental response costs incurred pursuant to section 9604 of this title. If sufficient funds are unavailable in the Hazardous Substance Superfund established under subchapter A of chapter 98 of Title 26 to make payments pursuant to such indemnification or if the Fund is repealed, there are authorized to be appropriated such amounts as may be necessary to make such payments.

(4) Requirements

An indemnification agreement may be provided under this subsection only if the President determines that each of the following requirements are met:

(A) The liability covered by the indemnification agreement exceeds or is not covered by insurance available, at a fair and reasonable price, to the contractor at the time the contractor enters into the contract to provide response action, and adequate insurance to cover such liability is not generally available at the time the response action contract is entered into.

(B) The response action contractor has made diligent efforts to obtain insurance coverage m non-Federal sources to cover such liability.

(C) In the case of a response action contract covering more than one facility, the response action contractor agrees to continue to make such diligent efforts each time the contractor begins work under the contract at a new facility.

(5) Limitations

(A) Liability covered

Indemnification under this subsection shall apply only to response action contractor liability which results m a release of any hazardous substance or pollutant or contaminant if such release arises out of response action activities.

(B) Deductibles and limits

An indemnification agreement under this subsection shall include deductibles and shall place limits on the amount of indemnification to be made available.

(C) Contracts with potentially responsible parties

(i) Decision to indemnify

In deciding whether to enter into an indemnification agreement with a response action contractor carrying out a written contract or agreement with any potentially responsible party, the President shall determine an amount which the potentially responsible party is able to indemnify the contractor. The President may enter into such an indemnification agreement only if the President determines that such amount of indemnification is inadequate to cover any reasonable potential liability of the contractor arising out of the contractor's negligence in performing the contract or agreement with such party. The President shall make the determinations in the preceding sentences (with respect to the amount and the adequacy of the amount) taking into account the total net assets and resources of potentially responsible parties with respect to the facility at the time of such determinations.

(ii) Conditions

The President may pay a claim under an indemnification agreement referred to in clause (i) for the amount determined under clause (i) only if the contractor has exhausted all administrative, judicial, and common law claims for indemnification against all potentially responsible parties participating in the clean-up of the facility with respect to the liability of the contractor arising out of the contractor's negligence in performing the contract or agreement with such party. Such indemnification agreement shall require such contractor to pay any deductible established under subparagraph (B) before the contractor may recover any amount m the potentially responsible party or under the indemnification agreement.

(D) RCRA facilities

No owner or operator of a facility regulated under the Solid Waste Disposal Act [42 U.S.C.A. § 6901 et seq.] may be indemnified under this subsection with respect to such facility.

(E) Persons retained or hired

A person retained or hired by a person described in subsection (e)(2)(B) of this section shall be eligible for indemnification under this subsection only if the President specifically approves of the retaining or hiring of such person.

(6) Cost recovery

For purposes of section 9607 of this title, amounts expended pursuant to this subsection for indemnification of any person who is a response action contractor with respect to any release or threatened release shall be considered a cost of response incurred by the United States Government with respect to such release.

(7) Regulations

The President shall promulgate regulations for carrying out the provisions of this subsection. Before promulgation of the regulations, the President shall develop guidelines to carry out this section. Development of such guidelines shall include reasonable opportunity for public comment.

(8) Study

The Comptroller General shall conduct a study in the fiscal year ending September 30, 1989, on the application of this subsection, including whether indemnification agreements under this subsection are being used, the number of claims that have been filed under such agreements, and the need for this subsection. The Comptroller General shall report the findings of the study to Congress no later than September 30, 1989.

(d) Exception

The exemption provided under subsection (a) of this section and the authority of the President to offer indemnification under subsection (c) of this section shall not apply to any person covered by the provisions of paragraph (1), (2), (3), or (4) of section 9607(a) of this title with respect to the release or threatened release concerned if such person would be covered by such provisions even if such person had not carried out any actions referred to in subsection (e) of this section.

(e) Definitions

For purposes of this section—

(1) Response action contract

The term "response action contract" means any written contract or agreement entered into by a response action contractor (as defined in paragraph (2)(A) of this subsection) with—

(A) the President;

(B) any Federal agency;

(C) a State or political subdivision which has entered into a contract or cooperative agreement in accordance with section 9604(d)(1) of this title; or

(D) any potentially responsible party carrying out an agreement under section 9606 or 9622 of this title;

to provide any remedial action under this chapter at a facility listed on the National Priorities List, or any removal under this chapter, with respect to any release or threatened release of a hazardous substance or pollutant or contaminant m the facility or to provide any evaluation, planning, engineering, surveying and mapping, design, construction, equipment, or any ancillary services thereto for such facility.

(2) Response action contractor

The term "response action contractor" means—

(A) any—

(i) person who enters into a response action contract with respect to any release or threatened release of a hazardous substance or pollutant or contaminant m a facility and is carrying out such contract; and[1]

(ii) person, public or nonprofit private entity, conducting a field demonstration pursuant to section 9660(b) of this title; and

(iii) Recipients[2] of grants (including sub-grantees) under section 9660a of this title for the training and education of workers who are or may be engaged in activities related to hazardous waste removal, containment, or emergency response under this chapter; and

(B) any person who is retained or hired by a person described in subparagraph (A) to provide any services relating to a response action; and

(C) any surety who after October 16, 1990, provides a bid, performance or payment bond to a response action contractor, and begins activities to meet its obligations under such bond, but only in connection with such activities or obligations.

(3) Insurance

The term "insurance" means liability insurance which is fair and reasonably priced, as determined by the President, and which is made available at the time the contractor enters into the response action contract to provide response action.

(f) Competition

Response action contractors and subcontractors for program management, construction management, architectural and engineering, surveying and mapping, and related services shall be selected in accordance with title IX of the Federal Property and Administrative Services Act of 1949 [40 U.S.C.A. § 541 et seq.]. The Federal selection procedures shall apply to appropriate contracts negotiated by all Federal governmental agencies involved in carrying out this chapter. Such procedures shall be followed by response action contractors and subcontractors.

(g) Surety bonds

(1) If under sections 3131 and 3133 of Title 40, surety bonds are required for any direct Federal procurement of any response action contract and are not waived pursuant to section 3134 of Title 40, they shall be issued in accordance with sections 3131 and 3133 of Title 40.

(2) If under applicable Federal law surety bonds are required for any direct Federal procurement of any response action contract, no right of action shall accrue on the performance bond issued on such response action contract to or for the use of any person other than the obligee named in the bond.

(3) If under applicable Federal law surety bonds are required for any direct Federal procurement of any response action contract, unless otherwise provided for by the procuring agency in the bond, in the event of a default, the surety's liability on a performance bond shall be only for the cost of completion of the contract work in accordance with the plans and specifications less the balance of funds remaining to be paid under the contract, up to the penal sum of the bond. The surety shall in no event be liable on bonds to indemnify or compensate the obligee for loss or liability arising m personal injury or property damage whether or not caused by a breach of the bonded contract.

(4) Nothing in this subsection shall be construed as preempting, limiting, superseding, affecting, applying to, or modifying any State laws, regulations, requirements, rules, practices or procedures. Nothing in this subsection shall be construed as affecting, applying to, modifying, limiting, superseding, or preempting any rights, authorities, liabilities, demands, actions, causes of action, losses, judgments, claims, statutes of limitation, or obligations under Federal or State law, which do not arise on or under the bond.

(5) This subsection shall not apply to bonds executed before October 17, 1990.

(Pub. L. No. 96–510, Title I, § 119, as added by Pub. L. No. 99–499, Title I, § 119, 100 Stat. 1662 (Oct. 17, 1986); and amended by Pub. L. No. 99–514, § 2, 100 Stat. 2095 (Oct. 22, 1986); Pub. L. No. 100–202, § 101(f) [Title II, § 201], 101 Stat. 1329–187, 1329–198 (Dec. 22, 1987); Pub. L. No. 101–584, § 1, 104 Stat. 2872 (Nov. 15, 1990); Pub. L. No. 102–484, Div. A, Title III, § 331(a), 106 Stat. 2373 (Oct. 23, 1992); Pub. L. No. 105–276, Title III, 112 Stat. 2497 (Oct. 21, 1998).)

[1] So in original. The word "and" probably should not appear.

[2] So in original. Probably should not be capitalized.

HISTORICAL AND STATUTORY NOTES

References in Text

The Solid Waste Disposal Act, referred to in subsec. (c)(5)(D), is Title II of Pub. L. No. 89–272, 79 Stat. 997 (Oct. 20, 1965), as amended generally by Pub. L. No. 94–580, § 2, 90 Stat. 2795 (Oct. 21, 1976), which is codified generally as chapter 82 (section 6901 et seq.) of this title. For complete classification of this Act to the Code, see Short Title of 1965 Acts note set out under section 6901 of this title and Tables.

Section 9660a of this title, referred to in subsec. (e)(2)(A)(iii), was in the original "section 126", probably meaning section 126 of Pub. L. No. 99–499, Title I, 100 Stat. 1690 (Oct. 17, 1986). Subsecs. (a) to (f) of section 126, which relate to worker protection standards, are set out as a note under section 655 of Title 29, Labor. Subsec. (g) of section 126, which relates to grants for training and education of workers who are or may be engaged in activities related to hazardous waste removal, etc., is codified as section 9660a of this title.

The Federal Property and Administrative Services Act of 1949, referred to in subsec. (f), is Act of June 30, 1949, c. 288, 63 Stat. 377. Title IX of the Act, which was codified generally as subchapter VI (§ 541 et seq.) of chapter 10 of former Title 40, Public Buildings, Property, and Works, was repealed and reenacted by Pub. L. No. 107–217, §§ 1, 6(b), 116 Stat. 1062, 1304 (Aug. 21, 2002), as chapter 11 (§ 1101 et seq.) of Title 40, Public Buildings, Property, and Works. For disposition of sections of former Title 40 to revised Title 40, see Table preceding section 101 of Title 40. For complete classification, see Tables.

Codifications

In subsec. (c)(3), "section 6301(a) and (b) of Title 41" substituted for "section 3732 of the Revised Statutes (41 U.S.C. 11)" on authority of Pub. L. No. 111–350, § 6(c), 124 Stat. 3854 (Jan. 4, 2011), which Act enacted Title 41, Public Contracts.

In subsec. (g)(1), "sections 3131 to 3133 of Title 40" substituted for "the Act of August 24, 1935 (40 U.S.C. 270a—270d), commonly referred to as the 'Miller Act' " on authority of Pub. L. No. 107–217, § 5(c), 116 Stat. 1301 (Aug. 21, 2002), which is set out as a note preceding 40 U.S.C.A. § 101. Pub. L. No. 107–217, § 1, enacted Title 40 into positive law. The Miller Act is Act of Aug. 24, 1935, c. 642, 49 Stat. 793, which was codified as former 40 U.S.C.A. §§ 270, 270a, 270b to 270d, 270d–1 prior to being repealed by Pub. L. No. 107–217, § 6(b), 116 Stat. 1309 (Aug. 21, 2002), and its substance reenacted as 40 U.S.C.A. §§ 3131 to 3133.

In subsec. (g)(1), "sections 3134 of Title 40" substituted for "the Act of April 29, 1941 (40 U.S.C. 270e—270f)", on authority of Pub. L. No. 107–217, § 5(c), 116 Stat. 1301 (Aug. 21, 2002), which is set out as a note preceding 40 U.S.C.A. § 101. Pub. L. No. 107–217, § 1, enacted Title 40 into positive law. Act of Apr. 29, 1941, c. 81, 55 Stat. 147, as amended, was codified as former 40 U.S.C.A. §§ 270e and 270f prior to being repealed by Pub. L. No. 107–217, § 6(b), 116 Stat. 1311 (Aug. 21, 2002), and its substance reenacted as 40 U.S.C.A. § 3134.

Effective and Applicability Provisions

1986 Acts. Section effective Oct. 17, 1986, see section 4 of Pub. L. No. 99–499, set out as a note under section 9601 of this title.

Delegation of Functions

Functions vested in the President by subsec. (c)(7) of this section, relating to the promulgation of regulations and guidelines, delegated to the Administrator of the Environmental Protection Agency, to be exercised in consultation with the National Response Team, see section 2(b) of Ex. Ord. No. 12580, 52 Fed. Reg. 2923 (Jan. 23, 1987), set out as a note under section 9615 of this title.

Functions vested in the President by this section delegated, with authority to redelegate, to the Director of the Federal Emergency Management Agency, to the extent such authority is needed to carry out certain other functions delegated to the Director by section 2(c)(1) of Ex. Ord. No. 12580, and subject to certain rulemaking authority of the Administrator of the Environmental Protection Agency, see sections 2(b), (c)(2), 11(g) of Ex. Ord. No. 12580, 52 Fed. Reg. 2923 (Jan. 23, 1987), set out as a note under section 9615 of this title.

Functions vested in the President by this section delegated, with authority to redelegate, (and subject to section 2(a), (b) and (c) of Ex. Ord. No. 12580) to the Secretaries of Defense and Energy, with respect to releases or threatened releases where either the release is on or the sole source of the release is m any facility or vessel under the jurisdiction, custody or control of their departments, respectively, including vessels bare-boat chartered and operated, with such functions to be exercised consistent with the requirements of section 9620 of this title, see sections 2(d), 11(g) of Ex. Ord. No. 12580, 52 Fed. Reg. 2923 (Jan. 23, 1987), set out as a note under section 9615 of this title.

Functions vested in the President by this section, subject to section 2(b) to (d) of Ex. Ord. No. 12580, delegated, with authority to redelegate, to the heads of Executive departments and agencies, with respect to releases or threatened releases where either the release is on or the sole source of the release is m any facility or vessel under the jurisdiction, custody or control of those departments and agencies, including vessels bare-boat chartered and operated, see sections 2(e)(2), 11(g) of Ex. Ord. No. 12580, 52 Fed. Reg. 2923 (Jan. 23, 1987), set out as a note under section 9615 of this title.

Functions vested in the President by this section, subject to section 2(a) to (e) of Ex. Ord. No. 12580, delegated, with authority to redelegate, to the Secretary of the Department in which the Coast Guard is operating ("the Coast Guard"), with respect to any release or threatened release involving the coastal zone, Great Lakes waters, ports, and harbors, see sections 2(f), 11(g) of Ex. Ord. No. 12580, 52 Fed. Reg. 2923 (Jan. 23, 1987), set out as a note under section 9615 of this title.

Functions vested in the President by this section, subject to section 2(a) to (f) of Ex. Ord. No. 12580, delegated, with authority to redelegate, to the Administrator of the Environmental Protection Agency, retroactive to the date of enactment of Pub. L. No. 99–499, which was approved Oct. 17, 1986, see sections 2(g), 11(g) of Ex. Ord. No. 12580, 52 Fed. Reg. 2923 (Jan. 23, 1987), set out as a note under section 9615 of this title.

Coordination of Titles I to IV of Pub. L. No. 99–499

Any provision of Titles I to IV of Pub. L. No. 99–499, imposing any tax, premium, or fee; establishing any trust fund; or authorizing expenditures m any trust fund, to have no force or effect, see section 531 of Pub. L. No. 99–499, set out as a note under section 1 of Title 26, Internal Revenue Code.

§ 9620. Federal facilities

[CERCLA § 120]

(a) Application of chapter to Federal Government

(1) In general

Each department, agency, and instrumentality of the United States (including the executive, legislative, and judicial branches of government) shall be subject to, and comply with, this chapter in the same manner and to the same extent, both procedurally and substantively, as any nongovernmental entity, including liability under section 9607 of this title. Nothing in this section shall be construed to affect the liability of any person or entity under sections 9606 and 9607 of this title.

(2) Application of requirements to Federal facilities

All guidelines, rules, regulations, and criteria which are applicable to preliminary assessments carried out under this chapter for facilities at which hazardous substances are located, applicable to evaluations of such facilities under the National Contingency Plan, applicable to inclusion on the National Priorities List, or applicable to remedial actions at such facilities shall also be applicable to facilities which are owned or operated by a department, agency, or instrumentality of the United States in the same manner and to the extent as such guidelines, rules, regulations, and criteria are applicable to other facilities. No department, agency, or instrumentality of the United States may adopt or utilize any such guidelines, rules, regulations, or criteria which are inconsistent with the guidelines, rules, regulations, and criteria established by the Administrator under this chapter.

(3) Exceptions

This subsection shall not apply to the extent otherwise provided in this section with respect to applicable time periods. This subsection shall also not apply to any requirements relating to bonding, insurance, or financial responsibility. Nothing in this chapter shall be construed to require a State to comply with section 9604(c)(3) of this title in the case of a facility which is owned or operated by any department, agency, or instrumentality of the United States.

(4) State laws

State laws concerning removal and remedial action, including State laws regarding enforcement, shall apply to removal and remedial action at facilities owned or operated by a department, agency, or instrumentality of the United States or facilities that are the subject of a deferral under subsection (h)(3)(C) of this section when such facilities are not included on the National Priorities List. The preceding sentence shall not apply to the extent a State law would apply any standard or requirement to such facilities which is more stringent than the standards and requirements applicable to facilities which are not owned or operated by any such department, agency, or instrumentality.

(b) Notice

Each department, agency, and instrumentality of the United States shall add to the inventory of Federal agency hazardous waste facilities required to be submitted under section 3016 of the Solid Waste Disposal Act [42 U.S.C.A. § 6937] (in addition to the information required under section 3016(a)(3) of such Act [42 U.S.C.A. § 6937(a)(3)]) information on contamination m each facility owned or operated by the department, agency, or instrumentality if such contamination affects contiguous or adjacent property owned by the department, agency, or instrumentality or by any other person, including a description of the monitoring data obtained.

(c) Federal Agency Hazardous Waste Compliance Docket

The Administrator shall establish a special Federal Agency Hazardous Waste Compliance Docket (hereinafter in this section referred to as the "docket") which shall contain each of the following:

(1) All information submitted under section 3016 of the Solid Waste Disposal Act [42 U.S.C.A. § 6937] and subsection (b) of this section regarding any Federal facility and notice of each subsequent action taken under this chapter with respect to the facility.

(2) Information submitted by each department, agency, or instrumentality of the United States under section 3005 or 3010 of such Act [42 U.S.C.A. § 6925, 6930].

(3) Information submitted by the department, agency, or instrumentality under section 9603 of this title.

The docket shall be available for public inspection at reasonable times. Six months after establishment of the docket and every 6 months thereafter, the Administrator shall publish in the Federal Register a list of the Federal facilities which have been included in the docket during the immediately preceding 6-month period. Such publication shall also indicate where in the appropriate regional office of the Environmental Protection Agency additional information may be obtained with respect to any facility on the docket. The Administrator shall establish a program to provide information to the public with respect to facilities which are included in the docket under this subsection.

(d) Assessment and evaluation

(1) In general

The Administrator shall take steps to assure that a preliminary assessment is conducted for each facility on the docket. Following such preliminary assessment, the Administrator shall, where appropriate—

(A) evaluate such facilities in accordance with the criteria established in accordance with section 9605 of this title under the National Contingency Plan for determining priorities among releases; and

(B) include such facilities on the National Priorities List maintained under such plan if the facility meets such criteria.

(2) Application of criteria

(A) In general

Subject to subparagraph (B), the criteria referred to in paragraph (1) shall be applied in the same manner as the criteria are applied to facilities that are owned or operated by persons other than the United States.

(B) Response under other law

It shall be an appropriate factor to be taken into consideration for the purposes of section 9605(a)(8)(A) of this title that the head of the department, agency, or instrumentality that owns or operates a facility has arranged with the Administrator or appropriate State authorities to respond appropriately, under authority of a law other than this chapter, to a release or threatened release of a hazardous substance.

(3) Completion

Evaluation and listing under this subsection shall be completed in accordance with a reasonable schedule established by the Administrator.

(e) Required action by department

(1) RI/FS

Not later than 6 months after the inclusion of any facility on the National Priorities List, the department, agency, or instrumentality which owns or operates such facility shall, in consultation with the Administrator and appropriate State authorities, commence a remedial investigation and feasibility study for such facility. In the case of any facility which is listed on such list before October 17, 1986, the department, agency, or instrumentality which owns or operates such facility shall, in consultation with the Administrator and appropriate State authorities, commence such an investigation and study for such facility within one year after October 17, 1986. The Administrator and appropriate State authorities shall publish a timetable and deadlines for expeditious completion of such investigation and study.

(2) Commencement of remedial action; interagency agreement

The Administrator shall review the results of each investigation and study conducted as provided in paragraph (1). Within 180 days thereafter, the head of the department, agency, or instrumentality concerned shall enter into an interagency agreement with the Administrator for the expeditious completion by such department, agency, or instrumentality of all necessary remedial action at such facility. Substantial continuous physical onsite remedial action shall be commenced at each facility not later than 15 months after completion of the investigation and study. All such interagency agreements, including review of alternative remedial action plans and selection of remedial action, shall comply with the public participation requirements of section 9617 of this title.

(3) Completion of remedial actions

Remedial actions at facilities subject to interagency agreements under this section shall be completed as expeditiously as practicable. Each agency shall include in its annual budget submissions to the Congress a review of alternative agency funding which could be used to provide for the costs of remedial action. The budget submission shall also include a statement of the hazard posed by the facility to human health, welfare, and the environment and identify the specific consequences of failure to begin and complete remedial action.

(4) Contents of agreement

Each interagency agreement under this subsection shall include, but shall not be limited to, each of the following:

(A) A review of alternative remedial actions and selection of a remedial action by the head of the relevant department, agency, or instrumentality and the Administrator or, if unable to reach agreement on selection of a remedial action, selection by the Administrator.

(B) A schedule for the completion of each such remedial action.

(C) Arrangements for long-term operation and maintenance of the facility.

(5) Annual report

Each department, agency, or instrumentality responsible for compliance with this section shall furnish an annual report to the Congress concerning its progress in implementing the requirements of this section. Such reports shall include, but shall not be limited to, each of the following items:

(A) A report on the progress in reaching interagency agreements under this section.

(B) The specific cost estimates and budgetary proposals involved in each interagency agreement.

(C) A brief summary of the public comments regarding each proposed interagency agreement.

(D) A description of the instances in which no agreement was reached.

(E) A report on progress in conducting investigations and studies under paragraph (1).

(F) A report on progress in conducting remedial actions.

(G) A report on progress in conducting remedial action at facilities which are not listed on the National Priorities List.

With respect to instances in which no agreement was reached within the required time period, the department, agency, or instrumentality filing the report under this paragraph shall include in such report an explanation of the reasons why no agreement was reached. The annual report required by this paragraph shall also contain a detailed description on a State-by-State basis of the status of each facility subject to this section, including a description of the hazard presented by each facility, plans and schedules for initiating and completing response action, enforcement status (where appropriate), and an explanation of any postponements or failure to complete response action. Such reports shall also be submitted to the affected States.

(6) Settlements with other parties

If the Administrator, in consultation with the head of the relevant department, agency, or instrumentality of the United States, determines that remedial investigations and feasibility studies or remedial action will be done properly at the Federal facility by another potentially responsible party within the deadlines provided in paragraphs (1), (2), and (3) of this subsection, the Administrator may enter into an agreement with such party under section 9622 of this title (relating to settlements). Following approval by the Attorney General of any such agreement relating to a remedial action, the agreement shall be entered in the appropriate United States district court as a consent decree under section 9606 of this title.

(f) State and local participation

The Administrator and each department, agency, or instrumentality responsible for compliance with this section shall afford to relevant State and local officials the opportunity to participate in the planning and selection of the remedial action, including but not limited to the review of all applicable data as it becomes available and the development of studies, reports, and action plans. In the case of State officials, the opportunity to participate shall be provided in accordance with section 9621 of this title.

(g) Transfer of authorities

Except for authorities which are delegated by the Administrator to an officer or employee of the Environmental Protection Agency, no authority vested in the Administrator under this section may be transferred, by executive order of the President or otherwise, to any other officer or employee of the United States or to any other person.

(h) Property transferred by Federal agencies

(1) Notice

After the last day of the 6-month period beginning on the effective date of regulations under paragraph (2) of this subsection, whenever any department, agency, or instrumentality of the United States enters into any contract for the sale or other transfer of real property which is owned by the United States and on which any hazardous substance was stored for one year or more, known to have been released, or disposed of, the head of such department, agency, or instrumentality shall include in such contract notice of the type and quantity of such hazardous substance and notice of the time at which such storage, release, or disposal took place, to the extent such information is available on the basis of a complete search of agency files.

(2) Form of notice; regulations

Notice under this subsection shall be provided in such form and manner as may be provided in regulations promulgated by the Administrator. As promptly as practicable after October 17, 1986, but not later than 18 months after October 17, 1986, and after consultation with the Administrator of the General Services Administration, the Administrator shall promulgate regulations regarding the notice required to be provided under this subsection.

(3) Contents of certain deeds

(A) In general

After the last day of the 6-month period beginning on the effective date of regulations under paragraph (2) of this subsection, in the case of any real property owned by the United States on which any hazardous substance was stored for one year or more, known to have been released, or disposed of, each deed entered into for the transfer of such property by the United States to any other person or entity shall contain—

(i) to the extent such information is available on the basis of a complete search of agency files—

(I) a notice of the type and quantity of such hazardous substances,

(II) notice of the time at which such storage, release, or disposal took place, and

(III) a description of the remedial action taken, if any;

(ii) a covenant warranting that—

(I) all remedial action necessary to protect human health and the environment with respect to any such substance remaining on the property has been taken before the date of such transfer, and

(II) any additional remedial action found to be necessary after the date of such transfer shall be conducted by the United States; and

(iii) a clause granting the United States access to the property in any case in which remedial action or corrective action is found to be necessary after the date of such transfer.

(B) Covenant requirements

For purposes of subparagraphs (A)(ii)(I) and (C)(iii), all remedial action described in such subparagraph has been taken if the construction and installation of an approved remedial design has been completed, and the remedy has been demonstrated to the Administrator to be operating properly and successfully. The carrying out of long-term pumping and treating, or operation and maintenance, after the remedy has been demonstrated to the Administrator to be operating properly and successfully does not preclude the transfer of the property. The requirements of subparagraph (A)(ii) shall not apply in any case in which the person or entity to whom the real property is transferred is a potentially responsible party with respect to such property. The requirements of subparagraph (A)(ii) shall not apply in any case in which the transfer of the property occurs or has occurred by means of a lease, without regard to whether the lessee has agreed to purchase the property or whether the duration of the lease is longer than 55 years. In the case of a lease entered into after September 30, 1995, with respect to real property located at an installation approved for closure or realignment under a base closure law, the agency leasing the property, in consultation with the Administrator, shall determine before leasing the property that the property is suitable for lease, that the uses contemplated for the lease are consistent with protection of human health and the environment, and that there are adequate assurances that the United States will take all remedial action referred to in subparagraph (A)(ii) that has not been taken on the date of the lease.

(C) Deferral

(i) In general

The Administrator, with the concurrence of the Governor of the State in which the facility is located (in the case of real property at a Federal facility that is listed on the National Priorities List), or the Governor of the State in which the facility is located (in the case of real property at a Federal facility not listed on the National Priorities List) may defer the requirement of subparagraph (A)(ii)(I) with respect to the property if the Administrator or the Governor, as the case may be, determines that the property is suitable for transfer, based on a finding that—

(I) the property is suitable for transfer for the use intended by the transferee, and the intended use is consistent with protection of human health and the environment;

(II) the deed or other agreement proposed to govern the transfer between the United States and the transferee of the property contains the assurances set forth in clause (ii);

(III) the Federal agency requesting deferral has provided notice, by publication in a newspaper of general circulation in the vicinity of the property, of the proposed transfer and of the opportunity for the public to submit, within a period of not less than 30 days after the date of the notice, written comments on the suitability of the property for transfer; and

(IV) the deferral and the transfer of the property will not substantially delay any necessary response action at the property.

(ii) Response action assurances

With regard to a release or threatened release of a hazardous substance for which a Federal agency is potentially responsible under this section, the deed or other agreement proposed to govern the transfer shall contain assurances that—

(I) provide for any necessary restrictions on the use of the property to ensure the protection of human health and the environment;

(II) provide that there will be restrictions on use necessary to ensure that required remedial investigations, response action, and oversight activities will not be disrupted;

(III) provide that all necessary response action will be taken and identify the schedules for investigation and completion of all necessary response action as approved by the appropriate regulatory agency; and

(IV) provide that the Federal agency responsible for the property subject to transfer will submit a budget request to the Director of the Office of Management and Budget that adequately addresses schedules for investigation and completion of all necessary response action, subject to congressional authorizations and appropriations.

(iii) Warranty

When all response action necessary to protect human health and the environment with respect to any substance remaining on the property on the date of transfer has been taken, the United States shall execute and deliver to the transferee an appropriate document containing a warranty that all such response action has been taken, and the making of the warranty shall be considered to satisfy the requirement of subparagraph (A)(ii)(I).

(iv) Federal responsibility

A deferral under this subparagraph shall not increase, diminish, or affect in any manner any rights or obligations of a Federal agency (including any rights or obligations under this section and sections 9606 and 9607 of this title existing prior to transfer) with respect to a property transferred under this subparagraph.

(4) Identification of uncontaminated property

(A) In the case of real property to which this paragraph applies (as set forth in subparagraph (E)), the head of the department, agency, or instrumentality of the United States with jurisdiction over the property shall identify the real property on which no hazardous substances and no petroleum products or their derivatives were known to have been released or disposed of. Such identification shall be based on an investigation of the real property to determine or discover the obviousness of the presence or likely presence of a release or threatened release of any hazardous substance or any petroleum product or its derivatives, including aviation fuel and motor oil, on the real property. The identification shall consist, at a minimum, of a review of each of the following sources of information concerning the current and previous uses of the real property:

(i) A detailed search of Federal Government records pertaining to the property.

(ii) Recorded chain of title documents regarding the real property.

(iii) Aerial photographs that may reflect prior uses of the real property and that are reasonably obtainable through State or local government agencies.

(iv) A visual inspection of the real property and any buildings, structures, equipment, pipe, pipeline, or other improvements on the real property, and a visual inspection of properties immediately adjacent to the real property.

(v) A physical inspection of property adjacent to the real property, to the extent permitted by owners or operators of such property.

(vi) Reasonably obtainable Federal, State, and local government records of each adjacent facility where there has been a release of any hazardous substance or any petroleum product or its derivatives, including aviation fuel and motor oil, and which is likely to cause or contribute to a release or threatened release of any hazardous substance or any petroleum product or its derivatives, including aviation fuel and motor oil, on the real property.

(vii) Interviews with current or former employees involved in operations on the real property.

Such identification shall also be based on sampling, if appropriate under the circumstances. The results of the identification shall be provided immediately to the Administrator and State and local government officials and made available to the public.

(B) The identification required under subparagraph (A) is not complete until concurrence in the results of the identification is obtained, in the case of real property that is part of a facility on the National Priorities List, m the Administrator, or, in the case of real property that is not part of a facility on the National Priorities List, m the appropriate State official. In the case of a concurrence which is required m a State official, the concurrence is deemed to be obtained if, within 90 days after receiving a request for the concurrence, the State official has not acted (by either concurring or declining to concur) on the request for concurrence.

(C) **(i)** Except as provided in clauses (ii), (iii), and (iv), the identification and concurrence required under subparagraphs (A) and (B), respectively, shall be made at least 6 months before the termination of operations on the real property.

(ii) In the case of real property described in subparagraph (E)(i)(II) on which operations have been closed or realigned or scheduled for closure or realignment pursuant to a base closure law described in subparagraph (E)(ii)(I) or (E)(ii)(II) by October 19, 1992, the identification and concurrence required under subparagraphs (A) and (B), respectively, shall be made not later than 18 months after October 19, 1992.

(iii) In the case of real property described in subparagraph (E)(i)(II) on which operations are closed or realigned or become scheduled for closure or realignment pursuant to the base closure law described in subparagraph (E)(ii)(II) after October 19, 1992, the identification and concurrence required under subparagraphs (A) and (B), respectively, shall be made not later than 18 months after the date by which a joint resolution disapproving the closure or realignment of the real property under section 2904(b) of such base closure law must be enacted, and such a joint resolution has not been enacted.

(iv) In the case of real property described in subparagraphs (E)(i)(II) on which operations are closed or realigned pursuant to a base closure law described in subparagraph (E)(ii)(III) or (E)(ii)(IV), the identification and concurrence required under subparagraphs (A) and (B), respectively, shall be made not later than 18 months after the date on which the real property is selected for closure or realignment pursuant to such a base closure law.

(D) In the case of the sale or other transfer of any parcel of real property identified under subparagraph (A), the deed entered into for the sale or transfer of such property by the United States to any other person or entity shall contain—

(i) a covenant warranting that any response action or corrective action found to be necessary after the date of such sale or transfer shall be conducted by the United States; and

(ii) a clause granting the United States access to the property in any case in which a response action or corrective action is found to be necessary after such date at such property, or such access is necessary to carry out a response action or corrective action on adjoining property.

(E) **(i)** This paragraph applies to—

(I) real property owned by the United States and on which the United States plans to terminate Federal Government operations, other than real property described in subclause (II); and

(II) real property that is or has been used as a military installation and on which the United States plans to close or realign military operations pursuant to a base closure law.

(ii) For purposes of this paragraph, the term "base closure law" includes the following:

(I) Title II of the Defense Authorization Amendments and Base Closure and Realignment Act (Public Law 100–526; 10 U.S.C. 2687 note).

(II) The Defense Base Closure and Realignment Act of 1990 (part A of title XXIX of Public Law 101–510; 10 U.S.C. 2687 note).

(III) Section 2687 of Title 10.

(IV) Any provision of law authorizing the closure or realignment of a military installation enacted on or after October 19, 1992.

(F) Nothing in this paragraph shall affect, preclude, or otherwise impair the termination of Federal Government operations on real property owned by the United States.

(5) Notification of States regarding certain leases

In the case of real property owned by the United States, on which any hazardous substance or any petroleum product or its derivatives (including aviation fuel and motor oil) was stored for one year or more, known to have been released, or disposed of, and on which the United States plans to terminate Federal Government operations, the head of the department, agency, or instrumentality of the United States with jurisdiction over the property shall notify the State in which the property is located of any lease entered into by the United States that will encumber the property beyond the date of termination of operations on the property. Such notification shall be made before entering into the lease and shall include the length of the lease, the name of person to whom the property is leased, and a description of the uses that will be allowed under the lease of the property and buildings and other structures on the property.

(i) Obligations under Solid Waste Disposal Act

Nothing in this section shall affect or impair the obligation of any department, agency, or instrumentality of the United States to comply with any requirement of the Solid Waste Disposal Act [42 U.S.C.A. § 6901 et seq.] (including corrective action requirements).

(j) National security

(1) Site specific Presidential orders

The President may issue such orders regarding response actions at any specified site or facility of the Department of Energy or the Department of Defense as may be necessary to protect the national security interests of the United States at that site or facility. Such orders may include, where necessary to protect such interests, an exemption m any requirement contained in this subchapter or under title III of the Superfund Amendments and Reauthorization Act of 1986 [42 U.S.C.A. § 11001 et seq.] with respect to the site or facility concerned. The President shall notify the Congress within 30 days of the issuance of an order under this paragraph providing for any such exemption. Such notification shall include a statement of the reasons for the granting of the exemption. An exemption under this paragraph shall be for a specified period which may not exceed one year. Additional exemptions may be granted, each upon the President's issuance of a new order under this paragraph for the site or facility concerned. Each such additional exemption shall be for a specified period which may not exceed one year. It is the intention of the Congress that whenever an exemption is issued under this paragraph the response action shall proceed as expeditiously as practicable. The Congress shall be notified periodically of the progress of any response action with respect to which an exemption has been issued under this paragraph. No exemption shall be granted under this paragraph due to lack of appropriation unless the President shall have specifically requested such appropriation as a part of the budgetary process and the Congress shall have failed to make available such requested appropriation.

(2) Classified information

Notwithstanding any other provision of law, all requirements of the Atomic Energy Act [42 U.S.C.A. § 2011 et seq.] and all Executive orders concerning the handling of restricted data and national security information, including "need to know" requirements, shall be applicable to any grant of access to classified information under the provisions of this chapter or under title III of the Superfund Amendments and Reauthorization Act of 1986 [42 U.S.C.A. § 11001 et seq.].

(Pub. L. No. 96–510, Title I, § 120, as added by Pub. L. No. 99–499, Title I, § 120(a), 100 Stat. 1666 (Oct. 17, 1986); and amended by Pub. L. No. 102–426, §§ 3–5, 106 Stat. 2175–2177 (Oct. 19, 1992); Pub. L. No. 104–106, Div. B, Title XXVIII, § 2834, 110 Stat. 559 (Feb. 10, 1996); Pub. L. No. 104–201, Div. A, Title III, §§ 330, 331, 334, 110 Stat. 2484, 2486 (Sept. 23, 1996).)

HISTORICAL AND STATUTORY NOTES

References in Text

This chapter, referred to in text, was in the original, "this Act", meaning Pub. L. No. 96–510, 94 Stat. 2767 (Dec. 11, 1980), as amended, known as the Comprehensive Environmental Response, Compensation, and Liability Act of 1980. For complete classification of this Act to the Code, see Short Title of 1980 Acts note set out under section 9601 of this title and Tables.

Section 2904(b) of such base closure law, referred to in subsec. (h)(4)(C)(iii), is Pub. L. No. 101–510, Div. B, Title XXIX, § 2904(b), 104 Stat. 1812 (Nov. 5, 1990), as amended, which is set out as a note under section 2687 of Title 10, Armed Forces.

Title II of the Defense Authorization Amendments and Base Closure and Realignment Act, referred to in subsec. (h)(4)(E)(ii)(I), is Pub. L. No. 100–526, Title II, 102 Stat. 2627 (Oct. 24, 1988), as amended, which is set out as a note under section 2687 of Title 10, Armed Forces.

The Defense Base Closure and Realignment Act of 1990, referred to in subsec. (h)(4)(E)(ii)(II), is Pub. L. No. 101–510, Part A, Title XXIX, §§ 2901 to 2910, 104 Stat. 1808 (Nov. 5, 1990), as amended, which is set out as a note under section 2687 of Title 10, Armed Forces.

The Solid Waste Disposal Act, referred to in subsec. (i), is Title II of Pub. L. No. 89–272, 79 Stat. 997 (Oct. 20, 1965), as amended generally by Pub. L. No. 94–580, § 2, 90 Stat. 2795 (Oct. 21, 1976), which is codified generally as chapter 82 (section 6901 et seq.) of this title. For complete classification of this Act to the Code, see Short Title of 1965 Acts note set out under section 6901 of this title and Tables.

Title III of the Superfund Amendments and Reauthorization Act of 1986, referred to in subsec. (j), is Title III (section 300 et seq.) of Pub. L. No. 99–499, 100 Stat. 1728 (Oct. 17, 1986), known as the Emergency Planning and Community Right-To-Know Act of 1986, which is codified principally as chapter 116 (section 11001 et seq.) of this title. For complete classification of the Emergency Planning and Community Right-To-Know Act of 1986 to the Code, see Short Title of 1986 Acts note set out under section 11001 of this title and Tables.

The Atomic Energy Act, referred to in subsec. (j)(2), probably means the Atomic Energy Act of 1954, Act of Aug. 30, 1954, c. 1073, § 1, 68 Stat. 919, as amended, which is codified principally as chapter 23 (section 2011 et seq.) of this title. For complete classification of this Act to the Code, see Short Title of 1954 Acts note set out under section 2011 of this title and Tables.

Coordination with Coast Guard

The Coast Guard Authorization Act of 2016, Pub. L. No. 114–120, § 534, 130 Stat. 75–76 (Feb. 8, 2016), as amended by Pub. L. No. 116–92, § 3514(e), 133 Stat. 1984–85, provided that:

"**(a) Environmental compliance.**—After the date on which the Secretary of the Interior conveys land under section 533 of this Act, nothing in this Act or any amendment made by this Act may be construed to affect or limit the application of or obligation to comply with any applicable environmental law, including section 120(h) of the Comprehensive Environmental Response, Compensation, and Liability Act of 1980 (42 U.S.C. 9620(h)), with respect to contaminants on such land prior to the date on which the land is conveyed.

"**(b) Liability.**—A person to which a conveyance is made under this subtitle shall hold the United States harmless from any liability with respect to activities carried out on or after the date of the conveyance of the real property conveyed. The United States shall remain responsible for any liability with respect to activities carried out before such date on the real property conveyed.

"**(c) Monitoring of known contamination.**—

"**(1) In general.**—To the extent practicable and subject to paragraph (2), any contamination in a Tract to be conveyed to the State or BSNC under this subtitle that—

"**(A)** is identified in writing prior to the conveyance; and

"**(B)** does not pose an immediate or long-term risk to human health or the environment; may be routinely monitored and managed by the State or BSNC, as applicable, through institutional controls.

"**(2) Institutional controls.**—Institutional controls may be used if—

"**(A)** the Administrator of the Environmental Protection Agency and the Governor of the State concur that such controls are protective of human health and the environment; and

"**(B)** such controls are carried out in accordance with Federal and State law."

Termination of Reporting Requirements

For termination, effective May 15, 2000, of provisions of law requiring submittal to Congress of any annual, semiannual, or other regular periodic report listed in House Document No. 103–7 (in which the report required by subsec. (e)(5) of this section is listed in item 5 on page 151), see Pub. L. No. 104–66, § 3003, as amended, and Pub. L. No. 106–554, § 1(a)(4) [div. A, § 1402(1)] set out as notes under 31 U.S.C.A. § 1113.

Identification of Uncontaminated Property at Installations to be Closed

Pub. L. No. 103–160, Div. B, Title XXIX, § 2910, 107 Stat. 1924 (Nov. 30, 1993), provided that: "The identification by the Secretary of Defense required under section 120(h)(4)(A) of the Comprehensive Environmental Response, Compensation, and Liability Act of 1980 (42 U.S.C. 9620(h)(4)(A)) [subsec. (h)(4)(A) of this section], and the concurrence required under section 120(h)(4)(B) of such Act [subsec. (h)(4)(B) of this section], shall be made not later than the earlier of—

"**(1)** the date that is 9 months after the date of the submittal, if any, to the transition coordinator for the installation concerned of a specific use proposed for all or a portion of the real property of the installation; or

"**(2)** the date specified in section 120(h)(4)(C)(iii) of such Act [subsec. (h)(4)(C)(iii) of this section]."

Congressional Findings

Section 2 of Pub. L. No. 102–426 provided that: "The Congress finds the following:

"**(1)** The closure of certain Federal facilities is having adverse effects on the economies of local communities by eliminating jobs associated with such facilities, and delay in remediation of environmental contamination of real property at such facilities is preventing transfer and private development of such property.

"**(2)** Each department, agency, or instrumentality of the United States, in cooperation with local communities, should expeditiously identify real property that offers the greatest opportunity for reuse and redevelopment on each facility under the jurisdiction of the department, agency, or instrumentality where operations are terminating.

"**(3)** Remedial actions, including remedial investigations and feasibility studies, and corrective actions at such Federal facilities should be expedited in a manner to facilitate environmental protection and the sale or transfer of such excess real property for the purpose of mitigating adverse economic effects on the surrounding community.

"**(4)** Each department, agency, or instrumentality of the United States, in accordance with applicable law, should make available without delay such excess real property.

"**(5)** In the case of any real property owned by the United States and transferred to another person, the United States Government should remain responsible for conducting any remedial action or corrective action necessary to protect human health and the environment with respect to any hazardous substance or petroleum product or its derivatives, including aviation fuel and motor oil, that was present on such real property at the time of transfer."

Limited Grandfather Provision

Section 120(b) of Pub. L. No. 99–499 provided that: "Section 120 of CERCLA [this section] shall not apply to any response action or remedial action for which a plan is under development by the Department of Energy on the date of enactment of this Act [Oct. 17, 1986] with respect to facilities—

"**(1)** owned or operated by the United States and subject to the jurisdiction of such Department;

"**(2)** located in St. Charles and St. Louis counties, Missouri, or the city of St. Louis, Missouri, and

"**(3)** published in the National Priorities List.

In preparing such plans, the Secretary of Energy shall consult with the Administrator of the Environmental Protection Agency."

§ 9621. Cleanup standards

[CERCLA § 121]

(a) Selection of remedial action

The President shall select appropriate remedial actions determined to be necessary to be carried out under section 9604 of this title or secured under section 9606 of this title which are in accordance with this section and, to the extent practicable, the national contingency plan, and which provide for cost-effective response. In evaluating the cost effectiveness of proposed alternative remedial actions, the President shall take into account the total short- and long-term costs of such actions, including the costs of operation and maintenance for the entire period during which such activities will be required.

(b) General rules

(1) Remedial actions in which treatment which permanently and significantly reduces the volume, toxicity or mobility of the hazardous substances, pollutants, and contaminants is a principal element, are to be preferred over remedial actions not involving such treatment. The offsite transport and disposal of hazardous substances or contaminated materials without such treatment should be the least favored alternative remedial action where practicable treatment technologies are available. The President shall conduct an assessment of permanent solutions and alternative treatment technologies or resource recovery technologies that, in whole or in part, will result in a permanent and significant decrease in the toxicity, mobility, or volume of the hazardous substance, pollutant, or contaminant. In making such assessment, the President shall specifically address the long-term effectiveness of various alternatives. In assessing alternative remedial actions, the President shall, at a minimum, take into account:

(A) the long-term uncertainties associated with land disposal;

(B) the goals, objectives, and requirements of the Solid Waste Disposal Act [42 U.S.C.A. § 6901 et seq.];

(C) the persistence, toxicity, mobility, and propensity to bioaccumulate of such hazardous substances and their constituents;

(D) short- and long-term potential for adverse health effects m human exposure;

(E) long-term maintenance costs;

(F) the potential for future remedial action costs if the alternative remedial action in question were to fail; and

(G) the potential threat to human health and the environment associated with excavation, transportation, and redisposal, or containment.

The President shall select a remedial action that is protective of human health and the environment, that is cost effective, and that utilizes permanent solutions and alternative treatment technologies or resource recovery technologies to the maximum extent practicable. If the President selects a remedial action not appropriate for a preference under this subsection, the President shall publish an explanation as to why a remedial action involving such reductions was not selected.

(2) The President may select an alternative remedial action meeting the objectives of this subsection whether or not such action has been achieved in practice at any other facility or site that has similar characteristics. In making such a selection, the President may take into account the degree of support for such remedial action by parties interested in such site.

(c) Review

If the President selects a remedial action that results in any hazardous substances, pollutants, or contaminants remaining at the site, the President shall review such remedial action no less often than each 5 years after the initiation of such remedial action to assure that human health and the environment are being protected by the remedial action being implemented. In addition, if upon such review it is the judgment of the President that action is appropriate at such site in accordance with section 9604 or 9606 of this title, the President shall take or require such action. The President shall report to the Congress a list of facilities for which such review is required, the results of all such reviews, and any actions taken as a result of such reviews.

(d) Degree of cleanup

(1) Remedial actions selected under this section or otherwise required or agreed to by the President under this chapter shall attain a degree of cleanup of hazardous substances, pollutants, and contaminants released into the environment and of control of further release at a minimum which assures protection of human health and the environment. Such remedial actions shall be relevant and appropriate under the circumstances presented by the release or threatened release of such substance, pollutant, or contaminant.

(2) (A) With respect to any hazardous substance, pollutant or contaminant that will remain onsite, if—

(i) any standard, requirement, criteria, or limitation under any Federal environmental law, including, but not limited to, the Toxic Substances Control Act [15 U.S.C.A. § 2601 et seq.], the Safe Drinking Water Act [42 U.S.C.A. § 300f et seq.], the Clean Air Act [42 U.S.C.A. § 7401 et seq.], the Clean Water Act [33 U.S.C.A. § 1251 et seq.], the Marine Protection, Research and Sanctuaries Act [16 U.S.C.A. § 1431 et seq., § 1447 et seq., 33 U.S.C.A. § 1401 et seq., § 2801 et seq.], or the Solid Waste Disposal Act [42 U.S.C.A. § 6901 et seq.]; or

(ii) any promulgated standard, requirement, criteria, or limitation under a State environmental or facility siting law that is more stringent than any Federal standard, requirement, criteria, or limitation, including each such State standard, requirement, criteria, or limitation contained in a program approved, authorized or delegated by the Administrator under a statute cited in subparagraph (A), and that has been identified to the President by the State in a timely manner,

is legally applicable to the hazardous substance or pollutant or contaminant concerned or is relevant and appropriate under the circumstances of the release or threatened release of such hazardous substance or pollutant or contaminant, the remedial action selected under section 9604 of this title or secured under section 9606 of this title shall require, at the completion of the remedial action, a level or standard of control for such hazardous substance or pollutant or contaminant which at least attains such legally applicable or relevant and appropriate standard, requirement, criteria, or limitation. Such remedial action shall require a level or standard of control which at least attains Maximum Contaminant Level Goals established under the Safe Drinking Water Act [42 U.S.C.A. § 300f et seq.] and water quality criteria established under section 304 or 303 of the Clean Water Act [33 U.S.C.A. § 1314 or 1313], where such goals or criteria are relevant and appropriate under the circumstances of the release or threatened release.

(B) (i) In determining whether or not any water quality criteria under the Clean Water Act [33 U.S.C.A. § 1251 et seq.] is relevant and appropriate under the circumstances of the release or threatened release, the President shall consider the designated or potential use of the surface or groundwater, the environmental media affected, the purposes for which such criteria were developed, and the latest information available.

(ii) For the purposes of this section, a process for establishing alternate concentration limits to those otherwise applicable for hazardous constituents in groundwater under subparagraph (A) may not be used to establish applicable standards under this paragraph if the process assumes a point of human exposure beyond the boundary of the facility, as defined at the conclusion of the remedial investigation and feasibility study, except where—

(I) there are known and projected points of entry of such groundwater into surface water; and

(II) on the basis of measurements or projections, there is or will be no statistically significant increase of such constituents m such groundwater in such surface water at the point of entry or at any point where there is reason to believe accumulation of constituents may occur downstream; and

(III) the remedial action includes enforceable measures that will preclude human exposure to the contaminated groundwater at any point between the facility boundary and all known and projected points of entry of such groundwater into surface water

then the assumed point of human exposure may be at such known and projected points of entry.

(C) **(i)** Clause (ii) of this subparagraph shall be applicable only in cases where, due to the President's selection, in compliance with subsection (b)(1) of this section, of a proposed remedial action which does not permanently and significantly reduce the volume, toxicity, or mobility of hazardous substances, pollutants, or contaminants, the proposed disposition of waste generated by or associated with the remedial action selected by the President is land disposal in a State referred to in clause (ii).

(ii) Except as provided in clauses (iii) and (iv), a State standard, requirement, criteria, or limitation (including any State siting standard or requirement) which could effectively result in the statewide prohibition of land disposal of hazardous substances, pollutants, or contaminants shall not apply.

(iii) Any State standard, requirement, criteria, or limitation referred to in clause (ii) shall apply where each of the following conditions is met:

(I) The State standard, requirement, criteria, or limitation is of general applicability and was adopted by formal means.

(II) The State standard, requirement, criteria, or limitation was adopted on the basis of hydrologic, geologic, or other relevant considerations and was not adopted for the purpose of precluding onsite remedial actions or other land disposal for reasons unrelated to protection of human health and the environment.

(III) The State arranges for, and assures payment of the incremental costs of utilizing, a facility for disposition of the hazardous substances, pollutants, or contaminants concerned.

(iv) Where the remedial action selected by the President does not conform to a State standard and the State has initiated a law suit against the Environmental Protection Agency prior to May 1, 1986, to seek to have the remedial action conform to such standard, the President shall conform the remedial action to the State standard. The State shall assure the availability of an offsite facility for such remedial action.

(3) In the case of any removal or remedial action involving the transfer of any hazardous substance or pollutant or contaminant offsite, such hazardous substance or pollutant or contaminant shall only be transferred to a facility which is operating in compliance with section 3004 and 3005 of the Solid Waste Disposal Act [42 U.S.C.A. §§ 6924 and 6925] (or, where applicable, in compliance with the Toxic Substances Control Act [15 U.S.C.A. § 2601 et seq.] or other applicable Federal law) and all applicable State requirements. Such substance or pollutant or contaminant may be transferred to a land disposal facility only if the President determines that both of the following requirements are met:

(A) The unit to which the hazardous substance or pollutant or contaminant is transferred is not releasing any hazardous waste, or constituent thereof, into the groundwater or surface water or soil.

(B) All such releases m other units at the facility are being controlled by a corrective action program approved by the Administrator under subtitle C of the Solid Waste Disposal Act [42 U.S.C.A. § 6921 et seq.].

The President shall notify the owner or operator of such facility of determinations under this paragraph.

(4) The President may select a remedial action meeting the requirements of paragraph (1) that does not attain a level or standard of control at least equivalent to a legally applicable or relevant and appropriate standard, requirement, criteria, or limitation as required by paragraph (2) (including subparagraph (B) thereof), if the President finds that—

(A) the remedial action selected is only part of a total remedial action that will attain such level or standard of control when completed;

(B) compliance with such requirement at that facility will result in greater risk to human health and the environment than alternative options;

(C) compliance with such requirements is technically impracticable m an engineering perspective;

(D) the remedial action selected will attain a standard of performance that is equivalent to that required under the otherwise applicable standard, requirement, criteria, or limitation, through use of another method or approach;

(E) with respect to a State standard, requirement, criteria, or limitation, the State has not consistently applied (or demonstrated the intention to consistently apply) the standard, requirement, criteria, or limitation in similar circumstances at other remedial actions within the State; or

(F) in the case of a remedial action to be undertaken solely under section 9604 of this title using the Fund, selection of a remedial action that attains such level or standard of control will not provide a balance between the need for protection of public health and welfare and the environment at the facility under consideration, and the availability of amounts m the Fund to respond to other sites which present or may present a threat to public health or welfare or the environment, taking into consideration the relative immediacy of such threats.

The President shall publish such findings, together with an explanation and appropriate documentation.

(e) Permits and enforcement

(1) No Federal, State, or local permit shall be required for the portion of any removal or remedial action conducted entirely onsite, where such remedial action is selected and carried out in compliance with this section.

(2) A State may enforce any Federal or State standard, requirement, criteria, or limitation to which the remedial action is required to conform under this chapter in the United States district court for the district in which the facility is located. Any consent decree shall require the parties to attempt expeditiously to resolve disagreements concerning implementation of the remedial action informally with the appropriate Federal and State agencies. Where the parties agree, the consent decree may provide for administrative enforcement. Each consent decree shall also contain stipulated penalties for violations of the decree in an amount not to exceed $25,000 per day, which may be enforced by either the President or the State. Such stipulated penalties shall not be construed to impair or affect the authority of the court to order compliance with the specific terms of any such decree.

(f) State involvement

(1) The President shall promulgate regulations providing for substantial and meaningful involvement by each State in initiation, development, and selection of remedial actions to be undertaken in that State. The regulations, at a minimum, shall include each of the following:

(A) State involvement in decisions whether to perform a preliminary assessment and site inspection.

(B) Allocation of responsibility for hazard ranking system scoring.

(C) State concurrence in deleting sites m the National Priorities List.

(D) State participation in the long-term planning process for all remedial sites within the State.

(E) A reasonable opportunity for States to review and comment on each of the following:

(i) The remedial investigation and feasibility study and all data and technical documents leading to its issuance.

(ii) The planned remedial action identified in the remedial investigation and feasibility study.

(iii) The engineering design following selection of the final remedial action.

(iv) Other technical data and reports relating to implementation of the remedy.

(v) Any proposed finding or decision by the President to exercise the authority of subsection (d)(4) of this section.

(F) Notice to the State of negotiations with potentially responsible parties regarding the scope of any response action at a facility in the State and an opportunity to participate in such negotiations and, subject to paragraph (2), be a party to any settlement.

(G) Notice to the State and an opportunity to comment on the President's proposed plan for remedial action as well as on alternative plans under consideration. The President's proposed decision regarding the selection of remedial action shall be accompanied by a response to the comments submitted by the State, including an explanation regarding any decision under subsection (d)(4) of this section on compliance with promulgated State standards. A copy of such response shall also be provided to the State.

(H) Prompt notice and explanation of each proposed action to the State in which the facility is located.

Prior to the promulgation of such regulations, the President shall provide notice to the State of negotiations with potentially responsible parties regarding the scope of any response action at a facility in the State, and such State may participate in such negotiations and, subject to paragraph (2), any settlements.

(2) (A) This paragraph shall apply to remedial actions secured under section 9606 of this title. At least 30 days prior to the entering of any consent decree, if the President proposes to select a remedial action that does not attain a legally applicable or relevant and appropriate standard, requirement, criteria, or limitation, under the authority of subsection (d)(4) of this section, the President shall provide an opportunity for the State to concur or not concur in such selection. If the State concurs, the State may become a signatory to the consent decree.

(B) If the State does not concur in such selection, and the State desires to have the remedial action conform to such standard, requirement, criteria, or limitation, the State shall intervene in the action under section 9606 of this title before entry of the consent decree, to seek to have the remedial action so conform. Such intervention shall be a matter of right. The remedial action shall conform to such standard, requirement, criteria, or limitation if the State establishes, on the administrative record, that the finding of the President was not supported by substantial evidence. If the court determines that the remedial action shall conform to such standard, requirement, criteria, or limitation, the remedial action shall be so modified and the State may become a signatory to the decree. If the court determines that the remedial action need not conform to such standard, requirement, criteria, or limitation, and the State pays or assures the payment of the additional costs attributable to meeting such standard, requirement, criteria, or limitation, the remedial action shall be so modified and the State shall become a signatory to the decree.

(C) The President may conclude settlement negotiations with potentially responsible parties without State concurrence.

(3) (A) This paragraph shall apply to remedial actions at facilities owned or operated by a department, agency, or instrumentality of the United States. At least 30 days prior to the publication of the President's final remedial action plan, if the President proposes to select a remedial action that does not attain a legally applicable or relevant and appropriate standard, requirement, criteria, or limitation, under the authority of subsection (d)(4) of this section, the President shall provide an opportunity for the State to concur or not concur in such selection. If the State concurs, or does not act within 30 days, the remedial action may proceed.

(B) If the State does not concur in such selection as provided in subparagraph (A), and desires to have the remedial action conform to such standard, requirement, criteria, or limitation, the State may maintain an action as follows:

(i) If the President has notified the State of selection of such a remedial action, the State may bring an action within 30 days of such notification for the sole purpose of determining whether the finding of the President is supported by substantial evidence. Such action shall be brought in the United States district court for the district in which the facility is located.

(ii) If the State establishes, on the administrative record, that the President's finding is not supported by substantial evidence, the remedial action shall be modified to conform to such standard, requirement, criteria, or limitation.

(iii) If the State fails to establish that the President's finding was not supported by substantial evidence and if the State pays, within 60 days of judgment, the additional costs attributable to meeting such standard, requirement, criteria, or limitation, the remedial action shall be selected to meet such standard, requirement, criteria, or limitation. If the State fails to pay within 60 days, the remedial action selected by the President shall proceed through completion.

(C) Nothing in this section precludes, and the court shall not enjoin, the Federal agency m taking any remedial action unrelated to or not inconsistent with such standard, requirement, criteria, or limitation.

(Pub. L. No. 96–510, Title I, § 121, as added by Pub. L. No. 99–499, Title I, § 121(a), 100 Stat. 1672 (Oct. 17, 1986).)

HISTORICAL AND STATUTORY NOTES

References in Text

The Solid Waste Disposal Act, referred to in subsecs. (b)(1)(B), (d)(2)(A)(i), is Title II of Pub. L. No. 89–272, 79 Stat. 997 (Oct. 20, 1965), as amended generally by Pub. L. No. 94–580, § 2, 90 Stat. 2795 (Oct. 21, 1976), which is codified generally as chapter 82 (section 6901 et seq.) of this title. Subtitle C of the Solid Waste Disposal Act, referred to in subsec. (d)(3)(B), is codified generally as subchapter III (section 6921 et seq.) of chapter 82 of this title. For complete classification of this Act to the Code, see Short Title of 1965 Acts note set out under section 6901 of this title and Tables.

The Toxic Substances Control Act, referred to in subsec. (d)(2)(A)(i), (3), is Pub. L. No. 94–469, 90 Stat. 2003 (Oct. 11, 1976), as amended, which is codified generally as chapter 53 (section 2601 et seq.) of Title 15, Commerce and Trade. For complete classification of this Act to the Code, see Short Title note set out under section 2601 of Title 15 and Tables.

The Safe Drinking Water Act, referred to in subsec. (d)(2)(A)(i), is Pub. L. No. 93–523, 88 Stat. 1660 (Dec. 16, 1974), as amended, which is codified principally as subchapter XII (section 300f et seq.) of chapter 6A of this title. For complete classification of this Act to the Code, see Short Title of 1974 Amendments note set out under section 201 of this title and Tables.

The Clean Air Act, referred to in subsec. (d)(2)(A)(i), is Act of July 14, 1955, c. 360, as amended generally by Pub. L. No. 88–206, 77 Stat. 392 (Dec. 17, 1963), and later by Pub. L. No. 95–95, 91 Stat. 685 (Aug. 7, 1977). The Clean Air Act was originally codified as chapter 15B (section 1857 et seq.) of this title. On enactment of Pub. L. No. 95–95, the Act was recodified as chapter 85 (section 7401 et seq.) of this title. For complete classification of this Act to the Code, see Short Title of 1955 Acts note set out under section 7401 of this title and Tables.

The Clean Water Act, referred to in subsec. (d)(2)(A)(i), (B)(i), is Act of June 30, 1948, c. 758, as amended generally by Pub. L. No. 92–500, § 2, 86 Stat. 816 (Oct. 18, 1972), also known as the Federal Water Pollution Control Act, which is codified generally as chapter 26 (section 1251 et seq.) of Title 33, Navigation and Navigable Waters. For complete classification of this Act to the Code, see Short Title note set out under section 1251 of Title 33 and Tables.

The Marine Protection, Research and Sanctuaries Act, referred to in subsec. (d)(2)(A)(i), probably means the Marine Protection, Research and Sanctuaries Act of 1972, Pub. L. No. 92–532, 86 Stat. 1052 (Oct. 23, 1972), as amended, which enacted chapters 32 (section 1431 et seq.) and 32A (section 1447 et seq.) of Title 16, Conservation, and chapters 27 (section 1401 et seq.) and 41 (section 2801 et seq.) of Title 33, Navigation and Navigable Waters. For complete classification of this Act to the Code, see Short Title note set out under section 1401 of Title 33 and Tables.

Effective and Applicability Provisions

1986 Acts. Section 121(b) of Pub. L. No. 99–499 provided that: "With respect to section 121 of CERCLA [this section], as added by this section—

"(1) The requirements of section 121 of CERCLA shall not apply to any remedial action for which the Record of Decision (hereinafter in this section referred to as the 'ROD') was signed, or the consent decree was lodged, before date of enactment [Oct. 17, 1986].

"(2) If the ROD was signed, or the consent decree lodged, within the 30-day period immediately following enactment of the Act [Oct. 17, 1986], the Administrator shall certify in writing that the portion of the remedial action covered by the ROD or consent decree complies to the maximum extent practicable with section 121 of CERCLA.

"Any ROD signed before enactment of this Act [Oct. 17, 1986] and reopened after enactment of this Act to modify or supplement the selection of remedy shall be subject to the requirements of section 121 of CERCLA [this section]."

Delegation of Functions

Functions vested in the President by subsec. (f)(1) of this section, relating to the promulgation of regulations and guidelines, delegated to the Administrator of the Environmental Protection Agency, to be exercised in consultation with the National Response Team, see section 2(b) of Ex. Ord. No. 12580, 52 Fed. Reg. 2923 (Jan. 23, 1987), set out as a note under section 9615 of this title.

Functions vested in the President by this section delegated, with authority to redelegate, (and subject to section 2(a), (b) and (c) of Ex. Ord. No. 12580) to the Secretaries of Defense and Energy, with respect to releases or threatened releases where either the release is on or the sole source of the release is from any facility or vessel under the jurisdiction, custody or control of their departments, respectively, including vessels bare-boat chartered and operated, with such functions to be exercised consistent with the requirements of section 9620 of this title, see sections 2(d), 11(g) of Ex. Ord. No. 12580, 52 Fed. Reg. 2923 (Jan. 23, 1987), set out as a note under section 9615 of this title.

Functions vested in the President by this section, subject to section 2(a) to (d) of Ex. Ord. No. 12580, delegated, with authority to redelegate, to the heads of Executive departments and agencies, with respect to remedial actions for releases or threatened releases which are not on the National Priorities List and removal actions other than emergencies, where either the release is on or the sole source of the release is from any facility or vessel under the jurisdiction, custody or control of those departments and agencies, including vessels bare-boat chartered and operated with the Administrator of the Environmental Protection Agency to define the term "emergency", solely for the purposes of section 2(e) of Ex. Ord. No. 12580, either by regulation or by a memorandum of understanding with the head of an Executive department or agency, see sections 2(e)(1), 11(g) of Ex. Ord. No. 12580, 52 Fed. Reg. 2923 (Jan. 23, 1987), set out as a note under section 9615 of this title.

Functions vested in the President by this section, subject to section 2(a) to (e) of Ex. Ord. No. 12580, delegated, with authority to redelegate, to the Secretary of the Department in which the Coast Guard is operating ("the Coast Guard"), with respect to any release or threatened release involving the coastal zone, Great Lakes waters, ports, and harbors, see sections 2(f), 11(g) of Ex. Ord. No. 12580, 52 Fed. Reg. 2923 (Jan. 23, 1987), set out as a note under section 9615 of this title.

Functions vested in the President by this section, subject to section 2(a) to (f) of Ex. Ord. No. 12580, delegated, with authority to redelegate, to the Administrator of the Environmental Protection Agency, see sections 2(g), 11(g) of Ex. Ord. No. 12580, 52 Fed. Reg. 2923 (Jan. 23, 1987), set out as a note under section 9615 of this title.

Termination of Reporting Requirements

For termination, effective May 15, 2000, of provisions of law requiring submittal to Congress of any annual, semiannual, or other regular periodic report listed in House Document No. 103–7 (in which the report required by subsec. (c) of this section is listed as item 15 on page 20), see Pub. L. No. 104–66, § 3003, as amended, set out as a note under 31 U.S.C.A. § 1113.

§ 9622. Settlements

[CERCLA § 122]

(a) Authority to enter into agreements

The President, in his discretion, may enter into an agreement with any person (including the owner or operator of the facility from which a release or substantial threat of release emanates, or any other potentially responsible person), to perform any response action (including any action described in section

9604(b) of this title) if the President determines that such action will be done properly by such person. Whenever practicable and in the public interest, as determined by the President, the President shall act to facilitate agreements under this section that are in the public interest and consistent with the National Contingency Plan in order to expedite effective remedial actions and minimize litigation. If the President decides not to use the procedures in this section, the President shall notify in writing potentially responsible parties at the facility of such decision and the reasons why use of the procedures is inappropriate. A decision of the President to use or not to use the procedures in this section is not subject to judicial review.

(b) Agreements with potentially responsible parties

(1) Mixed funding

An agreement under this section may provide that the President will reimburse the parties to the agreement from the Fund, with interest, for certain costs of actions under the agreement that the parties have agreed to perform but which the President has agreed to finance. In any case in which the President provides such reimbursement, the President shall make all reasonable efforts to recover the amount of such reimbursement under section 9607 of this title or under other relevant authorities.

(2) Reviewability

The President's decisions regarding the availability of fund financing under this subsection shall not be subject to judicial review under subsection (d) of this section.

(3) Retention of funds

If, as part of any agreement, the President will be carrying out any action and the parties will be paying amounts to the President, the President may, notwithstanding any other provision of law, retain and use such amounts for purposes of carrying out the agreement.

(4) Future obligation of Fund

In the case of a completed remedial action pursuant to an agreement described in paragraph (1), the Fund shall be subject to an obligation for subsequent remedial actions at the same facility but only to the extent that such subsequent actions are necessary by reason of the failure of the original remedial action. Such obligation shall be in a proportion equal to, but not exceeding, the proportion contributed by the Fund for the original remedial action. The Fund's obligation for such future remedial action may be met through Fund expenditures or through payment, following settlement or enforcement action, by parties who were not signatories to the original agreement.

(c) Effect of agreement

(1) Liability

Whenever the President has entered into an agreement under this section, the liability to the United States under this chapter of each party to the agreement, including any future liability to the United States, arising from the release or threatened release that is the subject of the agreement shall be limited as provided in the agreement pursuant to a covenant not to sue in accordance with subsection (f) of this section. A covenant not to sue may provide that future liability to the United States of a settling potentially responsible party under the agreement may be limited to the same proportion as that established in the original settlement agreement. Nothing in this section shall limit or otherwise affect the authority of any court to review in the consent decree process under subsection (d) of this section any covenant not to sue contained in an agreement under this section. In determining the extent to which the liability of parties to an agreement shall be limited pursuant to a covenant not to sue, the President shall be guided by the principle that a more complete covenant not to sue shall be provided for a more permanent remedy undertaken by such parties.

(2) Actions against other persons

If an agreement has been entered into under this section, the President may take any action under section 9606 of this title against any person who is not a party to the agreement, once the period for submitting a proposal under subsection (e)(2)(B) of this section has expired. Nothing in this section shall be construed to affect either of the following:

(A) The liability of any person under section 9606 or 9607 of this title with respect to any costs or damages which are not included in the agreement.

(B) The authority of the President to maintain an action under this chapter against any person who is not a party to the agreement.

(d) Enforcement

(1) Cleanup agreements

(A) Consent decree

Whenever the President enters into an agreement under this section with any potentially responsible party with respect to remedial action under section 9606 of this title, following approval of the agreement by the Attorney General, except as otherwise provided in the case of certain administrative settlements referred to in subsection (g) of this section, the agreement shall be entered in the appropriate United States district court as a consent decree. The President need not make any finding regarding an imminent and substantial endangerment to the public health or the environment in connection with any such agreement or consent decree.

(B) Effect

The entry of any consent decree under this subsection shall not be construed to be an acknowledgment by the parties that the release or threatened release concerned constitutes an imminent and substantial endangerment to the public health or welfare or the environment. Except as otherwise provided in the Federal Rules of Evidence, the participation by any party in the process under this section shall not be considered an admission of liability for any purpose, and the fact of such participation shall not be admissible in any judicial or administrative proceeding, including a subsequent proceeding under this section.

(C) Structure

The President may fashion a consent decree so that the entering of such decree and compliance with such decree or with any determination or agreement made pursuant to this section shall not be considered an admission of liability for any purpose.

(2) Public participation

(A) Filing of proposed judgment

At least 30 days before a final judgment is entered under paragraph (1), the proposed judgment shall be filed with the court.

(B) Opportunity for comment

The Attorney General shall provide an opportunity to persons who are not named as parties to the action to comment on the proposed judgment before its entry by the court as a final judgment. The Attorney General shall consider, and file with the court, any written comments, views, or allegations relating to the proposed judgment. The Attorney General may withdraw or withhold its consent to the proposed judgment if the comments, views, and allegations concerning the judgment disclose facts or considerations which indicate that the proposed judgment is inappropriate, improper, or inadequate.

(3) 9604(b) agreements

Whenever the President enters into an agreement under this section with any potentially responsible party with respect to action under section 9604(b) of this title, the President shall issue an order or enter into a decree setting forth the obligations of such party. The United States district court for the district in which the release or threatened release occurs may enforce such order or decree.

(e) Special notice procedures

(1) Notice

Whenever the President determines that a period of negotiation under this subsection would facilitate an agreement with potentially responsible parties for taking response action (including any action described in section 9604(b) of this title) and would expedite remedial action, the President shall so notify all such parties and shall provide them with information concerning each of the following:

(A) The names and addresses of potentially responsible parties (including owners and operators and other persons referred to in section 9607(a) of this title), to the extent such information is available.

(B) To the extent such information is available, the volume and nature of substances contributed by each potentially responsible party identified at the facility.

(C) A ranking by volume of the substances at the facility, to the extent such information is available.

The President shall make the information referred to in this paragraph available in advance of notice under this paragraph upon the request of a potentially responsible party in accordance with procedures provided by the President. The provisions of subsection (e) of section 9604 of this title regarding protection of confidential information apply to information provided under this paragraph. Disclosure of information generated by the President under this section to persons other than the Congress, or any duly authorized Committee thereof, is subject to other privileges or protections provided by law, including (but not limited to) those applicable to attorney work product. Nothing contained in this paragraph or in other provisions of this chapter shall be construed, interpreted, or applied to diminish the required disclosure of information under other provisions of this or other Federal or State laws.

(2) Negotiation

(A) Moratorium

Except as provided in this subsection, the President may not commence action under section 9604(a) of this title or take any action under section 9606 of this title for 120 days after providing notice and information under this subsection with respect to such action. Except as provided in this subsection, the President may not commence a remedial investigation and feasibility study under section 9604(b) of this title for 90 days after providing notice and information under this subsection with respect to such action. The President may commence any additional studies or investigations authorized under section 9604(b) of this title, including remedial design, during the negotiation period.

(B) Proposals

Persons receiving notice and information under paragraph (1) of this subsection with respect to action under section 9606 of this title shall have 60 days from the date of receipt of such notice to make a proposal to the President for undertaking or financing the action under section 9606 of this title. Persons receiving notice and information under paragraph (1) of this subsection with respect to action under section 9604(b) of this title shall have 60 days from the date of receipt of such notice to make a proposal to the President for undertaking or financing the action under section 9604(b) of this title.

(C) Additional parties

If an additional potentially responsible party is identified during the negotiation period or after an agreement has been entered into under this subsection concerning a release or threatened release, the President may bring the additional party into the negotiation or enter into a separate agreement with such party.

(3) Preliminary allocation of responsibility

(A) In general

The President shall develop guidelines for preparing nonbinding preliminary allocations of responsibility. In developing these guidelines the President may include such factors as the President considers relevant, such as: volume, toxicity, mobility, strength of evidence, ability to pay, litigative risks, public interest considerations, precedential value, and inequities and aggravating factors. When it would expedite settlements under this section and remedial action, the President may, after completion of the remedial investigation and feasibility study, provide a nonbinding preliminary allocation of responsibility which allocates percentages of the total cost of response among potentially responsible parties at the facility.

(B) Collection of information

To collect information necessary or appropriate for performing the allocation under subparagraph (A) or for otherwise implementing this section, the President may by subpoena require the attendance and testimony of witnesses and the production of reports, papers, documents, answers to questions, and other information that the President deems necessary. Witnesses shall be paid the same fees and mileage that are paid witnesses in the courts of the United States. In the event of contumacy or failure or refusal of any person to obey any such subpoena, any district court of the United States in which venue is proper shall have jurisdiction to order any such person to comply with such subpoena. Any failure to obey such an order of the court is punishable by the court as a contempt thereof.

(C) Effect

The nonbinding preliminary allocation of responsibility shall not be admissible as evidence in any proceeding, and no court shall have jurisdiction to review the nonbinding preliminary allocation of responsibility. The nonbinding preliminary allocation of responsibility shall not constitute an apportionment or other statement on the divisibility of harm or causation.

(D) Costs

The costs incurred by the President in producing the nonbinding preliminary allocation of responsibility shall be reimbursed by the potentially responsible parties whose offer is accepted by the President. Where an offer under this section is not accepted, such costs shall be considered costs of response.

(E) Decision to reject offer

Where the President, in his discretion, has provided a nonbinding preliminary allocation of responsibility and the potentially responsible parties have made a substantial offer providing for response to the President which he rejects, the reasons for the rejection shall be provided in a written explanation. The President's decision to reject such an offer shall not be subject to judicial review.

(4) Failure to propose

If the President determines that a good faith proposal for undertaking or financing action under section 9606 of this title has not been submitted within 60 days of the provision of notice pursuant to this subsection, the President may thereafter commence action under section 9604(a) of this title or take an action against any person under section 9606 of this title. If the President determines that a good faith proposal for undertaking or financing action under section 9604(b) of this title has not been submitted within 60 days after the provision of notice pursuant to this subsection, the President may thereafter commence action under section 9604(b) of this title.

(5) Significant threats

Nothing in this subsection shall limit the President's authority to undertake response or enforcement action regarding a significant threat to public health or the environment within the negotiation period established by this subsection.

(6) Inconsistent response action

When either the President, or a potentially responsible party pursuant to an administrative order or consent decree under this chapter, has initiated a remedial investigation and feasibility study for a particular facility under this chapter, no potentially responsible party may undertake any remedial action at the facility unless such remedial action has been authorized by the President.

(f) Covenant not to sue

(1) Discretionary covenants

The President may, in his discretion, provide any person with a covenant not to sue concerning any liability to the United States under this chapter, including future liability, resulting from a release or threatened release of a hazardous substance addressed by a remedial action, whether that action is onsite or offsite, if each of the following conditions is met:

(A) The covenant not to sue is in the public interest.

(B) The covenant not to sue would expedite response action consistent with the National Contingency Plan under section 9605 of this title.

(C) The person is in full compliance with a consent decree under section 9606 of this title (including a consent decree entered into in accordance with this section) for response to the release or threatened release concerned.

(D) The response action has been approved by the President.

(2) Special covenants not to sue

In the case of any person to whom the President is authorized under paragraph (1) of this subsection to provide a covenant not to sue, for the portion of remedial action—

(A) which involves the transport and secure disposition offsite of hazardous substances in a facility meeting the requirements of sections 6924(c), (d), (e), (f), (g), (m), (*o*), (p), (u), and (v) and 6925(c) of this title, where the President has rejected a proposed remedial action that is consistent with the National Contingency Plan that does not include such offsite disposition and has thereafter required offsite disposition; or

(B) which involves the treatment of hazardous substances so as to destroy, eliminate, or permanently immobilize the hazardous constituents of such substances, such that, in the judgment of the President, the substances no longer present any current or currently foreseeable future significant risk to public health, welfare or the environment, no byproduct of the treatment or destruction process presents any significant hazard to public health, welfare or the environment, and all byproducts are themselves treated, destroyed, or contained in a manner which assures that such byproducts do not present any current or currently foreseeable future significant risk to public health, welfare or the environment,

the President shall provide such person with a covenant not to sue with respect to future liability to the United States under this chapter for a future release or threatened release of hazardous substances from such facility, and a person provided such covenant not to sue shall not be liable to the United States under section 9606 or 9607 of this title with respect to such release or threatened release at a future time.

(3) Requirement that remedial action be completed

A covenant not to sue concerning future liability to the United States shall not take effect until the President certifies that remedial action has been completed in accordance with the requirements of this chapter at the facility that is the subject of such covenant.

(4) Factors

In assessing the appropriateness of a covenant not to sue under paragraph (1) and any condition to be included in a covenant not to sue under paragraph (1) or (2), the President shall consider whether the covenant or condition is in the public interest on the basis of such factors as the following:

(A) The effectiveness and reliability of the remedy, in light of the other alternative remedies considered for the facility concerned.

(B) The nature of the risks remaining at the facility.

(C) The extent to which performance standards are included in the order or decree.

(D) The extent to which the response action provides a complete remedy for the facility, including a reduction in the hazardous nature of the substances at the facility.

(E) The extent to which the technology used in the response action is demonstrated to be effective.

(F) Whether the Fund or other sources of funding would be available for any additional remedial actions that might eventually be necessary at the facility.

(G) Whether the remedial action will be carried out, in whole or in significant part, by the responsible parties themselves.

(5) Satisfactory performance

Any covenant not to sue under this subsection shall be subject to the satisfactory performance by such party of its obligations under the agreement concerned.

(6) Additional condition for future liability

(A) Except for the portion of the remedial action which is subject to a covenant not to sue under paragraph (2) or under subsection (g) of this section (relating to de minimis settlements), a covenant not to sue a person concerning future liability to the United States shall include an exception to the covenant that allows the President to sue such person concerning future liability resulting from the release or threatened release that is the subject of the covenant where such liability arises out of conditions which are unknown at the time the President certifies under paragraph (3) that remedial action has been completed at the facility concerned.

(B) In extraordinary circumstances, the President may determine, after assessment of relevant factors such as those referred to in paragraph (4) and volume, toxicity, mobility, strength of evidence, ability to pay, litigative risks, public interest considerations, precedential value, and inequities and aggravating factors, not to include the exception referred to in subparagraph (A) if other terms, conditions, or requirements of the agreement containing the covenant not to sue are sufficient to provide all reasonable assurances that public health and the environment will be protected from any future releases at or from the facility.

(C) The President is authorized to include any provisions allowing future enforcement action under section 9606 or 9607 of this title that in the discretion of the President are necessary and appropriate to assure protection of public health, welfare, and the environment.

(g) De minimis settlements

(1) Expedited final settlement

Whenever practicable and in the public interest, as determined by the President, the President shall as promptly as possible reach a final settlement with a potentially responsible party in an administrative or civil action under section 9606 or 9607 of this title if such settlement involves only a minor portion of the response costs at the facility concerned and, in the judgment of the President, the conditions in either of the following subparagraph (A) or (B) are met:

(A) Both of the following are minimal in comparison to other hazardous substances at the facility:

(i) The amount of the hazardous substances contributed by that party to the facility.

(ii) The toxic or other hazardous effects of the substances contributed by that party to the facility.

(B) The potentially responsible party—

(i) is the owner of the real property on or in which the facility is located;

(ii) did not conduct or permit the generation, transportation, storage, treatment, or disposal of any hazardous substance at the facility; and

(iii) did not contribute to the release or threat of release of a hazardous substance at the facility through any action or omission.

This subparagraph (B) does not apply if the potentially responsible party purchased the real property with actual or constructive knowledge that the property was used for the generation, transportation, storage, treatment, or disposal of any hazardous substance.

(2) Covenant not to sue

The President may provide a covenant not to sue with respect to the facility concerned to any party who has entered into a settlement under this subsection unless such a covenant would be inconsistent with the public interest as determined under subsection (f) of this section.

(3) Expedited agreement

The President shall reach any such settlement or grant any such covenant not to sue as soon as possible after the President has available the information necessary to reach such a settlement or grant such a covenant.

(4) Consent decree or administrative order

A settlement under this subsection shall be entered as a consent decree or embodied in an administrative order setting forth the terms of the settlement. In the case of any facility where the total response costs exceed $500,000 (excluding interest), if the settlement is embodied as an administrative order, the order may be issued only with the prior written approval of the Attorney General. If the Attorney General or his designee has not approved or disapproved the order within 30 days of this referral, the order shall be deemed to be approved unless the Attorney General and the Administrator have agreed to extend the time. The district court for the district in which the release or threatened release occurs may enforce any such administrative order.

(5) Effect of agreement

A party who has resolved its liability to the United States under this subsection shall not be liable for claims for contribution regarding matters addressed in the settlement. Such settlement does not discharge any of the other potentially responsible parties unless its terms so provide, but it reduces the potential liability of the others by the amount of the settlement.

(6) Settlements with other potentially responsible parties

Nothing in this subsection shall be construed to affect the authority of the President to reach settlements with other potentially responsible parties under this chapter.

(7) Reduction in settlement amount based on limited ability to pay

(A) In general

The condition for settlement under this paragraph is that the potentially responsible party is a person who demonstrates to the President an inability or a limited ability to pay response costs.

(B) Considerations

In determining whether or not a demonstration is made under subparagraph (A) by a person, the President shall take into consideration the ability of the person to pay response costs and still maintain its basic business operations, including consideration of the overall financial condition of the person and demonstrable constraints on the ability of the person to raise revenues.

(C) Information

A person requesting settlement under this paragraph shall promptly provide the President with all relevant information needed to determine the ability of the person to pay response costs.

(D) Alternative payment methods

If the President determines that a person is unable to pay its total settlement amount at the time of settlement, the President shall consider such alternative payment methods as may be necessary or appropriate.

(8) Additional conditions for expedited settlements

(A) Waiver of claims

The President shall require, as a condition for settlement under this subsection, that a potentially responsible party waive all of the claims (including a claim for contribution under this chapter) that the party may have against other potentially responsible parties for response costs incurred with respect to the facility, unless the President determines that requiring a waiver would be unjust.

(B) Failure to comply

The President may decline to offer a settlement to a potentially responsible party under this subsection if the President determines that the potentially responsible party has failed to comply with any request for access or information or an administrative subpoena issued by the President under this chapter or has impeded or is impeding, through action or inaction, the performance of a response action with respect to the facility.

(C) Responsibility to provide information and access

A potentially responsible party that enters into a settlement under this subsection shall not be relieved of the responsibility to provide any information or access requested in accordance with subsection (e)(3)(B) of this section or section 9604(e) of this title.

(9) Basis of determination

If the President determines that a potentially responsible party is not eligible for settlement under this subsection, the President shall provide the reasons for the determination in writing to the potentially responsible party that requested a settlement under this subsection.

(10) Notification

As soon as practicable after receipt of sufficient information to make a determination, the President shall notify any person that the President determines is eligible under paragraph (1) of the person's eligibility for an expedited settlement.

(11) No judicial review

A determination by the President under paragraph (7), (8), (9), or (10) shall not be subject to judicial review.

(12) Notice of settlement

After a settlement under this subsection becomes final with respect to a facility, the President shall promptly notify potentially responsible parties at the facility that have not resolved their liability to the United States of the settlement.

(h) Cost recovery settlement authority

(1) Authority to settle

The head of any department or agency with authority to undertake a response action under this chapter pursuant to the national contingency plan may consider, compromise, and settle a claim under section 9607 of this title for costs incurred by the United States Government if the claim has not been referred to the Department of Justice for further action. In the case of any facility where the total response costs exceed $500,000 (excluding interest), any claim referred to in the preceding sentence may be compromised and settled only with the prior written approval of the Attorney General.

(2) Use of arbitration

Arbitration in accordance with regulations promulgated under this subsection may be used as a method of settling claims of the United States where the total response costs for the facility concerned do not exceed $500,000 (excluding interest). After consultation with the Attorney General, the department or agency head may establish and publish regulations for the use of arbitration or settlement under this subsection.

(3) **Recovery of claims**

If any person fails to pay a claim that has been settled under this subsection, the department or agency head shall request the Attorney General to bring a civil action in an appropriate district court to recover the amount of such claim, plus costs, attorneys' fees, and interest from the date of the settlement. In such an action, the terms of the settlement shall not be subject to review.

(4) **Claims for contribution**

A person who has resolved its liability to the United States under this subsection shall not be liable for claims for contribution regarding matters addressed in the settlement. Such settlement shall not discharge any of the other potentially liable persons unless its terms so provide, but it reduces the potential liability of the others by the amount of the settlement.

(i) **Settlement procedures**

(1) **Publication in Federal Register**

At least 30 days before any settlement (including any settlement arrived at through arbitration) may become final under subsection (h) of this section, or under subsection (g) of this section in the case of a settlement embodied in an administrative order, the head of the department or agency which has jurisdiction over the proposed settlement shall publish in the Federal Register notice of the proposed settlement. The notice shall identify the facility concerned and the parties to the proposed settlement.

(2) **Comment period**

For a 30-day period beginning on the date of publication of notice under paragraph (1) of a proposed settlement, the head of the department or agency which has jurisdiction over the proposed settlement shall provide an opportunity for persons who are not parties to the proposed settlement to file written comments relating to the proposed settlement.

(3) **Consideration of comments**

The head of the department or agency shall consider any comments filed under paragraph (2) in determining whether or not to consent to the proposed settlement and may withdraw or withhold consent to the proposed settlement if such comments disclose facts or considerations which indicate the proposed settlement is inappropriate, improper, or inadequate.

(j) **Natural resources**

(1) **Notification of trustee**

Where a release or threatened release of any hazardous substance that is the subject of negotiations under this section may have resulted in damages to natural resources under the trusteeship of the United States, the President shall notify the Federal natural resource trustee of the negotiations and shall encourage the participation of such trustee in the negotiations.

(2) **Covenant not to sue**

An agreement under this section may contain a covenant not to sue under section 9607(a)(4)(C) of this title for damages to natural resources under the trusteeship of the United States resulting from the release or threatened release of hazardous substances that is the subject of the agreement, but only if the Federal natural resource trustee has agreed in writing to such covenant. The Federal natural resource trustee may agree to such covenant if the potentially responsible party agrees to undertake appropriate actions necessary to protect and restore the natural resources damaged by such release or threatened release of hazardous substances.

(k) **Section not applicable to vessels**

The provisions of this section shall not apply to releases from a vessel.

(*l*) **Civil penalties**

A potentially responsible party which is a party to an administrative order or consent decree entered pursuant to an agreement under this section or section 9620 of this title (relating to Federal facilities) or which is a party to an agreement under section 9620 of this title and which fails or refuses to comply with any term or condition of the order, decree or agreement shall be subject to a civil penalty in accordance with section 9609 of this title.

(m) Applicability of general principles of law

In the case of consent decrees and other settlements under this section (including covenants not to sue), no provision of this chapter shall be construed to preclude or otherwise affect the applicability of general principles of law regarding the setting aside or modification of consent decrees or other settlements.

(Pub. L. No. 96–510, Title I, § 122, as added by Pub. L. No. 99–499, Title I, § 122(a), 100 Stat. 1678 (Oct. 17, 1986); and amended by Pub. L. No. 107–118, Title I, § 102(b), 115 Stat. 2359 (Jan. 11, 2002).)

HISTORICAL AND STATUTORY NOTES

References in Text

The Federal Rules of Evidence, referred to in subsec. (d)(1)(B), are set out in the Appendix to Title 28, Judiciary and Judicial Procedure.

"This chapter", referred to in text, originally read "this Act", meaning Pub. L. No. 96–510, 94 Stat. 2767 (Dec. 11, 1980), as amended, known as the Comprehensive Environmental Response, Compensation, and Liability Act of 1980, which is codified principally as this chapter [42 U.S.C.A. § 9601 et seq.]; see Tables for complete classification.

Effective and Applicability Provisions

2002 Acts. Amendments made by Pub. L. No. 107–118, Title I, § 101 et seq., 115 Stat. 2356 to subsec. (g)(7) to (12) of this section (Jan. 11, 2002,) not applicable to and shall not in any way affect any settlement lodged in, or judgment issued by, a United States District Court, or any administrative settlement or order entered into or issued by the United States or any State, before Jan. 11, 2002, see Pub. L. No. 107–118, Title I, § 103, 115 Stat. 2360 (Jan. 11, 2002), set out as a note under 42 U.S.C.A. § 9607.

1986 Acts. Section effective Oct. 17, 1986, see section 4 of Pub. L. No. 99–499, set out as a note under section 9601 of this title.

Delegation of Functions

Functions vested in the President by subsec. (e)(3)(A) of this section, relating to development of regulations and guidelines, delegated to the Administrator of the Environmental Protection Agency, to be exercised in consultation with the Attorney General, see section 4(a) of Ex. Ord. No. 12580, 52 Fed. Reg. 2923 (Jan. 23, 1987), set out as a note under section 9615 of this title.

Functions vested in the President by this section, except for subsec. (b)(1), and subject to the delegation of functions by section 4(a) of Ex. Ord. No. 12580 (delegating functions vested in the President by subsec. (e)(3)(A) of this section), delegated, with authority to redelegate, to the heads of Executive departments and agencies, with respect to releases or threatened releases not on the National Priorities List where either the release is on or the sole source of the release is from any facility under the jurisdiction, custody or control of those Executive departments and agencies, with such functions to be exercised only with the concurrence of the Attorney General, see sections 4(b)(1) and 11(g) of Ex. Ord. No. 12580, 52 Fed. Reg. 2923 (Jan. 23, 1987), set out as a note under section 9615 of this title.

For delegation of functions vested in the President by provisions of section 9609 of this title relating to violations of this section, with authority to redelegate, see sections 4(b)(2), (c)(2), (d)(2), and 11(g) of Ex. Ord. No. 12580, 52 Fed. Reg. 2923 (Jan. 23, 1987), set out as a note under section 9615 of this title.

Functions vested in the President by this section delegated, subject to section 4(a), (b)(1) of Ex. Ord. No. 12580, and with authority to redelegate, to the Coast Guard with respect to any release or threatened release involving the coastal zone, Great Lakes waters, ports, and harbors, see sections 4(c)(1), 11(g) of Ex. Ord. No. 12580, 52 Fed. Reg. 2923 (Jan. 23, 1987), set out as a note under section 9615 of this title.

Functions vested in the President by this section delegated, subject to section 4(a), (b)(1) and (c)(1) of Ex. Ord. No. 12580, and with authority to redelegate, to the Administrator of the Environmental Protection Agency, see sections 4(d)(1), 11(g) of Ex. Ord. No. 12580, 52 Fed. Reg. 2923 (Jan. 23, 1987), set out as a note under section 9615 of this title.

Functions vested in the President by this section, except subsec. (b)(1), delegated, subject to section 4(a), (b)(1), of Ex. Ord. No. 12580, to the Secretary of the Interior, the Secretary of Commerce, the Secretary of

Agriculture, the Secretary of Defense, and the Secretary of Energy, to be exercised only with the concurrence of the Coast Guard, with respect to any release or threatened release in the coastal zone, Great Lakes waters, ports, and harbors, affecting (1) natural resources under their trusteeship, or (2) a vessel or facility subject to their custody, jurisdiction, or control, and with other exceptions and stipulations, see section 4(c)(3) of Ex. Ord. No. 12580, 52 Fed. Reg. 2923 (Jan. 23, 1987), as amended, set out as a note under section 9615 of this title.

Functions vested in the President by this section, except subsec. (b)(1), delegated, subject to section 4(a), (b) and (c)(1) of Ex. Ord. No. 12580, to the Secretary of the Interior, the Secretary of Commerce, the Secretary of Agriculture, the Secretary of Defense, and the Department of Energy, to be exercised only with the concurrence of the Administrator, with respect to any release or threatened release affecting (1) natural resources under their trusteeship, or (2) a vessel or facility subject to their custody, jurisdiction, or control, and with other exceptions and stipulations, see section 4(d)(3) of Ex. Ord. No. 12580, 52 Fed. Reg. 2923 (Jan. 23, 1987), as amended, set out as a note under section 9615 of this title.

Coordination of Titles I to IV of Pub. L. No. 99–499

Any provision of Titles I to IV of Pub. L. No. 99–499, imposing any tax, premium, or fee; establishing any trust fund; or authorizing expenditures from any trust fund, to have no force or effect, see section 531 of Pub. L. No. 99–499, set out as a note under section 1 of Title 26, Internal Revenue Code.

§ 9623. Reimbursement to local governments

[CERCLA § 123]

(a) Application

Any general purpose unit of local government for a political subdivision which is affected by a release or threatened release at any facility may apply to the President for reimbursement under this section.

(b) Reimbursement

(1) Temporary emergency measures

The President is authorized to reimburse local community authorities for expenses incurred (before or after October 17, 1986) in carrying out temporary emergency measures necessary to prevent or mitigate injury to human health or the environment associated with the release or threatened release of any hazardous substance or pollutant or contaminant. Such measures may include, where appropriate, security fencing to limit access, response to fires and explosions, and other measures which require immediate response at the local level.

(2) Local funds not supplanted

Reimbursement under this section shall not supplant local funds normally provided for response.

(c) Amount

The amount of any reimbursement to any local authority under subsection (b)(1) of this section may not exceed $25,000 for a single response. The reimbursement under this section with respect to a single facility shall be limited to the units of local government having jurisdiction over the political subdivision in which the facility is located.

(d) Procedure

Reimbursements authorized pursuant to this section shall be in accordance with rules promulgated by the Administrator within one year after October 17, 1986.

(Pub. L. No. 96–510, Title I, § 123, as added by Pub. L. No. 99–499, Title I, § 123(a), 100 Stat. 1688 (Oct. 17, 1986).)

HISTORICAL AND STATUTORY NOTES

Effective and Applicability Provisions

1986 Acts. Section effective Oct. 17, 1986, see section 4 of Pub. L. No. 99–499, set out as a note under section 9601 of this title.

Delegation of Functions

Functions vested in the President by this section delegated to the Administrator of the Environmental Protection Agency, see section 9(h) of Ex. Ord. No. 12580, 52 Fed. Reg. 2923 (Jan. 23, 1987), set out as a note under section 9615 of this title.

§ 9624. Methane recovery

[CERCLA § 124]

(a) In general

In the case of a facility at which equipment for the recovery or processing (including recirculation of condensate) of methane has been installed, for purposes of this chapter:

(1) The owner or operator of such equipment shall not be considered an "owner or operator", as defined in section 9601(20) of this title, with respect to such facility.

(2) The owner or operator of such equipment shall not be considered to have arranged for disposal or treatment of any hazardous substance at such facility pursuant to section 9607 of this title.

(3) The owner or operator of such equipment shall not be subject to any action under section 9606 of this title with respect to such facility.

(b) Exceptions

Subsection (a) of this section does not apply with respect to a release or threatened release of a hazardous substance from a facility described in subsection (a) of this section if either of the following circumstances exist:

(1) The release or threatened release was primarily caused by activities of the owner or operator of the equipment described in subsection (a) of this section.

(2) The owner or operator of such equipment would be covered by paragraph (1), (2), (3), or (4) of subsection (a) of section 9607 of this title with respect to such release or threatened release if he were not the owner or operator of such equipment.

In the case of any release or threatened release referred to in paragraph (1), the owner or operator of the equipment described in subsection (a) of this section shall be liable under this chapter only for costs or damages primarily caused by the activities of such owner or operator.

(Pub. L. No. 96–510, Title I, § 124, as added by Pub. L. No. 99–499, Title I, § 124(a), 100 Stat. 1688 (Oct. 17, 1986).)

HISTORICAL AND STATUTORY NOTES

Effective and Applicability Provisions

1986 Acts. Section effective Oct. 17, 1986, see section 4 of Pub. L. No. 99–499, set out as a note under section 9601 of this title.

§ 9625. Section 6921(b)(3)(A)(i) waste

[CERCLA § 125]

(a) Revision of hazard ranking system

This section shall apply only to facilities which are not included or proposed for inclusion on the National Priorities List and which contain substantial volumes of waste described in section 6921(b)(3)(A)(i) of this title. As expeditiously as practicable, the President shall revise the hazard ranking system in effect under the National Contingency Plan with respect to such facilities in a manner which assures appropriate consideration of each of the following site-specific characteristics of such facilities:

(1) The quantity, toxicity, and concentrations of hazardous constituents which are present in such waste and a comparison thereof with other wastes.

(2) The extent of, and potential for, release of such hazardous constituents into the environment.

(3) The degree of risk to human health and the environment posed by such constituents.

(b) Inclusion prohibited

Until the hazard ranking system is revised as required by this section, the President may not include on the National Priorities List any facility which contains substantial volumes of waste described in section 6921(b)(3)(A)(i) of this title on the basis of an evaluation made principally on the volume of such waste and not on the concentrations of the hazardous constituents of such waste. Nothing in this section shall be construed to affect the President's authority to include any such facility on the National Priorities List based on the presence of other substances at such facility or to exercise any other authority of this chapter with respect to such other substances.

(Pub. L. No. 96–510, Title I, § 125, as added by Pub. L. No. 99–499, Title I, § 125, 100 Stat. 1689 (Oct. 17, 1986).)

HISTORICAL AND STATUTORY NOTES

Effective and Applicability Provisions

1986 Acts. Section effective Oct. 17, 1986, see section 4 of Pub. L. No. 99–499, set out as a note under section 9601 of this title.

Delegation of Functions

Responsibility for the revision of the National Contingency Plan, and all other functions vested in the President by this section, delegated to the Administrator of the Environmental Protection Agency, see section 1(b)(1) of Ex. Ord. No. 12580, 52 Fed. Reg. 2923 (Jan. 23, 1987), set out as a note under section 9615 of this title.

§ 9626. Indian tribes

[CERCLA § 126]

(a) Treatment generally

The governing body of an Indian tribe shall be afforded substantially the same treatment as a State with respect to the provisions of section 9603(a) of this title (regarding notification of releases), section 9604(c)(2) of this title (regarding consultation on remedial actions), section 9604(e) of this title (regarding access to information), section 9604(i) of this title (regarding health authorities) and section 9605 of this title (regarding roles and responsibilities under the national contingency plan and submittal of priorities for remedial action, but not including the provision regarding the inclusion of at least one facility per State on the National Priorities List).

(b) Community relocation

Should the President determine that proper remedial action is the permanent relocation of tribal members away from a contaminated site because it is cost effective and necessary to protect their health and welfare, such finding must be concurred in by the affected tribal government before relocation shall occur. The President, in cooperation with the Secretary of the Interior, shall also assure that all benefits of the relocation program are provided to the affected tribe and that alternative land of equivalent value is available and satisfactory to the tribe. Any lands acquired for relocation of tribal members shall be held in trust by the United States for the benefit of the tribe.

(c) Study

The President shall conduct a survey, in consultation with the Indian tribes, to determine the extent of hazardous waste sites on Indian lands. Such survey shall be included within a report which shall make recommendations on the program needs of tribes under this chapter, with particular emphasis on how tribal participation in the administration of such programs can be maximized. Such report shall be submitted to Congress along with the President's budget request for fiscal year 1988.

(d) Limitation

Notwithstanding any other provision of this chapter, no action under this chapter by an Indian tribe shall be barred until the later of the following:

(1) The applicable period of limitations has expired.

(2) 2 years after the United States, in its capacity as trustee for the tribe, gives written notice to the governing body of the tribe that it will not present a claim or commence an action on behalf of the tribe or fails to present a claim or commence an action within the time limitations specified in this chapter.

(Pub. L. No. 96–510, Title I, § 126, as added by Pub. L. No. 99–499, Title II, § 207(e), 100 Stat. 1706 (Oct. 17, 1986).)

HISTORICAL AND STATUTORY NOTES

Effective and Applicability Provisions

1986 Acts. Section effective Oct. 17, 1986, see section 4 of Pub. L. No. 99–499, set out as a note under section 9601 of this title.

Delegation of Functions

Functions vested in the President by the second sentence of subsec. (b) of this section, to the extent they require permanent relocation of residents, businesses, and community facilities or temporary evacuation and housing of threatened individuals not otherwise provided for, delegated to the Director of the Federal Emergency Management Agency, with authority to redelegate, see sections 2(c)(1), 11(g) of Ex. Ord. No. 12580, 52 Fed. Reg. 2923 (Jan. 23, 1987), set out as a note under section 9615 of this title. Functions vested in the President by sections 9617(a), (c) and section 9619 of this title, to the extent such authority is needed to carry out the delegation of functions by section 2(c)(1) of Ex. Ord. No. 12580 (and subject to delegation of certain rulemaking authority to the Administrator of the Environmental Protection Agency), delegated to the Director, with authority to redelegate, see sections 2(b), (c)(2), 11(g) of Ex. Ord. No. 12580.

Functions vested in the President by subsec. (b) of this section, subject to section 2(a) to (f) of Ex. Ord. No. 12580, delegated, with authority to redelegate, to the Administrator of the Environmental Protection Agency, see sections 2(g), 11(g) of Ex. Ord. No. 12580, 52 Fed. Reg. 2923 (Jan. 23, 1987), set out as a note under section 9615 of this title.

Functions vested in the President by subsec. (c) of this section delegated to the Administrator of the Environmental Protection Agency, to be exercised in consultation with the Secretary of the Interior, see section 11(c) of Ex. Ord. No. 12580, 52 Fed. Reg. 2923 (Jan. 23, 1987), set out as a note under section 9615 of this title.

§ 9627. Recycling transactions

[CERCLA § 127]

(a) Liability clarification

(1) As provided in subsections (b), (c), (d), and (e) of this section, a person who arranged for recycling of recyclable material shall not be liable under sections 9607(a)(3) and 9607(a)(4) of this title with respect to such material.

(2) A determination whether or not any person shall be liable under section 9607(a)(3) of this title or section 9607(a)(4) of this title for any material that is not a recyclable material as that term is used in subsections (b) and (c), (d), or (e) of this section shall be made, without regard to subsections[1] (b), (c), (d), or (e) of this section.

(b) Recyclable material defined

For purposes of this section, the term "recyclable material" means scrap paper, scrap plastic, scrap glass, scrap textiles, scrap rubber (other than whole tires), scrap metal, or spent lead-acid, spent nickel-cadmium, and other spent batteries, as well as minor amounts of material incident to or adhering to the scrap material as a result of its normal and customary use prior to becoming scrap; except that such term shall not include—

(1) shipping containers of a capacity from 30 liters to 3,000 liters, whether intact or not, having any hazardous substance (but not metal bits and pieces or hazardous substance that form an integral part of the container) contained in or adhering thereto; or

(2) any item of material that contained polychlorinated biphenyls at a concentration in excess of 50 parts per million or any new standard promulgated pursuant to applicable Federal laws.

(c) Transactions involving scrap paper, plastic, glass, textiles, or rubber

Transactions involving scrap paper, scrap plastic, scrap glass, scrap textiles, or scrap rubber (other than whole tires) shall be deemed to be arranging for recycling if the person who arranged for the transaction (by selling recyclable material or otherwise arranging for the recycling of recyclable material) can demonstrate by a preponderance of the evidence that all of the following criteria were met at the time of the transaction:

(1) The recyclable material met a commercial specification grade.

(2) A market existed for the recyclable material.

(3) A substantial portion of the recyclable material was made available for use as feedstock for the manufacture of a new saleable product.

(4) The recyclable material could have been a replacement or substitute for a virgin raw material, or the product to be made from the recyclable material could have been a replacement or substitute for a product made, in whole or in part, from a virgin raw material.

(5) For transactions occurring 90 days or more after November 29, 1999, the person exercised reasonable care to determine that the facility where the recyclable material was handled, processed, reclaimed, or otherwise managed by another person (hereinafter in this section referred to as a "consuming facility") was in compliance with substantive (not procedural or administrative) provisions of any Federal, State, or local environmental law or regulation, or compliance order or decree issued pursuant thereto, applicable to the handling, processing, reclamation, storage, or other management activities associated with recyclable material.

(6) For purposes of this subsection, "reasonable care" shall be determined using criteria that include (but are not limited to)—

(A) the price paid in the recycling transaction;

(B) the ability of the person to detect the nature of the consuming facility's operations concerning its handling, processing, reclamation, or other management activities associated with recyclable material; and

(C) the result of inquiries made to the appropriate Federal, State, or local environmental agency (or agencies) regarding the consuming facility's past and current compliance with substantive (not procedural or administrative) provisions of any Federal, State, or local environmental law or regulation, or compliance order or decree issued pursuant thereto, applicable to the handling, processing, reclamation, storage, or other management activities associated with the recyclable material. For the purposes of this paragraph, a requirement to obtain a permit applicable to the handling, processing, reclamation, or other management activity associated with the recyclable materials shall be deemed to be a substantive provision.

(d) Transactions involving scrap metal

(1) Transactions involving scrap metal shall be deemed to be arranging for recycling if the person who arranged for the transaction (by selling recyclable material or otherwise arranging for the recycling of recyclable material) can demonstrate by a preponderance of the evidence that at the time of the transaction—

(A) the person met the criteria set forth in subsection (c) of this section with respect to the scrap metal;

(B) the person was in compliance with any applicable regulations or standards regarding the storage, transport, management, or other activities associated with the recycling of scrap metal that the Administrator promulgates under the Solid Waste Disposal Act [42 U.S.C.A. § 6901 et seq.] subsequent to November 29, 1999, and with regard to transactions occurring after the effective date of such regulations or standards; and

(C) the person did not melt the scrap metal prior to the transaction.

(2) For purposes of paragraph (1)(C), melting of scrap metal does not include the thermal separation of 2 or more materials due to differences in their melting points (referred to as "sweating").

(3) For purposes of this subsection, the term "scrap metal" means bits and pieces of metal parts (e.g., bars, turnings, rods, sheets, wire) or metal pieces that may be combined together with bolts or soldering (e.g., radiators, scrap automobiles, railroad box cars), which when worn or superfluous can be recycled, except for scrap metals that the Administrator excludes from this definition by regulation.

(e) Transactions involving batteries

Transactions involving spent lead-acid batteries, spent nickel-cadmium batteries, or other spent batteries shall be deemed to be arranging for recycling if the person who arranged for the transaction (by selling recyclable material or otherwise arranging for the recycling of recyclable material) can demonstrate by a preponderance of the evidence that at the time of the transaction—

(1) the person met the criteria set forth in subsection (c) of this section with respect to the spent lead-acid batteries, spent nickel-cadmium batteries, or other spent batteries, but the person did not recover the valuable components of such batteries; and

(2) **(A)** with respect to transactions involving lead-acid batteries, the person was in compliance with applicable Federal environmental regulations or standards, and any amendments thereto, regarding the storage, transport, management, or other activities associated with the recycling of spent lead-acid batteries;

(B) with respect to transactions involving nickel-cadmium batteries, Federal environmental regulations or standards are in effect regarding the storage, transport, management, or other activities associated with the recycling of spent nickel-cadmium batteries, and the person was in compliance with applicable regulations or standards or any amendments thereto; or

(C) with respect to transactions involving other spent batteries, Federal environmental regulations or standards are in effect regarding the storage, transport, management, or other activities associated with the recycling of such batteries, and the person was in compliance with applicable regulations or standards or any amendments thereto.

(f) Exclusions

(1) The exemptions set forth in subsections (c), (d), and (e) of this section shall not apply if—

(A) the person had an objectively reasonable basis to believe at the time of the recycling transaction—

(i) that the recyclable material would not be recycled;

(ii) that the recyclable material would be burned as fuel, or for energy recovery or incineration; or

(iii) for transactions occurring before 90 days after November 29, 1999, that the consuming facility was not in compliance with a substantive (not procedural or administrative) provision of any Federal, State, or local environmental law or regulation, or compliance order or decree issued pursuant thereto, applicable to the handling, processing, reclamation, or other management activities associated with the recyclable material;

(B) the person had reason to believe that hazardous substances had been added to the recyclable material for purposes other than processing for recycling; or

(C) the person failed to exercise reasonable care with respect to the management and handling of the recyclable material (including adhering to customary industry practices current at the time of the recycling transaction designed to minimize, through source control, contamination of the recyclable material by hazardous substances).

(2) For purposes of this subsection, an objectively reasonable basis for belief shall be determined using criteria that include (but are not limited to) the size of the person's business, customary industry practices (including customary industry practices current at the time of the recycling transaction designed to minimize, through source control, contamination of the recyclable material by hazardous substances), the price paid in the recycling transaction, and the ability of the person to detect the nature of the consuming facility's operations concerning its handling, processing, reclamation, or other management activities associated with the recyclable material.

(3) For purposes of this subsection, a requirement to obtain a permit applicable to the handling, processing, reclamation, or other management activities associated with recyclable material shall be deemed to be a substantive provision.

(g) Effect on other liability

Nothing in this section shall be deemed to affect the liability of a person under paragraph (1) or (2) of section 9607(a) of this title.

(h) Regulations

The Administrator has the authority, under section 9615 of this title, to promulgate additional regulations concerning this section.

(i) Effect on pending or concluded actions

The exemptions provided in this section shall not affect any concluded judicial or administrative action or any pending judicial action initiated by the United States prior to November 29, 1999.

(j) Liability for attorney's fees for certain actions

Any person who commences an action in contribution against a person who is not liable by operation of this section shall be liable to that person for all reasonable costs of defending that action, including all reasonable attorney's and expert witness fees.

(k) Relationship to liability under other laws

Nothing in this section shall affect—

(1) liability under any other Federal, State, or local statute or regulation promulgated pursuant to any such statute, including any requirements promulgated by the Administrator under the Solid Waste Disposal Act [42 U.S.C.A. § 6901 et seq.]; or

(2) the ability of the Administrator to promulgate regulations under any other statute, including the Solid Waste Disposal Act.

(*l*) Limitation on statutory construction

Nothing in this section shall be construed to—

(1) affect any defenses or liabilities of any person to whom subsection (a)(1) of this section does not apply; or

(2) create any presumption of liability against any person to whom subsection (a)(1) of this section does not apply.

(Pub. L. No. 96–510, Title I, § 127, as added by Pub. L. No. 106–113, Div. B, § 1000(a)(9) [Title VI, § 6001(b)(1)], 113 Stat. 1536, 1501A–599 (Nov. 29, 1999).)

[1] So in original. Probably should be "subsection."

HISTORICAL AND STATUTORY NOTES

References in Text

November 29, 1999, referred to in text, in the original read "the date of enactment of this section" and "the date of the enactment of this section", respectively, meaning the date of approval of Pub. L. No. 106–113, 113 Stat. 1501, which in Div. B, § 1000(a)(9), enacted into law S. 1948, which, among other changes, enacted this section.

Superfund Recycling Equity

Pub. L. No. 106–113, Div. B, § 1000(a)(9) [Title VI, § 6001(a)], 113 Stat. 1536, 1501A–599 (Nov. 29, 1999), provided that: "The purposes of this section [enacting this section and this note] are—

"(1) to promote the reuse and recycling of scrap material in furtherance of the goals of waste minimization and natural resource conservation while protecting human health and the environment;

"(2) to create greater equity in the statutory treatment of recycled versus virgin materials; and

"(3) to remove the disincentives and impediments to recycling created as an unintended consequence of the 1980 Superfund liability provisions [probably refers to the Comprehensive Environmental Response, Compensation, and Liability Act of 1980 [42 U.S.C.A. § 9601 et seq.], which is codified as this chapter]."

§ 9628. State response programs

[CERCLA § 128]

(a) Assistance to States

(1) In general

(A) States

The Administrator may award a grant to a State or Indian tribe that—

(i) has a response program that includes each of the elements, or is taking reasonable steps to include each of the elements, listed in paragraph (2); or

(ii) is a party to a memorandum of agreement with the Administrator for voluntary response programs.

(B) Use of grants by States

(i) In general

A State or Indian tribe may use a grant under this subsection to establish or enhance the response program of the State or Indian tribe.

(ii) Additional uses

In addition to the uses under clause (i), a State or Indian tribe may use a grant under this subsection to—

(I) capitalize a revolving loan fund for brownfield remediation under section 9604(k)(3) of this title;

(II) purchase insurance or develop a risk sharing pool, an indemnity pool, or insurance mechanism to provide financing for response actions under a State response program; or

(III) assist small communities, Indian tribes, rural areas, or disadvantaged areas in carrying out activities described in section 104(k)(7)(A) with respect to brownfield sites.

(iii) Small communities, Indian Tribes, rural areas, and disadvantaged areas.—

(I) In general.—To make grants to States or Indian tribes under clause (ii)(III), the Administrator may use, in addition to amounts available to carry out this subsection, not more than $1,500,000 of the amounts made available to carry out section 104(k)(7) in each fiscal year.

(II) Limitation.—Each grant made under subclause (I) may be not more than $20,000.

(III) Inclusion in other grants.—The Administrator may, at the request of a State or Indian tribe, include a grant under this clause in any other grant to the State or Indian tribe made under this subsection.

(iv) Definitions.—In this subparagraph:

(I) Disadvantaged area.—The term "disadvantaged area" means a community with an annual median household income that is less than 80 percent of the statewide annual median household income, as determined by the President based on the latest available decennial census.

(II) Small community.—The term "small community" means a community with a population of not more than 15,000 individuals, as determined by the President based on the latest available decennial census.

(2) Elements

The elements of a State or Indian tribe response program referred to in paragraph (1)(A)(i) are the following:

(A) Timely survey and inventory of brownfield sites in the State.

(B) Oversight and enforcement authorities or other mechanisms, and resources, that are adequate to ensure that—

(i) a response action will—

(I) protect human health and the environment; and

(II) be conducted in accordance with applicable Federal and State law; and

(ii) if the person conducting the response action fails to complete the necessary response activities, including operation and maintenance or long-term monitoring activities, the necessary response activities are completed.

(C) Mechanisms and resources to provide meaningful opportunities for public participation, including—

(i) public access to documents that the State, Indian tribe, or party conducting the cleanup is relying on or developing in making cleanup decisions or conducting site activities;

(ii) prior notice and opportunity for comment on proposed cleanup plans and site activities; and

(iii) a mechanism by which—

(I) a person that is or may be affected by a release or threatened release of a hazardous substance, pollutant, or contaminant at a brownfield site located in the community in which the person works or resides may request the conduct of a site assessment; and

(II) an appropriate State official shall consider and appropriately respond to a request under subclause (I).

(D) Mechanisms for approval of a cleanup plan, and a requirement for verification by and certification or similar documentation from the State, an Indian tribe, or a licensed site professional to the person conducting a response action indicating that the response is complete.

(3) Funding.—There is authorized to be appropriated to carry out this subsection $50,000,000 for each of fiscal years 2019 through 2023.

(b) Enforcement in cases of a release subject to State program

(1) Enforcement

(A) In general

Except as provided in subparagraph (B) and subject to subparagraph (C), in the case of an eligible response site at which—

(i) there is a release or threatened release of a hazardous substance, pollutant, or contaminant; and

(ii) a person is conducting or has completed a response action regarding the specific release that is addressed by the response action that is in compliance with the State program that specifically governs response actions for the protection of public health and the environment, the President may not use authority under this chapter to take an administrative or judicial enforcement action under section 9606(a) of this title or to take a judicial enforcement action to recover response costs under section 9607(a) of this title against the person regarding the specific release that is addressed by the response action.

(B) Exceptions

The President may bring an administrative or judicial enforcement action under this chapter during or after completion of a response action described in subparagraph (A) with respect to a release or threatened release at an eligible response site described in that subparagraph if—

(i) the State requests that the President provide assistance in the performance of a response action;

(ii) the Administrator determines that contamination has migrated or will migrate across a State line, resulting in the need for further response action to protect human health or the environment, or the President determines that contamination has migrated or is likely to migrate onto property subject to the jurisdiction, custody, or control of a department, agency, or instrumentality of the United States and may impact the authorized purposes of the Federal property;

(iii) after taking into consideration the response activities already taken, the Administrator determines that—

(I) a release or threatened release may present an imminent and substantial endangerment to public health or welfare or the environment; and

(II) additional response actions are likely to be necessary to address, prevent, limit, or mitigate the release or threatened release; or

(iv) the Administrator, after consultation with the State, determines that information, that on the earlier of the date on which cleanup was approved or completed, was not known by the State, as recorded in documents prepared or relied on in selecting or conducting the cleanup, has been discovered regarding the contamination or conditions at a facility such that the contamination or conditions at the facility present a threat requiring further remediation to protect public health or welfare or the environment. Consultation with the State shall not limit the ability of the Administrator to make this determination.

(C) Public record

The limitations on the authority of the President under subparagraph (A) apply only at sites in States that maintain, update not less than annually, and make available to the public a record of sites, by name and location, at which response actions have been completed in the previous year and are planned to be addressed under the State program that specifically governs response actions for the protection of public health and the environment in the upcoming year. The public record shall identify whether or not the site, on completion of the response action, will be suitable for unrestricted use and, if not, shall identify the institutional controls relied on in the remedy. Each State and tribe receiving financial assistance under subsection (a) of this section shall maintain and make available to the public a record of sites as provided in this paragraph.

(D) EPA notification

(i) In general

In the case of an eligible response site at which there is a release or threatened release of a hazardous substance, pollutant, or contaminant and for which the Administrator intends to carry out an action that may be barred under subparagraph (A), the Administrator shall—

(I) notify the State of the action the Administrator intends to take; and

(II) **(aa)** wait 48 hours for a reply from the State under clause (ii); or

(bb) if the State fails to reply to the notification or if the Administrator makes a determination under clause (iii), take immediate action under that clause.

(ii) State reply

Not later than 48 hours after a State receives notice from the Administrator under clause (i), the State shall notify the Administrator if—

(I) the release at the eligible response site is or has been subject to a cleanup conducted under a State program; and

(II) the State is planning to abate the release or threatened release, any actions that are planned.

(iii) Immediate Federal action

The Administrator may take action immediately after giving notification under clause (i) without waiting for a State reply under clause (ii) if the Administrator determines that one or more exceptions under subparagraph (B) are met.

(E) Report to Congress

Not later than 90 days after the date of initiation of any enforcement action by the President under clause (ii), (iii), or (iv) of subparagraph (B), the President shall submit to Congress a report describing the basis for the enforcement action, including specific references to the facts demonstrating that enforcement action is permitted under subparagraph (B).

(2) Savings provision

(A) Costs incurred prior to limitations

Nothing in paragraph (1) precludes the President from seeking to recover costs incurred prior to January 11, 2002, or during a period in which the limitations of paragraph (1)(A) were not applicable.

(B) Effect on agreements between States and EPA

Nothing in paragraph (1)—

(i) modifies or otherwise affects a memorandum of agreement, memorandum of understanding, or any similar agreement relating to this chapter between a State agency or an Indian tribe and the Administrator that is in effect on or before January 11, 2002 (which agreement shall remain in effect, subject to the terms of the agreement); or

(ii) limits the discretionary authority of the President to enter into or modify an agreement with a State, an Indian tribe, or any other person relating to the implementation by the President of statutory authorities.

(3) Effective date

This subsection applies only to response actions conducted after February 15, 2001.

(c) Effect on Federal laws

Nothing in this section affects any liability or response authority under any Federal law, including—

(1) this chapter, except as provided in subsection (b) of this section;

(2) the Solid Waste Disposal Act (42 U.S.C. 6901 et seq.);

(3) the Federal Water Pollution Control Act (33 U.S.C. 1251 et seq.);

(4) the Toxic Substances Control Act (15 U.S.C. 2601 et seq.); and

(5) the Safe Drinking Water Act (42 U.S.C. 300f et seq.).

(Pub. L. No. 96–510, Title I, § 128, as added by Pub. L. No. 107–118, Title II, § 231(b), 115 Stat. 2375 (Jan. 11, 2002); and amended by Pub. L. No. 115–141, tit. VII, §§ 14, 15, 132 Stat. 348, 1058, 1059 (Mar. 23, 2018).)

HISTORICAL AND STATUTORY NOTES

References in Text

"This chapter", referred to in subsecs. (b)(1)(A), (B) and (2)(B)(i), and (c)(1) originally read "this Act", meaning Pub. L. No. 96–510, 94 Stat. 2767 (Dec. 11, 1980), as amended, known as the Comprehensive Environmental Response, Compensation, and Liability Act of 1980, which is codified principally as this chapter [42 U.S.C.A. § 9601 et seq.]; see Tables for complete classification.

The Solid Waste Disposal Act, referred to in subsec. (c)(2), is Title II of Pub. L. No. 89–272, 79 Stat. 997 (Oct. 20, 1965), as amended generally by Pub. L. No. 94–580, § 2, 90 Stat. 2795 (Oct. 21, 1976), which is codified principally as chapter 82 of this title [42 U.S.C.A. § 6901 et seq.]. See Tables for complete classification.

The Federal Water Pollution Control Act, referred to in subsec. (c)(3), is Act of June 30, 1948, c. 758, as amended generally by Pub. L. No. 92–500, § 2, 86 Stat. 816 (Oct. 18, 1972), also known as the Clean Water Act, which is codified principally as chapter 26 of Title 33 [33 U.S.C.A. § 1251 et seq.]. See Tables for complete classification.

The Toxic Substances Control Act, referred to in subsec. (c)(4), is Pub. L. No. 94–469, 90 Stat. 2003 (Oct. 11, 1976), as amended, which is codified principally as chapter 53 of Title 15 [15 U.S.C.A. § 2601 et seq.]. See Tables for complete classification.

The Safe Drinking Water Act, referred to in subsec. (c)(5), is Pub. L. No. 93–523, 88 Stat. 1660 (Dec. 16, 1974), as amended, which is codified principally as subchapter XII of chapter 6A of this title [42 U.S.C.A. § 300f et seq.]. See Tables for complete classification.

SUBCHAPTER II—HAZARDOUS SUBSTANCE RESPONSE REVENUE

PART A—HAZARDOUS SUBSTANCE RESPONSE TRUST FUND

§§ 9631 to 9633. Repealed. Pub. L. No. 99–499, Title V, § 517(c)(1), 100 Stat. 1774 (Oct. 17, 1986).

HISTORICAL AND STATUTORY NOTES

Section 9631, Pub. L. No. 96–510, Title II, § 221, 94 Stat. 2801(Dec. 11, 1980); as amended by Pub. L. No. 99–499, Title II, § 204, 100 Stat. 1696 (Oct. 17, 1986), provided for establishment of a "Hazardous Substances Superfund", so redesignated by Pub. L. No. 99–499, § 204. See section 9507 of Title 26, Internal Revenue Code.

Section 9632, Pub. L. No. 96–510, Title II, § 222, 94 Stat. 2802 (Dec. 11, 1980), limited liability of United States to amount in Trust Fund.

Section 9633, Pub. L. No. 96–510, Title II, § 223, 94 Stat. 2802 (Dec. 11, 1980), prescribed administrative provisions.

Effective Date of Repeal

Sections repealed effective Jan. 1, 1987, see section 517(e) of Pub. L. No. 99–499, set out as an Effective Dates of 1986 Acts note under section 9507 of Title 26, Internal Revenue Code.

PART B—POST-CLOSURE LIABILITY TRUST FUND

§ 9641. Repealed. Pub. L. No. 99–499, Title V, § 514(b), 100 Stat. 1767 (Oct. 17, 1986).

HISTORICAL AND STATUTORY NOTES

Section, Pub. L. No. 96–510, Title II, § 232, 94 Stat. 2804 (Dec. 11, 1980), provided for establishment of a "Post-closure Liability Trust Fund" in the Treasury of the United States.

Effective Date of Repeal

Section repealed effective Oct. 1, 1983, with proviso that if refund or credit of any overpayment of tax resulting from application of this section be barred by any law or rule of law, refund or credit of such overpayment shall be made or allowed if claim therefor is filed before the date one year after Oct. 17, 1986, see section 514(c) of Pub. L. No. 99–499.

SUBCHAPTER III—MISCELLANEOUS PROVISIONS

§ 9651. Reports and studies

[CERCLA § 301]

(a) Implementation experiences; identification and disposal of waste

(1) The President shall submit to the Congress, within four years after December 11, 1980, a comprehensive report on experience with the implementation of this chapter including, but not limited to—

(A) the extent to which the chapter and Fund are effective in enabling Government to respond to and mitigate the effects of releases of hazardous substances;

(B) a summary of past receipts and disbursements from the Fund;

(C) a projection of any future funding needs remaining after the expiration of authority to collect taxes, and of the threat to public health, welfare, and the environment posed by the projected releases which create any such needs;

(D) the record and experience of the Fund in recovering Fund disbursements from liable parties;

(E) the record of State participation in the system of response, liability, and compensation established by this chapter;

(F) the impact of the taxes imposed by subchapter II of this chapter on the Nation's balance of trade with other countries;

(G) an assessment of the feasibility and desirability of a schedule of taxes which would take into account one or more of the following: the likelihood of a release of a hazardous substance, the degree of hazard and risk of harm to public health, welfare, and the environment resulting from any such release, incentives to proper handling, recycling, incineration, and neutralization of hazardous wastes, and disincentives to improper or illegal handling or disposal of hazardous materials, administrative and reporting burdens on Government and industry, and the extent to which the tax burden falls on the substances and parties which create the problems addressed by this chapter. In preparing the report, the President shall consult with appropriate Federal, State, and local agencies, affected industries and claimants, and such other interested parties as he may find useful. Based upon the analyses and consultation required by this subsection, the President shall also include in the report any recommendations for legislative changes he may deem necessary for the better effectuation of the purposes of this chapter, including but not limited to recommendations concerning authorization levels, taxes, State participation, liability and liability limits, and financial responsibility provisions for the Response Trust Fund and the Post-closure Liability Trust Fund;

(H) an exemption from or an increase in the substances or the amount of taxes imposed by section 4661 of Title 26 for copper, lead, and zinc oxide, and for feedstocks when used in the manufacture and production of fertilizers, based upon the expenditure experience of the Response Trust Fund;

(I) the economic impact of taxing coal-derived substances and recycled metals.

(2) The Administrator of the Environmental Protection Agency (in consultation with the Secretary of the Treasury) shall submit to the Congress (i)within four years after December 11, 1980, a report identifying additional wastes designated by rule as hazardous after the effective date of this chapter and pursuant to section 3001 of the Solid Waste Disposal Act [42 U.S.C.A. § 6921] and recommendations on appropriate tax rates for such wastes for the Post-closure Liability Trust Fund. The report shall, in addition, recommend a tax rate, considering the quantity and potential danger to human health and the environment posed by the disposal of any wastes which the Administrator, pursuant to subsection 3001(b)(2)(B) and subsection 3001(b)(3)(A) of the Solid Waste Disposal Act of 1980 [42 U.S.C.A. §§ 6921(b)(2)(B) and 6921(b)(3)(A)], has determined should be subject to regulation under subtitle C of such Act [42 U.S.C.A. § 6921 et seq.], (ii) within three years after December 11,

1980, a report on the necessity for and the adequacy of the revenue raised, in relation to estimated future requirements, of the Post-closure Liability Trust Fund.

(b) Private insurance protection

The President shall conduct a study to determine (1) whether adequate private insurance protection is available on reasonable terms and conditions to the owners and operators of vessels and facilities subject to liability under section 9607 of this title, and (2) whether the market for such insurance is sufficiently competitive to assure purchasers of features such as a reasonable range of deductibles, coinsurance provisions, and exclusions. The President shall submit the results of his study, together with his recommendations, within two years of December 11, 1980, and shall submit an interim report on his study within one year of December 11, 1980.

(c) Regulations respecting assessment of damages to natural resources

(1) The President, acting through Federal officials designated by the National Contingency Plan published under section 9605 of this title, shall study and, not later than two years after December 11, 1980, shall promulgate regulations for the assessment of damages for injury to, destruction of, or loss of natural resources resulting from a release of oil or a hazardous substance for the purposes of this chapter and section 1321(f)(4) and (5) of Title 33. Notwithstanding the failure of the President to promulgate the regulations required under this subsection on the required date, the President shall promulgate such regulations not later than 6 months after October 17, 1986.

(2) Such regulations shall specify (A) standard procedures for simplified assessments requiring minimal field observation, including establishing measures of damages based on units of discharge or release or units of affected area, and (B) alternative protocols for conducting assessments in individual cases to determine the type and extent of short- and long-term injury, destruction, or loss. Such regulations shall identify the best available procedures to determine such damages, including both direct and indirect injury, destruction, or loss and shall take into consideration factors including, but not limited to, replacement value, use value, and ability of the ecosystem or resource to recover.

(3) Such regulations shall be reviewed and revised as appropriate every two years.

(d) Issues, alternatives, and policy considerations involving selection of locations for waste treatment, storage, and disposal facilities

The Administrator of the Environmental Protection Agency shall, in consultation with other Federal agencies and appropriate representatives of State and local governments and nongovernmental agencies, conduct a study and report to the Congress within two years of December 11, 1980, on the issues, alternatives, and policy considerations involved in the selection of locations for hazardous waste treatment, storage, and disposal facilities. This study shall include—

(A) an assessment of current and projected treatment, storage, and disposal capacity needs and shortfalls for hazardous waste by management category on a State-by-State basis;

(B) an evaluation of the appropriateness of a regional approach to siting and designing hazardous waste management facilities and the identification of hazardous waste management regions, interstate or intrastate, or both, with similar hazardous waste management needs;

(C) solicitation and analysis of proposals for the construction and operation of hazardous waste management facilities by nongovernmental entities, except that no proposal solicited under terms of this subsection shall be analyzed if it involves cost to the United States Government or fails to comply with the requirements of subtitle C of the Solid Waste Disposal Act [42 U.S.C.A. § 6921 et seq.] and other applicable provisions of law;

(D) recommendations on the appropriate balance between public and private sector involvement in the siting, design, and operation of new hazardous waste management facilities;

(E) documentation of the major reasons for public opposition to new hazardous waste management facilities; and

(F) an evaluation of the various options for overcoming obstacles to siting new facilities, including needed legislation for implementing the most suitable option or options.

(e) Adequacy of existing common law and statutory remedies

(1) In order to determine the adequacy of existing common law and statutory remedies in providing legal redress for harm to man and the environment caused by the release of hazardous substances into the environment, there shall be submitted to the Congress a study within twelve months of December 11, 1980.

(2) This study shall be conducted with the assistance of the American Bar Association, the American Law Institute, the Association of American Trial Lawyers, and the National Association of State Attorneys General with the President of each entity selecting three members from each organization to conduct the study. The study chairman and one reporter shall be elected from among the twelve members of the study group.

(3) As part of their review of the adequacy of existing common law and statutory remedies, the study group shall evaluate the following:

(A) the nature, adequacy, and availability of existing remedies under present law in compensating for harm to man from the release of hazardous substances;

(B) the nature of barriers to recovery (particularly with respect to burdens of going forward and of proof and relevancy) and the role such barriers play in the legal system;

(C) the scope of the evidentiary burdens placed on the plaintiff in proving harm from the release of hazardous substances, particularly in light of the scientific uncertainty over causation with respect to—

(i) carcinogens, mutagens, and teratogens, and

(ii) the human health effects of exposure to low doses of hazardous substances over long periods of time;

(D) the nature and adequacy of existing remedies under present law in providing compensation for damages to natural resources from the release of hazardous substances;

(E) the scope of liability under existing law and the consequences, particularly with respect to obtaining insurance, of any changes in such liability;

(F) barriers to recovery posed by existing statutes of limitations.

(4) The report shall be submitted to the Congress with appropriate recommendations. Such recommendations shall explicitly address—

(A) the need for revisions in existing statutory or common law, and

(B) whether such revisions should take the form of Federal statutes or the development of a model code which is recommended for adoption by the States.

(5) The Fund shall pay administrative expenses incurred for the study. No expenses shall be available to pay compensation, except expenses on a per diem basis for the one reporter, but in no case shall the total expenses of the study exceed $300,000.

(f) Modification of national contingency plan

The President, acting through the Administrator of the Environmental Protection Agency, the Secretary of Transportation, the Administrator of the Occupational Safety and Health Administration, and the Director of the National Institute for Occupational Safety and Health shall study and, not later than two years after December 11, 1980, shall modify the national contingency plan to provide for the protection of the health and safety of employees involved in response actions.

(g) Insurability study

(1) Study by Comptroller General

The Comptroller General of the United States, in consultation with the persons described in paragraph (2), shall undertake a study to determine the insurability, and effects on the standard of care, of the liability of each of the following:

(A) Persons who generate hazardous substances: liability for costs and damages under this chapter.

(B) Persons who own or operate facilities: liability for costs and damages under this chapter.

(C) Persons liable for injury to persons or property caused by the release of hazardous substances into the environment.

(2) Consultation

In conducting the study under this subsection, the Comptroller General shall consult with the following:

(A) Representatives of the Administrator.

(B) Representatives of persons described in subparagraphs (A) through (C) of the preceding paragraph.

(C) Representatives (i) of groups or organizations comprised generally of persons adversely affected by releases or threatened releases of hazardous substances and (ii) of groups organized for protecting the interests of consumers.

(D) Representatives of property and casualty insurers.

(E) Representatives of reinsurers.

(F) Persons responsible for the regulation of insurance at the State level.

(3) Items evaluated

The study under this section shall include, among other matters, an evaluation of the following:

(A) Current economic conditions in, and the future outlook for, the commercial market for insurance and reinsurance.

(B) Current trends in statutory and common law remedies.

(C) The impact of possible changes in traditional standards of liability, proof, evidence, and damages on existing statutory and common law remedies.

(D) The effect of the standard of liability and extent of the persons upon whom it is imposed under this chapter on the protection of human health and the environment and on the availability, underwriting, and pricing of insurance coverage.

(E) Current trends, if any, in the judicial interpretation and construction of applicable insurance contracts, together with the degree to which amendments in the language of such contracts and the description of the risks assumed, could affect such trends.

(F) The frequency and severity of a representative sample of claims closed during the calendar year immediately preceding October 17, 1986.

(G) Impediments to the acquisition of insurance or other means of obtaining liability coverage other than those referred to in the preceding subparagraphs.

(H) The effects of the standards of liability and financial responsibility requirements imposed pursuant to this chapter on the cost of, and incentives for, developing and demonstrating alternative and innovative treatment technologies, as well as waste generation minimization.

(4) Submission

The Comptroller General shall submit a report on the results of the study to Congress with appropriate recommendations within 12 months after October 17, 1986.

(Pub. L. No. 96–510, Title III, § 301, 94 Stat. 2805 (Dec. 11, 1980); as amended by Pub. L. No. 99–499, Title I, § 107(d)(3), Title II, §§ 208, 212, 100 Stat. 1630, 1707, 1726 (Oct. 17, 1986); Pub. L. No. 99–514, § 2, 100 Stat. 2095 (Oct. 22, 1986).)

HISTORICAL AND STATUTORY NOTES

References in Text

This chapter, referred to in subsecs. (a)(1)(A), (E), (G), (c)(1), and (g)(1)(A), (B), (3)(D), (H), was in the original "this Act", meaning Pub. L. No. 96–510, 94 Stat. 2767 (Dec. 11, 1980), as amended, known as the Comprehensive Environmental Response, Compensation, and Liability Act of 1980, which enacted this chapter, section 6911a of this title, and sections 4611, 4612, 4661, and 4662 and former sections 4681 and 4682 of Title 26, Internal Revenue Code, amended section 6911 of this title, section 1364 of Title 33, Navigation and Navigable Waters, and section 11901 of Title 49, Transportation, and enacted provisions set out as notes under section 6911 of this title and sections 1 and 4611 of Title 26. For complete classification of this Act to the Code, see Short Title of 1980 Acts note set out under section 9601 of this title and Tables.

Subchapter II of this chapter, referred to in subsec. (a)(1)(F), was in the original, "Title II of this Act", meaning Title II of Pub. L. No. 96–510, 94 Stat. 2796 (Dec. 11, 1980), known as the Hazardous Substance Response Revenue Act of 1980, which enacted subchapter II of this chapter and sections 4611, 4612, 4661, 4662 and former sections 4681 and 4682 of Title 26, Internal Revenue Code. Sections 221 to 223 and 232 of Pub. L. No. 96–510, which were codified as sections 9631 to 9633 and 9641 of this title, comprising subchapter II of this chapter, were repealed by Pub. L. No. 99–499, Title V, §§ 514(6), 517(c)(1), 100 Stat. 1767, 1774 (Oct. 17, 1986). For complete classification of Title II to the Code, see Short Title of 1980 Amendments note set out under section 1 of Title 26 and Tables.

Subsection 3001(b)(2)(B) and subsection 3001(b)(3)(A) of the Solid Waste Disposal Act of 1980, referred to in subsec. (a)(2), probably mean section 3001(b)(2)(B) and (3)(A) of the Solid Waste Disposal Act, as amended by the Solid Waste Disposal Act Amendments of 1980, which enacted section 6921(b)(2)(B) and (3)(A) of this title.

The Solid Waste Disposal Act, referred to in subsecs. (a)(2) and (d)(C), is Title II of Pub. L. No. 89–272, 79 Stat. 997 (Oct. 20, 1965), as amended generally by Pub. L. No. 94–580, § 2, 90 Stat. 2795 (Oct. 21, 1976). Subtitle C of the Solid Waste Disposal Act is codified generally as subchapter III (section 6921 et seq.) of chapter 82 of this title. For complete classification of this Act to the Code, see Short Title of 1965 Acts note set out under section 6901 of this title and Tables.

Codifications

Subsec. (h) of this section, shown as omitted, which required the Administrator of the Environmental Protection Agency to submit an annual report to Congress of such Agency on the progress achieved in implementing this chapter during the preceding fiscal year, required the Inspector General of the Agency to review the report for reasonableness and accuracy and submit to Congress, as a part of that report, a report on the results of the review, and required the appropriate authorizing committees of Congress, after receiving those reports, to conduct oversight hearings to ensure that this chapter is being implemented according to the purposes of this chapter and congressional intent in enacting this chapter, terminated, effective May 15, 2000, pursuant to Pub. L. No. 104–66, § 3003, as amended, set out as a note under 31 U.S.C.A. § 1113 and the 5th item on page 164 of House Document No. 103–7.

Effective and Applicability Provisions

1986 Acts. Amendment by Pub. L. No. 99–499 effective Oct. 17, 1986, see section 4 of Pub. L. No. 99–499, set out as a note under section 9601 of this title.

Delegation of Functions

Responsibility for the revision of the National Contingency Plan, and all other functions vested in the President by subsec. (f) of this section, delegated to the Administrator of the Environmental Protection Agency, see section 1(b)(1) of Ex. Ord. No. 12580, 52 Fed. Reg. 2923 (Jan. 23, 1987), set out as a note under section 9615 of this title.

Functions vested in the President by subsec. (c) of this section delegated to the Secretary of the Interior, see section 11(d) of Ex. Ord. No. 12580, 52 Fed. Reg. 2923 (Jan. 23, 1987), set out as a note under section 9615 of this title.

§ 9652. Effective dates; savings provisions

[CERCLA § 302]

(a) Unless otherwise provided, all provisions of this chapter shall be effective on December 11, 1980.

(b) Any regulation issued pursuant to any provisions of section 1321 of Title 33 which is repealed or superseded by this chapter and which is in effect on the date immediately preceding the effective date of this chapter shall be deemed to be a regulation issued pursuant to the authority of this chapter and shall remain in full force and effect unless or until superseded by new regulations issued thereunder.

(c) Any regulation—

(1) respecting financial responsibility,

(2) issued pursuant to any provision of law repealed or superseded by this chapter, and

(3) in effect on the date immediately preceding the effective date of this chapter shall be deemed to be a regulation issued pursuant to the authority of this chapter and shall remain in full force and effect unless or until superseded by new regulations issued thereunder.

(d) Nothing in this chapter shall affect or modify in any way the obligations or liabilities of any person under other Federal or State law, including common law, with respect to releases of hazardous substances or other pollutants or contaminants. The provisions of this chapter shall not be considered, interpreted, or construed in any way as reflecting a determination, in part or whole, of policy regarding the inapplicability of strict liability, or strict liability doctrines, to activities relating to hazardous substances, pollutants, or contaminants or other such activities.

(Pub. L. No. 96–510, Title III, § 302, 94 Stat. 2808 (Dec. 11, 1980).)

§ 9653. Repealed. Pub. L. No. 99–499, Title V, § 511(b), 100 Stat. 1761 (Oct. 17, 1986).

HISTORICAL AND STATUTORY NOTES

Section, Pub. L. 96–510, Title III, § 303, 94 Stat. 2808 (Dec. 11, 1980), provided for termination of authority to collect taxes under this chapter.

Effective Date of Repeal

Section repealed effective Jan. 1, 1987, see section 511(c) of Pub. L. No. 99–499, set out as an Effective Dates of 1986 Acts note under section 4611 of Title 26, Internal Revenue Code.

§ 9654. Applicability of Federal water pollution control funding, etc., provisions [CERCLA § 304]

(a) Omitted

(b) One-half of the unobligated balance remaining before December 11, 1980, under subsection (k) of section 1321 of Title 33 and all sums appropriated under section 1364(b) of Title 33 shall be transferred to the Fund established under subchapter II of this chapter.

(c) In any case in which any provision of section 1321 of Title 33 is determined to be in conflict with any provisions of this chapter, the provisions of this chapter shall apply.

(Pub. L. No. 96–510, Title III, § 304, 94 Stat. 2809 (Dec. 11, 1980).)

HISTORICAL AND STATUTORY NOTES

References in Text

Subsection (k) of section 1321 of Title 33, referred to in subsec. (b), was repealed by Pub. L. No. 101–380, Title II, § 2002(b)(2), 104 Stat. 507 (Aug. 18, 1990).

Section 1364(b) of Title 33, referred to in subsec. (b), was repealed by Pub. L. No. 96–510, Title III, § 304(a), 94 Stat. 2809 (Dec. 11, 1980).

Subchapter II of this chapter, referred to in subsec. (b), was in the original, “Title II of this Act”, meaning Title II of Pub. L. No. 96–510, 94 Stat. 2796 (Dec. 11, 1980), known as the Hazardous Substance Response Revenue Act of 1980, which enacted subchapter II of this chapter and sections 4611, 4612, 4661, 4662 and former sections 4681 and 4682 of Title 26, Internal Revenue Code. Sections 221 to 223 and 232 of Pub. L. No. 96–510, which were codified as sections 9631 to 9633 and 9641 of this title, comprising subchapter II of this chapter, were repealed by

Pub. L. No. 99–499, Title V, §§ 514(b), 517(c)(1), 100 Stat. 1767, 1774 (Oct. 17, 1986). For complete classification of Title II to the Code, see Short Title of 1980 Amendments note set out under section 1 of Title 26 and Tables.

Codifications

Subsec. (a) of this section repealed section 1364(b) of Title 33, Navigation and Navigable Waters.

§ 9655. Legislative veto of rule or regulation

[CERCLA § 305]

(a) Transmission to Congress upon promulgation or repromulgation of rule or regulation; disapproval procedures

Notwithstanding any other provision of law, simultaneously with promulgation or repromulgation of any rule or regulation under authority of subchapter I of this chapter, the head of the department, agency, or instrumentality promulgating such rule or regulation shall transmit a copy thereof to the Secretary of the Senate and the Clerk of the House of Representatives. Except as provided in subsection (b) of this section, the rule or regulation shall not become effective, if—

(1) within ninety calendar days of continuous session of Congress after the date of promulgation, both Houses of Congress adopt a concurrent resolution, the matter after the resolving clause of which is as follows: "That Congress disapproves the rule or regulation promulgated by the _____ dealing with the matter of _____, which rule or regulation was transmitted to Congress on _____.", the blank spaces therein being appropriately filled; or

(2) within sixty calendar days of continuous session of Congress after the date of promulgation, one House of Congress adopts such a concurrent resolution and transmits such resolution to the other House, and such resolution is not disapproved by such other House within thirty calendar days of continuous session of Congress after such transmittal.

(b) Approval; effective dates

If, at the end of sixty calendar days of continuous session of Congress after the date of promulgation of a rule or regulation, no committee of either House of Congress has reported or been discharged from further consideration of a concurrent resolution disapproving the rule or regulation and neither House has adopted such a resolution, the rule or regulation may go into effect immediately. If, within such sixty calendar days, such a committee has reported or been discharged from further consideration of such a resolution, or either House has adopted such a resolution, the rule or regulation may go into effect not sooner than ninety calendar days of continuous session of Congress after such rule is prescribed unless disapproved as provided in subsection (a) of this section.

(c) Sessions of Congress as applicable

For purposes of subsections (a) and (b) of this section—

(1) continuity of session is broken only by an adjournment of Congress sine die; and

(2) the days on which either House is not in session because of an adjournment of more than three days to a day certain are excluded in the computation of thirty, sixty, and ninety calendar days of continuous session of Congress.

(d) Congressional inaction on, or rejection of, resolution of disapproval

Congressional inaction on, or rejection of, a resolution of disapproval shall not be deemed an expression of approval of such rule or regulation.

(Pub. L. No. 96–510, Title III, § 305, 94 Stat. 2809 (Dec. 11, 1980).)

HISTORICAL AND STATUTORY NOTES

Termination of Reporting Requirements

For termination, effective May 15, 2000, of reporting provisions of subsec. (a) of this section relating to proposed regulations to implement provisions of Title I of the Comprehensive Environmental Response,

Compensation, and Liability Act of 1980, see Pub. L. No. 104–66, § 3003, as amended, set out as a note under 31 U.S.C.A. § 1113, and the 15th item on page 164 of House Document No. 103–7.

For termination of reporting provisions of subsec. (a) of this section, effective May 15, 2000, see Pub. L. No. 104–66, § 3003, set out as a note under 31 U.S.C.A. § 1113, the 3rd item on page 59 of House Document No. 103–7, the 4th item on page 133 of House Document No. 103–7, the 2nd item on page 141 of House Document No. 103–7, and the 6th item on page 171 of House Document No. 103–7.

Transfer of Functions

Any reference in any provision of law enacted before Jan. 4, 1995, to a function, duty, or authority of the Clerk of the House of Representatives treated as referring, with respect to that function, duty, or authority, to the officer of the House of Representatives exercising that function, duty, or authority, as determined by the Committee on House Oversight of the House of Representatives, see section 2(1) of Pub. L. No. 104–14, set out as a note preceding section 21 of Title 2, The Congress.

§ 9656. Transportation of hazardous substances; listing as hazardous material; liability for release

[CERCLA § 306]

(a) Each hazardous substance which is listed or designated as provided in section 9601(14) of this title shall, within 30 days after October 17, 1986, or at the time of such listing or designation, whichever is later, be listed and regulated as a hazardous material under chapter 51 of Title 49.

(b) A common or contract carrier shall be liable under other law in lieu of section 9607 of this title for damages or remedial action resulting from the release of a hazardous substance during the course of transportation which commenced prior to the effective date of the listing and regulation of such substance as a hazardous material under chapter 51 of Title 49, or for substances listed pursuant to subsection (a) of this section, prior to the effective date of such listing: *Provided, however,* That this subsection shall not apply where such a carrier can demonstrate that he did not have actual knowledge of the identity or nature of the substance released.

(Pub. L. No. 96–510, Title III, § 306(a), (b), 94 Stat. 2810 (Dec. 11, 1980); as amended by Pub. L. No. 99–499, Title II, § 202, 100 Stat. 1695 (Oct. 17, 1986).)

HISTORICAL AND STATUTORY NOTES

References in Text

Chapter 51 of Title 49, referred to in text, is 49 U.S.C.A. § 5101 et seq.

Effective and Applicability Provisions

1986 Acts. Amendment by Pub. L. No. 99–499 effective Oct. 17, 1986, see section 4 of Pub. L. No. 99–499, set out as a note under section 9601 of this title.

§ 9657. Separability; contribution

[CERCLA § 308]

If any provision of this chapter, or the application of any provision of this chapter to any person or circumstance, is held invalid, the application of such provision to other persons or circumstances and the remainder of this chapter shall not be affected thereby. If an administrative settlement under section 9622 of this title has the effect of limiting any person's right to obtain contribution from any party to such settlement, and if the effect of such limitation would constitute a taking without just compensation in violation of the fifth amendment of the Constitution of the United States, such person shall not be entitled, under other laws of the United States, to recover compensation from the United States for such taking, but in any such case, such limitation on the right to obtain contribution shall be treated as having no force and effect.

(Pub. L. No. 96–510, Title III, § 308, 94 Stat. 2811 (Dec. 11, 1980); as amended by Pub. L. No. 99–499, Title I, § 122(b), 100 Stat. 1688 (Oct. 17, 1986).)

HISTORICAL AND STATUTORY NOTES

References in Text

This chapter, referred to in text, was in the original, "this Act", meaning Pub. L. No. 96–510, 94 Stat. 2767 (Dec. 11, 1980), as amended, known as the Comprehensive Environmental Response, Compensation, and Liability Act of 1980, which enacted this chapter, 6911a of this title, and sections 4611, 4612, 4661, 4662 and former sections 4681 and 4682 of Title 26, Internal Revenue Code, amended 6911 of this title, 1364 of Title 33, Navigation and Navigable Waters, and 11901 of Title 49, Transportation, and enacted provisions set out as notes under section 6911 of this title and sections 1 and 4611 of Title 26. For complete classification of this Act to the Code, see Short Title of 1980 Acts note set out under section 9601 of this title and Tables.

Effective and Applicability Provisions

1986 Acts. Amendment by Pub. L. No. 99–499 effective Oct. 17, 1986, see section 4 of Pub. L. No. 99–499, set out as a note under section 9601 of this title.

§ 9658. Actions under State law for damages from exposure to hazardous substances

[CERCLA § 309]

(a) State statutes of limitations for hazardous substance cases

(1) Exception to State statutes

In the case of any action brought under State law for personal injury, or property damages, which are caused or contributed to by exposure to any hazardous substance, or pollutant or contaminant, released into the environment from a facility, if the applicable limitations period for such action (as specified in the State statute of limitations or under common law) provides a commencement date which is earlier than the federally required commencement date, such period shall commence at the federally required commencement date in lieu of the date specified in such State statute.

(2) State law generally applicable

Except as provided in paragraph (1), the statute of limitations established under State law shall apply in all actions brought under State law for personal injury, or property damages, which are caused or contributed to by exposure to any hazardous substance, or pollutant or contaminant, released into the environment from a facility.

(3) Actions under section 9607

Nothing in this section shall apply with respect to any cause of action brought under section 9607 of this title.

(b) Definitions

As used in this section—

(1) Subchapter I terms

The terms used in this section shall have the same meaning as when used in subchapter I of this chapter.

(2) Applicable limitations period

The term "applicable limitations period" means the period specified in a statute of limitations during which a civil action referred to in subsection (a)(1) of this section may be brought.

(3) Commencement date

The term "commencement date" means the date specified in a statute of limitations as the beginning of the applicable limitations period.

(4) Federally required commencement date

(A) In general

Except as provided in subparagraph (B), the term "federally required commencement date" means the date the plaintiff knew (or reasonably should have known) that the personal injury or property damages referred to in subsection (a)(1) of this section were caused or contributed to by the hazardous substance or pollutant or contaminant concerned.

(B) Special rules

In the case of a minor or incompetent plaintiff, the term "federally required commencement date" means the later of the date referred to in subparagraph (A) or the following:

(i) In the case of a minor, the date on which the minor reaches the age of majority, as determined by State law, or has a legal representative appointed.

(ii) In the case of an incompetent individual, the date on which such individual becomes competent or has had a legal representative appointed.

(Pub. L. No. 96–510, Title III, § 309, as added by Pub. L. No. 99–499, Title II, § 203(a), 100 Stat. 1695 (Oct. 17, 1986).)

HISTORICAL AND STATUTORY NOTES

Effective and Applicability Provisions

1986 Acts. Section 203(b) of Pub. L. No. 99–499 provided that: "The amendment made by subsection (a) of this section [enacting this section] shall take effect with respect to actions brought after December 11, 1980."

§ 9659. Citizens suits

[CERCLA § 310]

(a) Authority to bring civil actions

Except as provided in subsections (d) and (e) of this section and in section 9613(h) of this title (relating to timing of judicial review), any person may commence a civil action on his own behalf—

(1) against any person (including the United States and any other governmental instrumentality or agency, to the extent permitted by the eleventh amendment to the Constitution) who is alleged to be in violation of any standard, regulation, condition, requirement, or order which has become effective pursuant to this chapter (including any provision of an agreement under section 9620 of this title, relating to Federal facilities); or

(2) against the President or any other officer of the United States (including the Administrator of the Environmental Protection Agency and the Administrator of the ATSDR) where there is alleged a failure of the President or of such other officer to perform any act or duty under this chapter, including an act or duty under section 9620 of this title (relating to Federal facilities), which is not discretionary with the President or such other officer.

Paragraph (2) shall not apply to any act or duty under the provisions of section 9660 of this title (relating to research, development, and demonstration).

(b) Venue

(1) Actions under subsection (a)(1)

Any action under subsection (a)(1) of this section shall be brought in the district court for the district in which the alleged violation occurred.

(2) Actions under subsection (a)(2)

Any action brought under subsection (a)(2) of this section may be brought in the United States District Court for the District of Columbia.

(c) Relief

The district court shall have jurisdiction in actions brought under subsection (a)(1) of this section to enforce the standard, regulation, condition, requirement, or order concerned (including any provision of an agreement under section 9620 of this title), to order such action as may be necessary to correct the violation, and to impose any civil penalty provided for the violation. The district court shall have jurisdiction in actions brought under subsection (a)(2) of this section to order the President or other officer to perform the act or duty concerned.

(d) Rules applicable to subsection (a)(1) actions

(1) Notice

No action may be commenced under subsection (a)(1) of this section before 60 days after the plaintiff has given notice of the violation to each of the following:

(A) The President.

(B) The State in which the alleged violation occurs.

(C) Any alleged violator of the standard, regulation, condition, requirement, or order concerned (including any provision of an agreement under section 9620 of this title).

Notice under this paragraph shall be given in such manner as the President shall prescribe by regulation.

(2) Diligent prosecution

No action may be commenced under paragraph (1) of subsection (a) of this section if the President has commenced and is diligently prosecuting an action under this chapter, or under the Solid Waste Disposal Act [42 U.S.C.A. § 6901 et seq.] to require compliance with the standard, regulation, condition, requirement, or order concerned (including any provision of an agreement under section 9620 of this title).

(e) Rules applicable to subsection (a)(2) actions

No action may be commenced under paragraph (2) of subsection (a) of this section before the 60th day following the date on which the plaintiff gives notice to the Administrator or other department, agency, or instrumentality that the plaintiff will commence such action. Notice under this subsection shall be given in such manner as the President shall prescribe by regulation.

(f) Costs

The court, in issuing any final order in any action brought pursuant to this section, may award costs of litigation (including reasonable attorney and expert witness fees) to the prevailing or the substantially prevailing party whenever the court determines such an award is appropriate. The court may, if a temporary restraining order or preliminary injunction is sought, require the filing of a bond or equivalent security in accordance with the Federal Rules of Civil Procedure.

(g) Intervention

In any action under this section, the United States or the State, or both, if not a party may intervene as a matter of right. For other provisions regarding intervention, see section 9613 of this title.

(h) Other rights

This chapter does not affect or otherwise impair the rights of any person under Federal, State, or common law, except with respect to the timing of review as provided in section 9613(h) of this title or as otherwise provided in section 9658 of this title (relating to actions under State law).

(i) Definitions

The terms used in this section shall have the same meanings as when used in subchapter I of this chapter.

(Pub. L. No. 96–510, Title III, § 310, as added by Pub. L. No. 99–499, Title II, § 206, 100 Stat. 1703 (Oct. 17, 1986).)

HISTORICAL AND STATUTORY NOTES

References in Text

The Solid Waste Disposal Act, referred to in subsec. (d)(2), is Title II of Pub. L. No. 89–272, 79 Stat. 997 (Oct. 20, 1965), as amended generally by Pub. L. No. 94–580, § 2, 90 Stat. 2795 (Oct. 21, 1976), which is codified generally as chapter 82 (section 6901 et seq.) of this title. For complete classification of this Act to the Code, see Short Title of 1965 Acts note set out under section 6901 of this title and Tables.

The Federal Rules of Civil Procedure, referred to in subsec. (f), are set out in Title 28, Judiciary and Judicial Procedure.

Effective and Applicability Provisions

1986 Acts. Section effective Oct. 17, 1986, see section 4 of Pub. L. No. 99–499, set out as a note under section 9601 of this title.

Delegation of Functions

Functions vested in the President by subsecs. (d) and (e) of this section, relating to the promulgation of regulations, delegated to the Administrator of the Environmental Protection Agency, see section 6(d) of Ex. Ord. No. 12580, 52 Fed. Reg. 2923 (Jan. 23, 1987), set out as a note under section 9615 of this title.

§ 9660. Research, development, and demonstration

[CERCLA § 311]

(a) Hazardous substance research and training

(1) Authorities of Secretary

The Secretary of Health and Human Services (hereinafter in this subsection referred to as the Secretary), in consultation with the Administrator, shall establish and support a basic research and training program (through grants, cooperative agreements, and contracts) consisting of the following:

(A) Basic research (including epidemiologic and ecologic studies) which may include each of the following:

(i) Advanced techniques for the detection, assessment, and evaluation of the effects on human health of hazardous substances.

(ii) Methods to assess the risks to human health presented by hazardous substances.

(iii) Methods and technologies to detect hazardous substances in the environment and basic biological, chemical, and physical methods to reduce the amount and toxicity of hazardous substances.

(B) Training, which may include each of the following:

(i) Short courses and continuing education for State and local health and environment agency personnel and other personnel engaged in the handling of hazardous substances, in the management of facilities at which hazardous substances are located, and in the evaluation of the hazards to human health presented by such facilities.

(ii) Graduate or advanced training in environmental and occupational health and safety and in the public health and engineering aspects of hazardous waste control.

(iii) Graduate training in the geosciences, including hydrogeology, geological engineering, geophysics, geochemistry, and related fields necessary to meet professional personnel needs in the public and private sectors and to effectuate the purposes of this chapter.

(2) Director of NIEHS

The Director of the National Institute for Environmental Health Sciences shall cooperate fully with the relevant Federal agencies referred to in subparagraph (A) of paragraph (5) in carrying out the purposes of this section.

(3) Recipients of grants, etc.

A grant, cooperative agreement, or contract may be made or entered into under paragraph (1) with an accredited institution of higher education. The institution may carry out the research or training under the grant, cooperative agreement, or contract through contracts, including contracts with any of the following:

(A) Generators of hazardous wastes.

(B) Persons involved in the detection, assessment, evaluation, and treatment of hazardous substances.

(C) Owners and operators of facilities at which hazardous substances are located.

(D) State and local governments.

(4) Procedures

In making grants and entering into cooperative agreements and contracts under this subsection, the Secretary shall act through the Director of the National Institute for Environmental Health Sciences. In considering the allocation of funds for training purposes, the Director shall ensure that at least one grant, cooperative agreement, or contract shall be awarded for training described in each of clauses (i), (ii), and (iii) of paragraph (1)(B). Where applicable, the Director may choose to operate training activities in cooperation with the Director of the National Institute for Occupational Safety and Health. The procedures applicable to grants and contracts under title IV of the Public Health Service Act [42 U.S.C.A. § 281 et seq.] shall be followed under this subsection.

(5) Advisory council

To assist in the implementation of this subsection and to aid in the coordination of research and demonstration and training activities funded from the Fund under this section, the Secretary shall appoint an advisory council (hereinafter in this subsection referred to as the "Advisory Council") which shall consist of representatives of the following:

(A) The relevant Federal agencies.

(B) The chemical industry.

(C) The toxic waste management industry.

(D) Institutions of higher education.

(E) State and local health and environmental agencies.

(F) The general public.

(6) Planning

Within nine months after October 17, 1986, the Secretary, acting through the Director of the National Institute for Environmental Health Sciences, shall issue a plan for the implementation of paragraph (1). The plan shall include priorities for actions under paragraph (1) and include research and training relevant to scientific and technological issues resulting from site specific hazardous substance response experience. The Secretary shall, to the maximum extent practicable, take appropriate steps to coordinate program activities under this plan with the activities of other Federal agencies in order to avoid duplication of effort. The plan shall be consistent with the need for the development of new technologies for meeting the goals of response actions in accordance with the provisions of this chapter. The Advisory Council shall be provided an opportunity to review and comment on the plan and priorities and assist appropriate coordination among the relevant Federal agencies referred to in subparagraph (A) of paragraph (5).

(b) Alternative or innovative treatment technology research and demonstration program

(1) Establishment

The Administrator is authorized and directed to carry out a program of research, evaluation, testing, development, and demonstration of alternative or innovative treatment technologies (hereinafter in this subsection referred to as the "program") which may be utilized in response actions to achieve more permanent protection of human health and welfare and the environment.

(2) Administration

The program shall be administered by the Administrator, acting through an office of technology demonstration and shall be coordinated with programs carried out by the Office of Solid Waste and Emergency Response and the Office of Research and Development.

(3) Contracts and grants

In carrying out the program, the Administrator is authorized to enter into contracts and cooperative agreements with, and make grants to, persons, public entities, and nonprofit private entities which are exempt from tax under section 501(c)(3) of Title 26. The Administrator shall, to the maximum extent possible, enter into appropriate cost sharing arrangements under this subsection.

(4) Use of sites

In carrying out the program, the Administrator may arrange for the use of sites at which a response may be undertaken under section 9604 of this title for the purposes of carrying out research, testing, evaluation, development, and demonstration projects. Each such project shall be carried out under such terms and conditions as the Administrator shall require to assure the protection of human health and the environment and to assure adequate control by the Administrator of the research, testing, evaluation, development, and demonstration activities at the site.

(5) Demonstration assistance

(A) Program components

The demonstration assistance program shall include the following:

(i) The publication of a solicitation and the evaluation of applications for demonstration projects utilizing alternative or innovative technologies.

(ii) The selection of sites which are suitable for the testing and evaluation of innovative technologies.

(iii) The development of detailed plans for innovative technology demonstration projects.

(iv) The supervision of such demonstration projects and the providing of quality assurance for data obtained.

(v) The evaluation of the results of alternative innovative technology demonstration projects and the determination of whether or not the technologies used are effective and feasible.

(B) Solicitation

Within 90 days after October 17, 1986, and no less often than once every 12 months thereafter, the Administrator shall publish a solicitation for innovative or alternative technologies at a stage of development suitable for full-scale demonstrations at sites at which a response action may be undertaken under section 9604 of this title. The purpose of any such project shall be to demonstrate the use of an alternative or innovative treatment technology with respect to hazardous substances or pollutants or contaminants which are located at the site or which are to be removed from the site. The solicitation notice shall prescribe information to be included in the application, including technical and economic data derived from the applicant's own research and development efforts, and other information sufficient to permit the Administrator to assess the technology's potential and the types of remedial action to which it may be applicable.

(C) Applications

Any person and any public or private nonprofit entity may submit an application to the Administrator in response to the solicitation. The application shall contain a proposed demonstration plan setting forth how and when the project is to be carried out and such other information as the Administrator may require.

(D) Project selection

In selecting technologies to be demonstrated, the Administrator shall fully review the applications submitted and shall consider at least the criteria specified in paragraph (7). The Administrator shall select or refuse to select a project for demonstration under this subsection within 90 days of receiving the completed application for such project. In the case of a refusal to select the project, the Administrator shall notify the applicant within such 90-day period of the reasons for his refusal.

(E) Site selection

The Administrator shall propose 10 sites at which a response may be undertaken under section 9604 of this title to be the location of any demonstration project under this subsection within 60 days after the close of the public comment period. After an opportunity for notice and public comment, the Administrator shall select such sites and projects. In selecting any such site, the Administrator shall take into account the applicant's technical data and preferences either for onsite operation or for utilizing the site as a source of hazardous substances or pollutants or contaminants to be treated offsite.

(F) Demonstration plan

Within 60 days after the selection of the site under this paragraph to be the location of a demonstration project, the Administrator shall establish a final demonstration plan for the project, based upon the demonstration plan contained in the application for the project. Such plan shall clearly set forth how and when the demonstration project will be carried out.

(G) Supervision and testing

Each demonstration project under this subsection shall be performed by the applicant, or by a person satisfactory to the applicant, under the supervision of the Administrator. The Administrator shall enter into a written agreement with each applicant granting the Administrator the responsibility and authority for testing procedures, quality control, monitoring, and other measurements necessary to determine and evaluate the results of the demonstration project. The Administrator may pay the costs of testing, monitoring, quality control, and other measurements required by the Administrator to determine and evaluate the results of the demonstration project, and the limitations established by subparagraph (J) shall not apply to such costs.

(H) Project completion

Each demonstration project under this subsection shall be completed within such time as is established in the demonstration plan.

(I) Extensions

The Administrator may extend any deadline established under this paragraph by mutual agreement with the applicant concerned.

(J) Funding restrictions

The Administrator shall not provide any Federal assistance for any part of a full-scale field demonstration project under this subsection to any applicant unless such applicant can demonstrate that it cannot obtain appropriate private financing on reasonable terms and conditions sufficient to carry out such demonstration project without such Federal assistance. The total Federal funds for any full-scale field demonstration project under this subsection shall not exceed 50 percent of the total cost of such project estimated at the time of the award of such assistance. The Administrator shall not expend more than $10,000,000 for assistance under the program in any fiscal year and shall not expend more than $3,000,000 for any single project.

(6) Field demonstrations

In carrying out the program, the Administrator shall initiate or cause to be initiated at least 10 field demonstration projects of alternative or innovative treatment technologies at sites at which a response may be undertaken under section 9604 of this title, in fiscal year 1987 and each of the succeeding three fiscal years. If the Administrator determines that 10 field demonstration projects under this subsection cannot be initiated consistent with the criteria set forth in paragraph (7) in any of such fiscal years, the Administrator shall transmit to the appropriate committees of Congress a report explaining the reasons for his inability to conduct such demonstration projects.

(7) Criteria

selecting technologies to be demonstrated under this subsection, the Administrator shall, consistent with the protection of human health and the environment, consider each of the following criteria:

(A) The potential for contributing to solutions to those waste problems which pose the greatest threat to human health, which cannot be adequately controlled under present technologies, or which otherwise pose significant management difficulties.

(B) The availability of technologies which have been sufficiently developed for field demonstration and which are likely to be cost-effective and reliable.

(C) The availability and suitability of sites for demonstrating such technologies, taking into account the physical, biological, chemical, and geological characteristics of the sites, the extent and type of contamination found at the site, and the capability to conduct demonstration projects in such a manner as to assure the protection of human health and the environment.

(D) The likelihood that the data to be generated from the demonstration project at the site will be applicable to other sites.

(8) Technology transfer

In carrying out the program, the Administrator shall conduct a technology transfer program including the development, collection, evaluation, coordination, and dissemination of information relating to the utilization of alternative or innovative treatment technologies for response actions. The Administrator shall establish and maintain a central reference library for such information. The information maintained by the Administrator shall be made available to the public, subject to the provisions of section 552 of Title 5 and section 1905 of Title 18, and to other Government agencies in a manner that will facilitate its dissemination; except, that upon a showing satisfactory to the Administrator by any person that any information or portion thereof obtained under this subsection by the Administrator directly or indirectly from such person, would, if made public, divulge—

(A) trade secrets; or

(B) other proprietary information of such person,

the Administrator shall not disclose such information and disclosure thereof shall be punishable under section 1905 of Title 18. This subsection is not authority to withhold information from Congress or any committee of Congress upon the request of the chairman of such committee.

(9) Training

The Administrator is authorized and directed to carry out, through the Office of Technology Demonstration, a program of training and an evaluation of training needs for each of the following:

(A) Training in the procedures for the handling and removal of hazardous substances for employees who handle hazardous substances.

(B) Training in the management of facilities at which hazardous substances are located and in the evaluation of the hazards to human health presented by such facilities for State and local health and environment agency personnel.

(10) Definition

For purposes of this subsection, the term "alternative or innovative treatment technologies" means those technologies, including proprietary or patented methods, which permanently alter the composition of hazardous waste through chemical, biological, or physical means so as to significantly reduce the toxicity, mobility, or volume (or any combination thereof) of the hazardous waste or contaminated materials being treated. The term also includes technologies that characterize or assess the extent of contamination, the chemical and physical character of the contaminants, and the stresses imposed by the contaminants on complex ecosystems at sites.

(c) Hazardous substance research

The Administrator may conduct and support, through grants, cooperative agreements, and contracts, research with respect to the detection, assessment, and evaluation of the effects on and risks to human health of hazardous substances and detection of hazardous substances in the environment. The Administrator shall coordinate such research with the Secretary of Health and Human Services, acting through the advisory council established under this section, in order to avoid duplication of effort.

(d) University hazardous substance research centers

(1) Grant program

The Administrator shall make grants to institutions of higher learning to establish and operate not fewer than 5 hazardous substance research centers in the United States. In carrying out the program under this subsection, the Administrator should seek to have established and operated 10 hazardous substance research centers in the United States.

(2) Responsibilities of centers

The responsibilities of each hazardous substance research center established under this subsection shall include, but not be limited to, the conduct of research and training relating to the manufacture, use, transportation, disposal, and management of hazardous substances and publication and dissemination of the results of such research.

(3) Applications

Any institution of higher learning interested in receiving a grant under this subsection shall submit to the Administrator an application in such form and containing such information as the Administrator may require by regulation.

(4) Selection criteria

The Administrator shall select recipients of grants under this subsection on the basis of the following criteria:

(A) The hazardous substance research center shall be located in a State which is representative of the needs of the region in which such State is located for improved hazardous waste management.

(B) The grant recipient shall be located in an area which has experienced problems with hazardous substance management.

(C) There is available to the grant recipient for carrying out this subsection demonstrated research resources.

(D) The capability of the grant recipient to provide leadership in making national and regional contributions to the solution of both long-range and immediate hazardous substance management problems.

(E) The grant recipient shall make a commitment to support ongoing hazardous substance research programs with budgeted institutional funds of at least $100,000 per year.

(F) The grant recipient shall have an interdisciplinary staff with demonstrated expertise in hazardous substance management and research.

(G) The grant recipient shall have a demonstrated ability to disseminate results of hazardous substance research and educational programs through an interdisciplinary continuing education program.

(H) The projects which the grant recipient proposes to carry out under the grant are necessary and appropriate.

(5) Maintenance of effort

No grant may be made under this subsection in any fiscal year unless the recipient of such grant enters into such agreements with the Administrator as the Administrator may require to ensure that such recipient will maintain its aggregate expenditures from all other sources for establishing and operating a regional hazardous substance research center and related research activities at or above the average level of such expenditures in its 2 fiscal years preceding October 17, 1986.

(6) Federal share

The Federal share of a grant under this subsection shall not exceed 80 percent of the costs of establishing and operating the regional hazardous substance research center and related research activities carried out by the grant recipient.

(7) Limitation on use of funds

No funds made available to carry out this subsection shall be used for acquisition of real property (including buildings) or construction of any building.

(8) Administration through the Office of the Administrator

Administrative responsibility for carrying out this subsection shall be in the Office of the Administrator.

(9) Equitable distribution of funds

The Administrator shall allocate funds made available to carry out this subsection equitably among the regions of the United States.

(10) Technology transfer activities

Not less than five percent of the funds made available to carry out this subsection for any fiscal year shall be available to carry out technology transfer activities.

(e) Report to Congress

At the time of the submission of the annual budget request to Congress, the Administrator shall submit to the appropriate committees of the House of Representatives and the Senate and to the advisory council established under subsection (a) of this section, a report on the progress of the research, development, and demonstration program authorized by subsection (b) of this section, including an evaluation of each demonstration project completed in the preceding fiscal year, findings with respect to the efficacy of such demonstrated technologies in achieving permanent and significant reductions in risk from hazardous wastes, the costs of such demonstration projects, and the potential applicability of, and projected costs for, such technologies at other hazardous substance sites.

(f) Saving provision

Nothing in this section shall be construed to affect the provisions of the Solid Waste Disposal Act [42 U.S.C.A. § 6901 et seq.].

(g) Small business participation

The Administrator shall ensure, to the maximum extent practicable, an adequate opportunity for small business participation in the program established by subsection (b) of this section.

(Pub. L. No. 96–510, Title III, § 311, as added by Pub. L. No. 99–499, Title II, § 209(b), 100 Stat. 1708 (Oct. 17, 1986); and amended by Pub. L. No. 99–514, § 2, 100 Stat. 2095 (Oct. 22, 1986).)

HISTORICAL AND STATUTORY NOTES

References in Text

The Public Health Service Act, referred to in subsec. (a)(4), is Act of July 1, 1944, c. 373, 58 Stat. 682, as amended, which is codified generally as chapter 6A (section 201 et seq.) of this title. Title IV of that Act is codified generally to subchapter III (section 281 et seq.) of chapter 6A of this title. For complete classification of this Act to the Code, see Short Title of 1944 Acts note set out under section 201 of this title and Tables.

The Solid Waste Disposal Act, referred to in subsec. (f), is Title II of Pub. L. No. 89–272, 79 Stat. 997 (Oct. 20, 1965), as amended generally by Pub. L. No. 94–580, § 2, 90 Stat. 2795 (Oct. 21, 1976), which is codified generally as chapter 82 (section 6901 et seq.) of this title. For complete classification of this Act to the Code, see Short Title of 1965 Acts note set out under section 6901 of this title and Tables.

Effective and Applicability Provisions

1986 Acts. Section effective Oct. 17, 1986, see section 4 of Pub. L. No. 99–499, set out as a note under section 9601 of this title.

Methamphetamine Remediation Research Act of 2007

Pub. L. No. 110–143, 121 Stat. 1809 (Dec. 21, 2007), provided that:

"Sec. 1. Short Title.

"This Act [this note] may be cited as the 'Methamphetamine Remediation Research Act of 2007'.

"Sec. 2. Findings.

"The Congress finds the following:

"(1) Methamphetamine use and production is growing rapidly throughout the United States.

"(2) Materials and residues remaining from the production of methamphetamine pose novel environmental problems in locations where methamphetamine laboratories have been closed.

"(3) There has been little standardization of measures for determining when the site of a closed methamphetamine laboratory has been successfully remediated.

"(4) Initial cleanup actions are generally limited to removal of hazardous substances and contaminated materials that pose an immediate threat to public health or the environment. It is not uncommon for significant levels of contamination to be found throughout residential structures after a methamphetamine laboratory has closed, partially because of a lack of knowledge of how to achieve an effective cleanup.

"(5) Data on methamphetamine laboratory-related contaminants of concern are very limited, and cleanup standards do not currently exist. In addition, procedures for sampling and analysis of contaminants need to be researched and developed.

"(6) Many States are struggling with establishing remediation guidelines and programs to address the rapidly expanding number of methamphetamine laboratories being closed each year.

"Sec. 3. Voluntary guidelines.

"(a) Establishment of voluntary guidelines.—Not later than one year after the date of enactment of this Act [Dec. 21, 2007], the Administrator of the Environmental Protection Agency (in this Act referred to as the 'Administrator'), in consultation with the National Institute of Standards and Technology, shall establish voluntary guidelines, based on the best currently available scientific knowledge, for the remediation of former methamphetamine laboratories, including guidelines regarding preliminary site assessment and the remediation of residual contaminants.

"(b) Considerations.—In developing the voluntary guidelines under subsection (a), the Administrator shall consider, at a minimum—

"(1) relevant standards, guidelines, and requirements found in Federal, State, and local laws and regulations;

"(2) the varying types and locations of former methamphetamine laboratories; and

"(3) the expected cost of carrying out any proposed guidelines.

"(c) States.—The voluntary guidelines should be designed to assist State and local governments in the development and the implementation of legislation and other policies to apply state-of-the-art knowledge and research results to the remediation of former methamphetamine laboratories. The Administrator shall work with State and local governments and other relevant non-Federal agencies and organizations, including through the conference described in section 5 [of this note], to promote and encourage the appropriate adoption of the voluntary guidelines.

"(d) Updating the guidelines.—The Administrator shall periodically update the voluntary guidelines as the Administrator, in consultation with States and other interested parties, determines to be necessary and appropriate to incorporate research findings and other new knowledge.

"Sec. 4. Research program.

The Administrator shall establish a program of research to support the development and revision of the voluntary guidelines described in section 3 [of this note]. Such research shall—

"(1) identify methamphetamine laboratory-related chemicals of concern;

"(2) assess the types and levels of exposure to chemicals of concern identified under paragraph (1), including routine and accidental exposures, that may present a significant risk of adverse biological effects, and the research necessary to better address biological effects and to minimize adverse human exposures;

"(3) evaluate the performance of various methamphetamine laboratory cleanup and remediation techniques; and

"(4) support other research priorities identified by the Administrator in consultation with States and other interested parties.

"Sec. 5. Technology transfer conference.

"(a) Conference.—Not later than 90 days after the date of enactment of this Act [Dec. 21, 2007], and at least every third year thereafter, the Administrator shall convene a conference of appropriate State agencies, as well as individuals or organizations involved in research and other activities directly related to the environmental, or biological impacts of former methamphetamine laboratories. The conference should be a forum for the Administrator to provide information on the guidelines developed under section 3 [of this note] and on the latest findings from the research program described in section 4 [of this note], and for the non-Federal participants to provide information on the problems and needs of States and localities and their experience with guidelines developed under section 3 [of this note].

"(b) Report.—Not later than 3 months after each conference, the Administrator shall submit a report to the Congress that summarizes the proceedings of the conference, including a summary of any recommendations or concerns raised by the non-Federal participants and how the Administrator intends to respond to them. The report shall also be made widely available to the general public.

"Sec. 6. Residual effects study.

"(a) Study.—Not later than 6 months after the date of enactment of this Act [Dec. 21, 2007], the Administrator shall enter into an arrangement with the National Academy of Sciences for a study of the status and quality of research on the residual effects of methamphetamine laboratories. The study shall identify research gaps and recommend an agenda for the research program described in section 4 [of this note]. The study shall pay particular attention to the need for research on the impacts of methamphetamine laboratories on—

"(1) the residents of buildings where such laboratories are, or were, located, with particular emphasis given to biological impacts on children; and

"(2) first responders.

"(b) Report.—Not later than 3 months after the completion of the study, the Administrator shall transmit to Congress a report on how the Administrator will use the results of the study to carry out the activities described in sections 3 and 4 [of this note].

"Sec. 7. Methamphetamine detection research and development program.

"The Director of National Institute of Standards and Technology, in consultation with the Administrator, shall support a research program to develop—

"(1) new methamphetamine detection technologies, with emphasis on field test kits and site detection; and

"(2) appropriate standard reference materials and validation procedures for methamphetamine detection testing.

"Sec. 8. Savings clause.

"Nothing in this Act [this note] shall be construed to affect or limit the application of, or any obligation to comply with, any State or Federal environmental law or regulation, including the Comprehensive Environmental Response, Compensation, and Liability Act of 1980 (42 U.S.C. 9601 et seq.) and the Solid Waste Disposal Act (42 U.S.C. 6901 et seq.).

"Sec. 9. Authorization of appropriations.

"(a) Environmental Protection Agency.—There are authorized to be appropriated to the Environmental Protection Agency to carry out this Act [this note] $1,750,000 for each of the fiscal years 2007 and 2008.

"(b) National Institute of Standards and Technology.—There are authorized to be appropriated to the National Institute of Standards and Technology to carry out this Act [this note] $750,000 for each of the fiscal years 2007 and 2008."

Congressional Statement of Purpose

Section 209(a) of Pub. L. No. 99–499 provided that: "The purposes of this section [enacting this section] are as follows:

"(1) To establish a comprehensive and coordinated Federal program of research, development, demonstration, and training for the purpose of promoting the development of alternative and innovative treatment technologies that can be used in response actions under the CERCLA program, to provide incentives for the development and use of such technologies, and to improve the scientific capability to assess, detect and evaluate the effects on and risks to human health from hazardous substances.

"(2) To establish a basic university research and education program within the Department of Health and Human Services and a research, demonstration, and training program within the Environmental Protection Agency.

"(3) To reserve certain funds from the Hazardous Substance Trust Fund to support a basic research program within the Department of Health and Human Services, and an applied and developmental research program within the Environmental Protection Agency.

"(4) To enhance the Environmental Protection Agency's internal research capabilities related to CERCLA activities, including site assessment and technology evaluation.

"(5) To provide incentives for the development of alternative and innovative treatment technologies in a manner that supplements or coordinates with, but does not compete with or duplicate, private sector development of such technologies."

Gulf Coast Hazardous Substance Research, Development, and Demonstration Center

Section 118(*l*) of Pub. L. No. 99–499 provided that:

"(1) Establishment of hazardous substance research, development, and demonstration center.—The Administrator shall establish a hazardous substance research, development, and demonstration center (hereinafter in this subsection referred to as the 'Center') for the purpose of conducting research to aid in more effective hazardous substance response and waste management throughout the Gulf Coast.

"(2) Purposes of the Center.—The Center shall carry out a program of research, evaluation, testing, development, and demonstration of alternative or innovative technologies which may be utilized in response actions or in normal handling of hazardous wastes to achieve better protection of human health and the environment.

"(3) Operation of Center.—(A) For purposes of operating the Center, the Administrator is authorized to enter into contracts and cooperative agreements with, and make grants to, a university related institute involved with the improvement of waste management. Such institute shall be located in Jefferson County, Texas.

"(B) The Center shall be authorized to make grants, accept contributions, and enter into agreements with universities located in the States of Texas, Louisiana, Mississippi, Alabama, and Florida in order to carry out the purposes of the Center.

"(4) Authorization of appropriations.—There are authorized to be appropriated to the Administrator for purposes of carrying out this subsection for fiscal years beginning after September 30, 1986, not more than $5,000,000."

Pacific Northwest Hazardous Substance Research, Development, and Demonstration Center

Section 118(*o*) of Pub. L. No. 99–499 provided that:

"(1) Establishment.—The Administrator shall establish a hazardous substance research, development, and demonstration center (hereinafter in this subsection referred to as the 'Center') for the purpose of conducting research to aid in more effective hazardous substance response in the Pacific Northwest.

"(2) Purposes of Center.—The Center shall carry out a program of research, evaluation, testing, development, and demonstration of alternative or innovative technologies which may be utilized in response actions to achieve more permanent protection of human health and welfare and the environment.

"(3) Operation of Center.—

"(A) Nonprofit entity.—For the purposes of operating the Center, the Administrator is authorized to enter into contracts and cooperative agreements with, and make grants to, a nonprofit private entity as defined in section 201(i) of Public Law 96–517 [probably means section 201(i) of Title 35, Patents, which was enacted by section 6(a) of Pub. L. No. 96–517, Dec. 12, 1980, 94 Stat. 3020] which entity shall agree to provide the basic technical and management personnel. Such nonprofit private entity shall also agree to provide at least two permanent research facilities, one of which shall be located in Benton County, Washington, and one of which shall be located in Clallam County, Washington.

"(B) Authorities.—The Center shall be authorized to make grants, accept contributions, and enter into agreements with universities located in the States of Washington, Oregon, Idaho, and Montana in order to carry out the purposes of the Center.

"(4) Hazardous waste research at the Hanford site.—

"(A) Interagency Agreements.—The Administrator and the Secretary of Energy are authorized to enter into interagency agreements with one another for the purpose of providing for research, evaluation, testing, development, and demonstration into alternative or innovative technologies to characterize and assess the nature and extent of hazardous waste (including radioactive mixed waste) contamination at the Hanford site, in the State of Washington.

"(B) Funding.—There is authorized to be appropriated to the Secretary of Energy for purposes of carrying out this paragraph for fiscal years beginning after September 30, 1986, not more than $5,000,000. All sums appropriated under this subparagraph shall be provided to the Administrator by the Secretary of Energy, pursuant to the interagency agreement entered into under subparagraph (A), for the purpose of the Administrator entering into contracts and cooperative agreements with, and making grants to, the Center in order to carry out the research, evaluation, testing, development, and demonstration described in paragraph (1).

"(5) Authorization of appropriations.—There is authorized to be appropriated to the Administrator for purposes of carrying out this subsection (other than paragraph (4)) for fiscal years beginning after September 30, 1986, not more than $5,000,000."

Termination of Advisory Councils

Advisory councils established after Jan. 5, 1973, to terminate not later than the expiration of the 2-year period beginning on the date of their establishment, unless, in the case of a council established by the President or an officer of the Federal Government, such council is renewed by appropriate action prior to the expiration of such 2-year period, or in the case of a council established by the Congress, its duration is otherwise provided by law. See sections 3(2) and 14 of Pub. L. No. 92–463, 86 Stat. 770, 776 (Oct. 6, 1972), set out in Appendix 2 to Title 5, Government Organization and Employees.

§ 9660a. Grant program

(1) Grant purposes

Grants for the training and education of workers who are or may be engaged in activities related to hazardous waste removal or containment or emergency response may be made under this section.

(2) Administration

Grants under this section shall be administered by the National Institute of Environmental Health Sciences.

(3) Grant recipients

Grants shall be awarded to nonprofit organizations which demonstrate experience in implementing and operating worker health and safety training and education programs and demonstrate the ability to reach and involve in training programs target populations of workers who are or will be engaged in hazardous waste removal or containment or emergency response operations.

(Pub. L. No. 99–499, Title I, § 126(g), 100 Stat. 1692 (Oct. 17, 1986).)

HISTORICAL AND STATUTORY NOTES

Codifications

Section was enacted as a part of the Superfund Amendments and Reauthorization Act of 1986, and not as a part of the Comprehensive Environmental Response, Compensation, and Liability Act of 1980, which is codified as this chapter.

§ 9661. Love Canal property acquisition

[CERCLA § 312]

(a) Acquisition of property in Emergency Declaration Area

The Administrator of the Environmental Protection Agency (hereinafter referred to as the "Administrator") may make grants not to exceed $2,500,000 to the State of New York (or to any duly constituted public agency or authority thereof) for purposes of acquisition of private property in the Love Canal Emergency Declaration Area. Such acquisition shall include (but shall not be limited to) all private property within the Emergency Declaration Area, including non-owner occupied residential properties, commercial, industrial, public, religious, non-profit, and vacant properties.

(b) Procedures for acquisition

No property shall be acquired pursuant to this section unless the property owner voluntarily agrees to such acquisition. Compensation for any property acquired pursuant to this section shall be based upon the fair market value of the property as it existed prior to the emergency declaration. Valuation procedures for property acquired with funds provided under this section shall be in accordance with those set forth in the agreement entered into between the New York State Disaster Preparedness Commission and the Love Canal Revitalization Agency on October 9, 1980.

(c) State ownership

The Administrator shall not provide any funds under this section for the acquisition of any properties pursuant to this section unless a public agency or authority of the State of New York first enters into a cooperative agreement with the Administrator providing assurances deemed adequate by the Administrator that the State or an agency created under the laws of the State shall take title to the properties to be so acquired.

(d) Maintenance of property

The Administrator shall enter into a cooperative agreement with an appropriate public agency or authority of the State of New York under which the Administrator shall maintain or arrange for the maintenance of all properties within the Emergency Declaration Area that have been acquired by any public agency or authority of the State. Ninety (90) percent of the costs of such maintenance shall be paid by the

Administrator. The remaining portion of such costs shall be paid by the State (unless a credit is available under section 9604(c) of this title). The Administrator is authorized, in his discretion, to provide technical assistance to any public agency or authority of the State of New York in order to implement the recommendations of the habitability and land-use study in order to put the land within the Emergency Declaration Area to its best use.

(e) Habitability and land use study

The Administrator shall conduct or cause to be conducted a habitability and land-use study. The study shall—

(1) assess the risks associated with inhabiting of the Love Canal Emergency Declaration Area;

(2) compare the level of hazardous waste contamination in that Area to that present in other comparable communities; and

(3) assess the potential uses of the land within the Emergency Declaration Area, including but not limited to residential, industrial, commercial and recreational, and the risks associated with such potential uses.

The Administrator shall publish the findings of such study and shall work with the State of New York to develop recommendations based upon the results of such study.

(f) Funding

For purposes of section 9611 of this title [and 9631(c) of this title], the expenditures authorized by this section shall be treated as a cost specified in section 9611(c) of this title.

(g) Response

The provisions of this section shall not affect the implementation of other response actions within the Emergency Declaration Area that the Administrator has determined (before October 17, 1986) to be necessary to protect the public health or welfare or the environment.

(h) Definitions

For purposes of this section:

(1) Emergency Declaration Area

The terms "Emergency Declaration Area" and "Love Canal Emergency Declaration Area" mean the Emergency Declaration Area as defined in section 950, paragraph (2) of the General Municipal Law of the State of New York, Chapter 259, Laws of 1980, as in effect on October 17, 1986.

(2) Private property

As used in subsection (a) of this section, the term "private property" means all property which is not owned by a department, agency, or instrumentality of—

(A) the United States, or

(B) the State of New York (or any public agency or authority thereof).

(Pub. L. No. 96–510, Title III, § 312, as added by Pub. L. No. 99–499, Title II, § 213(b), 100 Stat. 1727 (Oct. 17, 1986).)

HISTORICAL AND STATUTORY NOTES

References in Text

Section 9631 of this title, referred to in subsec. (f), was repealed by Pub. L. No. 99–499, Title V, § 517(c)(1), 100 Stat. 1774 (Oct. 17, 1986).

Effective and Applicability Provisions

1986 Acts. Section effective Oct. 17, 1986, see section 4 of Pub. L. No. 99–499, set out as a note under section 9601 of this title.

Coordination of Titles I to IV of Pub. L. No. 99–499

Any provision of Titles I to IV of Pub. L. No. 99–499, imposing any tax, premium, or fee; establishing any trust fund; or authorizing expenditures from any trust fund, to have no force or effect, see section 531 of Pub. L. No. 99–499, set out as a note under section 1 of Title 26, Internal Revenue Code.

Love Canal Property Acquisition; Congressional Findings

Section 213(a) of Pub. L. No. 99–499 provided that:

"(1) The area known as Love Canal located in the city of Niagara Falls and the town of Wheatfield, New York, was the first toxic waste site to receive national attention. As a result of that attention Congress investigated the problems associated with toxic waste sites and enacted CERCLA [this chapter] to deal with these problems.

"(2) Because Love Canal came to the Nation's attention prior to the passage of CERCLA and because the fund under CERCLA was not available to compensate for all of the hardships endured by the citizens in the area, Congress has determined that special provisions are required. These provisions do not affect the lawfulness, implementation, or selection of any other response actions at Love Canal or at any other facilities."

§ 9662. Limitation on contract and borrowing authority

Any authority provided by this Act, including any amendment made by this Act, to enter into contracts to obligate the United States or to incur indebtedness for the repayment of which the United States is liable shall be effective only to such extent or in such amounts as are provided in appropriation Acts.

(Pub. L. No. 99–499, § 3, 100 Stat. 1614 (Oct. 17, 1986).)

HISTORICAL AND STATUTORY NOTES

References in Text

This Act, referred to in text, is Pub. L. No. 99–499, 100 Stat. 1613 (Oct. 17, 1986), as amended, known as the Superfund Amendments and Reauthorization Act of 1986. For complete classification of this Act to the Code, see Short Title of 1986 Amendments note set out under section 9601 of this title and Tables.

Codifications

Section was enacted as part of the Superfund Amendments and Reauthorization Act of 1986, and not as part of the Comprehensive Environmental Response, Compensation, and Liability Act of 1980, which comprises this chapter.

Effective and Applicability Provisions

1986 Acts. Section effective Oct. 17, 1986, see section 4 of Pub. L. No. 99–499, set out as a note under section 9601 of this title.

SUBCHAPTER IV—POLLUTION INSURANCE

§ 9671. Definitions

[CERCLA § 401]

As used in this subchapter—

(1) Insurance

The term "insurance" means primary insurance, excess insurance, reinsurance, surplus lines insurance, and any other arrangement for shifting and distributing risk which is determined to be insurance under applicable State or Federal law.

(2) Pollution liability

The term "pollution liability" means liability for injuries arising from the release of hazardous substances or pollutants or contaminants.

(3) Risk retention group

The term "risk retention group" means any corporation or other limited liability association taxable as a corporation, or as an insurance company, formed under the laws of any State—

(A) whose primary activity consists of assuming and spreading all, or any portion, of the pollution liability of its group members;

(B) which is organized for the primary purpose of conducting the activity described under subparagraph (A);

(C) which is chartered or licensed as an insurance company and authorized to engage in the business of insurance under the laws of any State; and

(D) which does not exclude any person from membership in the group solely to provide for members of such a group a competitive advantage over such a person.

(4) Purchasing group

The term "purchasing group" means any group of persons which has as one of its purposes the purchase of pollution liability insurance on a group basis.

(5) State

The term "State" means any State of the United States, the District of Columbia, the Commonwealth of Puerto Rico, Guam, American Samoa, the Virgin Islands, the Commonwealth of the Northern Marianas, and any other territory or possession over which the United States has jurisdiction.

(Pub. L. No. 96–510, Title IV, § 401, as added by Pub. L. No. 99–499, Title II, § 210(a), formerly § 210, 100 Stat. 1716 (Oct. 17, 1986); and renumbered by Pub. L. No. 99–563, § 11(c)(1), 100 Stat. 3177 (Oct. 27, 1986).)

HISTORICAL AND STATUTORY NOTES

Effective and Applicability Provisions

1986 Acts. Section effective Oct. 17, 1986, see section 4 of Pub. L. No. 99–499, set out as a note under section 9601 of this title.

State Powers and Authorities under Risk Retention Amendments of 1986

Section 210(b) of Pub. L. No. 99–499, as added Pub. L. No. 99–563, § 11(c)(1), 100 Stat. 3177 (Oct. 27, 1986), effective Oct. 27, 1986, pursuant to Pub. L. No. 99–563, § 11(a), provided that: "For purposes of subsection (a) of this section [enacting this subchapter], the powers and authorities of States addressed by the Risk Retention Amendments of 1986 [for classification to the Code, see Short Title of 1986 Amendment note under section 3901 of Title 15, Commerce and Trade] are in addition to those of this Act [see Short Title of 1986 Amendments note set out under 9601 of this title]."

§ 9672. State laws; scope of subchapter

[CERCLA § 402]

(a) State laws

Nothing in this subchapter shall be construed to affect either the tort law or the law governing the interpretation of insurance contracts of any State. The definitions of pollution liability and pollution liability insurance under any State law shall not be applied for the purposes of this subchapter, including recognition or qualification of risk retention groups or purchasing groups.

(b) Scope of subchapter

The authority to offer or to provide insurance under this subchapter shall be limited to coverage of pollution liability risks and this subchapter does not authorize a risk retention group or purchasing group to provide coverage of any other line of insurance.

(Pub. L. No. 96–510, Title IV, § 402, as added by Pub. L. No. 99–499, Title II, § 210(a), formerly § 210, 100 Stat. 1716 (Oct. 17, 1986); and renumbered by Pub. L. No. 99–563, § 11(c)(1), 100 Stat. 3177 (Oct. 27, 1986).)

HISTORICAL AND STATUTORY NOTES

Effective and Applicability Provisions

1986 Acts. Section effective Oct. 17, 1986, see section 4 of Pub. L. No. 99–499, set out as a note under section 9601 of this title.

§ 9673. Risk retention groups

[CERCLA § 403]

(a) Exemption

Except as provided in this section, a risk retention group shall be exempt from the following:

(1) A State law, rule, or order which makes unlawful, or regulates, directly or indirectly, the operation of a risk retention group.

(2) A State law, rule, or order which requires or permits a risk retention group to participate in any insurance insolvency guaranty association to which an insurer licensed in the State is required to belong.

(3) A State law, rule, or order which requires any insurance policy issued to a risk retention group or any member of the group to be countersigned by an insurance agent or broker residing in the State.

(4) A State law, rule, or order which otherwise discriminates against a risk retention group or any of its members.

(b) Exceptions

(1) State laws generally applicable

Nothing in subsection (a) of this section shall be construed to affect the applicability of State laws generally applicable to persons or corporations. The State in which a risk retention group is chartered may regulate the formation and operation of the group.

(2) State regulations not subject to exemption

Subsection (a) of this section shall not apply to any State law which requires a risk retention group to do any of the following:

(A) Comply with the unfair claim settlement practices law of the State.

(B) Pay, on a nondiscriminatory basis, applicable premium and other taxes which are levied on admitted insurers and surplus line insurers, brokers, or policyholders under the laws of the State.

(C) Participate, on a nondiscriminatory basis, in any mechanism established or authorized under the law of the State for the equitable apportionment among insurers of pollution liability insurance losses and expenses incurred on policies written through such mechanism.

(D) Submit to the appropriate authority reports and other information required of licensed insurers under the laws of a State relating solely to pollution liability insurance losses and expenses.

(E) Register with and designate the State insurance commissioner as its agent solely for the purpose of receiving service of legal documents or process.

(F) Furnish, upon request, such commissioner a copy of any financial report submitted by the risk retention group to the commissioner of the chartering or licensing jurisdiction.

(G) Submit to an examination by the State insurance commissioner in any State in which the group is doing business to determine the group's financial condition, if—

(i) the commissioner has reason to believe the risk retention group is in a financially impaired condition; and

(ii) the commissioner of the jurisdiction in which the group is chartered has not begun or has refused to initiate an examination of the group.

(H) Comply with a lawful order issued in a delinquency proceeding commenced by the State insurance commissioner if the commissioner of the jurisdiction in which the group is chartered has failed to initiate such a proceeding after notice of a finding of financial impairment under subparagraph (G).

(c) Application of exemptions

The exemptions specified in subsection (a) of this section apply to—

(1) pollution liability insurance coverage provided by a risk retention group for—

(A) such group; or

(B) any person who is a member of such group;

(2) the sale of pollution liability insurance coverage for a risk retention group; and

(3) the provision of insurance related services or management services for a risk retention group or any member of such a group.

(d) Agents or brokers

A State may require that a person acting, or offering to act, as an agent or broker for a risk retention group obtain a license from that State, except that a State may not impose any qualification or requirement which discriminates against a nonresident agent or broker.

(Pub. L. No. 96–510, Title IV, § 403, as added by Pub. L. No. 99–499, Title II, § 210(a), formerly § 210, 100 Stat. 1717 (Oct. 17, 1986); and renumbered by Pub. L. No. 99–563, § 11(c)(1), 100 Stat. 3177 (Oct. 27, 1986).)

HISTORICAL AND STATUTORY NOTES

Effective and Applicability Provisions

1986 Acts. Section effective Oct. 17, 1986, see section 4 of Pub. L. No. 99–499, set out as a note under section 9601 of this title.

§ 9674. Purchasing groups

[CERCLA § 404]

(a) Exemption

Except as provided in this section, a purchasing group is exempt from the following:

(1) A State law, rule, or order which prohibits the establishment of a purchasing group.

(2) A State law, rule, or order which makes it unlawful for an insurer to provide or offer to provide insurance on a basis providing, to a purchasing group or its member, advantages, based on their loss and expense experience, not afforded to other persons with respect to rates, policy forms, coverages, or other matters.

(3) A State law, rule, or order which prohibits a purchasing group or its members from purchasing insurance on the group basis described in paragraph (2) of this subsection.

(4) A State law, rule, or order which prohibits a purchasing group from obtaining insurance on a group basis because the group has not been in existence for a minimum period of time or because any member has not belonged to the group for a minimum period of time.

(5) A State law, rule, or order which requires that a purchasing group must have a minimum number of members, common ownership or affiliation, or a certain legal form.

(6) A State law, rule, or order which requires that a certain percentage of a purchasing group must obtain insurance on a group basis.

(7) A State law, rule, or order which requires that any insurance policy issued to a purchasing group or any members of the group be countersigned by an insurance agent or broker residing in that State.

(8) A State law, rule, or order which otherwise discriminate[1] against a purchasing group or any of its members.

(b) Application of exemptions

The exemptions specified in subsection (a) of this section apply to the following:

(1) Pollution liability insurance, and comprehensive general liability insurance which includes this coverage, provided to—

(A) a purchasing group; or

(B) any person who is a member of a purchasing group.

(2) The sale of any one of the following to a purchasing group or a member of the group:

(A) Pollution liability insurance and comprehensive general liability coverage.

(B) Insurance related services.

(C) Management services.

(c) Agents or brokers

A State may require that a person acting, or offering to act, as an agent or broker for a purchasing group obtain a license from that State, except that a State may not impose any qualification or requirement which discriminates against a nonresident agent or broker.

(Pub. L. No. 96–510, Title IV, § 404, as added by Pub. L. No. 99–499, Title II, § 210(a), formerly § 210, 100 Stat. 1718 (Oct. 17, 1986); and renumbered by Pub. L. No. 99–563, § 11(c)(1), 100 Stat. 3177 (Oct. 27, 1986).)

[1] So in original. Probably should be "discriminates."

HISTORICAL AND STATUTORY NOTES

Effective and Applicability Provisions

1986 Acts. Section effective Oct. 17, 1986, see section 4 of Pub. L. No. 99–499, set out as a note under section 9601 of this title.

§ 9675. Applicability of securities laws

[CERCLA § 405]

(a) Ownership interests

The ownership interests of members of a risk retention group shall be considered to be—

(1) exempted securities for purposes of section 77e of Title 15 and for purposes of section 78*l* of Title 15; and

(2) securities for purposes of the provisions of section 77q of Title 15 and the provisions of section 78j of Title 15.

(b) Investment Company Act

A risk retention group shall not be considered to be an investment company for purposes of the Investment Company Act of 1940 (15 U.S.C. 80a–1 et seq.).

(c) Blue sky law

The ownership interests of members in a risk retention group shall not be considered securities for purposes of any State blue sky law.

(Pub. L. No. 96–510, Title IV, § 405, as added by Pub. L. No. 99–499, Title II, § 210(a), formerly § 210, 100 Stat. 1719 (Oct. 17, 1986); and renumbered by Pub. L. No. 99–563, § 11(c)(1), 100 Stat. 3177 (Oct. 27, 1986).)

HISTORICAL AND STATUTORY NOTES

References in Text

The Investment Company Act of 1940, referred to in subsec. (b), is Title I of Act of Aug. 22, 1940, c. 686, 54 Stat. 789, as amended, which is codified principally as subchapter I (section 80a–1 et seq.) of chapter 2D of Title 15, Commerce and Trade. For complete classification of this Act to the Code, see section 80a–51 of Title 15 and Tables.

Effective and Applicability Provisions

1986 Acts. Section effective Oct. 17, 1986, see section 4 of Pub. L. No. 99–499, set out as a note under section 9601 of this title.

EMERGENCY PLANNING AND COMMUNITY RIGHT-TO-KNOW

EMERGENCY PLANNING AND COMMUNITY RIGHT-TO-KNOW ACT OF 1986 [EPCRTKA § ______]

(42 U.S.C.A. §§ 11001 to 11050)

CHAPTER 116—EMERGENCY PLANNING AND COMMUNITY RIGHT-TO-KNOW

SUBCHAPTER I—EMERGENCY PLANNING AND NOTIFICATION

Sec.

SUBCHAPTER I—EMERGENCY PLANNING AND NOTIFICATION

§ 11001. Establishment of State commissions, planning districts, and local committees

[EPCRTKA § 301]

(a) Establishment of State emergency response commissions

Not later than six months after October 17, 1986, the Governor of each State shall appoint a State emergency response commission. The Governor may designate as the State emergency response commission one or more existing emergency response organizations that are State-sponsored or appointed. The Governor shall, to the extent practicable, appoint persons to the State emergency response commission who have technical expertise in the emergency response field. The State emergency response commission shall appoint local emergency planning committees under subsection (c) of this section and shall supervise and coordinate the activities of such committees. The State emergency response commission shall establish procedures for receiving and processing requests from the public for information under section 11044 of this title, including tier II information under section 11022 of this title. Such procedures shall include the designation of an official to serve as coordinator for information. If the Governor of any State does not designate a State emergency response commission within such period, the Governor shall operate as the State emergency response commission until the Governor makes such designation.

(b) Establishment of emergency planning districts

Not later than nine months after October 17, 1986, the State emergency response commission shall designate emergency planning districts in order to facilitate preparation and implementation of emergency plans. Where appropriate, the State emergency response commission may designate existing political subdivisions or multijurisdictional planning organizations as such districts. In emergency planning areas that involve more than one State, the State emergency response commissions of all potentially affected States may designate emergency planning districts and local emergency planning committees by agreement. In making such designation, the State emergency response commission shall indicate which facilities subject to the requirements of this subchapter are within such emergency planning district.

(c) Establishment of local emergency planning committees

Not later than 30 days after designation of emergency planning districts or 10 months after October 17, 1986, whichever is earlier, the State emergency response commission shall appoint members of a local emergency planning committee for each emergency planning district. Each committee shall include, at a minimum, representatives from each of the following groups or organizations: elected State and local officials; law enforcement, civil defense, firefighting, first aid, health, local environmental, hospital, and transportation personnel; broadcast and print media; community groups; and owners and operators of facilities subject to the requirements of this subchapter. Such committee shall appoint a chairperson and shall establish rules by which the committee shall function. Such rules shall include provisions for public notification of committee activities, public meetings to discuss the emergency plan, public comments, response to such comments by the committee, and distribution of the emergency plan. The local emergency planning committee shall establish procedures for receiving and processing requests from the public for information under section 11044 of this title, including tier II information under section 11022 of this title. Such procedures shall include the designation of an official to serve as coordinator for information.

(d) Revisions

A State emergency response commission may revise its designations and appointments under subsections (b) and (c) of this section as it deems appropriate. Interested persons may petition the State emergency response commission to modify the membership of a local emergency planning committee.

(Pub. L. No. 99–499, Title III, § 301, 100 Stat. 1729 (Oct. 17, 1986).)

HISTORICAL AND STATUTORY NOTES

Effective and Applicability Provisions

1986 Acts. Section effective Oct. 17, 1986, see section 4 of Pub. L. 99–499, set out as a note under section 9601 of this title.

Short Title

1986 Acts. Section 300(a) of Title III of Pub. L. No. 99–499 provided that: "This title [enacting this chapter] may be cited as the 'Emergency Planning and Community Right-To-Know Act of 1986'."

§ 11002. Substances and facilities covered and notification

[EPCRTKA § 302]

(a) Substances covered

(1) In general

A substance is subject to the requirements of this subchapter if the substance is on the list published under paragraph (2).

(2) List of extremely hazardous substances

Within 30 days after October 17, 1986, the Administrator shall publish a list of extremely hazardous substances. The list shall be the same as the list of substances published in November 1985 by the Administrator in Appendix A of the "Chemical Emergency Preparedness Program Interim Guidance".

(3) Thresholds

(A) At the time the list referred to in paragraph (2) is published the Administrator shall—

(i) publish an interim final regulation establishing a threshold planning quantity for each substance on the list, taking into account the criteria described in paragraph (4), and

(ii) initiate a rulemaking in order to publish final regulations establishing a threshold planning quantity for each substance on the list.

(B) The threshold planning quantities may, at the Administrator's discretion, be based on classes of chemicals or categories of facilities.

(C) If the Administrator fails to publish an interim final regulation establishing a threshold planning quantity for a substance within 30 days after October 17, 1986, the threshold planning quantity for the substance shall be 2 pounds until such time as the Administrator publishes regulations establishing a threshold for the substance.

(4) Revisions

The Administrator may revise the list and thresholds under paragraphs (2) and (3) from time to time. Any revisions to the list shall take into account the toxicity, reactivity, volatility, dispersability, combustability, or flammability of a substance. For purposes of the preceding sentence, the term "toxicity" shall include any short- or long-term health effect which may result from a short-term exposure to the substance.

(b) Facilities covered

(1) Except as provided in section 11004 of this title, a facility is subject to the requirements of this subchapter if a substance on the list referred to in subsection (a) of this section is present at the facility in an amount in excess of the threshold planning quantity established for such substance.

(2) For purposes of emergency planning, a Governor or a State emergency response commission may designate additional facilities which shall be subject to the requirements of this subchapter, if such designation is made after public notice and opportunity for comment. The Governor or State emergency response commission shall notify the facility concerned of any facility designation under this paragraph.

(c) Emergency planning notification

Not later than seven months after October 17, 1986, the owner or operator of each facility subject to the requirements of this subchapter by reason of subsection (b)(1) of this section shall notify the State emergency response commission for the State in which such facility is located that such facility is subject to the requirements of this subchapter. Thereafter, if a substance on the list of extremely hazardous substances referred to in subsection (a) of this section first becomes present at such facility in excess of the threshold planning quantity established for such substance, or if there is a revision of such list and the facility has present a substance on the revised list in excess of the threshold planning quantity established for such substance, the owner or operator of the facility shall notify the State emergency response commission and the local emergency planning committee within 60 days after such acquisition or revision that such facility is subject to the requirements of this subchapter.

(d) Notification of Administrator

The State emergency response commission shall notify the Administrator of facilities subject to the requirements of this subchapter by notifying the Administrator of—

(1) each notification received from a facility under subsection (c) of this section, and

(2) each facility designated by the Governor or State emergency response commission under subsection (b)(2) of this section.

(Pub. L. No. 99–499, Title III, § 302, 100 Stat. 1730 (Oct. 17, 1986).)

HISTORICAL AND STATUTORY NOTES

Effective and Applicability Provisions

1986 Acts. Section effective Oct. 17, 1986, see section 4 of Pub. L. No. 99–499, set out as a note under section 9601 of this title.

§ 11003. Comprehensive emergency response plans

[EPCRTKA § 303]

(a) Plan required

Each local emergency planning committee shall complete preparation of an emergency plan in accordance with this section not later than two years after October 17, 1986. The committee shall review such plan once a year, or more frequently as changed circumstances in the community or at any facility may require.

(b) Resources

Each local emergency planning committee shall evaluate the need for resources necessary to develop, implement, and exercise the emergency plan, and shall make recommendations with respect to additional resources that may be required and the means for providing such additional resources.

(c) Plan provisions

Each emergency plan shall include (but is not limited to) each of the following:

(1) Identification of facilities subject to the requirements of this subchapter that are within the emergency planning district, identification of routes likely to be used for the transportation of substances on the list of extremely hazardous substances referred to in section 11002(a) of this title, and identification of additional facilities contributing or subjected to additional risk due to their proximity to facilities subject to the requirements of this subchapter, such as hospitals or natural gas facilities.

(2) Methods and procedures to be followed by facility owners and operators and local emergency and medical personnel to respond to any release of such substances.

(3) Designation of a community emergency coordinator and facility emergency coordinators, who shall make determinations necessary to implement the plan.

(4) Procedures providing reliable, effective, and timely notification by the facility emergency coordinators and the community emergency coordinator to persons designated in the emergency plan, and to the public, that a release has occurred (consistent with the emergency notification requirements of section 11004 of this title).

(5) Methods for determining the occurrence of a release, and the area or population likely to be affected by such release.

(6) A description of emergency equipment and facilities in the community and at each facility in the community subject to the requirements of this subchapter, and an identification of the persons responsible for such equipment and facilities.

(7) Evacuation plans, including provisions for a precautionary evacuation and alternative traffic routes.

(8) Training programs, including schedules for training of local emergency response and medical personnel.

(9) Methods and schedules for exercising the emergency plan.

(d) Providing of information

For each facility subject to the requirements of this subchapter:

(1) Within 30 days after establishment of a local emergency planning committee for the emergency planning district in which such facility is located, or within 11 months after October 17, 1986, whichever is earlier, the owner or operator of the facility shall notify the emergency planning committee (or the Governor if there is no committee) of a facility representative who will participate in the emergency planning process as a facility emergency coordinator.

(2) The owner or operator of the facility shall promptly inform the emergency planning committee of any relevant changes occurring at such facility as such changes occur or are expected to occur.

(3) Upon request from the emergency planning committee, the owner or operator of the facility shall promptly provide information to such committee necessary for developing and implementing the emergency plan.

(e) Review by State emergency response commission

After completion of an emergency plan under subsection (a) of this section for an emergency planning district, the local emergency planning committee shall submit a copy of the plan to the State emergency response commission of each State in which such district is located. The commission shall review the plan and make recommendations to the committee on revisions of the plan that may be necessary to ensure coordination of such plan with emergency response plans of other emergency planning districts. To the maximum extent practicable, such review shall not delay implementation of such plan.

(f) Guidance documents

The national response team, as established pursuant to the National Contingency Plan as established under section 9605 of this title, shall publish guidance documents for preparation and implementation of emergency plans. Such documents shall be published not later than five months after October 17, 1986.

(g) Review of plans by regional response teams

The regional response teams, as established pursuant to the National Contingency Plan as established under section 9605 of this title, may review and comment upon an emergency plan or other issues related to preparation, implementation, or exercise of such a plan upon request of a local emergency planning committee. Such review shall not delay implementation of the plan.

(Pub. L. No. 99–499, Title III, § 303, 100 Stat. 1731 (Oct. 17, 1986).)

HISTORICAL AND STATUTORY NOTES

Effective and Applicability Provisions

1986 Acts. Section effective Oct. 17, 1986, see section 4 of Pub. L. 99–499, set out as a note under section 9601 of this title.

§ 11004. Emergency notification

[EPCRTKA § 304]

(a) Types of releases

(1) 11002(a) substance which requires CERCLA notice

If a release of an extremely hazardous substance referred to in section 11002(a) of this title occurs from a facility at which a hazardous chemical is produced, used, or stored, and such release requires a notification under section 103(a) of the Comprehensive Environmental Response, Compensation, and Liability Act of 1980 [42 U.S.C.A. § 9603(a)] (hereafter in this section referred to as "CERCLA") (42 U.S.C. 9601 et seq.), the owner or operator of the facility shall immediately provide notice as described in subsection (b) of this section.

(2) Other 11002(a) substance

If a release of an extremely hazardous substance referred to in section 11002(a) of this title occurs from a facility at which a hazardous chemical is produced, used, or stored, and such release is not subject to the notification requirements under section 103(a) of CERCLA [42 U.S.C.A. § 9603(a)], the owner or operator of the facility shall immediately provide notice as described in subsection (b) of this section, but only if the release—

(A) is not a federally permitted release as defined in section 101(10) of CERCLA [42 U.S.C.A. § 9601(10)],

(B) is in an amount in excess of a quantity which the Administrator has determined (by regulation) requires notice, and

(C) occurs in a manner which would require notification under section 103(a) of CERCLA [42 U.S.C.A. § 9603(a)].

Unless and until superseded by regulations establishing a quantity for an extremely hazardous substance described in this paragraph, a quantity of 1 pound shall be deemed that quantity the release of which requires notice as described in subsection (b) of this section.

(3) Non-11002(a) substance which requires CERCLA notice

If a release of a substance which is not on the list referred to in section 11002(a) of this title occurs at a facility at which a hazardous chemical is produced, used, or stored, and such release requires notification under section 103(a) of CERCLA [42 U.S.C.A. § 9603(a)], the owner or operator shall provide notice as follows:

(A) If the substance is one for which a reportable quantity has been established under section 102(a) of CERCLA [42 U.S.C.A. § 9602(a)], the owner or operator shall provide notice as described in subsection (b) of this section.

(B) If the substance is one for which a reportable quantity has not been established under section 102(a) of CERCLA [42 U.S.C.A. § 9602(a)]—

(i) Until April 30, 1988, the owner or operator shall provide, for releases of one pound or more of the substance, the same notice to the community emergency coordinator for the local emergency planning committee, at the same time and in the same form, as notice is provided to the National Response Center under section 103(a) of CERCLA [42 U.S.C.A. § 9603(a)].

(ii) On and after April 30, 1988, the owner or operator shall provide, for releases of one pound or more of the substance, the notice as described in subsection (b) of this section.

(4) Exempted releases

This section does not apply to any release which results in exposure to persons solely within the site or sites on which a facility is located.

(b) Notification

(1) Recipients of notice

Notice required under subsection (a) of this section shall be given immediately after the release by the owner or operator of a facility (by such means as telephone, radio, or in person) to the community emergency coordinator for the local emergency planning committees, if established pursuant to section 11001(c) of this title, for any area likely to be affected by the release and to the State emergency response commission of any State likely to be affected by the release. With respect to transportation of a substance subject to the requirements of this section, or storage incident to such transportation, the notice requirements of this section with respect to a release shall be satisfied by dialing 911 or, in the absence of a 911 emergency telephone number, calling the operator.

(2) Contents

Notice required under subsection (a) of this section shall include each of the following (to the extent known at the time of the notice and so long as no delay in responding to the emergency results):

(A) The chemical name or identity of any substance involved in the release.

(B) An indication of whether the substance is on the list referred to in section 11002(a) of this title.

(C) An estimate of the quantity of any such substance that was released into the environment.

(D) The time and duration of the release.

(E) The medium or media into which the release occurred.

(F) Any known or anticipated acute or chronic health risks associated with the emergency and, where appropriate, advice regarding medical attention necessary for exposed individuals.

(G) Proper precautions to take as a result of the release, including evacuation (unless such information is readily available to the community emergency coordinator pursuant to the emergency plan).

(H) The name and telephone number of the person or persons to be contacted for further information.

(c) Followup emergency notice

As soon as practicable after a release which requires notice under subsection (a) of this section, such owner or operator shall provide a written followup emergency notice (or notices, as more information becomes available) setting forth and updating the information required under subsection (b) of this section, and including additional information with respect to—

(1) actions taken to respond to and contain the release,

(2) any known or anticipated acute or chronic health risks associated with the release, and

(3) where appropriate, advice regarding medical attention necessary for exposed individuals.

(d) Transportation exemption not applicable

The exemption provided in section 11047 of this title (relating to transportation) does not apply to this section.

(e) Addressing source water used for drinking water.—

(1) Applicable State agency notification.—A State emergency response commission shall—

(A) promptly notify the applicable State agency of any release that requires notice under subsection (a);

(B) provide to the applicable State agency the information identified in subsection (b)(2); and

(C) provide to the applicable State agency a written followup emergency notice in accordance with subsection (c).

(2) Community Water System Notification.—

(A) In general.—An applicable State agency receiving notice of a release under paragraph (1) shall—

(i) promptly forward such notice to any community water system the source waters of which are affected by the release;

(ii) forward to the community water system the information provided under paragraph (1)(B); and

(iii) forward to the community water system the written followup emergency notice provided under paragraph (1)(C).

(B) Direct notification.—In the case of a State that does not have an applicable State agency, the State emergency response commission shall provide the notices and information described in paragraph (1) directly to any community water system the source waters of which are affected by a release that requires notice under subsection (a).

(3) Definitions.—In this subsection:

(A) Community water system.—The term "community water system" has the meaning given such term in section 1401(15) of the Safe Drinking Water Act.

(B) Applicable State agency.—The term "applicable State agency" means the State agency that has primary responsibility to enforce the requirements of the Safe Drinking Water Act in the State.

(Pub. L. No. 99–499, Title III, § 304, 100 Stat. 1733 (Oct. 17, 1986); as amended by Pub. L. No. 115–207, § 2018(a), 132 Stat. 3765, 3857–3858 (Oct. 23, 2018).)

HISTORICAL AND STATUTORY NOTES

References in Text

The Comprehensive Environmental Response, Compensation, and Liability Act of 1980, and CERCLA, referred to in subsec. (a)(1), is Pub. L. No. 96–510, 94 Stat. 2767 (Dec. 11, 1980), as amended, which is codified principally as chapter 103 (section 9601 et seq.) of this title. For complete classification of this Act to the Code, see Short Title of 1980 Acts note set out under section 9601 of this title and Tables.

Effective and Applicability Provisions

1986 Acts. Section effective Oct. 17, 1986, see section 4 of Pub. L. 99–499, set out as a note under section 9601 of this title.

§ 11005. Emergency training and review of emergency systems

[EPCRTKA § 305]

(a) Emergency training

(1) Programs

Officials of the United States Government carrying out existing Federal programs for emergency training are authorized to specifically provide training and education programs for Federal, State, and local personnel in hazard mitigation, emergency preparedness, fire prevention and control, disaster response, long-term disaster recovery, national security, technological and natural hazards, and emergency processes. Such programs shall provide special emphasis for such training and education with respect to hazardous chemicals.

(2) State and local program support

There is authorized to be appropriated to the Federal Emergency Management Agency for each of the fiscal years 1987, 1988, 1989, and 1990, $5,000,000 for making grants to support programs of State and local governments, and to support university-sponsored programs, which are designed to improve emergency planning, preparedness, mitigation, response, and recovery capabilities. Such programs shall provide special emphasis with respect to emergencies associated with hazardous chemicals. Such grants may not exceed 80 percent of the cost of any such program. The remaining 20 percent of such costs shall be funded from non-Federal sources.

(3) Other programs

Nothing in this section shall affect the availability of appropriations to the Federal Emergency Management Agency for any programs carried out by such agency other than the programs referred to in paragraph (2).

(b) Review of emergency systems

(1) Review

The Administrator shall initiate, not later than 30 days after October 17, 1986, a review of emergency systems for monitoring, detecting, and preventing releases of extremely hazardous substances at representative domestic facilities that produce, use, or store extremely hazardous substances. The Administrator may select representative extremely hazardous substances from the substances on the list referred to in section 11002(a) of this title for the purposes of this review. The Administrator shall report interim findings to the Congress not later than seven months after October 17, 1986, and issue a final report of findings and recommendations to the Congress not later than 18 months after October 17, 1986. Such report shall be prepared in consultation with the States and appropriate Federal agencies.

(2) Report

The report required by this subsection shall include the Administrator's findings regarding each of the following:

(A) The status of current technological capabilities to (i) monitor, detect, and prevent, in a timely manner, significant releases of extremely hazardous substances, (ii) determine the magnitude and direction of the hazard posed by each release, (iii) identify specific substances, (iv) provide data on the specific chemical composition of such releases, and (v) determine the relative concentrations of the constituent substances.

(B) The status of public emergency alert devices or systems for providing timely and effective public warning of an accidental release of extremely hazardous substances into the environment, including releases into the atmosphere, surface water, or groundwater from facilities that produce, store, or use significant quantities of such extremely hazardous substances.

(C) The technical and economic feasibility of establishing, maintaining, and operating perimeter alert systems for detecting releases of such extremely hazardous substances into the atmosphere, surface water, or groundwater, at facilities that manufacture, use, or store significant quantities of such substances.

(3) Recommendations

The report required by this subsection shall also include the Administrator's recommendations for—

(A) initiatives to support the development of new or improved technologies or systems that would facilitate the timely monitoring, detection, and prevention of releases of extremely hazardous substances, and

(B) improving devices or systems for effectively alerting the public in a timely manner, in the event of an accidental release of such extremely hazardous substances.

(Pub. L. No. 99–499, Title III, § 305, 100 Stat. 1735 (Oct. 17, 1986).)

HISTORICAL AND STATUTORY NOTES

Effective and Applicability Provisions

1986 Acts. Section effective Oct. 17, 1986, see section 4 of Pub. L. No. 99–499, set out as a note under section 9601 of this title.

Transfer of Functions

For transfer of functions of the Federal Emergency Management Agency, including existing responsibilities for emergency alert systems and continuity of operations and continuity of government plans and programs as constituted on June 1, 2006, including all of its personnel, assets, components, authorities, grant programs, and liabilities, and including the functions of the Under Secretary for Federal Emergency Management relating thereto, see 6 U.S.C.A. § 315.

For transfer of functions, personnel, assets, and liabilities of the Federal Emergency Management Agency, including the functions of the Director of the Federal Emergency Management Agency relating thereto, to the Secretary of Homeland Security, and for treatment of related references, see 6 U.S.C.A. §§ 313(1), 551(d), 552(d), and 557, and the Department of Homeland Security Reorganization Plan of November 25, 2002, as modified, set out as a note under 6 U.S.C.A. § 542.

SUBCHAPTER II—REPORTING REQUIREMENTS

§ 11021. Material safety data sheets

[EPCRTKA § 311]

(a) Basic requirement

(1) Submission of MSDS or list

The owner or operator of any facility which is required to prepare or have available a material safety data sheet for a hazardous chemical under the Occupational Safety and Health Act of 1970 [29 U.S.C.A. § 651 et seq.] and regulations promulgated under that Act shall submit a material safety data sheet for each such chemical, or a list of such chemicals as described in paragraph (2), to each of the following:

(A) The appropriate local emergency planning committee.

(B) The State emergency response commission.

(C) The fire department with jurisdiction over the facility.

(2) Contents of list

(A) The list of chemicals referred to in paragraph (1) shall include each of the following:

(i) A list of the hazardous chemicals for which a material safety data sheet is required under the Occupational Safety and Health Act of 1970 [29 U.S.C.A. § 651 et seq.] and regulations promulgated under that Act, grouped in categories of health and physical hazards as set forth under such Act and regulations promulgated under such Act, or in such other categories as the Administrator may prescribe under subparagraph (B).

(ii) The chemical name or the common name of each such chemical as provided on the material safety data sheet.

(iii) Any hazardous component of each such chemical as provided on the material safety data sheet.

(B) For purposes of the list under this paragraph, the Administrator may modify the categories of health and physical hazards as set forth under the Occupational Safety and Health Act of 1970 [29 U.S.C.A. § 651 et seq.] and regulations promulgated under that Act by requiring information to be reported in terms of groups of hazardous chemicals which present similar hazards in an emergency.

(3) Treatment of mixtures

An owner or operator may meet the requirements of this section with respect to a hazardous chemical which is a mixture by doing one of the following:

(A) Submitting a material safety data sheet for, or identifying on a list, each element or compound in the mixture which is a hazardous chemical. If more than one mixture has the same element or compound, only one material safety data sheet, or one listing, of the element or compound is necessary.

(B) Submitting a material safety data sheet for, or identifying on a list, the mixture itself.

(b) Thresholds

The Administrator may establish threshold quantities for hazardous chemicals below which no facility shall be subject to the provisions of this section. The threshold quantities may, in the Administrator's discretion, be based on classes of chemicals or categories of facilities.

(c) Availability of MSDS on request

(1) To local emergency planning committee

If an owner or operator of a facility submits a list of chemicals under subsection (a)(1) of this section, the owner or operator, upon request by the local emergency planning committee, shall submit the material safety data sheet for any chemical on the list to such committee.

(2) To public

A local emergency planning committee, upon request by any person, shall make available a material safety data sheet to the person in accordance with section 11044 of this title. If the local emergency planning committee does not have the requested material safety data sheet, the committee shall request the sheet from the facility owner or operator and then make the sheet available to the person in accordance with section 11044 of this title.

(d) Initial submission and updating

(1) The initial material safety data sheet or list required under this section with respect to a hazardous chemical shall be provided before the later of—

(A) 12 months after October 17, 1986, or

(B) 3 months after the owner or operator of a facility is required to prepare or have available a material safety data sheet for the chemical under the Occupational Safety and Health Act of 1970 [29 U.S.C.A. § 651 et seq.] and regulations promulgated under that Act.

(2) Within 3 months following discovery by an owner or operator of significant new information concerning an aspect of a hazardous chemical for which a material safety data sheet was previously submitted to the local emergency planning committee under subsection (a) of this section, a revised sheet shall be provided to such person.

(e) "Hazardous chemical" defined

For purposes of this section, the term "hazardous chemical" has the meaning given such term by section 1910.1200(c) of title 29 of the Code of Federal Regulations, except that such term does not include the following:

(1) Any food, food additive, color additive, drug, or cosmetic regulated by the Food and Drug Administration.

(2) Any substance present as a solid in any manufactured item to the extent exposure to the substance does not occur under normal conditions of use.

(3) Any substance to the extent it is used for personal, family, or household purposes, or is present in the same form and concentration as a product packaged for distribution and use by the general public.

(4) Any substance to the extent it is used in a research laboratory or a hospital or other medical facility under the direct supervision of a technically qualified individual.

(5) Any substance to the extent it is used in routine agricultural operations or is a fertilizer held for sale by a retailer to the ultimate customer.

(Pub. L. No. 99–499, Title III, § 311, 100 Stat. 1736 (Oct. 17, 1986).)

HISTORICAL AND STATUTORY NOTES

References in Text

The Occupational Safety and Health Act of 1970, referred to in subsecs. (a)(1), (2)(A)(i), (B), (d)(1)(B), is Pub. L. No. 91–596, 84 Stat. 1590 (Dec. 29, 1970), as amended, which is codified principally as chapter 15 (section 651 et seq.) of Title 29, Labor. For complete classification of this Act to the Code, see Short Title note set out under section 651 of Title 29 and Tables.

Effective and Applicability Provisions

1986 Acts. Section effective Oct. 17, 1986, see section 4 of Pub. L. No. 99–499, set out as a note under section 9601 of this title.

§ 11022. Emergency and hazardous chemical inventory forms

[EPCRTKA § 312]

(a) Basic requirement

(1) The owner or operator of any facility which is required to prepare or have available a material safety data sheet for a hazardous chemical under the Occupational Safety and Health Act of 1970 [29 U.S.C.A. § 651 et seq.] and regulations promulgated under that Act shall prepare and submit an emergency and hazardous chemical inventory form (hereafter in this chapter referred to as an "inventory form") to each of the following:

(A) The appropriate local emergency planning committee.

(B) The State emergency response commission.

(C) The fire department with jurisdiction over the facility.

(2) The inventory form containing tier I information (as described in subsection (d)(1) of this section) shall be submitted on or before March 1, 1988, and annually thereafter on March 1, and shall contain data with respect to the preceding calendar year. The preceding sentence does not apply if an owner or operator provides, by the same deadline and with respect to the same calendar year, tier II information (as described in subsection (d)(2) of this section) to the recipients described in paragraph (1).

(3) An owner or operator may meet the requirements of this section with respect to a hazardous chemical which is a mixture by doing one of the following:

(A) Providing information on the inventory form on each element or compound in the mixture which is a hazardous chemical. If more than one mixture has the same element or compound, only one listing on the inventory form for the element or compound at the facility is necessary.

(B) Providing information on the inventory form on the mixture itself.

(b) Thresholds

The Administrator may establish threshold quantities for hazardous chemicals covered by this section below which no facility shall be subject to the provisions of this section. The threshold quantities may, in the Administrator's discretion, be based on classes of chemicals or categories of facilities.

(c) Hazardous chemicals covered

A hazardous chemical subject to the requirements of this section is any hazardous chemical for which a material safety data sheet or a listing is required under section 11021 of this title.

(d) Contents of form

(1) Tier I information

(A) Aggregate information by category

An inventory form shall provide the information described in subparagraph (B) in aggregate terms for hazardous chemicals in categories of health and physical hazards as set forth under the Occupational Safety and Health Act of 1970 [29 U.S.C.A. § 651 et seq.] and regulations promulgated under that Act.

(B) Required information

The information referred to in subparagraph (A) is the following:

(i) An estimate (in ranges) of the maximum amount of hazardous chemicals in each category present at the facility at any time during the preceding calendar year.

(ii) An estimate (in ranges) of the average daily amount of hazardous chemicals in each category present at the facility during the preceding calendar year.

(iii) The general location of hazardous chemicals in each category.

(C) Modifications

For purposes of reporting information under this paragraph, the Administrator may—

(i) modify the categories of health and physical hazards as set forth under the Occupational Safety and Health Act of 1970 [29 U.S.C.A. § 651 et seq.] and regulations promulgated under that Act by requiring information to be reported in terms of groups of hazardous chemicals which present similar hazards in an emergency, or

(ii) require reporting on individual hazardous chemicals of special concern to emergency response personnel.

(2) Tier II information

An inventory form shall provide the following additional information for each hazardous chemical present at the facility, but only upon request and in accordance with subsection (e) of this section:

(A) The chemical name or the common name of the chemical as provided on the material safety data sheet.

(B) An estimate (in ranges) of the maximum amount of the hazardous chemical present at the facility at any time during the preceding calendar year.

(C) An estimate (in ranges) of the average daily amount of the hazardous chemical present at the facility during the preceding calendar year.

(D) A brief description of the manner of storage of the hazardous chemical.

(E) The location at the facility of the hazardous chemical.

(F) An indication of whether the owner elects to withhold location information of a specific hazardous chemical from disclosure to the public under section 11044 of this title.

(e) Availability of tier II information

(1) Availability to State commissions, local committees, and fire departments

Upon request by a State emergency response commission, a local emergency planning committee, or a fire department with jurisdiction over the facility, the owner or operator of a facility shall provide tier II information, as described in subsection (d) of this section, to the person making the request. Any such request shall be with respect to a specific facility.

(2) Availability to other State and local officials

A State or local official acting in his or her official capacity may have access to tier II information by submitting a request to the State emergency response commission or the local emergency planning committee. Upon receipt of a request for tier II information, the State commission or local committee shall, pursuant to paragraph (1), request the facility owner or operator for the tier II information and make available such information to the official.

(3) Availability to public

(A) In general

Any person may request a State emergency response commission or local emergency planning committee for tier II information relating to the preceding calendar year with respect to a facility. Any such request shall be in writing and shall be with respect to a specific facility.

(B) Automatic provision of information to public

Any tier II information which a State emergency response commission or local emergency planning committee has in its possession shall be made available to a person making a request under this paragraph in accordance with section 11044 of this title. If the State emergency response commission or local emergency planning committee does not have the tier II information in its possession, upon a request for tier II information the State emergency response commission or local emergency planning committee shall, pursuant to paragraph (1), request the facility owner or operator for tier II information with respect to a hazardous chemical which a facility has stored in an amount in excess of 10,000 pounds present at the facility at any time during the preceding calendar year and make such information available in accordance with section 11044 of this title to the person making the request.

(C) Discretionary provision of information to public

In the case of tier II information which is not in the possession of a State emergency response commission or local emergency planning committee and which is with respect to a hazardous chemical which a facility has stored in an amount less than 10,000 pounds present at the facility at any time during the preceding calendar year, a request from a person must include the general need for the information. The State emergency response commission or local emergency planning committee may, pursuant to paragraph (1), request the facility owner or operator for the tier II information on behalf of the person making the request. Upon receipt of any information requested on behalf of such person, the State emergency response commission or local emergency planning committee shall make the information available in accordance with section 11044 of this title to the person.

(D) Response in 45 days

A State emergency response commission or local emergency planning committee shall respond to a request for tier II information under this paragraph no later than 45 days after the date of receipt of the request.

(4) Availability to community water systems.—

(A) In general.—An affected community water system may have access to tier II information by submitting a request to the State emergency response commission or the local emergency planning committee. Upon receipt of a request for tier II information, the State commission or local committee shall, pursuant to paragraph (1), request the facility owner or operator for the tier II information and make available such information to the affected community water system.

(B) Definition.—In this paragraph, the term 'affected community water system' means a community water system (as defined in section 1401(15) of the Safe Drinking Water Act) that receives supplies of drinking water from a source water area, delineated under section 1453 of the Safe Drinking Water Act, in which a facility that is required to prepare and submit an inventory form under subsection (a)(1) is located.

(f) Fire department access

Upon request to an owner or operator of a facility which files an inventory form under this section by the fire department with jurisdiction over the facility, the owner or operator of the facility shall allow the fire department to conduct an on-site inspection of the facility and shall provide to the fire department specific location information on hazardous chemicals at the facility.

(g) Format of forms

The Administrator shall publish a uniform format for inventory forms within three months after October 17, 1986. If the Administrator does not publish such forms, owners and operators of facilities subject to the requirements of this section shall provide the information required under this section by letter.

(Pub. L. No. 99–499, Title III, § 312, 100 Stat. 1738 (Oct. 17, 1986); as amended by Pub. L. No. 115–270, § 2018(b), 132 Stat. 3765, 3858 (Oct. 23, 2018).)

HISTORICAL AND STATUTORY NOTES

References in Text

The Occupational Safety and Health Act of 1970, referred to in subsecs. (a)(1) and (d)(1)(A), (C)(i) is Pub. L. No. 91–596, 84 Stat. 1590 (Dec. 29, 1970), as amended, which is codified principally as chapter 15 (section 651 et seq.) of Title 29, Labor. For complete classification of this Act to the Code, see Short Title note set out under section 651 of Title 29 and Tables.

Effective and Applicability Provisions

1986 Acts. Section effective Oct. 17, 1986, see section 4 of Pub. L. No. 99–499, set out as a note under section 9601 of this title.

§ 11023. Toxic chemical release forms

[EPCRTKA § 313]

(a) Basic requirement

The owner or operator of a facility subject to the requirements of this section shall complete a toxic chemical release form as published under subsection (g) of this section for each toxic chemical listed under subsection (c) of this section that was manufactured, processed, or otherwise used in quantities exceeding the toxic chemical threshold quantity established by subsection (f) of this section during the preceding calendar year at such facility. Such form shall be submitted to the Administrator and to an official or officials of the State designated by the Governor on or before July 1, 1988, and annually thereafter on July 1 and shall contain data reflecting releases during the preceding calendar year.

(b) Covered owners and operators of facilities

(1) In general

(A) The requirements of this section shall apply to owners and operators of facilities that have 10 or more full-time employees and that are in Standard Industrial Classification Codes 20 through 39 (as in effect on July 1, 1985) and that manufactured, processed, or otherwise used a toxic chemical listed under subsection (c) of this section in excess of the quantity of that toxic chemical established under subsection (f) of this section during the calendar year for which a release form is required under this section.

(B) The Administrator may add or delete Standard Industrial Classification Codes for purposes of subparagraph (A), but only to the extent necessary to provide that each Standard Industrial Code to which this section applies is relevant to the purposes of this section.

(C) For purposes of this section—

(i) The term "manufacture" means to produce, prepare, import, or compound a toxic chemical.

(ii) The term "process" means the preparation of a toxic chemical, after its manufacture, for distribution in commerce—

(I) in the same form or physical state as, or in a different form or physical state from, that in which it was received by the person so preparing such chemical, or

(II) as part of an article containing the toxic chemical.

(2) Discretionary application to additional facilities

The Administrator, on his own motion or at the request of a Governor of a State (with regard to facilities located in that State), may apply the requirements of this section to the owners and operators of any particular facility that manufactures, processes, or otherwise uses a toxic chemical listed under subsection (c) of this section if the Administrator determines that such action is warranted on the basis of toxicity of the toxic chemical, proximity to other facilities that release the toxic chemical or to population centers, the history of releases of such chemical at such facility, or such other factors as the Administrator deems appropriate.

(c) Toxic chemicals covered

The toxic chemicals subject to the requirements of this section are—

(1) the chemicals on the list in Committee Print Number 99–169 of the Senate Committee on Environment and Public Works, titled "Toxic Chemicals Subject to Section 313 of the Emergency

Planning and Community Right-To-Know Act of 1986" [42 U.S.C.A. § 11023] (including any revised version of the list as may be made pursuant to subsection (d) or (e) of this section); and

(2) the chemicals included on such list under subsections (b)(1), (c)(1), and (d)(3) of section 7321 of the PFAS Act of 2019.

(d) Revisions by Administrator

(1) In general

The Administrator may by rule add or delete a chemical from the list described in subsection (c) of this section at any time.

(2) Additions

A chemical may be added if the Administrator determines, in his judgment, that there is sufficient evidence to establish any one of the following:

(A) The chemical is known to cause or can reasonably be anticipated to cause significant adverse acute human health effects at concentration levels that are reasonably likely to exist beyond facility site boundaries as a result of continuous, or frequently recurring, releases.

(B) The chemical is known to cause or can reasonably be anticipated to cause in humans—

(i) cancer or teratogenic effects, or

(ii) serious or irreversible—

(I) reproductive dysfunctions,

(II) neurological disorders,

(III) heritable genetic mutations, or

(IV) other chronic health effects.

(C) The chemical is known to cause or can reasonably be anticipated to cause, because of—

(i) its toxicity,

(ii) its toxicity and persistence in the environment, or

(iii) its toxicity and tendency to bioaccumulate in the environment,

a significant adverse effect on the environment of sufficient seriousness, in the judgment of the Administrator, to warrant reporting under this section. The number of chemicals included on the list described in subsection (c) of this section on the basis of the preceding sentence may constitute in the aggregate no more than 25 percent of the total number of chemicals on the list.

A determination under this paragraph shall be based on generally accepted scientific principles or laboratory tests, or appropriately designed and conducted epidemiological or other population studies, available to the Administrator.

(3) Deletions

A chemical may be deleted if the Administrator determines there is not sufficient evidence to establish any of the criteria described in paragraph (2).

(4) Effective date

Any revision made on or after January 1 and before December 1 of any calendar year shall take effect beginning with the next calendar year. Any revision made on or after December 1 of any calendar year and before January 1 of the next calendar year shall take effect beginning with the calendar year following such next calendar year.

(e) Petitions

(1) In general

Any person may petition the Administrator to add or delete a chemical from the list described in subsection (c) of this section on the basis of the criteria in subparagraph (A) or (B) of subsection (d)(2) of this section. Within 180 days after receipt of a petition, the Administrator shall take one of the following actions:

(A) Initiate a rulemaking to add or delete the chemical to the list, in accordance with subsection (d)(2) or (d)(3) of this section.

(B) Publish an explanation of why the petition is denied.

(2) Governor petitions

A State Governor may petition the Administrator to add or delete a chemical from the list described in subsection (c) of this section on the basis of the criteria in subparagraph (A), (B), or (C) of subsection (d)(2) of this section. In the case of such a petition from a State Governor to delete a chemical, the petition shall be treated in the same manner as a petition received under paragraph (1) to delete a chemical. In the case of such a petition from a State Governor to add a chemical, the chemical will be added to the list within 180 days after receipt of the petition, unless the Administrator—

(A) initiates a rulemaking to add the chemical to the list, in accordance with subsection (d)(2) of this section, or

(B) publishes an explanation of why the Administrator believes the petition does not meet the requirements of subsection (d)(2) of this section for adding a chemical to the list.

(f) Threshold for reporting

(1) Toxic chemical threshold amount

The threshold amounts for purposes of reporting toxic chemicals under this section are as follows:

(A) With respect to a toxic chemical used at a facility, 10,000 pounds of the toxic chemical per year.

(B) With respect to a toxic chemical manufactured or processed at a facility—

(i) For the toxic chemical release form required to be submitted under this section on or before July 1, 1988, 75,000 pounds of the toxic chemical per year.

(ii) For the form required to be submitted on or before July 1, 1989, 50,000 pounds of the toxic chemical per year.

(iii) For the form required to be submitted on or before July 1, 1990, and for each form thereafter, 25,000 pounds of the toxic chemical per year.

(2) Revisions

The Administrator may establish a threshold amount for a toxic chemical different from the amount established by paragraph (1). Such revised threshold shall obtain reporting on a substantial majority of total releases of the chemical at all facilities subject to the requirements of this section. The amounts established under this paragraph may, at the Administrator's discretion, be based on classes of chemicals or categories of facilities.

(g) Form

(1) Information required

Not later than June 1, 1987, the Administrator shall publish a uniform toxic chemical release form for facilities covered by this section. If the Administrator does not publish such a form, owners and operators of facilities subject to the requirements of this section shall provide the information required under this subsection by letter postmarked on or before the date on which the form is due. Such form shall—

(A) provide for the name and location of, and principal business activities at, the facility;

(B) include an appropriate certification, signed by a senior official with management responsibility for the person or persons completing the report, regarding the accuracy and completeness of the report; and

(C) provide for submission of each of the following items of information for each listed toxic chemical known to be present at the facility:

(i) Whether the toxic chemical at the facility is manufactured, processed, or otherwise used, and the general category or categories of use of the chemical.

(ii) An estimate of the maximum amounts (in ranges) of the toxic chemical present at the facility at any time during the preceding calendar year.

(iii) For each wastestream, the waste treatment or disposal methods employed, and an estimate of the treatment efficiency typically achieved by such methods for that wastestream.

(iv) The annual quantity of the toxic chemical entering each environmental medium.

(2) Use of available data

In order to provide the information required under this section, the owner or operator of a facility may use readily available data (including monitoring data) collected pursuant to other provisions of law, or, where such data are not readily available, reasonable estimates of the amounts involved. Nothing in this section requires the monitoring or measurement of the quantities, concentration, or frequency of any toxic chemical released into the environment beyond that monitoring and measurement required under other provisions of law or regulation. In order to assure consistency, the Administrator shall require that data be expressed in common units.

(h) Use of release form

The release forms required under this section are intended to provide information to the Federal, State, and local governments and the public, including citizens of communities surrounding covered facilities. The release form shall be available, consistent with section 11044(a) of this title, to inform persons about releases of toxic chemicals to the environment; to assist governmental agencies, researchers, and other persons in the conduct of research and data gathering; to aid in the development of appropriate regulations, guidelines, and standards; and for other similar purposes.

(i) Modifications in reporting frequency

(1) In general

The Administrator may modify the frequency of submitting a report under this section, but the Administrator may not modify the frequency to be any more often than annually. A modification may apply, either nationally or in a specific geographic area, to the following:

(A) All toxic chemical release forms required under this section.

(B) A class of toxic chemicals or a category of facilities.

(C) A specific toxic chemical.

(D) A specific facility.

(2) Requirements

A modification may be made under paragraph (1) only if the Administrator—

(A) makes a finding that the modification is consistent with the provisions of subsection (h) of this section, based on—

(i) experience from previously submitted toxic chemical release forms, and

(ii) determinations made under paragraph (3), and

(B) the finding is made by a rulemaking in accordance with section 553 of Title 5.

(3) Determinations

The Administrator shall make the following determinations with respect to a proposed modification before making a modification under paragraph (1):

(A) The extent to which information relating to the proposed modification provided on the toxic chemical release forms has been used by the Administrator or other agencies of the Federal Government, States, local governments, health professionals, and the public.

(B) The extent to which the information is (i) readily available to potential users from other sources, such as State reporting programs, and (ii) provided to the Administrator under another Federal law or through a State program.

(C) The extent to which the modification would impose additional and unreasonable burdens on facilities subject to the reporting requirements under this section.

(4) 5-year review

Any modification made under this subsection shall be reviewed at least once every 5 years. Such review shall examine the modification and ensure that the requirements of paragraphs (2) and (3) still justify continuation of the modification. Any change to a modification reviewed under this paragraph shall be made in accordance with this subsection.

(5) Notification to Congress

The Administrator shall notify Congress of an intention to initiate a rulemaking for a modification under this subsection. After such notification, the Administrator shall delay initiation of the rulemaking for at least 12 months, but no more than 24 months, after the date of such notification.

(6) Judicial review

In any judicial review of a rulemaking which establishes a modification under this subsection, a court may hold unlawful and set aside agency action, findings, and conclusions found to be unsupported by substantial evidence.

(7) Applicability

A modification under this subsection may apply to a calendar year or other reporting period beginning no earlier than January 1, 1993.

(8) Effective date

Any modification made on or after January 1 and before December 1 of any calendar year shall take effect beginning with the next calendar year. Any modification made on or after December 1 of any calendar year and before January 1 of the next calendar year shall take effect beginning with the calendar year following such next calendar year.

(j) EPA management of data

The Administrator shall establish and maintain in a computer data base a national toxic chemical inventory based on data submitted to the Administrator under this section. The Administrator shall make these data accessible by computer telecommunication and other means to any person on a cost reimbursable basis.

(k) Report

Not later than June 30, 1991, the Comptroller General, in consultation with the Administrator and appropriate officials in the States, shall submit to the Congress a report including each of the following:

(1) A description of the steps taken by the Administrator and the States to implement the requirements of this section, including steps taken to make information collected under this section available to and accessible by the public.

(2) A description of the extent to which the information collected under this section has been used by the Environmental Protection Agency, other Federal agencies, the States, and the public, and the purposes for which the information has been used.

(3) An identification and evaluation of options for modifications to the requirements of this section for the purpose of making information collected under this section more useful.

(*l*) Mass balance study

(1) In general

The Administrator shall arrange for a mass balance study to be carried out by the National Academy of Sciences using mass balance information collected by the Administrator under paragraph (3). The Administrator shall submit to Congress a report on such study no later than 5 years after October 17, 1986.

(2) Purposes

The purposes of the study are as follows:

(A) To assess the value of mass balance analysis in determining the accuracy of information on toxic chemical releases.

(B) To assess the value of obtaining mass balance information, or portions thereof, to determine the waste reduction efficiency of different facilities, or categories of facilities, including the effectiveness of toxic chemical regulations promulgated under laws other than this chapter.

(C) To assess the utility of such information for evaluating toxic chemical management practices at facilities, or categories of facilities, covered by this section.

(D) To determine the implications of mass balance information collection on a national scale similar to the mass balance information collection carried out by the Administrator under paragraph (3), including implications of the use of such collection as part of a national annual quantity toxic chemical release program.

(3) Information collection

(A) The Administrator shall acquire available mass balance information from States which currently conduct (or during the 5 years after October 17, 1986, initiate) a mass balance-oriented annual quantity toxic chemical release program. If information from such States provides an inadequate representation of industry classes and categories to carry out the purposes of the study, the Administrator also may acquire mass balance information necessary for the study from a representative number of facilities in other States.

(B) Any information acquired under this section shall be available to the public, except that upon a showing satisfactory to the Administrator by any person that the information (or a particular part thereof) to which the Administrator or any officer, employee, or representative has access under this section if made public would divulge information entitled to protection under section 1905 of Title 18, such information or part shall be considered confidential in accordance with the purposes of that section, except that such information or part may be disclosed to other officers, employees, or authorized representatives of the United States concerned with carrying out this section.

(C) The Administrator may promulgate regulations prescribing procedures for collecting mass balance information under this paragraph.

(D) For purposes of collecting mass balance information under subparagraph (A), the Administrator may require the submission of information by a State or facility.

(4) Mass balance definition

For purposes of this subsection, the term "mass balance" means an accumulation of the annual quantities of chemicals transported to a facility, produced at a facility, consumed at a facility, used at a facility, accumulated at a facility, released from a facility, and transported from a facility as a waste or as a commercial product or byproduct or component of a commercial product or byproduct.

(Pub. L. No. 99–499, Title III, § 313, 100 Stat. 1741 (Oct. 17, 1986), as amended by Pub. L. No. 116–92, § 7321(f), 133 Stat. 2281 (Dec. 20, 2019).)

HISTORICAL AND STATUTORY NOTES

Effective and Applicability Provisions

1986 Acts. Section effective Oct. 17, 1986, see section 4 of Pub. L. No. 99–499, set out as a note under section 9601 of this title.

References in Text

PFAS Act of 2019. The PFAS Act of 2019 referenced in § 11023(c) is Title LXXIII, §§ 7301–7361, of Pub. L. No. 116–92, 133 Stat. 2275–2290 (Dec. 20, 2019), codified at 15 U.S.C. §§ 2607(a)(7), 8901, 8911, 8921, 8931–8935, 8951, 8952, 8961, 8962.

Termination of Reporting Requirements

For termination of reporting provisions of this section pertaining to notice of intention to initiate rulemaking for modification in reporting frequency of chemical release forms, effective May 15, 2000, see Pub. L. No. 104–66, § 3003, as amended, set out as a note under 31 U.S.C.A. § 1113, and the 1st item on page 169 of House Document No. 103–7.

SUBCHAPTER III—GENERAL PROVISIONS

§ 11041. Relationship to other law

[EPCRTKA § 321]

(a) In general

Nothing in this chapter shall—

(1) preempt any State or local law,

(2) except as provided in subsection (b) of this section, otherwise affect any State or local law or the authority of any State or local government to adopt or enforce any State or local law, or

(3) affect or modify in any way the obligations or liabilities of any person under other Federal law.

(b) Effect on MSDS requirements

Any State or local law enacted after August 1, 1985, which requires the submission of a material safety data sheet from facility owners or operators shall require that the data sheet be identical in content and format to the data sheet required under subsection (a) of section 11021 of this title. In addition, a State or locality may require the submission of information which is supplemental to the information required on the data sheet (including information on the location and quantity of hazardous chemicals present at the facility), through additional sheets attached to the data sheet or such other means as the State or locality considers appropriate.

(Pub. L. No. 99–499, Title III, § 321, 100 Stat. 1747 (Oct. 17, 1986).)

HISTORICAL AND STATUTORY NOTES

Effective and Applicability Provisions

1986 Acts. Section effective Oct. 17, 1986, see section 4 of Pub. L. No. 99–499, set out as a note under section 9601 of this title.

§ 11042. Trade secrets

[EPCRTKA § 322]

(a) Authority to withhold information

(1) General authority

(A) With regard to a hazardous chemical, an extremely hazardous substance, or a toxic chemical, any person required under section 11003(d)(2), 11003(d)(3), 11021, 11022, or 11023 of this title to submit information to any other person may withhold from such submittal the specific chemical identity (including the chemical name and other specific identification), as defined in regulations prescribed by the Administrator under subsection (c) of this section, if the person complies with paragraph (2).

(B) Any person withholding the specific chemical identity shall, in the place on the submittal where the chemical identity would normally be included, include the generic class or category of the hazardous chemical, extremely hazardous substance, or toxic chemical (as the case may be).

(2) Requirements

(A) A person is entitled to withhold information under paragraph (1) if such person—

(i) claims that such information is a trade secret, on the basis of the factors enumerated in subsection (b) of this section,

(ii) includes in the submittal referred to in paragraph (1) an explanation of the reasons why such information is claimed to be a trade secret, based on the factors enumerated in subsection (b) of this section, including a specific description of why such factors apply, and

(iii) submits to the Administrator a copy of such submittal, and the information withheld from such submittal.

(B) In submitting to the Administrator the information required by subparagraph (A)(iii), a person withholding information under this subsection may—

(i) designate, in writing and in such manner as the Administrator may prescribe by regulation, the information which such person believes is entitled to be withheld under paragraph (1), and

(ii) submit such designated information separately from other information submitted under this subsection.

(3) Limitation

The authority under this subsection to withhold information shall not apply to information which the Administrator has determined, in accordance with subsection (c) of this section, is not a trade secret.

(b) Trade secret factors

No person required to provide information under this chapter may claim that the information is entitled to protection as a trade secret under subsection (a) of this section unless such person shows each of the following:

(1) Such person has not disclosed the information to any other person, other than a member of a local emergency planning committee, an officer or employee of the United States or a State or local government, an employee of such person, or a person who is bound by a confidentiality agreement, and such person has taken reasonable measures to protect the confidentiality of such information and intends to continue to take such measures.

(2) The information is not required to be disclosed, or otherwise made available, to the public under any other Federal or State law.

(3) Disclosure of the information is likely to cause substantial harm to the competitive position of such person.

(4) The chemical identity is not readily discoverable through reverse engineering.

(c) Trade secret regulations

As soon as practicable after October 17, 1986, the Administrator shall prescribe regulations to implement this section. With respect to subsection (b)(4) of this section, such regulations shall be equivalent to comparable provisions in the Occupational Safety and Health Administration Hazard Communication Standard (29 C.F.R. 1910.1200) and any revisions of such standard prescribed by the Secretary of Labor in accordance with the final ruling of the courts of the United States in United Steelworkers of America, AFL-CIO-CLC v. Thorne G. Auchter.

(d) Petition for review

(1) In general

Any person may petition the Administrator for the disclosure of the specific chemical identity of a hazardous chemical, an extremely hazardous substance, or a toxic chemical which is claimed as a trade secret under this section. The Administrator may, in the absence of a petition under this paragraph, initiate a determination, to be carried out in accordance with this subsection, as to whether information withheld constitutes a trade secret.

(2) Initial review

Within 30 days after the date of receipt of a petition under paragraph (1) (or upon the Administrator's initiative), the Administrator shall review the explanation filed by a trade secret claimant under subsection (a)(2) of this section and determine whether the explanation presents assertions which, if true, are sufficient to support a finding that the specific chemical identity is a trade secret.

(3) Finding of sufficient assertions

(A) If the Administrator determines pursuant to paragraph (2) that the explanation presents sufficient assertions to support a finding that the specific chemical identity is a trade secret, the Administrator shall notify the trade secret claimant that he has 30 days to supplement the explanation with detailed information to support the assertions.

(B) If the Administrator determines, after receipt of any supplemental supporting detailed information under subparagraph (A), that the assertions in the explanation are true and that the specific chemical identity is a trade secret, the Administrator shall so notify the petitioner and the petitioner may seek judicial review of the determination.

(C) If the Administrator determines, after receipt of any supplemental supporting detailed information under subparagraph (A), that the assertions in the explanation are not true and that the specific chemical identity is not a trade secret, the Administrator shall notify the trade secret claimant that the Administrator intends to release the specific chemical identity. The trade secret claimant has 30 days in which he may appeal the Administrator's determination under this subparagraph to the Administrator. If the Administrator does not reverse his determination under this subparagraph in such an appeal by the trade secret claimant, the trade secret claimaint[1] may seek judicial review of the determination.

(4) Finding of insufficient assertions

(A) If the Administrator determines pursuant to paragraph (2) that the explanation presents insufficient assertions to support a finding that the specific chemical identity is a trade secret, the Administrator shall notify the trade secret claimant that he has 30 days to appeal the determination to the Administrator, or, upon a showing of good cause, amend the original explanation by providing supplementary assertions to support the trade secret claim.

(B) If the Administrator does not reverse his determination under subparagraph (A) after an appeal or an examination of any supplementary assertions under subparagraph (A), the Administrator shall so notify the trade secret claimant and the trade secret claimant may seek judicial review of the determination.

(C) If the Administrator reverses his determination under subparagraph (A) after an appeal or an examination of any supplementary assertions under subparagraph (A), the procedures under paragraph (3) of this subsection apply.

(e) Exception for information provided to health professionals

Nothing in this section, or regulations adopted pursuant to this section, shall authorize any person to withhold information which is required to be provided to a health professional, a doctor, or a nurse in accordance with section 11043 of this title.

(f) Providing information to Administrator; availability to public

Any information submitted to the Administrator under subsection (a)(2) of this section or subsection (d)(3) of this section (except a specific chemical identity) shall be available to the public, except that upon a showing satisfactory to the Administrator by any person that the information (or a particular part thereof) to which the Administrator has access under this section if made public would divulge information entitled to protection under section 1905 of Title 18, such information or part shall be considered confidential in accordance with the purposes of that section, except that such information or part may be disclosed to other officers, employees, or authorized representatives of the United States concerned with carrying out this chapter.

(g) Information provided to State

Upon request by a State, acting through the Governor of the State, the Administrator shall provide to the State any information obtained under subsection (a)(2) of this section and subsection (d)(3) of this section.

(h) Information on adverse effects

(1) In any case in which the identity of a hazardous chemical or an extremely hazardous substance is claimed as a trade secret, the Governor or State emergency response commission established under section 11001 of this title shall identify the adverse health effects associated with the hazardous chemical or extremely hazardous substance and shall assure that such information is provided to any person requesting information about such hazardous chemical or extremely hazardous substance.

(2) In any case in which the identity of a toxic chemical is claimed as a trade secret, the Administrator shall identify the adverse health and environmental effects associated with the toxic chemical and shall assure that such information is included in the computer database required by section 11023(j) of this title and is provided to any person requesting information about such toxic chemical.

(i) Information provided to Congress

Notwithstanding any limitation[2] contained in this section or any other provision of law, all information reported to or otherwise obtained by the Administrator (or any representative of the Administrator) under this chapter shall be made available to a duly authorized committee of the Congress upon written request by such a committee.

(Pub. L. No. 99–499, Title III, § 322, 100 Stat. 1747 (Oct. 17, 1986).)

[1] So in original. Probably should be "claimant."

[2] So in original. Probably should be "limitation."

HISTORICAL AND STATUTORY NOTES

Effective and Applicability Provisions

1986 Acts. Section effective Oct. 17, 1986, see section 4 of Pub. L. No. 99–499, set out as a note under section 9601 of this title.

§ 11043. Provision of information to health professionals, doctors, and nurses [EPCRTKA § 323]

(a) Diagnosis or treatment by health professional

An owner or operator of a facility which is subject to the requirements of section 11021, 11022, or 11023 of this title shall provide the specific chemical identity, if known, of a hazardous chemical, extremely hazardous substance, or a toxic chemical to any health professional who requests such information in writing if the health professional provides a written statement of need under this subsection and a written confidentiality agreement under subsection (d) of this section. The written statement of need shall be a statement that the health professional has a reasonable basis to suspect that—

(1) the information is needed for purposes of diagnosis or treatment of an individual,

(2) the individual or individuals being diagnosed or treated have been exposed to the chemical concerned, and

(3) knowledge of the specific chemical identity of such chemical will assist in diagnosis or treatment.

Following such a written request, the owner or operator to whom such request is made shall promptly provide the requested information to the health professional. The authority to withhold the specific chemical identity of a chemical under section 11042 of this title when such information is a trade secret shall not apply to information required to be provided under this subsection, subject to the provisions of subsection (d) of this section.

(b) Medical emergency

An owner or operator of a facility which is subject to the requirements of section 11021, 11022, or 11023 of this title shall provide a copy of a material safety data sheet, an inventory form, or a toxic chemical release form, including the specific chemical identity, if known, of a hazardous chemical, extremely hazardous substance, or a toxic chemical, to any treating physician or nurse who requests such information if such physician or nurse determines that—

(1) a medical emergency exists,

(2) the specific chemical identity of the chemical concerned is necessary for or will assist in emergency or first-aid diagnosis or treatment, and

(3) the individual or individuals being diagnosed or treated have been exposed to the chemical concerned.

Immediately following such a request, the owner or operator to whom such request is made shall provide the requested information to the physician or nurse. The authority to withhold the specific chemical identity of a chemical from a material safety data sheet, an inventory form, or a toxic chemical release form under section 11042 of this title when such information is a trade secret shall not apply to information required to be provided to a treating physician or nurse under this subsection. No written confidentiality agreement or statement of need shall be required as a precondition of such disclosure, but the owner or operator disclosing such information may require a written confidentiality agreement in accordance with subsection (d) of this section and a statement setting forth the items listed in paragraphs (1) through (3) as soon as circumstances permit.

(c) Preventive measures by local health professionals

(1) Provision of information

An owner or operator of a facility subject to the requirements of section 11021, 11022, or 11023 of this title shall provide the specific chemical identity, if known, of a hazardous chemical, an extremely hazardous substance, or a toxic chemical to any health professional (such as a physician, toxicologist, or epidemiologist)—

(A) who is a local government employee or a person under contract with the local government, and

(B) who requests such information in writing and provides a written statement of need under paragraph (2) and a written confidentiality agreement under subsection (d) of this section.

Following such a written request, the owner or operator to whom such request is made shall promptly provide the requested information to the local health professional. The authority to withhold the specific chemical identity of a chemical under section 11042 of this title when such information is a trade secret shall not apply to information required to be provided under this subsection, subject to the provisions of subsection (d) of this section.

(2) Written statement of need

The written statement of need shall be a statement that describes with reasonable detail one or more of the following health needs for the information:

(A) To assess exposure of persons living in a local community to the hazards of the chemical concerned.

(B) To conduct or assess sampling to determine exposure levels of various population groups.

(C) To conduct periodic medical surveillance of exposed population groups.

(D) To provide medical treatment to exposed individuals or population groups.

(E) To conduct studies to determine the health effects of exposure.

(F) To conduct studies to aid in the identification of a chemical that may reasonably be anticipated to cause an observed health effect.

(d) Confidentiality agreement

Any person obtaining information under subsection (a) or (c) of this section shall, in accordance with such subsection (a) or (c) of this section, be required to agree in a written confidentiality agreement that he will not use the information for any purpose other than the health needs asserted in the statement of need, except as may otherwise be authorized by the terms of the agreement or by the person providing such information. Nothing in this subsection shall preclude the parties to a confidentiality agreement from pursuing any remedies to the extent permitted by law.

(e) Regulations

As soon as practicable after October 17, 1986, the Administrator shall promulgate regulations describing criteria and parameters for the statement of need under subsection[1] (a) and (c) of this section and the confidentiality agreement under subsection (d) of this section.

(Pub. L. No. 99–499, Title III, § 323, 100 Stat. 1750 (Oct. 17, 1986).)

[1] So in original. Probably should be "subsections."

HISTORICAL AND STATUTORY NOTES

Effective and Applicability Provisions

1986 Acts. Section effective Oct. 17, 1986, see section 4 of Pub. L. No. 99–499, set out as a note under section 9601 of this title.

§ 11044. Public availability of plans, data sheets, forms, and followup notices

[EPCRTKA § 324]

(a) Availability to public

Each emergency response plan, material safety data sheet, list described in section 11021(a)(2) of this title, inventory form, toxic chemical release form, and followup emergency notice shall be made available to the general public, consistent with section 11042 of this title, during normal working hours at the location or locations designated by the Administrator, Governor, State emergency response commission, or local emergency planning committee, as appropriate. Upon request by an owner or operator of a facility subject to the requirements of section 11022 of this title, the State emergency response commission and the appropriate local emergency planning committee shall withhold from disclosure under this section the location of any specific chemical required by section 11022(d)(2) of this title to be contained in an inventory form as tier II information.

(b) Notice of public availability

Each local emergency planning committee shall annually publish a notice in local newspapers that the emergency response plan, material safety data sheets, and inventory forms have been submitted under this section. The notice shall state that followup emergency notices may subsequently be issued. Such notice shall announce that members of the public who wish to review any such plan, sheet, form, or followup notice may do so at the location designated under subsection (a) of this section.

(Pub. L. No. 99–499, Title III, § 324, 100 Stat. 1752 (Oct. 17, 1986).)

HISTORICAL AND STATUTORY NOTES

Effective and Applicability Provisions

1986 Acts. Section effective Oct. 17, 1986, see section 4 of Pub. L. No. 99–499, set out as a note under section 9601 of this title.

§ 11045. Enforcement

[EPCRTKA § 325]

(a) Civil penalties for emergency planning

The Administrator may order a facility owner or operator (except an owner or operator of a facility designated under section 11002(b)(2) of this title) to comply with section 11002(c) of this title and section 11003(d) of this title. The United States district court for the district in which the facility is located shall have jurisdiction to enforce the order, and any person who violates or fails to obey such an order shall be liable to the United States for a civil penalty of not more than $25,000 for each day in which such violation occurs or such failure to comply continues.

(b) Civil, administrative, and criminal penalties for emergency notification

(1) Class I administrative penalty

(A) A civil penalty of not more than $25,000 per violation may be assessed by the Administrator in the case of a violation of the requirements of section 11004 of this title.

(B) No civil penalty may be assessed under this subsection unless the person accused of the violation is given notice and opportunity for a hearing with respect to the violation.

(C) In determining the amount of any penalty assessed pursuant to this subsection, the Administrator shall take into account the nature, circumstances, extent and gravity of the violation or violations and, with respect to the violator, ability to pay, any prior history of such violations, the degree of culpability, economic benefit or savings (if any) resulting from the violation, and such other matters as justice may require.

(2) Class II administrative penalty

A civil penalty of not more than $25,000 per day for each day during which the violation continues may be assessed by the Administrator in the case of a violation of the requirements of section 11004 of this title. In the case of a second or subsequent violation the amount of such penalty may be not more than $75,000 for each day during which the violation continues. Any civil penalty under this subsection shall be assessed and collected in the same manner, and subject to the same provisions, as in the case of civil penalties assessed and collected under section 2615 of Title 15. In any proceeding for the assessment of a civil penalty under this subsection the Administrator may issue subpoenas for the attendance and testimony of witnesses and the production of relevant papers, books, and documents and may promulgate rules for discovery procedures.

(3) Judicial assessment

The Administrator may bring an action in the United States District[1] court for the appropriate district to assess and collect a penalty of not more than $25,000 per day for each day during which the violation continues in the case of a violation of the requirements of section 11004 of this title. In the case of a second or subsequent violation, the amount of such penalty may be not more than $75,000 for each day during which the violation continues.

(4) Criminal penalties

Any person who knowingly and willfully fails to provide notice in accordance with section 11004 of this title shall, upon conviction, be fined not more than $25,000 or imprisoned for not more than two years, or both (or in the case of a second or subsequent conviction, shall be fined not more than $50,000 or imprisoned for not more than five years, or both).

(c) Civil and administrative penalties for reporting requirements

(1) Any person (other than a governmental entity) who violates any requirement of section 11022 or 11023 of this title shall be liable to the United States for a civil penalty in an amount not to exceed $25,000 for each such violation.

(2) Any person (other than a governmental entity) who violates any requirement of section 11021 or 11043(b) of this title, and any person who fails to furnish to the Administrator information required under section 11042(a)(2) of this title shall be liable to the United States for a civil penalty in an amount not to exceed $10,000 for each such violation.

(3) Each day a violation described in paragraph (1) or (2) continues shall, for purposes of this subsection, constitute a separate violation.

(4) The Administrator may assess any civil penalty for which a person is liable under this subsection by administrative order or may bring an action to assess and collect the penalty in the United States district court for the district in which the person from whom the penalty is sought resides or in which such person's principal place of business is located.

(d) Civil, administrative, and criminal penalties with respect to trade secrets

(1) Civil and administrative penalty for frivolous claims

If the Administrator determines—

(A) (i) under section 11042(d)(4) of this title that an explanation submitted by a trade secret claimant presents insufficient assertions to support a finding that a specific chemical identity is a trade secret, or

(ii) after receiving supplemental supporting detailed information under section 11042(d)(3)(A) of this title, that the specific chemical identity is not a trade secret; and

(B) that the trade secret claim is frivolous,

the trade secret claimant is liable for a penalty of $25,000 per claim. The Administrator may assess the penalty by administrative order or may bring an action in the appropriate district court of the United States to assess and collect the penalty.

(2) Criminal penalty for disclosure of trade secret information

Any person who knowingly and willfully divulges or discloses any information entitled to protection under section 11042 of this title shall, upon conviction, be subject to a fine of not more than $20,000 or to imprisonment not to exceed one year, or both.

(e) Special enforcement provisions for section 11043

Whenever any facility owner or operator required to provide information under section 11043 of this title to a health professional who has requested such information fails or refuses to provide such information in accordance with such section, such health professional may bring an action in the appropriate United States district court to require such facility owner or operator to provide the information. Such court shall have jurisdiction to issue such orders and take such other action as may be necessary to enforce the requirements of section 11043 of this title.

(f) Procedures for administrative penalties

(1) Any person against whom a civil penalty is assessed under this section may obtain review thereof in the appropriate district court of the United States by filing a notice of appeal in such court within 30 days after the date of such order and by simultaneously sending a copy of such notice by certified mail to the Administrator. The Administrator shall promptly file in such court a certified copy of the record upon which such violation was found or such penalty imposed. If any person fails to pay an assessment of a civil penalty after it has become a final and unappealable order or after the appropriate court has entered final judgment in favor of the United States, the Administrator may request the Attorney General of the United States to institute a civil action in an appropriate district court of the United States to collect the penalty, and such court shall have jurisdiction to hear and decide any such action. In hearing such action, the court shall have authority to review the violation and the assessment of the civil penalty on the record.

(2) The Administrator may issue subpoenas for the attendance and testimony of witnesses and the production of relevant papers, books, or documents in connection with hearings under this section. In case of contumacy or refusal to obey a subpoena issued pursuant to this paragraph and served upon any person, the district court of the United States for any district in which such person is found, resides, or transacts business, upon application by the United States and after notice to such person, shall have jurisdiction to issue an order requiring such person to appear and give testimony before the administrative law judge or to appear and produce documents before the administrative law judge, or both, and any failure to obey such order of the court may be punished by such court as a contempt thereof.

(Pub. L. No. 99–499, Title III, § 325, 100 Stat. 1753 (Oct. 17, 1986).)

[1] So in original. Probably should be "district."

HISTORICAL AND STATUTORY NOTES

Effective and Applicability Provisions

1986 Acts. Section effective Oct. 17, 1986, see section 4 of Pub. L. No. 99–499, set out as a note under section 9601 of this title.

§ 11046. Civil actions

[EPCRTKA § 326]

(a) Authority to bring civil actions

(1) Citizen suits

Except as provided in subsection (e) of this section, any person may commence a civil action on his own behalf against the following:

(A) An owner or operator of a facility for failure to do any of the following:

(i) Submit a followup emergency notice under section 11004(c) of this title.

(ii) Submit a material safety data sheet or a list under section 11021(a) of this title.

(iii) Complete and submit an inventory form under section 11022(a) of this title containing tier I information as described in section 11022(d)(1) of this title unless such requirement does not apply by reason of the second sentence of section 11022(a)(2) of this title.

(iv) Complete and submit a toxic chemical release form under section 11023(a) of this title.

(B) The Administrator for failure to do any of the following:

(i) Publish inventory forms under section 11022(g) of this title.

(ii) Respond to a petition to add or delete a chemical under section 11023(e)(1) of this title within 180 days after receipt of the petition.

(iii) Publish a toxic chemical release form under 11023(g)[1] of this title.

(iv) Establish a computer database in accordance with section 11023(j) of this title.

(v) Promulgate trade secret regulations under section 11042(c) of this title.

(vi) Render a decision in response to a petition under section 11042(d) of this title within 9 months after receipt of the petition.

(C) The Administrator, a State Governor, or a State emergency response commission, for failure to provide a mechanism for public availability of information in accordance with section 11044(a) of this title.

(D) A State Governor or a State emergency response commission for failure to respond to a request for tier II information under section 11022(e)(3) of this title within 120 days after the date of receipt of the request.

(2) State or local suits

(A) Any State or local government may commence a civil action against an owner or operator of a facility for failure to do any of the following:

(i) Provide notification to the emergency response commission in the State under section 11002(c) of this title.

(ii) Submit a material safety data sheet or a list under section 11021(a) of this title.

(iii) Make available information requested under section 11021(c) of this title.

(iv) Complete and submit an inventory form under section 11022(a) of this title containing tier I information unless such requirement does not apply by reason of the second sentence of section 11022(a)(2) of this title.

(B) Any State emergency response commission or local emergency planning committee may commence a civil action against an owner or operator of a facility for failure to provide information under section 11003(d) of this title or for failure to submit tier II information under section 11022(e)(1) of this title.

(C) Any State may commence a civil action against the Administrator for failure to provide information to the State under section 11042(g) of this title.

(b) Venue

(1) Any action under subsection (a) of this section against an owner or operator of a facility shall be brought in the district court for the district in which the alleged violation occurred.

(2) Any action under subsection (a) of this section against the Administrator may be brought in the United States District Court for the District of Columbia.

(c) Relief

The district court shall have jurisdiction in actions brought under subsection (a) of this section against an owner or operator of a facility to enforce the requirement concerned and to impose any civil penalty provided for violation of that requirement. The district court shall have jurisdiction in actions brought under subsection (a) of this section against the Administrator to order the Administrator to perform the act or duty concerned.

(d) Notice

(1) No action may be commenced under subsection (a)(1)(A) of this section prior to 60 days after the plaintiff has given notice of the alleged violation to the Administrator, the State in which the alleged violation occurs, and the alleged violator. Notice under this paragraph shall be given in such manner as the Administrator shall prescribe by regulation.

(2) No action may be commenced under subsection (a)(1)(B) or (a)(1)(C) of this section prior to 60 days after the date on which the plaintiff gives notice to the Administrator, State Governor, or State emergency response commission (as the case may be) that the plaintiff will commence the action. Notice under this paragraph shall be given in such manner as the Administrator shall prescribe by regulation.

(e) Limitation

No action may be commenced under subsection (a) of this section against an owner or operator of a facility if the Administrator has commenced and is diligently pursuing an administrative order or civil action to enforce the requirement concerned or to impose a civil penalty under this Act with respect to the violation of the requirement.

(f) Costs

The court, in issuing any final order in any action brought pursuant to this section, may award costs of litigation (including reasonable attorney and expert witness fees) to the prevailing or the substantially prevailing party whenever the court determines such an award is appropriate. The court may, if a temporary restraining order or preliminary injunction is sought, require the filing of a bond or equivalent security in accordance with the Federal Rules of Civil Procedure.

(g) Other rights

Nothing in this section shall restrict or expand any right which any person (or class of persons) may have under any Federal or State statute or common law to seek enforcement of any requirement or to seek any other relief (including relief against the Administrator or a State agency).

(h) Intervention

(1) By the United States

In any action under this section the United States or the State, or both, if not a party, may intervene as a matter of right.

(2) By persons

In any action under this section, any person may intervene as a matter of right when such person has a direct interest which is or may be adversely affected by the action and the disposition of the action may, as a practical matter, impair or impede the person's ability to protect that interest unless the Administrator or the State shows that the person's interest is adequately represented by existing parties in the action.

(Pub. L. No. 99–499, Title III, § 326, 100 Stat. 1755 (Oct. 17, 1986).)

[1] So in original. Probably should be preceded by "section."

HISTORICAL AND STATUTORY NOTES

References in Text

This Act, referred to in subsec. (e), is Pub. L. No. 99–499, 100 Stat. 1613 (Oct. 17, 1986), as amended, known as the Superfund Amendments and Reauthorization Act of 1986. For complete classification of this Act to the Code, see Short Title of 1986 Amendments note set out under section 9601 of this title and Tables.

The Federal Rules of Civil Procedure, referred to in subsec. (f), are set out in Title 28, Judiciary and Judicial Procedure.

Effective and Applicability Provisions

1986 Acts. Section effective Oct. 17, 1986, see section 4 of Pub. L. No. 99–499, set out as a note under section 9601 of this title.

§ 11047. Exemption

[EPCRTKA § 327]

Except as provided in section 11004 of this title, this chapter does not apply to the transportation, including the storage incident to such transportation, of any substance or chemical subject to the requirements of this chapter, including the transportation and distribution of natural gas.

(Pub. L. No. 99–499, Title III, § 327, 100 Stat. 1757 (Oct. 17, 1986).)

HISTORICAL AND STATUTORY NOTES

Effective and Applicability Provisions

1986 Acts. Section effective Oct. 17, 1986, see section 4 of Pub. L. No. 99–499, set out as a note under section 9601 of this title.

§ 11048. Regulations

[EPCRTKA § 328]

The Administrator may prescribe such regulations as may be necessary to carry out this chapter.

(Pub. L. No. 99–499, Title III, § 328, 100 Stat. 1757 (Oct. 17, 1986).)

HISTORICAL AND STATUTORY NOTES

Effective and Applicability Provisions

1986 Acts. Section effective Oct. 17, 1986, see section 4 of Pub. L. No. 99–499, set out as a note under section 9601 of this title.

§ 11049. Definitions

[EPCRTKA § 329]

For purposes of this chapter—

(1) Administrator

The term "Administrator" means the Administrator of the Environmental Protection Agency.

(2) Environment

The term "environment" includes water, air, and land and the interrelationship which exists among and between water, air, and land and all living things.

(3) Extremely hazardous substance

The term "extremely hazardous substance" means a substance on the list described in section 11002(a)(2) of this title.

(4) Facility

The term "facility" means all buildings, equipment, structures, and other stationary items which are located on a single site or on contiguous or adjacent sites and which are owned or operated by the same person (or by any person which controls, is controlled by, or under common control with, such person). For purposes of section 11004 of this title, the term includes motor vehicles, rolling stock, and aircraft.

(5) Hazardous chemical

The term "hazardous chemical" has the meaning given such term by section 11021(e) of this title.

(6) Material safety data sheet

The term "material safety data sheet" means the sheet required to be developed under section 1910.1200(g) of Title 29 of the Code of Federal Regulations, as that section may be amended from time to time.

(7) Person

The term "person" means any individual, trust, firm, joint stock company, corporation (including a government corporation), partnership, association, State, municipality, commission, political subdivision of a State, or interstate body.

(8) Release

The term "release" means any spilling, leaking, pumping, pouring, emitting, emptying, discharging, injecting, escaping, leaching, dumping, or disposing into the environment (including the abandonment or discarding of barrels, containers, and other closed receptacles) of any hazardous chemical, extremely hazardous substance, or toxic chemical.

(9) State

The term "State" means any State of the United States, the District of Columbia, the Commonwealth of Puerto Rico, Guam, American Samoa, the United States Virgin Islands, the Northern Mariana Islands, and any other territory or possession over which the United States has jurisdiction.

(10) Toxic chemical

The term "toxic chemical" means a substance on the list described in section 11023(c) of this title.

(Pub. L. No. 99–499, Title III, § 329, 100 Stat. 1757 (Oct. 17, 1986).)

HISTORICAL AND STATUTORY NOTES

Effective and Applicability Provisions

1986 Acts. Section effective Oct. 17, 1986, see section 4 of Pub. L. No. 99–499, set out as a note under section 9601 of this title.

§ 11050. Authorization of appropriations

[EPCRTKA § 330]

There are authorized to be appropriated for fiscal years beginning after September 30, 1986, such sums as may be necessary to carry out this chapter.

(Pub. L. No. 99–499, Title III, § 330, 100 Stat. 1758 (Oct. 17, 1986).)

HISTORICAL AND STATUTORY NOTES

Effective and Applicability Provisions

1986 Acts. Section effective Oct. 17, 1986, see section 4 of Pub. L. No. 99–499, set out as a note under section 9601 of this title.

POLLUTION PREVENTION

POLLUTION PREVENTION ACT OF 1990
[PPA § ______]

(42 U.S.C.A. §§ 13101 to 13109)

CHAPTER 133—POLLUTION PREVENTION

§ 13101. Findings and policy

[PPA § 6602]

(a) Findings

The Congress finds that:

(1) The United States of America annually produces millions of tons of pollution and spends tens of billions of dollars per year controlling this pollution.

(2) There are significant opportunities for industry to reduce or prevent pollution at the source through cost-effective changes in production, operation, and raw materials use. Such changes offer industry substantial savings in reduced raw material, pollution control, and liability costs as well as help protect the environment and reduce risks to worker health and safety.

(3) The opportunities for source reduction are often not realized because existing regulations, and the industrial resources they require for compliance, focus upon treatment and disposal, rather than source reduction; existing regulations do not emphasize multi-media management of pollution; and businesses need information and technical assistance to overcome institutional barriers to the adoption of source reduction practices.

(4) Source reduction is fundamentally different and more desirable than waste management and pollution control. The Environmental Protection Agency needs to address the historical lack of attention to source reduction.

(5) As a first step in preventing pollution through source reduction, the Environmental Protection Agency must establish a source reduction program which collects and disseminates information, provides financial assistance to States, and implements the other activities provided for in this chapter.

(b) Policy

The Congress hereby declares it to be the national policy of the United States that pollution should be prevented or reduced at the source whenever feasible; pollution that cannot be prevented should be recycled in an environmentally safe manner, whenever feasible; pollution that cannot be prevented or recycled should be treated in an environmentally safe manner whenever feasible; and disposal or other release into the environment should be employed only as a last resort and should be conducted in an environmentally safe manner.

(Pub. L. No. 101–508, Title VI, § 6602, 104 Stat. 1388–321 (Nov. 5, 1990).)

HISTORICAL AND STATUTORY NOTES

References in Text

This chapter, referred to in subsec. (a)(5), was in the original "this subtitle", meaning subtitle F (sections 6501, 6601 to 6610) of Title VI of Pub. L. No. 101–508, which is codified generally as this chapter. For complete classification of subtitle F to the Code, see Short Title of 1990 Acts note set out under this section and Tables.

Short Title

1990 Acts. Section 6601 of Pub. L. No. 101–508 provided that: This subtitle [subtitle F (sections 6501, 6601 to 6610) of Title VI of Pub. L. No. 101–508, enacting this chapter and section 4370c of this title] may be cited as the 'Pollution Prevention Act of 1990'."

Federal Compliance with Right-to-Know Laws and Pollution Prevention Requirements

For provisions requiring that all necessary actions be taken for the prevention of pollution with respect to the activities and facilities of each Federal agency, and for ensuring each such agency's compliance with pollution prevention and emergency planning and community right-to-know provisions established pursuant to all implementing regulations issued pursuant to chapters 116 [section 11001 et seq.] and 133 [section 13101 et seq.] of this title, and additional provisions for implementation, agency coordination, compliance, exemptions, etc., see Ex. Ord. No. 12856, 58 Fed. Reg. 41981 (Aug. 3, 1993), set out as a note under section 11001 of this title.

§ 13102. Definitions

[PPA § 6603]

For purposes of this chapter—

(1) The term "Administrator" means the Administrator of the Environmental Protection Agency.

(2) The term "Agency" means the Environmental Protection Agency.

(3) The term "toxic chemical" means any substance on the list described in section 11023(c) of this title.

(4) The term "release" has the same meaning as provided by section 11049(8) of this title.

(5) **(A)** The term "source reduction" means any practice which—

(i) reduces the amount of any hazardous substance, pollutant, or contaminant entering any waste stream or otherwise released into the environment (including fugitive emissions) prior to recycling, treatment, or disposal; and

(ii) reduces the hazards to public health and the environment associated with the release of such substances, pollutants, or contaminants.

The term includes equipment or technology modifications, process or procedure modifications, reformulation or redesign of products, substitution of raw materials, and improvements in housekeeping, maintenance, training, or inventory control.

(B) The term "source reduction" does not include any practice which alters the physical, chemical, or biological characteristics or the volume of a hazardous substance, pollutant, or contaminant through a process or activity which itself is not integral to and necessary for the production of a product or the providing of a service.

(6) The term "multi-media" means water, air, and land.

(7) The term "SIC codes" refers to the 2-digit code numbers used for classification of economic activity in the Standard Industrial Classification Manual.

(Pub. L. No. 101–508, Title VI, § 6603, 104 Stat. 1388–321 (Nov. 5, 1990).)

§ 13103. EPA activities

[PPA § 6604]

(a) Authorities

The Administrator shall establish in the Agency an office to carry out the functions of the Administrator under this chapter. The office shall be independent of the Agency's single-medium program offices but shall have the authority to review and advise such offices on their activities to promote a multi-media approach to source reduction. The office shall be under the direction of such officer of the Agency as the Administrator shall designate.

(b) Functions

The Administrator shall develop and implement a strategy to promote source reduction. As part of the strategy, the Administrator shall—

(1) establish standard methods of measurement of source reduction;

(2) ensure that the Agency considers the effect of its existing and proposed programs on source reduction efforts and shall review regulations of the Agency prior and subsequent to their proposal to determine their effect on source reduction;

(3) coordinate source reduction activities in each Agency Office[1] and coordinate with appropriate offices to promote source reduction practices in other Federal agencies, and generic research and development on techniques and processes which have broad applicability;

(4) develop improved methods of coordinating, streamlining and assuring public access to data collected under Federal environmental statutes;

(5) facilitate the adoption of source reduction techniques by businesses. This strategy shall include the use of the Source Reduction Clearinghouse and State matching grants provided in this chapter to foster the exchange of information regarding source reduction techniques, the dissemination of such information to businesses, and the provision of technical assistance to businesses. The strategy shall also consider the capabilities of various businesses to make use of source reduction techniques;

(6) identify, where appropriate, measurable goals which reflect the policy of this chapter, the tasks necessary to achieve the goals, dates at which the principal tasks are to be accomplished, required resources, organizational responsibilities, and the means by which progress in meeting the goals will be measured;

(8)[2] establish an advisory panel of technical experts comprised of representatives from industry, the States, and public interest groups, to advise the Administrator on ways to improve collection and dissemination of data;

(9) establish a training program on source reduction opportunities, including workshops and guidance documents, for State and Federal permit issuance, enforcement, and inspection officials working within all agency program offices.[3]

(10) identify and make recommendations to Congress to eliminate barriers to source reduction including the use of incentives and disincentives;

(11) identify opportunities to use Federal procurement to encourage source reduction;

(12) develop, test and disseminate model source reduction auditing procedures designed to highlight source reduction opportunities; and

(13) establish an annual award program to recognize a company or companies which operate outstanding or innovative source reduction programs.

(Pub. L. No. 101–508, Title VI, § 6604, 104 Stat. 1388–322 (Nov. 5, 1990).)

[1] So in original. Probably should not be capitalized.

[2] So in original. Subsec. (b) enacted without a paragraph (7).

[3] So in original. The period probably should be a semicolon.

§ 13104. Grants to States for State technical assistance programs

[PPA § 6605]

(a) General authority

The Administrator shall make matching grants to States for programs to promote the use of source reduction techniques by businesses.

(b) Criteria

When evaluating the requests for grants under this section, the Administrator shall consider, among other things, whether the proposed State program would accomplish the following:

(1) Make specific technical assistance available to businesses seeking information about source reduction opportunities, including funding for experts to provide onsite technical advice to business[1] seeking assistance and to assist in the development of source reduction plans.

(2) Target assistance to businesses for whom lack of information is an impediment to source reduction.

(3) Provide training in source reduction techniques. Such training may be provided through local engineering schools or any other appropriate means.

(c) Matching funds

Federal funds used in any State program under this section shall provide no more than 50 per centum of the funds made available to a State in each year of that State's participation in the program.

(d) Effectiveness

The Administrator shall establish appropriate means for measuring the effectiveness of the State grants made under this section in promoting the use of source reduction techniques by businesses.

(e) Information

States receiving grants under this section shall make information generated under the grants available to the Administrator.

(Pub. L. No. 101–508, Title VI, § 6605, 104 Stat. 1388–323 (Nov. 5, 1990).)

[1] So in original. Probably should be "businesses."

§ 13105. Source Reduction Clearinghouse

[PPA § 6606]

(a) Authority

The Administrator shall establish a Source Reduction Clearinghouse to compile information including a computer data base which contains information on management, technical, and operational approaches to source reduction. The Administrator shall use the clearinghouse to—

(1) serve as a center for source reduction technology transfer;

(2) mount active outreach and education programs by the States to further the adoption of source reduction technologies; and

(3) collect and compile information reported by States receiving grants under section 13104 of this title on the operation and success of State source reduction programs.

(b) Public availability

The Administrator shall make available to the public such information on source reduction as is gathered pursuant to this chapter and such other pertinent information and analysis regarding source reduction as may be available to the Administrator. The data base shall permit entry and retrieval of information to any person.

(Pub. L. No. 101–508, Title VI, § 6606, 104 Stat. 1388–324 (Nov. 5, 1990).)

§ 13106. Source reduction and recycling data collection [PPA § 6607]

(a) Reporting requirements

Each owner or operator of a facility required to file an annual toxic chemical release form under section 11023 of this title for any toxic chemical shall include with each such annual filing a toxic chemical source reduction and recycling report for the preceeding[1] calendar year. The toxic chemical source reduction and recycling report shall cover each toxic chemical required to be reported in the annual toxic chemical release form filed by the owner or operator under section 11023(c) of this title. This section shall take effect with the annual report filed under section 11023 of this title for the first full calendar year beginning after November 5, 1990.

(b) Items included in report

The toxic chemical source reduction and recycling report required under subsection (a) of this section shall set forth each of the following on a facility-by-facility basis for each toxic chemical:

(1) The quantity of the chemical entering any waste stream (or otherwise released into the environment) prior to recycling, treatment, or disposal during the calendar year for which the report is filed and the percentage change from the previous year. The quantity reported shall not include any amount reported under paragraph (7). When actual measurements of the quantity of a toxic chemical entering the waste streams are not readily available, reasonable estimates should be made based on best engineering judgment.

(2) The amount of the chemical from the facility which is recycled (at the facility or elsewhere) during such calendar year, the percentage change from the previous year, and the process of recycling used.

(3) The source reduction practices used with respect to that chemical during such year at the facility. Such practices shall be reported in accordance with the following categories unless the Administrator finds other categories to be more appropriate:

(A) Equipment, technology, process, or procedure modifications.

(B) Reformulation or redesign of products.

(C) Substitution of raw materials.

(D) Improvement in management, training, inventory control, materials handling, or other general operational phases of industrial facilities.

(4) The amount expected to be reported under paragraph[2] (1) and (2) for the two calendar years immediately following the calendar year for which the report is filed. Such amount shall be expressed as a percentage change from the amount reported in paragraphs (1) and (2).

(5) A ratio of production in the reporting year to production in the previous year. The ratio should be calculated to most closely reflect all activities involving the toxic chemical. In specific industrial classifications subject to this section, where a feedstock or some variable other than production is the primary influence on waste characteristics or volumes, the report may provide an index based on that primary variable for each toxic chemical. The Administrator is encouraged to develop production indexes to accommodate individual industries for use on a voluntary basis.

(6) The techniques which were used to identify source reduction opportunities. Techniques listed should include, but are not limited to, employee recommendations, external and internal audits, participative team management, and material balance audits. Each type of source reduction listed under paragraph (3) should be associated with the techniques or multiples of techniques used to identify the source reduction technique.

(7) The amount of any toxic chemical released into the environment which resulted from a catastrophic event, remedial action, or other one-time event, and is not associated with production processes during the reporting year.

(8) The amount of the chemical from the facility which is treated (at the facility or elsewhere) during such calendar year and the percentage change from the previous year. For the first year of reporting under this subsection, comparison with the previous year is required only to the extent such information is available.

(c) SARA provisions

The provisions of sections 11042, 11045(c), and 11046 of this title shall apply to the reporting requirements of this section in the same manner as to the reports required under section 11023 of this title. The Administrator may modify the form required for purposes of reporting information under section 11023 of this title to the extent he deems necessary to include the additional information required under this section.

(d) Additional optional information

Any person filing a report under this section for any year may include with the report additional information regarding source reduction, recycling, and other pollution control techniques in earlier years.

(e) Availability of data

Subject to section 11042 of this title, the Administrator shall make data collected under this section publicly available in the same manner as the data collected under section 11023 of this title.

(Pub. L. No. 101–508, Title VI, § 6607, 104 Stat. 1388–324 (Nov. 5, 1990).)

[1] So in original. Probably should be "preceding."

[2] So in original. Probably should be "paragraphs."

HISTORICAL AND STATUTORY NOTES

References in Text

SARA, referred to in the heading of subsec. (c), means the Superfund Amendments and Reauthorization Act of 1986, Pub. L. No. 99–499, 100 Stat. 1613 (Oct. 17, 1986), as amended. For complete classification of this Act to the Code, see Short Title of 1986 Amendments note set out under section 9601 of this title.

§ 13107. EPA report

[PPA § 6608]

(a) Biennial reports

The Administrator shall provide Congress with a report within eighteen months after November 5, 1990, and biennially thereafter, containing a detailed description of the actions taken to implement the strategy to promote source reduction developed under section 13103(b) of this title and of the results of such actions. The report shall include an assessment of the effectiveness of the clearinghouse and grant program established under this chapter in promoting the goals of the strategy, and shall evaluate data gaps and data duplication with respect to data collected under Federal environmental statutes.

(b) Subsequent reports

Each biennial report submitted under subsection (a) of this section after the first report shall contain each of the following:

(1) An analysis of the data collected under section 13106 of this title on an industry-by-industry basis for not less than five SIC codes or other categories as the Administrator deems appropriate. The analysis shall begin with those SIC codes or other categories of facilities which generate the largest quantities of toxic chemical waste. The analysis shall include an evaluation of trends in source reduction by industry, firm size, production, or other useful means. Each such subsequent report shall cover five SIC codes or other categories which were not covered in a prior report until all SIC codes or other categories have been covered.

(2) An analysis of the usefulness and validity of the data collected under section 13106 of this title for measuring trends in source reduction and the adoption of source reduction by business.

(3) Identification of regulatory and nonregulatory barriers to source reduction, and of opportunities for using existing regulatory programs, and incentives and disincentives to promote and assist source reduction.

(4) Identification of industries and pollutants that require priority assistance in multi-media source reduction[1]

(5) Recommendations as to incentives needed to encourage investment and research and development in source reduction.

(6) Identification of opportunities and development of priorities for research and development in source reduction methods and techniques.

(7) An evaluation of the cost and technical feasibility, by industry and processes, of source reduction opportunities and current activities and an identification of any industries for which there are significant barriers to source reduction with an analysis of the basis of this identification.

(8) An evaluation of methods of coordinating, streamlining, and improving public access to data collected under Federal environmental statutes.

(9) An evaluation of data gaps and data duplication with respect to data collected under Federal environmental statutes.

In the report following the first biennial report provided for under this subsection, paragraphs (3) through (9) may be included at the discretion of the Administrator.

(Pub. L. No. 101–508, Title VI, § 6608, 104 Stat. 1388–326 (Nov. 5, 1990).)

[1] So in original. Probably should be followed by a period.

HISTORICAL AND STATUTORY NOTES

References in Text

Section 13103(b) of this title, referred to in subsec. (a), was in the original "section 4(b)" and was translated as reading "section 6604(b)", meaning section 6604(b) of Pub. L. No. 101–508, because Pub. L. No. 101–508 has no section 4 but section 6604(b) of Pub. L. No. 101–508 relates to development of a strategy to promote source reduction.

Codifications

Reference in the original text of subsec. (a) of this section to "section 4(b)" has been translated in the codified text as "section 13103(b) of this title" to reflect the probable intent of Congress.

§ 13108. Savings provisions

[PPA § 6609]

(a) Nothing in this chapter shall be construed to modify or interfere with the implementation of title III of the Superfund Amendments and Reauthorization Act of 1986 [42 U.S.C.A. § 11001 et seq.].

(b) Nothing contained in this chapter shall be construed, interpreted or applied to supplant, displace, preempt or otherwise diminish the responsibilities and liabilities under other State or Federal law, whether statutory or common.

(Pub. L. No. 101–508, Title VI, § 6609, 104 Stat. 1388–327 (Nov. 5, 1990).)

HISTORICAL AND STATUTORY NOTES

References in Text

Title III of the Superfund Amendments and Reauthorization Act of 1986, referred to in subsec. (a), is Title III (section 300 et seq.) of Pub. L. No. 99–499, 100 Stat. 1728 (Oct. 17, 1986), known as the Emergency Planning and Community Right-To-Know Act of 1986, which is codified principally as chapter 116 (section 11001 et seq.) of this title. For complete classification of the Emergency Planning and Community Right-To-Know Act of 1986 to the Code, see Short Title of 1986 Acts note set out under section 11001 of this title and Tables.

§ 13109. Authorization of appropriations

[PPA § 6610]

There is authorized to be appropriated to the Administrator $8,000,000 for each of the fiscal years 1991, 1992, and 1993 for functions carried out under this chapter (other than State Grants[1]), and $8,000,000 for each of the fiscal years 1991, 1992, and 1993, for grant programs to States issued pursuant to section 13104 of this title.

(Pub. L. No. 101–508, Title VI, § 6610, 104 Stat. 1388–327 (Nov. 5, 1990).)

[1] So in original. Probably should not be capitalized.

TITLE 43

PUBLIC LANDS

FEDERAL LAND POLICY AND MANAGEMENT

FEDERAL LAND POLICY AND MANAGEMENT ACT OF 1976 [FLPMA § _____]

(43 U.S.C.A. §§ 1701 to 1787)

CHAPTER 35—FEDERAL LAND POLICY AND MANAGEMENT

SUBCHAPTER I—GENERAL PROVISIONS

SUBCHAPTER II—LAND USE PLANNING AND LAND ACQUISITION AND DISPOSITION

SUBCHAPTER III—ADMINISTRATION

SUBCHAPTER I—GENERAL PROVISIONS

§ 1701. Congressional declaration of policy

[FLPMA § 102]

(a) The Congress declares that it is the policy of the United States that—

(1) the public lands be retained in Federal ownership, unless as a result of the land use planning procedure provided for in this Act, it is determined that disposal of a particular parcel will serve the national interest;

(2) the national interest will be best realized if the public lands and their resources are periodically and systematically inventoried and their present and future use is projected through a land use planning process coordinated with other Federal and State planning efforts;

(3) public lands not previously designated for any specific use and all existing classifications of public lands that were effected by executive action or statute before October 21, 1976, be reviewed in accordance with the provisions of this Act;

(4) the Congress exercise its constitutional authority to withdraw or otherwise designate or dedicate Federal lands for specified purposes and that Congress delineate the extent to which the Executive may withdraw lands without legislative action;

(5) in administering public land statutes and exercising discretionary authority granted by them, the Secretary be required to establish comprehensive rules and regulations after considering the views of the general public; and to structure adjudication procedures to assure adequate third party participation, objective administrative review of initial decisions, and expeditious decisionmaking;

(6) judicial review of public land adjudication decisions be provided by law;

(7) goals and objectives be established by law as guidelines for public land use planning, and that management be on the basis of multiple use and sustained yield unless otherwise specified by law;

(8) the public lands be managed in a manner that will protect the quality of scientific, scenic, historical, ecological, environmental, air and atmospheric, water resource, and archeological values; that, where appropriate, will preserve and protect certain public lands in their natural condition; that will provide food and habitat for fish and wildlife and domestic animals; and that will provide for outdoor recreation and human occupancy and use;

(9) the United States receive fair market value of the use of the public lands and their resources unless otherwise provided for by statute;

(10) uniform procedures for any disposal of public land, acquisition of non-Federal land for public purposes, and the exchange of such lands be established by statute, requiring each disposal, acquisition, and exchange to be consistent with the prescribed mission of the department or agency involved, and reserving to the Congress review of disposals in excess of a specified acreage;

(11) regulations and plans for the protection of public land areas of critical environmental concern be promptly developed;

(12) the public lands be managed in a manner which recognizes the Nation's need for domestic sources of minerals, food, timber, and fiber from the public lands including implementation of the Mining and Minerals Policy Act of 1970 (84 Stat. 1876, 30 U.S.C. 21a) as it pertains to the public lands; and

(13) the Federal Government should, on a basis equitable to both the Federal and local taxpayer, provide for payments to compensate States and local governments for burdens created as a result of the immunity of Federal lands from State and local taxation.

(b) The policies of this Act shall become effective only as specific statutory authority for their implementation is enacted by this Act or by subsequent legislation and shall then be construed as supplemental to and not in derogation of the purposes for which public lands are administered under other provisions of law.

(Pub. L. No. 94–579, Title I, § 102, 90 Stat. 2744 (Oct. 21, 1976).)

HISTORICAL AND STATUTORY NOTES

References in Text

This Act, referred to in subsecs. (a)(1), (3) and (b), is Pub. L. No. 94–579, 90 Stat. 2743 (Oct. 21, 1976), as amended, known as the Federal Land Policy and Management Act of 1976. For complete classification of this Act to the Code, see Tables.

The Mining and Minerals Policy Act of 1970, referred to in subsec. (a)(12) is Pub. L. 91–631, 84 Stat. 1876 (Dec. 31, 1970), which is codified as section 21a of Title 30, Mineral Lands and Mining.

Savings Provisions

Section 701 of Pub. L. No. 94–579 provided that:

"(a) Nothing in this Act [see Short Title note under this section], or in any amendment made by this Act, shall be construed as terminating any valid lease, permit, patent, right-of-way, or other land use right or authorization existing on the date of approval of this Act [Oct. 21, 1976].

"(b) Notwithstanding any provision of this Act, in the event of conflict with or inconsistency between this Act and the Acts of August 28, 1937 (50 Stat. 874; 43 U.S.C. 1181a–1181j), and May 24, 1939 (53 Stat. 753), insofar as they relate to management of timber resources, and disposition of revenues from lands and resources, the latter Acts shall prevail.

"(c) All withdrawals, reservations, classifications, and designations in effect as of the date of approval of this Act [Oct. 21, 1976] shall remain in full force and effect until modified under the provisions of this Act or other applicable law.

"(d) Nothing in this Act, or in any amendments made by this Act, shall be construed as permitting any person to place, or allow to be placed, spent oil shale, overburden, or byproducts from the recovery of other minerals found with oil shale, on any Federal land other than Federal land which has been leased for the recovery of shale oil under the Act of February 25, 1920 (41 Stat. 437, as amended; 30 U.S.C. 181 et seq.).

"(e) Nothing in this Act shall be construed as modifying, revoking, or changing any provision of the Alaska Native Claims Settlement Act (85 Stat. 688, as amended; 43 U.S.C. 1601 et seq.).

"(f) Nothing in this Act shall be deemed to repeal any existing law by implication.

"(g) Nothing in this Act shall be construed as limiting or restricting the power and authority of the United States or—

"(1) as affecting in any way any law governing appropriation or use of, or Federal right to, water on public lands;

"(2) as expanding or diminishing Federal or State jurisdiction, responsibility, interests, or rights in water resources development or control;

"(3) as displacing, superseding, limiting, or modifying any interstate compact or the jurisdiction or responsibility of any legally established joint or common agency of two or more States or of two or more States and the Federal Government;

"(4) as superseding, modifying, or repealing, except as specifically set forth in this Act, existing laws applicable to the various Federal agencies which are authorized to develop or participate in the development of water resources or to exercise licensing or regulatory functions in relation thereto;

"(5) as modifying the terms of any interstate compact;

"(6) as a limitation upon any State criminal statute or upon the police power of the respective States, or as derogating the authority of a local police officer in the performance of his duties, or as depriving any State or political subdivision thereof of any right it may have to exercise civil and criminal jurisdiction on the national resource lands; or as amending, limiting, or infringing the existing laws providing grants of lands to the States.

"(h) All actions by the Secretary concerned under this Act shall be subject to valid existing rights.

"(i) The adequacy of reports required by this Act to be submitted to the Congress or its committees shall not be subject to judicial review.

"(j) Nothing in this Act shall be construed as affecting the distribution of livestock grazing revenues to local governments under the Granger-Thye Act (64 Stat. 85, 16 U.S.C. 580h), under the Act of May 23, 1908 (35 Stat. 260, as amended; 16 U.S.C. 500), under the Act of March 4, 1913 (37 Stat. 843, as amended; 16 U.S.C. 501), and under the Act of June 20, 1910 (36 Stat. 557)."

Severability of Provisions

Section 707 of Pub. L. No. 94–579 provided that: "If any provision of this Act [see Short Title note set out above] or the application thereof is held invalid, the remainder of the Act and the application thereof shall not be affected thereby."

Short Title

2009 Amendments. Pub. L. No. 111–88, Div. A, Title V, § 501, 123 Stat. 2968 (Oct. 30, 2009), provided that: "This title [Pub. L. No. 111–88, Div. A, Title V, §§ 501 to 503, 123 Stat. 2968 (Oct. 30, 2009), enacting 43 U.S.C.A. §§ 1748a, and 1748b] may be cited as the 'Federal Land Assistance, Management, and Enhancement Act of 2009' or 'FLAME Act of 2009'."

1988 Amendments. Pub. L. No. 100–409, § 1, 102 Stat. 1086 (Aug. 20, 1988), provided that: "This Act [enacting section 1723 of this title, amending section 1716 of this title and sections 505a, 505b, and 521b of Title 16, Conservation, and enacting provisions set out as notes under sections 751 and 1716 of this title] may be cited as the 'Federal Land Exchange Facilitation Act of 1988'."

1976 Acts. Section 101 of Pub. L. No. 94–579 provided that: "This Act [enacting this chapter and amending and repealing numerous other laws, which for complete distribution, see Tables Volume] may be cited as the 'Federal Land Policy and Management Act of 1976'."

Cooperative Action and Sharing of Resources by Secretaries of the Interior and Agriculture

Pub. L. No. 106–291, Title III, § 330, 114 Stat. 996 (Oct. 11, 2000), as amended by Pub. L. No. 109–54, Title IV, § 428, 119 Stat. 555 (Aug. 2, 2005); Pub. L. No. 111–8, Div. E, Title IV, § 418, 123 Stat. 747 (Mar. 11, 2009), which provided for the establishment of pilot programs involving the land management agencies referred to in this section to conduct projects, planning, permitting, leasing, contracting and other activities, either jointly or on behalf of one another; may co-locate in Federal offices and facilities leased by an agency of either Department; and promulgate special rules as needed to test the feasibility of issuing unified permits, applications, and leases, was editorially transferred to become section 1703 of this title.

Existing Rights-of-Way

Section 706(b) of Pub. L. No. 94–579 provided that: "Nothing in section 706(a) [see Tables for classification], except as it pertains to rights-of-way, may be construed as affecting the authority of the Secretary of Agriculture under the Act of June 4, 1897 (30 Stat. 35, as amended, 16 U.S.C. 551); the Act of July 22, 1937 (50 Stat. 525, as amended, 7 U.S.C. 1010–1212); or the Act of September 3, 1954 (68 Stat. 1146, 43 U.S.C. 931c)."

§ 1702. Definitions

[FLPMA § 103]

Without altering in any way the meaning of the following terms as used in any other statute, whether or not such statute is referred to in, or amended by, this Act, as used in this Act—

(a) The term "areas of critical environmental concern" means areas within the public lands where special management attention is required (when such areas are developed or used or where no development is required) to protect and prevent irreparable damage to important historic, cultural, or scenic values, fish and wildlife resources or other natural systems or processes, or to protect life and safety from natural hazards.

(b) The term "holder" means any State or local governmental entity, individual, partnership, corporation, association, or other business entity receiving or using a right-of-way under subchapter V of this chapter.

(c) The term "multiple use" means the management of the public lands and their various resource values so that they are utilized in the combination that will best meet the present and future needs of the American people; making the most judicious use of the land for some or all of these resources or related services over areas large enough to provide sufficient latitude for periodic adjustments in use to conform to changing needs and conditions; the use of some land for less than all of the resources; a combination of balanced and diverse resource uses that takes into account the long-term needs of future generations for renewable and nonrenewable resources, including, but not limited to, recreation, range, timber, minerals, watershed, wildlife and fish, and natural scenic, scientific and historical values; and harmonious and coordinated management of the various resources without permanent impairment of the productivity of the land and the quality of the environment with consideration being given to the relative values of the resources and not necessarily to the combination of uses that will give the greatest economic return or the greatest unit output.

(d) The term "public involvement" means the opportunity for participation by affected citizens in rulemaking, decisionmaking, and planning with respect to the public lands, including public meetings or hearings held at locations near the affected lands, or advisory mechanisms, or such other procedures as may be necessary to provide public comment in a particular instance.

(e) The term "public lands" means any land and interest in land owned by the United States within the several States and administered by the Secretary of the Interior through the Bureau of Land Management, without regard to how the United States acquired ownership, except—

> **(1)** lands located on the Outer Continental Shelf; and
>
> **(2)** lands held for the benefit of Indians, Aleuts, and Eskimos.

(f) The term "right-of-way" includes an easement, lease, permit, or license to occupy, use, or traverse public lands granted for the purpose listed in subchapter V of this chapter.

(g) The term "Secretary", unless specifically designated otherwise, means the Secretary of the Interior.

(h) The term "sustained yield" means the achievement and maintenance in perpetuity of a high-level annual or regular periodic output of the various renewable resources of the public lands consistent with multiple use.

(i) The term "wilderness" as used in section 1782 of this title shall have the same meaning as it does in section 1131(c) of Title 16.

(j) The term "withdrawal" means withholding an area of Federal land from settlement, sale, location, or entry, under some or all of the general land laws, for the purpose of limiting activities under those laws in order to maintain other public values in the area or reserving the area for a particular public purpose or program; or transferring jurisdiction over an area of Federal land, other than "property" governed by the Federal Property and Administrative Services Act, as amended from one department, bureau or agency to another department, bureau or agency.

(k) An "allotment management plan" means a document prepared in consultation with the lessees or permittees involved, which applies to livestock operations on the public lands or on lands within National Forests in the eleven contiguous Western States and which:

> **(1)** prescribes the manner in, and extent to, which livestock operations will be conducted in order to meet the multiple-use, sustained-yield, economic and other needs and objectives as determined for the lands by the Secretary concerned; and
>
> **(2)** describes the type, location, ownership, and general specifications for the range improvements to be installed and maintained on the lands to meet the livestock grazing and other objectives of land management; and
>
> **(3)** contains such other provisions relating to livestock grazing and other objectives found by the Secretary concerned to be consistent with the provisions of this Act and other applicable law.

(*l*) The term "principal or major uses" includes, and is limited to, domestic livestock grazing, fish and wildlife development and utilization, mineral exploration and production, rights-of-way, outdoor recreation, and timber production.

(m) The term "department" means a unit of the executive branch of the Federal Government which is headed by a member of the President's Cabinet and the term "agency" means a unit of the executive branch of the Federal Government which is not under the jurisdiction of a head of a department.

(n) The term "Bureau[1] means the Bureau of Land Management.

(o) The term "eleven contiguous Western States" means the States of Arizona, California, Colorado, Idaho, Montana, Nevada, New Mexico, Oregon, Utah, Washington, and Wyoming.

(p) The term "grazing permit and lease" means any document authorizing use of public lands or lands in National Forests in the eleven contiguous western States for the purpose of grazing domestic livestock.

(Pub. L. No. 94–579, Title I, § 103, 90 Stat. 2745 (Oct. 21, 1976).)

[1] So in original. Probably should have a close quote.

HISTORICAL AND STATUTORY NOTES

References in Text

This Act, referred to in the opening par. and in subsec. (k), is Pub. L. No. 94–579, 90 Stat. 2743 (Oct. 21, 1976), as amended, is known as the Federal Land Policy and Management Act of 1976. For complete classification of this Act to the Code, see Tables.

The general land laws, referred to in subsec. (j), are codified generally to this title.

The Federal Property and Administrative Services Act, referred to in subsec. (j), probably means the Federal Property and Administrative Services Act of 1949, Act of June 30, 1949, c. 288, 63 Stat. 377, which was substantially repealed and restated in chapters 1 to 11 of Title 40, Public Buildings, Property, and Works, and division C of subtitle I of Title 41, Public Contracts, by Pub. L. No. 107–217, §§ 1, 6(b), 116 Stat. 1062, 1304 (Aug. 21, 2002), which Act enacted Title 40, and Pub. L. No. 111–350, §§ 3, 7(b), 124 Stat. 3677, 3855 (Jan. 4, 2011), which Act enacted Title 41. For complete classification, see Short Title of 1949 Act note set out under section 101 of Title 41 and Tables. For disposition of sections of former Titles 40 and 41, see Disposition Tables preceding section 101 of Title 40 and section 101 of Title 41.

§ 1703. Cooperative action and sharing of resources by Secretaries of the Interior and Agriculture

In fiscal year 2012 and each fiscal year thereafter, the Secretaries of the Interior and Agriculture, subject to annual review of Congress, may establish programs to conduct projects, planning, permitting, leasing, contracting and other activities, either jointly or on behalf of one another; may co-locate in Federal offices and facilities leased by an agency of either Department; and may promulgate special rules as needed to test the feasibility of issuing unified permits, applications, and leases. The Secretaries of the Interior and Agriculture may make reciprocal delegations of their respective authorities, duties and responsibilities in support of the "Service First" initiative agency-wide to promote customer service and efficiency. Nothing herein shall alter, expand or limit the applicability of any public law or regulation to lands administered by the Bureau of Land Management, National Park Service, Fish and Wildlife Service, or the Forest Service or matters under the purview of other bureaus or offices of either Department. To facilitate the sharing of resources under the Service First initiative, the Secretaries of the Interior and Agriculture may make transfers of funds and reimbursement of funds on an annual basis, including transfers and reimbursements for multi-year projects, except that this authority may not be used to circumvent requirements and limitations imposed on the use of funds.

(Pub. L. No. 106–291, Title III, § 330, 114 Stat. 996 (Oct. 11, 2000); as amended by Pub. L. No. 109–54, Title IV, § 428, 119 Stat. 555 (Aug. 2, 2005); Pub. L. No. 111–8, Div. E, Title IV, § 418, 123 Stat. 747 (Mar. 11, 2009); Pub. L. No. 112–74, Div. E, Title IV, § 422, 125 Stat. 1045 (Dec. 23, 2011); Pub. L. No. 113–76, Div. G, Title IV, § 430, 128 Stat. 345 (Jan. 17, 2014).)

HISTORICAL AND STATUTORY NOTES

Codifications

Section was enacted as part of the Department of the Interior and Related Agencies Appropriations Act, 2001, and not as part of the Federal Land Policy and Management Act of 1976 which comprises this chapter.

Section was set out as a note under 43 U.S.C.A. § 1701 prior to editorial redesignation as this section.

Pub. L. No. 113–76, Div. G, § 430(1), which, in the first sentence of this section, directed the striking of "programs. involving the land management agencies referred to in this section" and the inserting of "programs", was executed by striking the language as quoted but without the period following the first word "programs" and inserting the language as directed, as the probable intent of Congress, since the text of this section did not have a period following that word "programs".

SUBCHAPTER II—LAND USE PLANNING AND LAND ACQUISITION AND DISPOSITION

§ 1711. Continuing inventory and identification of public lands; preparation and maintenance

[FLPMA § 201]

(a) The Secretary shall prepare and maintain on a continuing basis an inventory of all public lands and their resource and other values (including, but not limited to, outdoor recreation and scenic values), giving priority to areas of critical environmental concern. This inventory shall be kept current so as to reflect changes in conditions and to identify new and emerging resource and other values. The preparation and maintenance of such inventory or the identification of such areas shall not, of itself, change or prevent change of the management or use of public lands.

(b) As funds and manpower are made available, the Secretary shall ascertain the boundaries of the public lands; provide means of public identification thereof including, where appropriate, signs and maps; and provide State and local governments with data from the inventory for the purpose of planning and regulating the uses of non-Federal lands in proximity of such public lands.

(Pub. L. No. 94–579, Title II, § 201, 90 Stat. 2747 (Oct. 21, 1976).)

§ 1712. Land use plans

[FLPMA § 202]

(a) Development, maintenance, and revision by Secretary

The Secretary shall, with public involvement and consistent with the terms and conditions of this Act, develop, maintain, and, when appropriate, revise land use plans which provide by tracts or areas for the use of the public lands. Land use plans shall be developed for the public lands regardless of whether such lands previously have been classified, withdrawn, set aside, or otherwise designated for one or more uses.

(b) Coordination of plans for National Forest System lands with Indian land use planning and management programs for purposes of development and revision

In the development and revision of land use plans, the Secretary of Agriculture shall coordinate land use plans for lands in the National Forest System with the land use planning and management programs of and for Indian tribes by, among other things, considering the policies of approved tribal land resource management programs.

(c) Criteria for development and revision

In the development and revision of land use plans, the Secretary shall—

(1) use and observe the principles of multiple use and sustained yield set forth in this and other applicable law;

(2) use a systematic interdisciplinary approach to achieve integrated consideration of physical, biological, economic, and other sciences;

(3) give priority to the designation and protection of areas of critical environmental concern;

(4) rely, to the extent it is available, on the inventory of the public lands, their resources, and other values;

(5) consider present and potential uses of the public lands;

(6) consider the relative scarcity of the values involved and the availability of alternative means (including recycling) and sites for realization of those values;

(7) weigh long-term benefits to the public against short-term benefits;

(8) provide for compliance with applicable pollution control laws, including State and Federal air, water, noise, or other pollution standards or implementation plans; and

(9) to the extent consistent with the laws governing the administration of the public lands, coordinate the land use inventory, planning, and management activities of or for such lands with the land use planning and management programs of other Federal departments and agencies and of the States and local governments within which the lands are located, including, but not limited to, the statewide outdoor recreation plans developed under chapter 2003 of title 54, United States Code, and of or for Indian tribes by, among other things, considering the policies of approved State and tribal land resource management programs. In implementing this directive, the Secretary shall, to the extent he finds practical, keep apprised of State, local, and tribal land use plans; assure that consideration is given to those State, local, and tribal plans that are germane in the development of land use plans for public lands; assist in resolving, to the extent practical, inconsistencies between Federal and non-Federal Government plans, and shall provide for meaningful public involvement of State and local government officials, both elected and appointed, in the development of land use programs, land use regulations, and land use decisions for public lands, including early public notice of proposed decisions which may have a significant impact on non-Federal lands. Such officials in each State are authorized to furnish advice to the Secretary with respect to the development and revision of land use plans, land use guidelines, land use rules, and land use regulations for the public lands within such State and with respect to such other land use matters as may be referred to them by him. Land use plans of the Secretary under this section shall be consistent with State and local plans to the maximum extent he finds consistent with Federal law and the purposes of this Act.

(d) Review and inclusion of classified public lands; review of existing land use plans; modification and termination of classifications

Any classification of public lands or any land use plan in effect on October 21, 1976, is subject to review in the land use planning process conducted under this section, and all public lands, regardless of classification, are subject to inclusion in any land use plan developed pursuant to this section. The Secretary may modify or terminate any such classification consistent with such land use plans.

(e) Management decisions for implementation of developed or revised plans

The Secretary may issue management decisions to implement land use plans developed or revised under this section in accordance with the following:

(1) Such decisions, including but not limited to exclusions (that is, total elimination) of one or more of the principal or major uses made by a management decision shall remain subject to reconsideration, modification, and termination through revision by the Secretary or his delegate, under the provisions of this section, of the land use plan involved.

(2) Any management decision or action pursuant to a management decision that excludes (that is, totally eliminates) one or more of the principal or major uses for two or more years with respect to a tract of land of one hundred thousand acres or more shall be reported by the Secretary to the House of Representatives and the Senate. If within ninety days from the giving of such notice (exclusive of days on which either House has adjourned for more than three consecutive days), the Congress adopts a concurrent resolution of nonapproval of the management decision or action, then the management decision or action shall be promptly terminated by the Secretary. If the committee to which a resolution has been referred during the said ninety day period, has not reported it at the end of thirty calendar days after its referral, it shall be in order to either discharge the committee from further consideration of such resolution or to discharge the committee from consideration of any other resolution with respect to the management decision or action. A motion to discharge may be made only by an individual favoring the resolution, shall be highly privileged (except that it may not be made after the committee has reported such a resolution), and debate thereon shall be limited to not more than one hour, to be divided equally between those favoring and those opposing the resolution. An amendment to the motion shall not be in order, and it shall not be in order to move to reconsider the vote by which the motion was agreed to or disagreed to. If the motion to discharge is agreed to or disagreed to, the motion may not be made with respect to any other resolution with respect to the same management decision or action. When the committee has reprinted, or has been discharged from further consideration of a resolution, it shall at any time thereafter be in order (even though a previous motion to the same effect has been disagreed to) to move to proceed to the consideration of the resolution. The motion shall be highly privileged and shall not be debatable. An amendment to the motion shall not be in order, and it shall not be in order to move to reconsider the vote by which the motion was agreed to or disagreed to.

(3) Withdrawals made pursuant to section 1714 of this title may be used in carrying out management decisions, but public lands shall be removed from or restored to the operation of the Mining Law of 1872, as amended (R.S. 2318–2352; 30 U.S.C. 21 et seq.) or transferred to another department, bureau, or agency only by withdrawal action pursuant to section 1714 of this title or other action pursuant to applicable law: *Provided*, That nothing in this section shall prevent a wholly owned Government corporation from acquiring and holding rights as a citizen under the Mining Law of 1872.

(f) Procedures applicable to formulation of plans and programs for public land management

The Secretary shall allow an opportunity for public involvement and by regulation shall establish procedures, including public hearings where appropriate, to give Federal, State, and local governments and the public, adequate notice and opportunity to comment upon and participate in the formulation of plans and programs relating to the management of the public lands.

(Pub. L. No. 94–579, Title II, § 202, 90 Stat. 2747 (Oct. 21, 1976); as amended by Pub. L. No. 113–287, § 5(*l*)(6), 128 Stat. 3271 (Dec. 19, 2014).)

HISTORICAL AND STATUTORY NOTES

References in Text

This Act, referred to in subsecs. (a) and (c)(9), is Pub. L. No. 94–579, 90 Stat. 2743 (Oct. 21, 1976), as amended, known as the Federal Land Policy and Management Act of 1976. For complete classification of this Act to the Code, see Tables.

The Act of September 3, 1964 (78 Stat. 897), as amended, referred to in subsec. (c)(9), is Pub. L. No. 88–578, 78 Stat. 897 (Sept. 3, 1964), as amended, known as the Land and Water Conservation Fund Act of 1965, which is codified generally as part B (section 460*l*–4 et seq.) of subchapter LXIX of chapter 1 of Title 16, Conservation. For complete classification of this Act to the Code, see Short Title note set out under section 460*l*–4 of Title 16 and Tables volume.

The Mining Law of 1872, as amended, referred to in subsec. (e)(3), is Act of May 10, 1872, c. 152, 17 Stat. 91, as amended, which was incorporated into the Revised Statutes of 1878 as R.S. §§ 2319 to 2328, 2331, 2333 to 2337, and 2344, which are codified as sections 22 to 24, 26 to 28, 29, 30, 33 to 35, 37, 39 to 42, and 47 of Title 30, Mineral Lands and Mining. For complete classification of R.S. §§ 2318–2352, see Tables volume.

Termination of Reporting Requirements

For termination of reporting provisions of subsec. (e)(2) of this section, effective May 15, 2000, see Pub. L. No. 104–66, § 3003, as amended, set out as a note under 31 U.S.C.A. § 1113, and page 112 of House Document No. 103–7.

§ 1713. Sales of public land tracts

[FLPMA § 203]

(a) Criteria for disposal; excepted lands

A tract of the public lands (except land in units of the National Wilderness Preservation System, National Wild and Scenic Rivers Systems, and National System of Trails) may be sold under this Act where, as a result of land use planning required under section 1712 of this title, the Secretary determines that the sale of such tract meets the following disposal criteria:

(1) such tract because of its location or other characteristics is difficult and uneconomic to manage as part of the public lands, and is not suitable for management by another Federal department or agency; or

(2) such tract was acquired for a specific purpose and the tract is no longer required for that or any other Federal purpose; or

(3) disposal of such tract will serve important public objectives, including but not limited to, expansion of communities and economic development, which cannot be achieved prudently or feasibly on land other than public land and which outweigh other public objectives and values, including, but not limited to, recreation and scenic values, which would be served by maintaining such tract in Federal ownership.

(b) Conveyance of land of agricultural value and desert in character

Where the Secretary determines that land to be conveyed under clause (3) of subsection (a) of this section is of agricultural value and is desert in character, such land shall be conveyed either under the sale authority of this section or in accordance with other existing law.

(c) Congressional approval procedures applicable to tracts in excess of two thousand five hundred acres

Where a tract of the public lands in excess of two thousand five hundred acres has been designated for sale, such sale may be made only after the end of the ninety days (not counting days on which the House of Representatives or the Senate has adjourned for more than three consecutive days) beginning on the day the Secretary has submitted notice of such designation to the Senate and the House of Representatives, and then only if the Congress has not adopted a concurrent resolution stating that such House does not approve of such designation. If the committee to which a resolution has been referred during the said ninety day period, has not reported it at the end of thirty calendar days after its referral, it shall be in order to either discharge the committee from further consideration of such resolution or to discharge the committee from consideration of any other resolution with respect to the designation. A motion to discharge may be made only by an individual favoring the resolution, shall be highly privileged (except that it may not be made after the committee has reported such a resolution), and debate thereon shall be limited to not more than one hour, to be divided equally between those favoring and those opposing the resolution. An amendment to the motion shall not be in order, and it shall not be in order to move to reconsider the vote by which the motion was agreed to or disagreed to. If the motion to discharge is agreed to or disagreed to, the motion may not be made with respect to any other resolution with respect to the same designation. When the committee has reprinted, or has been discharged from further consideration of a resolution, it shall at any time thereafter be in order (even though a previous motion to the same effect has been disagreed to) to move to proceed to the consideration of the resolution. The motion shall be highly privileged and shall not be debatable. An amendment to the motion shall not be in order, and it shall not be in order to move to reconsider the vote by which the motion was agreed to or disagreed to.

(d) Sale price

Sales of public lands shall be made at a price not less than their fair market value as determined by the Secretary.

(e) Maximum size of tracts

The Secretary shall determine and establish the size of tracts of public lands to be sold on the basis of the land use capabilities and development requirements of the lands; and, where any such tract which is judged by the Secretary to be chiefly valuable for agriculture is sold, its size shall be no larger than necessary to support a family-sized farm.

(f) Competitive bidding requirements

Sales of public lands under this section shall be conducted under competitive bidding procedures to be established by the Secretary. However, where the Secretary determines it necessary and proper in order (1) to assure equitable distribution among purchasers of lands, or (2) to recognize equitable considerations or public policies, including but not limited to, a preference to users, he may sell those lands with modified competitive bidding or without competitive bidding. In recognizing public policies, the Secretary shall give consideration to the following potential purchasers:

(1) the State in which the land is located;

(2) the local government entities in such State which are in the vicinity of the land;

(3) adjoining landowners;

(4) individuals; and

(5) any other person.

(g) Acceptance or rejection of offers to purchase

The Secretary shall accept or reject, in writing, any offer to purchase made through competitive bidding at his invitation no later than thirty days after the receipt of such offer or, in the case of a tract in excess of two thousand five hundred acres, at the end of thirty days after the end of the ninety-day period provided in subsection (c) of this section, whichever is later, unless the offeror waives his right to a decision within such thirty-day period. Prior to the expiration of such periods the Secretary may refuse to accept any offer or may withdraw any land or interest in land from sale under this section when he determines that consummation of the sale would not be consistent with this Act or other applicable law.

(Pub. L. No. 94–579, Title II, § 203, 90 Stat. 2750 (Oct. 21, 1976).)

HISTORICAL AND STATUTORY NOTES

References in Text

This Act, referred to in subsecs. (a) and (g), is Pub. L. No. 94–579, 90 Stat. 2743 (Oct. 21, 1976), as amended, known as the Federal Land Policy and Management Act of 1976. For complete classification of this Act to the Code, see Tables.

Termination of Reporting Requirements

For termination of reporting provisions of subsec. (c) of this section, effective May 15, 2000, see Pub. L. No. 104–66, § 3003, as amended, set out as a note under 31 U.S.C.A. § 1113, and pages 112 and 114 of House Document No. 103–7.

§ 1714. Withdrawals of lands

[FLPMA § 204]

(a) Authorization and limitation; delegation of authority

On and after the effective date of this Act the Secretary is authorized to make, modify, extend, or revoke withdrawals but only in accordance with the provisions and limitations of this section. The Secretary may delegate this withdrawal authority only to individuals in the Office of the Secretary who have been appointed by the President, by and with the advice and consent of the Senate.

(b) Application and procedures applicable subsequent to submission of application

(1) Within thirty days of receipt of an application for withdrawal, and whenever he proposes a withdrawal on his own motion, the Secretary shall publish a notice in the Federal Register stating that the application has been submitted for filing or the proposal has been made and the extent to which the land is to be segregated while the application is being considered by the Secretary. Upon publication of such notice the land shall be segregated from the operation of the public land laws to the extent specified in the notice. The segregative effect of the application shall terminate upon (a) rejection of the application by the Secretary, (b) withdrawal of lands by the Secretary, or (c) the expiration of two years from the date of the notice.

(2) The publication provisions of this subsection are not applicable to withdrawals under subsection (e) hereof.

(c) Congressional approval procedures applicable to withdrawals aggregating five thousand acres or more

(1) On and after October 21, 1976, a withdrawal aggregating five thousand acres or more may be made (or such a withdrawal or any other withdrawal involving in the aggregate five thousand acres or more which terminates after such date of approval may be extended) only for a period of not more than twenty years by the Secretary on his own motion or upon request by a department or agency head. The Secretary shall notify both Houses of Congress of such a withdrawal no later than its effective date and the withdrawal shall terminate and become ineffective at the end of ninety days (not counting days on which the Senate or the House of Representatives has adjourned for more than three consecutive days) beginning on the day notice of such withdrawal has been submitted to the Senate and the House of Representatives, if the Congress has adopted a concurrent resolution stating that such House does not approve the withdrawal. If the committee to which a resolution has been referred during the said ninety day period, has not reported it at the end of thirty calendar days after its referral, it shall be in order to either discharge the committee from further consideration of such resolution or to discharge the committee from consideration of any other resolution with respect to the Presidential recommendation. A motion to discharge may be made only by an individual favoring the resolution, shall be highly privileged (except that it may not be made after the committee has reported such a resolution), and debate thereon shall be limited to not more than one hour, to be divided equally between those favoring and those opposing the resolution. An amendment to the motion shall not be in order, and it shall not be in order to move to reconsider the vote by which the motion was agreed to or disagreed to. If the motion to discharge is agreed to or disagreed to, the motion may not be made with respect to any other resolution with respect to the same Presidential recommendation. When the committee has reprinted, or has been discharged from further consideration of a resolution, it shall at any time thereafter be in order (even though a previous motion to the same effect has been disagreed to) to move to proceed to the consideration of the resolution. The motion shall be highly privileged and shall not be debatable. An amendment to the motion shall not be in order, and it shall not be in order to move to reconsider the vote by which the motion was agreed to or disagreed to.

(2) With the notices required by subsection (c)(1) of this section and within three months after filing the notice under subsection (e) of this section, the Secretary shall furnish to the committees—

(1) a clear explanation of the proposed use of the land involved which led to the withdrawal;

(2) an inventory and evaluation of the current natural resource uses and values of the site and adjacent public and nonpublic land and how it appears they will be affected by the proposed use, including particularly aspects of use that might cause degradation of the environment, and also the economic impact of the change in use on individuals, local communities, and the Nation;

(3) an identification of present users of the land involved, and how they will be affected by the proposed use;

(4) an analysis of the manner in which existing and potential resource uses are incompatible with or in conflict with the proposed use, together with a statement of the provisions to be made for continuation or termination of existing uses, including an economic analysis of such continuation or termination;

(5) an analysis of the manner in which such lands will be used in relation to the specific requirements for the proposed use;

(6) a statement as to whether any suitable alternative sites are available (including cost estimates) for the proposed use or for uses such a withdrawal would displace;

(7) a statement of the consultation which has been or will be had with other Federal departments and agencies, with regional, State, and local government bodies, and with other appropriate individuals and groups;

(8) a statement indicating the effect of the proposed uses, if any, on State and local government interests and the regional economy;

(9) a statement of the expected length of time needed for the withdrawal;

(10) the time and place of hearings and of other public involvement concerning such withdrawal;

(11) the place where the records on the withdrawal can be examined by interested parties; and

(12) a report prepared by a qualified mining engineer, engineering geologist, or geologist which shall include but not be limited to information on: general geology, known mineral deposits, past and present mineral production, mining claims, mineral leases, evaluation of future mineral potential, present and potential market demands.

(d) Withdrawals aggregating less than five thousand acres; procedure applicable

A withdrawal aggregating less than five thousand acres may be made under this subsection by the Secretary on his own motion or upon request by a department or an agency head—

(1) for such period of time as he deems desirable for a resource use; or

(2) for a period of not more than twenty years for any other use, including but not limited to use for administrative sites, location of facilities, and other proprietary purposes; or

(3) for a period of not more than five years to preserve such tract for a specific use then under consideration by the Congress.

(e) Emergency withdrawals; procedure applicable; duration

When the Secretary determines, or when the Committee on Natural Resources of the House of Representatives or the Committee on Energy and Natural Resources of the Senate notifies the Secretary, that an emergency situation exists and that extraordinary measures must be taken to preserve values that would otherwise be lost, the Secretary notwithstanding the provisions of subsections (c)(1) and (d) of this section, shall immediately make a withdrawal and file notice of such emergency withdrawal with both of those Committees. Such emergency withdrawal shall be effective when made but shall last only for a period not to exceed three years and may not be extended except under the provisions of subsection (c)(1) or (d), whichever is applicable, and (b)(1) of this section. The information required in subsection (c)(2) of this subsection shall be furnished the committees within three months after filing such notice.

(f) Review of existing withdrawals and extensions; procedure applicable to extensions; duration

All withdrawals and extensions thereof, whether made prior to or after October 21, 1976, having a specific period shall be reviewed by the Secretary toward the end of the withdrawal period and may be extended or further extended only upon compliance with the provisions of subsection (c)(1) or (d) of this section, whichever is applicable, and only if the Secretary determines that the purpose for which the withdrawal was first made requires the extension, and then only for a period no longer than the length of the original withdrawal period. The Secretary shall report on such review and extensions to the Committee on Natural Resources of the House of Representatives and the Committee on Energy and Natural Resources of the Senate.

(g) Processing and adjudication of existing applications

All applications for withdrawal pending on October 21, 1976 shall be processed and adjudicated to conclusion within fifteen years of October 21, 1976, in accordance with the provisions of this section. The segregative effect of any application not so processed shall terminate on that date.

(h) Public hearing required for new withdrawals

All new withdrawals made by the Secretary under this section (except an emergency withdrawal made under subsection (e) of this section) shall be promulgated after an opportunity for a public hearing.

(i) Consent for withdrawal of lands under administration of department or agency other than Department of the Interior

In the case of lands under the administration of any department or agency other than the Department of the Interior, the Secretary shall make, modify, and revoke withdrawals only with the consent of the head of the department or agency concerned, except when the provisions of subsection (e) of this section apply.

(j) Applicability of other Federal laws withdrawing lands as limiting authority

The Secretary shall not make, modify, or revoke any withdrawal created by Act of Congress; make a withdrawal which can be made only by Act of Congress; modify or revoke any withdrawal creating national monuments under chapter 3203 of title 54, United States Code; or modify, or revoke any withdrawal which added lands to the National Wildlife Refuge System prior to October 21, 1976, or which thereafter adds lands to that System under the terms of this Act. Nothing in this Act is intended to modify or change any provision of the Act of February 27, 1976 (90 Stat. 199; 16 U.S.C. 668dd(a)).

(k) Authorization of appropriations for processing applications

There is hereby authorized to be appropriated the sum of $10,000,000 for the purpose of processing withdrawal applications pending on the effective date of this Act, to be available until expended.

(*l*) Review of existing withdrawals in certain States; procedure applicable for determination of future status of lands; authorization of appropriations

(1) The Secretary shall, within fifteen years of October 21, 1976, review withdrawals existing on October 21, 1976, in the States of Arizona, California, Colorado, Idaho, Montana, Nevada, New Mexico, Oregon, Utah, Washington, and Wyoming of (1) all Federal lands other than withdrawals of the public lands administered by the Bureau of Land Management and of lands which, on October 21, 1976, were part of Indian reservations and other Indian holdings, the National Forest System, the National Park System, the National Wildlife Refuge System, other lands administered by the Fish and Wildlife Service or the Secretary through the Fish and Wildlife Service, the National Wild and Scenic Rivers System, and the National System of Trails; and (2) all public lands administered by the Bureau of Land Management and of lands in the National Forest System (except those in wilderness areas, and those areas formally identified as primitive or natural areas or designated as national recreation areas) which closed the lands to appropriation under the Mining Law of 1872 (17 Stat. 91, as amended; 30 U.S.C. 22 et seq.) or to leasing under the Mineral Leasing Act of 1920 (41 Stat. 437, as amended; 30 U.S.C. 181 et seq.).

(2) In the review required by paragraph (1) of this subsection, the Secretary shall determine whether, and for how long, the continuation of the existing withdrawal of the lands would be, in his judgment, consistent with the statutory objectives of the programs for which the lands were dedicated and of the other relevant programs. The Secretary shall report his recommendations to the President, together with statements of concurrence or nonconcurrence submitted by the heads of the departments or agencies which administer the lands. The President shall transmit this report to the President of the Senate and the Speaker of the House of Representatives, together with his recommendations for action by the Secretary, or for legislation. The Secretary may act to terminate withdrawals other than those made by Act of the Congress in accordance with the recommendations of the President unless before the end of ninety days (not counting days on which the Senate and the House of Representatives has adjourned for more than three consecutive days) beginning on the day the report of the President has been submitted to the Senate and the House of Representatives the Congress has adopted a concurrent resolution indicating otherwise. If the committee to which a resolution has been referred during the said ninety day period, has not reported it at the end of thirty calendar days after its referral, it shall be in order to either discharge the committee from further consideration of such resolution or to discharge the committee from consideration of any other resolution with respect to the Presidential recommendation. A motion to discharge may be made only by an individual favoring the resolution, shall be highly privileged (except that it may not be made after the committee has reported such a resolution), and debate thereon shall be limited to not more than one hour, to be divided equally between those favoring and those opposing the resolution. An amendment to the motion shall not be in order, and it shall not be in order to move to reconsider the vote by which the motion was agreed to or disagreed to. If the motion to discharge is agreed to or disagreed to, the motion may not be made with respect to any other resolution with respect to the same Presidential recommendation. When the committee has reprinted, or has been discharged from further consideration of a resolution, it shall at any time thereafter be in order (even though a previous motion to the same effect has been disagreed to) to move to proceed to the consideration of the resolution. The motion shall be highly privileged and shall not be debatable. An amendment to the motion shall not be in order, and it shall not be in order to move to reconsider the vote by which the motion was agreed to or disagreed to.

(3) There are hereby authorized to be appropriated not more than $10,000,000 for the purpose of paragraph (1) of this subsection to be available until expended to the Secretary and to the heads of other departments and agencies which will be involved.

(Pub. L. No. 94–579, Title II, § 204, 90 Stat. 2751 (Oct. 21, 1976); as amended by Pub. L. No. 103–437, § 16(d)(1), 108 Stat. 4594 (Nov. 2, 1994); Pub. L. No. 113–287, § 5(*l*)(7), 128 Stat. 3271 (Dec. 19, 2014).)

HISTORICAL AND STATUTORY NOTES

References in Text

On and after the effective date of this Act, referred to in subsecs. (a) and (k), probably means on and after the date of enactment of Pub. L. No. 94–579, which was approved Oct. 21, 1976.

The Act of June 8, 1906, referred to in subsec. (j), is Act of June 8, 1906, c. 3060, 34 Stat. 225, popularly known as the Antiquities Act of 1906, which is codified generally as sections 431, 432, and 433 of Title 16, Conservation. For complete classification of this Act to the Code, see Short Title note set out under section 431 of Title 16 and Tables volume.

The Act of February 27, 1976 (90 Stat. 199; 16 U.S.C. 668dd(a)), referred to in subsec. (j), is Pub. L. No. 94–223, 90 Stat. 199 (Feb. 27, 1976), which amended section 668dd of Title 16, Conservation. For complete classification of this Act to the Code, see Tables volume.

This Act, referred to in subsec. (j), is Pub. L. No. 94–579, 90 Stat. 2743 (Oct. 21, 1976), as amended, known as the Federal Land Policy and Management Act of 1976. For complete classification of this Act to the Code, see Tables volume.

The Mining Law of 1872 (17 Stat. 91, as amended; 30 U.S.C. 22 et seq.), referred to in subsec. (*l*)(1), is Act of May 10, 1972, c. 152, 17 Stat. 91, as amended, which was incorporated into the Revised Statutes of 1878 as R.S. §§ 2319 to 2328, 2331, 2333 to 2337, and 2344, which are codified as sections 22 to 24, 26 to 28, 29, 30, 33 to 35, 37, 39 to 42, and 47 of Title 30, Mineral Lands and Mining. For complete classification of such Revised Statutes sections to the Code, see Tables volume.

The Mineral Leasing Act of 1920 (41 Stat. 437, as amended; 30 U.S.C. 181 et seq.), referred to in subsec. (*l*)(1), is Act of Feb. 25, 1920, c. 85, 41 Stat. 437, as amended, which is codified principally as chapter 3A (section 181 et seq.) of Title 30, Mineral Lands and Mining. For complete classification of this Act to the Code, see Short Title note set out under section 181 of Title 30 and Tables volume.

Termination of Reporting Requirements

For termination of reporting provisions of subsec. (c) of this section, effective May 15, 2000, see Pub. L. No. 104–66, § 3003, as amended, set out as a note under 31 U.S.C.A. § 1113, and page 112 of House Document No. 103–7.

§ 1715. Acquisitions of public lands and access over non-Federal lands to National Forest System units

[FLPMA § 205]

(a) Authorization and limitations on authority of Secretary of the Interior and Secretary of Agriculture

Notwithstanding any other provisions of law, the Secretary, with respect to the public lands and the Secretary of Agriculture, with respect to the acquisition of access over non-Federal lands to units of the National Forest System, are authorized to acquire pursuant to this Act by purchase, exchange, donation, or eminent domain, lands or interests therein: *Provided*, That with respect to the public lands, the Secretary may exercise the power of eminent domain only if necessary to secure access to public lands, and then only if the lands so acquired are confined to as narrow a corridor as is necessary to serve such purpose. Nothing in this subsection shall be construed as expanding or limiting the authority of the Secretary of Agriculture to acquire land by eminent domain within the boundaries of units of the National Forest System.

(b) Conformity to departmental policies and land-use plan of acquisitions

Acquisitions pursuant to this section shall be consistent with the mission of the department involved and with applicable departmental land-use plans.

(c) Status of lands and interests in lands upon acquisition by Secretary of the Interior; transfers to Secretary of Agriculture of lands and interests in lands acquired within National Forest System boundaries

Except as provided in subsection (e) of this section, lands and interests in lands acquired by the Secretary pursuant to this section or section 1716 of this title shall, upon acceptance of title, become public lands, and, for the administration of public land laws not repealed by this Act, shall remain public lands. If such acquired lands or interests in lands are located within the exterior boundaries of a grazing district established pursuant to section 315 of this title, they shall become a part of that district. Lands and interests in lands acquired pursuant to this section which are within boundaries of the National Forest System may be transferred to the Secretary of Agriculture and shall then become National Forest System lands and subject to all the laws, rules, and regulations applicable thereto.

(d) Status of lands and interests in lands upon acquisition by Secretary of Agriculture

Lands and interests in lands acquired by the Secretary of Agriculture pursuant to this section shall, upon acceptance of title, become National Forest System lands subject to all the laws, rules, and regulations applicable thereto.

(e) Status and administration of lands acquired in exchange for lands revested in or reconveyed to United States

Lands acquired by the Secretary pursuant to this section or section 1716 of this title in exchange for lands which were revested in the United States pursuant to the provisions of the Act of June 9, 1916 (39 Stat. 218) or reconveyed to the United States pursuant to the provisions of the Act of February 26, 1919 (40 Stat. 1179), shall be considered for all purposes to have the same status as, and shall be administered in accordance with the same provisions of law applicable to, the revested or reconveyed lands exchanged for the lands acquired by the Secretary.

(Pub. L. No. 94–579, Title II, § 205, 90 Stat. 2755 (Oct. 21, 1976); as amended by Pub. L. No. 99–632, § 5, 100 Stat. 3521 (Nov. 7, 1986).)

HISTORICAL AND STATUTORY NOTES

References in Text

This Act, referred to in subsecs. (a) and (c), is Pub. L. No. 94–579, 90 Stat. 2743 (Oct. 21, 1976), as amended, known as the Federal Land Policy and Management Act of 1976. For complete classification of this Act to the Code, see Tables.

The public land laws, referred to in subsec. (c), are codified generally into this title.

The Act of June 9, 1916 (39 Stat. 218), referred to in subsec. (e), was not codified into the Code.

The Act of February 26, 1919 (40 Stat. 1179), referred to in subsec. (e), probably means Act of Feb. 26, 1919, c. 47, 40 Stat. 1179, which was not codified into the Code.

§ 1716. Exchanges of public lands or interests therein within the National Forest System

[FLPMA § 206]

(a) Authorization and limitations on authority of Secretary of the Interior and Secretary of Agriculture

A tract of public land or interests therein may be disposed of by exchange by the Secretary under this Act and a tract of land or interests therein within the National Forest System may be disposed of by exchange by the Secretary of Agriculture under applicable law where the Secretary concerned determines that the public interest will be well served by making that exchange: *Provided,* That when considering public interest the Secretary concerned shall give full consideration to better Federal land management and the needs of State and local people, including needs for lands for the economy, community expansion, recreation areas, food, fiber, minerals, and fish and wildlife and the Secretary concerned finds that the values and the objectives which Federal lands or interests to be conveyed may serve if retained in Federal ownership are not more than the values of the non-Federal lands or interests and the public objectives they could serve if acquired.

(b) Implementation requirements; cash equalization waiver

In exercising the exchange authority granted by subsection (a) of this section or by section 1715(a) of this title, the Secretary concerned may accept title to any non-Federal land or interests therein in exchange for such land, or interests therein which he finds proper for transfer out of Federal ownership and which are located in the same State as the non-Federal land or interest to be acquired. For the purposes of this subsection, unsurveyed school sections which, upon survey by the Secretary, would become State lands, shall be considered as "non-Federal lands". The values of the lands exchanged by the Secretary under this

Act and by the Secretary of Agriculture under applicable law relating to lands within the National Forest System either shall be equal, or if they are not equal, the values shall be equalized by the payment of money to the grantor or to the Secretary concerned as the circumstances require so long as payment does not exceed 25 per centum of the total value of the lands or interests transferred out of Federal ownership. The Secretary concerned and the other party or parties involved in the exchange may mutually agree to waive the requirement for the payment of money to equalize values where the Secretary concerned determines that the exchange will be expedited thereby and that the public interest will be better served by such a waiver of cash equalization payments and where the amount to be waived is no more than 3 per centum of the value of the lands being transferred out of Federal ownership or $15,000, whichever is less, except that the Secretary of Agriculture shall not agree to waive any such requirement for payment of money to the United States. The Secretary concerned shall try to reduce the amount of the payment of money to as small an amount as possible.

(c) Status of lands acquired upon exchange by Secretary of the Interior

Lands acquired by the Secretary by exchange under this section which are within the boundaries of any unit of the National Forest System, National Park System, National Wildlife Refuge System, National Wild and Scenic Rivers System, National Trails System, National Wilderness Preservation System, or any other system established by Act of Congress, or the boundaries of the California Desert Conservation Area, or the boundaries of any national conservation area or national recreation area established by Act of Congress, upon acceptance of title by the United States shall immediately be reserved for and become a part of the unit or area within which they are located, without further action by the Secretary, and shall thereafter be managed in accordance with all laws, rules, and regulations applicable to such unit or area.

(d) Appraisal of land; submission to arbitrator; determination to proceed or withdraw from exchange; use of other valuation process; suspension of deadlines

(1) No later than ninety days after entering into an agreement to initiate an exchange of land or interests therein pursuant to this Act or other applicable law, the Secretary concerned and other party or parties involved in the exchange shall arrange for appraisal (to be completed within a time frame and under such terms as are negotiated by the parties) of the lands or interests therein involved in the exchange in accordance with subsection (f) of this section.

(2) If within one hundred and eighty days after the submission of an appraisal or appraisals for review and approval by the Secretary concerned, the Secretary concerned and the other party or parties involved cannot agree to accept the findings of an appraisal or appraisals, the appraisal or appraisals shall be submitted to an arbitrator appointed by the Secretary from a list of arbitrators submitted to him by the American Arbitration Association for arbitration to be conducted in accordance with the real estate valuation arbitration rules of the American Arbitration Association. Such arbitration shall be binding for a period of not to exceed two years on the Secretary concerned and the other party or parties involved in the exchange insofar as concerns the value of the lands which were the subject of the appraisal or appraisals.

(3) Within thirty days after the completion of the arbitration, the Secretary concerned and the other party or parties involved in the exchange shall determine whether to proceed with the exchange, modify the exchange to reflect the findings of the arbitration or any other factors, or to withdraw from the exchange. A decision to withdraw from the exchange may be made by either the Secretary concerned or the other party or parties involved.

(4) Instead of submitting the appraisal to an arbitrator, as provided in paragraph (2) of this section, the Secretary concerned and the other party or parties involved in an exchange may mutually agree to employ a process of bargaining or some other process to determine the values of the properties involved in the exchange.

(5) The Secretary concerned and the other party or parties involved in an exchange may mutually agree to suspend or modify any of the deadlines contained in this subsection.

(e) Simultaneous issue of patents or titles

Unless mutually agreed otherwise by the Secretary concerned and the other party or parties involved in an exchange pursuant to this Act or other applicable law, all patents or titles to be issued for land or interests therein to be acquired by the Federal Government and lands or interest therein to be transferred out of Federal ownership shall be issued simultaneously after the Secretary concerned has taken any necessary steps to assure that the United States will receive acceptable title.

(f) New rules and regulations; appraisal rules and regulations; "costs and other responsibilities or requirements" defined

(1) Within one year after August 20, 1988, the Secretaries of the Interior and Agriculture shall promulgate new and comprehensive rules and regulations governing exchanges of land and interests therein pursuant to this Act and other applicable law. Such rules and regulations shall fully reflect the changes in law made by subsections (d) through (i) of this section and shall include provisions pertaining to appraisals of lands and interests therein involved in such exchanges.

(2) The provisions of the rules and regulations issued pursuant to paragraph (1) of this subsection governing appraisals shall reflect nationally recognized appraisal standards, including, to the extent appropriate, the Uniform Appraisal Standards for Federal Land Acquisitions: *Provided, however,* That the provisions of such rules and regulations shall—

(A) ensure that the same nationally approved appraisal standards are used in appraising lands or interest therein being acquired by the Federal Government and appraising lands or interests therein being transferred out of Federal ownership; and

(B) with respect to costs or other responsibilities or requirements associated with land exchanges—

(i) recognize that the parties involved in an exchange may mutually agree that one party (or parties) will assume, without compensation, all or part of certain costs or other responsibilities or requirements ordinarily borne by the other party or parties; and

(ii) also permit the Secretary concerned, where such Secretary determines it is in the public interest and it is in the best interest of consummating an exchange pursuant to this Act or other applicable law, and upon mutual agreement of the parties, to make adjustments to the relative values involved in an exchange transaction in order to compensate a party or parties to the exchange for assuming costs or other responsibilities or requirements which would ordinarily be borne by the other party or parties.

As used in this subparagraph, the term "costs or other responsibilities or requirements" shall include, but not be limited to, costs or other requirements associated with land surveys and appraisals, mineral examinations, title searches, archeological surveys and salvage, removal of encumbrances, arbitration pursuant to subsection (d) of this section, curing deficiencies preventing highest and best use, and other costs to comply with laws, regulations and policies applicable to exchange transactions, or which are necessary to bring the Federal or non-Federal lands or interests involved in the exchange to their highest and best use for the appraisal and exchange purposes. Prior to making any adjustments pursuant to this subparagraph, the Secretary concerned shall be satisfied that the amount of such adjustment is reasonable and accurately reflects the approximate value of any costs or services provided or any responsibilities or requirements assumed.

(g) Exchanges to proceed under existing laws and regulations pending new rules and regulations

Until such time as new and comprehensive rules and regulations governing exchange of land and interests therein are promulgated pursuant to subsection (f) of this section, land exchanges may proceed in accordance with existing laws and regulations, and nothing in the Act shall be construed to require any delay in, or otherwise hinder, the processing and consummation of land exchanges pending the promulgation of such new and comprehensive rules and regulations. Where the Secretary concerned and the party or parties involved in an exchange have agreed to initiate an exchange of land or interests therein prior to the day of enactment of such subsections, subsections (d) through (i) of this section shall not apply to such exchanges unless the Secretary concerned and the party or parties involved in the exchange mutually agree otherwise.

(h) Exchange of lands or interests of approximately equal value; conditions; "approximately equal value" defined

(1) Notwithstanding the provisions of this Act and other applicable laws which require that exchanges of land or interests therein be for equal value, where the Secretary concerned determines it is in the public interest and that the consummation of a particular exchange will be expedited thereby, the Secretary concerned may exchange lands or interests therein which are of approximately equal value in cases where—

(A) the combined value of the lands or interests therein to be transferred from Federal ownership by the Secretary concerned in such exchange is not more than $150,000; and

(B) the Secretary concerned finds in accordance with the regulations to be promulgated pursuant to subsection (f) of this section that a determination of approximately equal value can be made without formal appraisals, as based on a statement of value made by a qualified appraiser and approved by an authorized officer; and

(C) the definition of and procedure for determining "approximately equal value" has been set forth in regulations by the Secretary concerned and the Secretary concerned documents how such determination was made in the case of the particular exchange involved.

(2) As used in this subsection, the term "approximately equal value" shall have the same meaning with respect to lands managed by the Secretary of Agriculture as it does in the Act of January 22, 1983 (commonly known as the "Small Tracts Act").

(i) Segregation from appropriation under mining and public land laws

(1) Upon receipt of an offer to exchange lands or interests in lands pursuant to this Act or other applicable laws, at the request of the head of the department or agency having jurisdiction over the lands involved, the Secretary of the Interior may temporarily segregate the Federal lands under consideration for exchange from appropriation under the mining laws. Such temporary segregation may only be made for a period of not to exceed five years. Upon a decision not to proceed with the exchange or upon deletion of any particular parcel from the exchange offer, the Federal lands involved or deleted shall be promptly restored to their former status under the mining laws. Any segregation pursuant to this paragraph shall be subject to valid existing rights as of the date of such segregation.

(2) All non-Federal lands which are acquired by the United States through exchange pursuant to this Act or pursuant to other law applicable to lands managed by the Secretary of Agriculture shall be automatically segregated from appropriation under the public land law, including the mining laws, for ninety days after acceptance of title by the United States. Such segregation shall be subject to valid existing rights as of the date of such acceptance of title. At the end of such ninety day period, such segregation shall end and such lands shall be open to operation of the public land laws and to entry, location, and patent under the mining laws except to the extent otherwise provided by this Act or other applicable law, or appropriate actions pursuant thereto.

(Pub. L. No. 94–579, Title II, § 206, 90 Stat. 2756 (Oct. 21, 1976); as amended by Pub. L. No. 100–409, §§ 3, 9, 102 Stat. 1087, 1092 (Aug. 20, 1988).)

HISTORICAL AND STATUTORY NOTES

References in Text

This Act, referred to in subsecs. (a), (b), (d)(1), (e), (f)(1), (2)(B)(ii), (g), (h)(1), and (i), is Pub. L. No. 94–579, 90 Stat. 2743 (Oct. 21, 1976), as amended, known as the Federal Land Policy and Management Act of 1976. For complete classification of this Act to the Code, see Tables.

Act of January 22, 1983 (commonly known as the "Small Tracts Act"), referred to in subsec. (h)(2), is Pub. L. No. 97–465, 96 Stat. 2535 (Jan. 12, 1983), which enacted sections 521c to 521i of Title 16, Conservation, and amended section 484a of Title 16. For complete classification of this Act to the Code, see Tables.

The mining laws, referred to in subsec. (i), are codified generally into Title 30, Mineral Lands and Mining.

The public land laws, referred to in subsec. (i)(2), are codified generally into this title.

Savings Provisions

Section 5 of Pub. L. No. 100–409 provided that: "Nothing in this Act [see Short Title of 1988 Amendment note set out section 1701 of this title] shall be construed as amending the Alaska Native Claims Settlement Act (Public Law 92–203, as amended) [section 1601 et seq. of this title] or the Alaska National Interest Lands Conservation Act (Public Law 96–487, as amended) [Pub. L. No. 96–487, 94 Stat. 2371 (Dec. 2, 1980), see Short Title note set out under section 3101 of Title 16, Conservation] or as enlarging or diminishing the authority with regard to exchanges conferred upon either the Secretary of the Interior or the Secretary of Agriculture by either such Acts. If any provision of this Act or the application thereof is held invalid, the remainder of the Act and the application thereof shall not be affected thereby. Nothing in this Act shall be construed to change the discretionary nature of land exchanges or to prohibit the Secretary concerned or any other party or parties involved in a land exchange from withdrawing from the exchange at any time, unless the Secretary concerned and the other party or parties specifically commit otherwise by written agreement."

Congressional Statement of Findings and Purposes

Section 2 of Pub. L. No. 100–409 provided that:

"(a) Findings.—The Congress finds and declares that—

"(1) land exchanges are a very important tool for Federal and State land managers and private landowners to consolidate Federal, State, and private holdings of land or interests in land for purposes of more efficient management and to secure important objectives including the protection of fish and wildlife habitat and aesthetic values; the enhancement of recreation opportunities; the consolidation of mineral and timber holdings for more logical and efficient development; the expansion of communities; the promotion of multiple-use values; and fulfillment of public needs;

"(2) needs for land ownership adjustments and consolidation consistently outpace available funding for land purchases by the Federal Government and thereby make land exchanges an increasingly important method of land acquisition and consolidation for both Federal and State land managers and private landowners;

"(3) the Federal Land Policy and Management Act of 1976 [Pub. L. No. 94–579, see Short Title note set out under section 1701 of this title] and other laws provide a basic framework and authority for land exchanges involving lands under the jurisdiction of the Secretary of the Interior and the Secretary of Agriculture; and

"(4) such existing laws are in need of certain revisions to streamline and facilitate land exchange procedures and expedite exchanges.

"(b) Purposes.—The purposes of this Act [see Short Title of 1988 Amendment note set out under section 1701 of this title] are:

"(1) to facilitate and expedite land exchanges pursuant to the Federal Land Policy and Management Act of 1976 and other laws applicable to exchanges involving lands managed by the Departments of the Interior and Agriculture by—

"(A) providing more uniform rules and regulations pertaining to land appraisals which reflect nationally recognized appraisal standards; and

"(B) establishing procedures and guidelines for the resolution of appraisal disputes.

"(2) to provide sufficient resources to the Secretaries of the Interior and Agriculture to ensure that land exchange activities can proceed consistent with the public interest; and

"(3) to require a study and report concerning improvements in the handling of certain information related to Federal and other lands."

Land Exchange Funding Authorization

Section 4 of Pub. L. No. 100–409 provided that: "In order to ensure that there are increased funds and personnel available to the Secretaries of the Interior and Agriculture to consider, process, and consummate land exchanges pursuant to the Federal Land Policy and Management Act of 1976 [Pub. L. No. 94–579, see Short Title note set out under section 1701 of this title] and other applicable law, there are hereby authorized to be appropriated for fiscal years 1989 through 1998 an annual amount not to exceed $4,000,000 which shall be used jointly or divided among the Secretaries as they determine appropriate for the consideration, processing, and consummation of land exchanges pursuant to the Federal Land Policy and Management Act of 1976, as amended, and other applicable law. Such moneys are expressly intended by Congress to be in addition to, and not offset against, moneys otherwise annually requested by the Secretaries, and appropriated by Congress for land exchange purposes."

§ 1717. Qualifications of conveyees

[FLPMA § 207]

No tract of land may be disposed of under this Act, whether by sale, exchange, or donation, to any person who is not a citizen of the United States, or in the case of a corporation, is not subject to the laws of any State or of the United States.

(Pub. L. No. 94–579, Title II, § 207, 90 Stat. 2757 (Oct. 21, 1976).)

HISTORICAL AND STATUTORY NOTES

References in Text

This Act, referred to in text, is Pub. L. No. 94–579, 90 Stat. 2743 (Oct. 21, 1976), as amended, known as the Federal Land Policy and Management Act of 1976. For complete classification of this Act to the Code, see Tables.

§ 1718. Documents of conveyance; terms, covenants, etc.

[FLPMA § 208]

The Secretary shall issue all patents or other documents of conveyance after any disposal authorized by this Act. The Secretary shall insert in any such patent or other document of conveyance he issues, except in the case of land exchanges, for which the provisions of subsection[1] 1716(b) of this title shall apply, such terms, covenants, conditions, and reservations as he deems necessary to insure proper land use and protection of the public interest: *Provided*, That a conveyance of lands by the Secretary, subject to such terms, covenants, conditions, and reservations, shall not exempt the grantee from compliance with applicable Federal or State law or State land use plans: *Provided further*, That the Secretary shall not make conveyances of public lands containing terms and conditions which would, at the time of the conveyance, constitute a violation of any law or regulation pursuant to State and local land use plans, or programs.

(Pub. L. No. 94–579, Title II, § 208, 90 Stat. 2757 (Oct. 21, 1976).)

[1] So in original. Probably should be "section."

HISTORICAL AND STATUTORY NOTES

References in Text

This Act, referred to in text, is Pub. L. No. 94–579, 90 Stat. 2743 (Oct. 21, 1976), as amended, known as the Federal Land Policy and Management Act of 1976. For complete classification of this Act to the Code, see Tables.

§ 1719. Mineral interests; reservation and conveyance requirements and procedures

[FLPMA § 209]

(a) All conveyances of title issued by the Secretary, except those involving land exchanges provided for in section 1716 of this title, shall reserve to the United States all minerals in the lands, together with the right to prospect for, mine, and remove the minerals under applicable law and such regulations as the Secretary may prescribe, except that if the Secretary makes the findings specified in subsection (b) of this section, the minerals may then be conveyed together with the surface to the prospective surface owner as provided in subsection (b) of this section.

(b) **(1)** The Secretary, after consultation with the appropriate department or agency head, may convey mineral interests owned by the United States where the surface is or will be in non-Federal ownership, regardless of which Federal entity may have administered the surface, if he finds (1) that there are no known mineral values in the land, or (2) that the reservation of the mineral rights in the United States is interfering with or precluding appropriate nonmineral development of the land and that such development is a more beneficial use of the land than mineral development.

(2) Conveyance of mineral interests pursuant to this section shall be made only to the existing or proposed record owner of the surface, upon payment of administrative costs and the fair market value of the interests being conveyed.

(3) Before considering an application for conveyance of mineral interests pursuant to this section—

(i) the Secretary shall require the deposit by the applicant of a sum of money which he deems sufficient to cover administrative costs including, but not limited to, costs of conducting an exploratory program to determine the character of the mineral deposits in the land, evaluating the data obtained under the exploratory program to determine the fair market value of the mineral interests to be conveyed, and preparing and issuing the documents of conveyance: *Provided*, That, if the administrative costs exceed the deposit, the applicant shall pay the outstanding amount; and, if the deposit exceeds the administrative costs, the applicant shall be given a credit for or refund of the excess; or

(ii) the applicant, with the consent of the Secretary, shall have conducted, and submitted to the Secretary the results of, such an exploratory program, in accordance with standards promulgated by the Secretary.

(4) Moneys paid to the Secretary for administrative costs pursuant to this subsection shall be paid to the agency which rendered the service and deposited to the appropriation then current.

(Pub. L. No. 94–579, Title II, § 209, 90 Stat. 2757 (Oct. 21, 1976).)

§ 1720. Coordination by Secretary of the Interior with State and local governments

[FLPMA § 210]

At least sixty days prior to offering for sale or otherwise conveying public lands under this Act, the Secretary shall notify the Governor of the State within which such lands are located and the head of the governing body of any political subdivision of the State having zoning or other land use regulatory jurisdiction in the geographical area within which such lands are located, in order to afford the appropriate body the opportunity to zone or otherwise regulate, or change or amend existing zoning or other regulations concerning the use of such lands prior to such conveyance. The Secretary shall also promptly notify such public officials of the issuance of the patent or other document of conveyance for such lands.

(Pub. L. No. 94–579, Title II, § 210, 90 Stat. 2758 (Oct. 21, 1976).)

HISTORICAL AND STATUTORY NOTES

References in Text

This Act, referred to in text, is Pub. L. No. 94–579, 90 Stat. 2743 (Oct. 21, 1976), as amended, known as the Federal Land Policy and Management Act of 1976. For complete classification of this Act to the Code, see Tables.

§ 1721. Conveyances of public lands to States, local governments, etc.

[FLPMA § 211]

(a) Unsurveyed islands; authorization and limitations on authority

The Secretary is authorized to convey to States or their political subdivisions under the Recreation and Public Purposes Act (44 Stat. 741 as amended; 43 U.S.C. 869 et seq.), as amended, but without regard to the acreage limitations contained therein, unsurveyed islands determined by the Secretary to be public lands of the United States. The conveyance of any such island may be made without survey: *Provided, however*, That such island may be surveyed at the request of the applicant State or its political subdivision if such State or subdivision donates money or services to the Secretary for such survey, the Secretary accepts such money or services, and such services are conducted pursuant to criteria established by the Director of the Bureau of Land Management. Any such island so surveyed shall not be conveyed without approval of such survey by the Secretary prior to the conveyance.

(b) Omitted lands; authorization and limitations on authority

(1) The Secretary is authorized to convey to States and their political subdivisions under the Recreation and Public Purposes Act [43 U.S.C.A. §§ 869 to 869–4], but without regard to the acreage limitations contained therein, lands other than islands determined by him after survey to be public lands of the United States erroneously or fraudulently omitted from the original surveys (hereinafter referred to as "omitted lands"). Any such conveyance shall not be made without a survey: *Provided,* That the prospective recipient may donate money or services to the Secretary for the surveying necessary prior to conveyance if the Secretary accepts such money or services, such services are conducted pursuant to criteria established by the Director of the Bureau of Land Management, and such survey is approved by the Secretary prior to the conveyance.

(2) The Secretary is authorized to convey to the occupant of any omitted lands which, after survey, are found to have been occupied and developed for a five-year period prior to January 1, 1975, if the Secretary determines that such conveyance is in the public interest and will serve objectives which outweigh all public objectives and values which would be served by retaining such lands in Federal ownership. Conveyance under this subparagraph shall be made at not less than the fair market value of the land, as determined by the Secretary, and upon payment in addition of administrative costs, including the cost of making the survey, the cost of appraisal, and the cost of making the conveyance.

(c) Conformity with land use plans and programs and coordination with State and local governments of conveyances

(1) No conveyance shall be made pursuant to this section until the relevant State government, local government, and areawide planning agency designated pursuant to section 204 of the Demonstration Cities and Metropolitan Development Act of 1966 (80 Stat. 1255, 1262) [42 U.S.C.A. § 3334] and/or section 6506 of Title 31 have notified the Secretary as to the consistency of such conveyance with applicable State and local government land use plans and programs.

(2) The provisions of section 1720 of this title shall be applicable to all conveyances under this section.

(d) Applicability of other statutory requirements for authorized use of conveyed lands

The final sentence of section 1(c) of the Recreation and Public Purposes Act [43 U.S.C.A. § 869(c)] shall not be applicable to conveyances under this section.

(e) Limitations on uses of conveyed lands

No conveyance pursuant to this section shall be used as the basis for determining the baseline between Federal and State ownership, the boundary of any State for purposes of determining the extent of a State's submerged lands or the line of demarcation of Federal jurisdiction, or any similar or related purpose.

(f) Applicability to lands within National Forest System, National Park System, National Wildlife Refuge System, and National Wild and Scenic Rivers System

The provisions of this section shall not apply to any lands within the National Forest System, defined in the Act of August 17, 1974 (88 Stat. 476; 16 U.S.C. 1601), the National Park System, the National Wildlife Refuge System, and the National Wild and Scenic Rivers System.

(g) Applicability to other statutory provisions authorizing sale of specific omitted lands

Nothing in this section shall supersede the provisions of the Act of December 22, 1928 (45 Stat. 1069; 43 U.S.C. 1068), as amended, and the Act of May 31, 1962 (76 Stat. 89), or any other Act authorizing the sale of specific omitted lands.

(Pub. L. No. 94–579, Title II, § 211, 90 Stat. 2758 (Oct. 21, 1976).)

HISTORICAL AND STATUTORY NOTES

References in Text

The Recreation and Public Purposes Act, referred to in subsecs. (a) and (b)(1), is Act of June 14, 1926, c. 578, 44 Stat. 741, as amended, which is codified as sections 869 to 869–4 of this title. For complete classification of this Act to the Code, see Short Title note set out under section 869 of this title and Tables.

The Act of August 17, 1974 (88 Stat. 476; 16 U.S.C. 1601), referred to in subsec. (f), is Pub. L. No. 93–378, 88 Stat. 476 (Aug. 17, 1974), as amended, known as the Forest and Rangelands Renewable Resources Planning Act of 1974, which is codified generally as subchapter I (section 1600 et seq.) chapter 36 of Title 16, Conservation. The provisions of such Act defining the lands within the National Forest System are set out in section 1609 of Title 16. For complete classification of this Act to the Code, see Short Title note set out under section 1600 of Title 16 and Tables volume.

The Act of December 22, 1928 (45 Stat. 1069; 43 U.S.C. 1068), as amended, referred to in subsec. (g), is Act of Dec. 22, 1928, c. 47, 45 Stat. 1069, as amended, which is codified generally as chapter 25A (section 1068 et seq.) of this title. For complete classification of this Act to the Code, see Tables volume.

The Act of May 31, 1962, referred to in subsec. (g), is Pub. L. No. 87–469, 76 Stat. 89 (May 31, 1962), which is not codified into the Code.

Codifications

In subsec. (c)(1), "section 6506 of Title 31" was substituted for "Title IV of the Intergovernmental Cooperation Act of 1968 (82 Stat. 1098, 1103–4) [42 U.S.C.A. § 4231 et seq.]" on authority of Pub. L. No. 97–258, § 4(b), 96 Stat. 1067 (Sept. 13, 1982), the first section of which enacted Title 31, Money and Finance.

§ 1722. Sale of public lands subject to unintentional trespass

[FLPMA § 214]

(a) Preference right of contiguous landowners; offering price

Notwithstanding the provisions of the Act of September 26, 1968 (82 Stat. 870; 43 U.S.C. 1431–1435), hereinafter called the "1968 Act", with respect to applications under the 1968 Act which were pending before the Secretary as of the effective date of this subsection and which he approves for sale under the criteria prescribed by the 1968 Act, he shall give the right of first refusal to those having a preference right under section 2 of the 1968 Act [43 U.S.C.A. § 1432]. The Secretary shall offer such lands to such preference right holders at their fair market value (exclusive of any values added to the land by such holders and their predecessors in interest) as determined by the Secretary as of September 26, 1973.

(b) Procedures applicable

Within three years after October 21, 1976, the Secretary shall notify the filers of applications subject to paragraph (a) of this section whether he will offer them the lands applied for and at what price; that is, their fair market value as of September 26, 1973, excluding any value added to the lands by the applicants or their predecessors in interest. He will also notify the President of the Senate and the Speaker of the House of Representatives of the lands which he has determined not to sell pursuant to paragraph (a) of this section and the reasons therefor. With respect to such lands which the Secretary determined not to sell, he shall take no other action to convey those lands or interests in them before the end of ninety days (not counting days on which the House of Representatives or the Senate has adjourned for more than three consecutive days) beginning on the date the Secretary has submitted such notice to the Senate and House of Representatives. If, during that ninety-day period, the Congress adopts a concurrent resolution stating the length of time such suspension of action should continue, he shall continue such suspension for the specified time period. If the committee to which a resolution has been referred during the said ninety-day period, has not reported it at the end of thirty calendar days after its referral, it shall be in order to either discharge the committee from further consideration of such resolution or to discharge the committee from consideration of any other resolution with respect to the suspension of action. A motion to discharge may be made only by an individual favoring the resolution, shall be highly privileged (except that it may not be made after the committee has reported such a resolution), and debate thereon shall be limited to not more than one hour, to be divided equally between those favoring and those opposing the resolution. An amendment to the motion shall not be in order, and it shall not be in order to move to reconsider the vote by which the motion was agreed to or disagreed to. If the motion to discharge is agreed to or disagreed to, the motion may not be made with respect to any other resolution with respect to the same suspension of action. When the committee has reprinted, or has been discharged from further consideration of a resolution, it shall at any time thereafter be in order (even though a previous motion to the same effect has been disagreed to) to move to proceed to the consideration of the resolution. The motion shall be highly privileged and shall not be debatable. An amendment to the motion shall not be in order, and it shall not be in order to move to reconsider the vote by which the motion was agreed to or disagreed to.

(c) Time for processing of applications and sales

Within five years after October 21, 1976, the Secretary shall complete the processing of all applications filed under the 1968 Act and hold sales covering all lands which he has determined to sell thereunder.

(Pub. L. No. 94–579, Title II, § 214, 90 Stat. 2760 (Oct. 21, 1976).)

HISTORICAL AND STATUTORY NOTES

References in Text

The Act of Sept. 26, 1968, referred to in subsec. (a), is Pub. L. No. 90–516, 82 Stat. 870 (Sept. 26, 1968), which was codified generally as subchapter VII (section 1431 et seq.) of chapter 30 of this title, and was omitted from the Code pursuant to section 1435 of this title, which provided that the authority granted by that subchapter was to expire three years from September 26, 1968, with certain exceptions. For complete classification of this Act to the Code prior to omission, see Tables.

The effective date of this subsection, referred to in subsec. (a), probably means the date of the enactment of such subsection (a) by Pub. L. No. 94–579, which was approved Oct. 21, 1976.

§ 1723. Temporary revocation authority

[FLPMA § 215]

(a) Exchange involved

When the sole impediment to consummation of an exchange of lands or interests therein (hereinafter referred to as an exchange) determined to be in the public interest, is the inability of the Secretary of the Interior to revoke, modify, or terminate part or all of a withdrawal or classification because of the order (or subsequent modification or continuance thereof) of the United States District Court for the District of Columbia dated February 10, 1986, in Civil Action No. 85–2238 (National Wildlife Federation v. Robert E. Burford, et al.), the Secretary of the Interior is hereby authorized, notwithstanding such order (or subsequent modification or continuance thereof), to use the authority contained herein, in lieu of other authority provided in this Act including section 1714 of this title, to revoke, modify, or terminate in whole or in part, withdrawals or classifications to the extent deemed necessary by the Secretary to enable the United States to transfer land or interests therein out of Federal ownership pursuant to an exchange.

(b) Requirements

The authority specified in subsection (a) of this section may be exercised only in cases where—

(1) a particular exchange is proposed to be carried out pursuant to this Act, as amended, or other applicable law authorizing such an exchange;

(2) the proposed exchange has been prepared in compliance with all laws applicable to such exchange;

(3) the head of each Federal agency managing the lands proposed for such transfer has submitted to the Secretary of the Interior a statement of concurrence with the proposed revocation, modification, or termination;

(4) at least sixty days have elapsed since the Secretary of the Interior has published in the Federal Register a notice of the proposed revocation, modification, or termination; and

(5) at least sixty days have elapsed since the Secretary of the Interior has transmitted to the Committee on Natural Resources of the House of Representatives and the Committee on Energy and Natural Resources of the United States Senate a report which includes—

(A) a justification for the necessity of exercising such authority in order to complete an exchange;

(B) an explanation of the reasons why the continuation of the withdrawal or a classification or portion thereof proposed for revocation, modification, or termination is no longer necessary for the purposes of the statutory or other program or programs for which the withdrawal or classification was made or other relevant programs;

(C) assurances that all relevant documents concerning the proposed exchange or purchase for which such authority is proposed to be exercised (including documents related to compliance with the National Environmental Policy Act of 1969 [42 U.S.C.A. § 4321 et seq.] and all other applicable provisions of law) are available for public inspection in the office of the Secretary concerned located nearest to the lands proposed for transfer out of Federal ownership in furtherance of such exchange and that the relevant portions of such documents are also available in the offices of the Secretary concerned in Washington, District of Columbia; and

(D) an explanation of the effect of the revocation, modification, or termination of a withdrawal or classification or portion thereof and the transfer of lands out of Federal ownership pursuant to the particular proposed exchange, on the objectives of the land management plan which is applicable at the time of such transfer to the land to be transferred out of Federal ownership.

(c) Limitations

(1) Nothing in this section shall be construed as affirming or denying any of the allegations made by any party in the civil action specified in subsection (a) of this section, or as constituting an expression of congressional opinion with respect to the merits of any allegation, contention, or argument made or issue raised by any party in such action, or as expanding or diminishing the jurisdiction of the United States District Court for the District of Columbia.

(2) Except as specifically provided in this section, nothing in this section shall be construed as modifying, terminating, revoking, or otherwise affecting any provision of law applicable to land exchanges, withdrawals, or classifications.

(3) The availability or exercise of the authority granted in subsection (a) of this section may not be considered by the Secretary of the Interior in making a determination pursuant to this Act or other applicable law as to whether or not any proposed exchange is in the public interest.

(d) Termination

The authority specified in subsection (a) of this section shall expire either (1) on December 31, 1990, or (2) when the Court order (or subsequent modification or continuation thereof) specified in subsection (a) of this section is no longer in effect, whichever occurs first.

(Pub. L. No. 94–579, Title II, § 215, as added by Pub. L. No. 100–409, § 10, 102 Stat. 1092 (Aug. 20, 1988); and amended by Pub. L. No. 103–437, § 16(d)(2), 108 Stat. 4595 (Nov. 2, 1994).)

HISTORICAL AND STATUTORY NOTES

References in Text

This Act, referred to in subsecs. (a), (b)(1), and (c)(3), is Pub. L. No. 94–579, 90 Stat. 2743 (Oct. 21, 1976), as amended, known as the Federal Land Policy and Management Act of 1976. For complete classification of this Act to the Code, see Tables.

The National Environmental Policy Act of 1969, referred to in subsec. (b)(5)(C), is Pub. L. No. 91–190, 83 Stat. 852 (Jan. 1, 1970), as amended, which is codified generally as chapter 55 (section 4321 et seq.) of Title 42, The Public Health and Welfare. For complete classification of this Act to the Code, see Short Title note set out under section 4321 of Title 42 and Tables.

Savings Provisions; Severability of Provisions

Nothing in Pub. L. No. 100–409 construed as amending the Alaska Native Claims Settlement Act, Pub. L. No. 92–203, or the Alaska National Interest Lands Conservation Act, Pub. L. No. 96–487, as enlarging or diminishing the authority with regard to exchanges conferred upon either the Secretary of the Interior or the Secretary of Agriculture by either such Acts, or as changing the discretionary nature of land exchanges or prohibiting the Secretary concerned or any other party or parties involved in a land exchange from withdrawing from the exchange at any time, unless the Secretary concerned and the other party or parties specifically commit otherwise by written agreement, with any provision of Pub. L. No. 100–409 or the application thereof being held invalid not affecting the remainder of Pub. L. No. 100–409 and the application thereof, see section 5 of Pub. L. No. 100–409, set out as a note under section 1716 of this title.

SUBCHAPTER III—ADMINISTRATION

§ 1731. Bureau of Land Management

[FLPMA § 301]

(a) Director; appointment, qualifications, functions, and duties

The Bureau of Land Management established by Reorganization Plan Numbered 3, of 1946 shall have as its head a Director. Appointments to the position of Director shall hereafter be made by the President, by and with the advice and consent of the Senate. The Director of the Bureau shall have a broad background and substantial experience in public land and natural resource management. He shall carry out such functions and shall perform such duties as the Secretary may prescribe with respect to the management of lands and resources under his jurisdiction according to the applicable provisions of this Act and any other applicable law.

(b) Statutory transfer of functions, powers and duties relating to administration of laws

Subject to the discretion granted to him by Reorganization Plan Numbered 3 of 1950, the Secretary shall carry out through the Bureau all functions, powers, and duties vested in him and relating to the administration of laws which, on October 21, 1976, were carried out by him through the Bureau of Land Management established by section 403 of Reorganization Plan Numbered 3 of 1946. The Bureau shall administer such laws according to the provisions thereof existing as of October 21, 1976, as modified by the provisions of this Act or by subsequent law.

(c) Associate Director, Assistant Directors, and other employees; appointment and compensation

In addition to the Director, there shall be an Associate Director of the Bureau and so many Assistant Directors, and other employees, as may be necessary, who shall be appointed by the Secretary subject to the provisions of Title 5 governing appointments in the competitive service, and shall be paid in accordance with the provisions of chapter 51 and subchapter 3[1] of chapter 53 of such title relating to classification and General Schedule pay rates.

(d) Existing regulations relating to administration of laws

Nothing in this section shall affect any regulation of the Secretary with respect to the administration of laws administered by him through the Bureau on October 21, 1976.

(Pub. L. No. 94–579, Title III, § 301, 90 Stat. 2762 (Oct. 21, 1976).)

[1] So in original. Probably should be subchapter "III."

HISTORICAL AND STATUTORY NOTES

References in Text

The provision of Reorg. Plan No. 3 of 1946 establishing the Bureau of Land Management, referred to in subsec. (a), is section 403 of such Reorg. Plan. Section 403 of Reorg. Plan No. 3 of 1946, also referred to in subsec. (b), is set out as a note under section 1 of this title.

This Act, referred to in subsecs. (a) and (b), is Pub. L. No. 94–579, 90 Stat. 2743 (Oct. 21, 1976), as amended, known as the Federal Land Policy and Management Act of 1976. For complete classification of this Act to the Code, see Tables volume.

Reorg. Plan No. 3 of 1950, referred to in subsec. (b), is set out under section 1451 of this title.

The provisions of Title 5, governing appointments in the competitive service, referred to in subsec. (c), are codified as section 3301 et seq. of Title 5, Government Organization and Employees.

The General Schedule, referred to in subsec. (c), is set out under section 5332 of Title 5.

Use of Appropriated Funds For Protection of Lands and Surveys of Federal Lands in Alaska

Pub. L. No. 102–381, Title I, 106 Stat. 1378 (Oct. 5, 1992), provided in part: "That appropriations herein made, in fiscal year 1993 and thereafter, may be expended for surveys of Federal lands and on a reimbursable basis for surveys of Federal lands and for protection of lands for the State of Alaska[.]".

§ 1732. Management of use, occupancy, and development of public lands

[FLPMA § 302]

(a) Multiple use and sustained yield requirements applicable; exception

The Secretary shall manage the public lands under principles of multiple use and sustained yield, in accordance with the land use plans developed by him under section 1712 of this title when they are available, except that where a tract of such public land has been dedicated to specific uses according to any other provisions of law it shall be managed in accordance with such law.

(b) Easements, permits, etc., for utilization through habitation, cultivation, and development of small trade or manufacturing concerns; applicable statutory requirements

In managing the public lands, the Secretary shall, subject to this Act and other applicable law and under such terms and conditions as are consistent with such law, regulate, through easements, permits, leases, licenses, published rules, or other instruments as the Secretary deems appropriate, the use, occupancy, and development of the public lands, including, but not limited to, long-term leases to permit individuals to utilize public lands for habitation, cultivation, and the development of small trade or manufacturing concerns: *Provided*, That unless otherwise provided for by law, the Secretary may permit Federal departments and agencies to use, occupy, and develop public lands only through rights-of-way under section 1767 of this title, withdrawals under section 1714 of this title, and, where the proposed use and development are similar or closely related to the programs of the Secretary for the public lands involved, cooperative agreements under section 1737(b) of this title: *Provided further*, That nothing in this Act shall be construed as authorizing the Secretary concerned to require Federal permits to hunt and fish on public lands or on lands in the National Forest System and adjacent waters or as enlarging or diminishing the responsibility and authority of the States for management of fish and resident wildlife. However, the Secretary concerned may designate areas of public land and of lands in the National Forest System where, and establish periods when, no hunting or fishing will be permitted for reasons of public safety, administration, or compliance with provisions of applicable law. Except in emergencies, any regulations of the Secretary concerned relating to hunting and fishing pursuant to this section shall be put into effect only after consultation with the appropriate State fish and game department. Nothing in this Act shall modify or change any provision of Federal law relating to migratory birds or to endangered or threatened species. Except as provided in section 1744, section 1782, and subsection (f) of section 1781 of this title and in the last sentence of this paragraph, no provision of this section or any other section of this Act shall in any way amend the Mining Law of 1872 or impair the rights of any locators or claims under that Act, including, but not limited to, rights of ingress and egress. In managing the public lands the Secretary shall, by regulation or otherwise, take any action necessary to prevent unnecessary or undue degradation of the lands.

(c) Revocation or suspension provision in instrument authorizing use, occupancy or development; violation of provision; procedure applicable

The Secretary shall insert in any instrument providing for the use, occupancy, or development of the public lands a provision authorizing revocation or suspension, after notice and hearing, of such instrument upon a final administrative finding of a violation of any term or condition of the instrument, including, but not limited to, terms and conditions requiring compliance with regulations under Acts applicable to the public lands and compliance with applicable State or Federal air or water quality standard or implementation plan: *Provided*, That such violation occurred on public lands covered by such instrument and occurred in connection with the exercise of rights and privileges granted by it: *Provided further*, That the Secretary shall terminate any such suspension no later than the date upon which he determines the cause of said violation has been rectified: *Provided further*, That the Secretary may order an immediate temporary suspension prior to a hearing or final administrative finding if he determines that such a suspension is necessary to protect health or safety or the environment: *Provided further*, That, where other applicable law contains specific provisions for suspension, revocation, or cancellation of a permit, license, or other authorization to use, occupy, or develop the public lands, the specific provisions of such law shall prevail.

(d) Authorization to utilize certain public lands in Alaska for military purposes

(1) The Secretary of the Interior, after consultation with the Governor of Alaska, may issue to the Secretary of Defense or to the Secretary of a military department within the Department of Defense or to the Commandant of the Coast Guard a nonrenewable general authorization to utilize public lands in Alaska (other than within a conservation system unit or the Steese National Conservation Area or the White Mountains National Recreation Area) for purposes of military maneuvering, military training, or equipment testing not involving artillery firing, aerial or other gunnery, or other use of live ammunition or ordnance.

(2) Use of public lands pursuant to a general authorization under this subsection shall be limited to areas where such use would not be inconsistent with the plans prepared pursuant to section 1712 of this title. Each such use shall be subject to a requirement that the using department shall be responsible for any necessary cleanup and decontamination of the lands used, and to such other terms and conditions (including but not limited to restrictions on use of off-road or all-terrain vehicles) as the Secretary of the Interior may require to—

(A) minimize adverse impacts on the natural, environmental, scientific, cultural, and other resources and values (including fish and wildlife habitat) of the public lands involved; and

(B) minimize the period and method of such use and the interference with or restrictions on other uses of the public lands involved.

(3) **(A)** A general authorization issued pursuant to this subsection shall not be for a term of more than three years and shall be revoked in whole or in part, as the Secretary of the Interior finds necessary, prior to the end of such term upon a determination by the Secretary of the Interior that there has been a failure to comply with its terms and conditions or that activities pursuant to such an authorization have had or might have a significant adverse impact on the resources or values of the affected lands.

(B) Each specific use of a particular area of public lands pursuant to a general authorization under this subsection shall be subject to specific authorization by the Secretary and to appropriate terms and conditions, including such as are described in paragraph (2) of this subsection.

(4) Issuance of a general authorization pursuant to this subsection shall be subject to the provisions of section 1712(f) of this title, section 3120 of Title 16, and all other applicable provisions of law. The Secretary of a military department (or the commandant of the Coast Guard) requesting such authorization shall reimburse the Secretary of the Interior for the costs of implementing this paragraph. An authorization pursuant to this subsection shall not authorize the construction of permanent structures or facilities on the public lands.

(5) To the extent that public safety may require closure to public use of any portion of the public lands covered by an authorization issued pursuant to this subsection, the Secretary of the military department concerned or the Commandant of the Coast Guard shall take appropriate steps to notify the public concerning such closure and to provide appropriate warnings of risks to public safety.

(6) For purposes of this subsection, the term "conservation system unit" has the same meaning as specified in section 3102 of Title 16.

(Pub. L. No. 94–579, Title III, § 302, 90 Stat. 2762 (Oct. 21, 1976); as amended by Pub. L. No. 100–586, 102 Stat. 2980 (Nov. 3, 1988).)

HISTORICAL AND STATUTORY NOTES

References in Text

This Act, referred to in subsec. (b), is Pub. L. No. 94–579, 90 Stat. 2743 (Oct. 21, 1976), as amended, known as the Federal Land Policy and Management Act of 1976. For complete classification of this Act to the Code, see Tables.

The Mining Law of 1872, referred to in subsec. (b), is Act of May 10, 1872, c. 152, 17 Stat. 91, which was incorporated into the Revised Statutes of 1878 as R.S. §§ 2319 to 2328, 2331, 2333 to 2337, and 2344, which are codified as sections 22 to 24, 26 to 28, 29, 30, 33 to 35, 37, 39 to 42, and 47 of Title 30, Mineral Lands and Mining. For complete classification of such Revised Statutes sections to the Code, see Tables volume.

Transfer of Functions

For transfer of authorities, functions, personnel, and assets of the Coast Guard, including the authorities and functions of the Secretary of Transportation relating thereto, to the Department of Homeland Security, and for treatment of related references, see 6 U.S.C.A. §§ 468(b), 551(d), 552(d) and 557, and the Department of Homeland Security Reorganization Plan of November 25, 2002, as modified, set out as a note under 6 U.S.C.A. § 542.

Enforcement functions of Secretary or other official in Department of Interior related to compliance with land use permits for temporary use of public lands and other associated land uses, issued under sections 1732, 1761, and 1763 to 1771 of this title, with respect preconstruction, construction, and initial operation of transportation systems for Canadian and Alaskan natural gas were transferred to the Federal Inspector, Office of Federal Inspector for the Alaska Natural Gas Transportation System, until the first anniversary of date of initial operation of the Alaska Natural Gas Transportation System, see Reorg. Plan No. 1 of 1979, §§ 102(e), 203(a), 44 Fed. Reg. 33663, 33666, 93 Stat. 1373, 1376, effective July 1, 1979, set out in Appendix 1 to Title 5, Government Organization and Employees.

§ 1733. Enforcement authority

[FLPMA § 303]

(a) Regulations for implementation of management, use, and protection requirements; violations; criminal penalties

The Secretary shall issue regulations necessary to implement the provisions of this Act with respect to the management, use, and protection of the public lands, including the property located thereon. Any person who knowingly and willfully violates any such regulation which is lawfully issued pursuant to this Act shall be fined no more than $1,000 or imprisoned no more than twelve months, or both. Any person charged with a violation of such regulation may be tried and sentenced by any United States magistrate judge designated for that purpose by the court by which he was appointed, in the same manner and subject to the same conditions and limitations as provided for in section 3401 of Title 18.

(b) Civil actions by Attorney General for violations of regulations; nature of relief; jurisdiction

At the request of the Secretary, the Attorney General may institute a civil action in any United States district court for an injunction or other appropriate order to prevent any person from utilizing public lands in violation of regulations issued by the Secretary under this Act.

(c) Contracts for enforcement of Federal laws and regulations by local law enforcement officials; procedure applicable; contract requirements and implementation

(1) When the Secretary determines that assistance is necessary in enforcing Federal laws and regulations relating to the public lands or their resources he shall offer a contract to appropriate local officials having law enforcement authority within their respective jurisdictions with the view of achieving maximum feasible reliance upon local law enforcement officials in enforcing such laws and regulations. The Secretary shall negotiate on reasonable terms with such officials who have authority to enter into such contracts to enforce such Federal laws and regulations. In the performance of their duties under such contracts such officials and their agents are authorized to carry firearms; execute and serve any warrant or other process issued by a court or officer of competent jurisdiction; make arrests without warrant or process for a misdemeanor he has reasonable grounds to believe is being committed in his presence or view, or for a felony if he has reasonable grounds to believe that the person to be arrested has committed or is committing such felony; search without warrant or process any person, place, or conveyance according to any Federal law or rule of law; and seize without warrant or process any evidentiary item as provided by Federal law. The Secretary shall provide such law enforcement training as he deems necessary in order to carry out the contracted for responsibilities. While exercising the powers and authorities provided by such contract pursuant to this section, such law enforcement officials and their agents shall have all the immunities of Federal law enforcement officials.

(2) The Secretary may authorize Federal personnel or appropriate local officials to carry out his law enforcement responsibilities with respect to the public lands and their resources. Such designated personnel shall receive the training and have the responsibilities and authority provided for in paragraph (1) of this subsection.

(d) Cooperation with regulatory and law enforcement officials of any State or political subdivision in enforcement of laws or ordinances

In connection with the administration and regulation of the use and occupancy of the public lands, the Secretary is authorized to cooperate with the regulatory and law enforcement officials of any State or political subdivision thereof in the enforcement of the laws or ordinances of such State or subdivision. Such cooperation may include reimbursement to a State or its subdivision for expenditures incurred by it in connection with activities which assist in the administration and regulation of use and occupancy of the public lands.

(e) Uniformed desert ranger force in California Desert Conservation Area; establishment; enforcement of Federal laws and regulations

Nothing in this section shall prevent the Secretary from promptly establishing a uniformed desert ranger force in the California Desert Conservation Area established pursuant to section 1781 of this title for the purpose of enforcing Federal laws and regulations relating to the public lands and resources managed by him in such area. The officers and members of such ranger force shall have the same responsibilities and authority as provided for in paragraph (1) of subsection (c) of this section.

(f) Applicability of other Federal enforcement provisions

Nothing in this Act shall be construed as reducing or limiting the enforcement authority vested in the Secretary by any other statute.

(g) Unlawful activities

The use, occupancy, or development of any portion of the public lands contrary to any regulation of the Secretary or other responsible authority, or contrary to any order issued pursuant to any such regulation, is unlawful and prohibited.

(Pub. L. No. 94–579, Title III, § 303, 90 Stat. 2763 (Oct. 21, 1976); as amended by Pub. L. No. 101–650, Title III, § 321, 104 Stat. 5117 (Dec. 1, 1990).)

HISTORICAL AND STATUTORY NOTES

References in Text

This Act, referred to in subsecs. (a), (b), and (f), is Pub. L. No. 94–579, 90 Stat. 2743 (Oct. 21, 1976), as amended, known as the Federal Land Policy and Management Act of 1976. For complete classification of this Act to the Code, see Tables.

Change of Name

United States magistrate appointed under section 631 of Title 28, Judiciary and Judicial Procedure, to be known as United States magistrate judge after Dec. 1, 1990, with any reference to United States magistrate or magistrate in Title 28, in any other Federal statute, etc., deemed a reference to United States magistrate judge appointed under section 631 of Title 28, see section 321 of Pub. L. No. 101–650, set out as a note under section 631 of Title 28.

Modification of Regulations Relating to Mining Operations on Public Lands; Posting of Reclamation Bond for All Operations Involving Significant Surface Disturbance

Pub. L. No. 99–500, Title I, § 101(h) [Title I, § 100], 100 Stat. 1783–243 (Oct. 18, 1986); as amended by Pub. L. No. 99–591, Title I, § 101(h) [Title I, § 100], 100 Stat. 3341–243 (Oct. 30, 1986), provided: "That regulations pertaining to mining operations on public lands conducted under the Mining Law of 1872 (30 U.S.C. 22, et seq.) [30 U.S.C.A. §§ 22 to 24, 26 to 28, 29, 30, 33 to 35, 37, 39 to 42, 47] and sections 302, 303, and 603 of the Federal Land Policy and Management Act of 1976 (43 U.S.C. 1732, 1733, and 1782) [sections 1732, 1733, and 1782 of this title] shall be modified to include a requirement for the posting of reclamation bonds by operators for all operations which involve significant surface disturbance, (a) at the discretion of the authorized officer for operators who have a record of compliance with pertinent regulations concerning mining on public lands, and (b) on a mandatory basis only for operators with a history of noncompliance with the aforesaid regulations: *Provided further,* That surety bonds, third party surety bonds, or irrevocable letters of credits shall qualify as bond instruments: *Provided further,* That evidence of an equivalent bond posted with a State agency shall be accepted in lieu of a separate bond: *Provided further,* That the amount of such bonds shall be sufficient to cover the costs of reclamation as estimated by the Bureau of Land Management."

§ 1734. Fees, charges, and commissions

[FLPMA § 304]

(a) Authority to establish and modify

Notwithstanding any other provision of law, the Secretary may establish reasonable filing and service fees and reasonable charges, and commissions with respect to applications and other documents relating to the public lands and may change and abolish such fees, charges, and commissions.

(b) Deposits for payments to reimburse reasonable costs of United States

The Secretary is authorized to require a deposit of any payments intended to reimburse the United States for reasonable costs with respect to applications and other documents relating to such lands. The moneys received for reasonable costs under this subsection shall be deposited with the Treasury in a special account and are hereby authorized to be appropriated and made available until expended. As used in this section "reasonable costs" include, but are not limited to, the costs of special studies; environmental impact statements; monitoring construction, operation, maintenance, and termination of any authorized facility; or other special activities. In determining whether costs are reasonable under this section, the Secretary may take into consideration actual costs (exclusive of management overhead), the monetary value of the rights or privileges sought by the applicant, the efficiency to the government processing involved, that portion of the cost incurred for the benefit of the general public interest rather than for the exclusive benefit of the applicant, the public service provided, and other factors relevant to determining the reasonableness of the costs.

(c) Refunds

In any case where it shall appear to the satisfaction of the Secretary that any person has made a payment under any statute relating to the sale, lease, use, or other disposition of public lands which is not required or is in excess of the amount required by applicable law and the regulations issued by the Secretary, the Secretary, upon application or otherwise, may cause a refund to be made from applicable funds.

(Pub. L. No. 94–579, Title III, § 304, 90 Stat. 2765 (Oct. 21, 1976).)

HISTORICAL AND STATUTORY NOTES

Filing Fees for Applications for Non-competitive Oil and Gas Leases; Study and Report of Rental Charges on Oil and Gas Leases

Pub. L. No. 97–35, Title XIV, § 1401(d), 95 Stat. 748 (Aug. 13, 1981), provided that:

"**(1)** Notwithstanding any other provision of law, effective October 1, 1981, all applications for noncompetitive oil and gas leases shall be accompanied by a filing fee of not less than $25 for each such application: *Provided,* That any increase in the filing fee above $25 shall be established by regulation and subject to the provisions of the Act of August 31, 1951 (65 Stat. 290) [probably means Title V of that Act which was codified as section 483a of former Title 31, Money and Finance and was repealed and reenacted as section 9701 of Title 31 by Pub. L. No. 97–258] the Act of October 20, 1976 (90 Stat. 2765) [probably should be Oct. 21, 1976, meaning this chapter] but not limited to actual costs. Such fees shall be retained as a service charge even though the application or offer may be rejected or withdrawn in whole or in part.

"**(2)** The Secretary of the Interior is hereby directed to conduct a study and report to Congress within one year of the date of enactment of this Act [Aug. 13, 1981], regarding the current annual rental charges on all noncompetitive oil and gas leases to investigate the feasibility and effect of raising such rentals."

§ 1734a. Availability of excess fees

In fiscal year 1997 and thereafter, all fees, excluding mining claim fees, in excess of the fiscal year 1996 collections established by the Secretary of the Interior under the authority of section 1734 of this title for processing, recording, or documenting authorizations to use public lands or public land natural resources (including cultural, historical, and mineral) and for providing specific services to public land users, and which are not presently being covered into any Bureau of Land Management appropriation accounts, and not otherwise dedicated by law for a specific distribution, shall be made immediately available for program operations in this account and remain available until expended.

(Pub. L. No. 104–208, Div. A, Title I, § 101(d) [Title I], 110 Stat. 3009–182 (Sept. 30, 1996).)

HISTORICAL AND STATUTORY NOTES

Codifications

This section was enacted as part of the Department of the Interior and Related Agencies Appropriations Act, 1997, and not as part of the Federal Land Policy and Management Act of 1976, Pub. L. No. 94–579, which comprises this chapter.

§ 1735. Forfeitures and deposits

[FLPMA § 305]

(a) Credit to separate account in Treasury; appropriation and availability

Any moneys received by the United States as a result of the forfeiture of a bond or other security by a resource developer or purchaser or permittee who does not fulfill the requirements of his contract or permit or does not comply with the regulations of the Secretary; or as a result of a compromise or settlement of any claim whether sounding in tort or in contract involving present or potential damage to the public lands shall be credited to a separate account in the Treasury and are hereby authorized to be appropriated and made available, until expended as the Secretary may direct, to cover the cost to the United States of any improvement, protection, or rehabilitation work on those public lands which has been rendered necessary by the action which has led to the forfeiture, compromise, or settlement.

(b) Expenditure of moneys collected administering Oregon and California Railroad and Coos Bay Wagon Road Grant lands

Any moneys collected under this Act in connection with lands administered under the Act of August 28, 1937 (50 Stat. 874; 43 U.S.C. 1181a–1181j), shall be expended for the benefit of such land only.

(c) Refunds

If any portion of a deposit or amount forfeited under this Act is found by the Secretary to be in excess of the cost of doing the work authorized under this Act, the Secretary, upon application or otherwise, may cause a refund of the amount in excess to be made from applicable funds.

(Pub. L. No. 94–579, Title III, § 305, 90 Stat. 2765 (Oct. 21, 1976).)

HISTORICAL AND STATUTORY NOTES

References in Text

This Act, referred to in subsecs. (b) and (c), is Pub. L. No. 94–579, 90 Stat. 2743 (Oct. 21, 1976), as amended, known as the Federal Land Policy and Management Act of 1976. For complete classification of this Act to the Code, see Tables.

The Act of Aug. 28, 1937 (50 Stat. 874; 43 U.S.C. 1181a–1181j), referred to in subsec. (b), is Act of Aug. 28, 1937, c. 876, 50 Stat. 874, as amended, which enacted sections 1181a to 1181f of this title. Sections 1181f–1 to 1181f–4, included within the parenthetical reference to sections 1181a to 1181j, were enacted by Act of May 24, 1939, c. 144, 53 Stat. 753. Sections 1181g to 1181j, also included within the parenthetical reference to sections 1181a to 1181j, were enacted by Act of June 24, 1954, c. 357, 68 Stat. 270. For complete classification of these Acts to the Code, see Tables.

Service Charges, Deposits, and Forfeitures:

Pub. L. No. No. 113–76, 128 Stat. 290–91 (Jan. 17, 2014), provided that:

For administrative expenses and other costs related to processing application documents and other authorizations for use and disposal of public lands and resources, for costs of providing copies of official public land documents, for monitoring construction, operation, and termination of facilities in conjunction with use authorizations, and for rehabilitation of damaged property, such amounts as may be collected under Public Law 94–579 (43 U.S.C. 1701 et seq.), and under section 28 of the Mineral Leasing Act (30 U.S.C. 185), to remain available until expended: *Provided*, That, notwithstanding any provision to the contrary of section 305(a) of Public Law 94–579 (43 U.S.C. 1735(a)), any moneys that have been or will be received pursuant to that section, whether as a result of forfeiture, compromise, or settlement, if not appropriate for refund pursuant to section 305(c) of that Act (43 U.S.C. 1735(c)), shall be available and may be expended under the authority of this Act by the Secretary to improve, protect, or rehabilitate any public lands administered through the Bureau of Land Management which have been damaged by the action of a resource developer, purchaser, permittee, or any unauthorized person, without regard to whether all moneys collected from each such action are used on the exact lands damaged which led to the action: *Provided further*, That any such moneys that are in excess of amounts needed to repair damage to the exact land for which funds were collected may be used to repair other damaged public lands.

Similarly, Pub. L. No. No. 113–235, 128 Stat. 2398 (Dec. 16, 2014), provided that:

For administrative expenses and other costs related to processing application documents and other authorizations for use and disposal of public lands and resources, for costs of providing copies of official public land documents, for monitoring construction, operation, and termination of facilities in conjunction with use authorizations, and for rehabilitation of damaged property, such amounts as may be collected under Public Law 94–579 (43 U.S.C. 1701 et seq.), and under section 28 of the Mineral Leasing Act (30 U.S.C. 185), to remain available until expended: *Provided*, That, notwithstanding any provision to the contrary of section 305(a) of Public Law 94–579 (43 U.S.C. 1735(a)), any moneys that have been or will be received pursuant to that section, whether as a result of forfeiture, compromise, or settlement, if not appropriate for refund pursuant to section 305(c) of that Act (43 U.S.C. 1735(c)), shall be available and may be expended under the authority of this Act by the Secretary to improve, protect, or rehabilitate any public lands administered through the Bureau of Land Management which have been damaged by the action of a resource developer, purchaser, permittee, or any unauthorized person, without regard to whether all moneys collected from each such action are used on the exact lands damaged which led to the action: *Provided further*, That any such moneys that are in excess of amounts needed to repair damage to the exact land for which funds were collected may be used to repair other damaged public lands.

Similarly, Pub. L. No. 116–6, 133 Stat. 207–08 (Feb. 15, 2019), provided that:

For administrative expenses and other costs related to processing application documents and other authorizations for use and disposal of public lands and resources, for costs of providing copies of official public land documents, for monitoring construction, operation, and termination of facilities in conjunction with use authorizations, and for rehabilitation of damaged property, such amounts as may be collected under Public Law 94–579 (43 U.S.C. 1701 et seq.), and under section 28 of the Mineral Leasing Act (30 U.S.C. 185), to remain available until expended: Provided, That notwithstanding any provision to the contrary of section 305(a) of Public Law 94–579 (43 U.S.C. 1735(a)), any moneys that have been or will be received pursuant to that section, whether as a result of forfeiture, compromise, or settlement, if not appropriate for refund pursuant to section 305(c) of that Act (43 U.S.C. 1735(c)), shall be available and may be expended under the authority of this Act by the Secretary to improve, protect, or rehabilitate any public lands administered through the Bureau of Land Management which have been damaged by the action of a resource developer, purchaser, permittee, or any unauthorized person, without regard to whether all moneys collected from each such action are used on the exact lands damaged which led to the action: Provided further, That any such moneys that are in excess of amounts needed to repair damage to the exact land for which funds were collected may be used to repair other damaged public lands.

Similarly, Pub. L. No. 116–94, 133 Stat. 2688 (Dec. 20, 2019), provided that:

For administrative expenses and other costs related to processing application documents and other authorizations for use and disposal of public lands and resources, for costs of providing copies of official public land documents, for monitoring construction, operation, and termination of facilities in conjunction with use authorizations, and for rehabilitation of damaged property, such amounts as may be collected under Public Law 94–579 (43 U.S.C. 1701 et seq.), and under section 28 of the Mineral Leasing Act (30 U.S.C. 185), to remain available until expended: Provided, That notwithstanding any provision to the contrary of section 305(a) of Public Law 94–579 (43 U.S.C. 1735(a)), any moneys that have been or will be received pursuant to that section, whether as a result of forfeiture, compromise, or settlement, if not appropriate for refund pursuant to section 305(c) of that Act (43 U.S.C. 1735(c)), shall be available and may be expended under the authority of this Act by the Secretary to improve, protect, or rehabilitate any public lands administered through the Bureau of Land Management which have been damaged by the action of a resource developer, purchaser, permittee, or any unauthorized person, without regard to whether all moneys collected from each such action are used on the exact lands damaged which led to the action: Provided further, That any such moneys that are in excess of amounts needed to repair damage to the exact land for which funds were collected may be used to repair other damaged public lands.

Similarly, Pub. L. No. 116–260, 134 Stat. 1479–1480 (Dec. 27, 2020), provided that:

For administrative expenses and other costs related to processing application documents and other authorizations for use and disposal of public lands and resources, for costs of providing copies of official public land documents, for monitoring construction, operation, and termination of facilities in conjunction with use authorizations, and for rehabilitation of damaged property, such amounts as may be collected under Public Law 94–579 (43 U.S.C. 1701 et seq.), and under section 28 of the Mineral Leasing Act (30 U.S.C. 185), to remain available until expended: *Provided*, That notwithstanding any provision to the contrary of section 305(a) of Public Law 94–579 (43 U.S.C. 1735(a)), any moneys that have been or will be received pursuant to that section, whether as a result of forfeiture, compromise, or settlement, if not appropriate for refund pursuant to section 305(c) of that Act (43 U.S.C. 1735(c)), shall be available and may be expended under the authority of this Act by the Secretary of the Interior to improve, protect, or rehabilitate any public lands administered through the Bureau of Land Management which have been damaged by the action of a resource developer, purchaser, permittee, or any unauthorized person, without regard to whether all moneys collected from each such action are used on the exact lands damaged which led to the action: *Provided further*, That any such moneys that are in excess of amounts needed to repair damage to the exact land for which funds were collected may be used to repair other damaged public lands.

Of the unobligated balances from amounts collected in fiscal year 2015 or any prior fiscal year, $20,000,000 is permanently rescinded: *Provided*, That no amounts may be rescinded from amounts that were designated by the Congress as an emergency requirement pursuant to the Concurrent Resolution on the Budget or the Balanced Budget and Emergency Deficit Control Act of 1985.

Availability of Funds for Improvement, Protection, or Rehabilitation of Damaged Public Lands

Pub. L. No. 104–134, Title I, § 101(c) [Title I], 110 Stat. 1321–156, 1321–158 (Apr. 26, 1996); renumbered Title I by Pub. L. No. 104–140, § 1(a), 110 Stat. 1327 (May 2, 1996), provided in part: "That notwithstanding any provision to the contrary of section 305(a) of the Act of October 21, 1976 (43 U.S.C. 1735(a)), any moneys that have been or will be received pursuant to that section, whether as a result of forfeiture, compromise, or settlement, if not appropriate for refund pursuant to section 305(c) of that Act (43 U.S.C. 1735(c)), shall be available and may be expended under the authority of this or subsequent appropriations Acts by the Secretary to improve, protect, or rehabilitate any public lands administered through the Bureau of Land Management which have been damaged by the action of a resource developer, purchaser, permittee, or any unauthorized person, without regard to whether all moneys collected from each such forfeiture, compromise, or settlement are used on the exact lands damage to which led to the forfeiture, compromise, or settlement: Provided further, That such moneys are in excess of amounts needed to repair damage to the exact land for which collected."

Similar provisions were contained in the following Appropriations Acts:

Pub. L. No. 113–76, Div. G, Title I, 128 Stat. 291 (Jan. 17, 2014).

Pub. L. No. 112–74, Div. E, Title I, 125 Stat. 987 (Dec. 23, 2011).

Pub. L. No. 111–88, Div. A, Title I, 123 Stat. 2906 (Oct. 30, 2009).

Pub. L. No. 111–8, Div. E, Title I, 123 Stat. 703 (Mar. 11, 2009).

Pub. L. No. 110–161, Div. F, Title I, 121 Stat. 2099 (Dec. 26, 2007).

Pub. L. No. 109–54, Title I, 119 Stat. 502 (Aug. 2, 2005).

Pub. L. No. 108–447, Div. E, Title I, 118 Stat. 3042 (Dec. 8, 2004).

Pub. L. No. 108–108, Title I, 117 Stat. 1244 (Nov. 10, 2003).

Pub. L. No. 108–7, Div. F, Title I, 117 Stat. 219 (Feb. 20, 2003).

Pub. L. No. 107–63, Title I, 115 Stat. 418 (Nov. 5, 2001).

Pub. L. No. 106–291, Title I, 114 Stat. 925 (Oct. 11, 2000).

Pub. L. No. 106–113, Div. B, § 1000(a)(3) [Title I], 113 Stat. 1535, 1501A–138 (Nov. 29, 1999).

Pub. L. No. 105–277, Div. A, § 101(e) [Title I], 112 Stat. 2681–234 (Oct. 21, 1998).

Pub. L. No. 105–83, Title I, 111 Stat. 1545 (Nov. 14, 1997).

Pub. L. No. 104–208, Div. A, Title I, § 101(d) [Title I], 110 Stat. 3009–184 (Sept. 30, 1996).

Pub. L. No. 104–134, Title I, § 101(c)[Title I], 110 Stat. 1321–156, 1321–158 (Apr. 26, 1996); renumbered Title I by Pub. L. No. 104–140, § 1(a), 110 Stat. 1327 (May 2, 1996).

Pub. L. No. 103–332, Title I, 108 Stat. 2501 (Sept. 30, 1994).

Pub. L. No. 103–138, Title I, 107 Stat. 1381 (Nov. 11, 1993).

Pub. L. No. 102–381, Title I, 106 Stat. 1377 (Oct. 5, 1992).

Pub. L. No. 102–154, Title I, 105 Stat. 992 (Nov. 13, 1991).

Pub. L. No. 101–512, Title I, 104 Stat. 1917 (Nov. 5, 1990).

Pub. L. No. 101–121, Title I, 103 Stat. 703 (Oct. 23, 1989).

Pub. L. No. 100–446, Title I, 102 Stat. 1776 (Sept. 27, 1988).

Pub. L. No. 100–202, § 101(g) [Title I], 101 Stat. 1329–215 (Dec. 22, 1987).

§ 1736. Working capital fund

[FLPMA § 306]

(a) Establishment; availability of fund

There is hereby established a working capital fund for the management of the public lands. This fund shall be available without fiscal year limitation for expenses necessary for furnishing, in accordance with chapters 1 to 11 of Title 40 and division C (except sections 3302, 3307(e) 3501(b), 3509, 3906, 4710, and 4711) of subtitle I of Title 41, and regulations promulgated thereunder, supplies and equipment services in support of Bureau programs, including but not limited to, the purchase or construction of storage facilities, equipment yards, and related improvements and the purchase, lease, or rent of motor vehicles, aircraft, heavy equipment, and fire control and other resource management equipment within the limitations set forth in appropriations made to the Secretary for the Bureau.

(b) Initial funding; subsequent transfers

The initial capital of the fund shall consist of appropriations made for that purpose together with the fair and reasonable value at the fund's inception of the inventories, equipment, receivables, and other assets, less the liabilities, transferred to the fund. The Secretary is authorized to make such subsequent transfers to the fund as he deems appropriate in connection with the functions to be carried on through the fund.

(c) Payments credited to fund; amount; advancement or reimbursement

The fund shall be credited with payments from appropriations, and funds of the Bureau, other agencies of the Department of the Interior, other Federal agencies, and other sources, as authorized by law, at rates approximately equal to the cost of furnishing the facilities, supplies, equipment, and services (including depreciation and accrued annual leave). Such payments may be made in advance in connection with firm orders, or by way of reimbursement.

(d) Authorization of appropriations

There is hereby authorized to be appropriated a sum not to exceed $3,000,000 as initial capital of the working capital fund.

(Pub. L. No. 94–579, Title III, § 306, 90 Stat. 2766 (Oct. 21, 1976).)

HISTORICAL AND STATUTORY NOTES

Codifications

In subsec. (a), "chapters 1 to 11 of Title 40 and division C (except sections 3302, 3307(e) 3501(b), 3509, 3906, 4710, and 4711) of subtitle I of Title 41" was substituted for "the Federal Property and Administrative Services Act of 1949, as amended" on authority of Pub. L. No. 107–217, § 5(c), 116 Stat. 1303 (Aug. 21, 2002), which Act enacted Title 40, Public Buildings, Property, and Works, and Pub. L. No. 111–350, § 6(c), 124 Stat. 3854 (Jan. 4, 2011), which Act enacted Title 41, Public Contracts.

§ 1736a. Revolving fund derived from disposal of salvage timber

There is hereby established in the Treasury of the United States a special fund to be derived on and after October 5, 1992, from the Federal share of moneys received from the disposal of salvage timber prepared for sale from the lands under the jurisdiction of the Bureau of Land Management, Department of the Interior. The money in this fund shall be immediately available to the Bureau of Land Management without further appropriation, for the purposes of planning and preparing salvage timber for disposal, the administration of salvage timber sales, and subsequent site preparation and reforestation.

(Pub. L. No. 102–381, Title I, 106 Stat. 1376 (Oct. 5, 1992).)

HISTORICAL AND STATUTORY NOTES

Codifications

This section was enacted as part of the Department of the Interior and Related Agencies Appropriations Act, 1993, and not as part of the Federal Land Policy and Management Act of 1976, which comprises this chapter.

Distribution of Receipts

Title I of Pub. L. No. 102–381 provided in part that: "Nothing in this provision [this section] shall alter the formulas currently in existence by law for the distribution of receipts for the applicable lands and timber resources."

§ 1737. Implementation provisions

[FLPMA § 307]

(a) Investigations, studies, and experiments

The Secretary may conduct investigations, studies, and experiments, on his own initiative or in cooperation with others, involving the management, protection, development, acquisition, and conveying of the public lands.

(b) Contracts and cooperative agreements

Subject to the provisions of applicable law, the Secretary may enter into contracts and cooperative agreements involving the management, protection, development, and sale of public lands.

(c) Contributions and donations of money, services, and property

The Secretary may accept contributions or donations of money, services, and property, real, personal, or mixed, for the management, protection, development, acquisition, and conveying of the public lands, including the acquisition of rights-of-way for such purposes. He may accept contributions for cadastral surveying performed on federally controlled or intermingled lands. Moneys received hereunder shall be credited to a separate account in the Treasury and are hereby authorized to be appropriated and made available until expended, as the Secretary may direct, for payment of expenses incident to the function toward the administration of which the contributions were made and for refunds to depositors of amounts contributed by them in specific instances where contributions are in excess of their share of the cost.

(d) Recruitment of volunteers

The Secretary may recruit, without regard to the civil service classification laws, rules, or regulations, the services of individuals contributed without compensation as volunteers for aiding in or facilitating the activities administered by the Secretary through the Bureau of Land Management.

(e) Restrictions on activities of volunteers

In accepting such services of individuals as volunteers, the Secretary—

(1) shall not permit the use of volunteers in hazardous duty or law enforcement work, or in policymaking processes or to displace any employee; and

(2) may provide for services or costs incidental to the utilization of volunteers, including transportation, supplies, lodging, subsistence, recruiting, training, and supervision.

(f) Federal employment status of volunteers

Volunteers shall not be deemed employees of the United States except for the purposes of—

(1) the tort claims provisions of Title 28;

(2) subchapter 1[1] of chapter 81 of Title 5; and

(3) claims relating to damage to, or loss of, personal property of a volunteer incident to volunteer service, in which case the provisions of section 3721 of Title 31 shall apply.

(g) Authorization of appropriations

Effective with fiscal years beginning after September 30, 1984, there are authorized to be appropriated such sums as may be necessary to carry out the provisions of subsection (d) of this section, but not more than $250,000 may be appropriated for any one fiscal year.

(Pub. L. No. 94–579, Title III, § 307, 90 Stat. 2766 (Oct. 21, 1976); as amended by Pub. L. No. 98–540, § 2, 98 Stat. 2718 (Oct. 24, 1984); Pub. L. No. 101–286, Title II, § 204(c), 104 Stat. 175 (May 9, 1990).)

[1] So in original. Probably should be subchapter "I."

HISTORICAL AND STATUTORY NOTES

References in Text

The civil service classification laws, referred to in subsec. (d), probably should refer to civil service and classification laws. The civil service laws are set forth in Title 5, Government Organization and Employees. See, particularly, section 3301 et seq. of Title 5. The classification laws are set forth in chapter 51 and subchapter III of chapter 53 of Title 5.

The tort claims provisions of Title 28, referred to in subsec. (f), are the provisions of the Federal Tort Claims Act, which is codified generally as section 1346(b) and to chapter 171 (§ 2671 et seq.) of Title 28, Judiciary and Judicial Procedure.

§ 1738. Contracts for surveys and resource protection; renewals; funding requirements

[FLPMA § 308]

(a) The Secretary is authorized to enter into contracts for the use of aircraft, and for supplies and services, prior to the passage of an appropriation therefor, for airborne cadastral survey and resource protection operations of the Bureau. He may renew such contracts annually, not more than twice, without additional competition. Such contracts shall obligate funds for the fiscal years in which the costs are incurred.

(b) Each such contract shall provide that the obligation of the United States for the ensuing fiscal years is contingent upon the passage of an applicable appropriation, and that no payment shall be made under the contract for the ensuing fiscal years until such appropriation becomes available for expenditure.

(Pub. L. No. 94–579, Title III, § 308, 90 Stat. 2767 (Oct. 21, 1976).)

§ 1739. Advisory councils

[FLPMA § 309]

(a) Establishment; membership; operation

The Secretary shall establish advisory councils of not less than ten and not more than fifteen members appointed by him from among persons who are representative of the various major citizens' interests concerning the problems relating to land use planning or the management of the public lands located within the area for which an advisory council is established. At least one member of each council shall be an elected official of general purpose government serving the people of such area. To the extent practicable there shall be no overlap or duplication of such councils. Appointments shall be made in accordance with rules prescribed by the Secretary. The establishment and operation of an advisory council established under this section shall conform to the requirements of the Federal Advisory Committee Act (86 Stat. 770).

(b) Meetings

Notwithstanding the provisions of subsection (a) of this section, each advisory council established by the Secretary under this section shall meet at least once a year with such meetings being called by the Secretary.

(c) Travel and per diem payments

Members of advisory councils shall serve without pay, except travel and per diem will be paid each member for meetings called by the Secretary.

(d) Functions

An advisory council may furnish advice to the Secretary with respect to the land use planning, classification, retention, management, and disposal of the public lands within the area for which the advisory council is established and such other matters as may be referred to it by the Secretary.

(e) Public participation; procedures applicable

In exercising his authorities under this Act, the Secretary, by regulation, shall establish procedures, including public hearings where appropriate, to give the Federal, State, and local governments and the public adequate notice and an opportunity to comment upon the formulation of standards and criteria for, and to participate in, the preparation and execution of plans and programs for, and the management of, the public lands.

(Pub. L. No. 94–579, Title III, § 309, 90 Stat. 2767 (Oct. 21, 1976); as amended by Pub. L. No. 95–514, § 13, 92 Stat. 1808 (Oct. 25, 1978).)

HISTORICAL AND STATUTORY NOTES

References in Text

The Federal Advisory Committee Act (86 Stat. 770), referred to in subsec. (a), is Pub. L. No. 92–463, 86 Stat. 770 (Oct. 6, 1972), as amended, and is set out in Appendix 2 to Title 5, Government Organization and Employees.

This Act, referred to in subsec. (e), is Pub. L. No. 94–579, 90 Stat. 2743 (Oct. 21, 1976), as amended, known as the Federal Land Policy and Management Act of 1976. For complete classification of this Act to the Code, see Tables volume.

Termination of Advisory Councils

Advisory councils established after Jan. 5, 1973, to terminate not later than the expiration of the two-year period beginning on the date of their establishment, unless, in the case of a council established by the President or an officer of the Federal Government, such council is renewed by appropriate action prior to the expiration of such two-year period, or in the case of a council established by the Congress, its duration is otherwise provided for by law, see sections 3(2) and 14 of Pub. L. No. 92–463, 86 Stat. 770, 776 (Oct. 6, 1972), set out in Appendix 2 to Title 5, Government Organization and Employees.

§ 1740. Rules and regulations

[FLPMA § 310]

The Secretary, with respect to the public lands, shall promulgate rules and regulations to carry out the purposes of this Act and of other laws applicable to the public lands, and the Secretary of Agriculture, with respect to lands within the National Forest System, shall promulgate rules and regulations to carry out the purposes of this Act. The promulgation of such rules and regulations shall be governed by the provisions of chapter 5 of Title 5, without regard to section 553(a)(2). Prior to the promulgation of such rules and regulations, such lands shall be administered under existing rules and regulations concerning such lands to the extent practical.

(Pub. L. No. 94–579, Title III, § 310, 90 Stat. 2767 (Oct. 21, 1976).)

HISTORICAL AND STATUTORY NOTES

References in Text

This Act, referred to in text is Pub. L. No. 94–579, 90 Stat. 2743 (Oct. 21, 1976), as amended, known as the Federal Land Policy and Management Act of 1976. For complete classification of this Act to the Code, see Tables.

§ 1741. Annual reports

[FLPMA § 311]

(a) Purpose; time for submission

For the purpose of providing information that will aid Congress in carrying out its oversight responsibilities for public lands programs and for other purposes, the Secretary shall prepare a report in accordance with subsections (b) and (c) of this section and submit it to the Congress no later than one hundred and twenty days after the end of each fiscal year beginning with the report for fiscal year 1979.

(b) Format

A list of programs and specific information to be included in the report as well as the format of the report shall be developed by the Secretary after consulting with the Committee on Natural Resources of the House of Representatives and the Committee on Energy and Natural Resources of the Senate and shall be provided to the committees prior to the end of the second quarter of each fiscal year.

(c) Contents

The report shall include, but not be limited to, program identification information, program evaluation information, and program budgetary information for the preceding current and succeeding fiscal years.

(Pub. L. No. 94–579, Title III, § 311, 90 Stat. 2768 (Oct. 21, 1976); as amended by Pub. L. No. 103–437, § 16(d)(3), 108 Stat. 4595 (Nov. 2, 1994).)

HISTORICAL AND STATUTORY NOTES

Termination of Reporting Requirements

For termination of reporting provisions of subsec. (a) of this section, effective May 15, 2000, see Pub. L. No. 104–66, § 3003, as amended, set out as a note under 31 U.S.C.A. § 1113, and page 112 of House Document No. 103–7.

For termination, effective May 15, 2000, of provisions of law requiring submittal to Congress of any annual, semiannual, or other regular periodic report listed in House Document No. 103–7 (in which the 9th item on page 112 identifies a reporting provision which, as subsequently amended, is contained in this section), see Pub. L. No. 104–66, § 3003, as amended, set out as a note under 31 U.S.C.A. § 1113.

§ 1742. Search, rescue, and protection forces; emergency situations authorizing hiring

[FLPMA § 312]

Where in his judgment sufficient search, rescue, and protection forces are not otherwise available, the Secretary is authorized in cases of emergency to incur such expenses as may be necessary (a) in searching for and rescuing, or in cooperating in the search for and rescue of, persons lost on the public lands, (b) in protecting or rescuing, or in cooperating in the protection and rescue of, persons or animals endangered by an act of God, and (c) in transporting deceased persons or persons seriously ill or injured to the nearest place where interested parties or local authorities are located.

(Pub. L. No. 94–579, Title III, § 312, 90 Stat. 2768 (Oct. 21, 1976).)

§ 1743. Disclosure of financial interests by officers or employees

[FLPMA § 313]

(a) Annual written statement; availability to public

Each officer or employee of the Secretary and the Bureau who—

(1) performs any function or duty under this Act; and

(2) has any known financial interest in any person who (A) applies for or receives any permit, lease, or right-of-way under, or (B) applies for or acquires any land or interests therein under, or (C) is otherwise subject to the provisions of, this Act,

shall, beginning on February 1, 1977, annually file with the Secretary a written statement concerning all such interests held by such officer or employee during the preceding calendar year. Such statement shall be available to the public.

(b) Implementation of requirements

The Secretary shall—

(1) act within ninety days after October 21, 1976—

(A) to define the term "known financial interests" for the purposes of subsection (a) of this section; and

(B) to establish the methods by which the requirement to file written statements specified in subsection (a) of this section will be monitored and enforced, including appropriate provisions for the filing by such officers and employees of such statements and the review by the Secretary of such statements; and

(2) report to the Congress on June 1 of each calendar year with respect to such disclosures and the actions taken in regard thereto during the preceding calendar year.

(c) Exempted personnel

In the rules prescribed in subsection (b) of this section, the Secretary may identify specific positions within the Department of the Interior which are of a nonregulatory or nonpolicymaking nature and provide that officers or employees occupying such positions shall be exempt from the requirements of this section.

(d) Violations; criminal penalties

Any officer or employee who is subject to, and knowingly violates, this section, shall be fined not more than $2,500 or imprisoned not more than one year, or both.

(Pub. L. No. 94–579, Title III, § 313, 90 Stat. 2768 (Oct. 21, 1976).)

HISTORICAL AND STATUTORY NOTES

References in Text

This Act, referred to in subsec. (a)(1), (2), is Pub. L. No. 94–579, 90 Stat. 2743 (Oct. 21, 1976), as amended, known as the Federal Land Policy and Management Act of 1976. For complete classification of this Act to the Code, see Tables.

Termination of Reporting Requirements

For termination of reporting provisions of subsec. (b) of this section, effective May 15, 2000, see Pub. L. No. 104–66, § 3003, as amended, set out as a note under 31 U.S.C.A. § 1113, and page 108 of House Document No. 103–7.

For termination, effective May 15, 2000, of provisions in subsec. (b) requiring that the Secretary report to Congress on June 1 of each calendar year, see Pub. L. No. 104–66, § 3003, as amended, set out as a note under 31 U.S.C.A. § 1113, and the 2nd item on page 108 of House Document No. 103–7.

§ 1744. Recordation of mining claims

[FLPMA § 314]

(a) Filing requirements

The owner of an unpatented lode or placer mining claim located prior to October 21, 1976, shall, within the three-year period following October 21, 1976 and prior to December 31 of each year thereafter, file the instruments required by paragraphs (1) and (2) of this subsection. The owner of an unpatented lode or placer mining claim located after October 21, 1976 shall, prior to December 31 of each year following the calendar year in which the said claim was located, file the instruments required by paragraphs (1) and (2) of this subsection:

(1) File for record in the office where the location notice or certificate is recorded either a notice of intention to hold the mining claim (including but not limited to such notices as are provided by law to be filed when there has been a suspension or deferment of annual assessment work), an affidavit of assessment work performed thereon, on a detailed report provided by section 28–1 of Title 30, relating thereto.

(2) File in the office of the Bureau designated by the Secretary a copy of the official record of the instrument filed or recorded pursuant to paragraph (1) of this subsection, including a description of the location of the mining claim sufficient to locate the claimed lands on the ground.

(b) Additional filing requirements

The owner of an unpatented lode or placer mining claim or mill or tunnel site located prior to October 21, 1976 shall, within the three-year period following October 21, 1976, file in the office of the Bureau designated by the Secretary a copy of the official record of the notice of location or certificate of location, including a description of the location of the mining claim or mill or tunnel site sufficient to locate the claimed lands on the ground. The owner of an unpatented lode or placer mining claim or mill or tunnel site located after October 21, 1976 shall, within ninety days after the date of location of such claim, file in the office of the Bureau designated by the Secretary a copy of the official record of the notice of location or certificate of location, including a description of the location of the mining claim or mill or tunnel site sufficient to locate the claimed lands on the ground.

(c) Failure to file as constituting abandonment; defective or untimely filing

The failure to file such instruments as required by subsections (a) and (b) of this section shall be deemed conclusively to constitute an abandonment of the mining claim or mill or tunnel site by the owner; but it shall not be considered a failure to file if the instrument is defective or not timely filed for record under other Federal laws permitting filing or recording thereof, or if the instrument is filed for record by or on behalf of some but not all of the owners of the mining claim or mill or tunnel site.

(d) Validity of claims, waiver of assessment, etc., as unaffected

Such recordation or application by itself shall not render valid any claim which would not be otherwise valid under applicable law. Nothing in this section shall be construed as a waiver of the assessment and other requirements of such law.

(Pub. L. No. 94–579, Title III, § 314, 90 Stat. 2769 (Oct. 21, 1976).)

§ 1745. Disclaimer of interest in lands

[FLPMA § 315]

(a) Issuance of recordable document; criteria

After consulting with any affected Federal agency, the Secretary is authorized to issue a document of disclaimer of interest or interests in any lands in any form suitable for recordation, where the disclaimer will help remove a cloud on the title of such lands and where he determines (1) a record interest of the United States in lands has terminated by operation of law or is otherwise invalid; or (2) the lands lying between the meander line shown on a plat of survey approved by the Bureau or its predecessors and the actual shoreline of a body of water are not lands of the United States; or (3) accreted, relicted, or avulsed lands are not lands of the United States.

(b) Procedures applicable

No document or disclaimer shall be issued pursuant to this section unless the applicant therefor has filed with the Secretary an application in writing and notice of such application setting forth the grounds supporting such application has been published in the Federal Register at least ninety days preceding the issuance of such disclaimer and until the applicant therefor has paid to the Secretary the administrative costs of issuing the disclaimer as determined by the Secretary. All receipts shall be deposited to the then-current appropriation from which expended.

(c) Construction as quit-claim deed from United States

Issuance of a document of disclaimer by the Secretary pursuant to the provisions of this section and regulations promulgated hereunder shall have the same effect as a quit-claim deed from the United States.

(Pub. L. No. 94–579, Title III, § 315, 90 Stat. 2770 (Oct. 21, 1976).)

§ 1746. Correction of conveyance documents

[FLPMA § 316]

The Secretary may correct patents or documents of conveyance issued pursuant to section 1718 of this title or to other Acts relating to the disposal of public lands where necessary in order to eliminate errors. In addition, the Secretary may make corrections of errors in any documents of conveyance which have heretofore been issued by the Federal Government to dispose of public lands. Any corrections authorized by this section which affect the boundaries of, or jurisdiction over, land administered by another Federal agency shall be made only after consultation with, and the approval of, the head of such other agency.

(Pub. L. No. 94–579, Title III, § 316, 90 Stat. 2770 (Oct. 21, 1976); as amended by Pub. L. No. 108–7, Div. F, Title IV, § 411(e), 117 Stat. 291 (Feb. 20, 2003).)

HISTORICAL AND STATUTORY NOTES

Effective and Applicability Provisions

2003 Acts. Amendment by Pub. L. No. 108–7, Div. F, § 411(e), effective February 20, 2003, see Pub. L. No. 108–7, Div. F, Title IV, § 415, set out as a note under 16 U.S.C.A. § 539m.

§ 1747. Loans to States and political subdivisions; purposes; amounts; allocation; terms and conditions; interest rate; security; limitations; forebearance for benefit of borrowers; recordkeeping requirements; discrimination prohibited; deposit of receipts

[FLPMA § 317]

(1) The Secretary is authorized to make loans to States and their political subdivisions in order to relieve social or economic impacts occasioned by the development of minerals leased in such States pursuant to the Act of February 25, 1920, as amended [30 U.S.C.A. § 181 et seq.]. Such loans shall be confined to the uses specified for the 50 per centum of mineral leasing revenues to be received by such States and subdivisions pursuant to section 35 of such Act [30 U.S.C.A. § 191].

(2) The total amount of loans outstanding pursuant to this section for any State and political subdivisions thereof in any year shall be not more than the anticipated mineral leasing revenues to be received by that State pursuant to section 35 of the Act of February 25, 1920, as amended [30 U.S.C.A. § 191], for the ten years following.

(3) The Secretary, after consultation with the Governors of the affected States, shall allocate such loans among the States and their political subdivisions in a fair and equitable manner, giving priority to those States and subdivisions suffering the most severe impacts.

(4) Loans made pursuant to this section shall be subject to such terms and conditions as the Secretary determines necessary to assure the achievement of the purpose of this section. The Secretary shall promulgate such regulations as may be necessary to carry out the provisions of this section no later than three months after August 20, 1978.

(5) Loans made pursuant to this section shall bear interest equivalent to the lowest interest rate paid on an issue of at least $1,000,000 of tax exempt bonds of such State or any agency thereof within the preceding calendar year.

(6) Any loan made pursuant to this section shall be secured only by a pledge of the revenues received by the State or the political subdivision thereof pursuant to section 35 of the Act of February 25, 1920, as amended [30 U.S.C.A. § 191], and shall not constitute an obligation upon the general property or taxing authority of such unit of government.

(7) Notwithstanding any other provision of law, loans made pursuant to this section may be used for the non-Federal share of the aggregate cost of any project or program otherwise funded by the Federal Government which requires a non-Federal share for such project or program and which provides planning or public facilities otherwise eligible for assistance under this section.

(8) Nothing in this section shall be construed to preclude any forebearance[1] for the benefit of the borrower including loan restructuring, which may be determined by the Secretary as justified by the failure of anticipated mineral development or related revenues to materialize as expected when the loan was made pursuant to this section.

(9) Recipients of loans made pursuant to this section shall keep such records as the Secretary shall prescribe by regulation, including records which fully disclose the disposition of the proceeds of such assistance and such other records as the Secretary may require to facilitate an effective audit. The Secretary and the Comptroller General of the United States or their duly authorized representatives shall have access, for the purpose of audit, to such records.

(10) No person in the United States shall, on the grounds of race, color, religion, national origin, or sex be excluded from participation in, be denied the benefits of, or be subjected to discrimination under, any program or activity funded in whole or part with funds made available under this section.

(11) All amounts collected in connection with loans made pursuant to this section, including interest payments or repayments of principal on loans, fees, and other moneys, derived in connection with this section, shall be deposited in the Treasury as miscellaneous receipts.

(Pub. L. No. 94–579, Title III, § 317(c), 90 Stat. 2771 (Oct. 21, 1976); as amended by Pub. L. No. 95–352, § 1(f), Aug. 20, 1978, 92 Stat. 515.)

[1] So in original.

HISTORICAL AND STATUTORY NOTES

References in Text

The Act of February 25, 1920, as amended, referred to in par. (1), is Act of Feb. 25, 1920, c. 85, 41 Stat. 437, as amended, popularly known as the Mineral Leasing Act of 1920, which is codified principally as chapter 3A (section 181 et seq.) of Title 30, Mineral Lands and Mining. For complete classification of this Act to the Code, see Short Title note set out under section 181 of Title 30 and Tables.

Codifications

Section is comprised of subsec. (c) of section 317 of Pub. L. No. 94–579. Subsecs. (a) and (b) of section 317 of Pub. L. No. 94–579 are codified as section 191 of Title 30, Mineral Lands and Mining, and a note set out under that section; respectively.

§ 1748. Funding requirements

[FLPMA § 318]

(a) Authorization of appropriations

There are authorized to be appropriated such sums as are necessary to carry out the purposes and provisions of this Act, but no amounts shall be appropriated to carry out after October 1, 2002, any program, function, or activity of the Bureau under this or any other Act unless such sums are specifically authorized to be appropriated as of October 21, 1976 or are authorized to be appropriated in accordance with the provisions of subsection (b) of this section.

(b) Procedure applicable for authorization of appropriations

Consistent with section 1110 of Title 31, beginning May 15, 1977, and not later than May 15 of each second even numbered year thereafter, the Secretary shall submit to the Speaker of the House of Representatives and the President of the Senate a request for the authorization of appropriations for all programs, functions, and activities of the Bureau to be carried out during the four-fiscal-year period beginning on October 1 of the calendar year following the calendar year in which such request is submitted. The Secretary shall include in his request, in addition to the information contained in his budget request and justification statement to the Office of Management and Budget, the funding levels which he determines can be efficiently and effectively utilized in the execution of his responsibilities for each such program, function, or activity, notwithstanding any budget guidelines or limitations imposed by any official or agency of the executive branch.

(c) Distribution of receipts from Bureau from disposal of lands, etc.

Nothing in this section shall apply to the distribution of receipts of the Bureau from the disposal of lands, natural resources, and interests in lands in accordance with applicable law, nor to the use of contributed funds, private deposits for public survey work, and townsite trusteeships, nor to fund allocations from other Federal agencies, reimbursements from both Federal and non-Federal sources, and funds expended for emergency firefighting and rehabilitation.

(d) Purchase of certain public lands from Land and Water Conservation Fund

In exercising the authority to acquire by purchase granted by section 1715(a) of this title, the Secretary may use the Land and Water Conservation Fund to purchase lands which are necessary for proper management of public lands which are primarily of value for outdoor recreation purposes.

(Pub. L. No. 94–579, Title III, § 318, 90 Stat. 2771 (Oct. 21, 1976); as amended by Pub. L. No. 104–333, Div. I, Title III, § 310, 110 Stat. 4139 (Nov. 12, 1996).)

HISTORICAL AND STATUTORY NOTES

References in Text

This Act, referred to in subsec. (a), is Pub. L. No. 94–579, 90 Stat. 2743 (Oct. 21, 1976), as amended, known as the Federal Land Policy and Management Act of 1976. For complete classification of this Act to the Code, see Tables.

Codifications

In subsec. (b), "section 1110 of Title 31" was substituted for "section 607 of the Congressional Budget Act of 1974 [31 U.S.C.A. § 11c]" on authority of Pub. L. No. 97–258, § 4(b), 96 Stat. 1067 (Sept. 13, 1982), the first section of which enacted Title 31, Money and Finance.

Termination of Reporting Requirements

For termination of reporting provisions of subsec. (b) of this section, effective May 15, 2000, see Pub. L. No. 104–66, § 3003, as amended, set out as a note under 31 U.S.C.A. § 1113, and page 111 of House Document No. 103–7.

§ 1748a. FLAME Wildfire Suppression Reserve Funds

(a) Definitions

In this section:

(1) Federal land

The term "Federal land" means—

(A) public land, as defined in section 1702 of this title;

(B) units of the National Park System;

(C) refuges of the National Wildlife Refuge System;

(D) land held in trust by the United States for the benefit of Indian tribes or members of an Indian tribe; and

(E) land in the National Forest System, as defined in section 1609(a) of Title 16.

(2) FLAME Fund

The term "FLAME Fund" means a FLAME Wildfire Suppression Reserve Fund established by subsection (b).

(3) Relevant congressional committees

The term "relevant congressional committees" means the Committee on Appropriations, the Committee on Natural Resources, and the Committee on Agriculture of the House of Representatives and the Committee on Appropriations, the Committee on Energy and Natural Resources, and the Committee on Indian Affairs of the Senate.

(4) Secretary concerned

The term "Secretary concerned" means—

(A) the Secretary of the Interior, with respect to—

(i) Federal land described in subparagraphs (A), (B), (C), and (D) of paragraph (1); and

(ii) the FLAME Fund established for the Department of the Interior; and

(B) the Secretary of Agriculture, with respect to—

(i) National Forest System land; and

(ii) the FLAME Fund established for the Department of the Agriculture.

(b) Establishment of FLAME Funds

There is established in the Treasury of the United States the following accounts:

(1) The FLAME Wildfire Suppression Reserve Fund for the Department of the Interior.

(2) The FLAME Wildfire Suppression Reserve Fund for the Department of Agriculture.

(c) Purpose of FLAME Funds

The FLAME Funds shall be available to cover the costs of large or complex wildfire events and as a reserve when amounts provided for wildfire suppression and Federal emergency response in the Wildland Fire Management appropriation accounts are exhausted.

(d) Funding

(1) Credits to Funds

A FLAME Fund shall consist of the following:

(A) Such amounts as are appropriated to that FLAME Fund.

(B) Such amounts as are transferred to that FLAME Fund under paragraph (5).

(2) Authorization of appropriations

(A) Authorization of appropriations

There are authorized to be appropriated to the FLAME Funds such amounts as are necessary to carry out this section.

(B) Congressional intent

It is the intent of Congress that, for fiscal year 2011 and each fiscal year thereafter, the amounts requested by the President for a FLAME Fund should be not less than the amount estimated by the Secretary concerned as the amount necessary for that fiscal year for wildfire suppression activities of the Secretary that meet the criteria specified in subsection (e)(2)(B)(i).

(C) Sense of Congress on designation of FLAME Fund appropriations, supplemental funding request, and supplement to other suppression funding

It is the sense of Congress that for fiscal year 2011 and each fiscal year thereafter—

(i) amounts appropriated to a FLAME Fund in excess of the amount estimated by the Secretary concerned as the amount necessary for that fiscal year for wildfire suppression activities of the Secretary that meet the criteria specified in subsection (e)(2)(B)(i) should be designated as amounts necessary to meet emergency needs;

(ii) the Secretary concerned should promptly make a supplemental request for additional funds to replenish the FLAME Fund if the Secretary determines that the FLAME Fund will be exhausted within 30 days; and

(iii) funding made available through the FLAME Fund should be used to supplement the funding otherwise appropriated to the Secretary concerned for wildfire suppression and Federal emergency response in the Wildland Fire Management appropriation accounts.

(3) Availability

Amounts in a FLAME Fund shall remain available to the Secretary concerned until expended.

(4) Notice of insufficient funds

The Secretary concerned shall notify the relevant congressional committees if the Secretary estimates that only 60 days worth of funds remain in the FLAME Fund administered by that Secretary.

(5) Transfer authority

If a FLAME Fund has insufficient funds, the Secretary concerned administering the other FLAME Fund may transfer amounts to the FLAME Fund with insufficient funds. Not more than $100,000,000 may be transferred from a FLAME Fund during any fiscal year under this authority.

(e) Use of FLAME Fund

(1) In general

Subject to paragraphs (2) and (3), amounts in a FLAME Fund shall be available to the Secretary concerned to transfer to the Wildland Fire Management appropriation account of that Secretary to pay the costs of wildfire suppression activities of that Secretary that are separate from amounts for wildfire suppression activities annually appropriated to that Secretary under the Wildland Fire Management appropriation account of that Secretary.

(2) Declaration required

(A) In general

Amounts in a FLAME Fund shall be available for transfer under paragraph (1) only after that Secretary concerned issues a declaration that a wildfire suppression event is eligible for funding from the FLAME Fund.

(B) Declaration criteria

A declaration by the Secretary concerned under subparagraph (A) may be issued only if—

(i) in the case of an individual wildfire incident—

(I) the fire covers 300 or more acres; or

(II) the Secretary concerned determines that the fire has required an emergency Federal response based on the significant complexity, severity, or threat posed by the fire to human life, property, or resources; or

(ii) the cumulative costs of wildfire suppression and Federal emergency response activities for the Secretary concerned will exceed, within 30 days, all of the amounts previously appropriated (including amounts appropriated under an emergency designation, but excluding amounts appropriated to the FLAME Fund) to the Secretary concerned for wildfire suppression and Federal emergency response.

(3) State, private, and tribal land

Use of a FLAME Fund for emergency wildfire suppression activities on State land, private land, and tribal land shall be consistent with any existing agreements in which the Secretary concerned has agreed to assume responsibility for wildfire suppression activities on the land.

(f) Treatment of anticipated and predicted activities

For fiscal year 2011 and subsequent fiscal years, the Secretary concerned shall request funds within the Wildland Fire Management appropriation account of that Secretary for regular wildfire suppression activities that do not meet the criteria specified in subsection (e)(2)(B)(i).

(g) Prohibition on other transfers

The Secretary concerned may not transfer funds from non-fire accounts to the Wildland Fire Management appropriation account of that Secretary unless amounts in the FLAME Fund of that Secretary and any amounts appropriated to that Secretary for the purpose of wildfire suppression will be exhausted within 30 days.

(h) Accounting and reports

(1) Accounting and reporting requirements

The Secretary concerned shall account and report on amounts transferred from the respective FLAME Fund in a manner that is consistent with existing National Fire Plan reporting procedures.

(2) Annual report

The Secretary concerned shall submit to the relevant congressional committees and make available to the public an annual report that—

(A) describes the obligation and expenditure of amounts transferred from the FLAME Fund; and

(B) includes any recommendations that the Secretary concerned may have to improve the administrative control and oversight of the FLAME Fund.

(3) Estimates of wildfire suppression costs to improve budgeting and funding

(A) In general

Consistent with the schedule provided in subparagraph (C), the Secretary concerned shall submit to the relevant congressional committees an estimate of anticipated wildfire suppression costs for the applicable fiscal year.

(B) Independent review

The methodology for developing the estimates under subparagraph (A) shall be subject to periodic independent review to ensure compliance with subparagraph (D).

(C) Schedule

The Secretary concerned shall submit an estimate under subparagraph (A) during—

(i) the first week of March of each year;

(ii) the first week of May of each year;

(iii) the first week of July of each year; and

(iv) if a bill making appropriations for the Department of the Interior and the Forest Service for the following fiscal year has not been enacted by September 1, the first week of September of each year.

(D) Requirements

An estimate of anticipated wildfire suppression costs shall be developed using the best available—

(i) climate, weather, and other relevant data; and

(ii) models and other analytic tools.

(i) Termination of authority

The authority of the Secretary concerned to use the FLAME Fund established for that Secretary shall terminate at the end of the third fiscal year in which no appropriations to, or withdrawals from, that FLAME Fund have been made for a period of three consecutive fiscal years. Upon termination of such authority, any amounts remaining in the affected FLAME Fund shall be transferred to, and made a part of, the Wildland Fire Management appropriation account of the Secretary concerned for wildland suppression activities.

(Pub. L. No. 111–88, Div. A, Title V, § 502, 123 Stat. 2968 (Oct. 30, 2009).)

HISTORICAL AND STATUTORY NOTES

Codifications

This section was enacted as part of the Department of Interior, Environment, and Related Agencies Appropriations Act, 2010, and not as part of the Federal Land Policy and Management Act of 1976, which otherwise comprises this chapter.

§ 1748b. Cohesive wildfire management strategy

(a) Strategy required

Not later than one year after October 30, 2009, the Secretary of the Interior and the Secretary of Agriculture, acting jointly, shall submit to Congress a report that contains a cohesive wildfire management strategy, consistent with the recommendations described in recent reports of the Government Accountability Office regarding management strategies.

(b) Elements of strategy

The strategy required by subsection (a) shall provide for—

(1) the identification of the most cost-effective means for allocating fire management budget resources;

(2) the reinvestment in non-fire programs by the Secretary of the Interior and the Secretary of Agriculture;

(3) employing the appropriate management response to wildfires;

(4) assessing the level of risk to communities;

(5) the allocation of hazardous fuels reduction funds based on the priority of hazardous fuels reduction projects;

(6) assessing the impacts of climate change on the frequency and severity of wildfire; and

(7) studying the effects of invasive species on wildfire risk.

(c) Revision

At least once during each five-year period beginning on the date of the submission of the cohesive wildfire management strategy under subsection (a), the Secretary of the Interior and the Secretary of Agriculture shall revise the strategy to address any changes affecting the strategy, including changes with respect to landscape, vegetation, climate, and weather.

(Pub. L. No. 111–88, Div. A, Title V, § 503, 123 Stat. 2971 (Oct. 30, 2009).)

HISTORICAL AND STATUTORY NOTES

Codifications

This section was enacted as part of the Department of Interior, Environment, and Related Agencies Appropriations Act, 2010, and not as part of the Federal Land Policy and Management Act of 1976, which otherwise comprises this chapter.

§ 1748b-1. Wildfire Technology Modernization

(a) Purpose.—The purpose of this section is to promote the use of the best available technology to enhance the effective and cost-efficient response to wildfires—

(1) to meet applicable protection objectives; and

(2) to increase the safety of—

(A) firefighters; and

(B) the public.

(b) Definitions.—In this section:

(1) **Secretaries.**—The term "Secretaries" means—

(A) the Secretary of Agriculture; and

(B) the Secretary.

(2) **Secretary Concerned.**—The term "Secretary concerned" means—

(A) the Secretary of Agriculture, with respect to activities under the Department of Agriculture; and

(B) the Secretary, with respect to activities under the Department of the Interior.

(c) Unmanned Aircraft Systems.—

(1) **Defintions.**—In this subsection, the terms "unmanned aircraft" and "unmanned aircraft system" have the meanings given those terms in section 44801 of title 49, United States Code.

(2) **Establishment of Program.**—Not later than 180 days after the date of enactment of this Act, the Secretary, in consultation with the Secretary of Agriculture, shall establish a research, development, and testing program, or expand an applicable existing program, to assess unmanned aircraft system technologies, including optionally piloted aircraft, across the full range of wildland fire management operations in order to accelerate the deployment and integration of those technologies into the operations of the Secretaries.

(3) **Expanding Use of Unmanned Aircraft Systems in Wildfires.**—In carrying out the program established under paragraph (2), the Secretaries, in coordination with the Federal Aviation Administration, State wildland firefighting agencies, and other relevant Federal agencies, shall enter into an agreement under which the Secretaries shall develop consistent protocols and plans for the use on wildland fires of unmanned aircraft system technologies, including for the development of real-time maps of the location of wildland fires.

(d) Location Systems for Wildland Firefighters.—

(1) **In General.**—Not later than 2 years after the date of enactment of this Act, subject to the availability of appropriations, the Secretaries, in coordination with State wildland firefighting agencies, shall jointly develop and operate a tracking system (referred to in this subsection as the "system") to remotely locate the positions of fire resources for use by wildland firefighters, including, at a minimum, any fire resources assigned to Federal type 1 wildland fire incident management teams.

(2) **Requirements.**—The system shall—

(A) use the most practical and effective technology available to the Secretaries to remotely track the location of an active resource, such as a Global Positioning System;

(B) depict the location of each fire resource on the applicable maps developed under subsection (c)(3);

(C) operate continuously during the period for which any firefighting personnel are assigned to the applicable Federal wildland fire; and

(D) be subject to such terms and conditions as the Secretary concerned determines necessary for the effective implementation of the system.

(3) **Operation.**—The Secretary concerned shall—

(A) before commencing operation of the system—

(i) conduct not fewer than 2 pilot projects relating to the operation, management, and effectiveness of the system; and

(ii) review the results of those pilot projects;

(B) conduct training, and maintain a culture, such that an employee, officer, or contractor shall not rely on the system for safety; and

(C) establish procedures for the collection, storage, and transfer of data collected under this subsection to ensure—

(i) data security; and

(ii) the privacy of wildland fire personnel.

(e) **Wildland Fire Decision Support.**—

(1) **Protocol.**—To the maximum extent practicable, the Secretaries shall ensure that wildland fire management activities conducted by the Secretaries, or conducted jointly by the Secretaries and State wildland firefighting agencies, achieve compliance with applicable incident management objectives in a manner that—

(A) minimizes firefighter exposure to the lowest level necessary; and

(B) reduces overall costs of wildfire incidents.

(2) **Wildfire Decision Support System.**—

(A) **In General.**—The Secretaries, in coordination with State wildland firefighting agencies, shall establish a system or expand an existing system to track and monitor decisions made by the Secretaries or State wildland firefighting agencies in managing wildfires.

(B) **Components.**—The system established or expanded under subparagraph (A) shall be able to alert the Secretaries if—

(i) unusual costs are incurred;

(ii) an action to be carried out would likely—

(I) endanger the safety of a firefighter; or

(II) be ineffective in meeting an applicable suppression or protection goal; or

(iii) a decision regarding the management of a wildfire deviates from—

(I) an applicable protocol established by the Secretaries, including the requirement under paragraph (1); or

(II) an applicable spatial fire management plan or fire management plan of the Secretary concerned.

(f) **Smoke Projections from Active Wildland Fires.**—The Secretaries shall establish a program, to be known as the "Interagency Wildland Fire Air Quality Response Program", under which the Secretary concerned—

(1) to the maximum extent practicable, shall assign 1 or more air resource advisors to a type 1 incident management team managing a Federal wildland fire; and

(2) may assign 1 or more air resource advisors to a type 2 incident management team managing a wildland fire.

(Pub. L. No. 116–9, § 1114, 123 Stat. 615–17 (March 12, 2019).)

HISTORICAL AND STATUTORY NOTES

Codifications

This section was enacted as part of the John D. Dingell, Jr. Conservation, Management, and Recreation Act of 2019 and not as part of the Federal Land Policy and Management Act of 1976, which otherwise comprises this chapter.

SUBCHAPTER IV—RANGE MANAGEMENT

§ 1751. Grazing fees; feasibility study; contents; submission of report; annual distribution and use of range betterment funds; nature of distributions

[FLPMA § 401]

(a) The Secretary of Agriculture and the Secretary of the Interior shall jointly cause to be conducted a study to determine the value of grazing on the lands under their jurisdiction in the eleven Western States with a view to establishing a fee to be charged for domestic livestock grazing on such lands which is equitable to the United States and to the holders of grazing permits and leases on such lands. In making such study, the Secretaries shall take into consideration the costs of production normally associated with domestic livestock grazing in the eleven Western States, differences in forage values, and such other factors as may relate to the reasonableness of such fees. The Secretaries shall report the result of such study to the Congress not later than one year from and after October 21, 1976, together with recommendations to implement a reasonable grazing fee schedule based upon such study. If the report required herein has not been submitted to the Congress within one year after October 21, 1976, the grazing fee charge then in effect shall not be altered and shall remain the same until such report has been submitted to the Congress. Neither Secretary shall increase the grazing fee in the 1977 grazing year.

(b) **(1)** Congress finds that a substantial amount of the Federal range lands is deteriorating in quality, and that installation of additional range improvements could arrest much of the continuing deterioration and could lead to substantial betterment of forage conditions with resulting benefits to wildlife, watershed protection, and livestock production. Congress therefore directs that 50 per centum or $10,000,000 per annum, whichever is greater of all moneys received by the United States as fees for grazing domestic livestock on public lands (other than from ceded Indian lands) under the Taylor Grazing Act (48 Stat. 1269; 43 U.S.C. 315 et seq.) and the Act of August 28, 1937 (50 Stat. 874; 43 U.S.C. 1181d), and on lands in National Forests in the sixteen contiguous Western States under the provisions of this section shall be credited to a separate account in the Treasury, one-half of which is authorized to be appropriated and made available for use in the district, region, or national forest from which such moneys were derived, as the respective Secretary may direct after consultation with district, regional, or national forest user representatives, for the purpose of on-the-ground range rehabilitation, protection, and improvements on such lands, and the remaining one-half shall be used for on-the-ground range rehabilitation, protection, and improvements as the Secretary concerned directs. Any funds so appropriated shall be in addition to any other appropriations made to the respective Secretary for planning and administration of the range betterment program and for other range management. Such rehabilitation, protection, and improvements shall include all forms of range land betterment including, but not limited to, seeding and reseeding, fence construction, weed control, water development, and fish and wildlife habitat enhancement as the respective Secretary may direct after consultation with user representatives. The annual distribution and use of range betterment funds authorized by this paragraph shall not be considered a major Federal action requiring a detailed statement pursuant to section 4332(c) of Title 42.

(2) All distributions of moneys made under subsection (b)(1) of this section shall be in addition to distributions made under section 10 of the Taylor Grazing Act [43 U.S.C.A. § 315i] and shall not apply to distribution of moneys made under section 11 of that Act [43 U.S.C.A. § 315j]. The remaining moneys received by the United States as fees for grazing domestic livestock on the public lands shall be deposited in the Treasury as miscellaneous receipts.

(Pub. L. No. 94–579, Title IV, § 401(a), (b)(1), (2), 90 Stat. 2772 (Oct. 21, 1976); as amended by Pub. L. No. 95–514, § 6(b), 92 Stat. 1806 (Oct. 25, 1978).)

HISTORICAL AND STATUTORY NOTES

References in Text

The Taylor Grazing Act (48 Stat. 1269; 43 U.S.C. 315 et seq.), referred to in subsec. (b), is Act of June 28, 1934, c. 865, 48 Stat. 1269, as amended, which is codified principally as subchapter I (section 315 et seq.) of chapter 8A of this title. For complete classification of this Act to the Code, see Short Title note set out under section 315 of this title and Tables.

The Act of August 28, 1937, referred to in subsec. (b)(1), is Act of Aug. 28, 1937, c. 876, 50 Stat. 874, as amended, which is codified as sections 1181a to 1181f of this title. For complete classification of this Act to the Code, see Tables volume.

Codifications. Subsec. (b)(2) of this section is comprised of the second and third sentences of section 401(b)(2) of Pub. L. No. 94–579. The first sentence of such section 401(b)(2) amended section 315i(b) of this title.

Moratorium on Increase of Grazing Fee for 1978 Grazing Year

Pub. L. No. 95–321, 92 Stat. 394 (July 21, 1978), provided that in order to allow the Congress sufficient time to analyze the report and recommendations of the Secretaries of Interior and Agriculture under subsec. (a) of this section and to take appropriate action, provided that the 1978 grazing year fee was not to be raised by the Secretary of the Interior for the grazing of livestock on public lands nor by the Secretary of Agriculture for such grazing on lands under the jurisdiction of the Forest Service.

National Forest System

Pub. L. No. 116–6, 113 Stat. 242–43 (Feb. 15, 2019), provided that:

> For necessary expenses of the Forest Service, not otherwise provided for, for management, protection, improvement, and utilization of the National Forest System, and for hazardous fuels management on or adjacent to such lands, $1,938,000,000, to remain available through September 30, 2022: Provided, That of the funds provided, $40,000,000 shall be deposited in the Collaborative Forest Landscape Restoration Fund for ecological restoration treatments as authorized by 16 U.S.C. 7303(f): Provided further, That of the funds provided, $368,000,000 shall be for forest products: Provided further, That of the funds provided, $435,000,000 shall be for hazardous fuels management activities, of which not to exceed $15,000,000 may be used to make grants, using any authorities available to the Forest Service under the "State and Private Forestry" appropriation, for the purpose of creating incentives for increased use of biomass from National Forest System lands: Provided further, That $20,000,000 may be used by the Secretary of Agriculture to enter into procurement contracts or cooperative agreements or to issue grants for hazardous fuels management activities, and for training or monitoring associated with such hazardous fuels management activities on Federal land, or on non-Federal land if the Secretary determines such activities benefit resources on Federal land: Provided further, That funds made available to implement the Community Forestry Restoration Act, Public Law 106–393, title VI, shall be available for use on non-Federal lands in accordance with authorities made available to the Forest Service under the "State and Private Forestry" appropriations: Provided further, That notwithstanding section 33 of the Bankhead Jones Farm Tenant Act (7 U.S.C. 1012), the Secretary of Agriculture, in calculating a fee for grazing on a National Grassland, may provide a credit of up to 50 percent of the calculated fee to a Grazing Association or direct permittee for a conservation practice approved by the Secretary in advance of the fiscal year in which the cost of the conservation practice is incurred. And, that the amount credited shall remain available to the Grazing Association or the direct permittee, as appropriate, in the fiscal year in which the credit is made and each fiscal year thereafter for use on the project for conservation practices approved by the Secretary.

Similarly, Pub. L. No. 116–94, 133 Stat. 2724–25 (Dec. 20, 2019), provided that:

> For necessary expenses of the Forest Service, not otherwise provided for, for management, protection, improvement, and utilization of the National Forest System, and for hazardous fuels management on or adjacent to such lands, $1,957,510,000, to remain available through September 30, 2023: Provided, That of the funds provided, $40,000,000 shall be deposited in the Collaborative Forest Landscape Restoration Fund for ecological restoration treatments as authorized by 16 U.S.C. 7303(f): Provided further, That of the funds provided, $373,000,000 shall be for forest products: Provided further, That of the funds provided, $445,310,000 shall be for hazardous fuels management activities, of which not to exceed $15,000,000 may be used to make grants, using any authorities available to the Forest Service under the "State and Private Forestry" appropriation, for the purpose of creating incentives for increased use of biomass from National Forest System lands: Provided further, That $20,000,000 may be used by the Secretary of Agriculture to

> enter into procurement contracts or cooperative agreements or to issue grants for hazardous fuels management activities, and for training or monitoring associated with such hazardous fuels management activities on Federal land, or on non-Federal land if the Secretary determines such activities benefit resources on Federal land: Provided further, That funds made available to implement the Community Forestry Restoration Act, Public Law 106–393, title VI, shall be available for use on non-Federal lands in accordance with authorities made available to the Forest Service under the "State and Private Forestry" appropriations: Provided further, That notwithstanding section 33 of the Bankhead Jones Farm Tenant Act (7 U.S.C. 1012), the Secretary of Agriculture, in calculating a fee for grazing on a National Grassland, may provide a credit of up to 50 percent of the calculated fee to a Grazing Association or direct permittee for a conservation practice approved by the Secretary in advance of the fiscal year in which the cost of the conservation practice is incurred. And, that the amount credited shall remain available to the Grazing Association or the direct permittee, as appropriate, in the fiscal year in which the credit is made and each fiscal year thereafter for use on the project for conservation practices approved by the Secretary.

Similarly, Pub. L. No. 116–260, 134 Stat. 1517–18 (Dec. 27, 2020), provided that:

> For necessary expenses of the Forest Service, not otherwise provided for, for management, protection, improvement, and utilization of the National Forest System, and for hazardous fuels management on or adjacent to such lands, $1,786,870,000, to remain available through September 30, 2024: Provided, That of the funds provided, $13,787,000 shall be deposited in the Collaborative Forest Landscape Restoration Fund for ecological restoration treatments as authorized by 16 U.S.C. 7303(f): Provided further, That of the funds provided, $37,017,000 shall be for forest products: Provided further, That of the funds provided, $180,388,000 shall be for hazardous fuels management activities, of which not to exceed $12,454,000 may be used to make grants, using any authorities available to the Forest Service under the "State and Private Forestry" appropriation, for the purpose of creating incentives for increased use of biomass from National Forest System lands: Provided further, That $20,000,000 may be used by the Secretary of Agriculture to enter into procurement contracts or cooperative agreements or to issue grants for hazardous fuels management activities, and for training or monitoring associated with such hazardous fuels management activities on Federal land, or on non-Federal land if the Secretary determines such activities benefit resources on Federal land: Provided further, That funds made available to implement the Community Forestry Restoration Act, Public Law 106–393, title VI, shall be available for use on non-Federal lands in accordance with authorities made available to the Forest Service under the "State and Private Forestry" appropriations: Provided further, That notwithstanding section 33 of the Bankhead Jones Farm Tenant Act (7 U.S.C. 1012), the Secretary of Agriculture, in calculating a fee for grazing on a National Grassland, may provide a credit of up to 50 percent of the calculated fee to a Grazing Association or direct permittee for a conservation practice approved by the Secretary in advance of the fiscal year in which the cost of the conservation practice is incurred, and that the amount credited shall remain available to the Grazing Association or the direct permittee, as appropriate, in the fiscal year in which the credit is made and each fiscal year thereafter for use on the project for conservation practices approved by the Secretary: Provided further, That funds appropriated to this account shall be available for the base salary and expenses of employees that carry out the functions funded by the "Capital Improvement and Maintenance" account, the "Range Betterment Fund" account, and the "Management of National Forests for Subsistence Uses" account.

§ 1752. Grazing leases and permits

[FLPMA § 402]

(a) Terms and conditions

Except as provided in subsection (b) of this section, permits and leases for domestic livestock grazing on public lands issued by the Secretary under the Act of June 28, 1934 (48 Stat. 1269, as amended; 43 U.S.C. 315 et seq.) or the Act of August 28, 1937 (50 Stat. 874, as amended; 43 U.S.C. 1181a–1181j), or by the Secretary of Agriculture, with respect to lands within National Forests in the sixteen contiguous Western States, shall be for a term of ten years subject to such terms and conditions the Secretary concerned deems appropriate and consistent with the governing law, including, but not limited to, the authority of the Secretary concerned to cancel, suspend, or modify a grazing permit or lease, in whole or in part, pursuant to the terms and conditions thereof, or to cancel or suspend a grazing permit or lease for any violation of a grazing regulation or of any term or condition of such grazing permit or lease.

(b) Terms of lesser duration

Permits or leases may be issued by the Secretary concerned for a period shorter than ten years where the Secretary concerned determines that—

(1) the land is pending disposal; or

(2) the land will be devoted to a public purpose prior to the end of ten years; or

(3) it will be in the best interest of sound land management to specify a shorter term: *Provided*, That the absence from an allotment management plan of details the Secretary concerned would like to include but which are undeveloped shall not be the basis for establishing a term shorter than ten years: *Provided further*, That the absence of completed land use plans or court ordered environmental statements shall not be the sole basis for establishing a term shorter than ten years unless the Secretary determines on a case-by-case basis that the information to be contained in such land use plan or court ordered environmental impact statement is necessary to determine whether a shorter term should be established for any of the reasons set forth in items (1) through (3) of this subsection.

(c) First priority for renewal of expiring permit or lease

So long as (1) the lands for which the permit or lease is issued remain available for domestic livestock grazing in accordance with land use plans prepared pursuant to section 1712 of this title or section 1604 of Title 16, (2) the permittee or lessee is in compliance with the rules and regulations issued and the terms and conditions in the permit or lease specified by the Secretary concerned, and (3) the permittee or lessee accepts the terms and conditions to be included by the Secretary concerned in the new permit or lease, the holder of the expiring permit or lease shall be given first priority for receipt of the new permit or lease.

(d) Allotment management plan requirements

All permits and leases for domestic livestock grazing issued pursuant to this section may incorporate an allotment management plan developed by the Secretary concerned. However, nothing in this subsection shall be construed to supersede any requirement for completion of court ordered environmental impact statements prior to development and incorporation of allotment management plans. If the Secretary concerned elects to develop an allotment management plan for a given area, he shall do so in careful and considered consultation, cooperation and coordination with the lessees, permittees, and landowners involved, the district grazing advisory boards established pursuant to section 1753 of this title, and any State or States having lands within the area to be covered by such allotment management plan. Allotment management plans shall be tailored to the specific range condition of the area to be covered by such plan, and shall be reviewed on a periodic basis to determine whether they have been effective in improving the range condition of the lands involved or whether such lands can be better managed under the provisions of subsection (e) of this section. The Secretary concerned may revise or terminate such plans or develop new plans from time to time after such review and careful and considered consultation, cooperation and coordination with the parties involved. As used in this subsection, the terms "court ordered environmental impact statement" and "range condition" shall be defined as in the "Public Rangelands Improvement Act of 1978 [43 U.S.C.A. § 1901 et seq.]".

(e) Omission of allotment management plan requirements and incorporation of appropriate terms and conditions; reexamination of range conditions

In all cases where the Secretary concerned has not completed an allotment management plan or determines that an allotment management plan is not necessary for management of livestock operations and will not be prepared, the Secretary concerned shall incorporate in grazing permits and leases such terms and conditions as he deems appropriate for management of the permitted or leased lands pursuant to applicable law. The Secretary concerned shall also specify therein the numbers of animals to be grazed and the seasons of use and that he may reexamine the condition of the range at any time and, if he finds on reexamination that the condition of the range requires adjustment in the amount or other aspect of grazing use, that the permittee or lessee shall adjust his use to the extent the Secretary concerned deems necessary. Such readjustment shall be put into full force and effect on the date specified by the Secretary concerned.

(f) Allotment management plan applicability to non-Federal lands; appeal rights

Allotment management plans shall not refer to livestock operations or range improvements on non-Federal lands except where the non-Federal lands are intermingled with, or, with the consent of the permittee or lessee involved, associated with, the Federal lands subject to the plan. The Secretary concerned under appropriate regulations shall grant to lessees and permittees the right of appeal from decisions which specify the terms and conditions of allotment management plans. The preceding sentence of this subsection shall not be construed as limiting any other right of appeal from decisions of such officials.

(g) Cancellation of permit or lease; determination of reasonable compensation; notice

Whenever a permit or lease for grazing domestic livestock is canceled in whole or in part, in order to devote the lands covered by the permit or lease to another public purpose, including disposal, the permittee or lessee shall receive from the United States a reasonable compensation for the adjusted value, to be determined by the Secretary concerned, of his interest in authorized permanent improvements placed or constructed by the permittee or lessee on lands covered by such permit or lease, but not to exceed the fair market value of the terminated portion of the permittee's or lessee's interest therein. Except in cases of emergency, no permit or lease shall be canceled under this subsection without two years' prior notification.

(h) Applicability of provisions to rights, etc., in or to public lands or lands in National Forests

Nothing in this Act shall be construed as modifying in any way law existing on October 21, 1976, with respect to the creation of right, title, interest or estate in or to public lands or lands in National Forests by issuance of grazing permits and leases.

(Pub. L. No. 94–579, Title IV, § 402, 90 Stat. 2773 (Oct. 21, 1976); as amended by Pub. L. No. 95–514, §§ 7, 8, 92 Stat. 1807 (Oct. 25, 1978).)

HISTORICAL AND STATUTORY NOTES

References in Text

The Act of June 28, 1934, referred to in subsec. (a) is Act of June 28, 1934, c. 865, 48 Stat. 1269, as amended, known as the Taylor Grazing Act, which is codified principally as subchapter I (section 315 et seq.) of chapter 8A of this title. For complete classification of this Act to the Code, see Short Title note set out under section 315 of this title and Tables.

The Act of Aug. 28, 1937 (50 Stat. 874; 43 U.S.C. 1181a–1181j), referred to in subsec. (a), is Act of Aug. 28, 1937, c. 876, 50 Stat. 874, as amended, which enacted sections 1181a to 1181f of this title. Sections 1181f–1 to 1181f–4, included within the parenthetical reference to sections 1181a to 1181j, were enacted by Act of May 24, 1939, c. 144, 53 Stat. 753. Sections 1181g to 1181j, also included within the parenthetical reference to sections 1181a to 1181j, were enacted by Act of June 24, 1954, c. 357, 68 Stat. 270. For complete classification of these Acts to the Code, see Tables volume.

The Public Rangelands Improvement Act of 1978, referred to in subsec. (d), is Pub. L. No. 95–514, 92 Stat. 1803 (Oct. 25, 1978), which is codified principally as chapter 37 (section 1901 et seq.) of this title. For complete classification of this Act to the Code, see Short Title note set out under section 1901 of this title and Tables volume.

This Act, referred to in subsec (h), is Pub. L. No. 94–579, 90 Stat. 2743 (Oct. 21, 1976), as amended, known as the Federal Land Policy and Management Act of 1976. For complete classification of this Act to the Code, see Tables volume.

Reports to Congress on Grazing Permits

Pub. L. No. 108–108, Title III, § 325, 117 Stat. 1307 (Nov. 10, 2003), provided in part: "That beginning in November 2004, and every year thereafter, the Secretaries of the Interior and Agriculture shall report to Congress the extent to which they are completing analysis required under applicable laws prior to the expiration of grazing permits, and beginning in May 2004, and every two years thereafter, the Secretaries shall provide Congress recommendations for legislative provisions necessary to ensure all permit renewals are completed in a timely manner. The legislative recommendations provided shall be consistent with the funding levels requested in the Secretaries' budget proposals."

Reductions in Grazing Allotments on Public Rangelands

Pub. L. No. 102–381, Title I, 106 Stat. 1378 (Oct. 5, 1992), provided in part: "That an appeal of any reductions in grazing allotments on public rangelands must be taken within thirty days after receipt of a final grazing allotment decision. Reductions of up to 10 per centum in grazing allotments shall become effective when so designated by the Secretary of the Interior. Upon appeal any proposed reduction in excess of 10 per centum shall be suspended pending final action on the appeal, which shall be completed within two years after the appeal is filed[.]".

Similar provisions were contained in the following prior Appropriations Acts:

Pub. L. No. 102–154, Title I, 105 Stat. 993 (Nov. 13, 1991).

Pub. L. No. 101–512, Title I, 104 Stat. 1917 (Nov. 5, 1990).

Pub. L. No. 101–121, Title I, 103 Stat. 704 (Oct. 23, 1989).

Pub. L. No. 100–446, Title I, 102 Stat. 1776 (Sept. 27, 1988).

Pub. L. No. 100–202, § 101(g) [Title I], 101 Stat. 1329–216 (Dec. 22, 1987).

Pub. L. No. 99–591, Title I, § 101(h) [Title I, § 100], 100 Stat. 3341–245 (Oct. 30, 1986).

Pub. L. No. 99–500, Title I, § 101(h) [Title I, § 100], 100 Stat. 1783 (Oct. 18, 1986).

Pub. L. No. 99–190, § 101(d) [Title I, § 100], 99 Stat. 1226 (Dec. 19, 1985).

Pub. L. No. 98–473, Title I, § 101(c), 98 Stat. 1840 (Oct. 12, 1984).

Pub. L. No. 98–146, Title I, § 100, 97 Stat. 921 (Nov. 4, 1983).

Pub. L. No. 97–394, Title I, § 1, 96 Stat. 1968 (Dec. 30, 1982).

Pub. L. No. 97–100, Title I, § 100, 95 Stat. 1393 (Dec. 23, 1981).

Pub. L. No. 96–514, Title I, § 100, 94 Stat. 2959 (Dec. 12, 1980).

Pub. L. No. 96–126, Title I, § 100, 93 Stat. 956 (Nov. 27, 1979).

§ 1753. Grazing advisory boards

[FLPMA § 403]

(a) Establishment; maintenance

For each Bureau district office and National Forest headquarters office in the sixteen contiguous Western States having jurisdiction over more than five hundred thousand acres of lands subject to commercial livestock grazing (hereinafter in this section referred to as "office"), the Secretary and the Secretary of Agriculture, upon the petition of a simple majority of the livestock lessees and permittees under the jurisdiction of such office, shall establish and maintain at least one grazing advisory board of not more than fifteen advisers.

(b) Functions

The function of grazing advisory boards established pursuant to this section shall be to offer advice and make recommendations to the head of the office involved concerning the development of allotment management plans and the utilization of range-betterment funds.

(c) Appointment and terms of members

The number of advisers on each board and the number of years an adviser may serve shall be determined by the Secretary concerned in his discretion. Each board shall consist of livestock representatives who shall be lessees or permittees in the area administered by the office concerned and shall be chosen by the lessees and permittees in the area through an election prescribed by the Secretary concerned.

(d) Meetings

Each grazing advisory board shall meet at least once annually.

(e) Federal Advisory Committee Act applicability

Except as may be otherwise provided by this section, the provisions of the Federal Advisory Committee Act (86 Stat. 770) shall apply to grazing advisory boards.

(f) Expiration date

The provisions of this section shall expire December 31, 1985.

(Pub. L. No. 94–579, Title IV, § 403, 90 Stat. 2775 (Oct. 21, 1976); as amended by Pub. L. No. 95–514, § 10, 92 Stat. 1808 (Oct. 25, 1978).)

HISTORICAL AND STATUTORY NOTES

References in Text

The Federal Advisory Committee Act, referred to in subsec. (e), is Pub. L. No. 92–463, 86 Stat. 770 (Oct. 6, 1972), as amended, and is set out in Appendix 2 to Title 5, Government Organization and Employees.

SUBCHAPTER V—RIGHTS-OF-WAY

§ 1761. Grant, issue, or renewal of rights-of-way

[FLPMA § 501]

(a) Authorized purposes

The Secretary, with respect to the public lands (including public lands, as defined in section 1702(e) of this title, which are reserved from entry pursuant to section 24 of the Federal Power Act (16 U.S.C. 818)) and, the Secretary of Agriculture, with respect to lands within the National Forest System (except in each case land designated as wilderness), are authorized to grant, issue, or renew rights-of-way over, upon, under, or through such lands for—

(1) reservoirs, canals, ditches, flumes, laterals, pipes, pipelines, tunnels, and other facilities and systems for the impoundment, storage, transportation, or distribution of water;

(2) pipelines and other systems for the transportation or distribution of liquids and gases, other than water and other than oil, natural gas, synthetic liquid or gaseous fuels, or any refined product produced therefrom, and for storage and terminal facilities in connection therewith;

(3) pipelines, slurry and emulsion systems, and conveyor belts for transportation and distribution of solid materials, and facilities for the storage of such materials in connection therewith;

(4) systems for generation, transmission, and distribution of electric energy, except that the applicant shall also comply with all applicable requirements of the Federal Energy Regulatory Commission under the Federal Power Act, including part 1[1] thereof (41 Stat. 1063, 16 U.S.C. 791a–825r);[2]

(5) systems for transmission or reception of radio, television, telephone, telegraph, and other electronic signals, and other means of communication;

(6) roads, trails, highways, railroads, canals, tunnels, tramways, airways, livestock driveways, or other means of transportation except where such facilities are constructed and maintained in connection with commercial recreation facilities on lands in the National Forest System; or

(7) such other necessary transportation or other systems or facilities which are in the public interest and which require rights-of-way over, upon, under, or through such lands.

(b) Procedures applicable; administration

(1) The Secretary concerned shall require, prior to granting, issuing, or renewing a right-of-way, that the applicant submit and disclose those plans, contracts, agreements, or other information reasonably related to the use, or intended use, of the right-of-way, including its effect on competition, which he deems necessary to a determination, in accordance with the provisions of this Act, as to whether a right-of-way shall be granted, issued, or renewed and the terms and conditions which should be included in the right-of-way.

(2) If the applicant is a partnership, corporation, association, or other business entity, the Secretary concerned, prior to granting a right-to-way[3] pursuant to this subchapter, shall require the applicant to disclose the identity of the participants in the entity, when he deems it necessary to a determination, in accordance with the provisions of this subchapter, as to whether a right-of-way shall be granted, issued, or renewed and the terms and conditions which should be included in the right-of-way. Such disclosures shall include, where applicable: (A) the name and address of each partner; (B) the name and address of each shareholder owning 3 per centum or more of the shares, together with the number and percentage of any class of voting shares of the entity which such shareholder is authorized to vote; and (C) the name and address of each affiliate of the entity together with, in the case of an affiliate controlled by the entity, the number of shares and the percentage of any class of voting stock of that affiliate owned, directly or indirectly, by that entity, and, in the case of an affiliate which controls that entity, the number of shares and the percentage of any class of voting stock of that entity owned, directly or indirectly, by the affiliate.

(3) The Secretary of Agriculture shall have the authority to administer all rights-of-way granted or issued under authority of previous Acts with respect to lands under the jurisdiction of the Secretary of Agriculture, including rights-of-way granted or issued pursuant to authority given to the Secretary of the Interior by such previous Acts.

(c) Permanent easement for water systems; issuance, preconditions, etc.

(1) Upon receipt of a written application pursuant to paragraph (2) of this subsection from an applicant meeting the requirements of this subsection, the Secretary of Agriculture shall issue a permanent easement, without a requirement for reimbursement, for a water system as described in subsection (a)(1) of this section, traversing Federal lands within the National Forest System ("National Forest Lands"), constructed and in operation or placed into operation prior to October 21, 1976, if—

(A) the traversed National Forest lands are in a State where the appropriation doctrine governs the ownership of water rights;

(B) at the time of submission of the application the water system is used solely for agricultural irrigation or livestock watering purposes;

(C) the use served by the water system is not located solely on Federal lands;

(D) the originally constructed facilities comprising such system have been in substantially continuous operation without abandonment;

(E) the applicant has a valid existing right, established under applicable State law, for water to be conveyed by the water system;

(F) a recordable survey and other information concerning the location and characteristics of the system as necessary for proper management of National Forest lands is provided to the Secretary of Agriculture by the applicant for the easement; and

(G) the applicant submits such application on or before December 31, 1996.

(2) **(A)** Nothing in this subsection shall be construed as affecting any grants made by any previous Act. To the extent any such previous grant of right-of-way is a valid existing right, it shall remain in full force and effect unless an owner thereof notifies the Secretary of Agriculture that such owner elects to have a water system on such right-of-way governed by the provisions of this subsection and submits a written application for issuance of an easement pursuant to this subsection, in which case upon the issuance of an easement pursuant to this subsection such previous grant shall be deemed to have been relinquished and shall terminate.

(B) Easements issued under the authority of this subsection shall be fully transferable with all existing conditions and without the imposition of fees or new conditions or stipulations at the time of transfer. The holder shall notify the Secretary of Agriculture within sixty days of any address change of the holder or change in ownership of the facilities.

(C) Easements issued under the authority of this subsection shall include all changes or modifications to the original facilities in existence as of October 21, 1976, the date of enactment of this Act.

(D) Any future extension or enlargement of facilities after October 21, 1976, shall require the issuance of a separate authorization, not authorized under this subsection.

(3) **(A)** Except as otherwise provided in this subsection, the Secretary of Agriculture may terminate or suspend an easement issued pursuant to this subsection in accordance with the procedural and other provisions of section 1766 of this title. An easement issued pursuant to this subsection shall terminate if the water system for which such easement was issued is used for any purpose other than agricultural irrigation or livestock watering use. For purposes of subparagraph (D) of paragraph (1) of this subsection, non-use of a water system for agricultural irrigation or livestock watering purposes for any continuous five-year period shall constitute a rebuttable presumption of abandonment of the facilities comprising such system.

(B) Nothing in this subsection shall be deemed to be an assertion by the United States of any right or claim with regard to the reservation, acquisition, or use of water. Nothing in this subsection shall be deemed to confer on the Secretary of Agriculture any power or authority to regulate or control in any manner the appropriation, diversion, or use of water for any purpose (nor to diminish any such power or authority of such Secretary under applicable law) or to require the conveyance or transfer to the United States of any right or claim to the appropriation, diversion, or use of water.

(C) Except as otherwise provided in this subsection, all rights-of-way issued pursuant to this subsection are subject to all conditions and requirements of this Act.

(D) In the event a right-of-way issued pursuant to this subsection is allowed to deteriorate to the point of threatening persons or property and the holder of the right-of-way, after consultation with the Secretary of Agriculture, refuses to perform the repair and maintenance necessary to remove the threat to persons or property, the Secretary shall have the right to undertake such repair and maintenance on the right-of-way and to assess the holder for the costs of such repair and maintenance, regardless of whether the Secretary had required the holder to furnish a bond or other security pursuant to subsection (i) of this section.

(d) Rights-of-way on certain Federal lands

With respect to any project or portion thereof that was licensed pursuant to, or granted an exemption from, part I of the Federal Power Act [16 U.S.C.A. §§ 791a et seq.] which is located on lands subject to a reservation under section 24 of the Federal Power Act [16 U.S.C.A. § 818] and which did not receive a permit, right-of-way or other approval under this section prior to October 24, 1992, no such permit, right-of-way, or other approval shall be required for continued operation, including continued operation pursuant to section 15 of the Federal Power Act [16 U.S.C.A. § 808], of such project unless the Commission determines that such project involves the use of any additional public lands or National Forest lands not subject to such reservation.

(Pub. L. No. 94–579, Title V, § 501, 90 Stat. 2776 (Oct. 21, 1976); as amended by Pub. L. No. 99–545, § 1(b), (c), 100 Stat. 3047, 3048 (Oct. 27, 1986); Pub. L. No. 102–486, Title XXIV, § 2401, 106 Stat. 3096 (Oct. 24, 1992).)

[1] So in original. Probably should be "part I."

[2] So in original. The period preceding the semicolon probably should not appear.

[3] So in original. Probably should be "right-of-way."

HISTORICAL AND STATUTORY NOTES

References in Text

The Federal Power Act, referred to in text, is Act of June 10, 1920, c. 285, 41 Stat. 1063, as amended. Part I of the Federal Power Act is codified generally as subchapter I (section 791a et seq.) of chapter 12 of Title 16, Conservation. For complete classification of this Act to the Code, see section 791a of Title 16 and Tables.

This Act, referred to in subsec. (b)(1), is Pub. L. No. 94–579, 90 Stat. 2743 (Oct. 21, 1976), as amended, known as the Federal Land Policy and Management Act of 1976. For complete classification of this Act to the Code, see Tables.

Transfer of Functions

The Federal Power Commission was terminated and its functions, personnel, property, funds, etc., were transferred to the Secretary of Energy (except for certain functions which were transferred to the Federal Energy

Regulatory Commission) by sections 7151(b), 7171(a), 7172(a), 7291, and 7293 of Title 42, Public Health and Welfare.

Enforcement functions of the Secretary or other official in Department of Agriculture, insofar as they involve lands and programs under jurisdiction of that Department, related to compliance with land use permits for other associated land uses issued under sections 1761, and 1763 to 1771 of this title, and such functions of Secretary or other official in Department of Interior related to compliance with land use permits for temporary use of public lands and other associated land uses, issued under sections 1732, 1761, and 1763 to 1771 of this title, with respect to pre-construction, construction, and initial operation of transportation systems for Canadian and Alaskan natural gas were transferred to the Federal Inspector, Office of Federal Inspector for the Alaska Natural Gas Transportation System, until the first anniversary of date of initial operation of the Alaska Natural Gas Transportation System, see Reorg. Plan No. 1 of 1979, §§ 102(e), (f), 203(a), 44 Fed. Reg. 33663, 33666, 93 Stat. 1373, 1376, effective July 1, 1979, set out in Appendix 1 to Title 5, Government Organization and Employees.

§ 1762. Roads

[FLPMA § 502]

(a) Authority to acquire, construct, and maintain; financing arrangements

The Secretary, with respect to the public lands, is authorized to provide for the acquisition, construction, and maintenance of roads within and near the public lands in locations and according to specifications which will permit maximum economy in harvesting timber from such lands tributary to such roads and at the same time meet the requirements for protection, development, and management of such lands for utilization of the other resources thereof. Financing of such roads may be accomplished (1) by the Secretary utilizing appropriated funds, (2) by requirements on purchasers of timber and other products from the public lands, including provisions for amortization of road costs in contracts, (3) by cooperative financing with other public agencies and with private agencies or persons, or (4) by a combination of these methods: *Provided*, That, where roads of a higher standard than that needed in the harvesting and removal of the timber and other products covered by the particular sale are to be constructed, the purchaser of timber and other products from public lands shall not, except when the provisions of the second proviso of this subsection apply, be required to bear that part of the costs necessary to meet such higher standard, and the Secretary is authorized to make such arrangements to this end as may be appropriate: *Provided further*, That when timber is offered with the condition that the purchaser thereof will build a road or roads in accordance with standards specified in the offer, the purchaser of the timber will be responsible for paying the full costs of construction of such roads.

(b) Recordation of copies of affected instruments

Copies of all instruments affecting permanent interests in land executed pursuant to this section shall be recorded in each county where the lands are located.

(c) Maintenance or reconstruction of facilities by users

The Secretary may require the user or users of a road, trail, land, or other facility administered by him through the Bureau, including purchasers of Government timber and other products, to maintain such facilities in a satisfactory condition commensurate with the particular use requirements of each. Such maintenance to be borne by each user shall be proportionate to total use. The Secretary may also require the user or users of such a facility to reconstruct the same when such reconstruction is determined to be necessary to accommodate such use. If such maintenance or reconstruction cannot be so provided or if the Secretary determines that maintenance or reconstruction by a user would not be practical, then the Secretary may require that sufficient funds be deposited by the user to provide his portion of such total maintenance or reconstruction. Deposits made to cover the maintenance or reconstruction of roads are hereby made available until expended to cover the cost to the United States of accomplishing the purposes for which deposited: *Provided*, That deposits received for work on adjacent and overlapping areas may be combined when it is the most practicable and efficient manner of performing the work, and cost thereof may be determined by estimates: *And provided further*, That unexpended balances upon accomplishment of the purpose for which deposited shall be transferred to miscellaneous receipts or refunded.

(d) Fund for user fees for delayed payment to grantor

Whenever the agreement under which the United States has obtained for the use of, or in connection with, the public lands a right-of-way or easement for a road or an existing road or the right to use an existing road provides for delayed payments to the Government's grantor, any fees or other collections received by the Secretary for the use of the road may be placed in a fund to be available for making payments to the grantor.

(Pub. L. No. 94–579, Title V, § 502, 90 Stat. 2777 (Oct. 21, 1976).)

§ 1763. Right-of-way corridors; criteria and procedures applicable for designation

[FLPMA § 503]

In order to minimize adverse environmental impacts and the proliferation of separate rights-of-way, the utilization of rights-of-way in common shall be required to the extent practical, and each right-of-way or permit shall reserve to the Secretary concerned the right to grant additional rights-of-way or permits for compatible uses on or adjacent to rights-of-way granted pursuant to this Act. In designating right-of-way corridors and in determining whether to require that rights-of-way be confined to them, the Secretary concerned shall take into consideration national and State land use policies, environmental quality, economic efficiency, national security, safety, and good engineering and technological practices. The Secretary concerned shall issue regulations containing the criteria and procedures he will use in designating such corridors. Any existing transportation and utility corridors may be designated as transportation and utility corridors pursuant to this subsection without further review.

(Pub. L. No. 94–579, Title V, § 503, 90 Stat. 2778 (Oct. 21, 1976).)

HISTORICAL AND STATUTORY NOTES

References in Text

This Act, referred to in text, is Pub. L. No. 94–579, 90 Stat. 2743 (Oct. 21, 1976), as amended, known as the Federal Land Policy and Management Act of 1976. For complete classification of this Act to the Code, see Tables.

Transfer of Functions

Enforcement functions of Secretary or other official in Department of Agriculture, insofar as they involve lands and programs under jurisdiction of that Department, related to compliance with land use permits for other associated land uses issued under sections 1761, and 1763 to 1771 of this title, and such functions of Secretary or other official in Department of Interior related to compliance with land use permits for temporary use of public lands and other associated land uses, issued under sections 1732, 1761, and 1763 to 1771 of this title, with respect to pre-construction, construction, and initial operation of transportation systems for Canadian and Alaskan natural gas were transferred to the Federal Inspector, Office of Federal Inspector for Alaska Natural Gas Transportation System, until the first anniversary of date of initial operation of the Alaska Natural Gas Transportation System, see Reorg. Plan No. 1 of 1979, §§ 102(e), (f), 203(a), 44 Fed. Reg. 33663, 33666, 93 Stat. 1373, 1376, effective July 1, 1979, set out in Appendix 1 to Title 5, Government Organization and Employees.

§ 1764. General requirements

[FLPMA § 504]

(a) Boundary specifications; criteria; temporary use of additional lands

The Secretary concerned shall specify the boundaries of each right-of-way as precisely as is practical. Each right-of-way shall be limited to the ground which the Secretary concerned determines (1) will be occupied by facilities which constitute the project for which the right-of-way is granted, issued, or renewed, (2) to be necessary for the operation or maintenance of the project, (3) to be necessary to protect the public safety, and (4) will do no unnecessary damage to the environment. The Secretary concerned may authorize the temporary use of such additional lands as he determines to be reasonably necessary for the construction, operation, maintenance, or termination of the project or a portion thereof, or for access thereto.

(b) Terms and conditions of right-of-way or permit

Each right-of-way or permit granted, issued, or renewed pursuant to this section shall be limited to a reasonable term in light of all circumstances concerning the project. In determining the duration of a right-of-way the Secretary concerned shall, among other things, take into consideration the cost of the facility, its useful life, and any public purpose it serves. The right-of-way shall specify whether it is or is not renewable and the terms and conditions applicable to the renewal.

(c) Applicability of regulations or stipulations

Rights-of-way shall be granted, issued, or renewed pursuant to this subchapter under such regulations or stipulations, consistent with the provisions of this subchapter or any other applicable law, and shall also be subject to such terms and conditions as the Secretary concerned may prescribe regarding extent, duration, survey, location, construction, maintenance, transfer or assignment, and termination.

(d) Submission of plan of construction, operation, and rehabilitation by new project applicants; plan requirements

The Secretary concerned prior to granting or issuing a right-of-way pursuant to this subchapter for a new project which may have a significant impact on the environment, shall require the applicant to submit a plan of construction, operation, and rehabilitation for such right-of-way which shall comply with stipulations or with regulations issued by that Secretary, including the terms and conditions required under section 1765 of this title.

(e) Regulatory requirements for terms and conditions; revision and applicability of regulations

The Secretary concerned shall issue regulations with respect to the terms and conditions that will be included in rights-of-way pursuant to section 1765 of this title. Such regulations shall be regularly revised as needed. Such regulations shall be applicable to every right-of-way granted or issued pursuant to this subchapter and to any subsequent renewal thereof, and may be applicable to rights-of-way not granted or issued, but renewed pursuant to this subchapter.

(f) Removal or use of mineral and vegetative materials

Mineral and vegetative materials, including timber, within or without a right-of-way, may be used or disposed of in connection with construction or other purposes only if authorization to remove or use such materials has been obtained pursuant to applicable laws or for emergency repair work necessary for those rights-of-way authorized under section 1761(c) of this title.

(g) Rental payments; amount, waiver, etc.

The holder of a right-of-way shall pay in advance the fair market value thereof, as determined by the Secretary granting, issuing, or renewing such right-of-way. The Secretary concerned may require either annual payment or a payment covering more than one year at a time except that private individuals may make at their option either annual payments or payments covering more than one year if the annual fee is greater than one hundred dollars. The Secretary concerned may waive rentals where a right-of-way is granted, issued or renewed in consideration of a right-of-way conveyed to the United States in connection with a cooperative cost share program between the United States and the holder. The Secretary concerned may, by regulation or prior to promulgation of such regulations, as a condition of a right-of-way, require an applicant for or holder of a right-of-way to reimburse the United States for all reasonable administrative and other costs incurred in processing an application for such right-of-way and in inspection and monitoring of construction, operation, and termination of the facility pursuant to such right-of-way: *Provided, however,* That the Secretary concerned need not secure reimbursement in any situation where there is in existence a cooperative cost share right-of-way program between the United States and the holder of a right-of-way. Rights-of-way may be granted, issued, or renewed to a Federal, State, or local government or any agency or instrumentality thereof, to nonprofit associations or nonprofit corporations which are not themselves controlled or owned by profitmaking corporations or business enterprises, or to a holder where he provides without or at reduced charges a valuable benefit to the public or to the programs of the Secretary concerned, or to a holder in connection with the authorized use or occupancy of Federal land for which the United States is already receiving compensation for such lesser charge, including free use as the Secretary concerned finds equitable and in the public interest. Such rights-of-way issued at less than fair market value are not assignable except with the approval of the Secretary issuing the right-of-way. The moneys received for reimbursement of reasonable costs shall be deposited with the Treasury in a special account and are hereby authorized to be appropriated and made available until expended. Rights-of-way shall be granted, issued, or renewed, without rental fees, for electric or telephone facilities eligible for financing pursuant to the Rural Electrification Act of 1936, as amended [7 U.S.C.A. § 901 et seq.], determined without regard to any application requirement under that Act, or any extensions from such facilities: *Provided,* That nothing in this sentence shall be construed to affect the authority of the Secretary granting, issuing, or renewing the right-of-way to require reimbursement of reasonable administrative and other costs pursuant to the second sentence of this subsection.

(h) Liability for damage or injury incurred by United States for use and occupancy of rights-of-way; indemnification of United States; no-fault liability; amount of damages

(1) The Secretary concerned shall promulgate regulations specifying the extent to which holders of rights-of-way under this subchapter shall be liable to the United States for damage or injury incurred by the United States caused by the use and occupancy of the rights-of-way. The regulations shall also specify the extent to which such holders shall indemnify or hold harmless the United States for liabilities, damages, or claims caused by their use and occupancy of the rights-of-way.

(2) Any regulation or stipulation imposing liability without fault shall include a maximum limitation on damages commensurate with the foreseeable risks or hazards presented. Any liability for damage or injury in excess of this amount shall be determined by ordinary rules of negligence.

(i) Bond or security requirements

Where he deems it appropriate, the Secretary concerned may require a holder of a right-of-way to furnish a bond, or other security, satisfactory to him to secure all or any of the obligations imposed by the terms and conditions of the right-of-way or by any rule or regulation of the Secretary concerned.

(j) Criteria for grant, issue, or renewal of right-of-way

The Secretary concerned shall grant, issue, or renew a right-of-way under this subchapter only when he is satisfied that the applicant has the technical and financial capability to construct the project for which the right-of-way is requested, and in accord with the requirements of this subchapter.

(Pub. L. No. 94–579, Title V, § 504, 90 Stat. 2778 (Oct. 21, 1976); as amended by Pub. L. No. 98–300, 98 Stat. 215 (May 25, 1984); Pub. L. No. 99–545, § 2, 100 Stat. 3048 (Oct. 27, 1986); Pub. L. No. 104–333, Div. I, Title X, § 1032(a), 110 Stat. 4239 (Nov. 12, 1996).)

HISTORICAL AND STATUTORY NOTES

References in Text

The Rural Electrification Act of 1936, as amended, referred to in subsec. (g), is Act of May 20, 1936, c. 432, 49 Stat. 1363, as amended, which is codified generally as chapter 31 (section 901 et seq.) of Title 7, Agriculture. For complete classification of this Act to the Code, see section 901 of Title 7 and Tables.

Effective and Applicability Provisions

1996 Acts. Section 1032(b) of Title X of Div. I of Pub. L. No. 104–333 provided that: "The amendment made by subsection (a) [amending subsec. (g) of this section] shall apply with respect to rights-of-way leases held on or after the date of enactment of this Act [Nov. 12, 1996]."

Transfer of Functions

See note set out under section 1763 of this title.

§ 1765. Terms and conditions

[FLPMA § 505]

Each right-of-way shall contain—

(a) terms and conditions which will (i) carry out the purposes of this Act and rules and regulations issued thereunder; (ii) minimize damage to scenic and esthetic values and fish and wildlife habitat and otherwise protect the environment; (iii) require compliance with applicable air and water quality standards established by or pursuant to applicable Federal or State law; and (iv) require compliance with State standards for public health and safety, environmental protection, and siting, construction, operation, and maintenance of or for rights-of-way for similar purposes if those standards are more stringent than applicable Federal standards; and

(b) such terms and conditions as the Secretary concerned deems necessary to (i) protect Federal property and economic interests; (ii) manage efficiently the lands which are subject to the right-of-way or adjacent thereto and protect the other lawful users of the lands adjacent to or traversed by such right-of-way; (iii) protect lives and property; (iv) protect the interests of individuals living in the general area traversed by the right-of-way who rely on the fish, wildlife, and other biotic resources of the area for subsistence purposes; (v) require location of the right-of-way along a route that will cause least damage to the environment, taking into consideration feasibility and other relevant factors; and (vi) otherwise protect the public interest in the lands traversed by the right-of-way or adjacent thereto.

(Pub. L. No. 94–579, Title V, § 505, 90 Stat. 2780 (Oct. 21, 1976).)

HISTORICAL AND STATUTORY NOTES

References in Text

This Act, referred to in par. (a), is Pub. L. No. 94–579, 90 Stat. 2743 (Oct. 21, 1976), as amended, known as the Federal Land Policy and Management Act of 1976. For complete classification of this Act to the Code, see Tables.

Transfer of Functions

See note set out under section 1763 of this title.

§ 1766. Suspension or termination; grounds; procedures applicable

[FLPMA § 506]

Abandonment of a right-of-way or noncompliance with any provision of this subchapter condition of the right-of-way, or applicable rule or regulation of the Secretary concerned may be grounds for suspension or termination of the right-of-way if, after due notice to the holder of the right-of-way and, and[1] with respect to easements, an appropriate administrative proceeding pursuant to section 554 of Title 5, the Secretary concerned determines that any such ground exists and that suspension or termination is justified. No administrative proceeding shall be required where the right-of-way by its terms provides that it terminates on the occurrence of a fixed or agreed-upon condition, event, or time. If the Secretary concerned determines that an immediate temporary suspension of activities within a right-of-way for violation of its terms and conditions is necessary to protect public health or safety or the environment, he may abate such activities prior to an administrative proceeding. Prior to commencing any proceeding to suspend or terminate a right-of-way the Secretary concerned shall give written notice to the holder of the grounds for such action and shall give the holder a reasonable time to resume use of the right-of-way or to comply with this subchapter condition, rule, or regulation as the case may be. Failure of the holder of the right-of-way to use the right-of-way for the purpose for which it was granted, issued, or renewed, for any continuous five-year period, shall constitute a rebuttable presumption of abandonment of the right-of-way except that where the failure of the holder to use the right-of-way for the purpose for which it was granted, issued, or renewed for any continuous five-year period is due to circumstances not within the holder's control, the Secretary concerned is not required to commence proceedings to suspend or terminate the right-of-way.

(Pub. L. No. 94–579, Title V, § 506, 90 Stat. 2780 (Oct. 21, 1976).)

[1] So in original.

HISTORICAL AND STATUTORY NOTES

Transfer of Functions

See note under section 1763 of this title.

§ 1767. Rights-of-way for Federal departments and agencies [FLPMA § 507]

(a) The Secretary concerned may provide under applicable provisions of this subchapter for the use of any department or agency of the United States a right-of-way over, upon, under or through the land administered by him, subject to such terms and conditions as he may impose.

(b) Where a right-of-way has been reserved for the use of any department or agency of the United States, the Secretary shall take no action to terminate, or otherwise limit, that use without the consent of the head of such department or agency.

(Pub. L. No. 94–579, Title V, § 507, 90 Stat. 2781 (Oct. 21, 1976).)

HISTORICAL AND STATUTORY NOTES

Transfer of Functions

See note set out under section 1763 of this title.

§ 1768. Conveyance of lands covered by right-of-way; terms and conditions [FLPMA § 508]

If under applicable law the Secretary concerned decides to transfer out of Federal ownership any lands covered in whole or in part by a right-of-way, including a right-of-way granted under the Act of November 16, 1973 (87 Stat. 576; 30 U.S.C. 185), the lands may be conveyed subject to the right-of-way; however, if the Secretary concerned determines that retention of Federal control over the right-of-way is necessary to assure that the purposes of this subchapter will be carried out, the terms and conditions of the right-of-way complied with, or the lands protected, he shall (a) reserve to the United States that portion of the lands which lies within the boundaries of the right-of-way, or (b) convey the lands, including that portion within the boundaries of the right-of-way, subject to the right-of-way and reserving to the United States the right to enforce all or any of the terms and conditions of the right-of-way, including the right to renew it or extend it upon its termination and to collect rents.

(Pub. L. No. 94–579, Title V, § 508, 90 Stat. 2781 (Oct. 21, 1976).)

HISTORICAL AND STATUTORY NOTES

References in Text

The Act of November 16, 1973, referred to in text, is Pub. L. No. 93–153, 87 Stat. 576 (Nov. 16, 1973). For complete classification of this Act to the Code, see Tables.

Transfer of Functions

See note set out under section 1763 of this title.

§ 1769. Existing right-of-way or right-of-use unaffected; exceptions; rights-of-way for railroad and appurtenant communication facilities; applicability of existing terms and conditions [FLPMA § 509]

(a) Nothing in this subchapter shall have the effect of terminating any right-of-way or right-of-use heretofore issued, granted, or permitted. However, with the consent of the holder thereof, the Secretary concerned may cancel such a right-of-way or right-of-use and in its stead issue a right-of-way pursuant to the provisions of this subchapter.

(b) When the Secretary concerned issues a right-of-way under this subchapter for a railroad and appurtenant communication facilities in connection with a realinement[1] of a railroad on lands under his jurisdiction by virtue of a right-of-way granted by the United States, he may, when he considers it to be in the public interest and the lands involved are not within an incorporated community and are of approximately equal value, notwithstanding the provisions of this subchapter, provide in the new right-of-way the same terms and conditions as applied to the portion of the existing right-of-way relinquished to the United States with respect to the payment of annual rental, duration of the right-of-way, and the nature of the interest in lands granted. The Secretary concerned or his delegate shall take final action upon all applications for the grant, issue, or renewal of rights-of-way under subsection (b) of this section no later than six months after receipt from the applicant of all information required from the applicant by this subchapter.

(Pub. L. No. 94–579, Title V, § 509, 90 Stat. 2781 (Oct. 21, 1976).)

[1] So in original. Probably should be "realignment."

HISTORICAL AND STATUTORY NOTES

Transfer of Functions

See note set out under section 1763 of this title.

§ 1770. Applicability of provisions to other Federal laws

[FLPMA § 510]

(a) Right-of-way

Effective on and after October 21, 1976, no right-of-way for the purposes listed in this subchapter shall be granted, issued, or renewed over, upon, under, or through such lands except under and subject to the provisions, limitations, and conditions of this subchapter: *Provided,* That nothing in this subchapter shall be construed as affecting or modifying the provisions of sections 532 to 538 of Title 16 and in the event of conflict with, or inconsistency between, this subchapter and sections 532 to 538 of Title 16, the latter shall prevail: *Provided further,* That nothing in this Act should be construed as making it mandatory that, with respect to forest roads, the Secretary of Agriculture limit rights-of-way grants or their term of years or require disclosure pursuant to section 1761(b) of this title or impose any other condition contemplated by this Act that is contrary to present practices of that Secretary under sections 532 to 538 of Title 16. Any pending application for a right-of-way under any other law on the effective date of this section shall be considered as an application under this subchapter. The Secretary concerned may require the applicant to submit any additional information he deems necessary to comply with the requirements of this subchapter.

(b) Highway use

Nothing in this subchapter shall be construed to preclude the use of lands covered by this subchapter for highway purposes pursuant to sections 107 and 317 of Title 23.

(c) Application of antitrust laws

(1) Nothing in this subchapter shall be construed as exempting any holder of a right-of-way issued under this subchapter from any provision of the antitrust laws of the United States.

(2) For the purposes of this subsection, the term "antitrust laws" includes the Act of July 2, 1890 (26 Stat.[1] 15 U.S.C. 1 et seq.); the Act of October 15, 1914 (38 Stat. 730, 15 U.S.C. 12 et seq.); the Federal Trade Commission Act (38 Stat. 717; 15 U.S.C. 41 et seq.); and sections 73 and 74 of the Act of August 27, 1894 [15 U.S.C.A. §§ 8, 9].

(Pub. L. No. 94–579, Title V, § 510, 90 Stat. 2782 (Oct. 21, 1976).)

[1] So in original. Probably should be "26 Stat. 209,".

HISTORICAL AND STATUTORY NOTES

References in Text

This Act, referred to in subsec. (a), is Pub. L. No. 94–579, 90 Stat. 2743 (Oct. 21, 1976), as amended, known as the Federal Land Policy and Management Act of 1976. For complete classification of this Act to the Code, see Tables.

Act of July 2, 1890, referred to in subsec. (c)(2), is Act of July 2, 1890, c. 647, 26 Stat. 209, as amended, known as the Sherman Act, which is codified as sections 1 to 7 of Title 15, Commerce and Trade. For complete classification of this Act to the Code, see Short Title note set out under section 1 of Title 15 and Tables volume.

Act of October 15, 1914, referred to in subsec. (c)(2), is Act of Oct. 15, 1914, c. 323, 38 Stat. 730, as amended, known as the Clayton Act, which is codified generally as sections 12, 13, 14 to 19, 20, 21, and 22 to 27 of Title 15, Commerce and Trade, and sections 52 and 53 of Title 29, Labor. For further details and complete classification of this Act to the Code, see References in Text note set out under section 12 of Title 15 and Tables volume.

The Federal Trade Commission Act, referred to in subsec. (c)(2), is Act of Sept. 26, 1914, c. 311, 38 Stat. 717, as amended, which is codified generally as subchapter I (section 41 et seq.) of chapter 2 of Title 15, Commerce and Trade. For complete classification of this Act to the Code, see section 58 of Title 15 and Tables volume.

Sections 73 and 74 of the Act of August 27, 1894, referred to in subsec. (c), are sections 73 and 74 of Act Aug. 27, 1894, c. 349, 28 Stat. 570, which are codified as sections 8 and 9 of Title 15, Commerce and Trade.

Transfer of Functions

See note set out under section 1763 of this title.

§ 1771. Coordination of applications

[FLPMA § 511]

Applicants before Federal departments and agencies other than the Department of the Interior or Agriculture seeking a license, certificate, or other authority for a project which involve a right-of-way over, upon, under, or through public land or National Forest System lands must simultaneously apply to the Secretary concerned for the appropriate authority to use public lands or National Forest System lands and submit to the Secretary concerned all information furnished to the other Federal department or agency.

(Pub. L. No. 94–579, Title V, § 511, 90 Stat. 2782 (Oct. 21, 1976).)

HISTORICAL AND STATUTORY NOTES

Transfer of Functions

See note set out under section 1763 of this title.

§ 1772. Vegetation management, facility inspection, and operation and maintenance relating to electric transmission and distribution facility rights of way

[FLPMA § 512]

(a) Definitions.—In this section:

(1) Hazard tree.—The term "hazard tree" means any tree or part thereof (whether located inside or outside a right-of-way) that has been designated, prior to tree failure, by a certified or licensed arborist or forester under the supervision of the Secretary concerned or the owner or operator of a transmission or distribution facility to be—

(A) dead, likely to die within the routine vegetation management cycle, or likely to fail within the routine vegetation management cycle; and

(B) if the tree or part of the tree failed, likely to—

(i) cause substantial damage or disruption to a transmission or distribution facility; or

(ii) come within 10 feet of an electric power line.

(2) Owner; operator.—The terms "owner" and "operator" include contractors or other agents engaged by the owner or operator of an electric transmission or distribution facility.

(3) Plan.—The term "plan" means a vegetation management, facility inspection, and operation and maintenance plan that—

(A) is prepared by the owner or operator of 1 or more electric transmission or distribution facilities to cover 1 or more electric transmission and distribution rights-of-way; and

(B) provides for the long-term, cost-effective, efficient, and timely management of facilities and vegetation within the width of the right-of-way and abutting Federal land, including hazard trees, to enhance electric reliability, promote public safety, and avoid fire hazards.

(4) **Secretary concerned.**—The term "Secretary concerned" means—

(A) the Secretary, with respect to public lands; and

(B) the Secretary of Agriculture, with respect to National Forest System land.

(b) **Guidance.**—

(1) **In general.**—To enhance the reliability of the electric grid and reduce the threat of wildfire damage to, and wildfire caused by vegetation-related conditions within, electric transmission and distribution rights-of-way and abutting Federal land, including hazard trees, the Secretary concerned shall issue and periodically update guidance to ensure that provisions are appropriately developed and implemented for utility vegetation management, facility inspection, and operation and maintenance of rights-of-way, regardless of the means by which the rights-of-way are established (including by grant, special use authorization, and easement).

(2) **Limitation.**—The guidance issued under paragraph (1) shall be compatible with mandatory reliability standards established by the Electric Reliability Organization.

(3) **Considerations.**—The guidance issued under paragraph (1) shall take into account—

(A) all applicable law, including fire safety and electric system reliability requirements (including reliability standards established by the Electric Reliability Organization under section 215 of the Federal Power Act (16 U.S.C. 824*o*)); and

(B) the Memorandum of Understanding on Vegetation Management for Powerline Rights-of-Way between the Edison Electric Institute, Utility Arborist Association, the Department of the Interior, the Department of Agriculture, and the Environmental Protection Agency signed in 2016.

(4) **Requirements.**—The guidance issued under paragraph (1) shall—

(A) be developed in consultation with the owners of transmission and distribution facilities that hold rights-of-way;

(B) seek to minimize the need for case-by-case approvals for—

(i) routine vegetation management, facility inspection, and operation and maintenance activities; and

(ii) utility vegetation management activities that are necessary to control hazard trees; and

(C) provide for prompt and timely review of requests to conduct vegetation management activities that require approval of the Secretary concerned, especially activities requiring expedited or immediate action.

(c) **Vegetation management, facility inspection, and operation and maintenance plans.**—

(1) **Development and submission.**—Consistent with subsection (b), the Secretary concerned shall provide owners and operators of electric transmission or distribution facilities located on public lands and National Forest System land, as applicable, with the option to develop and submit a plan.

(2) **ERO Standards.**—Owners and operators subject to mandatory reliability standards established by the Electric Reliability Organization (or superseding standards) may use those standards as part of the plan.

(3) **Plan requirements.**—A plan developed under paragraph (1) shall—

(A) identify the applicable transmission or distribution facilities to be maintained;

(B) take into account operations and maintenance plans for the applicable transmission or distribution line;

(C) describe the vegetation management, inspection, and operation and maintenance methods that may be used to comply with all applicable law, including fire safety requirements and reliability standards established by the Electric Reliability Organization;

(D) include schedules for—

(i) the applicable owner or operator to notify the Secretary concerned about routine and major maintenance;

(ii) the applicable owner or operator to request approval from the Secretary concerned about undertaking routine and major maintenance; and

(iii) the Secretary concerned to respond to a request by an owner or operator under clause (ii); and

(E) describe processes for—

(i) identifying changes in conditions; and

(ii) modifying the approved plan, if necessary.

(4) Review and approval process.—

(A) In general.—The Secretary concerned shall jointly develop a consolidated and coordinated process for the review and approval of plans submitted under paragraph (1) that—

(i) includes timelines and benchmarks for—

(I) the submission of agency comments on the plans and schedules for final decision; and

(II) the timely review of modifications of the plans in cases in which modifications are necessary;

(ii) is consistent with applicable law; and

(iii) includes a process for modifications to a plan in a prompt manner if changed conditions necessitate a modification to a plan; and

(iv) ensures, to the maximum extent practicable, a prompt review and approval process not to exceed 120 days.

(B) Plan modification.—Upon reasonable advance notice to an owner or operator of an electric transmission or distribution facility of any changed conditions that warrant a modification to a plan, the Secretary concerned shall—

(i) provide an opportunity for the owner or operator to submit a proposed plan modification, consistent with the process described under subparagraph (A)(iii), to address the changed condition identified by the Secretary concerned;

(ii) consider the proposed plan modification consistent with the process described under paragraph (4)(A); and

(iii) allow the owner or operator to continue to implement any element of the approved plan that does not directly and adversely affect the condition precipitating the need for modification.

(5) Categories of actions not requiring environmental analysis.—With respect to the development and approval of plans submitted under paragraph (1), as well as with respect to actions carried out under such plans, the Secretary concerned shall identify categories of actions for which neither an environmental impact statement nor an environmental assessment shall be required under section 1508.4 of title 40, Code of Federal Regulations (or a successor regulation).

(d) Certain owners and operators.—

(1) In general.—The owner or operator of an electric transmission or distribution facility that is not subject to the mandatory reliability standards established by the Electric Reliability Organization or that sold less than or equal to 1,000,000 megawatt hours of electric energy for purposes other than resale during each of the 3 calendar years immediately preceding the date of enactment of this section may enter into an agreement with the Secretary concerned in lieu of a plan under subsection (c).

(2) Minimum requirements.—The Secretary concerned shall ensure that the minimum requirements for an agreement under paragraph (1)—

(A) reflect the relative financial resources of the applicable owner or operator compared to other owners or operators of an electric transmission or distribution facility;

(B) include schedules as described in subsection (c)(3)(D);

(C) are subject to modification requirements as described in subsection (c)(4)(B); and

(D) comply with applicable law.

(e) Emergency conditions.—If vegetation or hazard trees have contacted or present an imminent danger of contacting an electric transmission or distribution line from within or adjacent to an electric transmission or distribution right-of-way, the owner or operator of the electric transmission or distribution lines—

(1) may prune or remove the vegetation or hazard tree—

(A) to avoid the disruption of electric service; and

(B) to eliminate immediate fire and safety hazards; and

(2) shall notify the appropriate local agent of the Secretary concerned not later than 1 day after the date of the response to emergency conditions.

(f) Activities that require approval.—

(1) In general.—Except as provided under paragraph (3), the owner or operator of an electric transmission or distribution facility may conduct vegetation management activities that require approval of the Secretary concerned in accordance with a plan approved under subsection (c) or an agreement entered into under subsection (d) only with the approval of the Secretary concerned.

(2) Requirement to respond.—The Secretary concerned shall respond to a request for approval to conduct vegetation management activities in accordance with the applicable schedules in a plan approved under subsection (c) or an agreement entered into under subsection (d).

(3) Authorized activities.—The owner or operator of an electric transmission or distribution facility may conduct vegetation management activities that require approval of the Secretary concerned in accordance with a plan approved under subsection (c) or an agreement entered into under subsection (d) without the approval of the Secretary concerned if—

(A) the owner or operator submitted a request to the Secretary concerned in accordance with the applicable schedule in a plan approved under subsection (c) or an agreement entered into under subsection (d);

(B) the vegetation management activities, including the removal of hazard trees, proposed in the request under subparagraph (A) are in accordance with a plan approved under subsection (c) or an agreement entered into under subsection (d); and

(C) the Secretary concerned fails to respond to the request under subparagraph (A) in accordance with the applicable schedule in a plan approved under subsection (c) or an agreement entered into under subsection (d).

(g) Liability.—

(1) In general.—The Secretary concerned shall not impose strict liability for damages or injury resulting from—

(A) the Secretary concerned unreasonably withholding or delaying—

(i) approval of a plan under subsection (c); or

(ii) entrance into an agreement under subsection (d); or

(B) the Secretary concerned unreasonably failing to adhere to an applicable schedule in a plan approved under subsection (c) or an agreement entered into under subsection (d).

(2) **Damages.**—For the period ending 10 years after the date of the enactment of this subsection, the Secretary concerned shall not impose strict liability in an amount greater than $500,000 per incident for damages or injury resulting from activities conducted by an owner or operator in accordance with an approved agreement under subsection (d).

(3) **Rule of constructions.**—Nothing in paragraph (2) shall be construed to effect any liability imposed by the Secretary concerned under section 251.56(d) of title 36, Code of Federal Regulations (as in effect on the date of the enactment of this section) and section 2807.12 of title 43, Code of Federal Regulations (as in effect on the date of the enactment of this section), for activities conducted by an owner or operator in accordance with an approved plan under subsection (c).

(h) **Reporting requirement.**—

(1) **Activities that require approval.**—The Secretary concerned shall report requests and actions made under subsection (f) annually on the website of the Secretary concerned.

(2) **Liability.**—Not later than four years after the date of enactment of this subsection, the Secretary concerned shall prepare and submit a report to the Committee on Natural Resources of the House of Representatives and the Committee on Energy and Natural Resources of the Senate that describes the effect on the Treasury of the strict liability limitation established by subsection (g)(2).

(i) **Training and guidance.**—In consultation with the electric utility industry, the Secretary concerned is encouraged to develop a program to train personnel of the Department of the Interior and the Forest Service involved in vegetation management decisions relating to electric transmission and distribution facilities to ensure that the personnel—

(1) understand electric system reliability requirements as the requirements relate to vegetation management of transmission and distribution rights-of-way on Federal land, including reliability standards established by the Electric Reliability Organization and fire safety requirements;

(2) assist owners and operators of electric transmission and distribution facilities in complying with applicable electric reliability and fire safety requirements;

(3) encourage and assist willing owners and operators of electric transmission and distribution facilities to incorporate on a voluntary basis vegetation management practices to enhance habitats and forage for pollinators and for other wildlife if the practices are compatible with the integrated vegetation management practices necessary for reliability and safety; and

(4) understand how existing and emerging unmanned technologies can help electric utilities, the Federal Government, State and local governments, and private landowners—

(A) to more efficiently identify vegetation management needs;

(B) to reduce the risk of wildfires; and

(C) to lower ratepayer energy costs.

(j) **Implementation.**—The Secretary concerned shall—

(1) not later than 1 year after the date of enactment of this section, propose regulations, or amend existing regulations, to implement this section; and

(2) not later than 2 years after the date of enactment of this section, finalize regulations, or amend existing regulations, to implement this section.

(k) **Existing vegetation management, facility inspection, and operation and maintenance plans.**—Nothing in this section requires an owner or operator to develop and submit a new plan under this section if a plan consistent with this section has already been approved by the Secretary concerned before the date of enactment of this section.

(Pub. L. No. 94–579, Title V, § 511, 90 Stat. 2782 (Oct. 21, 1976); as added by Pub. L. No. 115–141, § 211(a), 132 Stat. 348, 1068–1073 (Mar. 23. 2018).)

SUBCHAPTER VI—DESIGNATED MANAGEMENT AREAS

§ 1781. California Desert Conservation Area

[FLPMA § 601]

(a) Congressional findings

The Congress finds that—

(1) the California desert contains historical, scenic, archeological, environmental, biological, cultural, scientific, educational, recreational, and economic resources that are uniquely located adjacent to an area of large population;

(2) the California desert environment is a total ecosystem that is extremely fragile, easily scarred, and slowly healed;

(3) the California desert environment and its resources, including certain rare and endangered species of wildlife, plants, and fishes, and numerous archeological and historic sites, are seriously threatened by air pollution, inadequate Federal management authority, and pressures of increased use, particularly recreational use, which are certain to intensify because of the rapidly growing population of southern California;

(4) the use of all California desert resources can and should be provided for in a multiple use and sustained yield management plant[1] to conserve these resources for future generations, and to provide present and future use and enjoyment, particularly outdoor recreation uses, including the use, where appropriate, of off-road recreational vehicles;

(5) the Secretary has initiated a comprehensive planning process and established an interim management program for the public lands in the California desert; and

(6) to insure further study of the relationship of man and the California desert environment, preserve the unique and irreplaceable resources, including archeological values, and conserve the use of the economic resources of the California desert, the public must be provided more opportunity to participate in such planning and management, and additional management authority must be provided to the Secretary to facilitate effective implementation of such planning and management.

(b) Statement of purpose

It is the purpose of this section to provide for the immediate and future protection and administration of the public lands in the California desert within the framework of a program of multiple use and sustained yield, and the maintenance of environmental quality.

(c) Description of Area

(1) For the purpose of this section, the term "California desert" means the area generally depicted on a map entitled "California Desert Conservation Area—Proposed" dated April 1974, and described as provided in subsection (c)(2) of this section.

(2) As soon as practicable after October 21, 1976, the Secretary shall file a revised map and a legal description of the California Desert Conservation Area with the Committees on Interior and Insular Affairs of the United States Senate and the House of Representatives, and such map and description shall have the same force and effect as if included in this Act. Correction of clerical and typographical errors in such legal description and a map may be made by the Secretary. To the extent practicable, the Secretary shall make such legal description and map available to the public promptly upon request.

(d) Preparation and implementation of comprehensive long-range plan for management, use, etc.

The Secretary, in accordance with section 1712 of this title, shall prepare and implement a comprehensive, long-range plan for the management, use, development, and protection of the public lands within the California Desert Conservation Area. Such plan shall take into account the principles of multiple use and sustained yield in providing for resource use and development, including, but not limited to, maintenance of environmental quality, rights-of-way, and mineral development. Such plan shall be completed and implementation thereof initiated on or before September 30, 1980.

(e) Interim program for management, use, etc.

During the period beginning on October 21, 1976, and ending on the effective date of implementation of the comprehensive, long-range plan, the Secretary shall execute an interim program to manage, use, and protect the public lands, and their resources now in danger of destruction, in the California Desert Conservation Area, to provide for the public use of such lands in an orderly and reasonable manner such as through the development of campgrounds and visitor centers, and to provide for a uniformed desert ranger force.

(f) Applicability of mining laws

Subject to valid existing rights, nothing in this Act shall affect the applicability of the United States mining laws on the public lands within the California Desert Conservation Area, except that all mining claims located on public lands within the California Desert Conservation Area shall be subject to such reasonable regulations as the Secretary may prescribe to effectuate the purposes of this section. Any patent issued on any such mining claim shall recite this limitation and continue to be subject to such regulations. Such regulations shall provide for such measures as may be reasonable to protect the scenic, scientific, and environmental values of the public lands of the California Desert Conservation Area against undue impairment, and to assure against pollution of the streams and waters within the California Desert Conservation Area.

(g) Advisory Committee; establishment; functions

(1) The Secretary, within sixty days after October 21, 1976, shall establish a California Desert Conservation Area Advisory Committee (hereinafter referred to as "advisory committee") in accordance with the provisions of section 1739 of this title.

(2) It shall be the function of the advisory committee to advise the Secretary with respect to the preparation and implementation of the comprehensive, long-range plan required under subsection (d) of this section.

(h) Management of lands under jurisdiction of Secretary of Agriculture and Secretary of Defense

The Secretary of Agriculture and the Secretary of Defense shall manage lands within their respective jurisdictions located in or adjacent to the California Desert Conservation Area, in accordance with the laws relating to such lands and wherever practicable, in a manner consonant with the purpose of this section. The Secretary, the Secretary of Agriculture, and the Secretary of Defense are authorized and directed to consult among themselves and take cooperative actions to carry out the provisions of this subsection, including a program of law enforcement in accordance with applicable authorities to protect the archeological and other values of the California Desert Conservation Area and adjacent lands.

(i) Omitted

(j) Authorization of appropriations

There are authorized to be appropriated for fiscal years 1977 through 1981 not to exceed $40,000,000 for the purpose of this section, such amount to remain available until expended.

(Pub. L. No. 94–579, Title VI, § 601, 90 Stat. 2782 (Oct. 21, 1976).)

[1] So in original. Probably should be "plan."

HISTORICAL AND STATUTORY NOTES

References in Text

This Act, referred to in subsecs. (c)(2) and (f), is Pub. L. No. 94–579, 90 Stat. 2743 (Oct. 21, 1976), as amended, known as the Federal Land Policy and Management Act of 1976. For complete classification of this Act to the Code, see Tables.

The United States mining laws, referred to in subsec. (f), are codified generally into Title 30, Mineral Lands and Mining.

Codifications

Subsec. (i) of this section, which required the Secretary to report annually to Congress on the progress in, and any problems concerning, the implementation of this section, terminated, effective May 15, 2000, pursuant to section 3003 of Pub. L. No. 104–66, as amended, set out as a note under 31 U.S.C.A. § 1113. See, also, the last item on page 107 of House Document No. 103097.

Change of Name

Committee on Interior and Insular Affairs of the House of Representatives changed to Committee on Natural Resources of the House of Representatives on Jan. 5, 1993, by House Resolution No. 5, One Hundred Third Congress.

The Committee on Interior and Insular Affairs of the Senate, referred to in subsec. (c)(2), was abolished and replaced by the Committee on Energy and Natural Resources of the Senate, effective Feb. 11, 1977. See Rule XXV of the Standing Rules of the Senate, as amended by Senate Resolution 4 (popularly cited as the "Committee System Reorganization Amendments of 1977"), approved Feb. 4, 1977.

Desert Lily Sanctuary

Pub. L. No. 103–433, Title I, § 107, 108 Stat. 4483 (Oct. 31, 1994), provided that:

"**(a) Designation.**—There is hereby established the Desert Lily Sanctuary within the California Desert Conservation Area, California, of the Bureau of Land Management, comprising approximately two thousand forty acres, as generally depicted on a map entitled 'Desert Lily Sanctuary', dated February 1986. The Secretary shall administer the area to provide maximum protection to the desert lily.

"**(b) Withdrawal.**—Subject to valid existing rights, all Federal lands within the Desert Lily Sanctuary are hereby withdrawn from all forms of entry, appropriation, or disposal under the public land laws; from location, entry, and patent under the United States mining laws; and from disposition under all laws pertaining to mineral and geothermal leasing, and mineral materials, and all amendments thereto."

Dinosaur Trackway Area of Critical Environmental Concern

Pub. L. No. 103–433, Title I, § 108, 108 Stat. 4483 (Oct. 31, 1994), provided that:

"**(a) Designation.**—There is hereby established the Dinosaur Trackway Area of Critical Environmental Concern within the California Desert Conservation Area, of the Bureau of Land Management, comprising approximately five hundred and ninety acres as generally depicted on a map entitled 'Dinosaur Trackway Area of Critical Environmental Concern', dated July 1993. The Secretary shall administer the area to preserve the paleontological resources within the area.

"**(b) Withdrawal.**—Subject to valid existing rights, the Federal lands within and adjacent to the Dinosaur Trackway Area of Critical Environmental Concern, as generally depicted on a map entitled 'Dinosaur Trackway Mineral Withdrawal Area', dated July 1993, are hereby withdrawn from all forms of entry, appropriation, or disposal under the public land laws; from location, entry, and patent under the United States mining laws; and from disposition under all laws pertaining to mineral and geothermal leasing, and mineral materials, and all amendments thereto."

§ 1781a. Acceptance of donation of certain existing permits or leases[1]

(1) During fiscal year 2012 and thereafter, the Secretary of the Interior shall accept the donation of any valid existing permits or leases authorizing grazing on public lands within the California Desert Conservation Area. With respect to each permit or lease donated under this paragraph, the Secretary shall terminate the grazing permit or lease, ensure a permanent end (except as provided in paragraph (2)), to grazing on the land covered by the permit or lease, and make the land available for mitigation by allocating the forage to wildlife use consistent with any applicable Habitat Conservation Plan, section 10(a)(1)(B) permit, or section 7 consultation under the Endangered Species Act of 1973 (16 U.S.C. 1531 et seq.).

(2) If the land covered by a permit or lease donated under paragraph (1) is also covered by another valid existing permit or lease that is not donated under such paragraph, the Secretary of the Interior shall reduce the authorized grazing level on the land covered by the permit or lease to reflect the donation of the permit or lease under paragraph (1). To ensure that there is a permanent reduction in the level of grazing on the land covered by a permit or lease donated under paragraph (1), the Secretary shall not allow grazing use to exceed the authorized level under the remaining valid existing permit or lease that is not donated.

(Pub. L. No. 112–74, Div. E, Title I, § 122(b), 125 Stat. 1013 (Dec. 23, 2011).)

[1] Editorially supplied.

HISTORICAL AND STATUTORY NOTES

References in Text

The Endangered Species Act of 1973, referred to in subsec. (1), is Pub. L. No. 93–205, 87 Stat. 884 (Dec. 28, 1973), as amended, which is codified principally as chapter 35 of Title 16, 16 U.S.C.A. § 1531 et seq. For complete classification, see Short Title note set out under 16 U.S.C.A. § 1531 and Tables.

Codifications

Section consists of subsec. (b) of section 122 of Pub. L. No. 112–74, Div. E. Subsec. (a) of such section was not codified into the Code.

§ 1782. Bureau of Land Management Wilderness Study

[FLPMA § 603]

(a) Lands subject to review and designation as wilderness

Within fifteen years after October 21, 1976, the Secretary shall review those roadless areas of five thousand acres or more and roadless islands of the public lands, identified during the inventory required by section 1711(a) of this title as having wilderness characteristics described in the Wilderness Act of September 3, 1964 (78 Stat. 890; 16 U.S.C. 1131 et seq.) and shall from time to time report to the President his recommendation as to the suitability or nonsuitability of each such area or island for preservation as wilderness: *Provided,* That prior to any recommendations for the designation of an area as wilderness the Secretary shall cause mineral surveys to be conducted by the United States Geological Survey and the United States Bureau of Mines to determine the mineral values, if any, that may be present in such areas: *Provided further,* That the Secretary shall report to the President by July 1, 1980, his recommendations on those areas which the Secretary has prior to November 1, 1975, formally identified as natural or primitive areas. The review required by this subsection shall be conducted in accordance with the procedure specified in section 3(d) of the Wilderness Act [16 U.S.C.A. § 1132(d)].

(b) Presidential recommendation for designation as wilderness

The President shall advise the President of the Senate and the Speaker of the House of Representatives of his recommendations with respect to designation as wilderness of each such area, together with a map thereof and a definition of its boundaries. Such advice by the President shall be given within two years of the receipt of each report from the Secretary. A recommendation of the President for designation as wilderness shall become effective only if so provided by an Act of Congress.

(c) Status of lands during period of review and determination

During the period of review of such areas and until Congress has determined otherwise, the Secretary shall continue to manage such lands according to his authority under this Act and other applicable law in a manner so as not to impair the suitability of such areas for preservation as wilderness, subject, however, to the continuation of existing mining and grazing uses and mineral leasing in the manner and degree in which the same was being conducted on October 21, 1976: *Provided,* That, in managing the public lands the Secretary shall by regulation or otherwise take any action required to prevent unnecessary or undue degradation of the lands and their resources or to afford environmental protection. Unless previously withdrawn from appropriation under the mining laws, such lands shall continue to be subject to such appropriation during the period of review unless withdrawn by the Secretary under the procedures of section 1714 of this title for reasons other than preservation of their wilderness character. Once an area has been designated for preservation as wilderness, the provisions of the Wilderness Act [16 U.S.C.A. § 1131 et seq.] which apply to national forest wilderness areas shall apply with respect to the administration and use of such designated area, including mineral surveys required by section 4(d)(2) of the Wilderness Act [16

U.S.C.A. § 1133(d)(2)], and mineral development, access, exchange of lands, and ingress and egress for mining claimants and occupants.

(Pub. L. No. 94–579, Title VI, § 603, 90 Stat. 2785 (Oct. 21, 1976); as amended by Pub. L. No. 102–154, Title I, 105 Stat. 1000 (Nov. 13, 1991); Pub. L. No. 102–285, § 10, 106 Stat. 171 (May 18, 1992).)

HISTORICAL AND STATUTORY NOTES

References in Text

The Wilderness Act of September 3, 1964, referred to in subsecs. (a) and (c), is Pub. L. No. 88–577, 78 Stat. 890 (Sept. 3, 1964), as amended, which is codified generally as chapter 23 (section 1131 et seq.) of Title 16, Conservation. For complete classification of this Act to the Code, see Short Title note set out under section 1131 of Title 16 and Tables.

This Act, referred to in subsec. (c), is Pub. L. No. 94–579, 90 Stat. 2743 (Oct. 21, 1976), as amended, known as the Federal Land Policy and Management Act of 1976. For complete classification of this Act to the Code, see Tables volume.

The mining laws, referred to in subsec. (c), are codified generally into Title 30, Mineral Lands and Mining.

Termination of Reporting Requirements

For termination of reporting provisions of subsec. (b) of this section, effective May 15, 2000, see Pub. L. No. 104–66, § 3003, as amended, set out as a note under 31 U.S.C.A. § 1113, and page 111 of House Document No. 103–7.

Change of Name

Pub. L. No. 102–285, § 10(a), 106 Stat. 171 (May 18, 1992), redesignated the Geological Survey and provided that on and after May 18, 1992, it shall be known as the United States Geological Survey. An earlier statute [Pub. L. No. 102–154, Title I, 105 Stat. 1000 (Nov. 13, 1991)] had provided for the identical change of name effective on and after Nov. 13, 1991. See note under section 31 of Title 43, Public Lands.

Pub. L. No. 102–285, § 10(b), 106 Stat. 172 (May 18, 1992), provided that, on and after May 18, 1992, the Bureau of Mines is redesignated and shall thereafter be known as the United States Bureau of Mines. See note under section 1 of Title 30, Mineral Lands and Mining.

Transfer of Functions

Pub. L. No. 104–134, Title I, § 101(c)[Title I], 110 Stat. 1321–165 (Apr. 26, 1996); renumbered Title I by Pub. L. No. 104–140, § 1(a), 110 Stat. 1327 (May 2, 1996), provided in part: "That the authority granted to the United States Bureau of Mines to conduct mineral surveys and to determine mineral values by section 603 of Public Law 94–579 [enacting this section] is hereby transferred to, and vested in, the Director of the United States Geological Survey."

§ 1783. Yaquina Head Outstanding Natural Area

(a) Establishment

In order to protect the unique scenic, scientific, educational, and recreational values of certain lands in and around Yaquina Head, in Lincoln County, Oregon, there is hereby established, subject to valid existing rights, the Yaquina Head Outstanding Natural Area (hereinafter referred to as the "area"). The boundaries of the area are those shown on the map entitled "Yaquina Head Area", dated July 1979, which shall be on file and available for public inspection in the Office of the Director, Bureau of Land Management, United States Department of the Interior, and the State Office of the Bureau of Land Management in the State of Oregon.

(b) Administration by Secretary of the Interior; management plan; quarrying permits

(1) The Secretary of the Interior (hereinafter referred to as the "Secretary") shall administer the Yaquina Head Outstanding Natural Area in accordance with the laws and regulations applicable to the public lands as defined in section 103(e) of the Federal Land Policy and Management Act of 1976, as amended (43 U.S.C. 1702) [43 U.S.C.A. § 1702(e)], in such a manner as will best provide for—

(A) the conservation and development of the scenic, natural, and historic values of the area;

(B) the continued use of the area for purposes of education, scientific study, and public recreation which do not substantially impair the purposes for which the area is established; and

(C) protection of the wildlife habitat of the area.

(2) The Secretary shall develop a management plan for the area which accomplishes the purposes and is consistent with the provisions of this section. This plan shall be developed in accordance with the provisions of section 202 of the Federal Land Policy and Management Act of 1976, as amended (43 U.S.C. 1712).

(3) Notwithstanding any other provision of this section, the Secretary is authorized to issue permits or to contract for the quarrying of materials from the area in accordance with the management plan for the area on condition that the lands be reclaimed and restored to the satisfaction of the Secretary. Such authorization to quarry shall require payment of fair market value for the materials to be quarried, as established by the Secretary, and shall also include any terms and conditions which the Secretary determines necessary to protect the values of such quarry lands for purposes of this section.

(c) Revocation of 1866 reservation of lands for lighthouse purposes; restoration to public lands status

The reservation of lands for lighthouse purposes made by Executive order of June 8, 1866, of certain lands totaling approximately 18.1 acres, as depicted on the map referred to in subsection (a) of this section, is hereby revoked. The lands referred to in subsection (a) of this section are hereby restored to the status of public lands as defined in section 103(e) of the Federal Land Policy and Management Act of 1976, as amended (43 U.S.C. 1702) [43 U.S.C.A. § 1702(e)], and shall be administered in accordance with the management plan for the area developed pursuant to subsection (b) of this section, except that such lands are hereby withdrawn from settlement, sale, location, or entry, under the public land laws, including the mining laws (30 U.S.C., ch. 2), leasing under the mineral leasing laws (30 U.S.C. 181 et seq.), and disposals under the Materials Act of July 31, 1947, as amended (30 U.S.C. 601, 602) [30 U.S.C.A. § 601 et seq.].

(d) Acquisition of lands not already in Federal ownership

The Secretary shall, as soon as possible but in no event later than twenty-four months following March 5, 1980, acquire by purchase, exchange, donation, or condemnation all or any part of the lands and waters and interests in lands and waters within the area referred to in subsection (a) of this section which are not in Federal ownership except that State land shall not be acquired by purchase or condemnation. Any lands or interests acquired by the Secretary pursuant to this section shall become public lands as defined in the Federal Land Policy and Management Act of 1976, as amended [43 U.S.C.A. § 1701 et seq.]. Upon acquisition by the United States, such lands are automatically withdrawn under the provisions of subsection (c) of this section except that lands affected by quarrying operations in the area shall be subject to disposals under the Materials Act of July 31, 1947, as amended (30 U.S.C. 601, 602) [30 U.S.C.A. § 601 et seq.]. Any lands acquired pursuant to this subsection shall be administered in accordance with the management plan for the area developed pursuant to subsection (b) of this section.

(e) Wind energy research

The Secretary is authorized to conduct a study relating to the use of lands in the area for purposes of wind energy research. If the Secretary determines after such study that the conduct of wind energy research activity will not substantially impair the values of the lands in the area for purposes of this section, the Secretary is further authorized to issue permits for the use of such lands as a site for installation and field testing of an experimental wind turbine generating system. Any permit issued pursuant to this subsection shall contain such terms and conditions as the Secretary determines necessary to protect the values of such lands for purposes of this section.

(f) Reclamation and restoration of lands affected by quarrying operations

The Secretary shall develop and administer, in addition to any requirements imposed pursuant to subsection (b)(3) of this section, a program for the reclamation and restoration of all lands affected by quarrying operations in the area acquired pursuant to subsection (d) of this section. All revenues received by the United States in connection with quarrying operations authorized by subsection (b)(3) of this section shall be deposited in a separate fund account which shall be established by the Secretary of the Treasury. Such revenues are hereby authorized to be appropriated to the Secretary as needed for reclamation and restoration of any lands acquired pursuant to subsection (d) of this section. After completion of such reclamation and restoration to the satisfaction of the Secretary, any unexpended revenues in such fund shall be returned to the general fund of the United States Treasury.

(g) Authorization of appropriations

There are hereby authorized to be appropriated in addition to that authorized by subsection (f) of this section, such sums as may be necessary to carry out the provisions of this section.

(Pub. L. No. 96–199, Title I, § 119, 94 Stat. 71 (Mar. 5, 1980).)

HISTORICAL AND STATUTORY NOTES

References in Text

The public land laws, referred to in subsec. (c), are codified generally as this title.

The mining laws, referred to in subsec. (c), are codified generally into Title 30, Mineral Lands and Mining.

Mineral leasing laws, referred to in subsec. (c), have been defined in sections 351, 505, 530, and 541e of Title 30 to mean Acts of Oct. 20, 1914, c. 330, 38 Stat. 741; Feb. 25, 1920, c. 85, 41 Stat. 437; Apr. 17, 1926, c. 158, 44 Stat. 301; and Feb. 7, 1927, c. 66, 44 Stat. 1057. The Act of Oct. 20, 1914, was repealed by Pub. L. No. 86–252, § 1, 73 Stat. 490 (Sept. 9, 1959). The Act of Feb. 25, 1920, is popularly known as the Mineral Lands Leasing Act and is codified principally as chapter 3A (section 181 et seq.) of Title 30. The Act of Apr. 17, 1926, is codified generally as subchapter VIII (section 271 et seq.) of chapter 3A of Title 30. The Act of Feb. 7, 1927, is codified principally as subchapter IX (section 281 et seq.) of chapter 3A of Title 30. For complete classification of these Acts to the Code, see Tables volume.

The Materials Act of July 31, 1947, as amended (30 U.S.C. 601, 602), referred to in subsecs. (c) and (d), is Act of July 31, 1947, c. 406, 61 Stat. 681, as amended, which is codified generally as subchapter I (section 601 et seq.) of chapter 15 of Title 30. For complete classification of this Act to the Code, see Short Title note set out under section 601 of Title 30 and Tables volume.

The Federal Land Policy and Management Act of 1976, as amended, referred to in subsec. (d), is Pub. L. No. 94–579, 90 Stat. 2743 (Oct. 21, 1976), as amended, which is codified principally as chapter 35 (section 1701 et seq.) of this title. For complete classification of this Act to the Code, see Short Title note set out under section 1701 of this title and Tables volume.

Codifications

Section was not enacted as part of the Federal Land Policy and Management Act of 1976 which enacted this chapter.

§ 1784. Lands in Alaska; designation as wilderness; management by Bureau of Land Management pending Congressional action

Notwithstanding any other provision of law, section 1782 of this title shall not apply to any lands in Alaska. However, in carrying out his duties under sections 1711 and 1712 of this title and other applicable laws, the Secretary may identify areas in Alaska which he determines are suitable as wilderness and may, from time to time, make recommendations to the Congress for inclusion of any such areas in the National Wilderness Preservation System, pursuant to the provisions of the Wilderness Act [16 U.S.C.A. § 1131 et seq.]. In the absence of congressional action relating to any such recommendation of the Secretary, the Bureau of Land Management shall manage all such areas which are within its jurisdiction in accordance with the applicable land use plans and applicable provisions of law.

(Pub. L. No. 96–487, Title XIII, § 1320, 94 Stat. 2487 (Dec. 2, 1980).)

HISTORICAL AND STATUTORY NOTES

References in Text

The Wilderness Act, referred to in text, is Pub. L. No. 88–577, 78 Stat. 890 (Sept. 3, 1964), as amended, which is codified generally as chapter 23 (§ 1131 et seq.) of Title 16, Conservation. For complete classification of this Act to the Code, see Short Title note set out under section 1131 of Title 16 and Tables.

Codifications

This section was enacted as part of the Alaska National Interest Lands Conservation Act and not as part of the Federal Land Policy and Management Act of 1976, which comprises this chapter.

Kenai Natives Association Land Exchange

Pub. L. No. 104–333, Div. I, Title III, § 311, 110 Stat. 4139 (Nov. 12, 1996); as amended by Pub. L. No. 106–176, Title I, § 105, 114 Stat. 25 (Mar. 10, 2000), provided that:

"(a) Short title.—This section [this note] may be cited as the 'Kenai Natives Association Equity Act Amendments of 1996'.

"(b) Findings and purpose.—

"(1) Findings.—The Congress finds the following:

"(A) The United States Fish and Wildlife Service and Kenai Natives Association, Inc., have agreed to transfers of certain land rights, in and near the Kenai National Wildlife Refuge, negotiated as directed by Public Law 102–458 [Pub. L. No. 102–458, 106 Stat. 2267 (Oct. 23, 1996)].

"(B) The lands to be acquired by the Service are within the area impacted by the Exxon Valdez oil spill of 1989, and these lands included important habitat for various species of fish and wildlife for which significant injury resulting from the spill has been documented through the EVOS Trustee Council restoration process. This analysis has indicated that these lands generally have value for the restoration of such injured natural resources as pink salmon, dolly varden, bald eagles, river otters, and cultural and archaeological resources. This analysis has also indicated that these lands generally have high value for the restoration of injured species that rely on these natural resources, including wilderness quality, recreation, tourism, and subsistence.

"(C) Restoration of the injured species will benefit from acquisition and the prevention of disturbances which may adversely affect their recovery.

"(D) It is in the public interest to complete the conveyances provided for in this section.

"(2) Purpose.—The purpose of this section is to authorize and direct the Secretary, at the election of KNA, to complete the conveyances provided for in this section.

"(c) Definitions.—For purposes of this section, the term—

"(1) 'ANCSA' means the Alaska Native Claims Settlement Act of 1971 (43 U.S.C. 1601 et seq.) [Pub. L. No. 92–203, 85 Stat. 688 (Dec. 18, 1971), as amended; for distribution of which to the Code, see Short Title note set out under section 1601 of this title and Tables];

"(2) 'ANILCA' means the Alaska National Interest Lands Conservation Act (Public Law 96–487; 94 Stat. 2371 et seq.) [Pub. L. No. 96–487, 94 Stat. 2371 (Dec. 2, 1980), as amended; for distribution of which to the Code, see Short Title note set out under section 3101 of Title 16, Conservation, and Tables];

"(3) 'conservation system unit' has the same meaning as in section 102(4) of ANILCA (16 U.S.C. 3102(4)) [section 3102(4) of Title 16];

"(4) 'CIRI' means the Cook Inlet Region, Inc., a Native Regional Corporation incorporated in the State of Alaska pursuant to the terms of ANCSA;

"(5) 'EVOS' means the Exxon Valdez oil spill;

"(6) 'KNA' means the Kenai Natives Association, Inc., an urban corporation incorporated in the State of Alaska pursuant to the terms of ANCSA;

"(7) 'lands' means any lands, waters, or interests therein;

"(8) 'Refuge' means the Kenai National Wildlife Refuge;

"(9) 'Secretary' means the Secretary of the Interior;

"(10) 'Service' means the United States Fish and Wildlife Service; and

"(11) 'Terms and Conditions' means the Terms and Conditions for Land Consolidation and Management in the Cook Inlet Area, as clarified on August 31, 1976, ratified by section 12 of Public

Law 94–204 (43 U.S.C. 1611 note) [Pub. L. No. 94–204, § 12, 89 Stat. 1150 (Jan. 2, 1976), as amended, set out as a note under section 1611 of this title].

"(d) Acquisition of lands.—

"(1) Offer to KNA.—

"(A) In general.—Subject to the availability of the funds identified in paragraph (2)(C), no later than 90 days after the date of enactment of this section [Nov. 12, 1996], the Secretary shall offer to convey to KNA the interests in land and rights set forth in paragraph (2)(B), subject to valid existing rights, in return for the conveyance by KNA to the United States of the interests in land or relinquishment of ANCSA selections set forth in paragraph (2)(A). Payment for the lands conveyed to the United States by KNA is contingent upon KNA's acceptance of the entire conveyance outlined herein.

"(B) Limitation.—The Secretary may not convey any lands or make payment to KNA under this section unless title to the lands to be conveyed by KNA under this section has been found by the United States to be sufficient in accordance with the provisions of section 355 of the Revised Statutes (40 U.S.C. 255) [see now 40 U.S.C.A. §§ 3111, 3112].

"(2) Acquisition lands.—

"(A) Lands to be conveyed to the United States.—The lands to be conveyed by KNA to the United States, or the valid selection rights under ANCSA to be relinquished, all situated within the boundary of the Refuge, are the following:

"(i) The conveyance of approximately 803 acres located along and on islands within the Kenai River, known as the Stephanka Tract.

"(ii) The conveyance of approximately 1,243 acres located along the Moose River, known as the Moose River Patented Lands Tract.

"(iii) The relinquishment of KNA's selection known as the Moose River Selected Tract, containing approximately 753 acres located along the Moose River.

"(iv) The relinquishment of KNA's remaining ANCSA entitlement of approximately 454 acres.

"(v) The relinquishment of all KNA's remaining overselections. Upon completion of all relinquishments outlined above, all KNA's entitlement shall be deemed to be extinguished and the completion of this acquisition will satisfy all of KNA's ANCSA entitlement.

"(vi) The conveyance of an access easement providing the United States and its assigns access across KNA's surface estate in the SW1/4 of section 21, T. 6 N., R. 9 W., Seward Meridian, Alaska.

"(vii) The conveyance of approximately 100 acres within the Beaver Creek Patented Tract, which is contiguous to lands being retained by the United States contiguous to the Beaver Creek Patented Tract, in exchange for 280 acres of Service lands currently situated within the Beaver Creek Selected Tract.

"(B) Lands to be conveyed to KNA.—The rights provided or lands to be conveyed by the United States to KNA, are the following:

"(i) The surface and subsurface estate to approximately 5 acres, subject to reservations of easements for existing roads and utilities, located within the city of Kenai, Alaska, identified as United States Survey 1435, withdrawn by Executive Order 2943 and known as the old Fish and Wildlife Service Headquarters site.

"(ii) The remaining subsurface estate held by the United States to approximately 13,651 acres, including portions of the Beaver Creek Patented Tract, the Beaver Creek Selected Tract, and portions of the Swanson River Road West Tract and the Swanson River Road East Tract, where the surface was previously or will be conveyed to KNA pursuant to this Act [this note] but excluding the SW1/4 of section 21, T. 6 N., R. 9 W., Seward Meridian, Alaska, which will be retained by the United States. The conveyance of these subsurface interests will be subject to the rights of CIRI to the coal, oil, gas, and to all rights CIRI, its successors, and assigns would have under paragraph 1(B) of the Terms and Conditions, including the right to sand and gravel, to construct facilities, to have rights-of-way, and to otherwise develop it subsurface interests.

"(iii) (I) The nonexclusive right to use sand and gravel which is reasonably necessary for on-site development without compensation or permit on those portions of the Swanson River Road East Tract, comprising approximately 1,738.04 acres; where the entire subsurface of the land is presently owned by the United States. The United States shall retain the ownership of all other sand and gravel located within the subsurface and KNA shall not sell or dispose of such sand and gravel.

"(II) The right to excavate within the subsurface estate as reasonably necessary for structures, utilities, transportation systems, and other development of the surface estate.

"(iv) The nonexclusive right to excavate within the subsurface estate as reasonably necessary for structures, utilities, transportation systems, and other development of the surface estate on the SW$^{1}/_{4}$, section 21, T. 6 N., R. 9 W., Seward Meridian, Alaska, where the entire subsurface of the land is owned by the United States and which public lands shall continue to be withdrawn from mining following their removal from the Refuge boundary under paragraph (3)(A)(ii). The United States shall retain the ownership of all other sand and gravel located within the subsurface of this parcel.

"(v) The surface estate of approximately 280 acres known as the Beaver Creek Selected Tract. This tract shall be conveyed to KNA in exchange for lands conveyed to the United States as described in paragraph (2)(A)(ii).

"(C) Payment.—The United States shall make a total cash payment to KNA for the above-described lands of $4,443,000, contingent upon the appropriate approvals of the Federal or State of Alaska EVOS Trustees (or both) necessary for any expenditure of the EVOS settlement funds.

"(D) National Register of Historic Places.—Upon completion of the acquisition authorized in paragraph (1), the Secretary shall, at no cost to KNA, in coordination with KNA, promptly undertake to nominate the Stephanka Tract to the National Register of Historic Places, in recognition of the archaeological artifacts from the original Dena'ina Settlement. If the Department of the Interior establishes a historical, cultural, or archaeological interpretive site, KNA shall have the exclusive right to operate a Dena'ina interpretive site on the Stephanka Tract under the regulations and policies of the department. If KNA declines to operate such a site, the department may do so under its existing authorities. Prior to the department undertaking any archaeological activities whatsoever on the Stephanka Tract, KNA shall be consulted.

"(3) [Omitted. Amended provisions set out as a note under section 668dd of Title 16]

"(e) [Omitted. Amended provisions set out as a note under section 1132 of Title 16]

"(f) Designation of Lake Todatonten Special Management Area.—

"(1) Purpose.—To balance the potential effects on fish, wildlife, and habitat of the removal of KNA lands from the Refuge System, the Secretary is hereby directed to withdraw, subject to valid existing rights, from location, entry, and patent under the mining laws and to create as a special management unit for the protection of fish, wildlife, and habitat, certain unappropriated and unreserved public lands, totaling approximately 37,000 acres adjacent to the west boundary of the Kanuti National Wildlife Refuge to be known as the 'Lake Todatonten Special Management Area', as depicted on the map entitled 'Proposed: Lake Todatonten Special Management Area', dated June 13, 1996, and to be managed by the Bureau of Land Management.

"(2) Management.—

"(A) Such designation is subject to all valid existing rights as well as the subsistence preferences provided under title VIII of ANILCA [subchapter II (section 3111 et seq.) of chapter 51 of Title 16]. Any lands conveyed to the State of Alaska shall be removed from the Lake Todatonten Special Management Area.

"(B) The Secretary may permit any additional uses of the area, or grant easements, only to the extent that such use, including leasing under the mineral leasing laws, is determined to not detract from nor materially interfere with the purposes for which the Special Management Area is established.

"(C) (i) The BLM shall establish the Lake Todatonten Special Management Area Committee. The membership of the Committee shall consist of 11 members as follows:

"(I) Two residents each from the villages of Alatna, Allakaket, Hughes, and Tanana.

"(II) One representative from each of Doyon Corporation, the Tanana Chiefs Conference, and the State of Alaska.

"(ii) Members of the Committee shall serve without pay.

"(iii) The BLM shall hold meetings of the Lake Todatonten Special Management Area Committee at least once per year to discuss management issues within the Special Management Area. The BLM shall not allow any new type of activity in the Special Management Area without first conferring with the Committee in a timely manner.

"(3) **Access.**—The Secretary shall allow the following:

"(A) Private access for any purpose, including economic development, to lands within the boundaries of the Special Management Area which are owned by third parties or are held in trust by the Secretary for third parties pursuant to the Alaska Native Allotment Act (25 U.S.C. 336) [probably means section 336 of Title 25, Indians]. Such rights may be subject to restrictions issued by the BLM to protect subsistence uses of the Special Management Area.

"(B) Existing public access across the Special Management Area. Section 1110(a) of ANILCA [section 3170(a) of Title 16] shall apply to the Special Management Area.

"(4) **Secretarial order and maps.**—The Secretary shall file with the Committee on Resources [now Natural Resources] of the House of Representatives and the Committee on Energy and Natural Resources and the Committee on Environment and Public Works of the Senate, the Secretarial Order and maps setting forth the boundaries of the Area within 90 days of the completion of the acquisition authorized by this section [this note]. Once established, this Order may only be amended or revoked by Act of Congress.

"(5) **Authorization of appropriations.**—There are authorized to be appropriated such sums as may be necessary to carry out the purposes of this section [this note]."

§ 1785. Fossil Forest Research Natural Area

(a) Establishment

To conserve and protect natural values and to provide scientific knowledge, education, and interpretation for the benefit of future generations, there is established the Fossil Forest Research Natural Area (referred to in this section as the "Area"), consisting of the approximately 2,770 acres in the Farmington District of the Bureau of Land Management, New Mexico, as generally depicted on a map entitled "Fossil Forest", dated June 1983.

(b) Map and legal description

(1) In general

As soon as practicable after November 12, 1996, the Secretary of the Interior shall file a map and legal description of the Area with the Committee on Energy and Natural Resources of the Senate and the Committee on Resources of the House of Representatives.

(2) Force and effect

The map and legal description described in paragraph (1) shall have the same force and effect as if included in this Act.

(3) Technical corrections

The Secretary of the Interior may correct clerical, typographical, and cartographical errors in the map and legal description subsequent to filing the map pursuant to paragraph (1).

(4) Public inspection

The map and legal description shall be on file and available for public inspection in the Office of the Director of the Bureau of Land Management, Department of the Interior.

(c) Management

(1) In general

The Secretary of the Interior, acting through the Director of the Bureau of Land Management, shall manage the Area—

(A) to protect the resources within the Area; and

(B) in accordance with this Act, the Federal Land Policy and Management Act of 1976 (43 U.S.C. 1701 et seq.), and other applicable provisions of law.

(2) Mining

(A) Withdrawal

Subject to valid existing rights, the lands within the Area are withdrawn from all forms of appropriation under the mining laws and from disposition under all laws pertaining to mineral leasing, geothermal leasing, and mineral material sales.

(B) Coal preference rights

The Secretary of the Interior is authorized to issue coal leases in New Mexico in exchange for any preference right coal lease application within the Area. Such exchanges shall be made in accordance with applicable existing laws and regulations relating to coal leases after a determination has been made by the Secretary that the applicant is entitled to a preference right lease and that the exchange is in the public interest.

(C) Oil and gas leases

Operations on oil and gas leases issued prior to November 12, 1996, shall be subject to the applicable provisions of Group 3100 of title 43, Code of Federal Regulations (including section 3162.5–1), and such other terms, stipulations, and conditions as the Secretary of the Interior considers necessary to avoid significant disturbance of the land surface or impairment of the natural, educational, and scientific research values of the Area in existence on November 12, 1996.

(3) Grazing

Livestock grazing on lands within the Area may not be permitted.

(d) Inventory

Not later than 3 full fiscal years after November 12, 1996, the Secretary of the Interior, acting through the Director of the Bureau of Land Management, shall develop a baseline inventory of all categories of fossil resources within the Area. After the inventory is developed, the Secretary shall conduct monitoring surveys at intervals specified in the management plan developed for the Area in accordance with subsection (e) of this section.

(e) Management plan

(1) In general

Not later than 5 years after November 12, 1996, the Secretary of the Interior shall develop and submit to the Committee on Energy and Natural Resources of the Senate and the Committee on Resources of the House of Representatives a management plan that describes the appropriate use of the Area consistent with this subsection.

(2) Contents

The management plan shall include—

(A) a plan for the implementation of a continuing cooperative program with other agencies and groups for—

(i) laboratory and field interpretation; and

(ii) public education about the resources and values of the Area (including vertebrate fossils);

(B) provisions for vehicle management that are consistent with the purpose of the Area and that provide for the use of vehicles to the minimum extent necessary to accomplish an individual scientific project;

(C) procedures for the excavation and collection of fossil remains, including botanical fossils, and the use of motorized and mechanical equipment to the minimum extent necessary to accomplish an individual scientific project; and

(D) mitigation and reclamation standards for activities that disturb the surface to the detriment of scenic and environmental values.

(Pub. L. No. 98–603, Title I, § 103, 98 Stat. 3156 (Oct. 30, 1984); as amended by Pub. L. No. 104–333, Div. I, Title X, § 1022(e), 110 Stat. 4213 (Nov. 12, 1996); Pub. L. No. 106–176, Title I, § 124, 114 Stat. 30 (Mar. 10, 2000).)

HISTORICAL AND STATUTORY NOTES

References in Text

November 12, 1996, referred to in subsecs. (b)(1), (c)(2)(C), (d), and (e)(1), was in the original "the date of enactment of this paragraph", "date of enactment of this subsection" and "the date of enactment of this Act", respectively. Such phrases were translated as Nov. 12, 1996, the date of approval of Pub. L. No. 104–333, section 1022(e) of which amended this section generally, as the probable intent of Congress.

This Act, referred to in subsecs. (b)(2) and (c)(1)(B), is the San Juan Basin Wilderness Protection Act of 1984, Pub. L. No. 98–603, 98 Stat. 3155 (Oct. 30, 1984), as amended. See Tables for complete classification.

The Federal Land Policy and Management Act of 1976, referred to in subsec. (c)(1)(B), is Pub. L. No. 94–579, 90 Stat. 2743 (Oct. 21, 1976), as amended, which is codified principally as chapter 35 (§ 1701 et seq.) of this title. For complete classification of this Act to the Code, see Short Title note set out under section 1701 of this title and Tables.

Mining laws, referred to in subsec. (c)(2)(A), are codified generally into Title 30, Mineral Lands and Mining.

Mineral leasing laws, referred to in subsec. (c)(2)(A), have been defined in sections 351, 505, 530, and 541e of Title 30, Mineral Lands and Mining, to mean Acts of Oct. 20, 1914, c. 330, 38 Stat. 741; Feb. 25, 1920, c. 85, 41 Stat. 437; Apr. 17, 1926, c. 158, 44 Stat. 301; and Feb. 7, 1927, c. 66, 44 Stat. 1057. The Act of Oct. 20, 1914, was repealed by Pub. L. No. 86–252, § 1, 73 Stat. 490 (Sept. 9, 1959). The Act of Feb. 25, 1920, is known as the Mineral Leasing Act and is codified generally as chapter 3A (section 181 et seq.) of Title 30. The Act of Apr. 17, 1926, is codified generally as subchapter VIII (section 271 et seq.) of chapter 3A of Title 30. The Act of Feb. 7, 1927, is codified principally as subchapter IX (section 281 et seq.) of chapter 3A of Title 30. For complete classification of these Acts to the Code, see Tables.

Geothermal leasing laws, referred to in subsec. (c)(2)(A), are codified principally into chapter 23 (section 1001 et seq.) of Title 30, Mineral Lands and Mining.

Codifications

This section was enacted as part of the San Juan Basin Wilderness Protection Act of 1984 and not as part of the Federal Land Policy and Management Act of 1976, which comprises this chapter.

Amendments by Pub. L. No. 106–176, Title I, § 124, 114 Stat. 30 (Mar. 10, 2000), were executed to this section as the probable intent of Congress, despite directory language referencing section 178 of this title; directory language correctly referred to laws which enacted and amended this section.

Change of Name

Committee on Resources of House of Representatives changed to Committee on Natural Resources of House of Representatives by House Resolution No. 6, One Hundred Tenth Congress, Jan. 5, 2007.

§ 1786. Piedras Blancas Historic Light Station

(a) Definitions

In this section:

(1) Light Station

The term "Light Station" means Piedras Blancas Light Station.

(2) Outstanding Natural Area

The term "Outstanding Natural Area" means the Piedras Blancas Historic Light Station Outstanding Natural Area established pursuant to subsection (c).

(3) Public lands

The term "public lands" has the meaning stated in section 103(e) of the Federal Land Policy and Management Act of 1976 (43 U.S.C. 1703(e)).[1]

(4) Secretary

The term "Secretary" means the Secretary of the Interior.

(b) Findings

Congress finds as follows:

(1) The publicly owned Piedras Blancas Light Station has nationally recognized historical structures that should be preserved for present and future generations.

(2) The coastline adjacent to the Light Station is internationally recognized as having significant wildlife and marine habitat that provides critical information to research institutions throughout the world.

(3) The Light Station tells an important story about California's coastal prehistory and history in the context of the surrounding region and communities.

(4) The coastal area surrounding the Light Station was traditionally used by Indian people, including the Chumash and Salinan Indian tribes.

(5) The Light Station is historically associated with the nearby world-famous Hearst Castle (Hearst San Simeon State Historical Monument), now administered by the State of California.

(6) The Light Station represents a model partnership where future management can be successfully accomplished among the Federal Government, the State of California, San Luis Obispo County, local communities, and private groups.

(7) Piedras Blancas Historic Light Station Outstanding Natural Area would make a significant addition to the National Landscape Conservation System administered by the Department of the Interior's Bureau of Land Management.

(8) Statutory protection is needed for the Light Station and its surrounding Federal lands to ensure that it remains a part of our historic, cultural, and natural heritage and to be a source of inspiration for the people of the United States.

(c) Designation of the Piedras Blancas Historic Light Station Outstanding Natural Area

(1) In general

In order to protect, conserve, and enhance for the benefit and enjoyment of present and future generations the unique and nationally important historical, natural, cultural, scientific, educational, scenic, and recreational values of certain lands in and around the Piedras Blancas Light Station, in San Luis Obispo County, California, while allowing certain recreational and research activities to continue, there is established, subject to valid existing rights, the Piedras Blancas Historic Light Station Outstanding Natural Area.

(2) Maps and legal descriptions

The boundaries of the Outstanding Natural Area as those shown on the map entitled "Piedras Blancas Historic Light Station: Outstanding Natural Area", dated May 5, 2004, which shall be on file and available for public inspection in the Office of the Director, Bureau of Land Management, United States Department of the Interior, and the State office of the Bureau of Land Management in the State of California.

(3) Basis of management

The Secretary shall manage the Outstanding Natural Area as part of the National Landscape Conservation System to protect the resources of the area, and shall allow only those uses that further the purposes for the establishment of the Outstanding Natural Area, the Federal Land Policy and Management Act of 1976 (43 U.S.C. 1701 et seq.), and other applicable laws.

(4) Withdrawal

Subject to valid existing rights, and in accordance with the existing withdrawal as set forth in Public Land Order 7501 (Oct. 12, 2001, Vol. 66, No. 198, Federal Register 52149), the Federal lands and interests in lands included within the Outstanding Natural Area are hereby withdrawn from—

(A) all forms of entry, appropriation, or disposal under the public land laws;

(B) location, entry, and patent under the public land mining laws; and

(C) operation of the mineral leasing and geothermal leasing laws and the mineral materials laws.

(d) Management of the Piedras Blancas Historic Light Station Outstanding Natural Area

(1) In general

The Secretary shall manage the Outstanding Natural Area in a manner that conserves, protects, and enhances the unique and nationally important historical, natural, cultural, scientific, educational, scenic, and recreational values of that area, including an emphasis on preserving and restoring the Light Station facilities, consistent with the requirements of subsection (c)(3).

(2) Uses

Subject to valid existing rights, the Secretary shall only allow such uses of the Outstanding Natural Area as the Secretary finds are likely to further the purposes for which the Outstanding Natural Area is established as set forth in subsection (c)(1).

(3) Management plan

Not later than 3 years after of[2] May 8, 2008, the Secretary shall complete a comprehensive management plan consistent with the requirements of section 202 of the Federal Land Policy and Management Act of 1976 (43 U.S.C. 1712) to provide long-term management guidance for the public lands within the Outstanding Natural Area and fulfill the purposes for which it is established, as set forth in subsection (c)(1). The management plan shall be developed in consultation with appropriate Federal, State, and local government agencies, with full public participation, and the contents shall include—

(A) provisions designed to ensure the protection of the resources and values described in subsection (c)(1);

(B) objectives to restore the historic Light Station and ancillary buildings;

(C) an implementation plan for a continuing program of interpretation and public education about the Light Station and its importance to the surrounding community;

(D) a proposal for minimal administrative and public facilities to be developed or improved at a level compatible with achieving the resources objectives for the Outstanding Natural Area as described in paragraph (1) and with other proposed management activities to accommodate visitors and researchers to the Outstanding Natural Area; and

(E) cultural resources management strategies for the Outstanding Natural Area, prepared in consultation with appropriate departments of the State of California, with emphasis on the preservation of the resources of the Outstanding Natural Area and the interpretive, education, and long-term scientific uses of the resources, giving priority to the enforcement of the Archaeological Resources Protection Act of 1979 (16 U.S.C. 470aa et seq.) and division A of subtitle III of title 54, United States Code within the Outstanding Natural Area.

(4) Cooperative agreements

In order to better implement the management plan and to continue the successful partnerships with the local communities and the Hearst San Simeon State Historical Monument, administered by the California Department of Parks and Recreation, the Secretary may enter into cooperative agreements with the appropriate Federal, State, and local agencies pursuant to section 307(b) of the Federal Land Management[3] Policy and Management Act of 1976 (43 U.S.C. 1737(b)).

(5) Research activities

In order to continue the successful partnership with research organizations and agencies and to assist in the development and implementation of the management plan, the Secretary may authorize within the Outstanding Natural Area appropriate research activities for the purposes identified in subsection (c)(1) and pursuant to section 307(a) of the Federal Land Policy and Management Act of 1976 (43 U.S.C. 1737(a)).

(6) Acquisition

State and privately held lands or interests in lands adjacent to the Outstanding Natural Area and identified as appropriate for acquisition in the management plan may be acquired by the Secretary as part of the Outstanding Natural Area only by—

(A) donation;

(B) exchange with a willing party; or

(C) purchase from a willing seller.

(7) Additions to the Outstanding Natural Area

Any lands or interest in lands adjacent to the Outstanding Natural Area acquired by the United States after May 8, 2008 shall be added to and administered as part of the Outstanding Natural Area.

(8) Overflights

Nothing in this section or the management plan shall be construed to—

(A) restrict or preclude overflights, including low level overflights, military, commercial, and general aviation overflights that can be seen or heard within the Outstanding Natural Area;

(B) restrict or preclude the designation or creation of new units of special use airspace or the establishment of military flight training routes over the Outstanding Natural Area; or

(C) modify regulations governing low-level overflights above the adjacent Monterey Bay National Marine Sanctuary.

(9) Law enforcement activities

Nothing in this section shall be construed to preclude or otherwise affect coastal border security operations or other law enforcement activities by the Coast Guard or other agencies within the Department of Homeland Security, the Department of Justice, or any other Federal, State, and local law enforcement agencies within the Outstanding Natural Area.

(10) Native American uses and interests

In recognition of the past use of the Outstanding Natural Area by Indians and Indian tribes for traditional cultural and religious purposes, the Secretary shall ensure access to the Outstanding

Natural Area by Indians and Indian tribes for such traditional cultural and religious purposes. In implementing this subsection, the Secretary, upon the request of an Indian tribe or Indian religious community, shall temporarily close to the general public use of one or more specific portions of the Outstanding Natural Area in order to protect the privacy of traditional cultural and religious activities in such areas by the Indian tribe or Indian religious community. Any such closure shall be made to affect the smallest practicable area for the minimum period necessary for such purposes. Such access shall be consistent with the purpose and intent of Public Law 95–341 (42 U.S.C. 1996 et seq.; commonly referred to as the "American Indian Religious Freedom Act").

(11) No buffer zones

The designation of the Outstanding Natural Area is not intended to lead to the creation of protective perimeters or buffer zones around[4] area. The fact that activities outside the Outstanding Natural Area and not consistent with the purposes of this section can be seen or heard within the Outstanding Natural Area shall not, of itself, preclude such activities or uses up to the boundary of the Outstanding Natural Area.

(e) Authorization of appropriations

There are authorized to be appropriated such sums as are necessary to carry out this section.

(Pub. L. No. 110–229, Title II, § 201, 122 Stat. 759 (May 8, 2008); as amended by Pub. L. No. 113–287, § 5(*l*)(8), 128 Stat. 3271 (Dec. 19, 2014).)

[1] So in original. Probably should be 1702(e)).

[2] So in original. The word "of" probably should not appear.

[3] So in original. The word "Management" probably should not appear.

[4] So in original. Probably should be followed by "the."

HISTORICAL AND STATUTORY NOTES

References in Text

The Federal Land Policy and Management Act of 1976, referred to in subsec. (c)(3), is Pub. L. No. 94–579, 90 Stat. 2743 (Oct. 21, 1976), as amended, which is codified principally as chapter 35 (section 1701 et seq.) of this title. Section 103(e), referred to in subsec. (a)(3), is codified as 43 U.S.C.A. § 1702(e). Section 202, referred to in subsec. (d)(3), is codified as 43 U.S.C.A. § 1712. Section 307, referred to in subsec. (d)(4), (5), is codified as 43 U.S.C.A. § 1737. For complete classification of this Act to the Code, see Short Title note set out under 43 U.S.C.A. § 1701 and Tables.

The Archaeological Resources Protection Act of 1979, referred to in subsec. (d)(3)(E), is Pub. L. No. 96–95, 93 Stat. 721 (Oct. 31, 1979), as amended, which is codified generally as chapter 1B (section 470aa et seq.) of Title 16. For complete classification of this Act to the Code, see Short Title note set out under 16 U.S.C.A. § 470aa and Tables.

The National Historic Preservation Act, referred to in subsec. (d)(3)(E), is Pub. L. No. 89–665, 80 Stat. 915 (Oct. 15, 1966), as amended, which is codified generally to subchapter II (section 470 et seq.) of chapter 1A of Title 16. For complete classification of this Act to the Code, see section 470(a) of Title 16 and Tables.

The American Indian Religious Freedom Act, referred to in subsec. (d)(10), is Pub. L. No. 95–341, 92 Stat. 469 (Aug. 11, 1978). For complete classification of this Act to the Code, see Short Title note set out under 42 U.S.C.A. § 1996 and Tables.

Codifications

Section was enacted as part of the Consolidated Natural Resources Act of 2008, and not as part of the Federal Land Policy and Management Act of 1976, which comprises this chapter.

§ 1787. Jupiter Inlet Lighthouse Outstanding Natural Area

(a) Definitions

In this section:

(1) Commandant

The term "Commandant" means the Commandant of the Coast Guard.

(2) Lighthouse

The term "Lighthouse" means the Jupiter Inlet Lighthouse located in Palm Beach County, Florida.

(3) Local Partners

The term "Local Partners" includes—

(A) Palm Beach County, Florida;

(B) the Town of Jupiter, Florida;

(C) the Village of Tequesta, Florida; and

(D) the Loxahatchee River Historical Society.

(4) Management plan

The term "management plan" means the management plan developed under subsection (c)(1).

(5) Map

The term "map" means the map entitled "Jupiter Inlet Lighthouse Outstanding Natural Area" and dated October 29, 2007.

(6) Outstanding Natural Area

The term "Outstanding Natural Area" means the Jupiter Inlet Lighthouse Outstanding Natural Area established by subsection (b)(1).

(7) Public land

The term "public land" has the meaning given the term "public lands" in section 103(e) of the Federal Land Policy and Management Act of 1976 (43 U.S.C. 1702(e)).

(8) Secretary

The term "Secretary" means the Secretary of the Interior.

(9) State

The term "State" means the State of Florida.

(b) Establishment of the Jupiter Inlet Lighthouse Outstanding Natural Area

(1) Establishment

Subject to valid existing rights, there is established for the purposes described in paragraph (2) the Jupiter Inlet Lighthouse Outstanding Natural Area, the boundaries of which are depicted on the map.

(2) Purposes

The purposes of the Outstanding Natural Area are to protect, conserve, and enhance the unique and nationally important historic, natural, cultural, scientific, educational, scenic, and recreational values of the Federal land surrounding the Lighthouse for the benefit of present generations and future generations of people in the United States, while—

(A) allowing certain recreational and research activities to continue in the Outstanding Natural Area; and

(B) ensuring that Coast Guard operations and activities are unimpeded within the boundaries of the Outstanding Natural Area.

(3) Availability of map

The map shall be on file and available for public inspection in appropriate offices of the Bureau of Land Management.

(4) Withdrawal

(A) In general

Subject to valid existing rights, subsection (e), and any existing withdrawals under the Executive orders and public land order described in subparagraph (B), the Federal land and any interests in the Federal land included in the Outstanding Natural Area are withdrawn from—

(i) all forms of entry, appropriation, or disposal under the public land laws;

(ii) location, entry, and patent under the mining laws; and

(iii) operation of the mineral leasing and geothermal leasing laws and the mineral materials laws.

(B) Description of Executive orders

The Executive orders and public land order described in subparagraph (A) are—

(i) the Executive Order dated October 22, 1854;

(ii) Executive Order No. 4254 (June 12, 1925); and

(iii) Public Land Order No. 7202 (61 Fed. Reg. 29758).

(c) Management plan

(1) In general

Not later than 3 years after May 8, 2008, the Secretary, in consultation with the Commandant, shall develop a comprehensive management plan in accordance with section 202 of the Federal Land Policy and Management Act of 1976 (43 U.S.C. 1712) to—

(A) provide long-term management guidance for the public land in the Outstanding Natural Area; and

(B) ensure that the Outstanding Natural Area fulfills the purposes for which the Outstanding Natural Area is established.

(2) Consultation; public participation

The management plan shall be developed—

(A) in consultation with appropriate Federal, State, county, and local government agencies, the Commandant, the Local Partners, and other partners; and

(B) in a manner that ensures full public participation.

(3) Existing plans

The management plan shall, to the maximum extent practicable, be consistent with existing resource plans, policies, and programs.

(4) Inclusions

The management plan shall include—

(A) objectives and provisions to ensure—

(i) the protection and conservation of the resource values of the Outstanding Natural Area; and

(ii) the restoration of native plant communities and estuaries in the Outstanding Natural Area, with an emphasis on the conservation and enhancement of healthy, functioning ecological systems in perpetuity;

(B) objectives and provisions to maintain or recreate historic structures;

(C) an implementation plan for a program of interpretation and public education about the natural and cultural resources of the Lighthouse, the public land surrounding the Lighthouse, and associated structures;

(D) a proposal for administrative and public facilities to be developed or improved that—

(i) are compatible with achieving the resource objectives for the Outstanding Natural Area described in subsection (d)(1)(A)(ii); and

(ii) would accommodate visitors to the Outstanding Natural Area;

(E) natural and cultural resource management strategies for the Outstanding Natural Area, to be developed in consultation with appropriate departments of the State, the Local Partners, and the Commandant, with an emphasis on resource conservation in the Outstanding Natural Area and the interpretive, educational, and long-term scientific uses of the resources; and

(F) recreational use strategies for the Outstanding Natural Area, to be prepared in consultation with the Local Partners, appropriate departments of the State, and the Coast Guard, with an emphasis on passive recreation.

(5) Interim plan

Until a management plan is adopted for the Outstanding Natural Area, the Jupiter Inlet Coordinated Resource Management Plan (including any updates or amendments to the Jupiter Inlet Coordinated Resource Management Plan) shall be in effect.

(d) Management of the Jupiter Inlet Lighthouse Outstanding Natural Area

(1) Management

(A) In general

The Secretary, in consultation with the Local Partners and the Commandant, shall manage the Outstanding Natural Area—

(i) as part of the National Landscape Conservation System;

(ii) in a manner that conserves, protects, and enhances the unique and nationally important historical, natural, cultural, scientific, educational, scenic, and recreational values of the Outstanding Natural Area, including an emphasis on the restoration of native ecological systems; and

(iii) in accordance with the Federal Land Policy and Management Act of 1976 (43 U.S.C. 1701 et seq.) and other applicable laws.

(B) Limitation

In managing the Outstanding Natural Area, the Secretary shall not take any action that precludes, prohibits, or otherwise affects the conduct of ongoing or future Coast Guard operations or activities on lots 16 and 18, as depicted on the map.

(2) Uses

Subject to valid existing rights and subsection (e), the Secretary shall only allow uses of the Outstanding Natural Area that the Secretary, in consultation with the Commandant and Local Partners, determines would likely further the purposes for which the Outstanding Natural Area is established.

(3) Cooperative agreements

To facilitate implementation of the management plan and to continue the successful partnerships with local communities and other partners, the Secretary may, in accordance with section 307(b) of the

Federal Land Management[1] Policy and Management Act of 1976 (43 U.S.C. 1737(b)), enter into cooperative agreements with the appropriate Federal, State, county, other local government agencies, and other partners (including the Loxahatchee River Historical Society) for the long-term management of the Outstanding Natural Area.

(4) Research activities

To continue successful research partnerships, pursue future research partnerships, and assist in the development and implementation of the management plan, the Secretary may, in accordance with section 307(a) of the Federal Land Policy and Management Act of 1976 (43 U.S. C. 1737(a)), authorize the conduct of appropriate research activities in the Outstanding Natural Area for the purposes described in subsection (b)(2).

(5) Acquisition of land

(A) In general

Subject to subparagraph (B), the Secretary may acquire for inclusion in the Outstanding Natural Area any State or private land or any interest in State or private land that is—

(i) adjacent to the Outstanding Natural Area; and

(ii) identified in the management plan as appropriate for acquisition.

(B) Means of acquisition

Land or an interest in land may be acquired under subparagraph (A) only by donation, exchange, or purchase from a willing seller with donated or appropriated funds.

(C) Additions to the Outstanding Natural Area

Any land or interest in land adjacent to the Outstanding Natural Area acquired by the United States after May 8, 2008, under subparagraph (A) shall be added to, and administered as part of, the Outstanding Natural Area.

(6) Law enforcement activities

Nothing in this section, the management plan, or the Jupiter Inlet Coordinated Resource Management Plan (including any updates or amendments to the Jupiter Inlet Coordinated Resource Management Plan) precludes, prohibits, or otherwise affects—

(A) any maritime security, maritime safety, or environmental protection mission or activity of the Coast Guard;

(B) any border security operation or law enforcement activity by the Department of Homeland Security or the Department of Justice; or

(C) any law enforcement activity of any Federal, State, or local law enforcement agency in the Outstanding Natural Area.

(7) Future disposition of Coast Guard facilities

If the Commandant determines, after May 8, 2008, that Coast Guard facilities within the Outstanding Natural Area exceed the needs of the Coast Guard, the Commandant may relinquish the facilities to the Secretary without removal, subject only to any environmental remediation that may be required by law.

(e) Effect on ongoing and future Coast Guard operations

Nothing in this section, the management plan, or the Jupiter Inlet Coordinated Resource Management Plan (including updates or amendments to the Jupiter Inlet Coordinated Resource Management Plan) precludes, prohibits, or otherwise affects ongoing or future Coast Guard operations or activities in the Outstanding Natural Area, including—

(1) the continued and future operation of, access to, maintenance of, and, as may be necessitated for Coast Guard missions, the expansion, enhancement, or replacement of, the Coast Guard High frequency antenna site on lot 16;

(2) the continued and future operation of, access to, maintenance of, and, as may be necessitated for Coast Guard missions, the expansion, enhancement, or replacement of, the military family housing area on lot 18;

(3) the continued and future use of, access to, maintenance of, and, as may be necessitated for Coast Guard missions, the expansion, enhancement, or replacement of, the pier on lot 18;

(4) the existing lease of the Jupiter Inlet Lighthouse on lot 18 from the Coast Guard to the Loxahatchee River Historical Society; or

(5) any easements or other less-than-fee interests in property appurtenant to existing Coast Guard facilities on lots 16 and 18.

(f) Authorization of appropriations

There are authorized to be appropriated such sums as are necessary to carry out this section.

(Pub. L. No. 110–229, Title II, § 202, 122 Stat. 763 (May 8, 2008).)

[1] So in original. The word "Management" probably should not appear.

HISTORICAL AND STATUTORY NOTES

References in Text

The Federal Land Policy and Management Act of 1976, referred to in subsec. (d)(1)(A)(iii), is Pub. L. No. 94–579, 90 Stat. 2743 (Oct. 21, 1976), as amended, which is codified principally as chapter 35 (section 1701 et seq.) of this title. Section 103(e), referred to in subsec. (a)(7), is codified as 43 U.S.C.A. § 1702(e). Section 202, referred to in subsec. (c)(1), is codified as 43 U.S.C.A. § 1712. Section 307, referred to in subsec. (d)(3), (4), is codified as 43 U.S.C.A. § 1737. For complete classification of this Act to the Code, see Short Title note set out under 43 U.S.C.A. § 1701 and Tables.

Codifications

This section was enacted as part of the Consolidated Natural Resources Act of 2008, and not as part of the Federal Land Policy and Management Act of 1976, which comprises this chapter.

APPENDIX A

OCCUPATIONAL SAFETY AND HEALTH ACT

(Selections from 29 U.S.C.A. §§ 651 et seq.)

CHAPTER 15—OCCUPATIONAL SAFETY AND HEALTH

Sec.

§ 651. Congressional statement of findings and declaration of purpose and policy

[OSH Act §§ 1, 2]

(a)[1] The Congress finds that personal injuries and illnesses arising out of work situations impose a substantial burden upon, and are a hindrance to, interstate commerce in terms of lost production, wage loss, medical expenses, and disability compensation payments.

(b) The Congress declares it to be its purpose and policy, through the exercise of its powers to regulate commerce among the several States and with foreign nations and to provide for the general welfare, to assure so far as possible every working man and woman in the Nation safe and healthful working conditions and to preserve our human resources—

(1) by encouraging employers and employees in their efforts to reduce the number of occupational safety and health hazards at their places of employment, and to stimulate employers and employees to institute new and to perfect existing programs for providing safe and healthful working conditions;

(2) by providing that employers and employees have separate but dependent responsibilities and rights with respect to achieving safe and healthful working conditions;

(3) by authorizing the Secretary of Labor to set mandatory occupational safety and health standards applicable to businesses affecting interstate commerce, and by creating an Occupational Safety and Health Review Commission for carrying out adjudicatory functions under this chapter;

(4) by building upon advances already made through employer and employee initiative for providing safe and healthful working conditions;

(5) by providing for research in the field of occupational safety and health, including the psychological factors involved, and by developing innovative methods, techniques, and approaches for dealing with occupational safety and health problems;

(6) by exploring ways to discover latent diseases, establishing causal connections between diseases and work in environmental conditions, and conducting other research relating to health problems, in recognition of the fact that occupational health standards present problems often different from those involved in occupational safety;

(7) by providing medical criteria which will assure insofar as practicable that no employee will suffer diminished health, functional capacity, or life expectancy as a result of his work experience;

(8) by providing for training programs to increase the number and competence of personnel engaged in the field of occupational safety and health;

(9) by providing for the development and promulgation of occupational safety and health standards;

(10) by providing an effective enforcement program which shall include a prohibition against giving advance notice of any inspection and sanctions for any individual violating this prohibition;

(11) by encouraging the States to assume the fullest responsibility for the administration and enforcement of their occupational safety and health laws by providing grants to the States to assist in identifying their needs and responsibilities in the area of occupational safety and health, to develop plans in accordance with the provisions of this chapter, to improve the administration and enforcement of State occupational safety and health laws, and to conduct experimental and demonstration projects in connection therewith;

(12) by providing for appropriate reporting procedures with respect to occupational safety and health which procedures will help achieve the objectives of this chapter and accurately describe the nature of the occupational safety and health problem;

(13) by encouraging joint labor-management efforts to reduce injuries and disease arising out of employment.

(Pub. L. No. 91–596, § 2, 84 Stat. 1590 (Dec. 29, 1970).)

[1] Section was enacted without subsec. (a) designation, which has been supplied editorially.

HISTORICAL AND STATUTORY NOTES

References in Text

This chapter, referred to in subsec. (b)(3), (11), and (12), was in the original "this Act", meaning Pub. L. No. 91–596, 84 Stat. 1590 (Dec. 29, 1970), as amended. For complete classification of this Act to the Code, see Short Title note under this section and Tables.

Effective and Applicability Provisions

1970 Acts. Section 34 of Pub. L. No. 91–596 provided that: "This Act [enacting this chapter and section 3142–1 of Title 42, The Public Health and Welfare, amending section 553 of this title, sections 5108, 5314, 5315, and 7902 of Title 5, Government Organization and Employees, sections 633 and 636 of Title 15, Commerce and Trade, section 1114 of Title 18, Crimes and Criminal Procedure, and section 1421 of Title 49, Transportation, and enacting provisions set out as notes under this section and section 1114 of Title 18] shall take effect one hundred and twenty days after the date of its enactment [Dec. 29, 1970]."

Short Title

1998 Amendments. Pub. L. No. 105–197, § 1, 112 Stat. 638 (July 16, 1998), provided that: "This Act [amending section 670 of this title] may be cited as the 'Occupational Safety and Health Administration Compliance Assistance Authorization Act of 1998'."

1970 Acts. Section 1 of Pub. L. No. 91–596 provided: "That this Act [enacting this chapter and section 3142–1 of Title 42, The Public Health and Welfare, amending section 553 of this title, sections 5108, 5314, 5315, and 7902 of Title 5, Government Organization and Employees, sections 633 and 636 of Title 15, Commerce and Trade, section 1114 of Title 18, Crimes and Criminal Procedure, and section 1421 of Title 49, Transportation, and enacting provisions set out as notes under this section and section 1114 of Title 18] may be cited as the 'Occupational Safety and Health Act of 1970'."

Occupational Safety and Health Programs

Occupational safety and health programs for federal employees and establishment of Federal Advisory Council on Occupational Safety and Health, see Ex. Ord. No. 12196, 45 Fed. Reg. 12769 (Feb. 26, 1980), as amended by Ex. Ord. No. 12223, 45 Fed. Reg. 45235 (June 30, 1980), set out as a note under section 7902 of Title 5, Government Organization and Employees.

§ 652. Definitions

[OSH Act § 3]

For the purposes of this chapter—

(1) The term "Secretary" mean[1] the Secretary of Labor.

(2) The term "Commission" means the Occupational Safety and Health Review Commission established under this chapter.

(3) The term "commerce" means trade, traffic, commerce, transportation, or communication among the several States, or between a State and any place outside thereof, or within the District of Columbia, or a possession of the United States (other than the Trust Territory of the Pacific Islands), or between points in the same State but through a point outside thereof.

(4) The term "person" means one or more individuals, partnerships, associations, corporations, business trusts, legal representatives, or any organized group of persons.

(5) The term "employer" means a person engaged in a business affecting commerce who has employees, but does not include the United States (not including the United States Postal Service) or any State or political subdivision of a State.

(6) The term "employee" means an employee of an employer who is employed in a business of his employer which affects commerce.

(7) The term "State" includes a State of the United States, the District of Columbia, Puerto Rico, the Virgin Islands, American Samoa, Guam, and the Trust Territory of the Pacific Islands.

(8) The term "occupational safety and health standard" means a standard which requires conditions, or the adoption or use of one or more practices, means, methods, operations, or processes, reasonably necessary or appropriate to provide safe or healthful employment and places of employment.

(9) The term "national consensus standard" means any occupational safety and health standard or modification thereof which (1),[2] has been adopted and promulgated by a nationally recognized standards-producing organization under procedures whereby it can be determined by the Secretary that persons interested and affected by the scope or provisions of the standard have reached substantial agreement on its adoption, (2) was formulated in a manner which afforded an opportunity for diverse views to be considered and (3) has been designated as such a standard by the Secretary, after consultation with other appropriate Federal agencies.

(10) The term "established Federal standard" means any operative occupational safety and health standard established by any agency of the United States and presently in effect, or contained in any Act of Congress in force on December 29, 1970.

(11) The term "Committee" means the National Advisory Committee on Occupational Safety and Health established under this chapter.

(12) The term "Director" means the Director of the National Institute for Occupational Safety and Health.

(13) The term "Institute" means the National Institute for Occupational Safety and Health established under this chapter.

(14) The term "Workmen's Compensation Commission" means the National Commission on State Workmen's Compensation Laws established under this chapter.

(Pub. L. No. 91–596, § 3, 84 Stat. 1591 (Dec. 29, 1970); as amended by Pub. L. No. 105–241, § 2(a), 112 Stat. 1572 (Sept. 29, 1998).)

[1] So in original. Probably should be "means."

[2] So in original. The comma probably should not appear.

HISTORICAL AND STATUTORY NOTES

References in Text

This chapter, referred to in introductory clause and pars. (2), (11), (13) and (14), was in the original "this Act", meaning Pub. L. No. 91–596, 84 Stat. 1590 (Dec. 29, 1970), as amended. For complete classification of this Act to the Code, see Short Title note set out under section 651 of this title and Tables.

Effective and Applicability Provisions

1970 Acts. Section effective 120 days after Dec. 29, 1970, see section 34 of Pub. L. No. 91–596, set out as a note under section 651 of this title.

Termination of Trust Territory of the Pacific Islands

For termination of Trust Territory of the Pacific Islands, see note set out under the heading for chapter 14 of Title 48, preceding 48 U.S.C.A. § 1681.

Termination of Advisory Committees

Advisory committees in existence on January 5, 1973, to terminate not later than the expiration of the two-year period following January 5, 1973, unless, in the case of a committee established by the President or an officer of the Federal Government, such committee is renewed by appropriate action prior to the expiration of such two-year period, or in the case of a committee established by the Congress, its duration is otherwise provided by law, see section 14 of Pub. L. No. 92–463, 86 Stat. 770 (Oct. 6, 1972), set out in Appendix 2 to Title 5, Government Organization and Employees.

§ 653. Geographic applicability; judicial enforcement; applicability to existing standards; report to Congress on duplication and coordination of Federal laws; workmen's compensation law or common law or statutory rights, duties, or liabilities of employers and employees unaffected

[OSH Act § 4]

(a) This chapter shall apply with respect to employment performed in a workplace in a State, the District of Columbia, the Commonwealth of Puerto Rico, the Virgin Islands, American Samoa, Guam, the Trust Territory of the Pacific Islands, Wake Island, Outer Continental Shelf lands defined in the Outer Continental Shelf Lands Act [43 U.S.C.A. § 1331 et seq.], Johnston Island, and the Canal Zone. The Secretary of the Interior shall, by regulation, provide for judicial enforcement of this chapter by the courts established for areas in which there are no United States district courts having jurisdiction.

(b) **(1)** Nothing in this chapter shall apply to working conditions of employees with respect to which other Federal agencies, and State agencies acting under section 2021 of Title 42, exercise statutory authority to prescribe or enforce standards or regulations affecting occupational safety or health.

(2) The safety and health standards promulgated under the Act of June 30, 1936, commonly known as the Walsh-Healey Act, the Service Contract Act of 1965, Public Law 91–54, Act of August 9, 1969,

Public Law 85–742, Act of August 23, 1958, and the National Foundation on Arts and Humanities Act [20 U.S.C.A. § 951 et seq.] are superseded on the effective date of corresponding standards, promulgated under this chapter, which are determined by the Secretary to be more effective. Standards issued under the laws listed in this paragraph and in effect on or after the effective date of this chapter shall be deemed to be occupational safety and health standards issued under this chapter, as well as under such other Acts.

(3) The Secretary shall, within three years after the effective date of this chapter, report to the Congress his recommendations for legislation to avoid unnecessary duplication and to achieve coordination between this chapter and other Federal laws.

(4) Nothing in this chapter shall be construed to supersede or in any manner affect any workmen's compensation law or to enlarge or diminish or affect in any other manner the common law or statutory rights, duties, or liabilities of employers and employees under any law with respect to injuries, diseases, or death of employees arising out of, or in the course of, employment.

(Pub. L. No. 91–596, § 4, 84 Stat. 1592 (Dec. 29, 1970).)

HISTORICAL AND STATUTORY NOTES

References in Text

This chapter, referred to in subsecs. (a) and (b), was in the original "this Act", meaning Pub. L. No. 91–596, 84 Stat. 1590 (Dec. 29, 1970), as amended. For complete classification of this Act to the Code, see Short Title note set out under section 651 of this title and Tables.

The Outer Continental Shelf Lands Act, referred to in subsec. (a), is Act of Aug. 7, 1953, c. 345, 67 Stat. 462, as amended, which is codified generally as subchapter III (section 1331 et seq.) of chapter 29 of Title 43, Public Lands. For complete classification of this Act to the Code, see Short Title note set out under section 1331 of Title 43 and Tables volume.

For definition of Canal Zone, referred to in subsec. (a), see section 3602(b) of Title 22, Foreign Relations and Intercourse.

Act of June 30, 1936, commonly known as the Walsh-Healey Act, referred to in subsec. (b)(2), is Act of June 30, 1936, c. 881, 49 Stat. 2036, which was codified principally as sections 35 to 45 of former Title 41, Public Contracts, and was substantially repealed and restated as chapter 65 (§ 6501 et seq.) of Title 41, Public Contracts, by Pub. L. No. 111–350, §§ 3, 7(b), 124 Stat. 3677, 3855 (Jan. 4, 2011). For complete classification, see Short Title of 1936 Act note set out under section 101 of Title 41 and Tables. For disposition of sections of former Title 41, see Disposition Table preceding section 101 of Title 41.

The Service Contract Act of 1965, referred to in subsec. (b)(2), was Pub. L. No. 89–286, 79 Stat. 1034 (Oct. 22, 1965), which was codified generally as chapter 6 (§ 351 et seq.) of former Title 41, Public Contracts, and was repealed and restated as chapter 67 (§ 6701 et seq.) of Title 41, Public Contracts, by Pub. L. No. 111–350, §§ 3, 7(b), 124 Stat. 3677, 3855 (Jan. 4, 2011). For complete classification, see Tables. For disposition of sections of former Title 41, see Disposition Table preceding section 101 of Title 41.

Public Law 91–54, Act of August 9, 1969, referred to in subsec. (b)(2), is Pub. L. No. 91–54, 83 Stat. 96 (Aug. 9, 1969), which amended sections 1 and 2 and added section 107 of Pub. L. No. 87–581, 76 Stat. 357 (Aug. 13, 1962). Sections 1 and 2 of Pub. L. No. 87–581 were set out as notes under section 327, and section 107 of Pub. L. 87–581 was codified as section 333, of former Title 40. Sections 1 and 2 of Pub. L. No. 87–581 were repealed, and section 107 of Pub. L. No. 87–581 was repealed and reenacted as 40 U.S.C.A. §§ 3704 and 3705 by Pub. L. No. 107–217, §§ 1, 6(b), 116 Stat. 1062, 1304 (Aug. 21, 2002).

Pub. L. No. 85–742, Act of August 23, 1958, referred to in subsec. (b)(2), is Pub. L. No. 85–742, 72 Stat. 835 (Aug. 23, 1958), which amended section 941 of Title 33, Navigation and Navigable Waters, and enacted provisions set out as a note under section 941 of Title 33. For complete classification of this Act to the Code, see Tables volume.

The National Foundation on Arts and Humanities Act, referred to in subsec. (b)(2), is Pub. L. No. 89–209, 79 Stat. 845 (Sept. 29, 1965), as amended, known as the National Foundation on the Arts and the Humanities Act of 1965, which is codified principally as subchapter I (section 951 et seq.) of chapter 26 of Title 20, Education. For complete classification of this Act to the Code, see Short Title note set out under section 951 of Title 20 and Tables volume.

The effective date of this chapter, referred to in subsec. (b)(2), (3), is the effective date of Pub. L. No. 91–596, which is 120 days after Dec. 29, 1970, see section 34 of Pub. L. No. 91–596, set out as an Effective Date note under section 651 of this title.

Effective and Applicability Provisions

1970 Acts. Section effective 120 days after Dec. 29, 1970, see section 34 of Pub. L. No. 91–596, set out as a note under section 651 of this title.

Termination of Trust Territory of the Pacific Islands

For termination of Trust Territory of the Pacific Islands, see note set out under the heading for chapter 14 of Title 48, preceding 48 U.S.C.A. § 1681.

EPA Administrator Not Exercising 'Statutory Authority' Under This Section in Exercising Any Authority Under the Toxic Substances Control Act

The EPA Administrator not to be considered to be exercising 'statutory authority' under subsec. (b)(1) of this section in exercising any authority under the Toxic Substances Control Act [Pub. L. No. 94–469, 90 Stat. 2003 (Oct. 11, 1976), as amended, which is codified as chapter 53 (2601 et seq.) of Title 15, Commerce and Trade], see section 15(b) of Pub. L. No. 101–637, set out as a note under section 2646 of Title 15.

§ 654. Duties of employers and employees

[OSH Act § 5]

(a) Each employer—

(1) shall furnish to each of his employees employment and a place of employment which are free from recognized hazards that are causing or are likely to cause death or serious physical harm to his employees;

(2) shall comply with occupational safety and health standards promulgated under this chapter.

(b) Each employee shall comply with occupational safety and health standards and all rules, regulations, and orders issued pursuant to this chapter which are applicable to his own actions and conduct.

(Pub. L. No. 91–596, § 5, 84 Stat. 1593 (Dec. 29, 1970).)

HISTORICAL AND STATUTORY NOTES

References in Text

This chapter, referred to in subsecs. (a) and (b), was in the original "this Act", meaning Pub. L. No. 91–596, 84 Stat. 1590 (Dec. 29, 1970), as amended. For complete classification of this Act to the Code, see Short Title note set out under section 651 of this title and Tables.

Effective and Applicability Provisions

1970 Acts. Section effective 120 days after Dec. 29, 1970, see section 34 of Pub. L. No. 91–596, set out as a note under section 651 of this title.

§ 655. Standards

[OSH Act § 6]

(a) Promulgation by Secretary of national consensus standards and established Federal standards; time for promulgation; conflicting standards

Without regard to chapter 5 of Title 5 or to the other subsections of this section, the Secretary shall, as soon as practicable during the period beginning with the effective date of this chapter and ending two years after such date, by rule promulgate as an occupational safety or health standard any national consensus standard, and any established Federal standard, unless he determines that the promulgation of such a standard would not result in improved safety or health for specifically designated employees. In the event of conflict among any such standards, the Secretary shall promulgate the standard which assures the greatest protection of the safety or health of the affected employees.

(b) Procedure for promulgation, modification, or revocation of standards

The Secretary may by rule promulgate, modify, or revoke any occupational safety or health standard in the following manner:

(1) Whenever the Secretary, upon the basis of information submitted to him in writing by an interested person, a representative of any organization of employers or employees, a nationally recognized standards-producing organization, the Secretary of Health and Human Services, the National Institute for Occupational Safety and Health, or a State or political subdivision, or on the basis of information developed by the Secretary or otherwise available to him, determines that a rule should be promulgated in order to serve the objectives of this chapter, the Secretary may request the recommendations of an advisory committee appointed under section 656 of this title. The Secretary shall provide such an advisory committee with any proposals of his own or of the Secretary of Health and Human Services, together with all pertinent factual information developed by the Secretary or the Secretary of Health and Human Services, or otherwise available, including the results of research, demonstrations, and experiments. An advisory committee shall submit to the Secretary its recommendations regarding the rule to be promulgated within ninety days from the date of its appointment or within such longer or shorter period as may be prescribed by the Secretary, but in no event for a period which is longer than two hundred and seventy days.

(2) The Secretary shall publish a proposed rule promulgating, modifying, or revoking an occupational safety or health standard in the Federal Register and shall afford interested persons a period of thirty days after publication to submit written data or comments. Where an advisory committee is appointed and the Secretary determines that a rule should be issued, he shall publish the proposed rule within sixty days after the submission of the advisory committee's recommendations or the expiration of the period prescribed by the Secretary for such submission.

(3) On or before the last day of the period provided for the submission of written data or comments under paragraph (2), any interested person may file with the Secretary written objections to the proposed rule, stating the grounds therefor and requesting a public hearing on such objections. Within thirty days after the last day for filing such objections, the Secretary shall publish in the Federal Register a notice specifying the occupational safety or health standard to which objections have been filed and a hearing requested, and specifying a time and place for such hearing.

(4) Within sixty days after the expiration of the period provided for the submission of written data or comments under paragraph (2), or within sixty days after the completion of any hearing held under paragraph (3), the Secretary shall issue a rule promulgating, modifying, or revoking an occupational safety or health standard or make a determination that a rule should not be issued. Such a rule may contain a provision delaying its effective date for such period (not in excess of ninety days) as the Secretary determines may be necessary to insure that affected employers and employees will be informed of the existence of the standard and of its terms and that employers affected are given an opportunity to familiarize themselves and their employees with the existence of the requirements of the standard.

(5) The Secretary, in promulgating standards dealing with toxic materials or harmful physical agents under this subsection, shall set the standard which most adequately assures, to the extent feasible, on the basis of the best available evidence, that no employee will suffer material impairment of health or functional capacity even if such employee has regular exposure to the hazard dealt with by such standard for the period of his working life. Development of standards under this subsection shall be based upon research, demonstrations, experiments, and such other information as may be appropriate. In addition to the attainment of the highest degree of health and safety protection for the employee, other considerations shall be the latest available scientific data in the field, the feasibility of the standards, and experience gained under this and other health and safety laws. Whenever practicable, the standard promulgated shall be expressed in terms of objective criteria and of the performance desired.

(6) **(A)** Any employer may apply to the Secretary for a temporary order granting a variance from a standard or any provision thereof promulgated under this section. Such temporary order shall be granted only if the employer files an application which meets the requirements of clause (B) and establishes that (i) he is unable to comply with a standard by its effective date because of unavailability of professional or technical personnel or of materials and equipment needed to come into compliance with the standard or because necessary construction or alteration of facilities cannot be completed by the effective date, (ii) he is taking all available steps to safeguard his employees against the hazards covered by the standard, and (iii) he has an effective program for coming into compliance with the standard as quickly as practicable. Any temporary order issued under this paragraph shall prescribe the practices, means, methods, operations, and processes which the employer must adopt and use while the order is in effect and state in detail his program for coming into compliance with the standard. Such a temporary order may be granted only after notice to employees and an opportunity for a hearing: *Provided,* That the Secretary may issue one interim order to be effective until a decision is made on the basis of the hearing. No temporary order may be in effect for longer than the period needed by the employer to achieve compliance with the standard or one year, whichever is shorter, except that such an order may be renewed not more than twice (I) so long as the requirements of this paragraph are met and (II) if an application for renewal is filed at least 90 days prior to the expiration date of the order. No interim renewal of an order may remain in effect for longer than 180 days.

(B) An application for a temporary order under this paragraph (6) shall contain:

(i) a specification of the standard or portion thereof from which the employer seeks a variance,

(ii) a representation by the employer, supported by representations from qualified persons having firsthand knowledge of the facts represented, that he is unable to comply with the standard or portion thereof and a detailed statement of the reasons therefor,

(iii) a statement of the steps he has taken and will take (with specific dates) to protect employees against the hazard covered by the standard,

(iv) a statement of when he expects to be able to comply with the standard and what steps he has taken and what steps he will take (with dates specified) to come into compliance with the standard, and

(v) a certification that he has informed his employees of the application by giving a copy thereof to their authorized representative, posting a statement giving a summary of the application and specifying where a copy may be examined at the place or places where notices to employees are normally posted, and by other appropriate means.

A description of how employees have been informed shall be contained in the certification. The information to employees shall also inform them of their right to petition the Secretary for a hearing.

(C) The Secretary is authorized to grant a variance from any standard or portion thereof whenever he determines, or the Secretary of Health and Human Services certifies, that such variance is necessary to permit an employer to participate in an experiment approved by him or the Secretary of Health and Human Services designed to demonstrate or validate new and improved techniques to safeguard the health or safety of workers.

(7) Any standard promulgated under this subsection shall prescribe the use of labels or other appropriate forms of warning as are necessary to insure that employees are apprised of all hazards to which they are exposed, relevant symptoms and appropriate emergency treatment, and proper conditions and precautions of safe use or exposure. Where appropriate, such standard shall also prescribe suitable protective equipment and control or technological procedures to be used in connection with such hazards and shall provide for monitoring or measuring employee exposure at such locations and intervals, and in such manner as may be necessary for the protection of employees. In addition, where appropriate, any such standard shall prescribe the type and frequency of medical examinations or other tests which shall be made available, by the employer or at his cost, to employees exposed to such hazards in order to most effectively determine whether the health of such employees is adversely affected by such exposure. In the event such medical examinations are in the nature of research, as determined by the Secretary of Health and Human Services, such examinations may be furnished at the expense of the Secretary of Health and Human Services. The results of such examinations or tests shall be furnished only to the Secretary or the Secretary of Health and Human Services, and, at the request of the employee, to his physician. The Secretary, in consultation with the

Secretary of Health and Human Services, may by rule promulgated pursuant to section 553 of Title 5, make appropriate modifications in the foregoing requirements relating to the use of labels or other forms of warning, monitoring or measuring, and medical examinations, as may be warranted by experience, information, or medical or technological developments acquired subsequent to the promulgation of the relevant standard.

(8) Whenever a rule promulgated by the Secretary differs substantially from an existing national consensus standard, the Secretary shall, at the same time, publish in the Federal Register a statement of the reasons why the rule as adopted will better effectuate the purposes of this chapter than the national consensus standard.

(c) Emergency temporary standards

(1) The Secretary shall provide, without regard to the requirements of chapter 5 of Title 5, for an emergency temporary standard to take immediate effect upon publication in the Federal Register if he determines (A) that employees are exposed to grave danger from exposure to substances or agents determined to be toxic or physically harmful or from new hazards, and (B) that such emergency standard is necessary to protect employees from such danger.

(2) Such standard shall be effective until superseded by a standard promulgated in accordance with the procedures prescribed in paragraph (3) of this subsection.

(3) Upon publication of such standard in the Federal Register the Secretary shall commence a proceeding in accordance with subsection (b) of this section, and the standard as published shall also serve as a proposed rule for the proceeding. The Secretary shall promulgate a standard under this paragraph no later than six months after publication of the emergency standard as provided in paragraph (2) of this subsection.

(d) Variances from standards; procedure

Any affected employer may apply to the Secretary for a rule or order for a variance from a standard promulgated under this section. Affected employees shall be given notice of each such application and an opportunity to participate in a hearing. The Secretary shall issue such rule or order if he determines on the record, after opportunity for an inspection where appropriate and a hearing, that the proponent of the variance has demonstrated by a preponderance of the evidence that the conditions, practices, means, methods, operations, or processes used or proposed to be used by an employer will provide employment and places of employment to his employees which are as safe and healthful as those which would prevail if he complied with the standard. The rule or order so issued shall prescribe the conditions the employer must maintain, and the practices, means, methods, operations, and processes which he must adopt and utilize to the extent they differ from the standard in question. Such a rule or order may be modified or revoked upon application by an employer, employees, or by the Secretary on his own motion, in the manner prescribed for its issuance under this subsection at any time after six months from its issuance.

(e) Statement of reasons for Secretary's determinations; publication in Federal Register

Whenever the Secretary promulgates any standard, makes any rule, order, or decision, grants any exemption or extension of time, or compromises, mitigates, or settles any penalty assessed under this chapter, he shall include a statement of the reasons for such action, which shall be published in the Federal Register.

(f) Judicial review

Any person who may be adversely affected by a standard issued under this section may at any time prior to the sixtieth day after such standard is promulgated file a petition challenging the validity of such standard with the United States court of appeals for the circuit wherein such person resides or has his principal place of business, for a judicial review of such standard. A copy of the petition shall be forthwith transmitted by the clerk of the court to the Secretary. The filing of such petition shall not, unless otherwise ordered by the court, operate as a stay of the standard. The determinations of the Secretary shall be conclusive if supported by substantial evidence in the record considered as a whole.

(g) Priority for establishment of standards

In determining the priority for establishing standards under this section, the Secretary shall give due regard to the urgency of the need for mandatory safety and health standards for particular industries, trades, crafts, occupations, businesses, workplaces or work environments. The Secretary shall also give due regard to the recommendations of the Secretary of Health and Human Services regarding the need for mandatory standards in determining the priority for establishing such standards.

(Pub. L. No. 91–596, § 6, 84 Stat. 1593 (Dec. 29, 1970); as amended by Pub. L. No. 96–88, Title V, § 509(b), 93 Stat. 695 (Oct. 17, 1979).)

HISTORICAL AND STATUTORY NOTES

References in Text

The effective date of this chapter, referred to in subsec. (a), is the effective date of Pub. L. No. 91–596, 84 Stat. 1590 (Dec. 29, 1970), which is 120 days after Dec. 29, 1970, see section 34 of Pub. L. No. 91–596, set out as an Effective Date note under section 651 of this title.

This chapter referred to in subsecs. (b)(1) and (e), was in the original "this Act", meaning Pub. L. No. 91–596, 84 Stat. 1590 (Dec. 29, 1970), as amended. For complete classification of this Act to the Code, see Short Title note set out under section 651 of this title and Tables volume.

Effective and Applicability Provisions

1970 Acts. Section effective 120 days after Dec. 29, 1970, see section 34 of Pub. L. No. 91–596, set out as a note under section 651 of this title.

Change of Name

"Secretary of Health and Human Services" was substituted for "Secretary of Health, Education, and Welfare" in subsecs. (b)(1), (6)(C), (7), and (g) pursuant to section 509(b) of Pub. L. No. 96–88 which is codified as section 3508(b) of Title 20, Education.

Termination of Advisory Committees

Advisory committees in existence on January 5, 1973, to terminate not later than the expiration of the two-year period following January 5, 1973, unless, in the case of a committee established by the President or an officer of the Federal Government, such committee is renewed by appropriate action prior to the expiration of such two-year period, or in the case of a committee established by the Congress, its duration is otherwise provided by law, see section 14 of Pub. L. No. 92–463, 86 Stat. 770 (Oct. 6, 1972), set out in Appendix 2 to Title 5, Government Organization and Employees.

Prohibition on Exposure of Workers to Chemical or Other Hazards for Purpose of Conducting Experiments

Pub. L. No. 102–394, Title I, § 102, 106 Stat. 1799 (Oct. 6, 1992), provided that: "None of the funds appropriated under this Act [Pub. L. No. 102–394, 106 Stat. 1792 (Oct. 6, 1992), the Departments of Labor, Health and Human Services, and Education, and Related Agencies Appropriations Act, 1993; for distribution of this Act to the Code, see Tables] or subsequent Departments of Labor, Health and Human Services, and Education, and Related Agencies Appropriations Acts shall be used to grant variances, interim orders or letters of clarification to employers which will allow exposure of workers to chemicals or other workplace hazards in excess of existing Occupational Safety and Health Administration standards for the purpose of conducting experiments on workers' health or safety."

Similar provisions were contained in the following prior appropriation acts:

Pub. L. No. 102–170, Title I, § 102, 105 Stat. 1114 (Nov. 26, 1991).

Pub. L. No. 101–517, Title I, § 102, 104 Stat. 2196 (Nov. 5, 1990).

Pub. L. No. 101–166, Title I, § 102, 103 Stat. 1165 (Nov. 21, 1989).

Pub. L. No. 100–202, § 101(h) [Title I, § 102], 101 Stat. 1329–256, 1329–263 (Dec. 22, 1987).

Pub. L. No. 99–500, § 101(i) [H.R. 5233, Title I, § 102], 100 Stat. 1783–287 (Oct. 18, 1986), and Pub. L. No. 99–591, § 101(i) [H.R. 5233, Title I, § 102], 100 Stat. 3341–287 (Oct. 30, 1986).

Pub. L. No. 99–178, Title I, § 102, 99 Stat. 1109 (Dec. 12, 1985).

Pub. L. No. 98–619, Title I, § 102, 98 Stat. 3311 (Nov. 8, 1984).

Promulgation of Regulations Concerning Occupational Exposure to Bloodborne Pathogens

Pub. L. No. 102–170, Title I, § 100, 105 Stat. 1113 (Nov. 26, 1991), provided that:

"(a) Notwithstanding any other provision of law, on or before December 1, 1991, the Secretary of Labor, acting under the Occupational Safety and Health Act of 1970 [Pub. L. No. 91–596, 84 Stat. 1590 (Dec. 29, 1970), as amended, codified principally as this chapter, for distribution of this Act to the Code, see Short Title note set out under section 651 of this title and Tables], shall promulgate a final occupational health standard concerning occupational exposure to bloodborne pathogens. The final standard shall be based on the proposed standard as published in the Federal Register on May 30, 1989 (54 FED. REG. 23042), concerning occupational exposures to the hepatitis B virus, the human immunodeficiency virus and other bloodborne pathogens.

"(b) In the event that the final standard referred to in subsection (a) is not promulgated by the date required under such subsection, the proposed standard on occupational exposure to bloodborne pathogens as published in the Federal Register on May 30, 1989 (54 FED. REG. 23042) shall become effective as if such proposed standard had been promulgated as a final standard by the Secretary of Labor, and remain in effect until the date on which such Secretary promulgates the final standard referred to in subsection (a).

"(c) Nothing in this Act [Pub. L. No. 102–170, 105 Stat. 1107 (Nov. 26, 1991), known as the Departments of Labor, Health and Human Services, and Education, and Related Agencies Appropriations Act, 1992, for distribution of this Act to the Code, see Tables] shall be construed to require the Secretary of Labor (acting through the Occupational Safety and Health Administration) to revise the employment accident reporting regulations published at 29 C.F.R. 1904.8."

Retention of Markings and Placards

Pub. L. No. 101–615, § 29, 104 Stat. 3277 (Nov. 16, 1990), provided that: "Not later than 18 months after the date of enactment of this Act [Nov. 16, 1990], the Secretary of Labor, in consultation with the Secretary of Transportation and the Secretary of the Treasury, shall issue under section 6(b) of the Occupational Safety and Health Act of 1970 (29 U.S.C. 655(b)) [subsec. (b) of this section] standards requiring any employer who receives a package, container, motor vehicle, rail freight car, aircraft, or vessel which contains a hazardous material and which is required to be marked, placarded, or labeled in accordance with regulations issued under the Hazardous Materials Transportation Act [49 App.U.S.C.A. § 1801 et seq.] to retain the markings, placards, and labels, and any other information as may be required by such regulations on the package, container, motor vehicle, rail freight car, aircraft, or vessel, until the hazardous materials have been removed therefrom."

Chemical Process Safety Management

Pub. L. No. 101–549, Title III, § 304, 104 Stat. 2576 (Nov. 15, 1990), provided that:

"(a) Chemical process safety standard.—The Secretary of Labor shall act under the Occupational Safety and Health Act of 1970 (29 U.S.C. 653) [Pub. L. No. 95–596, 84 Stat. 1590 (Dec. 24, 1970). which is codified principally as this chapter for complete distribution of this Act to the Code, see Short Title note set out under section 651 of this title and Tables] to prevent accidental releases of chemicals which could pose a threat to employees. Not later than 12 months after the date of enactment of the Clean Air Act Amendments of 1990 [Nov. 15, 1990], the Secretary of Labor, in coordination with the Administrator of the Environmental Protection Agency, shall promulgate, pursuant to the Occupational Safety and Health Act, a chemical process safety standard designed to protect employees from hazards associated with accidental releases of highly hazardous chemicals in the workplace.

"(b) List of highly hazardous chemicals.—The Secretary shall include as part of such standard a list of highly hazardous chemicals, which include toxic, flammable, highly reactive and explosive substances. The list of such chemicals may include those chemicals listed by the Administrator under section 302 of the Emergency Planning and Community Right to Know Act of 1986 [section 11002 of Title 42, The Public Health and Welfare]. The Secretary may make additions to such list when a substance is found to pose a threat of serious injury or fatality in the event of an accidental release in the workplace.

"(c) Elements of safety standard.—Such standard shall, at minimum, require employers to—

"(1) develop and maintain written safety information identifying workplace chemical and process hazards, equipment used in the processes, and technology used in the processes;

"(2) perform a workplace hazard assessment, including, as appropriate, identification of potential sources of accidental releases, an identification of any previous release within the facility which had a likely potential for catastrophic consequences in the workplace, estimation of workplace effects of a range of releases, estimation of the health and safety effects of such range on employees;

"(3) consult with employees and their representatives on the development and conduct of hazard assessments and the development of chemical accident prevention plans and provide access to these and other records required under the standard;

"(4) establish a system to respond to the workplace hazard assessment findings, which shall address prevention, mitigation, and emergency responses;

"(5) periodically review the workplace hazard assessment and response system;

"(6) develop and implement written operating procedures for the chemical process including procedures for each operating phase, operating limitations, and safety and health considerations;

"(7) provide written safety and operating information to employees and train employees in operating procedures, emphasizing hazards and safe practices;

"(8) ensure contractors and contract employees are provided appropriate information and training;

"(9) train and educate employees and contractors in emergency response in a manner as comprehensive and effective as that required by the regulation promulgated pursuant to section 126(d) of the Superfund Amendments and Reauthorization Act [of 1986] [Pub. L. No. 99–499, Title I, § 126(d), 100 Stat. 1691 (Oct. 17, 1986), set out as a note under this section];

"(10) establish a quality assurance program to ensure that initial process related equipment, maintenance materials, and spare parts are fabricated and installed consistent with design specifications;

"(11) establish maintenance systems for critical process related equipment including written procedures, employee training, appropriate inspections, and testing of such equipment to ensure ongoing mechanical integrity;

"(12) conduct pre-start-up safety reviews of all newly installed or modified equipment;

"(13) establish and implement written procedures to manage change to process chemicals, technology, equipment and facilities; and

"(14) investigate every incident which results in or could have resulted in a major accident in the workplace, with any findings to be reviewed by operating personnel and modifications made if appropriate.

"(d) State authority.—Nothing in this section may be construed to diminish the authority of the States and political subdivisions thereof as described in section 112(r)(11) of the Clean Air Act [section 7412(r)(11) of Title 42]."

Hazardous Waste Operations

Pub. L. No. 99–499, Title I, § 126(a)–(f), 100 Stat. 1690–1692 (Oct. 17, 1986), as amended by Pub. L. No. 100–202, § 101(f) [Title II, § 201], 101 Stat. 1329–187, 1329–198 (Dec. 22, 1987), provided that:

"(a) Promulgation.—Within one year after the date of the enactment of this section [Oct. 17, 1986], the Secretary of Labor shall, pursuant to section 6 of the Occupational Safety and Health Act of 1970 [this section], promulgate standards for the health and safety protection of employees engaged in hazardous waste operations.

"(b) Proposed standards.—The Secretary of Labor shall issue proposed regulations on such standards which shall include, but need not be limited to, the following worker protection provisions:

"(1) Site analysis.—Requirements for a formal hazard analysis of the site and development of a site specific plan for worker protection.

"(2) Training.—Requirements for contractors to provide initial and routine training of workers before such workers are permitted to engage in hazardous waste operations which would expose them to toxic substances.

"(3) Medical surveillance.—A program of regular medical examination, monitoring, and surveillance of workers engaged in hazardous waste operations which would expose them to toxic substances.

"(4) Protective equipment.—Requirements for appropriate personal protective equipment, clothing, and respirators for work in hazardous waste operations.

"(5) Engineering controls.—Requirements for engineering controls concerning the use of equipment and exposure of workers engaged in hazardous waste operations.

"(6) Maximum exposure limits.—Requirements for maximum exposure limitations for workers engaged in hazardous waste operations, including necessary monitoring and assessment procedures.

"(7) Informational program.—A program to inform workers engaged in hazardous waste operations of the nature and degree of toxic exposure likely as a result of such hazardous waste operations.

"(8) Handling.—Requirements for the handling, transporting, labeling, and disposing of hazardous wastes.

"(9) New technology program.—A program for the introduction of new equipment or technologies that will maintain worker protections.

"(10) Decontamination procedures.—Procedures for decontamination.

"(11) Emergency response.—Requirements for emergency response and protection of workers engaged in hazardous waste operations.

"(c) Final regulations.—Final regulations under subsection (a) shall take effect one year after the date they are promulgated. In promulgating final regulations on standards under subsection (a), the Secretary of Labor shall include each of the provisions listed in paragraphs (1) through (11) of subsection (b) unless the Secretary determines that the evidence in the public record considered as a whole does not support inclusion of any such provision.

"(d) Specific training standards.—

"(1) Offsite instruction; field experience.—Standards promulgated under subsection (a) shall include training standards requiring that general site workers (such as equipment operators, general laborers, and other supervised personnel) engaged in hazardous substance removal or other activities which expose or potentially expose such workers to hazardous substances receive a minimum of 40 hours of initial instruction off the site, and a minimum of three days of actual field experience under the direct supervision of a trained, experienced supervisor, at the time of assignment. The requirements of the preceding sentence shall not apply to any general site worker who has received the equivalent of such training. Workers who may be exposed to unique or special hazards shall be provided additional training.

"(2) Training of supervisors.—Standards promulgated under subsection (a) shall include training standards requiring that onsite managers and supervisors directly responsible for the hazardous waste operations (such as foremen) receive the same training as general site workers set forth in paragraph (1) of this subsection and at least eight additional hours of specialized training on managing hazardous waste operations. The requirements of the preceding sentence shall not apply to any person who has received the equivalent of such training.

"(3) Certification; enforcement.—Such training standards shall contain provisions for certifying that general site workers, onsite managers, and supervisors have received the specified training and shall prohibit any individual who has not received the specified training from engaging in hazardous waste operations covered by the standard. The certification procedures shall be no less comprehensive than those adopted by the Environmental Protection Agency in its Model Accreditation Plan for Asbestos Abatement Training as required under the Asbestos Hazard Emergency Response Act of 1986 [Pub. L. 99–519].

"(4) Training of emergency response personnel.—Such training standards shall set forth requirements for the training of workers who are responsible for responding to hazardous emergency situations who may be exposed to toxic substances in carrying out their responsibilities.

"(e) Interim regulations.—The Secretary of Labor shall issue interim final regulations under this section within 60 days after the enactment of this section [Oct. 17, 1986] which shall provide no less protection under this section for workers employed by contractors and emergency response workers than the protections contained in the Environmental Protection Agency Manual (1981) "Health and Safety Requirements for Employees Engaged in Field Activities" and existing standards under the Occupational Safety and Health Act of 1970 [29 U.S.C.A. § 651 et seq.] found in subpart C of part 1926 of title 29 of the Code of Federal Regulations. Such interim final regulations shall take effect upon issuance and shall apply until final regulations become effective under subsection (c).

"(f) Coverage of certain State and local employees.—Not later than 90 days after the promulgation of final regulations under subsection (a), the Administrator shall promulgate standards identical to those promulgated by the Secretary of Labor under subsection (a). Standards promulgated under this subsection shall apply to employees of State and local governments in each State which does not have in effect an approved State plan under section 18 of the Occupational Safety and Health Act of 1970 [section 667 of this title] providing for standards for the health and safety protection of employees engaged in hazardous waste operations."

§ 656. Administration

(a) National Advisory Committee on Occupational Safety and Health; establishment; membership; appointment; Chairman; functions; meetings; compensation; secretarial and clerical personnel

(1) There is hereby established a National Advisory Committee on Occupational Safety and Health consisting of twelve members appointed by the Secretary, four of whom are to be designated by the Secretary of Health and Human Services, without regard to the provisions of Title 5 governing appointments in the competitive service, and composed of representatives of management, labor, occupational safety and occupational health professions, and of the public. The Secretary shall designate one of the public members as Chairman. The members shall be selected upon the basis of their experience and competence in the field of occupational safety and health.

(2) The Committee shall advise, consult with, and make recommendations to the Secretary and the Secretary of Health and Human Services on matters relating to the administration of this chapter. The Committee shall hold no fewer than two meetings during each calendar year. All meetings of the Committee shall be open to the public and a transcript shall be kept and made available for public inspection.

(3) The members of the Committee shall be compensated in accordance with the provisions of section 3109 of Title 5.

(4) The Secretary shall furnish to the Committee an executive secretary and such secretarial, clerical, and other services as are deemed necessary to the conduct of its business.

(b) Advisory committees; appointment; duties; membership; compensation; reimbursement to member's employer; meetings; availability of records; conflict of interest

An advisory committee may be appointed by the Secretary to assist him in his standard-setting functions under section 655 of this title. Each such committee shall consist of not more than fifteen members and shall include as a member one or more designees of the Secretary of Health and Human Services, and shall include among its members an equal number of persons qualified by experience and affiliation to present the viewpoint of the employers involved, and of persons similarly qualified to present the viewpoint of the workers involved, as well as one or more representatives of health and safety agencies of the States. An advisory committee may also include such other persons as the Secretary may appoint who are qualified by knowledge and experience to make a useful contribution to the work of such committee, including one or more representatives of professional organizations of technicians or professionals specializing in occupational safety or health, and one or more representatives of nationally recognized standards-producing organizations, but the number of persons so appointed to any such advisory committee shall not exceed the number appointed to such committee as representatives of Federal and State agencies. Persons appointed to advisory committees from private life shall be compensated in the same manner as consultants or experts under section 3109 of Title 5. The Secretary shall pay to any State which is the employer of a member of such a committee who is a representative of the health or safety agency of that State, reimbursement sufficient to cover the actual cost to the State resulting from such representative's membership on such committee. Any meeting of such committee shall be open to the public and an accurate record shall be kept and made available to the public. No member of such committee (other than representatives of employers and employees) shall have an economic interest in any proposed rule.

(c) Use of services, facilities, and personnel of Federal, State, and local agencies; reimbursement; employment of experts and consultants or organizations; renewal of contracts; compensation; travel expenses

In carrying out his responsibilities under this chapter, the Secretary is authorized to—

(1) use, with the consent of any Federal agency, the services, facilities, and personnel of such agency, with or without reimbursement, and with the consent of any State or political subdivision thereof, accept and use the services, facilities, and personnel of any agency of such State or subdivision with reimbursement; and

(2) employ experts and consultants or organizations thereof as authorized by section 3109 of Title 5, except that contracts for such employment may be renewed annually; compensate individuals so employed at rates not in excess of the rate specified at the time of service for grade GS–18 under section 5332 of Title 5, including traveltime, and allow them while away from their homes or regular places of business, travel expenses (including per diem in lieu of subsistence) as authorized by section 5703 of Title 5 for persons in the Government service employed intermittently, while so employed.

(d) There is established a Maritime Occupational Safety and Health Advisory Committee, which shall be a continuing body and shall provide advice to the Secretary in formulating maritime industry standards and regarding matters pertaining to the administration of this Act related to the maritime industry. The composition of such advisory committee shall be consistent with the advisory committees established under subsection (b). A member of the advisory committee who is otherwise qualified may continue to serve until a successor is appointed. The Secretary may promulgate or amend regulations as necessary to implement this subsection.

(Pub. L. No. 91–596, § 7, 84 Stat. 1597 (Dec. 29, 1970); as amended by Pub. L. No. 96–88, Title V, § 509(b), 93 Stat. 695 (Oct. 17, 1979), Pub. L. No. 116–92, § 3510, 133 Stat. 1977–78 (Dec. 20, 2019).)

HISTORICAL AND STATUTORY NOTES

References in Text

This chapter, referred to in subsecs. (a)(2) and (c), was in the original "this Act", meaning Pub. L. No. 91–596, 84 Stat. 1590 (Dec. 29, 1970), as amended. For complete classification of this Act to the Code, see Short Title note set out under section 651 of this title and Tables.

Effective and Applicability Provisions

1970 Acts. Section effective 120 days after Dec. 29, 1970, see section 34 of Pub. L. No. 91–596, set out as a note under section 651 of this title.

Change of Name

"Secretary of Health and Human Services" was substituted for "Secretary of Health, Education, and Welfare" in subsecs. (a)(1), (2) and (b) pursuant to section 509(b) of Pub. L. No. 96–88 which is codified as section 3508(b) of Title 20, Education.

Termination of Advisory Committees

Advisory Committees in existence on January 5, 1973, to terminate not later than the expiration of the two-year period following January 5, 1973, unless, in the case of a committee established by the President or an officer of the Federal Government, such committee is renewed by appropriate action prior to the expiration of such two-year period, or in the case of a committee established by the Congress, its duration is otherwise provided by law, see section 14 of Pub. L. No. 92–463, 86 Stat. 770 (Oct. 6, 1972), set out in Appendix 2 to Title 5, Government Organization and Employees.

§ 657. Inspections, investigations, and recordkeeping

[OSH Act § 8]

(a) Authority of Secretary to enter, inspect, and investigate places of employment; time and manner

In order to carry out the purposes of this chapter, the Secretary, upon presenting appropriate credentials to the owner, operator, or agent in charge, is authorized—

(1) to enter without delay and at reasonable times any factory, plant, establishment, construction site, or other area, workplace or environment where work is performed by an employee of an employer; and

(2) to inspect and investigate during regular working hours and at other reasonable times, and within reasonable limits and in a reasonable manner, any such place of employment and all pertinent conditions, structures, machines, apparatus, devices, equipment, and materials therein, and to question privately any such employer, owner, operator, agent, or employee.

(b) Attendance and testimony of witnesses and production of evidence; enforcement of subpoena

In making his inspections and investigations under this chapter the Secretary may require the attendance and testimony of witnesses and the production of evidence under oath. Witnesses shall be paid the same fees and mileage that are paid witnesses in the courts of the United States. In case of a contumacy, failure, or refusal of any person to obey such an order, any district court of the United States or the United States courts of any territory or possession, within the jurisdiction of which such person is found, or resides or transacts business, upon the application by the Secretary, shall have jurisdiction to issue to such person an order requiring such person to appear to produce evidence if, as, and when so ordered, and to give testimony relating to the matter under investigation or in question, and any failure to obey such order of the court may be punished by said court as a contempt thereof.

(c) Maintenance, preservation, and availability of records; issuance of regulations; scope of records; periodic inspections by employer; posting of notices by employer; notification of employee of corrective action

(1) Each employer shall make, keep and preserve, and make available to the Secretary or the Secretary of Health and Human Services, such records regarding his activities relating to this chapter as the Secretary, in cooperation with the Secretary of Health and Human Services, may prescribe by regulation as necessary or appropriate for the enforcement of this chapter or for developing information regarding the causes and prevention of occupational accidents and illnesses. In order to carry out the provisions of this paragraph such regulations may include provisions requiring employers to conduct periodic inspections. The Secretary shall also issue regulations requiring that employers, through posting of notices or other appropriate means, keep their employees informed of their protections and obligations under this chapter, including the provisions of applicable standards.

(2) The Secretary, in cooperation with the Secretary of Health and Human Services, shall prescribe regulations requiring employers to maintain accurate records of, and to make periodic reports on, work-related deaths, injuries and illnesses other than minor injuries requiring only first aid treatment and which do not involve medical treatment, loss of consciousness, restriction of work or motion, or transfer to another job.

(3) The Secretary, in cooperation with the Secretary of Health and Human Services, shall issue regulations requiring employers to maintain accurate records of employee exposures to potentially toxic materials or harmful physical agents which are required to be monitored or measured under section 655 of this title. Such regulations shall provide employees or their representatives with an opportunity to observe such monitoring or measuring, and to have access to the records thereof. Such regulations shall also make appropriate provision for each employee or former employee to have access to such records as will indicate his own exposure to toxic materials or harmful physical agents. Each employer shall promptly notify any employee who has been or is being exposed to toxic materials or harmful physical agents in concentrations or at levels which exceed those prescribed by an applicable occupational safety and health standard promulgated under section 655 of this title, and shall inform any employee who is being thus exposed of the corrective action being taken.

(d) Obtaining of information

Any information obtained by the Secretary, the Secretary of Health and Human Services, or a State agency under this chapter shall be obtained with a minimum burden upon employers, especially those operating small businesses. Unnecessary duplication of efforts in obtaining information shall be reduced to the maximum extent feasible.

(e) Employer and authorized employee representatives to accompany Secretary or his authorized representative on inspection of workplace; consultation with employees where no authorized employee representative is present

Subject to regulations issued by the Secretary, a representative of the employer and a representative authorized by his employees shall be given an opportunity to accompany the Secretary or his authorized representative during the physical inspection of any workplace under subsection (a) of this section for the purpose of aiding such inspection. Where there is no authorized employee representative, the Secretary or his authorized representative shall consult with a reasonable number of employees concerning matters of health and safety in the workplace.

(f) Request for inspection by employees or representative of employees; grounds; procedure; determination of request; notification of Secretary or representative prior to or during any inspection of violations; procedure for review of refusal by representative of Secretary to issue citation for alleged violations

(1) Any employees or representative of employees who believe that a violation of a safety or health standard exists that threatens physical harm, or that an imminent danger exists, may request an inspection by giving notice to the Secretary or his authorized representative of such violation or danger. Any such notice shall be reduced to writing, shall set forth with reasonable particularity the grounds for the notice, and shall be signed by the employees or representative of employees, and a copy shall be provided the employer or his agent no later than at the time of inspection, except that, upon the request of the person giving such notice, his name and the names of individual employees referred to therein shall not appear in such copy or on any record published, released, or made available pursuant to subsection (g) of this section. If upon receipt of such notification the Secretary determines there are reasonable grounds to believe that such violation or danger exists, he shall make a special inspection in accordance with the provisions of this section as soon as practicable, to determine if such violation or danger exists. If the Secretary determines there are no reasonable grounds to believe that a violation or danger exists he shall notify the employees or representative of the employees in writing of such determination.

(2) Prior to or during any inspection of a workplace, any employees or representative of employees employed in such workplace may notify the Secretary or any representative of the Secretary responsible for conducting the inspection, in writing, of any violation of this chapter which they have reason to believe exists in such workplace. The Secretary shall, by regulation, establish procedures for informal review of any refusal by a representative of the Secretary to issue a citation with respect to any such alleged violation and shall furnish the employees or representative of employees requesting such review a written statement of the reasons for the Secretary's final disposition of the case.

(g) Compilation, analysis, and publication of reports and information; rules and regulations

(1) The Secretary and Secretary of Health and Human Services are authorized to compile, analyze, and publish, either in summary or detailed form, all reports or information obtained under this section.

(2) The Secretary and the Secretary of Health and Human Services shall each prescribe such rules and regulations as he may deem necessary to carry out their responsibilities under this chapter, including rules and regulations dealing with the inspection of an employer's establishment.

(h) Use of results of enforcement activities

The Secretary shall not use the results of enforcement activities, such as the number of citations issued or penalties assessed, to evaluate employees directly involved in enforcement activities under this chapter or to impose quotas or goals with regard to the results of such activities.

(Pub. L. No. 91–596, § 8, 84 Stat. 1598 (Dec. 29, 1970); as amended by Pub. L. No. 96–88, Title V, § 509(b), 93 Stat. 695 (Oct. 17, 1979); Pub. L. No. 105–198, § 1, 112 Stat. 640 (July 16, 1998).)

Validity

The United States Supreme Court has held Section 8(a) of the Occupational and Health Safety Act of 1970, unconstitutional insofar as it purports to authorize inspections of certain business premises without warrant or its equivalent. Marshall v. Barlow's, Inc., *436 U.S. 307, 98 S.Ct. 1816, 56 L.Ed.2d 305 (1978).*

HISTORICAL AND STATUTORY NOTES

References in Text

This chapter, referred to in subsecs. (a), (b), (c)(1), (d), (f)(2), (g)(2), and (h), was in the original "this Act", meaning Pub. L. No. 91–596, 84 Stat. 1590 (Dec. 29, 1970), as amended. For complete classification of this Act to the Code, see Short Title note set out under section 651 of this title and Tables.

Effective and Applicability Provisions

1970 Acts. Section effective 120 days after Dec. 29, 1970, see section 34 of Pub. L. No. 91–596, set out as a note under section 651 of this title.

Change of Name

"Secretary of Health and Human Services" was substituted for "Secretary of Health, Education, and Welfare" in subsecs. (c), (d), and (g) pursuant to section 509(b) of Pub. L. No. 96–88 which is codified as section 3508(b) of Title 20, Education.

Termination of Advisory Committees

Advisory committees in existence on January 5, 1973, to terminate not later than the expiration of the 2-year period following January 5, 1973, unless, in the case of a committee established by the President or an officer of the Federal Government, such committee is renewed by appropriate action prior to the expiration of such 2-year period, or in the case of a committee established by the Congress, its duration is otherwise provided by law, see section 14 of the Federal Advisory Committee Act, 5 App. 2 U.S.C.A. § 14.

References in Other Laws to GS–16, 17, or 18 Pay Rates

References in laws to the rates of pay for GS–16, 17, or 18, or to maximum rates of pay under the General Schedule, to be considered references to rates payable under specified sections of Title 5, see section 529 [Title I, § 101(c)(1)] of Pub. L. No. 101–509, set out in a note under 5 U.S.C.A. § 5376.

§ 658. Citations

[OSH Act § 9]

(a) Authority to issue; grounds; contents; notice in lieu of citation for de minimis violations

If, upon inspection or investigation, the Secretary or his authorized representative believes that an employer has violated a requirement of section 654 of this title, of any standard, rule or order promulgated pursuant to section 655 of this title, or of any regulations prescribed pursuant to this chapter, he shall with reasonable promptness issue a citation to the employer. Each citation shall be in writing and shall describe with particularity the nature of the violation, including a reference to the provision of the chapter, standard, rule, regulation, or order alleged to have been violated. In addition, the citation shall fix a reasonable time for the abatement of the violation. The Secretary may prescribe procedures for the issuance of a notice in lieu of a citation with respect to de minimis violations which have no direct or immediate relationship to safety or health.

(b) Posting

Each citation issued under this section, or a copy or copies thereof, shall be prominently posted, as prescribed in regulations issued by the Secretary, at or near each place a violation referred to in the citation occurred.

(c) Time for issuance

No citation may be issued under this section after the expiration of six months following the occurrence of any violation.

(Pub. L. No. 91–596, § 9, 84 Stat. 1601 (Dec. 29, 1970).)

HISTORICAL AND STATUTORY NOTES

References in Text

This chapter, referred to in subsec. (a), was in the original "this Act", meaning Pub. L. No. 91–596, 84 Stat. 1590 (Dec. 29, 1970), as amended. For complete classification of this Act to the Code, see Short Title note set out under section 651 of this title and Tables.

Effective and Applicability Provisions

1970 Acts. Section effective 120 days after Dec. 29, 1970, see section 34 of Pub. L. No. 91–596, set out as a note under section 651 of this title.

§ 659. Enforcement procedures

[OSH Act § 10]

(a) Notification of employer of proposed assessment of penalty subsequent to issuance of citation; time for notification of Secretary by employer of contest by employer of citation or proposed assessment; citation and proposed assessment as final order upon failure of employer to notify of contest and failure of employees to file notice

If, after an inspection or investigation, the Secretary issues a citation under section 658(a) of this title, he shall, within a reasonable time after the termination of such inspection or investigation, notify the employer by certified mail of the penalty, if any, proposed to be assessed under section 666 of this title and that the employer has fifteen working days within which to notify the Secretary that he wishes to contest the citation or proposed assessment of penalty. If, within fifteen working days from the receipt of the notice issued by the Secretary the employer fails to notify the Secretary that he intends to contest the citation or proposed assessment of penalty, and no notice is filed by any employee or representative of employees under subsection (c) of this section within such time, the citation and the assessment, as proposed, shall be deemed a final order of the Commission and not subject to review by any court or agency.

(b) Notification of employer of failure to correct in allotted time period violation for which citation was issued and proposed assessment of penalty for failure to correct; time for notification of Secretary by employer of contest by employer of notification of failure to correct or proposed assessment; notification or proposed assessment as final order upon failure of employer to notify of contest

If the Secretary has reason to believe that an employer has failed to correct a violation for which a citation has been issued within the period permitted for its correction (which period shall not begin to run until the entry of a final order by the Commission in the case of any review proceedings under this section initiated by the employer in good faith and not solely for delay or avoidance of penalties), the Secretary shall notify the employer by certified mail of such failure and of the penalty proposed to be assessed under section 666 of this title by reason of such failure, and that the employer has fifteen working days within which to notify the Secretary that he wishes to contest the Secretary's notification or the proposed assessment of penalty. If, within fifteen working days from the receipt of notification issued by the Secretary, the employer fails to notify the Secretary that he intends to contest the notification or proposed assessment of penalty, the notification and assessment, as proposed, shall be deemed a final order of the Commission and not subject to review by any court or agency.

(c) Advisement of Commission by Secretary of notification of contest by employer of citation or notification or of filing of notice by any employee or representative of employees; hearing by Commission; orders of Commission and Secretary; rules of procedure

If an employer notifies the Secretary that he intends to contest a citation issued under section 658(a) of this title or notification issued under subsection (a) or (b) of this section, or if, within fifteen working days of the issuance of a citation under section 658(a) of this title, any employee or representative of employees files a notice with the Secretary alleging that the period of time fixed in the citation for the abatement of the violation is unreasonable, the Secretary shall immediately advise the Commission of such notification, and the Commission shall afford an opportunity for a hearing (in accordance with section 554 of Title 5 but without regard to subsection (a)(3) of such section). The Commission shall thereafter issue an order, based on findings of fact, affirming, modifying, or vacating the Secretary's citation or proposed penalty, or directing other appropriate relief, and such order shall become final thirty days after its issuance. Upon a showing by an employer of a good faith effort to comply with the abatement requirements of a citation, and that abatement has not been completed because of factors beyond his reasonable control, the Secretary, after an opportunity for a hearing as provided in this subsection, shall issue an order affirming or modifying the abatement requirements in such citation. The rules of procedure prescribed by the Commission shall provide affected employees or representatives of affected employees an opportunity to participate as parties to hearings under this subsection.

(Pub. L. No. 91–596, § 10, 84 Stat. 1601 (Dec. 29, 1970).)

HISTORICAL AND STATUTORY NOTES

Codifications

Section 666 of this title, referred to in subsecs. (a) and (b), was in the original section 17 of Pub. L. No. 91–596. Subsecs. (a) to (g) and (i) to (*l*) of such section 17 are codified as section 666 of this title. Subsec. (h)(1) of such section 17 amended section 1114 of Title 18, Crimes and Criminal Procedure, and subsec. (h)(2) of section 17 enacted note set out thereunder.

Effective and Applicability Provisions

1970 Acts. Section effective 120 days after Dec. 29, 1970, see section 34 of Pub. L. No. 91–596, set out as a note under section 651 of this title.

§ 660. Judicial review

[OSH Act § 11]

(a) Filing of petition by persons adversely affected or aggrieved; orders subject to review; jurisdiction; venue; procedure; conclusiveness of record and findings of Commission; appropriate relief; finality of judgment

Any person adversely affected or aggrieved by an order of the Commission issued under subsection (c) of section 659 of this title may obtain a review of such order in any United States court of appeals for the circuit in which the violation is alleged to have occurred or where the employer has its principal office, or in the Court of Appeals for the District of Columbia Circuit, by filing in such court within sixty days following the issuance of such order a written petition praying that the order be modified or set aside. A copy of such petition shall be forthwith transmitted by the clerk of the court to the Commission and to the other parties, and thereupon the Commission shall file in the court the record in the proceeding as provided in section 2112 of Title 28. Upon such filing, the court shall have jurisdiction of the proceeding and of the question determined therein, and shall have power to grant such temporary relief or restraining order as it deems just and proper, and to make and enter upon the pleadings, testimony, and proceedings set forth in such record a decree affirming, modifying, or setting aside in whole or in part, the order of the Commission and enforcing the same to the extent that such order is affirmed or modified. The commencement of proceedings under this subsection shall not, unless ordered by the court, operate as a stay of the order of the Commission. No objection that has not been urged before the Commission shall be considered by the court, unless the failure or neglect to urge such objection shall be excused because of extraordinary circumstances. The findings of the Commission with respect to questions of fact, if supported by substantial evidence on the record considered as a whole, shall be conclusive. If any party shall apply to the court for leave to adduce additional evidence and shall show to the satisfaction of the court that such additional evidence is material and that there were reasonable grounds for the failure to adduce such evidence in the hearing before the Commission, the court may order such additional evidence to be taken before the Commission and to be made a part of the record. The Commission may modify its findings as to the facts, or make new findings, by reason of additional evidence so taken and filed, and it shall file such modified or new findings, which findings with respect to questions of fact, if supported by substantial evidence on the record considered as a whole, shall be conclusive, and its recommendations, if any, for the modification or setting aside of its original order. Upon the filing of the record with it, the jurisdiction of the court shall be exclusive and its judgment and decree shall be final, except that the same shall be subject to review by the Supreme Court of the United States, as provided in section 1254 of Title 28.

(b) Filing of petition by Secretary; orders subject to review; jurisdiction; venue; procedure; conclusiveness of record and findings of Commission; enforcement of orders; contempt proceedings

The Secretary may also obtain review or enforcement of any final order of the Commission by filing a petition for such relief in the United States court of appeals for the circuit in which the alleged violation occurred or in which the employer has its principal office, and the provisions of subsection (a) of this section shall govern such proceedings to the extent applicable. If no petition for review, as provided in subsection (a) of this section, is filed within sixty days after service of the Commission's order, the Commission's findings of fact and order shall be conclusive in connection with any petition for enforcement which is filed by the Secretary after the expiration of such sixty-day period. In any such case, as well as in the case of a noncontested citation or notification by the Secretary which has become a final order of the Commission under subsection (a) or (b) of section 659 of this title, the clerk of the court, unless otherwise ordered by the court, shall forthwith enter a decree enforcing the order and shall transmit a copy of such decree to the Secretary and the employer named in the petition. In any contempt proceeding brought to enforce a decree of a court of appeals entered pursuant to this subsection or subsection (a) of this section, the court of appeals may assess the penalties provided in section 666 of this title, in addition to invoking any other available remedies.

(c) Discharge or discrimination against employee for exercise of rights under this chapter; prohibition; procedure for relief

(1) No person shall discharge or in any manner discriminate against any employee because such employee has filed any complaint or instituted or caused to be instituted any proceeding under or related to this chapter or has testified or is about to testify in any such proceeding or because of the exercise by such employee on behalf of himself or others of any right afforded by this chapter.

(2) Any employee who believes that he has been discharged or otherwise discriminated against by any person in violation of this subsection may, within thirty days after such violation occurs, file a complaint with the Secretary alleging such discrimination. Upon receipt of such complaint, the Secretary shall cause such investigation to be made as he deems appropriate. If upon such investigation, the Secretary determines that the provisions of this subsection have been violated, he shall bring an action in any appropriate United States district court against such person. In any such action the United States district courts shall have jurisdiction, for cause shown to restrain violations of paragraph (1) of this subsection and order all appropriate relief including rehiring or reinstatement of the employee to his former position with back pay.

(3) Within 90 days of the receipt of a complaint filed under this subsection the Secretary shall notify the complainant of his determination under paragraph (2) of this subsection.

(Pub. L. No. 91–596, § 11, 84 Stat. 1602 (Dec. 29, 1970); as amended by Pub. L. No. 98–620, Title IV, § 402(32), 98 Stat. 3360 (Nov. 8, 1984).)

HISTORICAL AND STATUTORY NOTES

References in Text

This chapter, referred to in subsec. (c)(1), was in the original "this Act", meaning Pub. L. No. 91–596, 84 Stat. 1590 (Dec. 29, 1970), as amended. For complete classification of this Act to the Code, see Short Title note set out under section 651 of this title and Tables.

Codifications

Section 666 of this title, referred to in subsec. (b), was in the original section 17 of Pub. L. No. 91–596. Subsecs. (a) to (g) and (i) to (*l*) of such section 17 are codified as section 666 of this title. Subsec. (h) of such section 17 amended section 1114 of Title 18, Crimes and Criminal Procedure, and enacted note set out thereunder.

Effective and Applicability Provisions

1984 Acts. Amendment by Pub. L. No. 98–620 not to apply to cases pending on Nov. 8, 1984, see section 403 of Pub. L. No. 98–620, set out as a note under section 1657 of Title 28, Judiciary and Judicial Procedure.

1970 Acts. Section effective 120 days after Dec. 29, 1970, see section 34 of Pub. L. No. 91–596, set out as a note under section 651 of this title.

§ 661. Occupational Safety and Health Review Commission

[OSH Act § 12]

(a) Establishment; membership; appointment; Chairman

The Occupational Safety and Health Review Commission is hereby established. The Commission shall be composed of three members who shall be appointed by the President, by and with the advice and consent of the Senate, from among persons who by reason of training, education, or experience are qualified to carry out the functions of the Commission under this chapter. The President shall designate one of the members of the Commission to serve as Chairman.

(b) Terms of office; removal by President

The terms of members of the Commission shall be six years except that (1) the members of the Commission first taking office shall serve, as designated by the President at the time of appointment, one for a term of two years, one for a term of four years, and one for a term of six years, and (2) a vacancy caused by the death, resignation, or removal of a member prior to the expiration of the term for which he was appointed shall be filled only for the remainder of such unexpired term. A member of the Commission may be removed by the President for inefficiency, neglect of duty, or malfeasance in office.

(c) Omitted

(d) Principal office; hearings or other proceedings at other places

The principal office of the Commission shall be in the District of Columbia. Whenever the Commission deems that the convenience of the public or of the parties may be promoted, or delay or expense may be minimized, it may hold hearings or conduct other proceedings at any other place.

(e) Functions and duties of Chairman; appointment and compensation of administrative law judges and other employees

The Chairman shall be responsible on behalf of the Commission for the administrative operations of the Commission and shall appoint such administrative law judges and other employees as he deems necessary to assist in the performance of the Commission's functions and to fix their compensation in accordance with the provisions of chapter 51 and subchapter III of chapter 53 of Title 5 relating to classification and General Schedule pay rates: *Provided*, That assignment, removal and compensation of administrative law judges shall be in accordance with sections 3105, 3344, 5372, and 7521 of Title 5.

(f) Quorum; official action

For the purpose of carrying out its functions under this chapter, two members of the Commission shall constitute a quorum and official action can be taken only on the affirmative vote of at least two members.

(g) Hearings and records open to public; promulgation of rules; applicability of Federal Rules of Civil Procedure

Every official act of the Commission shall be entered of record, and its hearings and records shall be open to the public. The Commission is authorized to make such rules as are necessary for the orderly transaction of its proceedings. Unless the Commission has adopted a different rule, its proceedings shall be in accordance with the Federal Rules of Civil Procedure.

(h) Depositions and production of documentary evidence; fees

The Commission may order testimony to be taken by deposition in any proceeding pending before it at any state of such proceeding. Any person may be compelled to appear and depose, and to produce books, papers, or documents, in the same manner as witnesses may be compelled to appear and testify and produce like documentary evidence before the Commission. Witnesses whose depositions are taken under this subsection, and the persons taking such depositions, shall be entitled to the same fees as are paid for like services in the courts of the United States.

(i) Investigatory powers

For the purpose of any proceeding before the Commission, the provisions of section 161 of this title are hereby made applicable to the jurisdiction and powers of the Commission.

(j) Administrative law judges; determinations; report as final order of Commission

A[1] administrative law judge appointed by the Commission shall hear, and make a determination upon, any proceeding instituted before the Commission and any motion in connection therewith, assigned to such administrative law judge by the Chairman of the Commission, and shall make a report of any such determination which constitutes his final disposition of the proceedings. The report of the administrative law judge shall become the final order of the Commission within thirty days after such report by the administrative law judge, unless within such period any Commission member has directed that such report shall be reviewed by the Commission.

(k) Appointment and compensation of administrative law judges

Except as otherwise provided in this chapter, the administrative law judges shall be subject to the laws governing employees in the classified civil service, except that appointments shall be made without regard to section 5108 of Title 5. Each administrative law judge shall receive compensation at a rate not less than that prescribed for GS–16 under section 5332 of Title 5.

(Pub. L. No. 91–596, § 12, 84 Stat. 1603 (Dec. 29, 1970); as amended by Pub. L. No. 95–251, § 2(a)(7), 92 Stat. 183 (Mar. 27, 1978).)

[1] So in original. Probably should be "An."

HISTORICAL AND STATUTORY NOTES

References in Text

This chapter, referred to in subsecs. (a), (f), and (k), was in the original "this Act", meaning Pub. L. No. 91–596, 84 Stat. 1590 (Dec. 29, 1970), as amended. For complete classification of this Act to the Code, see Short Title note set out under section 651 of this title and Tables.

The General Schedule, referred to in subsec. (e), is set out under section 5332 of Title 5, Government Organization and Employees.

The Federal Rules of Civil Procedure, referred to in subsec. (g), are set out in Title 28, Judiciary and Judicial Procedure.

Codifications

Subsec. (c) of this section amended sections 5314 and 5315 of Title 5, Government Organization and Employees.

In subsec. (e), reference to section 5372 of Title 5 was substituted for reference to section 5362 on authority of Pub. L. No. 95–454, § 801(a)(3)(A)(ii), 92 Stat. 1221 (Oct. 13, 1978), which redesignated sections 5361 through 5365 of Title 5 as sections 5371 through 5375.

Effective and Applicability Provisions

1970 Acts. Section effective 120 days after Dec. 29, 1970, see section 34 of Pub. L. No. 91–596, set out as a note under section 651 of this title.

References in Other Laws to GS–16, 17, or 18 Pay Rates

References in laws to the rates of pay for GS–16, 17, or 18, or to maximum rates of pay under the General Schedule, to be considered references to rates payable under specified sections of Title 5, see section 529 [Title I, § 101(c)(1)] of Pub. L. No. 101–509, set out in a note under 5 U.S.C.A. § 5376.

§ 662. Injunction proceedings

[OSH Act § 13]

(a) Petition by Secretary to restrain imminent dangers; scope of order

The United States district courts shall have jurisdiction, upon petition of the Secretary, to restrain any conditions or practices in any place of employment which are such that a danger exists which could reasonably be expected to cause death or serious physical harm immediately or before the imminence of such danger can be eliminated through the enforcement procedures otherwise provided by this chapter. Any order issued under this section may require such steps to be taken as may be necessary to avoid, correct, or remove such imminent danger and prohibit the employment or presence of any individual in locations or under conditions where such imminent danger exists, except individuals whose presence is necessary to avoid, correct, or remove such imminent danger or to maintain the capacity of a continuous process operation to resume normal operations without a complete cessation of operations, or where a cessation of operations is necessary, to permit such to be accomplished in a safe and orderly manner.

(b) Appropriate injunctive relief or temporary restraining order pending outcome of enforcement proceeding; applicability of Rule 65 of Federal Rules of Civil Procedure

Upon the filing of any such petition the district court shall have jurisdiction to grant such injunctive relief or temporary restraining order pending the outcome of an enforcement proceeding pursuant to this chapter. The proceeding shall be as provided by Rule 65 of the Federal Rules, Civil Procedure, except that no temporary restraining order issued without notice shall be effective for a period longer than five days.

(c) Notification of affected employees and employers by inspector of danger and of recommendation to Secretary to seek relief

Whenever and as soon as an inspector concludes that conditions or practices described in subsection (a) of this section exist in any place of employment, he shall inform the affected employees and employers of the danger and that he is recommending to the Secretary that relief be sought.

(d) Failure of Secretary to seek relief; writ of mandamus

If the Secretary arbitrarily or capriciously fails to seek relief under this section, any employee who may be injured by reason of such failure, or the representative of such employees, might bring an action against the Secretary in the United States district court for the district in which the imminent danger is alleged to exist or the employer has its principal office, or for the District of Columbia, for a writ of mandamus to compel the Secretary to seek such an order and for such further relief as may be appropriate.

(Pub. L. No. 91–596, § 13, 84 Stat. 1605 (Dec. 29, 1970).)

HISTORICAL AND STATUTORY NOTES

References in Text

This chapter, referred to in subsec. (b), was in the original "this Act", meaning Pub. L. No. 91–596, 84 Stat. 1590 (Dec. 29, 1970), as amended. For complete classification of this Act to the Code, see Short Title note set out under section 651 of this title and Tables.

Rule 65 of the Federal Rules of Civil Procedure, referred to in subsec. (b), is set out in Title 28, Judiciary and Judicial Procedure.

Effective and Applicability Provisions

1970 Acts. Section effective 120 days after Dec. 29, 1970, see section 34 of Pub. L. No. 91–596, set out as a note under section 651 of this title.

§ 663. Representation in civil litigation

[OSH Act § 14]

Except as provided in section 518(a) of Title 28 relating to litigation before the Supreme Court, the Solicitor of Labor may appear for and represent the Secretary in any civil litigation brought under this chapter but all such litigations shall be subject to the direction and control of the Attorney General.

(Pub. L. No. 91–596, § 14, 84 Stat. 1606 (Dec. 29, 1970).)

HISTORICAL AND STATUTORY NOTES

References in Text

This chapter, referred to in text, was in the original "this Act", meaning Pub. L. No. 91–596, 84 Stat. 1590 (Dec. 29, 1970), as amended. For complete classification of this Act to the Code, see Short Title note set out under section 651 of this title and Tables.

Effective and Applicability Provisions

1970 Acts. Section effective 120 days after Dec. 29, 1970, see section 34 of Pub. L. No. 91–596, set out as a note under section 651 of this title.

§ 664. Disclosure of trade secrets; protective orders

[OSH Act § 15]

All information reported to or otherwise obtained by the Secretary or his representative in connection with any inspection or proceeding under this chapter which contains or which might reveal a trade secret referred to in section 1905 of Title 18 shall be considered confidential for the purpose of that section, except that such information may be disclosed to other officers or employees concerned with carrying out this chapter or when relevant in any proceeding under this chapter. In any such proceeding the Secretary, the Commission, or the court shall issue such orders as may be appropriate to protect the confidentiality of trade secrets.

(Pub. L. No. 91–596, § 15, 84 Stat. 1606 (Dec. 29, 1970).)

HISTORICAL AND STATUTORY NOTES

References in Text

This chapter, referred to in text, was in the original "this Act", meaning Pub. L. No. 91–596, 84 Stat. 1590 (Dec. 29, 1970), as amended. For complete classification of this Act to the Code, see Short Title note set out under section 651 of this title and Tables.

Effective and Applicability Provisions

1970 Acts. Section effective 120 days after Dec. 29, 1970, see section 34 of Pub. L. No. 91–596, set out as a note under section 651 of this title.

§ 665. Variations, tolerances, and exemptions from required provisions; procedure; duration

[OSH Act § 16]

The Secretary, on the record, after notice and opportunity for a hearing may provide such reasonable limitations and may make such rules and regulations allowing reasonable variations, tolerances, and exemptions to and from any or all provisions of this chapter as he may find necessary and proper to avoid serious impairment of the national defense. Such action shall not be in effect for more than six months without notification to affected employees and an opportunity being afforded for a hearing.

(Pub. L. No. 91–596, § 16, 84 Stat. 1606 (Dec. 29, 1970).)

HISTORICAL AND STATUTORY NOTES

References in Text

This chapter, referred to in text, was in the original "this Act", meaning Pub. L. No. 91–596, 84 Stat. 1590, as amended (Dec. 29, 1970). For complete classification of this Act to the Code, see Short Title note set out under section 651 of this title and Tables.

Effective and Applicability Provisions

1970 Acts. Section effective 120 days after Dec. 29, 1970, see section 34 of Pub. L. No. 91–596, set out as a note under section 651 of this title.

§ 666. Civil and criminal penalties

[OSH Act § 17]

(a) Willful or repeated violation

Any employer who willfully or repeatedly violates the requirements of section 654 of this title, any standard, rule, or order promulgated pursuant to section 655 of this title, or regulations prescribed pursuant to this chapter may be assessed a civil penalty of not more than $70,000 for each violation, but not less than $5,000 for each willful violation.

(b) Citation for serious violation

Any employer who has received a citation for a serious violation of the requirements of section 654 of this title, of any standard, rule, or order promulgated pursuant to section 655 of this title, or of any regulations prescribed pursuant to this chapter, shall be assessed a civil penalty of up to $7,000 for each such violation.

(c) Citation for violation determined not serious

Any employer who has received a citation for a violation of the requirements of section 654 of this title, of any standard, rule, or order promulgated pursuant to section 655 of this title, or of regulations prescribed pursuant to this chapter, and such violation is specifically determined not to be of a serious nature, may be assessed a civil penalty of up to $7,000 for each such violation.

(d) Failure to correct violation

Any employer who fails to correct a violation for which a citation has been issued under section 658(a) of this title within the period permitted for its correction (which period shall not begin to run until the date of the final order of the Commission in the case of any review proceeding under section 659 of this title initiated by the employer in good faith and not solely for delay or avoidance of penalties), may be assessed a civil penalty of not more than $7,000 for each day during which such failure or violation continues.

(e) Willful violation causing death to employee

Any employer who willfully violates any standard, rule, or order promulgated pursuant to section 655 of this title, or of any regulations prescribed pursuant to this chapter, and that violation caused death to any employee, shall, upon conviction, be punished by a fine of not more than $10,000 or by imprisonment for not more than six months, or by both; except that if the conviction is for a violation committed after a first conviction of such person, punishment shall be by a fine of not more than $20,000 or by imprisonment for not more than one year, or by both.

(f) Giving advance notice of inspection

Any person who gives advance notice of any inspection to be conducted under this chapter, without authority from the Secretary or his designees, shall, upon conviction, be punished by a fine of not more than $1,000 or by imprisonment for not more than six months, or by both.

(g) False statements, representations or certification

Whoever knowingly makes any false statement, representation, or certification in any application, record, report, plan, or other document filed or required to be maintained pursuant to this chapter shall, upon conviction, be punished by a fine of not more than $10,000, or by imprisonment for not more than six months, or by both.

(h) Omitted

(i) Violation of posting requirements

Any employer who violates any of the posting requirements, as prescribed under the provisions of this chapter, shall be assessed a civil penalty of up to $7,000 for each violation.

(j) Authority of Commission to assess civil penalties

The Commission shall have authority to assess all civil penalties provided in this section, giving due consideration to the appropriateness of the penalty with respect to the size of the business of the employer being charged, the gravity of the violation, the good faith of the employer, and the history of previous violations.

(k) Determination of serious violation

For purposes of this section, a serious violation shall be deemed to exist in a place of employment if there is a substantial probability that death or serious physical harm could result from a condition which exists, or from one or more practices, means, methods, operations, or processes which have been adopted or are in use, in such place of employment unless the employer did not, and could not with the exercise of reasonable diligence, know of the presence of the violation.

(*l*) Procedure for payment of civil penalties

Civil penalties owed under this chapter shall be paid to the Secretary for deposit into the Treasury of the United States and shall accrue to the United States and may be recovered in a civil action in the name of the United States brought in the United States district court for the district where the violation is alleged to have occurred or where the employer has its principal office.

(Pub. L. No. 91–596, § 17, 84 Stat. 1606, 1607 (Dec. 29, 1970); as amended by Pub. L. No. 101–508, Title III, § 3101, 104 Stat. 1388–29 (Nov. 5, 1990).)

HISTORICAL AND STATUTORY NOTES

References in Text

This chapter, referred to in text, was in the original "this Act", meaning Pub. L. No. 91–596, 84 Stat. 1590 (Dec. 29, 197), as amended. For complete classification of this Act to the Code, see Short Title note set out under section 651 of this title and Tables.

Codifications

Subsec. (h) of this section amended section 1114 of Title 18, Crimes and Criminal Procedure, and enacted note set out thereunder.

Effective and Applicability Provisions

1970 Acts. Section effective 120 days after Dec. 29, 1970, see section 34 of Pub. L. No. 91–596, set out as a note under section 651 of this title.

§ 667. State jurisdiction and plans

[OSH Act § 18]

(a) Assertion of State standards in absence of applicable Federal standards

Nothing in this chapter shall prevent any State agency or court from asserting jurisdiction under State law over any occupational safety or health issue with respect to which no standard is in effect under section 655 of this title.

(b) Submission of State plan for development and enforcement of State standards to preempt applicable Federal standards

Any State which, at any time, desires to assume responsibility for development and enforcement therein of occupational safety and health standards relating to any occupational safety or health issue with respect to which a Federal standard has been promulgated under section 655 of this title shall submit a State plan for the development of such standards and their enforcement.

(c) Conditions for approval of plan

The Secretary shall approve the plan submitted by a State under subsection (b) of this section, or any modification thereof, if such plan in his judgment—

(1) designates a State agency or agencies as the agency or agencies responsible for administering the plan throughout the State,

(2) provides for the development and enforcement of safety and health standards relating to one or more safety or health issues, which standards (and the enforcement of which standards) are or will be at least as effective in providing safe and healthful employment and places of employment as the standards promulgated under section 655 of this title which relate to the same issues, and which standards, when applicable to products which are distributed or used in interstate commerce, are required by compelling local conditions and do not unduly burden interstate commerce,

(3) provides for a right of entry and inspection of all workplaces subject to this chapter which is at least as effective as that provided in section 657 of this title, and includes a prohibition on advance notice of inspections,

(4) contains satisfactory assurances that such agency or agencies have or will have the legal authority and qualified personnel necessary for the enforcement of such standards,

(5) gives satisfactory assurances that such State will devote adequate funds to the administration and enforcement of such standards,

(6) contains satisfactory assurances that such State will, to the extent permitted by its law, establish and maintain an effective and comprehensive occupational safety and health program applicable to all employees of public agencies of the State and its political subdivisions, which program is as effective as the standards contained in an approved plan,

(7) requires employers in the State to make reports to the Secretary in the same manner and to the same extent as if the plan were not in effect, and

(8) provides that the State agency will make such reports to the Secretary in such form and containing such information, as the Secretary shall from time to time require.

(d) Rejection of plan; notice and opportunity for hearing

If the Secretary rejects a plan submitted under subsection (b) of this section, he shall afford the State submitting the plan due notice and opportunity for a hearing before so doing.

(e) Discretion of Secretary to exercise authority over comparable standards subsequent to approval of State plan; duration; retention of jurisdiction by Secretary upon determination of enforcement of plan by State

After the Secretary approves a State plan submitted under subsection (b) of this section, he may, but shall not be required to, exercise his authority under sections 657, 658, 659, 662, and 666 of this title with respect to comparable standards promulgated under section 655 of this title, for the period specified in the next sentence. The Secretary may exercise the authority referred to above until he determines, on the basis of actual operations under the State plan, that the criteria set forth in subsection (c) of this section are being applied, but he shall not make such determination for at least three years after the plan's approval under subsection (c) of this section. Upon making the determination referred to in the preceding sentence, the provisions of sections 654(a)(2), 657 (except for the purpose of carrying out subsection (f) of this section), 658, 659, 662, and 666 of this title, and standards promulgated under section 655 of this title, shall not apply with respect to any occupational safety or health issues covered under the plan, but the Secretary may retain jurisdiction under the above provisions in any proceeding commenced under section 658 or 659 of this title before the date of determination.

(f) Continuing evaluation by Secretary of State enforcement of approved plan; withdrawal of approval of plan by Secretary; grounds; procedure; conditions for retention of jurisdiction by State

The Secretary shall, on the basis of reports submitted by the State agency and his own inspections make a continuing evaluation of the manner in which each State having a plan approved under this section is carrying out such plan. Whenever the Secretary finds, after affording due notice and opportunity for a hearing, that in the administration of the State plan there is a failure to comply substantially with any provision of the State plan (or any assurance contained therein), he shall notify the State agency of his withdrawal of approval of such plan and upon receipt of such notice such plan shall cease to be in effect, but the State may retain jurisdiction in any case commenced before the withdrawal of the plan in order to enforce standards under the plan whenever the issues involved do not relate to the reasons for the withdrawal of the plan.

(g) Judicial review of Secretary's withdrawal of approval or rejection of plan; jurisdiction; venue; procedure; appropriate relief; finality of judgment

The State may obtain a review of a decision of the Secretary withdrawing approval of or rejecting its plan by the United States court of appeals for the circuit in which the State is located by filing in such court within thirty days following receipt of notice of such decision a petition to modify or set aside in whole or in part the action of the Secretary. A copy of such petition shall forthwith be served upon the Secretary, and thereupon the Secretary shall certify and file in the court the record upon which the decision complained of was issued as provided in section 2112 of Title 28. Unless the court finds that the Secretary's decision in rejecting a proposed State plan or withdrawing his approval of such a plan is not supported by substantial evidence the court shall affirm the Secretary's decision. The judgment of the court shall be subject to review by the Supreme Court of the United States upon certiorari or certification as provided in section 1254 of Title 28.

(h) Temporary enforcement of State standards

The Secretary may enter into an agreement with a State under which the State will be permitted to continue to enforce one or more occupational health and safety standards in effect in such State until final action is taken by the Secretary with respect to a plan submitted by a State under subsection (b) of this section, or two years from December 29, 1970, whichever is earlier.

(Pub. L. No. 91–596, § 18, 84 Stat. 1608 (Dec. 29, 1970).)

HISTORICAL AND STATUTORY NOTES

References in Text

This chapter, referred to in subsec. (a), was in the original "this Act", meaning Pub. L. No. 91–596, 84 Stat. 1590 (Dec. 29, 1970), as amended. For complete classification of this Act to the Code, see Short Title note set out under section 651 of this title and Tables.

Codifications

Section 666 of this title, referred to in subsec. (e), was in the original section 17 of Pub. L. No. 91–596. Subsecs. (a) to (g) and (i) to (*l*) of such section 17 are codified as section 666 of this title. Subsec. (h) of such section 17 amended section 1114 of Title 18, Crimes and Criminal Procedure, and enacted note set out thereunder.

Effective and Applicability Provisions

1970 Acts. Section effective 120 days after Dec. 29, 1970, see section 34 of Pub. L. No. 91–596, set out as a note under section 651 of this title.

§ 668. Programs of Federal agencies

[OSH Act § 19]

(a) Establishment, development, and maintenance by head of each Federal agency

It shall be the responsibility of the head of each Federal agency (not including the United States Postal Service) to establish and maintain an effective and comprehensive occupational safety and health program which is consistent with the standards promulgated under section 655 of this title. The head of each agency shall (after consultation with representatives of the employees thereof)—

(1) provide safe and healthful places and conditions of employment, consistent with the standards set under section 655 of this title;

(2) acquire, maintain, and require the use of safety equipment, personal protective equipment, and devices reasonably necessary to protect employees;

(3) keep adequate records of all occupational accidents and illnesses for proper evaluation and necessary corrective action;

(4) consult with the Secretary with regard to the adequacy as to form and content of records kept pursuant to subsection (a)(3) of this section; and

(5) make an annual report to the Secretary with respect to occupational accidents and injuries and the agency's program under this section. Such report shall include any report submitted under section 7902(e)(2) of Title 5.

(b) Report by Secretary to President

The Secretary shall report to the President a summary or digest of reports submitted to him under subsection (a)(5) of this section, together with his evaluations of and recommendations derived from such reports.

(c) Omitted

(d) Access by Secretary to records and reports required of agencies

The Secretary shall have access to records and reports kept and filed by Federal agencies pursuant to subsections (a)(3) and (5) of this section unless those records and reports are specifically required by Executive order to be kept secret in the interest of the national defense or foreign policy, in which case the Secretary shall have access to such information as will not jeopardize national defense or foreign policy.

(Pub. L. No. 91–596, § 19, 84 Stat. 1609 (Dec. 29, 1970); as amended by Pub. L. No. 97–375, Title I, § 110(c), 96 Stat. 1821 (Dec. 21, 1982); Pub. L. No. 105–241, § 2(b)(1), 112 Stat. 1572 (Sept. 29, 1998).)

HISTORICAL AND STATUTORY NOTES

Codifications

Subsec. (c) of this section amended section 7902 of Title 5, Government Organization and Employees.

Termination of Reporting Requirements

For termination of reporting provisions of subsec. (b) of this section, effective May 15, 2000, see Pub. L. No. 104–66, § 3003, as amended, set out as a note under 31 U.S.C.A. § 1113, and page 124 of House Document No. 103–7.

Occupational Safety and Health Programs for Federal Employees

Occupational safety and health programs for federal employees and continuation of Federal Advisory Council on Occupational Safety and Health, see Ex. Ord. No. 12196, 45 Fed. Reg. 12769 (Feb. 26, 1980), set out as a note under section 7902 of Title 5, Government Organization and Employees.

Safety Belt Use Requirements for Federal Employees

For provisions relating to safety belt use requirements for Federal employees, see Ex. Ord. No. 12566, 51 Fed. Reg. 34575 (Sept. 26, 1986), set out as a note under section 7902 of Title 5, Government Organization and Employees.

§ 669. Research and related activities

[OSH Act § 20]

(a) Authority of Secretary of Health and Human Services to conduct research, experiments, and demonstrations, develop plans, establish criteria, promulgate regulations, authorize programs, and publish results and industrywide studies; consultations

(1) The Secretary of Health and Human Services, after consultation with the Secretary and with other appropriate Federal departments or agencies, shall conduct (directly or by grants or contracts) research, experiments, and demonstrations relating to occupational safety and health, including studies of psychological factors involved, and relating to innovative methods, techniques, and approaches for dealing with occupational safety and health problems.

(2) The Secretary of Health and Human Services shall from time to time consult with the Secretary in order to develop specific plans for such research, demonstrations, and experiments as are necessary to produce criteria, including criteria identifying toxic substances, enabling the Secretary to meet his responsibility for the formulation of safety and health standards under this chapter; and the Secretary of Health and Human Services, on the basis of such research, demonstrations, and experiments and any other information available to him, shall develop and publish at least annually such criteria as will effectuate the purposes of this chapter.

(3) The Secretary of Health and Human Services, on the basis of such research, demonstrations, and experiments, and any other information available to him, shall develop criteria dealing with toxic materials and harmful physical agents and substances which will describe exposure levels that are safe for various periods of employment, including but not limited to the exposure levels at which no employee will suffer impaired health or functional capacities or diminished life expectancy as a result of his work experience.

(4) The Secretary of Health and Human Services shall also conduct special research, experiments, and demonstrations relating to occupational safety and health as are necessary to explore new problems, including those created by new technology in occupational safety and health, which may require ameliorative action beyond that which is otherwise provided for in the operating provisions of this chapter. The Secretary of Health and Human Services shall also conduct research into the motivational and behavioral factors relating to the field of occupational safety and health.

(5) The Secretary of Health and Human Services, in order to comply with his responsibilities under paragraph (2), and in order to develop needed information regarding potentially toxic substances or harmful physical agents, may prescribe regulations requiring employers to measure, record, and make reports on the exposure of employees to substances or physical agents which the Secretary of Health and Human Services reasonably believes may endanger the health or safety of employees. The Secretary of Health and Human Services also is authorized to establish such programs of medical examinations and tests as may be necessary for determining the incidence of occupational illnesses and the susceptibility of employees to such illnesses. Nothing in this or any other provision of this chapter shall be deemed to authorize or require medical examination, immunization, or treatment for those who object thereto on religious grounds, except where such is necessary for the protection of the health or safety of others. Upon the request of any employer who is required to measure and record exposure of employees to substances or physical agents as provided under this subsection, the Secretary of Health and Human Services shall furnish full financial or other assistance to such employer for the purpose of defraying any additional expense incurred by him in carrying out the measuring and recording as provided in this subsection.

(6) The Secretary of Health and Human Services shall publish within six months of December 29, 1970, and thereafter as needed but at least annually a list of all known toxic substances by generic family or other useful grouping, and the concentrations at which such toxicity is known to occur. He shall determine following a written request by any employer or authorized representative of employees, specifying with reasonable particularity the grounds on which the request is made, whether any substance normally found in the place of employment has potentially toxic effects in such concentrations as used or found; and shall submit such determination both to employers and affected employees as soon as possible. If the Secretary of Health and Human Services determines that any substance is potentially toxic at the concentrations in which it is used or found in a place of employment, and such substance is not covered by an occupational safety or health standard promulgated under section 655 of this title, the Secretary of Health and Human Services shall immediately submit such determination to the Secretary, together with all pertinent criteria.

(7) Within two years of December 29, 1970, and annually thereafter the Secretary of Health and Human Services shall conduct and publish industrywide studies of the effect of chronic or low-level exposure to industrial materials, processes, and stresses on the potential for illness, disease, or loss of functional capacity in aging adults.

(b) Authority of Secretary of Health and Human Services to make inspections and question employers and employees

The Secretary of Health and Human Services is authorized to make inspections and question employers and employees as provided in section 657 of this title in order to carry out his functions and responsibilities under this section.

(c) Contracting authority of Secretary of Labor; cooperation between Secretary of Labor and Secretary of Health and Human Services

The Secretary is authorized to enter into contracts, agreements, or other arrangements with appropriate public agencies or private organizations for the purpose of conducting studies relating to his responsibilities under this chapter. In carrying out his responsibilities under this subsection, the Secretary shall cooperate with the Secretary of Health and Human Services in order to avoid any duplication of efforts under this section.

(d) Dissemination of information to interested parties

Information obtained by the Secretary and the Secretary of Health and Human Services under this section shall be disseminated by the Secretary to employers and employees and organizations thereof.

(e) Delegation of functions of Secretary of Health and Human Services to Director of the National Institute for Occupational Safety and Health

The functions of the Secretary of Health and Human Services under this chapter shall, to the extent feasible, be delegated to the Director of the National Institute for Occupational Safety and Health established by section 671 of this title.

(Pub. L. No. 91–596, § 20, 84 Stat. 1610 (Dec. 29, 1970); as amended by Pub. L. No. 96–88, Title V, § 509(b), 93 Stat. 695 (Oct. 17, 1979).)

HISTORICAL AND STATUTORY NOTES

References in Text

This chapter, referred to in subsecs. (a)(2), (c), and (e), was in the original "this Act", meaning Pub. L. No. 91–596, 84 Stat. 1590 (Dec. 29, 1970), as amended. For complete classification of this Act to the Code, see Short Title note set out under section 651 of this title and Tables.

Effective and Applicability Provisions

1970 Acts. Section effective 120 days after Dec. 29, 1970, see section 34 of Pub. L. No. 91–596, set out as a note under section 651 of this title.

Change of Name

"Secretary of Health and Human Services" was substituted for "Secretary of Health, Education, and Welfare" in text pursuant to section 509(b) of Pub. L. No. 96–88 which is codified as section 3508(b) of Title 20, Education.

§ 669a. Expanded research on worker health and safety

The Secretary of Health and Human Services (referred to in this section as the "Secretary"), acting through the Director of the National Institute of Occupational Safety and Health, shall enhance and expand research as deemed appropriate on the health and safety of workers who are at risk for bioterrorist threats or attacks in the workplace, including research on the health effects of measures taken to treat or protect such workers for diseases or disorders resulting from a bioterrorist threat or attack. Nothing in this section may be construed as establishing new regulatory authority for the Secretary or the Director to issue or modify any occupational safety and health rule or regulation.

(Pub. L. No. 107–188, Title I, § 153, 116 Stat. 631 (June 12, 2002).)

HISTORICAL AND STATUTORY NOTES

Codifications

This section was enacted as part of the Public Health Security and Bioterrorism Preparedness and Response Act of 2002 and not as part of the Occupational Safety and Health Act of 1970, which comprises this chapter.

§ 670. Training and employee education

[OSH Act § 21]

(a) Authority of Secretary of Health and Human Services to conduct education and informational programs; consultations

The Secretary of Health and Human Services, after consultation with the Secretary and with other appropriate Federal departments and agencies, shall conduct, directly or by grants or contracts (1) education programs to provide an adequate supply of qualified personnel to carry out the purposes of this chapter, and (2) informational programs on the importance of and proper use of adequate safety and health equipment.

(b) Authority of Secretary of Labor to conduct short-term training of personnel

The Secretary is also authorized to conduct, directly or by grants or contracts, short-term training of personnel engaged in work related to his responsibilities under this chapter.

(c) Authority of Secretary of Labor to establish and supervise education and training programs and consult and advise interested parties

The Secretary, in consultation with the Secretary of Health and Human Services, shall (1) provide for the establishment and supervision of programs for the education and training of employers and employees in the recognition, avoidance, and prevention of unsafe or unhealthful working conditions in employments covered by this chapter, and (2) consult with and advise employers and employees, and organizations representing employers and employees as to effective means of preventing occupational injuries and illnesses.

(d) Compliance assistance program

(1) The Secretary shall establish and support cooperative agreements with the States under which employers subject to this chapter may consult with State personnel with respect to.—

(A) the application of occupational safety and health requirements under this chapter or under State plans approved under section 667 of this title; and

(B) voluntary efforts that employers may undertake to establish and maintain safe and healthful employment and places of employment.

Such agreements may provide, as a condition of receiving funds under such agreements, for contributions by States towards meeting the costs of such agreements.

(2) Pursuant to such agreements the State shall provide on-site consultation at the employer's worksite to employers who request such assistance. The State may also provide other education and training programs for employers and employees in the State. The State shall ensure that on-site consultations conducted pursuant to such agreements include provision for the participation by employees.

(3) Activities under this subsection shall be conducted independently of any enforcement activity. If an employer fails to take immediate action to eliminate employee exposure to an imminent danger identified in a consultation or fails to correct a serious hazard so identified within a reasonable time, a report shall be made to the appropriate enforcement authority for such action as is appropriate.

(4) The Secretary shall, by regulation after notice and opportunity for comment, establish rules under which an employer—

(A) which requests and undergoes an on-site consultative visit provided under this subsection;

(B) which corrects the hazards that have been identified during the visit within the time frames established by the State and agrees to request a subsequent consultative visit if major changes in working conditions or work processes occur which introduce new hazards in the workplace; and

(C) which is implementing procedures for regularly identifying and preventing hazards regulated under this chapter and maintains appropriate involvement of, and training for, management and non-management employees in achieving safe and healthful working conditions,

may be exempt from an inspection (except an inspection requested under section 657(f) of this title or an inspection to determine the cause of a workplace accident which resulted in the death of one or more employees or hospitalization for three or more employees) for a period of 1 year from the closing of the consultative visit.

(5) A State shall provide worksite consultations under paragraph (2) at the request of an employer. Priority in scheduling such consultations shall be assigned to requests from small businesses which are in higher hazard industries or have the most hazardous conditions at issue in the request.

(Pub. L. No. 91–596, § 21, 84 Stat. 1612 (Dec. 29, 1970); as amended by Pub. L. No. 96–88, Title V, § 509(b), 93 Stat. 695 (Oct. 17, 1979); Pub. L. No. 105–197, § 2, 112 Stat. 638 (July 16, 1998).)

HISTORICAL AND STATUTORY NOTES

References in Text

This chapter, referred to in text, was in the original "this Act", meaning Pub. L. No. 91–596, 84 Stat. 1590 (Dec. 29, 1970), as amended. For complete classification of this Act to the Code, see Short Title note set out under section 651 of this title and Tables.

Effective and Applicability Provisions

1970 Acts. Section effective 120 days after Dec. 29, 1970, see section 34 of Pub. L. No. 91–596, set out as a note under section 651 of this title.

Change of Name

"Secretary of Health and Human Services" was substituted for "Secretary of Health, Education, and Welfare" in subsecs. (a) and (c) pursuant to section 509(b) of Pub. L. No. 96–88, which is codified as section 3508(b) of Title 20, Education.

Retention of Training Institute Course Tuition Fees by OSHA

Pub. L. No. 109–149, Title I, 119 Stat. 2839 (Dec. 30, 2005), which provided in part that, notwithstanding 31 U.S.C. 3302, the Occupational Safety and Health Administration may retain up to $750,000 per fiscal year of training institute course tuition fees, otherwise authorized by law to be collected, and may utilize such sums for occupational safety and health training and education grants, was from the Departments of Labor, Health and Human Services, and Education, and Related Agencies Appropriations Act, 2006, and was repeated in subsequent Appropriations Acts but not set out in the Code.

Similar provisions were contained in the following prior Appropriations Acts:

Pub. L. No. 108–447, Div. F, Title I, 118 Stat. 3118 (Dec. 8, 2004).

Pub. L. No. 108–199, Div. E, Title I, 118 Stat. 232 (Jan. 23, 2004).

Pub. L. No. 108–7, Div. G, Title I, 117 Stat. 303 (Feb. 20, 2003).

Pub. L. No. 107–116, Title I, 115 Stat. 2182 (Jan. 10, 2002).

Pub. L. No. 106–554, § 1(a)(1) [Title I], 114 Stat. 2763, 2763A–8 (Dec. 21, 2000).

Pub. L. No. 106–113, Div. B, § 1000(a)(4) [Title I], 113 Stat. 1535, 1501A–222 (Nov. 29, 1999).

Pub. L. No. 105–277, Div. A, § 101(f) [Title I], 112 Stat. 2681–343 (Oct. 21, 1998).

Pub. L. No. 105–78, Title I, 111 Stat. 1474 (Nov. 13, 1997).

Pub. L. No. 104–208, Div. A, Title I, § 101(e) [Title I], 110 Stat. 3009–239 (Sept. 30, 1996).

Pub. L. No. 104–134, Title I, § 101(d) [Title I], 110 Stat. 1321–217 (Apr. 26, 1996); renumbered Title I by Pub. L. No. 104–140, § 1(a), 110 Stat. 1327 (May 2, 1996).

Pub. L. No. 103–333, Title I, 108 Stat. 2544 (Sept. 30, 1994).

§ 671. National Institute for Occupational Safety and Health

[OSH Act § 22]

(a) Statement of purpose

It is the purpose of this section to establish a National Institute for Occupational Safety and Health in the Department of Health and Human Services in order to carry out the policy set forth in section 651 of this title and to perform the functions of the Secretary of Health and Human Services under sections 669 and 670 of this title.

(b) Establishment; Director; appointment; term

There is hereby established in the Department of Health and Human Services a National Institute for Occupational Safety and Health. The Institute shall be headed by a Director who shall be appointed by the Secretary of Health and Human Services, and who shall serve for a term of six years unless previously removed by the Secretary of Health and Human Services.

(c) Development and establishment of standards; performance of functions of Secretary of Health and Human Services

The Institute is authorized to—

(1) develop and establish recommended occupational safety and health standards; and

(2) perform all functions of the Secretary of Health and Human Services under sections 669 and 670 of this title.

(d) Authority of Director

Upon his own initiative, or upon the request of the Secretary or the Secretary of Health and Human Services, the Director is authorized (1) to conduct such research and experimental programs as he determines are necessary for the development of criteria for new and improved occupational safety and health standards, and (2) after consideration of the results of such research and experimental programs make recommendations concerning new or improved occupational safety and health standards. Any occupational safety and health standard recommended pursuant to this section shall immediately be forwarded to the Secretary of Labor, and to the Secretary of Health and Human Services.

(e) Additional authority of Director

In addition to any authority vested in the Institute by other provisions of this section, the Director, in carrying out the functions of the Institute, is authorized to—

(1) prescribe such regulations as he deems necessary governing the manner in which its functions shall be carried out;

(2) receive money and other property donated, bequeathed, or devised, without condition or restriction other than that it be used for the purposes of the Institute and to use, sell, or otherwise dispose of such property for the purpose of carrying out its functions;

(3) receive (and use, sell, or otherwise dispose of, in accordance with paragraph (2)), money and other property donated, bequeathed or devised to the Institute with a condition or restriction, including a condition that the Institute use other funds of the Institute for the purposes of the gift;

(4) in accordance with the civil service laws, appoint and fix the compensation of such personnel as may be necessary to carry out the provisions of this section;

(5) obtain the services of experts and consultants in accordance with the provisions of section 3109 of Title 5;

(6) accept and utilize the services of voluntary and noncompensated personnel and reimburse them for travel expenses, including per diem, as authorized by section 5703 of Title 5;

(7) enter into contracts, grants or other arrangements, or modifications thereof to carry out the provisions of this section, and such contracts or modifications thereof may be entered into without performance or other bonds, and without regard to section 6101 of Title 41, or any other provision of law relating to competitive bidding;

(8) make advance, progress, and other payments which the Director deems necessary under this title without regard to the provisions of section 3324(a) and (b) of Title 31; and

(9) make other necessary expenditures.

(f) Annual reports

The Director shall submit to the Secretary of Health and Human Services, to the President, and to the Congress an annual report of the operations of the Institute under this chapter, which shall include a detailed statement of all private and public funds received and expended by it, and such recommendations as he deems appropriate.

(g) Lead-based paint activities

(1) Training grant program

(A) The Institute, in conjunction with the Administrator of the Environmental Protection Agency, may make grants for the training and education of workers and supervisors who are or may be directly engaged in lead-based paint activities.

(B) Grants referred to in subparagraph (A) shall be awarded to nonprofit organizations (including colleges and universities, joint labor-management trust funds, States, and nonprofit government employee organizations)—

(i) which are engaged in the training and education of workers and supervisors who are or who may be directly engaged in lead-based paint activities (as defined in title IV of the Toxic Substances Control Act [15 U.S.C.A. § 2681 et seq.]),

(ii) which have demonstrated experience in implementing and operating health and safety training and education programs, and

(iii) with a demonstrated ability to reach, and involve in lead-based paint training programs, target populations of individuals who are or will be engaged in lead-based paint activities.

Grants under this subsection shall be awarded only to those organizations that fund at least 30 percent of their lead-based paint activities training programs from non-Federal sources, excluding in-kind contributions. Grants may also be made to local governments to carry out such training and education for their employees.

(C) There are authorized to be appropriated, at a minimum, $10,000,000 to the Institute for each of the fiscal years 1994 through 1997 to make grants under this paragraph.

(2) Evaluation of programs

The Institute shall conduct periodic and comprehensive assessments of the efficacy of the worker and supervisor training programs developed and offered by those receiving grants under this section. The Director shall prepare reports on the results of these assessments addressed to the Administrator of the Environmental Protection Agency to include recommendations as may be appropriate for the revision of these programs. The sum of $500,000 is authorized to be appropriated to the Institute for each of the fiscal years 1994 through 1997 to carry out this paragraph.

(h) Office of Mine Safety and Health

(1) In general

There shall be permanently established within the Institute an Office of Mine Safety and Health which shall be administered by an Associate Director to be appointed by the Director.

(2) Purpose

The purpose of the Office is to enhance the development of new mine safety technology and technological applications and to expedite the commercial availability and implementation of such technology in mining environments.

(3) Functions

In addition to all purposes and authorities provided for under this section, the Office of Mine Safety and Health shall be responsible for research, development, and testing of new technologies and equipment designed to enhance mine safety and health. To carry out such functions the Director of the Institute, acting through the Office, shall have the authority to—

(A) award competitive grants to institutions and private entities to encourage the development and manufacture of mine safety equipment;

(B) award contracts to educational institutions or private laboratories for the performance of product testing or related work with respect to new mine technology and equipment; and

(C) establish an interagency working group as provided for in paragraph (5).

(4) Grant authority

To be eligible to receive a grant under the authority provided for under paragraph (3)(A), an entity or institution shall—

(A) submit to the Director of the Institute an application at such time, in such manner, and containing such information as the Director may require; and

(B) include in the application under subparagraph (A), a description of the mine safety equipment to be developed and manufactured under the grant and a description of the reasons that such equipment would otherwise not be developed or manufactured, including reasons relating to the limited potential commercial market for such equipment.

(5) Interagency working group

(A) Establishment

The Director of the Institute, in carrying out paragraph (3)(D) shall establish an interagency working group to share technology and technological research and developments that could be utilized to enhance mine safety and accident response.

(B) Membership

The working group under subparagraph (A) shall be chaired by the Associate Director of the Office who shall appoint the members of the working group, which may include representatives of other Federal agencies or departments as determined appropriate by the Associate Director.

(C) Duties

The working group under subparagraph (A) shall conduct an evaluation of research conducted by, and the technological developments of, agencies and departments who are represented on the working group that may have applicability to mine safety and accident response and make recommendations to the Director for the further development and eventual implementation of such technology.

(6) Annual report

Not later than 1 year after the establishment of the Office under this subsection, and annually thereafter, the Director of the Institute shall submit to the Committee on Health, Education, Labor, and Pensions of the Senate and the Committee on Education and the Workforce of the House of Representatives a report that, with respect to the year involved, describes the new mine safety technologies and equipment that have been studied, tested, and certified for use, and with respect to those instances of technologies and equipment that have been considered but not yet certified for use, the reasons therefore.

(7) Authorization of appropriations

There is authorized to be appropriated, such sums as may be necessary to enable the Institute and the Office of Mine Safety and Health to carry out this subsection.

(Pub. L. No. 91–596, § 22, 84 Stat. 1612 (Dec. 29, 1970); as amended by Pub. L. No. 96–88, Title V, § 509(b), 93 Stat. 695 (Oct. 17, 1979); Pub. L. No. 102–550, Title X, § 1033, 106 Stat. 3924 (Oct. 28, 1992); Pub. L. No. 109–236, § 6, 120 Stat. 498 (June 15, 2006).)

HISTORICAL AND STATUTORY NOTES

References in Text

The civil service laws, referred to in subsec. (e)(4), are set forth in Title 5, Government Organization and Employees. See, particularly, section 3301 et seq. of that title.

This chapter, referred to in subsec. (f), was in the original "this Act", meaning Pub. L. No. 91–596, 84 Stat. 1590 (Dec. 29, 1970), as amended. For complete classification of this Act to the Code, see Short Title note set out under section 651 of this title and Tables.

The Toxic Substances Control Act, referred to in subsec. (g), is Pub. L. No. 94–469, 90 Stat. 2003 (Oct. 11, 1976), as amended, which is codified generally as chapter 53 (section 2601 et seq.) of Title 15, Commerce and Trade. Title IV of such Act is codified as subchapter IV (section 2681 et seq.) of chapter 53 of Title 15. For complete classification of this Act to the Code, see Short Title note set out under section 2601 of Title 15 and Tables.

Codifications

In subsec. (e)(7), "section 6101 of Title 41"substituted for "section 3709 of the Revised Statutes, as amended (41 U.S.C. 5)," on authority of Pub. L. No. 111–350, § 6(c), 124 Stat. 3854 (Jan. 4, 2011), which Act enacted Title 41, Public Contracts.

In subsec. (e)(8), "section 3324(a) and (b) of Title 31" was substituted for "section 3648 of the Revised Statutes, as amended (31 U.S.C. 529)" on authority of Pub. L. No. 97–258, § 4(b), 96 Stat. 1067 (Sept. 13, 1982), the first section of which enacted Title 31, Money and Finance.

Effective and Applicability Provisions

1992 Acts. Except as otherwise provided, amendment by Pub. L. No. 102–550 effective Oct. 28, 1992, see section 2 of Pub. L. No. 102–550, set out as a note under section 5301 of Title 42, The Public Health and Welfare.

1970 Acts. Section effective 120 days after Dec. 29, 1970, see section 34 of Pub. L. No. 91–596, set out as a note under section 651 of this title.

Termination of Reporting Requirements

For termination, effective May 15, 2000, of provisions in subsec. (f) of this section relating to submitting annual report to Congress, see Pub. L. No. 104–66, § 3003, as amended, set out as a note under 31 U.S.C.A. § 1113, and House Document No. 103–7, page 97.

Change of Name

"Secretary of Health and Human Services" was substituted for "Secretary of Health, Education, and Welfare" in subsecs. (a) to (d) and (f) pursuant to section 509(b) of Pub. L. No. 96–88 which is codified as section 3508(b) of Title 20, Education.

§ 671a. Workers' family protection

(a) Short title

This section may be cited as the "Workers' Family Protection Act".

(b) Findings and purpose

(1) Findings

Congress finds that—

(A) hazardous chemicals and substances that can threaten the health and safety of workers are being transported out of industries on workers' clothing and persons;

(B) these chemicals and substances have the potential to pose an additional threat to the health and welfare of workers and their families;

(C) additional information is needed concerning issues related to employee transported contaminant releases; and

(D) additional regulations may be needed to prevent future releases of this type.

(2) **Purpose**

It is the purpose of this section to—

(A) increase understanding and awareness concerning the extent and possible health impacts of the problems and incidents described in paragraph (1);

(B) prevent or mitigate future incidents of home contamination that could adversely affect the health and safety of workers and their families;

(C) clarify regulatory authority for preventing and responding to such incidents; and

(D) assist workers in redressing and responding to such incidents when they occur.

(c) **Evaluation of employee transported contaminant releases**

(1) **Study**

(A) **In general**

Not later than 18 months after October 26, 1992, the Director of the National Institute for Occupational Safety and Health (hereafter in this section referred to as the "Director"), in cooperation with the Secretary of Labor, the Administrator of the Environmental Protection Agency, the Administrator of the Agency for Toxic Substances and Disease Registry, and the heads of other Federal Government agencies as determined to be appropriate by the Director, shall conduct a study to evaluate the potential for, the prevalence of, and the issues related to the contamination of workers' homes with hazardous chemicals and substances, including infectious agents, transported from the workplaces of such workers.

(B) **Matters to be evaluated**

In conducting the study and evaluation under subparagraph (A), the Director shall—

(i) conduct a review of past incidents of home contamination through the utilization of literature and of records concerning past investigations and enforcement actions undertaken by—

(I) the National Institute for Occupational Safety and Health;

(II) the Secretary of Labor to enforce the Occupational Safety and Health Act of 1970 (29 U.S.C. 651 et seq.);

(III) States to enforce occupational safety and health standards in accordance with section 18 of such Act (29 U.S.C. 667); and

(IV) other government agencies (including the Department of Energy and the Environmental Protection Agency), as the Director may determine to be appropriate;

(ii) evaluate current statutory, regulatory, and voluntary industrial hygiene or other measures used by small, medium and large employers to prevent or remediate home contamination;

(iii) compile a summary of the existing research and case histories conducted on incidents of employee transported contaminant releases, including—

(I) the effectiveness of workplace housekeeping practices and personal protective equipment in preventing such incidents;

(II) the health effects, if any, of the resulting exposure on workers and their families;

(III) the effectiveness of normal house cleaning and laundry procedures for removing hazardous materials and agents from workers' homes and personal clothing;

(IV) indoor air quality, as the research concerning such pertains to the fate of chemicals transported from a workplace into the home environment; and

(V) methods for differentiating exposure health effects and relative risks associated with specific agents from other sources of exposure inside and outside the home;

(iv) identify the role of Federal and State agencies in responding to incidents of home contamination;

(v) prepare and submit to the Task Force established under paragraph (2) and to the appropriate committees of Congress, a report concerning the results of the matters studied or evaluated under clauses (i) through (iv); and

(vi) study home contamination incidents and issues and worker and family protection policies and practices related to the special circumstances of firefighters and prepare and submit to the appropriate committees of Congress a report concerning the findings with respect to such study.

(2) Development of investigative strategy

(A) Task force

Not later than 12 months after October 26, 1992, the Director shall establish a working group, to be known as the "Workers' Family Protection Task Force". The Task Force shall—

(i) be composed of not more than 15 individuals to be appointed by the Director from among individuals who are representative of workers, industry, scientists, industrial hygienists, the National Research Council, and government agencies, except that not more than one such individual shall be from each appropriate government agency and the number of individuals appointed to represent industry and workers shall be equal in number;

(ii) review the report submitted under paragraph (1)(B)(v);

(iii) determine, with respect to such report, the additional data needs, if any, and the need for additional evaluation of the scientific issues related to and the feasibility of developing such additional data; and

(iv) if additional data are determined by the Task Force to be needed, develop a recommended investigative strategy for use in obtaining such information.

(B) Investigative strategy

(i) Content

The investigative strategy developed under subparagraph (A)(iv) shall identify data gaps that can and cannot be filled, assumptions and uncertainties associated with various components of such strategy, a timetable for the implementation of such strategy, and methodologies used to gather any required data.

(ii) Peer review

The Director shall publish the proposed investigative strategy under subparagraph (A)(iv) for public comment and utilize other methods, including technical conferences or seminars, for the purpose of obtaining comments concerning the proposed strategy.

(iii) Final strategy

After the peer review and public comment is conducted under clause (ii), the Director, in consultation with the heads of other government agencies, shall propose a final strategy for investigating issues related to home contamination that shall be implemented by the National Institute for Occupational Safety and Health and other Federal agencies for the period of time necessary to enable such agencies to obtain the information identified under subparagraph (A)(iii).

(C) Construction

Nothing in this section shall be construed as precluding any government agency from investigating issues related to home contamination using existing procedures until such time as a final strategy is developed or from taking actions in addition to those proposed in the strategy after its completion.

(3) Implementation of investigative strategy

Upon completion of the investigative strategy under subparagraph (B)(iii), each Federal agency or department shall fulfill the role assigned to it by the strategy.

(d) Regulations

(1) In general

Not later than 4 years after October 26, 1992, and periodically thereafter, the Secretary of Labor, based on the information developed under subsection (c) of this section and on other information available to the Secretary, shall—

(A) determine if additional education about, emphasis on, or enforcement of existing regulations or standards is needed and will be sufficient, or if additional regulations or standards are needed with regard to employee transported releases of hazardous materials; and

(B) prepare and submit to the appropriate committees of Congress a report concerning the result of such determination.

(2) Additional regulations or standards

If the Secretary of Labor determines that additional regulations or standards are needed under paragraph (1), the Secretary shall promulgate, pursuant to the Secretary's authority under the Occupational Safety and Health Act of 1970 (29 U.S.C. 651 et seq.), such regulations or standards as determined to be appropriate not later than 3 years after such determination.

(e) Authorization of appropriations

There are authorized to be appropriated from sums otherwise authorized to be appropriated, for each fiscal year such sums as may be necessary to carry out this section.

(Pub. L. No. 102–522, Title II, § 209, 106 Stat. 3420 (Oct. 26, 1992).)

HISTORICAL AND STATUTORY NOTES

References in Text

The Occupational Safety and Health Act of 1970, as amended, referred to in subsecs. (c)(1)(B)(i)(II) and (d)(2), is Pub. L. No. 91–596, 84 Stat. 1590 (Dec. 29, 1970), as amended, which is codified principally as this chapter. Section 18 of such Act, referred to in subsec. (C)(1)(B)(i)(III), is codified as section 667 of this title. For complete classification of this Act to the Code, see Short Title note set out under section 651 of this title and Tables.

Codifications

Section was enacted by Pub. L. No. 102–522 as part of the Fire Administration Authorization Act of 1992, and not as part of the Occupational Safety and Health Act of 1970, which comprises this chapter.

§ 672. Grants to States

[OSH Act § 23]

(a) Designation of State agency to assist State in identifying State needs and responsibilities and in developing State plans

The Secretary is authorized, during the fiscal year ending June 30, 1971, and the two succeeding fiscal years, to make grants to the States which have designated a State agency under section 667 of this title to assist them—

(1) in identifying their needs and responsibilities in the area of occupational safety and health,

(2) in developing State plans under section 667 of this title, or

(3) in developing plans for—

(A) establishing systems for the collection of information concerning the nature and frequency of occupational injuries and diseases;

(B) increasing the expertise and enforcement capabilities of their personnel engaged in occupational safety and health programs; or

(C) otherwise improving the administration and enforcement of State occupational safety and health laws, including standards thereunder, consistent with the objectives of this chapter.

(b) Experimental and demonstration projects

The Secretary is authorized, during the fiscal year ending June 30, 1971, and the two succeeding fiscal years, to make grants to the States for experimental and demonstration projects consistent with the objectives set forth in subsection (a) of this section.

(c) Designation by Governor of appropriate State agency for receipt of grant

The Governor of the State shall designate the appropriate State agency for receipt of any grant made by the Secretary under this section.

(d) Submission of application

Any State agency designated by the Governor of the State desiring a grant under this section shall submit an application therefor to the Secretary.

(e) Approval or rejection of application

The Secretary shall review the application, and shall, after consultation with the Secretary of Health and Human Services, approve or reject such application.

(f) Federal share

The Federal share for each State grant under subsection (a) or (b) of this section may not exceed 90 per centum of the total cost of the application. In the event the Federal share for all States under either such subsection is not the same, the differences among the States shall be established on the basis of objective criteria.

(g) Administration and enforcement of programs contained in approved State plans; Federal share

The Secretary is authorized to make grants to the States to assist them in administering and enforcing programs for occupational safety and health contained in State plans approved by the Secretary pursuant to section 667 of this title. The Federal share for each State grant under this subsection may not exceed 50 per centum of the total cost to the State of such a program. The last sentence of subsection (f) of this section shall be applicable in determining the Federal share under this subsection.

(h) Report to President and Congress

Prior to June 30, 1973, the Secretary shall, after consultation with the Secretary of Health and Human Services, transmit a report to the President and to the Congress, describing the experience under the grant programs authorized by this section and making any recommendations he may deem appropriate.

(Pub. L. No. 91–596, § 23, 84 Stat. 1613 (Dec. 29, 1970); as amended by Pub. L. No. 96–88, Title V, § 509(b), 93 Stat. 695 (Oct. 17, 1979).)

HISTORICAL AND STATUTORY NOTES

References in Text

This chapter, referred to in subsec. (a)(3), was in the original "this Act", meaning Pub. L. No. 91–596, 84 Stat. 1590 (Dec. 29, 1970), as amended. For complete classification of this Act to the Code, see Short Title note set out under section 651 of this title and Tables.

Effective and Applicability Provisions

1970 Acts. Section effective 120 days after Dec. 29, 1970, see section 34 of Pub. L. No. 91–596, set out as a note under section 651 of this title.

Change of Name

"Secretary of Health and Human Services" was substituted for "Secretary of Health, Education, and Welfare" in subsec. (c) pursuant to section 509(b) of Pub. L. No. 96–88 which is codified as section 3508(b) of Title 20, Education.

§ 673. Statistics

[OSH Act § 24]

(a) Development and maintenance of program of collection, compilation, and analysis; employments subject to coverage; scope

In order to further the purposes of this chapter, the Secretary, in consultation with the Secretary of Health and Human Services, shall develop and maintain an effective program of collection, compilation, and analysis of occupational safety and health statistics. Such program may cover all employments whether or not subject to any other provisions of this chapter but shall not cover employments excluded by section 653 of this title. The Secretary shall compile accurate statistics on work injuries and illnesses which shall include all disabling, serious, or significant injuries and illnesses, whether or not involving loss of time from work, other than minor injuries requiring only first aid treatment and which do not involve medical treatment, loss of consciousness, restriction of work or motion, or transfer to another job.

(b) Authority of Secretary to promote, encourage, or engage in programs, make grants, and grant or contract for research and investigations

To carry out his duties under subsection (a) of this section, the Secretary may—

(1) promote, encourage, or directly engage in programs of studies, information and communication concerning occupational safety and health statistics;

(2) make grants to States or political subdivisions thereof in order to assist them in developing and administering programs dealing with occupational safety and health statistics; and

(3) arrange, through grants or contracts, for the conduct of such research and investigations as give promise of furthering the objectives of this section.

(c) Federal share for grants

The Federal share for each grant under subsection (b) of this section may be up to 50 per centum of the State's total cost.

(d) Utilization by Secretary of State or local services, facilities, and employees; consent; reimbursement

The Secretary may, with the consent of any State or political subdivision thereof, accept and use the services, facilities, and employees of the agencies of such State or political subdivision, with or without reimbursement, in order to assist him in carrying out his functions under this section.

(e) Reports by employers

On the basis of the records made and kept pursuant to section 657(c) of this title, employers shall file such reports with the Secretary as he shall prescribe by regulation, as necessary to carry out his functions under this chapter.

(f) Supersedure of agreements between Department of Labor and States for collection of statistics

Agreements between the Department of Labor and States pertaining to the collection of occupational safety and health statistics already in effect on the effective date of this chapter shall remain in effect until superseded by grants or contracts made under this chapter.

(Pub. L. No. 91–596, § 24, 84 Stat. 1614 (Dec. 29, 1970); as amended by Pub. L. No. 96–88, Title V, § 509(b), 93 Stat. 695 (Oct. 17, 1979).)

HISTORICAL AND STATUTORY NOTES

References in Text

This chapter, referred to in subsecs. (a), (e), and (f), was in the original "this Act", meaning Pub. L. No. 91–596, 84 Stat. 1590 (Dec. 29, 1970), as amended. For complete classification of this Act to the Code, see Short Title note set out under section 651 of this title and Tables.

The effective date of this chapter, referred to in subsec. (f), means the effective date of Pub. L. No. 91–596, 84 Stat. 1590 (Dec. 29, 1970), which is 120 days after Dec. 29, 1970, see section 34 of Pub. L. No. 91–96, set out as an Effective Date note under section 651 of this title.

Effective and Applicability Provisions

1970 Acts. Section effective 120 days after Dec. 29, 1970, see section 34 of Pub. L. No. 91–596, set out as a note under section 651 of this title.

Change of Name

"Secretary of Health and Human Services" was substituted for "Secretary of Health, Education, and Welfare" in subsec. (a) pursuant to section 509(b) of Pub. L. No. 96–88 which is codified as section 3508(b) of Title 20, Education.

§ 674. Audit of grant recipient; maintenance of records; contents of records; access to books, etc.

[OSH Act § 25]

(a) Each recipient of a grant under this chapter shall keep such records as the Secretary or the Secretary of Health and Human Services shall prescribe, including records which fully disclose the amount and disposition by such recipient of the proceeds of such grant, the total cost of the project or undertaking in connection with which such grant is made or used, and the amount of that portion of the cost of the project or undertaking supplied by other sources, and such other records as will facilitate an effective audit.

(b) The Secretary or the Secretary of Health and Human Services, and the Comptroller General of the United States, or any of their duly authorized representatives, shall have access for the purpose of audit and examination to any books, documents, papers, and records of the recipients of any grant under this chapter that are pertinent to any such grant.

(Pub. L. No. 91–596, § 25, 84 Stat. 1615 (Dec. 29, 1970); as amended by Pub. L. No. 96–88, Title V, § 509(b), 93 Stat. 695 (Oct. 17, 1979).)

HISTORICAL AND STATUTORY NOTES

References in Text

This chapter, referred to in text, was in the original "this Act", meaning Pub. L. No. 91–596, 84 Stat. 1590 (Dec. 29, 1970), as amended. For complete classification of this Act to the Code, see Short Title note set out under section 651 of this title and Tables.

Effective and Applicability Provisions

1970 Acts. Section effective 120 days after Dec. 29, 1970, see section 34 of Pub. L. No. 91–596, set out as a note under section 651 of this title.

Change of Name

"Secretary of Health and Human Services" was substituted for "Secretary of Health, Education, and Welfare" in text pursuant to section 509(b) of Pub. L. No. 96–88 which is codified as section 3508(b) of Title 20, Education.

§ 675. Annual reports by Secretary of Labor and Secretary of Health and Human Services; contents

[OSH Act § 26]

Within one hundred and twenty days following the convening of each regular session of each Congress, the Secretary and the Secretary of Health and Human Services shall each prepare and submit to the President for transmittal to the Congress a report upon the subject matter of this chapter, the progress toward achievement of the purpose of this chapter, the needs and requirements in the field of occupational safety and health, and any other relevant information. Such reports shall include information regarding occupational safety and health standards, and criteria for such standards, developed during the preceding year; evaluation of standards and criteria previously developed under this chapter, defining areas of emphasis for new criteria and standards; an evaluation of the degree of observance of applicable occupational safety and health standards, and a summary of inspection and enforcement activity undertaken; analysis and evaluation of research activities for which results have been obtained under governmental and nongovernmental sponsorship; an analysis of major occupational diseases; evaluation of available control and measurement technology for hazards for which standards or criteria have been developed during the preceding year; description of cooperative efforts undertaken between Government agencies and other interested parties in the implementation of this chapter during the preceding year; a progress report on the development of an adequate supply of trained manpower in the field of occupational safety and health, including estimates of future needs and the efforts being made by Government and others to meet those needs; listing of all toxic substances in industrial usage for which labeling requirements, criteria, or standards have not yet been established; and such recommendations for additional legislation as are deemed necessary to protect the safety and health of the worker and improve the administration of this chapter.

(Pub. L. No. 91–596, § 26, 84 Stat. 1615 (Dec. 29, 1970); as amended by Pub. L. No. 96–88, Title V, § 509(b), 93 Stat. 695 (Oct. 17, 1979).)

HISTORICAL AND STATUTORY NOTES

References in Text

This chapter, referred to in text, was in the original "this Act", meaning Pub. L. No. 91–596, 84 Stat. 1590 (Dec. 29, 1970), as amended. For complete classification of this Act to the Code, see Short Title note set out under section 651 of this title and Tables.

Effective and Applicability Provisions

1970 Acts. Section effective 120 days after Dec. 29, 1970, see section 34 of Pub. L. No. 91–596, set out as a note under section 651 of this title.

Change of Name

"Secretary of Health and Human Services" was substituted for "Secretary of Health, Education, and Welfare" in text pursuant to section 509(b) of Pub. L. No. 96–88 which is codified as section 3508(b) of Title 20, Education.

Termination of Reporting Requirements

For termination, effective May 15, 2000, of provisions in this section relating to the transmittal to Congress of reports prepared by the Secretary of Labor and the Secretary of Health and Human Services, see Pub. L. No. 104–66, § 3003, as amended, set out as a note under 31 U.S.C.A. § 1113 and pages 98 and 124 of House Document No. 103–7.

Study of Occupationally Related Pulmonary and Respiratory Diseases; Study to be Completed and Report Submitted by September 1, 1979

Pub. L. 95–239, § 17, 92 Stat. 105 (Mar. 1, 1978), authorized the Secretary of Labor, in cooperation with the Director of the National Institute for Occupational Safety and Health, to conduct a study of occupationally related pulmonary and respiratory diseases and to complete such study and report the findings to the President and Congress not later than 18 months after Mar. 1, 1978.

§ 676. Omitted

HISTORICAL AND STATUTORY NOTES

Codifications

Section, Pub. L. No. 91–596, § 27, 84 Stat. 1616 (Dec. 29, 1970), provided for the establishment of a National Commission on State Workmen's Compensation Laws to make an effective study and evaluation of State workmen's compensation laws to determine whether such laws provide an adequate, prompt, and equitable system of compensation for injury or death, with a final report to be transmitted to President and Congress not later than July 31, 1972, ninety days after which the Commission ceased to exist.

§ 677. Separability

[OSH Act § 32]

If any provision of this chapter, or the application of such provision to any person or circumstance, shall be held invalid, the remainder of this chapter, or the application of such provision to persons or circumstances other than those as to which it is held invalid, shall not be affected thereby.

(Pub. L. No. 91–596, § 32, 84 Stat. 1619 (Dec. 29, 1970).)

HISTORICAL AND STATUTORY NOTES

References in Text

This chapter, referred to in text, was in the original "this Act", meaning Pub. L. No. 91–596, 84 Stat. 1590 (Dec. 29, 1970), as amended. For complete classification of this Act to the Code, see Short Title note set out under section 651 of this title and Tables.

Effective and Applicability Provisions

1970 Acts. Section effective 120 days after Dec. 29, 1970, see section 34 of Pub. L. No. 91–596, set out as a note under section 651 of this title.

§ 678. Authorization of appropriations

[OSH Act § 33]

There are authorized to be appropriated to carry out this chapter for each fiscal year such sums as the Congress shall deem necessary.

(Pub. L. No. 91–596, § 33, 84 Stat. 1620 (Dec. 29, 1970).)

HISTORICAL AND STATUTORY NOTES

References in Text

This chapter, referred to in text, was in the original "this Act", meaning Pub. L. No. 91–596, 84 Stat. 1590 (Dec. 29, 1970), as amended. For complete classification of this Act to the Code, see Short Title note set out under section 651 of this title and Tables.

Effective and Applicability Provisions

1970 Acts. Section effective 120 days after Dec. 29, 1970, see section 34 of Pub. L. No. 91–596, set out as a note under section 651 of this title.

APPENDIX B

CODE OF FEDERAL REGULATIONS

TITLE 40, CHAPTER V—COUNCIL ON ENVIRONMENTAL QUALITY NEPA REGULATIONS

Editor's Note for the 2021–2022 Volume: In July 2020, the Council on Environmental Quality promulgated comprehensive new regulations to implement the procedural provisions of the National Environmental Policy Act (NEPA). 85 Fed. Reg. 43,304 (July 16, 2020). As this volume goes to press, those 2020 regulations are still being implemented; however, they are the subject of litigation challenging their validity, the Biden Administration is reviewing all environmental regulations promulgated during the Trump Administration; and new CEQ Chair Brenda Mallory has confirmed that a review and potential update is underway. As a result, this section provides ***both*** the 2020 regulations and the prior regulations.

2020 CEQ NEPA REGULATIONS

PART 1500—PURPOSE AND POLICY

Sec.

Authority: 42 U.S.C. 4321–4347; 42 U.S.C. 4371–4375; 42 U.S.C. 7609; E.O. 11514, 35 FR 4247, 3 CFR, 1966–1970, Comp., p. 902, as amended by E.O. 11991, 42 FR 26967, 3 CFR, 1977 Comp., p. 123; E.O. 13807, 82 FR 40463, 3 CFR, 2017, Comp., p. 369.

Source: 85 Fed. Reg. 43,304 (July 16, 2020).

§ 1500.1 Purpose and policy.

(a) The National Environmental Policy Act (NEPA) is a procedural statute intended to ensure Federal agencies consider the environmental impacts of their actions in the decision-making process. Section 101 of NEPA establishes the national environmental policy of the Federal Government to use all practicable means and measures to foster and promote the general welfare, create and maintain conditions under which man and nature can exist in productive harmony, and fulfill the social, economic, and other requirements of present and future generations of Americans. Section 102(2) of NEPA establishes the procedural requirements to carry out the policy stated in section 101 of NEPA. In *43358 particular, it requires Federal agencies to provide a detailed statement on proposals for major Federal actions significantly affecting the quality of the human environment. The purpose and function of NEPA is satisfied if Federal agencies have considered relevant environmental information, and the public has been informed regarding the decision-making process. NEPA does not mandate particular results or substantive outcomes. NEPA's purpose is not to generate paperwork or litigation, but to provide for informed decision making and foster excellent action.

(b) The regulations in this subchapter implement section 102(2) of NEPA. They provide direction to Federal agencies to determine what actions are subject to NEPA's procedural requirements and the level of NEPA review where applicable. The regulations in this subchapter are intended to ensure that relevant environmental information is identified and considered early in the process in order to ensure informed decision making by Federal agencies. The regulations in this subchapter are also intended to ensure that Federal agencies conduct environmental reviews in a coordinated, consistent, predictable and timely manner, and to reduce unnecessary burdens and delays. Finally, the regulations in this subchapter promote concurrent environmental reviews to ensure timely and efficient decision making.

§ 1500.2 [Reserved].

§ 1500.3 NEPA compliance.

(a) Mandate. This subchapter is applicable to and binding on all Federal agencies for implementing the procedural provisions of the National Environmental Policy Act of 1969, as amended (Pub. L. 91–190, 42 U.S.C. 4321 et seq.) (NEPA or the Act), except where compliance would be inconsistent with other statutory requirements. The regulations in this subchapter are issued pursuant to NEPA; the Environmental Quality Improvement Act of 1970, as amended (Pub. L. 91–224, 42 U.S.C. 4371 et seq.); section 309 of the Clean Air Act, as amended (42 U.S.C. 7609); Executive Order 11514, Protection and Enhancement of Environmental Quality (March 5, 1970), as amended by Executive Order 11991, Relating to the Protection and Enhancement of Environmental Quality (May 24, 1977); and Executive Order 13807, Establishing Discipline and Accountability in the Environmental Review and Permitting Process for Infrastructure Projects (August 15, 2017). The regulations in this subchapter apply to the whole of section 102(2) of NEPA. The provisions of the Act and the regulations in this subchapter must be read together as a whole to comply with the law.

(b) Exhaustion. (1) To ensure informed decision making and reduce delays, agencies shall include a request for comments on potential alternatives and impacts, and identification of any relevant information, studies, or analyses of any kind concerning impacts affecting the quality of the human environment in the notice of intent to prepare an environmental impact statement (§ 1501.9(d)(7) of this chapter).

(2) The draft and final environmental impact statements shall include a summary of all alternatives, information, and analyses submitted by State, Tribal, and local governments and other public commenters for consideration by the lead and cooperating agencies in developing the draft and final environmental impact statements (§ 1502.17 of this chapter).

(3) For consideration by the lead and cooperating agencies, State, Tribal, and local governments and other public commenters must submit comments within the comment periods provided, and comments shall be as specific as possible (§§ 1503.1 and 1503.3 of this chapter). Comments or objections of any kind not submitted, including those based on submitted alternatives, information, and analyses, shall be forfeited as unexhausted.

(4) Informed by the submitted alternatives, information, and analyses, including the summary in the final environmental impact statement (§ 1502.17 of this chapter) and the agency's response to comments in the final environmental impact statement (§ 1503.4 of this chapter), together with any other material in the record that he or she determines relevant, the decision maker shall certify in the record of decision that the agency considered all of the alternatives, information, and analyses, and objections submitted by States, Tribal, and local governments and other public commenters for consideration by the lead and cooperating agencies in developing the environmental impact statement (§ 1505.2(b) of this chapter).

(c) Review of NEPA compliance. It is the Council's intention that judicial review of agency compliance with the regulations in this subchapter not occur before an agency has issued the record of decision or taken other final agency action. It is the Council's intention that any allegation of noncompliance with NEPA and the regulations in this subchapter should be resolved as expeditiously as possible. Consistent with their organic statutes, and as part of implementing the exhaustion provisions in paragraph (b) of this section, agencies may structure their procedures to include an appropriate bond or other security requirement.

(d) Remedies. Harm from the failure to comply with NEPA can be remedied by compliance with NEPA's procedural requirements as interpreted in the regulations in this subchapter. It is the Council's intention that the regulations in this subchapter create no presumption that violation of NEPA is a basis for injunctive relief or for a finding of irreparable harm. The regulations in this subchapter do not create a cause of action or right of action for violation of NEPA, which contains no such cause of action or right of action. It is the Council's intention that any actions to review, enjoin, stay, vacate, or otherwise alter an agency decision on the basis of an alleged NEPA violation be raised as soon as practicable after final agency action to avoid or minimize any costs to agencies, applicants, or any affected third parties. It is also the Council's intention that minor, non-substantive errors that have no effect on agency decision making shall be considered harmless and shall not invalidate an agency action.

(e) Severability. The sections of this subchapter are separate and severable from one another. If any section or portion therein is stayed or determined to be invalid, or the applicability of any section to any person or entity is held invalid, it is the Council's intention that the validity of the remainder of those parts shall not be affected, with the remaining sections to continue in effect.

§ 1500.4 Reducing paperwork.

Agencies shall reduce excessive paperwork by:

(a) Using categorical exclusions to define categories of actions that normally do not have a significant effect on the human environment and therefore do not require preparation of an environmental impact statement (§ 1501.4 of this chapter).

(b) Using a finding of no significant impact when an action not otherwise excluded will not have a significant effect on the human environment and therefore does not require preparation of an environmental impact statement (§ 1501.6 of this chapter).

(c) Reducing the length of environmental documents by means such as meeting appropriate page limits (§§ 1501.5(f) and 1502.7 of this chapter).

(d) Preparing analytic and concise environmental impact statements (§ 1502.2 of this chapter).

(e) Discussing only briefly issues other than significant ones (§ 1502.2(b) of this chapter).

(f) Writing environmental impact statements in plain language (§ 1502.8 of this chapter).

(g) Following a clear format for environmental impact statements (§ 1502.10 of this chapter).

(h) Emphasizing the portions of the environmental impact statement that are useful to decision makers and the public (e.g., §§ 1502.14 and 1502.15 of this chapter) and reducing emphasis on background material (§ 1502.1 of this chapter).

(i) Using the scoping process, not only to identify significant environmental issues deserving of study, but also to deemphasize insignificant issues, narrowing the scope of the environmental impact statement process accordingly (§ 1501.9 of this chapter).

(j) Summarizing the environmental impact statement (§ 1502.12 of this chapter).

(k) Using programmatic, policy, or plan environmental impact statements and tiering from statements of broad scope to those of narrower scope, to eliminate repetitive discussions of the same issues (§§ 1501.11 and 1502.4 of this chapter).

(*l*) Incorporating by reference (§ 1501.12 of this chapter).

(m) Integrating NEPA requirements with other environmental review and consultation requirements (§ 1502.24 of this chapter).

(n) Requiring comments to be as specific as possible (§ 1503.3 of this chapter).

(*o*) Attaching and publishing only changes to the draft environmental impact statement, rather than rewriting and publishing the entire statement when changes are minor (§ 1503.4(c) of this chapter).

(p) Eliminating duplication with State, Tribal, and local procedures, by providing for joint preparation of environmental documents where practicable (§ 1506.2 of this chapter), and with other Federal procedures, by providing that an agency may adopt appropriate environmental documents prepared by another agency (§ 1506.3 of this chapter).

(q) Combining environmental documents with other documents (§ 1506.4 of this chapter).

§ 1500.5 Reducing delay.

Agencies shall reduce delay by:

(a) Using categorical exclusions to define categories of actions that normally do not have a significant effect on the human environment (§ 1501.4 of this chapter) and therefore do not require preparation of an environmental impact statement.

(b) Using a finding of no significant impact when an action not otherwise excluded will not have a significant effect on the human environment (§ 1501.6 of this chapter) and therefore does not require preparation of an environmental impact statement.

(c) Integrating the NEPA process into early planning (§ 1501.2 of this chapter).

(d) Engaging in interagency cooperation before or as the environmental assessment or environmental impact statement is prepared, rather than awaiting submission of comments on a completed document (§§ 1501.7 and 1501.8 of this chapter).

(e) Ensuring the swift and fair resolution of lead agency disputes (§ 1501.7 of this chapter).

(f) Using the scoping process for an early identification of what are and what are not the real issues (§ 1501.9 of this chapter).

(g) Meeting appropriate time limits for the environmental assessment and environmental impact statement processes (§ 1501.10 of this chapter).

(h) Preparing environmental impact statements early in the process (§ 1502.5 of this chapter).

(i) Integrating NEPA requirements with other environmental review and consultation requirements (§ 1502.24 of this chapter).

(j) Eliminating duplication with State, Tribal, and local procedures by providing for joint preparation of environmental documents where practicable (§ 1506.2 of this chapter) and with other Federal procedures by providing that agencies may jointly prepare or adopt appropriate environmental documents prepared by another agency (§ 1506.3 of this chapter).

(k) Combining environmental documents with other documents (§ 1506.4 of this chapter).

(*l*) Using accelerated procedures for proposals for legislation (§ 1506.8 of this chapter).

§ 1500.6 Agency authority.

Each agency shall interpret the provisions of the Act as a supplement to its existing authority and as a mandate to view policies and missions in the light of the Act's national environmental objectives, to the extent consistent with its existing authority. Agencies shall review their policies, procedures, and regulations accordingly and revise them as necessary to ensure full compliance with the purposes and provisions of the Act as interpreted by the regulations in this subchapter. The phrase "to the fullest extent possible" in section 102 of NEPA means that each agency of the Federal Government shall comply with that section, consistent with § 1501.1 of this chapter. Nothing contained in the regulations in this subchapter is intended or should be construed to limit an agency's other authorities or legal responsibilities.

PART 1501—NEPA AND AGENCY PLANNING

Sec.

Authority: 42 U.S.C. 4321–4347; 42 U.S.C. 4371–4375; 42 U.S.C. 7609; E.O. 11514, 35 FR 4247, 3 CFR, 1966–1970, Comp., p. 902, as amended by E.O. 11991, 42 FR 26967, 3 CFR, 1977 Comp., p. 123; E.O. 13807, 82 FR 40463, 3 CFR, 2017, Comp., p. 369.

Source: 85 Fed. Reg. 43,304 (July 16, 2020).

§ 1501.1 NEPA thresholds.

(a) In assessing whether NEPA applies or is otherwise fulfilled, Federal agencies should determine:

(1) Whether the proposed activity or decision is expressly exempt from NEPA under another statute;

(2) Whether compliance with NEPA would clearly and fundamentally conflict with the requirements of another statute;

(3) Whether compliance with NEPA would be inconsistent with Congressional intent expressed in another statute;

(4) Whether the proposed activity or decision is a major Federal action;

(5) Whether the proposed activity or decision, in whole or in part, is a non-discretionary action for which the agency lacks authority to consider environmental effects as part of its decision-making process; and

(6) Whether the proposed action is an action for which another statute's requirements serve the function of agency compliance with the Act.

(b) Federal agencies may make determinations under this section in their agency NEPA procedures (§ 1507.3(d) of this chapter) or on an individual basis, as appropriate.

(1) Federal agencies may seek the Council's assistance in making an individual determination under this section.

(2) An agency shall consult with other Federal agencies concerning their concurrence in statutory determinations made under this section where more than one Federal agency administers the statute.

§ 1501.2 Apply NEPA early in the process.

(a) Agencies should integrate the NEPA process with other planning and authorization processes at the earliest reasonable time to ensure that agencies consider environmental impacts in their planning and decisions, to avoid delays later in the process, and to head off potential conflicts.

(b) Each agency shall:

(1) Comply with the mandate of section 102(2)(A) of NEPA to utilize a systematic, interdisciplinary approach which will ensure the integrated use of the natural and social sciences and the environmental design arts in planning and in decision making which may have an impact on man's environment, as specified by § 1507.2(a) of this chapter.

(2) Identify environmental effects and values in adequate detail so the decision maker can appropriately consider such effects and values alongside economic and technical analyses. Whenever practicable, agencies shall review and publish environmental documents and appropriate analyses at the same time as other planning documents.

(3) Study, develop, and describe appropriate alternatives to recommended courses of action in any proposal that involves unresolved conflicts concerning alternative uses of available resources as provided by section 102(2)(E) of NEPA.

(4) Provide for actions subject to NEPA that are planned by private applicants or other non-Federal entities before Federal involvement so that:

(i) Policies or designated staff are available to advise potential applicants of studies or other information foreseeably required for later Federal action.

(ii) The Federal agency consults early with appropriate State, Tribal, and local governments and with interested private persons and organizations when their involvement is reasonably foreseeable.

(iii) The Federal agency commences its NEPA process at the earliest reasonable time (§§ 1501.5(d) and 1502.5(b) of this chapter).

§ 1501.3 Determine the appropriate level of NEPA review.

(a) In assessing the appropriate level of NEPA review, Federal agencies should determine whether the proposed action:

(1) Normally does not have significant effects and is categorically excluded (§ 1501.4);

(2) Is not likely to have significant effects or the significance of the effects is unknown and is therefore appropriate for an environmental assessment (§ 1501.5); or

(3) Is likely to have significant effects and is therefore appropriate for an environmental impact statement (part 1502 of this chapter).

(b) In considering whether the effects of the proposed action are significant, agencies shall analyze the potentially affected environment and degree of the effects of the action. Agencies should consider connected actions consistent with § 1501.9(e)(1).

(1) In considering the potentially affected environment, agencies should consider, as appropriate to the specific action, the affected area (national, regional, or local) and its resources, such as listed species and designated critical habitat under the Endangered Species Act. Significance varies with the setting of the proposed action. For instance, in the case of a site-specific action, significance would usually depend only upon the effects in the local area.

(2) In considering the degree of the effects, agencies should consider the following, as appropriate to the specific action:

(i) Both short- and long-term effects.

(ii) Both beneficial and adverse effects.

(iii) Effects on public health and safety.

(iv) Effects that would violate Federal, State, Tribal, or local law protecting the environment.

§ 1501.4 Categorical exclusions.

(a) For efficiency, agencies shall identify in their agency NEPA procedures (§ 1507.3(e)(2)(ii) of this chapter) categories of actions that normally do not have a significant effect on the human environment, and therefore do not require preparation of an environmental assessment or environmental impact statement.

(b) If an agency determines that a categorical exclusion identified in its agency NEPA procedures covers a proposed action, the agency shall evaluate the action for extraordinary circumstances in which a normally excluded action may have a significant effect.

(1) If an extraordinary circumstance is present, the agency nevertheless may categorically exclude the proposed action if the agency determines that there are circumstances that lessen the impacts or other conditions sufficient to avoid significant effects.

(2) If the agency cannot categorically exclude the proposed action, the agency shall prepare an environmental assessment or environmental impact statement, as appropriate.

§ 1501.5 Environmental assessments.

(a) An agency shall prepare an environmental assessment for a proposed action that is not likely to have significant effects or when the significance of the effects is unknown unless the agency finds that a categorical exclusion (§ 1501.4) is applicable or has decided to prepare an environmental impact statement.

(b) An agency may prepare an environmental assessment on any action in order to assist agency planning and decision making.

(c) An environmental assessment shall:

(1) Briefly provide sufficient evidence and analysis for determining whether to prepare an environmental impact statement or a finding of no significant impact; and

(2) Briefly discuss the purpose and need for the proposed action, alternatives as required by section 102(2)(E) of NEPA, and the environmental impacts of the proposed action and alternatives, and include a listing of agencies and persons consulted.

(d) For applications to the agency requiring an environmental assessment, the agency shall commence the environmental assessment as soon as practicable after receiving the application.

(e) Agencies shall involve the public, State, Tribal, and local governments, relevant agencies, and any applicants, to the extent practicable in preparing environmental assessments.

(f) The text of an environmental assessment shall be no more than 75 pages, not including appendices, unless a senior agency official approves in writing an assessment to exceed 75 pages and establishes a new page limit.

(g) Agencies may apply the following provisions to environmental assessments:

(1) Section 1502.21 of this chapter—Incomplete or unavailable information;

(2) Section 1502.23 of this chapter—Methodology and scientific accuracy; and

(3) Section 1502.24 of this chapter—Environmental review and consultation requirements.

§ 1501.6 Findings of no significant impact.

(a) An agency shall prepare a finding of no significant impact if the agency *43361 determines, based on the environmental assessment, not to prepare an environmental impact statement because the proposed action will not have significant effects.

(1) The agency shall make the finding of no significant impact available to the affected public as specified in § 1506.6(b) of this chapter.

(2) In the following circumstances, the agency shall make the finding of no significant impact available for public review for 30 days before the agency makes its final determination whether to prepare an environmental impact statement and before the action may begin:

(i) The proposed action is or is closely similar to one that normally requires the preparation of an environmental impact statement under the procedures adopted by the agency pursuant to § 1507.3 of this chapter; or

(ii) The nature of the proposed action is one without precedent.

(b) The finding of no significant impact shall include the environmental assessment or incorporate it by reference and shall note any other environmental documents related to it (§ 1501.9(f)(3)). If the assessment is included, the finding need not repeat any of the discussion in the assessment but may incorporate it by reference.

(c) The finding of no significant impact shall state the authority for any mitigation that the agency has adopted and any applicable monitoring or enforcement provisions. If the agency finds no significant impacts based on mitigation, the mitigated finding of no significant impact shall state any enforceable mitigation requirements or commitments that will be undertaken to avoid significant impacts.

§ 1501.7 Lead agencies.

(a) A lead agency shall supervise the preparation of an environmental impact statement or a complex environmental assessment if more than one Federal agency either:

(1) Proposes or is involved in the same action; or

(2) Is involved in a group of actions directly related to each other because of their functional interdependence or geographical proximity.

(b) Federal, State, Tribal, or local agencies, including at least one Federal agency, may act as joint lead agencies to prepare an environmental impact statement or environmental assessment (§ 1506.2 of this chapter).

(c) If an action falls within the provisions of paragraph (a) of this section, the potential lead agencies shall determine, by letter or memorandum, which agency will be the lead agency and which will be cooperating agencies. The agencies shall resolve the lead agency question so as not to cause delay. If there is disagreement among the agencies, the following factors (which are listed in order of descending importance) shall determine lead agency designation:

(1) Magnitude of agency's involvement.

(2) Project approval or disapproval authority.

(3) Expertise concerning the action's environmental effects.

(4) Duration of agency's involvement.

(5) Sequence of agency's involvement.

(d) Any Federal agency, or any State, Tribal, or local agency or private person substantially affected by the absence of lead agency designation, may make a written request to the senior agency officials of the potential lead agencies that a lead agency be designated.

(e) If Federal agencies are unable to agree on which agency will be the lead agency or if the procedure described in paragraph (c) of this section has not resulted in a lead agency designation within 45 days, any of the agencies or persons concerned may file a request with the Council asking it to determine which Federal agency shall be the lead agency. A copy of the request shall be transmitted to each potential lead agency. The request shall consist of:

(1) A precise description of the nature and extent of the proposed action; and

(2) A detailed statement of why each potential lead agency should or should not be the lead agency under the criteria specified in paragraph (c) of this section.

(f) Any potential lead agency may file a response within 20 days after a request is filed with the Council. As soon as possible, but not later than 20 days after receiving the request and all responses to it, the Council shall determine which Federal agency will be the lead agency and which other Federal agencies will be cooperating agencies.

(g) To the extent practicable, if a proposal will require action by more than one Federal agency and the lead agency determines that it requires preparation of an environmental impact statement, the lead and cooperating agencies shall evaluate the proposal in a single environmental impact statement and issue a joint record of decision. To the extent practicable, if a proposal will require action by more than one Federal agency and the lead agency determines that it requires preparation of an environmental assessment, the lead and cooperating agencies should evaluate the proposal in a single environmental assessment and, where appropriate, issue a joint finding of no significant impact.

(h) With respect to cooperating agencies, the lead agency shall:

(1) Request the participation of each cooperating agency in the NEPA process at the earliest practicable time.

(2) Use the environmental analysis and proposals of cooperating agencies with jurisdiction by law or special expertise, to the maximum extent practicable.

(3) Meet with a cooperating agency at the latter's request.

(4) Determine the purpose and need, and alternatives in consultation with any cooperating agency.

(i) The lead agency shall develop a schedule, setting milestones for all environmental reviews and authorizations required for implementation of the action, in consultation with any applicant and all joint lead, cooperating, and participating agencies, as soon as practicable.

(j) If the lead agency anticipates that a milestone will be missed, it shall notify appropriate officials at the responsible agencies. As soon as practicable, the responsible agencies shall elevate the issue to the appropriate officials of the responsible agencies for timely resolution.

§ 1501.8 Cooperating agencies.

(a) The purpose of this section is to emphasize agency cooperation early in the NEPA process. Upon request of the lead agency, any Federal agency with jurisdiction by law shall be a cooperating agency. In addition, upon request of the lead agency, any other Federal agency with special expertise with respect to any environmental issue may be a cooperating agency. A State, Tribal, or local agency of similar qualifications may become a cooperating agency by agreement with the lead agency. An agency may request that the lead agency designate it a cooperating agency, and a Federal agency may appeal a denial of its request to the Council, in accordance with § 1501.7(e).

(b) Each cooperating agency shall:

(1) Participate in the NEPA process at the earliest practicable time.

(2) Participate in the scoping process (described in § 1501.9).

(3) On request of the lead agency, assume responsibility for developing information and preparing environmental analyses, including portions of the environmental impact statement or environmental assessment concerning which the cooperating agency has special expertise.

(4) On request of the lead agency, make available staff support to enhance *43362 the lead agency's interdisciplinary capability.

(5) Normally use its own funds. To the extent available funds permit, the lead agency shall fund those major activities or analyses it requests from cooperating agencies. Potential lead agencies shall include such funding requirements in their budget requests.

(6) Consult with the lead agency in developing the schedule (§ 1501.7(i)), meet the schedule, and elevate, as soon as practicable, to the senior agency official of the lead agency any issues relating to purpose and need, alternatives, or other issues that may affect any agencies' ability to meet the schedule.

(7) Meet the lead agency's schedule for providing comments and limit its comments to those matters for which it has jurisdiction by law or special expertise with respect to any environmental issue consistent with § 1503.2 of this chapter.

(8) To the maximum extent practicable, jointly issue environmental documents with the lead agency.

(c) In response to a lead agency's request for assistance in preparing the environmental documents (described in paragraph (b)(3), (4), or (5) of this section), a cooperating agency may reply that other program commitments preclude any involvement or the degree of involvement requested in the action that is the subject of the environmental impact statement or environmental assessment. The cooperating agency shall submit a copy of this reply to the Council and the senior agency official of the lead agency.

§ 1501.9 Scoping.

(a) Generally. Agencies shall use an early and open process to determine the scope of issues for analysis in an environmental impact statement, including identifying the significant issues and eliminating from further study non-significant issues. Scoping may begin as soon as practicable after the proposal for action is sufficiently developed for agency consideration. Scoping may include appropriate pre-application procedures or work conducted prior to publication of the notice of intent.

(b) Invite cooperating and participating agencies. As part of the scoping process, the lead agency shall invite the participation of likely affected Federal, State, Tribal, and local agencies and governments, the proponent of the action, and other likely affected or interested persons (including those who might not be in accord with the action), unless there is a limited exception under § 1507.3(f)(1) of this chapter.

(c) Scoping outreach. As part of the scoping process the lead agency may hold a scoping meeting or meetings, publish scoping information, or use other means to communicate with those persons or agencies who may be interested or affected, which the agency may integrate with any other early planning meeting. Such a scoping meeting will often be appropriate when the impacts of a particular action are confined to specific sites.

(d) Notice of intent. As soon as practicable after determining that a proposal is sufficiently developed to allow for meaningful public comment and requires an environmental impact statement, the lead agency shall publish a notice of intent to prepare an environmental impact statement in the Federal Register, except as provided in § 1507.3(f)(3) of this chapter. An agency also may publish notice in accordance with § 1506.6 of this chapter. The notice shall include, as appropriate:

(1) The purpose and need for the proposed action;

(2) A preliminary description of the proposed action and alternatives the environmental impact statement will consider;

(3) A brief summary of expected impacts;

(4) Anticipated permits and other authorizations;

(5) A schedule for the decision-making process;

(6) A description of the public scoping process, including any scoping meeting(s);

(7) A request for identification of potential alternatives, information, and analyses relevant to the proposed action (see § 1502.17 of this chapter); and

(8) Contact information for a person within the agency who can answer questions about the proposed action and the environmental impact statement.

(e) Determination of scope. As part of the scoping process, the lead agency shall determine the scope and the significant issues to be analyzed in depth in the environmental impact statement. To determine the scope of environmental impact statements, agencies shall consider:

(1) Actions (other than unconnected single actions) that may be connected actions, which means that they are closely related and therefore should be discussed in the same impact statement. Actions are connected if they:

(i) Automatically trigger other actions that may require environmental impact statements;

(ii) Cannot or will not proceed unless other actions are taken previously or simultaneously; or

(iii) Are interdependent parts of a larger action and depend on the larger action for their justification.

(2) Alternatives, which include the no action alternative; other reasonable courses of action; and mitigation measures (not in the proposed action).

(3) Impacts.

(f) Additional scoping responsibilities. As part of the scoping process, the lead agency shall:

(1) Identify and eliminate from detailed study the issues that are not significant or have been covered by prior environmental review(s) (§ 1506.3 of this chapter), narrowing the discussion of these issues in the statement to a brief presentation of why they will not have a significant effect on the human environment or providing a reference to their coverage elsewhere.

(2) Allocate assignments for preparation of the environmental impact statement among the lead and cooperating agencies, with the lead agency retaining responsibility for the statement.

(3) Indicate any public environmental assessments and other environmental impact statements that are being or will be prepared and are related to but are not part of the scope of the impact statement under consideration.

(4) Identify other environmental review, authorization, and consultation requirements so the lead and cooperating agencies may prepare other required analyses and studies concurrently and integrated with the environmental impact statement, as provided in § 1502.24 of this chapter.

(5) Indicate the relationship between the timing of the preparation of environmental analyses and the agencies' tentative planning and decision-making schedule.

(g) **Revisions**. An agency shall revise the determinations made under paragraphs (b), (c), (e), and (f) of this section if substantial changes are made later in the proposed action, or if significant new circumstances or information arise which bear on the proposal or its impacts.

§ 1501.10 Time limits.

(a) To ensure that agencies conduct NEPA reviews as efficiently and expeditiously as practicable, Federal agencies should set time limits appropriate to individual actions or types of actions (consistent with the time intervals required by § 1506.11 of this chapter).

(b) To ensure timely decision making, agencies shall complete:

(1) Environmental assessments within 1 year unless a senior agency official of the lead agency approves a longer *43363 period in writing and establishes a new time limit. One year is measured from the date of agency decision to prepare an environmental assessment to the publication of an environmental assessment or a finding of no significant impact.

(2) Environmental impact statements within 2 years unless a senior agency official of the lead agency approves a longer period in writing and establishes a new time limit. Two years is measured from the date of the issuance of the notice of intent to the date a record of decision is signed.

(c) The senior agency official may consider the following factors in determining time limits:

(1) Potential for environmental harm.

(2) Size of the proposed action.

(3) State of the art of analytic techniques.

(4) Degree of public need for the proposed action, including the consequences of delay.

(5) Number of persons and agencies affected.

(6) Availability of relevant information.

(7) Other time limits imposed on the agency by law, regulations, or Executive order.

(d) The senior agency official may set overall time limits or limits for each constituent part of the NEPA process, which may include:

(1) Decision on whether to prepare an environmental impact statement (if not already decided).

(2) Determination of the scope of the environmental impact statement.

(3) Preparation of the draft environmental impact statement.

(4) Review of any comments on the draft environmental impact statement from the public and agencies.

(5) Preparation of the final environmental impact statement.

(6) Review of any comments on the final environmental impact statement.

(7) Decision on the action based in part on the environmental impact statement.

(e) The agency may designate a person (such as the project manager or a person in the agency's office with NEPA responsibilities) to expedite the NEPA process.

(f) State, Tribal, or local agencies or members of the public may request a Federal agency to set time limits.

§ 1501.11 Tiering.

(a) Agencies should tier their environmental impact statements and environmental assessments when it would eliminate repetitive discussions of the same issues, focus on the actual issues ripe for decision, and exclude from consideration issues already decided or not yet ripe at each level of environmental review. Tiering may also be appropriate for different stages of actions.

(b) When an agency has prepared an environmental impact statement or environmental assessment for a program or policy and then prepares a subsequent statement or assessment on an action included within the entire program or policy (such as a project- or site-specific action), the tiered document needs only to summarize and incorporate by reference the issues discussed in the broader document. The tiered document shall concentrate on the issues specific to the subsequent action. The tiered document shall state where the earlier document is available.

(c) Tiering is appropriate when the sequence from an environmental impact statement or environmental assessment is:

(1) From a programmatic, plan, or policy environmental impact statement or environmental assessment to a program, plan, or policy statement or assessment of lesser or narrower scope or to a site-specific statement or assessment.

(2) From an environmental impact statement or environmental assessment on a specific action at an early stage (such as need and site selection) to a supplement (which is preferred) or a subsequent statement or assessment at a later stage (such as environmental mitigation). Tiering in such cases is appropriate when it helps the lead agency to focus on the issues that are ripe for decision and exclude from consideration issues already decided or not yet ripe.

§ 1501.12 Incorporation by reference.

Agencies shall incorporate material, such as planning studies, analyses, or other relevant information, into environmental documents by reference when the effect will be to cut down on bulk without impeding agency and public review of the action. Agencies shall cite the incorporated material in the document and briefly describe its content. Agencies may not incorporate material by reference unless it is reasonably available for inspection by potentially interested persons within the time allowed for comment. Agencies shall not incorporate by reference material based on proprietary data that is not available for review and comment.

PART 1502—ENVIRONMENTAL IMPACT STATEMENT

Sec.

Authority: 42 U.S.C. 4321–4347; 42 U.S.C. 4371–4375; 42 U.S.C. 7609; E.O. 11514, 35 FR 4247, 3 CFR, 1966–1970, Comp., p. 902, as amended by E.O. 11991, 42 FR 26967, 3 CFR, 1977 Comp., p. 123; E.O. 13807, 82 FR 40463, 3 CFR, 2017, Comp., p. 369.

Source: 85 Fed. Reg. 43,304 (July 16, 2020).

§ 1502.1 Purpose of environmental impact statement.

The primary purpose of an environmental impact statement prepared pursuant to section 102(2)(C) of NEPA is to ensure agencies consider the environmental impacts of their actions in decision making. It shall provide full and fair discussion of significant environmental impacts and shall inform decision makers and the public of reasonable alternatives that would avoid or minimize adverse impacts or enhance the quality of the human environment. Agencies shall focus on significant environmental issues and alternatives and shall reduce paperwork and the accumulation of extraneous background data. Statements shall be concise, clear, and to the point, and shall be supported by evidence that the agency has made the necessary environmental analyses. An environmental impact statement is a document that informs Federal agency decision making and the public.

§ 1502.2 Implementation.

(a) Environmental impact statements shall not be encyclopedic.

(b) Environmental impact statements shall discuss impacts in proportion to their significance. There shall be only brief discussion of other than significant issues. As in a finding of no significant impact, there should be only enough discussion to show why more study is not warranted.

(c) Environmental impact statements shall be analytic, concise, and no longer than necessary to comply with NEPA and with the regulations in this subchapter. Length should be proportional to potential environmental effects and project size.

(d) Environmental impact statements shall state how alternatives considered in it and decisions based on it will or will not achieve the requirements of sections 101 and 102(1) of NEPA as interpreted in the regulations in this subchapter and other environmental laws and policies.

(e) The range of alternatives discussed in environmental impact statements shall encompass those to be considered by the decision maker.

(f) Agencies shall not commit resources prejudicing selection of alternatives before making a final decision (see also § 1506.1 of this chapter).

(g) Environmental impact statements shall serve as the means of assessing the environmental impact of proposed agency actions, rather than justifying decisions already made.

§ 1502.3 Statutory requirements for statements.

As required by section 102(2)(C) of NEPA, environmental impact statements are to be included in every Federal agency recommendation or report on proposals for legislation and other major Federal actions significantly affecting the quality of the human environment.

§ 1502.4 Major Federal actions requiring the preparation of environmental impact statements.

(a) Agencies shall define the proposal that is the subject of an environmental impact statement based on the statutory authorities for the proposed action. Agencies shall use the criteria for scope (§ 1501.9(e) of this chapter) to determine which proposal(s) shall be the subject of a particular statement. Agencies shall evaluate in a single environmental impact statement proposals or parts of proposals that are related to each other closely enough to be, in effect, a single course of action.

(b) Environmental impact statements may be prepared for programmatic Federal actions, such as the adoption of new agency programs. When agencies prepare such statements, they should be relevant to the program decision and timed to coincide with meaningful points in agency planning and decision making.

(1) When preparing statements on programmatic actions (including proposals by more than one agency), agencies may find it useful to evaluate the proposal(s) in one of the following ways:

(i) Geographically, including actions occurring in the same general location, such as body of water, region, or metropolitan area.

(ii) Generically, including actions that have relevant similarities, such as common timing, impacts, alternatives, methods of implementation, media, or subject matter.

(iii) By stage of technological development including Federal or federally assisted research, development or demonstration programs for new technologies that, if applied, could significantly affect the quality of the human environment. Statements on such programs should be available before the program has reached a stage of investment or commitment to implementation likely to determine subsequent development or restrict later alternatives.

(2) Agencies shall as appropriate employ scoping (§ 1501.9 of this chapter), tiering (§ 1501.11 of this chapter), and other methods listed in §§ 1500.4 and 1500.5 of this chapter to relate programmatic and narrow actions and to avoid duplication and delay. Agencies may tier their environmental analyses to defer detailed analysis of environmental impacts of specific program elements until such program elements are ripe for final agency action.

§ 1502.5 Timing.

An agency should commence preparation of an environmental impact statement as close as practicable to the time the agency is developing or receives a proposal so that preparation can be completed in time for the final statement to be included in any recommendation or report on the proposal. The statement shall be prepared early enough so that it can serve as an important practical contribution to the decision-making process and will not be used to rationalize or justify decisions already made (§§ 1501.2 of this chapter and 1502.2). For instance:

(a) For projects directly undertaken by Federal agencies, the agency shall prepare the environmental impact statement at the feasibility analysis (go/no-go) stage and may supplement it at a later stage, if necessary.

(b) For applications to the agency requiring an environmental impact statement, the agency shall commence the statement as soon as practicable after receiving the application. Federal agencies should work with potential applicants and applicable State, Tribal, and local agencies and governments prior to receipt of the application.

(c) For adjudication, the final environmental impact statement shall normally precede the final staff recommendation and that portion of the public hearing related to the impact study. In appropriate circumstances, the statement may follow preliminary hearings designed to gather information for use in the statements.

(d) For informal rulemaking, the draft environmental impact statement shall normally accompany the proposed rule.

§ 1502.6 Interdisciplinary preparation.

Agencies shall prepare environmental impact statements using an interdisciplinary approach that will ensure the integrated use of the natural and social sciences and the environmental design arts (section 102(2)(A) of NEPA). The disciplines of the preparers shall be appropriate to the scope and issues identified in the scoping process (§ 1501.9 of this chapter).

§ 1502.7 Page limits.

The text of final environmental impact statements (paragraphs (a)(4) through (6) of § 1502.10) shall be 150 pages or fewer and, for proposals of unusual scope or complexity, shall be 300 pages or fewer unless a senior agency official of the lead agency approves in writing a statement to exceed 300 pages and establishes a new page limit.

§ 1502.8 Writing.

Agencies shall write environmental impact statements in plain language and may use appropriate graphics so that decision makers and the public can readily understand such statements. Agencies should employ writers of clear prose or editors to write, review, or edit statements, which shall be based upon the analysis and supporting data from the natural and social sciences and the environmental design arts.

§ 1502.9 Draft, final, and supplemental statements.

(a) Generally. Except for proposals for legislation as provided in § 1506.8 of this chapter, agencies shall prepare environmental impact statements in two stages and, where necessary, *43365 supplement them, as provided in paragraph (d)(1) of this section.

(b) Draft environmental impact statements. Agencies shall prepare draft environmental impact statements in accordance with the scope decided upon in the scoping process (§ 1501.9 of this chapter). The lead agency shall work with the cooperating agencies and shall obtain comments as required in part 1503 of this chapter. To the fullest extent practicable, the draft statement must meet the requirements established for final statements in section 102(2)(C) of NEPA as interpreted in the regulations in this subchapter. If a draft statement is so inadequate as to preclude meaningful analysis, the agency shall prepare and publish a supplemental draft of the appropriate portion. At appropriate points in the draft statement, the agency shall discuss all major points of view on the environmental impacts of the alternatives including the proposed action.

(c) Final environmental impact statements. Final environmental impact statements shall address comments as required in part 1503 of this chapter. At appropriate points in the final statement, the agency shall discuss any responsible opposing view that was not adequately discussed in the draft statement and shall indicate the agency's response to the issues raised.

(d) Supplemental environmental impact statements. Agencies:

(1) Shall prepare supplements to either draft or final environmental impact statements if a major Federal action remains to occur, and:

(i) The agency makes substantial changes to the proposed action that are relevant to environmental concerns; or

(ii) There are significant new circumstances or information relevant to environmental concerns and bearing on the proposed action or its impacts.

(2) May also prepare supplements when the agency determines that the purposes of the Act will be furthered by doing so.

(3) Shall prepare, publish, and file a supplement to a statement (exclusive of scoping (§ 1501.9 of this chapter)) as a draft and final statement, as is appropriate to the stage of the statement involved, unless the Council approves alternative procedures (§ 1506.12 of this chapter).

(4) May find that changes to the proposed action or new circumstances or information relevant to environmental concerns are not significant and therefore do not require a supplement. The agency should document the finding consistent with its agency NEPA procedures (§ 1507.3 of this chapter), or, if necessary, in a finding of no significant impact supported by an environmental assessment.

§ 1502.10 Recommended format.

(a) Agencies shall use a format for environmental impact statements that will encourage good analysis and clear presentation of the alternatives including the proposed action. Agencies should use the following standard format for environmental impact statements unless the agency determines that there is a more effective format for communication:

(1) Cover.

(2) Summary.

(3) Table of contents.

(4) Purpose of and need for action.

(5) Alternatives including the proposed action (sections 102(2)(C)(iii) and 102(2)(E) of NEPA).

(6) Affected environment and environmental consequences (especially sections 102(2)(C)(i), (ii), (iv), and (v) of NEPA).

(7) Submitted alternatives, information, and analyses.

(8) List of preparers.

(9) Appendices (if any).

(b) If an agency uses a different format, it shall include paragraphs (a)(1) through (8) of this section, as further described in §§ 1502.11 through 1502.19, in any appropriate format.

§ 1502.11 Cover.

The cover shall not exceed one page and include:

(a) A list of the responsible agencies, including the lead agency and any cooperating agencies.

(b) The title of the proposed action that is the subject of the statement (and, if appropriate, the titles of related cooperating agency actions), together with the State(s) and county(ies) (or other jurisdiction(s), if applicable) where the action is located.

(c) The name, address, and telephone number of the person at the agency who can supply further information.

(d) A designation of the statement as a draft, final, or draft or final supplement.

(e) A one-paragraph abstract of the statement.

(f) The date by which the agency must receive comments (computed in cooperation with EPA under § 1506.11 of this chapter).

(g) For the final environmental impact statement, the estimated total cost to prepare both the draft and final environmental impact statement, including the costs of agency full-time equivalent (FTE) personnel hours, contractor costs, and other direct costs. If practicable and noted where not practicable, agencies also should include costs incurred by cooperating and participating agencies, applicants, and contractors.

§ 1502.12 Summary.

Each environmental impact statement shall contain a summary that adequately and accurately summarizes the statement. The summary shall stress the major conclusions, areas of disputed issues raised by agencies and the public, and the issues to be resolved (including the choice among alternatives). The summary normally will not exceed 15 pages.

§ 1502.13 Purpose and need.

The statement shall briefly specify the underlying purpose and need for the proposed action. When an agency's statutory duty is to review an application for authorization, the agency shall base the purpose and need on the goals of the applicant and the agency's authority.

§ 1502.14 Alternatives including the proposed action.

The alternatives section should present the environmental impacts of the proposed action and the alternatives in comparative form based on the information and analysis presented in the sections on the affected environment (§ 1502.15) and the environmental consequences (§ 1502.16). In this section, agencies shall:

(a) Evaluate reasonable alternatives to the proposed action, and, for alternatives that the agency eliminated from detailed study, briefly discuss the reasons for their elimination.

(b) Discuss each alternative considered in detail, including the proposed action, so that reviewers may evaluate their comparative merits.

(c) Include the no action alternative.

(d) Identify the agency's preferred alternative or alternatives, if one or more exists, in the draft statement and identify such alternative in the final statement unless another law prohibits the expression of such a preference.

(e) Include appropriate mitigation measures not already included in the proposed action or alternatives.

(f) Limit their consideration to a reasonable number of alternatives.

§ 1502.15 Affected environment.

The environmental impact statement shall succinctly describe the environment of the area(s) to be affected or created by the alternatives under consideration, including the reasonably foreseeable environmental trends and planned actions in the area(s). The environmental impact statement may *43366 combine the description with evaluation of the environmental consequences (§ 1502.16), and it shall be no longer than is necessary to understand the effects of the alternatives. Data and analyses in a statement shall be commensurate with the importance of the impact, with less important material summarized, consolidated, or simply referenced. Agencies shall avoid useless bulk in statements and shall concentrate effort and attention on important issues. Verbose descriptions of the affected environment are themselves no measure of the adequacy of an environmental impact statement.

§ 1502.16 Environmental consequences.

(a) The environmental consequences section forms the scientific and analytic basis for the comparisons under § 1502.14. It shall consolidate the discussions of those elements required by sections 102(2)(C)(i), (ii), (iv), and (v) of NEPA that are within the scope of the statement and as much of section 102(2)(C)(iii) of NEPA as is necessary to support the comparisons. This section should not duplicate discussions in § 1502.14. The discussion shall include:

(1) The environmental impacts of the proposed action and reasonable alternatives to the proposed action and the significance of those impacts. The comparison of the proposed action and reasonable alternatives shall be based on this discussion of the impacts.

(2) Any adverse environmental effects that cannot be avoided should the proposal be implemented.

(3) The relationship between short-term uses of man's environment and the maintenance and enhancement of long-term productivity.

(4) Any irreversible or irretrievable commitments of resources that would be involved in the proposal should it be implemented.

(5) Possible conflicts between the proposed action and the objectives of Federal, regional, State, Tribal, and local land use plans, policies and controls for the area concerned. (§ 1506.2(d) of this chapter)

(6) Energy requirements and conservation potential of various alternatives and mitigation measures.

(7) Natural or depletable resource requirements and conservation potential of various alternatives and mitigation measures.

(8) Urban quality, historic and cultural resources, and the design of the built environment, including the reuse and conservation potential of various alternatives and mitigation measures.

(9) Means to mitigate adverse environmental impacts (if not fully covered under § 1502.14(e)).

(10) Where applicable, economic and technical considerations, including the economic benefits of the proposed action.

(b) Economic or social effects by themselves do not require preparation of an environmental impact statement. However, when the agency determines that economic or social and natural or physical environmental effects are interrelated, the environmental impact statement shall discuss and give appropriate consideration to these effects on the human environment.

§ 1502.17 Summary of submitted alternatives, information, and analyses.

(a) The draft environmental impact statement shall include a summary that identifies all alternatives, information, and analyses submitted by State, Tribal, and local governments and other public commenters during the scoping process for consideration by the lead and cooperating agencies in developing the environmental impact statement.

(1) The agency shall append to the draft environmental impact statement or otherwise publish all comments (or summaries thereof where the response has been exceptionally voluminous) received during the scoping process that identified alternatives, information, and analyses for the agency's consideration.

(2) Consistent with § 1503.1(a)(3) of this chapter, the lead agency shall invite comment on the summary identifying all submitted alternatives, information, and analyses in the draft environmental impact statement.

(b) The final environmental impact statement shall include a summary that identifies all alternatives, information, and analyses submitted by State, Tribal, and local governments and other public commenters for consideration by the lead and cooperating agencies in developing the final environmental impact statement.

§ 1502.18 List of preparers.

The environmental impact statement shall list the names, together with their qualifications (expertise, experience, professional disciplines), of the persons who were primarily responsible for preparing the environmental impact statement or significant background papers, including basic components of the statement. Where possible, the environmental impact statement shall identify the persons who are responsible for a particular analysis, including analyses in background papers. Normally the list will not exceed two pages.

§ 1502.19 Appendix.

If an agency prepares an appendix, the agency shall publish it with the environmental impact statement, and it shall consist of:

(a) Material prepared in connection with an environmental impact statement (as distinct from material that is not so prepared and is incorporated by reference (§ 1501.12 of this chapter)).

(b) Material substantiating any analysis fundamental to the impact statement.

(c) Material relevant to the decision to be made.

(d) For draft environmental impact statements, all comments (or summaries thereof where the response has been exceptionally voluminous) received during the scoping process that identified alternatives, information, and analyses for the agency's consideration.

(e) For final environmental impact statements, the comment summaries and responses consistent with § 1503.4 of this chapter.

§ 1502.20 Publication of the environmental impact statement.

Agencies shall publish the entire draft and final environmental impact statements and unchanged statements as provided in § 1503.4(c) of this chapter. The agency shall transmit the entire statement electronically (or in paper copy, if so requested due to economic or other hardship) to:

(a) Any Federal agency that has jurisdiction by law or special expertise with respect to any environmental impact involved and any appropriate Federal, State, Tribal, or local agency authorized to develop and enforce environmental standards.

(b) The applicant, if any.

(c) Any person, organization, or agency requesting the entire environmental impact statement.

(d) In the case of a final environmental impact statement, any person, organization, or agency that submitted substantive comments on the draft.

§ 1502.21 Incomplete or unavailable information.

(a) When an agency is evaluating reasonably foreseeable significant adverse effects on the human environment in an environmental impact statement, and there is incomplete or unavailable information, the agency shall make clear that such information is lacking.

(b) If the incomplete but available information relevant to reasonably foreseeable significant adverse impacts is essential to a reasoned choice among alternatives, and the overall costs of obtaining it are not unreasonable, the agency shall include the information in the environmental impact statement.

(c) If the information relevant to reasonably foreseeable significant adverse impacts cannot be obtained because the overall costs of obtaining it are unreasonable or the means to obtain it are not known, the agency shall include within the environmental impact statement:

(1) A statement that such information is incomplete or unavailable;

(2) A statement of the relevance of the incomplete or unavailable information to evaluating reasonably foreseeable significant adverse impacts on the human environment;

(3) A summary of existing credible scientific evidence that is relevant to evaluating the reasonably foreseeable significant adverse impacts on the human environment; and

(4) The agency's evaluation of such impacts based upon theoretical approaches or research methods generally accepted in the scientific community.

(d) For the purposes of this section, "reasonably foreseeable" includes impacts that have catastrophic consequences, even if their probability of occurrence is low, provided that the analysis of the impacts is supported by credible scientific evidence, is not based on pure conjecture, and is within the rule of reason.

§ 1502.22 Cost-benefit analysis.

If the agency is considering a cost-benefit analysis for the proposed action relevant to the choice among alternatives with different environmental effects, the agency shall incorporate the cost-benefit analysis by reference or append it to the statement as an aid in evaluating the environmental consequences. In such cases, to assess the adequacy of compliance with section 102(2)(B) of NEPA (ensuring appropriate consideration of unquantified environmental amenities and values in decision making, along with economical and technical considerations), the statement shall discuss the relationship between that analysis and any analyses of unquantified environmental impacts, values, and amenities. For purposes of complying with the Act, agencies need not display the weighing of the merits and drawbacks of the various alternatives in a monetary cost-benefit analysis and should not do so when there are important qualitative considerations. However, an environmental impact statement should at least indicate those considerations, including factors not related to environmental quality, that are likely to be relevant and important to a decision.

§ 1502.23 Methodology and scientific accuracy.

Agencies shall ensure the professional integrity, including scientific integrity, of the discussions and analyses in environmental documents. Agencies shall make use of reliable existing data and resources. Agencies may make use of any reliable data sources, such as remotely gathered information or statistical models. They shall identify any methodologies used and shall make explicit reference to the scientific and other sources relied upon for conclusions in the statement. Agencies may place discussion of methodology in an appendix. Agencies are not required to undertake new scientific and technical research to inform their analyses. Nothing in this section is intended to prohibit agencies from compliance with the requirements of other statutes pertaining to scientific and technical research.

§ 1502.24 Environmental review and consultation requirements.

(a) To the fullest extent possible, agencies shall prepare draft environmental impact statements concurrent and integrated with environmental impact analyses and related surveys and studies required by all other Federal environmental review laws and Executive orders applicable to the proposed action, including the Fish and Wildlife Coordination Act (16 U.S.C. 661 et seq.), the National Historic Preservation Act of 1966 (54 U.S.C. 300101 et seq.), and the Endangered Species Act of 1973 (16 U.S.C. 1531 et seq.).

(b) The draft environmental impact statement shall list all Federal permits, licenses, and other authorizations that must be obtained in implementing the proposal. If it is uncertain whether a Federal permit, license, or other authorization is necessary, the draft environmental impact statement shall so indicate.

PART 1503—COMMENTING ON ENVIRONMENTAL IMPACT STATEMENTS

Authority: 42 U.S.C. 4321–4347; 42 U.S.C. 4371–4375; 42 U.S.C. 7609; E.O. 11514, 35 FR 4247, 3 CFR, 1966–1970, Comp., p. 902, as amended by E.O. 11991, 42 FR 26967, 3 CFR, 1977 Comp., p. 123; E.O. 13807, 82 FR 40463, 3 CFR, 2017, Comp., p. 369.

Source: 85 Fed. Reg. 43,304 (July 16, 2020).

§ 1503.1 Inviting comments and requesting information and analyses.

(a) After preparing a draft environmental impact statement and before preparing a final environmental impact statement the agency shall:

(1) Obtain the comments of any Federal agency that has jurisdiction by law or special expertise with respect to any environmental impact involved or is authorized to develop and enforce environmental standards.

(2) Request the comments of:

(i) Appropriate State, Tribal, and local agencies that are authorized to develop and enforce environmental standards;

(ii) State, Tribal, or local governments that may be affected by the proposed action;

(iii) Any agency that has requested it receive statements on actions of the kind proposed;

(iv) The applicant, if any; and

(v) The public, affirmatively soliciting comments in a manner designed to inform those persons or organizations who may be interested in or affected by the proposed action.

(3) Invite comment specifically on the submitted alternatives, information, and analyses and the summary thereof (§ 1502.17 of this chapter).

(b) An agency may request comments on a final environmental impact statement before the final decision and set a deadline for providing such comments. Other agencies or persons may make comments consistent with the time periods under § 1506.11 of this chapter.

(c) An agency shall provide for electronic submission of public comments, with reasonable measures to ensure the comment process is accessible to affected persons.

§ 1503.2 Duty to comment.

Cooperating agencies and agencies that are authorized to develop and enforce environmental standards shall comment on statements within their jurisdiction, expertise, or authority within the time period specified for comment in § 1506.11 of this chapter. A Federal agency may reply that it has no comment. If a cooperating agency is satisfied that the environmental impact statement adequately reflects its views, it should reply that it has no comment.

§ 1503.3 Specificity of comments and information.

(a) To promote informed decision making, comments on an environmental impact statement or on a proposed action shall be as specific as possible, may address either the adequacy of the statement or the merits of the alternatives discussed or both, and shall provide as much detail as necessary to meaningfully participate and fully inform the agency of the commenter's position. Comments should explain why the issues raised are important to the consideration of potential environmental impacts and alternatives to the proposed action, as well as economic and employment impacts, and other impacts affecting the quality of the human environment. Comments should reference the corresponding section or page number of the draft environmental impact statement, propose specific changes to those parts of the statement, where possible, and include or describe the data sources and methodologies supporting the proposed changes.

(b) Comments on the submitted alternatives, information, and analyses and summary thereof (§ 1502.17 of this chapter) should be as specific as possible. Comments and objections of any kind shall be raised within the comment period on the draft environmental impact statement provided by the agency, consistent with § 1506.11 of this chapter. If the agency requests comments on the final environmental impact statement before the final decision, consistent with § 1503.1(b), comments and objections of any kind shall be raised within the comment period provided by the agency. Comments and objections of any kind not provided within the comment period(s) shall be considered unexhausted and forfeited, consistent with § 1500.3(b) of this chapter.

(c) When a participating agency criticizes a lead agency's predictive methodology, the participating agency should describe the alternative methodology that it prefers and why.

(d) A cooperating agency shall specify in its comments whether it needs additional information to fulfill other applicable environmental reviews or consultation requirements and what information it needs. In particular, it shall specify any additional information it needs to comment adequately on the draft statement's analysis of significant site-specific effects associated with the granting or approving by that cooperating agency of necessary Federal permits, licenses, or authorizations.

(e) When a cooperating agency with jurisdiction by law specifies mitigation measures it considers necessary to allow the agency to grant or approve applicable permit, license, or related requirements or concurrences, the cooperating agency shall cite to its applicable statutory authority.

§ 1503.4 Response to comments.

(a) An agency preparing a final environmental impact statement shall consider substantive comments timely submitted during the public comment period. The agency may respond to individual comments or groups of comments. In the final environmental impact statement, the agency may respond by:

(1) Modifying alternatives including the proposed action.

(2) Developing and evaluating alternatives not previously given serious consideration by the agency.

(3) Supplementing, improving, or modifying its analyses.

(4) Making factual corrections.

(5) Explaining why the comments do not warrant further agency response, recognizing that agencies are not required to respond to each comment.

(b) An agency shall append or otherwise publish all substantive comments received on the draft statement (or summaries thereof where the response has been exceptionally voluminous).

(c) If changes in response to comments are minor and are confined to the responses described in paragraphs (a)(4) and (5) of this section, an agency may write any changes on errata sheets and attach the responses to the statement instead of rewriting the draft statement. In such cases, only the comments, the responses, and the changes and not the final statement need be published (§ 1502.20 of this chapter). The agency shall file the entire document with a new cover sheet with the Environmental Protection Agency as the final statement (§ 1506.10 of this chapter).

PART 1504—PRE-DECISIONAL REFERRALS TO THE COUNCIL OF PROPOSED FEDERAL ACTIONS DETERMINED TO BE ENVIRONMENTALLY UNSATISFACTORY

Authority: 42 U.S.C. 4321–4347; 42 U.S.C. 4371–4375; 42 U.S.C. 7609; E.O. 11514, 35 FR 4247, 3 CFR, 1966–1970, Comp., p. 902, as amended by E.O. 11991, 42 FR 26967, 3 CFR, 1977 Comp., p. 123; E.O. 13807, 82 FR 40463, 3 CFR, 2017, Comp., p. 369.

Source: 85 Fed. Reg. 43,304 (July 16, 2020).

§ 1504.1 Purpose.

(a) This part establishes procedures for referring to the Council Federal interagency disagreements concerning proposed major Federal actions that might cause unsatisfactory environmental effects. It provides means for early resolution of such disagreements.

(b) Section 309 of the Clean Air Act (42 U.S.C. 7609) directs the Administrator of the Environmental Protection Agency to review and comment publicly on the environmental impacts of Federal activities, including actions for which agencies prepare environmental impact statements. If, after this review, the Administrator determines that the matter is "unsatisfactory from the standpoint of public health or welfare or environmental quality," section 309 directs that the matter be referred to the Council (hereafter "environmental referrals").

(c) Under section 102(2)(C) of NEPA (42 U.S.C. 4332(2)(C)), other Federal agencies may prepare similar reviews of environmental impact statements, including judgments on the acceptability of anticipated environmental impacts. These reviews must be made available to the President, the Council, and the public.

§ 1504.2 Criteria for referral.

Environmental referrals should be made to the Council only after concerted, timely (as early as practicable in the process), but unsuccessful attempts to resolve differences with the lead agency. In determining what environmental objections to the matter are appropriate to refer to the Council, an agency should weigh potential adverse environmental impacts, considering:

(a) Possible violation of national environmental standards or policies;

(b) Severity;

(c) Geographical scope;

(d) Duration;

(e) Importance as precedents;

(f) Availability of environmentally preferable alternatives; and

(g) Economic and technical considerations, including the economic costs of delaying or impeding the decision making of the agencies involved in the action.

§ 1504.3 Procedure for referrals and response.

(a) A Federal agency making the referral to the Council shall:

(1) Notify the lead agency at the earliest possible time that it intends to refer a matter to the Council unless a satisfactory agreement is reached;

(2) Include such a notification whenever practicable in the referring agency's comments on the environmental assessment or draft environmental impact statement;

(3) Identify any essential information that is lacking and request that the lead agency make it available at the earliest possible time; and

(4) Send copies of the referring agency's views to the Council.

(b) The referring agency shall deliver its referral to the Council no later than 25 days after the lead agency has made the final environmental impact statement available to the Environmental Protection Agency, participating agencies, and the public, and in the case of an environmental assessment, no later than 25 days after the lead agency makes it available. Except when the lead agency grants an extension of this period, the Council will not accept a referral after that date.

(c) The referral shall consist of:

(1) A copy of the letter signed by the head of the referring agency and delivered to the lead agency informing the lead agency of the referral and the reasons for it; and

(2) A statement supported by factual evidence leading to the conclusion that the matter is unsatisfactory from the standpoint of public health or welfare or environmental quality. The statement shall:

(i) Identify any disputed material facts and incorporate (by reference if appropriate) agreed upon facts;

(ii) Identify any existing environmental requirements or policies that would be violated by the matter;

(iii) Present the reasons for the referral;

(iv) Contain a finding by the agency whether the issue raised is of national importance because of the threat to national environmental resources or policies or for some other reason;

(v) Review the steps taken by the referring agency to bring its concerns to the attention of the lead agency at the earliest possible time; and

(vi) Give the referring agency's recommendations as to what mitigation alternative, further study, or other course of action (including abandonment of the matter) are necessary to remedy the situation.

(d) No later than 25 days after the referral to the Council, the lead agency may deliver a response to the Council and the referring agency. If the lead agency requests more time and gives assurance that the matter will not go forward in the interim, the Council may grant an extension. The response shall:

(1) Address fully the issues raised in the referral;

(2) Be supported by evidence and explanations, as appropriate; and

(3) Give the lead agency's response to the referring agency's recommendations.

(e) Applicants may provide views in writing to the Council no later than the response.

(f) No later than 25 days after receipt of both the referral and any response or upon being informed that there will be no response (unless the lead agency agrees to a longer time), the Council may take one or more of the following actions:

(1) Conclude that the process of referral and response has successfully resolved the problem.

(2) Initiate discussions with the agencies with the objective of mediation with referring and lead agencies.

(3) Obtain additional views and information.

(4) Determine that the issue is not one of national importance and request the referring and lead agencies to pursue their decision process.

(5) Determine that the referring and lead agencies should further negotiate the issue, and the issue is not appropriate for Council consideration until one or more heads of agencies report to the Council that the agencies' disagreements are irreconcilable.

(6) Publish its findings and recommendations (including, where appropriate, a finding that the submitted evidence does not support the position of an agency).

(7) When appropriate, submit the referral and the response together with the Council's recommendation to the President for action.

(g) The Council shall take no longer than 60 days to complete the actions specified in paragraph (f)(2), (3), or (5) of this section.

(h) The referral process is not intended to create any private rights of action or to be judicially reviewable because any voluntary resolutions by the agency parties do not represent final agency action and instead are only provisional and dependent on later consistent action by the action agencies.

PART 1505—NEPA AND AGENCY DECISION MAKING

Authority: 42 U.S.C. 4321–4347; 42 U.S.C. 4371–4375; 42 U.S.C. 7609; E.O. 11514, 35 FR 4247, 3 CFR, 1966–1970, Comp., p. 902, as amended by E.O. 11991, 42 FR 26967, 3 CFR, 1977 Comp., p. 123; and E.O. 13807, 82 FR 40463, 3 CFR, 2017, Comp., p. 369.

Source: 85 Fed. Reg. 43,304 (July 16, 2020).

§ 1505.1 [Reserved]

§ 1505.2 Record of decision in cases requiring environmental impact statements.

(a) At the time of its decision (§ 1506.11 of this chapter) or, if appropriate, its recommendation to Congress, each agency shall prepare and timely publish a concise public record of decision or joint record of decision. The record, which each agency may integrate into any other record it prepares, shall:

(1) State the decision.

(2) Identify alternatives considered by the agency in reaching its decision, specifying the alternative or alternatives considered environmentally preferable. An agency may discuss preferences among alternatives based on relevant factors including economic and technical considerations and agency statutory missions. An agency shall identify and discuss all such factors, including any essential considerations of national policy, that the agency balanced in making its decision and state how those considerations entered into its decision.

(3) State whether the agency has adopted all practicable means to avoid or minimize environmental harm from the alternative selected, and if not, why the agency did not. The agency shall adopt and summarize, where applicable, a monitoring and enforcement program for any enforceable mitigation requirements or commitments.

(b) Informed by the summary of the submitted alternatives, information, and analyses in the final environmental impact statement (§ 1502.17(b) of this chapter), together with any other material in the record that he or she determines to be relevant, the decision maker shall certify in the record of decision that the agency has considered all of the alternatives, information, analyses, and objections submitted by State, Tribal, and local governments and public commenters for consideration by the lead and cooperating agencies in developing the environmental impact statement. Agency environmental impact statements certified in accordance with this section are entitled to a presumption that the agency has considered the submitted alternatives, information, and analyses, including the summary thereof, in the final environmental impact statement (§ 1502.17(b)).

§ 1505.3 Implementing the decision.

Agencies may provide for monitoring to assure that their decisions are carried out and should do so in important cases. Mitigation (§ 1505.2(a)(3)) and other conditions established in the environmental impact statement or during its review and committed as part of the decision shall be implemented by the lead agency or other appropriate consenting agency. The lead agency shall:

(a) Include appropriate conditions in grants, permits, or other approvals.

(b) Condition funding of actions on mitigation.

(c) Upon request, inform cooperating or participating agencies on progress in carrying out mitigation measures that they have proposed and were adopted by the agency making the decision.

(d) Upon request, publish the results of relevant monitoring.

PART 1506—OTHER REQUIREMENTS OF NEPA

Sec.

Authority: 42 U.S.C. 4321–4347; 42 U.S.C. 4371–4375; 42 U.S.C. 7609; E.O. 11514, 35 FR 4247, 3 CFR, 1966–1970, Comp., p. 902, as amended by E.O. 11991, 42 FR 26967, 3 CFR, 1977 Comp., p. 123; and E.O. 13807, 82 FR 40463, 3 CFR, 2017, Comp., p. 369.

Source: 85 Fed. Reg. 43,304 (July 16, 2020).

§ 1506.1 Limitations on actions during NEPA process.

(a) Except as provided in paragraphs (b) and (c) of this section, until an agency issues a finding of no significant impact, as provided in § 1501.6 of this chapter, or record of decision, as provided in § 1505.2 of this chapter, no action concerning the proposal may be taken that would:

(1) Have an adverse environmental impact; or

(2) Limit the choice of reasonable alternatives.

(b) If any agency is considering an application from a non-Federal entity and is aware that the applicant is about to take an action within the agency's jurisdiction that would meet either of the criteria in paragraph (a) of this section, then the agency shall promptly notify the applicant that the agency will take appropriate action to ensure that the objectives and procedures of NEPA are achieved. This section does not preclude development by applicants of plans or designs or performance of other activities necessary to support an application for Federal, State, Tribal, or local permits or assistance. An agency considering a proposed action for Federal funding may authorize such activities, including, but not limited to, acquisition of interests in land (e.g., fee simple, rights-of-way, and conservation easements), purchase of long lead-time equipment, and purchase options made by applicants.

(c) While work on a required programmatic environmental review is in progress and the action is not covered by an existing programmatic review, agencies shall not undertake in the interim any major Federal action covered by the program that may significantly affect the quality of the human environment unless such action:

(1) Is justified independently of the program;

(2) Is itself accompanied by an adequate environmental review; and

(3) Will not prejudice the ultimate decision on the program. Interim action prejudices the ultimate decision on the program when it tends to determine subsequent development or limit alternatives.

§ 1506.2 Elimination of duplication with State, Tribal, and local procedures.

(a) Federal agencies are authorized to cooperate with State, Tribal, and local agencies that are responsible for preparing environmental documents, including those prepared pursuant to section 102(2)(D) of NEPA.

(b) To the fullest extent practicable unless specifically prohibited by law, agencies shall cooperate with State, Tribal, and local agencies to reduce duplication between NEPA and State, Tribal, and local requirements, including through use of studies, analysis, and decisions developed by State, Tribal, or local agencies. Except for cases covered by paragraph (a) of this section, such cooperation shall include, to the fullest extent practicable:

(1) Joint planning processes.

(2) Joint environmental research and studies.

(3) Joint public hearings (except where otherwise provided by statute).

(4) Joint environmental assessments.

(c) To the fullest extent practicable unless specifically prohibited by law, agencies shall cooperate with State, Tribal, and local agencies to reduce duplication between NEPA and comparable State, Tribal, and local requirements. Such cooperation shall include, to the fullest extent practicable, joint environmental impact statements. In such cases, one or more Federal agencies and one or more State, Tribal, or local agencies shall be joint lead agencies. Where State or Tribal laws or local ordinances have environmental impact statement or similar requirements in addition to but not in conflict with those in NEPA, Federal agencies may cooperate in fulfilling these requirements, as well as those of Federal laws, so that one document will comply with all applicable laws.

(d) To better integrate environmental impact statements into State, Tribal, or local planning processes, environmental impact statements shall discuss any inconsistency of a proposed action with any approved State, Tribal, or local plan or law (whether or not federally sanctioned). Where an inconsistency exists, the statement should describe the extent to which the agency would reconcile its proposed action with the plan or law. While the statement should discuss any inconsistencies, NEPA does not require reconciliation.

§ 1506.3 Adoption.

(a) Generally. An agency may adopt a Federal draft or final environmental impact statement, environmental assessment, or portion thereof, or categorical exclusion determination provided that the statement, assessment, portion thereof, or determination meets the standards for an adequate statement, assessment, or determination under the regulations in this subchapter.

(b) Environmental impact statements.

(1) If the actions covered by the original environmental impact statement and the proposed action are substantially the same, the adopting agency shall republish it as a final statement consistent with § 1506.10. If the actions are not substantially the same, the adopting agency shall treat the statement as a draft and republish it, consistent with § 1506.10.

(2) Notwithstanding paragraph (b)(1) of this section, a cooperating agency may adopt in its record of decision without republishing the environmental impact statement of a lead agency when, after an independent review of the statement, the cooperating agency concludes that its comments and suggestions have been satisfied.

(c) Environmental assessments. If the actions covered by the original environmental assessment and the proposed action are substantially the same, the adopting agency may adopt the environmental assessment in its finding of no significant impact and provide notice consistent with § 1501.6 of this chapter.

(d) Categorical exclusions. An agency may adopt another agency's determination that a categorical exclusion applies to a proposed action if the action covered by the original categorical exclusion determination and the adopting agency's proposed action are substantially the same. The agency shall document the adoption.

(e) Identification of certain circumstances. The adopting agency shall specify if one of the following circumstances is present:

(1) The agency is adopting an assessment or statement that is not final within the agency that prepared it.

(2) The action assessed in the assessment or statement is the subject of a referral under part 1504 of this chapter.

(3) The assessment or statement's adequacy is the subject of a judicial action that is not final.

§ 1506.4 Combining documents.

Agencies should combine, to the fullest extent practicable, any environmental document with any other agency document to reduce duplication and paperwork.

§ 1506.5 Agency responsibility for environmental documents.

(a) Responsibility. The agency is responsible for the accuracy, scope (§ 1501.9(e) of this chapter), and content of environmental documents prepared by the agency or by an applicant or contractor under the supervision of the agency.

(b) Information. An agency may require an applicant to submit environmental information for possible use by the agency in preparing an environmental document. An agency also may direct an applicant or authorize a contractor to prepare an environmental document under the supervision of the agency.

(1) The agency should assist the applicant by outlining the types of information required or, for the preparation of environmental documents, shall provide guidance to the applicant or contractor and participate in their preparation.

(2) The agency shall independently evaluate the information submitted or the environmental document and shall be responsible for its accuracy, scope, and contents.

(3) The agency shall include in the environmental document the names and qualifications of the persons preparing environmental documents, and conducting the independent evaluation of any information submitted or environmental documents prepared by an applicant or contractor, such as in the list of preparers for environmental impact statements (§ 1502.18 of this chapter). It is the intent of this paragraph (b)(3) that acceptable work not be redone, but that it be verified by the agency.

(4) Contractors or applicants preparing environmental assessments or environmental impact statements shall submit a disclosure statement to the lead agency that specifies any financial or other interest in the outcome of the action. Such statement need not include privileged or confidential trade secrets or other confidential business information.

(5) Nothing in this section is intended to prohibit any agency from requesting any person, including the applicant, to submit information to it or to prohibit any person from submitting information to any agency for use in preparing environmental documents.

§ 1506.6 Public involvement.

Agencies shall:

(a) Make diligent efforts to involve the public in preparing and implementing their NEPA procedures (§ 1507.3 of this chapter).

(b) Provide public notice of NEPA-related hearings, public meetings, and other opportunities for public involvement, and the availability of environmental documents so as to inform those persons and agencies who may be interested or affected by their proposed actions. When selecting appropriate methods for providing public notice, agencies shall consider the ability of affected persons and agencies to access electronic media.

(1) In all cases, the agency shall notify those who have requested notice on an individual action.

(2) In the case of an action with effects of national concern, notice shall include publication in the Federal Register. An agency may notify organizations that have requested regular notice.

(3) In the case of an action with effects primarily of local concern, the notice may include:

(i) Notice to State, Tribal, and local agencies that may be interested or affected by the proposed action.

(ii) Notice to interested or affected State, Tribal, and local governments.

(iii) Following the affected State or Tribe's public notice procedures for comparable actions.

(iv) Publication in local newspapers (in papers of general circulation rather than legal papers).

(v) Notice through other local media.

(vi) Notice to potentially interested community organizations including small business associations.

(vii) Publication in newsletters that may be expected to reach potentially interested persons.

(viii) Direct mailing to owners and occupants of nearby or affected property.

(ix) Posting of notice on and off site in the area where the action is to be located.

(x) Notice through electronic media (e.g., a project or agency website, email, or social media).

(c) Hold or sponsor public hearings, public meetings, or other opportunities for public involvement whenever appropriate or in accordance with statutory requirements applicable to the agency. Agencies may conduct public hearings and public meetings by means of electronic communication except where another format is required by law. When selecting appropriate methods for public involvement, agencies shall consider the ability of affected entities to access electronic media.

(d) Solicit appropriate information from the public.

(e) Explain in its procedures where interested persons can get information or status reports on environmental impact statements and other elements of the NEPA process.

(f) Make environmental impact statements, the comments received, and any underlying documents available to the public pursuant to the provisions of the Freedom of Information Act, as amended (5 U.S.C. 552).

§ 1506.7 Further guidance.

(a) The Council may provide further guidance concerning NEPA and its procedures consistent with Executive Order 13807, Establishing Discipline and Accountability in the Environmental Review and Permitting Process for Infrastructure Projects (August 5, 2017), Executive Order 13891, Promoting the Rule of Law Through Improved Agency Guidance Documents (October 9, 2019), and any other applicable Executive orders.

(b) To the extent that Council guidance issued prior to September 14, 2020 is in conflict with this subchapter, the provisions of this subchapter apply.

§ 1506.8 Proposals for legislation.

(a) When developing legislation, agencies shall integrate the NEPA process for proposals for legislation significantly affecting the quality of the human environment with the legislative process of the Congress. Technical drafting assistance does not by itself constitute a legislative proposal. Only the agency that has primary responsibility for the subject matter involved will prepare a legislative environmental impact statement.

(b) A legislative environmental impact statement is the detailed statement required by law to be included in an agency's recommendation or report on a legislative proposal to Congress. A legislative environmental impact statement shall be considered part of the formal transmittal of a legislative proposal to Congress; however, it may be transmitted to Congress up to 30 days later in order to allow time for completion of an accurate statement that can serve as the basis for public and Congressional debate. The statement must be available in time for Congressional hearings and deliberations.

(c) Preparation of a legislative environmental impact statement shall conform to the requirements of the regulations in this subchapter, except as follows:

(1) There need not be a scoping process.

(2) Agencies shall prepare the legislative statement in the same manner as a draft environmental impact statement and need not prepare a final statement unless any of the following conditions exist. In such cases, the agency shall prepare and publish the statements consistent with §§ 1503.1 of this chapter and 1506.11:

(i) A Congressional committee with jurisdiction over the proposal has a rule requiring both draft and final environmental impact statements.

(ii) The proposal results from a study process required by statute (such as those required by the Wild and Scenic Rivers Act (16 U.S.C. 1271 et seq.)).

(iii) Legislative approval is sought for Federal or federally assisted construction or other projects that the agency recommends be located at specific geographic locations. For proposals requiring an environmental impact statement for the acquisition of space by the General Services Administration, a draft statement shall accompany the Prospectus or the 11(b) Report of Building Project Surveys to the Congress, and a final statement shall be completed before site acquisition.

(iv) The agency decides to prepare draft and final statements.

(d) Comments on the legislative statement shall be given to the lead agency, which shall forward them along with its own responses to the Congressional committees with jurisdiction.

§ 1506.9 Proposals for regulations.

Where the proposed action is the promulgation of a rule or regulation, procedures and documentation pursuant to other statutory or Executive order requirements may satisfy one or more requirements of this subchapter. When a procedure or document satisfies one or more requirements of this subchapter, the agency may substitute it for the corresponding requirements in this subchapter and need not carry out duplicative procedures or documentation. Agencies shall identify which corresponding requirements in this subchapter are satisfied and consult with the Council to confirm such determinations.

§ 1506.10 Filing requirements.

(a) Agencies shall file environmental impact statements together with comments and responses with the Environmental Protection Agency (EPA), Office of Federal Activities, consistent with EPA's procedures.

(b) Agencies shall file statements with the EPA no earlier than they are also transmitted to participating agencies and made available to the public. EPA may issue guidelines to agencies to implement its responsibilities under this section and § 1506.11.

§ 1506.11 Timing of agency action.

(a) The Environmental Protection Agency shall publish a notice in the Federal Register each week of the environmental impact statements filed since its prior notice. The minimum time periods set forth in this section are calculated from the date of publication of this notice.

(b) Unless otherwise provided by law, including statutory provisions for combining a final environmental impact statement and record of decision, Federal agencies may not make or issue a record of decision under § 1505.2 of this chapter for the proposed action until the later of the following dates:

(1) 90 days after publication of the notice described in paragraph (a) of this section for a draft environmental impact statement.

(2) 30 days after publication of the notice described in paragraph (a) of this section for a final environmental impact statement.

(c) An agency may make an exception to the rule on timing set forth in paragraph (b) of this section for a proposed action in the following circumstances:

(1) Some agencies have a formally established appeal process after publication of the final environmental impact statement that allows other agencies or the public to take appeals on a decision and make their views known. In such cases where a real opportunity exists to alter the decision, the agency may make and record the decision at the same time it publishes the environmental impact statement. This means that the period for appeal of the decision and the 30-day period set forth in paragraph (b)(2) of this section may run concurrently. In such cases, the environmental impact statement shall explain the timing and the public's right of appeal and provide notification consistent with § 1506.10; or

(2) An agency engaged in rulemaking under the Administrative Procedure Act or other statute for the purpose of protecting the public health or safety may waive the time period in paragraph (b)(2) of this section, publish a decision on the final rule simultaneously with publication of the notice of the availability of the final environmental impact statement, and provide notification consistent with § 1506.10, as described in paragraph (a) of this section.

(d) If an agency files the final environmental impact statement within 90 days of the filing of the draft environmental impact statement with the Environmental Protection Agency, the decision-making period and the 90-day period may run concurrently. However, subject to paragraph (e) of this section, agencies shall allow at least 45 days for comments on draft statements.

(e) The lead agency may extend the minimum periods in paragraph (b) of this section and provide notification consistent with § 1506.10. Upon a showing by the lead agency of compelling reasons of national policy, the Environmental Protection Agency may reduce the minimum periods and, upon a showing by any other Federal agency of compelling reasons of national policy, also may extend the minimum periods, but only after consultation with the lead agency. The lead agency may modify the minimum periods when necessary to comply with other specific statutory requirements. (§ 1507.3(f)(2) of this chapter) Failure to file timely comments shall not be a sufficient reason for extending a period. If the lead agency does not concur with the extension of time, EPA may not extend it for more than 30 days. When the Environmental Protection Agency reduces or extends any period of time it shall notify the Council.

§ 1506.12 Emergencies.

Where emergency circumstances make it necessary to take an action with significant environmental impact without observing the provisions of the regulations in this subchapter, the Federal agency taking the action should consult with the Council about alternative arrangements for compliance with section 102(2)(C) of NEPA. Agencies and the Council will limit such arrangements to actions necessary to control the immediate impacts of the emergency. Other actions remain subject to NEPA review.

§ 1506.13 Effective date.

The regulations in this subchapter apply to any NEPA process begun after September 14, 2020. An agency may apply the regulations in this subchapter to ongoing activities and environmental *43373 documents begun before September 14, 2020.

PART 1507—AGENCY COMPLIANCE

Sec.

Authority: 42 U.S.C. 4321–4347; 42 U.S.C. 4371–4375; 42 U.S.C. 7609; E.O. 11514, 35 FR 4247, 3 CFR, 1966–1970, Comp., p. 902, as amended by E.O. 11991, 42 FR 26967, 3 CFR, 1977 Comp., p. 123; and E.O. 13807, 82 FR 40463, 3 CFR, 2017, Comp., p. 369.

Source: 85 Fed. Reg. 43,304 (July 16, 2020).

§ 1507.1 Compliance.

All agencies of the Federal Government shall comply with the regulations in this subchapter.

§ 1507.2 Agency capability to comply.

Each agency shall be capable (in terms of personnel and other resources) of complying with the requirements of NEPA and the regulations in this subchapter. Such compliance may include use of the resources of other agencies, applicants, and other participants in the NEPA process, but the agency using the resources shall itself have sufficient capability to evaluate what others do for it and account for the contributions of others. Agencies shall:

(a) Fulfill the requirements of section 102(2)(A) of NEPA to utilize a systematic, interdisciplinary approach that will ensure the integrated use of the natural and social sciences and the environmental design arts in planning and in decision making that may have an impact on the human environment. Agencies shall designate a senior agency official to be responsible for overall review of agency NEPA compliance, including resolving implementation issues.

(b) Identify methods and procedures required by section 102(2)(B) of NEPA to ensure that presently unquantified environmental amenities and values may be given appropriate consideration.

(c) Prepare adequate environmental impact statements pursuant to section 102(2)(C) of NEPA and cooperate on the development of statements in the areas where the agency has jurisdiction by law or special expertise or is authorized to develop and enforce environmental standards.

(d) Study, develop, and describe alternatives to recommended courses of action in any proposal that involves unresolved conflicts concerning alternative uses of available resources, consistent with section 102(2)(E) of NEPA.

(e) Comply with the requirements of section 102(2)(H) of NEPA that the agency initiate and utilize ecological information in the planning and development of resource-oriented projects.

(f) Fulfill the requirements of sections 102(2)(F), 102(2)(G), and 102(2)(I), of NEPA, Executive Order 11514, Protection and Enhancement of Environmental Quality, section 2, as amended by Executive Order 11991, Relating to Protection and Enhancement of Environmental Quality, and Executive Order 13807, Establishing Discipline and Accountability in the Environmental Review and Permitting for Infrastructure Projects.

§ 1507.3 Agency NEPA procedures.

(a) Where existing agency NEPA procedures are inconsistent with the regulations in this subchapter, the regulations in this subchapter shall apply, consistent with § 1506.13 of this chapter, unless there is a clear and fundamental conflict with the requirements of another statute. The Council has determined that the categorical exclusions contained in agency NEPA procedures as of September 14, 2020 are consistent with this subchapter.

(b) No more than 12 months after September 14, 2020, or 9 months after the establishment of an agency, whichever comes later, each agency shall develop or revise, as necessary, proposed procedures to implement the regulations in this subchapter, including to eliminate any inconsistencies with the regulations in this subchapter. When the agency is a department, it may be efficient for major subunits (with the consent of the department) to adopt their own procedures. Except for agency efficiency (see paragraph (c) of this section) or as otherwise required by law, agency NEPA procedures shall not impose additional procedures or requirements beyond those set forth in the regulations in this subchapter.

(1) Each agency shall consult with the Council while developing or revising its proposed procedures and before publishing them in the Federal Register for comment. Agencies with similar programs should consult with each other and the Council to coordinate their procedures, especially for programs requesting similar information from applicants.

(2) Agencies shall provide an opportunity for public review and review by the Council for conformity with the Act and the regulations in this subchapter before adopting their final procedures. The Council shall complete its review within 30 days of the receipt of the proposed final procedures. Once in effect, the agency shall publish its NEPA procedures and ensure that they are readily available to the public.

(c) Agencies shall adopt, as necessary, agency NEPA procedures to improve agency efficiency and ensure that agencies make decisions in accordance with the Act's procedural requirements. Such procedures shall include:

(1) Designating the major decision points for the agency's principal programs likely to have a significant effect on the human environment and assuring that the NEPA process begins at the earliest reasonable time, consistent with § 1501.2 of this chapter, and aligns with the corresponding decision points.

(2) Requiring that relevant environmental documents, comments, and responses be part of the record in formal rulemaking or adjudicatory proceedings.

(3) Requiring that relevant environmental documents, comments, and responses accompany the proposal through existing agency review processes so that decision makers use the statement in making decisions.

(4) Requiring that the alternatives considered by the decision maker are encompassed by the range of alternatives discussed in the relevant environmental documents and that the decision maker consider the alternatives described in the environmental documents. If another decision document accompanies the relevant environmental documents to the decision maker, agencies are encouraged to make available to the public before the decision is made any part of that document that relates to the comparison of alternatives.

(5) Requiring the combination of environmental documents with other agency documents. Agencies may designate and rely on one or more procedures or documents under other statutes or Executive orders as satisfying some or all of the requirements in this subchapter, and substitute such procedures and documentation to reduce duplication. When an agency substitutes one or more procedures or documents for the requirements in this subchapter, the agency shall identify the respective requirements that are satisfied.

(d) Agency procedures should identify those activities or decisions that are not subject to NEPA, including:

(1) Activities or decisions expressly exempt from NEPA under another statute;

(2) Activities or decisions where compliance with NEPA would clearly and fundamentally conflict with the requirements of another statute;

(3) Activities or decisions where compliance with NEPA would be inconsistent with Congressional intent expressed in another statute;

(4) Activities or decisions that are non-major Federal actions;

(5) Activities or decisions that are non-discretionary actions, in whole or in part, for which the agency lacks authority to consider environmental effects as part of its decision-making process; and

(6) Actions where the agency has determined that another statute's requirements serve the function of agency compliance with the Act.

(e) Agency procedures shall comply with the regulations in this subchapter except where compliance would be inconsistent with statutory requirements and shall include:

(1) Those procedures required by §§ 1501.2(b)(4) (assistance to applicants) and 1506.6(e) of this chapter (status information).

(2) Specific criteria for and identification of those typical classes of action:

(i) Which normally do require environmental impact statements.

(ii) Which normally do not require either an environmental impact statement or an environmental assessment and do not have a significant effect on the human environment (categorical exclusions (§ 1501.4 of this chapter)). Any procedures under this section shall provide for extraordinary circumstances in which a normally excluded action may have a significant environmental effect. Agency NEPA procedures shall identify when documentation of a categorical exclusion determination is required.

(iii) Which normally require environmental assessments but not necessarily environmental impact statements.

(3) Procedures for introducing a supplement to an environmental assessment or environmental impact statement into its formal administrative record, if such a record exists.

(f) Agency procedures may:

(1) Include specific criteria for providing limited exceptions to the provisions of the regulations in this subchapter for classified proposals. These are proposed actions that are specifically authorized under criteria established by an Executive order or statute to be kept secret in the interest of national defense or foreign policy and are in fact properly classified pursuant to such Executive order or statute. Agencies may safeguard and restrict from public dissemination environmental assessments and environmental impact statements that address classified proposals in accordance with agencies' own regulations applicable to classified information. Agencies should organize these documents so that classified portions are included as annexes, so that the agencies can make the unclassified portions available to the public.

(2) Provide for periods of time other than those presented in § 1506.11 of this chapter when necessary to comply with other specific statutory requirements, including requirements of lead or cooperating agencies.

(3) Provide that, where there is a lengthy period between the agency's decision to prepare an environmental impact statement and the time of actual preparation, the agency may publish the notice of intent required by § 1501.9(d) of this chapter at a reasonable time in advance of preparation of the draft statement. Agency procedures shall provide for publication of supplemental notices to inform the public of a pause in its preparation of an environmental impact statement and for any agency decision to withdraw its notice of intent to prepare an environmental impact statement.

(4) Adopt procedures to combine its environmental assessment process with its scoping process.

(5) Establish a process that allows the agency to use a categorical exclusion listed in another agency's NEPA procedures after consulting with that agency to ensure the use of the categorical exclusion is appropriate. The process should ensure documentation of the consultation and identify to the public those categorical exclusions the agency may use for its proposed actions. Then, the agency may apply the categorical exclusion to its proposed actions.

§ 1507.4 Agency NEPA program information.

(a) To allow agencies and the public to efficiently and effectively access information about NEPA reviews, agencies shall provide for agency websites or other means to make available environmental documents, relevant notices, and other relevant information for use by agencies, applicants, and interested persons. Such means of publication may include:

(1) Agency planning and environmental documents that guide agency management and provide for public involvement in agency planning processes;

(2) A directory of pending and final environmental documents;

(3) Agency policy documents, orders, terminology, and explanatory materials regarding agency decision-making processes;

(4) Agency planning program information, plans, and planning tools; and

(5) A database searchable by geographic information, document status, document type, and project type.

(b) Agencies shall provide for efficient and effective interagency coordination of their environmental program websites, including use of shared databases or application programming interface, in their implementation of NEPA and related authorities.

PART 1508—DEFINITIONS

Authority: 42 U.S.C. 4321–4347; 42 U.S.C. 4371–4375; 42 U.S.C. 7609; E.O. 11514, 35 FR 4247, 3 CFR, 1966–1970, Comp., p. 902, as amended by E.O. 11991, 42 FR 26967, 3 CFR, 1977 Comp., p. 123; and E.O. 13807, 82 FR 40463, 3 CFR, 2017, Comp., p. 369.

Source: 85 Fed. Reg. 43,304 (July 16, 2020).

§ 1508.1 Definitions.

The following definitions apply to the regulations in this subchapter. Federal agencies shall use these terms uniformly throughout the Federal Government.

(a) Act or NEPA means the National Environmental Policy Act, as amended (42 U.S.C. 4321, et seq.).

(b) Affecting means will or may have an effect on.

(c) Authorization means any license, permit, approval, finding, determination, or other administrative decision issued by an agency that is required or authorized under Federal law in order to implement a proposed action.

(d) Categorical exclusion means a category of actions that the agency has determined, in its agency NEPA procedures (§ 1507.3 of this chapter), normally do not have a significant effect on the human environment.

(e) Cooperating agency means any Federal agency (and a State, Tribal, or local agency with agreement of the lead agency) other than a lead agency that has jurisdiction by law or special expertise with respect to any environmental impact involved in a proposal (or a reasonable alternative) for legislation or other major Federal action that may significantly affect the quality of the human environment.

(f) Council means the Council on Environmental Quality established by title II of the Act.

(g) Effects or impacts means changes to the human environment from the proposed action or alternatives that are reasonably foreseeable and have a reasonably close causal relationship to the proposed action or alternatives, including those effects that occur at the same time and place as the proposed action or alternatives and may include effects that are later in time or farther removed in distance from the proposed action or alternatives.

(1) Effects include ecological (such as the effects on natural resources and on the components, structures, and functioning of affected ecosystems), aesthetic, historic, cultural, economic (such as the effects on employment), social, or health effects. Effects may also include those resulting from actions that may have both beneficial and detrimental effects, even if on balance the agency believes that the effect will be beneficial.

(2) A "but for" causal relationship is insufficient to make an agency responsible for a particular effect under NEPA. Effects should generally not be considered if they are remote in time, geographically remote, or the product of a lengthy causal chain. Effects do not include those effects that the agency has no ability to prevent due to its limited statutory authority or would occur regardless of the proposed action.

(3) An agency's analysis of effects shall be consistent with this paragraph (g). Cumulative impact, defined in 40 CFR 1508.7 (1978), is repealed.

(h) Environmental assessment means a concise public document prepared by a Federal agency to aid an agency's compliance with the Act and support its determination of whether to prepare an environmental impact statement or a finding of no significant impact, as provided in § 1501.6 of this chapter.

(i) Environmental document means an environmental assessment, environmental impact statement, finding of no significant impact, or notice of intent.

(j) Environmental impact statement means a detailed written statement as required by section 102(2)(C) of NEPA.

(k) Federal agency means all agencies of the Federal Government. It does not mean the Congress, the Judiciary, or the President, including the performance of staff functions for the President in his Executive Office. For the purposes of the regulations in this subchapter, Federal agency also includes States, units of general local government, and Tribal governments assuming NEPA responsibilities from a Federal agency pursuant to statute.

(*l*) Finding of no significant impact means a document by a Federal agency briefly presenting the reasons why an action, not otherwise categorically excluded (§ 1501.4 of this chapter), will not have a significant effect on the human environment and for which an environmental impact statement therefore will not be prepared.

(m) Human environment means comprehensively the natural and physical environment and the relationship of present and future generations of Americans with that environment. (See also the definition of "effects" in paragraph (g) of this section.)

(n) Jurisdiction by law means agency authority to approve, veto, or finance all or part of the proposal.

(*o*) Lead agency means the agency or agencies, in the case of joint lead agencies, preparing or having taken primary responsibility for preparing the environmental impact statement.

(p) Legislation means a bill or legislative proposal to Congress developed by a Federal agency, but does not include requests for appropriations or legislation recommended by the President.

(q) Major Federal action or action means an activity or decision subject to Federal control and responsibility subject to the following:

(1) Major Federal action does not include the following activities or decisions:

(i) Extraterritorial activities or decisions, which means agency activities or decisions with effects located entirely outside of the jurisdiction of the United States;

(ii) Activities or decisions that are non-discretionary and made in accordance with the agency's statutory authority;

(iii) Activities or decisions that do not result in final agency action under the Administrative Procedure Act or other statute that also includes a finality requirement;

(iv) Judicial or administrative civil or criminal enforcement actions;

(v) Funding assistance solely in the form of general revenue sharing funds with no Federal agency control over the subsequent use of such funds;

(vi) Non-Federal projects with minimal Federal funding or minimal Federal involvement where the agency does not exercise sufficient control and responsibility over the outcome of the project; and

(vii) Loans, loan guarantees, or other forms of financial assistance where the Federal agency does not exercise sufficient control and responsibility over the effects of such assistance (for example, action does not include farm ownership and operating loan guarantees by the Farm Service Agency pursuant to 7 U.S.C. 1925 and 1941 through 1949 and business loan guarantees by the Small Business Administration pursuant to 15 U.S.C. 636(a), 636(m), and 695 through 697g).

(2) Major Federal actions may include new and continuing activities, including projects and programs entirely or partly financed, assisted, conducted, regulated, or approved by Federal agencies; new or revised agency rules, regulations, plans, policies, or procedures; and legislative proposals (§ 1506.8 of this chapter).

(3) Major Federal actions tend to fall within one of the following categories:

(i) Adoption of official policy, such as rules, regulations, and interpretations adopted under the Administrative Procedure Act, 5 U.S.C. 551 et seq. or other statutes; implementation of treaties and international conventions or agreements, including those implemented pursuant to statute or regulation; formal documents establishing an agency's policies which will result in or substantially alter agency programs.

(ii) Adoption of formal plans, such as official documents prepared or approved by Federal agencies, which prescribe alternative uses of Federal resources, upon which future agency actions will be based.

(iii) Adoption of programs, such as a group of concerted actions to implement a specific policy or plan; systematic and connected agency decisions allocating agency resources to implement a specific statutory program or executive directive.

(iv) Approval of specific projects, such as construction or management activities located in a defined geographic area. Projects include actions approved by permit or other regulatory decision as well as Federal and federally assisted activities.

(r) Matter includes for purposes of part 1504 of this chapter:

(1) With respect to the Environmental Protection Agency, any proposed legislation, project, action or regulation as those terms are used in section 309(a) of the Clean Air Act (42 U.S.C. 7609).

(2) With respect to all other agencies, any proposed major Federal action to which section 102(2)(C) of NEPA applies.

(s) Mitigation means measures that avoid, minimize, or compensate for effects caused by a proposed action or alternatives as described in an environmental document or record of decision and that have a nexus to those effects. While NEPA requires consideration of mitigation, it does not mandate the form or adoption of any mitigation. Mitigation includes:

(1) Avoiding the impact altogether by not taking a certain action or parts of an action.

(2) Minimizing impacts by limiting the degree or magnitude of the action and its implementation.

(3) Rectifying the impact by repairing, rehabilitating, or restoring the affected environment.

(4) Reducing or eliminating the impact over time by preservation and maintenance operations during the life of the action.

(5) Compensating for the impact by replacing or providing substitute resources or environments.

(t) NEPA process means all measures necessary for compliance with the requirements of section 2 and title I of NEPA.

(u) Notice of intent means a public notice that an agency will prepare and consider an environmental impact statement.

(v) Page means 500 words and does not include explanatory maps, diagrams, graphs, tables, and other means of graphically displaying quantitative or geospatial information.

(w) Participating agency means a Federal, State, Tribal, or local agency participating in an environmental review or authorization of an action.

(x) Proposal means a proposed action at a stage when an agency has a goal, is actively preparing to make a decision on one or more alternative means of accomplishing that goal, and can meaningfully evaluate its effects. A proposal may exist in fact as well as by agency declaration that one exists.

(y) Publish and publication mean methods found by the agency to efficiently and effectively make environmental documents and information available for review by interested persons, including electronic publication, and adopted by agency NEPA procedures pursuant to § 1507.3 of this chapter.

(z) Reasonable alternatives means a reasonable range of alternatives that are technically and economically feasible, meet the purpose and need for the proposed action, and, where applicable, meet the goals of the applicant.

(aa) Reasonably foreseeable means sufficiently likely to occur such that a person of ordinary prudence would take it into account in reaching a decision.

(bb) Referring agency means the Federal agency that has referred any matter to the Council after a determination that the matter is unsatisfactory from the standpoint of public health or welfare or environmental quality.

(cc) Scope consists of the range of actions, alternatives, and impacts to be considered in an environmental impact statement. The scope of an individual statement may depend on its relationships to other statements (§ 1501.11 of this chapter).

(dd) Senior agency official means an official of assistant secretary rank or higher (or equivalent) that is designated for overall agency NEPA compliance, including resolving implementation issues.

(ee) Special expertise means statutory responsibility, agency mission, or related program experience.

(ff) Tiering refers to the coverage of general matters in broader environmental impact statements or environmental assessments (such as national program or policy statements) with subsequent narrower statements or environmental analyses (such as regional or basin-wide program statements or ultimately site-specific statements) incorporating by reference the general discussions and concentrating solely on the issues specific to the statement subsequently prepared.

§ 1508.2 [Reserved]

PRE-2020 CEQ NEPA REGULATIONS

PART 1500—PURPOSE, POLICY, AND MANDATE

Sec.

Authority: NEPA, the Environmental Quality Improvement Act of 1970, as amended (42 U.S.C. 4371 et seq.), sec. 309 of the Clean Air Act, as amended (42 U.S.C. 7609) and Executive Order 11514, Mar. 5, 1970, as amended by Executive Order 11991, May 24, 1977).

Source: 43 Fed. Reg. 55990 (Nov. 28, 1978), unless otherwise noted.

§ 1500.1 Purpose.

(a) The National Environmental Policy Act (NEPA) is our basic national charter for protection of the environment. It establishes policy, sets goals (section 101), and provides means (section 102) for carrying out the policy. Section 102(2) contains "action-forcing" provisions to make sure that federal agencies act according to the letter and spirit of the Act. The regulations that follow implement section 102(2). Their purpose is to tell federal agencies what they must do to comply with the procedures and achieve the goals of the Act. The President, the federal agencies, and the courts share responsibility for enforcing the Act so as to achieve the substantive requirements of section 101.

(b) NEPA procedures must insure that environmental information is available to public officials and citizens before decisions are made and before actions are taken. The information must be of high quality.

Accurate scientific analysis, expert agency comments, and public scrutiny are essential to implementing NEPA. Most important, NEPA documents must concentrate on the issues that are truly significant to the action in question, rather than amassing needless detail.

(c) Ultimately, of course, it is not better documents but better decisions that count. NEPA's purpose is not to generate paperwork—even excellent paperwork—but to foster excellent action. The NEPA process is intended to help public officials make decisions that are based on understanding of environmental consequences, and take actions that protect, restore, and enhance the environment. These regulations provide the direction to achieve this purpose.

§ 1500.2 Policy.

Federal agencies shall to the fullest extent possible:

(a) Interpret and administer the policies, regulations, and public laws of the United States in accordance with the policies set forth in the Act and in these regulations.

(b) Implement procedures to make the NEPA process more useful to decisionmakers and the public; to reduce paperwork and the accumulation of extraneous background data; and to emphasize real environmental issues and alternatives. Environmental impact statements shall be concise, clear, and to the point, and shall be supported by evidence that agencies have made the necessary environmental analyses.

(c) Integrate the requirements of NEPA with other planning and environmental review procedures required by law or by agency practice so that all such procedures run concurrently rather than consecutively.

(d) Encourage and facilitate public involvement in decisions which affect the quality of the human environment.

(e) Use the NEPA process to identify and assess the reasonable alternatives to proposed actions that will avoid or minimize adverse effects of these actions upon the quality of the human environment.

(f) Use all practicable means, consistent with the requirements of the Act and other essential considerations of national policy, to restore and enhance the quality of the human environment and avoid or minimize any possible adverse effects of their actions upon the quality of the human environment.

§ 1500.3 Mandate.

Parts 1500 through 1508 of this title provide regulations applicable to and binding on all Federal agencies for implementing the procedural provisions of the National Environmental Policy Act of 1969, as amended (P.L. 91–190, 42 U.S.C. 4321 et seq.) (NEPA or the Act) except where compliance would be inconsistent with other statutory requirements. These regulations are issued pursuant to NEPA, the Environmental Quality Improvement Act of 1970, as amended (42 U.S.C. 4371 et seq.) section 309 of the Clean Air Act, as amended (42 U.S.C. 7609) and Executive Order 11514, Protection and Enhancement of Environmental Quality (March 5, 1970, as amended by Executive Order 11991, May 24, 1977). These regulations, unlike the predecessor guidelines, are not confined to sec. 102(2)(C) (environmental impact statements). The regulations apply to the whole of section 102(2). The provisions of the Act and of these regulations must be read together as a whole in order to comply with the spirit and letter of the law. It is the Council's intention that judicial review of agency compliance with these regulations not occur before an agency has filed the final environmental impact statement, or has made a final finding of no significant impact (when such a finding will result in action affecting the environment), or takes action that will result in irreparable injury. Furthermore, it is the Council's intention that any trivial violation of these regulations not give rise to any independent cause of action.

§ 1500.4 Reducing paperwork.

Agencies shall reduce excessive paperwork by:

(a) Reducing the length of environmental impact statements (§ 1502.2(c)), by means such as setting appropriate page limits (§§ 1501.7(b)(1) and 1502.7).

(b) Preparing analytic rather than encyclopedic environmental impact statements (§ 1502.2(a)).

(c) Discussing only briefly issues other than significant ones (§ 1502.2(b)).

(d) Writing environmental impact statements in plain language (§ 1502.8).

(e) Following a clear format for environmental impact statements (§ 1502.10).

(f) Emphasizing the portions of the environmental impact statement that are useful to decisionmakers and the public (§§ 1502.14 and 1502.15) and reducing emphasis on background material (§ 1502.16).

(g) Using the scoping process, not only to identify significant environmental issues deserving of study, but also to deemphasize insignificant issues, narrowing the scope of the environmental impact statement process accordingly (§ 1501.7).

(h) Summarizing the environmental impact statement (§ 1502.12) and circulating the summary instead of the entire environmental impact statement if the latter is unusually long (§ 1502.19).

(i) Using program, policy, or plan environmental impact statements and tiering from statements of broad scope to those of narrower scope, to eliminate repetitive discussions of the same issues (§§ 1502.4 and 1502.20).

(j) Incorporating by reference (§ 1502.21).

(k) Integrating NEPA requirements with other environmental review and consultation requirements (§ 1502.25).

(*l*) Requiring comments to be as specific as possible (§ 1503.3).

(m) Attaching and circulating only changes to the draft environmental impact statement, rather than rewriting and circulating the entire statement when changes are minor (§ 1503.4(c)).

(n) Eliminating duplication with State and local procedures, by providing for joint preparation (§ 1506.2), and with other Federal procedures, by providing that an agency may adopt appropriate environmental documents prepared by another agency (§ 1506.3).

(*o*) Combining environmental documents with other documents (§ 1506.4).

(p) Using categorical exclusions to define categories of actions which do not individually or cumulatively have a significant effect on the human environment and which are therefore exempt from requirements to prepare an environmental impact statement (§ 1508.4).

(q) Using a finding of no significant impact when an action not otherwise excluded will not have a significant effect on the human environment and is therefore exempt from requirements to prepare an environmental impact statement (§ 1508.13).

[43 Fed. Reg. 55990 (Nov. 29, 1978); 44 Fed. Reg. 873 (Jan. 3, 1979).]

§ 1500.5 Reducing delay.

Agencies shall reduce delay by:

(a) Integrating the NEPA process into early planning (§ 1501.2).

(b) Emphasizing interagency cooperation before the environmental impact statement is prepared, rather than submission of adversary comments on a completed document (§ 1501.6).

(c) Insuring the swift and fair resolution of lead agency disputes (§ 1501.5).

(d) Using the scoping process for an early identification of what are and what are not the real issues (§ 1501.7).

(e) Establishing appropriate time limits for the environmental impact statement process (§§ 1501.7(b)(2) and 1501.8).

(f) Preparing environmental impact statements early in the process (§ 1502.5).

(g) Integrating NEPA requirements with other environmental review and consultation requirements (§ 1502.25).

(h) Eliminating duplication with State and local procedures by providing for joint preparation (§ 1506.2) and with other Federal procedures by providing that an agency may adopt appropriate environmental documents prepared by another agency (§ 1506.3).

(i) Combining environmental documents with other documents (§ 1506.4).

(j) Using accelerated procedures for proposals for legislation (§ 1506.8).

(k) Using categorical exclusions to define categories of actions which do not individually or cumulatively have a significant effect on the human environment (§ 1508.4) and which are therefore exempt from requirements to prepare an environmental impact statement.

(*l*) Using a finding of no significant impact when an action not otherwise excluded will not have a significant effect on the human environment (§ 1508.13) and is therefore exempt from requirements to prepare an environmental impact statement.

§ 1500.6 Agency authority.

Each agency shall interpret the provisions of the Act as a supplement to its existing authority and as a mandate to view traditional policies and missions in the light of the Act's national environmental objectives. Agencies shall review their policies, procedures, and regulations accordingly and revise them as necessary to insure full compliance with the purposes and provisions of the Act. The phrase "to the fullest extent possible" in section 102 means that each agency of the Federal Government shall comply with that section unless existing law applicable to the agency's operations expressly prohibits or makes compliance impossible.

PART 1501—NEPA AND AGENCY PLANNING

Sec.

Authority: NEPA, the Environmental Quality Improvement Act of 1970, as amended (42 U.S.C. 4371 et seq.), Sec. 309 of the Clean Air Act, as amended (42 U.S.C. 7609, and Executive Order 11514, Mar. 5, 1970, as amended by Executive Order 11991, May 24, 1977).

Source: 43 Fed. Reg. 55992 (Nov. 29, 1978), unless otherwise noted.

§ 1501.1 Purpose.

The purposes of this part include:

(a) Integrating the NEPA process into early planning to insure appropriate consideration of NEPA's policies and to eliminate delay.

(b) Emphasizing cooperative consultation among agencies before the environmental impact statement is prepared rather than submission of adversary comments on a completed document.

(c) Providing for the swift and fair resolution of lead agency disputes.

(d) Identifying at an early stage the significant environmental issues deserving of study and deemphasizing insignificant issues, narrowing the scope of the environmental impact statement accordingly.

(e) Providing a mechanism for putting appropriate time limits on the environmental impact statement process.

§ 1501.2 Apply NEPA early in the process.

Agencies shall integrate the NEPA process with other planning at the earliest possible time to insure that planning and decisions reflect environmental values, to avoid delays later in the process, and to head off potential conflicts. Each agency shall:

(a) Comply with the mandate of section 102(2)(A) to "utilize a systematic, interdisciplinary approach which will insure the integrated use of the natural and social sciences and the environmental design arts in planning and in decisionmaking which may have an impact on man's environment," as specified by § 1507.2.

(b) Identify environmental effects and values in adequate detail so they can be compared to economic and technical analyses. Environmental documents and appropriate analyses shall be circulated and reviewed at the same time as other planning documents.

(c) Study, develop, and describe appropriate alternatives to recommended courses of action in any proposal which involves unresolved conflicts concerning alternative uses of available resources as provided by section 102(2)(E) of the Act.

(d) Provide for cases where actions are planned by private applicants or other non-Federal entities before Federal involvement so that:

(1) Policies or designated staff are available to advise potential applicants of studies or other information foreseeably required for later Federal action.

(2) The Federal agency consults early with appropriate State and local agencies and Indian tribes and with interested private persons and organizations when its own involvement is reasonably foreseeable.

(3) The Federal agency commences its NEPA process at the earliest possible time.

§ 1501.3 When to prepare an environmental assessment.

(a) Agencies shall prepare an environmental assessment (§ 1508.9) when necessary under the procedures adopted by individual agencies to supplement these regulations as described in § 1507.3. An assessment is not necessary if the agency has decided to prepare an environmental impact statement.

(b) Agencies may prepare an environmental assessment on any action at any time in order to assist agency planning and decisionmaking.

§ 1501.4 Whether to prepare an environmental impact statement.

In determining whether to prepare an environmental impact statement the Federal agency shall:

(a) Determine under its procedures supplementing these regulations (described in § 1507.3) whether the proposal is one which:

(1) Normally requires an environmental impact statement, or

(2) Normally does not require either an environmental impact statement or an environmental assessment (categorical exclusion).

(b) If the proposed action is not covered by paragraph (a) of this section, prepare an environmental assessment (§ 1508.9). The agency shall involve environmental agencies, applicants, and the public, to the extent practicable, in preparing assessments required by § 1508.9(a)(1).

(c) Based on the environmental assessment make its determination whether to prepare an environmental impact statement.

(d) Commence the scoping process (§ 1501.7), if the agency will prepare an environmental impact statement.

(e) Prepare a finding of no significant impact (§ 1508.13), if the agency determines on the basis of the environmental assessment not to prepare a statement.

(1) The agency shall make the finding of no significant impact available to the affected public as specified in § 1506.6.

(2) In certain limited circumstances, which the agency may cover in its procedures under § 1507.3, the agency shall make the finding of no significant impact available for public review (including State and areawide clearinghouses) for 30 days before the agency makes its final determination whether to prepare an environmental impact statement and before the action may begin. The circumstances are:

(i) The proposed action is, or is closely similar to, one which normally requires the preparation of an environmental impact statement under the procedures adopted by the agency pursuant to § 1507.3, or

(ii) The nature of the proposed action is one without precedent.

§ 1501.5 Lead agencies.

(a) A lead agency shall supervise the preparation of an environmental impact statement if more than one Federal agency either:

(1) Proposes or is involved in the same action; or

(2) Is involved in a group of actions directly related to each other because of their functional interdependence or geographical proximity.

(b) Federal, State, or local agencies, including at least one Federal agency, may act as joint lead agencies to prepare an environmental impact statement (§ 1506.2).

(c) If an action falls within the provisions of paragraph (a) of this section the potential lead agencies shall determine by letter or memorandum which agency shall be the lead agency and which shall be cooperating agencies. The agencies shall resolve the lead agency question so as not to cause delay. If there is disagreement among the agencies, the following factors (which are listed in order of descending importance) shall determine lead agency designation:

(1) Magnitude of agency's involvement.

(2) Project approval/disapproval authority.

(3) Expertise concerning the action's environmental effects.

(4) Duration of agency's involvement.

(5) Sequence of agency's involvement.

(d) Any Federal agency, or any State or local agency or private person substantially affected by the absence of lead agency designation, may make a written request to the potential lead agencies that a lead agency be designated.

(e) If Federal agencies are unable to agree on which agency will be the lead agency or if the procedure described in paragraph (c) of this section has not resulted within 45 days in a lead agency designation, any of the agencies or persons concerned may file a request with the Council asking it to determine which Federal agency shall be the lead agency.

A copy of the request shall be transmitted to each potential lead agency. The request shall consist of:

(1) A precise description of the nature and extent of the proposed action.

(2) A detailed statement of why each potential lead agency should or should not be the lead agency under the criteria specified in paragraph (c) of this section.

(f) A response may be filed by any potential lead agency concerned within 20 days after a request is filed with the Council. The Council shall determine as soon as possible but not later than 20 days after receiving the request and all responses to it which Federal agency shall be the lead agency and which other Federal agencies shall be cooperating agencies.

[43 Fed. Reg. 55992 (Nov. 29, 1978); 44 Fed. Reg. 873 (Jan. 3, 1979).]

§ 1501.6 Cooperating agencies.

The purpose of this section is to emphasize agency cooperation early in the NEPA process. Upon request of the lead agency, any other Federal agency which has jurisdiction by law shall be a cooperating agency. In addition any other Federal agency which has special expertise with respect to any environmental issue, which should be addressed in the statement may be a cooperating agency upon request of the lead agency. An agency may request the lead agency to designate it a cooperating agency.

(a) The lead agency shall:

(1) Request the participation of each cooperating agency in the NEPA process at the earliest possible time.

(2) Use the environmental analysis and proposals of cooperating agencies with jurisdiction by law or special expertise, to the maximum extent possible consistent with its responsibility as lead agency.

(3) Meet with a cooperating agency at the latter's request.

(b) Each cooperating agency shall:

(1) Participate in the NEPA process at the earliest possible time.

(2) Participate in the scoping process (described below in § 1501.7).

(3) Assume on request of the lead agency responsibility for developing information and preparing environmental analyses including portions of the environmental impact statement concerning which the cooperating agency has special expertise.

(4) Make available staff support at the lead agency's request to enhance the latter's interdisciplinary capability.

(5) Normally use its own funds. The lead agency shall, to the extent available funds permit, fund those major activities or analyses it requests from cooperating agencies. Potential lead agencies shall include such funding requirements in their budget requests.

(c) A cooperating agency may in response to a lead agency's request for assistance in preparing the environmental impact statement (described in paragraph (b)(3), (4), or (5) of this section) reply that other program commitments preclude any involvement or the degree of involvement requested in the action that is the subject of the environmental impact statement. A copy of this reply shall be submitted to the Council.

§ 1501.7 Scoping.

There shall be an early and open process for determining the scope of issues to be addressed and for identifying the significant issues related to a proposed action. This process shall be termed scoping. As soon as practicable after its decision to prepare an environmental impact statement and before the scoping process the lead agency shall publish a notice of intent (§ 1508.22) in the Federal Register except as provided in § 1507.3(e).

(a) As part of the scoping process the lead agency shall:

(1) Invite the participation of affected Federal, State, and local agencies, any affected Indian tribe, the proponent of the action, and other interested persons (including those who might not be in accord with the action on environmental grounds), unless there is a limited exception under § 1507.3(c). An agency may give notice in accordance with § 1506.6.

(2) Determine the scope (§ 1508.25) and the significant issues to be analyzed in depth in the environmental impact statement.

(3) Identify and eliminate from detailed study the issues which are not significant or which have been covered by prior environmental review (§ 1506.3), narrowing the discussion of these issues in the statement to a brief presentation of why they will not have a significant effect on the human environment or providing a reference to their coverage elsewhere.

(4) Allocate assignments for preparation of the environmental impact statement among the lead and cooperating agencies, with the lead agency retaining responsibility for the statement.

(5) Indicate any public environmental assessments and other environmental impact statements which are being or will be prepared that are related to but are not part of the scope of the impact statement under consideration.

(6) Identify other environmental review and consultation requirements so the lead and cooperating agencies may prepare other required analyses and studies concurrently with, and integrated with, the environmental impact statement as provided in § 1502.25.

(7) Indicate the relationship between the timing of the preparation of environmental analyses and the agency's tentative planning and decisionmaking schedule.

(b) As part of the scoping process the lead agency may:

(1) Set page limits on environmental documents (§ 1502.7).

(2) Set time limits (§ 1501.8).

(3) Adopt procedures under § 1507.3 to combine its environmental assessment process with its scoping process.

(4) Hold an early scoping meeting or meetings which may be integrated with any other early planning meeting the agency has. Such a scoping meeting will often be appropriate when the impacts of a particular action are confined to specific sites.

(c) An agency shall revise the determinations made under paragraphs (a) and (b) of this section if substantial changes are made later in the proposed action, or if significant new circumstances or information arise which bear on the proposal or its impacts.

§ 1501.8 Time limits.

Although the Council has decided that prescribed universal time limits for the entire NEPA process are too inflexible, Federal agencies are encouraged to set time limits appropriate to individual actions (consistent with the time intervals required by § 1506.10). When multiple agencies are involved the reference to agency below means lead agency.

(a) The agency shall set time limits if an applicant for the proposed action requests them: *Provided,* That the limits are consistent with the purposes of NEPA and other essential considerations of national policy.

(b) The agency may:

(1) Consider the following factors in determining time limits:

(i) Potential for environmental harm.

(ii) Size of the proposed action.

(iii) State of the art of analytic techniques.

(iv) Degree of public need for the proposed action, including the consequences of delay.

(v) Number of persons and agencies affected.

(vi) Degree to which relevant information is known and if not known the time required for obtaining it.

(vii) Degree to which the action is controversial.

(viii) Other time limits imposed on the agency by law, regulations, or executive order.

(2) Set overall time limits or limits for each constituent part of the NEPA process, which may include:

(i) Decision on whether to prepare an environmental impact statement (if not already decided).

(ii) Determination of the scope of the environmental impact statement.

(iii) Preparation of the draft environmental impact statement.

(iv) Review of any comments on the draft environmental impact statement from the public and agencies.

(v) Preparation of the final environmental impact statement.

(vi) Review of any comments on the final environmental impact statement.

(vii) Decision on the action based in part on the environmental impact statement.

(3) Designate a person (such as the project manager or a person in the agency's office with NEPA responsibilities) to expedite the NEPA process.

(c) State or local agencies or members of the public may request a Federal Agency to set time limits.

PART 1502—ENVIRONMENTAL IMPACT STATEMENT

Sec.

Authority: NEPA, the Environmental Quality Improvement Act of 1970, as amended (42 U.S.C. 4371 et seq.), Sec. 309 of the Clean Air Act, as amended (42 U.S.C. 7609), and Executive Order 11514 (Mar. 5, 1970, as amended by Executive Order 11991, May 24, 1977).

Source: 43 Fed. Reg. 55994 (Nov. 29, 1978), unless otherwise noted.

§ 1502.1 Purpose.

The primary purpose of an environmental impact statement is to serve as an action-forcing device to insure that the policies and goals defined in the Act are infused into the ongoing programs and actions of the Federal Government. It shall provide full and fair discussion of significant environmental impacts and shall inform decisionmakers and the public of the reasonable alternatives which would avoid or minimize adverse impacts or enhance the quality of the human environment. Agencies shall focus on significant environmental issues and alternatives and shall reduce paperwork and the accumulation of extraneous background data. Statements shall be concise, clear, and to the point, and shall be supported by evidence that the agency has made the necessary environmental analyses. An environmental impact statement is more than a disclosure document. It shall be used by Federal officials in conjunction with other relevant material to plan actions and make decisions.

§ 1502.2 Implementation.

To achieve the purposes set forth in § 1502.1 agencies shall prepare environmental impact statements in the following manner:

(a) Environmental impact statements shall be analytic rather than encyclopedic.

(b) Impacts shall be discussed in proportion to their significance. There shall be only brief discussion of other than significant issues. As in a finding of no significant impact, there should be only enough discussion to show why more study is not warranted.

(c) Environmental impact statements shall be kept concise and shall be no longer than absolutely necessary to comply with NEPA and with these regulations. Length should vary first with potential environmental problems and then with project size.

(d) Environmental impact statements shall state how alternatives considered in it and decisions based on it will or will not achieve the requirements of sections 101 and 102(1) of the Act and other environmental laws and policies.

(e) The range of alternatives discussed in environmental impact statements shall encompass those to be considered by the ultimate agency decisionmaker.

(f) Agencies shall not commit resources prejudicing selection of alternatives before making a final decision (§ 1506.1).

(g) Environmental impact statements shall serve as the means of assessing the environmental impact of proposed agency actions, rather than justifying decisions already made.

§ 1502.3 Statutory requirements for statements.

As required by sec. 102(2)(C) of NEPA environmental impact statements (§ 1508.11) are to be included in every recommendation or report.

On proposals (§ 1508.23).

For legislation and (§ 1508.17).

Other major Federal actions (§ 1508.18).

Significantly (§ 1508.27).

Affecting (§§ 1508.3, 1508.8).

The quality of the human environment (§ 1508.14).

§ 1502.4 Major Federal actions requiring the preparation of environmental impact statements.

(a) Agencies shall make sure the proposal which is the subject of an environmental impact statement is properly defined. Agencies shall use the criteria for scope (§ 1508.25) to determine which proposal(s) shall be the subject of a particular statement. Proposals or parts of proposals which are related to each other closely enough to be, in effect, a single course of action shall be evaluated in a single impact statement.

(b) Environmental impact statements may be prepared, and are sometimes required, for broad Federal actions such as the adoption of new agency programs or regulations (§ 1508.18). Agencies shall prepare statements on broad actions so that they are relevant to policy and are timed to coincide with meaningful points in agency planning and decisionmaking.

(c) When preparing statements on broad actions (including proposals by more than one agency), agencies may find it useful to evaluate the proposal(s) in one of the following ways:

(1) Geographically, including actions occurring in the same general location, such as body of water, region, or metropolitan area.

(2) Generically, including actions which have relevant similarities, such as common timing, impacts, alternatives, methods of implementation, media, or subject matter.

(3) By stage of technological development including federal or federally assisted research, development or demonstration programs for new technologies which, if applied, could significantly affect the quality of the human environment. Statements shall be prepared on such programs and shall be available before the program has reached a stage of investment or commitment to implementation likely to determine subsequent development or restrict later alternatives.

(d) Agencies shall as appropriate employ scoping (§ 1501.7), tiering (§ 1502.20), and other methods listed in §§ 1500.4 and 1500.5 to relate broad and narrow actions and to avoid duplication and delay.

§ 1502.5 Timing.

An agency shall commence preparation of an environmental impact statement as close as possible to the time the agency is developing or is presented with a proposal (§ 1508.23) so that preparation can be completed in time for the final statement to be included in any recommendation or report on the proposal. The statement shall be prepared early enough so that it can serve practically as an important contribution to the decisionmaking process and will not be used to rationalize or justify decisions already made (§§ 1500.2(c), 1501.2, and 1502.2). For instance:

(a) For projects directly undertaken by Federal agencies the environmental impact statement shall be prepared at the feasibility analysis (go-no go) stage and may be supplemented at a later stage if necessary.

(b) For applications to the agency appropriate environmental assessments or statements shall be commenced no later than immediately after the application is received. Federal agencies are encouraged to begin preparation of such assessments or statements earlier, preferably jointly with applicable State or local agencies.

(c) For adjudication, the final environmental impact statement shall normally precede the final staff recommendation and that portion of the public hearing related to the impact study. In appropriate circumstances the statement may follow preliminary hearings designed to gather information for use in the statements.

(d) For informal rulemaking the draft environmental impact statement shall normally accompany the proposed rule.

§ 1502.6 Interdisciplinary preparation.

Environmental impact statements shall be prepared using an inter-disciplinary approach which will insure the integrated use of the natural and social sciences and the environmental design arts (section 102(2)(A) of the Act). The disciplines of the preparers shall be appropriate to the scope and issues identified in the scoping process (§ 1501.7).

§ 1502.7 Page limits.

The text of final environmental impact statements (e.g., paragraphs (d) through (g) of § 1502.10) shall normally be less than 150 pages and for proposals of unusual scope or complexity shall normally be less than 300 pages.

§ 1502.8 Writing.

Environmental impact statements shall be written in plain language and may use appropriate graphics so that decisionmakers and the public can readily understand them. Agencies should employ writers of clear prose or editors to write, review, or edit statements, which will be based upon the analysis and supporting data from the natural and social sciences and the environmental design arts.

§ 1502.9 Draft, final, and supplemental statements.

Except for proposals for legislation as provided in § 1506.8 environmental impact statements shall be prepared in two stages and may be supplemented.

(a) Draft environmental impact statements shall be prepared in accordance with the scope decided upon in the scoping process. The lead agency shall work with the cooperating agencies and shall obtain comments as required in Part 1503 of this chapter. The draft statement must fulfill and satisfy to the fullest extent possible the requirements established for final statements in section 102(2)(C) of the Act. If a draft statement is so inadequate as to preclude meaningful analysis, the agency shall prepare and circulate a revised draft of the appropriate portion. The agency shall make every effort to disclose and discuss at appropriate points in the draft statement all major points of view on the environmental impacts of the alternatives including the proposed action.

(b) Final environmental impact statements shall respond to comments as required in Part 1503 of this chapter. The agency shall discuss at appropriate points in the final statement any responsible opposing view which was not adequately discussed in the draft statement and shall indicate the agency's response to the issues raised.

(c) Agencies:

(1) Shall prepare supplements to either draft or final environmental impact statements if:

(i) The agency makes substantial changes in the proposed action that are relevant to environmental concerns; or

(ii) There are significant new circumstances or information relevant to environmental concerns and bearing on the proposed action or its impacts.

(2) May also prepare supplements when the agency determines that the purposes of the Act will be furthered by doing so.

(3) Shall adopt procedures for introducing a supplement into its formal administrative record, if such a record exists.

(4) Shall prepare, circulate, and file a supplement to a statement in the same fashion (exclusive of scoping) as a draft and final statement unless alternative procedures are approved by the Council.

§ 1502.10 Recommended format.

Agencies shall use a format for environmental impact statements which will encourage good analysis and clear presentation of the alternatives including the proposed action. The following standard format for environmental impact statements should be followed unless the agency determines that there is a compelling reason to do otherwise:

(a) Cover sheet.

(b) Summary.

(c) Table of contents.

(d) Purpose of and need for action.

(e) Alternatives including proposed action (sections 102(2)(C)(iii) and 102(2)(E) of the Act).

(f) Affected environment.

(g) Environmental consequences (especially sections 102(2)(C)(i), (ii), (iv), and (v) of the Act).

(h) List of preparers.

(i) List of Agencies, Organizations, and persons to whom copies of the statement are sent.

(j) Index.

(k) Appendices (if any).

If a different format is used, it shall include paragraphs (a), (b), (c), (h), (i), and (j), of this section and shall include the substance of paragraphs (d), (e), (f), (g), and (k) of this section, as further described in §§ 1502.11 through 1502.18, in any appropriate format.

§ 1502.11 Cover sheet.

The cover sheet shall not exceed one page. It shall include:

(a) A list of the responsible agencies including the lead agency and any cooperating agencies.

(b) The title of the proposed action that is the subject of the statement (and if appropriate the titles of related cooperating agency actions), together with the State(s) and county(ies)(or other jurisdiction if applicable) where the action is located.

(c) The name, address, and telephone number of the person at the agency who can supply further information.

(d) A designation of the statement as a draft, final, or draft or final supplement.

(e) A one paragraph abstract of the statement.

(f) The date by which comments must be received (computed in cooperation with EPA under § 1506.10).

The information required by this section may be entered on Standard Form 424 (in items 4, 6, 7, 10, and 18).

§ 1502.12 Summary.

Each environmental impact statement shall contain a summary which adequately and accurately summarizes the statement. The summary shall stress the major conclusions, areas of controversy (including issues raised by agencies and the public), and the issues to be resolved (including the choice among alternatives). The summary will normally not exceed 15 pages.

§ 1502.13 Purpose and need.

The statement shall briefly specify the underlying purpose and need to which the agency is responding in proposing the alternatives including the proposed action.

§ 1502.14 Alternatives including the proposed action.

This section is the heart of the environmental impact statement. Based on the information and analysis presented in the sections on the Affected Environment (§ 1502.15) and the Environmental Consequences (§ 1502.16), it should present the environmental impacts of the proposal and the alternatives in comparative form, thus sharply defining the issues and providing a clear basis for choice among options by the decisionmaker and the public. In this section agencies shall:

(a) Rigorously explore and objectively evaluate all reasonable alternatives, and for alternatives which were eliminated from detailed study, briefly discuss the reasons for their having been eliminated.

(b) Devote substantial treatment to each alternative considered in detail including the proposed action so that reviewers may evaluate their comparative merits.

(c) Include reasonable alternatives not within the jurisdiction of the lead agency.

(d) Include the alternative of no action.

(e) Identify the agency's preferred alternative or alternatives, if one or more exists, in the draft statement and identify such alternative in the final statement unless another law prohibits the expression of such a preference.

(f) Include appropriate mitigation measures not already included in the proposed action or alternatives.

§ 1502.15 Affected environment.

The environmental impact statement shall succinctly describe the environment of the area(s) to be affected or created by the alternatives under consideration. The descriptions shall be no longer than is necessary to understand the effects of the alternatives. Data and analyses in a statement shall be commensurate with the importance of the impact, with less important material summarized, consolidated, or simply referenced. Agencies shall avoid useless bulk in statements and shall concentrate effort and attention on important issues. Verbose descriptions of the affected environment are themselves no measure of the adequacy of an environmental impact statement.

§ 1502.16 Environmental consequences.

This section forms the scientific and analytic basis for the comparisons under § 1502.14. It shall consolidate the discussions of those elements required by sections 102(2)(C)(i), (ii), (iv), and (v) of NEPA which are within the scope of the statement and as much of section 102(2)(C)(iii) as is necessary to support the comparisons. The discussion will include the environmental impacts of the alternatives including the proposed action, any adverse environmental effects which cannot be avoided should the proposal be implemented, the relationship between short-term uses of man's environment and the maintenance and enhancement of long-term productivity, and any irreversible or irretrievable commitments of resources which would be involved in the proposal should it be implemented. This section should not duplicate discussions in § 1502.14. It shall include discussions of:

(a) Direct effects and their significance (§ 1508.8).

(b) Indirect effects and their significance (§ 1508.8).

(c) Possible conflicts between the proposed action and the objectives of Federal, regional, State, and local (and in the case of a reservation, Indian tribe) land use plans, policies and controls for the area concerned. (See § 1506.2(d).)

(d) The environmental effects of alternatives including the proposed action. The comparisons under § 1502.14 will be based on this discussion.

(e) Energy requirements and conservation potential of various alternatives and mitigation measures.

(f) Natural or depletable resource requirements and conservation potential of various alternatives and mitigation measures.

(g) Urban quality, historic and cultural resources, and the design of the built environment, including the reuse and conservation potential of various alternatives and mitigation measures.

(h) Means to mitigate adverse environmental impacts (if not fully covered under § 1502.14(f)).

[43 Fed. Reg. 55994 (Nov. 29, 1978); 44 Fed. Reg. 873 (Jan. 3, 1979).]

§ 1502.17 List of preparers.

The environmental impact statement shall list the names, together with their qualifications (expertise, experience, professional disciplines), of the persons who were primarily responsible for preparing the environmental impact statement or significant background papers, including basic components of the statement (§§ 1502.6 and 1502.8). Where possible the persons who are responsible for a particular analysis, including analyses in background papers, shall be identified. Normally the list will not exceed two pages.

§ 1502.18 Appendix.

If an agency prepares an appendix to an environmental impact statement the appendix shall:

(a) Consist of material prepared in connection with an environmental impact statement (as distinct from material which is not so prepared and which is incorporated by reference (§ 1502.21)).

(b) Normally consist of material which substantiates any analysis fundamental to the impact statement.

(c) Normally be analytic and relevant to the decision to be made.

(d) Be circulated with the environmental impact statement or be readily available on request.

§ 1502.19 Circulation of the environmental impact statement.

Agencies shall circulate the entire draft and final environmental impact statements except for certain appendices as provided in § 1502.18(d) and unchanged statements as provided in § 1503.4(c). However, if the statement is unusually long, the agency may circulate the summary instead, except that the entire statement shall be furnished to:

(a) Any Federal agency which has jurisdiction by law or special expertise with respect to any environmental impact involved and any appropriate Federal, State or local agency authorized to develop and enforce environmental standards.

(b) The applicant, if any.

(c) Any person, organization, or agency requesting the entire environmental impact statement.

(d) In the case of a final environmental impact statement any person, organization, or agency which submitted substantive comments on the draft.

If the agency circulates the summary and thereafter receives a timely request for the entire statement and for additional time to comment, the time for that requestor only shall be extended by at least 15 days beyond the minimum period.

§ 1502.20 Tiering.

Agencies are encouraged to tier their environmental impact statements to eliminate repetitive discussions of the same issues and to focus on the actual issues ripe for decision at each level of environmental review (§ 1508.28). Whenever a broad environmental impact statement has been prepared (such as a program or policy statement) and a subsequent statement or environmental assessment is then prepared on an action included within the entire program or policy (such as a site specific action) the subsequent statement or environmental assessment need only summarize the issues discussed in the broader statement and incorporate discussions from the broader statement by reference and shall concentrate on the issues specific to the subsequent action. The subsequent document shall state where the earlier document is available. Tiering may also be appropriate for different stages of actions. (Section 1508.28).

§ 1502.21 Incorporation by reference.

Agencies shall incorporate material into an environmental impact statement by reference when the effect will be to cut down on bulk without impeding agency and public review of the action. The incorporated material shall be cited in the statement and its content briefly described. No material may be incorporated by reference unless it is reasonably available for inspection by potentially interested persons within the time allowed for comment. Material based on proprietary data which is itself not available for review and comment shall not be incorporated by reference.

§ 1502.22 Incomplete or unavailable information.

When an agency is evaluating reasonably foreseeable significant adverse effects on the human environment in an environmental impact statement and there is incomplete or unavailable information, the agency shall always make clear that such information is lacking.

(a) If the incomplete information relevant to reasonably foreseeable significant adverse impacts is essential to a reasoned choice among alternatives and the overall costs of obtaining it are not exorbitant, the agency shall include the information in the environmental impact statement.

(b) If the information relevant to reasonably foreseeable significant adverse impacts cannot be obtained because the overall costs of obtaining it are exorbitant or the means to obtain it are not known, the agency shall include within the environmental impact statement:

(1) A statement that such information is incomplete or unavailable;

(2) a statement of the relevance of the incomplete or unavailable information to evaluating reasonably foreseeable significant adverse impacts on the human environment;

(3) a summary of existing credible scientific evidence which is relevant to evaluating the reasonably foreseeable significant adverse impacts on the human environment, and

(4) the agency's evaluation of such impacts based upon theoretical approaches or research methods generally accepted in the scientific community. For the purposes of this section, "reasonably foreseeable" includes impacts which have catastrophic consequences, even if their probability of occurrence is low, provided that the analysis of the impacts is supported by credible scientific evidence, is not based on pure conjecture, and is within the rule of reason.

(c) The amended regulation will be applicable to all environmental impact statements for which a Notice of Intent (40 CFR 1508.22) is published in the Federal Register on or after May 27, 1986. For environmental impact statements in progress, agencies may choose to comply with the requirements of either the original or amended regulation.

[51 Fed. Reg. 15625 (April 25, 1986).]

§ 1502.23 Cost-benefit analysis.

If a cost-benefit analysis relevant to the choice among environmentally different alternatives is being considered for the proposed action, it shall be incorporated by reference or appended to the statement as an aid in evaluating the environmental consequences. To assess the adequacy of compliance with section 102(2)(B) of the Act the statement shall, when a cost-benefit analysis is prepared, discuss the relationship between that analysis and any analyses of unquantified environmental impacts, values, and amenities. For purposes of complying with the Act, the weighing of the merits and drawbacks of the various alternatives need not be displayed in a monetary cost-benefit analysis and should not be when there are important qualitative considerations. In any event, an environmental impact statement should at least indicate those considerations, including factors not related to environmental quality, which are likely to be relevant and important to a decision.

§ 1502.24 Methodology and scientific accuracy.

Agencies shall insure the professional integrity, including scientific integrity, of the discussions and analyses in environmental impact statements. They shall identify any methodologies used and shall make explicit reference by footnote to the scientific and other sources relied upon for conclusions in the statement. An agency may place discussion of methodology in an appendix.

§ 1502.25 Environmental review and consultation requirements.

(a) To the fullest extent possible, agencies shall prepare draft environmental impact statements concurrently with and integrated with environmental impact analyses and related surveys and studies required by the Fish and Wildlife Coordination Act (16 U.S.C. 661 et seq.), the National Historic Preservation Act of 1966 (16 U.S.C. 470 et seq.), the Endangered Species Act of 1973 (16 U.S.C. 1531 et seq.), and other environmental review laws and executive orders.

(b) The draft environmental impact statement shall list all Federal permits, licenses, and other entitlements which must be obtained in implementing the proposal. If it is uncertain whether a Federal permit, license, or other entitlement is necessary, the draft environmental impact statement shall so indicate.

PART 1503—COMMENTING

Sec.

Authority: NEPA, the Environmental Quality Improvement Act of 1970, as amended (42 U.S.C. 4371 et seq.), sec. 309 of the Clean Air Act, as amended (42 U.S.C. 7609), and Executive Order 11514 (Mar. 5, 1970, as amended by Executive Order 11991, May 24, 1977).

Source: 43 Fed. Reg. 55997 (Nov. 29, 1978).

§ 1503.1 Inviting comments.

(a) After preparing a draft environmental impact statement and before preparing a final environmental impact statement the agency shall:

(1) Obtain the comments of any Federal agency which has jurisdiction by law or special expertise with respect to any environmental impact involved or which is authorized to develop and enforce environmental standards.

(2) Request the comments of:

(i) Appropriate State and local agencies which are authorized to develop and enforce environmental standards;

(ii) Indian tribes, when the effects may be on a reservation; and

(iii) Any agency which has requested that it receive statements on actions of the kind proposed.

Office of Management and Budget Circular A-95 (Revised), through its system of clearinghouses, provides a means of securing the views of State and local environmental agencies. The clearinghouses may be used, by mutual agreement of the lead agency and the clearinghouse, for securing State and local reviews of the draft environmental impact statements.

(3) Request comments from the applicant, if any.

(4) Request comments from the public, affirmatively soliciting comments from those persons or organizations who may be interested or affected.

(b) An agency may request comments on a final environmental impact statement before the decision is finally made. In any case other agencies or persons may make comments before the final decision unless a different time is provided under § 1506.10.

§ 1503.2 Duty to comment.

Federal agencies with jurisdiction by law or special expertise with respect to any environmental impact involved and agencies which are authorized to develop and enforce environmental standards shall comment on statements within their jurisdiction, expertise, or authority. Agencies shall comment within the time period specified for comment in § 1506.10. A Federal agency may reply that it has no comment. If a cooperating agency is satisfied that its views are adequately reflected in the environmental impact statement, it should reply that it has no comment.

§ 1503.3 Specificity of comments.

(a) Comments on an environmental impact statement or on a proposed action shall be as specific as possible and may address either the adequacy of the statement or the merits of the alternatives discussed or both.

(b) When a commenting agency criticizes a lead agency's predictive methodology, the commenting agency should describe the alternative methodology which it prefers and why.

(c) A cooperating agency shall specify in its comments whether it needs additional information to fulfill other applicable environmental reviews or consultation requirements and what information it needs. In particular, it shall specify any additional information it needs to comment adequately on the draft statement's analysis of significant site-specific effects associated with the granting or approving by that cooperating agency of necessary Federal permits, licenses, or entitlements.

(d) When a cooperating agency with jurisdiction by law objects to or expresses reservations about the proposal on grounds of environmental impacts, the agency expressing the objection or reservation shall specify the mitigation measures it considers necessary to allow the agency to grant or approve applicable permit, license, or related requirements or concurrences.

§ 1503.4 Response to comments.

(a) An agency preparing a final environmental impact statement shall assess and consider comments both individually and collectively, and shall respond by one or more of the means listed below, stating its response in the final statement. Possible responses are to:

(1) Modify alternatives including the proposed action.

(2) Develop and evaluate alternatives not previously given serious consideration by the agency.

(3) Supplement, improve, or modify its analyses.

(4) Make factual corrections.

(5) Explain why the comments do not warrant further agency response, citing the sources, authorities, or reasons which support the agency's position and, if appropriate, indicate those circumstances which would trigger agency reappraisal or further response.

(b) All substantive comments received on the draft statement (or summaries thereof where the response has been exceptionally voluminous), should be attached to the final statement whether or not the comment is thought to merit individual discussion by the agency in the text of the statement.

(c) If changes in response to comments are minor and are confined to the responses described in paragraphs (a)(4) and (5) of this section, agencies may write them on errata sheets and attach them to the statement instead of rewriting the draft statement. In such cases only the comments, the responses, and the changes and not the final statement need be circulated (§ 1502.19). The entire document with a new cover sheet shall be filed as the final statement (§ 1506.9).

PART 1504—PREDECISION REFERRALS TO THE COUNCIL OF PROPOSED FEDERAL ACTIONS DETERMINED TO BE ENVIRONMENTALLY UNSATISFACTORY

Sec.

Authority: NEPA, the Environmental Quality Improvement Act of 1970, as amended (42 U.S.C. 4371 et seq.), sec. 309 of the Clean Air Act, as amended (42 U.S.C. 7609), and Executive Order 11514 (Mar. 5, 1970, as amended by Executive Order 11991, May 24, 1977).

Source: 43 Fed. Reg. 55998 (Nov. 29, 1978), unless otherwise noted.

§ 1504.1 Purpose.

(a) This part establishes procedures for referring to the Council Federal interagency disagreements concerning proposed major Federal actions that might cause unsatisfactory environmental effects. It provides means for early resolution of such disagreements.

(b) Under section 309 of the Clean Air Act (42 U.S.C. 7609), the Administrator of the Environmental Protection Agency is directed to review and comment publicly on the environmental impacts of Federal activities, including actions for which environmental impact statements are prepared. If after this review the Administrator determines that the matter is "unsatisfactory from the standpoint of public health or welfare or environmental quality," section 309 directs that the matter be referred to the Council (hereafter "environmental referrals").

(c) Under section 102(2)(C) of the Act other Federal agencies may make similar reviews of environmental impact statements, including judgments on the acceptability of anticipated environmental impacts. These reviews must be made available to the President, the Council and the public.

§ 1504.2 Criteria for referral.

Environmental referrals should be made to the Council only after concerted, timely (as early as possible in the process), but unsuccessful attempts to resolve differences with the lead agency. In determining what environmental objections to the matter are appropriate to refer to the Council, an agency should weigh potential adverse environmental impacts, considering:

(a) Possible violation of national environmental standards or policies.

(b) Severity.

(c) Geographical scope.

(d) Duration.

(e) Importance as precedents.

(f) Availability of environmentally preferable alternatives.

§ 1504.3 Procedure for referrals and response.

(a) A Federal agency making the referral to the Council shall:

(1) Advise the lead agency at the earliest possible time that it intends to refer a matter to the Council unless a satisfactory agreement is reached.

(2) Include such advice in the referring agency's comments on the draft environmental impact statement, except when the statement does not contain adequate information to permit an assessment of the matter's environmental acceptability.

(3) Identify any essential information that is lacking and request that it be made available at the earliest possible time.

(4) Send copies of such advice to the Council.

(b) The referring agency shall deliver its referral to the Council not later than twenty-five (25) days after the final environmental impact statement has been made available to the Environmental Protection Agency, commenting agencies, and the public. Except when an extension of this period has been granted by the lead agency, the Council will not accept a referral after that date.

(c) The referral shall consist of:

(1) A copy of the letter signed by the head of the referring agency and delivered to the lead agency informing the lead agency of the referral and the reasons for it, and requesting that no action be taken to implement the matter until the Council acts upon the referral. The letter shall include a copy of the statement referred to in (c)(2) of this section.

(2) A statement supported by factual evidence leading to the conclusion that the matter is unsatisfactory from the standpoint of public health or welfare or environmental quality. The statement shall:

(i) Identify any material facts in controversy and incorporate (by reference if appropriate) agreed upon facts,

(ii) Identify any existing environmental requirements or policies which would be violated by the matter,

(iii) Present the reasons why the referring agency believes the matter is environmentally unsatisfactory,

(iv) Contain a finding by the agency whether the issue raised is of national importance because of the threat to national environmental resources or policies or for some other reason,

(v) Review the steps taken by the referring agency to bring its concerns to the attention of the lead agency at the earliest possible time, and

(vi) Give the referring agency's recommendations as to what mitigation alternative, further study, or other course of action (including abandonment of the matter) are necessary to remedy the situation.

(d) Not later than twenty-five (25) days after the referral to the Council the lead agency may deliver a response to the Council, and the referring agency. If the lead agency requests more time and gives assurance that the matter will not go forward in the interim, the Council may grant an extension. The response shall:

(1) Address fully the issues raised in the referral.

(2) Be supported by evidence.

(3) Give the lead agency's response to the referring agency's recommendations.

(e) Interested persons (including the applicant) may deliver their views in writing to the Council. Views in support of the referral should be delivered not later than the referral. Views in support of the response shall be delivered not later than the response.

(f) Not later than twenty-five (25) days after receipt of both the referral and any response or upon being informed that there will be no response (unless the lead agency agrees to a longer time), the Council may take one or more of the following actions:

(1) Conclude that the process of referral and response has successfully resolved the problem.

(2) Initiate discussions with the agencies with the objective of mediation with referring and lead agencies.

(3) Hold public meetings or hearings to obtain additional views and information.

(4) Determine that the issue is not one of national importance and request the referring and lead agencies to pursue their decision process.

(5) Determine that the issue should be further negotiated by the referring and lead agencies and is not appropriate for Council consideration until one or more heads of agencies report to the Council that the agencies' disagreements are irreconcilable.

(6) Publish its findings and recommendations (including where appropriate a finding that the submitted evidence does not support the position of an agency).

(7) When appropriate, submit the referral and the response together with the Council's recommendation to the President for action.

(g) The Council shall take no longer than 60 days to complete the actions specified in paragraph (f)(2), (3), or (5) of this section.

(h) When the referral involves an action required by statute to be determined on the record after opportunity for agency hearing, the referral shall be conducted in a manner consistent with 5 U.S.C. 557(d)(Administrative Procedure Act).

[43 Fed. Reg. 55998 (Nov. 29, 1978); 44 Fed. Reg. 873 (Jan. 3, 1979).]

PART 1505—NEPA AND AGENCY DECISIONMAKING

Sec.

Authority: NEPA, the Environmental Quality Improvement Act of 1970, as amended (42 U.S.C. 4371 et seq.), sec. 309 of the Clean Air Act, as amended (42 U.S.C. 7609), and Executive Order 11514 (Mar. 5, 1970, as amended by Executive Order 11991, May 24, 1977).

Source: 43 Fed. Reg. 55999 (Nov. 29, 1978), unless otherwise noted.

§ 1505.1 Agency decisionmaking procedures.

Agencies shall adopt procedures (§ 1507.3) to ensure that decisions are made in accordance with the policies and purposes of the Act. Such procedures shall include but not be limited to:

(a) Implementing procedures under section 102(2) to achieve the requirements of sections 101 and 102(1).

(b) Designating the major decision points for the agency's principal programs likely to have a significant effect on the human environment and assuring that the NEPA process corresponds with them.

(c) Requiring that relevant environmental documents, comments, and responses be part of the record in formal rulemaking or adjudicatory proceedings.

(d) Requiring that relevant environmental documents, comments, and responses accompany the proposal through existing agency review processes so that agency officials use the statement in making decisions.

(e) Requiring that the alternatives considered by the decisionmaker are encompassed by the range of alternatives discussed in the relevant environmental documents and that the decisionmaker consider the alternatives described in the environmental impact statement. If another decision document accompanies the relevant environmental documents to the decisionmaker, agencies are encouraged to make available to the public before the decision is made any part of that document that relates to the comparison of alternatives.

§ 1505.2 Record of decision in cases requiring environmental impact statements.

At the time of its decision (§ 1506.10) or, if appropriate, its recommendation to Congress, each agency shall prepare a concise public record of decision. The record, which may be integrated into any other record prepared by the agency, including that required by OMB Circular A-95 (Revised), part I, sections 6 (c) and (d), and part II, section 5(b)(4), shall:

(a) State what the decision was.

(b) Identify all alternatives considered by the agency in reaching its decision, specifying the alternative or alternatives which were considered to be environmentally preferable. An agency may discuss preferences among alternatives based on relevant factors including economic and technical considerations and agency statutory missions. An agency shall identify and discuss all such factors including any essential considerations of national policy which were balanced by the agency in making its decision and state how those considerations entered into its decision.

(c) State whether all practicable means to avoid or minimize environmental harm from the alternative selected have been adopted, and if not, why they were not. A monitoring and enforcement program shall be adopted and summarized where applicable for any mitigation.

§ 1505.3 Implementing the decision.

Agencies may provide for monitoring to assure that their decisions are carried out and should do so in important cases. Mitigation (§ 1505.2(c)) and other conditions established in the environmental impact statement or during its review and committed as part of the decision shall be implemented by the lead agency or other appropriate consenting agency. The lead agency shall:

(a) Include appropriate conditions in grants, permits or other approvals.

(b) Condition funding of actions on mitigation.

(c) Upon request, inform cooperating or commenting agencies on progress in carrying out mitigation measures which they have proposed and which were adopted by the agency making the decision.

(d) Upon request, make available to the public the results of relevant monitoring.

PART 1506—OTHER REQUIREMENTS OF NEPA

Sec.

Authority: NEPA, the Environmental Quality Improvement Act of 1970, as amended (42 U.S.C. 4371 et seq.), sec. 309 of the Clean Air Act, as amended (42 U.S.C. 7609), and Executive Order 11514 (Mar. 5, 1970, as amended by Executive Order 11991, May 24, 1977).

Source: 43 Fed. Reg. 56000 (Nov. 29, 1978), unless otherwise noted.

§ 1506.1 Limitations on actions during NEPA process.

(a) Until an agency issues a record of decision as provided in § 1505.2 (except as provided in paragraph (c) of this section), no action concerning the proposal shall be taken which would:

(1) Have an adverse environmental impact; or

(2) Limit the choice of reasonable alternatives.

(b) If any agency is considering an application from a non-Federal entity, and is aware that the applicant is about to take an action within the agency's jurisdiction that would meet either of the criteria in paragraph (a) of this section, then the agency shall promptly notify the applicant that the agency will take appropriate action to insure that the objectives and procedures of NEPA are achieved.

(c) While work on a required program environmental impact statement is in progress and the action is not covered by an existing program statement, agencies shall not undertake in the interim any major Federal action covered by the program which may significantly affect the quality of the human environment unless such action:

(1) Is justified independently of the program;

(2) Is itself accompanied by an adequate environmental impact statement; and

(3) Will not prejudice the ultimate decision on the program. Interim action prejudices the ultimate decision on the program when it tends to determine subsequent development or limit alternatives.

(d) This section does not preclude development by applicants of plans or designs or performance of other work necessary to support an application for Federal, State or local permits or assistance. Nothing in this section shall preclude Rural Electrification Administration approval of minimal expenditures not affecting the environment (e.g. long leadtime equipment and purchase options) made by non-governmental entities seeking loan guarantees from the Administration.

§ 1506.2 Elimination of duplication with State and local procedures.

(a) Agencies authorized by law to cooperate with State agencies of statewide jurisdiction pursuant to section 102(2)(D) of the Act may do so.

(b) Agencies shall cooperate with State and local agencies to the fullest extent possible to reduce duplication between NEPA and State and local requirements, unless the agencies are specifically barred from doing so by some other law. Except for cases covered by paragraph (a) of this section, such cooperation shall to the fullest extent possible include:

(1) Joint planning processes.

(2) Joint environmental research and studies.

(3) Joint public hearings (except where otherwise provided by statute).

(4) Joint environmental assessments.

(c) Agencies shall cooperate with State and local agencies to the fullest extent possible to reduce duplication between NEPA and comparable State and local requirements, unless the agencies are specifically barred from doing so by some other law. Except for cases covered by paragraph (a) of this section, such cooperation shall to the fullest extent possible include joint environmental impact statements. In such cases one or more Federal agencies and one or more State or local agencies shall be joint lead agencies. Where State laws or local ordinances have environmental impact statement requirements in addition to but not in conflict with those in NEPA, Federal agencies shall cooperate in fulfilling these requirements as well as those of Federal laws so that one document will comply with all applicable laws.

(d) To better integrate environmental impact statements into State or local planning processes, statements shall discuss any inconsistency of a proposed action with any approved State or local plan and laws (whether or not federally sanctioned). Where an inconsistency exists, the statement should describe the extent to which the agency would reconcile its proposed action with the plan or law.

§ 1506.3 Adoption.

(a) An agency may adopt a Federal draft or final environmental impact statement or portion thereof provided that the statement or portion thereof meets the standards for an adequate statement under these regulations.

(b) If the actions covered by the original environmental impact statement and the proposed action are substantially the same, the agency adopting another agency's statement is not required to recirculate it except as a final statement. Otherwise the adopting agency shall treat the statement as a draft and recirculate it (except as provided in paragraph (c) of this section).

(c) A cooperating agency may adopt without recirculating the environmental impact statement of a lead agency when, after an independent review of the statement, the cooperating agency concludes that its comments and suggestions have been satisfied.

(d) When an agency adopts a statement which is not final within the agency that prepared it, or when the action it assesses is the subject of a referral under Part 1504, or when the statement's adequacy is the subject of a judicial action which is not final, the agency shall so specify.

§ 1506.4 Combining documents.

Any environmental document in compliance with NEPA may be combined with any other agency document to reduce duplication and paperwork.

§ 1506.5 Agency responsibility.

(a) Information. If an agency requires an applicant to submit environmental information for possible use by the agency in preparing an environmental impact statement, then the agency should assist the applicant by outlining the types of information required. The agency shall independently evaluate the information submitted and shall be responsible for its accuracy. If the agency chooses to use the information submitted by the applicant in the environmental impact statement, either directly or by reference, then the names of the persons responsible for the independent evaluation shall be included in the list of preparers (§ 1502.17). It is the intent of this paragraph that acceptable work not be redone, but that it be verified by the agency.

(b) Environmental assessments. If an agency permits an applicant to prepare an environmental assessment, the agency, besides fulfilling the requirements of paragraph (a) of this section, shall make its own evaluation of the environmental issues and take responsibility for the scope and content of the environmental assessment.

(c) Environmental impact statements. Except as provided in §§ 1506.2 and 1506.3 any environmental impact statement prepared pursuant to the requirements of NEPA shall be prepared directly by or by a contractor selected by the lead agency or where appropriate under § 1501.6(b), a cooperating agency. It is the intent of these regulations that the contractor be chosen solely by the lead agency, or by the lead agency in cooperation with cooperating agencies, or where appropriate by a cooperating agency to avoid any conflict of interest. Contractors shall execute a disclosure statement prepared by the lead agency, or where appropriate the cooperating agency, specifying that they have no financial or other interest in the outcome of the project. If the document is prepared by contract, the responsible Federal official shall furnish guidance and participate in the preparation and shall independently evaluate the statement prior to its approval and take responsibility for its scope and contents. Nothing in this section is intended to prohibit any agency from requesting any person to submit information to it or to prohibit any person from submitting information to any agency.

§ 1506.6 Public involvement.

Agencies shall:

(a) Make diligent efforts to involve the public in preparing and implementing their NEPA procedures.

(b) Provide public notice of NEPA-related hearings, public meetings, and the availability of environmental documents so as to inform those persons and agencies who may be interested or affected.

(1) In all cases the agency shall mail notice to those who have requested it on an individual action.

(2) In the case of an action with effects of national concern notice shall include publication in the Federal Register and notice by mail to national organizations reasonably expected to be interested in the matter and may include listing in the 102 Monitor. An agency engaged in rulemaking may provide notice by mail to national organizations who have requested that notice regularly be provided. Agencies shall maintain a list of such organizations.

(3) In the case of an action with effects primarily of local concern the notice may include:

(i) Notice to State and areawide clearinghouses pursuant to OMB Circular A-95 (Revised).

(ii) Notice to Indian tribes when effects may occur on reservations.

(iii) Following the affected State's public notice procedures for comparable actions.

(iv) Publication in local newspapers (in papers of general circulation rather than legal papers).

(v) Notice through other local media.

(vi) Notice to potentially interested community organizations including small business associations.

(vii) Publication in newsletters that may be expected to reach potentially interested persons.

(viii) Direct mailing to owners and occupants of nearby or affected property.

(ix) Posting of notice on and off site in the area where the action is to be located.

(c) Hold or sponsor public hearings or public meetings whenever appropriate or in accordance with statutory requirements applicable to the agency. Criteria shall include whether there is:

(1) Substantial environmental controversy concerning the proposed action or substantial interest in holding the hearing.

(2) A request for a hearing by another agency with jurisdiction over the action supported by reasons why a hearing will be helpful. If a draft environmental impact statement is to be considered at a public hearing, the agency should make the statement available to the public at least 15 days in advance (unless the purpose of the hearing is to provide information for the draft environmental impact statement).

(d) Solicit appropriate information from the public.

(e) Explain in its procedures where interested persons can get information or status reports on environmental impact statements and other elements of the NEPA process.

(f) Make environmental impact statements, the comments received, and any underlying documents available to the public pursuant to the provisions of the Freedom of Information Act (5 U.S.C. 552), without regard to the exclusion for interagency memoranda where such memoranda transmit comments of Federal agencies on the environmental impact of the proposed action. Materials to be made available to the public shall be provided to the public without charge to the extent practicable, or at a fee which is not more than the actual costs of reproducing copies required to be sent to other Federal agencies, including the Council.

§ 1506.7 Further guidance.

The Council may provide further guidance concerning NEPA and its procedures including:

(a) A handbook which the Council may supplement from time to time, which shall in plain language provide guidance and instructions concerning the application of NEPA and these regulations.

(b) Publication of the Council's Memoranda to Heads of Agencies.

(c) In conjunction with the Environmental Protection Agency and the publication of the 102 Monitor, notice of:

(1) Research activities;

(2) Meetings and conferences related to NEPA; and

(3) Successful and innovative procedures used by agencies to implement NEPA.

§ 1506.8 Proposals for legislation.

(a) The NEPA process for proposals for legislation (§ 1508.17) significantly affecting the quality of the human environment shall be integrated with the legislative process of the Congress. A legislative environmental impact statement is the detailed statement required by law to be included in a recommendation or report on a legislative proposal to Congress. A legislative environmental impact statement shall be considered part of the formal transmittal of a legislative proposal to Congress; however, it may be transmitted to Congress up to 30 days later in order to allow time for completion of an accurate statement which can serve as the basis for public and Congressional debate. The statement must be available in time for Congressional hearings and deliberations.

(b) Preparation of a legislative environmental impact statement shall conform to the requirements of these regulations except as follows:

(1) There need not be a scoping process.

(2) The legislative statement shall be prepared in the same manner as a draft statement, but shall be considered the "detailed statement" required by statute; *Provided,* That when any of the following conditions exist both the draft and final environmental impact statement on the legislative proposal shall be prepared and circulated as provided by §§ 1503.1 and 1506.10.

(i) A Congressional Committee with jurisdiction over the proposal has a rule requiring both draft and final environmental impact statements.

(ii) The proposal results from a study process required by statute (such as those required by the Wild and Scenic Rivers Act (16 U.S.C. 1271 et seq.) and the Wilderness Act (16 U.S.C. 1131 et seq.)).

(iii) Legislative approval is sought for Federal or federally assisted construction or other projects which the agency recommends be located at specific geographic locations. For proposals requiring an environmental impact statement for the acquisition of space by the General Services Administration, a draft statement shall accompany the Prospectus or the 11(b) Report of Building Project Surveys to the Congress, and a final statement shall be completed before site acquisition.

(iv) The agency decides to prepare draft and final statements.

(c) Comments on the legislative statement shall be given to the lead agency which shall forward them along with its own responses to the Congressional committees with jurisdiction.

§ 1506.9 Filing requirements.

(a) Environmental impact statements together with comments and responses shall be filed with the Environmental Protection Agency, attention Office of Federal Activities, EIS Filing Section, Ariel Rios

Building (South Oval Lobby), Mail Code 2252–A, Room 7220, 1200 Pennsylvania Ave., NW., Washington, DC 20460. This address is for deliveries by US Postal Service (including USPS Express Mail).

(b) For deliveries in-person or by commercial express mail services, including Federal Express or UPS, the correct address is: US Environmental Protection Agency, Office of Federal Activities, EIS Filing Section, Ariel Rios Building (South Oval Lobby), Room 7220, 1200 Pennsylvania Avenue, NW., Washington, DC 20004.

(c) Statements shall be filed with the EPA no earlier than they are also transmitted to commenting agencies and made available to the public. EPA shall deliver one copy of each statement to the Council, which shall satisfy the requirement of availability to the President. EPA may issue guidelines to agencies to implement its responsibilities under this section and § 1506.10.

[70 Fed. Reg. 41148 (July 18, 2005).]

§ 1506.10 Timing of agency action.

(a) The Environmental Protection Agency shall publish a notice in the Federal Register each week of the environmental impact statements filed during the preceding week. The minimum time periods set forth in this section shall be calculated from the date of publication of this notice.

(b) No decision on the proposed action shall be made or recorded under § 1505.2 by a Federal agency until the later of the following dates:

(1) Ninety (90) days after publication of the notice described above in paragraph (a) of this section for a draft environmental impact statement.

(2) Thirty (30) days after publication of the notice described above in paragraph (a) of this section for a final environmental impact statement.

An exception to the rules on timing may be made in the case of an agency decision which is subject to a formal internal appeal. Some agencies have a formally established appeal process which allows other agencies or the public to take appeals on a decision and make their views known, after publication of the final environmental impact statement. In such cases, where a real opportunity exists to alter the decision, the decision may be made and recorded at the same time the environmental impact statement is published. This means that the period for appeal of the decision and the 30-day period prescribed in paragraph (b)(2) of this section may run concurrently. In such cases the environmental impact statement shall explain the timing and the public's right of appeal. An agency engaged in rulemaking under the Administrative Procedure Act or other statute for the purpose of protecting the public health or safety, may waive the time period in paragraph (b)(2) of this section and publish a decision on the final rule simultaneously with publication of the notice of the availability of the final environmental impact statement as described in paragraph (a) of this section.

(c) If the final environmental impact statement is filed within ninety (90) days after a draft environmental impact statement is filed with the Environmental Protection Agency, the minimum thirty (30) day period and the minimum ninety (90) day period may run concurrently. However, subject to paragraph (d) of this section agencies shall allow not less than 45 days for comments on draft statements.

(d) The lead agency may extend prescribed periods. The Environmental Protection Agency may upon a showing by the lead agency of compelling reasons of national policy reduce the prescribed periods and may upon a showing by any other Federal agency of compelling reasons of national policy also extend prescribed periods, but only after consultation with the lead agency. (Also see § 1507.3(d).) Failure to file timely comments shall not be a sufficient reason for extending a period. If the lead agency does not concur with the extension of time, EPA may not extend it for more than 30 days. When the Environmental Protection Agency reduces or extends any period of time it shall notify the Council.

[43 Fed. Reg. 56000 (Nov. 29, 1978); 44 Fed. Reg. 874 (Jan. 3, 1979).]

§ 1506.11 Emergencies.

Where emergency circumstances make it necessary to take an action with significant environmental impact without observing the provisions of these regulations, the Federal agency taking the action should consult with the Council about alternative arrangements. Agencies and the Council will limit such arrangements to actions necessary to control the immediate impacts of the emergency. Other actions remain subject to NEPA review.

§ 1506.12 Effective date.

The effective date of these regulations is July 30, 1979, except that for agencies that administer programs that qualify under section 102(2)(D) of the Act or under section 104(h) of the Housing and Community Development Act of 1974 an additional four months shall be allowed for the State or local agencies to adopt their implementing procedures.

(a) These regulations shall apply to the fullest extent practicable to ongoing activities and environmental documents begun before the effective date. These regulations do not apply to an environmental impact statement or supplement if the draft statement was filed before the effective date of these regulations. No completed environmental documents need be redone by reasons of these regulations. Until these regulations are applicable, the Council's guidelines published in the Federal Register of August 1, 1973, shall continue to be applicable. In cases where these regulations are applicable the guidelines are superseded. However, nothing shall prevent an agency from proceeding under these regulations at an earlier time.

(b) NEPA shall continue to be applicable to actions begun before January 1, 1970, to the fullest extent possible.

PART 1507—AGENCY COMPLIANCE

Sec.

Authority: NEPA, the Environmental Quality Improvement Act of 1970, as amended (42 U.S.C. 4371 et seq.), sec. 309 of the Clean Air Act, as amended (42 U.S.C. 7609), and Executive Order 11514 (Mar. 5, 1970, as amended by Executive Order 11991, May 24, 1977).

Source: 43 Fed. Reg. 56002 (Nov. 29, 1978), unless otherwise noted.

§ 1507.1 Compliance.

All agencies of the Federal Government shall comply with these regulations. It is the intent of these regulations to allow each agency flexibility in adapting its implementing procedures authorized by § 1507.3 to the requirements of other applicable laws.

§ 1507.2 Agency capability to comply.

Each agency shall be capable (in terms of personnel and other resources) of complying with the requirements enumerated below. Such compliance may include use of other's resources, but the using agency shall itself have sufficient capability to evaluate what others do for it. Agencies shall:

(a) Fulfill the requirements of section 102(2)(A) of the Act to utilize a systematic, interdisciplinary approach which will insure the integrated use of the natural and social sciences and the environmental design arts in planning and in decisionmaking which may have an impact on the human environment. Agencies shall designate a person to be responsible for overall review of agency NEPA compliance.

(b) Identify methods and procedures required by section 102(2)(B) to insure that presently unquantified environmental amenities and values may be given appropriate consideration.

(c) Prepare adequate environmental impact statements pursuant to section 102(2)(C) and comment on statements in the areas where the agency has jurisdiction by law or special expertise or is authorized to develop and enforce environmental standards.

(d) Study, develop, and describe alternatives to recommended courses of action in any proposal which involves unresolved conflicts concerning alternative uses of available resources. This requirement of section

102(2)(E) extends to all such proposals, not just the more limited scope of section 102(2)(C)(iii) where the discussion of alternatives is confined to impact statements.

(e) Comply with the requirements of section 102(2)(H) that the agency initiate and utilize ecological information in the planning and development of resource-oriented projects.

(f) Fulfill the requirements of sections 102(2)(F), 102(2)(G), and 102(2)(I), of the Act and of Executive Order 11514, Protection and Enhancement of Environmental Quality, Sec. 2.

§ 1507.3 Agency procedures.

(a) Not later than eight months after publication of these regulations as finally adopted in the Federal Register, or five months after the establishment of an agency, whichever shall come later, each agency shall as necessary adopt procedures to supplement these regulations. When the agency is a department, major subunits are encouraged (with the consent of the department) to adopt their own procedures. Such procedures shall not paraphrase these regulations. They shall confine themselves to implementing procedures. Each agency shall consult with the Council while developing its procedures and before publishing them in the Federal Register for comment. Agencies with similar programs should consult with each other and the Council to coordinate their procedures, especially for programs requesting similar information from applicants. The procedures shall be adopted only after an opportunity for public review and after review by the Council for conformity with the Act and these regulations. The Council shall complete its review within 30 days. Once in effect they shall be filed with the Council and made readily available to the public. Agencies are encouraged to publish explanatory guidance for these regulations and their own procedures. Agencies shall continue to review their policies and procedures and in consultation with the Council to revise them as necessary to ensure full compliance with the purposes and provisions of the Act.

(b) Agency procedures shall comply with these regulations except where compliance would be inconsistent with statutory requirements and shall include:

(1) Those procedures required by §§ 1501.2(d), 1502.9(c)(3), 1505.1, 1506.6(e), and 1508.4.

(2) Specific criteria for and identification of those typical classes of action:

(i) Which normally do require environmental impact statements.

(ii) Which normally do not require either an environmental impact statement or an environmental assessment (categorical exclusions (§ 1508.4)).

(iii) Which normally require environmental assessments but not necessarily environmental impact statements.

(c) Agency procedures may include specific criteria for providing limited exceptions to the provisions of these regulations for classified proposals. They are proposed actions which are specifically authorized under criteria established by an Executive Order or statute to be kept secret in the interest of national defense or foreign policy and are in fact properly classified pursuant to such Executive Order or statute. Environmental assessments and environmental impact statements which address classified proposals may be safeguarded and restricted from public dissemination in accordance with agencies' own regulations applicable to classified information. These documents may be organized so that classified portions can be included as annexes, in order that the unclassified portions can be made available to the public.

(d) Agency procedures may provide for periods of time other than those presented in § 1506.10 when necessary to comply with other specific statutory requirements.

(e) Agency procedures may provide that where there is a lengthy period between the agency's decision to prepare an environmental impact statement and the time of actual preparation, the notice of intent required by § 1501.7 may be published at a reasonable time in advance of preparation of the draft statement.

PART 1508—TERMINOLOGY AND INDEX

Sec.

Authority: NEPA, the Environmental Quality Improvement Act of 1970, as amended (42 U.S.C. 4371 et seq.), sec. 309 of the Clean Air Act, as amended (42 U.S.C. 7609), and Executive Order 11514 (Mar. 5, 1970, as amended by Executive Order 11991, May 24, 1977).

Source: 43 Fed. Reg. 56003 (Nov. 29, 1978), unless otherwise noted.

§ 1508.1 Terminology.

The terminology of this part shall be uniform throughout the Federal Government.

§ 1508.2 Act.

Act means the National Environmental Policy Act, as amended (42 U.S.C. 4321, et seq.) which is also referred to as "NEPA."

§ 1508.3 Affecting.

Affecting means will or may have an effect on.

§ 1508.4 Categorical exclusion.

Categorical Exclusion means a category of actions which do not individually or cumulatively have a significant effect on the human environment and which have been found to have no such effect in procedures adopted by a Federal agency in implementation of these regulations (§ 1507.3) and for which, therefore, neither an environmental assessment nor an environmental impact statement is required. An agency may decide in its procedures or otherwise, to prepare environmental assessments for the reasons stated in § 1508.9 even though it is not required to do so. Any procedures under this section shall provide for extraordinary circumstances in which a normally excluded action may have a significant environmental effect.

§ 1508.5 Cooperating agency.

Cooperating Agency means any Federal agency other than a lead agency which has jurisdiction by law or special expertise with respect to any environmental impact involved in a proposal (or a reasonable alternative) for legislation or other major Federal action significantly affecting the quality of the human environment. The selection and responsibilities of a cooperating agency are described in § 1501.6. A State or local agency of similar qualifications or, when the effects are on a reservation, an Indian Tribe, may by agreement with the lead agency become a cooperating agency.

§ 1508.6 Council.

Council means the Council on Environmental Quality established by title II of the Act.

§ 1508.7 Cumulative impact.

Cumulative impact is the impact on the environment which results from the incremental impact of the action when added to other past, present, and reasonably foreseeable future actions regardless of what agency (Federal or non-Federal) or person undertakes such other actions. Cumulative impacts can result from individually minor but collectively significant actions taking place over a period of time.

§ 1508.8 Effects.

Effects include:

(a) Direct effects, which are caused by the action and occur at the same time and place.

(b) Indirect effects, which are caused by the action and are later in time or farther removed in distance, but are still reasonably foreseeable. Indirect effects may include growth inducing effects and other effects related to induced changes in the pattern of land use, population density or growth rate, and related effects on air and water and other natural systems, including ecosystems.

Effects and impacts as used in these regulations are synonymous. Effects includes ecological (such as the effects on natural resources and on the components, structures, and functioning of affected ecosystems), aesthetic, historic, cultural, economic, social, or health, whether direct, indirect, or cumulative. Effects may also include those resulting from actions which may have both beneficial and detrimental effects, even if on balance the agency believes that the effect will be beneficial.

§ 1508.9 Environmental assessment.

Environmental Assessment:

(a) Means a concise public document for which a Federal agency is responsible that serves to:

(1) Briefly provide sufficient evidence and analysis for determining whether to prepare an environmental impact statement or a finding of no significant impact.

(2) Aid an agency's compliance with the Act when no environmental impact statement is necessary.

(3) Facilitate preparation of a statement when one is necessary.

(b) Shall include brief discussions of the need for the proposal, of alternatives as required by section 102(2)(E), of the environmental impacts of the proposed action and alternatives, and a listing of agencies and persons consulted.

§ 1508.10 Environmental document.

Environmental document includes the documents specified in § 1508.9 (environmental assessment), § 1508.11 (environmental impact statement), § 1508.13 (finding of no significant impact), and § 1508.22 (notice of intent).

§ 1508.11 Environmental impact statement.

Environmental impact statement means a detailed written statement as required by section 102(2)(C) of the Act.

§ 1508.12 Federal agency.

Federal agency means all agencies of the Federal Government. It does not mean the Congress, the Judiciary, or the President, including the performance of staff functions for the President in his Executive Office. It also includes for purposes of these regulations States and units of general local government and Indian tribes assuming NEPA responsibilities under section 104(h) of the Housing and Community Development Act of 1974.

§ 1508.13 Finding of no significant impact.

Finding of no significant impact means a document by a Federal agency briefly presenting the reasons why an action, not otherwise excluded (§ 1508.4), will not have a significant effect on the human environment and for which an environmental impact statement therefore will not be prepared. It shall include the environmental assessment or a summary of it and shall note any other environmental documents related to it (§ 1501.7(a)(5)). If the assessment is included, the finding need not repeat any of the discussion in the assessment but may incorporate it by reference.

§ 1508.14 Human environment.

Human environment shall be interpreted comprehensively to include the natural and physical environment and the relationship of people with that environment. (See the definition of "effects" (§ 1508.8).) This means that economic or social effects are not intended by themselves to require preparation of an environmental impact statement. When an environmental impact statement is prepared and economic or social and natural or physical environmental effects are interrelated, then the environmental impact statement will discuss all of these effects on the human environment.

§ 1508.15 Jurisdiction by law.

Jurisdiction by law means agency authority to approve, veto, or finance all or part of the proposal.

§ 1508.16 Lead agency.

Lead agency means the agency or agencies preparing or having taken primary responsibility for preparing the environmental impact statement.

§ 1508.17 Legislation.

Legislation includes a bill or legislative proposal to Congress developed by or with the significant cooperation and support of a Federal agency, but does not include requests for appropriations. The test for significant cooperation is whether the proposal is in fact predominantly that of the agency rather than another source. Drafting does not by itself constitute significant cooperation. Proposals for legislation include requests for ratification of treaties. Only the agency which has primary responsibility for the subject matter involved will prepare a legislative environmental impact statement.

§ 1508.18 Major Federal action.

Major Federal action includes actions with effects that may be major and which are potentially subject to Federal control and responsibility. Major reinforces but does not have a meaning independent of significantly (§ 1508.27). Actions include the circumstance where the responsible officials fail to act and that failure to act is reviewable by courts or administrative tribunals under the Administrative Procedure Act or other applicable law as agency action.

(a) Actions include new and continuing activities, including projects and programs entirely or partly financed, assisted, conducted, regulated, or approved by federal agencies; new or revised agency rules, regulations, plans, policies, or procedures; and legislative proposals (§§ 1506.8, 1508.17). Actions do not include funding assistance solely in the form of general revenue sharing funds, distributed under the State and Local Fiscal Assistance Act of 1972, 31 U.S.C. 1221 et seq., with no Federal agency control over the subsequent use of such funds. Actions do not include bringing judicial or administrative civil or criminal enforcement actions.

(b) Federal actions tend to fall within one of the following categories:

(1) Adoption of official policy, such as rules, regulations, and interpretations adopted pursuant to the Administrative Procedure Act, 5 U.S.C. 551 et seq.; treaties and international conventions or agreements; formal documents establishing an agency's policies which will result in or substantially alter agency programs.

(2) Adoption of formal plans, such as official documents prepared or approved by federal agencies which guide or prescribe alternative uses of Federal resources, upon which future agency actions will be based.

(3) Adoption of programs, such as a group of concerted actions to implement a specific policy or plan; systematic and connected agency decisions allocating agency resources to implement a specific statutory program or executive directive.

(4) Approval of specific projects, such as construction or management activities located in a defined geographic area. Projects include actions approved by permit or other regulatory decision as well as federal and federally assisted activities.

§ 1508.19 Matter.

Matter includes for purposes of part 1504:

(a) With respect to the Environmental Protection Agency, any proposed legislation, project, action or regulation as those terms are used in section 309(a) of the Clean Air Act (42 U.S.C. 7609).

(b) With respect to all other agencies, any proposed major federal action to which section 102(2)(C) of NEPA applies.

§ 1508.20 Mitigation.

Mitigation includes:

(a) Avoiding the impact altogether by not taking a certain action or parts of an action.

(b) Minimizing impacts by limiting the degree or magnitude of the action and its implementation.

(c) Rectifying the impact by repairing, rehabilitating, or restoring the affected environment.

(d) Reducing or eliminating the impact over time by preservation and maintenance operations during the life of the action.

(e) Compensating for the impact by replacing or providing substitute resources or environments.

§ 1508.21 NEPA process.

NEPA process means all measures necessary for compliance with the requirements of section 2 and title I of NEPA.

§ 1508.22 Notice of intent.

Notice of intent means a notice that an environmental impact statement will be prepared and considered. The notice shall briefly:

(a) Describe the proposed action and possible alternatives.

(b) Describe the agency's proposed scoping process including whether, when, and where any scoping meeting will be held.

(c) State the name and address of a person within the agency who can answer questions about the proposed action and the environmental impact statement.

§ 1508.23 Proposal.

Proposal exists at that stage in the development of an action when an agency subject to the Act has a goal and is actively preparing to make a decision on one or more alternative means of accomplishing that goal and the effects can be meaningfully evaluated. Preparation of an environmental impact statement on a proposal should be timed (§ 1502.5) so that the final statement may be completed in time for the statement to be included in any recommendation or report on the proposal. A proposal may exist in fact as well as by agency declaration that one exists.

§ 1508.24 Referring agency.

Referring agency means the federal agency which has referred any matter to the Council after a determination that the matter is unsatisfactory from the standpoint of public health or welfare or environmental quality.

§ 1508.25 Scope.

Scope consists of the range of actions, alternatives, and impacts to be considered in an environmental impact statement. The scope of an individual statement may depend on its relationships to other statements (§§ 1502.20 and 1508.28). To determine the scope of environmental impact statements, agencies shall consider 3 types of actions, 3 types of alternatives, and 3 types of impacts. They include:

(a) Actions (other than unconnected single actions) which may be:

(1) Connected actions, which means that they are closely related and therefore should be discussed in the same impact statement. Actions are connected if they:

(i) Automatically trigger other actions which may require environmental impact statements.

(ii) Cannot or will not proceed unless other actions are taken previously or simultaneously.

(iii) Are interdependent parts of a larger action and depend on the larger action for their justification.

(2) Cumulative actions, which when viewed with other proposed actions have cumulatively significant impacts and should therefore be discussed in the same impact statement.

(3) Similar actions, which when viewed with other reasonably foreseeable or proposed agency actions, have similarities that provide a basis for evaluating their environmental consequences together, such as common timing or geography. An agency may wish to analyze these actions in the same impact statement. It should do so when the best way to assess adequately the combined impacts of similar actions or reasonable alternatives to such actions is to treat them in a single impact statement.

(b) Alternatives, which include:

(1) No action alternative.

(2) Other reasonable courses of actions.

(3) Mitigation measures (not in the proposed action).

(c) Impacts, which may be:

(1) Direct;

(2) Indirect;

(3) Cumulative.

§ 1508.26 Special expertise.

Special expertise means statutory responsibility, agency mission, or related program experience.

§ 1508.27 Significantly.

Significantly as used in NEPA requires considerations of both context and intensity:

(a) Context. This means that the significance of an action must be analyzed in several contexts such as society as a whole (human, national), the affected region, the affected interests, and the locality. Significance varies with the setting of the proposed action. For instance, in the case of a site-specific action, significance would usually depend upon the effects in the locale rather than in the world as a whole. Both short- and long-term effects are relevant.

(b) Intensity. This refers to the severity of impact. Responsible officials must bear in mind that more than one agency may make decisions about partial aspects of a major action. The following should be considered in evaluating intensity:

(1) Impacts that may be both beneficial and adverse. A significant effect may exist even if the Federal agency believes that on balance the effect will be beneficial.

(2) The degree to which the proposed action affects public health or safety.

(3) Unique characteristics of the geographic area such as proximity to historic or cultural resources, park lands, prime farmlands, wetlands, wild and scenic rivers, or ecologically critical areas.

(4) The degree to which the effects on the quality of the human environment are likely to be highly controversial.

(5) The degree to which the possible effects on the human environment are highly uncertain or involve unique or unknown risks.

(6) The degree to which the action may establish a precedent for future actions with significant effects or represents a decision in principle about a future consideration.

(7) Whether the action is related to other actions with individually insignificant but cumulatively significant impacts. Significance exists if it is reasonable to anticipate a cumulatively significant impact on the environment. Significance cannot be avoided by terming an action temporary or by breaking it down into small component parts.

(8) The degree to which the action may adversely affect districts, sites, highways, structures, or objects listed in or eligible for listing in the National Register of Historic Places or may cause loss or destruction of significant scientific, cultural, or historical resources.

(9) The degree to which the action may adversely affect an endangered or threatened species or its habitat that has been determined to be critical under the Endangered Species Act of 1973.

(10) Whether the action threatens a violation of Federal, State, or local law or requirements imposed for the protection of the environment.

[43 Fed. Reg. 56003 (Nov. 29, 1978); 44 Fed. Reg. 874 (Jan. 3, 1979).]

§ 1508.28 Tiering.

Tiering refers to the coverage of general matters in broader environmental impact statements (such as national program or policy statements) with subsequent narrower statements or environmental analyses (such as regional or basinwide program statements or ultimately site-specific statements) incorporating by reference the general discussions and concentrating solely on the issues specific to the statement subsequently prepared. Tiering is appropriate when the sequence of statements or analyses is:

(a) from a program, plan, or policy environmental impact statement to a program, plan, or policy statement or analysis of lesser scope or to a site-specific statement or analysis.

(b) from an environmental impact statement on a specific action at an early stage (such as need and site selection) to a supplement (which is preferred) or a subsequent statement or analysis at a later stage (such as environmental mitigation). Tiering in such cases is appropriate when it helps the lead agency to focus on the issues which are ripe for decision and exclude from consideration issues already decided or not yet ripe.

Final Guidance for Federal Departments and Agencies on Establishing, Applying, and Revising Categorical Exclusions Under the National Environmental Policy Act

On December 6, 2010, 75 Fed. Reg. 75,628, the Council on Environmental Quality announced the availability of new guidance for federal agencies implementing NEPA with respect to categorical exclusions, applicable to 40 C.F.R. Parts 1500–1508. That announcement stated:

> This guidance provides methods for substantiating categorical exclusions, clarifies the process for establishing categorical exclusions, outlines how agencies should engage the public when establishing and using categorical exclusions, describes how agencies can document the use of categorical exclusions, and recommends periodic agency review of existing categorical exclusions. A categorical exclusion is a category of actions that a Federal agency determines does not normally result in individually or cumulatively significant environmental effects. This guidance clarifies the rules for establishing, applying, and revising categorical exclusions. It applies to categorical exclusions established by Federal agencies in accordance with CEQ regulations for implementing the procedural provisions of the National Environmental Policy Act. The guidance was developed to assist agencies in making their implementation of the National Environmental Policy Act (NEPA) more transparent and efficient.

Final Guidance for Federal Departments and Agencies on the Appropriate Use of Mitigation and Monitoring and Clarifying the Appropriate Use of Mitigated Findings of No Significant Impact

On January 21, 2011, 76 Fed. Reg. 3843, the Council on Environmental Quality announced the availability of new guidance to address federal agencies' implementation of NEPA, especially with respect to mitigation, applicable to 40 C.F.R. Parts 1500–1508. That announcement stated:

> The guidance was developed to modernize, reinvigorate, and facilitate and increase the transparency of NEPA implementation.
>
> This guidance outlines principles Federal agencies should apply in the development of their NEPA implementing regulations and procedures to guide their consideration of measures to mitigate adverse environmental impacts in EAs and EISs; their commitments to carry out mitigation made in related decision documents, such as the Record of Decision; the implementation of mitigation; and the monitoring of mitigation outcomes during and after implementation. This guidance also outlines principles agencies should apply to provide for public participation and accountability in the development and implementation of mitigation and monitoring efforts that are described in their NEPA documentation. Mitigation commitments should be explicitly described as ongoing commitments and should specify measurable performance standards and adequate mechanisms for implementation, monitoring, and reporting.
>
> In addition, this guidance affirms the appropriateness of what is traditionally referred to as a "mitigated Finding of No Significant Impact." Mitigated Findings of No Significant Impact (FONSIs) can result when an agency concludes its NEPA review with an EA that is based on a commitment to mitigate significant environmental impacts, so that a more detailed EIS is not required. As explained in this guidance, an agency does not have to prepare an EIS when the environmental impacts of a proposed action can be mitigated to a level where the agency can make a FONSI determination, provided that the agency or a project applicant commits to carry out the mitigation, and establishes a mechanism for ensuring the mitigation is carried out. When a FONSI depends on successful mitigation, the requisite mitigation commitments should be made public.

Final Guidance on Improving the Process for Preparing Efficient and Timely Environmental Reviews Under the National Environmental Policy Act

On March 12, 2012, 77 Fed. Reg. 14,473, the Council on Environmental Quality announced the availability of new guidance for the preparation of Environmental Assessments and Environmental Impact Statements, applicable to 40 C.F.R. Parts 1500–1508. That announcement stated:

> CEQ is issuing this guidance for Federal departments and agencies to emphasize and clarify that these techniques are available for all NEPA Environmental Assessments and Environmental Impact Statements. These techniques are consistent with a thorough and meaningful environmental review and agencies using these techniques should keep in mind the following basic principles: NEPA

encourages straightforward and concise reviews and documentation that are proportionate to potential impacts and effectively convey the relevant considerations in a timely manner to the public and decision makers, while rigorously addressing the issues presented; NEPA shall be integrated into project planning to ensure planning and decisions reflect environmental considerations, avoid delays later in the process, and anticipate and attempt to resolve issues, rather than be an after-the-fact process that justifies decisions already made; NEPA reviews should coordinate and take appropriate advantage of existing documents and studies, including through adoption and incorporation by reference; early and well-defined scoping can assist in focusing environmental reviews on appropriate issues that would be meaningful to a decision on the proposed action; agencies are encouraged to develop meaningful, predictable, and expeditious timelines for environmental reviews; and agencies should respond to comments in proportion to the scope and scale of the environmental issues raised. This guidance applies equally to the preparation of an Environmental Assessment or an Environmental Impact Statement consistent with legal precedent and agency NEPA experience and practice. This guidance does not change or substitute for any law, regulations, or any other legally binding requirement. It does provide CEQ's interpretation of existing regulations promulgated under NEPA.

PART 1515—FREEDOM OF INFORMATION ACT PROCEDURES

Authority: 5 U.S.C. 552, as amended by Pub. L. No. 93–502, Pub. L. No. 99–570, Pub. L. No. 104–231, Pub. L. No. 110–175; E.O. 13392; Pres. Mem. 74 Fed. Reg. 4685.

Source: 42 Fed. Reg. 65158 (Dec. 30, 1977); 75 Fed. Reg. 48590 (August 11, 2010), unless otherwise noted.

PURPOSE

§ 1515.1 FOIA procedures.

The Freedom of Information Act (5 U.S.C. 552), as amended, commonly known as FOIA, is a Federal law that creates a procedure for any person to request documents and other records from United States Government agencies. The law requires every Federal agency to make available to the public the material requested, unless the material falls under one of the limited exemptions stated in Section 552(b) of the Act. These procedures explain how the Council on Environmental Quality (CEQ)—one of several agencies in the Executive Office of the President—will carry out the FOIA. They are written from the standpoint of a FOIA requester and should be read together with the FOIA, which provides additional information about access to records maintained by CEQ. This information is furnished for the guidance of the public and in compliance with the requirements of Section 552 of title 5, United States Code, as amended.

ORGANIZATION OF CEQ

§ 1515.2 About the Council on Environmental Quality (CEQ).

The Council on Environmental Quality ("CEQ" or "the Council") was created by the National Environmental Policy Act of 1969, as amended (42 U.S.C. 4321 through 4347). The Council's authority is primarily derived from that Act, the Environmental Quality Improvement Act of 1970, as amended (42 U.S.C. 4371–4374), Reorganization Plan No. 1 of 1977 (July 15, 1977), and Executive Order 11514, "Protection and Enhancement of Environmental Quality," March 5, 1970, as amended by Executive Order 11991, May 24, 1977.

§ 1515.3 CEQ organization.

(a) The Council is made up of a Chair appointed by the President and subject to approval by the Senate who serves in a full-time capacity. Congress has allowed CEQ to consist of a Council of one member who serves as Chairman or Chair.

(b) The National Environmental Policy Act and the Environmental Quality Improvement Act give the Council the authority to hire any officers and staff that may be necessary to carry out responsibilities and functions specified in these two Acts. Also, the use of consultants and experts is permitted.

(c) In addition to the Chair, the Council has program and legal staff.

(d) The Council has no field or regional offices.

(e) The Council is located at 722 Jackson Place NW., Washington, DC 20503. Office hours are 9 a.m.–5:30 p.m., Monday through Friday, except Federal holidays. To meet with any of the staff, please write or phone ahead for an appointment. The main number is 202-456-6224.

§ 1515.4 CEQ FOIA Officials.

(a) The Chair shall appoint a Chief Freedom of Information Act Officer (Chief FOIA Officer) who is responsible for overseeing the Council's administration of the Freedom of Information Act and for receiving, routing and overseeing the processing of all Freedom of Information requests as set forth in these regulations. The Chair shall appoint an Appeals Officer, who is responsible for processing and acting upon any appeals and may designate one or more CEQ officials, as appropriate, as FOIA Officers authorized to oversee and process FOIA requests. The Chief FOIA Officer may serve as the Appeals Officer.

(b) The Chief FOIA officer shall designate a FOIA Public Liaison who is the supervisory official to whom a FOIA requester can raise concerns about the service the FOIA requester has received from the CEQ FOIA Center, described in Section 1515.5(a), following an initial response from the staff of the CEQ FOIA Center staff. The FOIA Public Liaison shall assist, as appropriate, in reducing delays and increasing understanding of the status of requests. The Chief FOIA officer shall also designate a CEQ FOIA Officer responsible for overseeing CEQ's day-to-day administration of the FOIA and for receiving, routing, and overseeing the processing of all FOIA requests.

PROCEDURES FOR REQUESTING RECORDS

§ 1515.5 Making a Freedom of Information Act request.

(a) Availability of records. The Council maintains a World Wide Web site, http://www.whitehouse.gov/administration/eop/ceq,[1] and an online Freedom of Information Act Requester Service Center ("Center"), http://www.whitehouse.gov/administration/eop/ceq/foia.[2] from the Center, a requester can find contact information regarding the CEQ's FOIA Public Liaison, as defined in Section 1515.4(b), and access CEQ's Online Reading Room where CEQ makes available records pertaining to matters within the scope of 5 U.S.C. 552(a)(2), as amended, and environmental issues and other documents that, because of the nature of their subject matter, are likely to be the subject of FOIA requests. To save both time and money, CEQ strongly urges requesters to review documents currently available from the Center's Online Reading Room before submitting a request.

(b) Requesting information from the Council.

(1) Requesters must make a Freedom of Information Act request in writing. For quickest possible handling, it should be sent via e-mail to: efoia@ceq.eop.gov and must include in the subject line of the e-mail message: "Freedom of Information Act Request." Written requests may also be faxed to (202) 456-0753 or addressed and mailed to: Council on Environmental Quality, Executive Office of the President, 722 Jackson Place NW., Washington, DC 20503. Requesters should mark both the request letter and the envelope "Freedom of Information Act Request" and include their name, address, and sufficient contact information to allow follow up regarding the scope and status of your request.

(2) The request should identify or reasonably describe the desired record. It should be as specific as possible, so that the item can be readily found. Blanket requests, such as requests for "all materials relating to" a specified subject are not recommended. Requesters should specify the preferred form or format (including electronic format) for the response. CEQ will accommodate such requests, if the record is readily reproducible in that form or format. Please be aware that FOIA requests and responses may themselves be made available for public inspection.

(3) The CEQ FOIA Officer is responsible for acting on all initial requests; however, he or she may consult and refer, pursuant to Section 552(a)(6)(B)(iii)(III) of the FOIA, with another agency if he or she determines that that agency is better able to act on the request. Whenever the CEQ FOIA Officer refers all or any part of the responsibility for responding to a request to another agency, he or she will notify the requester of the referral, the name of the agency and agency official to whom it has been referred, and which portion of the request has been referred. Unless a request is deemed "expedited" as set forth in Section 1515.7 below, the CEQ FOIA Officer will respond to requests in order of receipt. CEQ may use two or more processing tracks by distinguishing between simple and more complex requests based on the amount of time and work needed to process the request. CEQ may provide requesters on a slower track an opportunity to limit the scope of their request in order to qualify for faster processing.

(4) The Council will make a reasonable effort to assist with defining the request to eliminate extraneous and unwanted materials and to keep search and copying fees to a minimum. If budgetary constraints exist, the requester should indicate the maximum fee he or she is prepared to pay to acquire the information. (See also § 1515.11)

(5) The Freedom of Information Act does not require a government agency to create or research information; rather, it only requires that existing records be made available to the public.

§ 1515.6 CEQ's response to a request.

(a) Upon receipt of any written request for information or records, under the Act, the CEQ FOIA Officer or his or her designee, will make an initial determination on the request within 20 days (excepting Saturdays, Sundays and Federal holidays) from the date CEQ receives the request unless unusual or exceptional circumstances exist. The CEQ FOIA Officer will provide written notification of the

[1] The updated link to CEQ's website is: https://www.whitehouse.gov/ceq/.

[2] The updated link to the Center is: https://www.whitehouse.gov/ceq/foia/.

determination, including, if applicable, notification that the request has been referred to another agency for consultation as set forth above in § 1515.5(b)(3). CEQ may make one request to the requester for information and toll the 20-day period while it is awaiting such information that it has reasonably requested from the requester. It may also toll the 20-day period if necessary to clarify with the requester issues regarding fee assessment. In either case, CEQ's receipt of the requester's response to its request for information or clarification ends the tolling period.

(b) Requests received by the CEQ FOIA Officer or his or her designee will be assigned an individualized tracking number if they will take more than 10 days to process. Requesters may call the FOIA Public Liaison at (202) 456-6224 and, using the tracking number, obtain information about the request, including the date on which CEQ originally received the request and an estimated date on which CEQ will complete action on the request.

(c) If it is appropriate to grant the request, a staff member will immediately collect the requested materials in order to accompany, wherever possible, the Freedom of Information Officer's letter conveying decision.

(d) If a request is denied in part or in full, the letter conveying the decision will be signed by the CEQ FOIA Officer, and will include: The reasons for any denial, including any FOIA exemption(s) applied by the FOIA Officer in denying the request; an estimate of the volume of records or information withheld, in number of pages or in some other reasonable form of estimation. This estimate does not need to be provided, if the volume is otherwise indicated through exemptions on records disclosed in part or, if providing an estimate would harm an interest protected by an applicable exemption; and the procedure for filing an appeal.

§ 1515.7 Expedited processing.

(a) Requests and appeals will be taken out of order and given expedited treatment whenever it is determined that they involve:

(1) Circumstances in which the lack of expedited treatment could reasonably be expected to pose an imminent threat to the life or physical safety of an individual; or

(2) An urgency to inform the public about an actual or alleged Federal Government activity, if made by a person primarily engaged in disseminating information.

(b) A request for expedited processing may be made at the time of the initial request for records or at any later time.

(c) A requester who seeks expedited processing must submit a written statement, certified to be true and correct to the best of that person's knowledge and belief, explaining in detail the basis for requesting expedited processing. For example, a requester within the category described in paragraph (a)(2) of this section, if not a full-time member of the news media, must establish that he or she is a person whose main professional activity or occupation is information dissemination, though it need not be his or her sole occupation. A requester within the category (a)(2) of this section must also establish a particular urgency to inform the public about the government activity involved in the request, beyond the public's right to know about government activity generally. Formal certification may be waived as a matter of administrative discretion.

(d) Within 10 days of its receipt of a request for expedited processing, the CEQ FOIA Officer will decide whether to grant it and will notify the requester of the decision. If a request for expedited treatment is granted, the request will be placed in the expedited processing track, given priority, and processed as soon as practicable. If a request for expedited processing is denied, any appeal of that decision will be acted on expeditiously.

§ 1515.8 Appeals.

(a) The requester may appeal an adverse determination, in any respect, to the CEQ FOIA Appeals Officer. Any appeal must be received by CEQ within 60 days of the date on the CEQ letter denying the request.

(b) Appeals must be in writing and may be sent via e-mail to: efoia@ceq.eop.gov. They may also be sent via facsimile to: (202) 456-0753 or via U.S. mail addressed to: FOIA Appeals Officer, Council on Environmental Quality, Executive Office of the President, 722 Jackson Place NW., Washington, DC 20503.

(c) The appeal letter should specify the records requested and ask the Appeals Officer to review the determination made by the Freedom of Information Officer. The letter should explain the basis for the appeal.

(d) The Appeals Officer will make a final determination on an appeal within 20 working days (excepting Saturdays, Sundays and Federal holidays) from the date CEQ receives the appeal. The Appeals Officer (or designee) will send a letter to the requester conveying the decision as soon as it is made. If an appeal is denied, in part or in whole, the letter will also include the provisions for judicial review.

§ 1515.9 Extending CEQ's time to respond.

(a) In unusual circumstances as defined in paragraph (c) of this section, the time limits for responding to a request (§§ 1515.6(a) and 1515.8(d)) may be extended by the Council for not more than 10 working days. Extensions may be granted by the CEQ FOIA Officer in the case of initial requests and by the Appeals Officer in the case of any appeals. The extension period may be split between the initial request and the appeal but may not exceed 10 working days overall. Extensions will be confirmed in writing and set forth the reasons for the extension and the date that the final determination is expected.

(b) With respect to a request for which a written notice under this section extends the time limits prescribed under § 1515.6(a), the CEQ FOIA Officer will notify the requester, if the request cannot be processed within the time limit specified in § 1515.6(a) and provide an opportunity to limit the scope of the request, so that it may be processed within that time limit or an opportunity to arrange an alternative time frame for processing the request or a modified request. A requester's refusal to reasonably modify the request or arrange such an alternative time frame will be considered as a factor in determining whether exceptional circumstances exist for purposes of 5 U.S.C. 552(a)(6)(C). When CEQ reasonably believes that a requester, or a group of requesters, has submitted a request constituting a single request that would otherwise satisfy the unusual circumstances specified under this section, CEQ may aggregate those requests for purposes of this paragraph. Multiple requests involving unrelated matters will not be aggregated.

(c) The term "unusual circumstances" means:

(1) The need to search for and collect the requested records from establishments that are separate from the office processing the request;

(2) The need to search for, collect, and appropriately examine a voluminous amount of separate and distinct records which are demanded in a single request; or

(3) The need for consultation, which will be conducted with all practicable speed, with another agency having a substantial interest in the determination of the request or among two or more components of the agency having substantial subject-matter interest therein.

AVAILABILITY OF INFORMATION

§ 1515.10 Obtaining available information.

(a) When a request for information has been granted in whole or in part, CEQ will notify the requester in writing, inform the requester in the notice of any fee charged under § 1515.11 and will disclose records to the requester promptly on payment of any applicable fees. The requested material may be made available on CEQ's Online FOIA Center, http://www.whitehouse.gov/administration/eop/ceq/foia,[3] and also in the form or format requested if the record is readily reproducible in that form or format with reasonable effort. When a form or format of the response is not requested, CEQ will respond in the form or format in which the document is most accessible to CEQ. "Readily reproducible" means, with respect to electronic format, that the requested record or records can be downloaded or transferred intact to a computer disk or other electronic medium using equipment currently in use by CEQ.

(b) Records disclosed in part will be marked or annotated to show information deleted, unless doing so would harm an interest protected by an applicable exemption. The location of the information deleted will also be indicated in the record, if technically feasible.

[3] The updated link to the Center is: https://www.whitehouse.gov/ceq/foia/.

(c) The legislative history of the establishment of CEQ states that the Congress intended CEQ to be a confidential advisor to the President on matters of environmental policy. Therefore, members of the public should be aware that communications between CEQ and the President (including communications between their staff) may be confidential; they will usually fall, at a minimum, within Exemption 5 of the Act. The Freedom of Information Officer shall review each request to determine whether the record is exclusively factual or may have factual portions which may be reasonably segregated and made available to the requester. Furthermore, on the recommendation of the CEQ FOIA Officer or Appeals Officer, CEQ will consider the release of an entire record, even if it comes within an exemption or contains policy advice, if its disclosure would not impair Executive policymaking processes or CEQ's participation in decisionmaking.

COSTS

§ 1515.11 Definitions.

For purposes of these regulations:

Commercial use request means a request from or on behalf of a person who seeks information for a use or purpose that furthers the requester's or other person's commercial, trade, or profit interests.

Direct costs means those costs incurred in searching for and duplicating (and, in the case of commercial use requests, reviewing) documents to respond to a FOIA request. Direct costs include, for example, salaries of employees who perform the work and costs of conducting large-scale computer searches.

Duplicate means to copy records to be released to the FOIA requester. Copies can take the form of paper, audio-visual materials, or electronic records, among others.

Educational institution means a school that operates a program of scholarly research.

Non-commercial scientific institution means an institution that is not operated on a commercial basis and that operates solely for the purpose of conducting scientific research the results of which are not intended to promote any particular product or industry.

Representative of the news media means any person or entity that gathers information of potential interest to a segment of the public, uses its editorial skills to turn the raw materials into a distinct work, and distributes that work to an audience.

Review means to examine a record to determine whether any portion of the record may be withheld and to process a record for disclosure, including by redacting it.

Search means to look for and retrieve records covered by a FOIA request, including by looking page-by-page or line-by-line to identify responsive material within individual records.

§ 1515.12 Fees in general.

CEQ shall charge fees that recoup the full allowable direct costs it incurs in responding to FOIA requests. CEQ may assess charges for time spent searching for records even if CEQ fails to locate the records or if the records are located and determined to be exempt from disclosure. In general, CEQ shall apply the following fee schedule, subject to §§ 1515.13 through 1515.15:

(a) Manual searches. Time devoted to manual searches shall be charged on the basis of the salary of the employee(s) conducting the search (basic hourly rate(s) of pay for the employee(s), plus 16 percent).

(b) Electronic searches. Fees shall reflect the direct cost of conducting the search. This will include the cost of operating the central processing unit for that portion of operating time that is directly attributable to searching for and printing records responsive to the FOIA request and operator/programmer salary attributable to the search.

(c) Record reviews. Time devoted to reviewing records shall be charged on the same basis as under paragraph (a) of this section, but shall only be applicable to the review of records located in response to commercial use requests.

(d) Duplication. Fees for copying paper records or for printing electronic records shall be assessed at a rate of $.15 per page. For other types of copies such as disks or audio visual tapes, CEQ shall charge the direct cost of producing the document(s). If total costs are expected to exceed $25, the FOIA Officer shall provide the requester with an estimate in writing and, in return, obtain from the requester a commitment to pay the estimated fee. This does not apply if the requester has indicated in advance a willingness to pay fees as high as those anticipated. If a requester wishes to limit costs, the FOIA Officer shall provide the requester an opportunity to reformulate the request in order to reduce costs. If the requester reformulates a request, it shall be considered a new request and the 20-day period described in § 1515.6(a) shall be deemed to begin when the FOIA Officer receives the request.

(e) (1) Advance payments required. The FOIA Officer may require a requester to make an advance deposit of up to the amount of the entire anticipated fee before the FOIA Officer begins to process the request if:

(i) The FOIA Officer estimates that the fee will exceed $250; or

(ii) The requester has previously failed to pay a fee in a timely fashion.

(2) When the FOIA Officer requires a requester to make an advance payment, the 20-day period described in § 1515.6(a) shall begin when the FOIA Officer receives the payment.

(f) No assessment of fee. CEQ shall not charge a fee to any requester if:

(1) The cost of collecting the fee would be equal to or greater than the fee itself; or

(2) After the effective date of these regulations CEQ fails to comply with a time limit under the Freedom of Information Act for responding to the request for records where no unusual or exceptional circumstances apply.

§ 1515.13 Fees for categories of requesters.

CEQ shall assess fees for certain categories of requesters as follows:

(a) Commercial use requesters. In responding to commercial use requests, CEQ shall assess fees that recover the full direct costs of searching for, reviewing, and duplicating records.

(b) Educational and non-commercial scientific institutions. CEQ shall provide records to requesters in this category for the cost of duplication alone, excluding charges for the first 100 pages. To qualify for inclusion in this fee category, a requester must show that the request is authorized by and is made under the auspices of a qualifying institution and that the records are sought to further scholarly research, not an individual goal.

(c) Representatives of the news media. CEQ shall provide records to requesters in this category for the cost of duplication alone, excluding charges for the first 100 pages.

(d) All other requesters. CEQ shall charge requesters who do not fall within paragraphs (a) through (c) of this section fees that recover the full direct cost of searching for and duplicating records, excluding charges for the first 100 pages of reproduction and the first two hours of search time.

§ 1515.14 Other charges.

CEQ may apply other charges, including the following:

(a) Special charges. CEQ shall recover the full cost of providing special services, such as sending records by express mail, to the extent that CEQ elects to provide them in that manner.

(b) Interest charges. CEQ may begin assessing interest charges on an unpaid bill starting on the 31st day following the day on which the FOIA Officer sent the billing. Interest shall be charged at the rate prescribed in 31 U.S.C. 3717 and will accrue from the date of billing.

(c) Aggregating requests. When the FOIA Officer reasonably believes that a requester or a group of requesters acting in concert is attempting to divide a request into a series of requests for the purpose of avoiding fees, the FOIA Officer shall aggregate those requests and charge accordingly.

§ 1515.15 Payment and waiver.

(a) Remittances. Payment shall be made in the form of check or money order made payable to the Treasury of the United States. At the time the FOIA Officer notifies a requester of the applicable fees, the Officer shall inform the requester of where to send the payment.

(b) Waiver of fees. CEQ may waive all or part of any fee provided for in §§ 1515.12 and 1515.13 when the FOIA Officer deems that disclosure of the information is in the general public's interest because it is likely to contribute significantly to public understanding of the operations or activities of the government and is not primarily in the commercial interest of the requester. In determining whether a fee should be waived, the FOIA Officer may consider whether:

(1) The subject matter specifically concerns identifiable operations or activities of the government;

(2) The information is already in the public domain;

(3) Disclosure of the information would contribute to the understanding of the public-at-large as opposed to a narrow segment of the population;

(4) Disclosure of the information would significantly enhance the public's understanding of the subject matter;

(5) Disclosure of the information would further a commercial interest of the requester; and

(6) The public's interest is greater than any commercial interest of the requester.

§ 1515.16 Other rights and services.

Nothing in this subpart will be construed to entitle any person, as of right, to any service or to the disclosure of any record to which such person is not entitled under the FOIA.

§§ 1515.17 to 1515.19 [Reserved]

PART 1516—PRIVACY ACT IMPLEMENTATION

Sec.

Authority: 5 U.S.C. 552a; Pub. L. No. 93–579.

Source: 42 Fed. Reg. 32537 (June 27, 1977), unless otherwise noted.

§ 1516.1 Purpose and scope.

The purposes of these regulations are to:

(a) Establish a procedure by which an individual can determine if the Council on Environmental Quality (hereafter known as the Council) maintains a system of records which includes a record pertaining to the individual; and

(b) Establish a procedure by which an individual can gain access to a record pertaining to him or her for the purpose of review, amendment and/or correction.

§ 1516.2 Definitions.

For the purpose of these regulations:

(a) The term individual means a citizen of the United States or an alien lawfully admitted for permanent residence;

(b) The term maintain means maintain, collect, use or disseminate;

(c) The term record means any item or collection or grouping of information about an individual that is maintained by the Council (including, but not limited to, his or her employment history, payroll information, and financial transactions), and that contains his or her name, or an identifying number, symbol, or other identifying particular assigned to the individual such as a social security number;

(d) The term system of records means a group of any records under the control of the Council from which information is retrieved by the name of the individual or by some identifying number, symbol, or other identifying particular assigned to the individual; and

(e) The term routine use means with respect to the disclosure of a record, the use of such record for a purpose which is compatible with the purpose for which it was collected.

§ 1516.3 Procedures for requests pertaining to individual records in a record system.

An individual shall submit a written request to the Administrative Officer of the Council to determine if a system of records named by the individual contains a record pertaining to the individual. The individual shall submit a written request to the Administrative Officer of the Council which states the individual's desire to review his or her record. The Administrative Officer of the Council is available to answer questions regarding these regulations and to provide assistance in locating records in the Council's system of records.

[42 Fed. Reg. 32537 (June 27, 1977); 42 Fed. Reg. 35960 (July 13, 1977).]

§ 1516.4 Times, places, and requirements for the identification of the individual making a request.

An individual making a request to the Administrative Officer of the Council pursuant to § 1516.3 shall present the request at the Council's office, 722 Jackson Place NW., Washington, DC 20006, on any business day between the hours of 9 a.m. and 5 p.m. and should be prepared to identify himself by signature. Requests will also be accepted in writing if mailed to the Council's offices and signed by the requester.

§ 1516.5 Disclosure of requested information to the individual.

Upon verification of identity, the Council shall disclose to the individual the information contained in the record which pertains to that individual.

(a) The individual may be accompanied for this purpose by a person of his choosing.

(b) Upon request of the individual to whom the record pertains, all information in the accounting of disclosures will be made available.

[42 Fed. Reg. 35960 (July 13, 1977).]

§ 1516.6 Request for correction or amendment to the record.

The individual may submit a request to the Administrative Officer of the Council which states the individual's desire to correct or to amend his or her record. This request must be made in accordance with the procedures of § 1516.4 and shall describe in detail the change which is requested.

[42 Fed. Reg. 32537 (June 27, 1977). Redesignated at 42 Fed. Reg. 35960 (July 13, 1977).]

§ 1516.7 Agency review of request for correction or amendment of the record.

Within ten working days of the receipt of a request to correct or to amend a record, the Administrative Officer of the Council will acknowledge in writing such receipt and promptly either:

(a) Make any correction or amendment of any portion thereof which the individual believes is not accurate, relevant, timely, or complete; or

(b) Inform the individual of his or her refusal to correct or amend the record in accordance with the request, the reason for the refusal, and the procedure established by the Council for the individual to request a review of that refusal.

§ 1516.8 Appeal of an initial adverse agency determination on correction or amendment of the record.

An individual may appeal refusal by the Administrative Officer of the Council to correct or to amend his or her record by submitting a request for a review of such refusal to the General Counsel, Council on Environmental Quality, 722 Jackson Place NW., Washington, DC 20006. The General Counsel shall, not later than thirty working days from the date on which the individual requests such a review, complete such review and make a final determination unless, for good cause shown, the General Counsel extends such thirty day period. If, after his or her review, the General Counsel also refuses to correct or to amend the record in accordance with the request, the individual may file with the Council a concise statement setting forth the reasons for his or her disagreement with the General Counsel's decision and may seek judicial relief under 5 U.S.C. 552a(g)(1)(A).

§ 1516.9 Disclosure of a record to a person other than the individual to whom the record pertains.

The Council will not disclose a record to any individual other than to the individual to whom the record pertains without receiving the prior written consent of the individual to whom the record pertains, unless the disclosure either has been listed as a "routine use" in the Council's notices of its systems of records or falls within the special conditions of disclosure set forth in section 3 of the Privacy Act of 1974.

§ 1516.10 Fees.

If an individual requests copies of his or her record, he or she shall be charged ten cents per page, excluding the cost of any search for the record, in advance of receipt of the pages.

PART 1517—PUBLIC MEETING PROCEDURES OF THE COUNCIL ON ENVIRONMENTAL QUALITY

Sec.

Authority: 5 U.S.C. 552b(g); Pub. L. No. 94–409.

Source: 42 Fed. Reg. 20818 (Apr. 22, 1977), unless otherwise noted.

§ 1517.1 Policy and scope.

Consistent with the policy that the public is entitled to the fullest information regarding the decisionmaking processes of the Federal Government, it is the purpose of this part to open the meetings of the Council on Environmental Quality to public observation while protecting the rights of individuals and the ability of the Council to carry out its primary responsibility of providing advice to the President. Actions taken by the Chairman acting as Director of the Office of Environmental Quality and Council actions involving advice to the President when such advice is not formulated collegially during a meeting are outside the scope of this part. In addition to conducting the meetings required by this part, it is the Council's policy to conduct, open to public observation, periodic meetings involving Council discussions of Council business, including where appropriate, matters outside the scope of this part. This part does not affect the procedures set forth in Part 1515 pursuant to which records of the Council are made available to the public for inspection and copying, except that the exemptions set forth in § 1517.4(a) shall govern in the case of any request made to copy or inspect the transcripts, recording or minutes described in § 1517.7.

[47 Fed. Reg. 6277 (Feb. 11, 1982).]

§ 1517.2 Definitions.

For the purpose of this part:

(a) The term Council shall mean the Council on Environmental Quality established under title II of the National Environmental Policy Act of 1969 (42 U.S.C. 4321 through 4347).

(b) The term meeting means the deliberations of at least two Council members where such deliberations determine or result in the joint conduct or disposition of official collegial Council business, but does not include deliberations to take actions to open or close a meeting under §§ 1517.4 and 1517.5 or to release or withhold information under §§ 1517.4 and 1517.7. "Meeting" shall not be construed to prevent Council members from considering individually Council business that is circulated to them sequentially in writing.

(c) Director means the Chairman of the Council on Environmental Quality acting as the head of the Office of Environmental Quality pursuant to the Environmental Quality Improvement Act of 1970, Pub.L. 91–224, 42 U.S.C. 4371 through 4374.

[44 Fed. Reg. 34946 (June 18, 1979), as amended at 47 Fed. Reg. 6277 (Feb. 11, 1982).]

§ 1517.3 Open meeting requirement.

(a) Every portion of every meeting of the Council is open to public observation subject to the exemptions provided in § 1517.4. Members of the Council may not jointly conduct or dispose of the business of the Council other than in accordance with this part.

(b) The Council will conduct open to public observation periodic meetings involving Council discussions of Council business including where appropriate matters outside the scope of this part. Such meetings will be noticed pursuant to § 1517.6.

(c) Members of the public may attend open meetings of the Council for the sole purpose of observation and may not participate in or photograph any meeting without prior permission of the Council. Members of the public who desire to participate in or photograph an open meeting of the Council may request permission to do so from the General Counsel of the Council before such meeting. Members of the public may record open meetings of the Council by means of any mechanical or electronic device unless the Council determines such recording would disrupt the orderly conduct of such meeting.

[44 Fed. Reg. 34946 (June 18, 1979), as amended at 47 Fed. Reg. 6277 (Feb. 11, 1982).]

§ 1517.4 Exceptions.

(a) A meeting or portion thereof may be closed to public observation, and information pertaining to such meeting or portion thereof may be withheld from the public, if the Council determines that such meeting or portion thereof or disclosure of such information is likely to:

> **(1)** Disclose matters that are (i) specifically authorized under criteria established by an Executive order to be kept secret in the interest of national defense or foreign policy and (ii) in fact properly classified pursuant to that Executive order;
>
> **(2)** Relate solely to the internal personnel rules and practices of the Council;
>
> **(3)** Disclose matters specifically exempted from disclosure by statute (other than the Freedom of Information Act, 5 U.S.C. 552), provided that the statute: (i) Requires that the matters be withheld

from the public in such a manner as to leave no discretion on the issue, or (ii) establishes particular criteria for withholding or refers to particular types of matters to be withheld;

(4) Disclose the trade secrets and commercial or financial information obtained from a person and privileged or confidential;

(5) Involve accusing any person of a crime, or formally censuring any person;

(6) Disclose information of a personal nature if disclosure would constitute a clearly unwarranted invasion of personal privacy;

(7) Disclose investigatory records compiled for law enforcement purposes, or information which if written would be contained in such records, but only to the extent that the production of those records or information would:

(i) Interfere with enforcement proceedings,

(ii) Deprive a person of a right to a fair trial or an impartial adjudication,

(iii) Constitute an unwarranted invasion of personal privacy,

(iv) Disclose the identity of a confidential source and, in the case of a record compiled by a criminal law enforcement authority in the course of a criminal investigation, or by an agency conducting a lawful national security intelligence investigation, confidential information furnished only by the confidential source,

(v) Disclose investigative techniques and procedures, or,

(vi) Endanger the life or physical safety of law enforcement personnel;

(8) Disclose information contained in or related to examination, operating, or condition reports prepared by, on behalf of, or for the use of an agency responsible for the regulation or supervision of financial institutions;

(9) Disclose information the premature disclosure of which would be likely to significantly frustrate implementation of a proposed action of the Council. This exception shall not apply in any instance where the Council has already disclosed to the public the content or nature of the proposed action, or where the Council is required by law to make such disclosure on its own initiative prior to taking final action on the proposal; or

(10) Specifically concern the issuance of a subpoena by the Council, or the participation of the Council in a civil action or proceeding, an action in a foreign court or international tribunal, or an arbitration, or the initiation, conduct, or disposition by the Council of a particular case of formal adjudication pursuant to the procedures in 5 U.S.C. 554 or otherwise involving a determination on the record after opportunity for a hearing.

(b) Before a meeting is closed to public observation the Council shall determine whether or not the public interest requires that the meeting be open. The Council may open a meeting to public observation which could be closed under paragraph (a) of this section, if the Council finds it to be in the public interest to do so.

§ 1517.5 Procedure for closing meetings.

(a) A majority of the entire membership of the Council may vote to close to public observation a meeting or a portion or portions thereof, or to withhold information pertaining to such meeting. A separate vote of the members of the Council shall be taken with respect to each meeting of the Council, a portion or portions of which are proposed to be closed to the observation of the public or with respect to any information concerning such meetings or portion thereof. A single vote may be taken with respect to a series of meetings, a portion or portions of which are proposed to be closed to the public, or with respect to information concerning such series of meetings, so long as each meeting in such series involves the same particular matters and is scheduled to be held no more than thirty days after the initial meeting in such series. The vote of each member of the Council participating in a vote shall be recorded and no proxies shall be allowed.

(b) Whenever any person whose interest may be directly affected by a portion of a meeting requests that the Council close that portion to public observation for any of the reasons referred to in § 1517.4(a) the Council, upon request of any of the members of the Council, shall decide by recorded vote whether to close that portion of the meeting.

(c) For every meeting or portion thereof closed under this part, the General Counsel of the Council before such meeting is closed shall publicly certify that, in his or her opinion, the meeting may properly be closed to the public stating each relevant exemptive provision. The Council shall retain a copy of the General Counsel's certification, together with a statement from the presiding officer of the meeting setting forth the time and place of the meeting and listing the persons present.

(d) Within one day of any vote taken on a proposal to close a meeting, the Council shall make publicly available a record reflecting the vote of each member on the question. In addition, within one day of any vote which closes a portion or portions of a meeting to the public, the Council shall make publicly available a full written explanation of its closure action together with a list naming all persons expected to attend and identifying their affiliation, unless such disclosure would reveal the information that the meeting itself was closed to protect.

(e) Following any announcement that the Council intends to close a meeting or portion thereof, any person may make a request that the meeting or portion thereof be opened. Such request shall be made of the Chairman of the Council who shall ensure that the request is circulated to all members of the Council on the same business day on which it is received. The request shall set forth the reasons why the requestor believes the meeting should be open. The Council upon the request of any member or its General Counsel, shall vote on the request.

§ 1517.6 Notice of meetings.

(a) Except as otherwise provided in this section, the Council shall make a public announcement at least one week before a meeting, to include the following:

- **(1)** Time, place, and subject matter of the meeting;
- **(2)** Whether the meeting is to be open or closed; and
- **(3)** Name and telephone number of the official who will respond to requests for information about the meeting.

(b) A majority of the members of the Council may determine by recorded vote that the business of the Council requires a meeting to be called with less than one week's notice. At the earliest practicable time, the Council shall publicly announce the time, place and subject matter of the meeting, and whether or not it is to be open or closed to the public.

(c) If announcement of the subject matter of a closed meeting would reveal the information that the meeting itself was closed to protect, the subject matter shall not be announced.

(d) Following the public announcement required by paragraph (a) or (b) of this section:

- **(1)** A majority of the members of the Council may change the time or place of a meeting. At the earliest practicable time, the Council shall publicly announce the change.
- **(2)** A majority of the entire membership of the Council may change the subject matter of a meeting, or the determination to open or close a meeting to the public, if it determines by a recorded vote that the change is required by the business of the Council and that no earlier announcement of the change was possible. At the earliest practicable time, the Council shall publicly announce the change, and the vote of each member upon the change.

(e) Individuals or organizations having a special interest in activities of the Council may request the Council to place them on a mailing list for receipt of information available under this section.

(f) Following public announcement of a meeting, the time or place of a meeting may be changed only if the change is announced publicly at the earliest practicable time. The subject matter of a meeting or the determination to open or close a meeting may be changed following public announcement of a meeting only if both of the following conditions are met:

(1) There must be a recorded vote of a majority of the Council that the business of the Council requires the change and that no earlier announcement of such change was possible; and

(2) There must be a public announcement of the change and of the individual Council members' votes at the earliest practicable time.

(g) Immediately following each public announcement required by this section, the following information, as applicable, shall be submitted for publication in the Federal Register.

(1) Notice of the time, place, and subject matter of a meeting;

(2) Whether the meeting is open or closed;

(3) Any change in one of the preceding; and

(4) The name and telephone number of the official who will respond to requests for information about the meeting.

§ 1517.7 Records of closed meetings.

(a) A record of each meeting or portion thereof which is closed to the public shall be made and retained for two years or for one year after the conclusion of any Council proceeding involved in the meeting whichever occurs later. The record of any portion of a meeting closed to the public shall be a verbatim transcript or electronic recording. In lieu of a transcript or recording, a comprehensive set of minutes may be produced if the closure decision was made pursuant to § 1517.4(a)(8) or (10).

(b) If minutes are produced, such minutes shall fully and clearly describe all matters discussed, provide a full and accurate summary of any actions taken and the reasons expressed therefor, and include a description of each of the views expressed on any item. The minutes shall also reflect the vote of each member of the Council on any roll call vote taken during the proceedings and identify all documents produced at the meeting.

(c) The following documents shall be retained by the Council as part of the transcript, recording, or minutes of the meeting:

(1) Certification by the General Counsel that the meeting may properly be closed; and

(2) Statement from the presiding officer of the meeting setting forth the date, time, and place of the meeting and listing the persons present.

(d) The Council shall make promptly available to the public at its offices at 722 Jackson Place, NW., Washington, DC the transcript, electronic recording, or minutes maintained as a record of a closed meeting, except for such information as may be withheld under one of the provisions of § 1517.5. Copies of such transcript, minutes, or transcription of an electronic recording, disclosing the identity of each speaker, shall be furnished to any person at the actual cost of duplication or transcription.

(e) [Reserved]

(f) Requests to review or obtain copies of records other than transcripts, electronic recordings or minutes of a meeting will be processed under the Freedom of Information Act (5 U.S.C. 552) or, where applicable, the Privacy Act of 1974. (5 U.S.C. 552a). Nothing in these regulations authorizes the Council to withhold from any individual any record, including the transcripts or electronic recordings described in § 1517.8, to which the individual may have access under the Privacy Act of 1974 (5 U.S.C. 552a).

APPENDIX C

ADMINISTRATIVE PROCEDURE ACT

A. INTERNAL PROCEDURES

5 U.S.C.A., Chapter 5

CHAPTER 5—ADMINISTRATIVE PROCEDURE

SUBCHAPTER II—ADMINISTRATIVE PROCEDURE

[1] So in original. Does not conform to section catchline.

SUBCHAPTER II—ADMINISTRATIVE PROCEDURE

HISTORICAL AND STATUTORY NOTES

Short Title

1946 Acts. The provisions of this subchapter and chapter 7 of this title were originally enacted by Act of June 11, 1946, c. 324, 60 Stat. 237, popularly known as the "Administrative Procedure Act." That Act was repealed as part of the general revision of this title by Pub. L. No. 89–554 and its provisions incorporated into this subchapter and chapter 7 hereof.

§ 551. Definitions

For the purpose of this subchapter—

(1) "agency" means each authority of the Government of the United States, whether or not it is within or subject to review by another agency, but does not include—

(A) the Congress;

(B) the courts of the United States;

(C) the governments of the territories or possessions of the United States;

(D) the government of the District of Columbia;

or except as to the requirements of section 552 of this title—

(E) agencies composed of representatives of the parties or of representatives of organizations of the parties to the disputes determined by them;

(F) courts martial and military commissions;

(G) military authority exercised in the field in time of war or in occupied territory; or

(H) functions conferred by sections 1738, 1739, 1743, and 1744 of title 12; subchapter II of chapter 471 of title 49; or sections 1884, 1891–1902, and former section 1641(b)(2), of title 50, appendix;

(2) "person" includes an individual, partnership, corporation, association, or public or private organization other than an agency;

(3) "party" includes a person or agency named or admitted as a party, or properly seeking and entitled as of right to be admitted as a party, in an agency proceeding, and a person or agency admitted by an agency as a party for limited purposes;

(4) "rule" means the whole or a part of an agency statement of general or particular applicability and future effect designed to implement, interpret, or prescribe law or policy or describing the organization, procedure, or practice requirements of an agency and includes the approval or prescription for the future of rates, wages, corporate or financial structures or reorganizations thereof, prices, facilities, appliances, services or allowances therefor or of valuations, costs, or accounting, or practices bearing on any of the foregoing;

(5) "rule making" means agency process for formulating, amending, or repealing a rule;

(6) "order" means the whole or a part of a final disposition, whether affirmative, negative, injunctive, or declaratory in form, of an agency in a matter other than rule making but including licensing;

(7) "adjudication" means agency process for the formulation of an order;

(8) "license" includes the whole or a part of an agency permit, certificate, approval, registration, charter, membership, statutory exemption or other form of permission;

(9) "licensing" includes agency process respecting the grant, renewal, denial, revocation, suspension, annulment, withdrawal, limitation, amendment, modification, or conditioning of a license;

(10) "sanction" includes the whole or a part of an agency—

(A) prohibition, requirement, limitation, or other condition affecting the freedom of a person;

(B) withholding of relief;

(C) imposition of penalty or fine;

(D) destruction, taking, seizure, or withholding of property;

(E) assessment of damages, reimbursement, restitution, compensation, costs, charges, or fees;

(F) requirement, revocation, or suspension of a license; or

(G) taking other compulsory or restrictive action;

(11) "relief" includes the whole or a part of an agency—

(A) grant of money, assistance, license, authority, exemption, exception, privilege, or remedy;

(B) recognition of a claim, right, immunity, privilege, exemption, or exception; or

(C) taking of other action on the application or petition of, and beneficial to, a person;

(12) "agency proceeding" means an agency process as defined by paragraphs (5), (7), and (9) of this section;

(13) "agency action" includes the whole or a part of an agency rule, order, license, sanction, relief, or the equivalent or denial thereof, or failure to act; and

(14) "ex parte communication" means an oral or written communication not on the public record with respect to which reasonable prior notice to all parties is not given, but it shall not include requests for status reports on any matter or proceeding covered by this subchapter.

(Pub. L. No. 89–554, 80 Stat. 381 (Sept. 6, 1966); as amended by Pub. L. No. 94–409, § 4(b), 90 Stat. 1247 (Sept. 13, 1976); Pub. L. No. 103–272, § 5(a), 108 Stat. 1373 (July 5, 1994); Pub. L. No. 111–350, § 5(a)(2), 124 Stat. 3841 (Jan. 4, 2011).)

HISTORICAL AND STATUTORY NOTES

Codifications

Section 551 of former Title 5, Executive Departments and Government Officers and Employees, was transferred to 7 U.S.C.A. § 2242.

Effective and Applicability Provisions

1976 Acts. Amendment by Pub. L. No. 94–409 effective 180 days after Sept. 13, 1976, see section 6 of Pub. L. No. 94–409, set out as a note under section 552b of this title.

Study and Reports on Administrative Subpoenas.

Pub. L. No. 106–544, § 7, 114 Stat. 2719 (Dec. 19, 2000), provided that:

"(a) Study on use of administrative subpoenas.—Not later than December 31, 2001, the Attorney General, in consultation with the Secretary of the Treasury, shall complete a study on the use of administrative subpoena power by executive branch agencies or entities and shall report the findings to the Committees on the Judiciary of the Senate and the House of Representatives. Such report shall include—

"(1) a description of the sources of administrative subpoena power and the scope of such subpoena power within executive branch agencies;

"(2) a description of applicable subpoena enforcement mechanisms;

"(3) a description of any notification provisions and any other provisions relating to safeguarding privacy interests;

"(4) a description of the standards governing the issuance of administrative subpoenas; and

"(5) recommendations from the Attorney General regarding necessary steps to ensure that administrative subpoena power is used and enforced consistently and fairly by executive branch agencies.

"(b) Report on frequency of use of administrative subpoenas.—

"(1) In general.—The Attorney General and the Secretary of the Treasury shall report in January of each year to the Committees on the Judiciary of the Senate and the House of Representatives on the number of administrative subpoenas issued by them under this section and the identity of the agency or component of the Department of Justice or the Department of the Treasury issuing the subpoena and imposing the charges.

"(2) Expiration.—The reporting requirement of this subsection shall terminate in 3 years after the date of the enactment of this section [Dec. 19, 2000]."

§ 552. Public information; agency rules, opinions, orders, records, and proceedings

(a) Each agency shall make available to the public information as follows:

(1) Each agency shall separately state and currently publish in the Federal Register for the guidance of the public—

(A) descriptions of its central and field organization and the established places at which, the employees (and in the case of a uniformed service, the members) from whom, and the methods whereby, the public may obtain information, make submittals or requests, or obtain decisions;

(B) statements of the general course and method by which its functions are channeled and determined, including the nature and requirements of all formal and informal procedures available;

(C) rules of procedure, descriptions of forms available or the places at which forms may be obtained, and instructions as to the scope and contents of all papers, reports, or examinations;

(D) substantive rules of general applicability adopted as authorized by law, and statements of general policy or interpretations of general applicability formulated and adopted by the agency; and

(E) each amendment, revision, or repeal of the foregoing.

Except to the extent that a person has actual and timely notice of the terms thereof, a person may not in any manner be required to resort to, or be adversely affected by, a matter required to be published in the Federal Register and not so published. For the purpose of this paragraph, matter reasonably available to the class of persons affected thereby is deemed published in the Federal Register when incorporated by reference therein with the approval of the Director of the Federal Register.

(2) Each agency, in accordance with published rules, shall make available for public inspection in an electronic format—

(A) final opinions, including concurring and dissenting opinions, as well as orders, made in the adjudication of cases;

(B) those statements of policy and interpretations which have been adopted by the agency and are not published in the Federal Register;

(C) administrative staff manuals and instructions to staff that affect a member of the public;

(D) copies of all records, regardless of form or format—

(i) that have been released to any person under paragraph (3); and

(ii) **(I)** that because of the nature of their subject matter, the agency determines have become or are likely to become the subject of subsequent requests for substantially the same records; or

(II) that have been requested 3 or more times; and

(E) a general index of the records referred to under subparagraph (D);

unless the materials are promptly published and copies offered for sale. For records created on or after November 1, 1996, within one year after such date, each agency shall make such records available, including by computer telecommunications or, if computer telecommunications means have not been established by the agency, by other electronic means. To the extent required to prevent a clearly unwarranted invasion of personal privacy, an agency may delete identifying details when it makes available or publishes an opinion, statement of policy, interpretation, staff manual, instruction, or copies of records referred to in subparagraph (D). However, in each case the justification for the deletion shall be explained fully in writing, and the extent of such deletion shall be indicated on the portion of the record which is made available or published, unless including that indication would harm an interest protected by the exemption in subsection (b) under which the deletion is made. If technically feasible, the extent of the deletion shall be indicated at the place in the record where the deletion was made. Each agency shall also maintain and make available for public inspection in an electronic format current indexes providing identifying information for the public as to any matter issued, adopted, or promulgated after July 4, 1967, and required by this paragraph to be made available or published. Each agency shall promptly publish, quarterly or more frequently, and distribute (by sale or otherwise) copies of each index or supplements thereto unless it determines by order published in the Federal Register that the publication would be unnecessary and impracticable, in which case the agency shall nonetheless provide copies of such index on request at a cost not to exceed the direct cost of duplication. Each agency shall make the index referred to in subparagraph (E) available by computer telecommunications by December 31, 1999. A final order, opinion, statement of policy, interpretation, or staff manual or instruction that affects a member of the public may be relied on, used, or cited as precedent by an agency against a party other than an agency only if—

(i) it has been indexed and either made available or published as provided by this paragraph; or

(ii) the party has actual and timely notice of the terms thereof.

(3) **(A)** Except with respect to the records made available under paragraphs (1) and (2) of this subsection, and except as provided in subparagraph (E), each agency, upon any request for records which (i) reasonably describes such records and (ii) is made in accordance with published rules stating the time, place, fees (if any), and procedures to be followed, shall make the records promptly available to any person.

(B) In making any record available to a person under this paragraph, an agency shall provide the record in any form or format requested by the person if the record is readily reproducible by the agency in that form or format. Each agency shall make reasonable efforts to maintain its records in forms or formats that are reproducible for purposes of this section.

(C) In responding under this paragraph to a request for records, an agency shall make reasonable efforts to search for the records in electronic form or format, except when such efforts would significantly interfere with the operation of the agency's automated information system.

(D) For purposes of this paragraph, the term "search" means to review, manually or by automated means, agency records for the purpose of locating those records which are responsive to a request.

(E) An agency, or part of an agency, that is an element of the intelligence community (as that term is defined in section 3(4) of the National Security Act of 1947 (50 U.S.C. 401a(4))) shall not make any record available under this paragraph to—

(i) any government entity, other than a State, territory, commonwealth, or district of the United States, or any subdivision thereof; or

(ii) a representative of a government entity described in clause (i).

(4) (A) (i) In order to carry out the provisions of this section, each agency shall promulgate regulations, pursuant to notice and receipt of public comment, specifying the schedule of fees applicable to the processing of requests under this section and establishing procedures and guidelines for determining when such fees should be waived or reduced. Such schedule shall conform to the guidelines which shall be promulgated, pursuant to notice and receipt of public comment, by the Director of the Office of Management and Budget and which shall provide for a uniform schedule of fees for all agencies.

(ii) Such agency regulations shall provide that—

(I) fees shall be limited to reasonable standard charges for document search, duplication, and review, when records are requested for commercial use;

(II) fees shall be limited to reasonable standard charges for document duplication when records are not sought for commercial use and the request is made by an educational or noncommercial scientific institution, whose purpose is scholarly or scientific research; or a representative of the news media; and

(III) for any request not described in (I) or (II), fees shall be limited to reasonable standard charges for document search and duplication.

In this clause, the term "a representative of the news media" means any person or entity that gathers information of potential interest to a segment of the public, uses its editorial skills to turn the raw materials into a distinct work, and distributes that work to an audience. In this clause, the term "news" means information that is about current events or that would be of current interest to the public. Examples of news-media entities are television or radio stations broadcasting to the public at large and publishers of periodicals (but only if such entities qualify as disseminators of "news") who make their products available for purchase by or subscription by or free distribution to the general public. These examples are not all-inclusive. Moreover, as methods of news delivery evolve (for example, the adoption of the electronic dissemination of newspapers through telecommunications services), such alternative media shall be considered to be news-media entities. A freelance journalist shall be regarded as working for a news-media entity if the journalist can demonstrate a solid basis for expecting publication through that entity, whether or not the journalist is actually employed by the entity. A publication contract would present a solid basis for such an expectation; the Government may also consider the past publication record of the requester in making such a determination.

(iii) Documents shall be furnished without any charge or at a charge reduced below the fees established under clause (ii) if disclosure of the information is in the public interest because it is likely to contribute significantly to public understanding of the operations or activities of the government and is not primarily in the commercial interest of the requester.

(iv) Fee schedules shall provide for the recovery of only the direct costs of search, duplication, or review. Review costs shall include only the direct costs incurred during the initial examination of a document for the purposes of determining whether the documents must be disclosed under this section and for the purposes of withholding any portions exempt from disclosure under this section. Review costs may not include any costs incurred in resolving issues of law or policy that may be raised in the course of processing a request under this section. No fee may be charged by any agency under this section—

(I) if the costs of routine collection and processing of the fee are likely to equal or exceed the amount of the fee; or

(II) for any request described in clause (ii)(II) or (III) of this subparagraph for the first two hours of search time or for the first one hundred pages of duplication.

(v) No agency may require advance payment of any fee unless the requester has previously failed to pay fees in a timely fashion, or the agency has determined that the fee will exceed $250.

(vi) Nothing in this subparagraph shall supersede fees chargeable under a statute specifically providing for setting the level of fees for particular types of records.

(vii) In any action by a requester regarding the waiver of fees under this section, the court shall determine the matter de novo: *Provided*, That the court's review of the matter shall be limited to the record before the agency.

(viii)(I) Except as provided in subclause (II), an agency shall not assess any search fees (or in the case of a requester described under clause (ii)(II) of this subparagraph, duplication fees) under this subparagraph if the agency has failed to comply with any time limit under paragraph (6).

(II) **(aa)** If an agency has determined that unusual circumstances apply (as the term is defined in paragraph (6)(B)) and the agency provided a timely written notice to the requester in accordance with paragraph (6)(B), a failure described in subclause (I) is excused for an additional 10 days. If the agency fails to comply with the extended time limit, the agency may not assess any search fees (or in the case of a requester described under clause (ii)(II) of this subparagraph, duplication fees).

(bb) If an agency has determined that unusual circumstances apply and more than 5,000 pages are necessary to respond to the request, an agency may charge search fees (or in the case of a requester described under clause (ii)(II) of this subparagraph, duplication fees) if the agency has provided a timely written notice to the requester in accordance with paragraph (6)(B) and the agency has discussed with the requester via written mail, electronic mail, or telephone (or made not less than 3 good-faith attempts to do so) how the requester could effectively limit the scope of the request in accordance with paragraph (6)(B)(ii).

(cc) If a court has determined that exceptional circumstances exist (as that term is defined in paragraph (6)(C)), a failure described in subclause (I) shall be excused for the length of time provided by the court order.

(B) On complaint, the district court of the United States in the district in which the complainant resides, or has his principal place of business, or in which the agency records are situated, or in the District of Columbia, has jurisdiction to enjoin the agency from withholding agency records and to order the production of any agency records improperly withheld from the complainant. In such a case the court shall determine the matter de novo, and may examine the contents of such agency records in camera to determine whether such records or any part thereof shall be withheld under any of the exemptions set forth in subsection (b) of this section, and the burden is on the agency to sustain its action. In addition to any other matters to which a court accords substantial weight, a court shall accord substantial weight to an affidavit of an agency concerning the agency's determination as to technical feasibility under paragraph (2)(C) and subsection (b) and reproducibility under paragraph (3)(B).

(C) Notwithstanding any other provision of law, the defendant shall serve an answer or otherwise plead to any complaint made under this subsection within thirty days after service upon the defendant of the pleading in which such complaint is made, unless the court otherwise directs for good cause shown.

(D) Repealed. Pub. L. No. 98–620, Title IV, § 402(2), 98 Stat. 3357 (Nov. 8, 1984).

(E) **(i)** The court may assess against the United States reasonable attorney fees and other litigation costs reasonably incurred in any case under this section in which the complainant has substantially prevailed.

(ii) For purposes of this subparagraph, a complainant has substantially prevailed if the complainant has obtained relief through either—

(I) a judicial order, or an enforceable written agreement or consent decree; or

(II) a voluntary or unilateral change in position by the agency, if the complainant's claim is not insubstantial.

(F) **(i)** Whenever the court orders the production of any agency records improperly withheld from the complainant and assesses against the United States reasonable attorney fees and other litigation costs, and the court additionally issues a written finding that the circumstances surrounding the withholding raise questions whether agency personnel acted arbitrarily or capriciously with respect to the withholding, the Special Counsel shall promptly initiate a proceeding to determine whether disciplinary action is warranted against the officer or employee who was primarily responsible for the withholding. The Special Counsel, after investigation and consideration of the evidence submitted, shall submit his findings and recommendations to the administrative authority of the agency concerned and shall send copies of the findings and recommendations to the officer or employee or his representative. The administrative authority shall take the corrective action that the Special Counsel recommends.

(ii) The Attorney General shall—

(I) notify the Special Counsel of each civil action described under the first sentence of clause (i); and

(II) annually submit a report to Congress on the number of such civil actions in the preceding year.

(iii) The Special Counsel shall annually submit a report to Congress on the actions taken by the Special Counsel under clause (i).

(G) In the event of noncompliance with the order of the court, the district court may punish for contempt the responsible employee, and in the case of a uniformed service, the responsible member.

(5) Each agency having more than one member shall maintain and make available for public inspection a record of the final votes of each member in every agency proceeding.

(6) **(A)** Each agency, upon any request for records made under paragraph (1), (2), or (3) of this subsection, shall—

(i) determine within 20 days (excepting Saturdays, Sundays, and legal public holidays) after the receipt of any such request whether to comply with such request and shall immediately notify the person making such request of—

(I) such determination and the reasons therefor;

(II) the right of such person to seek assistance from the FOIA Public Liaison of the agency; and

(III) in the case of an adverse determination—

(aa) the right of such person to appeal to the head of the agency, within a period determined by the head of the agency that is not less than 90 days after the date of such adverse determination; and

(bb) the right of such person to seek dispute resolution services from the FOIA Public Liaison of the agency or the Office of Government Information Services; and

(ii) make a determination with respect to any appeal within twenty days (excepting Saturdays, Sundays, and legal public holidays) after the receipt of such appeal. If on appeal the denial of the request for records is in whole or in part upheld, the agency shall notify the person making such request of the provisions for judicial review of that determination under paragraph (4) of this subsection.

The 20-day period under clause (i) shall commence on the date on which the request is first received by the appropriate component of the agency, but in any event not later than ten days after the request is first received by any component of the agency that is designated in the agency's regulations under this section to receive requests under this section. The 20-day period shall not be tolled by the agency except—

(I) that the agency may make one request to the requester for information and toll the 20-day period while it is awaiting such information that it has reasonably requested from the requester under this section; or

(II) if necessary to clarify with the requester issues regarding fee assessment. In either case, the agency's receipt of the requester's response to the agency's request for information or clarification ends the tolling period.

(B) **(i)** In unusual circumstances as specified in this subparagraph, the time limits prescribed in either clause (i) or clause (ii) of subparagraph (A) may be extended by written notice to the person making such request setting forth the unusual circumstances for such extension and the date on which a determination is expected to be dispatched. No such notice shall specify a date that would result in an extension for more than ten working days, except as provided in clause (ii) of this subparagraph.

(ii) With respect to a request for which a written notice under clause (i) extends the time limits prescribed under clause (i) of subparagraph (A), the agency shall notify the person making the request if the request cannot be processed within the time limit specified in that clause and shall provide the person an opportunity to limit the scope of the request so that it may be processed within that time limit or an opportunity to arrange with the agency an alternative time frame for processing the request or a modified request. To aid the requester, each agency shall make available its FOIA Public Liaison, who shall assist in the resolution of any disputes between the requester and the agency, and notify the requester of the right of the requester to seek dispute resolution services from the Office of Government Information Services. Refusal by the person to reasonably modify the request or arrange such an alternative time frame shall be considered as a factor in determining whether exceptional circumstances exist for purposes of subparagraph (C).

(iii) As used in this subparagraph, "unusual circumstances" means, but only to the extent reasonably necessary to the proper processing of the particular requests—

(I) the need to search for and collect the requested records from field facilities or other establishments that are separate from the office processing the request;

(II) the need to search for, collect, and appropriately examine a voluminous amount of separate and distinct records which are demanded in a single request; or

(III) the need for consultation, which shall be conducted with all practicable speed, with another agency having a substantial interest in the determination of the request or among two or more components of the agency having substantial subject-matter interest therein.

(iv) Each agency may promulgate regulations, pursuant to notice and receipt of public comment, providing for the aggregation of certain requests by the same requestor, or by a group of requestors acting in concert, if the agency reasonably believes that such requests actually constitute a single request, which would otherwise satisfy the unusual circumstances specified in this subparagraph, and the requests involve clearly related matters. Multiple requests involving unrelated matters shall not be aggregated.

(C) (i) Any person making a request to any agency for records under paragraph (1), (2), or (3) of this subsection shall be deemed to have exhausted his administrative remedies with respect to such request if the agency fails to comply with the applicable time limit provisions of this paragraph. If the Government can show exceptional circumstances exist and that the agency is exercising due diligence in responding to the request, the court may retain jurisdiction and allow the agency additional time to complete its review of the records. Upon any determination by an agency to comply with a request for records, the records shall be made promptly available to such person making such request. Any notification of denial of any request for records under this subsection shall set forth the names and titles or positions of each person responsible for the denial of such request.

(ii) For purposes of this subparagraph, the term "exceptional circumstances" does not include a delay that results from a predictable agency workload of requests under this section, unless the agency demonstrates reasonable progress in reducing its backlog of pending requests.

(iii) Refusal by a person to reasonably modify the scope of a request or arrange an alternative time frame for processing a request (or a modified request) under clause (ii) after being given an opportunity to do so by the agency to whom the person made the request shall be considered as a factor in determining whether exceptional circumstances exist for purposes of this subparagraph.

(D) (i) Each agency may promulgate regulations, pursuant to notice and receipt of public comment, providing for multitrack processing of requests for records based on the amount of work or time (or both) involved in processing requests.

(ii) Regulations under this subparagraph may provide a person making a request that does not qualify for the fastest multitrack processing an opportunity to limit the scope of the request in order to qualify for faster processing.

(iii) This subparagraph shall not be considered to affect the requirement under subparagraph (C) to exercise due diligence.

(E) (i) Each agency shall promulgate regulations, pursuant to notice and receipt of public comment, providing for expedited processing of requests for records—

(I) in cases in which the person requesting the records demonstrates a compelling need; and

(II) in other cases determined by the agency.

(ii) Notwithstanding clause (i), regulations under this subparagraph must ensure—

(I) that a determination of whether to provide expedited processing shall be made, and notice of the determination shall be provided to the person making the request, within 10 days after the date of the request; and

(II) expeditious consideration of administrative appeals of such determinations of whether to provide expedited processing.

(iii) An agency shall process as soon as practicable any request for records to which the agency has granted expedited processing under this subparagraph. Agency action to deny or affirm denial of a request for expedited processing pursuant to this subparagraph, and failure by an agency to respond in a timely manner to such a request shall be subject to judicial review under paragraph (4), except that the judicial review shall be based on the record before the agency at the time of the determination.

(iv) A district court of the United States shall not have jurisdiction to review an agency denial of expedited processing of a request for records after the agency has provided a complete response to the request.

(v) For purposes of this subparagraph, the term "compelling need" means—

(I) that a failure to obtain requested records on an expedited basis under this paragraph could reasonably be expected to pose an imminent threat to the life or physical safety of an individual; or

(II) with respect to a request made by a person primarily engaged in disseminating information, urgency to inform the public concerning actual or alleged Federal Government activity.

(vi) A demonstration of a compelling need by a person making a request for expedited processing shall be made by a statement certified by such person to be true and correct to the best of such person's knowledge and belief.

(F) In denying a request for records, in whole or in part, an agency shall make a reasonable effort to estimate the volume of any requested matter the provision of which is denied, and shall provide any such estimate to the person making the request, unless providing such estimate would harm an interest protected by the exemption in subsection (b) pursuant to which the denial is made.

(7) Each agency shall—

(A) establish a system to assign an individualized tracking number for each request received that will take longer than ten days to process and provide to each person making a request the tracking number assigned to the request; and

(B) establish a telephone line or Internet service that provides information about the status of a request to the person making the request using the assigned tracking number, including—

(i) the date on which the agency originally received the request; and

(ii) an estimated date on which the agency will complete action on the request.

(8) **(A)** An agency shall—

(i) withhold information under this section only if—

(I) the agency reasonably foresees that disclosure would harm an interest protected by an exemption described in subsection (b); or

(II) disclosure is prohibited by law; and

(ii) **(I)** consider whether partial disclosure of information is possible whenever the agency determines that a full disclosure of a requested record is not possible; and

(II) take reasonable steps necessary to segregate and release nonexempt information; and

(B) Nothing in this paragraph requires disclosure of information that is otherwise prohibited from disclosure by law, or otherwise exempted from disclosure under subsection (b)(3).

(b) This section does not apply to matters that are—

(1) **(A)** specifically authorized under criteria established by an Executive order to be kept secret in the interest of national defense or foreign policy and

(B) are in fact properly codified pursuant to such Executive order;

(2) related solely to the internal personnel rules and practices of an agency;

(3) specifically exempted from disclosure by statute (other than section 552b of this title), if that statute—

(A) **(i)** requires that the matters be withheld from the public in such a manner as to leave no discretion on the issue; or

(ii) establishes particular criteria for withholding or refers to particular types of matters to be withheld; and

(B) if enacted after the date of enactment of the OPEN FOIA Act of 2009, specifically cites to this paragraph.

(4) trade secrets and commercial or financial information obtained from a person and privileged or confidential;

(5) inter-agency or intra-agency memorandums or letters that would not be available by law to a party other than an agency in litigation with the agency, provided that the deliberative process privilege shall not apply to records created 25 years or more before the date on which the records were requested;

(6) personnel and medical files and similar files the disclosure of which would constitute a clearly unwarranted invasion of personal privacy;

(7) records or information compiled for law enforcement purposes, but only to the extent that the production of such law enforcement records or information

(A) could reasonably be expected to interfere with enforcement proceedings,

(B) would deprive a person of a right to a fair trial or an impartial adjudication,

(C) could reasonably be expected to constitute an unwarranted invasion of personal privacy,

(D) could reasonably be expected to disclose the identity of a confidential source, including a State, local, or foreign agency or authority or any private institution which furnished information on a confidential basis, and, in the case of a record or information compiled by criminal law enforcement authority in the course of a criminal investigation or by an agency conducting a lawful national security intelligence investigation, information furnished by a confidential source,

(E) would disclose techniques and procedures for law enforcement investigations or prosecutions, or would disclose guidelines for law enforcement investigations or prosecutions if such disclosure could reasonably be expected to risk circumvention of the law, or

(F) could reasonably be expected to endanger the life or physical safety of any individual;

(8) contained in or related to examination, operating, or condition reports prepared by, on behalf of, or for the use of an agency responsible for the regulation or supervision of financial institutions; or

(9) geological and geophysical information and data, including maps, concerning wells.

Any reasonably segregable portion of a record shall be provided to any person requesting such record after deletion of the portions which are exempt under this subsection. The amount of information deleted, and the exemption under which the deletion is made, shall be indicated on the released portion of the record, unless including that indication would harm an interest protected by the exemption in this subsection under which the deletion is made. If technically feasible, the amount of the information deleted, and the exemption under which the deletion is made, shall be indicated at the place in the record where such deletion is made.

(c) **(1)** Whenever a request is made which involves access to records described in subsection (b)(7)(A) and—

(A) the investigation or proceeding involves a possible violation of criminal law; and

(B) there is reason to believe that (i) the subject of the investigation or proceeding is not aware of its pendency, and (ii) disclosure of the existence of the records could reasonably be expected to interfere with enforcement proceedings,

the agency may, during only such time as that circumstance continues, treat the records as not subject to the requirements of this section.

(2) Whenever informant records maintained by a criminal law enforcement agency under an informant's name or personal identifier are requested by a third party according to the informant's name or personal identifier, the agency may treat the records as not subject to the requirements of this section unless the informant's status as an informant has been officially confirmed.

(3) Whenever a request is made which involves access to records maintained by the Federal Bureau of Investigation pertaining to foreign intelligence or counterintelligence, or international terrorism, and the existence of the records is classified information as provided in subsection (b)(1), the Bureau may, as long as the existence of the records remains classified information, treat the records as not subject to the requirements of this section.

(d) This section does not authorize withholding of information or limit the availability of records to the public, except as specifically stated in this section. This section is not authority to withhold information from Congress.

(e) **(1)** On or before February 1 of each year, each agency shall submit to the Attorney General of the United States and to the Director of the Office of Government Information Services a report which shall cover the preceding fiscal year and which shall include—

(A) the number of determinations made by the agency not to comply with requests for records made to such agency under subsection (a) and the reasons for each such determination;

(B) **(i)** the number of appeals made by persons under subsection (a)(6), the result of such appeals, and the reason for the action upon each appeal that results in a denial of information; and

(ii) a complete list of all statutes that the agency relies upon to authorize the agency to withhold information under subsection (b)(3), the number of occasions on which each statute was relied upon, a description of whether a court has upheld the decision of the agency to withhold information under each such statute, and a concise description of the scope of any information withheld;

(C) the number of requests for records pending before the agency as of September 30 of the preceding year, and the median and average number of days that such requests had been pending before the agency as of that date;

(D) the number of requests for records received by the agency and the number of requests which the agency processed;

(E) the median number of days taken by the agency to process different types of requests, based on the date on which the requests were received by the agency;

(F) the average number of days for the agency to respond to a request beginning on the date on which the request was received by the agency, the median number of days for the agency to respond to such requests, and the range in number of days for the agency to respond to such requests;

(G) based on the number of business days that have elapsed since each request was originally received by the agency—

(i) the number of requests for records to which the agency has responded with a determination within a period up to and including 20 days, and in 20-day increments up to and including 200 days;

(ii) the number of requests for records to which the agency has responded with a determination within a period greater than 200 days and less than 301 days;

(iii) the number of requests for records to which the agency has responded with a determination within a period greater than 300 days and less than 401 days; and

(iv) the number of requests for records to which the agency has responded with a determination within a period greater than 400 days;

(H) the average number of days for the agency to provide the granted information beginning on the date on which the request was originally filed, the median number of days for the agency to provide the granted information, and the range in number of days for the agency to provide the granted information;

(I) the median and average number of days for the agency to respond to administrative appeals based on the date on which the appeals originally were received by the agency, the highest number of business days taken by the agency to respond to an administrative appeal, and the lowest number of business days taken by the agency to respond to an administrative appeal;

(J) data on the 10 active requests with the earliest filing dates pending at each agency, including the amount of time that has elapsed since each request was originally received by the agency;

(K) data on the 10 active administrative appeals with the earliest filing dates pending before the agency as of September 30 of the preceding year, including the number of business days that have elapsed since the requests were originally received by the agency;

(L) the number of expedited review requests that are granted and denied, the average and median number of days for adjudicating expedited review requests, and the number adjudicated within the required 10 days;

(M) the number of fee waiver requests that are granted and denied, and the average and median number of days for adjudicating fee waiver determinations;

(N) the total amount of fees collected by the agency for processing requests;

(O) the number of full-time staff of the agency devoted to processing requests for records under this section, and the total amount expended by the agency for processing such requests;

(P) the number of times the agency denied a request for records under subsection (c); and

(Q) the number of records that were made available for public inspection in an electronic format under subsection (a)(2).

(2) Information in each report submitted under paragraph (1) shall be expressed in terms of each principal component of the agency and for the agency overall.

(3) Each agency shall make each such report available for public inspection in an electronic format. In addition, each agency shall make the raw statistical data used in each report available in a timely manner for public inspection in an electronic format, which shall be made available—

(A) without charge, license, or registration requirement;

(B) in an aggregated, searchable format; and

(C) in a format that may be downloaded in bulk.

(4) The Attorney General of the United States shall make each report which has been made available by electronic means available at a single electronic access point. The Attorney General of the United States shall notify the Chairman and ranking minority member of the Committee on Oversight and Government Reform of the House of Representatives and the Chairman and ranking minority member of the Committees on Homeland Security and Governmental Affairs and the Judiciary of the Senate, no later than March 1 of the year in which each such report is issued, that such reports are available by electronic means.

(5) The Attorney General of the United States, in consultation with the Director of the Office of Management and Budget, shall develop reporting and performance guidelines in connection with reports required by this subsection by October 1, 1997, and may establish additional requirements for such reports as the Attorney General determines may be useful.

(6) **(A)** The Attorney General of the United States shall submit to the Committee on Oversight and Government Reform of the House of Representatives, the Committee on the Judiciary of the Senate, and the President a report on or before March 1 of each calendar year, which shall include for the prior calendar year—

(i) a listing of the number of cases arising under this section;

(ii) a listing of—

(I) each subsection, and any exemption, if applicable, involved in each case arising under this section;

(II) the disposition of each case arising under this section; and

(III) the cost, fees, and penalties assessed under subparagraphs (E), (F), and (G) of subsection (a)(4); and

(iii) a description of the efforts undertaken by the Department of Justice to encourage agency compliance with this section.

(B) The Attorney General of the United States shall make—

(i) each report submitted under subparagraph (A) available for public inspection in an electronic format; and

(ii) the raw statistical data used in each report submitted under subparagraph (A) available for public inspection in an electronic format, which shall be made available—

(I) without charge, license, or registration requirement;

(II) in an aggregated, searchable format; and

(III) in a format that may be downloaded in bulk.

(f) For purposes of this section, the term—

(1) "agency" as defined in section 551(1) of this title includes any executive department, military department, Government corporation, Government controlled corporation, or other establishment in the executive branch of the Government (including the Executive Office of the President), or any independent regulatory agency; and

(2) "record" and any other term used in this section in reference to information includes—

(A) any information that would be an agency record subject to the requirements of this section when maintained by an agency in any format, including an electronic format; and

(B) any information described under subparagraph (A) that is maintained for an agency by an entity under Government contract, for the purposes of records management.

(g) The head of each agency shall prepare and make available for public inspection in an electronic format, reference material or a guide for requesting records or information from the agency, subject to the exemptions in subsection (b), including—

(1) an index of all major information systems of the agency;

(2) a description of major information and record locator systems maintained by the agency; and

(3) a handbook for obtaining various types and categories of public information from the agency pursuant to chapter 35 of title 44, and under this section.

(h) (1) There is established the Office of Government Information Services within the National Archives and Records Administration. The head of the Office shall be the Director of the Office of Government Information Services.

(2) The Office of Government Information Services shall—

(A) review policies and procedures of administrative agencies under this section;

(B) review compliance with this section by administrative agencies; and

(C) identify procedures and methods for improving compliance under this section.

(3) The Office of Government Information Services shall offer mediation services to resolve disputes between persons making requests under this section and administrative agencies as a nonexclusive

alternative to litigation and may issue advisory opinions at the discretion of the Office or upon request of any party to a dispute.

(4) **(A)** Not less frequently than annually, the Director of the Office of Government Information Services shall submit to the Committee on Oversight and Government Reform of the House of Representatives, the Committee on the Judiciary of the Senate, and the President—

(i) a report on the findings of the information reviewed and identified under paragraph (2);

(ii) a summary of the activities of the Office of Government Information Services under paragraph (3), including—

(I) any advisory opinions issued; and

(II) the number of times each agency engaged in dispute resolution with the assistance of the Office of Government Information Services or the FOIA Public Liaison; and

(iii) legislative and regulatory recommendations, if any, to improve the administration of this section.

(B) The Director of the Office of Government Information Services shall make each report submitted under subparagraph (A) available for public inspection in an electronic format.

(C) The Director of the Office of Government Information Services shall not be required to obtain the prior approval, comment, or review of any officer or agency of the United States, including the Department of Justice, the Archivist of the United States, or the Office of Management and Budget before submitting to Congress, or any committee or subcommittee thereof, any reports, recommendations, testimony, or comments, if such submissions include a statement indicating that the views expressed therein are those of the Director and do not necessarily represent the views of the President.

(5) The Director of the Office of Government Information Services may directly submit additional information to Congress and the President as the Director determines to be appropriate.

(6) Not less frequently than annually, the Office of Government Information Services shall conduct a meeting that is open to the public on the review and reports by the Office and shall allow interested persons to appear and present oral or written statements at the meeting.

(i) The Government Accountability Office shall conduct audits of administrative agencies on the implementation of this section and issue reports detailing the results of such audits.

(j) **(1)** Each agency shall designate a Chief FOIA Officer who shall be a senior official of such agency (at the Assistant Secretary or equivalent level).

(2) The Chief FOIA Officer of each agency shall, subject to the authority of the head of the agency—

(A) have agency-wide responsibility for efficient and appropriate compliance with this section;

(B) monitor implementation of this section throughout the agency and keep the head of the agency, the chief legal officer of the agency, and the Attorney General appropriately informed of the agency's performance in implementing this section;

(C) recommend to the head of the agency such adjustments to agency practices, policies, personnel, and funding as may be necessary to improve its implementation of this section;

(D) review and report to the Attorney General, through the head of the agency, at such times and in such formats as the Attorney General may direct, on the agency's performance in implementing this section;

(E) facilitate public understanding of the purposes of the statutory exemptions of this section by including concise descriptions of the exemptions in both the agency's handbook issued under subsection (g), and the agency's annual report on this section, and by providing an overview, where appropriate, of certain general categories of agency records to which those exemptions apply;

(F) offer training to agency staff regarding their responsibilities under this section;

(G) serve as the primary agency liaison with the Office of Government Information Services and the Office of Information Policy; and

(H) designate 1 or more FOIA Public Liaisons.

(3) The Chief FOIA Officer of each agency shall review, not less frequently than annually, all aspects of the administration of this section by the agency to ensure compliance with the requirements of this section, including—

(A) agency regulations;

(B) disclosure of records required under paragraphs (2) and (8) of subsection (a);

(C) assessment of fees and determination of eligibility for fee waivers;

(D) the timely processing of requests for information under this section;

(E) the use of exemptions under subsection (b); and

(F) dispute resolution services with the assistance of the Office of Government Information Services or the FOIA Public Liaison.

(k) **(1)** There is established in the executive branch the Chief FOIA Officers Council (referred to in this subsection as the 'Council').

(2) The Council shall be comprised of the following members:

(A) The Deputy Director for Management of the Office of Management and Budget.

(B) The Director of the Office of Information Policy at the Department of Justice.

(C) The Director of the Office of Government Information Services.

(D) The Chief FOIA Officer of each agency.

(E) Any other officer or employee of the United States as designated by the Co-Chairs.

(3) The Director of the Office of Information Policy at the Department of Justice and the Director of the Office of Government Information Services shall be the Co-Chairs of the Council.

(4) The Administrator of General Services shall provide administrative and other support for the Council.

(5) **(A)** The duties of the Council shall include the following:

(i) Develop recommendations for increasing compliance and efficiency under this section.

(ii) Disseminate information about agency experiences, ideas, best practices, and innovative approaches related to this section.

(iii) Identify, develop, and coordinate initiatives to increase transparency and compliance with this section.

(iv) Promote the development and use of common performance measures for agency compliance with this section.

(B) In performing the duties described in subparagraph (A), the Council shall consult on a regular basis with members of the public who make requests under this section.

(6) **(A)** The Council shall meet regularly and such meetings shall be open to the public unless the Council determines to close the meeting for reasons of national security or to discuss information exempt under subsection (b).

(B) Not less frequently than annually, the Council shall hold a meeting that shall be open to the public and permit interested persons to appear and present oral and written statements to the Council.

(C) Not later than 10 business days before a meeting of the Council, notice of such meeting shall be published in the Federal Register.

(D) Except as provided in subsection (b), the records, reports, transcripts, minutes, appendices, working papers, drafts, studies, agenda, or other documents that were made available to or prepared for or by the Council shall be made publicly available.

(E) Detailed minutes of each meeting of the Council shall be kept and shall contain a record of the persons present, a complete and accurate description of matters discussed and conclusions reached, and copies of all reports received, issued, or approved by the Council. The minutes shall be redacted as necessary and made publicly available.

(*l*) FOIA Public Liaisons shall report to the agency Chief FOIA Officer and shall serve as supervisory officials to whom a requester under this section can raise concerns about the service the requester has received from the FOIA Requester Center, following an initial response from the FOIA Requester Center Staff. FOIA Public Liaisons shall be responsible for assisting in reducing delays, increasing transparency and understanding of the status of requests, and assisting in the resolution of disputes.

(m) **(1)** The Director of the Office of Management and Budget, in consultation with the Attorney General, shall ensure the operation of a consolidated online request portal that allows a member of the public to submit a request for records under subsection (a) to any agency from a single website. The portal may include any additional tools the Director of the Office of Management and Budget finds will improve the implementation of this section.

(2) This subsection shall not be construed to alter the power of any other agency to create or maintain an independent online portal for the submission of a request for records under this section. The Director of the Office of Management and Budget shall establish standards for interoperability between the portal required under paragraph (1) and other request processing software used by agencies subject to this section.".

(Pub. L. No. 89–554, 80 Stat. 383 (Sept. 6, 1966); as amended by Pub. L. No. 90–23, § 1, 81 Stat. 54 (June 5, 1967); Pub. L. No. 93–502, §§ 1 to 3, 88 Stat. 1561 to 1564 (Nov. 21, 1974); Pub. L. No. 94–409, § 5(b), 90 Stat. 1247 (Sept. 13, 1976); Pub. L. No. 95–454, Title IX, § 906(a)(10), 92 Stat. 1225 (Oct. 13, 1978); Pub. L. No. 98–620, Title IV, § 402(2), 98 Stat. 3357 (Nov. 8, 1984); Pub. L. No. 99–570, Title I, §§ 1802, 1803, 100 Stat. 3207–48, 3207–49 (Oct. 27, 1986); Pub. L. No. 104–231, §§ 3 to 11, 110 Stat. 3049 to 3054 (Oct. 2, 1996); Pub. L. No. 107–306, Title III, § 312, 116 Stat. 2390 (Nov. 27, 2002); Pub. L. No. 110–175, §§ 3, 4(a), 5, 6(a)(1), (b)(1), 7(a), 8 to 10(a), 12, 121 Stat. 2525 to 2530 (Dec. 31, 2007); Pub. L. No. 111–83, Title V, § 564(b), 123 Stat. 2184 (Oct. 28, 2009); Pub. L. No. 114–185, § 2, 130 Stat 538 (June 30, 2016).)

HISTORICAL AND STATUTORY NOTES

References in Text

The National Security Act of 1947, referred to in subsec. (a)(3)(E), is Act of July 26, 1947, c. 343, 61 Stat. 495, as amended, which was formerly codified principally as chapter 15 of Title 50, 50 U.S.C.A. § 401 et seq., prior to editorial classification in chapter 44 of Title 50, 50 U.S.C.A. § 3001 et seq. Section 3 of such Act is now codified as 50 U.S.C.A. § 3003. For complete classification, see Tables.

The date of enactment of the OPEN FOIA Act of 2009, referred to in subsec. (b)(3)(B), is the date of enactment of Pub. L. No. 111–83, which was approved Oct. 28, 2009.

Codifications

Section 552 of former Title 5, Executive Departments and Government Officers and Employees, was transferred to 7 U.S.C.A. § 2243.

Effective and Applicability Provisions

2016 Amendments. Pub. L. No. 114–185, § 6, 130 Stat. 544–45, provided that: "This Act, and the amendments made by this Act, shall take effect on the date of enactment of this Act and shall apply to any request for records under section 552 of title 5, United States Code, made after the date of enactment of this Act."

2007 Acts. Pub. L. No. 110–175, § 6(a)(2), 121 Stat. 2526 (Dec. 31, 2007), provided that: "The amendment made by this subsection [amending subsec. (a)(6)(A) of this section] shall take effect 1 year after the date of enactment of this Act [Dec. 31, 2007]."

Pub. L. No. 110–175, § 6(b)(2), 121 Stat. 2526 (Dec. 31, 2007), provided that: "The amendment made by this subsection [amending subsecs. (a)(4)(A) and (a)(6)(B)(ii) of this section] shall take effect 1 year after the date of enactment of this Act [Dec. 31, 2007] and apply to requests for information under section 552 of title 5, United States Code, filed on or after that effective date."

Pub. L. No. 110–175, § 7(b), 121 Stat. 2527 (Dec. 31, 2007), provided that: "The amendment made by this section [amending subsec. (a) by adding par. (7) to this section] shall take effect 1 year after the date of enactment of this Act [Dec. 31, 2007] and apply to requests for information under section 552 of title 5, United States Code, filed on or after that effective date."

Pub. L. No. 110–175, § 10(b), 121 Stat. 2530 (Dec. 31, 2007), provided that: "The amendments made by this section [adding subsecs. (h) to (*l*) of this section] shall take effect on the date of enactment of this Act [Dec. 31, 2007]."

1996 Acts. Section 12 of Pub. L. No. 104–231 provided that:

"(a) In general.—Except as provided in subsection (b), this Act [amending this section and enacting provisions set out as notes under this section] shall take effect 180 days after the date of the enactment of this Act [Oct. 2, 1996].

"(b) Provisions effective on enactment.—Sections 7 [enacting subsec. (a)(6)(D) of this section and amending subsec. (a)(6)(B) and (C) of this section] and 8 [enacting subsec. (a)(6)(E) and (F) of this section and amending subsec. (a)(6)(A)(i) of this section] shall take effect one year after the date of the enactment of this Act [Oct. 2, 1996]."

1986 Acts. Section 1804 of Pub. L. No. 99–570 provided that:

"(a) The amendments made by section 1802 [amending this section] shall be effective on the date of enactment of this Act [Oct. 27, 1986], and shall apply with respect to any requests for records, whether or not the request was made prior to such date, and shall apply to any civil action pending on such date.

"(b) (1) The amendments made by section 1803 [amending this section] shall be effective 180 days after the date of enactment of this Act [Oct. 27, 1986], except that regulations to implement such amendments shall be promulgated by such 180th day.

"(2) The amendments made by section 1803 [amending this section] shall apply with respect to any requests for records, whether or not the request was made prior to such date, and shall apply to any civil action pending on such date, except that review charges applicable to records requested for commercial use shall not be applied by an agency to requests made before the effective date specified in paragraph (1) of this subsection or before the agency has finally issued its regulations."

1984 Acts. Amendment by Pub. L. No. 98–620 not applicable to cases pending on Nov. 8, 1984, see section 403 of Pub. L. No. 98–620, set out as a note under section 1657 of Title 28, Judiciary and Judicial Procedure.

1978 Acts. Amendment by Pub. L. No. 95–454 effective 90 days after Oct. 13, 1978, see section 907 of Pub. L. No. 95–454, set out as a note under section 1101 of this title.

1976 Acts. Amendment by Pub. L. No. 94–409 effective 180 days after Sept. 13, 1976, see section 6 of Pub. L. No. 94–409, set out as a note under section 552b of this title.

1974 Acts. Section 4 of Pub. L. No. 93–502 provided that: "The amendments made by this Act [amending this section] shall take effect on the ninetieth day beginning after the date of enactment of this Act [Nov. 21, 1974]."

1967 Acts. Section 4 of Pub. L. No. 90–23 provided that: "This Act [amending this section] shall be effective July 4, 1967, or on the date of enactment [June 5, 1967], whichever is later."

Change of Name

Committee on Government Reform and Oversight of House of Representatives changed to Committee on Government Reform of House of Representatives by House Resolution No. 5, One Hundred Sixth Congress, Jan. 6, 1999. Committee on Government Reform of House of Representatives changed to Committee on Oversight and Government Reform of House of Representatives by House Resolution No. 6, 110th Congress, Jan. 5, 2007.

Committee on Governmental Affairs of Senate changed to Committee on Homeland Security and Governmental Affairs of Senate, effective Jan. 4, 2005, by Senate Resolution No. 445, 108th, Oct. 9, 2004.

Short Title

2016 Amendments. Section 1 of Pub. L. No. 114–185, 130 Stat. 538, provided that: "This act may be cited as the 'FOIA Improvement Act of 2016.' "

1996 Amendments. Section 1 of Pub. L. No. 104–231 provided that: "This Act [amending this section and enacting provisions set out as notes under this section] may be cited as the 'Electronic Freedom of Information Act Amendments of 1996'."

1986 Amendments. Section 1801 of Pub. L. No. 99–570 provided that: "This subtitle [subtitle N (sections 1801 to 1804) of Title I of Pub. L. No. 99–570, amending this section and enacting provisions set out as a note under this section] may be cited as the 'Freedom of Information Reform Act of 1986'."

1966 Acts. This section is popularly known as the "Freedom of Information Act" or the FOIA. A prior act, also popularly known as the Freedom of Information Act, Pub. L. No. 89–487, 80 Stat. 250 (July 4, 1966), which was codified as former 5 U.S.C.A. § 1002, was repealed by Pub. L. No. 90–23, § 3, 81 Stat. 54 (June 5, 1976). Section 1 of Pub. L. No. 90–23 generally amended this section to reflect Pub. L. No. 89–487.

Review and Issuance of Regulations

Pub. L. No. 114–185, § 3, 130 Stat. 544, provided that:

"(a) In General.—Not later than 180 days after the date of enactment of this Act, the head of each agency (as defined in section 551 of title 5, United States Code) shall review the regulations of such agency and shall issue regulations on procedures for the disclosure of records under section 552 of title 5, United States Code, in accordance with the amendments made by section 2.

"(b) Requirements.—The regulations of each agency shall include procedures for engaging in dispute resolution through the FOIA Public Liaison and the Office of Government Information Services."

Protected National Security Documents Act of 2009

Pub. L. No. 111–83, Title V, § 565, 123 Stat. 2184 (Oct. 28, 2009), provided that:

"(a) Short title.—This section [this note] may be cited as the 'Protected National Security Documents Act of 2009'.

"(b) Notwithstanding any other provision of the law to the contrary, no protected document, as defined in subsection (c), shall be subject to disclosure under section 552 of title 5, United States Code [this section] or any proceeding under that section.

"(c) Definitions.—In this section [this note]:

"(1) Protected document.—The term 'protected document' means any record—

"(A) for which the Secretary of Defense has issued a certification, as described in subsection (d), stating that disclosure of that record would endanger citizens of the United States, members of the United States Armed Forces, or employees of the United States Government deployed outside the United States; and

"(B) that is a photograph that—

"(i) was taken during the period beginning on September 11, 2001, through January 22, 2009; and

"(ii) relates to the treatment of individuals engaged, captured, or detained after September 11, 2001, by the Armed Forces of the United States in operations outside of the United States.

"(2) Photograph.—The term 'photograph' encompasses all photographic images, whether originals or copies, including still photographs, negatives, digital images, films, video tapes, and motion pictures.

"(d) Certification.—

"(1) In general.—For any photograph described under subsection (c)(1), the Secretary of Defense shall issue a certification if the Secretary of Defense determines that disclosure of that photograph would endanger citizens of the United States, members of the United States Armed Forces, or employees of the United States Government deployed outside the United States.

"(2) Certification expiration.—A certification and a renewal of a certification issued pursuant to subsection (d)(3) shall expire 3 years after the date on which the certification or renewal, is issued by the Secretary of Defense.

"(3) Certification renewal.—The Secretary of Defense may issue—

"(A) a renewal of a certification at any time; and

"(B) more than 1 renewal of a certification.

"(4) Notice to Congress.—The Secretary of Defense shall provide Congress a timely notice of the Secretary's issuance of a certification and of a renewal of a certification.

"(e) Rule of construction.—Nothing in this section [this note] shall be construed to preclude the voluntary disclosure of a protected document.

"(f) Effective date.—This section [this note] shall take effect on the date of enactment of this Act [Oct. 28, 2009] and apply to any protected document."

Findings

Pub. L. No. 110–175, § 2, 121 Stat. 2524 (Dec. 31, 2007), provided that:

"Congress finds that—

"(1) The Freedom of Information Act [Pub. L. No. 89–487, 80 Stat. 250 (July 4, 1966), which was codified as former 5 U.S.C.A. § 1002, which was repealed by Pub. L. No. 90–23, § 3, 81 Stat. 54 (June 5, 1976); section 1 of Pub. L. No. 90–23, generally amended this section to reflect Pub. L. No. 89–487] was signed into law on July 4, 1966, because the American people believe that—

"(A) our constitutional democracy, our system of self-government, and our commitment to popular sovereignty depends upon the consent of the governed;

"(B) such consent is not meaningful unless it is informed consent; and

"(C) as Justice Black noted in his concurring opinion in Barr v. Matteo (360 U.S. 564 (1959)), 'The effective functioning of a free government like ours depends largely on the force of an informed public opinion. This calls for the widest possible understanding of the quality of government service rendered by all elective or appointed public officials or employees.';

"(2) the American people firmly believe that our system of government must itself be governed by a presumption of openness;

"(3) the Freedom of Information Act establishes a 'strong presumption in favor of disclosure' as noted by the United States Supreme Court in United States Department of State v. Ray (502 U.S. 164 (1991)), a presumption that applies to all agencies governed by that Act;

"(4) 'disclosure, not secrecy, is the dominant objective of the Act,' as noted by the United States Supreme Court in Department of Air Force v. Rose (425 U.S. 352 (1976));

"(5) in practice, the Freedom of Information Act has not always lived up to the ideals of that Act; and

"(6) Congress should regularly review section 552 of title 5, United States Code (commonly referred to as the Freedom of Information Act), in order to determine whether further changes and improvements are necessary to ensure that the Government remains open and accessible to the American people and is always based not upon the 'need to know' but upon the fundamental 'right to know'."

Limitation

Pub. L. No. 110–175, § 4(b), 121 Stat. 2525 (Dec. 31, 2007), provided that: "Notwithstanding section 1304 of title 31, United States Code, no amounts may be obligated or expended from the Claims and Judgment Fund of the United States Treasury to pay the costs resulting from fees assessed under section 552(a)(4)(E) of title 5 [subsec. (a)(4)(E) of this section], United States Code. Any such amounts shall be paid only from funds annually appropriated for any authorized purpose for the Federal agency against which a claim or judgment has been rendered."

Nondisclosure of Certain Products of Commercial Satellite Operations

Pub. L. No. 108–375, Div. A, Title IX, § 914, 118 Stat. 2029 (Oct. 28, 2004), provided that:

"(a) Mandatory disclosure requirements inapplicable.—The requirements to make information available under section 552 of title 5, United States Code, shall not apply to land remote sensing information.

"(b) Land remote sensing information defined.—In this section [this note], the term 'land remote sensing information'—

"(1) means any data that—

"(A) are collected by land remote sensing; and

"(B) are prohibited from sale to customers other than the United States Government and United States Government-approved customers for reasons of national security pursuant to the terms of an operating license issued pursuant to the Land Remote Sensing Policy Act of 1992 (15 U.S.C. 5601 et seq.) [Pub. L. No. 102–555, 106 Stat. 4163 (Oct. 28, 1992), which is codified principally as chapter 82 of Title 15, 15 U.S.C.A. § 5601 et seq.]; and

"(2) includes any imagery and other product that is derived from such data and which is prohibited from sale to customers other than the United States Government and United States Government-approved customers for reasons of national security pursuant to the terms of an operating license described in paragraph (1)(B).

"(c) State or local government disclosures.—Land remote sensing information provided by the head of a department or agency of the United States to a State, local, or tribal government may not be made available to the general public under any State, local, or tribal law relating to the disclosure of information or records.

"(d) Safeguarding information.—The head of each department or agency of the United States having land remote sensing information within that department or agency or providing such information to a State, local, or tribal government shall take such actions, commensurate with the sensitivity of that information, as are necessary to protect that information from disclosure other than in accordance with this section and other applicable law.

"(e) Additional definition.—In this section [this note], the term 'land remote sensing' has the meaning given such term in section 3 of the Land Remote Sensing Policy Act of 1992 (15 U.S.C. 5602).

"(f) Disclosure to Congress.—Nothing in this section shall be construed to authorize the withholding of information from the appropriate committees of Congress."

Disclosure of Arson, Explosive, or Firearm Records

Pub. L. No. 108–7, Div. J, Title VI, § 644, 117 Stat. 473 (Feb. 20, 2003), provided that: "No funds appropriated under this Act [the Treasury and General Government Appropriations Act, 2003, Pub. L. No. 108–7, Div. J, 117 Stat. 428 (Feb. 20, 2003), which amended 2 U.S.C.A. § 1105, 5 U.S.C.A. §§ 8335, 9505, 19 U.S.C.A. §§ 1401, 1629, 20 U.S.C.A. § 4510, and 44 U.S.C.A. § 2112, enacted provisions set out as notes under 5 U.S.C.A. §§ 5304, 5305, 8335, 9505, 19 U.S.C.A. § 1629, and 42 U.S.C.A. § 3771, and amended provisions set out as notes under 3 U.S.C.A. § 102, 5 U.S.C.A. §§ 3101, 3104, 5343, 21 U.S.C.A. § 1702, 26 U.S.C.A. §§ 6103, 7443, 7804, 31 U.S.C.A. §§ 501, 1343, 33 U.S.C.A. § 776, 39 U.S.C.A. § 403, and 42 U.S.C.A. § 3771] or any other Act with respect to any fiscal year shall be available to take any action based upon any provision of 5 U.S.C. 552 [this section] with respect to records collected or maintained pursuant to 18 U.S.C. 846(b), 923(g)(3) or 923(g)(7), or provided by Federal, State, local, or foreign law enforcement agencies in connection with arson or explosives incidents or the tracing of a firearm, except that such records may continue to be disclosed to the extent and in the manner that records so collected, maintained, or obtained have been disclosed under 5 U.S.C. 552 prior to the date of the enactment of this Act [Feb. 20, 2003]."

Disclosure of Information on Japanese Imperial Government

Pub. L. No. 106–567, Title VIII, §§ 801 to 805, 114 Stat. 2864 (Dec. 27, 2000), as amended by Pub. L. No. 108–199, Div. H, § 163, 118 Stat. 452 (Jan. 23, 2004); Pub. L. No. 109–5, § 1, 119 Stat. 19 (Mar. 25, 2005), provided that:

"Sec. 801. Short title.

"This title [this note] may be cited as the 'Japanese Imperial Government Disclosure Act of 2000'.

"Sec. 802. Designation.

"(a) Definitions.—In this section:

"(1) Agency.—The term 'agency' has the meaning given such term under section 551 of title 5, United States Code.

"(2) Interagency Group.—The term 'Interagency Group' means the Nazi War Crimes and Japanese Imperial Government Records Interagency Working Group established under subsection (b).

"(3) Japanese Imperial Government records.—The term 'Japanese Imperial Government records' means classified records or portions of records that pertain to any person with respect to whom the United States Government, in its sole discretion, has grounds to believe ordered, incited, assisted, or otherwise participated in the experimentation on, and persecution of, any person because of race, religion, national origin, or political opinion, during the period beginning September 18, 1931, and ending on December 31, 1948, under the direction of, or in association with—

"(A) the Japanese Imperial Government;

"(B) any government in any area occupied by the military forces of the Japanese Imperial Government;

"(C) any government established with the assistance or cooperation of the Japanese Imperial Government; or

"(D) any government which was an ally of the Japanese Imperial Government.

"(4) Record.—The term 'record' means a Japanese Imperial Government record.

"(b) Establishment of Interagency Group.—

"(1) In general.—Not later than 60 days after the date of the enactment of this Act [Dec. 27, 2000], the President shall designate the Working Group established under the Nazi War Crimes Disclosure Act (Public Law 105–246; 5 U.S.C. 552 note) to also carry out the purposes of this title [this note] with respect to Japanese Imperial Government records, and that Working Group shall remain in existence for 6 years after the date on which this title [this note] takes effect. Such Working Group is redesignated as the 'Nazi War Crimes and Japanese Imperial Government Records Interagency Working Group'.

"(2) [Omitted. Amended section 2(b)(2) of Pub. L. No. 105–246, set out as a note under this section.]

"(c) Functions.—Not later than 1 year after the date of the enactment of this Act [Dec. 27, 2000], the Interagency Group shall, to the greatest extent possible consistent with section 803 [of this note]—

"(1) locate, identify, inventory, recommend for declassification, and make available to the public at the National Archives and Records Administration, all classified Japanese Imperial Government records of the United States;

"(2) coordinate with agencies and take such actions as necessary to expedite the release of such records to the public; and

"(3) submit a report to Congress, including the Committee on Government Reform and the Permanent Select Committee on Intelligence of the House of Representatives, and the Committee on the Judiciary and the Select Committee on Intelligence of the Senate, describing all such records, the disposition of such records, and the activities of the Interagency Group and agencies under this section.

"(d) Funding.—There is authorized to be appropriated such sums as may be necessary to carry out the provisions of this title [this note].

"Sec. 803. Requirement of disclosure of records.

"(a) Release of records.—Subject to subsections (b), (c), and (d), the Japanese Imperial Government Records Interagency Working Group shall release in their entirety Japanese Imperial Government records.

"(b) Exemptions.—An agency head may exempt from release under subsection (a) specific information, that would—

"(1) constitute an unwarranted invasion of personal privacy;

"**(2)** reveal the identity of a confidential human source, or reveal information about an intelligence source or method when the unauthorized disclosure of that source or method would damage the national security interests of the United States;

"**(3)** reveal information that would assist in the development or use of weapons of mass destruction;

"**(4)** reveal information that would impair United States cryptologic systems or activities;

"**(5)** reveal information that would impair the application of state-of-the-art technology within a United States weapon system;

"**(6)** reveal United States military war plans that remain in effect;

"**(7)** reveal information that would impair relations between the United States and a foreign government, or undermine ongoing diplomatic activities of the United States;

"**(8)** reveal information that would impair the current ability of United States Government officials to protect the President, Vice President, and other officials for whom protection services are authorized in the interest of national security;

"**(9)** reveal information that would impair current national security emergency preparedness plans; or

"**(10)** violate a treaty or other international agreement.

"**(c) Applications of exemptions.**—

"**(1) In general.**—In applying the exemptions provided in paragraphs (2) through (10) of subsection (b), there shall be a presumption that the public interest will be served by disclosure and release of the records of the Japanese Imperial Government. The exemption may be asserted only when the head of the agency that maintains the records determines that disclosure and release would be harmful to a specific interest identified in the exemption. An agency head who makes such a determination shall promptly report it to the committees of Congress with appropriate jurisdiction, including the Committee on the Judiciary and the Select Committee on Intelligence of the Senate and the Committee on Government Reform and the Permanent Select Committee on Intelligence of the House of Representatives.

"**(2) Application of Title 5.**—A determination by an agency head to apply an exemption provided in paragraphs (2) through (9) of subsection (b) shall be subject to the same standard of review that applies in the case of records withheld under section 552(b)(1) of title 5, United States Code [subsec. (b)(1) of this section].

"**(d) Records related to investigations or prosecutions.**—This section shall not apply to records—

"**(1)** related to or supporting any active or inactive investigation, inquiry, or prosecution by the Office of Special Investigations of the Department of Justice; or

"**(2)** solely in the possession, custody, or control of the Office of Special Investigations.

"Sec. 804. Expedited processing of requests for Japanese Imperial Government records.

"For purposes of expedited processing under section 552(a)(6)(E) of title 5, United States Code, any person who was persecuted in the manner described in section 802(a)(3) and who requests a Japanese Imperial Government record shall be deemed to have a compelling need for such record.

"Sec. 805. Effective date.

"The provisions of this title [this note] shall take effect on the date that is 90 days after the date of the enactment of this Act [Dec. 27, 2000]."

Nazi War Crimes Disclosure Act

Pub. L. No. 105–246, 112 Stat. 1859 (Oct. 8, 1998), as amended by Pub. L. No. 106–567, Title VIII, § 802(b)(2), 114 Stat. 2865 (Dec. 27, 2000), provided that:

"Sec. 1. Short Title.

"This Act [this note] may be cited as the 'Nazi War Crimes Disclosure Act'.

"Sec. 2. Establishment of Nazi War Criminal Records Interagency Working Group.

"(a) Definitions.—In this section the term—

"(1) 'agency' has the meaning given such term under section 551 of title 5, United States Code;

"(2) 'Interagency Group' means the Nazi War Criminal Records Interagency Working Group established under subsection (b);

"(3) 'Nazi war criminal records' has the meaning given such term under section 3 of this Act [section 3 of this note]; and

"(4) 'record' means a Nazi war criminal record.

"(b) Establishment of Interagency Group.—

"(1) In general.—Not later than 60 days after the date of enactment of this Act [Oct. 8, 1998], the President shall establish the Nazi War Criminal Records Interagency Working Group, which shall remain in existence for 3 years after the date the Interagency Group is established.

"(2) Membership.—The President shall appoint to the Interagency Group individuals whom the President determines will most completely and effectively carry out the functions of the Interagency Group within the time limitations provided in this section, including the Director of the Holocaust Museum, the Historian of the Department of State, the Archivist of the United States, the head of any other agency the President considers appropriate, and no more than 4 other persons who shall be members of the public, of whom 3 shall be persons appointed under the provisions of this Act in effect on October 8, 1998. The head of an agency appointed by the President may designate an appropriate officer to serve on the Interagency Group in lieu of the head of such agency.

"(3) Initial meeting.—Not later than 90 days after the date of enactment of this Act [Oct. 8, 1998], the Interagency Group shall hold an initial meeting and begin the functions required under this section.

"(c) Functions.—Not later than 1 year after the date of enactment of this Act [Oct. 8, 1998], the Interagency Group shall, to the greatest extent possible consistent with section 3 of this Act [section 3 of this note]—

"(1) locate, identify, inventory, recommend for declassification, and make available to the public at the National Archives and Records Administration, all classified Nazi war criminal records of the United States;

"(2) coordinate with agencies and take such actions as necessary to expedite the release of such records to the public; and

"(3) submit a report to Congress, including the Committee on the Judiciary of the Senate and the Committee on Government Reform and Oversight of the House of Representatives, describing all such records, the disposition of such records, and the activities of the Interagency Group and agencies under this section.

"(d) Funding.—There are authorized to be appropriated such sums as may be necessary to carry out the provisions of this Act [this note].

"Sec. 3. Requirement of disclosure of records regarding persons who committed Nazi war crimes.

"(a) Nazi war criminal records.—For purposes of this Act [this note], the term 'Nazi war criminal records' means classified records or portions of records that—

"(1) pertain to any person with respect to whom the United States Government, in its sole discretion, has grounds to believe ordered, incited, assisted, or otherwise participated in the persecution of any person because of race, religion, national origin, or political opinion, during the period beginning on March 23, 1933, and ending on May 8, 1945, under the direction of, or in association with—

"(A) the Nazi government of Germany;

"(B) any government in any area occupied by the military forces of the Nazi government of Germany;

"(C) any government established with the assistance or cooperation of the Nazi government of Germany; or

"(D) any government which was an ally of the Nazi government of Germany; or

"(2) pertain to any transaction as to which the United States Government, in its sole discretion, has grounds to believe—

"(A) involved assets taken from persecuted persons during the period beginning on March 23, 1933, and ending on May 8, 1945, by, under the direction of, on behalf of, or under authority granted by the Nazi government of Germany or any nation then allied with that government; and

"(B) such transaction was completed without the assent of the owners of those assets or their heirs or assigns or other legitimate representatives.

"(b) **Release of records.**—

(1) **In general.**—Subject to paragraphs (2), (3), and (4), the Nazi War Criminal Records Interagency Working Group shall release in their entirety Nazi war criminal records that are described in subsection (a).

"(2) **Exception for privacy, etc.**—An agency head may exempt from release under paragraph (1) specific information, that would—

"(A) constitute a clearly unwarranted invasion of personal privacy;

"(B) reveal the identity of a confidential human source, or reveal information about the application of an intelligence source or method, or reveal the identity of a human intelligence source when the unauthorized disclosure of that source would clearly and demonstrably damage the national security interests of the United States;

"(C) reveal information that would assist in the development or use of weapons of mass destruction;

"(D) reveal information that would impair United States cryptologic systems or activities;

"(E) reveal information that would impair the application of state-of-the-art technology within a United States weapon system;

"(F) reveal actual United States military war plans that remain in effect;

"(G) reveal information that would seriously and demonstrably impair relations between the United States and a foreign government, or seriously and demonstrably undermine ongoing diplomatic activities of the United States;

"(H) reveal information that would clearly and demonstrably impair the current ability of United States Government officials to protect the President, Vice President, and other officials for whom protection services, in the interest of national security, are authorized;

"(I) reveal information that would seriously and demonstrably impair current national security emergency preparedness plans; or

"(J) violate a treaty or international agreement.

"(3) Application of exemptions.—

"(A) **In general.**—In applying the exemptions listed in subparagraphs (B) through (J) of paragraph (2), there shall be a presumption that the public interest in the release of Nazi war criminal records will be served by disclosure and release of the records. Assertion of such exemption may only be made when the agency head determines that disclosure and release would be harmful to a specific interest identified in the exemption. An agency head who makes such a determination shall promptly report it to the committees of Congress with appropriate jurisdiction, including the Committee on the Judiciary of the Senate and the Committee on Government Reform and Oversight of the House of Representatives. The exemptions set forth in paragraph (2) shall constitute the only authority pursuant to which an agency head may exempt records otherwise subject to release under paragraph (1).

"(B) **Application of Title 5.**—A determination by an agency head to apply an exemption listed in subparagraphs (B) through (I) of paragraph (2) shall be subject to the same standard of review that applies in the case of records withheld under section 552(b)(1) of title 5, United States Code.

"(4) Limitation on application.—This subsection shall not apply to records—

"(A) related to or supporting any active or inactive investigation, inquiry, or prosecution by the Office of Special Investigations of the Department of Justice; or

"(B) solely in the possession, custody, or control of that office.

"(c) Inapplicability of National Security Act of 1947 Exemption.—Section 701(a) of the National Security Act of 1947 (50 U.S.C. 431) shall not apply to any operational file, or any portion of any operational file, that constitutes a Nazi war criminal record under section 3 of this Act [section 3 of this note].

"Sec. 4. Expedited processing of FOIA Requests for Nazi war criminal records.

"(a) Expedited processing.—For purposes of expedited processing under section 552(a)(6)(E) of title 5, United States Code, any requester of a Nazi war criminal record shall be deemed to have a compelling need for such record.

"(b) Requester.—For purposes of this section, the term 'requester' means any person who was persecuted in the manner described under section 3(a)(1) of this Act [section 3(a)(1) of this note] who requests a Nazi war criminal record.

"Sec. 5. Effective date.

"This Act [this note] and the amendments made by this Act [enacting this note] shall take effect on the date that is 90 days after the date of enactment of this Act [Oct. 8, 1998]."

[Committee on Government Reform and Oversight of House of Representatives changed to Committee on Government Reform of House of Representatives by House Resolution No. 5, One Hundred Sixth Congress, Jan. 6, 1999. Committee on Government Reform of House of Representatives changed to Committee on Oversight and Government Reform of House of Representatives by House Resolution No. 6, One Hundred Tenth Congress, Jan. 5, 2007.]

Classified National Security Information

For provisions relating to a response to a request for information under this section when the fact of its existence or nonexistence is itself classified or when it was originally classified by another agency, see Ex. Ord. No. 12958, § 3.7, 60 Fed. Reg. 19835 (April 17, 1995), set out as a note under section 435 of Title 50.

Congressional Statement of Findings and Purpose; Public Access to Information in Electronic Format

Section 2 of Pub. L. No. 104–231 provided that:

"(a) Findings.—The Congress finds that—

"(1) the purpose of section 552 of title 5, United States Code, popularly known as the Freedom of Information Act [this section], is to require agencies of the Federal Government to make certain agency information available for public inspection and copying and to establish and enable enforcement of the right of any person to obtain access to the records of such agencies, subject to statutory exemptions, for any public or private purpose;

"(2) since the enactment of the Freedom of Information Act in 1966 [Sept. 6, 1966], and the amendments enacted in 1974 and 1986, the Freedom of Information Act has been a valuable means through which any person can learn how the Federal Government operates;

"(3) the Freedom of Information Act has led to the disclosure of waste, fraud, abuse, and wrongdoing in the Federal Government;

"(4) the Freedom of Information Act has led to the identification of unsafe consumer products, harmful drugs, and serious health hazards;

"(5) Government agencies increasingly use computers to conduct agency business and to store publicly valuable agency records and information; and

"(6) Government agencies should use new technology to enhance public access to agency records and information.

"(b) Purposes.—The purposes of this Act [see Short Title of Amendments note set out under this section] are to—

"(1) foster democracy by ensuring public access to agency records and information;

"(2) improve public access to agency records and information;

"(3) ensure agency compliance with statutory time limits; and

"(4) maximize the usefulness of agency records and information collected, maintained, used, retained, and disseminated by the Federal Government."

Freedom of Information Act Exemption for Certain Open Skies Treaty Data

Pub. L. No. 103–236, Title V, § 533, 108 Stat. 480 (Apr. 30, 1994), provided that:

"(a) In general.—Data with respect to a foreign country collected by sensors during observation flights conducted in connection with the Treaty on Open Skies, including flights conducted prior to entry into force of the treaty, shall be exempt from disclosure under the Freedom of Information Act [this section]—

"(1) if the country has not disclosed the data to the public; and

"(2) if the country has not, acting through the Open Skies Consultative Commission or any other diplomatic channel, authorized the United States to disclose the data to the public.

"(b) Statutory construction.—This section constitutes a specific exemption within the meaning of section 552(b)(3) of title 5, United States Code [subsec. (b)(3) of this section].

"(c) Definitions.—For the purposes of this section—

"(1) the term 'Freedom of Information Act' means the provisions of section 552 of title 5, United States Code [this section];

"(2) the term 'Open Skies Consultative Commission' means the commission established pursuant to Article X of the Treaty on Open Skies; and

"(3) the term 'Treaty on Open Skies' means the Treaty on Open Skies, signed at Helsinki on March 24, 1992."

Treatment of Information in Catch a Serial Offender Program For Certain Purposes

Section 550 of Pub. L. No. 116–92, 133 Stat. 1379 (Dec. 20, 2019), provided that:

"**(a) Treatment under FOIA.**—Victim disclosures under the Catch a Serial Offender Program shall be withheld from public disclosure under paragraph (b)(3) of section 552 of title 5, United States Code (commonly referred to as the "Freedom of Information Act").

"**(b) Preservation of Restricted Report.**—The transmittal or receipt in connection with the Catch a Serial Offender Program of a report on a sexual assault that is treated as a restricted report shall not operate to terminate its treatment or status as a restricted report."

§ 552a. Records maintained on individuals

(a) Definitions.—For purposes of this section—

(1) the term "agency" means agency as defined in section 552(e) of this title;

(2) the term "individual" means a citizen of the United States or an alien lawfully admitted for permanent residence;

(3) the term "maintain" includes maintain, collect, use, or disseminate;

(4) the term "record" means any item, collection, or grouping of information about an individual that is maintained by an agency, including, but not limited to, his education, financial transactions, medical history, and criminal or employment history and that contains his name, or the identifying number, symbol, or other identifying particular assigned to the individual, such as a finger or voice print or a photograph;

(5) the term "system of records" means a group of any records under the control of any agency from which information is retrieved by the name of the individual or by some identifying number, symbol, or other identifying particular assigned to the individual;

(6) the term "statistical record" means a record in a system of records maintained for statistical research or reporting purposes only and not used in whole or in part in making any determination about an identifiable individual, except as provided by section 8 of title 13;

(7) the term "routine use" means, with respect to the disclosure of a record, the use of such record for a purpose which is compatible with the purpose for which it was collected;

(8) the term "matching program"—

(A) means any computerized comparison of—

(i) two or more automated systems of records or a system of records with non-Federal records for the purpose of—

(I) establishing or verifying the eligibility of, or continuing compliance with statutory and regulatory requirements by, applicants for, recipients or beneficiaries of, participants in, or providers of services with respect to, cash or in-kind assistance or payments under Federal benefit programs, or

(II) recouping payments or delinquent debts under such Federal benefit programs, or

(ii) two or more automated Federal personnel or payroll systems of records or a system of Federal personnel or payroll records with non-Federal records,

(B) but does not include—

(i) matches performed to produce aggregate statistical data without any personal identifiers;

(ii) matches performed to support any research or statistical project, the specific data of which may not be used to make decisions concerning the rights, benefits, or privileges of specific individuals;

(iii) matches performed, by an agency (or component thereof) which performs as its principal function any activity pertaining to the enforcement of criminal laws, subsequent to the initiation of a specific criminal or civil law enforcement investigation of a named person or persons for the purpose of gathering evidence against such person or persons;

(iv) matches of tax information (I) pursuant to section 6103(d) of the Internal Revenue Code of 1986, (II) for purposes of tax administration as defined in section 6103(b)(4) of such Code, (III) for the purpose of intercepting a tax refund due an individual under authority granted by section 404(e), 464, or 1137 of the Social Security Act; or (IV) for the purpose of intercepting a tax refund due an individual under any other tax refund intercept program authorized by statute which has been determined by the Director of the Office of Management and Budget to contain verification, notice, and hearing requirements that are substantially similar to the procedures in section 1137 of the Social Security Act;

(v) matches—

(I) using records predominantly relating to Federal personnel, that are performed for routine administrative purposes (subject to guidance provided by the Director of the Office of Management and Budget pursuant to subsection (v)); or

(II) conducted by an agency using only records from systems of records maintained by that agency;

if the purpose of the match is not to take any adverse financial, personnel, disciplinary, or other adverse action against Federal personnel;

(vi) matches performed for foreign counterintelligence purposes or to produce background checks for security clearances of Federal personnel or Federal contractor personnel;

(vii) matches performed incident to a levy described in section 6103(k)(8) of the Internal Revenue Code of 1986;

(viii) matches performed pursuant to section 202(x)(3) or 1611(e)(1) of the Social Security Act (42 U.S.C. 402(x)(3), 1382(e)(1));

(ix) matches performed by the Secretary of Health and Human Services or the Inspector General of the Department of Health and Human Services with respect to potential fraud, waste, and abuse, including matches of a system of records with non-Federal records; or

(x) matches performed pursuant to section 3(d)(4) of the Achieving a Better Life Experience Act of 2014.

(9) the term "recipient agency" means any agency, or contractor thereof, receiving records contained in a system of records from a source agency for use in a matching program;

(10) the term "non-Federal agency" means any State or local government, or agency thereof, which receives records contained in a system of records from a source agency for use in a matching program;

(11) the term "source agency" means any agency which discloses records contained in a system of records to be used in a matching program, or any State or local government, or agency thereof, which discloses records to be used in a matching program;

(12) the term "Federal benefit program" means any program administered or funded by the Federal Government, or by any agent or State on behalf of the Federal Government, providing cash or in-kind assistance in the form of payments, grants, loans, or loan guarantees to individuals; and

(13) the term "Federal personnel" means officers and employees of the Government of the United States, members of the uniformed services (including members of the Reserve Components), individuals[1] entitled to receive immediate or deferred retirement benefits under any retirement program of the Government of the United States (including survivor benefits).

(b) Conditions of disclosure.—No agency shall disclose any record which is contained in a system of records by any means of communication to any person, or to another agency, except pursuant to a written request by, or with the prior written consent of, the individual to whom the record pertains, unless disclosure of the record would be—

(1) to those officers and employees of the agency which maintains the record who have a need for the record in the performance of their duties;

(2) required under section 552 of this title;

(3) for a routine use as defined in subsection (a)(7) of this section and described under subsection (e)(4)(D) of this section;

(4) to the Bureau of the Census for purposes of planning or carrying out a census or survey or related activity pursuant to the provisions of title 13;

(5) to a recipient who has provided the agency with advance adequate written assurance that the record will be used solely as a statistical research or reporting record, and the record is to be transferred in a form that is not individually identifiable;

(6) to the National Archives and Records Administration as a record which has sufficient historical or other value to warrant its continued preservation by the United States Government, or for evaluation by the Archivist of the United States or the designee of the Archivist to determine whether the record has such value;

(7) to another agency or to an instrumentality of any governmental jurisdiction within or under the control of the United States for a civil or criminal law enforcement activity if the activity is authorized by law, and if the head of the agency or instrumentality has made a written request to the agency which maintains the record specifying the particular portion desired and the law enforcement activity for which the record is sought;

(8) to a person pursuant to a showing of compelling circumstances affecting the health or safety of an individual if upon such disclosure notification is transmitted to the last known address of such individual;

(9) to either House of Congress, or, to the extent of matter within its jurisdiction, any committee or subcommittee thereof, any joint committee of Congress or subcommittee of any such joint committee;

(10) to the Comptroller General, or any of his authorized representatives, in the course of the performance of the duties of the Government Accountability Office;

(11) pursuant to the order of a court of competent jurisdiction; or

(12) to a consumer reporting agency in accordance with section 3711(e) of title 31.

(c) Accounting of certain disclosures.—Each agency, with respect to each system of records under its control, shall—

(1) except for disclosures made under subsections (b)(1) or (b)(2) of this section, keep an accurate accounting of—

(A) the date, nature, and purpose of each disclosure of a record to any person or to another agency made under subsection (b) of this section; and

(B) the name and address of the person or agency to whom the disclosure is made;

(2) retain the accounting made under paragraph (1) of this subsection for at least five years or the life of the record, whichever is longer, after the disclosure for which the accounting is made;

(3) except for disclosures made under subsection (b)(7) of this section, make the accounting made under paragraph (1) of this subsection available to the individual named in the record at his request; and

(4) inform any person or other agency about any correction or notation of dispute made by the agency in accordance with subsection (d) of this section of any record that has been disclosed to the person or agency if an accounting of the disclosure was made.

(d) Access to records.—Each agency that maintains a system of records shall—

(1) upon request by any individual to gain access to his record or to any information pertaining to him which is contained in the system, permit him and upon his request, a person of his own choosing to accompany him, to review the record and have a copy made of all or any portion thereof in a form comprehensible to him, except that the agency may require the individual to furnish a written statement authorizing discussion of that individual's record in the accompanying person's presence;

(2) permit the individual to request amendment of a record pertaining to him and—

(A) not later than 10 days (excluding Saturdays, Sundays, and legal public holidays) after the date of receipt of such request, acknowledge in writing such receipt; and

(B) promptly, either—

(i) make any correction of any portion thereof which the individual believes is not accurate, relevant, timely, or complete; or

(ii) inform the individual of its refusal to amend the record in accordance with his request, the reason for the refusal, the procedures established by the agency for the individual to request a review of that refusal by the head of the agency or an officer designated by the head of the agency, and the name and business address of that official;

(3) permit the individual who disagrees with the refusal of the agency to amend his record to request a review of such refusal, and not later than 30 days (excluding Saturdays, Sundays, and legal public holidays) from the date on which the individual requests such review, complete such review and make a final determination unless, for good cause shown, the head of the agency extends such 30-day period; and if, after his review, the reviewing official also refuses to amend the record in accordance with the request, permit the individual to file with the agency a concise statement setting forth the reasons for his disagreement with the refusal of the agency, and notify the individual of the provisions for judicial review of the reviewing official's determination under subsection (g)(1)(A) of this section;

(4) in any disclosure, containing information about which the individual has filed a statement of disagreement, occurring after the filing of the statement under paragraph (3) of this subsection, clearly note any portion of the record which is disputed and provide copies of the statement and, if the agency deems it appropriate, copies of a concise statement of the reasons of the agency for not making the amendments requested, to persons or other agencies to whom the disputed record has been disclosed; and

(5) nothing in this section shall allow an individual access to any information compiled in reasonable anticipation of a civil action or proceeding.

(e) Agency requirements.—Each agency that maintains a system of records shall—

(1) maintain in its records only such information about an individual as is relevant and necessary to accomplish a purpose of the agency required to be accomplished by statute or by executive order of the President;

(2) collect information to the greatest extent practicable directly from the subject individual when the information may result in adverse determinations about an individual's rights, benefits, and privileges under Federal programs;

(3) inform each individual whom it asks to supply information, on the form which it uses to collect the information or on a separate form that can be retained by the individual—

(A) the authority (whether granted by statute, or by executive order of the President) which authorizes the solicitation of the information and whether disclosure of such information is mandatory or voluntary;

(B) the principal purpose or purposes for which the information is intended to be used;

(C) the routine uses which may be made of the information, as published pursuant to paragraph (4)(D) of this subsection; and

(D) the effects on him, if any, of not providing all or any part of the requested information;

(4) subject to the provisions of paragraph (11) of this subsection, publish in the Federal Register upon establishment or revision a notice of the existence and character of the system of records, which notice shall include—

(A) the name and location of the system;

(B) the categories of individuals on whom records are maintained in the system;

(C) the categories of records maintained in the system;

(D) each routine use of the records contained in the system, including the categories of users and the purpose of such use;

(E) the policies and practices of the agency regarding storage, retrievability, access controls, retention, and disposal of the records;

(F) the title and business address of the agency official who is responsible for the system of records;

(G) the agency procedures whereby an individual can be notified at his request if the system of records contains a record pertaining to him;

(H) the agency procedures whereby an individual can be notified at his request how he can gain access to any record pertaining to him contained in the system of records, and how he can contest its content; and

(I) the categories of sources of records in the system;

(5) maintain all records which are used by the agency in making any determination about any individual with such accuracy, relevance, timeliness, and completeness as is reasonably necessary to assure fairness to the individual in the determination;

(6) prior to disseminating any record about an individual to any person other than an agency, unless the dissemination is made pursuant to subsection (b)(2) of this section, make reasonable efforts to assure that such records are accurate, complete, timely, and relevant for agency purposes;

(7) maintain no record describing how any individual exercises rights guaranteed by the First Amendment unless expressly authorized by statute or by the individual about whom the record is maintained or unless pertinent to and within the scope of an authorized law enforcement activity;

(8) make reasonable efforts to serve notice on an individual when any record on such individual is made available to any person under compulsory legal process when such process becomes a matter of public record;

(9) establish rules of conduct for persons involved in the design, development, operation, or maintenance of any system of records, or in maintaining any record, and instruct each such person with respect to such rules and the requirements of this section, including any other rules and procedures adopted pursuant to this section and the penalties for noncompliance;

(10) establish appropriate administrative, technical, and physical safeguards to insure the security and confidentiality of records and to protect against any anticipated threats or hazards to their security or integrity which could result in substantial harm, embarrassment, inconvenience, or unfairness to any individual on whom information is maintained;

(11) at least 30 days prior to publication of information under paragraph (4)(D) of this subsection, publish in the Federal Register notice of any new use or intended use of the information in the system, and provide an opportunity for interested persons to submit written data, views, or arguments to the agency; and

(12) if such agency is a recipient agency or a source agency in a matching program with a non-Federal agency, with respect to any establishment or revision of a matching program, at least 30 days prior to conducting such program, publish in the Federal Register notice of such establishment or revision.

(f) Agency rules.—In order to carry out the provisions of this section, each agency that maintains a system of records shall promulgate rules, in accordance with the requirements (including general notice) of section 553 of this title, which shall—

(1) establish procedures whereby an individual can be notified in response to his request if any system of records named by the individual contains a record pertaining to him;

(2) define reasonable times, places, and requirements for identifying an individual who requests his record or information pertaining to him before the agency shall make the record or information available to the individual;

(3) establish procedures for the disclosure to an individual upon his request of his record or information pertaining to him, including special procedure, if deemed necessary, for the disclosure to an individual of medical records, including psychological records, pertaining to him;

(4) establish procedures for reviewing a request from an individual concerning the amendment of any record or information pertaining to the individual, for making a determination on the request, for an appeal within the agency of an initial adverse agency determination, and for whatever additional means may be necessary for each individual to be able to exercise fully his rights under this section; and

(5) establish fees to be charged, if any, to any individual for making copies of his record, excluding the cost of any search for and review of the record.

The Office of the Federal Register shall biennially compile and publish the rules promulgated under this subsection and agency notices published under subsection (e)(4) of this section in a form available to the public at low cost.

(g) (1) Civil remedies.—Whenever any agency

(A) makes a determination under subsection (d)(3) of this section not to amend an individual's record in accordance with his request, or fails to make such review in conformity with that subsection;

(B) refuses to comply with an individual request under subsection (d)(1) of this section;

(C) fails to maintain any record concerning any individual with such accuracy, relevance, timeliness, and completeness as is necessary to assure fairness in any determination relating to the qualifications, character, rights, or opportunities of, or benefits to the individual that may be made on the basis of such record, and consequently a determination is made which is adverse to the individual; or

(D) fails to comply with any other provision of this section, or any rule promulgated thereunder, in such a way as to have an adverse effect on an individual,

the individual may bring a civil action against the agency, and the district courts of the United States shall have jurisdiction in the matters under the provisions of this subsection.

(2) **(A)** In any suit brought under the provisions of subsection (g)(1)(A) of this section, the court may order the agency to amend the individual's record in accordance with his request or in such other way as the court may direct. In such a case the court shall determine the matter de novo.

(B) The court may assess against the United States reasonable attorney fees and other litigation costs reasonably incurred in any case under this paragraph in which the complainant has substantially prevailed.

(3) **(A)** In any suit brought under the provisions of subsection (g)(1)(B) of this section, the court may enjoin the agency from withholding the records and order the production to the complainant of any agency records improperly withheld from him. In such a case the court shall determine the matter de novo, and may examine the contents of any agency records in camera to determine whether the records or any portion thereof may be withheld under any of the exemptions set forth in subsection (k) of this section, and the burden is on the agency to sustain its action.

(B) The court may assess against the United States reasonable attorney fees and other litigation costs reasonably incurred in any case under this paragraph in which the complainant has substantially prevailed.

(4) In any suit brought under the provisions of subsection (g)(1)(C) or (D) of this section in which the court determines that the agency acted in a manner which was intentional or willful, the United States shall be liable to the individual in an amount equal to the sum of—

(A) actual damages sustained by the individual as a result of the refusal or failure, but in no case shall a person entitled to recovery receive less than the sum of $1,000; and

(B) the costs of the action together with reasonable attorney fees as determined by the court.

(5) An action to enforce any liability created under this section may be brought in the district court of the United States in the district in which the complainant resides, or has his principal place of business, or in which the agency records are situated, or in the District of Columbia, without regard to the amount in controversy, within two years from the date on which the cause of action arises, except that where an agency has materially and willfully misrepresented any information required under this section to be disclosed to an individual and the information so misrepresented is material to establishment of the liability of the agency to the individual under this section, the action may be brought at any time within two years after discovery by the individual of the misrepresentation. Nothing in this section shall be construed to authorize any civil action by reason of any injury sustained as the result of a disclosure of a record prior to September 27, 1975.

(h) **Rights of legal guardians.**—For the purposes of this section, the parent of any minor, or the legal guardian of any individual who has been declared to be incompetent due to physical or mental incapacity or age by a court of competent jurisdiction, may act on behalf of the individual.

(i) **(1)** **Criminal penalties.**—Any officer or employee of an agency, who by virtue of his employment or official position, has possession of, or access to, agency records which contain individually identifiable information the disclosure of which is prohibited by this section or by rules or regulations established thereunder, and who knowing that disclosure of the specific material is so prohibited, willfully discloses the material in any manner to any person or agency not entitled to receive it, shall be guilty of a misdemeanor and fined not more than $5,000.

(2) Any officer or employee of any agency who willfully maintains a system of records without meeting the notice requirements of subsection (e)(4) of this section shall be guilty of a misdemeanor and fined not more than $5,000.

(3) Any person who knowingly and willfully requests or obtains any record concerning an individual from an agency under false pretenses shall be guilty of a misdemeanor and fined not more than $5,000.

(j) General exemptions.—The head of any agency may promulgate rules, in accordance with the requirements (including general notice) of sections 553(b)(1), (2), and (3), (c), and (e) of this title, to exempt any system of records within the agency from any part of this section except subsections (b), (c)(1) and (2), (e)(4)(A) through (F), (e)(6), (7), (9), (10), and (11), and (i) if the system of records is—

(1) maintained by the Central Intelligence Agency; or

(2) maintained by an agency or component thereof which performs as its principal function any activity pertaining to the enforcement of criminal laws, including police efforts to prevent, control, or reduce crime or to apprehend criminals, and the activities of prosecutors, courts, correctional, probation, pardon, or parole authorities, and which consists of (A) information compiled for the purpose of identifying individual criminal offenders and alleged offenders and consisting only of identifying data and notations of arrests, the nature and disposition of criminal charges, sentencing, confinement, release, and parole and probation status; (B) information compiled for the purpose of a criminal investigation, including reports of informants and investigators, and associated with an identifiable individual; or (C) reports identifiable to an individual compiled at any stage of the process of enforcement of the criminal laws from arrest or indictment through release from supervision.

At the time rules are adopted under this subsection, the agency shall include in the statement required under section 553(c) of this title, the reasons why the system of records is to be exempted from a provision of this section.

(k) Specific exemptions.—The head of any agency may promulgate rules, in accordance with the requirements (including general notice) of sections 553(b)(1), (2), and (3), (c), and (e) of this title, to exempt any system of records within the agency from subsections (c)(3), (d), (e)(1), (e)(4)(G), (H), and (I) and (f) of this section if the system of records is—

(1) subject to the provisions of section 552(b)(1) of this title;

(2) investigatory material compiled for law enforcement purposes, other than material within the scope of subsection (j)(2) of this section: *Provided, however*, That if any individual is denied any right, privilege, or benefit that he would otherwise be entitled by Federal law, or for which he would otherwise be eligible, as a result of the maintenance of such material, such material shall be provided to such individual, except to the extent that the disclosure of such material would reveal the identity of a source who furnished information to the Government under an express promise that the identity of the source would be held in confidence, or, prior to the effective date of this section, under an implied promise that the identity of the source would be held in confidence;

(3) maintained in connection with providing protective services to the President of the United States or other individuals pursuant to section 3056 of title 18;

(4) required by statute to be maintained and used solely as statistical records;

(5) investigatory material compiled solely for the purpose of determining suitability, eligibility, or qualifications for Federal civilian employment, military service, Federal contracts, or access to classified information, but only to the extent that the disclosure of such material would reveal the identity of a source who furnished information to the Government under an express promise that the identity of the source would be held in confidence, or, prior to the effective date of this section, under an implied promise that the identity of the source would be held in confidence;

(6) testing or examination material used solely to determine individual qualifications for appointment or promotion in the Federal service the disclosure of which would compromise the objectivity or fairness of the testing or examination process; or

(7) evaluation material used to determine potential for promotion in the armed services, but only to the extent that the disclosure of such material would reveal the identity of a source who furnished information to the Government under an express promise that the identity of the source would be held in confidence, or, prior to the effective date of this section, under an implied promise that the identity of the source would be held in confidence.

At the time rules are adopted under this subsection, the agency shall include in the statement required under section 553(c) of this title, the reasons why the system of records is to be exempted from a provision of this section.

(l) **(1) Archival records.**—Each agency record which is accepted by the Archivist of the United States for storage, processing, and servicing in accordance with section 3103 of title 44 shall, for the purposes of this section, be considered to be maintained by the agency which deposited the record and shall be subject to the provisions of this section. The Archivist of the United States shall not disclose the record except to the agency which maintains the record, or under rules established by that agency which are not inconsistent with the provisions of this section.

(2) Each agency record pertaining to an identifiable individual which was transferred to the National Archives of the United States as a record which has sufficient historical or other value to warrant its continued preservation by the United States Government, prior to the effective date of this section, shall, for the purposes of this section, be considered to be maintained by the National Archives and shall not be subject to the provisions of this section, except that a statement generally describing such records (modeled after the requirements relating to records subject to subsections (e)(4)(A) through (G) of this section) shall be published in the Federal Register.

(3) Each agency record pertaining to an identifiable individual which is transferred to the National Archives of the United States as a record which has sufficient historical or other value to warrant its continued preservation by the United States Government, on or after the effective date of this section, shall, for the purposes of this section, be considered to be maintained by the National Archives and shall be exempt from the requirements of this section except subsections (e)(4)(A) through (G) and (e)(9) of this section.

(m) (1) Government contractors.—When an agency provides by a contract for the operation by or on behalf of the agency of a system of records to accomplish an agency function, the agency shall, consistent with its authority, cause the requirements of this section to be applied to such system. For purposes of subsection (i) of this section any such contractor and any employee of such contractor, if such contract is agreed to on or after the effective date of this section, shall be considered to be an employee of an agency.

(2) A consumer reporting agency to which a record is disclosed under section 3711(e) of title 31 shall not be considered a contractor for the purposes of this section.

(n) Mailing lists.—An individual's name and address may not be sold or rented by an agency unless such action is specifically authorized by law. This provision shall not be construed to require the withholding of names and addresses otherwise permitted to be made public.

(o) **Matching agreements.—(1)** No record which is contained in a system of records may be disclosed to a recipient agency or non-Federal agency for use in a computer matching program except pursuant to a written agreement between the source agency and the recipient agency or non-Federal agency specifying—

(A) the purpose and legal authority for conducting the program;

(B) the justification for the program and the anticipated results, including a specific estimate of any savings;

(C) a description of the records that will be matched, including each data element that will be used, the approximate number of records that will be matched, and the projected starting and completion dates of the matching program;

(D) procedures for providing individualized notice at the time of application, and notice periodically thereafter as directed by the Data Integrity Board of such agency (subject to guidance provided by the Director of the Office of Management and Budget pursuant to subsection (v)), to—

(i) applicants for and recipients of financial assistance or payments under Federal benefit programs, and

(ii) applicants for and holders of positions as Federal personnel,

that any information provided by such applicants, recipients, holders, and individuals may be subject to verification through matching programs;

(E) procedures for verifying information produced in such matching program as required by subsection (p);

(F) procedures for the retention and timely destruction of identifiable records created by a recipient agency or non-Federal agency in such matching program;

(G) procedures for ensuring the administrative, technical, and physical security of the records matched and the results of such programs;

(H) prohibitions on duplication and redisclosure of records provided by the source agency within or outside the recipient agency or the non-Federal agency, except where required by law or essential to the conduct of the matching program;

(I) procedures governing the use by a recipient agency or non-Federal agency of records provided in a matching program by a source agency, including procedures governing return of the records to the source agency or destruction of records used in such program;

(J) information on assessments that have been made on the accuracy of the records that will be used in such matching program; and

(K) that the Comptroller General may have access to all records of a recipient agency or a non-Federal agency that the Comptroller General deems necessary in order to monitor or verify compliance with the agreement.

(2) **(A)** A copy of each agreement entered into pursuant to paragraph (1) shall—

(i) be transmitted to the Committee on Governmental Affairs of the Senate and the Committee on Government Operations of the House of Representatives; and

(ii) be available upon request to the public.

(B) No such agreement shall be effective until 30 days after the date on which such a copy is transmitted pursuant to subparagraph (A)(i).

(C) Such an agreement shall remain in effect only for such period, not to exceed 18 months, as the Data Integrity Board of the agency determines is appropriate in light of the purposes, and length of time necessary for the conduct, of the matching program.

(D) Within 3 months prior to the expiration of such an agreement pursuant to subparagraph (C), the Data Integrity Board of the agency may, without additional review, renew the matching agreement for a current, ongoing matching program for not more than one additional year if—

(i) such program will be conducted without any change; and

(ii) each party to the agreement certifies to the Board in writing that the program has been conducted in compliance with the agreement.

(p) **Verification and opportunity to contest findings.—(1)** In order to protect any individual whose records are used in a matching program, no recipient agency, non-Federal agency, or source agency may suspend, terminate, reduce, or make a final denial of any financial assistance or payment under a Federal benefit program to such individual, or take other adverse action against such individual, as a result of information produced by such matching program, until—

(A) **(i)** the agency has independently verified the information; or

(ii) the Data Integrity Board of the agency, or in the case of a non-Federal agency the Data Integrity Board of the source agency, determines in accordance with guidance issued by the Director of the Office of Management and Budget that—

(I) the information is limited to identification and amount of benefits paid by the source agency under a Federal benefit program; and

(II) there is a high degree of confidence that the information provided to the recipient agency is accurate;

(B) the individual receives a notice from the agency containing a statement of its findings and informing the individual of the opportunity to contest such findings; and

(C) **(i)** the expiration of any time period established for the program by statute or regulation for the individual to respond to that notice; or

(ii) in the case of a program for which no such period is established, the end of the 30-day period beginning on the date on which notice under subparagraph (B) is mailed or otherwise provided to the individual.

(2) Independent verification referred to in paragraph (1) requires investigation and confirmation of specific information relating to an individual that is used as a basis for an adverse action against the individual, including where applicable investigation and confirmation of—

(A) the amount of any asset or income involved;

(B) whether such individual actually has or had access to such asset or income for such individual's own use; and

(C) the period or periods when the individual actually had such asset or income.

(3) Notwithstanding paragraph (1), an agency may take any appropriate action otherwise prohibited by such paragraph if the agency determines that the public health or public safety may be adversely affected or significantly threatened during any notice period required by such paragraph.

(q) **Sanctions.—(1)** Notwithstanding any other provision of law, no source agency may disclose any record which is contained in a system of records to a recipient agency or non-Federal agency for a matching program if such source agency has reason to believe that the requirements of subsection (p), or any matching agreement entered into pursuant to subsection (*o*), or both, are not being met by such recipient agency.

(2) No source agency may renew a matching agreement unless—

(A) the recipient agency or non-Federal agency has certified that it has complied with the provisions of that agreement; and

(B) the source agency has no reason to believe that the certification is inaccurate.

(r) **Report on new systems and matching programs.**—Each agency that proposes to establish or make a significant change in a system of records or a matching program shall provide adequate advance notice of any such proposal (in duplicate) to the Committee on Government Operations of the House of Representatives, the Committee on Governmental Affairs of the Senate, and the Office of Management and Budget in order to permit an evaluation of the probable or potential effect of such proposal on the privacy or other rights of individuals.

(s) **Biennial report.**—The President shall biennially submit to the Speaker of the House of Representatives and the President pro tempore of the Senate a report—

(1) describing the actions of the Director of the Office of Management and Budget pursuant to section 6 of the Privacy Act of 1974 during the preceding 2 years;

(2) describing the exercise of individual rights of access and amendment under this section during such years;

(3) identifying changes in or additions to systems of records;

(4) containing such other information concerning administration of this section as may be necessary or useful to the Congress in reviewing the effectiveness of this section in carrying out the purposes of the Privacy Act of 1974.

(t) (1) **Effect of other laws.**—No agency shall rely on any exemption contained in section 552 of this title to withhold from an individual any record which is otherwise accessible to such individual under the provisions of this section.

(2) No agency shall rely on any exemption in this section to withhold from an individual any record which is otherwise accessible to such individual under the provisions of section 552 of this title.

(u) Data Integrity Boards.—(1) Every agency conducting or participating in a matching program shall establish a Data Integrity Board to oversee and coordinate among the various components of such agency the agency's implementation of this section.

(2) Each Data Integrity Board shall consist of senior officials designated by the head of the agency, and shall include any senior official designated by the head of the agency as responsible for implementation of this section, and the inspector general of the agency, if any. The inspector general shall not serve as chairman of the Data Integrity Board.

(3) Each Data Integrity Board—

(A) shall review, approve, and maintain all written agreements for receipt or disclosure of agency records for matching programs to ensure compliance with subsection (*o*), and all relevant statutes, regulations, and guidelines;

(B) shall review all matching programs in which the agency has participated during the year, either as a source agency or recipient agency, determine compliance with applicable laws, regulations, guidelines, and agency agreements, and assess the costs and benefits of such programs;

(C) shall review all recurring matching programs in which the agency has participated during the year, either as a source agency or recipient agency, for continued justification for such disclosures;

(D) shall compile an annual report, which shall be submitted to the head of the agency and the Office of Management and Budget and made available to the public on request, describing the matching activities of the agency, including—

(i) matching programs in which the agency has participated as a source agency or recipient agency;

(ii) matching agreements proposed under subsection (*o*) that were disapproved by the Board;

(iii) any changes in membership or structure of the Board in the preceding year;

(iv) the reasons for any waiver of the requirement in paragraph (4) of this section for completion and submission of a cost-benefit analysis prior to the approval of a matching program;

(v) any violations of matching agreements that have been alleged or identified and any corrective action taken; and

(vi) any other information required by the Director of the Office of Management and Budget to be included in such report;

(E) shall serve as a clearinghouse for receiving and providing information on the accuracy, completeness, and reliability of records used in matching programs;

(F) shall provide interpretation and guidance to agency components and personnel on the requirements of this section for matching programs;

(G) shall review agency recordkeeping and disposal policies and practices for matching programs to assure compliance with this section; and

(H) may review and report on any agency matching activities that are not matching programs.

(4) (A) Except as provided in subparagraphs (B) and (C), a Data Integrity Board shall not approve any written agreement for a matching program unless the agency has completed and submitted to such Board a cost-benefit analysis of the proposed program and such analysis demonstrates that the program is likely to be cost effective.[2]

(B) The Board may waive the requirements of subparagraph (A) of this paragraph if it determines in writing, in accordance with guidelines prescribed by the Director of the Office of Management and Budget, that a cost-benefit analysis is not required.

(C) A cost-benefit analysis shall not be required under subparagraph (A) prior to the initial approval of a written agreement for a matching program that is specifically required by statute. Any subsequent written agreement for such a program shall not be approved by the Data Integrity Board unless the agency has submitted a cost-benefit analysis of the program as conducted under the preceding approval of such agreement.

(5) **(A)** If a matching agreement is disapproved by a Data Integrity Board, any party to such agreement may appeal the disapproval to the Director of the Office of Management and Budget. Timely notice of the filing of such an appeal shall be provided by the Director of the Office of Management and Budget to the Committee on Governmental Affairs of the Senate and the Committee on Government Operations of the House of Representatives.

(B) The Director of the Office of Management and Budget may approve a matching agreement notwithstanding the disapproval of a Data Integrity Board if the Director determines that—

(i) the matching program will be consistent with all applicable legal, regulatory, and policy requirements;

(ii) there is adequate evidence that the matching agreement will be cost-effective; and

(iii) the matching program is in the public interest.

(C) The decision of the Director to approve a matching agreement shall not take effect until 30 days after it is reported to committees described in subparagraph (A).

(D) If the Data Integrity Board and the Director of the Office of Management and Budget disapprove a matching program proposed by the inspector general of an agency, the inspector general may report the disapproval to the head of the agency and to the Congress.

(6) In the reports required by paragraph (3)(D), agency matching activities that are not matching programs may be reported on an aggregate basis, if and to the extent necessary to protect ongoing law enforcement or counterintelligence investigations.

(v) Office of Management and Budget responsibilities.—The Director of the Office of Management and Budget shall—

(1) develop and, after notice and opportunity for public comment, prescribe guidelines and regulations for the use of agencies in implementing the provisions of this section; and

(2) provide continuing assistance to and oversight of the implementation of this section by agencies.

(w) Applicability to Bureau of Consumer Financial Protection.—Except as provided in the Consumer Financial Protection Act of 2010, this section shall apply with respect to the Bureau of Consumer Financial Protection.

(Added Pub. L. No. 93–579, § 3, 88 Stat. 1897 (Dec. 31, 1974); and amended by Pub. L. No. 94–183, § 2(2), 89 Stat. 1057 (Dec. 31, 1975); Pub. L. No. 97–365, § 2, 96 Stat. 1749 (Oct. 25, 1982); Pub. L. No. 97–375, Title II, § 201(a), (b), 96 Stat. 1821 (Dec. 21, 1982); Pub. L. No. 97–452, § 2(a)(1), 96 Stat. 2478 (Jan. 12, 1983); Pub. L. No. 98–477, § 2(c), 98 Stat. 2211 (Oct. 15, 1984); Pub. L. No. 98–497, Title I, § 107(g), 98 Stat. 2292 (Oct. 19, 1984); Pub. L. No. 100–503, §§ 2 to 6(a), 7, 8, 102 Stat. 2507 to 2514 (Oct. 18, 1988); Pub. L. No. 101–508, Title VII, § 7201(b)(1), 104 Stat. 1388–334 (Nov. 5, 1990); Pub. L. No. 103–66, Title XIII, § 13581(c), 107 Stat. 611 (Aug. 10, 1993); Pub. L. No. 104–193, Title I, § 110(w), 110 Stat. 2175 (Aug. 22, 1996); Pub. L. No. 104–226, § 1(b)(3), 110 Stat. 3033 (Oct. 2, 1996); Pub. L. No. 104–316, Title I, § 115(g)(2)(B), 110 Stat. 3835 (Oct. 19, 1996); Pub. L. No. 105–34, Title X, § 1026(b)(2), 111 Stat. 925 (Aug. 5, 1997); Pub. L. No. 105–362, Title XIII, § 1301(d), 112 Stat. 3293 (Nov. 10, 1998); Pub. L. No. 106–170, Title IV, § 402(a)(2), 113 Stat. 1908 (Dec. 17, 1999); Pub. L. No. 108–271, § 8(b), 118 Stat. 814 (July 7, 2004); Pub. L. No. 111–148, Title VI, § 6402(b)(2), 124 Stat. 756 (Mar. 23, 2010); Pub. L. No. 111–203, Title X, § 1082, 124 Stat. 2080 (July 21, 2010); Pub. L. No. 113–295, § 102(d), 128 Stat. 4062 (Dec. 19, 2014).)

[1] So in original. Probably should be "and individuals."

[2] So in original. Probably should be "cost-effective."

HISTORICAL AND STATUTORY NOTES

References in Text

Section 552(e) of this title, referred to in subsec. (a)(1), was redesignated section 552(f) of this title by section 1802(b) of Pub. L. No. 99–570.

Section 6103 of the Internal Revenue Code of 1986, referred to in subsec. (a)(8)(B)(iv), (vii), is codified as 26 U.S.C.A. § 6103.

Sections 404, 464, and 1137 of the Social Security Act, referred to in subsec. (a)(8)(B)(iv), are codified as sections 604, 664, and 1320b–7, respectively, of Title 42.

For effective date of this section, referred to in subsecs. (k)(2), (5), (7), (*l*)(2), (3), and (m), see Effective Date of 1974 Acts note under this section.

Section 6 of the Privacy Act of 1974, referred to in subsec. (s)(1), is section 6 of Pub. L. No. 93–579, which was set out as a note under this section and was repealed by section 6(c) of Pub. L. No. 100–503.

For classification of the Privacy Act of 1974, referred to in subsec. (s)(4), see Short Title of 1974 Acts note under this section.

The Consumer Financial Protection Act of 2010, referred to in subsec. (w), is Title X of Pub. L. No. 111–203, § 1001 et seq., 124 Stat. 1955 (July 21, 2010), which enacted subchapter V of chapter 53 of Title 12, 12 U.S.C.A. § 5481 et seq., and enacted and amended numerous other sections and notes in the Code. For complete classification, see Short Title note set out under 12 U.S.C.A. § 5301 and Tables.

Codifications

Section 552a of former Title 5, Executive Departments and Government Officers and Employees, was transferred to 7 U.S.C.A. § 2244.

Effective and Applicability Provisions

2014 Act. Pub. L. No. 113–295, § 102(f)(1), 128 Stat. 4062 (Dec. 19, 2014), provided that "[t]he amendments made by this section shall apply to taxable years beginning after December 31, 2014.

2010 Acts. Pub. L. No. 111–203, § 1082, 124 Stat. 2080 (July 21, 2010), provided in part, that amendments made by such section are "[e]ffective on the date of enactment of this Act [July 21, 2010]".

Pub. L. No. 111–203, Title X, § 1100H, 124 Stat. 2113 (July 21, 2010), provided that: "Except as otherwise provided in this subtitle and the amendments made by this subtitle, this subtitle and the amendments made by this subtitle [subtitle H (§§ 1081–1100H) of Title X of Pub. L. No. 111–203, see Tables for classification], other than sections 1081 and 1082 [amending this section and 5 App. U.S.C.A. § 8G, and enacting provisions set out as a note under this section and 5 App. U.S.C.A. § 8G], shall become effective on the designated transfer date ."

[The term "designated transfer date" is defined in 12 U.S.C.A. § 5481(9) as the date established under 12 U.S.C.A. § 5582, which is July 21, 2011.]

1999 Acts. Amendment by section 402(a)(2) of Pub. L. No. 106–170 shall apply to individuals whose period of confinement in an institution commences on or after the first day of the fourth month beginning after December 1999, see section 402(a)(4) of Pub. L. No. 106–170, set out as a note under section 402 of Title 42.

1997 Acts. Amendment by Pub. L. No. 105–34 to apply to levies issued after Aug. 5, 1997, see section 1026(c) of Pub. L. No. 105–34, set out as a note under section 6103 of Title 26, Internal Revenue Code.

1996 Acts. Amendment of subsec. (a)(8)(B)(iv)(III) by Pub. L. No. 104–193 is effective July 1, 1997, with transition rules relating to State options to accelerate such date, rules relating to claims, actions, and proceedings commenced before such date, rules relating to closing out of accounts for terminated or substantially modified programs and continuance in office of Assistant Secretary for Family Support, and provisions relating to termination of entitlement under AFDC program, see section 116 of Pub. L. No. 104–193, set out as a note under section 601 of this title.

Amendment by Pub. L. No. 104–316 effective Oct. 19, 1996, see section 101(e) of Pub. L. No. 104–316, set out as a note under section 130c of Title 2, The Congress.

1993 Acts. Amendment by Pub. L. No. 103–66 effective Jan. 1, 1994, see section 13581(d) of Pub. L. No. 103–66, set out as a note under section 1395y of Title 42, The Public Health and Welfare.

1990 Acts. Pub. L. No. 101–366, Title II, § 206(d), 104 Stat. 442 (Aug. 15, 1990), provided that:

"(1) In the case of computer matching programs between the Department of Veterans Affairs and the Department of Defense in the administration of education benefits programs under chapters 30 and 32 of title 38 [section 1401 et seq. and section 1601 et seq. of Title 38, Veterans Benefits, respectively] and chapter 106 of title 10, United States Code [section 2131 et seq. of Title 10, Armed Forces], the amendments made to section 552a of title 5, United States Code, by the Computer Matching and Privacy Protection Act of 1988 [Pub. L. No. 100–503] (other than the amendments made by section 10(b) of that Act) [see Effective Date of 1988 Acts note under this section] shall take effect on October 1, 1990.

"(2) For purposes of this subsection, the term 'matching program' has the same meaning provided in section 552a(a)(8) of title 5, United States Code [subsec. (a)(8) of this section]."

1988 Acts. Section 10 of Pub. L. No. 100–503, as amended Pub. L. No. 101–56, § 2, 103 Stat. 149 (July 19, 1989), provided that:

"(a) In general.—Except as provided in subsections (b) and (c), the amendments made by this Act [amending this section and repealing provisions set out as a note under this section] shall take effect 9 months after the date of enactment of this Act [Oct. 18, 1988].

"(b) Exceptions.—The amendment made by sections 3(b), 6, 7, and 8 of this Act [amending this section and repealing provisions set out as a note under this section] shall take effect upon enactment.

"(c) Effective date delayed for existing programs.—In the case of any matching program (as defined in section 552a(a)(8) of title 5, United States Code [subsec. (a)(8) of this section], as added by section 5 of this Act) in operation before June 1, 1989, the amendments made by this Act (other than the amendments described in subsection (b)) shall take effect January 1, 1990, if—

"(1) such matching program is identified by an agency as being in operation before June 1, 1989; and

"(2) such identification is—

"(A) submitted by the agency to the Committee on Governmental Affairs of the Senate, the Committee on Government Operations of the House of Representatives, and the Office of Management and Budget before August 1, 1989, in a report which contains a schedule showing the dates on which the agency expects to have such matching program in compliance with the amendments made by this Act, and

"(B) published by the Office of Management and Budget in the Federal Register, before September 15, 1989."

[Any reference in any provision of law enacted before Jan. 4, 1995, to the Committee on Government Operations of the House of Representatives treated as referring to the Committee on Government Reform and Oversight of the House of Representatives, except that any reference in any provision of law enacted before Jan. 4, 1995, to the Committee on Government Operations of the House of Representatives treated as referring to the Committee on the Budget of the House of Representatives in the case of a provision of law relating to the establishment, extension, and enforcement of special controls over the Federal budget, see section 1(a)(6) and (c)(2) of Pub. L. No. 104–14, set out as a note preceding section 21 of Title 2, The Congress.]

1984 Acts. Amendment by Pub. L. No. 98–497 effective April 1, 1985, see section 301 of Pub. L. No. 98–497, set out as a note under section 2102 of Title 44, Public Printing and Documents.

Amendment by Pub. L. No. 98–477, effective Oct. 15, 1984 and applicable with respect to any request for records, whether or not such request was made prior to Oct. 15, 1984, and applicable to all civil actions not commenced prior to February 7, 1984, see section 4 of Pub. L. No. 98–477, set out as a note under section 431 of Title 50, War and National Defense.

1974 Acts. Section 8 of Pub. L. No. 93–579 provided that: "The provisions of this Act [enacting this section and provisions set out as notes under this section] shall be effective on and after the date of enactment [Dec. 31, 1974], except that the amendments made by sections 3 and 4 [enacting this section and amending analysis preceding section 500 of this title] shall become effective 270 days following the day on which this Act is enacted."

OMB Guidance on Electronic Consent and Access Forms

Section 3 of Pub. L. No. 116–50, 133 Stat. 1073–74 (Aug. 22, 2019), provided that:

"(a) Guidance.—Not later than 1 year after the date of the enactment of this Act, the Director shall issue guidance that does the following:

"(1) Requires each agency to accept electronic identity proofing and authentication processes for the purposes of allowing an individual to provide prior written consent for the disclosure of the individual's records under section 552a(b) of title 5, United States Code, or for individual access to records under section 552a(d) of such title.

"(2) Creates a template for electronic consent and access forms and requires each agency to post the template on the agency website and to accept the forms from any individual properly identity proofed and authenticated in accordance with paragraph (1) for the purpose of authorizing disclosure of the individual's records under section 552a(b) of title 5, United States Code, or for individual access to records under section 552a(d) of such title.

"(3) Requires each agency to accept the electronic consent and access forms described in paragraph (2) from any individual properly identity proofed and authenticated in accordance with paragraph (1) for the purpose of authorizing disclosure of the individual's records to another entity, including a congressional office, in accordance with section 552a(b) of title 5, United States Code, or for individual access to records under section 552a(d).

"(b) Agency Compliance.—Each agency shall comply with the guidance issued pursuant to subsection (a) not later than 1 year after the date on which such guidance is issued.

"(c) Definitions.—In this section:

"(1) Agency; Individual; Record.—The terms "agency", "individual", and "record" have the meanings given those terms in section 552a(a) of title 5, United States Code.

"(2) Director.—The term "Director" means the Director of the Office of Management and Budget."

Judicial Redress Act of 2015

Section 2 of Pub. L. No. 114–126, 130 Stat. 282–85 (Feb. 24, 2916), provided that:

"(a) Civil Action; Civil Remedies.—With respect to covered records, a covered person may bring a civil action against an agency and obtain civil remedies, in the same manner, to the same extent, and subject to the same limitations, including exemptions and exceptions, as an individual may bring and obtain with respect to records under—

"(1) section 552a(g)(1)(D) of title 5, United States Code, but only with respect to disclosures intentionally or willfully made in violation of section 552a(b) of such title; and

"(2) subparagraphs (A) and (B) of section 552a(g)(1) of title 5, United States Code, but such an action may only be brought against a designated Federal agency or component.

"(b) Exclusive Remedies.—The remedies set forth in subsection (a) are the exclusive remedies available to a covered person under this section.

"(c) Application of the Privacy Act with Respect to a Covered Person.—For purposes of a civil action described in subsection (a), a covered person shall have the same rights, and be subject to the same limitations, including exemptions and exceptions, as an individual has and is subject to under section 552a of title 5, United States Code, when pursuing the civil remedies described in paragraphs (1) and (2) of subsection (a).

"(d) Designation of Covered Country.—

"(1) In General.—The Attorney General may, with the concurrence of the Secretary of State, the Secretary of the Treasury, and the Secretary of Homeland Security, designate a foreign country or regional economic integration organization, or member country of such organization, as a "covered country" for purposes of this section if—

"(A) (i) the country or regional economic integration organization, or member country of such organization, has entered into an agreement with the United States that provides for appropriate privacy protections for information shared for the purpose of preventing, investigating, detecting, or prosecuting criminal offenses; or

(ii) the Attorney General has determined that the country or regional economic integration organization, or member country of such organization, has effectively shared information with the United States for the purpose of preventing, investigating, detecting, or prosecuting criminal offenses and has appropriate privacy protections for such shared information;

"(B) the country or regional economic integration organization, or member country of such organization, permits the transfer of personal data for commercial purposes between the territory of that country or regional economic organization and the territory of the United States, through an agreement with the United States or otherwise; and

"(C) the Attorney General has certified that the policies regarding the transfer of personal data for commercial purposes and related actions of the country or regional economic integration organization, or member country of such organization, do not materially impede the national security interests of the United States.

"(2) **Removal of Designation.**—The Attorney General may, with the concurrence of the Secretary of State, the Secretary of the Treasury, and the Secretary of Homeland Security, revoke the designation of a foreign country or regional economic integration organization, or member country of such organization, as a "covered country" if the Attorney General determines that such designated "covered country"—

"(A) is not complying with the agreement described under paragraph (1)(A)(i);

"(B) no longer meets the requirements for designation under paragraph (1)(A)(ii);

"(C) fails to meet the requirements under paragraph (1)(B);

"(D) no longer meets the requirements for certification under paragraph (1)(C); or

"(E) impedes the transfer of information (for purposes of reporting or preventing unlawful activity) to the United States by a private entity or person.

"(e) **Designation of Designated Federal Agency or Component.**—

"(1) **In General.**—The Attorney General shall determine whether an agency or component thereof is a "designated Federal agency or component" for purposes of this section. The Attorney General shall not designate any agency or component thereof other than the Department of Justice or a component of the Department of Justice without the concurrence of the head of the relevant agency, or of the agency to which the component belongs.

"(2) **Requirements for Designation.**—The Attorney General may determine that an agency or component of an agency is a "designated Federal agency or component" for purposes of this section, if—

"(A) the Attorney General determines that information exchanged by such agency with a covered country is within the scope of an agreement referred to in subsection (d)(1)(A); or

"(B) with respect to a country or regional economic integration organization, or member country of such organization, that has been designated as a "covered country" under subsection (d)(1)(B), the Attorney General determines that designating such agency or component thereof is in the law enforcement interests of the United States.

"(f) **Federal Register Requirement; Nonreviewable Determination.**—The Attorney General shall publish each determination made under subsections (d) and (e). Such determination shall not be subject to judicial or administrative review.

"(g) **Jurisdiction.**—The United States District Court for the District of Columbia shall have exclusive jurisdiction over any claim arising under this section.

"(h) **Definitions.**—In this Act:

"(1) **Agency.**—The term "agency" has the meaning given that term in section 552(f) of title 5, United States Code.

"(2) Covered Country.—The term "covered country" means a country or regional economic integration organization, or member country of such organization, designated in accordance with subsection (d).

"(3) Covered Person.—The term "covered person" means a natural person (other than an individual) who is a citizen of a covered country.

"(4) Covered Record.—The term "covered record" has the same meaning for a covered person as a record has for an individual under section 552a of title 5, United States Code, once the covered record is transferred—

"(A) by a public authority of, or private entity within, a country or regional economic organization, or member country of such organization, which at the time the record is transferred is a covered country; and

"(B) to a designated Federal agency or component for purposes of preventing, investigating, detecting, or prosecuting criminal offenses.

"(5) Designated Federal Agency or Component.—The term "designated Federal agency or component" means a Federal agency or component of an agency designated in accordance with subsection (e).

"(6) Individual.—The term "individual" has the meaning given that term in section 552a(a)(2) of title 5, United States Code.

"(i) Preservation of Privileges.—Nothing in this section shall be construed to waive any applicable privilege or require the disclosure of classified information. Upon an agency's request, the district court shall review in camera and ex parte any submission by the agency in connection with this subsection.

"(j) Effective Date.—This Act shall take effect 90 days after the date of the enactment of this Act."

Termination of Reporting Requirements

For termination, effective May 15, 2000, of provisions in subsec. (s) of this section, see Pub. L. No. 104–66, § 3003, as amended, set out as a note under 31 U.S.C.A. § 1113 and page 31 of House Document No. 103–7.

Change of Name

Committee on Governmental Affairs of Senate changed to Committee on Homeland Security and Governmental Affairs of Senate, effective Jan. 4, 2005, by Senate Resolution No. 445, 108th, Oct. 9, 2004.

Committee on Government Operations of House of Representatives treated as referring to Committee on Government Reform and Oversight of House of Representatives by section 1(a) of Pub. L. No. 104–14, set out as a note under section 21 of Title 2. Committee on Government Reform and Oversight of House of Representatives changed to Committee on Government Reform of House of Representatives by House Resolution No. 5, 106th Congress, Jan. 6, 1999. Committee on Government Reform of House of Representatives changed to Committee on Oversight and Government Reform of House of Representatives by House Resolution No. 6, 110th, Jan. 5, 2007.

Delegation of Functions

Functions of Director of Office of Management and Budget under this section delegated to Administrator for Office of Information and Regulatory Affairs by section 3 of Pub. L. No. 96–511, 94 Stat. 2825 (Dec. 11, 1980), set out as a note under section 3503 of Title 44, Public Printing and Documents.

Severability of Provisions

If any provision of Pub. L. No. 111–203, an amendment made by Pub. L. No. 111–203, or the application of such provision or amendment to any person or circumstance is held to be unconstitutional, the remainder of Pub. L. No. 111–203, the amendments made by Pub. L. No. 111–203, and the application of the provisions of such to any person or circumstance shall not be affected, see 12 U.S.C.A. § 5302.

Short Title

1990 Amendments. Section 7201(a) of Pub. L. No. 101–508 provided that: "This section [amending this section and enacting provisions set out as notes under this section] may be cited as the 'Computer Matching and Privacy Protection Amendments of 1990'."

1989 Amendments. Pub. L. No. 101–56, § 1, 103 Stat. 149 (July 19, 1989), provided that: "This Act [amending section 10 of Pub. L. No. 100–503, set out as a note under this section] may be cited as the 'Computer Matching and Privacy Protection Act Amendments of 1989'."

1988 Amendments. Section 1 of Pub. L. No. 100–503 provided that: "This Act [amending this section, enacting provisions set out as notes under this section and repealing provisions set out as a note under this section] may be cited as the 'Computer Matching and Privacy Protection Act of 1988'."

1974 Acts. Section 1 of Pub. L. No. 93–579 provided: "That this Act [enacting this section and provisions set out as notes under this section] may be cited as the 'Privacy Act of 1974'."

Designated Transfer Date Defined

For purposes of Pub. L. No. 111–203, not later than 60 days after July 21, 2010, a single calendar date shall be designated for the transfer of functions to the Bureau of Consumer Financial Protection which shall be not earlier than 180 days after July 21, 2010, nor later than 12 months after July 21, 2010, unless extended, see 12 U.S.C.A. § 5582.

Privacy and Data Protection Procedures

Pub. L. No. 108–447, Div. H, Title V, § 522, 118 Stat. 3268 (Dec. 8, 2004), relating to privacy and data protection procedures, was editorially redesignated 42 U.S.C.A. § 2000ee–2.

Codified National Security Information

For provisions relating to a response to a request for information under this section when the fact of its existence or nonexistence is itself codified or when it was originally codified by another agency, see Ex. Ord. No. 12958, § 3.7, 60 Fed. Reg. 19835 (April 17, 1995), set out as a note under section 435 of Title 50.

Publication of Guidance Under Subsection (p)(1)(A)(ii)

Section 7201(b)(2) of Pub. L. No. 101–508 provided that: "Not later than 90 days after the date of the enactment of this Act [Nov. 5, 1990], the Director of the Office of Management and Budget shall publish guidance under subsection (p)(1)(A)(ii) of section 552a of title 5, United States Code [subsec. (p)(1)(A)(ii) of this section], as amended by this Act."

Limitation on Application of Verification Requirement

Section 7201(c) of Pub. L. No. 101–508 provided that: "Section 552a(p)(1)(A)(ii)(II) of title 5, United States Code [subsec. (p)(1)(A)(ii)(II) of this section], as amended by section 2 [probably means section 7201(b)(1) of Pub. L. No. 101–508], shall not apply to a program referred to in paragraph (1), (2), or (4) of section 1137(b) of the Social Security Act (42 U.S.C. 1320b–7), until the earlier of—

"(1) the date on which the Data Integrity Board of the Federal agency which administers that program determines that there is not a high degree of confidence that information provided by that agency under Federal matching programs is accurate; or

"(2) 30 days after the date of publication of guidance under section 2(b) [probably means section 7201(b)(2) of Pub. L. No. 101–508, set out as a note under this section]."

Implementation Guidance for 1988 Amendments

Section 6(b) of Pub. L. No. 100–503 provided that: "The Director shall, pursuant to section 552a(v) of title 5, United States Code, develop guidelines and regulations for the use of agencies in implementing the amendments made by this Act [amending this section and repealing provisions set out as a note under this section] not later than 8 months after the date of enactment of this Act [Oct. 18, 1988]."

Construction of 1988 Amendments

Section 9 of Pub. L. No. 100–503 provided that: "Nothing in the amendments made by this Act [amending this section and repealing provisions set out as a note under this section] shall be construed to authorize—

"(1) the establishment or maintenance by any agency of a national data bank that combines, merges, or links information on individuals maintained in systems of records by other Federal agencies;

"(2) the direct linking of computerized systems of records maintained by Federal agencies;

"(3) the computer matching of records not otherwise authorized by law; or

"(4) the disclosure of records for computer matching except to a Federal, State, or local agency."

Congressional Findings and Statement of Purpose

Section 2 of Pub. L. No. 93–579 provided that:

"(a) The Congress finds that—

"(1) the privacy of an individual is directly affected by the collection, maintenance, use, and dissemination of personal information by Federal agencies;

"(2) the increasing use of computers and sophisticated information technology, while essential to the efficient operations of the Government, has greatly magnified the harm to individual privacy that can occur from any collection, maintenance, use, or dissemination of personal information;

"(3) the opportunities for an individual to secure employment, insurance, and credit, and his right to due process, and other legal protections are endangered by the misuse of certain information systems;

"(4) the right to privacy is a personal and fundamental right protected by the Constitution of the United States; and

"(5) in order to protect the privacy of individuals identified in information systems maintained by Federal agencies, it is necessary and proper for the Congress to regulate the collection, maintenance, use, and dissemination of information by such agencies.

"(b) The purpose of this Act [enacting this section and provisions set out as notes under this section] is to provide certain safeguards for an individual against an invasion of personal privacy by requiring Federal agencies, except as otherwise provided by law, to—

"(1) permit an individual to determine what records pertaining to him are collected, maintained, used, or disseminated by such agencies;

"(2) permit an individual to prevent records pertaining to him obtained by such agencies for a particular purpose from being used or made available for another purpose without his consent;

"(3) permit an individual to gain access to information pertaining to him in Federal agency records, to have a copy made of all or any portion thereof, and to correct or amend such records;

"(4) collect, maintain, use, or disseminate any record of identifiable personal information in a manner that assures that such action is for a necessary and lawful purpose, that the information is current and accurate for its intended use, and that adequate safeguards are provided to prevent misuse of such information;

"(5) permit exemptions from the requirements with respect to records provided in this Act only in those cases where there is an important public policy need for such exemption as has been determined by specific statutory authority; and

"(6) be subject to civil suit for any damages which occur as a result of willful or intentional action which violates any individual's rights under this Act."

Privacy Protection Study Commission

Section 5 of Pub. L. No. 93–579, as amended by Pub. L. No. 95–38, 91 Stat. 179 (June 1, 1977), which established the Privacy Protection Study Commission and provided that the Commission study data banks, automated data processing programs and information systems of governmental, regional and private organizations to determine standards and procedures in force for protection of personal information, that the Commission report to the President and Congress the extent to which requirements and principles of section 552a of title 5 should be applied to the information practices of those organizations, and that it make other legislative recommendations to protect the privacy of individuals while meeting the legitimate informational needs of government and society, ceased to exist on September 30, 1977, pursuant to section 5(g) of Pub. L. No. 93–579.

Guidelines and Regulations for Maintenance of Privacy and Protection of Records of Individuals

Section 6 of Pub. L. No. 93–579, which provided that the Office of Management and Budget shall develop guidelines and regulations for use of agencies in implementing provisions of this section and provide continuing assistance to and oversight of the implementation of the provisions of such section by agencies, was repealed by Pub. L. No. 100–503, § 6(c), 102 Stat. 2513 (Oct. 18, 1988).

Disclosure of Social Security Number

Section 7 of Pub. L. No. 93–579 provided that:

"(a) (1) It shall be unlawful for any Federal, State or local government agency to deny to any individual any right, benefit, or privilege provided by law because of such individual's refusal to disclose his social security account number.

"(2) the [The] provisions of paragraph (1) of this subsection shall not apply with respect to—

"(A) any disclosure which is required by Federal statute, or

"(B) the disclosure of a social security number to any Federal, State, or local agency maintaining a system of records in existence and operating before January 1, 1975, if such disclosure was required under statute or regulation adopted prior to such date to verify the identity of an individual.

"(b) Any Federal, State, or local government agency which requests an individual to disclose his social security account number shall inform that individual whether that disclosure is mandatory or voluntary, by what statutory or other authority such number is solicited, and what uses will be made of it."

Authorization of Appropriations to Privacy Protection Study Commission

Section 9 of Pub. L. No. 93–579, as amended by Pub. L. No. 94–394, 90 Stat. 1198 (Sept. 3, 1976), authorized appropriations for the period beginning July 1, 1975, and ending on September 30, 1977.

§ 552b. Open meetings

(a) For purposes of this section—

(1) the term "agency" means any agency, as defined in section 552(e) of this title, headed by a collegial body composed of two or more individual members, a majority of whom are appointed to such position by the President with the advice and consent of the Senate, and any subdivision thereof authorized to act on behalf of the agency;

(2) the term "meeting" means the deliberations of at least the number of individual agency members required to take action on behalf of the agency where such deliberations determine or result in the joint conduct or disposition of official agency business, but does not include deliberations required or permitted by subsection (d) or (e); and

(3) the term "member" means an individual who belongs to a collegial body heading an agency.

(b) Members shall not jointly conduct or dispose of agency business other than in accordance with this section. Except as provided in subsection (c), every portion of every meeting of an agency shall be open to public observation.

(c) Except in a case where the agency finds that the public interest requires otherwise, the second sentence of subsection (b) shall not apply to any portion of an agency meeting, and the requirements of subsections (d) and (e) shall not apply to any information pertaining to such meeting otherwise required by this section to be disclosed to the public, where the agency properly determines that such portion or portions of its meeting or the disclosure of such information is likely to—

(1) disclose matters that are (A) specifically authorized under criteria established by an Executive order to be kept secret in the interests of national defense or foreign policy and (B) in fact properly classified pursuant to such Executive order;

(2) relate solely to the internal personnel rules and practices of an agency;

(3) disclose matters specifically exempted from disclosure by statute (other than section 552 of this title), provided that such statute (A) requires that the matters be withheld from the public in such a manner as to leave no discretion on the issue, or (B) establishes particular criteria for withholding or refers to particular types of matters to be withheld;

(4) disclose trade secrets and commercial or financial information obtained from a person and privileged or confidential;

(5) involve accusing any person of a crime, or formally censuring any person;

(6) disclose information of a personal nature where disclosure would constitute a clearly unwarranted invasion of personal privacy;

(7) disclose investigatory records compiled for law enforcement purposes, or information which if written would be contained in such records, but only to the extent that the production of such records or information would (A) interfere with enforcement proceedings, (B) deprive a person of a right to a fair trial or an impartial adjudication, (C) constitute an unwarranted invasion of personal privacy, (D) disclose the identity of a confidential source and, in the case of a record compiled by a criminal law enforcement authority in the course of a criminal investigation, or by an agency conducting a lawful national security intelligence investigation, confidential information furnished only by the confidential source, (E) disclose investigative techniques and procedures, or (F) endanger the life or physical safety of law enforcement personnel;

(8) disclose information contained in or related to examination, operating, or condition reports prepared by, on behalf of, or for the use of an agency responsible for the regulation or supervision of financial institutions;

(9) disclose information the premature disclosure of which would—

(A) in the case of an agency which regulates currencies, securities, commodities, or financial institutions, be likely to (i) lead to significant financial speculation in currencies, securities, or commodities, or (ii) significantly endanger the stability of any financial institution; or

(B) in the case of any agency, be likely to significantly frustrate implementation of a proposed agency action,

except that subparagraph (B) shall not apply in any instance where the agency has already disclosed to the public the content or nature of its proposed action, or where the agency is required by law to make such disclosure on its own initiative prior to taking final agency action on such proposal; or

(10) specifically concern the agency's issuance of a subpena, or the agency's participation in a civil action or proceeding, an action in a foreign court or international tribunal, or an arbitration, or the initiation, conduct, or disposition by the agency of a particular case of formal agency adjudication pursuant to the procedures in section 554 of this title or otherwise involving a determination on the record after opportunity for a hearing.

(d) **(1)** Action under subsection (c) shall be taken only when a majority of the entire membership of the agency (as defined in subsection (a)(1)) votes to take such action. A separate vote of the agency members shall be taken with respect to each agency meeting a portion or portions of which are proposed to be closed to the public pursuant to subsection (c), or with respect to any information which is proposed to be withheld under subsection (c). A single vote may be taken with respect to a series of meetings, a portion or portions of which are proposed to be closed to the public, or with respect to any information concerning such series of meetings, so long as each meeting in such series involves the same particular matters and is scheduled to be held no more than thirty days after the initial meeting in such series. The vote of each agency member participating in such vote shall be recorded and no proxies shall be allowed.

(2) Whenever any person whose interests may be directly affected by a portion of a meeting requests that the agency close such portion to the public for any of the reasons referred to in paragraph (5), (6), or (7) of subsection (c), the agency, upon request of any one of its members, shall vote by recorded vote whether to close such meeting.

(3) Within one day of any vote taken pursuant to paragraph (1) or (2), the agency shall make publicly available a written copy of such vote reflecting the vote of each member on the question. If a portion of a meeting is to be closed to the public, the agency shall, within one day of the vote taken pursuant to paragraph (1) or (2) of this subsection, make publicly available a full written explanation of its action closing the portion together with a list of all persons expected to attend the meeting and their affiliation.

(4) Any agency, a majority of whose meetings may properly be closed to the public pursuant to paragraph (4), (8), (9)(A), or (10) of subsection (c), or any combination thereof, may provide by regulation for the closing of such meetings or portions thereof in the event that a majority of the members of the agency votes by recorded vote at the beginning of such meeting, or portion thereof, to close the exempt portion or portions of the meeting, and a copy of such vote, reflecting the vote of each member on the question, is made available to the public. The provisions of paragraphs (1), (2), and (3) of this subsection and subsection (e) shall not apply to any portion of a meeting to which such regulations apply: *Provided*, That the agency shall, except to the extent that such information is exempt from disclosure under the provisions of subsection (c), provide the public with public announcement of the time, place, and subject matter of the meeting and of each portion thereof at the earliest practicable time.

(e) **(1)** In the case of each meeting, the agency shall make public announcement, at least one week before the meeting, of the time, place, and subject matter of the meeting, whether it is to be open or closed to the public, and the name and phone number of the official designated by the agency to respond to requests for information about the meeting. Such announcement shall be made unless a majority of the members of the agency determines by a recorded vote that agency business requires that such meeting be called at an earlier date, in which case the agency shall make public announcement of the time, place, and subject matter of such meeting, and whether open or closed to the public, at the earliest practicable time.

(2) The time or place of a meeting may be changed following the public announcement required by paragraph (1) only if the agency publicly announces such change at the earliest practicable time. The subject matter of a meeting, or the determination of the agency to open or close a meeting, or portion of a meeting, to the public, may be changed following the public announcement required by this subsection only if (A) a majority of the entire membership of the agency determines by a recorded vote that agency business so requires and that no earlier announcement of the change was possible, and (B) the agency publicly announces such change and the vote of each member upon such change at the earliest practicable time.

(3) Immediately following each public announcement required by this subsection, notice of the time, place, and subject matter of a meeting, whether the meeting is open or closed, any change in one of the preceding, and the name and phone number of the official designated by the agency to respond to requests for information about the meeting, shall also be submitted for publication in the Federal Register.

(f) **(1)** For every meeting closed pursuant to paragraphs (1) through (10) of subsection (c), the General Counsel or chief legal officer of the agency shall publicly certify that, in his or her opinion, the meeting may be closed to the public and shall state each relevant exemptive provision. A copy of such certification, together with a statement from the presiding officer of the meeting setting forth the time and place of the meeting, and the persons present, shall be retained by the agency. The agency shall maintain a complete transcript or electronic recording adequate to record fully the proceedings of each meeting, or portion of a meeting, closed to the public, except that in the case of a meeting, or portion of a meeting, closed to the public pursuant to paragraph (8), (9)(A), or (10) of subsection (c), the agency shall maintain either such a transcript or recording, or a set of minutes. Such minutes shall fully and clearly describe all matters discussed and shall provide a full and accurate summary of any actions taken, and the reasons therefor, including a description of each of the views expressed on any item and the record of any rollcall vote (reflecting the vote of each member on the question). All documents considered in connection with any action shall be identified in such minutes.

(2) The agency shall make promptly available to the public, in a place easily accessible to the public, the transcript, electronic recording, or minutes (as required by paragraph (1)) of the discussion of any item on the agenda, or of any item of the testimony of any witness received at the meeting, except for such item or items of such discussion or testimony as the agency determines to contain information which may be withheld under subsection (c). Copies of such transcript, or minutes, or a transcription of such recording disclosing the identity of each speaker, shall be furnished to any person at the actual cost of duplication or transcription. The agency shall maintain a complete verbatim copy of the transcript, a complete copy of the minutes, or a complete electronic recording of each meeting, or portion of a meeting, closed to the public, for a period of at least two years after such meeting, or until one year after the conclusion of any agency proceeding with respect to which the meeting or portion was held, whichever occurs later.

(g) Each agency subject to the requirements of this section shall, within 180 days after the date of enactment of this section, following consultation with the Office of the Chairman of the Administrative Conference of the United States and published notice in the Federal Register of at least thirty days and opportunity for written comment by any person, promulgate regulations to implement the requirements of subsections (b) through (f) of this section. Any person may bring a proceeding in the United States District Court for the District of Columbia to require an agency to promulgate such regulations if such agency has not promulgated such regulations within the time period specified herein. Subject to any limitations of time provided by law, any person may bring a proceeding in the United States Court of Appeals for the District of Columbia to set aside agency regulations issued pursuant to this subsection that are not in accord with the requirements of subsections (b) through (f) of this section and to require the promulgation of regulations that are in accord with such subsections.

(h) **(1)** The district courts of the United States shall have jurisdiction to enforce the requirements of subsections (b) through (f) of this section by declaratory judgment, injunctive relief, or other relief as may be appropriate. Such actions may be brought by any person against an agency prior to, or within sixty days after, the meeting out of which the violation of this section arises, except that if public announcement of such meeting is not initially provided by the agency in accordance with the requirements of this section, such action may be instituted pursuant to this section at any time prior to sixty days after any public announcement of such meeting. Such actions may be brought in the district court of the United States for the district in which the agency meeting is held or in which the agency in question has its headquarters, or in the District Court for the District of Columbia. In such actions a defendant shall serve his answer within thirty days after the service of the complaint. The burden is on the defendant to sustain his action. In deciding such cases the court may examine in camera any portion of the transcript, electronic recording, or minutes of a meeting closed to the public, and may take such additional evidence as it deems necessary. The court, having due regard for orderly administration and the public interest, as well as the interests of the parties, may grant such equitable relief as it deems appropriate, including granting an injunction against future violations of this section or ordering the agency to make available to the public such portion of the transcript, recording, or minutes of a meeting as is not authorized to be withheld under subsection (c) of this section.

(2) Any Federal court otherwise authorized by law to review agency action may, at the application of any person properly participating in the proceeding pursuant to other applicable law, inquire into violations by the agency of the requirements of this section and afford such relief as it deems appropriate. Nothing in this section authorizes any Federal court having jurisdiction solely on the basis of paragraph (1) to set aside, enjoin, or invalidate any agency action (other than an action to close a meeting or to withhold information under this section) taken or discussed at any agency meeting out of which the violation of this section arose.

(i) The court may assess against any party reasonable attorney fees and other litigation costs reasonably incurred by any other party who substantially prevails in any action brought in accordance with the provisions of subsection (g) or (h) of this section, except that costs may be assessed against the plaintiff only where the court finds that the suit was initiated by the plaintiff primarily for frivolous or dilatory purposes. In the case of assessment of costs against an agency, the costs may be assessed by the court against the United States.

(j) Each agency subject to the requirements of this section shall annually report to the Congress regarding the following:

(1) The changes in the policies and procedures of the agency under this section that have occurred during the preceding 1-year period.

(2) A tabulation of the number of meetings held, the exemptions applied to close meetings, and the days of public notice provided to close meetings.

(3) A brief description of litigation or formal complaints concerning the implementation of this section by the agency.

(4) A brief explanation of any changes in law that have affected the responsibilities of the agency under this section.

(k) Nothing herein expands or limits the present rights of any person under section 552 of this title, except that the exemptions set forth in subsection (c) of this section shall govern in the case of any request made pursuant to section 552 to copy or inspect the transcripts, recordings, or minutes described in subsection (f) of this section. The requirements of chapter 33 of title 44, United States Code, shall not apply to the transcripts, recordings, and minutes described in subsection (f) of this section.

(l) This section does not constitute authority to withhold any information from Congress, and does not authorize the closing of any agency meeting or portion thereof required by any other provision of law to be open.

(m) Nothing in this section authorizes any agency to withhold from any individual any record, including transcripts, recordings, or minutes required by this section, which is otherwise accessible to such individual under section 552a of this title.

(Added by Pub. L. No. 94–409, § 3(a), 90 Stat. 1241 (Sept. 13, 1976); and amended by Pub. L. No. 104–66, Title III, § 3002, 109 Stat. 734 (Dec. 21, 1995).)

HISTORICAL AND STATUTORY NOTES

References in Text

Section 552(e) of this title, referred to in subsec. (a)(1), was redesignated section 552(f) of this title by section 1802(b) of Pub. L. No. 99–570.

180 days after the date of enactment of this section, referred to in subsec. (g), means 180 days after the date of enactment of Pub. L. No. 94–409, which was approved Sept. 13, 1976.

Effective and Applicability Provisions

1976 Acts. Section 6 of Pub. L. No. 94–409 provided that:

"(a) Except as provided in subsection (b) of this section, the provisions of this Act [see Short Title of 1976 Acts note set out under this section] shall take effect 180 days after the date of its enactment [Sept. 13, 1976].

"(b) Subsection (g) of section 552b of title 5, United States Code, as added by section 3(a) of this Act [subsec. (g) of this section], shall take effect upon enactment [Sept. 13, 1976]."

Short Title

1976 Acts. Section 1 of Pub. L. No. 94–409 provided: "That this Act [enacting this section, amending sections 551, 552, 556, and 557 of this title, section 10 of Pub. L. No. 92–463, set out in Appendix 1 to this title, and section 410 of Title 39, Postal Service, and enacting provisions set out as notes under this section] may be cited as the 'Government in the Sunshine Act'." This Act is also popularly known as the Open Meetings Act.

Termination of Reporting Requirements

For termination, effective May 15, 2000, of provisions of law requiring submittal to Congress of any annual, semiannual, or other regular periodic report listed in House Document No. 103–7 (in which the report required by subsec. (j) of this section is listed on page 151), see Pub. L. No. 104–66, § 3003, as amended, set out as a note under 31 U.S.C.A. § 1113.

Termination of Administrative Conference of United States

For termination of Administrative Conference of United States, see provisions of title IV of Pub. L. No. 104–52, set out as a note preceding section 591 of this title.

Declaration of Policy and Statement of Purpose

Section 2 of Pub. L. No. 94–409 provided that: "It is hereby declared to be the policy of the United States that the public is entitled to the fullest practicable information regarding the decision making processes of the Federal Government. It is the purpose of this Act [see Short Title of 1976 Acts note set out under this section] to provide the public with such information while protecting the rights of individuals and the ability of the Government to carry out its responsibilities."

§ 553. Rule making

(a) This section applies, according to the provisions thereof, except to the extent that there is involved—

(1) a military or foreign affairs function of the United States; or

(2) a matter relating to agency management or personnel or to public property, loans, grants, benefits, or contracts.

(b) General notice of proposed rule making shall be published in the Federal Register, unless persons subject thereto are named and either personally served or otherwise have actual notice thereof in accordance with law. The notice shall include—

(1) a statement of the time, place, and nature of public rule making proceedings;

(2) reference to the legal authority under which the rule is proposed; and

(3) either the terms or substance of the proposed rule or a description of the subjects and issues involved.

Except when notice or hearing is required by statute, this subsection does not apply—

(A) to interpretative rules, general statements of policy, or rules of agency organization, procedure, or practice; or

(B) when the agency for good cause finds (and incorporates the finding and a brief statement of reasons therefor in the rules issued) that notice and public procedure thereon are impracticable, unnecessary, or contrary to the public interest.

(c) After notice required by this section, the agency shall give interested persons an opportunity to participate in the rule making through submission of written data, views, or arguments with or without opportunity for oral presentation. After consideration of the relevant matter presented, the agency shall incorporate in the rules adopted a concise general statement of their basis and purpose. When rules are required by statute to be made on the record after opportunity for an agency hearing, sections 556 and 557 of this title apply instead of this subsection.

(d) The required publication or service of a substantive rule shall be made not less than 30 days before its effective date, except—

(1) a substantive rule which grants or recognizes an exemption or relieves a restriction;

(2) interpretative rules and statements of policy; or

(3) as otherwise provided by the agency for good cause found and published with the rule.

(e) Each agency shall give an interested person the right to petition for the issuance, amendment, or repeal of a rule.

(Pub. L. No. 89–554, 80 Stat. 383 (Sept. 6, 1966).)

HISTORICAL AND STATUTORY NOTES

Codifications

Section 553 of former Title 5, Executive Departments and Government Officers and Employees, was transferred to 7 U.S.C.A. § 2245.

§ 554. Adjudications

(a) This section applies, according to the provisions thereof, in every case of adjudication required by statute to be determined on the record after opportunity for an agency hearing, except to the extent that there is involved—

(1) a matter subject to a subsequent trial of the law and the facts de novo in a court;

(2) the selection or tenure of an employee, except a[1] administrative law judge appointed under section 3105 of this title;

(3) proceedings in which decisions rest solely on inspections, tests, or elections;

(4) the conduct of military or foreign affairs functions;

(5) cases in which an agency is acting as an agent for a court; or

(6) the certification of worker representatives.

(b) Persons entitled to notice of an agency hearing shall be timely informed of—

(1) the time, place, and nature of the hearing;

(2) the legal authority and jurisdiction under which the hearing is to be held; and

(3) the matters of fact and law asserted.

When private persons are the moving parties, other parties to the proceeding shall give prompt notice of issues controverted in fact or law; and in other instances agencies may by rule require responsive pleading. In fixing the time and place for hearings, due regard shall be had for the convenience and necessity of the parties or their representatives.

(c) The agency shall give all interested parties opportunity for—

(1) the submission and consideration of facts, arguments, offers of settlement, or proposals of adjustment when time, the nature of the proceeding, and the public interest permit; and

(2) to the extent that the parties are unable so to determine a controversy by consent, hearing and decision on notice and in accordance with sections 556 and 557 of this title.

(d) The employee who presides at the reception of evidence pursuant to section 556 of this title shall make the recommended decision or initial decision required by section 557 of this title, unless he becomes unavailable to the agency. Except to the extent required for the disposition of ex parte matters as authorized by law, such an employee may not—

(1) consult a person or party on a fact in issue, unless on notice and opportunity for all parties to participate; or

(2) be responsible to or subject to the supervision or direction of an employee or agent engaged in the performance of investigative or prosecuting functions for an agency.

An employee or agent engaged in the performance of investigative or prosecuting functions for an agency in a case may not, in that or a factually related case, participate or advise in the decision, recommended decision, or agency review pursuant to section 557 of this title, except as witness or counsel in public proceedings. This subsection does not apply—

(A) in determining applications for initial licenses;

(B) to proceedings involving the validity or application of rates, facilities, or practices of public utilities or carriers; or

(C) to the agency or a member or members of the body comprising the agency.

(e) The agency, with like effect as in the case of other orders, and in its sound discretion, may issue a declaratory order to terminate a controversy or remove uncertainty.

(Pub. L. No. 89–554, 80 Stat. 384 (Sept. 6, 1966); as amended by Pub. L. No. 95–251, § 2(a)(1), 92 Stat. 183 (Mar. 27, 1978).)

[1] So in original.

HISTORICAL AND STATUTORY NOTES

Codifications

Section 554 of former Title 5, Executive Departments and Government Officers and Employees, was transferred to 7 U.S.C.A. § 2246.

§ 555. Ancillary matters

(a) This section applies, according to the provisions thereof, except as otherwise provided by this subchapter.

(b) A person compelled to appear in person before an agency or representative thereof is entitled to be accompanied, represented, and advised by counsel or, if permitted by the agency, by other qualified representative. A party is entitled to appear in person or by or with counsel or other duly qualified representative in an agency proceeding. So far as the orderly conduct of public business permits, an interested person may appear before an agency or its responsible employees for the presentation, adjustment, or determination of an issue, request, or controversy in a proceeding, whether interlocutory, summary, or otherwise, or in connection with an agency function. With due regard for the convenience and necessity of the parties or their representatives and within a reasonable time, each agency shall proceed to conclude a matter presented to it. This subsection does not grant or deny a person who is not a lawyer the right to appear for or represent others before an agency or in an agency proceeding.

(c) Process, requirement of a report, inspection, or other investigative act or demand may not be issued, made, or enforced except as authorized by law. A person compelled to submit data or evidence is entitled to retain or, on payment of lawfully prescribed costs, procure a copy or transcript thereof, except that in a nonpublic investigatory proceeding the witness may for good cause be limited to inspection of the official transcript of his testimony.

(d) Agency subpenas authorized by law shall be issued to a party on request and, when required by rules of procedure, on a statement or showing of general relevance and reasonable scope of the evidence sought. On contest, the court shall sustain the subpena or similar process or demand to the extent that it is found to be in accordance with law. In a proceeding for enforcement, the court shall issue an order requiring the appearance of the witness or the production of the evidence or data within a reasonable time under penalty of punishment for contempt in case of contumacious failure to comply.

(e) Prompt notice shall be given of the denial in whole or in part of a written application, petition, or other request of an interested person made in connection with any agency proceeding. Except in affirming a prior denial or when the denial is self-explanatory, the notice shall be accompanied by a brief statement of the grounds for denial.

(Pub. L. No. 89–554, 80 Stat. 385 (Sept. 6, 1966).)

HISTORICAL AND STATUTORY NOTES

Codifications

Section 555 of former Title 5, Executive Departments and Government Officers and Employees, was transferred to 7 U.S.C.A. § 2247.

§ 556. Hearings; presiding employees; powers and duties; burden of proof; evidence; record as basis of decision

(a) This section applies, according to the provisions thereof, to hearings required by section 553 or 554 of this title to be conducted in accordance with this section.

(b) There shall preside at the taking of evidence—

(1) the agency;

(2) one or more members of the body which comprises the agency; or

(3) one or more administrative law judges appointed under section 3105 of this title.

This subchapter does not supersede the conduct of specified classes of proceedings, in whole or in part, by or before boards or other employees specially provided for by or designated under statute. The functions of presiding employees and of employees participating in decisions in accordance with section 557 of this title shall be conducted in an impartial manner. A presiding or participating employee may at any time disqualify himself. On the filing in good faith of a timely and sufficient affidavit of personal bias or other disqualification of a presiding or participating employee, the agency shall determine the matter as a part of the record and decision in the case.

(c) Subject to published rules of the agency and within its powers, employees presiding at hearings may—

(1) administer oaths and affirmations;

(2) issue subpenas authorized by law;

(3) rule on offers of proof and receive relevant evidence;

(4) take depositions or have depositions taken when the ends of justice would be served;

(5) regulate the course of the hearing;

(6) hold conferences for the settlement or simplification of the issues by consent of the parties or by the use of alternative means of dispute resolution as provided in subchapter IV of this chapter;

(7) inform the parties as to the availability of one or more alternative means of dispute resolution, and encourage use of such methods;

(8) require the attendance at any conference held pursuant to paragraph (6) of at least one representative of each party who has authority to negotiate concerning resolution of issues in controversy;

(9) dispose of procedural requests or similar matters;

(10) make or recommend decisions in accordance with section 557 of this title; and

(11) take other action authorized by agency rule consistent with this subchapter.

(d) Except as otherwise provided by statute, the proponent of a rule or order has the burden of proof. Any oral or documentary evidence may be received, but the agency as a matter of policy shall provide for the exclusion of irrelevant, immaterial, or unduly repetitious evidence. A sanction may not be imposed or rule or order issued except on consideration of the whole record or those parts thereof cited by a party and supported by and in accordance with the reliable, probative, and substantial evidence. The agency may, to the extent consistent with the interests of justice and the policy of the underlying statutes administered by the agency, consider a violation of section 557(d) of this title sufficient grounds for a decision adverse to a party who has knowingly committed such violation or knowingly caused such violation to occur. A party is entitled to present his case or defense by oral or documentary evidence, to submit rebuttal evidence, and to conduct such cross-examination as may be required for a full and true disclosure of the facts. In rule making or determining claims for money or benefits or applications for initial licenses an agency may, when a party will not be prejudiced thereby, adopt procedures for the submission of all or part of the evidence in written form.

(e) The transcript of testimony and exhibits, together with all papers and requests filed in the proceeding, constitutes the exclusive record for decision in accordance with section 557 of this title and, on payment of lawfully prescribed costs, shall be made available to the parties. When an agency decision rests on official notice of a material fact not appearing in the evidence in the record, a party is entitled, on timely request, to an opportunity to show the contrary.

(Pub. L. No. 89–554, 80 Stat. 386 (Sept. 6, 1966); as amended by Pub. L. No. 94–409, § 4(c), 90 Stat. 1247 (Sept. 13, 1976); Pub. L. No. 95–251, § 2(a)(1), 92 Stat. 183 (Mar. 27, 1978); Pub. L. No. 101–552, § 4(a), 104 Stat. 2737 (Nov. 15, 1990).)

HISTORICAL AND STATUTORY NOTES

Effective and Applicability Provisions

1976 Acts. Amendment by Pub. L. No. 94–409 effective 180 days after Sept. 13, 1976, see section 6 of Pub. L. No. 94–409, set out as a note under section 552b of this title.

Sunset Provisions

The termination of amendments by Pub. L. No. 101–552 and authority to use dispute resolution proceedings on Oct. 1, 1995, provided by section 11 of Pub. L. No. 101–552, set out as a note under section 571 of this title, was repealed by section 9 of Pub. L. No. 104–320.

Hearing Examiners Employed by Department of Agriculture

Functions vested by this subchapter in hearing examiners employed by Department of Agriculture not included in functions of officers, agencies, and employees of that Department transferred to Secretary of Agriculture by 1953 Reorg. Plan No. 2, § 1, eff. 18 Fed. Reg. 3219, 67 Stat. 633 (June 4, 1953), set out in Appendix 1 to this title.

Hearing Examiners Employed by Department of Commerce

Functions vested by this subchapter in hearing examiners employed by Department of Commerce not included in functions of officers, agencies, and employees of that Department transferred to Secretary of Commerce by 1950 Reorg. Plan No. 5, § 1, 15 Fed. Reg. 3174, 64 Stat. 1263 (eff. May 24, 1950), set out in Appendix 1 to this title.

Hearing Examiners Employed by Department of Justice

Functions vested by this subchapter in hearing examiners employed by Department of Justice not included in functions of officers, agencies, and employees of that Department transferred to Attorney General by 1950 Reorg. Plan No. 2, § 1, 15 Fed. Reg. 3173, 64 Stat. 1261 (eff. May 24, 1950), set out in Appendix 1 to this title.

Hearing Examiners Employed by Department of Labor

Functions vested by this subchapter in hearing examiners employed by Department of Labor not included in functions of officers, agencies, and employees of that Department transferred to Secretary of Labor by 1950 Reorg. Plan No. 6, § 1, 15 Fed. Reg. 3174, 64 Stat. 1263 (eff. May 24, 1950), set out in Appendix 1 to this title.

Hearing Examiners Employed by Department of The Interior

Functions vested by this subchapter in hearing examiners employed by Department of the Interior not included in functions of officers, agencies, and employees of that Department transferred to Secretary of the Interior by 1950 Reorg. Plan No. 3, § 1, 15 Fed. Reg. 3174, 64 Stat. 1262 (eff. May 24, 1950), set out in Appendix 1 to this title.

Hearing Examiners Employed by Department of The Treasury

Functions vested by this subchapter in hearing examiners employed by Department of the Treasury not included in functions of officers, agencies, and employees of that Department transferred to Secretary of the Treasury by 1950 Reorg. Plan, No. 26, § 1, 15 Fed. Reg. 4935, 64 Stat. 1280 (eff. July 31, 1950), set out in Appendix 1 to this title.

§ 557. Initial decisions; conclusiveness; review by agency; submissions by parties; contents of decisions; record

(a) This section applies, according to the provisions thereof, when a hearing is required to be conducted in accordance with section 556 of this title.

(b) When the agency did not preside at the reception of the evidence, the presiding employee or, in cases not subject to section 554(d) of this title, an employee qualified to preside at hearings pursuant to section 556 of this title, shall initially decide the case unless the agency requires, either in specific cases or by general rule, the entire record to be certified to it for decision. When the presiding employee makes an initial decision, that decision then becomes the decision of the agency without further proceedings unless there is an appeal to, or review on motion of, the agency within time provided by rule. On appeal from or review of the initial decision, the agency has all the powers which it would have in making the initial decision except as it may limit the issues on notice or by rule. When the agency makes the decision without having presided at the reception of the evidence, the presiding employee or an employee qualified to preside at hearings pursuant to section 556 of this title shall first recommend a decision, except that in rule making or determining applications for initial licenses—

(1) instead thereof the agency may issue a tentative decision or one of its responsible employees may recommend a decision; or

(2) this procedure may be omitted in a case in which the agency finds on the record that due and timely execution of its functions imperatively and unavoidably so requires.

(c) Before a recommended, initial, or tentative decision, or a decision on agency review of the decision of subordinate employees, the parties are entitled to a reasonable opportunity to submit for the consideration of the employees participating in the decisions—

(1) proposed findings and conclusions; or

(2) exceptions to the decisions or recommended decisions of subordinate employees or to tentative agency decisions; and

(3) supporting reasons for the exceptions or proposed findings or conclusions.

The record shall show the ruling on each finding, conclusion, or exception presented. All decisions, including initial, recommended, and tentative decisions, are a part of the record and shall include a statement of—

(A) findings and conclusions, and the reasons or basis therefor, on all the material issues of fact, law, or discretion presented on the record; and

(B) the appropriate rule, order, sanction, relief, or denial thereof.

(d) **(1)** In any agency proceeding which is subject to subsection (a) of this section, except to the extent required for the disposition of ex parte matters as authorized by law—

(A) no interested person outside the agency shall make or knowingly cause to be made to any member of the body comprising the agency, administrative law judge, or other employee who is or may reasonably be expected to be involved in the decisional process of the proceeding, an ex parte communication relevant to the merits of the proceeding;

(B) no member of the body comprising the agency, administrative law judge, or other employee who is or may reasonably be expected to be involved in the decisional process of the proceeding, shall make or knowingly cause to be made to any interested person outside the agency an ex parte communication relevant to the merits of the proceeding;

(C) a member of the body comprising the agency, administrative law judge, or other employee who is or may reasonably be expected to be involved in the decisional process of such proceeding who receives, or who makes or knowingly causes to be made, a communication prohibited by this subsection shall place on the public record of the proceeding:

(i) all such written communications;

(ii) memoranda stating the substance of all such oral communications; and

(iii) all written responses, and memoranda stating the substance of all oral responses, to the materials described in clauses (i) and (ii) of this subparagraph;

(D) upon receipt of a communication knowingly made or knowingly caused to be made by a party in violation of this subsection, the agency, administrative law judge, or other employee presiding at the hearing may, to the extent consistent with the interests of justice and the policy of the underlying statutes, require the party to show cause why his claim or interest in the proceeding should not be dismissed, denied, disregarded, or otherwise adversely affected on account of such violation; and

(E) the prohibitions of this subsection shall apply beginning at such time as the agency may designate, but in no case shall they begin to apply later than the time at which a proceeding is noticed for hearing unless the person responsible for the communication has knowledge that it will be noticed, in which case the prohibitions shall apply beginning at the time of his acquisition of such knowledge.

(2) This subsection does not constitute authority to withhold information from Congress.

(Pub. L. No. 89–554, 80 Stat. 387 (Sept. 6, 1966); as amended by Pub. L. No. 94–409, § 4(a), 90 Stat. 1246 (Sept. 13, 1976).)

HISTORICAL AND STATUTORY NOTES

Codifications

Section 557 of former Title 5, Executive Departments and Government Officers and Employees, was transferred to 7 U.S.C.A. § 2207.

Section 557a of former Title 5, Executive Departments and Government Officers and Employees, was transferred to 7 U.S.C.A. § 2208.

Effective and Applicability Provisions

1976 Acts. Amendment by Pub. L. No. 94–409 effective 180 days after Sept. 13, 1976, see section 6 of Pub. L. No. 94–409, set out as a note under section 552b of this title.

§ 558. Imposition of sanctions; determination of applications for licenses; suspension, revocation, and expiration of licenses

(a) This section applies, according to the provisions thereof, to the exercise of a power or authority.

(b) A sanction may not be imposed or a substantive rule or order issued except within jurisdiction delegated to the agency and as authorized by law.

(c) When application is made for a license required by law, the agency, with due regard for the rights and privileges of all the interested parties or adversely affected persons and within a reasonable time, shall set and complete proceedings required to be conducted in accordance with sections 556 and 557 of this title or other proceedings required by law and shall make its decision. Except in cases of willfulness or those in which public health, interest, or safety requires otherwise, the withdrawal, suspension, revocation, or annulment of a license is lawful only if, before the institution of agency proceedings therefor, the licensee has been given—

(1) notice by the agency in writing of the facts or conduct which may warrant the action; and

(2) opportunity to demonstrate or achieve compliance with all lawful requirements.

When the licensee has made timely and sufficient application for a renewal or a new license in accordance with agency rules, a license with reference to an activity of a continuing nature does not expire until the application has been finally determined by the agency.

(Pub. L. No. 89–554, 80 Stat. 388 (Sept. 6, 1966).)

HISTORICAL AND STATUTORY NOTES

Codifications

Section 558 of former Title 5, Executive Departments and Government Officers and Employees, was transferred to 7 U.S.C.A. § 2209.

§ 559. Effect on other laws; effect of subsequent statute

This subchapter, chapter 7, and sections 1305, 3105, 3344, 4301(2)(E), 5372, and 7521 of this title, and the provisions of section 5335(a)(B) of this title that relate to administrative law judges, do not limit or repeal additional requirements imposed by statute or otherwise recognized by law. Except as otherwise required by law, requirements or privileges relating to evidence or procedure apply equally to agencies and persons. Each agency is granted the authority necessary to comply with the requirements of this subchapter through the issuance of rules or otherwise. Subsequent statute may not be held to supersede or modify this subchapter, chapter 7, sections 1305, 3105, 3344, 4301(2)(E), 5372, or 7521 of this title, or the provisions of section 5335(a)(B) of this title that relate to administrative law judges, except to the extent that it does so expressly.

(Pub. L. No. 89–554, 80 Stat. 388 (Sept. 6, 1966); as amended by Pub. L. No. 90–623, § 1(1), 82 Stat. 1312 (Oct. 22, 1968); Pub. L. No. 95–251, § 2(a)(1), 92 Stat. 183 (Mar. 27, 1978); Pub. L. No. 95–454, Title VIII, § 801(a)(3)(B)(iii), 92 Stat. 1221 (Oct. 13, 1978).)

HISTORICAL AND STATUTORY NOTES

Effective and Applicability Provisions

1978 Acts. Amendment by Pub. L. No. 95–454 effective on the first day of the first applicable pay period beginning on or after the 90th day after Oct. 13, 1978, see section 801(a)(4) of Pub. L. No. 95–454, set out as a note under section 5361 of this title.

1968 Acts. Amendment by Pub. L. No. 90–623 intended to restate without substantive change the law in effect on Oct. 22, 1968, see section 6 of Pub. L. No. 90–623, set out as a note under section 5334 of this title.

SUBCHAPTER V—ADMINISTRATIVE CONFERENCE OF THE UNITED STATES

HISTORICAL AND STATUTORY NOTES

Codifications

This subchapter, sections 591 through 596 of this title, was formerly set out as subchapter III of this chapter, sections 571 through 576 of this title, prior to redesignation by Pub. L. No. 102–354, § 2(1), (2), 106 Stat. 944 (Aug. 26, 1992).

Appropriations; Termination of Administrative Conference of United States

Pub. L. No. 104–52, Title IV, 109 Stat. 480 (Nov. 19, 1995), provided in part that: "For necessary expenses of the Administrative Conference of the United States, established under subchapter V of chapter 5 of title 5, United States Code [this subchapter], $600,000: *Provided,* That these funds shall only be available for the purposes of the prompt and orderly termination of the Administrative Conference of the United States by February 1, 1996."

B. JUDICIAL REVIEW

5 U.S.C.A., Chapter 7

CHAPTER 7—JUDICIAL REVIEW

HISTORICAL AND STATUTORY NOTES

Short Title

1946 Acts. The provisions of sections 551 to 559 of this title and this chapter were originally enacted by Act of June 11, 1946, c. 423, 60 Stat. 237, popularly known as the "Administrative Procedure Act". That Act was repealed as part of the general revision of this title by Pub. L. No. 89–554 and its provisions incorporated into sections 551 to 559 of this title and this chapter.

§ 701. Application; definitions

(a) This chapter applies, according to the provisions thereof, except to the extent that—

(1) statutes preclude judicial review; or

(2) agency action is committed to agency discretion by law.

(b) For the purpose of this chapter—

(1) "agency" means each authority of the Government of the United States, whether or not it is within or subject to review by another agency, but does not include—

(A) the Congress;

(B) the courts of the United States;

(C) the governments of the territories or possessions of the United States;

(D) the government of the District of Columbia;

(E) agencies composed of representatives of the parties or of representatives of organizations of the parties to the disputes determined by them;

(F) courts martial and military commissions;

(G) military authority exercised in the field in time of war or in occupied territory; or

(H) functions conferred by sections 1738, 1739, 1743, and 1744 of title 12; subchapter II of chapter 471 of title 49; or sections 1884, 1891–1902, and former section 1641(b)(2), of title 50, appendix; and

(2) "person", "rule", "order", "license", "sanction", "relief", and "agency action" have the meanings given them by section 551 of this title.

(Pub. L. No. 89–554, 80 Stat. 392 (Sept. 6, 1966); as amended by Pub. L. No. 103–272, § 5(a), 108 Stat. 1373 (July 5, 1994); Pub. L. No. 111–350, § 5(a)(3), 124 Stat. 3841 (Jan. 4, 2011).)

HISTORICAL AND STATUTORY NOTES

References in Text

Sections 1891 to 1902 of title 50, appendix, referred to in subsec. (b)(1)(H), have been omitted from the Code as executed.

§ 702. Right of review

A person suffering legal wrong because of agency action, or adversely affected or aggrieved by agency action within the meaning of a relevant statute, is entitled to judicial review thereof. An action in a court of the United States seeking relief other than money damages and stating a claim that an agency or an officer or employee thereof acted or failed to act in an official capacity or under color of legal authority shall not be dismissed nor relief therein be denied on the ground that it is against the United States or that the United States is an indispensable party. The United States may be named as a defendant in any such action, and a judgment or decree may be entered against the United States: *Provided*, That any mandatory or injunctive decree shall specify the Federal officer or officers (by name or by title), and their successors in office, personally responsible for compliance. Nothing herein (1) affects other limitations on judicial review or the power or duty of the court to dismiss any action or deny relief on any other appropriate legal or equitable ground; or (2) confers authority to grant relief if any other statute that grants consent to suit expressly or impliedly forbids the relief which is sought.

(Pub. L. No. 89–554, 80 Stat. 392 (Sept. 6, 1966); as amended by Pub. L. No. 94–574, § 1, 90 Stat. 2721 (Oct. 21, 1976).)

§ 703. Form and venue of proceeding

The form of proceeding for judicial review is the special statutory review proceeding relevant to the subject matter in a court specified by statute or, in the absence or inadequacy thereof, any applicable form of legal action, including actions for declaratory judgments or writs of prohibitory or mandatory injunction or habeas corpus, in a court of competent jurisdiction. If no special statutory review proceeding is applicable, the action for judicial review may be brought against the United States, the agency by its official title, or the appropriate officer. Except to the extent that prior, adequate, and exclusive opportunity for judicial review is provided by law, agency action is subject to judicial review in civil or criminal proceedings for judicial enforcement.

(Pub. L. No. 89–554, 80 Stat. 392 (Sept. 6, 1966); as amended by Pub. L. No. 94–574, § 1, 90 Stat. 2721 (Oct. 21, 1976).)

§ 704. Actions reviewable

Agency action made reviewable by statute and final agency action for which there is no other adequate remedy in a court are subject to judicial review. A preliminary, procedural, or intermediate agency action or ruling not directly reviewable is subject to review on the review of the final agency action. Except as otherwise expressly required by statute, agency action otherwise final is final for the purposes of this section whether or not there has been presented or determined an application for a declaratory order, for any form of reconsideration, or, unless the agency otherwise requires by rule and provides that the action meanwhile is inoperative, for an appeal to superior agency authority.

(Pub. L. No. 89–554, 80 Stat. 392 (Sept. 6, 1966).)

§ 705. Relief pending review

When an agency finds that justice so requires, it may postpone the effective date of action taken by it, pending judicial review. On such conditions as may be required and to the extent necessary to prevent irreparable injury, the reviewing court, including the court to which a case may be taken on appeal from or on application for certiorari or other writ to a reviewing court, may issue all necessary and appropriate process to postpone the effective date of an agency action or to preserve status or rights pending conclusion of the review proceedings.

(Pub. L. No. 89–554, 80 Stat. 393 (Sept. 6, 1966).)

§ 706. Scope of review

To the extent necessary to decision and when presented, the reviewing court shall decide all relevant questions of law, interpret constitutional and statutory provisions, and determine the meaning or applicability of the terms of an agency action. The reviewing court shall—

(1) compel agency action unlawfully withheld or unreasonably delayed; and

(2) hold unlawful and set aside agency action, findings, and conclusions found to be—

(A) arbitrary, capricious, an abuse of discretion, or otherwise not in accordance with law;

(B) contrary to constitutional right, power, privilege, or immunity;

(C) in excess of statutory jurisdiction, authority, or limitations, or short of statutory right;

(D) without observance of procedure required by law;

(E) unsupported by substantial evidence in a case subject to sections 556 and 557 of this title or otherwise reviewed on the record of an agency hearing provided by statute; or

(F) unwarranted by the facts to the extent that the facts are subject to trial de novo by the reviewing court.

In making the foregoing determinations, the court shall review the whole record or those parts of it cited by a party, and due account shall be taken of the rule of prejudicial error.

(Pub. L. No. 89–554, 80 Stat. 393 (Sept. 6, 1966).)

HISTORICAL AND STATUTORY NOTES

Abbreviation of Record

Pub. L. No. 85–791, 72 Stat. 941 (Aug. 28, 1958), which authorized the abbreviation of the record on the review of enforcement of orders of administrative agencies and review on the original papers, provided, in section 35 thereof, that: "This Act [which added section 2112 of Title 28, Judiciary and Judicial Procedure, and amended sections 1036 and 1037(c) of former Title 5, [now sections 2346 and 2347(c) of Title 28], sections 8, 9, 193(c), 194(b) to (d), (h), 1115(c), 1599(c), 1600, and 1601 of Title 7, Agriculture, section 1848 of Title 12, Banks and Banking, sections 21, 45(b)–(d), 77i(a), 78y(a), 79x(a), 80a–42(a), 80b–13(a), and 717r(a), (b) of Title 15, Commerce and Trade, section 825 *l*(a), (b) of Title 16, Conservation, sections 81r(c) and 1641(b) of Title 19, Customs Duties, section 277(b) of Title 20, Education, sections 346a(i)(2), (3), 371(f)(1), (3) of Title 21, Food and Drugs, section 1631f(b) of Title 22, Foreign Relations and Intercourse, section 204(h) of Title 27, Intoxicating Liquors, sections 160(d) to (f) and 210(a) of Title 29, Labor, section 576 [now section 6212(f)] of former Title 39, The Postal Service, section 291j(b)(1), (2) of Title 42, the Public Health and Welfare, section 315(f) of Title 45, Railroads, section 1181(b) of Title 46, Appendix, Shipping, section 402(d) of Title 47, section 646(c) of former Title 49, Transportation, and sections 793(a), 820(e), 821(c), (d) of Title 50, War and National Defense] shall not be construed to repeal or modify any provision of the Administrative Procedure Act."

APPENDIX D

EQUAL ACCESS TO JUSTICE ACT

5 U.S.C. § 504 and 28 U.S.C. § 2412

Editorial Note: *Many federal environmental statutes provide for attorney fees in their citizen suit provisions, and prevailing plaintiffs suing under those provisions can request their attorney fees and costs directly under the citizen suit provisions. Citizen suit provisions, however, by definition involve court actions. Prevailing plaintiffs in adjudications that occur within agencies rely on the Equal Access to Justice Act, 5 U.S.C. § 504, to claim their costs and attorney fees. In turn, prevailing parties in non-citizen suit lawsuits with the federal government—for example, lawsuits brought pursuant to the federal Administrative Procedure Act—claim their costs and attorney fees pursuant to 28 U.S.C. § 2412.*

5 U.S.C. § 504. Costs and fees of parties

(a) **(1)** An agency that conducts an adversary adjudication shall award, to a prevailing party other than the United States, fees and other expenses incurred by that party in connection with that proceeding, unless the adjudicative officer of the agency finds that the position of the agency was substantially justified or that special circumstances make an award unjust. Whether or not the position of the agency was substantially justified shall be determined on the basis of the administrative record, as a whole, which is made in the adversary adjudication for which fees and other expenses are sought.

(2) A party seeking an award of fees and other expenses shall, within thirty days of a final disposition in the adversary adjudication, submit to the agency an application which shows that the party is a prevailing party and is eligible to receive an award under this section, and the amount sought, including an itemized statement from any attorney, agent, or expert witness representing or appearing in behalf of the party stating the actual time expended and the rate at which fees and other expenses were computed. The party shall also allege that the position of the agency was not substantially justified. When the United States appeals the underlying merits of an adversary adjudication, no decision on an application for fees and other expenses in connection with that adversary adjudication shall be made under this section until a final and unreviewable decision is rendered by the court on the appeal or until the underlying merits of the case have been finally determined pursuant to the appeal.

(3) The adjudicative officer of the agency may reduce the amount to be awarded, or deny an award, to the extent that the party during the course of the proceedings engaged in conduct which unduly and unreasonably protracted the final resolution of the matter in controversy. The decision of the adjudicative officer of the agency under this section shall be made a part of the record containing the final decision of the agency and shall include written findings and conclusions and the reason or basis therefor. The decision of the agency on the application for fees and other expenses shall be the final administrative decision under this section.

(4) If, in an adversary adjudication arising from an agency action to enforce a party's compliance with a statutory or regulatory requirement, the demand by the agency is substantially in excess of the decision of the adjudicative officer and is unreasonable when compared with such decision, under the facts and circumstances of the case, the adjudicative officer shall award to the party the fees and other expenses related to defending against the excessive demand, unless the party has committed a willful violation of law or otherwise acted in bad faith, or special circumstances make an award unjust. Fees and expenses awarded under this paragraph shall be paid only as a consequence of appropriations provided in advance.

(b) **(1)** For the purposes of this section—

(A) "fees and other expenses" includes the reasonable expenses of expert witnesses, the reasonable cost of any study, analysis, engineering report, test, or project which is found by the agency to be necessary for the preparation of the party's case, and reasonable attorney or agent fees (The amount of fees awarded under this section shall be based upon prevailing market rates for the kind and quality of the services furnished, except that (i) no expert witness shall be compensated at a rate in excess of the highest rate of compensation for expert witnesses paid by the agency involved, and (ii) attorney or agent fees shall not be awarded in excess of $125 per hour unless the agency determines by regulation that an increase in the cost of living or a special factor, such as the limited availability of qualified attorneys or agents for the proceedings involved, justifies a higher fee.);

(B) "party" means a party, as defined in section 551(3) of this title, who is (i) an individual whose net worth did not exceed $2,000,000 at the time the adversary adjudication was initiated, or (ii) any owner of an unincorporated business, or any partnership, corporation, association, unit of local government, or organization, the net worth of which did not exceed $7,000,000 at the time the adversary adjudication was initiated, and which had not more than 500 employees at the time the adversary adjudication was initiated; except that an organization described in section 501(c)(3) of the Internal Revenue Code of 1986 (26 U.S.C. 501(c)(3)) exempt from taxation under section 501(a) of such Code, or a cooperative association as defined in section 15(a) of the Agricultural Marketing Act (12 U.S.C. 1141j(a)), may be a party regardless of the net worth of such organization or cooperative association or for purposes of subsection (a)(4), a small entity as defined in section 601;

(C) "adversary adjudication" means (i) an adjudication under section 554 of this title in which the position of the United States is represented by counsel or otherwise, but excludes an adjudication for the purpose of establishing or fixing a rate or for the purpose of granting or renewing a license, (ii) any appeal of a decision made pursuant to section 7103 of title 41 before an agency board of contract appeals as provided in section 7105 of title 41, (iii) any hearing conducted under chapter 38 of title 31, and (iv) the Religious Freedom Restoration Act of 1993;

(D) "adjudicative officer" means the deciding official, without regard to whether the official is designated as an administrative law judge, a hearing officer or examiner, or otherwise, who presided at the adversary adjudication;

(E) "position of the agency" means, in addition to the position taken by the agency in the adversary adjudication, the action or failure to act by the agency upon which the adversary adjudication is based; except that fees and other expenses may not be awarded to a party for any portion of the adversary adjudication in which the party has unreasonably protracted the proceedings; and

(F) "demand" means the express demand of the agency which led to the adversary adjudication, but does not include a recitation by the agency of the maximum statutory penalty (i) in the administrative complaint, or (ii) elsewhere when accompanied by an express demand for a lesser amount.

(2) Except as otherwise provided in paragraph (1), the definitions provided in section 551 of this title apply to this section.

(c) **(1)** After consultation with the Chairman of the Administrative Conference of the United States, each agency shall by rule establish uniform procedures for the submission and consideration of applications for an award of fees and other expenses. If a court reviews the underlying decision of the adversary adjudication, an award for fees and other expenses may be made only pursuant to section 2412(d)(3) of title 28.

(2) If a party other than the United States is dissatisfied with a determination of fees and other expenses made under subsection (a), that party may, within 30 days after the determination is made, appeal the determination to the court of the United States having jurisdiction to review the merits of the underlying decision of the agency adversary adjudication. The court's determination on any appeal heard under this paragraph shall be based solely on the factual record made before the agency. The court may modify the determination of fees and other expenses only if the court finds that the failure to make an award of fees and other expenses, or the calculation of the amount of the award, was unsupported by substantial evidence.

(d) Fees and other expenses awarded under this subsection shall be paid by any agency over which the party prevails from any funds made available to the agency by appropriation or otherwise.

(e) **(1)** Not later than March 31 of the first fiscal year beginning after the date of enactment of the John D. Dingell, Jr. Conservation, Management, and Recreation Act, and every fiscal year thereafter, the Chairman of the Administrative Conference of the United States, after consultation with the Chief

Counsel for Advocacy of the Small Business Administration, shall submit to Congress and make publicly available online a report on the amount of fees and other expenses awarded during the preceding fiscal year under this section.

(2) Each report under paragraph (1) shall describe the number, nature, and amount of the awards, the claims involved in the controversy, and any other relevant information that may aid Congress in evaluating the scope and impact of such awards.

(3) **(A)** Each report under paragraph (1) shall account for all payments of fees and other expenses awarded under this section that are made pursuant to a settlement agreement, regardless of whether the settlement agreement is sealed or otherwise subject to a nondisclosure provision.

(B) The disclosure of fees and other expenses required under subparagraph (A) shall not affect any other information that is subject to a nondisclosure provision in a settlement agreement.

(f) As soon as practicable, and in any event not later than the date on which the first report under subsection (e)(1) is required to be submitted, the Chairman of the Administrative Conference of the United States shall create and maintain online a searchable database containing, with respect to each award of fees and other expenses under this section made on or after the date of enactment of the John D. Dingell, Jr. Conservation, Management, and Recreation Act, the following information:

(1) The case name and number of the adversary adjudication, if available, hyperlinked to the case, if available.

(2) The name of the agency involved in the adversary adjudication.

(3) A description of the claims in the adversary adjudication.

(4) The name of each party to whom the award was made as such party is identified in the order or other court document making the award.

(5) The amount of the award.

(6) The basis for the finding that the position of the agency concerned was not substantially justified.

(g) The online searchable database described in subsection (f) may not reveal any information the disclosure of which is prohibited by law or a court order.

(h) The head of each agency shall provide to the Chairman of the Administrative Conference of the United States in a timely manner all information requested by the Chairman to comply with the requirements of subsections (e), (f), and (g).

(i) No award may be made under this section for costs, fees, or other expenses which may be awarded under section 7430 of the Internal Revenue Code of 1986.

(Added by Pub. L. No. 96–481, § 203(a)(1), (c), 94 Stat. 2325, 2327 (Oct. 21, 1980); and revived and amended by Pub. L. No. 99–80, §§ 1, 6, 99 Stat. 183, 186 (Aug. 5, 1985); and amended by Pub. L. No. 99–509, § 6103(c), 100 Stat. 1948 (Oct. 21, 1986); Pub. L. No. 99–514, § 2, 100 Stat. 2095 (Oct. 22, 1986); Pub. L. No. 100–647, Title VI, § 6239(b), 102 Stat. 3746 (Nov. 10, 1988); Pub. L. No. 103–141, § 4(b), 107 Stat. 1489 (Nov. 16, 1993); Pub. L. No. 104–121, Title II, § 231, 110 Stat. 862 (Mar. 29, 1996); Pub. L. No. 111–350, § 5(a)(1), 124 Stat. 3841 (Jan. 4, 2011); Pub. L. No. 116–9, § 4201(a)(1), 133 Stat. 762–63 (March 12, 2019).)

28 U.S.C. § 2412. Costs and fees

(a) **(1)** Except as otherwise specifically provided by statute, a judgment for costs, as enumerated in section 1920 of this title, but not including the fees and expenses of attorneys, may be awarded to the prevailing party in any civil action brought by or against the United States or any agency or any official of the United States acting in his or her official capacity in any court having jurisdiction of such action. A judgment for costs when taxed against the United States shall, in an amount established by statute, court rule, or order, be limited to reimbursing in whole or in part the prevailing party for the costs incurred by such party in the litigation.

(2) A judgment for costs, when awarded in favor of the United States in an action brought by the United States, may include an amount equal to the filing fee prescribed under section 1914(a) of this title. The preceding sentence shall not be construed as requiring the United States to pay any filing fee.

(b) Unless expressly prohibited by statute, a court may award reasonable fees and expenses of attorneys, in addition to the costs which may be awarded pursuant to subsection (a), to the prevailing party in any civil action brought by or against the United States or any agency or any official of the United States acting in his or her official capacity in any court having jurisdiction of such action. The United States shall be liable for such fees and expenses to the same extent that any other party would be liable under the common law or under the terms of any statute which specifically provides for such an award.

(c) **(1)** Any judgment against the United States or any agency and any official of the United States acting in his or her official capacity for costs pursuant to subsection (a) shall be paid as provided in sections 2414 and 2517 of this title and shall be in addition to any relief provided in the judgment.

(2) Any judgment against the United States or any agency and any official of the United States acting in his or her official capacity for fees and expenses of attorneys pursuant to subsection (b) shall be paid as provided in sections 2414 and 2517 of this title, except that if the basis for the award is a finding that the United States acted in bad faith, then the award shall be paid by any agency found to have acted in bad faith and shall be in addition to any relief provided in the judgment.

(d) **(1)** **(A)** Except as otherwise specifically provided by statute, a court shall award to a prevailing party other than the United States fees and other expenses, in addition to any costs awarded pursuant to subsection (a), incurred by that party in any civil action (other than cases sounding in tort), including proceedings for judicial review of agency action, brought by or against the United States in any court having jurisdiction of that action, unless the court finds that the position of the United States was substantially justified or that special circumstances make an award unjust.

(B) A party seeking an award of fees and other expenses shall, within thirty days of final judgment in the action, submit to the court an application for fees and other expenses which shows that the party is a prevailing party and is eligible to receive an award under this subsection, and the amount sought, including an itemized statement from any attorney or expert witness representing or appearing in behalf of the party stating the actual time expended and the rate at which fees and other expenses were computed. The party shall also allege that the position of the United States was not substantially justified. Whether or not the position of the United States was substantially justified shall be determined on the basis of the record (including the record with respect to the action or failure to act by the agency upon which the civil action is based) which is made in the civil action for which fees and other expenses are sought.

(C) The court, in its discretion, may reduce the amount to be awarded pursuant to this subsection, or deny an award, to the extent that the prevailing party during the course of the proceedings engaged in conduct which unduly and unreasonably protracted the final resolution of the matter in controversy.

(D) If, in a civil action brought by the United States or a proceeding for judicial review of an adversary adjudication described in section 504(a)(4) of title 5, the demand by the United States is substantially in excess of the judgment finally obtained by the United States and is unreasonable when compared with such judgment, under the facts and circumstances of the case, the court shall award to the party the fees and other expenses related to defending against the excessive demand, unless the party has committed a willful violation of law or otherwise acted in bad faith, or special circumstances make an award unjust. Fees and expenses awarded under this subparagraph shall be paid only as a consequence of appropriations provided in advance.

(2) For the purposes of this subsection—

(A) "fees and other expenses" includes the reasonable expenses of expert witnesses, the reasonable cost of any study, analysis, engineering report, test, or project which is found by the court to be necessary for the preparation of the party's case, and reasonable attorney fees (The amount of fees awarded under this subsection shall be based upon prevailing market rates for the kind and quality of the services furnished, except that (i) no expert witness shall be compensated at a rate in excess of the highest rate of compensation for expert witnesses paid by the United

States; and (ii) attorney fees shall not be awarded in excess of $125 per hour unless the court determines that an increase in the cost of living or a special factor, such as the limited availability of qualified attorneys for the proceedings involved, justifies a higher fee.);

(B) "party" means (i) an individual whose net worth did not exceed $2,000,000 at the time the civil action was filed, or (ii) any owner of an unincorporated business, or any partnership, corporation, association, unit of local government, or organization, the net worth of which did not exceed $7,000,000 at the time the civil action was filed, and which had not more than 500 employees at the time the civil action was filed; except that an organization described in section 501(c)(3) of the Internal Revenue Code of 1986 (26 U.S.C. 501(c)(3)) exempt from taxation under section 501(a) of such Code, or a cooperative association as defined in section 15(a) of the Agricultural Marketing Act (12 U.S.C. 1141j(a)), may be a party regardless of the net worth of such organization or cooperative association or for purposes of subsection (d)(1)(D), a small entity as defined in section 601 of Title 5;

(C) "United States" includes any agency and any official of the United States acting in his or her official capacity;

(D) "position of the United States" means, in addition to the position taken by the United States in the civil action, the action or failure to act by the agency upon which the civil action is based; except that fees and expenses may not be awarded to a party for any portion of the litigation in which the party has unreasonably protracted the proceedings;

(E) "civil action brought by or against the United States" includes an appeal by a party, other than the United States, from a decision of a contracting officer rendered pursuant to a disputes clause in a contract with the Government or pursuant to chapter 71 of title 41;

(F) "court" includes the United States Court of Federal Claims and the United States Court of Appeals for Veterans Claims;

(G) "final judgment" means a judgment that is final and not appealable, and includes an order of settlement;

(H) "prevailing party", in the case of eminent domain proceedings, means a party who obtains a final judgment (other than by settlement), exclusive of interest, the amount of which is at least as close to the highest valuation of the property involved that is attested to at trial on behalf of the property owner as it is to the highest valuation of the property involved that is attested to at trial on behalf of the Government; and

(I) "demand" means the express demand of the United States which led to the adversary adjudication, but shall not include a recitation of the maximum statutory penalty (i) in the complaint, or (ii) elsewhere when accompanied by an express demand for a lesser amount.

(3) In awarding fees and other expenses under this subsection to a prevailing party in any action for judicial review of an adversary adjudication, as defined in subsection (b)(1)(C) of section 504 of title 5, or an adversary adjudication subject to chapter 71 of title 41, the court shall include in that award fees and other expenses to the same extent authorized in subsection (a) of such section, unless the court finds that during such adversary adjudication the position of the United States was substantially justified, or that special circumstances make an award unjust.

(4) Fees and other expenses awarded under this subsection to a party shall be paid by any agency over which the party prevails from any funds made available to the agency by appropriation or otherwise.

(5) **(A)** Not later than March 31 of the first fiscal year beginning after the date of enactment of the John D. Dingell, Jr. Conservation, Management, and Recreation Act, and every fiscal year thereafter, the Chairman of the Administrative Conference of the United States shall submit to Congress and make publicly available online a report on the amount of fees and other expenses awarded during the preceding fiscal year pursuant to this subsection.

(B) Each report under subparagraph (A) shall describe the number, nature, and amount of the awards, the claims involved in the controversy, and any other relevant information that may aid Congress in evaluating the scope and impact of such awards.

(C) **(i)** Each report under subparagraph (A) shall account for all payments of fees and other expenses awarded under this subsection that are made pursuant to a settlement agreement, regardless of whether the settlement agreement is sealed or otherwise subject to a nondisclosure provision.

(ii) The disclosure of fees and other expenses required under clause (i) shall not affect any other information that is subject to a nondisclosure provision in a settlement agreement.

(D) The Chairman of the Administrative Conference of the United States shall include and clearly identify in each annual report under subparagraph (A), for each case in which an award of fees and other expenses is included in the report—

(i) any amounts paid under section 1304 of title 31 for a judgment in the case;

(ii) the amount of the award of fees and other expenses; and

(iii) the statute under which the plaintiff filed suit.

(6) As soon as practicable, and in any event not later than the date on which the first report under paragraph (5)(A) is required to be submitted, the Chairman of the Administrative Conference of the United States shall create and maintain online a searchable database containing, with respect to each award of fees and other expenses under this subsection made on or after the date of enactment of the John D. Dingell, Jr. Conservation, Management, and Recreation Act, the following information:

(A) The case name and number, hyperlinked to the case, if available.

(B) The name of the agency involved in the case.

(C) The name of each party to whom the award was made as such party is identified in the order or other court document making the award.

(D) A description of the claims in the case.

(E) The amount of the award.

(F) The basis for the finding that the position of the agency concerned was not substantially justified.

(7) The online searchable database described in paragraph (6) may not reveal any information the disclosure of which is prohibited by law or a court order.

(8) The head of each agency (including the Attorney General of the United States) shall provide to the Chairman of the Administrative Conference of the United States in a timely manner all information requested by the Chairman to comply with the requirements of paragraphs (5), (6), and (7).

(e) The provisions of this section shall not apply to any costs, fees, and other expenses in connection with any proceeding to which section 7430 of the Internal Revenue Code of 1986 applies (determined without regard to subsections (b) and (f) of such section). Nothing in the preceding sentence shall prevent the awarding under subsection (a) of this section of costs enumerated in section 1920 of this title (as in effect on October 1, 1981).

(f) If the United States appeals an award of costs or fees and other expenses made against the United States under this section and the award is affirmed in whole or in part, interest shall be paid on the amount of the award as affirmed. Such interest shall be computed at the rate determined under section 1961(a) of this title, and shall run from the date of the award through the day before the date of the mandate of affirmance.

(June 25, 1948, c. 646, 62 Stat. 973; as amended by Pub. L. No. 89–507, § 1, 80 Stat. 308 (July 18, 1966); Pub. L. 96–481, Title II, § 204(a), (c), 94 Stat. 2327, 2329 (Oct. 21, 1980); Pub. L. 97–248, Title II, § 292(c), 96 Stat. 574 (Sept. 3, 1982); Pub. L. 99–80, §§ 2, 6(a), (b)(2), 99 Stat. 184, 186 (Aug. 5, 1985); Pub. L. No. 99–514, § 2, 100 Stat. 2095 (Oct. 22, 1986); Pub. L. No. 102–572, Title III, § 301(a), Title V, §§ 502(b), 506(a), Title IX, § 902(b)(1), 106

Stat. 4511–4513, 4516 (Oct. 29, 1992); Pub. L. No. 104–66, Title I, § 1091(b), 109 Stat. 722 (Dec. 21, 1995); Pub. L. No. 104–121, Title II, § 232, 110 Stat. 863 (Mar. 29, 1996); Pub. L. No. 105–368, Title V, § 512(b)(1)(B), 112 Stat. 3342 (Nov. 11, 1998); Pub. L. No. 111–350, § 5(g)(9), 124 Stat. 3848 (Jan. 4, 2011); Pub. L. No. 116–9, § 4201(a)(2)–(3), 133 Stat. 763–64 (March 12, 2019).).)

HISTORICAL AND STATUTORY NOTES

References in Text

Chapter 71 of title 41, referred to in subsec. (d)(2)(E), (3), is codified as 41 U.S.C.A. § 7101 et seq.

Section 7430 of the Internal Revenue Code of 1986, referred to in subsec. (e), is codified as section 7430 of Title 26, Internal Revenue Code.

Effective and Applicability Provisions

1998 Acts. Amendment by Pub. L. No. 105–368 effective on the first day of the first month beginning more than 90 days after Nov. 11, 1998, see section 513 of Pub. L. No. 105–368, set out as a note under section 7251 of Title 38.

1996 Acts. Amendment by Pub. L. No. 104–121 applicable to civil actions and adversary adjudications commenced on or after March 29, 1996, see section 233 of Pub. L. No. 104–121, set out as a note under section 504 of Title 5, Government Organization and Employees.

1992 Acts. Section 506(b) of Pub. L. No. 102–572 provided that: "The amendment made by subsection (a) [amending subsec. (d)(2)(F) of this section] shall apply to any case pending before the United States Court of Veterans Appeals on the date of the enactment of this Act [Oct. 29, 1992], to any appeal filed in that court on or after such date, and to any appeal from that court that is pending on such date in the United States Court of Appeals for the Federal Circuit."

Section 506(d) of Pub. L. No. 102–572 provided that: "This section, and the amendment made by this section [amending subsec. (d)(2)(F) of this section and enacting provisions set out as notes under this section], shall take effect on the date of the enactment of this Act [Oct. 29, 1992]."

Amendment by section 902(b)(1) of Pub. L. No. 102–572 effective Oct. 29, 1992, see section 911 of Pub. L. No. 102–572, set out as a note under section 171 of this title.

Amendments by sections 301(a) and 502(b) of Pub. L. No. 102–572 effective Jan. 1, 1993, see section 1101(a) of Pub. L. No. 102–572, set out as a note under section 905 of Title 2, The Congress.

1985 Acts. Amendment by Pub. L. 99–80 applicable to cases pending on or commenced on or after Aug. 5, 1985, but with provision for additional applicability to certain prior cases and to prior board of contracts appeals cases, see section 7 of Pub. L. 99–80, set out as a note under section 504 of Title 5, Government Organization and Employees.

1982 Acts. Amendment by Pub. L. No. 97–248 applicable to civil actions or proceedings commenced after Feb. 28, 1983, see section 292(e)(1) of Pub. L. No. 97–248, as amended, set out as a note under section 7430 of Title 26, Internal Revenue Code.

1980 Acts. Amendment by section 204(a) of Pub. L. No. 96–481 to take effect on Oct. 1, 1981, and applicable to any adversary adjudication, as defined in section 504(b)(1)(C) of Title 5, and to civil actions and adversary adjudications described in this section, which are pending on, or commenced on or after, Oct. 1, 1981, see section 208 of Pub. L. No. 96–481, as amended, set out as a note under section 504 of Title 5, Government Organization and Employees.

Section 204(c) of Pub. L. No. 96–481 which provided in part that effective Oct. 1, 1984, subsec. (d) of this section is repealed, except that the provisions of subsec. (d) shall continue to apply through final disposition of any adversary adjudication initiated before the date of repeal, was repealed by Pub. L. No. 99–80, § 6(b)(2), Aug. 5, 1985, 99 Stat. 186.

1966 Acts. Section 3 of Pub. L. No. 89–507 provided that: "These amendments [to this section and section 2520 of this title] shall apply only to judgments entered in actions filed subsequent to the date of enactment of this Act [July 18, 1966]. These amendments [to this section and section 2520 of this title] shall not authorize the reopening or modification of judgments entered prior to the enactment of this Act [July 18, 1966]."

Savings Provisions

Section 206 of Pub. L. No. 96–481, as amended by Pub. L. No. 99–80, § 3, 99 Stat. 186 (Aug. 5, 1985), provided that:

> **"(a)** Except as provided in subsection (b), nothing in section 2412(d) of title 28, United States Code, as added by section 204(a) of this title [subsec. (d) of this section], alters, modifies, repeals, invalidates, or supersedes any other provision of Federal law which authorizes an award of such fees and other expenses to any party other than the United States that prevails in any civil action brought by or against the United States.
>
> **"(b)** Section 206(b) of the Social Security Act (42 U.S.C. 406(b)(1)) [section 406(b) of Title 42, The Public Health and Welfare] shall not prevent an award of fees and other expenses under section 2412(d) of title 28, United States Code [subsec. (d) of this section]. Section 206(b)(2) of the Social Security Act [section 406(b)(2) of Title 42] shall not apply with respect to any such award but only if, where the claimant's attorney receives fees for the same work under both section 206(b) of that Act [section 406(b) of Title 42] and section 2412(d) of title 28, United States Code [subsec. (d) of this section], the claimant's attorney refunds to the claimant the amount of the smaller fee."

Congressional Findings and Purposes

For Congressional findings and purposes relating to 1980 amendment of this section, see section 202 of Pub. L. No. 96–481, set out as a note under section 504 of Title 5, Government Organization and Employees.

Fees Awarded to Non-attorney Practitioners

Pub. L. No. 107–330, Title IV, § 403, 116 Stat. 2833 (Dec. 6, 2002), provided that: "The authority of the United States Court of Appeals for Veterans Claims to award reasonable fees and expenses of attorneys under section 2412(d) of title 28, United States Code [Subsec. (d) of this section], shall include authority to award fees and expenses, in an amount determined appropriate by the United States Court of Appeals for Veterans Claims, of individuals admitted to practice before the Court as non-attorney practitioners under subsection (b) or (c) of Rule 46 of the Rules of Practice and Procedure of the United States Court of Appeals for Veterans Claims."

Fee Agreements

Section 506(c) of Pub. L. No. 102–572 provided that: "Section 5904(d) of title 38, United States Code [section 5904(d) of Title 38, Veterans' Benefits], shall not prevent an award of fees and other expenses under section 2412(d) of title 28, United States Code [subsec. (d) of this section]. Section 5904(d) of title 38, United States Code, shall not apply with respect to any such award but only if, where the claimant's attorney receives fees for the same work under both section 5904 of title 38, United States Code, and section 2412(d) of title 28, United States Code, the claimant's attorney refunds to the claimant the amount of the smaller fee."

Nonliability of Judicial Officers for Costs

Pub. L. No. 104–317, Title III, § 309(a), 110 Stat. 3853 (Oct. 19, 1996), provided that: "Notwithstanding any other provision of law, no judicial officer shall be held liable for any costs, including attorney's fees, in any action brought against such officer for an act or omission taken in such officer's judicial capacity, unless such action was clearly in excess of such officer's jurisdiction."

Revival of Previously Repealed Provisions

For revival of subsec. (d) of this section effective on or after Aug. 5, 1985, as if it had not been repealed by section 204(c) of Pub. L. No. 96–481, and repeal of section 204(c) of Pub. L. No. 96–481, see section 6 of Pub. L. No. 99–80, set out as a note under section 504 of Title 5, Government Organization and Employees.